Who's Who in America®

Published by Marquis Who's Who®

Titles in Print

Who's Who in America®
Who Was Who in America®
  Historical Volume (1607–1896)
  Volume I (1897–1942)
  Volume II (1943–1950)
  Volume III (1951–1960)
  Volume IV (1961–1968)
  Volume V (1969–1973)
  Volume VI (1974–1976)
  Volume VII (1977–1981)
  Volume VIII (1982–1985)
  Volume IX (1985–1989)
  Volume X (1989–1993)
  Volume XI (1993–1996)
  Volume XII (1996–1998)
  Index Volume (1607–1998)
Who's Who in the World®
Who's Who in the East®
Who's Who in the Midwest®
Who's Who in the South and Southwest®
Who's Who in the West®
Who's Who in American Art™
Who's Who in American Education®
Who's Who in American Law®
Who's Who in American Nursing®
Who's Who in American Politics®
Who's Who in Entertainment®
Who's Who in Finance and Industry®
Who's Who in Medicine and Healthcare™
Who's Who in Religion™
Who's Who in Science and Engineering®
Who's Who in the Media and Communications™
Who's Who of American Women®
Who's Who of Emerging Leaders in America®
Index to Marquis Who's Who® Publications
The *Official* ABMS Directory of Board Certified Medical Specialists®

Available on CD-ROM

The Complete Marquis Who's Who® on CD-ROM
ABMS Medical Specialists *PLUS*™

Who's Who in America®

2000

Millennium Edition

Since 1899

54th Edition

Volume 1
A–K

MARQUIS
Who's Who® 121 Chanlon Road
New Providence, NJ 07974 U.S.A.

Who'sWho in America®

Marquis Who's Who®

Managing Director Thomas M. Bachmann

Editorial Director Fred Marks   **Managing Editor** Robert Docherty

Editorial

Senior Editor	Maurice Brooks
Assistant Editors	Danielle M.L. Barry
	Donald Bunton
	Josh Samber
	Mary San Giovanni
	Elissa Strell
	Paul M. Zema

Editorial Services

Managers	Karen Chassie
	Debra Krom
Creative Project Manager	Michael Noerr
Assistant Creative Project Managers	William R. Miller
Production Supervisor	Jeanne Danzig

Editorial Support

Manager	Debby Nowicki
Coordinator	J. Hector Gonzalez
Clerk	Sola Osofisan

Mail Processing

Supervisor	Kara A. Seitz
Staff	Betty Gray
	Jill S. Terbell

Database Operations

Director, Production & Training	Mark Van Orman
Assistant Managing Editor	Matthew O'Connell
Assistant Manager	Patrick Gibbons

Research

Senior Managing Research Editor	Lisa Weissbard
Freelance Coordinator	Debra Ayn
Associate Research Editors	Susan Eggleton
	Oscar Maldonado
Assistant Research Editor	Stephen J. Sherman

Published by Marquis Who's Who, a member of the Lexis-Nexis Group.

President and Chief Executive Officer Lou Andreozzi

Vice President and Publisher Randy H. Mysel

Vice President, Database Production Dean Hollister

Marquis Who's Who
121 Chanlon Road
New Providence, New Jersey 07974
1-908-464-6800
www.marquiswhoswho.com

WHO'S WHO IN AMERICA is a registered trademark of Reed Publishing (Nederland) B.V., used under license.
Library of Congress Catalog Card Number 49-48186
International Standard Book Number   0-8379-0199-5 (set, Classic Edition)
                                         0-8379-0200-2 (volume 1, Classic Edition)
                                         0-8379-0203-7 (set, Deluxe Edition)
                                         0-8379-0204-5 (volume 1, Deluxe Edition)
Internationl Standard Serial Number   0083-9817

Manufactured in the United States of America

Table of Contents

Preface

"WHO'S WHO IN AMERICA *shall endeavor to list those individuals who are of current national reference interest and inquiry either because of meritorious achievement or because of the positions they hold."*

Albert Nelson Marquis
Founder, 1899

A Standard Reference Work

When the first edition of *Who's Who in America* appeared in 1899, it presented itself as a new and untried experiment in the field of American reference book publishing. It was the first publication ever issued which claimed to be, in any comprehensive degree, a general biographical directory of notable American contemporaries. During the generations that have passed, *Who's Who in America* has garnered a worldwide reputation for presenting the most accurate, current biographical data available. Quickly establishing itself as a standard reference work, it has grown steadily in public favor, and today is recognized globally as the premier reference pertaining to notable living Americans.

Continuing a century-long tradition, the Millennium Edition upholds the guiding principle set forth by A.N. Marquis in 1899: The editors of *Who's Who in America* continue to strive to identify and chronicle the achievements of men and women who have become the leaders in our society's political, cultural, and economic affairs.

One Principle Governs Selection

In 1899, Marquis Biographees numbered 8,602, or one person per 10,000 of U.S. population. In this Millennium Edition, Marquis Who's Who proudly presents the biographies of over 120,000 outstanding individuals. While our Biographees have grown in number, our selection standards remain stringent. Fewer than four in 10,000 people are included in *Who's Who in America*.

Selection is based solely on reference value. Individuals become eligible for listing by virtue of their positions and/or noteworthy achievements that have proven to be of significant value to society. An individual's desire to be listed is not sufficient reason for inclusion. Similarly, wealth or social position are not criteria. Of course, Marquis Who's Who has never charged a fee for publishing a biography, nor is purchase of the book ever a factor in the selection of Biographees.

Compiling the Most Accurate Biographical Data

Through fifty-four issues, the basic *Who's Who in America* compilation process has remained unchanged. Potential Biographees are identified by Marquis researchers and editors. Candidates are sent data forms and are invited to submit complete biographical and career information. These data are reviewed to confirm that candidates meet the stringent selection criteria. Sketches are then prepared and sent to Biographees for prepublication checking.

In some cases, Marquis staff members compile and/or verify the biographical data through independent research. Sketches compiled in this manner are denoted by asterisks. For a small number of cases, where detailed information is not available at publication, the editors have written brief sketches with current career information; these are also indicated by asterisks.

To maintain its reputation for currency, and at the same time to adhere to space limitations, *Who's Who in America* undergoes meticulous review of selection criteria with each edition. Deletion of some names is inevitable; such deletion is not arbitrary. For example, if a Biographee has retired from active participation in a career or public life, the sketch may be excluded. In large part, it is career development that determines inclusion and continuation.

Annual publication enables *Who's Who in America* to bring users more new names and update more existing entries each edition. In all, over 30,000 new names appear in the Millennium Edition.

Responding to Your Reference Needs

Who's Who in America provides a number of useful reference features. As a complement to the biographical profiles, the Geographic and Professional Indexes make *Who's Who in America* an even more productive research tool. Through these indexes, users can identify and locate individuals in any of thirty-eight categories, as well as by country, state, or city.

This edition also contains a cumulative Retiree Index of persons whose names were deleted from the 51st through 53rd Editions because they have retired from active work. This index enables the user to locate the last published biographical sketch of each listee.

There is also a Necrology of Biographees whose sketches appeared in the previous Edition and whose deaths were reported prior to the closing of this edition. The sketches have been removed from the book. (For those Biographees whose deaths were reported prior to May 1998, complete biographical information, including date of death and place of interment, can be found in Volume XII of *Who Was Who in America*.)

Finally, many of the women and men profiled in *Who's Who in America* have included in their biographies a listing of their avocations, thus providing additional insights into their personal lives and interests. Some of the sketches also end with an italicized feature, "Thoughts on My Life." The statement is written by the Biographees and reflects their own principles, goals, ideals, and values that have been guidelines for their success and achievement.

Our Challenge

Putting together a reference source as comprehensive as *Who's Who in America* is a monumental challenge. Over our long history, Marquis Who's Who researchers and editors have exercised diligent care in preparing each sketch for publication. Despite all precautions, however, errors do occasionally occur. Users of this directory are invited to notify the publisher of any such errors so that corrections can be made in a subsequent edition.

Board of Advisors

Marquis Who's Who gratefully acknowledges the following distinguished individuals who have made themselves available for review, evaluation, and general comment with regard to the publication of the Millennium Edition of *Who's Who in America*. The advisors have enhanced the reference value of this edition by the nomination of outstanding individuals for inclusion. However, the Board of Advisors, either collectively or individually, is in no way responsible for the selection of names appearing in this volume, nor does the Board of Advisors bear responsibility for the accuracy or comprehensiveness of the biographical information or other material contained herein.

Standards of Admission

The foremost consideration in determining who will be admitted to the pages of *Who's Who in America* is the extent of an individual's reference interest. Reference value is based on either of two factors: 1) the position of responsibility held or 2) the level of significant achievement attained in a career of noteworthy activity. The majority of Biographees qualify for admission on the basis of the first factor, a specific position of responsibility. Incumbency in the position makes the person someone of high reference interest. The factor of position includes the following categories:

1. High-ranking members of the executive, legislative, and judicial branches of the United States government. This group includes, for example, the President of the United States, members of Congress, cabinet secretaries, chief administrators of selected federal agencies and commissions, and justices of the federal courts.

2. Military officers on active duty with the rank of Major General or higher in the Army, Air Force, and Marine Corps, and of Rear Admiral or higher in the U.S. Navy.

3. Specified state government officials. Among these are governors, lieutenant governors, secretaries of state, attorneys general, and treasurers. Also included under this standard are presidents of state senates, state university system administrators, chief state health officers, and officials of American territories.

4. Judges of state and territorial courts of the highest appellate jurisdiction.

5. High-level officials of principal cities, based on population. These officials include mayors, police chiefs, school superintendents, and other selected positions.

6. Leading government officials of Canada and Mexico. In Canada, this group includes the prime minister, premiers of the provinces, ministers of departments of the federal government, and justices of the highest courts. Examples in the Mexican government are the president of the country and cabinet secretaries of the national government.

7. Principal officers of major national and international businesses as defined by several quantitative criteria.

8. Ranking administrative officials of major universities and colleges. Some of the officers included in this category are president, provost, dean, and selected department heads.

9. Heads of leading philanthropic, cultural, educational, professional, and scientific institutions and associations. These institutions include, for example, selected foundations, museums, symphony orchestras, libraries, and research laboratories.

10. Selected members of certain honorary and professional organizations, such as the National Academy of Sciences, the National Academy of Design, the American College of Trial Lawyers, and the Royal Society of Canada.

11. Chief ecclesiastics of the principal religious denominations.

12. Recipients of major national and international awards, such as the Nobel and Pulitzer Prizes, the Academy Awards and the Antoinette Perry, or Tony Awards. Also included are winners of important professional awards, such as the American Institute of Architecture's Gold Medal for Architecture.

Admission by the second factor—significant achievement—is based on the application of objective criteria established for each field. An artist whose works are included in major museums qualifies for admission for noteworthy accomplishment. The professor who has made important research contributions in his field is of reference interest because of his outstanding achievements. Qualitative standards determine eligibility for every field.

In many instances there is considerable overlap between the two factors used for inclusion in *Who's Who in America*. For example, the head of a major library is in the book because of position, but reaching that responsibility also signifies important achievement. Similarly, a state governor not only holds a position that warrants inclusion; attaining that post also represents significant achievement in the political world. In both cases, the reference value of the biographical sketch is significant. Whether the person has been selected because of position or as a mark of achievement, the Biographee in *Who's Who in America* has noteworthy accomplishments beyond those of the vast majority of contemporaries.

viii

Key to Information

[1] **GIBSON, OSCAR JULIUS, [2]** physician, medical educator; **[3]** b. Syracuse, N.Y., Aug. 31, 1937; **[4]** s. Paul Oliver and Elizabeth H. (Thrun) G.; **[5]** m. Judith S. Gonzalez, Apr. 28, 1968; **[6]** children: Richard Gary, Matthew Cary, Samuel Perry. **[7]** BA magna cum laude, U. Pa., 1960; MD, Harvard U., 1964. **[8]** Diplomate Am. Bd. Internal Medicine, Am. Bd. Preventive Medicine. **[9]** Intern Barnes Hosp., St. Louis, 1964-65, resident, 1965-66; clin. assoc. Nat. Heart Inst., NIH, Bethesda, Md., 1966-68; chief resident medicine U. Okla. Hosps., 1968-69; asst. prof. community health Okla. Med. Ctr., 1969-70, assoc. prof., 1970-74, prof., chmn. dept., 1974-80; dean U. Okla. Coll. Medicine, 1978-82; v.p. med. staff affairs Bapt. Med. Ctr., Oklahoma City, 1982-86, exec. v.p., 1986-88, chmn., 1988-95, chmn, CEO, 1995—; **[10]** mem. governing bd. Ambulatory Health Care Consortium, Inc., 1979-80; mem. Okla. Bd. Medicolegal Examiners, 1985—; mem. Okla. Bd. of Medical Ethics, 1994—. **[11]** Contrb. articles to profl. jours. **[12]** Bd. dirs., v.p. Okla. Arthritis Found., 1982—; trustee North Central Mental Health Ctr., 1985—. **[13]** Served with U.S. Army, 1955-56. **[14]** Recipient R.T. Chadwick award NIH, 1968; Am. Heart Assn. grantee, 1985-86, 88, 1995-96. **[15]** Fellow Assn. Tchrs. Preventive Medicine; mem. Am. Fedn. Clin. Research, Assn. Med. Colls., AAAS, AMA, Masons, Shriners, Sigma Xi. **[16]** Republican. **[17]** Roman Catholic. **[18]** Avocations: swimming, weight lifting, travel. **[19]** Home: 6060 N Ridge Ave Oklahoma City OK 73126 **[20]** Office: Bapt Med Ctr 1986 Cuba Hwy Oklahoma City OK 73120

KEY

- **[1]** Name
- **[2]** Occupation
- **[3]** Vital statistics
- **[4]** Parents
- **[5]** Marriage
- **[6]** Children
- **[7]** Education
- **[8]** Professional certifications
- **[9]** Career
- **[10]** Career-related
- **[11]** Writings and creative works
- **[12]** Civic and political activities
- **[13]** Military
- **[14]** Awards and fellowships
- **[15]** Professional and association memberships, clubs and lodges
- **[16]** Political affiliation
- **[17]** Religion
- **[18]** Avocations
- **[19]** Home address
- **[20]** Office address

Table of Abbreviations

The following abbreviations and symbols are frequently used in this book.

*An asterisk following a sketch indicates that it was researched by the Marquis Who's Who editorial staff and has not been verified by the Biographee.

A Associate (used with academic degrees only)

AA, A.A. Associate in Arts, Associate of Arts

AAAL American Academy of Arts and Letters

AAAS American Association for the Advancement of Science

AACD American Association for Counseling and Development

AACN American Association of Critical Care Nurses

AAHA American Academy of Health Administrators

AAHP American Association of Hospital Planners

AAHPERD American Alliance for Health, Physical Education, Recreation, and Dance

AAS Associate of Applied Science

AASL American Association of School Librarians

AASPA American Association of School Personnel Administrators

AAU Amateur Athletic Union

AAUP American Association of University Professors

AAUW American Association of University Women

AB, A.B. Arts, Bachelor of

AB Alberta

ABA American Bar Association

ABC American Broadcasting Company

AC Air Corps

acad. academy, academic

acct. accountant

acctg. accounting

ACDA Arms Control and Disarmament Agency

ACHA American College of Hospital Administrators

ACLS Advanced Cardiac Life Support

ACLU American Civil Liberties Union

ACOG American College of Ob-Gyn

ACP American College of Physicians

ACS American College of Surgeons

ADA American Dental Association

a.d.c. aide-de-camp

adj. adjunct, adjutant

adj. gen. adjutant general

adm. admiral

adminstr. administrator

adminstrn. administration

adminstrv. administrative

ADN Associate's Degree in Nursing

ADP Automatic Data Processing

adv. advocate, advisory

advt. advertising

AE, A.E. Agricultural Engineer

A.E. and P. Ambassador Extraordinary and Plenipotentiary

AEC Atomic Energy Commission

aero. aeronautical, aeronautic

aerodyn. aerodynamic

AFB Air Force Base

AFL-CIO American Federation of Labor and Congress of Industrial Organizations

AFTRA American Federation of TV and Radio Artists

AFSCME American Federation of State, County and Municipal Employees

agr. agriculture

agrl. agricultural

agt. agent

AGVA American Guild of Variety Artists

agy. agency

A&I Agricultural and Industrial

AIA American Institute of Architects

AIAA American Institute of Aeronautics and Astronautics

AIChE American Institute of Chemical Engineers

AICPA American Institute of Certified Public Accountants

AID Agency for International Development

AIDS Acquired Immune Deficiency Syndrome

AIEE American Institute of Electrical Engineers

AIM American Institute of Management

AIME American Institute of Mining, Metallurgy, and Petroleum Engineers

AK Alaska

AL Alabama

ALA American Library Association

Ala. Alabama

alt. alternate

Alta. Alberta

A&M Agricultural and Mechanical

AM, A.M. Arts, Master of

Am. American, America

AMA American Medical Association

amb. ambassador

A.M.E. African Methodist Episcopal

Amtrak National Railroad Passenger Corporation

AMVETS American Veterans of World War II, Korea, Vietnam

ANA American Nurses Association

anat. anatomical

ANCC American Nurses Credentialing Center

ann. annual

ANTA American National Theatre and Academy

anthrop. anthropological

AP Associated Press

APA American Psychological Association

APGA American Personnel Guidance Association

APHA American Public Health Association

APO Army Post Office

apptd. appointed

Apr. April

apt. apartment

AR Arkansas

ARC American Red Cross

arch. architect

archeol. archeological

archtl. architectural

Ariz. Arizona

Ark. Arkansas

ArtsD, ArtsD. Arts, Doctor of

arty. artillery

AS American Samoa

AS Associate in Science

ASCAP American Society of Composers, Authors and Publishers

ASCD Association for Supervision and Curriculum Development

ASCE American Society of Civil Engineers

ASHRAE American Society of Heating, Refrigeration, and Air Conditioning Engineers

ASME American Society of Mechanical Engineers

ASNSA American Society for Nursing Service Administrators

ASPA American Society for Public Administration

ASPCA American Society for the Prevention of Cruelty to Animals

assn. association

assoc. associate

asst. assistant

ASTD American Society for Training and Development

ASTM American Society for Testing and Materials

astron. astronomical

astrophys. astrophysical

ATLA Association of Trial Lawyers of America

ATSC Air Technical Service Command

AT&T American Telephone & Telegraph Company

atty. attorney

Aug. August

AUS Army of the United States

aux. auxiliary

Ave. Avenue

AVMA American Veterinary Medical Association

AZ Arizona

AWHONN Association of Women's Health Obstetric and Neonatal Nurses

B. Bachelor

b. born

BA, B.A. Bachelor of Arts

BAgr, B.Agr. Bachelor of Agriculture

Balt. Baltimore

Bapt. Baptist

BArch, B.Arch. Bachelor of Architecture

BAS, B.A.S. Bachelor of Agricultural Science

BBA, B.B.A. Bachelor of Business Administration

BBB Better Business Bureau

BBC British Broadcasting Corporation

BC, B.C. British Columbia
BCE, B.C.E. Bachelor of Civil Engineering
BChir, B.Chir. Bachelor of Surgery
BCL, B.C.L. Bachelor of Civil Law
BCLS Basic Cardiac Life Support
BCS, B.C.S. Bachelor of Commercial
    Science
BD, B.D. Bachelor of Divinity
bd. board
BE, B.E. Bachelor of Education
BEE, B.E.E. Bachelor of Electrical
    Engineering
BFA, B.F.A. Bachelor of Fine Arts
bibl. biblical
bibliog. bibliographical
biog. biographical
biol. biological
BJ, B.J. Bachelor of Journalism
Bklyn. Brooklyn
BL, B.L. Bachelor of Letters
bldg. building
BLS, B.L.S. Bachelor of Library Science
BLS Basic Life Support
Blvd. Boulevard
BMI Broadcast Music, Inc.
BMW Bavarian Motor Works (Bayerische
    Motoren Werke)
bn. battalion
B.&O.R.R. Baltimore & Ohio Railroad
bot. botanical
BPE, B.P.E. Bachelor of Physical Education
BPhil, B.Phil. Bachelor of Philosophy
br. branch
BRE, B.R.E. Bachelor of Religious
    Education
brig. gen. brigadier general
Brit. British, Brittanica
Bros. Brothers
BS, B.S. Bachelor of Science
BSA, B.S.A. Bachelor of Agricultural Science
BSBA Bachelor of Science in Business
    Administration
BSChemE Bachelor of Science in Chemical
    Engineering
BSD, B.S.D. Bachelor of Didactic Science
BSEE Bachelor of Science in Electrical
    Engineering
BSN Bachelor of Science in Nursing
BST, B.S.T. Bachelor of Sacred Theology
BTh, B.Th. Bachelor of Theology
bull. bulletin
bur. bureau
bus. business
B.W.I. British West Indies

CA California
CAA Civil Aeronautics Administration
CAB Civil Aeronautics Board
CAD-CAM Computer Aided
    Design–Computer Aided Model
Calif. California
C.Am. Central America
Can. Canada, Canadian
CAP Civil Air Patrol
capt. captain
cardiol. cardiological
cardiovasc. cardiovascular
CARE Cooperative American Relief
    Everywhere
Cath. Catholic
cav. cavalry
CBC Canadian Broadcasting Company
CBI China, Burma, India Theatre of
    Operations
CBS Columbia Broadcasting Company
C.C. Community College
CCC Commodity Credit Corporation

CCNY City College of New York
CCRN Critical Care Registered Nurse
CCU Cardiac Care Unit
CD Civil Defense
CE, C.E. Corps of Engineers, Civil Engineer
CEN Certified Emergency Nurse
CENTO Central Treaty Organization
CEO chief executive officer
CERN European Organization of Nuclear
    Research
cert. certificate, certification, certified
CETA Comprehensive Employment Training
    Act
CFA Chartered Financial Analyst
CFL Canadian Football League
CFO chief financial officer
CFP Certified Financial Planner
ch. church
ChD, Ch.D. Doctor of Chemistry
chem. chemical
ChemE, Chem.E. Chemical Engineer
ChFC Chartered Financial Consultant
Chgo. Chicago
chirurg. chirurgical
chmn. chairman
chpt. chapter
CIA Central Intelligence Agency
Cin. Cincinnati
cir. circle, circuit
CLE Continuing Legal Education
Cleve. Cleveland
climatol. climatological
clin. clinical
clk. clerk
C.L.U. Chartered Life Underwriter
CM, C.M. Master in Surgery
CM Northern Mariana Islands
CMA Certified Medical Assistant
cmty. community
CNA Certified Nurse's Aide
CNOR Certified Nurse (Operating Room)
C.&N.W.Ry. Chicago & North Western
    Railway
CO Colorado
Co. Company
COF Catholic Order of Foresters
C. of C. Chamber of Commerce
col. colonel
coll. college
Colo. Colorado
com. committee
comd. commanded
comdg. commanding
comdr. commander
comdt. commandant
comm. communications
commd. commissioned
comml. commercial
commn. commission
commr. commissioner
compt. comptroller
condr. conductor
Conf. Conference
Congl. Congregational, Congressional
Conglist. Congregationalist
Conn. Connecticut
cons. consultant, consulting
consol. consolidated
constl. constitutional
constn. constitution
constrn. construction
contbd. contributed
contbg. contributing
contbn. contribution
contbr. contributor
contr. controller
Conv. Convention

COO chief operating officer
coop. cooperative
coord. coordinator
CORDS Civil Operations and Revolutionary
    Development Support
CORE Congress of Racial Equality
corp. corporation, corporate
corr. correspondent, corresponding,
    correspondence
C.&O.Ry. Chesapeake & Ohio Railway
coun. council
CPA Certified Public Accountant
CPCU Chartered Property and Casualty
    Underwriter
CPH, C.P.H. Certificate of Public Health
cpl. corporal
CPR Cardio-Pulmonary Resuscitation
C.P.Ry. Canadian Pacific Railway
CRT Cathode Ray Terminal
C.S. Christian Science
CSB, C.S.B. Bachelor of Christian Science
C.S.C. Civil Service Commission
CT Connecticut
ct. court
ctr. center
ctrl. central
CWS Chemical Warfare Service
C.Z. Canal Zone

D. Doctor
d. daughter
DAgr, D.Agr. Doctor of Agriculture
DAR Daughters of the American Revolution
dau. daughter
DAV Disabled American Veterans
DC, D.C. District of Columbia
DCL, D.C.L. Doctor of Civil Law
DCS, D.C.S. Doctor of Commercial Science
DD, D.D. Doctor of Divinity
DDS, D.D.S. Doctor of Dental Surgery
DE Delaware
Dec. December
dec. deceased
def. defense
Del. Delaware
del. delegate, delegation
Dem. Democrat, Democratic
DEng, D.Eng. Doctor of Engineering
denom. denomination, denominational
dep. deputy
dept. department
dermatol. dermatological
desc. descendant
devel. development, developmental
DFA, D.F.A. Doctor of Fine Arts
D.F.C. Distinguished Flying Cross
DHL, D.H.L. Doctor of Hebrew Literature
dir. director
dist. district
distbg. distributing
distbn. distribution
distbr. distributor
disting. distinguished
div. division, divinity, divorce
divsn. division
DLitt, D.Litt. Doctor of Literature
DMD, D.M.D. Doctor of Dental Medicine
DMS, D.M.S. Doctor of Medical Science
DO, D.O. Doctor of Osteopathy
docs. documents
DON Director of Nursing
DPH, D.P.H. Diploma in Public Health
DPhil, D.Phil. Doctor of Philosophy
D.R. Daughters of the Revolution
Dr. Drive, Doctor
DRE, D.R.E. Doctor of Religious Education
DrPH, Dr.P.H. Doctor of Public Health,
    Doctor of Public Hygiene

D.S.C. Distinguished Service Cross
DSc, D.Sc. Doctor of Science
DSChemE Doctor of Science in Chemical
    Engineering
D.S.M. Distinguished Service Medal
DST, D.S.T. Doctor of Sacred Theology
DTM, D.T.M. Doctor of Tropical Medicine
DVM, D.V.M. Doctor of Veterinary Medicine
DVS, D.V.S. Doctor of Veterinary Surgery

E, E. East
ea. eastern
E. and P. Extraordinary and Plenipotentiary
Eccles. Ecclesiastical
ecol. ecological
econ. economic
ECOSOC Economic and Social Council (of
    the UN)
ED, E.D. Doctor of Engineering
ed. educated
EdB, Ed.B. Bachelor of Education
EdD, Ed.D. Doctor of Education
edit. edition
editl. editorial
EdM, Ed.M. Master of Education
edn. education
ednl. educational
EDP Electronic Data Processing
EdS, Ed.S. Specialist in Education
EE, E.E. Electrical Engineer
E.E. and M.P. Envoy Extraordinary and
    Minister Plenipotentiary
EEC European Economic Community
EEG Electroencephalogram
EEO Equal Employment Opportunity
EEOC Equal Employment Opportunity
    Commission
E.Ger. German Democratic Republic
EKG Electrocardiogram
elec. electrical
electrochem. electrochemical
electrophys. electrophysical
elem. elementary
EM, E.M. Engineer of Mines
EMT Emergency Medical Technician
ency. encyclopedia
Eng. England
engr. engineer
engring. engineering
entomol. entomological
environ. environmental
EPA Environmental Protection Agency
epidemiol. epidemiological
Episc. Episcopalian
ERA Equal Rights Amendment
ERDA Energy Research and Development
    Administration
ESEA Elementary and Secondary Education
    Act
ESL English as Second Language
ESPN Entertainment and Sports
    Programming Network
ESSA Environmental Science Services
    Administration
ethnol. ethnological
ETO European Theatre of Operations
Evang. Evangelical
exam. examination, examining
Exch. Exchange
exec. executive
exhbn. exhibition
expdn. expedition
expn. exposition
expt. experiment
exptl. experimental
Expy. Expressway
Ext. Extension

F.A. Field Artillery
FAA Federal Aviation Administration
FAO Food and Agriculture Organization (of
    the UN)
FBA Federal Bar Association
FBI Federal Bureau of Investigation
FCA Farm Credit Administration
FCC Federal Communications Commission
FCDA Federal Civil Defense Administration
FDA Food and Drug Administration
FDIA Federal Deposit Insurance
    Administration
FDIC Federal Deposit Insurance Corporation
FE, F.E. Forest Engineer
FEA Federal Energy Administration
Feb. February
fed. federal
fedn. federation
FERC Federal Energy Regulatory
    Commission
fgn. foreign
FHA Federal Housing Administration
fin. financial, finance
FL Florida
Fl. Floor
Fla. Florida
FMC Federal Maritime Commission
FNP Family Nurse Practitioner
FOA Foreign Operations Administration
found. foundation
FPC Federal Power Commission
FPO Fleet Post Office
frat. fraternity
FRS Federal Reserve System
FSA Federal Security Agency
Ft. Fort
FTC Federal Trade Commission
Fwy. Freeway

G-1 (or other number) Division of General
    Staff
GA, Ga. Georgia
GAO General Accounting Office
gastroent. gastroenterological
GATE Gifted and Talented Educators
GATT General Agreement on Tariffs and
    Trade
GE General Electric Company
gen. general
geneal. genealogical
geod. geodetic
geog. geographic, geographical
geol. geological
geophys. geophysical
geriat. geriatrics
gerontol. gerontological
G.H.Q. General Headquarters
GM General Motors Corporation
GMAC General Motors Acceptance
    Corporation
G.N.Ry. Great Northern Railway
gov. governor
govt. government
govtl. governmental
GPO Government Printing Office
grad. graduate, graduated
GSA General Services Administration
Gt. Great
GTE General Telephone and
    ElectricCompany
GU Guam
gynecol. gynecological

HBO Home Box Office
hdqs. headquarters

HEW Department of Health, Education and
    Welfare
HHD, H.H.D. Doctor of Humanities
HHFA Housing and Home Finance Agency
HHS Department of Health and Human
    Services
HI Hawaii
hist. historical, historic
HM, H.M. Master of Humanities
HMO Health Maintenance Organization
homeo. homeopathic
hon. honorary, honorable
Ho. of Dels. House of Delegates
Ho. of Reps. House of Representatives
hort. horticultural
hosp. hospital
H.S. High School
HUD Department of Housing and Urban
    Development
Hwy. Highway
hydrog. hydrographic

IA Iowa
IAEA International Atomic Energy Agency
IATSE International Alliance of Theatrical
    and Stage Employees and Moving Picture
    Operators of the United States and Canada
IBM International Business Machines
    Corporation
IBRD International Bank for Reconstruction
    and Development
ICA International Cooperation
    Administration
ICC Interstate Commerce Commission
ICCE International Council for Computers in
    Education
ICU Intensive Care Unit
ID Idaho
IEEE Institute of Electrical and Electronics
    Engineers
IFC International Finance Corporation
IGY International Geophysical Year
IL Illinois
Ill. Illinois
illus. illustrated
ILO International Labor Organization
IMF International Monetary Fund
IN Indiana
Inc. Incorporated
Ind. Indiana
ind. independent
Indpls. Indianapolis
indsl. industrial
inf. infantry
info. information
ins. insurance
insp. inspector
insp. gen. inspector general
inst. institute
instl. institutional
instn. institution
instr. instructor
instrn. instruction
instrnl. instructional
internat. international
intro. introduction
IRE Institute of Radio Engineers
IRS Internal Revenue Service
ITT International Telephone & Telegraph
    Corporation

JAG Judge Advocate General
JAGC Judge Advocate General Corps
Jan. January
Jaycees Junior Chamber of Commerce
JB, J.B. Jurum Baccalaureus

JCB, J.C.B. Juris Canoni Baccalaureus
JCD, J.C.D. Juris Canonici Doctor, Juris Civilis Doctor
JCL, J.C.L. Juris Canonici Licentiatus
JD, J.D. Juris Doctor
jg. junior grade
jour. journal
jr. junior
JSD, J.S.D. Juris Scientiae Doctor
JUD, J.U.D. Juris Utriusque Doctor
jud. judicial

Kans. Kansas
K.C. Knights of Columbus
K.P. Knights of Pythias
KS Kansas
K.T. Knight Templar
KY, Ky. Kentucky

LA, La. Louisiana
L.A. Los Angeles
lab. laboratory
L.Am. Latin America
lang. language
laryngol. laryngological
LB Labrador
LDS Latter Day Saints
LDS Church Church of Jesus Christ of Latter Day Saints
lectr. lecturer
legis. legislation, legislative
LHD, L.H.D. Doctor of Humane Letters
L.I. Long Island
libr. librarian, library
lic. licensed, license
L.I.R.R. Long Island Railroad
lit. literature
litig. litigation
LittB, Litt.B. Bachelor of Letters
LittD, Litt.D. Doctor of Letters
LLB, LL.B. Bachelor of Laws
LLD, L.L.D. Doctor of Laws
LLM, L.L.M. Master of Laws
Ln. Lane
L.&N.R.R. Louisville & Nashville Railroad
LPGA Ladies Professional Golf Association
LPN Licensed Practical Nurse
LS, L.S. Library Science (in degree)
lt. lieutenant
Ltd. Limited
Luth. Lutheran
LWV League of Women Voters

M. Master
m. married
MA, M.A. Master of Arts
MA Massachusetts
MADD Mothers Against Drunk Driving
mag. magazine
MAgr, M.Agr. Master of Agriculture
maj. major
Man. Manitoba
Mar. March
MArch, M.Arch. Master in Architecture
Mass. Massachusetts
math. mathematics, mathematical
MATS Military Air Transport Service
MB, M.B. Bachelor of Medicine
MB Manitoba
MBA, M.B.A. Master of Business Administration
MBS Mutual Broadcasting System
M.C. Medical Corps
MCE, M.C.E. Master of Civil Engineering
mcht. merchant
mcpl. municipal
MCS, M.C.S. Master of Commercial Science

MD, M.D. Doctor of Medicine
MD, Md. Maryland
MDiv Master of Divinity
MDip, M.Dip. Master in Diplomacy
mdse. merchandise
MDV, M.D.V. Doctor of Veterinary Medicine
ME, M.E. Mechanical Engineer
ME Maine
M.E.Ch. Methodist Episcopal Church
mech. mechanical
MEd., M.Ed. Master of Education
med. medical
MEE, M.E.E. Master of Electrical Engineering
mem. member
meml. memorial
merc. mercantile
met. metropolitan
metall. metallurgical
MetE, Met.E. Metallurgical Engineer
meteorol. meteorological
Meth. Methodist
Mex. Mexico
MF, M.F. Master of Forestry
MFA, M.F.A. Master of Fine Arts
mfg. manufacturing
mfr. manufacturer
mgmt. management
mgr. manager
MHA, M.H.A. Master of Hospital Administration
M.I. Military Intelligence
MI Michigan
Mich. Michigan
micros. microscopic, microscopical
mid. middle
mil. military
Milw. Milwaukee
Min. Minister
mineral. mineralogical
Minn. Minnesota
MIS Management Information Systems
Miss. Mississippi
MIT Massachusetts Institute of Technology
mktg. marketing
ML, M.L. Master of Laws
MLA Modern Language Association
M.L.D. Magister Legnum Diplomatic
MLitt, M.Litt. Master of Literature, Master of Letters
MLS, M.L.S. Master of Library Science
MME, M.M.E. Master of Mechanical Engineering
MN Minnesota
mng. managing
MO, Mo. Missouri
moblzn. mobilization
Mont. Montana
MP Northern Mariana Islands
M.P. Member of Parliament
MPA Master of Public Administration
MPE, M.P.E. Master of Physical Education
MPH, M.P.H. Master of Public Health
MPhil, M.Phil. Master of Philosophy
MPL, M.P.L. Master of Patent Law
Mpls. Minneapolis
MRE, M.R.E. Master of Religious Education
MRI Magnetic Resonance Imaging
MS, M.S. Master of Science
MS, Ms. Mississippi
MSc, M.Sc. Master of Science
MSChemE Master of Science in Chemical Engineering
MSEE Master of Science in Electrical Engineering

MSF, M.S.F. Master of Science of Forestry
MSN Master of Science in Nursing
MST, M.S.T. Master of Sacred Theology
MSW, M.S.W. Master of Social Work
MT Montana
Mt. Mount
MTO Mediterranean Theatre of Operation
MTV Music Television
mus. museum, musical
MusB, Mus.B. Bachelor of Music
MusD, Mus.D. Doctor of Music
MusM, Mus.M. Master of Music
mut. mutual
MVP Most Valuable Player
mycol. mycological

N. North
NAACOG Nurses Association of the American College of Obstetricians and Gynecologists
NAACP National Association for the Advancement of Colored People
NACA National Advisory Committee for Aeronautics
NACDL National Association of Criminal Defense Lawyers
NACU National Association of Colleges and Universities
NAD National Academy of Design
NAE National Academy of Engineering, National Association of Educators
NAESP National Association of Elementary School Principals
NAFE National Association of Female Executives
N.Am. North America
NAM National Association of Manufacturers
NAMH National Association for Mental Health
NAPA National Association of Performing Artists
NARAS National Academy of Recording Arts and Sciences
NAREB National Association of Real Estate Boards
NARS National Archives and Record Service
NAS National Academy of Sciences
NASA National Aeronautics and Space Administration
NASP National Association of School Psychologists
NASW National Association of Social Workers
nat. national
NATAS National Academy of Television Arts and Sciences
NATO North Atlantic Treaty Organization
NATOUSA North African Theatre of Operations, United States Army
nav. navigation
NB, N.B. New Brunswick
NBA National Basketball Association
NBC National Broadcasting Company
NC, N.C. North Carolina
NCAA National College Athletic Association
NCCJ National Conference of Christians and Jews
ND, N.D. North Dakota
NDEA National Defense Education Act
NE Nebraska
NE, N.E. Northeast
NEA National Education Association
Nebr. Nebraska
NEH National Endowment for Humanities
neurol. neurological
Nev. Nevada
NF Newfoundland

NFL National Football League
Nfld. Newfoundland
NG National Guard
NH, N.H. New Hampshire
NHL National Hockey League
NIH National Institutes of Health
NIMH National Institute of Mental Health
NJ, N.J. New Jersey
NLRB National Labor Relations Board
NM New Mexico
N.Mex. New Mexico
No. Northern
NOAA National Oceanographic and
    Atmospheric Administration
NORAD North America Air Defense
Nov. November
NOW National Organization for Women
N.P.Ry. Northern Pacific Railway
nr. near
NRA National Rifle Association
NRC National Research Council
NS, N.S. Nova Scotia
NSC National Security Council
NSF National Science Foundation
NSTA National Science Teachers Association
NSW New South Wales
N.T. New Testament
NT Northwest Territories
nuc. nuclear
numis. numismatic
NV Nevada
NW, N.W. Northwest
N.W.T. Northwest Territories
NY, N.Y. New York
N.Y.C. New York City
NYU New York University
N.Z. New Zealand

OAS Organization of American States
ob-gyn obstetrics-gynecology
obs. observatory
obstet. obstetrical
occupl. occupational
oceanog. oceanographic
Oct. October
OD, O.D. Doctor of Optometry
OECD Organization for Economic
    Cooperation and Development
OEEC Organization of European Economic
    Cooperation
OEO Office of Economic Opportunity
ofcl. official
OH Ohio
OK Oklahoma
Okla. Oklahoma
ON Ontario
Ont. Ontario
oper. operating
ophthal. ophthalmological
ops. operations
OR Oregon
orch. orchestra
Oreg. Oregon
orgn. organization
orgnl. organizational
ornithol. ornithological
orthop. orthopedic
OSHA Occupational Safety and Health
    Administration
OSRD Office of Scientific Research and
    Development
OSS Office of Strategic Services
osteo. osteopathic
otol. otological
otolaryn. otolaryngological

PA, Pa. Pennsylvania

P.A. Professional Association
paleontol. paleontological
path. pathological
PBS Public Broadcasting System
P.C. Professional Corporation
PE Prince Edward Island
pediat. pediatrics
P.E.I. Prince Edward Island
PEN Poets, Playwrights, Editors, Essayists
    and Novelists (international association)
penol. penological
P.E.O. women's organization (full name not
    disclosed)
pers. personnel
pfc. private first class
PGA Professional Golfers' Association of
    America
PHA Public Housing Administration
pharm. pharmaceutical
PharmD, Pharm.D. Doctor of Pharmacy
PharmM, Pharm.M. Master of Pharmacy
PhB, Ph.B. Bachelor of Philosophy
PhD, Ph.D. Doctor of Philosophy
PhDChemE Doctor of Science in Chemical
    Engineering
PhM, Ph.M. Master of Philosophy
Phila. Philadelphia
philharm. philharmonic
philol. philological
philos. philosophical
photog. photographic
phys. physical
physiol. physiological
Pitts. Pittsburgh
Pk. Park
Pky. Parkway
Pl. Place
P.&L.E.R.R. Pittsburgh & Lake Erie
    Railroad
Plz. Plaza
PNP Pediatric Nurse Practitioner
P.O. Post Office
PO Box Post Office Box
polit. political
poly. polytechnic, polytechnical
PQ Province of Quebec
PR, P.R. Puerto Rico
prep. preparatory
pres. president
Presbyn. Presbyterian
presdl. presidential
prin. principal
procs. proceedings
prod. produced (play production)
prodn. production
prodr. producer
prof. professor
profl. professional
prog. progressive
propr. proprietor
pros. atty. prosecuting attorney
pro tem. pro tempore
PSRO Professional Services Review
    Organization
psychiat. psychiatric
psychol. psychological
PTA Parent-Teachers Association
ptnr. partner
PTO Pacific Theatre of Operations, Parent
    Teacher Organization
pub. publisher, publishing, published
pub. public
publ. publication
pvt. private

quar. quarterly
qm. quartermaster

Q.M.C. Quartermaster Corps
Que. Quebec

radiol. radiological
RAF Royal Air Force
RCA Radio Corporation of America
RCAF Royal Canadian Air Force
RD Rural Delivery
Rd. Road
R&D Research & Development
REA Rural Electrification Administration
rec. recording
ref. reformed
regt. regiment
regtl. regimental
rehab. rehabilitation
rels. relations
Rep. Republican
rep. representative
Res. Reserve
ret. retired
Rev. Reverend
rev. review, revised
RFC Reconstruction Finance Corporation
RFD Rural Free Delivery
rhinol. rhinological
RI, R.I. Rhode Island
RISD Rhode Island School of Design
Rlwy. Railway
Rm. Room
RN, R.N. Registered Nurse
roentgenol. roentgenological
ROTC Reserve Officers Training Corps
RR Rural Route
R.R. Railroad
rsch. research
rschr. researcher
Rt. Route

S. South
s. son
SAC Strategic Air Command
SAG Screen Actors Guild
SALT Strategic Arms Limitation Talks
S.Am. South America
san. sanitary
SAR Sons of the American Revolution
Sask. Saskatchewan
savs. savings
SB, S.B. Bachelor of Science
SBA Small Business Administration
SC, S.C. South Carolina
SCAP Supreme Command Allies Pacific
ScB, Sc.B. Bachelor of Science
SCD, S.C.D. Doctor of Commercial Science
ScD, Sc.D. Doctor of Science
sch. school
sci. science, scientific
SCLC Southern Christian Leadership
Conference
SCV Sons of Confederate Veterans
SD, S.D. South Dakota
SE, S.E. Southeast
SEATO Southeast Asia Treaty Organization
SEC Securities and Exchange Commission
sec. secretary
sect. section
seismol. seismological
sem. seminary
Sept. September
s.g. senior grade
sgt. sergeant
SHAEF Supreme Headquarters Allied
    Expeditionary Forces
SHAPE Supreme Headquarters Allied Powers
    in Europe
S.I. Staten Island

S.J. Society of Jesus (Jesuit)
SJD Scientiae Juridicae Doctor
SK Saskatchewan
SM, S.M. Master of Science
SNP Society of Nursing Professionals
So. Southern
soc. society
sociol. sociological
S.P.Co. Southern Pacific Company
spkr. speaker
spl. special
splty. specialty
Sq. Square
S.R. Sons of the Revolution
sr. senior
SS Steamship
SSS Selective Service System
St. Saint, Street
sta. station
stats. statistics
statis. statistical
STB, S.T.B. Bachelor of Sacred Theology
stblzn. stabilization
STD, S.T.D. Doctor of Sacred Theology
std. standard
Ste. Suite
subs. subsidiary
SUNY State University of New York
supr. supervisor
supt. superintendent
surg. surgical
svc. service
SW, S.W. Southwest
sys. system

TAPPI Technical Association of the Pulp and Paper Industry
tb. tuberculosis
tchg. teaching
tchr. teacher
tech. technical, technology
technol. technological
tel. telephone
Tel. & Tel. Telephone & Telegraph
telecom. telecommunications
temp. temporary
Tenn. Tennessee
Ter. Territory
Ter. Terrace
TESOL Teachers of English to Speakers of Other Languages
Tex. Texas
ThD, Th.D. Doctor of Theology
theol. theological

ThM, Th.M. Master of Theology
TN Tennessee
tng. training
topog. topographical
trans. transaction, transferred
transl. translation, translated
transp. transportation
treas. treasurer
TT Trust Territory
TV television
TVA Tennessee Valley Authority
TWA Trans World Airlines
twp. township
TX Texas
typog. typographical

U. University
UAW United Auto Workers
UCLA University of California at Los Angeles
UDC United Daughters of the Confederacy
U.K. United Kingdom
UN United Nations
UNESCO United Nations Educational, Scientific and Cultural Organization
UNICEF United Nations International Children's Emergency Fund
univ. university
UNRRA United Nations Relief and Rehabilitation Administration
UPI United Press International
U.P.R.R. United Pacific Railroad
urol. urological
U.S. United States
U.S.A. United States of America
USAAF United States Army Air Force
USAF United States Air Force
USAFR United States Air Force Reserve
USAR United States Army Reserve
USCG United States Coast Guard
USCGR United States Coast Guard Reserve
USES United States Employment Service
USIA United States Information Agency
USMC United States Marine Corps
USMCR United States Marine Corps Reserve
USN United States Navy
USNG United States National Guard
USNR United States Naval Reserve
USO United Service Organizations
USPHS United States Public Health Service
USS United States Ship
USSR Union of the Soviet Socialist Republics
USTA United States Tennis Association

USV United States Volunteers
UT Utah

VA Veterans Administration
VA, Va. Virginia
vet. veteran, veterinary
VFW Veterans of Foreign Wars
VI, V.I. Virgin Islands
vice pres. vice president
vis. visiting
VISTA Volunteers in Service to America
VITA Volunteers in Technical Assistance
vocat. vocational
vol. volunteer, volume
v.p. vice president
vs. versus
VT, Vt. Vermont

W, W. West
WA Washington (state)
WAC Women's Army Corps
Wash. Washington (state)
WATS Wide Area Telecommunications Service
WAVES Women's Reserve, US Naval Reserve
WCTU Women's Christian Temperance Union
we. western
W. Ger. Germany, Federal Republic of
WHO World Health Organization
WI Wisconsin
W.I. West Indies
Wis. Wisconsin
WSB Wage Stabilization Board
WV West Virginia
W.Va. West Virginia
WWI World War I
WWII World War II
WY Wyoming
Wyo. Wyoming

YK Yukon Territory
YMCA Young Men's Christian Association
YMHA Young Men's Hebrew Association
YM & YWHA Young Men's and Young Women's Hebrew Association
yr. year
YT, Y.T. Yukon Territory
YWCA Young Women's Christian Association

zool. zoological

Alphabetical Practices

Names are arranged alphabetically according to the surnames, and under identical surnames according to the first given name. If both surname and first given name are identical, names are arranged alphabetically according to the second given name.

Surnames beginning with De, Des, Du, however capitalized or spaced, are recorded with the prefix preceding the surname and arranged alphabetically under the letter D.

Surnames beginning with Mac and Mc are arranged alphabetically under M.

Surnames beginning with Saint or St. appear after names that begin Sains, and are arranged according to the second part of the name, e.g. St. Clair before Saint Dennis.

Surnames beginning with Van, Von, or von are arranged alphabetically under the letter V.

Compound surnames are arranged according to the first member of the compound.

Many hyphenated Arabic names begin Al-, El-, or al-. These names are alphabetized according to each Biographee's designation of last name. Thus Al-Bahar, Neta may be listed either under Al- or under Bahar, depending on the preference of the listee.

Also, Arabic names have a variety of possible spellings when transposed to English. Spelling of these names is always based on the practice of the Biographee. Some Biographees use a Western form of word order, while others prefer the Arabic word sequence.

Similarly, Asian names may have no comma between family and given names, but some Biographees have chosen to add the comma. In each case, punctuation follows the preference of the Biographee.

Parentheses used in connection with a name indicate which part of the full name is usually deleted in common usage. Hence Chambers, E(lizabeth) Anne indicates that the usual form of the given name is E. Anne. In such a case, the parentheses are ignored in alphabetizing and the name would be arranged as Chambers, Elizabeth Anne. However, if the name is recorded Chambers, (Elizabeth) Anne, signifying that the entire name Elizabeth is not commonly used, the alphabetizing would be arranged as though the name were Chambers, Anne. If an entire middle or last name is enclosed in parentheses, that portion of the name is used in the alphabetical arrangement. Hence Chambers, Elizabeth (Anne) would be arranged as Chambers, Elizabeth Anne.

Where more than one spelling, word order, or name of an individual is frequently encountered, the sketch has been entered under the form preferred by the Biographee, with cross-references under alternate forms.

Who'sWho in America®

Biographies A–K

AABERG, THOMAS MARSHALL, SR., academic administrator, ophthalmology educator; b. St. Paul, Sept. 5, 1936; m. Judith S. Young, June 17, 1961; children: Thomas M. Jr., Leigh, Sarah. BA, Dartmouth Coll., 1958, MS, 1959; MD, Harvard U., 1961; MS in Preventative Medicine, U. Okla., 1968. Diplomate Am. Bd. Ophthalmology. Asst. prof. ophthalmology Med. Coll. Wis., Milw., 1969-71, assoc. prof. ophthalmology, 1971-76, prof. ophthalmology, 1976-88; chmn. dept. ophthalmology Sch. Medicine Emory U., Atlanta, 1988—. Surgeon USPHS, 1966-68. Office: Emory Eye Ctr Ste B 4405 1365 Clifton Rd NE Atlanta GA 30322-1013

AADLAND, THOMAS VERNON, minister; b. Mpls., Dec. 24, 1950; s. Otto Sidney and Dorothy Jean (Holmquist) A.; m. Mary Joanne Pratt, June 27, 1981; children: Evangeline Faith, Brigitta Hope, Andrew Paul, Marian Joy. AB in Philosophy, Wheaton Coll., 1973; MDiv, Luther Theol. Sem., 1980. Ordained to ministry Am. Luth. Ch., 1980. Assoc. pastor Christ Luth. Ch., Duluth, Minn., 1980-91, sr. pastor, 1991—; sec. Am. Assn. Luth. Chs., Mpls., 1987-93; min. Christ. Luth. Ch., 1981—. Presiding pastor, Amer. Assn. of Lutheran Chs., 1999—, bd. dirs. Lake Superior Life Care Ctr., Duluth, Minn., 1987-90, pres. Lake Superior Chap., Lutherans for Life, 1996—. Home: 2409 Ensign St Duluth MN 55811-2927 Office: Christ Luth Ch 2415 Ensign St Duluth MN 55811-2927 *I believe Americans cannot escape the religous question. The enjoyment of our freedoms—in some vitally important sense—depends upon a humble and grateful recognition that the source of our fundamental rights to life, liberty and property is transcendent: they derive not from the generosity of the State but from the magnanimity of God, in Whose image we are created.*

AADNESEN, CHRISTOPHER, railroad company executive, consultant; b. Salt Lake City, Nov. 2, 1948; s. Grant C. and Helen Jane (Ray) A.; m. Helen Elizabeth Twelves, Aug. 14, 1973 (div. 1988); children: Aric Paul, Brian James, Nicholas Twelves; m. Betty Jean DeLeon, Aug. 19, 1988; children: Brooke Bingham, Brad Bingham. BA in English, U. Utah, 1971, MBA, 1973; PMD, Harvard U., 1990. Gen. mgr. and founder Thaddeus Duncan Co., Salt Lake City, 1968-72; divsn. supt. Western Pacific R.R., Sacramento, 1978-82; gen. supt. of transp. Mo. Pacific R.R., Spring, Tex., 1983-84; asst. gen. mgr. So. Region Union Pacific R.R., Spring, Tex., 1984-88; gen. dir. pers. svcs. Union Pacific R.R., Omaha, 1988-89, asst. v.p. ops. adminstrn., 1989-90, asst. v.p. employee devel. and involvement, 1990-91, sr. asst. v.p. field ops., 1992-93, sr. asst. v.p. transp., 1993-95, pres. captiol city group, pres. capitol city mgmt. assocs., 1996—; chief oper. officer Transp. Ferroviara Mexicana, S.A. de C.V., 1996-99, exec. v.p., 1999—; bd. dirs. Brownsville and Matamoros Bridge Co., Brownsville, Tex., 1992-95. Campaign mgr. County Commr., Quincy, Calif., 1978. With USN, 1967-69. Mem. Am. Assn. R.R. Supts., Field Club of Omaha, Happy Hollow Country Club, Berry Creek Country Club, Greater Austin C. of C., Round Rock C. of C., Georgetown C. of C., Beta Theta Pi. Republican. Episcopalian. Avocations: guitar, piano, golf, fishing, bowling. Home: 30205 Oak Tree Dr Georgetown TX 78628-1143 Office: The Capitol City Group 3007 Dawn Dr Ste 10403 Georgetown TX 78628 also: TFM SA de CV, Av Manuel C Barragan, 4850 Norte Col Hidalgo, Monterrey Mexico

AALFS, JANET ELIZABETH, poet, writer, martial arts educator; b. Elmira, N.Y., Aug. 14, 1956; d. John Linden and Joanne Elizabeth (Wilkinson) A.; life ptnr. Janis A. Totty. BA, U. Mass., 1979; MFA in Poetry, Sarah Lawrence Coll., 1990. Dir., head instr. Valley Women's Martial Arts, Easthompton, Mass., 1982—; founder, mem. Orogeny Press; instr. self-def. video Fighting Back, Fighting Forward, 1995 (Mass. Cmty. TV award). Author: (poetry) Against the Odds, 1992, Full Open, 1996; contbr. poems to various lit. publs. Mem. organizing com. Undoing Racism Workshops, Northampton, Mass., 1995—; self-def. instr., social change activist for numerous social and civic orgns., including youth, elders, disabled on local, nat. and internat. level, 1980—; cons., self-def. instr. Girl Scouts U.S.A., 1996. Named One of 125 Alumni To watch, U. Mass.; recipient Woman of Distinction award Girl Scouts U.S.A., 1996. Mem. Nat. Women's Martial Arts Fedn. (founder), Valley Lesbian Writing Group (founder). Avocations: karate (4th degree black belt), hiking, swimming, cross-country skiing, knot tying. Office: Valley Women's Martial Arts Inc PO Box 1064 One Cottage St Easthampton MA 01027

AALL, CHRISTIAN BERGENGREN, software company executive; b. St. Louis, Dec. 7, 1955; s. Christian Hiorth Aall and Ruth (Bergengren) Perkins; m. Esther Drugowitsch, Aug. 5, 1983; children: Christian Daniel, Nathalie Caroline. MME, Swiss Fed. Inst. Tech., Zürich, Switzerland, 1980; MBA, Internat. Mgmt. Devel. Inst., Lausanne, Switzerland, 1987. Project mgr. Cementos Apasco S.A., Apasco, Mex., 1981-82; cons. Holderbank (Switzerland) Mgmt. & Cons. Ltd., 1982-86; mgr. systems and strategic planning GM Europe Parts and Accessories, Zürich, 1988-91; comptr. GM Europe Parts & Accessories, Ruesselsheim, Germany, 1991-92; comptr. sales Adam Opel AG, Ruesselsheim, Germany, 1992-95; mng. dir. Opel Master Lease GmbH, Ruesselsheim, Germany, 1996-98; pres. Daidalos Cons., Wellesley, Mass., 1998—; dir. internat. ops. Daidalos Unternehmensberatung GmbH, Wolfratshausen, Germany, 1998—. Bd. trustees Frankfurt Internat. Sch., 1995-97, chmn. bldgs. and grounds com., treas., chmn. fin. com. 1997-98; treas. IMD Alumni Deutschland e.V., 1997-98. Office: Diadalos Cons PO Box 81058 Wellesley MA 02481

AALTO, MADELEINE, library director. BA, Wellesley Coll., 1964; BLS, U. Toronto, 1967. Clerical asst. Toronto Pub. Libr., 1964-66, children's libr. Parkdale br., 1968-69, collection libr. Spaced Out libr., 1969-73, br. head Annette St. br., 1973-74, coord. adult svcs., 1974-75; chief libr. East York Pub. Libr., 1975-84, Greater Victoria Pub. Libr., 1984-88; dir. Vancouver (B.C.) Pub. Libr., Can., 1988—. Contbr. intro. to A Geography for Children (Philippe du Fresnoy), 1968. Recipient Commerative medal 125th Anniversary Confederation Can., 1993. Mem. B.C. Libr. Assn. Office: Vancouver Pub Libr, 350 W Georgia St, Vancouver, BC Canada V6B 6B1*

AAMODT, ROGER LOUIS, federal agency administrator; b. San Francisco, Dec. 9, 1941; s. Rodney Lee and Barbara Helen (Quinn) A.; m. Janet Roberta Hall, Sept. 15, 1962 (div. 1995); children: Sandra Marie, Aaron Lee; m. Diane Sue Dwyer, Apr. 27, 1997. Student, Antioch Coll., 1959-60; BS cum laude, U. Utah, 1966; PhD, U. Rochester, 1972. Rsch. asst. dept. radiol. health U. Utah, Salt Lake City, 1965-66; sect. chief dept. nuclear medicine Clin. Ctr., NIH, Bethesda, Md., 1971-83; grants assoc. NIH, Bethesda, 1983-84; program dir. cancer diagnosis br. Nat. Cancer Inst., NIH, Rockville, Md., 1984-96, chief resources devel. br. cancer diagnosis program, 1997—. Author: (with others) Textbook of Nuclear Medicine, 1978; contbr. reference tables to Human Health and Disease, 1977, over 43 articles to profl. jours. Pres. Calvin Park Civic Assn., Rockville, 1974—. Spl. Health Physics fellow U.S. Atomic Energy Commn., 1966-69, NDEA fellow, 1969-71. Mem. AAAS, Am. Soc. Investigative Pathology, Internat. Soc. Analytical Cytology, N.Y. Acad. Sci., NIH Microcomputer Club (sec.-treas. 1983-84). Democrat. Methodist. Achievements include research on zinc absorption and metabolism in humans; organization of the NCI Cooperative Human Tissue Network and Cooperative Breast Cancer Tissue Resource. Office: Nat Cancer Inst EPN 700 6130 Executive Blvd Rockville MD 20852-4910

AANSTOOS, CHRISTOPHER MICHAEL, psychology educator; b. Saipan Island, U.S. Trust, U.S. Trust Ter., Apr. 4, 1952; s. Anthony Matthew and Frances Henrietta (Jambrick) A.; children: Megan, Elizabeth, Lucas Matthew. BA, Mich. State U., 1974; MA, Duquesne U., 1976, PhD, 1982. Instr. Pa. State U., McKeesport, 1979-82; asst. prof. psychology State U. West Ga., Carrollton, 1982-87, assoc. prof., 1987-92, prof., 1992—, chmn., 1995-96; contracted rschr. Pitts. Sch. Dist., 1979; manuscript reviewer Harcourt, Brace, Jovanovich, N.Y., 1983, New Ideas in Psychology, 1984-85, Saybrook Inst., 1986, Metaphor and Symbolic Activity, 1985-88, Sage, 1989, Guilford, 1990; nat. adv. panel Existential-Humanistic Inst.; adv. coun. Ctr. Study Psychology Psychiatry. Editor: Exploring the Lived World, 1984, The World of the Infant, 1987, Human Growth and Development, 1990, Studies in Humanistic Psychology, 1991, Jour. Humanistic Psychologist, 1984—; assoc. editor Jour. Theoretical Philos. Psychology, 1986-89; cons. editor Jour. Phenomenological Psychology, 1982—, Jour. Humanistic Psychology, 1989—, Psychotherapy Patient, 1996—, Ethical Human Scis. Svcs., 1999—; contbr. over 70 articles to profl. publs. Vol. West Ga. Coll. Spkrs. Bur., 1983—; coord. fund drive Am. Heart Assn., State U. West Ga., 1985. Faculty Rsch. grantee State U. West Ga., 1983-85, 89-90, 92-93. Fellow APA (exec. bd. divs. 24, 32, program chmn. divsn. 24 1991, pres. divsn. 32 1997-98); mem. AAUP, Human Sci. Rsch. Assn. (program chmn. 1984), Southeastern Psychol. Assn., Assn. Qualitative Rsch. Psychology (dchmn. program com. 1987-97), Chess Fedn. West Ga., Phi Beta Kappa. Home: 2175 Hog Liver Rd Carrollton GA 30117-9308 Office: State U West Ga Psychology Dept Carrollton GA 30118

AARESTAD, JAMES HARRISON, retired educational administrator, army officer; b. Mpls., Dec. 3, 1924; s. Selmer Emil and Myrthel Perline (Olson) A.; m. Mary-Jo Finn, Oct. 20, 1951; 1 child, Elizabeth Boe. BA, U. Minn., 1949; MA, Georgetown U., 1959; postgrad., Commd. and Gen. Staff Coll., Ft. Leavenworth, Kans., 1960-61, Nat. War Coll., Washington, 1970-71. Commd. 2d lt. U.S. Army, 1949, advanced through grades to col., 1970; comdr. 2d Squadron, 11th Cav., U.S. Army, Vietnam, 1969; dir. strategy and policy War Plans Div., Washington, 1970; chief staff Hdqrs. 1st Armored Div., Fed. Republic Germany, 1971-72; comdr. 2d Brigade, 3d Armored Div., Fed. Republic Germany, 1972-74; dir. nat. security seminar Army War Coll., Carlisle Barracks, Pa., 1974-76; ret., 1976; dep. dir. indsl. devel. N.C. Dept. Commerce, Raleigh, 1976-79; sec., bus. mgr. Dover (Pa.) Area Sch. Dist., 1979-92; ret., 1992; sr. strategy cons. Ketron Corp., Malvern, Pa., 1980—. Bd. dirs., vice chmn. York County Indsl. Devel. Corp., 1980-84, chmn. bd., 1986-88, treas., 1988-96, dir. emeritus, 1997—; chmn. mgmt. com. CYPER Ctr., York, 1990-97; bd. dirs., mem. exec. com. Better York, 1989-97; bd. dirs. Susquehanna Conf.; vet. WWII, Korea, Vietnam wars. Decorated Silver Star, Legion of Merit with 3 oak leaf clusters, DFC, Bronze Star, Air medal with 9 oak leaf clusters, Presdl. Unit Citation; recipient cert. of appreciation Gov. State of N.C., 1976, 79, resolution of appreciation York County Indsl. Devel. Corp., 1988. Mem. Nat. Assn. Sch. Bus. Ofcls. (registered sch. bus. adminstr.), Pa. Assn. Sch. Bus. Ofcls. (regional pres. 1982-83, citation 1986), Ends of Earth Club (N.Y.C.), Cavalry and Guards Club (London), Army-Navy Country Club (Arlington, Va.), Officers of the First Divsn. 11th Cavalry Vets. of Vietnam and Cambodia, Rotary, Sigma Alpha Epsilon. Republican. Episcopalian. Avocations: golf, gardening, military history, travel. Home: 1200 Stratford Dr Carlisle PA 17013-3543 Office: York County Indsl Devel Corp 160 Roosevelt Ave Ste 300 York PA 17404-3333

AARESTAD, NORMAN O., oncologist; b. Minot, N.D., Nov. 19, 1933; s. Gerhard and Gustava (Lee) A.; m. Margaret Anne Helling, Aug. 21, 1966; children: David, Tor. BA, Concordia Coll., Moorhead, Minn., 1955; BS in Medicine, U. N.D., 1957; MD, Harvard U., Boston, 1959; MS in Radiologic Biology, U. Rochester, 1966. Diplomate Am. Bd. Radiology. Intern U. Oreg. Med. Sch. Hosp. and Clinics, Portland, 1959-60, resident, 1960-63; asst. chief radiation oncology Walter Reed Med. Ctr., Washington, 1968-69; chief radiation oncology Letterman Gen. Hosp., San Francisco, 1969-71, St. Luke's Hosp., Denver, 1971-89; med. dir. R.R. Hart Regional Radiation Ctr., Boulder, Colo., 1988-93; med. dir. radiation oncology Swedish Med. Ctr., Englewood, Colo., 1992—; med. dir. radiation oncology Columbia (Colo. divsn.), Denver, 1994—, chmn. oncology adv. bd., 1995-98; chmn. cancer com. Swedish Med. Ctr., 1993—; med. advisor radiation oncology therapy tng. program Cmty. Coll. Denver, 1985-97. Mem. exec. com., pres. Colo. divsn. Am. Cancer Soc., Denver, 1973-98; bd. dirs. Marie Droste Svcs., Denver, 1992—, Ebenezer Luth. Health, Brush, Colo., 1990-98, also v.p.; bd. divsn. ch. and soc. Evang. Luth. Ch. Am., 1997—; pres. Augustana Found., Denver, 1992-98. Lt. col. U.S. Army, 1963-71. Fellow Am. Coll. Radiology; mem. AMA, Am. Soc. Therapeutic Radiation Oncology, Am. Coll. Radiation Oncology, Internat. Soc. Stereotactic Radiosurgery, Arapahoe Med. Soc., Colo. Med. Soc. (del. 1994-96). Lutheran. Avocations: skiing, travel, music, singing (choir), reading. Office: 799 E Hampden Ave Ste 100 Englewood CO 80110-2757

AAROE, PAUL MORRIS, retired superior court judge; b. Oxford, N.J., Dec. 24, 1913; s. Morris and Sadie (Little) A.; m. Marjorie Monroe, July 1, 1952 (div.); m. Eileen O'Rourke Day, May 10, 1958 (dec. Aug. 1979); m. Flora Van Hecke Simmons, Nov. 6, 1983; 1 child, Paul II; 12 stepchildren. AB, Lafayette Coll., Easton, Pa., 1935; LLB, Rutgers U., 1949. Bar: N.J. 1949. Asst. mgr. Sears Roebuck & Co., N.Y.C., 1938-46; assoc. Townsend & Doyle, Jersey City, 1949-52; pvt. practice Warren County, N.J., 1952-72; judge Superior Ct. N.J., Belvidere, 1972-83, 87—; pvt. practice Belvidere, 1983-87. Col. ORD and JAG, U.S. Army, 1942-46, Normandy Invasion, 1944, Battle of the Bulge. Decorated Bronze Star medal. Mem. ABA, JAG Assn., VFW, N.J. Bar Assn., Warren County Bar Assn., Am. Judicature Soc., Am. Legion, Travellers Century Club. Republican. Avocations: travel, chess, music.

AARON, BENJAMIN, law educator, arbitrator; b. Chgo., Sept. 2, 1915; s. Henry Jacob and Rose (Weinstein) A.; m. Eleanor Opsahl, May 24, 1941; children: Judith, Louise. A.B., U. Mich., 1937; LL.B., Harvard U., 1940; postgrad., U. Chgo., 1940-41. With Nat. War Labor Bd., 1942-45; mem. labor adv. com. to Supreme Comdr. Allied Powers, Tokyo, 1946; research assoc. Inst. Indsl. Relations; lectr. labor law, dept. econs. UCLA, 1946-51, assoc. dir., 1957-60, dir., 1960-75, prof. law, 1960-86, prof. emeritus, 1986—; faculty mem. Salzburg (Austria) Seminar in Am. Studies, 1958, 67; arbitrator labor-mgmt. disputes, 1946—; pub. mem. WSB, Washington, 1951-52; mem. Statutory Arbitration Bd. in R.R. Dispute, 1963-64; chmn. Calif. Farm Labor Panel, 1965-66; mem. Nat. Commn. on Tech., Automation and Economic Progress, 1965-66; pub. mem. Adv. Council on Employee Welfare and Pension Benefit Plans, 1966-68; vis. prof. Harvard U., 1972, U. Mich., 1979; mem. pub. rev. bd. U.A.W., 1975—; mem. arbitration services adv. com. Fed. Mediation and Conciliation Service, 1974-82; mem. ILO Com. of Experts on Application of Convs. and Recommendations, 1986-94; charter emeritus fellow Coll. of Labor and Employment Lawyers, 1996—. Author: Legal Status of Employee Benefit Rights Under Private Pension Plans, 1961; Editor: The Employment Relation and The Law, 1957, Labor Courts and Grievance Settlement in Western Europe, 1970, Comparative Labor Law jour, 1979-85; co-editor: Industrial Conflict: A Comparative Legal Survey, 1972; Public-Sector Bargaining, 1979; editorial bd., Internat. Labor Law Reps., 1974—. Fellow Center for Advanced Study in Behavioral Sciences, 1966-67; vis. fellow Clare Hall, Cambridge (Eng.) U., 1973; named First Southwestern Legal Found. Research Fellows' Disting. Scholar in Residence, 1971; first Howard W. Wissner Meml. Lectr. Tulane U., 1971; Phi Beta Kappa vis. scholar, 1978-79. Mem. ABA (sec. sect. labor rels. law 1975-76), AAUP, Internat. Soc. Labor Law and Social Security (chmn. U.S. nat. com., internat. exec. com. 1967-83, v.p. N.Am. region 1982-85, pres. 1985-88, hon. pres. 1988—), Nat. Acad. Arbitrators (pres. 1962, bd. govs.), Indsl. Rels. Rsch. Assn. (exec. bd. 1965-68, pres. 1972, mem. CCH labor law reports panel of experts 1987-92), Am. Arbitration Assn. (mem. adv. coun. L.A. 1975-76, Disting. Svc. award 1981). Home: 316 18th St Santa Monica CA 90402-2406 Office: UCLA 405 Hilgard Ave Los Angeles CA 90095-9000

AARON, BERTRAM DONALD, corporation executive; b. Newport News, Va., Jan. 10, 1922; s. Harry and Lillian (Blackman) A.; BS in Elec. Engring., Va. Poly. Inst., 1943; children: Harry, Cynthia, Jill; m. Marcia Kurke, 1952 (dec. Nov. 1974); m. Judith Goldstein, Dec. 28, 1985 (dec. May 1993); m. Gladys Cohen, June, 1998. Aero. rsch. scientist Nat. Adv. Com. for Aeros., Langley AFB, Va., 1946-50; pres. Aaron Investors, Inc., 1948-98; elec. engr. Signal Corps Supply Agy., Phila., 1950-53; propr. Bertram D. Aaron and Co., L.A., 1953-58, pres., Plainview, N.Y., 1958-91, Aaron Tech. Cons., 1990—; pres. Microwave Instrumentation Labs., 1959-80, HAL Antenna Products, Inc., Aaron Tech. Market, Inc. Dir. devel. Va. Breast Cancer Found., 1993, organizer, chmn. symposium Primary Care Perspectives, 1995; founder, chmn. Williamsburg Va. Symphony Soc., 1998—; bd. dirs. Va. Symphony, 1998—. Commnr., Junes City Co., Wiliamsburg Commn. of the Arts, 1999—, Served to capt., Signal Corps, U.S. Army, 1943-46. Registered profl. engr., N.Y., Pa., Va. Mem. IEEE (various offices), Electronic Reps. Assn. (pres., chmn. bd., nat. del. MY chpt.), Assn. of Old Crows (pres. Tidewater, Va. chpt. 1993-95). Jewish. Author: Hydrogen Thyratron Circuitry Considerations, 1953; Surveillance Under Low Light Level Conditions, 1971; editor Procs. of Integration Com. on Hydrogen Thyratrons, 1951-53; patentee antenna. Home and Office: Aaron Tech Cons Inc 212 Burtcher Ct Williamsburg VA 23185-8905

AARON, CYNTHIA G., judge; b. Mpls., May 3, 1957; d. Allen Harold and Barbara Lois (Perlman) A.; m. Craig D. Higgs, May 15, 1993. Student, Brandeis U., 1975-77; BA with honors and distinction, Stanford U., 1979; JD cum laude, Harvard U., 1984. Bar: Calif. 1984, U.S. Dist. Ct. (so. dist.) Calif. 1984, U.S. Ct. Appeals (9th cir.) 1984, U.S. Dist. Ct. (no. dist.) Calif. 1986, U.S. Dist. Ct. (ctrl. dist.) Calif. 1988, U.S. Supreme Ct. 1991. Rsch. asst. to Prof. Alan Dershowitz Law Sch. Harvard U., 1982-83; trial atty. Fed. Defenders San Diego, Inc., 1984-88; ptnr. Aaron & Cortez, 1988-94; U.S. magistrate judge U.S. Dist. Ct. (so. dist.) Calif., San Diego, 1994—; instr. pacific regional program Nat. Inst. for Trial Advocacy, 1988-91, instr. deposition skills workshop, 1993; adj. prof. Calif. We. Sch. Law, San Diego, 1990-93; instr. advocacy trial skills acad. Inst. for Criminal Def., San Diego, 1992-94; adj. prof. law sch. U. San Diego, 1993, 95. Mem. Nat. Assn. Women Judges, Lawyers Club San Diego, City Club San Diego, Phi Beta Kappa. Office: US Dist Ct (So Dist) Calif Ste 1185 940 Front St San Diego CA 92101-8940*

AARON, DAVID L., diplomat; b. Chgo., Aug. 21, 1938; m. Chloe W. Aaron; 1 child. BA, Occidental Coll., PhD (hon.); MA, Princeton U. With Fgn. Svc., 1962—; polit. and econ. officer Fgn. Svc., Guayaquil, Ecuador; internat. rels. officer Dept. of State, 1964-66; polit. officer NATO, Paris, 1966; with Arms Control and Disarmament Agy.; sr. staff mem. Nat. Security Coun., 1972-74; legis. asst. Senator Walter F. Mondale, Minn., 1974-75; task force leader select com. intelligence U.S. Senate, 1975-76; dep. asst. to pres. for nat. security, 1977-81; v.p. Oppenheimer and Co., Inc., 1981-85; writer, lectr. Lantz-Harris Agy., 1985-93; sr. advisor Mondale Presdl. Campaign, 1984; cons. 20th Century Fund, 1990-92, sr. fellow, 1992-93; bd. dirs. quest value dual purpose fund Oppenheimer Capital Corp.; U.S. rep. Orgn. Econ. Cooperation and Devel., Paris, 1996.; presdl. spl. envoy for cryptography, 1996; undersec. internat. trade dept. Commerce, 1997. Author: State Scarlet, Agent of Influence, Crossing By Night; contbr. articles to profl. jours. Staff mem. Carter-Mondale Presdl. Campaign. Decorated Nat. Def. medal. Mem. Nat. Dem. Inst. Internat. Affairs (bd. dirs.), Coun. Fgn. Rels., Overseas Devel. Coun., Internat. League Human Rights (bd. dirs.), Authors Guild. Office: US Dept Commerce Rm 3850 14th & Constitution Ave NW Washington DC 20230

AARON, HENRY JACOB, economics educator; b. Chgo., June 16, 1936; s. David and Betty (Cooper) A.; m. Ruth Kotell, May 5, 1963; children: Jeffrey, Melissa. AB, UCLA, 1958; MA, Harvard U., 1960, PhD, 1963. Assoc. prof. econs. U. Md., 1967-75, prof., 1975-77, 79-89; sr. fellow Brookings Instn., 1968-78, 96—, 1996—, dir. econ. studies, 1990-96; asst. sec. planning and evaluation HEW, Washington, 1977-78; sr. staff economist Pres.'s Coun. Econ. Advisers, 1966-67; mem. Gov. Md. Coun. Econ. Advisers, 1968-75; vis. prof. econs. Harvard U., 1974; mem. bd. dirs. Abt Assocs., 1979—, Ctr. on Budget and Policy Priorities, 1994—; chmn. Adv. Coun. on Social Security, 1978-79; trustee Tchrs. Ins. and Annuity Assn., 1984-87; trustee Georgetown U., 1995-97, bd. dirs.; mem. vis. com. dept. econs. Harvard U., 1985-89; mem. Inst. Medicine, 1986—, mem. com. on econ. future of baseball, 1990-92; rsch. adv. coun. Joint Ctr. Polit. Studies, 1984-89; v.p. Nat. Acad. Social Ins., 1986-96, chmn. bd. dirs., 1998—; rsch. adv. bd. Com. Econ. Devel., 1988-92; mem. adv. com. Stanford Inst. for Econ. Policy Rsch. Stanford U., 1991—. Author: Who Pays the Property Tax?, 1974, Politics and the Professors, 1978, Serious and Unstable Condition: Financing America's Health Care; co-author: The Peculiar Problem of Taxing Life Insurance Companies, 1983, The Economic Effects of Social Security, 1984, The Painful Prescription: Rationing Hospital Care, 1984, Assessing Tax Reform, 1985, Can America Afford To Grow Old?, 1988, (with Robert Reischauer) Countdown to Reform: The Great Social Security Debate; editor: Setting National Priorities: Policies for the Nineties, 1990, Serious and Unstable Condition: Financing America's Health Care, 1991; co-editor: Setting Domestic Priorities: What Can Government Do?, 1992, Values and Public Policy, 1994. Economic Effects of Fundamental Tax Reform (edited with William Gale), 1996, (with Robert D. Reischauer) Countdown to Reform: The Great Social Security Debate, 1998, Jour. Econ. Perspectives, Jour. Pub. Econs., Jour. Health Econs.; contbr. articles to profl. jours. Mem. adv. com. Ctr. for Econ. Policy Rsch., Stanford U. Ctr. for Advanced Study in the Behavioral Scis. fellow, 1996-97, Guggenheim fellow, 1996-97. Mem. Am. Econ. Assn. (exec. com. 1978-81, v.p. 1991), Am. Acad. Arts and Scis., Assn. Pub. Policy and Mgmt. (pres. 1998-99). Home: 1326 Hemlock St NW Washington DC 20012-1551 Office: 1775 Massachusetts Ave NW Washington DC 20036-2188

AARON, HENRY L. (HANK AARON), professional baseball team executive; b. Mobile, Ala., Feb. 5, 1934; s. Herbert and Estella A.; children: Gail, Hank, Lary, Gary (dec.), Dorinda; m. Billye Suber, Nov. 1973; 1 child, Ceci. Ed. pub. schs. Former semi-pro baseball player; baseball player Milw. Braves (became Atlanta Braves 1966), 1954-74, v.p. player devel., 1976-89, sr. v.p., asst. to pres., 1989—, also bd. dirs.; player Milw. Brewers, 1974-76; bd. dirs. Turner Broadcasting. Author: (autobiography) I Had A Hammer: The Hank Aaron Story, 1991. Pres. No Greater Love, 1974; state chmn. Wis. Easter Seal Soc., 1975; nat. sports chmn. Nat. Easter Seal Soc., 1974; nat. chmn. Friends of Fisk for Athletics; organizer Hank Aaron Scholarship Fund, 1974; sponsor Hank Aaron Celebrity Bowling Tournament for Sickle Cell Anemia, 1972; mem. exec. bd. PUSH; mem. nat. bd. Big Bros./Big Sisters Am., NAACP; mem. Atlanta bd. Am. Cancer Soc.; mem. sterling com. Morehouse Coll.; active Leukemia Soc. Atlanta. Mem. Nat. League All-Star Team, 1955-74, Am. League All-Star Team, 1975, World Series Championship Team, 1957; Most Valuable Player, Nat. League, 1957; named Player of Yr. Sporting News, 1956, 63; inducted into Baseball Hall of Fame, 1982; broke Babe Ruth's career home run record with 715th home run, April 8, 1974; holder major league record for most home runs, most runs batted in. Office: care Atlanta Braves PO Box 4064 Atlanta GA 30302-4064*

AARON, HUGH, writer; b. Worcester, Mass., Nov. 30, 1924; s. Barnet and Gertrude Rose Aaron; m. Joyce Charlotte Gomberg, June 19, 1955 (div. June 1988); children: Suzanne Ruth, Andrew Mark, Elizabeth Ann; m. Ann Marie Stein, Apr. 29, 1989. AB, U. Chgo., 1951. Supr. Apex Tire & Rubber Co., Pawtucket, R.I., 1955-57, Elfskin Corp., Worcester, 1958-60; mgr. Plastic Materials Inc., Slatersville, R.I., 1960-65; pres. Customcolor Inc., Cumberland, R.I., 1966-85; writer Belfast, Maine, 1985—. Author: Business Not as Usual, 1993, When Wars Were Won, 1995, It's All Chaos, 1996, Letters from the Good War, 1997, Driven, Notes of a Neurotic Entrepreneur, 1995, Go West Old Man, 1996, Suzy, Fair Suzy (a children's story), 1998; author of essays, short stories, letters. With USN, 1943-45. Mem. Nat. Writers Union, Maine Writers and Pubs. Alliance. Avocations: reading, sailing, gardening, hiking. Home: 71 Congress St Belfast ME 04915-6312

AARON, KENNETH ELLYOT, lawyer; b. Phila., Nov. 3, 1948; s. Neal L. and Dorothea G. Aaron; m. Phyllis A. Carroll, May 29, 1969; children: Seth Joel, Joshua Scott. BS in Econs., U. Pa., 1970, JD, 1973. Bar: Pa. 1973, U.S. Dist. Ct. (ea. dist.) Pa. 1973, (we. dist.) Pa., 1993, U.S. Ct. Appeals (3rd cir.) 1974, U.S. Supreme Ct. 1977; cert. bus. bankruptcy law specialist, Am. Bankruptcy Bd. Cert. Assoc. Astor & Weiss, Phila., 1973-76; ptnr. Casper & Davidson, P.C., Phila., 1976-80; pvt. practice Phila., 1980-83; ptnr. Garfinkel & Volpicelli, Phila., 1983-86, Mesirov, Gelman, Jaffe, Cramer & Jamieson, Phila., 1986-91, Buchanan Ingersoll P.C., Phila., 1991—. Author: Foreclosure and Repossession, 1989, (chpt.) Bus. Lawyer's Bankruptcy Guide, 1992, BNA's Environmental Due Diligence Guide, 1992, Matthew Bender's Environmental Law Practice Guide, 1992. Commr. Haverford (Pa.) Twp. Planning Bd., 1976-80, mem. lower Merion zoning bd., 1993—; chmn. Indian Creek Homeowners Assn., Wynnewood, Pa., 1985—; mem. Lower Merion steering com., Wynnewood, 1987; campaign chmn. Alan Kessler for Twp. Commr., Wynnewood, 1987, 91, 95; mem. Ea. Dist. of Pa. Bankruptcy Conf., vice chmn. edn. com., 1991, co-chmn. edn. com., 1992, co-chmn. legis. com. 1993; planning commr. Lower Merion Twp. Planning Bd., Ardmore, Pa., 1992; trustee Phila. Bar Found., 1997-99. Recipient Tax Writing award Nat. Assn. Accts., 1970, Am. Jr. award in Creditors' Rights, 1973. Mem. Phila. Bar Assn. (chmn. com. on insolvency issues in real estate 1989—), Phila. Bar Found. (trustee 1997—), Rotary (pres. Haverford Twp. chpt. 1982-83), Hais & Coun. (v.p. 1999—). Avocations: sports, camping, golfing. Office: Buchanan Ingersoll PC Eleven Penn Ctr 14th Fl Philadelphia PA 19103

AARON, M. ROBERT, electrical engineer; b. Phila., Aug. 21, 1922; s. Edward A. and Beatrice A.; m. Wilma Spiegelman, Nov. 18, 1944; children—Richard, James. B.S.E.E., U. Pa., 1949, M.S.E.E., 1951. Research engr. Franklin Inst. Research Labs., Phila., 1949-51; with Bell Telephone Labs. Inc., Murray Hill, N.J., 1951-89; supr. Bell Telephone Labs. Inc., 1954-68, dept. head, 1968-89; ret., 1989, cons., 1989—; lectr., tchr. in field. Mem. adv. com. Whippany (N.J.) Sch. Bd., 1950's. Guest editor for tech. jours., 1971-99; contbr. articles to profl. jours., poems to various jours. Tutor NAACP Program, Red Bank, N.J., 1966-68. Served to lt. (j.g.) USCG, 1942-45. Co-recipient computers and communications prize Found. for Computers and Communications Promotion, 1988. Fellow IEEE (mem. fin. bd. 1976-77, awards bd. 1987-89, 93, co-recipient Alexander Graham Bell medal 1978, Centennial medal 1984); mem. Nat. Acad. Engring., IEEE Circuits and Systems Soc. (assoc. editor 1969-71, pres. 1973), IEEE Comm. Soc. (chmn. awards bd. 1975-79, 80-84, bd. govs. 1986-89, Meritorious Svc. award 1985, fellow evaluation 1992-96, disting. lectr. 1995, lifetime svc. award 1997), Soc. of Cable Telecom. Engrs. Patentee in field. Home and Office: Apt 901 2427 Presidential Way West Palm Beach FL 33401-1838

AARON, MARCUS, II, lawyer; b. Pitts., Oct. 24, 1929; s. Marcus Lester and Maxine (Goldmark) A.; m. Barbara Goldman, Feb. 6, 1955; children: Susan, Judith, Barbara. AB, Princeton U., 1950; JD, Harvard U., 1953. Bar: Pa. 1953, D.C. 1953, U.S. Dist. Ct. (we. dist.) Pa. 1956, U.S. Supreme Ct. 1969, U.S. Ct. Appeals (3d cir.) 1971. Assoc. Glick, Berkman & Engel, Pitts., 1956-64; ptnr. Klett, Lieber, Rooney & Schorling, P.C., Pitts., 1965—; asst. solicitor City of Pitts., 1957-67; bd. dirs. Homer Laughlin China Co., Newell, W.Va., 1967—, sec., 1972-88, v.p., 1980-88, pres., treas., 1989—. Trustee Western Pa. Sch. for Blind Children, Pitts., 1969—, pres., 1982-90; bd. dirs. Blue Cross of Western Pa., Pitts., 1972-86, sec., 1984-86; bd. dirs. Centre Engring., Inc., State College, Pa., 1984-92; trustee Rodef Shalom Congregation, Pitts., 1991—, treas., 1996-98, v.p., 1998—. Mem. ABA, Pa. Bar Assn., Allegheny County Bar Assn., Concordia Club, Rivers Club, HYP Pitts. Club. Democrat. Jewish. Home: 1925 Wightman St Pittsburgh PA 15217-1537 Office: Klett Lieber Rooney & Schorling 1 Oxford Ct Fl 40 Pittsburgh PA 15219-6498

AARON, MELISSA D., education educator; b. Oct. 31, 1964. BA, Sarah Lawrence Coll., 1986; MA, Cambridge U., 1988; MS, Ind. U., 1990; PhD, U. Wis., 1998. Rehearsal asst. Lyric Opera of Chgo., 1990-91; lectr. U. Mich., Ann Arbor, 1990—; admissions officer Meadville/Lombard Theol. Sch., Chgo., 1991-92; lectr., tchg. asst. U. Wis., Madison, 1993-98. E-mail: mdaaron@umich.edu.

AARON, PAUL, film and television producer and director. BFA, Bennington Coll.; PhD (hon.), Internat. Fine Arts Coll. Dir.: (films) A Different Story, 1978, A Force of One, 1979, Maxie, 1985, (TV movies) The Miracle Worker, 1979, Thin Ice, 1981, Maid in America, 1982, When She Says No, 1984, In Love and War, 1987, (creator, exec. producer) Laurel Ave., 1993, (creator, exec. prodr., writer) Under One Roof, 1995, (exec. prodr.) Grand Ave., 1996, (Broadway musicals) '70 Girls '70, The Burnt Flower Bed, A Dream Out of Time, (play) That's Entertainment. Recipient Christopher award, 1979, Monte Carlo award for Best Dir., 1979, Emmy for Best Film, 1980. Office: Elsboy Entertainment 1581 N Crescent Heights Blvd Los Angeles CA 90046-2405*

AARON, ROY HENRY, entertainment company executive; b. Los Angeles, Apr. 8, 1929; s. Samuel Arthur and Natalie (Krakauer) A.; m. Theresa Gesas, Dec. 20, 1953; 1 child, Jill. BA, U. Calif.-Berkeley, 1951; LLB, U. So. Calif., 1956. Bar: Calif. 1957. Mem. Pacht, Ross, Warne, Bernhard & Sears, Inc., L.A., 1957-79, of counsel, 1979-83; sr. v.p., gen. counsel Plitt Theatres, Inc. and Plitt Theatre Holdings, Inc., L.A., 1978-80, pres., COO, 1980-85; pres. Plitt Entertainment Group, Inc., L.A., 1985—; pres., chief exec. officer Showscan Corp., L.A., 1985-93; chmn., CEO Intra-Asia Ent. Corp., 1998—; lectr. Calif. Continuing Edn. of Bar; lectr. continuing legal edn. Loyola U. Law Sch., Los Angeles. Mem. editorial bd. U. So. Calif. Law Rev., 1954-56. Trustee, mem. exec. com. Vista Del Mar Child-Care Svc., 1968-80, Reiss-Davis Child Study Ctr., 1977-80, Plitt So. Theaters Inc., Employees Trust, 1978-97; bd. dirs. Rape Found.; mem. adv. bd. dirs. Rape Treatment Ctr. of Santa Monica, UCLA Med. Ctr.; pres. UCLA Royce Two Seventy, 1986-88; mem. UCLA Found., pres. 1996-98, chmn., 1998—, bd. dirs. Fellow Am. Bar Found. (life), L.A. County Bar Found. (life); mem. ABA, State Bar Calif., L.A. County Bar Assn. (trustee 1977-83, v.p. 1979-80, sr. v.p. 1980-81, pres.-elect 1982-83, pres. 1982-83, Shattuck-Price Meml. award 1996), U. Calif.-Berkeley Alumni Assn., UCLA Alumni Assn., Found. Motion Pictures Pioneers (bd. dirs.), So. Calif. Tennis Assn. (bd. dirs.).

AARON, STEVEN P., publishing executive. Sr. v.p., pub. Premiere, N.Y.C., 1996—. Office: Premiere 1633 Broadway New York NY 10019-6708

AARONS-HOLDER, CHARMAINE MICHELE, lawyer; b. Kingston, Jamaica, Jan. 24, 1959; came to U.S., 1982; d. Alan and Berly-Mae Aarons; m. Lisle Anthony Holder, 1982. LLB honors, U. W.I., Barbados, 1980; Cert. Legal Edn., Norman Manley Law Sch., Kingston, 1982; JD cum laude, U. Houston, 1987. Bar: Barbados 1982, Tex. 1987, U.S. Dist. Ct. (so. dist.) Tex. 1988, U.S. Ct. Appeals (5th cir.) 1996. Participating assoc. Fulbright & Jaworski, Houston, 1987-94; atty. Wickliff & Hall, Houston, 1994-99; sr. atty. Equiva Svcs., LLC, Houston, 1999—; bd. dirs. Houston Lawyer Referral Svcs., 1997—. Co-editor, co-author: The Texas Environmental Law Handbook, 1989, 2nd edit., 1990, 3rd edit., 1993. Mem. ABA, Tex. Bar Assn., Houston Bar Assn. (chair campaign for homeless com. 1996-97), Houston Young Lawyers Assn. (chair hunger relief com. 1994-95), Order of Coif, Order of Barons. Democrat. Avocations: swimming, sailing. Office: Equiva Services LLC 910 Louisiana St Houston TX 77002

AARONSON, DAVID ERNEST, lawyer, educator; b. Washington, Sept. 19, 1940; s. Edward Allan and May (Rosett) A.; m. Laura Dine, 1991; stepchildren: Dara Prushansky, Jared Prushansky. B.A. in Econs, George Washington U., 1961, M.A., 1964, Ph.D., 1970; LL.B., Harvard U., 1964; LL.M. (E. Barrett Prettyman fellow), Georgetown U., 1965. Bar: D.C. bar 1965, Md. bar 1975, U.S. Supreme Ct. bar 1969. Research asst. Office of Commr., Bur. Labor Stats., U.S. Dept. Labor, Washington, 1961; staff atty. legal intern program Georgetown Grad. Law Center, Washington, 1964-65; research asso. patent research project dept. econs. George Washington U., Washington, 1966; asso. firm Aaronson and Aaronson, Washington, 1965-67; ptnr. Aaronson and Aaronson, 1967-70; prof., B.J. Tennery Scholar Am. U. Law Sch., Washington, 1970—; prof. Sch. Justice, Coll. Public and Internat. Affairs, 1981-92; dep. dir. Law and Policy Inst., Jerusalem, Israel, summer, 1978; interim dir. clin. programs Md. Criminal Justice Clinic, 1971-73, founder prosecutor criminal litigation clinic, 1972, co-dir. trial practice litigation program, 1982—; vis. prof. Law Sch. of Hebrew U., Jerusalem, summer, 1978; trustee Montgomery-Prince George's Continuing Legal Edn. Inst., 1983—. Author: Maryland Criminal Jury Instructions and Commentary, 1975, (with N.N. Kittrie and D. Saari) Alternatives to Conventional Criminal Adjudication: Guidebook for Planners and Practitioners, 1977, (with B. Hoff, P. Jaszi, N.N. Kittrie and D. Saari) The New Justice: Alternatives to Conventional Criminal Adjudication, 1977, (with C.T. Dienes and M.C. Musheno) Decriminalization of Public Drunkenness: Tracing the Implementation of a Public Policy, 1981, Public Policy and Police Discretion: Processes of Decriminalization, 1984, (with R. Simon) The Insanity Defense: A Critical Assessment of Law and Policy in the Post-Hinckley Era, 1988, Maryland Criminal Jury Instructions and Commentary, 2d rev. edit., 1988; contbr. articles to legal and public policy jours. Mem. council Friendship Heights Village Council, 1979. Recipient Outstanding Community Service award, 1980; Outstanding Tchr. award Am. U. Law Sch., 1978, 81, Scholar/Tchr. of the Year award Am. U., 1989; Pauline Ruyle Moore scholar in Pub. Law, 1983. Mem. ABA (mem. criminal justice sect. rules of cr. prof. and evid. com. 1991—), D.C. Bar Assn. (chmn. criminal code rev. com. 1971-73), Md. State Bar Assn. (criminal law sect. coun. 1984—, chairperson 1989-90), Assn. Am. Law Schs. (elected to sect. coun., criminal justice sect. 1992-97), Montgomery County (Md.) Bar Assn., Soc. for Reform of Criminal Law, Am. Law Inst., Phi Beta Kappa. Office: Am U Law Sch 4801 Massachusetts Ave NW Washington DC 20016-8180*

AARONSON, ROBERT JAY, aviation executive; b. Temple, Tex., June 8, 1942; s. Leonard and Ruth (Lader) A.; m. Louise Elaine Loia, June 6, 1967; children: Steven Bradford, Suzanne Denise. AB, Brown U., 1964; M in Govtl. Adminstrn., Wharton Sch., U. Pa., 1965. Spl. asst. Southeastern Pa. Transp. Authority, Phila., 1965-67; transp. rep. Urban Mass Transp. Adminstrn., Washington, 1967-69; transp. adviser HUD, 1969-71; aviation adminstr. Md. Dept. Transp., Balt., 1972-78; asso. adminstr. for airports FAA, Washington, 1978-81; dir. aviation Port Authority of N.Y. and N.J., N.Y.C., 1981-89; pres. Air Transport Assn. Am., Washington, 1989-92; exec. v.p. Lockheed Air Terminal, Inc., Burbank, Calif., 1993-94, Airport Group Internat., Inc., Glendale, Calif., 1995-97; pres. Strategies For Airports, Inc., Encino, Calif., 1997—; lectr. Royal Aero. Transport Course, Oxford U. Samuel S. Fels fellow, 1964-65. Mem. Nat. Assn. State Aviation Ofcls. (pres. 1978), Airport Operators Coun. Internat. (chmn. 1987-88), Am. Assn. Airport Execs., Wings Club (pres. 1992), Mountaingate Country Club. Home: 16477 Oldham St Encino CA 91436-3701 Office: Ste 1245 16133 Ventura Blvd Encino CA 91436

AARS, RALLIN JAMES, management, business development, marketing communications executive, consultant; b. Clifton, Tex., Sept. 28, 1941; s. C. Pernell and Rosalie (Rueter) A.; m. Barbara Ann Zuehlke, June 13, 1964; children: Christian, James, Michael. BA, Baylor U., 1964; MA, Mich. State U., 1970; Grad. with honors, Indsl. Coll. of the Armed Forces, 1980. Commd. USAF, 1964, advanced through grades to col., 1980; ops. officer HQ USAF Armed Forces Radio and TV Svc.-Europe, Wiesbaden, Germany, 1964-66; comdr. Am. Forces TV, Berlin, 1966-69; chief of pub. affairs Bergstrom AFB Austin, Tex., 1970-72; chief of info. and liaison Armed Forces Radio and TV, L.A., 1972-76; exec. officer Joint Casualty Resolution Ctr., U'Tapao, Thailand, 1976-77; dir. pub. affairs Electronic Security Command USAF, San Antonio, Tex., 1977-80; dir. plans and resources, office of pub. affairs, sec. of the Air Force Washington, 1980-82; dir. pub. affairs UN Command Seoul, Korea, 1982-84; ret. USAF, 1984; v.p. Gurasich, Spence, Darilek & McClure, Dallas, 1984-86, The Oakley Co., Dallas, 1986-87; v.p. comm. PARTNERS Nat. Health Plans, Irving, Tex., 1987-90, Aetna Health Plans, Irving, Tex., 1990-93; v.p. mktg. and communications Aetna Profl. Mgmt. Corp., Irving, Tex., 1993-94; health plan mgr., exec. dir. bus. devel. Kaiser Found. Health Plan of Tex., Dallas, 1994-96; pres., CEO Strategic Advantage, 1996-99; vice chmn. bd. dirs. Hastings Fin. Corp., 1997—; pres. Assured Indoor Air Quality, LP, 1999—. Prodr. (TV documentary) Berlin: Freedom's Island, 1968 (George Washington honor medal 1968), Airlift Anniversary, 1969 (George Washington honor medal 1969), Money Box (Golden Tops award 1988), Healthwise Today Newsletter (Dallas Press Club KATIE award 1988), Perfect Health Plan (Silver Tops award 1989, Bronze Tops award 1989), Super Dave Ad Campaign (Golden Tops award 1990), Preventive Health Care Campaign (four gold and two silver awards Health Mgmt. Rev. 1992). Bd. dirs. chmn. profl. devel. com. Tex. Assn. Health Plans; co-chmn. managed care task force Dallas/Ft.Worth Health Industry Coun.; pres. Internat. Luth. Ch., Seoul, 1983; v.p. New Life In Christ Luth. Ch., Dallas, 1986-88. Decorated Legion of Merit; Nat. Order Mil. Merit (Republic of Korea); recipient 3 gold and 2 silver awards for significant achievement in healthcare advt. Health Mgmt. Rev. mag., 1992; named to Tex. Hall of Fame, 1995. Mem. VFW, Am. Legion, Nat. Assn. Govt. Communicators, Am. Managed Care and Rev. Assn. (chmn. pub. affairs com.), Am. Mktg. Assn. (sr. exec. mem.), Pub. Rels. Soc. Am. (accredited, v.p. San Antonio chpt. 1979-80), Tex. Pub. Rels. Assn., Aviation and Space Writers Assn., Armed Forces Broadcasters Assn. (golden anniversary com), Air Force Assn., Assn. U.S. Army, Ret. Officers Assn., Air Force Pub. Affairs Alumni Assn. (charter life mem.), LaCima Club. Avocation: photography. Office: 1254 Whispering Oaks Dr De Soto TX 75115

AARSLEFF, HANS, linguistics educator; b. Rungsted Kyst, Denmark, July 19, 1925; came to U.S., 1948, naturalized, 1964; s. Einar Faber and Inger (Lotz) A. B.A., U. Copenhagen, 1945; Ph.D., U. Minn., 1960. Instr. English U. Minn., 1952-56; instr. Princeton U., 1956-60, asst. prof., 1960-65, assoc. prof., 1965-72, prof., 1972-97. Author: The Study of Language in England 1780-1860, 1967, From Locke to Saussure: Essays on the Study of Language and Intellectual History, 1982, Introduction to Wilhelm von Humboldt, On Language, 1988; assoc. editor: The Historiography of Linguistics; bd. editors: Jour. History Ideas, 1979—; contbr. articles to jours. and books. Jr. fellow Council of Humanities Princeton U., fall 1962; fellow Am. Council Learned Socs., 1964-65, 72-73, NEH, 1975-76. Fellow Am. Acad. Arts and Scis.; mem. Am. Philos. Soc., Soc. d'histoire de l'épistemologie des sci. du lang. (Paris), Royal Danish Acad. Scis. and Letters (fgn.). Office: Princeton U Dept English Princeton NJ 08544

AARSTOL, MICHAEL PATRICK, economics educator; b. Aug. 4, 1967. BA, BS, Washington and Lee U., 1989; PhD, Stanford U., 1996. Asst. prof. econs. U. Ga., Athens, 1996—. E-mail: aarstol@rigel.econ.uga.edu.

AASEN, LAWRENCE OBERT, public relations executive; b. Gardner, N.D., Dec. 5, 1922; s. Theodore and Clara Olina (Brenden) A.; m. Martha Ann McMullan, Nov. 25, 1954; children—David Lawrence, Susan Clare. Ph.B., U. N.D., 1947; M.S., Boston U., 1949. With McGraw Hill Publishing Co., N.Y.C., 1952-54; with N.Y. Life Ins. Co., 1954-67, asst. v.p., 1965-67; exec. sec. Better Vision Inst., N.Y.C., 1967-87; pres. Publicity, Inc., Westport, Conn., 1988—. Dem. commiteeman Westport; elected mem. Representative Town Meeting, 1970. With AUS, 1943-45. Mem. Public Relations Soc. Am., Am. Soc. Assn. Execs. Congregationalist. Home: 31 Ellery Ln Westport CT 06880-5203

AASEN-HULL, AUDREY AVIS, music educator; b. Coquille, Oreg., July 9, 1916; d. John Lawrence and Orra Amy (Kelley) Aasen; m. James Byrne Hull, Sept. 15, 1962. BA, U. Oreg., 1939; MA, Stanford U., 1946. Music tchr. Monroe (Oreg.) H.S., 1939-40, Estacada (Oreg.) Union Sch., 1940-41; performer of solo violin program Sta. KOOS, Coos Bay, Oreg., 1941-43; supr. instrumental music San Francisco Pub. Schs., 1944-45; tchr. violin and piano Menlo Sch. & Coll., Menlo Park, Calif., 1947-48, Sacred Heart Convent Sch., Menlo Park, Calif., 1948-49. Performances of string quartets, trios, quintets and sextets for San Francisco Musical Club and Palo Alto Fortnightly Music Club, 1947-89; performed with People's Symphony, San Francisco, 1945, Calif. Mfrs. Assn., San Francisco, 1950, Palo Alto String quartet, 1958, String Orch. Televised Concert, Innsbruck, Austria, 1982, Queen Elizabeth Hall, Belgium, Internat. String Tchrs. Workshop, Brussels, 1984, and numerous others; soloist at Soroptimist Internat. Conv. for Am. Fedn. Soroptimist Clubs, Can., 1954; concertmistress Penisula Symphony, 1958-59; most recent performances include recital Menlo Park, Calif., 1997, performances at Fortnightly Music Club, 1997, 98, U. Oreg., 1997. Adv. bd. mem. Calif. Summer Music at Pebble Beach, initiating mem., 1996—; patron San Francisco Symphony, underwriter violin chair position, 1989—. Recipient citation for Disting. Svc. USO, 1943-44, 45-46. Mem. Am. Fed. Musicians (life), Am. String Tchrs. Assn., Soroptomist Club (life), Fortnightly Music Club. Avocations: gardening, studying French, dancing, cooking.

AASLESTAD, HALVOR GUNERIUS, college dean, retired; b. Birmingham, Ala., Sept. 6, 1937; s. Knut and Geraldine (Dobson) A.; m. Barbara Wohn, July 30, 1960; children: Katherine, Karen, Peter, Lauren. BS, La. State U., 1960, PhD, 1965; MS, Pa. State U., 1961. Asst. prof. U. Ga., Athens, 1968-70; rsch. scientist Wistair Inst., Phila., 1970-73; sr. scientist Frederick (Md.) Cancer Rsch. Ctr., 1973-76; exec. sec. NIH, Bethesda, Md., 1976-81, rev. chief, 1981-85; dir. rsch. grants Sch. Medicine Yale U., New Haven, 1985-95, asst. dean Sch. Medicine, 1987-89, assoc. dean, retired, 1989-96; sr. mem. Rsch. and Review Svcs., Staunton, Va., 1996-98; sr. assoc. United Info. Sys., Inc., Bethesda, Md., 1998—; cons. NIH, Bethesda, 1985—. NIH rsch. grantee and fellow, 1965—.

ABADI, FRITZIE, artist, educator; b. Aleppo, Syria, Mar. 10, 1915; came to U.S., 1924; d. Matloub and Esther (Nahum) A.; m. Al Hidary, Feb. 11, 1934 (div. 1955); children: Annette Hidary Goldman, Esther Louise Friedberg (dec.); m. Lewis Ginsburg, Feb. 24, 1963. Student, Art Students League, 1947-48. Contbr. art data, Smithsonian Instn., Washington, 1980; exhibited group shows, Yeshiva U., N.Y.C., 1971-79, Whitney Mus. Am. Art, N.Y.C., Butler Art. Inst., ten one-woman shows. Recipient awards in oil painting, collage, assemblage. Mem. Am. Soc. Comtemporary Artists (pres. 1971-73, dir., advisor), Hudson River Contemporary Artists, Nat. Assn. Women Artists, Artists Equity. Democrat. Jewish. *Born in Aleppo, Syria, I came to America at the age of eight. Life in my new country was both exciting and frightening. I remember sitting in front of the mirror, practicing proper English. I was unable to get a proper education. At the ageof 29 I went to the Art Students League and found a new interest and goal in art. I am still actively pursuing my art and find it brings great joy and fulfillment.**

ABARBANEL, GAIL, social service administrator, educator; b. Los Angeles, Apr. 17, 1944; d. Sam and Sylvia (Cramer) A.; m. Stephen P. Klein, Jan. 31, 1975. BA magna cum laude, UCLA, 1966; MSW, U. So. Calif., 1968. Lic. clin. social worker. Clin. social worker Mental Health Agy., L.A., 1968-74; founder, dir. Rape Treatment Ctr. and Dept. Social Svcs. Santa Monica (Calif.) Hosp. Med. Ctr., L.A., 1974—; cons., educator in field. Contbr. articles to profl. jours.; author successful legislation to change rape laws; producer films about campus rape. Bd. dirs. Clare Found., 1975-77; atty. gen. task force Violence Against Women Act, 1995; active Am. Cancer Soc., 1975-79; Child Trauma Coun., 1978-81; Sr. Health Ctr., 1981-87. Recipient Gov.'s Victim Svcs. award, 1985, Coro Found. Pub. Affairs award, 1985, Woman of Year Leadership award YWCA, 1980, 82, Status of Women award AAUW, 1978, Nat. Outstanding Achievement award Am. Cancer Soc., 1977, Disting. Citizen award L.A. County Bar Assn., 1988, Humanitarian award Nat. Conf. Christians and Jews, 1987, Soc. for Clin. Social Work award, 1989, DOJ award for Outstanding Svc. on Behalf of Victims of Crime, Pres. of U.S., 1991, Woman of Distinction award Soroptimist Internat., 1992, Excellence in Prof. Achievement Alumni award, UCLA, 1994, Outstanding Corp. Citizen award Pub. Rels. Soc. Am. La. chpt., 1997; named Outstanding Alumni, U. So. Calif., 1979, one of Heroes of 1988 L.A. mag. Fellow Soc. for Clin. Social Work; mem. Nat. Assn. Social Workers (Agy. of Yr. award 1977, Social Worker of Yr. award 1995), Nat. Orgn. for Victim Assistance (Exemplary Program award 1985), NCASA (Nat. Coal. Against Sex. Ass.) ; NOVA (Nat. Org. for Vic. Assis.) Phi Beta Kappa, Pi Gamma Mu. Office: Santa Monica-UCLA Med Ctr 1250 16th St Santa Monica CA 90404-1249

ABARBANELL, GAYOLA HAVENS, financial planner; b. Chgo., Oct. 21, 1939; d. Leonard Milton and Lillian Love (Leviten) Havens; m. Burton J. Abarbanell, June 1, 1965 (div. 1972); children: Jeffrey J. Reddick, Dena Reddick Lamb. Student, UCLA, 1975; student, San Joaquin Coll. Law, 1976-77. CFP; lic. real estate rep. Calif.; lic. life ins. broker, Calif., Wash., Nev., N.Y., Ill., S.C.; lic. securities broker. Postal clk. Van Nuys, Calif., 1966-69; regional mgr. Niagara Cyclo Massage, Fresno, Calif., 1969-72; owner, mgr. AD Enterprises, Fresno, 1970-72; agt., field supr. Equitable of Iowa, Fresno, 1972-73; rep. Ciba Pharms., Fresno, 1973-75; owner, operator Creativity Unltd., Fresno, 1975-76; registered fin. advisor Univ. Securities Corp., L.A., 1976-83, Fin. Network Inv. Corp., Santa Monica, 1983-99, Nat. Planning corp., Santa Monica, 1999—; lectr. seminars for civic orgns.; mem. adv. bd. Financial Network, Torrance, Calif., 1985-88. Co-author: Guidelines to Feminist Consciousness Raising, 1985. Mem. bus. adv. bd. of 2d careers. Recipient award Women in Ins., 1972. Mem. Bus. and Profl. Assn., L.A. Internat. Assn. Fin. Planners (bd. dirs. 1993-94), Inst. Cert. Fin. Planners, So. Calif. Socially Responsible Investment Profls., ACLU, NOW (nat. consciousness raising coord. 1975-76), Gay Acad. Union, Nat. Gay Task Force, Culver City C. of C., Internat. Assn. Fin. Planners, Social Investment Forum, Rotary (founding mem. L.A. Westside Sunrise Club sgt. at arms 1990-91, community svc. chair 1991-94, v.p. 1992-93, found. chair 1993-94). Democrat. Jewish. Avocations: photography, ceramics, painting, design. Home: 57124 Mono Wind Way North Fork CA 93643-9797 Office: Nat Planning Corp Ste 103 5625 Green Valley Cir Culver City CA 90230-7120

ABATE, FRANK SALVATORE, JR., mental health services professional; b. Jamestown, N.Y., June 4, 1939; s. Frank and Theresa (Andrea) A. BA, Gannon U., Erie, Pa., 1969, MEd, 1971. Cert. profl. counselor, Md.; nat. cert. counselor; cert. forensic counselor, lic. profl. counselor. Asst. rsch. psychologist Nat. Inst. Mental Health, Bethesda, Md., 1970-73; personnel psychologist U.S. Patent and Trademark Office, Arlington, Va., 1973-88; cons. Person-System Integration, Alexandria, Va., 1976-88; asst. psychologist Lorain Correctional Inst., Grafton, Ohio, 1990-94; dir. mental health svcs. St. Mary's Co. Detention Ctr., Leonardtown, Md., 1994-98; pvt. practice therapist, Washington, 1980—; sr. clinician Psychotherapeutic Svcs., Great Mills, Md., 1996—; psychotherapist del. People-to People Assn., Washington, 1982. Contbr. articles to profl. jours. Vol. psychologist D.C. Homeless Ctr. for Creative Non-violence, 1986-87; cons., counselor At-Risk Youth, Pa. and Ohio, 1989-91; drug counselor Y.A.R.C., Rockville, Md., 1971-72. Master degree fellow Gannon U., 1969-70; recipient Internat. Man of Achievement award, Washington, 1975. Mem. APA (assoc.), Am. Coll. Forensic Examiners (bd. dirs. 1996—), Am. Mental Health Counseling Assn., D.C. Psychol. Assn. (assoc., treas. 1987-88, cert. recognition 1982), Internat. Soc. Polit. Psychology. Avocations: travel, cooking, exercise.

ABATEMARCO, FRED, editor in chief; b. N.Y.C., Oct. 13, 1949; s. Michael and Phyllis (Guidone) A.; m. Natalie DeMartino, Oct. 27, 1973;

children: Daniel, Diane. BA in Journalism, L.I. U., 1973. Wire asst., copy clk. Wall Street Jour., N.Y.C., 1966-69; chief desk asst. Sta. WCBA Newsradio, N.Y.C., 1971-73; new and broadcast mgr. Sta. WGMF/WXXY Radio, Watkins Glen and Elmira, N.Y., 1973-74; reporter Elmira State Gazette, 1974-75; section editor Home Furnishings Daily, N.Y.C., 1975-77; assoc. editor Newsweek Internat., N.Y.C., 1977-84; became editor-in-chief Personal Computing, Hasbrouck Heights, N.J., 1984; now editor-in-chief, v.p. Popular Science, N.Y.C. With U.S. Army, 1969-71, Vietnam. Mem. Am. Soc. Mag. Editors, Computer Press Assn. Office: Popular Science Times Mirror Mags Inc 9th Fl Two Park Ave New York NY 10016*

ABAUNZA, DONALD RICHARD, lawyer; b. New Orleans, Oct. 25, 1945; s. Alfred E. and Virginia (White) A.; m. Carolyn Thompson; 1 child, Richard. BA, Vanderbilt U., 1966; JD, Tulane U., 1969. Bar: La. 1969, U.S. Dist. Ct. (ea. dist.) La. 1969, U.S. Dist. Ct. (we. dist.) La. 1980, U.S. Supreme Ct. 1986. Assoc. Lemle, Kelleher, Kohlmeyer, Dennery, Hunley, Moss & Frilot, New Orleans, 1969-76; ptnr. Liskow & Lewis, New Orleans, 1977-96, mng. ptnr., 1996—; adj. faculty Tulane Sch. Law, 1981-89. Fellow Am. Coll. Trial Lawyers; mem. La. Bar Assn. (Pres.'s award 1988). Office: Liskow & Lewis 1 Shell Sq 50th Fl 701 Poydras St New Orleans LA 70139-5099

ABBADO, CLAUDIO, conductor; b. Milan, Italy, June 26, 1933. Hon. degree, Aberdeen, 1986, Ferrara, 1990, Cambridge, 1994. Music dir. Teatro alle Scala Milano, 1968-86, London Symphony Orch., 1979-88, Vienna (Austria) State Opera, 1986-91; generalmusikdirektor City of Vienna, 1987—; artistic dir., prin. condr. Berlin Philharm. Orch., 1989—; founder European Commn. Youth Orch., 1978; founder, artistic dir. Gustav Mahler Jugend Orch., 1988, WIEN MODERN Festival Contemporary Art, 1988, Encounters in Berlin Chamber Music Festival, 1992, Competitions of the Salzburg Easter Festival, 1994; artistic advisor Chamber Orch. of Europe; artistic dir. Easter Festival Salzburg, 1994. Recipient Mozart medal Mozart Gemeinde, Vienna, 1973, Golden Nicolai medal Vienna Philharm. Orch., 1980, Std. Opera award Covent Garden, London, 1989, Gold medal Internat. Mahler Soc., 1985, internat. prizes for recs.; decorated with Gran Croce of the Italian Rep., 1984, French Legion D'Honneur, 1988, Bundesverdienstkreuz, Germany, 1992, Ehrenring der Stadt Wien, 1994, Goldenes Ehrenzeichen Österreich. Office: Berliner Philharm Orch, Matthaikirchstrasse 1, D-10785 Berlin Germany also: care Columbia Artists Man Inc 165 W 57th St New York NY 10019-2201*

ABBAMONDI, JOHN GABRIEL, lawyer; b. Phila., Mar. 30, 1947; s. Almerico and Maria Antonia Abbamondi; m. Theresa Cecelia Blatteau, Aug. 24, 1968; children: John Gabriel Jr., Theresa Marie, Almerico Anthony. BA, LaSalle U., 1969; MS, Ctrl. Mo. State U., 1975; JD, U. Okla., 1997. Bar: Okla. Commd. officer USAF, 1969, advanced through grades to capt., ret., 1990; emergency mgmt. tng. officer State Okla., Oklahoma City, 1990-93; pvt. practice emergency mgmt. cons. Choctaw, Okla., 1993-94; pvt. practice law Oklahoma City, 1997—; vol. pro bono atty. Legal Aid Western Okla., Oklahoma City, 1997—. Vol. Com. to Elect Susan Caswell, Oklahoma City, 1998. Decorated Meritorious Svc. medal USAF, 1981, 89, Air Force Commendation medals, USAF, 1985, 86. Mem. ABA, Okla. Bar Assn., Oklahoma County Bar Assn., Choctaw Kiwanis (v.p. 1997-98). Republican. Roman Catholic. Avocations: golf, photography. E-mail: jabbamond@aol.com. Home: 13356 Fairway Dr Choctaw OK 73020 Office: Ste 245 4200 Perimeter Ctr Oklahoma City OK 73112

ABBAN, ANDREW PAUL, laboratory coordinator; b. Boston, July 14, 1966; s. Joseph Butler and Geraldine Ann (Lennon) A. BS, U. Mass., Boston, 1992; M of Liberal Arts, Harvard U., 1996. Curatorial asst. MCZ Harvard U., Cambridge, Mass., 1994, rsch. asst. Earth & Planetary Scis., 1994-96, lab. coord., 1997—. Infantryman U.S. Army, 1984-88. Mem. Geol. Soc. Am., Am. Assn. Petroleum Geologists, Soc. Sedimentary Geology. Office: Earth & Planetary Scis 20 Oxford St Cambridge MA 02138-2902

ABBASCHIAN, REZA, materials science and engineering educator; b. Zanjan, Iran, Jan. 23, 1944; came to U.S., 1966; s. Ebrahim and Motahreh Abbaschian; m. Janette S. Johnson, Sept. 6, 1973; children: Lara S., Cyrus E. BS, U. Tehran, Iran, 1965; MS, Mich. Tech. U., 1968; PhD, U. Calif., Berkeley, 1971. Rsch. analyst U.S. Steel Corp., Gary, Ind., 1967; rsch. asst. U. Calif., 1968-71; asst. prof. Shiraz (Iran) U., 1972-74, assoc. prof., 1974-80; with U. Fla., Gainesville, 1980—, acting chmn., 1986-87, chmn., prof., 1987—; vis. assoc. prof. dept. metallurgy and mining engring. U. Ill., Urbana, 1976-78; vis. scientist MIT, Cambridge, 1980, NASA Space Processing Lab., Marshall Space Flight Ctr., Huntsville, Ala., 1981; chmn. Shiraz U., 1974-76; mem. Nat. Materials Adv. Bd., 1996—. Co-author: Physical Metallurgy Principles, 1992; editor: Grain Refinement in Castings and Welds, 1983, Solidification Processing of Eutectic Alloys, 1988, Modeling and Control of Casting, 1988 (TMS Outstanding Educator award 1998, TMS Leadership award 1999, Structural Materials Divsns. Disting. Scientist/Engr. award 1998). Grantee NSF, NASA, 1984—. Office: U Fla Dept Materials Sci and Engring PO Box 116400 Gainesville FL 32611-6400

ABBASI, TARIQ AFZAL, psychiatrist, educator; b. Hyderabad, India, Aug. 13, 1946; came to U.S., 1976, naturalized, 1983; s. Shujaat Ali and Salma Khatoon (Siddiqui) A.; m. Kashifa Khatoon, Nov. 10, 1972; children—Sameena, Omar, Osman. B.S., Madrasa-I-Aliya, Hyderabad, 1964; M.B.B.S., Osmania Med. Coll., Hyderabad, 1970; Diploma in Psychol. Medicine, St. John's Hosp., U. Sheffield (Eng.), 1976. Diplomate Am. Bd. Psychiatry and Neurology; diplomate in psychiatry Royal Coll. Physicians of Eng. Sr. house officer St. John's Hosp., Lincoln, Eng., 1972-73, registrar, 1973-76; resident in psychiatry Rutgers Med. Sch., Piscataway, N.J., 1976-79, chief resident, 1979, dir. adult in-patient services Community Mental Health Ctr., Rutgers Med. Sch., also asst. prof. psychiatry, 1979-82; staff psychiatrist Northville Regional Psychiat. Hosp. (Mich.), 1982-83, div. dir., 1983—; cons. psychiatrist Rahway State Prison (N.J.), 1979-82; clin. instr. psychiatry Wayne State U. Med. Sch., Detroit. Mem. Am. Psychiat. Assn., Mich. Psychiat. Soc. Office: Northville Regl Psychiat Hosp 41001 7 Mile Rd Northville MI 48167-2655 also: 33200 Dequindre Rd Ste 200 Sterling Heights MI 48310-5916 also: 53950 Van Dyke Ave Shelby Township MI 48316-1813

ABBE, COLMAN, investment banker; b. N.Y.C., Sept. 24, 1932; s. Leo Theodore and Beatrice (Shiff) A.; m. Nancy Adele Hyams, June 23, 1963; children: Elizabeth, Leo, Richard. BS in Acctg., Bucknell U., 1953; MBA, NYU, 1962. CPA, N.Y. Ptnr. Belsky & Abbe CPAs, N.Y.C., 1960-70; stockbroker Loeb Rhoades, N.Y.C., 1971-72; pres. Sagittarius Fund, N.Y.C., 1973, OCG Tech. Inc., N.Y.C., 1973, Profl. Mediquip Inc., Scarsdale, N.Y., 1974-80, Abbe & Co., Inc., 1984—; mng. dir. corp. fin. Evans & Co. Inc., N.Y.C., 1985-87, Reich & Co., Inc., N.Y.C., 1988-90; vice chmn., sr. mgr., dir. investment banking Laidlaw Internat. Inc., N.Y.C., 1991-93; chmn. AB Capital Markets, N.Y.C., 1993-94. Trustee Heart Rsch. Found., N.Y.C., 1982-92, pres., 1986; pres. Am. Friends of HAIFA Med. Ctr., 1989-93. Mem. AICPA, N.Y. State Soc. CPAs. Democrat. Jewish. Office: Abbe & Co Inc 26 Lawrence Rd Scarsdale NY 10583-7209

ABBE, ELFRIEDE MARTHA, sculptor, graphic artist; b. Washington; d. Cleveland Jr. and Frieda (Dauer) A. Student, Art Inst. Chgo., 1937; B.F.A., Cornell U., 1940; postgrad., Syracuse U., 1947. Author and illustrator: books including The Plants of Virgil's Georgics, 1965; One-woman exhbns. include Carnegie-Mellon U., 1962, 69, Cornell U., 1963, Trinity Coll., Hartford, 1964, Arts Club of Washington, 1972, Cornell Club of N.Y., 1977, Copley Soc. Boston, 1978, Woods-Gerry Gallery, R.I. Sch. Design, 1983; represented in permanent collections Met. Mus. Art., Watson Library, Boston Mus. Fine Arts, Cin. Art Mus., Dumbarton Oaks, Washington, Houghton Library, Harvard U., Hunt Library, Carnegie-Mellon U., N.Y. Pub. Library, Rosenwald Collection Nat. Gallery, Kew Gardens Library, Royal Bot. Garden, Edinburgh, Nat. Library, Canberra, Australia; sculpture placed in Mann Library, Kroch Library and Morrison Hall, Cornell U., McGill U., N.Y. Bot. Gardens, Hunt Library, Pitts., Pres.'s Office, Keene (N.H.) State Coll., Herzog August Bibliothek, Wolfenbüttel, Fed. Republic Germany (bronze bust of founder). Recipient Gold medals Pen and Brush, N.Y.C., 1964, Margaret Sussman Meml. award 1987, Gold medals Nat. Arts Club, 1970, Gold medals Acad. Artists Assn., Springfield, Mass., 1976, Founders' Prize Pen and Brush, 1977; Bd. Dirs. award Salmagundi Club N.Y., 1978; Elliot Liskin award, 1979, Catherine Lorillard Wolfe Club award, 1993. Fellow Nat. Sculpture Soc. (Barrett-Colea prize 1984); mem. Nat. Soc. Mural Painters.

ABBETT, WILLIAM S., dean. Dean Mich. State U. Coll. Human Medicine, East Lansing. Office: Mich State U A110 E Fee Hall East Lansing MI 48824*

ABBEY, G(EORGE) MARSHALL, lawyer, former health care company executive, general counsel; b. Dunkirk, N.Y., July 24, 1933; s. Ralph Ambrose and Grace A. (Fisher) A.; m. Sue Carroll, July 13, 1974; children: Mark, Steven, Michael, Lincoln. BA with high distinction, U. Rochester, 1954; JD with distinction, Cornell U., 1957. Bar: N.H. 1957, Ill. 1965. Atty. McLane, Carleton, Graf, Greene & Brown, Manchester, N.H., 1957-65; atty. Baxter Internat. Inc., Deerfield, Ill., 1965-69, gen. counsel, 1969-72, sec., gen. counsel, 1972-75, v.p., sec., gen. counsel, 1975-82, sr. v.p., gen. counsel, 1985-90, sr. v.p., sec., gen. counsel, 1990-93; pvt. practice, 1993-97; of counsel Bell Boyd & Lloyd, Chgo., 1997—. Editor Cornell Law Rev., 1956-57. Mem. vis. com. Law Sch., U. Chgo., 1978-81; dir. Coun. Puerto Rico-U.S. Affairs, 1988-92; mem. indsl. adv. coun. U. P.R.; dir. P.R.-USA Found., 1975-93, B.U.I.L.D., Chgo., 1980-84, bus. adv. com. B.U.I.L.D. Inc.; bd. dirs. Hundred Club of Lake County, Ill., 1976-86; dir. Food and Drug Law Inst., 1975-93; bd. dirs. Evanston Inventure, 1986-88; former trustee Winnetka Congl. Ch.; dir. Nat. Com. for Quality Health Care, 1988-93; mem. Northwestern U. Corp. Coun. adv. bd., 1976-93; dir. P.R. Cmty. Found., 1986-94; bd. dirs. Better Bus. Bur. Chgo. and No. Ill., 1991-93; mem. Conf. Bd's. Coun. Chief Legal Officers and Legal Quality Coun., 1991-93. Mem. ABA, Ill. Bar Assn., Lake County Bar Assn., Chgo. Bar Assn., Health Industry Mfrs. Assn. (chmn. legal/regulatory affairs 1976-78, bd. dirs. 1978-80, chmn. govt. affairs com. 1980-81), Univ. Club, Exmoor Country Club, Bankers Club (P.R.), Order of the Coif, Phi Beta Kappa. Office: GM Abbey, Bell, Boyd & Lloyd 3 Parkway N Ste 110 Deerfield IL 60015-2548

ABBEY, GEORGE W. S., space center executive; b. Seattle, Aug. 21, 1932; children: George, Joyce, Suzanne, James, Andrew. BS in Gen. Sci., U.S. Naval Acad., 1954; MSEE, Air Force Inst. Tech., 1959. Commd. 2d lt. USAF, 1954, advanced through grades to maj., 1965; detailed to Johnson Space Ctr. (formerly Manned Spacecraft Ctr.), Houston, 1964-67, tech. asst. to mgr. Apollo Spacecraft program, 1967-69, tech. asst. to dir., 1969-76, dir. flight ops., 1976-85, dir. flight crew ops., 1985-88; dep. assoc. adminstr. for space flight NASA Hdqs., Washington, 1988-90, dep. for ops. for synthesis group, 1990-91; sr. dir. for civil space policy Nat. Space Coun., Exec. Office Pres., Washington, 1991-92; spl. asst. to adminstr. NASA, Washington, 1992-94; dep. dir. Johnson Space Ctr., 1994-95, acting dir., 1995, dir., 1996—. Recipient Medal of Freedom, Pres. of U.S., 1970, Exceptional Performance award Fed. Women Program, 1973, Civil Servant of Yr. award managerial and exec. category Fed. Bus. Assn., 1974, Space Flight award Am. Astron. Soc., 1983, Al Merito Della Repulica Italiana award, 1996, Quasar award, 1997, Clear Lake Econ. Devel. Found. award for excellence, 1997, Rotary Nat. award for Space Achievement Found., 1997; named Sr. Exce. Svc. Presdl. rank, meritorious, 1989, disting., 1994, Nassau Bay Citizen of Yr., 1999. Fellow Am. Astronautical Soc.; mem. U.S. Naval Inst. Office: Lyndon B Johnson Space Ctr 2101 Nasa Rd 1 Houston TX 77058-3607

ABBOT, QUINCY SEWALL, retired insurance executive; b. Wilkes-Barre, Pa., Apr. 24, 1932; s. Theodore S. and Alice (Howell) A.; m. Zelia Gillam, Jan. 12, 1957; children: Elizabeth, Susan, Rebecca, Jayne. AB, Williams Coll., 1954. Actuarial student Conn. Gen. Life Ins. Co., Hartford, 1954-55, 59-64, asst. actuary, 1964-67, assoc. actuary, 1967-70, dir. taxes, 1970-75, v.p., 1975-82; v.p. CIGNA, Hartford, Conn., 1982-85, sr. v.p., 1985-91; ret., 1991. Pres. Hartford Assn. Retarded Citizens, 1975-76, Conn. Assn. Retarded Citizens, 1981-83, Corp. Ind. Living, Hartford, 1980-81, Corp. Supported Employment, 1985-88, Communitas, 1990—; v.p. The Arc of U.S., 1994-96, pres., 1996-98; vice chair Conn. Cmty. Care, Inc., 1992-95; chmn. Inst. for Human Resources Devel., 1988-90. Gov.'s Coun. Mental Retardation, 1990-96; trustee Wyo. Sem., 1990-93. 1st lt. U.S. Army, 1955-58. Fellow Soc. Actuaries; mem. Am. Ins. Assn. (chmn. tax com. 1986-87), Tax Execs. Inst. (chpt. pres. 1970-71), Ins. Assn. Conn. (chmn. tax com. 1975-83), Am. Council Life Ins. (chmn. tax com. 1975-77, 88-89). Republican. Mem. United Ch. of Christ. Home: 52 Sunrise Hill Dr Hartford CT 06107-3350

ABBOT, WILLIAM WRIGHT, history educator; b. Louisville, Ga., May 20, 1922; s. William Wright and Lillian (Carswell) A.; m. Eleanor Pearre, Mar. 31, 1958; children—William Wright, John Pearre. Student, Davidson (N.C.) Coll., 1939-41; AB, U. Ga., 1943; MA, Duke U., 1949, PhD, 1953; LittD, Coll. William and Mary, 1998. Tchr. Louisville Acad., 1946-47, McCallie Sch., 1951-52; from asst. prof. to prof. history Coll. William and Mary, 1953-58, 59-66; assoc. prof. Northwestern U., 1958-59, Rice U., 1961-63; James Madison prof. history U. Va., 1966-92, emeritus, 1992—; chmn. history dept. 1972-74. Author: The Royal Governors of Georgia, 1754-1775, 1957, The Colonial Origins of the United States, 1607-1763, 1975; editor in chief: The Papers of George Washington, 1977-92 , Colonial Series, Vols. I-X, Revolutionary War Series, Vols. I-VI, Confederation, Vols. I-VI, 1992-97, Presidential, Vols. I-V, Retirement Series, Vols. I-IV, 1998; editor Jour. So. History, 1961-63; book rev. editor William and Mary Quar., 1955-61, editor, 1963-66; bd. editors Va. Quarterly Rev., 1971-90. Served to lt. USNR, 1943-46. Mem. Inst. Early Am. History and Culture (coun. 1976-79), So. Hist. Assn. (exec. coun. 1978-81), Mass. Hist. Soc., Am. Antiquarian Soc., Va. Hist. Soc. (hon.), Gridiron Club (U. Ga.), Raven Soc. (U. Va.), Phi Beta Kappa (pres. Alpha chpt. 1984-87). Home: 804 Rugby Rd Charlottesville VA 22903-1629

ABBOTT, ALDEN FRANCIS, lawyer, government official, educator; b. Bethesda, Md., Nov. 10, 1951; s. Roger Sloane and Suzanne Jeanne (Dupuy) Abbott; m. Ljubica Visich, May 3, 1980; 1 child, Roger Visich. Cert., U. Madrid, 1972; BA, U.Va., 1974; JD, Harvard U., 1977; MA in Econ., Georgetown U., 1984. Bar: D.C. 1977, U.S. Supreme Ct. 1992. Atty. Office of Legal Policy FTC, Washington, 1977-80; atty. Fried, Frank, Harris, Shriver & Kampelman, Washington, 1980-82; spl. counsel Office of Legal Policy U.S. Dept. Justice, Washington, 1982-84, spl. asst. to asst. atty. gen. antitrust divsn., 1984-86, sr. counsel Office of Legal Counsel, 1987-89; counsellor to gen. counsel U.S. Dept. Commerce, Washington, 1989-92, chief counsel Nat. Telecomm. and Info. Adminstrn., 1992-94, asst. gen. counsel fin. and litigation, 1994—; adj. prof. Sch. Law George Mason U., Arlington, Va., 1991—. Comment and note editor Harvard Internat. Law Jour.; contbr. numerous articles to profl. jours. Mem. Fed. Comms. Bar Assn. (internat. sect.), U.S. Supreme Ct. Bar, Henry Simons Soc., Phi Eta Sigma, Phi Beta Kappa. Avocations: foreign languages and travel, swimming, reading, skiing. Home: 1611 Westmoreland St Mc Lean VA 22101-5166 Office: US Dept Commerce General Counsel 14th St NW # 5896 Washington DC 20011-8107

ABBOTT, ANN AUGUSTINE, social worker, educator; b. Green Bay, Wis., July 6, 1943; d. Walter A. and Ethel D. Augustine. BS in Psychology, St. Norbert Coll., W. DePere, Wis., 1965; MSS in Social Work (U.S. Children's Bur. fellow), Bryn Mawr Coll., 1969, PhD (NIMH fellow), 1977; postgrad. in Higher Edn. Adminstrn., Higher Edn. Resource Sevcs. Summer Inst. for Women, Bryn Mawr (Pa.) Coll., 1978. Acad. tutor, counselor Devereux Schs., Devon, Pa., 1965-67; psychol. clinic coord. Pa. State U., University Park, 1969-71; social worker Tidewater Mental Health Clinic, Williamsburg, Va., 1971-72; adj. prof. Pa. State U., King of Prussia, 1973-75; vis. lectr. Community Coll. of Phila., 1975-76; asst. prof. dir. social work, community psychology Widener U., Chester, Pa., 1976-81, project dir. Univ. Yr. for Action, 1976-81, project cons. Adult Competency Tng. Grant, 1976-81; with sch. social work Rutgers U., Camden, N.J., 1981—, assoc. prof., 1987—, assoc. dean, 1993—; faculty fellow NIAAA/NIDA/OSAP, 1990-93. Tennis coach Nat. Jr. Tennis League, Phila., 1974-76; budget rev. bd. United Way, vice-chair allocations com., 1979-86. Trustee Ins. Trust, 1995-98, chair, 1996-98. Vocation Rehab. Tng. grantee, 1964. Fellow Am. Orthopsychiat. Assn., Coll. Physicians of Phila.; mem. NASW (nat. bd. mem. region IV 1988-91, del. assembly rep. 1978-89, pres. Pa. state chpt. 1987-89, nat. pres.-elect 1992-93, nat. pres. 1993-95), Coun. on Social Work Edn. (commn. on accreditation 1997—), Am. Group Psychotherapy Assn., Internat. Fed. of Social Workers (v.p. for N. Am. 1994-96). Home: PO Box 637 Villanova PA 19085-0637 Office: Rutgers U Social Work Dept 327 Cooper St Camden NJ 08102-1519

ABBOTT, BEVERLY STUBBLEFIELD, artist; b. Greensboro, N.C., Dec. 12, 1940; d. Robert L. and Helen W. Stubblefield; m. Ira H.A. Abbott, May 7, 1960; children: Ira Robert, Leslie Ann. Represented by Gallery Jamel, Waldorf, Md., Blue Skies Gallery, Hampton, Va., Gray Wolf Gallery, Woodbridge, Va., Rappahannock Hang-Ups, Kilmarnock, Va. Exhibited in group shows at Leigh Yawkey Woodson Art Mus., 1996, 97, Seaside Art Gallery Internat. Art Show, 1996, 97, 98, Village Gallery Internat. Show, 1997, 98, 99. Mem. Hampton Arts League (Merit award 1997), Atlantic Wildfowl Heritage Mus. (Appreciation award 1990), James River Camera Club (pres. 1994), Langley Kennel Club (life, show chmn. 1977, 84). Avocations: traveling, photography. Home: 13 Delta Cir Newport News VA 23601-3117

ABBOTT, BOB, state supreme court justice; b. Kans., Nov. 1, 1932. BS, Emporia State U.; JD, Washburn U.; LLM, U. Va. Bar: Kans. 1960. Pvt. practice Junction City, Kans., from 1960; former chief judge Kans. Ct. Appeals; justice Kans. Supreme Ct., 1990—. Office: Kansas Supreme Court 374 Kansas Judicial Ctr Topeka KS 66612-1599*

ABBOTT, BOYCE, temporary help company executive; b. Aug. 5, 1945. BS, Ind. State U.; MBA, Northwestern U. Rep. Hong Kong Trade Coun., Chgo. and, Hong Kong; dir. Conf. Bd., N.Y.C. and Chgo.; v.p. Kelly Internat., Chgo. and Taipei, Taiwan. Office: 3340 Dundee Rd Ste 2C3 Northbrook IL 60062

ABBOTT, CHARLES FAVOUR, lawyer; b. Sedro-Wolley, Wash., Oct. 12, 1937; s. Charles Favour and Violette Doris (Boulter) A.; m. Oranee Harward, Sept. 19, 1958; children: Patricia, Stephen, Nelson, Cynthia, Lisa, Alyson. BA in Econs., U. Wash., 1959, JD, 1962. Bar: Calif. 1962, Utah 1981. Law clk. Judge M. Oliver Koelsch, U.S. Ct. Appeals (9th cir.), San Francisco, 1963; assoc. Jones, Hatfield & Abbott, Escondido, Calif., 1964; pvt. prarctice Escondido, 1964-77, Provo, Utah, 1983-93; of counsel Mueller & Abbott, Escondido, 1997—; ptnr. Abbott, Thorn & Hill, Provo, 1981-83, Abbott & Abbott, Provo, 1993—. Author: How to Do Your Own Legal Work, 1976, 2d edit., 1981, How to Win in Small Claims Court, 1981, How to Be Free of Debt in 24 Hours, 1981, How to Hire the Best Lawyer at the Lowest Fee, 1981, The Lawyers's Inside Method of Making Money, 1979, The Millionaire Mindset, 1987, How to Make Big Money in the Next 30 Days, 1989, Business Legal Manual and Forms, 1990, How to Make Millions in Marketing, 1990, Telemarketing Training Course, 1990, How to Form A Corporation in Any State, 1990, The Complete Asset Protection Plan, 1990, Personal Injury and the Law, 1997, Fen-Phen Fallout--The Medical and Legal Crisis, 1998; mem. editl. bd. Wash. Law Rev. and State Bar Assn. Jour., 1961-62; bd. editors Phen-fen Litigation Strategist, 1998—; contbr. articles to profl. jours. Mem. ATLA, Utah Bar Assn., Calif. Bar Assn., U.S. Supreme Ct. Bar Assn. Home: 2830 N Marrcrest Circle Provo UT 84058 Office: 3651 N 100 E Ste 300 Provo UT 84604-4598

ABBOTT, CORINNE, fundraiser; b. Bryan, Tex., Feb. 3, 1968; d. Edwin Hunt and Ann (Quain) A. BA, Tufts U., 1990; MPA, George Mason U., 1996. Adminstrv. asst. Trinity Coll., Washington, 1991; asst. dir. ednl. found. No. Va. C.C., Annandale, 1991-95; mgr. ann. fund Am. Assn. Blood Banks, Bethesda, Md., 1995-96; assoc., disaster fundraising Am. Red Cross, Washington, 1996-98; major gifts officer ARC, Washington, 1998—. Vol. Mark Warner, Senate, Falls Church, Va., 1996. Mem. Women's Info. Network. Avocations: tennis, Yoga, wine tasting. Office: American Red Cross 430 17th St NW Washington DC 20006-5307

ABBOTT, DAVID HENRY, manufacturing company executive; b. Milton, Ky., July 6, 1936; s. Carl and Rachael (Miles) A.; m. Joan Shefchik, Aug. 14, 1976; children—Kristine, Gina, Beth, Linsey. B.S., U. Ky., 1960, M.B.A., 1961. With Ford Motor Co., Louisville, Mpls. and Dearborn, Mich., 1961-69; div. controller J I Case Co., Racine, Wis., 1970-73, gen. mgr. service parts supply div., 1973-75, v.p., 1975, v.p. and gen. mgr. constrn. equipment div., 1975-77; v.p., gen. mgr. Drott div. J I Case Co., Wausau, Wis., 1977-79, exec. v.p. worldwide constrn. equipment, 1979-81; pres., chief operating officer Portec, Inc., Oak Brook, Ill., 1981-87, also dir.; pres., chief exec. officer, dir. E.D. Etnyre & Co., Oregon, Ill., 1988—; dir. Oak Brook Bank, 1982-88. Served with U.S. Army, 1958. Mem. Constrn. Industry Mfrs. Assn. (bd. dirs. 1979-81, 82—, chmn. 1992—), Am. Rd. and Transpn. Builders Assn. (dir. 1988—). Republican. Home: 2690 W Pines Rd Oregon IL 61061-9068 Office: E D Etnyre & Co 1333 S Daysville Rd Oregon IL 61061-9778

ABBOTT, DOUGLAS EUGENE, engineering educator; b. Glendale, Calif., Apr. 20, 1934; s. Richard Edward and Eva (Pogue) A.; m. Doris Bernice Newmark, Dec. 16, 1956; children: Sandra Lee, Jodi Frances, Shari Evalinis, Traci Bernice. B.M.E., Stanford U., 1956, M.M.E., 1957, Ph.D., 1961. Asst. head fluid mechanics sect. Vidya div. Itek Corp., Palo Alto, Calif., 1960-64; lectr. Stanford U., 1963-64; asso. prof. Purdue U., 1964-69, prof., 1969-77, dir. thermal scis. and propulsion center, 1972-77; prof., chmn. dept. mech. engring. and mechanics, dir. computer-aided design/computer-aided mfg. ednl. program Lehigh U., Bethlehem, Pa., 1977-83; vice provost for computing and info. services Lehigh U., 1983-85; assoc. vice chancellor for info. technologies U. Mass.-Amherst, 1985-96; cons. in comms. technologies Amherst, 1996—; Staff cons. Midwest Applied Sci. Corp., Lafayette, Ind., 1964-72; energy controls div. Bendix Corp., South Bend, Ind., 1967-75, Westinghouse Research and Devel. Center, Pitts., 1970-75, ERDA, 1975-77; chmn. air breathing propulsion adv. com. Air Force Office of Sci. Research, 1973-83, Tech. Concepts, Inc., Sudbury, Mass., 1985-88; bd. dirs. Univ. Programs in Computer Aided Engring., Design and Mfg., 1984-91. Mem. governing bd. Five Coll. Libr., 1991-96. Hon. research fellow Sci. Research Council, U.K., 1971-72. Fellow AAAS, Am. Phys. Soc.; mem. ASME, AIAA, N.Y. Acad. Scis., Nat. Computer Graphics Assn. (bd. dirs. 1985-87, treas. 1987-89), Nat. Computer Graphics Assn. Ednl. Found. (bd. dirs. 1989-92), Trout Unltd. (bd. dirs. Pioneer Valley chpt. 1995—), Pi Tau Sigma. Home: 307 Shutesbury Rd Amherst MA 01002-1268

ABBOTT, EDNA ELEANOR, nurse, retired; b. Horton Bay, Mich., Dec. 23, 1920; d. John Adolph and Ruth Caroline (Ekstrom) Koteskey; m. Dearl Wesley Abbott, June 9, 1945; children: James, David, Jeanne, Daryl. Diploma in nursing, W.A. Foote Meml. Hosp., 1946; BA, Seattle Pacific U., 1953. Tchr. Kenya Highland Bible Coll.; tchr. psychiat. nursing Norton Meml. Infirmary, Louisville; sch. tchr. Mich. Dept. Edn.; nurse coord. VA Med. Ctrs., Lexington, Ky., retired, 1983. Author: Twice Around and More, 1993, Poems & Stories for the Heart, 1994, The Counters, 1995, If You Can't Sing...Humm, 1997, Spreading the Good News, 1998. Recipient Ky. Col. award, 1973. Republican. Avocations: writing, poems and stories, travel. Home: 501 Bellevue Ave Wilmore KY 40390-1013

ABBOTT, EDWARD LEROY, finance executive; b. Dayton, Ohio, Dec. 18, 1930; s. Roy Edward and Mildred Eileen (Filler) A.; m. Elizabeth Joan Grahame, June 8, 1957; children: Jay Edward, Julie Beth Abbott Holland. A.B., Wittenberg U., 1952; postgrad., Ohio State U., 1952-53. With Northwestern Mut. Life Ins. Co., 1956-73; regional mgr. Northwestern Mut. Life Ins. Co., Washington, 1970-73; with Acacia Mut. Life Ins. Co., Washington, 1973-83; exec. v.p., treas. Acacia Mut. Life Ins. Co., 1978-83; vice chmn., exec. v.p. CenTrust Savs. Bank, Miami, Fla., 1983-87; chmn., pres., chief exec. officer Capital-Union Savs., Baton Rouge, 1987-90; pres., chief exec. officer, dir. Firstate Fin., Orlando, Fla., 1992-97, Heritage Hll Farms, 1998—. Served with U.S. Army, 1954-55. Mem. Alpha Tau Omega. Republican.

ABBOTT, ERNEST B., emergency management administrator. BA, Swarthmore Coll.; JD, Harvard U., MA. Atty. Hogan & Hartson, Washington; atty.-advisor Interstate Commerce Commn.; spl. asst. for legis. devel. U.S. EPA; mng. atty. Tenneco Energy, Houston, prin. dep. gen. counsel, dir., v.p.; gen. counsel Fed. Emergency Mgmt. Agy., Washington, 1997—; mem. adv. com. Am. Arbitration Assn. Office: Fed Emergency Mgmt Agy Office Gen Counsel 500 C St SW Washington DC 20472

ABBOTT, FRANK HARRY, lawyer; b. Lansdowne, Pa., May 6, 1919; s. Harry J. and Eva E. (LaGasse) A.; m. Elisabeth Dunigan, Jan. 29, 1943;

children—Terence, Richard, Francis Harry Jr. B.E.E., Villanova U., 1941; J.D., Temple U., 1949. Bar: Pa. 1950. Electronics engr. RCA, Camden, N.J., 1941-46; assoc. Schnader, Harrison, Segal & Lewis, Phila., 1949-59, ptnr., 1959—. Served to lt. comdr. USNR, 1942-46, PTO. Mem. ABA, Pa. Bar Assn., Phila. Bar Assn. Republican. Roman Catholic. Clubs: Merion Golf (Ardmore, Pa.); Lawyers, Union League (Phila.); Rehoboth Beach Country. Avocations: golf, shooting, tennis. Office: Schnader Harrison Segal et al 1600 Market St Ste 3600 Philadelphia PA 19103-7240

ABBOTT, GAYLE ELIZABETH, human resources consultant; b. Cleve., July 7, 1954; d. Olcott Rutherford and Eleanor Francis (Norley) A.; 1 child, Elizabeth Laura. BA, Am. U., 1976; MBA, Loyola Coll., Balt., 1983. Cert. sr. profl. in human resources. Personnel mgmt. specialist Food and Drug Adminstrn., Washington, 1975-77; personnel mgr. Computer Network Corp., Washington, 1977-78; dir. human resources STSC, Inc., Rockville, Md., 1978-84; compensation cons. Comm. Satellite Corp., Washington, 1984-85; pres., founder HURECO, Inc. dba Century Solutions, Herndon, Va., 1985—; lectr., adj. faculty Marymount U., Arlington, Va., 1990-95, Am. U., Washington, 1995—; spkr. profl. assns. and confs. Co-author: Deflecting Workplace Violence, 1994; contbr. articles to profl. jours. Chmn. pers. com. Lewinsville Presbyn. Ch., 1987-91; troop leader Brownie Girl Scout Troop, 1996-97. Recipient Lodestar award Am. U., 1992. Mem. AAUW (bd. rec. sec. 1987, v.p. membership 1988-89), Soc. for Human Resource Mgmt. (dir. Va. state coun. 1991), No. Va. Soc. for Human Resource Mgmt. (legis. rep. 1987-88, v.p. programs 1988, pres. 1989-90, dir. 1991-93, Disting. Leadership award 1991), Am. U. Alumni Assn. (v.p. 1988-90, pres. 1990-92, bd. dirs. 1993-97). Unity. Office: 2455 Horse Pen Rd Ste 220-a Herndon VA 20171-3426

ABBOTT, GEORGE LINDELL, librarian; b. Rutland, Vt., July 11, 1941; s. F. George and Eva Marie (Fields) A.; m. Sandra Jean Baker, Aug. 6, 1966; 1 child, Brian George. BA in Math., St. Michael's Coll., 1963; MLS, Syracuse U., 1966. Cataloguer St. Michael's Coll., Winooski, Vt., 1963-64; cataloguer libr. Syracuse (N.Y.) U., 1966-70, media librarian, 1970-80, head dept. media svcs., 1980—; cons. in field. Contbr. articles to various publs.; editor Videodisc/VideoTex jour., 1980-82. Mem. ALA, Am. Soc. Info. Sci. (bd. dirs. 1981-85), Libr. and Info. Tech. Assn. (bd. dirs. 1985-88), Soc. Motion Picture and TV Engrs., Beta Phi Mu. Avocations: microcomputing, cinema. Office: Syracuse Univ Libr 222 Waverly Ave Syracuse NY 13210-2412

ABBOTT, GREGORY ANDREW, lawyer; b. Omaha, Nebr., Feb. 10, 1964; s. Jon B. Abbott and Sandra Joan (Walenz) Vanderpool; m. Lynn Murphy, Nov. 5, 1994. BA, Augustana Coll., 1987; JD, U. Iowa, 1990. Bar: Minn. 1990, Tex. 1994, U.S. Supreme Ct. 1997. Assoc. Popham, Haik, Schnobrich & Kaufman, Mpls., 1990-92; instr. U. Tex., Austin, 1992-93; ptnr. Abbott & Baruch, Ltd., Mpls., 1993-98, Weinblatt and Gaylord, PLC, St. Paul, 1998—. Chair Mpls. Dem. Farmer Labor Party, 1997-98. Mem. ABA, Fed. Bar Assn., Minn. State Bar Assn., Tex. State Bar., Computer Law Assn., Minn. Software Assn.

ABBOTT, HIRSCHEL THERON, JR., lawyer; b. Clarksdale, Miss., Jan. 11, 1942; s. Hirschel Theron Sr. and Ona Belle (Williamson) A.; m. Mimi Eugenia DuPre, June 14, 1969; children: Barkley, Chip. BBA in Acct., U. Miss., Oxford, 1964; JD, U. Va., Charlottesville, 1971. Bar: La. 1971, Miss. 1971, U.S. Dist. Ct. (ea. dist.) La. 1971, U.S. Ct. Appeals (5th cir.) 1981, U.S. Tax Ct. 1988; bd. cert. tax law specialist. Lawyer Stone, Pigman, Walther, Wittmann & Hutchinson, New Orleans, 1971-75, ptnr., 1975—. Bd. dirs. Episcopal Housing for Srs., Inc., Lambeth House, Inc.; past trustee, sec. Preservation Resource Ctr., New Orleans; past bd. mem., chmn. Trinity Episcopal Sch. Bd. Trustees; past trustee, treas. La. Civil Svc. League; past bd. mem. Uptown Neighborhood Improvement Assn.; past mem., chmn. Jefferson Scholarship Selection Com. U. Va.; past regional chmn. U. Va. Law Sch. Annual Giving Fund; past mem. of vestry Trinity Episcopal Ch.; past mem. Adv. Bd. Jr. League New Orleans. Recipient Monte M. Lemann award, La. Civil Svc. League, 1989. Fellow Am. Coll. Trust and Estate Counsel (mem. charitable planning & exempt orgns. com.), La. Bar Found.; mem. ABA (tax sect., bus. law sect., real property trusts probate sect.), La. Bar Assn. (chmn. tax law specialization comm., tax sect., corp. sect., successions, donations and trusts sect.), Miss. State Bar Assn., New Orleans Estate Planning Coun., Assn. Employee Benefit Planners. Republican. Epicopalian. Office: Stone Pigman Walther et al 546 Carondelet St Ste 100 New Orleans LA 70130-3588

ABBOTT, ISABELLA AIONA, biology educator, retired; b. Hana, Maui, Hawaii, June 20, 1919; d. Loo Yuen and Annie Patseu (Chung) Aiona; m. Donald P. Abbott, Mar. 3, 1943 (dec.); 1 dau., Ann Kaiue Abbott. A.B., U. Hawaii, 1941; M.S., U. Mich., 1942; Ph.D., U. Calif., Berkeley, 1950. Prof. biology Stanford U., 1972-82; G.P. Wilder prof. botany U. Hawaii, 1978-98, ret., 1998; vis. research biologist and tchr., Japan and Chile. Author: (with G.J. Hollenberg) Marine Algae of California, 1976, La'au Hawaii, traditional Hawaiian uses of plants, 1992; contbr. articles to profl. jours. Co-recipient N.Y. Bot. Garden award for best book in botany, 1978; recipient Merit award Bot. Soc. Am., 1995, G.M. Smith medal Nat. Acad. Scis., 1997. Fellow AAAS; mem. Internat. Phycological Soc. (treas. 1964-68), Western Soc. Naturalists (sec. 1962-64, pres. 1977), Phycological Soc. Am., Brit. Phycological Soc., Hawaiian Bot. Soc. Office: U Hawaii Botany Dept 3190 Maile Way Honolulu HI 96822-2232

ABBOTT, JAMES SAMUEL, III, marketing executive; b. Cleve., Nov. 19, 1918; s. James Samuel and Dorothy (Wilbor) A.; m. Mary Margaret Torrance, Oct. 13, 1957; 1 child, James Samuel. Student, Cornell U., 1941. Sales engr. Nat. Acme Co., Cleve., Chgo., 1945-63; chief sales engr. Nat. Acme Co., Cleve., 1963-67; sales mgr. Nat. Acme Co., 1967-69; mktg. mgr. Cleveland Twist Drill Co., Cleve., 1969-83; pres. James S. Abbott Consulting, Inc., Gates Mills, Ohio, 1983—. Contbr. articles to profl. jours. Mem. pk. bd. Village of Gates Mills, Ohio, 1979-86. Capt. USAF, 1941-45. Mem. Soc. Founders-Patriots (gov. 1968-69), Soc. Colonial Wars, Western Res. Hist. Soc., Clev. Mus. Natural History, U.S. Horse Cavalry Assn., Mayfield Country Club. Avocations: Am. history, antiques, fly fishing, golf, tennis, vintage cars. Home: 7059 Hillcreek Ln Gates Mills OH 44040-9629

ABBOTT, JIM, member of Canadian parliament; b. Toronto, Ontario, Can., Aug. 18, 1943. Mem. parliament rep. Kootenay E. House of Commons, Ottawa, Ontario, Can., 1993-97; mem. parliament rep. Kootenay-Columbia House of Commons, Ottawa, Can., 1997—. mem. standing com. pub. accts., 1993-97, standing com. on fin. 1993-97, standing com. on environ., standing com. on natural resources, 1993-97; 1st vice chair standing com. on Canadian Heritage, 1997—. Mem. Reform Party Can. Office: House of Commons, 915 Confed Bldg, Ottawa, ON Canada KIA086 Other Address: 35 Carnbrook St N, Cranbrook, BC Canada VIC 3P7*

ABBOTT, JOHN RODGER, electrical engineer; b. L.A., Aug. 2, 1933; s. Carl Raymond and Helen Catherine (Roche) A.; m. Theresa Andrea McQuaide, Apr. 20, 1968. BS with honors, UCLA, 1955; MSEE, U. So. Calif., 1957. Registered profl. engr. Calif.; cert. tchr. Calif. Advanced study engr. Lockheed Missile Systems, L.A., 1955-56; B-58 aircraft doppler radar systems engr. Hughes Aircraft Co., L.A., 1956-59; devel. engr. F-104 aircraft air data computer Garrett Airesearch Co., L.A., 1959-63, instr. in-plant tng. program, 1962-63; asst. project engr. Litton Industries, L.A., 1963; space power systems engr. pioneer 6 TRW Systems, L.A., 1963-65; engr. specialist L.A. Dept. Water and Power, 1965-92, Abtronix, 1992—; frequency coordination chmn. Region X, Utilities Telecommunications Coun., 1977-79, sec.-treas. Utilities Telecommunication Coun., 1979-80; instr. amateur radio course L.A. City Schs., Birmingham High Sch., Van Nuys, Calif., 1965-66, Los Feliz Elem. Sch., Hollywood, Calif., 1990—. Author, pub.: Ride The Airways with Alfa & Zulu and DIT & DAH Card and Dice Games; contbr. articles to profl. jours. Mem. IEEE, Am. Radio Relay League (Tau Beta Pi award 1971), Tau Beta Pi. Office: Abtronix PO Box 220066 Santa Clarita CA 91322-0066

ABBOTT, JOHN SHELDON, law school dean and chancellor emeritus; b. Detroit, May 10, 1926; s. Arthur James and Florence E. (Allen) A.; m. Karen Filline Ackerman; children—Laura Kathryn, John Sheldon Jr. A.B., Kalamazoo Coll., 1950; J.D., Detroit Coll. Law, 1953, LL.D. (hon.); LL.M., U. Mich., 1954. Bar: Mich. 1954. Individual practice law Detroit, 1954-59; prof. law Detroit Coll. Law, 1959-70, assoc. dean, 1970-72, dean, chief adminstrv. officer, 1972-86, chancellor, 1986-87, dean emeritus, 1987—; commr. State Bar Mich., 1982-85; chmn. Mich. Jud. Tenure Commn., 1987-88; chmn. Assn. Ind-Colls. and Univs., 1985; trustee Lawrence Tech. U. Author: Organizing Small Business Enterprises, 1962. Served with USN, 1944-45. Fellow Am. Bar Found.; mem. ABA, Mich. Bar Assn., Royal Poinciana Golf Club of Naples. Home: 825 Bentwood Dr Naples FL 34108-8204*

ABBOTT, LAWRENCE E., lawyer; b. Miami, Fla., May 18, 1944. BA, St. Edward's U., 1967; JD, Tulane U. La., 1972. Bar: La. 1972, U.S. Dist. Ct. (ea. dist.) La. 1972, U.S. Dist. Ct. (we. dist.) La. 1974, U.S. Dist. Ct. (mid. dist.) La. 1975, U.S. Supreme Ct. 1979, U.S. Ct. Appeals (5th cir.) 1981, U.S. Ct. Appeals (11th cir.) 1984, Tex. 1996. D.C. 1996. Mem. Abbott, Simses, Album & Kaister, Houston. Mem. ABA (products, gen. liability and consumer law com., rail and motor carrier law com., toxic and hazardous substances and environ. law com. 1995—), Maritime Law Assn. U.S. (mem. internat. law sea com. 1984—, mem. subcom. offshore exploration and devel. 1984—, mem. com. river and ocean towing 1985—), Average Adjusters Assn. U.S. (assoc.), La. State Bar Assn. (asst. examiner com. on bar admissions 1994—), La. Assn. Def. Counsel, New Orleans Bar Assn., New Orleans Def. Counsel Assn., Southeastern Admiralty Law Inst., Def. Rsch. Inst., Inc., La. Bar Found., La. Assn. R.R. Trial Counsel, Am. Arbitration Assn., La. Assn. Bus. and Industry, Phi Delta Phi. Office: Abbott Simses Album & Kaister 1360 Post Oak Blvd Ste 1700 Houston TX 77056-3062*

ABBOTT, LENICE C., education educator, administrator; b. Dec. 11, 1953. BA in Elem. Edn., Wheaton (Ill.) Coll., 1976; MS in Adult Edn., Nat.-Louis U., Evanston, Ill., 1992. Dir. prior learning assessment Nat.-Louis U., Wheaton, 1986—. Email: labb@whe2.nl.edu. Office: Assessment Ctr 200 S Naperville Rd Wheaton IL 60187

ABBOTT, LINDA JOY, stained glass artisan, educator; b. Hempstead, N.Y., Oct. 10, 1943; d. Edward Morton Brandstatter and Evalyne Manchik; divorced 1971; children: David Edward Black, Adam Michael Black. AAS in Design, SUNY at FIT, N.Y.C., 1963; Cert. paralegal, Tarrant County C.C., Fort Worth, Tex., 1983. Fashion designer Alyssa/Little Craft, N.Y.C., 1963-65; bus. owner Virgin Islands Diving Sch., St. Thomas, V.I., 1972-76; stained glass artisan Creative Glass, Salt Lake City, 1978-81, Linda Abbott Glass Art, Willow Park, Tex., 1981-86; stained glass artisan, instr. Crystal Rainbow Glass Studio, Dania, Fla., 1986-99; stained glass artisan Linda Abbott Glass Studio, 1999—; freelance calligrapher various colls., Covina, Calif., 1968-71; freelance artist, Lancaster, Calif., 1976-78; cons. various stained glass cos., 1989—; product cons. various stained glass equipment mfrs., 1994—; instr. sem. for glass craft expo, Las Vegas, 1994—, Lake Geneva, Wis., 1997, sem. instr. Internat. Art Glass Supplies Assn., 1994—, coord. for seminars, chairperson, 1995, 1996-98, mem. seminar com., 1999; mem. steering com. Art Glass Am., Tampa, Fla., 1998. Co-author: (books) Hot & Wired, 1993, Some Things Fishy, 1993, Rainforest, 1994, Stargazing, 1995, Image is Everything, 1996; contbr. articles to mags. in field. Recipient Best in Show award Calif. City Art Assn., 1978, Glass Expo, Salt Lake City, 1982. Mem. So. Fla. Ferret Club, Internat. Art Glass Suppliers Assn. (com. chair 1996—), Internat. Stained Glass Designers Assn. (pres. 1995—), Art Glass Guild Artisans (dir. 1996—), Art Glass Am. (founder), Edn. Consumer Conf. Jewish. Avocations: scuba diving, white water rafting, animal welfare causes. Office: Linda Abbott Glass Studio 11280 NW 14th Ct Pembroke Pines FL 33026-2631

ABBOTT, MARY ELAINE, photographer, lecturer, researcher; b. LaGrange, Ill., Apr. 23, 1922; d. Vergil and Goldie (Wright) Schwarzkopf; m. Harry Edward Abbott, Oct. 8, 1949; children: John Edward, Jane Ann. BA in English, Psychology, U. Iowa, 1944, student. With child welfare dept. Montgomery County Children's Home, Dayton, Ohio, 1944-47, Mich. Children's Inst., Ann Arbor, 1947-49; photographer, lectr., rschr., 1978—; participant Taft Confs., Eagle's Nest, Oregon, Ill.; lectr. on Lorado Taft. Photographer St. Paul's Ch. history, History of Jackson County, History of Queens Cath. Ch., History of Music in Jackson County, Mich. Living, Victorian Living; photodocumentary of homes in Jackson Hist. Dist., homes and blds. of Claire Allen; commd. Taft Sculpture, Sculpture Jackson County; author: The Wondrous Works of Claire Allen, 1997; photography and artistic dir. James Agee's Knoxville, Summer 1915 in concert; commd. by Jackson Historic Dist. Commn. and State Hist. Soc., Mich. Dance Assn.; hist. dist. commn. advisor Dance for the Handicapped, Savs. and Loan "40 Doors", Amitech, Jackson Alliance of Businessmen; represented in permenant collections Ella Sharp Mus., Jackson Symphony, St. Paul's Episcopal Ch., Carnegie Libr., others; exhibited in one-woman and group shows; slides included in archives Midwest Alliance, Commn. on Art in Pub. Places, Carnegie Libr., Nat. Endowment Arts, U. Ill., Eagle's Nest. Mem. Jr. League, Jackson Chorale, Nat. Trust for Hist. Preservation; panel participant on creative process Ella Sharp Mus.; advisor Jackson Hist. Commn.; tchr. U. Chgo. Gt. Books Found.; active enrichment for advanced children, Save Outdoor Sculpture for Nat. Inst. Conservation Cultural Property, Smithsonian Instn. Recipient Photography award Ella Sharp Mus., Hist. Trinity Ch., Detroit, Cert. of Honor, Spl. Recognitions Excellence Luth. Ctr. Assn.; included in Funk and Wagnall Encyclopedia. Mem. Internat. Platform Assn. (mem. arts com., arts adv. bd., photography award, Juror's Choice in art exhibit, Inner Cir. Merit award 1993, 2d prize for photography 1994, 1st prize art show 1996), Log Cabin Soc. Mich., Internat. Platform Assn. (2d prize 1997), Nat. Mus. Women in Arts, Arts Midwest, Kappa Alpha Theta. Republican. Episcopalian. Avocations: music, history, reading, walking, Indian and frontier history. Home and Office: 721 Oakridge Dr Jackson MI 49203-3914

ABBOTT, REBECCA PHILLIPS, museum director, art consultant; b. Giessen, Germany, Jan. 10, 1950; d. Charles Leonard and Janet Alice (Praeger) Phillips. BA, Emory and Henry Coll., 1973; postgrad., Georgetown U., 1975, Am. U., 1982-88. Assoc. univ. registrar Am. U., Washington, 1977-81, assoc. dir. adminstrv. computing, 1981-84, dir. adminstrv. computing, 1984-88; dir. membership Nat. Mus. of Women in the Arts, Washington, 1988-89, dir., 1989-98; cons. in fine arts, 1998—; fine arts photographer. Selected solo exhbns., Includes Anton Gallery, Public Places Private Views, 1992, The Wind, 1994, Canal Views, 1996, Burton Marinkovich Fine Art, Shadows at 18th and K, 1998; Selected group exhbns. includes The Annex Gallery, Metaphysical Landscapes,1989, Embassy of Japan: East Meets West, 1995, Nippon Gallery, Assimilations, 1997. Mem. Am. Assn. Mus., Mid-Atlantic Assn. Mus. Art Table.

ABBOTT, REGINA A., neurodiagnostic technologist, consultant, business owner; b. Haverhill, Mass., Mar. 5, 1950; d. Frank A. and Ann (Drelick) A. Student, Pierce Bus. Sch., Boston, 1967-70, Seizure Unit Children's Hosp. Med. Ctr. Sch. EEG Tech., Boston, 1970-71. Registered technologist. Tech. dir. electrodiagnostic labs. Salem Hosp., 1972-76; lab. dir. clin. neurophysiology Tufts U. New Eng. Med. Ctr., Boston, 1976-78; clin. instr. EEG program Laboure Coll., Boston, 1977-81; adminstrv. dir. dept. Neurology Mt. Auburn Hosp., Cambridge, Mass., 1978-81; tech. dir. clin. neurophysiology Drs. Diagnostic Service, Virginia Beach, Va.; tech. dir. neurodiagnostic ctr. Portsmouth Psychiatric Ctr., 1981-87; founder, pres., owner Commonwealth Neurodiagnostic Services, Inc., 1986—; co-dir. continuing edn. program EEG Tech., Boston, 1977-78; mem. adv. com. sch. neurodiagnostic tech. Laboure Coll., 1977-81, Sch. EEG Tech. Children's Hosp. Med. Ctr., Boston, 1980-81; assoc. examiner Am. Bd. Registration of Electroencephalographic Technologists, 1977-83; mem. guest faculty Oxford Medilog Co., 1986; cons. Nihon Kohden Am., 1981-83; cons., educator Teca Corp., Pleasantville, N.Y., 1981-87; allied health profl. staff mem. Virginia Beach Gen. Hosp., Humana Hosp. Bayside, Virginia Beach; clin. evaluator Calif. Coll. for Health Scis., 1995—. Contbr. articles to profl. jours. EIL scholar, Poland/USSR, 1970; recipient Internat. Woman of Yr. award in bus. and sci. Internat. Biographical Ctr., London, 1993-94, Woman of Yr. award Am. Biographical Inst., 1993. Mem. NAFE, Am. Soc. Electroneurodiagnostic Technologists, New Eng. Soc. EEG Technologists (bd. dirs., sec., tng. and edn. com., faculty tng. and edn.), Am. Assn. Electrodiagnostic Technologists, Epilepsy Soc. Mass. Avocations: running, art collecting, photography, reading, investing. Office: Commonwealth Neurodiagnostic Svcs Inc 400 Biltmore Ct Virginia Beach VA 23454-3459

ABBOTT, ROBERT CARL, management company executive; b. Riverside, Calif., Oct. 20, 1955; s. Orville Hancock and Erna Adella (Sparber) Whitney; m. Diane Alicia Sallstrom, Aug. 5, 1978 (div. May 1999); children: Ryan Christian, Aaron Matthew, Kalen James. MBA, Century U., 1993. Ordained to ministry Calvary Grace Christian, 1976; firefighter, Wash., Emergency Med. Tech., first aid instr. and survival instr.; reg. hypnotherapist Am. Bd. Hypnotherapists, Wash. State Dept. of Health; lic. massage therapist, Oreg. Affirmative action officer State of Wash., Spokane, Wash., 1976-77; personnel supr. Key Tronic Corp., Spokane, 1977-80; personnel mgr. ISC Systems Corp., Spokane, 1980-84; fire chief Millwood Fire Dept., Millwood, Wash., 1982-88; pres. and CEO Total Mgmt. Systems, Inc., Millwood, 1984-88; gen. mgr. Ptarmigan Village, Whitefish, Mont., 1988-91, Unitech Composites, Inc., Hayden Lake, Idaho, 1991-93; CEO Total Mgmt Sys., Rathdrum, Idaho, 1993-94; dir. staffing and employee devel. N.W. Natural Gas Co., 1994-97; human resources mgr. Great Western Chem., Portland, Oreg., 1997—; dir. Northwest Psychic Rsch., Oregon City, Oreg. Mem. Gov.'s Com. of Vet. Bus., Washington, 1983-84; chmn. Whitefish Fire Svcs. Area Commn., 1989-91; mem. CAP. Named Most Influential for the Year, Millwood Fire Dept., 1984. Christian. Avocations: karate (black belt), backpacking, scuba diving, juggling, fishing. Home: 17957 S Greenfield Dr Oregon City OR 97045-7848 Office: 808 SW 15th Ave Portland OR 97205-1907

ABBOTT, ROBERT DEAN, education scientist; b. Twin Falls, Idaho, Dec. 19, 1946; s. Charles Dean and Billie June (Moore) A.; m. Sylvia Patricia Keim, Dec. 16, 1967; children: Danielle, Matthew. B.A., Calif. Western U., San Diego, 1967; M.S., U. Wash., 1968, Ph.D., 1970. Asst. prof., assoc. prof. Calif. State U.-Fullerton, 1970-75; asst. prof., prof. ednl. psychology U. Wash., Seattle, 1975—; dir. Ctr. Inst. Devel. and Research, Seattle, 1983-92. Author: Elementary Multivariate Statistics, 1983; contbr. articles to profl. jours. Calif. State scholar, 1964-67. Fellow Am. Psychol. Assn.; mem. Am. Ednl. Research Assn., Am. Stats. Assn., Psychometric Soc. Methodist. Office: Ednl Psych 312 Miller PO Box 353600 Seattle WA 98195-3600

ABBOTT, THOMAS BENJAMIN, speech educator; b. Washington County, Pa., June 27; s. Thomas Rankin and Emma Elizabeth (Behling) A.; m. Lee M. Parsons, Dec. 29, 1945; children—John Parsons, Amy Parsons Quinn. B.A., Muskingum Coll., New Concord, Ohio, 1943; M.A., Case Western Res. U., 1947; Ph.D., U. Fla., 1957. Lectr. U. So. Calif., 1957-58; prof. speech Baylor U., 1958-63; prof. speech U. Fla., 1963-90, prof. emeritus, 1991—, chmn. dept. speech, 1978-86, acting assoc. dean Grad. Sch., 1990; cons. Westinghouse Elec. Corp. Health Systems, 1978-85, Kuwait U., 1988—. Bd. dirs. Fla. Easter Seal Soc., 1969—, Nat. Easter Seal Soc., 1978-86. Served with AUS, 1942-45. Recipient Disting. Alumni award Case Western Res. U., 1990. Fellow Am. Speech-Lang.-Hearing Assn. (cert., legis. coun.); mem. Fla. Lang.-Speech-Hearing Assn. (honors award), U. Fla. Faculty Club (past pres.). Democrat. Episcopalian. Office: U Fla 356 Dauer Hall Gainesville FL 32611-2005

ABBOTT, VERLIN LEROY, sales executive; b. St. Joseph, June 24, 1954; s. Verlin M. and Mary Lou (Johnston) A.; m. Kathleen Marie Girou, Aug. 10, 1974 (div.); 1 child, Crystal Lynn; m. Margaret Rose Svetlik, Aug. 2, 1996. BS, U. Mo., 1976; MS, The Johns Hopkins U., 1988. Commd. 2d lt. U.S. Army, 1976, advanced through grades to lt. col., 1993, platoon leader, 1977-78, battalion S2, 1978-79, exec. officer, 1979-80, detachment commdr., 1981-82, comp. commdr., 1982-84, chief rsch. team, 1984-85, program coord. R&D, 1985-87, program mgr. R&D, 1988-93, chief ops. staff, 1993-95, dep. comdr., 1995-96, R&D divsn. chief, 1995-96, ret., 1997; v.p. sales Resort Condominiums Internat., Indpls., 1997—. Contbr. numerous articles to profl. publs. Fund raiser, neighborhood capt. March of Dimes, Columbia, Md., 1986, 89, 90, 94; v.p. Cedar Crossing Home Owners Assn., 1989-97. Mem. Urban Land Inst., Am. Resort Devel. Assn., Am. Hotel & Motel Assn., Nat Ski Area Assn., Materials Rsch. Soc., Assn. of Old Crows, Am. Legion. Avocations: reading, scuba/snorkling, cars. Home: 13702 Thistlewood Dr E Carmel IN 46032-5132 Office: Resort Condominiums Internat 3502 Woodview Trce Indianapolis IN 46268-1195

ABBOTT, VICKY LYNN, educational administrator; b. Evansville, Ind., Aug. 27, 1951; d. Irl Raymond and Juanita Joyce (Becker) Hicks; m. Bill David Abbott, Aug. 4, 1973. BS in Elem. Edn., Ind. State U., 1972; MA in Elem. Edn., U. S.C., 1979, postgrad., 1988. Cert. elem. tchr., mid. sch. sci. tchr., S.C. Tchr. math. Dade Christian Sch., Hialeah, Fla., 1972-73, Alice Drive Mid. Sch., Sumter, S.C., 1973-84; staff developer Sumter Sch. Dist. 17, Sumter, 1984-89, coord. instrn., 1989—; condr. insvc. workshops. Mem. sch. bd. Sumter Christian Sch., 1983-85; treas. Alice Dr. Mid. Sch. PTA, 1983-84; chmn. Sumter County Clemson Extension Adv. Coun., 1989; bd. dirs. Sumter YMCA. Named mem. 1992 Citizen Amb. Program to Russia and Estonia; honoree Tribute to Women in Industry, 1990. Mem. ASCD (assoc.), NSTA, Nat. Coun. Tchrs. Math., S.C. Coun. Tchrs. Math., S.C. Coun. Suprs. Math. (sec.), S.C. ASCD, S.C. Sci. Coun., S.C. Sci. Suprs. Assn., U. S.C. Alumni Assn., Ind. State U. Alumni Assn., Phi Delta Kappa (newsletter editor 1991-93, rsch. rep. 1994, pres. 1995), Delta Kappa Gamma (treas.). Republican. Baptist. Avocation: astronomy. Home: 709 White Pine Way Sumter SC 29154-6210 Office: Sumter Sch Dist 17 PO Box 1180 Sumter SC 29151-1180

ABBOTT, WILLIAM THOMAS, claim specialist; b. Guthrie, Okla., Jan. 6, 1938; s. Benjamin Franklin and Eva Mae (Lattin) A.; m. Jerri Evelyn Stacy, Apr. 20, 1974. BS, Cen. State U., Okla., 1960; Casualty Claim Law Assoc., Am. Ednl. Inst., 1975. Cert. Fraud Examiner, Assn. Cert. Fraud Examiners, 1996. Claim adjuster Crawford and Co., Lubbock, Tex., 1964-67, Tulsa, 1967-70; sr. claim specialist State Farm Ins. Co., Tulsa, 1970—; bd. dirs. Okla. Arson Adv. Coun., chmn., 1996—. Mem. Young Reps., 1967, Tulsa Met. Ministries, 1971-75, Tulsa Mental Health Hotline, 1971-73, Okla. Hist. Soc. With USMC, 1960-64. Mem. Am. Legion, Internat. Assn. Arson Investigators (bd. dirs. Okla. chpt. 1985-93, pres. 1991), Assn. Cert. Fraud Examiners (Tulsa chpt.), Tulsa Claims Assn. (pres. 1981, Claimsman of Yr. 1979), pres. Mt Carmel Cemetery Assn., Noble Co., Okla., Internat. Assn. Spl. Investigation Units (bd. dirs. Okla. chpt. 1998—), Profls. Against Confidence Crime (assoc.), Investigative Reporters and Editors (assoc.), Santa Fe Trail Assn., Blue Goose, Fire Marshal Assn. Okla. (assoc.), League Am. Bicyclists (life), Adventure Cyclists, Tulsa Bicycle Club, Nat. Off-Road Bicycle Assn., Adventure Club N.Am. Republican. Methodist. Avocations: bicycling, state and regional history, writing. Office: State Farm Ins Co 12222 State Farm Blvd Tulsa OK 74146-5402

ABBOTT-LYON, FRANCES DOWDLE, journalist, civic worker; b. Rome, Ga., Mar. 21, 1924; d. John Wesley and Lucille Elizabeth (Field) Dowdle; m. Jackson Miles Abbott, May 15, 1948; children: Medora Frances, David Field, Elizabeth Stockton, Robert Jackson; m. Archibald W. Lyon, Oct. 15, 1993. Student, Draughon's Bus. Coll., Columbia, S.C. Feature writer, Mt. Vernon corr. Alexandria Gazette, Va., 1967-75; libr. rsch. assoc. Gadsby's Tavern Mus., Alexandria, 1977-99. Chmn. ann. George Washington Birthnight Ball, Mt. Vernon, 1974-82; sec. George Washington 250th Birthday Celebration Commn., 1979-82; mem. steering com. Neighborhood Friends Hist. Mt. Vernon, 1988-92; chmn. publicity Waynewood Woman's Club, Waynewood Citizens Assn.; treas. Mt. Vernon Citizens Assn., 1967-82; dist. chmn. Mt. Vernon March of Dimes, 1960-62; sec. Waynewood Sch. PTA, 1962-64; tchr. 1st aid Girl Scouts U.S., 1964-65; den mother Cub Scouts, 1966; registar DAR, 1968-77; chmn. publicity Mt. Vernon Women's Rep. Club, 1955. Named Mfrs. Waynewood by Cmty. Vote, 1969. Mem. The Nature Conservancy, Nat. Trust Hist. Preservation. Episcopalian. Home: 9013 Delancey Cir East Charleston SC 29406

ABBOUD, ALFRED ROBERT, banker, consultant, investor; b. Boston, May 29, 1929; s. Alfred and Victoria (Karam) A.; m. Joan Grover, June 11, 1955; children: Robert G., Jeanne Frances, Katherine Jane. B.S. cum laude, Harvard U., 1951, LL.B., 1956, M.B.A., 1958. Bar: Mass. 1957, Ill. 1959. Asst. cashier First Nat. Bank of Chgo., 1960-62, asst. v.p., 1962-64, v.p., 1964-69, sr. v.p., 1969-72, exec. v.p., 1972-73, vice chmn. bd., 1973-74, dep. chmn. bd., 1974-75, chmn. bd., CEO, 1975-80; pres., COO Occidental Petroleum Corp., L.A., 1980-84; pres. A. Robert Abboud & Co., Fox River Grove, Ill., 1984—, Braeburn Capital, Inc., Fox River Grove, Ill., 1984-92; chmn., CEO First City Bancorp. of Tex. Inc., Houston, 1988-91; bd. dirs. Hartmarx Corp., Chgo., Inland Steel Co., Chgo., AAR Corp., Elk Grove Village, Alberto-Culver Co. Author: Money in the Bank: How Safe Is It?, 1988. Capt. USMC, 1951-53. Decorated Purple Heart, Bronze Star; Baker scholar, 1958. Mem. Econ. Comml. Club, The Chgo. Club, Harvard Club

Chgo., Harvard Club N.Y.C., Barrington Hills Country Club. Home: 209 Braeburn Rd Barrington Hills IL 60010-9637 Office: 212 Stone Hill Ctr Fox River Grove IL 60021-0033

ABBOUD, FRANCOIS MITRY, physician, educator; b. Cairo, Egypt, Jan. 5, 1931; came to U.S., 1955, naturalized, 1963; s. Mitry Y. and Asma (Habac) A.; m. Doris Evelyn Khal, June 5, 1955; children: Mary Agnese, Susan Marie, Nancy Louise, Anthony Lawrence. Student, U. Cairo, 1948-52; M.B., B.Ch., Ein Chams U., 1955; D (hon.), U. Lyon, France, 1991; DSc (hon.), Med. Coll. Wis., 1994. Diplomate Am. Bd. Internal Medicine, Am. Bd. Cardiovascular Disease (bd. govs. 1987-93). Intern Demerdash Govt. Hosp., Cairo, 1955; resident Milw. County Hosp., 1955-58; Am. Heart Assn. research fellow cardiovascular labs. Marquette U., 1958-60; Am. Heart Assn. advanced research fellow U. Iowa, 1960-62, asst. prof., 1961-65, assoc. prof. medicine, 1965-68, prof. medicine, 1968—, prof. physiology and biophysics, 1975—, Edith King Pearson prof. cardiovascular rsch., 1988—; dir. cardiovascular div., 1970-76, chmn. dept. internal medicine, 1976—, dir. cardiovascular center, 1974—; attending physician U. Iowa Hosps., 1961—, VA Hosp., Iowa City, 1963—; chmn. rsch. rev. com. Nat. Heart, Lung and Blood Inst., 1978-80, adv. coun., 1995—. Editor Circulation Rsch., 1981-86, Procs. of the Assn. Am. Physicians, 1995—; assoc. editor Advances in Internal Medicine, 1991-96; editl. bd. Medicine, 1992—. Recipient European Traveling fellowship French Govt., 1948, NIH Career Devel. award, 1962-71. Master ACP; mem. Inst. Medicine NAS, AMA, Am. Soc. Clin. Investigation, Ctrl. Soc. for Clin. Rsch. (pres. elect 1984-85, pres. 1985-86), Soc. Exptl. Biology and Medicine, Am. Heart Assn. (bd. dirs. 1977-80, past chmn. rsch. coms., award of Merit 1982, Disting. Achievement award 1988, CIBA award for hypertension rsch. 1990, pres. elect 1989-90, pres. 1990-91, Gold Heart award 1995), Am. Fedn. Clin. Rsch. (pres. 1971-72), Assn. Univ. Cardiologists, Assn. Profs. Medicine (Robert H. Williams Disting. Chmn. of Medicine award 1993, bd. dirs. 1993-97), Assn. Am. Physicians (treas. 1979-84, councillor 1984-89, 89—, pres.-elect 1989-90, pres. 1990-91), Am. Physiol. Soc. (chmn. circulation group 1979-80, chmn. clin. physiology sect. 1979-83, publ. com. 1987-90, Wiggers award 1988), Am. Clin. and Climatological Assn. (councillor 1992), Am. Soc. Pharmacology and Exptl. Therapeutics (award exptl. therapeutics 1972), Internat. Soc. Hypertension (Merck Sharp & Dohme Internat. award for rsch. in hypertension 1994), Am. Acad. Arts and Scis., Sigma Xi, Alpha Omega Alpha (bd. dirs. 1989—). Achievements include research and publications in cardiovascular physiology on neurohumoral control of circulation and mechanisms of baroreceptor activation. Home: 24 Kennedy Pky Iowa City IA 52246-2780 Office: U Iowa Coll Medicine SE 308 General Hosp Dept Internal Medicine Iowa City IA 52242*

ABBOUD, G. JASON, telecommunications executive, consultant, engineer; b. Tripoli, Lebanon, May 28, 1955; came to U.S., 1973; s. Nassry and Minerva (Keyrouz) A. BSME, Lehigh U., 1977; MBA, Columbia U., 1992. With tech. sales and mktg. Worthington Group, Mountainside, N.J., 1977-81; sales mgr. Dorr-Oliver, Stamford, Conn., 1981-83; mgr. internat. rels. div. MCI Internat., Rye Brook, N.Y., 1983-85, dir. internat. rels., 1985-87; v.p. mktg. devel. Internat. 800 Telecom, Stamford, 1987-88, with office of the pres., 1988-89; dir. global strategy NYNEX Corp., White Plains, N.Y., 1989-93; pres. Telecom line Unisys Corp., Blue Bell, Pa., 1993-95; prin. Concepts in Technology, New Canaan, Conn., 1995-97; v.p. mktg. and bus. devel. Wavtrace, Inc., Bellevue, Wash., 1997—. Office: Wavtrace Inc 1555 132nd Ave NE Bellevue WA 98005-2265

ABBOUD, JOSEPH M., fashion designer; b. Boston, May 5, 1950; s. Joseph and Lila (Sallah) A.; m. Lynn Weinstein, June 6, 1976. BA cum laude, U. Mass, 1972. Buyer, merchandiser Louis of Boston, 1972-80; salesman, designer Polo-Ralph Lauren, N.Y.C., 1980-84; designer, cons. Chanel, Paris, 1984-86; designer, prin. Joseph Abboud Co., N.Y.C., 1986—. Recipient men's knitwear design award Woolknit Assocs., 1986, Cutty Sark award as most promising menswear designer, 1987, Woolmark award as best designer of menswear, 1988, Spl. Achievement award Neckwear Assn. Am., Inc., 1994; named Menswear Designer of Yr., Coun. Fashion Designers Am., 1989, 90. Avocations: tennis, squash, running, fiction. Office: 650 5th Ave Fl 27 New York NY 10019-6108

ABBRUZZESE, JAMES LEWIS, medical oncologist; b. Hartford, Conn., Nov. 22, 1952; s. Carmine Thomas and Dorothy Elizabeth (Brown) A.; m. Marie Cristiano, Oct. 6, 1976; 1 child, Jason Lewis. BS summa cum laude, Fairfield U., 1974; MD with honors, U. Chgo., 1978. Staff physician Boston VA Hosp. Med. Ctr., Boston, 1983-84; staff Marquette (Mich.) Gen. Hosp., 1984-86; asst. internist U. Tex. M.D. Anderson Cancer Ctr., Houston, 1986-90, assoc. internist, sect. chief, dep. head, dep. dept. chmn., 1990-97, prof., internist, 1997—, chmn. dept. gastrointestinal med. oncology/digestive disease, 1996—. Fellow ACP; mem. AAAS, Am. Soc. Clin. Oncology, Am. Assn. for Cancer Rsch., Am. Pancreatic Assn., European Soc. Med. Oncology, Alpha Epsilon Delta (treas. 1974), Alpha Omega Alpha. Home: 4405 Valerie St Bellaire TX 77401-5626 Office: U Tex MD Anderson Cancer Ctr 1515 Holcombe Blvd Houston TX 77030-4009

ABCARIAN, HERAND, surgeon, educator; b. Ahvaz, Iran, Jan. 23, 1941; came to U.S., 1966; s. Joseph and Stella (Banki) A.; m. Karen Jane Berger, May 10, 1969; children: Gregory, Ariane, Margot. MD, Teheran U., 1965. Diplomate Am. Bd. Colon and Rectal Surgery (exec. dir., sec.-treas.). Intern Cook County Hosp., Chgo., 1966-67, resident in gen. surgery, 1967-71, resident in colon and rectal surgery, 1971-72, chmn. colon and rectal surgery, 1972-93; head dept. surgery, Turi Josephson prof. U. Ill. Coll. Med., Chgo., 1989—; mem. Am. Bd. Colon and Rectal Surgery, exec. dir., 1987—; mem. Am. Bd. Med. Spltys., exec. com., 1993-96. Assoc. editor Diseases of Colon and Rectum, 1981-95. Fellow ACS (various coms. and offices), Am. Soc. Colon and Rectal Surgeons (sec. 1985-87, pres. 1988-89); mem. Am. Surg. Assn., Soc. Am. Gastroendoscopic Surgeons (founder), Sydney Soc. Colon and Rectal Surgeons (hon.). Republican. Roman Catholic. Avocations: visual arts, music, philately. Office: U Ill 840 S Wood St # 518 Chicago IL 60612-7317*

ABDEL-GHANY, MOHAMED, family economics educator; b. Cairo, Mar. 24, 1940; came to U.S., 1965; s. Ibrahim Abdel-Ghany and Aischa Hassanen; m. Nancy Jean Evans; children from a previous marraige: Tamara, Sonya, Mary Katherine. BS, Cairo U., 1962; diploma, Inst. Nat. Planning, Cairo, 1963; MS, Iowa State U., 1972; PhD, U. Mo., 1974. Asst prof. consumer sci. U. N.C., Greensboro, 1974-78; assoc. prof., head dept. consumer sci. U. Ala., Tuscaloosa, 1978-82, prof., chmn. consumer sci. dept., 1982-90, prof. consumer sci., dir. internat. affairs, Coll. Human Environ. Scis., 1990—; vis. prof. Chiba U., Japan, 1990; mem. econ. rsch. group USDA, 1991, U. Qatar, Doha, 1991, U. B.C., Can., 1992, 93, 95, 97, 98, U. Pertanian, Malaysia, 1993; cons. Agy. Internat. Devel., Cairo, 1980, U. Ga., 1996. Contbr. articles to profl. jours. Mem. Am. Assn. Family and Consumer Scis. (chair rsch. sect. 1984-86, assoc. editor 1996—, Family Econs. Rsch. award 1998), Assn. Consumer Rsch. (policy bd. Jour. Consumer Rsch. 1983-85), Am. Coun. Consumer Interest (bd. dirs. 1977-79, treas. 1997—, Disting. Fellow award 1999). Avocations: chess, karate, ballroom dancing. Office: U Ala Dept Consumer Scis Box 870158 Tuscaloosa AL 35487-0158

ABDEL-KHALIK, SAID IBRAHIM, nuclear and mechanical engineering educator; b. Alexandria, Egypt, Aug. 9, 1948; came to U.S., 1969; s. Ibrahim Saad and Esha Farag (Ahmad) A.-K.; m. Sharon Lora Duncan; 1 child, Faith Austen Khalik. B.S. summa cum laude, Alexandria U., 1967; M.S. in Mech. Engring., U. Wis.-Madison, 1971, Ph.D. in Mech. Engring., 1973. Postdoctoral fellow in chem. engring. U. Wis., Madison, 1973-74, asst. prof. nuclear engring., 1976-78, assoc. prof., 1978-82, prof., 1982-87; Ga. Power disting. prof. nuclear engring. Ga. Inst. Tech., Atlanta, 1987-89, assoc. dir. sch. mech. engring., 1990-92, so. nuclear disting. prof., 1993—; instr. Alexandria U., 1967-69; sr. engr. Babcock & Wilcox, Lynchburg, Va., 1975; guest research scientist Nuclear Research Ctr., Karlsruhe, Fed. Republic Germany, 1979; vis. prof. EPFL, Inst. de Genie Atomique, Lausanne, Switzerland, 1982; cons. Kewaunee Nuclear Plant, Green Bay, Wis., 1983—, numerous research orgns. and govtl. agys.; bd. dirs. Rechargeable Battery Industries Corp., Middleton, Wis. Contbr. articles to profl. jours. Fellow Am. Nuclear Soc.; mem. ASME, Profl. Reactor Operators Soc., Am. Inst. Physics, Assn. Egyptian-Am. Scholars, Sigma Xi, Phi Kappa Phi. Achievements include three patents for gaseous control system for nuclear reactors. Home: 3579 Midvale Cv Tucker GA 30084-3210 Office: Sch Mech Engring Ga Inst Tech Atlanta GA 30332

ABDELLAH, FAYE GLENN, retired public health service executive; b. N.Y.C., Mar. 13; d. H.B. and Margaret (Glenn) A. BS in Teaching, Columbia U., 1945, MA in Teaching, 1947, EdD, 1955; LLD (hon.), Case Western Res. U., 1967, Rutgers U., 1973; DSc (hon.), U. Akron, 1978, Cath. U. Am., 1981, Monmouth Coll., 1982, Ea. Mich U., 1987, U. Bridgeport, 1987, Georgetown U., 1989; D in Pub. Svc. (hon.), Am. U., 1987; LHD (hon.), Georgetown U., 1989, U. S.C., 1991; D in Pub. Svc., U. S.C., 1991. RN, N.Y., D.C. Commd. officer USPHS, Rockville, Md., 1949, advanced through grades to rear adm., 1970, asst. surgeon gen., chief nurse officer, 1970-87, dep. surgeon gen., 1981-89, chief nursing edn. br., divsn. nursing, 1949-59; surgeon gen. USPHS, 1989; chief rsch. grants br. Bur. Health Manpower Edn., NIH, HEW, Rockville, 1959-69; dir. Office Rsch. Tng. Nat. Ctr. for Health Svcs. R & D, Health Svcs. Mental Health Adminstrn., Rockville, 1969; acting dep. dir. Nat. Ctr. for Health Svcs. R & D, Rockville, 1971, Bur. Health Svcs. Rsch. and Evaluation, Health Resources Adminstrn., Rockville, 1973; dir. Office Long-Term Care, Office Asst. Sec. for Health, HEW, Rockville, 1973-80; exec. dir. grad. sch. nursing uniformed svcs., dean, prof. U. Health Scis., Bethesda, Md., 1993—; prof. nursing, Emily Smith chair U. S.C., Columbia, 1990-91; dean, prof. Grad. Sch. Nursing, Uniformed Svcs. U. Health Scis., 1993—. Author: Effect of Nurse Staffing on Satisfactions with Nursing Care, 1959, Patient Centered Approaches to Nursing, 1960, Better Patient Care Through Nursing Research, 1965, 2d edit., 1979, 3d edit., 1986, Intensive Care, Concepts and Practices for Clinical Nurse Specialists, 1969, New Directions in Patient Centered Nursing, 1972, Preparing Nursing Research for the 21st Century, 1994; contbr. articles to profl. jours. Recipient Mary Adelaide Nutting award, 1983, hon. recognition ANA, 1986, Oustanding Leadership award U. Pa., 1987, 99, Disting. Svc. award, 1973-89, Surgeon Gen.'s medal and medallion, 1989, Allied-Signal Achievement award in aging, 1989, Gustav O. Lienhard award Inst. Medicine, NAS, 1992. Fellow Am. Acad. Nursing (charter, past v.p., pres.); mem. APA, AAAS, Assn. Mil. Surgeons U.S., Sigma Theta Tau (Disting. Rsch. Fellow award 1989), Phi Lambda Theta. Home: 3713 Chanel Rd Annandale VA 22003-2024

ABDEL-RAHMAN, MOHAMED, international agribusiness consultant; b. Cairo, Egypt, July 3, 1941; came to U.S., 1965; m. Janine Neerdaels, Dec. 21, 1967 (div. 1989); children: Magda, Susan; m. NaimaA.K. Abdel-Ghany, May 8, 1994. BS, Ain-Shams U., 1962, MS in Plant Pathology, 1964; PhD in Hort., U. Fla., 1970; postgrad., Cornell U., 1971-72. Instr. Ain-Shams Coll. Agr., 1962-65; rsch. assoc. U. Fla. Coll. Agrl., Gainesville, 1968-70; product devel. mgr., planning & devel. mgr., bus. mgr. Agway Inc., Syracuse, N.Y., 1972-82; v.p. rsch. devel. Food Source Inc., Larkspur, Calif., 1982-83; dir. Agri-Intelligence Doane Inc., Princeton, N.J., 1983-85; pres. I.A-M Corp., Trenton, N.J., 1985-89; mktg. product mgr. fungicides and herbicides BASF, Inc., Rsch. Triangle Park, N.C., 1989-95; v.p. HAAN Internat., Chapel Hill, N.C., 1995-98; sec. gen. PGRWG, 1977-79; pres. I.A.M. Corp., Trenton, N.J., 1985-89. Author: Agway Chemical and CropProtection Guides, 1972-82; contbr. over 240 articles to profl. jours. Vol. Flood Relief Orgn., N.Y., 1972. Recipient Nat. award Excellence, Egyptian Govt., 1962, 1st pl. award Am. Mktg. Assn., 1991, Best Ad award Agrl. Mktg. Assn., 1992. Mem. Am. Soc. Hort. Sci. (program chmn. 1970-76), Am. Phytopathological Soc. (numerous exec. positions 1971—), Plant Growth Regulator Soc. Am. (numerous exec. positions 1973—). Muslim. Achievements include patent for the fungicide glyodin; devel. 2 new plant growth regulators; developed several fungicides, herbicides, and plant growth regulators. Home: 23 Beechtree Ct Durham NC 27713-1942

ABDELSAMAD, MOUSTAFA HASSAN, dean; b. Mar. 12, 1941. B in Commerce with honors, Cairo U., 1961; MBA, George Washington U., 1965, DBA, 1970. Assoc. dean Va. Commonwealth U., Richmond, Va., 1977-88; dean, finance prof. U. Mass., N. Dartmouth, Mass., 1988-91; prof. fin. Tex. A&M U., Corpus Christi, Tex., 1991—, dean Coll. Bus., 1991—; cons. in field. Editor-in-chief Jour. Soc. Advanced Mgmt., 1985—. Mem. Fin. Mgmt. Assoc., Soc. Advancement Mgmt. (mgmt. excellence award, 1991, 1998, pres. excellence award, 1996, Phil Carroll Advancement Mgmt. finance award, 1989, internat. pres. 1983-86, 96—), Tex. Coun. Coll. Bus. Edn., So. Bus. Adminstrn. Assoc. Office: Dean Coll Business Tex A&M U Corpus Christi Corpus Christi TX 78412

ABDELSAYED, WAFEEK HAKIM, accounting educator; b. Fayoum, Egypt, Aug. 16, 1958; came to U.S., 1970; s. Fr. Gabriel H. and Tahani (Mikhael) A. BBA, Hofstra U., 1979; MBA, Adelphi U., 1983, MS, 1984; PhD, U. Conn., 1996. CPA Fla., N.Y.; cert. fraud examiner Assn. of Cert Fraud Examiners; cert. fin. mgr. Staff acct. KPMG Peat Marwick, L.I., N.Y., 1981-82, Deloitte & Touche, L.I., 1983-84; prof. acctg. dept. So. Conn. State U., New Haven, 1984—. Contbr. rsch. papers to profl. publs. (Competitive Paper award 1991, Becker's Outstanding Rsch. award 1991). Mem. bd. deacons Virgin Mary Coptic Orthodox Ch. Recipient scholarship N.Y. State Soc. CPAs, 1983. Mem. AICPA, N.E. Bus. and Econs. Assn. (bd. dirs.), Am. Acctg. Assn., Inst. Mgmt. Accts. (cert. mgmt. acct., cert. fin. mgmt.), Inst. Internal Auditors (cert. internal auditor), Cert. Govt. Financial Mgr., Assn. of Govt. Accts, Conn. Soc. CPAs, Beta Gamma Sigma, Beta Alpha Psi. Egyptian/Christian Orthodox. Avocations: coin and stamp collecting, photography. Home: PO Box 170 North Haven CT 06473-0170 Office: So Conn State U Sch Bus 501 Crescent St New Haven CT 06515-1330

ABDO, DEBORAH J., school administrator; b. Syracuse, N.Y., Aug. 13, 1954; d. Kamal George and Betty J. (King) A. BSEd cum laude, SUNY, Fredonia, 1976; MSEd cum laude, SUNY, Cortland, 1982; EdS, Barry U., 1997. Cert. adminstr., Fla., N.Y. Tchr. E. Syracuse (N.Y.) Minoa Sch. Dist., 1976-79; trainer, bookkeeper Winn Dixie Store, Inc., Pompano Beach, Fla., 1985-86; asst. dir. Angel's Ark Presch., West Palm Beach, Fla., 1985-86; tchr. Palm Beach County Sch. Dist., West Palm Beach, 1986-92, resource tchr. Title I, 1992-94, lang. arts specialist, 1994-96, magnet coord., 1996-98, performance devel. specialist, 1998—; ednl. cons. Houghton Miflin, Boston, 1995—, Grolier Classrrom Publs., Danbury, Conn., 1995-96. Author: Florida Professional Educators Exam Review, 1996; reviewer Houghton Miflon Lang. Series, Grade 3, 1997. Mem. ASCD, Palm Beach County Reading Coun. (pres. 1995-96, treas. 1996—), Fla. Reading Assn., Internat. Reading Assn., Nat. Coun. Tchrs. of English, Phi Delta Kappa, Delta Kappa Gamma (sec., 2nd v.p. 1988—). Avocations: quilting, cross-stitch, cooking, piano. Office: Palm Beach Co Sch Dist 3308 Forest Hill Blvd #C124 West Palm Beach FL 33406-5869

ABDOU, MOHAMED A., mechanical, aerospace, and nuclear engineering educator; b. Dissouk, Egypt, July 10, 1945; came to U.S., 1969; s. Abdelaziz Ahmed A.; 1 child, Shareef. BS, Alexandria (Egypt) U., 1967; MS, U. Wis., 1971, PhD, 1973. Rsch. engr. Argonne (Ill.) Nat. Lab., 1974-75, system mgr., 1976-77, sect. head applied physics, 1979-83, assoc. dir. fusion program, 1979-83; assoc. prof. Ga. Inst. Tech., Atlanta, 1978-79; prof. mech., aerospace, nuclear engring. UCLA, 1983—; nuclear system leader for INTOR, Internat. Atomic Energy Agy., Vienna, Austria, 1980-83; leader testing program for internat. reactor U.S. Dept. Energy, Internat. Atomic Energy Agy., Garching, Germany, 1987-90; leader JAERL neutronics program U.S. Dept. Energy, L.A., 1984-94, leader advanced power estraction, 1998—; dir. Inst. Plasma & Fusion Rsch., 1996—. Contbr. numerous articles to profl. jours. Recipient Disting. Assoc. award U.S. Dept. Energy, 1988. Fellow Am. Nuclear Soc. (recipient Young Mems. Engring. Achievement award 1982, Outstanding Achievement award fusion energy div. 1988), Furian Power Assn. (Leadership award 1996). Office: UCLA 44-114 Eng 4 Los Angeles CA 90024

ABDOU, NABIH I., physician, educator; b. Cairo, Oct. 11, 1934; came to U.S., 1962, naturalized, 1972; s. Ibrahim and Galila (Azer) A.; m. Nancy L. Layle, Aug. 26, 1939; children—Mark L., Marie L. MD, Cairo U., 1958; PhD, McGill U., 1969. Intern then resident Cairo Univ. Hosp., 1959-62; resident, fellow in allergy and immunology Hosp. U. Pa., 1963-65, Mayo Clinic, 1965-67, Royal Victoria Hosp., Montreal, Que., Can., 1967-69; asst., assoc. prof. U. Pa., 1969-75; assoc. prof. medicine U. Kans. Med. Ctr., Kansas City, 1975-78, prof. medicine, 1978-89; pvt. practice Ctr. for Rheumatic Disease and Ctr. for Allergy Immunology, Kansas City, 1989—; clin. prof. medicine U. Mo., 1989—. Fulbright scholar, 1962-65. Fellow ACP, Am. Acad. Allergy, Am. Coll. Rheumatology; mem. Am. Assn. Immunologists, Cen. Soc. Clin. Rsch., Clin. Immunology Soc. Office: Ctr for Rheumatic Disease and Ctr Allergy Immunology 4330 Wornall Rd Ste 40 Kansas City MO 64111-3217

ABDUL-BAKI, AREF ASAD, physiologist, researcher; b. Einbal, Shoof, Lebanon, Apr. 9, 1932; came to U.S., 1960; s. Asad Mahmoud and Hadiah Husein (Abdul-Baki) Abdul-Baki; children: Mei, Heitham. BS in Agr., Am. U. Beirut, Lebanon, 1956; MS in Agr., U. Ill., 1962, PhD in Agr., 1964. Asst. prof. biology Ea. Mich. U., Ypsilanti, 1964; rsch. assoc. U. Mich., Ann Arbor, 1965-66, U. Calif., Santa Cruz, 1966-67; rsch. scientist USDA, Beltsville, Md., 1967-80; dir. Am.-Saudi Agr. Rsch. Program Riyadh, Saudi Arabia, 1980-82; sci. advisor Lebanese Nat. Coun. for Scientific Rsch., Beirut, 1982-87; rsch. physiologist Veg. Lab. USDA, 1987—; ednl. advisor Govt. of Libya, Tripoli, 1956-60; cons. Food and Agr. Orgn./UN, Syria, 1977-78, Internat. Ctr. for Agr. Rsch. in Dry Areas, Syria, Yemen Arab. Rep., 1984-86; v.p. adv. bd. Orgn. for Internat. Cooperation and Devel.-Seed Scheme, 1979. Author, co-author 6 books on biology and agr.; contbr. more than 70 articles to profl. jours.; assoc. editor: Jour. Am. Soc. for Hort. Sci., HortSci. Jour. Mentor Agrl. Rsch. Svc./Beltsville program, 1992-94. Fellow Beltsville Agrl. Rsch. Ctr., 1997; recipient Mid.-East Silver award Mid.-East Jour., 1985, ARS-Tech. Transfer award USDA, 1994, Disting. Performance awards, 1992-97, Fed. Labs. Consortium award, 1995, Nat. Canners Assn. award, 1972, named Man of Yr., 1996, Friend of the Small Farmer Nat. award, 1995, Nat. Award for Environ. Protection, 1997; named Hon. Citizen, State of Tenn., 1964. Mem. Am. Soc. Plant Physiology (pres. 1976), Phi Sigma, Sigma Xi. Achievements include developing vigor and deterioration tests for seed quality measurements and sustainable vegetable production systems, environmental stress in the date growing region of hot, dry southwest California desert. Home: 11910 Franklin St Beltsville MD 20705-1120 Office: U S Dept Agriculture Beltsville Agr Rsch Ctr Vegetable Lab Beltsville MD 20705

ABDULEZER, SUSAN BETH, communications educator; b. N.Y.C., Sept. 27, 1949; d. George and Cecelia Irene Pomerantz; m. Loren Abdulezer, Aug. 30, 1987. BA in English, CUNY, 1971; MA in Deaf Edn., Columbia U., 1974; MA in Indsl. Tech., NYU, 1983. Lic. tchr. of deaf and hard of hearing, indsl. tech., N.Y.C. Tchr. of deaf N.J. Spl. Svcs., 1974-78; tchr. graphic arts N.Y.C. Pub. Sch. for Deaf, 1979-94; multimedia coord. N.Y.C. Pub. Schs., 1994—; multimedia cons. Apple Computer, Inc., Calif., 1994—; mem. adv. bd. Digital Clubhouse Network, N.Y.C., 1997—; freelance feature writer Converge. Author: (software) Street Signs: A City Kid's Guide to American Sign Language, 1996, The Virtual Alphabet Book, 1997; author, prodr., editor: (CD-rom digital documentaries) Exemplary Programs, 1998-99; contbr. articles to profl. jours. Recipient Hero in Edn. award Reader's Digest, 1996; winner innovation in tech., edn. and academia award Computerworld-Smithsonian Instn., 1996, 97; Christa McAuliffe fellow, 1994-95, fellow Smithsonian Mus. Am. History, summer 1997. Jewish. Avocation: celtic fiddling. Office: NYC Pub Schs Multimedia Ctr 225 E 23d St New York NY 10010

ABDUL-JABBAR, KAREEM (LEWIS FERDINAND ALCINDOR), retired professional basketball player, sports commentator; b. N.Y.C., Apr. 16, 1947; s. Ferdinand Lewis and Cora Alcindor; m. Habiba (Janice Brown), 1971 (div. 1973); children: Habiba, Kareem, Sultana, Amir. B.A., UCLA, 1969. Basketball player with Milw. Bucks, 1969-75, Los Angeles Lakers, 1975-89; owner Kareem Productions; now commentator ESPN, Bristol, Ct. Became NBA all-time leading scorer, 1984; appeared on TV in episodes of Mannix, The Man from Atlantis, Diff'rent Strokes, Tales from the Darkside, Pryor's Place, The ABC Afterschool Spl.; appeared in movies: The Fish that Saved Pittsburgh, 1979, Airplane, 1980, Fletch, 1985; author: (with Peter Knobler) Giant Steps: An Autobiography of Kareem Abdul-Jabbar, 1983, (with Mignon McCarthy) Kareem, 1990. Named Rookie of Year NBA, 1970; recipient Maurice Podoloff Cup; named Most Valuable Player NBA, 1971, 72, 74, 76, 77, 80; player NBA All-Star game, 1970-87, 89; named to NBA 35th Anniversary All-Time Team, 1980; NBA Playoff Most Valuable Player, 1971, 85; mem. NBA Championship Team, 1971, 80, 82, 85, 87, 88, NCAA Championship Team, 1967, 68, 69; named NCAA Tournament Most Outstanding Player, 1967, 68, 69. Muslim. Avocation: jazz. Office: 10100 Santa Monica Blvd Los Angeles CA 90067 also: Kareem Productions Ste 2200 1999 Avenue Of The Stars Los Angeles CA 90067-4699

ABDULLAH, NINA JUNAINA, psychologist; b. Bogor, Indonesia, June 1, 1970; d. Abdullah and Hindun (Bawazir) Al-Batati; m. Omar Hisham Altalib, July 26, 1992. BA, George Mason U., 1995. Receptionist Mar-Jac Investments, Herndon, Va., 1990-91; hotline listener No. Va. Hotline, Arlington, 1996; acctg. asst. Dulles Networking, Chantilly, Va., 1996; publs. asst. IIIT, Herndon, Va., 1997—; tutor Pengajian Indonesia, Chgo., 1993; sec. Muslim Social Scientist Group, Chgo., 1994. Tchr. Imaam Sunday sch., Rockville, Md., 1997; fundraiser Minaret of Freedom, Bethesda, 1997. Mem. Am. Psychol. Assn., Islamic Soc. of N.Am., Assn. for Humanist Psychology. Avocations: quranic tutoring, world travel. Home: 11926 Safa Ct Herndon VA 20170-2324 Office: Internat Inst Islamic Thought 580 Herndon Pkwy Ste 500 Herndon VA 20170-5236

ABDUL-RAHIM, SHAREEF, professional basketball player; b. Dec. 11, 1976. Forward, guard Vancouver Grizzlies. Named to NBA All-Rookie Firest Team, 1996-97, Third Team All-Am., AP. Avocations: pool, collecting basketball jerseys, movies. Office: Vancouver Grizzlies, 800 Griffiths Way, Vancouver, BC Canada V6B 6G1*

ABE, YOSHIHIRO, ceramic engineering educator, materials scientist; b. Aichi-ken, Japan, Jan. 13, 1935; s. Kiichi and Shige Abe; m. Keiko Itoh, Mar. 27, 1966; children: Masanari, Kenshi, Hiroyuki. BS, Nagoya Inst. Tech., Japan, 1958; Deng, Nagoya U., Japan, 1977. Rschr. Nippon Mineral Fibers Co., Kanagawa, Japan, 1958-61; instr. ceramic engring. Nagoya (Japan) Inst. Tech., 1961-66, lectr., 1966-76, assoc. prof., 1976-79, prof., 1979-98; prof. Chubu U., 1998—; vis. prof. U. Fla., 1980-81. Co-author: Topics in Phosphorus Chemistry, Vol. 11 1983, Phosphate Materials, 1989; editor: Superconducting Glass-Ceramics in Bi-Sr-Ca-Cu-O, 1997, procs. 2d Internat. Symposium on Inorganic Phosphate Mateirlas; patentee unidirectional crystalli, phosphate glasses and supercond. glass ceramics; inventor castable dental crowns made of calcium phosphate glass-ceramics; contbr. over 200 articles to profl. jours. including Nature, Phys. Rev., Jour. Am. Ceramic Soc. Recipient New Tech. Devel. award Ichimura Found., 1978, Acad. award Ceramic Soc. Japan, 1980, Acad. award Japan Assn. Inorganic Phosphorus Chemistry, 1993, The 20th Century award for Achievement, 1993, Acad. award Chem. Soc. Japan, 1998. Mem. N.Y. Acad. Scis., Am. Ceramic Soc., Am. Chem. Soc., Ceramic Soc. Japan (trustee, chmn. divsn. glass 1994—), N.Y. Acad. Scis., Japan Soc. Biomaterial, Internat. Dental Assn. Achievements include authority on glass-ceramics in calcium phosphate biomaterials and in Bi-based super-conductors, and on protonic conduction in glasses; discovered crystallization of some glasses below glass transition temperatures; developed castable dental crown in calcium phosphate glass-ceramics and superprotonic glassy conductors. Home: 6-1705 Higashiyama, Nisshin-City Aichi-Ken 470-01, Japan Office: Chubu U, Matsumoto-cho Kasugai-city, Aichi 487-8501, Japan

ABEEL, SAMANTHA LYNN, juvenile fiction author; b. Forks, Wash., Dec. 29, 1977; d. David Nelson and Elizabeth Ann (Pringle) A. Student pub. schs., Traverse City, Mich. Speaker Learning Disabilities Assn. Mich. Ann. Conf., 1993, Walloon Inst., Petoskey, Mich., 1993, 94, N.Y. Orton Dyslexia Soc., N.Y.C., 1994, Carroll Sch., Boston, 1994; keynote speaker Ceya Inst., U. Wis., Platteville, 1994. Author: What One Was White, 1994 (repub. as Reach for the Moon) (Margot Marek book award N.Y. Orton Dyslexia Soc. 1994); participant video Hidden Gifted. Speaker to civic groups on learning disabilities, 1993; numerous presentations to ch. groups on writing and learning differences, 1993—. Recipient 1st regional and 2d place state writer's award DAR, 1992, award of excellence Learning Disabilities Assn., 1993. Avocations: early American history, hiking, skiing, music. Home: 216 W 7th St Traverse City MI 49684-2427

ABEGG, MARTIN GERALD, retired university president; b. Alliance, Nebr., Oct. 3, 1925; s. Frank and Mary Anna (Newberry) A.; m. Barbara Louise Chamberlain, June 29, 1946; children: Martin Gerald, Robert Miles. B.S. in Gen. Engring, Bradley U., 1947; M.S. in Civil Engring, U.

Colo., 1951; Ph.D. in Civil Engring, Rensselaer Poly. Inst., 1960; LL.D. (hon.), Ill. Coll., 1982; L.H.D. (hon.), Bradley U., 1993. Registered profl. engr., Ill. registered land surveyor, Ill. Instr. engring. Bradley U., 1947-50, asst. prof., 1950-55, asso. prof., 1955-60, prof., 1960—, head dept. civil engring., 1960-63, dean Coll. Engring. and Tech., 1963-70, pres., 1971-92, pres. emeritus, 1992—; engring. aide Ill. Div. Hwys., Dixon, 1946, civil engr., Peoria, Ill., 1948; park dist. engr., Peoria, 1953-55; cons. engr. Norman Porter & Assos., N.Y.C., 1956-57, 59. Served to lt. (j.g.) USNR, 1943-46. Recipient Putnam award Bradley U., 1961, Disting. Engring Alumnus award U. Colo., 1986, Disting. Alumnus award Bradley U., 1992. Mem. Am. Soc. C.E., Sigma Xi, Sigma Tau, Phi Kappa Phi, Omicron Delta Kappa, Tau Beta Pi, Chi Epsilon. Home: PO Box 429 Fish Creek WI 54212-0429

ABEL, ANNE ELIZABETH SUTHERLAND, pediatrician; b. Milw., June 16, 1945; d. David Hollingsworth and Mildred June (Nees) Sutherland; m. Francis Lee Abel; 1 child, Jonathan Earl. BA, Pasadena Coll., 1967; MS, Ind. U., Indpls., 1969, MD, 1973. Diplomate Am. Bd. Pediatrics. Resident in pediat. Meth. Hosp., Indpls., 1973-75, Richland Meml. Hosp., Columbia, S.C., 1975-76; pediatrician Moncrief Army Hosp., Ft. Jackson, S.C., 1976-80; child and adolescent psychiatry fellow William S. Hall Psychiat. Inst., Columbia, 1981, 82-83, U. B.C.-Vancouver Gen. Hosp., 1982; pvt. practice Columbia, S.C., 1983—; pediatrician Children's Rehabilitative Svcs., Orangeburg, S.C., 1984-91, 92—; chief med. sect. Columbia Area Mental Health Ctr., 1987-92; assoc. prof. neuropsychiatry, behavioral sci. and pediats. Sch. Medicine U. S.C., Columbia, 1992—; mental health dir. Abuse Recovery Ctr., Columbia, 1994-95; cons. behavioral pediatrics Epworth Children's Home, Columbia, 1983-86, 90-97; med. dir. Abuse Recovery Ctr., Columbia, 1996—; mem. med. adv. com., children's health rehabilitative svcs. S.C. Dept. Health & Environ. Control, Columbia, 1986-92, mem. maternal and child health adv. com., 1989-91; behavioral/devel. pediatrician Orangeburg Health Dept., 1994—. Contbr. articles to profl. jours. Mem. S.C. Gov.'s Youth Unemployment Coun., Columbia, 1987. Recipient Alumni award Pasadena Coll., 1977, Vol. of Yr. award Mayor's Com. Employment Handicapped, 1988; grantee Ctr. Family Soc., U. S.C., 1993—. Fellow Am. Acad. Pediatrics; mem. AMA, Am. Acad. Cerebral Palsy and Devel. Medicine, Am. Profl. Soc. on Abuse of Children, S.C. Med. Assn., S.C. Pediatric Soc., Columbia Med. Soc. Avocations: music, boating, hiking, fishing, reading. Office: 1 Harbison Way Ste 108 Columbia SC 29212-3408

ABEL, C. HOUSTON, federal judge; b. 1930. BS, Miss. State U., 1957; JD, U. Tex., 1964. Asst. U.S. atty., 1968-79; spl. judge Upshur County Ct.; magistrate judge ea. dist. U.S. Dist. Ct. Tex., 1979-85, apptd. bankruptcy judge ea. dist., 1985. Fax: (903) 592-7273. Office: 1st Fl 200 E Ferguson St Fl 1 Tyler TX 75702-5999

ABEL, CARLOS ALBERTO, immunologist; b. Buenos Aires, May 7, 1930; came to U.S., 1959, naturalized, 1969; s. Carlos Alberto and Rosa Blanca (Molinero) A.; m. Amalia Carmen Minieri, June 15, 1959. BS, M. Belgrano Coll., 1948; MD, U. Buenos Aires, 1957. Intern St. Joseph's Hosp., Providence, 1959-60; resident in pediatrics U. Md. Hosp., 1964-66; fellow in pediatrics U. Md., Balt., 1960-64, resident in pediatrics, 1964-66; advanced rsch. fellow Scripps Clinic, La Jolla, Calif., 1966-69; vis. scientist U. Oxford, Eng., 1969-70; mem. div. basic immunology Nat. Jewish Hosp., Denver, 1970-84; sr. scientist Med. Rsch. Inst., San Francisco, 1984-92; dir. immunochemistry ICR/Med. Rsch. Inst., 1986-89; chmn. sci. coun. Med. Rsch. Inst., 1993—; biotech. cons.; vis. scholar U. Calif.-Berkeley, 1982. Contbr. articles to profl. jours. Mem. Am. Assn. Immunologists, Am. Assn. Pathologists, Biochem. Soc. (Eng.), British Soc. for Immunology, Sociedad Argentina de Immunologia, Assn. Latino Americana Immunologia, Soc. Clin. Immunology. Democrat. Roman Catholic. Achievements include research in structure and function of glycoproteins from the surfaces of lymphocytes; study of their role in cell-cell interactions, structure of antibodies, glycobiology. Home: 523 Cragmont Ave Berkeley CA 94708-1205

ABEL, ELIE, reporter, broadcaster, educator; b. Montreal, Que., Can., Oct. 17, 1920; s. Jacob and Rose (Savetsky) A.; children: Mark, Suzanne; m. Charlotte Page Abel, July 2, 1995. B.A., McGill U., 1941, LL.D., 1971; M.S. in Journalism, Columbia U., 1942; LL.D., U. Western Ont., 1976. Reporter Windsor (Ont.) Star, 1941; asst. city editor Montreal Gazette, 1945-46; fgn. corr. N.Am. Newspaper Alliance, Berlin, 1946-47; UN corr. Overseas News Agy., 1947-49; nat., fgn. corr. N.Y. Times, 1949-59; Washington bur. chief Detroit News, 1959-61; with NBC, 1961-69, chief London bur., 1965-67; diplomatic corr. NBC News, Washington, 1967-69; Godfrey Lowell Cabot prof., also dean Grad. Sch. Journalism, Columbia U., N.Y.C., 1969-79; Harry and Norman Chandler prof. Stanford U., 1979-91; Bd. govs. Am. Stock Exchange, 1974-78. Author: The Missile Crisis, 1966, (with Marvin Kalb) Roots of Involvement, The U.S. in Asia 1784-1971, 1971, (with Averell Harriman) Special Envoy to Churchill and Stalin, 1941-46, 1975, Leaking: Who Does It? Who Benefits? At What Cost?, 1987, The Shattered Bloc: Behind the Upheaval in Eastern Europe, 1990; editor: What's News: The Media in American Society, 1981. Recipient George Foster Peabody award for outstanding radio news, 1968; Overseas Press Club award for best interpretation of fgn. news, 1969. Mem. Coun. Fgn. Rels., Cosmos Club (Washington). Home: 4101 Cathedral Ave NW Apt 904 Washington DC 20016-3585

ABEL, FRANCIS LEE, physiology educator; b. Iowa City, Apr. 12, 1931; s. Earl Lester A.; m. Evelyn Joyce Reischauer, Sept. 11, 1954 (div. Mar. 1974); children: Wanda, Donna, Carolyn; m. Anne Elizabeth Sutherland, June 9, 1974; 1 child, Jonathan. AA, Creston Jr. Coll., 1950; BA in Physics, U. Kans., 1952; MD, Harvard U., 1957; PhD in Physiology, U. Wis., 1960. Postdoctoral fellow, postdoctoral trainee Wis. Heart Assn. USPHS, Madison, 1958-60; intern in pediatrics Children's Hosp., L.A., 1960-61; from asst. prof. to prof. dept. physiology Sch. Medicine Ind. U., Indpls., 1962-75; prof., chmn. dept. physiology Sch. Medicine U. S.C., Columbia, 1975-98, disting. prof. dept. pharm. and physiology, 1998-99, interim dean Sch. Medicine, 1976, assoc. dean basic sci. affairs Sch. Medicine, 1976-78; vis. prof. dept. biomed. engring. U. So. Calif., L.A., 1970; vis. prof. dept. kinesiology Simon Fraser U., Burnaby, B.C., Can., 1982; vis. prof. dept. physiology U. Limburg, Maastricht, The Netherlands, 1989-90; cons. Eli Lilly & Co., Indpls., 1965-68, VA Hosp., Columbia, 1976-80. Co-author: Basic Physiology for the Health Sciences, 1975, Cardiovascular Function, Principles and Applications, 1979, Functional Aspects of the Normal Hypertrophied and Failing Heart, 1984. Recipient Career Devel. award NIH, 1968-73, Nat. Rsch. Svc. award NIH, 1989-90. Fellow Cardiovascular sect. Am. Physiol. Soc.; mem. IEEE (life), Am. Physiol. Soc., Am. Heart Assn., Biomed. Engring. Soc. (sr.), Shock Soc. (councillor 1980-82). Avocations: fishing, hiking, water and snow skiing. Office: USC Dept Physiology Columbia SC 29208

ABEL, HAROLD, psychologist, educator, academic administrator; b. N.Y.C., July 31, 1926; s. Felix N. and Jennie (Schaefer) A.; m. Iris Tash, Jan. 30, 1949; children: Lawrence William, Matthew Robert. AB, Syracuse U., 1949, MA, 1951, PhD, 1958; DLitt (hon.), Hanyang U., Republic of Korea, 1979. Tchr. mentally retarded Syracuse and Rochester, N.Y., 1950-52; asst. instr. Syracuse U., 1952-56; assoc. prof. to prof. depts. psychology and home econs. and dir. child devel. lab. U. Nebr., 1956-65, chmn. dept. human devel., 1963-65; dir. divsn. psycho-ednl. studies, prof. edn. U. Oreg., 1965-68, assoc. dean, prof. ednl. psychology Coll. Edn., 1968-70; pres. Castleton State Coll., 1970-75; pres. Cen. Mich. U., 1975-85, prof. psychology and ednl. adminstrn., 1985-93; pres. Walden U., Mpls., 1988-91, Grad. Sch. Am., Mpls., 1993-95; chancellor Grad. Sch. Am. (now Capella U.), Mpls., 1995—. With AUS, 1945-46. Mem. AAAS, Am. Psychol. Assn., Soc. Rsch. in Child Devel., Sigma Xi, Phi Delta Kappa.

ABEL, KATE, researcher; b. Rahway, N.J., Nov. 5, 1969; d. Robert R. and Helen E. (Carter) A. B of Engring., Stevens Inst. Tech., 1991, M of Mgmt., 1993. Grad. asst. to dean student affairs Stevens Inst. Tech., Hoboken, N.J., 1991-96, rsch. asst., 1996—; pres., dir. The New Stevens Rathskeller, Hoboken, 1993—. Mem. Am. Soc. Profl. Engrs., Nat. Dirs. Assn. Avocations: weightlifting, waterskiing. Office: Stevens Inst of Tech Castle Point on Hudson Hoboken NJ 07030

ABEL, MARK R., federal judge; b. 1944. BA, Ohio U., 1966; JD, Ohio State U., 1969. Law clk. to Hon. Judge Joseph Kinneary, 1969-71; magistrate judge U.S. Dist. Ct. (so. dist.) Ohio, Columbus, 1971—. Mem. ABA, Fed. Bar Assn., Ohio Bar Assn., Columbus Bar Assn. Fax: (614) 469-5666. Office: US Dist Ct So Dist Ohio 208 US Courthouse 85 Marconi Blvd Columbus OH 43215

ABEL, MARY ELLEN KATHRYN, quality control executive, chemist; b. Cleve., Nov. 3, 1949; d. Arthur L. and Dorothy Virginia (DeLura) Jaklic; m. Burton E. Abel, June 22, 1990; 2 stepchildren: Stephanie, Russell E.; 1 child, Matthew Anthony. AA with honors, Lakeland C.C., 1985; BS in Chemistry magna cum laude, Lake Erie Coll., Painesville, Ohio, 1991. Lab technician W.S. Tyler Inc., Cleve., 1969-71, C-E Tyler, Cleve., 1974-76; quality control mgr., environ. coord. Morton Salt, Painesville, 1977—. Treas. com. mem. Boy Scouts Am., 1988-90, sr. mem. explorer scouts marksmanship post, 1987-90, sec. local com., 1987-90; mem. Lake County Indsl. Cmty. Awareness Emergency Response Adv. Panel, 1987-90. Mem. NAFE, AAUW, Am. Chem. Soc., Gold Wing Road Riders Assn. Republican. Roman Catholic. Avocations: traveling, photography, tutoring math. Home: 391 Manhattan Pkwy Painesville OH 44077-5024 Office: Morton Salt Divsn Morton Internat Inc PO Box 428 Grand River OH 44045-0428

ABEL, ROBERT BERGER, science administrator; b. Providence, July 21, 1926; s. Abraham Lincoln and Betty Ruth (Berger) A.; m. Nancy Marilyn Klein, Oct. 4, 1953; children: Alan Stewart, Deborah Jane. BS in Chemistry, Brown U., 1947; MEA, George Washington U., 1961; PhD, Am. U., 1972. Chemist Woods Hole (Mass.) Oceanographic Inst., 1947-50; oceanographer U.S. Navy Hydrographic Office, Suitland, Md., 1950-55; asst. to dir. U.S. Navy Hydrog. Office, 1955-60; asst. research coordinator Office Naval Research, Washington, 1961-64; exec. sec. Interagy. Com. Oceanography, 1960-67; asst. exec. sec. Nat. Council Marine Resources and Engring. Devel., 1967-68; dir. Nat. Sea Grant Program, Dept. Commerce, 1966-77; asst. v.p. Tex. A&M U., 1977-78; v.p. N.J. Marine Scis. Consortium, Fort. Hancock, 1979-81; pres. N.J. Marine Scis. Consortium, 1981-93; sr. sci. Stevens Inst. Tech., Hoboken, N.J., 1993—, Tex. A&M U., 1993—; instr. oceanography USNR Officers Sch., 1960-65, Fairleigh Dickinson U., 1966-83, U. Va., 1976-77; instr. ocean mgmt. Rutgers U., 1980-84; dir. Israel Oceanographic and Limnol. Rsch. Ltd., Inc.; mem. panel Nat. Acad. Scis.; mem. N.J. Dept. Agr. Adv. Bd.; mgr. Cooperative Marine Tech. Program for Middle East, 1993—; chmn. Shrewsbury N.J. Zoning Bd., 1990—; mem. N.J. Marine Fisheries Coun., 1993—. Pres. Cris-Mar Manor Civic Assn., 1957-61; bd. dirs. Tantallon Civic Assn., 1973-74, Ctr. Ocean Law and Policy; v.p. Jewish Congregation. With USNR, 1944-46. Recipient Spl. award Prince of Monaco, 1952, Superior Civilian Svc. award Navy Dept., 1963, Disting. Svc. award, 1967, Disting. Alumnus award George Washington U., 1983, Compass Disting. Svc. award, 1987, Disting. Svc. award Egyptian Nat. Inst. Oceanography and Fisheries; Gold medal Dept. Commerce, 1973; named Man of Yr. Nat. Sea Grant Program, 1977; decorated Order Jules Richard, Monaco, 1951. Mem. Am. Chem. Soc., Rsch. Soc. Am. (past pres. chpt.), Marine Tech. Soc. (pres. 1974-75), Am. Geophys. Union, Am. Soc. Oceanography (pres. 1971-72), Gulf and Caribbean Fisheries Inst. (bd. dirs.), Cosmos Club (Washington), Brown Club (N.J.). Jewish. Home: 55 Queen Ann Dr Shrewsbury NJ 07702-4127 Office: Stevens Inst Tech Davidson Labs 711 Hudson St Hoboken NJ 07030

ABELE, LAWRENCE GORDON, biology educator, university administrator; b. Balt., Mar. 1, 1946; m. Linda Abele; children: Lawrence Robert, Kenneth Paul. AA, Miami Dade C.C., 1966; BS in Biology, Fla. State U., 1968, MS in Biology, 1970; PhD, U. Miami (Fla.), 1972. Postdoctoral fellow Smithsonian Instn., Washington, 1972-73; asst. prof. Fla. State U., Tallahassee, 1973-78, assoc. prof., 1978-82, prof., 1983—, assoc. chair dept., 1979-82, chair, 1983-91, dean Coll. Arts and Scis., 1991-94, provost, vp. for acad. affairs, 1994—; vis. prof. Marine Sci. Consortium U. System Ala. State U. Fellow AAAS; mem. Am. Soc. Zoologists, Biol. Soc. Washington, Soc. Systematic Zoology, Crustacean Soc. (pres. 1983-87). Home: 841 Maderia Cir Tallahassee FL 32312-1831 Office: Fla State U Office of Provost Tallahassee FL 32306-3020

ABELE, ROBERT CHRISTOPHER, lawyer; b. Boonville, Mo., Mar. 24, 1958; s. William Arved and Joyce (Gowan) A. AB, U. Mo., 1980; JD, U. Mo., Kansas City, 1983. Bar: Mo. 1983, U.S. Dist. Ct. (we. dist.) Mo. 1983, U.S. Ct. Appeals (8th cir.) 1983, U.S. Ct. Appeals (10th cir.) 1985, U.S. Supreme Ct. 1991, U.S. Ct. Appeals (11th cir.) 1993. Law clk. to judge U.S. Ct. Appeals (8th cir.), 1983-85; assoc. Morrison, Hecker, Curtis, Kuder & Parrish, Kansas City, Mo., 1985-90, ptnr., 1990-91; ptnr. Morrison & Hecker, Kansas City, 1991-95, Badger & Levings, Kansas City, 1995—; adj. prof. U. Mo. Kansas City Sch. Law, 1988. Chmn. Mo. Coun. on Arts, 1989-94; trustee U. Mo.-Kansas City Law Found., 1986-99, pres., 1997-98; bd. dirs. Mid.-Am. Arts Alliance, 1989-98, treas. Nat. Assembly of State Art Agys, 1994-95, 95-96. Recipient Decade award U. Mo.-Kansas City Law Found., 1991. Republican. Avocation: classical vocal music. Home: 4616 Wyoming St Kansas City MO 64112-1136 Office: Badger & Levings 1101 Walnut St Ste 1207 Kansas City MO 64106-2183

ABELES, CHARLES CALVERT, retired lawyer; b. Norfolk, Va., Nov. 3, 1929; s. Charles T. and Sally (Taylor) A.; m. Mehitable Mackay-Smith, Sept. 30, 1961; children—Nathaniel C., Damaris S., Jessica A.K. A.B., Harvard U., 1952; J.D., U. Va., 1958. Bar: Va. 1958, D.C. 1958, U.S. Dist. Ct. (D.C. dist.) 1958, U.S. Ct. Appeals 1958. Assoc. Hogan & Hartson, Washington, 1958-62; assoc. Kieffer & Moroney, Washington, 1962-64, ptnr., 1964-69; ptnr. Lichtman, Abeles, Anker & Nagle, Washington, 1969-77, Wald, Harkrader & Ross, Washington, 1977-85, Piper & Marbury, Washington, 1986-95; bd. dirs. D&D Ventures Corp.; trustee Corina Higginson Trust. Author articles in field. Served to lt. (j.g.) USN, 1952-55. Mem. D.C. Bar, Transplant Recipients Internat. Orgn. (sec., nat. bd. dirs., past pres. local chpt.). Democrat. Club: Metropolitan (Washington). Home: 4531 Dexter St NW Washington DC 20007-1116

ABELES, JAMES DAVID, manufacturing company executive; b. N.Y.C., Mar. 24, 1916; s. James A. and Williemene H. (Kirtland) A.; m. Elizabeth Brunet, Aug. 24, 1940 (dec. 1978); children: James B. and Elizabeth K. (twins); m. Mary E. Ballantyne, Dec. 11, 1982. Student, Stevens Inst. Tech., 1935-36, M.I.T., 1936-37. Tool and die apprentice Electrolux Co., 1934-35; erecting engr. U.S. Fire Protection Co., 1937-38; sales engr. Thomas F. Mason Co., 1938-39; time study engr. Waterbury Button Co., 1939-40; with Purolator, Inc., Rahway, N.J., 1940-87; dir. Purolator, Inc., 1954-87, pres., 1955-70, chmn. exec. com., 1970-73; pres., dir. Interpace Corp., 1973-74, chmn. bd. dirs., 1974-76. Mem. Jockey Hollow Fish and Game Protective Assn., Chi Phi. Clubs: Somerset Hills Country (Bernardsville, N.J.); Seal Harbor (Maine) Yacht. Home: 4113 Fellowship Rd Basking Ridge NJ 07920-3906

ABELES, KIM VICTORIA, artist; b. Richmond Heights, Mo., Aug. 28, 1952; d. Burton Noel Wright and Frances Elizabeth (Sander) Hoffman. BFA in Painting, Ohio U., 1974; MFA in Studio Art, U. Calif., Irvine, 1980. Free-lance artist L.A., 1975—; lectr. varius schs. and art ctrs., 1980—; vis. disting. artist Calif. State U., Fullerton, 1985-87; asst. prof. Calif. State U., Northridge, 1998—. Author, illustrator: Crafts, Cookery and 'Country Living, 1976; author, photographer: Impressions, 1979, work featured in Artery, 1979, Pacific Poetry and Fiction Review, 1980, Fiction Internat., 1985; one-woman shows include U. Calif., Irvine, 1979, 80, Mcpl. Art Gallery, L.A., 1981, L.A. City Hall, 1982, Phyllis Kind Gallery, Chgo., 1983, Karl Bornstein Gallery, Santa Monica, Calif., 1983, 85, 87, Pepperdine U., Malibu, Calif., 1985, A.I.R. Gallery, N.Y.C., 1986, Chapman Coll., Orange, Calif., 1986, Mount St. Mary's Coll., L.A., 1987, Atlanta Pavilion, 1990, Calif. Mus. of Sci. and Industry, L.A., 1991, Laguna Art Mus. Satellite Gallery, Costa Mesa, Calif., 1991, Turner-Krull Gallery, L.A., 1992, Lawrence Miller Gallery, N.Y.C., 1992, Santa Monica Mus. Art (15 yr. survey), L.A., 1993, Nat. Mus. Fine Arts, Santiago, Chile, 1996, Mus. Modern Art, Rio de Janeiro, 1996, Cmplejo Cultural Recoleta, Buenos Aires, 1986, Centro Cutural Consolidado, Caracus, 1997, Cepa Gallery, Buffalo, 1998, ARt, Inc., N.Y.C., 1989. Honored for Outstanding Student Rsch. & Creative Achievement U. Calif., 1979; recipient U.S. Steel award Exhbn. of the Associated Artists of pitts., 1977, Clean Air award Air Quality Mgmt. Dist., Calif., 1992; hand Hollow Found. fellow, 1984, Design Team fellow Panorama City Libr., Calif., 1992-93, J. Paul Getty Trust Fund for the Visual Arts fellow, 1994; Pollock-Krasner Found. grantee, 1990, Calif. Arts Coun. grantee, 1990, L.A. Cultural Affairs grantee, 1991, 95, 96, U.S. Info. Agy. grantee, 1995-97; commissioned by Panorama City Pub. Libr., L.A., 1993, Met. Transp. Authority, L.A., 1995.

ABELES, NORMAN, psychologist, educator; b. Vienna, Austria, Apr. 15, 1928; came to U.S., 1939, naturalized, 1944; s. Felix and Bertha (Gronich) A.; m. Jeanette Bueller, Apr. 14, 1957; children: Linda, Mark. BA, NYU, 1949; MA, U. Tex., 1952, PhD, 1958. Diplomate: Am. Bd. Profl. Psychology (Midwest regional bd. 1972-78, chmn. regional bd. 1975-77; nat. trustee 1975-77). Fellow in counseling U. Tex., Austin, 1956-57; instr. Mich. State U., East Lansing, 1957-59; asst. prof. Mich. State U., 1959-64, asso. prof., 1964-67, prof. psychology, 1968—, dir. psychol. clinic, 1978—, co-dir. clin. tng., 1981-96, asst. dir. counseling center, 1965-71; U.S. State Dept. ednl. exch. prof. U. Utrecht, Netherlands, 1969, vis. prof., 1975; cons. Peace Corps, 1965-69; vocat. cons. Social Security Office of Hearings and Appeals, 1962—; med. advisor Social Security Office of Hearings and Appeals, 1986—; mem. Mich. Commn. Cert. of Psychologists, 1962-77, chmn., 1966-68; mem. coun. Nat. Register Health Svc. Providers in Psychology, 1974—, vice chmn., 1975-80; del. White House Conf. on Aging, 1995. Editor: Acad. Psychology bull., 1978-82; cons. editor Jour. Personality Assessment, 1988—, Clin. Psychology: Sci. and Practice, 1994—, Clin. Psychology Rev., 1995-98, Profl. Psychology: Rsch. and Practice, 1979-81, 89—, editor, 1983-88; contbr. articles to profl. jours. Served with U.S. Army, 1954-56. Fulbright-Hays grantee, 1969; recipient Disting. Psychologist award Mich. Soc. Clin. Psychologists, 1984; Disting. Practitioner, Nat. Acad. Practice, 1982; Arthur Furst Ethics Lectureship medal Pacific Grad. Sch. Psychology, 1996; Dept. Vets. Affairs Spl. Contbns. award, Battle Creek Mich., 1997. Fellow APA (coun. reps. 1972-75, 77-79, 89-91, 93-95, policy and planning bd. 1975-79, chmn. 1976, rec. sec. 1980-86, chmn. edn. and tng. bd. 1988, pres.-elect divsn. clin. psychology 1989, pres. divsn. psychotherapy and divsn. clin. psychology 1990, publs. and comm. bd. 1990-96, chmn. 1995, pres.-elect 1996, pres. 1997, past pres. 1998, Disting. Prof. divsn. psychotherapy 1996), Coun. Sci. Socs. Pres.; mem. Midwestern Psychol. Assn. (exec. bd. Coun. Sci. Soc. Pres.'s 1999), Mich. Psychol. Assn. (legis. chmn. 1964-72, pres. 1971-72, Disting. Psychologist 1974), Sigma Xi. Home: 953 Rosewood Ave East Lansing MI 48823-3126 Office: Mich State U Dept Psychology 129 Psychology Research East Lansing MI 48824-1117

ABELES, SIGMUND M., artist, printmaker; b. N.Y.C., Nov. 6, 1934; s. Samuel and Henrietta (Banner) A.; m. Anne Merck (div. 1998); children: David Paul, Shoshanna Lynn, Maxwell Merck Abeles. Student, Pratt Inst., 1952-53, Art Students' League, 1954, Skowhegan Sch. (scholar), 1955-56, Bklyn. Mus. Sch. (Graphics scholar), 1956-57; AB in Art, U. S.C., 1955; MFA, Columbia U., 1957. Faculty Swain Sch. Design, New Bedford, Mass., 1961-64; resident artist Wellesley (Mass.) Coll., 1964-69; asst. prof. art Boston U., 1969-70; prof. U. N.H., 1970-87, prof. emeritus, 1987—; artist-in-residence U. So. Maine, Gorham, 1990; instr. workshop Acad. Realist Art, Seattle, 1995, Art Students League, N.Y.C., 1997—; instr. advanced drawing workshop Nat. Acad. Sch. Fine Arts, N.Y.C., 1997-98; bd. dirs. Artist Fellowship, N.Y.C. Represented in permanent collections including Albert & Victoria Mus., London, The Brit. Mus., London, Libr. Congress, Washington, Mus. Modern Art, N.Y.C., Met. Mus. Art, N.Y.C., Museo de Arte, Ponce, P.R., Phila. Mus. Art, Mus. Find Art, Boston, Fitz William Mus., Cambridge, England, Munson-Proctor-Williams Inst., Ithaca, N.Y.; vis. sculptor Johnson Atelier, Tech. Inst. for Sculpture, 1977; traveling retrospective exhbn. New Eng. Coll., Henniker, N.H., McKissick Mus., U. S.C., Columbia, Checkwood Mus. Art, Nashville, Fitchburg (Mass.) Mus. Art, 1992-93; (subject of) The Observant Hand, Forty Years of the Drawing of Sigmund Abeles, So. Meth. U. Gallery, Dallas, 1998. Nat. Inst. Arts and Letters grantee, 1965, Nat. Coun. Arts and Humanities sabbatical grantee, 1966, Louis Comfort Tiffany Found. grantee, 1967, U. N.H. Grad. Sch. Sculpture grantee, 1973, Am. Jewish Com. grantee for acad. seminar in Israel, 1981, Florsheim Found. grantee, 1992; recipient Am. Master/Printmaking award Am. Artist mag., 1996; subject of "Sigmund Abeles, A Monograph" essays by Charles Simic and Robert Doty, 1992. Mem. NAD (Leo Meisner prize 1983, academician 1990, mem. coun., corr. sec. 1991—), Soc. Am. Graphic Artists, Pastel Soc. Am. Studio: 630 9th Ave Ste 1102A New York NY 10036-3708 *I strive to observe life with a penetrating eye that I hope can go beyond surface reality to reveal psychological and visual truth, even some magic.*

ABEL HOROWITZ, MICHELLE SUSAN, advertising executive; b. Detroit, Mar. 31, 1950; d. Martin Louis and Phyllis (Berkowitz) A.; m. H. Jay Abel Horowitz, July 11, 1976; children—Jordan Michael, Stefanie Jennifer. Student Goucher Coll., 1967-70; B.A. in Econs., U. Mich., 1971; postgrad. in econs. U. Calif.-San Diego, 1973; M.A. in Econs., U. Detroit, 1974-76. Planning group supr. Hill Holliday Connors, Cosmopolus, Mass., 1976-78; econ. analyst Data Resources, Boston, 1978-79; v.p., media dir. Barkley & Evergreen, Southfield, Mich., 1979-80; v.p., dir. mktg. and media Yaffe/Berline, Southfield, Mich., 1980-82; pres., ptnr., corp. treas. Berline Group, Birmingham, Mich., 1982—; instr. Oakland U., Rochester, Mich., 1982; trustee, chairperson mktg. com. Harbinger Dance Co., Farmington, Mich., 1983—. Named Advt. Woman of Yr., Women's Ad Club Detroit, 1982. Mem. Adcraft Club Detroit, Women in Communications. Democrat. Jewish. Office: The Berline Group 6100 N Adams Bloomfield Hills MI 48304

ABELL, DAVID ROBERT, lawyer; b. Raleigh, N.C., Nov. 24, 1934; s. De Witt Sterling and Edna Renilde (Doughty) A.; children: David Charles, Elizabeth A. Harrington, Kimberly A. Creasman, Hilary Ayres, Glenn Bryan; m. Ellen Penrod Hackmann, July 27, 1985. BA, Denison U., 1956; JD (Internat. fellow), Columbia U., 1963. Bar: Pa. 1963, Ill. 1973. Assoc. Ballard, Spahr, Andrews & Ingersoll, Phila., 1963-68; sec., counsel Hurst Performance, Inc., Warminster, Pa., 1969-70; sec., gen. counsel STP Corp., Des Plaines, Ill., 1970-72; ptnr. David R. Abell Ltd., Winnetka, Ill., 1974—, Rooks, Pitts & Poust, Chgo., 1996—. Author: Residential Real Estate System, 1977, 2d edit., 1990. Trustee Music Inst. Chgo., 1988-96; bd. govs. Winnetka Cmty. House, 1993-96. Aviator USMCR, 1956-60. Mem. ABA, Ill. Bar Assn., Chgo. Bar Assn., Rotary (pres. Winnetka 1977-78). Episcopalian. Home: 740 Oak St Winnetka IL 60093-2521 Office: Rooks Pitts & Poust 560 Green Bay Rd Ste 407 Winnetka IL 60093-2243

ABELL, JAN MEISTERHEIM, architect; b. Chgo.; d. Philip and Dolores (Krumdick) Meisterheim. BArch, Ohio U., 1969. Registered architect, N.Y., Fla. Architect apprentice Verster, Djikstra, Cannegieter, Amsterdam, The Netherlands, 1970-72, Stevens, Bertin, O'Connell, Rochester, N.Y., 1972-76; architect McElvy, Jennewein Stefany, Howard, Tampa, Fla., 1976-79; prin., owner Abell Garcia Partnership Architects, Tampa, 1980—; adj. faculty mem. U. South Fla., Tampa, 1989-96; Beinecke Reeves disting. chair in Archtl. Preservation, U. Fla., 1995-97. Prin. works include Port Tampa City Libr. (Fla. Trust Outstanding Preservation Project award), B.C. Graham Elem. Sch. (Outstanding Preservation Project award), restoration of Sunrise Theatre, Ft. Pierce, Fla., restoration of St. Paul AME Ch. (Fla. Trust Outstanding Preservation Project award), Leiman Wilson House (Gt. Am. Home award Nat. Trust for Hist. Preservation, Outstanding Preservation Project award Hillsborough County Planning Commn.), Edson Keith Estate, Sarasota, Fla. (Fla. Preservation award), Founder's House, Koreshan State Hist. Park, Estero, Fla. (Outsanding award for Restoration, Fla. Trust for Hist. Preservation), master plan for Hist. Tampa Bay Hotel, Writers Studio (Hillsborough County Planning award 1995); exhbns. include Women in Arch., Washington, 1987, Fla./Caribbean Arch., San Juan, P.R. Recipient numerous awards for arch., 1979—, Women of Achievement award Bus. and Profl. Women's Assn., 1982, Fla. Trust award, 1995. Fellow AIA (juror Broward County chpt. Honor awards 1990, Nat. AIA Honor awards 1993, Nat. Com. on Design co-chmn. publs., Medal of Honor Fla. Cen. chpt. 1990), AIA Fla. Assn. (Comty. Svc. award 1979). Office: Abell Garcia Architects 2201 W Dekle Ave Tampa FL 33606-3118

ABELL, MURRAY RICHARDSON, retired medical association administrator; b. Aylmer, Ont., Can., Oct. 14, 1920; came to U.S., 1952, naturalized, 1958; s. Murray C. and Alta May (Richardson) A.; m. Ruth Barbara Sommers, May 1, 1944; children: David, Cathy, Michael, Grant. Student, Aylmer Collegiate Inst., 1939; MD, U. Western Ont., London, 1944, PhD, 1951. Diplomate Am. Bd. Pathology. Instr. pathology U. Mich., Ann Arbor, 1952-53, asst. prof., 1953-56, assoc. prof., 1956-59, prof., 1959-80, prof. emeritus, 1980—; exec. dir. Am. Bd. Pathology, Tampa, Fla., 1979-93; clin. prof. U. South Fla., Tampa, 1979—; hon. lectr. numerous confs. Author: (with W.M. Thurlbeck) The Lung—Structure, Function, and Disease, 1978; series editor: (with H.J. Norris and A.T. Hertig) The Uterus, 1973; (with J.E. Edwards) The Heart, 1974; (with J. Rebuck) The Reticuloendothelial System, 1975; (with L.V. Ackerman and J.J. Spjut) Diseases of Bones and Joints, 1977; contbr. numerous articles to profl. jours. Bd. dirs. S.W. Fla. Blood Bank, Tampa, 1979—. Capt. Royal Can. Army M.C., 1943-46. Recipient Elizabeth C. Crosby award, 1963; B'nai B'rith fellow, 1942. Fellow Coll. Am. Pathologists, Am. Soc. Clin. Pathologists, U.S. & Can. Acad. Pathology (pres. 1974-75), Fla. West Coast Assn. Pathologists (past pres.).

ABELL, RICHARD BENDER, lawyer, federal judicial official; b. Phila., Dec. 2, 1943; s. Ernest George and Charlotte Amelia (Bender) A.; m. Lucia del Carmen Lombana-Cadavid, Dec. 2, 1968; children: David, Christian, Rachel. BA in Internat. Affairs, George Washington U., 1966, JD, 1974. Bar: Pa. 1974. Vol. Peace Corps, Colombia, 1967-69; assoc. Reilly & Fogwell, West Chester, Pa., 1974-80; asst. dist. atty. Chester County, Pa., 1974-79; staff mem. U.S. Senator Richard Schweiker, Washington, 1979-80; dir. Office of Program Devel. Peace Corp., Washington, 1981-83; dep. asst. atty. gen. U.S. Dept. Justice, Washington, 1983-86, asst. atty. gen., 1986-90; special master U.S. Ct. Fed. Claims, 1991—; mem. adj. faculty Del. Law Sch., Wilmington, 1975-77, West Chester State U., 1976; bd. dirs. Fed. Prison Industries, Inc., 1985-91; chmn. Nat. Crime Prevention Coalition, 1986-90; mem. adv. bd. Nat. Inst. Corrections, 1986-90; co-chmn. adv. com. Nat. Ctr. for State and Local Law Enforcement Tng., 1987-90; vice chmn. rsch. and devel. rev. bd. Dept. Justice, 1987-89; mem. nat. drug policy bd. Enforcement Coordinating Group and Coordinating Group for Drug Abuse Prevention and Health, The White House, Washington, 1988-89. Author: Peter Smith of Westmoreland County, Va. (Died 1741) and Some Descendents, 1996, Sojourns of a Patriot: Field and Prison Papers of An Unreconstructed Confederate, 1998. Chmn. Young Rep. Nat. Fedn., Washington, 1979-81; mem. exec. com. Rep. Nat. Com., 1979-81; mem. fed. coordinating coun. on Juvenile Justice and Delinquency Prevention, 1986-90; mem. Pres.'s Task Force on Adoption, 1987-88; mem. Pres.'s Commn. on Agrl. Workers, 1988-93. With U.S. Army, 1969-71. Decorated Purple Heart, Army Commendation medal for heroism, Air medal. Episcopalian. Home: 8209 Chancery Ct Alexandria VA 22308-1514

ABELLA, MARISELA CARLOTA, business executive; b. Havana, Cuba, Feb. 5, 1943; d. Carlos and Angela (Acosta) A.; m. Alberto Herrera Nogueira, Apr. 6, 1968 (div. Apr. 1986); 1 child, Carlos Alberto Herrera Abella. Asst. to v.p. and gen. mgr. bonding dept. Manuel San Juan (P.R.) Co. Inc., 1962-64; asst. corp. sec. and exec. sec. to pres. and stockholder Interstate Gen. Corp., Hato Rey, P.R., 1964-72, corp. sec. and pvt. sec. to corp. pres., 1972-79; sec.-treas., dir. A. H. Enterprises Inc., Caparra Heights, P.R., 1979-86; v.p., sec., bd. dirs. El Viajero Inc.; bd. dirs. A. H. Enterprises Inc., San Juan; pres. Marisela Abella Mktg. and Selling Promotional Items and Ideas, Caparra Heights, 1986—. Roman Catholic. Clubs: Caribe Hilton Swimming and Tennis, Barry U. Alumnae Assn. Home: 909 Borinquen Towers 2 Caparra Heights PR 00920 Office: PO Box 10510 Caparra Heights San Juan PR 00922-0510

ABELLA-DOMINICIS, ESTEBAN MARTIN, pediatrician, educator; b. Havana, Cuba, Feb. 11, 1961; came to U.S., 1961; s. Manuel and Alicia (Dominicis) Abella; m. Beth I. Wheeler, May 16, 1981; children: Isabel, Alicia, Carmen, Margarita. Student, U. Pa., 1980; MD, U. Cen. del Este, San Pedro de Macoris, 1985. Diplomate Am. Bd. Pediats. and Pediat. Hematology/Oncology; lic. physician Mich., lic. pharmacist, Mich. Resident in pediats. Wayne State U., Detroit, 1985-91, fellow in hematology, 1988-91; assoc. hematologist Wayne State Children's Hosp. of Mich., Detroit, 1991-98; asst. prof. Wayne State U., Detroit, 1991-96, assoc. prof. medicine/pediats., 1997—; assoc. bone marrow transplant faculty Karmanos Cancer Inst., Detroit, 1992—, clin. dir. pediat. BMT, 1995—, pediat. hospice dir., 1997—; med. dir. pediat. hospice Children's Hosp. of Mich., Detroit, 1996-98; presenter in field. Contbr. articles and abstracts to profl. jours. Mem. med. adv. group J. P. McCarthy Found., Detroit, 1995—; state of Mich. bone marrow transplant adv. group CON, Lansing, Mich., 1996-97; med. dir., bd. dirs. Spl. Days Camp, Lansing, 1997—. Children's Leukemia Found. Fellowship grantee, Ford/Lincoln Mercury Divsn. grantee, 1988-91. Roman Catholic. Avocations: motorcycles, dogs, children. Office: Children's Hosp of Mich Divsn Hematology Oncology 3901 Beaubien St Detroit MI 48201-2119

ABELMAN, ARTHUR F., lawyer; b. N.Y.C., June 12, 1933; s. Bert and Myra (Dickoff) A. A.B., Harvard U., 1954, J.D., 1957. Bar: N.Y. 1958, U.S. Dist. Ct. (so. and ea. dist.) N.Y. 1958, U.S. Ct. Appeals (2d cir.) 1958. Assoc. Casey Lane & Mittendorf, N.Y.C., 1957-59; counsel Am. Petroleum Inst., N.Y.C., 1959-61; corp. sec. Pocket Books, Inc., N.Y.C., 1961-65; assoc. Weil Gotshal Manges, N.Y.C., 1965-79; counsel Moses & Singer, N.Y.C., 1979—; pres. Millan House, Inc., N.Y.C., 1982—. Pres., Sculpture Ctr., Inc., N.Y.C., 1979-85, trustee, 1971—, exec. com. 1988—, treas., 1991—; trustee Neighbors of the Seventh, Inc., Norman Rockwell Art Collection Trust, E.E. Cummings Trust; trustee James Beard Found., Inc., mem. exec. com., 1995—. Mem. ABA, N.Y. Bar Assn., Assn. of Bar of City of N.Y. Republican. Jewish. Club: Harvard. Home: 116 E 68th St New York NY 10021-5905 Office: Moses & Singer LLP 1301 Avenue Of The Americas New York NY 10019-6022

ABELN, MAURA, plastics company executive; b. Reading, Pa., Oct. 3, 1955; d. Henry J. and Lynn B. (Blashe) Abeln; children: Gwendolyn, Karl. BA, Vassar Coll., 1977; MPhil, Oxford (Eng.) U., 1979; JD, U. Miami, 1982. Bar: Fla. 1982. Assoc. Steel Hector & Davis, Miami, Fla., 1982-87; ptnr. Baker & McKenzie, Miami, 1987-91; gen. counsel GE Plastics, Pittsfield, Mass., 1991—, v.p., 1993-98; sr. vice pres., gen. couns. and sec. Owens Corning, Toledo, OH, 1998—. Rhodes Scholar, 1977-79. Rhodes scholar, 1977. Mem. Phi Beta Kappa. Avocations: horseback riding, tennis, skiing. Office: Owens Corning One Owens Corning Pkwy Toledo OH 43659

ABELOFF, MARTIN DAVID, medical administrator, educator, researcher; b. Shenandoah, Pa., Apr. 4, 1942; s. Aaron Harry and Cele (Freid) A.; m. Diane Kaufman, Jan. 7, 1967; children: Elisa, Jennifer. Student, Franklin and Marshall Coll., 1959-61; AB, Johns Hopkins U., 1963, MD, 1966. Diplomate Am. Bd. Internal Medicine, subspecialty in med. oncology. Intern U. Chgo. Hosps. and Clinics, 1966-67; clin. assoc. Balt. Cancer Rsch. Ctr., 1967-69; sr. asst. resident in medicine Beth Israel Hosp., Boston, 1969-70; fellow in clin. hematology New Eng. Med. Ctr., Boston, 1970-71; fellow in clin. oncology Sch. Medicine Johns Hopkins U., Balt., 1971-72, instr. in medicine, 1972-75, asst. prof. oncology, 1974-79, asst. prof. medicine, 1975-80, prof. medicine, 1980—; Eli Kennerly Mashall Jr. prof. oncology Johns Hopkins U.; prof. & dir. Johns Hopkins Oncology Ctr., 1992; numerous vis. professorships and lectrs. including INstitut Jules Bordet, Brussels, Milton S. Hershey Med. Ctr., Nat. Cancer Inst., U. Ariz., SUNY, Stony Brook, U. So. Calif., U. Chgo., U. Md., Boston U., Mayo Clinic, others; advisor St. George's Soc., Am. Cancer Soc., 1974-84; chmn. psychosocial com. Ea. Coop. Oncology Group, 1979-83; cons. reviewer for clin. oncology rev. com. divsn. cancer treatment Nat. Cancer Inst., Bethesda, Md., 1980—. Editorial bd. Lung Cancer, 1985—, PDQ, NCI, 1986-88, Cancer Rsch., 1993; assoc. editor Jour. Clin. Oncology, 1987-96, Oncology, 1987—; assoc. editor, editorial bd. Cancer Treatment Reports, 1980-83; editor Clin. Oncology, 1992—, Oncology News Internat.; sect. editor Annals of Surg. Oncology, 1993—; adv. bd. The Med. Letter, 1991—; mem. editorial adv. bd. Health After 50, 1989—; contbr. numerous articles to profl. jours., chpts. to books. Bd. dirs. Md. divsn. Am. Cancer Soc., 1985-86. Mem. Am. Soc. Clin. Oncology (mem. ednl. com. 1978-80, mem. program com. 1981-83, chmn. program 1983-84, bd. dirs. 1984-87, chmn. com. on patterns of care 1986-87, chmn. ad-hoc com. for FDA liaison 1988-89, pres. 1991-92), Am. Assn. Cancer Rsch., Internat. Assn. for Study of Lung Cancer, Am. Assn. Cancer Edn., Phi Beta Kappa. Office: Johns Hopkins Oncology Ctr 600 N Wolfe St Rm 157 Baltimore MD 21287-0005

ABELOV, STEPHEN LAWRENCE, uniform clothing company executive, consultant; b. N.Y.C., Apr. 1, 1923; s. Saul S. and Ethel (Esterman) A.; B.S., NYU, 1945, M.B.A., 1950; m. Phyllis S. Lichtenson, Nov. 18, 1945; children—Patricia C. (Mrs. Marvin Demoff), Gary M. Asst. div. mgr. Nat. Silver Co., N.Y., 1945; sales rep. Angelica Uniform Co., N.Y., 1945-50; asst. sales mgr., 1950-56, western regional mgr., Los Angeles, 1956-66, v.p. Angelica Uniform Co. of Calif., 1958-66, nat. v.p. sales, 1966-72, v.p. Angelica Corp. 1958-88, cons., 1988—, group v.p. mktg., 1972-80, exec. v.p., chief mktg. officer Angelica Uniform Group, 1980-88; vis. lectr. mktg. NYU Grad. Sch. Bus. Adminstrn. Vice comdr. Am. Legion; mem. vocational adv. bd. VA.; adv. bd. Woodcraft Rangers; bd. dirs. Univ. Temple. Served with USAF, 1942-44. Mem. Am. Assn. Contamination Control (dir.), Am. Soc. for Advancement Mgmt. (chpt. pres.), Am. Mktg. Assn., Health Industries Assn. Am. (dir.), Inst. Environ. Scis., various trade assns., St. Louis Coun. on World Affairs, Sales Execs. Club (bd. dirs.), NYU Alumni Assn., B'nai B'rith (past pres.), Coast Guard Aux. (Flotilla comdr.), Lake of the Ozarks Yachting Assn., Men's Club (exec. v.p.), Town Hall Club, NYU Club, Aqua Sierra Sportsmen Club, Moorings Yacht Club (v.p.), Phi Epsilon Pi (treas.). Contbr. articles to profl. jours. Home: 9821 Log Cabin Ct Saint Louis MO 63124-1133

ABELOVE, HENRY, historian, literary critic; b. Montgomery, Ala., Jan. 18, 1945; s. Leo and Bernice (Kasover) A. AB, Harvard U., 1966; PhD, Yale U., 1978. Assoc. prof. history Wesleyan U., Middletown, Conn., 1979-90, assoc. prof. English, 1990-91, prof. English, 1991—; instr. history Wesleyan U., 1972-73, lectr. history, 1973-78, asst. prof. history, 1978-79; vis. assoc. prof. history Brown U., Providence, 1990; vis. prof. English, Trinity Coll., Hartford, Conn., 1992; Disting. vis. prof. English, U. Alta., Edmonton, Can., 1995. Author: The Evangelist of Desire: John Wesley and the Methodists, 1990; editor: The Lesbian and Gay Studies Reader, 1993 (Lambda prize 1993), Visions of History, 1983. Fellow John Simon Guggenheim Found., 1995-96, Nat. Endowment Humanities fellow Inst. Advanced Study, 1995-96. Mem. MLA (del. assembly 1994-96, exec. com. divsn. late 18th century English lit. 1996—), Am. Hist. Assn., Am. Soc. Eighteenth-Century Studies, Am. Studies Assn. Office: Dept English Wesleyan Univ Middletown CT 06459

ABELS, ROBERT FREDERICK, tax consultant; b. West Palm Beach, Fla., Nov. 18, 1926; s. John Frederick and Nelly (Bulfin) A.; m. Shirley Mae Larsen, May 31, 1953; children: Robert Frederick, Steven John, Richard Alan. Student, U. S.C., 1946-47; ed. flight tng. program, Naval Air Sta., Pensacola, Fla., 1947-49; BS, Naval Postgrad. Sch., Monterey, Calif., 1965; MBA in Fin., U. West Fla., 1971. Enlisted USN, 1944, commd. ensign, 1949, advanced through grades to comdr., 1963, radar operator PT boats, 1945-46, radar and radio operator PT Boats World War II; aviator USN, Republic of Korea, 1950-51, 53, Pensacola, Fla., Vietnam, 1962-63, 65-66; ret. USN, 1969; tchr. math. and bus. Skyline H.S., Lemon Grove, Calif., 1971-83, 1983; past ptnr., salesman area real estate co.; enrolled agent IRS, Washington, 1984. Decorated Bronze Star, Air medal, Vietnamese Cross Gallantry. Mem. Nat. Assn. Enrolled Agts., Inland Soc. Tax. Cons., Nat. Assn. Tax Consultors. Republican. Lutheran.

ABELSON, ALAN, columnist; b. N.Y.C., Oct. 12, 1925; s. Harry Carl and Vivian (Finkelstein) A.; m. Virginia Eloise Peterson, Sept. 1, 1951; children—Justin Adams, Reed Vivian. BS in Chemistry and English, CCNY, 1946; MA in Creative Writing, U. Iowa, 1947. Reporter N.Y. Jour. Am., N.Y.C., 1949-56; stock market columnist N.Y. Jour. Am., 1952-56; with Barron's, The Dow Jones Bus. and Fin. Weekly, N.Y.C., 1956—, mng. editor, 1965-81, editor, 1981-93; columnist Up & Down Wall St., 1966—; bus. corres. NBC-TV News at Sunrise, 1982-90. Office: Barron's 200 Liberty St New York NY 10281-0083*

ABELSON, HAROLD, electrical engineer, educator. Prof. elec. engring. MIT, Cambridge, Mass., 1990—. Recipient MIT Convocation Program award, 1992. E-mail: Hal@mit.edu. Office: MIT Dept Elec Engring 545 Tech Sq Cambridge MA 02139-4301*

ABELSON, HERBERT TRAUB, pediatrician, educator; b. St. Louis, Feb. 19, 1941; s. Benjamin J. and Ann (Traub) A.; m. Constance Faye Caldwell, May 17, 1968; children: Matthew, Rebecca, Jonathan and Daniel (twins). AB with high honors, U. Ill., 1962; MD, Washington U., St. Louis, 1966. Diplomate Am. Bd. Pediatrics (examiner 1988—, bd. dirs. 1992-97, sec.-treas. 1995, chmn.-elect 1995-96, chmn. 1996-97), Am. Bd. Pediatric Hematology-Oncology. Intern pediatrics U Colo. Med. Ctr., Denver, 1966-67; resident Boston Children's Hosp., 1969-71; staff assoc. Nat. Cancer Inst. NIH, Bethesda, Md., 1967-69; Jane Childs Meml. Fund for Med. Rsch. fellow NIH, 1971, spl. postdoctoral fellow, 1972; teaching fellow Med. Sch. Harvard Coll., Boston, 1970-71, instr. pediatrics, 1973-74, asst. prof., 1974-79; tutor in med. scis., 1977-79; assoc. prof. Harvard Coll., Boston, 1979-83; vis. prof., Ctr. for Cancer Rsch. MIT, Cambridge, 1982-83; prof., chmn. dept. pediatrics Med. Sch. U. Wash., Seattle, 1983-95; prof., chmn., physician-in-chief dept. pediatrics U. Chgo., 1995—; rsch. fellow in hematology Children's Hosp. Med. Ctr., Boston, 1971-73; rsch. assoc. in biology MIT, 1971-73; mem. pediatric residency rev. com. Accreditation Coun. for Grad. Med. Edn.; mem. exec. com. Am. Med. Sch. Pediatric Dept. Chmn. Contbr. articles to profl. jours. Lt. comdr. USPHS, 1967-69. Recipient Rsch. Career Devel. award NIH, 1975-80. Fellow Am. Acad. Pediatrics; mem. Am. Soc. Hematology (mem. sci. subcom. on pediatric hematology 1987-91), Am. Assn. Cancer Rsch., Am. Soc. Clin. Oncology, Soc. Pediatric Rsch., Am. Pediatric Soc., Am. Bd. Med. Spltys. (fin. com.). Office: Univ Chgo Dept Pediatrics 5841 S Maryland Ave # Mc1051 Chicago IL 60637-1463*

ABELSON, JOHN NORMAN, biology educator; b. Grand Coulee Dam, Wash., Oct. 19, 1938. B.S., Wash. State U., 1960; Ph.D., Johns Hopkins U., 1965; postgrad., Lb. Molecular Biology, Cambridge, Eng., 1965-68. Asst. prof. dept. chemistry U. Calif.-San Diego, 1968-73, assoc. prof., 1973-77, prof., 1977-82; prof. biology Calif. Inst. Tech., Pasadena, 1982—, chmn. dept., 1989-95; founding bd. dirs. Agouron Inst. (La Jolla), Calif., 1979—; co-founder Agouron Pharmaceuticals, Inc. Asst. editor: Analytical Biochemistry, 1980—; mem. editorial bd. Jour. Biol. Chemistry, 1981-85; mem. editorial com. Ann. Rev. Inc., 1982-86, Ann. Rev. Biochemistry; editor Methods in Enzymology; contbr. numerous articles to profl. jours. Mem. Am. Soc. Biol. Chemists, Am. Chem. Soc., Nat. Acad. Scis., Am. Acad. Arts and Scis. Home: 1233 Arden Rd Pasadena CA 91106-4135 Office: Calif Inst Tech 147-75 1200 E Calif Blvd Pasadena CA 91125*

ABELSON, PHILIP HAUGE, physicist; b. Tacoma, Wash., Apr. 27, 1913; s. Ole Andrew and Ellen (Hauge) A.; m. Neva Martin, Dec. 30, 1936; 1 child, Ellen Hauge Abelson Cherniavsky. BS, Wash. State Coll., 1933, MS, 1935; PhD, U. Calif., 1939; DS, Yale U., 1964, So. Meth. U., 1969, Tufts U., 1976, Duke U., 1981, Oregon State U., 1995; DHL, U. Puget Sound, 1968. Asst. physicist Carnegie Instn. of Washington, 1939-41, chmn. biophysics sect. dept. terrestrial magnetism, 1946-53, dir. Geophysics Lab., 1953-71, pres. instn., 1971-78; trustee from, 1978—; assoc. physicist Naval Research Lab, Washington, 1941-42, physicist, 1942-44, sr. physicist, 1944-45, prin. physicist, 1945; civilian in charge Naval Research Lab. br. Navy Yard, Phila., 1944-45; resident fellow Resources for the Future Inc., Washington, 1985-88; Chmn. com. on radiation cataracts NRC, 1949-57, sub-com. on shock, 1950-53, mem. Plowshare adv. com., 1959-63; gen. adv. com. AEC, 1960-63; mem. biophysics and biophys. chemistry study sect. Nat. Inst. Arthritis and Metabolic Diseases, NIH, 1956-59, mem. phys. biology tng. grants com. 1958-60, bd. sci. counselors, 1960-63; cons. NASA, 1960-63; sci. advisor AAAS, from 1985, acting exec. dir., 1989. Author: Energy for Tomorrow, 1975, Enough of Pessimism, 1985; mem. adv. bd. Jour Nat. Cancer Inst., 1947-52; editor: Researches in Geochemistry, 1959, Vol. 2, 1967; Energy: Use, Conservation and Supply, 1974, Food: Politics, Economics, Nutrition, and Research, 1975; Materials: Renewable and Nonrenewable, 1976, Electronics: The Continuing Revolution, 1977; co-editor Jour. Geophys. Research, 1959-65; editor Sci. mag., 1962-85, dep. editor for engring. and applied scis., from 1985. Recipient Disting. Civilian Service medal, 1945, ann. award phys. sci. Washington Acad. Sci., 1950, Disting. Alumnus award Wash. State U., 1962, Hillebrand award Chem. Soc. Washington, 1962, Modern Medicine award, 1967, Mellon award Carnegie-Mellon U., 1970, Joseph Priestley award Dickinson Coll., 1973, Sci. Achievement award AMA, 1974, Hon. Scroll award D.C. Inst. Chemists, 1976, Kalinga prize UNESCO, 1972, Disting. Pub. Service award NSF, 1984, Nat. Medal Sci., 1989, Vannevar Bush award, 1996, PublicWelfare Medal, NAS, 1992. Fellow Am. Phys. Soc., Geol. Soc. Am., Mineral. Soc. Am., Geol. Soc. Washington, Am. Acad. Arts and Scis.; mem. Am. Nuclear Soc., Seismol. Soc. Am., Internat. Union Geol. Scis. (pres. 1972-76), Brit. Biochem. Soc., Brit. Mineral. Soc., Am. Chem. Soc., Am. Philos. Soc., Soc. Am. Bacteriologists, Am. Geophys. Union (pres. 1972-74), Am. Assn. Petroleum Geologists, Geochem. Soc., Washington Acad. Scis., Biophys. Soc., Philos. Soc. Washington, Phi Beta Kappa (senator-at-large 1972—), Sigma Xi, Nat. Acad. Scis., Nat. Inst. Medicine (sr.). Club: Cosmos (pres. 1972). Office: AAAS 1200 New York Ave NW Ste 100 Washington DC 20005-3941

ABELSON, ROBERT PAUL, psychologist, educator; b. N.Y.C., Sept. 12, 1928; s. Miles Arthur and Margaret (Coble) A.; m. Willa Dinwoodie, June 11, 1955; children: John, William. BS, MIT, 1948, MS, 1950; PhD, Princeton, 1953. Psychometric fellow Princeton U., 1950-52; mem. faculty Yale U., 1952—, prof., 1963—, Eugene Higgins prof. psychology, 1969—, prof. polit. sci., 1985-94, prof. psychology and polit. sci. emeritus, 1994—; dir. Simulmatics Corp., 1961-67. Co-author: Candidates, Issues and Strategies, 1965, Theories of Cognitive Consistency, 1968, Scripts, Plans, Goals and Understanding, 1977, Knowledge Structures, 1986; author: Statistics as Principled Argument, 1995. Fellow Center Advanced Study Behavioral Scis., 1957-58, 65-66. Fellow Am. Psychol. Assn. (disting. sci. contbn. award 1986), Am. Statis. Assn., Am. Acad. Arts and Scis., Soc. for Exptl. Social Psychology (Disting. Scientist award 1990), Internat. Soc. Polit. Psychology (Disting. Sci. Contbn. to Polit. Psychology award 1996). Home: 1155 Whitney Ave Hamden CT 06517-3434

ABELT, RALPH WILLIAM, bank executive; b. Elmhurst, Ill., Feb. 16, 1929; s. P. Alfred and Clara S. (Springhorn) A.; m. Patricia Mitchell, Feb. 2, 1952; children: Susan E., Christopher M., Leslie A. BS, U. Colo., 1952; MBA, Ind. U., 1953. Acct. Marion Hutchinson, C.P.A., Denver, 1952; v.p. comml. banking Continental Ill., Chgo., 1953-77; pres., chief exec. officer, dir. Bank One of Northeastern Ohio, NA, Painesville, 1977-83; chmn., chief exec. officer Bank One Cleve., NA, 1983-86; pres., chief exec. officer Work in N.E. Ohio Council, 1988-91; bd. dirs. Plasticolors, Inc., Ashtabula, Ohio; trustee Thomas L. Conlan Found., Cin. Past pres., mem. exec. bd., area v.p. N.E. Ohio coun. Boy Scouts Am., Painesville, 1981; trustee Holden Arboretum, Kirtland, Ohio, 1982; corp. dir. Ohio Motorists Assn. Served with USMC, 1946-48. Mem. Kirtland Country Club. Home: 4711 Figgie Dr Willoughby OH 44094-7947

ABENROTH, DONNA JEAN, community health nurse; b. Excelsior Springs, Mo., Feb. 1, 1948; d. J.E. and Florence M. Dorst; m. Dennis M. Abenroth, July 2, 1971; children: James, Timothy. Cert. with honors, Letterman Army Hosp., San Francisco, 1971; AA in Nursing with honors, DeAnza Jr. Coll., 1975; BSN with honors, U. Phoenix, 1987. Lic. vocat. nurse; RN, Calif.; cert. diabetes educator. Hypertension and diabetes educator Permanente Med. Group, Milpitas, Calif., 1976-85, staff nurse III, triage nurse, case mgr. occpl. medicine, 1975-83, 1996—, hypertension and diabetes nurse instr., 1976—; clinic staff nurse III Permanete Med. Group, Milpitas, Calif., 1983—; emergency room staff nurse II, Kaiser Hosp., Santa Clara, Calif., 1975-76, Santa Teresa Hosp., San Jose, Calif., 1986; pres. Milpitas Nursing Quality Assurance Com., 1988-91, chair profl. performance com., 1991-98, chief nurse rep., 1993—, labor contract negotiator, 1993-98. With U.S. Army, 1970-72. Mem. Calif. Nurses Assn. (pres. region 10 1994—), Emergency Nurses Assn. (past county pres.). Home: 2998 Cropley Ave San Jose CA 95132-1620

ABER, JOHN DAVID, global ecosystem research scientist; b. L.A., Mar. 3, 1949; s. Otto Schultz and Esther Louise (Guy) A.; m. Lynn Marie Buckley, Mar. 30, 1971; children: Patrick, Colleen, Caitlin. BS, Yale U., 1971, M.F.S., 1973, PhD, 1976. Post-doctoral research assoc. Ecosystem Ctr., Marine Biol. Lab., Woods Hole, Mass., 1976-77; asst. prof. U. Va., Charlottesville, 1977-78, U. Wis., Madison, 1978-82; assoc. prof. U. Wis., 1982-87; assoc. prof. U. N.H., Durham, 1987-90, prof., 1990—; dir. Complex Systems Research Ctr., Durham, 1989-97; chair natural resources PhD program, 1991—; panel mem. Ecosystem Studies Program, NSF, Washington, 1987-90; cons. Jet Propulsion Lab., Pasadena, 1984-87; Bullard fellow Harvard U., 1996. Editor: Restoration Ecology, 1987; assoc. editor: Biogeochemistry, 1984-87, Can. Jour. Forest Rsch., 1995-98; author: Introduction to Forest Science, 1987, Terrestrial Ecosystems, 1991; mem. edit. bd.: Trees: Structure and Function, 1986-90, Can. Jour. Forest Rsch., 1996-98, Jour. Near Infared Reflectance Spectroscopy, 1995—; contbr. articles to profl. jours. councilor Town of Durham, 1994-97; chair bd. trustees Durham Pub. Libr., 1998—. Recipient Pound award for Excellence in Rsch., U. Wis., Madison, 1984; rsch. grantee NSF, NASA, EPA, U.S. Forest Svc., 1978—; Romnes Faculty fellow U. Wis., Madison, 1985. mem. Ecol. Soc. Am., Am. Insts. Biol. Scis., Tau Beta Pi. Home: 4 Sumac Ln Durham NH 03824-3214 Office: U NH Inst for Study Earth Oceans and Space Durham NH 03824

ABER, JOHN WILLIAM, finance educator; b. Canonsburg, Pa., Sept. 9, 1937; s. John William and Rose (Lauda) A.; m. Cynthia Louise Sousa, Nov. 24, 1962; children: John, Valerie, Alexander. BS, Pa. State U., 1959; MBA, Columbia U., 1965; BDA, Harvard U., 1972. Cons. Univ. Affiliates, Inc., Boston, 1969-71; asst. prof. fin. Ga. State U., Atlanta, 1971-72; asst. prof. fin. Boston U., 1972-78, assoc. prof., 1978-97, prof., 1997—; chmn. dept. fin. and econs., 1991-97; fin. and bank mgmt. cons., dir. Mgrs. Funds, 1999—. McKinsey scholar Columbia U.; Bus. Sch. leadership fellow, Divsn. of Rsch. fellow. Home: 51 Columbia St Brookline MA 02446-2407 Office: Boston U 595 Commonwealth Ave Boston MA 02215-1704

ABERCROMBIE, CHARLOTTE MANNING, reading specialist, supervisor; b. Swampscott, Mass., Oct. 25, 1915; d. Fredric Wilbur and Mary Sayer (Delano) Manning; m. Alexander Vaughan Abercrombie, Oct. 17, 1937; children: Lois A. Street, Paul M., David M., Lucia A. Harvilchuck. BA, Marietta Coll., 1937; MA, Columbia U., 1974, EdD, 1976. Cert. tchr. R.I., Wash., Wis., N.J.; cert. reading specialist, supr. N.J. Tchr. elem. schs. Tacoma (Wash.) Pub. Schs., 1958-62, Warwick (R.I.) Pub. Schs., 1957; tchr., reading specialist Milw. Pub. Schs., 1966-69; elem. tchr. and reading specialist, supr. East Orange (N.J.) Pub. Schs., 1969-79; dir. Fla. Ctr. for Philosophy for Children, Pensacola, 1994—. Mem. Nat. Assn. Congregational Chs. (exec. com. 1980-84). Mem. AAUW (v.p. Marco Island, Fla. chpt. 1988-89, bd. dirs. State of Fla. 1990, bd. dirs. Pensacola br. Coll. Univ., 1992). Repulican. Avocations: reading, swimming, walking the beach. Home: 10100 Hillview Rd Apt 616 Pensacola FL 32514-5460

ABERCROMBIE, NEIL, congressman; s. G. Don and Vera June (Giersdorf) A.; m. Nancie Ellen Caraway, July 18, 1981; BA Union Coll., 1959, MA U. Hawaii, 1964, PhD in Am. Studies, 1974; Mem. Hawaii state legislature, 1974-86; elected to U.S. Congress, 1986, 91—, mem. Resources subcom. on Energy & Mineral Resources; mem. Nat. Security Com., Honolulu City Coun., 1988-90. Democrat. Office: US Ho of Reps 1233 Longworth Bldg Washington DC 20515-1101

ABERCROMBIE, STANLEY, magazine editor; b. Cedartown, Ga., Feb. 18, 1935; s. Stanley and Frances (Howard) A.;. BS in Architecture, Ga. Inst. Tech., 1957; BArch, MIT, 1961; MArch (Urban Design), Columbia U., 1967. Draftsman Marcel Breuer & Assocs., N.Y.C., 1962-65; sr. designer John Carl Warnecke & Assoc., N.Y.C., 1968-72; sr. editor Architecture Plus, N.Y.C., 1973-74; editor-in-chief Interiors, N.Y.C., 1975-77; editor Abitare in America, N.Y.C., 1978-79; sr. editor, architecture AIA Jour., Washington, 1980-83; chief editor Interior Design, N.Y.C., 1983-95, editorial dir., 1996—; publ. advisor Inst. for Urban Design, Purchase, N.Y., 1978-89, Mcpl. Art Soc., N.Y.C., 1979-89. Author: Ferrocement, 1977, Gwathmey Siegel, 1981, Architecture As Art, 1984, A Philosophy of Interior Design, 1990, George Nelson: The Design of Modern Design, 1994. Trustee Design Industries Foun. for AIDS, N.Y.C., 1985-89; bd. dirs. Interior Designers for Legis. in N.Y., 1988—. Lt. (j.g.) USN, 1957-59. Loeb fellow for advanced environ. studies Harvard Grad. Sch. Design, 1973-74. Fellow AIA (bd. dirs. N.Y. chpt., chmn. arch. selection com.), Am. Acad. in Rome, Am. Soc. Interior Designers (hon., steering com. 1988—); mem. Soc. Archtl. Historians (bd. dirs.), Archs. and Planners for Social Responsibility (bd. dirs. 1988—), Internat. Assn. Interior Designers (hon.), Inst. Bus. Designers (hon.).

ABERCROMBIE, STONEY ALTON, family physician; b. Six Mile, S.C., Dec. 9, 1949; s. William Morris and Mildred Marette (Ellenburg) A.; m. Donna Gay Underwood, June 17, 1973; children: Jonathan Edward, Kristina Katherine. BS, Clemson U., 1972; MD, Med. U. S.C., 1976. Diplomate Am. Bd. Family Practice; lic. physician, S.C. Family practice intern Greenville (S.C.) Hosp. System, 1976, family practice resident, 1979-80; pvt. practice Seneca (S.C.) Med. Assocs., 1981-88; asst. residency dir. Self Meml.

Hosp., Greenwood, 1989-90; residency dir. and dir. med. edn. Med. U. S.C., Charleston, 1990—; prof. family medicine MUSC, 1995—; staff physician Oconee Meml. Hosp., Seneca, 1981-88, chief of staff, 1988, bd. trustees, 1987-88; mem. utilization rev. com. Oconee Geriatric Ctr., 1981-87; asst. med. dir. Greenwood Health Care Ctr., 1990—, chmn. utilization rev. com., 1990—; med. dir. Greenbrook Manor Nursing Home, 1989-93; lectr. in field. Contbr. articles to profl. jours. Founder Oconee County Prenatal Clinic for Indigent OB Patients, 1983; mem. Upstate S.C. Emergency Svcs. Coun., 1981-84, Upstate S.C. Perinatal Adv. Com., 1981-84, Teen Pregnancy Prevention Coun., Oconee, 1988; mem. Gov.'s Task Force on Primary Health Care in Oconee County, 1984, Med.-Industry Com. for Health Care in Oconee County, 1984-85; bd. visitors Lander U., Greenwood, 1991-93, Med. U. S.C., 1997-98; bd. advisors Vocat. Rehab. Ctr., Greenwood, 1991-94; bd. trustees Greenwood Literacy Coun., 1994-97, chmn., 1996, mem. century club Clemson U., 1981—, mem. IPTAY, 1981—, alumni loyalty fund vol., 1984; active Gideon's Internat., 1984—. Recipient Dist. Svc. to Mankind award Rotary, 1995, Halford award excellence in humane medicine S.C. AHEC, 1996. Fellow Am. Bd. Family Practice; mem. AMA, Am. Acad. Family Physicians (reviewer Huffington Libr. 1991—, pub. com. 1994-96, S.C. alt. del. 1998—), S.C. Acad. Family Physicians (bd. trustees 1987—, editor S.C. Family Physician, v.p. 1995, pres. 1996, 97, chair bd. dirs. 1998), Soc. of Tchrs. Family Practice, S.C. Med. Assn. (liability case reviewer 1990—, assoc. chmn. CME com. 1995-97, chmn. 1997—), Greenwood Med. Soc. (pres. 1992-93), Clemson Alumni Physicians Soc. (charter), Med. U.S.C. Alumni Assn. (Alumni Assn. Centennial Recognition List 1992), Assn. of Family Practice Residency Dirs. (charter, S.C. chpt. chmn. 1994-96), Emerald City Rotary Club (bd. dirs. 1989-96, pres. 1992-93). Republican. Ch. of God. Avocations: baseball card collecting, reading, coaching youth league sports. Office: Self Meml Hosp Family Practice Residency 160 Academy Ave Greenwood SC 29646-3808

ABERLE, DAVID FRIEND, anthropologist, educator; b. St. Paul, Nov. 23, 1918; s. David Winfield and Lisette (Friend) A.; m. Eleanor Kathleen Gough, Sept. 5, 1955 (dec. Sept. 1990); 1 son. A.B. summa cum laude, Harvard U., 1940; Ph.D. in Anthropology, Columbia U., 1950; postgrad., U. N.Mex., summers 1938-40, No. Ariz. U., summers 1971, 73, Harvard U., 1946-47. Instr. dept. social rels. Harvard U., Cambridge, Mass., 1947-50, rsch. assoc. Sch. Pub. Health, 1948-50; vis. assoc. prof. Page Sch., Johns Hopkins U., Balt., 1950-52; assoc. prof., then prof. dept. sociology and dept. anthropology U. Mich., Ann Arbor, 1952-60; fellow Ctr. Advanced Study in Behavioral Scis., Stanford, Calif., 1955-56; Simon vis. prof. and hon. research assoc. dept. social anthropology Manchester U., Eng., 1960-61; prof., chmn. dept. anthropology Brandeis U., Waltham, Mass., 1961-63; prof. dept. anthropology U. Oreg., Eugene, 1963-67; prof. dept. anthropology and sociology U. B.C., Vancouver, Can., 1967-83, prof. emeritus, 1983—; cons. Inst. Devel. Anthropology, Inc., Binghamton, N.Y., 1978-79; cons. to attys. Navajo Tribe, 1976-77; disting. lectr. at ann. meeting Am. Anthrop. Assn., 1986. Author: The Peyote Religion Among the Navaho, 1966, (with Isidore Dyen) Lexical Reconstruction, the Case of the Proto-Athapaskan Kinship System, 1974; contbr. articles on anthropological theory and Navajo Indians to scholarly jours.; rev. editor: Am. Anthropologist, 1952-55. Served with U.S. Army, 1942-46. Recipient Social Sci. Research Council Demobilization award, 1946; Harvard U. Nat. scholar; NIMH grantee; USPHS grantee; Wenner-Gren Found. grantee, 1954-63; NSF grantee, 1965-72; Can. Council grantee, 1969-77; Social Scis. and Humanities Research Council Can., 1978-80, 84-86. Fellow Royal Soc. Can., Royal Anthropol. Inst. of Gt. Britain and Ireland; mem. Am. Anthropol. Assn. (mem. panel on Navajo-Hopi land dispute 1973-95), Am. Sociol. Assn., Soc. Applied Anthropology, Am. Ethnol. Assn., Can. Anthropology Soc., Soc. Lesbian and Gay Anthropologists, Phi Beta Kappa. Jewish. Office: U BC Dept Anthropology, 6303 NW Marine Dr, Vancouver, BC Canada V6T 2B2

ABERLE, ELTON DAVID, dean; b. Sabetha, Kans., Aug. 30, 1940; s. Alphia Henry and Irene Judith A.; n. Carrie Rae Campbell, Sept. 11, 1965; children: Krista Kaye, Barbara Ann. BS, Kans. State U., 1962; MS, Mich. State U., 1965, DPhil, 1967. Asst. prof. Purdue U., West Lafayette, Ind., 1967-71, assoc. prof., 1971-76, prof., 1976-83; prof., dept. head U. Nebr., Lincoln, 1983-98; dean, dir., prof. U. Wis., Madison, 1998—. Author: Principles of Meat Science, 1975, 3d edit., 1994; contbr. articles to profl. jours. Fellow Am. Soc. Animal Sci. (pres. 1994-95, Meat Rsch. award 1982, Signal Svc. award 1998); mem. Am. Meat Sci. Assn. (dir. 1979-80, pres. 1985-86, Disting. Teaching award 1983, Disting. Rsch. award 1986), Inst. Food Tech., Coun. Agrl. Sci. & Tech. (dir. 1996-99), Kiwanis. Avocations: golf, fishing, hunting. Home: 5810 Windsona Cir Madison WI 53711 Office: U Wis Office of Dean 1450 Linden Dr Madison WI 53706-1562

ABERMAN, ARNOLD, dean. Dean faculty medicine U. Toronto, 1995—. Office: Univ Toronto, 215 Huron St, Toronto, ON Canada M5S 1A1 Office: Univ Toronto Med Scis Bldg, 1 Kings College Cir Rm 2109, Toronto, ON Canada*

ABERMAN, HAROLD MARK, veterinarian; b. Chgo., Aug. 5, 1956; s. Howard Oscar and Goldie Esther Aberman. BS, Purdue U., 1979, MSE, 1987, BSE, 1986, DVM, 1983. NIH postdoctoral fellow Purdue U., W. Lafayette, 1983-87; sr. rsch. scientist Howmedica Inc. subsidiary of Pfizer, Rutherford, N.J., 1987-88; prin. rsch. scientist Howmedica div. Pfizer, Rutherford, N.J., 1988-90, asst. dir., 1990-96, dir., 1996—; adj. prof. N.C. State U., Raleigh, 1988—, Miss. State U., Starkville, Miss., 1990—, Purdue U., 1991—. Contbr. articles to profl. jours. Mem. ASME, Am. Vet. Med. Assn., Am. Animal Hosp. Assn., Ortho. Rsch. Soc., Soc. Biomechanics, Acad. Surg. Rsch. Jewish. Home: 530 Valley Rd Apt 3X Montclair NJ 07043-2724 Office: Howmedica 359 Veterans Blvd Rutherford NJ 07070-2584

ABERNATHY, BARBARA EUBANKS, counselor; b. Mobile, Ala., Aug. 28, 1963; d. Hardy Millard and Sarah Louise (Pate) Eubanks; m. James Abernathy Jr., Dec. 15, 1984. BS, Northwestern U., 1984; MS, U. South Ala., 1986; MS in Biol. Sci., Fla. Atlantic U., 1995. Lic. mental health counselor. Mental health worker 11 Charter Southland Hosp., Mobile, 1985-86; counselor Indian River Community Mental Health, Ft. Pierce, Fla., 1986-87; family counselor Youth Svc. Bur., Palm Beach County, Fla., 1987-93; adj. prof. South Coll., 1997-98; therapy cons. Alt. Family Care, Jupiter, Fla., 1995-98; pediat. oncology therapist St. Mary's Med. Ctr., 1998—; owner Wet Dreams Scuba, Inc., Palm Beach Gardens, Fla., 1988—, Healthy Minds Counseling and Wellness, Inc., 1998—; behavior mgmt. cons. Okeechobee (Fla.) Sch. Sys., 1987; cons. Palm Beach County Sch. Bd., 1989—; instr., adj. prof. Palm Beach C.C., Palm Beach Gardens, 1990—; case mgmt. supr. Parent-Child Ctr., West Palm Beach, 1993-95; therapy cons. Comprehensive AIDS Program, West Palm Beach, 1995—. Counselor Rape Crisis Ctr., Mobile, 1985-86, Contact Mobile, 1985-86; troop leader Girl Scouts Chgo., 1982-84; dir. marine mammal rsch. South Fla. Sci. Mus., West Palm Beach, 1995—; vol. counselor disaster mental health team ARC, 1998—. Mem. APA, ACA, Nat. Bd. Cert. Counselors, Child Life Coun., Kappa Delta Pi. Avocations: scuba diving, photography, reading. Office: 5325 Greenwood Ave Ste 305 West Palm Beach FL 33407

ABERNATHY, CHARLES OWEN, toxicologist; b. Brunswick, Ga., Nov. 18, 1941; s. William Owen and Marcelle Louise (Francony) A.; m. Mary Mella Dees, Nov. 18, 1973. AB, Asbury Coll., Wilmore, Ky., 1964; MS, U. Ky., 1966; PhD, N.C. State U., 1970. Postdoctoral fellow U. Calif., Berkeley, 1970-73; pharmacologist VA Med. Ctr., Washington, 1973-84; pharmacologist office of toxic substances EPA, Washington, 1984-86; toxicologist Office Water, EPA, Washington, 1986—; rsch. toxicologist VA Med. Ctr., Washington, 1984-89. Contbr. numerous articles to sci. jours., chpts. to books; co-editor 4 books. Vol. tutor Bapt. Boys Home, Raleigh, N.C., 1967-69; vol. blood drive ARC, Washington, 1978. Recipient Employee Recognition award EPA, 1988, bronze medal, 1993, 96, 97, 98, Nat. Environ. Edn. Achievement awardee, 1997. Mem. Soc. Toxicology (chmn. awards com. risk assessment sect. 1989-90), Soc. for Exptl. Biology and Medicine, N.Y. Acad. Scis., Soc. Environ. Geochemistry and Health, Internat. Soc. Study of Xenobiotics. Achievements include rsch. on selective toxicity of pyrethroids, reversal of cholestatic effects of steroids by cholic acid derivatives; developed hypothesis on neonates and cholestasis, risk assessment of essential trace elements. Home: 4718 River Rd Bethesda MD 20816-3035 Office: EPA 401 M St SW Washington DC 20460-0002

ABERNATHY, FREDERICK HENRY, mechanical engineering educator; b. Denver, Colo., June 30, 1930; s. Henry James and Irene Sarah (Lehman) A.; m. AnnaMaria Herbert, June 18, 1961; children: Sarah, Marian, Pauline. BSME, Newark Coll. Engring., 1951; postgrad., Oak Ridge Sch. Reactor Tech., 1952; SM, Harvard U., 1954, PhD, 1959. Gordon McKay prof. mech. engring. Harvard U., Cambridge, Mass., 1963—, Abbott and James Lawrence prof. mech. engring., 1995—; dir. engring. divsn. NSF, Washington, 1972-73, dir. energy-realted rsch., 1973-74; dir. Textile/Clothing Tech. Corp., Cambridge, 1985-87, Harvard Ctr. for Textile and Apparel Rsch., 1991—. Fellow Am. Phys. Soc., Am. Acad. Arts and Scis.; mem. ASME, Am. Soc. Engring. Edn., Sigma Xi. Home: 45 Islington Rd Auburndale MA 02466-1005 Office: Harvard Univ Divsn Engring/Applied Sci Pierce Hall Cambridge MA 02138

ABERNATHY, JAMES LOGAN, public relations executive; b. Kansas City, Mo., Jan. 23, 1941; s. James Logan and Caryl (Nicolson) A. ; m. Kevin Kearns, Sept. 12, 1981; 1 child, Nell Logan. Student, Brown U., 1959-64. Assoc. dir. investor relations CBS Inc., N.Y.C., 1967-72; v.p. investor relations Warner Communications Inc., N.Y.C., 1972-74; v.p. investor relations ABC Inc., N.Y.C., 1974-79, v.p. corp. affairs, 1979-84; chmn. Abernathy/MacGregor Group Inc., N.Y.C., 1984—. Trustee, chmn., dir. Caron Found., Wernersville, Pa., 19836; trustee Hackley Sch., Tarrytown, N.Y., 1982-89; overseer Brown U. Sch. Medicine, 1996—. Mem. Investor Relations Assn. (pres. 1979-80), Nat. Investor Relations Inst., Knickerbocker Club (N.Y.C.), Doubles Club (N.Y.C.), Devon Yacht Club (L.I.). Home: 130 E End Ave New York NY 10028-7553 Office: Abernathy MacGregor Group Inc 501 Madison Ave New York NY 10022-5602

ABERNETHY, IRENE MARGARET, civic worker, retired county official; b. Ord, Nebr., Mar. 28, 1924; d. Glen Dayton and Margaret Lillian (Jones) Auble; m. Don R. Abernethy, Aug. 8, 1954 (dec. Nov. 1980); children: Jill Adele Abernethy Johnson, Ted Verne. BA cum laude, Hastings Coll., 1946; postgrad., U. Nebr., 1950-53. Tchr. Ord High Sch., 1946-50, Scottsbluff (Nebr.) High Sch., 1950-55, Grand Island (Nebr.) Sr. High Sch., 1961-62; mem. Hall County Bd. Suprs., Grand Island, 1979-98, chmn., 1984, 95; ret., 1998. Vice chair Hall County Rep. Ctrl. Com., Grand Island, 1971-73; chair campaign Congresswoman Virginia Smith for Hall County, 1974-80; sr. v.p. Nebr. Rep. Founders Day, Lincoln, 1981; chair Gov.'s Juv. Justice Adv. Group, Lincoln, 1981-91; mem. Nebr. Commn. on Law Enforcement and Criminal Justice, Lincoln, 1970-91; mem. Nebr. Commn. on Local Govt. Innovation and Restructuring; bd. dirs. Head Start, 1979—, Hall County Leadership Tomorrow, 1990-94, Indsl. Found., 1991, College Park, 1991-98, Community Help Ctr., 1991-96, Family Violence Coalition, 1993—, Midland Area Agy. on Aging, 1993-95; adv. com. Region III Mental Health Adv. Bd., mem. quality rev. team, 1996—; active Nat. Coalition State Juvenile Justice Adv. Groups, 1981-91, Partners in Community Planning, 1994-97, Grand Island Area Edn. 2000; mem. task force on needs Heartland United Way; mem. Grand Island Bd. of Edn., 1998—; mem. Grand Island Bd. Edn., 1998—. Named Woman of Yr., Grand Island Independent, 1980, Bus. and Profl. Woman, Grand Island, 1980, Beta Sigma Phi, 1982, Nebr. chpt. NASW, 1983; recipient Svc. to Mankind award Sertoma, 1983-84, recognition award PTA, 1988, Outstanding Cmty. Svc. award Rotary, 1985, Cmty. Leadership award Ak-Sar-Ben, 1995, Outstanding Alumni award Hastings Coll., 1996, Hall County Rep. Hall of Fame award, 1997, Disting. Citizenship award Grand Island Elks, 1997, cert. of appreciation Grand Island-Hall County Dept. Health, 1998. Mem. LWV (local pres. 1962-64, state bd. dirs. 1965-69), AAUW (local pres. 1966-68, state bd. dirs. 1970-71), YWCA (local pres. 1974-75, Woman of Distinction award 1988), Nebr. Assn. County Ofcls. (pres. 1985, Pres.'s award for Disting. Leadership 1997, County Ofcl. of Yr. award 1998), Assn. Child Abuse Prevention, Grand Island Area C. of C. (bd. dirs. 1992-94, Disting. Svc. award 1999), Philanthropic Ednl. Orgn. (local pres. 1970-71), Woodland Golf Club Ladies Assn. (champion 1961, 63, 64, loca pres. 1963), Riverside Golf Club (champion 1969), Pi Lambda Theta. Republican. Methodist. Avocations: travel, music, photography, golf, spectator sports. Home: 707 S Blaine St Grand Island NE 68803-6146

ABERNETHY, ROBERT JOHN, real estate developer; b. Indpls., Feb. 28, 1940; s. George Lawrence and Helen Sarah (McLandress) A. BA, Johns Hopkins U., 1962; MBA, Harvard U., 1968; cert. in real estate fin. and constrn., UCLA, 1974. Asst. to chief scientist Phoenix missile program Hughes Aircraft Co., L.A., 1966-69, asst. program mgr. Iroquois night fighter and night tracker program, 1969-71, asst. to contr. space and comm. group, 1971-72, contr. tech. divsn., 1972-74; pres. Am. Std. Devel. Co., L.A., 1974—, Transit Cmty. Devel. Corp., 1997—; bd. dirs., chmn. audit com. Pub. Storage, Inc., Glendale, Calif., Marathon Nat. Bank, L.A., L.A. Bancorp, Met. Water Dist., So. Calif., Met. Transp. Authority, L.A. County; pres. Self Svc. Storage Assn., San Francisco, 1978-83. Asst. to dep. campaign mgr. Humphrey for Pres., Washington, 1968; commr. L.A. Planning Commn., 1984-88, L.A. Telecom. Commn., 1992-93; vice chmn. L.A. Econ. Devel. Coun., 1988-93; chmn. Ctr. for Study Dem. Inst., Santa Barbara, Calif., 1986—; bd. dirs. Met. Transp. Authority Los Angeles County, South Bay Civic Light Opera, World Children's Transplant Fund, French Found. for Alzheimers Rsch., Pacific Coun. on Internat. Policy; adv. bd. mem. Peabody Conservatory, 1992—, Ctr. Talented Youth, 1992—, Nitse Sch. Advanced Internat. Studies, 1993—, Harvard Ptnrs., 1996—, Inst. Acad. Achievement of Youth, 1999—; bd. vis. Davidson Coll.; bd. dirs. L.A. Theatre Ctr., 1986-92, YMCA; trustee Johns Hopkins U., 1991—; mem. Coun. on Fgn. Rels., L.A. Com. on Fgn. Rels. Lt. USNR, 1962-66. Mem. So. Calif. Planning Congress (bd. dirs.), Parker Found. (bd. dirs.), Californian Club, St. Francis Yacht Club, Jonathan Club, Calif. Yacht Club, Alpha Lambda. Home: 5800 W Century Blvd Los Angeles CA 90009-5600 Address: 5221 W 102nd St Los Angeles CA 90045

ABERSON, LESLIE DONALD, lawyer; b. St. Louis, May 30, 1936; s. Hillard and Adele (Wenneker) A.; m. Regene Jo Lowenstein, Oct. 16, 1960; children—Karen, Angie, Leslie. BS, U. Ky., 1957, JD, 1960. Bar: Ky. 1960, U.S. Dist. Ct. (we. dist.) Ky. 1964, U.S. Tax Ct. 1968, U.S. Supreme Ct. 1975. Assoc. Washer, Kaplan, Rothschild, Aberson & Miller, Louisville, 1963-65, ptnr., 1965—; dir. Bank of Louisville. Bd. dirs. Ky. Athletic Hall of Fame, 1965—, Jewish Hosp. Louisville, 1978—, Louisville Med. Rsch. Found., 1975—, NCCJ; bd. dirs., past pres. B'rith Sholom Temple; bd. dirs., past v.p. Jewish Community Fedn. Louisville; bd. dir. Louisville Free Pub. Libr. Found. Recipient Louis Cole Young Leadership award Louisville C. of C. Mem. Ky. Bar Assn., Louisville Bar Assn., Ky. Trial Lawyers Assn., Am. Trial Lawyers Assn., Louisville C. of C. (instl. rev. com.), U. Ky. Law Sch. Alumni Assn. (bd. dirs.). Home: 2306 Merrick Rd Louisville KY 40207-1255 Office: Washer Kaplan Rothschild Aberson & Miller Ky Home Life Bldg 239 S 5th St Fl 17 Louisville KY 40202-3213

ABETTI, PIER ANTONIO, consulting electrical engineer, technology management and entrepreneurship educator; b. Florence, Italy, Feb. 7, 1921; came to U.S., 1946; s. Giorgio and Anna (Garino) A.; m. Elizabeth Burr Nelson, June 11, 1948; children: George E., Frank A. Student, Poly. Inst., Turin, Italy, 1940-44; D of Indsl. Engring., U. Pisa, Italy, 1945; MSEE, Ill. Inst. Tech., Chgo., 1948; PhD in Elec. Engring., Ill. Inst. Tech., 1953. Registered profl. engr., Mass. Advanced devel. engr. Gen. Electric Co., Pittsfield, Mass., 1948-56, mgr. project EHV, 1957-62; mgr. pvt. telephone sys. Gen. Electric Co., Lynchburg, Va., 1971-73; mgr. Europe strategic planning Gen. Electric Co., Brussels, 1974-79; cons. R & D Gen. Electric Co., Schenectady, N.Y., 1980-81; dep. gen. mgr. UNIVAC-Europe, Lausanne, Switzerland, 1963-64; prof. mgmt. of tech. and entrepreneurship Rensselaer Poly. Inst., Troy, N.Y., 1982—, dir. Ctr. for Entrepreneurship New Tech. Ventures, 1988-92; adj. prof. MIT, Troy, N.Y., 1951-52, Berkshire C.C., Pittsfield, Mass., 1958-60; cons. Tech. Assessment Group, Schenectady, 1980—, UN Program Devel., Mex., Indonesia, South Korea, China, Poland, 1989, USIA, Ukraine, 1991-93, Internat. Atomic Energy Commn., Chile, 1994, OAS, Venezuela, 1994; vis. prof. U. Calgary, Can., 1986-87, U. Tech., Compiègne, France, 1988-92, Internat. U., Japan, 1991, 93, Helsinki Sch. Econs. and Bus. Adminstrn., 1994-99, U. Oulu, Finland, 1997, Korean Advanced Inst. Sci. and Tech., 1995-97, U. Stellenbosch, South Africa, 1994, Gordon Inst. Tufts U., 1987-99, Duxx Sch. Bus. Leadership, Monterrey, Mex., 1997-98, Queensland U. Technol., Brisbane, Australia, 1998, Nat. Coll. of Ireland, Dublin, 1998, Navick Technol. U., 1999, Technol. Inst. of Coclarice, 1999. Author: Linking Technology and Business Strategy, 1990, (with J. Maldifassi) The Defense Industries of Argentina, Brazil, Chile, 1994; author more than 100 tech. and mgmt. papers in 5 langs. Pres. Berkshire Mycol. Soc., Pittsfield, 1954-59; pres. Berkshire Film Soc., 1955-58. Recipient Coffin award GE, 1952, Internat. prize Montefiore Inst., 1953, Recognition award Italian Hist. Soc. Am., 1953, Kaufmann Found. award Entrepreurship Educator of Yr. Finalist, 1993. Fellow IEEE (chmn. Volta scholarship 1961-66, mem. awards bd. 1984-86, chmn. scholarship awards 1984-86); mem. Am. Mgmt. Assn. (R&D coun. 1985-92), Italian Soc. for Sci. Progress (hon.), Eta Kappa Nu (Recognition award 1953), Tau Beta Pi. Office: Rensselaer Poly Inst Sch Mgmt Troy NY 12180-3590 *In my life I have always tried to learn from my predecessors in science and technology and innovate based on their teaching and my original thinking.*

ABHYANKAR, SHREERAM S., mathematics and industrial engineering educator; b. Ujjain, India, July 22, 1930; came to U.S., 1951, naturalized, 1989; s. Shankar Keshav and Uma (Tamhankar) A.; m. Yvonne Margit Kraft, June 5, 1958; children: Hari Shreeram, Kashi Shreeram. BSc, Bombay U., 1951; AM, Harvard U., 1952, PhD, 1955; DHD (hon.), U. Angers, 1998. Rsch. instr. Columbia U., N.Y.C., 1955-56, vis. asst. prof., 1956-57; asst. prof. Cornell U., Ithaca, N.Y., 1957-58; vis. asst. prof. Princeton (N.J.) U., 1958-59; assoc. prof. Johns Hopkins U., Balt., 1959-63; pres. math. Purdue U., West Lafayette, Ind., 1963-67, Marshall disting. prof. math., 1967—, prof. indsl. engring., 1987—, prof. computer scis., 1988—; vis. lectr. Harvard U., 1960-61; vis. prof. Munster U., Erlangen U., summer 1963, Matsci., Madras, India, fall 1963, Tata Inst., Bombay, 1969-70, 75-76, spring 1974, Kyoto U., fall 1976, U. Ky., fall 1978, U. Paris, spring 1980, ENS St. Cloud, France, spring 1982, U. Nice, spring 1983, U. Sydney, spring 1986, U. Strasbourg, spring 1991, Ohio State U., spring 1995; vis. assoc. prof. Yale U., spring 1963; spkr. numerous profl. meetings, univ., insts., symposia, confs., and congresses, 1960—. Author: Ramification Theoretic Methods in Algebraic Geometry, 1959, Local Analytic Geometry, 1964, Resolution of Singularities of Embedded Algebraic Surfaces, 1966, 2d enlarged edit. 1998, A Glimpse of Algebraic Geometry, 1971, Algebraic Space Curves, 1971, Lectures on Expansion Techniques in Algebraic Geometry, 1977, Weighted Expansions for Canonical Desingularization, 1982, Enumerative Combinatorics of Young Tableaux, 1988, Algebraic Geometry for Scientists and Engineers, 1990; also over 150 articles. Recipient Herbert Newby McCoy award Purdue U., 1973, Medal of Honor, U. Valliadolid, Spain, 1990; grantee NSF, 1960-87, 89-91, 89-99, Office Naval Rsch., 1986-90, Army Rsch. Office, 1988-90, Nat. Security Agy., 1992-99; rsch. fellow Alfred P. Sloan Found., 1958-60. Fellow Indian Nat. Sci. Acad., Indian Acad. Scis.; mem. Am. Math. Soc., Math. Assn. Am. (Lester R. Ford prize 1977, Chauvenet award 1978), Phi Beta Kappa. Achievements include research in algebraic geometry, commutative and local algebra, theory of functions of several complex variables, quantum electrodynamics, circuit and invariant theory, combinatorics, computer aided design, and robotics. Home: 111 Waldron St West Lafayette IN 47906-2836 Office: Purdue U Div Math Sci West Lafayette IN 47907

ABID, ANN B., art librarian; b. St. Louis, Mar. 17, 1942; d. Clarence Frederick and Luella (Niehaus) Bartelsmeyer; m. Amor Abid (div. 1969); children: Rod, Kady; m. Cleon R. Yohe, Aug. 10, 1974 (div.); m. Roldo S. Bartimole, Feb. 1, 1991. Cert. in Librarianship, Washington U., St. Louis, 1976. Asst. to libr. St. Louis Art Mus., 1963-68, libr., 1968-85; head libr. Cleve. Mus. Art, 1985—; vis. com. univ. librs. Case We. Res.U., 1987-90, cochairperson, 1990. Co-author: Documents of Surrealism, 1918-1942, 1981, Planning for Automation of the Slide and Photograph Collections at the Cleveland Museum of Art: A Draft Marc Visual Materials Record, 1998; contbr. articles to profl. jours. Grantee Mo. Coun. Arts, 1978, Mo. Com. Humanities, 1980, Nat. Hist. Pubs. and Records Commn., 1981, Reinberger Found., 1987, Japan Found., 1996. Mem. ALA, Art Librs. Soc. N.Am. (chmn. mus.-type-of-libr. group nat. and Ohio chpts. 1979-81, chmn. New Orleans 1980, nominating com. 1980, 84, Wittenborn awards com. 1981, 90, v.p., pres.-elect 1987-88, pres. 1988-89, past pres. 1989-90, chmn. N.Am. art libr. resources com. 1991-93, search com. new exec. dir. 1993-94, chmn. fin. com. 1996-98, presenter numerous papers, chmn. nominating com. 1999—, co-chair conf. program com. 1999—), Soc. Am. Archivists, Midwest Mus. Conf. (co-chmn. program com. ann. meeting 1982), Spl. Librs. Assn., Rsch. Librs. Group (shares exec. group 1996-98, shares participation com. 1997-99). Office: Cleve Mus of Art 11150 East Blvd Cleveland OH 44106-1711

ABILDSKOV, J. A., cardiologist, educator; b. Salem, Utah, Sept. 22, 1923; s. John and Annie Marie (Peterson) A.; m. Mary Helen McKell, Dec. 4, 1944; children—Becky, Alan, Mary, Marilyn. B.A., U. Utah, 1944, M.D., 1946. Diplomate Am. Bd. Internal Medicine. Intern Latter-day Saints Hosp., Salt Lake City, 1947-48; resident Charity Hosp. La., New Orleans, 1948-51; instr. Tulane U., New Orleans, 1954-54; asst. prof. to prof. SUNY-Syracuse, 1955-68; prof. medicine U. Utah, Salt Lake City, 1968—; dir. Nora Eccles Harrison Cardiovascular Rsch. and Tng. Inst., Salt Lake City, 1970-94. Contbr. articles to profl. jours. Served to capt. USAR, 1954-56. Recipient Disting. Research award U. Utah, 1976. Fellow Am. Coll. Cardiology; mem. Assn. Am. Physicians, Am. Soc. Clin. Investigation (emeritus), Assn. Univ. Cardiologists (founding), Western Assn. Physicians, Venezuelan Cardiology Soc. (hon.), Cardiology Soc. Peru (corresponding). Republican. Mormon. Home: 1506 Canterbury Dr Salt Lake City UT 84108-2833 Office: U Utah Bdlg 500 Salt Lake City UT 84112

ABISH, CECILE, artist; b. N.Y.C.; m. Walter Abish. B.F.A., Bklyn. Coll., 1953. Instr. art Queens Coll.; vis. artist U. Mass, Amherst, Cooper Union, Harvard U. Solo exhbns. include Newark Coll. Engring., 1968, Inst. Contemporary Art, Boston, 1974, U. Md., 1975, Alessandra Gallery, N.Y.C., 1977, Wright State U., Dayton, Ohio, 1978, Carpenter Ctr., Cambridge, Mass., 1979, Anderson Gallery, Va. Commonwealth U., Richmond, 1981, SUNY-Stony Brook, 1982, Ctr. for Creative Photography, Tucson, 1984, Books & Co., N.Y.C., 1996; group exhbns.: Detroit Inst. Art, 1969, Aldrich Mus. Art, 1971, 10 Bleecker St., N.Y.C., 1972, Lakeview Ctr. Arts, Peoria, Ill., 1972, Bykert Gallery, N.Y.C., 1971-74, Michael Walls Gallery, N.Y.C., 1975, Fine Arts Bldg. Gallery, N.Y.C., 1976, Mus. Modern Art, N.Y.C., 1976, Hudson River Mus., 1979, Atlanta Arts Festival, 1980, New Mus., N.Y.C., 1980, 81, Kuntsgebaude, Stuttgart, Fed. Republic Germany, 1981, Long Beach (Calif.) Mus., 1983, Edith C. Blum Art Inst., Bard Coll., Annandale-on-Hudson, N.Y., 1984, Mus. Modern Kunst, Vienna, Austria, 1985, U. R.I., Kingston, 1985, Art Defense Galleries, Paris, 1993, Architektur Zentrum, Vienna, 1993, Artists Space, N.Y.C., 1994, Islip Art Mus., N.Y., 1995; numerous commns.; represented in permanent collections; published photo works: Firsthand, 1978, Chinese Crossing, 1986, 99: The New Meaning, 1990. Nat. Endowment Arts fellow, 1975, 77, 80; CAPS fellow, 1975. Mem. Coll. Art Assn. Office: Cooper Station PO Box 485 New York NY 10276-0485

ABIZAID, JOHN P., career officer; b. Redwood City, Calif., Apr. 1, 1951. Commd. 2nd lt. U.S. Army, 1973, advanced through grades to brig. gen., 1997; comdt. cadets U.S. Mil. Acad., West Point, N.Y., 1997—. Office: US Mil Acad West Point NY 10996

ABLARD, CHARLES DAVID, lawyer; b. Enid, Okla.; s. Charles Ross and Mary M. (Pattie) A.; m. Doris Maria Perl, Nov. 14, 1959; children—Jennifer, Jonathan, Catherine. BA, U. Okla., 1952, JD, 1954; LLM, George Washington U., 1959. Bar: D.C. Jud. officer U.S. Post Office Dept., Washington, 1958-60; ptnr. Ablard and Harrison, Washington, 1960-63; v.p., counsel Mag. Pubs. Assn., Washington, 1963-69; gen. counsel USIA, Washington, 1969-72; assoc. dep. atty. gen. Dept. Justice, Washington, 1972-74; assoc. dean Vt. Law Sch., South Royalton, 1974; gen. counsel Dept. Army, Washington, 1975-77; ptnr. Gage and Tucker, Washington, 1979-92, Faegre and Benson, Washington and Mpls., 1992-97, Perkins, Smith, Cohen & Crowe, Washington and Boston, 1997—; adj. prof. Cath. U., Washington, 1984; mem. Fgn. Srv. Grievance Bd. Contbr. articles to profl. jours. Bd. dirs. Hist. Alexandria Found., Pub. Diplomacy Found.; commr. Alexandria Hist. Restoration and Preservation Commn.; mem. coun. Adminstrv. Conf. U.S., Washington, 1970-73; mem. Bd. Internat. Broadcasting, Washington, 1980-84; bd. dirs. Radio Free Europe/Radio Liberty, Washington, 1983-84. With USAF, 1954-56. Fellow Ctr. for Internat. Studies, Cambridge U., Eng., 1974; recipient Profl. Achievement award George Washington U., 1976, Disting. Civilian Service award Dept. Army, 1975, 76. Fellow Am. Bar Found. (life); mem. ABA (chmn. adminstrv. law sect. 1984-85), English Speaking Union U.S. (bd. dirs.). Republican. Episcopalian. Clubs: Cosmos (Washington); Army-Navy Country (Arlington, Va.); Small Point (Maine).

Home: 803 Hall Pl Alexandria VA 22302-3405 Office: 1001 Pennsylvania Ave NW Washington DC 20004-2505

ABLE, EDWARD H., association executive. BA in Chemistry, Emory U., 1967; MBA, George Washington U., 1973. Cert. assn. exec. Staff aide to U.S. Senator Richard B. Russell, 1967-68, staff aide to U.S. Senator Mike Mansfield, 1968; acct. exec. Exec. Cons., Inc., Washington, 1971-73; asst. dir. resident assoc. program Smithsonian Instn., Washington, 1973-77; exec. v.p. Am. Soc. Landscape Architects, Washington, 1977-86; pres., CEO Am. Assn. Mus., Washington, 1986—; lectr. in field. Author: (with others) Principles of Association Management, 1988. Bd. dirs. Nat. Humanities Alliance, 1986—, officer, 1990—, Nat. Cultural Alliance, 1991—; mem. founding bd. dirs. Nat. Ctr. Non-profit Bds., 1987—, vice chair, 1993—; coun. mem. U.S. Com. World Heritage, 1988—; bd. mem. Nat. Ctr. for Non-Profit Enterprise. Capt. U.S. Army, 1968-71. Decorated Bronze Star. Fellow Am. Soc. Assn. Execs. (bd. dirs. 1987-90, chmn. mgmt. conf. 1988, instr. 1985—, frequent speaker meetings and convs. 1981—, chmn. grad. studies commn. 1986-87, mem. nat. edn. com. 1984-86, vice-chmn. 1985, chmn. 1986, bd. dirs. membership dirs. sect. 1982-83, Key award 1990, vice-chmn. fellows 1987-88, chmn. 1988-89), bd. dirs., 1994—; Greater Washington Soc. Assn. Execs. (chief exec. officer conf. com. 1982-83), Univ. Club (Washington). Office: Am Assn Museums 1575 I St NW Ste 400 Washington DC 20005-1113

ABLE, JAMES AUGUSTUS, JR., writer; b. Decatur, Ill., Dec. 30, 1928; s. James Augustus and Florence Elizabeth (Gerhardt) A.; m. Martha Frances Collins, Feb. 10, 1952 (div. Apr. 1972); children: James B., Cynthia L. Able Singh, Robert G., Cheryl A. Able Moulton; m. Mary Louise Mathews, Apr. 26, 1972; children: Stephanie Ann, Victoria Ann. Student, James Millikin U., 1946, 49-50, USAF Inst., 1946-49; LLB, Atlanta Law Sch., 1953, LLM, 1954. Bar: Ga. 1955. Reporter Decatur Herald-Rev., 1943-46, 49-50; regional legal counsel Assocs. Investment Co., Atlanta, 1955-61; pvt. practice law Atlanta, 1961-70; security supr. State of Ga., Atlanta, 1970-72; pvt. investigator Advance Indsl. Security, Atlanta, 1972-75; freelance writer Tampa, Fla., 1975—; spkr., advisor on writing and careers Hillsborough County Sch. Sys., Tampa, 1993—. Author: (novel) Victims, 1979; (nonfiction) Inside Swing, 1987, Writing Nostalgia, 1988; contbr. columns, numerous features, articles and short stories to lit. publs. and mags. Campaign aide various polit. campaigns, 1960s and 70s. Sgt. U.S. Army, 1946-49, 50-51. Mem. Tampa Writers Alliance (pres. 1986-89, publicity/pub. rels. dir. 1992—, workshop instr./coord. 1990—, 10-yr. Meritorious Svc. plaque 1996). Methodist. Avocation: listening, collecting, and chronicling jazz and swing music. Home: 4408 W Harbor View Ave Tampa FL 33611-1132 Office: PO Box 13982 Tampa FL 33681-3982

ABLE, KENNETH PAUL, biology educator; b. Louisville, Feb. 5, 1944; s. William Morris and Viola (Bridwell) A.; m. Mary Allen, Jan. 27, 1967; 1 child, Joshua. BS, U. Louisville, 1966, MS, 1968; PhD, U. Ga., 1971. Asst. prof. SUNY, Albany, 1971-77, assoc. prof., 1977-84, prof., 1984—. NSF grantee, 1974—. Fellow Animal Behavior Soc., Am. Ornithologists' Union (treas. 1981-85, William Brewster medal 1996); mem. Internat. Soc. Behavioral Ecology, Am. Soc. Naturalists, Am. Birding Assn. (dir. 1986-95). Office: Univ at Albany-SUNY Dept Biology 1400 Washington Ave Albany NY 12222-0100

ABLE, WARREN WALTER, natural resource company executive, physician; b. Seymour, Ind., Mar. 3, 1932; s. Walter Cudwith and Edith (Harmon) A.; m. Joan Graham, May 6, 1956; children: Susan, Nancy, Cynthia, Wally. AB, Ind. U., 1953, MD, 1956, JD, 1968. Bar: Ind. 1968. Intern Indpls. Gen. Hosp., 1956-57; surgeon USPHS, 1957-59; pres. Able Ventures, Inc., Evansville, Ind., 1968—; bd. dirs. Salin Bank & Trust. Editor: Lawyer's Medical Cyclopedia, 1967-68. Bd. dirs. Bartholomew Consol. Sch. Corp., Columbus, 1970-74; trustee Christian Theol. Sem., 1991—. Mem. AMA, Ind. Med. Soc., ABA, Ind. Bar Soc., Nat. Benevolent Assn. (bd. dirs. 1983-90). Democrat. Mem. Disciples of Christ Ch. Avocations: aviation, farming. Home: 4253 E Windsor Ln Columbus IN 47201-9681 Office: Able Ventures Inc 101 Court St Evansville IN 47708-1164

ABLER, RONALD FRANCIS, geography educator; b. Milw., May 30, 1939; s. Ambrose Francis and Lucille Bernice (Chartraw) A.; m. Barbara Ruth Bailey, Apr. 23, 1983; children: Frederick F., Kenneth J. BA, U. Minn., Mpls., 1963, MA, 1966, PhD, 1968. Prof. Pa. State U., University Park, 1967-95; exec. dir. Assn. Am. Geographers, Washington, 1990—; dir. geography program NSF, Washington, 1984-88; vis. prof. Stockholm Sch. Econs., 1982-83, U. Minn., Mpls., 1972-74, U. B.C., Vancouver, 1971. Editor: A Comparative Atlas of America's Great Cities, 1976; co-editor: Atlas of Pennsylvania, 1989, Geography's Inner Worlds, 1992. Councilman State College (Pa.) Borough, 1978-82. Recipient Publ. award Geog. Soc. Chgo., 1976, Centenary medal Royal Scottish Geog. Soc., 1990, Spl. Recognition award NSF, Washington, 1988, Victoria medal Royal Geog. Soc./Inst. British Geographers, 1996. Fellow AAAS, Assn. Am. Geographers (pres. 1985-86, exec. dir. 1990—, honors 1995), Cosmos Club, Internat. Geographical Union (v.p. 1996—). Avocation: beekeeping. Home: 2246 N Pollard St Arlington VA 22207-3805 Office: Assn Am Geographers 1710 16th St NW Washington DC 20009-3104

ABLESON, DONALD WILLIAM, automobile industry executive; b. Ypsilanti, Mich., May 24, 1937; s. Guy Franklin and Katherine Ann (Pratt) A.; m. Muriel Ruth Studt, Aug. 22, 1959; children: Michael, Bruce, Christopher, Kimberly. B of Ind. Engring., Kettering U., Flint, Mich., 1960; MBA, Mich. State U., 1978. Registered profl. engr., Mich. Engr. in charge GMC-Fisher Body, Warren, Mich., 1972-78; gen. supt. GMC-Fisher Body, Livonia, Mich., 1978-80, GMC-Pontiac, Mich., 1980-84; plant mgr. GM-Chevrolet-Pontiac-Canada, Pontiac, 1984-87, Tarrytown, N.Y., 1987-90; program mgr. GM-Chevrolet-Pontiac-Canada, Warren, Mich., 1990-96; dir. specialty vehicles GM-Mid/Luxury Car Group, Warren, 1997-98, NA Car Group, Warren, 1999—. Chmn., dir. Westchester C.C. Found., Mt. Pleasant, N.Y., 1988-94; dir. GMI Alumni Bd., Flint, 1980; chmn. Birmingham (Mich.) Mid. Sch. Com., 1983, West Bloomfield (Mich.) Cable TV Com., 1985. Recipient citation Birmingham Sch. Bd., 1983, proclamation Westchester County, 1990. Mem. Soc. Automotive Engring. (bd. dirs. 1987-90, chmn. 1965-68, chmn. Detroit sect. 1982-83, chmn. sects. bd. 1987-88, chmn. strategic planning com. 1990-91, chmn. bd. trustees SAe Found. 1992-98, chmn. fin. com. 1994-97, pres. elect 1999-2000). Avocations: skiing, sailing, photography, wildlife, hiking. Office: GM Corp 480-210-251 30001 Van Dyke Ave Warren MI 48093-2350

ABLIN, RICHARD JOEL, immunologist, educator; b. Chgo., May 15, 1940; s. Robert Benjamin and Minnie Edith (Gordon) A.; m. Linda Lee Lutwack; 1 son, Michael David. AB, Lake Forest Coll., 1962; PhD in Microbiology, SUNY, Buffalo, 1967. Diplomate Am. Bd. Clin. Immunology and Allergy; cert. specialist in pub. health and med. lab. microbiology Nat. Registry Microbiologists of Am. Acad. Microbiology. Grad. asst. dept. biology SUNY-Buffalo, 1963-65, research asst., summer 1963, research fellow, 1965-66; USPHS postdoctoral fellow dept. microbiology Sch. Medicine, lectr., lab instr., 1966-68; instr., research asst. Rosary Hill Coll., 1965-66; research cons. program med. edn. AID, Paraguay, 1968; dir. div. immunology Millard Fillmore Hosp. Rsch. Inst., Buffalo, 1968-70; head sect. immunology, renal unit Meml. Hosp. of Springfield, 1970-73; dir. sect. immunobiology div. urology dept. surgery Cook County Hosp. and Hektoen Inst. for Med. Research, Chgo., 1973-75, sr. sci. officer div. immunology, 1976-83; sr. mem. sci. staff, clin. immunologist Cook County Hosp., 1973-75; asst. prof. medicine So. Ill. U., 1971-73; assoc. prof. microbiology Univ. Health Sci. (Chgo. Med. Sch.), 1973-74; research assoc. prof. urology, dir. immunology unit dept. urology SUNY, Stony Brook, 1983-89; pres., dir. Robert Benjamin Ablin Found. for Cancer Rsch., Evergreen Park, Ill., 1979—; dir. sci. investigation Innapharma, Inc., Upper Saddle River, N.J., 1991—; mem. Univ. Senate, 1986-89, 89-92, Univ. Governing Coms., 1984-92; acad. del. United Univ. Professions, 1986-88, 88-90; organizer, presenter, instr., participant numerous nat. and internat. profl. meetings, symposia, seminars. Editor: Allergologia et Immunopathologia, 1980-84; contbg. editor: Current Perspectives in Allergology and Immunopathology, 1974-84; assoc. editor Jour. Investigational Allergology and Clin. Immunology (formerly Allergologia et Immunopathglia), 1985-95, Seminars in Immunopathology and Oncology, Ill. Med. Jour., 1975-88; adv. editor: Jour. Cancer, 1976—; assoc. editor: Low Temperature Medicine, 1975—; mem. internat. editl. staff: Medikon, 1974—; mem. editl. bd. Advances in Therapy, 1999—, Bratislava Med. Jour., 1999—, Current Oncology, 1998—, Immunology and Allergy Practice, 1979-95, Am. Jour. Reproductive Immunology and Microbiology, 1980-91, Cellular and Molecular Biology, 1985-87, Early Pregnancy: Biology and Medicine, 1995—; mem. sci. bd.: Chemistry Today, 1991-97, TumorDiagnostik and Therapie, 1980-98; mem. editl. acad. Internat. Jour. of Oncology, 1996—; mem. editl. adv. bd. Med. Sci. Rsch., 1984—; contbr. numerous articles to profl. jours. and texts. Chief Sangamo Nation Y-Indian Guides, Springfield, 1972-73; mgr. Skokie Indians' Boys' Baseball, Ill., 1973-74, 77, 80, 81, bd. dirs., 1979-83, exec. v.p., 1981-82; mgr. Little League Three Villages, Setauket, N.Y., 1986; cubmaster N.W. Suburban coun. Boy Scouts Am., 1974-78, asst. scoutmaster, 1975-77; mem. exploring divsn. Suffolk County coun. Boy Scouts Am., 1985-88; pres., dir. Spirit of Chgo. Hockey Club Found., Skokie, Ill., 1982—. Recipient Nat. Pres. Leader's Dist. Boy Scouts Am., 1975; named Cubmaster of Yr. Boy Scouts Am., 1977. Fellow Am. Coll. Allergy and Immunology, Am. Coll. Cryosurgery (v.p. 1977-79, parliamentarian 1977-79, adv. bd. 1977-78, 80-81, 84-99), Indian Cryogenics Coun. (hon.), Assn. Clin. Scientists; mem. AAAS, Am. Assn. Cancer Rsch., Am. Assn. Immunologists, Am. Soc. Microbioogy, Assn. Med. Lab. Immunologists, Brit. Assn. Surg. Oncology, Buffalo Collegium Immunology, Internat. Soc. Andrology, Internat. Soc. Chronobiology, Internat. Soc. Cryosurgery (pres. 1977-80, hon. life pres.), Internat. Soc. Immunology Reprodn., Japan Soc. Low Temperature Medicine, N.Y. Acad. Scis., Soc. Leukocyte Biology, Soc. Cryobiology, Soc. Protozoologists, Soc. Study Reprodn., Soc. Exptl. Biology and Medicine, Transplantation Soc., Cryoimmunotherapeutic Study Group (chmn.), Sigma Xi. Achievements include identification of prostate specific antigen (PSA), used as tumor marker (diagnosis) in prostate cancer, and of human thymic specific antigen providing means for differentiation of thymic lymphocytes from other lymphoid cells and the development of antithymocyte globulin (selectively immunosuppressive for thymocytes) used in renal allograft (transplant) recipients; and development of concept of cryoimmunotherapy for treatment of cancer. *One of the saddest things in life, is to have the opportunity to do something, and not to take advantage of it.*

ABLONCZY, DIANE, member Canadian parliament; b. 1949; married; 1 child. BEd, U. Calgary, 1973, LLB, 1980. Tchr. elem. sch., 1969-74, grain farmer, 1973-86, pvt. practice atty., 1981-91, asst. to leader Reform Party, 1991-93, mem. Can. Parliament for Calgary-Nose Hill, 1993—; Opposition critic human resources devel., mem. Reform shadow cabinet, chair Reform human resources devel. critics com., mem. standing com. on human resources devel., mem. Reform Party strategy com., mem. Reform family caucus, former dep. justice critic, Atlantic issues critic, human resources devel. critic, Reform Party caucus whip, Can. Parliament. Founding mem., mem. 1st exec. coun., 2-term chmn. Reform Party. Office: Ho of Commons, 217 W Block, Ottawa, ON Canada K1A 0A6

ABLOW, JOSEPH, artist, educator; b. Salem, Mass., Aug. 16, 1928; s. Benjamin and Eva (Smith) A.; m. Roselyn Karol, June 23, 1956; 1 child, Rachel. BA, Bennington Coll., 1954; MA, Harvard U., 1955. Instr. Middlebury (Vt.) Coll., 1955-58; asst. prof. Bard Coll., Annandale, N.Y., 1959-61, Wellesley (Mass.) Coll., 1962-63; assoc. prof. Boston U., 1972-95, chmn. div. of art, 1964-67, prof. of art, 1972-95, prof. emeritus, 1996—; vis. assoc. prof. MIT, Cambridge, 1969-70; vis. prof. Amherst (Mass.) Coll., 1975-76; vis. scholar Cambridge (Mass.) Humanities Seminar, MIT, 1973-82; mem. adv. com. Bunting Inst., Radcliffe Coll., Cambridge, 1984-87; lectr. Amherst Coll., 1975, 78, 82, Univ. N.H., 1980, 82, Inst. of Contemporary Art, Boston, 1980, Nieman Found., Harvard Univ., 1982, 83, MIT, 1984, St. John's Univ., Collegeville, Minn., 1986, Fitchburg Art Mus., 1987, Salve Regina Coll., Newport, R.I., 1990, and others. One-man shows include Boris Mirski Gallery, Boston, 1961, 65, 69, Pucker/Safari Gallery, Boston, 1979, 81, 83, 87, 91, 94, The Trustman Art Gallery, Simmons Coll., Boston, 1983, Fitchburg Art Mus., Miami U., Oxford, Ohio, 1987, others; represented in permanent collections Bard Coll., Middlebury Coll., DeCordova and Dana Mus., Univ. Mass. Harbor Campus, Mead Art Gallery, Amherst Coll., Rose Art Mus., Brandeis U., others; contbg. editor Bostonia Mag., Boston, 1986-89; contbr. articles to profl. jours. Mem. bd. dirs. Jewish Cultural Endowment, Boston Univ., 1988—. Recipient Paige traveling fellowship Mus. Fine Arts, Boston, 1951, Fulbright grant in painting, Paris, 1958-59, Silver medal award for best article of the yr. Coun. for Advancement and Support of Edn., 1987, Boston U. Sch. for the Arts disting. faculty award, 1996. Avocation, music. Home: 16 Monmouth Ct Brookline MA 02446-5634 Office: Boston U Sch Visual Art 855 Commonwealth Ave Boston MA 02215-1303

ABLOW, KEITH RUSSELL, psychiatrist, journalist, author; b. Boston, Nov. 23, 1961; s. Allan Murray and Jeanette Norma (Mezansky) A. ScB, Brown U., 1983; MD, Johns Hopkins U., 1987. Reporter Newsweek, N.Y.C., 1984; columnist Balt. Evening Sun, Boston Herald, 1985-89, Washington Post, 1990—; intern in psychiatry Tufts U.-New Eng. Med. Ctr. Hosps., Boston, 1987-88, resident, 1988-91; chief resident 1991—, 1991-92; columnist Washington Post, 1990—; cons. psychiatrist WCVB TV, Boston, 1992—; med. dir. Tri-City Mental Health Ctr., 1992-94; assoc. med. dir. Heritage Health Systems, 1993-94; corr. Med. News Network, 1993—; med. dir. FHC New Eng., 1994-96; outpatient psychiatrist Boston Regional Med. Ctr., 1996—; med. editor Lifetime Med. TV, L.A. and Astoria, N.Y., 1986-89. Author: Medical School: Getting In, Staying In, Staying Human, 1987, How to Cope With Depression, 1989, To Wrestle With Demons, 1992, Anatomy of a Psychiatric Illness, 1993, The Strange Case of Dr. Kappler, 1994, Denial, 1997; columnist Mental Health Infosource Website, 1996—. Trustee White Pines Coll., Chester, N.H., 1989-91. Recipient Optimate award Am. Soc. Profl. Italians, 1990. Mem. AAAS, AMA (sr. editor, creative cons. Pulse 1986-87, Jerry L. Pettis award 1987), Am. Psychiat. Assn., Am. Med. Writers Assn. (Will Solimene award 1991, 92, Best Trade Book, 1993). Democrat. Avocation: writing fiction. Home: 4 Breakwater Dr Chelsea MA 02150-4038

ABLOW, RONALD CHARLES, hospital executive; b. Salem, Mass., June 1, 1932; s. Benjamin and Eva (Smith) A.; m. Judith Ablow. AB in Physics cum laude, Harvard U., 1954, MBA, 1956, MD, U. Rochester, 1962; MA (hon.), Yale U., 1974. Diplomate Am. Bd. Radiology. Instr. radiology, assoc. attending radiologist Yale U., New Haven, 1966-67, asst. prof. radiology, attending radiologist, 1967-69, prof. radiology and pediatrics, 1973-84; dir. radiology New Haven unit Yale New-Haven Hosp., 1973-75; chief pediatric radiology Yale-New Haven Hosp., 1974-84; asst. clin. prof. radiology U. Calif., San Francisco, 1971-73, Stanford (Calif.) U., 1971-73; assoc. CEO of radiology Mt. Zion Hosp./Med. Ctr., San Francisco, 1969-73; dir. radiology St. Luke's-Roosevelt Hosp. Ctr., N.Y.C., 1984-97, pres., CEO, 1996-98; prof. radiology Coll. Physicians and Surgeons Columbia U., N.Y.C., 1984—; cons. dir. radiology Beth Israel Med. Ctr., N.Y.C., 1991-94, chmn. radiology, 1994-96; mem. com. on practice of commn. on physics and radiation proction Am. Bd. Radiology, 1985-87, examiner, Louisville, 1987-88; specialist site visitor Accreditation Coun. for Grad. Med. Edn., 1988—. Contbr. articles to profl. jours. Timothy Dwight Coll. fellow Yale U., 1977-84. Fellow Am. Coll. Radiology, N.Y. Acad. Medicine; mem. Am. Roentgen Ray Soc., Radiol. Soc. N.Am., N.Y. Acad. Scis., N.Y. Roentgen Ray Soc. (pres. 1993-94), Conn. Radiology Soc., Assn. Univ. Radiologists, Silverman Soc., Soc. Pediatric Radiology, Soc. Thoracic Radiology. Office: St Lukes's-Roosevelt Hosp Ctr Corp Adminstrn 1111 Amsterdam Ave New York NY 10025-1716

ABNEE, A. VICTOR, trade association executive; b. Lexington, Ky., June 12, 1923; s. A. Victor and Irene Sarah (Brogle) A.; m. Doris Heuck, Dec. 28, 1946 (deceased); children: Janice Lee Abnee Williams, A. Victor III. BA, U. Cin., 1948. With U.S. Gypsum Co., Chgo., 1948-63, dir. advt. and promotion, 1961-64; with Gypsum Assn., Evanston, Ill., 1964—, exec. v.p., 1964-83, pres., 1983-88; cons., 1988—. Served to capt. C.E., AUS, 1943-46, PTO. Named Alumna of Yr., U. Cin., 1967, Constrn. Industry Man of Yr. Wall and Ceiling Industries Assn., 1980. Mem. Nat. Assn. Mfrs. (councilman 1983—), Am. Soc. Assn. Execs., Exec. Svc. Corps, Internat. Exec. Svc. Corps., Chgo. Soc. Assn. Execs. (hon. life), Les Cheneaux Islands Assn. (pres. 1986-87), Bohemian Club, Sigma Chi (Significant Sig award 1986). Clubs: Les Cheneaux Yacht (bd. dirs. 1982-85), Foundation (Chgo.) (pres. 1985), University (Chgo.) (pres. 1981-83), Adventurers (Chgo.), University (Evanston) (pres. 1984-85), Skokie Country (Glencoe, Ill.), Skyline Country (Tucson), Gyro Internat. Lodge: Shriners, Masons. Office: Gypsum Assn 1603 Orrington Ave Evanston IL 60201-3841

ABNEY, FREDERICK SHERWOOD, lawyer; b. Brownwood, Tex., Dec. 2, 1919; s. DeWitt Fleetwood and Margaret (Lyles) A.; m. Jeanne Elizabeth Larson, Feb. 28, 1942; children: Stephen Frederick, James Lorntz. B.A., U. Tex., Austin, 1942, LL.B., 1947. Bar: Tex. bar 1947, U.S. Supreme Ct. bar 1963. Pvt. practice Brownwood, 1948-49, Dallas, 1949-94. Served with USAAF, 1942-45. Mem. Am., Dallas bar assns., State Bar Tex., Am. Judicature Soc., Southwestern Legal Found., Dallas Bar Found., Tex. Bar Found. (life fellow), Delta Tau Delta, Phi Delta Phi. Mem. Unity Ch. Home and Office: 6730 Orchid Ln Dallas TX 75230-4137

ABNEY, STEPHEN DOUGLAS, civilian military employee; b. Scott AFB, Ill., Sept. 15, 1952; s. Jessie and Ruth Alice (Broadley) A.; m. Nancy Lee Funck, Apr. 4, 1987; children: Margaret Joy, Ann Chapman. BA, U. Ky., 1974; postgrad., U. Ga., 1974-76, U. S.C., 1989. Info. and editl. intern Forces Command, Atlanta, 1976-78; advt. and info. specialist 5th U.S. Army, San Antonio, 1978-79; advt. specialist Army S.W. Recruiting Region, San Antonio, 1979-80; chief advt. and sales promotion Army Dist. Recruiting Command, Ft. Monmouth, N.J., 1980-84; dep., pub. affairs officer U.S. Army Recruiting Command, Ft. Sheridan, Ill., 1984-87; chief pub. affairs U.S. Army Depot Sys. Command, Chambersburg, Pa., 1987-95; pub. affairs officer Joint Logistics Support Command, Port-au-Prince, Haiti, 1994; chief pub. affairs U.S. Army Indsl. Ops. Command, Rock Island, Ill., 1996—. Contbr. articles to mags. Pres. Edward White PTA, Eldridge, Iowa, 1996-98; mem. supt.'s adv. coun. North Scott Comty. Sch., Eldridge, 1995-98; deacon chair Monmouth Bapt. Ch., Eatontown, N.J., 1983-84; chair resolutions com. Young Dems. of Ga., Atlanta, 1976. Mem. Pub. Rels. Soc. Am., Assn. of U.S. Army (chpt. v.p. 1987-94). Methodist. Home: 620 N 6th St Eldridge IA 52748-1173 Office: HQIOC Attn: AMSIO-PA Bldg 390 2d Fl SW Rock Island IL 61299-6000

ABO, RONALD KENT, architect; b. Rupert, Idaho, July 10, 1946; s. Isamu and Ameria (Hachiya) A.; m. Lisa A. Wiesley; children: Tamiko N., Reiko D., Ryan A. BArch, U. Colo., 1969. Lic. architect, Colo. Designer SLP & Ptnrs., Denver, 1968-71; dir. Community Design Ctr., Denver, 1971-72; assoc. Barker, Rinker, Seacat, Denver, 1972-76; pvt. practice Denver, 1976-80; pres. Abo Gude Architects, Denver, 1980-84, Ron Abo Architects, Denver, 1984-91, Abo Architects PC, Denver, 1991-94, Abo Copeland Architecture, 1995—; design instr., thesis advisor U. Colo., Denver. Prin. works include Morrison Horticultre Ctr., 1983 (W.O.O.D. Inc. citation 1983), Highland Square, 1982 (AIA citation 1983), Roxborough Elem. Sch., 1990, Tropical Discovery Ctr. Denver Zoo, 1992, New Denver Internat. Airport Concourse Bldgs., 1993, Nederland Middle/H.S., 1996, Julesburg Welcome Ctr., 1997, Rocky Mountain Mfg. Acad., 1998. Active Denver Comty. Leadership Forum, 1986, Colfax-on-the-Hill, 1988—, U. Colo. Alumni Bd., Workforce Devel. Bd., 1990—. Recipient Design Excellence award W.O.O.D. Inc., Denver, 1982, Martin Luther King Bus. Social Responsibility award, 1998. Mem. AIA (bd. dirs., pres.-elect Denver chpt. 1990, pres. 1991, pres.-elect Colo. chpt. 1997, pres. 1998), Asian C. of C. (pres. 1998), Colo. Aikido Assn. (head instr. Denver Buddhist Temple Aikido). Democrat. Avocation: Aikido (4th degree black belt). Office: Abo Copeland Architecture 1600 Downing St Ste 700 Denver CO 80218-1540

ABOLINS, MARIS ARVIDS, physics researcher and educator; b. Liepaja, Latvia, Feb. 5, 1938; came to U.S., 1949, naturalized, 1956; s. Arvids Gustavs and Olga Elizabete (Grintals) A.; m. Frances Delano, Dec. 19, 1959. B.S. magna cum laude, U. Wash., 1960; M.S., U. Calif.-San Diego, 1962, Ph.D., 1965. Research asst. U. Calif.-San Diego, 1960-65; physicist Lawrence Berkeley Lab., 1965-68; assoc. prof. physics Mich. State U., East Lansing, 1968-73, prof. physics, 1973—; cons. U.S. Dept. Energy; sci. assoc. CERN, Geneva, 1976-77; vis. research scientist, Saclay, France, 1977, Fermi Nat. Accelerator Lab., 1990-92, Saclay, France, 1997; mem. tech. adv. com. Argonne Nat. Lab., 1971-72; mem. prep. com. Fermilab, 1978-79; chmn. Fermilab Users' Exec. Com., 1982-83; mem. SSC Users Exec. Com., 1988-91; chmn. bd. dirs. ATLAS Trigger/DAQ Instnl., 1997-99. NSF research grantee, 1971—; Disting. Faculty award 1998. Fellow Am. Phys. Soc. (exec. com. div. particles and fields 1984-86); mem. AAAS, Patria, Phi Beta Kappa, Sigma Xi. Home: 1430 Fairoaks Ct East Lansing MI 48823-1812 Office: Mich State U Dept Physics And Astro East Lansing MI 48824

ABORN, FOSTER LITCHFIELD, insurance company executive; b. Providence, July 8, 1934; s. John Russell and Helene Cecile (Hesse) A.; m. Sara Holbrook; children: Justin, Hilary. BA, Dartmouth Coll., 1956; MBA, 1957. Asst. v.p. Mellon Bank, N.A., Pitts., 1957-68; vice chmn. chief investment officer John Hancock Mut. Life Ins. Co., Boston, 1968—; bd. dirs. John Hancock Capital Corp., Hancock Venture Ptnrs., Inc., Boston, John Hancock Subs., Inc., Independence Investment Assocs., 1987—, John Hancock Mut. Life Ins. Co., John Hancock Funds, Mass. Bus. Devel. Corp.; mem. adv. com. One Liberty Ventures. Trustee John Hancock Asset Mgmt., Beth Israel Deaconess Med. Ctr. Mem. Univ. Club Boston. Republican. Unitarian. Home: 121 Main St Hingham MA 02043-2506 Office: John Hancock Mut Life Ins PO Box 111 Boston MA 02117-0111

ABOU-KHALIL, BASSAM MICHAEL, cardiothoracic surgeon; b. Beirut, Lebanon, Mar. 20, 1963; came to U.S., 1985; s. Michael and Claude (Khoury) A.-K. BS in Chemistry, Am. U. Beirut, 1983; MD, Med. U. S.C., 1987. Resident in gen. surgery SUNY Downstate, Bklyn., 1987-92; resident in cardiothoracic surgery Med. U. S.C., Charleston, 1992-95; attending surgeon Ctrl. Bapt. Hosp., Lexington, Ky., 1995—, chief intensive care com., 1996-97. Contbr. articles to profl. jours.; presenter in field. Mem. Soc. Thoracic Surgeons, Ky. Med. Assn. Roman Catholic. Office: 168 Burt Rd Lexington KY 40517

ABPLANALP, GLEN HAROLD, civil engineer; b. Youngsville, N.Y., Nov. 9, 1914; s. William P. and Elizabeth (Tremper) A.; m. Marion Clark, Sept. 5, 1937; children: Diane Abplanalp Guimmule, Jeffrey. C.E., Rensselaer Poly. Inst., 1936; J.D., Fordham U., 1943. Bar: N.Y. 1943; registered profl. engr., N.Y., N.J., Pa., Mich., Wis., Md. Asst. dist. mgr. Wallace & Tiernan Co. Inc., Newark, 1936-43; sec-treas. Glenwal Co., Inc., Ridgewood, N.J., 1946-47; cons. engr. Havens & Emerson, Inc., N.Y.C. and Saddle Brook, N.J., 1947—; prin. engr. Havens & Emerson, Inc., 1955-59, gen. partner, 1959-70, vice chmn., 1970-77, v.p., 1977-80, staff cons., 1980-91; lectr. in field; head coop. research project on upper Passaic River, 1965—; cons. N.J. Commr. Health, 1964—; mem., past chmn. Engrs. Joint Contract Documents Com. Contbr. articles to profl. jours.; legal editor: The Specifier, 1960-64. Dir. Met. Youth for Christ. Served with USNR, 1943-46; to lt. comdr. USNR. Recipient Pres's. plaque Constrn. Specifications Inst., 1963, 64, 67, 77, Meritorious Svc. award Profl. Engrs. in Constrn., 1993. Fellow Constrn. Specifications Inst. (pres. 1960-61, hon. mem. 1985—), ASCE (life), Am. Cons. Engrs. Council (past chmn. contract documents com.); mem. NSPE (past com. chmn.), Am. Arbitration Assn. (past chmn. nat. constrn. industry arbitration com.), Am. Water Works Assn. (past chmn. engring. and constrn. div., tech. and profl. council, hon. and life mem. 1987, Fuller award), Water Pollution Control Fedn. (life), Am. Acad. Environ. Engrs. (diplomate, past trustee), VFW, Am. Legion, Pi Kappa Alpha. Pentecostal. Home and Office: 539 Grove St Ridgewood NJ 07450-5428*

ABRAHAM, F(AHRID) MURRAY, actor, educator; b. Pitts., Oct. 24, 1939; s. Fahrid and Josephine Abraham; m. Kate Hannan, 1962; two children. Student, U. Tex., El Paso, 1959-61. Actor Broadway, Off-Broadway, children's theater, musicals, film, TV; prof. Bklyn. Coll., 1985—; dir. No Smoking Please, N.Y.C., Time & Space Ltd. Theatre, N.Y.C. Profl. stage debut in The Wonderful Ice Cream Suit, Coronet Theatre, L.A., 1965;Broadway debut in The Man in the Glass Booth, Royale Theatre, 1968; appeared in numerous Broadway plays including 6 Rms RivVu, 1972-73, Bad Habits, 1974, The Ritz, 1976-76, Teibele and Her Demon, 1979; other stage appearences include Landscape of the Body, 1977, The Master and Margarita, 1978, The Golem, 1984, King Lear, 1981, Frankie and Johnny in the Claire de Lune, 1987, A Month in the Country, 1995; films include They Might Be Giants, 1971, Serpico, 1974, The Sunshine Boys, 1975, All the President's Men, 1976, The Ritz, 1976, The Big Fix, 1979, Scarface, 1983, Amadeus, 1984 (Academy award best actor 1984, Golden Globe award best actor 1984), The Name of the Rose, 1986, Russicum, 1989, An Innocent Man, 1989, Bonfire of the Vanities, 1990, Cadence, 1991, Mobsters, 1991, National Lampoon's Loaded Weapon I, 1993, By the Sword, 1993, Last Action Hero, 1993, Surviving the Game, 1994, The Case, 1994, Nostradamus, 1994, Jamila, 1994, Fresh, 1994, Mighty Aphrodite, 1995, Dillinger and Capone, 1995, Baby Face Nelson, 1995, Looking for Richard, 1996, Children of the Revolution, 1996, Mimic, 1997, Eruption, 1997, Laurel and Hardy: For Love or Mummy, 1998, Star Trek IX, 1998, Falcone, 1999, Esther, 1999; narrator Herman Melville, Damned in Paradise, PBS, 1985; appeared in PBS Masterpiece Theatre prodn.: Silas Marner, 1987, Noah's Ark, 1999, Star Trek: Insurrection, 1998; TV mini-series Larry McMurtry's Dead Man's Walk, 1996; TV Spl. Einstein Revealed (voice), 1996, TV movie Sex and the Married Woman, 1977, Color of Justice, 1997; TV series Love of Life. Recipient Obie award for Uncle Vanya 1984; Los Angeles Film Critics award, 1985. Mem. Actors Equity, AFTRA, Screen Actors Guild. Office: care Paradigm F Murray Abraham Agt 10100 Santa Monica Blvd #2500 Los Angeles CA 90067*

ABRAHAM, HENRY JULIAN, political science educator; b. Offenbach am Main, Germany, Aug. 25, 1921; s. Fredrick and Louise (Kullmann) A.; m. Mildred Kosches, Apr. 13, 1954; children: Philip F., Peter D. AB summa cum laude, Kenyon Coll., 1948, LHD (hon.), 1972; MA, Columbia U., 1949; PhD, U. Pa., 1952; LLD (hon.), U. Hartford, 1982, Knox Coll., 1982; LittD (hon.), St. Joseph's U., 1987; LLD (hon.), Old Dominion U., 1996. Mem. faculty U. Pa., 1949-72, prof. polit. sci., 1962-72; Doherty prof. govt. and fgn. affairs U. Va., 1971-78, James Hart prof., 1978—; vis. prof. Swarthmore Coll., CCNY, Colo. U., Columbia U., U. Richmond Law Sch., U. Copenhagen, U. Stockholm, Aarhus U., Lund U., U. Göteborg, U. Oslo, U. Helsinki, U. Uppsala, U. Amsterdam, U. London; cons. in field, 1956; Fulbright prof., Denmark, 1959-60. Author: Compulsory Voting, 1955, Government as Entrepreneur, 1956, Courts and Judges, 1959, Elements of Democratic Government, 1964, Essentials of National Government, 1971, American Democracy, 1990, Justices, Presidents and Senators, 1999, The Judiciary, 1997, The Judicial Process, 1998, Freedom and the Court, 1998. Mem. com. on non-discrimintion Phila. Bd. Edn., 1962; mem. vis. com. on govt. Lehigh U., 1967-71; trustee fedn. Jewish Agys. Greater Phila., 1970-72, Kenyon Coll., 1987-93; mem. Va. Commn. on Bicentennial of Constn. of U.S., 1985-92. Recipient award excellence undergrad. teaching U. Pa., 1959, 67, Kite and Key Teaching award, 1967, award excellence undergrad. teaching U. Va., 1978, Thomas Jefferson award U. Va., 1983, U. Va. Alumni Teaching award, 1986, Disting. Svc. award Va. Social Sci. Assn., 1982, Disting. Prof. award U. Va. Alumni Assn., 1986, First Lifetime Achievement award, org. sec. on law & courts, Am. polit., sci. Assn., 1993, others; NEH, 1975, 76, 78, 80, 81, NSF fellow, 1965, fellow Am. Philos. Soc., 1961-67, 79, Rockefeller Found. fellow, 1978, Earhart fellow, 1984, Bradley Found., 1989-97. Mem. Fellows in Am. Studies (pres. 1966), Am. Polit. Sci. Assn. (v.p. 1980-82), Raven Soc., Am. Soc. for Legal History, So. Polit. Sci. Ass. (rec. sec. 1980-81), Soc. of Fellows, Met. Opera Guild, Nat. Trust, Golden Key, Greencroft Club (v.p. 1985-87, Charlottesville, Va.), Z Club (U. Va.), Imp Club (U. Va.), Yale Club (N.Y.C.), Phi Beta Kappa (vis. scholar 1970-71), Pi Sigma Alpha, Pi Gamma Mu, Omicron Delta Kappa. Fax: 804-924-3359. Home: 906 Fendall Ter Charlottesville VA 22903-1617 Office: Univ Va 232 Cabell Hall Charlottesville VA 22903 *Basically—a commitment to hard work; to discipline; to a maintenance of a sense of humour; to a rejection of pompousness and egomania; to a resolute embrace of merit. Above all, an abiding faith in drawing a viable line between the rights and obligations of individuals and those of society without which the democratic process can neither work nor survive.*

ABRAHAM, KATHARINE GAIL, economics educator; b. Dayton, Ohio, Aug. 28, 1954; d. William Hamilton and Roberta Taylor (Grannis) A.; m. Graham Neil Horkley, May 25, 1985; children: Ian Robert Horkley, Benjamin William Horkley. Student, Carleton Coll., 1972-74; BS, Iowa State U., 1976; PhD, Harvard U., 1982. Asst. prof. Sloan Sch. Mgmt. MIT, Cambridge, Mass., 1980-85; rsch. assoc. Brookings Inst., Washington, 1985-87; assoc. prof. econs. U. Md., College Park, 1987-91, prof. econs., 1991-97; commnr. labor stats. U.S. Bur. Labor Stats., 1993—; rsch. assoc. Nat. Bur. Econ. Rsch., 1987-95. Author 2 books; assoc. editor Quar. Jour. Econs., 1985-92; bd. reviewers Indsl. Rels., 1984-93; contbr. articles to profl. jours. Named Outstanding Young Alumnus Iowa State U., 1988; grad. fellow NSF, 1977-80. Mem. Am. Econ. Assn., Indsl. Rels. Rsch. Assn., Com. on the Status Women in the Econs. Profession. Office: US Bur Labor Stats 2 Massachusetts Ave NE Washington DC 20212-0022

ABRAHAM, LYNNE M., district attorney; b. Phila., 1941. BA, Temple U., 1962, JD, 1965. Mem. reg. counsel's office U.S. Dept. HUD, 1965-67; asst. dist. atty. City and County of Phila., 1967-72, 73-74, dist. atty., 1991—; exec. dir. Phila. Redevel. Authority, 1972-73; legis. cons. Phila. County Coun., 1974-76; rsch. assoc. Ct. Common Please/Ct. Adminstr. of Pa., 1974-77; judge Phila. Mcpl. Ct., 1976-80, Ct. Common Pleas/Phila. County, 1980-91. Office: City and County of Phila 1421 Arch St Philadelphia PA 19102-1507*

ABRAHAM, NICHOLAS ALBERT, lawyer, real estate developer; b. Boston, Sept. 17, 1941; s. Nicholas and Ida (Ghiz) A.; m. Evie Stathopoulos, June 30, 1968; children: Annise, Nicholas. BS, Boston U., 1963, JD, 1966. Bar: Mass. 1966, U.S. Dist. Ct. Mass. 1968, U.S. Ct. Appeals (1st cir.) 1971. Sr. ptnr. Abraham-Hanna, P.C., Boston, 1968-88; CEO Boston Investors Fund, Inc., 1988-93; pres., CEO Abraham Properties Inc., Boston, 1993—; CEO., chmn., founder STOR/GARD, Inc., 1996—. Author: Doing Business in Egypt, 1979, Doing Business in Saudi Arabia, 1980, Doing Business in Kuwait, 1982. Bd. of trustees Boston U. Coll. of Bus. Adminstrn., 1968; chmn. fund raising com. Boy Scouts Am., 1968; coach Weston Little League; founder of Weston Youth Hockey League, 1985. Served with U.S. Army, 1966-67; to lt. comdr. USN, 1967-74. Republican. Eastern Orthodox. Home: 21 Buckskin Dr Weston MA 02493-1129 Office: Abraham Properties Inc 581 Boylston St Fl 3 Boston MA 02116-3608

ABRAHAM, REBECCA JACOB, finance educator; b. Calcutta, India, Nov. 4, 1962; came to U.S., 1986; d. Connayil Mani and Susan (Varugis) Jacob; m. Anthony Zikiye, May 10, 1989 (dec. Jan. 1994); 1 child, Mark. BS in Chemistry, Women's Christian Coll., Madras; MBA, U.S. Internat., San Diego, 1984, D in Bus. Adminstrn., 1989. Asst. prof. Nova S.E. Univ., Ft. Lauderdale, Fla., 1989-94; assoc. prof. Nova S.E. Univ., Ft. Lauderdale, 1994—. Corr. South Fla. Bus., Ft. Lauderdale, 1995, Broward Times, Ft. Lauderdale, 1995; contbr. articles to profl. jours. Recipient Nat. Collegiate Bus. award, 1987. Mem. Acad. Mgmt. Avocations: reading, traveling, badminton. Office: Nova SE Univ 3301 College Ave Fort Lauderdale FL 33314-7721

ABRAHAM, SPENCER, senator; b. Lansing, Mich., June 12, 1952. BA in Social Sci.and Polit. Sci., Mich. State U., 1974; JD, Harvard U., 1979. Asst. prof. law Thomas M. Cooley Law Sch., 1981-83; chmn. Mich. Republican Party, 1983-90; dep. chief of staff to Vice President Dan Quayle, 1990-91; co-chair Nat. Republican Congressional Com., 1991-93; of counsel Canfield, Paddock & Stone, 1993-94; U.S. senator from Mich., 1994—; mem. budget com., 1995—, judiciary com., 1997—, subcom. on immigration, 1997—, commerce sci. and transp. com., 1996—, subcom. on mfg. and competitiveness, 1997—, subcom. on aviation, 1999—, small bus. com., 1999—. Office: US Senate 329 Dirksen Senate Bldg Washington DC 20510-2203*

ABRAHAM, TAJAMA, basketball player; b. Sept. 27, 1975. Grad., George Washington U., 1997. Ctr. WNBA - Sacramento Monarchs, 1997-98, WNBA - Detroit Shock, 1999—. Named Atlantic 10 Conf. Player of Yr., 1996-97, Kodak Al-Am. Team, 1997. Office: Detroit Shock 2 Championship Dr Auburn Hills MI 48326*

ABRAHAM, TONSON, chemist, researcher; b. Bombay, Dec. 21, 1948; came to U.S., 1970; s. Thykadavil Jorge and Annie (Joseph) A.; m. Iona Marianne Joseph, June 17, 1978; children: Akash, Kavi. B in Tech., Indian Inst. Tech., Kanpur, India, 1970; PhD in Organic Chemistry, Cath. U. Am., 1976. Fellow NRC, Washington, 1976-78; postdoctoral fellow No. Ill. U., DeKalb, 1978-79; vis. asst. prof. Ill. State U., Normal, 1979-80; polymer scientist Wright-Patterson Air Force Base, Fairborn, Ohio, 1980-86; sr. scientist Owens-Corning Fiberglas, Granville, Ohio, 1986; R & D assoc. B.F. Goodrich Co., Brecksville, Ohio, 1987-94; polymer chemist Argonne (Ill.) Nat. Lab., 1994-96; sr. rsch. specialist Advanced Elastomer Sys., Akron, Ohio, 1996—. Contbr. articles to profl. jours. Mem. Am. Chem. Soc. Roman Catholic. Achievements include patents in synthetic polymer and organic chemistry; research in the synthesis and applications of thermoplastic elastomers, biodegradable polymers, water swellable and water soluble polymers, synthesis of high temperature, oil resistent elastomers, fluoroelastomers, hydrogenation of polymers, homogeneous hydrogenation catalysts, thermosetting resin precursors for aerospace composites and in the chemistry of indoles. Home: 16936 Deer Path Dr Strongsville OH 44136-6260 Office: Advanced Elastomer Sys 388 S Main St Ste 600 Akron OH 44311-1065

ABRAHAM, WILLIAM JOHN, JR., lawyer; b. Chgo., Jan. 17, 1948; s. William John and Constance (Dudley) A.; m. Linda Omeis, Aug. 31, 1968; children: Richard S., Heidi K. BA with honors, U. Ill., 1969; JD magna cum laude, U. Mich., Arbor, 1972. Bar: Wis. 1973, U.S. Supreme Ct. 1975. Jud. clk. U.S. Ct. Appeals (D.C. Cir.), Washington, 1972-73; ptnr. Foley & Lardner, Milw., 1973—, former mem. mgmt. com., chmn. bus. law dept; bd. dirs. The Vollrath Co., The Printery, Global Sourcing Ptnrs. Ltd., Market St. Investors Inc., Windway Capital Corp., Sirco, Inc., Park Bank, TransPro, Inc., Indus, Inc. Past bd. dirs. United Way of Greater Milw., Family Svc. of Milw.; bd. dirs. Milw. Zool. Soc.; chmn. Children's Hosp. Found., chmn. fin. com. All-Am. Big 10 Fencing Champion, 1968-69, Greater Milw. Com., Children's Hosp. of Milw.; mem. adv. bd. Marquette U. Bus. Sch. Mem. ABA, State Bar of Wis. (chmn. legis. com.), Milw. Bar Assn., Tripoli Country Club (bd. dirs., pres.), Milw. Athletic Club, Univ. Club, Desert Mountain Country Club. Office: Foley & Lardner 777 E Wisconsin Ave Ste 3800 Milwaukee WI 53202-5367

ABRAHAMS, ATHOL DENIS, geography researcher, geography educator; b. Sydney, New South Wales, Australia, Mar. 10, 1946; came to U.S., 1977; s. Alfred George and Muriel Clare (McTaggart) A.; m. Lesley Jane Hungerford, June 9, 1968 (div. 1975); 1 child, Katharine Jane; m. Helen Lorraine Oak, Jan. 3, 1976; 1 child, Geoffrey James. BA with honors, U. Sydney, 1966, PhD, 1971. Killam post-doctoral fellow U. Alta., Edmonton, Can., 1971-73; lectr. U. New South Wales, Sydney, 1973-77; assoc. prof. SUNY-Buffalo, 1977-84, prof., 1984—, chmn. dept. geography, 1988-91; Disting. vis. prof. Ariz. State U., 1988; dir. 16th Ann. Geomorphology Symposium, Buffalo. Editor: Hillslope Processes, 1985; co dir. 22d Ann. Geomorphology Symposium, Buffalo. Co-editor: Periglacial Geomorphology, 1992; co-editor: Overland Flow: Hydraulics and Erosion Mechanics, 1992, Geomorphology of Desert Environments, 1994; assoc. editor jour. Annals of the Assn. of Am. Geographers, 1982-87. Contbr. articles to profl. jours. Tchrs. Coll. scholar New South Wales Edn. Dept., 1963-66, Commonwealth scholar, 1967-71; NSF grantee, 1985, 86, 88, 90, 92, 94, 96, NATO grantee 1985, 87, 89, 93, EPA grantee, 1997, Assn. Am. Geographers honors, 1992. Fellow Geol. Soc. Am. (Gladys W. Cole Research award 1985); mem. Assn. Am. Geographers (G.K. Gilbert award 1985, Honors 1992), Am. Geophys. Union, Brit. Geomorphological Research Group, Internat. Geog. Union Commn. on Gemorphological Response to Environ. Change. Avocations: skiing, squash. Office: SUNY Buffalo Dept Geography Buffalo NY 14261

ABRAHAMS, JIM, film director; b. Shorewood, Wis., May 10, 1944. Dir., writer, exec. prodr.: Airplane!/Flying High, 1980, Top Secret!, 1984; dir., writer: Hot Shots!, 1991, Hot Shots: Part Deux, 1993, Jane Austen's Mafia, 1998; dir.: Ruthless People, 1986, Big Business, 1988, Welcome Home, Roxy Carmichael, 1990; dir. (TV series) Police Squad, 1988; writer, exec. prodr.: The Naked Gun, 1988, Naked Gun 2 1/2: The Smell of Fear, 1991, Naked Gun 33 1/3: The Final Insult, 1994; writer, actor: Kentucky Fried Movie, 1977; exec. prodr.: Cry-Baby, 1990. Office: c/o Zucker Bros Prodns 1351 4th St Ste 300 Santa Monica CA 90401 and: c/o DGA 7920 Sunset Blvd Los Angeles CA 90046*

ABRAHAMSON, A. CRAIG, lawyer; b. Washington, May 24, 1954; s. Joseph Labe and Helen Dorothy (Selis) A.; m. Mary Ellen Bernard, Dec. 29, 1979; children: Nicholas Eric, Amy Nicole. BA, U. Minn., 1976; JD, U. Tulsa, 1979. Bar: Minn. 1979, U.S. Dist. Ct. Minn. 1979, Okla. 1982, U.S. Dist. Ct. (no. and ea. dists.) Okla. 1983, Mo. 1991. Assoc. Law Office of Joseph L. Abrahamson, Mpls., 1979-82, Freese & March, Tulsa, 1982-83, Barlow & Cox, Tulsa, 1983-86; pvt. practice Tulsa, 1986-95; ptnr. Levinson, Smith & Abrahamson, Tulsa, 1995—. V.p. program com. Youth Svcs., Tulsa, Inc., Leadership Tulsa Class XVII, 1989-92; sec. Great Expectations Educators, Inc., 1995—. Recipient Am. Jurisprudence Evidence award Lawyers Co-operative Pub. Co. Bancroft-Whitney Co., 1978. Mem. ABA (litigation sect.), Okla. Bar Assn. (family law sect.), Assn. Trial Lawyers Am., Okla. Trial Lawyers Assn., Tulsa County Bar Assn. (profl. responsibility com.). Democrat. Jewish. Lodge: Masons. Avocations: fishing, camping, travel, tennis. Home: 7518 S 107th East Ave Tulsa OK 74133-2530 Office: Levinson Smith & Abrahamson 35 E 18th St Tulsa OK 74119-5201 also: PO Box 3366 Tulsa OK 74101-3366

ABRAHAMSON, SHIRLEY SCHLANGER, state supreme court chief justice; b. N.Y.C., Dec. 17, 1933; d. Leo and Ceil (Sauerteig) Schlanger; m. Seymour Abrahamson, Aug. 26, 1953; 1 son, Daniel Nathan. AB, NYU, 1953; JD, Ind. U., 1956; SJD, U. Wis., 1962. Bar: Ind. 1956, N.Y. 1961, Wis. 1962. Asst. dir. Legis. Drafting Research Fund, Columbia U. Law Sch., 1957-60; since practiced in Madison, Wis., 1962-76; mem. firm LaFollette, Sinykin, Anderson & Abrahamson, 1962-76; justice Supreme Ct. Wis., Madison, 1976-96, chief justice, 1996—; prof. U. Wis. Sch. Law, 1966-92; bd. visitors Ind. U. Sch. Law, 1972—, U. Miami Sch. Law, 1982-97, U. Chgo. Law Sch., 1988-92, Brigham Young U., Sch. Law, 1986-88, Northwestern U. Law Sch., 1989-94; chmn. Wis. Rhodes Scholarship Com., 1992-95; chmn. nat. adv. com. on ct.-adjudicated and ct.-ordered health care George Washington U. Ctr. Health Policy, Washington, 1993-95; mem. DNA adv. bd. FBI, U.S. Dept. Justice, 1995—; bd. dirs. Inst. Jud. Adminstrn., Inc., NYU Sch. Law; chair Nat. Inst. Justice's Commn. Future DNA Evidence, 1997—. Editor: Constitutions of the United States (National and State) 2 vols, 1962. Mem. study group program of rsch., mental health and the law John D. and Catherine T. MacArthur Found., 1988-96; mem. coun. fund for rsch. on dispute resolution Ford Found., 1987-91; bd. dirs. Wis. Civil Liberties Union, 1968-72; mem. ct. reform adv. panel Internat. Human Rights Law Group Cambodia Project, 1995-97. Mem. ABA (coun., sect. legal edn. and admissions to bar 1976-86, mem. commn. on undergrad. edn. in law and the humanities 1978-79, standing com. on pub. edn. 1991-95, mem. commn. on access to justice/2000 1993—, mem. adv. bd. Ctrl. and East European law initiative 1994—, mem. consortium on legal svcs. and the public 1995—, vice-chair ABA Coalition for Justice 1997—), Wis. Bar Assn., Dane County Bar Assn., 7th Cir. Bar Assn., Nat. Assn. Women Judges, Am. Law Inst. (mem. coun. 1985—). Home: 2012 Waunona Way Madison WI 53713-1616 Office: Wis Supreme Ct 231 East Capitol PO Box 1688 Madison WI 53701-1688

ABRAHM, JANET LEE, hematologist, oncologist, educator; b. San Francisco, Mar. 14, 1949; d. Paul Milton and Helen Lesser Abrahm; m. David Rytman Slavitt, Apr. 16, 1978. Student, U. Calif., Berkeley, 1969; BA, U. Calif., San Francisco, 1970, MD, 1973. Diplomate Am. Bd. Internal Medicine, Hematology & Oncology. Intern and resident medicine Mass. Gen. Hosp., Boston, 1973-75, hematology fellow, 1975-76; chief resident medicine Moffitt Hosp. U. Calif., San Francisco, 1976-77; hematology/oncology fellow Hosp. U. Pa., Phila., 1977-80; postdoctoral fellow medicine U. Pa., Phila., 1977-78, postdoctoral trainee medicine, 1977-80, asst. prof. medicine, 1980-86; asst. prof. medicine Hosp. U. Pa. and VA Med. Ctr., Phila., 1986-89, assoc. prof. medicine, 1989—; attending physician Hosp. U. Pa., Phila., 1980-93, 98—; staff physician Phila. VA Med. Ctr., 1982—, dir. Hematology/Oncology Clinic, 1983-94, chief hematology and oncology sect., 1984-94, med. oncologist Hospice Consultation Team, 1993-97, chief med. svc., 1994-97, faculty scholar Project Death in Am., 1997—; med. dir. Wissahickon Hospice UPHS, 1998—; prin. investigator Palliative Care Fellowship Grant, 1996-2001; mem. concensus panel on End-of-Life Care, ACP, 1997—; chmn. adv. com. Cancer Care VA Dist. 4, 1987-90; sec. subspecialty bd. hematology Am. Bd. Internal Medicine, 1987-92, sec. SEP subcom. hematology, 1993-95; vis. asst. prof. medicine Med. Coll. Pa., 1988-97; adj. asst. prof. clin. pharmacy Phila. Coll. Pharmacy and Sci., 1988—; mem. tech. adv. group Cancer Care Region 1, 1990-95; med. oncology cons. cancer pain consultation panel Ctr. for Continuing Edn. U. Pa. Sch. Nursing, 1990—; mem. quality of life and cancer edn. com. Pa. Cancer Adv. Bd., 1994-97; mem. human resources coun. of VHA VISN, 1996-97, councillor Region 1, AVOCOM, 1996-97; invited lectr. Mt. Zion Med. Ctr. U. Calif., San Francisco, 1992, 95, Women in Medicine, Phila., 1993, 98, Med. Coll. Pa., Phila., 1993-96, Family Practice Group Bryn Mawr (Pa.) Hosp., 1994, Pa. Cancer Control Program, Phila., 1994, Hospice Conf. Phila. VA Med. Ctr., 1994, Washington VA Med. Ctr., 1994, Phila. Corp. for Aging, 1994, Mercy Cath. Med. Ctr., 1995, Mt. Sinai Med. Ctr., Miami, 1995, U. Chgo. Med. Sch., 1995, Northwestern U. Sch. Medicine, Chgo., 1995, U. Calif., San Diego, 1995, Stanford U., 1995, Tulane U. Sch. Med., 1996, Lehigh Valley Hosp., 1997, U. Oklahoma Med. Sch., 1997, Bethlehem, Pa., 1998, Coatesville, Pa., 1998, Columbia U. Coll. Physicians Surgeons, 1998, others. Author: (with others) Handbook of experimental Pharmacology, 1980, Vivo and In Vitro Erythropoiesis: The Friend System, 1980, Clinical Care of the Terminal Patient, 1982, Yearbook of Medicine, 1984, Yearbook of Cancer, 1984, Vitamins and Cancer - Human Cancer Prevention by Vitamins and Micronutrients, 1985, Biological Regulation of Cell Proliferation, vol. 34, 1986, Pain Management in Hematology: Basic Principles and Practice, 1990, 94, 99, Internal Medicine for Dentistry, 2d edit., 1990, Pain Management in Kelley W. Textbook of Internal Medicine, 1996, Anemia, Pain Management in Geriatric Secrets, 1996; contbr. (booklets) Caring for the Terminally Ill Patient at Home - A Guide for Family Caregivers, 1986, Caring for the Cancer Patient at Home - A Guide for Patients and Families, 1986; reviewer JAMA, Cancer, Archives Internal Medicine, Annals Internal Medicine, Jour. Cancer Edn., Resident and Staff Physician; contbr. numerous articles to profl. jours. Vol. lectr. Am. Cancer Soc. Pain Control in Cancer Patients; mem. edn. com. Greater Phila. Pain Soc., 1993. Recipient Manual award Merck, 1973; Fife Medicine scholar, 1973. Fellow ACP (lectr. Pa. chpt. 1994, consensus panelist on end-of-life care 1997—); mem. Am. Soc. Hematology, Am. Fedn. Clin. Rsch., Am. Soc. Clin. Hypnosis, Am. Soc. Clin. Oncology, Am. Assn. Cancer Edn. (program com. 1993), Am. Pain Soc., Am. Assn. Hospice and Palliative Medicine, Phi Beta Kappa, Alpha Omega Alpha. Home: 523 S 41st St Philadelphia PA 19104-4501 Office: 514 Maloney Bldg Hosp U Pa 3400 Spruce St Philadelphia PA 19104

ABRAM, DONALD EUGENE, federal magistrate judge; b. Des Moines, Feb. 8, 1935; s. Irwin and Freda Phyllis (Gibson) A.; m. Frances Jennette Cooley, Apr. 22, 1962; children: Karen Lynn, Susan Ann, Scott Alan, Diane Jennette. BS in Bus., U. Col., 1957, JD, 1963. Ptnr. Phelps, Fonda, Hays, Abram and Shaw (now Peterson & Fonda, PC), Pueblo, Colo., 1963-75; dist. judge Colo. 10th Jud. Dist., Pueblo, 1975-81; chief U.S. magistrate judge U.S. Dist. Ct. State of Colo., 1981—; lectr. law in criminal procedure U. Denver Sch. of Law, 1983-90; adj. prof. sociology, instr. bus. law U. So. Colo., Pueblo, 1977-81. Mng. editor, bd. dir. Colo. Law Review, 1961-63. Vice chmn. Pueblo County Rep. Party, 1973-75; city councilman Pueblo, 1970-73; pres. Pueblo city coun., 1972-73, Pueblo Goodwill Industries, 1965, Pueblo United Fund, 1968; chmn. consolidation planning com. Pueblo County Sch. Dists. 60, 70, 1968-70; mem. gov's. milit. affairs adv. com., 1975-78; mem. gov's. commn. children and families, 1978-80. Lt. (j.g.) USN, 1957-60, capt. Res. ret. Recipient Disting. Svc. award Colo. Jaycee, 1970, Disting. Citizen Svc. award, Pueblo Rotary, 1975. Mem. Fed. Magistrate Judges Assn. (pres. 1990-91), Pueblo C. of C.(bd. dirs. 1972, chmn. edn. com. 1970-71), Colo. Bar Assn. (1st v.p. 1975-76), Nat. Coun. U. S. Magistrates (dir., officer 1984-89), Juvenile Judges Assn. Colo. (chmn. 1979-80), Colo. Navy League (state pres. 1976-78). Lutheran. Office: US Dist Ct US Courthouse C-566 1929 Stout St Denver CO 80294-0001

ABRAM, MORRIS BERTHOLD, lawyer, educator, diplomat; b. Fitzgerald, Ga., June 19, 1918; s. Sam and Irene (Cohen) A.; m. Jane Maguire, Dec. 23, 1943 (div. 1974); children: Ruth, Ann, Morris Berthold, Jonathan Adam, Joshua Anthony; m. Carlyn Feldman Fisher, Jan. 25, 1975 (div. 1987); m. Bruna Molina, Aug. 26, 1990. AB summa cum laude, U. Ga., 1938; JD, U. Chgo., 1940; BA (Rhodes scholar), Oxford U., 1948, MA, 1953; LLD, Davidson Coll., Kings Coll., 1972, Yeshiva U., 1975, Adelphi U., 1989; HHD, Hebrew Union Coll., 1986; LLD (hon.), Emory U., 1996. Ptnr. Paul, Weiss, Rifkind, Wharton & Garrison, N.Y.C., 1962-68, 1970-89, ret., 1989; counsel Paul, Weiss, Rifkind, Wharton & Garrison, 1993—; pres. Brandeis Univ., Waltham, Mass., 1968-70; amb. to UN European office Geneva, 1989-93; chmn. UN Watch, Geneva, 1993—; pros. staff Internat. Mil. Tribunal, Nurnberg, Germany, 1946; asst. to dir. Com. for Marshall Plan, 1948; regional counsel WSB; gen. counsel Peace Corps, 1961; mem. subcom. on prevention of discrimination and protection of minorities UN, 1963-65; U.S. rep. UN Commn. Human Rights, 1965-68; co-chmn. planning conf. White House Conf. on Civil Rights, 1965; mem. exec. com. President's Nat. Com. Community Relations, 1964-68; chmn. Moreland Act Commn. on Nursing Homes and Residential Facilities, 1975-76, Pres.'s Commn. for Study of Ethics in Medicine and Biomed. and Behavioral Research, 1979-83; chmn. Nat. Conf. on Soviet Jewry, 1983-88; chmn. Conf. of Presidents of Major Am. Jewish Orgns., 1986-88; vice chmn. U.S. Commn. Civil Rights, 1984-86; chief U.S. del. Conf. on Security and Cooperation in Europe, Paris, 1989. lectr. Oxford U. (Eng.). Author: The Day is Short, 1982; co-author: How to Stop Violence in Your Community, 1950. Pres. Family Service Soc. of, Fulton, DeKalb, Cobb counties, 1957-59; chmn. Atlanta Citizens Crime Com., 1958-60; nat. pres. Am. Jewish Com., 1963-68; bd. dirs. 20th Century Fund; pres. Field Found., 1965-82; bd. dirs. Morehouse Coll., 1959-85; Inst. Internat. Edn., Council Fgn. Relations; trustee Sarah Lawrence Coll., 1971-74, Inst. Internat. Edn., 1969-74; chmn. United Negro Coll. Fund, 1970-79; founding chmn. bd. Benjamin N. Cardozo Law Sch., Yeshiva U., 1976-79; mem. Nat. Adv. Council Econ. Opportunity, 1967-68. Served to maj. USAAF, 1941-45. Decorated Legion of Merit, 1946. Fellow Am. Acad. Arts & Scis. (hon.), Am. Coll. Trial Lawyers, Pembroke Coll., Oxford U.; found. mem. Lawyers Comm. for Civil Rights Under the Law; mem. ABA, N.Y. State Bar Assn., Ga. Bar Assn., Lawyers Club Atlanta, Assn. Bar City N.Y., D.C. Bar Assn., Phi Beta Kappa, Omicron Delta Kappa, Phi Kappa Phi. Office: Quai Gustave Ador 56, 1207 Geneva Switzerland also: PO Box 402 Green Farms CT 06436-0402 Address: Paul Weiss Rifkind Wharton & Garrison 1285 Ave of the Americas New York NY 10019 *It is often personally distressing to stand by an unpopular cause but if there were not those who do, it would be a poorer world.**

ABRAMOVITZ, ANITA ZELTNER BROOKS (MRS. MAX ABRAMOVITZ), writer; b. Long Island, N.Y., January 7, 1914; d. Charles Frederick and Amelia (Koch) Zeltner. grad. Sarah Lawrence Coll., 1932, BA, 1962; m. Thomas Vail Brooks, Sept. 25, 1937 (div. July 1957); children: Antoinette Brooks-Floyd, Cora Vail Brooks, Henry Stanford Brooks II; m. Max Abramovitz, Feb. 29, 1964. Editl. asst. The New Yorker mag., N.Y.C., 1943-46; editor alumni mag. Sarah Lawrence Coll., 1947-48, asst. to prof. history, 1958-60, asst. in writing to lectr. courses, 1960-62; tchr. remedial reading, 1950; asst. to dir. Sarah Lawrence Paris Summer Sch., 1963. Democratic Party Insp. 18th Dist. Hastings-on-Hudson, N.Y., 1958-61; founding mem. Village League, 1950. Author series Picture Aids to World Geography, Picture Book of Fisheries, 1961, Picture Book of Tea and Coffee, 1962, Picture Book of Grains, 1963, Picture Book of Salt, 1964, Picture Book of Oil, 1965, Picture Book of Timber, 1966, A Small Bird Sang, 1967, Winifred, 1970, Picture Book of Metals, 1972, People and Spaces: A View of History Through Architecture, 1979; contbr. stories to children's books. Home: 176 Honey Hollow Rd Pound Ridge NY 10576-1105

ABRAMOVITZ, MAX, architect; b. Chgo., May 23, 1908; s. Benjamin and Sophia (Maimon) A.; m. Anne Marie Causey, Sept. 4, 1937 (div.); children: Michael John, Katherine Paul; m. Anita Zeltner Brooks, Feb. 29, 1964. BS, U. Ill., 1929; MS, Columbia U., 1931; postgrad., Ecole des Beaux Arts, 1932-34; DFA (hon.), U. Pitts., 1961, U. Ill., 1970. Ptnr. firm Harrison & Abramovitz, Architects, 1945-76, Abramovitz-Harris-Kingsland, Architects, N.Y.C., 1976-85, 85—; asso. prof. Yale U. Sch. Fine Arts, 1939-42; dep. dir. UN Hdqrs. Planning Office, 1947-52; Cons. Brandeis U., U. Pitts. Prin. works include U.S. Steel Bldg, Pitts., Nationwide Ins, Columbus, Ohio, Assembly Hall and Krannert Center Performing Arts, U. Ill.-Urbana; chapels Brandeis U; major campus devel. La Banque Rothschild, Paris, France, Groupe des Assurances Nationales, LaDefense, France, Jewish Chapel, U.S. Mil. Acad., West Point, N.Y., Rockeller U. Rsch. Lab., N.Y.C.;. Served with C.E. AUS, 1942-45; col. 1950-52; spl. asst. to asst. sec. air force Mar. 1952-July 1952. Recipient Legion of Merit; fellow Brandeis U., 1963; Achievement award U. Ill. Alumni Assn., 1963. Fellow AIA; mem. Am. Soc. C.E., Regional Plan Assn. (chmn. bd. 1966-68), Archtl. League N.Y. Club: Century Assn. (N.Y.C.). Home: 176 Honey Hollow Rd Pound Ridge NY 10576-1105

ABRAMOVITZ, MICHAEL JOHN, lawyer; b. N.Y.C., Feb. 7, 1939; s. Max and Anne (Causey) A.; m. Patricia Carson, 1959 (div. 1968); 1 child, Deborah Woodbury; m. Frances Koncilja, Nov. 12, 1972 (div. 1983); 1 child, Nicholas; m. Carol Lay, May 24, 1988; 1 child, Alexandra. AB, Harvard U., 1961; MA in Maths., U. Calif., 1967; postgrad., U. Calif., Berkeley; JD,

U. Colo., 1972. Bar: Colo. 1972, U.S. Dist. Ct. Colo. 1972, U.S. Ct. Appeals (10th cir.) 1973, U.S. Tax Ct. 1973, U.S. Supreme Ct. 1975, U.S. Ct. Claims 1977. Law clk. to presiding justice Colo. Supreme Ct., Denver, 1972-73; ptnr. Drexler, Wald & Abramovitz, Denver, 1973-84, Berenbaum & Weinshienk, Denver, 1984-86, Abramovitz, Merriam & Shaw, Denver, 1987-94, Abramovitz & Merriam, Denver, 1994—. Mem. ABA (taxation sect., civil and criminal tax penalties com., litigation sect.), Colo. Bar Assn. Office: Abramovitz & Merriam 1625 Broadway Ste 770 Denver CO 80202-4717

ABRAMOWICZ, ALFRED L., retired bishop; b. Chgo., Jan. 27, 1919. Ed., St. Mary Sem., Mundelein, Ill.; J.C.L., Gregorian U., Rome. Ordained priest Roman Cath. Ch., 1943; papal chamberlain, very rev. msgr. and officials Chgo. Archdiocesan Ct. when named titular bishop of paestum and aux. of Chgo., 1968, consecrated bishop, 1968, ret., 1995. Home: 6101 S 75th Ave Summit Argo IL 60501-1628

ABRAMOWICZ, JANET, painter, print-maker; b. N.Y.C.; children: Alex, Anna. Student, Art Students League, 1948-50, Columbia U., 1948-50; BFA, Accademia di Belle Arti, Bologna, Italy, 1952, MFA, 1953. Teaching asst. to Giorgio Morandi Acad. di Belle Art, 1953-55; instr. dept. art and architecture U. Ill., 1955-57, Sch. Worcester, Mass., 1957-58; sr. lectr. fine arts Harvard U., Cambridge, Mass., 1971-91; former lectr. on spl. exhibits Mus. Fine Arts, Boston; vis. artist Am. Acad. Rome, 1984, 85, 94; fellow Japan Found., 1979-80; advisor Calcografia Nazionale, Rome, 1989-90; hon. fellow Accademia Clementina, Bologna, Italy, 1990—. Contbg. editor: Opera Grafiche di Morandi, 1990; contbr. articles to profl. jours. Sr. Fulbright fellow, 1977-79, 89, Rockefeller Found., 1989—, Am. Coun. Learned Socs. fellow, 1990, John Simon Guggenheim fellow, 1992. Democrat. *

ABRAMOWITZ, MORTON I., former ambassador; b. Lakewood, N.J., Jan. 20, 1933; s. Mendel and Dora (Smith) A.; m. Sheppie Glass, Sept. 13, 1959; children: Michael, Rachel. BA, Stanford U.; MA, Harvard U., 1955. Joined U.S. Fgn. Service, 1960; 3d sec., vice consul Taipei, Formosa, 1960-62; with Fgn. Area and Lang. Tng. Ctr., Taichung, Taiwan, 1962-63; consul, polit. officer Hong Kong, 1963-66; assigned Bur. Econ. Affairs, 1966-68; Sr. Inter dept. Group, 1968-69; spl. asst. under-sec. state, 1969-71; research assoc. Inst. for Strategic Studies, 1971; asst. to sec. of def., 1972-73; polit. adviser to Comdr.-in-Chief Pacific, 1973-78; also dep. asst. sec. def. for Inter-Am., E. Asia and Pacific, 1974-78, amb. to Thailand, Bangkok, 1978-83; U.S. rep. to Mutual and Balanced Force Reduction Negotiations Vienna, 1983-85; dir., asst. sec. Bur. of Intelligence and Rsch., 1985-89; amb. to Turkey, 1989-91. Author: (with Richard Moorsteen) Remaking China Policy, 1972, Moving the Glacier, the Two Koreas and the Powers, 1972, East Asian Actors and Issues, China, Can We Have a Policy, 1997; contbr. articles to jours. and newspapers. Pres. Carnegie Endowment for Internat. Peace, Washington, 1991-97, Internat. Crisis Group, 1997— (sr. fellow century found., 1998, sr. fellow coun. foreign rels., 1999—); bd. dirs. Internat. Rescue Com., Nat. Endowment for Democracy, Open Soc. Inst., Freedom House. With AUS, 1957. Recipient Disting. Pub. Svc. award Dept. Def., 1976, Sec. Def. Disting. Svc. award, 1978, Joseph C. Wilson award, 1980, Pres.'s award for Disting. Fed. Svc., 1981, 85, 88, Nat. Intelligence Disting. medal, 1989. Mem. Am. Acad. Arts and Scis., Phi Beta Kappa.

ABRAMOWITZ, ROBERT LESLIE, lawyer; b. Phila., May, 1950; s. Nathan P. and Lucille H. (Rader) A.; m. Susan Margaret Stewart, Dec. 1, 1974; children: David, Catherine. BA, Yale U., 1971; JD, Harvard U., 1974. Bar: Pa. 1974, N.J. 1975. Assoc. Ballard, Spahr, Andrews & Ingersoll, Phila., 1974-81, ptnr., 1981-90; ptnr. Morgan Lewis & Bockius, LLP, Phila., 1990—; adj. prof. law Villanova U., 1986—. Trustee Moorestown (N.J.) Friends Sch., 1981-90, Rock Sch. of Pa. Ballet, 1990—. Mem. ABA, Pa. Bar Assn., Phila. Bar Assn. (exec. com. probate sect. 1982-85, pension com. 1985-94, chair, 1987-89), Yale Club, Merion Cricket Club. Home: 623 Pembroke Rd Bryn Mawr PA 19010-3613 Office: Morgan Lewis & Bockius LLP 1701 Market St Philadelphia PA 19103-2903

ABRAMS, ARTHUR JAY, physician; b. Camden, N.J., Apr. 9, 1938; s. Morris and Sophia Sarah (Kates) A.; m. Marianne Ritto Abrams, June 8, 1963; children: Suzanne Beth, Cheryl Lyn, Robert Dwight. BA, Rutgers U., Camden, N.J., 1959; MD, Hahnemann U., 1963. Diplomate Am. Bd. Dermatology. Intern Madigan Army Med. Ctr., Tacoma, Wash., 1963-64; resident, chief resident Letterman Army Med. Ctr., San Francisco, 1964-67; dermatologist, Far East cons. 249th Gen. Hosp. U.S. Army, Tokyo, 1967-69; asst. chief dermatologist Tripler Army Med. Ctr., Honolulu, 1969-70; staff dermatologist El Camino Hosp., Mountain View, Calif., 1970—; clin. assoc. prof. dermatology Stanford U. Med. Ctr., 1979—; dermatology cons. San Jose (Calif.) State U., 1994—; maj. U.S. Army, 1963-70. Mem. AMA, Calif. Med. Assn., Pacific Dermatol. Assn., San Francisco Dermatol. Soc. Avocation: volleyball, walking. Office: 763 Altos Oaks Dr Ste 4 Los Altos CA 94024-5400

ABRAMS, BERNARD WILLIAM, construction manufacturing and property development executive; b. West Palm Beach, Fla., Jan. 21, 1925; s. Alfred Robert and Sara Lee (Kaufman) A.; children: David Louis, Janet Beth, Judith Frances. B.S., U.S. Mil. Acad., 1947. With Abrams Industries, Inc., Atlanta, 1952—, chmn. bd., chief exec. officer, 1972-95, also bd. dirs., 1952—, chmn. exec. com., 1995-97, chmn. emeritus exec. com., chmn. emeritus, 1997-98; dir. Bank South Corp., Atlanta, 1982-95. Nat. keynote speaker ARC campaign, 1953; chmn. appointments com. Armed Forces Acads., 5th Congressional Dist. of Ga., 1968-70; bd. dirs. Hank Aaron Scholarship Fund, 1974-76; co-chmn. Atlanta Com. for Devel. U.S. Army Inf. Mus., Ft. Benning, Ga., 1976; gen. chmn. United Way campaign, 1975-76; pres. Atlanta Area council Boy Scouts Am., 1977-79, chmn. adv. bd., 1980-81; active USO Council Greater Atlanta, 1979; mem. adv. com. Ga. Tech. Inst. Coll. Indsl. Mgmt., 1978; active Jewish Welfare Fedn., 1975-78; civilian aide to Sec. of Army, 1978-85, civilian aide emeritus, 1985 ; mem. Ga. Gov.'s Edn. Commn., chmn. definition com., 1983-84; trustee West Point Cadet Jewish Chapel, 1966—; mem. funds com. West Point Assn. of Grads., 1987; liaison to White House for Jewish War Vets. U.S.A., 1991, 92, 93; mem. funds com. West Point Assn. of Grads. Served to capt. U.S. Army, 1947-53, Korea. Decorated Silver Star, Bronze Star with V, Purple Heart with oak leaf cluster, Expert Rifleman and Combat Inf. badges; recipient MOWW Patrick Henry medallion, 1994, Silver Beaver award Boy Scouts Am., 1972, Disting. Svc. award United Way, 1975, USO World Bd. Govs. award, 1984, Outstanding Civilian medal Dept. of Army, 1985, Citation as Disting. Citizen Ga., Gov. of Ga., 1985, Brotherhood award Nat. Conf. Christians and Jews, 1997. Mem. Assn. U.S. Army (pres. 3d region 1966-67, cert. of appreciation 1965, citation 1978, Gen. Creighton W. Abrams medal 1990), Ga. Bus. and Industry Assn. (Appreciation award 1972), Atlanta Assn. for Corp. Growth (pres. 1981), West Point Soc. of Atlanta (pres. 1959-62), Assn. Grads. U.S. Mil. Acad. (trustee 1959-62), Commerce Club, Ga. Alliance of Pvt. Clubs, B'nai Brith (Outstanding Lodge Pres. citation 1972), Phi Eta Sigma. Republican. Office: Abrams Industries Inc PO Box 724728 Atlanta GA 31139-1728

ABRAMS, EDWARD MARVIN, construction company executive; b. South Bend, Ind., Mar. 13, 1927; s. Alfred Robert and Sara Lee (Kaufman) A.; m. Ann Uhry, Oct. 11, 1953; children: Alan Ralph, Laurie, James Andrew. Student, Ga. Inst. Tech., 1947-48; B.S. cum laude, U. Notre Dame, 1950; grad., Naval Officer Candidate Sch., 1951. Pres. Abrams Industries, Inc., Atlanta, 1953-95; chmn. bd. dirs. Abrams Industries, Inc., 1995-98, chmn. exec. com., 1998—; mem. faculty Univ. of Shopping Ctrs., Ga. adv. bd. Liberty Mut. Ins. Co. Mem. interreligious affairs com. Am. Jewish Com., 1969—, chmn. Atlanta chpt., 1971-73, mem. nat. task force on social club discrimination; mem. adv. council Coll. Arts and Letters, U. Notre Dame, 1972—, chmn., 1977-78; co-chmn. Ga. region NCCJ, 1977-78; active United Way Metro Atlanta. Served with USN, 1945-47, 50-52. Mem. Internat. Council Shopping Centers, Ga. Engring. Soc., Atlanta C. of C. (chmn. aviation task force com. 1981, adv. bd. 1999—), Notre Dame Alumni Assn., Commerce Club (Atlanta), Notre Dame Club (Atlanta). Home: 3770 Paces Ferry Rd NW Atlanta GA 30327-3004 Office: 1945 The Exchange SE Ste 300 Atlanta GA 30339-2040

ABRAMS, ELLIOTT, think-tank executive, writer, foreign affairs analyst; b. N.Y.C., Jan. 24, 1948; s. Joseph and Mildred (Kauder) A.; m. Rachel Decter, Mar. 9, 1980; children: Jacob, Sarah, Joseph. BA, Harvard U., 1969, JD, 1973; MS in Econs, London Sch. Econs., 1970. Assoc. Breed, Abbott & Morgan, N.Y.C., 1974-75; asst. counsel U.S. Senate Permanent Subcom. on Investigations, Washington, 1975; spl. counsel Sen. Henry M. Jackson, 1975-76; spl. counsel Sen. Daniel P. Moynihan, 1977-78, chief of staff, 1978-79; atty. Verner, Liipfert, Bernhard & McPherson, Washington, 1979-80; asst. sec. for internat. orgn. affairs U.S. Dept. State, Washington, 1981, asst. sec. for human rights and humanitarian affairs, 1981-85, asst. sec. for InterAm. affairs, 1985-89; sr. fellow Hudson Inst., Washington, 1990-96; pres. Ethics and Pub. Policy Ctr., Washington, 1996—. Author: Undue Process, 1992, Security and Sacrifice, 1995, Faith or Fear, 1997; contbg. editor Nat. Rev. Mag. Chmn. bd. Nicaraguan Resistance Ednl. Found., Marroquin Found.; mem. Coun. Fgn. Rels., U.S. Commn. Internat. Religious Freedom. Office: Ethics & Pub Policy Ctr 1015 15th St NW Ste 900 Washington DC 20005-2605

ABRAMS, FLOYD, lawyer; b. N.Y.C., July 9, 1936; s. Isidore and Rae (Eberlin) A.; m. Efrat Surasky, Dec. 25, 1963; children: Daniel, Ronnie. B.A., Cornell U., 1956; LL.B., Yale U., 1960. Bar: N.Y. 1961. Research asst. dept. politics Princeton U., 1960-61; law clk. to Paul Leahy U.S. Dist. Ct., Wilmington, Del., 1961-63; assoc. firm Cahill Gordon & Reindel, N.Y.C., 1963-70, ptnr., 1970—; vis. lectr. Yale U., 1974-79, 86-89; assoc. in journalism Grad. Sch. Journalism, Columbia U., 1980, William J. Brennan Jr. vis. prof., 1993—; lectr. Law Sch., Columbia U., 1981-85. Mem. bd editors: N.Y. Law Jour., 1983—, Legal Times, 1989—. Bd. dirs. Mexican Am. Legal Def. and Ednl. Fund, Dalton Sch., 1978-81; bd. dirs. Dalton Sch., 1978-84, v.p., 1982-83; bd. dirs. media and soc. seminars, 1980-90 , vice chmn., 1983-90. Mem. ABA (chmn. rights of expression com. individual rights sect. 1976-79, Ross essay prize, chmn. freedom of speech and press com. litigation sect. 1977-79, mem. forum com. 1979-80, amicus curiae com. 1980-82), Assn. Bar City N.Y. (state legal com. 1965-67, chmn. comm. com. 1992-94). Home: 1136 5th Ave New York NY 10128-0122 Office: Cahill Gordon & Reindel 80 Pine St Fl 17 New York NY 10005-1790*

ABRAMS, GEORGE, type designer, executive; b. Bklyn., Sept. 3, 1919; s. Morris and Millie (Rosenberg) Abrahams; m. Marion Estelle Cordes, Feb. 25, 1947 (dec. 1971); children: Jeffrey, Vicki Hertz, Nancy, Lauren; m. Joan Allen Walker, Aug. 26, 1983. Pres. Alphabets, Inc., N.Y.C., 1948-89, Expert Alphabets Internat. Ltd., Great Neck, N.Y., 1996—; prof. type design, Columbia U. Tchrs. Coll., N.Y.C., 1964, Parsons, New Sch., N.Y.C., 1996, Berghs Coll., Stockholm, 1997. Creator logotype mastheads Sports Illustrated, 1954, Newsweek, 1968, Saturday Evening Post, 1965, House Beautiful Mag., 1949, Ladies Home Jour., Holiday Mag., Calif. Home Mag., Am. Home Mag., Sat. Review, The Singer Co., B. Altman Co., Reed and Barton, Ballantine, Godiva; published type designs: Abrams Venetian, Abrams Augereau, Abrams Joan Walker. Invited to testify U.S. Ho. of Reps. 2223 Hearings on Type Design Copyright Law Revision, 1975. With USAF, 21st Weather Liaison, 3d Armored Divsn., 1942-45, ETO. Decorated 5 Battle Stars; recipient Caen (France) Meml. Invasion Medal, 1995, hon. cert. Royal Danish Soc., Copenhagen, 1987; named hon. fellow London Soc. Typographic Design. Fellow Pierpont Morgan Libr.; Internat. Assn. Bibliophiles (France), Stockholm Typographic Guild (corr.), Assn. Typographic Internat. (A Type I), Typophiles (N.Y.), The Grolier Club (membership com. 1978—). Avocations: sports cars, rare books, ethnic sculpture, photography, fine art. Home and Office: 10 Shore Dr Great Neck Est New York NY 11021

ABRAMS, GERALD DAVID, physician, educator; b. Detroit, Apr. 27, 1932; s. Arthur and Esther (Kushner) A.; m. Gloria Sandra Turner, June 6, 1954; children—Kathryn, Nancy. A.B., Wayne U., 1951; M.D., U. Mich., 1955. Diplomate Am. Bd. Pathology. House officer pathology U. Mich., Ann Arbor, 1955-59, instr. pathology, 1959-60; asst. prof. pathology U. Mich., 1963-66, assoc. prof., 1966-69, prof., 1969—, dir. anatomic pathology, 1985-89; asst. chief dept. exptl. pathology Walter Reed Army Inst. Research, 1961-62; dep. med. examiner, Washtenaw County, Mich., 1963—; cons. physician Ann Arbor VA Hosp., 1970—. Served to capt. M.C., U.S. Army, 1961-62. Markle scholar John and Mary Markle Found., 1963-68; recipient Elizabeth Crosby Teaching award U. Mich., 1969, 87, 96, Kaiser-Permanente Teaching award U. Mich., 1978. Mem. AAAS, Internat. Acad. Pathology, Mich. Soc. Pathologists. Office: U Mich Dept Pathology Ann Arbor MI 48109

ABRAMS, HAROLD EUGENE, lawyer; b. Pensacola, Fla., Jan. 18, 1933; s. Samuel Ralph and Sadie (Gerhardt) A.; m. Nancy Gray, June 22, 1958; children: Shari Abrams Marx, Eric Gray. BA, U. Mich., 1954; JD, Harvard U., 1957. Bar: Ga. 1958, D.C. 1976, U.S. Supreme Ct. 1970. Law clk. to presiding judge U.S. Ct. Appeals (5th cir.), Atlanta, 1957-58; assoc. Kilpatrick & Cody, Atlanta, 1958-63; ptnr. Kilpatrick Stockton, Atlanta, 1963—; pres. Atlanta Tax Forum, 1990-91, Atlanta Estate Planning Coun., 1991-92; bd. dirs. Randall Bros., Inc., Atlanta, Selig Enterprises, Inc., Atlanta. Contbr. articles on tax and estate planning to profl. publs. Pres. Buckhead Little League, Atlanta, 1972-73; bd. dirs. Atlanta chpt. Am. Jewish Com., 1987—, Atlanta Jewish Fedn., 1996—; sec. Ronald McDonald's Children's Charities, Atlanta, 1988—. With U.S. Army, 1957-58. Fellow Am. Coll. Tax Counsel; mem. State Bar of Ga. (chmn. tax sect. 1964-65), So. Fed. Tax Inst. (trustee 1964—, pres. 1970-71, treas. 1986-95), Peachtree Club, Atlanta Lawyers Club. Avocations: tennis, travel. Office: Kilpatrick Stockton LLP 1100 Peachtree St NE Ste 2800 Atlanta GA 30309-4501

ABRAMS, HERBERT E., artist; b. Greenfield, Mass., Mar. 20, 1921; s. Adolph and Mathilda (Schaer) A.; m. Lois Kathryn Miller, June 5, 1954; children: Kathryn Ann Abrams Bindert, William Frederick. Student, Norwich (Conn.) Art Sch., 1939-40; cert. with honors, Pratt Inst., Bklyn., 1946; studies with DuMond, Art Students' League, N.Y.C., 1948-53; LHD (hon.), Johns Hopkins U., 1997. tchr. pvt. classes, Warren, Conn., 1953-75; instr. art U.S. Mil. Acad., West Point, N.Y., 1953-74. Prin. works include portraits of Pres. Jimmy Carter, The White House, Washington, 1983, Govs. Meskill and Grasso, Conn. State Libr. Mus., Hartford, 1974, 83, Gens. Westmoreland, Abrams and Palmer, Pentagon, Washington, 1973, 75, 76, Sen. Baker, U.S. Senate, 1985, Treasury Sec. Regan, Treasury, Washington, 1986 Alan S. Boyd, Nat. Trust for Hist. Preservation, Washington, 1989, Amb. Wilkey, Washington, 1992, Pres. George Bush, The White House, 1994, First Lady Barbara Bush, The White House, 1995, others; represented in permanent collection Dept. Mil. History, Washington, 1972, U.S. Mil. Acad. Mus., West Point, N.Y.; designer aircraft insignia USAF, 1942. Del. Dem. State Conv., Hartford, Conn., 1978-80; chmn. Dem. Town Commn., Warren, 1978-79. Lt. USAF, 1941-45. Mem. Artists Equity Assn., Kent Art Assn., Art Students League. Avocations: tennis, gardening, golf. Home and Office: 178 Kent Rd Warren CT 06754-1607

ABRAMS, HERBERT KERMAN, physician, educator; b. Chgo., 1913. BS, Northwestern U.; MD, MS, U. Ill., 1940; MPH, Johns Hopkins U., 1947. Intern Cook County Hosp., Chgo., 1940-41; chief Bur. of Adult Health, Calif. Health Dept., 1947-52; dir. Chgo. Union Health Service, 1952-66; prof., chair dept. community medicine Chgo. Med. Sch.-Mt. Sinai Hosp., Chgo., 1966-68; prof., head dept. family community medicine U. Ariz., Tucson, 1968-78, prof. emeritus, 1990—; dir. Ariz. Ctr. for Occupl. Safety and Health, 1978-83. Surgeon USPHS, 1942-46. Mem. AMA, APHA (v.p. 1981-82), Ariz. Med. Assn., Assn. Tchrs. Preventive Medicine, Am. Coll. Occupational Environ. Medicine, Physicians for Social Responsibility, Internat. Physicians Prevention Nuclear War. Office: U Ariz Dept Family and Community Medicine Ariz Health Scis Center Tucson AZ 85724

ABRAMS, HERBERT LEROY, radiologist, educator; b. N.Y.C., Aug. 16, 1920; s. Morris and Freda (Sugarman) A.; m. Marilyn Spitz, Mar. 23, 1943; children: Nancy, John. BA, Cornell U., 1941; MD, Downstate Med. Ctr., N.Y., 1946. Diplomate Am. Bd. Radiology. Intern L.I. Coll. Hosp., 1946-47; resident in internal medicine Montefiore Hosp., Bronx, N.Y., 1947-48; resident in radiology Stanford (Calif.) U. Hosp., 1948-51; practice medicine specializing in radiology Stanford U., Calif., 1951-67; mem. faculty Sch. Medicine Stanford U., 1951-67, dir. divsn. diagnostic roentgenology Sch. Medicine, 1961-67, prof. radiology Sch. Medicine, 1962-67; Philip H. Cook prof. radiology Harvard U., 1967-85, now prof. emeritus, chmn. dept. radiology, 1967-80; prof. radiology Stanford U. Sch. Medicine, 1985-90, prof. emeritus, 1990—; clin. prof. U. Calif. Sch. Medicine, San Francisco, 1986—; radiologist-in-chief Peter Bent Brigham Hosp., Boston, 1967-80; chmn. dept. radiology Brigham and Women's Hosp., Boston, 1981-85; radiologist-in-chief Sidney Farber Cancer Inst., Boston, 1974-85; R.H. Nimmo vis. prof. U. Adelaide, Australia; mem.-in-residence Ctr. for Internat. Security and Arms Control Stanford U., 1985—; mem. radiation study sect. NIH, 1962-66; cons. to hosps., profl. socs.; mem. com. disability U.S. Presidents, 1995—. Author: (with others) Angiocardiography in Congenital Heart Disease, 1956, Congenital Heart Disease, 1965, Coronary Arteriography: A Practical Approach, 1983, Brigham Guide to Diagnostic Imaging, 1986, Assessment of Diagnostic Technology in Health Care; editor: Abrams' Angiography, 3rd edit., 1983; author: The President Has Been Shot: Confusion, Disability and the 25th Amendment, 1992, 94, The History of Cardiac Radiology, 1996; mem. editl. bd. Investigative Radiology; editor-in-chief, founder Cardiovasc. and Interventional Radiology, 1978-88, Postgrad. Radiology, 1983—. Nat. Cancer Inst. fellow, 1950; Spl. Rsch. fellow Nat. Heart Inst., 1960, 73-74; David M. Gould Meml. lectr. Johns Hopkins, 1964; William R. Whitman Meml. lectr., 1968; Leo G. Rigler lectr. Tel Aviv U., 1969; Holmes lectr. New England Roentgen Ray Soc., Boston, 1970; Ross Golden lectr. N.Y. Roentgen Ray Soc., N.Y.C., 1971; Stauffer Meml. lectr. Phila. Roentgen Ray Soc., 1971; J.M.T. Finney Fund lectr. Md. Radiol. Soc., Ocean City, 1972; Aubrey Hampton lectr. Mass. Gen. Hosp., Boston, 1974; Kirklin-Weber lectr. Mayo Clinic, 1974; Crookshank lectr. Royal Coll. Radiology, 1980; Alpha Omega Alpha lectr., vis. prof. U. Calif. Med. Sch., San Francisco, 1961-65; W.H. Herbert lectr. U. Calif.; Caldwell lectr. Am. Roentgen Ray Soc., 1982; Percy lectr. McMaster Med. Sch., 1983; Charles Dotter lectr. Soc. Cardiovasc. and Interventional Radiology, 1988; Philip Hodes lectr. Jefferson Med. Coll., 1988; David Gould Meml. lectr. Johns Hopkins U., 1991, Hymer Friedell lectr. Western Res. Sch. Medicine, 1993, Felix Fheischner Memmal lectr. Harvard Med. Sch., 1997, Charles Dotter Meml. lectr. Am. Heart Assn., 1998; Henry J. Kaiser sr. fellow Ctr. for Advanced Study in Behavioral Sci., 1980-81. Hon. fellow Royal Coll. Radiology (Gt. Britain), Royal Coll. Surgery (Ireland), Am. Coll. Radiology, Am. Coll. Cardiology; mem. Assn. Univ. Radiologists (Gold medal 1984), Inst. Medicine, Am. Heart Assn., Am. Soc. Nephrology, Radiol. Soc. N.Am. (Gold medal 1995), N.Am. Soc. Cardiac Radiology (pres. 1979-80), Internat. Physicians for Prevention of Nuc. War (founding v.p., participant Nobel Peace prize 1985), Soc. Cardiovasc. Radiology, Soc. Chmn. Acad. Radiology Depts. (pres. 1970-71), Nat. Coun. Health Tech. Assessment, Inst. of Medicine, NAS, NIH (chmn. consensus panel on MRI, internat. blue ribbon panel radiation effects rsch. found. Hiroshima 1996, mem. working group on disability of U.S. pres. 1995—), Phi Beta Kappa, Alpha Omega Alpha. Home: 714 Alvarado Stanford CA 94305 Office: Stanford U Sch Medicine Stanford CA 94305

ABRAMS, JOHN N., career officer; b. Sept. 3, 1946. Commd. U.S. Army, advanced through grades to gen. Office: Tradoc 7 Fenwick Rd Fort Monroe VA 23651-1049

ABRAMS, LEE NORMAN, lawyer; b. Chgo., Feb. 28, 1935; s. Saul E. and Evelyn (Cohen) A.; m. Myrna Parker, Dec. 26, 1965; 1 dau., Elana Shira. A.B., U. Mich., 1951, J.D., 1957. Bar: Ill. 1957, U.S. Tax Ct. 1972, U.S. Supreme Ct. 1961. Assoc. firm Mayer, Brown & Platt and predecessors, Chgo., 1957-66, ptnr., 1966—; bd. dirs. Perkins Mgmt. Co. Mem. visitors com. U. Mich. Law Sch., 1970—; bd. assocs. Nat. Coll. Edn., Chgo., 1973-80. Recipient gold medal Am. Inst. C.P.A.s, 1958. Mem. ABA (coun. antitrust sect. 1975-77, fin. officer 1977-81, program chair antitrust sect. 1988-91, vice chair antitrust sect. 1991-92, chmn. forum on franchising 1982-85, chmn. antitrust com. sect. bus. law 1995—), Chgo. Bar Assn. (antitrust law com. 1970—), Ill. State Bar Assn. (antitrust section coun. 1994—), U.S. C. of C. (antitrust and trade regulation com. 1974-80), Royal and Ancient Golf Club of St. Andrews (Scotland). Office: Mayer Brown & Platt 190 S La Salle St Ste 3100 Chicago IL 60603-3441

ABRAMS, MARC, lawyer, state political party executive; b. N.Y.C., Mar. 23, 1957; s. Stephen Robert and Virginia Ornstein Abrams; m. Barbara Christopher, 1981; 1 child, Lawrence Christopher. BA magna cum laude, Wesleyan U., Middletown, Conn., 1978; MA, JD, U. Mich., 1981. Bar: Conn. 1982, N.Y. 1986, D.C. 1987, Pa. 1987, Oreg. 1989, U.S. Dist Ct. (so. dist.) N.Y. 1986, U.S. Dist. Co. (ea. dist.) Pa. 1988, U.S. Dist. Ct. Mont. 1989, U.S. Cir. Ct. (3d, 4th and 9th cirs.), U.S. Dist. Ct. Oreg. 1989, U.S. Supreme Ct. Asst. prof. U. Oreg., 1981-83; exec. dir. Student Press Law Ctr., 1983-85; pvt. practice, 1985—. Co-author: Law of the Student Press, 1983, Confronting Wrongful Discharge Under Oregon and Washington Law, 1989. Vice chair Lane County (Oreg.) Dem. Ctrl. Com., 1981-82, Multnomah County (Oreg.) Dem. Ctrl. Com., 1991-92; mem. Oreg. Dem. State Ctrl. Com., 1981-82, 91—, Multnomah Edn. Svc. Dist. Bd., 1993-97, chmn., 1996-97; fin. chair Oreg. State Dem. Party, 1993-95, vice chair, 1994-97, chmn., 1997—; mem. Portland Sch. Bd., 1995—, vice chair, 1998—; treas. Assn. State Dem. Chairs, 1998—. Recipient Johnnie Phelps medal Vets. for Human Rights, 1995. Jewish. Office: 1753 NW Aspen Ave Portland OR 97210-1208

ABRAMS, MEYER HOWARD, English language educator; b. Long Branch, N.J., July 23, 1912; s. Joseph and Sarah (Shanes) A.; m. Ruth Gaynes, Sept. 1, 1937; children: Jane, Judith. A.B., Harvard U., 1934, M.A., 1937, Ph.D., 1940; postgrad. (Henry fellow), Cambridge (Eng.) U., 1934-35; D.H.L. (hon.), U. Rochester, 1978, Northwestern U., 1981, U. Chgo., 1982, Western Md. Coll., 1985, Le Moyne Coll., 1993. Instr. Harvard, 1938-42; research asso. psycho-acoustic lab. Harvard U., 1942-45; asst. prof. English, Cornell U., Ithaca, N.Y., 1945-47; asso. prof. Cornell U., 1947-53, prof., 1953-60, Frederic J. Whiton prof. English,, 1960-73, Class of 1916 prof. English, 1973-83; prof. emeritus, 1983—; adv. editor W.W. Norton & Co., Inc., 1961—; bd. editors various Cornell publs. Hon. sr. fellow Sch. Criticism and Theory, Cornell U.; Fulbright lectr. Royal U. Malta, Cambridge U., 1953; Roache lectr. U. Ind., 1963; Alexander lectr. U. Toronto, 1964; Ewing lectures UCLA, 1975; Cecil Green lectr. U BC., 1980; Lamont lectures Union Coll., 1995; Mem. founders group Nat. Humanities Ctr.; mem. coun. of scholars Libr. of Congress, 1980—, chmn. coun. of scholars, 1984—. Author: The Milk of Paradise, 1934, 2d edit., 1970, The Mirror and the Lamp: Romantic Theory and the Critical Tradition, 1953, A Glossary of Literary Terms, 1957, 7th edit., 1998, Natural Supernaturalism: Tradition and Revolution in Romantic Literature, 1971, The Correspondent Breeze: Essays on English Romanticism, 1984, Doing Things with Texts: Essays in Criticism and Critical Theory, 1989, also publs. on mil. communications; editor: The Poetry of Pope, 1954; Editor: Literature and Belief, 1958, The Romantic Poets: Modern Essays in Criticism, 1960, rev. edit., 1975, The Norton Anthology of English Literature, 1962, 7th edit., 1999, Wordsworth: A Collection of Critical Essays, 1972, (with others) Wordsworth's Prelude: Norton Critical Edition, 1979. Recipient Christian Gauss prize Phi Beta Kappa, 1954, James Russell Lowell prize, 1971, Am. Acad. award humanistic studies, 1984, Disting. Scholar award Keats-Shelley Assn., 1987, Am. Acad. and Inst. Arts and Letters award for lit., 1990; Rockefeller fellow, 1946; Ford fellow, 1952; Guggenheim fellow, 1958, 60-61; fellow Center for Advanced Study in the Behavioral Scis., Palo Alto, Calif., 1967-68; vis. fellow All Soul's Coll., Oxford, 1977. Mem. AAUP, MLA (exec. council 1961-64), Am. Acad. Arts and Scis., Am. Philos. Soc., Brit. Acad. (corr. fellow), Phi Beta Kappa, Sigma Xi. Home: 378 Savage Farm Dr Ithaca NY 14850-6505

ABRAMS, NORMAN, law educator, university administrator; b. Chgo., July 7, 1933; s. Harry A. and Gertrude (Dick) A.; m. Toshka Alster, 1977; children: Marshall David, Julie, Hanna, Naomi. AB, U. Chgo., 1952, JD, 1955. Bar: Ill. 1956, U.S. Supreme Ct. 1967. Assoc. in law Columbia U., 1955-57; rsch. assoc. Harvard U., 1957-59; sec. Harvard-Brandeis Coop. Rsch. for Israel's Legal Devel., 1957-58, dir., 1959; mem. faculty law sch. UCLA, 1959—, prof. law, 1964—, assoc. dean law, 1989-91, vice chancellor acad. pers., 1991—, interim exec. v. chancellor, spring 1998, co-dir. Ctr. for internat. and strategic studies, 1982-83, chmn. steering com., 1985-87, 88-89; vis. prof. Hebrew U., 1969-70, Forchheimer vis. prof., 1986; vis. prof. Bar Ilan U., 1970-71, 78, U. So. Calif., 1972, 73, Stanford U., 1977, U. Calif. at Berkeley, 1977, Loyola U., Los Angeles, summers 1974, 75, 76, 79; spl. asst. to U.S. atty. gen., also prof.-in-residence criminal div. Dept. Justice, 1966-67; reporter for So. Calif. indigent accused persons study Am. Bar Found., 1963; cons. Gov. Calif. Commn. L.A. Riots, 1965, Pres.'s Commn. Law Enforcement and Adminstrn. Justice, 1966-67, Nat. Commn. on Reform of Fed. Criminal Laws, 1967-69, Rand Corp., 1968-74, Ctr. for Adminstrv. Justice, ABA, 1973-77, Nat. Advs. Commn. on Criminal Justice Stds., Organized Crime Task Force, 1976; spl. hearing officer conscientious objector cases Dept. Justice, 1967-68; vis. scholar Inst. for Advanced Studies, Hebrew U., summer, 1994. Author: (with others) Evidence, Cases and Materials, 7th edit., 1983, 8th edit., 1988, 9th edit., 1997, Federal Criminal Law and Its Enforcement, 1986, 2d edit. (with S. Beale), 1993; mem. editorial bd. Criminal Law Forum, 1990—. Chmn. Jewish Conciliation Bd., L.A., 1975-81; bd. dirs. Bet Tzedek, 1975-85, L.A. Hillel Coun., 1979-82, Shalhevet High Sch.; chmn. So. Calif. region Am. Profs. for Peace in Middle East, 1981-83; bd. dirs. met. region Jewish Fedn., 1982-88, v.p. 1982-83; pres. Westwood Kehillah Congregation, 1985. Mem. Soc. for Reform of Criminal Law (mem. exec. com. 1994—), Phi Beta Kappa. Office: UCLA 405 Hilgard Ave Los Angeles CA 90095-9000

ABRAMS, OSSIE EKMAN, fundraiser; b. Olofström, Blekinge, Sweden, Jan. 8, 1952; came to the U.S., 1972; d. Ossian B. and Margit A. (Adolfsson) Ekman; m. Howard L. Abrams, Nov. 17, 1973 (div. Sept. 1983); m. David B. Orser, Aug. 1992. Student, Lärarhögskolan, 1972, New Sch. for Social Rsch., 1975; BA (hon.), Rocky Mountain Coll., 1994. Dental asst., sec. Samuel Meyer DDS, N.Y.C., 1973-74; office mgr., adminstr. Irving Peress DDS, N.Y.C., 1974-81; chief adminstr. Allen Kozin DDS, N.Y.C., 1981-87; head devel. Rocky Mountain Coll., Billings, Mont., 1991-92; owner, operator Davoss Ranch, Park City, Mont.; bd. mem. Mental Health Found., Billings, 1991, 92, bd. pres., 1993, 94. Active in Met. Opera Guild, N.Y.C., N.Y.C. Ballet Guild, N.Y. Philharm. Soc.; supporter Alberta Bair Theater, Billings Symphony, Billings Studio Theater; mem. selection com. Orser Chair, Coll. Bus., Mont. State U., Bozeman, 1988-99; fundraiser ann. campaign Yellowstone Art Ctr., Billings, 1989; fundraiser bus. drive Rocky Mountain Coll., Billings, 1990, vol. Rocky Mountain Coll. Black Tie Blue Jeans Ball, mem. auction com. 1990-93, chair auction com. 1994, 95, chair ball, 1996, chair sponsor com., 1997; mem. nat. adv. coun. Rocky Mountain Coll., 1993-99; mem. sponsor com. Salute to Women, YMCA, 1997; mem. subscription dr. Billings Symphony, 1996, 97. Recipient Alumni Hall of Fame award Rocky Mountain Coll., 1993, Leadership award Mental Health Found., Billings, 1994. Home: 1420 Granite Ave Billings MT 59102-0716 Office: Davoss Ranch 804 Valley Creek Rd Park City MT 59063

ABRAMS, PAMELA NADINE, magazine editor; b. Ithaca, N.Y., Dec. 23, 1957; d. Kenneth Theodore and Madeline Laura (Cantor) Abrams; m. Robert S. Steiner, Oct. 11, 1984; children: Mickey, Jamie. BA, SUNY, Purchase, 1981. Pub. assoc. Nuclear Times, N.Y.C., 1982-83; assoc. editor Harper's Mag., N.Y.C., 1983-88; exec. editor Parents Mag., N.Y.C., 1988-95; editor-in-chief Child Mag., N.Y.C., 1995—; adv. bd. War, Peace and the News Media, NYU, 1983-88; judge Olive Br. Awards, Editor's Organizing Com., N.Y.C., 1983-90. Contbr. articles to profl. jours.; author/reviewer Chgo. Tribune, 1989. Vol. Parents as Reading Ptnrs., Pub. Schs. 321, Bklyn., 1995-98; mem. parent adv. bd. Children's Def. Fund, Washington, 1996; judge Heart of Am. Awards, 1998. Mem. Am. Soc. Mag. Editors (screener Nat. Mag. Awards 1997, 98). Avocations: cooking, reading. Home: 86 Prospect Park W Brooklyn NY 11215-3575 Office: Child Magazine 375 Lexington Ave New York NY 10017-5514*

ABRAMS, REID ALLEN, surgeon, educator; b. San Antonio, July 26, 1955. BA in Biology, Lawrence U., 1977; MD, U. Colo., 1982. Diplomate Am. Bd. Orthopaedic Surgery, with cert. of added qualifications in hand surgery; lic. physician, Calif., Colo., Washington. Intern then resident in orthopedic surgery U. Colo. Health Scis. Ctr., Denver, 1982-87; fellow pediatric orthopedics Children's Hosp. and Health ctr., San Diego, 1987-88; fellow hand and microvascular surgery Brigham and Women's Hosp., Boston, 1988-89; gen. orthopedist Group Health Coop. Puget Sound, 1989-90; assoc. prof. clin. orthopedics U. Calif. Med. Ctr., San Diego, 1990—, chief hand and microvascular surgery, 1990—. Contbr. numerous articles to profl. jours. Mem. Western Orthopedic Assn., Acad. Orthopaedic Soc., Am. Acad. Orthopaedic Surgeons, Am. Soc. Surgery of the Hand, Kiros Soc., Phi Sigma. Avocations: music, back-packing, snow skiing. Office: U Calif Med Ctr Orthopedic Surgery 200 W Arbor Dr San Diego CA 92103-1911

ABRAMS, RICHARD LEE, physicist; b. Cleve., Apr. 20, 1941; s. Morris S. and Corinne (Tobias) A.; m. Jane Shack, Aug. 12, 1962; children: Elizabeth, Laura. B. Engring. Physics, Cornell U., Ithaca, N.Y., 1964, Ph.D., 1968. Mem. tech. staff Bell Telephone Labs., Whippany, N.J., 1968-71; sect. head Hughes Rsch. Labs., Malibu, Calif., 1971-75, dept. mgr., 1975-83; chief scientist Space and Comm. Group Hughes Aircraft Co., El Segundo, Calif., 1983-89; chief scientist Hughes Rsch. Labs., Malibu, Calif., 1989-96, cons., 1997—; program co-chmn. Conf. on Laser Engring. and Applications, Washington, 1979; chmn. Conf. on Lasers and Electro-Optics, Phoenix, 1982. Assoc. editor: Optics Letters, 1979-82; patentee in field. Fellow IEEE (assoc. editor Jour. Quantum Electronics 1980-83, bd. editors Proc. 1987-89, Centennial medal 1989), Optical Soc. Am. (bd. dirs. 1982-85, v.p. 1988, pres. 1990); mem. IEEE Quantum Electronics and Applications Soc. (adminstrve. com. 1980-83, v.p. 1982, pres. 1983), Tau Beta Pi, Phi Kappa Phi. Club: Riviera Country (Pacific Palisades, Calif.). E-mail: abrams@hrl.com. Home: 922 Enchanted Way Pacific Palisades CA 90272-2823

ABRAMS, ROBERT, lawyer, former state attorney general; b. Bronx, N.Y., July 4, 1938; s. Benjamin and Dorothy (Kaplan) A.; m. Diane B. Schulder, Sept. 15, 1974; children: Rachel Schulder, Becky Schulder. B.A., Columbia U., 1960; J.D., NYU, 1963; LL.D. (hon.), Hofstra U., 1979; Lugum Doctoris (hon.), Yeshiva U., 1984; LLD (hon.), L.I. U., 1989, Pace U., 1991. Mem. N.Y. State Assembly, 1965-69; pres. Borough of Bronx, 1970-78; atty. gen. State of N.Y., 1979-93; ptnr. Stroock & Stroock & Lavan, N.Y.C., 1994—; panel mem. of disting. neutrals CPR Inst. Contbr. articles to profl. publs.; writer column Nat. Law Jour., N.Y. Law Jour., N.Y. Times, N.Y. Newsday, N.Y. Post, N.Y. Daily News, Buffalo News, Albany Times Union, Ganette Suburban Newspapers, The Harvard Environ. Law Rev., NYU Law Rev., Columbia Jour. Environ. Law, Pace Environ. Law Rev., Washburn Law Rev., Albany Law Rev., Pace Law Rev., The Jour. of State Gov. Del. Dem. Nat. Conv., 1972, 76, 80, 84, mem. platform com., 1988; elector Electoral Coll., 1988. Recipient Adam Clayton Powell Pub. Svc. award, Interfaith award Coun. Chs., N.Y.C., Bronx Community Coll. medallion for Svc., Scroll of Honor plaque United Jewish Appeal, Benjamin Cardozo award for legal excellence Jewish Lawyers Guild, Brotherhood award B'nai B'rith, Man of Yr. award NAACP, Alumni Achievement award NYU Sch. Law, Environmentalist of Yr. award Environ. Planning Lobby N.Y., Disting. Pub. Svc. Citation Bus. Coun. N.Y. State, N.Y. State Sheriff's Assn. award, Nat. Crime Victims award, Torch of Liberty award Anti-Defamation League, Anatoly Scharansky Freedom award N.Y. Conf. Soviet Jewry, Environmentalist of Yr. award L.I. Pine Barrens Soc., Il Leone de San Marco Hon. Italian Am. award, Cavaliere medal Pres. Italy, Pres. award Marist Coll., Hubert Humphrey Humanitarian award United Fedn. Tchrs., Law Day award N.Y. State Trial Lawyers Assn., Contbns. to Urban Law award Fordham Law Jour., Deans medal Law Sch. NYU, Margaret Sanger award N.Y. State Family Planning Advocates, Lehman/LaGuardia Civic Achievement award Anti-Defamation League B'nai B'rith and Commn. on Social Justice of the Order of Sons of Italy, Father of the Yr. award Nat. Father's Day Com., B'nai Zion Bill of Rights award, Avodah award Jewish Tchr's. Assn., Man of the Yr. award N.Y. State Consumer Assembly, Rodef Tzedek Pursuer of Justice award Restructionist Rabbinical Coll., Humanitarian award Rochester Labor and Religious Coalition, Special Recognition award Profl. Women in Construction and Allied Industries, Humanitarian award Long Island Assn. for Children with Learning Disabilities, Man of the Yr. award Mental Ilness Found., N.Y. State Ct's. Man of the Yr. award Shamrai Tzedek Soc., Grand Marshall award Schenectady Labor Coun. Labor Day Parade, Louis Brandeis award Zionist Orgn. Am., Lubavich Tzivos Hashem award, Chassidius in Am. Exemplary Leadership award Bostoner Chassidum, Recognition for Pub. Svc. award Greater Buffalo AFL-CIO Coun., Effort on Behalf of the Elderly award Workmen's Circle Home & Infirmary For the Aged, Dedication Concerning Reproductive Rights award N.Y. Coun. of Jewish Women, Citation of Appreciation N.Y. State Assn. of Architects, Pesach-Tikvah Hope Developer award, Pub. Svc. award N.Y. Soc. Clin. Psychologists, Cmty. Achievement award Am. Orthodox Fedn., State Svc. award Nat. Columbus Day Com., Environmentalist of the Yr. award Sierra Club, Svc. award N.Y. State Jewish War Veterans, Cadet award N.Y.C. Mission Soc., Disting. Achievement award AMIT Women, Man of the Yr. award Nassau County Police Res. Assn., Ann. award Lubavitch Youth Orgn., Appreciation award Japanese C. of C. of N.Y., Friend of the Cmty. award Empire State Pride Agenda, Roland Smith award Capital Region chpt. N.Y. Civil Liberties Union, Scharansky Freedom award L.I. Com. on Soviet Jewry, Cert. of Honor award N.Y. League of Histadrut, Scouting For the Handicapped Outstanding Svc. award Greater N.Y. Coun. of Boy Scouts of Am., Citizen of the Yr. award We. N.Y. Labor Coalition, Svc. award Citizen's Coun. for the Cmty. of Mentally Retarded, Rockland Hosp. Guild, Man of the Yr. award The Shield Inst. for Retarded Children, Maccabean Svc. award N.Y. Bd. of Rabbis, Thurgood Marshall award Bridge Builders Albany, Pro Choice award Naral N.Y., Dist. Humanitarian award Insts. Applied Human Dynamics, Life-Long Dedication award Holocaust Meml. Com.; named Man of Yr. St. Patrick's Home Aged and Infirm, Man of Yr. State Israel Bonds. Mem. N.Y. State Bar Assn. (Environ. Acheivement award), Nat. Assn. of Attys. Gen. (pres. 1988-89, chmn. environ. protection com. 1982-85, chmn. antitrust com. 1985-88, chmn. civil rights com. 1990-92, chmn. ea. regional conf. of attys. gen. 1983-84, Wyman award for Outstanding Atty. Gen. in the Nation 1991). Democrat. Office: Stroock & Stroock & Lavan 180 Maiden Ln New York NY 10038-4925*

ABRAMS, ROBERTA BUSKY, hospital administrator, nurse; b. Bklyn., Feb. 16, 1937; d. Albert H. and Gladys Busky; m. Robert L. Abrams, June 28, 1959 (div. 1977); children: Susan Abrams Federman, David B. BSN, U. Rochester, 1959; MA, Fairfield U., 1977. Asst. head nurse Jewish Hosp., Bklyn., 1959-60; instr. medicine/surgery Bklyn. Hosp., 1960-62, U. Rochester, N.Y., 1963-64; instr. ob-gyn Malden (Mass.) Hosp. Sch. Nursing, 1965-66; instr. prospective parents ARC, San Rafael, Calif., 1968-69; instr. ob-gyn SUNY, Farmingdale, 1970-71; instr. maternal/child health Stamford (Conn.) Hosp., 1971-75; clinician maternal/child health Lawrence Hosp., Bronxville, N.Y., 1975-78; asst. prof. nursing Ohio Wesleyan U., Delaware, 1981-84; dir. Elizabeth Blackwell Hosp. at Riverside Meth., Columbus, Ohio, 1978-86; dir. nursing Henry Ford Hosp., Detroit, 1986-87, assoc. adminstr. nursing, 1988-92; sr. ptnr. Health Cuard, Inc., 1997—; sr. ptnr. Health Quad, Inc., 1997—; cons. maternal/child nursing currents Ross Labs., 1984-94; state coord. maternal/child health First Am. Home Care Co., 1994-95; dir. women's and children's health Arcadia Health Systems, 1995-96; lectr., cons. in field. Contbr. articles to profl. jours. Mem. LWV, Greater Detroit Orgn. Nurses Execs., Lamaze Internat., Sigma Theta Tau. Home and Office: 32478 Dunford St Farmington Hills MI 48334

ABRAMS, ROGER IAN, law educator, arbitrator; b. Newark, July 30, 1945; s. Avel S. and Myrna (Posner) A.; m. Frances Elise Kovitz, June 1, 1969; children: Jason, Seth. BA, Cornell U., 1967; JD, Harvard U., 1970. Bar: Mass. 1970, U.S. Dist. Ct. Mass. 1971, U.S. Ct. Appeals (1st cir.) 1971. Law clk. to Judge Frank M. Coffin U.S. Ct. Appeals (1st cir.), Boston, 1970-71; assoc. Foley, Hoag & Eliot, Boston, 1971-74; prof. law Law. Sch. Case Western Res. U., Cleve., 1974-86; dean Law Ctr. Nova U., Ft. Lauderdale, Fla., 1986-93; dean Law Sch. Rutgers U., Newark, 1993-1998; prof. law sch. Rutger U., Newark, 1993—; Herbert J. Hannuch scholar Rutgers U., Newark, 1998—; labor arbitrator Fed. Mediation Svc., 1975—; mem. gender bias report implementation com. Fla. Supreme Ct.; prof. law Law Sch., Rutgers U., 1993—. Author: Legal Bases: Baseball and the Law, 1998; contbr. articles to law jours. Bd. dirs. Inst. for Continuing Legal Edn., N.J., 1993—. Recipient Gen. Counsel's Advocacy award NAACP, Boston, 1974; inductee Union N.J. Hall of Fame, 1995. Mem. Am. Law Inst., Am. Bar Found., Am. Arbitration Assn. (labor arbitrator). Democrat. Jewish. Avocations: swimming, distance walking, reading. Office: Rutgers U Sch Law 15 Washington St Newark NJ 07102-3105

ABRAMS, RUTH IDA, state supreme court justice; b. Boston, Dec. 26, 1930; d. Samuel and Matilda A. BA, Radcliffe Coll., 1953; LLB, Harvard U., 1956; hon. degree, Mt. Holyoke Coll., 1977, Suffolk U., 1977, New Eng. Sch. Law, 1978. Bar: Mass. 1957. Ptnr. Abrams Abrams & Abrams, Boston, 1957-60; asst. dist. atty. Middlesex County, Mass., 1961-69; asst. atty. gen. Mass., chief appellate sect. criminal div., 1969-71; spl. counsel Supreme Jud. Ct. Mass., 1971-72; assoc. justice Supreme Jud. Ct. Mass., Boston, 1977—, Superior Ct. Commonwealth of Mass., 1972-77; mem. Gov.'s Commn. on Child Abuse, 1970-71, Mass. Law Revision Commn. Proposed Criminal Code for Mass., 1969-71; trustee Radcliffe Coll., from 1981. Editor: Handbook for Law Enforcement Officers, 1969-71. Recipient Radcliffe Coll. Achievement award, 1976, Radcliffe Grad. Soc. medal, 1977. Mem. ABA (com. on proposed fed. code from 1977), Mass. Bar Assn., Am. Law Inst., Am. Judicature Soc. (dir. 1978), Am. Judges Assn., Mass. Assn. Women Lawyers. Office: Supreme Jud Ct Mass 1300 New Courthouse Pemberton Square Boston MA 02108*

ABRAMS, SAM, humanities educator; b. N.Y.C., Nov. 18, 1935; s. Morris and Miriam (Rosenfeld) A.; m. Barbara Odette Leeb, Dec. 10, 1958; two children. AB, Bklyn. Coll., 1958; MA, U. Ill., 1959. Instr. classics U. Ill., Urbana, 1950-60, Fla. State U., Tallahassee, 1960-61, Wheaton Coll., Madison, N.J., 1961-65, Drew U., Enfield, N.H., 1965-68; workshop leader St. Mark's Poetry Project, N.Y.C., 1965-68; communal farmer Stone Acad., Enfield, 1969-77; prof. Rochester (N.Y.) Inst. Technology, 1978—. Author: Barbara, 1966; editor: The Neglected Walt Whitman, 1993. Coord. Poets Caravan Angry Arts Against the War in Vietnam, 1966-68. Office: Rochester Inst Technology 92 Lomb Memorial Dr Rochester NY 14623-5604

ABRAMS, SYLVIA FLECK, religious studies educator; b. Buffalo, Apr. 5, 1942; d. Abraham and Ann (Hanf) Fleck; m. Ronald M. Abrams, June 30, 1963; children—Ruth, Sharon. BA magna cum laude, Western Res. U., 1963, MA, 1964, PhD, 1988; BHL, Cleve. Coll. Jewish Studies, 1976, MHL, 1983; postgrad. U. Haifa, 1975, Yad Va Shem Summer Inst., Hebrew U., 1983. Hebrew tchr. The Temple, 1959-77, Hebrew coord., 1973-77; tchr. Beachwood H.S., 1964-66; tchr. Hebrew and social studies Agnon Sch., Cleve., 1975-77, social studies resource tchr., 1976-77; ednl. dir. Temple Emanu El, Cleve., 1977-85; asst. dir. Cleve. Bur. Jewish Edn., 1985-92, acting exec. v.p., 1993-94, exec. dir. ednl. svcs. Jewish Edn. Ctr. Cleve., 1994-99, dean cleve. Coll. Jewish Studies, 1999—; chmn. ednl. dirs. coun. Cleve. Bd. Jewish Edn., 1982-85. Appointed to Ohio Coun. Holocaust Edn., 1986. Recipient Elbert J. Benton award Western Res. U., 1963; Fred and Rose Rosenwasser Bible award Coll. Jewish Studies, 1974; Emmanuel Gamoran Meml. Curriculum award Nat. Assn. Temple Educator, 1978; Samuel Lipson Meml. award Coll. Jewish Studies, 1981 Bingham fellow Case Western Res. U., 1984-86. Mem. ASCD, Nat. Assn. Temple Educators (bd. dirs. 1984-88), Coun. Jewish Edn. (bd. dirs. 1991—, v.p. 1995), Assn. Dirs. Ctrl. Agys. (sec./treas. 1995-98), Coalition for Advancement of Jewish Edn. (bd. mem. at large 1989-93, chair 1996—), Union Am. Hebrew Congregations (Israel curriculum task force), Cleve. Bur. Jewish Edn. (chmn. ednl. dirs. coun. 1982-85), Nat. Coun. Jewish Women (life), Phi Beta Kappa. Jewish. Club: Hadassah (life). Editor: You and Your Schools, 1972. Office: Jewish Edn Ctr of Cleve 2030 S Taylor Rd Cleveland OH 44118-2605

ABRAMS-COLLENS, VIVIEN, artist; b. Cleve., BFA, Carnegie-Mellon U.; MFA, Instituto Allende, San Miguel de Allende, Mex. Art tchr. Biblioteca Publica, San Miguel de Allende, Mex., 1969, Cleve. Mus. Art, 1971-72; instr. watercolor Dept. Community Svcs., Cleveland Heights, Univ. Heights, Ohio, 1974; instr. drawing Cuyahoga C.C., Cleve., 1974; design instr. Manhattanville Coll., Purchase, N.Y., 1985-86; artist-in-residence Bennington (Vt.) Coll., 1980; vis. artist in painting SUNY, Purchase, N.Y., 1983; lectr. in field. One-woman shows include Akron (Ohio) Art Inst., 1976, The New Gallery Contemporary Art, Cleve., 1977, 80, Luise Ross Gallery, N.Y.C., 1984, Coup de Grâce Gallery, N.Y.C., 1992, 100 Church Street, N.Y.C., 1992, Lisa Stern Gallery, Mountainville, N.Y., 1993, Lycian Ctr. Galleries, Sugarloaf, N.Y., 1994, Mus. Hudson Highlands, Cornwall-on-Hudson, N.Y., 1995; selected group exhbns. include Butler Inst. Am. Art, Ohio, 1976, 77, Cleve. Mus. Art, 1976, 77, 79, 81, 84 (1st Prize in Painting 1981), Akron Inst. Art, 1977, Harbourfront Gallery, Toronto, 1978, Marilyn Pearl Gallery, N.Y.C., 1978, 82, Phoenix Mus. Art, 1979, Soho Ctr. Visual Artists, N.Y.C., 1979, Washington Sq. East Galleries, N.Y.C., 1980, Little Rock (Ark.) Art Mus., 1982, Steven Rosenberg Gallery, N.Y.C., 1983, Ericson Gallery, N.Y.C., 1983, Sculpture Ctr., N.Y.C., 1983, A.I.R. Gallery, N.Y.C., 1983, Aldrich Mus. Contemporary Art, Ridgefield, Conn., 1984, 86, 92, Luise Ross Gallery, 1984, Mus. of the Hudson Highlands, 1985, City Gallery, N.Y.C., 1987, Squibb Gallery, Princeton, N.J., 1988, Cleve. Inst. Art, 1988, Mansfield Art Ctr., Ohio, 1989, OIA Salon, N.Y.C., 1991, Middletown Art Ctr., 1994 (Oil/Acrylic award 1994), Dietrich Contemporary Arts, N.Y.C., 1994, Cleve. Ctr. for Contemporary Art, 1994, Mansfield (Ohio) Art Ctr., 1995; permanent collections include Cleve. Found., Cleve. Art Assn., The Currier Gallery Art, Home Ins. Co., We. Electric, J.P. Morgan & Co., Continental Corp., Progressive Ins. Co., Nat. City Bank Cleve., Sohio, Walter & Samuels, Inc., Columbus Mus. Arts & Scis., Cleve. Mus. Art, Aldrich Mus. Contemporary Art; commns. include AT&T Longlines. Mem. fellows exec. com. MacDowell Colony, 1982-85. Cleve. Found. grantee, 1976, Athena Found. grantee, 1984; Hand Follow Found. fellow, 1983, fellow MacDowell Colony, Peterborough, N.H., 1979, 81, 85; recipient 1st prize Cleve. Mus. Art 62nd May Show, 1981, award Middletown Art Ctr., 1994; named to Shaker Heights H.S. Hall of Fame, 1994. Office: 196 Mountain Rd Cornwall On Hudson NY 12520-1803*

ABRAMSON, ARTHUR SEYMOUR, linguistics educator, researcher; b. Jersey City, Jan. 26, 1925; s. Seymour Vallie (Olshan) A.; m. Ruby Melamed, June 27, 1952 (div. May 1985); children: Joseph B., David N. Student, Rutgers U., 1942-43; BA, Yeshiva U., 1949; MA, Columbia U., 1950, PhD, 1960. Tchr. English and French Pub. High Schs., Jersey City, 1950-53; research staff Haskins Labs., N.Y.C., 1959-63, 64-65, research assoc., 1963-64, 65—; assoc. prof. speech CUNY, 1963-64, prof. communication arts and scis., 1965-67; prof. linguistics U. Conn., Storrs, 1967-92, prof. emeritus, 1992—, head dept. linguistics, 1967-74; Fulbright tchr. Bangkok and Songkhla, Thailand, 1953-55; vis. prof. Lady Davis Fellowship Trust, Jerusalem, 1981. Author: The Vowels and Tones of Standard Thai: Acoustical Measurements and Experiments; editor Language and Speech, 1975-87; contbr. numerous articles to profl. jours. With U.S. Army, 1943-46, ETO. Am. Coun. Learned Socs. fellow, 1973-74, Ford Found. fellow, Thailand, 1973-74. Fellow Acoustical Soc. Am., Internat. Soc. Phonetic Scis. (v.p. 1985-91); mem. MLA, Permanent Coun. for Orgn. Internat. Congresses of Phonetic Scis., Linguistic Soc. Am. (sec.-treas. 1974-78, v.p. 1982, pres. 1983), Internat. Phonetic Assn. (coun. 1986-90), Am. Soc. Phonetic Scis., S.E. Asian Linguistics Soc., Siam Soc., Conn. Acad. Arts. and Scis. Democrat. Jewish. E-mail: abramson@uconnvm.uconn.edu. Home: 43 Timber Dr Storrs Mansfield CT 06268-1210 Office: U Conn Dept of Linguistics U-145 341 Mansfield Rd Storrs Mansfield CT 06269-1145 also: Haskins Labs 270 Crown St New Haven CT 06511-6695

ABRAMSON, HANLEY NORMAN, pharmacy educator; b. Detroit, June 10, 1940; s. Frederick Jacob and Lillian (Kampner) A.; m. Young Hee Kim, Aug. 4, 1967; children: Nathaniel, Deborah, Stephen. BS in Pharmacy, Wayne State U., 1962; MS in Pharm. Chemistry, U. Mich., 1963, PhD in Pharm. Chemistry, 1966. Registered pharmacist. Rsch. assoc. The Hebrew U., Jerusalem, Israel, 1966-67; asst. prof. Wayne State U., Detroit, 1967-73, assoc. prof., 1973-78, prof., 1978—, chmn. dept. pharm. sci., 1986-95, interim dean Coll. of Pharmacy and Allied Health Professions, 1987-88, assoc. provost, 1991-95, assoc. dean, 1996—. Author numerous published articles in field of medicinal chemistry. Bd. trustees 1st Bapt. Ch. of Oak Park, Mich., 1974-78; deacon Bloomfield Hills (Mich.) Bapt. Ch., 1986-89; dir. Met. Detroit Alliance for Minority Participation, 1994—. Recipient rsch. grants Mich. Heart Assn., Detroit, 1967-76, Nat. Cancer Inst., Bethesda, Md., 1982-91. Mem. AAAS, Am. Chem. Soc., Am. Pharm. Assn., Am. Assn. Colls. Pharmacy. Baptist. Avocations: astronomy, numismatics, baseball history, classical music. Home: 5530 Hammersmith Dr West Bloomfield MI 48322-1452 Office: Wayne State U 125 Shapero Hall Detroit MI 48202

ABRAMSON, HAROLD C., federal judge; b. 1928. Student, Ga. inst. Tech., 1944-45; BBA, U. Tex., 1948, LLB with honors, 1949. Bar: Tex. 1949, U.S. Dist. Ct. (no. dist.) Tex. 1951. Pvt. practice, 1952-85; bankruptcy judge U.S. Dist. Ct. (no. dist.) Tex., Dallas, 1985—. With USN, 1948-52. Mem. Nat. Assn. Bankruptcy Judges, Dallas Bar Assn. Fax: (214) 753-2149. Office: US Dist Ct (no dist) Tex 1100 Commerce St Rm 12A24 Dallas TX 75242-1496

ABRAMSON, HYMAN NORMAN, engineering and science research executive; b. San Antonio, Mar. 4, 1926; s. Nathan and Pearl (Westerman) A.; m. Idelle Rebecca Ringel, Apr. 20, 1947; children—Phillip David, Mark Donald. BSME, Stanford U., 1950, MS in Engring. Mechanics, 1951; Ph.D. in Engring. Mechanics (So. Fellowship Fund fellow), U. Tex., Austin, 1956. Engr. U.S. Naval Air Missile Test Center, Point Mugu, Calif., 1947-48; project engr. Chance Vought Aircraft Co., Dallas, 1951-52; assoc. prof. aero. engring. Tex. A&M U., 1952-55; sect. mgr., dept. dir. S.W. Research Inst., San Antonio, 1956-72, v.p. div. engring. scis., 1972-85, exec. v.p., 1985-91, also bd. dirs.; mem. many research adv. coms. U.S. Govt.; bd. dirs. Broadway Nat. Bank. Author: An Introduction to the Dynamics of Airplanes, 1958, reprinted, 1971; contbr. numerous articles to profl. publs.; editor: (with others) Applied Mechanics Surveys, 1966, The Dynamic Behavior of Liquids in Moving Containers, 1966; assoc. editor: (with others) Applied Mechanics Revs, 1954-85; editorial adv. bd.: (with others) Jour. Computers and Structures, 1970—, Aeros. and Astronautics, 1975-80. Mem. Greater San Antonio C. of C., and City of San Antonio Market Sq. Adv. Com., 1973-77; mem. U.S. Bicentennial Com. of San Antonio, 1975-76; mem. adv. bd. dirs. U.S. Alamo, Inc., 1985—. Served with USN, 1943-45. Fellow AIAA (Disting. Service award 1973, dir., Structures, Structural Dynamics and Materials award 1991), ASME (v.p., gov., hon. mem.); mem. Nat. Acad. Engring., Soc. Naval Architects and Marine Engrs., Nat. Acad. Engring. Mexico, AAAS, Sigma Xi. Republican. Jewish. Home: 1511 Spanish Oaks San Antonio TX 78213-1635 Office: SW Research Inst PO Box 28510 San Antonio TX 78228-0510

ABRAMSON, JILL, newspaper publishing executive. AB in History and Lit., Harvard U., 1976. Stringer Time mag., 1974-76, Boston bur. mgr., reporter, 1976-77; with NBC News Election Unit, 1979-81; sr. writer Am. Lawyer, 1981-88; editor Legal Times, 1986-88; with New York Times, Washington, 1988—, Chernoff Silver, 1988-97; dep. bur. chief The Wall Street Jour., 1993-97; enterprise editor Washington bur. New York Times, 1997—. Co-author: Where Are They Now: The Story of Women of Harvard Law 1974, 1976, Where They Are Now, 1986, Strange Justice, 1994. Office: New York Times 1627 I St NW Ste 700 Washington DC 20006-4085*

ABRAMSON, PAUL ROBERT, political scientist, educator; b. St. Louis, Nov. 28, 1937; s. Harry Benjamin and Hattie Abramson; m. Janet Carolyn Schwartz, Sept. 11, 1966; children—Lee Jacob, Heather Lyn. B.A., Washington U., St. Louis, 1959; M.A., U. Calif.-Berkeley, 1961, Ph.D., 1967. Asst. prof. polit. sci. Mich. State U., East Lansing, 1967-71, assoc. prof. polit. sci., 1971-77, prof. polit. sci., 1977—; Lady Davis vis. prof. Hebrew U. Jerusalem, 1994. Author: Generational Change in American Politics, 1975, The Political Socialization of Black Americans, 1977, Political Attitudes in America, 1983; co-author: Change and Continuity in the 1980 Elections, 1982, rev. edit., 1983, Change and Continuity in the 1984 Elections, 1986, rev. edit., 1987, Change and Continuity in the 1988 Elections, 1990, rev. edit., 1991, Change and Continuity in the 1992 Elections, 1994, rev. edit., 1995, Value Change in Global Perspective, 1995, Change and Continuity in the 1996 Elections, 1998, Change and Continuity in the 1996 and 1998 Elections, 1999; contbr. articles to profl. jours. Served to lt. U.S. Army, 1960-62. Woodrow Wilson fellow, 1959-60; Ford Found. faculty research fellow, 1972-73; Fulbright grantee sr. lectr. Hebrew U. of Jerusalem, 1987-88. Mem. Am. Polit. Sci. Assn., Midwest Polit. Sci. Assn., So. Polit. Sci. Assn., Am. Sociol. Assn., Internat. Polit. Sci. Assn., Phi Beta Kappa. Home: 2697 Linden Dr East Lansing MI 48823-3813 Office: Mich State U Dept Polit Sci East Lansing MI 48824-1032

ABRAMSON, SARA JANE, radiologist, educator; b. New Orleans, La., May 12, 1945; m. Walter Sayre; children: Harrison, Russell, Zachary, Andrew. BA, Sarah Lawrence Coll., 1967; postgrad., Tulane U., 1967-69; MD, Mt. Sinai Sch. Medicine, 1971. Diplomate Am. Bd. Radiology, cert. added qualifications pediat. radiology. Intern in pediatrics Mt. Sinai Hosp., N.Y.C., 1971-72, resident in pediatrics, 1972-73; resident in radiology St. Luke's Children's Mercy Hosp., Kansas City, Mo., 1973-76; asst. prof. radiology U. Mo., 1976-79, Harvard U. Med. Sch., Cambridge, Mass., 1979-81; fellow in pediatric radiology Children's Hosp., Boston, 1979-81; asst. prof. radiology Columbia Coll. Physicians & Surgeons, N.Y.C., 1981-88, assoc. prof. radiology, 1988-93; assoc. attending radiologist Babies Hosp. Columbia Presbyn. Med. Ctr., N.Y.C., 1981-93, dep. dir. Div. Pediatric Radiology, 1992-93; assoc. prof. radiology Med. Coll. Cornell U., Ithaca, N.Y., 1993—; assoc. attending radiologist, assoc. mem. Mem. Sloan-Kettering Cancer Ctr. Mem. Hosp., N.Y.C., 1993—; mem. radiology elective program Columbia U. Med. Sch., N.Y.C., 1981-93, radiology residency program reevaluation, 1984-93, program coord. affiliated hosps. teaching program, 1991-93, med. student advisor, 1991-93; mem. faculty coun. Columbia U., 1987-93; cons. in pediatric radiology Blythedale Children's Hosp., 1982—, Bet Israel Hosp.,

N.Y.C., 1983—, Harlem Hosp., N.Y.C., 1983—, N.Y. Foundling Hosp., 1988—, Lenox Hill Hosp., 1990—, Morristown Meml. Hosp., 1990—; lectr., presenter in field. Contbr. over 40 articles to profl. jours., chpts. to books. Named Radiology Tchr. of Yr., Columbia Coll. Physicians and Surgeons, 1992. Fellow Am. Coll. Radiology (del. N.Y. chpt. 1991—, alt. del. 1984-91); mem. AMA, Soc. for Pediat. Radiology, Radiology Soc. N.Am., European Soc. for Pediat. Radiology, Soc. Thoracic Radiology, Am. Assn. Ultrasound in Medicine, Am. Assn. Women in Radiology, N.Y. Roentgen Soc. (sec.-treas. 1991-94, v.p. 1996-97, pres.-elect 1997-98, pres. 1998—, moderator, pediat. program chair spring conf. 1991, guest lectr. spring conf. 1990-97), Nat. Children's Cancer Study Group, Caffey Soc., Neuhauser Soc., Kirkpatrick Soc. Office: Sloan-Kettering Cancer Ctr 1175 York Ave New York NY 10021-7169

ABRAMSON, STEPHANIE W., lawyer; b. Dec. 24, 1944. BA, Radcliffe Coll., 1966; JD, NYU, 1969. Bar: N.Y. 1969. Mem. Morgan, Lewis & Bockius, N.Y.C.; Exec Vice Pres & Gen Counsel Young & Rubicam Inc, N.Y.C. Office: Young & Rubicam Inc 285 Madison Ave New York NY 10017-6486*

ABRAVANEL, ALLAN RAY, lawyer; b. N.Y.C., Mar. 11, 1947; s. Leon and Sydelle (Berenson) A.; m. Susan Ava Paikin, Dec. 28, 1971; children: Karen, David. BA magna cum laude, Yale U., 1968; JD cum laude, Harvard U., 1971. Bar: N.Y. 1972, Oreg. 1976. Assoc. Paul, Weiss, Rifkind, Wharton & Garrison, N.Y.C., 1971-72, 74-76; fellow Internat. Legal Ctr., Lima, Peru, 1972-74; from assoc. to ptnr. Stoel, Rives, Boley, Fraser & Wyse, Portland, Oreg., 1976-83; ptnr. Perkins Coie, Portland, 1983—. Editor, pub. Abravanel Family Newsletter. Mem., dep. chair Oreg. Internat. Trade Com., Oreg. Dist. Export Coun. Mem. ABA, Portland Met. C. of C. Office: Perkins Coie 1211 SW 5th Ave Portland OR 97204-3713

ABREU, SUE HUDSON, physician, army officer; b. Indpls., May 24, 1956; d. M.B. Hudson and Wilma (Jones) Hudson Black. BS in Engring., Purdue U., 1978; MD, Uniformed Services U., 1982. Grad. U.S. Army Command & Gen. Staff Coll, 1988, Armed Forces Staff Coll., 1990. Commd. 2d lt. U.S. Army, 1978, advanced to lt. col., 1993; intern Walter Reed Army Med. Ctr., Washington, 1982-83, resident in diagnostic radiology, 1983-85, fellow in nuclear medicine, 1985-87, staff nuclear medicine physician, 1987-88, med. rsch. fellow, 1988-89, chief nuclear medicine svc., 1990-96; chief dept. radiology Womack Army Med. Ctr., Ft. Bragg, N.C., 1991-92, 96-98; med. dir. quality assurance, 1998—. Fellow Am. Coll. Nuclear Physicians; mem. Am. Coll. Radiology, Soc. Nuclear Medicine, Soc. Women Engrs., Am. Soc. Nuclear Cardiology, U.S. Parachute Assn., Tau Beta Pi, Omicron Delta Kappa, Phi Kappa Phi. Avocations: calligraphy, parachuting. Home: 613 Saddlebred Ln Raeford NC 28376-5535 Office: Quality Svcs Divsn Womack Army Med Ctr Fort Bragg NC 28307

ABROMSON, IRVING JOEL, financial services professional; b. Lewiston, Maine, Aug. 15, 1938; s. John and Ada (Meltzer) A.; m. Linda Joan Elowitch, Aug. 23, 1959; children: Lori Abromson Yohann, Leslie Abromson Sherman, Eric. AB, Bowdoin Coll., 1960. Registered rep. Nat. Assn. Securities Dealers. From sales rep. to pres. Maine Rubber Internat., Westbrook, Maine, 1960-85; pres. InterTrade Corp., South Portland, Maine, 1986-88; nat. mktg. dir. Cumberland Advisors, Inc., Vineland, N.J., 1988-91, sr. assoc., 1991—; senator State of Maine, 1994—; mem. Boston Dist. Export Coun., 1982-92, Maine Gov.'s Adv. Com. on World Trade, Augusta, 1986-92. Chmn. Combined Jewish Appeal, Portland, Maine, 1968; nat. chmn. Young Leadership Cabinet, United Jewish Appeal, N.Y.C., 1976; mem. Portland Com. on Fgn. Rels., 1980-97; trustee, corporator Maine Med. Ctr.; mem. exec com. Spurwink Sch., Portland, 1988-92; trustee, pres., 1987-88; corporator Girls and Boys Club Greater Portland, pres. 1975; pres., alumni coun. Bowdoin Coll. Alumni Coun., 1985-86, chmn. alumni fund, 1992, overseer, 1994-97, trustee, 1997—. Recipient Israel Leadership award State of Israel Bonds, 1966, Herbert Lehman Young Leadership award Nat. United Jewish Appeal, 1977, E award for exporting Pres. of U.S. and Dept. Commerce, 1977, Operation Moses award Jewish Fedn. Portland, 1985, Golden Boy award Girls and Boys Club Greater Portland, 1975, bronze keystone Boys Clubs Am., 1986, Alumni Svc. award Bowdoin Coll., 1993. Republican. Jewish. Avocations: photography, golf, travel.

ABSHER, DAN, construction executive; b. Apr. 30, 1958. BA in Polit. Sci., Stanford U., 1980; JD, U. Notre Dame, 1983. Pvt. practice, 1983-85; corp. atty. Absher Constrn. Co., Puyallup, 1985-90, pres., 1990—; mediator Pierce County Small Claims Ct., 1987-89. Asst. basketball coach Mercer Island H.S., 1984-90; youth group leader St. Andrew's Cath. Ch., 1985-89, group facilitator, 1992-95; mem. Supt. Pub. Instrns. Sch. Facility Cost Adv. Bd., 1993-96. Mem. Wash. State Bar Assn. (pub. procurement and pvt. constrn. law sect.), Tacoma/Pierce County Bar Assn. (bd. mem. young lawyers divsn. 1989-91, sec. young lawyers divsn. 1990), Associated Gen. Contractors Wash. (union negotiating team 1986—, chair state facilities com. 1990-92, trustee 1990—, chair govt. affairs coun. 1992-94, pres. 1996, Contractor of the Yr. 1991), Am. Arbitration Assn. (arbitrator). Office: Absher Constrn Co 1001 Shaw Rd Puyallup WA 98372

ABSHIRE, DAVID MANKER, diplomat, research executive; b. Chattanooga, Apr. 11, 1926; s. James Ernest and Phyllis (Patten) A.; m. Carolyn Lamar Sample, Sept. 7, 1957; children: Lupton Patten, Anna Lamra Abshire Bowman, Mary Lee Sample Abshire Jensvold, Phyllis Anderson Abshire d'Hoop, Carolyn. Student, U. Chattanooga, 1945; BS, U.S. Mil. Acad., 1951; PhD, Georgetown U., 1959; DHL, Va. Theol. Sem., 1992; DCL (hon.), U. of the South, 1994. Mem. minority staff U.S. Ho. Reps., 1958-60; dir. spl. projects Am. Enterprise Inst., Washington, 1961-62; from exec. dir. to vice chmn. Center Strategic and Internat. Studies Georgetown U., 1962-99; vice chmn. Center Strategic and Internat. Studies, Georgetown U., 1999—; ambassador, U.S. permanent rep. North Atlantic Council, 1983-87; spl. counsellor to pres. White House, 1987, vice chmn., bd. trustees; pres., CEO Ctr. for the Study of the Presidency, 1999—; asst. sec. state for congl. rels., 1970-73; presdl. appointee Congl. Commn. on Orgn. of Govt. for Conduct of Fgn. Policy, 1973-75; chmn. U.S. Bd. for Internat. Broadcasting, 1974-77; dir. nat. security group Transition Office of Pres.-Elect Reagan, 1980-81; dir. Ogden Corp., 1987-96; mem. adv. bd. BP Am., President's Task Force on U.S. Government Internat. Broadcasting, 1991, bd. Procter and Gamble; adj. prof. Georgetown U., 1973-83,. Author: The South Rejects a Prophet: The Life of Senator D.M. Key, 1967, International Broadcasting: A New Dimension of Western Diplomacy, 1976, Foreign Policy Makers: President vs. Congress, 1979, The Growing Power of Congress, 1981, Preventing World War III: A Realistic Grand Strategy, 1988, (with others) Detente, 1965, Vietnam Legacy, 1976, The Global Economy, 1990; editor: National Security, 1963, Portuguese Africa, 1969, Research Resources for the Seventies, 1971; co-editor Washington Quar., 1977-83; co-author: Putting America's House in Order, 1996. Mem. adv. bd. Naval War Coll., 1975-79; vice-chmn. bd. Youth for Understanding, 1979-80; trustee Baylor Sch., 1980—; mem. Pres.'s Fgn. Intelligence Adv. Bd., 1981-83; bd. dirs. Spaak Found. (Brussels). With AUS, 1945-46; 1st lt. 1951-56; capt. Res. ret. Decorated Bronze Star with oak leaf cluster, with V for Valor, V commendation ribbon with metal pendant; Order of Crown, comdr. Order of Leopold (Belgium); grand ofcl. Order of Republic of Italy; recipient medal of Pres. of Italian Republic, Senate, Parliament and Govt. and of Pio Manzu Ctr.; recipient John Carroll award, Dept. Def. disting. pub. svc. medal, 1988, Presdl. Citizens medal, 1989, medal of diplomatic merit Republic of Korea, 1993; First Class Order of The Lion of Finland insignia of the Comdr., 1994, U.S. Military Acad. Castle award, 1994. Mem. Coun. Am. Ambs., Coun. on Competitiveness, Coun. Fgn. Rels., Inst. Strategic Studies, Trinity Nat. Leadership Roundtable (co-founder), Gold Key Soc., Alfalfa Club, Met. Club, Cosmos Club, Alibi Club, Phi Alpha Theta. Republican. Episcopalian. Home: 311 S St Asaph St Alexandria VA 22314-3745 Office: Ctr Strategic & Internat Studies 1800 K St NW Ste 400 Washington DC 20006-2202

ABSTON, DUNBAR, JR., management executive; b. Memphis, Jan. 26, 1931; s. Dunbar and Esther (Cook) A.; m. Constance Condon, Apr. 29, 1978; children—Lauri Abston Arnold, Dunbar III, Linda Abston Larsen, Frank Norfleet; stepchildren—Selden Early Popwell, Martha McKellar Early, William Cole Early III, Elizabeth Early Gore. AB, Princeton U., 1953; MBA, Harvard U., 1955; M.Phil., Oxford U., 1989. Joined Parts Inc., Memphis, 1959, chmn., 1979; pres. parent co. Parts Industries Corp., Memphis, 1981-83, pres., chief exec. officer, 1983-87; pres., proprieter Abston Mgmt. Co., Memphis, 1987—; pres. Tract-O-Land Plantation; ptnr. Abston Farms, Lake Coromorant, Miss., Abston-Norfleet Realty Co., Memphis. Past chmn. Memphis Symphony Orch., Memphis Plough Community Found.; trustee Rhodes Coll., Lawrenceville Sch. Baker scholar Harvard U., 1954. Mem. Automotive Warehouse Distbrs. Assn. (past chmn.), Memphis Econ. Club (past chmn.), Phi Beta Kappa. Republican. Presbyterian. Home: 228 E Chickasaw Pky Memphis TN 38111-2536 Office: Abston Mgmt Co 4727 Spottswood Ave Memphis TN 38117-4818

ABT, CLARK C., social scientist, executive, engineer, publisher, educator; b. Cologne, Germany, Aug. 31, 1929; came to U.S., 1937, naturalized, 1945; m. Wendy Peter, Nov. 3, 1971; children: Thomas, Emily. BS, MIT, 1951, PhD, 1965; MA, Johns Hopkins U., 1952. Instr. Johns Hopkins U., Balt., 1951-52; mgr. advanced systems dept. Raytheon Co., Bedford, Mass., 1957-64; pres., treas. Abt Assocs., Inc., Cambridge, Mass., 1965-86, chmn., 1986—; pres., publisher Abt Books Inc., Cambridge, 1987-94; prof., dir. Ctr. for Study of Small States Boston U., 1991-93, rsch. prof. internat. rels., 1991-94, dir. Def. Tech. Conversions Ctr., 1993-96; vis. lectr. Harvard U., 1968-69; vis. prof. SUNY, Binghamton, 1975-76; adj. prof. mgmt. U. Mass., 1991-93; dir. Russian Am. Boston Workshop on Def. Tech. Conversion, 1992, dir. Moscow Workshop, 1993; faculty dir. Moscow Entrepreneurial Workshop, 1993, 95; assoc. Ctr. for Sci. and Internat. Affairs Harvard U., 1991—. Author: Serious Games, 1970, The Evaluation of Social Programs, 1977, The Social Audit for Management, 1977, Applied Research for Social Policy: The U.S. and the Federal Republic of Germany Compared, 1978, Costs and Benefits of Applied Social Research, 1979, A Strategy for Terminating a Nuclear War, 1985, AIDS and the Courts, 1990, Drugs and Crime CD-ROM Library, 1990, International Drug Library CD-ROM, 1990, National Portrait Gallery Permanent Collection of Notable Americans on CD-ROM, 1990, others. Served with USAF, 1952-57. Recipient grand prize Thoreau award for landscape architecture, 1975. Clubs: Cosmos, MIT of Boston. Home: 19 Follen St Cambridge MA 02138-3502 also: Abt Assocs Inc 55 Wheeler St Cambridge MA 02138-1192

ABT, JEFFREY, art and art history educator, artist, writer; b. Kansas City, Mo., Feb. 27, 1949; s. Arthur and Lottie (Weinman) A.; m. Mary Kathleen Paquette, July 16, 1972; children: Uriel, Danya. BFA, Drake U., 1971, MFA, 1977. Curator collections Wichita (Kans.) Art Mus., 1977-78; gen. mgr. Billy Hork Galleries, Ltd., Chgo., 1978-80; exhbns. coordinator U. Chgo. Libr., 1980-86; asst. dir. David & Alfred Smart Gallery, U. Chgo., 1986-87, acting dir., 1987-89; assoc. prof. dept. art and art history Wayne State U., Detroit, 1989—, dept. chair, 1989-94, mem. adv. bd. Humanities Ctr., 1993-95. Author: exhbn. catalogues The Printer's Craft, 1982, The Book Made Art, 1986; one-man shows include Cliff Dwellers, 1997, Cary Gallery, 1998; editor ann. Book and Paper Group Am. Inst. for Conservation, 1985-86; mem. editl. bd. Wayne State U. Press, 1990-96, chmn. editl. bd., 1996—; illustrator: Water: Sheba's Story, 1997; contbr. articles and book revs. to profl. jours., chpts. to books and encys. Bd. dirs. Hyde Pk. Jewish Comty. Ctr., Chgo., 1988-89, Detroit Artists Market, 1994—, sec., 1996-99, pres. and chmn. bd. dirs., 1999—; trustee Ragdale Found., Lake Forest, Ill., 1985—; mem. intercultural programs com., 1990-92, libr. adv. com., 1990-96, Detroit Inst. Arts, mem. edn. adv. com., 1992-95; mem. visual arts com. Detroit Festival of the Arts, 1989-92; juror numerous art exhbns., 1986—. Recipient numerous purchase prizes, awards and commns. for artistic work, 1974—; Hebrew Union Coll.-Jewish Inst. Religion fellow, Jerusalem, 1971-72; grantee IMS, NEA, NEH, Rockefeller Archive Ctr., Rockefeller U., Logan Found., Wayne State U. Humanities Ctr., Kaufman Meml. Trust. Mem. Am. Assn. Mus., Coll. Art Assn. Office: Wayne State U Dept Art and Art History 150 Art Bldg Detroit MI 48202

ABT, RALPH EDWIN, lawyer; b. Chgo., Apr. 9, 1960; s. Wendel Peter and Hedi Lucie (Wieder) A. BA, Loyola U., Chgo., 1982; JD, John Marshall Law Sch., Chgo., 1987. Bar: Ill. 1987, U.S. Dist. Ct. (no. dist.) Ill. 1987, U.S. Ct. Appeals (7th cir.) Ill. 1988. Pvt. practice Chgo., 1987-88; staff atty. Sec. of State's Office, Chgo., 1988-95, Ill. Dept. Pub. Aid, Chgo., 1995—. Poll watcher, Chgo., 1981, 83, precinct capt., 1983, 93—. Mem. ABA, Ill. Bar Assn., Chgo. Bar Assn., Trade Law Assn. (charter mem., chmn. charter membership drive 1986), Phi Alpha Delta. Lutheran. Avocations: reading, tennis, bicycling, weight lifting. Home: 5067 W Balmoral Ave Chicago IL 60630-1547 Office: Ill Dept Pub Aid 32 W Randolph St Chicago IL 60601-3405

ABT, SYLVIA HEDY, dentist; b. Chgo., Oct. 7, 1957; d. Wendel Peter and Hedi Lucie (Wieder) A. Student, Loyola U., Chgo., 1975-77; cert. dental hygiene, Loyola U., Maywood, Ill., 1979, DDS, 1983. Registered dental hygienist. Dental asst. Office Dr. Baran and Dr. O'Neill, DDS, Chgo., 1977-78; dental hygienist Drs. Spiro, Sudakoff, Kadens, Weidman, DDS, Skokie, Ill., 1979-83, Dr. Laudando, DiFranco, Rosemont, Ill., 1980-83; gen. practice dentistry Chgo., 1983—. Vol. Community Health Rotations, VA Hosps., grammar schs., convalescent ctrs., mental health ctrs., Maywood, Ill. and Chgo., 1978-82. Recipient 1st Pl. award St. Apollonia Art Show Loyola U., 1982. Mem. ADA, PETA, Ill. Dental Soc., Chgo. Dental Soc., Loyola Dental Alumni Assn. (golf outing registration chmn. 1987, awards in golf and tennis 1987), Ill. Dentists 99th Club (legis. interest com.), Psi Omega (historian, editor Kappa chpt.). Avocations: art, singing, dancing, bicycling, jogging. Office: 6509 W Higgins Ave Chicago IL 60656-2204

ABTS, HENRY WILLIAM, banker; b. Columbus, Nebr., July 3, 1918; s. Matthew C. and Irene (Xanders) A.; m. Virginia Lung, Nov. 7, 1942; children: Bruce M., Susan A. (Mrs. J. Farnham). B.S., Butler U., 1941. Asst. mgr. indsl. relations Union Carbide Co., Kokomo, Ind., 1945-54; personnel mgr. Union Carbide Co., N.Y.C., 1954-56; dir. indsl. relations Union Carbide Co., South Charleston, W.Va., 1956-60; v.p. personnel Cummins Engine Co., Inc., Columbus, Ind., 1960-68; v.p. adminstrn., sec. Cummins Engine Co., Inc., 1968-82, ret., 1982; v.p. Columbus Bank and Trust, 1982-87, pres., chief exec. officer, 1987-88; ret., 1988; mem. regional adv. bd. Liberty Mut. Ins. Co. Served to capt. USAAF, 1941-45. Recipient Disting. Alumnus award Butler U., 1981; named Outstanding Young Man Kokomo Jr. C. of C., 1951, Boss of Year Columbus Jr. C. of C., 1963, Athletic Hall of Fame, Butler U., 1963. Mem. Ind. C. of C., Ind. Golf Assn. (past pres., dir.), Phi Delta Theta. Mem. Christian Ch. Clubs: Otter Creek Golf (past pres.), Harrison Lakes Country (past pres.); Columbus Rotary (past pres.). Home: 9544 Raintree Dr S Columbus IN 47201-4817

ABUALSAMID, AHMAD ZUHAIR, software scientist, researcher; b. Irbid, Jordan, Aug. 15, 1970; came to U.S., 1992; s. Zuhair A. and Hayat I. (Issa) A. BSc in Elec. Engring., Jordan U. Sci. and Tech., Irbid, 1991; MSc in Elec. Engring., U. Wis., 1993, 94, postgrad., 1994—. R & D engr. Gen. Computers and Electronics, Amman, Jordan, 1991-92; advanced computing specialist U. Wis., Madison, 1992-96, dir. model advanced facility, 1996-97; R & D team leader EPIC Systems Corp., Madison, 1997—; COO Coffee Computing Corp., Madison, 1995—. Contbr. articles to profl. jours., confs. in field. Moslem. Avocations: golf, racquetball, software development, reading. Office: EPIC Systems Corp 5301 Tokay Blvd Madison WI 53711-1027

ABUBAKR, SAID MOHAMMED, chemical engineering educator; b. Irbid, Jordan, Sept. 23, 1948; came to U.S., 1977; s. Abdellatif and Khaireh (Hrais) A.; m. Doha M. Serieh, Jan. 24, 1984; children: Haniene, Tamer, Maher, Majdy. BS in Petroleum Engring., Moscow Inst. Petrochems., 1974; MSChemE, Mich. State U., 1981, PhD in Chem. Engring., 1982. Prodn. engr. Jordan Petroleum Refinery, Zarga, 1974-77; instr. Mich. State U., East Lansing, 1977-82; asst. prof. Yarmouk U., Irbid, 1982-84; asst. prof. U. Wis., Stevens Point, 1984-87, from assoc. prof. to prof., 1987-93; project leader USDA Forest Products Lab., Madison, Wis., 1993—; mem. adv. bd. U. Wis.-Stevens Point Gesell Inst., 1988-93, U. Wis.-Stevens Point, 1993—. Editor: Anthology of Paper Recycling, 1996; contbr. more than 100 sci. papers to profl. publs., author/co-author four books. Recipient Tchg. Excellence award U. Wis., 1987, Sec.'s Honor award USDA, 1995-97, Tech. Transfer award Forest Svc. Chief, 1997. Fellow TAPPI (mem. divsn. coun. forestry bd. 1997—, vice chair fiber recycling 1997—); mem. AIChE. Achievements include research in area of paper recycling and removal of contaminants from recycled paper using enzymatic deinking, fiber loading and fractionation; inventions in field. Office: USDA Forest Products Lab One Gifford Pinchot Dr Madison WI 53705

ABUL-HAJ, SULEIMAN KAHIL, pathologist; b. Palestine, Apr. 20, 1925; came to U.S., 1946, naturalized, 1955; s. Sheik Khalil and S. Buteina (Oda) Abul-H.; m. Elizabeth Abood, Feb. 11, 1948; children: Charles, Alan, Cary. BS, U. Calif. at Berkeley, 1949; M.S. at San Francisco, U. Calif., 1951, MD, 1955. Intern Cook County Hosp., Chgo., 1955-56; resident U. Calif. Hosp., San Francisco, 1949, Brooke Gen Hosp., 1957-59; chief clin. and anatomic pathology Walter Reed Army Hosp., Washington, 1959-62; assoc. prof. U. So. Calif. Sch. Medicine, Los Angeles, 1963-69; sr. surg. pathologist L.A. County Gen. Hosp., 1963; dir. dept. pathology Cmty. Meml. Hosp., Ventura, Calif., 1964-80, Gen. Hosp. Ventura County, 1966-74; dir. Pathology Service Med. Group, 1970—; cons. Calif. Tumor tissue Registry, 1962-96, Camarillo State Hosp., 1964-70, Tripler Gen. Hosp., Hawaii, 1963-67, Armed Forces Inst. Pathology, 1960-69. Contbr. articles to profl. jours. Bd. dirs. Tri-Counties Blood Bank, Am. Cancer Soc. Served to maj., M.C., U.S. Army, 1956-62. Recipient Borden award Calif. Honor Soc., 1949; Achievement cert. Surgeon Gen. Army, 1962. Fellow Am. Soc. Clin. Pathogists, Coll. Am. Pathologist; mem. Internat. Coll. Srgeons, World Affairs Coun. Achievements include research in cardiovascular disease, endocrine, renal, skin diseases, also cancer. Home and Office: 105 Encinal Way Ventura CA 93001-3317

ABU-LUGHOD, JANET LIPPMAN, sociologist, educator; b. Newark, Aug. 3, 1928; d. Irving O. and Tessie Lippman; m. Ibrahim Abu-Lughod, Dec. 8, 1951 (div. 1992); children: Lila, Mariam, Deena, Jawad. BA, U. Chgo., 1947, MA, 1950; PhD (NSF fellow), U. Mass., 1966. Dir. research Am. Soc. Planning Ofcls., 1950-52; sociologist-cons. Am. Council to Improve Our Neighborhoods, 1953-57; asst. prof. sociology Am. U., Cairo, 1958-60, Smith Coll., 1963-66; assoc. prof. Northwestern U., Evanston, Ill., 1967-71; prof. sociology, urban affairs Northwestern U., 1971-87, dir. comparative urban studies program, 1974-77, dir. urban studies program, 1984-87; emerita, 1987; prof. sociology Grad. Faculty The New Sch. for Social Research, N.Y.C., 1986-98; dir. Rsch. Ctr. on Lower Manhattan, N.Y.C., 1988-91, chmn. dept. of sociology, 1990-92; emerita, 1999; cons. UN, 1971—, UNESCO, 1979-80. Author: (with Nelson Foote, others) Housing Choices and Constraints, 1960, Cairo-1001 Years of the City Victorious, 1971, (with Richard Hay, Jr.) Third World Urbanization, 1977, Rabat: Urban Apartheid in Morocco, 1980, Before European Hegemony, 1989, Changing Cities, 1991, From Urban Village to East Village, 1994, New York, Chicago, Los Angeles, 1999, Sociology For the 21st Century, 1999; contbr. chpts. to books, articles, revs. to profl. jours.; also monographs. Radcliffe Inst. scholar, 1963-64; Ford Faculty fellow, 1971-72, Simon Guggenheim fellow, 1976-77, NEH fellow, 1977-78, ACLS fellow, 1994; Getty Sr. scholar, 1994-96; H.F. Guggenheim fellow, 1997-98. Mem. Internat. Sociol. Assn., Am. Sociol. Assn. (governing coun. 1994-97, Robert and Helen Lynd award for disting. career achievement in urban sociology 1999), Phi Beta Kappa. Office: New Sch for Social Rsch Grad Faculty 65 5th Ave New York NY 10003-3089

ABU-MOSTAFA, AYMAN SAID, computer consultant; b. Giza, Egypt, June 1, 1953; came to U.S., 1978; s. Said S. Abu-Mostafa and Faiza A. Ibrahim. BME, Cairo U., 1976; MS in Mech. and Aerospace Engring., Okla. State U., 1980, PhD, 1984. Tchg. asst. Cairo U., Giza, Egypt, 1978; tchg. asst. Okla. State U., Stillwater, 1978-79, rsch. assoc., 1979-81; software engr. SEAM Internat. Corp., Palos Verdes, Calif., 1984-87; computing and networking cons. Calif. State U., Los Alamitos, 1987-92; sr. sys. analyst Allied Signal Aerospace, Torrance, Calif., 1992-93; pres., CEO NeuroDollars, Inc., Huntington Beach, Calif., 1993-97; sr. program analyst Softnet Systems, Irvine, Calif., 1997—. Author papers, articles in field. Undergrad. fellow Ministry of Higher Edn., Cairo, 1971, 72, 76; NASA/Ames grantee, 1979-81. Mem. AIAA, IEEE, Assn. for Computing Machinery. Avocations: reading, computers, languages, music. Office: Softnet Systems 18662 Macarthur Blvd Ste 300 Irvine CA 92612-1215

ABUT, CHARLES C., lawyer; b. Jan. 11, 1944. BA, Columbia U., 1969; JD, Cornell U., 1972. Bar: N.J. 1972, U.S. Supreme Ct. 1976, D.C. 1979, N.Y. 1980; cert. matrimonial atty. Assoc. Hannoch & Weisman, Newark, 1972-74; arbitrator Am. Arbitration Assn., 1978—; lectr. Inst. CLE, 1989-98. Author: Celebrity Goodwill, 1989. With Mil. Police, U.S. Army, 1964-67. Fellow Am. Acad. Matrimonial Attys.; mem. ABA, ATLA, N.J. Trial Lawyers Assn., Masons, Psi Upsilon. E-mail: ccaesq@counsel.com. Office: 1 Executive Dr Fort Lee NJ 07024-3309

ABUZAAKOUK, ALY RAMADAN, publishing executive; b. Misurata, Libya, Sept. 12, 1942; came to U.S., 1977; s. Ramadan Khalil and Umm Khatirha A. (Balam) A.; m. Fawzia Faraj Al Nahly, July 17, 1972; children: Asmaa, Ahmad, Anas, Aalaa. BA in Journalism, U. Cairo, 1968; MA in Comm., Stanford U., 1971; MA in Middle East Studies, U. Mich., 1980, postgrad., 1977-81. Lectr. Faculty Arts, U. Benghazi, Libya, 1972-76; dir. Internat. Muslim House, Ann Arbor, Mich., 1977-80; pres. New Era Publs., Ann Arbor, 1980-81; dir. info. NSFL, Chgo., 1981-87; dir. publs. Internat. Inst. Islamic Thought, Herndon, Va., 1987-93; publs. mgr. amana publ., Beltsville, Md., 1994-98; exec. dir. Am. Muslim Coun., Washington, 1998—; elected mem. Faculty Arts Acad. Coun., Libya, 1973-75, U. Benghazi Acad. Coun., Libya, 1974-75; chmn. 1st Congress of the Libyan Students in N.Am., 1980; founding mem. Nat. Front for the Salvation of Libya, 1981; pres. N.Am. News Media, Fairfax, Va., 1993. Editor-in-chief: AL INQATH, 1981-86. Mem., founder Nat. Front for the Salvation of Libya, 1980, Libyan League for Human Rights, Geneva, 1990; founder, bd. dirs. Libyan Studies Ctr., Oxford, Eng., Ctr. for Devel. of Mughrib, Montreal, 1994; mem. Amnesty Internat., 1983; mem. Am. Muslim Coun., Washington, 1997-98, exec. dir. 1998—; bd. dirs., v.p. Minaret of Freedm Inst., Bethesda, Md.; bd. dirs. United Assn. for Studies and Rsch., Annandale, Va., 1998—. Mem. Assn. Muslim Social Scientists, Fgn. Press Ctr., bd. dirs. The Minaret of Freedom Inst. Avocations: soccer, swimming, traveling. Fax: 703-425-3280. E-mail: arab@erols.com. Office: North Am News Media PO Box 7148 Fairfax Station VA 22039-7148

ABZUG, MALCOLM, flight mechanics engineer; b. N.Y., Apr. 13, 1920. BS, Mass. Inst. Tech., 1941; MS, Univ. Calif., 1959, PhD, 1962. Asst. aeronautical engr. aircraft lab. U.S. Air Corps, 1941-43; project engr. flight control dept. Sperry Gyroscope Co., 1949-52; aerodyn. engr. stability & control group Douglas Co., 1946048, design specialist, 1952-55, supr., 1955-62; chief astrodyn. br. Missile & Space Systems Divsn., Santa Monica, 1963-64; sr. staff engr. TRW System, Inc., 1962-67; cons., 1976—; cons. Cambridge Univ. Press, 1951-57, guest lectr. Univ. Calif., L.A., 1958; adj. prof. Univ. Southern Calif., 1980-86. Recipient Douglas Aircraft Co. award, 1957, 64. Fellow Am. Inst. Aeronautical & Astronautical; mem. Nat. Acad. Engring. Home: 14951 Camarosa Dr Pacific Palisades CA 90272-4428*

ACAMPORA, RALPH JOSEPH, brokerage firm executive; b. N.Y.C., Oct. 2, 1941; s. Ralph J. and Teresa (Fusco) A. BA, St. Joseph's Sem., Yonkers, N.Y., Iona Coll. With Harris, Upham & Co. (merged with Smith Barney), N.Y.C., 1969-80; sr. v.p., tech. analyst Kidder Peabody & Co., N.Y.C., 1980-90, Prudential Securities, N.Y.C., 1990—; tchr. N.Y. Inst. Fin., 1970—; panelist on TV show Wall St. Week with Louis Rukeyser. Mem. Market Technicians Assn. (chartered, founder 1970s, pres. 1979-80, founder assn. libr. 1975, hon. award 1987), Internat. Fedn. Technician Analysts (founder, former and first chmn. 1986-92), N.Y. Soc. Security Analysts (bd. dirs.). Republican. Roman Catholic. Avocation: study of World War II. Home: 350 Albany St Ph 1 New York NY 10280-1415 Office: Prudential Securities 1 New York Plz New York NY 10004-1901

ACCARDI, JAMES ROY, prosecutor; b. Berea, Ohio, Aug. 31, 1949; s. Roy R. Accardi; m. Marian Elizabeth Hollon, June 24, 1989; 1 child, Thomas Burns. BS, U. North Ala., 1971; JD, U. Ala., Tuscaloosa, 1974. Bar: Ala. 1974, U.S. Dist. Ct. (no. dist.) 1975, U.S. Ct. Appeals (11th cir.) 1981. Pvt. practice Huntsville, 1980-81; asst. dist. atty. Madison County Office of Dist. Atty., Huntsville, 1974-80, 81-91, chief trial atty., 1991-93, dep. dist. atty., 1993—. Author: The Abridged Significant Historie, 1979, Amber Aspects, 1988, numerous essays and profiles, 1981—. Pres. bd. dirs. Family Svcs. Ctr., Huntsville, 1991-92. Office: Dist Atty Madison County 100 Northside Sq Huntsville AL 35801-4800

ACCARDI, JOSEPH RONALD, accountant; b. Bklyn., July 29, 1960; s. Joseph Anthony and Mary Catherine (Masotti) A.; m. Colette Possert, Oct. 9, 1988; children: Joseph Theodore, Nicolette Barbara. BS, St. John's U.,

1982. CPA N.Y., N.J. Staff acct. Pannell Kerr Forster, N.Y.C., 1982-84; sr. acct. KPMG Peat Marwick, N.Y.C., 1984-87; sr. acct. Siemens Corp., N.Y.C., 1987-90, mgr. fin. acctg., 1990-92; mgr. bus. adminstrn. Siemens Corp., Iselin, N.J., 1992-97; mgr. bus. planning & fin. analysis Siemens Transp. Systems, Inc., Iselin, N.J., 1998—. Mem. AICPA, N.J. State Soc. CPAs, St. John's Alumni Assn., Inst. Mgmt. Accts. Roman Catholic. Avocations: aerobics, football, baseball, music. Home: 315 Church St Woodbridge NJ 07095-2437 Office: Siemens Transp Systems Inc 186 Wood Ave S Iselin NJ 08830-2704

ACCARDO, PASQUALE J., pediatrician, educator; b. Bklyn., Oct. 22, 1943; s. Annunziato and Julia (Vitola) A.; m. Patricia Leahy, June 8, 1968; children: Jennifer, Matthew, Claire. BS, St. John's U., Bklyn., 1965; MD, SUNY, Bklyn., 1969. Intern in pediats. Bklyn.-Cumberland Med. Ctr., 1969-70; resident in pediats. James Whitcomb Riley Hosp. Children, Ind., 1972-74; fellow in devel. pediats. John F. Kennedy Inst., Balt., 1974-76; instr. Johns Hopkins U., Balt., 1976-77, asst. prof., 1977-81; assoc. prof. St. Louis U. Sch. Medicine, 1981-90, prof., 1990-96; prof. N.Y. Med. Coll., Valhalla, 1997—. Author: A Neurodevelopmental Perspective on Specific Learning Disabilities: Monographs in Developmental Pediatrics, vol. 3, 1980, Diagnosis and Detection: The Medical Iconography of sherlock Holmes, 1987, The Medical Almanac: A Calendar of Dates of Significance to the Profession of Medicine including Fascinating Illustrations, Medical Milestones, Dates of Birth and Death of Notable Physicians, Brief Biographical Sketches, Quotations, Assorted Medical curiosities and Trivia, 1992, The Invisible Disability: Understanding Learning Disabilities in the Context of Health and Education, 1996; co-author: Primitive Reflex Profile Monographs in Developmental Pediatrics, vol. 1, 1978, The Pediatrician and the Developmentally Delayed Child: A Clinical Textbook on Mental Retardation, Monographs in Developmental Pediatrics, vol. 2, 1979, Dictionary of Developmental Disabilities: An Interdisciplinary Introduction to Multidisciplinary Terminology, 1996; editor/co-editor: Failure to Thrive in Infancy and Early Childhood: A Multidisciplinary Team Approach, 1982, When A Parent is Mentally Retarded, 1990, Developmental Disabilities in Infancy and Childhood, 1991, Attention Deficit Disorders and Hyperactivity in Children, Monographs in Pediatric Habilitation, vol. 7, 1991, Attention Deficit Disorders and Learning Disabilities, 1994, Developmental Disabilities in Infancy and Childhood, 2 vols., 2d edit., 1996, Behavior Belongs in the Brain, 1997. Capt. USAF, 1970-72. Roman Catholic. Avocations: Sherlockian, Chestertonian, Dantean, Carrollian. Home: 67 Underhill Rd Ossining NY 10562-5103 Office: WIHD/WCMC Main St Valhalla NY 10595

ACCURSO, CATHERINE JOSEPHINE, asset manager; b. Kansas City, Mo., Jan. 3, 1955; d. Anthony Carl and Josephine Blaze (Mancuso) A.; m. Kenneth E. Deffenbaugh; children: Joanna Nicole, Anthony Michael. Assoc. Liberal Arts, Penn Valley Community Coll., Kansas City, 1975; BFA, U. Kans., 1980. Sales Macy's Dept. Store, Kansas City, 1972-82; dept. mgr. Macy's Dept. Store, 1982, dir. bridal registry, 1982-85; asset mgr. Exec. Hills, Inc., Kansas City, 1985-98; pres. Tri-D Concrete, Inc., Blue Springs, Mo., 1992—. Mem. Kansas City Comets Connection (bd. dirs. 1984-87), Nat. Assn. Interior Designers. Avocations: exercise, fashion designing, sewing, reading, dancing. Home: 3300 E 51st Ter Blue Springs MO 64015-3906

ACE, KATHERINE, artist; b. Chgo., Jan. 31, 1953; d. Karl Peak and Evelyn (Schmitt) Zerfoss; m. Brian Corbett, Apr. 25, 1987 (div. 1980); m. Mark Ace, Dec. 10, 1983; 1 child, Corinna. BA cum laude, Knox Coll., 1975. Illustrator, 1979-92; illustrator Women of the American West, Native Am. series, 1983-92, Silver Burdette Composer series; numerous other illustrations for publs.; recipient comms. in field; collections held by U. Oreg., Vintage Plz. Hotel, Portland, Mario's, Seattle, Theoz, Seattle, Ambac Corp., N.Y.C., Children's Hosp., Oakland, Calif., Corestates Fin. of Phila. Bank, Dieber, Lazar, Paccar/Seattle, Stroup, MDPA, Fla., DuPont Pvt. Collection, Fla., Temple Sinai, Oakland; fine arts pub. Pomegranate Pub.-Cards Calendars, Anagrama, Spain. One-woman shows include So. Oreg. State Coll./The OtherArt Gallery, Ashland, 1992, U. Portland, 1993, Stanford U., Palo Alto, Calif., 1993, Shoreline Coll., Seattle, 1993, Paccar Corp., Seattle, 1994, Pacific U., Oreg., 1995, Grants Pass Mus. Art, 1994, Oreg. Sch. Art and Craft, 1994, Cultural Forum U. Oreg., Eugene, 1995, Maude Kerns Art Ctr., 1995, Acanthus Gallery, 1995, 97, Phinney Art Ctr., 1996, Portland State U., Green River C.C., Mark Woolley Gallery, Portland, 1997, Cornish Coll. Arts, Seattle, 1998, Seattle, Wash., 1997, Woodside/Braseth, Seattle, 1997, 99, The Cliff Dwellers, Chgo., 1997, Oreg. Health Sci. U., Portland, 1997, Vorpal Gallery, San Francisco, 1997, Cornish Coll. Art, Seattle, 1998, Pacific U., Oreg., 1999; group exhbns. include Parliament for World's Religions, Chgo., 1993, Belleview Art Mus., 1995, Hoyt Nat., 1994, Bumbershoot Seattle, 1995, 96, Whatcom Mus., 1996, Vorpol Gallery, 1997, 98, 99, Maryhill Mus., 1998, 99, Margo Jacobsen, Portland, 1999. Recipient numerous awards in field including Portland Symphony Program Cover, 1997, Student Choice award Seattle U., 1995, Northwest Poets and Artists Calendar runner-up, Bainbridge Island, Wash., 1994, 95, Spirit Echoes Gallery, Austin, Tex., 1992, 1st pla. Invitational Christmas competition, Sacramento Mag., 1987, Grumbacher Gold Medallion award Batavia Soc. Artists 3rd Ann. Nat. Exhbn., Calif., 1985, numerous others. E-mail: katace@europa.com. Studio: 4017 SW 41st Pl Portland OR 97221-3704

ACERRA, MICHELE (MIKE ACERRA), engineering and construction company executive; b. Messina, Italy, Apr. 15, 1937; came to U.S., 1978; s. Luigi and Matilde Mazzullo A.; m. Elena Fino, May 31, 1975; children—Marco Eugenio, Matilde Enrica Jennifer. Dr. Chem. Engring., Politecnico, Milan, Italy, 1962. Vessels designer Foster Wheeler Italiana, Milan, 1962, asst. mgr. drawing office, 1963, project engr., 1963-70, project mgr., 1970-74; pres. Glitsch Italiana, Rome, 1974-78; pres., chief oper. officer, dir. 8 subs. cos. Glitsch, Inc., Dallas, 1978-86; pres., chief exec. officer Foster Wheeler USA Corp., Perryville, N.J., 1986-89; corp. v.p. indsl. and environ. group Foster Wheeler Corp., Perryville, N.J., 1989-94; v.p. Foster Wheeler Energy Internat. Inc., 1994-97; dir. 4 subs.; v.p., mgr. BOC JV Foster Wheeler Power Sys., 1997—; dir. 2 subs. cos. Roman Catholic. Avocations: reading; swimming; gardening; jogging. Office: Foster Wheeler Corp Perryville Corp Park Clinton NJ 08809

ACERS, PATSY PIERCE, financial seminars company executive; b. Muskogee, Okla., Mar. 10, 1933; d. Claude James and Clara B. (Chaney) Pierce; m. Thomas Edward Acers, Apr. 9, 1955 (div. Feb. 1980); children: Alison Ann, Angela Lynn, Ann Pierce, Ashley French. BA, U. Okla., 1955. Tchr. Oklahoma City Pub. Schs., 1955-58; dir. spl. events Am. Cancer Soc., 1980-86, dir. legacies and planned giving, 1983-86; ins. agt. life and health Conn. Mut., Oklahoma City, 1986-90; pres., owner Bag Lady Fin. Svcs., Inc., Oklahoma City, 1987—. Developer slide seminars: Do You Really Want to Be a Bag Lady, 1987, The Bag Lady Returns With Who Do You Trust, 1991, There Is Financial Life for Singles, 1989. Mem. Women Life Underwriters (pres. 1989-90), High Noon Profl. Women (pres. 1990-91), Women's Exec. Network (pres. 1988-89), Million Dollar Round Table, Am. Bus. Women's Assn., Okla. Spkrs. Assn., Nat. Spkrs. Assn., Nat. Leaders Club. Methodist. Avocations: aerobics, movies, canoeing, gardening. Home: 1413 Sims Ave Edmond OK 73013-6355 Office: Bag Lady Fin Seminars Inc PO Box 20213 Oklahoma City OK 73156-0213

ACETO, VINCENT JOHN, librarian, educator; b. Schenectady, N.Y., Feb. 5, 1932; s. Henry and Gilda (Maietta) A.; m. Jean Louise Rasey, Aug. 27, 1955 (div. 1974); children: David, Paul, Andrew; m. Kveta Urbanova, June 16, 1993. AB, SUNY, 1953, MA, 1953; MLS, 1959; postgrad. Case Western Res. U., 1959, 62, 65-66. Tchr., Scotia (N.Y.)-Glenville Ctrl. Schs., 1956-57; high sch. libr. Burnt Hills (N.Y.)-Ballston Lake Ctrl. Schs., 1957-59; library dir. Town Ballston Pub. Libr., Burnt Hills, 1958-60; Fulbright lectr. U. Dacca, East Pakistan, 1964-65; asst. prof. Sch. Libr. Sci., SUNY, Albany, 1959-62, assoc. prof. library sci., 1963-69, prof., 1969—, assoc. dean, 1987-93, interim dean, 1993-95, co-dir. film and TV documentation ctr., 1983—, pres. SUNY-WIDE Faculty Senate, 1995—. Joint editor: Film Lit. Index; contbr. articles to profl. jours. Pres., Filmdex Part II, Inc., 1973-90; library cons. various pub. schs., N.Y. State Edn. Dept., U.S. Dept. Edn., USIA, Govt. Bangladesh, 1965, Govt. Cypress, 1992, 94; dir. U.S. Office Edn. insts. and traineeships; bd. dirs. Freedom Forum, Schenectady, 1970-78, chmn., 1976-78; trustee Shenendehowa Pub. Libr., 1995—, v.p., 1996-97, pres., 1997—. Served with AUS, 1954-56. Collins fellow U. Albany, 1997. Collins fellow, 1997. Mem. ALA, NEA, Pakistan Libr. Assn., East Pakistan Libr. Assn., N.Y. Libr. Assn., Hudson-Mohawk Library Assn. (v.p. 1964-66), Am. Soc. Indexers, Am. Soc. Info. Scis., Soc. Cinema Studies, Idaka Forum, Kappa Phi Kappa, Phi Delta Kappa. Democrat. Unitarian. Office: SUNY System Adminstrn SUNY Plz Albany NY 12246

ACEVEDO, ELIZABETH MORRISON, special education educator; b. Kittanning, Pa., Apr. 22, 1938; d. Thomas L. and Ethel (Morrison) McKelvey; m. Ruben Acevedo, Oct. 11, 1963; children: Thomas B., Samantha Jo Acevedo-Fox, Holly Elizabeth. BA, Muskingum Coll., 1960; MS, Pepperdine U., 1980; postgrad., Claremont Grad. Sch., 1988-90, Azusa-Pacific U. Lifetime credentials in English and spl. edn., Calif., Pa.; credential in resource specialist, Calif.; cert. adminstr., Calif. Tchr. Armstrong Sch. Dist., Ford City, Pa., 1970-77; tchr. Glendora (Calif.) Unified Sch. Dist., 1979-80, resource specialist, 1980-97; adj. prof., field supervisor Grad. Sch. of Edn., Azusa-Pacific U., Azusa, Calif., 1997—; cons. reading program The Acevedo Advantage, Glendora, 1986—. Contbr. articles to profl. jours. Bd. dirs. christian edn. Ch. Brethren, Glendora, 1989—. Grantee Claremont (Calif.) Grad. Sch., 1989. Mem. Assn. Supervision and Curriculum Devel., Calif. Assn. Resource Specialists, Pi Lambda Theta (membership com.). Democrat. Mem. Ch. Brethren. Avocations: reading, jogging, sewing, refinishing antique wood pieces. Home: 643 N Wabash Ave Glendora CA 91741-2116

ACEVEDO-VILA, ANIBAL, state legislator, lawyer; b. Río Piedras, P.R., Feb. 13, 1962; s. Salvador Acevedo-Colón and Elba Vilá; m. Luisa Gándara, June 29, 1987; children: Gabriela, Juan-Carlos. BA, U. P.R., 1982, JD, 1985; LLM, Harvard U., 1987. Law clk. to Hon. Hernández Denton Supreme Ct. of P.R., San Juan, 1985-86; law clk. to Hon. Campbell U.S. Ct. Appeals (1st cir.), Boston, 1987-88; legis. affairs aide Gov. P.R., San Juan, 1989-92; mem. at-large P.R. Ho. of Reps., San Juan, 1993—, ho. minority leader, 1997—; pres. Popular Dem. Party, 1997—. Editor-in-chief Law Jour., U. P.R., 1984-85; columnist El Nuevo Dia, 1993—. Mem. governing bd. Popular Dem. Party, San Juan, 1995—. Mem. P.R. Bar Assn. Avocation: reading. Office: House of Representatives Capitol Bldg San Juan PR 00901

ACHAMPONG, FRANCIS KOFI, law educator, consultant; b. Kumasi, Ghana, Feb. 18, 1955; came to U.S., 1981; s. John Wilberforce and Salome (Mensa) A.; m. Nicole Victoria Blache. LLB, U. Ghana, 1976; LLM, U. London, 1977, PhD, 1981; LLM, Georgetown U., 1985. Bar: N.Y. 1986, Va. 1988, U.S. Dist. Ct. (ea. dist.) Va. 1988, U.S. Ct. Appeals (4th cir.) 1988, U.S. Supreme Ct. 1990. Adj. lectr. George Washington U., Washington, 1981-82; asst. prof. Howard U., Washington, 1981-85; prof. Norfolk (Va.) State U., 1985—, chair dept. entrepreneurial studies, 1998—; of counsel Shelton & Malone, Norfolk, 1998—; cons. Aetna Life & Casualty, Hartford, Conn., 1981-82, Profl. Ins. Assn. of Md., Pa., 1986, Shapiro, Meiselman & Greene, P.C., Rockville, Md., 1987, Crowell & Moring, Washington, 1988, Clark & Stant, Virginia Beach, Va., 1988. Author: Workplace Sexual Harassment, 1999; contbr. articles to profl. jours. Mem. Am. Risk and Ins. Assn., Acad. Legal Studies in Bus. Avocations: gospel music, exercise, reading, movies. FAX: 757-683-2506. Home: 1509 Colebrook Dr Virginia Beach VA 23464-7206 Office: Norfolk State U 2401 Corprew Ave Norfolk VA 23504-3993

ACHATZ, JOHN, lawyer; b. Detroit, Jan. 11, 1948. AB, U. Mich., 1975, JD, 1978. Bar: Mass. 1978, U.S. Dist. Ct. Mass. 1979. Assoc. Brown, Rudnick, Freed & Gesmer, Boston, 1978-85, ptnr., 1986—. Co-author: Massachusetts Condominium Law. Dir. Emmanuel Music Inc., 1993—; trustee Boston Opera Theater, Inc., 1989-93. Office: Brown Rudnick Freed Gesmer 1 Financial Ctr Ste 1802 Boston MA 02111-2600*

ACHAUER, BRUCE MICHAEL, plastic surgeon. MD, Baylor U., 1967. Intern San Francisco Gen. Hosp., 1967-68; resident in gen. surgery U. Calif., Irvine, 1970-74, rsch. in plastic surgery, 1974-76, adj. prof. surgery, 1994—; fellow in plastic surgery Queen Victoria Hosp., East Grinstead, U.K., 1976; pvt. practice U. Calif. Irvine Med. Ctr., Orange, 1977—; mem. staff St. Joseph Hosp., 1977—; mem. active staff Children's Hosp. of Orange County, 1977—; pvt. practice plastic surgery Orange; mem. courtesy staff Med. Ctr. of GGG, 1985—; dir. Am. Bd. Plastic Surgery, 1995—. Fellow Am. Acad. Pediatrics; mem. AMA, Am. Assn. Plastic Surgeons, Am. Cleft Palate Assn., Am. Soc. Surgery of the Hand, Am. Soc. Plastic and Reconstructive Surgeons (sec. ednl. found.). Office: 1140 W La Veta Ave Ste 810 Orange CA 92868-4230

ACHEAMPONG, ROBERT KWABENA, investment consultant; b. Nyakrom, Ghana, Sept. 17, 1962; came to U.S., 1982; s. Yeboa and Hanna (Hayford) A.; m. Dina Cardoso, May 27, 1989; children: Bobby Simao, Celicia Hanna. BSBA, Berea (Ky.) Coll., 1985; MBA, U. Dayton, 1992; postgrad., Case Western Res. U., Cleve., 1995-96. CPA, Ohio. Mgr. trainee Kobacker Cos., Columbus, Ohio, 1985-87; fin. advisor/account rep. Horace Mann Cos., Columbus, 1988-93; agy. mgr./exclusive agt. Allstate Ins. Cos., Columbus, 1992-93; bus. opportunity cons. AT&T Corp., Cleve., 1994-96; mng. cons. Monymax Cons. Group, Cleve., 1995—; adj. faculty Bryant & Stratton Coll., Cleve., 1997—; prin. Acheampong & Assocs., CPAs, Cleve., 1996—. Bus. advisor Minority Owned Bus., Cleve., 1994—; cons. advisor Watoes Outreach Program, Canton, Ohio, 1994—. Recipient Nkrumah Parker Leadership award Berea Coll., 1985. Mem. AICPAs, Ohio Soc. CPAs, N.E. Ohio Soc. CPAs (minority devel. com. 1996—). Avocations: reading, travel. Home: 2121 Brandywine Dr Euclid OH 44143-1614 Office: Moneymax Consulting Group PO Box 43011 Richmond Hts OH 44143-0011

ACHEBE, CHINUA, writer, humanities educator; b. Ogidi, Nigeria, November 16, 1930; s. Isaiah Okafo and Janet N. (Iloegbunam) A.; m. Christie Chinwe Okoli, Sept. 10, 1961; children: Chinelo, Ikechukwu, Chidi, Nwando. Student Univ. Coll., Ibadan, Nigeria, 1948-52; BA, U. London, 1953; DUniv Stirling U., U.K., 1975, Open U., U.K., 1989; DLitt (hon.), Dartmouth Coll., 1972, U. Southampton, Eng., 1975, U. Ife, Nigeria, 1978, U. Nigeria, Nsukka, 1981, U. Kent, Canterbury, Eng., 1982, Mt. Allison U., Sackville, Can., 1984, U. Guelph, Can., 1984, Franklin Pierce Coll., 1985, Ibadan (Nigeria) U., 1989, Skidmore Coll., 1991, CCNY, 1992, Fitchburg State Coll., 1994, DLitt Harvard U., 1996, Binghamton U., 1996, Bates Coll., 1996, Syracuse U., 1997, Brown U., 1998; LLD (hon.), U. Prince Edward Island, Can., 1976, Georgetown U., 1990, Port Harcourt (Nigeria) U., 1991; LHD (hon.), U. Mass., 1977, Westfield Coll., 1989, New Sch. for Social Rsch., 1991, Hobart and William Smith Coll., 1991, Marymount Manhattan Coll., 1991, Colgate U., 1993, Brown U., 1998. Prodr., contr., dir. Nigerian Broadcasting Co., Lagos, 1954-66; sr. rsch. fellow in African studies, U. Nigeria, 1967-72, prof. dept. English, 1976-81, emeritus prof., 1985—; vis. prof. English, U. Mass., Amherst, 1972-75, 88, U. Conn., Storrs, 1975-76, Afro-Am. studies, U. Mass., Amherst, 1987-88; pro-chancellor Anambra State U. of Tech., Enugu, Nigeria, 1986-88; Regents' lectr. UCLA, 1984; dir. Heinemann Ednl. Books (Nigeria) Ltd.; vis. fellow and Ashby lectr. Clare Hall, Cambridge (Eng.) U., 1993. Mem. coun. Lagos (Nigeria) U., 1966; mem. East Ctrl. State Libr. Bd., 1971-72, Anambra State Arts Coun., 1977-79. Recipient Lit. award New Statesman, 1965; Commonwealth Poetry prize, 1973; Rockefeller fellow, 1960-61; UNESCO fellow, 1963. Fellow MLA (hon.), Royal Soc. Lit. (London); mem. Am. Acad. Arts and Letters (hon.), Nonino Risit D'Aur, 1994. Author: (novels) Things Fall Apart, 1958, No Longer at Ease, 1960, Arrow of God, 1964, A Man of the People, 1966, Anthills of the Savannah, 1988; (poetry) Christmas in Biafra, 1975; (short stories) Girls at War, 1972; (essays) Morning Yet on Creation Day, 1975; (children's stories) The Flute, 1978, The Drum, 1978; The Trouble with Nigeria, 1983, Hopes and Impediments-Selected Essays 1965-87, 1988; (essays and poems) Another Africa, 1998. Office: Bard Coll Dept Lang and Lit Annandale On Hudson NY 12504

ACHEE, ROLAND JOSEPH, lawyer; b. New Orleans, Dec. 12, 1922; s. Benjamin Elphege and Marie Josephine (Cazenave) A.; m. Jean Winifred Lant, Feb. 19, 1955; 1 child, Marie Alaine Achee Mayo. BA, Centenary Coll., 1944; JD, La. State U., 1949. Bar: La. 1949, U.S. Dist. Ct. (we. dist.) La. 1950, U.S. Ct. Appeals (5th cir.) 1960. Atty. Rountree, Cox, Guin & Achee, Shreveport, La. Editor-in-chief La. Law Review, 1948-49. Chmn. Selective Svc. Bd. No. 10, Shreveport, 1965. Lt. (j.g.) USNR, 1944-46, PTO. Named Outstanding Asst. City Atty. U.S., Nat. Inst. Mcpl. Officers, 1988. Fellow Am. Coll. Trial Lawyers; mem. ABA, Internat. Assn. Def. Counsel, La. Stat Bar Assn. (past chmn. profl. responsibility, legal ethics adv. com. 1991—), Shreveport Bar Assn. (chmn. ethics com. 1975-77, pres. 1984), Harry V. Booth Inn of Ct. (master of bench), Am. Legion (comdr. 1961), Elks (life, Exalted Ruler 1958), Order of Coif. Home: 182 Bruce Ave Shreveport LA 71105-3711 Office: Rountree Cox Guin & Achee PO Box 1807 400 Travis St Ste 1200 Shreveport LA 71101-5565

ACHENBACH, JAN DREWES, engineering educator, scientist; b. Leeuwarden, Netherlands, Aug. 20, 1935; came to U.S., 1959, naturalized, 1978; s. Johannes and Elizabeth (Schipper) A.; m. Marcia Graham Fee, July 15, 1961. Candidate engr., Tech. U. Delft, 1959; PhD, Stanford U., 1962. Preceptor Columbia U., 1962-63; asst. prof. Northwestern U., Evanston, Ill., 1963, assoc. prof., 1966-69, prof. dept. civil engring., 1969—, Walter P. Murphy prof. civil engring., mech. engring. and applied math., 1981—, dir. Ctr. for Quality Engring. and Failure Prevention, 1986—; vis. assoc. prof. U. Calif., San Diego, 1969; vis. prof. Tech. U. Delft, 1970-71; prof. Huazhong Inst. Sci. and Tech., 1981; mem. at large U.S. Nat. Com. Theoretical and Applied Mechanics, 1972-78, 86—. Author: Wave Propagation in Elastic Solids, 1973, A Theory of Elasticity with Microstructure for Directionally Reinforced Composites, 1975, (with A.K. Gautesen and H. McMaken) Ray Methods for Waves in Elastic Solids, 1982, (with Y. Rajapakse) Solid Mechanics Research for Quantitative Non-Destructive Evaluation, 1987; editor: (with J. Miklowitz) Modern Problems in Elastic Wave Propagation, 1978 (with S.K. Datta and Y.S. Rajapakse) Elastic Waves and Ultrasonic Nondestructive Testing, 1990; editor-in-chief: Wave Motion, 1979—. Recipient award C. Gelderman Found., 1970, C.W. McGraw Rsch. award Am. Soc. Engring. Edn., 1975, Tempo All-Professor Team, Sciences, Chicago Tribune, 1993, Model of Excellence award McDonnell-Douglas, 1996, Disting. Svc. medal Am. Acad. Mechanics, 1997. Fellow AAAS, Am. Acad. Arts Scis., ASME (Timoshenko medal 1992), Acoustical Soc. Am.; mem. IEEE, U.S. Nat. Acad. Scis., Am. Geophys. Union, U.S. Nat. Acad. Engring., Am. Soc. Nondestructive Testing. Home: 711 Roslyn Ter Evanston IL 60201-1721 Office: Northwestern U Room 324 2137 N Sheridan Catalysis Bldg Evanston IL 60208

ACHENBACK, NANCY BANKS, pediatric nurse; b. Balt., Dec. 5, 1931; d. Harry Whittington Jr. and Gladys Rebecca (Lynch) Banks; m. James Richard Achenback, Sept. 19, 1953; children: Donna Achenback Forrester, Juli Achenback Pastrana, Allison Achenback Blackburn. Diploma in nursing, Union Meml. Hosp., Balt., 1953. RN, Md.; cert. pediatric nurse ANCC.; cert. in pediatric advanced life support. Office nurse pvt. doctor's office, Annapolis, Md., 1953-55; nurse pediatic unit Anne Arundel Med. Ctr., Annapolis, 1955—, supr., 1998—. Mem. ethics com. City of Annapolis, 1996—; vol. ASPCA; mem. Anne Arundel Med. Ctr. Aux. Mem. Soc. Pediatric Nusrses, Union Meml. Hosp. Alumni Assn. Democrat. Methodist. Avocations: church activities, cats, her grandchildren, learning to play piano. Home: 225 Gibson Rd Annapolis MD 21401-2224 Office: Anne Arundel Med Ctr Franklin and Cathedral Sts Annapolis MD 21401

ACHENBAUM, ALVIN ALLEN, marketing and management consultant; b. N.Y.C., Dec. 11, 1925; s. Benjamin and Dora (Dworin) A.; m. Barbara Ann Greenwald, June 24, 1951 (dec. Apr. 1992); children: Jonathan Peter, Lisa Jane, Martha Beth; m. Leila Lebendig, June 6, 1994. BS, UCLA, 1950; MS, Columbia U., 1951. Mgr. market rsch. McCann-Erickson, N.Y.C., 1951-57; exec. v.p., sec., dir. Grey Advt., Inc., N.Y.C., 1957-71; exec. v.p. J. Walter Thompson Co., 1971-74; chmn. bd. dirs. Canter, Achenbaum, Assocs., Inc., N.Y.C., 1974-89; vice chmn. bd. dirs. Backer, Spielvogel, Bates Worldwide, N.Y.C., 1989-93; pres. Achenbaum Assocs. Inc., N.Y.C., 1992-95; chmn. Achenbaum Bogda Assocs. Inc., N.Y.C., 1996—; bd. dirs. MARC, Inc. Mem. edit. bd. Jour. Advt. Rsch. Mem. Citizens Adv. Com. of Irvington, 1970—; mem. Middle Eastern affairs com. Anti-Defamation League; adv. com. Assn. Consumer Research.; Trustee Mktg. Sci. Inst. With USAAF, 1944-46. Named to Market Research Hall of Fame. Mem. Market Rsch. Coun. N.Y., Copy Rsch. Coun. N.Y., Am. Mktg. Assn. (v.p. global mktg. div., bd. dirs., found. trustee), Am. Econ. Assn., Assn. Pub. Opinion Rsch., Beta Gamma Sigma. Home: 225 Central Park W New York NY 10024-6026 Office: Achenbaum Bogda Assocs Inc 225 Central Park W Apt 723 New York NY 10024-6033

ACHESON, ALLEN MORROW, retired engineering executive; b. Tanta, Egypt, June 12, 1926; s. Samuel Irvine and Hazel Lenore (Welker) A.; m. Mary Jean Baird, Aug. 5, 1950 (div. May 1978); children: Rebecca R., Jennifer E., Scott A., Jon M.; m. Judith H. Buwalda, May 29, 1983. BS in Mech. Engring., Iowa State U., 1950; LLD, Tarkio Coll., 1985. Registered profl. engr., Mo. Sta. supt. Iowa Pub. Svc. Co., Carroll, 1950-54; engr. Proctor & Gamble Co., 1954-55, Iowa-Ill. Gas & Electric Co., 1955-56; mgr. City Power & Light Co., Independence, Mo., 1956-60; mgmt. adviser Yanhee Electricity Authority, Bangkok, Thailand, 1960-63; exec. v.p. Black & Veatch Internat., Kansas City, Mo., 1964-73, pres., 1973-88, chmn., 1989-91; gen. ptnr. Black & Veatch, Kansas City, Mo., 1974-75; exec. ptnr. Black & Veatch, 1975-91; ret., 1991. Trustee Tarkio (Mo.) Coll., 1964-77, chmn., 1975-77; elder Trinity and Rolling Hills United Presbyn. Ch. With USNR, 1944-46. Recipient Profl. Achievement citation Coll. Engring., Iowa State U., 1976, Marston medal, 1992. Mem. Am. Cons. Engrs. Coun. (chmn. internat. engring. divsn., past pres. award 1992); mem. ASME (life). Home: 224 W 124th St Kansas City MO 64145-1704

ACHESON, DAVID CAMPION, lawyer, author, policy analyst; b. Washington, Nov. 4, 1921; s. Dean G. and Alice (Stanley) A.; m. Patricia Castles, May 1, 1943; children: Eleanor Dean, David Campion, Peter Wesley. BA, Yale U., 1942; LLB, Harvard U., 1948. Bar: D.C., Pa., U.S. Supreme Ct. With Office Gen. Counsel AEC, 1948-49; with firm Covington & Burling, Washington, 1950-61; mem. firm Covington & Burling, 1958-61; U.S. atty. for D.C., 1961-65, spl. asst. to sec. treasury, 1965-67; v.p., sr. v.p., gen. counsel Communications Satellite Corp., 1967-74; ptnr. Jones, Day, Reavis & Pogue, Washington, 1974-78, Drinker Biddle & Reath, Phila. and Washington, 1978-87; bd. dirs. Dulles Access Rapid Transit Inc. Author: (with others) Effective Washington Representation, 1983, Acheson Country: A Memoir, 1993; co-author: (CSIS report) A More Effective Civil Space Program, 1988; editor: This Vast External Realm, 1973, (with David McLellan) Among Friends, 1980. Mem. presdl. commn. on Challenger accident, 1986; pres. Atlantic Coun. U.S., 1993—. Mem. Met. Club. Episcopalian. Home: 2700 Calvert St NW Washington DC 20008-2621 Office: 910 17th St NW Ste 1000 Washington DC 20006-2601

ACHESON, ELEANOR DEAN, federal government official. Asst. atty. gen. Office of Policy Devel., Dept. of Justice, 1993—. Address: Office of Policy Devel Dept of Justice 950 Pennsylvania Ave NW Washington DC 20530-0001*

ACHESON, LOUIS KRUZAN, JR., aerospace engineer and systems analyst; b. Brazil, Ind., Apr. 2, 1926; s. Louis Kruzan and Irene Ruth (Morrison) A.; m. Hyla Armstrong Cook, July 12, 1958; children: Mari Ruth, William Louis. B.S. in E.E., Case Inst. Tech., 1946; Ph.D. in Theoretical Physics, MIT, 1950. Mem. tech. staff Hughes Aircraft Co., L.A., 1950-89, chief scientist systems design lab Space and Communications Group, 1985-89; with Inst. Def. Analyses, Washington, 1958-59. Contbr.: articles to profl. pubs. Mem. AIAA, ISPE, IEEE, Am. Phys. Soc., Mensa, World Federalists, Worldview Exploration Seminar, Unity-and-Diversity Coun., Bertrand Russell Soc., Sigma Xi, Tau Beta Pi, Eta Kappa Nu, Theta Tau (Alumni Hall of Fame), Sigma Chi. Home: 17721 Marcello Pl Encino CA 91316-4328

ACHESON, ROY MALCOLM, epidemiologist, educator; b. Belfast, Ireland, Aug. 18, 1921; emigrated to U.S., 1962, naturalized, 1968; s. Malcolm King and Dorothy (Rennoldson) A.; m. Fiona Marigo O'Brien, Mar. 16, 1950 (div.); children: Malcolm O'Brien, Vincent Rennoldson, Marigo Fiona. BA, Trinity Coll., Dublin, Ireland, 1945, MA, 1949, ScD, 1962; BA, U. Oxford, Eng., 1948, MA, 1951, BM, BChir, 1951, DM, 1954; MA (hon.), Yale U., 1964. Intern, then resident internal medicine Radcliffe Infirmary, Oxford, 1951-55; lectr. social medicine U. Dublin (Ireland), 1955-59; reader social and preventive medicine U. London, Eng., 1959-62; mem. faculty Yale Sch. Medicine, 1962-75, prof. epidemiology, 1964-72; fellow Jonathan Edwards Coll., 1966-75; dir. Center for Tng. in Community Medicine, London (Eng.) Sch. Hygiene and Tropical Medicine, 1972-76; prof. health services studies U. London, 1974-76; prof. community medicine U. Cambridge, Eng.,

1976-88; prof. emeritus U. Cambridge, 1988—; life fellow Churchill Coll., 1976—; R. Samuel McLaughlin vis. prof. in residence Med. Sch. McMaster U., Hamilton, Ont., Can., 1976-77; Mem. expert com. health statistics WHO, 1966; cons., tech. adviser epidemiology and med. edn. Pan-Am. Health Orgn., in Peru, Venezuela, P.R., Argentina, India and Colombia, 1964-82; cons. med. edn. AID, East Pakistan, 1963; cons. epidemiology NIH, 1963-72; mem. nat. adv. com. thrombosis Nat. Heart Inst., 1968-70; mem. epidemiology study sect. Nat. Inst. Gen. Med. Scis., 1970-72; cons. epidemiology WHO, Europe, 1973, adv. health services research, Geneva, 1978-87; mem. Gen. Med. Coun., 1979-89, exec. com., edn. com., 1979-89; mem. Gen. Dental Council, 1984-89, exec. com., 1984; gov. Action in Internat. Medicine, 1988-91. Author: History of Education in Public Health, 1991; also articles in profl. jours., chpts. in book; editor Comparability in International Epidemiology, 1965, Seminars in Community Medicine, Vol. 1, 1976, Vol. 2, 1977, Jour. Epidemiology and Community Health, 1977-89. Served with Brit. Army, 1940-45. Rockefeller traveling fellow medicine, 1955-56; Commonwealth Fund travelling fellow, 1968-69; fellow Trinity Coll., Dublin, 1957-59. Fellow Royal Coll. Physicians (faculty occupational medicine, faculty community medicine, v.p. 1986-89, Eng.), Internat. Epidemiol. Assn. (council 1964-74, gen. sec. 1964-68, ednl. sec. 1968-74). Office: Churchill Coll, Cambridge CB3 ODS, England

ACHGILL, RALPH KENNETH, retired research scientist; b. Indpls., June 17, 1938; s. Kenneth and Lois Ann (Philips) A.; m. Virginia Ann Swisher, July 21, 1956 (dec. Nov. 1992); children: Kenneth Edward, Douglas Alan, Kerry Wayne, Bridget Marie; m. Diane K. McCauley, Dec. 26, 1993. Student, Purdue U., 1956-60. Rsch. scientist Eli Lilly & Co., Indpls., 1956-93, internat. tech. coord., 1974-93; ret., 1993. Patentee in field. Mem. Masons (past master), Optimist Club (charter pres.). Republican. Avocation: philatelic dealer. Home: PO Box 6508 Lafayette IN 47903-6508

ACHINSTEIN, PETER JACOB, philosopher, educator; b. N.Y.C., June 30, 1935; s. Asher and Betty (Comras) A.; children: Jonathan, Sharon, Betty. AB, Harvard, 1956, AM, 1958, PhD, 1961; postgrad. (Knox Traveling fellow), Oxford U., Eng., 1959-60. Asst. prof. U. Iowa, Iowa City, 1961-62; asst. prof. philosophy Johns Hopkins Balt., 1962-64; asso. prof., 1964-68, prof., 1968—, chmn. dept. philosophy, 1968-77; vis. prof. M.I.T., Cambridge, 1965-66, Stanford (Calif.) U., 1967, City U. N.Y., 1973; mem. adv. panel NSF, 1968-70, 79-81; Lady Davis vis. prof. Hebrew U., Jerusalem, spring 1976. Author: Concepts of Science, 1968, Law and Explanation, 1971, The Nature of Explanation, 1983, Particles and Waves: Historical Essays in the Philosophy of Science, 1991 (Lakatos award 1993); editor: (with Stephen Barker) The Legacy of Logical Positivism, 1969, The Concept of Evidence, 1983, (with Laura J. Snyder) Scientific Methods, 1994; mem. editl. bd. Philosophy of Sci., 1973. Guggenheim fellow, 1966-67. Fellow AAAS (chair history and philosophy of sci. sect. L 1995); mem. Philosophy of Sci. Assn. (bd. govs.), Internat. Union History and Philosophy (del. U.S. 1967-73, 79-86), Phi Beta Kappa. Office: Johns Hopkins U Dept Philosophy Baltimore MD 21218

ACHORD, JAMES LEE, gastroenterologist, educator; b. Dayton, Ohio, Sept. 24, 1931; s. Lonnie M. and Ethel E. (Collins) A.; m. Patsy Jane Moore, Dec. 18, 1954; children: J. Michael, Ann Elizabeth, Andrew P. Student, Emory U., 1949-52, MD, 1956. Intern Emory Hosp., 1956-57; resident Emory U., Atlanta, 1959-62, instr., assoc. prof., 1962-71; med. dir. Med. Ctr. Cen. Ga., Macon, 1971-75; assoc. dean, prof. East Tenn. State Sch. Medicine, Johnson City, 1975-76; prof., dir. div. digestive diseases U. Miss. Med. Ctr., Jackson, 1976-98. Editor(book revs.) Am. Jour. Gastroenterology, 1985-91, Dig. Dis. Sci., 1994-96; contbr. numerous articles and editorials to profl. jours. and chpts. to books. Capt. U.S. Army, 1957-59. Fellow ACP (gov. Miss. chpt. 1993-97), Am. Coll. Gastroenterology (pres. 1983-84); mem. Am. Assn. Subspecialty Profs., Am. Assn. Study Liver Disease, Am. Gastroent. Assn., Am. Soc. Gastroenterologic Endoscopy. Office: U Miss Med Ctr 2500 N State St Jackson MS 39216-4500

ACHORN, ROBERT COMEY, retired newspaper publisher; b. Westboro, Mass., Mar. 31, 1922; s. Edward Welt and Mabel (Comey) A.; m. Jean Mary Berlo, Sept. 23, 1950 (dec. 1980); children: Nancy Louise (Mrs. Eric Engberg), Susan Jean, Edward Christopher, Judith Joyce (Mrs. Albert Berry), Carole Lee (Mrs. Ralph Abislaiman); m. Ann Bouvier, Aug. 20, 1982. AB, Brown U., 1943. Reporter Worcester (Mass.) Telegram, 1946-53; editorial writer Evening Gazette, Worcester, 1953-60; mng. editor Evening Gazette, 1964-67; editor editorial pages Worcester Telegram & Gazette, 1964-67, assoc. editor, 1967-70, editor, 1970-73, v.p., editor, 1973-81, assoc. pub., exec. v.p., 1981-82, pub., 1982-87, dir., 1982-88, pres., 1986-87; pres. Beacon Communications Corp., 1984-85, vice chmn., 1985-87; pres. Worcester Telegram & Gazette, Inc., 1985-87; bd. dirs. Bank of Boston-Worcester, 1994-95, Blackstone Valley Regional Devel. Corp., 1991—; mem. newspaper adv. bd. UPI, 1974-78. Pres. United Way Ctrl. Mass., Worcester, 1973-75; v.p. The Meml. Hosp., 1976; vice chmn. Ctr. Mass. chpt. ARC, 1976-84, chmn., 1984-86; media chmn. Mass. Bar-Press Com., 1976-77; chmn. trustees Worcester Found. Exptl. Biology, 1984-87; trustee Old Sturbridge Village, 1986—, U. Mass. Med. Ctr. Found., 1991-98, Sutton Coun. on Aging, 1993—, U. Mass. Meml. Found., 1998—. Fellow Acad. New Eng. Journalists; mem. UPI New Eng. Newspaper Editors (pres. 1969), Am. Soc. Newspaper Editors, New Eng. Newspaper Assn. (pres. 1986-87), New Eng. Soc. Newspaper Editors (pres. 1968), New Eng. AP News Execs. Assn. (pres. 1971), Am. Antiquarian Soc., Soc. Profl. Journalists, Worcester Club, Worcester Econ. Club (pres. 1975), Bohemian Club, Nat. Press Club, St. Wulstan Soc., Phi Beta Kappa.

ACHTEL, ROBERT ANDREW, pediatric cardiologist; b. Bklyn., May 5, 1941; s. Murray and Amelia (Ellian) A.; m. Erica Noel Woods, Mar. 10, 1963; children: Bergen Alison, Roland Hugh. BA, Adelphi U., 1963; MD, U. Cin., 1967. Diplomate Am. Bd. Pediat. Cardiology. Intern Cin. Children's Hosp., 1967-68; resident in pediat. Yale U., 1968-69, fellow in pediat. cardiology, 1969-71; clin. instr. pediat. U. Calif., Davis, 1972-73, clin. asst. prof., 1977-83; asst. prof. U. Ky., 1973-76; dir. pediat. ICU Sutter Meml. Hosp., Sacramento, 1977-85, dir. pediat. cardiology, 1982—, chmn. instl. rev. com., 1981-85, 96—; chmn. dept. pediat. Mercy Hosp., Sacramento, 1981-83, 97—, dir. pediat. ICU, 1982-83, vice chmn. pediat., 1983-85, 95—; dir. Laurel Hills Devel. Ctr., 1985-89; chmn. rsch. com. Sutter Inst. for Med. Rsch., 1989—; trustee, mem. exec. com. Sutler Hosps. Found., vice chmn., 1992-93; vice chmn. CEO Access Care, 1994-95; med. dir. FastServe Med. Group, 1995; vice chmn. dept. pediat. Mercy Hosp., 1995-97, chmn., 1997—; mem. tech. adv. com. pediat. cardiology State of Calif.; CEO Access Care, 1993-97; chmn. regional instl. rev. bd. Sutter/CHS Ctrl., 1996; mem. quality assurance com., mem. pharmacy com. Omni Health Plan; lectr. Mooney Aircraft Pilots Assn., FAA; bd. dirs. Mooney Aircraft Pilots Assn. Safety Found.; mem. FAA Safety Coun., 1997—. Contbr. articles on aviation safety to cassette Pilots Audio Update; contbr. articles on cardiovasc. rsch. to profl. publs.; contbr. monthly editl. to Mooney Airplane Pilots Assn. Log. Bd. dirs. Sutter Meml. Hosp. Found., 1986—; bd. dirs. Sutter Found., 1989, trustee, 1989—. Maj. M.C., USAF, 1971-73. Grantee, U. Ky. Tobacco and Health Fsch. Found. Mem. Am. Heart Assn. (bd. dirs. Sacramento chpt., mem. couns. on congenital heart disease and atherosclerosis and cardiovasc. surgery, grantee), Am. Coll. Chest Physicians, Am. Acad. Pediat., S.W. Pediat. Cardiology Soc., So. Soc. Pediat. Rsch. Office: Perinatal and Pediatric Subspecialist Med Group 5609 J St Ste A Sacramento CA 95819-3948

ACHTENBERG, ROBERTA, former federal official; b. L.A., July 20, 1950; d. Louis and Beatrice A.; 1 child. AB, U. Calif., Berkeley, 1972; postgrad., U. Calif., San Francisco, 1972-73; JD, U. Utah, 1975. Bar: Calif., U.S. Dist. Ct. (no. dist.) Calif., U.S. Ct. Appeals (9th cir.). Exec. dir. Nat. Ctr. Lesbian Rights, 1989-90; of counsel Lilienthal & Fowler, 1991-93, Weller & Drucker, 1992-93; asst. sec. fair housing and equal opportunity HUD, Washington, 1993-95, Sr. Adv. to Sec., 1995—; sr. v.p. pub. policy dept. San Francisco C. of C. Assoc. editor Jour. Contemporary Law. Commr. San Francisco County Transp. Authority; mem. County Bd. Suprs., City and County of San Francisco; bd. dirs. Bay Area Air Quality Mgmt. Dist., 1991-93. Mem. Order of Coir, Phi Beta Kappa. Office: San Francisco C of C Pub Policy Dept 465 California St San Francisco CA 94104*

ACHTERMAN, GAIL LOUISE, lawyer; b. Portland, Oreg., Aug. 1, 1949. AB in Econs. with distinction, Stanford U., 1971; MS in Natural Resource Policy and Mgmt., U. Mich., 1975, JD cum laude, 1974. Bar: Oreg. 1974, U.S. Dist. Ct. Oreg. 1978, U.S. Supreme Ct. 1978, U.S. Ct. Appeals (fed. and 10th cirs.). Atty.-advisor U.S. Dept. Interior, 1975-78; asst. for natural resources Gov. Neil Goldschmidt, 1987-91; mem. Stoel Rives LLP, Portland; adj. prof. Lewis & Clark Law Sch., 1978-83; adj. prof. forest policy, Coll. Forestry, Oreg. State U., 1991-98; adj. prof. pub. adminstrn. Portland State U., 1998—. Mem. Oreg. Water Resources Comm., 1981-85; chair Strategic Water Mgmt. Group, 1987-91, Gov.'s Growth Task Force, 1998. Mem. bd. dirs. Sustainable Ecosystems Inst., Am. Leadership Forum, Oreg. Women's Forum, Portland C. of C. (bd. dirs. 1996—). Office: Stoel Rives LLP 900 SW 5th Ave Ste 2300 Portland OR 97204-1232

ACHUFF, STEPHEN CHARLES, physician; b. St. Louis, Mar. 12, 1943; m. Cary Williams Lipscomb, Dec. 27, 1970; children: Catherine Elise, Jeanne Ann, Charles Walter. BA in Religion, Philosophy, Wesleyan U., 1964; MD, U. Mo., 1969. Diplomate Am. Bd. Internal Medicine, Am. Bd. Cardiovasc., Am. Bd. Med. Examiners. Intern, jr. asst. resident John Hopkins Hosp., 1969-71, fellow medicine, 1971-73, chief resident medicine, 1973-74, asst. dir. Adult Cardia Catheterization Lab., 1975-77, cardiologist Lipid Rsch. Clinic, 1975-84, dir. Adult Cardiology Clin. Program, 1980—; instr. medicine John Hopkins U., 1973-74, from asst. prof. to assoc. prof., 1975-90, prof., 1990—; rsch. fellow Am. Heart Assn., 1971-73; rsch. fellow, hon. sr. registrar dept. cardiology Royal Infirmary Edinburgh, Scotland, 1974-75; mem. adv. bd. John Hopkins U., 1979-80; vis. prof. Guy's Hosp., London, 1990. Mem. editl. bd. Audiovisual Programs Continuing Edn., John Hopkins U., 1976-92; contbr. articles to profl. jours. Recipient Oustanding Grad. award Mo. State Med. Assn., 1969, Pfizer award U. Mo., 1968; USPHS fellow U. Mo., 1966-67. Fellow Am. Coll. Cardiology, Am. Heart Assn. (mem. coun. clin. cardiology 1979, v.p., bd. dirs. 1979-80); mem. Internat. Soc. Heart Tranplantation, Alpha Omega Alpha. Home: 114 Croydon Rd Baltimore MD 21212

ACKELL, EDMUND FERRIS, university president; b. Danbury, Conn., Nov. 29, 1925; s. Ferris M. and Barbara (Elias) A.; m. Judith S. Fox, Oct. 13, 1995. BS, Holy Cross Coll., Worcester, Mass., 1949; DMD, Tufts U., 1953; MD, Case Western Res. U., 1962; postgrad., U. Pa., 1955-57. Intern Bellevue Hosp., N.Y.C., 1962-63; resident Meadowbrook Hosp., 1963-66; pvt. practice medicine, specializing in oral and maxillofacial surgery; prof. medicine and dentistry U. Fla. Med. and Dental Sch., 1966-69; dean Sch. Dentistry, 1966-69, univ. v.p. health affairs, 1969-74; v.p. health affairs U. So. Calif., 1974-78; pres. Va. Commonwealth U., Richmond, 1978-90, pres. emeritus, 1990—; chmn. Keswick Group, Inc., 1997—. Served with USNR, 1943-46. Mem. AMA, ADA, Soc. Health and Human Values, Am. Public Health Assn., Va. Med. Assn., Va. Dental Assn. Clubs: Commonwealth, Country of Va., Keswick. Home: 4098 Wood Ln Keswick VA 22947-2900*

ACKER, ANN, lawyer; b. Chgo., July 21, 1948. BA, St. Mary's Coll.; JD, Loyola U. Bar: Ill. 1973. Mem. Chapman and Cutler, Chgo. Office: Chapman and Cutler 111 W Monroe St Ste 1700 Chicago IL 60603-4006

ACKER, FREDERICK GEORGE, lawyer; b. Defiance, Ohio, May 7, 1934; s. Julius William and Orah Louise (Dowler) A.; m. Cynthia Ann Wayne, Dec. 1, 1962; children: Frederick Wayne, Mary Katherine, Richard Hoghton, Jennifer Ruth. Student, Ind. U., 1952-54; BA, Valparaiso U., 1956; MA, Harvard U., 1957, JD, 1961; postgrad., U. Manchester (Eng.), 1957-58. Bar: Ill. 1961, Ind. 1961. Ptnr. Winston & Strawn, Chgo., 1961-88, McDermott, Will & Emery, Chgo., 1988—; co-chmn. Joint Prin. and Income Act. com., Chgo., 1976-81. Co-author: (portfolio) Generation-Skipping Tax, 1991; contbr. articles to profl. jours. Bd. dirs. Max McGraw Wildlife Found., Dundee, Ill., 1984—, chmn., pres. 1997—; trustee L.S. Wood Ednl. Trust, Chgo., 1975—, The Nature Conservancy Ill. chpt., Chgo., 1981-90; chmn.1986-90). Danforth Found. fellow, 1956; Fulbright scholar, 1957. Fellow Am. Coll. Trust and Estate Counsel; mem. ABA, Ill. Bar Assn., Trout Unlimited, Fulbright Assn. (bd. dirs. 1994—), Met. Chgo. Club, Anglers Club, Chgo. Farmers Club. Lutheran. Avocations: hunting, fishing. Home: 543 N Madison St Hinsdale IL 60521-3213 Office: McDermott Will & Emery 227 W Monroe St Ste 3100 Chicago IL 60606-5096

ACKER, FREDERICK WAYNE, lawyer; b. Chgo., Feb. 28, 1966; s. Frederick George and Cynthia Ann (Wayne) A.; m. Anette Kjeldaas, June 3, 1988; children: Chelsea Kirsten, Ingrid Noelle. BA, St. Olaf Coll., 1988; JD, U. Notre Dame, 1992; Splty. Degree, U. Oslo, Norway, 1993. Bar: Mich. 1993, Ill. 1994, U.S. Dist. Ct. (no. dist.) Ill. 1995, U.S. Ct. Appeals (7th cir.) 1997, U.S. Ct. Appeals (fed. cir.) 1997. Vis. scholar Notre Dame Law Sch., South Bend, Ind., 1993; atty. Stamos & Trucco, Chgo., 1994-98, Hahn, Loeser & Parks, Columbus, OH, 1998—. Author: The MBA and the Magic Lamp, 1994, (novella) The Curse of Agnes Larsen, 1996; columnist Minn. Spectator, 1988-90; mem. Notre Dame Law Rev. Campaign mgr. Gilbertson for Congress, Mpls., 1988, Fintzen for Rep., Geneva, Ill., 1997; pres. Notre Dame Federalist Soc., 1991-92. Thomas J. White scholar, 1989. Mem. ABA, Chgo. Bar Assn. (internat. fgn. law com. 1995-98, comml. fin. and transactions com. 1995-98, YLS intellectual property law com. 1995-98). Republican. Evangelical Christian. Avocations: fiction and editorial writing, Scandinavian languages and history, fishing, theology. Office: Hahn, Loeser & Parks Ste 1800 One Columbus 10 West Broad St Columbus OH 43215

ACKER, JOSEPH EDINGTON, retired cardiology educator; b. Knoxville, Tenn., Oct. 19, 1918; s. Joseph Edwand and Kate Loubelle (Edington) A.; m. Elizabeth Chase Gutch, Nov. 14, 1942; children: Joseph Edington III, Judith Ann Acker Mitchell, Julia Chase Acker Van Mol, John Howard, Janet Acker Fox; m. Mary (Polly) Winters Phillips, Apr. 22, 1991. BS, U. Tenn., 1941, MD, 1941. Diplomate Am. Bd. Internal Medicine. Intern Kansas City Gen. Hosp., 1941-42; resident Cleve. City Hosp., 1946-48; pvt. practice internal medicine Knoxville, 1948-55, pvt. practice cardiology, 1955-84; mem. Knoxville Cardiovascular Group, 1962-85; chief cardiac work evaluation clinic Knoxville Gen. Hosp., 1948-56; chief cardiac work evaluation clinic U. Tenn., 1956-72, prof. clin. medicine Meml. Rsch. Ctr. and Hosp., 1957-84; dir. cardiac outpatient rehab. programs U. Tenn. Meml. Hosp., 1977-84, St. Mary's Hosp., 1977-83, Fort Sanders Presbyn. Hosp., 1977-93. Author: (with Erb and Mann) Physicians Handbook for Evaluation of Cardiovascular and Physical Fitness, 1970; editor Newsletter Internat. Soc. Cardiology, 1972-80. Served to lt. comdr. USNR, 1942-46. Fellow ACP, Coun. Clin. Cardiology, Am. Heart Assn., Am. Coll. Cardiology; mem. East Tenn. Heart Assn. (pres. 1956), Tenn. Heart Assn. (pres. 1961-63), internat. Soc. Cardiology (rehab. coun. 1968-79). Home: 1276 Old Weisgarber Rd Knoxville TN 37909-2639

ACKER, LOREN CALVIN, medical instrument company executive; b. Lamar, Colo., Mar. 3, 1934; s. John C. and Ada M. (Ecton) A.; m. Judy N. Willms, Sept. 17, 1955 (dec. Oct. 1968); children: Cheryl Acker Hoge, Keith B., Karen Acker Kime; m. Darla C. Copeland, July 24, 1976. BS in Mech. Engrng., Fresno State Coll., 1956; Bus. and Mgmt. cert., U. Calif., Berkeley, 1961; MBA, U. Santa Clara, 1966. Flight test technician NASA, Edwards, Calif., 1954-56; engrng. mgr. Westinghouse, Sunnyvale, Calif., 1956-69; assoc. dir. Kitt Peak Nat. Obs., Tucson, Ariz., 1969-73; chmn., CEO founder SEBRA-Engr. & Rsch. Assocs., Inc. (SEBRA), Tucson, 1973—; gen. ptnr. Winged Foot Assocs., Tucson, 1974—; dir., founder NYPA Inc., Tucson, 1988—. Patentee in field. Chmn. park and recreation City of Cupertino, Calif., 1968, Bioindustry Greater Tucson econ. coun., 1994—; dir. So. Ariz. Leadership Coun., 1997—, Sonoran Sea Aquarium, 1999—; mem. agrl. and biosys. coun. U. Ariz., 1999—. Entrepreneurial fellow U. Ariz., 1999—. Mem. Am. Assn. Blood Banks, Am. Soc. Apherises, Internat. Soc. for Hematotherapy and Graft Engring. Republican. Avocations: skiing, tennis. Home: 4831 E Winged Foot Pl Tucson AZ 85718-1727 Office: 100 N Tucson Blvd Tucson AZ 85716-4412

ACKER, MARTIN HERBERT, psychotherapist, educator; b. N.Y.C., Dec. 15, 1921; s. Irving and Rose Martha (Katz) A.; m. Joan Elise Robinson, Apr. 29, 1948; children—Michael Christopher, David, Jonathon, Steven Anthony; m. Julia Ann Payne, Feb. 14, 1976. Ph.D., NYU, 1963. Lic. psychologist, Oreg. Prof. counseling and psychology U. Oreg., Eugene, 1961-86, prof. emeritus, 1986—, chmn. counseling, 1963-68; vis. prof. Fed. City Coll., Washington, 1968-69, U. Victoria, B.C., Can., 1974, Fredrich Karls U., Tübingen, Germany, 1987; psychotherapist, Eugene, 1974—; dir. BeBusk Meml. Clinic, 1983-85. Mem. adv. com. Lane County Adult Corrections; bd. dirs. Lane Mental Health Assn., Pearl Buck Ctr.; mem. budget com. Sch. Dist. 4J, Eugene, 1994—. Mem. Am. Pers. and Guidance Assn. (bd. dirs. 1967-68), Soc. Sci. Study Sex, Oreg. Psychol. Assn., Am. Rehab. Counselors Assn. (pres. 1968-69), Men's Studies Assn. (co-chair 1986-90), Lane County Psychologists Assn. (pres. 1985-86), Friars Club. Home: 1310 Barber Dr Eugene OR 97405-4400

ACKER, NATHANIEL HULL, retired educational administrator; b. Manistee, Mich., July 29, 1927; s. Carmon M. and Cathryn (Keiser) A.; m. Mary Anne Brawley, June 6, 1951; children: Kristan, Nathaniel Hull Jr., Amy. B.S. in Bus. Adminstrn., Miami U., Oxford, Ohio, 1951. Sales rep. Proctor and Gamble Co., 1951-52, Peninsular Steel Co., Dayton, Ohio, 1952-53; with Mutschler Bros. Co., Nappanee, Ind., 1953-70; v.p. Mutschler Midwest, Inc., Chgo., 1963-68; regional mgr. Ohio-Ky.-Mich., 1968-70; dir. Am. Peace Corps Office Vol. Placement Midwest Region, Chgo., 1970-71; assoc. dir. Northern region, New Delhi, India, 1971-72; exec. officer New Delhi, 1972-73; dir. estate planning St. Lawrence U., Canton, N.Y., 1973-78; v.p. instl. devel. Hampden-Sydney (Va.) Coll., 1978-84; dir. devel. Episcopal High Sch., Alexandria, Va., 1984-91, ret., 1991. Park commr., Lake Bluff, Ill., 1965-68, pres., 1967-68; mem. Citizen's Com. for Lake Forest-Lake Bluff High Sch., 1966, Sch. Caucus, 1963-64, Village Bd. Caucus, 1966-68, Citizens' Com. for Rockland Park, 1964; chmn. Lake Bluff United Fund, 1962-63. Mem. Sigma Alpha Epsilon. Home: 1280 Taquaka Rd Frankfort MI 49635-9510

ACKER, ROBERT FLINT, microbiologist; b. Chgo., Aug. 24, 1920; s. Robert Booth and Mary (Flint) A.; m. Phyllis Catharine Fry, Jan. 2, 1948; children: Catharine Elizabeth, Barbara Fenner, Robert Macdonald, James Christopher. B.A., Ind. U., 1942, M.A., 1948; Ph.D., Rutgers U., 1953. Asst. prof. Iowa State U., Ames, 1954-59; asst. chief cancer chemotherapy dept., chief quality control dept. Microbiol. Assocs., Inc., Bethesda, Md., 1959-61; chief dept. cell and media prodn. Microbiol. Assocs., Inc., 1961-62; dir. microbiology program Office of Naval Research, Dept. Navy, Washington, 1962-69; dir. fed. program devel., asst. dean faculties for research, prof. biol. scis. Northwestern U., Evanston, Ill., 1969-74; exec. dir. Am. Soc. Microbiology, Washington, 1974-81, Nat. Found. Infectious Disease, Bethesda, Md., 1981-86; pres. Bionox Corp., Tucson, 1985-92. Author: (with R.R. Jennings) The Protistan Kingdom, 1970; editor: Proc. 24th Internat. Congress on Marine Corrosion and Fouling, 1972; editorial bd.: Applied Microbiology, 1962-73. V.p., bd. dirs. Iona House Sr. Svc. Ctr., Washington, 1978-79, pres., 1979-81; trustee Massanetta Conf. Ctr., 1983-86; bd. dirs. Am. Type Culture Collection, 1983-89; pres. Sunrise Mountain Ridge Homeowners Assn., 1994-95; bd. elders Potomac United Presbyn. Ch., Md., 1967-69, Winnetka (Ill.) Presbyn. Ch., 1972-74, Nat. Presbyn. Ch., Washington, 1983-86, St. Andrew's Presbyn. Ch., Tucson, 1989-91, 1998—. Eli Lilly & Co. postdoctoral fellow, 1953-54. Fellow Am. Acad. Microbiology, Soc. for Indsl. Microbiology (pres. 1986-87); mem. Am. Soc. for Microbiology, Am. Inst. Biol. Sci. (coun. 1983-91), Cosmos Club. Home and Office: 6890 E Loma Del Bribon Tucson AZ 85750-6372

ACKER, RODNEY, lawyer; b. Jacksonville, Tex., Sept. 29, 1949; s. Mike and Dorothy (Kennedy) A.; m. Judy Bruyere, Sept. 2, 1972; children: Amy, Shelley, Rachel, Sam. BBA, U. Tex., Arlington, 1971; JD with honors, Tex. Tech, 1974. Bar: Tex. 1974, U.S. Dist. Ct. (no., so., ea., we. dists.) Tex., U.S. Ct. Appeals (5th and 11th cirs.), U.S. Supreme Ct.; cert. in civil trial law. Law clk. to Hon. Eldon Mahon, U.S. Dist. Ct., Ft. Worth, 1974-76; assoc. Kendrick, Kendrick & Bradley, Dallas, 1976; assoc. Jenkens & Gilcrist, Dallas, 1976-79, ptnr., then shareholder, 1979—. Fellow Am. Bar Found., Tex. Bar Found., Dallas Bar Found.; mem. ABA, Am. Coll. Trial Lawyers, State Bar Tex., Dallas Bar Assn., Patrick Higginbotham Am. Inns of Ct., Phi Delta Phi. Baptist. Home: 9639 Hilldale Dr Dallas TX 75231-2705 Office: Jenkens & Gilcrist 1445 Ross Ave Ste 3200 Dallas TX 75202-2799

ACKER, VIRGINIA MARGARET, nursing educator; b. Madison, Wis., Aug. 11, 1946; d. Paul Peter and Lucille (Klein) A. Diploma in nursing, St. Mary's Med. Ctr., Madison, 1972; BSN, Incarnate Word Coll., San Antohio, 1976; MS in Health Professions, S.W. Tex. State U., 1980; postgrad., U. Tex., 1992-93. RN, Tex. Staff nurse St. Mary's Hosp., Milw., 1972-73, Kenosha (Wis.) Meml. Hosp., 1973-74, S.W. Tex. Meth. Hosp., San Antonio, 1974-75, Met. Gen. Hosp., San Antonio, 1975-76; instr. Bapt. Meml. Hosp. Sys. Sch. Nursing, San Antonio, 1976-83; DON, Meml. Hosp., Gonzales, Tex., 1983-84; instr., DON, Victoria Coll., Cuero, Tex., 1984-86; DON, Rocky Knoll Health Care Facility, Plymouth, Wis., 1986-87, Unicare Health Facilities, Milw., 1987-88; coord. nursing edn. St. Nicholas Hosp., Sheboygan, Wis., 1989-90; instr. U. Wis., Oshkosh, 1990-92, St. David's Hosp., Austin, Tex., 1992-95; coord. quality improvement Bailey Square Surgery Ctr., Austin, 1995-98; coord. regulation compliance South Austin Hosp., 1998—; nursing educator; b. Madison, Wis., Aug. 11, 1946; d. Paul Peter and Lucille (Klein) A. Diploma in nursing, St. Mary's Med. Ctr., Madison, 1972; BSN, Incarnate Work Coll., San Antonio, 1976; MS in Health Professions, S.W. Tex. State U., 1980; postgrad., U. Tex., 1992-93. RN, Wis., Tex. Staff nurse St. Mary's Hosp., Milw., 1972-73, Kenosha (Wis.) Meml. Hosp., 1973-74, S.W. Tex. Meth. Hosp., San Antonio, 1974-75, Met. Gen. Hosp., San Antonio, 1975-76; instr. Bapt. Meml. Hosp. Sys. Sch. Nursing, San Antonio, 1976-83; DON Meml. Hosp., Gonzales, Tex., 1983-84; instr., DON Victoria Coll., Cuero, Tex., 1984-86; DON Rocky Knoll Health Care Facility, Plymouth, Wis., 1986-87, Unicare Health Facilities, Milw., 1987-88; coord. nursing edn. St. Nicholas Hosp., Sheboygan, Wis., 1989-90; instr. U. Wis., Oshkosh, 1990-92, Bailey Sq. Surgery Ctr., 1995—, St. David's Hosp., Austin, Tex. , 1992-95, quality improvement coord. Roman Catholic. Avocations: cross-stitching, reading, camping, fishing. Roman Catholic. Avocations: cross-stitching, reading, camping, fishing. Home: 2605 Cascade Falls Dr Austin TX 78733-5300

ACKER, WILLIAM MARSH, JR., federal judge; b. Birmingham, Ala., Oct. 25, 1927; s. William Marsh and Estelle (Lampkin) A.; m. Martha Walters, 1957; children—William Marsh III, Stacey Reed. BA, Birmingham So. Coll., 1949; LLB, Yale U., 1952. Bar: Ala. 1952. Assoc. Graham, Bibb, Wingo & Foster, Birmingham, Ala., 1952-57, Smyer, White, Reid & Acker, 1957-72, Dominick, Fletcher, Yeilding, Acker, Wood & Lloyd, Birmingham, 1972-82; judge U.S. Dist. Ct. (no. dist.) Ala., 1982-96, sr. judge, 1996—. Mem. Ala. Republican Exec. Com.; del. to Repub. Nat. Convention, 1972, 76, 80. Mem. Birmingham Bar Assn. Office: 481 Hugo L Black Courthouse 1729 5th Ave N Birmingham AL 35203-2000*

ACKER, WOODROW LOUIS (LOU ACKER), retired security and protection professional; b. Amarillo, Tex., Mar. 24, 1937; s. Doyle and Jewel (Talley) A.; m. Peggy Ann Thompson, Jan. 1, 1959, 1 child, Kelly Michael Kennedy. Cert. protection profl., lic. peace officer, Tex. BS in Police Sci., Sam Houston State U., 1974; BA in History, U. Tex., Dallas, 1985; grad. U.S. Army Command & Gen. Staff Coll., 1989. Dir. adminstrv. services bur. Dallas County Sheriffs Dept., 1965-76; chief campus police dept. North Lake Coll., Irving, Tex., 1977-84; ops. mgr. for security cos., Dallas, 1984-87; pvt. investigator, acad. dir. Dear & Assoc., DeSoto, Tex., 1987-90; acad. dir., co-owner Acker and Acker Tng. Acad., Mesquite, Tex., 1990-91; chief police, Cockrell Hill, Tex., 1992; chief instr. Lakeside Tng. Acad., Dallas, 1994—. Scoutleader Boy Scouts Am., Dallas; mem. CAP, Mesquite; bd. dirs. Shekinah Messianic Ministries. With AUS, 1955-57; maj. Tex. State Guard. South Found. fellow. Fellow Confederate Hist. Inst.; mem. Internat. Police Assn. (Tex. div.), NRA (life), Tex. Rifle Assn. (life), Sons Am. Revolution, Sons of Confederate Vets. (life), Milt. Order Stars and Bars (life), Soc. Order of So. Cross (life), Confederate Meml. Assn., Clan Sutherland Soc. of North Am.

ACKERLEY, BARRY, professional basketball team executive, communications company executive. Student, U. Iowa, 1956. Exec. v.p. Advan, Inc.; owner Golden West Outdoor Advt., 1968-75; chmn., CEO Ackerley Comm., Inc., 1975—; owner, chmn. bd. dirs. Seattle SuperSonics, 1984—. Office: Seattle SuperSonics 190 Queen Anne Ave N Ste 200 Seattle WA 98109-9711 also: Ackerley Group 1301 5th Ave Ste 4000 Seattle WA 98101-2603*

ACKERLY, BENJAMIN CLARKSON, lawyer; b. Lexington, Va., Aug. 25, 1942; s. John Paul Jr. and Marguerite Emmetta (Clarkson) A.; m. Lucille Wiltshire Moore; children: Benjamin, Cabell, Burns, Stewart. BA, U. Va., 1965, LLB, 1968. Bar: Va. 1968, U.S. Dist. Dist. Ct. (ea. dist.) Va. 1970, U.S. Ct. Appeals (4th cir.) 1976, U.S. Supreme Ct. 1976, U.S. Ct. Claims 1978. Assoc. Hunton & Williams, Richmond, Va., 1970-77, ptnr., 1977—; lectr. T.C. Williams Law Sch. U. Richmond, 1979; lectr. law Sch. of Law U.

Va., 1992—. Pres., trustee, chmn. bd. dirs. Hist. Richmond Found., 1972-87; bd. dirs. Richmond Goodwill Industries, 1971-76. Served to capt. U.S. Army. 1968-70. Mem. ABA, Va. Bar Assn. (chmn. bankruptcy sect. 1992-93, chmn. subcom. bankruptcy and creditors rights), Richmond Bar Assn. (pres. bankruptcy sect. 1986-87), Am. Coll. Bankruptcy, Country Club of Va., Fishing Bay Yacht Club. Episcopalian. Avocations: sailing, skiing, gardening. Home: 6106 Three Chopt Rd Richmond VA 23226-2732 Office: Hunton & Williams Riverfront Pla E Tower 951 E Byrd St Richmond VA 23219*

ACKERLY, WENDY SAUNDERS, construction company executive; b. Chgo., July 23, 1960; d. Robert S. Jr. and Linda Ackerly. BS in Atmospheric Sci., U. Calif., Davis, 1982; postgrad., U. Nev., Reno, 1985. Programmer U. Calif, Davis, 1982-83; cons. software Tesco, Sacramento, 1983; software engr. Bently Nev. Corp., Minden, Nev., 1984-85; mgr. computer scis. Jensen Electric Co., Reno, 1985-86; software engr. Jensen Electric Co., Cameron Park, Calif., 1986-89; sr. engr. Aerojet, Sacramento, 1989-96, test ops. specialist, 1996-98; dir. design and devel. Kerry King Constrn., Inc., 1998—, sec.-treas., 1991—. Mem. Nat. Space Soc., Am. Meteorol. Soc., Planetary Soc., U.S. Tennis Assn., Calif. Aggie Alumni Assn. Republican. Avocations: tennis, hiking, travel, piano. Office: PO Box 269 Rescue CA 95672-0269

ACKERMAN, ANDY, television director. Dir. (TV series) Cheers, 1988-91, Roc, 1991-92, Wings, 1991-93, Flying Blind, 1992, Frasier, 1993, Seinfeld, 1996 (Comedy Series award 1996), (TV pilot) Big Wave Dave's, 1993. Office: care Kaplan-Stahler Agy 8383 Wilshire Blvd Ste 923 Beverly Hills CA 90211-2408*

ACKERMAN, ARLENE ALICE, accountant, business consultant, artist, writer; b. Omaha, Mar. 24, 1936; d. Walter Nelson and Mildred Eleanor (Krimlofski) A. BA in Social Sci. and Econs., San Francisco State U., 1962; MA in Polit. Sci., Purdue U., 1967; grad., U.S. Dept. Def. Info. Sch., 1973, U.S. Army Command-Gen. Staff Coll., 1977. CPA, Ind. Acct., adminstr. Peeples & MacDonald, CPAs, Sacramento, 1961-66; acct. chief acct.'s office Purdue U., West Lafayette, Ind., 1966-67; adj. gen. and info. officer, editor newspaper 123d Army Res. Command, Ind., 1972-75; mng. ptnr. Piano Showcase, Indpls., 1975-83; adminstr. Bennett Thrasher & Co. CPAs, Atlanta, 1983-86, Melvin Belli Law Offices, San Francisco, 1990; bus. cons. Ackerman & Assocs., Indpls., 1986-90; acctg. mgr., acting CFO Lera Dynalectric, San Francisco, 1991-94; CFO Nat. Home Bus. Assn., St. Helena, Calif., 1994-96; prin. Ackerman & Assocs., Fairfax, Calif. Editor Mus. Indian Heritage Newsletter, Indpls., 1971-77; exhibited in group shows at Marin Agrl. Land Trust, San Rafael, Calif., 1993, Marin County Fair & Exposition, San Rafael, 1993, 96, Marin Soc. Artists, Ross, Calif., 1993, 94, Monterey Peninsula Mus. Art Christmas Miniature Show, 1993, Artisans Gallery, Mill Valley, Calif., 1993-95, Sonoma-Marin Fair, Petaluma, Calif., 1993-94, San Mateo (Calif.) County Fair, 1992-94, Sonoma County Fair, Santa Rosa, Calif., 1993-95; contbr. articles to Army profl. jours. Officer U.S. Army, 1956-61, 67-71; col. USAR. Mem. Soc. Children's Book Writers and Illustrators (assoc.), Marin Soc. Artist, San Francisco Early Music Soc., Nat. Assn. Miniature Enthusiasts. Avocations: classical piano, painting, drawing, writing children's stories, miniature artist. Home: 5134 Cribari Pl San Jose CA 95135

ACKERMAN, BRUCE ARNOLD, lawyer, educator; b. N.Y.C., Aug. 19, 1943; s. Nathan and Jean (Rosenberg) A.; m. Susan Gould Rose, May 29, 1967; children: Sybil Rose, John Mill. BA summa cum laude, Harvard U., 1964; LLB with honors, Yale U., 1967. Bar: Pa. 1970. Law clk. U.S. Ct. Appeals (2d cir.), New York, 1967-68; law clk. to assoc. justice John M. Harlan U.S. Supreme Ct., Washington, 1968-69; prof. law and public policy analysis U. Pa., Phila., 1969-74; prof. law Yale U., New Haven, 1974-82, Sterling prof. law and polit. sci., 1987—; Beekman prof. law and philosophy Columbia U., N.Y.C., 1982-87. Author: Private Property and the Constitution, 1977, Social Justice in the Liberal State, 1980 (Gavel award ABA), (with Hassler) Clean Coal/Dirty Air, 1981, Reconstructing American Law, 1984, We the People: Foundations, 1991, The Future of Liberal Revolution, 1992, (with Golove) Is NAFTA Constitutional?, 1995, We the People: Transformations, 1998, (with others) The Uncertain Search for Environmental Quality, 1974 (Henderson prize Harvard Law Sch.). Guggenheim fellow, 1985. Fellow Am. Acad. Arts and Scis.; mem. Am. Law Inst. Office: Yale U Law Sch PO Box 208215 New Haven CT 06520-8215*

ACKERMAN, EUGENE, biophysics educator; b. Bklyn., July 8, 1920; s. Saul Benton and Dorothy (Salwen) A.; m. Dorothy Hopkirk, June 5, 1943; children— Francis H., Emmanuel T., Amy R. Ackerman de Canésie. B.A., Swarthmore Coll., 1941; Sc.M., Brown U., 1943; Ph.D., U. Wis., 1949; postgrad., U. Pa., 1949-51, fellow, 1957-58. Instr. Brown U., 1943; from asst. prof. to prof. biophysics Pa. State U., 1951-60; mem. faculty U. Minn. Mayo Grad. Sch. Medicine, 1960-67, prof. biophysics, 1965-91; Hill Family Found. prof. biomed. computing, prof. biometry also computer scis. U. Minn. Mayo Grad. Sch. Medicine, Mpls., 1967-79; prof. dept. lab. medicine and pathology U. Minn. Mayo Grad. Sch. Medicine, 1969-91, prof. emeritus, 1991—, dir. div. health computer sci., 1969-79; staff cons. biophysics Mayo Found. and Mayo Clinic, 1960-67; dir. computer facility Mayo Found., 1964-65; Cons. bioacoustics USAF, 1957-62; mem. epidemiology and biometry tng. com. NIH, 1963-67, spl. study sect. ultrasonic applications, 1965-67, spl. study sect. lab. med. scis., 1967-69, computer and biomath. sci. study sect., 1969-73; dir. nat. resource for simulation of stochastic micropopulation models, 1983-90. Author: Biophysical Science, 1962, (with L. Ellis and L. Williams), 2d edit., 1979; (with L. Gatewood) Math Models in the Health Sciences, 1979, (with L. Elveback and J. Fox) Infectious Disease: Simulation of Epidemics and Vaccination Strategies, 1984; editor Biophys. Jour., 1983-87; also articles, tech. reports, chpts. in books. Rsch. grantee Am. Cancer Soc., 1953-56, NSF, 1958-64, NIH, 1954-90. Mem. Biophys. Soc., Am. Physiol. Soc., Assn. Computing Machinery, IEEE, Phi Beta Kappa, Sigma Xi, Gamma Alpha. Mem. Soc. of Friends. Home: 11301 Park Ridge Dr W Minnetonka MN 55305-2551 Office: U Minn Health Ctr Box 511 UMHC 420 Delaware St SE Minneapolis MN 55455-0374

ACKERMAN, F. DUANE, utility company executive; b. 1942; married. BS, Rollins Coll., MS. With So. Bell Telephone & Telegraph Co., Atlanta, 1964-83; with BellSouth Corp., Atlanta, 1983-85, past v.p., vice chmn., now pres., CEO, 1997; exec. v.p. BellSouth Svcs., Inc., Atlanta, 1985-89, chmn., CEO, 1998—. Office: BellSouth Corp 1155 Peachtree St NE Atlanta GA 30309-3610*

ACKERMAN, F. KENNETH, JR., health facility administrator; b. Mansfield, Ohio, Apr. 2, 1939; m. Patricia Ackerman, Dec. 17, 1960; children: Franklin Kenneth III, Robert Christian, Peter Jonathan. BS in Biology, Denison U., 1961; MHA, U. Mich., 1963. Adminstrv. resident Henry Ford Hosp., Detroit, 1963-64; from asst. adminstrv. dir. to pres. Geisinger Med. Ctr., Danville, Pa., 1964-94; sr. v.p. adminstrv. affairs Geisinger Found., Danville, Pa., 1981-94; prin. assoc. McManis Assocs., Washington, 1994-97, v.p., 1997—; bd. dirs. Pa. Millers Mut. Ins. Co., Wilkes-Barre. Bd. dirs. Pa. Chamber of Bus. and Industry, Harrisburg, 1977-90, Nat. Com. for Quality Healthcare, Washington, 1985—, Healthcare R&D Inst., Pensacola, Fla., 1990—; mem. Nat. Adv. Com. on Rural Health, Washington, 1988-94; bd. trustees Suburban Hosp. and Health Sys., Bethesda, Md., 1995—. Recipient Adminstr. Yr. award Am. Group Practice Assn., 1988, Polit. Action Com. award Hosp. Assn. Pa., 1982, 85, 86, 88, 90, 91, Nat. Merit award Duke U. Hosp. and Health Adminstrn. Alumni Assn., 1991, Harry Harwick award for Excellence, 1994, Article of Yr. award Am. Coll. Med. Practice Execs., 1994. Mem. Am. Coll. Healthcare Execs. (regents adv. coun. 1989—, Hudgens' Meml. Award 1975). Office: McManis Assocs Inc 1900 K St NW Ste 700 Washington DC 20006-1112*

ACKERMAN, FRANKLIN KENNETH, health services administrator; b. Danville, Pa., Feb. 11, 1966; s. F. Kenneth Jr. and Patricia (Driscoll) A.; m. Michelle Reese, Dec. 31, 1997. BA, Franklin and Marshall Coll., 1988; MHA, Duke U., 1991. Adminstrv. fellow Thomas Jefferson U. Hosp., Phila., 1991-92; sr. adminstrv. fellow Henry Ford Health Sys., Detroit, 1992-93, mgr. managed care spl. projects, 1993-94; exec. asst. to the CEO Thomas Jefferson U. Hosp., 1994-96, adminstr. Digestive Disease Inst., 1996—; mem. adv. bd. Phila. Coll. Pharmacy and Sci., 1997—; chmn. career devel. com. Greater Phila. Health Assembly, 1995-97. Contbr. articles to profl. jours. Key campaigner United Way, Phila., 1994—; vol. Habitat for Humanity, Phila., 1997; vol., coach Spl. Olympics, Durham, N.C., 1991; co. leader Metro Detroit Am. heart Walk, Detroit, 1992; exec. com. Greater Phila. Health Assembly, 1995—. Mem. Am. Coll. Healthcare Execs. (diplomate), Am. Coll. Med. Practice Execs., Med. Group Mgmt. Assn., Duke U. Health and Hosp. Adminstrn. Alumni Assn., Am. Coll. of Healthcare Execs. (regent's adv. coun. 1999—, Early Career award 1999). Republican. Episcopalian. Avocations: reading, travel, sports. Office: Thomas Jefferson U Hosp Digestive Disease Inst 132 S 10th St Ste 480 Philadelphia PA 19107-5244

ACKERMAN, GARY LEONARD, congressman; b. Brooklyn, N.Y., Nov. 19, 1942; s. Max and Eva (Barnett) A.; m. Rita Tewel, May 27, 1967; children: Lauren Meredith, Corey Brian, Ari David. B.A., Queens Coll., 1965. Tchr. N.Y.C. Pub. Schs., 1966-70; founder Queens (N.Y.) Tribune, 1970—; owner Multi Media, Queens, 1972—; mem. N.Y. Senate, 1979-83, 98th-105th Congresses from 5th N.Y. dist., Washington, D.C., 1983—; mem. internat. rels. com., mem. banking and fin. svcs. com. Mem. Queens Coll. Alumni Assn. Democrat. Office: Ho of Reps 2243 Rayburn Bldg Washington DC 20515-3205*

ACKERMAN, GERALD MARTIN, art historian, consultant; b. Alameda, Calif., Aug. 21, 1928; s. Alois M. and Eva L. (Sadler) A. BA, U. Calif.-Berkeley, 1952; postgrad., U. Munich, Germany, 1955-58; PhD, Princeton U., 1964. Instr. Bryn Mawr Coll., Pa., 1960-64; asst. prof. Stanford U., Calif., 1964-70; assoc. prof. dept. art Pomona Coll., Claremont, Calif., 1970-75, prof., 1975-89, chmn. dept. art, 1972-82; prof. emeritus, 1989—; Fulbright prof. U. Leningrad, 1980; prof. Florence (Italy) Acad. Art, 1996—. Author: (plays) Family and Friends, 1979, The Surfer, 1981, The Life and Work of J.L. Gerome, 1986, American Orientalists, 1994, Les Orientalistes de l'Ecole britannique, 1991; contbr. articles to profl. jours. Appleton eminent scholar Fla. State U., 1994. Democrat. Home: 360 S Mills Ave Claremont CA 91711-5331

ACKERMAN, HAROLD A., federal judge; b. 1928. Student, Seton Hall U., 1945-46, 48; LL.B., Rutgers U., 1951. Bar: N.J. 1951. Adminstrv. asst. to Commr. of Labor and Industry, State of N.J., 1955-56; judge of compensation State of N.J., 1956-62, supervising judge of compensation, 1962-65; judge Union County Dist. Ct., 1965-70, presiding judge, 1966-70; judge Union County Ct., 1970-73, Superior Ct. law div., 1973-75, Superior Ct. Chancery div., 1975-79; judge U.S. Dist. Ct., Dist. of N.J., 1979—, now sr. judge; mem. Supreme Ct. Com. on Revision of Rules, 1967; chmn. Supreme Ct. Com. on County Dist. Cts., 1968; mem. faculty Nat. Jud. Coll., 1978. Sgt. U.S. Army, 1946-48. Recipient Disting. Alumni award Rutgers U. Sch. Law, 1980. Fellow ABA; mem. Order of Coif. Office: US Dist Ct PO Box 999 Newark NJ 07101-0999

ACKERMAN, HELEN PAGE, librarian, educator; b. Evanston, Ill., June 30, 1912; d. John Bernard and Florence Page. B.A., Agnes Scott Coll., Decatur, Ga., 1933; B.L.S., U. N.C., 1940. Cataloger Columbia Theol. Sem., 1942-43; post librarian U.S. Army, Aberdeen Proving Ground, Md., 1943-45; asst. librarian Union Theol. Sem., Richmond, Va., 1945-49; reference librarian UCLA, 1949-54, asst. univ. librarian, 1954-65, asso. univ. librarian, 1965-73, univ. librarian, 1973-77, prof. Sch. Info. and Library Sci., 1973-77, 82, 83; vis. prof. Sch. Librarianship, U. Calif., Berkeley, 1978, 80. Recipient award of distinction in libr. sci. UCLA Alumnae Assn., 1977, Disting. Career Citation, Assn. Coll. and Rsch. Librs., 1989. Mem. ALA, AAUW (Status of Women award 1973), Calif. Libr. Assn., Coun. on Libr. Resources (bd. dirs. 1975-90). Home: 310 20th St Santa Monica CA 90402-2414

ACKERMAN, JACK ROSSIN, investment banker; b. N.Y.C., Feb. 8, 1931; s. Robert M. and Florence (Rossin) A.; m. Dana Lowenthal, Nov. 29, 1974; children: Ellen, Jay, Robin, Bradley. BA, Harvard U., 1953, MBA, 1955. With Bache Halsey Stuart Shields, Inc., N.Y.C., 1955-80; mng. dir. Drexel Burnham Lambert, Inc., N.Y.C., 1980-88; pres. Bond Review Inc., N.Y.C., 1988-91; mng. dir. Ladenburg Thalmann & Co. Inc., N.Y.C., 1991-93, Brill Securities, 1993-94; Burnham Securities, Inc., 1994-96. Trustee Jewish Bd. Family and Children's Services, 1980; bd. dirs. Jewish Found. Edn. Women, 1980. Clubs: Century, Country (Purchase, N.Y.), Harvard Club N.Y.C.

ACKERMAN, JAMES SLOSS, fine arts educator; b. San Francisco, Nov. 8, 1919; s. Lloyd S. and Louise (Sloss) A.; m. Mildred Rosenbaum, Apr. 11, 1947 (dec. Jan. 10, 1986); children: Anne, Anthony, Sarah; m. Jill Slosburg, Aug. 1987; 1 child, Jesse August. AB, Yale U., 1941; MA, NYU, 1947, PhD, 1952; LHD, Kenyon Coll., 1961; DFA, Md. Inst., 1972, Mass. Coll. Art, 1984; LHD, U. Md., 1976; DArch, U. Venice, 1985. Part-time instr. Yale U., 1946-48; rsch. fellow Am. Acad. in Rome, 1949-52; from asst. prof. to prof. U. Calif., 1952-60; editor in chief Art Bull., 1956-60; prof. fine arts Harvard U., 1960—, chmn. dept. fine arts, 1963-68, 82-84, Arthur Kingsley Porter prof. fine arts, 1984-90, prof. emeritus, 1990; Slade prof. fine art, fellow King's Coll., Cambridge U., 1969-70; vis. fellow Coun. Humanities, Princeton, 1960-61; fellow Am. Coun. Learned Socs., 1964-65, N.Y. Humanities Inst., spring 1992; vis. prof. fine arts NYU, 1992; sr. fellow NEH, 1974-75; Mellon lectr. Nat. Gallery Art, 1985; Schapiro prof. art history Columbia U., 1989-90, 91; vis. prof. Architecture, MIT, 1996, Harvard, 1996-97. Author: The Cortile del Belvedere, 1954, The Architecture of Michelangelo, 1961 (winner Alice D. Hitchcock award Soc. Archtl. Historians 1961, Charles R. Morey award 1963), (with Rhys Carpenter) Art and Archaeology, 1963, Palladio, 1967, Palladio's Villas, 1967, The Villa: Form and Ideology of Country Houses, 1990, Distance Points, 1991, The Reinvention of Architectural Drawing 1250-1550, 1998; editor: Annali d'Architettura, 1992-95; films Looking for Renaissance Rome (with Kathleen Weil-Garris), 1975, Palladio the Architect and His Influence in America. Trustee The Artists Found., pres., 1977-79; mem. council of scholars Library of Congress, 1980-82. Recipient medal for svc. in art edn. Nat. Gallery Art, 1966, Centennial citation U. Calif., 1968, Honors AIA 1987, Gold medal Inst. per la Storia dell'Arte Lombarda, 1987, Archtl. History award AIA, 1991, Paul Oskar Kristeller Lifetime Achievement award Renaissance Soc. Am., 1998; decorated grand officer Order of Merit, Republic of Italy, 1985, Premio Daria Borghese, 1995; Guggenheim fellow, 1992-93. Fellow Am. Acad. Arts and Scis., Brit. Acad., Accademia Olimpica (corr.), Royal Acad. Arts and Scis., Accademia of St. Luca (Rome, hon.), Ateneo Veneto, Royal Acad. Uppsala (corr.), Bavarian Acad. Scis. (corr.). Home: 12 Coolidge Hill Rd Cambridge MA 02138-5510 Office: Harvard U Sackler Mus Cambridge MA 02138

ACKERMAN, JEROME LEONARD, radiology educator; b. Bklyn., Jan. 4, 1950. BS in Chemistry, SUNY, Stony Brook, 1971; PhD in Physical Chemistry, MIT, Cambridge, 1976. Postdoctoral fellow U. Calif., Berkeley, 1976-77; asst. prof. chemistry U. Cin., 1977-82, assoc. prof. chemistry, 1982-85; asst. prof. radiology Harvard Med. Sch., Boston, 1985-95, assoc. prof. radiology, 1995—; dir. NMR spectroscopy Mass. Gen. Hosp., Charlestown, 1985—; cons. in field. Editor: (book) Advanced Tomographic Imaging Methods for the Analysis of Materials, 1991; contbr. numerous articles to profl. jours. Mem. Internat. Soc. for Magnetic Resonance in Medicine, Experimental Nuclear Magnetic Resonance Conf. (mem. exec. com. 1991—, conf. chair-elect 1998). Office: Biomaterials Lab NMR Ctr Mass Gen Hosp Rm 2301 149 13th St Charlestown MA 02129-2020*

ACKERMAN, JOHN HENRY, health services consultant, physician; b. Fond du Lac, Wis., Feb. 27, 1925; s. Henry Theodore and Clara Frances (Voss) A.; m. Eugenia Ellen Mulligan, May 22, 1948 (dec. 1996); children: H. John, Mary, Lisa, Paul. Student, Cornell U., 1943-44, Ind. U., 1944; M.D., Marquette U., 1948; M.P.H., Johns Hopkins U., 1955. Intern St. Agnes Hosp., Fond du Lac, 1948-49; family practice medicine Clarksville, Iowa, 1949-51; commd. officer USPHS, 1951-70; dep. chief tng. program Center Disease Control, Atlanta, 1970; ret. as capt. Center Disease Control, 1970; dep. dir. Ohio Dept. Health, Columbus, 1970-75; dir. Ohio Dept. Health, 1975-83; utilization rev. cons. Grant Med. Ctr., Columbus, Ohio, 1985-88; med. dir. Ohio Health Choice Plan, 1985-88; dir. med. affairs CRT, Inc., 1988-92; med. dir. Co. Rehab. Svcs.; med. cons. EBMC, 1991-95; clin. prof. preventive medicine Ohio State U.; cons. WHO; med. cons. EBMC, Inc., ACMS, Inc., 1989-95. Served with AUS, 1943-46. Fellow APHA, Am. Coll. Preventive Medicine, Royal Soc. Health; mem. Commd. Officers Assn., N.Y. Acad. Sci., Ohio Med. Assn., Columbus Acad. Medicine, Alpha Kappa Kappa. Roman Catholic. Home: 4183 Reedbury Ln Columbus OH 43220-3946

ACKERMAN, KENNETH DAVID, federal agency administrator. BA, Brown U., 1973; JD, Georgetown U., 1976. Minority staff counsel U.S. Senate Com. on Govtl. Affairs, Washington, 1976-81, Commodity Futures Trading Commn., Washington, 1981-88; spl. counsel U.S. Senate Com. on Agr., Nutrition, and Forestry, Washington, 1988-93; mgr. Fed. Crop Ins. Corp., 1993—; adminstr. Risk Mgmt. Agy. USDA, Washington, 1996—. Author: The Gold Ring: Jim Fisk, Jay Gould and Black Friday 1869; contbr. articles to profl. jours. Office: Risk Mgmt Agy Dept Agr 14th & Independence Ave Washington DC 20250

ACKERMAN, KENNETH EDWARD, lawyer, educator; b. Bronx, N.Y., May 25, 1946; s. Kenneth L. and Anna (McCarthy) A.; m. Kathryn H. Hartnett, July 10, 1972; children—Andrew, Carl, Sheila, Edward, Daniel, Kenneth. Student Talladega Coll., 1966; B.A., Fordham Coll., 1968; J.D. Cornell U., 1971. Bar: N.Y. 1972, Pa. 1994, U.S. Dist. Ct. (no. dist.) N.Y. 1975, U.S. Ct. Appeals (2d cir.) 1975, U.S. Supreme Ct. 1976. Clk. legal dept. Port Authority N.Y. and N.J., 1969; Clk. legal dept. IBM, 1970; ptnr. Mackenzie, Smith, Lewis, Michell & Hughes, Syracuse, N.Y., 1971—; adj. prof. banking law and negotiable instruments Am. Inst. Banking program Onondaga Community Coll., 1984—, Syracuse U. Coll., lectr. Author: Alcoholism-Prognosis for Recovery in the Reconstituted Soviet Republics, 1991; contbr. article to profl. jour. Chmn. Central N.Y. chpt. March of Dimes, 1972-82; mem. A.A.-USSR Travel Group, 1987; bd. dirs. Central N.Y. Health Systems Agy., Inc., 1982-83, Syracuse Sr. Citizens Housing Corp, 1992—. Mem. ABA, N.Y. State Bar Assn. (chmn. com. lawyer alcoholism and drug abuse 1993-95), Onondaga County Bar Assn. (bd. dirs. 1990-93). Office: 600 Onondaga Savs Bank Bldg Syracuse NY 13202

ACKERMAN, LENNIS CAMPBELL, management consultant retired; b. L.A., July 28, 1917; s. Lennis Howard and Ethel (Campbell) A.; m. Barbara Bohlken, July 27, 1941; children: Nancy (Mrs. Michael H. Burnaugh), Janet (Mrs. Robert W. Lesser), John, Barbara (Mrs. H.D. Arnold), George. AB, UCLA, 1940. With Texaco Co., L.A., 1940-43, Schenley Distillers, San Francisco, 1945-48; merchandiser Richfield Oil Corp., San Francisco, 1949-52; sales rep. Walker Mfg. Co., 1952-56, mktg. adminstr., 1956-58; v.p., gen. mgr. Can. subs. Galt Metal Industries, 1958-63, v.p. internat. ops. parent co., 1963-65, v.p. mktg., 1965, pres., 1966-68; pres., chief exec. officer Newport News Shipbldg. and Dry Dock Co., 1969-73; exec. v.p. Tenneco, Inc., 1972-73; group v.p. Questor Corp., 1973-78; assoc. dean Sch. Bus. Adminstrn. Coll. William and Mary, Williamsburg, Va., 1978-83. Sec. Va. Port Authority, 1971-73; mem. Sch. Bus. Adminstrn. Sponsors, Inc., Coll. William and Mary, 1970-79, chmn., 1970-72. Served with USAAF, 1943-45. Mem. Soc. Automotive Engrs., Pine Valley Golf Club, Beta Gamma Sigma (hon.), Alpha Sigma Phi. Episcopalian. Home and Office: Apt 129 5700 Williamsburg Landing Dr Williamsburg VA 23185-3779

ACKERMAN, MARSHALL, publishing company executive; b. N.Y.C., Jan. 22, 1925; s. Albert and Beatrice (Munstuk) A.; m. Carol Lipman, June 8, 1948; children: Stark, Scott, A. Marc. AB, Harvard U., 1949; MS in Journalism, Northwestern U., 1950. Dir. employee relations Gimbel Bros., N.Y.C., 1950-51; account exec. Leonard Wolf & Assoc. (advt. agy.), N.Y.C., 1951-54; with Rodale Press, Inc., 1954-91, exec. v.p., 1967-91, vice chmn. bd., 1978-91; pub. Prevention mag., 1977-86; pub. Theatre Crafts mag., 1967-78, vice chmn., Western divsn., 1986-91; ind. cons. health food industry, health media, 1992—. Pres. bd. assocs. Cedar Crest Coll., Allentown, Pa., 1976-78, trustee, 1983-87; pres. Pa. Stage Co., Allentown, 1978-80; chmn. Santa Barbara chpt. Am. Inst. Wine and Food, 1998—; mem. comm. dept. adv. bd. U. Calif. Santa Barbara, 1993—, vice chmn., 1998. Charge de Presse, Confrerie de la Chaine des Rotisseurs, Bailliage de Santa Barbara, 1998—; Decorated Bronze Star, Purple Heart. Home and Office: 894 Toro Canyon Rd Santa Barbara CA 93108-1642

ACKERMAN, MELVIN, investment company executive; b. Bronx, N.Y., Feb. 6, 1937; s. Norman Ackerman and Lilly (Ostreicher) Warshaw; m. Jennie Wang, Sept. 19, 1964; children: Lori, Julie, Melissa. Student, Bklyn. Coll., 1956, 59. Trader Myron A. Lomasney & Co., N.Y.C., 1960-62; sr. v.p. E.F. Hutton & Co., N.Y.C., 1963-88; exch. arbitrator Am. Stock Exch., N.Y.C., 1984-88; mem. options adv. com. Phila. Stock Exch., 1980-88, Am. Stock Exch., 1975-88; ind. cons., 1988—; dir. BBFD Investment Co.; ptnr. Breckenridge Holding Co. With USMC, 1956-58. Mem. Securities Traders Assn. N.Y., Securities Industry Assn. (credit div., options and derivative products com., 1983-88). Jewish.

ACKERMAN, MICHAEL W., career officer; b. Dec. 17, 1946. Commd. U.S. Army, advanced through grades to maj. gen., 1997. Office: 1700 Army Pentagon Washington DC 20310-1700

ACKERMAN, MITCHELL, television executive; b. N.Y.C., Apr. 16, 1949. BS, SUNY, Buffalo, 1971; MA, U. Md., 1973. Dir. prodn. Lorimar Prodns., Los Angeles, 1975-85; sr. v.p. TV prodn. Walt Disney TV, Burbank, Calif., 1985-95, exec. v.p. TV prodn., 1995—. Producer: (TV film) Washington Mistress, 1983, (TV pilots) House Detective, 1984, Rock Hopper, 1985. Mem. Dirs. Guild Am. Office: Walt Disney TV 500 S Buena Vista St Burbank CA 91521-0004

ACKERMAN, PAUL ADAM, pharmacist; b. Cleve., Oct. 6, 1945; s. Kenneth Edwin and Jane (Hand) A.; m. Charity Reba Schierhorst, June 5, 1971; 1 child, Adam. BS, U. Fla., 1969. Lic. pharmacist, Fla., Ga. Pharmacist Robalo Pharmacy, Lake Park, Fla., 1969-73, Tru Valu Drugs, Lake Worth, 1973-77, Village Pharmacy, Tequesta, Fla., 1977-79, Shoppers Drug Mart, Palm Beach Garden, Fla., 1979-86; pharmacy mgr. Walgreen's, Palm Beach Garden, 1986—. Member Airports and Aviation Adv. Com., Palm Beach County, Fla., 1985—; mem. adv. bd. Coll. of Pharmacy, U. Fla., 1986—; bd. dirs. Am. Cancer Soc., Palm Beach County, 1983-89. Recipient Pharmacy Disting. Svc. Alumnus award U. Fla., 1991. Mem. Am. Pharmacy Assn., Fla. Pharmacy Assn. (exec. com. Tallahassee chpt. 1984-85, 88, chmn. Acad. Pharmacy Practice 1987-88, bd. dirs. ho. of dels. 1988-90, vice-speaker 1991, speaker 1992, pres. 1997-98, Practitioner Merit award 1990), Palm Beach County Pharmacy Assn. (pres. West Palm Beach, Fla. chpt. 1983-85, Joe Price Pharmacist of Yr. 1985), Fla. Aero Club, Jupiter Elks, Palm Beach Gardens Moose, Masons, Shriners, Phi Lambda Sigma. Republican. Avocations: swimming, flying. Home: 12931 Inshore Dr West Palm Beach FL 33410-2005 Office: Walgreens 7170 Fairway Dr West Palm Beach FL 33418-3763

ACKERMAN, PHILIP CHARLES, utility executive, lawyer; b. Kenmore, N.Y., Feb. 14, 1944; s. Harold Lewis and Marion (Ehrhardt) A.; m. Nancy Margaret Weig, Sept. 11, 1967; children: David Philip, Kathryn Elizabeth. BS in Acctg., SUNY, Buffalo, 1965; LLB, Harvard U., 1968. Bar: N.Y. 1968. Atty. Iroquois Gas Corp., Buffalo, 1968-72, asst. sec., 1972-74; asst. sec. Nat. Fuel Gas Distbn. Corp., Buffalo, 1974-75, sec., 1975-84, gen. counsel, 1978-84, sr. v.p., 1983-84, exec. v.p., 1989-95, pres., 1995—, also bd. dirs.; sr. v.p. Nat. Fuel Gas Supply Corp., 1984-88, exec. v.p., 1988-90, 94—; v.p. Nat. Fuel Gas Co., Buffalo, 1980-89, sr. v.p., 1989—, dir., 1994—; v.p. Seneca Resources Corp., 1978-89, pres., 1989-96, also bd. dirs.; mem. Buffalo regional bd. Chase Manhattan Bank N.A., 1985-98. Mem. Am. Gas Assn. (bd. dirs. 1999—), N.Y. State Bar Assn., Pa. Gas Assn. (chmn. 1997-98), N.Y. Gas Group (exec. com. 1996—, chmn. 1998—), Buffalo Soc. Natural Sci. (bd. mgrs. 1982—, vice chmn. 1990-99, chmn. 1999—), Audubon Soc., Sitzmarker Ski Club (bd. dirs.). Office: Nat Fuel Gas Co 10 Lafayette Sq Buffalo NY 14203-1824

ACKERMAN, RAYMOND BASIL, advertising agency executive; b. Pitts., Aug. 7, 1922; s. Charles Raymond and Teresa Jane (Grasinger) A.; m. Lucille Frances Flanagan, June 14, 1948; children: Patricia Ann Mehring, Ann Carol Adams, Ray K., Susan Marie Fuller, Mark, Amy Lou Shaver. BS, Oklahoma City U., 1951, PhD (hon.), 1996. Mem. display advt. staff Okla. Pub. Co., Oklahoma City, 1947-52; account exec. Knox-Ackerman Advt., Oklahoma City, 1952-53; pres. Ackerman Assos., Oklahoma City, 1954-74; chmn. bd. Ackerman McQueen, Inc., advt. agy., Oklahoma City, Tulsa, Dallas, Washington, 1975-92; chmn. emeritus Ackerman McQueen, Inc., 1992—; bd. dirs. LSB Industries. Author: Tomorrow

Belongs to Oklahoma, 1964. Pres., gen. chmn. Oklahoma City United Appeal, 1964-66, trustee, 1967—; chmn. Oklahoma City Salvation Army, 1968; pres. Oklahoma City Better Bus. Bur., 1966; gen. chmn. Nat. Finals Rodeo Oklahoma City, 1965-84; past bd. dirs. Jr. Achievement, Oklahoma City, Okla. Water Devel. Found.; past pres., bd. dirs. St. Anthony Hosp. Found.; past pres. Omniplex Sci. Mus., Oklahoma City; past trustee Oklahoma City Youth Park; campaign chmn., pres. Allied Arts Found., Oklahoma City, 1986-88, mem. exec. com., 1989—, Oklahoma City Cmty. Coun., 1989—; bd. dirs. Kirkpatrick Ctr. Mus. Complex, Oklahoma City, 1986—, pres. 1990-92; trustee, mem. exec. com., Oklahoma City U., 1988—; bd. dirs. Red Earth Indian Ctr., 1987—, Oklahoma City Pub. Sch. Found., 1990—, Last Frontier Coun. Boy Scouts Am., 1989—; adv. bd. Enterprise Sq., 1994—. Rear adm. USNR, ret. Recipient Silver medal Am. Adv. Fedn., 1982, lifetime svc. award Oklahoma City United Appeal, 1992, Pathfinder award Oklahoma County Hist. Soc., 1992, Outstanding Grad. award, Oklahoma City U., 1964, Disting. Alumnus award, 1991; named Humanitarian of Yr. Oklahoma County Arthritis Found., 1992; elected to Okla. Hall of Fame, 1993, Okla. Commerce and Industry Hall of Honor, 1998. Mem. Naval Res. Assn. (nat. pres. 1969-71), Navy League (nat. bd. dirs. 1972-76, pres. Okla. chpt. 1974-76), Okla. Heritage Assn. (bd. dirs. 1993—), Oklahoma City C. of C. (bd. dirs., chmn. 1991), Oklahoma City Advt. Club (pres. 1954, Disting. Svc. award 1964). Home: 12905 Laurel Valley Ct Oklahoma City OK 73142-5167 Office: 1100 The Tower 1601 NW Expressway St Oklahoma City OK 73118-1467

ACKERMAN, ROBERT KEITH, journalist; b. Passaic, N.J., Dec. 11, 1954; s. John Warren and Alba Ackerman; m. Beth Ann Anthony, Nov. 17, 1979 (div. Mar. 1988); m. Aileen Mary Natrella, June 22, 1991; children: Katherine Aileen, Abigail Mary. Student, Boston U., 1972-77. Pub. rels. coord Commonwealth Hist. Preservation Trust, Boston, 1979-80; press aide Anderson for Pres., Washington, 1980; press sec. McClaughrgy for U.S. Senate, Montpelier, Vt., 1982; staff reporter The Monitor, Washington, 1986; assoc. editor Signal Mag., Fairfax, Va., 1987-90, sr. editor, 1990-98, editor-in-chief, 1998—; project coord. Tippets-Abbett-McCarthy-Stratton, Boston, 1978-79. Mem. Fairfax County Airports adv. com., Fairfax, 1991—; writer, dir., cameraman Boston Cable Access Found., 1984-86; media coord. Ford/Dole campaign, Boston, 1976. Mem. Soc. of Profl. Journalists, Soc. of Aerospace Comms., Aircraft Owners and Pilots Assn. Avocations: flying, political memorabilia collecting. E-mail: arka@us.net.

ACKERMAN, ROBERT LLOYD, chemical engineer, environmental tree farmer; b. Greensburg, Pa., Sept. 3, 1925; s. Lloyd William and Anne Stella (Saul) A.; m. Margaret Dorothy Ansty, May 30, 1959; children: Julia Anne Ackerman Glenister, Janet Deborah Ackerman Fuhrmeister, Robert Peter. BSChE, U. Pitts., 1947. Tech. supr. Pittsburgh Plate Glass Co., Creighton, Pa., 1948-52; chem. engr. Koppers Co., Inc., Pitts., 1952-57; sr. chem. engr. Arabian Am. Oil Co., N.Y.C., also Saudi Arabia, 1957-75; sr. commg. engr. 8 oil desalting plants Oil Svc. Co. of Iran, Ahwas, Iran, 1975-77; sr. design-commg. engr. Balikpapan oil refinery, Murchison and Beryl B Northsea oil/gas producing platforms, also Ok Tedi gold/copper refinery, Bechtel Internat., Inc., London, Indonesia, Papua New Guinea, 1978-84; tree farmer New Alexandria, Pa., 1984—. Author: A Short History of Andrico, A Coal Patch. Patentee mfg. device used in glass industry; inventor of a graphical method used as a basis to plan and control daily operating parameters for an oil refinery-marine shipping complex. V.p. Westmoreland Woodlands Improvement Assn., Greensburg, Pa., 1990—; assoc. dir. Westmoreland Conservation Dist., Greensburg, 1993—; treas. Penn West conf. United Ch. of Christ, Greensburg, 1994—; active Amnesty Internat., The Wilderness Soc., Sierra Club, Baltzer Meyer Hist. Soc., German Am. Nat. Congress. Recipient Maurice K. Goddard State award Pa. Assn. Conservation Dists., 1993. Mem. AIChE, Sigma Tau. Mem. United Ch. of Christ. Avocations: reading, hunting, hiking, genealogy. Home: PO Box 339 New Alexandria PA 15670-0339

ACKERMAN, ROBERT WALLACE, steel company executive; b. N.Y.C., Sept. 14, 1938; s. Emory Graham and Margaret Wallace A.; m. Margaret Tracy Dealy, Dec. 30, 1964; children: Ashley, Graham, Todd. BS, Yale U., 1960; MBA, Harvard U., 1962. CPA, N.Y. Cons. Arthur Young & Co., N.Y.C., 1962-66; asst. prof. Harvard Bus. Sch., Boston, 1968-72, lectr., 1972-74; v.p. fin. and adminstrn. Preco, Inc., West Springfield, Mass., 1974-78; pres., bd. dirs. Premoid Corp., West Springfield, Mass., 1979-86, Whitman Products Ltd., West Warwick, R.I., 1977-86; sr. research fellow Harvard Bus. Sch., 1986-88; pres., chief exec. officer Lincoln Pulp & Paper, Inc., 1988-92, Sheffield Steel Corp., 1992—; dir. Gulf State Steel Corp.; trustee The Baupost Fund. Author: The Social Challenge to Business, 1975, (with Hugo Uyterhoeven and John Rosenblum) Strategy and Organization, Text and Cases, General Management, 1973, 2d. edit., 1977, (with Raymond Bauer) Corporate Social Responsiveness, 1976. Deacon, mem. exec. council 1st Ch. in Cambridge Congl., 1970—; bd. dirs. Wildlife Conservation Trust, 1977—. Served with AUS, 1963. Mem. AICPA, Timber Owners of New Eng. (pres. 1977—, bd. dirs.), Am. Acad. Mgmt. (gov. 1972-73), N.Y. State Soc. CPA's, Steel Mfrs. Assn. (chmn. 1998—), Yale Club (N.Y.C.), Weston (Mass.) Golf Club. Home: 229 Ash St Weston MA 02493-1940 Office: 220 Jefferson St Sand Springs OK 74063-7914

ACKERMAN, ROGER G., ceramic engineer; m. Maureen Ackerman; 4 children. Grad., Rutgers U., D (hon.); PMD program, Harvard U. Engr., sales, mgmt. positions Corning (N.Y.) Inc., 1962-72, pres. Corhart Refractories Co., 1972-75, gen. mgr., v.p. Ceramic Products Divsn., 1975-80, sr. v.p., 1980-81, dir. Mfg. and Engring. Divsn., 1981-83, pres. MetPath Inc., 1983-85, pres. Specialty Materials, 1985-90, pres., COO, 1990-96, chmn., CEO, 1996—. Bd. dirs. Pittston Co., Mass. Mutual Life Ins. Co., Dow Corning Corp.; trustee Corning Inc. Found., Corning Mus. Glass; mem. bd. overseers Rutgers U. Found. Office: Corning Inc. One Riverfront Plaza Corning NY 14831

ACKERMAN, VALERIE B., sports association executive; m. Charlie Rappaport; children: Emily, Sally. Grad., U. Va., 1981; degree in law, UCLA, 1985. Assoc. Simpson, Thacher & Bartlett, N.Y.C.; staff atty. NBA, 1988, spl. asst. to commr., 1990-92, dir. bus. affairs, 1992, v.p. bus. affairs, 1994; bd. dirs. Women's Basketball Hall of Fame; USA Basketball; bd. trustees Naismith Meml. Basketball Hall of Fame. Office: Olympic Tower 645 Fifth Ave New York NY 10022-5910 also: WNBA Enterprises LLC 450 Harmon Meadow Blvd Secaucus NJ 07094*

ACKERMANN, KAREN, publishing executive. BA, U. Md. Pres. Heritage Books Ind., Bowie, Md., 1991—. *

ACKERMANN, RUSSELL ALBERT, manufacturing company executive; b. Cin., Aug. 14; s. Russell Albert and Jennie Agatha (Brockmeier) A.; m. Mildred Arlene Streicher, July 24, 1948; children: Layne Anne Seifert, Kristie Allison Clepper, Leslie Arlene Bickel. Student, U. Cin., 1944-47. Registered profl. engr., Ohio. Rsch. assoc. CHMR Rsch. Inst., Cin., 1947-54; adminstrv. svc. mgr. Cin. Milacron, 1954-76; mktg. mgr. Dresser Ind., Niagara Falls, N.Y., 1976-87; pres. Ackermann & Assoc., Cin., 1987-89; chmn. Internat. Abrasives Corp., Nashville, 1989-91, Ackermann & Assocs., Cin., 1991—; cons. Colonial Abrasives, Aberdeen, N.C., 1987-89; chmn., CEO Greater Cin. Info. Svcs., Inc. (d.b.a. Net Results), 1996; chmn. Genesis Materials Internat., 1997—. Author: Laboratory Techniques, 1954; contbr. numerous articles to profl. jours.; patentee grinding wheels. Mem. Rep. Cen. Com., 1960-65; mem. city coun., Madeira, Ohio, 1965-76; mem. regional coun. Boy Scouts Am., Cin., 1955-60, Econ. Dev. and Export Coun., Pinehurst, N.C., 1988. Mem. American Water Works Assoc., Water Pollution Control Fed., Grinding Wheel Inst. (committee mem. 1986-89), Abrasive Grain Assoc. (committee mem. 1976-86), Abrasive Eng. Soc. (dir.), Germania Soc., Sons of Union Veterans of the Civil War, Alpha Phi Omega, Masons, Acacia Fraternity. Mem. United Ch. of Christ. Avocations: painting, coin collecting, golf, writing, geneology. Home: 1352 Rambling Hills Dr Cincinnati OH 45230-2359 Office: Ackermann & Assocs 2961 Madison Rd Cincinnati OH 45209-2027

ACKERSON, BARRY JAMES, social worker; b. Ogdensburg, N.Y., June 24, 1953; s. Gerald Wilson and Mary Agnes (Brown) A.; m. Linda Carol Graves, Aug. 15, 1976; 1 child, Sean Eric. BA in Sociology, U. Ala., 1975, MSW, 1978, PhD, 1998. Lic. clin. social worker, Ala. Psychiat. social work asst. I non-instl. care and svcs. dept Bryce Hosp., Tuscaloosa, Ala., 1975-76; dir. Alpha Program Bryce Hosp., Tuscaloosa, 1982-85, dir. dept. non-instl. care and svcs., 1985-90; rsch. asst. Coll. of Cmty. Health Scis. U. Ala., Tuscaloosa, 1978; dir. Russellville Transitional Home Riverbend Mental Health Ctr., Florence, Ala., 1979-80; group home coord., aftercare therapist Indian Rivers Mental Health Ctr., Tuscaloosa, 1980-82; acting dir. cmty. placement Ala. Dept. Mental Health-Mental Retardation, Tuscaloosa, 1990-92, mental health specialist III, 1992-97; asst. prof. U. Ill., Urbana, 1998—; adj. faculty U. Ala. Sch. Social Work, 1994-98. Recipient Outstanding Svc. award Boys Club of Tuscaloosa, 1974. Mem. NASW, Coun. on Social Work Edn., Alliance for Mentally Ill (nat. and Ala.), Mental Health Assn. of Tuscaloosa, U. Ala. Social Work Soc. (coun. social work edn.), Phi Beta Kappa, Phi Kappa Phi. Avocations: organic gardening, maritial arts. E-mail: backerso@uiuc.edu.

ACKERSON, BRADLEY KENT, physician; b. Fort Wayne, Ind., Apr. 30, 1956; s. Benjamin Ralph and Beverly Ann (Preston) A. BA in Biology, UCLA, 1978, MD, 1982. Intern in pediatrics Harbor-UCLA, 1982-83, residency in Pediatrics, 1983-85, fellowin infectious disease, 1985-86; pediatrician Kaiser Permanente, Harbor City, Calif, 1986—; asst. chief pediatrician Kaiser Permanente, Harbor City, Calif., 1987-93. contbr. articles to profl. jours. Excellence in Rsch., U Calif. San Diego, 1982—, UCLA fellow, 1994-97. Mem. Infectious Disease Soc., Pediat. Infectious Disease Soc., L.A. Pediat. Soc., Habitat for Humanity, Sierra Club, Nature Conservancy. Avocations: piano, bicycling, hiking. Office: Kaiser Permanente 25825 Vermont Ave Harbor City CA 90710-3599

ACKERSON, CHARLES STANLEY, minister, social worker; b. St. Louis, June 19, 1935; s. Charles Albert and Glenda Mae (Brown) A.; m. Carol Jean Stehlick, Aug. 18, 1957; children: Debra Lynn, Charles Mark, Heather Sue. AB, William Jewell Coll., 1957; MDiv, Colgate Rochester Div. Sch., 1961. Ordained to ministry Am. Bapt. Ch., 1961; lic. clin. social worker. Pastor Glens Falls (N.Y.) Friends Meeting, 1961-65; assoc. pastor Delmar Bapt. Ch., St. Louis, 1965-68; resource dir. Block Partnership, St. Louis, 1968-71; group home supr. St. Louis Juvenile Ct., 1973-74; program dir. Youth Opportunities Unltd., casework supr. St. Louis County Juvenile Ct., 1974-83; youth svcs. specialist St. Louis County Dept. Human Svcs., 1985-94; assoc. dir. Gen. Protestant Children's Home, 1994-99; residential dir. Mo. Bapt. Children's Home, 1999—; instr. adminstrn. of justice and human svcs. Mo. Bapt. Coll., St. Louis, 1980—; asst. pastor St. Jordan's and St. John's United Chs. of Christ, 1976—; exhibit coord. Dog Mus., 1989-91; cons. Am. Youth Found., 1990—; mem. ordination coun. area V, Great Rivers region Am. Bapt. Chs. U.S.A., 1982-84; chmn. youth focus group Interfaith Partnership Met. St. Louis, 1985-88; chmn. St. Louis Area Youth Svcs. Network, 1987-89. Chmn. group home com. Mo. Coun. on Criminal Justice, 1973-75; chmn. cts. and instns. subcom. Juvenile Delinquency Task Force for Gov. Mo. Action Plan for Pub. Safety, 1976. Mem. Nat. Coun. Juvenile and Family Ct. Judges, Mo. Juvenile Justice Assn. (v.p., chmn. tng. com.), Am. Correctional Assn., Nat. Audubon Soc., Smithsonian Instn. Assn., Cairn Terrier Club Am., Three Rivers Kennel Club of Mo. (past pres.), mo. Conservation Fedn., Lambda Chi Alpha. Democrat. Baptist. Home: 1221 Havenhurst Rd Ballwin MO 63011-4402

ACKERSON, DUANE WRIGHT, JR., author; b. N.Y.C., Oct. 17, 1942; s. Duane Wright and Virginia Gale (Rabe) A.; m. Catherine Eleanor McFarland, Aug. 19, 1967; 1 child, Elizabeth. Student, George Washington Univ., 1960-63; BA, Univ. Oreg., 1964, MFA, 1967. Instr. English Salem Coll., Winston-Salem, N.C., 1967-68; asst. prof. English Idaho State Univ., Pocatello, 1968-74; writer-in-residence Willamette Univ., Salem, Oreg., 1976-78; rsch. analyst Oreg. Vocat. Rehab. Divsn., Salem, 1978-80; employment economist Oreg. Employment Dept., Salem, 1980—; part-time instr. Chemeketa C.C., Salem, 1976-92; union officer, shop steward, activist Oreg. Pub. Employees Union, 1978-93. Author: Weathering, 1973, The Eggplant and Other Absurdities, 1978, The Bird at the End of the Universe, 1997; co-editor: 54 Prose Poems, 1974; vis. writer State Arts Orgn., various states, 1970-78. Creative Writing fellow NEA, 1974-75, Arts Adminstrn. fellow, 1975; recipient Rhysling award Sci. Fiction Poetry Assn., 1978, 79. Avocations: musical theater research. Home: 1850 Corina Dr SE Salem OR 97302-1624 Office: Oreg Employment Dept 875 Union St NE Salem OR 97311-0800

ACKERSON, NELS J(OHN), lawyer; b. Indpls., Apr. 12, 1944; s. Ralph D. and Mariel F. (Maze) A.; m. Sharon Carroll Ackerson, June 11, 1983; children by previous marriage: Betsy Virginia, Peter Nels; stepchildren: Stacia Carroll Loveall, Joshua Michael Loveall. BS with distinction, Purdue U., 1967, M in Pub. Policy, 1971; JD cum laude, Harvard U., 1971. Bar: Ind. 1971, U.S. Dist. Ct. (so. dist.) Ind. 1971, U.S. Ct. Appeals (7th cir.) 1971, D.C. 1985, U.S. Ct. Appeals (D.C. cir.) 1985, U.S. Supreme Ct. 1989, U.S. ct. Internat. Trade, 1991, U.S. Ct. Appeals (6th cir.), 1996. Advisor Harvard Adv. Mission to Republic of Columbia, 1970; assoc. Barnes, Hickam, Pantzer & Boyd, Indpls., 1971-76; chief counsel U.S. Senate Subcom. Constl. Amendments, Washington, 1976-77; chief counsel, exec. dir. U.S. Senate Subcom. on Constn., Washington, 1977-79; ptnr. Campbell, Kyle & Proffitt, Noblesville, Ind., 1979-82, Sidley, Austin & Naguib, Cairo, 1982-84, Sidley & Austin, Cairo, Washington, 1982-91; chmn. Ackerson & Bishop Chartered, The Ackerson Group, Chartered, Washington, 1991—. Bd. editors Harvard Law Rev., 1968-71. Dem. nominee for U.S. Congress, 5th dist., Ind., 1980. Mem. ABA (litigation sect., bus. and banking sect., internat. law sect., adminstrv. law sect.), Am. Agrl. Law Assn., Ctr. Nat. Policy, Nat. Policy Assn. (food and agr. com.), Am. C. of C. in Egypt (pres. 1984), Assn. Trial Lawyers Am. Presbyterian. Office: 700 13th St NW Ste 525 Washington DC 20005-3976

ACKLEY, KATHERINE ANNE, English educator, writer; b. Columbia City, Ind., Oct. 1, 1943; d. Walter Eugene and Phyllis Elizabeth (Phend) Mitchell; m. Allan David White, June 14, 1965 (div. 1978); children: Heather Anne, Laurel Leigh, Jeremy Aaron; m. Richard Cameron Ackley, Jan. 9, 1988. BA, Ball State U., 1965, PhD, 1978; MA, Purdue U., 1969. Lectr. in English Ball State U., Muncie, Ind., 1974-78, U. Wis., Whitewater, 1978-79; asst. prof. English U. Wis., Steven Point, 1979-86, assoc. prof., 1986-90, prof. English, 1990—, coord. women's studies, 1982-92, asst. dean grad. studies, 1990-95; leader semester abroad program U. Wis.-Stevens Point, London, spring 1992, 96; presenter and lectr. in field. Author: The Novels of Barbara Pym, 1989; author, editor: Perspectives on Contemporary Issues: Readings Across the Disciplines, 1996, 2nd edit., 1999; editor: Women and Violence in Literature: An Essay Collection, 1990, Misogyny in Literature: An Essay Collection, 1992, Essays from Contemporary Culture, 1992, 2nd edit., 1995, 3rd edit., 1998; contbr. articles to profl. jours. Del. U.S./China Joint Conf. on Women's Issues, People to People, Beijing, 1995. Grantee Wis. Humanities Com. Insights, 1983, 87, NEH Summer Seminar, 1985, 89, 91. Mem. Midwest MLA, Nat. Coun. Tchrs. English, Am. Soc. for Eighteenth-Century Studies, 18th and 19th-Century Brit. Women Writers Assn., Conf. on Coll. Composition and Comm., The Barbara Pym Soc. (life), Dorothy L. Sayers Soc., Internat. Dickens Fellowship, Bus. and Profl. Women (pres. Stevens Point chpt. 1985-87, Woman of the Yr. 1990), Phi Eta Sigma. Democrat. Methodist. Home: 8675 County Hwy Q Custer WI 54423 Office: Dept English Univ Wis Stevens Point WI 54481

ACKLEY, ROBERT O., lawyer; b. Chgo., July 24, 1952; s. William O. and Jeannette E. (Mitchell) A.; m. Patricia Ann Cerney, May 24, 1980; children: Matthew, Allison, Elizabeth, Anne, Kathryn, Kimberly. BA, No. Ill. U., 1974; MA., No. Mich. U., 1977; JD, John Marshall Law Sch., Chgo., 1988. Bar: Ill. 1988, U.S. Dist. Ct. (no. dist.) Ill. 1988. Adminstrv. intern, asst. to city mgr. City of Marquette, Mich., 1976-77; adminstrv. asst. to town mgr. Town of Glastonbury, Conn., 1978; supr. Continental Bank, Chgo., 1979; chief methods analyst dept. fin. City of Chgo., 1980-81, chief supr. ops. dept. revenue, 1981-84; pres. Ackley & Assocs., Chgo., 1984-88; law clk., adminstrv. asst. to chief justice Thomas J. Moran Supreme Ct. of Ill., Lake Forest, 1988-90; atty. Cassiday, Schade & Gloor, Chgo., 1990-91; pvt. practice Chgo., 1991—; bd. dirs. Ill. Pro Bono Ctr.; adj. prof. Roosevelt U., Chgo., 1989-90; mem. panel arbitrators Cir. Ctr. of 19th Jud. Cir., 1991-97, Cir. Ct. Cook County, 1993-97; detention screening atty. pretrial svcs. Cir. Ct. of Cook County, 1991—; drugs panel atty. Office of State Appellate Defender, 1992—. Bd. dirs. Bryn Mawr-Broadway Ridge Mchts. Assn., Chgo., 1984-87; panel mem. Capital Resource Ctr., 1991, Community Econ. Devel. Law Project. Fellow Ill. Bar Found.; mem. ABA, Nat. Assn. Counsel Children, Ill. Bar Assn., Chgo. Bar Assn., Lake County Bar Assn., Ill. Appellate Lawyers Assn., Acad. Polit. Sci. (life). Home: 606 Buckingham Pl Libertyville IL 60048-3326 Office: 500 N Lake St Ste 109 Mundelein IL 60060-1860

ACKMAN, LAURESS V., lawyer; b. Charles City, Iowa, Sept. 4, 1920; s. John B. and Emma C. (Frevert) A.; m. Chloe Doerr, June 6, 1945; children: C. Stuart, Delia C., Lauress M. Student, Cornell Coll., 1938-40; BSL, U. Minn., 1942, JD, 1945. Bar: Minn. 1946, U.S. Dist. Ct. Minn. 1949. Asst. prof. law U. Wyo., Laramie, 1945-46; mem. faculty U. Minn., Mpls., 1947-49; ptnr. Vennum, Newhall, Ackman, Goetz, Mpls., 1949-68, Lindquist & Vennum, Mpls., 1968—; bd. dirs. numerous private cos. Councilman Wayzata (Minn.) City Coun., 1953-55; bd. dirs. various civic orgns., including Minn. Soc. Fine Arts. Lt. USNR, 1943-46. Mem. ABA, Minn. Bar Assn. Hennepin County Bar Assn. (sec. 1954), The Minn. Club (pres. 1989-90), Woodhill Country Club (sec. 1986-91), LaJolla Country Club. Avocations: golf, tennis, squash, reading. Home: 217 Northgate Rd Wayzata MN 55391-1066 Office: Lindquist & Vennum 4200 IDS Ctr 80 S 8th St Ste 4200 Minneapolis MN 55402-2274

ACKMAN, PAUL JEFFREY, wholesale distribution executive, researcher; b. Richmond, Va., July 4, 1955; s. Barry A. and Elaine F. (Shapiro) A. SB in Physics, MIT, 1977; postgrad., U. Calif., San Diego, 1977-79; MS in Sys. Mgmt., U. So. Calif., 1985; postgrad., U. San Diego, 1986, 87. Programmer, analyst air corrections divsn. UOP, Darien, Conn., 1976; applied physics assoc. Eastman Kodak, Rochester, N.Y., 1977; assoc. tech. staff aerophysics The Aerospace Corp., El Segundo, Calif., 1979-82; project engr. TRW, Redondo Beach, Calif., 1982-85; ret., 1985; v.p., dir. Lewis Supply Co. Inc., Richmond, Va., 1991—; researcher in field. Contbr. article to profl. jour. mem. ednl. coun. MIT, Cambridge, Mass., 1979—; mem. events com. Friends of Art Va. Mus. Fine Arts, Richmond, 1993-96. Officer Civil Air Patrol, 1970-77. Regents fellow U. Calif., 1977-78. Mem. Sigma Xi. Democrat. Jewish. Avocations: travel, American folk dancing, nieces and nephews, Eastern European culture. Home: 1006 Baywood Ct Richmond VA 23226-1525 Office: Lewis Supply Co Inc PO Box 24268 Richmond VA 23224-0268

ACKOFF, RUSSELL LINCOLN, systems sciences educator; b. Phila., Feb. 12, 1919; s. Jack and Fannie (Weitz) A.; m. Alexandra Makar, July 17, 1949 (dec. Feb. 1987); children: Alan W., Karen B., Karla S.; m. Helen Wald, Dec. 20, 1987. BArch, U. Pa., 1941, PhD in Philosophy, 1947; DSc, U. Lancaster, 1967, Washington U., 1993; DSc (hon.), Washington U., St. Louis, Mo., 1993; DL (hon.), U. New Haven, 1997; Doctor honoris causa, Pontificia U. Cath. del Peru, Lima, 1999. Asst. instr. philosophy U. Pa., Phila., 1941-42, 46-47; Silberberg prof. systems scis. U. Pa., 1964-86, Anheuser-Busch prof. emeritus of mgmt. scis., 1986—, chmn. dept. statistics and operations research, 1964-66, chmn. grad. faculty ops. research, 1964-69, dir. Mgmt. Sci. Ctr., 1964-67, 69-70, chmn. social systems scis. unit, 1974-78, 86—, chmn. Busch Ctr., 1970-74, 76-79; asst. prof. philosophy and math. Wayne U., Detroit, 1947-51; assoc. prof., prof. operations research Case Inst. Tech., Cleve., 1951-64; chmn. INTERACT: The Inst. Interactive Mgmt., 1986—; methodological cons. U.S. Bur. Census, 1950-51; cons. Eastern Airlines, Emerson Electric Co., Gen. Foods Co., Mobil Oil Co., Nat. Acad. Scs., Nat. U. Mex., Sci. and Tech. Rsch. Coun., Turkey, Western Electric Co.; bd. dirs. Mantual Indsl. Devel. Corp.; August A. Busch Jr. vis. prof. mktg. Washington U., St. Louis, 1989-95; mem. core faculty Union Inst., Cin., 1989-91. Author: (with C.W. Churchman) Psychologistics, 1946, Methods of Inquiry, 1950, (with C.W. Churchman and M. Wax) Measurement of Consumer Interest, 1947, The Design of Social Research, 1953, (with C.W. Churchman and E.L. Arnoff) Introduction to Operations Research, 1957, Progress in Operations Research, I, 1961, Scientific Method, 1962, (with P. Rivett) A Manager's Guide to Operations Research, 1963, (with M. Sasieni) Fundamentals of Operations Research, 1968, A Concept of Corporate Planning, 1970, (with F.E. Emery) On Purposeful Systems, 1972, Redesigning The Future, 1974, (with T.A. Cowan et al) Designing a National Scientific and Technological Communication System, 1976, The Art of Problem Solving, 1978, Creating the Corporate Future, 1981, (with E. V. Finnel, J. Gharajedaghi) A Guide to Controlling Your Corporation's Future, 1984, (with P. Broholm and R. Snow) Revitalizing Western Economics, 1984, Management in Small Doses, 1986, Ackoff's Fables, 1991, The Democratic Corporation, 1994, Exploring Personality: An Intellectual Odyssey, 1998, Ackoff's Best, 1999, Re-Creating the Corporation, 1999; editor: Management Science, 1965-70, Systems and Mgmt. Ann, 1974; assoc. editor Ops. Rsch., 1953-65, Conflict Resolution, 1964-70; book rev. editor Philosophy of Science, 1947-53; mem. abstracting staff: Biological Abstracts, 1950-51; adv. editor mgmt. sci. John Wiley & Sons, 1964-86; mem. adv. bd. Math. Spectrum, 1968-86; mem. editorial bd. Management Decision, 1968-86, The Soc. Orgnl. Learning; editorial assoc. European Jour. Operational Research; contbr. articles to profl. jours. Bd. dirs. Tallberg Found., Sweden, 1997—, Ctr. for Quality Mgmt., Cambridge, Mass., 1996—; mem. UN Devel. Adv. Coun., 1996—;. Recipient Am. Soc. for Tng. and Devel. award, 1993. Fellow Am. Statis. Assn., Ops. Rsch. Soc. Am. (v.p., pres. 1956-57), Internat. Acad. Mgmt., Inst. Mgmt. Cons.; mem. Internat. Acad. Mgmt., Russian Acad. Natural Scis. (fgn. mem.), Inst. Mgmt. Scis. (v.p. 1965), Operational Rsch. Soc. (U.K.) (Silver medal 1971), Soc. Gen. Systems Rsch. (pres. 1987-88), Oprational Rsch. Soc. India, Peace Rsch. Soc., Sigma Xi, Tau Sigma Delta. Home: Benson House 101 930 Montgomery Ave Rosemont PA 19010-3044 Office: INTERACT Ste 200 6 S Bryn Mawr Ave Bryn Mawr PA 19010-3215

ACKOUREY, PETER PAUL, lawyer; b. Scranton, Pa., Dec. 18, 1954; s. Paul Peter and Regina Helene (Dorris) A.; m. Christine Marie Van Wert, Aug. 6, 1977; children: Abigail Regina, Kenneth Jamal, Jemeille Irene, Mary Rose. BA in History, U. Scranton, 1974; JD, Harvard U., 1977. Bar: Pa. 1977, N.J. 1989. Assoc. Drinker Biddle & Reath, Phila., 1977-83; assoc. counsel Mellon Bank Corp., Phila., 1983-88; ptnr. Drinker Biddle & Reath LLP, Princeton, N.J., 1988—. Mem. ABA, Pa. Bar Assn., N.J. Bar Assn., Phila. Bar Assn. Avocations: reading and research Am. History, baseball. Office: Drinker Biddle & Reath LLP PO Box 627 105 College Rd E Princeton NJ 08542-0627

ACLIN, KEITH ANDREW, technicial service executive, educator; b. Meridan, Conn., May 9, 1960; s. John Joseph and Anne (Barr) A.; m. Jean Anne Taylor, May 28, 1983. BA in Psychology, Rutgers U., 1983; MS in Meteorology, Tex. A&M U., 1995. Navigator tng. USAF, Mather AFB, Calif., 1983-86; navigator USAF, Carswell AFB, Tex., 1986-88, radar navigator, 1988-91; radar navigator USAF, K.I. Sawyer AFB, Mich., 1991-92; radar meteorologist TVR Comms., Oklahoma City, 1995-96; sr. field support technician Oklahoma City Clinic, 1997-98; network computer engr. Coll. Edn. U. Ctrl. Okla., 1998-99; tech. svcs. mgr., tech. instr. ExecuTrain of Oklahoma City, 1999—. Comdr. Edmond Composite Squadron, CAP, 1995—. NSF grantee, 1993-95. Mem. DAV, Am. Meteorol. Soc., Masons, Scottish Rite. Avocations: scuba diving, flying, camping, reading. Home: 604 Harrier Hawk Edmond OK 73003-3185

ACOBA, SIMEON RIVERA, JR., judge; b. Honolulu, Mar. 11, 1944; s. Simeon R. and Martina (Domingo) A. BA, U. Hawaii, 1966; JD, Northwestern U., 1969. Bar: Hawaii 1969, U.S. Dist. Ct. Hawaii, U.S. Ct. Appeals (9th cir.). Law clk. Hawaii Supreme Ct., Honolulu, 1969-70; housing officer U. Hawaii, Honolulu, 1970-71; dep. atty. gen., Honolulu, 1971-73; pvt. practice, Honolulu, 1973-80; judge 1st Cir. Ct., State of Hawaii, Honolulu, 1980-94; judge Intermediate Ct. of Appeals, State of Hawaii, 1994—; atty. on spl. contract Div. OSHA, Dept. Labor, Honolulu, 1975-77, Pub. Utilities Div., State of Hawaii, 1976-77, Campaign Spending Com., State of Hawaii, 1976; staff atty. Hawaii State Legislature, 1975. Bd. dirs. Hawaii Mental Health Assn., 1975-77, Nuuanu YMCA, 1975-78, Hawaii Youth at Risk, 1990-91; mem. Gov.'s Conf. on Yr. 2000, Honolulu, 1970, Citizens Com. on Adminstrn. of Justice, 1972, State Drug Abuse Commn., 1975-76, Com. to Consider the Adoption of ABA Model Rules of Profl. Conduct, 1989-91; subcom. chmn. Supreme Ct. Com. Pattern Jury Instrns., 1990-91; mem. Hawaii Supreme Ct. Ad Hoc Com. Jury Master List, 1991-92, Judicial Edn. Com., 1992-93, Hawaii State Bar Assn. Jud. Adminstrn. Com., 1992-94, Permanent Com. Rules of Penal Procedure and Cir. Ct. Rules, 1992-96; instr. criminal law Hawaii Pacific U., 1992—. Recipient Liberty Bell award, 1964. Mem. ABA, ATLA, Hawaii State Bar Assn. (dir. young lawyers sect. 1973), Am. Judicature Soc. Office: Intermediate Ct of Appeals State of Hawaii PO Box 2560 Honolulu HI 96804-2560

ACOMB, FREDERICK ALLAN, lawyer; b. Warsaw, Ind., May 18, 1962; s. Dwight Earl and Joan Lois (Schultz) A.; m. Andrea Rebecca Kast, Aug. 15, 1987; children: Matthew Joseph, Peter Christian, Micaela Sophia. BMus, Northwestern U., 1984; JD, U. Calif., San Francisco, 1990. Bar: Mich. Atty. Miller, Canfield, Paddock & Stone, Detroit, 1991—. Mem. staff Hastings Law Jour.; contbr. articles to profl. jours. Trustee Fanclub for the Arts, Southfield, Mich., 1995-96, 20-30 Club, Southfield, 1995-96; bd. dirs. Kaleidoscope Concerts, Bloomfield Hills, Mich., 1993-96. Mem. ABA, State Bar Mich., Detroit Met. Bar Assn., The Detroit Club. Avocations: running, reading, travel. Office: Miller Canfield et al 15 W Jefferson Ave Ste 2500 Detroit MI 48226-4428

ACOMB, ROBERT BAILEY, JR., lawyer, educator; b. New Orleans, July 28, 1930; s. Robert Bailey and Catherine (Ryan) A.; m. Greta LeBlanc, Apr. 25, 1953; children: Robert III, Dwight J., Greta, William Ryan, John. BBA, Tulane U., 1951, JD, 1953. Bar: La. 1953, U.S. Dist. Ct. (ea. and mid. dist.) La. 1953, U.S. Ct. Appeals (5th cir.) 1955, U.S. Supreme Ct. 1967, U.S. Ct. Appeals (7th cir.) 1976, U.S. Ct. Appeals (11th cir.) 1981, U.S. Dist. Ct. (we. dist.) La. 1989. Assoc. Jones, Walker, Waechter, Poitevent, Carrere & Denegre, New Orleans, 1953-56, ptnr., 1956, sr. ptnr., 1968—; adj. prof. law Tulane U., New Orleans, 1969—; bd. dirs. Attys. Liability Assurance Soc. Ltd., Hamilton, Bermuda, 1979—; pres. bd. dirs. Christian Bros. Found., Inc., New Orleans, 1976-78; trustee Christian Bros. Retirement Fund, New Orleans, 1989—. Author: Maritime Personal Injury & Death, 4th edit., 1993; editor: Damages Recovered, 1984; contbr. articles to profl. jours.; chmn. adv. editors: Tulane Maritime Law Jour., 1976-93. Chmn. Archbishop's Community Appeal, New Orleans, 1993; pres. Tulane U. Assocs., New Orleans, 1990-92. Decorated knight cmdr. Equestrian Order of Holy Sepulchre of Jerusalem. Fellow Am. Coll. Trial Lawyers (state chair 1972—), Am. Bar Found.; mem. ABA (mem. standing com. on admiralty, chmn. 1979-83), Tulane Maritime Law Ctr. (chmn. 1982—), Maritime Law Assn. U.S. (proctor, mem. exec. com. 1981-84), Tulane Maritime Law Inst. (chmn. 1991—), Tulane U. Alumni Assn. (pres. 1989-90, Vol. of Yr. 1992), Navy League U.S. (pres. New Orleans chpt. 1987-88, state pres. 1994), Assn. Average Adjusters U.S. (chmn. 1992-93), New Orleans Country Club, Boston Club, Pickwick Club, Stratford Club, Order of St. Louis, New Orleans Bar Assn. (Disting. Maritime Lawyer 1996). Roman Catholic. Avocations: photography, travel, sports, teaching. Home: 3450 Vincennes Pl New Orleans LA 70125-4350 Office: Jones Walker Waechter Poitevent Carrere & Denegre 201 Saint Charles Ave Ste 5200 New Orleans LA 70170-5100

ACORD-SKELTON, BARBARA BURROWS, counselor, educator, artist; b. L.A., Dec. 26, 1928; d. Harry and Sophia (Dittman) Burrows; m. Benjamin Raddatz, June 11, 1949 (div. Dec. 1970); children: Randolph, Marjorie, Thomas, Deborah; m. William A. Acord, Feb. 26, 1974 (dec.); m. Gerald Skelton, 1989. AA, Riverside City Coll., 1956; BA, Calif. State U., San Bernardino, 1970; MA, Pacific Oaks Coll., 1974; postgrad., Claremont Coll., 1976-91. Lic. marriage, family and child counselor, Calif., 1974. Dir. pvt. nursery sch. Headstart, Riverside, Calif., 1964-66; career devel., coord. Riverside County Head Start and Corono Norco Sch. Dist., Riverside, 1966-72; instr. Chaffey Community Coll., Alta Loma, Calif., 1971-82; class room coord., family counselor Casa Colina Hosp., Pomona, Calif., 1973-79; counselor LaVerne (Calif.) Ctr. for Edn. Counseling, 1976-82; social worker III San Andreas Regional Ctr., Salinas, Calif., 1984-87; pvt. practice family and individual counseling Medford, 1987-92; cons. Pomona U. Sch. Dist., Calif., 1973-80, San Gabriel Valley Regional Ctr., Covina, Calif., 1976-82, Nat. Council Alcoholism, Covina, 1980-82; instr. U. LaVerne, 1976-82. Author: On Learning and Growing, 1974; co-author: Parent Advocacy Training, 1977, Creative Competency, 1978. Vol. Day Springs Hospice, Medford, 1987-90; bd. dirs. Gold Coast Arab Horse Assn., Santa Clara County, Calif., 1983-85. Riverside County Headstart scholar, 1967, Ednl. Profl. Devel. Act scholar, 1971-74. Mem. Am. Assn. Marriage and Family Therapists, Upper Rogue Art Assn., Arab Horse Assn. (So. Oreg. bd. dirs. 1988, pres. 1989), Women Artists Cascades Mountains, Region III Arab Horse Assn. (bd. dirs. 1983-85). Avocations: painting, stained glass, sewing, fishing. Home: 13856 Weowna Way White City OR 97503-8535

ACOSTA, CRISTINA PILAR, artist; b. L.A., Sept. 23, 1959; d. Joaquin Enrique and Sandra Diane (Wisner) A.; m. Randall Scott Barna, May 25, 1991; 1 child, Isabella Pilar Acosta Barna. AA, Ctrl. Oreg. C.C., 1984; BFA, U. Oreg., 1988. Freelance comml. sign painter, window graphics Bend and Eugene, Oreg., 1985-92; sign maker Safeway Corp., Bend and Eugene, Oreg., 1987-88; billboard, mural & lettering artist Carlson Sign, Bend, Oreg., 1989-91; instr. Ctrl. Oreg. C.C., Bend, 1990-96; comml. artist, fine artist Bend, 1990—; designer ceramic tile. One-woman shows include Pinkney Gallery, Bend, 1987, Upper Gallery, Sunriver, Oreg., 1992, The Welcome Ctr., Bend, 1992, North Gallery, Grants Pass, Oreg., 1995; group shows include Sunriver Juried Art Show, 1987, Gallery 141, Eugene, Oreg., 1989, Sunbird Gallery, Bend, 1992, Ramskull Gallery, Hood River, Oreg., 1991-92, Columbia Art Gallery, Hood River, 1991-93, City Hall, Bend, 1992-93, Beaverton (Oreg.) Arts Commn. Juried Show, 1992-93, Wickman Gallery, Redmond, Oreg., 1992, Linn Benton C,C,m 1992, Blue Sky Gallery, Bend, 1993, Ctrl. Oreg. C.C., Bend, 1995, Works of Faith, Portland, 1995, others, illustrator, "When Woman Became Sea", 1998; contbr. art to mags. and books. Mem. Ctrl. Oreg. Arts Assn. (bd. dirs. 1992-93), Tile Heritage Found., Graphic Artists Guild. Studio: Cristina Acosta Art Studio PO Box 923 Bend OR 97709-0923

ACOSTA, JULIO BERNARD, obstetrician, gynecologist; b. Loreto, Peru, July 29, 1927; came to U.S., 1955, naturalized, 1960; s. Miguel and Flor Maria (Solis) A.; m. Mary Jane Aedinvice, Aug. 30, 1974; children: Raul, Luis-Miguel, Patricia, Silvia, Douglas, Jill. MD, St. Marcos U., Peru, 1955. Diplomate Am. Bd. Obstetrics and Gynecology. Intern St. Alexis Hosp., Cleve., 1955-56, resident, 1956-57; resident St. Ann Hosp., Cleve., 1957-59; pvt. practice medicine specializing in obstetrics and gynecology Livonia, Mich., 1964-86; chief staff Plymouth Gen. Hosp., Detroit, 1970-73, chief gynecologic sect., 1974-83, med. dir.; active staff St. Mary Hosp., Livonia, 1964-86, Grace-Harper Hosp., Detroit, 1973-86; clin. instr. Wayne State U. Sch. Medicine, 1983-87; sr. physician Kaiser Permanente Med. Ctr., Walnut Creek, Calif., 1986—; clin. faculty U. Calif., San Francisco, 1988—. Contbr. articles to profl. jours. Capt. M.C., USAR, 1959-62. Fellow ACOG, Am. Fertility Soc., Am. Soc. Colposcopy and Cervical Pathology, Am. Soc. Abdominal Surgeons; mem. Peruvian-Am. Med. Soc. Home: 170 F Alamo Plaza # 241 Alamo CA 94507-1550 Office: 1515 Newell Ave Walnut Creek CA 94596-5120 also: Kaiser Permanente Med Ctr Dept Ob Gyn 1425 S Main St Dept Ob Walnut Creek CA 94596-5318

ACOSTA, RAYMOND LUIS, federal judge; b. N.Y.C., May 31, 1925; s. Ramon J. and Carmen J. (Acha-Jimenez) Acosta-Colon; m. Marie Hatcher, Nov. 2, 1957; children: Regina, Gregory, Ann Marie. Student, Princeton U., 1948; JD, Rutgers U., 1951. Bar: N.J. 1953, U.S. Supreme Ct. 1956, P.R. 1959. Sole practice Hackensack, N.J., 1953-54; spl. agt. FBI, San Diego, Washington, Miami, Fla., 1954-58; asst. U.S. atty. San Juan, P.R., 1958-61; sole practice San Juan, 1961-67; trust officer Banco Credito y Ahorro Ponceno, San Juan, 1967-80; U.S. atty. Dist. P.R., Hato Rey, 1980-82; judge U.S. Dist. Ct. P.R., San Juan, 1982—; Alt. del. U.S.-P.R. Commn. on Status, 1962-63; mem. Gov.'s Spl. Com. to Study Structure and Orgn. Police Dept., P.R., 1969. Contbr. articles to profl. jours. Pres. United Fund, P.R., 1979. Served with USN, 1943-46. Recipient Merit cert. Mayor of San Juan, 1973. Mem. Fed. Bar Assn. (pres., P.R. 1967), P.R. Bankers Assn. (chmn. trust div. 1971, 75, 77), P.R. Bar Assn., Soc. Former Spl. Agts. FBI. Office: US Dist Ct Chase Manhattan Bldg 1200C 254 Ave Munoz Rivera San Juan PR 00918-1900

ACOSTA, URSULA, psychologist; b. Hannover, Germany, Jan. 14, 1933; came to U.S., 1954, naturalized, 1958; d. Johannes Karl and Irma (Ulrich) Schmidt; BA, U. P.R., 1971, ME, 1973; PhD in Psychology, Gutenberg U., Mainz, Germany, 1979; m. Sebastian Acosta-Ronda, June 12, 1954; children: Johann, Dennis, Peter. Various occupations, 1954-66; from instr. to asst. prof., assoc. prof. then prof. psychology U. P.R., Mayagüez, 1973-95, ret. 1995. Chairperson appeal bd. SSS. Mem. LWV (unit chair 1977-78, 86-88), Puerto Rican Geneal. Soc. (editor jour.). Active Puerto Rican Statehood Movement. Co-author: Cabo Rojo (History prize Ateneo Puertorriqueno de New York 1983); author: Quien era Cofresi?, 1984, New Voices of Old: Five Centuries of Puerto Rican Cultural History, 1987, Cofresi y Ducoudray: Dos Hombres Al Margen de la Historia, 1991; co-author: Cabo Rojo: Notas para su historia, 1985; editor: Boletín de la Sociedad Puertorriquéna de Genealogía, 1994—; Named Adopted Daughter of Cabo Rojo, PR, 1999; contbr. articles to various jours. and newspapers. Republican. Office: PO Box 8 Hormigueros PR 00660-0008

ACREE, G. HARDY, airport executive. Mgr., dep. dir. aviation Bush Intercontinental Airport, Houston, TX, 1995—. Office: Bush Intercontinental Airport/Houston Dept Aviation PO Box 60106 Houston TX 77205-0106*

ACREE, WILMA KATHERYN, retired secondary school educator; b. Ripley, W.Va., July 16, 1942; d. Mote Jackson and Emma Roseanne (McHenry) Stanley; m. Frank H. Acree Sr., Sept. 26, 1975 (dec. Oct. 1990). BA in Edn., Glenville State Coll., 1965; MA in Edn., W.Va. U., 1971. Tchr. English Wood County Schs., Parkersburg, W.Va., 1965-97, ret., 1997; presenter workshop W.Va. Writers' Conf., Ripley, 1995, 96. Author: About Bee Robbing and Other Things, 1995; contbr. poems to lit. publs.; editor children's poetry Gambit Lit. Mag., Parkersburg, W.Va., 1986. Citizen rep. Jackson Jr. H.S. Local Sch. Improvement Assn., Vienna, W.Va., 1997-99; advisor Jackson Jr. H.S. Writers' Club, 1995-99; mem. adv. bd. Confluence lit. mag., Marietta (Ohio) Coll., 1996-99. Mem. W.Va. Writers, Inc. (pres. 1997-99, 3rd pl. narrative poetry 1991), Ohio Valley Lit. Group (exec. dir. 1993-99), Wood County Ret. Tchrs. Assn. Avocations: writing, reading, walking, dogs, computers. Home: 1024 28th St Vienna WV 26105-1475

ACRIVOS, ANDREAS, chemical engineering educator; b. Athens, Greece, June 13, 1928; m. Juana Vivo, Sept. 1, 1956. BSChemE, Syracuse U., 1950; MS, U. Minn., 1951, PhD, 1954. Instr. U. Calif., Berkeley, 1954-55, asst. prof., 1955-59, assoc. prof., 1959-62; prof. Stanford (Calif.) U., 1962-88; Einstein prof. CCNY, 1988—. Contbr. articles to profl. jours. Guggenheim Found. fellow, 1959, 76; recipient Bingham Medal, 1994, Soc. Rheology. Fellow AIChE (awards 1963, 68, 84), Am. Phys. Soc. (Fluid Dynamics prize 1991); mem. NAS, NAE, Am. Acad. Arts and Scis., Am. Chem. Soc., Soc. Rheology. Office: CCNY Levich Inst 138th St at Convent Ave New York NY 10031

ACS, JOSEPH STEVEN, transportation engineering consultant; b. Budapest, Hungary, Apr. 26, 1936; came to U.S., 1957; s. Gyula Istvan and Gizella (Sztanek) A.; m. Eva Hegedus, Apr. 18, 1960; 1 child, Joseph S. Jr. BS in Civil Engring., Kvassay Jeno Kozlekedes Ipari Technikum, Budapest, 1956. With Balt. & Ohio R.R. Co., Cin., 1957-68; project engr. Balt. & Ohio Chgo. Terminal R.R. Co., 1968-75, terminal engr., 1975-88; pub. projects engr. CSX Transp., Chgo., 1988-92; prin. Allied Consulting Svcs., Ltd., Chgo., 1992—. Author: The Eleuthero Line, 1999; contbr. articles to profl. jours. Mem. NSPE, ASCE, AREMA, Am. Rlwy. Engring. and Maintenance Assn. (chmn. com. 14/yard and terminals 1989-92, Profl. Svcs. award 1992), Am. Rlwy. Bridge and Bldg. Assn., Am. Right of Way Assn., Roadmasters and Maintenance of Way Assn., Chicago Heights Country Club, Eagles, Lions, Am. Legion, KC. Republican. Roman Catholic. Fax: 815-437-2041. Home: 45 Fairoaks Dr Putnam IL 61560-9614 Office: Allied Consulting Svcs Ltd PO Box 277945 Chicago IL 60827-7945

ACTON, DAVID, lawyer; b. Phila., Feb. 13, 1933; s. Kenneth Davis and Mary (Musselman) A.; m. Barbara Ann Sullivan, June 18, 1955; children—Lauren Doane, Paul Bodine; m. Jane Thomas Young, June 24, 1978. Grad., Episcopal Acad., 1951; A.B., Yale, 1955; J.D., U. Pa., 1960. Assoc. Krusen, Evans & Byrne, Phila., 1960-63; asst. sec., asst. gen. counsel Leeds & Northrup Co., Phila., 1963-65; sec., gen. counsel Leeds & Northrup Co., North Wales, Pa., 1965-71; v.p., gen. counsel K.S. Sweet Assos., King of Prussia, Pa., 1971-75; practice in Bryn Mawr, Pa., 1975-77; v.p. Crockett Mortgage Co., Valley Forge, Pa.; gen. mgr. Hershey's Mill, 1977-82; exec. v.p. Ultec, Inc., Exton, Pa., 1982-85; arbitrator and mediator, 1986—. Mem. Bd. Friends Independence Nat. Hist. Park. Mem. Phila. Bar Assn., Colonial Soc. Pa., Mensa, Union League Club, Merion Cricket Club, Yale Club (Phila., pres. class of 1955), Chevaliers du Tastevin. Home and Office: 233 Righters Mill Rd Gladwyne PA 19035-1532

ACTON, DAVID L(AWRENCE), automobile company executive; b. Detroit, Apr. 12, 1949; s. Lawrence E. and Johannah (Cassimatis) A.; m. Dianne Patience McNeill, Sept. 5, 1981; children: Andrew, Stephen, Amy. BME, Gen. Motors Inst., Flint, Mich., 1973; MBA, U. Mich., 1978. Assoc. engr. Hydra-matic div. GM, Ypsilanti, Mich., 1973-74, project engr., 1974-77, supr. indsl. engring., 1977-78, asst. supt. indsl. engring., 1978-81; asst. supt. progress tracking, quality and reliability GM, Detroit, 1981-83, sr. administr., 1983-85, mgr. program planning B-O-C car group, 1985, program mgr. Allanté elec. test system, 1985-87; mgr. elec. design and processing Cadillac Motor Car Co., Detroit, 1987-91, mgr. electrical product systems, 1991-93; chief engr. elec./electronics Cadillac luxury car divsn. GM, Flint, Mich., 1993-96, dir. elec. engring. mid-luxury car group, 1996-97; dir. elec. engring. N.Am. ops. GM, Warren, Mich., 1997-98; chief vehicle engr. on-star divsn. GM, Troy, Mich., 1998—. Mem. SAE. Office: GM 888 W Big Beaver Rd Ste 200 Troy MI 48084

ACTON, NORMAN, international organization executive; b. Denver, Oct. 29, 1918; s. Norman Erwin and Mildred (Welch) A.; m. Katherine E. Brown, June 9, 1946; 1 child, Mary Ann. B.S. in Journalism, U. Ill., 1939; ScD (hon.), L.I. U., 1973. Engaged in advt. and pub. relations, 1939-43; chief econs. and labor sect. Gifu Mil. Govt. Team, Japan, 1947-49; exec. dir. U.S. Com. Resettlement Physically Disabled, 1950-51; asst. sec. gen. Internat. Soc. Welfare Cripples, 1951-54; exec. dir. U.S. com. for UNICEF, 1954-59, bd. dirs., 1967-69; dep. sec. gen. World Vets. Fedn., 1959-61, sec. gen., 1961-67; sec. gen. Rehab. Internat., N.Y.C., 1967-84; pres. Acton Internat., Miles, Va., 1984-88; Chmn. non-govtl. organ com. UNICEF, 1952-54, cons., 1957; chmn. conf. group U.S. orgns. for UN, 1958; pres. Internat. Working Group on Sports for Disabled, 1961-64; mem. Pres.'s Com. Employment Handicapped, 1952-57, 63-93, chmn. internat. com., 1985-87; chmn. Internat. Council on Disability (formerly Conf. World Orgns. Interested in Handicapped), 1964-67, 69-88; pres. Internat. Sports Orgn. for Disabled, 1965-66; cons. UN, 1981—, Internat. Labour Office, 1988. Author: Rehabilitation of the Physically Handicapped, 1953. Bd. dirs. Inst. de la Vie, 1961-67, Am. Impact Found., 1986-88; bd. dirs. Nat. Ctr. for Appropriate Tech., 1987-91, chmn. bd. APTEK Internat., 1987-88. Capt AUS, 1943-47. Mem. Soc. Internat. Devel., World Future Soc., Overseas Press Club Am., Phi Gamma Delta. Home and Office: 31 Lemington Ct Homosassa FL 34446-3978

ACZÉL, JÁNOS DEZSÖ, mathematics educator; b. Budapest, Hungary, Dec. 26, 1924; s. Dezsö and Irén (Adler) A.; m. Susan Kende, Dec. 14, 1946; children: Catherine, Julie. MA, U. Budapest, 1947, PhD, 1947; DSc, Hungarian Acad. Sci., 1957; Dr. honoris causa, U. Karlsruhe, 1990, U. Graz, 1995, Silesian U. Katowice, 1996, Tech. U. Miskole, 1999. Faculty U. Szeged, Hungary, 1948-50; prof. math. Tech. U., Miskolc, 1950-52, Kossuth U., Debrecen, Hungary, 1952-65, U. Waterloo, Ont., Can., 1965-93; disting. prof. U. Waterloo, 1969-93, disting. prof. emeritus, 1993—; vis. prof. U. Fla., Gainesville, 1963-64, 81, Stanford U., 1964, U. Koln, Germany, 1965, U. Giessen, 1966, 70, Ruhr U., 1968, Fla. Atlantic U., 1968, U. Pavia, 1968, 69, Ist. Naz. Alta Matematica, Rome, 1971, Monash U., Clayton, Victoria, Australia, 1972, Ahmadu Bello U., Zaria, Nigeria, 1975-76, Calif. Inst. Tech., 1978, Karl-Franzens U., Graz, Austria, 1979, 86, 91, 93, 99, Okayama U. (Japan), 1984, U. Milan, 1985, 91, U. Hamburg, 1985, U. Politécnica Catalunya, Barcelona, 1986, 92, U. Berne, Switzerland, 1986, U. Karlsruhe, Germany, 1992, 98, U. Calif., Irvine, 1994, 96—; cons. Naval Ocean Systems Ctr., San Diego, 1979-81; chmn. Internat. Symposium Functional Equations, 1962-96, hon. chmn., 1997—;. Author: (with S. Golab) Funktionalgleichungen der Theorie der geometrischen Objekte, 1960, Vorlesungen über Funktionalgleichungen und ihre Anwendungen, 1961, Ein Blick auf Funktionalgleichungen und ihre Anwendungen, 1962, Lectures on Functional Equations and Their Applications, 1966, On Applications and Theory of Functional Equations, 1969, (with Z. Daróczy) On Measures of Information and Their Characterizations, 1975, A Short Course on Functional Equations Based Upon Recent Applications to Social and Behavioral Sciences, 1987, (with J. Dhombres) Functional Equations in Several Variables with Applications to Mathematics, Information Theory and to the Natural and Social Sciences, 1989; editor: Functional Equations: History, Applications and Theory, 1984, Aggregating Clones, Colors, Equations, Iterates, Numbers and Tiles, 1995; editor jours. Rendiconti di Matematica e delle sue Applicazioni, Inequalities and their Applications, Mathematica Japonica, Results of Mathematics, Mathware and Soft Computing; hon. editor-in-chief Aequationes Mathematicae; editor: Theory and Decision Library, Series B; also numerous articles. Recipient M. Beke award J. Bolyai Math. Soc., 1961, Hungarian Acad. Scis. award, 1962, Cajal medal Spanish Nat. Council Sci. Research, 1988. Fellow Royal Soc. Can., Hungarian Acad. Scis. (fgn.); mem. Can. Math. Soc., Am. Math. Soc., N.Y. Acad. Scis., Austrian Math. Soc. Initiated modern theory of functional equations; gave gen. theorems and applications to geometry, algebra, analysis, econs., mathematical psychology, utility, decision, probability, and info. theory; theories of mean values, measurement, and webs. Home: 97 McCarron Cres, Waterloo, ON Canada N2L 5M9 Office: U Waterloo, Pure Math Dept, Waterloo, ON Canada N2L 3G1

ACZEL, MOLLIE GOODMAN, educational administrator; b. Houston, Aug. 7, 1939; d. Aaron and Bess (Kaminsky) Goodman; m. Thomas Aczel (dec.); children: Joseph, Stephen, Elisabeth A. Aczel Wallock, Bettina V. Aczel Prober. BS in Edn., U. Houston, 1961, MEd in Spl. Edn., 1967. Cert. tchr., Tex., N.J. Prin., supr. secular studies Irvin M. Shlenker Sch., Houston, 1985-88; instr., supr. student tchrs. Kean Coll., Union, N.J., 1989-91; founding head of sch. Alfred and Adele Davis Acad., Atlanta, 1992—. Office: Davis Acad 8105 Roberts Dr Atlanta GA 30350-4120

ADAIR, CHARLES ROBERT, JR., lawyer; b. Narrows, Va., Sept. 29, 1914; s. Charles Robert and Margaret (Davis) A.; m. Lillian Adele Duffee, Sept. 19, 1942 (dec. 1993). B.S., U. Ala., 1942, LL.B., 1948, J.D., 1969. Bar: Ala. bar 1948. Since practiced in Dadeville; solicitor Tallapoosa County, 1955-73; vice chmn. Ala. Securities Commn., 1969-71; mem., chmn. Ala. Jud. Compensation Commn., 1984—; v.p., bd. dirs. Dadeville Industries, Inc.; bd. dirs. Bank of Dadeville, Ala.. Chmn. Dadeville One Drive, 1960; chmn. Horseshoe Bend Regional Library, 1960-65; mem., sec. planning commn. City of Dadeville, 1965-80; hon. life mem. Bethel Vol. Fire Dept. and Rescue Service, Jackson's Gap Vol. Fire Dept. and Rescue Service; trustee Ala. Law Inst., Ala. Bar Found. Served as officer USAAF, World War II. Mem. Ala. Bar Assn. (past v.p.), Tallapoosa Bar (past pres.), 5th Cir. Bar Assn. (pres.), Farrah Law Soc., VFW, Am. Legion, East Ala. Peace Officers Assn. (hon. life), The Club, Capital City Club, Quarterback Club (past capt.), Masons, Kiwanis, Scabbard and Blade, Omicron Delta Kappa, Delta Tau Delta, Phi Alpha Delta. Presbyterian. Home: Duffee's Hill Dadeville AL 36853 Office: Old Bank Of Dadeville Dadeville AL 36853

ADAIR, CHARLES VALLOYD, retired physician; b. Lorain, Ohio, Apr. 20, 1923; s. Waite and Ella Jane (Robertson) A.; m. Contance Dean, Apr. 1, 1944; children: Allen V., Richard D. AB, Hobart Coll, Geneva, N.Y., 1944; MD, Western Res. U., 1947. Diplomate Am. Bd. Internal Medicine. Intern, then asst. resident in medicine Rochester Gen. Hosp., N.Y., 1947-49; fellow in medicine Univ. Hosps., Syracuse, N.Y., 1949-51; practice medicine specializing in internal medicine Mansfield, Ohio, 1953-85; ret., 1985; mem. staffs Mansfield Gen. Hosp., Peoples Hosp., Richland Neuropsychiat. Hosp.; mem. Mansfield City Bd. Health to 1985; trustee, past. pres. Mansfield Meml. Homes. Served to capt. AUS, 1943-46, 51-53. Fellow ACP; mem. AMA, Am. Soc. Internal Medicine, Ohio Med. Assn., Richland County Med. Soc., Our Club, Westbrook Country Club. Republican. Congregationalist. Home: 1010 Woodland Rd Mansfield OH 44907-2242

ADAIR, DWIGHT RIAL, film director, educator; b. Winters, Tex., Mar. 1, 1950; s. J.P. and Beth (Clayton) A.; m. Sandra Estrin, Mar. 11; children: Marshall Clayton, Holly AshLyn. BA, Southwestern U., 1972; MA, Claremont Coll., 1975; ABD in Film, U. Tex., 1978. Dir. TV series Dallas, Dynasty, 1983-90; dialogue coach for various films and TV programs, including Urban Cowboy, 1979-80, Oldest Living Graduate, 1981, Member of the Wedding, 1982, A River Runs Through It, 1992; prodr. (movie) She Fought Alone, 1995. Chmn. Entertainment Industry Task Force Austin C. of C., 1994-97. Mem. SAG, Dirs. Guild Am. Democrat. Methodist. Home: 11511 Queens Way Austin TX 78759-4468 Office: Granite House Inc 1411 W 6th St Austin TX 78703-5140

ADAIR, LAWRENCE R., army officer; b. West Point, N.Y., Sept. 8, 1951. BS, U.S. Mil. Acad.; MS, Webster U. Commd. 2d lt. U.S. Army, 1974, advanced through grades to brig. gen.; served in Germany, 1980-83; detailed to U.S. Army Command and Gen. Staff Coll., 1983; pers. staff officer Office of Dep. Chief of Staff for Pers., Washington, 1983-85; aide to Sec. of Army, Washington, 1985-86; bn. exec. officer Ft. Hood, Md., 1986-88; team chief Readiness Group, Ft. Sam Houston, Tex., 1988-90; served in Operation Desert Shield/Deesert Storm, Saudi arabia, 1990-91; detailed to Nat. War Coll., Washington, 1993; spl. asst. to Sec. of Army, 1993-94; comdr. 2d Armord Divsn. Arty., Ft. Hood, 1994-96; exec. asst. to comdr.-in-chief U.S. Atlantic Command and Supreme Allied Comdr. Atlantic, Norfolk, Va., 1996-98; dep. comdg. gen. for tng. U.S. Army field Arty. Ctr. and U.S. Army Field Arty. Sch., Ft. Sill, Okla., 1998—. Decorated Legion of Merit, Bronze Star medal, Army Commendation medals, others. Office: US Army Fielt Arty Ctr and Sch Fort Sill OK 73503-5600

ADAIR, LESLIE GAYLE, marketing professional; b. Ft. Wayne, Ind., Aug. 20, 1970; d. Roger D. and Doris E. (Meyr) Pflughaupt; m. Eric T. Adair, Apr. 20, 1996. BBA, Ind. U., 1993. Rep. consumer prods. Lever Bros. Co., Chgo., 1993-94; pharms. rep. Schwarz Pharma, Ft. Wayne, 1994-95; brand mgr. Dana Corp., Auburn, Ind., 1995-96; mktg. mgr. Eaton Corp., Auburn, Ind., 1997-98; mktg. comms. adminstr. Eaton Corp., Auburn, 1998—; sec. Communication coun. Dana Eaton Corp., Toledo, 1995-97. Mem. Parents of Multiples, 1998—. Mem. Alpha Chi Omega. Luth. Avocations: running, biking, aerobics, baking. Office: Eaton Corp 201 Brandon St Auburn IN 46706-1643

ADAIR, ROBERT KEMP, physicist, educator; b. Fort Wayne, Ind., Aug. 14, 1924; s. Robert Cleland and Margaret (Wiegman) A.; m. Eleanor Reed, June 21, 1952; children—Douglas McVeigh, Margaret Guthrie, James Cleland. Ph.B., U. Wis., 1947, Ph.D., 1951, DSc (hon.), 1994. Instr. physics U. Wis., Madison, 1950-53; physicist Brookhaven (N.Y.) Nat. Lab., 1953-58; mem. faculty Yale U., New Haven, 1958—, prof. physics, 1961-72, Eugene Higgins prof. physics, 1972-88, Sterling prof. physics, 1988—, chmn. dept. physics, 1967-70, dir. div. phys. scis., 1977-80, Sterling prof. emeritus, 1994—, sr. rsch. scientist, 1994—; assoc. dir. for high energy and nuclear physics Brookhaven Nat. Lab., Upton, N.Y., 1987-88; physicist Nat. Baseball League, 1987-89. Author: (with Earle C. Fowler) Strange Particles, 1963; Concepts in Physics, 1969, The Great Design, 1987, The Physics of Baseball, 1990; assoc. editor Phys. Rev., 1963-66; assoc. editor Phys. Rev. Letters, 1974-76, editor, 1978-84. Served with inf. AUS, 1943-46. Guggenheim fellow, 1954; Ford Found. fellow, 1962-63; Sloane Found. fellow, 1962-63. Fellow Am. Phys. Soc. (chmn. divsn. particles and fields 1972-73), Am. Acad. Arts and Scis.; mem. NAS (chmn. physics sect. 1986-89, sec. class phys. scis. 1989-92, chmn. class phys. scis. 1992-94). Home: 50 Deepwood Dr Hamden CT 06517-3415 Office: Yale U Dept Physics Sloane Physics Lab 217 Prospect St New Haven CT 06520-8120*

ADAIR, TOBY WARREN, JR., minister; b. Beaumont, Tex., Sept. 8, 1922; s. Toby Warren and Mildred Lee (Muldrow) A.; m. Ann Ivareese Redden, May 8, 1943; 1 child, Robin Lee Adair. BS, Centenary Coll., 1947; MDiv, Golden Gate Bapt. Theol. Sem., 1973, MA, 1974; ThD, Internat. Sem., 1990. Ordained to ministry So. Bapt. Conv., 1973. Commd. 2d lt. USAF, 1944, advanced through grades to maj., 1959, command pilot, 1967-70, ret., 1967; founding pastor South Reno (Nev.) Bapt. Ch., 1973-77; pastor Bancroft Bapt. Ch., Spring Valley, Calif., 1977-81, Mt. Zion Bapt. Ch., Praireville, La., 1982-85, Forrest Park Bapt. Ch., Pine Bluff, Ark., 1986-93; pres. pastor's conf. San Diego (Calif.) So. Bapt. Assn., 1981, Ascension So. Bapt. Assn., Praireville, 1984, Harmony So. Bapt. Assn., Pine Bluff, 1988. Prayertime host Radio Sta. KNIS, Reno-Carson City, Nev., 1974-76. Bd. dirs. Pine Bluff-Jefferson County Hist. Mus. Guild, 1991-92, mem. adminstrv. bd. trustees 1992—, chmn. 1995—. Decorated Army Commendation medal USAF, Japan, 1950, DFC Air Medal with 2 oak leaf clusters USAF, Korea, 1951, USAF Commendation medal, USAF, USA, 1959. Named Boss of the Yr., Am. Bus. Women Assn., Reno, 1975. Mem. Jefferson County Clergy Conf. (treas.), Confedn. Air Forces (chaplain Razor Base wing), Kemper Mil. Sch. and Coll. Alumni Assn. (bd. dirs. 1991—, trustee 1993—), Rotary (Pine Bluff, bd. dirs. 1988-91, pres. 1991-92, dist. gov.'s rep. 1992-93, dist. gov. 1995-96). Republican. Home: 803 W 12th Ave Pine Bluff AR 71601-5631

ADAIR, TREVOR, soccer coach; b. Belfast, Ireland; came to U.S., 1972; BS in Econs., Lock Haven State Coll., 1982. Asst. men's soccer coach U. S.C., 1982-90; head coach Brown U., R.I., 1990-94, Clemson (S.C.) U., 1994—; asst. coach U.S. Under 20 Nat. Team; staff coach, instr. U.S. Soccer Fedn.; staff coach Nat. Soccer Coaches Assn. Am., U.S. Youth Soccer Assn. Region III; head coach S.C. Olympic Devel. State Team, 1984-90. Office: Clemson U PO Box 31 Clemson SC 29633-0031*

ADAIR, WENDELL HINTON, JR., lawyer; b. Ft. Benning, Ga., Mar. 17, 1944; s. Wendell H. Sr. and Jacqueline (Moore) A.; children: Elizabeth Carroll, John Michael, Benjamin David. BA, Emory U., 1966, postgrad., 1966-67; JD, U. Chgo., 1969. Bar: Ill. 1969. Assoc. Ross, Hardies, O'Keefe, Babcock & Parsons, Chgo., 1969-72; ptnr. Mayer, Brown & Platt, Chgo., 1972-89, McDermott, Will & Emery, Chgo., 1989—. Bd. dirs. ARC Mid-Am. chpt. 1991—, Chgo. Opera Theatre, 1993—; mem. Evanston Zoning Amendment Com., 1980-83. Mem. ABA (bus. sect., natural resources sect., pub. utilities sect.), Ill. Bar Assn., Fed. Energy Bar Assn. (bd. dirs. 1985-87, program chmn. 1990-91), Am. Gas Assn. (bd. dirs. legal sect. 1986-89), Turnaround Mgmt. Assn. (program and publs. coms.). Republican. Club: Econ. (Chgo.), Chicago. Home: 5682 Sawyer Rd Sawyer MI 49125-9249 Office: McDermott Will & Emery 227 W Monroe St Ste 3100 Chicago IL 60606-5096*

ADAM, CORNEL See LENGYEL, CORNEL ADAM

ADAM, JOHN, JR., insurance company executive emeritus; b. Braintree, Mass., Dec. 14, 1914; s. John and Harriet E. (Hubley) A.; m. Ruth E. Maddock, Dec. 27, 1945. A.B., Oberlin Coll., 1937; LL.D. (hon.), Clark U., 1974. Underwriter Glens Falls Ins. Co., 1938-39, mgr. inland marine dept., 1939-40; with Central Mut. Ins. Co., 1940-60, v.p., 1957-60; v.p. Worcester Mut. Ins. Co., 1960, pres., 1960-79; also dir. pres., dir. Hanover Ins. Cos., 1969-79, dir., 1979, pres. emeritus, 1979—; pres. Heald, Inc., 1979-87; chmn. adv. com. Mich. Investment Fund, M.B.W. Venture Ptnrs. Author: More Sales for You, 1949, also articles. Chmn. Mass. Bd. Higher Edn., 1972-77; past pres. Greater Worcester Community Found. Mem. Worcester C. of C. (past pres., dir.), Worcester County Music Assn. (past pres.), C.P.C.U. Soc. (nat. pres. 1967, dir.), Worcester Econ. Club (past pres.), Boston Sales Execs. Club (past pres.).

ADAM, NANCY ELIZABETH, library and information manager; b. Mar. 22, 1960. BA, Suffolk (Eng.) Coll., 1981; MEd, London Montessori Inst. & Coll, 1985; MLS, Cath. U. Am., 1996. Intern The Sugar Assoc. Inc. & Olivera Lima Libr., 1995; info. records mgr. Environ. Protection Agy., Washington, 1995; librarian, book store mgr. U. So. Calif., Washington, 1996—. E-mail: nadam@uscdc.edu. Home: 2235 Beacon Lane Falls Church VA 22043 Office: USC Washington Ctr 512 10th St NW Washington DC 20004

ADAM, ORVAL MICHAEL, retired financial executive, lawyer; b. Detroit, Apr. 25, 1930; s. Edgar Michael and Beatrice Rose (White) A.; m. Mary P. Knowles, Dec. 29, 1956 (dec. Jan. 1996); children: Margaret, Celine, Sarah, Mary Katherine, Charles, Bridget; m. Mary D. Yeo, Aug. 29, 1998. BBA, Canisius Coll., 1953; LLB, Georgetown U., 1956. Bar: N.Y. 1956, Ill. 1961, U.S. Dist. Ct. (all dists.) Ill. 1961, U.S. Ct. Appeals (7th and 10th cirs.) 1961, U.S. Tax Ct. 1961. Atty. IRS, Washington, 1956-60, Atchison, Topeka & Santa Fe Ry. Co., Chgo., 1960-73; asst. v.p. law Santa Fe Industries, Chgo., 1970-75, asst. v.p., tax counsel, 1975-76, v.p., tax counsel, 1977-83, sr. v.p. fin., tax counsel, 1983-84; v.p., treas., chief fin. officer Santa Fe Pacific Corp., Chgo., 1984-87, sr. v.p., chief fin. officer, 1988-90, ret., 1990; bd. dirs. Santa Fe Pacific Pipelines, Santa Fe Pacific Holdings, Inc. Bd. editors Georgetown Law Jour., 1955-56. Bd. dirs., pres. Homeowners' Civic Assn., Flossmoor, Ill., 1966-71; mem. zoning bd. appeals Village of Flossmoor, 1967-73, trustee, 1973-79; mem. fiscal bd. Infant Jesus of Prague Cath. Ch., Flossmoor, 1973-74. Mem. ABA, Fed. Bar Assn., Olympia Fields Country Club, Lake Geneva Country Club, Union League Club Chgo. Republican.

ADAM, PATRICIA A., state legislator; b. Mobridge, S.D., May 22, 1936; d. George T. and Madge Mickelson; m. Thomas C. Adam, Aug. 28, 1959; children: Kathleen Bykowski, Paula Adam-Burchill, Karlton Adam, Sarah Adam Axtman. BA in Speech Pathology, U. S.D., MA in Speech Pathology. Dir. 1st Nat. Bank, Selby, S.D.; sec. S.D. State Senate; Bd. dirs. Cmty. 1st Bancshares. Bd. dirs. AAUW Nursery Sch., 1965—, YMCA, Children's Care Hosp. and Sch., Sioux Falls, S.D., U. S.D. Found., Vermillion, Oahe Found., S.D., Pierre Sch. Found.; pres. Pierre Sch. Bd., 1977-86; bd. dirs. Sch. Bd. Assn., pres.; mem. City of Pierre Pk. and Recreation Bd.; pres. bd. trustees S.D. State Hist. Soc. Office: State Capitol Pierre SD 57501

ADAM, PAUL JAMES, engineering company executive, mechanical engineer; b. Kansas City, Mo., Oct. 26, 1934; s. Paul James and Adrienne (Zimmerman) A.; m. Barbara Ann Mills, Dec. 18, 1956; children: Paul James, Blair Dodderidge, Matthew Mills. BSME, U. Kans., 1956. Registered profl. engr. Mo., Kans., Colo. Mech. engr. Black & Veatch, Engrs.-Architects, Kansas City, 1956, 59-74, ptnr. asst. head power divsn., 1975-78, exec. ptnr., head power divsn., 1978-88, vice-chmn., CEO energy group, 1989-92, chmn., CEO, 1993-98, chmn., 1998—. Engring. adv. bd. U. Kans., 1982—; chmn. World Energy Coun. Exec. Assembly, 1998—; trustee U. Kans. Endowment Assn., 1994—. Fellow ASME; mem. NSPE, Mo. Soc. Profl. Engrs., Am. Nuclear Soc., U. Kans. Alumni Assn. (chmn.), Greater Kansas City C. of C. (vice-chmn.), Mission Hills Country Club, Saddle and Sirloin Club, Kansas City Club, River Club, U.S. Energy Assn. (chmn. 1996-98), Tau Beta Pi, Sigma Tau, Pi Tau Sigma, Omicron Delta Kappa, Alpha Tau Omega. Episcopalian. Office: Black & Veatch PO Box 8405 8400 Ward Pkwy Kansas City MO 64114-2031

ADAMANY, DAVID WALTER, law and political science educator; b. Janesville, Wis., Sept. 23, 1936; s. Walter Joseph and Dora Marie (Mutter) A. AB, Harvard U., 1958, JD, 1961; MS, U. Wis., 1963, PhD in Polit. Sci., 1967; LLD (hon.), Adrian Coll., 1984; AAS (hon.), Schoolcraft Coll., 1986; D. Engring. (hon.), Mich. Tech. U., 1987; D in Pub. Svc. (hon.), Ea. Mich. U., 1997. Bar: Wis. 1961. Spl. asst. to atty. gen. State of Wis., Madison, 1961-63, exec. pardon counsel, 1963; commr. Wis. Public Service Commn., 1963-65; instr. polit. sci. Wis. State U., Whitewater, 1965-67; asst. prof., then assoc. prof. Wesleyan U., Middletown, Conn., 1967-72; dean coll. Wesleyan U., 1969-71; assoc. prof., then prof. polit. sci. U. Wis., Madison, 1972-77; v.p. acad. affairs, prof. Calif. State U., Long Beach, 1977-80, U. Md., College Park, 1980-82; disting. prof. law and polit. sci. Wayne State U., Detroit, 1982—, pres., 1982-97, pres. emeritus, 1997; CEO Detroit Pub. Schs., 1999; chmn. Wis. Coun. Criminal Justice, 1973-75, Wis. Elections Bd., 1976-77; sec. Wis. Dept. Revenue, 1973-75; advisor to Gov. Patrick J. Lucey, State of Wis., 1972; bd. dirs. Caraco Pharm. Ltd., Thyssen Inc. Author: Financing Politics, 1969, Campaign Finance in America, 1972; co-author Borzoi Reader in American Politics, 1972, American Government: Democracy and Liberty in Balance, 1975, Political Money, 1975; editorial bd.: Social Sci. Quarterly, 1973—, State and Local Govt. Rev., 1974-80; contbr. articles to profl. jours. Mem. exec. com. Detroit Med. Ctr., 1982-97; chmn. Mich. Bicentennial of U.S. Constrn. Commn., 1986-88; bd. dirs. Detroit Inst. Arts Founders Soc., 1983-92, Detroit Symphony Orch., 1983-89, Detroit Econ. Growth Corp., 1984-92, Karmanos Cancer Inst., 1982-97, New Detroit, 1982-95, Blue Cross Blue Shield Found. Mich., 1995—, Gilmour Fund, 1996—, HOPE Fund of Cmty. Found. of S.E. Mich., 1995—; mem. Wis. Gov.'s Commn. on Campaign Fin. Reform, 1996-97; mem. Mich. Civil Svc. Commn., 1996—. Mem. ACLU, ABA (commn. on coll. and univ. legal studies 1992-95), Wis. Bar Assn., Am. Polit. Sci. Assn., Pres.'s Coun. State Univs. (chmn. 1986-88), Can.-U.S. Fulbright Commn. (bd. dirs. 1993-97), Nat. Adv. Com. on Institutional Quality and Integrity (U.S. dept. edn.). Democrat. Office: Wayne State U Law Sch Detroit MI 48202

ADAMEC, JOSEPH VICTOR, bishop; b. Bannister, Mich., Aug. 13, 1935. Ed., Mich. State U., Nepomucene Coll., Lateran U., Rome. Ordained priest Roman Cath. Ch. (for Nitra Diocese, Slovak Republic), 1960, ordained bishop of Altoona-Johnstown, Pa., 1987. Asst. pastor Diocese of Saginaw, Mich., 1960-65, notary, 1965-69, sec. to bishop, master of ceremonies, 1969-72, chancellor, 1972-77; pastor St. Hyacinth Ch., All Saints Cath. High Sch., Bay City, Mich., 1977-84, Sts. Peter and Paul Parish, Bay City, 1984-87; bishop Altoona-Johnstown, Pa., 1987—. Episcopal moderator Slovak Cath. Fedn. Mem. Nat. Conf. Cath. Bishops (joint com. Orthodox and Roman Cath. Bishops, ad hoc com. for aid to the Ch. in Cen. and Ea. Europe and USSR). Avocations: photography, sailing, writing. Address: The Chancery 126 Logan Blvd Hollidaysburg PA 16648-2604*

ADAMEK, CHARLES ANDREW, lawyer; b. Chgo., Dec. 24, 1944; s. Stanley Charles and Virginia Marie (Budzban) A.; m. Lori Merriel Klein; children: Donald Steven, Elizabeth Jean. BA with honors, U. Mich., 1966, JD, 1969. Bar: Ill. 1969, Calif. 1978. Clk. U.S. Dist. Judge U.S. Fed. Cts., Chgo., 1969-71; assoc. atty. Lord Bissell & Brook, Chgo., 1971-77, ptnr., 1977-78; ptnr. Lord Bissell & Brook, L.A., 1978—. Mem. ABA, Ill. State Bar Assn., State Bar Calif., Nat. Assn. Railroad Trial Counsel (Western Region exec. com. 1985—). Roman Catholic. Avocations: Bluegrass banjo, sr. ice hockey. Office: Lord Bissell & Brook 300 S Grand Ave Ste 800 Los Angeles CA 90071-3119

ADAMIAN, GREGORY HARRY, academic administrator; b. Somerville, Mass., Sept. 17, 1926; s. Adam K. and Sandy (Martin) A.; m. June Mouradian, July 6, 1958 (dec. Jan. 1967); children: Douglas, Daniel; m. Deborah Murdza, Jan. 1, 1978. AB, Harvard, 1947; then MPA; JD, Boston U., 1951, LLD (hon.), 1991; DCS (hon.), Bentley Coll., 1991. Bar: Mass. 1951. Since practiced in Cambridge; lectr. law and econs. Suffolk U., 1953-54; prof. law Bentley Coll., Waltham, Mass., 1955-67; chmn. dept. law Bentley Coll., 1968-70, pres. coll., 1970-91; chancellor Bentley Coll., Waltham, Mass., 1991—; lectr. real estate law Am. Savs. and Loan Inst. Trustee Bentley Coll.; bd. dirs. Joan Fabrics Corp.; bd. dirs. St. Nerses Sem. Lt. USN, 1944-47. Recipient Boyan Humanity award Armenian Students Assn., 1973, Silver Shingle Disting. Svc. award Boston U. Law Sch., 1986, Humanities award, 1990, Significant SIG medal, 1997. Mem. ABA, Mass. Bar Assn., Boston Bar Assn., Am. Bus. Law Assn., Nat. Assn. Armenian Studies and Rsch. (bd. dirs.), Masons, Shriners, Oakley Country Club, Addison-Reserve Country Club, Algonquin Club Boston, Sigma Chi. Mem. Armenian Apostolic Ch. Home: 22 9th St Apt 804 Medford MA 02155-5166 Office: Bentley Coll Office of Chancellor Waltham MA 02452

ADAMKIN, DAVID HOWARD, pediatric medicine educator; b. N.Y.C., Apr. 4, 1948; s. Joseph and Julie (Termin) A.; m. Carol Ann Seyfferth, Aug. 18, 1979; children: Stephanie Merete, Michelle Rachel, Matthew David. BS in cum laude, Ohio State U., 1970; MD, Upstate Med. Coll., 1974. Diplomate Am. Bd. Pediatrics; diplomate Sub-Bd. Neonatal-Perinatal Medicine, Am. Bd. Pediatrics. Pediatric resident Upstate Med. Ctr., Syracuse, N.Y., 1974-76; neonatalology fellow U. Louisville (Ky.) Sch. Med., 1976-78, asst. prof. pediatrics, asst. prof. obstetrics, 1978-85, assoc. prof. pediatrics, assoc. prof. obstetrics, 1985—, prof. pediatrics, 1992—; vis. prof. U. Ill., Chgo., 1984, Ind. U., Riley-Children's Hosp. and the Ind. Perinatal Assn., Indpls., 1985, La. State U., Baton Rouge, 1987; mem. adv. com. Gov.'s Conf. on Infant Mortality, Frankfort, Ky., 1989; dir. Divsn. Neonatal Medicine, U. Louisville, 1994—; dir. nurseries Kosair Children's Hosp., Louisville, Women's Pavilion, The Norton Hosp., Louisville, 1994—; staff mem. U. Louisville (Ky.) Hosp.; various coms. and adv. positions Kosair Children's Hosp., 1980—; presenter in field. Contbr. chpts. to books and textbooks and articles to profl. jours.; manuscript reviewer Jour. of Perin, Ped Rsch., Jour. of Am. Coll. of Nutrition; med. reviewer AMA. Active March of Dimes State Coun., Mid-Am. Region for Maternal and Child Health, 1989—, rev. panel for Phys. and Devel. Environ. of High Risk Inf.; bd. dirs. Ronald McDonald House, 1996. Grantee Abbott Labs., 1978-83, 85, 87, 91, WHAS Crusade for Children, 1979, 82, 87, 88, 90, 92-98, Travenol Labs., 1981, Mead Johnson, 1982, 91, 92, 93, Ross Labs., 1984, 85, 87, 90, 96, 98, Nat. Eye Inst. NIH, 1989, Alliant Cmty. Trust, 1990, 93, Wyeth-Ayerst, 1995, 96. Fellow Am. Coll. Nutrition; mem. Am. Pediatric Soc., Am. Acad. Pediatrics, Subsection Neonatal/Perinatal Medicine-Am. Acad. Pediatrics, Am. Soc. for Parenteral and Enteral Nutrition (Pediatric planninc com. 1989), Nat. Perinatal Assn. (coun. 1989-91), So. Soc. for Pediatric Rsch. (instn. rep. 1982—), Ky. Perinatal Assn. (organizer 1988, first pres. 1988-91, Disting. Leadership award 1991, Outstanding Leadership and Founder award 1993), Ky. Sect. Acad. Pediatrics, Ky. Med. Assn., Jefferson County Med. Soc. Jewish. Avocations: jogging, basketball, sports events, volleyball, cooking. Home: 9109 Brookwood Path Louisville KY 40241-2417 Office: 571 S Floyd St Ste 300 Louisville KY 40202-3830

ADAMLE, MIKE, sports commentator; b. Oct. 4, 1949. Grad., Northwestern U., 1971. Fullback Kansas City Chiefs, 1971-72, N.Y. Jets, 1973-74, Chgo. Bears, 1975-77; host SportsWorld, reporter NBC Sports, 1977-83; sports anchor WLS TV, Chgo., 1983-89; host Am. Gladiators, 1989-95; studio host ESPN, 1996—. Office: ESPN 935 Middle St No 2 Bristol CT 06010*

ADAMO, KENNETH R., lawyer; b. Staten Island, N.Y., Sept. 27, 1950. BS, ChE, Rensselaer Polytech. Inst., 1972; JD, Union U., Albany, 1975; LLM, John Marshall Law Sch., 1989. Bar: Ill. 1975, N.Y. 1976, Ohio 1984, Tex. 1988, U.S. Patent and Trademark Office. Ptnr. Jones, Day, Reavis & Pogue, Cleve. Mem. Internat. Bar Assn. Office: Jones Day Reavis & Pogue N Point 901 Lakeside Ave Cleveland OH 44114

ADAMS, A. JOHN BERTRAND, public affairs consultant; b. Liverpool, Eng., Nov. 22, 1931; came to U.S., 1962, naturalized, 1971; s. Wilfrid and Francine Sophia (Bertrand) A.; m. Vibeke Dinsen, June 3, 1963 (div. 1975); m. Judith Ann Duff, Oct. 15, 1978; 1 dau., Caroline Louise. Corr. London Daily Telegraph, 1952-56; editor, bur. chief, asst. dir. news Radio Free Europe, Bonn and Munich, W.Ger., 1956-62; Africa corr. ABC News, 1963; writer, exec. CBS News, N.Y.C., 1964-70; assoc. dir. advt. and pub. rels. Investment Co. Inst., 1971-72; dir. pub. affairs U.S. Price Commn., Washington, 1972-73; pres. John Adams Assocs., Inc., Washington, 1973—; founding chmn. The WORLDCOM Group, N.Y.C., London, Tokyo, 1987; bd. dirs. King Comm. Group, Washington. Author: (with J.M. Burke) Civil Rights: A Current Guide to the People, Organizations and Events, 1970; editor: Energy Policy: Industry Perspectives, 1975. Bd. dirs. Psychiat. Inst. Found., Washington, 1974-79, Nat. Coun. Fireworks Safety, 1986-96, Radio Free Europe Radio Liberty Fund, 1987—, Am. Com. for Aid to Poland, 1989-97, Am. Friends of Queen Mary Coll., U. London, 1990—, Friends of Benjamin Franklin House, London, 1990—; exec. dir. Eviron. Industry Coun., 1975-80; mem adv. bd. Gallaudet Coll. for Deaf, Washington, 1977-79. Lt. King's Shropshire Light Inf., Brit. Army, 1951-52, Korea. Recipient Knight's Cross, Order of Merit, Govt. of Poland, 1998, Disting. Svc. award U.S. Price Commn., 1973. Mem. Pub. Rels. Soc. Am. (Silver anvil award 1978, 84), Nat. Press Club, Fed. City Club (Washington), Severn River Yacht Club (Annapolis, Md.). Home: 12204 Meadow Creek Ct Potomac MD 20854-1408 Office: John Adams Assocs 655 National Press Building Washington DC 20045-1601

ADAMS, ALBERT WILLIE, JR., lubrication company executive; b. Detroit, Nov. 22, 1948; s. Albert Willie and Goldie Inez (Davis) A.; m. Linda Maureen North, Sept. 2, 1972; children—Nichole Leahna, Albert Willie III, Melanie Rachel, Kimberly Monet. BA in Elem. Edn., Harris Tchrs. Coll., St. Louis, 1970; MBA, So. Ill. U., Edwardsville, 1974. Recreation leader City of St. Louis, 1967-69; recreation supr. Mo. Hills Home for Boys, 1969-70; tchr. spl. edn. St. Louis Bd. Edn., 1968-71; personnel asst. Equal Opportunity Adminstrn., Seven-Up Co., St. Louis, 1971-75; corporate equal opportunity adminstr. Equal Opportunity Adminstrn., Seven-Up Co., 1975-80, sr. employee relations adminstr., 1980-81, personnel mgr., 1981-82, mgr. indsl. relations, 1982-83, mgr. personnel programs and services, 1983-85, mgr. personnel ops., 1985-87; regional mgr. A. L. Williams, St. Louis, 1987-89; staff v.p. human resources Citicorp Mortgage Inc., St. Louis, 1989-91; v.p. human resources and quality Lincoln Indsl., Pentair Co., 1991—; residence counselor Magdala Found., halfway house, 1971-77. Community-at-large mem. Affirmative Action Commn. Minorities St. Louis U., 1974-76; chmn. St. Louis corp. solicitation United Negro Coll. Fund, 1972; mem. adv. com. Statewide Job Placement Svc., 1979-84, Project Search, 1980-85; mem. Family and Children's Svc. N.W. Community Adv. Coun., 1982-85; mem. allocations com. United Way, 1985-90, bd. dirs., 1989-93; apptd. commr. St. Louis Civil Rights Enforcement Agy., 1988; bd. dirs. Vanderschmidt Sch., 1989-98, Habitat for Humanity, St. Louis, 1996-98, Pentair Found., 1998—. U.S. Naval Acad. nominee, 1965; St. Louis Post-Dispatch scholar, 1971; Parsons-Blewett Meml. scholar tchrs., 1971; recipient Jr. Achievement scholarship award, 1966, St. Louis Sales and Mktg. Execs. award, 1966, St. Louis Sentinel achiever award, 1980. Mem. AAIM (bd. dirs. 1998—), St. Louis Indsl. Relations Assn., Assn. M.B.A. Execs., Kappa Alpha Psi. Baptist. Home: 2331 Albion Pl Saint Louis MO 63104-2524

ADAMS, ALFRED BERNARD, JR., environmental engineer; b. Asbury Park, N.J., Oct. 15, 1920; s. Alfred Bishop and Julia Ruth (Wiseman) A.; m. Claudia Neff, Dec. 28, 1942; children: Alfred B. III, Tamara Adams Harris, Carla Adams York. BSChemE, Ga. Inst. Technol., 1943; postgrad., Wayne State U., 1946-48, U. Ala., Birmingham, 1986-88, Jefferson State C.C., 1989-95. Registered profl. engr., Ala., Mich., Fla., Ga., N.C.; Diplomate in Am. Acad. Environ. Engrs. Project engr. Pennwalt, Wyandotte, Mich., 1946-50; sales mgr., design engr. Goslin-Birmingham Div., Birmingham, Ala., 1950-61; field engr. & Sales Elmco Corp., Birmingham, Ala., 1961-62; prin. engr. Morton-Thiokol Corp., Brunswick, Ga., 1962-64; tech. mgr. Rust Internat., Birmingham, 1964-86; pres., owner Adams Cons. & Engring. Svcs., Birmingham, 1986—; cons. in field. Contbr. tech. papers to profl. publs. Pres. Woodhaven Lakes Property Owners Assn., Pinson, Ala., 1980-82, Lake Park Neighborhood Assn., 1996-98; mem. Pub. Health Com., Birmingham, 1975-78. 2d lt. U.S. Army Chem. Corps, 1943-53. Mem. Air & Waste Mgmt. Assn., Tech. Assn. Pulp & Paper Industries. Presbyterian. Avocations: travel, photography, golf. Fax number: (205) 824-3955. Home and Office: Adams Cons & Engring Svcs 2084 Montreat Cir Birmingham AL 35216-3902

ADAMS, ALFRED GRAY, lawyer; b. Winston-Salem, N.C., Feb. 28, 1946; s. Carlton Noble and Elizabeth (Walker) A.; m. Elizabeth Lark; children: Alfred Gray Jr., Amanda Laing. BA, Wake Forest U., 1968, JD, 1973. Bar: N.C. 1973; cert. specialist residential, bus., comml., and indsl. real property transactions. Ptnr. Van Winkle, Buck, Wall, Starnes & Davis, P.A., Asheville, N.C., 1973-94, Kilpatrick Stockton L.L.P, Winston-Salem, 1994—; adj. prof. law Wake Forest U., 1996—. Assoc. editor Wake Forest Law Rev., 1972. Chmn. Buncombe County Tax Adv. Com., Asheville, 1983. James Mason scholar Wake Forest U., 1972. Mem. ABA, N.C. Bar Assn. (bd. govs. 1987-90, real property sect. vice chmn. 1982-83, chmn. 1983-84, writer, lectr. real property and future interests bar rev. course 1981-83, mem. real property curriculum adv. com. 1984-91, chmn. 1988-91, seminar planner and lectr. real property 1987-98, chmn. continuing legal edn. com. 1991-93), Am. Coll. Real Estate Lawyers, Am. Coll. Mortgage Attys. (state chair 1995—, bd. regents 1996-98, sec. 1998—), Biltmore Forest Country Club (bd. govs. 1993-94), Forsyth Country Club, Old North State Club, Rhododendron Royal Brigade Guards Club (capt. Ensign Class 1986). Democrat. Methodist. Home: 115 Sullivan Way Winston Salem NC 27104 Office: 1001 W 4th St Winston Salem NC 27101-2410

ADAMS, ALFRED HUGH, college president; b. Punta Gorda, Fla., Mar. 8, 1928; s. Alfred and Irene (Gatewood) A.; m. Joyce Morgan, Nov. 10, 1954; children: Joy, Al, Paul. A.A., U. Fla., 1948; B.S., Fla. State U., 1950, M.S., 1956, Ed.D., 1962; L.H.D., Fla. Atlantic U., 1972. Asst. coach varsity football Fla. State U., 1955-58, asst. dir. housing, instr. edn., 1958-62, asst. dean men, asst. prof. edn., 1962-64; supt. pub. instrn. Charlotte County, Fla., 1965-68; pres. Broward Community Coll., Ft. Lauderdale, Fla., 1968-87; exec. dir. Performing Arts Ctr. Authority, Ft. Lauderdale, 1987-88; pres. Broward Performing Arts Found., Ft. Lauderdale, 1990-91; bd. dirs. Am. Council on Edn.; vis. lectr. in higher edn. Inst. Higher Edn., U. Fla.; also mem. com. on internat. edn. relations, com. on mil-higher edn. relations; mem. adv. com. Inst. Internat. Edn.; dir. Sun Bank/South Fla., N.A.; Vice chmn. Gov. Fla. Commn. Quality Edn., 1968-70; mem. Gov.'s Adv. Com. Edn., 1966-70; mem. regional council Southeastern Edn. Corp., 1966-69; mem. commn. adminstrv. affairs Am. Council on Edn., 1973; pres. Pub. Instns. Higher Learning in So. States, 1975; mem. adv. com. Joint Council on Econ. Edn.; chmn. AACJC Internat./Intercultural Consortium, S.E. Fla. Ednl. Consortium; chmn. council pres. Fla. Community Colls.; Trustee South Fla. Edn. Center, Pub. Service TV. Mem. editorial bd., Soc. for Coll. and Univ. Planning. Pres. United Way, 1973; bd. dirs. local chpt. ARC, 1971; bd. dirs. local State U. Sports Hall of Fame; bd. dirs. Opera Guild, Ft. Lauderdale, pres., 1983-85; bd. dirs. Coll. Consortium Internat. Studies; exec. dir. Performing Arts Ctr. Authority, Ft. Lauderdale; pres. Broward Performing Arts Found., Ft. Lauderdale. Served to comdr. USNR, 1945-46, 52-55. Decorated knight Internat. Constantinian Order, 1971; recipient Liberty Bell award, 1975, Patriot award Freedoms Found., Disting. Alumnus award Fla. State U., A. Hugh Adams Coll. Gold Key. cert. of recognition Fla. Ho. of Reps., Disting Omicron Delta Kappa Alumnus of Yr., 1987; named Patriot Fla. Bicentennial Commn. Mem. Fla. Tchr. Edn. Adv. Council, Fla. Edn. Council Ethics Com. Sch. Adminstrs., Am. Assn. Sch. Adminstrs., Ft. Lauderdale C. of C. (v.p.), Profl. Practices Commn., Fla. Assn. Colls. and Univs. (pres. 1975), Naval Res. Assn., Res. Officers Assn., U.S. Naval Inst. (life), Broward Minutemen (pres.), Fla. Inter-agy. Law Enforcement Planning Council, Omicron Delta Kappa, Phi Theta Kappa. Methodist. Clubs: Gulfstream Sailing, Fort Lauderdale; Tower (gov. 1985-86). Lodge: Kiwanis.

ADAMS, ALGALEE POOL, college dean, art educator; b. Columbia, Mo., Nov. 6, 1919; d. William I. and Anna Ethelene (Dunning) Pool; 1 dau., Judith Dean Adams. B.S. in Art and English, U. Mo., 1941, M.A. in Art, 1951; Ed.D. in Fine Arts and Art Edn, Pa. State U., 1960; postgrad. Inst. Adminstrv. Advancement, for Women, U. Mich.; postgrad., Inst. Ednl. Mgmt., Harvard U. Tchr. art Cuba (Mo.) High Sch., 1941-42, Hickman High Sch., Columbia, 1942-43; art specialist elementary schs. St. Joseph, Mo., 1943-45; tchr. art St. Clair (Mo.) High Sch., 1946-49; pub. sch. art supr. Webb City, Mo., 1949-51; instr. dept. of art St. Cloud (Minn.) State Coll., 1951-58, asst. prof., 1958-60, assoc. prof., 1960-63, prof., 1963-64, chmn. dept. art, 1959-64; prof. art edn. Mass. Coll. Art, Boston, 1964-77; also chmn. div. of edn. Mass. Coll. Art, 1967-70, dir. tchr. placement, 1964-70, dir. grad. programs in edn., 1970-77; chmn. grad. council, 1970-74; dean Firelands Coll. Bowling Green State U., Huron, Ohio, 1977-85; owner Adams Miniature Fiber Arts, Columbia, Mo., 1989; liaison with bus. and industry; mem. gov.'s adv. commn. on edn. in arts, 1958, 67; asso. dir. Project Renewal Mass. State Coll. System, 1974-76; art curriculum cons. to numerous pub. schs. in Minn., 1951-64; art cons. to Minn. Ins. Info. Center, 1960-62; chmn. Eastern Arts Student Conf., N.Y.C., 1968; participant Internat. Conf., Notre Dame U., 1968; field reader HEW, 1966-70. Vol. tutor state literacy program; docent Detroit Inst. Arts. Recipient Artisian Status award Internat. Guild Miniature Artisians, 1991, Fellow status award, 1995, Citation of Merit for Outstanding Achievement and Meritorius Svc. to Edn. Alumni Bd. U. Mo., 1997. Club: Zonta. Home: 2604 Grant Ln Columbia MO 65203-0652 *Early in my teaching career, I was conscious of the differences between creative teaching and other more traditional philosophies and methods. This awareness and concern led to the development of my professional goal "to have a broad impact on improving the quality of teaching."*

ADAMS, ALICE, sculptor; b. N.Y.C., Nov. 16, 1930; d. Charles P. and Loretto G. (Tobin) A.; m. William D. Gordy, Feb. 7, 1969; 1 dau., Katherine Adams Gordy. Student, Adelphi Coll., 1948-50; BFA, Columbia U., 1953; postgrad. (French Govt. fellow), 1953-54; postgrad. Fulbright Travel grantee, L'Ecole Nat d'Art Decoratif, Aubusson, France, 1953-54. Lectr. Manhattanville Coll., Purchase, N.Y., 1960-79; instr. sculpture Sch. Visual Arts, 1980-87. One-woman shows N.Y.C., 1972, 74, 75, Hal Bromm Gallery, N.Y.C., 1979, 80; group shows include Whitney Mus. Am. Art, N.Y.C., 1971, 73, Indpls. Mus. Art, 1974, Nassau County Mus. Fine Arts, Roslyn, N.Y., 1977, Wave Hill, Riverdale, N.Y., 1979, Mus. Modern Art, N.Y.C., 1984; represented in permanent collections Weatherspoon Gallery U. N.C., Greensboro, U. Nebr., Everson Mus., Syracuse, N.Y., Haags Gemetemuseum, The Hague, Netherlands, Am. Craft Mus., N.Y.C., Edwin I. Ulrich Mus., Wichita, Kans.; pub. commissions include Bot. Garden, Toledo, Ohio, Design Team Seattle Transit Project, St. Louis Metro-Link Project, Midland Metro, Birmingham, Eng., Port Authority of N.Y. and N.J., Thomas Jefferson U., Phila., N.Y.C. Bd. Edn., State of Conn., Denver Internat. Airport, N.Y.C. Metro. Transp. Authority, U. Tex. San Antonio, Broward County, Fla., U. Del., Newark. Creative Artists Pub. Service grantee, 1973-74, 76-77; Nat. Endowment for Arts Artists grantee, 1978-79; Guggenheim fellow, 1981-82; Am. Acad. of Arts and Letters grantee, 1984. Home: 3370 Fort Independence St Bronx NY 10463-4502

ADAMS, ALICE, writer; b. Fredericksburg, Va., Aug. 14, 1926; d. Nicholson Barney and Agatha Erskine (Boyd) A.; 1 son, Peter Adams Linenthal. A.B., Radcliffe Coll., 1946. Author: (novels) Careless Love, 1966, Families and Survivors, 1975, Listening to Billie, 1978, Rich Rewards,

1980, Superior Women, 1984, Second Chances, 1988, Caroline's Daughters, 1991, Almost Perfect, 1993, A Southern Exposure, 1995, Medicine Men, 1997; (short story collections) Beautiful Girl, 1979, To See You Again, 1982, Return Trips, 1985, After You've Gone, 1989, The Last Lovely City, 1999, (travel) Mexico: Some Travels and Travellers There, 1991; editor: Best American Short Stories, 1991; contbr. short stories to New Yorker mag., others. Recipient Best Am. Short Stories award, 1976, 92, 96, O. Henry awards, 1971-82, 84-96, Acad. and Inst. award in lit. Am. Acad. and Inst. of Arts and Letters, 1992; grantee NEA, 1976; Guggenheim fellow, 1978-79. Mem. PEN. Democratic Socialist. Office: Alfred A Knopf Inc Press Rels 201 E 50th St New York NY 10022-7703

ADAMS, ANDREW JOSEPH, army officer; b. Rose Hill, Ala., Aug. 29, 1909; s. Alfred E. and Eunice (Clements) A.; m. DeLellis Frances Shramek, Oct. 25, 1934; children—Carol (Mrs. Charles E. Lucier), Andrew Joseph, Elizabeth Adams Robison. B.S., U.S. Mil. Acad., 1931; grad., Inf. Sch., 1938, Command and Gen. Staff Coll., 1942, Air Command and Gen. Staff Sch., 1946, Indsl. Coll. Armed Forces, 1953. Commd. 2d lt. U.S. Army, 1931, advanced through grades to maj. gen., 1956; chief staff, combat comdr. 7th Armored Div. ETO, 1944-45; instr. Air Command Staff Coll., 1946-49; adviser Peruvian Army, 1950-52; chief mgmt. div. Office Comptroller, U.S. Army, 1953; comdr. 23d Inf. Regt., also sr. adviser to comdg. gen. 2d Republic of Korea Army, 1954-55; dir. personnel, also dir. supply operations Office Dep. Chief Staff for Logistics, Dept. Army, 1955-59; dep. chief staff for logistics Hdqtrs. U.S. Army, Europe, 1959-61; dep. comdg. gen. 7th U.S. Army; also comdg. gen. 7th U.S. Support Command and Mobile Land Force, Allied Forces Europe, 1961-62; comdg. gen. XIX U.S. Army Corps, 1962-63; dep. chief staff logistics Hdqrs. U.S. Army Pacific, 1963-66, U.S. Continental Army Command, 1966-67; chief exec. and sec. Am. Battle Monuments Commn., Washington, 1967-92; bd. dirs. Ft. Rucker Nat. Bank., 1968-85, Army Stock Fund, 1957-59, U.S. Army Pacific Stock Fund, 1963-66, U.S. Army CONARC Stock Fund, 1966; chmn. bd. dirs. Pacific Army-Air Force Exchange System, 1964-66. Decorated D.S.M., Silver Star, Legion of Merit with oak leaf cluster, Bronze Star, Army Commendation medal with oak leaf cluster; Legion of Honor; Croix de Guerre with palm France; Ulchi medal with gold star Korea; Mil. Order Ayachucho Peru). Home: 3412 Chiswick Ct Silver Spring MD 20906-1602*

ADAMS, ARLIN MARVIN, lawyer, arbitrator, mediator, retired judge; b. Phila., Apr. 16, 1921; s. Aaron M. and Mathilda (Landau) A.; m. Neysa Cristol, Nov. 10, 1942; children: Carol (Mrs. Howard Kirshner), Judith A., Jane C. BS in Econs. with highest honors, Temple U., 1941; LLB with honors, U. Pa., 1947, MA in Econs., 1950; DHL (hon.), Temple U., 1964; DSc (hon.), Phila. Coll. Optometry, 1965; LLD (hon.), Phila. Coll. Textiles, 1966, Susquehanna U., 1985, Muhlenberg Coll., 1986, Villanova U., 1987, U. Pa., 1998. Bar: Pa. 1947; U.S. Ct. Appeals (3rd cir.), 1969. Law clk., Chief Justice Horace Stern Pennsylvania Supreme Ct., 1947; assoc. firm Schnader, Harrison, Segal & Lewis, Phila., 1947-50, sr. partner, 1950-63, 66-69; sec. pub. welfare Commonwealth of Pa., Phila., 1963-66; judge U.S. Ct. Appeals (3d cir.), Phila., 1969-87; counsel Schnader, Harrison, Segal & Lewis, Phila., 1987—; apptd. ind. counsel to investigate Dept. HUD, 1990-95; apptd. spl. counsel Pa. Commn. of Police, 1994-95; instr. Am. Inst. Banking, Phila., 1949-52; lectr. fed. practice Law Sch., U. Pa., Phila., 1952-56, lectr. constl. law, 1972-97. Author: Law and Religion, 2 vols., 1991, A Nation Dedicated to Religious Liberty, 1990; Editor-in-chief Law Review U. Penn., 1947; contbr. articles to profl. jours. Pres. Annenberg Inst., 1988-91; chmn. bd. dirs. Moss Rehab. Hosp., Phila., 1962-63; trustee U. Pa., 1985—; chmn. U.S. Supreme Ct. Jud. Fellows Commn., 1987-93, Fels Inst. Govt., Phila., 1967-77, Sch. of Social Work, Bryn Mawr (Pa.) Coll., 1967-78, Diagnostic and Rehab. Ctr., Phila., 1971-72; chmn. overseers U. Pa. Law Sch., 1985-92; trustee Med. Coll. of Pa., 1974-80, hon. trustee, 1981—; trustee German Marshall Meml. Fund, 1972-84, Lewis H. Stevens Trust, Bryn Mawr Coll., 1972-78, Columbia U. Ctr. for Law and Econ. Studies, U. of Pa. Inst. for Law and Econs., William Penn Found.; hon. trustee Phila. Mus. Art, 1998—. With U.S. Naval Reserve, 1942-45, North Pacific. Recipient Disting. Service award U. Pa. Law Sch., 1981, Justice award Am. Jud. Soc., 1982, John Murray award DePaul U., 1987, Cresset award Rosemont Coll., 1988, Gold Medallion award Chapel of Four Chaplains, Founders award Temple U., 1997, Phila. award, 1997; U. Pa. scholar, 1941. Mem. ABA (del. ho. of dels. 1966-67, 75-77, chmn. trade assn. com.), Am. Law Inst., Am. Bar Found., Pa. Bar Assn. (pres. 1950, del. ho. of dels. 1967-71), Phila. Bar Assn. (chancellor 1967), Am. Judicature Soc. (pres. 1975-77), Am. Philos. Soc. (sec. 1980-83, v.p. 1987-92, pres. 1993), Am. Acad. Arts & Scis., Phila. Club, Union League, Sun. Breakfast Club, Legal Club (pres. 1986-91), Jr. Legal Club, Order of Coif, Beta Gamma Sigma. Office: Schnader Harrison Segal & Lewis LLP 36th Flr 1600 Market St Fl 36 Philadelphia PA 19103-7240

ADAMS, BARBARA, English language educator, poet, writer; b. N.Y.C., Mar. 23, 1932; d. David S. Block and Helen (Taxter) Block Tyler; m. Elwood Adams, June 6, 1952; (dec. 1993); children: Steven, Amy, Anne, Samuel. BS, SUNY, New Paltz, 1962, MA, 1970; PhD, NYU, 1981. Prof. English Pace U., N.Y.C., 1984—, dir. bus. comm., 1984—; poet in residence Cape Cod Writers' Conf., 1988. Author: Double Solitaire, 1982, The Enemy Self: The Poetry & Criticism of Laura Riding, 1990, Hapax legomena, 1990, Negative Capability, 1999 (1st Prize for Fiction); contbr. poems, stories, articles to various mags. and jours. Recipient 1st prize for poetry NYU and Acad. Am. Poets, 1975; Penfield fellow NYU, 1977. Mem. PEN, Poetry Soc. Am., Assn. Bus. Comm., Poets and Writers. Home: 59 Coach Ln Newburgh NY 12550-3818 Office: Pace U Pace Plz New York NY 10038

ADAMS, BARBARA, artist, designer; b. Bronx, N.Y., Sept. 23, 1935; d. Morris and Anna (Waltzer) Bittleman; m. Eugene Joseph Adams, July 3, 1958 (div. Apr. 1991); children: Jeffrey Mark, Richard Michael, Julia Leslie. Student, Sch. Visual Arts, N.Y.C., 1954-56, Arts Students League, N.Y.C., 1956-58. Designer Needlework Arts, Spring Valley, N.Y., 1975-85; prin. Barbara Adams Designs, Orangeburg, N.Y., 1993—. Vol. Edward Hopper Found., Nyack, N.Y., 1984—; group leader h.s. chpt. B'nai Brith, Rockland County, N.Y., 1960-62; bd. dirs. women's divsn. United Jewish Appeal, Rockland county, 1970-75; trustee, bd. dirs. Jewish Cmty. Ctr. Sisterhood, Spring Valley, N.Y., 1963—; life mem., vol. nat. woman com. Brandeis U., 1972—. Mem. Nat. Museum of Women in Arts (charter), Hadassah. Democrat. Jewish. Avocations: interior design, gardening, swimming, woodworking. Office: 103 S Greenbush Rd Orangeburg NY 10962-1322

ADAMS, BARBARA KAREN, special education teacher, real estate agent; b. Mexico, Mo., June 23, 1950; d. Robert Lee Benskin and Wilma Lee Lewis Hase; m. Randall Dean Adams, Apr. 11, 1970; children: Kristen Lee, Darren Douglas. BA in Comms., Columbia Coll., 1990, BA in Edn., 1990; MEd, U. Mo., 1995. Proofreader Standard Pub., Columbia, Mo., 1972-75; export svc. corrs. A.B. Chance Co., Emerson Elec., Centralia, Mo., 1975-87; spl. edn. tchr. Mexico (Mo.) Pub. Schs., 1990-92; spl. reading tchr. Sturgeon (Mo.) R-V Sch. Dist., 1993—; sales assoc. Adams Realty, Centralia, 1984—. Recipient award Sundance Co., Md., 1999. Mem. Internat. Reading Assn., Supervision and Curr. Devel., Cmty. Tchrs. Assn. Avocations: European travel, gardening, golf, reading, bike riding. E-mail: adamsrealt@socket.net. Home: 526 Orchard St Centralia MO 65240-1207 Office: 122 N Allen St Centralia MO 65240

ADAMS, BEEJAY (MEREDITH ELISABETH JANE J. ADAMS), sales executive; b. Jefferson Barracks, Mo., June 9, 1920; d. Alden Humphrey and Louise Marion (Banta) Seabury; m. Merlin Francis Adams, July 10, 1948 (dec. 1977); children; S(tephen) Kent, Mark Francis. AB, Bradley U., 1942. Svc. editor Peoria (Ill.) Jour. Star, 1942-46; women's program dir. Sta. WEEK-AM, Peoria, 1946-47; on air personality Sta. KSD-AM, St. Louis, 1948; lectr. Sch. Assembly Svc., Chgo., 1948-49; pres. M.F. Adams, Inc., Quincy, Ill., 1977-85; commodities broker Quincy, 1985-87; pres. MarKent, Inc., Quincy, 1975—; sec., treas. Miss. Belle Distbn. Co., Inc., Quincy, 1976—, v.p., treas., 1979—. Active Quincy Svc. League, 1949-57, local polit. campaigns, co-chmn. local presdl. campaigns, 1952-77; founder, past pres. Quincy Jr. Theatre, 1953-78; charter mem. Quincy Community Theatre; co-chmn. coll. fund drive Quincy Coll., 1988, chmn. 1989. Mem. Quincy C. of C., Adams County Red Cross Bd., Sales and Mktg. Execs. Club, Quincy Art Club, Atlantis Study Club, Quincy Country Club, Phi Beta Phi. Anglican. Avocations: golf, reading, home repair, traveling, politics. Home: 2303 Jersey St Quincy IL 62301-4343 Office: Miss Belle Distbn Co Inc PO Box 768 Quincy IL 62306-0768

ADAMS, BELINDA JEANETTE SPAIN, nursing administrator; b. Rome, Ga., Dec. 5; d. Oscar Joe and Eleanor (Camacho) Spain. Diploma, Ga. Bapt. Hosp. Sch. Nursing, Atlanta, 1974; BS in Nursing, Med. Coll. Ga., Augusta, 1976; MS in Nursing, Ga. State U., Atlanta, 1980, PhD in Human Resource Devel., 1998. Cert. clin. specialist in med.-surg. nursing, intravenous nurse. Critical care flight nurse Critical Care Medflight, Inc., Atlanta, 1984-88; intravenous therapy coord. DeKalb Gen. Hosp., Atlanta, 1974-81; asst. prof. Mercer U., Atlanta, 1981-87; corp. dir. infusion/high tech. svcs. Kimberly Quality Care, Atlanta, 1988-92; cons. Profl. Learning Systems, 1992—; asst. prof. Clayton State Coll., Morrow, Ga., 1992-94, Ga. Bapt. Coll. Nursing, Atlanta, 1994-95; clin. examiner State of N.Y.-Regents Coll., 1995—. Mem. ANA, Intravenous Nurses Soc. (rsch. com., entrepreneur com.), Ga. Nurses Assn. Home and Office: 4542 Ferncroft Rd Mercer Island WA 98040

ADAMS, BERNARD SCHRODER, retired college president; b. Lancaster, Pa., July 20, 1928; s. Martin Ray and Charlotte (Schroder) A.; m. Natalie Virginia Stout, June 2, 1951; children: Deborah Rowland, David Schroder. B.A., Princeton, 1950; M.A., Yale, 1951; Ph.D., U. Pitts., 1964; LL.D. (hon.), Lawrence U., 1967; cert., Inst. for Ednl. Mgmt., Harvard U., 1975. Asst. dir. admissions, instr. English Princeton, 1953-57; dir. admissions and student aid U. Pitts., 1957-60, spl. asst. to chancellor, 1960-64; dean students, lectr. English Oberlin (Ohio) Coll., 1964-66; pres. Ripon (Wis.) Coll., 1966-85, Ft. Lewis Coll., Colo., 1985-87; ednl. cons. pvt. practice, Colo. Springs, 1987-88; v.p. resources Goodwill Industries, Colorado Springs, Colo., 1988-94; dir. Wis. Power & Light Co., Newton Funds, 1970-85; cons., examiner Commn. on Instns. Higher Edn., North Cen. Assn. Colls. and Secondary Schs., 1972-87, exec. commr., 1981-86; bd. dirs. Four Corners Opera Assn., 1985-87, pres., 1986-87. Contbr. articles to profl. jours. Bd. dirs. Keep Colorado Springs Beautiful, 1990—, Colo. chpt. Nat. Assn. Rundraising Execs., 1990-94, Tradition of Excellence Found., 1991—, Colorado Springs Symphony Vols., 1992—, Ctr. for Prevention of Domestic Violence, 1995—. 1st lt. USAF, 1951-53. Woodrow Wilson fellow, 1951. Mem. Assoc. Colls. Midwest (bd. dirs. 1966-85, pres. 1973-75), Wis. Assn. Ind. Colls. and Univs. (bd. dirs. 1966-85, pres. 1969-71, 83-85). Home: 90 Ellsworth St Colorado Springs CO 80906-7954

ADAMS, BEVERLY JOSEPHINE, data processing specialist; b. Kansas City, Kans., Nov. 29, 1951; d. Cecil and Eula Laverne (Lynch) Brown; m. Theodore Lavern Adams, Sept. 20, 1969; children: Theodore Lavern Jr., Terry Levar, Traveon LeVar. AA in Data Processing, Kansas City Kans. Community Coll., 1980; BS in Mgmt. and Computers, Park Coll., Parkville, Mo., 1986; postgrad., Rockhurst Coll.; MA, Webster U., 1991. Sr. data processor AT&T, Kansas City, Mo., 1984-86, computer programmer, 1987—; profl. devel. and career devel. facilitator tng. orgn. AT&T, 1991-96; v.p. ops. AT&T Alliance; lectr. in field. Editor: (newspaper) Courier, 1969, (newsletter) Kansas City Link, 1987. Cons. Youth of Am., Kansas City, 1983; mem. Kansas City Chief's Football, 1968-72, Coalition Labor Union Women, Washington, 1984, AFL-CIO City Labor Coun., Kansas City, 1984; dir. ch. adult and youth choir, Kansas City, 1982—; Kans. state advisor Young Women's Christian Coun. Named one of Outstanding Young Women of Am., 1981-96, SCLC Achiever in Industry and Bus., 1997. Mem. NAFE, Alliance AT&T Employees (chairperson 1987, treas. 1988-89, regional dir., v.p. ops. 1998—), Profl. Women's Fedn., Young People's Willing workers, Nat. Alliance (nat. outstanding mem. award), Alpha Kappa Alpha (exec. bd., philacter, chairperson Debutante Ball), Gamma Mu Gamma (program chmn. 1985, exec. bd., pres.). Republican. Pentacostal. Clubs: Wecomo (svcs. award 1983), Young Adults Action (bd. dirs., Leadership award 1980), YWCA (Kansas City). Avocations: golf, sewing, singing. Home: 701 NE Lake Point Dr Lees Summit MO 64064-1392 Office: AT&T Comms 2121 E 63rd St Kansas City MO 64130-3493

ADAMS, BILL, principal. Prin. Portland (Mich.) Mid. Sch. Office: Portland Middle Sch 745 Storz Ave Portland MI 48875-1805*

ADAMS, BRENDA KAY, publications administrator, consultant; b. Chickasha, Okla., Dec. 5, 1954; d. William Opal and Frances Mahota (Greer) Pettigrew; m. Phillip Wayne Haney, May 29, 1976 (div. Feb. 1995); children: Kristin Lea, Phillip Kollin, Kasey Kay; m. Warren Lynn Adams, Feb. 3, 1996; stepchildren: Lindsay Nichelle, London Reed. BA, U. Sci. and Arts of Okla., 1976. Photographer, reporter Chickasha Daily Express, 1974, lifestyles editor, 1974-78, advt. dir., 1978-88, pub., 1992-95; pub. Pauls Valley (Okla.) Democrat, 1988-92, Real Estate Exec., Chickasha, 1996-97, Builder/Architect, Chickasha, 1996-97; publs. dir. Nat. Rural Water Assn., Duncan, Okla., 1997—; pub. cons. Adams Assocs., Ninnekah, Okla., 1995—. Contbr. articles to profl. jours. Bd. dirs. Grady County Family YMCA, Chickasha, 1993-96, United Way of Grady County, Chickasha, 1993-96; v.p., treas. Cmty. Edn. Adv. Coun., Pauls Valley, 1990-92; bd. dirs. (alumni) U. Sci. and Arts of Okla., Chickasha, 1993-96, bd. dirs. (found.), 1993-96; founding bd. dirs. Festival of Light, Chickasha, 1993-96. Mem. Okla. Press Assn. (better newspaper contest com. chair 1992-95, newspaper in edn. com. chmn. 1992-95, advt. com. chmn. 1993-95, conv. com. 1993-95, 1st place in sales promotion 1991-92, 1st place in cmty. leadership 1991-92), Pauls Valley C. of C. (bd. dirs. 1988-92). Democrat. Christian Ch. Avocations: antiques, photography, travel, country crafts, gardening. Home: RR 2 Box 6 Ninnekah OK 73067-9504 Office: Nat Rural Water Assn 2915 S 13th St Duncan OK 73533-9786

ADAMS, BRYAN, vocalist, composer; b. Kingston, Ont., Can., Nov. 5, 1959. Vocalist, 1976—; composer various bands including Prism, Bachman-Turner Overdrive, Bob Welch, Kiss, 1977—. Albums include Bryan Adams, 1980, You Want It, You Got It, 1982, Cuts Like a Knife, 1983, Reckless, 1985, Into the Fire, 1987, Waking Up the Neighbors, 1991, So Far, So Good, 1993, Live! Live! Live!, 1994; singles include Straight from the Heart, Cuts Like a Knife, 1983, Heaven, One Night Love Affair, It's Only Love, 1985, Heat of the Night, Victim of Love, Only the Strong Survive, Hearts On Fire, 1987, Thought I Died and Gone to Heaven, 1991, (Everything I Do) I Do It for You (Acad. award nominee for best original song 1992), Can't Stop This Thing We Started, There Will Never Be Another Tonight, (with Michael Kamen and Robert John Lange, from Don Juan DeMarco) Have You Ever Loved a Woman, 1995 (Acad. award nominee for best original song 1996); contbr. to soundtracks: Robin Hood: Prince of Thieves, The Three Musketeers (with Rod Stewart & Sting), Don Juan DeMarco. Decorated with Order of B.C., Order of Canada; recipient multi-platinum record, #1 single in Am., Can., U.K., Sweden, Finland, Denmark, Norway; named Artist of Decade, Canadian Recording Industry; nominated for 6 Grammys and 7 Juno awards, 1992, many other awards in music.

ADAMS, C. LEE, marketing executive; b. Houston, Dec. 5, 1940; s. Carl Adams and Ruth (Carroll) Adams McGraw; BBA, Tex. A&M U., 1963; m. Betty Leatherwood, June 1, 1963; children: Diana, Carroll Ann. Export sales service asst. Comet Rice Mills, Inc., Houston, 1963-64, asst. export sales mgr., 1964-67, export sales mgr., 1967-68; gen. mgr. Country Cupboard Foods Divsn., Comet Rice Mills, 1968-71; sales mgr. Childers Mfg. Co., Houston, 1971-75; export sales mgr. Am. Rice, Inc., Houston, 1975-76, v.p. internat. mktg., 1976-80, group v.p. mktg., 1980-85, group v.p. internat. mktg., 1986-93, sr. v.p., 1993—; bd. dirs. USA Rice Fedn., mem. rice com. New Orleans Commodity Exchange, 1981-84. Bd. dirs. Harris County Water Control and Improvement Dist. 93, 1974-76; mem. Chelford One Mcpl. Utility Dist. Appraisal Rev. Bd., 1982-85. Served with USMCR, 1960-66. Mem. Am. Arab C. of C. (dir. 1978-81), TAMU 12th Man Found. (bd. dirs. 1987—), USA Rice Coun. (bd. dirs. 1995—), Rice Millers Assn. (dir. 1983—, pres. 1986-87), Assn. Former Students Tex. A&M U. Roman Catholic. Clubs: Elsik High Sch. Ram Rods (pres. 1984-85), Sweetwater Country. Lodge: K.C., Am. Legion. Office: Am Rice Inc PO Box 2587 Houston TX 77252-2587

ADAMS, CARL FILLMORE, JR., finance company executive; b. Muskogee, Okla., Feb. 8, 1950; s. Carl Fillmore Sr. and Lillian Elizabeth (Rozelle) A.; m. Katharine Ann Turley, Dec. 28, 1990. BA, U. Okla., 1968-72; MBA, NYU, 1975-81. Asst. v.p. economist Moody's Investors Svc., Inc., N.Y.C., 1976-85; pres., founder Strategic Rsch. Internat., Inc., N.Y.C., 1985, pres., 1988-90; mng. dir. Carl Marks & Co., Inc., N.Y.C., 1986-88; mng. dir. Strategic Global Rsch. Dun & Bradstreet Corp., N.Y.C., 1990-91; dr. credit, global mgr. Merrill Lynch & Co., N.Y.C., 1991—; dir., chmn. of credit com. Merrill Lynch Internat. Bank; chmn. Capital Markets Credit Analysts Soc.; bd. dirs. Internat. Adv. Coun., Murray Hill, N.J. Contbr. articles to profl. jours. Mem. N.Y. Soc. Internat. Investors, Info. Industry Assn., Asia Soc. (Merrill Lynch & Co.), Econ. Roundtable (Dun & Bradstreet, founder), Japan Soc. Republican. Avocations: American Indian history, travel, international relations policy. Office: Merrill Lynch & Co Inc World Fin Ctr South Tower 7th Fl Corp Credit Div New York NY 10080-6107

ADAMS, CAROL JEAN, educator; b. Sept. 25, 1955. BA, Calif. State U., Sacramento, 1977. Tchr. Benicia (Calif.) Unified Sch. Dist., 1978-81, 89—, 1st Hosp. Vallejo, 1986-87, John Suett Unified Sch. Dist., Crockett, Calif., 1987-89. Home: 520 West St Crockett CA 94525

ADAMS, CHARLES FRANCIS, advertising and real estate executive; b. Detroit, Sept. 26, 1927; s. James R. and Bertha C. (DeChant) A.; m. Helen R. Harrell, Nov. 12, 1949; children: Charles Francis, Amy Ann, James Randolph, Patricia Duncan. BA, U. Mich., 1948; postgrad., U. Calif., Berkeley, 1949. With D'Arcy-MacManus & Masius, Inc., 1947-80, exec. v.p., dir., 1970-76, pres., chief operating officer, 1976-80; pres. Adams Enterprises, 1971—; exec. v.p., dir. Washington Office, Am. Assn. Advt. Agys., 1980-84; chmn., chief exec. officer Wajim Corp., Detroit; past mem. steering com. Nat. Advt. Rev. Bd.; mem. mktg. com. U.S. Info. Agy.; pres. Internat. Visitors Ctr. of the Bay Area, 1988-89. Author: Common Sense in Advertising, 1965, Heroes of the Golden Gate, 1987, California of the Year 2000, 1992, The Magnificent Rogues, 1998. Past chmn. exec. com. Oakland U. Mem. Am. Assn. Advt. Agys. (dir., mem. govt. relations com.), Advt. Fedn. Am. (past dir.), Nat. Outdoor Advt. Bur. (past chmn.), Theta Chi, Alpha Delta Sigma (hon.). Republican. Roman Catholic. Clubs: Bloomfield Hills Country; Carmel Valley Ranch (Calif.); Nat. Golf Links Am. (Southampton, L.I.); Olympic, The Family (San Francisco). Home: 2240 Hyde St San Francisco CA 94109-1509 also: 25450 Loma Robles Dr Carmel CA 93923-8409 Office: 10 W Long Lake Rd Bloomfield Hills MI 48304-2707

ADAMS, CHARLES GILCHRIST, pastor; b. Detroit, Dec. 13, 1936. Student, Fisk U., 1954-56; BA with honors, U. Mich., 1958; MDiv. with honors, Harvard U., 1964; DD (hon.), Birmingham Bapt. Coll., 1976, Shaw Coll., Detroit, 1980, Morris Coll., 1980, Morehouse Coll., 1984; LHD (hon.), Marygrove Coll., 1985; LLD (hon.), Dillard U., 1985; D Hum (hon.), U. Mich., 1986; DD (hon.), Edward Waters Coll., 1987; LHD (hon.), Kalamazoo Coll., 1994. Pastor Concord Bapt. Ch., Boston, 1962-69, Hartford Meml. Bapt. Ch., Detroit, 1970—; instr. theology Boston U., Andover Newton Sch. Theology, Ctrl. Bapt. Sem., Kansas City, Iliff Sch. Theology, Denver; invited speaker UN, 1989, World Congress of Bapt. World Alliance, Seoul, Korea, 1990, 7th Gen. assembly of World Coun. Chs., Canberra, Australia, 1991, Evian, France, 1992; conf. preacher Hampton (Va.) U. Ministers Conf., 1993-94. Doctoral fellow Union Theol. Sem., N.Y.C.; named One of Ebony's Top 100 Influential Black Ams., 1990-94, One of 15 Greatest Black Preachers, 1993-94. Office: Hartford Memorial Baptist Church 18700 James Couzens Hwy Detroit MI 48235-2573*

ADAMS, CHARLES HENRY, retired animal scientist, educator; b. Burdick, Kans., Nov. 7, 1918; s. Henry Lory and Bertha Frances (Westbrook) A.; m. Eula Mae Peters, Apr. 29, 1943. BS, Kans. State U., 1941, MS, 1942; PhD, Mich. State U., 1964. Instr. Kans. State U., Manhattan, 1946-47; asst. prof. U. Nebr., Lincoln, 1947-64, assoc. prof., 1964-70, prof. animal sci., 1970-83, prof. emeritus, 1983—; asst. dean Coll. Agr., U. Nebr., Lincoln, 1973-83. Contbr. articles to profl. jours. 1st lt. AUS, 1943-46. Recipient Disting. Teaching awards Gamma Sigma Delta, 1969, U. Nebr., 1971, Am. Meat Sci. Assn., 1969, Am. Soc. Animal Sci., 1972; Disting. Svc. award U. Nebr. Lincoln Alumni Assn., 1989; named to Nebr. Hall of Agrl. Achievement, 1990. Fellow AAAS, Am. Soc. Animal Sci.; mem. Am. Meat Sci. Assn. (R.C. Pollock award 1992), Inst. Food Technologists, Nebr. Acad. Sci., Am. Legion, VFW, Rotary, Sigma Xi, Gamma Sigma Delta, Alpha Zeta, Alpha Gamma Rho. Republican. Mem. Christian Ch. (Disciples of Christ). Home: 7101 Colby St Lincoln NE 68505-1428

ADAMS, CHARLES JAIRUS, lawyer; b. Randolph, Vt., Feb. 17, 1917; s. Charles B. and Jeanette E. (Metzger) A.; m. Mary E. Tobey, July 5, 1942; children: Mary Jean, Carol Ann. B.S. in Elec. Engring, Norwich U., 1939; LL.B., Boston U., 1951. Bar: Vt. 1951. Student engr. Gen. Electric Co., also New Eng. Power Co., 1939-41; plant supt. Demeritt Co., Waterbury, Vt., 1946-48; practiced in Montpelier and Waterbury, 1951-98; partner firm Adams, Darby & Laundon, 1980-86; of counsel Darby, Laundon, Stearns, Thorndike & Kolter, 1987-98; treas. Vt. Bar Assn., 1951-55; atty. gen. State of Vt., 1962-63; chmn. State of Vt. Legis. Apportionment Bd., 1972-80; mem. adv. com. on civil rules Vt. Supreme Ct., 1971-82. Trustee Village of Waterbury, 1956-57, 88-90, pres., 1958; moderator Town of Waterbury, 1961; mem. Waterbury Pub. Libr. Assn., 1961-93. Mem. Am. Legion, Norwich U. Gen. Alumni Assn. (pres. 1960-61, bd. fellows), Masons. Congregationalist. Home: 290 Whitewater Cir Williston VT 05495-9484

ADAMS, CHARLES LYNFORD, English language educator; b. Joliet, Ill., May 11, 1929; s. Charles Lynford and Eloise A. (Henault) A.; m. Joan Marie Johnson, June 6, 1953; children—Rebecca Lynn, Stephen Thomas. B.A., Mich. State U., 1951; M.A., U. Ill., 1952; Ph.D., U. Oreg., 1959. Instr. English U. Ore., 1959-60; asst. prof. U. Nev., Las Vegas, 1960-65; assoc. prof. U. Nev., 1965-67, prof. English, 1967-96, prof. emeritus English, 1996—; Las Vegas rep. U. Nev. System Grad. Sch., 1964-66, coordinator grad. studies, 1966-68, dean grad. studies, 1968-71. Editor: Studies in Frank Waters. Mem. adv. com. Univ. Mus. Soc. Served with AUS, 1954-56. Mem. MLA, Nat. Coun. Tchrs. English, Nev. Coun. Tchrs. English, So. Nev. Coun. Tchrs. English, Rocky Mountain MLA, Conf. Coll. Composition and Comm., AAUP, Nat. Soc. Profs., Frank Waters Soc., Phi Kappa Phi. Home: 1921 E St Louis Ave Las Vegas NV 89104-3805 Office: 4505 S Maryland Pkwy Las Vegas NV 89154-9900

ADAMS, CHRISTINE BEATE LIEBER, psychiatrist, educator; b. Greensboro, N.C., June 20, 1949; d. Paul Lieber Adams and Marjorie Pinckney (Quackenbos) Ould; 1 child, Justin McKendree Adams-Tucker. Student, Agnes Scott Coll., 1967-69; BA in English Lit. with honors, U. Fla., 1971, MD, 1976. Diplomate Am. Bd. Psychiatry and Neurology (examiner 1985), Am. Bd. Child Psychiatry (examiner 1984, 91), Nat. Bd. Med. Examiners. Resident in gen. psychiatry U. Louisville Sch. Medicine, 1976-78, fellow in child psychiatry, 1978-80, asst. clin. prof. dept. psychiatry and behavioral scis., 1981—, attending psychiatrist consultation-liaison svc., 1992, 93; pvt. practice, Louisville, 1980—; med. advisor Social Security Adminstrn., HHS, Louisville, 1986—; child psychiatry cons. Seven Counties Svcs., Ky. Dept. Human Resources, 1989, 93; physician advisor Nat. Health Svcs., Louisville, 1993—; reviewer Am. Jour. Psychiatry, 1983—; cons. So. Ind. Mental Health and Guidance Ctr., Jeffersonville, 1981-83, U. Fla., 1982; presenter in field. Contbr. articles to med. jours., chpts. to books. Bd. dirs. Gainesville (Fla.) Women's Health Ctr., 1973-75; mem. Jefferson County (Ky.) Juvenile Justice Commn., 1982-86. Recipient award Nat. Psychiat. Endowment Fund, 1980. Fellow Am. Acad. Child and Adolescent Psychiatry (com. on rights and legal matters 1984-92); mem. Am. Psychiat. Assn. (mem. com. family violence and child sexual abuse 1987-94), Am. Orthopsychiat. Assn., Am. Acad. Psychiatry and Law, Nat. Com. for Prevention Child Abuse, Ky. Psychiat. Assn., Ky. Acad. Child Psychiatry (sec.-treas. 1980-81, pres.-elect 1981-82, pres. 1982-83). Office: Med Arts Bldg Ste 3364 1169 Eastern Pky Louisville KY 40217-1417

ADAMS, CHRISTINE HANSON, advertising executive; b. Hackensack, N.J., May 24, 1950; d. Kenwood Alwin and Doris (Rogers) Hanson; m. L. Ashby Adams III, June 1, 1974 (div. Aug. 1993); 1 child, Nathaniel Kaufman. BA, Lafayette Coll., 1972; MBA, Duke U., 1979. Med. sales rep. Hoffman-LaRoche, Nutley, N.J., 1972-75; sr. market rsch. analyst Burroughs Wellcome Co., Research Triangle Park, N.C., 1976-77, product planner, 1978; dir. market research Sterling Drug Inc., N.Y.C., 1979-81; group product mgr. Pfizer Inc., N.Y.C., 1981-83; account supr. Kallir Philips Ross Inc., N.Y.C., 1983, v.p., account group supr., 1984-86; v.p., account supr. Baxter Gurian and Mazzei Inc., Beverly Hills, Calif., 1987-89, account group v.p., 1990-91, sr. v.p. account group, supr., 1991-93, sr. v.p. mgmt. supr., 1994; sr. v.p. group acct. dir. Kallir Philips Ross Inc, N.Y., 1994-96; sr. v.p.

mgmt. supr. Torre Lazur Comm., Parsippany, N.J., 1996-98; v.p., mgmt. supr. Integrated Comm. Corp., Lawrenceville, N.J., 1998—; cons. advt. Wellness Cmty., Santa Monica, Calif., 1988-92. Active membership com. St. Michael's Episcopal Ch., Studio City, Calif., 1987-93, altar guild, 1988-93, tchr. Sunday sch., 1990-91. Named Young Career Woman Bus. Profl. Women's Assn., Chapel Hill, N.C., 1978. Mem. Healthcare Mktg. and Comms. Coun., Healthcare Businesswomen's Assn. Republican. Avocations: fashion design, sewing, music, 19th-century English literature. Home: 8 Villa Dr Princeton Junction NJ 08550-1241 Office: Integrated Comm Corp 989 Lenox Dr Ste 300 Lawrenceville NJ 08648-2315

ADAMS, CHRISTOPHER PAUL, journalist; b. Covington, Ga., Mar. 19, 1957; s. Paul and Jeanne (Shropshire) Adams; m. Tina-Marie Armstrong, Oct. 19, 1996; children: Anderson Scot, Susan Margaret, Creighton Paul. BS, Purdue U., 1978. Asst. sports editor Jour. and Courier, Lafayette, Ind., 1978-84; sports editor Daily Jour., Marietta, Ga., 1984-85, Kankakee, Ill., 1985-90; sports editor Union, Sacramento, 1990, The Free Press, Burlington, Vt., 1990-92, The News-Record/News Dispatch, Pitts., 1992-95, The News Jour., Wilmington, Del., 1995-96; mng. editor The News Sun, Waukegan, Ill., 1996-98; exec. editor Copley Chgo. Newspapers, 1998—. Named Best Columnist Women's Sports Found., 1988, Nat. Newspaper Assn., 1989; recipient Top Ten Sports Section, AP Sports Editors, 1992, 93, Best Sports Sect., Nat. Newspaper Assn., 1987, 88, 92. Avocations: writing, reading, golf, personal fitness.

ADAMS, CHRISTOPHER STEVE, JR., retired defense electronics corporation executive, former air force officer; b. Shreveport, La., July 8, 1930; s. Christopher Steve and Armenda Lee (Tanner) A.; m. Mary Alene Mitchell, Aug. 22, 1953; children: Cynthia, Charlotte, Cheri, Christopher III. A.S., Tarleton State U., 1950; B.S., East Tex. State U., 1952. Commd. U.S. Air Force, 1952, advanced through grades to maj. gen., 1979; B-36 pilot 95th Bombardment Wing, Ramey AFB, P.R.; dir. plans and policy J-5, Def. Nuclear Agy., Washington, 1970-73; vice comdr., then comdr. 90th Strategic Missile Wing, 1973-75; comdr. 12th Air Div., 1975-78; dep. chief staff, ops. plans Hdqrs. SAC; chief of staff SAC, 1982-83; ret., 1983; assoc. dir. U. Calif. Los Alamos Nat. Lab., 1983-86; exec. v.p. Sci. Commn., Inc., Dallas, 1986-87; v.p. bus. devel. Andrew Corp., Dallas, 1987-94, ret., 1994. Contbr. articles to profl. jours. Bd. dirs. ARC, 1976-78, Mid-Am. Council Boy Scouts Am., 1976-81. Decorated D.S.M., Def. Superior Service medal, Legion of Merit, Air Force Commendation medal; recipient Disting. Alumnus award Tarleton State U., 1990, Disting. Alumnus award E. Tex. State U., 1991. Presbyterian. Home: 101 Skyview Ln Liberty Hill TX 78642-6008 *America the beautiful. I have dedicated my life through service to preserve our freedom. There is no better place on earth—I know, I've been there.*

ADAMS, CLINTON, artist, historian; b. Glendale, Calif., Dec. 11, 1918; s. Merritt Cooley and Effie (Mackenzie) A.; m. Mary Elizabeth Atchison, Jan. 9, 1943; 1 child, Michael Gerald. Ed.B., UCLA, 1940, M.A., 1942. Instr. art UCLA, 1946-48, asst. prof., 1948-54; prof. art, head dept. U. Ky.; also dir. Art Gallery, 1954-57; prof. art, head dept. U. Fla., 1957-61; dean Coll. Fine Arts U. N.Mex., Albuquerque, 1961-76, asso. provost, dean faculties, 1976-77; dir. Tamarind Inst., 1970-85; asso. dir. Tamarind Lithography Workshop, Los Angeles, 1960-61, program cons., 1961-70. Represented in permanent collections Bklyn. Mus., Art. Inst. Chgo., Brit. Mus., Australian Nat. Gallery, Mus. Modern Art, Los Angeles County Art Mus., and others; author: (with Garo Antreasian) The Tamarind Book of Lithography: Art and Techniques, 1970, American Lithographers, 1900-1960: The Artists and Their Printers, 1983, (with others) Lasting Impressions: Lithography As Art, 1988, Printmaking in New Mexico, 1880-1990, 1991, Crayonstone: The Life and Work of Bolton Brown, 1993, Nineteenth-Century Lithography in Europe, 1998; editor The Tamarind Papers, 1974-90, Second Impressions: Modern Prints and Printmakers Reconsidered, 1996; subject: bibliography Clinton Adams: Paintings and Watercolors 1945-87; exhbn. catalogue Albuquerque: University of New Mexico Art Mus., 1987; biography A Spectrum of Innovation: Color in American Printmaking, 1890-1990, 1990. Recipient Gov.'s award for outstanding contbns. to arts of N.Mex., 1985. Mem. NAD (academician), Nat. Coun. Fine Arts Deans (chmn. 1965-67). Home: 1917 Morningside Dr NE Albuquerque NM 87110-4927

ADAMS, COREY EMILE, planner, analyst; b. Saginaw, Mich., Mar. 5, 1971; s. George W. and Marilyn A. Adams. BA, Morehouse Coll., 1995. Sales and svc. rep. Ameritech, Saginaw, 1995-97; rsch. asst. EPA/Nat. Assn. Sch. Pub. Affairs and Adminstrn., Atlanta, 1998; asst. Fulton County, Atlanta, Ga., 1998-99, planner II, 1999—. Mem. ASPA, Nat. Forum Black Pub. Adminstrs. (Atlanta chpt. student bd. rep. 1998—), Conf. Minority Pub. Adminstrs., Clark Atlanta U. Pub. Adminstrn. Student Assn. (pres. 1998—), Morehouse Coll. Alumni Assn., Alpha Phi Alpha. Avocations: sports, dancing, computers. E-mail: CAdams11@CompuServe.com. Home: 4021 Lakemont Dr Apt 7T College Park GA 30337 Office: Fulton County 141 Pryor St Ste 5001 Atlanta GA 30303

ADAMS, CORLYN HOLBROOK, nursing facility administrator; b. Beloit, Kans., Sept. 28, 1926; d. Charles Benjamin and Hazel Marian (Brokaw) Holbrook; m. Henry Robert Adams, Oct. 28, 1961; 1 child, Charles Paul. Student, U. Kans., 1944-45, 48. Lic. nursing facility adminstr. Clk. bd. edn. Beloit (Kans.) City Schs., 1945-48; adminstr. Stanford Conv. Ctrs., Fort Worth, 1973-79; adminstr., owner Four Nursing Homes, Fort Worth, 1979-84. Author, editor: The Jose Family, 1994. Mem. Order of Ea. Star, DAR, Nat. Soc. New England Women (sec. 1975), Nat. Hugenot Soc., Gen. Soc. Mayflower Descendents, Daus. of Utah Pioneers. Republican. Avocations: geneaology, music-playing piano.

ADAMS, CRAIG DAVID, environmental engineering educator; b. St. Paul, Minn., Apr. 25, 1958; married; 4 children. BS in Chem. Engring., U. Kans., 1983, MS in Environ. Engring., 1988, PhD, 1991. Registered profl. engr., Kans. Product devel. engr. Optical Coating Lab., Inc., Santa Rosa, Calif., 1983-87; grad. rsch. asst. Dept. Environ. Engring. U. Kans., Lawrence, 1987-91; asst. prof. environ. sys. engring. Clemson (S.C.) U., 1991-95; John & Susan Mathers prof. environ. engring. U. Mo., Rolla, 1995—, assoc. prof. civil engring., 1995—; dir. environ. rsch. ctr. U. Mo., 1995—, sr. investigator Ctr. Environ. Sci. & Tech., 1995—; cons. in field, 1993—. Contbr. articles to profl. jours. Recipient Young Investigator award NSF, Arlington, Va., 1992-97. Mem. AIChE, Am. Water Works Assn., Internat. Ozone Assn. (dir., internat. bd. dirs. 1993—), Water Environment Fedn., Assn. Environ. Engring. Profs. (membership com. 1991—), Tau Beta Pi (life). Achievements include development of products and technology related to environmental chemistry, ozone and advanced oxidation processes for air, water, wastewater and hazardous waste treatment and air pollution control. Office: Univ Mo Rolla Environ Engring Program 202 Civil Engring Bldg Rolla MO 65409

ADAMS, DANIEL CLIFFORD, music educator; b. Miami, Fla., June 28, 1956; s. Joseph Peter and Molly (Smith) A.; m. Elise Ruth Benjamin, Dec. 21, 1985 (div. Aug. 1994). MusB, La. State U., 1978; MusM, U. Miami, Coral Gables, Fla., 1981; D Mus. Arts, U. Ill., 1985. Adj. faculty Miami-Dade C.C., 1985-88, U. Miami, Coral Gables, 1986-88; mem. music faculty Tex. So. U., Houston, 1988—. Contbr. articles to profl. jours. Recipient music composition awards ASCAP, N.Y.C., 1985-98, Percussive Arts Soc., 1989. Mem. Soc. Composers, Inc. (nat. coun. 1995-97), Coll. Music Soc. (treas. South Ctrl. chpt. 1994—), South Fla. Composers Alliance (bd. dirs. 1985-88), Houston Composers Alliance (bd. dirs. 1991—), Phi Mu Alpha Sinfonia. Avocations: travel, fishing, scuba diving. Home: 5620 Chimney Rock Rd Apt 10 Houston TX 77081-1942 Office: Tex So U 3100 Cleburne St Houston TX 77004-4501

ADAMS, DANIEL FENTON, law educator; b. Reading, Pa., July 29, 1922; s. Daniel Snyder and Carrie Betsy (Vought) A.; m. Eloise Williams, Sept. 6, 1968. A.B., Dickinson Coll., 1947; LL.B., Dickinson Sch. Law, 1949. Bar: Pa. 1951, Ark. 1984. Prof. law Sch. Law Dickinson U., Carlisle, Pa., 1949-65, asst. to dean, 1952-54, 56-60, acting dean, 1954-56, asst. dean, 1960-65; prof. Sch. Law U. Ark., Little Rock, 1965-70, 77-93, prof. emeritus, 1993—; asst. dean U. Ark. Sch. Law, Little Rock, 1966-70, acting dean, 1981-82, interim dean, 1989-91; prof. U. Miss. Sch. Law, Oxford, 1970-77; vis. prof. Stetson U. Sch. Law, St. Petersburg, Fla., 1976-77, U. Tenn. Coll. Law, 1993. Contbr. articles to profl. jours. Served with U.S. Army, 1943-44. Mem. ABA, Pa. Bar Assn., Ark. Bar Assn. Home: 32571 River Rd Orange Beach AL 36561-5713

ADAMS, DANIEL LEE, lawyer; b. Beaver, Ohio, Oct. 3, 1936; s. Paul D. and Margaret (Rhea) A.; m. Julianne Faller, Aug. 13, 1960; children: Cristin Ann, Meghan Kathleen. BA, Ohio State U., 1957, JD, 1960. Bar: Fla. 1962. Atty. Attys.' Title Services, Inc., Ft. Lauderdale, Fla., 1960-62, also bd. dirs.; atty. Attys. Title Ins. Fund, Inc., 1962-69; ptnr. English, McCaughan and O'Bryan, Ft. Lauderdale, 1969—; trustee, dir. 17th Jud. Cir. of Attys.' Title Ins. Fund, Orlando, Fla.; mem. MRTA Commn., Tallahassee, 1985-86; dir. Atty.'s Title Guaranty Fund, Inc., Colo. Mem. ABA, Broward County Bar Assn., Fla. Bar Assn. (exec. coun. real property, probate and trust law sect., grievance com.), Broward County Club 100 (pres. 1992-93, bd. dirs. 1988-94). Democrat. Roman Catholic. Avocations: bicycling, reading, wood working. Home: 600 Petunia Dr Fort Lauderdale FL 33317-1926 Office: English McCaughan & O'Bryan 100 NE 3rd Ave Ste 1100 Fort Lauderdale FL 33301-1144

ADAMS, DARLENE AGNES, secondary education educator; b. Prague, Okla., Aug. 23, 1952; d. Carney and Bertha Ellen (Capps) A. AS, Murray State Coll., 1972; BA, East Ctrl. State Coll., 1974, MEd, 1978. Cert. libr. media specialist. Tchr., libr. Carney Pub. Schs., 1974-75, Paden (Okla.) Pub. Schs., 1975—; staff devel com. Paden Pub. Schs., 1985-90, curriculum guidelines com., 1985—, career counseling com., 1990—, gifted and talented com., 1993—, sponsor jr. and sr. class plays and proms. Pres. The Chem. People, Paden, 1983—; sponsor Beta Club, 1990-91, 95-96. Mem. ALA, NEA, Okla. Library Asnn., Okla. Edn. Assn., Smithsonian, Phi Theta Kappa. Republican. Pentacostal. Avocations: photography, painting, fishing, hiking, reading. Home: 300 E Kerr McGee Rd Paden OK 74860-9766 Office: Paden Pub Schs PO Box 370 Paden OK 74860-0370

ADAMS, DARLENE W., computer services administrator; b. New Orleans, La., Dec. 3, 1958; d. Sam and Ida Rose (Johnson) Wilson; m. Anthony Joseph Adams Sr., Sept. 13, 1980; children: Simone Nicole, Anthony Joseph, Shedrenna Marie. BA, U. New Orleans, 1976. Waitress Grants Dept. Store, New Orleans, 1975, K-Mart, New Orleans, 1976; cashier Bonanza Steak House, Gretna, La., 1976; student unit clerk Charity Hosp., New Orleans, 1977-79; cashier, asst. office mgr. Maison Blanche, Gretna, 1979-82; clerk, supervisor Food For Families, New Orleans, 1987-89, computer coord., 1989-97, assoc. dir. computer svcs., 1997—. Editorial asst.: (newsletter) The Crew Connection, 1997. Vol. Senator Paulette Iron, New Orleans, 1992; coach Athlete For Christ, 1997. Mem. Phi Beta Lambda Soc. Democrat. Avocations: sewing, playing baseball and basketball, computers, singing. Home: 630 Manhattan Blvd Harvey LA 70058-4446 Office: Food For Families 8326 Apricot St New Orleans LA 70118-3126

ADAMS, DAVID GRAY, lawyer; b. Tyler, Tex., Feb. 18, 1961; s. Ralph Judson and Laura (George) A. BBA, U. Tex., 1983; M in Taxation, Baylor U., 1987; JD, U. Houston, 1995. CPA, Tex. Acct. Grant Thornton, Dallas, 1983-85; tax mgr. Ernst & Young, Dallas, 1987-91; jud. law clk. to Hon. Joe J. Fisher U.S. Dist. Ct. (ea. dist.) Tex., 1995-96; jud. law clk. to Hon. Robert M. Parker U.S. Ct. Appeals (5th cir.), 1996-97; atty. Baker & Botts, L.L.P., Dallas, 1997—; mem. Tex. Bd. Pub. Acctg. Mem. AICPA, ABA, State Bar Tex. Episcopalian. Avocations: golf, tennis, snow skiing.

ADAMS, DAVID PARRISH, historian, educator; b. Jacksonville, Fla., Aug. 2, 1958; s. David Parrish and Gloria Ann (Nesmith) A.; m. Teri Ann Becker, Aug. 31, 1985; 1 child, Morgan Becker. BA, Emory U., 1980; AM, Washington U., St. Louis, 1982; PhD, U. Fla., 1987; MPH, Ohio State U., 1994. Resource faculty dept. family medicine U. Fla., Gainesville, 1983-87; assoc. prof. dept. humanities Columbus (Ohio) State C.C., 1987-95; rsch. dir. Cabarrus Family Medicine Residence Program, Concord, N.C., 1995—; cons. assoc. dept. cmty. and family medicine Duke Med. Ctr., Durham, N.C., 1996—; adj. faculty dept. history Ohio Dominican Coll., Columbus, 1987-95; adj. asst. prof. dept. family medicine Ohio State U., Columbus, 1990-95, post-doctoral rschr. AHEC program, 1995, lectr. dept. history, 1995; adj. asst. prof. dept. family medicine Ponce (P.R.) Sch. Medicine, 1993; rsch. dir. Cabarrus Family Practice Residence program Cabarrus Meml. Hosp., Concord, N.C.; cons. assoc. dept. cmty. and family medicine Duke U., 1995—; vis. asst. prof. med. humanities program Davidson Coll., 1996—; adj. asst. prof. Coll. Nursing, U. Tenn.-Knoxville; adj. asst. prof. dept. family medicine Quillen Coll. Medicine, Ea. Tenn. State U., 1998—; cons. in field. Author: The Greatest Good to the Greatest Number: Penicillin Rationing on the American Home Front, 1940-45, 1991; contbr. articles to profl. jours. Med. Humanities fellow U. Ill., Chgo., 1992; grant-in-aid U. Wis., 1985; grantee NIH, 1989, Ohio Acad. Family Physicians, 1991. Mem. APHA, Am. Assn. History of Medicine, Am. Hist. Assn., Orgn. Am. Historians, Soc. Tchrs. Family Medicine, Am. Soc. Tropical Medicine and Hygiene. Democrat. Mem. United Ch. of Christ. Achievements include research in general and family practice; evolution of family practice; penicillin, dentistry and SBE; wartime penicillin policy; community oriented primary care. Home: 8827 Ryegate Dr Knoxville TN 37922-1427 Office: Cmty Health Rsch Group U Tenn-Knoxville Knoxville TN 37996

ADAMS, DAVID PORTERFIELD, III, business appraiser; b. Nashville, Oct. 10, 1961; s. David Porterfield Adams and Elizabeth (Morgan) Spiegel; m. Pamela Beverforden, Oct. 12, 1991; children: Porter, Trevor. BS in Mech. Engring., Ga. Inst. Tech., 1986, MBA, 1988. CPA. From cons. to mgr. KPMG Peat Marwick, Atlanta, 1988-94; mgr. Coopers & Lybrand, Atlanta, 1994-96; pres. Adams Capital Inc., Atlanta, 1996—. Co-author: Closely Held Business Valuation, 1995, Minority Interests & Discounts, 1995. Fellow Ga. Soc. CPAs; mem. AICPAs, Am. Soc. Appraisers, The Georgian Club. Avocations: skiing, hiking, reading, building. Office: Adams Capital Inc 100 Galleria Pkwy SE Ste 400 Atlanta GA 30339-3122

ADAMS, (LEWIS) DEAN, theater director; b. Seattle, July 22, 1957; s. Brockman and Mary Elizabeth (Scott) A.; m. Kristin Cook Gilbert, June 20, 1981. BA in Drama and English, Tufts U., 1980; MA in TV-Film, U. Md., 1986. Stage prodn. mgr. Shakespeare and Co., Washington, 1975-79; asst. stage mgr. Arena Stage, Washington, 1976; tech. dir. St. Albans Sch., Washington, 1980-82; dir. theater Loomis Chaffee Sch., Windsor, Conn., 1982-88, Westminster Sch., Simsbury, Conn., 1989—; artistic dir. Centennial Theater Festival, Simsbury, 1989—. Dir. (U.K. tour) Dining Room, 1985; dir., producer (1st Chinese tour of Am. mus.) Once Upon a Mattress, 1987. Bd. dirs. Farmington Valley Music Found. Grantee Ford Found., 1984; scholar Tufts U., 1978-80. Mem. Internat. Brotherhood Magicians, Soc. Am. Magicians, Soc. of Stage Dirs. and Choreographers, New Eng. Presenters, Assn. of Performing Arts Presenters. Democrat. Episcopalian. Home: PO Box 342 Weatogue CT 06089-0342 Office: Westminster Sch 995 Hopmeadow St Simsbury CT 06070-1880

ADAMS, DEBORAH ROWLAND, lawyer; b. Princeton, N.J., July 28, 1952; d. Bernard S. and Natalie S. Adams; m. Charles L. Campbell, June 16, 1990. BA, Colo. Coll., Colorado Springs, 1974; JD, U. Colo., 1978. Bar: Ind. 1978, Colo. 1978, U.S. Dist. Ct. Colo. 1978. Atty. Legal Svcs. Orgn. Ind., Indpls., 1978-79, Pikes Peak Legal Svcs., Colorado Springs, 1979-80, Pub. Defender's Office, Colorado Springs, 1980-81; assoc. Ranson, Thomas, Cook and Livingston, Colorado Springs, 1982-84, Ranson, Thomas, Adams, Petinga and Yukawa, Colorado Springs, 1984; pvt. practice Colorado Springs, 1985—; mem. state Jud. Nominating Commn. for 4th Jud. Dist., 1994-2000; Colo. state grievance com., 1997-2000. Bd. dirs. Domestic Violence Prevention Ctr., 1980-86, pres., 1982-84; bd. dirs. Pikes Peak Legal Svcs., 1983-88, pres., 1986-87, pro bono advocacy sch. faculty, 1990-92; co-chairperson Colo. Springs Devel. Com., Colo. Women's Found., 1987, mem. grant selection com., 1988, 90; bd. dirs. Vis. Nurses Assn., 1989-91; bd. dirs. Chins Up, 1991-97, pres., 1997-98; co-chairperson El Paso County sect. COLTAF Fundraising Com. for benefit of Colo. Legal Aid Found., 1991-99, chairperson, 1994-95; mem. state bd. dirs. Legal Aid Found., 1994—, v.p., 1997-98. Recipient Pro Bono award Pikes Peak Legal Svcs., 1988; named Atty of Yr. El Paso County Legal Secs. Assn., 1990; selected to attend Colo. Springs Leadership Class, Colorado Springs Leadership Inst., 1997. Mem. Colo. Bar Assn. (family law sect. 1991-99, conciliation panel subcom. of profls. com. 1992, bd. govs. 1994-97, exec. com. 1995-97, nominating com. 1996), Colo. Bar Found., Colo. Women's Bar Assn., El Paso County Bar Assn. (pres.-elect 1994-95, pres. 1995-96, Trial Advocacy Sch. faculty 1990, 94, Moot Ct. judge 1992, 95, fee arbitration dispute com. 1990-95), Women Lawyer's Assn. Fourth Jud. Dist.(chairperson jud. nominating com. 1991-93, Portia award 1992), Zonta Club Colorado Springs (pres. 1989-90, co-chairperson dist. 12 regional conf. 1991-92, Zontian of Yr. 1990-91). Democrat. Avocations: reading, skiing, tennis, running, mountain biking. Office: 324 S Cascade Ave Colorado Springs CO 80903-3804

ADAMS, DENNIS PAUL, artist; b. Des Moines, Nov. 15, 1948; s. Paul Thomas Adams and Stella Vernita (Kirkland) MacGregor; 1 child, Todd Dennis Haffner; m. Jody Rodman Walker, Oct. 8, 1981; 1 child, Jack Walker Adams. BFA, Drake U., 1969; MFA, Tyler Sch. Art, Phila., 1971. Assoc. prof. MIT, Cambridge, 1996—; vis. prof. Parsons Sch., N.Y.C., 1990-94, Cooper Union, N.Y.C., 1988-90, Ecole Des Beaux-Arts, Paris, 1992, Rijksakademie, Amsterdam, 1992-94, Akademie Der Bildenden Künst, Munich, 1993-94, MIT, Cambridge, 1994—; asst. prof. Tyler Sch. Art, 1976, Ohio Sch. Art, Athens, 1972-75. Numerous one-man shows include de Appel Found., Amsterdam, The Netherlands, 1988, The Clocktower, N.Y.C., 1988, Galerie Meert-Rihoux, Brussels, 1989, John Weber Gallery, N.Y.C., 1989, Galerie Gabrielle Maubrie, Paris, 1990, Kent Fine Art, N.Y.C., 1990, Hirschhorn Mus., Washington, 1990, Mus. Modern Art, N.Y.C., 1991, Fundacio la Caixa, Barcelona, Spain, 1992, Portikus, Frankfurt, Germany, 1993, Muhka, Antwerpen, 1994, Contemporary Arts Mus., Houston, 1994, Queens Mus., N.Y.C., 1996; contbr. articles to profl. jours. Bd. govs. N.Y. Found. for Arts, N.Y.C., 1989-92. NEA fellowship grantee, 1984, 88, 95; recipient Visual Artists Project award N.Y. State Coun. on Arts, 1984. Home: 42 Walker St New York NY 10013-3514

ADAMS, DIANE LORETTA, physician; b. St. Louis, Nov. 3, 1948; m. William McKinley Adams; children: Kareem McKinley, Dawn Caron, Akeem Michael. BS, Howard U., 1969; MD, N.J. Med. Sch., 1976; MPH, Johns Hopkins U., 1980. Resident in family practice Howard U. Hosp., Washington, 1976-79; chief med. officer USCG Shipyard, Curtis Bay, Md., 1980-83, Bur. Engraving and Printing, Washington, 1983-85; med. officer St. Elizabeth Hosp., Washington, 1985-86; rsch. analyst Office Asst. Sec. Health, Rockville, Md., 1987-90; chief minority health svcs. rsch. program Agy. Health Care Policy and Rsch., Rockville, 1990-93; congl. fellow office of Congressman Louis Stokes U.S. Ho. of Reps., Washington, 1990; sr. med. adv. Agy. Health Care Policy and Rsch., Dept. Health/Human Svcs., Rockville, 1993—; clin. assoc. prof. dept. phys. therapy U. Md.; cons. rep. AIDS Task Force, 1987-93; lectr. intensive bioethics Georgetown U. Kennedy Inst. Ethics, 1991. Editor: Health Issues for Women of Color: A Cultural Diversity Perspective, 1995. Recipient Adminstrs. Outstanding Cmty. Svc. award Agy. Health Care Policy and Rsch., 1996; inductee Md. Women's Hall of Fame, 1997. Mem. Am. Coll. Preventive Medicine, Alpha Kappa Alpha (Outstanding Comt. Svc. award 1981-85). Avocation: equitation. Home: 17032 Barn Ridge Dr Silver Spring MD 20906-1106

ADAMS, DONALD EDWARD, biotechnology and pharmaceutical patent examiner; b. Pitts., June 4, 1964; s. George Oliver and Norma Shirley (Whetton) A.; m. Daria Ann Novekosky, Oct. 21, 1989; children: Tasha Novekosky, Kyla Daria Ann. BS in Chemistry and Biology, Geneva Coll., 1986; PhD in Microbiology, U. Ala., Birmingham, 1991; JD, George Mason U., 1997. Bar: Va. Teaching asst. Geneva Coll., Beaver Falls, Pa., 1985-86; rsch. scientist Sch. Medicine, U. Ala., Birmingham, 1986-91; supervisory patent examiner biotech. U.S. Dept. Commerce, Patent & Trademark Office, Arlington, Va., 1991—; adj. prof. sci. Marymount U., 1991-93; judge Patent and Trademark Office Regional Sci. Fair. Contbr. articles to scholarly and profl. jours. Recipient Bronze medal Dept. Commerce; NIH grantee, 1986; U. Ala. fellow, 1987. Mem. ABA, AIPLA, Patent and Trademark Office Soc., Va. Bar Assn. Achievements include discovery of a novel cell cycle regulated protein kinase and its potential application for the diagnosis of acute lymphoblastic leukemia; discovery of a novel pathway for control of cell division utilizing a glycosyltransferase associated protein kinase. Office: US Dept Commerce Patent and Trademark Office Crystal Mall Rm 9a01 Arlington VA 22202

ADAMS, DONALD ELWIN, cultural and organization development consultant; b. Sioux Falls, S.D., July 13, 1953; s. James Robert and Louise (Lewis) A.; m. Arlene Frances Goldbard, Dec. 1, 1978. Student, U. S.D., 1971-74; MA in Arts Adminstrn., Sangamon State U., 1976. Cmty. devel. dir. Arts and Humanities Coun., Baton Rouge, 1975-76; dep. dir. Calif. Arts Coun., Sacramento, 1976-77; ptnr. Adams & Goldbard, Seattle, 1978—; dir. Inst. for Cultural Democracy, Seattle, 1987—; writer-in-residence Blue Mountain Ctr., Blue Mountain Lake, N.Y., 1982, Rockefeller Found., Bellagio, Italy, 1994. Author: Crossroads: Reflections on the Politics of Culture, 1990. Dir. Webster's World of Cultural Democracy, Seattle, 1995—; treas. Congregation Eitz Or, 1998—. Fellow Nat. Endowment for the Arts, Washington, 1976. E-mail: icd@wwcd.org. Office: PO Box 30061 Seattle WA 98103-2061

ADAMS, DONALD SCOTT, engineer, pharmacist; b. Covington, Ky., Apr. 29, 1960; s. Donald Ray and Joan Marie (Hunter) A.; m. Carol Jean Hausfeld, Mar. 30, 1985; children: Samuel Scott, Michelle Elizabeth, Allison Marie. A Applied Sci. in Pharm., U. Cinn., 1980, A Sci. Info. Sys. magna cum laude, 1991, BS in Info. Sys. magna cum laude, 1994. Pharmacy tech. Jewish Hosp., Cin., 1980-81; rsch. tech. Procter & Gamble Co., Cin., 1981-90, rsch. scientist, 1991-94, engr., 1995-99; sr. engr. Procter & Gamble Co., 1999—. Mem. Progressive Citizens Orgn., St. Bernard, Ohio, 1985—. Mem. Assn. Pharmacy Tech. (advisor 1984—, treas. 1980-82), Ohio Valley Football Ofcls. Assn., Assn. Profl. Engrs., Am. Chem. Soc., Eagles, Alpha Sigma Lambda, Delta Tau Kappa, Delta Mu Delta, Golden Key Nat. Hon. Soc. Achievements include 9 patents applied for. Home: 4705 Heger Dr Cincinnati OH 45217-1413 Office: Procter & Gamble 5299 Spring Grove Ave Cincinnati OH 45217

ADAMS, DOUGLAS NOEL, writer; b. Cambridge, England, Mar. 11, 1952; s. Christopher Douglas and Janet (Donovan) A.; m. Jane Belson, 1991; 1 child, Polly Jane Rocket. BA and MA in English Lit., Cambridge (Eng.) U., 1974. Author: The Hitchhiker's Guide to the Galaxy, 1979 (Best books for Young adults list ALA 1980), The Restaurant at the End of the Universe, 1980, Life, The Universe and Everything, 1982, So Long, And Thanks for All the Fish, 1984, The Original Hitchhiker's Radio Scripts, 1985, Dirk Gently's Holistic Detective Agency, 1987, The Long Dark Tea Time of the Soul, 1988, More Than Complete Hitchhiker's Guide, 1990, (with Mark Carwardine) Last Chance to See..., 1990, Mostly Harmless, 1992, The Illustrated Hitchhiker's Guide to the Galaxy, 1994; (with John Lloyd) The Meaning of Liff, 1983, The Deeper Meaning of Liff, 1993; (with others) Not 1982: Not the Nine O'Clock News Rip Off Annual, 1981; editor (with Peter Fincham) The Utterly Utterly Merry Comic Relief Christmas Book, 1986; freelance comedy scriptwriter for BBC Radio; script editor TV series Doctor Who, 1978-80; creator, author: (CD Rom) Starship Titanic, 1998. Office: c/o The Digital Village Ltd, 11 Maiden Ln, London WC2E 7NA, England

ADAMS, DOUGLASS FRANKLIN, radiologist, educator, medical ethicist; b. Lewiston, Maine, Aug. 5, 1935; s. Shirah Devoy and Olive (Colburn) A.; m. Eleanor Pohleven, Aug. 15, 1954; children: Stanford, Jennifer, Jason. BA, Stetson U., 1957; BS, Wake Forest Coll., Winston-Salem, N.C., 1957; MD, Bowman Gray Sch. Medicine, Winston-Salem, 1960; SM, MIT, 1974; AM, Harvard U., 1990. Intern Phila. Gen. Hosp., 1960, resident in radiology, 1961; resident in radiology, then fellow Am. Cancer Soc., Stanford U. Hosp., 1963-66; radiologist Peter Bent Brigham Hosp., Boston, 1967-79, Brigham and Women's Hosp., Boston, 1981—; instr. Stanford U. Med. Sch., 1966-67; mem. faculty Harvard U. Med. Sch., 1967-79, 81—, assoc. prof. radiology, 1976-82, prof. radiology, 1982—; prof. radiology, chmn. dept. U. Mich. Med. Sch., 1979-81. Mem. editl. bd. profl. jours. Capt. M.C., USAF, 1961-63. Sloan fellow MIT, 1974; James Picker Found. scholar, 1967-70. Mem. Am. Coll. Radiology, Assn. Univ. Radiologists, Radiol. Soc. N.Am., Alpha Omega Alpha. Home: 9 Riverview Ter Dover MA 02030-2249 Office: 75 Francis St Boston MA 02115-6110

ADAMS, EARL WILLIAM, JR., economics educator; b. Lansing, Mich., Nov. 13, 1937; s. Earl William and V. Crystal (Woodruff) A.; m. Barbara Joan Charlton, Aug. 4, 1964; children: Earl William, III, Nicholas Charlton. B.A., U. Mich., 1959; Ph.D., Mass. Inst. Tech., 1971. Asst. prof. econs. Amherst Coll., 1963-66, U. Pitts., 1966-72; Andrew Wells Robertson prof. econs. Allegheny Coll., Meadville, Pa., 1972—; vis. asst. prof. U. Mass., 1966; rsch. dir. bus. taxation Pa. Tax Commn., 1979-81; mem. adv. coun. Pa. Blue Shield, 1980-82, mem. corp., 1982. Contbr. to profl. publs. Woodrow Wilson fellow, 1959. Mem. Am. Econs. Assn., Pa. Econs. Assn., Phi Beta

Kappa, Phi Kappa Phi. Home: 187 Grandview Ave Meadville PA 16335-1415 Office: Allegheny Coll Dept Econs Meadville PA 16335

ADAMS, EDDIE, company executive; b. 1958. With Greater Atlanta Printing, 1979-85; pres. Adams Land Co., Leachville, Ark., 1985—. Office: Adams Land Co N Main St Leachville AR 72438*

ADAMS, EDMUND JOHN, lawyer; b. Lansing, Mich., June 6, 1938; s. John Edmund and Helen Kathryn (Pavlick) A.; m. Mary Louise Riegler, Aug. 11, 1962. BA, Xavier U., 1960; LLB, U. Notre Dame, 1963. Bar: Ohio 1963. Assoc. Paxton & Seasongood, Cin., 1965-70; assoc. Frost & Jacobs, 1970-71, exec. com., 1985-88, 1990-96, ptnr., 1971-94, mng. ptnr., 1994-96, chmn., 1996—. Author: Catholic Trails West, The Founding Catholic Families of Pennsylvania, Vol. 1, 1988, Vol. 2, 1989. Trustee Jewish Hosp., 1995—; Southwest Ohio Regional Transit Authority, 1980-91, pres. 1983, 88; trustee Sister Cities Assn. of Greater Cin., 1984-91, chmn., 1984-90; trustee Cin. Internat. Visitors Ctr., 1989-91, Japan Am. Soc. Greater Cin., 1988-96, Ursuline Acad., 1992-94; trustee Greater Cin. Ctr. for Econ. Edn., 1996—, mem. exec. com., 1999—; chmn. USTA Nat. Father amd Son Clay Ct. Tennis Championships, 1990-92, Hamilton County Rep. Exec. Com., mem., 1982—, Hamilton County Rep. Fin. Com., 1990—, chmn. 1992-94. 1st lt. U.S. Army, 1963-65. Mem. ABA, Ohio Bar Assn., Cin. Bar Assn., Cin. Tennis Club (trustee 1990-98, treas. 1992-93, sec. 1994-95, pres. 1996-98), Queen City Club, Met. Club (dir. 1996—). Roman Catholic. Home: 3210 Columbia Pky Cincinnati OH 45226-1042 Office: Frost & Jacobs 2500 PNC 201 E 5th St Ste 2500 Cincinnati OH 45202-4182

ADAMS, EDWARD A., legal journalist; b. South Bend, Ind., Sept. 28, 1963; s. Richard E. and Louise M. (Augustine) A.; m. Eliza A. Dolin, Dec. 31, 1988. PhB, Miami U., Oxford, Ohio, 1985; JD, Columbia U., 1988. Metro intern Cin. Enquirer, summer 1983; reporter intern Am. Lawyer, N.Y.C., winter 1984; rschr. intern Cable News Network, Washington, summer 1984; features intern Cleve. Plain Dealer, summer 1985; reporter intern Nat. Law Jour., N.Y.C., summers 1986-87; bus. intern U.S. News & World Report, Washington, summer 1988; TV reporter N.Y. Post, N.Y.C., 1988; law firm reporter N.Y. Law Jour., N.Y.C., 1989-97, on line editor, 1997—. Co-editor book: Inside the Law Schools, 1991. Mem. Investigative Reporters and Editors. Office: NY Law Jour 345 Park Ave S New York NY 10010-1707

ADAMS, EDWARD THOMAS (EDDIE ADAMS), photographer; b. New Kensington, Pa., June 12, 1933; s. Edward I. and Adelaide (Suprano) A.; children: Susan Ann, Edward II, Amy Marie; m. Alyssa Ann Adkins; 1 child, August Everhett. Grad. H.S., New Kensington. Staff photographer New Kensington Daily Dispatch, 1950-58, Battle Creek, Mich.; Enquirer & News, 1958, Phila. Eve. Bull., 1958-62, A.P., 1962-72, Time mag., 1972-76; spl. corr. A.P., 1976-80; free-lance photographer, 1980—; prof. emeritus Daytona Beach (Fla.) C.C., 1984; lectr. in field; creator ann. photojournalism workshop for America's most talented young photographers The Eddie Adams Workshop, sponsored by Eastman Kodak and Nikon, Inc., 1988—. Served with USMC, 1951-54. Recipient Pulitzer prize in photography, 1969; Grand prize World Press Photography, 1969, 1st pl. award, 1972; named 3d place World Photo Reporter, 1969; 2nd place World Photo Reporter, 1970; recipient Sigma Delta Chi award, 1969, 78, 80, several Overseas Press Club Am. awards, 1969, 74, George Polk Meml. award, 1969, 78, 79, Nat. Press Photographer award, 1969; 1st place AP Mng. Editors, 1968, 79; Best Pictures in Book or Mag. award Overseas Press Club, 1975; named Photographer of Year N.Y. Press Photographers, 1966, 67, 70, 72; Mid. Atlantic States, 1958, 59; Phila. Art Dirs. award, 1961; Nat. Headliners award, 1973; World Press Photo award, (7 times) 1974-85; Mag. Photographer of Yr. U. Mo.-Nat. Press Photographers Assn., 1975; Joseph Sprague Meml. award Nat. Press Photographers Assn., 1976; Silver Prix award Japan Advt. Assn., 1978; Robert Capa Meml. award, 1978; Am. Soc. Mag. Photographers Ann. award, 1980; W. Ger. Photokina award, 1978; 1st Pl. Hollywood Reporters Key Art English Lang. Movie Poster "Unforgiven" award, 1993; others; named Profl. Photographer of Yr., Photog. Mfrs. and Dealers Assn., 1996. Office: 538 E 11th St New York NY 10009 *I always hope that everytime I squeeze the shutter on my camera and once the photographs are published—that something good will happen to the subjects portrayed—or their cause.*

ADAMS, EDWIN MELVILLE, former foreign service officer, actor, author, lecturer; b. Gridley, Ill., Sept. 28, 1914; s. Edwin Melville and Crystal (Montgomery) A. A.B., U. Ill., 1936, LL.B., 1939; postgrad., The Hague Acad. Internat. Law, summer 1951. Bar: Ill. 1939. Atty. State Farm Ins. Cos., Bloomington, Ill., 1939-42; officer charge Brazil area World Trade intelligence div., State Dept., Washington, 1942-43; negotiator German external assets agreements with neutral countries World Trade intelligence div., State Dept., 1946-48; successively assigned by State Dept. to, London, Paris, Bern and Frankfort; as U.S. negotiator at internat. econ. confs., 1948-50; econ. attache Am. embassy, The Hague, 1950-52; charge Italian econ. affairs State Dept., 1952-55; dep. chief mut. def. affairs, 2d sec. Am. embassy, Rome, Italy, 1955-58; chief mut. def. affairs, 1st sec. Am. embassy, 1958-61; officer in charge econ. affairs for N. Africa Dept. State, 1961-64, career mgmt. officer, 1964-65; spl. asst. to dep. under sec. state, 1965-67; asso. dean Fgn. Service Inst., 1967-68; cons. Dept. State, 1968-72. Host: radio show Passport, WAMU, 1972—; author-narrator radio show, NBC-TV show, Venice, My Love, 1972; pub. broadcasting The Social Responsibility of Business; radio shows My Beloved Italy; star radio shows, CBS-TV show, The Empty Frame, 1973; appeared in films The Last Detail, 1974, Airport, 1975, Three Days of the Condor, 1975, Franklin and Eleanor, The Other Side of Midnight, Company, The Seduction of Joe Tynan, Justice for All, First Monday in October, BBC's Double Image. U.S. del. Conf. of African States on Devel. of Edn. in Africa, 1961. Served to lt. (j.g.) USNR, 1943-46, PTO. Decorated cavaliere ufficiale Order of Merit of Italian Republic. Mem. Screen Actors Guild, AFTRA, Actors Equity, Phi Delta Phi, Phi Kappa Sigma. Espicopalian. Lodge: Masons (Washington).

ADAMS, ELAINE, art agent, publicist, writer; b. L.A., Sept. 15, 1960; d. Mikhael Nikitovich Periev-Shelby and Emma (Davidian) Shelby; m. Peter Seitz Adams, Mar. 12, 1990. BA in Econs. and Math., U. So. Calif., 1982. Stock broker Crowell, Weedon & Co., L.A., 1983-89; art agt., artist rep. Peter Adams Studio, Pasadena, Calif., 1990—; publicity chmn. Calif. Art Club, Pasadena, 1993. Editor Calif. Art Club newsletter, 1994—; art reviewer Art-Talk. Assoc. trustee Pacific Asia Mus., Pasadena, 1993, chmn. Festival of Autumn Moon, 1994; bd. dirs. Pasadena Symphony, 1994; cofounder, sec. exec. bd. Calif. Art Acad. and Mus., Pasadena, 1997. Mem. Am. Art Coun. (steering com.). Republican. Russian Orthodox. Avocations: art and antique collecting, gourmet cooking. Office: Calif Art Club PO Box 92555 Pasadena CA 91109-2555

ADAMS, ELAINE PARKER, college administrator. BA in Spanish Edn., Xavier U., 1961; MS in Libr. Sci., La. State U., 1966; PhD in Libr. Sci., U. So. Calif., 1973. Cert. learning resources specialist. Dist. catalog libr. Grossmont Union High Sch. Dist., La Mesa, Calif., 1971; mid. sch. libr. Upper St. Clair (Pa.) Sch. Dist., 1972-73; vis. asst. prof. U. Md., College Park, 1973; media specialist U. So. Calif., L.A., 1974-75; coord. Learning Resources Ctr. Tex. So. U., Houston, 1976-80; supr. libr. svcs. and tech. tng. Getty Oil Rsch. Ctr., Houston, 1980-83; assoc. v.p. acad. svcs. and planning Prairie View (Tex.) A&M U., 1983-85, v.p. student affairs, 1985-89; asst. commr. Edn. Opportunity Planning Tex. Higher Edn. Coordinating Bd., Austin, 1989-91; pres. N.E. Coll. Houston C.C. System, 1991-96; interim pres. Central Coll., Houston, 1997; vice chancellor ednl. devel. Houston C.C. Sys., 1997-98; lectr. Sch. Profl. Edn. U. Houston-Clear Lake, summers 1977-79; planner Honors Coll. Prairie View A&M U., 1983-84, user coord. bldg. cons. libr., 1984-88; cons. Libr./Pharmacy Addition Xavier U., New Orleans, 1989; evaluator Mid States Assn. Commn. on Higher Edn., Phila., 1988—, So. Assn. Colls. and Schs., 1991—. Co-editor: Media and the Young Adult, 1981; contbr. articles to profl. jours. Trustee Xavier U., 1990-95, Lon Morris Coll., 1993-94, bd. mem. Tex. Trailblazers, Preservation, 1993—, Fifth Ward Enrichment Prog., mem. ACE Commn. on Leadersip Devel., 1994-96; bd. dirs. Friends, 1998—, Houston Pub. Lib., 1998—. Recipient Bonita St. House of Hope award, 1997, Silver Scholar award TAPHE, 1998; fellow U. So.. Calif., 1968-71; scholar Xavier U., 1957-61, AT&T scholar Harvard U. Inst. for Edn. Mgmt. Mem. ALA, Am. Assn. C.C.s, Am. Assn. Women in C.C.s, Nat. Assn. Student Pers. Adminstrs. (editl. bd. 1988-90), Am. Assn. for Higher Edn. (Black Caucus exec. bd. 1990-96), Nat. Assn. Women in Edn. (mem. editl. bd. Initiatives 1999—), Nat. Coalition of 100 Black Women (bd. dirs. Houston chpt., Makeda award 1993), Xavier Univ. Alumni Assn. (nat. pres. 1990-91, Alumna of Yr.). Office: Houston C C Sys PO Box 7849 Houston TX 77270-7849

ADAMS, ELINOR RUTH, retired laboratory technician; b. Irby, Wash., May 26, 1921; m. Curtis Edward Adams, Sept. 14, 1940 (dec. Oct. 1987); children: Curtis Joseph, Anna May, Neal Edward, Janice Helen. Grad. h.s., Spokane, Wash. Apprentice lab. technician Hollister-Stier Labs., Spokane, 1962-63, mgr. animal rm., 1962-73, raised animals, 1972-79. Author: Santa and the Testy Troll, 1998; contbr. poetry to anthologies. Active People Pet Program, Coeur d'Alene, Idaho, 1989—; vol. Kootenai Med. Ctr., Coeur d'Alene, 1990—. Recipient Golden Poet award World of Poetry, 1987-92, other awards; named to Nat. Poetry Hall of Fame, 1998. Mem. Phi Sigma Alpha (program chmn., Woman of Yr. 1987). Republican. Roman Catholic. Avocations: reading, writing, fishing, camping, music. Home: 2115 N 8th St Coeur D Alene ID 83814-4705

ADAMS, ELIZABETH HERRINGTON, banker; b. Tulsa, May 25, 1947; d. James Dillon and Helen (Allderdice) Herrington; m. Phillip Hollis Hackney, Mar. 5, 1977 (dec. Jan. 1990); m. Keith R. Adams, Sept. 4, 1993. Student, No. Ariz. U., 1965-67, 68-69. With Coldwater (Kans.) Nat. Bank, summers 1964-67; with The Ariz. Bank, Phoenix, 1969, Flagstaff, 1970-71; asst. cashier The Wilmore (Kans.) State Bank, 1972—; asst. cashier The Coldwater Nat. Bank, 1974-83, cashier, ops. officer, 1984—; v.p. The Coldwater (Kans.) Nat. Bank, 1998—; dir. The Coldwater Nat. Bank, 1972—, The Wilmore State Bank, 1970—. Bd. dirs. Pioneer Lodge Nursing Home, Coldwater, 1984-89; mem. sch. site coun., 1993-94; life mem. Girl Scouts, chmn. Neighborhood Cookie Drive, 1991-95; bd. dirs., mem. strategic planning com. Wheatbelt Area Girl Scout Coun., 1994-96—; elder 1st Presbyn. Ch., Coldwater; Kans. Lung Assn. Vol. Speakers Bur., 1998—. Mem. Fin. Women Internat., Community Bankers Assn. Kans. (membership com. 1991-94, INPAC com. 1992-93), Kans. Ind. Bankers (gen. svcs. com. 1986-87), PEO, Alpha Omicron Pi, Church Session Bd., Coldwater, KS, 1994—, Comm. Hlth. Assessment Prog., Comanche County, KS 1996—. Republican. Avocation: music (pianist). Office: Coldwater Nat Bank PO Box 726 Coldwater KS 67029-0726

ADAMS, F. GERARD, economist, educator; b. Apr. 28, 1929; s. Walter and Margot Adams; m. Heidi Vernon; children: Leslie, Colin, Loren, Mark. B.A., U. Mich., 1949, M.A., 1951, Ph.D., 1956. Instr. dept. econs. U. Mich., Ann Arbor, 1952-56; economist Calif. Tex. Oil Corp., N.Y.C., 1956-59; cons. economist, mgr. gen. econs. dept. Compagnie Française des Pétroles, N.Y.C. and Paris, 1959-61; mem. faculty U. Pa., Phila., 1961-98, prof. econs. and fin.; McDonald prof. Northeastern U., Boston, 1998—; dir. Econs. Research Unit, 1961-98, chmn. Faculty Senate, 1987-88; chmn. profl. bd. WEFA Group, Phila., 1969-91. Author: (with others) An Econometric Analysis of International Trade, 1969, (with J.R. Behrman) Econometric Models of World Agricultural Commodity Markets, 1976, Commodity Exports and Economic Development, 1982, (with L.R. Klein) Industrial Policies for Growth and Competitiveness, 1983, The Business Forecasting Revolution, 1986; editor: (with S.A. Klein) Stabilizing World Commodity Markets - Analysis, Practice and Policy, 1978, The Macroeconomic Dimensions of Arm Reduction, 1992, Economic Activity, Trade and Industry in the U.S.-Japan-World Economy, 1993, East Asian Development: Will the Miracle Survive?, 1998; Public Policies in East Asian Development: Facing New Challenges, 1999. Home: 39 Stafford Rd Newton Center MA 02459-1818

ADAMS, FAYE ANN, musician, educator; b. Allentown, Pa., Mar. 24, 1952; d. Lester H. and Anna M. (Arndt) Meck; m. Ronald G. Adams, Oct. 19, 1974; children: David (dec.), Megan, Mandy. BS in Music Edn., Mansfield State U., 1974; MEd in Elem. Edn., Kutztown U., 1983. Cert. music specialist, Pa. Owner, instr. Willing Hearts, Hands and Voices Music Studio, Lenhartsville, Pa., 1968—; music specialist classrm., vocal and instrumental music City Sch. Dist. of Reading, Pa., 1974-78; soloist German dialect svcs., profl. soprano, pianist; spkr. on Berks county history, historic churches and cemeteries, church life, education, Indian life, genealogy, other topics. Author: Events at Allemangel, 1995. Sec. Jerusalem (Red) Ch. (The Allemangel Ch.), 1994—; sec., Sunday sch. tchr., rschr. Frieden's Luth. Ch. (The New Allemangel Ch.), 1991-94. Home and Office: 42 George Rd Lenhartsville PA 19534-9696

ADAMS, FRANK, education specialist; b. Cleve., Sept. 11, 1948; s. Frank Albin and Helen (Coleman) Kovacevic. BS in Bus. Adminstrn., Bowling Green (Ohio) State U., 1970, MEd in Phys. Edn., 1978. Tech. writer Soldier Phys. Fitness Sch., Ft. Ben Harrison, Ind., 1983-85; edn. specialist Directorate of Tng. and Doctrine, Ft. Huachuca, Ariz., 1985-90, Dept. Tactics Intelligence Mil. Sci., Ft. Huachuca, 1990-93, 111th Mil. Intelligence Brigade, Ft. Huachuca, 1993-97; staff Directorate Continuous Learning U.S. Army Intelligence Ctr., 1998—; mem. steering com. tng. and doctrine command, staff and faculty devel. divsn., El Paso, Tex., 1987. Co-author: (field manual) Physical Fitness Training, 1984, (Internet site) Total Fitness; contbr. articles to profl. jours. and local newspapers. Recipient Civilian Achievement medal Dept. Army, Ft. Huachuca 1993, Comdr.'s award, 1995, Superior Civilian Svc. award, 1999. Mem. AAHPERD (life), Mil. Intelligence Corp., Self-Realization Fellowship. Avocations: internal martial arts, reading, Reiki master-teacher. Home: 4838 Corte Vista Sierra Vista AZ 85635-5738 Office: Directorate of Continuous Learning Advanced Individual Skills Divsn Fort Huachuca AZ 85613-6000

ADAMS, G. ROLLIE, museum executive; b. El Dorado, Ark., Sept. 11, 1941; s. George Donaghey and Floy (Kinard) A.; m. Diana Murphy, Dec. 19, 1982; children: Sara Ann, Amy Kristina Hee Sook. BA in Social Sci. Edn., La. Tech. U., 1963, MA in Social Sci. Edn., 1967; PhD in Am. History, U. Ariz., 1983. Tchr. El Dorado Sr. High Sch., 1963-67; libr. U. Ariz. Libr., Tucson, 1968-71; instr. U. Ariz. Continuing Edn. Dept., Tucson, 1973; dir. nat. hist. landmarks Am. Assn. State & Local Hist., Nashville, 1973-78, dir. edn. divsn., 1978-82, dir. planning & devel., 1982-83; exec. dir. Buffalo & Erie County Hist. Soc., 1984-85; dir. La. State Mus., New Orleans, 1986-87; pres., chief exec. officer The Strong Mus., Rochester, N.Y., 1987—; mem. faculty Colonial Williamsburg Hist. Adminstrn. Seminar, 1987-88, 90-96; mem. parks adv. com. Rockefeller Inst. Govt., Albany, 1992-93; chair exec. com. N.Y. Hist. Records Adv. Bd., Albany, 1992-95, mem. 1992-98; chair N.Y. State Commr. Edn. Mus. Task Force, Albany, 1994-95. Coauthor: Nashville: A Pictorial History, 1981, rev. edit. 1988; co-editor: Ordinary People and Everyday Life, 1983, The American Indian, Past and Present, 1971. Mem. Steering com. Goals for a Greater Rochester, 1990-95; vice chair bd. dirs. Greater Rochester Vis. Assn., 1991-97; chair, bd. dirs. Family Svcs., Rochester, 1993-96; bd. dirs. Rochester Downtown Devel. Corp., 1995—, East End Alliance, 1997—. Funded seminars grantee U.S. Hist. NEH, 1980, hist. interpretation, NEH, 1979, 80, 81, Mus. Exhibit Workshops NEH, 1980-82, Local Govt. Records Com. NEH, 1981-83. Mem. Mus. Assn. N.Y. (v.p. 1995-96, chair strategic planning com. 1996-97, pres. 1997), Am. Assn. Mus. (mem. vis. team, accreditation commn., Washington 1988, 90, 92-97; bd. dirs. 1997—), Am. Assn. State and Local History (audit com. 1995—), Orgn. Am. Historians, Assn. Youth Mus., Western Hist. Assn. Avocations: photography, baseball. Office: The Strong Museum One Manhattan Square Rochester NY 14607*

ADAMS, GARY LEE, systems engineer; b. Clearfield, Pa., May 23, 1947; s. William Ellsworth and Ethel Mae (Ling) A.; m. Rebecca Estelle Peppers, Dec. 29, 1967; children: William Matthew, Preston Lee. BSEE, Tulane U., 1969; Grad. of Theology, Bapt. Bible Coll., 1974. Assoc. engr. Westinghouse Electric Corp., Balt., 1969-71; asst. prin., dean edn. Hollywood (Fla.) Christian Sch., 1974-79; assoc. engr. Martin Marietta Corp., Orlando, Fla., 1979-80, engr., 1980-82, sr. engr., 1982-84, group engr., 1984-85; sr. lead engr. Harris Corp., Orlando, Fla., 1985, engring. sect. head, 1985-89; engring. br. mgr. PEI Electronics, Inc., Huntsville, Ala., 1989-98, lead systems engr., 1998—; vice chmn. Nat. Indsl. Assn. MATE Users Group Test Program Set Com., Washington, 1986-88. Deaf interpreter First Bapt. Ch., Hollywood, 1974-79, Tabernacle Bapt. Ch., Orlando, 1979-89, Triana Village Bapt. Ch., Huntsville, 1989-93; deacon Granite Bapt. Ch., Glen Burnie, Md., 1970-71, Friendship Bapt. Ch., Huntsville, 1995—. Recipient Jung scholarship Tulane U., 1965-68. Mem. IEEE, Assn. U.S. Army. Republican. Baptist. Avocations: coin collecting, camping, roller skating, home computing. Home: 13436 Wendy Dr Madison AL 35757-6530

ADAMS, GEORGE BELL, lawyer; b. N.Y.C., Sept. 16, 1930; s. George Bell and Mary Josephine (Smith) A.; m. Lucy Elizabeth Ahearn, Sept. 10, 1952; children—Lucy S., Marea F., George B. Jr., Alison E. BA, Yale U., 1952; LLB cum laude, Harvard U., 1957. Bar: N.Y. 1957, U.S. Dist. Ct. (so. and ea. dists.) N.Y. 1965, U.S. Ct. Appeals (2d cir.) 1973. Assoc. Debevoise, Plimpton, Lyons & Gates, N.Y.C., 1957-65; ptnr. Debevoise & Plimpton, N.Y.C., 1966-97, chmn. corp. dept., 1988-93, of counsel, 1998—; mng. ptnr. Debevoise & Plimpton, London, 1993-96; pres. Greater N.Y. Fund, N.Y.C., 1981-84, also bd. dirs. Trustee Sarah Lawrence Coll., Bronxville, N.Y., 1977—, chmn. bd. trustees, 1987-91, vice chmn., chmn. exec. com., 1981-87; bd. dirs. United Way of N.Y.C., 1982-95; dir. Lawyers Alliance for World Security, 1989-98; fellow Pierpont Morgan Libr., N.Y.C., 1977—, coun. of fellows, 1983-87; mem. Yale U. Coun., 1983-90, chmn. Yale alumni publs., 1979-83; trustee Am. Trust for the Brit. Libr., 1998—; bd. dirs. New Amsterdam Singers, 1997—. 1st lt. U.S. Army, 1952-54. Fellow Davenport Coll., Yale U., 1983-90. Fellow Am. Bar Found.; mem. ABA, Assn. of Bar of City of N.Y., Internat. Bar Assn., Am. Arbitration Assn. (mem. panel arbitrators), Pilgrim Soc., Am. Assn. Internat. Com. on Jurists (dir. 1996—), Law Soc. (Eng. affiliate mem.), Cosmos Club, Racquet & Tennis Club. Office: Debevoise & Plimpton 875 3rd Ave Fl 23 New York NY 10022-6256

ADAMS, GORDON MERRITT, federal agency administrator; b. Chico, Calif., Oct. 1, 1941; s. Harlen M. and Lois C. Adams; m. Glenda E. Adams; 1 child, Caitlin; m. Phyllis Jane Goodnow, Aug. 25, 1987; children: David, Timothy. BA, Stanford U., 1963; Cert. and Diploma, Coll. Europe, Bruges, Belgium, 1964; MA, PhD, Columbia U., 1970. Asst. prof. polit. sci. Columbia U., N.Y.C., 1970-72; mem. sr. profl. staff Social Sci. Rsch. Coun., N.Y.C., 1972-74; internat. affairs fellow Coun. Fgn. Rels., N.Y.C., 1974-75; dir. mil. rsch. Coun. Econ. Priorities, N.Y.C., 1976-78, sr. rsch. assoc., 1980-83; asst. prof. polit. sci. Rutgers U., Newark, N.J., 1978-80; dir. Def. Budget Project, Washington, 1983-93; assoc. dir. nat. security and internat. affairs Office Mgmt. and Budget, Washington, 1993-97; dep. dir. Internat. Inst. Strategic Studies, London, 1998—. Author: The Iron Triangle: The Politics of Defense Contracting, 1982; co-author: Defense Spending and the American Economy, 1990. Mem. Coun. Fgn. Rels., Social Sci. Rsch. Coun. (mem. com. internat. peace and security). Avocations: running, singing, theater. Office: Internat Inst Strategic Studies, 23 Tavistock St, London WC2E 7NQ, UK*

ADAMS, HARLENE, speech communications educator; b. Chico, Calif., Oct. 18, 1939; d. Harlen Martin and Lois Vivian (Carman) A.; m. George Byron Beattie, Dec. 22, 1961 (div. June 1987); children: Dresden Elizabeth Beattie, Denver Michelle Beattie, Ryan Amery Beattie. BA, Stanford U., 1960; MA, San Francisco State U., 1965; postgrad., McGeorge Sch. Law, 1972. Legis. asst. Calif. State Senate, Sacramento, 1961-63; asst. dir. internat. programs Calif. State U., San Francisco, Calif., 1963-68; instr. Calif. State U., Sacramento, 1982—, Yuba Coll., Marysville, Calif., 1988-89, Sierra Coll., Rocklin, Calif., 1989-99; instr. European divsn. U. Md., Germany, Iceland, England, 1994-95; instr. Cosumnes River Coll. El Dorado Ctr., Placerville, 1992—, Sacramento City Coll., 1981-99, Am. River Coll., Sacramento, 1981-99, Folsom Lake Ctr., 1999—; keynote spkr. Calif. Employment Devel. Dept., Sacramento, 1991; workshop dir., presenter Calif. Jour. Inst. for Pub. Policy Rev., Sacramento, 1991. Pres., v.p., clk. San Juan Unified Sch. Dist. Bd. Edn., Sacramento, 1975-79; mem. scholarship com. AAUW, Sacramento, 1970-72; mem. program planning com., actor Sacramento Civic Theater and Eleanor McClatchy Performing Arts Ctr., 1975—. Recipient Outstanding Professor award Delta Gamma Sorority, 1992. Avocations: writing, travel, photography, reading, piano.

ADAMS, HAROLD LYNN, architect; b. Palmer, Tex., May 15, 1939; s. Charles Roy and Lola (Beck) A.; m. Janice Lindhurst, Aug. 29, 1963; children: Harold Lynn, Abigail, Ashley, Sam. B.S. in Architecture, Tex. A&M U., 1962. Registered architect 44 states and U.K.; 1st class registered architect Japan. Draftsman Pratt Box Henderson, Dallas, 1960; intern William B. Tabler & Assocs., N.Y.C., 1961-62; architect John Carl Warnecke & Assocs., Washington, 1962-66; pres. RTKL Assocs., Inc., Balt., 1967-87, chmn. bd., 1987—; regent Am. Archtl. Found., 1989—; cons. Nat. Caital Planning Commn., 1992. Contbg. author: Current Techniques in Architectural Practice, Representative Am. Speeches, 1987-88, Technology: Trap or Triumph. Chmn. archtl. divsn. United Fund Drive, 1972; mem. task force on econ. devl. Balt. C. of C., 1975; pres. Econ. Devel. Coun. of Balt.; exec. com. Mt. Washington Country Sch. for Boys, 1976-77; bd. mgrs. Black Rock YMCA, 1971; vice chmn. GBC Found.; mem. Greater Balt. Com. on Edn., 1977-80, Com. on Planning, 1980-82; bd. dirs. Greater Balt. Com., 1983-90; mem. devel. coun. Tex. A&M U., 1982-90; mem. vis. com. Dept. Architecture U. Md., 1985-87; trustee Md. Inst. Coll. Art, Balt., 1984—, Maryvale Prep. Sch., Brooklandville, Md., 1985-89, Peale Mus., Balt., 1985-92, Balt. City Life Mus., 1985-92; regent Morgan State U., Balt., 1985-87, Am. Architecture Found., 1989—; trustee Balt. Fgn. Rels. Coun., 1987-93, Walter Gallery Art, 1987—; Balt. Metro. YMCA, 1987-90; chmn. World Trade Ctr. Inst., Md., 1990—; mem. svcs. policy adv. com. U.S. Trade Rep., 1990—; bd. dirs. Internat. Visitors Ctr., 1990-92; mem. U.S.-China Bus. Coun., U.S.-Korea Bus. Coun.; adv. bd. Korea Econ. Inst. of Am.; vice chair Nat. Bldg. Mus.; chmn. Downtown Partnership Balt.; commr. Md. Econ. Devel. Comm.; chmn. bd. trustees Nat. Bldg. Mus., 1996—. Recipient Featherlite Design award Tex. A&M U., 1962; recipient Davidson Design award Tex. A&M U., 1962, Alpha Rho Chi medal, 1962, Tau Sigma Delta Gold medal Assn. Collegiate Schs. Architecture, 1993, Gov.'s award World Trade Ctr. Md., 1996, Outstanding Alumni award Tex. A&M U., 1998. 03340785IA (pres. Balt. chpt. 1973-74, chmn. large firm roundtable 1984—, chancellor Coll. of Fellows 1997-98, Kemper medal 1997); mem. Urban Land Inst., Am. Inst. Architects (chmn. large firm roundtable 1984—), Soc. Am. Mil. Engrs. (Urban medal 1997), Bursar Coll. of Fellows (vice chancellor), Royal Inst. Brit. Architects, Japan Inst. Architects, Crescent Club (Dallas), Center Club (Balt.), Met. Club (Washington), Cosmos Club, Caves Valley Golf Club (Balt.), The Athenaeum (London). Democrat. Baptist. Home: 1601 The Terraces Baltimore MD 21209-3636

ADAMS, HAZARD SIMEON, English educator, author; b. Cleve., Feb. 15, 1926; s. Robert Simeon and Mary (Thurness) A.; m. Diana White, Sept. 17, 1949; children: Charles Simeon, Perry White. A.B., Princeton, 1948; M.A., U. Wash., 1949, Ph.D., 1953. Instr. English Cornell U., 1952-56; asst. prof. U. Tex., 1956-59; vis. assoc. prof. Washington U., St. Louis, 1959; from assoc. prof. to prof. Mich. State U., 1959-64; Fulbright lectr. U. Dublin, 1962-63; prof. U. Calif.-Irvine, 1964-77, founding chmn. English dept., 1964-69; dean Sch. Humanities, 1970-72, vice chancellor acad. affairs, 1972-74; co-dir. Sch. Criticism and Theory, 1975-77; sr. fellow, 1975-88, hon. sr. fellow, 1988—; prof. comparative lit. U. Wash., Seattle, 1977—, Byron W. and Alice L. Lockwood prof. humanities, 1988—; prof. English U. Calif., Irvine, 1990-94. Author: Poems by Robert Simeon Adams, 1952, Blake and Yeats: The Contrary Vision, 1955, 2d edit., 1969, The Contexts of Poetry, 1963, William Blake: A Reading of the Shorter Poems, 1963, Poetry: An Introductory Anthology, 1968, The Horses of Instruction, 1968, Fiction as Process, 1968, The Interests of Criticism, 1969, William Blake: Jerusalem, Selected Poems and Prose, 1970, The Truth About Dragons, 1971, Critical Theory Since Plato, 1971, rev. edit., 1992, Lady Gregory, 1973, The Academic Tribes, 1976, 2d edit., 1988, Philosophy of the Literary Symbolic, 1983, Joyce Cary's Trilogies, 1983, Critical Theory Since 1965, 1986, The Book of Yeats's Poems, 1991, Antithetical Essays, 1991, Critical Essays on William Blake, 1991, The Book of Yeats's Vision, 1995,The Farm at Richwood and Other Poems, 1997, Many Pretty Toys, 1999; mem. editl. bd. Epoch, 1954-56, Tex. Studies Lit. and Lang., 1957-68, Studies in Romanticism, 1966—, Blake Studies, 1969-80, Modern Lang. Quar., 1977-84. Served to 1st lt. USMCR, 1943-45, 51. Guggenheim fellow, 1974-75. Mem. Internat. Assn. Univ. Profs. English, Am. Conf. for Irish Studies, Phi Beta Kappa. Home: 3930 NE 157th Pl Seattle WA 98155-6730 Office: U Wash PO Box 354338 Seattle WA 98195-4338

ADAMS, HENRY LEE, JR., federal judge; b. 1945. BS in Polit. Sci., Fla. A&M U., 1966; JD, Howard U., 1969. Staff atty. Duval County Legal Aid Assn., 1969-70; asst. pub. defender, pub. defender's office 4th Jud. Cir., 1970-72; with Sheppard, Fletcher, Hand & Adams, Jacksonville, 1972-76, Marshall & Adams, Jacksonville, 1976-79; judge 4th Jud. Cir., 1979-93, U.S.

Dist. Ct. (mid. dist.) Fla., 1993—. Active Tots N' Teens; mem. adv. bd. Fla. Augustus Secure Care Unit; mem. Habijax Adv. Bd.; mem. local sch. adv. coun. Mid. W. Gilbert Mid. Sch. Mem. NAACP, Nat. Bar Assn., Fla. Bar Assn., Fla. Conf. Circuit Judges (mem. legis. com.), Jacksonville Bar Assn., D.W. Perkins Bar Assn., Kappa Alpha Psi. Office: US Dist Ct Gibbons US Courthouse 801 N Florida Ave Tampa FL 33602-4509*

ADAMS, HERBERT RYAN, management consultant, retired clergyman, actor, director, educator, publishing executive; b. Phila., Apr. 19, 1932; s. Leander Hampton and Helen Marguerite (Richards) A.; m. Carol Anne Levine, Aug. 27, 1956; children: Ashley Pozefsky, Joshua, Lee Hampton, Rachel Ellis; m. Mary Ryan, Aug. 20, 1977. AB, Colby Coll., 1954; EdD, Harvard U., 1972; student Harvard Div. Sch., 1955-56, Kent State U., 1957, Boston U., 1963. Ordained to ministry Congregationalist Ch., 1952, Unitarian Universalist Assn., 1968; minister Fairfield and Pine Point, Maine, 1950-56, Chelsea, Mass., 1962-66. Lexington, Mass., 1967-75, Winnetka, Ill., 1978-87, West Paris, Maine, 1988-94, South Paris and Norway, Maine, 1991-94, ret., 1994, Iterim, Ithaca, N.Y., 1997-1998, Santa Fe, NM 1998-99; editor Allyn and Bacon, Boston, 1959-62; sr. editor Ginn and Co., Boston, 1962-68; v.p. mktg. Visual Learning Corp., Cambridge, Mass., 1968-71; dir. Sci. Rsch. Assocs. div. IBM, Chgo., 1975-83; v.p. Laidlaw Bros., River Forest, Ill., 1983-84, pres., CEO, 1984-87; pres. Ryan-Adams Cons. Svcs., Center Lovell, Maine, 1994—. bd. dirs. Learning Design Assocs., Mystery Cafe, Mpls.; tchr. Greenville (Pa.) High Sch., 1956-58, Euclid (Ohio) High Sch., 1958-59, Lexington (Mass.) High Sch., 1968-69, Harvard Grad. Sch. Edn., 1971-72, Oxford Hills (Maine) High Sch., 1987-88; prin. Oxford Hills Jr. High Sch, 1988-91, life mem., Girard Coll., Alumni Assn. Recipient Coe Found. award DePauw U., 1958, Cert. of Merit VFW, 1989, Disting. Pres. award Norway-Paris Kiwanis, 1996. Mem. Oxford Hills Retired Tchrs. Assn., Oxford Hills Clergy Assn., Unitarian Universalist Ret. Mins. Assn., Lake Kezar Country Club, Lovell Land Trust, Lovell Historical Society, Jefferson Group. Author: Poetry on Film, 1970; Project Listening, 1975; Listening Your Way to Management Success, 1983; contbr. numerous articles to profl. jours. Home and Office: PO Box 302 Center Lovell ME 04016-0302 *My deeds must be my life. When I am dead, my actions must speak for me.*

ADAMS, HILARY SHIELS, theater director; b. Washington, Nov. 3, 1972; d. Lawrence Curtis and Barbara (Johnston) A. BA, Evergreen State Coll., 1995. Dir.: (theatrical prodns.) Women of Manhattan, 100 Variations of a Family Theme, 70 Scenes of Halloween, What Neighbors Are For, Stills, It's Called the Sugar Plum, Office Work, Showboats, Rain, Packing; asst. dir.: Aida (Disney Theatrical Prodns.), Titanic, The Fastest Clock in the Universe, Griller, Bedfellows; author, dir.: Whiskey Talking. Avocations: camping, hiking, poetry, writing.

ADAMS, HOOVER, newspaper founder; b. Dunn, N.C., Mar. 6, 1920; m. Mellicent Stalder; children: Brent, Maere Kay Adams Lashmight, Bart. Grad., Dunn H.S., 1937; D of Humanity (hon.), Campbell U. Reporter Charlotte Observer; reporter, editor, ptnr. Dunn Dispatch; owner, editor Daily Record, ret. Past pres. Dunn Area C. of C.; former chmn. Raleigh Fed. Svs. Bank; presdl. bd. advs. Campbell U.; bd. trustees Heritage Bible Coll., Dunn; former chmn. bd. Ea. Carolina Regional Housing Authority, Goldsboro; pres. Gen. William C. Lee Airborne Mus.; chmn. Dunn Alcoholic Beverage Control Bd.; press cons., campaign aide to former U.S. Sen. Robert Morgan; bd. dirs. Airborne Mus., Fayetteville. With U.S. Army, ETO. Named Man of the Yr. City of Dunn's, 1980. Mem. Rotary (former pres., Paul Harris fellow), Masons, Shriners, Am. Legion, VFW. Home: PO Box 1448 Dunn NC 28335-1448

ADAMS, J. PHILLIP, oil industry executive. CEO Flying J. Inc., Brigham City, Utah. Office: Flying J Inc PO Box 678 Brigham City UT 84302-0678*

ADAMS, JACK, film company executive, screenwriter, producer, educator; b. Lakehurst, N.J., Sept. 15, 1952; s. John Carey and Dorothy Jeanne (Conover) A.; m. Shirley Janulewicz, June 28, 1975; children: Carey Miller, Chanine Angelina, Mikael Walter, Jozef Conover. MusB in Music Edn., U. Del., 1974. Pres. Koala Studio, Valencia, Calif., 1977—; v.p. devel. Unifilms, Inc., North Hollywood, Calif., 1984—; instr. film, TV writing and script analysis Coll. of Canyons, Valencia, 1988—, L.A. City Coll., 1989—, EveryWoman's Village, Van Nuys, Calif., 1990—, Info. Exch., L.A., 1990—, Learning Tree U., Chatsworth, Calif., 1990—, U. Wis., Madison, 1991—, U. Hawaii, 1992—, USIA, Washington, 1991—, Info. Network, South Pasadena, Calif., 1990—, Moorpark Coll., 1991—, Oxnard Coll., 1991—, Northwestern U., Evanston, Ill., 1991—, Glendale (Calif.) Community Coll., 1991—; co-founder ScripTip, 1990, Classes Unlimited, 1992—, Johnson County Community Coll., Kansas City, 1993, Univ. Wis., Milwaukee, 1993, Irvine (Calif.) Valley Coll., 1992—, Shenandoah Valley Writer's Guild, Front Royal, Va., 1993—, Rancho Santiago Coll., Santa Ana, Calif., 1993—, Orange Coast Coll., Costa Mesa, Calif., 1993—; script cons. Wis. Screenwriters Forum; mem. KNX Speakers Bur., CBS Radio, 1989—, Story Bd. Devel. Group, Paramount Studios, 1989—; pres. NBC Writers Workshop; mem. Larry Wilson Devel. Workshop, Paramount Studios, Le Group, Paramount Studios; founding mem., officer, bd. dirs. L.A. Filmmakers Workshop, 1989-91; founder Santa Clarita Scriptwriters Workshop, Writers Anonymous, 1988; pres. Entertainment Writers' Workshop, 1990, Adams Entertainment, 1993; ptnr. Flying Cow, 1994; co-founder: Weasels in My Pants Prodns., 1996; mem. Ind. Feature Project West; presenter numerous seminars and workshops. Composer (film) Eat, 1980 (Filmex award 1981, best short film award Cinemagic mag. 1981); writer, co-creator sitcom pilot Lola, Universal Studios, 1991; writer, developer sitcom pilot Fat Farm; writer, producer, dir. sitcom pilot Box # 22; line producer sitcom pilots Zebra, It's Not My Fault; creator: Screenwriting Warriors: Basic Training, 1988; columnist: Creative Screenwriting Mag., 1994—; TV editor Freelance Screenwriters' Forum Newsletter; columnist ScreenWrite Now mag.; creator (audiotapes) Top 50 Script Marketing Tips, Get An Agent to Sell Your Script, Write To Get Past the Script Reader, Pitch Your Film and Television Projects. Mem. Indian Guides/Princesses Program, chief Apache tribe YMCA, 1990—, produced annual haunted house fundraiser for Santa Clarita Family YMCA, 1991-94, participate in annual fundraising campaign, 1990, Am. Youth Soccer Orgn. AYSO, 1988. Mem. Am. Film Inst. (alumni assn. writers workshop), Scriptwriters Network (bd. advisors), Film Artists Network, Ind. Writers So. Calif. Scriptwriters Caucus, Assn. Info. Systems Profls. (bd. dirs. 1983), Freelance Screenwriter's Forum (founding), Comedy Writers Co-op (founding ABC), Wis. Screenwriters Forum (advisor 1989—). Avocations: tennis, still photography, music. Home and Office: 22931 Sycamore Creek Dr Santa Clarita CA 91354-2050

ADAMS, JAMES ALFRED, natural science educator; b. Columbia, Miss., Dec. 17, 1949; s. Joseph Quincy and Bernice (Jackson) A.; 1 child, Jasmine Denise; m. Candy Marilyn Morrell, July 10, 1993. BS, Alcorn State U., 1970; MS, U. So. Miss., 1971; PhD, U. Pitts., 1975. Asst. prof. biology Tenn. State U., Nashville, 1975-80, assoc. prof. biology, 1981-86, prof. biology, 1986-94; chmn. dept. natural sci. U. Md.-Ea. Shore, Princess Anne, 1988-94; prof., chmn. biology dept. Fla. A&M U., Tallahassee, 1994—; mem. exec. com. grad. toxicology program U. Md., Balt., 1988—; mem. exec. com. Minority Inst. Marine Sci. Program, Jackson, Miss., 1989—; cons. State U. System of Fla., Tallahassee, 1992—. Contbr. articles to profl. jours. Mem. Men Inspiring Students to Enjoy Reading, Salisbury, Md., 1991—. Macy fellow Corp. Marine Biol. Lab., 1976, 77, 79, Westinghouse fellow, 1990; grantee NIH-Nat. Inst. Environ. Health Sci., 1991, NSF, 1992. Fellow Tenn. Acad. Scis.; mem. AAAS, N.Y. Acad. Scis., 100 Black Men of Md./Am. Democrat. Bapist. Achievements include discovery that Reagent grade Acetone can induce metamorphosis in Anuran Amphibian, that glutathione can induce budding in Hydra. Office: Fla A & M U Dept Biology Tallahassee FL 32308

ADAMS, JAMES BLACKBURN, former state government official, former federal government official, lawyer; b. Corsicana, Tex., Dec. 21, 1926; s. Lynn and Florence (Blackburn) A.; m. Ione Winistorfer, Sept. 3, 1955; children—James Blackburn, Elizabeth, Martha. Student, La. State U., 1944, Yale U., 1944-45; B.A., Baylor U., 1950, LL.B., 1949, J.D., 1969. Bar: Tex. bar 1949, U.S. Supreme Ct. bar 1965. Asst. county atty. Limestone County, Tex., 1950; mem. Tex. Ho. of Reps., 1951; spl. agt. FBI, Seattle and San Francisco offices, 1951-53; supervisory spl. agt. FBI (Hdqrs.), 1953-59; asst. spl. agt. in charge FBI (Mpls. field div.), 1959-61, asst. chief personnel sect., 1961-65, chief personnel sect., 1965-71; exec. asst. to asst. to dir. adminstrn. FBI, Washington, 1971-72; spl. agt. in charge FBI, San Antonio (Tex.) div., 1972-74; asst. dir., head Office of Planning and Evaluations, Washington, 1974; asst. to dir. FBI, 1974-78, assoc. dir., 1978-79, ret., 1979; mem. Gov.'s Task Force on Drug Abuse; exec. dir. criminal justice div. Gov.'s Office, State of Tex., 1979-80; dir. Dept. Public Safety, 1980-87; guest lectr. various U.S. and fgn. law enforcement, intelligence and bus. groups, 1974-79. Served with U.S. Army, 1945-46, PTO. Recipient numerous govt. achievement awards, 1953-79, Atty. Gen.'s award for Disting. Service, 1978; Nat. Intelligence Disting. Service medal, 1979. Mem. U.S. Supreme Ct. Bar, Tex. Bar Assn., Tex. Police Assn., Soc. Former Spl. Agts. of FBI. Presbyterian.

ADAMS, JAMES FREDERICK, psychologist, educational administrator; b. Andong, Korea, Dec. 27, 1927; s. Benjamin Nyce and Phyllis Irene (Taylor) A.; m. Carol Ann Wagner, Jan. 17, 1980; children—James Edward, Dorothy Lee Adams Vanderhorst, Robert Benjamin. B.A. In Psychology, U. Calif.-Berkeley, 1950; Ed.M. in Counseling and Psychology, Temple U., 1951; Ph.D. in Exptl. Psychology, Wash. State U., 1959. Cert. psychologist, Wash., Pa.; lic. psychologist, Pa. Psychometrician Measurement and Research Ctr., Temple U., Phila., 1951-52; asst. prof. psychology Whitworth Coll., Spokane, Wash., 1952-55; teaching and research asst. State U. Wash., 1955-57; research assoc. Miami U., Oxford, Ohio, 1957-59; asst. prof. psychology Coll. Liberal Arts, Temple U., 1959-62, assoc. prof., 1962-66, prof., 1966-80, chmn. dept. counseling psychology, 1969-72; vis. prof. psychology Coll. Soc. Scis., U. P.R., Rio Piedras, 1963-64, Coll. Scis., Cath. U., Ponce, P.R., 1971-72; chmn. dept. counseling psychology Coll. Edn., Temple U., 1973-77, coordinator div. ednl. psychology, 1974-76; grad. dean, prof. psychology Grad. Coll., U. Nev., Las Vegas, 1980-85; acad. (sr.) v.p. Longwood Coll., Farmville, Va., 1985-86. Author: Problems in Counseling: A Case Study Approach, 1962, Instructors Manual for Understanding Adolescence, 1969; (exhbn. catalogue with J. D. Selig) Colonial Spanish Art of the Americas, 1976; (comml. pamphlet with C. L. Davis) The Use of the Vu-graph as an Instructional Aid, 1960; editor: Counseling and Guidance: A Summary View, 1965, Understanding Adolescence: Current Developments in Adolescent Psychology, 1968, 4th edit., 1980, Human Behavior in a Changing Society, 1973, Songs that had to be Sung (by B. N. Adams), 1979; contbr. chpts., articles, tests and book revs. to profl. publs. Served to cpl. USMC, 1945-46. Recipient Alexander Meiklejohn award AAUP, 1984; James McKean Cattell research fund grantee Miami U., Oxford, Ohio, 1958, Bolton fund research grantee Temple U., 1960, 62, faculty research grantee Temple U., 1961, 63, Commonwealth of Pa. research grantee Temple U., 1969, 70, 71, 72, summer research fellow Temple U., 1979; recipient scholarship U. Munich, 1955. Fellow Am. Psychol. Assn. (divs. 26, 17); mem. Eastern Psychol. Assn., Western Psychol. Assn., Interam. Soc. Psychology, Sigma Xi, Psi Chi. Avocations: art collecting; art restoring. Scholarship established in his name at U. Nev., Las Vegas. Home: 130 Palacio Rd Corrales NM 87048-9648

ADAMS, JAMES MERVYN, JR., pediatrician, neonatologist, educator; b. Dallas, Oct. 25, 1943; s. James Mervyn and Mary (Holmes) A.; m. Elizabeth Cecile Cowen, July 1, 1967; children: James Scott, Karen Lynn. BS cum laude, Southwestern U., 1966; MD, Baylor U., 1970. Diplomate Am. Bd. Pediatrics, Am. Bd. Neonatal/Perinatal Medicine. Rotating intern Ben Taub Gen. Hosp., Houston, 1970-71; resident in pediatrics Baylor Affiliated Hosps., Houston, 1971-73; fellow in neonatology newborn sect. dept pediatrics Baylor Coll. Medicine, Houston, 1973-75, asst. prof. pediatrics, 1976-84, assoc. prof., 1985—; med. dir. neonatal ICU Tex. Children's Hosp., Houston, 1976—, med. dir. neonatal transport and nurse practitioner program, 1978—; clin. prof. nursing U. Tex. Sch. Nursing, Houston, 1992—; mem. active staff Tex. Children's Hosp., 1976—, The Woman's Hosp. of Tex., 1976—, St. Luke's Episcopal Hosp., 1977—, Meth. Hosp., 1983—; attending neonatologist St. Luke's Episcopal/Tex. Children's Hops., 1977—; officer numerous coms. with Tex. Children's Hosp., including chmn. perinatal adv. com., mem. cardiopulmonary resuscitation com., accreditation review com., med. exec com. 1987-88, capital planning com., pharmacy and therapeutics com.; mem. med. exec com. Woman's Hosp. of Tex., 1986-87; mem. neonatology task force Tex. Crippled Children's Program, 1987-88; mem. perinatal adv. com. State Tex. Dept. Health, 1988-89; mem. perinatal morbidity/mortality com. St. Luke's Episcopal Hosp. Contbr. numerous articles to sci. and profl. jours. Fellow Am. Acad. Pediatrics; mem. AMA, Tex. Med. Assn., Am. Acad. Pediatrics, So. Soc. Pediatric Rsch., Harris County Med. Soc., Tex. Perinnatal Assn. (com. neonatal transport 1980-81), Tex. Pediatric Soc. Methodist. Avocations: photography, outdoor sports. Office: Tex Childrens Hosp 6621 Fannin St Houston TX 77030-2303

ADAMS, JAMES MICHAEL, nuclear physicist; b. Brookline, Mass., Dec. 5, 1957; s. Michael James and Elizabeth (Corchary) A.; m. Linda Gail Sheehan Adams, Dec. 26, 1990; children: Kelley Marie, Megan Marie. AB, Coll. of the Holy Cross, Worcester, Mass., 1979; MS, Pa. State U., 1990, PhD, 1995. Lt. sr. grade USN, Washington, 1979-84; sr. engr. Westinghouse Electric Corp., Pitts., 1984-88; rsch. asst. Pa. State U., University Park, 1988-94; rsch. fellow U. Mich., Ann Arbor, Mich., 1995-96; guest rschr., physics lab. Nat. Inst. Stds. and Tech., Gaithersburg, Md., 1995-96; rsch. physicist Neutron Interactions & Dosimetry Group Physics Lab. Nat. Inst. Stds. and Tech., Gaithersburg, 1996—. Contbr. articles to profl. jours. including Phys. Rev., Applied Physics Letters, Surface Sci., Hyperfine Interactions, Ferroelectrics, Materials Sci. and Engring., Nuclear Tech. Vol. Alpha Cmty. Ambulance Svc., State College, Pa., 1994; asst. scoutmaster Boy Scouts Am., Framingham, Mass., 1975. Lt. USN, 1979-84. Recipient Grad. scholarships Am. Nuclear Soc., 1990-93; named Inst. of Nuclear Power Op. scholar, 1988-89, Pa. State U. Grad. fellow The Pa. State U., 1991-92, Deans fellow, 1988-90. Mem. ASTM (sec., mem. com.), Am. Phys. Soc., Am. Nuc. Soc., Sigma Xi, Sigma Pi Sigma, Tau Beta Pi, Alpha Nu Sigma. Achievements include research in hyperfine interactions, surface physics, fundamental neutron physics, neutron spectroscopy and dosimetry, neutron source calibrations, and nuclear reactor analysis. Avocations: mountaineering, triathelon, scuba diving, musician. Home: 21503 Fox Field Cir Germantown MD 20876-5944 Office: Nat Inst Stds and Tech 100 Bureau Dr Mail Stop 8461 Gaithersburg MD 20899

ADAMS, JAMES MILLS, retired chemicals executive; b. Sioux Falls, S.D., Aug. 4, 1936; m. Sherrill D.; 2 children. BSChemE, S.D. Sch. Mines and Tech., 1958; MS in Engring., U. Wash., 1961, PhD in Chem. Nuclear Engring., 1962. Sr. engring. specialist aerophysics rsch. Aerojet-Gen. Corp., Sacramento, 1962-68; sr. spectroscopist Hoffmann La Roche, Inc., Nutley, N.J., 1968-70, sr. scientist applied scis. dept., 1970-73, mgr. CVA engring., 1974-76; plant mgr. aroma chem. plant Haarmann and Reimer Corp., Springfield, N.J., 1976-79, v.p., gen. mgr. aroma chem. div., 1978-85, exec. v.p., 1979-80, pres., 1980-96, CEO, 1985-96; ret.; adv. bd. Cook Coll., Rutgers U., 1985-92; corp. v.p. Miles, Inc., 1989-91; chmn. bd. dirs. Creations Aromatiques, Inc., 1990-96; bd. dirs. Florasynth, Inc., 1995-96. Assoc. editor Pyrodynamics, 1966-69; contbr. over 40 articles to profl. jours.; patentee in fields of med. instrumentation, emission spectrometry, pyrometry, remote sensing, others. Mem. Charleston County Aviation Commn., 1978-79; internat. adv. coun. Monell Ctr., 1990-97. H.L. Doherty Ednl. Found. scholar 1954-58; W. Alton Jones fellow, 1959-60; recipient Centennial 100 Alumni award, S.D. Sch. Mines and Tech., 1985, Eric Bruell award for excellence U.S. Fragrance Industry, 1998. Mem. AAAS, Am. Phys. Soc., Am. Mgmt. Assn., Flavor and Extract Mfrs. Assn. (bd. govs. 1985-94, v.p., sec. 1989-90, pres. elect 1990, pres. 1992-93), Fragrance Materials Assn. (bd. dirs. 1985-96, pres. 1988-92), Rsch. Inst. for Fragrance Materials (chmn. bd. dirs. 1984-89, vice chmn. 1989-90), Cosmetic, Toiletries and Fragrance Assn. (bd. dirs. 1984-98), Internat. Fragrance Assn. (bd. dirs. 1990-98, pres. 1996-98), N.J. C. of C., Pres. Assn., Optimists Club (pres. Watchung chpt. 1984-85), Sigma Xi (pres. Roche Rsch. Club 1973-74). Home: 5131 Cheltenham Terr San Diego CA 92130-1416 Office: H&R Zlorasyuth PO Box 175 Springfield NJ 07081-0175

ADAMS, JAMES R., electronics company executive; b. June 1939. BA, Tex. A&M, 1961; MBA, U. Tex., 1965. With Southwestern Bell, 1965-92, pres., 1988-92; group pres. FBC Comms., 1992-95; bd. dirs. Tex. Instruments, Dallas, 1987—, chmn. bd., 1996-98. Office: Texas Instruments Inc 13510 N Central Expy Dallas TX 75243-1108*

ADAMS, JAMES THOMAS, surgeon; b. Rochester, N.Y., Mar. 28, 1930; s. Thomas and Sarah A.; m. Jacqueline K. Stemmler, July 7, 1952; children—Pamela, Mark, Sari Lynn. A.B., Washington U., St. Louis, 1951, M.D., 1955. Intern, then resident in surgery Barnes Hosp., St. Louis, 1955-60; mem. faculty U. Rochester Med. Sch., 1962—, prof. surgery, 1977—. Author papers in field, chpts. in books. Served as officer M.C. USAR, 1960-62. Mem. Am. Surg. Assn., Soc. Internat. de Chirurgie, Soc. U. Surgeons, Central Surg. Assn., Soc. Vascular Surgery, Am. Gastroenterol. Assn., Soc. Surgery Alimentary Tract, Am. Assn. Surgery Trauma, Phi Beta Kappa, Sigma Xi, Alpha Omega Alpha. Club: Oak Hill Country (Rochester). Co-designer inferior vena cava clip.

ADAMS, JAMES WILLIAM, retired chemist; b. Conover, Wis., Oct. 29, 1921; s. Aldred Henry and Pauline (Evertson) A.; m. Joyce Marie Braatz, Oct. 27, 1944 (div. Oct. 1986); children: Judy R. Adams Swank, Neal J.; m. Barbara A. Backlund, Apr. 4, 1987. BS in Chemistry, U. Wis., 1943. Analytical chemist U.S. Rubber Co., Institute, W.Va., 1943-47; rsch. chemist U.S. Rubber Co., Naugatuck, Conn., 1947-52; sr. scientist Marathon Corp., Rothschild, Wis., 1952-53, rsch. group leader, 1953-57; sr. rsch. assoc. Am. Can Co., Rothschild, 1957-80; rsch. fellow Reed Lignin Inc., Rothschild, 1980-89; retired, 1989; chemistry specialist J&B Cons., Schofield, Wis., 1989—. Contbr. articles to Chem. and Engring. Progress, Indsl. and Engring. Chemistry, Applied Polymer Symposium, Radiochem. Radioanalytical Letters. Alderman Schofield City Coun., 1958-74; vol. Wausau Nordic Ski Club. Recipient Meritorious Svc. award City of Schofield, 1976, Vol. of Yr. award Badger State Games, 1991. Mem. Am. Chem. Soc. (tour speaker 1986—, chmn. Ctr. Wis. sect. 1995), Am. Inst. Chemists, N.Y. Acad. Scis. Achievements include 20 patents for using Wood Pulping Liquor in Animal Feed, Process for Making Superabsorbent Fibers, Modified Wood Pulp Fibers for Plant Growth Medium, and others on industrial products and processes; development of test for measuring road wear qualities of tire rubber. Home: 2008 Clarberth St Schofield WI 54476-1211

ADAMS, JANE MILLER, retired psychotherapist; b. Shreveport, La., June 10, 1922; d. Charles Frederick and Lucile Elizabeth (Day) Miller; m. James Franklin Adams, June 8, 1946. BA, La. State U., 1950, MSW, 1960. Bd. cert. social worker La.; bd. cert. diplomat. Am. Bd. of Examiners of Clin. Social Work, emeritus. Clin. social worker Ctrl. La. State Hosp., Pineville, 1957-62, Forest Glen Mental Health Outpatient Clinic, Pineville, 1962-64; med. social worker La. Pub. Health, Alexandria, 1964-67; adminstr., therapist Alexandria Outpatient Alcoholism Clinic, 1967-73; psychotherapist Episcopal Diocese La., Pineville, 1974-82, pvt. practice, Pineville, 1982-92; cons. and spkr. in field. Pink lady vol. Huey P. Long Regional Hosp., Pineville, 1982-85; vol. to cons. Cmty. Mental Health Day Care Ctr., Alexandria, 1984-85; staff cons. Ctrl. La. Alcoholism Clinic, Alexandria, 1975-78; alcoholism cons. Forest Glen Mental Health Outpatient Clinic, 1975-78. Democrat. Episcopalian. Avocations: gardening, poetry. Home: 404 Hiawatha Trl Pineville LA 71360-4407

ADAMS, JEANNE MASTERS, community health nurse, consultant; b. N.Y.C., Oct. 1, 1934; d. Thomas J. Coleman and Ann Mahon; children: Timothy, Christopher, Annmarie, Jeanne, Martin. AAS, Bergen Community Coll., 1974; BSN, Dominican Coll., 1976; MS in Nursing, Hunter Grad. Sch. of Nursing, 1976; PhD, CUNY, 1995. Occupational health nurse med. dept. N.Y. Daily News, N.Y.C.; asst. prof. sch. of nursing Hunter Coll., N.Y.C.; lectr., clin. instr. Bergen Community Coll., Paramus, N.J.; surg. nurse Columbia Presbyn. Hosp., N.Y.C.; educator, coord. health promotion Fashion Inst. Tech., N.Y.C., 1989—. Mem. N.Y. Acad. Sci., Sociologist Practice Assn., ANA. Home: 340 W 11th St Ship Bottom NJ 08008-6314

ADAMS, JEFFREY ALAN, web developer, writer; b. Flint, Mich., June 25, 1968; s. William and Linda Suzanne (Montgomery) A.; m. William R. Knauss, Sept. 7, 1997. BA in Journalism, U. Ala., 1991. Editl. asst. Randall Pub. Co., Tuscaloosa, Ala., 1989-90; assoc. editor Equipment World Mag., Tuscaloosa, Ala., 1990-91, Overdrive Mag., Tuscaloosa, Ala., 1990-93; mng. editor Equipment World Mag., 1991-93, TVRO Dealer Mag., Fortuna, Calif., 1993-97; staff writer Satellite TV Week Mag., Fortuna, Calif., 1993-96, mng. editor, 1996-98; mng. editor Satellite Choice Mag., Fortuna, Calif., 1996-98; web developer Dobbin/Bolgla Assocs., N.Y.C., 1998—; contbg. editor Equipment World Mag., Tuscaloosa, Ala., 1993—. Co-editor, co-pub. The First Line Literary Mag., Bklyn., N.Y., Plano, Tex. Sec. Ferndale (Calif.) Repertory Theater, 1994-95, bd. mem., 1993-94, media rels., 1994-97, photographer, 1993-98, publicist, web developer Redwood Curtian Theatre Consortium, 1997—. Recipient Robert F. Boger Feature Writing award, Constrn. Writers Assn., 1993. Mem. Soc. Profl. Journalists. Avocations: acting, theater, travel, music, Internet. Office: Dobbin Bolgla Assocs 24 E 21st 3d fl New York NY 10010

ADAMS, JEFFREY PAUL, insurance agent, insurance company executive; b. Boca Raton, Fla., Oct. 1, 1944; s. Crawford W. and Barbara (Simpkins) A.; m. Carolyn Green, Aug. 28, 1982; children: Carolyn G. Gwynn, Ashley R., Jeffrey P. Jr. BA, U. N.C., Chapel Hill, 1967. CLU; ChFC. Field underwriter Mutual of N.Y., Nashville, 1967-69, asst. mgr., 1969-73, mgr., 1973-85; pres. Adams & Assocs., Inc., Mobile, Ala., 1986—. Contbr. article to profl. jour. Chmn. South Ala. Arthritis Found., Mobile, 1991-92, Ala. Arthritis Found., 1995; vice-chmn. Am.'s Jr. Miss, Mobile, Ala., 1994-96, bd. dirs., 1997-99; chmn. Better Bus. Bur., Mobile, 1994-95, officer, bd. rep., 1997. Mem. Am. Soc. CLU, Ala. Assn. Life Underwriters (pres. 1977-78, Life Underwriter of Yr. 1992), Mobile Assn. Life Underwriters (Life Underwriter of Yr. 1982), Mobile Touchdown Club (sec. 1997-98, v.p. 1999-2000), Sales and Mktg. Execs. (pres. 1982-83), Mobile Soccer Club Inc. (pres. 1998—). Roman Catholic. Avocations: saltwater, fishing. Office: Adams & Assocs Inc 3 Dauphin St Mobile AL 36602-3707

ADAMS, JIMMY WAYNE, osteopath; b. Rockymount, Va., July 21, 1953; s. Mose Chitwood and Nellie June (Hall) A.; m. Mary Virginia Hunter, May 19, 1996. BA in Psychology, Roanoke Coll., Salem, Va., 1982; DO, Kirksville Coll. Osteo. Med., 1991. Diplomate Am. Bd. Osteo. Med. Examiners, Am. Acad. Pain Mgmt. Family med. intern Doctors Hosp., Columbus, Ohio, 1991-92, resident in diagnostic radiology and nuclear medicine, 1992-94; resident in phys. medicine and rehab. Med. Coll. Va., Richmond, 1994-96, attending physician episodic care unit, emergency dept., 1994-95; med. dir. Commonwealth Diagnostics and Rehab., Richmond, 1995-98; attending physician in pain mgmt. Albemarle Pain Ctr., 1996—; attending physician Family Practice Specialists Richmond, 1997—; mental helth therapist Roanoke Valley Psychiat. Ctr., Salem, 1982-85; clin. instr, Ohio U. Coll. Osteo. Medicine, Columbus, 1993-94. Squadron comdr. North Ctrl. Mo. Composite Squadron, CAP USAF Aux., Kirksville, Mo., 1988-90. Mem. AMA, Am. Osteo. Assn., Christian Med. and Dental Soc., Am. Osteo. Acad. Sports Medicine, Am. Acad. Phys. Medicine and Rehab., Va. Osteo. Med. Assn., Am. Acad. Pain Mgmt., Am. Pain Soc., Albemarle County Med. Soc., Am. Coll. Osteo. Family Practitioners, Med. Soc. Va., Soc. Pain Practice Mgmt., Psy Chi, Pi Gamma Mu, Iota Tau Sigma. Roman Catholic. Avocations: flying, running, hiking, canoeing, photographer. Home and Office: 2401 Dorothea Ln Maidens VA 23102-2627

ADAMS, JO-ANN MARIE, lawyer; b. L.A., May 27, 1949; d. Joseph John and Georgia S. (Wein) A.; AA, Pasadena City Coll., 1968; BA, Pomona Coll., 1970; MA, Calif. State U., L.A., 1971; MBA, Pacific Luth. U., 1983; cert. in Telecomm. and Info. Resource Mgmt., U. Hawaii, 1993; JD, Santa Clara U., 1996. Secondary tchr. South Pasadena (Calif.) Unified Schs., 1970-71; appraiser Riverside County (Calif.) Assessor's Office, 1972-74; systems and procedures analyst Riverside County Data Processing Dept., 1974-76, supervising systems analyst, 1976-79; systems analyst computer Boeing Computer Svcs. Co., Seattle, 1979-81; sr. systems analyst Thurston County Central Svcs., Olympia, Wash., 1981-83, data processing systems mgr., 1983-84; data processing systems engr. IBM Corp., 1984-87; realtor-assoc., Dower Realty, 1987-92; corp. sales rep. UniGlobe Met. Travel, 1988-89; project mgr. Servco Pacific, 1989-90, Scott Software Systems, 1990-91; systems analyst Dept. Atty. Gen., 1991-93; cons. in field, 1993—; pvt. practice, 1996—; law clerk HiTech Law, 1995-96, Law Offices Thomas R. Hogan, 1995; instr. Riverside City Coll., 1977-79; vis. lectr. Santa Clara U., 1997—. Chair legis. task force Riverside/San Bernardino chpt. NOW, 1975-76, chpt. co-chair, 1978; mem. ethics com. Calif. NOW Inc., 1978; alt. del. Calif Dem. Caucus, 1978. Mem. ABA, SCCBA, NAFE, Pomona Coll. Alumni Assn., Santa Clara U. Alumni Assn. Home: 1200 Ranchero Way Apt 80 San Jose CA 95117-3155 Office: 19925 Stevens Creek Blvd Cupertino CA 95014-2305

ADAMS, JOEY, comedian, author; b. N.Y.C., Jan. 6, 1911; s. Nathan and Ida (Chonin) Abramowitz; m. Cindy Heller, Feb. 14, 1952. Student, CCNY, 1931, Dr. Comedy (hon.), 1952; Dr. Comedy (hon.), Columbia, 1950, NYU, 1959; spl. hon. degree, L.I. U.; LLD (hon.), Chung-Aug U., Korea; PhD (hon.), Fu-Jen U., Taipei, Taiwan. Ind. author, comedian, goodwill ambassador, 1931—. Nightclub and vaudeville entertainer throughout U.S., 1930—; motion pictures include Ringside, 1945, Singing in the Dark; also producer motion pictures; theatrical appearances include The Gazebo, 1959, Guys and Dolls, 1960; radio-TV programs include Sez Who, 1958, Person to Person, 1959, Joey Adams Show, 1956-58, Gags to Riches, 1958; also guest appearances, also radio show for Sta. WEVD Syndicate, recs. for Coral Records, MGM, Roulette Records, State Dept. rep. to entertain soldiers around world, 1958, Pres.'s goodwill ambassador; syndicated columnist Strictly for Laughs, N.Y. Post; author: From Gags to Riches (entire proceeds given to Damon Runyon Cancer Fund), 1946, The Curtain Never Falls, 1949, Strictly For Laughs, 1955, Joey Adams Joke Book, 1952, Joke Dictionary, 1961, Round the World Joke Book, 1964, Cindy and I, 1957, It Takes One to Know One, 1959, On the Road for Uncle Sam, 1963, L.B.J.'s Texas Laughs, 1964, The Borscht Belt, Encyclopedia of Humor, Son of Encyclopedia of Humor, 1971, Laugh Your Calories Away, 1971, The God Bit, 1973, Speakers Bible of Humor, 1973, Joey Adams Ethnic Humor, Here's to the Friars, Joey Adams Joke Diary, 1979, Brother Billy the Pain from Plains, 1979, Strictly for Laughs, 1981, Live Longer Through Laughter, 1984, The Roast of the Town, 1986, 2d rev. edit., 1987, Guaranteed To Make You Laugh, 1989; also mysteries; weekly columnist The Star. Dir. Central State Bank.; Dep. commr. N.Y.C. Youth Bd., chmn. entertainment com. for youth, 1959—, commr. youth, N.Y.C.; del. Allied Entertainment Unions, 1959—; bd. dirs. Theatre Authority, 1959—; chmn. spl. events com. March of Dimes, 1955; pres. Am. Guild Variety Artists, 1959—, pres. retirement found., chmn. youth fund; pres. Actors Youth Fund, Sr. Citizens of Am. Fund, personal rep. of Pres. U.S. as entertainer to, Asia, Africa, 1961. Named Man of Year of March of Dimes, 1958, Man of Year City of Hope, 1959, Man of Year N.Y.C. Police Dept., 1960; recipient Humanitarian awards Yiddish Theatrical Alliance, 1960, Humanitarian awards Am. Cancer Soc., 1952, Humanitarian awards Crusade for Freedom, 1956; Pope's Medal, 1971; honored by Israeli Govt. for work in United Jewish Appeal and Israel Bond drives, 1952; also numerous citations Am. Guild Variety Artists created; Joey Awards for talent in variety field, 1960. Mem. Screen Actors Guild, AFTRA, Actors Equity Assn. Office: NY Post 210 South St New York NY 10002-7807 *As the "adopted son" and protege of the late mayor of New York City, Fiorello LaGuardia, I have always lived by his words to me when I was 6 years old: "Don't worry about people knowing you, make yourself worth knowing," and by the words of Mary Baker Eddy: "A dose of joy is a spiritual cure."**

ADAMS, JOHN ANDREW, physicist, engineering company executive; b. Cin., Feb. 15, 1946; s. John Andrew and Joan Loretta (Rasfeld) A.; m. Sally Ann Howard, June 6, 1969; children: John Michael and Sarah Louise (twins). BS in Physics, U. San Diego, 1968; PhD in Physics, Ariz. State U., Tempe, 1978. Project mgr., staff sr. scientist IRT Corp., San Diego, 1978-81, mgr. logging svcs., 1981-84, mgr. tech. devel., 1984-86; co-founder, chief scientist Four Pi Systems, San Diego, 1986-94, chief scientist, dir. engring., 1991-94; chief scientist Athens Corp., Phoenix, 1994—, Internat. Process Equipment Co., Phoenix. Patentee automated laminography, automated inspections. With USN, 1969-73. Recipient IR100 award R&D Mag., 1984. Avocation: amateur radio.

ADAMS, JOHN BRETT, investment banker, company executive; b. Tiverton, U.K., Dec. 6, 1940; came to U.S., 1972; s. Harold Coates and Mildred B. (Jones) A.; m. Laura Marie Schneider, July 15, 1970; children: Alexa, Caroline. BA, Oxford U., Eng., 1962; MBA, Stanford U., 1964. Exec. dir. S.G. Warburg & Co., Ltd., London, 1964-72; dir. Singer & Friedlander, Ltd., London, 1972-74; sr. v.p. White, Weld & Co., Inc., N.Y.C., 1974-78; mng. dir. Merrill Lynch Capital Markets, N.Y.C., 1978-85; ptnr. M.J.H. Nightingale & Co., N.Y.C., 1986-89; v.p. corp. devel., Am. Home Products Corp., 1991—; dir. Am. Swiss Assn., N.Y.C.; mem. internat. com. Securities Industry Assn., N.Y.C. Bd. dirs. Brit. Schs. and Univs. Found., Inc., N.Y.C., 1982-98; treas. Am. Friends of the Warburg Inst. Clubs: Racquet and Tennis (N.Y.C.), Maidstone (East Hampton, N.Y.), Devon Yacht Club (Amagansett, N.Y.). Avocations: golf, racquet sports, art, theater. Home: 224 E 68th St New York NY 10021-6001

ADAMS, JOHN CARTER, JR., insurance executive; b. Williston, Fla., June 13, 1936; s. John Carter and Katharine Anna (Beall) A.; m. Leila Nora Johnson, Nov. 28, 1958; children: Julia Katharine, Ruth Anne. BSBA, U. Fla., 1958. Agt. Pan Am Ins. Co., 1958-59; acct. exec. Guy B. Odum & Co., Inc., 1959-63, v.p., 1963-66, exec. v.p., 1966-71, pres., 1971-76; pres. Jay Adams & Assocs., Inc., Daytona Beach, 1976-85, Hilb Rogal & Hamilton Co., Daytona Beach, ., 1986-89; chmn., CEO Hilb Rogal & Hamilton Co., 1989-93, bd. dirs., 1987-95; mem. exec. com. Hilb Rogal & Hamilton Co., Richmond, Va., 1988-95, chmn. operating com., 1987-93, sr. v.p. ops., 1989-90, exec. v.p. sales and mktg., 1991-93, exec. v.p., COO, 1993-94, exec. v.p. ops., 1994-99; exec. v.p. Poe & Brown Inc., Daytona Bch., Fla., 1999—; bd. dirs. Westside Atlantic Bank, 1972-76, First Atlantic Nat. Bank, 1976-81, Heritage Fed. Savings & Loan, 1981-85, Daytona Beach, 1985-90, Am. Pioneer Savings Bank, Fla., 1985-90, Consol. Tomoka Land Co., 1976—; chmn. adv. bd. Daytona Beach region Am. Pioneer Savings Bank, Orlando, Fla., 1986-90; chmn. compensation com. Consol. Tomoka Land Co., 1990—. Mem. bd. visitors Embry-Riddle Aero. U., Daytona Beach, 1967-79, trustee, 1969—, mem. exec. com., 1972—, vice chmn. bd. 1981—, chmn. exec. com, 1983—, devel. coun. chmn. fund drive Hunt Meml. Libr. Embry-Riddle Aero U., 1985; chmn. Commitment 2000 Fund Drive Embry-Riddle Aero U.; campaign chmn. Easter Seal Soc., 1969, trustee, 1970-73, pres., 1972-73; bd. dirs. YMCA, Daytona Beach, 1968-76, 78—, treas., 1970, v.p., 1971-82, pres., 1983; mem. Metro Bd. Daytona Beach YMCA, 1992-95; dir. Futures, Inc., 1985-93, Nat. Intercollegiate Sports Festival, 1985-87; gen. campaign chmn. United Way of Volusia County, Fla., 1977, pres., 1979, dir., 1976-82, trustee, 1985—; chmn. Civic League of Halifax Area, 1983-84, exec. com., 1977-92, chmn. 1981-82; chmn. Fla. Internat. Festivals, Inc., 1990-91, bd. dirs. 1987—, chmn. Lively Arts Corp., 1997—, mem. Tourist Devel. Coun. Volusia County 1983-85, Halifax Advt. Authority, 1985; bd. dirs. Volusia County Bus. Deve. Coun., 1984-92; Daytona Beach Community Found., 1984-87, Fla. State C. of C., 1985-86. Served with USNR, 1953-61. Recipient Disting. Service award Bd. visitors Embry-Riddle Aero. U., 1975, Champion Higher Ind. Edn. in Fla. award Ind. Colls. and Univs. of Fla., 1973, 1st Ann. Herbert M. Davidson Community. Svc. award United Way of Volusia County, 1992; established John C. Adams Community Svc. award Embry-Riddle Aero U., 1990. Mem. Daytona Beach C. of C. (bd. govs. 1968-70, v.p. bus. and govt. 1970, pres. 1975, gen. campaign chmn. devel. fund drive 1984, Louis Fuchs Man of Yr. award 1985), Volusia County Insurors Assn. (pres. 1971-72), Fla. Assn. Ins. Agts. (bd. dirs. 1978-81), Coun. Ins. Agts. and Brokers (bd. dirs. 1989-83, bd. dirs. coun. of ins. agents and brokers 1993—, co-chmn. exec. liasion com., mem. fin. and audit com. 1993-94, sec. 1994-95, treas. 1995-96, vice chmn. 1996-97, chmn. 1997-98, co-chmn. nominating com. 1998—), Rotary (bd. dirs. 1989-91). Republican. Episcopalian. Home: 1616 S Peninsula Dr Daytona Beach FL 32118-4948 Office: Poe & Brown Inc PO Box 2412 220 S Ridgewood Ave Daytona Beach FL 32115

ADAMS, JOHN DAVID VESSOT, manufacturing company executive; b. Ottawa, Ont., Can., Jan. 7, 1934; s. Albert Oliver and Estelle Priscilla (Vessot) A.; m. Dorothy Marion Blyth, June 27, 1959; children: Nancy, Joel, Louis. Student Carleton U., 1950-51; B in Engring., McGill U., 1955; MBA, U. Western Ont., 1958. Registered profl. engr., Ont. Project engr. Abitibi Paper Co., Toronto, Ont., 1962-63, Cockshutt Farm Equipment Co. Ltd., Brantford, Ont., 1958-62, Can. Industries Ltd., Kingston, Ont., 1955-58; mgr. fin. analysis and planning Rio Tinto Zinc Group, London, 1963-66; mgr. adminstrn. and planning Can. Gypsum Co. Ltd., Toronto, 1966-72; mgr. logistics and fin. Massey Ferguson Co. Ltd., Toronto, 1972-79; pres. Can. Spool & Bobbin Co. Ltd., Walkerton, Ont., 1979-88, pres. Quality Performance Engring., Inc., 1988—; consulting, mfg., Hanover, Ont., Can. Mem. Assn. Profl. Engrs. Province Ont. Mem. Rotary. Home: 386 14th Ave, Hanover, ON Canada N4N 2Y1 Office: Quality Performance Engring Inc, 800 12th St, Hanover, ON Canada N4N 1W8

ADAMS, JOHN HAMILTON, lawyer; b. N.Y.C., Feb. 15, 1936; s. John and Barbara (Johnston) A.; m. Patricia Brandon Smith, Sept. 30, 1963; children: Katherine L., John H., Ramsay W. B.A., Mich. State U., 1959; LL.B., Duke U., 1962. Bar: N.Y. 1963. Assoc. Cadwalader, Wickersham & Taft, N.Y.C., 1962-65; asst. U.S. atty. So. Dist. N.Y., N.Y.C., 1965-69; exec. dir. Nat. Resources Def. Coun., Inc., N.Y.C., 1970—; chmn. Open Space Inst., N.Y.C., 1979—. Bd. dirs. Catskill Ctr. for Conservation, Arkville, N.Y., 1974—, Hudson River Found. Sci. and Environ. Rsch., Inc., 1981—, Winston Found. World Peace, 1984—, World Resources Inst., 1987—. Recipient As They Grow award Parents mag., 1989, Frances K. Hutchinson award Garden Club Am., 1990, Disting. Alumni award Duke U., 1991. Mem. Am. Conservation Assn. (bd. dirs. 1985—), Century Assn. Home: RR 1 Garrison NY 10524-9801 Office: Natural Resources Def Coun Inc 40 W 20th St New York NY 10011-4211*

ADAMS, JOHN HANLY, retired magazine editor, writer, consultant; b. Sikeston, Mo., Nov. 2, 1918; s. Laurence B. and Mary B. (O'Connell) A.; m. Helen Lorraine Pollard, Apr. 18, 1942; children: John Bruce, Barbara Alison, Lawrence Kirby. BA in Econs.; BJ, U. Mo., 1940. Reporter Eugene (Oreg.) Daily News, 1940; mem. news staff U.S. News & World Report, Washington, 1940-79; asso. exec. editor U.S. News & World Report, 1968-70, mng. editor, 1970-76, exec. editor, 1976-79, dir., 1973-79; contbg. editor Nation's Bus. mag., 1981-82; editorial cons. Ernst & Whinney, 1980-82, Tax Found., Inc., 1983-89. Served with USNR, 1943-46. Mem. Nat. Press Club. Home: 3700 N Edison St Arlington VA 22207-1832*

ADAMS, JOHN HURST, bishop; b. Columbia, S.C., Nov. 27, 1929; s. Eugene Avery and Charity A. (Nash) A.; m. Dolly Desselle, Aug. 25, 1956; children: Gaye Desselle, Jann Hurst, Madelyn Rose. AB, Johnson C. Smith Coll., 1948; STB, Boston U., 1951, STM, 1953; DD, Wilberforce U., 1956, Paul Quinn Coll., 1972. Ordained to ministry A.M.E. Ch. as deacon, 1948, elder, 1952, bishop, 1972. Pastor Bethel A.M.E. Ch., Lynn, Mass., 1950-52; prof. Wilberforce (Ohio) U., 1952-56; pres. Paul Quinn Coll., Waco, Tex., 1956-62, chmn. bd., 1972—; pastor 1st A.M.E. Ch., Seattle, 1962-68, Grant A.M.E. ch., L.A., 1968-72; 87th A.M.E. bishop 10th Dist. Tex. councils chs., from 1972; bishop 2d Dist., 1986-89; sr. bishop Atlanta, 1989-92, 7th Episcopal Dist., Columbia, S.C., 1992—. Author: Ethnic Education in Black Church, 1970. Bd. dirs. Nat. Tex. couns. chs., Nat. Conf. Black Churchmen, Nat. Bd. Black United Funds, Nat. Coun. Chs., PUSH (People United to Save Humanity). Named Man of Yr., B'nai B'rith, 1964, Urban League, Seattle, 1965. Mem. Boulé, Alpha Phi Alpha. Office: African Meth Episc Ch 110 Pisgah Church Rd Columbia SC 29203-9351*

ADAMS, JOHN L., retired career officer, federal agency administrator; b. Saint John, N.B., Can., May 31, 1942; s. Lawrence Hugh and Jean Marjorie (Poley) A.; m. Marilyn Walton, July 23, 1966; children: Derek, Ryan, Erin. B in Engring., Royal Mil. Coll., 1965; BA, Oxford U., 1967. Advanced through grades to maj.-gen., 1990; project officer Office Dir. Gen. Milt. Engring. and Ops. Nat. Def. Hdqs., Ottawa, Can., 1970-71; dir. constrn. engring. requirements Nat. Def. Hdqs., Ottawa, 1982; assoc. asst. dep. min. Nat. Def. Hdqs., 1992, asst. dep. min. infrastructure and environment, 1993-98; commdg. officer 3 Field Engr. Squadron, Chilliwack, B.C., Can., 1974; sr. staff officer adminstrn. Brigade Hdqs. Staff, Calgary, Alta., Can.; sr. staff officer Works in Tng. Sys. Hdqs., Trenton, Ont., Can., 1978; dep. comdr. Spl. Svc. Force, Can. Forces Base, Petawawa, Ont., 1985; chief staff foreign and def. policy secretariat Privy Coun. Office, 1987; chief constrn. and properties Nat. Def. Hdqs., 1990; ret., 1993. Rhodes scholar Oxford U., 1965-67. Office: Nat Def Hdqs Commr Can CG, 200 Kent, Ottawa, ON Canada K1A 0E6

ADAMS, JOHN M., library director; b. Chicago, Ill., June 10, 1950; s. Merlin J. and Esther (Bohn) A.; m. Nancy Ileen Coultas, June 12, 1970; 1 child, Arwen Lee. B.A. in English, U. Ill., 1972, M.L.S., 1973. Grad. asst. U. Ill. Libr., Urbana, 1972-73; libr.-reference Sherman Oaks Libr., L.A., 1973-75; libr. philosophy dept. L.A. Pub. Libr., 1975-77, head gen. reading svc., 1977-78; dir. Moline Pub. Libr., Ill., 1978-83, Tampa (Fla.)-Hillsborough County Pub. Libr. System, 1983-91; dir., county librarian Orange County (Calif.) Public Library System, 1991—; dir. Tampa Bay Libr. Consortium, Fla., 1983-91, Santiago Libr. System, 1991—; mem. adv. com. on pub. librs. OCLC, 1992-95. Contbr. articles to profl. jours. Bd. dirs. Planned Parenthood of Tampa, 1984. Recipient Frontier award ALA Mag., 1981; named Outstanding Young Man, Moline Jaycees, 1983. Mem. ALA (J.C. Dana award 1982, 93), Calif. Libr. Assn., Calif. County Librs. Assn., Orange County C. of C. Avocations: music; tennis. Office: Orange County Pub Libr 1501 E Saint Andrew Pl Santa Ana CA 92705-4930

ADAMS, JOHN MARSHALL, lawyer; b. Columbus, Ohio, Dec. 6, 1930; s. H.F. and Ada Margaret (Gregg) A.; m. Janet Hawk, June 28, 1952; children: John Marshall, Susan Lynn, William Alfred. B.A., Ohio State U., 1952; J.D. summa cum laude, 1954. Bar: Ohio 1954. Mem. Cowan & Adams, Columbus, 1954-55; asst. city atty. City of Columbus, 1955-56; mem. Knepper, White, Richards & Miller, 1956-63; practiced in Columbus, 1963-74; ptnr. Porter, Wright, Morris & Arthur, Columbus, 1975-91, of counsel, 1992—; vice chmn. Ohio Bar Liability Ins. Co., 1990-93, chmn., 1994—; trustee Ohio Legal Ctr. Inst., 1976-81, Ohio Lawpac, 1980-89. Fellow Am. Coll. Trial Lawyers, Am. Bar Found., Ohio Bar Found. (trustee 1975-84); mem. ABA, Ohio State Bar Assn. (exec. com. 1975-80, pres. 1978-79), Columbus Bar Assn. (bd. govs. 1970-76, pres. 1974-75), Lawyers Club (pres. 1968-69, 6th cir. jud. conf. life mem., Ohio Bar medal 1994), Order of Coif, Grey Oaks Country Club (Naples, Fla.), Scioto Country Club, Masons, Delta Upsilon, Phi Delta Phi. Republican. Home: 2535 Canterbury Rd Columbus OH 43221-3081 Office: 41 S High St Columbus OH 43215-6101

ADAMS, JOHN PLETCH, orthopaedic surgeon; b. Ashburn, Md., Feb. 22, 1922; s. John William and Norm Emma (Pletch) A.; m. Nancy Ellen Murphy; 1 child, John P., Jr. BS, U. Mo., 1943; MD, Washington U., St. Louis, 1945; MPH, Harvard U., 1978. Diplomate Am. Bd. Orthopaedic Surgery. Intern Wilmington (Del.) Gen. Hosp., 1945-46; resident Duke U., Durham, N.C., 1949-52; prof. and dept. chmn. George Washington U. Sch. of Medicine, Washington, 1953-87, prof. emeritus, 1987—. Councilman Lewes, Del., 1990-92, Mayor, 1992-94; chmn. Gov.'s Coun. Long Term Care Facilities, 1990-94. Capt. USPHSR, 1946-49. Named Am.-Brit. Exchange fellow, 1959. Fellow Am. Acad. Orthopaedic Surgery, Am. Coll. Surgeons, So. Surgical Assn.; mem. Am. Orthopaedic Assn., Am. Soc. for Surgery of the Hand (pres. 1971), Cosmos Club, Alpha Omega Alpha (chmn. gov.'s coun. long term care facilities 1990-94). Republican. Episcopalian. Avocations: sailing, tennis. Home and Office: 804 Bay Ave Lewes DE 19958-1005

ADAMS, JOHN QUINCY, economist, educator; b. Dallas, Mar. 7, 1938; s. John Quincy and Ruby (Withrow) A.; m. Adele Ingwersen; children by previous marriage: Jennifer Lynn, Lara Jill, John Michael. AB, Oberlin Coll., 1960; PhD, U. Tex., 1966. Prof. U. Md., College Park, 1980-90; prof., chair Northeastern U., Boston, 1990-98; vis. fellow Inst. of Devel. Studies Univ. Sussex, U.K., 1973. Author: Black Homelands of South Africa, 1977, Exports, Politics, and Economic Development, 1983, Economics as Social Science, 1989; editor: Institutional Economics, 1980. Fulbright prof. Bangalore U., 1967-68. Mem. Phi Beta Kappa.

ADAMS, JOHN QUINCY, educator, consultant; b. Gary, Ind., Sept. 6, 1950; s. John Quincy and Fannie (Simpson) A.; m. Becky Jo Yonan (div. 1978); m. Pearlie Mae Strother, June 26, 1980; children: Leia, Jabari. PhB, Grand Valley State Coll., 1975; MA, Ind. U., 1977; PhD, U. Ill., 1989. Tchr. Ctr. for World Studies, Grand Rapids, Mich., 1975-77, Catalyst H.S., Peoria, Ill., 1977-78; asst. prof. Ill. State U., Normal, 1978-83; tchg. asst. U. Ill., Urbana, 1983-84; dir. Minority and Intercultural Affairs, Joliet (Ill.) Jr. Coll., 1985-88; asst. prof. Western Ill. U., Macomb, 1988-93, dir. edn. opportunity, 1993-97, prof., 1997—; prof. PBS teleclass Dealing with Diversity, 1992, 99. Co-author (CD Rom) Multicultural Prism, 1999; co-editor (anthology) Multicultural Education: Strategies for Implementation in Colleges and Universities, vol. 1-5, 1991-96, (anthology and video) Multicultural Prism: Voices from the Field, 1994. Mem. adv. bd. Golden Apple Orgn., Chgo. Cpl. USMC, 1970-74. Recipient Pacesetter award for multicultural edn. Ill. State Bd. Edn., 1981, Leadership award Ill. Com. on Black Concerns in Higher Edn., 1989, Connections 2000 award Ill. State Bd. Edn., 1993. Mem. ASCD, Ill. Staff and Curriculum Developers Assn. (pres. 1992-94, adv. bd. 1995—, Leadership award 1994), Phi Kappa Phi. Avocations: Frisbee golf, poetry, music. E-mail: jabari@macomb.com. FAX: 309-298-2222. Home: 1 Bacon Woods Macomb IL 61455 Office: Western Ill Univ 1 University Cir Macomb IL 61455

ADAMS, JOHN STEPHEN, geography educator; b. Mpls., Sept. 7, 1938; s. Edward Francis and Ellen Cecilia (Cullen) A.; m. Judith Estelle Nielsen, Sept. 1, 1962; children: John D., Ellen Anastasia, Martin Francis, David Joseph Cullen. BA, U. St. Thomas, 1960; MA, U. Minn., 1962, PhD, 1966. Rsch. asst., rsch. fellow Upper Midwest Econ. Study, Mpls., 1960-64; teaching asst. dept. geography U. Minn., Mpls., 1964-66, assoc. prof., then prof. geography, 1970—, now prof. geography, planning and pub. affairs, dir. Sch. Pub. Affairs and H.H. Humphrey Inst. Pub. Affairs, 1976-79, chmn. dept. geography, 1981-84, 92-93, 99—; asst. prof. geography Pa. State U., State College, 1966-70; rsch. asst. N. Star Rsch. and Devel., Inc., Mpls., 1964; Fulbright prof. geog. Econ. U. Vienna, Austria, 1975-76; vis. prof. geography U. Wash., Seattle, 1979; vis. prof. geography and environ. engring. U.S. Mil. Acad., West Point, N.Y., 1990-91; vis. prof. geography and earth scis. Marie Curie-Sklodowska U., Lublin, Poland, 1997; mem. nat. adv. com. H.H. Humphrey N.-S. Fellowship Program, Inst. Internat. Edn., N.Y.C., 1979-81, coord. at U. Minn., 1981-87, 89-90; econ. geographer in residence Bank of Am., San Francisco, 1980-81; mem. exec. com. Nat. Com. Rsch. on 1980 census Social Sci. Rsch. Coun., N.Y.C., 1981-88; bd. dirs. Consortium of Social Sci. Assns., Washington, 1983-85, Kattner FVD Dist. Energy Inc.; mem. geography panel Coun. for Internat. Exchange of Scholars, Washington, 1983-85, chair, 1986, mem. Soviet-Eastern European panel, 1990-93; mem. geography div. adv. com. U.S. Bur. Census, Washington, 1985; Bush sabbatical fellow, 1987-88, Fulbright prof. geography Moscow State U., 1988. Author: (with R. Abler and P. Gould) Spatial Organization, 1971, (with Abler, Gould and K. Lee) A Comparative Atlas of America's Great Cities, 1976 (Geog. Soc. Chgo. award 1977), Housing America in the 1980's, 1987); editor: Contemporary Metropolitan America, 4 vols., 1976, Urban Policy Making and Metropolitan Dynamics, 1976, (with B. Van Drasek) Minneapolis-St. Paul People, Place and Public Life, 1993; mem. editl. bd. Geographia Polonica, 1998—; editl. adv. bd. jours. Govt. and Policy, Urban Geography, Post-Soviet Geography and Economics, Geographia Polonica. Bd. dirs. Newman Ctr., Mpls., 1983-88, Citizens League, Mpls., 1985-88, 94—. Sr. Scientist Rsch. fellow NSF, Berkeley, Calif., 1980-81. Mem. Assn. Am. Geographers (nat. sec. 1975-78, v.p. 1981-82, pres. 1982-83, honors award 1988, editorial bd. Annals), Nat. Coun. Geog. Edn., Mpls. Com. Fgn. Rels. Democrat. Roman Catholic. Avocations: photography, numismatics, gardening. Home: 2611 W 49th St Minneapolis MN 55410-1902 Office: U Minn Dept Geography 267 19th Ave S Minneapolis MN 55455-0499

ADAMS, JONATHAN L., computer programmer; b. Portland, Maine, Mar. 7, 1956. BA in Music, U. Lowell, 1981; MEd in Instructional Design Media, U. Mass., 1991; EdD in Curriculum and Tchg. Ednl. Media, Boston U., 1995. Cert. tchr., Mass. Instr. Boston U., 1991-95; mus. staff, cons. Boston Mus. Sci., 1992-97; prin. cons., developer Pilot Media Inc., Arlington, Mass., 1992—; instr. U. Mass., Lowell, 1993-99; asst. prof. Boston Univ., Boston, MA, 1998—; faculty Softbank Interactive 95, L.A., 1995, Softbank Interactive 96, Atlanta, 1996; authorized developer Macromedia, Inc., 1996-97. Author: Salon Pilot, 1997, Pilot Catalog Builder, 1997, Protector, 1997, Slide Pilot, 1997, Test Pilot, 1998; co-editor Macromedia User Jour., 1995-97; contbr. articles to profl. jours. Mem. Phi Delta Kappa, Pi Lambda Theta. Avocation: long distance cycling. Fax: (781) 646-9191. Office: Pilot Media Inc PO Box 440494 Somerville MA 02144-0005

ADAMS, JOSEPH KEITH, lawyer; b. Provo, Utah, Apr. 3, 1949; s. Joseph S. and Marian (Bellows) A.; m. Myrle June Overly, Sept. 2, 1971; children: Derek J., Bret K., Stephanie, Julie K., Scott J., Laura. BA summa cum laude, Brigham Young U., 1973; JD, Harvard U., 1976. Bar: Utah 1976, U.S. Dist. Ct. Utah 1976, U.S. Tax Ct. 1983. Assoc. Van Cott, Bagley, Cornwall & McCarthy, Salt Lake City, 1976-82, shareholder, 1982-98; also bd. dirs. Van Cott, Bagley, et al, Salt Lake City, 1993-97, chmn. tax and estate planning sect., 1995-98; ptnr. Stoel, Rives, LLP, Salt Lake City, 1998—; adj. faculty Brigham Young U. Law Sch., Provo, 1993. Co-author: Practical Estate Planning Techniques, 1990. Planned giving com. Restoration Cathedral Madeleine, Salt Lake City, 1991-93; pres. Utah Planned Giving Roundtable, Salt Lake City, 1994, Salt Lake City Estate Planning Coun.; planned giving com. U. Utah Hosp. Found., 1994; bd. dirs. Salt Lake C.C. Found., 1982-98; stake pres. LDS Ch. David O. Mackay scholar Brigham Young U., 1967-73. Fellow Am. Coll. Trust and Estate Counsel; mem. ABA (real property, probate and trust sect., taxation sect.), Utah State Bar (exec. com., past chmn. estate planning probate sect.), Harvard Alumni Assn. Utah (chair bd. dirs. 1980-90), Harvard Law Sch. Assn. Utah (vice chair). Republican. Mem. LDS Ch. Avocations: skiing, reading, golfing. Office: Stoel Rives LLP 201 S Main St Ste 1100 Salt Lake City UT 84111-4904

ADAMS, JOSEPH LEE, JR., history educator, mayor; b. Kansas City, Mo., Jan. 5, 1944; s. Joseph L. and Thelma L. (O'Neal) A.; children: Joseph L. III, Patrick J. BA, U. Mo., Kansas City, 1970, MA, 1971; postgrad., Washington U., 1977-80. Prof. history St. Louis C.C.-Meramec, Kirkwood, Mo., 1971—. City coun. mem. City University City, Mo., 1974-95, mayor pro-tem, 1986-95, mayor, 1995—; mem. Mo. Citizens for Rsch. and Ext., 1980-88, v.p., 1983-85; mem. Midland and Pathfinder Dist. Com., Boy Scouts Am., 1981-86, vice-chmn., 1985-86, chmn. Friends of Scouts Fund Raising Pathfinder Dist., 1985-86; steering com. transp. planning for small and medium cmtys. NRC, 1982-83; chmn. fin. com. Episcopal Ch. of the Holy Communion, 1985-89, chairperson bldg. fund, 1986-88, vestry-sr. warden, 1992-95; mem. Gov. Mo. Commn.on Intergovernmental Co-Operation, 1985—, vice-chair, 1995—; mem. Citizens for Modern Transit Bd. Dirs., 1993-97, by laws rev. com., 1995; mem. Young Audiences Bd. Dirs., 1996—; chmn. transp. com. St. Louis County Mcpl. League. Mem. Nat. League Cities (transp. and comm. policy com. 1979-81, transp. and comm. steering com. 1982-91, vice chair transp. and comm. steering com. 1988, chair telecom. subcom. 1991, alt. resolution com. 1991, bd. dirs. 1991-93, bd. rep. to transp. and comm. 1993, policy com. bd. dirs. 1993, adv. coun. 1993—, adv. coun. rep. transp. and com. 1993, resolution com. 1995, vice chair 1994-95), Mo. Mcpl. League (cmty. devel. com. 1978-81, nominating com. mem. 1980, 91, bd. dirs. 1981-86, 97-98, v.p. 1998-99, pres. 1999—, fin. and taxation com. 1981-84, chair bds. league fin. com. 1984-86, chair league intergovernmental rel. com. 1987-92, resolution com. 1987-91, 96-97, chair resolution com. 1995-96). Avocation: golf. Home: 924 Wild Cherry Ln University City MO 63130-2724 Office: 6801 Delmar Blvd University City MO 63130

ADAMS, KELLY LYNN, emergency physician; b. High Point, N.C., Oct. 17, 1959; d. Roger Lee and Kathryn Maxine (Floyd) A. AA in Gen. Studies, U. Md., 1979; BA in Biology, Va. Intermont Coll., 1980; DO, Southeastern Coll. Osteo. Med., 1988. Cert. Am. Coll. Osteopathic Family Physicians. Emergency physician Humana South Broward, Hollywood, Fla., 1989-91; family practice physician Adams and Herzog, DO, PA, Plantation, Fla., 1990-91; emergency physician Homestead (Fla.) AFB, 1991-92, Mariners Hosp., Tavernier, Fla., 1991-93, Meml. Hosp., Pembroke Pines, Fla., 1992-96, Comp Health, Salt Lake City, 1996-98, 99—, St. Francis Med. Ctr., Honolulu, 1998-99, Hawaii EMI Med. Svcs., Honolulu, 1998-99. Recipient Cert. of Merit, State of Fla. and Fla. N.G., 1992, Physicians Recognition award, AMA, 1995, 98. Mem. AMA, Am. Osteo. Assn., Am. Coll. Osteo. Emergency Physicians (publ. com.), Am. Coll. Osteo. Family Physicians, Fla. Osteo. Med. Assn., Assn. Emergency Physicians, Am. Assn. Physician Specialists, Mensa. Republican. Avocations: reading, hiking. Home and Office: 11751 SE 16th Ln Morriston FL 32668

ADAMS, KENNETH FRANCIS, automobile manufacturing company executive; b. Danbury, Conn., Feb. 4, 1946; s. Donald and Evelyn Trocola (Mulvihill) A.; m. Annette Talarico, Sept. 28, 1968; children: Amy, Ella Louise, Elizabeth. Student Mt. St. Mary's Coll., 1964-68. C.P.A., Conn. Mgr., Price Waterhouse & Co., Bridgeport, Conn., 1968-74; v.p. fin. and adminstrn., dir. Saab Cars USA, Inc., Norcross, Ga., 1974—; pres. SaabFin. Svcs, Corp. Served with USAR, 1968-74. Mem. AICPA, Conn. Soc. CPAs, Fin. Exec. Inst., Inst. Mgmt. Accts.. Roman Catholic. Office: Saab Cars USA Inc 4405 International Blvd Ste A Norcross GA 30093-3205

ADAMS, KENNETH ROBERT, gaming analyst, writer, consultant, historian; b. Carson City, Nev., Sept. 8, 1942; s. Maurice Adams and Gertrude Aloha (Wilson) Burke; children: John Anthony, James. Prin. Ken Adams and Assoc., Sparks, Nev., 1990—; coord. gaming history series of the oral history program U. Nev., continuing edns. gaming mgmt. program adv. com., 1988-97, chmn., 1988. Co-author: Playing the Cards That Are Dealt, 1992, Always Bet on the Butcher, 1994, War Stories, 1995; publ., assoc. editor: Nev. Gaming Almanac, 1991-97, Nev. Gaming Directory, 1993-97, The Adams Report. Chmn. mktg. com. Downtown Improvement Assn., 1994—; steering com., chmn. gaming com. Festival Reno, 1984-86; mem. adv. bd. Leadership Reno Alumni Assn., 1995-97. Mem. Internat. Platform Assn. Fax: (702) 322-7806. Office: Ken Adams and Assocs 210 Marsh Ave Ste 103 Reno NV 89509-1625

ADAMS, KENNETH STANLEY, JR. (BUD ADAMS), energy company executive, football executive; b. Bartlesville, OK, Jan. 3, 1923; s. Kenneth Stanley and Blanch (Keeler) A.; m. Nancy Neville, Oct. 26, 1946; children: Susan (Mrs. Thomas S. Smith), Amy, Kenneth Stanley III. Student, Menlo Coll., 1940-41, U. Kans., 1941-44. Chmn. bd. Adams Resources & Energy, Inc., Houston; vp. Travel House of Houston; owner Bud Adams Ranches, KSA Industries, Inc.; owner, pres. Houston Oilers, 1946-97, Tenn. Titans, Inc., Nashville, 1997—; owner Southwest Lincoln-Mercury, Inc., Southwest Motor Leasing; from adv. dir. to owner First City Nat. Bank Houston, Houston, TX; adv. dir. Am. Bank & Trust Co. Houston., Houston, TX. Mem. exec. bd. Sam Houston Area council Boy Scouts Am.; trustee Profl. Football Hall Fame. Served with USNR, 1943-46. Named Houston Salesman of Year, 1960, Mr. Sportsman of 1961, Westerner of Year, 1969. Mem. Tex. Ind. Producers and Royalty Owners Assn., Ind. Petroleum Assn., Am., Houston Assn. Petroleum Landmen, Houston Geol. Soc., Sigma Chi (named Significant Sig 1963). Clubs: River Oaks Country, Houston, Petroleum, 100 of Houston. Office: care Tenn Titans Baptist Sports Park 460 Great Circle Rd Nashville TN 37228*

ADAMS, LAURA ANN, critical care nurse; b. Thibodaux, La., Mar. 17, 1960; d. John Anthony Sr. and M. Elma Theresa (Dufrene) A. AD, Nicholls State U., Thibodaux, 1981, BSN, 1988. RNC, La.; cert. neonatal intensive care. Staff nurse South La. Med. Ctr. (now Leonard J. Chabert Med. Ctr.), Houma, 1981-89, 90-94, Earl K. Long Med. Ctr. (now LSU/Earl K. Long Med. Ctr.), Baton Rouge, 1992—. Mem. ANA, Nat. Assn. Neonatal Nurses, Nat. League of Nurses, La. League Nurses, La. State Nurses Assn. Home: PO Box 356 Cut Off LA 70345-0356

ADAMS, LAWRENCE EARL, educator; b. Radford, Va., Mar. 3, 1953; s. Charles Robet A. and Susan Elizabeth Anderson; m. Elizabeth Gordon Rector, Aug. 7, 1976; children: Katherine Virginia, Rachel Elizabeth, Charles Nathaniel. BA, U. Richmond, 1975; MA, U. Va., 1984, PhD, 1987. Policy analyst U.S. Ho. of Reps., Budget Com., Washington, 1987-89; dir. rsch. Inst. Religion & Democracy, Washington, 1989-93; assoc. prof. politics North Park U., Chgo., 1993-96; program, rsch. dir. ctr. univ. programs U. Va., Charlottesville, 1996—; cons. in field. Mem. Am. Polit. Sci. Assn., Christian in Polit. Sci. Episcopalian. Office: U Va 104 Midmont Ln Charlottesville VA 22903

ADAMS, LEE STEPHEN, lawyer, banker; b. St. Louis, June 3, 1949; s. Albert L. and Margaret C. (Donoghue) A. A.B., Rutgers Coll., 1971; J.D., Georgetown U., 1974. Bar: D.C. 1975, Mo. 1975, Ohio 1982, Calif. 1995. Asst. dean Georgetown U. Law Ctr., Washington, 1974-76, adj. prof. law, 1973-76; sr. counsel to bd. govs. FRS, Washington, 1976-81; v.p., gen. counsel Fed. Res. Bank, Cleve., 1981-82, sr. v.p., gen. counsel, 1982-86; dep. gen. counsel Bank One Corp., Columbus, Ohio, 1986-95, v.p., gen. counsel, 1986-91; of counsel Morrison & Foerster, San Francisco, 1995-98, Washington, 1999—; lectr. law Cath. U. Law Sch., Washington, 1977-81. Mem. Athletic Club (Columbus), Columbus Country Club. Home: 4309 Torchlight Cir Bethesda MD 20816 Office: Morrison & Foerster 2000 Pennsylvania NW Washington DC 20006

ADAMS, LEE TOWNE, lawyer; b. Chatham, Ont., Can., July 12, 1922; came to U.S., 1923; s. Lee Eugene and Josephine Towne A.; m. Muriel Kathryn Stang, June 29, 1946; children: Nancy Louise, Carol Josephine, Jane Bertha. BA, U. Rochester, 1943; JD, Yale U., 1949. Atty. pvt. practice, Forestville, N.Y., 1949-72; mcpl. atty. various towns and villages, 1955-72; judge State of N.Y., Chautauqua County, 1992-93; retired, 1993—. Trustee Presbytery of Western N.Y., 1970-796; dir., vice chmn. Presbyn. Homes N.Y., 1984-90. Lt. USN, 1943-46. Mem. VFW, Am. legion, Submarine Vets. WWII, Masons, Jamestown Consistory, Ismaila Temple, Phi Beta Kappa. Republican. Avocations: gardening, reading. Home: 21 Pearl St PO Box 306 Forestville NY 14062

ADAMS, LESLIE, composer; b. Cleve., Dec. 30, 1932; s. Harrison and Jessie (Manease) A. MusB, Oberlin Conservatory, 1955; MusM, Long Beach State U., 1964; PhD in Music, Ohio State U., 1974. Composer opera Blake, (premiered by the Municipal Opera Co. of Balt., Inc., Oct. 24, 1997), numerous orchestral works performed by Cleve. Orch., Buffalo Philharm., Indpls. Symphony, Savannah Symphony, Detroit Symphony, Prague Radio Symphony, Iceland Symphony. E-mail: CreativeArts@webtv.net. Home: 9409 Kempton Ave Cleveland OH 44108-2940

ADAMS, LILIANA OSSES, music performer, harpist; b. Poznan, Poland, May 16, 1939; came to U.S., 1978, naturalized, 1990; d. Sylwester and Helena (Koswenda) O.; m. Edmund Pietryk, Sept. 4, 1965 (div. Aug. 1970); m. Bruce Meredith Adams, Feb. 3, 1978. MA, Music Acad. Poznan, Poland, 1971. Prin. harpist Philharm. Orch. of Szczecin, Poland, 1964-72, Imperial Opera and Ballet Orch., Tehran, Iran, 1972-78; pvt. music tchr. Riyadh, Saudi Arabia, 1979-81; soloist Austrian Radio, 1981-86; solo harpist, pvt. tchr. harp and piano Antioch, Calif., 1986—; music cons. Schs. and Librs., Calif., 1991—. Contbr. articles to profl. jours. Mem. Am. Fedn. of Musicians, Am. Harp Soc., Music Tchrs. Assn. Calif., Internat. Soc. of Harpers, U.K. Harp Assn., Internat. Harp Ctr. (Switzerland). Fax: 925-778-0174. E-mail: harpliliana@home.com. Home: PO Box 233 Antioch CA 94509-0023

ADAMS, LINAS JONAS, gastroenterologist; b. Akron, Ohio, May 2, 1955; s. Vladas and Veronika (Somkaite) A.; m. Elaine Kay Bulchik, Aug. 30, 1980; children: Jillian, Jonas, Nikolas, Madeline. MD, U. Autonoma of Guadalajara, Mex., 1978. Diplomate Am. Bd. Internal Medicine with subspecialty in gastroenterology; lic. physician, Tenn., Ky. Rotating intern St. Thomas Hosp. Med. Ctr., Akron, 1978-79; intern in internal medicine Tijuana BC Mex./Mexican Social Svc., 1979-80; resident Akron City Hosp., 1980-83; fellow in gastroenterology U. Ky. Med. Ctr., Lexington, 1983-86, clin. scholar, 1985-86; staff physician VA Hosp., Lexington, 1985-88; asst. prof. medicine U. Ky. Med. Ctr., Lexington, 1986-88; clin. asst. prof. medicine U. Tenn. Med. Ctr., Knoxville, 1988-89, asst. prof. medicine, 1989-94, assoc. prof. medicine, 1994—; physician dir. nutritional support team VA Med. Ctr., Lexington, 1984-86, fellowship dir. divsn. digestive diseases and nutrition, 1985-86, dir. therapeutic endoscopy, 1985-88, med. supr. D.R.G. allocations, 1985-88; co-dir. drug studies divsn. digestive diseases and nutrition U. Ky., 1985-88; dir. gastroenterology clinic U. Tenn. Med. Ctr., Knoxville, 1988—, dir. gastro-intestinal endoscopic, diagnostic and therapeutic lab., 1989—, chief divsn. gastroenterology and nutrition, 1989—; med. cons. Contbr. numerous articles to profl. jours., chpts. to books. Grantee U. Tenn. Physicians Med. Edn. and Rsch. Found., 1993—, Karl Storz Endoscopy-Am., Inc., 1990-91, VA, 1987-88, Smith, Kline and French, 1986-88, VA Coop. Studies Program, 1986-90, Upjohn Co., 1986-87, Eli Lilly and Co., 1985-87. Fellow Am. Coll. Gastroenterology; mem. ACP, Nat. Assn. Residents and Interns, Am. Gastroenterology Assn., Am. Soc. Parenteral and Enteral Nutrition, Am. Soc. Gastrointestinal Endoscopy, Ky. Soc. Gastrointestinal Endoscopy, Knoxville Acad. Medicine, Tenn. Med. Assn., tenn. Soc. Gastrointestinal Endoscopy, Crohn's Colitis Found. Am., Am. Soc. Internal Medicine, So. Med. Assn., Internat. Assn. Pancreatology, Am. Lithotripsy Soc., Am. Endosonography Club. Avocations: fishing, camping. Office: University Gastroenterology Physicians Office Bldg 1924 Alcoa Hwy # 100 Knoxville TN 37920-1511

ADAMS, LORETTA, marketing executive. BS in Internat. Mktg., Am. U., 1962; postgrad. in Econs., U. Panama, Panama City, 1963-64. Mgmt. trainee Sears Roebuck & Co., Panama City, Panama, 1962-63, mgmt. pers., 1963-65; supr. internat. advertising projects Kenyon & Eckhardt Advertising, Inc., N.Y.C., 1965-68; asst. rsch. dir. divsn. L.Am. and Far E. Richardson-Vicks Internat., Mexico City and Wilton, Conn., 1968-69, rsch. dir. divsn. Mex. and L.Am., 1969-75, mem. top mgmt. strategic planning team, 1975-78; founder, pres. Mkt. Devel., Inc., San Diego, 1978—. Contbr. articles to profl. jours. Mem. Am. Mktg. Assn., European Soc. for Opinion & Market Rsch., Advt. Rsch. Found., Coun. Am. Survey Rsch. Orgns., Market Rsch. Assn. Office: Market Devel Inc 600 B St Ste 1600 San Diego CA 92101-4584

ADAMS, LORRAINE, reporter. BA in English, Princeton U., 1981; MA in English, Columbia U., 1982. With The Concord (N.H.) Monitor, 1983, 84, The Dallas Morning News, 1984-92; with The Washington Post, 1992-93, projects reporter, 1993—. Recipient Pulitzer Prize for investigative reporting, 1992. Office: Washington Post 1150 15th St NW Washington DC 20071-0002*

ADAMS, MARGARET BERNICE, retired museum official; b. Toronto, Ont., Can., Apr. 29, 1936; came to U.S., 1948, naturalized, 1952; d. Robert Russell and Kathleen Olive (Buffin) A.; m. Alberto Enrique Sánchez-Quiñonez, Nov. 30, 1956 (div. 1960). AA, Monterey Peninsula Coll., 1969; BA, San Jose State U., 1971; MA, U. Utah, 1972. Curator ethnic arts Civic Art Gallery, San Jose, 1971; staff asst. Utah Mus. Fine Arts, Salt Lake City, 1972; lectr./curator Coll. Seven, U. Calif., Santa Cruz, 1972-74; part-time educator Cabrillo Coll., Aptos, Calif., 1973, Monterey Peninsula Coll., 1973-84; dir. U.S. Army Mus., Presidio of Monterey, 1974-83; chief. mus. br. Ft. Ord Mil. Complex, 1983-88; Guest curator Am. Indian arts Monterey Peninsula Mus. Art, 1975-88. Author: Indian Tribes of North America and Chronology of World Events in Prehistoric Pueblo Times, 1975, Historic Old Monterey, 1976; cntbg. editor Indian Am., (exhibit catalogue) Writing on the Wall: WWII Patriotic Posters, 1987; contbr. articles to jours. Mem. native Am. adv. panel AAAS, Washington, 1972-78; mem. rev. and adv. com. Project Media, Nat. Indian Edn. Assn., Mpls., 1973-78; working mem. Program for Tng. Am. Indian Counsellors in Alcoholism Counselling and Rehab. Programs, 1972-74; mem. hist. adv. com. Montery County Bd. Suprs., 1987-89. Grad. fellow, dean's scholar U. Utah, 1972; dean's scholar Monterey (Calif.) Peninsula Coll., 1969, San Jose (Calif.) State U., 1971. Mem. Am. Anthrop. Assn., Am. Assn. Museums, Soc. for Applied Anthropology, Soc. Am. Archeology, Am. Ethnol. Soc., Nat., Calif., Indian edn. assns. Home: PO Box 51983 Pacific Grove CA 93950-6983

ADAMS, MARILYN KAY, music educator; b. Feb. 18, 1935. BA, Miami U., Oxford, Ohio, 1982, MA, 1984. Pvt. practice music educator, 1960—; dir. mus. activities MidFest Internat., 1988-91. Pres. Furukawa Japan Sister City Orgn., Middletown, Ohio, 1992—; U.S. rep. to Internat. Sister City Summit, Sendai, Japan, 1997. Mem. Music Tchrs. Nat. Assn. (nat. cert. tchr. piano and organ), Ohio Music Tchrs. Assn. (chmn. student activities 1968-70), Phi Beta Kappa, Phi Eta Sigma, Alpha Kappa Delta.

ADAMS, MARK, coach. BA in History, Western Mich. U., 1987; M in Counseling and Human Devel., Hardin-Simmons U., 1992. m. Kim Adams; children: MacKenzie, Liam. Asst. men's basketball coach Hardin-Simmons U., 1988-89, head coach, 1989-93; asst. coach Baylor U., 1993-94; asst. coach U. Calif., Irvine, 1995-97, head coach, 1997—. Named Coach of Yr. Tex. Intercollegiate Athletic Assn., 1993. Office: U Calif Irvine Womens Athletic Dept Crawford Hall-Athletics Irvine CA 92697-4500*

ADAMS, MARK, retail executive. CFO Hechinger Investments, Largo, Md. Office: Hechinger Investments 1801 Mccormick Dr Largo MD 20774-5326*

ADAMS, MARK A., city manager; b. Lewiston, Maine, Sept. 3, 1963; s. David E. and Virginia S. (Gardner) A.; m. Katerine A. Penley, Aug. 3, 1985; chidlren: Tucker A., Tanner A. BA in Public Mgmt., U. Maine, 1985. Adminstrv. officer City of Lewiston, Maine, 1985-87, asst. city adminstr., 1987-95; asst. city mgr. City of Auburn, Maine, 1995—; chair Lewiston-Auburn Transit Com., 1988—, Lake Auburn Waterstd. Commn., 1993—; mem. St. Mary's Hosp. Found., 1994—, Ctrl. Maine Tech. Coll. Bd., Auburn, 1990—. Mem. Internat. City Mgmt. Assn. Office: City of Auburn 45 Spring St Auburn ME 04210-6907

ADAMS, MARK DAVID, molecular biologist; b. Chapel Hill, N.C., Aug. 26, 1962; s. John Berry and Mary Elizabeth (Goslin) A.; m. Kathryn Colville Betts, Aug. 2, 1986; children: Harrison, Jocelyn. BA in Chemistry, Warren Wilson Coll., 1984; MS in Biol. Chemistry, U. Mich., 1986, PhD in Biol. Chemistry, 1990. IRTA fellow Nat. Inst. Neurol. Disorders and Stroke/NIH, Bethesda, Md., 1990-92, staff fellow, 1992; asst. investigator Inst. for Genomic Rsch., Rockville, Md., 1992-96; investigator, head dept. eukaryotic genomics Inst. for Genomic Rsch., Rockville, 1996-98; v.p. for genome programs Celera Genomics, Rockville, 1998—. Editor: Automated DNA Sequencing, 1994; contbr. articles to profl. publs. Democrat. Office: Celera Genomics Corp 45 W Gude Dr Rockville MD 20850-1159

ADAMS, MARY RAPRICH, retired nursing education administrator; b. Lonoke, Ark., July 25, 1918; d. Fred A. and Katie (Kittler) Raprich; children: Richard, Dorothy A. Grad., St. Vincent Infirmary, Little Rock; BSN, Case Western Res. U., 1951, MSN, 1953. Sr. asst. nurse officer USPHS, 1944-48; head nurse, supr. Ohio USPHS, Ohio, 1954-58; instr. nursing edn. Akron (Ohio) City Hosp. Sch. Nursing, 1954-58, Akron Gen. Hosp. Sch. Nursing, 1958-60; dir. nursing edn. affiliate program pediatrics Children's Hosp., Akron, 1961-83, ret. Sr. asst. nurse officer USPHS, 1944-48. Mem. Nat. League for Nursing, Sigma Theta Tau. Home: 1146 Raprich Rd Lonoke AR 72086-9271

ADAMS, MENDLE EUGENE, minister; b. Bath County, Va., July 1, 1938; s. Earl and Margaret M. (Godsey) A.; m. N. Ruth Williams, Feb. 2, 1957; children: David Mendle, Brian Richard, Josef Wayne, Vicki Ruth. AB, Ind. Wesleyan U., 1967; MA in Religion, Christian Theol. Sem., 1969; postgrad., Aquinas Coll., 1977, Harvard U., 1978. Ordained to ministry Meth. Ch. as deacon, 1968, as min., United Ch. of Christ, 1981; orders accepted The Old Cath. Order, 1993. Pastor Windfall (Ind.) Pilgrim Ch., 1960-63, Mt. Olive Meth. Ch., Marion, Ind., 1963-67, Mt. Comfort United Meth. Ch., Indpls., 1967-69, United Meth. Cir., Donnybrook, Maxbass, Lansford, N.D., 1979, Hope Congl. United Ch. of Christ, Granville, N.D., 1980-82, 1st Congl. United Ch. of Christ, McPherson, Kans., 1982-87; chaplain ecumenical campus Okla. State U., Stillwater, 1987-91; interim pastor Peace United Ch. of Christ, Loyal, Okla., 1988, 1st Christian Ch. (Disciples of Christ), Stillwater, 1990, Bethel Congl. Ch., Edmond, Okla., 1991; organizing min. High Point United Ch. of Christ, Boone County, Ky., 1991-99; pastor St. Peter's United Ch. of Christ, Cin., 1997—; ednl. trips to Israel-Palestine, 1980, Nicaragua, 1983, The Philippines, 1985. Co-author: Touching Center Adventures in Christ Consciousness, 1990. Mem. Ind. Ho. of Reps., 1975-76, Ind. Solid Waste Com., 1976; mem. Ind. and Okla. group for Equal Rights Ammendment to U.S. Constn., 1977, 81; bd. dirs. McPherson Family Life Ctr., 1983-84, Interfaith Chapel, Cin./No. Ky. Internat. Airport, 1992—; chmn. com. McPherson Community Nursing Home, 1984; mem. Gov.'s Task Force on AIDS, Okla., 1987-88, Gov.'s Cabinet on Children's Issues, 1988-91, Ecumenical Coun. on Maternal and Infant Health, So. Gov.'s Leadership Coun., 1989-91; cert. mediator Okla. Dispute Resolution, Supreme Ct. Okla., 1991; mem. Chs. Uniting in Global Mission, 1992—; co-chmn. United Ch. Assembly of Greater Cin. Recipient Honored Legislator citation Ind. Coun. Chs., 1976. Mem. Masons. Democrat. Home: 6113 Webbland Pl Cincinnati OH 45213-1405 *Upon being ordained Deacon, Bishop Richard Raines counseled, "The Divine call is where your abilities intersect human needs." I have sought to discern that call and respond in Christ's name; trusting in Providence for a spiritual legacy.*

ADAMS, MICHAEL FRED, university president, political communications specialist; b. Montgomery, Ala., Mar. 25, 1948; s. Hubert W. and Jean (Taylor) A.; m. Mary Lynn Ethridge, June 7, 1969; children: David Winston, Stephen Taylor. BA, Lipscomb U., 1970; MA, Ohio State U., 1971, PhD, 1973. Asst. prof. Ohio State U., 1973-74; chief of staff for Sen. Howard Baker, Washington, 1975-79; advisor to gov. State of Tenn., Nashville, 1981-82; v.p. Pepperdine U., Malibu, Calif., 1982-88; pres. Centre Coll. Ky., Danville, 1988-97, U. Ga., Athens, 1997—; chmn. Nat. Assn. Ind. Colls. and Univs., 1995-96; bd. dirs. Ky. Ctr. Pub. Issues, Assoc. Colls. of South; mem. coun. for advancement and support of edn. NCAA Pres. Commn., 1992-94; chmn. Commn. on Colls. of So. Assn. Colls. and Schs.; vice chmn. task force that founded Coun. for Higher Edn. Accreditation; bd. dirs. Am. Coun. on Edn. Author: Rhetorical Strategies of Howard Baker, 1973; contbr. articles to various publs. Pres. Circle K Internat., Chgo., 1970; nominee for U.S. Congress, Nashville, 1980; mem. site host com. 1984 Olympiad, L.A.; elder Christian Ch. Recipient Bronze Quill award Internat. Assn. Bus. Communicators, 1986, Excellence award Nat. Sch. Pub. Relations Soc., 1985; Ohio State U. grad. fellow, 1970-73. Mem. Young Pres. Orgn., Speech Comm. Assn., Ctr. for Study of Presidency, Univ. Club (N.Y.C.). Republican. Avocations: golf, reading, travel. Office: U Ga Lustrat House Athens GA 30602

ADAMS, MICHAEL JOHN, air force non-commissioned officer; b. Buffalo, May 20, 1958; s. Raymond Francis and Ruth Margaret A.; m. Heidi Luise Gehling, June 5, 1998. AS in Bus. Adminstrn., Onondaga C.C., Syracuse, N.Y., 1980; AS in Comm. Ops. Tech., Community Coll. of the Air Force, 1983. Enlisted USAF, 1981, advanced through grades to tech. sgt., 1996; operator giant talk radio ops. 2006th Communications Group, SAC, Incirlik Air Base, Turkey, 1982-83; frequency mgr. combat crew communications 2019th Communications Squadron, Griffiss AFB, N.Y., 1983-85; frequency mgr. info. network USAF in Europe, Comiso Air Sta., Sicily, Italy, 1985-86; supr. mil. affiliate radio system 2045th Communications Group, Andrews AFB, Md., 1986-87, supr. ops. satellite communications, 1987-89; unit tng. mgr. 2045th Communications Group, 1989-91; sr. operator Global Command and Control Sta., 1956th Communications Group, Yokota Air Base, Japan, 1991-93; mgr. unit tng. 374th Comm. Squadron (PACAF), Yokota AFB, Japan, 1993-95; unit tng. mgr. 374th Maintenance Squadron, Yokota AFB, Japan, 1995-96; noncommd. officer-in-charge tng. systems mgmt., distance lng., civilian pers. tng. 3d Comm. Squadron, Elmendorf AFB, Alaska, 1996—, interactive video teletng. coord., 1998—. Vol. local food bank. Mem. VFW, Am. Soc. Tng. and Devel., U.S. Distance Learning Assn., Air Force Sgts. Assn., Assn. for Quality and Participation, Internat. Pers. Mgmt. Assn., Am. Legion. Republican. Lutheran. Avocations: computers, fishing, hunting.

ADAMS, MORGAN GOODPASTURE, lawyer; b. Nashville, Feb. 2, 1964; s. David Porterfield Jr. and Elizabeth Devereux (Morgan) Spiegel. BA, Bowdoin Coll., 1985; JD, Ga. State U., 1989. Bar: Ga. 1989, Tenn. 1989, D.C. 1990, U.S. Ct. Mil. Appeals 1990, U.S. Dist. Ct. (ea. dist.) Tenn. 1994, U.S. Ct. Vets. Appeals 1994, U.S. Supreme Ct. 1997. Litigation assoc. Luther Anderson Cleary & Ruth, Chattanooga, 1993-95; litig. ptnr. Hatfield, Van Cleave, Akers & Adams, Chattanooga, 1995-97; pvt. practice Chattanooga, 1997—. Contbg. editor ABA Family Law Lit. newsletter. Pres. Advantage Hunter, Hunter Mus., Chattanooga, 1994-95; vice chmn. Hamilton County Rep. Com., Chattanooga, 1997-99. With USMC, 1989-93; maj. USMCR, 1983-89, 93—. Bosch-Duisberg scholar Ga. State U. Coll. Law, Germany, 1989. Mem. Army Navy Club. Pachyderm Club (pres. 1997-98). Avocations: rugby, tennis, running. Office: Law Office Morgan Adams 410 McCallie Ave Chattanooga TN 37402

ADAMS, NANCY ANN, school system administrator; b. Syracuse, N.Y., Mar. 20, 1932; d. Percival William Normand and Marion Vivian (Arnold) Taylor; m. Walter Adams, June 19, 1959 (div. 1970); children: Norman, Laurie. BEd, U. Miami, Coral Gables, 1957; MEd, Fla. Atlantic U., 1969; PhD, U. Wyoming, 1981. Cert. tchr., Fla. Tchr. Broward County Schs., Ft. Lauderdale, Fla., 1957-62, rsch. asst., 1969-73, counselor high sch. srs., 1973-79, counselor adults, 1980-81, coord. adult program, 1981-94. Mem. Fla. Adminstrs. Adult Edn. (vice chmn. 1984-86, state chmn. 1994-96), Adult and Cmty. Educators of Fla. (bd. dirs. 1988-98), Am. Assn. Adult and Continuing Edn., Fla. Sch. Counselor Assn. (v.p. 1987), Adult and Cmty. Educators of Fla. (bd. dirs.). Democrat. Home: 800 NW 6th Ter Boca Raton FL 33486-3506 Office: NE Adult Ctr 700 NE 56th Ste Oakland Park FL 33334

ADAMS, NANCY R., nurse, military officer. BSN, Cornell U., N.Y. Hosp. Sch. Nursing; MSN, Cath. U. Am.; grad., Command and Gen. Staff Coll., U.S. Army War Coll. Commd. Nurse Corps, U.S. Army, 1968, advanced through grades to maj. gen., 1991; chief nurse Army Regional Med. Ctr., Frankfurt, Germany, 1987-89; nursing adminstr. various locations; nurse cons. to U.S. Surgeon Gen., 1989-91; chief Army Nurse Corps Comdr. Ctr. for Health Prom. and Prev. Medicine, U.S. Army, 1991-95; asst. surgeon gen., comdr. Ctr. for Health Promotion and Preventive Medicine, U.S. Army, 1993-95; cmdr. Tripler Army Medical Ctr., 1998—. Author textbooks; contbr. articles to profl. jours. Fellow Am. Acad. Nursing; mem. ANA, Assn. Mil. Surgeons of U.S., Am. Orgn. Nurse Execs., Sigma Theta Tau. Office: 1 Jarrett White Rd Tripler Army Medical Center HI 96859-5000

ADAMS, PAMELA JEANNE, nurse, flight nurse; b. West Palm Beach, Fla., Aug. 7, 1959; d. Walter Maxim and Dorothy Althea (Mitchell) Carlisle; m. Timothy Weldon Adams, July 1, 1978; children: Rebecca Jeanne, Brian Peter, Holly Suzanne. ASN, Palm Beach C.C., 1981. Cert. paramedic, Fla. Vol. Good Samaritan Med. Ctr., West Palm Beach, Fla., 1973-75, RN LORP and antepartum unit, 1983-95, maternal transport coord., 1992-95; emergency med. technician Atlantic P.B. Ambulance, West Palm Beach, Fla., 1979-82; RN emergency dept. Bethesda Meml. Hosp., Boynton Beach, Fla., 1981-83; asst. childbirth educator Palm Beach Med. Group, West Palm Beach, Fla., 1985-88; clin. instr. paramedics Palm Beach C.C., Lake Worth, Fla., 1986-91; RN labor and delivery Meml. Mission Hosp., Asheville, N.C., 1995—; cons., legal nurse cons. obstetric malpractice cases, Fla., 1995—; adv. com. for merger Good Samaritan Med. Ctr. and St. Mary's Hosp., 1995. Author: O.B. STAT Maternal Transport Manual, 1992; co-author: Flight Nurse Association Core Curriculum, 1996. Mem. Nat. Flight Nurses Assn., Nat. Flight Spl. Interest Group for Maternal Transports. Prebyterian. Avocations: marine aquariums, hiking, white water rafting, gardening. Home: 23 Turnberry Dr Arden NC 28704-2637

ADAMS, PAT, artist, educator; b. Stockton, Calif., July 8, 1928; d. Roy Alanson and Minerva Matilda (Smith) A.; m. Vincent John Longo, Apr. 21, 1951 (div. 1969); children: Matthew Adams, Jason Rice; m. R. Arnold Ricks III, June 24, 1972. BA, U. Calif., Berkeley, 1949; student, Calif. Coll. Arts and Crafts, 1945, Chgo. Art Inst., 1947, Bklyn. Mus. Art Sch., 1950-51. Mem. art faculty Bennington Coll., Vt., 1964-93; vis. critic of painting Sch. Art Yale U., New Haven, 1971-72, 76, 79, 82-83, Yale-Norfolk, Conn., 1987, vis. prof. painting fall semesters 1990-95; vis. lectr. Queens Coll., N.Y.C., 1972; mem. vis. faculty RISD, 1980; vis. artist U. Iowa, 1976, U. N.Mex., 1978, U. Western Ky., 1978, Columbia U., 1979, Cornell U., 1984, Mills Coll., Calif., 1987, RISD, 1989, U. Mass., Amherst, 1989, Skidmore Coll., Saratoga Springs, N.Y., 1992, Vt. Studio Ctr., 1986, 94, 97, 98, 99; artist-in-residence Dartmouth Coll., Hanover, N.H., 1994; vis. critic Vt. Coll., 1995; lectr. Marlboro Coll., Vt., 1995; colloquium Douglas Coll., Rutgers U., 1995; mem. Coll. Art Assn. Panel, 1996, Silvermine Guild Inst. for Visual Artists, 1997, Mass. Coll. of Art, 1997. One-woman shows Zabriskie Gallery, N.Y.C., biannually 1954—, Williams Coll. Mus. of Art, 1972, Rutgers U. Art Mus., 1978, Contemporary Art Ctr., Cin., 1979, Columbia Mus. Art and Sci., S.C., 1982, Va. Commonwealth U., 1982, Haggin Mus., Stockton, Calif., 1986, U. Va., 1986, N.Y. Acad. Scis., 1988, AAAS, Washington, 1988, Addison-Ripley Galleries, Washington, 1988, Pat Adams Paintings 1968-88, Berkshire Mus., 1988-89, Jaffe Friede Strauss Galleries Dartmouth Coll., Hanover, N.H., 1994; exhibited in group travelling show New Eng. Art Now; also exhibited in group shows, Montclair Art Mus., N.J., Berkshire Mus., Pittsfield, Mass., 1981, Boston Mus. Fine Arts., 1982, Mus. Fine Arts, Houston, 1982, U. Hawaii-Hilo, 1983, Lehigh U., 1983, Chrysler Mus., Norfolk, Va., 1983, Hassam Purchase Fund of Am. Acad. and Inst. Arts and Letters, 1983, 85, 89, Md. Inst. Coll. Art Meyerhoff Gallery, 1986, Yale Sch. Art Faculty, 1950-90, Marilyn Pearl Gallery, N.Y.C., 1990, Brattleboro Art Ctr., 1991, 99, Webb-Parsons Gallery, Burlington, Vt., 1991, Williams Coll. Art Mus., Mass., 1991, Bennington Coll. Usdan Gallery, Vt., 1993, Zabriskie, Paris, 1992, Nat. Acad. Mus., N.Y.C., 1992, 93, 94, 95, Associated Am. Artists Gallery, N.Y.C., 1993, Art in Embassies Program, Mexico City, 1994-97, Berne, Switzerland, 1996—, Jane Vorhees Zimmerli Art Mus., Rutgers U., N.J., 1994-95, A&A Gallery, Yale Sch. of Art, 1995, Am. Acad. Arts and Scis. Invitational Exhbn., 1996, Beth Urdang Gallery, Boston, 1997, Rider U. Art Gallery Lawrenceville, N.J., 1997, Silvermine Guild of

Art Ctr., 1998. Mem. Yaddo Found., 1972—, bd. dirs., 1980-96, vice chmn., 1985-88; trustee Vt. Coun. for Arts, 1977-81, Williamstown Regional Art Conservation Lab., 1985-86. Recipient award Nat. Coun. for Arts, 1968, Achievement award Stockton Arts Commn., 1985, award in art Am. Acad. and Inst. Arts and Letters, 1986, Jimmy Ernst award, 1996; Fulbright scholar, 1956; grantee Yaddo Found., 1954, 64, 69, 70, McDowell Colony, 1968, 72, Nat. Endowment for Arts, 1976, 87. Fellow Vt. Acad. Arts and Scis.; mem. Coll. Art Assn. (bd. dirs. 1986-90, Disting. Teaching of Art award 1984), Nat. Assn. Women Artists (hon. vice chmn. 1992), Nat. Acad. (assoc. 1992, academician 1993, 170th ann. exhbn. 1995 Andrew Carnegie prize for painting), Vt. Coun. on the Arts (Gov.'s award for Excellence in the Arts 1995), Phi Beta Kappa, Delta Epsilon. Home: 370 Elm St Bennington VT 05201-2214

ADAMS, PATRICK O., career officer; b. Cape Gireadeau, Mo.; m. Jean Marie Means; children: Patrick Jr., Christine. BS in Pub. Adminstrn., U. Mo., 1968; MS in Internat. Rels., Auburn U., 1983. Commd. 2d lt. USAF, 1968; advanced through grades to brig. gen., 1995; personnel officer Air U., Maxwell AFB, Ala., 1969-71; aide-de-camp mil. assistance and adv. group Hdqs. Command, Tehran, Iran, 1971-72; personnel officer De Nang Air Base, Republic South Vietnam, 1972-73, Udorn Royal Thai Air Base, Thailand, 1973; chief field activities Air Force Mil. Personnel Ctr., Randolph AFB, Tex., 1991, mem. air staff tng. program, 1973-75; personnel officer office asst. for col. assignments Hdqs. USAF, Washington, 1975-78, dir. svc., 1995—; personnel officer office asst. for col. assignments Air Force Manpower and Personnel Ctr., Randolph AFB, Tex., 1978-80, asst. exec., exec. officer to comdr., 1980-82; chief mil. personnel Tinker AFB, Okla., 1983-84; exec. officer to comdr. in chief Mil. Airlift Command, Scott AFB, Ill., 1985-87, dir. personnel programs, asst. sr. officer matters, 1988-90; comdr. 3440th Tech. Tng. Group Lowry Tech. Tng. Ctr., Colo., 1987-88; dir. personnel Air Mobility Command, Scott AFB, Ill., 1993-94, spl. asst. to comdr., 1994-95; chief Mil. Liaison Team Bulgaria European Command, Sofia, 1994; dir. manpower and personnel Joint Staff/J1, Washington, 1995—. Decorated Legion of Merit with oak leaf cluster, Airman's medal, Bronze Star medal. Office: Joint Staff/J1 Rm 1E948 1000 Joint Staff Pentagon Washington DC 20318-1000

ADAMS, PAUL WINFREY, lawyer, business executive; b. Ozark, Ark., July 10, 1913; s. Robert Montague and Myrtle (Johnson) A.; m. Louise Forbes Barnes, Mar. 21, 1942; children: Sally B. (Mrs. T. V. O'Connor), Thomas Fuller, Edward Montague. BS, Trinity Coll., Hartford, Conn., 1935; JD, Yale, 1938. Bar: Conn. 1938, N.Y. 1964. Practiced in Hartford, 1938-42, 45-50; asst. dean Yale Law Sch., New Haven, 1956-58; pvt. practice New Haven, 1958-64, N.Y.C., 1964-72, various locations, Conn., 1972-95; counsel Mfrs. Assn. Conn., 1939-42; pres. The Norden Labs. Corp., 1949-55. Pres. Pope-Brooks Found., 1949-89; trustee Trinity Coll., 1958-64, St. Margaret's Sch., 1967-71; founding trustee Southborough Sch., 1971-74; trustee Stone Found., 1967-92; pres. Atlantic Round, Inc., 1976-92. Served as lt. USNR, 1942-45. Dubbed Knight of White Rose by Pres. of Finland, 1993. Mem. Mountain Lake Colony (Fla.), Country Club (Fairfield, Conn.), N.Y. Yacht Club (N.Y.C.), Cruising Club of Am., N.Am. Sta. of Royal Scandinavian Yacht Clubs, Nylandska Jaktklubben (hon., Finland), Kongelig Dansk Yacht Club (hon., Denmark), Gothenburg Royal Yacht Club (hon.), Royal Norwegian Yacht Club. Home: PO Box 832 Lake Wales FL 33859-0832

ADAMS, PERRY RONALD, former college administrator; b. Parkersburg, W.Va., Sept. 16, 1921; s. Russell Douglas and Beulah Grace (Cunningham) A.; m. Ann Mallory Gillespie, Dec. 25, 1943; children—Suzanne Adams Markwell, Sally Adams Barrios. A.B., U. Ky., 1943, M.A., 1948; Ed.D., U. Fla., 1965. Instr. U. Ky., 1948-53; dir. music; U. Fla., 1953-65; dean instruction Polk Jr. Coll., Winter Haven, Fla., 1965-69; provost No. Va. Community Coll., Annandale, 1969-70; pres. Paul D. Camp Community Coll., Franklin, Va., 1970-79; vice chancellor Va. Community Coll. System, Richmond, 1979-86; ret., 1986. Served with USN, 1942-47. Kellogg fellow, 1963-65. Mem. Assn. Supervision and Curriculum Devel., Am. Assn. Higher Edn., Am. Vocat. Assn., Phi Mu Alpha (nat. councilman), Phi Delta Kappa, Kappa Delta Pi. Home: 2376 Carefree Cv Tallahassee FL 32308-5748

ADAMS, PETER FREDERICK, university president, civil engineer; b. Halifax, N.S., Can.; m. Barbara Adams, Oct. 11, 1957; 3 sons. B.Eng., N.S. Tech. Coll., 1958, M.Engr., 1961; Ph.D., Lehigh U., 1966. With Internat. Nickel Co. Can., 1958-59, Dominion Bridge Co., 1974-75; mem. faculty U. Alta., Edmonton, 1960-89, prof. civil engring., 1971-89; dean Faculty of Engring., 1976-84; pres. Ctr. for Frontier Engring. Research, 1984-89, Tech. U. N.S., Halifax, 1989-92, Can. Inst. Petroleum Industry Devel., Edmonton, Alta., Can., 1992—; dir. Churchill Corp., 1993—; lectr. in field. Author: (Krentz & Kulak) Canadian Structural Steel Design, 1973, (Krentz & Kulak) Limit States Design in Structural Steel, 1977. Past pres. Aspen Gardens Community League;past chmn. Salvation Army Red Shield Appeal. Fellow Can. Soc. Civil Engring. (Sanderson award 1986), Can. Acad. Engring., Engring. Inst. Can.; mem. ASCE (A.B. Anderson award 1986), Internat. Assn. Bridge & Structural Engring. (hon.), Can. Stds. Assn., Toastmasters (past pres.). Office: Canadian Inst Petroleum, 100 Spring Wood Ct, Edmonton, AB Canada T6E 6A1

ADAMS, PHOEBE, sculptor; b. Greenwich, Conn., 1953. BFA, Phila. Coll. Art, 1972; postgrad., Skowhegan Sch. Painting, Maine, 1977; MFA, SUNY, Albany, 1978. Solo shows include Lawrence Oliver Gallery, Phila., 1984, 86, 90, Curt Marcus Gallery, N.Y.C., 1987, 90, 94, Pence Gallery, Santa Monica, Calif., 1988, 91, Locks Gallery, Phila., 1993; exhibited in group shows at Sophia's House, Morris Gallery, Pa. Acad. Fine Arts, Phila., 1983, New Horizons in Am. Art, Exxon Nat. Exhibit, Solomon R. Guggenheim Mus., N.Y.C., 1985, Sculpture on the Wall, Aldrich Mus. Contemporary Art, Ridgefield, Conn., 1987, Sculpture Inside/Out (with catalog) Walker Art Ctr., Mpls., 1988, Works on Paper, 92, Curt Marcus Gallery, N.Y.C., 1993, Process to Presence: Issues in Sculpture 1960-1990, 1992, Les Objects d'artistes: Objects of Domestic Elegence for the Home, Locks Gallery, Phila., 1994, Small Sculpture Triennial 1993 (with catalog) Walker Hill Art Ctr., Seoul, Korea, 1993; two person exhibit Ind. U. Pa., 1993, N.S. Art and Design, Halifax, 1994, others; works in permanent collections at Solomon R. Guggenheim Met. Mus. Art, N.Y.C., Bklyn. Mus., AT&T, Chgo., Pa. Acad. Fine Arts, Phila., Pa. Conv. Ctr., Phila. Mus. Art, Storm King Art Ctr., Mountainville, N.Y., Prudential Ins. Co., Walker Art Ctr., Mpls., Harn Mus., Fla., others; commns. include: Sculpture for outdoor garden, Walker Art Ctr., Mpls., 1988, Intaglio print, Friends of the Phila. Mus. Art, 1991, sculpture Pa. Conv. Ctr., Phila., 1993. Recipient Pa. Coun. Arts awards, 1982, 84, Guggenheim Sculptor in Residence award, Chesterwood, Stockbridge, Mass., 1986; Nat. Endowment Arts fellow, 1986. Office: c/o Bellas Artes 653 Canyon Rd Santa Fe NM 87501*

ADAMS, PHOEBE-LOU, journalist; b. Hartford, Conn., Dec. 18, 1918; d. Harold Irving and Alice (Burlingame) A. A.B. cum laude, Radcliffe Coll., 1939. Reporter Hartford Courant, 1942-45; with editorial staff Atlantic Monthly, Boston, 1945—. Author: A Rough Map of Greece, 1965. Office: The Atlantic 77 N Washington St Ste 500 Boston MA 02114-1916

ADAMS, RACHEL ELIZABETH, English language educator; b. Nov. 9, 1968. BA in English summa cum laude, U. Calif., Berkeley; MA, U. Mich., 1992; PhD, U. Calif., Santa Barbara, 1997. Mng. editor Camera Obscura, Santa Barbara, 1997-97; asst. prof. English, Columbia U., N.Y.C., 1997—. E-mail: rea15@columbia.edu. Office: Columbia U Dept English 1150 Amsterdam Ave New York NY 10027

ADAMS, RANALD TREVOR, JR., retired air force officer; b. Ft. Sill, Okla., Mar. 7, 1925; s. Ranald Trevor and Mary (King) A.; m. Jeannette Malloy Chichester, May 3, 1947; children: Ranald T. III, Mary M., Jeannette M. Student, Va. Poly. Inst., 1941-43; B.S., U.S. Mil. Acad., 1946; M.S., George Washington U., 1966. Commd. 2d lt. USAF, 1946, advanced through grades to lt. gen., 1978; served in Korean conflict, 1950-51, Vietnam, 1968-69; comdr. 408 Fighter Group, 1969-71; asst. dep. chief staff ops. N.Am. Air Def. Command, 1971-73; comdr. 26 N.Am. Air Def. Command Region/Air Div. Luke AFB, Ariz., 1973-74; dep. insp. gen. inspection and safety Norton AFB, Calif., 1974-77; dir. InterAm. Def. Coll., Ft. McNair, D.C., 1977-78; chmn. Interam. Def. Bd., Washington, 1978-81; ret. Interam. Def. Bd., 1981; cons., 1981-91. Decorated Legion of Merit, Meritorious Service medal, D.S.M., D.F.C., Air medal. Mem. Air Force Assn., Order Daedalians (flight capt. 1973). Home and Office: 1002 Emerald Dr Alexandria VA 22308-2626

ADAMS, RENEE BLEDSOE, elementary school educator; b. Louisville, Mar. 7, 1947; d. Charles Henry and Irene (Russell) Bledsoe; m. Neil Douglas Adams, Apr. 13, 1968; children: Krista Lynn, Shawnda Renee. BA, U. Ky., 1970; MA, Murray State U., 1980. Cert. rank I tchr., Ky. Tchr. 1st grade Anderson County Schs., Lawrenceburg, Ky.; tchr. sci. kindergarten through 6th grades Paducah (Ky.) Ind. Schs.; presenter workshops on space and environ. edn., performance assessment. Publs. com. Childhood Edn. mag. Mem. NEA, Assn. Childhood Ednl. Internat. (pres. Ky. chpt. 1987-89, 92-94, pres. pres. coun. 1998—), Assn. Childhood Edn. (pub. com. 1988-91), Nat. Sci. Tchrs. Assn., Ky. Edn. Assn., Ky. Instrnl. Results Info. System (sci. cons. adv. com.), Ky. Ednl. Reform Act (assessment fellow), Partnership in Reform Initiative in Sci. and Math. (primary level curriculum devel. specialist), Alpha Delta Kappa, Phi Delta Kappa.

ADAMS, REX, dean; m. Ellen Cates; three children. BA in Polit. Sci. magna cum laude, Duke U., 1962. Govt. rels. trainee Mobil Internat., London, 1965-70; dir. employee and govt. rels. Mobil Oil, Libya, 1970-72; pers. dir. European ops. Mobil Oil, London, 1972-75; mgr. recruitment and placement Mobil Oil Corp., 1975-79, mgr. employee rels. exploration and producing divsn., 1979-84; v.p. employee rels. Mobil Corp., 1984-88; v.p. adminstrn. Mobil Oil Corp. and Mobil Corp., 1988-96; prof. bus. adminstrn., dean Fuqua Sch. Bus. Duke U., 1996—; bd. dirs. Pub./Pvt. Ventures, Inc., Labor Policy Assn.; chair bd. dirs. Ctr. for Econ. Policy Rsch.; trustee Com. for Econ. Devel. and Woods Holes Oceanog. Instn.; mem. Pers. Round Table Group, Bus. Round Table's Employee Rels. Com.; former trustee Duke U. and Va. Union U. Rhodes scholar Merton Coll., Oxford U., 1962. Fellow Nat. Acad. Human Resources; mem. Phi Beta Kappa. Office: Fuqua Sch Bus Duke Univ Box 90120 Durham NC 27708-0120*

ADAMS, REX M., telecommunications executive; b. Peoria, Ill., July 27, 1961; s. Kenneth E. and Ann (Meils) A.; m. Ritsuko Bates, May 25, 1987; 1 child, Miles. BS, U.S. Mil. Acad., 1983; MBA, Harvard U., 1990. Cons. Monitor Co., Cambridge, Mass., 1990-94; chief strategist Bell South Corp., Atlanta, 1994-96; v.p. Bell South Long Distance, Atlanta, 1996—. Capt. U.S. Army, 1983-88. Baptist. Home: 12155 Oak Hollow Way Alpharetta GA 30005-7280

ADAMS, RICHARD EUGENE, aerospace engineer, project manager; b. Medford, Mass., Sept. 22, 1959; s. Eugene Henry and Martha Caroline (Brown) A.; m. Shari Renée Schneider, Apr. 29, 1960; children: Brian David, Robyn Lynn. BS in Aeronautical Engring., Embry-Riddle Aeronautical U., 1983; MS in Engring. Mgmt., Drexel U., 1995. Aerospace engr. Naval Air Devel Ctr., Warminster, Pa., 1983-96; project mgr. Naval Warfare Ctr. Aircraft Divsn., Patuxent River, Md., 1996—. Recipient Navy Meritorious Civilian Svc. award 1999. Mem. AIAA (chmn. Lighter-than-Air tech. com. 1985-87), Assn. Unmanned Vehicle Syss. Achievements include contributions to development of unmanned air vehicles including Predator and Global Hawk systems, expertise in lighter than air vehicle design. Avocations: model aircraft, sailing, flying. Office: NAWCAD 22541 Millstone Rd Patuxent River MD 20670-1606

ADAMS, RICHARD GEORGE, writer; b. Newbury, Berkshire, Eng., May 9, 1920; s. Evelyn George Beadon and Lilian Rosa (Button); m. Elizabeth Acland, Sept. 26, 1949; children: Juliet Vera Lucy, Rosamond Beatrice Elizabeth. M.A., Oxford U., 1948. With Brit. Home Higher Civil Svc. Ministry Housing and Local Govt., 1948-74; asst. sec. Dept. Environ., 1968-74; writer-in-residence U. Fla., 1975, Hollins Coll., 1976. Author: Watership Down, 1972 (Guardian award Children's Lit. 1972, Carnegie Medal 1972), Shardik, 1974, (with Max Hooper) Nature Through the Seasons, 1975, The Tyger Voyage, 1976, The Adventures and Brave Deeds of the Ship's Cat on the Spanish Main: Together with the Most Lamentable Losse of the Alcestis and Triumphant Firing of the Port of Chagres, 1977, The Plague Dogs, 1977, (with Max Hooper) Nature Day and Night, 1978, Introduction to Faithful Ruslan, 1979, The Unbroken Web: Stories and Fables, 1980, Voyage Through the Antarctic, 1982, The Girl in a Swing, 1980, Maia, 1985, The Bureaucats, 1985, A Nature Diary, 1985, The Legend of Te Tuna, 1986, Traveller, 1988, The Day Gone By, 1990, Tales from Watership Down, 1996; editor, contbr. Occasional Poets, 1986. Served with Brit. Army, 1940-46. Fellow Royal Soc. Lit., Royal Soc. Arts; mem. Royal Soc. for Prevention of Cruelty to Animals (former pres.). Mem. Ch. of Eng. Home: 26 Church St, Whitechurch Hampshire, England

ADAMS, ROBERT B., financial services company executive. AB, Boston Coll., 1961; JD, NYU, 1965. Bar: N.Y. 1965. Dep. county atty. Nassau County, N.Y., 1965-67; assoc. Cullen & Dykman, 1968-70; v.p., asst. gen. counsel Chase Manhattan Corp., 1971-86; sr. v.p., dep. gen. counsel Chase Manhattan Corp., N.Y.C., 1986-97; ptnr. Kelley, Drye & Warren, N.Y.C., 1998—. Office: Kelley Drye & Warren 101 Park Ave New York NY 10178

ADAMS, ROBERT EDWARD, journalist; b. Geneseo, Ill., Apr. 27, 1941; s. Horace Mann and Florence (Beidelman) A. BS, U. Ill., 1963. Reporter Champaign-Urbana Courier, 1962-64; reporter, city staff St. Louis Post-Dispatch, 1966-72, Washington corr., 1972-93, asst. Washington bur. chief, 1981-83, Washington bur. chief, 1983-93; Washington commentator Sta. KMOX, St. Louis, 1984—; founding mem. St. Louis Journalism Rev., 1970. Recipient reporting award Nat. Civil Service League, 1975, polit. reporting award Lincoln U., Jefferson City, Mo., 1984, Raymond Clapper Meml. award for Washington Corr., 1987, citation for excellence Overseas Press Club, for series on Soviet Union, 1988; co-recipient Fgn. Corr. award Overseas Press Club Am., 1984, Nat. Headliner award, 1986. Mem. Nat. Press Club, Internat. Platform Assn., Com. to Protect Journalists, Washington Ind. Writers, The Gridiron Club, Sigma Delta Chi (Outstanding Young Reporter award St. Louis chpt. 1969). Roman Catholic. Home: 2500 Wisconsin Ave NW Washington DC 20007-4504 Office: 529 14th St NW Washington DC 20045-1000

ADAMS, ROBERT GRANVILLE, marketing professional; b. Indpls., July 2, 1927; s. Jack and Iris (Trippeer) A.; m. Marilyn Howe (div.); m. Ilona Molnar (div.); children: Lynn, Victoria, Amy. BS, Ind. U., 1953. Capt. USAF, 1945-65; various assignments as pilot Adams Mktg., Inc.; horse rancher Am. Quarter Horse Assn., Scottsdale, Ariz., 1965-88; wholesaler Nat. Home Furnishings Assn., Scottsdale, 1988—; pres. Adams Mktg., Inc., Scottsdale, 1980—. Bd. dirs. Desert Caballeros, Wickenburg, Ariz., Rancheros Visitadores, Santa Barbara, Calif. Mem. Desert Caballeros (Wickenburg, Ariz., bd. dirs.), Rancheros Visitadores (Santa Barbara, Calif.), Sigma Chi (life Loyal Sig). Avocations: horse breeding, training, riding. Office: PO Box 14350 Scottsdale AZ 85267-4350

ADAMS, ROBERT MCCORMICK, anthropologist, educator; b. Chgo., July 23, 1926; s. Robert McCormick and Janet (Lawrence) A.; m. Ruth Salzman Skinner, July 24, 1953; 1 dau., Megan. PhB, U. Chgo., 1947, MA, 1952, PhD, 1956; DSc (hon.), U. Pitts., 1985, Dartmouth Coll., 1989; LHD (hon.), Hunter Coll., CUNY, 1986, Coll. William and Mary, 1989, Brandeis U., 1992; LD (hon.), Harvard U., 1992. Archaeol. field tng. in Jarmo, Iraq, 1950-51, Yucatan, Mex., 1953; field studies history irrigation and urban settlement Iraq, Saudi Arabia and Iran, 1956-77; reconnaissance and excavation ancient Mayan settlement patterns Chiapas, Mex., 1958-61; mem. faculty dept. anthropology Oriental Inst. U. Chgo., 1955-84, assoc. prof. Oriental Inst., 1961-62, prof., 1962-84, dir. Oriental Inst., 1962-68, 81-83, dean div. social scis., 1970-74, 79-80, provost, 1982-84; sec. Smithsonian Instn., Washington, 1984-94; Homewood prof. dept. anthropology and near ea. studies Johns Hopkins U., 1984-94; adj. prof. U. Calif., San Diego, 1993—; fellow Inst. for Advanced Study, Berlin, 1995-96; resident dir. Baghdad Sch., Am. Schs. Oriental Rsch., 1968-69; chmn. assembly behavioral and social scis. NRC, 1972-76, chmn. commn. on behavioral and social scis. and edn., 1987-93. Author: Land Behind Baghdad, 1965, The Evolution of Urban Society, 1966, (with H.J. Nissen) The Uruk Countryside, 1972, Heartland of Cities, 1981, Paths of Fire, 1996; Editor: (with C. H. Kraeling) City Invincible: A Symposium on Urbanization and Cultural Development in the Ancient Near East, 1960, (with C.S. Schelling) Corners of a Foreign Field, 1979, (with N.J. Smelser and D.J. Treiman) Behavioral and Social Science Research: A National Resource, 1982, Paths of Fire: An Anthropologist's Inquiry Into Western Technology, 1996. Trustee Nat. Opinion Ctr., 1970-94, Nat. Humanities Ctr., 1976-83, Russell Sage Found., 1978-91, Santa Fe Inst., 1984—, Am. U. Beirut, 1989-94, Morehouse Coll, 1989-94, German Am. Acad. Coun., 1993-99. Recipient medal UCLA, 1989, Great Cross of Vasco Nuñez de Balboa, Panama, 1993. Fellow AAAS, Am. Anthrop. Assn., Am. Acad. Arts and Scis., Mid. East Studies Assn., Iraqi Acad. (assoc.); mem. NAS, Soc. Am. Archaeology (Disting. Svc. award 1996), German Archaeol. Inst., Am. Philos. Soc., Coun. Fgn. Rels., Soc. Antiquaries of London, Sigma Xi.

ADAMS, ROBERT WAUGH, state agency administrator, economics educator; b. Johnstown, Pa., Oct. 26, 1936; s. Robert Waugh and Mary Louise (Pyle) A.; m. Karen Day, June 13, 1964; children: Robert W. and Tara Anne Adams Mason. BS in Acctg., Pa. State U., 1958; MBA, U. Louisville, 1967. Acct., comptroller, v.p. lending Citizens Fidelity Bank, Louisville, Ky., 1959-77; dir. fin., planning, and from dep. exec. dir. to exec. dir. Ky. Housing Corp., Frankfort, 1977-96; owner Adams Consulting Co., Louisville, 1996—; past pres. Bank Adminstrv. Inst., 1966, Planning Exec. Inst., 1970, Fin. Exec. Inst., 1974. Bd. dirs. Habitat for Humanity. Capt. U.S. Army Infantry, 1958-62. Mem. Louisville Boat Club (pres.). Republican. Roman Catholic. Home and Office: Adams Cons 5210 Tamerlane Rd Louisville KY 40207-1160

ADAMS, ROGER C., lawyer. BA cum laude, Bowdoin Coll., 1966; JD, Boston Coll., 1969. With criminal divsn. U.S. Dept. Justice, 1972-93, counsel to dep. atty. gen., 1993-97, acting pardon atty., 1997, pardon atty., 1998—. Mem. Maine Bar Assn. Office: US Dept Justice 4th Fl 500 1st St NW Washington DC 20530

ADAMS, RONALD EMERSON, army officer; b. Lancaster, Pa., Dec. 28, 1943; s. Robert Harvey and Margaret May (Freeman) A.; m. Ardeelou Ann Christy, Sept. 6, 1970. MBA, Pa. State U., 1972; postgrad., Command and Gen. Staff Coll., Ft. Leavenworth, Kans., 1974-75; cert. in advanced mgmt., Carnegie-Mellon U., 1989. Commd. 2d lt. U.S. Army, 1965, advanced through grades to lt. gen., 1998; various field assignments, 1965-77; mil. asst., aide Office Sec. Army, Washington, 1977-81; bn. comdr. 2d Inf. Divsn., Republic of Korea, 1981-82; chief aviation br. U.S. Army Mil. Pers. Ctr., Alexandria, Va., 1982-84; grad. student Nat. War Coll., Washington, 1984-85; brigade comdr. 25th Inf. Div., Schofield Barracks, Hawaii, 1985-87; exec. asst., chief of staff U.S. Pacific Command, Camp Smith, Hawaii, 1987-89; asst. div. comdr. 101st Airborne Div., Ft. Campbell, Ky., Saudi Arabia, Iraq, 1989-91; dir. requirements Hdqrs. Dept. Army, Washington, 1991-94; comdg. gen. U.S. Army Aviation Ctr. and Ft. Rucker, Fort Rucker, Ala., 1994-96; asst. dep. chief staff for ops. and plans hdqs. U.S. Army, 1996-98; dep. comdr./chief staff Allied Land Forces Europe, 1998—. Decorated D.S.M., Bronze Star (3), Def. Superior Svc. medal, Legion of Merit (5); recipient Tenn. Outstanding Achievement award, 1991. Mem. Assn. U.S. Army, Army Aviation Assn. Am. (nat. bd. dirs.), Armor Assn., 101st Airborne Divsn. Assn. Methodist. Avocations: sailing, golf, reading. Home: 9 Concord Str PHV, Heidelberg Germany Office: Hdqs LANDCENT Unit 29101 Box 24 APO AE 09099-9101

ADAMS, RONALD G., middle school educator; b. Boston, July 7, 1948; s. Russell Lawrence and Alice Gertrude (LeCorn) A.; m. Patricia Marie Sullivan, Mar. 15, 1950; children: Ronald Patrick, Michael Joseph, Kevin Russell. BS, U. Mass., 1975; MEd, Cambridge Coll., 1992. Cert. tchr. Eng., reading, adult basic edn., Mass. Tchr. Eng. Quincy (Mass.) Pub. Sch., 1975-81, tchr. grade 7, 1983—; tchr. grade 7/8 Lincoln (Mass.) Pub. Schs., 1981-83; mem. adv. bd. Mass. Carnegie Coun.: Turning Points, Dept. Edn., Mass., 1991-93; founding mem. Internat. Space Educators Coun., Huntsville, Ala., 1992-93. Prodr. TV documentary Quincy Shipbuilding, 1989 (award Dept. Edn. 1990); co-author: (booklet) Not Me, I Can Handle It, 1985 (Gov.'s award 1986); cons. TV series A Century of Women, TBS, 1994 (A&E Cable award 1992). Founder Winnie the Welder Day, City of Quincy, 1991-93; coach Houghs Neck Women's Softball League, Quincy, 1980-85; vol. Cub Scouts, Weymouth, Mass., 1989-93; mem. edn. steering com. Amnesty Internat., Somerville, Mass., 1989-93; mem. adv. bd. U.S. Naval Shipbldg. Mus., Quincy, 1992-93. Recipient Nat. Ednl. award Cable in Classroom, 1992, George Washington medal Freedoms Found., 1992, Young Prodr.'s award Continental Cablevision, 1992, A World of Difference Tchr. award Anti-Defamation League, 1994, Giraffe award, Reebok Internat. Youth-in-Action Human Rights award, 1995, Minn. Advocates for Human Rights award, 1997, Domestic Partnership award US AID, 1998, Anti-defamation League's Global Activism award 1998, 99, Darryl Williams Human Rights Leadership award Northeastern U., 1999; named Tchr. of Yr., Mass. Dept. Edn., 1992, Nat. Consumers League Trumpeter award, 1998. Fellow Mass. Acad. Tchrs. (history coord. 1992-93), Boston Writing Project; mem. NEA, Nat. State Tchrs. of Yr., Nat. Coun. Social Studies, Nat. Coun. Tchrs. English, Mass. Tchrs. Assn. (Human Rights award 1991), Quincy Edn. Assn. (exe. bd. 1980-81). Avocation: N.Y. Giants football. Home: 8 Coolidge Ave Weymouth MA 02188-3605 Office: Broad Meadows Middle Sch 50 Calvin Rd Quincy MA 02169-2516

ADAMS, SALVATORE CHARLES, lawyer, speaker, financial consultant, radio and television commentator; b. Bklyn., July 10, 1934; s. Charles Joseph and Rose (Scala) A.; m. Ann Shepherdson, Aug. 3, 1957 (div. Feb. 1973); children: Mark, Scott, David, Christopher; m. Mary Jo Comstock, Dec. 8, 1990. BCE, Rensselaer Poly. Inst., 1955; MS, U. Conn., 1961; JD, U. Miami, 1968. Bar: Fla 1968, U.S. Dist. Ct. (so. dist.) Fla. 1969, U.S. Tax Ct. 1990, U.S. Ct. Appeals (11th cir.) 1974, U.S. Supreme Ct., 1974; registered profl. engr., N.Y., Conn. Pres. Motivation Cons., Miami, Fla., 1965-68; v.p. Exposition Corp., Miami, 1968-72; gen. counsel City of Pompano Beach, Fla., 1972-76; mcpl. judge Broward County, Fla., 1974-76; corp. counsel Five Star Industries, Hialeah, Fla., 1976-80; chmn., CEO Atlantic Svcs. Group, Ft. Lauderdale, Fla., 1977-86; prin. S. Charles Adams & Assocs., Ft. Lauderdale, 1986—; dir. Good Steward Ministries, 1992—; investment advisor U.S. SEC; gen. coun. Planned Giving Found., 1993—, Morgan, Howeh & Co., 1993—; dir. Planned Giving Roundtable, 1994—, Minute Man Found., 1994—, In God We Trust, 1994—. Author: Your Fiscal Fitness; creator radio commentary Your Fiscal Fitness; host talk show The Bus. Round Table; pub. Timely Tax and Money Strategies Newsletter. Bd. dirs., pres. Planned Giving Coun., 1993-96, Fla. Bar Mgmt. Sect.; del. White House Conf. on Small Bus., Washington, 1986; apptd. to joint Presdl.-Congl. Com. by Pres. Reagan, 1984; pres. Broward Planned Giving Coun., 1994-95, Broward Estate Planning Coun., endowment com. Broward Performing Arts Ctr., planned giving com. United Way, 1992—, fin. com. Honda Classic, 1988—; bd. dirs. Minute Man Found., 1995—, In God We Trust Ministries. Recipient Pres.'s award Broward County Bar Assn., 1975. Mem. Nat. Soc. Fundraising Execs. (bd. dirs. 1991—), North Broward County Bar Assn. (treas., bd. dirs.), Broward County Mcpl. Judges Assn., Nat. Inst. Mcpl. Law Officers (chmn. ethics com.), Rensselaer Poly. Inst. Alumni Assn. (pres. South Fla. chpt.), Christian Stewardship Assn., Christian Legal Soc. Republican. Avocations: golf, tennis, racquetball, sailing, travel. Office: Adams & Assocs PO Box 30488 Fort Lauderdale FL 33303-0488

ADAMS, SANDRA LYNN, principal; b. Barbourville, Ky., Oct. 29, 1948; d. Frank Walter and Mildred Opalee (Cupp) Dozier; m. Ronnie Pascal Lillard, June 13, 1970 (div. 1988); 1 child, Randolph; m. Robert Randall Adams, June 15, 1991. BA, U. Ky., 1970; MA, No. Ky. U., 1975. Tchr. English, Spanish Grant County H.S., Dry Ridge, Ky., 1970-96; sophomore vice prin. Boone County H.S., Florence, Ky., 1996—; bd. dirs. Appalachia Ednl. Lab., Charleston, W.Va., 1987-95, pres. 1994, v.p., 1993, chair Ky. caucus, 1989, 90, chair classroom instrn. com., 1988, 90. Recipient alumni award No. Ky. U., 1995, Milken Nat. Educator Award, 1993-94. Mem. Nat. Coun. Tchrs. English, Ky. Coun. Tchrs. Lang. Arts, Boone County Edn. Assn., Phi Delta Kappa, Kappa Delta Pi, Pi Lambda Theta, Sigma Delta Pi. Avocations: golf, reading. Home: 10717 Crown Pointe Dr Union KY 41091-9253 Office: Boone County HS 7056 Burlington Pike Florence KY 41042-1681

ADAMS, SARAH VIRGINIA, family counselor; b. San Francisco, Oct. 23, 1955; d. Marco Tulio and Helen (Jorge) Zea; separated; children: Mark Vincent, Elena Giselle, Johnathan Richard. BA, Calif. State U., Long Beach, 1978, MS in Psychology, 1980; MA in Christian Leadership, 1997; postgrad., Fuller Sem., 1996—. Lic. marriage, family, child counseling. Tutor math. and sci.

Montebello, Calif., 1979-82; behavioral specialist Cross Cultural Psychol. Corp., L.A., 1979-80; psychol. asst. Legal Psychology, L.A., 1980-82, Eisner Psychol. Assocs., L.A., 1982-83; assoc. dir. Legal Psychodiagnosis and Forensic Psychology, L.A., 1982-83; adminstrv. dir. Diagnostic Clinic, Calif., 1983-85; dir. Diagnostic Clinic of West Covina, Calif., 1985-87; owner Adams Family Counseling Inc., Calif., 1987—; with Health Group Psychol. Svcs., 1994—; tchr. piano, Montebello, 1973-84; ins. agent Am. Mut. Life Ins., Des Moines, 1982-84. Fellow Am. Assn. Marriage and Family Therapists, Am. Psychol. Assn.; mem. NAFE, Calif. Assn. Marriage and Family Therapists, Calif. State Psychol. Assn., Calif. Soc. Indsl. Medicine and Surgery, Western Psychol. Assn., Psi Chi, Pi Delta Phi. Republican. Roman Catholic. Avocations: piano, creative writing, drawing, collecting coins. Office: Adams Family Counseling 260 S Glendora Ave Ste 103 West Covina CA 91790-3041

ADAMS, SCOTT, cartoonist; b. Windham, N.Y.; s. Paul and Virginia Adams. MBA in Econs., Hartwick Coll., 1979. Engr. Pacific Bell, San Ramon, Calif., 1986-95; cartoonist United Features Syndicate, 1989—. Author: The Dilbert Future: Thriving on Stupidity in the 21st Century, Dogbert's Top Secret Management Handbook; creator Dilbert cartoon (syndicated in 1,550 newspapers in 35 countries worldwide). Office: c/o United Feature Syndicate 200 Madison Ave New York NY 10016-3903*

ADAMS, SHARON FARRELL, financial analyst; b. Aug. 24, 1951; d. Vincent J. and Louise (Gulick) Farrell; children: William Z., David C.; m. Charles Adams. BS in Math., Columbus State U., 1973, MPA, 1996. Cert. fin. officer, Ga. Fin. analyst Muscogee County Sch. Dist., Columbus, Ga., 1989—; participant Student Govt. Assn. Leadership Conf., Columbus State U., 1995. Bd. dirs. Columbus State U. Alumni Assn., 1984-88, 96—, sec./treas. 1985, 88, 97—, 1st v.p. 1986, 2nd v.p. 1987; sec. MPA Assn., Columbus State U., 1994—. Regents grantee U. System of Ga., 1995-96, 96-97. Mem. Govt. Fin. Officers Assn., Ga. Govt. Fin. Officers Assn., Ga. Assn. Sch. Bus. Ofcls., Pi Kappa Pi, Pi Alpha Alpha.

ADAMS, SHELBY LEE, photographer; b. Hazard, Ky., Oct. 24, 1950. BFA in Photography, Cleve. Inst. of Art, 1974; MA in Photography, U. Iowa, 1975; MFA, Mass. Coll. of Art, Boston, 1989. Instr. Cin. Art Acad., 1979, No. Ky. U., 1979; freelance photographer Pittsfield, Mass., 1980-87; head photography instr. Ill. Ctrl. Coll., East Peoria, 1981-84; asst. prof., head photography dept. Salem (Mass.) State Coll., 1985-92; comml., fine art free lance photographer Pittsfield, Mass., 1992—; workshop presenter Appalachian Environ. Photo Workshop, Pa. State U., 1993, Portrait Photography, Anderson Ranch Arts Ctr., Aspen, Colo., 1994, Environ. Portraiture, Santa Fe (N. Mex.) Photographic Workshop, 1995, Portraiture, FotoGalerie, Amsterdam, The Netherlands, 1995. Photographer: solo exhbns. include U. Ill. Chgo. Campus, 1985, Mass. Coll. of Art, Boston, 1987, Harvard Fogg Mus., Cambridge, Mass., 1989, U. Notre Dame, Ind., 1993, Internat. Ctr. Photography, Midtown Permanent Collection Gallerys, N.Y.C., 1994, Cleve. Mus. of Art, 1995, Internat. Travelling Exhbns, 1999; two person exhibits: In Pursuit of the Human Spirit (with Nicholas Nixon), Second Street Gallery, Charlottesville, Va., 1988, From the Inside (with Larry Fink), Catherine Edelman Gallery, Chgo., 1992; group exhbns.: An American Place, Chgo., 1984, Kansas City (Mo.) Art Inst., 1987, Selections 5 Polaroid Internat. Exhbn. traveling througout Europe, 1990-92, A Photographic Bestiary, Robert Koch Gallery, San Francisco, 1994; works are included in permanent collections of the Mus. of Contemporary Photography, Columbia Coll., Chgo., Art. Inst. of Chgo., Boca Raton (Fla.) Mus. of Art, L.A. County Mus. of Art, San Francisco Mus. of Modern Art, Mus. of Fine Arts, Houston, Polaroid Collection, Cambridge, Mass., Mus. of Photographic Arts, San Diego, Bayly Art Mus., U. Va.; photography used in ednl. TV prodns., Miss. Ednl. Network, 1994, Nat. PBS Broadcast, 1995; (books of photograpy) Appalachian Portraits, 1993, Appalachian Legacy, 1998. Recipient Excellence award Soc. for Contemporary Photography, Kansas City Art Inst., 1987, Gold medal Coun. for Advancement and Support of Edn., N.Y.C., 1987, Finalist award Mass. Artist Fellowship program, 1989, Finalist award Mother Jones Internat. Documentary Photography Competition, San Francisco, 1990, fellowship NEA, 1992; grantee: Elizabeth Firestone Graham Found., Akron, 1990, Polaroid Corp., 1989, 90, 91, 92. Home and Office: 3 S Church St Pittsfield MA 01201-6103

ADAMS, THOMAS LAWRENCE, lawyer; b. Jersey City, Apr. 14, 1948; s. Lawrence Ignatius and Dorothy Tekla (Halgas) A.; m. Elizabeth Anne Russell, June 14, 1969 (div. 1981); children: Thomas, Katherine; m. Deanna Louise Mollo, July 30, 1983; stepchildren: Kathy, Kerry. BS, N.J. Inst. of Tech., 1969; JD, Seton Hall U., 1975. Bar: N.J. 1975, N.Y. 1976, U.S. Dist. Ct. N.J. 1975, U.S. Patent Office 1975. Systems engr. Grumman Aerospace, Bethpage, N.Y., 1969-71; sr. engr. Weston Instruments, Newark, 1971-74; with patent staff RCA Corp., Princeton, N.J., 1974-75; corp. atty. Otis Elevator, N.Y.C., 1975-77; ptnr. Goebel & Adams, Morristown, N.J., 1978-80, Behr & Adams, Morristown & Edison, N.J., 1981—. Councilman Twp. Council, Livingston, N.J., 1985-88, dep. mayor, 1987; commr. Environ. Commn., Livingston, 1984-87; chmn. Livingston Rep. County com., 1992-98. Mem. N.J. Patent Law Assn., Morris County Bar Assn., Trial Attys. of N.J., N.J. State Bar Assn. (chair patent, trademark, copyright law and unfair competition 1991), Seton Hall Law Rev., Tau Beta Pi, Eta Kappa Nu. Roman Catholic. Lodges: K.C. (Grand Knight 1980).

ADAMS, THOMAS LYNCH, JR., lawyer; b. Fayette County, Ky., Nov. 22, 1941; s. Thomas Lynch and Amanda (Keith) A.; m. Anne Randolph, Aug. 13, 1974 (div. 1992); children: Thomas Lynch III, Randolph T., Alexander K., Andrew D. BA in History, U. Va., 1963; JD, Vanderbilt U., 1970. Bar: Ky. 1970, D.C. 1970, Tenn. 1970. Appellate atty. U.S. Dept. Justice, Washington, 1970-72; minority counsel U.S. Senate Commerce Commn., Washington, 1972-75; legal counsel SBA, Washington, 1975; asst. gen. counsel FTC, Washington, 1975-77; with govt. rels. Rep. Steel Corp., Washington, 1977-83; dep. gen. counsel U.S. EPA, Washington, 1983-86, asst. adminstr., presdl. appointee, 1986-89; ptnr. Dechert, Price & Rhoads, 1989-93; environ. dir. Internat. Paper, 1993; counsel to pres. America's Clean Water Found., 1994-95; of counsel Perkins Coie, Washington, 1995—. Lt. (j.g.) USNR, 1963-67. Mem. ABA, Ky. Bar Assn., D.C. Bar Assn., Met. Club, Beta Theta Pi.

ADAMS, THOMAS MERRITT, lawyer; b. St. Louis, Sept. 27, 1935; s. Galen Edward and Chloe (Merritt) A.; m. Sarah McCardell Davis, June 6, 1959; children: Mark Merritt, John Harrison, William Shields, Thomas Bondurant. AB, Washington U., St. Louis, 1956, JD, 1960; postgrad., London Sch. Econs., 1957; LLM, George Washington U., 1966. Bar: Mo. 1960, Calif. 1971. Atty. SEC, Washington, 1964-66; asst. dir., asst. gen. counsel Investment Bankers Assn., Washington, 1966-68; pres. Transamerica Investment Svcs., 1969-80; ptnr. Lanning Adams & Peterson, 1980—. Author: State and Local Pension Funds, 1968; contbr. articles to profl. jours. Chmn. Salina (Kans.) Community Ambassador program, 1961. Served to capt. USAF, 1960-63. Decorated Air Force Commendation medal. Mem. Phi Beta Kappa. Episcopalian. Office: Lanning Adams & Peterson 11777 San Vicente Blve #750 Los Angeles CA 90049-5067

ADAMS, THOMAS TILLEY, lawyer; b. Orchard Park, N.Y., Oct. 9, 1929; s. Floyd Tilley and Clara Elizabeth (Potter) A.; m. Virginia Rives Smith, Sept. 1, 1956; children: Julia, Janet, Claire, Douglas. BA, U. Buffalo, 1951; JD, Cornell U., 1957. Bar: N.Y. 1957, U.S. Ct. Appeals (2d cir.) 1962, U.S. Supreme Ct. 1962, Conn. 1964. Tchr. Lake Shore Cen. Sch., Angola, N.Y., 1953-54; assoc. Davies, Hardy & Schenck, N.Y.C., 1957-63; prin. Gregory & Adams P.C., Wilton, Conn. and N.Y.C., 1963—; lectr. Cornell U. Law Sch., Ithaca, N.Y., 1962-65, emeritus mem. adv. coun., 1990—; adj. assoc. prof. law Fordham U., N.Y.C., 1973-76; adviser Dana Fund Internat. and Comparative Legal Studies, Toledo, 1976-91; assoc. bd. dirs. Union Trust Co., Stamford, Conn., 1982-94; mem. adv. bd. Norwalk Savs. Soc., 1993-97. Town counsel Town of Wilton, 1966-71; pres. Five Town Found., Norwalk, Conn., 1983-85, trustee, 1989-91; chmn. bldg. com. Wilton High Sch., 1966; bd. dirs. Woodcock Nature Ctr., Wilton-Ridgefield, Conn., 1997—. Recipient Silver Beaver award Boy Scouts Am., 1980, Disting. Alumnus award Cornell Law Sch., 1990. Mem. ABA, Am. Judicature Soc. (dir. 1991-92), Norwalk/Wilton Bar Assn. (pres. 1990), Stamford/Norwalk Regional Bar Assn. (bd. dirs. 1991-93), Conn. Bar Assn. (ethics com. 1970-75, 92-93, mem. coun. bar pres.'s 1988-90), N.Y. Bar Assn., Silver Spring Country Club (gov. 1998—), Cornell Club (N.Y.), Phi Delta Phi. Episcopalian. Fax: 203 834-1628. Home: 55 Deer Run Rd Wilton CT 06897-1204 also: Rogers Rock Clb Ticonderoga NY 12883 Office: Gregory & Adams PC 190 Old Ridgefield Rd Wilton CT 06897-4023

ADAMS, THOMAS WAYNE, chemistry educator; b. Warsaw, Ind., Jan. 3, 1945; s. Leo Wayne and Mary Francis (Ball) A.; m. Rebecca Ann Bodenmiller, Aug. 20, 1967; 1 child, Robyn Michelle Axel-Adams. BS in Chemistry, Manchester Coll., 1967; MS in Sci. Edn., Fla. State U., 1969; MS in Chemistry, Purdue U., 1987, PhD in Chem. Edn., 1990. Chemistry tchr. Fla. State U. Lab. Sch., Tallahassee, 1969-70; chemistry and math. tchr. Lakeland H.S., LaGrange, Ind., 1970-73, Woodlan (Ind.) H.S., 1973-84; vis. prof. chemistry Manchester Coll., North Manchester, Ind., 1990-91; chemistry instr. Ind. Acad. for Sci., Math. and Humanities, Muncie, 1991—, chair sci. divsn., 1992-99; reviewer Jour. Chem. Edn., 1992—; mentor U.S. Nat. Chemistry Olympiad, 1994-96; reader AP chemistry Coll. Bds., 1995—; mem. H.S. test com. ACS Exams. Inst., 1997—. Contbr. articles to profl. publs. V.p., pres. Lions Club, Woodburn, 1974-84. Recipient Outstanding Sci. Tchr. award N.E. Ind. chpt. Nat. Sci. Rsch. Soc., 1982, 95, Outstanding Chemistry Tchr. award N.E. Ind. sect. Am. Chem. Soc., 1983, Tandy prize for excellence Tandy Corp., 1997. Mem. Nat. Sci. Tchrs. Assn., Am. Chem. Soc. (Cen. Regional award in h.s. chemistry tchg. 1999), Ind. Acad. Sci., Ind. Alliance Chemistry Tchrs. (pres. 1995), Hoosier Assn. Sci. Tchrs., Inc. Avocations: building/construction, mysteries, sports. Home: 6600 N CR800 W Yorktown IN 47396 Office: Ind Acad Sci Math and Humanities Ball State U Muncie IN 47306

ADAMS, TODD PORTER, financial and investment advisor; b. Nyack, N.Y., Oct. 11, 1955; s. Edmond Robert and Georgina (Porter) A.; m. Catherine Elizabeth Jarboe, Dec. 26, 1982 (div. Dec. 1985); 1 child, Danielle Elyce; m. Janine Marilyn Leduc, Jan. 29, 1994. BS, St. Thomas Aquinas Coll., 1977; MBA, SUNY, Buffalo, 1981. CFP. Acct. trainee Allied Chem., Syracuse, N.Y., 1977-78; from acct. to supr. of acctg. %, Buffalo, 1978-80; pvt. practice fin. cons. Buffalo, 1980-81; account exec. Dean Witter Reynolds, Cape Coral, Fla., 1981-82, E.F. Hutton & Co., Cape Coral, 1982-85; v.p. investments Advest, Inc., Ft. Myers, Fla., 1985-90; rep. Linsco/Pvt. Ledger, Ft. Myers, 1990—; v.p. Mills-Price & Assoc., Inc., Ft. Myers, 1990-96, 97—; investment and inf. commentator WINK-TV, 1989-94. Chmn. Jr. Olympic Torch Run, Lee County, Fla., 1990. Mem. Inst. CFPs, Nat. Assn. Investors Corp., Am. Assn. Ind. Investors, Assn. MBA Execs., Kiwanis (life, v.p. house South Ft. Myers chpt. 1984—, Kiwanian of Yr. award 1983, 95). Republican. Presbyterian. Avocations: all sports, stamp and coin collecting. Office: Mills-Price & Assoc Inc 6700 Winkler Rd Ste 3 Fort Myers FL 33919-7235

ADAMS, VICTORIA ELEANOR, retired realty company executive; b. San Francisco, Feb. 8, 1941; d. George Mulford and Sarah Louise (Dearborn) A.; m. Gene M. Richardson, 1965 (div. 1972); 1 child, Raymond; m. Franklin Carlisle Boosman, 1972 (div. 1990); 1 child, Eric; m. Harold Glen Kirchner, Mar. 14, 1992. AA, Palomar Coll., 1976; BBA summa cum laude, Nat. U., 1978. Sales adminstr. Evergreen Internat. Airlines, McMinnville, Oreg., 1983; corp. adminstr. N.N. Jaeschke, Inc., San Diego, 1984—; adminstrv. mgr. Tomlinson Agy., Inc., Spokane, Wash., 1980-86; v.p. Champion Realty Inc., Spokane, 1987-93; pub. dir. Champion Pubs., 1987-93. Editor: Bravura, 1976; (text) Science Among Us, 1965, Principles in Action Newsletter, 1992-98; author: No More than 4 Ingredients Cookbook, 1994; designer Astrology game, 1974; contbr. articles to profl. jours. Solicitor Am. Heart Assn., 1985. Recipient cert. real estate sales achievement, 1978, 82, 85, 86, 88, 89, 91; cert. outstanding contbn. to real estate edn., 1980. Avocations: writing, educational research, fishing, camping, travel. Home and Office: # 30 815 124th St SW Trlr 30 Everett WA 98204-5671

ADAMS, WARREN LYNN, publisher, business consultant; b. Clarksville, Ark., Jan. 11, 1955; s. Warren Earnest Adams and Doris Anita (Reed) Crandall; m. Pamela Jo Sullivan, Sept. 9, 1978 (div. 1995); children: Lindsay Nichelle, London Reed; m. Brenda Kay Pettigrew, Feb. 3, 1996; children: Kristin Lea Haney, Phillip Kollin Haney, Kasey Kay Haney. BA, U. Ctrl. Okla., 1978, BS, 1994; MBA, Oklahoma City U., 1996. Dir. pub. rels. Oklahoma City Zoo, 1979-80; dir. sports info. Oklahoma City U., 1980-82; chief operating officer Fite-Davis & Assocs., Oklahoma City, 1982-84; pres., CEO Lynn Adams & Assocs., Oklahoma City, 1984-88; pub. rels. technician Runkle-Moroch Advertising, Oklahoma City, 1988-89; chief operating officer Jim Fite Mktg. and Mgmt. Resources, Edmond, Okla., 1989-92; administrator Okla. Ctr. for Alcohol and Drug-Related Studies, Oklahoma City, 1992—; publ. cons. First Baptist Ch., Oklahoma City, 1984-95; bus. cons. Adams Assocs., Ninnekah, Okla., 1995—; pub., bus. mgr. Real Estate Exec. Mag., Chickasha, Okla., 1996—, Builder/Architect Mag., Chickasha, 1996—. Contbr. articles to profl. jours. Master mason Ancient, Free & Accepted Masons, Oklahoma City, 1981—; 32 Mason Okla. Scottish Rite, Guthrie, 1982—; recreation coord. First Baptist Ch., 1984-95; sec., bd. deacons 1988-90. Named Gov.'s Non-Profit Corp. of Yr., Okla. Fedn. of Parents for Drug-Free Youth, Oklahoma City, 1994. Mem. Outstanding Young Men of Am. (named Outstanding Young Men of Am. 1987, 88, 89, 92; mem. nat. nom. com.), U. Okla. Health Scis. Ctr. (OUHSC) Staff Senate. Democrat. First Christian. Avocations: antiques, science fiction, team sports participation, travel, numismatics. Home: RR 2 Box 6 Ninnekah OK 73067-9504 Office: Okla Ctr for Alcohol & Drug-Related Studies 800 NE 15th St Ste 410 Oklahoma City OK 73104-4602

ADAMS, WAYNE VERDUN, pediatric psychologist, educator; b. Rhinebeck, N.Y., Feb. 24, 1945; s. John Joseph and Lorena Pearl (Munroe) A.; m. Nora Lee Swindler, June 12, 1971; children: Jennifer, Elizabeth. BA, Houghton Coll., 1966; MA, Syracuse U., 1969, PhD, 1970; postgrad., U. N.C., Chapel Hill, 1975. Diplomate Am. Bd. Profl. Psychology. Asst. prof. Colgate U., Hamilton, N.Y., 1970-75; chief psychologist Alfred I. DuPont Inst., Wilmington, Del., 1976-86; dir. divsn. psychology, dept. pediat. DuPont Hosp. for Children (formerly Alfred I. DuPont Inst.), Wilmington, 1987—; mem. Del. Bd. Licensure in Psychology, 1983-86, bd. pres., 1986; assoc. prof. pediat. Thomas Jefferson Coll. Medicine, Phila., 1995-99; prof. psychology George Fox U., Newberg, Oreg., 1999—. Cons. editor Jour. Pediatric Psychology, 1980-83, guest reviewer, 1984—; co-author 4 nationally used psychol. tests in field; contbr. articles to profl. jours. Fellow Am. Psychol. Assn.; mem. Soc. Pediatric Psychology, Del. Psychol. Assn. (exec. com. 1979-82, pres. 1981-82). Office: George Fox U Dept Psychology Newberg OR 97132

ADAMS, WESTON, diplomat, lawyer; b. Columbia, S.C., Sept. 16, 1938; s. Robert and Helen Hayes (Calhoun) A.; m. Elizabeth Nicholson Nelson, Mar. 2, 1962; children—Robert VI, Weston III, Daniel Wallace, Julian Calhoun II. A.B. in History, U. S.C., 1960, LL.B., 1962. Bar: S.C. 1962. Research dir. S.C. Republican Orgn., Columbia, 1966-67; trust officer S.C. Nat. Bank, Columbia, 1967-70; assoc. counsel Select Com. on Crime, U.S. Ho. of Reps., Washington, 1970-71; sole practice Columbia, 1971-84, 86—; ambassador to Malawi U.S. Dept. of State, Lilongwe, 1984-86; mem. global policy coun. Nat. Security Caucus U.S. Congress. Mem. S.C. House of Reps., 1972-74; presdl. elector U.S. Electoral Coll., S.C., 1980; del. Rep. Nat. Conv., Kansas City, Mo., 1976, New Orleans, 1988, Houston, 1992, alt. del., Detroit, 1980, San Diego, 1996; mem. diplomatic adv. com. and exec. com. bus./industry adv. com. Am. Bicentennial Presdl. Inaugural, 1989; mem. U.S. presdl. del. to inauguration of Pres. of Dominican Republic, 1982; United Nations Day Chmn. for the State of S.C., honoring its 50th Anniversary, 1995; mem. UNESCO, 1982-84; active Global Policy Coun. Nat. Security Caucus of the U.S. Congress. Served to capt. USAF, 1963-66. Recipient Order of Palmetto, Gov. S.C., 1974. Mem. S.C. Bar, Richland County Bar Assn., U. S.C. Alumni Assn., S.C. Hist. Soc., U. South Carolina Hist. Soc., S.C. Geneal. Soc., S.C. Soc. of Cincinnati, Order First Families N.C., Magna Charta Barons (Somerset chpt.), St. Andrews Soc., Soc. Colonial Wars, Huguenot Soc. of S.C., Soc. Lower Richland, St. David's Soc., Jamestowne Soc., Welcome Soc. Pa., The Society of First Families of S.C. 1670-1700, The Internat. Rep. Inst., Most Venerable Order Hosp. St. John Jerusalem, Coun. Am. Ambs. Episcopalian. Club: Palmetto Columbia). Home: 303 Saluda Ave Columbia SC 29205-3032 Office: 1705 Richland St PO Box 291 Columbia SC 29202-0291*

ADAMS, WILBURN CLIFTON, communication educator; b. Huntsville, Ala., Feb. 14, 1943; s. Wilburn Clifton and Pauline Marie (Pennington) A.; m. Sara Ruth Shook, July 25, 1970; 1 child, Ami Rhae. BA, U. Ala., 1968; MS, Fla. State U., 1970, PhD, 1973. Asst. prof. Ctrl. Mo. State U., Warrensburg, 1972-77, assoc. prof., 1977-82, prof., 1982—; chmn. curriculum com. Ctrl. Mo. State U., 1987-88, chmn. stds. com., 1992-93, sponsor speech comm. soc., 1979-99, co-dir. 1st nat. officiated debate tournament, 1993. Contbr. articles to profl. jours. and local newspapers; creater games Sieze, Communication Activities Clock. Sgt. U.S. Army, 1964-66. Named Outstanding Tchr. Speech and Theatre Assn. of Mo., 1975; receipient Podium of Honor, Ctrl. Mo. Forensics Squad, 1996. Mem. Elks (trustee 1997-99, exalted ruler 1989-90). Office: Dept Comm Ctrl Mo State U Warrensburg MO 64093

ADAMS, WILLIAM D., university president; b. Pontiac, Mich., Aug. 18, 1947; s. Waldemar Harmon Adams and Charlotte Elizabeth (Drea) Rising; m. Catherine Spaulding Bruce, Oct. 10, 1993; children: Sean Douglass Vallant, Carmen Milena. BA magna cum laude, The Colo. Coll., 1972; PhD, U. Calif., Santa Cruz, 1982. Vis. asst. prof. dept. polit. sci. U. N.C., Chapel Hill, 1983-84, U. Santa Clara, Calif., 1984-85; instr. gt. works in western culture program Stanford U., Calif., 1985-86, program coord. gt. works in western culture program, 1986-88; exec. asst. to pres. Wesleyan U., Middletown, Conn., 1988-93, v.p., sec., 1993-95; pres. Bucknell U., Lewisburg, Pa., 1995—. Contrb. articles to profl. jours. 1st lt. U.S. Army, 1966-69. Home: 103 University Ave Lewisburg PA 17837-2113 Office: Bucknell U Office Pres 219 Marts Hall Lewisburg PA 17837

ADAMS, WILLIAM GILLETTE, lawyer; b. Dallas, Tex., July 26, 1940; s. Dwight B. and Ruth L. (Gillette) A.; m. Barbara A. Picoli, Jan. 24, 1970. BA in Econs., Stanford U., 1963; JD, U. Utah, 1968. Bar: Calif. 1969; registered Conseil Juridique, France. Vol. Peace Corps, Morocco, 1963-65; assoc. O'Melveny & Myers, L.A., 1968-75; ptnr. O'Melveny & Myers, 1979—; resident ptnr. O'Melveny & Myers, Paris, 1979-84; ptnr. Erickson, Zerfas & Adams, L.A., 1975-79; bd. dir. Valentine Enterprises, Inc., 1983—. Editor-in-chief Utah Law Rev., 1967-68. With USCG, 1957-58. Mem. ABA, Orange County Bar Assn., L.A. Bar Assn., Calif. Bar Assn., Cercle Union Interalliee, Big Canyon Country Club, Order of Coif, Phi Kappa Phi, Phi Delta Phi. Office: O'Melveny & Myers 610 Newport Center Dr Ste 1700 Newport Beach CA 92660-6429 also: O'Melveny & Myers 499 S Hope St Los Angeles CA 90071-1903*

ADAMS, WILLIAM HENSLEY, ecologist, educator; b. Nashville, Aug. 14, 1929; s. William Hensley and Mary Pauline (Vaughn) A.; children: Deska Lee, Norma Dee, Anita Rice, Patricia Lynn. AB, U. Tenn., 1951; postgrad., U. Okla., 1951, Tulane U., 1953-54; MS, La. State U., 1956; PhD, Auburn U., 1959. Grad. research asst. Auburn U., 1956-59; sr. research biologist Tenn. Game and Fish Commn., 1959-60; chmn. dept. biology, prof. biology Tenn. Wesleyan Coll., 1960-64, dean Coll. Arts and Scis.; prof. biology Tenn. Technol. U., Cookeville, 1964-66; with div. pre-coll. edn. in sci. NSF, 1966-68, div. undergrad. edn. in sci., 1969-73, div. higher edn. in sci., 1973-75, div. sci. edn. devel. and research, 1975-77, div. sci. improvement, 1977-81; cons., 1981—; pres. BIADA Constrn. Devel. Co. and Empire Realty Investment Co., Vienna, Va., 1990-92; broker Shipyard Real Estate, Hilton Head, S.C., 1992—; mem. NSF Research Participation for Coll. Tchrs. Highlands Biol. Sta., 1961, NSF Summer Inst. Radiation Biology Oak Ridge Inst. Nuclear Studies, 1961, NSF Summer Inst. Comparative Anatomy Harvard, 1962, NSF Summer Inst. Marine Biology Duke Marine Lab., 1963, NSF-Tenn. Acad. Sci. Vis. Scientist Program, 1962-66; dir. NSF Coop. Coll.- Sch. Sci. Program, 1963-65; mem. Commn. Undergrad. Edn. in Biol. Scis. Southeastern Regional Conf., 1965, Advanced Placement Reader in Biology, 1965; Oak Ridge Inst. Nuclear Scis. Radiation Biology Conf., 1965. Mem. Savanah River Site Citizens Adv. Bd. Served to lt. col. Med. Service Corps, USAF, 1951-53, 68-69. Recipient Sigma Xi-Research Engring. Soc. Am. grant-in-aid, 1960-61, Tenn. Wesleyan Coll. Faculty award, 1962, Tenn. Technol. U. faculty research grant, 1966. Fellow Explorers Club; mem. Am. Soc. Mammalogists (honorarium 1959), Am. Ornithologists Union, Cooper Ornithol. Soc., Wilson Ornithol. Soc., Wildlife Soc. Home: 4 Field Sparrow Ct Hilton Head Island SC 29926-1881 Office: 110 Executive Ctr Hilton Head Island SC 29928-4724 *Increasingly, people in positions of responsibility are abdicating their concomitant role as respected leaders and thereby failing to set good examples for young people to follow, especially at a time when they need high standards for self-emulation. Therefore I challenge young people to set forceful leadership as their highest personal goal in life and remember, as I have, that attainment of this goal will require the stamina necessary to remount their white chargers each time and no matter how often they are unseated.*

ADAMS, WILLIAM JOHNSTON, financial and tax consultant; b. Detroit, Nov. 24, 1934; s. William Montgomery and Sara Emogene (Johnston) A.; m. Lynn Laviolette, Aug. 24, 1957 (div. Sept. 1976); 1 child, William David; m. Donna Wolcott, Apr. 24, 1977. BBA, U. Mich., 1957, MBA, 1958. CPA, Mich. Staff acct. Arthur Andersen & Co., Detroit, 1958-62, tax mgr., 1962-70, tax ptnr., 1970-90, corp. dir., fin. and tax cons., 1990—; arbitrator Am. Arbitration Assn., 1994—; bd. dirs. Detroit Exec. Svc. Corps. Trustee, sec., treas., pres. Grosse Pointe (Mich.) Pub. Sch., 1969-72; chmn. Greater Detroit Fgn. Trade Zone, Inc., 1983—; mem. adv. bd. Paton Fund, 1988-96; bd. dirs. Civic Searchlight, Detroit, 1985—, 2d v.p., 1989-92, pres., 1992—; bd. dirs. Civic Inc., 1992; chmn. bd. for advancement of acctg. edn. U. Mich. Bus. Sch., 1996—. Named Outstanding Young Man of Yr. Grosse Pointe Jaycees, 1970; named to Pres.' Club U. Mich., Ann Arbor, 1975. Mem. AICPA, Mich. Assn. CPAs (bd. dirs. 1997—, Disting. Svc. award 1992), Tappan Soc., Detroit Regional Yachting Assn. (exec. com. 1993—, commodore 1996-97), Detroit Club (bd. dirs. 1998—), Detroit Boat Club (bd. dirs., treas. 1985-87, com. 1986), Detroit Yacht Club. Congregationalist. Home: 1453 Iroquois St Detroit MI 48214-2715

ADAMS, WILLIAM ROGER, historian; b. Mpls., Nov. 4, 1935; s. Jacob Anthony and Clara Louise (Jordan) A.; m. LaVonne May Turgeon, June 24, 1961; children: James Jacob, April Louise. B.A., U. Minn., 1961, M.A., 1967; Ph.D., Fla. State U., 1974. Analyst USIS, 1964-69; asst. prof. history Fla. State U., 1972-75; exec. dir. Fla. Bicentennial Commn., 1975-77; dir. Historic St. Augustine (Fla.) Preservation Bd., 1977-85; pres., prin. cons. Historic Property Assocs.; bd. dirs. Fla. Trust Historic Preservation, 1979-81, Fla. Hist. Soc., 1980-88. Served with AUS, 1955-57. Office: Historic Property Assocs PO Box 1002 Saint Augustine FL 32085-1002

ADAMS, WILLIAM WHITE, retired manufacturing company executive; b. Dubuque, Iowa, May 14, 1934; s. Waldo and Therese (White) A.; m. Susan Joanne Cole, Dec. 29, 1956; children: Nancy, Sara, Mark, Catherine. BS in Indsl. Adminstrn., Iowa State U., 1956; LHD (hon.), Millersville U., 1990, Lebanon Valley Coll., 1990; LittD, Franklin & Marshall, 1991. With Armstrong World Industries, Inc., Lancaster, Pa., 1956-94, gen. sales mgr. residential ceiling systems div., 1975-80, group v.p. bldg. products ops., 1981, exec. v.p., 1982-88, chmn., pres., CEO, 1988-93, chmn., 1993-94; exec.-in-residence U. Tenn. Grad. Sch. Bus. Adminstrn.; bd. dirs. High Industries, Irex Corp., Specialty Products & Insulation, Inc.; chmn. Lancaster Alliance; dir. emeritus Bell Atlantic Corp. Chmn. adv. bd. Lancaster-Lebanon coun. Boy Scouts Am., 1970—; bd. dirs. United Way Lancaster County, Pa., 1977-82, WITF Pub. Broadcasting, 1986-88; bd. dirs. Lancaster Symphony Assn., 1978-87, pres., 1983-84; dir. Lancaster Health Alliance, 1988-96; bd. dirs. Pa. 2000, 1990-95. Recipient Silver Beaver award Boy Scouts Am., 1979. Mem. Nat. Assn. Corp. Dirs. (dir.), Caves Valley Golf Club, Lancaster Country Club (dir. 1978-84).

ADAMSKI, RICHARD FRANKLYN, writer, mental health consultant, technical theatre assistant; b. Waterbury, Conn., Apr. 5, 1961; s. Chester Edward and Cecelia Agnes Adamski. AS, Mattatuck C.C., Waterbury, Conn., 1989; student, U. Conn., 1989-98. Envmerator U.S. Dept. Commerce, U.S. Census Bur., Hartford, Conn., 1989; usher Shubert Performing Arts Ctr., New Haven, 1991-93; sound asst. Seven Angles Theatre, Conn., 1993; pub. rels. Portland (Conn.) Theatre, 1994; processer K-Mart Corp., Waterbury, 1996-97; TV telethon worker Conn. Pub. TV, Hartford, 1997; warmline hotline operator State Conn. Dept. Mental Health and Addiction Svc., Waterbury, 1997—; spkr. in field. Contbr. articles to profl. jours. Contbg. mem. Dem. Nat. Com., 1989, 92, campaign worker Dukasis for Pres.,1989; mem. Nat. Trust Historic Preservation, 1996, Ams. for Dem. Action, 1995. Mem. Nat. Alliance for the Mentally Ill., Counterculture-Mattatuck Mus., Poets and Writers Inc., Libr. Congress (assoc.) Conn. Pub. TV (contbg.), Americans for Dem. Action, 1977 (contbg.). Democrat.

Roman Catholic. Avocations: attending art galleries, historical sites and theatre, postcard collecting, astronomy. Home: 500 Waterville Street Waterbury CT 06710 Office: 115 South Main St Waterbury CT 06720

ADAMSON, ARTHUR WILSON, chemistry educator; b. Shanghai, China, Aug. 15, 1919; s. Arthur Quintin and Ethel (Rhoda) A.; m. Virginia Louise Dillman, Mar. 24, 1942; children—Carol Ann, Janet Louise, Jean Elizabeth. B.S. with honors, U. Calif.-Berkeley, 1940; Ph.D. in Phys. Chemistry, U. Chgo., 1944; PhD (hon.), U. Ferrara, Italy, 1993. Research assoc. Manhattan Project, Oak Ridge, 1944-46; asst. prof. U. So. Calif., 1946-49, assoc. prof., 1949-53, prof., 1953-89, prof. emeritus, 1989—, chmn. dept. chemistry, 1972-75; Foster lectr. U. Buffalo, 1970; Venable lectr. U. N.C., 1975; Bikerman lectr. Case Western U., 1982; Reilly lectr. Notre Dame U., 1984. Author: Concepts of Inorganic Photochemistry, 1975, Understanding Physical Chemistry, 1980, Textbook of Physical Chemistry, 1986, Physical Chemistry of Surfaces, 1997; editor Langmuir Am. Chem. Soc., 1984-89; editor emeritus, 1990—; contbr. articles to profl. jours. Recipient Creative Scholarship and rsch. award U. So. Calif., 1971, Excellence in Teaching award, 1979, Raubenheimer award, 1984, Disting. Emeritus award, 1991; Alexander von Humboldt Sr. Scientist award, 1971, others; Gold medal Am. Inst. Chemists, 1994, Monie A. Ferst award Sigma Xi, 1999. Fellow Am. Inst. Chemists (Gold medal 1994); mem. Am. Chem Soc. (councillor So. Calif. sect. 1964-80, chmn. 1964, Tolman award 1967, Kendall award 1979, Langmuir lectr. 1981, Disting. Svc. in Inorganic Chemistry award 1982, Chem. Edn. award 1984, Agnes Ann Green Disting Svc. award 1989, Harry and Carol Mosher award 1990, Arthur W. Adamson Award for Disting. Svc. in Advancement of Surface Chemistry established in his honor 1992), Palos Verdes Tennis Club. Republican. Avocations: tennis; photography. Office: U So Calif Dept of Chemistry U Park Los Angeles CA 90089-0744

ADAMSON, DAN KLINGLESMITH, science association executive; b. Vernon, Tex., Oct. 12, 1939; s. Earl Larkin and Edith (Klinglesmith) A.; m. Eva Diane Pope, Aug. 18, 1962; children: Larkin, Rebecca, Amy, Sarah. Student, U. Mo., 1958-59; B.A. in History, Southwestern U., Georgetown, Tex., 1962. Tchr. pub. schs., Jefferson County, Colo., 1962-64; asst. dir. Soc. Petroleum Engrs., Dallas, 1964-67, editor jour., 1967-71, gen. mgr., 1972-79, exec. dir., 1979—. Mem. Am. Soc. Assn. Execs., Council Engring. Sci. Soc. Execs. Republican. Methodist. Office: Soc Petroleum Engrs PO Box 833836 222 Palisades Creek Dr Richardson TX 75080-2097

ADAMSON, HEIDI BETH, English educator; b. Binghamton, N.Y., Aug. 16, 1967; d. John Leslie and Irene Coleman Adamson. BA in English, George Mason U., 1988, MA in English Linguistics, 1989, postgrad., 1994—. Tchr. ESL Fairfax (Va.) County Pub. Schs., 1991-92; instr. ESL No. Va. C.C., Manassas, 1992-94, head dept. ESL, 1992-94, asst. prof., 1994-97, assoc. prof. ESL/English, 1997—, head dept. fgn. langs. and ESL, 1997-98, asst. divsn. chair ESL, 1998—; cons. in pvt. industry; presenter, spkr. in field. Contbr. articles to profl. jours. No. Va. C.C. Ednl. Found. grantee, 1997. Mem. Nat. Assn. C.C. Educators, Washington Area Tchrs. English to Spkrs. of Other Langs. Avocations: child and adult language acquisition, masculine/feminine leadership in higher education, using technology to facilitate learning, travel. E-mail: HAdamson@nv.cc.va.us. Office: No Va CC 6901 Sudley Rd Manassas VA 20109

ADAMSON, JAMES B., business executive; b. 1948. Various positions The Gap, 1975-84; exec. v.p. mktg. Revco Inc., 1984-91; various positions, CEO Burger King Corp., 1991-95; chmn., pres., CEO Advantica Restaurant Group, Spartanburg, S.C., 1995—. Office: Advantica Restaurant Group 203 E Main St Spartanburg SC 29319-0001*

ADAMSON, JANICE LYNNE, fundraiser, grant writer, event coordinator; b. New Braunfels, Tex., Sept. 28, 1965; d. Cameron and Lavaughn (Davis) A. BA in Philosophy, St. Andrews Coll., Laurinburg, N.C., 1988. Trust asst. Ctrl. Carolina Bank, Durham, N.C., 1988-89; sales asst. Shearson Lehmann Hutton, Durham, 1989-90; devel. asst. Houston Food Bank, 1990-93; devel. dir. Houston SPCA, 1993-96; grant writer Lee Coll., Baytown, Tex., 1996-98; dir. major gifts and capital campaign The Coun. on Alcohol and Drug Abuse, Houston, 1998—; mem. adv. bd. Endangered Species Media Project, St. Andrews Press, 1991—, Aldine Youth, Houston, 1991—. Contbr. poetry to Currents Mag., St. Andrews Rev. mem. Houston Corp. Recycling Coun.; mem. Nat. Com. on Resource Devel., 1996—. Recipient Cmty. Outreach award Houston Corp. Recycling Coun., 1994, 95. Mem. Clan Mackintosh N.A. Republican. Methodist. Avocations: golf, literature, art. Home: 5292 Memorial Dr A-3 Houston TX 77007 Office: Coun Alcohol & Drugs 303 Jackson Hill Houston TX 77007

ADAMSON, JOHN WILLIAM, hematologist; b. Oakland, Calif., Dec. 28, 1936; s. John William and Florence Jean Adamson; m. Susan Elizabeth Wood, June 16, 1960; children: Cairn Elizabeth, Loch Rachael; m. Christine Fenyvest, Sept. 1, 1989. BA, U. Calif., Berkeley, 1958; MD, UCLA, 1962. Intern, resident in medicine U. Wash. Med. Ctr., Seattle, 1962-64, clin. and rsch. fellow hematology, 1964-67, faculty, 1969-90, prof. hematology, 1978-90, head divsn. hematology, 1981-89; pres. N.Y. Blood Ctr., N.Y.C., 1989-97; dir. Lindsley F. Kimball Rsch. Inst., N.Y.C., 1989-98; exec. v.p. rsch., dir. Blood Rsch. Inst. Blood Ctr./Southeastern Wis., Milw., 1998—; Josiah Macy Jr. Found. scholar, vis. scientist Nuffield dept. clin. medicine, U. Oxford, Eng., faculty medicine, 1976-77. Author papers in field, chpts. in books. With USPHS, 1967-69. Recipient Rsch. Career Devel. award NIH, 1972-77, Rsch. grant, 1976-95. Fellow AAAS; mem. Am. Soc. Hematology (pres. 1995-96), Assn. Am. Physicians, Am. Soc. Clin. Investigation, Western Assn. Physicians. Office: Blood Rsch Inst PO Box Milwaukee WI 10021-6273

ADAMSON, JUDY, theater educator; b. Burlington, Iowa, Sept. 10, 1945; d. Victor Emanuel Lauer and Alma House; m. David A. Adamson, May 27, 1967. BA, U. No. Iowa, 1967. Costumer Unto These Hills, Cherokee, N.C., 1972-78; costumer U. N.C., Chapel Hill, 1976-80, costume dir., 1993—; draper Ala. Shakespeare Festival, Anniston, 1980; draper asst. Barbara Matera Ltd., N.Y.C., 1980-90, draper, 1990—; costume coord. Carolina Ballet, Raleigh, N.C., 1998—. Editor, author (electronic pub.) Survey Costume Programs U.S. Active mother's march March of Dimes, Chapel Hill, 1997, 99. Mem. U.S. Inst. Theatre Tech. (vice-commr. costume symposium 1995), U.S. Inst. Theatre Tech. S.E., Costume Soc. Am., Southea. Theatre Conf., Theta Alpha Pi. Office: U NC CB # 3230 Ctr Dramatic Art Chapel Hill NC 24599-3230

ADAMSON, MARY ANNE, geographer, systems engineer; b. Berkeley, Calif., June 25, 1954; d. Arthur Frank and Frances Isobel (Key) A.; m. Richard John Harrington, Sept. 20, 1974. BA with highest honors, U. Calif., Berkeley, 1975, MA, 1976, postgrad., 1976-78. Cert. tchr. earth scis., Calif.; cert. cave rescue ops. and mgmt., Calif.; lic. EMT, Contra Costa (Calif.) County, 1983. Tchg. asst. dept. geography U. Calif., Berkeley, 1976; geographer, environ. and fgn. area analyst Lawrence Livermore (Calif.) Nat. Lab., 1978-83, cons., 1983-86; sys. engr. ESL, Sunnyvale, Calif., 1986-90; rsch. analyst, rsch. devel. and analysis Pacific Gas & Electric Co., San Francisco, 1993-93, adminstrv. asst. internal audit dept., 1993—. Asst. editor Vulcan's Voice, 1982; contbr. articles to profl. jours. Staff mem. ARC/Am. Trauma Soc./Sierra Club Urgent Care and Mountain Medicine seminars, 1983-98. With USNR, 1983—, comdr., 1999—. Recipient Navy Achievement medal, 1992. Mem. Assn. Am. Geographers (life), Assn. Pacific Coast Geographers, Nat. Speleol. Soc. (geology, geography sects., sec., editor newsletter Diablo Grotto chpt. 1982-86), Toastmasters Internat. Club (adminstrv. v.p. Blue Monday Club 1991), Sierra Club (life), Nature Conservancy (life), U. Calif. Alumnae Assn., Phi Beta Kappa. Home: 4603 Lakewood St Pleasanton CA 94588-4342 Office: PG&E Corp Dept Internal Auditing 245 Market St San Francisco CA 94105-1702

ADAMSON, OSCAR CHARLES, II, lawyer; b. St. Paul, June 9, 1924; s. Oscar Charles and Dorothy M. (Garlock) A.; m. Mary Rae Josephson, Oct. 1, 1977. BSL, U. Minn., 1949, JD, 1951. Bar: Minn. 1951, U.S. Supreme Ct 1960. Since practiced in Mpls.; partner Meagher, Geer, Markham, Anderson, Adamson, Flaskamp & Brennan, 1960—; adj. prof. law U. Minn. Law Sch., 1962-63, prof. law, 1963-66; mem. Minn. Supreme Ct. Adv. Com., 1965-84. Author: (with James L. Hetland, Jr.) Minnesota Practice, Civil Rules Annotated, 1970. Served with USAAF, 1942-45. Decorated D.F.C., Purple Heart, Air medal. Mem. Am., Minn., Hennepin County bar assns. Clubs: Pool and Yacht (St. Paul), North Oaks Golf (St. Paul). Home: 14 Evergreen Rd North Oaks Saint Paul MN 55127 also: 4401 Lower Honoapiilani Rd Lahaina HI 96761-9207 Office: 4200 Multifoods Towers Minneapolis MN 55402*

ADAMSON, THOMAS CHARLES, JR., aerospace engineering educator, consultant; b. Cicero, Ill., Mar. 24, 1924; s. Thomas Charles and Helen Emily (Koubek) A.; m. Susan Elizabeth Huncilman, Sept. 16, 1949; children: Thomas Charles III, William Andros, Laura Elizabeth. BS, Purdue U., 1949; MS, Calif. Inst. Tech., 1950, PhD, 1954. Rsch. engr. Jet Propulsion Lab., Pasadena, Calif., 1952-54; assoc. research engr. U. Mich., Ann Arbor, 1954-56, asst. prof., 1956-57, assoc. prof., 1957-61, prof., 1961-93; prof. emeritus, 1993—; chmn. dept. aerospace engring. U. Mich., Ann Arbor, 1983-91; chmn. François-Xavier Bagnoud Aerospace Prize Bd., 1992—. Editor: (with M.F. Platzer) Transonic Flow Problems in Turbo Machinery, 1977; contbr. articles to profl. jours. With U.S. Army, 1943-46, ETO. Guggenheim fellow, 1950-52; recipient Disting. Faculty Achievement award U. Mich., 1980. Fellow AIAA; mem. Combustion Inst., Am. Phys. Soc., Francois-Xavier Bagnoud U.S. Found., Sigma Xi. Episcopalian. Home: 667 Worthington Pl Ann Arbor MI 48103-6138 Office: U Mich Dept Aerospace Engring 1320 Beal Ave Ann Arbor MI 48109-2140

ADAMSONS, ULDIS, government official; b. Zwittau, Czechoslovakia, Jan. 2, 1945; s. Osvalds V. and Austra Agnes (Osis) A.; m. Janene Adelle Sward; children: Kari Lee, Ryan Erik. BA in Econs., U. Minn., Duluth, 1973; student, DePaul U., 1969-70; grad., Nat. Def. U., 1984. Cert. mgmt. acct. Supr. GAO, Chgo., 1968-75; team leader GAO, Honolulu, 1975-79; group dir. GAO, Washington, 1980-91, asst. dir. def. environ. issues, 1992—; broadcaster classical music radio program worldwide. Mem. Congl. Squadron, Civil Air Patrol. Recipient Outstanding Achievement award, 1987, Exceptional Svc. award, 1988; named Alumnus of Notable Achievement Coll. Liberal Arts U. Minn., 1995. Mem. AAAS, Am. Def. Preparedness Assn., World Affairs Coun., Inst. Cert. Mgmt. Accts. Lutheran. Avocations: travel, music, ham radio, flying, astronomy. Home: 7230 Ashview Dr Springfield VA 22153-1520 Office: GAO 441 G St NW Rm 4a12 Washington DC 20548-0001

ADANTI, MICHAEL J., academic administrator. Pres. So. Conn. State U., New Haven, 1994—. Office: So Conn State U 501 Cresecent St New Haven CT 06515-0901*

ADASKIN, MURRAY, composer; b. Toronto, Ont., Can., Mar. 28, 1906; s. Samuel and Nisha (Perstnyov) A.; m. Frances James, July 16, 1931 (dec. Aug. 1988); m. Asta Dorothea Larsen, May 7, 1989. Student, Royal Conservatory Music, Toronto, Can. and Paris, Music Acad. West; student of Darius Milhaud, Aspen (Colo.) Sch. Music; LLD (hon.), U. Lethbridge, Alta., Can., 1970; DMus (hon.), Brandon U., 1972, U. Windsor, Ont., 1977, U. Victoria, B.C., 1984; LLD (hon.), U. Saskatoon, Saskatoon, 1984. Prof. music, chair dept. U. Sask., Saskatoon, 1952-66, composer in residence, 1966-73; mem. Can. Coun., 1966-69; violinist Toronto Symphony Orch., 10 yrs. Composer (opera) Warden of the Plains, also over 120 orchestral, chamber and solo works including Man and the Universe; commd. by CBC for Exp. 1967, premier Concerto for Orch. with Victoria Symphony, 1990, premier Rivka Golani Concerto for Solo Viola and Orch., 1991, Woodwind Quintet No. 2, 1993, String Quartet No. 2 (La Cadenza), Lafayette String Quarter, 1994, Concerto for Viola and Orch. No. 2, 1995, String Quintet (for Lafayette Quartet adn Gary Karr, bass), 1995, The Travelling Musician for Narrator/Singer and Chamber by Orch., 1997, String Quartet No. 3, The Vecchi Amici, 1998; subject CBC broadcasts, 1971, 89, Sta. CJRT-FM broadcast, 1993; 2 CDs included in the Adaskin Collection; contbr. over 90 scores published by Adlar Publs. Bd. dirs. Saskatoon Arts Ctr., 1966-67. Decorated officer Order of Can., 1980; named Saskatoon Citizen of Yr., 1969; recipient Lifetime award for excellence in the arts Sask. Arts Bd., 1991; Sr. Arts fellow Can. Coun., 1960-61; Can. Coun. grantee U. Sask. Mem. Royal Soc. Arts, Can. League Composers (founding), Saskatoon Musician's Assn. (hon. life), Toronto Musician'a Assn. (hon. life).

ADASKO, MARY HARDY, speech pathologist; b. Miss., Jan. 6, 1920; d. B.F. and Margaret Elizabeth (Walker) Hardy; m. Herbert I. Adasko, Sept. 21, 1944; children: H. Hardy, Laura A. Lenzner. BA, CUNY, 1969, MS, 1976. Berard cert. in Auditory Integration Tng. Tchr. speech improvement Day Elem. Schs., N.Y.C. Bd. Edn., 1972-92; pvt. practice speech/lang. cons. N.Y.C., 1992—. v.p. United Parents Assn., N.Y.C., 1960-64; pres. Madison High Sch. Parent Assn., 1962-64. Mem. Am. Speech-Hearing-Lang. Assn. (clin. competence cert./speech lang.), N.Y. State Speech-Hearing-Lang. Assn. (lic. speech lang. pathologist N.Y. state), N.Y.C. Speech-Hearing-Lang. Assn. (officer), Coun. for Exceptional Children, Bi-lingual Lang.-Speech-Hearing Assn., N.Y. Acad. Sci., Autism Rsch. Rev. Internat., Children and Adults with Attention Deficit Disorder, Autism Soc. Am., Soc. Auditory Integration Tng., Am. Tinnitus Assn., Orton Duslexic Soc. (del. and presenter Conf. on Exceptionality, Beijing 1995, South Africa 1996). Avocations: traveling, gardening. Home: 1797 E 22nd St Brooklyn NY 11229-1524

ADATO, PERRY MILLER, documentary producer, director, writer; b. Yonkers, N.Y.; d. Perry and Ida (Block) Miller; m. Neil M. Adato, Sept. 11, 1955; children: Laurie, Michelle. Student, Marshalov Sch. Drama, N.Y.C., New Sch. Social Rsch.; LHD (hon.), Ill. Wesleyan U., 1984. Film rsch. coord. CBS-TV, N.Y.C., 1959-64, prodr., 1964; assoc. prodr. NET, N.Y.C., 1964-68, prodr., dir., 1968-92; lectr. Fairfield U., Conn., 1974-75; writer Sta. WNET-TV, 1989, 96-97; exec. prodr. Alvin H. Perlmutter Inc./Ind. Prodn. Fund, 1992-96; guest lectr. on film Harvard U., Columbia U., NYU, Yale U., U. Ill., others, 1970—; mem. film award jury Am. Film Inst., Beverly Hills, Calif., 1974; judge film award Creative Artists Pub. Svc., N.Y.C., 1976; first chmn. UN Women in the Arts Film Com., 1976-77; pres. jury Montreal Internat. Film Festival, 1990; mem. jury Pompidou Ctr., Paris Internat. Festival of Films on Art, 1994. Producer, dir.: (TV documentary films) Dylan Thomas: The World I Breathe, 1968 (Emmy award for outstanding achievement in cultural documentary 1968), Gertrude Stein: When This You See, Remember Me, 1970 (Montreal Festival Diplome d'Excellence 1970, Am. Film Festival Blue Ribbon award 1970, 2 Emmy nominations for outstanding direction and outstanding achievement in cultural documentary 1971), The Great Radio Comedians, 1972 (Am. Film Festival Red Ribbon award 1975), An Eames Celebration: Several Worlds of Charles and Ray Eames, 1973 (Chgo. Internat. Film Festival Silver Hugo award 1973, Am. Film Festival Red Ribbon award 1973), Mary Cassatt: Impressionist From Philadelphia, 1974 (Women in Communications Clarion award 1974), Georgia O'Keeffe, 1977 (Dirs. Guild Am. award for documentary achievement 1977-1st woman to receive any Dirs. Guild Am. award, NCCJ Christopher award 1978, Com. for Internat. Events Golden Eagle award 1978, Women in Communications Clarion award 1978, Alfred I. DuPont/Columbia U. citation 1978), Frankenthaler: Toward a New Climate, 1978 (Am. Film Festival Blue Ribbon award in fine arts 1979), Picasso: A Painter's Diary, 1980 (Dirs. Guild Am. award for directorial achievement in TV documentary 1980, Alfred I. DuPont/Columbia U. award for excellence in broadcast journalism 1980, Com. for Internat. Events Golden Eagle award 1980, Am. Film Festival Blue Ribbon award in fine arts 1980, Montreal Internat. Festival of Films on Art First prize for Best Biography of an Artist 1981), Carl Sandburg: Echoes and Silences, 1982 (Women in Communications Matrix award 1982, American Women in Radio and TV Pinnacle award for TV documentary 1982, Dirs. Guild Am. award for achievement in TV documentary 1983), Eugene O'Neill: A Glory of Ghosts, 1984-85, Broadcast, 1986 (Most Outstanding Achievement in TV Documentary award Dirs. Guild Am. 1986, Spl. Jury award San Francisco Film Festival 1985, Internat. Film and TV Festival of N.Y. Silver medal 1986); exec. producer (TV series) Women in Art, 1974-78, Art of the Western World, 1985-89; producer, dir., writer: A White Garment of Churches, 1989 (Clarion award 1990, Silver Plaque award Chgo. Internat. Film Festival 1990, Silver Cindy award 1990); exec. prodr. rsch. and devel. 3 part series Asian Art, 1990-94; prodr., dir. Great Tales in Asian Art, 1994-96; writer Dream Journeys-Nature in East Asian Art, 1994-95; prodr. R & D Alfred Stieglitz, 1996-97, (working title) Writer, Alfred Stieglitz, 1996-97. Hon. bd. dirs. Weston-Westport (Conn.) Arts Coun., 1981-89. Poynter fellow Yale U., 1976; grantee NEA, 1977-78, 93, NEH, 1980, 83, 91, 93; Calhoun Coll. assoc. fellow Yale U., 1993—; subject tribute, Montreal Internat. Art Film Festival, 1990; recipient Westport (Conn.) Arts Coun. Lifetime Achievement award in visual arts category, 1996; film retrospective Nat. Gallery Art, Washington, 1998. Mem. NATAS, Dirs. Guild Am., Writers Guild Am., Women in Communications, N.Y. Women in Film and TV.

ADAWI, IBRAHIM HASAN, physics educator; b. Palestine, Apr. 18, 1930; came to U.S., 1951, naturalized, 1961; s. Hasan and Dabella (Miari) A.; children: Omar, Nadia, Yasmin, Rhonda, Tariq. B.S. in Engring. Physics, Washington U., St. Louis, 1953; Ph.D. in Engring. Physics, Cornell U., 1957. Mem. tech. staff RCA Labs., Princeton, N.J., 1956-60; research cons. Battelle Meml. Inst., Columbus, Ohio, 1960-68; adj. prof. elec. engring. Ohio State U., 1965-68; prof. physics U. Mo., Rolla, 1968-97, emeritus prof. physics, 1997—; vis. prof. U. Hamburg, W.Ger., winter 1977, Sch. Math. and Physics, U. East Anglia, Norwich, Eng., fall 1982; Fulbright lectr. Rabat, Morocco, 1982; sr. scientist Motorola, Phoenix, summer 1979; rsch. leader Internat. Ctr. Theoretical Physics, Trieste, Italy, summers 1982, 83, 85. Jr. fellow Cornell U., 1953-54; J. McMullen scholar, 1954-55; Sigma Xi fellow, 1955-56. Mem. Am. Phys. Soc. Home: 10540 County Road 3010 Rolla MO 65401-7754 Office: U Mo-Rolla Dept Physics Rolla MO 65401 *Goals in science, and perhaps in life, are seldom reached; they are only approached asymptotically. The higher we soar the more dazzling is the panorama, but the wider is the horizon, and the frontiers of knowledge keep expanding.*

ADCOCK, ANTHONY GREEN, health education educator; b. Madison, Tenn., Apr. 23, 1942; s. Paul Joseph and Mildred Hortense (Green) A.; m. Alice Arnelle Sweatt, June 4, 1967; 1 child, Matthew Joseph. BS, David Lipscomb Coll., Nashville, 1964; MA, George Peabody Coll., 1966; D Health and Safety, Ind. U., 1971. Cert. health edn. specialist Nat. Commn. for Health Edn. Cert. Instr. David Lipscomb Coll., 1964-69; teaching assocc. Ind. U., Bloomington, 1969-71; asst. prof. Memphis State U., 1971-73; prof. health, head dept. Freed-Hardeman Coll., Handerson, Tenn., 1973-86; prof. Troy (Ala.) State U., 1986—; mem. steering com. Tenn. Health Curriculum Guide Project, Nashville, 1978-83; co-dir. Ala. Adolescent Student Health Survey Project, 1987—; paper presenter at nat. and regional confs. Contbr. articles to profl. jours., chpt. to book. Recipient Disting. Faculty award Freed-Hardeman Coll., 1984, Outstanding Tchr. educator award Troy State U., 1988. Mem. Am. Sch. Health Assn. (life), Assn. for Advancement Health Edn. (life), Health Educators Assn. Ala. (Ala. Health Educator of the Yr. 1990), Ala. Assn. Tchr. Educators, Ala. Assn. Health, Phys. Edn., Recreation and Dance (v.p. for health 1989-90), Tenn. Assn. Health, Phys. Edn., Recreation and Dance (v.p. for health 1980-82, honor award 1982), Phi Delta Kappa. Mem. Ch. of Christ. Avocation: gardening. Office: Troy State U University Ave Troy AL 36081

ADCOCK, DAVID FILMORE, radiologist, educator; b. Columbia, S.C., Sept. 19, 1938; s. David Filmore and Eloise (Daniel) A. BS, U. S.C., 1958, MPH, 1986; MD, Med. Coll. S.C., 1962. Diplomate Am. Bd. Radiology, Am. Bd. Nuclear Medicine, Am. Bd. Preventive Medicine. Asst. prof. radiology U. N.C.-Chapel Hill, 1970-72, assoc. prof., 1972-73; dir. nuclear medicine Richard Meml. Hosp., Columbia, 1974-79; prof., chmn. dept. radiology U. S.C.-Columbia, 1979—; cons. in field. Contbr. articles to profl. jours. Served as capt. U.S. Army, 1963-66. Fellow Am. Coll. Preventive Medicine; mem. Radiol. Soc. N.Am., Assn. Univ. Radiologists, Soc. Chmn. Acad. Radiology Depts., Alpha Omega Alpha. Office: U SC Sch Medicine Dept Radiology Columbia SC 29208

ADCOCK, RICHARD PAUL, lawyer; b. Chgo., May 14, 1955; s. Horace John and Louise Kathreen (Gallagher) A. AB with distinction in Econs., U. Ill., 1977; JD, Columbia U., 1980. Bar: Calif., 1980. Assoc. Lawler, Felix & Hall, L.A., 1980-82; corp. counsel Technicolor, Inc., L.A., 1982-83; assoc. counsel Nat. Med. Enterprises, L.A., 1983-85, sr. assoc. counsel, 1985-86, asst. gen. counsel, 1986-87; v.p., sec., gen. counsel The Hillhaven Corp., Tacoma, Wash., 1987-90; sr. v.p., sec., gen. counsel The Hillhaven Corp., Tacoma, 1990-95; chmn. legal subcom. Am. Health Care Assn., Washington, 1993-95. Mem. ABA, Am. Corp. Counsel Assn., Nat. Health Lawyers Assn.

ADCOCK, WILLIS ALFRED, electrical engineer, educator; b. St. Johns, Que., Can., Nov. 25, 1922; came to U.S., 1936, naturalized, 1944; s. William Arthur and Luella (White) A.; m. Sara McCoy Whiddon, Dec. 28, 1970; children by previous marriage: William John, Robert Charles, Edward James, Margaret Eleanor Adcock Corrie. B.S. cum laude, Hobart Coll., 1943; Ph.D., Brown U., 1948; M.L.A., So. Meth. U., 1975; ScD (hon.), Hobart Coll., 1989. Mem. staff Woods Hole (Mass.) Oceanographic Inst., 1943-44; mem. tech. staff Clinton Labs., Oak Ridge, 1944-46, Stanolind Oil & Gas Co., Tulsa, 1948-53; mgr. devel. dept., mgr. integrated circuits dept. Tex. Instruments, Inc., Dallas, 1953-64; tech. dir. Sperry Semicondr., Norwalk, Conn., 1964-65; mgr. advanced planning, tech. devel. areas Tex. Instruments Inc., Dallas, 1965-75; asst. v.p. consumer products activity Tex. Instruments Inc., 1975-78, prin. fellow, asst. v.p. corp. research devel. and engring., 1978-82, v.p. corp. staff, 1982-86; sr. lectr., asst. chmn. dept. elec. and computer engring. U. Tex., Austin, 1986-87, Cockrell Family Regent Chair in Engring. prof., 1987-93; emeritus, 1993—. Contbr. articles to profl. jours. Fellow IEEE, AAAS; mem. Nat. Acad. Engring., Am. Chem. Soc., Phi Beta Kappa, Sigma Xi. Episcopalian. Patentee in field. Home: 3414 Mt Bonnell Dr Austin TX 78731-5729 Office: U Tex Dept Elec & Computer Engring ENS 143 Austin TX 78712

ADCOX, MARY SANDRA, dietitian, consultant; b. Portsmouth, Ohio, Dec. 4, 1939; d. Philip Henry and Bertha Mae (Hansgen) Riddinger; m. Steve Jordan Jr., Dec. 5, 1962 (dec. May 1972); 1 child, Michael Philip; m. Henry Lonzo Adcox Jr., Sept. 30, 1972. BS in Food and Nutrition, U. Cin., 1961; MEd, S.W. Tex. State U., 1984. Lic. dietitian, Tex.; registered dietitian Commn. on Dietetic Registration. Rsch. dietitian U.S. Army Inst. Surg. Rsch., Ft. Sam Houston, 1964-65; chief dietitian Luth. Gen. Hosp., San Antonio, 1966-67; dir. dietetics Santa Rosa Med. Ctr., San Antonio, 1967-72, San Antonio Cmty. Hosp., 1972-75; adult edn. instr. San Antonio Coll., 1973-84; food svc. supr. San Antonio Ind. Sch. Dist., 1975-96, ret., 1996; sch. food svc. cons., San Antonio, 1996—. Author: Dietetic Assistant Program, 1983, Diet Manual: San Antonio Community Hospital, 1st edit., 1973, Diet Manual: Santa Rosa Medical Center, 4th edit., 1969. Former den mother cub scouts, Boy Scouts Am. 1st lt. U.S. Army, 1962-64. Mem. Am. Dietetic Assn., San Antonio Dietetic Assn., U. Cin. Alumni Assn., S.W. Tex. State U. Alumni Assn., Tex. State Nutrition Coun., San Antonio Area Ret. Tchrs. Assn., Delta Zeta. Baptist. Avocations: piano, organ, herb gardening. Home: 5503 Oo-Loo-Te-Ka Dr San Antonio TX 78218-5041

ADCROFT, PATRICE GABRIELLA, editor; b. Scranton, Pa., Apr. 15, 1954; d. Joseph Raymond and Patricia Ann (Ryan) A. BA In Mag. Journalism and Creative Writing, Syracuse U., 1976. Editor-in-chief Carbondale (Pa.) Miner Mid Valley Gazette, 1976-77; staff writer Good Housekeeping Mag., N.Y.C., 1978-80; mng. editor Family Media/Alive and Well, N.Y.C., 1980-81; freelance writer, editor N.Y.C., 1981-82; sr. editor CBS Mags. Family Weekly, N.Y.C., 1982-84; sr. editor Omni Mag., N.Y.C., 1984-85, exec. editor, 1985-86, editor-in-chief, 1986-90; Editor-in-Chief Seventeen Magazine, 1998—; vis. prof. Syracuse U., 1992-93. Editor-in-chief Omni Future Medical Almanac, 1987; contbr. writer Arthur C. Clarke's 2019, 1986, Omni Book of Continuum, 1982; author: (novel) Every Day Doughnuts. Bd. advisors SCI Ctr. for Advanced Studies in Mgmt., Wharton Sch., U. Pa. Roman Catholic. Office: Seventeen Magazine Primedia Corp 200 Madison Ave New York NY 10016*

ADDAMS, ROBERT JEAN, finance executive; b. Salt Lake City, Sept. 24, 1942; s. Harvey J. and Virginia (Dutson) A.; m. Elizabeth Addams; children: Ryan, Kelley, Amy, Michael. BS, U. Utah, 1968, MBA, 1969. Dir. budgets & cost control Western Airlines, Inc., L.A., 1976-80; v.p., gen. mgr. Ball Bros., Inc., Everette, Wash., and Anchorage, 1980-82; pres., cons. Addams & Assocs., Woodinville, Wash., 1982-89; contr. Lafayette Fisheries, Seattle, 1990-93; CFO Internat. Integrators, Seattle; CFO Mountain High Knitting, Seattle and San Diego, 1995-98; v.p. ISSI Bus. Solutions, Bothell, Wash., 1999—. Author: Care and Handling of Wetsalted Cod Fish, 1984; also articles on budgeting and business plans to nat. monthly newsletter. Scoutmaster, Explorer advisor Gt. Salt Lake and L.A. councils Boy Scouts Am., 1973-75; served 2-yr. mission for Ch. Jesus Christ of Latter-day Saints, 1962-64. Served with U.S. Army, 1961-62. Named Outstanding Grad., Coll. Bus., 1968, Beehive Honor Soc., 1969. Mem. U. Utah Alumni

Assn. (pres. So. Calif. chpt. 1976-80), U. Utah Coll. of Bus. Alumni (pres. So. Calif. group 1978-79), Alpha Kappa Psi. Republican. Home: 3028 177th Ave NE Redmond WA 98052

ADDERLEY, TERENCE E., corporate executive; b. 1933; married. BBA, U. Mich., 1951, BMA, 1956. Former fin. analyst Standard Oil Co. of N.J., 1956-57; with Kelly Services, Inc., Troy, Mich., 1957—, v.p., 1961-65, exec. v.p., 1965-67, pres., COO, 1967—, also dir., chmn., pres., CEO, 1998—. Office: Kelly Svcs Inc 999 W Big Beaver Rd Troy MI 48084-4716*

ADDICOTT, BEVERLY JEANNE, elementary school educator; b. Youngstown, Ohio, Nov. 9, 1948; m. Gerald Leslie Addicott, Mar. 30, 1974; 1 child, Katherine Elizabeth. BS in Edn., Youngstown State U., 1971, cert. media specialist, 1978; cert. in ESL, Brevard U., 1995. Cert. tchr., Ohio, Fla. Tchr. Mathews Sch. Dist., Vienna, Ohio, 1972-75, media specialist, 1975-78, supr. media, 1978-79; media specialist Brevard County Schs., Melbourne, Fla., 1987-91, tchr., 1991—. Chef du jour Haven for Children, Melbourne, 1989-94; vol. Habitat for humanity, Melbourne, 1993, University Park PTO, Melbourne, 1989—. Mem. Melbourne Alumnae Panhellenic (chair fundraiser 1992), Jr. League of South Brevard (parent educator 1992-95). Avocations: cross-stitch, knitting, crocheting. Office: University Park Elem Sch 500 W University Blvd Melbourne FL 32901-6999

ADDICOTT, FREDRICK TAYLOR, retired botany educator; b. Oakland, Calif., Nov. 16, 1912; s. James Edwin and Ottilia Katherine Elizabeth (Klein) A.; m. Alice Holmes Baldwin, Aug. 11, 1935; children: Donald James, Jean Alice, John Fredrick, David Baldwin. AB in Biology, Stanford U., 1934; PhD in Plant Physiology, Calif. Inst. Tech., 1939. Instr. to asst. prof. Santa Barbara (Calif.) State Coll., 1939-46; assoc. physiologist emergency rubber project USDA, Salinas, Calif., 1942-44; asst. prof. to prof. UCLA, 1946-60; prof. agronomy U. Calif., Davis, 1961-72, prof. botany, 1972-77, prof. emeritus, 1977—; vis. prof. U. Adelaide, Australia, 1966, U. Natal, Pietermaritzburg, Republic South Africa, 1970. Author: Abscission, 1982; editor, author: Abscisic Acid, 1983; contbr. articles to profl. jours. Fulbright rsch. scholar Victoria U., N.Z., 1957, Royal Bot. Garden, U.K., 1976; vis. fellow Australian Nat. U., 1983. Fellow AAAS; mem. Am. Soc. Plant Physiologists (Charles Reid Barnes Life Membership award 1990), Australian Soc. Plant Physiologists, Bot. Soc. Am., Internat. Plant Growth Substance Assn., Internat. Soc. Plant Morphologists, South African Assn. Botanists. Avocations: backpacking, cabinet making. Home and Office: 1003 Pine Ln Davis CA 95616-1764

ADDICOTT, WARREN OLIVER, retired geologist, educator; b. Fresno, Calif., Feb. 17, 1930; s. Irwin Oliver and Astrid (Jensen) A.; m. Suzanne Aubin, Oct. 2, 1976; m. Susanne Smith, Aug. 20, 1955 (div. 1974); children: Eric Oliver, Carol. BA cum laude, Pomona Coll., Calif., 1951; MA, Stanford U., Calif., 1952; PhD, U. Calif.-Berkeley, 1956. Teaching asst. U. Calif.-Berkeley, 1952-54; paleontologist Standard Oil Co. Calif., 1953; geologist Mobil Oil Co., 1954-62; research geologist U.S. Geol. Survey, Menlo Park, Calif., 1962-94; cons. prof. Stanford U., Calif., 1970-81; dep. chmn. Circum-Pacific Map Project, Menlo Park, Calif., 1979-82, gen. chmn., 1982-86, project advisor, 1986—; adj. prof. So. Oreg. U., 1989-97; bd. dirs. Circum-Pacific Coun. Energy and Mineral Resources, 1983-86. Contbr. articles to profl. jours. Fellow AAAS, Geol. Soc. Am., Calif. Acad. Scis.; mem. Paleontol. Soc. (pres. 1979-80), Am. Assn. Petroleum Geologists, Paleontol. Res. Instn. (bd. dirs. 1980-81). Unitarian. Home: 2260 Old Siskiyou Hwy Ashland OR 97520

ADDIE, HARVEY WOODWARD, retired secondary education educator, music director; b. Birmingham, Ala., June 14, 1930; s. LeRoy and Frances (Driscoll) A.; m. Gwendolyn Marie Mendes, June 5, 1955; children: Cynthia Marie Corra, Julie Ann Lorch, Mary Elizabeth Dunaway. MusB, Coll. Pacific, 1959; MusM, U. Pacific, 1970. Cert. life music tchr., Calif. Mgr. dept. S.H. Kress and Co., Santa Monica and Stockton, Calif., 1953-55; head produce, mgr. area Safeway Stores Inc., Lodi, Stockton, Calif., 1955-61; tchr. music Manteca (Calif.) Elem. Sch. Dist., 1959-61, San Joaquin County Sch. Music Office, Stockton, 1961-71; mgr. store Bill's Music Sales, Stockton, 1971-73; dir. music El Dorado High Sch., Placerville, Calif., 1973, Stockton Unified Sch. Dist., 1973-89; pres. San. Joaquin County Band Dirs. Assn., Stockton, 1984-86, Stagg High Sch. Faculty Assn., 1984-85. 1st. v.p. San Joaquin Concert Ballet Assn., Stockton, 1966; bd. dirs. Stockton opera Assn., 1968, Stockton Concert Band Assn., 1986-88. Served to cpl. U.S. Army, 1951-53, Korea. Mem. Assn. Jazz Edn., Calif. Music Educators Assn. (bd. dirs. 1983-87), Stockton Tchrs. Assn. (treas. 1986-89), Am. Fedn. Musicians (life mem., bd. dirs., sec.-treas. 1992—, pres. 1995—), Calif. Tchrs. Assn. (state coun. 1986-89), Noble Grand Fraternal Order of Odd Fellows (dist. dep. Grand Master Calif., trustee Saratoga Home 1994-97). Democrat. Methodist. Avocations: fishing, golf, computers. Home: 1426 W Euclid Ave Stockton CA 95204-2903 Office: Stockton Musicians' Assn 33 W Alpine Ave Stockton CA 95204-3607

ADDIS, DEBORAH JANE, management consultant, editor; b. Rahway, N.J., Jan. 29, 1950; d. Emmanuel and Stella (Oles) Addis; m. James Eldin Reed, Apr. 14, 1983. BA, Bowling Green State U., 1972; MA in Orgn., Mgmt. and Pub. Policy, Lesley Coll., Cambridge, Mass., 1992. Pub. info. officer Dept. Transp., State of Ohio, 1972-73; dir. pub. info. and edn. Dept. Commerce, State of Ohio, 1973-75; press sec. Atty. Gen., State of Ohio, 1975-77; dep. press sec. Office of Gov., Commonwealth of Mass., Boston, 1978-79; sr. account exec. Miller Communications, Boston, 1979-80; v.p., prin. Addis & Reed Cons., Inc., Boston, 1981-91, pres., 1992—; adj. faculty Lesley Coll. Grad. Sch., 1992—; bd. dirs. Can. Inst. Internat. Affairs, Boston. Author monograph and numerous articles, congl. testimony; mng. editor The American Canada Watch, 1995—. Bd. govs. Women's City Club of Boston, 1982-85; mem. Ohio Task Force on Domestic Violence, Columbus, 1976. Mem. New Eng.-Can. Bus. Coun. (bd. dirs. 1994-98), Harvard Club of Boston. Democrat. Avocations: photography, herpetology (turtles), hiking. Home: 25 Holly Ln Chestnut Hill MA 02467-2156 Office: Addis & Reed Cons Inc PO Box 85 Chestnut Hill MA 02467

ADDIS, KAY TUCKER, newspaper editor. AB in English, Coll. of William and Mary, 1970. Editor The Virginian-Pilot, Norfolk, 1996—. Office: The Virginian-Pilot 150 W Brambleton Ave Norfolk VA 23510-2075*

ADDIS, LAIRD CLARK, JR., philosopher, educator, musician; b. Bath, N.Y., Mar. 25, 1937; s. Laird Clark and Dora Ersel (Webber) A.; m. Patricia Karen Peterson, Dec. 20, 1962; children—Kristin, Karin. B.A., U. Iowa, 1959, Ph.D., 1964; M.A. (Woodrow Wilson fellow), Brown U., 1960. Instr. U. Iowa, Iowa City, 1963-64; asst. prof. U. Iowa, 1964-68, asso. prof., 1968-74, prof. philosophy, 1974—, also chmn. dept. philosophy., 1977-85; Sr. Fulbright lectr. State U. Groningen, Netherlands, 1970-71. Author: (with Douglas Lewis) Moore and Ryle: Two Ontologists, 1965, The Logic of Society, 1975, Natural Signs, 1989, Of Mind and Music, 1999; contbr. articles to profl. jours. Mem. Am. Philos. Assn., Philosophy of Sci. Assn., Am. Soc. for Aesthetics, Quad City Symphony Orch. (ret.). Home: 20 W Park Rd Iowa City IA 52246-2304 Office: U Iowa Dept Philosophy Iowa City IA 52242

ADDIS, RICHARD BARTON, lawyer; b. Columbus, Ohio, April 9, 1929; s. Wilbur Jennings and Leila Olive (Grant) A.; m. Marguerite C. Christjohn, Feb. 9, 1957; children: Jacqueline Carol, Barton David. BA, Ohio State U., 1954, JD, 1955. Bar: Ohio 1956, U.S. Dist. Ct. (no. dist.) Ohio 1957, N.Mex. 1963, U.S. Dist. Ct. N.Mex. 1963, Laguna Pueblo (N.Mex.) Tribal Ct. 1986. Pvt. practice, Canton, Ohio, 1956-63, Albuquerque, 1963—, Laguna Pueblo, 1986—. Co-developer The Woodlands Subdivsn., Albuquerque; co-owner Cerro del Oro Mine, Valencia County, N.Mex., 1977—. With USMC, 1946-48, 50-52. Mem. Ohio Bar Assn., N.Mex. Bar Assn. Office: PO Box 25923 Albuquerque NM 87125-0923

ADDIS, THOMAS HOMER, III, professional golfer; b. San Diego, Nov. 30, 1945; s. Thomas H. and Martha J. (Edwards) A.; m. Susan Tera Buckley, June 13, 1966; children: Thomas Homer IV, Bryan Michael. Student, Foothill Jr. Coll., 1963, Grossmont Jr. Coll., 1965; degree in profl. golf mgmt. (hon.), Ferris State U. Head golf prof., mgr. Sun Valley Golf Course, La Mesa, Calif., 1966-67; head golf prof., dir. golf Singing Hills Country Club and Lodge, 1969-98; sr. v.p. Golfstar Mgmt., 1998-99; v.p. Full Swing Golf, San Diego, 1999—; gen. chmn. Nat. Jr. Golf Championship, U.S. Golf Assn., 1973-89; lectr., owner Golf Cons. & Design, Rocky Mountain Chocolate Factory, Mammoth; spkr. in field. Contbr. articles to profl. jours. Pres. Calif. State Open, 1980-84; chmn. Nat. Com. Liaison for Physically Challenged, 1984-88; dir. Cuyamaca Coll. Found.; mem. internat. golf com. Spl. Olympics. Recipient Retailer award Golf Industry mag., 1985; named to Lady Aztec San Diego State U. Hall of Fame. Mem. PGA (pres. San Diego chpt. 1978-79, pres. sect. 1980-82, bd. dirs. sect. 1974-90, spkr., chmn. mem. svc. com. 1986-87, bd. dirs. San Diego sect. 1974-90, assn. coord. bus. schs. and seminars, named Profl. of Yr. So. Calif. sect. 1979, 89, Horton Smith award So. Calif. sect. 1980-81, 89, PGA Golf Profl. of Yr. 1989, Nat. Horton Smith awarwd 1981, Resort Merchandiser of Yr., So. Calif. sect. 1978, 83, mem. nat. bd. control 1978-85, chmn. nat. bd. control 1991-92, membership com. 1978, 89-90, nat. edn. com. 1980-85, 89-90, nat. bd. dirs. 1986-88, rules com. 1986-90, championship com. 1986—, hon. life mem. So. Calif. sect. and San Diego PGA, sec. PGA Am. 1991, 92, v.p. PGA Am. 1993, 94, pres. 1994-96), So. Calif. PGA Hall of Fame, Nat. Golf Found. (Joe Graffis award 1988), Nat. Amputee Golf Assn. (hon.), San Diego Jr. Golf Assn. (pres. 1997-98), Assn. Golf Educators, Golf Collector's Soc., Rotary. Office: 11413 W Bernardo Ct San Diego CA 92127

ADDISON, ALONZO CHURCH, graphics visualization executive, educator, consultant; b. Berkeley, Calif., 1965; s. John West Jr. and Mary Ann A. BS in Engring., Princeton U., 1988; MArch, U. Calif., Berkeley, 1992, postgrad., 1994. Computer graphics programmer ALK Assocs., Princeton, N.J., 1988-89; strategic tech. cons. ACA Group, El Cerrito, Calif., 1989—; project dir. U. Calif., Berkeley, 1992; v.p. CYRA Technologies, Inc., Oakland, Calif., 1993—; mem. corp. found. rels. com. U. Calif., Berkeley, 1995—; mng. dir., co-founder Mus. of Future Consortium, Berkeley, Milan, 1994—; panel chair, author ACM Siggraph Internat. Conf., 1994, 95; chmn., founder, Asterix Tech. and Design, Inc., Berkeley, 1996; cons., web strategist Bus. Internat. Networks, Inc., Virginia Beach, 1996-97; conf. chair Internat. Workshop on Cities, Design and Internet, 1996, 97, 98; mem. adv. bd. ARCH Found, Salzburg, 1998—. Adv. bd. Berkeley Contemporary Opera, 1994-97; asst. scoutmaster Mt. Diablo coun. Boy Scouts Am., 1984—. Recipient AIA award, 1992; fellow U. Calif., 1994; rsch. grantee Taisei Am. Corp, 1992-94, Dai Nippon Printing Corp., 1996. Mem. Assn. Computing Machinery Siggraph, Assn. Computer Aided Design in Architecture. Home: 7927 Terrace Dr El Cerrito CA 94530-3024

ADDISON, DAVID DUNHAM, lawyer; b. Richmond, Va., Aug. 23, 1941; s. Grafton Dulany and Anne (Withers) A.; m. Marion Lee Wood, Aug. 21, 1965; children: David Dunham Jr., Marion Lee, Elizabeth Townshend. BA, Hampden-Sydney Coll., 1964; LLB, U. Va., 1967. Bar: Va. 1967. Assoc. Browder, Russell, Morris & Butcher, Richmond, 1967-72; ptnr., dir. Browder & Russell, P.C., Richmond, 1972-90; mem. firm, shareholder Williams, Mullen, Christian & Dobbins, P.C., Richmond, 1990—. Contbr. articles to profl. jours. Profl. adv. bd. Richmond Cmty. Found., 1988—, Massie Cancer Ctr., Richmond, 1988-91. Fellow Am. Coll. Trust and Estate Counsel (state chmn. 1986-92); mem. ABA (com. chmn. 1987-94), S.R., Va. Bar Assn., Richmond Bar Assn., Estate Planning Coun. Richmond (pres. 1987-88), Richmond Trust Adminstrs. Coun. (pres. 1986-87), Kiwanis Club of Richmond (pres. 1998-99), Country Club of Va., Commonwealth Club. Episcopalian. Avocations: travel, tennis, golf. Office: Williams Mullen Christian & Dobbins 2 James Center 1021 E Cary St Richmond VA 23219-4000

ADDISON, HERBERT JOHN, publishing executive; b. Berkeley, Calif., Nov. 21, 1932; s. Herbert and Clara Virginia (Mason) A.; m. Geraldyne Elaine Harvey, Aug. 17, 1957; children: Bradley Thomas, Gregory James. B.A., U. Calif.-Berkeley, 1958; M.A., NYU, 1959. Office-personnel mgr. Thomas Y. Crowell Co., N.Y.C., 1958-65; editor-in-chief coll. dept. Holt, Rinehart & Winston, Inc., N.Y.C., 1965-70; v.p., gen. mgr. coll. dept. Thomas Y. Crowell Co., N.Y.C., 1970-74; exec. editor coll. dept. John Wiley & Sons, Inc., N.Y.C., 1974-78; gen. mgr. coll. dept. Oxford U. Press, Inc., N.Y.C., 1978-82, v.p., exec. editor bus. and econs., 1982—; adj. lectr. NYU, 1977-83. Author: Books and Bucks: The Business of College Textbook Publishing, 1980. Trustee Adult Sch. Montclair, N.J., 1976-80; mem. Civic Conf. Com., Glen Ridge, N.J., 1974-77. Served with U.S. Army, 1953-55. Mem. Acad. Mgmt., Strategic Mgmt. Soc., Am. Econ. Assn., Cornell Club. Home: 46 Sherman Ave Glen Ridge NJ 07028-1441 Office: Oxford U Press Inc 198 Madison Ave Fl 9 New York NY 10016-4314

ADDISON, WILLIAM B.C., JR., state senate employee; b. Prince Georges County, Md., Oct. 11, 1951. BA, U. S.C., 1973. Sec. Md. State Senate, Annapolis, 1998—. Office: Md State Senate State House Rm H105 Annapolis MD 21401-1991

ADDLESTONE, NATHAN SIDNEY, metals company executive; b. Charleston, S.C., Jan. 16, 1913; s. Abram and Rachel (Lader) A.; m. Marlene Kronsberg, Apr. 27, 1982; children by previous marriage: Carole Anita, Susan Lader. Grad. pub. high sch.; LittD (hon.), Coll. Charleston, 1989. With Sumter (S.C.) Iron & Metal Co., 1932-45, pres., 1938-45; founding pres. Addlestone & Co., Sumter, 1945-66, Addlestone Steel Corp., 1945-66; pres. Columbia Steel & Metal Co., 1951-88; founder, chmn. bd. Steelmet, Inc., Charleston, 1961-73; pres., treas., dir. Metro Iron & Metal Corp., 1964-74; founder, pres., chmn. bd. Raw Materials Corp., 1969-80, Addlestone Internat. Corp., Charleston, 1973—; founder, chmn. bd. Allied Steel Corp., Charleston, 1984-89; v.p., treas. Ramkin, Inc., 1985-94; pres. Ramkin, Inc., Jacksonville, Fla., 1994—; pres., chmn. bd. Assoc. Iron & Metals Co., Jacksonville, Fla., 1985-88, N. Goldberg Co., Inc., Charleston, 1986-88; pres. Dreyfus Assocs., 1988—; President Ramkin, Inc., 1994-present; President & CEO & Treasurer Addlestone International, 1973-present; President & Treasurer 5705 Hwy Ave Corporation, 1993-present; founder, chmn. bd., pres. Addlestone Export Corp., 1974-88; founder, chmn., pres. Addlestone Recycling Corp., Metter, Ga., 1993-97, Addlestone & Co., Jacksonville, Fla., 1993-97. Mem., del. Bur. Internat. de la Recuperation, 1973-85; bd. dirs. Jewish Community Ctr., Charleston, Nations Bank S.C., 1991-93; pres. Addlestone Hebrew Acad. Trust, 1976-89; mem. Trident Area Commn. for Tech. Edn., 1976-87, chmn. bd., 1981-86; pres., chmn. bd. Nathan S. and Marlene Addlestone Found., Inc., 1979—. Mem. C. of C. Sumter (past pres.), Nat. Assn. Secondary Materials (past bd. dirs.), Inst. Scrap Iron and Steel (past bd. dirs., mem. fgn. trade com. 1965-90, vice chmn. 1970-71). Jewish. Clubs: Rotarian, Elk, Mason, Shriner. Home: 330 Concord St Apt 10bc Charleston SC 29401-1549 Office: 288 Meeting St Charleston SC 29401-1570

ADDUCCI, JOSEPH EDWARD, obstetrician, gynecologist; b. Chgo., Dec. 1, 1934; s. Dominee Edward and Harriet Evelyn (Kneppreth) A.; m. Mary Ann Tiertje, 1958; children—Christopher, Gregory, Steven, Jessica, Tobias. B.S., U. Ill., 1955; M.D., Loyola U., Chgo., 1959. Diplomate Am. Bd. Ob-Gyn., Nat. Bd. Med. Examiners. Intern Cook County Hosp, Chgo., 1959-60; resident in ob-gyn Mt. Carmel Hosp., Detroit, 1960-64; practice medicine specializing in obstetrics and gynecology Williston, N.D., 1966—; chief staff, chmn. obstetrics dept. Mercy Hosp., Williston, mem. governing bd., 1996; clin. prof. U. N.D. Med. Sch., 1973—; mem. gov. bd. Mercy Hosp. Cath. Health Corp. Mem. N.D. Bd. Med. Examiners, 1974—, past chmn.; project dir. Tri County Family Planning Svc.; past pres. Tri County Health Planning Coun.; mem. governing bd. Mercy Hosp., Williston, N.D. With Med. Corps, AUS, 1964-66. Fellow Am. Soc. Abdominal Surgeons, ACS (regent N.D. 1990—), Am. Coll. Obstetrics and Gynecologists (sect. chmn. N.D.), Internat. Coll. Surgeons (regent 1972-74, 88-89), Am. Fertility Soc., Am. Assn. Internat. Lazar Soc., Gynecol. Lataropists, N.D. Obstetricians and Gynecologists Soc. (pres. 1966, 76); mem. Am. Soc. for Colposcopy and Colpomicroscopy, Am. Soc. Cryosurgery, Am. Soc. Contemporary Medicine and Surgery, Am. Assn. Profl. Ob-Gyn., Pan Am. Med. Assn., Am. Coll. Surgeons (regent 1989— N.D.). Lodge: Elks. Home: 1717 Main St Williston ND 58801-4244 Office: Medical Ctr OB GYN Williston ND 58801

ADDUCCI, REGINA MARIE, medical/surgical nurse; b. Flushing, N.Y., Jan. 1, 1956; d. Robert Philip and Brenda Claire (Guinan) Hosey; m. Joseph Anthony Adducci, June 30, 1990 (div. June 14, 1995); 1 child, Sarah Elizabeth. BS, Mount St. Mary Coll., Newburgh, N.Y., 1978. RN, Conn. Staff nurse med./surg. unit Danbury (Conn.) Hosp., 1979-88, staff nurse ob./gyn./urology unit, 1988-89, asst. nurse mgr. gynecology/urology unit, 1989-92, asst. nurse mgr. general surgery unit, 1992-93, coord. quality improvement med. svcs., 1993-95, asst. dir. nursing, 1995—.

ADDY, ALVA LEROY, mechanical engineer; b. Dallas, S.D., Mar. 29, 1936; s. Alva Isaac and Nellie Amelia (Brumbaugh) A.; m. Sandra Ruth Turney, June 8, 1958. BS, S.D. Sch. Mines and Tech., 1958; MS, U. Cin., 1960; PhD, U. Ill., 1963. Engr. Gen. Electric Co., Cin., also Lancaster, Calif., 1958-60; prof. mech. engring. U. Ill., Urbana, 1963-98, prof. emeritus, 1998—, dir. mech. engring. lab., 1965-97, assoc. head mech. engring. dept., 1980-87, head, 1987-98; aerodynamics cons. U.S. Army Missile Command, Redstone Arsenal, Ala., summers 1965-98; cons. U.S. Army Research Office, 1964—; cons. in high-speed fluid dynamics to indsl. firms, 1963—; vis. research prof. U.S. Army, 1976; lectr. Von Karman Inst. Fluid Dynamics, Brussels, 1968, 75, 76. Fellow ASME, AIAA (assoc.), Am. Soc. for Engring. Edn. (Ralph Coates Roe award 1990); mem. Sigma Xi, Pi Tau Sigma, Sigma Tau. Home: 1706 Golfview Dr Urbana IL 61801-1111 Office: U Ill 1206 W Green St Urbana IL 61801-2906

ADDY, FREDERICK SEALE, retired oil company executive; b. Boston, Jan. 1, 1932; s. William R. and Edith (Seale) A.; m. Joyce Marilyn Marshall, Mar. 26, 1954; children: Deborah, William, Brian. BA, Mich. State U., 1953; MBA, 1957. With Amoco Corp. and its subs., 1957-94; exec. v.p., chief fin. officer, dir. Amoco Corp., Chgo., 1990-94; interim chmn., pres., CEO Enserch Exptl. Inc., 1996-97; bd. dirs. Baker Fentress & Co., JPM Funds, EEX, Inc. Served with USAF, 1954-56.

ADDY, JAN ARLENE, clinical nurse, educator; b. Balt., Apr. 16, 1951; d. James Anderson and June Annette (Windsor) Briggle; m. Rick Edward Addy, Feb. 26, 1988; children: Brittany Anissa, Richard Michael. AA in Nursing, Essex Community Coll., Balt., 1972; BSN, U. San Francisco, 1976; MS, U. Md., Balt., 1979; postgrad., Nova Southeastern U. Cert. sch. health nurse, pub. health nurse. Sr. staff nurse Francis Scott Key Med. Ctr., Balt., 1980-87; clin. instr. Harford Community Coll., Bel Air, Md., 1987-88; primary nurse and nurse educator U. Md., Balt., 1987—; asst. prof. Baltimore City C.C., 1994—; mem. rev. faculty for Nat. State Bd. Exam. for Nursing; mem. adj. faculty Catonsville C.C., 1994; instr. jr. students St. Joseph's Hosp. Sch. Nursing, Towson, Md., 1979-80; clin. instr., skills instr. Essex C.C., 1978-79; mem. U. Md. Med. Sys. Partnership Program, Frederick Douglas H.S. Contbr. articles to profl. jours. Mem. ASCD, Nat. Soc. Trauma Nurses, Nat. Nursing Staff Devel. Orgn., Emergency Nurses Assn., C.A.R.E., Sigma Theta Tau (program com. Pi chpt.).

ADE, BARBARA JEAN, secondary education educator; b. Youngstown, Ohio, Nov. 6, 1951; d. Donald Eugene Sr. and Louise Ann (Bodnark) Kihm; m. Robert Randal Ade, Mar. 17, 1973. BS in Edn., Youngstown State U., 1975, MS in Edn., 1987. High sch. media specialist Springfield Local High Sch., New Middletown, Ohio, 1975—. Active Youngstown Area YWCA. Grad. Sch. scholar Youngstown State U., 1986-87; named Woman of the Yr., Youngstown Area YWCA, 1993. Mem. NEA, AAUW, Ohio Ednl. Libr./Media Assn., Ohio Edn. Assn., Delta Kappa Gamma, Phi Delta Kappa. Democrat. Roman Catholic. Avocations: reading, antique collecting, golf, painting. Office: Springfield Local High Sch 11335 Youngstown-Pittsburgh Rd New Middletown OH 44442-9738

ADEBONOJO, FESTUS O., medical educator; b. Lagos, Nigeria, May 6, 1931; came to U.S., 1952; naturalized, 1989; s. Samuel A. and Regina O. Adebonojo; m. Leslie J. Goodale, Nov. 26, 1987; children: William, David, Andrew, Geoffrey. B.S., Yale U., 1956, M.D., 1960. Diplomate Am. Bd. Pediatrics. Intern in pediatrics Yale New Haven (Conn.) Hosp., 1960-61, resident in pediatrics, 1961-63; pediatrician Permanente Med. Group, San Rafael, Calif., 1964-71; asst. prof. pediatrics U. Pa., Phila., 1971-76; assoc. prof. U. Pa, Phila., 1976-77; prof. pediatrics, chmn. U. Ife, Ile-Ife, Nigeria, 1977-78, dean Sch. Medicine, 1978-80; sr. research fellow J. Stokes Research Inst., Children's Hosp., Phila., 1980-82; prof. pediatrics Cornell U., N.Y.C., 1982-84; prof., chmn. pediatrics Meharry Med. Coll, Nashville, 1984-88, James H. Quillen Coll. Medicine, East Tenn. State U., Johnson City, 1988—. Author: How Baby Grows, 1985. Bd. dirs. Family Service Agy., Marin County, Calif., 1965-71; bd. dirs. Econ. Opportunity Council, Marin County, 1966-71, chmn., 1970-71; mem. Gov.'s Task Force on Healthy Children, Tenn., 1984-87. Mem. Am. Pediatric Soc., Sigma Xi. Office: East Tenn State U James H Quillen Coll Medicine PO Box 70578 Johnson City TN 37614-0984

ADEL, GARRY DAVID, lawyer; b. N.Y.C., June 7, 1956; s. Seymour and Ruth (Moskowitz) A.; m. Terry Linn Cole, June 21, 1980. BS, Fla. State U., 1978, JD, 1982. Bar: Fla. 1982, U.S. Dist. Ct. (mid. dist.) Fla. 1983, U.S. Dist. Ct. (no. dist.) Fla. 1987, U.S. Dist. Ct. (so. dist) Fla. 1989, U.S. Ct. Appeals (11th cir.) 1986, U.S. Supreme Ct. 1988. Assoc. Bond, Arnett & Phelan PA, Ocala, Fla., 1983-85, Blanchard Custureri, Merriam PA, Ocala, 1986-87; ptnr. Blanchard, Merriam, Adel & Kirkland, P.A., Ocala, 1987—. Mem. Asn. Trial Lawyers Am., Acad. Fla. Trial Lawyers, Am. Acad. Trial Lawyers, Fl. Criminal Defense Lawyers Assn., Lions. Avocations: sports, fishing, reading. Address: 4 SE Broadway St Ocala FL 34471-2132

ADELBERG, ARNOLD MELVIN, mathematics educator, researcher; b. Bklyn., Mar. 17, 1936; s. David and Evelyn (Brass) A.; m. Harriet Diamond, June 30, 1962; children: Danielle Hamill, Erica. BA, Columbia U., 1956; MA, Princeton U., 1959, PhD, 1996. Instr. Columbia U., N.Y.C., 1959-62; instr., asst. prof., assoc. prof., prof. Grinnell (Iowa) Coll., 1962—, Myra Steele prof. math., 1991—; chair math. dept., sci. div. several times, chmn. faculty Grinnell Coll., 1974-76. Contbr. articles to profl. jours. Mem. Math. Assn. Am., Am. Math. Soc. Avocations: bridge, chess. Home: 1930 Manor Cir Grinnell IA 50112-1136 Office: Grinnell Coll Math Dept PO Box 805 Grinnell IA 50112-0805

ADELBERG, ARTHUR WILLIAM, lawyer; b. Oakland, Calif., Aug. 18, 1951; s. Edward Allen and Mary (Sanders) A.; m. Lisa Sheprow, Feb. 5, 1994; children: Jeffrey, Sarah. BA, Yale U., 1973; JD, U. N.C., 1976. Bar: Conn. 1976, D.C. 1977, Maine 1985. Gen. atty. FTC, Washington, 1976-80; assoc. Pepper Hamilton & Scheetz, Washington, 1980-84, ptnr., 1984-85; gen. counsel Ctrl. Maine Power Co., Augusta, 1985-91, v.p., gen. counsel, 1988-91, v.p. law and pub. affairs, 1991-92, sr. v.p. law and pub. affairs, 1992-93; sr. v.p. law and govt. rels. Maine Power Co., Augusta, 1993-97; exec. v.p. CMP Group, Inc., Augusta, 1997—; lectr. U. Maine Law Sch., Portland, 1987-88; adv. com. Profls. Responsible to Maine Supreme Ct., 1990-96; cons. U.S.Agy. for Internat. Devel. and World Bank, 1993—. Chmn. Maine Milk Commn., 1988-91; mem. adv. panel Coun. on Econ. Regulation, 1990—; trustee Susan Curtis Found., 1994—. Mem. ABA, Fed. Energy Bar Assn., Fed. Bar Assn. (chmn. YLD 1986-87, officer, bd. dirs. 1984-86). Home: 44 Winthrop St Hallowell ME 04347-1228 Office: CMP Group Inc 85 Edison Dr Augusta ME 04336

ADELL, HIRSCH, lawyer; b. Novogrodek, Poland, Mar. 11, 1931; came to U.S., 1937; s. Nathan and Nachama (Wager) A.; m. Judith Audrey Fuss, Feb. 8, 1963; children—Jeremiah, Nikolas, Balthasar, Valentine. Student, CCNY, 1949-52; B.A., UCLA, 1955, LL.B., 1963. Bar: Cal. bar 1963. Adminstrv. asst. to State Senator Richard Richards, 1956-60; ptnr. Warren & Adell, Los Angeles, 1963-75, Reich, Adell, Crost & Cvitan, L.A., 1975—; counsel AFTRA, Los Angeles. Served with AUS, 1953-55. Mem. ABA (labor and employment law sect.). Home: 545 S Norton Ave Los Angeles CA 90020-4610 Office: Reich Adell Crost & Cvitan 501 Shatto Pl Ste 100 Los Angeles CA 90020-1792

ADELMAN, ANDREW A., city manager; married; 2 children. BSCE, U. Calif., Berkeley, BS in Nuclear Engring., MS in Structural Engring.; cert. in mgmt., Harvard U. Registered profl. engr., Calif., Ariz., Nev. Engr. Impel Corp. and-Quadrex Corp., San Francisco, 1979-81; lead engr. Cygna Corp., San Francisco, 1981-83; chief engr. Panel Clip/Lumberlok, Hayward, Calif., 1983-84; plans and permit divsn. mgr., chief plan check engr. City of Fremont, Calif., 1984-92; chief bldg. offcl., dep. dir. Dept. Planning Bldg. and Code Enforcement, City of San Jose, Calif., 1992-97; gen. mgr. bldg. safety dept. Bldg. and Code Enforcement, City of San Jose, 1997—; adj. prof. engring. Saginaw Valley State Coll., Mich., 1982. Mem. Inverness Ridge Homeowners Assn., Mission Meadows Homeowners Assn. Recipient numerous awards. Mem. Delta Chi, Tau Beta Pi, Chi Epsilon. Office: Bldg and Safety Dept City of Los Angeles 201 N Figueroa St Rm 1000 Los Angeles CA 90012-2623*

ADELMAN, HOWARD, philosophy educator; b. Toronto, Jan. 7, 1938; s. Harry Adelman and Frances (Duviner) Bromstein; m. Margaret Dorothy Smith, May 31, 1960; children: Jeremy Ian, Shonagh Eva, Rachel Esther, Eric Reuben; m. Nancy Jean Garrett, June 15, 1985; children: Daniel Jacob, Gabriel Benjamin. BA, U. Toronto, 1961, MA, 1963, PhD, 1971. From asst. prof. to assoc. prof. philosophy York U., North York, Ont., 1966-80, prof., 1981-83, acting dean Atkinson Coll., 1973-74, dir. grad. programme in philosophy, 1980-83, 95-96, dir. Ctr. for Refugee Studies, 1986-93, chmn. senate, 1981-82; Lady Davis vis. prof. Hebrew U., 1977-78; conf. presenter, workshop presenter in field. Author: Beds of Academe, 1970, The Holiversity, 1973, Canada and the Indochinese Refugees, 1982, (monograph) Palestinian Refugees and Durable Solutions, 1987; co-author: Early Warning and Conflict Management: The Genocide in Rwanda, 1996; editor: Refugee Policy: Canada and the United States, 1991, Legitimate and Illegitimate Discrimination: New Issues in Migration, 1993; co-editor: African Refugees, 1994, Immigration and Refugee Policy: Australia and Canada Compared, 1994, (with John Simpson) Multiculturalism, Jews and Canandian Identity, 1996, Immigration and Refugee Policy: Canada and Europe, 1998, The Path of a Genocide: The Rwanda Crisis from Uganda to Zaire, 1998; editor Refuge, 1982-93; contbr. numerous articles to profl. publs. Harvard Harvey Harnick scholar, Queen Elizabeth II scholar, Can. Coun. writing scholar; grad. fellow Province of Ont.; grantee Ctrl. Mortgage and Housing Corp., Slater Found., 1980, SSHRC, 1983, 90-93, 91, 93, Aktinson Coll., 1982-84, 85-86, CIDA, 1991, UNESCO, 1991, CEIC, 1982, 86-93, Ford Found., 1984, 86-88, 89, IDRC, 1982, ICMC, 1982, Ditchley Conf., 1983, IDRC, 1992, OECD, 1995; recipient Gerstein award, 1996, Marvin Gelber award, 1996, European Task Force award, 1996, John Holmes Found. award, 1997, SSHRC, 1997. Home: 64 Wells Hill Ave, Toronto, ON Canada M5R 3A8 Office: York U Philosophy Dept, 4700 Keele St, North York, ON Canada M3J 1P3

ADELMAN, IRMA GLICMAN, economics educator; b. Cernowitz, Rumania, Mar. 14, 1930; came to U.S., 1949, naturalized, 1955; d. Jacob Max and Raissa (Ettinger) Glicman; m. Frank L. Adelman, Aug. 16, 1950 (div. 1979); 1 son, Alexander. BS, U. Calif., Berkeley, 1950, MA, 1951, PhD, 1955. Teaching assoc. U. Calif., Berkeley, 1955-56; instr. U. Calif., 1956-57, lectr. with rank asst. prof., 1957-58; vis. asst. prof. Mills Coll., 1958-59; acting asst. prof. Stanford, 1959-61, asst. prof., 1961-62; assoc. prof. Johns Hopkins, Balt., 1962-65; prof. econs. Northwestern U., Evanston, Ill., 1966-72, U. Md., 1972-78; prof. econs. and agrl. econs. U. Calif. at Berkeley, 1979-94; prof. emeritus, 1994—; cons. divsn. indsl. devel. UN, 1962-63, AID U.S. Dept. State, Washington, 1963-72, World Bank, 1968—, ILD, Geneva, 1973—. Author: Theories of Economic Growth and Development, 1961, (with A. Pepelasis and L. Mears), Economic Development: Analysis and Case Studies, 1961, (with Eric Thorbecke) The Theory and Design of Economic Development, 1966, (with C.T. Morris) Society, Politics and Economic Development—A Quantitative Approach, 1967, Practical Approaches to Development Planning-Korea's Second Five Year Plan, 1969, (with C.T. Morris) Economic Development and Social Equity in Developing Countries, 1973, (with Sherman Robinson) Planning for Income Distribution, 1977-78, (with C. T. Morris) Comparative Patterns of Economic Growth, 1850-1914, 1987, (J. Edward Taylor) Village Economies: Design, Estimation and Application of Village Wide Economic Models, 1996, Institutions and Development Strategies: Selected Essays of Irma Adelman Vol. I, 1994, Vol. II, 1994, Selected Essays (in Spanish), 1994, (with Irma and Song Byung Nak) The South Korean Miracle: How Replicable Is It?, 1999. Fellow Center Advanced Study Behavioral Scis., 1970-71; named Women's Hall Fame U. Calif., Berkeley, 1994. Fellow Am. Acad. Arts and Scis., Econometric Soc., Royal Soc. Encouragement Arts, Mfgs. & Commerce (Berkeley citation 1996); mem. Am. Econ. Assn. (mem. exec. com., v.p. 1969-71). Office: Univ Calif Dept Agr & Natural Resources 207 Giannini Hall Spc 3310 Berkeley CA 94720-3310

ADELMAN, JONATHAN REUBEN, political science educator, consultant; b. Washington, Oct. 30, 1948; s. Benjamin and Kitty (Sandler) A.; m. Agota Kuperman, Aug. 3, 1997. BA, Columbia U., 1969, MA, 1972, M in Philosophy, 1974, PhD, 1976. Vis. asst. prof. Columbia U., N.Y.C., 1977; vis. asst. prof. U. Ala., Tuscaloosa, 1977-78; asst. prof. Grad. Sch. Internat. Studies U. Denver, 1978-85, assoc. prof., 1985-92, prof. polit. sci., 1992—; sr. rsch. analyst Sci. Applications, Inc., Denver, 1981-87, 96—; hon. prof. People's U., Beijing, 1996—, Beijing U., 1996—; cons., 1988-89, 96—; Lady Davis vis. assoc. prof. Hebrew U., Jerusalem, 1986; vis. fellow Soviet Acad. Scis., 1989, 90, Chinese Inst. Contemporary Internat. Rels., Beijing, 1988, People's U., Beijing, 1990, 94, 96, 97, 98, 99; vis. prof. Beijing U., 1989, 98, U. Haifa, Israel, 1990; vis. spkr. Soviet Acad. Scis., 1990, Barcelona (Spain) U. and Complutense U., 1990, Cambridge (Eng.) U., 1991, Nat. Taiwan U., 1998, 99; vis. lectr., Japan, India, Hong Kong, Yugoslavia, Spain, 1990, 91, Germany, 1991, Bulgaria, 1991; vis. spkr. Conf. for Study of European Ideas, Aalborg U., Denmark, 1992; vis. prof. People's U., Beijing, 1990, 97, Janus Pannonius U., Pecs, Hungary, 1981. Author: The Revolutionary Armies, 1980, Revolution, Armies and War, 1986, Prelude to the Cold War: Tsarist, Soviet and U.S. Armies in Two World Wars, 1988, Torrents of Spring: Soviet and Post Soviet Politics, 1994; co-author: The Dynamics of Soviet Foreign Policy, 1988; editor: Communist Armies in Politics, 1982, Terror and Communist Politics, 1984, Superpowers and Revolution, 1986; co-editor: Contemporary Soviet Military Affairs: The Legacy World War II, 1989; contbr. numerous articles in fieod to profl. jours. Charles Phelps Taft fellow U. Cin., 1976-77; Am. Philos. Soc. grantee, 1980. Mem. Am. Polit. Sci. Assn., Am. Assn. Advancement Slavic Studies. Democrat. Jewish. Office: U Denver Grad Sch Internat Studies Denver CO 80208

ADELMAN, LYNN S., United States district judge; b. Milw., Oct. 1, 1939; s. Albert B. and Edith Margoles Adelman; m. Elizabeth Halmbacher, 1976; children: Lisa, Mia. AB, Princeton U., 1961; LLB, Columbia U., 1965. State senator dist. 28 State of Wis., Milw., 1977-97; U.S. dist. judge Ea. Dist. of Wis., Milw., 1997—; chmn. judiciary and consumer affairs com. Wis. State Senate; pvt. practice as atty. Mem. Berlin Hist. Soc. Democrat. Office: 33725 Janesville Dr Mukwonago WI 53149-8909 also: U.S.Courthouse & Fed Bldg 517 E Wisconsin Ave Milwaukee WI 53202-4500

ADELMAN, PAMELA BERNICE KOZOLL, education educator; b. Milw., Dec. 26, 1945; d. Harry and Rebecca (Sharp) Kozoll); m. Steven H. Adelman, June 30, 1968; children: David, Robert. BS, U. Wis., Madison, 1967; MA, Northwestern U., 1972, PhD, 1982. Cert. tchr., Ill. Shair edn. dept. Barat Coll., Lake Forest, Ill., 1986-97; tchr. Peckham Jr. High Sch., Milw., 1967-68, Fairview Sch., Skokie, Ill., 1968-70; learning disabilities specialist Sch. Dist 28, Northbrook, Ill., 1971-77; instr., rsch. asst. Northwestern U., Evanston, Ill., 1977-80; lectr., asst. prof., then assoc. prof. Barat Coll., Lake Forest, Ill., 1977-90, prof. edn., 1990—, dir. learning opportunities program, 1985—, chmn. edn. dept., 1986-97, grad. dean, 1997—, chmn. edn. dept., 1986-97; cons. Deerfield (Ill.) Pub. Schs., 1986-90; proposal reviewer State of N.J., Trenton, 1986-87; mem. Pres.'s Com. on Hiring of Disabled, 1990; mem. higher edn. adv. coun. State of Ill.; mem. Coun. Chgo. Area Deans of Edn., 1992—, chair, 1998-99; mem. comprehensive sys. of pers. devel. adv. com. Ill. State Bd. Edn.; presenter at profl. confs. Co-author: Learning Disabilities, Graduate School, and Careers, 1990; co-editor: Success for College Students with Learning Disabilities, 1993; consulting editor Learning Disabilities Focus, 1989-92, Jour. Developmental Edn., 1990-98, Jour. of Postsecondary Edn. and Disabilities, 1991—; contbr. articles to ednl. publs. Chair Sch. Dist. 107 Caucus, Highland Park, Ill., 1982; bd. dirs. Jewish Children's Bur., Chgo., 1985—, pres., 1994-96; co-author brochure for Ill. Dept. Human Rights, Chgo., 1986; bd. dirs. Jewish Fedn. Met. Chgo., 1996—. Paul A. Witty fellow Northwestern U., 1978-80; grantee Lloyd A. Fry Found., 1985-86, McDonald's Corp., Chgo., 1986, Kraft Corp., Chgo., 1989, Thorn River Found., 1990—. Fellow Internat. Acad. for Rsch. in Learning Disabilities; mem. Coun. Exceptional Children, Learning Disabilities Assn. Am., Coun. Learning Disabilities, Orton Dyslexia Soc., Assn. on Higher Edn. and Disabilities. Avocations: reading, walking, music, swimming. Office: Barat Coll 700 E Westleigh Rd Lake Forest IL 60045-3263

ADELMAN, RICHARD CHARLES, gerontologist, educator; b. Newark, Mar. 10, 1940; s. Morris and Elanor (Wachman) A.; m. Lynn Betty Richman, Aug. 18, 1963; children—Mindy Robin, Nicole Ann. A.B., Kenyon Coll., 1962; M.A., Temple U., 1965, Ph.D., 1967. Postdoctoral fellow Albert Einstein Coll. Medicine, Bronx, N.Y., 1967-69; from asst. prof. to prof. Temple U., Phila., 1969-82, dir. inst. aging, 1978-82; prof. biol. chemistry U. Mich., Ann Arbor, 1982—, dir. inst. gerontology, 1982-97; mem. study sect. NIH, 1975-78; adv. coun. VA, 1981-85; chmn. Gordon Rsch. Conf. Biol. Aging, 1976; adv. com. VA, 1981-91; chmn. VA Geriatrics and Gerontology Adv. Com., 1987-91. Mem. various editorial bds. biomed. research jours., 1972—. Bd. dirs. Botsford Continuing Care Ctrs., Inc., Farmington Hills, Mich., 1984-88. Recipient Medalist award Intrasci. Research Found., 1977; grantee NIH, 1970—; established investigator Am. Heart Assn., 1975-78. Fellow Gerontol. Soc. Am. (v.p. 1976-77, pres. elect 1986-87, Kent award 1990); mem. Am. Soc. Biol. Chemists, Gerontol. Soc. Am. (pres. 1986-87), Am. Chem. Soc., AAAS, Phila. Biochemists (pres.), Practicioners in Aging. Jewish.

ADELMAN, RICK, professional basketball coach; b. June 16, 1946; m. Mary Kay Adelman; children: Kathryn Mary, Laura, R.J., David. Master's, Loyola Marymount U. Profl. basketball player San Diego, 1968-70; profl. basketball player Portland (Oreg.) Trail Blazers, 1970-73, asst. coach, 1983-89, head coach, 1989-94; basketball player Chgo., New Orleans, Kansas City, and Omaha, 1973-75; head coach Chemeketa Community Coll., Salem, Oreg., 1975-83, Golden State Warriors, Oakland, Calif., 1995-97. Office: Sacramento Kings ARCO Arena One Sports Parkway Sacramento CA 95834*

ADELMAN, ROBERT PAUL, retired construction company executive, lawyer; b. N.Y.C., Dec. 7, 1930; s. Saul and Eva (Ochs) A.; m. Renee Gratum, June 7, 1953; children: Michael, Susan, John; m. Judith A. Turner, Jan. 9, 1999. BA, Columbia U., 1952, JD, 1954. Bar: N.Y. 1954, U.S. Supreme Ct. 1960. Assoc. Winthrop, Stimson, Putnam & Roberts, N.Y.C., 1956-64; with Celanese Corp., N.Y.C., 1964-71; v.p., treas., gen. counsel Calina Industries, Inc., N.Y.C., 1971-73; chief fin. officer Rockefeller Group, Inc., N.Y.C., 1975-84; chmn., chief exec. officer, pres. Rogers Group, Inc., Nashville, 1984-88, chmn., 1988-92, vice chmn., 1992—; mem. Fin. Execs. Inst., 1973-84, Conf. Bd. Exec. Coun., 1985-90; bd. dirs. N. European Oil Royalty Trust, Fundamental Mgmt. Corp. Treas. and chief fin. officer N.Y. State Urban Devel. Corp., 1973-75; trustee The Jackson Lab., 1981—. Served with U.S. Army, 1954-56, instr. Corps of Cadets U.S. Mil. Acad., West Point, N.Y. Mem. University Club (N.Y.C.), Amelia Island Club. Avocations: sailing, tennis, golf.

ADELMAN, RODNEY LEE, federal agency administrator; b. Washington, Sept. 21, 1950; s. Charles H. and Vivian Fern (Sleek) A.; widowed; 2 children. BS, U. Md., 1972. Staff Senator Robert P. Griffin, Mich., 1970-73; fin. mgr. labor mgmt. svcs. adminstrn. Dept. of Labor, 1973-78; budget officer Congress of Micronesia, 1978-79, Federated States Micronesia, 1979-80; dir. budget and grants mgmt. Trust Territory of the Pacific Islands, 1980-85; comptroller Def. Personnel Support Ctr. Def. Logistics Agy., 1985-86; dir. Washington Liaison Office, Juneau, Alaska, 1986-92; dep. asst. adminstr. Power Mktg. Liaison Office, 1992-96; Alaska power adminstr. Dept. of Energy, Juneau, 1996—.

ADELMAN, STANLEY JOSEPH, lawyer; b. Devils Lake, N.D., May 20, 1942; s. Isadore Russell Adelman and Eva Claire (Robins) Stoller; m. Mary Beth Petchaft, Jan. 30, 1972; children: Laura E., Sarah A. BS, U. Wis., 1964, JD, 1967. Bar: Ill. 1967, U.S. Dist. Ct. (no. dist.) Ill. 1967, Wis. 1968, U.S. Ct. Appeals (7th cir.), U.S. Dist. Ct. (ea. dist.) Wis. 1979, U.S. Supreme Ct. 1982, U.S. Ct. Appeals (10th cir.) 1984, U.S. Ct. Appeals (fed. cir.) 1987. Assoc. Sonnenchein, Carlin, Nath & Rosenthal, Chgo., 1967-75, ptnr., 1975-85; co-chmn. litigation dept. Rudnick & Wolfe, Chgo., 1985-91, 96-97, ptnr., 1985—; profl. responsibility ptnr. Rudnick & Wolfe, 1992-94, mem. mgmt. policy com., 1985-97, co-chmn. complex litigation practices group, 1997-98. Bd. dirs. Legal Assistance Found., Chgo., 1982-83. Fellow Nat. Inst. Trial Advocacy; mem. Chgo. Bar Assn., Chgo. Coun. Lawyers, Am. Inns of Ct. (pres. Markey/Wigmore chpt.), Law Club Chgo., Order of Coif. Jewish. Home: 115 Crescent Dr Glencoe IL 60022-1303 Office: Rudnick & Wolfe 203 N La Salle St Ste 1800 Chicago IL 60601-1225

ADELMAN, STEVEN ALLEN, theoretical physical chemist, chemistry educator; b. Chgo., July 4, 1945; s. Hyman and Sarah Adelman; m. Barbara Stolberg, May 13, 1974. BS, Ill. Inst. Tech., 1967; Ph.D., Harvard U., 1972. Postdoctoral fellow MIT, Cambridge, 1972-73; postdoctoral fellow U. Chgo., 1973-74; asst. prof. chemistry Purdue U., West Lafayette, Ind., 1975-77, assoc. prof., 1977-82, prof., 1982—; cons. Exxon Rsch. Co., Los Alamos Nat. Lab.; vis. prof. U. Paris, 1985; nominator 1994 Nobel Prize in Chemistry, Royal Swedish Acad. Scis. Contbr. articles to profl. jours. Vol. U.S. Peace Corp., Ankara, Turkey, 1969-70. Fellow Alfred P. Sloan Found., 1976-78, Guggenheim Found., 1982-83; NSF grantee, 1976—; named Outstanding Sr. in Chemistry, Am. Inst. Chemistry, 1967. Fellow Am. Phys. Soc.; mem. AAAS, Am. Chem. Soc., Am. Statis. Assn., Math. Assn. Am., Sigma Xi. Avocations: long-distance running, bicycling, Turkish language and literature. Home: 3037 Courthouse Dr W Apt 2C West Lafayette IN 47906-1035 Office: Purdue U Dept Chemistry West Lafayette IN 47907

ADELMAN, STEVEN HERBERT, lawyer; b. Chgo., Dec. 21, 1945; s. Irving and Sylvia (Cohen) A.; m. Pamela Bernice Kozoll, June 30, 1968; children: David, Robert. BS, U. Wis.-Madison, 1967; JD, DePaul U., 1970. Bar: Ill. 1970, U.S. Dist. Ct. (no. dist.) Ill. 1970, U.S. Ct. Appeals (7th cir.) 1975. Ptnr. Keck, Mahin & Cate, Chgo., 1970-93, Lord, Bissell & Brook, Chgo., 1993—. Contbr. chpts. to books, articles to profl. jours. Bd. dirs. Bur. Jewish Employment Problems, Chgo., 1983—, pres. 1991, 92; employment relations com. Chgo. Assn. Commerce and Industry, 1982-90. Mem. Chgo. Bar Assn. (chmn. labor and employment law com. 1988-89), ABA (Silver Key award 1969), Ill. State Bar Assn., Chgo. Council Lawyers, Decalogue Soc. Office: Lord Bissell & Brook 115 S La Salle St Ste 3200 Chicago IL 60603-3972

ADELMAN, TERRY I., federal judge. Magistrate judge U.S. Dist. Ct. (ea. dist.) Mo., St. Louis, 1993—; adj. prof. Washington U. Sch. Law. Office: 106 Fed Ct and Custom House 114 N Market St Saint Louis MO 63102

ADELMAN, WILLIAM JOHN, university labor and industrial relations educator; b. Chgo., July 26, 1932; s. William Sidney and Annie Teresa (Goan) A.; m. Nora Jill Walters, June 26, 1952; children: Michelle, Marguerite, Marc, Michael, Jessica. Student, Lafayette Coll., 1952; BA, Elmhurst Coll., 1956; MA, U. Chgo., 1964. Tchr. Whitecross Sch., Hereford, Eng., 1956-57, Jefferson Sch., Berwyn, Ill., 1957-60, Morton High Sch., Berwyn, 1960-66; mem. faculty dept. labor and indsl. relations U. Ill., Chgo., 1966-91, prof., 1978-91, prof. emeritus, 1991—; coordinator Chgo. Labor Edn. Program, 1981-87; lectr. Road Scholar Program, Ill. Humanities Coun., 1997. Author: Touring Pullman, 1972, Haymarket Revisited, 1976, Pilsen and the West Side, 1981; writer: film Packingtown U.S.A., 1968; narrator: Palace Cars and Paradise: Pullman's Model Town, 1983. Bd. dirs. Chgo. Regional Blood Program, 1977-80; mem. Ill. State Employment Security Adv. Bd., 1974-75; Democratic candidate U.S. Ho. of Reps. from 14th dist. Ill., 1970; organizer Haymarket Centennial Events, 1986; chmn. Jane Addams' Hull House Adv. Bd., 1991—. Ill. Humanities Council grantee, 1977; German Marshall Fund U.S. grantee, 1977; recipient Tradition of Excellence award Oak Park/River Forest H.S., 1993, Eugene V. Debs award Midwest Labor Press assn., 1995. Mem. Ill. Labor History Soc. (founding mem., v.p., Union Hall of Honor 1993), Am. Fedn. Tchrs., Doris Humphrey Soc. (v.p. 1990—). Unitarian. Home and Office: 613 S Highland Ave Oak Park IL 60304-1524

ADELSBERG, HARVEY, hospital administrator; b. Bronx, N.Y., Aug. 5, 1931; s. Joseph and Becky (Rindner) A.; BA, NYU, 1953, MPA, 1960, postgrad., 1960-65; m. Miriam Levine, June 20, 1964; children: Jonathan, Risa, Seth. Adminstrv. resident Beth David Hosp., N.Y.C., 1953-54; adminstrv. asst. Met. Jewish Geriatric Center, Bklyn., 1954-58; asst. dir. Kingsbrook Jewish Med. Center, Bklyn., 1958-61; asst. dir. Hosp. for Joint Diseases, N.Y.C., 1961-64; exec. dir. Theresa Grotta Center for Restorative Services, Caldwell, N.J., 1964-70; asst. dir. Mt. Sinai Hosp., N.Y.C., 1970-72; cons. med. care and svcs. to aged Fedn. Jewish Philanthropies, N.Y.C., 1972-74; exec. dir. Daus. of Miriam Center for Aged, Clifton, N.J., 1974-76, exec. v.p., 1977-95, exec. v.p. emeritus, 1996; adj. asst. prof. health care adminstrn., Bernard M. Baruch Coll., Mt. Sinai Sch. Medicine, CUNY, 1973—, U. Medicine and Dentistry, N.J., 1995; mem. adv. com. Rutgers U., 1969—; mem. adj. prof. N.J. Grad. Sch. Pub. Health, 1995; cons. Consulting Svcs. Inst., 1995, mem. N.J. Licensing Bd. for Nursing Home Adminstrs., 1969—, vice chmn., 1969-77; mem. Adv. Council on Aging, Livington, N.J., 1977—. Trustee Hosp. and Council Met. N.J., 1967-70, Health and Hosp. Council So. N.Y., 1972-74, N.J. Assn. Non-Profit Homes for Aging, 1976—, Jewish Community Housing Corp., Paterson, N.J., 1975—; trustee tng. Dist, 1199J, 1990; agt. Daus. of Miriam Found., 1984; v.p. Solomon Schechter Day Sch. of Essex and Union, 1980—; trustee Synagogue of Suburban Torah Center, Livingston, 1978—; bd. govs. Greater N.Y. Hosp. Assn., 1972-74; v.p. Temple Beth Shalom, Livingston, 1970-71, 73, trustee, 1968-70, 75—; mem. governing com. Camp Ramah, Wingdale, N.Y., 1979—; exec. bd. Jewish Communal Svc. Assn. 1993—. Fellow Am. Coll. Hosp. Adminstrs., Am. Coll. Nursing Home Adminstrs., Am. Geriatric Soc., Am. Pub. Health Assn.; mem. Am., N.J. hosp. assns., Hosp. Exec. Club. Mem. B'nai B'rith (v.p. 1960-64). Home: 27 Tuxedo Dr Livingston NJ 07039-2452 Office: 155 Hazel St Clifton NJ 07011-3423

ADELSBERGER, DONNA L., lawyer, educator; b. Phila., July 19, 1954; married; 2 children. AA, Pa. State U., 1982; BA, Temple U., 1984, JD, 1988. Assoc. Krusen Evans & Byrne, Phila., 1988-95, ptnr., 1995; pvt. practice Donna Adelsberger & Assoc., Glenside, Pa., 1996—. Vol. lawyer Support Ctr. for Child Advocates, Phila., 1989—. Mem. Pa. Bar Assn., Montgomery County Bar Assn. Avocation: classical pianist. Office: Donna Adelsberger & Assocs PO Box 530 Glenside PA 19038-0530

ADELSMAN, (HARRIETTE) JEAN, newspaper editor; b. Indpls., Oct. 21, 1944; d. Joe and Beatrice Irene (Samuel) A. BS in Journalism, Northwestern U., 1966, MS in Journalism, 1967. Copy editor Chgo. Sun-Times, 1967-75, fin. news editor, 1975-77, entertainment editor, 1977-80, asst. mng. editor features, 1980-84; now mng. editor Daily Breeze, Torrance, Calif. Office: Daily Breeze 5215 Torrance Blvd Torrance CA 90503-4077*

ADELSON, DUFFIE ANN, music school administrator; b. Evanston, Ill., Oct. 13, 1951; d. Bernard H. and Martha Adelson. MusB, Lawrence U., 1973; MusM, U. Wis., 1979. Tchr. music Niagara (Wis.) Pub. Schs., 1973-74; string instr. Needham (Mass.) String Program, 1976-82; string tchr. Groton (Mass.) Pub. Schs., 1977-79, Quincy (Mass.) Pub. Schs., 1979-82; coord. met. area Urban Gateways, Chgo., 1982-83; strings coord. U. Chgo. Lab. Sch., 1983-86; assoc. dir. Merit Music Program, Chgo., 1986-93, exec. dir., 1993—; coord., initiator Six City String Festival, Mass., 1980-81; founder, coord. March String Fest, Boston, 1982; co-organizer Bay State String Camp, Hanson, Mass., 1981; review panelist Chgo. Office Fine Arts, 1989-91; mem. Chgo. com. Nat. Classical Music Month, 1994-96; adv. bd. Interface Ensemble Chgo., 1995-96, Chgo. Commons, 1995-97; pressenter in field. Charter mem. bd. dirs. Found. for Advancement String Edn., Boston, 1979-82; bd. dirs. Bus. and Profl. Assn. Chgo. Symphony, 1985-94, Chgo. Music Alliance, 1993-97; bd. dirs. Hyde Park Youth Sinfonia, Chgo., 1986-94, v.p., 1991-92, mem. adv. bd. 1994—. Mem. Am. String Tchrs. Assn. (sec. Chgo. chpt. 1985-88, coord. chamber music workshop 1985, nat. urban outreachcom. 1992—). Avocation: amateur violist University of Chicago Symphony Orchestra. Office: The Merit Music Program 47 W Polk St Chicago IL 60605-2000

ADELSON, MERV LEE, entertainment and communication industry executive; b. Los Angeles, Oct. 23, 1929; s. Nathan and Pearl (Schwarzman) A.; m. Thea Nesis, May 25, 1993; 1 child, Lexi Rose; children from previous marriage: Ellen, Gary, Andrew. Student, Menlo Park Jr. Coll. Pres. Markettown Supermarket and Builders Emporium, Las Vegas, 1953-63; mng. ptnr. Paradise Devel., Las Vegas, 1958—; pres. Realty Holdings, 1962—, La Costa, Inc., 1963-87; chmn. bd. dirs. Lorimar Inc., Culver City, Calif., 1969-86; chmn. bd. dirs., chief exec. officer Lorimar Telepictures Corp., Culver City, 1986-89; vice chmn. Warner Communications, 1989—; chmn. East-West Capital Assocs., Inc., 1989—; bd. dirs. Time-Warner Inc. Co-founder Nathan Adelson Hospice Found. Recipient Sherill Corwin Human Relations award Am. Jewish Com., 1987. Mem. Am. Film Inst. (trustee), Am. Mus. of Moving Images (trustee), Entertainment Industries Council (trustee), Acad. Motion Pictures Arts and Scis., Acad. TV Arts and Sciences, Nat. Acad. Cable Programming, Alliance for Capital Access (bd. dirs.), Com. Publicly Owned Cos. (bd. dirs.).

ADELSON, ROGER DEAN, history educator, editor, historian; b. Abilene, Kans., July 11, 1942; s. Orlie Austin and Winnifred Graham (McClure) A.; m. Sally Isabelle Squires, Sept. 1966 (div. Apr. 1978). BA, George Washington U., 1964; MA, Washington U., 1967, PhD, 1972; BLitt, Oxford (Eng.) U., 1970. Danforth fellow Washington U., St. Louis, 1964-67; sr. rsch. fellow St. Antony's Coll., Oxford U., 1972-73; lectr. history Harvard U., Cambridge, Mass., summer 1974; asst. prof. Ariz. State U., Tempe, 1974-78, assoc. prof., 1978-95, prof., 1996—; editor Historian, 1990-95, cons. editor, 1995—; vis. prof. Am. Grad. Sch. Internat. Mgmt., Glendale, Ariz., 1980s, Pepperdine U., Malibu, Calif., 1994, 95, 96; dir. Global History Project, 1995-97. Author: Mark Sykes: Portrait of an Amateur, 1975, London and the Invention of the Middle East, 1995, Speaking of History, 1996. Founding. pres. Soc. for Internat. Devel., Ariz., 1983; charter mem. Coun. Fgn. Rels., Phoenix, 1976. Mem. Conf. Hist. Jours. (pres. 1995-97), Phi Alpha Theta (historian 1990-95). Avocations: cycling, swimming, gardening, entertaining. Office: Ariz State U Dept History PO Box 872501 Tempe AZ 85287-2501

ADELSTEIN, S(TANLEY) JAMES, physician, educator; b. N.Y.C., Jan. 24, 1928; s. George and Belle (Schild) A.; m. Mary Charlesworth Taylor, Sept. 20, 1957; children: Joseph Burrows, Elizabeth Dunster. BS, MIT, 1949, MS, 1949, PhD in Biophysics, 1957; MD, Harvard U., 1953. Med. house officer Peter Bent Brigham Hosp., Boston, 1953-54, sr. asst. resident physician, 1957-58, chief resident, 1959-60; fellow Howard Hughes Med. Inst., 1957-58, Henry A. and Camilus Christian fellow, 1959-60; Moseley travel fellow Harvard U. Med. Sch., Boston, 1958-59, instr. anatomy, then asst. prof., 1961-68, assoc prof. radiology, 1968-72, prof., 1972-89, Paul C. Cabot prof. med. biophysics, 1989-97, prof. pathology, Daniel S. Tosteson univ. prof., 1997—, dean for acad. program, 1978-97; mem. Nat. Coun. for Radiation Protection Measurements, 1978—, dir., 1980—, v.p. 1982—; cons. Med. Found. fellow, 1960-63; Walter Dahdy lectr. John Hopkins U., 1996. Mem. editl. bd. Investigative Radiology, 1972-80, Postgrad. Radiology, Radiation Rsch., 1990-94; assoc. editor Jour. Nuc. Medicine, 1975-81; contbr. articles to profl. jours. Trustee Am. Bd. Nuc. Medicine, 1972-78; mem. fellowship adv. com. Whitaker Found., 1991-97. NIH Career Devel. awardee, 1965-68; Nat. Found. fellow MIT, 1957; Fogarty Sr. Internat. fellow, 1976. Fellow AAAS, Am. Coll. Nuc. Physicians; mem. Am. Chem. Soc., Biophys. Soc., Assn. for Radiation Rsch., Radiation Rsch. Soc. (councillor 1975-78), Soc. Nuc. Medicine (trustee 1970-74, Blumgart award 1983, Aebersold award 1986, Dr. Hevesy award 1999), Boylston Med. Soc., Inst. Medicine, Sigma Xi, Tau Beta Pi, Alpha Omega Alpha. Office: Harvard Med Sch 25 Shattuck St Boston MA 02115-6027

ADENAIKE, CAROLYN KEYES, historian, educator; b. Suffern, N.Y., Aug. 26, 1962; d. John Oliver and Leona Rose Keyes; m. David Olurotini Adenaike, Apr. 16, 1992; 1 child, Michael Jayeola. BA, Mt. Holyoke Coll., 1985; lic., U. Paris X, 1986; MA, U. Wis., 1988, PhD, 1993. Asst. prof. Hunters Coll., N.Y.C., 1994, Johns Hopkins U., Balt., 1996, Vassar Coll., Poughkeepsie, N.Y., 1996-97, U. Memphis, 1997—; assoc. mem. Inst. African Studies, U. Ibadan, Nigeria, 1989-92; rsch. scholar U. Lagos, Nigeria, 1995. Co-editor: (with J. Vansina) In Pursuit of History: Historical Fieldwork in Africa, 1996; contbr. articles to profl. jours. Recipient Summer stipend NEH, 1999; IIE/Fulbright fellow, Nigeria, 1989-90, Scholars-in-Residence fellow Schomburg Ctr. for Sch. in Black Culture, N.Y.C., 1999—; CIES Fulbright Scholars grantee African Regional Rsch. Program, Nigeria, 1995. Mem. AAUP, Am. Hist. Assn., African Studies Assn. Office: Schomburg Ctr for Rsch in Black Culture 515 Malcolm X Blvd New York NY 10037

ADERHOLD, H. RANDOLPH, prosecutor. U.S. atty. Mid. Dist. Ga., Macon, to 1998, chief civil divsn., 1998—. Office: US Atty Mid Dist Ga 433 Cherry St Macon GA 31201-7919*

ADERHOLT, ROBERT B., congressman; b. Haleyville, Ala., July 22, 1965. Mem. 105th Congress from 4th Ala. dist., 1996—. Office: 1007 Longworth Bldg Washington DC 20515-0104*

ADERMAN, RALPH MERL, English educator; b. Malinta, Ohio, May 27, 1919; s. Rudolph Ernest and Stella Barbara (Litzenberg) A.; m. Alice Coralyn Rath, Nov. 26, 1942; 1 child, Jeffrey Alan. B of Edn., U. Toledo, 1941, MA, 1945; PhD, U. Wis., 1951. Tchr. high sch. Henry County, Ohio, 1941-45; grad. teaching asst. U. Wis., Madison, 1945-47; instr. English Milw. State Tchrs. Coll., 1947-52, Wis. State Coll., Milw., 1952-56; assoc. prof. English U. Wis., Milw., 1956-59, prof. English, 1959-85, prof. emeritus, 1985—; Fulbright lectr. U. Bucharest, 1965-66. Editor: The Letters of James Kirke Paulding, 1962 (translation) Ion, 1967, Washington Irving Reconsidered; A Symposium, 1969, The Quest for Social Justice, 1983, From Trading Post to Metropolis: A History of Milwaukee County, 1987, Papa Floribunda: A Biography of Eugene S. Boerner, 1989, Critical Essays on Washington Irving, 1990; co-editor: (with Elizabeth M. Kerr) Aspects of American English, 1971 (with Herbert L. Kleinfield, Jenifer S. Banks) The Letters of Washington Irving, Vol. I 1802-1823, 1978, Vol. II 1823-1838, 1979, Vol. III 1839-1845, 1982, Vol. IV 1846-1859, 1982, (with Alice R. Aderman) A Genealogy of the Irvings of New york: Washington Irving, His Brothers and Sisters, and Their Descendants, 1983. Dir. Milw. County Hist. Soc., 1953-85. Am. Philos. Soc. grantee, 1954, 57. Mem. Wis. Acad. Scis., Arts & Letters, Modern Lang. Assn., Melville Soc., Poe Soc., Thoreau Soc., Manuscript Soc., Sigma Tau Delta, Phi Kappa Phi. Avocations: stamp collecting, gardening, reading. Home: 8706 W Oklahoma Ave West Allis WI 53227

ADERSON, SANFORD M., lawyer; b. Pitts., July 15, 1949; s. Sanford C. and Marjorie S. (Stern) A.; m. Leslie S. Sertner, Aug. 12, 1972; children: Benjamin, Jonathan. BSBA, Boston U., 1971, JD, 1974. Bar: Pa. 1974, U.S. Dist. Ct. (we. dist.) Pa. 1974, U.S. Tax Ct. 1978, U.S. Ct. Appeals (3d cir.) 1986. Law clk. to judge Ct. of Common Pleas, Pitts., 1974-83; with Aderson, Frank, Steiner & Blechman, Pitts., 1976—. Bd. dirs. Jewish Cmty. Ctr. of Pitts., 1993-98, chmn. sports, fitness and recreation com., bd. dirs. Mem. ABA, Pa. Bar Assn., Allegheny County Bar Assn. (bankruptcy sect. mem. of coun. 1993-98), Westmoreland Country Club (bd. dirs. 1987—, chmn. legal adv. com., chmn. greens com. 1992-96, v.p. 1997—). Office: 2300 Grant Bldg Pittsburgh PA 15219-2302

ADERTON, JANE REYNOLDS, lawyer; b. Riverside, Calif., Dec. 22, 1913; d. Charles Low and Verna Mae (Marshall) Reynolds; m. Robert Granville Johnson (div. 1959); children: Marshall Fallon, Jeannette Townsend; m. Thomas Radcliffe Aderton, Oct. 18, 1964. BS in Merchandising, U. So. Calif., 1935; JD, Southwestern U., L.A., 1965. Bar: Calif. 1968. Jud. sec. Dist. Ct. Appeals, Los Angeles, 1960-65; pvt. practice Beverly Hills, Calif., 1968-70; assoc. Wyman, Bautzer, Rothman & Kuchel, 1970-79; pvt. practice Riverside, 1979—; del. Calif. Bar Conf., 1976, 77, 78. Mem. Founders' Club, Riverside Community Hosp., 1980—; women's aux. Salvation Army, 1980—, pres., 1981-83, adv. bd., 1983—, sec. 1985-87; mem. World Affairs Coun. Inland So. Calif., 1981—, Mus. Photography, 1985—; mem. Affiliates U. Calif., Riverside, 1983—, bd. dirs., 1990—; mem. Art Alliance Riverside Art Mus., 1982—, pres., 1985-86; mem. Riverside Hospice, 1983—, Riverside Opera Guild, 1989—; bd. dirs. Friends of Mission Inn, 1986-89, sec., 1987-89; bd. dirs. San Gorgonio Girl Scouts U.S.A., 1987-93. Mem. ABA, Calif. Bar Assn., Riverside Bar Assn., Beverly Hills Bar Assn. (bd. govs. 1976-79, chmn. probate and trust com. 1975-77, chmn. del. to Calif. bar conf. 1978), Calif. Mus. Photography, Victoria Country Club, Newport Harbor Yacht Club, Soroptomist Internat., Phi Alpha Delta, Pi Beta Phi (pres. Riverside Alumnae Club 1981-83, 88-89, v.p. 1990-92). Home: 5190 Stonewood Dr Riverside CA 92506-1567

ADETORO, OLALEKAN OLAYIWOLA, obstetrician, gynecologist, educator; b. Ikirun, Osun, Nigeria, June 15, 1947; s. Salami Adio Adetoro and Raliat Abebi Adebayo; m. Bernice Oladunni Ibironke; 5 children. BSc in Med. Sci. in Anatomy with honors, U. Ibadan, Nigeria, 1971, MB, BChir, 1975; specialist in ob-gyn. cert., Nat. Postgrad. Med. Coll., Nigeria, 1982; cert. in gynecol. endoscopy, Univ. Coll. Hosp., Ibadan, 1982, cert. in fertility treatment, 1982. Cert. in gen. medicine and surgery; cert. specialist in ob-gyn.; cert. gynecol. endoscopist, 1983; cert. in infertility treatment; cert. in treatment of sexually transmitted diseases, 1983. Demonstrator dept. human anatomy U. Ibadan, 1971-72; house officer, then sr. house officer dept. ob-gyn. Univ. Coll. Hosp., Ibadan, 1975-78; med. officer Mil. Hosp., Kano, 1976-77; registrar, then sr. registrar dept. ob-gyn. Univ. Coll. Hosp., Ibadan, 1978-83; rsch. fellow dept. ob-gyn. Univ. Hosp. South Manchester, Eng., 1980-81; lectr., then sr. lectr., cons. U. Ilorin, Nigeria, 1983-91, assoc. prof., 1991-92; prof. reproductive health Moi U., Kenya, 1992; prof. ob-gyn. Ogun State U., Ago-Iwoye, Nigeria, 1992—, dean faculty clin. scis. Obafemi Awolowo Coll. Health Scis., 1992—; sr. residents staff sec., cons. dept. ob-gyn. Univ. Coll. Hosp., 1982-83; mem. acad. staff for cmty. oriented based med. edn. svcs. posting faculty health scis. U. Ilorin, 1984-91, faculty rep. bd. appointment and promotion for jr. staff, 1987-91, acting head dept. ob-gyn., mem. senate, 1988-90; mem. senate Ogun State U., 1992—, external examiner Coll. Health Scis., 1990-91; mem. faculty ob-gyn., mem. faculty bd. Nat. Postgrad. Med. Coll. Nigeria, 1987—, examiner, 1988—; examiner West African Postgrad. Med. Coll., 1987—; vis. sr. obstetrician lectr./cons. U. Sokoto (Nigeria) Tchg. Hosp., 1986-87; vis. sr. lectr. Coll. Health Scis. U. Sokoto, 1986-88; vis. sr. lectr. Coll. Med. Scis. U. Maiduguri, 1988-89, external examiner, 1993—; vis. sr. lectr./cons. U. Maiduguri Tchg. Hosp., 1988-89; external examiner Coll. Med. Scis. U. Benin, Benin City, 1990-91, Coll. Medicine U. Lagos, Araba, 1991-92, U. Jos, 1992-93, U. Ibadan, 1994—; invited lectr. Obafemi Awolowo U., Ile-Ife, Nigeria, 1988, external examiner, 1991-92; invited advisor to tech. working group on prevention and better mgmt. of postpartum hemorrhage WHO, Geneva, 1989; resource person St. Vincent Continued Med. Edn. Program, Ibadan, 1990; mem. resource staff nat. postgrad. revision course Obafemi Awolowo U. Tchg. Hosp., 1995; participant, presenter many confs. and workshops. Contbr. chpts. to: Syndromes of Head and Neck, 1985, 2 other books; mem. editl. bd. Tropical Jour. Health Scis., 1987-91; contbr. over 60 articles to profl. publs. Pfizer travel fellow, 1985. Fellow West African Coll. Surgeons (mem. faculty bd. ob-gyn. 1988—, sec. bd. ob-gyn. 1990-92); mem. Nigerian Med. Assn., Soc. Gynecology and Obstetrics Nigeria (mem. organizing conf. 1987), African Union Venereal Diseases and Treponamioses, Orgn. Gestosisa Internat. Soc. for Study of Pathophysiology of Pregnancy, Internat. Soc. for Study of Hypertension in Pregnancy, Internat. Fedn. Gynecology and Obstetrics. Avocations: reading, travel, jogging. Home: 83 Amola St, Ikirun Osun, Nigeria Office: Ogun State Univ Tchg Hosp, PMB 2001, Sagamu Ogun, Nigeria

ADEWUYI, YUSUF GBADEBO, chemical engineering educator, researcher, consult; b. Offa, Kwara, Nigeria, Nov. 26, 1952; came to U.S., 1975; s. Alhaji Kadiri and Sifawu (Oguntundun) A.; m. Janice Hughes, Jan. 16, 1987; 1 child, Kasim Adesegun. BSChemE, Ohio U., 1978; MSChemE, U. Iowa, 1980, PhD, 1985. Postdoc. resident assoc. Boston Coll., 1986-87; postdoc. resident fellow U. Ill., Urbana-Champaign, 1987-88; sr. staff engr. Mobil R & D Corp., Paulsboro, N.J., 1988-91, rsch. engr., 1991-93; assoc. prof. chem. engring. N.C. A & T State U., Greensboro, N.C., 1994—; cons. Air Purification Inc., N.Y., 1996—; rev. panelist NSF, Washington, 1996—. Contbr. articles to Atmospheric Environment, Environ. Sci. Tech., Jour. Geophysics Rsch., Chem. Engring. Comms., Applied Catalysis, others. Named to environ. del. to China by Citizen Ambassador's Program, Spokane, Wash., 1994. Mem. AAAS, AIChE (sec. Triad sect. 1996-97, pres. 1997), Am. Chem. Soc., Sigma Xi Sci. Rsch. Soc. Achievements include patent for Riser cracking for maximum C3 and C4 Olefin yields; for fluidized catalytic cracking. Home: 3916 Brass Cannon Ct Greensboro NC 27410-9229 Office: NC Agrl Tech State Univ Dept Chem Engring 1601 E Market St Dept Chem Greensboro NC 27401-3209

ADEY, WILLIAM ROSS, physician; b. Adelaide, Australia, Jan. 31, 1922; s. William James and Constance Margaret (Weston) A.; m. Alwynne Sidney Morris (div. 1970); children: John, Susan, Geoffrey. MB and BS, U. Adelaide, Australia, 1943, MD, 1949. Sr. lectr. and reader, Dept. Anatomy U. Adelaide, Australia, 1947-53; sr. lectr., Dept. Anatomy U. Melbourne, Australia, 1955-56; prof. anatomy and physiology UCLA, 1957-77; dir. Space Biology Lab UCLA Space Biology Lab., 1965-77; dir. rsch. VA Med. Ctr., Loma Linda, Calif., 1977-97; adj. prof. biochemistry U. Calif., Riverside, 1997—; cons. Office of Sci. and Tech. Policy, Washington, 1964—, NIH, 1961—, NAS, 1965—. Author: Nonlinear Electrodynamics in Biological Systems, 1984, Magnetic Resonance Imaging of the Brain, Head and Neck, 1984. Surgeon lt. Australian Navy, 1944-46, South Pacific. Fellow IEEE, Royal Soc. and Nuffield Found. (London), AAAS, Am. Electroencephalographic Soc., Royal Soc. Medicine (London), Am. Assn. Neurolog. Surgeons. Avocations: radiophysics, radioastronomy, marathon running, backpacking. Home: Rte 1 Box 615 31866 3rd Ave Redlands CA 92374-8237

ADEYIGA, ADEYINKA A., engineering educator; b. Irolu-Remo, Nigeria, Jan. 20, 1946; s. adeyiga and Oladunni (Opadiya) Osinbowale; m. Abidemi Janet Adibi-Adeyiga, Dec. 21, 1975; children: Adeleke, Adebunmi, Adetayo. BSChemE, Tenn. Tech. U., 1974; MSChemE, U. Mo., Columbia, 1976; PhDChemE, Okla. State U., 1980. Rsch. engr. E.I. DuPont Denemours Co., Seaford, Del., 1981-82; reservoir engr. Shell Petroleum Devel. Co., Lagos, Nigeria, 1982-84; asst. prof. Va. State U., Petersburg, 1984-85; from assoc. prof. to prof. Hampton (Va.) U., 1985—, chmn. engring., 1986-96; pres. Interex Inc., Yorktown, Va., 1997—; chair dean's adv. bd. NSF, U. Calif., Berkeley, 1994-95; chief cons. Padson Constrn., Lagos, 1982-84. Mem. AIChE, Am. Chem. Soc., Order Engrs. Orgn., Am. Soc. Engring. Edn., Omega Chi Epsilon. Home: 126 Chinquapin Orch Yorktown VA 23693-2321 Office: Hampton U E Queen St Hampton VA 23668

ADICKES, LOUIS WYCKOFF, educator; b. Somerville, N.J., Oct. 9, 1948; s. Ernest Norman and Dorothy (Wyckoff) A.; m. Maria Polczyk, May 20, 1989. BA in Lit., Rutgers U., 1971; MA in Adminstrn., Rider Coll., 1977; postgrad., Drew U., 1997—. Cert. instr. N.J. State Police Tng. Commn. Adj. instr. mgmt. Middlesex County Coll., Edison, N.J., 1980—, cons., trainer, 1985—; dir. customized tng. Ocean County Coll., Toms River, N.J., 1995—; mem. coun. for adj. faculty devel. Middlesex County Coll., 1989-96; bus. adv. com. Ocean County Coll., 1995—, Middlesex County Coll.,1 997—; mem. QNJ Higher Edn. Roundtable, 1996—. Bd. dirs. Literacy Vols. Am., Ocean City, 1997—, Homes for All, Shore Region Tourism Coun.; bd. dirs., vice pres., Big Brothers/Big Sisters, Ocean Cty., 1998—, mem. planning com. Big Bros./Big Sisters, Eatontown, N.J., 1996—; mem. USCG Aux., 1991—; mem. com. Monmouth Ocean Devel. Coun., 1995—; mem. Bound Brook Fire Dept., Watchung Co. # 3, 1980, former v.p., trustee. Mem. Am. Soc. Quality, Assn. for Quality and Participation (v.p. program devel. 1996-97), bd. dirs., Shore Reg. Tourism Councl., Jersey Shore Quality Coun. (chmn. exec. bd. 1995—). Home: 549 Washington St Bound Brook NJ 08805-1336 Office: Ocean County Coll College Dr CN 2001 Toms River NJ 08754

ADIELE, NKWACHUKWU MOSES, state official; b. Umuahia, Abia, Nigeria, June 22, 1951; came to U.S. 1973; s. Robert O. and Virginia A. Adiele; m. Vickie I. Eseonu, July 7, 1984; children: Elizabeth, Robert, Casey. BS, Ga. Inst. Tech., 1976; MD, Howard U., 1980; MPH, Johns Hopkins U., 1981. Diplomate Nat. Bd. Med. Examiners, Fed. Licensure Examiners Med. Bd. House officer Howard U. Hosp., Washington, 1981-84, intern in family practice, 1981-82, resident in family practice, 1982-84; asst. dir. pub. health Va. State Health Dept., Richmond, 1984-86; dist. health dir. Va. State Health Dept., Boydton, 1986-87; pub. health officer, clinician Va. State Health Dept., Richmond, 1987-90; cons., dir. med. support svcs. Va. State Dept. Med. Asst. Svcs., Richmond, 1990—; cons. Internat. United Black Fund, Washington, 1984-90. Role model youth edn. Richmond Redevel. and Housing Authority, 1984; vol. physician Richmond Area High Blood Pressure Ctr., 1985-90. Lt. col. USAR, 1996—, cmdr. 4215th U.S. Army Hosp., Richmond, Va., 1997—. Named Outstanding Resident Physician, Howard U. Hosp., Washington, 1982. Fellow Am. Acad. Family Physicians (recognition award 1991), Am. Coll. Med. Quality (recognition award 1992); mem. AMA (physician recognition award 1984, 89, 91, 97), Am. Coll. Physician Execs. (Recognition award 1998), Assn. African Physicians in N.Am. (pres. 1982-84, recognition award 1991), Va. Pub. Health Assn. Avocations: running, reading, volleyball, singing. Home: 1305 Cedar Crossing Trl Midlothian VA 23113-3148 Office: Va State Dept Med Asst Svcs 600 E Broad St Ste 1300 Richmond VA 23219-1856

ADIK, STEPHEN PETER, energy company executive; b. Elizabeth, N.J., Apr. 17, 1943; s. Stephen Peter and Stella (Laschuk) A.; m. Victoria Rita Pyle, June 26, 1965; Gwynn, Jeffrey. BME, Stevens Inst. Tech., 1964; MBA in Fin., Northwestern U., 1971. With ops. mgmt. dept. Chessie System, Balt., 1964-68, C&NW Transp. Co., 1968-74; v.p. Lehigh Valley R.R., Bethlehem, 1974-83; asst. treas. Am. Natural Resources Co., Detroit, 1983-85, treas., 1985-86; v.p. audit Am. Natural Resources Co., Detroit, 1986-87; v.p., gen. mgr. No. Ind. Pub. Svc. Co., Hammond, 1987-91, sr. v.p., gen. mgr. fin. and acctg., 1991; v.p., sec., treas. Nipsco Industries, Inc., Hammond, 1988-91, sr. v.p., chief fin. officer, treas., 1991-94, exec. v.p., CFO, treas., 1994—; pres. Nipsco Devel. Co., Hammond, 1989—; bd. dirs. Chgo. SouthShore & South Bend R.R., Bank One, Merrillville, Ind., No. Ind. Fuel & Light, Kokomo Gas Co., IWC Resources Corp.; mem. dean's bus. adv. coun., trustee Ind. U. N.W., 1995—. Chmn. bd. suprs. Hanover Twp., Pa., 1977-80, commr. Planning Commn., 1976; rep. Coun. Govts., Northampton County, Pa., 1977-83; trustee Lake Area United Way, Griffin, Ind., 1989—, vice chmn., 1992, chmn., 1993; trustee Cath. Charities, 1992—, vice chmn., 1994; pres. Lake County divsn. Am. Heart Assn., 1995; bd. dirs. Porter County Cmty. Found., 1997—; mem. economists bd. The Times, 1997—. Mem. Am. Gas Assn., Midwest Gas Assn., Ind. Electric Assn., Ind. Soc. Chgo., Edison Electric Inst., Woodmar Country Club, Sand Creek Country Club, Traffic Club Chgo. Roman Catholic. Home: 488 Wexford Rd Valparaiso IN 46385 Office: Nipsco Industries Inc 801 E 86th Ave Merrillville IN 46410-6272

ADILETTA, DEBRA JEAN OLSON, business analyst consultant; b. Gloucester, Mass., Oct. 1, 1959; d. Melvin Porter Jr. and Ruth Margaret (Dahlmer) Olson; m. Mark Anthony Adiletta, Aug. 25, 1984; children: Christopher Michael, Nichole Brianna, Mark Andrew. BA, Coll. of Holy Cross, Worcester, Mass., 1981; MBA, U. Rochester, 1986. Systems analyst Eastman Kodak Co., Rochester, N.Y., 1981-85, infosystems specialist, 1985-86, personal computer area mgr., 1986-87, bus. analyst cons., 1987—. seminar instr., Rochester, 1987. Fin. advisor Sts. Peter and Paul Ch., Rochester, 1985-86; div. chairperson United Way, Rochester, 1987. Mem. Assn. Systems Mgmt., Holy Cross Alumni Assn. (class agt. 1981—, sec. 1983-84, treas. 1984-88, v.p. 1988-90, pres. 1990-91, bd. dirs. 1992—). Avocations: snow and water skiing, horseback riding. Office: Eastman Kodak Co 343 State St Rochester NY 14650-0001

ADIZES, ICHAK, management consultant, author. *Spouse, Nurit Adizes. Children are Atalya, Topaz, Shoham, Nimmy, Chaan, Sapphir.* PhD, Columbia U. With Hebrew U., Jerusalem, Tel Aviv U., Stanford (Calif.) U., Columbia U., N.Y.C.; founder, profl. dir. Adizes Inst., Santa Barbara, Calif., 1975—; acad. dean Adizes Inst., L.A.; adj. assoc. prof. ULCA John Anderson Grad. Sch. Mgmt.; lectr. in field. *Ichak Adizes is consultant to the Bank of America and governments of Brazil, Isrel, Sweden, Macedonia, Greece, Ghana and others.* Author: Self-Management, 1975, How to Solve the Mismanagement Crisis, 1979, Corporate Lifecycles: How and Why Corporations Grow and Die and What to Do About It, 1988, Mastering Change; The power of Mutual Trust and Respect in Personal Life, Business and Society, 1992, The Pursuit of Prime, 1996, Managing Corporate Life Cycles, 1999; contbr. articles to profl. jours., newspapers. Fax: (805) 565-9796. E-mail: adius@adres.com. Office: Adizes Inst 2815 E Valley Rd Santa Barbara CA 93108

ADJENIAN, ROBERT, publisher. Mgr. Vedanta Press, Hollywood, Calif. Office: Vedanta Press 1946 Vedanta Pl Hollywood CA 90068-3920*

ADKINS, BEN FRANK, management and engineering consultant; b. West Liberty, Ky., Mar. 6, 1938; s. Stuart Kendall Adkins and Dorothy Elizabeth (Shaver) Indes; m. Judith Ann Williams, Mar. 14, 1959; children: Michelle Rene, Lori Lee. BS in Indsl. Engring., Ariz. State U., 1964; MBA, Western New Eng. Coll., Springfield, Mass., 1971; MS in Systems Mgmt., U. So. Calif., 1983. Registered profl. engr. Enlisted USAF, 1955, commd. 2d lt., 1964, advanced through grades to maj., 1975, ret., 1979; internal cons., mgr. State of Wash., Olympia, 1979-87; mgmt. and engring. cons. Olympia, 1987-88; sr. rsch. sci. Battelle Pacific N.W. Labs., Richland, Wash., 1988-89; mng. prin. Ben Adkins & Assocs., Olympia, 1989—. Decorated Bronze star USAF. Mem. Inst. Indsl. Engrs. (sr. mem., bd. dirs. Puget Sound chpt. 1984-86, asst. dir. and dir. govt. div. 1979-83, v.p. Washington chpt. 1969-76). Avocations: skiing, sailing, photography, reading. Home: 6606 Miner Dr SW Olympia WA 98512-7257 Office: Ben Adkins & Assocs PO Box 7613 Olympia WA 98507-7613

ADKINS, CHARLES M., JR., United States marshall; b. East Lynn, W.Va., Oct. 26, 1939. Diploma Police Adminstrn. Sch., Marshall U., 1960; diploma, Fed. Law Enforcement Tng. Acad, 1967. U.S. marshall U.S. Marshall Svc., W.Va., 1993—. Office: Fed Bldg 300 Virginia St Rm 3602 Charleston WV 25301

ADKINS, DEAN PHILLIP, painter; b. Royal Oak, Mich., Dec. 4, 1962; s. Phillip Ray and Marcia Ann (Egan) A.; m. Kimberly Chapple, June 9, 1990 (div. Feb. 1992). Student, Purdue U., 1981-84; BFA, Ohio U., 1988; MA, George Washington U., Washington, 1991. Intern Smithsonian Instn., Washington, 1988; asst. dir. Tech 2000, Washington, 1988-89, dep. dir., 1989-92; dir. exhbn. design Spear ED, Tampa, 1992-95; dir. KTR Inc., Ashtabula, Ohio, 1995-97, Still Nat. Osteopathic Mus., Kirksville, Mo., 1998—; exhbn. designer Ars Electronics, Linz, Austria, 1992-93. Recipient award Hoosier Art Patron's Assn., 1981, award of excellence Photographer's Forum, 1983, 84, 85. Mem. Am. Assn. Museums, Nat. Assn. Museum Exhbns., Rare Breed Soc., Ducks Unltd., Delta Waterfowl. Democrat. Home: 1618 E Washington St Kirksville MO 63501-3362

ADKINS, DERRICK RALPH, Olympic athlete; b. Bklyn., July 2, 1970. BS in Engring., Ga. Tech. U., 1993. Recipient Gold medal 400 meter hurdles Atlanta Olympics, 1996; winner U.S. Jr. Championships, Pan Am. Jr. Championships, World Univ. Games, 1991, 93, USA Mobil Championships, 1995, 2d place USA Mobil Championships, 1993. Office: USA Track & Field PO Box 120 Indianapolis IN 46206-0120*

ADKINS, EDWARD CLELAND, lawyer; b. Montgomery County, Iowa, Aug. 11, 1926; s. Esse Clarence and Elsie Mae (Cline) A.; m. Claudia Kangas, Sept. 17, 1955; children—Pamela, Philip, Paul. B.S., U.S. Naval Acad., 1949; J.D., U. Mich., 1957. Bar: Ohio 1957, U.S. Supreme Ct. 1961, Fla. 1963, Mich. 1965, U.S. Ct. Appeals (5th cir.) 1973, U.S. Ct. Appeals (8th cir.) 1974, U.S. Ct. Appeals (11th cir.) 1982, U.S. Ct. Appeals (3d cir.) 1991. Assoc. Arter & Hadden, Cleve., 1957-64; trial counsel, Gen. Motors Corp., 1964-70; ptnr. litigation Adkins & Diaco, PA, Tampa, Fla., 1970—. Served to capt. USNR. Mem. ABA, Fla. Bar, Mich. Bar. Republican. Lutheran. Clubs: Palma Ceia Golf and Country, University. Home: 3938 Venetian Way Tampa FL 33634-7424 Office: Adkins Kise & Diaco PA 3938 Venetian Way Tampa FL 33634-7424 *Replace wrong with justice.**

ADKINS, EDWARD JAMES, lawyer; b. Annapolis, Md., Oct. 18, 1947; s. Lee William and Lottie Elizabeth (Stevenson) A.; m. Cheryl Lynne Walcroft, Aug. 24, 1968; children: Helen Elizabeth, Susan Eileen. AB, U. N.C., 1969; JD, U. Md., 1972. Bar: Md. 1972, D.C. 1988, U.S. Mil. Ct. Appeals 1973, U.S. Dist. Ct. Md. 1974, U.S. Supreme Ct. 1976. Assoc. Smith, Somerville & Case, Balt., 1972-75; assoc. Venable, Baetjer & Howard, Balt., 1975-80, ptnr., 1980-81; ptnr. Miles & Stockbridge, P.C., Balt., 1982-93, prin., 1994—; sr. cons. Yaffe & Offutt Assocs., Balt., 1981-82; adj. prof. Loyola Coll., Balt., 1980-83. Mem. Pension Oversight Commn., Anne Arundel County, Md., 1985; bd. dirs. United Way Cen. Md., Balt., 1980, Children's Home, 1997, Archbishop's Spalding High Sch., 1996; bd. dirs., v.p. YMCA, Anne Arundel County, 1985. Served to capt. USAF, 1973. Named one of Outstanding Young Marylanders Jaycees, 1972. Mem. ABA, Md. Bar Assn., Balt. City Bar Assn., Order of Coif. Democrat. Presbyterian. Office: Miles & Stockbridge PC 10 Light St Ste 1100 Baltimore MD 21202-1487*

ADKINS, GREGORY D., higher education administrator; b. Charleston, W.Va., May 20, 1941; s. Wondel Lafayette and Corda Christenia (Carnes) A.; m. Dolores June Lowe, Sept. 9, 1961; children: Christenia Lea, Angela Dawn. BS, U. Charleston, 1962; MEd, Fla. Atlantic U., 1966; M.C.S., U. Miss., 1968, EdD, 1970. Assoc. prof. edn. Palm Beach Atlantic Coll., West Palm Beach, Fla., 1972-74, chair dept. edn., 1972-73, chair div. profl. studies, dir. tchr. edn., 1973-74; assoc. dean career edn. W.Va. No. Community Coll., Wheeling, 1974-75, dean acad. affairs, 1975-79; coordinator instrn. and planning Colo. State Bd. C.C.s. and Occupational Edn., Denver, 1979-81; pres. So. W.Va. Community Coll., Logan, 1981-88, Bluefield (W.Va.) State Coll., 1988-93, Franklin County Schs., Frankfort, Ky., 1993-94, Jefferson Coll., Hillsboro, Mo., 1994—; vice chmn. adv. coun. of pres. W.Va. Bd. Regents, 1986-87; chair legis. affairs com., 1986-87; bd. dirs. Missourians for Higher Edn., Mo. Coordinating Bd. for Higher Edn. Com. on Transfer and Articulation, 1997—, Jefferson Coll. Found. Inc. Mem. Gov.'s Labor/Mgmt. Coun., Charleston, 1986-93, W.Va. Enterprise Zone Authority, Charleston, 1987-93, Mercer County Econ. Devel. Authority, 1989-93; bd. dirs. Bluefield Regional Med. Ctr., 1988-89, W.Va. Joint Commn. for Vocat. and Occupational Edn., 1989-93, Missourians for Higher Edn., 1996—; mem. coms. on transfer and articulation Mo. Coordinating Bd. for Higher Edn., 1996—. Recipient Alumnus of Yr. award U. Charleston, 1984, award VFW, Chapmanville, 1987; NSF grad. fellow 1967-68, Richard Weaver fellow Intercollegiate Studies Inst., 1969-70. Mem. W.Va. Assn. Coll. and Univ. Pres. (pres. 1984-85), W.Va. C.C. Assn. (pres. 1985-86), Mo. C.C. Assn. (bd. dirs. 1995-97, adv. coun. of pres. 1994—), North Ctrl. Assn. (cons., evaluator 1984—, commr.-at-large 1984-90), Kiwanis, Rotary Internat., Chi Beta Phi (pres.). Mem. Ch. of Christ. Avocations: outdoor sports, gardening. Office: Jefferson Coll 1000 Viking Dr Hillsboro MO 63050-2440

ADKINS, TERRY R., artist; b. Washington. BS, Fisk U., 1975; MS, Ill. State U., 1977; MFA, U. Ky., 1979. instr. Norfolk (Va.) State U., 1981; artist-in-residence The Studio Mus. in Harlem, N.Y.C., 1982, Spl. Arts Svcs. NYSCA, N.Y.C., 1988; studio artist Nat. Program Pub. Sch. 1, Queens, N.Y., 1984; guest artist KOPROD Internat., Zurich, 1989, Calif. State U. at Humboldt, Arcata, Calif., 1995; vis. prof. Calif. State U., Chico, 1991; guest lectr. U. Calif., Davis, 1991, Montclair (N.J.) State Coll., 1992, U. Pa., Phila., 1993, Brown U., Providence, 1994; vis. artist Learning Through Art Program, Guggenheim Mus., N.Y.C., 1993; Falk vis. artist Weatherspoon Gallery, U. N.C., Greensboro, 1993; asst. prof. SUNY, New Paltz, N.Y., 1993-96, assoc. prof., 1996—. One person shows include James Wise Gallery, Norfolk State U., 1980, Arts and Humanities Ctr., Richmond, Va., 1981, Galerie Emmerich-Baumann, Zurich, 1987, Liz Harris Gallery, Boston, 1988, Galerie Andy Jllien, Zurich, 1989, Valencia C.C., Miami, 1990, Anderson Galery, Va. Commonwealth U., Richmond, 1991, LedisFlam, N.Y.C., 1992, The Chrysler Mus., Norfolk, 1993, The Hammonds House Gallery, Atlanta, 1995, Whitney Mus. Am. Art, 1995, William Benton Mus. Art, Storrs, Conn, 1997, N.J. State Mus., 1998, Sculpture Ctr., N.Y.C., 1998; represented in group exhbns. Miss. Mus. Art, Jackson, 1980, Kenkeleba Gallery, N.Y.C., 1983, 89, 92, William Patterson Coll., Wayne, N.J., 1984, The High Mus., Atlanta, 1984, The Clocktower, N.Y.C., 1984, Longwood Arts Project, N.Y.C., 1986, Salama-Caro Gallery, London, 1987, Kulturhaus Palazzo, Basel, 1987, Projekt Binz 39, Zurich, 1987, Galerie Emmerich-Baumann, Basel, 1987, S.E.C.C.A., Winston-Salem, N.C., 1989, 91, Bermans Van Eck Gallery, N.Y.C., 1989, Williams Coll. Mus. Art, 1989, The Meml. Arch, Prospect Park, Bklyn., 1990, Studio Mus. in Harlem, N.Y.C., 1990, 95, Washington Project for Arts, Washington, 1980, 90, LedisFlam, N.Y.C., 1990, 91, Carnegie Mellon Art Gallery, Pitts., 1991, The New Mus. Contemporary Art, N.Y.C., 1991, Dart Gallery, Chgo., 1991, Philippe Briet, N.Y.C., 1991, U. Wis., 1992, Hunter Mus. Art, Chattanooga, 1992, Franklin Parrasch Gallery, N.Y.C., 1992, Cin. Contemporary Arts Ctr., 1992, Orlando (Fla.) Mus. Art, 1992, Hillwood Art Mus., Brookville, N.Y., 1992, 93, Snug Harbor Cultural Ctr., S.I., N.Y., 1993, David Klein Gallery, Birmingham, Miss., 1993, Mus. for African Art, Brookville, 1994, Cleve. Ctr. for Contemporary Art, 1994, John Berggruen Gallery, San Francisco, 1994, Exit Art, N.Y.C., 1994, Mus. Arti Et Amicitiae, Amsterdam, 1995; represented in permanent collections Met. Mus. Art, N.Y.C., Hirshhorn Mus. and Sculpture Garden, Washington, High Mus. Art, Atlanta, Chrysler Mus., Norfolk, The New Sch., N.Y.C., Bank Julius Bar, Zurich, Fisk U., Nashville, Tougaloo (Miss.) Coll., Atlanta Life Ins. Co., AT&T, N.Y.C.; performances at Wash. Project of the Arts, Washington, 1981, U. Cin. Sch. Fine Arts, 1982, New Music Am. Festival, Washington, 1983, P.S. 1 Inst. Art and Urban Resources, N.Y.C., 1985, Kulturzentrum Rote Fabrik, Zurich, 1987, The Inst. Contemporary Art, London, 1988, Koprod Internat., Zurich, 1989, Rigiblick Theatre, Zurich, 1989, Valencia C. C. Black Box

Theatre, Orlando, Fla., 1990, Hall of Sci., N.Y.C., 1991, Calif. State U., Chico, 1991; featured in numerous newspapers, mags. and catalogues. Fellow Va. Mus., 1980, Nat. Endowment for Arts, 1986, SECCA 7, 1989, Joan Mitchell Found., 1994, artist exch. fellow Projekt Binz 39, Zurich, 1986. *

ADKINS, THOMAS SAMUEL, library director; b. Portsmouth, Ohio, Oct. 24, 1965; s. Millard Elwood and Ruth Caroline (Shultz) A. BS, Ohio U., 1988; MLS, Kent (Ohio) State U., 1993. Tchr. Cmty. Action Agy., Portsmouth, Ohio, 1988, Scioto County Schs., Portsmouth, 1988-89; ext. svcs. coord. Portsmouth Pub. Libr., 1989-95; dir. G.A. Wilson Pub. Libr., Waverly, Ohio, 1996—; chairperson Libr. Adv. Coun., Wellston, Ohio, 1997. Author: Lucasville Cemeteries, 1988; editor: A Backward Glance, vol. 1, 1987, vol. 2, 1990. Mem. Cmty. Svcs. Coun., Waverly, Ohio, 1996—; treas. Lucasville (Ohio) Hist. Soc., 1986—; mem. Valley Alumni Scholarship Com., Lucasville, 1990—. Recipient Diana Vescelius Meml. award, 1998. Mem. ALA (Emerging Leaders 2000), Ohio Libr. Coun., Rotary Club Pike County, Pike County C. of C. (bd. dirs.). A. Avocations: book collecting, local history, movies, travel.

ADKINS, WILLIAM LLOYD, state official; b. Emporia, Kans., May 19, 1959; s. James Lloyd and Elaine (Staples) A.; m. Sheri Jo Brown, May 19, 1984; children: Brian Patrick, Erica Michelle. BA in Psychology, Washburn U., Topeka, Kans., 1981; MA in Adminstrn. of Justice, Wichita State U., 1996. Toll collector Kans. Turnpike Authority, Topeka, 1976-79; biofeedback technician VA, Topeka, 1979-81; career counselor U. Kans., Lawrence, 1981; resdl. coord. Dodge City (Kans.) Mental Health, 1982-83; vault adminstr. Kans. Lottery, Topeka, 1987-88; corrections officer Kans. Dept. Corrections, Lansing, 1988-91; corrections specialist I Kans. Dept. Corrections, El Dorado, 1991, corrections counselor II, 1991—. Contbr. articles to profl. jours. Crisis counselor Headquarters, Inc., Lawrence, 1981-83; cadet advisor Towanda Law Enforcement, 1993—; jail steering com. Botler County, El Dorado, 1995-96; CPR and first aid instr. ARC. Mem. VFW, Hostage Negotiators of Am., Kans. Correctional Assn. (facility rep. 1991—), Correctional Peace Officers Found., Kans. Peace Officers Assn., Am. Correctional Assn. (pub. screening com. 1991—), Charles F. Menninger Soc. Avocation: walking dog. Office: El Dorado Correctional Facility PO Box 311 El Dorado KS 67042-0311

ADKINSON, N. FRANKLIN, JR., clinical immunologist; b. Forest City, N.C., May 18, 1943; s. N. Frank and Estelle (Stembridge) A.; m. Judy F. Hyder, Aug. 20, 1966; children: Anna Estelle, Carter F. BA with highest honors, U. N.C., Chapel Hill, 1965; MD, Johns Hopkins U., 1969. Intern, resident in internal medicine Johns Hopkins U., Balt., 1969-71, asst. prof. medicine, 1973-81, assoc. prof., 1981-87, prof. medicine, 1987—; co-dir. div. allergy and clin. immunology Johns Hopkins Sch. of Medicine, Balt., 1991—, program dir. grad. tng. program in clin. investigation, 1992—; mem. immunolog. scis. study sect. NIH, Bethesda, Md., 1982-86, allergy immunology rev. com., 1987-91; clin. assoc. Lab. of Immunology, NIH, 1971-73. Editor: Allergy: Principles and Practice, 5th edit., 1998; mng. editor: Updates in Allergy and Immunology, 1989-94; contbr. more than 250 articles to profl. jours. Lt. comdr. USPHS, 1971-73. Recipient Allergic Disease Acad. award Nat. Inst. Allergy and Infectious Disease, 1975. Fellow Am. Acad. Allergy and Immunology; mem. Am. Soc. Clin. Investigation, Collegium Allergologica Internat., Am. Clin. and Climatological Assn. Episcopalian. Office: Johns Hopkins Allergy & Asthma Ctr 5501 Hopkins Bayview Cir Baltimore MD 21224-6821

ADKISON, LINDA RUSSELL, geneticist, consultant; b. Columbia, S.C., Apr. 28, 1951; d. George Palmer Russell, Jr. and Annie Frances (Ingram) White; m. Daniel Lee Adkison, Jan. 28, 1978; children: Emily Kathleen, Seth Adams Russell. BS, Ga. So. U., 1973, MS, 1977; PhD, Tex. A&M U., 1986. Lab. tech. VA Hosp., Gainesville, 1973-75, Shands Teaching Hosp., Gainesville, Fla., 1973-75; grad. teaching asst. Ga. So. U., Statesboro, 1975-77; rsch. assoc. U. South Ala. Med. Sch., Mobile, 1978-80; instr. St. Mary's Dominican Coll., New Orleans, 1980-81; grad. rsch. asst. Tulane Med. Sch., New Orleans, 1980-82, Tex. A&M U., College Station, 1982-86; postdoctoral fellow Jackson Lab., Bar Harbor, Maine, 1986-89; asst. prof. genetics Mercer U. Sch. Medicine, Macon, Ga., 1989-94, assoc. prof. genetics, 1994-99; prof. genetics, 1999—; assoc. prof. ob-gyn. Mercer U. Sch. Medicine, Macon, Ga., 1995—, asst. prof. ob-gyn., 1991-95, assoc. prof. ob-gyn., 1995—. contbr. more than 40 articles to profl. jours. Vol. Girl Scouts Mid. Ga., Macon, 1990—, Abnaki Girl Scout Coun., Bar Harbor, 1986-89, Ctrl. Ga. Boy Scouts, Macon, 1993—. Elam fellow, 1999. Mem. AAAS, Am. Coll. Med. Genetics, Am. Soc. Human Genetics, Grad. Women in Sci., Internat. Mammalian Genome Soc., S.E. Regional Genetics Group, Genetics Soc. Ga. (bd. dirs. 1990-97, sec. 1997—), Ga. Acad. Sci., Sigma Xi. Achievements include research in gene mapping mutational analyses, Chromosome 2 physical mapping, X-inactivation. Avocations: running, gardening, softball. Home: 1699 Wesleyan Bowman Rd Macon GA 31210-1037 Office: Mercer Univ Sch Medicine 1550 College St Macon GA 31207-1500

ADKISSON, GREGORY HUGH, anesthesiologist; b. Wurzburg, Germany, July 2, 1952; s. Glenn William and Phyllis Victoria (Trax) A.; m. Kathryn Lynn Wallin, Aug. 8, 1982; children: Matthew William, Casey Lee. BS, U.S. Naval Acad., 1974; MD, U. Ariz., 1978; MA, Naval War Coll., 1996. Diplomate Am. Bd. Anesthesiology; qualified diving dr., U.K.; lic. physician, Calif., U.K. Commd. ensign USN, 1974—, advanced through grades to capt., 1994; intern Naval Hosp., San Diego, 1978-79; acting flight surgeon NAS, Guantanamo Bay, Cuba, 1979; gen. med. officer NTC, San Diego, 1979; comdr. submarine group 5 med. officer and med. officer USS Dixon, San Diego, 1980-82; comdr., med. officer Submarine Devel. Group 1, Detachment Bravo, San Diego, 1982-85, sr. med. officer, 1985-87; exch. officer in underwater medicine Inst. of Naval Medicine, Alverstoke, Eng., 1987-89; resident in anesthesiology Naval Med. Ctr., San Diego, 1989-92, staff anesthesiologist, head quality assurance, 1992-94, staff anesthesiologist, spl. asst. to commanding officer, 1994-95; student Naval War Coll., Newport, R.I., 1995-96; dep. comdr. Def. Med. Readiness Tng. Inst., 1996-97; commdg. officer def. med. readiness Fort Sam Houston, Tex., 1997-99; commdg. officer Naval Health Care New England, Newport, R.I., 1999—. Contbr. numerous articles to profl. jours.; inventor in field. Cubmaster Pack 20, Boy Scouts Am., Mission Hills, Calif., 1992-95, Pack 2, Newport, 1995-96, Troop 23, Fort Sam Houston, 1996-99. Decorated Navy Commendation medal (2), Meritorious Svc. medal, Navy Achievement medal, Stephen B. Luce award Naval War Coll., Def. Superior Svc. medal. Roman Catholic. Avocations: diving, scouting.

ADKISSON, PERRY LEE, university system chancellor; b. Hickman, Ark., Mar. 11, 1929; s. Robert Louis and Imogene (Perry) A.; m. Frances Rozelle, Dec. 29, 1956 (dec. 1995); m. Gloria Ray, May 16, 1998; 1 dau., Jean Amanda. BS, U. Ark., 1950, MS, 1954; PhD in Entomology, Kans. State U., 1956; DS (hon.), U. Ark., 1997. Asst. prof. entomology U. Mo., 1956-58; assoc. prof. Tex. A&M U., 1958-63, prof., 1963-67, Disting. prof. entomology, 1967—, head dept. entomology, 1967-78, v.p. for agr. and renewable resources, 1978-80, dep. chancellor for agr., 1980-83, dep. chancellor, 1983-86, chancellor, 1986-91, regent's prof., 1991-95; cons. Internat. AEC, Vienna, 1969-74; chmn. sci. adv. panel Gov. Tex. on Agrl. Chems., 1970-72; chmn. Tex. Pesticide Adv. Com., 1972; mem. panel experts on integrated pest control UN/FAO, Rome, 1971-78, chmn., 1992-96; mem. Structural Pest Control Bd., Tex., 1972-78, NRC World Food and Nutrition Study Team, 1977; chmn. com. biology pest species NRC, 1974; mem. environ. studies bd., study group problems pest control NAS-NRC, 1973-75; mem. U.S. directorate UNESCO Man and the Biosphere Program, 1975-77; mem. bd. on agr. NRC, 1985-87, mem. Nat. Sci. Bd., 1985-96; mem. governing bd. Internat. Crops Rsch. Inst. for Semi-Arid Tropics, 1982-88; mem. rsch. adv. com. Agr. for Internat. Devel., 1986; mem. com. on life scis. NRC, 1985-85; mem. Tex. Sci. and Tech. Coun., 1986-88; mem. Standing Com. for Internat. Plant Protection Congresses, 1984—, adv. dir. Export-Import Bank U.S., 1987. Mem. editorial com. Ann. Rev. Entomology, 1973-78; contbr. articles to profl. jours. Exec. dir. G.H.W. Bush Presdl. Libr. Ctr. and Bush Libr. Found., 1991-93. With M.C., U.S. Army, 1951-53. Recipient Faculty Disting. Achievement award for rsch. Tex. A&M U., 1965, Alexander Von Humboldt award, 1980; Disting. Svc. award Am. Registry Prof. Entomology, 1979, Disting. Scientist of Yr. award Tex. Acad. Scis., 1982, Disting. Alumnus Svc. award Kans. State U., 1980, Disting. Svc. award Am. Inst. Biol. Sci., 1987, Nat. 4-H Alumni award, 1988, Outstanding Alumnus award Coll. of Agr. and Home Econs., U. Ark., 1990, Disting. Alumni award U. Ark., 1990, Disting. Svc. award Am. Agrl. Editors Assn., 1992, Wolfe Prize in Agriculture, 1994-95, World Food prize, 1997; USPHS postdoctoral fellow Harvard U., 1963-64; Tex. Heritage Hall of Honor, 1998. Fellow AAAS, Entomol. Soc. Am. (governing bd. 1971-75, pres. 1974, Bussart Meml. award 1967, Founders Meml. lectr. 1985); mem. Am. Acad. Arts and Scis., Kans. Entomol. Soc., Internat. Orgn. Biol. Control, Am. Registry Profl. Entomologists (governing council 1976-78, pres. 1977), Nat. Acad. Scis., Phi Kappa Phi, Sigma Xi. Office: Tex A&M U Dept Entomology College Station TX 77843-2475

ADKISSON, RANDALL LYNN, minister; b. Atlanta, May 28, 1957; s. John Earl and Mearl (Cox) A.; m. Salee Robin Smith, Nov. 7, 1981; children: Katheryn Lynsey, Keith Alan. BA in Journalism, U. Ga., 1979; MDiv, Southwestern Bapt. Theol. Sem., Ft. Worth, 1985; PhD, New Orleans Bapt. Theol. Sem., 1990. Ordained to ministry So. Bapt. Conv., 1979. Min. of youth Bethel Bapt. Ch., Good Hope, Ga., 1976-79; assoc. pastor Orange Hill Bapt. Ch., Austell, Ga., 1979-82; pastor Shifalo Bapt. Ch., Kiln, Miss., 1985-88; pastor 1st Bapt. Ch., Foxworth, Miss., 1988-91, Monroeville, Ala., 1991-98; sr. pastor 1st Bapt. Ch., Cookeville, Tenn., 1998—; tchg. fellow New Orleans Bapt. Theol. Sem., 1985-86. Bd. dirs. Judson Coll., 1994-98, Romanian-Am. Missions, 1998—. Mem. Marion Bapt. Assn. (pastoral ministries dir. 1990-91, pres. min.'s conf. 1990-91), Nat. Assn. Bapt. Profs. Religion, Soc. Bibl. Lit., Alumni Assn. New Orleans Bapt. Theol. Seminary (v.p. to pres.-elect Ala. chpt., 1993, pres. 1994), Am. Assn. Christian Counselors. Office: 1st Bapt Ch 18 S Walnut Ave Cookeville TN 38501-3284 *Christian faith is not a faith that can be separated from action and ethic. To be a "believer" must by necessity impact every area of conduct as well as attitude.*

ADLARD, CAROLE RECHTSTEINER, adoption educational agency executive; b. Cin., Jan. 8, 1952; d. Carl John and Ruth Francis (Hucke) Rechtsteiner; m. Ed Joseph Adlard, Sept. 9, 1978; children: Tara, Chase, Bret, Eric. Diploma in bus. adminstrn. mgmt., U. Notre Dame, 1974. Sales rep. Burroughs/UNYSIS, Boston, 1973-76; acct. exec. Young Rubican, Cin., 1976-77; advt. mgr. Cincom Sys., Cin., 1977-79; cons. B. Cross Assocs., Indpls., 1979-88; exec. dir. Adoption Option, Cin., 1986—; bd. dirs. Common Ground Network, Washington. Editor Up-Downtowners, 1976-83. Mem. Ohio Child Conservation League, Kindervelt, Cin., 1990—. Grantee State of Ohio, 1990—, Greater Cin. Found., 1993, Helen Steiner Rice Found., 1994; named Up-Downtowner of Yr., Ohio Child Conservation League Citizen of Yr. Mem. Child and Family First, Adoption Awareness Alliance. Roman Catholic. Avocations: hiking, biking, swimming, boating, water skiing. Home: 9990 Zig Zag Rd Cincinnati OH 45242-6339 Office: Adoption Option Inc PO Box 429327 Cincinnati OH 45242-9327

ADLER, CHARLES SPENCER, psychiatrist; b. N.Y.C., Nov. 27, 1941; s. Benjamin H. and Anne (Greenfield) A.; m. Sheila Noel Morrissey, Oct. 8, 1966 (dec.); m. Peggy Dolan Bean, Feb. 23, 1991. BA, Cornell U., 1962; MD, Duke U., 1966. Diplomate Nat. Bd. Med. Examiners, Am. Bd. Psychiatry and Neurology. Intern Tucson Hosps. Med. Edn. Program, 1966-67; psychiat. resident U. Colo. Med. Sch., Denver, 1967-70; pvt. practice medicine specializing in psychiatry and psychosomatic medicine Denver, 1970—; chief divsn. psychiatry Rose Med. Ctr, 1982-87; co-founder Applied Biofeedback Inst., Denver, 1972-75; prof. pro tempore Cleve. Clinic, 1977; asst. clin. prof. psychiatry U. Colo. Med. Ctr., 1986—, chief psychiatry and psychophysiology Colo. Neurology and Headache Ctr., 1988-95; med. dir. Colo. Ctr. for Biobehavioral Health, Boulder, 1994—; bd. dirs. Acad. Cert. Neurotherapists. Author: (with Gene Stanford and Sheila M. Adler) We Are But a Moment's Sunlight, 1976, (with Sheila M. Adler and Russell Packard) Psychiatric Aspects of Headache, 1987; contbr. (with S. Adler) sect. biofeedback med. and health ann. Ency. Britannica, 1986; chpts. to books, articles to profl. jours.; mem. editorial bd. Cephalalgia: an Internat. Jour. of Headache, Headache Quar. Emeritus mem. Citizen's Adv Bd. Duke U. Ctr. Aging and Human Devel. Recipient Award of Recognition, Nat. Migraine Found., 1981; N.Y. State regents scholar, 1958-62. Fellow Am. Psychiat. Assn.; mem. AAAS (rep. of AAPB to med. sect. com.), Am. Assn. Study Headache, Internat. Headache Soc. (chmn. subcom. on classifying psychiat. headaches), Am. Acad. Psychoanalysis (sci. assoc.), Colo. Psychiat. Soc., Biofeedback Soc. Colo. (pres. 1977-78), Assn. for Applied Psychophysiology and Biofeedback (rep. to AAAS, chmn. ethics com. 1983-87, bd. dirs. 1990-93, Sheila M. Adler cert. honor 1988). Jewish. Office: 955 Eudora St Apt 1605 Denver CO 80220-4341

ADLER, DALE ANN, artist; b. Birmingham, Ala., Aug. 16, 1943; d. Oliver Fraser and Marjorie Neola (Deakin) Atkins; m. David Parker Wheeler, Oct. 5, 1966 (div. Aug. 1983); children: Traci Pendelton, Steven Parker; m. Leonard Adler, Sept. 27, 1987. BS, Radford U., 1966. Mem. Greater Reston Arts Assn. Avocations: horseback riding, sailing, skiing. E-mail: Adler33@pressroom.com. Home and Studio: 12209 Thoroughbred Rd Oak Hill VA 20171

ADLER, DAVID NEIL, lawyer; b. Bklyn., Apr. 11, 1955; s. Leonard Howard and Elaine (Holder) A. Student, Colgate U., 1973-75; BA, NYU, 1977; JD, St. John's U., 1980. Bar: N.Y. 1981, U.S. Dist. Ct. (ea. and so. dists.) N.Y. 1986, U.S. Tax Ct. 1989. Pvt. practice Kew Gardens, N.Y., 1982—. Contbr. articles to profl. jours. Mem. Queens County Bar Assn. (com. chmn. 1983—, co-editor Queens Bar Bull. 1987—, bd. mgrs. 1989—, officer 1993—, pres. 1998), N.Y. State Bar Assn. (exec. com. trusts and estates). Office: 12510 Queens Blvd Kew Gardens NY 11415-1519

ADLER, EDWARD ANDREW KOEPPEL, lawyer; b. N.Y.C., Apr. 12, 1948; s. H. Henry and Geraldine (Koeppel) A.; m. Karen Stapf, Apr. 15, 1973; children: Heather, Trevor. BA, Trinity Coll., Hartford, Conn., 1969; JD, Columbia U., 1972. Bar: N.Y. 1973, U.S. Dist. Ct. (ea. and so. dists.) N.Y. 1973, U.S. Supreme Ct. 1977. Counsel Koeppel & Koeppel, N.Y.C., 1972—. Trustee Sands Point (N.Y.) Civic Assn., 1982—, also pres., 1986-90; trustee Buckley Country Day Sch., Roslyn, N.Y., 1984—, chmn., 1993-96, also treas., 1987-93; trustee, bldg. commr. Village of Sands Point, 1991—; dir. Port Washington Libr. Found., 1996—; dir. Greenwich House, Inc., 1997—, chmn., 1998—. Mem. ABA, N.Y. State Bar Assn., N.Y. County Lawyers Assn., Manhasset Bay Yacht Club, N.Y. Yacht Club. Avocations: sailing, skiing. Home: 86 Barkers Point Rd Port Washington NY 11050-1328

ADLER, EDWARD I., media and entertainment company executive; b. N.Y.C., Jan. 12, 1954; s. Walter S. and Justine (Rosenberg) P.; m. Shari Goldman; children: Alexander Justin, Jillian Haly. BA, Vassar Coll., 1976; MA in Journalism, NYU, 1979. Reporter Time Mag. subs. Time Inc, N.Y.C., 1976-79; sports programming exec. Home Box Office Inc. subs. Time Inc., N.Y.C., 1979-81; news editor TV-Cable Week Mag. subs. Time Inc., N.Y.C., 1981-83; sr. assoc. corp. pub. affairs Time Inc., N.Y.C., 1983-88; mgr. media rels. corp. communications Time Warner Inc., N.Y.C., 1989-93, dir. media rels. corp. comm., 1993-97, v.p. corp. comm., 1997—. Democrat. Office: Time Warner Inc 75 Rockefeller Plz New York NY 10019-6990

ADLER, ERWIN ELLERY, lawyer; b. Flint, Mich., July 22, 1941; s. Ben and Helen M. (Schwartz) A.; m. Stephanie Ruskin, June 8, 1967; children: Lauren, Michael, Jonathan. B.A., U. Mich., 1963, LL.M., 1967; J.D., Harvard U., 1966. Bar: Mich. 1966, Calif. 1967. Assoc. Pillsbury, Madison & Sutro, San Francisco, 1967-73; assoc. Lawler, Felix & Hall, L.A., 1973-76, ptnr., 1977-80; ptnr. Rogers & Wells, L.A., 1981-83, Richards, Watson & Gershon, L.A., 1983—. Bd. dirs. Hollywood Civic Opera Assn., 1975-76, Children's Scholarships Inc., 1979-80. Mem. ABA (vice chmn. appellate advocacy com. 1982-87), Calif. Bar Assn., Phi Beta Kappa, Phi Kappa Phi. Jewish. Office: Richards Watson & Gershon 333 S Hope St Bldg 38 Los Angeles CA 90071-1406

ADLER, FRED PETER, electronics company executive; b. Vienna, Austria, Mar. 29, 1925; came to U.S., 1942, naturalized, 1947; s. Michael and Ellida (Bronner) A.; m. Alicia Gulkis, 1950; children: Michael Steven, Andrew David; m. Adrienne Wilcox, 1991. BSEE with honors, U. Calif., Berkeley, 1945; MEE (Charles A. Coffin fellow), Calif. Inst. Tech., 1948, PhD magna cum laude, 1950. Elec. engr. GE Rsch. and Cons. Labs., 1945-47; project engr. Jet Propulsion Lab., 1950; with Hughes Aircraft Co., 1950-70, sr. staff physicist, dept. mgr., 1954-57, mgr. advanced planning, 1957-59, dir. advanced projects labs., 1959-61, v.p., mgr. space systems div., 1961-66, v.p., asst. group exec. Aerospace Group, 1966-70; pres. Nadgeco Ltd., 1970-72, chmn. bd., 1973-77; v.p., group exec. aerospace groups Hughes Aircraft Co., 1973-81, sr. v.p., pres. electro-optical and data sys. group, 1981-87; dir. Jefferson Ctr. for Character Edn., Monvovia, Calif., 1973—, chmn. bd., 1988—. Co-author: text Guided Missile Engineering, 1959; also articles tech. jours. Fellow AIAA; mem. N.Y. Acad. Scis., Sigma Xi, Tau Beta Pi. Office: Jefferson Ctr for Character Edn 112 E Lemon Ave Monrovia CA 91016-2808

ADLER, FREDA SCHAFFER (MRS. G. O. W. MUELLER), criminologist, educator; b. Phila., Nov. 21, 1934; d. David and Lucia G. (de Wolfson) Schaffer; children by previous marriage: Mark, Jill, Nancy. B.A., U. Pa., 1956, M.A., 1968, Ph.D. (fellow), 1971. Instr. dept. psychiatry Temple U., Phila., 1971; research coordinator Addiction Scis. Center, 1971-72; research dir. sect. on drug and alcohol abuse Med. Coll. Pa., 1972-74, asst. prof. psychiatry, 1972-74; assoc. prof. criminal justice Rutgers U., Newark, 1974-79; prof. Rutgers U., 1979-82, disting. prof., 1982—, acting dean grad. sch. criminal justice, 1986-87; bd. dirs. Internat. Sci. and Profl. Adv. Coun. UN Programs in Crime Prevention and Criminal Justice, Consortium of Social Sci. Assns., 1994—, The Police Found., 1996—; vis. fellow Yale U., 1976; cons. to Nat. Commn. on Marijuana and Drug Abuse, 1972-73, NYU Sch. Law, 1972-74; mem. faculty Nat. Jud. Coll., U. Nev., 1973—, Nat. Coll. Criminal Def. Lawyers and Pub. Defenders U. Houston, 1975; mem. adv. com. Gen. Fedn. Women's Clubs, 1975-77; UN rep. Internat. Prisoner Aid Assn., 1973-75, Centro Nat. di Prevenzione e Difesa Sociale, 1989—, Internat. Soc. Social Def., regional sec. gen., 1991—, bd. dirs.; sec. bd. dirs. Inst. for Continuous Study of Man, 1974-77, v.p., 1977—. Author: Sisters in Crime, 1975, The Incidence of Female Criminality in the Contemporary World, 1981, Nations Not Obsessed with Crime, 1983; co-author: A Systems Approach to Drug Treatment, 1975, Medical Lollypop, Junkie Insuline or what?, 1974, Criminology of Deviant Women, 1978, Outlaws of the Ocean, 1985, Criminology, 1991, 2d edit., 1995, 3d edit., 1998, Criminal Justice, 1993, Criminal Justice: The Core, 1996; contbr. numerous articles on criminology and psychiatry to profl. jours.; editor Advances in Criminological Theory, 1987—; mem. editl. bd. Criminology, 1971-73, Jour. Criminal Law and Criminology, 1971-73, 97—, Jour. Criminal Law and Criminology, 1982—; co-editor: Politics, Crime and the International Scene, 1972, Revue Internationale de Droit Penal, 1974, Advances in Crimonological Theory, 1987—; assoc. editor LAE Jour., 1977-85; cons. editor Jour. Criminal Law and Criminology. Recipient (with G.O.W. Mueller) Beccaria medal in Gold Deutsche Kriminologische Gesellschaft, 1979; fellow Max Planck Inst. Fgn. and Internat. Law and Criminology, 1984, Am. Soc. Criminology, 1994. Mem. Am. Soc. Criminology (pres. 1994-95, Herbert Bloch award 1972), Am. Sociol. Assn., Internat. Assn. Penal Law, U. Pa. Alumnae Assn. (bd. dirs. 1974-77), Chi Omega. Home: 30 Waterside Plz Apt 37J New York NY 10010-2628 Office: Rutgers U Sch Criminal Justice 15 Washington St New York NY 10004-1005

ADLER, FREDERICK RICHARD, lawyer, financier; b. N.Y.C., Apr. 4, 1926; s. Samuel and Rose (Axelrod) A.; m. Catherine R. George, Apr. 25, 1986; Christopher Wells, Frederick George Richard; children by previous marriage: Barbara Ilene, James Richard, Susan Ruth Chapman, Elizabeth Anne Wertheimer. BA, Bklyn. Coll., 1948; JD magna cum laude, Harvard U., 1951; hon. doctorate, Isr. Inst. of Tech., 1998. Bar: N.Y. 1952. Assoc. Reavis & McGrath, N.Y.C., 1951-58, ptnr., 1959-89; ptnr. Fulbright, Jaworski, Reavis & McGrath, N.Y.C., 1989-91; ret. sr. ptnr. Fulbright & Jaworski, N.Y.C., 1991-95, of counsel, 1996—; dir., chmn. exec. com. Data Gen. Corp., Westbo, Mass., 1968—; mng. ptnr. VENAD Assocs., Adler & Co.; chmn. bd., dir. Shells Seafood Restaurants, Inc., Tampa, Fla., 1995—; bd. dirs. USA Detergents, Inc., New Brunswick, N.J. Trustee Tchrs. Ins. and Annuity Assn., 1977-95; bd. mgrs./overseers Meml. Sloan-Kettering Cancer Ctr.; chmn. bd. dirs. Intracoastal Health Sys., Inc., Palm Beach, Fla.; bd. visitors Harvard Law Sch. With U.S. Army, 1943-45. Mem. Rockefeller Ctr. Club, Harvard Club, Met. Club, Maroon Creek Club (Aspen, Colo.), Univ. Club (N.Y.), Atlantic Golf Club (Southampton, N.Y.), Palm Beach Country Club (Palm Beach, Fla.). Office: 239 S County Rd Palm Beach FL 33480-4255

ADLER, HOWARD, JR., lawyer; b. Chgo., Jan. 25, 1925; s. Howard and Martha (Grossman) A.; m. Mary E. Williamson, Oct. 30, 1955; children: Martine, Karla, Elizabeth. MA in Econs., U. Chgo., 1951, JD, 1951. Bar: Ill. 1952. Atty. U.S. Dept. Justice, Washington, 1952-54, law clk., 1954-55; ptnr. Bergson, Borkland, Margolis & Adler, Washington, 1956-85, Davis, Graham & Stubbs, Washington, 1986-96; of counsel Baker & McKenzie, Washington, 1996—. 1st lt. USAAF, 1946, PTO. Fellow Am. Bar Found.; mem. ABA (vice chmn. coun. 1978-79, sect. on antitrust law 1973-77). Home: 3711 Morrison St NW Washington DC 20015-1733

ADLER, HOWARD BRUCE, lawyer; b. N.Y.C., Apr. 29, 1951; s. Mandel and Dora (Rosenblatt) A.; m. Tanya Jean Potter; 1 child, Alexandra. BA, Johns Hopkins U., 1972; JD, NYU, 1975. Bar: N.Y. 1976, U.S. Dist. Ct. (ea. and so. dists.) N.Y. 1976, D.C. 1979, U.S. Dist. Ct. D.C., 1979, U.S. Ct. Appeals (D.C. cir.) 1979. Assoc. Shearman & Sterling, N.Y.C., 1975-79, Arnold & Porter, Washington, 1979-82; mng. counsel Mellon Bank N.A., Pitts., 1982-84; exec. v.p., gen. counsel The Riggs Nat. Bank of Wash. D.C., Riggs Nat. Corp., 1984-87; ptnr. Gibson, Dunn & Crutcher LLP, Washington, 1987—. Contbr. articles to profl. jours. Mem. ABA (banking law com.), Fed. Bar Assn. (exec. coun. banking law com. 1990-98), D.C. Bar (treas. 1996-97, steering com. corp., fin. and securities law sect., 1991-96, chmn. 1994-95, vice chmn. 1993-94, budget com. 1996-97, chmn. task force of lawyers for econ. redevel. of D.C.), Archdiocesan Legal Network of Washington (adv. bd.), Met. Club, Knight of Malta. Avocation: Civil War history. Home: 9517 Eagle Ridge Dr Bethesda MD 20817-3916 Office: Gibson Dunn & Crutcher LLP 1050 Connecticut Ave NW Washington DC 20036-5303

ADLER, IRA JAY, lawyer; b. N.Y.C., Jan. 1, 1942; s. Ralph and Beatrice (Rosenblum) A.; m. Laraine Sheila Garfinkel, July 4, 1965; children: Jodi, Michael. BA, NYU, 1963, JD, 1966. Bar: N.Y. 1966. Ptnr. Certilman, Balin, Adler & Hyman, LLP, East Meadow, N.Y., 1973—; bd. dirs. Queens County Builders and Contractors, Flushing, N.Y. Contbr. to profl. publs. Mem. ABA, N.Y. State Bar Assn., Nassau County Bar Assn., L.I. Builders Inst. (bd. dirs. 1985—), Real Estate Inst. C.W. Post (bd. dirs. 1986—), N.Y. State Builders Assn. (bd. dirs. 1988—). Office: Certilman Balin Adler & Hyman LLP 90 Merrick Ave East Meadow NY 11554-1571

ADLER, IRVING, mathematician; b. N.Y.C., Apr. 27, 1913; s. Marcus and Celia (Kress) A.; m. Ruth Relis, June 2, 1935 (dec. 1968); children: Stephen L., Peggy A.; m. Joyce Lifshutz, Sept. 16, 1968. BS, CCNY, 1931; MA, Columbia U., 1938, PhD, 1961; DSc (hon.), St. Michael's Coll., 1990. Tchr. pub. high schs., N.Y.C., 1932-46; chmn. dept. math. Textile High Sch., N.Y.C., 1946-52; instr. math. Columbia U., N.Y.C., 1957-60, Bennington Coll., North Bennington, Vt., 1961, So. Vt. Coll., Bennington, 1983; researcher in math. biology North Bennington, 1972—; lectr. in field. Author 49 books; co-author 34 books; contbr. numerous articles to profl. jours.; contbg. editor Sci. and Society, 1981—; mem. editorial bd. Sci. and Nature, 1978-89. Recipient awards for outstanding sci. books for children Children's Book Coun. and Nat. Sci. Tchrs. Assn., 1972, 75, 80, 90, Townsend Harris medal for outstanding achievement CCNY Alumni Assn., 1993. Fellow AAAS, Vt. Acad. Arts and Sci.; mem. Am. Math. Soc., Math. Assn. Am., Nat. Council Tchrs. Math., Soc. for Indsl. and Applied Math., Authors League, Townsend Harris Hall of Fame, 1996, Phi Beta Kappa, Sigma Xi. Democrat. Jewish. Avocations: vegetable gardening. Home: RR 1 Box 532 North Bennington VT 05257-9748

ADLER, JAMES BARRON, publisher; b. N.Y.C., Mar. 8, 1932; s. George G. and Mollie (Barron) A.; m. Esthy Lehmann, June 26, 1956; children: Laura Frances, Eric Stephen. A.B. magna cum laude, Harvard U., 1953. With NBC, N.Y.C., 1956-57, R.R. Bowker Co., N.Y.C., 1957-61, Random House, Inc., N.Y.C., 1961-64, G.P. Putnam's Sons, N.Y.C., 1964-67; founder James B. Adler, Inc., 1967; founder, pres., chmn. Congressional Info. Service, Inc., Washington, 1969-81; mng. partner Adler Assos., 1981—; pres. Adler & Adler Pubs., 1983—; chmn. Greenwood Press, Inc., 1976-79; mem. U.S. Nat. Advisory Commn. Internat. Documentation Fedn., 1972-73. Served with U.S. Army, 1954-55. Recipient Profl. award Spl. Libraries Assn., 1972; Product of Yr. award Info. Industry Assn., 1971, 76. Mem. ALA, Am. Soc. Info. Sci. Clubs: Cosmos, Nat. Press. Home: 5600 Wisconsin Ave Bethesda MD 20815-4405 Office: 5530 Wisconsin Ave Chevy Chase MD 20815-4404

ADLER, JEFFREY D., political consultant, public affairs consultant, crisis management expert; b. Cleve., July 10, 1952; s. Bennett and Edythe Joy (Eisner) A.; m. Colleen Ann Bentley, May 29, 1983. BS in Journalism, Northwestern U., 1975. Porter, waiter, bartender Amtrak, Chgo., 1975-76; reporter Enterprise-Courier, Oregon City, Oreg., 1977, Las Vegas Sun, 1977-80, O.C. Daily Pilot, Costa Mesa, Calif., 1982-85; v.p. pub. affairs Englander Comm., Newport Beach, Calif., 1985-86; pres. Adler Wilson Campaign Svcs., Laguna Hills, Calif., 1990-95, Adler Pub. Affairs, Long Beach, Calif., 1987—. Mem. Am. Assn. Polit. Cons. Democrat. Jewish. Home: 33 Pomona Ave Long Beach CA 90803-3426 Office: Adler Pub Affairs 200 Pine Ave Ste 300 Long Beach CA 90802-3038

ADLER, JOHN HERBERT, lawyer, state legislator; b. Phila., Aug. 23, 1959; s. John Herbert and Mary Louise (Beatty) A.; m. Shelley Arlene Levitan, Sept. 1, 1985; children: Jeffrey David, Alexander Samuel, Andrew Neal. AB, Harvard U., 1981, JD, 1984. Bar: N.J. 1984. Assoc. atty. Archer & Greiner, Haddonfield, N.J., 1984-87, McCarter & English, Cherry Hill, N.J., 1987-89, Gerstein Cohen & Grayson, Haddonfield, 1989-92; mem. N.J. Senate, Trenton, 1992-98; ptnr. Adler & Gold, P.C., Cherry Hill, 1992-98; sr. mem. Cozen & O'Connor, Cherry Hill, 1998—. Councilman, Cherry Hill Twp., 1988-89. Democrat. Jewish. Home: 61 Cameo Dr Cherry Hill NJ 08003-5127 Office: NJ Senate 231 Route 70 E Cherry Hill NJ 08034-2406

ADLER, JULIUS, biochemist, biologist, educator; b. Edelfingen, Germany, Apr. 30, 1930; came to U.S., 1938, naturalized, 1943; s. Adolf and Irma (Stern) A.; m. Hildegard Wohl, Oct. 15, 1963; children: David Paul, Jean Susan. AB, Harvard U., 1952; MS, U. Wis., 1954, PhD, 1957; postdoctoral fellow, Washington U., St. Louis, 1957-59, Stanford U., 1959-60; hon. doctorate, U. Tübingen, Germany, 1987, U. Regensburg, Germany, 1995. Asst. prof. biochemistry and genetics U. Wis., Madison, 1960-63, assoc. prof., 1963-66, prof., 1966-96; prof. emeritus U.Wis., Madison, 1996—; Edwin Bret Hart prof. biochemistry and genetics U. Wis., Madison, 1972, Steenbock prof. microbiol. scis., 1982-92; recipient hon. symposium on behavior and signaling in microorganisms, 1995. Research, publs. in field. Recipient Otto-Warburg medal German Soc. Biol. Chemistry, 1986, R.H. Wright award Simon Fraser U., 1988, Hilldale award U. Wis., 1988, Abbott-Am. Soc. Microbiology Lifetime Achievment award, 1995, William C. Rose award Am. Soc. Biochemistry and Molecular Biology, 1996. Mem. NAS (Selman A. Waksman Microbiology award 1980), Am. Acad. Arts and Scis., Am. Philos. Soc., Wis. Acad. Scis., Arts and Letters. Home: 1234 Wellesley Rd Madison WI 53705-2232 Office: U Wis Dept Biochemistry Madison WI 53706

ADLER, KARL PAUL, medical educator, academic administrator; b. Paterson, N.J., July 9, 1939. MD, Georgetown U., 1966. Diplomate Am. Bd. Internal Medicine. Intern 2d med. div. Bell Hosp., Cornell U., 1966-67, jr. asst. resident 2d med. div., 1967-68; jr. asst. resident Meml. Hosp., 1967-68; sr. asst. resident Cornell Cooperating Hosps., 1968-69, chief resident in medicine, 1969-70; sr. asst. resident North Shore Hosp., Manhasset, N.Y., 1968-69, chief resident in medicine, 1969-70, assoc. dir. dept. medicine, 1972-74, chief nephrology, 1972-74; med. dir. dept. emergency services Kings County Hosp. Ctr., Bklyn., 1974-77, med. dir. dept. medicine, 1974-77; asst. prof. medicine Cornell U., 1971-74; asst. prof. medicine SUNY Med. Sch., Bklyn., 1974-76, assoc. prof. clin. medicine, 1976-77; chief dept. medicine Ellis Hosp., 1977-81; vice chmn. at Albany Med., 1977-81, assoc. prof. med., 1977-81; chief dept. medicine Met. Hosp. Ctr., 1981-87; dean N.Y. Med. Coll., 1987-94, prof. medicine, 1981—, v.p. for med. affairs, 1990-94; pres., CEO St. Vincent's Hosp. and Med. Ctr., N.Y.C., 1994—; pres. Assoc. Med. Schs. N.Y., 1991-93. Mem. ACP, Am. Assn. Med. Colls., Alpha Omega Alpha. Office: St Vincents Hosp & Med Ctr 153 W 11th St New York NY 10011-8397

ADLER, KRAIG (KERR), biology educator; b. Lima, Ohio, Dec. 6, 1940; s. William Charles and Jennie Belle (Noonan) A.; m. Dolores Rose Pochocki, Mar. 25, 1967; 1 child, Todd David. BA, Ohio Wesleyan U., 1962; MS, U. Mich., 1965, PhD, 1968. Asst. prof. biology U. Notre Dame, Ind., 1968-72; assoc. prof. biology Cornell U., Ithaca, N.Y., 1972-80, prof., 1980—, chmn. dept. neurobiology and behavior, 1976-79, 91-94, vice provost life scis., 1998—; Baer Meml. lectr. Milw. Pub. Mus., 1977; Hefner lectr. Miami U., Oxford, Ohio, 1980; Anderson Meml. lectr. Rutgers U., 1982; vis. prof. zoology Ariz. State U., 1980; vis. scholar U. Cambridge, 1985; Am. del. 16th Internat. Ethological Congress, Vancouver, 1979, 1st Herpetological Congress of Socialist Countries, Budapest, 1981; disting. scholar China Program, Nat. Acad. Scis., 1984-85; sec. gen. First World Congress Herpetology Internat., 1982-89; disting lectr. USSR Acad. Scis., 1986; bd. dirs. Declining Amphibian Populations Task Force, 1994—; mem. bd. govs. Great Lakes Rsch. Consortium, 1998—, N.Y. Sea Grant, 1999—; mem. Univ. Corp. for Atmospheric Rsch., 1998—. Author: History of Herpetology, 1989; co-author Handbook to Middle East Amphibians and Reptiles, 1992, Herpetology of China, 1993, Encyclopedia of Reptiles and Amphibians, 1986; editor: Herpetological Studies in Eastern U.S., 1978, Herpetological Explorations in the Great American West, 1978, Herpetology: Current Research on Biology of Amphibians and Reptiles, 1992; co-editor: Captive Management and Conservation of Amphibians and Reptiles, 1994; contbr. articles to profl. jours. Grantee NSF, 1971-83, NIH, 1983-87, USDA, 1975—. Fellow Acad. Zoology, AAAS; mem. Soc. Study Amphibians and Reptiles (pres. 1982), Animal Behavior Soc., Am. Soc. Naturalists, Soc. Study Evolution. Office: Cornell U Dept Neurobiology and Behavior Seeley G Mudd Hall Ithaca NY 14853-2702

ADLER, LARRY, marketing executive; b. Frankfort, Ind., Dec. 18, 1938; s. Leon Sidney and Roslyn Jane (Woolf) A.; m. Ruthlee Figlure, Oct. 9, 1960; children: Laurie Kaye, Mark Allan, Joy Ellen. B.S. in Mktg. and Journalism, Ind. U., 1960. Asst. circulation and promotion mgr. McCall Corp., 1960-61; circulation and promotion mgr. Bartell-Media, Inc., 1961-63; sales promotion mgr. Golden Press, Inc., 1963-64; audio-visual dir., licensing mdse. dir., periodical publs. dir., advt. sales and mktg. dir. periodical div. Western Pub. Co., N.Y.C., 1964-74; v.p., pub., dir., treas. Washingtonian mag. and books Washington Mag., Inc., 1974-79; pres. Am. Program Bur., 1980; communications cons., 1980; pres., chmn. Adler Enterprises Ltd., 1981—, Adler Media, Inc., 1981—; pres. Bergen Cablevision, Inc., Bergen County, N.J., 1970-72; asso. profl. lectr. Pubs. Specialists program George Washington U., 1977-79. Creator, host: TV show Toy Fair News, 1968-73. Pres. Englewood (N.J.) Jaycees, 1965-66; mem. bd. edn. High Sch. Planning Com., Tenafly, N.J., 1969; program chmn. Tenafly Action Conf. on Edn., 1969; exec. bd. Maughan Sch. P.T.A., Tenafly, 1968-70; mem. steering com., long range planning com. Tenafly Bd. Edn., 1971-72; chmn. Tenafly Citizens Communications Com., 1971-72, Tenafly Townwide Com., 1972-73; chmn. bd. dirs. Capital Children's Mus., 1977-83; Bd. dirs. Englewood Boys Club, 1967-69. Mem. City and Regional Mag. Assn. (founder, pres., treas.), Ind. U. Alumni Assn., Alpha Delta Sigma, Zeta Beta Tau (v.p. 1960). Office: 6849 Old Dominion Dr Mc Lean VA 22101

ADLER, LEE, artist, educator, marketing executive; b. N.Y.C., May 22, 1926; s. Isidore and Anne (Blasser) A.; m. Florence Blumenkrantz, Dec. 28, 1956; 1 child, Derek Jonathan Tristan. B.A., Syracuse U., 1948; M.B.A., N.Y. U., 1960. Research account exec. Amos Parrish & Co., N.Y.C., 1954-56; dir. mktg. Lewin, Williams & Saylor, Inc., N.Y.C., 1956-57; with Interpub. Group Cos., Inc., N.Y.C., 1958-68; client service dir. Marplan, 1958-63; market devel. McCann-Erickson, Inc., N.Y.C., 1963-64; v.p. research and planning Pritchard, Wood, Inc., N.Y.C., 1964-65; v.p. mktg. services McCann-ITSM, Inc., N.Y.C., 1966-67; dir. research Market Planning Corp., N.Y.C., 1967-68; pres. Flouton, Adler & Assos., N.Y.C., 1969-70; dir. mktg. research RCA Corp., N.Y.C., 1970-74; prof. mktg. Fairleigh Dickinson U., Madison, N.J., 1974-80; ptnr. Machlin-Adler Realty Co., Bklyn., 1978-82, Adler Realty Co., Bklyn., 1982—; owner, operator beef cattle ranch Climax, N.Y.; guest lectr. Columbia, Emory U., N.Y. U., U. Conn., St. John's U.; bd. govs., v.p., chmn. research com. Bklyn. Heights Assn.; trustee Mktg. Communications Research Ctr. Author, editor: Attitude Research at Sea, 1966, Plotting Marketing Strategy, 1967, Attitude Research on the Rocks, 1968, Managing the Marketing Research Function, 1977; also articles; contbg. author Modern Marketing Strategy, 1964, Handbook Modern Marketing, 1970, others; one man shows include, Ruth White Gallery, N.Y.C., 1968, Salpeter Gallery, N.Y.C., 1967, N.Y.C. Community Coll., 1967, NYU, 1972, New Bertha Schaefer Gallery, N.Y.C., 1973, 74, Hagley Mus., Wilmington, Del., 1974, Mickelson Gallery, Washington, 1975, Norton Gallery, St. Louis, 1974, Fairleigh Dickinson U., 1975, John Leech Gallery, Auckland, New Zealand, 1975, Poster Place, N.Y.C., 1975, Dallas, 1975, Canterbury Soc. Arts, Christ Church, New Zealand, 1975, Pub. Art Gallery, Dunedin, New Zealand, 1975, Waikato Art Gallery, Hamilton, New Zealand, 1975, Terrain Gallery, N.Y.C., 1975, Warwick (Eng.) Gallery, 1976, L.I. U., Bklyn., 1976, Kingpitcher Gallery, Pitts., 1976, Graham Gallery, N.Y.C., 1976, Instituto de Cultura Hispanica, Madrid, Spain, 1976, Mus. Modern Art, Mexico City, 1976, Universidad Autonoma de Nuevo Leon, Monterrey, Mex., 1976, Galeria de Arte, Saltillo, Mexico, 1976, Unidad de la Ciudadela, Monterrey, 1976, U. Monterrey, 1976, Instituto Tecnologico, Monterrey, 1976, USIA, Monterrey, 1976, Mus. Art, Torréon, Mexico, 1976, Albert White Gallery, Toronto, Ont., 1977, Centro de Arte Moderno, Guadalajara, Mexico, 1977, Mint Mus. Art, Charlotte, N.C., 1978, Heritage Found. Mus., 1978-79, Aldrich Mus. Contemporary Art, 1979, Gertrud Dorn Gallery, Stuttgart, W. Ger., 1979, Ulrich Mus. Art, Wichita, Kans. U., 1980, numerous others; exhibited in group shows, Museo de Arte Contemporanea, Bogota, Colombia, Whitney Mus. Am. Art, N.Y.C., State U. N.Y., Rochester, Bklyn. Mus., Am. Acad., Mus. Modern Art, São Paulo, Brazil, N.A.D., Soc. Am. Graphic Artists, Fine Arts, Springfield, Mass., New Eng. Exhbn., Butler Inst. Am. Art, Youngstown, Ohio, numerous others; represented in many permanent collections including Whitney Mus. Am. Art, Met. Mus. Art, Brit. Mus., Art Inst. Chgo., Corcoran Gallery, Washington, Fogg Art Mus., Harvard, Mus. Contemporary Art, São Paulo, Bklyn. Mus., Seattle Art Mus., Albion (Mich.) Coll., Andrew Dickson White Mus. Art, Ithaca, N.Y., Butler Inst. Am. Art, Indpls. Mus. Art, Columbia Tchrs. Coll., Cin. Art Mus., N.Y. U., N.Y.C., Community Coll., Jersey City Mus., DeCordova Mus., Lincoln, Mass., Syracuse Art Mus., Ithaca Art Mus., Detroit Inst. Art, Mus. Modern Art, Sao Paulo, Mus. Fine Arts, Montreal, Phila. Mus. Art, Municipal Art Gallery, Dublin, Ireland, Hagley Mus., Wilmington, Del. Art Mus., Wilmington, Art Gallery Ont., Toronto, Auckland Art Mus., Fairleigh Dickinson U., Madison, N.J., L.I. U., Bklyn., Printmakers Workshop Collection, N.Y.C., Wichita State U., Larry Aldrich Mus., Ridgefield, Conn., Colgate U., Munson-Williams-Proctor Inst., Utica, N.Y., N.Y. Pub. Library, Instituto de Cultura Hispanica, Madrid, Edwin A. Ulrich Mus. Art, Wichita, Kans., Nat. Acad. Health and Safety, Beckley, W.Va., Civic Mus., Udine, Italy, Neuberger Mus., Pratt Graphics Center, SUNY, Purchase, Weatherspoon Art Gallery at U. N.C., Mint Mus. Art, Charlotte, N.C., USIA. Recipient Burndy Corp. award, 1969; Grumbacher award, 1968; Purchase award Soc. Am. Graphic Artists, 1979; won Childe Hassam Fund competition, 1969. Mem. Am. Mktg. Assn. (v.p. 1970-71, dir. 1968-70, chmn. attitude research com. 1963-65), Am. Assn. Pub. Opinion Research, Am. Sociol. Assn., N.Y. U. Grad. Sch. Bus. Adminstrn. Alumni Assn. (dir. 1964-67). Home: Lime Kiln Farm Climax NY 12042

ADLER, LEWIS GERARD, lawyer; b. N.Y.C., Sept. 13, 1960; s. Sherman and Esther (Weiss) A.; m. Kim Adler, Sept. 5, 1988; children: Craig, Stephanie, Katie, Samantha. AS, Vanderbilt U., 1981; JD, Rutgers U., 1985. Bar: N.J. 1986, Pa. 1985, U.S. Dist. Ct. N.J. 1986, U.S. Dist. Ct. Pa. 1990, U.S. Supreme Ct. 1990. Solicitor Gloucester County Constrn. Bd. Appeals, Woodbury, N.J., 1987-88; atty. Gloucester County Sr. Citizen Will Program, Woodbury, 1987-88; pvt. practice Woodbury, N.J., 1989—; spl. counsel Gloucester County, 1990—; pub. defender Deptford Township, 1996, zoning bd. solicitor, 1997—. Designer computer software. Mem. ABA, N.J. Bar Assn., Gloucester County Bar Assn., Phila. Trial Lawyers, Pa. Bar Assn. Democrat. Avocations: water and snow skiing, spelunking, chess, bicycling, rappelling. Home: 215 Douglass Ave Haddonfield NJ 08033-1626 Office: 57 Euclid St Woodbury NJ 08096-4633

ADLER, LOUISE DECARL, bankruptcy judge; b. 1945. BA, Chatham Coll., Pitts.; JD, Loyola U., Chgo. Bar: Ill., 1970, Calif., 1972. Practicing atty. San Diego, 1972-84; standing trustee Bankruptcy Ct. So. Dist. Calif., San Diego, 1974-79, chief judge bankruptcy, 1996—. Mem. editorial bd. Calif. Bankruptcy Jour., 1991-92. Fellow Am. Coll. Bankruptcy; mem. San Diego County Bar Assn. (chair bus. law study sect. 1979, fed. ct. com. 1983-84), Lawyers Club of San Diego (bd. dirs. 1972-73, treas. 1972-75, sec. 1972-74, v.p. 1974-75), San Diego Bankruptcy Forum (bd. dirs. 1989-92), Nat. Conf. Bankruptcy Judges (bd. dirs. 1989-91, sec. 1992-93, v.p. 1993-94, pres. 1994-95). Office: US Bankruptcy Ct 325 W F St Rm 2 San Diego CA 92101-6017

ADLER, MADELEINE WING, academic administrator; d. George and Bette Wing; m. Frederick S. Lane; children: J. Peter Adler, Rand Lane, Cary Lane. BA in Polit. Sci., Northwestern U., 1962; MA in Polit. Sci., U. Wis., 1963, PhD in Polit. Sci., 1969. Asst. prof. polit. sci. Am. U., Washington, 1965-67; cons. Charles Nelson Assoc., N.Y.C., 1967-68; asst. prof. Queens Coll. CUNY, N.Y.C., 1969-74, assoc. prof. Queens Coll., 1974-86, assoc. dean, 1983-86; v.p. acad. affairs, prof. polit. sci. Framingham (Mass.) State Coll., 1986-92; pres. West Chester (Pa.) U., 1993—; staff mem. Joint Com. Orgn. Congress, Washington, 1965-66; vis. asst. prof. Pa. State U., summers 1967-71; dir. profl. staff recruitment N.Y.C. Urban Acad., 1975-78; pres. Ctr. Applied Rsch. and Analysis Social Scis., Inc., 1976-86; mem. crosscutting rsch. panel, office rsch. and evaluation U.S. HEW, 1978-80; program coord. N.E. region Soc. Coll. and Univ. Planning, 1987-89; mem. exec. bd. Am. Coun. Edn./Nat. Identification Project, State of Mass., 1987-92, vice chair exec. bd., 1991—. Author: (with Harold Savitch) Decentralization at the Grassroots: Political Innovation in New York City and London, 1974; contbr. article to profl. jours. Mem. Comty. Bd. 14, Bklyn., 1978-81, Gov.'s Award Panel for Humanities, 1993—, Gov.'s Comty. Svc. Adv. Bd., 1994—, Chester County Comty. Found., 1994—; appointee Bklyn. Econ. Devel. Corp., 1982-86; bd. advisors Acad. Search Consultation Svcs., 1994—. Mem. Pa. Assn. Colls. and Univs. (com. acad. issues 1993—). Home: 100 E Rosedale Ave West Chester PA 19382-4927 Office: Office of Pres West Chester University West Chester PA 19383

ADLER, MARGOT SUSANNA, journalist, radio producer; b. Little Rock, Apr. 16, 1946; d. Kurt Alfred and Freyda (Nacque) A. BA, U. Calif.-Berkeley, 1968, MS, Columbia U., 1970. Newscaster Sta. WBAI-FM, N.Y.C., 1968-71, host talk show, 1972-90; chief Washington bur. Pacifica News Svc. Network, 1971-72; corr., prodr. All Things Considered, Morning Edit., Nat. Pub. Radio, N.Y.C., 1978—; instr. radio comms. Goddard Coll., Plainfield, Vt., 1977; instr. religion and ecology Inst. for Social Ecology, Vt., 1986-93. Author: Drawing Down the Moon, 1979, Heretic's Heart, 1997. Co-prodr., dir. (radio drama) War Day, 1985. Contbr. articles to jours. Nieman fellow Harvard U., 1982. Mem. Phi Beta Kappa. Avocations: swimming, bird watching, science fiction. Home: 333 Central Park W New York NY 10025-7145 Office: Nat Pub Radio 801 2nd Ave Rm 701 New York NY 10017-4781

ADLER, MICHAEL S., control systems and electronic technologies executive; b. Detroit, July 13, 1943; s. Gerald and Edna (Paananen) A.; m. Virginia Louise Dohring, July 31, 1965; children—Emily, Gerald. BSEE, MIT, 1965, MSEE, 1967, PhD in Elec. Engring., 1971. Staff mem. Gen. Electric Corp. Research and Devel., Schenectady, N.Y., 1971-79, mgr. archival memory program, 1979-80, mgr. device unit, 1980-82, mgr. power sem. condr. br., 1982-84, mgr. power electric lab., 1984-89, mgr. Electronic Tech. Lab., 1989-93, mgr. Controls Systems and Electronic Tech. Lab., 1993—. Author: Design of High Voltage Semiconductor Devices; contbr. articles to profl. jours., tech. meeting procs.; inventor. Recipient IR100 award Indsl. Research Mag., 1982, 83, 84; Dushman award Gen. Electric, 1983, 85. Fellow IEEE (Region I award 1980, chmn. internat. electronic devices mtg., 1982, pres. electron device soc. 1992-93, bd. dirs. 1996-97, v.p. tech. activities 1999). Club: Adirondack Mountain. Avocations: sailing; hiking; skiing. Office: Gen Electric Corp Rsch and Devel Dept 1 Rsch Circle Niskayuna NY 12309

ADLER, MORTIMER JEROME, philosopher, author; b. N.Y.C., Dec. 28, 1902; s. Ignatz and Clarissa (Manheim) A.; m. Caroline Sage Pring, 1963. Ph.D., Columbia U., 1928; B.A., Columbia Coll., 1983. Instr. Columbia U., 1923-30; asst. dir. People's Inst., N.Y.C., 1927-29; assoc. prof. philosophy of law U. Chgo., 1930-42, prof., 1942-52; dir. Inst. for Philos. Research, 1952-95; pres. San Francisco Prodns., Inc., 1954-94; chmn. bd. editors Ency. Brit., 1974-95; chmn. emeritus, 1995—; hon. chair, co-founder Ctr. for the Study of Great Ideas, 1990—; vis. lectr. St. John's Coll., Md., 1937—, visitor emeritus, 1985—; university prof. U. N.C., Chapel Hill, 1988-91; hon. trustee The Aspen Inst., 1973—. Author: Dialectic, 1927, (with Jerome Michael) Crime, Law and Social Science, 1933, (with Maude Phelps Hutchins) Diagrammatics, 1932, Art and Prudence, 1937, What Man Has Made of Man, 1938, 94, How To Read a Book, 1940 (with Charles Van Doren), rev. edit., 1972, Problems for Thomists, The Problems of Species, 1940, A Dialectic of Morals, 1941, How to Think About War and Peace, 1944, 95, (with Louis Kelso) The Capitalist Manifesto, 1958, 75, The New Capitalists, 1961, 75, (with Milton Mayer) The Revolution in Education, 1958, The Idea of Freedom, Vol. I, 1958, Vol. II, 1961, Great Ideas from the Great Books, 1961, The Conditions of Philosophy, 1965, The Difference of Man and the Difference It Makes, 1967, 1993, The Time of Our Lives, 1970, 95, The Common Sense of Politics, 1971, 95, (with William Gorman) The American Testament, 1975, Some Questions About Language, 1976, 1991, Philosopher at Large, 1977, 1992, Reforming Education, 1977, Aristotle for Everybody, 1978, 1991, How To Think About God, 1980, 91, Six Great Ideas, 1981, The Angels and Us, 1982, The Paideia Proposal, 1982, Paideia Problems and Possibilities, 1983, How to Speak/How to Listen, 1983, 1985, The Paideia Program, 1984, A Vision of the Future, 1984, Ten Philosophical Mistakes, 1985, 87, A Guidebook to Learning, 1986, We Hold These Truths, 1987, Reforming Education: The Opening of the American Mind, 1989, Intellect: Mind Over Matter, 1990, 93, Truth in Religion, 1990, Haves Without Have-Nots, 1991, Desires Right and Wrong, 1991, A Second Look in the Rearview Mirror, 1992, 94, The Great Ideas: A Lexicon of Western Thought, 1992, The Four Dimensions of Philosophy, 1993, Art, the Arts, and the Great Ideas, 1994, 95, Adler's Philosophical Dictionary, 1995; editor: (with Charles Van Doren) Great Treasury of Western Thought, 1977; assoc. editor: Great Books of the Western World, 1945-52, editor in chief 2d edit., 1990, Syntopicon, 1952, 90; gen. editor: The Idea of Happiness, The Idea of Justice, The Idea of Love, The Idea of Progress, 1967; editor in chief: The Annals of America, 21 vols., through 1986. Mem. Am. Catholic philos. assn., Am. Maritain Assn, Internat. Listening Assn. Home: 555 Laurel Ave Apt 510 San Mateo CA 94401-4153 Office: Ctr for Study of Great Ideas 325 W Huron St Chicago IL 60610-3636

ADLER, NADIA C., lawyer; b. Salford, Lancashire, Eng., Feb. 26, 1945; came to U.S., 1948; d. David Colin and Rose (Bolton) Cohen; m. David J. Adler, Mar. 1977 (div. 1992); m. Robert Bernstein, May, 1997. BA, CCNY, 1966; JD, N.Y.U., 1973. Bar: N.Y. 1974, U.S. Dist. Ct. (so. and ea. dists.) N.Y. 1974, U.S. Ct. Appeals (2d cir.) 1975, U.S. Supreme Ct. 1983. Assoc. Rosenman Colin Freund Lewis & Cohen and predecessor firms, N.Y.C., 1973-82; ptnr. Rosenman & Colin, N.Y.C., 1983-87; v.p., gen. counsel Montefiore Med. Ctr., N.Y.C., 1987-89, sr. v.p., gen. counsel, 1989-98; v.p., gen. counsel, corp. sec. C.R. Bard, Inc., Murray Hill, N.J., 1999—; mem. legal affairs com. Greater N.Y. Hosp. Assn., N.Y.C., 1987-99; mem. bioethics task force, subcoms. on patient decision making, reproductive techs. and physician-assisted suicide, commn. women's equality Am. Jewish Congress, N.Y.C., 1989—; mem. bd. ethics Village Briarcliff Manor, N.Y., 1997—. Bd. dirs. Berkeley-in-Scarsdale (N.Y.) Assn., 1989-91. Mem. ABA (mem. forum on health care), Assn. of Bar of City of N.Y., Am. Health Lawyers Assn. and predecessor assns., N.Y. State Bar Assn. (co-chair in-house counsel com. health law sect., mem. exec. com. health law sect. 1996-99). Democrat. Office: C R Bard Inc 730 Central Ave Murray Hill NJ 07974

ADLER, NANCY ELINOR, psychologist, educator. BA, Wellesley Coll., 1968; MA, Harvard U., 1971, PhD, 1973. Asst. prof. psychology U. Calif., Santa Cruz, 1972-76, assoc. prof. psychology, 1976-77; assoc. prof. med. psychology dept. psychiatry and pediat. U. Calif., San Francisco, 1977-84, prof. med. psychology depts. psychiatry and pediat., 1984—, dir. health psychology program, 1988—, program dir. NIMH tng. program, 1991—, vice chair dept. psychiatry, 1994—; dir. Ctr. for Health and Cmty., 1998—; vis. asst. rsch. psychologist Inst. Personality Assessment and Rsch., U. Calif., Berkeley, 1975; mem. peer rev. panel Ad Hoc Sci. Study Sects., Nat. Inst. Child Health and Human Devel., 1977—, Nat. Heart, Lung and Blood Inst., 1993; adv. com. for five-yr. plan Demographic and Social Scis. Br., Ctr. for Population RSch., Nat. Inst. Child Health and Human Devel., 1986-87, adv. com., 1991; sr. rsch. scientist in psychology Yale U., New Haven. 1994-95; review com. Intramural Rsch. NIMH, 1997, sci. adv. bd. Ctr. Advancement Health, Washington, 1995-96, bd. trustees, 1996—; grant reviewer NSF, Social Scis. and Humanities Rsch. Coun. Can., Soc. Behavioral Medicine, March of Dimes, Ctrs. for Disease Control, Econ. and Social Rsch. Coun.; presenter in field. Author: (with others) Health Psychology-A Handbook: Theories, Applications, and Challenges of a Psychological Approach to the Health Car System, 1979, Preventing Preterm Birth: A Parent's Guide, 1988; adv. bd. Ency. Mental Health, 1995—; assoc. editor Health Psychology, 1984-90, Women's Health: Research in Gender, Behavior and Policy, 1994-98; mem. editl. bd. Jour. Population and Environment, 1982-88, Health Psychology, 1994—; manuscript reviewer Jour. Personality and Social Psychology, Jour. Nervous and Mental Disease, Personality and Social Psychology Bull., Jour. Health and Social Behavior, Jour. Applied Social Psychology, Basic and Applied Social Psychology, Psychology Women Quarterly, The Western Jour. Medicine, Jour. Am. Med. Assn., Am. Jour. Pub. Health, many others; contbr. articles in field. Recipient Best Rsch. Paper award Soc. for Adolescent Medicine, 1984; NSF fellow, 1968-72, U. Calif. Regents Summer fellow, 1974; grantee in field. Fellow APA (sec.-treas. divsn. 34 1975-78, pres. divsn. 34 1979-80, chairperson fellow com. divsn. 34 1982-86, planning com. for nat. conf. on tng. in health psychology 1982-83, participant Arden House conf. on edn. and tng. in health psychology 1983, chairperson nominations com., mem. expert panel on psychol. effects of abortion 1989-90, task force on promotion of population psychology 1992-97), A m. Psychol. Soc., Soc. Exptl. Social Psychology, Internat. Assn. Applied Psychology, Soc. Advancement Social Psychology, assn. Med. Sch. Profs. Psychology, Soc. for Rsch. on Adolescence, Inst. Medicine, Sigma Xi, Phi Beta Kappa. Office: U of CA at San Francisco Health Psychology Program 3333 California St San Francisco CA 94118-1944

ADLER, RAPHAEL, educator emeritus, speech pathologist; b. N.Y.C., Feb. 21, 1922; s. Marcus and Celia (Kress) A.; m. Minna Adler, Sept. 23, 1948; children: Ava Dee, Roxanne, Margo Celeste. BA, Wayne State U., 1953, M in Edn., 1962; PhD, Walden U., 1981. Cert. tchr. secondary schs., Mich.; cert. speech pathologist Am. Speech and Hearing Assn. Tchr. dept. English/speech Berkley (Mich.) Sch. Dist., 1954-68; prof. Oakland C.C., Union Lake, Mich., 1968-92; prof. emeritus Oakland C.C., Union Lake, 1992—; dir. speech and hearing St. Joseph Mercy Hosp., Pontiac, Mich.,1965-84; owner, dir., pres. Speech Pathology Svcs., Southfield, Mich., 1972-86; cons. hosps., nursing homes, VNA, S. Oakland County Health Dept.; bd. dirs. Motion Picture Inst. Mich. Com. mem. Am. Heart Assn. of Mich.; chmn., bd. trustees State of Mich . Stroke Com. Recipient many speaking citations and awards, 1953-62, Toastmasters Internat. 1971, Mrs. Horace Elgin Dodge award Am. Heart Assn. Mich., 1989, 92, 95. Avocations: reading, dancing, gardening, volunteering, writing. Office: Oakland Cmty Coll 7350 Cooley Lake Rd Waterford MI 48327-3864

ADLER, RICHARD, composer, lyricist; b. N.Y.C., Aug. 3, 1921; s. Clarence and Elsa (Richard) A.; children by previous marriage: Andrew H., Christopher E. (dec.). A.B., U. N.C., 1943. Mem. advt. dept. Celanese Corp. Am., 1946-50; White House cons. on the arts, 1965-69; cons. on arts gov. N.C. Adv. bd. Inst. Outdoor Drama, 1968-83, N.C. School arts, 1963—; commd. by Harvard U. to write a march for 50th Anniversary of Neiman Found. Journalist Soc., 1989. Collaborator (with Jerry Ross); on music and lyrics for musicals John Murray Anderson's Almanac, 1953, Pajama Game, 1954, Damn Yankees, 1955; composer, lyricist Kwamina, 1961, TV prodns. Little Women, 1959, Gift of the Magi, 1959; produced and staged White House Press Corrs. and Photographers show for Pres. Kennedy and Prime Minister MacMillan, 1962, N.Y.'s Birthday Salute for Pres. Kennedy, 1962, Inaugural Anniversary Salute to Pres. Kennedy, 1963, Salutes to Pres. Johnson, 1964, Inaugural Gala for Pres. Lyndon Johnson, 1965; producer, composer, lyricist: ABC-TV Stage 67 Musical Olympus 7-0000, fall 1966; composer, lyricist: A Mother's Kisses, 1968; producer: revival Pajama Game, 1973; producer: Rex, 1976; co-producer-composer: Music Is, 1976, Yellowstone Overture (Pulitzer prize nomination); commd. by Dept. of Interior to write Wilderness Suite (Pulitzer prize nomination), 1983, recorded by Utah Symphony; commd. by Statue of Liberty/Ellis Island Found. to write The Lady Remembers (Pulitzer prize nomination), recorded by Detroit Symphony, Retrospectrum (Pulitzer prize nomination); commd. by Chgo. City Ballet to write Eight by Adler, 1984 (Emmy award for TV version 1985); commd. by City of Chgo. to write (ballet) Chicago for sesquicentennial, 1987; commd. by Olympic Com. to write fanfare and overture for U.S. Olympic Festival, 1987, commd. by U. N.C. to write suite to commemorate bi-centennial, 1993, recorded by London Symphony Orch.; (author, autobiography) You Gotta Have Heart, 1990; collaborator lyrics, composer: Off Key, 1995. Trustee John F. Kennedy Ctr. for Performing Arts, 1964-77, exec. com., 1975-77; bd. dirs. Southampton Cultural Com. Lt. (j.g.) USNR, 1943-46. Recipient Antoinette Perry award, Donaldson award, Variety Critics Poll for Pajama Game 1954, Damn Yankees 1955, Antoinette Perry nomination Kwamina 1962, Pulitzer Prize nomination Retrospectrum 1980, Yellowstone Overture 1981; Pulitzer prize nominee for rec. The Statue of Liberty Suite; named to Songwriters Hall of Fame, 1984; Hon. Park Ranger award Nat. Park Service, 1984. Mem. Dramatists Guild (exec. coun. 1958-68), Songwriters Guild Am. (bd. dirs., exec. com., exec. v.p. 1985—), New Dramatists (bd. dirs. 1974—), Nat. Hypertension Assn. (bd. dirs. 1978—). Address: 8 E 83rd St New York NY 10028-0418

ADLER, RICHARD MELVIN, architect, planner; b. N.Y.C., Mar. 25, 1928; s. Jacob Wiliam and Betty (Uffer) A.; children—Robin Sheryl, Joy Lois; m. Marie Fusco Cusano, 1986. B.Arch., Pratt Inst., 1948. Registered architect, N.Y. and others, Airport architect, Port Authority of N.Y., 1952-58; ptnr. Brodsky Hoff & Adler, N.Y.C., 1959-71; pres. B, H, A Architects & Engrs., 1971-75, Brodsky & Adler, N.Y.C., 1975-80, R.M. Adler & Assocs., Peterborough, N.H., 1993—, Adler, Goodman A Kolab For Architects & Engrs., Great Neck, 1993—; chmn. bd. Geller Termotto & Adler, Teaneck, N.J., 1982—, Clendening Adler, Arlington, Tex., 1983—; elected budget com. Peterborough, 1998—. Served to 1st lt., N.Y. N.G., 1948-63. Recipient Disting. Service award Engrs. News Record, 1974; Creative Design award ASCE, 1973. Mem. AIA (Merit award 1977, bd. dirs. Long Island chpt. 1988, chair for profl. practice Long Island), N.Y. Soc. Architects, Wings Club, Constrn. Specifications Inst., Queens C. of C. Republican. Jewish.

ADLER, ROBERT, electronics engineer; b. Vienna, Austria, Dec. 4, 1913; came to U.S., 1940, naturalized, 1945; s. Max and Jenny (Herzmark) A.; m. Mary F. Buehl, 1946 (dec. Jan. 1993); m. Ingrid C. Koch, 1998. Ph.D. in Physics, U. Vienna, 1937. Asst. to patent atty. Vienna, 1937-38; lab. Sci. Acoustics, Ltd., London, Eng., 1939-40, Assoc. Research, Inc., Chgo., 1940-41; research group Zenith Radio Corp., Chgo., 1941-52; assoc. dir. research Zenith Radio Corp., 1952-63, v.p., 1959-77, dir. research, 1963-77; dir. research EXTEL Corp., Northbrook, Ill., 1978-79; v.p. research EXTEL Corp., 1979-82; tech. cons. Zenith Electronics Corp., 1982-97, Elo Touch Systems, Motorola, 1997—. Contbr. numerous articles profl. publs. Fellow IEEE (Edison medal 1980); mem. Nat. Acad. Engring. Achievements include 180 patents: invention of ultrasonic remote control for TV sets, first electromechanical I.F. filter, electron beam parametric amplifier, ultrasonic touch system. Home: 1380 Ridge Rd Northbrook IL 60062-4626

ADLER, ROBERT, advertising executive. Exec. v.p., co-dir. media Gotham Inc., N.Y.C. Office: Gotham Inc 100 5th Ave New York NY 10011-6903*

ADLER, ROBERT MARTIN, lawyer; b. Toledo, Ohio, Oct. 2, 1943; s. Charles J. and Barbara (Sechback) A.; m. Andrea Rosenberg, June 12, 1966; children: Rebecca J., David C. BA, Oberlin Coll., 1965; JD, U. Mich., 1968. Bar: D.C. 1969. Trial atty. tax divsn. U.S. Dept. Justice, Washington, 1968-74; ptnr. Stiller, Adler & Schwartz, Washington, 1974-81; pvt. practice Law Offices Robert M. Adler, Washington, 1981-91; sr. ptnr. Drinker Biddle & Reath, Washington, 1991-96; ptnr. O'Connor & Hannon, L.L.P., Washington, 1996—. Chmn. Stiller Meml. Found., Washington, 1979-91. Avocation: sailing. Office: O'Connor & Hannan LLP Ste #800 1919 Pennsylvania Ave NW Washington DC 20006-3404*

ADLER, SAMUEL HANS, retired conductor, composer; b. Mannheim, Fed. Republic of Germany, Mar. 4, 1928; came to U.S., 1939, naturalized, 1945; s. Hugo Chaim and Selma (Rothschild) A.; m. Carol Ellen Stalker, Feb. 14, 1960 (div. 1989); children: Deborah Ruth, Naomi Leah; m. Emily Freeman Brown, June 8, 1991. MusB, Boston U., 1948; MA, Harvard U., 1950; MusD (hon.), So. Methodist U., 1969; DFA (hon.), Wake Forest U.; D.F.A. (hon.), St. Mary's Coll., Ind., 1986; DMus (hon.), St. Louis Conservatory, 1986. Music dir. Temple Emanu-El, Dallas, 1953-66; prof. composition North Tex. State U., Denton, 1957-66; Eastern regional dir. contemporary music project Ford Found., 1966-70; prof. composition Eastman Sch. Music, U. Rochester, N.Y., 1966-94; hon. prof. U. Wales, Cardiff, 1984-89; ret., 1994; tchr. Julliard Sch. Music, N.Y.C.; lectr., condr. throughout world. Condr. Dallas Chorale, 1954-57, Dallas Lyric Theatre, 1955-59; composer 6 symphonies, 4 operas, 8 string quartets, sonatas for piano, violin (4), cello, flute, viola, guitar, oboe, clarinet, organ, saxophone, concertos for piano (2), violin, cello, flute, saxophone quartet, organ, woodwind quintet, guitar, viola, also for orch. and band, chamber and choral works, songs; author: Choral Conducting, 1971, 2d revised edit., 1985, Sight Singing, 1979, 2d revised edit., 1996, The Study of Orchestration, 1982, 2d edit., 1989. Served with AUS, 1950-52. Grantee Nat. Endowment Arts, Ford Found., Rockefeller Found.; recipient 6 1st prizes Tex. Composers Contest, Charles Ives award, 1965, Lillian Fairchild award, 1968, Deems Taylor award, 1983, Am. Acad. and Inst. Arts and Letters award, 1990; Guggenheim fellow, 1984-85. Mem. Music Educators Nat. Conf., Music Tchrs. Nat. Assn., ASCAP (awards 1960—), Phi Mu Alpha Sinfonia, Phi Beta Kappa. Jewish.

ADLER, SARA, arbitrator, mediator; b. Chgo., Jan. 26, 1942; d. Matthew Michael and Mildred Paula (Eckhaus) Lewison; m. James N. Adler, Aug. 19, 1967; children: Michael, Philip, Matthew. AB, U. Chgo., 1961; JD, UCLA, 1969. Bar: Calif. Cons. Inst. Criminal Justice Adminstrn. U. Calif., Davis, 1969-71; assoc. Law Office of Sara Radin, L.A., 1971-72; assoc. dir. Paralegal Tng. Inst. U. So. Calif., L.A., 1972-74; assoc. Wyman, Bautzer, et al, L.A., 1974-78; arbitrator, mediator Dispute Resolution Svcs., L.A., 1978—. Fellow Coll. Labor and Employment Lawyers; mem. ABA (neutral co-chair ADR in Labor/employment Law 1995-98), Am. Arbitration Assn. (bd. dirs., exec. com., mem. employment law task force), Nat. Acad. Arbitrators (regional chair 1994-96), Indsl. Rels. Rsch. Assn. (pres. so. Calif. 1991-92), L.A. County Bar Assn. (chmn. labor and employment sect. 1997-98). Avocations: travel, theater, bridge. Office: Dispute Resolution Svcs 1034 Selby Ave Los Angeles CA 90024-3106

ADLER, SEYMOUR JACK, social services administrator; b. Chgo., Oct. 22, 1930; s. Michael L. and Sarah (Pasnick) A.; m. Barbara Fingold, Mar. 24, 1958; children: Susan Lynn Hoke, Karen Sandra Adler-Marder, Michelle Lauren Adler-Morrison. BS, Northwestern U., Evanston, Ill., 1952; MA, U. Chgo., 1958. Caseworker Cook County Dept. Pub. Aid, Chgo., 1955; juv. officer Cook County Sheriff's Office, 1955-56; U.S. probation-parole officer U.S. Dist. Ct., Chgo., 1958-68; exec. dir. Youth Guidance, Chgo., 1968-73; dir. court svcs. Juv. Ct. Cook County, Chgo., 1973-75; exec. dir. Meth. Youth Svcs., Chgo., 1975-85; program mgr. Dept. Social Svcs., Kenosha, Wis., 1985-91, dir., 1992-95; dir. Dept. Human Svcs., Kenosha, 1996—; mem. Ill. Law Enforcement Commn., 1969-72; instr. corrections program Chgo. State U., 1972-75; instr. Harper Coll., 1977, St. Joseph's Coll., 1978; case developer Nat. Ctr. on Instns. and Alternatives, 1985-86; mem. soc. sci. adv. com. Carthage Coll., 1997—. Bd. dirs. Child Care Assn. Ill., 1979-84; exec. bd. Kenosha br. NAACP, 1998—, W-2 steering com., 1998—, Workforce Investment Bd., Kenosha, 1999—. Served to 1st lt. USMCR, 1952-55. Recipient Meritorious Svc. award Chgo. City Colls., 1968. Mem. Ill. Acad. Criminology (pres. 1972, Morris J. Wexler award 1975, Pres.'s award 1997), Nat. Assn. Social Workers (del. Assembly 1977, 79, 81, 84, 87, chmn. Chgo. dist. 1978-80, com. inquiry Wis. chpt. 1990—, chmn. group for action planning childrens svcs. 1980-84, Disting. Svc. award Criminal Justice Coun. 1978 Ill. NASW, chmn. population study group Kenosha Jail 1993-95), Ill. Probation, Parole and Correctional Assn., Internat. Half-way House Assn. (Ill. dir.), Alpha Kappa Delta, Tau Delta Phi. Home: 232 Grandview Ln Twin Lakes WI 53181-9572 Office: Kenosha Dept Human Svcs 714 52nd St Kenosha WI 53140-3426

ADLER, STEPHEN LOUIS, physicist; b. N.Y.C., Nov. 30, 1939; s. Irving and Ruth (Relis) A.; children: Jessica Wendy, Victoria Stephanie, Anthony Curtis; m. Sarah C. Brett-Smith, 1995. A.B. summa cum laude, Harvard U., 1961; Ph.D., Princeton U., 1964. Jr. fellow Soc. of Fellows Harvard U., 1964-66; research assoc. Calif. Inst. Tech., 1966; mem. Inst. for Advanced Study, Princeton, N.J., 1966-69; prof. Sch. Natural Scis., Inst. for Advanced Study, 1969-79, N.J. Albert Einstein prof., 1979—; vis. lectr. dept. physics Princeton U., 1969—; cons. in field. Author: (with R.F. Dashen) Current Algebras, 1968, Quaternionic Quantum Mechanics and Quantum Fields, 1995; contbr. articles to profl. jours. Recipient J.J. Sakurai prize Am. Phys. Soc., 1988, Dirac medal Internat. Ctr. Theoretical Physics, Trieste, Italy, 1998. Fellow Am. Acad. Arts and Scis., AAAS, Am. Phys. Soc.; mem. Nat. Acad. Scis., Phi Beta Kappa, Sigma Xi. Home: 287A Nassau St Princeton NJ 08540-4618 Office: Inst for Advanced Study Sch Natural Scis Olden Ln Princeton NJ 08540

ADLER, THOMAS WILLIAM, real estate executive; b. Rochester, N.Y., Dec. 21, 1940; s. Richard H. and Margaret (Freund) A.; m. Joann Seidenfeld, July 1, 1962; children: Peggy Lynn, Sally Ann, William Richard. BS, U. Wis., 1962. Salesman Cragin Lang Free Co., Cleve., 1962-65, Cragin Lang Free and Smythe, Cleve., 1965-67; ptnr. Cragin Lang Free & Smythe, Cleve., 1967-79, chmn. exec. com., 1975-79; prin. Adler Galvin Rogers, Cleve., 1979-86; pres. Grubb Ellis Instnl. Investment Group, 1988-90; chmn. The Hadley Group, Cleve., 1991; prin. Cleve. Real Estate Ptnrs., 1992-98; mng. ptnr. NewGar Ltd., Cleve., 1999—; pres. Clevetrust Realty Advisors, 1971-73, Nat. City Realty Corp., Cleve., 1973-75; trustee Nat. Assn. Real Estate Investment Trust, Washington, 1971-75; bd. dirs., mem. exec. com. Highwoods Properties, Inc., 1994—; vis. com. Sch. Bus. Cleve. State U. Author: Industrial Real Estate, 1971. Bd. dirs. Leadership Cleve., Am. Jewish Com., Jewish Cmty. Fedn. Cleve., Planned Parenthood of Cleve., Playhouse Sq. Found., Nat. Crime Prevention Coun., Downtown Devel. Coords., Greater Cleve. Growth Assn., United Way Cleve. Mem. Am. Soc. Real Estate Counselors (bd. govs.), Soc. Indsl. and Office Realtors (pres. 1990), Friends Shaker Sq., Union Club, Oakwood Club (pres. 1996-98). Jewish. Avocations: golf, fishing, sailing. Home: 2851 Winthrop Rd Cleveland OH 44120-1825 Office: NewGar Ltd Ste 735 629 Euclid Ave Cleveland OH 44114

ADLERSHTEYN, LEON, naval architect, engineer, educator, researcher; b. St. Petersburg, Russia, Oct. 28, 1925; s. Tsalim and Judith (Shusterovich) A.; m. Irina Bereznaya, Feb. 24, 1962. MS in Shipbuilding, Shipbuilding Inst., St. Petersburg, 1951; DSc in Engring., Ctr. Rsch. Inst. Shipbuilding Tech., St. Petersburg, 1970. Foreman, dep. chief of the hull shop Baltic Shipyard, St. Petersburg, 1951-63; chief technologist Ctrl. Rsch. Inst. for Shipbuilding Tech., St. Petersburg, 1963-65, leader of the team, 1965-74, chief rschr., 1993-94; head of the dept. Acad. of Shipbuilding, St. Petersburg, 1974-88, prof., 1988-94; ret., 1994; chmn. state examination commn. State Marine Tech. U., St. Petersburg, 1989-94; coun. mem. Acad. of Shipbuilding, St. Petersburg, 1974-94, Ctrl. Rsch. Inst. for Shipbuilding Tech., St. Petersburg, 1963-94. Co-author, author 11 books on shipbuilding technology; contbr. over 140 articles to profl. jours. Chmn. coun. sect. Union of Scientists and Engrs., St. Petersburg, 1992-94, mem. bd., 1990-94. Pvt. Russian Army, 1943-45, WWII veteran. Decorated 11 mil. awards Pres. of USSR Supreme Soviet and Pres. of Russian Fedn., 1945-97, 2 mil. medals Am. Legion, 1995-96; recipient Order of the Patriotic War 1st Class Pres. USSR Supreme Soviet, 1985, Medals Russian Nat. Indsl. Exhbn., 1955-93. Fellow Inst. of Marine Engrs. (U.K.); mem. The Soc. of Naval Architects and Marine Engrs. (US), Union of Scientists and Engrs., Russian Soc. of Shipbuilders (Nat. Indsl. Exhbn. medals 1955-93), Am. Assn. Invalids and Vets. of WWII from the former USSR. Achievements include 9 Russian patents on shipbuilding technology; creation and leadership in development of the theory of accuracy in ship hull manufacturing; designed and developed mechanized means for ship manufacturing. Home: 72 Montgomery St Apt 1510 Jersey City NJ 07302-3827

ADMIRE, JOHN H., career officer; b. Tulsa, Okla.; m. Susan B. Moss; 1 child, Katelyn Eileen. BA, Univ. Okla, 1964, MA in journalism, 1965; MA in military history, Old Dominion Univ., 1982; MA in internat. rels., Salve Regina Newport Coll., 1988; MA in nat. security, Naval War Coll., 1991. Infantry platoon leader Co. M 3d Battalion 3d Marines, Vietnam, 1966-67; infantry co. commander Co. M 3d Battalion 28th Marines, Camp Pendleton, Calif., 1967-68, Co. H 2d Battalion 8th Marines, Camp LEjeune, N.C., 1973-74; commanding officer Third Reconnaissance Battalion, Okinawa, Japan, 1983-84; commander Contingency MAGTF 3-88, Persian Gulf, 1988; commanding officer 3d Marine Regiment, Kaneohe Bay, Hawaii, 1990-91; command general 1st Marine Divsn., 1995-98; instr. Armed Forces Staff Coll., Norfolk, Va., 1980-82. Decorated Defense Disting. Svc. medal, Legion of Merit with Combat V, Bronze Star with Combat V (2), Purple Heart, Def. Meritorious Svc. medal (2), Meritorious Svc. medal, Combat Action Ribbon (2). Office: First Marine Divsn Camp Pendleton CA 92055*

ADNET, JACQUES JIM PIERRE, astronautical and electrical engineer, consultant; b. Sermaize-les-Bains, Marne, France, Dec. 12, 1929; came to U.S., 1947; s. Julien Charles and Aline Georgette (Klein) A.; m. Mildred Ann Pruet, June 8, 1952 (div. Apr. 1982); children: Denise E., Lisa A., Paul A.; m. Helen Ilene Milam, Nov. 3, 1990. BA with honors, U. Fla., 1951, BEE with honors, 1960; MS in Astronautics, AF Inst. Tech., 1965; student, Indsl. Coll. of Armed Forces, 1972. Enlisted USAF, 1951, commd. 2d lt., 1952, advanced through grades to lt. col., 1968; elec. warfare officer USAF, Wiesbaden, Germany, 1954-57; with Radar Evaluation Flt./Air Def. Command, Griffiss AFB, N.Y., 1957-58; flight test engr. USAF Systems Command, Hanscom Field, Mass., 1960-61, subsystem devel. engr., 1961-63; site implementation engr. USAF Systems Command, France, Belgium, Italy, 1968; chief space systems divsn. USAF Fgn. Tech. Divsn., Dayton, 1968-71; R&D dir. aero. sys. divsn. USAF Systems Command, Dayton, Ohio, 1971-73; ret., 1973; instr., course dir. Air Force Acad., Colorado Springs, Colo., 1974-81; tech. cons. and tech. translator Adnetech, Colorado Springs, 1973—; dir. Dept. Def. Protocol Office Paris Internat. Air and Space Show, 1969, 71, 73, 75, 77. Contbr. articles to profl. jours. Dir. of protocol 1986 World Cycling Championships, Colorado Springs, 1985-86; mem. Tri-Lakes (Colo.) Comprehensive Plan Com.; co-founder Am. Air Mus. Britain; mem. Air Force Acad. Environ. Coun., 1999—. Decorated Air Force Meritorious Svc. medal, Air Force Commendation medal; recipient Ordre National Du Mérite French Govt., Paris, 1982. Mem. AIAA, VFW, Nat. Space Soc., Am. Legion, Air Force Assn., The Ret. Officers' Assn., USAF Acad. École de l'Air Exch. Assn. (hon., exec. sec.), U. Fla. Alumni Assn. Roman Catholic. Achievements include numerous design modifications and conceptual design of electronic warfare equipment; direction of analysis of foreign space systems and equipment; design of unique passively heated solar homes. E-mail: adnet@divide.net. Fax: 719-481-0082. Home and Office: Adnetech 4360 Diamondback Dr Colorado Springs CO 80921-2364

ADOLFAE, MICHAEL H., municipal government official; b. 1944. BA, Gonzaga U. From city planner II to sr. planner City of Spokane, Wash., 1973-80, dir. of cmty. devel., 1981—. Mem. Inland New Bus. Devel. Co., Cert. Comml. Investor Real Estate Inst. Office: City of Spokane 808 W Spokane Falls Blvd Spokane WA 99201-3333*

ADOLPH, ROBERT J., physician, medical educator; b. Chgo., May 12, 1927; s. Abe and Ina Adolph; m. Ivadean Lair, July 12, 1986. PhB, U. Chgo., 1947; BS, U. Ill., 1950, MD, 1952. Diplomate Am. Bd. Internal Medicine (chmn. com. cardiovascular diseases 1979-81). Instr., then asst. prof. medicine U. Ill. Med. Sch., 1958-60, asst. dir. med. clinics, Rsch. and Edn. Hosps., 1958-60; spl. rsch. fellow NIH U. Wash. Med. Sch., Seattle, 1960-62; mem. faculty U. Cin. Med. Sch., 1962—, now prof. medicine, 1970—, dir. div. cardiology, 1986-90; cons. VA, U. Cin. hosps.; dir. cardiac clinic, U.cin. Hosp. Author papers, abstracts in field; mem. editorial bds. profl. jours. Mem. ACP, AAAS, Am. Heart Assn. (adv. bds., sects. and couns., trustee Southwest Ohio chpt.), Assn. Univ. Cardiologists, Am. Coll. Cardiology (gov. Ohio chpt. 1982-85, chmn. bd. govs. 1984-85, mem. various coms.), Cin. Soc. Internal Medicine (pres. 1982-83), Laennec Soc. (pres. 1978-79), Am. Coll. Cardiology (trustee 1986-91), Sigma Xi, Alpha Omega Alpha, Pi Kappa Epsilon. Office: 231 Bethesda Ave Cincinnati OH 45229-2827

ADOMFEH, CHARLES N., internist; b. Kumasi, Ghana, 1959; s. Charles Akwasi and Akosua (Amoabeng) A.; m. Abena Mansah Adomfeh, May 30, 1987; children: Emmanuel, Gabriel, Michael, JeanAnne. BSc, Med. Sch. U. Sci. and Tech., Kumasi, 1982, MD, 1985; PhD, U. Nottingham, 1992. Diplomate Am. Bd. Internal Medicine. Intern Komfo Anokye Tchg. Hosp., Kumasi, 1985-89; resident N.Y. Med. Coll./Our Lady of Mercy Med. Ctr., Bronx, 1992-95; fellow in geriatrics Albert Einstein Coll. Medicine/L.I. Jewish Med. Ctr., 1995-96; phys. diagnosis preceptor Albert Einstein Coll. Medicine, Bronx, 1995-96; clin. medicine preceptor Albany (N.Y.) Med. Coll., 1996—. Mem. Assemblies of God Health Svcs. Adv. Bd., Accra, Ghana, 1988-89. Recipient Med. Elective awrd The Assn. of Commonwealth Univs., 1984, British Tech. Cooperation award, 1989, AMA Physician's Recognition award, 1998—. Fellow ACP-Am. Soc. Internal Medicine; mem. AMA (Physician's Recognition award 1998—), Ghana Med. Assn., Full Gospel Bus. Men's Fellowship Internat. Christian. Office: Clifton Park Internal Med & Geriatrics 1741 Route 9 Clifton Park NY 12065-2420 Office: Clifton Park Internal Medicine & Geriatrics PLLC 1741 Rte 9 Clifton Park NY 12065

ADOQUEI, SAM, art educator, artist; b. Accra, Ghana, Jan. 20, 1962; came to U.S., 1981; s. Tetteh Adoquei and Adjeley Adjei. Diploma, Ghanatta Coll. Arts, 1978; grad., Opportunities Indsl. Ctr., Ghana, 1986; student, Art Student League N.Y., 1986. Artist N.Y.C., 1986—; art instr. Ghanatta Coll. Fine Arts; mem. faculty Nat. Acad. Design, N.Y.C., Ednl. Alliance, N.Y.C.; represented by Portrait Inc.; instr. Ednl. Allience, N.Y.C., 1995—, Nat. Acad. Design, N.Y.C., 1993—, N.Y. Acad. Art, 1997—. Exhibited in shows including Salmagundi Art Club, Allied Artists Am., Knickerbocker Artists, Hudson Valley Art Assn., Nat. Acad. Design BiAnn. Exch.; designer textbook covers; contbr. articles to profl. jours. Recipient Honorable Mention award Nat. Portrait Competition Artists Mag., 1989, 3rd place award in portrait competition Artists Mag., Grumbacher Gold medal award Knickerbocker Artists 41st Ann. Award of Best Traditional Oil Painting Nat. Open Exhibition, 1991. Mem. Salmagundi Art Club, Knickerbocker Club. Home: 46-36 Oceania St Bayside NY 11361 Studio: 32 Union Sq E New York NY 10003-3209

ADORNO, MONICA S., taxpayer representative; d. Frank Joseph and Dorothy Beatrice Negri Serra; m. Marshall S. Adorno, Oct. 30, 1977. BSBA, U. Hartford, 1988. CPA, Conn.; lic. enrolled agt. U.S. Treas. Dept. Ptnr. Marshall S. & Monica S. Adorno, CPA's, Torrington, Conn., 1996—; v.p. Just-WRite Systems, Inc., Torrington, 1980—; enrolled agt. IRS, 1987—. Author: Shower Songs and Car Poems; A Collection of Words From My Heart. Charter mem. Rep. Presdl. Task Force, Washington; mem. Mus. Modern Art, N.Y.C.; Spl. Master Accountant, Tax Session of the Superior Ct., Spl. Masters Program; Conn. Soc. of CPA's, Fed. Taxation Divsn. Individual Taxation Com., PCPS Task Force on value added peer reviews. Mem. Conn. Soc. CPAs, Inst. Cert. Mgmt. Accts., Nat. Assn. Tax Practitioners. Avocations: poetry, writing, investment portfolio analysis. Office: Marshall S Adorno CPA 1144 E Main St Torrington CT 06790-3912

ADOVASIO, J. M., anthropologist, archeologist, educator; b. Youngstown, Ohio. BA in Anthropology magna cum laude, U. Ariz., 1965, postgrad., 1965-66; PhD in Anthropology, U. Utah, 1970; DSc (hon.), Washington & Jefferson U., 1983. From instr. to asst. prof. anthropology Youngstown State U., 1966-68, 70-71; from asst. prof. to prof. anthropology, Latin Am. studies U. Pitts., Pa., 1972-90; chmn. dept. anthropology U. Pitts., 1980-89, dir. Cultural Resource Mgmt. Program, 1976-89, prof. geology and planetary scis., 1985-90; John E. Boyle prof. anthropology and archaeology, prof. geology Mercyhurst Coll., Erie, Pa., 1990—, dir. anthropology and archaeology dept., 1990—, dir. geology dept., 1991—; dir. archaeology rsch. program So. Meth. U., Dallas, 1990-93; adj. assoc. prof. Youngstown State U., 1976-78; rsch. assoc. Smithsonian Instn., 1974—, Carnegie Mus., 1978—; expert witness Archaeol. Resources Protection Act cases U.S. Govt., Ariz., N.Mex., 1987—; exec. dir. Mercyhurst Archaeol. Inst., 1990—; commr. Pa. Hist. and Mus. Commn., 1995—; bd. dirs. Preservation Pa., Pa. State Hist. Preservation Bd.; presenter in field. Reviewer Libr. Jour., 1973—; contbr. numerous book revs. and articles to profl. jours. Mem. Pa. Hist. and Mus. Commn., 1995—. Nat. Def. Edn. Act fellow, 1968-70, Smithsonian Instn. Post-Doctoral Rsch. fellow, 1971-72; recipient Cert. for Academic Achievement, Smithsonian Instrn., 1972, J. Alden Mason award for lifetime contbns. to Pa. Archaeology, 1997; numerous grants from 1969—. Fellow Am. Anthrop. Assn.; mem. AAAS, Soc. Am. Archaeology, Current Anthropology, Am. Quaternary Assn., Soc. Pa. Archaeology, N.Y. Acad. Scis., Knight of Malta, Sigma Xi, Phi Beta Kappa, Phi Eta Sigma. Home: 4676 White Pine Dr Erie PA 16506-1546 Office: Mercyhurst Coll Anthropology and Archaeology Dept Erie PA 16546

ADREON, BEATRICE MARIE RICE, pharmacist; b. Huntington, W.Va., July 23, 1929; d. Lloyd Emerson and Beatrice (Odell) Rice; student Mary Washington Coll., 1947-49; B.S. in Pharmacy, Med. Coll. Va., 1952; M.A. in Spl. Studies and Women's Studies, George Washington U., 1976; m. Harry Barnes Adreon, Jr., Dec. 27, 1952. Summer vol. worker pharmacies De Paul Hosp., Norfolk, Va., 1949, U.S. Marine Hosp., Norfolk, 1950; pharmacist Washington Clinic, 1954-71; counselor George Washington U., 1976-77, cons. gerontology health scis. dept., 1977—; cons. medicine control traffic patterns nursing homes Cross & Adreon, Washington, 1962-87; founder, pres. Pharmacy Counseling Services, Inc., 1978—. Instr. advanced first aid ARC, 1952—, civil def. instr., 1952—; vol. Spanish Edn. Devel. Center, Washington, 1972; mem. Arlington (Va.) Community Services Bd., 1980-83; chmn. com. substance abuse. Recipient Arnold and Marie Schwartz award in pharmacy, 1980. Mem. Acad. Pharmacy Practice and Mgmt., Am. Pharm. Assn., Va. Pharm. Assn., Potomac Pharmacists Assn., Am. Inst. History of Pharmacy, Nat. Council Patient Info. and Edn. (task force pub. info.), Panhellenic Assn., Kappa Epsilon. Episcopalian (mem. bishop's com. neighborhood services 1967-69, chmn. services for aged div. 1967-69). Contbr. articles in field to profl. jours. Home: 4524 19th Rd N Arlington VA 22207-2352

ADREON, HARRY BARNES, architect; b. Norfolk, Va., July 18, 1929; s. Harry Barnes and Helen Rae (Medairy) A.; m. Beatrice Marie Rice, Dec. 27, 1952. MS in Architecture, Va. Poly. Inst. and State U., 1952; postgrad., George Mason U. Law Sch., 1977-78; grad., USMC Pack and Equitation Sch., U.S. Army Engr. Sch., Ft. Belvoir, Va. Registered architect, Va., Md., D.C. Pvt. practice architect in Va., Md. and Washington; ptnr. Cross & Adreon, Architects, Washington, Va., 1961-87; prin. Harry B. Adreon, Architect, Arlington, Va., 1987—. Pres. Arlington Kiwanis Club, 1984; mem. com. on mgmt. Arlington YMCA, 1982-84; mem. Arlington Commn. on Physically Disabled Persons, 1987-93, Arlington County Fire Prevention Code Appeals Bd., 1990; chmn. Arlington County chpt. ARC, 1990-92, damage assessment technician Disaster Svcs. Human Resources Sys. Capt. USMCR, 1952. Recipient Dorothy Brunsman Outstanding Svc. award ARC, 1997. Mem. AIA (commr., dir. D.C. Met. chpt. 1978-79, Nat. Design Honor award 1968), Constrn. Specifications Inst. (pres. D.C. Met. chpt. 1972-74, Nat. Pres.'s plaque 1974, Carl Ebert award D.C. Met. chpt. 1990, cert. constrn. specifier). Episcopalian (Vestryman 1961, 67, 71). Home and office: 4524 N 19th Rd Arlington VA 22207-2352

ADRI (ADRI STECKLING COEN), fashion designer; b. St. Joseph, Mo.. Ed., Sch. Fine Arts, Washington U., St. Louis, Parson Sch. Design. With B.H. Wragge; owner, pres. Adri Studio, Ltd., N.Y.C., 1983—; with Claire McCardell in 2-person showing, Innovative Contemporary Fashion, Smithsonian Instn., Washington, 1971. Two-woman show (with Claire McCardell) Smithsonian Instn., Washington, 1972. Recipient Coty award, 1982, Internat. Best Five award, Tokyo, 1986. Office: Adri 143 W 20th St New York NY 10011-3630

ADRIAN, CHARLES RAYMOND, political science educator; b. Portland, Oreg., Mar. 12, 1922; s. Harry Raymond and Helen K. (Petersen) A.; m. Audrey Jean Nelson, Apr. 2, 1946; children: Kristin, Nelson. B.A., Cornell (Iowa) Coll., 1947, LL.D., 1973; M.A., U. Minn., 1948, Ph.D., 1950; postdoctoral fellow, U. Copenhagen, Denmark, 1954-55. Instr., then asst. prof. govt. Wayne State U., 1949-55; from asst. prof. to prof. polit. sci. Mich. State U., 1955-66, chmn. dept., 1963-66; dir. Inst. Community Devel., 1958-63; prof. polit. sci. U. Calif.-Riverside, 1966-88, prof. emeritus, 1988—, chmn. dept., 1966-70, acad. asst. to v.p. acad. affairs, 1973-74; cons. fed., state and local govt. ABC; research cons. Mich. Constl. Conv., 1961-62; Adminstrv. asst. to gov. Mich., 1956-57; mem. Meridian Twp. (Mich.) Planning Commn., 1957-60. Author: (with O. P. Williams) Four Cities: A Comparative Study in Community Politics, 1963, State and Local Governments, 2d edit., 1967, 3d edit., 1971, 4th edit., 1976, (with Charles Press) American Political Process, 1965, 2d. edit., 1969, Governing Urban America, 4th edit., 1972, 5th edit., 1977, American Politics Reappraised, 1974, (with E.S. Griffith) History of American City Government 1775-1870, 1976, History of American City Government, 1920-45, 1987, (with Michael Fine) State and Local Politics, 1990; also articles. Mem. Riverside Environ. Protection Commn., 1976-78, Riverside Mayor's Charter Revision Commn., 1985. Served with USAAF, 1943-46, PTO. Faculty fellow Fund Advancement Edn., 1954-55; mem. Phi Beta Kappa. Home: 606 Peachwood Pl Riverside CA 92506-6502

ADRIAN, DONNA JEAN, librarian; b. Morden, Man., Can., Aug. 28, 1940; d. William Gordon and Dorothy Jean (Gregory) Frazer; m. James Ross Adrian, July 17, 1965. B.A., Brandon (Man.) Coll., 1962; B.L.S., McGill U., Montreal, 1963, M.L.S., 1969; master tutor cert., Laubach Literacy Can., 1984. Librarian Laurenvale Sch. Bd., Rosemere, Que., 1963-66; librarian, then library coordinator Rosemere High Sch., 1966-74; library coordinator North Island Regional Sch. Bd., Laval, Que., 1974-79; pedagogical cons. Laurenval Sch. Bd., Laval, 1979—97, now also literacy tutor; lectr. Concordia U., Montreal; mem. Laval Mayor's Library Com., 1975-84. Mem. adv. bd. Canadian Materials, Emergency Librarian. Mem. copyright com. Que. Dept. Edn., 1989-97. Mem. Canadian Library Assn., Que. Assn. Sch. Librarians, Que. Library Assn., Corp. Profl. Librarians Que., Assn. for Tchr.-Librarianship in Can. Home: 194 Roi du Nord Ste Rose, Laval, PQ Canada H7L 1W5

ADRIAN, GEORGE PANAITISOR, graphic designer; b. Bucharest, Mar. 27, 1956; came to U.S., 1990; s. George and Maria (Dumitrescu) Panatisor; m. Mona Florea, Mar. 26, 1983; 1 child, Monica Maria. BSEE, Polytechnic Acad., Constantza, Romani, 1980; BFA in Painting, The Fine Arts Ctr., Bucharest, Romania, 1987; BFA in Graphic Design, U. Conn., 1995. Registered profl. elec. engr., Bucharest. Elec. engr. Navrom/Constantza, Romania and Athens, 1980-88; freelance artist Athens, 1988-90; store mgr. Freshens Yougurt, Manchester, Conn., 1990-92; freelance designer/artist Conn. Repertory Theatre, Storrs, 1992-95; graphic designer Ford Folios Design, Colchester, Conn., 1995-96; layout artist C.M. Almy & Son, Greenwich, Conn., 1996—. Mem. Stamford Art Assn., Glastoubury Art Guild, Conn. Art Dirs. Club, Silvermine Arts Ctr./Conn. Republican. Avocations: cinema, music, action sports, knife collector. Home: 277 Hartford Ave Wethersfield CT 06109-1256 Office: CM Almy & Son Inc 3 Maerican Ln Greenwich CT 06830

ADRIAN, MANUELLA, research scientist, administrator. BA, McGill U., Montreal, Can., 1968; MS in Hygiene, U. Pitts., 1973. Cons. Orgn. Controle Endemies en Afrique Ctrl., Ctrl. African Republic, Chad and Cameroon, 1973; prof. Coll. Algonquin, Ottawa, Ont., 1973-74; policy analyst Ministry State Sci. and Tech., Ottawa, 1974-75; rsch. economist, sociologist Dept. Health and Welfare Can., Ottawa, 1975-78; sr. scientist, head statistical rsch. program Addiction Rsch. Found., Toronto, 1978-96; sr. rsch. scientist, dir. health behavior rsch., dir. rsch. Kans. Health Inst., Topeka, 1996-98; with dept. health svcs. rsch. U. Kans., Overland Park, 1998—; bd. dirs. Metro Credit, Toronto, 1983-96, Social Planning Coun. Met. Toronto, 1979-81; cons. WHO, Geneva, 1982-95, Pan Am. Health Orgn., 1988; adj. rsch. prof. dept. preventive medicine U. Kans., Wichita, 1996-98, lectr. dept. anthropology U. Kans., Lawrence, 1996—. Author, editor: (textbook) Canadian Women's Use of Tobacco, Alcohol and Other Drugs, 1996; guest editor: Jour. Substance Use and Misuse, spl. issue, 1996; contbr. articles to profl. jours., Can. World Almanac, Ency. of Alcoholism, State of Health Atlas. Mem. com. United Way, Toronto. Grantee Nat. Health and Rsch. Devel. Program, Can. Mem. Am. Pub. Heatlh Assn. (rev. Alcohol, Tobacco and Other Drugs 1991-99). Office: 300 Bayview Dr Ste 1507 Sunny Isles Beach FL 33160-4746

ADRIANCE, BRENDA, broadcast executive. V.p. Stas. KHKS-KBFB, Dallas. Office: Stas KHKS-KBFB 8235 Douglas Ave Ste 300 Dallas TX 75225-6002

ADRIANOPOLI, BARBARA CATHERINE, librarian; b. Fort Dodge, Iowa, Jan. 27, 1943; d. Daniel Joseph and Mary Dolores (Coleman) Hogan; m. Carl David Adrianopoli, June 28, 1968; children: Carlin, Laurie. BS, Mundeline Coll., 1966; MLS, Rosary Coll., 1975. Tchr. Father Bertrand H.S., Memphis, 1966-68; caseworker Dept. Pub. Aid, Chgo., 1968; tchr. North Chgo. Jr. H.S., 1968-70, Austin Mioddle Sch., Chgo., 1970-73; libr. Barrington (Ill.) Pub. Libr., 1976-79, Schaumburg Twp. (Ill.) Dist. Libr., 1979—; Mem. diversity com. N. Suburban/Suburban Libr. Sys., Wheeling, Ill., 1995—. Columnist local newspaper, 1995—; contbr. articles to profl. jours. Mem. com. Schaumburg Twp. Disabled, 1981—; historian Village of Hoffman Estates, 1986-99; adv. com. Hoffman Estates Sister Cities, 1988-96; advisor Boy Scout Am. handicapped badge, Schaumburg Twp., 1981—; mem. adv. bd. Cmty. Nutrition Network, 1994—; organizer, mem. Northwest Corridor-St. Patrick's Day Parade com., 1986—; bd. dirs. Children's Mus. and Imaginasium, 1990-93; trainer A World of Difference Anti-Defamation League, 1994; spkr. on libr. outreach svcs., 1995—; me. Com. For Choices For Success-Seminars For Young Women, 1996—. Grantee Sears Cmty. Project for Literacy, Choices for the 21st Century, 1998; recipient Hoffman Estates Citizen of Yr. award VFW, 1995, Libr. Advocate award North Suburban Libr. Sys., 1998. Mem. ALA, Ill. Libr. Assn.úú. Democrat. Roman Catholic. Home: 1105 Kingsdale Rd Schaumburg IL 60194-2378 Office: Schaumburg Twp Pub Libr 730 S Rosedale Rd Schaumburg IL 60193

ADRION, WILLIAM RICHARDS, academic administrator, computer and information sciences educator, author; b. Nov. 2, 1943; s. Vernon Richards and Mary Leone (Carlock) A.; m. Jacqueline Cotner, July 3, 1971; children; Carrie Buchanan, Emily Richards. BS, Cornell U., 1966, ME, 1967; PhD, U. Tex., 1971. Computer engr. Honeywell EDP, Waltham, Mass., 1969-70; asst. prof. U. Tex., Austin, 1971-72; area chmn., asst. prof. Oreg. State U., Corvallis, 1972-78; program dir. NSF, Washington, 1976-78, 80-85, dep. divsn. dir., 1985-86, chief scientist computer rsch., 1986; group mgr. Nat. Bur. Stds., 1978-80; prof. U. Mass., Amherst, 1986—, chmn. computer scis., 1986-94, dir. Ctr. Realtime Intelligent Complex Computing Sys., 1988—; chmn. bd. dirs., pres. Applied Computing Sys. Inst. of Mass., inc., 1989—, Applied Computing Sys. Inst. of Mass., Inc. Labs., 1990—; cons. Applied Theory Assocs., Corvallis, 1973-78, Tektronix, Portland, Oreg., 1974-76, Lawrence Livermore (Calif.) Labs., 1985-88, Radio Free Europe/Radio Liberty, Munich, 1981-82; prof., lectr. Am. U., Washington, 1978; vis. prof. U. Calif., Berkeley, 1984-85, U. Paris-Sud, 1992—; adj. rsch. prof. Georgetown U., 1985-86; gen. chair internat. conf. on Software Engring, 1994, 97. Contbr. articles to profl. jours. Named Outstanding Young Faculty, Am. Soc. Engring. Edn., 1973; recipient Disting. Svc. award ACM/Spl. Interst Group on Software Engring., 1996. Fellow AAAS, Assn. Computing Machinery (editor-in-chief ACM Trans. on Software Engring. and Methodology 1989-95); mem. IEEE, Soc. Indsl. and Applied Math., N.Y. Acad. Scis., Computer Rsch. Assn. (bd. dirs. 1988-96, chmn. govt. ops. 1990-94), CSNET (exec. com. 1986-89), Sigma Xi, Phi Kappa Phi. Home: 104 Wildflower Dr Amherst MA 01002-3447 Office: U Mass Dept Computer Sci 307 LGRT PO Box 34610 Amherst MA 01003-4610

ADROUNIE, V. HARRY, public health administrator, scientist, educator, environmentalist; b. Battle Creek, Mich., Apr. 29, 1915; s. Haroutune Asadour and Dorthy (Kalaidjian) A.; m. Emalea Riley, June 1943 (div. Jan. 1980); children: Harry Michael, Vee Patrick; m. Agnes M. Slone, June 26, 1981. BS, St. Ambrose U., 1940, BA, 1959; MS in Environ. Health, Western States U. Profl. Studies, 1984, PhD in Environ. Health, 1984, PhD in Pub. Health, 1984. Diplomate Am. Bd. Indsl. Hygiene, Am. Acad. Sanitarians; registered sanitarian, Calif., Mich., Pa. Enlisted U.S. Army, 1941, commd. 2nd. lt., 1943; advanced through grades to lt. col. USAF, ret., 1968; tech. dir. ARA Environ. Svcs., 1968-70; dir. environ. health div. Chester County (Pa.) Health Dept., 1970-75, Berrien County (Mich.) Health Dept., 1975-78; prof. environ. health Sch. Pub. Health U. Hawaii, Manoa, 1978-80; dean, prof. Sch. Pub. Health, Western States U. Profl. Studies, Mo., 1980-83; ret., 1983; vis. prof. environ. and pub. health Am. U., Armenia, 1995; USAF rep. U.S. Interdepartmental Com. on Nutrition for Nat. Def., 1959-61; cons. Health Mobilization Program USPHS Surgeon Gen., 1957-61; mem. USAF Surgeon Gen.'s med. goodwill tour all S.Am. countries, 1960; chmn., vis. assoc. prof. dept. environ. health Am. U. Beirut, 1963-66, chmn. dept. environ. health, 1964-66; charter mem. RSH-UN Welfare Relief Agy. Pub. Health Examining Bd. for Mid. East, 1963-66, UNWRA cons., 1964-66; founder, coord. 1st and 2d Environ. Health Symposium of Mid. East, 1965-66; mem. Mich. Hazardous Waste Policy Com., 1990-91, Mich. Mustfa Fin. Policy Bd., 1994—; adj. instr., mem. adv. com. environ. health Ferris State Coll., Big Rapids, Mich., 1974-75, 77-78. Contbr. numerous articles to profl. jours.; author many manuals and tng. booklets for USAF and several books. Chmn. Barry County Solid Waste Planning and Oversight com., 1981—; mem. Barry County Family Independence Agy., 1996—; vice chmn. Hastings City Planning Commn., 1984—; mem., co-founder sci. adv. and policy bd. Mich. Ground Water Survey, Inc., 1983-90, chmn., 1988-91; chmn. adv. coun. South Ctrl. Mich. Commn. on Aging, 1981-91; charter mem. UL Underwriters adv. coun. environ. and pub. health, 1996—; past adult leader Boy Scouts Am. Decorated Legion of Merit, USAF; named Alumnus of Yr., Hastings H.S., 1961; recipient Walter S. Mangold award Nat. Environ. Health Assn., 1963, spl. recognition Mich. Environ. Health Assn., 1980, Concerned Citizen award World Safety Orgn., 1992, Safety Person of World Safety Orgn., 1992, Safety Person of Yr. award World Safety Orgn., 1991, State of Mich. White Pine award, 1998. Mem. VFW (life), APHA (emeritus v.p., emeritus conf. 1993, pres.-elect 1994-95, pres. 1995-97), Mich. Assn. Local Environ. Health Adminstrs. (pres., founder 1976), Nat. Environ. Health Assn. (life, pres. 1961-62), Assn. Mil. Surgeons U.S. (life), Internat. Pub. Health Soc. (charter-emeritus), Nat. Coun. Internat. Health, NRA (life, cert. rifle marksmanship instr.), World Safety Orgn. (bd. dirs. 1986-95, cert. bd. 1987—, editl. bd. 1988—), Mich. Environ. Health Assn. (pres. 1991-92), Air Force Assn., Am. Legion (comdr. 1989-90), Indonesian Environ. Health Assn. (co-founder 1979), Global Health Assn., Lions, Elks (life), Moose, Kiwanis (pres. 1985-86). Home: 1905 N Broadway Hastings MI 49058-1086

ADSIT, RUSSELL ALLAN, landscape architect; b. Syracuse, N.Y., June 11, 1952. B of Landscape Arch., U. Ga., 1975; M of Agribus. Mgmt., Miss. State U., 1997. Registered landscape arch., Ala., Ark., Ga., Miss., Tenn.; lic. pest control operator. Landscape designer Landscape Svcs., Birmingham, Ala., 1975-76; pres., owner, gen. mgr. Adsit Landscape and Design Firm, Inc., Memphis, 1976-94; owner Natural Design Solutions, Memphis, 1995-98; prin. Fisher & Arnold, Inc., Memphis, 1998—; instr. Toro U., 1990-91, Tenn. Fedn. Garden Clubs, 1990-92, Miss. State U., 1995-98; spkr. Hinds C.C., Jackson, Miss. Active BBB, Intern Program at Cobelskill Program, 1991-92, Co-op Program at Miss. State U., 1980-92, Econs. Amenities Task Force, 1982; mem. finance com. Asbury Meth. Ch., 1991-92. Named Outstanding Small Bus. of Yr., Memphis Bus. Jour., 1981, Outstanding Bus. Vol., Memphis Bot. Garden Found., 1988. Fellow Am. Soc. Landscape Archs. (chmn. membership application rev. com. 1978-80, water mgmt. ednl. seminar 1979, pres. Tenn. chpt. 1980-81, 84-85, chmn. nat. coun. chpt. pres. 1981, judges panel Miss. ann. awards 1981, spkr. nat. conv. Cin. 1985, Tenn. trustee 1987-93, judges facilitator Okla. ann. awards 1987, mem. ann. conf. organizing com. Tenn. chpt. 1989, chpt. membership com. 1989-91, publs. bd. 1991-92, fin. and adminstrn. com. 1991-92, merit award 1979, 80, honor award 1981); mem. Assn. Turf and Ornamental Mgrs. (charter, pres. 1986), Assoc. Landscape Contractors Am. (distinction award 1990, 92, 93, merit award 1991), So. Nurserymen's Assn., Memphis Bot. Garden Found. (bd. dirs. 1984-92, chmn. master plan selection com. 1987, 2d v.p. 1989-90), West Tenn. Nursery and Landscape Assn., Tenn. Nursery Assn., Memphis Hort. Soc., Memphis Assn. Bldg. Owners and Mgrs., Memphis C. of C. (small bus. coun., chmn. small bus. connection 1992). Office: 3205 Players Club Pkwy Memphis TN 38125

ADUBATO, RICHARD ADAM (RICHIE ADUBATO), professional basketball coach; b. East Orange, NJ, Nov. 23, 1937; m. Carol Begerow, July 25, 1989; children: Beth, Scott, Adam. Grad., William Paterson Coll., Wayne, NJ, postgrad. degree. Head coach Our Lady of the Valley High Sch., Orange, NJ; asst. coach Upsala Coll., East Orange, NJ, 1969-72, head coach, 1972-78; asst. coach Detroit Pistons, Detroit, MI, 1978-79, head coach, 1979-80; scout Atlanta Hawks, Atlanta, GA, 1980-82; asst. coach New York Knicks, N.Y.C., NY, 1982-86; asst. coach Dallas Mavericks, Dallas, TX, 1986-89, head coach, 1989-93; asst. coach Cleveland Cavaliers, 1993-96; head coach Orlando Magic, 1996-97, New York Liberty (WNBA), 98-. Named to William Paterson Hall Fame. Office: New York Liberty 2 Penn Plaza New York NY 10121

ADUDDLE, LARRY STEVEN, marketing and sales executive, consultant; b. Miami Beach, Fla., Oct. 21, 1946; s. William Allen and Bernice Elizabeth (Newlon) A.; m. Susan Carol Dominiak, Nov. 27, 1982; 1 child, Melissa Sue. BBA, Lake Forest Coll., 1982; MBA, Lake Forest Sch. Mgmt., 1984. Supr. Rexnord, Inc., Milw., 1974-77, product mgr., 1977-79, sales mgr., 1979-81; mktg. mgr. V/R Wesson, Fansteel, Inc., Waukegan, Ill., 1981-82; v.p. Metropolymer Labs, Inc., Milw., 1983—, bd. dirs.; bd. dirs., treas. Metromark, Inc.; v.p., sec. Metropolymer Labs, Inc.; cons. in field, Milw., 1982-83. Patentee insert for drill stabilizers. vice chmn. United Fund Campaign, Milw., 1975; adv. Jr. Achievement, Milw., 1980. Served to capt. U.S. Army, 1965-69, Vietnam. Decorated Bronze Star. Mem. Reserve Officers Assn. (sec. 1977-78), Assn. Internat. Mktg. Execs. Republican. Lutheran. Avocations: golf, tennis, boating. Home: 825 S Butterfly Ct Nixa MO 65714-7167 Office: Metropolymer Labs Inc PO Box 1467 Nixa MO 65714-1467

AEBI, CHARLES JERRY, minister, educator; b. Webster, Pa., Feb. 15, 1931; s. Jerry and Madeline (Stipes) A.; m. Imogene D. McDonough, Aug. 5, 1955; children: Ruth, Joy, Mark, Mary. BS, Pa. State U., 1952; MA, Abilene Christian U., 1959; PhD, Ohio U., 1972. Part-time minister Ch. of Christ, Vanceville, Pa., 1954-55; minister Ch. of Christ, Coraopolis, Pa., 1956-61, Sistersville, W.Va., 1962-64, Vienna, W.Va., 1971-82, Parkersburg, W.Va., 1964-70, 82—; chmn. Bible Dept. Ohio Valley Coll., Parkersburg, W.Va., 1964-70, v.p., acad. dean, 1970-85; prof. Bible and religion Ohio Valley Coll., Parkersburg, 1985—; cons., evaluator North Cen. Assn. Colls. and Schs. Author: Old Testament Survey, 1964; Herzberg's Job Satisfaction Theory, 1972; Lamp to My Feet, A Thorough Study of the Bible, 1978; New Testament Survey, 1984; editor: The New Birth and Its Implications, 1980; Educating to Service, OVC Self Study, 1977, 2d edit, 1982, New Testament Thought, 1990. Mem. Am. Assn. Higher Edn., W.Va. Coun. Acad. Deans, Phi Delta Kappa, Kiwanis. Home: RR 1 Vincent OH 45784-9801 Office: Ohio Valley Coll College Pky Parkersburg WV 26101

AEHLERT, BARBARA JUNE, health services executive; b. San Antonio, June 17, 1956; d. Bobby Ray and Ronella Su (Light) Mahoney; m. Dean A. Aehlert, Sept. 6, 1980; children: Andrea, Sherri. AA in Nursing, Glendale (Ariz.) C.C., 1976; BS in Profl. Arts, St. Joseph's Coll., Windham, Maine, 1997. Cert. ACLS instr., affiliate faculty, BLS instr., Basic Trauma Life Support instr., emergency med. tng./paramedic instr., ATLS course coord. Gen. mgr. Hosp. Ambulance Svc., Phoenix, 1982-83; critical care nurse Samaritan Health Svcs., Phoenix, 1978-80, coord. patient transp., 1980-82, mgr. clin. programs, 1983-92; dir. emergency med. svcs. edn. EMS Edn. and Rsch., 1992-97; pres. S.W. EMS Edn. Inc., Glendale, Ariz., 1997—. Author: ACLS Quick Review Study Guide, 1994, ACLS Quick Review Slide Set, 1994, ACLS Quick Review Study Cards, 1994, PALS Study Guide, 1994, ECGs Made Easy, 1995, ECGs Made Easy Lesson Plans, 1996, Mosby's Computerized Paramedic Test Generator, 1996, Aehlert's EMT Basic Study Guide, 1997. Republican.

AELION, C. MARJORIE, adult education educator. BS summa cum laude, U. Mass., 1980; MSCE, MIT, 1983; PhD, U. N.C., 1988. Park ranger Nat. Park Svc., Cape Cod Nat. Seashore, South Wellfleet, Mass., 1976-78; biologist, resource assessment divsn. Nat. Marine Fisheries, Woods Hole, Mass., 1978-84; rsch. asst. MIT, Cambridge, Mass., 1981-83, U. Mass.-Amherst, Amherst, Peru, 1983-84; rsch. asst. U. N.C., Chapel Hill, 1986-88, teaching asst., 1987; hydrologist U.S. Geol. Survey, Water Resources Divsn., Columbia, S.C., 1988-91, faculty mem., 1991-97; asst. prof. dept. environ. health scis. U. S.C., Columbia, 1991-97, assoc. prof., 1997—; presenter in field. contbr. articles to profl. jours. Fulbright-Hayes scholar, 1980-81; Bd. Govs.' fellow U. N.C., 1984-86, Dissertation fellow, 1988, NSF fellow in engring., 1993; grantee U.S. EPA, 1991-93, Hazardous Waste Mgmt. Rsch. Fund, 1991-94, Nat. Geographic Soc., 1992, S.C. Dept. Health and Environ. Control and Hazardous Waste Mgmt. Rsch. Fund, 1991-94, U. S.C., 1993-94, NSF, 1993—; recipient Grad. Student Travel award U. N.C., 1988, James A. Keith Excellence in Tchg. award U. S.C., 1998. Mem. Am. Chem. Soc., Am. Soc. Microbiology, Assn. for Women in Sci. (sec. S.C. chpt. 1996-97, pres. S.C. chpt. 1997-98), Soc. Women Engrs., Soc. Environ. Toxicology and Chemistry, Phi Kappa Phi, Delta Omega. Office: U SC Environ Health Scis Dept Columbia SC 29208

AELMORE, DONALD K., systems engineer; b. Greensburg, Kans., Aug. 25, 1952; s. Martin A. and Mary I. (Whalen) A.; m. Dorothy A. Hansen, Aug. 19, 1978; children; Timothy B., Jeffrey A., Matthew D. AA, Hutchinson Community Coll., 1973; BS, Pittsburg State Coll., 1976. Svc. engr. RCA Svc. Co., Chgo., 1976-78; design engr. NCR Corp., Dayton, Ohio, 1978-92; sys. engr. Mueller Industries, Wichita, Kans., 1992-95; dir. info. tech. Interex Computer Products, Wichita, 1995-96; sys. analyst Raytheon Aircraft Co., Wichita, 1996—. Moderator Ctrl. Assn. of Kans. Okla. Conf. of United Ch. of Christ, Wichita, 1991-95. Mem. IEEE (tech. com. of computer comm.), Internat. Alliance Theatrical State Employees and Moving Picture Machine Operators, Lions, Masons. Avocations: gardening, remodeling, handy work, children. Home: 4278 Eagle Lake Ct Wichita KS 67220-1719 Office: Raytheon Aircraft Wichita KS 67209

AERTS, CINDY SUE, nurse; b. Green Bay, Wis., Oct. 18, 1946; d. John and Winon (Kazilek) A. RN, St. Mary's Sch. Nursing, 1967; BSN, U. Wis., 1985; MSN in Critical Care Nursing, Med. Coll. Wis., 1987. CCRN; cert. ACLS instr.; CEN; cert. pediat. advanced life support; cert. emergency nurse pediat. course. Dir. coronary care unit St. Vincent Hosp., Green Bay, Wis., 1970-85; dir. critical care nursing Mary Washington Hosp., Fredericksburg, Va., 1986, L.W. Blake Hosp., Brodenton, Fla., 1988; RN Sarasota Mem. Hosp. Health Care Pers., Sarasota, Fla., Manatee Meml. ECC. Recipient Linda Daniels Award 1985, Vol. of Year Am. Health Assn., Green Bay 1978. Mem. AACN (Northeastern Wis. chpt. pres. 1976, 77, manasota chpt. pres. 1991, 92), Emergency Nurses Assn. Home: 4513 Park Lake Ter S Bradenton FL 34209-6221

AFFELDT, JOHN ELLSWORTH, physician; b. Lansing, Mich., May 26, 1918; s. John Ferdin and Pearl Heald (Gardner) A.; m. Nancy Faye Spomer, Sept. 2, 1942; children—John C., Elizabeth Affeldt Westberg, Cindy L. B.S., Andrews U., Berrian Springs, Mich., 1939; M.D., Loma Linda (Calif.) U., 1944. Intern Detroit Gen. Hosp., 1943-44; resident in internal medicine White Meml. Hosp., Los Angeles, 1946-49; fellow in pulmonary physiology Harvard Sch. Pub. Health, 1949-51; med. dir. Rancho Los Amigos Hosp., Downey, Calif., 1956-64, Los Angeles County Dept. Hosps., 1964-72, Los Angeles County Dept. Health Services, 1972-77; pres. Joint Commn. Accreditation Hosps., Chgo., 1977-86; med. advisor Beverly Enterprises, Fort Smith, Ark., 1986-97. Served with AUS, 1944-47. Mem. AMA, ACP, Am. Congress Rehab. Medicine, Inst. Medicine Western Soc. Clin. Rsch., L.A. County Med. Assn., Calif. Assn. Med. Dirs. (pres. 1993-94). Home: 5140 Bareback Sq PO Box 8432 Rancho Santa Fe CA 92067-8432

AFFENS, STEVEN CHARLES, television photojournalist; b. Bklyn., Dec. 25, 1947; s. Wilbur Allen and Ruth Affens; m. Patricia Susan Schultz, Nov. 30, 1970; 1 child, Scott Matthew Affens. Student, U. Okla., 1990, U. Md., 1965-69, U. Okla., 1990. TV photojournalist WJLA-TV, Washington, 1968—; pres. AFFCOM Corp. Web Site Devel.; speaker in field. TV photojournalist covered Rep. Nat. Conv., 1972, 76, 80, Dem. Nat. Conv., 1976, 84. Recipient White House News Photographers Assn. Camerman of Yr. award, 1985-89, Nat. Acad. of TV Arts and Scis. Emmy awards 1982, 88, 89, 90, 91, 97, 98, Ted Yates award, 1990. Mem. White House News Photographers (exec. bd. 1987-89, Life Achievement award 1999), Nat. Acad. of TV Arts and Sci., (exec. bd. Washington chpt. 1989-90), Nat. Press Photographers Assn., Washington Automotive Press Asn., U.S. Senate and House Press Galleries; faculty U. Okla. TV Workshop, 1991; Nat. Press Photographers Assn. Nat. TV Contest 1991. Avocations: amateur radio (K3SA), travel, computers, seminars, photography. Office: Sta WJLA-TV 3007 Tilden St NW Washington DC 20008-3008

AFFLECK, BEN, actor. Actor; appeared in films School Ties, 1992, Mallrats, 1995, Going All the Way, 1997, Chasing Amy, 1997, Armegeddon, 1998, Reindeer Games, 1999, Forces of Nature, 1999, Dogma, 1999, 200 Cigarettes, 1999, Daddy and Them, 1999, The Boiler Room, 1999; actor, writer: Good Will Hunting, 1997 (Oscar award Best Writing Screenplay Written Directly for Screen, 3d pl. Boston Soc. Film Critics award Best Screenplay, Broadcast Film Critics Assn. award Best Original Screenplay, Fla. Film Critics Cir. award Newcomer of Yr., Golden Globe award Best Screenplay-Motion Picture, Golden Satellite award Best Motion Picture Screenplay-Original, London Critics Cir. award Screenwriter of Yr., others). Office: Creative Artists Agency 9830 Wilshire Blvd Beverly Hills CA 90212*

AFFLECK, JULIE KARLEEN, accountant; b. Upland, Calif., Dec. 23, 1944; d. Karl W. and Juliette O. (Oppegaard) Hall; m. William J. Affleck, Aug. 29, 1964; children: Stephen, Tamara. BS in Bus., U. Colo., 1967; MBA, U. Denver, 1972. CPA, Colo. Cost acct. IBM, Boulder, Colo., 1967-71; audit supr. Ernst & Young, Denver, 1972-79, Rosemary E. Weiss & Co., Denver, 1979-80; ptnr. Affleck, Melaragno, Gilman & Co., Denver, 1980—; tchr. Colo. Soc. CPA's., U. Denver; dir., corp. sec. Better-Way Electric, Inc. Treas., bd. dirs. Bal Swan Children's Ctr. for Handicapped, Broomfield, Colo. Mem. Am. Inst. CPA's., Colo. Soc. CPA's., Am. Soc. Women Accts. (pres. chpt. 1980-81), Nat. Assn. Women Bus. Owners (treas., dir., pres. 1988-89). Republican. Lutheran. Home: 1270 Elmwood Ct Broomfield CO 80020-7609

AFFLECK, MARILYN, sociology educator; b. Logan, Utah, July 1, 1932; d. Clark B. and Velda (Bryson) A.; children: Michelle Alisa, Kimberly Kay, Lacey Dawn. B.A., U. Okla., 1954; M.A., Brigham Young U., 1957; Ph.D., UCLA, 1966. Instr., Central State Coll., Edmond, Okla., 1958-60; asst. prof. Fla. State U., Tallahassee, 1966-68; asst. prof. sociology U. Okla., Norman, 1968-70; asso. prof. U. Okla., 1971-90, interim dean Grad. Coll., 1978-79, asst. dean, 1976-82. Editor Free Inquiry in Creative Sociology Jour., 1984-90. Recipient AMOCO Good Teaching award U. Okla., 1974. Mem. Okla. Sociol. Assn. (pres. 1974-75), South Ctrl. Women's Studies Assn. (treas. 1979-83), Phi Beta Kappa. Democrat. Mormon. Home: 6395 Corky Dr Norman OK 73026-3135

AFFONSO, DYANNE D., dean, nursing educator. BSN, U. Hawaii, 1966; MN in Nursing, U. Wash., 1967; MA in Clin. Psychology, U. Ariz., 1980, PhD in Clin. Psychology, 1982. Asst. prof. sch. nursing U. Miss., 1967-68; OB staff nurse, night charge nurse Kinchloe AFB Hosp., Mich., 1968-70; instr. sch. nursing U. Hawaii, 1970-73; asst. prof. coll. nursing U. Ariz., 1974-77, assoc. prof. coll. nursing, 1978, coord. psychiatric mental health nursing coll. nursing, 1982-84, joint appointment in psychology dept. psychology, 1983; assoc. prof. sch. nursing U. Calif., San Francisco, 1984-87, prof. sch. nursing, 1988; prof., dean sch. nursing Emory U., Atlanta, 1993-98, assoc. prof. women's & children's divsn. sch. pub. health, 1993—; prof. sch. nursing Emory U., Atlanta, 1998—. Contbr. articles to profl. jours.; presenter in field. Mem. NAS (mem. inst. medicine 1994), NIH (mem. adv. coun. nat. inst. child health & human devel. 1979-83, mem. agenda com. nat. inst. child health & human devel. 1982, mem. scientific rev. com. nat. ctr. nursing rsch. 1986, mem. adv. coun. nat. ctr. nursing rsch. 1986-88, mem. steering com. rsch. patient outcomes nat. ctr. nursing rsch. 1991, sec.'s conf. 1993, charter mem. adcv. coun. office rsch. on women's health 1995). Office: Emory U Sch Nursing 531 Asbury Cir Atlanta GA 30322*

AFFRON, MIRELLA JONA, academic administrator. BA magna cum laude, Mt. Holyoke Coll., 1958; PhD, Yale U., 1964. Dir. Classrooms Abroad in Italy, U. Florence, 1962-71; chancellor's faculty fellow office acad. affairs CUNY, 1980-81; chair dept. performing and creative arts Coll. S.I./CUNY, 1977-80, 82-83, 84-87, dean divsn. humanities and social scis., 1987-94, v.p. for acad. affairs, provost, 1994—; asst.-in-instrn. in Italian, Yale U., 1959-61; lectr. French and Italian, New Eng. Conservatory of Music, 1963-65; asst. prof. French and Italian, Stern Coll., Yeshiva U., 1965-69, Richmond Coll., 1969-73; assoc. prof. French and Italian, cinema studies Coll. of S.I./Richmond Coll., 1973-85; prof. cinema studies The Grad. Sch./CUNY, 1994—, Coll. of S.I./CUNY, 1985—. Co-author: (with Charles Affron) Sets in Motion: Art Direction and Film Narrative, 1994; assoc. editor: Cinema Jour., 1984-87, mem. editl. bd., 1981-83; contbr. articles to profl. jours. Fellow AAUP, 1961-62, Bardwell fellow, 1958-59. Mem. AAUW, MLA, CUNY Film Soc., Soc. for Cinema Studies (co-chair ann. conf. 1995, chair tenure and promotions com. 1993-96, mem. promotion and tenure com. 1992-95, mem. exec. com. 1981-83), Phi Beta Kappa. Fax: (718) 982-2442. Office: Coll of S I/CUNY 2800 Victory Blvd Staten Island NY 10314

AFFRONTI, LEWIS FRANCIS, SR., microbiologist, educator; b. Rochester, N.Y., Aug. 12, 1928; s. John and Mary (Least) A.; m. Aileen Ledford, June 2, 1956; children: John, Lewis, Mary Louise, Eileen. BA, U. Buffalo, 1950, MA, 1951; PhD, Duke U., 1958. Rsch. assoc. Buffalo VA Hosp., 1951-52, Roswell Meml. Cancer Inst., 1954, TB Henry Phipps Inst. U. Pa., 1957-58; asst. prof. Sch. Medicine, George Washington U., Washington, 1962-65, assoc. prof., 1965-72, prof. microbiology, 1972-93, prof. emeritus, 1994—, chmn. dept. microbiology, 1973-93; cons. AVCO Rsch. Corp., VA Hosp., Martinsburg, W.Va., VA Hosp. Ctr., Wilmington, Del.; U.S. rep. WHO Conf. on Skin Test Antigens and Vaccines, Geneva, 1966; mem. med. adv. bd. VA, Wilmington. Mem. editl. bd. Infection and Immunity, 1972-78. Bd. dirs. Lynchburg (Va.) unit Am. Cancer Soc., 1996. Commd. officer USPHS, 1958-62; with USAF, 1952-54. NIH Spl. fellow, 1969; Nat. Tb fellow for Internat. Conf. on Tb Moscow, 1971; Nat. Tb fellow for Internat. Conf. on Tb Tokyo, 1973; Washington Acad. Sci. fellow; Recipient WHO Exch. Rsch. Workers award, 1970, Scientist Emeritus award Soc. Expl. Biology and Mecicine, Washington, 1994; interacad. exch. program award NAS, 1980. Fellow Am. Acad. Microbiology, Assn. Med. Sch. Microbiology Chmn. (sec.-treas. 1976-86, bd. dirs. 1976-86), Washington Acad. Sci.; mem. Am. Soc. Microbiology, Am. Assn. Immunologists, Reticuloendothelial Soc., Am. Thoracic Soc., Assembly on Microbiologists and Immunologists (sec. 1971-72), The Protein Soc., Toastmasters Internat. (Atlanta), KC, Sigma Xi (local pres. 1986-87). Office: George Washington U Med Ctr Dept Microbiology 2300 I St NW Washington DC 20037-2336

AFIELD, WALTER EDWARD, psychiatrist, service executive; b. N.Y.C., Dec. 28, 1935; s. Walter Edward and Mollie Evelyn (MCGovern) A.; m. Nancy Browning, Dec. 27, 1973; children: Walter Edward, Neva Browning. AB, U. Pa., 1956; MD, Johns Hopkins U., 1960. Intern Grady Meml. Hosp., Atlanta, 1960-61; fellow in psychiatry Harvard U., Cambridge, Mass., 1961-64, 66-67; asst. prof. psychiatry Johns Hopkins U., Balt., 1967-70, dir. dept. child psychiatry, 1967-70; prof. U. South Fla. Coll. Medicine, 1970-74, chmn. dept. psychiatry, 1970-74; exec. dir. Tampa Bay Neuropsychiat. Inst., Tampa, Fla., 1970—; chmn., chief exec. officer The Mental Health Programs Corp., Tampa, 1985-92. Author: The Children of Resurrection City, 1970; contbr. articles to profl. jours. Pres. Fla. Lyric Opera, 1976—. Capt. USAF, 1964-66. Fellow Am. Coll. Psychiatrists; mem. AMA, Am. Acad. Neurology, University Club, Tampa Yacht Club. Republican. Roman Catholic. Home: 4619 W Bay To Bay Blvd Tampa FL 33629-7610 Office: 5820 W Cypress St Ste B Tampa FL 33607-1785

AFIFI, ABDELMONEM A., biostatistics educator, academic dean; b. El-Menia, Egypt, Aug. 7, 1939; came to U.S., 1960; s. Abdelaziz A. and Nazira (Afifi) A.; m. Beverly L. Coppage, June 30, 1962 (div. 1974); children: Osama A., Mostafa A.; m. Marianne H. Blimlinger, Mar. 4, 1977. BS in Math., Cairo U., 1959; MS in Stats., U. Chgo., 1962; PhD in Stats., U. Calif., Berkeley, 1965. Demonstrator math. dept. Cairo U., 1959-60; prof. biostats. Sch. Pub. Health UCLA, 1965—, dean Sch. Pub. Health, 1987—; vis. asst. prof. U, Wis., Madison, 1965; pres. Western Consortium for Pub. Health, Berkeley, 1987—; stats. cons. numerous orgns., U.S. and abroad, 1965—. Author: Statistical Analysis, 1979, Computer Aided Multivariate Analysis, 3d edit, 1995; contbr. numerous sci. articles to jours. Fulbright scholar, 1960-64, guest scholar Internat. Inst. Systems Analysis, Laxenburg, Austria, 1974-75, 76-77. Fellow Am. Statis. Assn.; mem. Am. Pub. Health Assn. Democrat. Avocations: classical music, photography, travel. Office: UCLA Sch Pub Health PO Box 951772 Los Angeles CA 90095-1772

AFIFI, ADEL KASSIM, physician; b. Akka, Palestine, Oct. 19, 1930; came to U.S., 1984; naturalized, 1988; s. Kassim and Zeinnab (Akki) A.; m. Larryanna Patten, June 17, 1960; children: Rema, Walid. MD, Am. U., Beirut, 1957; MS, U. Iowa, 1965. Intern Am. U. of Beirut, 1956-57, resident in internal medicine, 1959-61; resident in neurology U. Iowa, 1962-64, fellow in neuroanatomy, 1961-62; fellow in neurology N.Y. Neurol. Inst., 1964-65; fellow in electron microscopy Johns Hopkins U., Balt., 1967-68; asst. prof. Am. U., Beirut, 1965-69, assoc. prof., 1969-74, prof., 1974-84, asst. dean Coll. Medicine, 1969-78, chmn. Dept. Human Morphology, 1969-84; prof. U. Iowa, Iowa City, 1984—. Author: Atlas of Microscopic Anatomy, 1974, 89, Basic Neuroscience, 1980, 86, Compendium of Anatomical Variation, 1988, Atlas of Human Anatomy, 1991; contbr. articles to jours. in field. Trustee Diana Tamari Sabbagh Found., Beirut, 1979—, Med. Welfare Fund, Switzerland, 1991—; mem. King Faisal Internat. Prize in Medicine, Riyadh, Saudi Arabia, 1981-85. Fulbright scholar U. Iowa, 1980-81. Mem. Am. Neurol. Assn., Am. Acad. Neurology, Child Neurology Soc., Soc. for Neurosci., Alpha Omega Alpha. Home: 1147 Penkridge Dr Iowa City IA 52246-4933 Office: U Iowa Coll Medicine Dept Anatomy Iowa City IA 52242

AFLAGUE, JOHN M., mental health nurse, educator, administrator; s. N.G. and Helen (Morris) A. Diploma in Nursing, Mt. Auburn Hosp. Sch. Nursing, Cambridge, Mass., 1977; BSN magna cum laude, Northeastern U., Boston, 1980; MS in Psychiat. and Mental Health Nursing, Boston U., 1987; postgrad., 1992—, U. R.I., 1998—. RN, Mass. Staff nurse Mt. Auburn Hosp., Cambridge, 1977-80, Tobey Hosp., Wareham, Mass., 1980-81, Northeastern U., Boston, 1981-95, Mass. Gen. Hosp., Boston, 1984-95; dir., asst. prof., coord. psychiat. mental health nursing Lasell Coll., Newton, Mass., 1995-98; asst. prof. R.I Coll., Providence, 1998—; instr., clin. supr. Medford (Mass.) Pub. Schs., 1979; lectr., clin. instr. Shepard-Gill Sch. Practical Nursing, Mass. Gen. Hosp., 1982-84, Laboure Coll., 1987, 92-94, Quincy (Mass.) Coll., 1991-94, Mass. Bay C.C., Wellesley Hills, 1991-94; clin. instr. acad. advisor Boston U. Sch. Nursing, 1987-88; lectr., lab. instr. Roxbury C.C., Boston, 1991-94; baccalaureate curriculum com. Northeastern U., Boston, 1979-80, psychiat. clin. nurse specialist, 1994-95, coord. psychiat. /mental health svcs., 1994-95; patient tchg. com. Mass. Gen. Hosp., 1984-85; instr. Simmons Coll., Boston, 1992-94; psychosocial cons. Curry Coll., Milton, Mass., 1993-94; cons. and lectr. in field. Vol. local chpt. Am. Cancer Soc., action com. AIDS, Boston. Thorne Found. scholar, 1976. Mem. ANA (cert. clin. specialist adult psychiat./mental health nursing 1988), Nat. League for Nursing, Mass. Nurses Assn., Upper Cape Cod RN's Assn. (scholar 1977), Mt. Auburn Hosp. Nurses Alumnae Assn. (v.p. 1977-78, scholar for clin. and acad. excellence 1977), Nat. League for Nursing, Sigma Theta Tau (pres.-elect 1998—). Home: 148 Lagrange St Boston MA 02132-3023 Office: RI Coll Providence RI 02908

AFRICK, LANCE M., federal judge; b. 1951. BA, U. N.C., 1973, JD, 1975. With Normann & Normann, 1967-77; law clk. to Hon. James Gulotta La. Ct. Appeals (4th cir.), 1975-76; asst. dist. atty. Orleans Parish, 1977-80; assoc. Kierr, Gainsburgh, Benjamin, Fallon & Lewis, 1980-81, McDermott Inc., 1981-82; asst. U.S. atty. U.S. Dist. Ct. (ea. dist.) La., 1983-90; magistrate judge U.S. Dist. Ct. (ea. dist.) La., New Orleans, 1990—; instr. U. New Orleans, 1986—. Fax: (504) 589-3781. Office: US Dist Ct (ea dist) La Rm B-345 500 Camp St New Orleans LA 70130

AFRICK, STEVEN ALLEN, physicist; b. N.Y.C., Mar. 2, 1945; s. David and Ida (Liben) A.; m. Joan Patricia Handley, July 23, 1967; children: Daniel Jason, Michael Lawrence. AB in Physics, Cornell U., 1965; PhD in Physics, Brown U., 1971. Sci., sr. sci. Bolt Beranek & Newman, Inc., Cambridge, Mass., 1972-84; v.p. Atlantic Applied Rsch. Corp., Burlington, Mass., 1984-94, pres., 1994-97; pres. Prodyne Corp., Newton, Mass., 1996—; prin. rsch. scientist Phys. Scis., Inc., Andover, Mass., 1997—. basketball coach Newton (Mass.) Athletic Assn., 1981-86. Mem. Acoustical Soc. of Am. Avocation: music publishing, scuba diving. Office: Phys Scis Inc 20 New England Bus Ctr Andover MA 01810-1022

AFTERMAN, ALLAN B., accountant, educator, researcher, consultant; b. Chgo., Jan. 25, 1944; s. Joseph and Ruth Gertrude (Jacobson) A.; m. Joan Elaine Hoffman, Apr. 30, 1974; children: Debra, Lori, Julie, Robin. BBA, Roosevelt U., 1964; PhD, U. Birmingham, Eng., 1989. CPA, Calif. Asst. dir. securities exchange com. practices Alexander Grant & Co., Chgo., 1967-70; nat. staff mgr. Touche Ross & Co., Chgo., 1970-73; nat. tech. dir. Practice Devel. Inst., Chgo., 1977-82; acctg. prof. U. Ill., Chgo., 1983-88, dir. exec. edn.; mem. faculty grad. sch. bus. U. Chgo., 1992—; cons. to govts. Author: Accounting and Auditing Disclosure Manual, 1982, Compilation and Review, 1983, Accounting and Auditing Update, 1984, SEC Accounting and Reporting Update, 1985, GAAP Practice Manual, 1985 (best loosleaf bus. reference award profl. and scholastic divsn. Assn. Am. Pubs. 1985), Accounting and Tax Highlights, 1986, Handbook of SEC Accounting and Disclosure, 1987, Credit Analyst's Report, 1988, Financial Reporting and Disclosure Manual in the United Kingdom, 1989, Public Accounting Practice Manual, 1990, Governmental Accounting & Auditing Disclosure Manual, 1991, Nonprofit Accounting and Auditing Disclosure Manual, 1992, Auditing Standards and Practices in Poland, 1993, SEC Regulation of Public Companies, 1994, International Financial Accounting, Reporting & Analysis, 1994, U.S. Securities Regulation of Foreign Issuers, 1995, Charities Accounting and Auditing Disclosure Manual in the United Kingdom, 1996, Nonprofit GAAP Practice Manual, 1998. Mem. AICPA, Am. Acctg. Assn., Practicing Law Inst., N.Y. Soc. CPAs. Jewish. Home: 3900 Mission Hills Rd Apt 302 Northbrook IL 60062-5721 Office: 3330 Dundee Rd Ste N6 Northbrook IL 60062-2329

AFTOORA, PATRICIA JOAN, transportation executive; b. Cleve., Jan. 2, 1940; d. Joseph Patrick and Frances Dolores (Fabis) Hunady; m. Albert B. Aftoora, Feb. 17, 1989; 1 child, Christopher Hunady; stepchildren: Melissa, Matthew, Richard. Student, Fenn Coll., Cleve., 1957-59, UCLA, 1959-61, John Carroll U., Cleve., 1961-63. Various positions Chesapeake and Ohio Ry. Co., Balt. and Ohio R.R. Co., Cleve., 1962-73; asst. corp. sec. Chessie System, Inc., Cleve., 1973-79; dept. corp. sec. Chessie System Inc. and Affiliates, Cleve., 1979-80; corp. sec. Chesapeake and Ohio Ry. Co., Balt. and Ohio R.R. Co., Cleve., 1980-87, CSX Transp. Inc., Balt., 1986-87; asst. v.p., asst. corp. sec. CSX Corp., Richmond, Va., 1987-89, v.p., corp. sec., from 1989; now v.p., corp. sec. CSX Transp., Inc., Jacksonville, Fla. Mem. Am. Soc. Corp. Secs. Inc., Nat. Assn. Records Mgrs. and Adminstrs. Home: 1211 Creek View Way Ponte Vedra Beach FL 32082-2509 Office: CSX Transp Inc 500 Water St Jacksonville FL 32202-4423

AFULEZI, UJU N., economic association administrator, professor, librarian, author, consultant; b. Umuohiagu, Nigeria, Dec. 24, 1945; came to U.S., 1970; s. Nkwocha Mgbeke and Igbegu (Oparaku) A.; m. Carol Ahunna, Feb. 12, 1972; children: Chidi, Ugochukwu, Ijeoma, Nzoputa, Udodiri. BS, U. Oreg., 1973, MS, 1974; PhD, U. Mo., Columbia, 1977; MLS, Pratt Inst., Bklyn., 1992. Sr. lectr. Coll. Edn., Owerri, Nigeria, 1978-81; exec. dir. Imo State C. of C., Owerri, Nigeria, 1984-88; exec. dir., CEO Ctr. African Devel., N.Y.C., 1993—; chmn. State Broadcasting Sta., Owerri, 1979-81, chmn. Coll. Agr., 1981-83, mem. planning commn. Imo State U., 1979-82, mem. adv. com. on tech. edn., 1984-88. Author: In the Unbeginning, The Igbo Question, 1997; inventor. Chmn. Igbo Orgn., N.Y.C., 1992, Igbo Elders Coun., N.Y.C., 1996, Ngor-Okpala Union, N.Y./N.J., 1991. Fabian/Zikist scholar. Mem. ALA, World Future Soc., Soc. Strategic and Long-Range Planning, KC. Roman Catholic. Avocations: golf, swimming, lawn tennis. Home: # 5L 98-25 Horace Harding Expwy Corona NY 11368

AGAJANIAN, GILDA, pianist; b. Apr. 3; d. Oganes and Azatuhi (Tosunian) A. BA, U. So. Calif., 1973, Grad. Study, 1974-76; Diploma, Am. Coll. of Musicians, Austin, Tex., 1981, Artist Diploma, 1984. Russian educator Calif., 1976-81; music educator Gilda Agajanian Piano Studio, La Habra Heights, Calif., 1987—; profl. classical pianist Calif., 1985—; entrepreneur, ptnr. Aggie's Restaurants, Calif., 1981-89. *Gilda Agajanian is active as a performer specializing on the works of American Composer, Alan Hovhaness. She is very well known in La Habra Heights, California, for her talent of teaching literally hundreds of children and adults the piano for more than a decade. Her students are frequent winners of district and state sponsored competitions. Ms. Agajanian uses her own teaching method. With this method, she has been very successful in making the average piano student, no matter what age, appear to be a prodigy. The advantage of beginning piano at age 2 1/2, 3 or 4 is emphasized at her studio.* Mem. Westshore Musicians Club (pres. 1992-95), Music Tchrs. Nat. Assn., Calif. Assn. of Profl. Music Tchrs. (chmn. recitals 1992—), Dominant Club (sec. 1994-96), nat. Guild of Piano Tchrs., AAUW, Woman's Club of Hollywood. Avocations: Slavic langs. and lits., exotic birds, dogs, cats, horticulture. Office: Gilda Agajanian Piano Studio 2039 N Cypress St La Habra Heights CA 90631

AGAR, JOHN RUSSELL, JR., school district administrator; b. Camden, N.J., July 25, 1949; s. John R. and Evva L. (Wilhelm) A.; m. Beatrice A. B.; children: Rebekah A., Sarah L. BA with high honors, Rutgers U., 1971; MS, U. Pa., 1973, MS in Edn., 1975; EdD with distinction, Temple U., 1983; postgrad., U. Pa., 1989. Cert. secondary educator, supr., prin., dist. supt., Pa., NJ. Lectr. in chemistry U. Pa., Phila., 1974-75; sci. dept. head West Cath. Girls' High Sch., Phila., 1974-79; chemistry tchr. Moorestown (N.J.) Friends' Sch., 1979-82, West Deptford High Sch., Westville, N.J., 1982-84; visiting asst. prof. Temple U., Phila., 1983-88; lectr. in edn. U. Pa., Phila., 1988-90; sci. supr. Marple Newtown Sch. Dist., Newtown Sq., Pa., 1984—; mem. SEPUP staff U. Calif., Berkeley, 1991-96; mem. tchrs. industry environment com. Pa. Chem. Industry Coun., 1992-95; mem. writing team for "Teaching Issue-Oriented Science", 1991; dir. Pa. Devel. Ctr. for "Issues, Evidence and You", 1995. NIH fellow U. Pa., 1973-74, CEPUP/CHEM/NSF fellow U. Calif., Berkeley, 1990-91; recipient Nat. Tchr. award CEPUP, U. Calif., Berkeley, 1992. Mem. Nat. Sci. Tchrs. Assn., Phi Lambda Upsilon, Phi Delta Kappa. Avocations: travel, backpacking, scuba diving, weightlifting, studying the Bible.

AGARD, NANCEY PATRICIA, nursing administrator; b. Amsterdam, N.Y., Mar. 3, 1955; d. Richard Edward and Jean Elizabeth (Sweet) A.; m. Robert Frank Whittaker, Nov. 16, 1991. Diploma, St. Mary's Hosp. Sch. Nursing, 1976; BS, SUNY, 1981; MS, Syracuse U., 1986. RN N.Y. Staff nurse St. Mary's Hosp., Amsterdam, N.Y., 1976-77; nurse teaching & rsch. SUNY Health Sci. Ctr., Syracuse, N.Y., 1977-80; staff nurse St. Luke's Hosp., Utica, N.Y., 1980-81; clin. edn. specialist SUNY Health Sci. Ctr., 1981-84, lectr., 1984-90, nurse tchg. and rsch. ctr., 1984-90, cons., 1986; assoc. dir. nursing practice N.Y. State Nurses Assn., Latham, N.Y., 1990—; ANA del., 1992—; mem. ANA Inst. on Nursing Practice, 1998—; mem. turning point initiative com. N.Y. State Dept. Health, 1997-98; mem. immunization action plan com. N.Y. State Dept. Health, Albany, 1993—, mem. immunization info. sys. com., 1994—, mem. adult immunization coalition, 1997—, mem. medicaid managed care adv. com., 1993-96; mem. health family com. N.Y. State Fedn. to Prevent Child Abuse, 1993-96; mem. workplace violence com. Healthcare Assn. of N.Y. State, 1998—, mem. latex allergy workgroup, 1998; mem. regional activities com. N.Y. Emergency Med. Svcs. Vol. Karen Burstein and Mary Eileen Callan Campaigns, Albany, 1994-96. Rural immunization grantee Merck Vaccine Div., 1992-93. Mem. ANA, AACN, N.Y. State Nurses Assn., Emergency Nurses Assn. (liaison 1996—), Nat. Assn. Clin. Nurse Specialists, N.E. Safety Coun., Rural Nurse Orgn., Sigma Theta Tau (media award 1993). Democrat. Avocations: piano, pets, plants. Office: NY State Nurses Assn 11 Cornell Rd Latham NY 12110-1402

AGARWAL, GYAN CHAND, engineering educator; b. Bhagwanpur, India, Apr. 22, 1940; came to U.S., 1960; s. Hari Chand and Ramrati (Jindal) A.; m. Sadhna Garg, July 7, 1965; children: Monika, Mudita. BS, Agra U., India, 1957; BE with honors, U. Roorkee, India, 1960; MSEE, Purdue U., Ind., 1962, PhD, 1965. Lic. profl. engr. Ill., Wis. Asst. prof. engring. U. Ill., Chgo., 1965-69, assoc. prof. engring., 1969-73, prof. engring., 1973—, dir. grad. studies, 1975-79, 82-85, 91—; vis. prof. Rush Med. Coll., Chgo., 1976—; vis. prof. Indian Inst. Sci., Bangalore, 1971, Indian Inst. Tech., Kanpur, 1972; cons. FDA, Washington, 1979—; mem. study sect. NIH, 1990-94. Co-editor: Biomaterials, 1969; cons. editor Jour. Motor Behavior, 1981-93; assoc. editor IEEE Transactions on Biomed. Engring., 1988-96, Jour. Electromyography and Kinesiology, 1994—; contbr. articles to profl. jours. U. Roorkee merit scholar, 1958-60; NSF, NIH, NASA, VA, Wright-Patterson AFB rsch. grantee. Fellow AAAS, IEEE, Am. Inst. for Med. and Biol. Engring. (founding); mem. Soc. Neurosci., Sigma Xi, Phi Kappa Phi, Eta Kappa Nu. Home: 947 Lathrop Ave River Forest IL 60305-1448 Office: U Ill Coll Engring Dept Elec Engring 851 S Morgan St Rm 1120 SEO Chicago IL 60607-7042

AGARWAL, SUMAN KUMAR, editor; b. Bolpur, India, Jan. 21, 1945; came to U.S., 1980; s. Hari Prasad and Rukmini (Modi) A.; m. Tracy L. Krainock, Mar. 21, 1998; children: Tripti, Samantha Rani. BSc with honors, Visva-Bharati, Santiniketan, India, 1966; MSc, Delhi U., India, 1971; PhD, U. Paris, 1975, DSc, 1979. Rsch. scholar Atomic Energy Commn. of France, Saclay, 1976-80; rsch. assoc. Purdue U., West Lafayette, Ind., 1980-82; sr. sci. info. analyst Chem. Abstracts Svc., Columbus, Ohio, 1982—; pres. Commodities Internat. Ltd. Inc., Columbus, Ohio, 1992—. Contbr. articles to profl. jours. Vol. Columbus Schs., 1984, 85, Ohio State U. TV, Columbus, 1986, 87, 88. Scholar Govt. of France, 1973-76. Mem. Am. Chem. Soc. Avocations: bridge, photography, tennis.

AGASAR, RONALD JOSEPH, mortgage banker; b. Phila., Nov. 27, 1946; s. Francis Robert and Penny Dolores (Alahverde) A.; m. Eleanor Joan Smith, Aug. 30, 1969 (div. Jan. 1982); m. Elizabeth Katherine Muhr, Apr. 20, 1989. BS, La Salle Coll., Phila., 1970; MBA in Mortgage Banking, Northwestern U., 1978. Regional v.p. Colonial Mortgage Svc. Co., Elkins Park, Pa., 1976-80, City Fed. Mortgage Corp., Cherry Hill, N.J., 1980-83; sr. v.p. Chase Manhattan Mortgage Corp., Cherry Hill, 1983-96; N.E. regional v.p. CTX Mortgage Co., Cherry Hill, 1996—. Mem. Mortgage Bankers Assn. N.J. (bd. govs. 1996—), Pa. Mortgage Bankers Assn., Phila. Young Mortgage Bankers Assn. (chmn. 1983-84, vice-chmn. wholesale lending com. 1992). Republican. Roman Catholic. Avocations: antique cars, coin collecting, racquetball, power boating. Office: CTX Mortgage Co 51 Haddonfield Rd Ste 338 Cherry Hill NJ 08002-4801

AGASSI, ANDRE KIRK, tennis player; b. Las Vegas, Nev., Apr. 29, 1970; s. Mike and Elizabeth Agassi; m. Brooke Shields, April 19, 1997 (div. 1999). Mem. U.S. Davis Cup team, 1988—. Owner found. for children. Winner tournaments including Itaparica, 1987, Memphis, 1988, Charleston, 1988, Forest Hills, 1988, Stuttgart, 1988, Stratton Mountain, 1988, Livingston, 1988, Orlando, 1989, San Francisco, 1990, Key Biscayne, 1990, Washington, 1990, ATP Tour World Championship-Frankfurt, 1990, Orlando, 1991, Washington, 1991; Wimbledon champion, 1992, U.S. Open champion, 1994, Australian Open champion, 1995; gold medal U.S. Olympics, 1996; winner French Open/Grand Slam, 1999. Address: International Mgmt Group One Erieview Plaza Ste 1300 Cleveland OH 44114*

AGATA, BURTON C., lawyer, educator; b. N.Y.C., Feb. 7, 1928; s. Max and Augusta (Steger) A.; m. Dale S. Granirer, Dec. 24, 1955; children: Seth Hugh, Abby Fran. AB, U. Mich., 1947, JD, 1950; LLM in Trade Regulation, NYU, 1951. Bar: N.Y. 1951. Counsel div. N.Y. State Banking Dept., 1955-59; ptnr. firm Burstein & Agata, Mineola and N.Y.C., 1959-61; prof. Mont. U., 1961-62, N.Mex. U., 1962-63, Houston U., 1963-69; counsel Nat. Commn. on Reform Fed. Criminal Laws, 1968-70; prof. law Hofstra U., 1970—, Max Schmertz disting. prof. law, 1982—, interim dean, 1989; mem. faculty Nat. Inst. Trial Advocacy, 1977-81; dir. N.E. Regional Program, 1981-84; spl. counsel N.Y. City Charter Revision Commn., 1987-89, N.Y. State Senate Minority, 1982-87; cons. Fed. Jud. Center, 1972, Inst. Jud. Adminstrn., 1973, HEW, 1971, White House Spl. Action Office Drug Abuse Prevention, 1973, N.Y. State Temp. Com. on Constitl. Revision, 1993-95; Chmn. N.Y. State Task Force, Standards and Go als for Prosecution and Def., 1977-79; cons. Adv. Com. on Qualifications of Counsel, 2d Ct., 1977; bd. dirs. Nassau Economic Opportunity Commn., 1972-73; reporter-cons. action unit on criminal justice system N.Y. State Bar Assn., 1986-90. Contbr. articles to law jours. With JAGC U.S. Army, 1951-54. Food Law fellow NYU, 1951, fellow U. Wis., 1963. Fellow Am. Bar Found. (life); mem. Am. Law Inst., ABA (state antitrust law commn. 1980—, vice chair com. on professionalism sr. lawyers divsn. 1996—), N.Y. State Bar Assn. (exec. com. criminal justice sect., chmn. com. rev. of criminal law 1987—, spl. com. on pre-sentence reports 1989—, Donnelly Act com. 1990—), Assn. of Bar of City of N.Y. (criminal cts. com. 1970-73, penology com. 1973-76, criminal justice council 1983-85, antitrust com. 1986-89), Fed. Jud. Council, Assn. Am. Law Schs. (chmn. criminal law sect. 1973). Home: PO Box 727 Hudson NY 12534-0727 Office: Hofstra U School Law Hempstead NY 11549

AGBETSIAFA, DOUGLAS KOFI, financial and management consultant; b. Anloga, Volta, Ghana; came to the U.S., 1976; s. Benjamin K. Agbetsiafa and Rebecca Afafa Agbakpe; m. Patricia Ann Williams. BS, U. Ghana, 1971, MS, 1975; MA, Western Ontario, 1976; PhD, U. Notre Dame, 1980. Secondary sch. tchr. Mininstry Edn., Accra, Ghana, 1966-68; instr. Univ. Western Ontario, London, 1973-75, Univ. Notre Dame, 1976-80; prof. econs., acad. senate pres., spl. asst. to chancellor Ind. Univ., South Bend. Contbr. articles and revs. to profl. jours. Sec., treas. United Way St. Joe County, bd. dirs., 1987—; trustee Urban League, South Bend, 1988; bd. dirs., trustee Urban League of South Bend and St. Joseph's County, 1996—. Mem. Am. Econ. Assn. Am. Statis Assn., Internat. Bus. Assn., Western Econ. Internat., Midwest Econ. Assn., Midsouth Acad. Econs. and Fin. (bd. dirs.), Ind. Acad. Soc. Sci., Bus. Assn. Latin Am. Studies, Assn. for Global Bus. (program dir. 1993-94, v.p. program dir. 1995—), South Bend-Mishawaka C. of C. (bd. dirs., mem. minority bus. devel. task force), U. Notre Dame Alumni Assn. Avocations: raquetball, reading poetry, gardening, traveling. Home: 224 N Sunnyside Ave South Bend IN 46617-3332 Office: Ind U 1700 Mishawaka Ave South Bend IN 46615-1400

AGEE, BOB R., university president, educator, minister; b. Brownsville, Tenn., Sept. 30, 1938; s. Edwin L. and Katie L. (Stewart) A.; m. Nelle Rose; children—Nancy Denise, Robyn Janelle. B.A., Union U., Tenn., 1960; M.Div., So. Bapt. Theol. Sem., 1964, D.Min., 1974; Ph.D., Vanderbilt U., 1986. Ordained to ministry Baptist Ch. Pastor Shively Heights Bapt. Ch., Louisville, 1964-70; pastor Ardmore Bapt. Ch., Memphis, 1970-75; dean, v.p. religious affairs Union U., Jackson, Tenn., 1975-82; pres. Okla. Bapt. U., Shawnee, 1982-98, pres. emeritus, 1998—; mem. edn. commn. So. Bapt. Conv., 1985-93, chmn., 1987-90; bd. dirs. Co-op Svcs. Internat. Edn. Consortium, chmn., 1988-90; cons. evaluator North Ctrl. Assn. Colls. and Univs., 1987—; bd. dirs. Nat. Assn. Ind. Colls. and Univs., 1986-90, 93—. Author Bibl. study materials and articles. Mem. human relations com. Memphis Bd. Edn., 1972-74; mem. Memphis Mayor's Crime Commn., 1973-75; mem. Okla. Ind. Coll. Found., 1982-98, chmn., 1985-87. Mem. Soc. Coll. and Univ. Planning, Shawnee C. of C. (bd. dirs. 1983-98), So. Bapt. Theol. Sem. Alumni Assn. (nat. pres. 1985-86), AAUP, Am. Assn. Univ. Adminstrs., Nat. Assn. Ind. Colls. and Univs. (bd. dirs. 1988-97), Coalition of Christian Colls. and Univs. (bd. dirs. 1997-98), Assn. So. Bapt. Colls. and Schs. (exec. dir. 1998—, exec. dir. consortium global edn.). Republican. Avocations: racquetball; golf; fishing; writing. Office: PO Box 11655 Jackson TN 38308-0127

AGEE, CLAUDIA, clerk, receptionist, tax consultant; b. Selma, Ala., Nov. 11, 1939; d. Claude and M. Marie (McConico) Thomas; m. Cleveland Agee Jr. (dec.); children: Debbie K., Danita McCary, Cleveland III (dec.), La Shondria, Ed'Keia, Mondena, Tocara, Lil Freddie, Mondeno Agee. Student, Booker T. Washington, 1973, Birmingham Bapt. Bible Coll., 1989, Bessemer Tech., 1992; AA in Office Adminstrn., Bessemer State Tech. Coll., 1997. Bookkeeper Thomas Deli, Birmingham, AmSouth Corp. Revolving Credit Rsch., Birmingham; garment mgr. NLS, Birmingham; svc. clk., bookkeeper Minority Literacy Expo; office mgr., personal sec. Ross Gardner, ENT Specialist. Mem. The Bidders Orgn. (sec.), Order Ea. Star (sec. Lodge 385), Zeta Phi Lambda, Beta Psi. Home: 1346 45th St W Birmingham AL 35208-1919

AGEE, KEVIN JEROME, minister; b. Washington, Dec. 20, 1960; s. Charles Henry Jr. and Emma Abbie (Light) A.; m. Gwendolyn Jean McAllister, June 28, 1997. BA, U. Md., 1982; MDiv, Wesley Theol. Sem., 1990; postgrad., Hartford Sem., 1991—. Lic. to ministry Christian Meth. Episcopal Ch., 1987; deacon, 1988; elder, 1989. Asst. pastor Israel Met. Christian Meth. Episcopal Ch., Washington, 1987-89; fellow Nat. Fellowship Program for Black Pastors Congress Nat. Black Chs., Washington, 1988-89; pastor St. Paul and Williams Temple Christian Meth. Episcopal Chs., Halifax, Va., 1989-90; dir. youth ctr. Good Shepherd Ministries, Washington, 1989-90; pastor Christ Christian Meth. Episcopal Ch., Waterbury, Conn., 1990-94; sub. tchr. City of Waterbury Dept. Edn., 1990-91; vocat. instr. Rehab. Ctr. of Greater Waterbury (Easter Seals), 1993-94; pastor Russell Temple Christian Meth. Episcopal Ch., Bridgeport, Conn., 1994—; mem. interch. rels. task force Christian Conf. Conn., Hartford, 1990-91; co-chair Commn. on Social Concerns, 1992—; bd. dirs. Christian Conf. of Conn., 1992—, mem. exec. com., 1992—; mem. pub. rels. com. Waterbury Area Coun. Chs., 1991-94; mem. Interdenominational Ministerial Alliance of Greater Bridgeport, 1994—, chair social and polit. action com., 1996-98, vp., 1999—; commr. Bridgeport Redevel. Agy./Housing site Devel. Agy., City of

Bridgeport, 1996—. Bd. dirs. Green Cmty. Svcs., 1991-94; mem. ch. missions com. Coun. Chs. of Greater Bridgeport, 1995—, bd. dirs., 1996—, pres., 1998—; bd. dirs., chair pub. rels. com. Interfaith Hunger Svcs., 1995—; mem. 100 Black Men of Bridgeport, 1996—; mem. adv. bd. Pride Inc., Waterbury, 1991; mem. bd. mgrs. Ralphola Taylor Ctr. YMCA, Bridgeport, 1994—; commr. Bridgeport Redevel. Agy./Housing Site Devel. Agy., City of Bridgeport, 1996—; mem. pastoral care adv. com. Bridgeport Hosp., 1997—. Delaplain scholar Wesley Theol. Sem., 1990. Mem. NAACP, Interfaith Clergy Assn., Toastmasters Internat. (Competent Toastmaster award 1986, pres. 1985-87). Democrat. Home: 228 Ridgefield Ave Bridgeport CT 06610-2815 Office: Russell Temple Christian Meth Episcopal Ch 555 Connecticut Ave Bridgeport CT 06607-1021 *One who truly loves the Lord loves his/her neighbor as well. If we all loved our neighbors, racism, sexism, classism, war, violence, poverty, homelessness and other societal ills would be non existent.*

AGEE, LYNNE, university head basketball coach. BS in Health and Phys. Edn., Longwood Coll., 1971; MS in Ednl. Adminstrn., Radford U., 1981. Coach William Fleming H.S., 1971-78, Roanoke Coll., 1978-81; head coach U. N.C., Greensboro, 1981—; women's basketball rules com. NCAA, divsn. I east region selection com. NCAA Tournament; assoc. dir. internal affairs, sr. women's adminstr. Office: U NC Greensboro Athletics PO Box 26168 Greensboro NC 27412-6168*

AGEE, WARREN KENDALL, journalism educator; b. Sherman, Tex., Oct. 23, 1916; s. Frederic M. and Minnie E. (Logsdon) A.; m. Edda Robbins, June 1, 1941; children: Kim Kendall Schmidman, Robyn Kendall Ansley. BA cum laude, Tex. Christian U., 1937; MA, U. Minn., 1949, PhD, 1955. Mem. editorial staff Ft. Worth Star-Telegram, 1937-48; instr. journalism Tex. Christian U., 1948-50, asst. prof., 1950-55, asso. prof., 1955-57, prof., 1957-58, chmn. dept., 1950-58, faculty adviser student publs., 1949-58; prof. journalism, dean sch. journalism W.Va U., 1958-60; mem. ednl. adv. com. WJPB-TV, Fairmont and Weston, W.Va., 1959-60; nat. exec. officer Soc. Profl. Journalists, Sigma Delta Chi, 1960-62; prof. journalism, dean Evening Coll., Tex. Christian U., Ft. Worth, 1962-65; dean William Allen White Sch. Journalism, U. Kans., Lawrence, 1965-69; dean Henry W. Grady Coll. Journalism and Mass Communication U. Ga., 1969-75, prof. journalism, 1975-87, dean and prof. emeritus, 1987—; vis. scholar U. Tex., fall 1975; copy editor Atlanta Constn., summer 1977; combat corr. USCG Res., 1941-44; pub. info. specialist USCG Res. Hdqrs., 1944-45; mem. adv. screening com. journalism, com. internat. exchange of persons Conf. Bd. Assn. Rsch. Couns., Washington, 1958-62; mem. Am. Coun. Edn. for Journalism and Mass Communication, 1958-60, 65-67, mem. accrediting com., 1969-76, vice chmn., 1973-74, chmn., 1974-76, chmn. appeals bd., 1977, 79, 81, 83; mng. dir. William Allen White Found., 1965-69, trustee, 1970—; mng. dir. George Foster Peabody Radio and TV awards, 1969-75, Sigma Delta Chi Nat. Journalism Awards, 1960-62; assoc. James M. Cox Jr. Ctr. Internat. Mass Comm. Tng. and Research, U. Ga., 1985—. Author: (with Edwin Emery and Phillip H. Ault) Introduction to Mass Communications, 1960, 12th rev. edit., 1997, Reporting and Writing the News, 1983, (with Dennis L. Wilcox, Ault) Public Relations: Strategies and Tactics, 1986, rev. edit., 1989, 3d edit., 1992, 4th edit., 1995, 5th edit., 1997(with Nelson Traquina) O Quarto Poder Frustrado: Os Meios de Comunicacão Social No Portugal Pós-Revolucionário, 1988; also articles.; editor: The Press and the Public Interest, 1968, Mass Media In A Free Society, 1969, (with Emery and Ault) Perspectives on Mass Communications, 1982, Maincurrents in Mass Communications, 1986, rev. edit., 1989; assoc. editor, bus. mgr.: The Quill, 1960-62; press rev. columnist, contbg. editor, 1977-82; adv. editorial bd.: Journalism Quar, 1955-60. Mem. Athens (Ga.) Internat. Rels. Cmty. Coun., pres., 1980-82; pres. Friends of Mus. Art U. Ga., 1974-75; mem. Howard Blakeslee Media Awards judging com. Am. Heart Assn., 1976-94, chmn. judging com., 1980-94. Recipient Journalism award Fort Worth Press, 1936; Outstanding News Writing award Ft. Worth Profl. chpt. Sigma Delta Chi, 1946; Carl Towley award Journalism Edn. Assn., 1969; Outstanding Achievement award U. Minn., 1973; Wells Meml. key Sigma Delta Chi, 1978, Disting. Teaching award Soc. Profl. Journalists, 1987; Fulbright grantee to Portugal, 1982, 85. Mem. Assn. Edn. in Journalism and Mass Communication (pres. 1958), Am. Soc. Journalism Sch. Adminstrs. (pres. 1956), Am. Studies Assn., Southwestern Journalism Congress (sec. 1957-58), Soc. Profl. Journalists, Sigma Delta Chi (pres. Fort Worth profl. chpt. 1954-55, sec. Tex. 1957-58, nat. v.p. campus chpt. affairs 1966-69, leader council 1982—, v.p. N.E. Ga. profl. chpt. 1978-79, pres. 1979-80), Kappa Tau Alpha (50 yr. journalism edn. service award 1987), Alpha Chi, Phi Kappa Sigma, Alpha Sigma Lambda, Phi Beta Delta. Presbyterian. Club: Gridiron (Ft. Worth). Lodge: Rotary. Home: 130 Highland Dr Athens GA 30606-3212 Office: U Ga Henry W Grady Coll Journalism and Mass Communication Athens GA 30602 *One abiding goal has been to spread and deepen public understanding of the fundamentals of our democratic society as embodied in the Bill of Rights in general and the First Amendment in particular. That public understanding has been seriously eroded in recent decades. Only through a renewed, vastly broadened national effort to teach these principles in our schools and other social institutions, and through the media of mass communication, will this erosion be halted and our nation, as we have known it, survive.*

AGEMA, GERALD WALTON, broadcasting company executive; b. Rockford, Ill., Sept. 9, 1947; s. Samuel W. and Lillian (Walton) A.; m. Marcia L. Vander Meer, June 14, 1969; children: Jerry, Matt and Mike (twins). BS in Acctg., No. Ill. U., 1970; MBA, U. Chgo., 1984. CPA, Ill. Staff/sr. auditor Price Waterhouse, Chgo., 1971-76, audit mgr., 1976-79; audit mgr. Tribune Co., Chgo., 1979-80, asst. controller, 1980-85; dir., chief fin. officer Tribune Broadcasting Co., Chgo., 1985-86, v.p., chief fin. officer, 1986-88, v.p. ops., chief fin. officer, 1988-97, v.p. adminstrn., chief fin. officer, 1997—. Bd. dirs. Mus. of Broadcast Comms., Chgo., 1986—, treas., 1986-97. Mem. AICPA, Ill. Soc. CPAs, Broadcast Cable Fin. Mgmt. Assn. (bd. dirs. 1987-89, 91-95). Avocations: reading, boating, fishing, travel. Office: Tribune Broadcasting Co 435 N Michigan Ave Ste 1800 Chicago IL 60611-4066

AGERSBORG, HELMER PARELI K., pharmaceutical company executive, researcher; b. Decatur, Ill., Dec. 2, 1928; s. Helmer Pareli and Jennie E. (Dunbar) A.; m. Marcella Felchlia; children—Eric, Kristin, Karen. B.A., Harvard U., Cambridge, 1949; B.S., So. Ill. U., Carbondale, 1953; Ph.D., U. Tenn., Memphis, 1957. Asst. physiology U. Tenn., Memphis, 1954-57, instr. physiology, 1957-58; clin. physiologist Wyeth Labs., Phila., 1958-61, mgr. toxicology, 1961-69, assoc. dir. research, 1969-76, v.p. research and devel., 1976-85, sr. v.p. research and devel., 1985-87; pres. Wyeth Ayerst Research, 1987-91; CEO, pres. Fieldcastle, Inc., Wayne, Pa., 1991—, Afferon Corp., 1991—, Maret Corp., 1994—. Mem. Am. Soc. Pharmacology and Exptl. Therapy, Am. Physiol. Soc., Am. Soc. Zoology, Soc. Toxicology. Home: 336 St Andrews Pl Blue Bell PA 19422 Office: Fieldcastle Inc 200 Eagle Rd Wayne PA 19087-3115

AGERWALA, TILAK KRISHNA MAHESH, computer company executive; b. New Delhi, India, Mar. 8, 1950; came to U.S. 1971; s. Krishna Mahesh and Manorama (Vaish) A.; m. Geeta Heble, Jan. 6, 1974; children: Arjun Mahesh, Suneel Mahesh. B.Tech., Indian Inst. of Tech., Kanpur, India, 1971; PhD, The Johns Hopkins U., Balt., 1975. Asst. prof. U. Tex., Austin, 1975-79; rsch. staff mem. IBM Watson Rsch. Ctr., Yorktown Heights, N.Y., 1979-80, various mgmt. positions, 1980-85, dir. symbolic and numeric processing, 1985-87; mem. corp. tech. com. IBM Corp. Hdqrs., Armonk, N.Y., 1987-89; dir. future systems tech., advanced workstation div. IBM Corp., Austin, Tex., 1989-91, dir. tech., personal systems, 1991-92; dir. parallel architechture and systems design, power parallel systems IBM Corp., Poughkeepsie, N.Y., 1992-97, dir. server arch. and sys. strategy, server devel., 1997—; mem. adv. com. Ctr. for Supercomputer Applications, U. Ill., Urbana-Champaign, 1985-88; mem. vis. com. dept. elec. engring. U. Tex., Austin, 1987-89, dept. of computer scis., 1989-93; mem. sci. coun. U. Space Rsch. Assn., Washington, 1988-90. Contbr. numerous articles to profl.jours., chpts. to books, IBM rsch. reports. Recipient best presentation award Internat. Conf. on Parallel Processing, 1978. Fellow IEEE (chmn. fellows com. 1988-89, disting. visitor, chmn. tech. com. on computer architecture, cert. appreciation 1976, 82, W. Wallace McDowell award 1998); mem. Assn. for Computing Machinery (Samuel Alexander award 1974). Office: IBM 522 South Rd Poughkeepsie NY 12601-5400*

AGESA, RICHARD UGUNZI, economics educator; b. Aug. 18, 1961. PhD, U. Wis., Milw., 1996. Asst. prof. of econ. North Carolina A&T State U., Greensboro. E-mail: agesa@ncat.edu. Office: 2506 Glen Meadow Dr Greensboro NC 27455-2483

AGGARWAL, SURESH KUMAR, mechanical and aerospace engineering educator; b. India, Aug. 22, 1949; came to U.S., 1973; m. Veena Gupta, Dec. 12, 1980; children: Sonal, Monika. PhD, Ga. Inst. Tech., 1979. Rsch. fellow Princeton (N.J.) U., 1978-79; rsch. engr. Carnegie-Mellon U., Pitts., 1979-82, sr. rsch. engr., 1983-84; asst. prof. mech. engring. U. Ill., Chgo., 1984-88, assoc. prof. mech. engring., 1989-94; prof. mech. engring., 1995—; cons. NASA, Cleve., 1988. Assoc. editor AIAA; contbr. articles to profl. jours. Named one of the Outstanding Young Men of Am.; U. Ill. scholar; Am. Soc. Engring. Edn./USN sr. faculty fellow, 1994. Fellow AIAA (assoc., assoc. editor AIAA Jour.); mem. Gas Turbine Inst. Home: 6428 Waterford Ct Hinsdale IL 60521-5438 Office: U Ill Dept Mech Engring Chicago IL 60607

AGGER, JAMES H., lawyer; b. 1936; married. A.B., St. Joseph's U., 1958; J.D., U. Pa., 1961. Mem. Krusen, Evans & Byrne, 1965-69; gen. counsel Catalytic Inc., Air Products and Chems. Inc., 1969-77; asst. gen. counsel Air Products and Chems. Inc., Trexlertown, Pa., 1977-80, gen. counsel, 1980—, v.p., 1982-97, corp. sec., 1990, sr. v.p., 1997-99, ret., 1999. Office: Air Products & Chems Inc 7201 Hamilton Blvd Allentown PA 18195-1526

AGGERGAARD, STEVEN PAUL, journalist, musician; b. LeSueur, Minn., May 1, 1967; m. Lana Rosario, Aug. 8, 1998;. BA, Augsburg Coll., Mpls., 1989; MSJ, Northwestern U., 1992. Newspaper reporter Ft. Dodge (Iowa) Messenger, 1989-90, weekend news editor, 1990-91; newspaper reporter-intern Chgo. Tribune, 1992; newspaper designer, copy editor Duluth (Minn.) News-Tribune, 1992-96, newspaper city editor, 1996-98; news editor St. Paul Pioneer Press, 1998—; freelance editor/writer, 1989—; sect. leader Arrowhead Chorale, Duluth, 1997-98, tenor vocalist, 1993—; guest journalism lectr. various high schs. and colls., 1994—; classical music reviewer Duluth News-Tribune, 1992-98. Classrm. vol. Jr. Achievement, Duluth, 1995-98. Avocations: running, swimming, American literature, classical music, travel. Home: 1064 Dayton Ave Saint Paul MN 55104-6503 Office: St Paul Pioneer Press 345 Cedar St Saint Paul MN 55101-1057

AGGOR, FRANCIS KOMLA, language educator; b. Anfoega, Ghana, Feb. 24, 1959; came to U.S., 1987; s. Joseph Komla and Mercy Afua (Dakpo) A.; m. Dale Marcia Callender, Aug. 27, 1988; children: Aseye, Eli. Diploma, U. Complutense, Madrid, 1982; BA with honors, U. Ghana, 1984; MA, U. Western Ont., 1987; PhD, UCLA, 1992. Tchg. asst. U. Ghana, Accra, 1984-85; tchg. asst. U. Western Ont., London, 1986-87; tchg. assoc. UCLA, 1988-90, tchg. fellow, 1990-92; asst. prof. John Carroll U., Cleve., 1992-98; assoc. prof. John Carroll U., 1998—; coord. Spanish studies John Carroll U., 1997—; dir. cultural exch. program dept. classical and modern langs. John Carroll U., 1997—. Author: Eros en la poesia de Miguel Hernández, 1994; contbr. articles to profl. jours. Recipient George E. Grauel faculty fellowship John Carroll U., 1996, Del Amo Dissertation fellowship UCLA, 1990, Del Amo grad. fellowship UCLA, 1987; named to Outstanding Young Man of Am., 1996. Mem. Assn. Internacional de Hispanistas, Hispanic Assn. for the Humanities, Assn. de Amigos de Miguel Hernández, Am. Assn. Tchrs. of Spanish and Portuguese, Bishop Herman Old Boys Union. Avocations: music, tennis, entertaining friends. Office: Dept Classical & Modern Langs & Cultures John Carroll U University Heights OH 44118-4520

AGGREY, ORISON RUDOLPH, former ambassador, university administrator; b. Salisbury, N.C., July 24, 1926; s. J.E. Kwegyir and Rose Rudolph (Douglass) A.; m. Francoise Fratacci, Nov. 5, 1966; 1 dau., Roxane Rose. BS, Hampton Inst., 1946; MS, Syracuse U., 1948; fellow Ctr. for Internat. Affairs, Harvard U., 1964-65; LLD, Livingstone Coll., 1977. Publicity asst. United Negro Coll. Fund, 1947, 50; reporter Cleve. Call and Post, 1948-49; corr. Chgo. Defender, 1949; info. officer, vice consul Am. Consulate Gen., Lagos, Nigeria, 1951-53; asst. dir. USIS, Lille, France, 1953-54; asst. cultural affairs officer Am. embassy, Paris, 1954-57; dir. USIS Cultural Ctr., Paris, 1957-60; dep. pub. affairs adviser for Africa Dept. State, 1961-64; acting chief French br. Voice of Am., 1965; 1st sec., dep. pub. affairs officer Am. embassy, Kinshasa, Democratic Republic of Congo, 1966-68; program mgr. Motion Picture and TV Service, USIA, 1968-70; dir. West African affairs Dept. State, 1970-73; ambassador to The Gambia and Senegal, 1973-77, ambassador to Romania, 1977-81, career min. info., 1979, career min., 1981; Dept. State fgn. affairs sr. fellow, rsch. prof. diplomacy Georgetown U., Washington, 1981-83; spl. asst. Office Analysis Soviet Union and Eastern Europe Dept. State, Washington, 1983-84; internat. rels. cons., 1984-87, 94—; dir. Patricia Roberts Harris pub. affairs program Howard U., 1987-90; acting dir. Howard U. Press, 1988-90, dir., 1990-94; mem. adv. coun. Joint Ctr. for Polit. and Econ. Studies. Decorated grand officer Senegalese Nat. Order of Lion; recipient Meritorious Svc. award USIA, 1955, Superior Svc. award, 1960; Hampton Inst. Alumni award, 1961, Meritorious Svc. award Pres. of U.S., 1984, Chancellor's medal Syracuse U., 1984, Meritorious Achievement award Fla. A&M U., 1985, Disting. Achievement award Dillard U., 1987. Mem. Atlantic Coun. (exec. com.), Soc. Prodigal Sons State of N.C., Acad. Jazz Paris (hon.), Fed. City Club, Alpha Phi Alpha, Sigma Delta Chi, Alpha Kappa Mu, Sigma Pi Phi. Home: Apt 1406 2301 Jefferson Davis Hwy Arlington VA 22202-3817

AGHABEGIAN, DIANA E. BORTNOWSKY, English language educator, publisher; b. Santa Monica, Calif., Apr. 25, 1963; d. Michael and Lillian Kristine (Panka) Bortnowsky; m. Armond Aghabegian, Mar. 7, 1986; children: Alex Michael, Nicole Eugenia. BA in English Lit., UCLA, 1984; MA in English Lit., Calif. State U., Carson, 1988. Cert. lifetime tchg. credential, Calif. Instr. English, West Los Angeles Coll., Culver City, Calif., 1989-93, El Camino Coll., Torrance, 1990-91, Santa Monica Coll., 1990—; pub. Blue Rabbit Press, West Hills, Calif., 1997—. Editor Full Moon lit. mag., 1997—; contbr. poetry to lit. mags. Mem. Santa Monica Coll. Concert Chorale. Mem. MLA, L.A. Libr. Assn., UCLA Alumni Assn. Democrat. Roman Catholic. Avocations: choral singing, writing poetry, cycling. E-mail: aghabegianúdiana@smc.edu. Office: Santa Monica Coll 1900 Pico Blvd Santa Monica CA 90405

AGHAJANIAN, GEORGE KEVORK, medical educator; b. Beirut, Apr. 14, 1932; Am. parents; s. Ghevont M. and Araxi (Movsessian) A.; m. Anne E. Hammond, Jan. 10, 1959; children: Michael, Andrew, Carol, Laura. AB, Cornell U., 1954; MD, Yale U., 1958. Asst. prof. psychiatry Sch. of Medicine Yale U., New Haven, 1965-68, assoc. prof. psychiatry Sch. of Medicine, 1968-70, assoc. prof. psychiatry and pharmacology Sch. of Medicine, 1970-74, prof. psychiatry and pharmacology Sch. of Medicine, 1974—, founds. fund prof. Sch. of Medicine, 1985. Contbr. more than 275 articles to profl. jours. Capt. U.S. Army, 1963-65. Recipient Founds. Fund Rsch. prize Am. Psychiat. Assn., 1981, Scheele medal Swedish Acad. Pharmacy, 1981, Merit award NIH, 1990-2000, Hillarp award Internat. Amine Group, 1996, Lieber prize NARSAD, 1998. Fellow Am. Coll. Neuropsychopharmacology (Efron award 1975); mem. Soc. for Pharmacology and Exptl. Therapeutics, Soc. for Neurosci., Internat. Brain Rsch. Orgn. Achievements include research in electrophysiological and pharmacological properties of brain serotonergic, noradrenergic, and dopaminergic neurons. Office: 34 Park St New Haven CT 06519-1109

AGHASSI, WILLIAM J., mechanical engineer, consultant; b. N.Y.C., July 3, 1948; s. Norman H. and Violette (Solomon) A.; m. Marion Weston, June 17, 1979; children: Rachel, Eli. BSME, Polytech. U. Bklyn., 1969; MS in Environ. Engring., N.J. Inst. Tech., 1975. Registered profl. engr., N.Y.; cert. asbestos investigator, N.Y.C. Engr. Combustion Engring., Windsor, Conn., 1969-71, City of N.Y., 1971-74, Leeds and Northrup Co., N.Y.C., 1974-82; prin. W.J. Aghassi Cons. Engrs., N.Y.C., 1982—; developer engring. curricula for h.s. Recipient Environ. Quality award EPA, 1998. Mem. ASME, ASHRAE, Am. Water Works Assn. Avocations: hiking, biking, outdoor activities. Home: 771 West End Ave New York NY 10025-5572

AGHIORGOUSSIS, MAXIMOS DEMETRIOS See MAXIMOS, METROPOLITAN

AGISIM, PHILIP, advertising and marketing company executive; b. Newark, Jan. 12, 1919; s. Isidore and Jennie (Socket) A.; m. Blanche Tedlow, June 14, 1942; children: Leslie Wayne, Elliot Steven. B.S., Rutgers U., 1941; M.B.A., N.Y. U., 1949. Asst. market research dir. Crowell-Collier Pub. Co., N.Y.C., 1945-49; asso. market research dir. Cowles Pub. Co., N.Y.C., 1949-54; research and planning dir. J.B. Williams Co., N.Y.C., 1954-59, v.p., advt. dir., 1970-71; research dir. Parkson Advt. Agy., N.Y.C., 1959-63, v.p., 1963-69, exec. v.p., 1971-72, vice chmn., 1972-77, pres., 1978—, chief exec. officer, 1980-84, also bd. dirs.; vice chmn. Ohlmeyer Advt., 1984; pres. Product Opportunities Unltd., Inc., 1985-92; ptnr. Ron Meyer and Assocs.; bd. dirs. Trevor, Cole, Reid & Monroe Inc., TCRM Advisors Inc. Contbr. articles in field to profl. jours. Mem. Acad. Health Svcs. Mktg., Nat. Acad. TV Arts and Scis., Am. Mktg. Assn., Friars Club. Jewish. Home: 650 Park Ave New York NY 10021-6115 Office: Trevor Cole Reid & Monroe 515 Madison Ave New York NY 10022-5403

AGLER, BRIAN, professional basketball coach; m. Robin Agler; children: Bryce, Taylor. BA, Wittenberg U.; MEd, Pittsburg (Kans.) State U. Profl. basketball player Blackpool, Eng., 1980-81; coach Northeastern Okla. A&M U., U. Mo., Kansas City; head women's basketball coach Kans. State U.; head coach Columbus Quest; head coach, gen. mgr. Minn. Lynx, Mpls., 1998—. Inductee Wittenberg U. Athletic Hall of Honor, 1995; named ABL Ea. Conf. All-Star head coach, 1997, 98, ABL Coach of the Yr., 1996-97. Mem. Women's Basketball Coaches Assn. Office: Minnesota Lynx Target Ctr 600 First Ave N Minneapolis MN 55403*

AGLER, RICHARD DEAN, rabbi; b. N.Y.C., May 11, 1952; s. Eugene and Sylvia (Spieler) A.; m. Mindy Steinberg, June 19, 1976; children: Jesse Allen, Talia Faith, Sarah Suzan. BA in Polit. Sci., NYU, 1973; MA in Hebrew Lit., Hebrew Union Coll.-Jewish Inst. Religion, 1976. Ordained rabbi, 1978. Rabbi Stephen Wise Free Synagogue, N.Y.C., 1978-80, Temple Beth Shalom, Vero Beach, Fla., 1980-82, Temple Beth El, Boca Raton, Fla., 1982-84; founding rabbi Congregation Bnai Israel, Boca Raton, 1984—; Palm Beach County rep. So. Fla. Conf. on Soviet Jewry, Miami, 1983-91; bd. mem. Am. Friends Hebrew U., Boca Raton, Anti Defamation League, Palm Beach County. V.p. Handgun Control of Palm Beach County, Fla., 1983-93; cofounder Boca Raton Black-Jewish Fellowship, 1984—; facilitating founder Barton's Boosters, Boca Raton, 1986—; founder Ctr. for Justice, Boca Raton, 1989—; co-founder Black-Jewish Coalition Quality Pub. Edn. Named Outstanding Young Man Am., 1989. Mem. Ctr. Conf. Am. Rabbis, South Palm Beach County Rabbinical Assn. (pres. 1991-93), S.E. Assn. Ctrl. Conf. Am. Rabbis (spirituality chair 1984—), Assn. Reform Zionists of Am. (life, bd. dirs.), Am. Jewish Congress (bd. dirs.). Avocations: literature, athletics, sailing. Office: Congregation Bnai Israel 2200 Yamato Rd Boca Raton FL 33431-4325

AGLI, STEPHEN MICHAEL, English language educator, literature educator; b. Yonkers, N.Y., Feb. 11, 1942; s. Michael Joseph and Pauline Joanna (Perrone) A. AB summa cum laude, Fordham Coll., 1965; AM, Harvard U., 1968, EdM, 1972; postgrad., CUNY, 1995—. Cert. secondary sch. English tchr., N.Y. Resident tutor Quincy House, Harvard Coll., Cambridge, Mass., 1968-73; instr. humanities Berklee Coll. Music, Boston, 1971-73; mem. curriculum devel. com., teaching fellow in expository writing Harvard U., Cambridge, 1973-77, tutor in expository writing Bur. of Study Counsel, 1977-81; tchr., chmn. English dept. Jewish H.S. South Fla., North Miami Beach, 1982-83, St. Sergius H.S., N.Y.C., 1983-84; tchr. secondary sch. English Columbia Grammar and Prep. Sch., N.Y.C., 1984-85; coll. counselor, ednl. adminstr. St. Sergius Acad., 1994-95; bd. Freshman advisers Harvard Coll., 1970-77; counselor, ednl. cons., Cambridge, Mass., N.Y.C., 1977-82; ednl. rsch. and cons., N.Y.C., 1985—; adj. instr. English N.J. Inst. Tech., Newark, 1987-88, CUNY, 1992—; conf. session chmn. Soc. for Textual Scholarship, 1993; presenter rsch. papers Rockhurst Coll., Kansas City, Mo., 1989, St. Louis U., Gerard Manley Hopkins Centennial Celebration, 1989, Malone Soc. Centennial Conf., Stratford-upon-Avon, Eng., 1990; spkr. St. Sergius H.S. commencement, 1992-93. Alumni rep. Harvard U., 1982-90. Recipient Woodrow Wilson fellowship Woodrow Wilson Found. to Harvard U., 1965-66, CUNY travel and rsch. awards to confs. and librs. in U.S. and Europe, 1988-90, 95; fellow NDEA Dept. Celtic Langs. and Lit., Harvard U., 1967-70, CUNY, 1986-90, N.E. MLA, London and Oxford, 1990. Mem. MLA, N.E. MLA, Celtic Studies Assn. N. Am. (speaker annual meeting 1989), Phi Beta Kappa. Home: 65 Central Park Ave Apt 1M Yonkers NY 10705-4743

AGNELLI, GIOVANNI, industrial executive; b. Turin, Italy, Mar. 12, 1921; s. Edoardo and Princess Virginia Bourbon del Monte Agnelli; m. Princess Marella Caracciolo di Castagneto; children: Edoardo, Margherita. LLD, U. Torino. With Fiat Co., 1943—, vice chmn. bd., 1945-63, mng. dir., 1963-66, chmn., 1966-96, hon. chmn., 1996—; chmn. IFI Istituto Finanziario Industriale, Exor Group S.A.; chmn. Giovanni Agnelli Found; bd. dirs. Eurafrance; internat. adv. coun. Chase Manhattan Corp. Mem. adv. bd. Bilderberg Meetings; hon. co-chmn. Coun. for the U.S. & Italy; assoc. mem. Moral and Polit. Scis. Acad. of Inst. de France; life mem. Italian Senate; chmn. Editrice La Stampa Spa. With Italian Army, 1941-43. Decorated Cross Mil. Valour, Grand Cross of the Royal Order of the No. Star. Mem. Italian Stock Cos. Assn. (dir.), Turin Indsl. Assn. (dir.), Confedn. Italian Industry (mem. exec. bd.), Assn. Monetary Union Europe (hon. v.p.). Office: Fiat Spa, Via Nizza 250, 10126 Turin Italy

AGNES, GREGORY STEPHEN, engineering educator, military officer; b. Balt., June 8, 1967; s. Janet Thelma (Avery) A.; m. Susan Regina Carney, June 23, 1990; 1 child, Courtney Janet. BS in Aero. Engring., Rensselaer Poly. Inst., 1989; MS in Aerospace Engring., U. Md., 1991; PhD in Engring. Mechanics, Va. Tech., 1997. Commd. 2d. lt. USAF, 1989, advanced through grades to capt., 1993; aerospace rsch. engr. USAF Wright Lab., Wright Patterson AFB, Ohio, 1991-94; asst. prof. aero. engring. Air Force Inst. Tech., Wright Patterson AFB, 1997—. Contbr. articles to profl. jours. Advanced through grades to capt. USAF, 1989—. Recipient Achievement medal USAF, 1992, Commendation medal, 1994. Mem. AIAA, ASME, Wings Lacrosse Club of Dayton (v.p. 1993-94). Avocations: lacrosse, woodworking. Office: AFIT/ENY 2950 P St Bldg 640 Wright Patterson AFB OH 45433

AGNEW, CHRISTOPHER MACK, minister, historian; b. Santa Barbara, Calif., Aug. 7, 1944; s. Jack and Agnes Emma (Mack) A.; m. Suzanne Marie Souder, June 1, 1974 (div.); m. Elizabeth Lewis Lyddane, Apr. 25, 1998. AB, Bucknell U., Lewisburg, Pa., 1967; MA, U. Del., Newark, 1975, PhD, 1980; STM, Gen. Theol. Sem., N.Y.C., 1991. Ordained to ministry Episcopal Ch. as deacon, 1991, as priest, 1992. Reference libr. Dover (Del.) Pub. Libr., 1969-72; tchg. asst. dept. history U. Del., Newark, 1972-76; manuscript libr. Hist. Soc. Del., 1979-81; asst. prof. history and Can. studies SUNY, Plattsburgh, 1981-84; registrar Diocese of Del., Wilmington, 1985-89; deacon St. Thomas' Ch., Newark, 1991-92; assoc. ecumenical officer Episcopal Ch., N.Y.C., 1989-94; priest assoc. All Angels Ch., N.Y.C., 1992-95; interim rector All Hallows, Wyncote, Pa., 1995, St. Michael's, Litchfield, Conn., 1995-97, Ch. of the Ascension, Norfolk, Va., 1997, St. Peter's in Great Valley, Paoli, Pa., 1997—; mem. staff Anglican-Roman Cath. Consultation, Standing Commn. Ecumenical Rels., 1989-94, Episcopal Russian Orthodox Joint Coord. Com., 1990-94; mem. Faith and Order Commn., 1991-95; mem. NCC Christian-Muslim Rels. Commn., 1989-91, NCC Christian-Jewish Rels. Commn., 1989—, chmn. 1991—; mem. Parliament of the Worlds Religions, 1993, NCC Interfaith Working Group, 1990-95, Interfaith Rels. Commn., 1996—, Planning Com., Nat. Workshop on Christian Unity, 1990-94. Editor: The Ecumenical Bull., 1989-94, Anglican Statements on the Church: Selected Documentary Sources for a Study of Anglican Ecclesiology, 1994; author: God With Us, 1986; contbr. articles to profl. jours. Mem. Nat. Episc. Historians Assn., Hist. Soc. Episc. Ch., Order Crown Charlemagne U.S. (asst. chaplain 1997—), Orgn. Am. Historians, Am. Hist. Assn., N.Am. Acad. Ecumenists, Can. Hist. Assn., Assn. Can. Studies in U.S., Mil. Order of Loyal Legion of U.S. (chaplain-in-chief 1995—), Mil. Order of Stars and Bars, Soc. Colonial Wars, N.Am. Guild of Change Ringers. Home: 1007 Charleston Grn Malvern PA 19355-2460 Office: PO Box 334 Paoli PA 19301-0334

AGNEW, HAROLD MELVIN, physicist; b. Denver, Mar. 28, 1921; s. Sam E. and Augusta (Jacobs) A.; m. Beverly Jackson, May 2, 1942; children: Nancy E. Agnew Owens, John S. AB, U. Denver, 1942; MS, U. Chgo., 1948, PhD, 1949; PhD (hon.), Coll. Santa Fe, 1980, U. Denver, 1992. With Los Alamos Sci. Lab., 1943-46, alt. div. leader, 1949-61, leader weapons div.,

1964-70, dir., 1970-79; pres. Gen. Atomics, San Diego, 1979-85, also bd. dirs., 1985—; sci. adviser Supreme Allied Comdr. in Europe, Paris, 1961-64; chmn. Army Sci. Adv. Panel, 1965-70, San Diego County adv. bd.; mem. aircraft panel President's Sci. Adv. Com., 1965-73; mem. USAF Sci. Adv. Bd., 1957-69, Def. Sci. Bd., 1965-70, Gov. of N.Mex.'s Radiation Adv. Coun., 1959-61; sec. N.Mex. Health and Social Svcs., 1971-73; chmn. gen. adv. com. ACDA, 1974-77, mem., 1977-81; mem. aerospace safety adv. panel NASA, 1964-70; mem. U.S. Army Sci. Bd., 1978-80, White House Sci. Coun., 1982-89; adj. prof. U. Calif., San Diego, 1988—. Mem. council engring. NRC, 1978-82; mem. Los Alamos Bd. Ednl. Trustees, 1950-55, pres., 1955; trustee San Diego Mus. Art, 1983-87; mem. Woodrow Wilson Nat. Fellowship Found., 1973-80; N.Mex. State senator, 1955-61; sec. N.Mex. Legis. Council, 1957-61; chmn. N.Mex. Senate Corp. Commn., 1957-61; mem. Fed. Emergency Agy., 1982-88; bd. dirs. Fedn. Rocky Mountain States, Inc., 1975-77, Charles Lee Powell Found., 1993—; chmn. U. Calif. San Diego Chancellors Assocs., 1998—. Recipient Ernest Orlando Lawrence award AEC, 1966,; Enrico Fermi award Dept. Energy, 1978. Fellow Am. Phys. Soc., AAAS; mem. Nat. Acad. Scis., Nat. Acad. Engring., Council on Fgn. Relations, Phi Beta Kappa, Sigma Xi, Omicron Delta Kappa. Home: 322 Punta Baja Dr Solana Beach CA 92075-1720

AGNEW, JANET BURNETT, secondary education educator; b. Spartanburg, S.C., Aug. 29, 1936; d. James and Ruby Evelyne (Burnett) A.; 1 child, James Gilmour. BA, U. N.C., Greensboro, 1958; MA in Teaching, Converse Coll., Spartanburg, S.C., 1966; postgrad., Clemson (S.C.) U., 1970-72, U. S.C., Columbia, 1990—. Cert. tchr., prin., math. supr. Tchr. gen. math. and algebra Greensboro Schs.-Aycock, 1958-60; tchr. coll. prep. math. Air Force Dependent H.S., Stevenville, Nfld., Can., 1960-61; tchr. gen. math. and algebra Roebuck H.S. Spartanburg Schs. #6, 1962; tchr. gen. phys. sci. Campobello Sch. Spartanburg Schs., 1962-63, tchr. math. and algebra, 1965-68, substitute tchr., 1975-76; tchr. gen. math. and algebra Pacolet & Broome H.S., 1976-98; corp. sec. Delagrave Co., Spartanburg, 1963-75; instr. math. Spartanburg Meth. Coll., 1968-75; ret., 1998; cons., 1998—. Contbr. articles to profl. jours. Pres. Gen. Fedn. Women's Clubs-S.C., Columbia, 1978-80, chmn. trustees, 1985-87, 88-91, 91-97, chmn. scholarship com., 1991-93, 95-97, 98-04, sec.-treas. so. region, 1990-92, v.p., 1992-94, pres. 1994-96. Recipient Svc. award Spartanburg March of Dimes, 1967, 68. Mem. Nat. Coun. Tchrs. Math., S.C. Edn. Assn. (life, del. assembly 1987-98), S.C. Tchrs. Math. (life), Spartanburg County Assn. Educators (dist. dir. 1988-91, v.p, pres. elect 1991-92, pres. 1992-93), Spartanburg Country Club Woman's Golf Assn., Spartanburg Coun. Federated Woman's Clubs (pres. 1989-92), Jubilee Club (pres. 1996—), Piedmont Jr. Woman's Clubs (pres. 1974, 76, Clubwoman of Yr. 1974, 75, 76), Delta Kappa Gamma. Democrat. Presbyterian. Avocations: crafts, travel. Home: 140 Burnett Dr Spartanburg SC 29302-3402

AGNEW, PETER TOMLIN, employee benefit consultant; b. Orange, N.J., Nov. 20, 1948; s. William Harold and Janet Elisabeth (Gittinger) A.; m. Linda W. Seyffarth; children: Jonathan, Stephen, Douglas, Karen; 1 step child, Kristin Seyffarth. BA in English cum laude, Amherst Coll., 1971; MBA in Fin., NYU, 1976. CLU. Asst. investment officer Mutual Benefit Life, Newark, 1971-78; exec. v.p., bd. dir., prin. Post & Kurtz, Inc., N.Y.C., 1978-85, exec. v.p., prin., 1993—, also bd. dirs., pres., treas., 1998—; sr. regional dir. Minet, N.Y.C., 1985-92; pres. P. Tomlin Agnew Assocs., Glen Ridge, N.J., 1982—; mem. pension com. Croda, Inc. Contbr. articles to profl. jours. Capt. United Way, Newark, 1978; assoc. class agt. Amherst Coll. Alumni Fund, 1980—, class agt., 1993—; mem. exec. bd. Rep. Congl. Leadership Coun., 1988-92; mem. Rep. Nat. Com. Pres.'s Club, 1992—; vice chair Civic Conf. Com. of Glen Ridge, 1998—, Glen Ridge Rep. Club; asst. treas. Glen Ridge Congl. Ch. Fellow Life Mgmt. Inst.; mem. Soc. CLU (com. chmn. N.Y. chpt. 1984), Assn. Advanced Life Underwriters, Nat. Assn. Securities Dealers, Yale Ins. Group (chmn. 1988-90), Glen Ridge Country Club, Downtown Assn., Williams Club. Avocations: swimming, bridge, skiing, music. golf. Home: 503 Ridgewood Ave Glen Ridge NJ 07028-1821

AGNEW, SAMUEL GERARD, orthopaedic traumatologist; b. New Orleans, Oct. 22, 1958; s. Thomas A. and Elizabeth (De la Houssaye) A.; m. Denise Kachler, May 3, 1986; children: Taylor Frances, Caroline Elizabeth. BS, U. S.C., 1980; MD, Tulane U., 1984. Diplomate Am. Bd. Orthopaedic Surgeons. Chief trauma orthopedic dept. orthopedics, asst. prof. U. Miss. Med. Ctr., Jackson, 1990-91; chief orthopedic trauma, asst. prof. U. Ark. for Med. Scis., Little Rock, 1991-95; chief orthopedic trauma, assoc. prof. U. Fla., Jacksonville, 1995—; vis. lectr. Hennepin County Med., 1994, Pa. Orthopaedic, 1994. Author: Orthopedic Clinics of North America, 1992. Fellow Am. Acad. Orthopaedics; mem. ACS, Orthopedic Trauma Assn., Am. Assn. for Surgery of Trauma, Assn. for Advancement of Automotive Medicine. Office: U Fla Health Scis Ctr 653-1 W 8th St Jacksonville FL 32209-6511

AGNEW, THEODORE LEE, JR., historian, educator; b. Ogden, Ill., Dec. 21, 1916; s. Theodore Lee and Agnes (Faris) A.; m. Jeanne Starrett LeCaine, Dec. 25, 1942; children: Theodore (dec.), Theodore Lee III, Susan Elizabeth (Mrs. Tom Balestreri), Hugh LeCaine, Peter Wallace, Marion Jeanne. B.A., U. Ill., 1937, M.A., 1938; A.M., Harvard U., 1939; Ph.D., Harvard, 1954. Grad. research asst. U. Ill., 1938; asst prof. history Okla. State U., Stillwater, 1947-54, assoc. prof., 1954-60, prof., 1960-84, prof. emeritus, 1984—; vis. prof. history Emory U., summer 1964, 66-67; adj. prof. Meth. history Phillips Grad. Sem., Tulsa, 1992, 94; mem. World Meth. Coun., 1976-91, 96—, exec. com., 1981-86; del. United Meth. Gen. Conf. and South Ctrl. Judisdictional Conf., 1976, 80, 84, 88, 92, 96, mem. gen. commn. on archives and history, 1972-80, commn. to study ministry, 1972-76, 88-92, commn. on Christian unity and interreligious concerns United Meth. Ch., 1980-88, gen. coun. on ministries, 1984-88; mem. bds. South Ctrl. Jurisdiction and Okla. Ann. Conf., Okla. Conf. of Churches; lay mem. Okla. Ann. Conf., 1971—, mem. joint adminstrv. bd. Meth. Theol. Sch. in Ohio and United Theol. Sem.; lay consultation coun. St. Paul Sch. Theology; bd. dirs. Frances E. Willard Home, Tulsa. Author: The South Central Jurisdiction 1939-1972, 1973,; contbr. articles to profl. jours. Served from ensign to lt. USNR, 1942-46, comdr. Res. ret. Mem. AAUP (mem. coun. 1960-63), Am. Hist. Assn., Orgn. Am. Historians, So. Hist. Assn., Am. Soc. Ch. History, Am. Studies Assn., Midcontinent Am. Studies Assn. (pres. 1982), Okla. and Ill. Hist. Socs., Phi Beta Kappa, Phi Kappa Phi, Phi Alpha Theta, Alpha Kappa Lambda. Democrat. Home: 1216 N Lincoln St Stillwater OK 74075-2749

AGNEW, WILLIAM HAROLD, insurance company executive; b. Passaic, N.J., Aug. 25, 1920; s. Arthur Maurice and Marion Kingsley (Tomlin) A.; m. Mar. 29, 1947; children: Peter, Nancy, Susan, Elisabeth. AB, Amherst Coll., 1943; MBA, U. Pa., 1949. CLU. Assoc. Post & Kurtz Inc., N.Y.C., 1947-53; salesman Ludlow Mfg. Co., Boston, 1953-58; v.p. Post & Kurtz Inc., N.Y.C., 1958-76, pres., 1976-85; chmn. bd. Osborne Post & Kurtz Inc., N.Y.C., 1976-85; sr. regional dir. Minet Profl. Svcs. (formerly Osborne Post & Kurtz Inc.), N.Y.C., 1985-93; pres. Post & Kurtz, Inc., N.Y.C., 1993—. Warden Calvary Episc. Ch., Summit, N.J., 1970-74; trustee Police Athletic League, Summit, 1975-77; v.p. Wilson Sch. PTA, Summit, 1975; chmn. Boy Scout Am. Troop Com., Summit, 1961-64. Maj. USMC, 1942-46, PTO. Decorated Silver Star, Purple Heart. Mem. Assn. of Advanced Life Underwriters, Canoe Brook Country Club. Republican. Episcopalian. Avocations: bridge, golf, platform tennis, reading. Office: Post & Kurtz 111 John St Rm 2400 New York NY 10038-3101

AGNICH, RICHARD JOHN, lawyer, electronics company executive; b. Eveleth, Minn., Aug. 24, 1943; s. Frederick J. and Ruth H. (Welton) A.; m. Victoria Webb Trescher, Apr. 19, 1969; children: Robert Frederick, Michael McCord, Jonathon Welton. A.B. in Econs., Stanford U., 1965; J.D., U. Tex., 1969. Bar: Tex. 1969. Legis. asst., legal counsel to John G. Tower U.S. Senate, 1969-70, adminstrv. asst. to John G. Tower, 1971-72; asst. counsel Tex. Instruments Inc., Dallas, 1973-78, asst. gen. counsel, 1978-82, v.p., sec., gen. counsel, 1982—, sr v.p., sec. gen. counsel, 1988—. Bd. dirs. U.S. Com. of Pacific Basin Econ. Coun., U.S.-Korea Bus. Coun. Mem. ABA (com. corp. law depts.) Tex. Bar Assn., Dallas Bar Assn., Am. Soc. Corp. Secs., Southwestern Legal Found. (adv. bd. Internat. and Comparative Law Ctr.), Assn. Gen. Counsel. Republican. Presbyterian. Home: 19 Downs Lake Cir Dallas TX 75230-1900 Office: Tex Instruments Inc PO Box 660199 MS 8658 Dallas TX 75266-0199 also: Tex Instruments Inc 8505 Forest Ln # Ms8658 Dallas TX 75243-4136

AGNO, JOHN G., management consultant; b. Gloversville, N.Y., Dec. 8, 1940; s. John G. and Margretta (Luff) Anagnostopulos; m. Lynn Airey Mar. 30, 1968 (div. Oct. 1979); children; J. Robert, Constance Blythe, Randy R.; m. Karen Clark Mikus, June 29, 1985; 1 stepchild, Luke Ravlin. BBA, U. Fla., 1962. Mktg. specialist Eastman Kodak Co., Rochester, N.Y., 1965-73; gen. mgr. sanitation appliance divsn. Thetford Corp., Ann Arbor, Mich., 1973-80; v.p. mktg. and adminstrn. Stirling Power Systems Corp. divsn. McDonnell Douglas Corp., Ann Arbor, 1980-87; pres. Signature, Inc., Ann Arbor, 1983—. Deacon First Presbyn. Ch., Ann Arbor; bd. dirs. Washtenaw United Way, 1991-95; bd. dirs. YMCA, 1995—. 1st lt. U.S. Army, 1963-65. Mem. ASTD, Recreational Vehicle Industry Assn. (chmn. mktg. commn. 1978-82, bd. dirs. 1981-83), Turnaround Mgmt. Assn., Ann Arbor Country Club, Rotary. Republican. Home: 4701 Midway Dr Ann Arbor MI 48103-9427 Office: Signature Inc PO Box 2086 Ann Arbor MI 48106-2086

AGOGINO, GEORGE ALLEN, anthropologist, educator; b. West Palm Beach, Fla., Nov. 18, 1920; s. Andrew and Beulah Mae A.; m. Mercedes Merner, Dec. 1, 1952; children: Alice, Karen. BA, U. N.Mex., 1948, MA, 1951; PhD, Syracuse U., 1958; postgrad., Harvard U., 1962-63. Asst. prof. anthropology Syracuse U., N.Y., 1956-58; asst. prof. anthropology, acting dir. mus. U. S.D., Vermillion, 1958-59; asst. prof. anthropology U. Wyo., Laramie, 1959-61; Wenner-Gren postdoctoral fellow Harvard U., Cambridge, Mass., 1961-62; assoc. prof. Baylor U., Waco, Tex., 1962-63; assoc. prof. anthropology Ea. N.Mex. U., Portales, 1963-68, prof., 1968-85, disting. rsch. prof. anthropology, 1985-91, emeritus disting. rsch. prof., 1991—, disting. (tchg.) prof., 1995—, dir. Paleo-Indian Inst., 1963—, founding dir. Anthropology Mus., Blackwater Draw Mus., Miles Mus., 1967-86, chmn. dept. anthropology, 1963-80, dir. spl. programs, 1972-73, dir. humanities div., 1973-74; cons. forensic phys. anthropology U.S. Bur. Reclamation, 1984—; cons. to mags. Am. Antiquity, Plains Anthropologist, Nat. Geog., Pursuit, Smithsonian. Author monographs in field including (with C. V. Haynes) Smithsonian Contributions in Anthropology, No. 32; contbr. more than 580 articles on Mex. anthropology, Paleo Indian archaeology, primative religion and folklore to profl. jours. With Signal Corps, U.S. Army, Special Assignment, 1942-46. Recipient Pres.'s award Eastern N.Mex. U., 1971, numerous rsch. grants; proclaimed Ofcl. Eminent Scholar by State of N.Mex. Fellow Explorers Club Am., Am. Anthrop. Assn., AAAS, Instituto Interamericana. Home: 1600 S Main Ave Portales NM 88130-7331

AGOOS, JEFF, professional soccer player. Student, U. Va. Defender DC United, Herndon, Va.; mem. U.S. Under-15, Under-17, Under-20, World Univ. and Indoor Nat. Teams; competitor 13 internat. matches in 1996, scoring winning goal in 2d internat. appearance, Guatemala, mem. silver-medal U.S. Futsai Nat. Team, Hong Kong, 1992; helped lead DC United to inaugural MLS Cup title and 1996 U.S. Open Cup championship. Vol. asst. coach, Bruce Arena, U. Va., 1995. Named one of Soccer Am.'s 11 most valuable players, 1989, Soccer Am.'s co-freshman of yr., 1986. Office: US Soccer Fedn 1801-1811 S Prairie Ave Chicago IL 60616 and: DC United 13832 Redstein Dr Herndon VA 20171*

AGOSIN, MOISES KANKOLSKY, zoology educator; b. Marseilles, France, Dec. 1, 1922; came to U.S., 1968, naturalized, 1973; s. Abraham W. and Rachel S. (Kankolsky) A.; m. Frida Halpern, June 19, 1948; children—Cynthia Regina, Marjorie Stella, Mario Daniel. M.D., U. Chile, 1948. Intern Salvador Hosp., Santiago, Chile, 1946; resident parasitology and med. entomology Salvador Hosp., 1948; Rockefeller Found. fellow NIH, Bethesda, Md., 1952-54; research assoc. NIH, 1955; head biochemistry sect., dept. parasitology U. Chile, 1957-59, chmn. dept. chemistry, prof. chemistry, 1960-67; research prof. zoology U. Ga., Athens, 1968—; vis. prof. U. Calif., Berkeley, 1960, U. London, 1964; hon. prof. U. Cayetano Heredia, Peru, 1984 cons. in field. Contbg. author: The Physiology of Insecta, 1974, Comprehensive Insect Biochemistry, Physiology, Pharmacology, 1985; mem. editorial bd.: Exptl. Parasitology, 1967-73, Archives Insect Biochemistry and Physiology, 1982-86; contbr. articles to profl. jours. Recipient Lamar Dodd award for creativity in rsch. U. Ga., 1989; grantee USPHS, 1958—, WHO, 1963-67, Wellcome Trust, 1966, NSF, 1974, U.S.-Israel bi-nat. Sci. Found., 1976, Conicit, Chile, 1996; Fulbright scholar, Peru, 1991, Fondecit (Chile) grant, 1996. Fellow Am. Acad. Microbiology; mem. Am. Soc. Biol. Chemists, Biochem. Soc. (London), AAAS, N.Y. Acad. Scis., Am. Soc. Parasitology (Bueding-von Brand Meml. award 1990), Chilean Acad. Scis.(rsch. prof. emeritus 1992). Home: 177 Deertree Dr Athens GA 30605-4501 Office: U Ga 623 Biol Scis Bldg Athens GA 30602 *Perhaps the most important driving force in my career has always been the need to find out not how phenomena occur but why. This has been coupled to my belief that there are only two types of research, good and bad, regardless of whether they are considered basic or applied.*

AGOSTA, VITO, mechanical and aerospace engineering educator; b. N.Y.C., July 26, 1923; s. John and Elizabeth (Alvares) A.; m. Mary Frago, Aug. 9, 1952; children: John, Diana, Charles. M.S. in Engring., U. Mich., 1949; Ph.D., Columbia, 1959. Registered profl. engr., N.Y. Thermodynamicist DeLaval Steam Turbine Co., 1946-47; mem. faculty Poly. Inst. N.Y., Bklyn., 1950—, prof. mech. and aerospace engring., 1962—, prof. emeritus, 1986—; pres. Propulsion Scis., Inc., Huntington, N.Y., 1966-75, Fuels Systems Design Corp., Huntington, N.Y., 1975-94, Propulsion Scis. Co., Huntington, 1989—; researcher combustion instability in rocket motors, supersonic combustion of two phase systems, air and thermal pollution, heat transfer analysis in reacting fuels. Inventor non-miscible liquid emulsifier, modulating oil burner; designer and mfr. of modulating fuel emulsifier systems for engines and boilers. Served with AUS, 1943-45. Mem. AIAA, Combustion Inst., ASME, Sigma Xi, Tau Beta Pi. Home: 42 Cherry Ln Huntington NY 11743-2945 Office: Propulsion Scis Co 300 Broadway Huntington Station NY 11746

AGOSTA, WILLIAM CARLETON, chemist, educator; b. Dallas, Jan. 1, 1933; s. Angelo N. and Helen Carleton (Jones) A.; m. Karin Solveig Engstrom, July 2, 1958; children—Jennifer Ellen, Christopher William. BA, Rice Inst., 1954; AM, Harvard U., 1955, PhD, 1957. NRC postdoctoral fellow Oxford (Eng.) U., 1957-58; Pfizer postdoctoral fellow U. Ill., Urbana, 1958-59; asst. prof. U. Calif., Berkeley, 1959-61; liaison scientist U.S. Navy, Frankfurt, Germany, 1961-63; asst. prof. chemistry Rockefeller U., N.Y.C., 1963-67, assoc. prof., 1967-74, prof., 1974-98, prof. emeritus, 1998—; vis. prof. U. Innsbruck, 1995, Princeton U., 1996; cons. in field; officer Chiron Press, Inc., 1977-85; mem. NRC Associateship Programs Chem. Scis. Panel, 1997—. Author: Chemical Communication, 1992, Bombardier Beetles and Fever Trees, 1996; mem. editl. adv. bd. Jour. Organic Chemistry, 1984-88; contbr. articles to profl. jours. John Angus Erskine fellow U. Canterbury (N.Z.), 1981. Fellow AAAS; mem. Chem. Soc. London, Am. Chem. Soc., Interam. Photochem. Soc., European Photochemistry Assn., Am. Soc. Photobiology, Internat. Soc. for Chem. Ecology, Phi Beta Kappa, Sigma Xi. Home: PO Box 1547 Friday Harbor WA 98250-1547 Office: U Wash Friday Harbor Labs Friday Harbor WA 98250

AGOSTINELLI, ROBERT FRANCESCO, investment banker; b. Rochester, N.Y., May 21, 1953. BS, St. John Fisher Coll., 1976; MBA, Columbia U., 1981. Assoc. J. Rothschild & Co., London, 1981-82; v.p. investment banking Goldman, Sachs & Co., N.Y.C. and London, 1982-87; mng. dir. investment banking Lazard Frères & Co. LLC, N.Y.C., 1987-96; bd. dirs. Rhone Group/Rhone Capital, N.Y.C., 1996—; supervisory bd. mem. Lazard GmbH; dir. Lazard Spa; non-exec. mem. adv. com. Frontera S.A.; vice chmn. Coun. for U.S. and Italy; mem. Coun. on Fgn. Rels.; dir. European Inst., The Am.-Italian Cancer Found.; non-resident fellow The Pierpont Morgan Libr. Bd. dirs. Soc. des Amis du Musee d'Art Moderne; supporting fellow The Frick Collection; mem. N.Y.-Rome Sister City Adv. Com. Office: Rhone Group 630 Fifth Ave New York NY 10021

AGOSTINI, ROSEMARIE CONIGLIO, human services administrator; b. N.Y.C., Aug. 13, 1939; d. Louis and Frances (Licata) Coniglio; m. Remo P. Agostini, Oct. 24, 1959; children: Peter L. Agostini, Francesca G. Agostini. Cert. cmty. svc. profl. gerontologist, bereavement counselor/Lazarus min.; cert. mentor trainer. Exec. dir. Dept. Aging, Parsippany, N.J., 1973-91, Sussex County (N.J.) Office on Aging, 1991-93; del. Nat. coun. Aging., NISC. Author, pub. (newsletter) Golden Gazette, 1974—; producer, host (cable TV) Horizons Unltd., 1976—, Sincerely Yours, 1991—. Bd. dirs., trustee Hospice of Morris County, N.J., 1982—; founder, leader Parkinsons and Caregiver Support Group, Parsippany, 1980; co-founder Parsippany Area Legis. Task Force, 1980; founder chpt. 3070 AARP, Parsippany, 1976; chair interdenominational com. of Parsippany; chair cmty. rels. St. Christophers Ch., chair cmty. svc.; candidate for mayor Parsippany-Troy Hills, N.J., 1993; mem. bd. dirs. Mental Health Assn., Parsippany Day Care Ctr., United Way, Morris County Libr. Found.; bd. mgrs., v.p., treas. Am. Cancer Soc., 1994—; mem. Twp. Coun., 1996—; mem. Twp. Coun.; eucharistic min.; bd. trustees Craftsman Farms; assessment mgr. United Way Agy., 1999—, mem. leadership initiative, agy. team mgr., evaluator; team leader mentoring program 200 Club pub. rels. chair. Named Woman of Distinction Cath. War Vets., 1988. Mem. N.J. Assn. Sr. Ctr. Dirs. (founder, pres.), Jaycees (Disting. Svc. 1976, Outstanding Pub. Health award 1980), N.J. Gerontol. Soc. (bd. dirs.), Morris County Svc. Providers (founder, chair), LWV (pres. Parsippany chpt.), Rotary Club (Outstanding Citizen 1978), Unico Nat. (co-founder 1976, Citizen of Yr. 1986), Human Svcs. Assn. Avocations: church lector, travel, cooking, singing. Home: 79 Jean Ter Parsippany NJ 07054-1719

AGRANOFF, BERNARD WILLIAM, biochemist, educator; b. Detroit, June 26, 1926; s. William and Phyllis (Pelavin) A.; m. Raquel Betty Schwartz, Sept. 1, 1957; children: William, Adam. MD, Wayne State U., 1950; BS, U. Mich., 1954. Intern Robert Packer Hosp., Sayre, Pa., 1950-51; commd. surgeon USPHS, 1954-60; biochemist Nat. Inst. Neurol. Diseases and Blindness, NIH, Bethesda, Md., 1954-60; mem. faculty U. Mich., Ann Arbor, 1960—, prof. biochemistry, 1965—; R.W. Gerard prof. of neurosci. in psychiatry, 1991; rsch. biochemist Mental Health Rsch. Inst., 1960—, assoc. dir., 1977-83, dir. 1983-95, dir. neurosci. lab., 1983—; vis. scientist Max Planck Inst. Zellchemie, Munich, 1957-58, Nat. Inst. Med. Rsch., Mill Hill, Eng., 1974-75; Henry Russel lectr. U. Mich., 1987; cons. pharm. industry, govt. Contbr. articles to profl. jours. Fogarty scholar-in-residence NIH, Bethesda, Md., 1989-95; named Mich. Scientist of Yr. Mus. of Sci., Lansing, 1992. Fellow AAAS, N.Y. Acad. Sci., Am. Coll. Neuropsychopharmacology; mem. Am. Soc. Biochemistry and Molecular Biology, Am. Chem. Soc., Inst. Medicine, Internat. Soc. Neurochemistry (treas. 1985-89, chmn. 1989-91), Am. Soc. Neurochemistry (pres. 1973-75). Achievements include research in brain lipids, biochem. basis of learning, memory and regeneration in the nervous system, human brain imaging. Home: 1942 Boulder Dr Ann Arbor MI 48104-4164 Office: U Mich Neurosci Lab 1103 E Huron St Ann Arbor MI 48104-1630

AGRANOFF, GERALD NEAL, lawyer; b. Detroit, Nov. 24, 1946; s. Carl and Frances (Solomon) A.; children—Lindsay Sara, Dana Jill. B.S., Wayne State U., 1969, J.D., 1972; LL.M., NYU, 1973. Bar: N.Y. 1975, Mich. 1973, U.S. Tax Ct. 1974, U.S., Ct. Claims 1974. Atty.-advisor U.S. Tax Ct., Washington, 1973-75; assoc. law firm Baker & McKenzie, N.Y.C., 1975-79, Baer Marks & Upham, N.Y.C., 1979-80; counsel Pryor, Cashman et al, N.Y.C., 1980-82; gen. counsel Arbitrage Securities Co., Plaza Securities Co., N.Y.C., 1982—; gen. ptnr. Edelman Securities Co., N.Y.C., 1984—, Plaza Securities Co., N.Y.C., 1987-96; trustee, Mgmt. Assistance Inc., Liquidating Trust; bd. dirs. Canal Capital Corp., N.Y.C., Bull Run Corp., Datapoint Corp., Atlantic Gulf Cmtys., Am. Energy Group, Ltd.; adj. instr. NYU Inst. on Fed. Taxation, 1980-81. Bd. dirs. Soho Repertory Theatre, N.Y.C., 1982; mem. N.Y. com. UNICEF. Office: The Edelman Cos 717 5th Ave New York NY 10022-8101

AGRAWAL, DHARMA PRAKASH, engineering educator; b. Balod, India, Apr. 12, 1945; came to U.S., 1976; s. Saryoo Prasad and Chandra K. Agrawal; m. Purnima Agrawal, June 7, 1971; children: Sonali, Braj. BE, Ravishankar U., Raipur, India, 1966; ME with honors, Roorkee (India) U., 1968; DSc in Tech., Fed. Inst. Tech., Lausanne, Switzerland, 1975. Lectr. M.N.R. Engring. Coll., Allahabad, India, 1968-72, Roorkee U., 1972-73; asst. Fed. Inst. Tech., Lausanne, 1973-75; instr., postdoctoral work So. Meth. U., Dallas, 1976-77; asst. prof., then assoc. prof. Wayne State U., Detroit, 1977-82; assoc. prof. N.C. State U., Raleigh, 1982-84, prof., 1984-98; OBR Disting. prof. U. Cin., 1998—; gen. co-chair Advanced Computing Conf., 1997, 98; keynote spkr. Internat. Conf. on Parallel and Distributed Sys., 1997. Book editor: Advanced Computer Architecture, 1986, Advances in Distributed System Reliability, 1990, Distributed Computing Network Reliability, 1990; editor: Jour. Parallel and Distg. Computing, 1984, Computer mag., 1986-91, Internat. Jour. High Speed Computing, IEEE Transactions on Computers, 1992-96, IEEE Computer Soc. Press Tutorials, 1992-94. Fellow IEEE (chair tech. com. on computer architecture, IEEE Computer Soc. 1991-94, chair McDowell Award and Harry Grode Award coms. 1991—, program chair internat. conf. on parallel processing 1994, workshop chair internat. conf. on parallel processing 1995, gen. chair fourth internat. workshop on modeling analysis and simulation of computer and telecom. sys. 1996), Assn. for Computing Machinery; mem. Soc. for Indsl. and Applied Math. Office: U Cin ECE&CS PO Box 210030 Cincinnati OH 45221-0030

AGRAWAL, HARISH CHANDRA, neurobiologist, researcher, educator; b. Allahabad, Uttar Pradesh, India; came to U.S., 1970, naturalized, 1982; s. Shambhu and Rajmani Devi A.; m. Daya Kumari Bhushan, Feb. 6, 1960; children—Sanjay, Sanjeev. B.Sc., Allahabad U., 1957, M.Sc., 1959, Ph.D., 1964. Med. research assoc. Thudichum Psychiat. Lab., Galesburg, Ill., 1964-68; lectr. dept. biochemistry Charing Cross Hosp., London, 1968-70; prof. neurology Washington U. Sch. Medicine, St. Louis, 1970—; mem. neurology study sect. NIH, 1979-82. Author: Handbook of Neurochemistry, 1969, Developmental Neurobiology, 1970, Biochemistry of Developing Brain, 1971, Membranes and Receptors, 1974, Proteins of the Nervous System, 1980, Biochemistry of Brain, 1980, Handbook of Neurochemistry, 1984; contbr. numerous papers on various aspects of myelin proteins and their role in demyelinating disrders. Jr. research fellow Council Sci. and Indsl. Research, New Delhi, 1960-62, sr. research fellow, 1963-64; Research Career Devel. award Nat. Inst. Neurol. and Communicative Disorders, 1974-79. Mem. Internat. Soc. Neurochemistry, Internat. Brain Rsch. Orgn., Am. Soc. Neurochemistry, Am. Soc. Biol. Chemists and Molecular Biologists, Am. Soc. Physiology. Home: 11 Morwood Ln Saint Louis MO 63141 Office: Washington U Dept Neurology 660 S Euclid Ave Dept Saint Louis MO 63110-1093

AGRAWAL, KRISHNA CHANDRA, pharmacology educator; b. Calcutta, India, Mar. 15, 1937; naturalized; s. Prasadi Lal and Asarfi Devi (Agrawal) A.; m. Mani Agrawal, Dec. 2, 1960; children—Sunil, Lina, Nira. B.S. in Pharmacy, Andhra U., Waltair, India, 1959, M.S., 1960; Ph.D., U. Fla., 1965. Cert. in pharm. chemistry. Research assoc. dept. pharmacology Yale U. Sch. Medicine, New Haven, 1966-69, instr., 1969-70, asst. prof., 1970-76, assoc. prof., 1976; assoc. prof. dept. pharmacology Tulane U. Sch. Medicine, New Orleans, 1976-81, prof., 1981—, interim chmn., 1996—; cons. mem. Southeastern Cancer Study Group, 1980-85; mem. adv. com. on instnl. grants Am. Cancer Soc., 1980-85; mem. AIDS and Related Rsch. Rev. Group NIH, 1989-94. Conbr. articles to profl. jours.; patentee radiosensitizers for hypoxic tumor cells and compositions; novel AZT analogs. Grantee Nat. Cancer Inst., 1976-89, WHO, 1979-82, La. Bd. Regents, 1981-82, Nat. Inst. Allergy and Infectious Diseases, 1987—, Dept. Def., 1994-96, Nat. Heart Lung and Blood Inst., 1997—. Fellow Am. Inst. Chemists; mem. Am. Chem. Soc., Am. Assn. Cancer Rsch., Internat. Soc. Antiviral Rsch., Radiation Rsch. Soc., Am. Soc. Pharmacology and Exptl. Therapeutics, Am. Soc. Hematology, Sigma Xi. Home: 26 Olympic Ct New Orleans LA 70131-8614 Office: Tulane U Sch Medicine Dept Pharmacology New Orleans LA 70112

AGRAWAL, SURENDRA P., accountant, educator; b. Chandausi, India, Jan. 21, 1936; came to U.S., 1969; s. Sohan and Janakdulari (Gupta) A.; m. Vijaya Gupta, Feb. 18, 1961; three children. B in Commerce, Agra U., 1954, LLB, 1956; MA, U. Fla., 1971, PhD, 1973. CPA. Asst. Price Waterhouse, Calcutta, India, 1958-66; dep. dir. rsch. Inst. Chartered Accts. India, New Delhi, 1966-69; from asst. to assoc. prof. Fla. Internat. U., Miami, 1973-77; assoc. prof. Wright State U., Dayton, Ohio, 1977-79; vis. assoc. prof. Ohio State U., Columbus, 1979-82; prof. U. Memphis, 1982—; vis. sr. fellow Nat. U. Singapore, 1991-92. Author: Advanced Financial Accounting, 1993, Introduction to Financial Accounting, 1996; contbr. articles to profl. jours. Trustee India Assn. Memphis, 1989-92. Fulbright scholar, Fort Hare U., South Africa, 1999. Fellow Inst. Chartered Accts. India; mem. AICPAs, Am. Acctg. Assn., Inst. Mgmt. Accts. Hindu. Avocations: bridge, reading, walking, golf. Home: 1272 Brookfield Rd Memphis TN 38119-5012

AGRE, JAMES COURTLAND, physical medicine and rehabilitation educator; b. Northfield, Minn., May 2, 1950; s. Courtland Leverne and Ellen Violet (Swedberg) A.; m. Patti Dee Soderberg, Aug. 6, 1982. MD, U. Minn., 1976, PhD, 1985. Diplomate Nat. Bd. Med. Examiners; bd. cert. Am. Acad. Phys. Medicine and Rehab. Rsch. fellow dept. phys. medicine and rehab. U. Minn., Mpls., 1979-80, instr. dept. phys. medicine and rehab., 1980-84; asst. prof. dept. phys. medicine and rehab. U. Wis., Madison, 1984-90, assoc. prof. dept. rehab. medicine, 1990-93, chmn. dept. rehab. medicine, 1991-97, prof. dept. rehab. medicine, 1993-97; practitioner in svc. Howard Young Med. Ctr., Woodruff, Wis., 1997—. Mem. editorial bd. and contbr. articles to Archives of Phys. Medicine and Rehab. Ski coord. Wis. Ski for Light, Madison, 1985-95. Fellow Am. Acad. Phys. Medicine and Rehab. (Elizabeth and Sidney Licht award 1989, Excellence in Sci. Writing award 1990), Am. Coll. Sports Medicine (New Investigator award 1991); mem. Assn. Acad. Physiatrists. Office: Howard Young Med Ctr PO Box 470 Woodruff WI 54568-0470*

AGREEN, LINDA KERR, secondary eduacation educator; b. Washington, Aug. 29, 1949; d. Elton Clare and Barbara Ann (Wilson) Kerr; m. Russell Warren Agreen, June 26, 1971. BS, U. Md., 1971, MEd, 1974. Cert. secondary math. tchr., Md. Tchr. Marley Jr. H.S., Glen Burnie, Md., 1971-75, DuVal H.S., Seabrook, Md., 1975-76; math. tchr. coord. Eleanor Roosevelt H.S., Greenbelt, Md., 1976-96; coach math. team, Greenbelt, 1975-98; team leader Sch. Based Supervision Team, Greenbelt, 1976-98; mem., chmn. Faculty Adv. Com., Greenbelt, 1976-98; math. tchr. Queen Anne's County H.S., Centreville, Md., 1996-98; math. coord. Kent Island H.S., Stevensville, Md., 1998—, NHS advisor, 1998—. Choir mem. Unitd Bapt. Ch., New Carrollton, Md., 1988-98; choir, Sunday Sch. tchr., supt. Trinity Bapt. Ch., Adelphi, Md., 1966-88. Named Agnes Meyer Outstanding Tchr., Washington Post, 1984, Outstanding Educator, Cornell U., Ithaca, N.Y., 1990; recipient Presidential award NSF, Washington, 1990. Mem. Nat. Coun. Tchrs. Math. (publicity com.), ASCD, Math. Assn. Am., NEA, Md. Coun. Tchrs. Math. (local arrangements chair competitions com. 1989), Md. Assn. Tchr. Educators, Prince George's County Educators Assn., Queen Anne's County Educators Assn. Democrat. Avocations: needlepoint, golf, skiing, reading, music. Office: Kent Island HS 900 Love Point Rd Stevensville MD 21666

AGRES, THEODORE JOEL, editor; b. Chgo., July 6, 1949; s. Morris A. and Lee (Frank) A.; m. Rosetta Maria Agres, Aug. 22, 1982; children: Jason Maxwell, Michael Antonio. BA, U. Chgo., 1971; MS with honors, Johns Hopkins U., 1993. Asst. editor R & D Mag., Chgo., 1973-75; features editor The News World, N.Y.C., 1976-78, news editor, 1978-79; Washington Bur. chief The News World, 1979-82; asst. mng. editor The Washington Times, 1982-97, dep. mng. editor, 1997—. Contbg. editor R & D Mag., 1990—; contbr. articles to profl. jours. Recipient Edward J. Stegnan CPA Meml. award Johns Hopkins U., 1993. Mem. Soc. Profl. Journalists (pres. Washington chpt. 1985-86), Investigative Reporters and Editors, Nat. Assn. Sci. Writers, Newspaper Assn. Am. Unificationist. Avocations: classical music, amateur radio operator. Office: The Washington Times 3600 New York Ave NE Washington DC 20002-1996

AGRESTO, JOHN, college president. AB in Polit. Sci/History magna cum laude, Bost. Coll.; PhD in Govt., Cornell U., 1974; LHD (hon.), Kenyon Coll., 1989. Vis. lectr. U. Toronto, 1971-72; asst. prof. Kenyon Coll., Gambier, Ohio, 1972-78; projects dir. Nat. Humanities Ctr., Triangle Park, N.C., 1979-82; asst. chmn. NEH, Washington, 1982-85, acting chmn., 1985-86, dep. chmn., 1985-89; pres. St. John's Coll., Santa Fe, 1989—; vis. assoc. prof. Duke U., Durham N.C.; mem. faculty New Sch. for Social Rsch., N.Y.C., 1988-89; pres. Madison Ctr., Washington, 1989. Author: The Supreme Court and Constitutional Democracy, 1984; editor, contbr. Liberty and Equality Under the Constitution, 1983; editor (with Peter Riesenberg) The Humanist as Citizen: Essays on the Uses of the Humanities, 1982; contbr. numerous articles to profl. jours.; speaker, panelist in field. Trustee Pontifical Coll. Josephinum; former mem. Ind. Commn. Arts; former mem. Columbian Quincentenary Commn. Nat. Humanities Ctr. fellow, 1978-79. Mem. Am. Polit. Sci. Assn., Nat. Assn. Scholars, Sons of Italy in Am., Am. Acad. Liberal Edn. (founding chmn.). Home: 1040 Camino San Acacio Santa Fe NM 87501-5955 Office: St John's College 1160 Camino Cruz Blanca Santa Fe NM 87501-4599*

AGRICOLA, DIANNE G., secondary education educator, tutor; b. Portsmouth, Va.; d. James H. and Vermelle E. (Pinnix) Griffin; m. William Edward Agricola, Apr. 19, 1975; 1 child, William Edward Jr. AA, Chowan Coll., 1974; BA in Journalism, U. S.C., 1982; BA in English, Christopher Newport U., 1988. Cert. English, journalism educator. Asst. acct. Va. Nat. Bank, Norfolk, 1970-75; mortgage loan assoc. Bank of Va., Richmond, 1976, VNB Mortgage Corp., Richmond, Va., 1975; legal sec. Wilmeth & DeLoach, Hartsville, S.C., 1976-80; reporter Tidewater News, Franklin, Va., 1984; subs. tchr. Franklin Schs., 1984-85, Southampton County Schs., Courtland, Va., 1985-86; summer sch. tchr. Franklin H.S., 1988; tchr. English and journalism Greensville County H.S., Emporia, Va., 1988-98; tchr. English, Hunt-Mapp Mid. Sch., Portsmouth, Va., 1998—. Mem. Journalism Educators Assn., Chowan Coll. Alumni Assn. (v.p. 1989-94, pres. 1995), Christopher Newport U. Edn. Found. Alumni Assn., Sigma Tau Delta, Alpha Epsilon Rho, Beta Sigma Phi. Methodist. Avocations: reading, bowling, swimming, home decorating and design, shopping. Home: 18553 Lakeside Dr Courtland VA 23837-2631 Office: Hunt-Mapp Middle School 3701 Willett Dr Portsmouth VA 23707-1201

AGRIOS, GEORGE NICHOLAS, plant pathology educator; b. Galarinos, Halkidiki, Greece, Jan. 16, 1936; s. Nicholas and Olga (Kotsioudi) A.; m. Annette Braynard, Nov. 11, 1962; children: Nicholas, Anthony, Alexander. BS in Horticulture, U. Thessaloniki, Greece, 1957; PhD in Plant Pathology, Iowa State U., 1960. Prof. plant pathology U. Mass., Amherst, 1963-88; prof., chmn. plant pathology dept. U. Fla., 1988—. Author: Plant Pathology, 1969, 2d edit., 1978, 3d edit., 1988, 4th edit., 1997; contbr. articles to profl. jours.; editor-in-chief APS Press Books, 1984-87. Served to 2d lt. Engring. Corps, Greek Army, 1961-62. Fellow Am. Phytopathol. Soc.; mem. AAAS, Can. Phytopathol. Soc., Am. Phytopathological Soc. (v.p., pres.-elect, pres., 1988-91). Greek Orthodox. Avocations: reading; outdoor activities.

AGRUSS, NEIL STUART, cardiologist; b. Chgo., June 2, 1939; s. Meyer and Frances (Spector) A.; B.S., U. Ill., 1960, M.D., 1963; children—David, Lauren, Michael, Joshua, Susan. Intern, U. Ill. Hosp., Chgo., 1963-64, resident in internal medicine, 1964-65, 67-68; fellow in cardiology, Cin. Gen. Hosp., 1968-70, dir. coronary care unit, 1971-74, dir. echocardiography lab., 1972-74; dir. cardiac diagnostic labs., Central DuPage Hosp., Winfield, Ill., 1974—; asst. prof. medicine, U. Cin., 1970-74, Rush Med. Coll., 1976—. Chmn. coronary care com. Heart Assn. DuPage County, 1974-76; active Congregation Beth Shalom, Naperville, Ill. Served to capt. M.C. U.S. Army, 1965-67. Diplomate Am. Bd. Internal Medicine. Fellow ACP, Am. Coll. Cardiology, Am. Coll. Chest Physicians, Council Clin. Cardiology, Am. Heart Assn.; mem. AMA, DuPage County, Ill. State Med. Socs., Am. Fedn. Clin. Research, Chgo. Heart Assn. Author and co-author publs. in field. Office: 454 Pennsylvania Ave Glen Ellyn IL 60137-4418

AGUAYO, ALBERT JUAN, neuroscientist. MD, U. Cordoba, Argentina, 1959; Dr. Honoris Causa, U. Lund, Sweden. Cert. specialist in neurology, Que., cert. EEG specialist, Que. Intern Port Arthur Gen. Hosp., 1960-61; resident in neurology Toronto Gen. Hosp., 1961-62, resident in medicine, 1962-63; resident in neurology Montreal Gen. Hosp., 1964-65; prof. neurology and physiology McGill U., 1977—; prof. medicine McGill U. and Montreal Gen. Hosp. Rsch. Inst., 1976—, asst. dept. physiology, 1981—, dir. Ctr. for Rsch. in Neurosci., 1985—; dir. Can. Network of Ctrs. of Excellence for the study of Neural Regeneration; mem. sci. adv. bds. and coms. including Med. Rsch. Can., Howard Hughes Med. Inst., Am. Paraplegic Assn., Ipsen Found., Max Planck Inst., Munich, Germany, Friedrich Miescher-Inst., Basle, Switzerland. Co-editor Current Opinion in Neurobiology; mem. editorial bd. European Jour. Neurosci., Experimental Brain Rsch., Brain Rsch., Synapse, Jour. of Neural Transplantation, Jour. of Chemical Transplantation, Jour. Neurobiology; mem. adv. bd. Neuroscis. Rsch.; mem. internat. adv. bd. NeuroReport. Decorated Order of Can.; recipient Gairdner Found. Internat. award, Ipsen award on Neural Plasticity, WH Helmerich III award for Outstanding Achievement in retina rsch., Leo Parizeau Prize in Biology Assn. Canadienne-Française pour l'Avancement des Sciences, 1993; rsch. fellow Banting Inst., U. Toronto, 1963-64, Montreal Gen. Hosp., 1965-66, traveling fellow McLaughlin Found., 1966-67. Fellow Royal Soc. Can.; mem. Inst. Medicine of the NAS (U.S), N-Am. Soc. for Neurosci. (pres.), Can. Neurol. Sco. (pres.), Can. Assn. of Neuroscientists (pres.), Third World Congress of the Internat. Brain Rsch. Orgn. (pres.). Office: Ctr Rsch in Neurosci, 1650 Cedar Ave, Montreal, PQ Canada H3G 1A4*

AGUIAR, ADAM MARTIN, chemist, educator; b. Newark, Aug. 11, 1929; s. Joaquim Ramahlo and Emilea Andrada (Nunes) A.; m. Laura E. Brand, Sept. 2, 1980; children: Justine Diane, David Laurence, Adam Albert, Erick Arthur, Aaron Benjamin, Evan Joaquim. BS, Fairleigh Dickinson U., 1955; MA, Columbia U., 1957, PhD, 1960. Chemist Otto B. May, Newark, 1948-55; asst. prof. Fairleigh Dickinson U., Rutherford, N.J., 1959-63; asst. prof. chemistry Tulane U., New Orleans, 1963-65, assoc. prof., 1965-67, prof., 1967-72, head dept. chemistry Newcomb Coll. div., 1970; dean grad. and research programs William Paterson Coll., Wayne, N.J., 1972-73; research prof. Rutgers U., Newark, 1973-75; prof. chemistry Fairleigh Dickinson U., Madison, N.J., 1975-93, chmn. dept. chemistry/geol. scis., 1984-89; pres. Seltox Corp., N.J., 1980—; adj. prof. chemistry Monmouth U., West Long Branch, N.J., 1993—; cons. chem. firms in La. and N.J. Contbr. articles to profl. jours. Union Carbide fellow, 1957; NIH fellow, 1959; recipient other grants. Mem. AAUP, Am. Chem. Soc., AAAS, N.Y. Acad. Sci., Ctr. for Profl. Advancement, Sigma Xi, Phi Lambda Epsilon, Phi Omega Epsilon. Home: 37 Wyncrest Ln Neptune NJ 07753-7421

AGUIAR, SARAH APPLETON, English language educator, writer; b. Providence, Oct. 11, 1957; d. Daniel Day Appleton and Janice Gardner Normand; m. Jesse J. Aguiar, Nov. 29, 1980; children: Sam, Jillian. BA, R.I. Coll., 1989; MA, U. R.I., 1991; PhD, U. Conn., 1995. Asst. prof. English Murray (Ky.) State U., 1995—. Contbr. articles to profl. jours. E-mail: sarah.aguiar@murraystate.edu. Office: Murray State U Dept English Murray KY 42071

AGUILAR, JULIA ELIZABETH, real estate associate, writer; b. Organal, Mex., Feb. 16, 1943; came to U.S., 1965; d. Felix and Leticia (Rodriguez) Vergara; m. Aaron Aguilar, Feb. 1, 1964; children: Juan Antonio, Elizabeth, Alex. Grad., San Fernando (Calif.) Adult Sch., 1980; Real Estate Assoc., Anthony Real Estate Sch., Sepulveda, Calif., 1985. Real estate assoc. ERA Rocking Horse Realty, San Fernando, 1986-98; owner Home Sweet Home Realty, San Fernando, 1998—. Author poetry, cooking recipes, song lyrics, 1996, Musical Poetry, 1997. Democrat. Roman Catholic. Avocations: writing, gardening, knitting. Home: 626 Newton St San Fernando CA 91340-2107 Office: Home Sweet Home Realty 563 S Brand Blvd San Fernando CA 91340

AGUILAR, MELISSA WARD, newspaper editor; b. Houston, Mar. 30, 1960; d. Darrell Nielsen and Afton (Hall) Ward; children: Tessa Nicole, Dylan Michael. BS in Journalism, U. Tex., 1982. Fact checker Tex. Monthly Press, Austin, 1982; copy editor Houston Chronicle, 1982-83, weekend preview editor, 1983-86, entertainment editor, 1986—. Active Girl Scouts U.S.A. Mem. Am. Assn. Sunday and Features Editors, Soc. Newspaper Design, Am. Press Inst. Avocations: photography, running. Office: Houston Chronicle PO Box 4260 Houston TX 77210-4260*

AGUILAR-BRYAN, LYDIA, medical educator, medical researcher; b. Mexico City, Feb. 25, 1951; m. Joseph Bryan; 1 child. MD, U. Nacional Autonoma de Mex., 1975; PhD in Population Studies, U. Tex., 1985. Rsch. assoc. Inst. Biomed. Rsch., U. Nacional Autonoma de Mex., Mexico City, 1985-86; rsch. assoc. Baylor Coll. of Medicine, Dept. of Medicine, Divsn. of Endocrinology, Houston, 1987-88, postdoctoral fellow, 1988-90, instr., 1990-91, asst. prof., 1991—. Contbr. articles to profl. jours. Postdoctoral fellow Juvenile Diabetes Found., 1988-90. Mem. AAAS, Am. Diabetes Assn. (Rsch. grantee 1995—), Biophys. Soc., Endocrine Soc. Office: Baylor Coll of Medicine Divsn Endocrinology 1 Baylor Plz Rm 537E Houston TX 77030-3411*

AGUILERA, DONNA CONANT, psychologist, researcher; b. Kinmundy, Ill.; d. Charles E. and Daisy L. (Frost) Conant; m. George Limon Aguilera; children: Bruce Allen, Craig Steven. B.S., UCLA, 1963, M.S., 1965; Ph.D., U. So. Calif., 1974. Teaching asst. UCLA, 1965, grad. rsch. asst., 1965-66; prof. Calif. State U., L.A., 1966-81; cons. crisis intervention Didi Hirsch Community Mental Health Ctr., L.A., 1967-82; mem. Def. Adv. Com. Women in the Services, 1978-82; originator, project dir. Project Link Lab. U. Author: Crisis Intervention: Theory and Methodology, 1974, 8th edit., 1998 (pub. in 14 langs., braille and tapes), Review of Psychiatric Nursing, 1977, 7th edit., 1978, Crisis Intervention: Therapy for Psychological Emergencies, 1983; contbr. articles to profl. jours. Docent Huntington Libr. San Marino, Calif. 1991—; mem., mgr. disaster mental health svcs. ARC. NIH fellow, 1972-75. Fellow Am. Acad. Nursing (sec. 1976-77, pres. 1977-78), Acad. Psychiat. Nurse Specialists, Internat. Acad. Eclectic Psychotherapists (pres. 1987-89); mem. Am. Nurses Assn., Faculty Women's Assn., Am. Psychol. Assn., Calif. Psychol. Assn., AAUP, Alpha Tau Delta, Sigma Theta Tau. Home: 3924 Dixie Canyon Ave Sherman Oaks CA 91423-4830 Office: 450 N Bedford Dr Ste 210 Beverly Hills CA 90210-4306

AGUILERA, RICHARD WARREN (RICK AGUILERA), baseball player; b. San Gabriel, Calif., Dec. 31, 1961. Student, Brigham Young U. Pitcher N.Y. Mets, 1985-89, Minn. Twins, 1989-95, 96—, Boston Red Sox, 1995; player Am. League All-Star Game, 1991-93. Ranked 2nd in Am. League in saves, 1992. Office: Minn Twins 34 Kirby Puckett Pl Minneapolis MN 55415-1596*

AGUINSKY, RICHARD DANIEL, software and electronics engineer; b. Buenos Aires, Dec. 26, 1958; s. Elias Lorenzo and Rosa Isabel (Grille) A.; m. Adriana Faiman. Electronics Engr., U. Técnica Nacional, Avellaneda, Buenos Aires, 1984; MSEE, San Jose State U., 1991. Serial prodn. technician Norman S.A., Buenos Aires, 1978-80; electronics lab. technician U. Técnologica Nacional, Avellaneda, Buenos Aires, 1980-84; instr. digital technics, 1985; project engr. No. Telecom, Santa Clara, Calif., 1986—; mentor adelante program San Jose City Coll. Contbr. articles to Revista Telegrafica Electronica, No. Telecom., Am. Nat. Std. Telecomms. Avocations: travel, camping, windsurfing, skiing, sky diving. Office: Nortel Networks 2305 Mission College Blvd Santa Clara CA 95054-1521

AGUIRRE, PAMELA A., manufacturing executive; d. Hank A.; 3 children. CEO, chmn. bd. Mexican Industries, Detroit, 1994—. Bd. mem. Small Bus. Assn., 1996. Recipient Hispanic Bus. Alliance award, 1996; Mem. Econ. Club of Detroit, (bd. dirs.), Mich. Minority Bus. Devel. Coun., (bd. dirs.), U.S. Hispanic C. of C., (bd. dirs.), Hank Aguire Cancer Awareness Found., (bd. dirs.), the Chidren's Ctr., (bd. dirs.) and numerous others. Fax: 313-963-6217. Officd: Mexican Industries Aguirre Plaza 1801 Howard St Detroit MI 48216-1920

AGUIRRE, VUKOSLAV ENEAS, environmental engineer; b. Santiago, Chile, Nov. 2, 1941; came to U.S., 1960; s. Eneas and Tonka (Domic) A.; m. Emma Jeannette Bendana, Nov. 15, 1970; children: Sergio Eneas, Tonka Lily. BS, U. S. Mil. Acad., 1964; MS, U. Ill., 1965, postgrad., 1966-67. Registered profl. engr. Pa., Va., Md., Mich., D.C., Colo., Ill., Utah, Wyo., Ariz., N.Mex. Project engr. Ackenheil Assocs., Pitts., 1965-69; soils specialist Harza Internat., Chgo., 1969-70; project mgr. Law Engring. Testing, Washington, 1971-74; pres. Colo. Testing Lab., Denver, 1974-75, Geotek Inc., Denver, 1974-77; pres., owner Aguirre Engrs. Inc., Englewood, Colo., 1977—. Mem. Internat. Soc. Soil Mechanics and Found. Engring., Internat. Soc. Soil Mechanics, ASCE, Assn. Soil and Found. Engrs., Colo. Cons. Engrs. Council. Roman Catholic. Avocation: skiing. Office: Aguirre Engrs Inc PO Box 3814 Englewood CO 80155-3814*

AGUIRRE-BACA, FRANCISCO, publisher; b. León, Nicaragua, Jan. 7, 1920; came to U.S., 1947; s. Horacio and Pilar (Baca) Aguirre-Muñoz; m. Gladys Sacasa Aguirre, Dec. 27, 1941; children: Gladys, Francisco Xavier, Mariangeles, Rafael Eugenio, Guiomar, Alejandra. Co-pub. Diario Las Americas, Miami, Fla.; internam. cons. Ambassador Extraordinary and Pleinpotenciary of Nicaragua in Spl. Missions. Republican. Roman Catholic. Home: 4951 Rockwood Pkwy NW Washington DC 20016-3247

AGUIRRE-BATTY, MERCEDES, Spanish and English language and literature educator; b. Cd Juarez, Mex., Dec. 20, 1952; came to U.S., 1957.; d. Alejandro M. and Mercedes (Péon) Aguirre; m. Hugh K. Batty, Mar. 17, 1979; 1 child, Henry B. BA, U. Tex., El Paso, 1974, MA, 1977. Cert. online tchr., Calif. Instr. ESL Paso del Norte- Prep Sch., Cd Juarez, 1973-74; tchg. asst. ESL and English U. Tex., El Paso, 1974-77; instr. ESL English Lang. Svcs., Bridgeport, Conn., 1977-80; instr. Spanish and English, coord. modern lang. Sheridan (Wyo.) Coll., 1980—, pres. faculty senate, 1989-90; pres. faculty senate, chair dist. coun. No. Wyo. C.C. Dist., 1995-96; mem. planning com. No. Wyo. C.C. Dist., 1996-97; mem. advanced placement faculty Spanish cons. Coll. Bd. Ednl. Testing Svc., 1996-99; adj. prof. Spanish, U. Autonoma Cd Juarez, 1975; adj. prof. Spanish and English, Sacred Heart U., Fairfield, Conn., 1977-80; spkr. in field. Bd. dirs. Wyo. Coun. for the Humanities, 1988-92; translator county and dist. cts., Sheridan; vol. Wmen's Ctr.; translator Sheridan County Meml. Hosp.; del. Citizen Ambassador Program, People to People-India, 1996. NEH fellow, 1991, 92; Wyo. State Dept. Edn. grantee, 1991. Mem. MLA (del. assembly 1998—), Wyo. Fgn. Lang. Tchrs. Assn. (pres. 1990-92), Am. Assn. Tchrs. Spanish and Portuguese (founder, 1st pres. Wyo. chpt. 1987-90), TESOL, Sigma Delta Mu (v.p. 1992—), Sigma Delta Pi (pres. 1974-75). Avocations: traveling, reading, archeology, languages, geography. Office: Sheridan Coll NWCCD 3059 Coffeen Ave Sheridan WY 82801-9133

AGUIRRE-SACASA, FRANCISCO XAVIER, international banker, diplomat; b. Managua, Nicaragua, Sept. 4, 1944; s. Francisco and Gladys (Sacasa) A.; m. Maria de los Angeles, Oct. 6, 1968; children: Rafael Ignacio, Roberto Francisco, Georgiana Eugenia. BS in Fgn. Svc., Georgetown U., 1966; JD, Harvard U., 1969. Contributing writer Christian Sci. Monitor, Boston Herald Traveler, Boston Globe, Wall Street Jour., 1968—; young profl. and loan officer The World Bank, Washington, 1969-76, div. chief, 1977-86, asst. dir., 1986-87, sr. ops. advisor, 1987-88, dir., external affairs, 1988-90, dir. Africa region, 1990-95, dir. ops. evalutation dept., 1995-97; ambassador to U.S. govt. Nicaragua, Washington, 1997—. OAS scholar Harvard U., 1966-68. Mem. Nat. Press Club, Congl. Country Club (Bethesda, Md.), Harvard Club of Washington, Univ. Club (Washington). Roman Catholic. Avocations: carpentry, golf, farming. Home: 4739 Tilden St NW Washington DC 20016-2327 also: Valhalla Farm 11302 Obannons Mill Rd Boston VA 22713-4132 Office: Embassy of Nicaragua 1627 New Hampshire Ave NW Washington DC 20009-2573*

AGUIRRE-SACASA, RAFAEL EUGENIO, marketing executive; b. Washington, Dec. 31, 1951; s. Francisco and Gladys (Sacasa) A.; m. Patricia Duque Estrada, July 9, 1976; children: Javier Eugenio, Francisco Eduardo. BS in Fgn. Svc., Georgetown U., 1973; grad., Air Command and Staff Coll., 1983. With U.S. Air Force, 1973-83; dir. internat. sales P. Beretta SpA, Washington, 1983-87; dir. govt. rels. Beretta USA Corp., Washington, 1986-87; dir. mktg. Beretta USA Corp., Accokeek, Md., 1987-98; exec. v.p. Inter Internat., Washington, 1998—; spl. advisor for internat. polit. and mil. affairs to Fgn. Minister of Nicaragua. Mem. OAS Presidential Electoral Com., Ecuador, 1969, Pan-Am. Devel. Found. Emergency Earthquake Relief Team, Managua, Nicaragua, 1972; vice chmn. Rep. Nat. Hispanic Assembly, Washington, 1983.; bd. dirs. Am. Firearms Coun., 1994-98, Nat. Shooting Sports Found. Mktg. Coun., 1996-98; spl. advisor Fgn. Min. Internat. Polit. & Mil. Affairs, 1997—. Maj. USAF, 1973-83. Decorated Air Force Commendation with oak leaf cluster, Meritorious Svc. medal with oak leaf cluster; ROTC scholar Georgetown U., 1971-73. Mem. Am. Mktg. Assn., Congl. Country Club, Army-Navy Club. Roman Catholic. Avocations: reading, jogging, hunting. Home: 7900 Greentree Rd Bethesda MD 20817-1302 Office: Inter Internat 4835 Yuma St NW Washington DC 20016-2061

AGUS, ZALMAN S., physician, educator; b. Chgo., Apr. 3, 1941; s. Jacob B. and Miriam (Shore) A.; m. Sondra L. Lebow, June 26, 1963; children: David, Joel, Michael. BA, Johns Hopkins U., 1961; MD, U. Md., 1965; MA (hon., U. Pa., 1979. Diplomate Am. Bd. Internal Medicine, Am. Bd. Nephrology. Resident med. sch. U. Md., Balt., 1965-68; fellow nephrology U. Pa. Hosp., Phila., 1968-71, asst. prof., 1973-79, assoc. prof., 1979-86, chief renal sect., 1979-88, prof., 1986—. Contbr. over 100 articles to profl. jours. Chmn. bd. dirs. Harry B. Kellman Acad., Cherry Hil, N.J., 1981-83; bd. dirs. Congragation Beth El, Cherry Hill, 1978—; chmn. bd. Solomon Schecter Day Sch., San Antonio, 1972-73. Served to maj. USAF, 1971-73. Recipient Clin. Investigator award VA, 1973-76, Research Career Devel. award NIH, 1977-82. Fellow ACP; mem. Am. Heart Assn. (exec. com. coun. on the kidney 1984—, chmn. 1990-92), Am. Soc. for Clin. Investigation, Nat. Kidney Found. (regional v.p. 1987-89, Disting. Svc. award 1985). Democrat. Jewish. Office: Va Med Ctr Med Svc University and Woodland Ave Philadelphia PA 19104

AHALT, MARY JANE, management consultant; b. Elizabethville, Pa., Oct. 11, 1914; d. George Lewis and Grace Eva (Cooper) Zeigler; m. Arthur Montraville Ahalt, Mar. 29, 1935 (dec. Sept. 1958); children: Mary Jane Ahalt Barker, Arthur Montraville Monty. Student, U. Md., 1949-51, 63-65. Relief tchr., dir. Calvert Nursery Sch., Riverdale, Md., 1943-45; off-campus housemother U. Md., College Park, 1939-93, typist, 1951-58; prin. stenographer U. Md. Coll. Agr., College Park, 1958-59; sec. I, III, and IV U. Md. Coll. Edn., College Park, 1959-78; sec. to dean U. Md., College Park, 1960-76; sec., bookkeeper Entomology Soc. Am., College Park & Washington, 1951-53; cons. office practice and mgmt. College Park, 1978—; panel mem. College Park Bus. and Profl. Women, St. Louis, 1994, College Park, 1995; cons. Project Return, Prince George's County Mental Health Assn., 1970-72. Historian archivist History of Maryland Business and Professional Women, 1983-86; co-prodr. cable TV program Women's Changing Roles: Finding a Balance, 1991. Sec. coun. Hope Luth. Ch., College Park, 1956-61, 69-74, pres. Luth. Ch. Women, 1952, 74, 87, mem. adv. bd. dist. bd., 1975-87; mem. Prince George's County Internat. Women's Task Force, 1974-76; mem. aux. Nat. Luth. Home for Aged, 1960-98; asst. leader Jr. H.S. Girl Scout troop, 1951-54; co-chair publicity com. Prince George's County Internat. Women's Yr. Task Force, 1974-76, mem. recognition of woman of month com., 1974-76; mem. by-laws com. Women's Action Coalition of Prince George's County, 1976-77; chair parish-staff rels. com. Hope Luth. Ch., 1988; judge Most Beautiful Youth, Prince George's County; coord. archives com. Charlestown Cmty. Inc., 1998—. Named Prince Georgian of Yr., Prince George County Citizens, 1989, Womanof Hist. Note Prince George County Bus. and Profl. Women, 1988, Woman of Achievement in Prince George's County History, 1994; named to Women's Hall of Fame, Prince George's County, Commn. for Women, 1990; recipient Beautification award Com. for a Better Environ., College Park, 1990. Mem. College Park Bus. and Profl. Women (charter, historian, archivist 1964-93, mem. Cable TV 1983-89, 89—, pres. 1966-68, Woman of Yr. award 1976), Md. Fedn. Bus. and Profl. Women's Clubs (bd. mem. 1967—, pres. 1973-74, BPW Woman of Yr. award 1976), Nat. Fedn. Bus. and Profl. Women's Clubs (nat. bd. 1973-74, founder career advancement scholar com. 1975-76). Avocations: landscaping, sewing, reading, card games, volunteering. Home: 717 Maiden Choice Ln Apt St215 Catonsville MD 21228-6137

AHARONOV, YAKIR, physicist, educator; b. Haifa, Israel, July 28, 1932. BS, Technion U., 1956, Dr, 1992; PhD, Bristol U., 1960; DSc, U. S.C., 1993. Rsch. assoc. Brandeis U., 1960-61; from asst. prof. to prof. Yesiva U., 1964-73; Miller prof. U. Calif., Berkeley, 1988-90; prof. Tel Aviv U., 1967—, U. S.C., 1973—; vis. prof. Boston U., 1991-92. Recipient Weizmann prize, 1984, Rothschild prize, 1984, Nat. Physics prize, Israel, 1989. Fellow Am. Physics Soc.; mem. Nat. Acad. Sci., Nat. Acad. Sci. Israel. *

AHART, ALAN M., bankruptcy judge; b. 1949. AB, U. Calif., Berkeley, 1970; JD, SUNY, 1975; LLM, U. Pa., 1979. Judge U.S. Bankrupty Ct. Cen. Dist. Calif., L.A., 1988—. Contbr. articles to profl. jours. Office: US Bankruptcy Ct Calif Edward R Roybal Bldg 255 E Temple St Ste 1382 Los Angeles CA 90012-3334

AHART, JAN FREDRICK, electrical manufacturing company executive; b. U.S.A., May 13, 1941; s. Frank Lyle and Deloris Ruth (Solum) A.; m.

Patricia Louise Heffner, Sept. 1, 1962 (dec. July 1997); children—Erik Christopher, Wendy Kristine. B.B.A., Tex. A&M U., 1962; M.B.A., Harvard U., 1971. Bar: C.P.A., Va., Tex. Comml. auditor Arthur Andersen & Co., Houston, 1962-66; asst. controller Esso Standard Eastern (Far East), Tokyo, 1966-69; asst. v.p. Reynolds Metals Co., Richmond, Va., 1971-79; treas. Raymond Internat., Inc., Houston, 1979-83; v.p., treas. Datapoint Corp., San Antonio, 1983-86; pres. Penta*Med Group, Inc. (formerly Med-Call, Inc.), Comfort, Tex., 1986-89; v.p., chief fin. officer, sec.-treas. Powell Industries, Inc., Houston, 1989—, also bd. dirs. Mem. editorial bd. Va. Acct., 1976-79. Served to capt., inf. AUS, 1963-65. Mem. Am. Inst. CPAs, Tex. CPAs. Home: 1002 Leslie Ln Friendswood TX 77546-4841 Office: Powell Industries Inc PO Box 12818 8550 Mosley Rd Houston TX 77075-1116*

AHEARN, JAMES, newspaper columnist; b. S. Bend, Ind., Dec. 26, 1931; s. Francis T. and Loretto (Lorden) A.; m. Mary Ann Boesch, June 7, 1954; children—Michael James, Mary Elizabeth, Sarah Katharine, Margaret Ann. B.A., Amherst Coll., 1953; Nieman fellow, Harvard U., 1970-71. Reporter UPI, Boston, Newark and Trenton, N.J., 1957-61; state house corr. The Record, Hackensack, N.J., 1961-65; editorial writer, then editor editorial page The Record, 1965-77, mng. editor, 1977-87, assoc. editor, 1987-91, contbg. editor, 1993—. Served with USNR, 1953-57. Office: 150 River St Hackensack NJ 07601-7110

AHEARN, JOHN FRANCIS, JR., retired oil and gas company executive; b. Waterbury, Conn., May 19, 1921; s. John Francis and Anna Elizabeth (Kane) A.; m. Mary Louise Gardner, Jan. 7, 1956 (dec. Aug. 1985); m. Margaret Bloch Bagby, Feb. 23, 1991. A.B., Brown U., 1944; M.B.A., Stanford U., 1955. Mgr. agrl. mktg. Kern County Land Co., Bakersfield, Calif., 1955-62; mgr. corp. planning Kern County Land Co., San Francisco, 1962-65; dir. corp. planning J.I. Case, Racine, Wis., 1965-67, Kern County Land Co., 1968; v.p. corp. planning Sonat Inc., Birmingham, Ala., 1968-82, sr. v.p. corp. planning, 1982-85. Served to lt. USNR, 1944-46, 50-53. Republican. Roman Catholic. Clubs: Mountain Brook (Ala.); Shoal Creek (Ala.). Avocations: traveling, tennis; trout fishing; walking. Home: Eagle View Shoal Creek AL 35242

AHEARNE, DOUGLAS, state legislator; b. Aug. 25, 1968; s. Daniel Paul and Germaine (Sirois) A. BA, Worcester State Coll., 1990. Rep. dist. 149 Maine Ho. Reps., 1993, rep. dist. 150, 1994—; chmn. state and local govt. com. Maine House Rep. Mem. Rotary, K. of C. Office: House of Reps State House Augusta ME 04330

AHEARNE, JOHN FRANCIS, scientific research administrator, researcher; b. New Britain, Conn., June 14, 1934; s. Daniel Paul and Balbena Marian (Baloski) A.; m. Barbara Helen Drezek, June 19, 1956; children: Thomas, Paul, Mary Ann, Robert, Patricia. B of Engring. Physics, Cornell U., 1957, MS in Physics, 1958; MA, Princeton U., 1963, PhD, 1966. Nuclear weapons analyst USAF, 1959-61; assoc. prof. physics USAF Acad., 1964-69; from analyst to dir. tactical air Office Asst. Sec. Def. for Systems Analysis, 1969-72; dep. asst. sec. def. for gen. purpose programs, 1972-74, prin. dep. sec. def. manpower and res. affairs, 1974-76; staff White House Energy Office, 1977; dep. asst. sec. Dept. Energy, 1978; commr. U.S. Nuclear Regulatory Commn., 1978-83, chmn., 1980-81; mgmt. cons. Comptr. Gen of U.S., 1983-84; v.p., sr. fellow Resources for the Future, 1984-89; exec. dir. Sigma Xi, The Sci. Rsch. Soc., Research Triangle Park, N.C., 1989-96; dir. Sigma Xi Ctr., 1995—; adj. fellow Resources for the Future, 1992—; lectr. pub. policy Duke U., Durham, N.C., 1995—; adj. prof. civil and environ. engring. Duke U., 1996—; adj. prof. U. Colo., 1966-69; adj. fellow Resources for the Future, 1992—; mem. Nat. Rsch. Coun. Bd. on Radioactive Waste Mgmt., 1993—, vice-chmn. 1997—; chmn. adv. com. on nuclear facility safety U.S. Dept. Energy, 1988-91, environ. mgmt. adv. bd., 1994—, co-chmn. adv. com. on external regulation, 1995-96, nuclear rsch. adv. com., 1998—; chmn. risk perception and comm. com. NAS, 1987-89, chmn. future nuclear power com., 1990-93, com. on tech. bases for Yucca Mountain Stds., 1993-96, com. on risk characterization, 1994-97, dual use techs. and export controls com., electrometallurg. tech. com., co-chmn. forum on the environment, 1995-97, vice-chmn. com. risk assessment and mgmt. marine sys., 1996-98, com. on battlefield radiation exposure, 1996—, chmn. com. to rev. rsch. under EPACT, 1997—; mem. pres.'s coun. for nat. labs. U. Calif., 1992—; vice-chmn. U.S. Commn. for IIASA, 1992-93, chmn., 1994-98; adv. coun. Princeton Plasma Physics Nat. Lab., 1993-98; co-chmn. NAS Panel on Opportunities in Plasma Sci. Tech., 1992-96; mem. NAS Reactor Panel for Disposition of Weapons Plutonium, 1992-96; bd. dirs. Wis. Energy Corp.; lectr. Colo. Coll., 1966-69; mem. pres. com. adv. S&T Energy R&D panel, 1997-98; USGAO exec. coun. Info. Mgmt. and Tech., 1997—. Bd. dirs. Woodstock Theol. Ctr., chmn., 1980-85. Gen. Electric Coffin fellow, 1957-58; recipient Dept. Def. Disting. Civilian Service medal and bronze palm, Sec. Def. Meritorious Svc. medal; named Boss of Year D.C. chpt. Nat. Secs. Assn., 1976. Fellow AAAS, Am. Phys. Soc. (chmn. forum on physics and soc. 1996-97, panel on pub. affairs), Am. Acad. Arts and Scis.; mem. Am. Nuclear Soc., Soc. for Risk Analysis, Nat. Acad. Engring., Sigma Xi. Democrat. Roman Catholic.

AHERIN, DARREL WILLIAM, lawyer; b. Colfax, Wash., July 11, 1946; s. Don Lewis and Leona Margaret (Edwards) A. m. Freda jean Kieffer, June 27, 1968 (dec.); children: Daniel Winston, Dustin Wynne; m. Michelle Rae Messley, June 26, 1982; children: Alex William. BA, Lewis Clark State Coll., 1969; JD, U. Idaho, 1973. Pvt. practice Lewiston, Idaho, 1973—; ptnr. Aherin, Rice & Anegon (formerly Aherin, Rice & Brown), Lewiston, 1973—. Active Planning & Zoning Com., Genesee, Idaho, 1996—. Mem. ATLA (gov. 1996—), Idaho Trial Lawyers Assn. (sec., treas., pres.), Western Trial Lawyers (gov. 1995—), Lewis Clark State Coll. Alumni (pres.). Home: PO Box 337 Genesee ID 83832-0337 Office: Aherin Rice & Anegon 1212 Idaho St Lewiston ID 83501-1941

AHERN, JOSEPH A., television station executive. Pres., gen. mgr. WLS-TV, Chgo. Office: WLS-TV 190 N State St Ste 1100 Chicago IL 60601-3379*

AHERN, JOSEPH A., television station executive. Pres., gen. mgr. WLS-TV, Chgo., 1996-97; sr. v.p., mng. dir. Walt Disney Internat., London, 1997-98; pres., gen. mgr. KGO-TV, San Francisco, 1998—. Office: KGO-TV 900 Front St San Francisco CA 94111*

AHERN, MAUREEN JEANNE, museum director, artist; b. Salem, Mass., Oct. 7, 1947; d. Joseph John and Marie Jeanne (Letourneau) A.; m. William J. Knorr, Nov. 11, 1977. BFA, U. Mass., 1961; MA, SUNY, Albany. Art dir. Jewish Cmty. Ctr. Boston, Brighton, Mass., 1969-70; curator Albany Inst. History and Art, 1973-81; dir. Thorne Sagendorph Art Gallery, Keene, N.H., 1981—; pres. N.H. Visual Arts Coalition, 1992-96. Trustee Mt. Caesar Union Libr., Swanzey, N.H., 1996—. Mem. Am. Assn. Museums, New ENg. Mus. Assn., Am. Craft Coun. Office: Thorne Sagendorph Art Gallery Keene State Coll Keene NH 03435-3201

AHERN, RICHARD FAVOR, state legislator; b. Concord, N.H., Aug. 21, 1912; s. William J. Jr. and Catherine (Favor) A.; m. Arlene M. Campbell, 1941 (dec. Aug. 1997); children: Richard C., Judith Fay (dec.). BS, U. N.H., 1934. Mem. N.H. Ho. of Reps., 1975-96, 99—; clk. Manchester Ward II; treas. Dem. Ward II Com., Manchester; dep. collector Bur. Internal Revenue, 1943-52, agt., 1952-71, chief rev. staff, 1971-72, ret. Mem. N.H. Sr. Golfers Assn. (pres. 1986), Derryfield Country Club, Sigma Alpha Epsilon. Address: 191 North St Manchester NH 03104-3232

AHL, ALWYNELLE SELF, zoology, ecology and veterinary medical executive; b. Leesville, La., Mar. 18, 1941; d. Clyde and Fariebee Margaret (Parker) Self; m. James Gilmore Ahl, May 29, 1963; children—Robert C., Laura J. B.S., Centenary Coll., La., 1961; M.S., U. Wyo., 1963, Ph.D., 1967; DVM, Mich. State U., 1987. Research asst. U. Wyo., 1965-67; mem. faculty Mich. State U., East Lansing, 1967—, assoc. prof. natural scis., 1971-77, prof., 1977-87; vet. ednl. specialist USDA/Animal and Plant Health Inspection Service/Vet. Svcs., 1987-89, dep. dir. recruitment and devel. for animal health and care tng., 1989-91; head risk analysis sect. USDA/Animal and Plant Health Inspection Service/Policy and Program Devel., Riverdale, Md., 1991-94; chief planning and risk sys. Riverdale, Md., 1994-95; dir. Office of Risk Assessment and Cost-Benefit analysis USDA, Washington, 1995—. Contbr. articles to profl. jours. Recipient Mich. State U. tchr. scholar award, 1971; fellow NDEA, 1961-64, NSF, 1964-65, NIH summer fellow, 1963. Fellow AAAS, Coun. Excellence in Govt.; mem. AVMA, Soc. for Risk Analysis, Soc. Tropical Vet. Medicine, Sigma Xi. Episcopalian. Home: 7001 Mayfair Rd Laurel MD 20707-5235 Office: USDA/ORACBA Ste 5248-S Stop 3811 1400 Independence Ave SW Washington DC 20250-0002

AHL, DAVID HOWARD, writer, editor; b. N.Y.C., May 17, 1939; s. G. W. Howard and Muriel (Schillinger) A.; m. Sandra June Perrott, July 14, 1962 (div. Nov. 1981); children—Detta June, Darcy Allison, Derek Howard; m. Elizabeth Baumann Staples, June 18, 1988. B.E.E., Cornell U., 1961; M.S., Carnegie-Mellon U., 1963. Cons. Mgmt. Sci. Assocs., Pitts., 1965-69; ednl. mktg. mgr. Digital Equipment Corp., Maynard, Mass., 1969-74; mktg. mgr. AT&T, Morristown, N.J., 1974-78; founder, editor-in-chief Creative Computing, Morris Plains, N.J., 1974-86; pub. Atari Explorer and Atarian mags., 1986-90; pres. SBI Cons., 1990—; pub., editor Mil. Vehicles Mag.; coordinator student fair Nat. Computer Conf., 1977; cons. U. Ala., Birmingham, 1985; speaker numerous ednl. confs. Author: Basic Computer Games, 1972; author computer programs, 20 books on ednl. and recreational use of computers, numerous articles. Served as 1st lt. U.S. Army, 1961-63. Recipient Outstanding Service award Data Processing Mgmt. Assn., 1977, Recognition award SE Asia Computer Confedn., 1978, 84, Achievement award U. Wis., 1979, Computer Pioneer award Sybex, 1984. Mem. Nat. Council Tchrs. Math., Assn. for Computing Machinery, World Future Soc. Republican. Mem. Christian Missionary Alliance. Avocations: philately; hiking. Home: 12 Indianhead Rd Morristown NJ 07960-4802

AHLEM, LLOYD HAROLD, psychologist; b. Moose Lake, Minn., Nov. 7, 1929; s. Harold Edward and Agnes (Carlson) A.; m. Anne T. Jensen, Dec. 29, 1952; children: Ted, Dan, Mary Jo, Carol, Aileen. A.A., North Park Coll., 1948; A.B., San Jose State Coll., 1952, M.A., 1955; Ed.D., U. So. Calif., 1962. Tchr. retarded children Fresno County (Calif.) Pub. Schs., 1953-54; psychologist Baldwin Park (Calif.) Sch. Dist., 1955-62; prof. psychology Calif. State U., Stanislaus (formerly Stanislaus State Coll.), Turlock, Calif., 1962-70; pres. North Park Coll., Chgo., 1970-79; dir. North Park Coll., 1966-70; exec. dir. Covenant Village Retirement Center, Turlock, 1979-89; dir. spl. projects Covenant Retirement Communities, Chgo., 1989-93; dir. Emanuel Med. Ctr., Turlock, Calif., 1984-99, Merced Mut. Ins. Co., Atwater, Calif., 1993—; chmn. Capital Corp. of West, Merced, Calif., 1995—. Author: Do I Have To Be Me, 1974, How to Cope: Managing Change, Crisis and Conflict, 1978, Help for the Families of the Mentally Ill, 1983, Living and Growing in Later Years, 1992; columnist Covenant Companion, 1972-90. Decorated comdr. Order of Polar Star Sweden; recipient Disting. Alumnus award North Park Coll., 1966. Mem. Assn. Colls. Ill. (vice chmn. 1975-79). Mem. Covenant Ch. Club: Rotary (Paul Harris fellow 1987). Home: 1165 La Sombra Ct Turlock CA 95380-3631

AHLER, KENNETH JAMES, physician; b. Meadryville, Ind., Aug. 4, 1940; s. James and Bernadine (Benner) A.; m. Margaret Ann Ahler, Aug. 24, 1963; children: John, Mary Margaret, James. AB in Biology magna cum laude, St. Joseph's Coll., Rensselaer, Ind., 1962; LLD (hon.), St. Joseph's Coll., 1988; MD, Ind. U., 1966. Diplomate Am. Bd. Family Practice. Intern St. Joseph's Hosp., South Bend, Ind., 1966-67, resident in gen. medicine, 1967-68; mem. med. staff Jasper County Hosp., Rensselaer, 1968—, George Ade Nursing Facility, Brook, Ind.; Med. dir. Rensselaer Care Ctr.; sr. assoc. Clinic of Family Medicine; assoc. clin. prof. of family medicine Ind. U. Sch. of Medicine; mem. gov.'s commn. Newborn Inborn Errors of Metabolism, 1978; asst. physician Boy Scouts Am. Nat. Jamboree at A.P. Hill, Va., 1985, and 89, chief physician subcamp 2, Nat. Jamboree, 1993, 97; bd. dirs. First of Am. Bank, Rensselaer; mem. utilization & quality assurance com. Arnett HMO, 1992, 93, 94; exec. com., bd. trustees St. Joseph's Coll. Rensselaer. Mem. St. Augustine Cath. Ch., Rensselaer, exec. bd. Sagamore coun. Boy Scouts Am., pres. 1984-86; asst. scoutmaster Troop 409 Boy Scouts Am. Jamboree, Australia, 1988, v.p. program Area 4 Ctrl. Region Boy Scouts Am., 1987-98, explorer adv. post 2152, 1995-98, mem. Nat. Coun. 1990-98, mem. ctrl. region exec. bd., mem. exec. bd.; trustee St. Joseph Coll. Rensselaer; pres. Jasper County Indsl. Found., Inc., 1987-90, v.p. devel. 1993-98; coroner Jasper County, 1973-81, chief dep. coroner, 1996—; others. Fellow Am. Acad. Family Physicians, Royal Soc. Medicine, Royal Soc. Medicine (London); mem. AMA, Am. Diabetes Assn. (profl. section), Ind. State Med. Assn. (disting.), Jasper County Med. Soc. (pres. 1987-98), Am. Geriatrics Soc., Am. Med. Dirs. Assn., Rotary (pres. Rensselaer club 1984-85), K.C., Am. Med. Dirs. Assn. (cert. med. dir.). Avocations: reading, gardening, community activities, cooking. Home: 703 W Milroy Ave Rensselaer IN 47978-2756 Office: 1103 E Grace St Rensselaer IN 47978-3210

AHLERS, DOUGLAS, communications company executive. Mgr. product devel. CUC Internat., 1976-81; founding ptnr. Modem Media Poppe Tyson, Saughtuck, Conn., 1981—. Office: Modem Media Poppe Tyson 230 East Ave Norwalk CT 06855*

AHLERS, GLEN-PETER, SR., law library director, educator, consultant; b. N.Y.C., Mar. 15, 1955; s. LeGrande Jacob and Joan (Stoltz) A.; m. Sondra Sue Wadley, May 17, 1987; children: Glen-Peter II, Sandia Marie, Gavin Patrick, Sierra Le Ann Rose. BS, U. N.Mex., Albuquerque, 1979; MA, U. of South Fla., 1983; JD, Washburn U., 1987. Bar: Kans. 1987, U.S. Dist. Ct. Kans. 1987, U.S. Ct. Mil. Appeals 1988, D.C. 1990. Reference asst. U. N.Mex. Sch. Law, Albuquerque, 1979-83; asst. dir. Washburn Sch. Law Libr., Topeka, Kans., 1983-87; assoc. libr. dir. Wake Forest U., Winston-Salem, N.C., 1987-90; libr. dir., assoc. prof. D.C. Sch. Law, Washington, 1990-92, U. Ark., Fayetteville, 1992—; computer and libr. cons. Ctr. for R&D in Law-Related Edn., Winston-Salem, 1987-90; adj. prof. Sch. of Law Wake Forest U., Winston-Salem, N.C., 1987-90; bd. dirs. Mid-Am. Law Sch. Libr. Consortium, 1992—, Consortium of Southestern Law Librs., 1988-90. Author: Election Laws of the United States, 1995; co-author: Notary Law and Practice, 1997; editor The Scrivener, 1992—; tech. editor Washburn Law Jour., 1985-86; contbr. articles to profl. jours. Mediator N.C. Neighborhood Justice Ctr., Winston-Salem, 1989-90. Mem. ABA, ALA, Ark. Bar Assn., Am. Assn. Law Librs., Southwestern Assn. Law Librs. (pres. 1995-97), Mid Am. Assn. Law Librs., Scribes (exec. dir. 1997—), Phi Kappa Phi, Kappa Delta Pi, Beta Phi Mu. Avocation: writing. Home: 2139 Revere Ln Fayetteville AR 72701-2711 Office: U Ark Leflar Law Ctr Fayetteville AR 72701-1201

AHLERS, GUENTER, physicist, educator; b. Bremen, Germany, Mar. 28, 1934; came to U.S., 1951; s. William Carl and Ida Pauline (Cornelson) A.; m. June Bly, Aug. 24, 1964. BS, U. Calif., Riverside, 1958; PhD, U. Calif., Berkeley, 1963. Mem. tech. staff Bell Labs., Murray Hill, N.J., 1963-79; prof. physics U. Calif.-Santa Barbara, 1979—. Contbr. numerous articles to profl. jours. Recipient Fritz London award in low temperature physics, 1978. Fellow AAAS, Am. Phys. Soc.; mem. NAS. Home: 523 Carriage Hill Ct Santa Barbara CA 93110-2022 Office: U Calif Dept Of Physics Santa Barbara CA 93106

AHLERS, ROLF WILLI, philosopher, theologian; b. Hamburg, Fed. Republic of Germany, June 22, 1936; came to U.S., 1966; s. Arthur W. and Ilse F. (Freund) A.; m. Luise Kuse, July 1965; children: Christoph Matthias, Marcus Andreas. B.A., Drew U., 1958; M.Div., Princeton Theol. Sem., 1961; Dr. Theol., U. Hamburg, 1966. Wissenschaftlicher Ass. Seminar Für Systematische Theologie und Sozialethik, U. Hamburg, Fed. Republic Germany, 1962-66; asst. prof. religion Ill. Coll., Jacksonville, 1966-72; Reynolds prof. philosophy and religion Russell Sage Coll., Troy, N.Y., 1973—. Author: The Barmen Declaration of 1934: Archeology of a Confessional Text, 1986, The Community of Freedom: Karl Barth and Presuppositionless Theology, 1989. NEH grantee, 1972-73; Soc. for Health and Human Values grantee, 1975. Mem. Hegel Soc. Am., Am. Acad. Religion, Am. Philos. Soc. Presbyterian. Home: 3 Academy Rd Albany NY 12208-3102 Office: Russell Sage Coll Philosophy Dept Troy NY 12180 *The cunning of history, pure grace and keen sense of self made me the person who I am.*

AHLGREN, CHARLES STEPHEN, business and public policy consultant; b. Appleton, Wis., Sept. 22, 1938; s. Theodore Carl Ahlgren and Valery Dorothey (Vanevenhoven) Knox; m. Marianne Collins, Oct. 19, 1972; children: Ingrid, Theodore. BA, Loras Coll., 1960; MIA, Johns Hopkins U., 1967; MPA, Harvard U., 1978. Comml. attache Am. Embassy, Singapore, 1974-77; consul Am. Consulate, Cape Town, South Africa, 1978-80; econ. officer Am. Embassy, South Africa, 1980-81; econ. counselor Am. Embassy, Wellington, New Zealand, 1981-84; vis. prof. U.S. Mil. Acad., West Point, N.Y., 1984-86; consul-gen. Am. Consulate-Gen., Chiangmai, Thailand, 1986-89; vis. prof. U.S. Naval War Coll., Newport, R.I., 1989-92, U.S. Army War Coll., Carlisle, Pa., 1992-93; econ. counselor Am. Embassy, Caracas, Venezuela, 1993-96; Dept. State advisor Air U., Montgomery, Ala., 1996-97; cons. internat. bus. and pub. policy, 1997—. Mem. Am. Fgn. Svc. Assn., Soc. Historians of Am. Fgn. Rels. Avocations: hiking, philately. Home: 136 Arnold Ave Cranston RI 02905-3816

AHLGREN, GIBSON-TAYLOR, real estate broker; b. Memphis, Sept. 7, 1940; s. Frank Richard and Nona Elizabeth (Alley) A. B.S., U. Md., 1967; J.D., Western State U., San Diego, 1978. Legis. clk. U.S. Senate, Washington, 1963-67, spl. asst., 1970-71; legis. rep. Associated Gen. Contractors, Washington, 1971-73, San Diego, 1973-74; campaign dir. Brown for Gov. Calif., 1974; mgmt. cons. Ahlgren, Peters & Assocs., La Jolla, Calif., 1975-77; v.p., dir. pub. affairs Gt. Am. First Savs. Bank, San Diego, 1977-84; polit. cons., 1984-85; real estate broker, 1986—. Served to lt. USN, 1967-70; Vietnam. Mem. Pi Kappa Alpha.

AHLQUIST, JEFFREY, strategy consultant; b. Council Bluffs, Iowa, Nov. 20, 1965; s. Larry Bernard and Jane Ellen Ahlquist; m. Stephanie Renee Fountain, May 26, 1990; children: Matthew, Connor. BA in Polit. Sci., Calif. Poly. State U., San Luis Obispo, 1989; M in Internat. Mgmt., Am. Grad. Sch. Internat. Mgmt., 1990. Mgr. fin. Cigna Healthplan Ariz., Phoenix, 1990-92; dir. corp. strategy group United Parcel Svc. Am., Inc., Atlanta, 1992-99; strategy cons. Ernst & Young LLP, Atlanta, 1999—. Mem. Global Bus. Network, Corp. Strategy Bd. Republican. Lutheran. Avocations: running, tennis, martial arts, reading. E-mail: jsahlquist@aol.com and Jeffrey.Ahlquist@ey.com. Office: Ernst & Young LLP 600 Peachtree St Atlanta GA 30308

AHLQUIST, PAUL GERALD, molecular biology researcher, educator; b. Des Moines, Jan. 9, 1954; s. Irving Elmer and Sigrun Evelyn (Eidbo) A. BS in Physics, Iowa State U., 1976; PhD in Biophysics, U. Wis., 1981. Asst. sci. in biophysics U. Wis., Madison, 1981-84, asst. prof. biophysics and plant pathology, 1984-87, assoc. prof. molecular virology and plant pathology, 1987-91, prof., 1991—, prof. molecular virology, oncology and plant pathology, 1997—, chmn. molecular virology, 1996-97; investigator Howard Hughes Med. Inst., 1997—; mem. exec. com. Internat. Commn. Taxonomy of Viruses, 1987-93; van Arkel hon. faculty chair in biochemistry Leiden (The Netherlands) U., 1995. Editor: RNA Genetics, vols. I, II, III, 1988, Molecular Biology of Plant-Microbe Interactions, 1989; assoc. editor Virology, 1988-93, Molecular Plant-Microbe Interactions, 1988-95, Plant Molecular Biology, 1987-90; contbr. articles to profl. jours. Recipient Presdl. Young Investigator award NSF, 1985-90, Romnes Faculty Fellowship award, 1988, Shaw Faculty Scholar award Milw. Found., 1985-90, Allen Rsch. award Am. Phytopathology Soc., 1988, Pound Rsch. award, 1987, WARF Mid-Career Rsch. award, 1995, NIH Merit award, 1995—. Mem. NAS, Am. Soc. Virology (mem. exec. coun. 1993-96), Internat. Soc. Plant Molecular Biology (bd. dirs. 1989-93), Am. Soc. for Microbiology, Genetics Soc. Am.

AHLRICHS, NANCY SURRATT, marketing professional; b. Harrisburg, Pa., Oct. 13, 1952; d. Joe Free and Mary Alice (Norris) Surratt; m. Karl J. Ahlrichs, Sept. 10, 1983. BA in Anthropology, Purdue U., 1974, MS in Phys. Anthropology, 1976. With dept. prodn. Steuben Printing Co., Angola, Ind., 1977-78; project specialist A.B. Dick Co., Chgo., 1978-81, sr. instructional designer, 1981-82; mgr. tng. and devel. Equitable Relocation Mgmt. Corp., Chgo. and Orlando, 1982-83; v.p. Todd Persons Communications, Inc., Orlando, 1984-87, Gary Bitner Pub. Rels., Orlando, 1987-89; v.p. client svcs. Right Assocs., San Diego, 1989-90; v.p. profl. svcs. Right Assocs., Indpls., 1992-94; mktg. cons., entrepreneur Indpls., 1994—; sr. orgn. devel. cons. RCI, Indpls., 1995—; v.p. bus. devel. Dimensions, LLC, 1997—. Producer videotape: The Big Push, 1983; author/ghost writer over 50 mag. and trade jour. articles; writer, producer, dir. over 50 corp. videotapes. Vol. Steve Goldsmith for Mayor, Indpls., 1991; major gifts chmn. Am. Heart Assn., San Diego, 1990-91. Recipient Pres.'s award Cen. Fla. Zool. Soc., 1988. Mem. Kiwanis Indpls. (bd. dirs. 1995—, mktg. com., chmn. downtown program 1994-95, numerous other coms. 1994-95), Phi Kappa Phi. Democrat. Lutheran. Avocations: anthropology, psychology, reading, gardening, gourmet cooking. Office: 6160 N Meridian St Indianapolis IN 46208-1536

AHLSTEDT, N. STAFFAN, immunologist; b. Göteborg, Sweden, Apr. 29, 1946; s. Stig Nils Ernst Bertil and Inga (Orstadius) A.; divorced; children; Susanne, Erika, Sara. PhD, U. Göteborg, 1973. Rsch. mgr. Astra, Sodertalje, 1975-81; sr. scientist Pharmacia Diagnostics, Uppsala, 1981-92, dir. asthma unit, 1992-95; dir. sci. mktg. Pharmacia Upjohn Diagnostics, Uppsala, 1995-97; prof. Göteborg U., 1978—; mgr. sci. affairs Pharmacia Upjohn Diagnostics, Kalamazoo, 1997-99; sci. advisor $D, Uppsala, Sweden, 1999—. Editor: Clinical Impact of the Monitoring of Allergic Inflammation, 1990, In Vitro Monitoring of Asthma, Suppl. Allergy, 1993. Active Pharmacia Rsch. Found. Mem. AAAS, Am. Acad. Allergy Clin. Immun., Am. Thoracic Soc., Am. In vitro Allergy/Immunology Soc., Clin. Immunology Soc., European Respiratory Soc., European Acad. Allergy Clin. Immunology, N.Y. Acad. Scis., Collegium Internat. Allergologicum, Allergy Soc. South Africa (hon.), Scandinavian Soc. Immunology. Office: Pharmacia Upjohn Diagnostic, Rapsgatan 7, S-75182 Uppsala Sweden

AHLSTROM, CALLIS BLYTHE, university official; b. Oct. 1, 1933. BS, Utah State U., 1958; postgrad., Rutgers U., 1959-62; MA, Columbia U., 1961. Exec. asst. to pres. Calif. State U., Chico, 1971-79; asst. prof. history Utah State U., Logan, 1964-71, asst. to pres., 1979-86, asst. provost, 1986—. E-mail: blythea@champ.usu.edu. Home: 1661 East 1650 North Logan UT 84341 Office: Utah State U Provost's Office Logan UT 84322-1435

AHLSTROM, MICHAEL JOSEPH, lawyer; b. N.Y.C., June 1, 1953; s. Albert Warren and Bernadette Patricia (Flynn) A.; m. Mary Lou Donnelly, Apr. 19, 1980; 1 child, Courtney Leigh. BS, St. Francis Coll., 1975; JD, U. San Francisco, 1978. Bar: N.Y. 1980, U.S. Dist. Ct. (so. and ea. dists.) N.Y. 1980, Ga. 1982, U.S. Dist. Ct. (no. dist.) Ga. 1983, U.S. Ct. Appeals (11th cir.) 1984, U.S. Supreme Ct. 1987. Counsel Gear Design, Inc., N.Y.C., 1979-80; ptnr. Ahlstrom & Ahlstrom, N.Y.C., 1981-83; gen. counsel Network Rental, Inc., Atlanta, 1984-87; assoc. John Marshall and Assocs., P.C., Atlanta, 1987; ptnr. Marshall & Ahlstrom, P.C., Atlanta, 1987-88; mng. atty. UAW-GM-Ford Chrysler Legal Plan Ga., Atlanta, 1993-96; pvt. practice, Marietta, Ga., 1988-92, 96—; arbitrator NASD. Arbitrator Superior Ct. Fulton County, Ga., 1987—, Ga. Lemon Law, 1991—; panel atty. Cobb County Cir. Defender; spl. master Cobb County Superior Ct., mediator, 1996—, Ga. Registered Neutral, 1997—; mediator, domestic cases, Fulton County Superior Ct., 1998—. Named one of Outstanding Young Men Am. U.S. Jaycees, 1986. Mem. N.Y. Bar Assn., Ga. Bar Assn. (pub. rels. com. 1989-91), Cobb County Bar Assn., Am. Corp.Counsel Assn. (program chmn. 1986-87), Am. Arbitration Assn. (comml. panel 1987—), KC, Phi Delta Phi, Alpha Kappa Psi. Republican. Roman Catholic. Avocations: fishing, hunting, tennis, golf, croquet. Home: 613 Fairway Ct Marietta GA 30068-4159

AHLSTROM, RONALD GUSTIN, artist; b. Chgo., Jan. 17, 1922; s. Frederick Karl and Gertrude (Gustin) A.; m. Nancy Costa; 1 son, Arn Gustin. Ed., U. Chgo., Art Inst. Chgo.; B.F.A., 1955. Asst. dir. McCormick Pl. Gallery, 1960-63; dir. Tacoma Art Mus., 1963—. One-man shows include Barat Coll., Lake Forest, Ill., 1958, Blackhawk Restaurant, Chgo., 1961, collages at Main St. Galleries, Chgo., 1969, J. Faulkner Galleries, Chgo., 1970, 71, Spiesberger Gallery, Skokie, Ill., 1975, Zriny-Hayes Gallery, Chgo., 1978; group shows include Chgo. and vicinity ann., Art Inst. Chgo., 1955, 56, 59, 61, 62, 64, other shows at Art Inst., 1957, 58, Inst. Jewish Studies, 1956, 1020 Art Ctr., 1957, Navy Pier, 1957, 58, Old Town Art Center, 1959, B.C. Holland Gallery, 1961, McCormick Pl. Art Gallery, 1961, 62, 63, Hyde Park Art Ctr., 1963, Studio 22, 1970, all Chgo., C. McNider Mus., Mason City, Iowa, 1971, Touchstone Gallery, N.Y.C., 1973; exhibited in Chgo. Artists European Tour Exhibit, USIA, 1957-59, Festival of Fine Arts, Lake Forest, 1958, Soc. of Four Arts Exhibit, West Palm Beach, Fla., 1959, E. Mich. Coll. at Ypsilanti, 1960, Corcoran Gallery Art, Washington, 1961, Tacoma Art Mus., 1963, 5 Abstractionists, Main St. Galleries, 1968; represented in permanent collections Tacoma Art Mus., Barat Coll. Gallery, Gutenberg Mus., Mainz, Germany, Art Inst. Chgo., Blue Cross, Chgo., Atlantic-Richfield, Chgo., Ill. Bell Telephone, Container Corp. Am., Chgo., also in numerous pvt. collections; work represented in book Collage and Foundation Art (Meilach and Ten Hoor), 1964, Collage and Assemblage, Trend and Techniques (Meilach and Ten Hoor), 1973. Served with U.S. Army, 1942-46. Recipient Clyde M. Carr prize for painting, 1955, Alumni of Sch. Art Inst. prize, 1959, Jane Broadus Clark prize, 1958; both Nvay Pier; Abel Fagan prize Festival Fine Arts, Lake Forest, 1958; Ford Found. purchase prize Seattle Art Mus., 1964. Represented in The Art of Collage (Gerald F. Brommer Davis) 1978. Home: 121 W Park Dr Lombard IL 60148-3320

AHLUWALIA, BRIJ M. SINGH, neurologist, educator; b. India, Oct. 22, 1939; children: Sandeep, Samita. Student, Delhi U., 1955-56; MB, BChir, Punjab (India) U., 1961; MD, Punjabi (India) U., 1966. Diplomate Am. Bd. Psychiatry and Neurology. Rotating intern Rajindra Hosp.-Govt. Med. Coll., Patiala, India, 1961; resident internal medicine Rajindra Hosp.-Govt. Med. Coll., Patiala, 1962, casualty med. officer, emergency room resident, 1963; rsch. officer dept. medicine Indian Coun. Med. Rsch., Govt. Med. Coll., 1963-67; resident internal medicine Beekman-Downtown Hosp., N.Y.C., 1968; resident neurology N.Y. Med. Coll., Valhalla, 1969-72, instr. neurology, 1972-74, asst. prof. neurology, 1974-79, assoc. prof. clin. neurology, 1979-82, assoc. prof. neurology, 1982-86, prof. clin. neurology, 1986-88, tenured prof. clin. neurology, 1988—, acting co-chmn. dept. neurology, 1987-90, vice chmn. dept. neurology, 1991—; asst. attending physician Met. Hosp. Ctr., N.Y.C., 1972-77, attending physician, 1977—, chief neurology, 1977-86, dir. EEG lab., 1977-86; asst. attending physician Flower & Fifth Ave. Hosps., N.Y.C., 1972-78, Cabrini Med. Ctr., 1978-82; assoc. attending physician Westchester County Med. Ctr., Valhalla, 1982-85, attending physician, 1985—, dir. neurology, 1986—; attending physician Lincoln Hosp. Ctr., Bronx, 1981—, Mt. Vernon (N.Y.) Hosp., 1987—, Our Lady of Mercy Med. Ctr., Bronx, 1988—, St. Agnes Hosp., White Plains, N.Y., 1989—; presenter in field. Contbr. articles to profl. jours. Named Dr. of the Yr., Dr. I Fund Found., 1992; grantee NIH, Dr. I Fund Found.; rsch. fellow Indian Coun. Med. Rsch., 1963-67. Mem. Assn. for Rsch. in Nervous and Mental Disease, Neurovascular Soc. N.Am. (founder), Am. Acad. Clin. Neurophysiology, Am. Heart Assn. (fellow stroke coun. 1987, profl. edn. task force 1998—, bd. dirs. Westchester/Putnam chpt. 1991—, pres. 1998—), Am. Coll. Physician Execs., N.Y. State Med. Soc., Amyotrophic Lateral Sclerosis Assn. (med. adv. bd. Hudson Valley Support Group 1987—). Fax: 914-594-4295. Office: NY Med Coll Dept Neurology Munger Pavilion 4th Fl Valhalla NY 10595

AHMAD, ANWAR, radiologist; b. Peshawar, Pakistan, Apr. 15, 1945; s. Shams and Amtulaziz (Lateef) A.; m. Amtur R. Hameed, May 20, 1970; children: Attiya, Ghazala, Iftekhar. FSc, Islamia Coll., Peshawar, 1962; MBBS, Khyber Med. Sch., Peshawar, 1968. Cert. Am. Bd. Radiology. Gen. practice medicine Govt. Pakistan, Peshawar, 1968-71; med. missionary Ahmadiyya Mission, Banjul, The Gambia, 1971-75; attending physician VA Hosp., Hines, Ill., 1975-85, Mercy Hosp., Benton Harbor, Mich., 1985—; clin. instr. Chgo. Med. Sch., North Chicago, Ill., 1978—; program dir. residency tng., VA Hosp., Hines, 1982-85. Pres. suburban chpt. Ahmadiyya Muslim Mission, Glen Ellyn, Ill., 1982-85. Mem. AMA, Am. Soc. Therapeutic Radiology and Oncology, Am. Soc. Clin. Oncology, Am. Coll. Radiology, Radiol. Soc. N.Am., Am. Endocurie Therapy Soc., European Soc. Therapeutic Radiology and Oncology, Am. Endocurietherapy Soc., Internat. Assn. Study of Lung Cancer. Avocations: bridge, tennis, photography, reading. Home: 1515 Cardinal Dr Saint Joseph MI 49085-9748 Office: PO Box 273 Saint Joseph MI 49085-0273

AHMAD, IMAD ALDEAN, astronomer, consultant; b. shipboard Atlantic Ocean, Aug. 11, 1948; s. Hassan and Qudsia (Holazada) A.; m. France Eddy, June 11, 1980. BA, Harvard U., 1970; PhD, U. Ariz., 1975. Rsch. assoc. Harvard Univ., Cambridge, Mass., 1975-76; staff scientist Am. Sci. and Engring., Cambridge, 1976-77; sr. scientist Univ. Md., College Park, 1977-79; sr. staff scientist Andrulis Rsch Corp, Bethesda, Md., 1979-81; pres. Imad-Ad-Dean, Inc., Bethesda, 1981—; mem. orgn. com. Washington Area Astronomers, College Park, 1986-96. Author: Signs in the Heavens: A Muslim Astronomer's Perspective on Religion and Science; contbr. articles to Astrophysical Jour.; Astronomers & Astrophysics; co-author: Islam and the Discovery of Freedom; co-editor: Islam and the West: A Dialog. Nat. com. mem. Libertarian Party, Washington, 1983-93; pres. East Bethesda (Md.) Citizens Assn., 1989-91, 93-95, 98—; chmn. Med. Libertarian Party, Bethesda, 1990-92. Harvard scholar, 1966; recipient Samual Chase Freedom award Md. Libertarian Party, Balt., 1990, Montgomery County Civic Fedn. Sentinel award, 1997, Champion of Democracy award Marylanders for Democracy, 1998. Mem. Am. Astron. Soc., Internat. Astronomers Union. Muslim. Achievements include invention of unified global Islamic calendar. Office: Imad-Ad-Dean Inc 4232 Rosedale Ave Bethesda MD 20814-4750

AHMAD, IRFAN SALEEM, agricultural engineer, researcher; b. Rawalpindi, Punjab, Pakistan, Aug. 7, 1958; came to U.S., 1989; s. Ahmad Khan Qureshi and Farrukh Ahmad; m. Raheela Yasmin Irfan, Sept. 12, 1985; children: Umair Irfan, Roveiza Irfan. BSc, U. Agr., Faisalabad, Pakistan, 1980; MS, U. Ill., 1992, PhD, 1997. Registered profl. engr., Pakistan. Asst. scientist Pakistan Agrl. Rsch. Coun., Islamabad, Pakistan, 1980-84, sr. scientist, 1985-89; tech. sales mgr. Sayyed Machinery Ltd., Lahore, Pakistan, 1984; training, indusl. extension specialist Swiss Devel. Coop., Mardan, Pakistan, 1984-85; rsch. scholar U.S. Agy. Internat. Devel., Washington, 1989-91; rsch. asst. U. Ill., Urbana, 1992-97, postdoctoral rsch. assoc., 1997—; cons. Hagler Bailley/ENERCON, Islamabad, Swiss Devel. Coop., Islamabad. Reviewer articles for profl. jours. Bd. dir. Ctrl. Ill. Mosque and Islamic Ctr., Urbana, 1995-97, coord. 1996-99; active Internat. Com. for Bosnia, Urbana, 1993-97. Recipient Food and Agr. Orgn. award Islamabad, England, 1982; USAID-PARC scholar Washington, Islamabad, 1989-91. Mem. Am. Soc. Agrl. Engrs. (v. chair machine vision com.). Avocations: reading, international politics, technology, travel. Fax: 217-244-0323. E-mail: i-ahmad1@uiuc.edu. Home: 2103 202 Hazelwood Dr Urbana IL 61801 Office: Univ Ill 338 AESB 1304 W Penn Ave Urbana IL 61801

AHMAD, JAMEEL, civil engineer, researcher, educator; b. Lahore, Punjab, Pakistan, May 22, 1941; came to U.S. 1962; s. Naseer and Iftikhar (Dean) Bakhsh; m. Rosalba Quiroz, March 31, 1983; 1 child, Monica. BSc, Punjab U., Lahore, 1962; MS, U. Hawaii, 1964; PhD, U. Pa., 1967. East-west ctr. fellow U. Hawaii, Honolulu, 1962-65; rsch. fellow U. Pa., Phila., 1965-67; asst. prof. Widener U., Chester, Pa., 1967-68; asst. prof. Cooper Union, N.Y.C., 1968-71, assoc. prof., 1971-80, chmn. civil engring., 1980—, prof. civil engring., 1979—; dir. rsch. Cooper Union Rsch. Found., N.Y.C., 1983—; dir. High Techs., Inc., N.Y.C., 1986—; bd. dirs. Consortium of N.Y.C. Engring. Colls. and Univs., Mayor's Office of Constrn., 1994—. V.p. Vilmanor Community Assn., N.Y.C., 1992, West Side Community Assn., N.Y.C., 1976. Mem. ASCE (Outstanding Svc. award 1985), Pakistan League of Am. (bd. dirs., Abdus Salam medal for disting. rsch. in engring. scis. 1993). Achievements include patents for fleximech reinforcement system, asphalt reinforcement system. Office: Cooper Union Coll 51 Astor Pl New York NY 10003-7132 *My philosophy of life is best exemplified by the great 19th century industrialist/philanthropist Peter Cooper - concentrate on giving something back to society. As the founder of the only tuition-free private college in America, his legacyhas benefited generations of young people since 1849.*

AHMAD, KAMAL M., lawyer; b. Dacca, Bangladesh, Mar. 28, 1965; came to U.S., 1980; s. Kamaluddin and Nahar Ahmad. AB in Govt., Harvard U., 1988; JD, U. Mich., 1996. Bar: N.Y. 1998. Rschr. World Bank, Washington, 1988-89; Warren Weaver fellow Rockefeller Found., N.Y.C., 1989-91; jr. profl. officer UNICEF, N.Y.C. and Harare, Zimbabwe, 1991-93; corp. assoc. Fried Frank Harris Shriver & Jacobson, N.Y.C., 1996—; study co-dir. task force on higher edn. & soc. World Bank/UNESCO, 1997—; cons. nutrition divsn. UNICEF Hdqs., N.Y.C., 1994. Founder, exec. dir. Overseas Devel. Network, 1983-86; trustee, v.p. bd. Internat. Devel. Conf., Washington, 1986-93; trustee Ctr. for Global Edn. and Devel., Cambridge, Mass., 1996—. Recipient Paul G. Hoffman award for outstandingly significant work in nat. and internat. devel. Paul G. Hoffman Awards Fund, UN, 1984, Coll. Achievement award Time Mag., 1987. Mem. Coun. Fgn. Rels., Harvard Club N.Y. Home: PO Box 621 New York NY 10274-0621

AHMAD, MIRZA MUZAFFAR, economic advisor; b. Qadian, India, Feb. 28, 1913; came to U.S., 1972; d. Mirza and Sarwar (Sultana) Bashir; m. Amatul Q. Ahmad, May 8, 1939; 1 child, Zahir Ahmad. BA, Gov. Coll., Lahore, India, 1933; BA wtih honors, London U., 1935; postgrad. law, Middle Temple, London, 1935; postgrad., Corpus Christie Coll., Oxford, London, 1938. Several govt. positions India, 1944-59; additional chief sec. West Pakistan Province, 1959-62; sec. commerce Govt. of Pakistan, 1962, sec. fin., 1963-66, dep. chmn. planning commn., 1966-70, econ. adviser, fin. adviser to the pres., 1970-71, adviser for fgn. loans and consortium, 1971-72; exec. dir. bd. World Bank, 1972-74; dep. exec. sec., staff mem., con. Joint Ministerial Com. of Bd. Govs. World Bank and IMF, 1974-93; mem. Pakistan del. to Commonwealth Prime Ministers' Conf., 1962, 64; negotiator with World Bank for Indus Basin Devel. Fund, 1964; leader Pakistan del. to 8th consortium meeting, Washington, 1966, Pakistan del. to meetings of Econ. Coun. of Indonesia-Pakistan Econ. and Cultural Cooperation, 1966-69, Pakistan del to ministerial meetings Colombo Plan Conf., Geneva, 1987, Pakistan del. to People's Republic of China, 1967; chmn. ministerial meetings 17th Colombo Plan Conf., 1966. Amir/pres. Ahmadiya Movement in Islam, Inc. Recipient Hilal Quaid Azam award, Sitari Pakistan award Pres. of Pakistan. Muslim. Home: 9920 New London Dr Potomac MD 20854-4845 Office: Ahmadiya Movement in Islam Baitur Rahman 15000 Good Hope Rd Silver Spring MD 20905-4120

AHMAD, MIRZA NASIR, plastic and reconstructive surgeon; b. Simla, India, Aug. 6, 1943; came to U.S., 1967; s. Hafix and Mubaraka Abdus-Salam; married June 21, 1969; children: Jameel, Shameem. MB BS, King Edward Med. Coll., Lahore, Pakistan, 1965; cert. profl. photography, N.Y. Inst. Photography, 1994. House surgeon May Hosp., Lahore, 1965-66; intern Meml. Hosp., Albany, N.Y., 1967-68; resident in surgery Meml. Hosp., Worcester, Mass., 1968-69, Bronx-Lebanon Hosp. Ctr., 1969-72; resident in plastic surgery Wilmington (Del.) Med. Ctr., 1972-74; plastic surgeon St. Thomas Hosp., Akron, Ohio, 1974-77, Aultman Hosp., Mercy Hosp., Canton, Ohio, 1977—; sr. attending physician Aultman Hops., Canton, 1983—; plastic surgeon Mercy Med. Ctr., Canton, 1991—. Plastic surgeon charity work, Honduros, Calif., 1993. Mem. Am. Soc. Plastic and Reconstructive Surgery, Ohio State Med. Soc., Stark County Med. Soc. Moslem. Avocations: photography, computer imaging. Office: 4782 Munson St NW Canton OH 44718

AHMAD, NASEER, pharmaceutical sales executive; b. Karachi, Pakistan, Jan. 9, 1954; came to U.S., 1975; s. Munir and Sadiqa (Begum) A.; m. Nasrin Ahmad, July 4, 1989; 1 child, Tahir. BS in Pharmacy, U. Karachi, 1974. Cert. med. rep. Asst. mgr. The Custom Shop, N.Y.C., 1980-84; med. rep. Mead Johnson & Co., N.Y.C., 1985-87; field trainer Burroughs Wellcome, N.Y.C., 1987-91; med. rep. Ciba-Geigy Corp., N.Y.C., 1991-94; regional sales trainer Concensys, Inc., N.Y.C., 1994-97; dist. mgr. Innovex, Inc., Parsippany, N.J., 1997—; reader adv. panel pharm. rep. news mag. Mem. Nat. Assn. of Sales Profls. Avocations: collecting autographed photographs of world leaders, tennis, walking, reading religion and politics. Fax: 516-579-0207. Home: 137 Blacksmith Rd Levittown NY 11756-3127

AHMAD, SALAHUDDIN, nuclear scientist; b. Sylhet, Bangladesh, Nov. 25, 1954; arrived in Can., 1978; came to U.S., 1990; s. Jalal and Momtaz (Begum) A.; m. Munawar Sultana, June 1, 1978; 1 child, Nahid Rubaba. MSc, Dhaka U., Bangladesh, 1975; PhD, U. Victoria, B.C., Can., 1981. Lectr. Dhaka U., 1978; postdoctoral rsch. assoc. U. Victoria, 1981; rsch. scientist U. Paris South, Orsay, France, 1982-83; profl. rsch. assoc. U. Sask., Saskatoon, Can., 1983-84; rsch. assoc. Triumf Nat. Lab., Vancouver, 1984-86, U. B.C., Vancouver, 1987-89; faculty fellow Rice U., Houston, 1990-96; rsch. assoc. MD Anderson Cancer Ctr., U. Tex., Houston, 1996-98; instr. radiology Baylor Coll. Medicine, Houston, 1999—; physicist VA Med. Ctr., Houston, 1999—. Contbr. more than 120 articles to sci. jours. and conf. procs., including Physics Letters, Phys. Rev., Phys. Rev. Letters. Bangladeshi rep. World Muslim Youth Conf., Abha, Saudi Arabia, 1977; founder, pres. Bangladesh-Can. Cultural Assn., Vancouver, 1988-89, Bangladesh-Am. Lit., Art and Cultural Assn., Houston, 1992-95, 98—. Raja Kalinarayan scholar U. Dhaka, 1974-75; fellow Can. Commonwealth Fellowship Com., 1978-81. Mem. Am. Assn. Physicist in Medicine (jr.). E-mail: sahmad@bcm.tmc.edu. Office: VA Med Ctr Radiotherapy (190) 2002 Holcombe Blvd Houston TX 77030

AHMAD, SHAIR, mathematics educator; b. Kabul, Afghanistan, June 19, 1934; s. Mir and Fatima Ahmad; m. Carol Fulton, Aug. 26, 1974; children: Taj M., Soraya, Schaud. B.S., U. Utah, 1960, M.S., 1962; Ph.D., Case Western Res. U., 1968. Instr. S.D. State U., 1962-64; asst. prof. U. N.D., 1965-66; instr. Case Western Res. U., 1966-68; mem. faculty Okla. State U., Stillwater, 1968-80; prof. math Okla. State U., 1975-78, chmn. dept., 1978-79; prof., chmn. dept. U. Miami, Coral Gables, Fla., 1980-86; dean coll. arts and scis. U. West Fla., Pensacola, 1986-87; chmn. dept. U. Miami, 1987-89; dir. div. math. and stats. U. Tex., San Antonio, 1989-95, prof. math., 1995-98; head dept. math and stats. Miss. Staet U., Mississippi State, 1999—. Recipient nat. and internat. awards and honors for research and teaching. Mem. Math. Assn. Am., Am. Math. Soc. Office: Miss State U Dept Math and Stats Mississippi State MS 39762

AHMAD, SYEDA SULTANA, physician; b. Dacca, Pakistan; d. Syed Wakil and Syeda (Begum) A. B in Medicine and Surgery, Punjab U., Lahore, Pakistan, 1977; MD, Ednl. Commn. Fgn. Med. Grads., Phila., 1982. Resident pediatrics Narain Das Mool Chand Children Hosp., Lahore, 1978; resident ob-gyn. U. Punjab, Sir Ganga Ram Hosp., Lahore, 1978-79; med. officer ob-gyn. Fertility Svcs. and Tng. Ctr., Dhaka, Bangladesh, 1980; clin. attachment staff S. Georgia Med. Ctr., Amarillo, Tex., 1983-84, Pvt. Clinic, Bedford, Tex., 1985-89; rschr. U. Tex. South Western Med. Ctr., Dallas, 1989; resident pathology U. Okla., Oklahoma City, 1989-90; resident pediatrics U. Tenn., Le Bonheur Childrens Med. Ctr., Memphis, 1990-92; resident in pediats. Tex. A&M U. and Scott and White Hosp., Temple, 1992-94, Scott and White Hosp., 1992-94. Mem. Am. Acad. Pediatrics. Avocations: traveling, reading, bicycling. Office: 2831 W 15th St Ste A Plano TX 75075-7527

AHMANN, JOHN STANLEY, psychology educator; b. Struble, Iowa, Oct. 17, 1921; s. Henry Frank and Philomena (Wictor) A.; children—Sandi Ann, Sheri Kay, Gregory Steven, Shelly Joan. *A descendant of Adolf Otto Ahmann of Marl, Germany, John Stanley Ahmann was born and raised in midwestern United States. His four children are: daughter Sandi (Ahmann) Ashley, BS Colorado State U., EdS U. of Kansas, a mental health counselor in Montana; daughter Sheri (Ahmann) Carmon, BA U. of Northern Colorado, is a real estate associate in Colorado; son Steve Ahmann, BS Montana State U., a teacher in Montana; and daughter Shelly Ahmann, BA and MD U of Colorado, a surgeon in Georgia. Each has an abiding love of the Rocky Mountain west and its environment.* BA, Trinity Coll., 1943; BS, Iowa State U., 1947, MS, 1949, PhD, 1951. Instr. profl. studies Iowa State U., 1949-51; asst. prof. div. ednl. psychology and psychol. measurement Cornell U., 1951-54, asso. prof., 1954-58, prof., 1958-60; prof. psychology Colo. State U., 1960-75; also asso. dir. Human Factors Research Lab., 1969-71, asst. to pres., 1961-64, head dept. psychology, 1962-64, acad. v.p., 1964-69; prof. edn. and psychology Iowa State U., Ames, 1975—; disting. prof. edn. Iowa State U., 1981—, chmn. dept. profl. studies, 1975-84; adj. prof. psychology and edn. U. Denver, 1971-76; vis. prof. Colo. State U., 1951, Wash. State U., 1960, Western Wash. U., 1970; Cons. research programs U.S. Dept. of Edn.; cons. for evalu. of ednl. programs in Colo., N.Y., La., Tex., Ark., Hawaii, Ga., Ariz., Ohio, Minn., Iowa; project dir. Nat. Assessment of Ednl. Progress, 1971-75; dir. various fed. and state sponsored research projects; honor lectr. Mid-Am. State U. Assn., 1976-77. Author: Statistical Methods in Educational and Psychological Research, 1954, Evaluating Student Progress, 6th edit, 1981, Evaluating Elementary School Pupils, 1960, Testing Student Achievements and Aptitudes, 1962, Measuring and Evaluating Educational Achievement, 2d edit, 1975, How Much Are Our Young People Learning?, 1976, Needs Assessment for Program Planning in Vocational Education, 1979, Academic Achievements of Young Americans, 1983; assoc. editor: Ednl. Studies, 1975-79. Served with USNR, 1943-46, PTO. Recipient Laureate award Iowa State U., 1975. Fellow AAAS, Am. Psychol. Assn.; mem. Am. Ednl. Research Assn., Nat. Council on Measurement in Edn., Sigma Xi, Phi Kappa Phi, Phi Delta Kappa, Phi Lambda Upsilon, Alpha Chi Sigma, Psi Chi. Home: 11630 N Rio Vista Dr Sun City AZ 85351-3665 Office: Iowa State Univ N 243 Quadrangle Ames IA 50011

AHMANN, MATHEW HALL, social action organization administrator, consultant; b. St. Cloud, Minn., Sept. 10, 1931; s. Norbert T. and Chlotild (Hall) A.; m. Margaret Cunningham, Sept. 18, 1954; children: Elizabeth, Thomas, Teresa, Timothy, Ruth, Katherine. BA, St. John's U., 1952; postgrad., U. Chgo., 1953-54. Social worker Chgo. Dept. Welfare, 1954-56; bus. and circulation mgr. Today mag., 1956-57; field rep. Catholic Interracial Council, Chgo., 1957-59; asst. and acting dir. Catholic Interracial Council, 1959-69; exec. dir. Nat. Cath. Conf. Interracial Justice, 1959-68, Commn. on Ch. and Society, Archdiocese San Antonio, 1969-73; assoc. dir. for govtl. relations Cath. Charities USA, 1973-89; organizer, exec. sec. Nat. Conf. Religion and Race, 1962-63; pvt. practice social svcs., non-profit mgmt. cons. Washington, 1989—. Editor: The New Negro, 1961, Race: Challenge to Religion, 1963, (with Margaret Roach) The Church and the Urban Racial Crisis. Home and Office: 4112 Legation St NW Washington DC 20015-2920

AHMED, JIMMIE, health facility administrator; b. Memphis, Nov. 26, 1946; d. George and Cora (Sias) Stockley; children: Michael, Donald, Eric. Grad., Kingsborough Community Coll., 1973; student, Hunter Coll.; BS in Community Health, Empire State Coll., 1983; cert. in infection control, Winthrop U. Hosp., 1988; cert. Cath. hosp. adminstrv. program, St. John's U., 1990. RN, N.Y. Head nurse gerontology Margaret Tietz Ctr. for Nursing Care, Jamaica, N.Y., 1976-80; staff nurse Mary Immaculate Hosp., Jamaica, 1980-84; asst. dir. field ops. Social Concern Home Attendant Agy., Laurelton, N.Y., 1980-82; nursing care coord. ambulatory care Bklyn./Caledonian Hosp., 1982-85; night adminstrv. supr. M.I.H., Jamaica, 1985-87; infection control practitioner Cath. Med. Ctr. M.I.H., 1987-89; adminstr. infection control Cath. Med. Ctr. Bklyn. and Queens, Inc., Jamaica, 1989—; psychiat. nurse St. Claire Hosp., 1982-93; lectr. Am. Lung Assn. Queens, also others. Author abstracts in field. Mem. ANA, N.Y. State Nurses Assn., Assn. Practitioners in Infection Control (cert.), Empire State Coll. Alumni Assn., N.C. A&T State U. Alumni Assn. Home: 17809 132nd Ave Jamaica NY 11434-5843

AHMED, LEILA NADINE, religious studies educator; b. Cairo, May 29, 1940; d. Abdel Aziz and Ikbal A. BA with honors, U. Cambridge, Eng., 1961, MA, 1966, PhD, 1971. Asst. prof. U. Mass., Amherst, 1980-86, assoc. prof., 1986-91, prof., 1991-99; prof. women's studies, religion Harvard U., 1999—. Author: E.W. Lane and British Ideas of the Middle East, 1978, Women and Gender in Islam, 1992, A Border Passage, 1999. Fellow NEH, 1981-82, Bunting Inst., 1985-86. Home: 9 Ellery St Apt 36 Cambridge MA 02138-5325

AHMED, M. BASHEER, psychiatrist, educator; b. Hyderbad, India, June 7, 1935; came to U.S., 1968; s. M. Qamaruddin and Aziz Fatima Ahmed; m. Shakila Khatoon, Dec. 7, 1967; children: Sameer, Araj. Osmania U., Hyderabad, 1954; MD, Dow Med. Coll., 1960. Diplomate Am. Bd. Psychiatry and Neurology, Am. Bd. Geriatric Psychiatry. Dir. psychiat. dept. St. Louis County Gen. Hosp., Clayton, Mo., 1969-71; dir. sound view Throngs Neck Community Mental Health Ctr., Bronx, N.Y., 1971-76; chief psychiatry VA Hosp., Dayton, Ohio, 1976-78; dir. psychiat. dept. John Peter Smith Hosp., Ft. Worth, 1978-82; pvt. practice, Ft. Worth, 1984—; dir. dept. psychiatry St. Joseph Hosp., Ft. Worth, 1985-89; chief staff Care Unit Hosp., Ft. Worth, 1989-94; dir. psych. geriatric unit Med. Plaza Hosp., Ft. Worth, 1992-96; med. dir. New Horizon PHP Program, Ft. Worth, 1997—; asst. prof. Albert Einstein Coll. Medicine, N.Y.C., 1971-76; prof. Wright State U. Med. Sch., Dayton, 1976-78, U. Tex. Southwestern Med. Sch., Dallas, 1978-88, U. Tex. Health Sci. Ctr., Ft. Worth, 1982-98; chmn. dept. psychiatry Plaza Med. Ctr. East, 1995-97, Med. Direct New Horizon Mental Health Ctr., Ft. Worth, 1997—. Contbg. author: Group Counseling and Psychotherapy, 1976, Administration of Mental Health, 1980. Life mem. Rep. Presdl. Task Force, Washington, 1986—. Hogg Found. grantee, 1980-81, U. Tex. Health Sci. Ctr. grantee, 1981. Fellow Am. Psychiat. Assn.; mem. AMA (Physician's Recognition award 1971—), Tex. Med. Assn., Tex. Soc. Psychiat. Physicians (pres. Tarrant County chpt. 1989-90), Tarrant County Med. Soc. (task force for homeless 1989-90), Islamic Med. Assn. (pres. 1978-79), Internat. Inst. Islamic Medicine. Home: 10 Home Place Ct Arlington TX 76016-3913 Office: 1125 College Ave Fort Worth TX 76104-4514

AHMED, S. BASHEER, research company executive, educator; b. Kurnool, Andhra, India, Jan. 1, 1934; s. S. M. and K.A. (Bee) Hussain; m. Alice Cordelia Pearce; 1 child, Ivy Amina. BA, Osmania Coll., Kurnool, 1955; MA, Osmania U., Hyderabad, India, 1957; MS, Tex. A&M U., 1963, PhD, 1966. Asst. prof. Tenn. Tech. U., Cookeville, 1966-68, Ohio U., Athens, 1968-70; vis. fellow Princeton U., N.J., 1977-78; prof. Western Ky. U., Bowling Green, 1970-80; prof. Mgmt. Scis. Lubin Grad. Sch. Bus., dir. doctoral program Pace U., N.Y.C., 1982-92; prof. emeritus Pace U., 1993—; pres. Princeton Econ. Rsch., Inc., 1980—; cons. Oak Ridge (Tenn.) Nat. Lab., 1969-77, Inst. for Energy Analysis, Oak Ridge, 1975, Honeywell Corp., Mpls., 1985. Author: Quantitative Methods for Business, 1974, Nuclear Fuel and Energy Policy, 1979; author, editor: Technology, International Stability, and Growth, 1984. Mem. cirs. bd. The Kennedy Ctr., 1997—. Recipient Achievement award Oak Ridge Nat. Lab., 1977, IEEE Centennial Medal, 1983. Fellow AAAS, Systems, Man, and Cybernetics Soc. (pres. 1980-82). Republican. Moslem. Home: 10209 Fleming Ave Bethesda MD 20814-2133

AHMED, SALEEM, management consultant; b. Agra, India, Mar. 16, 1945; came to U.S., 1969; s. Mohammed Wasi and Iqbal Begum Uddin; m. Joumana Chebbani, Nov. 7, 1962; children: Nadeem Saleem, Asmahan Saleem, Nabeel Saleem. AEPT in Power Tech., Karachi Polytech Inst., Pakistan, 1965; BA in Math, U. Karachi, Pakistan, 1965; BSME, Detroit Inst. Tech., 1971; MBA in Systems Approach, Baldwin Walace Coll., 1980; PhD in Mktg. and Mgmt., Calif. Coast U., Santa Ana, 1985. Cert. plant engr.; cert. mfg. engr. Project engr. Union Carbide Corp., Westlake, Ohio, 1977-85; mgmt. cons. Saleem & Assocs., Detroit, 1986-89; pres. Mich. Ctr. For Excellence, Inc., Dearborn, Mich., 1990—, Soc. for Profl. Advancement, Inc., Dearborn, Mich., 1991—. Author: Project Mgmt. Systems Approach for Plastics Engrs., 1990, The Excellence in Sales for Executives, 1991, Multi-Level Marketing, 1991, The Psychology of Winning, 1992, The Job Connection, 1992, How to Close Sale Every Time, 1992, others. Mem. ASTD. Avocations: wood working, photography. Home: 2024 N Silvery Ln Dearborn MI 48128-1021 Office: Soc Profl Advancement Inc PO Box 1727 Dearborn MI 48121-1727

AHMED, SYED Z., anthropologist; b. Meerut, India, Aug. 19, 1923; s. Syed Riazuddin and Shah Jehan Begum; m. Susan Ahmed, Feb. 20, 1944; 1 child, Suraiya. PhD, Eng. Leader Sahara Recon Expdn., North Africa; prodr. 40 scientific documentary films for TV, Europe; pres., exec. prodr. Xploration Internat.; rschr., traveler numerous expdns. worldwide. Author: Twilight of an Empire in India, Twilight of an Empire in China, Twilight on the Silk Road, Ruwenzori: A Land Journey Through Europe to Central Africa, Twilight on Caucausus, Incredible Journeys Around the World, Tales of Imperial China and Asia, 1997, Travel in Shangri-La, 1998, East of Tien Shan, 1998, An Imperial Affair, 1999, I Was a Geisha, 1999. Islamic.

AHN, JAMES JONGHO, legislative aide; b. Bristol, Pa., Jan. 17, 1973; s. Sei Hyun and Eu Sook (Lee) A. BA in English, Oberlin Coll., 1994; postgrad., U. Del., 1995—. Rsch. asst. DE Pub., Newark, 1995; rsch. asst. New Castle County Exec. Office, Wilmington, Del., 1995, legis. aide, 1995—; county coun. rep. Libr. Adv. and Rev. Bd., Wilmington, 1995-97. Co-editor: (book) Registry of Abnormal Karyotypes, 1991. Vol. H.O.S.T.S., Wilmington, 1995-97, Del. Diversity Network, Newark, 1995-97; sec.-treas. Del.'s Dem. Future, Wilmington, 1996-97; grad., class spkr. Citizenolice Acad., Wilmington, 1996-97; mem. Police Adv. Coun., Newark, Delaware, 196-97. Mem. Am. Soc. for Pub. Adminstrn., Del. Assn. for Pub. Adminstrn., Pi Alpha Alpha. Democrat. United Methodist. Avocations: guitar, jazz. Home: 51 Tenby Chase Dr Newark DE 19711-2440 Office: New Castle County Coun 800 N French St Ste 100 Wilmington DE 19801-3590

AHN, PETER PYUNG-CHOO, dean; b. Chor-won, Korea, May 21, 1917; came to U.S., 1948; s. Kyung-sam and Ok-bong (Lee) A.; m. Grace Chung, June 10, 1950; children: David Kyu-young and John Avery (twins). Diploma, St. Paul's U., Tokyo, 1944; BD, Garrett Theol. Sem., 1949; MA, Northwestern U., 1951; PhD, Boston U., 1962. Ordained to ministry United Meth. Ch., 1954. Pastor San Francisco Korean Meth. Ch., 1953-60, various United Meth. Chs., Calif., 1965-82; asst. prof. L.A. Pacific Coll., 1963-65; dean Korean Christian Acad., Oakland, Calif., 1986-92; trustee Calif.-Nev. annual conf. United Meth. Ch., San Francisco, 1970-73, chair div. higher edn., 1973-76. Compiler: English-Korean and Koran-English dictionaries, 1947-48; translator: New American Standard Bible, 1965-70; rsch. dir. New Am. Standard Bible Exhaustive Concordance, 1970-76. Hon. mem. bd. dirs. Lockman Found., 1992. Mem. Soc. Biblical Lit. Republican. Home: 608 Princeton Dr Sunnyvale CA 94087-1851 Office: Lockman Found 900 S Euclid St La Habra CA 90631-6893 *Our joy of life should be shared with others in service with compassion and understanding. Our Christian journey has worth when we remember our responsibility to witness our love amid the world's materialistic temptation.*

AHO, ERIC, artist; b. Melrose, Mass., Oct. 20, 1966; s. David A.and Carolyn E. (Blatchford) A. BFA, Mass. Coll. Art, 1988, postgrad., 1988-89; postgrad., Inst. Superior de Arte, Havana, Cuba, 1989, Lahti Art Inst., Finland. Faculty visual arts The Putney (Vt.) Sch., 1989-98, U. Lapland, Rovaniemi, Finland, 1997—; vis. lectr. Burren Coll. Art, County Clare, Ireland, 1996. Works in collections at Fine Arts Mus. of San Francisco, Fleming Mus./U. Vt., U.S. Embassy, Helsinki, Fidelity Investment Corp., Boston, Union Bank of Scandinavia, N.Y.C., The Uhlmann Corp., Kansas City, Mo., Fleming Mus. U. Vt., Oulu City Art Mus., Finland. Grantee Vt. Arts Coun., NEA, 1997, Finlandia Found., N.Y.C., 1997; Pollock-Krasner Found. fellow, 1994, Am.-Scandinavian Found. fellow, 1993, Fulbright fellow, 1991-92. Home and Office: PO Box 436 Saxtons River VT 05154-0436

AHR, PETER, academic administrator. AB in Classics and Philosophy, Seton Hall U., 1962; grad. studies in theology, U. Innsbruck, Austria, 1962-64; PhD in History of Theology, U. St. Michael's Coll., Toronto, Ont., Can., 1970. Instr. theology Seton Hall U., 1964-68; tchg. fellow religious knowledge U. Toronto, 1966-68; asst. prof. theology Seton Hall U., 1968-71, assoc. prof. religious stdies, 1971—, asst. dean Coll. Arts and Scis., 1972-81; faculty fellow N.J. Dept. Higher Edn., 1984-85; assoc. dean Coll. Arts and Scis. Seton Hall U., 1981-87, dean freshman studies, 1987-96, interim dean Coll. Arts and Scis., 1997, interim provost, 1997-98, assoc. prof. religious studies, 1998—. Contbr. papers to profl. jours. and confs. Mem. Commn. on Christian Unity, Archdiocese Newark, 1988—, Commn. on Ecumenical and Interreligious Affairs of Archdiocese Newark, 1975-86, South Orange Comty. Rels. Com., 1980—, South Orange Beautification Com., 1974-80; chair Our Lady of Sorrows Parish Liturgical Renovation Com., 1984-87. NJDHE grantee Seton Hall U., 1985, Computers in Humanities Edn. grantee Assn. Am. Colls., 1982-83; faculty fellow N.J. Dept. Higher Edn., 1984-85. Mem. AAUP, Nat. Acad. Advising Assn. (Outstanding Instnl. Advising Program award 1991). E-mail: ahrpeter@shu.edu. Office: Seton Hall U 400 S Orange Ave South Orange NJ 07079

AHRARI, M. EHSAN, political science educator, researcher, consultant; b. Hyderabad, India, Nov. 24, 1945; came to U.S. 1968; s. Mohammed Hashmatullah and Sayyeda Ahrari; m. Sharon Leyland Ahrari. BA, Ea. Ill. U., 1971, MA, 1972; PhD, So. Ill. U., 1976. Grants specialist Jackson County Housing, Murpheesboro, Ill., 1977; vis. asst. prof. Ea. Ill. U., Charleston, 1977-79, Kean Coll. N.J., Union, 1980; asst. prof. polit. sci. Eastern Carolina U., Greenville, 1980-86; assoc. prof. polit. sci. Miss. State U., 1986-90; prof. Middle East and Southwestn Asian Studies Air War Coll., Maxwell AFB, Ala., 1990-94; prof. internat. security and strategy Armed Forces Coll., Norfolk, Va., 1994—, assoc. dean of joint and combined warfighting sch., 1995-96; sr. rsch. fellow Ctr. for Internat. Security and Strategic Studies, Miss. State U. Author: The Dynamics of Oil Diplomacy, 1980, OPEC-The Failing Giant, 1986, Ethnic Groups and U.S. Foreign Policy, 1987, The Gulf and International Security: The 1980's and Beyond, 1989, the Persian Gulf After the Cold War, 1993, The Middle East in Transition, 1994, Change in the Continuity in the Middle East, 1996, The New Great Game in Central Asia, 1996; contbr. book revs. and articles to profl. jours. NEH fellow, 1979, 84-85. Mem. Am. Polit. Sci. Assn., Am. Soc. Pub. Adminstrn. (bd. dirs. Ea. N.C. chpt. 1985-86, pres. Ea. N.C. chpt. 1985-86, editl. bd. Internat. Jour. Pub. Adminstrn.), Pi Sigma Alpha, Pi Alpha Alpha. Democrat. Muslim. Avocations: photography, tennis, fishing, racquetball, travel. Home: 100 E Ocean View Ave Apt 907 Norfolk VA 23503-1634

AHRENS, CLIFFORD H., judge; b. Hannibal, Mo., Dec. 19, 1945; s. Clifford L. and Doris O. (Kessler) A.; married, June 10, 1968; children: Todd, Joe, Ann. BS cum laude, U. Mo., 1967, JD, 1969. Atty. Rendlen, Ahrens & Rendlen, Hannibal, Mo., 1969-91; judge Mo. Ct. Appeals (ea. dist.), St. Louis, 1991—; vice chair Mo. Ct. Automation Com., St. Louis; mem. Mo. Jud. Records Com., St. Louis. Mem. Planning Commn., Hannibal, 1979-83, chair, 1983-86; pres. United Way Hannibal, 1977-78, YMCA, Hannibal, 1981-83. Avocations: amateur radio, computers, reading. Office: Mo Ct Appeals Ea Dist 111 N 7th St Rm 350 Saint Louis MO 63101-2136

AHRENS, EDWARD HAMBLIN, JR., physician; b. Chgo., May 21, 1915; s. Edward Hamblin and Pauline (Forsyth) A.; m. Gertrude A. Fobes, Sept. 12, 1940; children: Sandra H., Peter Forsyth, Burgess. Grad., Hotchkiss Sch., 1933; BS magna cum laude, Harvard U., 1937, MD cum laude, 1941; MD (hon.), U. Lund, Sweden, 1976, U. Edinburgh, Scotland, 1988. Diplomate Am. Bd. Pediat. Intern Babies Hosp. of N.Y., 1942-43, chief resident, 1951-52; rsch. asst. Rockefeller U., 1946-49, from assoc. to prof., 1952-85; prof. emeritus, 1985—. Pres. Mountain Top Arboretum, 1977-97, chmn., 1997—; bd. mgrs. N.Y. Bot. Garden, 1981-93. Mem. NAS, Am. Soc. Biol. Chemists, Assn. Am. Physicians, Am. Soc. Clin. Investigation, Assn. Patient-Oriented Rsch. (bd. dirs.), Phi Beta Kappa. Office: Rockefeller U 66th St and York Ave New York NY 10021

AHRENS, FRANKLIN ALFRED, veterinary pharmacology educator; b. Leigh, Nebr., Apr. 27, 1936; s. Alfred Henry and Agnes Elizabeth (Higgins) A.; m. Katherine Aldene Henning, May 8, 1960; children—Jeffrey, Gregory, Matthew, Kristin. D.V.M., Kans. State U., 1959; M.S., Cornell U., 1965, Ph.D., 1968. Instr. U. Minn.-St. Paul, 1959-60; asst. prof. pharmacology Coll. Vet. Medicine, Iowa State U., Ames, 1968-70; assoc. prof. pharmacology Coll. Vet. Medicine, Iowa State U., 1970-75, prof. pharmacology, 1975—, chmn. dept. vet. physiology and pharmacology, 1982-90. Served as capt. USAF, 1960-63, lt. col. Air N.G., 1971-91. Recipient Norden Disting. Tchr. award Iowa State U., 1981; NIH spl. research fellow Cornell U., 1967-68. Mem. AVMA, N.Y. Acad. Scis., Assn. Mil. Surgeons U.S., Sigma Xi. Democrat. Lutheran. Office: Iowa State U Dept Vet Physiology & Pharmacology Ames IA 50011

AHRENS, HENRY WILLIAM, art educator, consultant, puppeteer; b. Bklyn., Apr. 11, 1918; s. Otto Conrad and Caroline Johanna (Schoneck) A.; BFA, Pratt Inst., Bklyn., 1941; MA, Columbia U., 1943; EdD, NYU, 1964; m. Marjorie June Brooks, Dec. 18, 1965. Art tchr. Lincoln Sch., Tchrs. Coll., Columbia U., N.Y.C., 1941-42; art supr. Bd. Edn., South River, N.J., 1946-47; art tchr. Bd. Edn., Elizabeth, N.J., 1947-52; assoc. prof. SUNY, Buffalo, 1952-57; prof. art The Coll. of N.J., 1957-83 chmn. art dept., 1965-70, 72-75, ret., 1983, prof. emeritus, 1987—; cons. Thomas A. Edison State Coll., Trenton, 1975-93; exchange prof. U. Frankfurt, Frankfurt Am Main, W. Ger., 1970-71; lectr. in field. Served alt. mil. duty Civilian Pub. Svc., 1943-46. Recipient Frank A. Rexford medal for Cooperation in Govt., 1937. Mem. Art Educators N.J. (hon. life, 1st v.p., pres.), Puppeteers of Am. (religious cons. 1969-76), Mercer County Ret. Tchrs. Assn. (life mem.), N.J. Edn. Assn. (life mem.), NEA (life mem.), Union Internat. Del La Marionettes, The Greater Phila. Area Puppetry Guild (hon. life), Phi Delta Kappa (life), Puppeteers of Am., Original puppet prodns. in Can., Europe and U.S., 1947—; Mem. Religious Soc. Friends (Quakers). Home and Office: 139 N Main St Yardley PA 19067-1322

AHRENS, KENT, museum director, art historian; b. Martinsburg, W.Va.; s. Fred E. and Mary C. (Routzahn) A. A.B., Dartmouth Coll., 1961; M.A., U. Md., 1966; Ph.D., U. Del., 1972. Mem. faculty Fla. State U., Tallahassee, 1971-74, Randolph-Macon Woman's Coll., Lynchburg, Va., 1974-77; mem. curatorial staff Wadsworth Atheneum, Hartford, Conn., 1977-78; mem. faculty Georgetown U., Washington, 1979-82; dir. Everhart Mus., Scranton, Pa., 1982-90, Rockwell Mus., Corning, N.Y., 1990-95, Civic Fine Arts Ctr., Sioux Falls, S.D., 1996-97, Kennedy Mus. of Art, Ohio U., Athens, 1997—; mem. task force on art activities Lynchburg Bicentennial Commn., 1975-76; project evaluator Md. Com. Humanities, 1980-82; mem. adv. panel The Lucan Ctr., Scranton, Pa., 1983-84; mem. mus. adv. com. Pa. Hist. and Mus. Commn., 1984-86; trustee Williamstown (Mass.) Regional Art Conservation Lab., Inc., 1984-92; mem. art mus. adv. panel Pa. Coun. on Arts, 1984-87; mem. adv. panel Pa. Fedn. Mus. and Hist. Orgns., 1989-90; mem. adv. com. on exhbns. at Pa. Gov.'s residence, 1987-90; juror Regional Art '89, Marywood Coll. Art Galleries, Scranton, 1989, Regional 1991, Arnot Art Mus., Elmira, 1991, Cmty. Cultural Ctr,. Brookings, S.D., 1996; bd. dirs. Mus. West, 1990-95; juror Fiber and Textile Exhibn. Civic Fine Arts Ctr., Sioux Falls, S.D., 1996, Wilbur Stilwell Student Awards Exhibn., U. S.D., Vermillion, 1997; adj. prof. Sch. Art, Ohio U., Athens, 1997—, mem. percent for art com., 1997—. Author: (with others) Rembrandt in the National Gallery of Art, 1969; contbg. author: American Paintings and Sculpture: Illustrated Catalogue, Nat. Gallery of Art, 1970, Wadsworth Atheneum Paintings: The Netherlands and German-speaking Countries, 1978, Dictionary of Women Artists, 1997; author: The Drawings and Watercolors by Truman Seymour (1824-1891), Everhart Mus. 1986; co-author: Frederic C. Knight (1898-1979), Everhart Mus., 1987; author: The Oils and Watercolors by Edward D. Boit (1840-1915), Everhart Mus., 1990, Cyrus E. Dallin: His Small Bronzes and Plasters, Rockwell Mus., 1995. Vol. Bosnia-Herzegovina Heritage Rescue, London, 1995—. Served as 1st lt. U.S. Army, 1962-64. Recipient grant-in-aid Am. Philos. Soc., 1975; Samuel H. Kress fellow Nat. Gallery of Art, 1968-69; Chester Dale fellow Nat. Gallery Art, 1970-71; NEH fellow, 1973-74, Mus. Mgmt. Inst., J. Paul Getty Trust, 1991. Mem. Coll. Art Assn., Am. Assn. Mus. (on-site surveyor mus. assessment program 1984-89, 92—, accreditation com. 1986, 90—), Mus. Assn. Pa. (chmn. 1984-90), Mid-Atlantic Assn. Mus., Rotary. Office: Kennedy Mus Art Ohio Univ Athens OH 45701

AHRENS, LYNN, lyricist; m. Neil Costa. Author book, lyricist: Once On This Island, 1995 (Olivier award best musical, Tony nominations for best book and score, NAACP award for best playwright), Lucky Stiff (Helen Hayes award for best musical); lyricist: My Favorite Year, Ragtime (Grammy nomination, Tony award 1998, Drama Test award 1998, Outer Critics Cir. award 1998), Anastasia (Acad. award nomination, 2 Golden Globe awards); co-author/lyricist: A Christmas Carol; TV work includes Schoolhouse Rock (Emmy award, 4 Emmy nominations). Mem. ASCAP, Dramatists Guild Coun. Office: Ford Ctr for Performing Arts 213 W 42d St New York NY 10036*

AHRENS, THOMAS H., production company executive; b. N.Y.C., Oct. 25, 1919. B.A. magna cum laude, U. Buffalo, 1938; J.D., Harvard U., 1941; certificate in Culinary Arts, N.Y.C. Tech. Coll., 1953. Bar: N.Y. 1944. Dir. Edward F. Gallaher Prodns., 1946—; lectr. wines and beverages N.Y.C. Tech. Coll., 1953-55, prof. hotel and restaurant mgmt., 1971—; dir. rsch., security analyst Templeton, Dobbrow and Vance, 1962-64; pres. Chef Phillip, Inc., 1956-69. Author radio and TV scripts on wines, gastronomy and music, 1946—. Mem. chmn.'s coun. Lincoln Ctr. for Performing Arts. 2d lt. AUS, 1942-45. Decorated officer Chaine des Rotisseurs; Confrerie Saint Etienne d'Alsace; Chevaliers du Tastevin; Commanderie des Cordons Bleus de France; Medaille de la Ville de Paris, 1976. Mem. ABA, N.Y. Soc. Security Analysts, Phi Beta Kappa. Clubs: Harvard, Paris-American, Met., Met. Opera (all N.Y.C.); Travellers, Cercle de l'Union Interalliée (Paris). Home: 333 E 69th St New York NY 10021-5549 Office: 300 Jay St Brooklyn NY 11201-1909

AHRENS, THOMAS J., geophysicist; b. Wichita Falls, Tex., Apr. 25, 1936; s. Eric and Therese Ahrens. BS in Geology-Geophysics, MIT, 1957; MS in Geophysics, Calif. Inst. Tech., 1958; PhD in Geophysics, Rensselaer Poly. Inst., 1962. Geophysicst Pan Am. Petroleum Corp., Menlo Park, Calif., 1958-59; geophysicist, head geophysics sect. Poulter Lab., Stanford Rsch. Inst., Pasadena, Calif., 1962-67; assoc. prof. Calif. Inst. Tech., 1967-76, W.M. Keck prof. earth scis., prof. geophysics, 1976—; mem. earth. scis. adv. com. NSF, 1973-76, adv. com. divsn. earth scis., 1979-82; chmn. geophysics Gordon Rsch. Conf., 1974; convenor mineral physics workshop Am. Geophys. Union, 1988, chmn. Macelwane award com., 1992-94; vis. com. dept. terrestrial magnetism and geophys. lab. Carnegie Inst. Washington, 1989, dept. geology and geophysics Princeton U., 1990—, Max Planck Inst. Chemistry, Mainz, Germany, 1993—, divsn. phys. sci. U. Chgo., 1993—. Editor: AGU, Handbook of Physical Constants, Vol. I, II, III, 1995; assoc. editor Rev. Sci. Instruments, 1972-74, Jour. Geophys. Rsch., 1972-74; adv. editor Physics and Chemistry of Minerals, 1976—; mem. editl. bd. Surveys in Geophysics, 1984-94; contbr. more than 300 sci. papers to profl. publs. 1st lt. U.S. Army, 1959-60. Recipient Shock Compression Sci. award Am. Phys. Soc., 1995, Arthur L. Day medal Geol. Soc. Am., 1995, Barringer award Meteoritical Soc., 1997; Geochem. fellow Geochem. Soc. and Geochem. Soc. of Europe, 1998; asteroid named after him/Main Belt Asteroid --4739, Tomahrens, 1985 by discoverer Theodore Bowell. Fellow AAAS (Newcomb-Cleveland prize 1984), Am. Geophys. Union (Harry H. Mess medal 1996); mem. U.S. Nat. Acad. Sci. Achievements include patents in shock consolidation of cubic boron nitride with whiskers of silicon compounds; method for measuring fracture toughness of brittle media; polycrystalline diamond and method for forming same. Office: Calif Inst Tech Seismological Lab 252-21 Pasadena CA 91125

AHRENS, WILLIAM HENRY, architect; b. N.Y.C., May 12, 1925; s. John Karl and Sophie (Hashage) A.; m. Joyce Nolan, Mar. 27, 1951. Student, R.I. Sch. Design, 1946; A.B. in Architecture, Princeton U., 1950, M.F.A. in Arch. and Urban Planning, 1953; postgrad., Tehran U., 1960. Chief architect Litchfield, Whiting, Bowne, Iran, 1958-61, Rome, 1961-64; dir. internat. ops. Whiting Assos., Rome, 1964-67; architect William H. Ahrens, AIA, Rome, Italy. Prin. archtl. works include ITT Sheraton Hotels, Tunisia and Iraq, Marriott Hotels, Egypt and Iran, Esso Hotels, Bologna, Italy and Bordeaux, France, Holiday Inn at Salalah Oman, Univ. of Dallas Rome Campus, various projects for NATO, Pontifical N.Am. Coll., Vatican Cuty State. Trustee John Cabot U.; mem. adv. bd. U. Dallas, U. Rome; bd. regents Marymount Internat. Sch., Rome. With USAAF, World War II, PTO. Recipient award AIA, 1953, Pub. Svc. award Tehran Lions Club, 1961, Rector's award Pontifical N.Am. Coll., Rome, 1994. Mem. AIA, Princeton Club (N.Y.C.), John's Island Club, Circolo del Golf Club (Rome), Knight of Malta, Knight of St. Gregory, Met. Club (N.Y.C.). Home: John's Island 371 Silver Moss Dr Vero Beach FL 32963-3430

AHRENSFELD, THOMAS FREDERICK, lawyer; b. Bklyn., June 30, 1923; s. Frederick Herman and Madeline Florence (Moffett) A.; m. Joan Ann McGowan, Mar. 17, 1944; 1 child, Thomas Frederick. A.B., Bklyn. Coll., 1948; LL.B., Columbia U., 1948. Bar: N.Y. 1948. Assoc., then ptnr. Conboy, Hewitt, O'Brien & Boardman, N.Y.C., 1948-58; sec., assoc. gen. counsel Philip Morris Inc., N.Y.C., 1959-70, v.p., gen. counsel, 1970-76, sr. v.p., gen. counsel, 1976-85; sr. v.p., gen. counsel Philip Morris Cos., Inc., N.Y.C., 1985-88; pvt. practice law Pleasantville, N.Y., 1988—. Trustee Trinity-Pawling Sch. Corp., 1976-98; elder Presbyn. Ch. 1st lt. USAAF, 1942-45. Decorated D.F.C., Air medal with oak leaf clusters. Mem. ABA, N.Y.C. Bar Assn., N.Y. Athletic Club, Mt. Kisco (N.Y.) Country Club, Johns Island (Fla.) Club. Home and Office: 85 Nannahagan Rd Pleasantville NY 10570-2314

AHSAN, OMAR FARUK, computer engineer, manager, consultant; b. Suri, India, Feb. 20, 1964; came to U.S., 1981; s. Mohammad and Masuda (Gowas) A.; m. Angela Rahim, August 4, 1991. BS, Rensselaer Poly. Inst., 1986, MS in Computer Systems Engrng., 1987. Coop. student IBM, Atlanta, 1984-85; coop. student Factron, Latham, N.Y., 1985-87, design engr., 1987-88; lead design engr. Schlumberger, Simi Valley, Calif., 1988-90, new product introduction project mgr., 1990-92, product mgr. diagnostic systems, 1992-93, product mgr. diagnostic systems and well svcs., 1993-94, product mgr. diagnostic systems, well svcs., front end mfg., 1994-95, product mgr. test systems, 1995-97, program mgr. diagnostic sys., 1997-98; program mgr. test and transactions Schlumberger, Simi Valley, 1998—; con. Omega Rsch. & Applications, Valencia, Calif., 1989—; instr. Calif. Luth. U., 1991—. Recipient scholarship Rensselaer Poly. Inst., 1981-85, Nat. Honor Soc., 1981. Mem. Am. Prodn. and Inventory Control Soc., World Affairs Coun., Eta Kappa Nu. Office: Schlumberger Techs 85 Moreland Rd Simi Valley CA 93065-1662

AH-TYE, KIRK THOMAS, lawyer; b. L.A., Mar. 31, 1951; s. Thomas and Ruth Elizabeth (Liu) Ah-T.; m. Deborah Ann Wells, Jan. 31, 1981; 1 child, Torrey Ann. BA, U. Calif., Santa Barbara, 1973; JD, Boston Coll., 1976. Bar: Calif. 1977, U.S. Dist. Ct. (cen. dist.) Calif. 1978, U.S. Dist. Ct. (ea. dist.) Calif. 1994, U.S. Ct. Appeals (9th cir.) 1978, U.S. Supreme Ct. 1981. Co-exec. dir., mng. atty. Channel Counties Legal Svcs. Assn., Santa Barbara, 1977—; expert witness Assembly Com. on Edn., Calif. Legis., Sacramento; panelist Ctr. for the Study of Dem. Instns., Santa Barbara; panelist, instr. CLE approved classes; past legal cons. Santa Barbara chpt. calif. Assn. Bilingual Educators; inaugural prodr., moderator Santa Barbara Law, Sta. KTMS-AM, 1994—. Editor (bar newsletter) The Quibbler, 1992-93, (monthly legal series) Santa Barbara News-Press; contbr. articles to profl. jours. Trustee Montessori Ctr. Sch., Santa Barbara, 1991-93; bd. dirs., v.p. Santa Barbara Internat. Film Festival, 1991-93; chair adv. bd. Santa Barbara Regional Health Authority, 1985; mem. blue-ribbon com. County Bd. Suprs., Santa Barbara, 1988; chair Santa Barbara County Affirmative Action Commn., 1987-88; mem. grant-making com. Fund for Santa Barbara, 1988-92. Recipient Local Hero award Santa Barbara Ind., 1988. Master Santa Barbara Am. Inns of Ct.; mem. State Bar Calif. (state resolutions com. to state bar conf. of dels. 1994-96, exec. com. to conf. dels. 1997, ann. legal svcs. achievement award for so. Calif. 1997, Achievement award for legal svc. 1997), Santa Barbara County Bar Assn. (jud. svc. award com. 1992, chmn. pro bono com. 1993, bd. dirs., sec., CFO 1992—, pres. 1997-98), Lawyer Referral Svc. Santa Barbara (bd. dirs., pres. 1992). Avocations: sports, film, literature, weights, tennis. Office: Channel Counties Legal Svcs Assn 324 E Carrillo St Ste B Santa Barbara CA 93101-7438

AHUJA, JAGDISH CHAND, mathematics educator; b. Rawalpindi, West Pakistan, Dec. 24, 1927; came to U.S., 1966, naturalized 1972; s. Nihal Chand and Ishwardai (Chhabra) A.; m. Sudarshan Sachdeva, May 18, 1955; children—Naina, Anita. B.A., Banaras U., 1953, M.A., 1955; Ph.D., U. B.C., 1963. Sr. math. tchr. D.A.V. High Sch., Nairobi, Kenya, 1955-56; tchr. math. Tanzania, 1956-58; teaching asst. U. B.C., 1958-61, teaching fellow, 1961-63, stats. lab. instr., 1959-61, lectr. stats., 1961-63; asst. prof. math. U. Calgary, Can., 1963-66; assoc. prof. math. Portland State U., Oreg., 1966-69, prof. math., 1969—. Contbr. articles to profl. jours.; referee profl. jours., reviewer profl. jours. Mem. Inst. Math. Stats. Home: 4016 Orchard Dr Lake Oswego OR 97035-2406 Office: Portland State U Dept Math PO Box 751 Portland OR 97207-0751

AIBEL, HOWARD J., lawyer; b. N.Y.C., Mar. 24, 1929; m. Katherine Webster, June 6, 1952; children: David Webster, Daniel Walter, Jonathan Brown. AB magna cum laude, 1950; JD cum laude, Harvard U., 1951. Bar: N.Y. 1952. Assoc. White & Case, N.Y.C., 1952-57; trade regulation counsel GE, 1957-60, spl. litigation counsel elec. equipment antitrust cases, 1960-64; antitrust counsel ITT Corp., N.Y.C., 1964-66, v.p., assoc. gen. counsel, 1966-68, sr. v.p., gen. counsel, 1968-87, exec. v.p., gen. counsel, 1987-92, exec. v.p., chief legal officer, 1992-94; ptnr. LeBoeuf Lamb Greene & MacRae, N.Y.C., 1994-99, of counsel, 1999—; bd. dirs. Farrel Corp., Transparancy, Internat.-USA; vice chmn. Fund for Modern Cts., 1985-95, Conn. Appleseed Ctr. for Law and Justice, 1999—; mem. AAA/ABA/AMA Com. Health Care Dispute Resolution, 1997—. Mem. vis. com. Northwestern U. Law Sch., 1984-90; mem. adv. com. Corp. Counsel Ctr., chmn., 1986-87; bd. dirs. Alliance of Resident Theatres, N.Y., 1986—, chmn., 1989—; trustee Lawyers Com. for Civil Rights, 1991-95; trustee U. Bridgeport, 1989-91, chmn. adv. com. Sch. Law, 1987-92; cons. trustee Westport Nature Ctr. for Environ. Activities; bd. dirs., 1st v.p. Westport Arts Ctr., 1993-96. Fellow Am. Bar Found. (life); mem. ABA Bus. Law Section Com. on Corporate Governance, Amer. Law Inst. Corporate Governance Project, 1984-94, v.p. Bar Assn. NY, 1988-89, mem. ABA (bus. law com. corp. governance 1994-98), Am. Law Inst., Am. Arbitration Assn. (chmn. exec. com. 1992-95, chmn. bd. dirs. 1995-98), Assn. Gen. Counsel, pres. Harvard Law Sch. Assn. NY, 1992-94, v.p. Harvard Law Sch. Assn., 1994—. Home: 183 Steep Hill Rd Weston CT 06883-1924 Office: LeBoeuf Lamb Greene & MacRae 125 W 55th St New York NY 10019-5369

AIDINOFF, M(ERTON) BERNARD, lawyer; b. Newport, R.I., Feb. 2, 1929; s. Simon and Esther (Miller) A.; m. Celia Spiro, May 30, 1956 (dec. June 28, 1984); children: Seth G., Gail M.; m. Elsie V. Newburg, Nov. 29, 1996. BA, U. Mich., 1950; LLB, Harvard U., 1953. Bar: D.C. 1953, N.Y. 1954. Law clk. to Judge Learned Hand, U.S. Ct. of Appeals, N.Y.C., 1955-56; with Sullivan & Cromwell, N.Y.C., 1956-63, ptnr., 1963-96, sr. counsel, 1997—; dir. Am. Internat. Group Inc., Gibbs & Cox, Inc.; adv. com. to IRS commr., 1979-80, 85-86. Editor in chief The Tax Lawyer, 1974-77. Trustee Spence Sch., 1971-79; mem. adv. com. Gibbs Bros. Fedn., 1965-94; mem. vis. com. Harvard U. Law Sch., 1976-82; adv. dir. Met. Opera Assn., 1989—; chmn. bd. dirs. St. Luke's Chamber Ensemble, 1988—. 1st lt. JAGC, AUS, 1953-55. Recipient Judge Learned Hand Human Rels. award Am. Jewish Com., 1997. Mem. ABA (vice-chmn. sect. taxation 1974-77, chmn.-elect 1981-82, chmn. 1982-83, chmn. commn. taxpayer compliance 1983-88, Ho. of Dels. 1988-91), N.Y. State Bar Assn., Assn. Bar of City of N.Y. (exec. com. 1974-78, chmn. exec. com. 1977-78, v.p. 1978-79, chmn. taxation com. 1979-81, chmn. govt. ethics com. 1988-90), East Hampton Hist. Soc. (trustee 1983-89, 90-95), Am. Law Inst. (cons. fed. income tax project 1974—, chmn. tax program com. 1988—, John Minor Wisdom award 1995), Found. for a Civil Soc. (bd. dirs. 1994—, vice chmn. 1997-98, chmn. 1999—), Coun. Fgn. Rels., Guild Hall (trustee1989-94, 95—, treas. 1993-94, 95—), Lawyers Com. for Human Rights (bd. dirs. 1986—, treas. 1997—), Confrerie des Chevaliers du Tavestin, Commanderie de Bordeaux, The Parks Coun. (bd. dirs. 1995-97), Century Assn., India House, Met. Club, Phi Beta Kappa. Home: 980 5th Ave New York NY 10021-0126 Office: Sullivan & Cromwell 125 Broad St New York NY 10004-2489

AIELLO, DANNY, actor; b. N.Y.C., May 20, 1933; s. Daniel Louis A. and Frances (Pietrocova) A.; m. Sandy Cohen, Jan. 8, 1955; children: Danny, Rick, Jaime, Stacey. Actor: (stage prodns.) Lampost Reunion, 1975 (Theatre World award 1976), Wheelbarrow Closers, 1976, Gemini, 1977, (Obie award 1977), Knockout, 1979, The Floating Light Bulb, 1981, A Destiny with Half Moon Street, 1982, Hurlyburly, 1985 (L.A. OCC Best Actor award), The House of Blue Leaves, 1986, (feature films) Bang the Drum Slowly, 1973, The Godfather II, The Front, 1976, Blood Brothers, 1979, Defiance, 1980, Hide in Plain Sight, 1980, Fort Apache, The Bronx, 1981, Chu Chu and the Philly Flash, 1981, Once Upon a Time in America, 1984, Old Enough, 1984, The Purple Rose of Cairo, 1985, Key Exchange, 1985, The Stuff, 1985, The Protector, 1985, Death Mask, 1986, Man on Fire, 1987, Radio Days, 1987, Moonstruck, 1988, Do The Right Thing, 1989 (Boston Critics award, Chgo. critics award, L.A. critics award, nom. best supporting actor Acad. Award, nom. Golden Globe award), Russicum, 1989, Harlem Nights, 1989, Jacob's Ladder, 1990, Once Around, 1991, Hudson Hawk, 1991, The Closer, 1991, 29th Street, 1991, Mistress, 1992, Ruby, 1992, The Pickle, 1992, The Cemetery Club, 1992, The Professional, 1994, Ready to Wear (Prêt-à-Porter), 1994, City Hall, 1995; (theatre) That Championship Season (Faberge award); (TV movies) The Last Tenant, 1978, Lovey: A Circle of Children, Part II, 1978, The Unforgivable Secret, 1982, A Question of Honor, 1982, Blood Feud, 1983, Lady Blue, 1985, Daddy, 1987, Alone in the Neon Jungle, 1988, The Preppie Murder, 1989, A Family of Strangers, 1993 (Emmy award), Showtime movie Lieberman in Love, 1995. Léon, 1994; Power of Attorney, 1995; Lieberman in Love, 1995; Brother's Destiny (tv), 1995; Unforgotten: Twenty-Five Years After Willowbrook, 1996; Mojave Moon, 1996; Two Much, 1996; 2 Days in the Valley, 1996; A Brooklyn State of Mind, 1997; The Last Don (mini tv series), 1997; Del-laventura (tv series), 1997; Bring me the Head of Mavis Davis, 1998; The Last Don II (tv mini series), 1998; Dust, 1999. Office: William Morris Agency 151 S El Camino Dr Beverly Hills CA 90212-2775*

AIELLO, GENNARO C., insurance company executive; b. Ridgway, Pa., Dec. 16, 1953; s. Victor C. and Victoria I. (Bevacqua) A.; m. Cynthia K. Medvid, Sept. 20, 1975; children: Erin M., Kathryn T. BS, Gannon U., 1975; postgrad., Pa. State U, 1974-76. Lic. ins. agt., real estate agt. Sales rep. Met. Ins. Co., DuBois, Pa., 1975-80; owner, agt. Ins. Mktg. Assocs., Ridgway, 1980-86; acct. exec. The Pa. Mfrs. Assn. Group, Ridgway, 1986-94; acct. mgr. EBI Cos., Erie, Pa., 1994-98; comml. account mgr., ptnr.

Anderson and Kime Ins., Inc., Ridgway, 1998—; gen. mgr. Wolf Run Marina, Warren, Pa., 1978-79; controller U.S. Coal, Inc., Ridgway, 1981-83; realtor Anderson and Kime, St. Marys, Pa., 1983—. Bd. dirs., v.p. Ridgway Action for Community Enhancement, 1986-88; chmn. St. Leo's Home and Sch. Assn., Ridgway, 1989-91; bd. dirs. St. Leo's Parish Coun., 1986-90, pres. sports assn., 1988-91; pres. Elk County Coun. on the Arts, 1991-92, v.p., 1990-91, pres., 1991-92; pres. Ridgway Independence Festival Inc., 1990—; v.p., bd. dirs. Ridgway Community Nurses Svc. Inc., 1991—, Outdoor Companions Inc., 1991, Citizens Against Phys., Sexual and Emotional Abuse, 1992-93; bd. dirs. Ridgway Heritage Coun., 1997—. Mem. Johnsonburg C. of C. (bd. dirs., pres. 1989—), Elk-Cameron Bd. Realtors, Jaycees (pres. local chpt. 1986-87), Ducks Unltd. (spons. chmn. 1987-88), Elk County Country Club (bd. dirs. 1991-95, v.p. 1992-93, pres. 1993—), Rotary (pres. Johnsonburg lodge 1980-81), K.C. (3d degree). Avocations: hunting, fishing, archery, boating, golf. Home: 220 Montmorenci Ave Ridgway PA 15853-1615 Office: Anderson and Kime Ins PO Box 507 Ridgway PA 15853-0507

AIELLO, STEPHEN, public relations executive. BA in History, NYU; MA in History, Columbia U.; PhD in Urban Studies, Union Grad. Sch. Former adminstr. N.Y.C. Bd. Edn., pres., 1974-80; former prof. Fordham U., N.Y.C.; spl. asst. ethnic affairs White House, Washington, 1980-81; exec. dir. N.Y.C. Ednl. Constrn. Fund; v.p., dir., civic affairs Burson-Marsteller, 1983-86, exec. v.p., pub. affairs, 1987-89, dir. pub. affairs, 1991-92; exec. v.p., gen. mgr. Cohn & Wolfe, N.Y.C., 1989-90, exec. v.p., gen. mgr. N.Y., 1992-93, pres., CEO, 1993—. Chair ethnic/urban coun. Nat. Dem. Com.; former chmn. N.Y. Urban Coalition. Office: Cohn & Wolfe 225 Park Ave S Fl 17 New York NY 10003-1653*

AIG, DENNIS IRA, writer, film producer; b. Bklyn., Jan. 15, 1950; s. Irving and Judith (Gran) A.; m. Ann Therese Bertagnolli, Nov. 26, 1983; children: Hannah Elena, Leah Isabella, Aaron Anthony (dec.). BA, CUNY, Flushing, 1971; MA, Ohio State U., 1973, PhD, 1983. Founder, co-exec. dir., pres. bd. trustees Community Film Assn., Columbus, Ohio, 1979-81; ind. writer, producer, 1981-83; staff writer, producer Chem. Abstracts Service, Columbus, 1983-89; asst. prof. Montana State U., Bozeman, 1989-95, assoc. prof., 1995—; instr. continuing edn. Ohio State U., 1978; writer Frontier Press Columbus, 1980-81; media cons. Ridihalgh and Eggers, 1981-82; producer, dir. KUSM Pub. TV, Mont. State U., 1989—; pres. The Hunter Neil Co., Bozeman, 1996—. Screenwriter, exec. prodr.: KAZ vs. the Gypsy Moth, 1984 (Cert. of Excellence 1984), CAS-the World Resource, 1986 (Cine Golden Eagle award 1986); exec. prodr.: A Heartbeat Away: Health Care in Three Forks Montana, 1991 (Coll. TV award, The Mainstreet Show TV series; co-prodr./dir.: Shadow Casting: The Making of "A River Runs Through It", 1993 (Gold Hugo award, Chris award, Gold Apple award); co-dir., co-prodr.: Sacred Journey of Nez Perce, 1996 (winner Gold award N.Y. Festivals, Crystal award, Communicator awards, Regional Emmy award), Black Hawk Waltz: Tales of a Rocky Mountain Town, 1996 (Telly award); exec. prodr.: Confessions of a Stand-Up, 1994 (Regional Emmy award), Base Camp, 1999; dir., co-prodr.: Test Pilots of the Body, 1997; exec. prodr.: Bridgehampton Suite, 1998; prod., dir., exec. prodr.: Visions of Grace: Robert Redford and The Horse Whisperer, 1998, Electronic Press Kit, The Horse Whisperer, 1998. Trustee Nat. Hall of Fame for Persons with Disabilities, Columbus, 1981-84; co-chmn. (photo exhibit) Anne Frank In The World: 1929-45, Columbus, 1987. Rockefeller Found. travel grantee, 1990. Mem. Univ. Film and Video Assn., Assn. Ind. Video and Filmmakers. Jewish. Avocations: photography, reading, weight training. Home: 8111 Rolling Hills Dr Bozeman MT 59715-9346 Office: KUSM Pub TV Dept Media Theatre Art Bozeman MT 59717 also: The Hunter Neil Co PO Box 1245 PO Box 1-c Bozeman MT 59771-1245

AIGNER, B. ROBERT, neurologist; b. Fürth-in-Ward, Germany, Mar. 24, 1928; came to U.S., 1929; s. Alois and Josefine Aigner; m. Martha Ann Wagner, June 24, 1952; children: Susan, Robert, David, Paul, Sarah. Student, St. Martins Coll., 1945-48; MD, St. Louis U., 1952. Resident in neurology Mayo Clinic, Rochester, Minn., 1956-59; pvt. practice neurology Seattle, 1960-97; chief of staff Providence Hosp., 1989-90. Pres. Amigos, Seattle, 1982; trustee St. Martin's Coll., Lacey, Wash., 1967-94, pres., 1987. Lt. USAF, 1954-56. Mem. AMA, Am. Acad. Neurology, Wash. State Med. Soc. (mem. com.), King County Med. Soc. (mem. com.), North Pacific Soc. Neurology and Psychiatry (pres. 1981). Avocations: travel, birding, photography. Office: Panel of Cons Med Dental Bldg 509 Olive Way Seattle WA 98004

AIGNER, DENNIS JOHN, economics educator, consultant; b. L.A., Sept. 27, 1937; s. Herbert Lewis and Della Geraldine (Balasek) A.; m. Vernita Lynne White, Dec. 21, 1957 (div. May 1977); children: Mitchell A., Annette N., Anita L., Angela D.; m. Gretchen Camille Bertolet, Dec. 22, 1992. B.S., U. Calif.-Berkeley, 1959, M.A., 1962, Ph.D., 1963. Asst. prof. econs. U. Ill., Urbana, 1962-67; from assoc. prof. to prof. U. Wis., Madison, 1967-76; prof., chmn. dept. econs. U. So. Calif., L.A., 1976-88; dean grad. sch. mgmt. U. Calif., Irvine, 1988-97, prof. grad. sch. mgmt., 1988—; assoc. dean sch. environ. sci. and mgmt. U. Calif., Santa Barbara, 1998—; pres. Dennis Aigner Inc., L.A., 1978—; dir. Analysis Group Econs. Author: Introduction to Statistical Decision Making, 1968, Basic Econometrics, 1971; editor: Latent Variables in Socio-Economic Models, 1977; co-editor: Jour. Econometrics, 1972-91. Fulbright fellow Belgium, 1970, Israel, 1983, Bren fellow U. Calif. Santa Barbara, 1998—; NSF grantee, 1968-70, 70-72, 73-76, 79-81, 84-86. Fellow Econometric Soc.; mem. Am. Statis. Assn., Am. Econ. Assn. Office: U Calif-Irvine Grad Sch Mgmt Irvine CA 92697-3130

AIGNER, EMILY BURKE, lay worker; b. Henrico, Va., Oct. 28, 1920; d. William Lyne and Susie Emily (Willson) Burke; m. Louis Cottrell Aigner, Nov. 27, 1936; children: Lyne, Betty, D. Muriel (dec.), Willson, Norman, William, Randolph, Dorothy. Cert. in Bible, U. Richmond, 1969; postgrad., So. Bapt. Sem. Extension, Nashville, 1987, Va. Commonwealth U., 1981; diploma in Bible, Liberty Home Bible Inst., 1992. Cert. telephone counseling. Deacon Four Mile Creek Bapt. Ch., Richmond, Va., 1972—, trustee, 1991, dir. Woman's Missionary Union, 1986-94, treas., 1984-89, dir. Sunday sch., 1969-78, 84-85, 1989-93; spl. edn. tchr., 1993—; acctg. tech., 1959-80. Prodr. Dial-A-Devotion for pub. by telephone, 1978-85. Solicitor ARC, Henrico County, 1947-49, induction ctr. vol., 1994-97; solicitor, United Givers' Fund, Henrico County, 1945-48; sec.-treas. soliciting funds Bible Edn. in Varina Sch., 1946-49; singer Bellwood Choir, Chesterfield County, Va., 1965-70; telephone counselor Richmond Contact, 1980-82, Am. Cancer Soc., Richmond, 1980-82; program chmn. Varina (Va.) Home Demonstration Club, 1950-53; worker Vol. Visitor Program Westport Convalescent Home, 1983—; vol. patient rep. Richmond Meml. Hosp., 1994-98; jail min. Richmond City Jail, 1973—; chaplain Richmond Meml. Hosp., 1996-97. Named Woman of Yr., Henrico Farm Bur., 1996. Mem. Gideons Internat. (sec. Va. aux. 1977-80, 82-84, new mem. plan rep. 1981, 85, 91, 94, zone leader 1988-89, 90-91, state cabinet rep. 1989-90, pres. Richmond N.E. Camp 1976-78, sec.-treas. 1980-82, 93, scripture sec. 1973-75, 87-89, v.p., 1997-98, chmn. Va. state widows com. 1993-97), Henrico Farm Bur. (women's com. 1994—), Alpha Phi Sigma. Home: 9717 Varina Rd Richmond VA 23231-8428 *Forgive or not to forgive. I choose to forgive that I may not become bitter and cynical within but have peace and love to share with others with whom I encounter.*

AIJIAN, HAIG SCHUYLER, pathologist, educator; b. Detroit, Apr. 2, 1919; s. Misak Michael and Mabel Maude (Schuyler) A.; m. Ethel Louise Johnson, May 14, 1948 (dec. Jan. 1998); children: Paul S., Mark M., Peter C., Lane Louise, Maria V. (adopted). BS, UCLA, 1940; MD, USC, 1945. Diplomate Am. Bd. Pathology, anatomical and clin. Mem. faculty USC Sch. of Medicine, L.A., 1945—; asst. pathologist St. Luke Hosp., Pasadena, Calif., 1952-57; pathologist St. Francis Hosp., Lynwood, Calif., 1957-68, Meth. Hosp. So. Calif., Arcadia, Calif., 1968-83, Goleta Valley Hosp., Santa Barbara, 1983-87, St. Francis Hosp., Santa Barbara, 1983-87; insp. blood bank Am. Assn. Blood Banks, Chgo., Med. Technician Schs., Am. Soc. Clin. Pathologists Bd. of Schs., Chgo.; mem. joint generalist com. ASCP Bd. of Schs., Chgo. Mem. Santa Barbara County Reps. Avocations: reading, teaching. Home: 956 Via Fruteria Santa Barbara CA 93110-2322

AIKAWA, JERRY KAZUO, physician, educator; b. Stockton, Calif., Aug. 24, 1921; s. Genmatsu and Shizuko (Yamamoto) A.; m. Chitose Aihara, Sept. 20, 1944; 1 son, Ronald K. AB, U. Calif., 1942; MD, Wake Forest Coll., 1945. Intern, asst. resident N.C. Baptist Hosp., 1945-47; NRC fellow in med. scis. U. Calif. Med. Sch., 1947-48; NRC, AEC postdoctoral fellow in med. scis. Bowman Gray Sch. Medicine, 1948-50, instr. internal medicine, 1950-53, asst. prof., 1953; established investigator Am. Heart Assn., 1952-58; exec. officer lab. service Univ. Hosps., 1958-61, dir. lab. services, 1961-83, dir. allied health program, 1969—, assoc. dean allied health program, 1983—, pres. med. bd.; assoc. dean clin. affairs asst. prof. U. Colo. Sch. Medicine, 1953-60, assoc. prof. medicine, 1960-67, prof., 1967—, prof. biometrics, 1974—, assoc. dean clin. affairs, 1974—; Pres. Med. bd. Univ. Hosps. Fellow ACP, Am. Coll. Nutrition; mem. Western Soc. Clin. Research, So. Soc. Clin. Research, Soc. Exptl. Biology and Medicine, Am. Fedn. Clin. Research, AAAS, Central Soc. Clin. Research, AMA, Assn. Am. Med. Colls., Phi Beta Kappa, Sigma Xi, Alpha Omega Alpha. Home: 3233 Lake Albano Cir San Jose CA 95135-1467 Office: U Colo Sch Medicine 4200 E 9th Ave Denver CO 80220-3706

AIKEN, JOAN (DELANO), author; b. Rye, Sussex, Eng., Sept. 4, 1924; d. Conrad Potter and Jessie (MacDonald) A.; m. Ronald George Brown, July 7, 1945 (dec. 1955); children: John Sebastian, Elizabeth Delano; m. Julius Goldstein, Sept. 2, 1976. Mem. staff BBC, London, 1942-43; libr. UN Info. Ctr., London, 1943-49; sub-editor, features editor Argosy mag., London, 1955-60; copywriter J. Walter Thompson, London, 1960-61. Author: (juvenile fiction) All You've Ever Wanted and Other Stories, 1953, The Kingdom and The Cave, 1960, Black Hearts in Battersea, 1964, The Whispering Mountain, 1968 (Guardian award, 1969), Night Fall (Mystery Writer's of Am. award, 1972), Winterthing: A Child's Play, 1970, The Cuckoo Tree, 1971, All and More, 1971, A Harp of Fishbones and Other Stories, 1972, The Skin Spinners, 1976, The Spiral Stair, 1979, The Shadow Guests, 1980, Up The Chimney Down, 1985, Give Yourself a Fright, 1989, A Foot in the Grave, 1990, Is, 1992, A Creepy Company, 1993, numerous others; (adult fiction) The Silence of Herondale, 1964, Beware of the Boquet, 1966, The Ribs of Death, 1967, The Embroidered Sunset, 1970, Castle Barebane, 1976, Last Movement, 1977, The Smile of the Stranger, 1978, The Weeping Ash, 1980, Foul Matter, 1983, Mansfield Revisted, 1984, If I Were You, 1987, Blackground, 1989, Jane Fairfax, 1990, The Shoemaker's Boy, 1991, The Midnight Moropus, 1993, Cold Shoulder Road, 1995, A Handful of Gold, 1995, Emma Watson, 1996, The Cockatrice Boys, 1996, The Jewel Seed, 1997, Moon Caie, 1998, The Youngest Miss Ward, 1998, others; (trans.) The Angel Inn, (Contessa de Ségur, 1976), Moon Cake, 1998, The Youngest Miss Ward, 1998, The Way to Write for Children, 1998, Dangerous Games, 1999. Address: The Hermitage, East St Petworth, West Sussex GU28 0AB, England

AIKEN, LEWIS ROSCOE, JR., psychologist, educator; b. Bradenton, Fla., Apr. 14, 1931; s. Lewis Roscoe and Vera Irene (Hess) A.; M. Dorothy Ree Grady, Dec. 16, 1956; children: Christopher, Timothy. BS, Fla. State U., Tallahassee, 1955, MA, 1956; PhD, U. N.C., 1960. Assoc. prof. psychology U. N.C., Greensboro, 1960-65; prof. Guilford Coll., Greensboro, 1966-74, Sacred Heart Coll., Belmont, N.C., 1974-76, U. Pacific, Stockton, Calif., 1977-79, Pepperdine U., Malibu, Calif., 1979. Author: General Psychology, 1969, Psychological and Educational Testing, 1971, Readings in Psychological and Educational Testing, 1973, Psychological Testing and Assessment, 1976, 9th edit., 1997, Later Life, 1978, 3rd edit., 1989, Dying, Death and Bereavement, 1985, 3rd edit., 1994, Assessment of Intellectual Functioning, 1987, 96, Personality Assessment Method and Practices, 1989, 94, 99, Personality: Theories, Research and Applications, 1993, Aging: An Introduction to Gerontology, 1994, Rating Scales and Checklists, 1996, Assessment of Adult Personality, 1997, Questionnaires and Inventories, 1997, Human Development in Adulthood, 1998, Tests and Examinations, 1998, Human Differences, 1999; contbr. articles to profl. jours. Sgt. USMC, 1951-54. Fla. Lewis scholar, 1949-51, Gen. scholar, 1954-56; Emory U. fellow, 1957-58, U.S. Office Edn. postdoctoral fellow, 1968-69; NAS-NRC postdoctoral resident rsch. assoc., 1963-64. Fellow APA, Am. Psychol. Soc.; mem. Am. Ednl. Rsch. Assn., Sigma Xi. Office: Pepperdine U Social Sci Divsn Malibu CA 90263

AIKEN, LINDA HARMAN, nurse, sociologist, educator; b. Roanoke, Va., July 29, 1943; d. William Jordan and Betty Philips (Warner) Harman; children: June Elizabeth, Alan James. BSN, U. Fla., 1964, M in Nursing, 1966; PhD in Sociology, U. Tex., 1973. Nurse Med. Ctr. U. Fla., Gainesville, 1964-65, instr. coll. nursing, 1966-67; instr. sch. of nursing U. Mo., Columbia, 1967-70, clin. nurse specialist sch. of nursing, 1967-70; program officer Robert Wood Johnson Found., Princeton, N.J., 1974-76, dir. rsch., 1976-79, asst. v.p., 1979-81, v.p., 1981-87; Claire M. Fagin Leadership prof. nursing, prof. sociology U. Pa., Phila., 1988—, dir. Ctr. for Health Svcs. and Policy Rsch., 1988—; rsch. assoc. population studies ctr. U. Pa.; mem. Sec. Health and Human Svcs. Commn. on Nursing, 1988, Pres. Clinton's Nat. Health Care Reform Task Force, 1993; commr. Physician Payment Rev. Commn. nat. adv. coun. U.S. Agy. for Health Care Policy and Rsch. Author: Health Policy and Nursing Practice, 1981, Nursing in the 1980s, 1982, Applications of Social Science to Clinical Medicine and Health Policy, 1986, Evaluation Studies Rev. Ann., 1985, Charting Nursing's Future, 1991, Hospital Restructuring in North America and Europe, 1997; contbr. articles to profl. jours. Mem. Adv. Council Social Security, 1982-83. Recipient Joint Secretarial commendation U.S. Dept. Health and Human Services and HUD, 1987; NIH Nurse Scientist fellow, 1970-73. Mem. ANA (Jessie M. Scott award 1984), Am. Acad. Arts and Scis., Assn. Health Svcs. Rsch. (Disting. Investigator), Inst. Medicine, Nat. Acad. Scis., Nat. Acad. Social Ins., Am. Acad. Nursing (pres. 1979-80), Am. Sociol. Assn. (chair med. sociology sect. 1983-84), Sociol. Rsch. Assn., Coun. Nurse Rschrs. (Nurse Scientist of Yr. 1991), Sigma Theta Tau, Phi Kappa Phi. Home: 2209 Lombard St Philadelphia PA 19146-1107 Office: U Pa 420 Service Dr Philadelphia PA 19104-4210

AIKEN, MICHAEL DEWAYNE, lawyer; b. Independence, Kans., May 27, 1954; s. Marvin Ray and Myra Jo (Hattan) A.; m. Linda Jean Olson, July 20, 1974; children: Jason Michael, David Bruce, Sarah Jean. BA in Econs., Wash. State U., 1976; JD, U. Kans., 1979. Bar: Kans. 1979, Wash. 1980, U.S. Ct. Appeals (9th cir.) 1980, U.S. Dist. Ct. Kans. 1980, U.S. Dist. Ct. (ea. dist.) Wash. 1980. Pub. defender Grant County, Ephrata, Wash., 1980-88; pvt. practice Ephrata, 1988—. Mem. Citizens Task Force, Moses Lake, Wash., 1996—; scoutmaster Boy Scouts Am., Moses Lake, 1981-98; Superior Ct. jud. candidate, 1992, 96; Superior Ct. commr. pro tem, 1997-99; guardian ad litem qualified, 1994—. Mem. Wash. Assn. Criminal Def. Lawyers, Wash. Assn. Trial Lawyers (10 Yr. Svc. award), Moose. Democrat. Avocations: golf, hunting, fishing, hiking, camping. Home: 403 Biggs Rd Moses Lake WA 98837-3109 Office: 54 Basin St SW PO Box 1189 Ephrata WA 98823-1189

AIKEN, MICHAEL THOMAS, academic administrator; b. El Dorado, Ark., Aug. 20, 1932; s. William Floyd and Mary (Gibbs) A.; m. Catherine Comet, Mar. 28, 1969; 1 child, Caroline R. BA, U. Miss., 1954; MA, U. Mich., 1955, PhD, 1964. Asst. prof. U. Wis., Madison, 1963-67, assoc. prof., 1967-70, prof., 1970-84, assoc. dean coll. arts and scis., 1980-82; prof. U. Pa., Phila., 1984-93, dean sch. arts and scis., 1985-87, provost, 1987-93; chancellor U. Ill., Urbana, 1993—, Champaign/Urbana, 1993—. Author: (with others) The Dynamics of Idealism, 1971, Economic Failure, Alienation, and Extremism, 1968; editor: (with others) Complex Organizations: Critical Perspectives, 1981, The Structures of Community Power, 1970. Mem. Am. Sociol. Assn. (sec. 1986-89). Office: U Ill 320 Swanlund Adminstrn Bldg 601 E John St Champaign IL 61820-5711

AIKEN, ROBERT MCCUTCHEN, retired chemical company executive, management consultant; b. Washington, Pa., Nov. 8, 1930; s. Robert Wilson and Helen (McCutchen) A.; m. Brenda Jean Ashton, Nov. 6, 1957; children: Jennifer Ann, Robert Ashton. BS in Mech. Engring., Case Inst. Tech., Cleve., 1952. With E.I. duPont Co., 1952—; planning mgr. plastics dept. E.I. duPont Co., Wilmington, Del., 1967-69; dist. sales mgr. E.I. duPont Co., Atlanta, 1969-70; asst. plant mgr. E.I. duPont Co., Victoria, Tex., 1970-71; mgr. polymer intermediates ops. E.I. duPont Co., Cape Fear, N.C., 1971-74; dir. Caustic-Chlorine div. E.I. duPont Co., Wilmington, 1974-75; asst. dir. L.Am. divsn. E.I. duPont, Wilmington, 1975-76; dir. internat. E.I. duPont Co., Wilmington, 1976-78; gen. mgr. internat. dept. E.I. duPont Co., 1978-81; v.p. internat. E.I. du Pont Co., Wilmington, 1981-83, group v.p. petrochems., 1983-91; ret., 1991, mgmt. cons. safety and environ. leadership, 1991—. Lt. j.g. USN, 1955-58. Mem. World Affairs Council, Wilmington Club, Wilmington Country Club. Republican. Home and Office: Linden Farm 1225 Birmingham Rd West Chester PA 19382-8201

AIKEN, V. FRED, legislative staff member; b. Atlanta, Jan. 30, 1938. LLB, Atlanta Law Sch., 1965; cert. grad., La. State U., 1969. Banker Nat. Bank Ga., Bank Smyrna, Cobb Bank and Trust; mem. Ga. Gen. Assembly, 1979-91; dist. rep. Spkr. Newt Gingrich, 1991-94; dist. dir. Rep. Bob Barr, Marietta, Ga., 1994—. Bd. mem. SafePath Child Advocacy Ctr.; active No. Ga. Svcs. for Blind and Vision, Cancer Crusade, March of Dimes. Mem. Cobb City C. of C. (past pres.), Jaycees. Office: Office US Rep Bob Barr Ste 13 499 Whitlock Ave Marietta GA 30064*

AIKENS, C(LYDE) MELVIN, anthropology educator, archaeologist; b. Ogden, Utah, July 13, 1938; s. Clyde Walter and Claudia Elena (Brown) A.; m. Alice Hiroko Endo, Mar. 23, 1963; children: Barton Hiroyuki, Quinn Yoshihisa. A.S., Weber Coll., 1958; B.A., U. Utah, 1960; M.A., U. Chgo., 1962, Ph.D., 1966. Curator U. Utah Mus. Anthropology, Salt Lake City, 1963-66; asst. prof. U. Nev., Reno, 1966-68; asst. prof. anthropology U. Oreg., Eugene, 1968-72, assoc. prof., 1972-78, prof., 1978—, dir. U. Oreg. Mus. Natural History, 1996—. Author: Fremont Relationships, 1966, Hogup Cave, 1970, Great Basin Archaeology, 1978, The Last 10,000 Years in Japan and Eastern North America, 1981, From Asia to America: The First Peopling of the New World, 1990, Archaeology of Oregon, 1993; co-author: Prehistory of Japan, 1982, Great Basin Numic Prehistory, 1986, Early Human Occupation in Far Western North America, 1988; editor: Archaeological Studies Willamette Valley, 1975; co-editor: Prehistoric Hunter-Gatherers in Japan, 1986, Pacific Northeast Asia in Prehistory, 1992, Archaeological Researches in the Northern Great Basin, 1994. NSF research grantee, 1970, 73, 78-80, 84; NSF Sci. Faculty fellow Kyoto U., Japan, 1971-72; Japan Found. research fellow Kyoto U., 1977-78, Tokyo U., 1986. Fellow Am. Anthrop. Assn., AAAS; mem. Soc. for Am. Archaeology. Home: 3470 Mcmillan St Eugene OR 97405-3317 Office: U Oreg Dept Anthropology Eugene OR 97403-1218

AIKIN, JUDITH POPOVICH, languages educator, academic administrator; b. L.A., Aug. 6, 1946; d. Milosh and Jeanne (Hartman) Popovich; m. Roger Cushing Aikin, Dec. 27, 1966; 1 child, Thomas. BA, U. Oreg., 1968, MA, 1969; PhD, U. Calif., Berkeley, 1974. Asst. prof. U. Iowa, Iowa City, 1975-81, assoc. prof., 1981-88, prof., 1988—, assoc. dean liberal arts, 1990-92, interim dean liberal arts, 1992-93, dean liberal arts, 1993-97, prof. German, 1988—. Author: The Mission of Rome in the Dramas of Daniel Casper von Lohenstein: Historical Tragedy as Prophecy and Polemic, 1978, German Baroque Drama, 1982, Scaramutza in Germany: The Dramatic Works of Caspar Stieler, 1989; contbr. articles to profl. jours. Fellow NEH, 1988, Am. Coun. Learned Socs., 1988-89. Mem. MLA (chair exec. com. divsn. German lit. to 1700, 1989), Soc. for German Renaissance and Baroque Lit. (pres. 1985), Lessing Soc. E-mail: judith-aikin/uiowa.edu. Office: U Iowa Dept German 528 PH Iowa City IA 52242

AIKMAN, ALBERT EDWARD, lawyer; b. Norman, Okla., Mar. 11, 1922; s. Albert Edwin and Thelma Annette (Brooke) A.; m. Shirley Barnes, June 24, 1944; children: Anita Gayle, Priscilla June, Rebecca Brooke. B.S., Tex. A&M U., 1947; J.D. cum laude, So. Meth. U., 1948, LL.M., 1954. Bar: Tex. (no. dist.) 1948, U.S. Supreme Ct. 1956, U.S. Ct. Appeals (5th dist.), U.S. Tax Ct. Staff atty. Phillips Petroleum Co., Amarillo, Tex., 1948-49; sole practice, Amarillo, 1949-53; tax counsel Magnolia Petroleum Co. (Mobil) Dallas, 1953-56; ptnr. Locke, Purnell, Boren, Laney & Neely, Dallas, 1956-71; sole practice, Dallas, 1973-81; of counsel Pickens Energy Corp., Dallas, 1981-96; couns. Ptnrs. In Exploration, LLC, Dallas, 1997—. Served with inf. U.S. Army, 1943-45. Mem. ABA, Tex. Bar Assn., Dallas Bar Assn. Methodist. Contbr. articles in field to profl. jours.

AIKMAN, CAROL CHIDESTER, education educator; b. Lexington, Ky., July 25, 1943; d. Charles B. and Jean B. (Hensley) Chidester; m. Donald M. Aikman, Oct. 10, 1964; children: Jeanne, Andrea. BS in Edn., Ind. U., Bloomington, 1965; MS in Edn., Ind. U., Ft. Wayne, 1977, EdD, 1985. Ednl. cons., Ft. Wayne; tchr. English, Ft. Wayne Community Schs.; asst. dir. transitional studies Ind.-Purdue U., Ft. Wayne, asst. prof. secondary edn. Contbr. articles to profl. publs. Recipient scholarships. Mem. ASCD, Nat. Coun. Tchrs. English, Tchrs. English to Speakers Other Langs., Am. Assn. Adult and Continuing Edn., Ind. Assn. Devel. Educators, Nat. Assn. Devel. Edn., Internat. Reading Assn. Home: 1721 Traders Xing Fort Wayne IN 46845-1535

AIKMAN, TROY, professional football player; b. West Covina, Calif., Nov. 21, 1966. Student, Okla. U., UCLA. Quarterback Dallas Cowboys, 1989—. Named to Sporting News Coll. All-Am. team, 1988, Pro Bowl team, 1991, 92, 93, 94, 96, Sporting News NFL All-Pro team, 1993; Super Bowl Most Valuable Player, 1992. Mem. Super Bowl Championship Team, 1992, 93, 95. Office: Dallas Cowboys One Cowboys Pkwy Irving TX 75063*

AIKMAN, WILLIAM FRANCIS, venture capitalist; b. Darby, Pa., Aug. 1, 1945; s. John Earl and Phyllis Rose (Miller) A. AB, Brown U., 1967; student, Harvard Law Sch., 1970-72; JD, U. Pa., Phila., 1972. Bar: Mass. 1972. Counsel Mass. Law Reform Inst., Boston, 1969-73; pres. Mass. Ctr. for Pub. Interest Law, Boston, 1973-76, Mass. Tech. Devel. Corp., Boston, 1979-84; mng. gen. ptnr. Gryphon Ventures Ltd. Partnerships, Boston, 1984—; under sec. of econ. affairs Commonwealth of Mass., Boston, 1976-79; pres. Gryphon Mgmt. Co., Boston, 1984—; of counsel Chin, Wright & Branson, Boston, 1994—; bd. dirs. Optex Comms. Corp., Rockville, Md.; chmn. bd. Geltech, Inc., Orlando, Fla., SeasCape Realty, Inc., Boston. Bd. dirs. Fedn. for Children with Spl. Needs, Boston, Mass. Cert. Devel. Corp., Boston; bd. overseers, Mus. of Sci., Boston. Mem. Harvard Club Boston, Brown Club Boston, Union Club Boston. Presbyterian. Home: 179 Beacon St Boston MA 02116-1423 also: Bayberry Rd Truro MA 02666-1186 Office: Gryphon Mgmt Co 222 Berkeley St Ste 1600 Boston MA 02116-3772

AILES, ROGER EUGENE, television producer, consultant; b. Warren, Ohio, May 15, 1940; s. Robert Eugene and Donna Marie (Cunningham) A. B.F.A., Ohio U., 1962, D in Communications (hon.), 1989. Assoc. dir. Sta. KYW-TV, Cleve., 1962-63; prodr., dir. Sta. KYW-TV, 1963-65; prodr. Mike Douglas Show Westinghouse Broadcasting Corp., Phila., 1965-67; exec. prodr. Westinghouse Broadcasting Corp., 1967-68; exec. prodr. TV for Richard M. Nixon, 1968; chmn. Ailes Comm., Inc., N.Y.C., 1969—; exec. v.p. TV News Inc., N.Y.C., 1975-76; pres. CNBC, N.Y.C., 1993-96, America's Talking, N.Y.C., 1993; chmn., CEO, Fox News, N.Y.C., 1996—; cons. WCBS-TV, 1978—; communications cons. to polit. and bus. leaders; v.p. Conf. Personal Mgrs. Author: You Are the Message: Secrets of the Master Communicators, 1987; producer Broadway mus. Mother Earth, 1972; (play) Hot-L Baltimore, 1973-76; exec. producer, dir. TV spl. The Last Frontier, 1974, Television and the Presidency, 1984 (Emmy award); producer, dir. TV spl. Fellini: Wizards, Clowns and Honest Liars (Emmy nominee 1977); exec. producer The Rush Limbaugh Show, 1992—. Polit. cons. Reagan '84, Bush '88. Recipient award for Shakespeare prodn. Fine Arts Mag., 1964; Liberty Bell award Advt. Alliance of Phila., 1971; Commendation award for contbn. to communications Ohio U., 1972; 4 Obie awards for Hot-L Baltimore, 1973. Mem. AFTRA, Dirs. Guild Am., Radio and TV News Dirs. Assn. Office: Fox News 1211 Ave of Americas New York NY 10036

AILLONI-CHARAS, DAN, marketing executive; b. Ploiesti, Rumania, May 22, 1930; came to U.S., 1950, naturalized, 1960; s. Max and Felicia (Lupescu) Charas; m. Miriam C. Taytelbaum, Oct. 8, 1957; children: Ethan, Benjamin, Orrin, Adam. AB with honors, U. Calif., Berkeley, 1952, MA, 1953; PhD, NYU, 1968. Mem. editl. staff San Francisco Coll. Bull., 1953-54; exec. sec. TAHAL, 1955-57; project dir. Marplan divsn. Interpub., N.Y.C., 1958-60; supr. advt. studies NBC, N.Y.C., 1960-62; dir. consumer and comm. rsch. Forbes Rsch., Inc., N.Y.C., 1962; mgr. market rsch. Chesebrough-Pond's, Inc., N.Y.C., 1963-64, new products mgr., 1964-68, mgr. internat. mktg. services dept., 1968-69; pres. Stratmar Sys., Inc., Port Chester, N.Y., 1969-91, chmn., CEO, 1991—; asst., then prof. mktg. Pace U., 1963-85; mem. adv. bd. Premium Incentive Show, 1986-92, Nat. Premium Incentive Show, 1987-92; lectr. Israel Inst. Tech., 1956-58, dir. extension divsn. no. region, 1956-58. Author: Promotion: A Guide to Effective Promotional Planning, Strategies and Execution, 1984; editor: Mktg. Rev., 1960-63, Proc. 1st Ann. Conf. on Rsch. Design, 1964, New Directions in Research Design, 2d Conf., 1965, Planning, 1968-71; bd. editors Jour.

Consumer Mktg., 1982—, Jour. of Brand and Product Mgmt., 1991—, Jour. Svc. Mktg., 1992—; contbr. to Brandweek, Marketime News, Chain Drug Rev., MMR, New Product News. Trustee Inst. Advanced Mktg. Studies, 1965-66, Philharmonic Symphony of Westchester, 1977-80; bd. dirs. Young Men's Bd. Trade, 1960-63, state dir., N.Y. StatJr. C. of C., 1962-63; bd. advisers Ad Expo, 1978; 1st v.p. Student World Affairs Coun. Northern Calif., 1953-54, chmn. conf., 1954; founder Israel Assn. Grads. Social Scis. & Humanities, 1955; pres. Haifa Jr. C. of C., 1956-57. Coro Found. fellow, 1953; Univ. honors scholar NYU, 1968. Mem. Am. Mktg. Assn. (pres. N.Y. chpt. 1965-66, nat. v.p. 1970-71), Promotion Mktg. Assn. Am. (bd. dirs. 1978-98, chmn. edn. com. 1979-81, 82-91, chmn. premium show com. 1982-91, exec. com. 1986-87, 89-93, 94-95, 96-97, chmn. nat. conf. 1988, 96, v.p. 1989-93, 94-95, chmn. retailers and mfrs. conf. 1992, 93, chmn. in-store mktg. coun. 1993-94), N.Am. Soc. Corp. Planning (bd. dirs. 1970-72), Nat. Assn. Chain Drug Stores (nat. industry adv. bd. 1992—), Soc. Profl. Journalists, The Deadline Club, Coro Alumni Assn. (nat. bd. dirs. 1989-95), Sigma Delta Chi, Phi Sigma Alpha. Home: 23 Woodland Dr Rye Brook NY 10573-1723 Office: Stratmar Bldg 109 Willett Ave Port Chester NY 10573-4232

AIN, SANFORD KING, lawyer; b. Glen Cove, N.Y., July 24, 1947; s. Herbert and Victoria (Ben Susan) A.; m. Miriam Luskin, July 12, 1980; children: David Lloyd, Daniel Jason. BA cum laude, U. Wis., 1969; JD, Georgetown U., 1972. Bar: Va. 1972, D.C. 1973, Md. 1982. Ptnr. Sherman, Meehan, Curtin & Ain P.C., Washington, 1972—; mem. faculty continuing legal edn. program State Bar Va., D.C. Bar, Md. Bar. Fellow Am. Acad. Matrimonial Lawyers (pres. D.C. chpt. 1991-94), Am. Coll. Family Trial Lawyers, Va. Trial Lawyers Assn., Md. Bar Assn. Office: Sherman Meehan Curtin & Ain PC 1900 M St NW Ste 600 Washington DC 20036-3565

AINGE, DANNY RAY, professional basketball coach; b. Eugene, Oreg., Mar. 17, 1959; m. Michele Ainge; children: Ashlee, Austin, Tanner, Taylor, Cooper, Crew. Grad., Brigham Young U., 1981. Basketball player Boston Celtics, 1981-89, Sacramento, 1989-90, Portland Trailblazers, 1990-92; basketball player Phoenix Suns, 1992-95, head coach, 1996—; player Celebrity Golf Assn. Tour. Active Cildren's Miracle Network, Spl. Olympics. Holder of record for most 3-pointers mde and attempted in playoffs; one of 4 players in NBA history to make 1,000 or more career 3-pointers. Avocation: golf. Office: Phoenix Suns Am West Arena 201 E Jefferson St Phoenix AZ 85004-2412*

AINSA, FRANCIS SWINBURNE, lawyer; b. El Paso, Tex., Jan. 7, 1915; s. Frank S. and Roselle (McNamee) A.; m. Evelyn Fraser, Jan. 14, 1941; children: Dorothy, Francis Jr., Michael, Mary, Kathleen, Richard, Barbara, Stephen. AB, Georgetown U., 1936; LLB, Harvard U., 1940; postgrad., U.S. Army Sch. Mil. Govt.; postgrad ethnology, archaeology, U. Tex., El Paso. Legal officer sup. hq. AEF Mission to Luxembourg, 1944-45; pvt. practice law El Paso, Tex., 1947—. Bd. chmn. Mary L. Peyton Found., El Paso, 1955-77; mem. zoning bd. of adjustment, El Paso, 1960. Maj. U.S. Army Cavalry, 1942-46 ETO. Decorated Bronze Star, 1946, Croix de Guerre (Luxembourg), 1946; named Officer Order of Couronne de Chene (Luxembourg), Officer Order of Leopold II (Belgium), 1946, Knight of St Gregory, Holy See, 1965, Knight Grand Comdr. Equestrian Order of Holy Sepulchre Jerusalem, 1985. Roman Catholic. Avocations: photography, firearms, automotive. Home and Office: 525 Corto Way El Paso TX 79902-3817

AINSCOUGH, THOMAS LEE, JR., business educator, internet marketing consultant; b. Washington, Pa., Nov. 2, 1962; s. Thomas Lee and Carolyn Martha Ainscough; m. Michelle Parrish, Dec. 28, 1985; children: Kira Michelle, Andrew Thomas, Elena Jean. BS, Brigham Young U., 1987; MBA, Idaho State U., 1990; PhD in Bus. Admistrn., U. Ga., 1994. Instr. dept. mktg. U. Ga., Athens, 1991-94; asst. prof. mktg. and bus. info. sys. U. Mass., Dartmouth, 1994—; condr. seminars in field, 1995—; conf. presenter in field, including Acad. Mktg. Sci. Conf., Coral Gables, Fla., 1997, Mktg. Sci. Conf., U. Calif., Berkeley, 1997, Am. Soc. Bus. and Behavioral Scis., Las Vegas, Nev., 1998, Mktg. Sci. Conf., INSEAD, Fonainebleau, France, 1998, Assn. for Consumer Rsch. 1998 Conf., Montreal, Que., Can. Author: Multimedia Resource Guide, 1997; contbr. articles to profl. jours. Cohen fellow U. Ga., 1990-94, Comer fellow, 1990-92; Chancellor's Com. on Innovation in Tchg. grantee U. Mass., 1995, President's Office grantee, 1996; grantee Healey Found., 1996. Fax: 508-999-8646. E-mail: tainscough@umassd.edu. Office: U Mass Dartmouth Charleton Coll Bus North Dartmouth MA 02747-2300

AINSLIE, GEORGE WILLIAM, psychiatrist, behavioral economist; b. Ithaca, N.Y., Sept. 19, 1944; s. George William and Elizabeth Lee Ainslie; m. Elizabeth Boyd Keeney, June 25, 1966; children: Matthew Forrest, Roger Scott, Eleanor Ruth. BA, Yale Coll., 1965; MD, Harvard Med. Sch., 1969. Diplomate Am. Bd. Psychiatry and Neurology; cert. adult psychiatry. Intern Mary Imogene Bassett Hosp., Cooperstown, N.Y., 1969-70; resident in psychiatry Mass. Mental Health Ctr., Boston, 1970-71, 73-75; fellow Harvard U. Health Svcs., Cambridge, Mass., 1975-76; asst. clin. dir. Mass. Mental Health Ctr., Boston, 1976-79; psychiatrist VA Med. Ctr., Coatesville, Pa., 1979-90, chief psychiatrist, 1990—; asst. prof. Jefferson Med. Coll., Phila., 1979-85, assoc. prof., 1985-92; clin. prof. Temple U. Med. Coll., Phila., 1992—; rsch. assoc. Harvard Lab. Exptl. Psychology, Cambridge, Mass., 1967-78. Author: Picoeconomics: The Strategic Interaction of Successive Motivational States Within The Person, 1992; contbr. articles on motivational conflict to profl. jours. Surgeon, USPHS, 1971-73. Mem. Players Club Swarthmore (stage dir.), Phi Beta Kappa. Avocations: dramatics, writing fiction. Office: Dept Psychiatry VA Med Ctr 116A Coatesville PA 19320*

AINSLIE, KIMBLE FLETCHER, scholar, research consultant, writer; b. London, Ont., Can., May 5, 1951; came to U.S., 1995; s. Bryan Harold and Alice Jean Ainslie; m. Robin Elizabeth Nixon, Apr. 27, 1954. BA with honors, U. Western Ont., London, 1974; MPA, Queens U., Kingston, Ont., 1976; PhD, York U., Toronto, 1987; postgrad., Harvard U. Exec. asst. Town of Whitby, Ont., 1976-77; cons. Nordex Group, Toronto, 1977-80; lectr. U. Western Ont., 1980-83; prin. cons. Nordex Group, London, Ont., 1983-85; pres. Nordex Rsch., London, Ont., 1985-95, Nordex Rsch. Internat., Ft. Lauderdale, Sarasota, Fla., 1995—; rsch. assoc. Kennedy Sch./Harvard U., Cambridge, Mass., 1999—. Author: The Big State and Small Business, 1999; editor: Conservative Corrections, 1993; co-editor: Understanding Entrepreneurship, 1988; contbr. articles to profl. jours. Mem. exec. bd. Inst. of Pub. Adminstrn. of Can., Toronto; advisor to min. of small bus. Govt. of Can., Ottawa, 1989; leader, pres. Ont. Reform Party, 1994-95. 2d lt. Can. Army, 1986-88. Recipient Regional Leader award London Free Press, 1990, Rotary Leadership award, 1968; named Outstanding Young Londoner, West London Jaycees, 1988; Queen's Grad. scholar, 1975; Can. Fedn. Ind. Bus. doctoral fellow, 1980. Mem. Mktg. Rsch. Assn. (dir. Fla. chpt. 1999—), Can.-Am. Bus. Alliance (exec. mem.), So. Econ. Devel. Coun., Coun. for Urban Econ. Devel. Avocations: reading, sailing, travel, writing. Office: Nordex Rsch Internation Inc PO Box 4045 Sarasota FL 34230

AINSWORTH, CYNTHEA LEE, folklorist; b. Sept. 6, 1953. BA in Clssical Studies, U. Mo., 1981, MA in English, 1989; PhD in Folklore, U. Ind., 1997. Adj. faculty U. Alaska, Tok, Glennallen, 1986—; folklorist, fieldworker Ind. Arts Coun., 1984; folklorist Mentasta Cultural Enhancement Project, 1992-93; cons. Yukon Native Lang. Ctr., 1992-98; dir. Tanacross Oral History/Photo Project, 1995-96; project dir. ANA Lang. Planning Grant, 1995-97; grant dir. Athabascan Lang. Devel. Mt. Sanford Tribal Consortium, Alaska, 1995—; dir. Mt. Sanford Tribal Consortium Lang. Ctr. Project, 1999; presenter in field. Author: Ethnographic Overview of Ahtna Indians, 1996-99; author, videographer: Mentasta Community History, 1996-99, Chistochina Community History, 1996-99, Mentasta Remembers, 1996-99. E-mail: rfcla@aurora.alaska.edu. Office: Star Route 560 Gakona AK 99586

AINSWORTH, HARRIET CRAWFORD, journalist, public relations consultant; b. Columbus, Ohio, Nov. 27, 1914; d. Harry Hoskins and Pansy Lucy (Graham) Crawford; m. J. Gordon Ainsworth, Oct. 6, 1945; children: J. Gordon Jr., Adeline Ainsworth Forrest. BA, Ohio Wesleyan U., 1934; postgrad., Columbia U. Sch. Journalism, 1934-35, Gonzaga U., 1940, Calif. Coll. Arts and Crafts, 1968; life adult edn.-C.C. tchg. credential, U. Calif., Berkeley, 1967. Reporter Portland Oregonian, 1936-37; ind. pub. rels. writer, 1937-42; fgn. corr. Oakland Tribune, Indpls. Star, Japan, China, The Philippines, 1946; pub. info. dir. Am. Cancer Soc., Contra Costa County, Calif., 1958-89; cons. Calif. divsn. Am. Cancer Soc., 1965-77; pres. Ainsworth-Powell Pub. Rels., 1965-77, Corp. Identity Assocs., Orinda, Calif., 1966—; columnist (Sunbeams), feature writer Contra Costa Sun, Contra Costa Times, 1990—. Co-author: The Road Back, 1968; contbr. articles to profl. jours., newspaper columns. Mem. Citizen's Recreation Commn., dist. 6, Orinda, 1974-79; founder, pres. Orinda Found., 1975; chmn. spl. events Calif. Shakespeare Festival Amphitheater campaign, 1988-92. Lt. comdr. USNR, 1942-58. Named Orinda Citizen of Yr., 1976; recipient Plaque and Resolution Commendation Recreation Dist. 6, Orinda, 1979, Recognition award Plaque Pres. U.S. People-to-People Sports Com. Mem. San Francisco Pub. Rels. Round Table, Contra Costa Press Club, East Bay Women's Press Club (past pres.), Orinda Country Club, Orindawoods Tennis Club, Orinda Tennis Club, Kappa Alpha Theta (co-founder Diablo Valley chpt.). Avocations: tennis.

AINSWORTH, JOAN HORSBURGH, university development director; b. Cleve., Dec. 30, 1942; d. Donald Francis and Elaine Mildred Horsburgh; m. Richard B. Ainsworth Jr., Oct. 30, 1965; children: Richard B. III, Alison. BA, Wells Coll., 1965; MBA, Case Western Res. U., 1986. Cert. fund raising exec. 1994. Social worker San Diego County (Calif.) Welfare Dept., 1966-68; social worker, vol. coord. Washtenaw County (Mich.) Juvenile Ct., Ann Arbor, 1968-70; adminstrv. asst. to pres. Med. Ventures, Ltd., Cleve., 1985-86; dir. Project MOVE, Office of Mayor City of Cleve., 1986-89; dir. devel. and pres.'s programs Case Western Res. U., Cleve., 1989-97, dir. spl. gifts and prin. projects, 1997-98, dir. devel. Coll. Arts and Scis., 1998—. Trustee, v.p. Children's Aid Soc., Cleve., 1989—, pres., 1997; trustee, chair devel. Project: LEARN, Cleve., 1990-96; past trustee, cmty. vol. Jr. League Cleve., Inc., 1971—; mem. Vol. Ohio, 1987—. Named Hon. Mayor City of Cleve., 1989. Mem. Nat. Assn. Fundraising Execs. (cert.; chair publicity Greater Cleve. chpt. 1994-96), Coun. for Advancement and Support of Edn. Avocations: flying, tennis, boating, travel. Home: 2023 Lyndway Rd Cleveland OH 44121-4265 Office: Case Western Res U 10900 Euclid Ave Cleveland OH 44106-1712

AINSWORTH, KIMBERLY E., federal employee; b. Aug. 21, 1969. BA, U. Mass., 1991; MS, Northeastern U., 1996. Exec. dir. Greater Boston Fed. Exch. Bd., Boston, 1996—. Email: kim.ainsworth@gsa.gov. Office: 10 Causeway St Ste 1075 Boston MA 02222-1047

AISENBERG, ALAN C., physician, educator, researcher; b. N.Y.C., Dec. 7, 1926; s. Jacob and Celia (Able) A.; m. Nadya Margulies, Oct. 2, 1952; children: James, Margaret. SB, Harvard U., 1945, MD, 1950; PhD, U. Wis., 1956. Diplomate Am. Bd. Internal Med. Internship and resident Presbyn. Hosp., N.Y.C., 1950-53; instr. medicine Harvard Med. Sch., Boston, 1956-62, asst. prof., 1962-69, assoc. prof., 1969-84, prof., 1984—; asst. physician Mass. Gen. Hosp., Boston, 1959-69, assoc. physician, 1969-84, physician, 1984—; mem. Clin. Trials Com. Nat. Cancer Inst., Bethesda, Md., 1977-82. Author: Glycolysis and Respiration of Tumors, 1961, Malignant Lymphoma: Biology , Natural History and Treatment, 1991; contbr. over 150 articles on rsch. in oncology to profl. jours. Recipient Guggenheim Fellowship, Guggenheim Found. Nat. Inst. for Med. Research, London, 1964-65. Mem. Am. Coll. of Physicians, Am. Soc. of Clin. Oncology, Am. Assn. Immunologists. Home: 124 Chestnut St Boston MA 02108-3318 Office: Mass Gen Hosp Fruit St Boston MA 02114-2620

AISENBERG, BENNETT S., lawyer; b. Feb. 17, 1931; s. Joseph Samuel and Minna Ruth (Cohan) A. BA, Brown U., 1952; JD, Harvard U., 1955. Bar: Mass. 1955, Colo. 1958, U.S. Dist. Ct. Colo. 1958, U.S. Ct. Appeals (10th cir.) 1958. Ptnr. Gorsuch, Kirgis, Denver, 1958-80; pvt. practice Denver, 1980—. Mem. Nat. Acad. Arbitrators, Colo. Trial Lawyers Assn. (pres. 1984-85), Denver Bar Assn. (trustee 1982-85, 86-89, pres. 1991-92), Colo. Bar Assn. (pres. 1998-99). Office: Colorado State Bank Bldg 1600 Broadway Ste 2350 Denver CO 80202-4921

AISENBERG, IRWIN MORTON, lawyer; b. Worcester, Mass., Aug. 8, 1925; s. William and Esther (Lewis) A.; m. Lois P., Sept. 4, 1955 (div. Apr. 1986); children: Karen Sue Portner, Sondra Lee, David Craig, Steven Bennett. BS in Chem Engring., Carnegie Mellon U., 1946; JD, Georgetown U., 1957. Bar: D.C. 1958, U.S. Ct. of Customs and Patent Appeals 1958, U.S. Ct. Appeals (D.C. cir.) 1958, U.S. Supreme Ct. 1964, N.J. 1965, Va. 1969, U.S. Ct. Appeals (fed. cir.) 1982; registered profl. engr., Mass. Patent examiner U.S. Patent and Trademark Office, Washington, 1954-57; assoc. atty. Wenderoth, Lind & Ponack, Washington, 1957-63; chief patent counsel Sandoz, Inc., Hanover, N.J., 1963-67; pvt. practice Washington, 1967-75; ptnr. Berman, Aisenberg & Platt, Washington, 1975-91, mng. ptnr., 1980-85; ptnr. Jacobson, Price, Holman & Stern, Washington, 1991—; lectr. Franklin Pierce Law Sch., Concord, N.H., 1980-88; mem. appeal bd. Nat. Register of Health Svc. Providers in Psychology, 1987-89. Mem. editl. adv. bd. IDEA, Jour. Law and Tech., 1981-95; author: Attorney's Dictionary of Patent Claims, 1985, Patent Law Precedent, 1991, 2d edit., 1992, Modern Patent Law Precedent, 3d edit., 1997, 4th edit., 1999; contbr. articles to profl. jours.; patentee in field. Served to cpl. U.S. Army, 1950-52. Mem. ABA, Internat. Assn. Protection Indsl. Property, Am. Intellectual Property Law Assn., Am. Arbitration Assn. (mem. panel arbitrators). Jewish. Club: Kenwood Golf and Country, Am. Contract Bridge League (life master). Home: 6402 Kirby Rd Bethesda MD 20817-5524 Office: Jacobson Price Holman & Stern Jenifer Bldg 400 7th St NW Washington DC 20004

AISENBREY, STUART KEITH, trust company official; b. Huron, S.D., Feb. 4, 1942; s. Amandus Ernest and Alma Olive (Hins) A.; m. Beverly K. Walker, June 6, 1964. BA, Yale U., 1964; MBA, Pace U., 1985. From jr. position to sr. v.p. U.S. Trust Co. of N.Y., N.Y.C., 1964—; bd. dirs. Diaz Corp., N.Y.C., U.S. Trust Cayman, U.S. Trust N.J., U.S. Trust N.Y. Internat. Corp.; chmn. Corp. Fiduciary Counsel, N.Y.C. Served with U.S. Army, 1966-68. Mem. N.Y. State Bankers Assn. (chmn. trust and estate tng. com. 1979-85), Yale Club (N.Y.C.), Hudson Nat. Golf Club (founder). Congregationalist. Office: US Trust Co of New York 114 W 47th St Ste C-1 New York NY 10036-1594

AISHMAN, SHARON KAY, science educator; b. Ft. Smith, Ark., Oct. 12, 1953; d. Richard Eugene and Geraldine (Bradley) Goff; m. Tom J. Aishman, Dec. 23, 1971; children: Vanessa Meagher, Samantha, Erica. RN, Westark C.C., Ft. Smith, 1976; BSEd, Northeastern State U., Tahlequah, Okla., 1988, MEd, 1992. Cert. tchr., adminstr., Okla.; RN, Ark. RN, CPR instr. St. Edward Mercy Med. Ctr., Ft. Smith, 1976-77; sci. tchr. Spiro (Okla.) Pub. Schs., 1988—; mem. curriculum devel. com. Spiro Mid. Sch., 1996-98. Pres. Spiro Band Boosters, 1996-97. Grantee Spiro Found. for Acad. Excellence, 1997, 99. Mem. Okla. Edn. Assn., Delta Kappa Gamma. Avocations: sewing, reading. Office: Spiro Pub Schs 600 W Broadway St Spiro OK 74959-2428

AISNER, JOSEPH, oncologist, physician; b. Munich, Jan. 5, 1944; came to U.S., 1948; s. Philip and Faye Aisner; m. Seena Feldman, Aug. 31, 1969; children: Dara Lianna, Leon Andrew. BS in Chemistry, Wayne State U., 1965, MD, 1970. Intern Sinai Hosp. Detroit, 1970-71; resident Georgetown U. Hosp., Washington, 1971-72; commd. med. officer USPHS, 1972, advanced through grades to rank 05; clin. assoc. Nat. Cancer Inst., Balt., 1972-75, sr. investigator, 1975-78, chief med. oncology, 1978-81; resigned USPHS, 1981; chief med. oncology U. Md. Cancer Ctr., Balt., 1981-92, dep. dir. clin. affairs, 1982-88, ctr. dir., 1988-93; prof. medicine U. Medicine and Dentistry of N.J., New Brunswick, 1995—, prof. environ. and cmty. medicine, 1996—; prof. medicine U. Md., 1982-95, prof. oncology, 1982-95, prof. pharmacology, 1985-95, prof. clin. pharmacy, 1987-95, prof. epidemiology preventive medicine, 1993-95; mem. N.J. Legis. Commn. Pain Mgmt., 1998. Editor books; contbr. numerous chpts. to books and articles and abstracts to profl. jours. Bd. dirs. Md. Chpt. Am. Cancer Soc., 1988-94, Am. Assn. Cancer Edn., 1990; exec. com. Md. Cancer Consortium, chmn. breast cancer sect., 1992-93, chmn., 1993-95,; mem. Gov.'s Coun. Cancer Prevention, 1991, exec. com., 1991-95; bd. dirs. Md. Children's Cancer Found., 1991-95. nat. Cancer Inst. grantee, 1982-95. Fellow ACP; mem. Am. Fedn. Clin. Rsch., Am. Soc. Clin. Oncology (edn. program 1985-86, bd. dirs. 1991-94), Am. Assn. Cancer Rsch., Cancer Leukemia Group B (bd. dirs. 1982-95, vice chair breast sect. 1980-86), Am. Radium Soc. (sci. program com. 1993-94), Ea. Cooperation Oncology Group (prin. investigation com. 1996—). Home: 6 Cotswold Ln Warren NJ 07059-6900 Office: Cancer Institute of NJ 195 Little Albany St New Brunswick NJ 08901-1914

AITAY, VICTOR, concert violinist, music educator; b. Budapest, Hungary; came to U.S., 1946, naturalized, 1952; s. Sigmund and Irma (Fazekas) A.; m. Eva Vera Kellner; 1 child, Ava Georgianna. Pvt. studies with father; entered, Royal Acad. Music at age 7; studies with Bela Bartok, studies with Ernest von Dohnanyi, studies with Leo Weiner, studies with Zoltan Kodaly; artist diploma, Franz Liszt Royal Acad. Music, Budapest, 1939; DFA, Lake Forest Coll., 1986. prof. 1st Internat. String Congress; prof. violin DePaul U., Chgo., 1962—. Organizer, leader Aitay String Quartet, European tour, recitals; also solo symphony orchs.; concertmaster Met. Opera Assn., N.Y.C., 948-54, Chgo. Symphony Orch., 1954—; leader Chgo. Symphony String Quartet; condr., music dir. Lake Forest (Ill.) Symphony Orch.; numerous performances Casals Festival by invitation of Pablo Casals. Office: Chgo Symphony Assn 220 S Michigan Ave Chicago IL 60604-2501*

AITCHISON, KENNETH W., health facility administrator; b. Can., Dec. 16, 1942. BS in Bus. and Pub. Adminstrn., U. N.D., 1965, MS in Bus. and Pub. Adminstrn., 1969; MS in Pub. Health, U. Mich., 1977. Pres., CEO Kessler Rehab. Corp., West Orange, N.J., 1979—. Office: 300 Executive Dr West Orange NJ 07052

AITKEN, DOUG, artist. Student, Marymount Coll., Palos Verdes, Calif., 1986-87; BFA, Art Ctr. Coll. Design, Pasadena, Calif., 1991. One-man shows include AC Project Room, N.Y.C., 1993, 303 Gallery, N.Y.C., 1994, 97, 98, Pasco Art Ctr., Holiday, Fla., 1994, Taka Ishil Gallery, Tokyo, 1996, 98, Gallery Side Two, Tokyo, 1998, Jiri Svestka Gallery, Prague, Czech Republic, 1998, Doug Lawing Gallery, Houston, 1999, Victoria Miro Gallery, London, 1999, Dallas Mus. Art, 1999, Pitti Discovery Series, Florence, Italy, 1999; group shows include AC Project Room, N.Y.C., 1991, 93, 98, Stux Gallery, N.Y.C., 1992, New Museum Contemporary Art, N.Y.C., 1992, Christopher Middendorf Gallery, Washington, 1992, Rushmore Estate, 1993, 303 Gallery, 1993, Santa Monica Mus. Art, 1994, Ma'nes Space, Prague, 1994, Espace Montjoie, Paris, 1994, Flash Art Mus., Trevi, Italy, 1994, Lisson Gallery, London, 1994, Mus. Lab. Art Contemporanea, Rome, 1995, Musee Art Ville Paris, 1995, Elga Wimmer Gallery, N.Y.C., 1996, Lauren Wittles Gallery, N.Y.C., 1996, Basilico Fine Arts, N.Y.C., 1996, Bard Ctr. Curatorial Studies, Annandale-on-Hudson, 1996, Kunsthalle N.Y., 1996, Kunstraum Vienna, 1996, Galleria Civica Art Modern Contemporanes Turin, Italy, 1996, Bonnefanten Mus., Maastricht, The Netherlands, 1996, Modern Gallery, Ljubljiana, 1997, Tivoli Gallery, 1997, San Casciano Dei Bagni, Italy, 1997, Taka Ishii Galley, Tokyo, 1997, Galleri Index, Stockholm, 1997, Cubitt Gallery, 1997 Whitney Mus. Am. Art, N.Y.C., 1997, Photographer's Gallery, 1998, Mus. Ludwig, Cologne, Germany, 1998, Walker Art Ctr., 1998, Long Beach (Calif.) Mus. Art, 1998, Galerie Peter Kilchmann, Zurich, Switzerland, 1998. Office: c/o 303 Gallery 525 W 22nd St New York NY 10011

AITKEN, ROSEMARY THERESA, financial planner, consultant; b. June 26, 1946; d. John Francis and Mary Helen (Kinslow) A.; m. Frank Furch, June 24, 1983. AA, Mundelein Coll., 1976. CLU. Mktg. cons. Anchor Orgn., Chgo., 1974-76; assoc. dir. Big Bros.-Big Sisters of Chgo., 1975-76; fin. planner Phoenix Co., Chgo., 1976—; chmn bd. Lincoln Equities, Inc., Chgo., 1985-88, also bd. dirs.; pres. Capital Interests, Inc., Chgo., 1984-87, Aitken Assocs., Chgo., 1980—; speaker, instr. Chgo. Women's Network, 1984—; cons., columnist Chgo. Tribune, 1980—, Chgo. Sun-Times, 1981—; lectr. Midwest Life Underwriters Assns., 1982—, lectr., instr. Mundelein Coll., Northwestern Univ., Oakton Community Coll., Loyola U. Contbr. articles to profl. jours. Bd. dirs. Loop YWCA, 1974-81. Mem. Women Life Underwriters Conf. (bd. dirs., 1st v.p. 1984-85), Chgo. Assn. Life Underwriters (chmn., bd. dirs. 1984—), Million Dollar Roundtable (life and qualifying mem.), Internat. Asns. Fin. Planners, East Bank Club. Republican. Roman Catholic. Avocations: marathon running, sailing, photography. Fax: (847) 795-8239. Home: Morningside Island 26884 W Maple Ave Mundelein IL 60060 Office: Aitken Assocs 10600 W Higgins Rd Ste 606 Rosemont IL 60018-3720

AITKEN, THOMAS DEAN, lawyer; b. Coffeyville, Kans., July 9, 1939; s. Arthur E. and Kathleen Lucille (Bressie) A.; m. Molly Alexandrea Coston, Dec. 17, 1960; children: Molly Kym Aitken Wright, Michele Bressie Aitken McKinney. BBA, U. Okla., 1961, LLB, 1964; LLM in Taxation, NYU, 1965. Bar: Okla. 1964, Fla. 1966. Assoc. Carlton, Fields, Ward, Emmanuel, Smith & Cutler, P.A., Tampa, Fla., 1965-70, ptnr., 1971-96; of counsel Trenam, Kemker, Scharf, Barkin, Frye, O'Neill & Mullis, P.A., Tampa, Fla., 1996—. Contbr. articles, speaker NYU Tax Inst., 1972; editor NYU Intramural Law Rev., 1964-65; mng. editor Okla. Law Rev., 1963-64; articles editor ABA jour. The Tax Lawyer, 1987. Bd. dirs. ARC, Tampa, 1984-87; pres., bd. dirs. Met. Ministries, Tampa, 1979-80. Fellow Am. Coll. Trust and Estate Counsel; mem. Fla. Bar (tax sect. exec. coun. 1970-82), Tampa Bay Estate Planning Coun. (pres. 1975-76), Beta Gamma Sigma, Phi Eta Sigma. Democrat. Methodist. Avocations: choral music, opera, baritone soloist, clarinetist. Office: Trenam Kemker Scharf Barkin Frye ONeill & Mullis PA 2700 Barnett Plz 101 E Kennedy Blvd Tampa FL 33602-5179

AIUTO, RUSSELL, science education consultant; b. Monroe, Mich., July 13, 1934; s. Crispino and Maria (d'Aiuto) A.; m. Nancy Jane Obenauf, Dec. 17, 1955 (dec. 1980); children: Mary T. Carroll, Susan M. Summa; m. Beverly Bradley, Jan. 3, 1981. BA, Ea. Mich. U., 1958, U. Mich., 1995; MA, U. N.C., 1963, PhD, 1971. Tchr. speech, drama Monroe High Sch., Mich., 1958-61; prof. biology Albion Coll., Mich., 1966-82, provost, 1982-85; pres. Hiram Coll., Ohio, 1985-88; div. dir. tchr. preparation and enhancement NSF, Washington, 1988-90; program mgr. Nat. Sci. Tchrs. Assn., Washington, 1990-93, Coun. Ind. Colls., 1993-95; cons. Gygi Found., Dundee, Mich., 1984—. Author: Mencken and Sara, 1980, Ring Lardner's America, 1984, Dorothy Parker, 1986; co-author: Science Interactions, 3 vols., 1993; contbr. articles to profl. jours. Vice chmn. Albion Improvement Com., 1983-85. NSF grantee, 1968. Mem. Sigma Xi, Omicron Delta. Episcopalian. Avocation: collecting books. Home: 5701 Trailview Ct # C22 Frederick MD 21703-5110

AIZEN, RACHEL K., clinical psychologist; b. Tel-Aviv, Israel. MA, U. Ill., 1968, PhD, 1970; postgrad. in clin. psychology, U. Mass., 1980-83. Lic. psychologist, Mass.; nat. cert. sch. psychologist. Asst. prof. Tel-Aviv U., 1972-73; psychologist Northampton (Mass.) State Hosp., 1971-72; clin. psychologist Amherst (Mass.) Sch. System, 1974—; pvt. practice Amherst, Mass, 1974—; intern VA Med. Ctr., Northampton, 1982-83; clin. psychologist Shieba Med. Ctr., Israel, 1985-86; fellow in neuropsychology Mass. Mental Health Hosp., Boston, 1987-88; cons. psychologist Mass. Rehab., 1974—, various local agys. and cts. Cons. editor The Am. Psychologist, 1974; co-author: Psychological Counseling: Principles, Strategies and Intervention, 1990; contbr. articles to profl. jours. Mem. APA (divsn. clin. and psychoanalysis), NEA, Nat. Assn. Sch. Psychologists. Avocations: travel, art. Office: 48 N Pleasant St Ste 204 Amherst MA 01002-1740

AIZENMAN, MICHAEL, mathematics and physics educator, researcher; b. Aug. 28, 1945; m. Marta Beatriz Gershanik; children: Nurith Celina, Ya'ir Gideon. BS, Hebrew U., Jerusalem, Israel, 1969; PhD, Yeshiva U., 1975. Postdoctoral vis. mem. Courant Inst. Math. Scis. Courant Inst. Math. Scis. NYU, 1974-75, prof., 1987-90; postdoctoral position to asst. prof. physics Princeton (N.J.) U., 1975-82, prof. math. and physics, 1990—; from assoc. prof. to prof. math. and physics Rutgers U., New Brunswick, N.J., 1982-87; vis. prof. Institut des Hautes Etudes Scientifiques, Bures-sur-Yvette, U. Paris, 1984-85, Inst. Advanced Study, 1991. Mem. Nat. Acad. Scis., 1997. Sloan fellow, 1981-84, Guggenheim fellow, 1984-85; Fairchild scholar, 1992; recipient Giudo Stampacchia prize Scuola Normale Superior di Pisa, 1982, Excellence in Rsch. award Rutger U. Bd. Trustees, 1987, Norbert Wiener award Am. Math. Soc. and Soc. Indsl. and Applied Math., 1990. Achievements include rsch. in physics and math. with focus on math. analysis of issues arrising in statis. mechanics, quantum field theory, theory of Schrödinger operators and disorder effects. Office: Princeton U 1204 Fine Hall Washington Rd Princeton NJ 08544-0708*

AJAX, ERNEST THEODORE, neurology educator; b. Salt Lake City, Oct. 11, 1926; s. William Theodore and Kathryn Fleming Ajax; m. Gwendolyn

Quilico, June 9, 1950; children: Ted J., Katherine Ajax Steinberg, Wendy, E. Todd. BS in Basic Biol. Scis., U. Utah, 1949, MD, 1951; postgrad., Northwestern U., 1952-55. Diplomate Am. Bd. Psychiatry and Neurology. Chief neurology svc. VA Med. Ctr., Salt Lake City, 1962-86; asst. prof. neurology U. Utah, Salt Lake City, 1962-67, asst. prof. psychiatry, 1965-72, assoc. prof. neurology, 1967-71, prof. neurology, 1971-87, assoc. prof. psychiatry, 1972-87, prof. emeritus neurology, 1987—; assoc. prof. psychiatry emeritus; vis. prof. Multiple Care Facilities, 1976-80; examiner Am. Bd. Psychiatry and Neurology, 1970, 76, 80, 81, 83. Contbr. articles to profl. publs. Capt. USAF, 1955-57. Mem. AMA, Am. Acad. Neurology, Am. Clin. Neurophysiology Soc., Salt Lake County Med. Soc., Utah State Med. Assn. Avocations: reading, travel, hunting, fishing, marksmanship.

AJAX, ERNEST TODD, neurologist; b. Salt Lake City, Aug. 12, 1964; s. Ernest Theodore and Gwendolyn Ajax; m. Denise Edna Zumbach, Dec. 23, 1995. BS in Psychology, U. Utah, 1987, MD, 1991. Diplomate Nat. Bd. Med. Examiners, Am. Bd. Psychiatry and Neurology, Am. Bd. Electrodiagnostic Medicine. Intern in internal medicine U. Iowa, 1991-92, resident in neurology, 1992-95, fellowship movement disorders and clin. electromyography, 1995-97; neurologist McFarland Clinic, Ames, Iowa, 1997—. Contbr. articles to profl. jours. Fellow Am. Acad. Neurology; mem. Movement Disorder Soc., Iowa Med. Soc., Story County Med. Soc. Avocations: bicycling, golfing. E-mail: t.ajax@gateway.net. Office: McFarland Clinic PO Box 3014 Ames IA 50010-3014

AJAY, ABE, artist; b. Altoona, Pa., Mar. 24, 1919; s. William and Mary (Simmons) A.; m. Betty Raymond, Dec. 16, 1947; children—Alexander, Stephen, Robin. Student, public schs., Altoona. With WPA Fed. Art Project, 1939; staff artist newspaper PM, 1942-44; free-lance artist for New York Times, Fortune, Sports Illustrated, other publs., 1946-64; prof. visual arts SUNY, Purchase, 1973—. Exhibited in one-man shows in, N.Y.C., Los Angeles, others, 1964—; represented in permanent collections, Met. Mus. Art, N.Y.C., Solomon R. Guggenheim Mus., N.Y.C., Hirshhorn Mus. and Sculpture Garden, Washington, others; illustrated biography: Abe Ajay (Lee Hall), 1989. With inf. AUS, 1945. SUNY faculty research fellow, 1979. Home: 40 Walnut Hill Rd Bethel CT 06801-1306 *The studio is my workshop and cathedral. No sanity exists outside its walls and no order but that which comes from my hand each day.**

AJELLO, EDITH H., state legislator; b. Apr. 26, 1944; d. Kenneth Aaron and Rozella Christina (Ewoldt) Hanover; children: Linell, Aaron. BA, Bucknell U., 1966. Store mgr. V George Rustigian Rugs, Inc., 1981-93, 94—; interim exec. dir. Providence Schs., 1993; mem. R.I. Ho. of Reps., 1993—; with V. George Rustigian Rugs, 1994—. Democrat. Home and Office: 29 Benefit St Providence RI 02904-2743*

AJEMIAN, CHERYL BLOOM, audit consultant; b. Norwalk, Conn., June 26, 1950; d. Norman R. and June E. (Stiles) Bloom; m. Robert Ajemian, Aug. 15, 1987. AA with high honors, Mohegan Coll., Norwich, Conn., 1984, AS in Psychology with high honors, 1984; ADN with honors, Mohegan Coll., Norwich, 1986; BGS in Human Resource Mgmt. high honors, Eastern Conn. State U., Willimantic, 1993; MBA, Rensselaer Poly. Inst., 1997. RN, Conn.; CEN; cert. ACLS, TNCC. Staff nurse med.-surg. and orthopaedic units W.W. Backus Hosp., Norwich, 1986-87; staff nurse ICU-CCU, Windham Hosp., Willimantic, Conn., 1987-89, staff nurse emergency room, 1989-93; nursing supr. Windham Hills, Willimantic, Conn., 1992-93; nursing supr., asst. dir. nursing Mediplex of Newington, Conn., 1993-94; mgr. patient care Windham Hosp., Willimantic, Conn., 1994-97; audit cons. Aetna Inc., Hartford, Conn., 1997—. Mem. Leadership Hon. Soc., Phi Theta Kappa, Omicron Delta Kappa. Home: 3 Roger Foote Rd Lebanon CT 06249-2423

AJMANI, RANJEET SINGH, educator; b. Indore, India, Oct. 7, 1963; came to U.S., 1995; s. Mohan S. and Shahni Devi Ajmani; m. Manpreet Kaur, June 2, 1996; 1 child, Baani. BSD, Holkar Sci., Indore, 1983, BS, MS, 1985; PhD, Bombay, 1994. Asst. prof. U. Indore, 1985-86; program assoc. Govt. India, Indore, 1988-89; rsch. fellow Sch., Bombay, 1989-94; rsch. asst. Indian Inst. Tech., Bombay, 1994-95; vis. fellow NIH, Balt., 1995—. Avocations: writing, hiking, reading, drama. Home: 6044 E Pratt St Baltimore MD 21224 Office: NIH Gerontology Rsch Ctr 5600 Nathan Shock Dr Baltimore MD 21224-6825

AJZENBERG-SELOVE, FAY, physicist, educator; b. Berlin, Feb. 13, 1926; came to U.S., 1940, naturalized, 1946; d. Mojzesz A. and Olga (Naiditch) A.; m. Walter Selove, Dec. 18, 1955. BS in Engring., U. Mich., 1946; MS, U. Wis., 1949, PhD, 1952; DSc (hon.), Smith Coll., 1995, Mich. State U., 1997, Haverford Coll., 1999—. Rsch. fellow Calif. Inst. Tech., 1952, 54; lectr. Smith Coll., 1952-53; cons., fellow Mass. Inst. Tech., 1952-53; from asst. prof. to asso. prof. Boston U., 1953-57; mem. faculty Haverford Coll., 1957-70, prof. physics, 1962-70, acting chmn. dept. physics, 1967-69; rsch. prof. U. Pa., 1970-73, prof. physics, 1973—, assoc. chairperson, 1989-93; vis. asst. prof. Columbia, summer 1955, Nat. U. Mexico, summer 1955; lectr. U. Pa., 1957; cons. in field, 1962-63; vis. assoc. Calif. Inst. Tech., 1973-74; Exec. sec. com. physics faculties in colls. Am. Inst. Physics, 1962-65, mem. adv. com. manpower, 1963-68, adv. com. vis. scientists program, 1963-67; commr. Commn. on Coll. Physics, 1968-71; exec. sec. ad hoc panel on nuclear data compilations NAS-NRC, 1971-75; mem. Commn. on Nuclear Physics, Internat. Union Pure and Applied Physics, 1972-78, chairperson. 1978-81; mem. U.S. del. low energy nuclear physics to USSR, AEC, 1966; mem. Distinguished Faculty Awards Commn. Commonwealth of Pa., 1976; mem. nuclear sci. adv. com. Dept Energy-NSF, 1977-80; mem. numerical data adv. bd., assembly math. and phys. scis. NRC, 1977-79; lectr. U. Minn., 1994. Author: A Matter of Choice, Memoirs of a Female Physicist, 1994; editor: Nuclear Spectroscopy, vol. A and B, 1960; bd. editors Phys. Rev. C., 1981-83. Mem. Bower awards com. Franklin Nat. Meml., 1993. Recipient Christian R. and Mary F. Lindback award for disting. teaching, 1991; Smith-Mundt fellow, 1955; Guggenheim fellow, 1965-66. Fellow AAAS (mem. governing coun. 1974-80, mem. com. on coun. affairs 1977, 78), Am. Phys. Soc. (chairperson divsn. nuclear physics 1973-74); mem. AAUP, NRC (mem. phys. scis. panel, associateship program 1988-91), Am. Inst. Physics (mem. com. on pub. edn. and info. 1980-83), Phi Beta Kappa, Sigma Xi (nat. lectr. 1973-74). Home: 118 Cherry Ln Wynnewood PA 19096-1209 Office: U Pa Philadelphia PA 19104-6396

AKAKA, DANIEL KAHIKINA, senator; b. Honolulu, Sept. 11, 1924; s. Kahikina and Annie (Kahoa) A.; m. Mary Mildred Chong, May 22, 1948; children: Millannie, Daniel, Gerard, Alan, Nicholas. BEdn, U. Hawaii, 1952, MEdn, 1966. Tchr. Hawaii, 1953-60; vice prin., then prin. Ewa Beach Elem. Sch., Honolulu, 1960-64; prin. Pohakea Elem. Sch., 1964-65, Kaneohe Elem. Sch., 1965-68; program specialist Hawaii Compensatory Edn., 1978-79, from 1985; dir. Hawaii OEO, 1971-74; spl. asst. human resources Office Gov. Hawaii, 1975-76; mem. 95th-101st Congresses from 2d Dist., Hawaii, 1977-90; U.S. senator from Hawaii, 1990—, mem. energy and natural resources com., mem. govt. affairs com., mem. Indian affairs com., mem. Indian affairs com., mem. vets. affairs com., mem. Senate dem. policy com.; chmn. Hawaii Principals' Conf. Bd. dirs. Hanahauoli Sch.; mem. Act 4 Ednl. Adv. Council, Library Adv. Council.; Trustee Kawaiahao Congl. Ch. Served with U.S. Army, 1945-47. Mem. NEA, Musicians Assn. Hawaii. Democrat. Office: US Senate 720 Senate Hart Office Bldg Washington DC 20510-1103

AKALIN, ROBERTA ANN, education counselor; b. Fond Du Lac, Wis., Oct. 21, 1945; d. Emil Jacob and Teresa Cecilia (Thill) Steiner; m. Semsettin Akalin, Feb. 7, 1976; 1 child, Fahri John. BA in Math. and Art, Alverno Coll., 1968; MS in Edn. Psychology and Counseling, Winona State U., 1973; cert. administrational leadership, U. Wis., Milw., 1977. Tchr. math. St. Gregory High Sch., St. Nazianz, Wis., 1968-70; tchr. math., art John F. Kennedy Prep. Sch., St. Nazianz, 1968-72; counselor Lincoln Jr. High Sch., Kenosha, Wis., 1973-75; dean of students Lance Jr. High Sch., Kenosha, 1975-84, counselor, 1985-97, peer helper advisor, 1990-97; tchr. math. summer sch., cons. Kenosha Unified Sch. Dist., 1987-96; sch. counselor Tremper H.S., 1997—; mem. Drug Awareness Week Com., Kenosha, 1990-95; dist. coord. Midwest Talent Search, Kenosha, 1987—; tchr. mentor Regional Devel. Ctr., Kenosha, 1989-90. Sec., historian Prairie Lane PTA Bd., Kenosha, 1987-92; treas. Kenosha PTA Coun., 1989-93; sec. St. Mark Religious Edn. Rep. Bd., Kenosha, 1989-99; bd. dirs. cultural awareness leadership bd. U. Wis.-Parkside, Kenosha, 1990-91; advisor African Hispanic Asia Native Am., Cultural Awareness Leadership Coun., 1992-97, pre-coll. Stepping Stones Advisor, 1997—. Recipient Excellence award Wis. Career Info. System U. Wis., Madison, 1990, Bronze Horn Kenosha/Racine (Wis.) Boy Scouts Am., 1991. Mem. NEA, Wis. Edn. Assn., Wis. Sch. Counselors Assn., Kenosha Edn. Assn. (bd. dirs. 1991-93, rep. 1994-96); Kenosha-Racine Reading Coun., Wis. State Counselors Assn., Am. Sch. Counseling Assn., Southeastern Wis. Assn. for Counseling Devel., Nat. Coun. Tchrs. Math., Wis. Math. Coun., Kenosha Family Connection (editor 1998—), St. Mark Women's Club, Delta Kappa Gamma (scholarship chair 1989-94, yearbook editor 1994—). Democrat. Roman Catholic. Avocations: gardening, calligraphy, walking. Home: 320 116th St Pleasant Prairie WI 53158-5317 Office: Tremper HS 8560-26 Ave Kenosha WI 53143-7446

AKARD, JOHN C., federal judge; b. 1933. BBA, Tex. A&M U., 1954; JD, U. Tex., 1957. Atty. El Paso (Tex.) Natural Gas Co., 1957-60; ptnr. Akard & Kirk, El Paso, 1960-86; bankruptcy judge U.S. Bankruptcy Ct. (no. dist.) Tex., Lubbock, 1986—; trustee El Paso divsn. U.S. Bankruptcy Ct. (we. dist.) , Midland-Odessa Divsn., 1965-86. Office: US Dist Ct (no dist) Tex Fed Bldg 1205 Texas Ave Rm C-110 Lubbock TX 79401

AKASOFU, SYUN-ICHI, geophysicist; b. Nagano-Ken, Japan, Dec. 4, 1930; came to U.S., 1958, naturalized, 1986; s. Shigenori and Kumiko (Koike) A.; m. Emiko Endo, Sept. 25, 1961; children: Ken-Ichi, Keiko. B.S., Tohoku U., 1953, M.S., 1957; Ph.D., U. Alaska, 1961. Sr. research asst. Nagasaki U., 1953-55; research asst. Geophys. Inst., U. Alaska, Fairbanks, 1958-61, mem. faculty, 1961—, prof. geophysics, 1964—, dir. Geophys. Inst., 1986—. Author: Polar and Magnetospheric Substorms (Russian edit. 1971), 1968, The Aurora: A Discharge Phenomenon Surrounding the Earth (in Japanese), 1975, Physics of Magnetospheric Substorms, 1977, Aurora Borealis: The Amazing Northern Lights (Japanese edit. 1981), 1979; co-author: Sydney Chapman, Eighty, 1968, Solar-Terrestrial Physics (Russian edit. 1974); editor: Dynamics of the Magnetosphere, 1979; co-editor: Physics of Auroral Arc Formation, 1980—, The Solar Wind and the Earth, 1987; editorial bd.: Planet and Earth Sci; co-editor: Space Sci. Revs. Recipient Chapman medal Royal Astron. Soc., 1976, award Japan Acad., 1977; named Disting. Alumnus U. Alaska, 1980, Centennial Alumnus Nat. Assn. State Univs. and Land Grant Colls., 1987; recipient Japanese Fgn. Minister award, 1993. Fellow Am. Geophys. Union (John Adam Fleming medal 1977); mem. AAAS, Sigma Xi. *As a researcher of earth sciences, I feel that an artist and a scientist have something very much in common. Both watch carefully a natural object such as the aurora, a glacier, migrating birds, the Arctic Ocean, etc., and abstract whatever they feel the most essential part from the object. Then, an artist paints his abstraction on a canvas, while a scientist puts his abstraction into the form of equations.*

AKAZAWA-EGUCHI, MIYUKI REI REAL, landscape architect, environmental artist; b. Toronto, Ont., Canada, Feb. 2, 1955; m. Barbara L. Flanagan-Eguchi; children: Jahra Jo Nami Typhina Akazawa-Eguchi, Marlise Satori Alyssa Akazawa-Eguchi. B of Tech. Architectural Science, Ryerson Polytechnic U., Toronto, Ont., 1983; M of Landscape Architecture, U. Guelph, Ont., 1986; BA, Fine Arts/Literature, York U., Toronto, Ont., 1987. Designer, landscape architect held positions with several architecture, planning, and landscape architecture firms, Toronto, 1978-90; mng. prin., creative dir. Eguchi Assocs. Landscape Architects, Toronto, 1990—; dir. Design with Nature Inc., Toronto, 1990—; juror, Toronto Real Estate Bd., Annual Garden Competition, Toronto, 1992-94. Projects include Yan Tai Resort Area, China, WindReach Farm, Ashburn, Ont., Can., Blue Danube Non-Profit Housing, Scarborough, Ont., Regional Parks Pre-Devel. Master Plan, Kuwait, Abu Dhabi Corniche, United Arab Emirates, Revolution/Resolution, Toronto, Can., Earth/Home, Toronto, Can., Children's Garden - - An Environmental Transformation, Toronto, Can., St. Patrick Catholic Secondary Sch., Toronto, Can., Seniors' Residence and Nursery, Glad Tidings Pentecostal Church, Burlington, Can., many others, and pvt. residences. Founding mem., chairperson Cmty. Conservation Ctr., East York, 1984; founding mem. adv. com. on environ. Borough of East York, Can., 1984, 96; landscape architect rep./team mem. cmty. assist. for an urban study effort program of the Ont. Assn. Architects, Orangeville; mem. Presteign Heights Sch. Coun., Toronto, 1996—. U. Guelph scholar, 1985-86; recipient Honor cert. Am. Soc. Landscape Archs., 1986, Prize winner Borough East York Ann. Garden Competition, 1993, 2nd Place award Nat. Assn. Japanese Cans., 1994, 1st Place award Am. Soc. Landscape Archs. 6th Ann Visionary Landscapes Competition, 1994, finalist, Mississauga City Centre Park Competition, 1995. Mem. Can. Soc. Landscape Archs., Ont. Assn. Landscape Archs. Nature, spirituality, community development, parenting, aesthetics. Office: 39 Ferris Rd, Toronto, ON Canada M4B 1G2

AKEEL, HADI ABU, robotics executive; b. Cairo, Egypt, Apr. 9, 1938; came to U.S., 1961; s. Kobaisi Aly Abu-Akeel and Zeinab Makhlouf; m. Sofia Sarwat; children: Shereef, Nezar. BS in Mech. Engring., Cairo U., 1959; MS in Applied Mechanics, UCLA, 1963; PhD in Mech. Engring., U. Calif., Berkeley, 1966. Cert. mfg. engr. Acting instr. U. Calif., Berkeley, 1963-66; analytical specialist Bendix Corp., South Bend, Ind., 1966-69; assoc. prof. Ain Shams U., Cairo, 1969-74; sr. staff engr. GM Mfg., Warren, Mich., 1974-76; program mgr. GM Corp., Warren, 1976-78; dept. head mfg. staff GM, Warren, 1978-80, chief engr. flexible automation systems, 1980-82; v.p., chief engr. GMFanuc Robotics Corp., Auburn Hills, Mich., 1982-92; sr. v.p. Fanuc U.S.A., 1992-96; gen. mgr. Berkeley Lab. Fanuc Am. Corp., Union City, Calif., 1992—; sr. v.p. Fanuc Robotics N.A., Inc., 1996-98, also bd. dirs., vice chmn., 1992-98; tech. advisor FANUC Ltd., Japan, 1992—; advisor Mgmt. of Tech. Program U. Calif., Berkeley, 1988-92; chmn. bd. dirs. Robotics Internat. of SME, Dearborn, Mich., 1992-93;. Author: Machine Design, 1972; contbr. articles to profl. jours.; holds over 55 U.S. and fgn. patents. Soccer coach Am. Youth Soccer Orgn.; mem. bd. advisors Sch. Engring., U. Mich., Dearborn, 1991—; chmn. bd. advisors Sch. Engring., Oakland U., 1991-92. Recipient Joseph F. Engleberger award Robotic Industries Assn., 1989, Mich. Sci. Trailblazer award State Mich., 1989. Fellow ASME, Soc. Mfg. Engrs. (internat. bd. dirs.); mem. Nat. Acad. Engring. Republican. Muslim. Avocations: tennis, swimming, camping, travel, machine shop. Office: Fanuc Robotics Corp 3900 W Hamlin Rd Rochester Hills MI 48309

AKEL, OLLIE JAMES, oil company executive; b. Harlan, Ky., Aug. 14, 1933; s. William M. and Jameleh (Raffih) A.; m. Mona, June 11, 1966; children: Omar James, Amanda Dalal, Roanna Lyn. BSME, U. Ky., 1954; M in Aero. Engring., Rensselaer Polytech. Inst., 1955; MS in Mgmt., Mass. Inst. Tech., 1967. Thermodynamic engr. North Am. Aviation, Columbus, Ohio, 1958-59; engr. Middle East Airlines, Beirut, Lebanon, 1959-65, Exxon Corp., N.Y., London, Arabia, 1967-80; pres. Exxon Chem. Mideast and Africa, Brussels, 1981-86, Exxon Chem. Belgium, Brussels, 1986-88; dir. corp. comm. Exxon Chem. Internat., Brussels, 1988-89; pres. Exxon Saudi Arabia, Riyadh, 1989-92; pres. Exxon Mexicana, Mex., 1993-96, ret., 1997. Author: Driving According to Oliver, 1999, Prisoners of Circumstances, 1999. Dir. United Way, Brussels, 1988-89. 2d lt. U.S. Army, 1956-58. Mem. Am. C.C. Mex. (bd. dirs., pres. 1995), Am. Businessmen's Group of Riyadh (steering com. 1979-81, 90-92), Tau Beta Pi, Pi Tau Sigma. Protestant.

AKENSON, DONALD HARMAN, historian, educator; b. Mpls., May 22, 1941; s. Donald Nels and Fern L. (Harman) A. BA, Yale U., 1962; PhD, Harvard U., 1967; LittD (hon.), McMaster U., 1995; HHD (hon.), U. Lethbridge, 1996. Allston Burr sr. tutor Dunster House, Harvard U., 1966-67; asst. prof. history, asst. dean Yale Coll., 1967-70; assoc. prof. history Queens U., Kingston, Ont., Can., 1970-74, prof., 1974—; Beamish rsch. prof. migration studies U. Liverpool, Eng., 1997—; hon. rsch. fellow Queens U., Belfast, 1976-77, sr. rsch. fellow, 1995-96; hon. prof. edn. Trinity Coll., Dublin, 1976-77; hon. lectr. Australian Nat. U., 1985; Cecil H. Green disting. vis. prof. Green Coll., U. B.C., 1995; owner, pub. Langdale Press; guest artist Yaddo Colony, 1985; writer-in-residence Bellagio Ctr., Lake Como, Italy, 1993. Author: The Irish Education Experiment: The National System of Education in the Nineteenth Century, 1970, The Church of Ireland: Ecclesiastical Reform and Revolution 1800-1885, 1971, Education and Enmity: The Control of Schooling in Northern Ireland 1920-50, 1973, The United States and Ireland, 1973, A Mirror to Kathleen's Face: Education in Independent Ireland 1922-60, 1975, Local Poets and Social History: James Orr, Bard of Ballycarry, 1977, Between Two Revolutions: Islandmagee, County Antrim, 1798-1920, 1979, The Lazar House Notebooks, 1981, A Protestant in Purgatory: Richard Whately, Archbishop of Dublin, 1981, The Irish in Ontario, 1984, Brotherhood Week in Belfast, 1984, Being Had: Historians, Evidence, and the Irish in North America, 1985, The Orangeman: The Life and Times of Ogle Gowan, 1986, The Edgerston Audit, 1987, Small Differences: Irish Catholics and Irish Protestants, 1815-1922, 1988, Half the World from Home; Perspectives on the Trial in New Zealand, 1990, At Face Value: The Life and Times of Eliza McCormack/John White, 1990 Occasional Papers on the Irish in South Africa, 1991, God's Peoples: Covenant and Land in South Africa, Israel and Ulster, 1992, The Irish Diaspora A Primer, 1993, Conor: A Biography of Conor Cruise O'Brien, 1994, If the Irish Ruled thr World: Montserrat 1630-1730, 1997, Surpassing Wonder. The Invention fo the Bible and the Talmuds; editor: Canadian Papers in Rural History, 1978-96; sr. editor McGill-Queen's U. Press, 1982—. Recipient rsch. award Can. Coun., 1974-83, 91-94, Am. Coun. Learned Socs., 1976-77, Chalmers prize, 1985, Landon prize, 1987, Grawemeyer award for improving world order, 1993, Biography medal U. B.C., 1994, Trillium prize, 1995, Molson Laureate, 1996; Guggenheim fellow, 1981-85, John David Stout rsch. fellow Victoria U., 1988-89, Univ. fellow Rhodes U., 1990. Fellow Royal Soc. Can., Royal Hist. Soc. (U.K.); mem. Am. Conf. Irish Studies, Phi Beta Kappa. Office: Queens U, Dept History, Kingston, ON Canada K7L 3N6

AKER, SUSAN K., elementary education educator; b. Bklyn., Aug. 4, 1951; d. Mike and Rose Kriegsman; m. David Aker, Sept. 1, 1974; children: Michael, Jessica. BA, CUNY, 1973, MS, 1975; MS, Long Island U., 1976, Long Island U., 1991, Coll. New Rochelle, 1998. Cert. in early childhood edn., elem. edn., spl. edn., libr. sci., sch. adminstrn. and supervision. Tchr. 4th grade Yeshiva of Crown Heights, Bklyn., 1974-75; tchr. 6th grade Hebrew Acad. of Nassau County, Bethpage, N.Y., 1975-76; libr. Jericho (N.Y.) Jewish Ctr., 1978-81, Half-Hollow Hills Pub. Libr., Dix Hills, N.Y., 1978-81; libr. media specialist Uniondale (N.Y.) Free Sch. Dist., 1989-90, Hempstead (N.Y.) Union Free Sch. Dist., 1990-92; tchr. P.S. 105 N.Y.C. Bd. Edn., Bronx, 1993—; internal geography cons. N.Y.C. Bd. Edn., 1996—, staff devel. workshop presenter, 1996—. Contbr. articles to TeacherLink. Grantee United Fedn. Tchrs., 1997, N.Y. Geographic Alliance, 1998, 99. Mem. ASCD, N.Y. Geographic Alliance, N.Y. Reading Assn. Home: 23 Southern Rd Hartsdale NY 10530-2128

AKERA, TAI, pharmacologist; b. Tokyo, July 13, 1932; came to U.S., 1971; s. Jibusuke and Ayako (Omata) A.; m. Chiseko Masuda, Apr. 10, 1962; children—Atsushi, Yukako, Chikako. M.D., Keio U., Tokyo, 1958, Ph.D. in Pharmacology, 1965. From instr. to asst. prof. Keio U., Tokyo, 1960-71; vis. asst. prof. dept. pharmacology Mich. State U., East Lansing, 1967-70, prof. dept. pharmacology and toxicology, 1974-87; dir. med. rsch. ctr. Nat. Children's Hosp., Tokyo, Japan, 1987-91; v.p. Merck Sharp and Dohme Rsch. Labs., Tokyo, 1991—; head, R&D Banyu Pharm. Co., 1995—; vis. prof. Tokai U., Isehara, Japan, 1977, prof. Sch. Medicine, 1990-97; adj. prof. Sch. Medicine, Keio U., 1988—. Contbr. articles to profl. jours.; assoc. editor: Pharmacol. Revs. Mem. Am. Soc. for Pharmacology and Exptl. Therapeutics, Japanese Pharm. Soc., Internat. Soc. for Heart Rsch. Home: 3-7-10 Jingumae, Shibuya-ku, Tokyo 150, Japan Office: Banyu Pharm Co, 2-3 Nihombashi-Honcho, Chuo-Ku Tokyo 103-8416, Japan

AKERLOF, CARL WILLIAM, physics educator; b. New Haven, Mar. 5, 1938; s. Gosta Carl and Rosalie Clara (Hirschfelder) A.; m. Carol Irene Ruska, Sept. 4, 1965; children—Karen Louise, William Gustav. B.A., Yale U., 1960; Ph.D., Cornell U., 1967. Research assoc. U. Mich., Ann Arbor, 1966-68, asst. prof., 1968-72, assoc. prof., 1972-78, prof. physics, 1978—. Contbr. articles to profl. jours. Incorporator Ann Arbor Hands-On Mus. Fellow Am. Phys. Soc.; mem. Am. Astron. Soc. Office: U Mich Randall Lab Physics Dept Physics Ann Arbor MI 48109

AKERS, JAMES ERIC, medical practice marketing executive; b. Jonesboro, Ark., Oct. 14, 1945; s. Ward Eldridge and Dorothy Catherine (Erb) A.; 1 child, William Eric; m. Marie Oreigr, Aug. 31, 1991. BA in Social Sci., Vanderbilt U., 1968; MDiv in Strategic Planning, Louisville Presbyn. Theol. Sem, 1971. Gen. mgr. TGI Fridays, Nashville, 1972-73, Annie Tigues Restaurant & Bar, Jacksonville, Fla., 1973-77; sales rep. Northwestern Mut. Life Ins. Co., Jacksonville, 1977-79, Peter Gregg Mercedes-Benz, Jacksonville, 1979-80; dir. life flight Bapt. Med. Ctr., Jacksonville, 1980-83, dir. spl. projects, 1983-84; dir. mktg. Jacksonville Faculty Practice Assn., 1984-88, v.p. planning, devel. and mktg., 1988—; v.p. mktg. Profl. Biling Systems Inc. subs. JFPA, 1986—, Fin.-Med. Mgmt. Svcs., 1989—, Physician Bus. Svcs. Inc., 1990; pres. Healthcare Mktg. Cons., Jacksonville, 1990—. Master of ceremonies Children's Miracle Network Telethon, Jacksonville, 1983, 84, 89, Am. Heart Assn., Jacksonville, 1988-90; chief auctioneer Sta. WJCT-TV, PBS, Jacksonville, 1983-98; campaign mgr. Senator Bill Bankhead, Jacksonville, 1984; pres. bd. dirs. Suicide Prevention Svcs., Jacksonville, 1983-89. Col. U.S. Army, 1966-96. Mem. Med. Group Mgmt. Assn., Acad. Practice Assembly, Am. Soc. Hosp. Based Emergency Air Med. Svcs. (bd. dirs.), Am. Coll. Healthcare Mktg., Alliance for Healthcare Strategy and Mktg., Acad. Health Svcs. Mktg., N.G. Officers Assn., Ye Mystic Revellers (team leader), Rotary (sec. Mandarin, Fla. 1983-84, Paul Harris fellow 1990). Republican. Presbyterian. Avocations: mountain climbing, flying, whitewater rafting. Home: 8629 Royalwood Dr Jacksonville FL 32256-8447 Office: U Fla. Jacksonville Healthcare Inc PO Box 44008 Jacksonville FL 32231-4008

AKERS, MICHELLE ANNE, soccer player; b. Santa Clara, Calif., Feb. 1, 1966. BS in Liberal Studies and Health, U. Ctrl. Fla., 1989. Forward Tyreso Football Club, Sweden, 1990, 92, 94, Orlando (Fla.) Calibre Soccer Club, 1993, U.S. Women's Nat. Soccer Team, Chgo., 1985—. Author: Face to Face with Michelle Akers: Standing Fast; columnist Soccer Jr. mag., 1995—, Sidekicks mag., 1994, 95. Recipient Hermann Trophy, Golden Boot award FIFA Women's World Championship, 1991, Silver Ball award, 1991, Gold medal Atlanta Olympics, 1996; named All-Am., Ctrl. Fla. Athlete of Yr., 1988-89, MVP CONCACAF Qualifying Championship, 1994, U.S. Soccer Female Athlete of Yr., 1990, 91; named ESPN Athlete of Yr., 1985. Mem. Soccer Outreach Internat. (founder 1998), U.S. Soccer Fedn. (nat. bd. dirs. 1990-95), Women's Sports Found. (adv. bd. 1992—). Office: US Soccer Fedn US Soccer House 1801 S Prairie Ave Chicago IL 60616-1357*

AKERS, OTTIE CLAY, lawyer, publisher; b. Huntsville, Ala., Sept. 4, 1949; s. Merrideth Townsend and Mary Lois (Reed) A.; m. Marcia Bradley Ligon, Mar. 21, 1971; 1 child, Katie Virginia. BA, U. Alabama, Birmingham, 1972, MA, 1976; JD, Samford U., Birmingham, 1985. Bar: Ala. 1985. Assoc. Haskell, Slaughter, Young & Lewis, Birmingham, 1985-86; pub., chief exec. officer Clay-Bradley, Washington, 1986-90; prin. Ottie Akers Law Offices, Birmingham, 1986—. Mem. adminstrv. bd., fin. com. East Lake United Meth. Ch., 1996—; bd. dirs. Bankhead Trail Trust, 1996—. Mem. ABA, Am. Judicature Soc., Assn. Trial Lawyers Am., Ala. Bar Assn., Exch. Club (bd. dirs. Birmingham chpt. 1986, child abuse prevention ctr. 1985-86, 94-96, v.p. fin. 1995-96), Friends of Ala. Sch. Fine Arts Theatre (pres. 1989-90). Home: PO Box 2038 Buckingham VA 23921 Office: PO Box 610462 Birmingham AL 35261-0462

AKERS, SAMUEL LEE, lawyer; b. Chattanooga, Oct. 20, 1943; s. Shelby Russell and Helen Louise (Crumley) A.; m. Mercedes Lilia Vuksanovic, Mar. 13, 1967; children: Bradford Lee, Camby Leigh. BA, Berry Coll., 1966; JD, Memphis State U., 1974. Bar: Tenn. 1974, U.S. Dist. Ct. (ea. dist.) Tenn. 1976, U.S. Ct. Appeals (6th cir.) 1985, U.S. Supreme Ct. 1987, U.S. Dist. Ct. (mid. dist.) Tenn. 1989. Trust examiner Office of the Compt. of the Currency, Memphis, 1975-76; assoc. Luther, Anderson, Cleary & Ruth, Chattanooga, 1976-78, 81-84, ptnr., 1985-93; ptnr. Hatfield Van Cleave & Akers, Chattanooga, 1994, Hatfield Van Cleave Akers & Adams, P.L.C., Chattanooga, 1995-96; spl. agt. FBI, Orlando, Fla., 1978-81; clk. and master Chancery Ct. Hamilton County, 11th Jud. Dist., Chattanooga, 1996—; mem. comml. panel Am. Arbitration Assn., N.Y.C., 1986-96. Asst. instr. SCUBA cert. Lt. comdr. USNR, 1967-71. Named Outstanding Young Man of Am. Jaycees, 1977. Mem. Tenn. Bar Assn., Chattanooga Bar Assn. (bd. govs. 1995-96, sec.-treas. 1997, pres.-elect 1998, pres. 1999—), Soc. Former Spl. Agts. of the FBI (Chmn. Chattanooga chpt. 1987-88, 95-96). Republican. Roman Catholic. Avocations: jogging, bicycling, hiking, tennis, scuba diving. Home: 106 Westwood Dr Signal Mountain TN 37377-2525 Office: Chancery Ct Tenn 300 Courthouse Hamilton Co Chattanooga TN 37402

AKERS, TOM, JR., cotton broker, consultant; b. Woodford, Okla., May 1, 1919; s. George Tom and Sadie Dean (Jones) A.; m. Eleanor Hoskins, Dec. 23, 1971; children: Tom, Alyce, Peggy, John. B.S., Okla. A&M Coll., 1946; postgrad., Stanford U., 1966. Cotton classer Chickasha Cotton Oil Co., (Okla.), 1936-41; exec. v.p. Calcot. Ltd., Bakersfield, Calif., 1946-80; owner, ptnr. Tom Akers-Cotton, Bakersfield, 1980—; cons. Algodonera Comercial Mexicana, 1980—, Central Cooperativa Nacional, Asuncion, Paraguay, 1982, Cooperativa Agropecuaria, Tegucigal, Paraguay, 1983, Algodonera Del Sur, Honduras, 1983, cons., Cotton Trading Corp., Goondiwindi, Queensland, 1990, cons. Zimbabwe Cotton Mktg. Bd., Harare, Zimbabwe, 1994, cons., ACDI/VOCA Cooperative Union Project Addis Ababa, Ethiopia, 1998. Campaign chmn. 18th Congl. Dist. Jimmy Carter for Pres., 1976-80; campaign chmn. Kern County for Tom Bradley for Gov., 1982; mem. Kern County Democratic Central Com, 1978—. Served to maj. inf. AUS, 1941-46, PTO. Named Rotarian of Yr. East Bakersfield Rotary, 1974. Mem. Nat. Cotton Mktg. Study Group of U.S. Congress, Nat. Cotton Adv. Com. Democrat. Congregationalist. Club: Bakersfield Trade (dir. 1960-70). Lodge: East Bakersfield Rotary. Home: 4 Greenfair Ct Bakersfield CA 93309-2423 Office: Tom Akers-Cotton 1716 Oak St Rm 7 Bakersfield CA 93301-3040

AKERS-PARRY, DEBORAH, lawyer; b. Troy, N.Y., Apr. 27, 1949; d. Samuel Lansing and Audrey (Relyea) Rowley. AB, Washington U., St. Louis, 1971; JD, Cleve. State U., 1976. Bar: Ohio 1976. Assoc. Wm. F. Manlove Co., L.P.A.; ptnr. Manlove, Manlove, Rowley & Fuhry, Chagrin Falls, Ohio, 1976-79; pvt. practice Avon Lake, Ohio, 1979-84; assoc. Schwarzwald, Robiner, Wolf & Rock, L.P.A., Cleve., 1984-88; prin. Wolf & Akers, L.P.A., Cleve., 1988—; mem. faculty Ohio CLE Inst., 1985-87, 89-93, Ohio Supreme Ct. Jud. Coll. Teleconf., 1991. Co-author: Disqualification, Family Advocate, vol. 9, #3, 1987; mem. editorial bd. The Domestic Rels. Jour. of Ohio. Trial referee Medina County Ct. of Common Pleas, 1983-84; mem. Profl. Edn. systems, 1990-91; appointee 8th Ohio Appellate Dist. Jud. Conf., 1991, 98, Bench Bar Conf., 1990, 94. Fellow Am. Acad. Matrimonial Lawyers; mem. ABA (family law sect., property divsn. com., 1992—, litigation sect., 1989—, participant Advanced Family Law Advocacy Inst. 1987, faculty 1992-94, 97, vice chmn. family law ethics 1990-91), Nat. Inst. Trial Advocacy (participant Teacher Training Program, Harvard Law Sch., 1993); Ohio State Bar Assn. (vice chmn. family law com. 1992-93, chmn. 1994-96, chmn. legis. drafting subcom. 1989-93, del. coun. of dels. 1990—), Cuyahoga County Bar Assn. (chmn. family law com. 1992-93, trustee 1986-87, mem. grievance com. 1986-96, faculty Trial Advocacy Inst. 1988-89, co-chmn. 1990-91, chmn. 1993), Cleve. Bar Assn. (chmn. family law sect. 1989-90, profl. ethics com. 1986-93), Medina County Bar Assn. (lectr. 1983, 84, 87), Ohio Family Law Inst., Akron Bar Assn., Wayne County Bar Assn., Geauga County Bar Assn., Cleveland-Marshall Coll. of Law Alumni Assn. (trustee 1991-96, chmn. CLE com. 1994-96). Episcopalian. Office: 1515 East Ohio Bldg 1717 E 9th St Cleveland OH 44114-2803

AKESON, WAYNE HENRY, orthopedic surgeon, orthopedic educator; b. Sioux City, Iowa, May 5, 1928; m. June Austin, Mar. 1969; children: Jeffrey, Mark, Cheryl, Gregory. BS, State U. Iowa, 1948; MD, U. Chgo., 1953; MD (hon.), U. Gothenburg, 1995. Intern, Billings Hosp., U. Chgo., 1953-54, fellow, 1954-55, resident, 1954-58; instr. orthopedics U. Chgo., 1957-58; instr. orthopedics U. N.C., Chapel Hill, N.C., 1958-59, asst. prof. orthopedics, 1959-61; asst. prof. orthopedics, Creighton U., Omaha, 1961; prof. orthopedics U. Wash., Seattle, 1961-70; mem. faculty U. Calif., San Diego, 1970—, prof., head orthopedics, 1970-96, acting chmn. dept. surgery, 1981-83, chmn. faculty, 1984-85, acting dean sch. medicine, 1986-88; practice medicine specializing in orthopedic surgery, San Diego; mem. staff U. Calif. San Diego Med Ctr., 1970—; chmn. acad. senate U. Calif. San Diego, 1991-92. Mem. rsch. adv. bd. Shriners Hosp. for Crippled Children, 1980-86; v.p., bd. trustees Orthopedic Rsch. and Ednl. Found., Chgo., 1981-90; mem. rsch. adv. com. Arthritis Found., Atlanta, 1982—; trustee L.A. Orthopedic Hosp., 1999—. Editor: Am. Acad. Orthopedic Surg. Symposium on Heritable Disorders, 1982; editor Jour. Orthopedic Rsch., 1983-92. Served to cpl. U.S. Army, 1946-48. Recipient Nicolas Andry award Assn. Bone and Joint Surgeons, 1966; Kappa Delta award 3X for rsch. excellence, 1967; award for Distinction in Sports Medicine Rsch., Am. Orthopedic Soc. Sports Medicine, 1983, Bristol Meyers/Zimmer award for disting. rsch. career, 1989, Merit award NIH, 1989—, Alumni Disting. Svc. award U. Chgo., 1992, U. Calif., San Diego, 1998. Mem. Orthopedic Research and Ednl. Found. (trustee 1978-85; v.p. 1982-90), Am. Acad. Orthopedic Surgeons, Am. Orthopedic Assn., Orthopedic Rsch. Soc. (sec./treas. Sirot 1992-99, pres. 1999—, co-editor Jour. Ortho Rsch. 1980-93), Academic Orthopaedic Soc. (pres. 1995). Fax: (619) 552-4350. E-mail: wakeson@ucsd.edu. Office: U Calif San Diego Med Ctr Dept Orthopaedics 200 W Arbor Dr Dept 8894 San Diego CA 92103-8894

AKESSON, NORMAN BERNDT, agricultural engineer, emeritus educator; b. Grandin, N.D., June 12, 1914; s. Joseph Berndt and Jennie (Nonthen) A.; m. Margaret Blasing, Dec. 14, 1946; children: Thomas Ryan (dec.), Judith Elizabeth. BS in Agrl. Engring., N.D. State U., 1940; MS in Agrl. Engring, U. Idaho, 1942. Registered profl. engr., Calif. Research fellow U. Idaho, 1940-42; physicist U.S. Navy, Bremerton, Wash., 1942-47; asst. prof. agrl. engring. U. Calif., Davis, 1947-56; assoc. prof. U. Calif., 1956-62, prof., 1962-84, prof. emeritus, 1984—; engring. cons., 1984—; cons. United Fruit Honduras, 1959, Israel, 1968, WHO Mosquito Control, 1969-84, FAO Aircraft in Agr., 1971-84, Japan, 1972, Egypt, 1980, China, 1985, Can. Forest Svc. Herbicide Application, 1987, U. Fla. Aircraft Application Herbicides, 1987; chmn. expert com. on vector control equipment WHO, 1976; chmn. com. on aircraft for agr. Coun. for Agrl. Sci. and Tech., 1982; pres. Calif. Weed Control Conf., 1966. Author: The Use of Aircraft in Agriculture, 1974, Pesticide Application Equipment and Techniques, 1979, Aircraft Use for Mosquito Control, 1981; contbr. over 330 articles to profl. jours. Recipient research and devel. award FAO, 1973-74, research and devel. award WHO, 1978; Fulbright fellow, Eng. and East Africa, 1957-58. Fellow Am. Soc. Agrl. Engrs. (chmn. Pacific region 1965, dir. 1972-74, assoc. editor tech. publs. 1983-93); mem. ASTM (chair E35-22 1982-84), Am. Chemical Soc., Nat. Agrl. Aviation Assn., Calif. Agrl. Aviation Assn., Nat. Mosquito Control Assn., Entomol. Soc. Am., Weed Sci. Soc. Am. (editl. bd. 1968-70), Western Weed Soc. (hon.), Calif. Weed Sci. Soc. (hon.), Farmers Club (London), Sigma Xi, Phi Kappa Phi, Alpha Zeta, Alpha Gamma Rho. Republican. Home: 748 Elmwood Dr Davis CA 95616-3517 Office: U Calif Bio-Agr Engring Dept Davis CA 95616-5294

AKEY, STEVEN JOHN, public relations executive; b. West Springfield, Mass.; m. Joyce Carrier; children: Kendall, Logan. Student, Boston U. Various comm. positions Gov. Michael Dukakis' Adminstrn., 1983-87; dep. nat. press sec. Dukakis' Presdl. Campaign, 1987-88; v.p. Rasky & Co., Boston, 1989-92; search mgr./pub. affairs White House Presdl. Pers.; dir. pub. affairs Fed. Hwy. Adminstrn., 1993-95; asst. to the secd. and dir. pub. affairs U.S. Dept. Transp., 1995-99; William Schulz asst. to the sec., dir. pub. affairs Edelman Pub. Rels., Washington, 1999—. Office: Edelman Pub Rels Pub Affairs Office 1420 K St NW 6th Fl Washington DC 20005*

AKHAVI, SHAHROUGH, educator; b. Tehran, Iran, June 10, 1940. BA, Brown U., 1962; MA, Harvard U., 1964; PhD, Columbia U., 1969. Lectr. U. Calif., Davis, 1970-73; asst. prof. U. S.C., Columbia, 1973-77, assoc. prof., 1977-84, prof., 1984—. Editor Mid-East series SUNY Press, Albany, 1981—. Recipient Postdoctoral Rsch. award Am. Coun. Learned Socs. & Am. Rsch. Ctr., N.Y.C., 1980, Russell Rsch. award U. S.C., 1984; Fulbright scholar, 1991, Social Sci. Rsch. Coun. Sr. scholar, 1998. Mem. Soc. Iranian Studies (book rev. editor 1981-96), Mid-East Studies Assn., Mid-East Inst. Office: U SC Dept Govt & Internat Study Gambrell Hall Columbia SC 29208-0001

AKHTER, MOHAMMAD NASIR, physician, government public health administrator; b. Jullandur, Punjab, India, June 6, 1944; came to U.S., 1970, naturalized, 1975; s. Mohammad and Fazal (Bibi) Sharif; m. Jeanette E. Easton, Sept. 26, 1970; 1 dau., Sarah. F.Sc., Govt. Coll. Lahore, Pakistan, 1962; M.B.B.S., King Edwards Med. Coll., Lahore, Pakistan, 1967; M.P.H., Johns Hopkins U., 1973. Diplomate: Am. Bd. Preventive Medicine. Resident and fellow Mt. Sinai Med. Sch., N.Y.C., 1973-76; chief div. emergency med. service Ill. Dept. Pub. Health, Springfield, Ill., 1976-78, Mich. Dept. Pub. Health, Lansing, 1978-80; dir. health State of Mo., Jefferson City, 1980-82, dep. dir. med. affairs, 1982-84; pres. Mo. Patient Care Rev. Found., 1984-86, prof., 1987-90; dean Coll. Community Medicine, Lahore, Pakistan, 1990-91; commr. Commn. Pub. Health, Washington, 1991-94; sr. advisor HHS Agy. Health Care Policy and Rsch., 1994-97; exec. dir. Am. Pub. Health Assn., Washington, 1997—. Home: 1920 S St NW Washington DC 20009-1124 Office: Am Pub Health Assn 1015 15th St NW Washington DC 20005-2605

AKIL, HUDA, neuroscientist, educator, researcher; b. Damascus, Syria, May 19, 1945; came to U.S., 1968; d. Fakher and Widad (Al-Imam) A.; m. Stanley Jack Watson Jr., Dec. 21, 1972; children: Brendon Omar, Kathleen Tamara. BA, Am. U., Beirut, Lebanon, 1966, MA, 1968; PhD, UCLA, 1972. Postdoctoral fellow Stanford U., Palo Alto, Calif., 1974-78; from asst. prof. to prof. psychiatry and neuroscience U. Mich., Ann Arbor, 1979—; mem. adv. bd. Neurex Corp., Menlo Park, Calif., 1986—, Neurobiol. Techs., Inc., 1994-97; sec. Internat. Narcotics Rsch. Conf., 1990-94. Editor: Pain and Headache: Neurochemistry of Pain, 1990; co-editor: Handbook of Experimental Pharmacology, 1990-91; contbr. over 300 articles to profl. jours. including 10 to Science and Nature, 1971-97. Recipient Pacesetter award Nat. Inst. Drug Abuse, 1993, Pasarow award Pasarow Found., 1994, Bristol-Myers Squibb award, 1998, Edward Sachar award Columbia U., 1998; Rockefeller scholar, Beirut, 1963-66; Alfred P. Sloan fellow, Stanford, Calif., 1974-78; grantee Nat. Inst. Drug Abuse, Washington, 1978—, NIMH, Washington, 1980—, Markey Found., U. Mich., 1988-97. Fellow Am. Coll. Neuropsychopharmacology (pres. 1997-98), U. Mich. Soc. Fellows; mem. Inst. Medicine/NAS. Achievements include first to produce physiological evidence for existence of naturally occurring opiate-like substances (endorphins) in brain; described phenomenon of stress-induced analgesia; described functions and regulation of endorphins in brain and pituitary gland; contributed to understanding of biological mechanisms of morphine tolerance and physical dependence; (with colleagues) cloned two main types of opiate receptors, described critical brain circuits relevant to stress and depression. Office: Mental Health Rsch Inst 205 Zina Pitcher Ann Arbor MI 48109-2214

AKIN, CEM, internist; b. Istanbul, Turkey, Nov. 25, 1964; came to U.S., 1989; s. Rifat and Ozden Akin. MD, Istanbul U., 1988; PhD, U. Louisville, 1995. Diplomate Am. Bd. Internal Medicine. Intern, then resident U. Louisville Hosps., 1993-96; fellow in allergy and immunology NIH Clin. Ctr., 1996—; clin. assoc. NIH, Bethesda, Md., 1996—. Contbr. articles to profl. jours. U. Louisville fellow, 1989-93. Mem. ACP, Am. Acad. Allergy, Am. Soc. Hematology, Asthma and Immunology. Avocations: travel, photography, music, cooking. Office: NIAID/NIH 10 Center Dr Rm 11C210 Bethesda MD 20892

AKIN, JOHN STEPHEN, economics educator; b. Carrollton, Ga., Mar. 10, 1945; s. Lewis Washington and Ruby (Wallis) A.; m. Ella Jane Davis, June 6, 1965; 1 child, John Stephen Jr. BA, Emory U., 1967; PhD, U. Mich., 1971. Vis. asst. prof. econs. U. Wis., Madison, 1971-73; econ. policy fellow Brookings Instn., Washington, 1975-76; sr. economist World Bank, Washington, 1985-87, 96-97; asst. prof. U. N.C., Chapel Hill, 1973-78; assoc. prof. U. N.C., 1978-83, prof., 1983—; vis. scholar London Sch. Econs., summer 1977. Co-author: The Demand for Primary Health Care in the Third World, 1985 (named one of 10 best books in health econs. Health Policy and Planning 1985); contbr. articles to profl. jours. Woodrow Wilson (Found.) fellow, 1967. Fellow Carolina Population Ctr. (mem. exec. com. 1990-95. Democrat. Methodist. Avocations: soccer, gardening, home repair, running, travel. Home: 116 Breckenridge Pl Chapel Hill NC 27514-3253 Office: Univ NC Dept Econs Gardner Hall CB 3305 Chapel Hill NC 27516

AKIN, JONATHAN ANDREW, educator; b. Fairfax, Va., Aug. 13, 1970; s. James Paul A. and Barbara Regine Melms. BS, Coll. William & Mary, 1992; PhD, U. Southwestern La., 1998. Teaching asst. U. Southwestern La., Lafayette, 1992-98, instr., 1998—. Office: U Southwestern La Dept Biology Billeaud Hall 300 E St Mary Lafayette LA 70504-2451

AKIN, STEVEN PAUL, financial company executive; b. Hackensack, N.J., Apr. 6, 1945; s. Richard Ernest and Lucille F. (Mosher) A.; m. Jane Goddard, Nov. 24, 1973; children: Kyla, Susan. BA in Econs., Ohio Wesleyan U., 1969; postgrad., Columbia U., Harriman, N.Y., 1986. Lic. series 7 and 24, NASD, NYSE. Mgmt. trainee customer svc. mgmt. N.Y. Telephone, 1969-78; asst. v.p. customer svc. United Tel. Co. Ohio, Mansfield, 1978-85; v.p. ops. United Tel. Co. Ind., Warsaw, 1985-86, United Tel. Co. Midwest, Overland Park, Kans., 1986-87; sr. v.p., then pres. US Sprint, Kansas City, Mo., 1987-92; pres. Fidelity Retail Investor Svcs., Boston, 1992-95, Fidelity Brokerage Svcs., Inc., Boston, 1995-97, Fidelity Retail Customer Svcs., Boston, 1995-96; pres., chief info. officer Fidelity Investments Sys. Co., Boston, 1997-99; pres. Fidelity Capital, 1999—. Pres. Mansfield Symphony, 1985-86, Lyric Opera, Kansas City, Kans., 1991-92. Office: Fidelity Investments Sys Co Customer Svcs R23A 82 Devonshire St Boston MA 02109

AKINAKA, ASA MASAYOSHI, lawyer; b. Honolulu, Jan. 19, 1938; s. Arthur Yoshinori and Misako (Miyoshi) A.; m. Betsy Yoshie Kurata, Oct. 7, 1967; children—David Asa Yoshio, Sarah Elizabeth Sachie. B.A. magna cum laude, Yale U., 1959; postgrad. (Rotary Found. fellow), Trinity Coll., Oxford U., 1959-60, Yale Law Sch., 1960-61; LL.B., Stanford Law Sch., 1964. Bar: Hawaii bar 1964. Research asst. U.S. Senator Oren Long, Washington, 1961-62; pvt. practice law Honolulu, 1964—. Bd. visitors Stanford Law Sch., 1971-74. Mem. Am. Bar Assn., Hawaii State Bar Assn. (pres. 1977), Nat. Conf. Bar Presidents, Pacific Club, YMCA (bd. dirs., v.p. 1970-81). Democrat. Episcopalian. Office: PO Box 1035 Honolulu HI 96808-1035

AKINGBEMI, BENSON TOKUNBO, biomedical scientist, veterinarian, educator; b. Ode-Aye, Ondo, Nigeria, Dec. 16, 1957; s. Rufus Onetine and Oluwafemi (Adegbayemu) A.; m. Victoria Oyekunbi Ajayi, Aug. 3, 1985. DVM, U. Ibadan, Nigeria, 1980, MSc, 1988, PhD, 1997. Pub. veterinarian Ondo Civil Svc., 1981-86; lectr. Usman Dan Fodio U., Sokoto, Nigeria, 1986-90, U. Ibadan, 1990-92, U. Zimbabwe, Harare, 1992-97; internat. rsch. fellow Population Coun., N.Y.C., 1997—. Contbr. articles to profl. jours. Sec., Ode-Aye Devel. Assn., Akure, Nigeria, 1983-84. Recipient 2d prize European Acad. Andrology, 1997; German Acad. Exch. Program fellow, Berlin, 1994, Fogarty Internat. Ctr./NIH fellow, 1997. Mem. World Assn. Vet. Anatomists Soc. for Study of Reprodn., Soc. for Study of Fertility, Endocrine Soc., Assn. Nigerians Resident in Zimbabwe (sec. 1995-96), Nigerian Vet. Med. Assn. (sec. Ondo br. 1984-85). Christian. Office: Population Coun 1230 York Ave New York NY 10021-6307

AKINS, GEORGE CHARLES, accountant; b. Willits, Calif., Feb. 22, 1917; s. Guy Brookins and Eugenie (Swan) A.; A.A., Sacramento City Coll., 1941; m. Jane Babcock, Mar. 27, 1945. Accountant, auditor Calif. Bd. Equalization, Dept. Finance, Sacramento, 1940-44; controller-treas. DeVons Jewelers, Sacramento, 1944-73, v.p., controller, 1973-80, v.p., chief fin. officer, dir., 1980-84; individual accounting and tax practice, Sacramento, 1944—. Accountant, cons. Mercy Children's Hosp. Guild, Sacramento, 1957-77. Served with USAAF, 1942. Mem. Soc. Calif. Pioneers, Nat. Soc. Accts., U.S. Navy League, Calif. Hist. Soc., Drake Navigators Guild, Internat. Platform Assn., Mendocino County Hist. Soc. (life), Sacramento County Hist. Soc. (life), Northwestern Pacific Railroad Hist. Soc., Crocker Art Mus. (life). Republican. Roman Catholic. Clubs: Commonwealth of Calif., Comstock. Contbg. author: Portfolio of Accounting Systems for Small and Medium-Sized Business, 1968, rev., 1977. Home and Office: 96 S Humboldt St Willits CA 95490-3539

AKINS, MARILYN PARKER, interior designer; b. Oak Park, Ill., Dec. 28, 1932; d. Clifford and Evelyn (Davenport) Parker; children: Tamlyn Akins, Caryn A., Lauralyn A. Kimont, Sharyn A. Student, Beloit Coll., 1951-53; Cert. of Grad., Harrington Inst. Interior Des., 1971. Owner/interior designer Marilyn Akins Interiors, Hinsdale, Ill., 1969-90, Akins & Assocs., Ltd., Hinsdale, 1990—. Projects pub. in Accessory Mag., Chgo. Tribune, Traditional Homes, Chgo. Home and Garden, New Ideas for Decorating, Perfect Home, Furnishings Daily, Met. Home, 1001 Home Ideas, N.Y. Times, numerous others. Mem. designer adv. bd. Burlington House, 1983-86; adv. bd. dirs. Ray Sch. Design, Chgo., 1987-90; design del. People's Rep. of China, 1985. Mem. Am. Soc. Interior Design (Young Mem. award Ill. 1979, Presdl. citation Ill. chpt. 1984, Medal of Honor 1986). Republican. Avocations: tennis, travel. Home: 424 S Garfield Ave Hinsdale IL 60521-4419 Office: 26 E 1st St Hinsdale IL 60521-4102

AKINS, VAUGHN EDWARD, retired engineering company executive; b. Gowanda, N.Y., Sept. 28, 1934; s. Elsworth D. and Alice (Carlton) A.; grad. pub. schs.; student U.S. Naval Schs., 1956-57, IBM Engring. Sch., 1961-65; m. Muriel M. Hoglund, May 15, 1960 (dec. 1992); children: Sonja L., Coleen R., Joseph E.; m. Beverly J. Martin, Apr. 5, 1997. Lab. specialist IBM, Poughkeepsie, N.Y., Boulder, Colo. and East Fishkill, N.Y., 1959-69; test engr. Semi, Phoenix, 1969-74; mgr. computer-aided mfg. and test engring. semiconductor process research and devel. Motorola Corp., Mesa, Ariz., 1974-84; applications mgr. (CIM) Motorola Corp. New Enterprises Group, Mesa, Ariz., 1984-86, mgr. computer integrated mfg. semiconductor products sector, Phoenix, 1986-87; with start-up team SEMATECH, Inc., Austin, Tex., 1988-93, dir. internat. standards programs, 1989-93, mgr. incubator programs, 1992; mgr. strategic integration Motorola Ctr. Advanced Computer Products, Austin, Tex., 1992-98; mgr. mktg. support Motorola Wireless Syss. Ctr., Austin, Tex. Precinct committeeman N.Y. State Conservative Party, 1963; instr. first aid ARC, 1971-78; chair U.S. exec.com. S.E.M.I., Inc., mem. exec. com. internat. standard program. With USNR, 1956-59. Mem. IEEE (sr.), Mensa, NRA, Electrochem. Soc. (cons. to exec. bd.; founding com. chmn. Automation in Mfg. chpt., exec. com. electronics divsn. 1985-92). Republican. Fundamentalist. Patentee in field. Home: 270 West Oak Loop Cedar Creek TX 78612

AKINS, ZANE VERNON, association executive; b. Bethel, Kans., Apr. 13, 1940; s. Gerald Vernon and Vesta Jean (Rutherford) A.; m. Kay Ellen Cowan, Aug. 17, 1963; children: Michael Scott, Deborah Lynn, Christine Sue. BS in Agriculture, U. Mo., 1962. Farmer, 1962-64; svc. technician No. Ohio Breeders Assn., Tiffin, 1964-66; program dir. Holstein Assn. Am., Brattleboro, Vt., 1966-73; mgr. sire devel. svc. Holstein Assn. Am., 1973-77, adminstrv. asst., 1977-78, CEO, 1978-90; exec. v.p. Holstein-Friesian Svcs., Inc., Brattleboro, 1978-90; pres. Zane Akins and Assocs., West Brattleboro, 1991—; pres., chmn. bd. dirs. Nat. Integrated Techs. Inc., 1996—; bd. dirs. Earthwide Assocs., Inc., pres. 1994—; pres. A&S Assocs., Ltd., 1995—; bd. dirs. Vt. Nat. Bank, Earthwide Sys. Inc., v.p., 1995—; v.p. Earthwide Products Corp., 1996—; bd. dirs. Vt. Fin. Svcs., 1987—, chmn. exec. com., 1995-96, chmn. audit com., 1996-97, chmn. loan com., 1997-98; chmn. bd. dirs. Anitech Internat. Inc., Boulder, Colo., 1991-92; trustee N.E. Delta/Vt. Dental Soc., Inc., 1990—, chmn., 1995—. Bd. dirs. Windham County United Way, 1980-84; corporator Brattleboro Meml. Hosp., 1980—, chmn. pub. rels. com., 1982-83, bd. dirs., 1983-86; pres. Windham County Humane Soc., 1992-93; bd. dirs. Brattleboro Area Boys & Girls Club, 1998—, treas., 1999—. Sears & Roebuck scholar, Freshman Curators scholar, Borden's scholar, U. Mo., 1958-59, Sophomore Curators scholar, Campus Chest scholar, 1958-60; recognized as Man of the Yr. Tri-State Breeders Coop., 1984; recipient Citation of Merit U. Mo., 1986. Mem. Purebred Dairy Cattle Assn. (bd. dirs. 1978-90, Recognition award 1991), Nat. Soc. Livestock Records Assn. (v.p. 1982-84), Nat. Pedigree Livestock Coun. (pres. 1984-86, sec., treas. 1989—, Disting. Svc. award 1993), Nat. Coop. Dairy Herd Improvement Programs (policy bd. 1980-90), Geonomics Inst., Boston Dist. Export Coun., Brattleboro C. of C. (bd. dirs. 1979-81), Alpha Zeta (Centennial Honor Roll 1997), Alpha Gamma Rho (regional v.p. 1980-84, bd. dirs. 1984-90, grand pres. 1986-89, Man of Yr. award Chgo. Alumni chpt. 1991), Brattleboro Rotary Club (bd. dirs. 1993-94). Congregationalist. Home and Office: 272 Meeting House Ln Brattleboro VT 05301-8987

AKIYAMA, CAROL LYNN, motion picture industry executive. BA magna cum laude, U. So. Calif., 1968, JD, 1971. Bar: Calif. Atty. NLRB, Los Angeles, 1971-75, ABC-TV, Hollywood, Calif., 1975-79, So. Calif. Edison, Rosemead, 1980-81; asst. gen. atty. CBS Inc., Los Angeles, 1981-82; sr. v.p. Alliance of Motion Picture and TV Producers, Sherman Oaks, Calif., 1982-88; ind. producer and writer TV, motion pictures and multimedia/new techs., Woodland Hills, Calif., 1988—; cons. entertainment industry; founding ptnr. Bierstedt, Akiyama and Assocs., Woodland Hills, 1988—. Mem. Los Angeles County Bar Assn. (chmn. labor law sect. 1981-82, exec. com. 1975-85), Phi Kappa Phi, Phi Beta Kappa.

AKIYAMA, MASAYASU, chemistry educator; b. Okayama, Japan, June 28, 1937; s. Shizuo and Teruko (Tokuda) A.; m. Hiroko Matsuda, June 12, 1969; children: Takuo, Yuko. BS, Okayama, 1960; MS, Tokyo Inst. Tech., 1962, DSc, 1965. Rsch. assoc. Tokyo Inst. Tech., 1965-70; postdoctoral fellow Northwestern U., Evanston, Ill., 1968-70; assoc. prof. Tokyo U. Agr. and Tech., Koganei, Tokyo, 1970-82, prof., 1982—, chief libr. faculty br., 1983-85; vis. scholar Harvard U., Cambridge, Mass., 1986; chmn. dept. grad. course of biol. & chem. sci. Tokyo U. Agr. and Tech., 1991-92; chmn. dept. applied chemistry Tokyo U. Agr. and Tech., 1998; mem. editorial bd. Chem. Soc. Japan, Tokyo, 1988-90. Contbr. articles to profl. jours. Mem. AAAS, Chem. Soc. Japan, Am. Chem. Soc., Royal Soc. Chemistry, N.Y. Acad. Sci., Nat. Geographic Soc. Achievements include polymerization of p-cyanobenzonitrile N-oxide; preparation of N-Hydroxymaleimide; catalytic activity of 2-substituted imidazoles for hydrolysis of acyl derivatives; design and synthesis of artificial siderophores; synthesis and properties of N-hydroxy Peptides. Home: 3-20-11 Nanyodai, Hachioji 192-0371, Japan Office: Tokyo U Agriculture & Tech, 2-24-16 Naka-cho, Koganei 184-8588, Japan *In science, I have tried to be faithful and obedient to Nature and to myself; but in society, faithful to others.*

AKIYAMA, TOSHIO, cardiologist, educator, researcher; b. Shimizu, Japan, Mar. 10, 1941; came to U.S., 1968; MD, Kyoto Prefectural U. Med., 1966. Cert. in internal medicine, specialty in cardiovasc. disease. Intern Rochester Gen. Hosp., 1968-69, resident in medicine, 1969-70; resident in medicine Strong Meml. Hosp.-U. Rochester, 1970-71, resident in cardiology, 1972-73; fellow in cardiology Emory U., Atlanta, 1971-72, U. Chgo., 1973-75; dir. arrhythmia monitoring and pacemaker svc. Strong Meml. Hosp., Rochester; prof. medicine with unltd. tenure U. Rochester Sch. Medicine, 1993—; reviewer NIH study sect. Biomed. Tech. Spl. Emphasis Panel; cons. Exec. com. for Japanese Med. Specialist Joint commn. Editl. bd. Jour. Electrocardiology, Japanese Circulation Jour., Acta Medica Biologica; contbr. papers to 140 profl. jours. Chmn. Rochester Hamamatsu Sister City Com., chmn., 1998-2000. Fellow Am. Coll. Cardiology; mem. Am. Heart Assn., N.Am. Soc. of Pacing and Electrophysiology, Japanese Med. Soc. (exec. com. joint commn. med. specialist sys.), Japanese Clin. Cardiology Soc. Fax: 716-271-7667. Office: U Rochester Med Ctr Dept Cardiology 601 Elmwood Ave Box 679 Rochester NY 14642-8679

AKKARA, JOSEPH AUGUSTINE, biochemist; b. Feb. 22, 1938; came to U.S., 1964; naturalized, 1980; s. Augustine Aippu Akkara and Theresa Anthony Kolapran; m. Mary Ann Malaickel, Aug. 18, 1969; children: Augustine Viju, Jeena Theresa. PhD in Biochemistry, U. Mo., 1969. Med. rschr. Med. Coll. Trivandrum, Kerala, India, 1959-61; tech. asst. Ctrl. Food Technol. Rsch. Inst., Mysore, India, 1961-64; grad. asst., rsch. assoc. Sch. Medicine U. Mo., Columbia, 1964-69; rsch. assoc. Rockefeller U., N.Y.C., 1969-71; rsch. assoc. Brookdale Hosp. Med. Ctr., Bklyn., 1971-73, chief radioassay, 1973-80; sr. scientist Med. Rsch. Inst., Worcester, Mass., 1980-81; biochemist stat. Txicology Svc. Boston, 1981-84; rsch. chemist U.S. Army Natick Rsch. and Engring. Ctr., 1984—; program dir. NSF, 1999—; adj. faculty Framingham State Coll., 1996—; mem. biotechnology adv. bd. Mass. Bay Coll.; advisor NRC; bd. dirs. Invention Evaluation. Recipient R&D award U.S. Army, 1992, 96, Inventor of Yr. award U.S. Army Soldier Sys. commd., 1998. Mem. Materials Rsch. Soc., Am. Chem. Soc., N.Y. Acad. Scis., Kerala Assn. New Eng. (pres. 1986-87), Indian Assn. Greater Boston (sec. 1986-88, 1st v.p. 1988-89), Lions Club, Sigma Xi (pres. Natick chpt. 1998—). Roman Catholic. Achievements include patents and publications in synthesis, modification and characterization of polymers bioengineered materials for electro-optic and high performance multifunctional applications, enzymology, nutrition, endocrinology, analytical biochemistry. Home: 18 Temi Rd Holliston MA 01746-1220 Office: NSF Arlington VA 22230

AKKERMAN, CHARLOTTE ANN, principal; b. Sioux Falls, S.D., Sept. 25, 1950; d. Adrin Winfield and Arlene Edna Jackson; m. Larry Akkerman, Aug. 13, 1972; children: Jessica Akkerman Anderson, Laura. Student, No. State Coll., 1970, BS in Secondary Edn., 1972; MS in Secondary Adminstrn., No. State U., 1990. Tchr. Ctrl. H.S., Aberdeen, S.D., 1972-90; asst. prin. Ctrl. H.S., Aberdeen, 1990—; computer coord. Aberdeen Sch. Dist., 1985-90; team chair NCA OA accreditation Huron (S.D.) H.S., 1997-99. Mem., officer Family and Consumer Edn. Group, Bath, S.D., 1976-99; 4-H leader Dakota Sharpshooters 4-H Club and Dual Doers, Bath, 1984-99; ch. coun.

mem., Sunday sch. tchr. Bethlehem Luth. Ch., Aberdeen, 1985-88. Named S.D. Asst. Prin. of the Yr., McDonalds, S.D. Assn. Secondary Sch. Prins. and Nat. Assn. Secondary Sch. Prins., 1999. Mem. ASCD, Nat. Assn. Secondary Sch. Prins., S.D. Assn. Secondary Sch. Prins., Phi Delta Kappa, Delta Kappa Gamma. Avocations: rodeo, sports, music, gardening, travel. E-mail: cakkerman@aberdeen.K12.sd.us. Home: 39849 127th St Columbia SD 57433 Office: Ctrl HS 225 3rd Ave SE Aberdeen SD 57401

AKOS, FRANCIS, violinist; b. Budapest, Hungary, Mar. 30, 1922; came to U.S., 1954; s. Karoly and Rose (Reti) Weinberg; m. Phyllis Malvin Sommers, June 7, 1981; children from previous marriage—Katherine Elizabeth, Judith Margaret. Baccalaureate, Budapest, 1941; M.A., Franz Liszt Acad. Music, Budapest, 1940, Ph.D., 1941. Concertmaster, Budapest Symphony Orch., 1945-46, Royal Opera and Philharmonic Soc., Budapest, 1947-48, Gothenburg (Sweden) Symphony Orch., 1948-50, Municipal Opera, West Berlin, Ger., 1950-54, Mpls. Symphony Orch., 1954, asst. concertmaster, Chgo. Symphony Orch., 1955—, concertmaster emeritus, 1997—, also performed as soloist; performed at Salzburg Festival, 1948, Scandinavian Festival, Helsinki, Finland, 1950, Berlin Festival, 1951, Prades Festival, 1953, Bergen Festival, 1962, Vienna Festival, 1962, founder, condr., Chgo. Strings, chamber orch., 1961, condr., Fox River Valley Symphony, Aurora, Ill., 1965-73, Chicago Heights (Ill.) Symphony, 1975-79, Highland Park Strings, 1979—. Prizewinner Hubay competition, Budapest, 1939, Remenyi competition, Budapest, 1939. Home: 1310 Maple Ave Evanston IL 60201-4325 Office: 220 S Michigan Ave Chicago IL 60604-2501

AKRE, DONALD J., school system administrator. Supt. Selby (S.D.) Area Sch. Dist. State finalist Nat. Supt. Yr., 1992. Office: Selby Area Sch Dist PO Box 324 Selby SD 57472-0324

AKRIDGE, WILLIAM DAVID, hotel management company executive; b. Mobile, Ala., Aug. 14, 1961; s. William Emory Akridge III and Benita Marie (DeVan) Parnell. BS, Tampa Coll., 1989. Asst. mgr. So. Host Inns, Bay Minette, Ala., 1978-79; ops. mgr. Sheraton Inn, Mobile, 1979-82; front office mgr. Ramada Inn-South, Mobile, 1982-83; gen. mgr. Joli Hospitalities, New Bern, N.C., 1984-86; v.p. GAP Mgmt. Co., Clearwater, Fla., 1986—. Mem. Nat. Assn. Real Estate Appraisers. Republican. Methodist. Home: PO Box 920232 Norcross GA 30010-0232 Office: Ocean Hospitalities Inc 1000 Market St Portsmouth NH 03801-4646*

AKSEN, GERALD, lawyer, educator, arbitrator; b. N.Y.C., Feb. 16, 1930; s. David and Bess (Stein) A.; m. Phyllis Schwadron, June 3, 1957 (dec.); 1 child, Lisa Susan. AB, CCNY, 1951; MA, Columbia U., 1952; LLB, NYU, 1958. Bar: N.Y. 1959, U.S. Dist. Ct. (so. and ea. dist.) N.Y. 1961, U.S. Supreme Ct. 1964. Assoc. Flood & Purvin, N.Y.C., 1958-61; assoc. gen. counsel Am. Arbitration Assn., N.Y.C., 1962-63, gen. counsel, 1964-80; ptnr. Reid & Priest L.L.P., N.Y.C., 1981-98, Thelen Reid & Priest L.L.P., N.Y.C., 1998—; adj. prof. NYU, N.Y.C., 1968—; mem. First Dept. Jud. Screening Com., 1983-93; bd. dirs. U.S. Coun. Internat. Bus., 1982—; ICC Inst. Internat. Bus. Law and Practice, 1992—. Bd. dirs. Nat. Inst. Consumer Justice, 1971-72, World Arbitration Inst. 1984—; adv. bd. Internat. and Comparative Law Ctr. of Southwestern Legal Found., 1988—; pvt. adjudications com. Ctr. for Pub. Resources, 1988—. 1st lt. U.S. Army, 1952-55. Fellow Am. Bar Found; mem. ABA (ho. of dels. 1985-87, chmn. sect. internat. law and practice 1982-83), N.Y. State Bar Assn., Assn. Bar City of N.Y. (chmn. adv. com. on ADR 1992-93), London Ct. Internat. Arbitration, Am. Arbitration Assn. (bd. dirs. 1982-95), Citizens Union (bd. dirs. 1983-86), Am. Soc. Internat. Law. Office: Thelen Reid & Priest LLP 40 W 57th St Fl 28 New York NY 10019-4097

AKSOY, ZEYNEL, manufacturing professional; b. Istanbul, Apr. 20, 1964; s. Muharrem and Selvi (Tanik) A.; m. Mehtap Aksoy, July 7, 1991; 1 child, Evran. BS, Tech. U. Istanbul, 1994; MS, Wayne State U., 1997. Cert. ISO auditor Registrar Accredition Bd. Indsl./quality engr. Star Gasket Corp., Mt. Clemens, Mich., 1988-90, process engr., 1990-92, dir. engring., 1992-93, dir. quality mfg., 1993-94; mfg. cons. EDS, Troy, Mich., 1994—. Mem. Am. Soc. for Quality (cert. quality engr., cert. quality auditor), Am. Productivity and Inventory Control Soc. Avocations: soccer, volleyball, wallyball, table tennis. Home: 47075 Cherry Valley Dr Macomb MI 48044-2832 Office: EDS 300 Big Beaver Troy MI 48089

AKUBUILO, FRANCIS EKENECHUKWU, secondary school educator; b. Ebe-Udi, Enugu, Nigeria, Mar. 25, 1952; came to U.S., 1984; d. Robert O. and Regina N. (Agada) A.; m. Assumpta Ify Chinegwu, Aug. 22, 1987; children: Frank-Roberts, Olivia, Nneoma, Christopher-Daniel. AS, Fachhochschule, Stuttgart, Fed. Republic of Germany, 1983; MArch, Fachhochschule, Frankfurt, Fed. Republic of Germany, 1984; D in Bus., Pacific State U., 1985; M in Adminstrn., Nat. U., San Diego, 1989. BDB, Germany; cert. tchr. bus. & indsl. mgmt., basic edn., bus. edn., social sci., vocat. tng. Asst. archtl. engr. Albrecht Assocs., Stuttgart, 1978-83; asst. lectr. Fachhochschule, Frankfort, 1981-83; legal researcher Control Data, L.A., 1984; legal edn. researcher Am. Legal Systems, L.A., 1984-86; head para-lega litigation, supr. Chase, Rotchford, et. al., L.A., 1986—; adj. faculty prof. Coll. of Canyons, Valencia, Calif., 1990—; tchr. Calif. Youth Authority, Whittier, Calif., 1992—, Hacienda/ La Puente Sch., Whittier, Calif., 1992-93; cons. Udi Div. Schs., Udi-Enugu, Nigeria, 1981-83, Frank's Consulting Svcs., L.A., 1988—; dir., pres. Okuli Enterprises, L.A., 1991—; dir. Enugu Cultural Assn., L.A., 1992—. Mem. German Architects Engrs. Assn. Roman Catholic. Avocations: table tennis, soccer, jogging. Home: 7122 Bon Villa Cir La Palma CA 90623-1167

AKUJUOBI, CAJETAN MADUABUCHUKWU, systems engineer, electrical engineering educator, researcher; b. Umuahia, Abia, Nigeria, Apr. 18, 1950; came to U.S., 1977; s. John Ohiri and Roseline (Amadi) A.; m. Caroline Chioma Njoku, May 8, 1982; children: Obinna Chukwuemeka, Chijoke Eze. BSEE, So. Univ., 1980; MSEE, Tuskegee (Ala.) Inst., 1983; MBA, Hampton U., 1987; PhD, George Mason U., 1995. Asst. prof. elec. engr. Norfolk State U., Va., 1983-96; R&D engr. Austin Product Ctr., Schlumberger Inc., 1996-97; engr. sr. design and devel. Data Race, Inc., San Antonio, 1997—; rsch./systems engr., cons. Advanced Hardware Architectures, Inc., Pullman, Wash., 1998—; assoc. prof., rschr. NASA ctr. space radiation Prairie View A&M U., Prairie View, Tex., 1998—; assoc. prof. electr. engrng. Praire View A&M Univ., Praire View, TX, 1998—; adj. assoc. prof. U. D.C., 1989-90; rsch. fellow NASA, Langley, Va., 1987; tech. staff AT&T Bell Labs., Holmdel, N.J., 1986, 88, 90, 91; prin. engr. Spectrum Engrng. & Tech., Washington, 1991-92; rschr. George Mason U., Fairfax, Va., 1991-94; engr. Intelsat, Washington, 1993; session chmn. Modeling and Simulation Conf., Pitts., 1986-90; judge Tidewater Sci. Fair, Southampton H.S., Courtland, Va., 1994; chief judge sr. engring. design projects Tidewater Sci. Fair, 1996, head jusge, 1995; faculty rsch. participant Argonne Nat. Lab., 1995-96. Mem. SPIE, IEEE (award 1982, 83, counselor 1977—, judge 1986), Instrument Soc. Am. (chmn. digital sys. 1986, session organizer 1986—), Am. Soc. Engring. Edn. (campus rep. 1983—), Soc. Indsl. and Applied Math., Sigma Xi, Alpha Kappa Mu. Roman Catholic. Avocations: soccer, tennis, swinning, volleyball, table tennis. Home: 5023 Cairnleigh Dr Houston TX 77084 Office: Prairie View A&M U Dept Elec Engring PO Box 2117 Prairie View TX 77446-2117

AKUKWE, CHINUA, public health physician, health service executive; b. Aug. 7, 1962. MD, U. Nigeria, Enugu, 1985; M in Pub. Health, Hebrew U., Jerusalem, Israel, 1991. Sci. coord. NIH, D.C. Initiative, Washington, 1992-97; sr. policy and planning advisor to dir. D.C Dept Health, Washington, 1997-98; assoc. prof. U. Md., College Park, 1997—, George Washington U. Dept. Pub. Health, Washington, 1998—, U. D.C., Washington, 1998—; conductor Global Health Seminars, George Washington U., Washington, 1994-97; vice chmn. Nat. Coun. for Internat. Health, Washington, 1997-98, chmn. strategic planning com., 1997-98; guest lectr. Global Health, SUNY, Rennselaer, 1998, HIV/AIDS, Cornell U., Ithaca, N.Y., 1998; workshop expert minority health Dept. Health Columbia, S.C., 1998. Author or co-author 7 monographs on D.C. Health Svcs. Bd. dirs. Christian Connections for Internat. Health. Fellow Royal Soc. of Health (Eng.); mem. Am. Coll. Epidemiology, Am. Pub. Health Assn. (co-chair 125th anniversary conf. 1997), Am. Soc. for Pub. Adminstrn. Avocations: current affairs, soccer, reading biographies, health books. Office: PBS Internat Devel Group 901 W Washington St Alexandria VA 22300

AKUTAGAWA, DONALD, psychologist, educator; b. Grace, Idaho, June 7, 1923; s. Fred T. and Shizue (Oyama) A.; children: Trina Bortko, Murray, Doran. MA, U. Chgo., 1951; PhD, U. Pitts., 1956. Group counselor Orthogenic Sch., U. Chgo., 1951-52; clin. psychologist Inst. Pa. Hosp., Phila., 1959-67; pvt. practice Phila., 1957—, Bellevue, Wash., 1968—; chief community services Eastside Community Mental Health Center, Bellevue, 1968-72; clin. prof. psychology U. Wash., Seattle, 1974-90. Served with AUS, 1944-46. Fellow Am. Orthopsychiat. Assn. Office: Family Treatment Ctr 10845 Main St Bellevue WA 98004-6362 *Ideal: To so live my life that the world is better for my having been a part of it.*

AKUTSU, YOSHIHIRO, communications educator; b. Utsunomiya, Tochigi, Japan, Apr. 13, 1932; s. Miyoshi and Fumi (Owada) A.; m. Masako Ota, May 3, 1963. BA, Internat. Christian U., Mitaka, Tokyo, 1958, MA in Edn., 1960; PhD in Communication, Mich. State U., 1969. Instr. Internat. Christian U., 1969-71, asst. prof., 1971-74, assoc. prof., 1974-77, prof., 1977—; chmn. divsn. edn. Internat. Christian U., 1980-82, dir. pub. info. office, 1985-87, dean of students, 1988-90, dean Coll. of Liberal Arts, 1991-93. Co-author: Explorations in Mass Communication, 1970, Public Communication, 1975; editor Jour. Communication, 1976. Advisor social edn. Mitaka-City, 1983-91. Mem. Japan Soc. for Study of Audio-Visual Edn. (bd. dirs. 1972-94), Japan Soc. for Study of Radio-TV Edn. (bd. dirs. 1977-94), Japan Soc. Ednl. Sociology (bd. councillors 1987-97), Japan Assn. for Ednl. Media Study (bd. dirs. 1994—), Japan Soc. for Child Study (bd. dirs. 1994—). Avocations: Noh song, Go. Home: 4-12-11 Josuiminami, Kodaira Tokyo 187-0021, Japan Office: Internat Christian U, 3-10-2 Osawa, Mitaka Tokyo 181-8585, Japan

ALABISO, VINCENT, photojournalist. Exec. photo editor AP, N.Y.C. Office: Associated Press 50 Rockefeller Plz Fl 6 New York NY 10020-1666*

ALADEEN, LARY JOE, secondary school educator; b. St. Joseph, Mo., Oct. 17, 1946; s. Joseph Harold and Hilda Marie (Bowman) A.; m. Donna Marlene Hill, July 1, 1972 (div.); 1 child, Juliana Hill. BA, Calif. Bapt. Coll., Riverside, 1971; MA, Calif. State U., Hayward, 1989. Cert. secondary tchr., cmty. coll. tchr., Calif. Tchr. Norbridge H.S., Castro Valley, Calif., 1974-75, Foothill H.S., Pleasanton, Calif., 1975—; cons. George Lucas Edn. Found., Mill Valley, Calif., 1992; reader Golden State exam. Calif. Dept. Edn., Sacramento, 1994-96; mem. social studies curriculum rev. com. Pleasanton (Calif.) Unified Sch. Dist., 1989-90; presenter seminar workshop Calif. Coun. for Social Studies Conv., 1993. Editor: Supplemental Readings for A.P. U.S. History, 1994. Media rep. Dem. Campaign Com., Riverside, 1972; vol. Dem. Election campaigns, Pleasanton, 1976-94, Love, Inc., San Mateo, Calif., 1992—. With USMC, 1967-70. Recipient Outstanding Svc. award Amador Valley Secondary Edn. Assn., Pleasanton, 1982-83; Mentor Tchr., Pleasanton Unified Sch. Dist., 1985-86, Master Tchr., 1988-91. Mem. Orgn. Am. Historians, Nat. Coun. for the Social Studies, Calif. Coun. for the Social Studies. Democrat. Presbyterian. Avocations: golf, writing, travel. Home: PO Box 993 Pleasanton CA 94566-0099 Office: Foothill High Sch 4375 Foothill Rd Pleasanton CA 94588-9720

ALAFOUZO, ANTONIA, marketing professional; b. Cairo, Egypt, Oct. 13, 1952; came to U.S., 1982; d. Pano Antony and Agni-Maria (Ranos) A.; m. Thomas D'Ambola Jr., May 29, 1988; 1 child. BSC in Econs., Brunel U., London, 1975; Diploma in Econs. and Politics, Oxford (Eng.) U., 1977, M of Philosophy, PhD, 1980. Staff reporter The Economist, London, 1973-75, contbg. writer, 1975-82; mktg. exec. Rubenstein, Wolfson Co., N.Y.C., 1982-87; founder, pres. Markcom Ltd., N.Y.C., 1987—; contbg. writer Fin. Report, London, 1975-82; cons. writer Fin. Times, London, 1980-82; cons. communications and econs. World Gold Council, N.Y.C., 1982—. Contbr. reports to fin. publs. Mem. Inst. Journalism Internat., Oxford Union Soc. Avocations: travel, languages, tennis, marksmanship. Office: Markcom Ltd 599 Broadway New York NY 10007-2001

ALAGEM, BENY, former electronics executive; b. 1952. Grad., Calif. Polytechnical U., 1979. With Cal Circuit Abco, Inc., Woodland Hills, Calif., 1979-86; chmn., CEO, pres. Packard Bell NEC Inc., Sacramento, Calif., 1986-98. *

ALAIMO, ANTHONY A., federal judge; b. 1920. AB, Ohio No. U.; JD, Emory U. Bar: Ga. 1948, Ohio 1948. Assoc. Reuben A. Garland, 1949-51, 53-56; pvt. practice, Atlanta, 1967-63; ptnr. Highsmith, Highsmith, Alaimo & Knox, Brunswick, Ga., 1963-67, Cowart, Sapp, Alaimo & Gale, Brunswick, 1963-67, Alaimo, Taylor & Bishop, Brunswick, 1967-71; judge U.S. Dist. Ct. (so. dist.) Ga., Brunswick, 1971—, now sr. judge. Office: US Dist Ct PO Box 944 Brunswick GA 31521-0944*

ALAIN, ROBERT, foundation administrator. LLL, Laval U., Quebec, Can., 1966. Bar: Quebec 1967. Exec. dir. E.J.L.B. Found., Montreal, Que., Can., 1994—. Office: EJLB Found, 1350 Sherbrooke St W Ste 1050, Montreal, PQ Canada H3G 1J1*

ALALA, JOSEPH BASIL, JR., lawyer, accountant; b. Aleppo, Syria, Apr. 29, 1933; s. Joseph Basil and Waheda (Tall) A.; m. Nell Powers, Dec. 19, 1954; children: Sharon J., Tracy M., Joseph B. BSBA, U. N.C., 1957, JD cum laude, 1959. Bar: N.C. 1959. Acct. Arthur Andersen & Co., Charlotte, N.C., 1959-92; pres. Garland & Alcala, P.A., Gastonia, N.C., 1992-97; of counsel Alala Mullen Holland & Cooper, P.A., Gastonia, 1997—; bd. dirs. Branch Banking & Trust Co.; lectr. in field. Contbr. articles to profl. jours. Bd. dirs., past pres. Community Found. Gaston County, Inc.; mem., past pres. Law Sch. Bd. U. N.C.; bd. dirs. Belmont Abbey Coll.; past trustee, chmn. fin. com. St. Michael's Cath. Ch.; pres. Jaycees, 1964. With MPs U.S. Army, 1954-55, Korea. Mem. ABA, AICPA, Am. Coll. Tax Lawyers, Law Found. (bd. dirs., past pres.), Am. Judicature Soc., Am. Assn. Atty.-CPAs, N.C. Bar Assn., Gaston County Bar Assn., N.C. Assn. CPAs, Nat. Assn. Accts. (planning com., bd. U. N.C. tax symposium), Gaston Country Club (bd. dirs., past pres.), Knights of Malta, Rotary (bd. dirs. Gastonia chpt.). Home: 1216 S South St Gastonia NC 28052-7536 Office: 301 S York St Gastonia NC 28052-4051 *I believe everyone has four areas of responsibility in life: to his family, his church, his job and his community. My goal in life is to serve these areas with dignity and charity.*

ALAMIN, KHOSROW, pathologist; b. Tehran, Iran, June 6, 1932; came to U.S., 1960; s. Abdol and Talat (Kazemi) A.; m. Julie Ann Hurst, Oct. 24, 1964; children: Todd, Raud. MD, Tehran U., 1959; postgrad., U. Cin., 1969. Intern Coney Is. Hosp., Bklyn., 1960-61; chief resident U. Cin., 1968-69; dir. lab. St. George Hosp., Cin., 1970-93; dir. labs. Franciscan Health Sys., St. Francis/St. George & Providence, Cin., 1982-93; pathologist Franciscan Health Sys. Western Hill Co., Cin., 1993—, dir., 1998—; asst. prof. U. Cin., 1975—. Cancer liaison Am. Cancer Soc., Cin., 1996—. Fellow Am. Soc. Clin. Pathology, Coll. Am. Pathologists; mem. Ohio Soc. Pathology, Cin. Soc. Pathology (pres. 1989), Acad. Medicine. Avocations: skiing, tennis, golf. Home: 5725 Drewry Farm Ln Cincinnati OH 45243-3401 Office: 3131 Queen City Ave Cincinnati OH 45238-2316

ALANIZ, MIGUEL JOSÉ CASTAÑEDA, library director; b. L.A., Oct. 21, 1944; s. Francisco and Amalia (Castañeda) A.; m. Mercedes P., June 7, 1980. AA, Chabot C.C., 1972; BS in Child/Human Devel., Calif. State U., Hayward, 1974; MS in LS, Calif. State U., Fullerton, 1975; MS Pub. Admnstrn., Calif. State U., San Bernardino, 1988. Spanish svcs. libr. Alameda County Libr., Hayward, 1975-77; branch mgr. San Jose Pub. Libr., 1977-78, Santa Ana (Calif.) Pub. Libr., 1978-79; divsn. chief, tech. process San Bernardino (Calif.) County Libr., 1979-84; city libr. Azusa City (Calif.) Libr., 1984-92; libr. dir. Inglewood Pub. (Calif.) Libr., 1992—. With U.S. Army, 1965-71. Recipient Grad. Rsch. Fellow Clif. State U., 1974. Mem. ALA, Calif. Libr. Assn., Reforma, Am. Heart Assn., Nat. Exch Club. Avocations: automobiles, golf, reading, investments. Office: City of Inglewood Public Library 101 W Manchester Blvd Inglewood CA 90301-1753

ALANIZ, THEODORA VILLARREAL, elementary education educator; b. Mercedes, Tex., Feb. 16, 1951; d. Alejandro and Maria (Villarreal) A. BS in Elem. Edn., Pan Am. U., 1979; MEd, Tex. A&I U., 1984; cert. in counseling, U. Tex., 1992. Cert. vocat. counselor, Level I and II lic. chem. dependency counselor, South Tex. C.C. Asst. tchr. Mercedes Ind. Sch. Dist., 1973-78; tchr. Pharr (Tex.)-San-Juan-Alamo Ind. Sch. Dist., 1979-91, Edcouch-Elsa (Tex.) Ind. Sch. Dist., 1991-93; counselor Donna Ind. Sch. Dist., 1993—. Census rep. Diocese of Brownsville, 1974-75; choir mem. Sacred Heart Ch., Mercedes, Tex., 1974-78, 3rd grade tchr., 1975-78; rep. Cancer Soc., Mercedes, 1980-81, Assn. Tex. and Profl. Educators to Pharr and Elsa Ind. Sch. Dists. Scholar Title VII Bilingual/Bicultural, 1978-79. Roman Catholic. Avocations: photography, pencil drawing, sight seeing. Address: RR 4 Box 161-c Mercedes TX 78570-9802

ALANO, ERNESTO OLARTE, secondary education educator; b. Naga City, Philippines, Aug. 2, 1948; s. Pedro Quirante and Nieves (Olarte) A.; m. Arsenia Paulino Monedera, June 18, 1972; children: Jose Paulo Monedera Alano, Dionessa Monedera Alano. BA, Ateneo de Naga Coll., Philippines, 1969; MA, Loyola Marymount U., L.A., 1979. Classroom tchr. Ateneo de Naga, Philippines, 1969-74, Xavier H.S., Truk, 1974-79; dir. Diocesan Catechetical Program, Caroline/Marshall Islands, 1979-81; classroom tchr. Acad. of Our Lady, Guam, 1981-83; social worker Cath. Social Svc., Guam, 1983-86; classroom tchr. Hopwood Jr. H.S., Northern Marianas, 1986—; pres. Commonwealth Accreditation Network, Northern Marianas, 1994-95. Editor, advisor Book of Poems, Vols., 1, 2, 3, 1989-95. V.p. Filipino Cmty., Inc., No. Marianas, 1989-95; sec. Fedn. of Filipino Assns., No. Marianas, 1994-95. Recipient Nat. New Hero award Bagong Bayani Found., Philippines, 1994; named Outstanding Pacific Educator, Pacific Region Ednl. Lab., Hawaii, 1994. Mem. Nat. State Tchrs. of Yr. (state rep. 1994-95), Kappa Delta Pi. Roman Catholic. Avocations: reading, jogging, playing basketball. Home: PO Box 4009 Agana GU 96932-4009 Office: San Juan Bautista Ch PO Box 49 Hagatna GU 96932-0049

ALARCON, ARTHUR LAWRENCE, federal judge; b. L.A., Aug. 14, 1925; s. Lorenzo Marques and Margaret (Sais) A.; m. Sandra D. Paterson, Sept. 1, 1979; children—Jan Marie, Gregory, Lance. B.A. in Polit. Sci, U. So. Calif., 1949, J.D., 1951. Bar: Calif. 1952. Dep. dist. atty. L.A. County, 1952-61; exec. asst. to Gov. Pat Brown State of Calif., Sacramento, 1962-64, legal adv. to gov., 1961-62; judge L.A. Superior Ct., 1964-78; assoc. justice Calif. Ct. Appeals, L.A., 1978-79; judge U.S. Ct. Appeals for 9th Circuit, L.A., 1979—. Served with U.S. Army, 1943-46, ETO. Office: US Ct Appeals 9th Cir 1607 US Courthouse 312 N Spring St Los Angeles CA 90012-4701

ALARCON, RAUL, JR., broadcast executive. Former pres., CEO Sta. KXED, L.A.; pres. Sta. WSKQ, N.Y.C. Office: Sta WSKQ 26 W 56th St New York NY 10019-3801*

ALARCON, RICHARD, state senator, former councilman; m. Corina; children: Armando, Antonio, Claudia, Andrea. Sr. mgmt. analyst Criminal Justice Planning Office, L.A.; sr. personnel analyst occupl. health and safety divsn. L.A. Personnel Dept.; San Fernando Valley coord. Mayor's Office; city councilman City of L.A., 1993-98; state senator Calif. State Sen., Sacramento, 1998-, majority whip, 1998-; chmn. Pub. Works Com.; vice chmn. Govt. Efficiency Com.; mem. Cmty. Redevel. and Housing Com. Adminstrv. dir. Cmty. Youth Gang Svc.; chmn. N.E. Cmty. Action Project; mem. United Way, MADD, AHA, Women's Care Cottage, Habitat for Humanity, Meet Each Need With Dignity. Office: California State Senate State Capitol Sacramento CA 95814-4906 Office: 6150 Van Nuys Blvd #400 Van Nuys CA 91401*

ALARCON, ROGELIO ALFONSO, physician, researcher; b. Yungay, Nuble, Chile, Feb. 14, 1926; came to U.S., 1954; s. Alfredo and Carmen Rosa (Carrasco) A. BS, U. Chile, Concepcion, 1943; MD, U. Chile, Santiago, 1950. Staff physician internal medicine U. Chile Hosp. Salvador, Santiago, 1951-52, Hosp. Gonzalez Cortez, Santiago, 1952-54; resident medicine Meml. Ctr. for Cancer and Allied Diseases, N.Y.C., 1955-56; fellow internal medicine George Washington U. Hops., George Washington Sch. Medicine, Washington, 1956-57; resident internal medicine Lemuel Shattuck Hosp., Boston, 1957-58; rsch. fellow pathology Children's Cancer Rsch. Found., Children's Hosp. Med. Ctr., Boston, 1958-60; rsch. assoc. Children's Cancer Rsch. Found., Boston, 1960-74, Harvard Med. Sch., Boston, 1962-76, Cancer Rsch. Inst., New Eng. Deaconess Hosp., Boston, 1974-76; staff physician Boston Children's Hosp. Med. Ctr., Wrentham, Mass., 1977-79; staff physician VA Med. Ctr., Phila., 1979-80, Bedford, Mass., 1980—. Contbr. articles to profl. jours. Mem. Am. Assn. for Cancer Rsch., N.Y. Acad. Scis., Nat. Assn. VA Physicians. Roman Catholic. Achievements include discovery of the enzymatic generation of acrolein, a highly cytotoxic aldehyde, from biogenic polyamines; development of a fluorometric method to measure minimal amounts of acrolein; research in the growth inhibitory effects of oxidized spermine on mammalian cells, research involving acrolein in cell growth regulation, and identification of acrolein as a metabolite of cyclophosphamide and related chemotherapeutic agents. Home: 33 Pond Ave Apt B-915 Brookline MA 02445-7128 Office: Bedford VA Med Ctr 200 Springs Rd Bedford MA 01730-1114

ALARCON, TERRY QUENTIN, judge; b. New Orleans, July 6, 1948; s. Frederick Joseph and Ann Marie (Quentin) A.; m. Mollie Ann McCullough, June 2, 1972; children: Joseph McCullough, Joshua Holland. BS, Spring Hill Coll., 1970; MSW, U. Ala., 1974; JD, Loyola U., New Orleans, 1979. Bar: La. 1979. Asst. to criminal sheriff Orleans Parish, New Orleans, 1974-78, asst. dist. atty., 1978-83; asst. dist. atty. Jefferson Parish, Gretna, La., 1983-86; ptnr. Brandt, Alarcon & McDonald, Metairie, La., 1983-86; judge Traffic Ct. City of New Orleans, 1991-96, judge Criminal Dist. Ct., 1996—; trial adv. lectr. Tulane U. Sch. Law, New Orleans, 1981-90; exec. counsel to mayor, New Orleans 1986-90; chief of staff, 1989-90; elected judge Traffic Ct., City of New Orleans, 1990, Criminal Dist. Ct., 1996; apptd. by Pres. U.S. to Nat. Inst. Justice. Mem. ABA, La. Bar Assn. Democrat. Roman Catholic. Home: 6225 St Bernard Ave New Orleans LA 70122-1327 Office: 2950 Energy Ctr 2700 Tulane Ave New Orleans LA 70119

ALARID, LEANNE FIFTAL, criminal justice educator; b. Niskiyuna, N.Y., Sept. 16, 1967; d. Conrad Franklin Fiftal and Jean Louise Fiftal Buchan; m. Raymond Alarid Jr. BA in Psychology magna cum laude, U. No. Colo., 1989; MA in Criminal Justice, Sam Houston State U., 1993, PhD in Criminal Justice, 1996. Group home counselor Daybreak Girls Home, Denver, 1989; case mgr. for adult felons Williams St. Ctr. Halfway House, Denver, 1989-91; rsch./tng. asst. Sam Houston State U., Huntsville, 1991-94, instr., 1994-96; asst. prof. U. Mo., Kansas City, 1996—; reviewer Jour. Rsch. in Crime and Delinquency, 1996—; rschr. Kansas City Police Dept., 1997—; rschr. Mo. Dept. Corrections, Jefferson City, 1997—. Contbr. articles to profl. jours., chpt. to book. Scholar psychology dept. U. No. Colo., 1989; rsch. grantee U. Mo.-Kansas City, 1997. Mem. Acad. Criminal Justice Scis., Am. Soc. Criminology. Avocations: reading, music, chess, billiards, weight lifting. Office: U Mo Kansas City Dept Sociology and Criminology 5100 Rockhill Rd Kansas City MO 64110-2446

ALARIE-ANDERSON, PEGGY SUE, physician assistant; b. Flint, Mich., Feb. 8, 1957; d. Albert Joseph Jr. and Elizabeth Anna (Eksten) A.; m. John L. McAttee III, Oct. 3, 1980 (div. Aug. 1987); m. Donn P. Anderson, Aug. 23, 1997. AAS, Mott C.C., 1983; BS, Mich. State U., 1988; MS, U. Detroit-Mercy, 1994. Physician asst. supr. emergency rm. Hurley Med. Ctr., Flint, Mich., 1996—. Fellow Am. Acad. Physician Assts., Mich. Acad. Physician Assts.; mem. Soc. Emergency Physician Assts., Sigma Theta Tau. Avocations: dance (ballet, ballroom, tap, jazz). Home: 2769 Brandon St Flint MI 48503-3469 Office: Hurley Med Ctr 1 Hurley Plz Flint MI 48503-5902

ALATIS, JAMES EFSTATHIOS, university dean emeritus; b. Weirton, W.Va., July 13, 1926; s. Efstathios and Vasiliki (Galanoudis) A.; m. Penelope Mastorides, Dec. 30, 1951; children: William, Stephen, Anthony. B.A., W.Va. U., 1948; M.A., Ohio State U., 1953; Ph.D., 1966. Fulbright lectr. English U., Athens, 1955-57; English testing and teaching specialist Dept. State, 1959-61; specialist for lang. research U.S. Office Edn., 1961-65, chief lang. sect., 1965-66; assoc. dean Sch. Langs. and Linguistics, Georgetown U., Washington, 1966-73, dean, 1973-94; dean emeritus Georgetown U., Washington, 1994—, sr. advisor to exec. v.p. internat. lang. programs and rsch., 1994—; assoc. prof. linguistics Sch. Langs. and Linguistics, Georgetown U., Washington, 1966-75; disting. prof. linguistics and modern Greek Georgetown U., Washington, 1994—; exec. sec. TESOL, 1966-82, exec. dir. emeritus, 1982—; pres. Joint Nat. Com. for Langs., 1980-88. Editor: Studies in Honor of Albert H. Marckwardt, 1972, (with Kristie Twaddell) English as a Second Language in Bilingual Education, 1976, (with Ruth Crymes) Human Factors in ESL, 1977, (with Gerli and Brod) Language in American

Life, 1978, Internat. Dimensions of Bilingual Education, 1978, (with G. R. Tucker) Language in Public Life, 1979, Current Issues in Bilingual Education, 1980, (with others) The Second Language Classroom: Directions for the 1980s, 1981, Applied Linguistics and the Preparation of Second Language Teachers: Toward a Rationale, 1983, (with John J. Staczek) Perspectives on Bilingualism and Bilingual Education, 1985, (with Deborah Tannen) Language and Linguistics: The Interdependence of Theory, Data, and Application, 1986, Language Teaching, Testing, and Technology: Lessons from the Past with a View Toward the Future, 1989, Linguistics, Language Teaching and Language Acquisition: The Interdependence of Theory, Practice, and Research, 1990, Quest for Quality: The First 21 Years of TESOL, 1991, Linguistics and Language Pedagogy: The State of the Art, 1991, Language, Communication and Social Meaning, 1993, Strategic Interaction and Language Acquisition: Theory, Practice and Research, 1993; contbr. articles to profl. jours. Served with USNR, 1944-46. Recipient N.E. Conf. award, 1985, Pres.'s award Nat. Assn. for Bilingual Edn., 1987. Mem. MLA, Am. Coun. on Teaching Fgn. Langs., Linguistic Soc. Am (del. 1966-69), Nat. Assn. Fgn. Student Affairs (dir. 1965-66), Def. Lang. Inst. (bd. visitors), Phi Beta Kappa. Home: 5108 Sutton Pl Alexandria VA 22304-2704 Office: Georgetown U Int'l Langs Prog & Rsch 37th & 0 St Washington DC 20057-1042*

ALATZAS, GEORGE, delivery service company executive; b. Salonika, Greece, Sept. 30, 1940; came to U.S., 1954; s. Gus Alatzas and Georgia Karayanidou; m. Ida Elizabeth Feldman, Sept. 26, 1965; children: Dennis, Ari. AA in Liberal Arts, Middlesex Community Coll., 1979; student, Rutgers U. Dept. mgr. Bamberger's N.J. div. Macy's Dept. Store, Newark, 1959-61, 63-65; buyer Koos Bros., Rahway, N.J., 1965-67; sales rep. Bassett (Va.) Furniture, 1967-69; store mgr. W&J Sloane, Union, N.J., 1969-72, Steinbach & Co., Freehold, N.J., 1972-78; owner, pres. Lawyers & Corp. Messenger Svc., Middlesex, N.J., 1978-84; pres., chief exec. officer Pegasus Delivery Systems, Inc., Somerville, N.J., 1984—; pres. Just In Time Inc. fin. mgmt. & support svcs. Instr. swimming Am. Legion Children's Camp, Newburgh, N.Y., 1957-58; instr. marksmanship reservation Boy Scouts Am., Yards Creek, and Blairstown, N.J., 1980-83; pres. Office Condominium Assn. Ctr. at Raritan. With U.S. Army, 1961-63; Command Sgt. Maj. USAR, 1973—. Paul Harris fellow. Mem. Assn. U.S. Army, Nat. Alliance Businessmen, 78th Divsn. NCO Assn., 78th Divsn. Vets. Assn., N.J. Bus. and Industry Coun., Rotary (Somerville chpt. bd. dir.). Greek Orthodox. Avocations: tennis, golf, walking. Office: Pegasus Delivery Systems Inc 1124 Us Highway 202 Ste B14 Raritan NJ 08869-1475

ALAUPOVIC, ALEXANDRA VRBANIC, artist, educator; b. Slatina, Yugoslavia, Dec. 21, 1921; d. Joseph and Elizabeta (Papp) Vrbanic; m. Peter Alaupovic, Mar. 22, 1947; 1 child, Betsy. Student Bus. Sch., Zagreb, Yugoslavia, 1940-41, Acad. Visual Arts, Zagreb, Yugoslavia, 1944-48; postgrad. Acad. Visual Arts, Prague, Czechoslovakia, 1949, Art Sch., U. Ill., 1959-60; MFA, U. Okla., 1966; came to U.S., 1958. Sec., Arko Liquer & Yeast Factory and Distillery, Zagreb, 1941-44; instr. U. Okla., Norman, 1964-66; instr. three dimensional design sculpture Oklahoma City U., 1969-77, Okla. Sci. Found., Oklahoma City, 1969-75; one-woman shows at Okla. Art Ctr., Oklahoma City, U. Okla. Mus. Art, Norman, La Mandragore Internat. Galerie d'Art, Paris, 1984; exhibited art in group shows retrospective 50 yrs. Struggle, Growth and Whimsy, 1987-88, Okla. Art Ctr., Springfield (Mo.) Art Mus., Okla. U. Mus., Norman, 7th Ann. Temple Emanuel Brotherhood Arts Festival, Dallas, Salon des Nation, Paris, 1983; since statehood twevle Okla. artists Art. Mus., Okla. 1996; represented in permanent collections Okla. U. Art Mus., Okla. State Art Collection, Okla. Art Ctr., Mercy Health Ctr. Recipient Jacobson award U. Okla., 1964; hon. mention in sculpture Philbrook Art Ctr., Tulsa, 1967; 1st sculpture award Philbrook Art Ctr., Tulsa, 1970; biography included in Virginia Watson Jones' Contemporary American Women Sculptors, 1986, Jules and Nancy Heller's North American Women Artists of 20th Century, 1995; State of Okla. Art commemdation, 1996. Mem. Internat. Sculpture Center, Lausanne, Suisse, Prestige de la Peinture et de la Sculpture d'Aujourd'hui dans le Monde, 1992, Paris, 1995. Home and Office: 11908 N Bryant Ave Oklahoma City OK 73131-4823

ALAUPOVIC, PETAR, biochemist, educator; b. Prague, Czechoslovakia, Aug. 3, 1923; came to U.S., 1957; married, 1947; 1 child. ChemE, U. Zagreb, 1948, PhD in Chemistry, 1956; DHC (hon.), U. Lille, France, 1987, U. Buenos Aires, 1994, U. Goteborg, 1999. Rschr. pharms. rsch. lab. Chem Corp, Prague, 1948-49; rschr. organic lab. Inst. Indsl. Rsch., Yugoslavia, 1949-50; asst. agrl. faculty U. Zagreb, 1951-54, asst. chem. inst. med. faculty, 1954-56; rsch. biochemist U. Ill., 1957-60; with cardiovascular sect. Okla. Med. Rsch. Found., Oklahoma City, 1960—, head lipoprotein lab., 1972-92, also head Lipid and Lipoprotein Lab.; prof. rsch. biochemistry, sch. med. U. Okla., 1960—. Assoc. editor Lipids, 1974-78. Named Disting. Career Scientist Okla. Med. Rsch. Fund, 1990; NIH grantee, 1961-95. Mem. AAAS, Am. Soc. Biol. Chemists, Am. Chem. Soc., Am. Heart Assn. (Spl. Recognition award 1994), Am. Oil Chemistry Soc. Achievements include research on chemistry of naturally occuring macromolecular lipid compounds such as serum and tissue lipoproteins and bacterial endotoxins, on biochemistry of red cell membranes; isolation and characterization of tissue lipases. Office: Okla Med Rsch Found Lipid and Lipoprotein Lab 825 NE 13th St Oklahoma City OK 73104-5005

ALAWANA See WALDMAN, ALAN I.

ALAZRAKI, JAIME, Romance languages educator; b. La Rioja, Argentina, Jan. 26, 1934; came to U.S., 1962, naturalized, 1971; s. Leon and Clara A. (Bolomo) A.; children: Daphne G., Adina L. B.A., Hebrew U., Jerusalem, 1962; M.A., Columbia U., 1964, Ph.D., 1967. Instr. Columbia U., N.Y.C., 1964-67; asst. prof. U. Calif.-San Diego, 1967-68, assoc. prof., 1968-71, prof., 1971-77; prof. dept. romance langs. Harvard U., Cambridge, Mass., 1977-87; prof. dept. Spanish and Portuguese Columbia U., N.Y.C., 1987—, chair, 1988-91; vis. prof. U. Wis., 1972, UCLA, 1975-76, Autonomous U. Barcelona, Spain, 1985-86; spl. advisor Guggenheim Found., 1981-91. Author: Poética y poesía de P. Neruda, 1965, La prosa narrativa de J.L. Borges, 1968, 74, 84, En busca del unicornio: Los cuentos de J. Cortázar, 1983, Jorge Luis Borges, 1971, Versiones, inversiones, reversiones, 1977, Critical Essays on J.L. Borges, 1987, Borges and the Kabbalah and Other Essays on His Fiction and Poetry, 1988, Hacia Cortázar: Aproximaciones a su obra, 1994; editor: (with I. Ivask) The Final Island: The Fiction of J. Cortázar, 1978, J.L. Borges: el escritor y la crítica, 1976, 84, 86, 87, Julio Cortazar, Obra crítica/2, 1994, J. Cortázar, Final del Juego, 1995; co-editor: Revista Hispánica Moderna, 1988—; mem. editorial bd. Jour. Spanish Studies, 1973-76, Hispanic Review, 1977—, La Torre 1977-95, Revista Iberoamericana, 1977-81, Hispanic Jour., 1980—, Hispania, 1980-85, Confluencia, 1987—. Recipient Nieto gold medal Argentina, 1970; NEH fellow, 1976; Guggenheim Found. fellow, 1971-72, 82-83. Mem. MLA (mem. adv. bd. Publs. of MLA of Am. 1980-84), Internat. Inst. Ibero-Am. Lit., Am. Assn. Tchrs. Spanish and Portuguese (Huntington prize 1964), Internat. Assn. Hispanists. Home: 161 W 61st St Apt 21G New York NY 10023-7461 Office: Columbia U Dept Spanish and Portuguese 612 W 116th St New York NY 10027-7009

ALBA, BENNY, artist; b. Columbus, Ohio, May 7, 1949. Student, Kent State U., 1968-70; BA in Psychology, U. Mich., 1982. artist-in-residence St. Charles Boy's Pres. Sch., Columbus, 1982-85; lectr. Columbus Cultural Arts Ctr., 1983, 84, 93; presenter workshops in field; panelist Calif. Inst. for Intergral Studies, San Francisco, 1995. Solo shows include Columbus Cultural Arts Ctr., 1993, Apprentice Alliance, San Francisco, 1994, Las Vegas (Nev.) Mus., 1994, Artist TV Access, San Francisco, 1994, Western Wyo. Coll., Rock Springs, 1994, A Gallery in the Clock Tower, San Francisco, 1994, Ctr. for Psychol. Studies, Albany, Calif., 1994, Idyllwild (Calif.) Sch. Music and Art, 1995, Merced (Calif.) Coll. Art G., 1997, N. Country Mus. of Art, Park Rapids, Minn., 1997, Martinez (Calif.) City Hall, 1997, Martinez Arts and Culture Com., 1997, Office of Sup. Contra County Ct., Martinez, 1997, State Bd., Sacramento, Calif., 1997, Saginaw (Mich.) Art Mus., 1998, Met. Transp. Co., Oakland, Calif., 1998, Commonwealth Club, San Francisco, 1998, San Francisco State U. Club, 1998, Zen Ctr., San Francisco, 1998, Hastings Coll. Law, San Francisco, 1999, U. Oreg., Eugene, 1999, U. Berkeley (Calif.), 1999; exhibited in group shows at Informative Edge, San Francisco, 1992, YWCA Youngstown, Ohio, 1992, Mus. Without Walls, Bemis Pt., N.Y., 1993, Davis (Calif.) Art Ctr., 1993, Kunst für Begegnungen, Munich, 1993, Ednl. Testing Svc., Emeryville, Calif., 1993-94, Diablo (Calif.) Valley Coll. Gallery, 1994, N. Mex. Art League, Albuquerque, 1995, Nat. Congress Art & Design, Salt Lake City, 1995, Danville (Calif.) Fine Arts, 1995, Lillian Paley Ctr. Visual Arts, Oakland, 1995, Lamar U., Beaumont, Tex., 1996, John Jay Coll. of Criminal Justice, N.Y., 1996, Serra House, Stanford U., 1996, Fed. Bldgs. Window Project, Oakland, 1996, Civic & Cultural Ctr., Brea, Calif., 1997, Palm Springs (Calif.) Desert Mus., 1997, Downey (Calif.) Mus. Art, 1997, Mus. Downtown L.A., 1998, Sun Gallery, Hayward, Calif., 1998, Hoyt Inst. Fine Arts, New Castle, Pa., 1998, Maude Kers Art Ctr., Eugene, 1998, Bolinas (Calif.) Mus., 1998, George Ohr Mus., Biloxi, 1998, Galesburg (Ill.) Civic Art Ctr., 1999, Coll. Notre Dame Md., Balt., 1999, others; represented in private and public collections Nat. Mus. Women in Arts, Ark. A Ctr., Little Rock, U. Mich. Mus. Art, Kalamazoo (Mich.) Inst. Arts, Greenpeace, Ulli Wachter (Germany), Las Vegas Art Mus., Ctr. for Psychol. Studies, Albany, Calif., Birmingham (Ala.) Mus. Art, Portland (Oreg.) Art Mus., Tyler (Mich.) Mus. Art, others. Bd. dirs. No. Calif. Women's Caucus for Art, 1991, sec. 1991-92, phone liaison, 1991-93. Recipient Lenore Miles award North Platte Valley Art Gallery, 1991, Body of Work award Women Artists, A Celebration, 1990, Merit award San Francisco Women Artist Gallery, 1986, Dr. S. Mackoff award Palm Springs Desert Mus., 1997. Mem. Women's Caucus for Art (bd. dirs. No. Calif. 1991-94, sec. 1991, 92), Calif. Soc. Printmakers (v.p. 1999). Studio: 4219 M L King Jr Way Oakland CA 94609-2321

ALBA, SAMUEL, federal judge; b. 1947. BS, Utah State U., 1969; JD, Ariz. State U., 1972. Dep. fed. pub. defender Dist. Ariz., 1972-77; atty. Gama, Iniquez & Alba, Phoenix, 1977-80; asst. U.S. atty. Dept. Justice, Salt Lake City, 1980-87; atty. Prince, Yeates & Geldzahler, Salt Lake City, 1987-92; magistrate judge U.S. Dist. Ct. Utah, Salt Lake City, 1992—. Office: 350 S Main St Ste 260 Salt Lake City UT 84101-2130

ALBACH, RICHARD ALLEN, microbiology educator; b. Chgo., Mar. 31, 1930; s. Maurice and Martha (Silverman) A.; m. Janice Elaine Boewe, Jan. 23, 1962; children: Michael, Karren, Kimala, David, Brian, Julie, Barry. B.S., U. Ill., 1956, M.S., 1958; Ph.D., Northwestern U., 1963. Asst. prof. U. Health Scis., Chgo. Med. Sch., 1968-69, North Chicago, Ill., assoc. prof., 1969-73, prof., 1973—, vice chmn., 1975-82, acting chmn., 1982-83; editl. cons. Yearbook Med. Pubs., Chgo., 1975-81; vis. prof. St. George's U. Sch. Medicine, Grenada, 1992—. Contbr. articles to profl. jours. With U.S. Army, 1953-55. Recipient Trustees Rsch. award Chgo. Med. Sch., 1968, Tchg. Prof. of Yr. award, 1976, 78, 82; Fellow Abbott Found., 1961; grantee NIH, 1965-78. Fellow Am. Acad. Microbiology; mem. Am. Soc. Microbiology, Soc. Protozoologists (exec. com. 1984-89, chmn. awards com. 1995—), Am. Soc. Parasitologists, Ill. Soc. Microbiology (membership chmn. 1969-70) Research in biology of parasitic protozoa. Office: U Health Sci Chgo Med Sch 3333 Green Bay Rd North Chicago IL 60064-3037

ALBAGLI, LOUISE MARTHA, psychologist; b. Queens, N.Y., Jan. 15, 1954; d. Meyer Nathan and Leah (Bleier) Greenberg; m. Eli S. Albagli, July 31, 1977. BA in Psychology summa cum laude, CUNY, 1976; D of Clin. Psychology, Rutgers U., 1983. Cert. Reiki master. Clin. psychology intern Postgrad. Ctr. Mental Health, N.Y.C., 1980-81; staff psychologist Queens County Neuropsychiat. Inst., Jackson Heights, N.Y., 1981-83, Bklyn. Community Counseling Ctr., 1981-84; sr. clin. psychologist Richard Hall Community Mental Health Ctr., Bridgewater, N.J., 1984-86; pvt. practice specializing in women's reproductive health issues cen. N.J., 1985—; mem. adj. faculty Rutgers U., 1990-93; Jin Shin Jyutsu practitioner, 1995—, self-help tchr., 1996—. Mem. Nat. Register Health Care Providers, Am. Psychol. Assn., N.J. Psychol. Assn. (com. inter-profl. rels.), Internat. Childbirth Edn. Assn., RESOLVE, Raritans, Phi Beta Kappa.

ALBAN, ROGER CHARLES, construction equipment distribution executive; b. Columbus, Ohio, Aug. 3, 1948; s. Charles Ellis and Alice Jacqueline (Hosfeld) A.; children: Allison Ann, Roger Charles II, Charles Michael (dec. June 1998); m. Linda Bayer Lusk, Aug. 30, 1997. Student pub. schs. With Alban Equipment Co., Columbus, 1963—, sales mgr., 1972-75, gen. mgr., 1975-85, treas., 1978-85, v.p., 1980-85, pres., 1985—. Mem. Grandview Heights Bd. Edn., Columbus, 1978-85, pres., 1979, v.p., 1982, legis. liaison, 1978-79, 83-84, re-elected mem., 1992-93; elected Grandview Heights City Coun., 1986; mem. Met. Ednl. Coun., Columbus Area Leadership PRogram, 1982-83; trustee Builders Exch. Benefit Trust, 1987-98, chmn., 1996. Mem. Assoc. Equipment Distbrs. (lt. dir. region 6 1980, 85, 86, 88, dir. 1989-91, chmn. light equipment dist. com. 1985, chmn. sales and mktg. com. 1988, elected dir. region 6 1989-92, chmn. lt. equipment steering com. 1998), Ohio Sch. Bds. Assn. (all-ctrl. region bd. 1984), Bldg. Industry Assn. Ctrl. Ohio, Am. Rental Assn., Builders Exch. Ctrl. Ohio (dir. 1990—, elected treas. 1996, 2nd v.p. 1996, v.p. 1997—, pres. 1998), Am. Mgmt. Assn., Nat. Right to Work Com., Nat. Fedn. Ind. Bus., Ohio Equipment Distbrs. Assn. (dir. 1982, 84-91, pres. 1983), Roundtable, Mensa (chpt. exec. com. 1979-80), Rotary (elected Columbus dir. 1994), Downtown Columbus Club. Home: 1482 McCoy Rd Upper Arlngton OH 43220-4931 Office: 1825 Mckinley Ave Columbus OH 43222-1003

ALBANI, SUZANNE BEARDSLEY, lawyer; b. Albany, N.Y., Sept. 28, 1943; d. Alling Prudden and Carol Elizabeth (Rossiter) Beardsley; m. Thomas J. Albani, Sept. 3, 1966; children: Karin, Steven. BA, Smith Coll., Northampton, Mass., 1965; JD, St. John's U., Jamaica, N.Y., 1978. Bar: Conn. 1978, U.S. Dist. Ct. 1979, U.S. Tax Ct. 1982. Ptnr. Cummings & Lockwood, Stamford, Conn., 1978-92, Levett, Rockwood & Sanders P.C., Westport, Conn., 1992—. Bd. dirs. ABC in Darien, Inc., 1981—, Darien (Conn.) Arts Coun., 1990. Mem. Real Estate Exch.: A Forum for Women in Comml. Real Estate, Conn. Women in Healthcare Mgmt., Inc., ABA, Conn. Bar Assn. Office: Levett, Rockwood & Sanders 33 Riverside Ave Ste 1 Westport CT 06880-4237

ALBANO, ANTHONY WILLIAM, retired career officer, secondary school educator; b. Atlanta, Dec. 6, 1953; s. Rocco Louis and Ida Elizabeth (White) A. AA, Manatee Jr. Coll., 1973; BA, U. Fla., 1975; MA, Cen. Mich. U., 1979. Commd. 2d lt. USAF, 1975, advanced through grades to maj., 1979, ret., 1993; tchr. Venice (Fla.) Area Mid. Sch., 1995—. Scoutmaster Boy Scouts Am., Rochester, N.H., 1984-86, Ramstein AB, Germany, 1986-88, asst. dist. commr., Mt. Holly, N.J., 1988-92; vestry mem. St. Albans Episcopal. Congregation, Ramstein AB, 1986-88. Mem. Air Force Assn., Order Daedalians, Mil Order of World Wars, Elks. Republican. Avocations: hiking, skiing, water skiing, camping, boating, travel. Home: 711 Albee Farm Rd N Nokomis FL 34275-2411

ALBANO, MICHAEL J., mayor; m. Michele Garreffi; children: Jonathan, Michael, Christopher. BS, Springfield Coll., 1974; MS, Am. Internat. Coll., 1976; MPA, U. Hartford, 1981. Probation officer Westfield Dist. Ct., 1974-82; mem. staff Office of the State Auditor, 1994-95; spl. parole bd. mem., 1993-94, mem. Mass. parole bd., 1982—; mayor City of Springfield, Mass., 1996—; adj. faculty mem. Asnutuck C.C., Enfield, Conn., 1979-81, 92-94, Springfield Tech. C.C., 1977-81, U. Mass., 1992; vis. lectr. criminal justice Westfield State Coll./Suffolk U., Boston. Springfield Youth commr., 1980-81; mem. Springfield Sch. com., 1985-90; commr. Springfield Conservation, 1990-92; mem. Springfield City Coun., 1991—, pres., 1994-95. Home: 36 Florentine Gdns Springfield MA 01108-2508 Office: City of Springfield 36 Court St Springfield MA 01103-1687*

ALBAUGH, JOHN CHARLES, hospital executive; b. Cedar Rapids, Iowa, Oct. 30, 1938; s. Charles Alden and Helen Martha (Johnson) A.; m. Betty Alice Hardie, July, 1955 (div. Oct. 1972); children: John Charles Jr., Benjamin Alden, James Patrick, Susan Marie; m. Janette Carol Osland, Jan. 1974. B in Bus. Adminstrn., Wake Forest U., 1960; M in Health Care Adminstrn., U. Minn., 1979; PhD, Walden U., 1997. Oper. dist. mgr. Firestone Co., Des Moines, Iowa, 1960-67; asst. adminstr. St. Gabriel's Hosp., Little Falls, Minn., 1967-75; exec. dir. Monticello-Big Lake Community Hosp. and Nursing Home, Minn., 1975-78; adminstr. Worthington (Minn.) Regional Hosp., 1978-84; pres. Ft. Atkinson (Wis.) Meml. Hosp., 1984—; bd. dirs. Bank Ft. Atkinson, Joint Venture Managed Care Inc., sec.; former Hosp. Dist. Pres. Minn.; former preceptor hosp. adminstrn. program Concordia Coll., ISPHA program U.Minn.; preceptor health care adminstrn. program U. Wis., Madison, 1993—; preceptor pub. adminstrn. program U. Wis. Whitewater, 1993—. Pres. Land of Blackhawk United Way, Ft. Atkinson, 1991-92, bd. dirs.; vice chmn. Rep. Party, Jefferson County, 1993, sec., 1988-92; moderator 1st Congl. United Ch. Christ; past bd. dirs. Health Systems Agy. Fellow Am. Coll. Health Care Execs.; mem. Wis. Hosp. Assn. (shared svc. dir. 1993, trustee 1999, dist. pres. 1991-92), U. Minn. Alumni Assn. (program health care adminstrn.), Rotary Club (pres. 1990), Ft. Atkinson C. of C. (pres. 1991-92, project leader, facilitator 1992-94). Avocations: golf, skiing, travel, community activities. Office: Fort Atkinson Memorial Hospital 611 Sherman Ave E Fort Atkinson WI 53538-1960

ALBEE, ARDEN LEROY, geologist, educator; b. Port Huron, Mich., May 28, 1928; s. Emery A. and Mildred (Tool) A.; m. Charleen H. Ettenheim, 1978; children: Janet, Margaret, Carol, Kathy, James, Ginger, Mary, George. B.A., Harvard, 1950, M.A., 1951, Ph.D., 1957. Geologist U.S. Geol. Survey, 1950-59; prof. geology Calif. Inst. Tech., 1959—; chief scientist Jet Propulsion Lab., 1978-84, dean grad. studies, 1984—, project scientist Mars Observer and Global Surveyor Missions, 1984; cons. in field, 1950; chmn. lunar sci. rev. panel NASA, 1972-77, mem. space sci. adv. com., 1976-84; mem. exam. bd. T.O.E.F.L. (Test of English as a Foreign Lang.), 1995-97; mem. Grad. Record Exam. Bd., 1995-98; mem. exec. com. Assn. Grad. Schs., 1995—. Assoc. editor Jour. Geophys. Rsch., 1976-82, Ann. Rev. Earth Space Scis., 1978—; contbr. numerous articles to profl. jours. Bd. regents L.A. Chiropractic Coll., 1990-98. Recipient Exceptional Sci. Achievement medal NASA, 1976. Fellow Mineral Soc. Am. (assoc. editor Am. Mineralogist 1972-76), Geol. Soc. Am. (assoc. editor bull. 1972-89, councilor 1989-92), Am. Geophys. Union. Office: Calif Inst Tech Mail Code 02 31 Pasadena CA 91125

ALBEE, EDWARD FRANKLIN, author, playwright; b. Mar. 12, 1928; s. Reed A. and Frances (Cotter) Albee. Student, Trinity Coll., 1946-47. Messenger Western Union, 1955-58; lectr. Brandeis U., Johns Hopkins U., Webster U., others. Plays written include The Zoo Story, 1958, The Death of Bessie Smith, 1959, The Sandbox, 1959, The American Dream, 1960, Who's Afraid of Virginia Woolf?, 1961-62, The Ballad of the Sad Cafe (adaption of Carson McCullers' novella), 1963, Tiny Alice, 1964, Malcolm, 1966, A Delicate Balance, 1966 (Pulitzer Prize for drama 1967), Everything in the Garden, 1968, Box, Quotations from Chairman Mao, 1970, All Over, 1971, Seascape, 1975 (Pulitzer prize for drama 1975), Counting the Ways, 1976, Listening, 1977, The Man Who Had Three Arms, 1983, The Lady from Dubuque, 1978-79; adaptation of Lolita (Nabokov), 1980, Finding the Sun, 1982, Marriage Play, 1986-87, Three Tall Women, 1990-91 (Pulitzer Prize for drama 1994), Fragments, 1993, The Play about the Baby, 1996; dir. plays, including Happy Days, 1993, Alley Theatre, Houston, 1991. pres. Edward F. Albee Found. Recipient gold medal in drama Am. Acad. and Inst. Arts and Letters, 1980; inducted into Theater Hall of Fame, 1985, Nat. Medal of Arts, 1996; Kennedy Ctr. honoree, 1996. Mem. Nat. Inst. Arts and Letters, Dramatists Guild Coun., Internat. Theatre Inst. (pres.). Address: 14 Harrison St New York NY 10013-2842

ALBEE, GEORGE WILSON, psychology educator; b. St. Marys, Pa., Dec. 20, 1921; s. George W. amd Maude (Allen) A.; m. Constance Impallaria, Aug. 6, 1955 (dec.); children: Alexander, Luke, Maud, Sarah; m. Margaret Moon-Mui Tong, Dec. 20, 1985. AB, Bethany Coll., 1943, ScD (hon.), 1969; MS, U. Pitts., 1947, PhD, 1949; PhD (hon.), Stirling U., Scotland, 1998. Rsch. psychologist Western Psychiat. Inst., Pitts., 1949-51; asst. exec. sec. Am. Psychol. Assn., Washington, 1951-53; Fulbright prof. Helsinki (Finland) U., 1953-54; assoc. prof. psychology Western Res. U., Cleve., 1954-56, prof., 1957-71, chmn. dept. psychology, 1957-60, 63-66, Ladd disting. prof. psychology, 1959-71; prof. psychology U. Vt., Burlington, 1971-92, prof. emeritus, 1992—; courtesy prof. Fla. Mental Health Inst. U. South Fla., Tampa, 1994—; cons. VA, Surgeon Gen. of Army, Pres.'s Com. on Mental Retardation, Peace Corps, 1962-65. Author: Mental Health Manpower, 1959, Emerging Concepts of Mental Disorder, 1969, The Uncertain Future of Clinical Psychology, 1970, The Future of Psychology, 1974, The Protestant Ethic, Sex, and Psychotherapy, 1978; editor: Primary Prevention of Psychopathology, 1977; gen. editor: (with Justin M. Joffe) series of books on primary prevention of psychopathology; contbr. articles to profl. jours. Mem. Vt. Psychology Licensing Bd., 1972-75; dir. task force on manpower Joint Commn. Mental Illness and Health, Cambridge, Mass., 1957-59; program com. Nat. Assn. for Mental Health, 1968-70; dir. task group in prevention Pres.'s Commn. Mental Health, 1977-78; com. on prevention Nat. Mental Health Assn., 1985-86; bd. dirs. Internat. Coun. Psychologists, 1985-88; prevention com. World Fedn. Mental Health, 1992—, Biennial Albee lectr. on prevention. Fellow APA (bd. profl. affairs, coun. reps., bd. dirs. 1965-70, 77-80, pres. div. clin. psychology 1967, nat. pres. 1969-70, policy and planning bd. 1972-75, chairperson com. on human resources 1973-76, mem. com. on sci. and profl. ethics 1990-92, Disting. Profl. Contbn. award 1975, Gold medal for lifetime contbns. in the public interest 1993); mem. AAAS, AAUP, Am. Bd. Profl. Psychology (bd. dirs. 1975-78, treas. 1976-80), Am. Psychol. Soc., Ea. Psychol. Assn., Midwestern Psychol. Assn., Ohio Psychol. Assn. (pres. 1963-64), Vt. Psychol. Assn., New Eng. Psychol. Assn. (pres. 1978-79, Disting. Contbn. award 1997), Am. Assn. Applied and Preventive Psychology (1st pres. 1990-92, Lifetime Achievement award in prevention psychology 1997), Psychologists for Social Responsibility (pres.-elect 1998), Phi Beta Kappa, Sigma Xi, Psi Chi. Home: 7157 Longboat Dr N Longboat Key FL 34228-1047

ALBER, RICHARD LAWRENCE, quality assurance professional; b. Troy, N.Y., Aug. 5, 1947; s. Norman Lawrence and Jane Frances (Procak) A.; m. Janet Carol Pakatar, Oct. 28, 1967; children: Michael, David. AS, Hudson Valley C.C., Troy, 1975; grad. mgmt. devel., Rensselaer Polytechnic Inst., 1992. Cert. lead quality auditor. Machinist Watervliet (N.Y.) Arsenal, 1966-72; intern quality assurance specialist Dept. Army, Washington, 1972-75; quality assurance specialist Watervliet Arsenal, 1975-86, supr. quality assurance specialist, 1986—. Mem. Am. Soc. for Quality (cert.), U.S. Water Polo (referee), Mt. Zion Free and Accepted Masons Lodge #311 (master 1992-93). Avocations: swimming, biking, travel, Greek language, computers. Home: 42 Whiteview Rd Wynantskill NY 12198-7832 Office: SIOWV-ODP-M Watervliet Arsenal Watervliet NY 12189

ALBERG, TOM AUSTIN, investment company executive, lawyer; b. San Francisco, Feb. 12, 1940; s. Thomas A. and Miriam A. (Twitchell) A.; m. Mary Ann Johnke, June 8, 1963 (div. July 1989); children: Robert, Katherine, John; m. Judith Beck, Aug. 8, 1989; children: Carson, Jessica. AB, Harvard Coll., 1962; JD, Columbia U., 1965. Bar: N.Y. 1965, Wash. 1967. Assoc. Cravath, Swaine & Moore, N.Y.C., 1965-67; assoc. Perkins, Cole, Stone, Olsen & Williams, Seattle, 1967-71, ptnr., 1971-90, chmn. exec. com., 1986-90; exec. v.p. legal and corp. affairs McCaw Cellular Comm. Inc., Kirkland, Wash., 1990-95; pres., CEO, dir. Personal Connect Comm. Corp., Kirkland, 1995—; prin. Madrona Investment Group, 1996—; pres., COO, dir. Lin Broadcasting Inc., Kirkland, 1991-95; bd. dirs. Active Voice Corp., VISIO Corp., Emeritus Corp., Amazon Com., Inc.; pres. Seattle Legal Svcs., 1973-74; lectr. on securities and fin. law. Editor Law Rev., Columbia U. Contbr. articles to profl. jours. Pres. Intiman Theatre, Seattle, 1981-83, Pacific Sci. Ctr. Found., Seattle, 1982-84; chmn. Discovery Inst., 1991—, Seattle Commons, 1991-94; trustee Children's Hosp. Found., 1992-95, Pacific Sci. Ctr., 1994—, U. Puget Sound, 1994—, Sta. KING-FM, 1994—. Stone scholar Columbia U., 1963-65. Mem. ABA, Wash. State Bar Assn. (chmn. corp. sect. 1975-76, securities com. 1974-75), Univ. Club, Seattle Yacht Club. Office: Madrona Investment Group LLC 1000 2nd Ave Ste 3700 Seattle WA 98104-1053

ALBERGA, ALTA WHEAT, artist; b. Ala.; d. James Richard and Leila Savannah (Sullivan) Wheat; BA, MA, Wichita State U., 1954; BFA, Washington U., St. Louis, 1961; MFA, U. Ill., 1964; m. Alvyn Clyde Alberga, Dec. 3, 1930. Mem. faculty Wichita (Kans.) State U., 1955-56, Webster Coll., St. Louis, 1969. art tchr. Ossining (N.Y.) High Sch., 1968; asst. prof., head visual arts Presbyn. Coll., Clinton, S.C., 1969-74; pvt. art tchr., Greenville, S.C., 1972—; substitute tchr. Greenville County Schs.; tchr. painting Tempo Gallery Sch., Greenville, 1974—, Greenville County Mus. Sch., 1975—, Tryon (N.C.) Fine Arts Ctr., 1975; 1986 (merit award 1987); tchr. Tri-County Tech. Coll., Pendleton, S.C., 1975. One-woman shows include Greenville County Mus., 1979, Greenville Artists Guild Gallery, 1979, 83, Wichita State U., 1954, St. Louis Artists Guild, 1956, N.C. State U., 1965, 66, Met. Arts Council, Greenville, 1980, 83, 85, Tryon Fine Arts Ctr., 1988, S.C. State U., 1992, 93; exhibited in group shows at Pickens County Mus., 1979, 88-89, Internation, Washington, 1981-82, Greenville Artists Guild, 1982, 88, Art/7, Washington, 1983, N.C. Univ., Charlotte invitational, 1989, Furman U. Women's Show, 1989, S.C. State U., 1992, Upstate Visual Arts, 1993, S.C.

State U., 1993, Rolling Green Gallery, 1993, Internationale Grafiek Biennale, Maastricht, the Netherlands, 1993, S.C. Watercolor Soc., 1994 (award), Greenville County Mus. Art, 1995, Embry Found., Peace Ctr. Greenville, 1997, Gov.'s Sch. Art, BMW, Greenville, 1997; represented in permanent collections S.C. State Mus., Columbia, S.C. Arts Commn., Pickens County Mus.; represented in pvt. collections; bd. dirs. Greenville Artists Guild, 1977-79, pres., 1985; bd. dirs. Guild Gallery, 1978, Guild Greenville Symphony, 1989-90. Recipient Richard K. Weil award St. Louis Mus., 1957; Purchase prize S.C. Arts Commn., 1972; Merritt award Greenville Mus., 1986, Pickens County Mus., 1987, 88; Cash award S.C. Water Color Assn., 1994. Mem. Artists Equity (pres. St. Louis chpt. 1962), Internat. Platform Assn. (life), Art Students League (life), Guild Greenville Artists (pres. 1984-85), S.C. Artists Guild, Southeastern Council Printmakers, Greenville Symphony Guild, Mus. Assn. (invited Greenville County Mus. 1993), Kappa Pi, Kappa Delta Pi. Democrat. Home: 11 Overton Ave Greenville SC 29617-7513 *In this innovating age, we must be constantly evaluating and chosing in order to make valuable decisions. In my field, the fine arts, the exciting ideas; concepts that are so open; with an abundance of materials to work with, endless international styles and a climate of freedom; all breed quality and originality in today's art.*

ALBERGER, WILLIAM RELPH, lawyer, government official; b. Portland, Oreg., Oct. 11, 1945; s. Relph Griffin and Ferne (Ahlstrom) A.; m. Joyce Alberger; children: Eric Griffin, Blake Eugene. BA, Willamette U., 1967; MBA, U. Iowa, 1971; JD, Georgetown U., 1973. Bar: D.C. 1974. Spl. asst. to U.S. Senator Bob Packwood, 1969-71; legis. asst. U.S. Rep. Al Ullman, Washington, 1972-75; adminstrv. asst. U.S. Rep. Al Ullman, 1975-77, House Com. on Ways and Means, 1977; mem. U.S. Internat. Trade Commn., Washington, 1977-82, vice-chmn., 1978-80, chmn., 1980-82; ptnr. Ball Janik, L.L.P., Washington, 1995—. Mem. ABA (chmn. standing com. customs law 1983-85), D.C. Bar Assn., Internat. Bar Assn. Democrat. Office: 1725 Stonebridge Rd Alexandria VA 22304

ALBERGHETTI, ANNA MARIA, singer, actress; b. Rhodes, Italy, May 15, 1936; d. Daniele and Vittoria (Ricci) A.; m. Claudio Guzman (div. Feb. 1973); children: Alexandra, Pilar. Appeared in films Here Comes the Groom, 1950, The Stars Are Singing, 1952, The Last Command, 1955, 10, 000 Bedrooms, 1956, Cinderella, 1958, The Medium, also in Broadway musical Carnival, 1961 (Tony award). Roman Catholic.

ALBERS, CHARLES EDGAR, investment manager; b. Flushing, N.Y., Nov. 30, 1940; s. Edwin M. and Olive F. (Van Dyke) A.; m. Judy Mae Hite, Dec. 18, 1961 (dec. June 1998); children: Robert, Karin, Laura. AB, Kenyon Coll., 1962; MBA, Columbia U., 1967. CFA. Securities analyst Arnold Bernhard & Co., N.Y.C., 1963-66; fin. analyst Baker Industries, Newark, 1967-68; securities analyst Wertheim & Co., N.Y.C., 1968-69; asst. portfolio mgr. Am. Standard, Inc., N.Y.C., 1969-71; sr. v.p. equity securities Guardian Life Ins. Co., N.Y.C., 1971-98; portfolio mgr. Guardian Park Avenue Fund, Inc., N.Y.C., 1972-98; pres. Guardian Stock Fund, N.Y.C., 1983-98; sr. v.p. Oppenheimer Funds, 1998—; portfolio mgr. Oppenheimer Main St. G&I Fund, 1998—. Named to honor roll Forbes Mut. Fund 9 times, Variable Annuity Mgr. of Yr. Morningstar, 1996; Woodrow Wilson fellow, 1962-63. Mem. Am. Fin. Assn., Assn. for Investment Mgmt. and Rsch., N.Y. Soc. Security Analysts, Fin. Mgmt. Assn., Beacon Hill Club. Episcopalian. Avocations: platform tennis, reading, mountain hiking. Office: Oppenheimer Funds Inc 2 World Trade Ctr New York NY 10048

ALBERS, EDWARD JAMES, SR., retired secondary school educator; b. Centralia, Wash., July 6, 1922; s. Otto Johnson and Nell Genevieve Albers; m. Caroline Constance Cochran, July 30, 1944; 1 child, Edward James Jr. Student, Wash. State Coll., 1942, U. Ariz., 1949-51; BA, U. Nebr., Omaha, 1959; MA, Rolliins Coll., 1966. Cert. tchr., Fla. Commd. 2d lt. USAF, 1944, advanced through grades to maj., 1961, pilot, 1944-65, served command pilot SAC, ret., 1965; tchr. social studies Winter Park (Fla.) H.S., 1966-96, chmn. dept. social studies, 1973-88, ret., 1996. Decorated Yun-Hui medal, Chinese pilot wings. Mem. Nat. Geog. Soc., Air Force Assn., Burma Star (England), Mil. Order of the World Wars (commdr.), Exptl. Aircraft Assn. and Warbirds, Ret. Officers' Assn. (commdr.), China-Burma-India Vets. Assn., Santa Ana Calif. AAF Alumni, Train Collectors Assn., Lionel Collectors Assn., Officers' Club, Patrick AFB, Hump Pilots' Assn., Corvette Club Ctrl. Fla., Daedalians, Sigma Phi Epsilon. Democrat. Episcopalian. Avocations: antique toy train collecting, golfing, scuba diving, snow and water skiing, flying.

ALBERS, LUCIA BERTA, land developer; b. Guatemala, Feb. 10, 1943; d. Jose Luis De Leon Polanco and Maria Marta (Vasquez) De Leon; m. Ray Cisneros, Nov. 2, 1968 (div. 1972); 1 child, Elizabeth Ann Albers Cisneros; m. Monte Dean Albers, June 12, 1974; 1 child, Monte Roberto. Grad. in Acctg., Sacred Heart, Guatemala, 1963; student in Econs., San Carlos, Guatemala, 1964; student, Diablo Valley Coll., 1975, 76. Chief acct. Discovery Bay, Byron, Calif., 1971-76; asst. fin. dir. City of Pittsburg, Calif., 1976-78; corporate contr. Conco Cement, Concord, Calif., 1981-90; land developer Contra Costa County, Calif., 1990—. Mem. adv. coun. City of Byron, Calif., 1991-94; dir. Ctr. for New Ams., Concord, 1994—. Mem. Nat. Assn. Accts., Nat. Assn. Exec. Women, Nat. Assn. Women, Mex.-Am. Polit. Assn. Home: 9601 Deer Valley Rd Brentwood CA 94513-4907

ALBERSHEIM, PETER, biology educator; b. N.Y.C., Mar. 30, 1934; s. Walter Julius and Alberta (Green) A.; children: Renee, Jim, Stephi. B.S., Cornell U., 1956; Ph.D., Calif. Inst. Tech., 1959. NSF postdoctoral research fellow Swiss Fed. inst. Tech., Zurich, Switzerland, 1959; instr. biology Harvard, Cambridge, Mass., 1960-61; asst. prof. Harvard, 1961-64; asso. prof. biochemistry, dept. chemistry U. Colo., Boulder, 1964-67; prof. U. Colo., 1967-85, prof. molecular, cellular, developmental biology, 1970-85; rsch. prof. biochemistry, chemistry, botany and plant pathology, dir. Complex Carbohydrate Rsch. Ctr. U. Ga., Athens, 1985—; co-dir. ctr. for plant and microbial complex carbohydrates Dept. Energy, Athens, 1987—; dir. resource ctr. for biomed. complex carbohydrates NIH, Athens, 1989—; Faculty Rsch. lectr. U. Colo. Coun. on Rsch. and Creative Work, 1980; Storrer Life Scis. lectr. U. Calif., Davis, 1977; Dupont lectr. Tex. A&M U., 1978; vis. prof. U. Tex., 1978. Author: (with others) Twenty-six Afternoons of Biology - An Introductory Lab Manual, 1966; mem. editl. bd. Carbohydrate Rsch., Plant and Cell Physiology, Physiol. and Molecular Plant Pathology, Glycoconjugate Jour.; referee other jours.; contbr. over 275 articles to sci. jours. Recipient Robert L. Stearns award for contbns. to progress U. Colo., 1979; grantee NIH, 1960-65, 87—, NSF, 1966-67, 71-86, AEC-ERDA-Dept. Energy, 1964—, Herman Frasch Found., 1972-77, Rockefeller Found., 1975-83, USDA, 1975-78. Fellow AAAS; Mem. Am. Chem. Soc., Am. Soc. Biol. Chemists, Am. Soc. Plant Physiology (mem. exec. com. 1978—, Charles A. Shull award 1973), The Biochem. Soc., Am. Phytopathol. Soc., Sigma Xi, others. Office: U Ga Complex Carbohydrate Rsch Ctr 220 Riverbend Rd Athens GA 30602-1511

ALBERT, DANIEL MYRON, ophthalmologist, educator; b. Newark, Dec. 19, 1936; s. Maurice I. and Flora Albert; m. Eleanor Kagle, June 26, 1960; children: B. Steven, Michael. BS, Franklin and Marshall Coll., 1958; MD, U. Pa., 1962; MA (hon.), Harvard U., 1976; D honoris causa, Louis Pasteur U., Strasbourg, 1992; MS, U. Wis., Madison, 1997. Diplomate: Am. Bd. Ophthalmology. Intern Hosp. U. Pa., 1962-63, resident, 1963-66; surgeon USPHS, 1966-68; NIH spl. fellow in ophthalmic pathology Armed Forces Inst. Pathology, 1968-69; practice medicine specializing in ophthalmology; assoc. surgeon Mass. Eye and Ear Infirmary, 1976-86, surgeon, 1986-92, dir. David G. Cogan eye pathology lab., 1979-92, surgeon, 1986-92; asst. prof. ophthalmology Yale U. Sch. Medicine, 1969-70, assoc. prof., 1970-75, prof., 1975-76; prof. ophthalmic pathology Harvard U. Med. Sch., 1976-84, David G. Cogan prof. ophthalmology, 1984-92; Frederick Allison Davis prof., chmn. dept. ophthalmology U. Wis., Madison, 1992—. Author: (with Scheie) A History of Ophthalmology at the University of Pennsylvania, 1965, Textbook of Ophthalmology, 8th edit. 1969, 9th edit. 1977; co-author: Jaegar's Atlas of Ophthalmology, 1972, (with Puliafito) Foundations of Ophthalmology, 1979, Men of Vision, 1993, (with Jakobiec) Atlas of Clinical Ophthalmology, 1996; (with Edwards) History of Ophthalmology, 1996; editor: (with Edwards) The History of Ophthalmology, 1996, John Jeffres' Lectures on the Diseases of the Eye, 1998, Ophthalmic Surgery: Principles and Techniques, 1998; co-editor Principles and Practice of Ophthalmology, 1994; editor Archives of Ophthalmology, 1994—; contbr. articles to profl. jours. Recipient Oliver Meml. medal U. Pa., 1962, Friedenwald award, 1981, Von Sallmann award in vision and ophthalmology Internat. Conf. for Eye Rsch., 1988, award Humboldt Found., 1991, MacKenzie medal Scottish Ophthal. Soc., 1992, Lighthouse Pisart Vision award The Lighthouse Inc., 1997; Lorenze E. Zimmerman (WARF) professorship, 1999; William and Mary Greve scholar, 1978-79, scholar Alcon Rsch. Inst., 1984-85. Fellow ACS; mem. Am. Assn. Ophthalmic Pathology (Zimmerman medal 1993), Am. Acad. Ophthalmology (Jackson Meml. lectr. 1996), Am. Bd. Ophthalmology (dir. 1997—). Jewish. Home: 1106 Wellesley Rd Madison WI 53705-2230 Office: U Wis Hosp and Clinics Dept Ophthalmology F4/334 600 Highland Ave Madison WI 53792-0001

ALBERT, EDDIE (EDWARD ALBERT HEIMBERGER), actor; b. Rock Island, Ill., Apr. 22, 1908; s. Frank and Julia (Jones) Heimberger; m. Maria Margarita Guadelupe Teresa Estella Bolado Castilla y O'Donnell (profl. name Margo) (dec.); children: Edward, Maria. Student, U. Minn., 1927-29. With singing trio, Mpls., 1930; then to St. Louis, Cin., to N.Y.C., 1935 for radio show Grace and Eddie; acted in Broadway version radio show No Hard Feelings, 1973; organized for making ednl. films Edward Prodns., Inc., 1945; appeared in motion pictures including The Teahouse of August Moon, 1956, Miracle of the White Stallions, 1963, Brother Rat, Carrie, 1976, Roman Holiday (nominated for Acad. award 1955), Oklahoma, 1955, Sun Also Rises, 1957, Roots of Heaven, 1958, Attack, 1958, Longest Day, 1962, Captain Newman, 1964, The Heartbreak Kid, 1972 (Academy award nominee), The Longest Yard, 1974, Escape to Witch Mountain, 1975, Yes, Giorgio, 1981, Take This Job and Shove It, 1981, Dreamscape, 1984, Head Office, 1984, Stitches, 1985, Getting Even, 1986 The Big Picture, 1989, Headless, 1994; toured night-club act with wife, 1954; star of TV series Green Acres, 1965-71, Switch, 1975-78; TV appearances include Studio One, 1948-57, The Outer Limits, Show of Shows, also TV movies Peter and Paul, 1981, Rooster, 1982, Dress Gray, 1986, Mercy or Murder, 1986, Brenda Starr, 1986, Girl From Mars, 1986, War and Remembrance, 1989, Return From Green Acres, 1990, Highway to Heaven, Falcon Crest, Twilight Zone, Murder She Wrote, General Hospital, thirtysomething, Ray Bradbury Theatre, Golden Palace, Time Trax, Barefoot Executive, 1995, Dr. Quinn: Medicine Woman, 1995, others; Broadway appearances include O, Evening Star, Brother Rat, Room Service, Boys from Syracuse, Miss Liberty, Music Man; appeared with Circus Moderno, Mexico, 1941, Hagenbeck Circus, Europe, 1965, San Francisco Opera, 1982; conducted lecture tour on ecology, 1969-70; chmn. emeritus Plaza de la Raza. Participant World Hunger Conf., Rome, 1974; dir. U.S. Commn. on Refugees; bd. dirs. Film Council; trustee Nat. Recreation and Parks Assn., Alaska-Pacific U., Nat. Arbor Day Found.; nat. conservation chmn.; bd. dirs. solar lobby, mem. consumer adv. bd. Dept. Energy, Washington; chmn. Eddie Albert World Trees Found. Am. Recipient Nat. Film Critics award, 1972, Presdl. award World Without Hunger, 1984. Club: Bohemian (San Francisco). Office: Edward Prodns Inc 719 Amalfi Dr Pacific Palisades CA 90272-4509*

ALBERT, GARETT J., lawyer; b. Sept. 7, 1943; m. Eleanor Lanier Culbertson, Oct. 2, 1971. BA cum laude, Columbia U., 1965; postgrad., Harvard U. Bus. Sch., 1967-68; JD, Harvard U., 1968. Bar: D.C. 1969, N.Y. 1970. Atty. U.S. Atomic Energy Commn., 1968; assoc. Hughes Hubbard & Reed, N.Y.C., 1969-77; ptnr. Hughes Hubbard & Reed, LLP, N.Y.C., 1977—. Contbr. articles to various publs. including James Joyce Quar. Bd. dirs. Nat. Acad. Design, Nat. Corp. Fund for Dance, Paul Taylor Dance Found. Winner U.S. Nat. Powerlifting Championship, Nat. Physique com., Tournament of Champions, 1996, Mr. USA, 1996, Kevin Levrone Bodybuilding Classic, 1995, and other masters powerlifting and bodybuilding championships. Mem. Union Club. Office: Hughes Hubbard & Reed LLP 1 Battery Park Plz Fl 12 New York NY 10004-1482

ALBERT, HARRY FRANCIS, investments executive; b. Phila., Mar. 14, 1935; s. James J. Albert and Mary A. (Miller) Mannes; m. Anna Cosmina Rago, Sept. 5, 1955; children: Anne Marie Borneman, Harry F. Jr., Steven J. Student, Drexel Inst. Tech., 1952-56; student, U. Pa., 1958. Exec. v.p. Health Corp. Am., Wayne, Pa., 1975-80; pres., chmn. Annin, Inc., Berwyn, Pa., 1980-93; v.p. Prudential Investments, 1993—. Mem. Nat. Right to Life, Delaware County, Pa., 1978—; mem., officer Rotary Internat., Springfield, Pa., 1966-71; bd. dirs. Trevor's Campaign for the Homeless. Recipient Thomas Lovejoy Cup, Manhattan Cos., N.Y., 1985. Mem. Internat. assn. Fin. Planners, Nat. Assn. Variable Annuities, Nat. Assn. Security Dealers, World Trade Club N.Y.C. Republican. Roman Catholic. Avocations: boating, fishing, golf, reading, tennis. Home and Office: PO Box 180 145 Port Herman Dr Chesapeake City MD 21915-1658

ALBERT, JACK, communications company executive. Sr. v.p., gen. mgr. Loral Skynet, Inc., Bedminister, N.J. Office: Loral Skynet Inc 500 Hills Dr PO Box 7018 Bedminister NJ 07921

ALBERT, JANYCE LOUISE, business educator, banker; b. Toledo, July 27, 1932; d. Howard C. And Glenola Mae (Masters) Blessing; m. John R. Albert, Aug. 7, 1954; children: John R., James H. Student, Ohio Wesleyan U., 1949-51; BA, Mich. State U., 1953; MS, Iowa State U., 1980. Asst. pers. mgr./tng. sup. Sears, Roebuck & Co., Toledo, 1953-56; tchr. adult edn. Tenafly Pub. Schs. (N.J.), 1966-70; pers. officer, tng. officer, tng. and edn. mgr. Iowa Dept. Transp., Ames, 1974-77; coll. recruiting coord. Rockwell Internat., Cedar Rapids, Iowa, 1977-79, engring. adminstrn. mgr., 1979-80; employee rels. and job evaluation analyst Phillips Petroleum Co., Bartlesville, Okla., 1980-81; v.p., dir. pers. Rep. Bancorp, Tulsa, 1981-83; sr. v.p. and dir. human resources First Nat. Bank, Rockford, Ill., 1983-94; dir. bus. divsn. Rock Valley Coll., Rockford, Ill., 1994—; advisor to Nat. Profl. Secs. Assn.; bd. dirs. Riverside Community Bank, 1995—. Bd. dirs. Rocvale Children's Home, 1986-97, 99—, pres. 1991-94; v.p. bd. dirs. United Way of Ames, 1976-77; mem. employee svc. comm., Rockford Pub. Schs., 1988-92; account exec. United Way Rockford, 1993-98, account sec. head, 1996; bd. dirs. Rockford Human Resources Cmty. Action Program; chair legis. com. Rockford Human Svcs. Dept.; chair Rockford State of Ill. Job Svcs. Employers Coun., 1990-97; publicity chmn. Tenafly 300th Ann. Celebration, 1969; mem. task force Rockford Bd. Edn., 1993-94; mem. gala com. Janet Wattles Mental Health Ctr., 1990; deacon Presbyn. Ch., Ames, 1972-75; mem. adv. coun. Rockford YWCA, bd. dirs., 1986, mem. fund drive task force, 1998-99, co-chair YWCA Leader Luncheon, 1986—; advisor Rockford chpt. ARC, 1991—; mem. Mayor's Task Force for Rockford Project Self-Sufficiency, 1986-89, chmn. adv. coun., 1991; chair info. and referral com., bd. dirs. United Way of Rockford and Contact, 1994—, account exec., 1993—; bd. dirs. Rockford Symphony Orch., 1992-95, sec. 1994-95; bd. dirs. Rockford Leadership Found., 1994-96, Contact, 1998—; chair pers. com. Rockford Ctrl. Area Comm., 1997-99, v.p., bd. dirs.; mem. fund drive taskforce Blackhawk Day Nursery, 1998-99. Pres.'s scholar Mich. State U., 1951-53; recipient YWCA Kate O'Connor award for Women in Labor Force, 1984; named Bd. Mem. of Yr. Rockford Human Resources Community Action Program, 1992. Mem. Rockford Network (past chairperson 1985, 86, awards com. 1995, 96—), Rockford C. of C. (transp. com., human resources com., leadership program 1989, pres. coun. 1991-92, pres. 1992-94, mem. internat. bus. coun. 1999—, Athena award 1991), Rockford Pers. Assn. (co-chmn. programs 1985-86, adv. coun. 1983—), Crusader Clin. Found. (bd. dirs. 1997—), Am. Soc. Pers. Adminstrn. (co-chair awards com. 1998), Employee Benefits Assn. No. Ill. (membership chmn.), Womenspace (bd. dirs. 1993-95, mktg. com. 1993-99, awards com. 1995, 96-98), Rockford Personal and Profl. Power Coalition, P.E.O., Rockford Panhellenic Coun. (sec. 1992-93, treas. 1993-94, v.p. 1994-95, pres. 1995-96, Woman of Yr. award 1994), World Trade Coun. (bd. dirs. 1994-97), Ill. Consortium Internat. Travel (mentor The Netherlands 1997), Sigma Epsilon, Alpha Gamma Delta, Phi Kappa Phi. Home: 5587 Thunderidge Dr Rockford IL 61107-1756 Office: Rock Valley Coll Bus Divsn 3301 N Mulford Rd Rockford IL 61114-5640

ALBERT, LEONARD, religious organization executive. Dir. of lay ministries Ch. of God, Cleve.; exec. dir. of lay ministries Ch. of God, Cleve., Tenn., 1974. Office: Ch of God PO Box 2430 Cleveland TN 37320-2430*

ALBERT, MARGARET COOK, communications executive; b. Madison, Wis., Aug. 25, 1933; d. Hulet Hall and Esther Frances (Marhoefer) Cook; m. Walter E. Albert, Jan. 24, 1959; children: Jennifer Ann, Bryan Walter. AB in Journalism, Ind. U., 1955; postgrad., U. Bordeaux, France, 1957-58. Reporter Daily Herald-Telephone, Bloomington, Ind., 1953-55, 59-60; copy editor Cosmopolitan Mag., N.Y.C., 1955-57; copy chief, coll. advt. Houghton Mifflin, Boston, 1960-62, freelance writer, 1962-70; pub. rels. coord., editor Allegheny County Med. Soc., Pitts., 1970-75; dir. pub. info. Urban League Pitts., 1975-86; pres., owner Matrix Comms. Assocs., Pitts., 1986—; cons. West Penn Hosp.; James I. McGuire Antiquity Ctr., Pitts., 1989-91; cons., sr. writer Comms. 2000, Agy. for Instnl. Tech., Bloomington, 1994—; cons. Family Comms., Pitts., 1992—; writer, editor 651-Arts, Bklyn. Acad. Music, 1992-95. Rschr., ghost writer: Day Breakers: The Story of the Urban League of Pittsburgh, 1983 (Matrix award 1984); author: A Practical Vision: The Story of Blue Cross of West Pennsylvania, 1987; contbr. articles to profl. publs.; prodr. computer graphics program African-Am. Computer Graphics, 1994; guest editor Mademoiselle Mag., 1955. Bd. dirs. Health Sys. Agy. of S.W. Pa., Pitts., 1976-86, Pa. Med. Care Found., Camp Hill, 1981-86, Animal Rescue League of S.W. Pa., Pitts., 1988-93; mem. Pa. Blue Shield Corp., Camp Hill, 1982-90. Fulbright scholar, 1957-58; recipient Disting. Svc. award Urban League of Pitts., 1977, Harold B. Gardner Citizens award Allegheny County Med. Soc., 1981, 1st place award Women in Comms., Inc., Pa. Assn. for Nonprofit Homes for Aging, Brotherhood award. Mem. Phi Beta Kappa. Democrat.

ALBERT, MARV, sportscaster, program director; b. N.Y.C., June 12, 1944; s. Max and Alida (Kahn) A.; children: Kenny, Jackie, Denise, Brian. Student, Syracuse U., 1960-63; BS in Journalism, NYU, 1964. Announcer Sta. WOLF, Syracuse, N.Y., 1961-64; sports dir. Sta. WHN, N.Y.C., 1967-73; announcer N.Y. Knicks basketball team, 1967—, N.Y. Rangers hockey team, 1967—; basketball, football and boxing announcer, host baseball pre-game show NBC Sports Network, 1977—; sports dir. Sta. WNBC-TV, N.Y.C., 1974-88. Author: Yes--A Guide to Sportscasting, 1981, Marv Albert's Quiz Book, 1976, Krazy About the Knicks, 1970, I'd Love To But I Have a Game, 1993. Recipient Global Ace award for Play-by-Play, 1990, Emmy award, 1990, 93, 6-time recipient Cable Ace award Play-by-Play sportscasting; named Sports Personality of Yr. Spl. Olympics, N.Y.C., 1983. Mem. Nat. Sportscaster and Sportswriters Assn. (Sportscaster of Yr. 1971-90), Internat. Boxing Writers Assn. Office: NBC Sports 30 Rockefeller Plz Rm 1445 New York NY 10112-0002*

ALBERT, MILTON JOHN, retired chemist, microbiologist; b. St. Louis, Oct. 27, 1917; s. Fredrich and Mary (Kuchenmeister) A.; m. Arline Louise Bolle, Mar. 30, 1946; children: Mary Louise, Kathleen Marie, Barbara Jean, Patricia Lee. BS, U. Ill., 1948. Plant mgr. Lucky Club Flavors, St. Louis, 1950-53; quality control Vestal Labs., St. Louis, 1953-57; microbiologist Rexall Drug Co., St. Louis, 1957-64; quality control Falstaff Brewing Co., St. Louis, 1964-67; dept. head Morton Frozen Food, Russellville, Ark., 1967-81; quality control Ga.-Pacific, Crossett, Ark., 1981-82; cons. Russellville, 1982—; vol. Vols. in Tech. Assistance, Arlington, Va., 1981—; tech. advisor Ark. Valley Vocat. Tech. Sch., Ozark, 1985-87. With U.S. Army, 1942-46, World War II. Mem. Am. Soc. Microbiology, Inst. Food Tech., Am. Chem. Soc. Home: 240 S Inglewood Ave Apt 224 Russellville AR 72801-3355

ALBERT, NEALE MALCOLM, lawyer; b. N.Y.C., Dec. 18, 1937; s. J. Louis and Sadie (Korn) A.; m. Margaret Morgan, Apr. 11, 1981; children: Deborah Beth, Miriam Susan. BA, Princeton U., 1958; LLB, Yale U., 1961. Ptnr. Paul, Weiss, Rifkind, Wharton & Garrison, N.Y.C., 1959—. Office: Paul Weiss Rifkind Wharton 30th Fl 1285 Ave of the Americas New York NY 10019-6028*

ALBERT, ROBERT ALAN, lawyer; b. Boston, May 29, 1933; s. James and Mildred (Levine) A.; m. Revel Guest, Aug. 22, 1963; children: Justin Thomas, Corisande Charlotte. AB, Harvard U., 1955; LLB, Columbia U., 1960. Bar: N.Y. 1960. Assoc. Casey, Lane and Mittendorf, N.Y.C., 1960-63; resident sr. counsel Casey, Lane and Mittendorf, London, 1963-67; ptnr. Albert, Homet and Albert, London, 1967-75, Sidley & Austin, London, 1975-86, Finley, Kumble, Wagner et al, London, 1986-88; sr. ptnr. The Albert Partnership, London, 1988-90; cons. Alsop Wilkinson, London, 1990-92; mng. dir., chief exec. officer Covent Garden Pioneer FSP Ltd., 1992-95; chmn. TransAtlantic Films, London. Trustee Internat. Youth Found.; dep. dist. leader Yorkville Dem. Party, N.Y.C., 1960-63. Served to 1st lt. U.S. Army, 1955-57. Fellow Royal Soc. Arts; mem. ABA, Internat. Bar Assn., Assn. Bar City of N.Y. Clubs: Garrick, Queen's (London); Harvard (N.Y.C.). Avocations: tennis, shooting, golf. Home: Cabalua Whiting-on-Wye, Herefordshire HR3 6EX, England Office: The Albert Partnership, Studio 1 3 Brandenbury Rd, London England W6 OBE

ALBERT, SARAH CATHLEEN, public policy specialist; b. Jan. 2, 1974. BA in Law and Society, Am. U., 1996, MPA, 1998. Pub. policy dir. The Gen. Fedn. of Women's Clubs, Washington, 1998—. Email: legislation@gfwc.org.

ALBERT, SIDNEY PAUL, philosophy and drama educator; b. Syracuse, N.Y., Apr. 11, 1914; s. Simon and Gertrude Dora (Siskin) A.; m. Lucy Ann Schroeder, Oct. 30, 1955 (div.); children: Vivian Risa Albert Shemesh, Alan Edward, Laurence David. AB, Syracuse U., 1934; PhD in Philosophy, Yale U., 1939; postgrad. in drama and theatre, Carnegie Inst. Tech., Northwestern U., Stanford U., U. Ill., 1950-53; postgrad., U. Ill., 1953-54, Columbia U., 1954-56. Instr. philosophy U. Conn., Storrs, 1946, Syracuse (N.Y.) U., 1946; asst. prof., philosophy Triple Cities Coll./Syracuse U., 1946-50, SUNY, 1950-53; part time instr. speech dept. U. Ill., 1953-54; asst. prof., philosophy L.A. State Coll., 1956-60, assoc. prof., philosophy, 1960-64; prof., philosophy Calif. State U., L.A., 1964-79, prof. emeritus, 1979—; chair dept. philos., Calif. State U., L.A., 1960-63, assoc. chair 1967-68, acad. senate, 1962-64; first chair assembly sch. letters and sci., 1966-67, mem.-at-large, 1966-68. Dir. first Triple Cities Coll. theatre prodn., 1947; directed coll. and cmty. theatre prodns.; contbr. numerous articles and reviews about George Bernard Shaw to profl. jours. Pres. West San Gabriel (Calif.) Dem. Club, 1960-64; mem. Calif. Dem. State Ctrl. Com., 1960-62; mem. L.A. County Dem. Ctrl. Com., 1962-64; mem. state human rels. com. Calif. Dem. Coun., 1963-64. Warrant officer (j.g.) U.S. Army, 1941-46. Fellow Syracuse U., 1934-35; scholar Yale U., 1935-36; Hon. Rsch. fellow Yale U., 1940-41; Rsch. grantee, 1964-65, 66-67, 69, 73-74; Sidney P. Albert/George Bernard Shaw Collection established at John Hay Libr., Brown Univ., 1991. Mem. MLA, AAUP (sec. and treas. Triple Cities Coll. chpt 1947-48, pres. Harpur Coll. chpt. 1950-51, treas. L.A. State Coll. chpt. 1959-61, mem. exec. com. 1960-61, 63-64, pres. 1962-63, del. 1963; state coll. rep. exec. com. So. Calif. Conf. 1963-64, chair com. Emeriti and retirement issues, ex-officio mem. exec. com. Calif. Conf., 1980—, awarded nat. cert. 50 years of distinguished membership, advisor nat. retirement com. 1997), CSULA Emeriti Assn. (founder, 1978, v.p., 1983-84, pres. 1984-85), Am. Philos. Assn., Am. Soc. Aesthetics (v.p. Calif. divsn. 1962-63, pres. 1963-64), Modern Lang. Assn., Am. Soc. Theatre Rsch. (mem. nominating com. 1971), Theatre Libr. Assn., Assn. Calif. State Univ. Profs. (v.p. L.A. state coll. chpt. 1959-60), Shaw Soc. (London), Bernard Shaw Soc. (N.Y.C.), Shaw Soc. Calif. (bd. dirs. 1959-65, mem. editorial bd. Shaw Review, 1968-80, Shaw: The Annual of Bernard Shaw Studies, 1981-85), Shaw Soc. (Japan, lect. 1976, 80), Calif. State U. Emeritus and Ret. Faculty Assn. (founder, pres. 1985-87), Royal Inst. Philosophy (pres. 1963-64), Phi Beta Kappa, Phi Kappa Phi, Pi Gamma Mu. Avocations: collecting B. Shaw books, manuscripts, memorabilia; attending concerts, opera, theater, motion pictures. Home: 847 Eaton Dr Pasadena CA 91107-1837

ALBERT, SUSAN WITTIG, writer, English educator; b. Maywood, Ill., Jan. 2, 1940; d. John H. and A. Lucille (Franklin) Webber; m. William Albert, 1986; children by previous marriage: Robert, Robin, Michael. BA, U. Ill., 1967; PhD, U. Calif.-Berkeley, 1972. Instr. U. San Francisco, 1969-71; asst. prof. to assoc. prof. U. Tex., Austin, 1971-79; assoc. dean Grad. Sch., U. Tex., Austin, 1977-79; dean Sophie Newcomb Coll., New Orleans, 1979-81; dean of faculty, grad. dean S.W. Tex. State U., San Marcos, 1981-82, v.p. acad. affairs, 1982-86, prof. English, 1981-87; founder Story Circle Network, Inc. Author: Work of Her Own, Writing From Life, 8 China Bayles mystery novels, 6 Robin Page Victorian mystery novels. Danforth grad. fellow, 1967-72. Home: Drawer M Bertram TX 78605

ALBERTERNST, JUDITH ANN, pension administrator; b. Highland, Ill., Oct. 26, 1963; d. Joseph Bernard and Luetta Elizabeth (Seefeldt) A. Student, Kaskaskia Coll., 1992—. Bookkeeper William B. Kealey & Co., Belleville, Ill., 1981-86, office mgr., 1986-92; sr. pension administr. Qualified Plan Svcs., Highland, Ill., 1992—. Contbr. poems published to publs. Roman Catholic. Avocations: stamp collecting, beadwork, cross-stich, geneology, gardening.

ALBERT-GALTIER, ALEXANDRE, literature and language educator; b. Graveson, France, June 3, 1960; came to U.S., 1989; BA, U. Lyon II, 1981, MA with honors, 1982, PhD with honors, 1988. Tech. dir. Festival D'Avignon, France, 1983-90; Dia Art Found., N.Y.C., 1989-90; chargé de cours U. Lyon II, 1986-88; vis. instr. U. Oreg., Eugene, 1990-91; vis. asst. prof. U. Oreg., 1991-93, assoc. prof., 1996—; asst. prof. Mt. Holyoke Coll., 1993-94. Author: (poetry book) La Connaissance des Corps, 1995, La Traversée du Pacifique, 1998; contbr. articles to profl. jours.; invited spkr. Le Festival d'Avignon, U. Mass., 1994, others. Mem. MLA, Soc. d'Etudes du XVIIème Siè, Coll. de France, N.Am. Assn. for 17th Century French Lit., S.E. Am. Soc. for French 17th Century Studies, Centre Méridional de Rencontres sur le XVIIème Siècle, Soc. Internat. d' Etudes Yourcenariennes, Assn. des Amis d'André Gide, Assn. des Amis de Lancelot Desquais (pres.). Office: U Oreg Romance Langs 2450 Spring Blvd Eugene OR 97403-1658

ALBERTI, PETER WILLIAM, otolaryngologist; b. Coblenz, Germany, Aug. 23, 1934; arrived in Can., 1967; s. William Peter and Edith Elizabeth (Lachmann) A.; m. Elizabeth Margery Smith, Aug. 5, 1961; children: Andrew Peter, Fiona Elizabeth, Kathryn Penelope. MB, BS, U. Durham, Newcastle, Eng., 1957; PhD, Washington U., St. Louis, 1963. Intern Royal Victoria Infirmary, Newcastle upon Tyne, Eng., 1957-58, resident, 1958-60, 63-66; 1st asst. otolaryngology U. Newcastle, 1964-67; clin. tchr. U. Toronto, Ont., Can., 1967-68, asst. prof., 1968-70, assoc. prof., 1970-77, prof., 1977—, chmn. dept. otolaryngology, 1982-92; otolaryngologist-in-chief Mt. Sinai Hosp., Toronto, 1970-88, Toronto Gen. Hosp., 1982-89; sr. staff otolaryngologist Toronto Gen. Hosp., 1982—; exec. bd. Hearing Internat., 1992—. Editor: Personal Hearing Protection in Industry, 1981; co-author: An Atlas of Otoscopy, 1984, 2d edit., 1990, Otological Medicine and Surgery, 1988; co-editor Proc. Centennial Conf. on Laryngeal Cancer, 1976. Fellow Royal Coll. Surgeons (London), Royal Coll. Surgeons Can.; mem. Can. Otolaryngol. Soc. (pres. 1988-89), Triological Soc. (v.p. ea. sect. 1988-89), Collegium Oto-Rhino-Laryngologicorum Amicitae Sacrum (dep. sec. 1991-96, pres. 1996-97), Acoustical Soc. Am.; hon. mem. Brazilian Otolaryngol. Soc., Assn. Otolaryngologists of India, Irish Otolaryngol. Soc., Internat. Fedn. Otolaryngol. Socs. (sec.-gen. 1991—), Kenyan Ear, Nose and Throat Soc. Anglican. Home: 10 Deer Park Crescent, Toronto, ON Canada M4V 2C2 Office: 7-229 EN 200 Elizabeth St, Toronto, ON Canada M5G 2C4

ALBERTINI, STEPHEN ANTHONY, public relations and advertising executive. BS in Journalism, Temple U., 1972. Assoc. editor South Phila. Rev., Phila., 1971-72; editor Indsl. Distributor News, Phila., 1973-78; sr. counselor Lewis, Gilman & Kynett, 1978-83; account group mgr./PR S&A; v.p. Spiro & Assocs., 1985-87, EPB, 1987-89; v.p., gen. mgr. Earle Palmer Brown & Spiro, 1988-89; sr. v.p., gen. mgr. Earle Palmer Brown, Phila., 1989-94, exec. v.p., ptnr., 1994-98; sr. v.p., dir. pub. rels. Lev Lane Advt. and Pub. Rels., Bala Cynwyd, Pa., 1998—. Office: Lev Lane Advt and Pub Rels 1 Belmont Ave Bala Cynwyd PA 19004-1617

ALBERTINI, WILLIAM OLIVER, telecommunications industry executive; b. Mt. Carmel, Pa., June 29, 1943; s. William F. and Phyllis (Newman) A.; m. Katherine M. Keliher, Aug. 27, 1966; children: Elizabeth M., William O. Jr. BS, U. Notre Dame, 1965; MBA, Lehigh U., 1967; MS, MIT, 1982. With Bell of Pa., Harrisburg, 1967-83; dist. sales mgr. Bell of Pa., Allentown, 1973-74, dist. plant mgr., 1974-77; div. mgr. customer services Bell of Pa., Harrisburg, 1979-81; gen. pub. relations supr. community relations Bell of Pa., Phila., 1982-83; acctg. mgr. AT&T Co., Basking Ridge, N.J., 1977-79; dir. investor relations Bell Atlantic Corp., Phila., 1983-85; asst. v.p. bus. planning and fin. mgmt. network services div. Bell Atlantic Corp., Arlington, Va., 1985; v.p., sec., treas. Bell Atlantic Corp., Phila., 1985—; exec. v.p., CFO Bell Atlantic Global Wireless, Phila., 1989-99. Bd. dirs. United Cerebal Palsy Campaign, Harrisburg, 1979-81, pres., 1980-81. Served as staff sgt. USAF, 1967-68. Fellow Soc. Sloan Fellows (bd. govs. 1982-86); mem. Stockholder Relations Soc. N.Y. (adv. bd. 1985—), Fin. Execs. inst. (adv. bd. 1985—, com. investment employee benefit assets). Republican. Roman Catholic. Clubs: Eagles Mere (Pa.) Country (bd. dirs. 1976—, pres. 1986—); Merion Golf (Ardmore, Pa.). Avocations: golfing, tennis, platform tennis. Office: Bell Atlantic Corp 1717 Arch St Philadelphia PA 19103-2713*

ALBERTO, PAMELA LOUISE, oral and maxillofacial surgeon, educator; b. Somerville, Mass., Apr. 13, 1954; d. Louis Leon and Pamela Marie (Spera) A.; m. Gregory John Wroclawski, Aug. 4, 1979; children: Daniel Alberto, Catherine Marie. BS, Rensselaer Poly. Inst., 1976; DMD, U. Pa., 1980. Cert. oral and maxillofacial surgeon; diplomate Am. Bd. Forensic Dentistry. Clin. asst. prof. dept. oral/maxillofacial surgery N.J. Dental Sch., Newark, 1983-89, clin. assoc. prof. dept. oral/maxillofacial surgery, 1989—, dir. predoctoral edn. dept. oral/maxillofacial surgery, 1989—; pvt. practice Sparta, N.J., 1984—; dir. CPR N.J. Dental Sch., Newark, 1985-90; dir. Dental Implant Ctr. Wallkill Valley Hosp., Sussex, N.J., 1988—. Recipient Outstanding Clin. Dentistry award Acad. Gen. Dentistry, 1980. Fellow Am. Assn. Oral and Maxillofacial Surgery, Am. Coll. Oral/Maxillofacial Surgery; mem. ADA, AAUP, Am. Assn. Dental Anesthesiology, Internat. Congress Oral Implantology, Psi Omega. Avocations: tennis, skiing, photography, scuba diving, jewelry making. Home: 549 Cherry Tree Ln Kinnelon NJ 07405-2229 Office: 171 Woodport Rd Sparta NJ 07871-2637

ALBERTS, ALAN RICHARD, rheumatologist; b. N.Y.C., July 29, 1960; s. Phillip and Elaine (Pollock) A.; m. Nancy Maxine Rozenberg, Nov. 19, 1988; children: Melissa Beth, Jonathan Scott. BA, Boston U., 1982; MD, Sackler Sch. of Medicine, Tel Aviv, 1988. Diplomate Am. Bd. Internal Medicine, Am. Bd. Internal Medicine and Rheumatology. Intern, resident, fellow North Shore U. Hosp., Manhasset, N.Y., 1988-94; dir. rheumatology Jamaica (N.Y.) Hosp., 1994—. Fellow Am. Coll. Rheumatology; mem. ACP. Jewish. Avocations: collecting fountain pens and watches. Home: 59 Concord Ave Oceanside NY 11572-5415 Office: Jamaica Hosp 8900 Van Wyck Expy Jamaica NY 11418-2832

ALBERTS, BRUCE MICHAEL, federal agency administrator, foundation administrator, biochemist; b. Chicago, Ill., Apr. 14, 1938; s. Harry C. and Lillian (Surasky) A.; m. Betty Neary, June 14, 1960; children: Beth L., Jonathan B., Michael B. AB in Biochemical Scis. summa cum laude, Harvard Coll., 1960; PhD in Biophysics, Harvard U., 1965. Postdoctoral fellow NSF Institut de Biologie Moleculaire, Geneva, 1965-66; asst. prof. dept. chemistry Princeton (N.J.) U., 1966-73, assoc. prof. dept. biochemical scis., 1971-73, Damon Pfeiffer prof. life scis., 1973-76; prof., vice chmn. dept. biochemistry and biophysics U. Calif., San Francisco, 1976-81, Am. Cancer Soc. Rsch. prof., 1981-85, prof., chmn., 1985-90, Am. Cancer Soc. Rsch. prof. of biochemistry, 1990-93; pres. NAS, Washington, 1993—; chrm. NRC, Washington, 1993—; trustee Cold Spring Harbor Lab., 1972-75; adv. panel human cell biology NSF, 1974-76; adv. coun. dept. biochemical scis. and molecular biology Princeton U., 1979-85; chmn. vis. com. dept. biochemistry and molecular biology Harvard Coll., 1983-86; chmn. mapping and sequencing the human genome Nat. Rsch. Coun. Com., 1986-88; bd. sci. couns. divsn. arthritis and metabolic diseases NIH, 1974-78, molecular cytology study sect. 1982-86, chmn. 1984-86; program adv. com. NIH Human Genome Project, 1988-91; sci. adv. bd. Jane Coffin Childs Meml. Fund for Med. Rsch., 1978-85, Markey Found., 1984—, Fred Hutchinson Cancer Rsch. Ctr., Seattle, 1988—; com. mem. corp. vis. dept. biology MIT, 1978—, dept. embryology Carnegie Inst., Washington, 1983—; faculty rsch. lectr. U. Calif., San Francisco, 1985; sci. adv. com. Marine Biological Lab., Woods Hole, Mass., 1988—; bd. dirs. Genentech Rsch. Found., Fed. Am. Socs. for Experimental Biology; adv. bd. Bethesda Rsch. Labs. Life Tech. Inc., Nat. Sci. Resources Ctr., Smithsonian Inst., 1990—; com. mem. adolescence and young adulthood/sci. standards, Nat. Bd. Profl. Teaching Standards, 1991—. Co-author: The Molecular Biology of the Cell, 1989; editor: Mechanistic Studies of DNA Replication and Genetic Recombination, 1980; editorial bd. Jour. Biological Chemistry, 1976-82, Jour. Cell Biology, 1984-87; assoc. editor Annual Reviews Cell Biology, 1984—; essay editor Molecular Biology of th Cell, 1991—; contbr. numerous articles to profl. jours. including Saunders Sci. Publ., Current Sci., Ltd. Fellow NSF, 1960-65; recipient Eli Lilly award in biological chemistry Am. Chemical Soc., 1972, Baxter award for Disting. Rsch. in Biomedical Scis. Assn. Am. Med. Colls., 1992; named Lifetime Rsch. Prof. Am. Cancer Soc., 1980, Outstanding Vol. Coord. Calif. Sch. Vol. Partnership, 1993. Gairdner Foundation InternationalAward, 1995. Fellow AAAS; mem. NAS (commn. life scis. Nat. Rsch. Coun. 1988—, chmn. 1988-93, adv. bd. Nat. Sci. Resources Ctr. 1990—, Nat. Com. Sci. Edn. Standards and Assessment 1992—, com. mem. Nat. Edn. Support System for Tchrs. and Schs. 1992—, U.S. Steel Found. award 1975), Am. Chemical Soc., Am. Soc. for Cell Biology, Am. Soc. for Microbiology, Genetics Soc. Am., Am. Soc. Biochemistry and Molecular Biology (councilor 1984—), Am. Philos. Soc., European Molecular Biology Orgn. (assoc.), Phi Beta Kappa. Office: National Academy of Sciences Office of the President 2101 Constitution Ave NW Washington DC 20418-0007*

ALBERTS, DAVID, artistic director, mime; b. Akron, Ohio, Nov. 14, 1946; married (div. 1972); 1 child, Morgan Elizabeth; married (div. 1992); children: Sarah Aimee, Samantha Kaitlin Wynne. BA in Music, Kent State U., 1972; MA in Theatre, West Va. U., 1978; PhD in Theatre, Bowling Green State U., 1989. Instr. Akron (Ohio) U., 1970-71, W.Va. U., 1978, Va. Commonwealth U., Richmond, 1979-81, Calif. State U., Turlock, Calif., 1981-83, Kent (Ohio) State U., 1986-87, Bowling Green (Ohio) State U., 1987-89; artistic dir. Theatre of the One Actor, San Diego, 1995—; mime artist in field. Author: Pantomime: Exercises and Elements, 1971, Talking About Mime, 1994 (San Diego Book award 1994), Rehearsal Management for Directors, 1995, The Expressive Body: Physical Characterization for the Actor, 1997, (play) Death by Arrangement, 1981; contbr. articles to profl. jours. Recipient Founders award Internat. Thespian Soc., 1972, Directing award Am. Coll. Theatre Festival, 1982. Mem. Internat. Mimes and Pantomimes, Assn. for Theatre in Higher Edn., Speech Comms. Assn.

ALBERTS, DAVID SAMUEL, physician, pharmacologist, educator; b. Milw., Dec. 30, 1939; m. Heather Alberts; children: Tim, Sabrina. BS, Trinity Coll., Hartford, Conn., 1962; MD, U. Va., 1966. Dir. clin. pharmacology Ariz. Cancer Ctr., Tucson, 1975—, prof. medicine and pharmacology, 1982—, dir. cancer prevention and control, 1988—, dep. dir., 1989-96, assoc. dean rsch. Coll. Medicine, 1996—, acting chief hematology and oncology, 1998-99; external advisor U. Chgo. Cancer Ctr., 1993-98, Tulane U. Cancer Ctr., New Orleans, 1993-96, M.D. Anderson Cancer Ctr., Houston, 1994—, Norris Cotton Cancer Ctr., Hanover, 1995—; mem. bd. sci. counselors divsn. Cancer Prevention and Control, Nat. Cancer Inst., NIH, 1990-94, chmn. chemoprevention external com. divsn. cancer prevention, 1997—; chmn. gynecologic cancer com. S.W. Oncology Group, 1977—; mem. monitoring and adv. panel Nat. Prostate Lung-Colon-Ovary Cancer Study, NCI-NIH, 1994—; chmn. cancer prevention com. Gynecologic Oncology Group, 1995—; chmn. oncologic adv. com. U.S. FDA, 1982-84, spl. cons., 1984-86. Sr. editor Cancer, Epidemiology, Biomarkers and Prevention, 1997—; assoc. editor Cancer Rsch., 1989—, Cancer Chemother. and Pharmacol., 1992—, Clin. Cancer Rsch., 1994-96, Neoplasia, 1998—; contbr. articles to profl. jours.; inventor azamitosene and anthracene anticancer agts., tumorimeter, hypodermic needle with automatic retracting point; tropical DFMO two step carcinogen/HIV chemical deactivation system; method and composition for deactivating HIV infected blood and anticancer drugs. Grantee NIH, 1975—, Nat. Cancer Inst.-NIH, 1987—. Mem. Am. Soc. for Clin. Pharmacology and Therapeutics, Am. Soc. Clin. Oncology, Am. Soc. Preventive Oncology, Am. Assn. for Cancer Rsch., Soc. Gynecologic Oncologists. Office: Ariz Cancer Ctr 1501 N Campbell Ave Tucson AZ 85724-0001

ALBERTS, HAROLD, lawyer; b. San Antonio, Tex., Apr. 3, 1920; s. Bernard H. and Rose Alberts; m. Rose M. Gaskin, Mar. 25, 1945; children—Linda Rae, Barry Lawrence. LL.B., U. Tex.-Austin, 1942. Bar: Tex. 1943, U.S. Supreme Ct. 1950, U.S. Ct. Mil. Apls. 1959. Tchr., U. Tex. 1942; instr., U. Tex., Austin, 1941-42; legal officer Chase Field, 1944; sole practice, Corpus Christi, Tex. Pres. Jewish Welfare Fund, Corpus Christi, 1948; chmn. Southwest Regional Anti-Defamation League, Tex. and Okla., 1970-71, chmn., 1969-72, chmn. Brotherhood Week, 1957; chmn. Nueces County (Tex.) Red Cross, 1959-61; mem. campaign exec. com., chmn. meetings United Community Services, 1961; v.p. Little Theatre, Corpus Christi, 1964; chmn. Corpus Christi NCCJ, 1967-69, nat. dir., 1974-76; bd. dirs. Tex. State Assn. Mental Health; pres. Combined Jewish Apl., Corpus Christi, 1974-76; moderator Friday Morning Group, 1975, 96. Served to lt. (sr. grade) USNR, 1942-46. Mem. ABA, Tex. Bar Assn., Corpus Christi Bar Assn. Clubs: Kiwanis (pres. 1962), B'nai B'rith (pres. 1955), Mason (32d degree). Home: 5314 Hulen Dr Corpus Christi TX 78413-2247 Office: PO Box 271477 Corpus Christi TX 78427-1477

ALBERTS, HENRY CELLER, real estate company executive; b. N.Y.C., Aug. 23, 1927; s. Alfred Edward and Helen (Masch) A.; m. Renée Mira Miller, Jan. 13, 1950; children: Jo Lee Lord, Nina Sue Charnley, Hope Anne Megonigal, Jody Beth Naleppa. BS in Physics/Math., Queens Coll., N.Y.C., 1949; MS in Physics/Math., U. Del., Newark, 1956; PhD in Sys. Sci., City U., London, 1995. Cert. mem. Def. Acquisition Corps (Level III), Level III Sys. Planning, rsch., Devel., Engring. and Test. Physicist USAF/U.S. Army, 1949-56; head ops. rsch. Avco Corp., Wilmington, Mass., 1956-60; dir. mktg./rsch. Nat. Co., Inc., Malden, Mass., 1960-62; sr. sci. staff Stanford Rsch. Inst., Menlo Park, Calif., 1962-69; pres., CEO Vertex Corp., McLean, Va., 1969-76; prin. scientist Gen. Rsch. Corp., McLean, 1975-80; dir. instrument dept. Arcata Assocs., Monterey, Calif., 1980-81; mem. tech. staff MRJ Inc., Fairfax, Va., 1981-83; prof. engring. mgmt. U.S. Govt./Dept. of Def./Def. Sys. Mgmt. Coll., Ft. Belvoir, Va., 1983-98; pres. Alco Realty Corp., McLean, Va.; adj. prof. U. Md. Grad. Sch., 1998—, mem. com. on def. mfg. in yrs. 2010 and beyond NRC, 1997-98; lectr. in field; spl. lectr. on indsl. issues and analysis methodologies CIA, 1984—; mem. U.S. del. to NATO, 1996; mem. adv. bd. Inst. for Strategic tech. and Innovative Leadership, Coll. Engring., U. Tex., 1996; sr. fellow Inst. for Pub. Policy, George Mason U. Electronic Commerce rsch. Ctr., 1994—; cons. in field. Contbr. articles to profl. jours. Mem. oversight bd. Fairfax County Govt., 1988-89. Recipient George Mason medal Commonwealth of Va./George Mason U., 1995, Dept. Defense Superior Civilian Svc. award, 1998. Mem. Internat. Coun. on Sys. Engring. (charter, bd. dirs. Wash. chpt., mem. tech. com. redefining sys. engring.), Internat. Test and Evaluation Assn. (charter, mem. nat. edn. com., chpt. pres. 1988-91, other coms.), Ops. rsch. Soc. Am. (chmn. def. acquisition processes session 1992, chmn. advanced mgmt. and math. session 1992), Inst. Mgmt. Sci., Soc. Logistics Engrs., Internat. Sys. Sci. Soc. Avocations: music, art, jewelry making and design. Office: 5842 Hilldon St Mc Lean VA 22101-3324

ALBERTS, MARION EDWARD, physician; b. Hastings, Nebr., Mar. 14, 1923; s. Eddie and Mary Margaret (Hilbers) A.; m. Jeannette McDaniel, Dec. 25, 1944; children: Kathryn (dec.), Brian, Deborah, Timothy. BA, U. Nebr., 1944, MD, 1948. Lic. Am. Bd. Pediatrics. Intern Iowa Methodist Hosp., Des Moines, 1948-49; resident in pediatrics Raymond Blank Hosp. Children, Des Moines, 1949-50, 52-53; practice medicine specializing in pediatrics Des Moines, 1953-88; chief pediatrics Mercy Hosp., 1953-69, 74-78, chief med. staff, 1966; mem. med. staff Iowa Luth. Hosp., 1953-88, Iowa Meth. Hosp., 1953-88, Broadlawns Polk County Hosp., 1983-88; instr. clin. pediatrics Coll. Osteo. Medicine and Surgery, 1970-82. Sci. editor Iowa Medicine, 1971-97. Contbr. articles to profl. jours. Pres. Polk County Tb and Respiratory Diseases Assn., 1965, 66, 70. Comdr. USNR, 1943-45, 50-52 (ret.) 1983. Recipient Whitaker Interstate Teaching award Interstate Postgrad. Med. Assn., 1980; Service award Sisters of Mercy, 1978. Fellow Am. Acad. Pediatrics, AMA (recognition awards 1969—), Iowa Med. Soc.; mem. Masons, Kiwanis. Presbyterian (elder). Home: 5991 Pommel Cir West Des Moines IA 50266-6324

ALBERTS, ROBERT W., federal judge; b. 1938. AB, Brown U., 1960; LLB, NYU, 1963. With Sulmeyer & Kupetz, Sulmeyer, Kupetz & Alberts, 1965-73; pvt. practice, 1978; with Alberts & Miner, 1983, Rutan & Tucker, 1992; apptd. bankruptcy judge cen. dist. U.S. Dist. Ct. Calif., 1992. Office: 3420 12th St Riverside CA 92501-3801

ALBERTSON, CHRISTIERN GUNNAR (CHRIS ALBERTSON), broadcaster, music critic, writer; b. Reykjavik, Iceland, Oct. 18, 1931; came to U.S., 1957, naturalized, 1963; s. Thordur and Yvonne (Broberg) A.; m. Hanne Elisabeth Christensen, 1954 (div. 1958). Student, Kent Coll., Canterbury, England, 1947-49; grad., Acad. Merc. Art, Copenhagen, 1952. Gen. mgr. Storyville Club, Copejhagen, 1952-54; producer, writer U.S. Armed Forces Radio and TV, Iceland, 1954-57, WCAU Radio, Phila., 1957-58; disc jockey WHAT-RM Radio, Phila., 1958-60; producer Riverside Records, N.Y.C., 1960-62; continuity dir. WNEW Radio, N.Y.C., 1963-64; gen. mgr. WBAI-FM Radio, N.Y.C., 1964-66; dir. BBC programs HArtwest Prodns., N.Y.C., 1966-67; co-producer, host weekly TV series The Jazz Set , PBS Network, 1972-73; pres. Video One, Inc., 1976-79; producer, co-host weekly cable TV series Doin' It, 1976-77; entertainment editor Beauty Trade Mag., 1978-79; producer Bessie Smith blues series Columbia Records, 1970; U.S. jazz reporter Danish Radio, 1972-75; U.S. music corr. Berlingske Tidende, Copenhagen, 1960-64; talent cons. Dupont Show of Week, 1961. Author: Bessie-The Life of Bessie Smith, 1972, Empress of the Blues, 1974; contbg. author: Bluesland, 1992; co-editor: Oxford Biographical Encyclopedia of Jazz, 1998; writer story and script The Alberta Hunter Story, TV mini-series, 1980, (film) Really The Blues, 997, (TV documentary) My Castle's Rockin', 1988, The Story of Jazz, 1994; contbg. editor Stereo Review, 1973-99, A Plus Mag., 1983-96, Sound & Vision, 1999—; editl. cons. Routes Mag., 1978-80, 91-95; contbr. articles to Down Beat, Saturday Rev., Rolling Stone, N.Y. Times, Jazz Forum, Sound & Image, MacWeek, N.Y. Amsterdam News, Timeline, others; assoc. producer, cons. (film) Bessie, 1974; music cons. (film) Buddy Can You Spare A Dime, 1974. Mem. adv. bd. N.Y. Jazz Mus., 1972-75. Recipient Grand Prix du Disque, Montreal Jazz Festival, 1971, Trendsetter of Yr. award Billboard, 1971, CEBA award for distinction, 1964, Critics Poll Best Liner Notes award Living Blues MAg., 1993. Mem. Nat. Acad. Rec. Arts & Scis. (Grammy award 1971, Trustees award 1971, Grammy nominations 1977, 97). E-mail: fugl@earthlink.net. Address: 444 Central Park W New York NY 10025-4378

ALBERTSON, CHRISTOPHER ADAM, librarian; b. Oak Park, Ill., Dec. 10, 1951; s. Charles J. and Eve M. (Kosawick) A.; m. Sarah Ann Daugherty, Dec. 29, 1973; children: Julia, Stephanie, Matthew. Student, U. New Orleans, 1969-70; BA magna cum laude, U. Tex.-Arlington, 1972; MLS, N. Tex. State U., 1973. Cataloger, Orange (Tex.) Pub. Libr., 1974-75, asst. libr., 1975-79, city libr., 1979-81; city libr. Tyler (Tex.) Pub. Libr., 1981—. Mem. Am. Library Assn., Am. Soc. Pub. Adminstrn., Am. Mgmt. Assn., Am. Soc. Info. Sci., Tex. Libr. Assn. Presbyterian. Club: Rotary. Contbr. articles to profl. jours. Home: 3100 Pounds Ave Tyler TX 75701-8034 Office: Tyler Pub Library 201 S College Ave Tyler TX 75702-7381

ALBERTSON, GARY DAVID, marketing executive, consultant; b. Paterson, N.J., July 4, 1962; s. Benjamin Albertson and Helene Krehm; m. Judy Sue Kagan, aug. 22, 1993; 1 child, Helene Binyamina. BA, Rutgers U., Newark, 1985; MBA, N.H. Coll., 1991. Mgmt. trainee ITT Consumer Fin., Inc., Mpls., 1986-87; account mgr. Healthcare Svcs. Group, Inc., Huntington Valley, Pa., 1987-89; advt. mgr. Callsoft, Inc., Somerset, N.J., 1992-94; account specialist Bell Atlantic Mobile, Orangeburg, N.Y., 1994-96; account exec. Douglas Samuel Advt., Montville, N.J., 1996-97; mktg. mgr. Prochem/BioCoordination Scis., N.Y.C., 1997—; cons. Waksman Biotech. Inst., Piscataway, N.J., 1992-93, Timbrel Med. Devel., Inc., Glen Rock, N.J., 1997—, Johnson, Smith, Knisely, Inc., N.Y.C., 1993, Internat. Discount Telecom., Hackensack, N.J., 1996. Capt. Roseland (N.J.) Emergency Med. Svc., 1984, pres., 1986, trustee, advisor, 1987, treas., 1987. Recipient Capt.'s Achievement award Roseland Emergency Med. Svc., 1984, Honorable Svc. award, 1984, 85, Pres.'s Achievement award, 1986, Goldstar sales award Nynex Mobile Comms., Inc., 1994. Mem. Am. Mktg. Assn., Am. Mgmt. Assn., Assn. MBA Execs., Soc. for Advancement of Mgmt. Avocations: computers, bicycling, automobiles, high technology, sports. Home: 3130 Grand Concourse Apt 5E Bronx NY 10458-1225 Office: Prochem/BioCoordination Scis Inc 425 Park Ave Fl 27 New York NY 10022-3506

ALBERTSON, SUSAN L., retired federal government official; b. Washington, Dec. 3, 1929; d. J. Mark and Alice (Myers) A. BS, Purdue U., 1952; postgrad., George Washington U., 1956-58. Numerous profl. positions CIA, Washington, 1952-88; ret., 1988. Republican. Avocations: piano, cooking, swimming.

ALBERTSON, TERRY L., lawyer; b. Montebello, Calif., Nov. 15, 1946; s. Vern G. and June L. (Wodei) A.; m. Kathleen A. Blackburn, June 3, 1968; children: Sarah, Andrew. AB, Georgetown U., 1968; AM, Yale U., 1969; JD, Harvard U., 1974. Ptnr. Crowell & Moring, Washington, 1974—. Contbr. articles to profl. jours. Sgt. U.S. Army, 1969-71, Vietnam. Office: Crowell & Moring 1001 Pennsylvania Ave NW Fl 10 Washington DC 20004-2595

ALBERTY, ROBERT ARNOLD, chemistry educator; b. Winfield, Kans., June 21, 1921; s. Luman Harvey and Mattie (Arnold) A.; m. Lillian Jane Wind, May 22, 1944; children—Nancy Lou, Steven Charles, Catherine Ann. B.S., U. Nebr., 1943, M.S., 1944, D.Sc., 1967; Ph.D., U. Wis., 1947; D.Sc., Lawrence U., 1967. Engaged in research blood plasma fractionation for U.S. Govt., 1944-46; mem. faculty U. Wis., 1947-67, prof. chemistry, 1955-67, assoc. dean letters and sci., 1961-63; dean U. Wis. (Grad. Sch.), 1963-67; prof. chemistry MIT, 1967-91, 96—, prof. emeritus, 1991—, dean Sch. Sci., 1967-82; cons. NSF, 1958-83, NIH, 1962-72; chmn. commn. on human resources NRC, 1974-77; dir. Colt Industries, 1978-88, Inst. for Def. Analysis, 1980-86; pres. phys. chemistry div. Internat. Union Pure and Applied Chemistry, 1991-93. Co-author: Physical Chemistry, 1997, Experimental Physical Chemistry, 3d edit., 1970. Guggenheim fellow Calif. Inst. Tech., 1950-51; recipient Eli Lilly award biol. chemistry, 1955. Fellow AAAS; mem. NAS, Inst. Medicine, Am. Chem. Soc. (chmn. com. on chemistry and pub. affairs 1978-80), Am. Acad. Arts and Scis. (coun. 1991-94), Phi Beta Kappa, Sigma Xi. Home: 931 Massachusetts Ave Cambridge MA 02139 Office: MIT 77 Massachusetts Ave Rm 6-215 Cambridge MA 02139-4307*

ALBICKER, ROBERT, federal official; m. Susan, children: Katie, Kristen. BA, SUNY, 1973; postgrad., 1999—. Tax auditor IRS, Newark, 1974-96; deputy chief info. officer Dept. of Treasury, Washington, 1996—. Office: Dept of Treasury 1111 Constitution Ave NW Washington DC 20224-0001

ALBIN, LESLIE OWENS, biology educator; b. Spur, Tex., Jan. 8, 1940; s. John Leslie and Ottie Maude (Lassetter) A.; m. Monta Kay Gragg, Sept. 3, 1961 (div. 1982); children: Leslie Susan Albin Gann, Kimberly Ann Albin. BA, McMurry Coll., Abilene, 1962; MA, N. Tex. State U., 1969. Instr. biology E. Cen. State U., Ada, Okla., 1969-71; rsch. assoc. M.D. Andrson Hosp. & Tumor Inst., Houston, 1971; asst. prof. biology Western Tex. Coll., Snyder, 1971-74, assoc. prof. biology, 1974-77; prof. Austin (Tex.) C.C., 1977—, chmn. divsn. natural scis., 1978-95, head dept. biology, 1977-97. NDEA fellow, 1968. Mem. Am. Inst. Biol. Scis., Faculty Assn. Western Tex. Coll. (pres. 1973-74), Faculty Assn. Austin C.C. (pres. 1987-88), Faculty Senate Austin C.C., Tex. C.C. Tchrs. Assn., Tex. Acad. Sci., Am. Soc. for Microbiology, Alpha Chi. Office: Austin Community Coll Cypress Creek Campus 1555 Cypress Creek Rd Cedar Park TX 78613-4490

ALBINAK, MARVIN JOSEPH, chemistry educator; b. Detroit, June 21, 1928; s. Alfred S. and Katherine (Smulson) A.; m. Gloria Ann Galamb, Aug. 26, 1961; children: Stephen, Anne, Alexandra. AB, U. Detroit, 1949, MS, 1952; PhD, Wayne State U., 1959. Rsch. chemist Ethyl Corp., Detroit, 1952-54; instr. to asst. prof. U. Detroit, 1954-58, 59-61; rsch. fellow Wayne State U., Detroit, 1958-59; sr. rsch. scientist Elec. Autolite Corp., Toledo, Ohio, 1961-62; rsch. chemist Owens-Ill., Inc., Toledo, 1962-65; asst. to assoc. prof. Wheeling (W.Va.) Coll., 1965-68; assoc. prof. to prof. chemistry and adminstr. Essex Community Coll., Balt., 1968-96, prof. emeritus, 1997. 7 U.S. patents; contbr. articles to profl. jours. Mem. Am. Chem. Soc., Sigma Xi, Phi Lambda Upsilon. Democrat. Avocations: music, theatre, books, environmental activities. Home: 819 Providence Rd Baltimore MD 21286-2964

ALBINO, GEORGE ROBERT, business executive; b. Boston, 1929; m. Julianne E. Albino; children: William, Robert, George. A.B., Columbia U., 1950; M.B.A., Harvard U., 1954. Ret. chmn., CEO Rio Algom Ltd., Toronto, Ont., Can.; also bd. dirs. Served to capt. USMC, 1950-52. Mem. Toronto Club, York Club, Sara Bay Country CLub.

ALBINO, JUDITH ELAINE NEWSOM, university president; b. Jackson, Tenn.; m. Salvatore Albino; children: Austin, Adrian. BJ, U. Tex., 1967, PhD, 1973. Mem. faculty sch. dental medicine SUNY, Buffalo, 1972-90, assoc. provost, 1984-87, dean sch. arch. and planning, 1987-89, dean grad.

sch., 1989-90; v.p. acad. affairs and rsch, dean system grad. sch. U. Colo., Boulder, 1990-91, pres., 1991-95, pres. emerita, prof. psychiatry, 1995-97; pres. Calif. Sch. Profl. Psychology, San Francisco, 1997—. Contbr. articles to profl. jours. Acad. Adminstrn. fellow Am. Coun. on Edn., 1983; grantee NIH. Fellow APA (treas., bd. dirs.); mem. Behavioral Scientists in Dental Rsch. (past pres.), Am. Assn. Dental Rsch. (bd. dirs.). Office: Calif Sch Profl Psychology Office of the Pres 2728 Hyde St San Francisco CA 94109-1223

ALBINSKI, HENRY STEPHEN, academic research center director, writer; b. Chgo., Dec. 31, 1931; m. Nan Bowman Albinski, Feb. 11, 1984. BA with highest honors, UCLA, 1953, MA, 1955; PhD, U. Minn., 1959. Vis. fellow Australian Nat. U., Canberra, 1963-64; cons. Rsch. Analysis Corp., McLean, Va., 1968-70; vis. prof. U. Queensland, Brisbane, Australia, 1970; cons. Ctr. Strategic and Internat. Studies, Washington, 1972-73; vis. prof. Flinders U., Adelaide, Australia, 1974, U. Sydney, Australia, 1974-75; cons. U.S. Dept. State, Washington, 1977, 93-94; vis. fellow Australian Nat. U., 1978-79, 95; cons. U.S. Fgn. Svc. Inst., Alexandria, Va., 1980; advisor Asian agenda program The Asia Found., N.Y.C., 1982; cons. ESSO Corp., Houston, 1983-84, U.S. Dept. Def., Washington, 1984-85; vis. prof. U. Melbourne, Australia, 1985-86, Australian Def. Force Acad., Canberra, 1988-89; advisor U. Hawaii, Honolulu, 1989-91; cons. Inst. Fgn. Policy Analysis, Washington, 1991-92; prof. polit. sci. and Australian and New Zealand studies and dir. Australia-New Zealand Studies Ctr. Pa. State U., University Park, 1982-98, prof. emeritus, 1998—; Haydn Williams and Curtin Internat. Inst. fellow Curtin U., Perth, 1995-96; vis. prof. U. Western. Ont., London, Can., 1969, Australian Def. Force Acad., 1992, U. Sydney, 1999—; cons. Inst. Def. Analyses, Washington, 1969, Frost & Sullivan, Syracuse, N.Y., 1983-89, Pacific Forum, Honolulu, 1984-85; rsch. counselor, 1986-91; cons. Ellen Raider Internat., N.Y.C., Deakin U. Geelong, Victoria, Australia, 1992-94; advisor Nat. Coun. Fgn. Lang. and Internat. Studies, N.Y.C., 1980, East-West Ctr., Honolulu, 1987-93, Australia-Am. Study Com. on Comprehensive Security, Honolulu, 1989-91, Inst. Internat. Edn., N.Y.C., 1991-92, Coun. Internat. Coop., E. Lansing, Mich., 1992-94; vis. fellow Australian Nat. U., 1995; cons. Interlink Internat., 1998; vis. prof., fellow Rsch. Inst. for Asia and the Pacific. Author: Australian Policies and Attitudes Toward China, 1965, Politics and Foreign Policy in Australia: The Impact of Vietnam and Conscription, 1969, Canadian and Australian Politics in Comparative Prespective, 1973, Australian External Policy Under Labor: Content, Process and the National Debate, 1977, The Australian-American Security Relationship: A Regional and Transregional Perspective, 1982; (monographs) The Australian Labor Party and Aid to Parochial Schools Controversy, 1966, Australia in Southeast Asia: Interest, Capacity and Acceptability, 1970, ANZUS, The United States and Pacific Security, 1987, The Australian-American Alliance: Prospects for the 1990s, 1990; Australia's Evolving American Relationship: Interests, Processes and Prospects for Australian Influence, 1995; author and co-editor: European Political Processes: Essays and Readings, 1968, 74; author and editor: Asian Political Processes Essays and Readings, 1971, Australia and the United States: Strategic and Defence Cooperation Futures, 1993; contbr. 100 book chpts. and articles to profl. jours. Advisor Am.-Australian Bicentennial Found., Washington, 1984-88; cons. Australian Nat. Maritime Mus., Sydney NSW, 1988. Travel fellow Rockefeller Found., 1963-64, New Zealand-U.S. Edn. Found., 1979; fellow Hoover Instn., 1984; sr. scholar Fulbright-Hays, 1974-75, 78-79, Fulbright Travel fellow, New Zealand, 1979. Mem. Australian Studies Assn. N. Am. (charter chair 1990-91, exec. bd. overseas mem. 1986-92), Australian Polit. Studies Assn., Australian and New Zealand Assn. Canadian Studies, Am. Assn. Univ. Profs. (past pres. Pa. State U. chpt.), Am. Polit. Sci. Assn., U.S. Naval Inst., Mid. Atlantic Conf. Can. Studies (pres. 1983-84), New Zealand Polit. Studies Assn., Brit. Australian Studies Assn., Can. Polit. Sci. Assn., Assn. Can. Studies in U.S., Internat. Studies Assn., Inter-Univ. Seminar Armed Forces and Soc., Can. Inst. Strategic Studies, Phi Beta Kappa, Pi Sigma Alpha, Pi Kappa Delta, Pi Sigma Mu, Alpha Mu Gamma, Phi Eta Sigma, Omicron Delta Kappa. Avocation: music. Fax: 61 2 9351 3624. E-mail: henrya@bullwinkle.econ.usyd.edu.au. Office: U Sydney, Dept Govt, Sydney NSW 2006, Australia

ALBOM, MICHAEL JONATHAN, surgeon, educator; b. Hartford, Conn., Oct. 2, 1944; s. Milton Jeramiah and Clare (Marcus) A.; m. Lia Shuster, Jan. 22, 1983; children: Blair Ruth, Mark Jeffrey. BA, U. Conn., 1966; MD, Boston U., 1970. Diplomate Am. Bd. Dermatology, Am. Bd. Med. Examiners, Am. Bd. Mohs Micrographic Surgery and Cutaneous Oncology. Med. intern Hartford Hosp., 1970-71; resident in dermatology Boston U., 1971-74; fellow in skin cancer surgery NYU, N.Y.C., 1974-75; asst. prof. dermatology NYU Med. Ctr., 1976-83, head skin and cancer unit surgery sect., 1979-85, clin. assoc. prof., 1983-93, clin. prof., 1993—; pvt. practice, N.Y.C.; attending surgeon dept. plastic surgery Manhattan Eye Ear and Throat Hosp., N.Y. Eye and Ear Infirmary, Lenox Hill Hosp.; co-dir. Interspecialty Facial Surgery Congress, N.Y.C., 1983, 85. Contbg. editor Jour. Dermatologic Surgery; contbr. articles to med. jours., chpts. to books. Fellow Am. Soc. Dermatologic Surgery (bd. dirs. 1980-83, 88-91), Am. Coll. Mohs Micrographic Surgery and Cutaneous Oncology (bd. dirs. 1987-90, sec.-treas. 1990-92, v.p. 1992-94, pres. 1994-96), Am. Acad. Dermatology (task force dermatol. surgery 1979—, dir. advanced surgery course 1979-86, dir. surg. forum 1986-91); mem. AMA, Internat. Soc. Dermatologic Surgery (charter). Office: 33 E 70th St New York NY 10021-4941

ALBOM, MITCH DAVID, sports columnist; b. Passaic, N.J., May 23, 1958; s. Ira and Rhoda Albom. BA in Sociology, Brandeis U., 1979; M in Journalism, Columbia U., 1981, M in Bus. Adminstrn., 1982. Editor Queens Tribune, Flushing, N.Y., 1981-82; contbrg. writer Sport Mag., Phila. Inquirer, Geo Mag., 1982-83; sports columnist Ft. Lauderdale News and Sun Sentinel, Fort Lauderdale, Fla., 1983-85, Detroit Free Press, 1985—; sports dir. Sta. WLLZ Radio, Detroit, 1985—; sports columnist Sta. WDIV-TV, Detroit, 1987—; host Sta. WLLZ radio talk show, 1988—. Author: (book) The Live Album, 1988; co-author Bo The Bo Schembecher Story, 1989. Chmn. Hospice Mich. Fundraising, 1987—; speaker, vol. Heart Assn. Mich., 1985—, Am. Cancer Soc. Mich. Pub. Broadcasting, 1985—. Named #1 Sports Columnist in U.S.A. AP Sports Editors, 1987, 88, 89, #1 Sports Columnist in Mich. AP and UPI, 1985, 86, 87, 88, #1 Sports News Story in U.S.A., 1985, #1 Sports Columnist in Mich. United Press Internat., 1986, 87, 88, #1 Sports Columnist in Mich. Nat. Assn. Sportswriters and Broadcasters, 1988, 89, #2 Outstanding Writer Nat. Headliners award, 1989. Mem. Baseball Writers Am., Football Writers Am., Tennis Writers Am. Avocation: former musician. Office: Detroit Free Press Inc 600 W 4th St Detroit MI 48226*

ALBRECHT, ALBERT PEARSON, electronics engineer, consultant; b. Bakersfield, Calif., Aug. 23, 1920; s. Albert Waldo and Elva (Shuck) A.; m. Muriel Elizabeth Grenell, June 15, 1942 (dec. Apr. 1943); m. Edith J. Dorner, July 18, 1944. BSEE, Calif. Inst. Tech., 1942; MSEE, U. So. Calif., L.A., 1947. Registered profl. engr., Calif. Rsch. assoc. radiation lab. MIT, Cambridge, 1942-43; chief engr. Gilfillan Bros., L.A., 1943-58; v.p. Space Gen. Corp., El Monte, Calif., 1958-68; exec. v.p. Telluran Cons., Santa Monica, Calif., 1968-72; dir. systems evaluation Office of Asst. Sec. of Def. for Intelligence, Washington, 1972-76; assoc. adminstr. FAA, Washington, 1976-86; cons., prin. AP Albrecht-Cons., Bellingham, Wash., 1986—; bd. dirs. Air Traffic Control Assn.; mem. exec. bd. RADIO Tech. Commn. for Aeronautics, Washington, 1980-86; mem. aeronautics adv. com. NASA, Washington, 1980-90. Co-author: Electronic Designers Handbook-Design Compendium, 1957, 2d edit., 1974; editor Air Traffic Control Quar. Fellow AIAA (adv. com. Aerospace Am. 1984—), IEEE (Engr. Mgr. of the Yr. 1989). Achievements include technical leadership of the replacement and automation of the nation's air traffic control system. Home and Office: 3224 Eagleridge Way Bellingham WA 98226-7821

ALBRECHT, BEVERLY JEAN, special education educator; b. Dixon, Ill., Sept. 8, 1936; d. Harold Ivan Foster and Grace Gertrude Tracy Freed; m. Marvin Blackert Albrecht, Aug. 13, 1960; children: Bradley K., Brent D., Kimberly S. Albrecht Schluns. BS, Manchester Coll., North Manchester, Ind., 1958; MS, No. Ill. U., 1978. Cert. in elem. edn., educable mentally handicapped, learning disabled, supervision and early childhood edn., Ill. Kindergarten tchr. Sch. Dist. 300, Carpentersville, Ill, 1958-60; thcr. 5th grade Sch. Dist. 5, Sterling, Ill., 1960-61, 64-65, kindergarten tchr., 1962-64, substitute tchr., 1965-71, 97—; dir. nursery sch. Sterling YWCA, 1971-75; program dir. Ctr. for Human Devel., Sterling, 1975-76; family advocate Ill. Dept. Child and Family Svcs., Rock Falls, 1977-78; learning disablities and behavior disorders spl. edn. tchr. Sch. Dist. 289, Mendota, Ill., 1978-84, devel. pre-sch. tchr., 1984-89; clinician, case mgr., family preservation Sinnissippi Ctrs. Inc., Sterling, 1989-97; replication specialist PEECH project U. Ill., Champaign, 1985-88; supervisory faculty Ill. State U., Normal, 1983-85, Ill. Valley C.C., Oglesby 1985-89. Host family Rock River Valley Internat. Fellowships, Sterling, 1975-98; chair coun. on edn. United Meth. Ch., Rock Falls, 1973-75, supt., tchr. ch. sch., 1968-88; Rock River Valley Hospice vol. United Ch. Women's Bd.; vol. Pub. Action to Deliver Shelter, 1997-99; vol. tutor for Ill. Cmty. Sch. Dist. # 5, 1997. Spl. Edn. fellow Ill. Office of Pub. Instrn., 1966; name grant honoree United Meth. Women, Rock Falls. Republican. Avocations: tennis, golf, travel. Home: 3254 Mineral Springs Rd Sterling IL 61081-4107

ALBRECHT, CAROL HEATH, artist, educator; b. Lafayette, Ind., May 26, 1921; d. Donald Leroy and Zula Elpha (Whicker) Heath; m. Edward Mathews Albrecht, May 25, 1944; children: Lynn, Catherine. Grad. high sch., Lafayette, Ind. Sec. U.S. Maritime Commn., San Francisco, 1941-44; mem. faculty art dept. Pensacola (Fla.) Jr. Coll., 1984-86, Eastern Shore Fine Arts Acad., Fairhope, Ala., 1986-91; presenter workshops in field, including oriental brush painting workshop/seminar, Sarasota, Fla., Clearwater, Fla., Pensacola. One-woman shows include Maison Le Cel, Ft. Walton Beach, Fla., 1976, 77, Whiting Gallery, Fairhope, 1989, Estate Gallery, Pensacola, 1991, Elliott Mus., Stuart, Fla., 1983; group shows include Fla. Watercolor Soc., Tallahassee, 1982, Pensacola Mus. Art, 1983-93, Sumi-e Soc. Am., Washington, 1982-94, Fla. Gulf Coast Art Ctr., Belleair, 1983, Asheville (N.C.) Mus. Art, 1983, Yosemite (Calif.) Renaissance Nat. Art Exhibit, 1987. Recipient purchase award Elliot Mus., 1983. Mem. Sumi-e Soc. Am. (2d v.p., pres. White Lotus chpt., Best in Show award 1990, Grumbacher gold medal 1991, Winsor-Newton award 1992, Sarasota chpt. award 1993, Shaffer award for brush mastery 1994, Reba Dickerson Hill Meml. award 1994, Am. Frome award 1998). Home and Studio: 510 Smithridge Park Reno NV 89502

ALBRECHT, DONNA G., author; b. Bridgeton, N.J., Feb. 26, 1949; d. Walter S. and Helen Louise (McCabe) Garrison; m. Michael C. Albrecht, Aug. 16, 1970; children: Katherine (dec.), Abigail. BA, Antioch U., San Francisco, 1983. Tchr. U. Calif. Ext.; lectr. in field; cons. in field. Author: Deals and Discounts: If You're 50 or Older, 1990, Buying a Home When You're Single, 1994, Raising A Child Who Has A Physical Disability, 1995, Overcoming the Four Deceptions: In Career Relationships (with Dwaine L. Canova), 1995, Promoting Your Business with Free (or Almost Free) Publicity, 1997, I Love to Tell the Story, 1999; contbr. over 400 articles to mags., including Entrepreneur Mag. (columnist), Ms., Modern Maturity, Real Estate Today, Calif. Bus., San Francisco Bus. Times, San Francisco Examiner, Contra Costa Times, Writer's Digest, Sharing Ideas, Exceptional Parent, Accent on Living, others. Pres. exec. com. No. Calif. chpt. Muscular Dystrophy Assn., 1992. Mem. Am. Soc. Journalists and Authors (founding co-chmn. for regional symposium 1992, chmn. 1994, chpt. pres. 1991-93, 98-99, nat. bd. dirs. 1994-98), Author Guild, Assn. for Care of Children's Health, Am. Med. Writers Assn. Lutheran. Office: PO Box 21423 Concord CA 94521-0423

ALBRECHT, DUANE TAYLOR, veterinarian; b. Sioux City, Iowa, Nov. 7, 1927; s. Carl Frederick Albrecht and Mildred Ida (Taylor) Chapin; m. Elinor Gaylord, Mar. 22, 1952; children: Steven Gaylord, Stanley Taylor, Susan Elaine Albrecht O'Neil, Duane Taylor Jr. DVM, Iowa State U., 1950. Intern Angell Meml. Animal Hosp., Boston, 1950-51; instr. Iowa State U., Ames, 1951-52; founding pres. Aspenwood Animal Hosp., P.C., Denver, 1952-90; sec. Colo. State Bd. Vet. Medicine, 1970-80; pres. Am. Assn. Vet. State Bds., 1975-76; mem. Nat. Bd. Vet. Medicine, 1973-87, chmn. com. 1980-81; mem. Ednl. Commn. Fgn. Vet. Grads.; bd. dirs. Citizens Bank of Glendale. Designer Aspenwood Animal Hosp., P.C., 1976 (Design Merit award Vet. Econs. Jour.); contbr. articles to profl. jours. Sponsor Vet. Explorer Scout Post Boy Scouts Am.; endowment fund bd. dirs. Colo. State U. Coll. Vet. Medicine and Biomed. Scis., 1985-88; alumni advisor Beta Theta Pi, U. Denver, 1955-56; bd. dirs. AVMA Found., 1993—, treas., 1996-98. Recipient Stange award meritorius svc. vet. medicine Iowa State U., 1982, Disting. Svc. award Ohio Vet. Med. Assn., 1984, Centennial Merit award U. Pa. Sch. Vet. Medicine, 1984. Mem. AVMA (dist. IX rep., exec. bd. 1978-82, pres. 1983-84), Nat. Acad. Practice in Vet. Medicine (Disting. Practitioner 1986—), Colo. Vet. Med. Assn. (rep. bd. control 1958-60, named Vet. of Yr. 1980), Denver Area Vet. Med. Soc. (life, pres. 1956-57), Am. Animal Hosp. Assn. (Outstanding Svc. award region IV 1980), Iowa State U. Alumni Assn. (pres. 1957, Svc. award 1958), Shriners, Rotary, Denver Athletic Club, Cherry Hills Country Club, Phi Zeta. Presbyterian. Avocations: flying (comml. instrument and balloon pilot), skiing, golf, gardening. Home: 9 Huntwick Ln Englewood CO 80110-7110

ALBRECHT, KATHE HICKS, art historian, visual resources manager; b. Ann Arbor, Mich., Aug. 21, 1952; d. Richard Brian and Mafalda (Brasile) Hicks; m. Mark Jennings Albrecht, July 20, 1973; children: Nicole, Alexander, Olivia. BA in Art History, UCLA, 1975; MA in Art History, Am. U., 1989. Slide libr. asst. Am. U., Washington, 1986-88, visual resources mgr., 1991—; panel mem. Forum on Career Options in Art History, Am. Univ., 1994; co-coord. Mus. Ednl. Site Licensing Project (Nat. Initiative Getty), 1994; presenter Southeastern Coll. Art Conf., 1995, 97; mem. Conf. on Fair Use (Dept. of Commerce) VRA rep. to Digital Future Coalition, 1996—; mem. Nat. Initiative for a Networked Cultural Heritage (NINCH), 1996—. Vol. Fairfax County Pub. Sch. System, 1980—; re-election com. Rep. Nat. Com., Washington, 1984; Rep. precinct worker Mason dist., 1980s. Grantee: Getty Art History Info. Program, 1994-97; Am. U. (image processing, database devel.), 1995 (2). Mem. Art Librs. Soc. N. Am., Coll. Art Assn., Mus. Computer Network, Southeastern Coll. Art Conf., Visual Resources Assn. (pres. Mid-Atlantic region 1995-96, chair nat. membership com., 1995-97, co-chair intellectual property rights com. 1996—). Presbyterian. Avocations: antique and prints collectin. Office: Am Univ 4400 Massachusetts Ave NW Washington DC 20016-8001

ALBRECHT, RICHARD RAYMOND, airplane manufacturing company executive, lawyer; b. Storm Lake, Iowa, Aug. 29, 1932; s. Arnold Louis and Catherine Dorothea (Boettcher) A.; m. Constance Marie Berg, June 16, 1957; children: John Justin, Carl Arnold, Richard Louis, Henry Berg. BA, U. Iowa, 1958, JD with highest honors, 1961. Bar: Wash. 1961. Assoc. Perkins, Coie, Stone, Olsen & Williams, Seattle, 1961-67; ptnr. Perkins, Coie, Stone, Olsen & Williams, 1968-74; gen. counsel U.S. Dept. Treasury, Washington, 1974-76; v.p., gen. counsel, sec. Boeing Co., Seattle, 1976-81, v.p. fin., contracts and internat. bus., 1981-83, v.p., gen. mgr. Everett div., 1983-84; exec. v.p. Boeing Comml. Airplane Group, 1984-97, sr. advisor, 1997—; dir. Esterline Technologies Corp. Bd. regents Wash. State U., 1987—. With AUS, 1955-58. Recipient Outstanding Citizen of Yr. award Seattle-King County Municipal League, 1968-69. Mem. ABA, Wash. State Bar Assn., Seattle-King County Bar Assn., Am. Judicature Soc., Order of Coif, Sigma Nu, Omicron Delta Kappa, Phi Delta Phi. Club: Rainier (Seattle). Home: 1940 Shenandoah Dr E Seattle WA 98112-2326 Office: Boeing Comml Airplane Group M/S 10-23 PO Box 3707 Seattle WA 98124-2207

ALBRECHT, RONALD LEWIS, financial services executive; b. Derby, Conn., Dec. 30, 1935; s. Lewis Davis and Gladys Imogene (Spear) A.; m. Mikyong Kim, Dec. 28, 1968; children: Rondi Kim, Kathryn Lynn, Karen Ann. BS in Agr., U. Vt., 1957; BBA in Bus. Mgmt., Baylor U., 1966; MA in Bus. Mgmt., Cen. Mich. U., 1975. Commd. 2d lt. USAF, 1957, advanced through grades to lt. col., 1973; comdr. detachment USAF, Sioux City AB, Iowa, 1957-60; air traffic control officer USAF, Cheveston, Eng., 1960-62; dir. air traffic control HQ12 USAF, Waco, Tex., 1962-66; comdr. detachment USAF, Kimpo AB, Korea, 1967-68; comdr. squadron Sewart AFB USAF, Tenn., 1969-70; comdr. squadron Holloman AFB USAF, N.Mex., 1970-73; staff officer, air traffic control HQ air force systems command USAF, Andrews AFB, 1973-75; dep. comdr. group USAF, Pentagon, 1975-77; staff officer electronics HQ joint staff USAF, Yongson, Korea, 1977-79; staff officer air traffic control communications area USAF, Rome, N.Y., 1979-80; retired USAF, 1980; real estate broker Bangor, Maine, 1980—; retirement, investment and fin. planning exec. Bangor (Maine) Savs. Bank, 1981-87; pres. Maine Fin. Mgmt. Svcs.,Inc. and Albrecht Fin. Svcs., Bangor, 1987—; instr. Los Angeles Community Coll., Seoul, Korea, 1977-79, Husson Coll. Bangor, 1981-84. Mem. loaned exec. bd. div. planning com. United Way of Penobscot Valley, Bangor, 1981—, Rep. Party, Bangor, 1981—. Hood Dairy scholar U. Vt., 1955. Mem. Internat. Assn. Fin. Planning (v.p. programs, co-founder 1985, pres. Maine chpt. 1988-89), Inst. Cert. Fin. Planners, Internat. Cert. Fin. Planners (bd. standards and practices), Ret. Officers Assn., Am. Assn. Ret. Persons, Air TrafficControl Assn., Armed Forces Communications Electronics Assn., Kiwanis (2d and 1st v.p. Bangor Club, pres. 1987-88), Masons, Anah Temple, Valley of Tokyo, Orientof Japan and Korea. Avocations: reading, hiking, gardening, travel. Home: 98 Judson Blvd Bangor ME 04401-2542

ALBRECHT, RONDI KIM, financial services executive; b. Holloman AFB, N.Mex., July 9, 1971; d. Ronald Lewis and Mi Kyong (Kim) A. BS, U. Maine, 1993. Adminstrv. asst. A.G. Edwards, Bangor, Maine, 1992-93; mktg. rep. Fidelity Investments Instl. Svcs., Boston, 1993-94; nat. sales rep. Boston Capital, 1994-95; fin. svcs. exec. Commonwealth Equity Svcs., Bangor, 1995—. Fellow Internat. Assn. Fin. Planning, Eastern Maine Assn. Life Underwriters; mem. Alpha Phi (treas. 1996—, fin. advisor 1995—). Avocations: hiking, skiing, reading, biking. Home: PO Box 1075 Bangor ME 04402-1075 Office: Albrecht Fin Svcs 992 Union St Ste 3 Bangor ME 04401-3057

ALBRECHT, WILLIAM PRICE, economist, educator, government official; b. Pitts., Jan. 7, 1935; s. William Price and Jane Lanier (Moses) A.; m. Alice Annette Cooper, June 14, 1956 (div. Nov. 1975); children—William, Alison, Jonathan, Jeffrey; m. Fran Jaecques, July 4, 1976. AB, Princeton U., 1956; MA, U. S.C., 1962, Yale U., 1963; PhD, Yale U., 1965. Asst. prof. U. Iowa, Iowa City, 1965-70, assoc. prof., 1970-82, prof. econs., 1982-88, assoc. dean Coll. Bus. Adminstrn., 1984-88; self-employed antitrust cons., 1978-88; commr. Commodity Futures Trading Commn., Washington, 1988-93; prof. econs. U. Iowa, Iowa City, 1993—; dir. Inst. for Internat. Bus. U. Iowa, 1998—; TV fin. advisor. Author: Economics, 1974, 4th edit., 1986, Black Employment, 1970, Microeconomic Principles, 1979, Macroeconomic Principles, 1979. Candidate U.S. Ho. of Reps., 1970; legis. asst. U.S. Senator Dick Clark, 1974. Served to lt. USN, 1956-61. Mem. Am. Econ. Assn., Midwest Econ. Assn. (v.p. 1981-82). Avocations: tennis; farming. Home: 5770 NE Morse Rd Solon IA 52333-8806 Office: U Iowa Dept Econs Iowa City IA 52242

ALBRECHTSON, RICK, psychologist; b. LaCrosse, Wis., Mar. 31, 1945; s. Richard Milton and Marie (Young) A.; m. Barbara Ann Conk, Dec. 26, 1971. BS, U. Wis., LaCrosse, 1973, MS in Edn., 1976. Lic. sch. psychologist, Wis. Sch. psychologist Sparta (Wis.) Area Schs., 1975-85, Sch. dist. LaCrosse, 1985—; adj. prof. U. Wis., LaCrosse, 1987-96. With USAF, 1966-70. Mem. Nat. Assn. Sch. Psychologists, Wis. Sch. Psychologist Assn., Coulee Region assn. Psychologists in the Schs. (pres., sec.). Avocations: sports car auto racing, running, photography. Home: N2841 County Road FA La Crosse WI 54601-3029 Office: Central High Sch 1801 Losey Blvd S La Crosse WI 54601-6866

ALBRIGHT, ALAN D., federal judge; b. 1959. BA, Trinity U., 1981; JD, U. Tex., 1984. Briefing atty. to James R. Nowlin we. dist. U.S. Dist. Ct. Tex., 1984-86; with Akin, Gump, Strauss, Hauer & Feld, 1988-92, McGinnis, Lochridge & Kilgore, 1986-88; apptd. magistrate judge we. dist. U.S. Dist. Ct. Tex., 1993. Fax: (512) 916-5668. Office: 200 W 8th St Austin TX 78701-2325

ALBRIGHT, DANIEL, English educator; b. Chgo., Oct. 29, 1945; s. Frank J. and Leone Hinze Albright; m. Karin Larson, June 19, 1977; 1 child, Christopher Torrey. BA, Rice U., 1967; MPhil, Yale U., 1969, PhD, 1970. Assoc. prof. English U. Va., Charlottesville, 1970-75, 1975-81, prof. English, 1981-87; prof. english U. Rochester, N.Y., 1987—, Richard L. Turner prof. in humanities, 1995—; vis. prof. U. Munich, 1986-87; affiliate dept. musicology Eastman Sch. Music, 1998—. Author: The Myth Against Myth, 1972, Representation and the Imagination, 1981, Quantum Poetics, 1998; editor: W.B. Yeats: The Poems, 1990, others. Fellow NEH, 1973, Guggenheim Found., 1976. Mem. Phi Beta Kappa. Home: 121 Van Voorhis Rd Pittsford NY 14534 Office: U Rochester Dept English Rochester NY 14627

ALBRIGHT, JACK LAWRENCE, animal science and veterinary educator; b. San Francisco, Mar. 14, 1930; s. George Clarence and Elizabeth Ann (Murphy) A.; m. Lorraine Aylmer Hughes, Aug. 17, 1957; children: Maryann A. Williams, Amy Elizabeth. BS with honors, Calif. State Poly. U., 1952; MS, Wash. State U., 1954, PhD, 1957. Rsch. asst. Wash. State U., 1952-54, 55-57, acting instr., 1954-55; instr. Calif. State Poly. U., 1955, 57-59; asst. prof. U. Ill., Urbana, 1959-63; assoc. prof. Purdue U., West Lafayette, Ind., 1963-66, prof. animal sci. Sch. Agr., 1966-96, prof. animal mgmt. and behavior Sch. Vet. Medicine, 1974-96, prof. emeritus animal sci. and vet. medicine, 1996—; mem. Ctr. Applied Ethology and Human-Animal Interactions Purdue U., 1982-96, Purdue Interdisciplinary Undergrad. Program in Animal Welfare and Societal Concerns, 1992-96, Purdue Animal Care and Use com., 1989-92, Ctr. for Rsch. on Well-Being in Food Animals, 1992-96; vis. prof. U. Ariz., Tucson, 1995, vis. prof. N.Mex. State U., Las Cruces, 1995; vis. prof. U. Ill., Urbana, 1988-89; vis. prof. pure and applied zoology U. Reading, Eng., 1977-78; vis. scientist N.Z. Dept. Agr., Ruakura, Hamilton, 1971-72, Dairy Shrine, Ft. Atkinson, Wis., 1958—; cons., lectr. in field, animal mgmt., behavior, care and welfare; mem. Ind. Commn. Farm Animal Care, 1981-99. Author papers, revs., chpts., guidelines, and books; reviewer sci. jours. Vestryman St. John's Episcopal Ch., West Lafayette, 1979-82; bellringer Salvation Army, 1964—; mem. judging teams Cal Poly Dairy Cattle, Dairy Products and Livestock. Fulbright scholar, N.Z., 1971-72; NSF Animal Behavior grantee, summer 1964; USDA/FAS/ICD Sci. and Tech. Exch. Program awardee to Rep. of Ireland, 1994; recipient Guardian award Ind. Vet. Med. Assn., 1995, Sci., Edn. and Tech. award dept. animal scis. Washington State U., 1996; one of 7 named to inaugaral Renaissance Acad. Hall of Fame, Paso Robles H.S., 1998. Fellow AAAS, Am. Dairy Sci. Assn., Ind. Acad. Sci.; mem. Am. Dairy Sci. Assn. (sec. 1972-73, chmn. profl. coun. 1973-74, Dairy Mgmt. Rsch. award 1986, invited lectrs. ann. meeting, 1982, 86-87, 92, 94, found. charter 1992), Animal Behavior Soc. (charter), Am. Soc. Animal Sci. (chmn. animal behavior com. 1970, 76, 85, Animal Mgmt. Rsch. award 1988, Found. charter 1993, animal care com. 1994-96), Am. Registry Profl. Animal Sci. (dairy and animal behavior 1993—), Am. Coll. Animal Behavior Sci. (cert., charter, diplomate 1995), Am. Soc. Vet. Ethology (charter), Internat. Soc. Applied Ethology, Chillingham Wild Cattle Assn. (life), Soc. Study Ethics and Animals, Scientist's Ctr. Animal Welfare (corr.), Univs. Fedn. for Animal Welfare, Hooved Animal Humane Soc., Los Lecheros Dairy Club Calif. STate Poly. U. (hon.), Kiwanis (pres. Lafayette club 1969-70, sec. found. 1976-77), Blue Key, Delta Soc., Sigma Xi, Alpha Zeta, Gamma Sigma Delta, Farm House. Republican. Home: 188 Blueberry Ln West Lafayette IN 47906-4810 Office: Purdue Univ Poul Bldg Dept Animal Scis West Lafayette IN 47907-1026

ALBRIGHT, JAMES AARON, orthopedist, surgeon; b. Terre Haute, Ind., Dec. 19, 1928; m. Merrilee G. Albright; children: Susan L., Daniel J., Linda L. BS, U. Ill., 1950; MD, U. Ill., Chgo., 1954. Diplomate Am. Bd. Orthop. Surgery. Intern U. Ill. Rsch. & Edn. Hosp., Chgo., 1954-55; resident in gen. practice U. Colo., Denver, 1958-60; resident in orthop. surgery Yale U. Sch. Medicine, New Haven, Conn., 1960-63; fellow in orthop. surgery Pub. Health Tng. Grant, 1963-66; from instr. to asst. prof. orthop. surgery Yale U. Sch. Medicine, New Haven, Conn., 1962-69, assoc. prof. orthop. surgery, 1970-77; attending orthop. surgery Yale-New Haven Hosp., Conn., 1963-77; asst. attending orthop. surgery Newington (Conn.) Children's Hosp., 1965-77, dir. Osteogenesis Imperfecta Clinic, 1976-77; prof., head dept. orthop. surgery La. State U. Sch. Medicine, Shreveport, 1978—; cons. West Haven (Conn.) Vets. Adminstrn. Hosp., 1963-77, Windham Meml. Hosp., Willimantic, Conn., 1965-77, Gaylord Rehab. Hosp., Wallingford, Conn., 1966-77; mem. med. adv. bd., cons. New Haven (Conn.) Rehab. Ctr., 1971-77; mem. med. adv. bd. Nat. Osteogenesis Imperfecta Found., 1972—; dir. annual postgraduate course Yale U., 1974-77; mem. dean's administrv. com. La. State U. Sch. Medicine, Shreveport, 1980-82, chmn. faculty promotions com., 1981, mem. faculty promotions com., 1985—; judge Internat. Sci. and Engring. Fair, 1985; chmn. N.W. La. Orthop. Rsch. & Edn. Found., 1986—; med. coord. bioengring. confs.; guest lectr., presenter numerous hosps., colls., confs., seminars. Cons. reviewer Jour. of Bone and Joint Surgery, 1979—; author, contbr. numerous articles, procs. to profl. jours. Flight surgeon USAF, 1955-58, Eng., Germany. Mem. AMA, AAAS, ASME, Am. Acad. Orthop. Surgeons (mem. psychomotor skills com. 1976-85, mem. basic sci. com. 1976—), Am. Orthop. Assn., Assn. Orthop. Chmn., Am. Assn. Tissue

Banks, Orthop. Rsch. Soc., So. Med. Assn., La. Orthop. Assn., Shreveport Med. Soc., Shreveport Orthop. Assn., Sigma Xi. Office: La State Med Ctr 1501 Kings Hwy Shreveport LA 71103-4228

ALBRIGHT, JOHN D., emergency room and telemetry nurse; b. Pine Bluff, Ark., June 6, 1944; s. John D. and Nettie (Pitts) A.; m. Carol Lennie, Jan. 16, 1991. BS, U. Ark., Monticello, 1970; lic. practical nurse diploma, Bapt. Lic. Practical Nurse Sch., Little Rock, 1977; BSN, Fla. Internat. U., 1984. RN, Fla. Staff relief nurse All Better Nursing, Miami, Fla. Sgt. USAF, 1966-70. Home: 15432 SW 17th Cir Ln Miami FL 33143

ALBRIGHT, JOSEPH WILLIAM, army officer; b. Chillicothe, Ohio, Feb. 3, 1954; s. Herman LeRoy and Catherine Regina (Rieder) A.; m. Deanna Wells, Aug. 13, 1989; children: Andrea Lyn, Jason Michael; stepchildren: Jennifer Charlene, Tammy Darlene. BME, U. Dayton, 1976. Commd. 2nd lt. Ordnance br. U.S. Army, 1976; advanced through grades to col. Ordnance br. U.S. Army, 1999; accountable officer 9th ordnance co. 9th Ordnance Co., Germany, 1977-79, ops. officer, 1979-80; rsch. engr., chief integrated logistic support office large caliber weapon sys. lab., 1980-82; material officer 3rd ordnance bn. 59th ordnance brigade 3d Ordnance Bn., 59th Ordnance Brigade, 1982-85; Dept. of Army coord. for ammunition logistics Dept. of Army, 1985-87; asst. exec. officer to dep. commanding gen. Material Readiness Army Material Commd., 1987-88; commdr. 96th ordnance co. 96th Ordnance Co., 1988-90; inspector gen. Tech. Insp. divsn. Army Material Command Tech. Insp. divsn. Army Materiel Command, 1990-93, chief program mgmt. divsn., 1993-94; comdr. Milan Army Ammunition Plant Milan Army Ammunition Plant, Tenn., 1994-96; dep. support ops. officer 3rd corps support command V U.S. Army Corps, 1996-98; depot maintenance project chief, hdqs. dept. U.S. Army Hdqrs., Dept. of Army, 1998—. Decorated Legion of Merit, Meritorious Svc. medal with 4 oak leaf clister, Army Commendation medal with oak leaf cluster, Army Achievement medal; named Disting. Mil. Grad., 1976, Disting. Grad. Ordnance Officer Advanced Course, 1980. Mem. ASME, Pi Sigma Tau. Home: 219 Diamond Dr Walkersville MD 21793-9145 Office: Dep Chief Staff Logistics Supply & Maintenance Direct 500 Army Pentagon Washington DC 20310-0500

ALBRIGHT, JUDITH ANNE, writer; b. Toldeo, Ohio; d. Matthew M. and Margaret Fern McMahon; m. Bill Eugene Albright, Aug. 15, 1964; children: Mary Sheila, Michael James. Tchr. Concord Sch. System, Elkhart, Ind., 1965-67, Dows Ln. Sch., Irvington, N.Y., 1967-69, Capistrano Unified Schs., San Juan Capistrany, Calif., 1980-89; owner, dir. Albright Presch., Mission Viejo, Calif., 1984-86; tchr. St. Edwards Sch., Dana Point, Calif., 1986-87; cons., spkr. in field of religion. Author: Our Lady of Medjugorje, 1988, Neustra Senora de Medjugorje, 1988, Mary and the Children of Medjugorje, 1989, Our Lady of Garabandal, 1992. Roman Catholic. Avocations: travel, reading, writing, boating. Home: 201 Internat Dr #313 Cape Canaveral FL 32920

ALBRIGHT, JUSTIN W., lawyer; b. Lisbon, Iowa, Oct. 14, 1908; m. Mildred Carlton, 1935; 1 child, Carlton J. B.S.C., U. Iowa, 1931, J.D., 1933. Bar: Iowa 1933. Former counsel firm Simmons, Perrine, Albright & Ellwood, P.L.C., Cedar Rapids, Iowa, ret. Editor: Iowa Law Rev, 1932-33. Past trustee, bd. trustees YMCA of Met. Cedar Rapids; bd. dirs. Cedar Rapids Symphony Orch.; founding mem., past pres. St. Paul's United Meth. Ch. Found., Cedar Rapids. Served with AUS, World War II. Mem. ABA, Iowa Bar Assn., Linn County Bar Assn. (life), Am. Judicature Soc., Hoover Presdl. Libr. Assn., Cedar Rapids C. of C., Phi Delta Phi. Clubs: Cedar Rapids Country, Pickwick (Cedar Rapids) (past pres.). Lodges: Masons (32 deg.), Shriners, Rotary (Paul Harris fellow). Office: Simmons Perrine Albright & Ellwo 115 3rd St SE Ste 1200 Cedar Rapids IA 52401-1266

ALBRIGHT, LYLE FREDERICK, chemical engineering educator; b. Bay City, Mich., May 3, 1921; s. William Edward and Isabella (Sidebotham) A.; m. Jeanette Van Belle, Mar. 4, 1950; children: Christine, Diane. B.S. in Chem. Engring, U. Mich., 1943, M.S. in Chem. Engring, 1944, Ph.D. in Chem. Engring, 1950. Lab. technician Dow Chem. Co., Midland, Mich., 1939-41; chem. engr. E.I. duPont de Nemours & Co., Hanford, Wash., 1944-46; research chem. engr. Colgate-Palmolive Co., Jersey City, 1950-51; asst. prof. U. Okla., Norman, 1951-54; assoc. prof. U. Okla., 1954-55, Purdue U., West Layette, Ind., 1955-58; prof. chem. engring. Purdue U., 1958—; cons. to numerous chem. petroleum cos., 1960—. Author: Industrial and Laboratory Pyrolyses, 1976, Industrial and Laboratory Alkylations, 1977, Coke Formation on Metals, 1982, Pyrolysis: Theory and Industrial Practice, 1983, Processes for Major Addition Type Plastics and Their Monomers, 2d edit., 1985, Novel Production Methods for Ethylene, Light Hydrocarbons, and Aromatics, 1992, Nitrations: Recent Laboratory and Industrial Developments, 1996. Recipient Shreve prize Purdue U., 1960, 70, 88, Potter award for best instr. Schs. of Engring. Purdue U., 1988. Fellow Am. Inst. Chem. Engrs. (dir. 1982-84); mem. Am. Chem. Soc., Internat. Brotherhood Magicians, Sigma Xi, Tau Beta Pi. Methodist. Home: 4750N N 250 W West Lafayette IN 47906-5525 Office: Purdue Univ Sch Chem Engring West Lafayette IN 47907

ALBRIGHT, MADELEINE KORBEL, federal official, diplomat, political scientist; b. Prague, Czechoslovakia, May 15, 1937; d. Josef and Anna (Speeglova) Korbel; m. Joseph Medill Patterson Albright, June 11, 1959 (div. 1983); children: Anne Korbel, Alice Patterson, Katharine Medill. BA with honors, Wellesley Coll., 1959; MA, Columbia U., 1968; cert., Russian Inst., 1968, PhD, 1976. Washington coord. Maine for Muskie, 1975-76; chief legis. asst. to U.S. Senator Muskie, 1976-78; mem. staff NSC, 1978-81; sr. fellow in Soviet and Eastern European Affairs Ctr. for Strategic and Internat. Studies, Ctr. for Strategic and Internat. Studies, 1981; fellow Woodrow Wilson Internat. Ctr. for Scholars, Washington, 1981-82; Research prof. internat. affairs, dir. women in fgn. service Sch. Fgn. Service Georgetown U., 1982-93; pres. Ctr. for Nat. Policy, 1985-93; fgn. policy coord. Mondale for Pres. campaign, 1984, to Geraldine A. Ferraro, 1984; vice chmn. Nat. Dem. Inst. for Internat. Affairs, Washington, 1984-93; perm. rep. of the U.S. UN, N.Y.C., 1993-97; Sec. U.S. Dept. of State, 1997—; sr. fgn. policy advisor Dukakis for Pres. Campaign, 1988; mem. Pres.'s Cabinet, Nat. Security Coun. Author: Poland: The Role of the Press in Political Change, 1983; contbr. articles to profl. jours., chpts. to books. Bd. dirs. Beauvoir Sch., Washington, 1968-76, chmn., 1978-83; trustee Black Student Fund, 1969-78, 82-93, Dem. Forum, 1976-78, Williams Coll., 1978-82, Wellesley Coll., 1983-89; mem. exec. com. D.C. Citizens for Better Pub. Edn., 1975-76; bd. dirs. Washington Urban League, 1982-84, Atlantic Coun., 1984-93, Ctr. for Nat. Policy, 1985-93, Chatham House Fedn., 1986-88. Mem. Council Fgn. Relations, Am. Polit. Sci. Assn., Czechoslovak Soc. Arts and Scis. Am., Atlantic Council U.S. (dir.), Am. Assn. for Advancement Slavic Studies. Office: Office of the Secretary of State 2201 C St NW Washington DC 20520-0001*

ALBRIGHT, MINDY SUE, college health and geriatrics nurse; b. Wooster, Ohio, June 29, 1955; d. Ernest Clyde and Miriam Jean (Leighty) Yates; m. Jerrold Arden Albright, Aug. 27, 1974; children: Franz, Emil, Ewen. Student, Kent State U., Canton, Ohio, 1973-74, Aultman Hosp. Sch. Nursing, Canton, 1973-75; AAS with honors, North Cen. Tech. Coll., Mansfield, Ohio, 1986. RNC (coll. health nurse); cert. hypnotherapist; cert. Reiki master tchr., cert. Universal Spiritual Energy Healing Instr. Staff nurse Altercare of Millersburg, Ohio, 1986-87, Emerald Svcs., Lodi, Ohio, 1988—; supr. Good Shepherd Home, Ashland, Ohio, 1987-90; staff nurse Coll. of Wooster, 1988-93; supr. Shady Lawn Nursing Home, Wooster, Ohio, 1990-97; camp nurse Wooster Outdoor Ctr., Perrysville, Ohio, 1993—; owner Wellness Success Ctr., Wooster; part-time faculty dept. continuing edn. Wayne Coll., Akron U., Orrveille, Ohio, 1996—. Mem. Am. Coll. Health Assn., Ohio Coll. Health Assn. Home: 3441 Lattasburg Rd Wooster OH 44691-9223 Office: Coll of Wooster Hygeia Hall Wooster OH 44691

ALBRIGHT, RAYMOND JACOB, government official; b. Reading, Pa., Apr. 7, 1929; s. Raymond Wolf and Mary Catherine (Sherr) A.; m. Ruthmarie Reich, Sept. 13, 1952; children: Raymond Jacob, David Reich. B.A., Yale, 1951; Fulbright scholar, U. Vienna, Austria, 1951-52; M.A., Harvard, 1954, Ph.D.; in Polit. Sci., 1961. Fgn. affairs officer (Nat. Security Council affairs and policy planning) Office Asst. Sec. Def. (Internat. Security Affairs), 1954-61; with Office Asst. Sec. State (European affairs), 1961-62; nat. security affairs adviser Treasury Dept., 1962-67; asst. to sec. treasury (Nat. Security Affairs) Office Sec. Treasury, 1967-69; counselor for econ. affairs Am. embassy, Belgrade, Yugoslavia, 1969-72; fgn. service res. officer Dept. State, 1969-73; v.p. Export-Import Bank U.S., 1973-92, sr. v.p., 1992-95; mng. dir. Lange, Mullen & Bohn, LLC/Global Fin. Solutions; Lectr. Yale, 1959, George Washington U., 1960, George Mason U., 1997. Author: (with others) Forging a New Sword, 1958. Pres. Fgn. Policy Discussion Group, Washington. Club: Yale (Washington) (bd. dirs., chmn. Yale and govt. com. 1966-69). Home: 3609 Dunlop St Chevy Chase MD 20815-5926

ALBRIGHT, TERRILL D., lawyer; b. Lebanon, Ind., June 23, 1938; s. David Henry and Georgia Pauline (Doty) A.; m. Judith Ann Stoelting, June 2, 1962; children: Robert T., Elizabeth A. AB, Ind. U., 1960, JD, 1965. Bar: Ind. 1965, U.S. Dist. Ct. (so. dist.) Ind. 1965, U.S. Dist. Ct. (no. dist.) Ind. 1980, U.S. Ct. Appeals (7th cir.) 1981, U.S. Ct. Appeals (3d and D.C. cirs.) 1982, U.S. Supreme Ct. 1972; cert. arbitrator for large complex cse program constrn. and internat. commercial cases Am. Arbitration Assn., cert. mediator. Assoc. Baker and Daniels Law Firm, Indpls., 1965-72; ptnr. Baker and Daniels Law Firm, 1972—. Bd. dirs., pres. Christamore House, Indpls., 1979-86; bd. dirs. Greater Indpls. YMCA, 1980-82; chmn. Jordan YMCA, Indpls., 1982; pres. Community Ctrs. Indpls., 1987-90. 1st lt. U.S. Army, 1960-62. Fellow Am. Bar Found., Ind. Bar Found., Indpls. Bar Found., Am. Coll. Trial Lawyers; mem. Nat. Conf. Bar Presidents (exec. coun. 1995-98), Ind. State Bar Assn. (chmn. young lawyer sect. 1971-72, rep. 11th dist. 1983-85, bd. dirs., v.p. 1991-92, pres. elect 1992-93, pres. 1993-94), Ind. U. Law Alumni Assn. (bd. dirs. 1974-80, pres. 1979-80). Democrat. Office: Baker & Daniels 300 N Meridian St Ste 2700 Indianapolis IN 46204-1782

ALBRIGHT, TOWNSEND SHAUL, investment banker; b. Anderson, Ind., May 1, 1942; s. Townsend S. and Maxine Aree (Zimmerman) A.; m. Eileen Therese Argent, Aug. 30, 1968; children—Megan Eileen, Alexandra Michele. B.A., Wabash Coll., 1964; M.B.A., U. Mich., 1966. With Mead Corp., Cin. and Chgo., 1966-69; mcpl. bond underwriter No. Trust Co., Chgo., 1969-71; v.p. Channer Newman Securities Co., Chgo., 1971-80; v.p., treas., dir., Croake Roberts, Inc., Chgo., 1980-86; v.p. instl. sales John Nuveen & Co., Chgo., 1986-90, prin. Fin. Forum, 1991—; sr. program adminstr. Ill. Devel. Fin. Authority, Chgo., 1995—; faculty mem. Loyola U., 1990—. Bd. dirs., mem. adv. council Urban Gateways, Chgo., 1976—; dean Mcpl. Bond Sch. Chgo; with Inst. Entrepreneurial Studies U. Ill., Chgo. Served with USAR, 1966-72. Mem. Mcpl. Bond Club Chgo., Chgo. Assn. Wabash Men, U. Mich. Alumni Assn., Phi Gamma Delta (Chgo. grad. chpt. bd. dirs.). Presbyterian. Clubs: Economic (Chgo.). Home: 2019 Beechwood Ave Wilmette IL 60091-1503

ALBRITTON, DANIEL LEE, atmospheric scientist; b. Camden, Ala., June 8, 1936. BS in Elec. Engring., Ga. Inst. Tech., 1959, MS in Physics, 1963, PhD in Physics, 1967. Dir. Aeronomy Lab. Environ. Rsch. Labs. NOAA, Boulder, Colo., 1986—; leader atmospheric chemistry project Climate and Global Change Program NOAA; co-chmn. sci. assessments of stratospheric ozone U.N. Environ. Programme; mem. sci. working group Intergovtl. Panel on Climate Change; lectr. in atm scis. and policy/sci. interface. Former mem. editl. adv. bd. Jour. Molecular Spectroscopy; former co-editor Jour. Atmospheric Chemistry; contbr. 150 articles to profl. jours. Recipient pres. rank svc. award, 1990, gold medal Dept. Commerce, 1977, 93, sci. freedom and responsibility award AAAS, 1993, sci. assessments award Am. Meteorol. Soc., 1993, stratospheric ozone protection award EPA, 1994, UN environ. programme ozone award, 1995. Fellow Am. Phys. Soc., Am. Geophys. Union. Achievements include research in laboratory investigation of atmospheric ion-molecular reactions and theoretical studies of diatomic molecular structure, investigation of atmospheric trace-gas photochemistry, sci. advisor in ozone depletion and climate change policy. Office: NOAA Aeronomy Lab 325 Broadway St Boulder CO 80303-3337*

ALBRITTON, WILLIAM HAROLD, III, federal judge; b. Andalusia, Ala., Dec. 19, 1936; s. Robert Bynum and Carrie (Veal) A.; m. Jane Rollins Howard, June 2, 1958; children: William Harold IV, Benjamin Howard, Thomas Bynum. A.B., U. Ala., 1959, LL.B., 1960. Bar: Ala. 1960. Assoc. firm Albrittons & Rankin, Andalusia, 1962-66, ptnr., 1966-76; ptnr. firm Albrittons & Givhan, Andalusia, 1976-86; ptnr. Albrittons, Givhan & Clifton, Andalusia, 1986-91; judge U.S. Dist. Ct. (mid. dist.) Ala., Montgomery, 1991-97, chief judge, 1998—. Pres. Ala. Law Sch. Found., 1988-91, Ala. Law Inst. Fellow Am. Coll. Trial Lawyers, Am. Bar Found.; mem. ABA, Fed. Judges Assn. (bd. dirs. 1999—), Ala. State Bar (commr. 1981-89, disciplinary commn. 1981-84, v.p. 1985-86, pres.-elect 1989-90, pres. 1990-91), Am. Judicature Soc., Am. Inns of Ct., Bluewater Bay Sailing Club, Bluewater Bay Country Club, Phi Beta Kappa, Phi Delta Phi, Omicron Delta Kappa, Alpha Tau Omega. Office: US Dist Ct S Court St Rm 311 Montgomery AL 36104-4009

ALBRITTON, WILLIAM HAROLD, IV, lawyer; b. Tuscaloosa, Ala., Mar. 21, 1960; s. William Harold III and Jane Rollins (Howard) A.; m. Lucille Smith, July 23, 1983; 1 child, Elizabeth Rollins. BA, U. Ala., Tuscaloosa, 1982, JD, 1985. Ptnr. Albrittons Clifton Alverson and Moody P.C., Andalusia, Ala., 1985—; bd. dirs. Colonial Bank, Andalusia; judge Mcpl. Ct. Andalusia, 1989—. Bd. dirs. Covington County Arts Coun., Andalusia, 1986-90, Andalusia City Schs. Found., 1991—, Andalusia Area C. of C., 1986-89; elder 1st Presbyn. Ch., Andalusia, 1990—. Mem. ABA, Ala. Bar Assn. (sec. pres.'s adv. task force 1986-88, chmn. com. on local bar activities 1990, task force on minority opportunity 1990-96, character and fitness com. 1991-96, chmn. 1993-96, chmn. com. solo practitioners & small firms 1997—), Ala. Def. Lawyers Assn. (bd. dirs. young lawyers sect. 1991-96, amicus curiae com. 1992—), Internat. Assn. Def. Counsel, Am. Inns of Ct., Kiwanis. Avocations: scuba diving, music, photography, travel, sailing. Home: 723 Albritton Rd Andalusia AL 36420-4601 Office: Albrittons Clifton Alverson & Moody PC 109 Opp Ave Andalusia AL 36420-3812

ALBUM, JERALD LEWIS, lawyer; b. Monroe, La., Oct. 18, 1947; s. Natt B. and Rose Marie (Pickens) A.; m. Joan Abbey Lurie, July 30, 1983; children: Nicole, Jeffrey. BS, Tulane U., 1969, JD, 1973. Bar: La. 1973, Colo. 1990, Tex. 1992, U.S. Dist. Ct. (ea. dist.) La. 1975, U.S. Dist. Ct. (mid. dist.) La. 1980, U.S. Dist. Ct. (we. dist.) La. 1983, U.S. Ct. Appeals (5th cir.) 1976. Assoc. Mmahat, Gagliano, Duffy & Giordano, Metairie, La., 1973-79; assoc. to ptnr. Lemle, Kelleher, Hunley, Moss & Frilot, New Orleans, 1980-85; shareholder Abbott Simses, Album & Knister, New Orleans, 1985-96; ptnr. Album, Stovall, Radecker & Giordano, New Orleans. Mem. La. Assn. of Def. Counsel, New Orleans Bar Assn., La. State Bar Assn. Avocations: golf, volleyball, gardening. Home: 4637 Southshore Dr Metairie LA 70002-1430 Office: Album Stovall Radecker & Giordano 3850 N Causeway Blvd Ste 1130 Metairie LA 70002-7247*

ALBUQUERQUE, EDSON XAVIER, pharmacology educator; b. Recife, Pernambuco, Brazil, Jan. 22, 1938. BS, Salesiano Coll., Recife, Brazil, 1953; MD, U. Recife, 1959; PhD, Fed. U. Pernambuco, U. Sao Paulo, U. Ill., 1962. Lectr. anatomy and physiology U. Recife, Pernambuco, Brazil, 1954-59; instr. pharmacology U. Ill., 1964-65; asst. prof. pharmacology U. Lund (Sweden), 1965-67; rsch. asst. prof. dept. pharmacology Schs. Medicine and Dentistry SUNY, Buffalo, 1968-69, assoc. prof. pharmacology, 1969-72, prof. pharmacology, 1972-73, prof., acting chmn., 1973-74; prof., chmn. dept. pharmacology and exptl. therapeutics U. Md., Balt., 1974—; titular prof. Fed. U. Rio de Janeiro; dir. molecular pharmacology tng. program Joint U. Md./Fed. U. Rio de Janeiro. Mem. editl. bd. and contbr. articles to profl. jours. C.A.P.E.S. fellow, 1959-62, Rockefeller Found. fellow, 1962-63, 63-64; Neuropharmacology grantee Nat. Inst. Neurological Diseases and Blindness, 1964-65; Neuropharmacology fellow Swedish Med. Rsch. Coun., IBRO/Unesco, 1965-67; Order of Grand Cross, Pres. of Brazil, 1995, Order of Rio Branco, 1996. Mem. AAAS, Am. Physiol. Soc., Am. Soc. Pharmacology and Exptl. Therapeutics (Otto Krayer award 1996), Am. Men and Women of Sci., Biophys. Soc. Am., Internat. Soc. Myochemistry, Internat. Brain Rsch. Orgn. (Latin Am. delegation), Latin Am. Soc. Physiol. Sci., Brazilian Pharmacology Soc., Soc. Toxicology, Soc. Neurosci., Third World Acad. Scis., Brazilian Acad. Sci. Office: U Md Sch Medicine Dept Pharmacology & Exptl Therapeutics 655 W Baltimore St Baltimore MD 21201*

ALBURTUS, MARY JO, social worker, consultant, trainer; b. Jersey City, Oct. 31, 1949; d. Wilson Vincent and Mary Therese (O'Neill) A. BA, Jersey City State U., 1973; MSW, Fordham U., 1982. Lic. clin. social worker, N.J. Mgmt. analyst U.S. Dept. of Labor, N.Y.C., 1973-76; social worker/specialist Monmouth Family Ctr., Freehold, N.J., 1976-83; social work supr. Monmouth Family Ctr., Asbury Park, N.J., 1983-85; founder, group therapist Monmouth County Sexual Abuse Groups, Monmouth County, N.J., 1983-89; supr. cmty. and program devel. Monmouth County Bd. Social Svcs., Neptune, N.J., 1985-90; pvt. practice clin. social worker, cons. Shrewsbury, N.J., 1988—; founder Monmouth County Sexual Abuse Coalition, 1981; social work specialist Family Svcs. Monmouth County Bd. Social Svcs., Neptune, 1990-91; adv. bd. Sexual Abuse Treatment Prog., Red Bank, 1983-89. Grantee Nat. Ctr. on Abuse and Neglect, 1980. Mem. NASW, Acad. Cert. Social Workers (diplomate social work), Mental Health Assn., Monmouth County Sexual Abuse Coalition, Task Force on Women and Alcohol, N.J. Soc. for Study of Dissociation. Office: 21 White St Shrewsbury NJ 07702-4440

ALBYN, RICHARD KEITH, retired architect; b. Detroit, Apr. 8, 1927; s. Walter Harris and Corrine Henrietta (Miller) A.; m. Nancy Jane Cosby; children: Keith Cosby, Lisa Benton Albyn Drummond. Student, U. Ill., 1945-49. Registered architect, Mich., Ohio, Fla., Md., W.Va., N.C. Prin. dir. Linn Smith Assocs., Inc., Birmingham, Mich., 1962-64, TMP Assocs., Inc., Bloomfield Hills, Mich., 1964-82, HEPY Assocs., Inc., Southfield, Mich., 1982-86; ret., 1986. Co-author: Buildings of Michigan, 1987; also articles in profl. jours. and hist. publs.; illustrator: A Handbook for the Amateur Archaeologist, 1967, The Archaeologists Coloring Book, 1964. Mem. Preservation N.C., Transylvania County Arts Coun., Transylvania County Hist. Soc., Asheville Art Mus., Greenville Art Mus. Recipient citation Am. Assn. Sch. Adminstrs., 1964, 70, 1st pl. award Ch. Architects Guild, 1965, others. Fellow AIA (pres. Detroit chpt. 1971, treas. 1968, sec. 1969, mem. past pres. com. 1971—, host chpt. com. nat. conv. 1971, pres. Detroit archtl. found. 1971, mem. vocat.-tech. edn. svc. study com. 1976, lectr. 1961-65, honor award 1964, 71, 77, award of merit 1971); mem. AIA N.C., Transylvania County Hist. Soc. (bd. dirs. 1991-94), Transylvania County Joint Hist. Preservation Commn. (chmn. 1993-96), Archaeol. Soc. N.C. Presbyterian. Avocations: painting, archaeology, geneology, photography, writing. Home: 60 Kentwood Ln Pisgah Forest NC 28768-9511

ALCALAY, ALBERT S., artist, design educator; b. Paris, Aug. 11, 1917; came to U.S., 1951, naturalized, 1956; s. Samuel and Lepa (Afar) A.; m. Vera Eskenazi, Nov. 11, 1950; children: Leor, Ammiel. Student in Paris, Rome. Lectr. design Carpenter Center, Harvard U., 1960—. One man shows, De Cordova and Dana Mus., Lincoln, Mass., 1968, Swetzoff Gallery, Pucker-Safrai Gallery, Pace Gallery, others; retrospective, Carpenter Ctr., Harvard U., 1982; group shows, Inst. Contemporary Art, Boston, 1960, Venice (Italy) Biennale, Mus. Modern Art., 1955, Whitney Mus. Am. Art, 1956, 58, 60, U. Ill., Urbana, Pa. Acad. Fine Arts, 1960; represented in permanent collections, Mus. Modern Art, N.Y.C., Boston Mus. Fine Arts, Fogg Art Mus., DeCordova and Dana Mus., Phillips Acad., Mus. Am. Art, Brandeis U. Rose Art Mus., U. Mass. Mus., Wellesley Coll. Mus., Colby Coll. Mus., Smith Coll., Rome Mus. Modern Art, U. Rome, Brockton Art Mus., Tufts U., Medford, Mass., Boston Pub. Library, Smithsonian Inst. Archives of Am. Artists. Guggenheim fellow, 1959-60; recipient prize Boston Arts Festival, 1960. Home: 66 Powell St Brookline MA 02446-3929 Office: Harvard U Carpenter Ctr Cambridge MA 01238

ALCANTARA, THEO, conductor; b. Cuenca, Castile, Spain, 1941; student Real Conservatorio de Musica, Madrid; grad. Akademie Mozarteum, Salzburg, Austria, 1964; m. Susan Alcantara; children: Rafael, Carlos. Conducting debut with Teatro de la Zarzuela, Madrid; condr. Frankfurt Opera Theatre Orch., 1964-66; dir. orchs. U. Mich., Ann Arbor, 1968-73; music dir., condr. Grand Rapids Symphony, 1973-78; music dir., prin. condr. Phoenix Symphony Orch., from 1978; music dir., condr. Music Acad. of West Summer Festival, Santa Barbara, Calif., 1981-85, prin. condr. Pitts. Opera, 1987—; artistic dir., prin. condr. Bilbao Symphony, Spain, 1993—; prin. guest condr. Nat. Orch. Spain, 1994—; guest condr. numerous orchs. including: world premier Christopher Columbus, Teatro Colon, Buenos Aires, Met. Opera, Pitts. Opera, Washington Opera, Am. Symphony, orchs. of Paris, Berlin, Madrid, Barcelona, Mexico City, Montevideo, New Orleans, Detroit, Pitts., Rochester (N.Y.) Philharm., Oreg. Symphony, Utah Symphony. Office: ICM Artists Ltd 40 W 57th St New York NY 10019-4001

ALCENA, VALIERE, internist, hematologist, educator, television producer, broadcast journalist. Student, Hunter Coll., 1963-67; BA, Queens Coll., 1970; MD, Albert Einstein Coll. Medicine, 1973. Diplomate Am. Bd. Internal Medicine. Intern Montefiore Hosp. and Med. Ctr., Bronx, N.Y., 1973-74, resident, 1974-75, chief resident, 1975-76, fellow in hematology, 1976-77, fellow in oncology, 1977-78, med. dir. methadone clinic, 1978-79, asst. attending physician medicine, 1978-87, asst. attending physician oncology, 1978-91, adj. attending physician medicine, 1987-93, assoc. attending physician medicine, 1993—; asst. attending physician internal medicine and hematology White Plains (N.Y.) Hosp., 1978-83, assoc. attending physician internal medicine and hematology, 1983-85, attending physician internal medicine, 1985—; clin. instr. medicine Albert Einstein Coll. Medicine, Bronx, 1978-88, teaching attending physician, 1994—, assoc. clin. prof. medicine, 1995—; teaching attending physician, asst. attending physician medicine North Ctrl. Bronx Hosp., 1978—; teaching attending physician Montefiore Hosp., Bronx, 1978—; asst. attending physician internal medicine, hematology and med. oncology St. Agnes Hosp., White Plains, 1978-83, assoc. attending physician, 1983-89, attending physician medicine and oncology, 1989—, dir. gen. medicine, hematology and med. oncology clinic, 1993; asst. attending physician, teaching attending physician Harlem Hosp., N.Y.C., 1979-81; attending physician employee health clinic, teaching attending physician N.Y. Hosp. Westchester divsn., Cornell Med. Sch., 1979-85; clin. assoc. N.Y. Hosp. Med. Ctr. Westchester divsn., White Plains, 1979-89; clin. instr. Cornell U. Med. Ctr., N.Y.C., 1979-89; attending physician St. Barnabas Hosp., Bronx, 1981-90; teaching attending physician Columbia U. Coll. Physicians & Surgeons, White Plains Hosp. Med. Residency Program, 1994—; founder and exec. dir. Alcena Africa Hunger Relief Fund, 1992—; pres. Alcena Med. Commm., Inc., 1992—; adj. asst. clin. prof. medicine N.Y. Med. Coll., Valhalla, N.Y., 1992-96, adj. assoc. prof., 1996—. Author: The Status of Health of Blacks in the United States of America, A Prescription for Improvement, 1992, The Third World Tropical Diet, Health Maintenance and Medical Management Program, 1992, AIDS The Expanding Epidemic, What the Public Needs to Know-Multi Cultural Overview, 1994, The African-American Health Book, 1994, 2d edit., 1996; contbr. articles to profl. jours. Founder, chmn. minority affairs com. Albert Einstein Coll. Medicine, Bronx, 1969-73; med. dir. Ronald-Fraser Neighborhood Health Ctr., Bronx, 1979-80; founder, med. dir. Ann. Health Fair for Cancer Screening, White Plains, 1979—; founder Sam Seifter Ann. Lectureship (Minority Health Care Issues), Albert Einstein Coll. Medicine, Bronx, 1989; founder, chmn., pres. White Plains Cmty. Health Fair, Inc., 1996; founder, pres. Westchester United Sickle Cell Anemia Support Group, 1997; cmty. activist, philanthropist. King-Kennedy scholar Albert Einstein Coll. Medicine, Yeshiva U., 1968-69; named Cmty. Man of Yr., Seventh Day Adventist Ch., White Plains; recipient Commendation for Cmty. Work, N.Y. State Senate, 1989, Disting. Svc. award Calvery Bapt. Ch., White Plains, 1989, Cert. of Merit, Pub. Edn. award Am. Cancer Soc., 1989, 90, Man of Yr. award Nat. Assn. Negro Bus. and Profl. Women's Clubs, Inc., Westchester, 1990, Pres.'s Vol. award, Nominee award, 1990, Cmty. Svc. award City of White Plains, 1996, congressional proclamation U.S. Congress, 1996; Dr. Valiere Alcena Day proclaimed by Westchester Bd. Legislators; cited for cmty. svc. N.Y. State Assembly, 1996. Fellow ACP, Interamerican Coll. Physicians and Surgeons, N.Y. Acad. Medicine, N.Y. Acad. Sci., Westchester Acad. Medicine; mem. AAAS, NAACP, Assn. Acad. Minority Physicians, Eastern Cancer Oncology Group, Internat. Platform Assn., Montefiore Hosp. Alumni and Med. Staff Assn., Nat. Med. Assn., N.Y. Black Journalists, Westchester Black Journalists Assn. Office: 37 Davis Ave White Plains NY 10605-1003

AL-CHALABI, MARGERY LEE, economic development services company executive; b. Tarentum, Pa., Oct. 20, 1938; d. Stephen and Margaretta E. (Wuerfel) Pupach; m. Suhail al-Chalabi, Mar. 9, 1965. BArch, Carnegie-Mellon U., 1961; MSc, Athens Technol. Inst., 1965. Architect, planner Doxiadis Assocs., Athens, Greece, 1962-65; regional planner HUD, Chgo., 1965-67; sr. planner Dept. Urban Renewal, Chgo., 1967-70; planning cons.,

Chgo., 1970-71; sr. planner Bauer Engring., Chgo., 1971-79; v.p. Real Estate Rsch. Corp., 1979-81; mgr. dir. real estate Laventhol & Horwath, Chgo., 1981-82; mayor's office coord. city devel. City of Chgo., 1982-83, asst. commr. dept. planning, 1982-83; pres. al-Chalabi Group Ltd., Chgo., 1983—; planning team Third Airport for Chgo., 1986—. Author numerous plans on urban and econ devel., numerous transp. plans for rail, bridges, tollroads, airports and their econ. impacts. Prepared financing/restoration plan, secured funds, restored landmark Chgo. Theater, 1984-86, operated theater, 1989-95. Recipient numerous restoration awards, 1985-95. Mem. Urban Land Inst., World Soc. Ekistics, Landmarks Preservation Coun. Ill., Nat. Trust Hist. Preservation, Women's Transp. Seminar, Lambda Alpha (hon.). Home: 330 W Diversey Pkwy Apt 2708 Chicago IL 60657-6209 also: 718 Wilson Ave Beverly Shores IN 46301-0232 Office: al-Chalabi Group Ltd 330 W Diversey Pky # 1403 Chicago IL 60657-6206

AL-CHALABI, SUHAIL ABDUL-JABBAR, transportation executive; b. Baghdad, Iraq, July 14, 1940; came to the U.S., 1965; s. Abdul Jabbar and Wajeeha Al-Chalabi; m. Margery Lee Pupach, Mar. 9, 1965. BArch, MIT, 1962; MSc, Athens (Greece) Tech. Inst., 1965. Planner, arch. Doxiadis Assocs., Athens, 1963-65, Skidmore Owings & Merrill, Chgo., 1965-67; rsch. dir. Northeastern Ill. Planning Commn., Chgo., 1967-74; exec. dep. dir. Chgo. Area Transp. Study, 1974-81; spl. advisor to mayor City of Chgo., 1981-82, commr. dept. econ. devel., 1982-83; exec. v.p., CFO The al Chalabi Group, Ltd., Chgo., 1983—. Rsch. and forecast adv. com. Northeastern Ill. Planning Commn., Chgo., 1992—. Mem. World Soc. Ekistics, Am. Assn. Airport Execs. (corp.), Chgo. Southland C. of C., Lambda Alpha. E-mail: acgtran@aol.com. Address: 330 W Diversey Pky Apt 2708 Chicago IL 60657 Office: Ste 1403 330 W Diversey Pkwy Chicago IL 60657

ALCINDOR, LEWIS FERDINAND See **ABDUL-JABBAR, KAREEM**

ALCOCK, CHARLES BENJAMIN, materials science consultant; b. London, Oct. 24, 1923; s. Arthur Charles and Margaret (Francis) A.; m. Valerie Robinson, Aug. 20, 1949; children—Deborah Susan, Martin Charles, James Benjamin. BSc, Imperial Coll., London, 1944, PhD, 1955; DSc, U. London, London, 1965. With BISRA, London, Eng., 1948-50; investigator Nuffield Research Group Royal Sch. Mines, London, Eng., 1950-53; mem. faculty metall. dept. Imperial Coll., 1953-69, lectr., 1953-61, reader, 1961-65, prof. metall. chemistry, 1965-69; prof., chmn. dept. metallurgy and materials sci. U. Toronto, Ont., Can., 1969-76, prof. emeritus, 1986—; vis. prof. Carnegie Inst. Tech., 1961, N.C. State U., 1965, Imperial Coll., 1992—; vis. com. mem. chem. engring. div. Argonne Nat. Lab., 1977-82; chmn. Can. Nat. Com. for CODATA, 1982-88, exec. com. mem., 1988-90; Ford vis. prof. U. Pa., 1968; Freimann vis. prof. U. Notre Dame, 1986, Freimann chaired prof., 1987-94, prof. emeritus, 1994—; dir. Ctr. for Sensor Materials, U. N.D., 1987-94. Recipient Paul Lebeau medal, 1975, Kroll medal, 1983. Fellow Royal Soc. Arts, Royal Inst. Chemistry, Instn. Mining and Metallurgy (London), Royal Soc. Can., Am. Inst. Metall. Engrs., N.Y. Acad. Scis. Office: U Toronto, Dept Metallurgy & Materials Sci, Toronto, ON Canada M5S 3E4

ALCOCK, CHARLES ROGER, science educator; b. Windsor, Eng., June 15, 1951; came to U.S., 1973; BS in Physics and Math., U. Auckland, 1972; PhD in Astronomy and Physics, Calif. Inst. Tech., 1977. Long-term mem. Inst. for Advanced Study, Princeton, N.J., 1977-81; assoc. prof. dept. physics MIT, Cambridge, 1981-86; head Astrophysics Ctr., Inst. Geophysics & Planetary Physics Lawrence Livermore (Calif.) Nat. Lab., 1986-97, head Inst. Geophysics and Planetary Physics, 1994-98, dep. assoc. dir. for sci. in the physics directorate, 1998—; vis. prof. Niels Bohr Inst., Copenhagen, 1979; vis. fellow Australian Nat. U., Canberra, 1983; adj. prof. dept. astronomy U. Calif., Berkeley. Recipient R&D 100 award, 1993, E.O. Lawrence award, 1996; Earle C. Anthony fellow Caltech, 1973-79, Alfred P. Sloan Rsch. fellow MIT, 1983-86. Office: Lawrence Livermore Nat Lab Univ Calif PO Box 808 L-413 Livermore CA 94551-0808*

ALCOCK, GEORGE LEWIS, JR. (PETER ALCOCK), investor, business strategist; b. Boston, Feb. 26, 1940; s. George Lewis and Louise Hall Alcock; m. Louise Stewart Bachelder, Sept. 29, 1984; children: Peter L., Caroline S. BS, Northeastern U., Boston, 1962. Prodn. supr. J.H. Winn, Winchester, Mass., 1963-65; sales staff Liberty Mutual Ins., Boston, 1966-68; fin. staff Nat. Med. Leasing, Cambridge, Mass., 1968-69; cons. Innovative Mgmt., Cambridge, Mass., 1970-73; treas. Devel. Mgmt. Consultants, Boston, 1973-80; chmn. M.B. Claff & Sons Inc., Brockton, Mass., 1980—; corp. fin. staff Alcock Investments, Watertown, Mass., 1980-87; pres., CEO U.S. Repeating Arms Co., New Haven, Conn., 1987-90; gen. ptnr. Alcock Ltd. Ptnrs., Weston, Mass., 1991—; pres. S. Bent & Bros. Inc., Gardner, Mass., 1992—; v.p. Assn. for Corp. Growth, Boston, 1991-98. Dir. The Nat. Coun. Northeastern U., Boston, 1989—, Gardner (Mass.) C. of C., 1992-95. Mem. Turnaround Mgmt. Assn., Strategic Leadership Forum, Assn. for Corp. Growth, Newcomen Soc. U.S. Avocation: outdoor sports. Office: Alcock Ltd Ptnrs 105 Cherry Brook Rd Weston MA 02493-1347

ALCON, SONJA LEE DE BEY GEBHARDT RYAN, retired medical social worker; b. Orange City, Iowa, Aug. 2, 1937; d. Albert Lee Gerard and Clarice Victoria (Brown) deBey; m. Richard J. Bebhardt, June 6, 1959; children: Russell, Cheryl, Kurt Gebhardt Ryan; m. George W. Ryan, Dec. 28, 1968; 1 child, Alanna (dec.); m. David E. Alcon, July 20, 1985. BA, Western Md. Coll., 1959; MSW, U. Md., 1973. Caseworker Springfield State Hosp., Sykesville, Md., 1959-61; dir. social work dept. Hanover (Pa.) Gen. Hosp., 1966-96; ret., 1996; part-time worker Matthews Hallmore Store, Hanover, 1997—; field instr. Western Md. Coll., 1967-96; clin. assoc. prof. sch. social work and social planning U. Md., 1987-92; cons. Golden Age Nursing Home, Hanover, 1973-76, Carlisle (Pa.) Hosp., 1974-78, Hanover Vis. Nurse Assn., 1977-83, emergency svcs. Mental Health Clinic, 1972; chmn. profl. adv. com. Vis. Nurse Assn. Hanover and Spring Grove, Inc., 1986-89; mem. social work adv. coun. Western Md. Coll., 1979-81, 84-86. Bd. dirs. Hospice of York, 1980-82, Hanover chpt. ARC, 1976-79, Adams-Hanover Mental Health, 1973-76; pres. Human Svcs. Orgn., 1980, v.p., 1985-86; mem. adv. coun. Hanover Hospice, 1982-85; treas. Hanover Cmty. Progress Com., 1976-80; mem. Adams-Hanover Sheltered Workshop Com., 1968-70; bd. dirs. Hanover Cmty. Players, 1974-77, sec., 1982; organizer local chpt. Make Today County and Preemie Parent Support Group, 1979; initiator, co-trustee Children's Cardiac Fund, 1979-92; mem. Hanover Oratorio Soc., 1964-85; adv. bd. United Cerebral Palsy South Ctrl. Pa., 1989-90; active YWCA, 1979-84, 96-98; co-organizer Adams-Hanover chpt. Compassionate Friends, 1983; mem. vestry All Saints Episcopal Ch., 1973-74, 76-79, 83-86, 97, vestry sec., 1975, diocesan del. Ctrl. Pa., 1978, 80-86, mem. altar guild, 1968-86, 92—, treas. ch. women, 1979-83, ch. choir, soloist, 1975—; life mem. Hanover Gen. Hosp. Aux., Harmony Ct. No 146, Order Amarnth, 1996, Hanover Chpt. No. 378, Order of the Eastern Star; mem. adv. group Inst. Pastoral Care, 1976-77; mem. adv. coun. Parents Anonymous, 1976-79, 85-92; adminstr. Hanover Gen. Hosp. Spl. Needs Fund, 1986-96; cmty. adv. com. Healthsouth Rehab. York, 1995-96; co-facilitator I Can Cope classes Am. Cancer Soc., 1989-92; active Cmty. Needs Coalition, 1990-96, South Ctrl. Pa. Coalition for Organ/Tissue Donation, 1994—; mem. Case Mgmt. Network South Ctrl. Pa., 1994-96; vol. Hanover Gen. Hosp., South Ctrl. Pa. Coalition Organ/Tissue Donation, Hanover Area Coun. Chs. Recipient York Daily Record Exceptional Citizen award, 1979, Spl. Recognition cert. Col. Richard Mcallister chpt. DAR, 1980; finalist YWCA Salute to Women, 1986, 87. Mem. NASW, Acad. Cert. Social Workers (lic. social worker, cert.), Md. Alumni Assn. (bd. dirs. 1983), Order Eastern Star (worthy matron 1985-86), Order of Amaranth (royal patron 1988-89, royal matron 1995-96, 99—, grand historian, 1998— Harmony Court), Order of the White Shrine of Jerusalem (life mem. Material Objective, worthy high priestess 1994-95, watchman of shepherds 1999-2000, Supere Hearld 1999-2000—), Commandery Ladiees Aux. (pres. 1989-90). Home: RR 3 Box 3305-m Tamarind Dr Spring Grove PA 17362-9457

ALCONE, MATT, advertising executive; b. 1953. BS in Biology, U. Calif., Irvine, BA in Bus. Adminstrn. CEO Alcone Mktg. Group, Irvine, Calif., 1975—, also chmn. bd. dirs. Office: Alcone Mktg Group 15 Whatney Irvine CA 92618-2808*

ALCORN, JAMES M., state insurance administrator. BS in Bus., Eastern Ill. U., 1967, postgrad. in econs. Owner various ind. property and casualty ins. agys., Idaho, 1970—; investigator, various other positions to dep. dir. Idaho Dept. Ins., Boise, 1989—, acting dir., 1994-96, dir., 1996-98; mgr. Idaho State Ins. Fund, Boise, 1998—; Cert. Ins. Counselor, 1981. Mem. Gooding County (Idaho) Fair bd.; chmn. hosp. adv. bd. Walker Ctr. of Gooding; founding bd. dirs. Payette (Idaho) Recreation Dist.; mem. CIC Edn. Com. Idaho. With USMC Inf., Vietnam. Recipient Outstanding Cmty. Achievement award, 1979. Mem. Ind. Agts. Assn., Profl. Ins. Agts. Assn., Gooding (Idaho) C. of C., Gooding Rotary Club. Office: Idaho Stae Ins Fund PO Box 83720 Boise ID 83720-0044*

ALCORN, WALLACE ARTHUR, minister; b. Milw., Aug. 29, 1930; s. William Keith and Dora Mildred (Brazee) A.; m. Ann Margaret Carmichael, June 5, 1958; children: John Mark, Allison Alcorn-Oppedahl, Stephen Paul. Student, Marquette U., 1950; AB, Wheaton Coll., 1952; MDiv, Grand Rapids Bapt. Theol. Sem., 1959; AM, Wheaton Grad. Sch. Theology, 1959; postgrad., Mich. State U., 1959-60, U. Mich., 1960-61; ThM, Princeton Theol. Sem., 1965; PhD, NYU, 1974; cert. in clin. pastoral edn., Fitzsimons Army Med. Ctr., 1975; postgrad., U. Minn., 1980-81. Ordained to ministry Gen. Assn. Regular Bapt. Chs., 1957. Pastor Caddy Vista Bapt. Ch., Caldonia, Wis., 1955-57, Bloomfield Hills (Mich.) Bapt. Ch., 1960-61, Community Bapt. Ch. Shark River Hills, Neptune, N.J., 1961-67, 1st Bapt. Ch., Austin, Minn., 1976-83; prof. bible Moody Bible Inst., Chgo., 1967-73; assoc. prof. N.T. N.W. Bapt. Sem., Tacoma, 1974-76; affiliate chaplain Madigan Army Med. Ctr., Tacoma, 1974-76; police chaplain Tacoma, 1974-76, Austin, Minn., 1976—; prin. Wallace Alcorn Assocs., Austin, 1983—; pastoral counselor New Life Family Svcs., Rochester, Minn., 1987-92; radio tchr. Moody Radio Network, 1968-74; radio commentator Sta. KTIS and Northwestern Coll. Network, 1987-98;- syndicated newspaper columnist, 1993—; adj. faculty Riverland C.C., 1994—; chmn. Minn. Assn. Regular Bapt. Chs., 1980-83; pres. Faith Acad., Fridley, Minn., 1986. Author: The Bible as Literature, 1965, Elijah, Prophet of God, 1972, The Life of Christ Visualized, 1973, Knowing and Using the Bible, 1975, Momentum, 1986; nat. editor Christian Life, 1956-59, Mil. Life, 1983-86; N.T. editor Living Bible Commentary, 1974-76; contbr. Wycliffe Bible Ency., 1974, Tyndale Family Bible Ency., 1976, New Commentary on the Whole Bible, 1990, The Book We Love, 1994; contbr. numerous articles to profl. jours. Mem. citizen's adv. coun. Neptune (N.J.) Bd. Edn., 1965-67; chair Austin Human Rights Commn., 1989-98; mem. profl. adv. coun. Pub. Edn. Religion Studies Ctr., Wright State U., 1972-76; pub. mem. 10th Jud. Dist. Ethics. Com., 1993—; dir. The Good News Hour, Austin, 1976-83, Minn. Human Rights Commn., Coop. Solutions Mediation Ctr., Austin, Minn., 1995—. With USNR, 1947-52, U.S. Army, 1952-54, USAR, 1954-57, chaplain, col., 1957-90. Mem. Evang. Theol. Soc., Evang. Press Assn., Nat. Assn. Religious Broadcasters, Soc. of Profl. Journalists, Assn. of Former Intelligence Officers, Mil. Chaplains Assn. (pres. Chgo. chpt. 1970-74), hist. socs. Wis., Ohio, S.C. E-mail: waalcorn@wolf.co.net. Home: 1010 7th Ave NW Austin MN 55912-2153 Office: PO Box 733 Austin MN 55912-0733

ALCOSSER, LOIS HARMON, cultural organization administrator; b. N.Y.C., June 15, 1926; d. Harry and Bertha (Lambert) Harmon; m. Albert Alcosser, Mar. 25, 1962; children: Melinda, Andrew. BA, Barnard Coll., 1948. Creative dir. Altman-Stoller, N.Y.C., 1960s; copywriter various advt. agys., N.Y.C., Fairfield, Conn., 1970s; dir. Voluntary Action Ctr., Norwalk, Conn., 1987-91; dir. devel. Coun. Chs. and Synagogues, Stamford, Conn., 1992-96; corporator Griffin Hosp., Derby, Conn. Editor (newsletter) Perspective on Addiction, 1990-97, Council Counsel, 1997—; newspaper columnist Woman, 1985-95, Gardener's Gazette, 1990—. Mem. Conn. Life, Westport Minutemen. Avocations: writing, painting, human development. Home: 11 Willow Rd Weston CT 06883-2534

ALCOTT, AMY STRUM, professional golfer; b. Kansas City, Mo., Feb. 22, 1956; d. Eugene Yale and Leatrice (Strum) A. Profl. golfer Ladies Profl. Golf Assn., 1975—; spokesperson Countrywide Funding Corp., 1980—; winner U.S. Golf Assn. Jr. Girl's Title, 1973; winner 32 profl. titles including Can. Open-Peter Jackson Classic, 1979, Women's U.S. Open, 1980, Nabisco-Dinah Shore Invitational, 1980, 88, Mitsukoshi Ladies Open, 1982, Tucson Open, 1985, Moss Creek Invitational, 1985, World Championship of Women's Golf, 1985, Mazda Champions, 1986, Mazda Hall of Fame Championship, LPGA Nat. Pro-Am., 1986-88. Named Rookie of Year Ladies Profl. Golf Assn., 1975, Player of Yr. Ladies Profl. Golf Assn., 1980; Player of Year Golf mag., 1980; Jewish Athlete of Year, 1980; named to Calif. Golf Writers Hall of Fame, 1987, World Golf Hall of Fame, 1999; recipient Seagrams Seven Crown of Sports award, 1980, Vare Trophy, 1980, Ladies Pro Golf Assn. Founders Cup award, 1986, Humanitarian award Jr. C. of C., 1995. Winner U.S. Golf Assn. Jr. Girl's Title, 1971, 30 profl. titles including Can. Open-Peter Jackson Classic, 1979, Women's U.S. Open, 1980, Nabisco-Dinah Shore Invitational, 1983, 88, 91, Tucson Open, 1985, Moss Creek Invitational, 1985, World Championship of Women's Golf, 1985, Mazda Champions, 1986, Mazda Hall of Fame Championship, LPGA Nat. Pro-Am., 1986, Boston Five Classic, 1988. Office: Ladies Profl Golf Assn 100 International Golf Dr Daytona Beach FL 32124-1082 also: LPGA PO Box 956 Pacific Palisades CA 90272-0956*

ALCOTT TEMPEST TEMPLE, LESLIE, artist; b. Oklahoma City, 1951; d. William Joseph and Gretta Atkinson; m. George Arthur Carlson, July 18, 1974 (div. Feb. 1981); children: Solon Emil Carlson, Andra Sean Carlson. Student, Colo. Women's Coll., U. Denver, 1969-70; BS, Oklahoma City U., 1973; postgrad., U. Ctrl. Okla., Edmond, 1973-74; studied sculpture with, Bruno Lucchesi, N.Y., Italy; studied painting, sculpture, and anatomy with, Jon Zahourek. Cert. in concrete work City of Denver and State of Colo.; cert. tchr. elem. edn., Okla. Multi-medium artist, 1965—; adult reading tchr. Oscar Rose Jr. Coll., Midwest City, Okla., 1971; author, 1971—; art tchr. Oklahoma City Fine Arts Mus., 1972; bus. mgr. and mktg. dir. for artist George Carlson Elizabeth and Frankton, Colo., 1974-80; tchr. art and art history 2d grade Our Lady of Lourdes Sch., 1988, tchr. Tarahumara, AABTT, 1997—; pres., CEO SLA Concrete Constrn., Inc., 1990-96; pres. S L A Arch/Couture, Inc., Denver, 1981—; mem. adv. com. Colo. Dept. Transp., 1991-92; lectr. art, human sci. of relations. Author: The Tarahumara, 1977, Body of Work, 1981, Amer. Art Dir., 1999, Portrait of a Mus., 1989, Natl. Libr. of Poetry, 1997, Art in Process, 1990: exhibited in shows including Catherine Lorillard Wolfe 92d Ann., N.Y.C., N.Am. Sculpture Exhbn., High Plains Sculpture Exhbn., Greely Invitation (Best of Show 1983), Am. Artists Profl. League 60th Grand Nat. Exhbn., Salmagundi Club, N.Y., 1988; represented in corp. and pvt. collections including Nat. Jewish Med. and Rsch. Ctr., JRS Exploration Co. LTD, Calgary, Geoevalaciones, So. America, Founders Corp., N.Y.C., J. Serrano, Mexico City & Fla., The Andrews Group Internat., Inc., Houston, No. Geophys., Inc., Anchorage, Patricia Ellison, MD, World Summit of the Eight,Founders Corp. Coll., 5 State Profl. Photography Exhibition, 1997, 99, 1st Natl. Denver Dark Room, 1998, Museo de las Americas, 1997, Tarahumara Indian Exhibit, 1997-98, others; featured in permanent collection monumental sculptor Western history dept. Denver Pub. Libr., Mus. Outdoor Art; contbr. to Nat. Libr. Poetry. Mem. audience devel. and pub. rels. coms. Denver Art Mus., 1993—; vol. Denver Safe House, 1980—, Oklahoma City Fine Arts Mus., also tchr.; Spkr.'s Bur. of Heart Paths, Head Start Program, 1969-74, Denver Indian Ctr., Denver Pub. Sch. Sys., Denver Christian H.S., others; inner-active trustee Denver Art Mus., 1993-94, audience devel. com.; tribal diplomat govt. offices and Native Am. tribal leaders, 1981—; mem. mktg. com. Artists of Am. Exhbn., 1997, 99, docent, 1998; tribal diplomat, adv. civil, women's, and children's rights, 1981—. Summer scholar Oklahoma City U., North Amer. Poetry Competition Finalist, 1997. Mem. Museo de las Ams., Denver Art Mus., Denver Art Students League, Sister Cities Internat., Natural History Mus., Women Constrn. Owners and Execs. (founding mem., officer), Artists of Am. (mktg. com. 1999). Avocations: art philosophy as life, research in psychology, physics, symbolism, ethnology and ethnography. Fax: (303) 282-9202. Home and Studio: 2088 S Pennsylvania Denver CO 80210 Office: Am Assn Benefit Tarahumara Ind. 501 C-3 dba AABTT Tara Humana 2088 S Pennsylvania Denver CO 80210-4034 also: Forest Fenn Pvt Dealer 1021 Old Sante Fe Trail Santa Fe NM 87501

ALDA, ALAN, actor, writer, director; b. N.Y.C., Jan. 28, 1936; s. Robert and Joan (Browne) A.; m. Arlene Weiss; children: Eve, Elizabeth, Beatrice. BS, Fordham U., 1956, hon. degree, 1978; hon. degree, Drew U., 1979, Columbia U., 1979, Conn. Coll., 1980, Kenyon Coll., 1982. Ind. actor stage, screen, TV, 1956—; tchr. Compass Sch. Improvisation. Actor: (Broadway plays) including The Apple Tree (nominated Tony award), The Owl and the Pussycat, Purlie Victorious, Fair Game for Lovers, Jakes Women (Tony award nominee), Art, (films) including Gone Are the Days, 1963, The Moonshine War, Paper Lion, 1968, The Extraordinary Seaman, 1968, Jenny, 1970, The Mephisto Waltz, 1971, To Kill a Clown, 1972, California Suite, 1978, Same Time, Next Year, 1978, Crimes and Misdemeanors, 1989 (D.W. Griffith award, N.Y. Film Critics award), Whispers in the Dark, 1992, Manhattan Murder Mystery, 1993, Canadian Bacon, 1995, Flirting With Disaster, 1996, Everyone Says I Love You, 1996, Murder at 1600, 1997, Mad City, 1997, The Object of My Affection, 1998; (TV movies) include The Glass House, 1972, Marlo Thomas and Friends in Free to be...You and Me, 1974, 6 Rms Riv Vu, 1974, Kill Me If You Can, And The Band Played On, 1993 (Emmy nomination, Supporting Actor - Special, 1994), White Mile, 1994; star: (TV series, as Benjamin Franklin "Hawkeye" Pierce) M*A*S*H, 1972-83 (5 Emmy awards, 5 Golden Globe awards, Humanitas award for writing); creator: (TV series) We'll Get By, 1975, The Four Seasons; writer,(narrator) Scientific American Frontiers, 1993—, actor: (film) The Seduction of Joe Tynan, 1979; actor, writer, dir.: (films) The Four Seasons, 1981, Sweet Liberty, 1986, A New Life, 1987, Betsy's Wedding, 1990. Presdl. appointee Nat. Commn. for Observance of Internat. Women's Yr., 1976; co-chair Nat. ERA Countdown Campaign, 1982; trustee Mus. of TV and Radio, 1985, Rockefeller Found., 1989. Recipient Theatre World award for Fair Game for Lovers, 7 People's Choice awards; elected to TV Acad. Hall of Fame, 1994. Mem. AFTRA, Dirs. Guild Am. (awards 1977, 82), Writers Guild Am. (award 1977), Screen Actors Guild, Actors Equity Assn.

ALDAG, RAMON JOHN, management and organization educator; b. Beccles, Suffolk, Eng., Feb. 11, 1945; came to U.S., 1947; s. Melvin Frederick and Joyce Evelyn (Butcher) A.; m. Hollis Maura Jellinek, June 11, 1977; children—Elizabeth, Katherine. B.S., Mich. State U., 1966, M.B.A., 1968, Ph.D., 1974. Thermal engr. Bendix Aerospace div., Ann Arbor, Mich., 1966-70; teaching asst., instr. Mich. State U., East Lansing, Mich., 1966-73; asst. prof. mgmt. U. Wis., Madison, 1973-78, assoc. prof., 1978-82, prof. mgmt. and orgn., 1982—, chmn. dept. mgmt., 1986-88, assoc. dir. Indsl. Rels. Rsch. Inst., 1977-83, co-dir. Ctr. for Study of Orgnl. Performance, 1982—, faculty senator, 1980-84, Pyle Bascom prof. leadership, 1992—, student advisor, 1979—, chmn. dept. mgmt. and human resources Sch. Bus., 1995—; mgmt. cons. various businesses and industries, 1973—. Author: Task Design and Employee Motivation, 1979, Managing Organizational Behavior, 1981, Introduction to Business, 1984, (now titled Business in a Changing World), 3d edit., 1993, 4th edit., 1996, Management, 1987, 2d edit., 1991; contbr. articles to profl. jours.; cons. editor for mgmt. South-Western Pub. Co., 1987—; assoc. editor Jour. Bus. Rsch., 1988—; essays co-editor Jour. Mgmt. Inquiry. Bd. dirs. Family Enhancement Program, Madison, 1981—. Grantee U. Wis., HEW, 1975-85; recipient Adminstrv. Rsch. Inst. award, 1976, Jerred Disting. Svc. award, 1993; U. Wis. faculty rsch. fellow, 1985-88; Fellow. Acad. of Mgmt. (div. chmn. 1971—, bd. govs. 1986—, v.p. and program chair 1989—, pres. elect 1990, pres. 1991, past pres. 1992—, recipient Disting Svc. award, 1995); mem. Midwest Acad. Mgmt. (pres. 1973—), Decision Scis. Inst. (track chmn. 1975—), Indsl. Rels. Rsch. Assn. (elections commn. 1980—), Found. Adminstrn. Rsch. (pres. 1992—), Pi Tau Sigma, Tau Beta Pi, Sigma Iota Epsilon, Beta Gamma Sigma, Alpha Iota Delta. Avocations: running; gardening; fishing. Home: 2818 Van Hise Ave Madison WI 53705-3620 Office: U Wis 3112 Grainger Hall 975 University Ave Madison WI 53706-1324

ALDAVE, BARBARA BADER, law educator, lawyer; b. Tacoma, Dec. 28, 1938; d. Fred A. and Patricia W. (Burns) Bader; m. Ralph Theodore Aldave, Apr. 2, 1966; children—Anna Marie, Anthony John. BS, Stanford U., 1960; JD, U. Calif.-Berkeley, 1966. Bar: Oreg. 1966, Tex. 1982. Assoc. law firm Eugene, Oreg., 1967-70; asst. prof. U. Oreg., 1970-73; vis. prof. U. Calif., Berkeley, 1973-74; from vis. prof. to prof. U. Tex., Austin, 1974-89, coholder James R. Dougherty chair for faculty excellence, 1981-82, Piper prof., 1982, Joe A. Worsham centennial prof., 1984-89, Liddell, Sapp, Zivley, Hill and LaBoon prof. banking financial and comml. law, 1989; dean Sch. Law, prof. St. Mary's U., San Antonio, 1989-98, Ernest W. Clemens prof. corp. law, 1996-98; vis. prof. Northeastern U., 1985-88, 98; vis. prof. Boston Coll. 1999; ABA rep. to Coun. Inter-ABA, 1995—; NAFTA chpt. 19 panelist, 1994-96. Pres. NETWORK, 1985-89; chair Gender Bias Task Force of Supreme Ct. Tex., 1991-94; bd. dirs. Tex. Alliance Children's Rights, Assn. Religiously Affiliated Law Schs., Lawyer's com. for Civil Rights Under Law of Tex. Recipient tchg. excellence award U. Tex. Student Bar Assn., 1976, Appreciation awards Thurgood Marshall Legal Soc. of U. Tex., 1979, 81, 85, 87, Tchg. Excellence award Chicano Law Students Assn. of U. Tex., 1984, Hermine Tobolowsky award Women's Law Caucus of U. Tex., 1985, Ethics award Kugle, Stewart, Dent & Frederick, 1988, Leadership award Women's Law Assn. St. Mary's U., 1989, Ann. Inspirational award Women's Advocacy Project, 1989, Appreciation award San Antonio Black Lawyers Assn., 1990, Spl. Recognition award Nat. Conv. Nat. Lawyers Guild, 1990, Spirit of the Am. Woman award J. C. Penney Co., 1992, Sarah T. Hughes award Women and the Law sect. State Bar Tex., 1994, Ann. Tchg. award Soc. Am. Law Tchrs., 1996, Legal Svcs. award Mexican-Am. Legal Def. and Ednl. Fund, 1996, Woman of Justice award NETWORK, 1997, Ann. Peacemaker award Camino a la Paz, 1997, Outstanding Profl. in the Cmty. award Dept. Pub. Justice, St. Mary's U., 1997, Charles Hamilton Houston award Black Allied Law Students Assn. St. Mary's U., 1998, Woman of Yr. award Tex. Women's Polit. Caucus, 1998, award Clin. Legal Edn. Assn., 1998, lifetime achievement award Jour. Law and Religion, 1998. Mem. ABA (com. on corp. laws sect., banking and bus. law 1982-88), Bexar County Women's Bar Assn. (Belva Lockwood Outstanding Lawyer award 1991), San Antonio Bar Assn., World Affairs Coun. San Antonio, Harlan Soc., Tex. Women's Forum, Stanford U. Alumni Assn., Alamo Telecomms. coun., Tex. Appleseed, Tex.-Mexico Bar Assn., San Antonio Bar Found., Order of Coif, Phi Delta Phi, Iota Sigma Pi, Omicron Delta Kappa, Delta Theta Phi (Outstanding Law Prof. award St. Mary's U. chpt. 1990, 91). Roman Catholic. Home: 323 W Woodlawn Ave San Antonio TX 78212-3312 Office: 950 Massachusetts Ave # 517 Cambridge MA 02139

ALDCROFT, GEORGE EDWARD, guidance counselor; b. Toronto, Ont., Can., Nov. 29, 1941; s. George and Margaret Aldcroft; BS in Edn., Wayne State U., 1966; MS in Guidance and Counseling, U. Mich., 1971; postgrad. Gestalt Center L.I.; m. Bernadette M. Cartoski, Nov. 27, 1971; children: Allison Marie, Bonnie Christine. Nat. cert. counselor, nat. cert. sch. counselor; cert. leader developing capable people. Elem. and jr. high sch. tchr. Ctr. Line (Mich.) Pub. Sch. System, 1967-72; summer camp counselor and vol. worker Boys' Clubs Met. Detroit, 1967-69; guidance dir. Shelter Island (N.Y.) Union Free Sch. Dist., 1972-83; sch. counselor Westhampton Beach (N.Y.) Union Free Sch. Dist., 1983-89; sch. counselor Mattituck Cutchogue Sch. Dist., 1989—. Mem. Shelter Island Drug Edn. Com., 1974, Southold Union Free Sch. Dist. Bd. Edn., 1983-86; bd. dirs. Human Understanding and Growth Seminars (H.U.G.S.), 1985—, pres. bd. dirs. 1991-92. Recipient Outstanding Vol. Leader award Boys' Clubs Detroit, 1968. Mem. N.Y. State Counseling Assn., N.Y. State Sch. Counselor's Assn. (region VI gov.), East End Counselors Assn. (pres. 1995-97), Am. Sch. Counselors Assn., U. Mich. Alumni Assn., Outward Bound Assn., N.Y. State United Tchrs. Roman Catholic. Home: PO Box 431 Peconic NY 11958-0431 Office: Mattituck-Cutchogue Sch Dist Main Rd Cutchogue NY 11935

ALDEN, PETER CHARLES, author, naturalist; b. Concord, Mass., July 8, 1944; s. John Coppins and Evelyn Elizabeth (Engborg) A. BA in Geography, L.Am. Studies, U. Ariz., 1967. Internat. tour leader Mass. Audubon Soc., Lincoln, 1968-82; with Lindblad Travel, Inc., Westport, Conn., 1982-89; dir. ecotourism Overseas Adventure Travel, Cambridge, Mass., 1991-94; internat. tour leader Harvard U./Friends of Harvard Mus. Natural History, Cambridge, 1992—. Author: Finding Birds in Western Mexico, 1969, Finding Birds Around the World, 1981, Peterson First Guide to Mammals, 1987, Field Guide to African Wildlife, 1995, F. G. to New England, 1998, F. G. to Florida, 1998, F. G. to California, 1998, F. G. to Pacific Northwest, 1998, F. G. to Rocky Mountains, 1999, F. G. to Southwest, 1999, F. G. to Southeast, 1999, F. G. to Middle Atlantic, 1999, (video) Gone Birding: The VCR Game, 1989. Mem. Am. Birding Assn., Nuttall Ornithol. Club, Harvard Travellers Club (v.p. 1980-82). Democrat. Achievements include founding of Biodiversity Day, 1998. Avocations: bird watching, world travel, photography. Home: 11 Riverside Ave Concord MA 01742-3026

ALDEN, STEVEN MICHAEL, lawyer; b. Los Angeles, May 19, 1945; s. Herbert and Sylvia Zina (Hochman) A.; m. Evelyn Mae Subotky, Dec. 31, 1977; children: Carissa Louise, Bramley Marshall, Darym Alexander. AB,

UCLA, 1967; JD, U. Calif.-Berkeley, 1970. Bar: Calif. 1971, N.Y. 1971. Assoc. Debevoise & Plimpton, N.Y.C., 1971-78, ptnr., 1979—; lectr., seminar panelist Practising Law Inst., N.Y.C., 1981—; panelist, lectr. N.Y. State Bar, Albany, 1984. Contbr. articles to profl. jours., 1982-83. Mem. ABA (real estate fin. com.), Assn. of Bar of City of N.Y. (com. real property law), Am. Land Title Assn. (assoc. lender's counsel group), Am. Coll. Real Estate Lawyers, Order of Coif, Phi Beta Kappa. Republican. Club: Board Room (N.Y.C.). Office: Debevoise & Plimpton 875 3rd Ave Fl 23 New York NY 10022-6256

ALDEN, VERNON ROGER, corporate director, trustee; b. Chgo., Apr. 7, 1923; s. Arvid W. and Hildur Pauline (Johnson) A.; m. Marion Frances Parson, Aug. 18, 1951; children: Robert Parson, Anne Elizabeth, James Malcolm, David Douglas. AB magna cum laude, Brown U., 1945; MBA, Harvard, 1950; LLD (hon.), Brown U., 1964, Emerson Coll., 1957, Ohio Wesleyan U., 1964, R.I. Coll., 1965, William Jewell Coll., 1965, Loyola U., 1966, Wilberforce U., 1970, Ottawa U., 1970, Babson Coll., 1972; LHD, North Park Coll., 1965; LittD, Ohio U., 1969; DPS, Bowling Green U., 1969; LittD, Bethany Coll., 1970. Admission officer Brown U., 1946-48; asst. dir. admissions Northwestern U., 1950-51; dir. fin. aid Harvard Grad. Sch. Bus. Adminstrn., assoc. dean, faculty, 1951-61; ednl. dir. U. Hawaii Advanced Mgmt. Program, summer 1960, Keio U. Advanced Mgmt. Program, Tokyo, summers 1960-61; pres. Ohio U., Athens, 1962-69; chmn. bd., chmn. exec. com. Boston Co. and subsidiary Boston Safe Deposit & Trust Co., 1969-78; bd. dirs. Colgate-Palmolive Co., Digital Equipment Corp., Intermet Corp., Sonesta Internat. Hotels Corp., Tax-Free Trust Funds Hawaii, Oreg. and Rhode Island, ML-Lee Fund, Ind. Gen. Ptnrs.; hon. consul-gen. Kingdom of Thailand. Chmn. Pres.' Task Force Job Corps Program, com. Future of U. Mass, 1971, chmn. Mass. Coun. Arts/Humanities, 1972-84, Mass. Bus. Devel. Coun./Fgn. Bus. Coun., 1978-83; life trustee Boston Symphony Orch., Mus. Sci., Boston; chmn. arts facilities com. MIT; fellow emeritus Brown U.; chmn. exec. com., life trustee French Libr., Boston; adv. com. Harvard Program Japan-U.S. Rels. Lt. USNR, 1943-46. Recipient Gov.'s award State Ohio, 1969; Founder's citation Ohio U., 1969; Bus. Statesman award Harvard Grad. Sch. Bus., 1975; named Hon. Consul-Gen. Kingdom of Thailand; decorated Order Rising Sun, Star (Japan), Most Noble Order of the Crown of Thailand, Disting. Civilian Svc. medal U.S. Army, Most Exalted Order of the White Elephant (Thailand). Mem. Nat. Assn. Japan-Am. Socs. (chmn.), Japan Soc. of Boston (chmn.), Somerset Club (Boston), Edgartown Yacht Club (Martha's Vineyard), Country Club (Brookline), Farm Neck Golf Club (Martha's Vineyard), Mariner Sands (Fla.) Country Club, Phi Beta Kappa, Phi Kappa Phi, Phi Delta Theta, Beta Gamma Sigma. Episcopalian. Avocations: golf, tennis, reading. Home: 37 Warren St Brookline MA 02445-5925 Office: 20 Park Plz Ste 1010 Boston MA 02116-4398

ALDER, BERNI JULIAN, physicist; b. Duisburg, Germany, Sept. 9, 1925; came to U.S., 1941, naturalized, 1944; s. Ludwig and Ottilie (Gottschalk) A.; m. Esther Berger, Dec. 28, 1956; children—Kenneth, Daniel, Janet. B.S., U. Calif., Berkeley, 1947, M.S., 1948; Ph.D., Calif. Inst. Tech., 1951. Instr. chemistry U. Calif., Berkeley, 1951-54; theoretical physicist Lawrence Livermore Lab., Livermore, Calif., 1955-93; prof. dept. applied sci. U. Calif., Davis, 1987-93, prof. emeritus, 1993; van der Waals prof. U. Amsterdam, Netherlands, 1971; prof. associé U. Paris, 1972; G.N. Lewis lectr. U. Calif., Berkeley, 1984, Hinshelwood prof., Oxford, 1986, Lorentz prof., Leiden, 1990, Kistiakowsky lectr. Harvard U., 1990, Royal Soc. lectr., 1991. Author: Methods of Computational Physics, 1963; editor: Jour. Computational Physics, 1966-91. Served with USN, 1944-46. Guggenheim fellow, 1954-55; NSF sr. postdoctoral fellow, 1963-64, Japanese Promotion of Sci. fellow, 1989. Fellow Am. Phys. Soc.; mem. Nat. Acad. Scis., Am. Chem. Soc. (Hildebrand award 1985). Republican. Jewish. Office: Lawrence Livermore Lab PO Box 808 Livermore CA 94550

ALDERDICE, CYNTHIA LOU, artist; b. Des Moines, Mar. 16, 1932; d. Charles Lloyd and Marion Maxine (Hinn) Sandahl; m. Lee Edward Alderdice, Jan. 30, 1954; children: Cheryl Lynn, Kirk Bryan. BA, U. Tex., 1957. Pres. Am. Art Assocs., Inc., Bethesda, Md., 1966-92; v.p. Am. Art Make-A-Frame, Inc., Rockville, Md., 1972-97; pres. Am. Art Assocs., Inc., Annapolis, Md., 1997—; v.p., bd. dirs. Pyramid Atlantic, Inc., Riverdale, Md., 1994—; com. mem. Jewelry from Walters Art Gallery and Zucker Family Collection, 1987, Greek Gold from Beenaki Mus., 1991; com. mem. tarnished vistas Hist. Annapolis, Md., 1988. One-woman shows include: Touchstone Gallery, Washington, 1993, 95, Marion Price Contemporary Fine Art Gallery, Centreville, Md., 1995, U. Md., University College, Annapolis, 1996, Md. Fedn. of Art, Annapolis, 1997, Touchstone Gallery, Washington, 1997, Robert C. Williams Am. Museum of Papermaking, Atlanta, 1998, Richards Gallery, Westbrook Gallery, Robert Ferst Ctr. for the Arts, Atlanta, 1998, Air Gallery, Annapolis, 1998, Zaruba Gallery, Rockville, Md., 1999, others; exhibited in group shows Mus. Contemporary Art, Chamalieres, France, 1991, Walters Art Gallery, Balt., 1991, Inst. of the Arts George Mason U., Fairfax, Va., 1995, Montpelier Cultural Arts Ctr., Laurel, Md., 1995, Tarrytown Gallery, Austin, Tex., 1995, Fairbanks Arts Assn., Alaska, 1997, Melvin Art Gallery, Lakeland, Fla., 1997, Towson State U., Md., 1997, Montgomery Coll., Rockville, Md., 1997, Corcoran Mus. Art, Washington, 1997, Fernbank Mus. of Natural History, Atlanta, 1997, 98, Ann Arundel C.C., Annapolis, Md., 1997, 98, Tallahassee Museum of Natural History, 1998, Fed. Res. Bd., Washington, 1998, Washington Arts Club, 1998, Manhattan Graphics Ctrs., N.Y.C., Loyola Coll. Art Gallery, Five Md. Printmakers, Md., The Arts Club Washington, Md. Hall for Creative Arts, Annapolis, Howard County Ctr. for Arts, Ellicott City, Md., Mary Condon hodges Gallery, Frederick, Md., Cade Fine Arts Ctr. Gallery, Annapolis, McLean Project for Arts, Va.; numerous others; permanent collections include Musee d'Art Contemporain of Chamalieres, France, Artist Book Collection Balt. Mus. Art, Md. Fedn. Art, 1991, Internat. Monetary Fund Collection, Washington, Freddie Mac's Collection Honoring Washington Artists, U. Md., The Jane Voorhees Silmmerli Art Mus., N.J., Robert C. Williams Am. Mus. Papermaking, Ga. Tech. Univ. Recipient individual artist award Md. Arts Coun., 1992. Mem. Md. Fedn. Art (pres., bd. dirs. 1985-87), Md. Printmakers, So. Graphics Art Coun., Friends Cardinal Gallery (hon.), Friends of Dard Hunter. Avocations: tennis, swimming, reading, working on computer. Studio: Annapolis Bus Pk 2104 Renard Ct Annapolis MD 21401-6748

ALDERDICE, DOUGLAS ALAN, secondary education educator; b. Buffalo, May 26, 1964; s. Lawrence Gilchrist and Carol Isabelle (Maas) A. BA, Susquehanna U., 1986; MS in Edn., Canisius Coll., 1993. Cert. secondary math. tchr., N.Y. Tchr. computers, coord. computer svcs. Buffalo Bd. Edn., 1986—. Mem. Am. Radio Relay League, Antique Telephone Collectors Assn., Buffalo Amateur Radio Repeater Assn. (v.p. 1988-89, pres. 1989-94, editor jour. 1994—), Lafayette High Sch. Alumni Assn. (alumni liaison 1987—), Morse Telegraph Club. Republican. Presbyterian. Avocations: amateur radio, photography, model railroading, classical organ playing. Office: Lafayette High Sch 370 Lafayette Ave Buffalo NY 14213-1494

ALDERFER, CLAYTON PAUL, organizational psychologist, educator, author, consultant, administrator; b. Sellersville, Pa., Sept. 1, 1940; s. Joseph Paul and Ruth Althea (Buck) A.; m. Charleen Judith Frankenfield, July 14, 1962; children: Kate, Benjamin. BS with high honors, Yale U., 1962, PhD, 1966. Cert. Am. Bd. Profl. Psychology. Asst. prof. Cornell U., Ithaca, N.Y., 1966-68; asst. prof. Yale U., New Haven, 1968-70, assoc. prof., 1970-78; prof. Sch. Orgn. Mgmt., Yale U., New Haven, 1978-92, assoc. dean, 1982-84; prof. Grad. Sch. Applied and Profl. Psychology Rutgers U., 1992—, dir. Orgnl. Psychology program, 1992—. Author: Existence, Relatedness and Growth, 1972, Learning from Changing, 1975; contbr. articles to profl. jours.; mem. editl. bd. Jour. Applied Behavioral Sci., 1978-89, editor, 1990—; mem. editl. bd. Family Bus. Rev., 1987—, Jour. Orgnl. Behavior, 1988-92; editor: Advances in Experiential Social Processes, vol. 1, 1979, vol. 2, 1980. Bd. dirs. NTL Inst., Arlington, Va., 1975-78, DATA, New Haven, 1989-92. Grantee Office Naval Research, 1970-74, 79-80, 82-86; recipient Cattell award, 1972, McGregor award, 1979, Levinson award, 1997, Helus award, 1999. Fellow Am. Psychol. Assn., Soc. Applied Anthropology, Am. Psychol. Soc.; mem. Sigma Xi, Tau Beta Pi. Independent. Lutheran. Office: Rutgers Grad Sch Applied Profl Psychology 152 Frelinghuysen Rd Piscataway NJ 08854-8020

ALDERMAN, BISSELL, architect; b. Holyoke, Mass., Sept. 19, 1912; s. George P. B. and Hortense B. (Goslee) A.; m. Mary Evelyn Compton, Nov. 16, 1935 (dec. Jan. 1995); children: Jean A. Hazen, Mary A. Lord, Holly C. BArch, MIT, 1935, MArch, 1937, traveling fellow, 1937-38. Registered architect, N.H. Mem. faculty MIT, 1938, 41-43, U. Wash., 1939-41; ptnr. Alderman & Mac Neish, 1951-78; trustee Williston Acad., 1952-68. Important works (in Mass.) include Weymouth Libr., Medford Libr., Mohawk Trail Regional H.S., Buckland, Minnechaug H.S., Wilbraham, Algonquin H.S., Northboro, Assabet Regional H.S., Marlboro, Thorton W. Burgess Sch., Hampden, Dudley/Charlton Regional H.S., North Shore Regional Vocat. H.S., Beverly; also Monadnock Bank, Jaffrey, N.H., Korea-Vietnam Meml. Park, Jaffrey, Berger-Lahr Mfg. Plant, Jaffrey, Alderman Park, Jaffrey, Hutter Co. Hdqrs., New Ipswich, N.H., Millard Corp. Hdqrs., Peterborough, N.H., Jaffrey Bible Ch. Trustee Williston Acad., 1952-68; trustee, past pres. Sharon (N.H.) Arts Ctr. With USAAF, 1943-45. Decorated Medal of Freedom; recipient hon. mention William and Mary Festival Theater Competition, 1938, Smithsonian Art Gallery Competition, 1939. Fellow AIA (past pres. Western Mass. chpt.); mem. Mass. Assn. Architects (past pres.), Boston Soc. Architects, Tau Sigma Delta, Kappa Sigma. Congregationalist. Home: 183 Old Dublin Rd Peterborough NH 03458

ALDERMAN, CHARLES WAYNE, university dean; b. Mobile, Ala., Oct. 10, 1950; s. Charles B. and E. Mae (Henderson) A.; m. Mary Noel Perritt. BS, Auburn U., 1971, MBA, 1972; D in Bus. Adminstrn., U. Tenn., 1977. CPA, cert. internal auditor. Sr. auditor Ernst & Young, Birmingham, Ala., 1973-75; asst. prof. U. Tex., 1978-79; asst. prof. Auburn (Ala.) U., 1979-82, assoc. prof., 1982-87, Coopers & Lybrand prof., dir. Sch. Accountancy, 1987-89, assoc. dean Coll. Bus., 1990-93, dean bus., south trust endowed prof., 1993—; bd. dirs. Auburn Bank. Co-author: Accounting Information Systems, 1982, 86, 90, Auditing, 1987, 90, 93, 96, 99; contbr. articles to profl. jours. Ernst & Young grantee, 1976-77. Mem. AICPA (bd. examiners 1995-98), Ala. Soc. CPAs, Am. Acctg. Assn., Mortar Board, Omicron Delta Kappa, Phi Gamma Delta (faculty advisor 1982—). Presbyterian. Office: Auburn U Coll Bus Auburn AL 36849

ALDERMAN, MINNIS AMELIA, psychologist, educator, small business owner; b. Douglas, Ga., Oct. 14, 1928; d. Louis Cleveland Sr. and Minnis Amelia (Wooten) A. AB in Music, Speech and Drama, Ga. State Coll., Milledgeville, 1949; MA in Supervision and Counseling Psychology, Murray State U., 1960; postgrad. Columbia Pacific U., 1987—. Tchr. music Lake County Sch. Dist., Umatilla, Fla., 1949-50; instr. vocal and instrumental music, dir. band, orch. and choral Fulton County Sch. Dist., Atlanta, 1950-54; instr. English, speech, debate, vocal and instrumental music, dir. drama, band, choral and orch. Elko County Sch. Dist., Wells, Nev., 1954-59; tchr. English and social studies Christian County Sch. Dist., Hopkinsville, Ky., 1960; instr. psychology, counselor critic prof. Murray (Ky.) State U., 1961-63, U. Nev., Reno, 1963-67; owner Minisizer Exercising Salon, Ely, Nev., 1969-71, Knit Knook, Ely, 1969—, Minimimeo, Ely, 1969—, Gift Gamut, Ely, 1977—; prof. dept. fine arts Wassuk Coll., Ely, 1986-91, assoc. dean, 1986-87, dean, 1987-90; counselor White Pine County Sch. Dist., Ely, 1960-68; dir. Child and Family Ctr., Ely Indian Tribe, 1988-93, Family and Cmty. Ctr., Ely Shoshone Indian Tribe, 1988-93, Family Resource Ctr., Great Basin Rural Nev. Youth Cabinet, 1996—; adv. Ely Shoshone Tribal Youth Coun., 1990-93, Budge Stanton Meml. Scholarship, 1991-93, Budge Stanton Meml. Living Mus. and Cultural Ctr., 1991-93; fin. aid contracting officer Ely Shoshone Tribe, 1990-93; instr. No. Nev. C.C., 1995—; supr. testing Ednl. Testing Svc., Princeton, N.J., 1960-68, Am. Coll. Testing Program, Iowa, 1960-68, U. Nev., Reno, 1960-68; chmn. bd. White Pine Sch. Dist. Employees Fed. Credit Union, Ely, 1961-69; psychologist mental hygiene div. Nev. Pers., Ely, 1969-75, dept. employment security, 1975-80; sec.-treas. bd. dirs. Gt. Basin Enterprises, Ely, 1969-71; speaker at confs.; rep. Ely/East Ely Bus. Coun., 1997—; mem. Econ. Devel. Bd., 1998—. Author various news articles, feature stories, pamphlets, handbooks and grants in field. Pvt. instr. piano, violin, voice and organ, Ely, 1981—; dir. Family Resource Ctr. (Great Basin Rural Nev. Youth Cabinet), 1996—; bd. dirs. band Sacred Heart Sch., Ely, 1982—; mem. Gov.'s Mental Health State Commn., 1963-65, Ely Shoshone Tribal Youth Camp, 1991-92, Elys Shoshone Tribal Unity Conf., 1991-92, Tribal Parenting Skills Coord., 1991; bd. dirs. White Pine County Sch. Employees Fed. Credit Union, 1961-68, pres., 1963-68; 2d v.p. White Pine Community Concert Assn., 1965-67, pres., 1967, 85—, treas., 1975-79, dr. chmn., 1981-85; chmn. of bd., 1984; bd. dirs. White Pine chpt. ARC, 1978-82; mem. Nev. Hwy. Safety Leaders Bd., 1979-82; mem. Gov.'s Commn. on Status Women, 1968-74, Gov.'s Nevada State Juvenile Justice Adv. Commn., 1992-94, White Pine Overall Econ. Devel. Plan Coun., 1992-99; sec.-treas. White Pine Rehab. Tng. Ctr. for Retarded Persons, 1973-75; mem. Gov.'s Commn. on Hwy. Safety, 1979-81, Gov.'s Juvenile Justice Program; sec.-treas. White Pine County Juvenile Problems Cabinet, 1994—; dir. Ret. Sr. Vol. Program, 1973-74; vice chmn. Gt. Basin Health Coun., 1973-75, Home Extension Adv. Bd., 1977-80; sec.-treas. Great Basin chpt. Nev. Employees Assn.; bd. dirs. United Way, 1970-76; vice chmn. White Pine Coun. on Alcoholism and Drug Abuse, 1975-76, chmn., 1976-77, White Plains County Bus. Coun., 1998—; grants author 3 yrs. Indian Child Welfare Act, State Hist. Preservation, Fair and Recreation Bd. Centennial Fine Arts Ctr.; originator Community Tng. Ctr. for Retarded People, 1972, Ret. Sr. Vol. Program, 1974, Nutrition Program for Sr. Citizens, 1974, Sr. Citizens Ctr., 1974, Home Repairs for Sr. Citizens, 1974, Sr. Citizens Home Assistance Program, 1977, Creative Crafters Assns., 1976, Inst. Current World Affairs, 1989, Victims of Crime, 1990-92, grants author Family Resource Ctr., 1995; bd. dirs. Family coalition, 1990-92, Sacred Heart Parochial Sch., 1982—, dir. band, 1982—; candidate for diaconal ministry, 1982-93; dir. White Pine Community Choir, 1962— invited performer Branson Jubilee Nat. Ch. Choir Festival, Mo., Ely Meth. Ch. Choir, 1960-84; choir dir., organist Sacred Heart Ch., 1984—. Precinct reporter ABC News 1966; speaker U.S. Atty. Gen. Conf. Bringing Nev. Together; bd. dirs. White Pine Juvenile Cabinet, 1993—, Ely/East Ely Bus. Coun., 1997—, Econ. Devel. Bd., 1998—. Recipient Recognition rose Alpha Chi State Delta Kappa Gamma, 1994; mem. adv. com. William Bee Ririe Hosp., 1996—, Ea. Nev. Child and Family Svcs., 1996—. Fellow Am. Coll. Musicians, Nat. Guild Piano Tchrs.; mem. NEA (life), UDC, DAR, Nat. Fedn. Ind. Bus. (dist. chair 1971-85, nat. guardian coun. 1985—, state guardian coun. 1987—), AAUW (pres. Wells br. 1957-58, pres. White Pine br. 1965-66, 86-87, 89-91, 93—, bd. dirs. 1965-87, rep. edn. 1965-67, implementation chair 1967-69, area advisor 1969-73, 89-91), Nat. Fedn. Bus. and Profl. Women (1st v.p. Ely chpt. 1965-66, pres. Ely chpt. 1966-68, 74-76, 85—, bd. dirs. Nev. chpt. 1966—, 1st v.p. Nev. Fedn. 1970-71, pres. Nev. chpt. 1972-73, nat. bd. dirs. 1972-73), White Pine County Mental Health Assn. (pres. 1960-63, 78—), Mensa (supr. testing 1965—), Delta Kappa Gamma (br. pres. 1968-72, 94—, state bd. 1967—, chpt. parliamentarian 1974-78, state 1st v.p. 1967-69, state pres. 1969-71, nat. bd. 1969-71, state parliamentarian 1971-73, 95—, chmn. state nominating com. 1995-97, workshop presenter on aging S.W. Regional Conf. San Francisco 1995), White Pine Knife and Fork Club (1st v.p. 1969-70, pres. 1970-71, bd. dirs. 1979—), Soc. Descendants of Knights of Most Noble Order of Garter, Nat. Soc. Magna Charta Dames, Delta Kappa Gamma. Office: PO Box 150457 East Ely NV 89315-0457 *My mission in this life: To use to the fullest good, the talents and abilities that have been given me in order to productively help whenever and wherever the opportunity arises.*

ALDERMAN, RHENUS HOFFARD, III, investment company executive; b. Roanoke, Va., Dec. 16, 1926; s. Rhenus Hoffard Jr. and Virginia (Allen) A.; m. Mary Elizabeth Malin, Dec. 28, 1957; children: Elizabeth Allen, Rhenus H. IV, Sarah Malin. BS, Ga. Inst. Tech., 1953; MBA, U. Mich., 1963. Trainee GE Co., Lynn, Mass., 1953-54; sales exec. John Hancock Mut. Life Ins. Co., Boston, 1954-64; asst. v.p. Citibank N.A., N.Y.C., 1964-80; sr. v.p. The Merchants Bank & Trust Co., Norwalk, Conn., 1980-90; pres. Investors Capital Mgmt., Inc., Rowayton, Conn., 1990—. Past pres., treas. Alcoholism & Drug Dependency Coun., Westport, Conn., 1995-96. With U.S. Army, 1944-45. Mem. Am. Pension Conf., Am. Arbitration Assn., Norwalk Yacht Club. Home: 156 Mariomi Rd New Canaan CT 06840-3311 Office: Investors Capital Mgmt Inc 71 Rowayton Ave Norwalk CT 06853-1644

ALDERMAN, WALTER ARTHUR, JR., computer company and corporate rescue executive; b. Stoneham, Mass., July 29, 1945; s. Walter Arthur and Ida Ellen (Patchett) A.; m. Sandra May Johnston, Aug. 23, 1969; children: Walter Arthur III, Deborah Ellen. BSBA with honors, Northeastern U., 1968; MBA, Harvard U., 1971. Divisional controller Anken Industries, Williamstown, Mass., 1971-73; treas., controller James Hunter Machine Co., North Adams, Mass., 1973-78; gen. mgr. Petricca Industries, Pittsfield, Mass., 1978-80; chmn., pres. Alderman Assocs. Inc., Coral Springs, Fla., 1980-85, Bedford Computer Corp., 1985-90; owner, pres. Paragon Pub. Systems, Bedford, 1990—; bd. dirs. Mahoney and Assocs., Inc., Springfield, Mass.; instr., mem. adv. bd. North Adams (Mass.) State Coll., 1976-78; registered rep. First New England Securities, Stockbridge, Mass., 1968-74. Bd. dirs. Mass. C. of C., 1976-78, YMCA, 1976-78; sect. leader United Fund, Mass., 1977; mem. N.H. Industry and Tech. Partnership, 1992—. Recipient Outstanding Svc. award C. of C., 1978, Community Svc. award United Fund, 1977, Blue Chip Enterprise award U.S. C. of C., 1993; named Turnaround Entrepreneur of Yr., Arthur Young and Venture mag., 1987, New Eng. and N.H. Small Bus. Exporter of Yr., SBA, 1992, Master Entrepreneur, Ernst & Young, Merrill Lynch and Inc. mag., 1991. Mem. Turnaround Mgmt. Assn., Phi Kappa Phi, Beta Gamma Sigma. Avocations: sports, coaching, bridge, chess, reading. Office: Paragon Pub Sys Bedford NH 03110

ALDERN, ROBERT JUDSON, architectural, liturgical and landscape artist; b. Sioux Falls, S.D., Jan. 16, 1929; s. John Olson and Emma (Dahl) A.; m. Joey Marlys Grunwald, Dec. 27, 1951; children: Bradley (dec.), Marlys, Noreen, Jared. Student, Augustana Coll., Sioux Falls, S.D., 1947-51; BFA, U. Hartford, 1957. Draftsman Spitznagel, Inc., Sioux Falls, 1957-61; dir. Civic Fine Arts Ctr., Sioux Falls, 1963-66; artist-in-residence S.D. State U., Brookings, 1966-68; prof. art U. S.D., Vermillion, 1968-80, chmn. art dept., 1968-73; chmn. dept. art Augustana Coll., 1980-88, prof. art, 1988-91, artist-in-residence, 1991—; dir. Liturgical Resource Ctr., 1991—; dir.; owner, operator Aldern Art Studio, Sioux Falls, 1957—; liturgical artist-cons. St. Michael's Cath. Ch., Gloria Dei Luth. Ch., Holy Spirit Cath. Ch., Sioux Falls. Prin. works include sound baffle design St. Mary's Cath. Ch., Sioux Falls, 1959 (Silver medal N.Y. Archtl. League), (murals) Our Savior's Luth. Ch., Sioux Falls, Grace Luth. Ch., Sturgis, S.D., Plains Clinic, Sioux Falls, First Luth. Ch., St. Peter, Minn., Augustana Coll. Chapel, Sioux Falls, Luther Ctr., Uermillion, Sch. of Mines and Tech., Rapid City, King of Glory Luth. Ch., Dallas, Sioux Valley Hosp., Sioux Falls, Good Samaritan Corp. Offices, Sioux Falls, McKennan Hosp., Sioux Falls, Gloria Dei Luth. Ch., Sioux Falls, Christ the King Catholic Church, Sioux Falls, St. John the Bapt. Cath. Ch., Groton, S.D. Bd. dirs. S.D. Art Mus., Brookings, 1995—, Civic Fine Arts Ctr., Sioux Falls, 1998—. Active USAF, 1951-54. S.D. Arts Coun. grantee, 1985; recipient Silver medal N.Y. Archtl. League, 1959, , Alumni Achievement award Augustana Coll., Sioux Falls, 1977, Creative Achievement award Gov. of S.D., 1997, Spitznagel award, 1997. Lutheran. Office: Augustana Coll 29th and Summit Sioux Falls SD 57197

ALDERSON, GLORIA FRANCES DALE, rehabilitation specialist; b. Rainelle, W.Va., May 11, 1945; d. Orval Rupert and Juanita Rose (Nelson) Dale; m. Grayson Raines Alderson, June 3, 1964; children: John Grayson, James Leslie. ADN, U. Charleston; BS, W.Va. U. Diplomate Am. Bd. Disability Analysts. DON Charleston Area Med. Ctr., Charleston, 1977-84; head nurse Eye & Ear Clinic, Charleston, 1981-84; owner, operator ABZ Nursing, Kanawha County, W.Va., 1983-87; rehab. specialist W.Va., 1983—; bd. dirs. Profl. and Social Com. on Nursing. Bd. dirs. Urban Politics Symposium, Charleston, 1978; election campaign mgr. Rep. Party, Charleston. Bd. Regents scholar, W.Va. U., 1974-77; named Woman of Yr., Am. Biographical Assn., 1996-97, Internat. Ambassador with hn. title HE, Cambridge, Eng. and the Crown, 1998. Mem. AAUW, Am. Rehab. Profls., Am. Bd. Disability Analysts (cert., life), Internat. Soc. Poets (Nominee Poet of Yr. 1997), Internat. Platform Assn., Menniger Soc., Order Ea. Star. Avocations: painting, writing. Home and Office: 1089 Highland Dr Saint Albans WV 25177-3675

ALDERSON, PHILIP OTIS, radiologist, educator; b. San Francisco, Aug. 11, 1944; s. Lloyd I. and Helen (Boekemeier) A.; m. Marjorie Jean Hawkins, June 13, 1970; children: Lisa Joanne, Kelly Suzanne. AB in Zoology, Washington U., St. Louis, 1966, MD, 1970. Diplomate Am. Bd. Nuclear Medicine, Am. Bd. Radiology (Diagnosis). Intern Jewish Hosp., Washington U. Med. Sch., St. Louis, 1970-71, resident in radiology and nuclear medicine, 1971-74; instr. in radiology Mallinckrodt Inst., Washington U. Med. Sch., St. Louis, 1974-75; from asst. to assoc. prof., dept. radiology Johns Hopkins Med. Inst., Balt., 1977-80; prof. radiology Columbia-Presbyn. Med. Ctr., N.Y.C., 1980—, James Picker prof., chmn. dept. radiology, 1990—; cons. Bur. Radiol. Health, FDA, Rockville, Md., 1980-82, mem. radiopharm. adv. com., 1980-82; trustee Am. Bd. Radiology, 1998—, Am. Bd. Nuclear Medicine, 1989-95; invited spkr. numerous internat. confs.; holder 6 named lectureships. Author 4 books; contbr. numerous scientific articles to profl. jours. Maj. USAF, 1975-77. Recipient Alumni Achievement award Wash. U. Med. Sch., 1995; NIH grantee, 1974—. Fellow Am. Coll. Radiology (bd. chancellors 1993—), Am. Coll. Nuclear Physicians, N.Y. Acad. Medicine; mem. Fleischner Soc. (sec. 1989-92, treas. 1996-99), N.Y. City Roentgen Soc. (v.p. 1989-90, pres. 1991-92), N.Y. State Radiol. Soc. (sec.-treas. 1991-93, pres. 1993-94), Soc. Nuclear Medicine (v.p. 1984-85, chmn. sci. program com. 1984-86), Assn. Univ. Radiologists (sec.-treas. 1994-95, pres. 1996-97), Assn. Residency Program Dirs. in Radiology (sec.-treas. 1996-97, pres. 1998-99), Am. Roentgen Ray Soc. (chmn. exec. coun. 1997-98), Acad. Radiology Rsch. (sec. 1998—), Soc. Chmn. Acad. Radiology Depts. (rep. Coun. Acad. Socs. of Am. Assn. Med. Colls. 1990-95, pres. 1994-95), Omicron Delta Kappa. Office: Columbia-Presbyn Med Ctr Dept Radiology 630 W 168th St New York NY 10032-3702

ALDINGER, WILLIAM F., III, banker; b. 1947. BA, CUNY, 1969. With U.S. Trust Co., N.Y.C., 1969-75, Citibank Corp., N.Y.C., 1975-76; exec. v.p. Wells Fargo Bank NA, San Francisco, 1986-98; CEO Household Internat., Inc., 1994—, chmn. bd. dirs., 1996-97. Office: Wells Fargo Bank 464 California St Ste 100 San Francisco CA 94104-1287 Office: Household Internat 2700 Sanders Rd Prospect Heights IL 60070-2701*

ALDISERT, RUGGERO JOHN, federal judge; b. Carnegie, Pa., Nov. 10, 1919; s. John S. and Elizabeth (Magnacca) A.; m. Agatha Maria DeLacio, Oct. 4, 1952; children: Lisa Maria, Robert, Gregory. B.A., U. Pitts., 1941, J.D., 1947. Bar: Pa. bar 1947. Gen. practice law Pitts., 1947-61; judge Ct. Common Pleas, Allegheny County, 1961-68; judge U.S. Ct. Appeals (3d cir.), Pitts., 1968-84, chief judge, 1984-87; sr. judge U.S. Ct. Appeals (3d cir.), Pitts., Sanat Barbara, Calif., 1987—; adj. prof. law U. Pitts. Sch. Law, 1964-87 ; faculty Appellate Judges Seminar, NYU, 1971-85 , assoc. dir., 1979-85 ; lectr. internat. seminar legal medicine U. Rome, 1965, Law Soc. London, 1967, Internat. seminar comparative law, Rome, 1971; chmn. Fed. Appellate Judges Seminar; bd. dirs. Fed. Jud. Center, Washington, 1974-79; mem. Pa. Civil Procedural Rules Com., 1965-84 Jud. Conf. Com. on Adminstrn. Criminal Law, 1971-77; chmn. adv. com. on bankruptcy rules Jud. Conf. U.S., 1979-84; lectr. univs. in U.S. and abroad. Author: Il Ritorno al Paese, 1966-67, The Judicial Process, Readings, Materials and Cases, 1976, Logic for Lawyers: A Guide to Clear Legal Thinking, 1989, Opinion Writing, 1990, Winning on Appeal, 1992. Allegheny dist. chmn. Multiple Sclerosis Soc., 1961-68; pres. ISDA, Cultural Heritage Found., 1965-68; trustee U. Pitts., 1968—; chmn. bd. visitors Pitts. Sch. Law, 1978—. Served to maj. USMCR, 1942-46. Recipient Outstanding Merit award Allegheny County Acad. Trial Lawyers, 1964. Mem. Inst. Jud. Adminstrn., Am. Law Inst., Italian Sons and Daus. of Am. (nat. pres. 1954-68), Italian Sons and Daus. Am. Fraternal Assn. (nat. pres. 1960-68), Phi Beta Kappa, Phi Alpha Delta, Omicron Delta Kappa. Democrat. Roman Catholic. Home: PO Box 3810 Santa Barbara CA 93130-3810 Office: US Ct Appeals 120 Cremona Dr Ste D Santa Barbara CA 93117-5511*

ALDISS, BRIAN (WILSON), writer; b. East Dereham, Norfolk, Eng., Aug. 8, 1925; s. Stanley and May (Wilson) A.; children from previous marriage: Clive, Caroline Wendy; m. Margaret Christie Manson, Dec. 11, 1965 (div. Nov. 1997); children: Timothy Nicholas, Charlotte May. Lit. editor Oxford Mail, 1957-69; editor sci. fiction novels Penguin Books Ltd., London, 1961-64; art corr. The Guardian, London, 1971-80; judge Booker-McConnell Prize, 1981; v.p. West Buckland Sch., 1997—. Author: (novels) The Brightfount Diaries, 1955, Non-Stop, 1958 (Prix Jules Verne 1977), Starship, 1959, Vanguard from Alpha, 1959, Bow Down to Nul (published in Eng. as The Interpreter, 1961), 1960, The Male Response, 1961, The Primal Urge, 1961, The Long Afternoon of Earth (published in Eng. as Hothouse, 1962), 1962 (Hugo award for best short fiction World Sci. Fiction Conv. 1962), The

Dark Light Years, 1964, Greybeard, 1964, Earthworks, 1965, The Saliva Tree, and Other Strange Growths, 1966 (Nebula award for best novella Sci. Fiction Writers Am. 1966), An Age, 1967 (published as Cryptozoic!, 1968), Report on Probability A, 1968, A Brian Aldiss Omnibus, 1969, Barefoot in the Head: A European Fantasia, 1969, The Hand-Reared Boy, 1970, A Soldier Erect, 1971, Brian Aldiss Omnibus 2, 1971, Frankenstein Unbound, 1973, The Eighty-Minute Hour: A Space Opera, 1974, The Malacia Tapestry, 1976, Brothers of the Head, 1977, A Rude Awakening, 1978, Enemies of the System: A Tale of Homo Uniformis, 1978, Life in the West, 1980, Moreau's Other Island, 1980 (published as An Island Called Moreau 1981), Helliconia Spring, 1982 (John W. Campbell Meml. award for best novel 1982, Brit. Sci. Fiction Assn. award for best fiction 1982, Kurd Lasswitz award 1984), Helliconia Summer, 1983, Helliconia Winter, 1985 (BSFA award best novel 1986), The Year Before Yesterday: A Novel in Three Acts, 1987, Ruins, 1987, Forgotten Life, 1988, Cracken at Critical: A Novel in Three Acts, 1989, Dracula Unbound, 1992, Remembrance Day, 1993, Somewhere East of Life, 1994; (non-fiction) Cities and Stones: A Traveller's Yugoslavia, 1966, The Shape of Further Things, 1970, Billion Year Spree: The History of Science Fiction, 1973 (BSFA Spl. award 1974, Coneta D'Argento Italy, 1977, Eurocon III award 1976), Science Fiction Art, 1975, This World and Nearer Ones: Essays Exploring the Familiar, 1979, Pile: Petals from St. Klaed's Computer, 1979, The Pale Shadow of Science, 1985, ...And the Lurid Glare of the Comet, 1986, (with David Wingrove) Trillion Year Spree: The History of Science Fiction, 1986, Bury My Heart at W.H. Smith's, 1990 (Hugo award Best Nonfiction 1987, Locus award Best Nonfiction 1987, J. Lloyd Eaton Meml. award Best Critical Work of Yr. 1988), Home Life with Cats, 1992, At the Caligula Hotel, 1995, The Detached Retina, 1995, Songs from the Steppes of Central Asia, 1996, The Twinkling of an Eye, 1998, When the Feast if Finished, 1999, The Squire Quartet, 1999; (story collections) Space, Time and Nathaniel, 1957, The Canopy of Time, 1959, No Time Like Tomorrow, 1959, Galaxies Like Grains of Sand, 1960, The Airs of Earth, 1963, Starswarm, 1964, Best Science Fiction Stories of Brian Aldiss, 1965 (published as Who Can Replace a Man?, 1966), Intangibles Inc., and Other Stories: Five Novellas, 1969, Neanderthal Planet, 1969, The Moment of Eclipse, 1971 (Brit. Sci. Fiction Assn. award 1972), The Book of Brian Aldiss, 1972 (published in Eng. as Comic Inferno, 1973), Last Orders and Other Stories, 1977, New Arrivals, Old Encounters, 1979, Foreign Bodies, 1981, Seasons in Flight, 1984, Best Science Fiction Stories of Brian W. Aldiss, 1988, Science Fiction Blues: The Show that Brian Aldiss Took on the Road, 1988, A Tupolev Too Far, 1993, The Secret of This Book, 1995, Common Clay, 1996; co-editor several anthologies including SF Master series, 1976-79, Best Science Fiction annuals, 1967-75, Decades SF, 1975-77, World Omnibus of Science Fiction, 1986; played roadshow Science Fiction Blues, 1986-95; appeared in play Kindred Blood, Kensington Gate, Fla. and London, 1992; contbr. numerous stories to periodicals and books. Served Brit. Army, Indian Army, 1943-46. Decorated Burma Star; recipient Observer award for sci. fiction, 1956, Ditmar award for world's best contemporary sci. fiction author, 1970, James Blish award for excellence in sci. fiction criticism, 1977, Internat. Assn. for Fantastic in the Arts Disting. Scholarship award, 1986; named Most Promising New Author of Yr., World Sci. Fiction Conv., 1958. Fellow Royal Soc. Lit.; mem. Internat. Inst. Study of Time, Internat. Assn. for the Fantastic in Arts, World Sci. Fiction Soc. (pres. 1982-84), Brit. Sci. Fiction Assn. (pres. 1960-64, Britain's Most Popular Sci. Fiction Author Spl. award 1964), Sci. Fiction Writers Am., Sci. Fiction Rsch. Assn. (Pilgrim award 1978), Soc. Authors (chmn. 1977-78, Arts Coun. Gt. Britain (lit. panelist 1978-80), Cultural Exchs. Com. (chmn.), Sci. Fiction Theatre of Liverpool (officer mem.), H.G. Wells Soc. (pres. 1994—). Office: Hambelden, 39 St Andrews Rd Old Headington, Oxford OX3 9DL, England

ALDOVER-AYON, MARTA, critical care nurse; b. Batangas City, Philippines, Jan. 19, 1951; d. Aurelio T. and Vicenta C. (Espino) Aldover; m. Lucito P. Ayon, Mar. 31, 1984; children: Oliver, April. BSN, Pamantasan ng Lungsod ng Maynila, Manila, Philippines, 1972. RN, Pa., N.J.; cert. critical care nurse, basic cardiac life support, instr. advanced cardiac life support. Staff nurse Bapt. Med. Ctr., Little Rock; charge nurse Parkview Hosp., Phila., 1975-77; clin. nurse II, advanced staff nurse, clin. staff nurse III Thomas Jefferson U. Hosp., Phila., 1977-88; adminstrn. nursing supr. Thomas Jefferson Univ. Hosp., Phila., 1988—. Recipient Full Scholarship, 1967-72, Outstanding Staff Nurse award, 1987. Mem. Am. Assn. Critical Care Nurses. Home: 12 Knoll Ct Sewell NJ 08080-3218

ALDREDGE, THEONI VACHLIOTIS, costume designer; b. Athens, Greece, Aug. 22, 1932; d. Gen. Athanasios and Meropi (Gregoriades) Vachliotis; m. Thomas E. Aldredge, Dec. 10, 1953. Student, Am. Sch., Athens, 1949-53, Goodman Theatre, Chgo.; LHD, De Paul U., 1985. Mem. design staff Goodman Theatre, 1951-53; head designer N.Y. Shakespeare Festival, 1962—. Designer numerous Broadway and off Broadway shows, ballet, opera, TV spls.; films include Girl of the Night, You're a Big Boy Now, No Way to Treat a Lady, Uptight, Last Summer, I Never Sang for My Father, Promise at Dawn, The Great Gatsby (Brit. Motion Picture Acad. award 1976), Network, The Cheap Detective, The Fury, The Eyes of Laura Mars (Acad. Sci. Fiction Films award), The Champ, Semi-Tough, The Rose, Monsignor, Annie, Ghostbusters, Moonstruck, We're No Angels, Stanley and Iris, Other People's Money, Night and the City, Addams Family Values, Milk Money, Mrs. Winterbourne, The Mirror Has Two Faces, The First Wives Club; over 100 Broadway shows include A Chorus Line (Theatre World award 1976), Annie (Tony award 1977), Barnum (Tony award 1979), Dream Girls, Woman of the Year, Onward Victoria, La Cage Aux Folles (Tony award 1984), 42d Street, A Little Family Business, Merlin, Private Lives, The Corn Is Green, The Rink, Blithe Spirit, Chess, Gypsy (1989 revival), Oh, Kay, The Secret Garden, Nick and Nora, High Rollers, Putting It Together, Annie Warbucks, The Flowering Peach, School for Scandal, Taking Sides, The Three Sisters, St. Louis Woman, "EFX" MGM Grand. Recipient Obie award for Disting. Svc. to Off-Broadway Theatre Village Voice, Maharam award for Peer Gynt, N.Y.C. Liberty medal, 1986, numerous Drama Desk and Critic awards; inducted into Theatre Hall of Fame. Mem. United Scenic Artists, Costume Designers Guild, Acad. Motion Picture Arts Scis. (Oscar award Great Gatsby 1975).

ALDRICH, ANN, federal judge; b. Providence, June 28, 1927; d. Allie C. and Ethel M. (Carrier) A.; m. Chester Aldrich, 1960 (dec.); children: Martin, William; children by previous marriage: James, Allen; m. John H. McAllister III, 1986. BA cum laude, Columbia U., 1948; LLB cum laude, NYU, 1950, LLM, 1964, JSD, 1967. Bar: D.C. bar, N.Y. bar 1952, Conn. bar 1966, Ohio bar 1973, Supreme Ct. bar 1956. Research asst. to mem. faculty N.Y. U. Sch. Law; atty. IBRD, 1952; atty., rsch. asst. Samuel Nakasian, Esq., Washington, 1952-53; mem. gen. counsel's staff FCC, Washington, 1953-60; U.S. del. to Internat. Radio Conf., Geneva, 1959; practicing atty. Darien, Conn., 1961-68; asso. prof. law Cleve. State U., 1968-71, prof., 1971-80; judge U.S. Dist. Ct. (no. dist.) Ohio, Cleveland, 1980—; bd. govs. Citizens' Communications Center, Inc., Washington; mem. litigation com.; guest lectr. Calif. Inst. Tech., Pasadena, summer 1971. Mem. Fed. Bar Assn., Nat. Assn. of Women Judges, Fed. Communications Bar Assn., Fed. Judge Assn. Episcopalian. Office: US Dist Ct 201 Superior Ave E Cleveland OH 44114-1201

ALDRICH, BAILEY, federal judge; b. Boston, Apr. 23, 1907; s. Talbot and Eleanor (Little) A.; m. Elizabeth Perkins, Aug. 13, 1932; children: Jonathan, David. AB, Harvard U., 1928, LLB, 1932. Bar: Mass. 1932. With Choate, Hall & Stewart, Boston, 1932-54; judge U.S. Dist. Ct. Mass., 1954-59, U.S. Ct. Appeals, 1959-64; chief judge U.S. Ct. Appeals (1st cir.), 1965-72, now sr. judge, 1972—. Mem. Am. Law Inst., Am. Acad. Arts and Scis. Home: 120 Brattle St Cambridge MA 02138-3423 Office: US Courthouse 1 Courthouse Way Ste 8740 Boston MA 02210

ALDRICH, C. ELBERT, real estate broker; b. Rosebud, Tex., Sept. 12, 1923; s. Murdock Collins and Mamie (Mock) A.; m. Dorothy Ann Cox, June 30, 1947; children: Ann Aldrich Dunn, Amy Aldrich Thomas. Student, Temple Jr. Coll., 1946-47. Co-owner M.C. Aldrich & Son, Temple, Tex., 1946-65; pres. Elbert Aldrich Realtor, Inc., Temple, 1965—; bd. dirs. 1st Fed. Savs. & Loan, Temple, Temple Indsl. Found. Served with USN, 1942-46, PTO. Decorated D.F.C.; named Realtor of Yr., Temple Bd. Realtors, 1971, 73, 77, Farm and Land Broker of Yr., Tex. chpt. Farm and Land Inst., 1979. Mem. Realtors Land Inst. (regional v.p. 1977-79, pres. Tex. chpt. 1978), Soc. Indsl. Realtors (pres. South Cen. Tex. chpt. 1989-90), Realtors Nat. Mktg. Inst. (cert.), Tex. Assn. Realtors (bd. dirs. 1965), Nat. Assn. Realtors, Temple C. of C. (v.p. 1973-75), Sons of Republic of Tex. Baptist. Lodges: Rotary, Masons, Shriners, Descendents of San Jacinto. Home: 510 Blackfoot Dr Temple TX 76504-3727 Office: 18 N 3rd St Temple TX 76501-7617

ALDRICH, DAVID ALAN, accountant; b. West Haven, Conn., Jan. 14, 1958; s. Harold and Janet (Candia) A. BS in Fin. Acctg., U. New Haven, 1980; BS in Profl. Acctg., Tampa Coll., 1990. CPA, Fla. Acct. State Nat. Bank of Conn., Bridgeport, 1981-82, Coordinated Benefit Plans Inc., Tampa, Fla., 1984-85, N.Am. Telephone, Tampa, 1986; acctg. mgr. Coordinated Benefit Plans Inc., Tampa, 1987-90; acct. Payroll Transfers, Inc., Tampa, 1991—. Mem. AICPA, Fla. Inst. CPAs. Home: 11261 Riddle Dr Spring Hill FL 34609-3439

ALDRICH, DAVID LAWRENCE, public relations executive; b. Lakehurst Naval Air Sta., N.J., Feb. 21, 1948; s. Clarence Edward and Sarah Stiles (Andrews) A.; m. Benita Susan Massler, Mar. 17, 1974. BA in Communications, Calif. State U.-Dominguez Hills, 1976. Pub. info. technician City of Carson (Calif.), 1973-77; pub. rels. dir./adminstrv. asst. Calif. Fed. Savs., L.A., 1977-78; v.p., group supr. Hill & Knowlton, L.A., 1978-81; v.p., mgr. Ayer Pub. Rels. western div. N.W. Ayer, L.A., 1981-84; pres. Aldrich and Assocs. Inc., L.A., 1984—; bd. dirs., exec. com. Drum Corps Internat. Bd. dirs. Long Beach (Calif.) Housing Devel. Co.; mayor's task force for strategic planning Long Beach; docent Long Beach Aquarium of the Pacific. Home: 25 15th Pl Unit 704 Long Beach CA 90802-6061 Office: Aldrich & Assocs 110 Pine Ave Ste 620 Long Beach CA 90802-4423

ALDRICH, FRANK NATHAN, banker; b. Jackson, Mich., June 8, 1923; s. Frank Nathan and Marion (Butterfield) A.; m. Edna Dora DeJan, Nov. 21, 1956; children: Marion Dolores, Clinton Pershing. Student, U. Md., summer 1943; A.B. in Govt, Dartmouth Coll., 1948; postgrad., Harvard U., summer 1948. Sub-mgr. First Nat. Bank of Boston, Havana, Cuba, 1949-60, Rio de Janeiro, Brazil, 1961-62; sub-mgr. First Nat. Bank of Boston, Sao Paulo, Brazil, 1963-64, mgr., 1965, exec. mgr. Rio de Janeiro, 1966, v.p. Brazilian brs., 1966-69; v.p. overseas ops. First Nat. Bank of Boston, Boston, 1969-70; v.p. Latin Am.-Asia-Africa-Middle East div., Boston, 1970-73; sr. v.p. Latin Am. div., Boston, 1973-88; pres., CEO McLaughlin Bank N.V., Netherland Antilles, 1989-96; CEO Amicorp N.V., Netherlands Antilles, 1996—; dir. Paradigm Fin. Svcs., Netherlands Antilles. Trustee Pan Am. Devel. Found., Washington. With USAAF, 1943-46. Decorated Air medal with 4 oak leaf clusters, D.F.C. U.S.; Medalha Marechal Candido Mariano da Silva Rondon (Brazil); Ordem Nacional do Cruzeiro do Sul (Brazil). Fellow Brit. Interplanetary Soc.; mem. Air Force Assn., Res. Officers Assn., Confederate Air Force, Inst. Navigation, Royal Astron. Soc. Can., Soc. of the Cin., Sphinx Soc., Vets of Battle of the Bulge, Squadron A Assn. of N.Y., Disting. Flying Cross Soc., Harvard Club (Boston), Dartmouth Coll. Club, Yale Club (N.Y.C.), Army and Navy Club (Washington), Wellesley (Mass.) Country Club, Wellesley Coll. Club, Masons, Shriners., Beta Theta Pi. Home: 3 Indian Spring Rd Dover MA 02030-2331

ALDRICH, FRANKLIN DALTON, research physician; b. Detroit, Jan. 25, 1929; s. George Franklin and Ruth Markham (Dalton) A.; m. Margaret Joan Pearson, Mar. 22, 1952; children: Allison Aldrich Cobb, Janet D., George P.; m. Gertrude Suydam Melsom, Mar. 24, 1984. BS, Mich. State U., 1950; MA, Oreg. State U., 1953, PhD, 1954; MD, Case Western Res. U., 1962. Diplomate Am. Bd. Med. Toxicology. Intern U. Iowa Hosps., Iowa City, 1962-63; fellow in medicine U. Colo., Boulder, 1964-65; resident and chief resident Lemuel Shattuck Hosp., Boston, 1969-71; physician Colo. Dept. Pub. Health, Denver, 1966-69; asst. med. dir. MIT, Cambridge, 1971-76; med. dir. Climax (Colo.) Molybdenum Co., 1976-77; health effects research mgr. IBM, Boulder, Colo., 1977-92, ret., 1992; cons. Boulder, 1992—; mem. com. mil. environ. rsch. Nat. Acad. Scis., 1976-80; mem. toxicology adv. com. U.S. Consumer Product Safety Com., 1982-85; clin. assoc. prof. medicine U. Colo. Health Scis. Ctr., Denver. Contbr. articles to profl. jours. Served with AUS, 1954-56. Case Meml. scholar, Mich. State Coll., 1948. Fellow ACP (Mead Johnson resident scholar 1970), Am. Acad. Clin. Toxicology (pres. 1980-82). Episcopalian. Avocations: fishing, amateur radio.

ALDRICH, HARL PRESLAR, JR., retired civil engineer, consultant; b. Spokane, Wash., June 21, 1923; s. Harl Preslar and Lucy Matilda (Cooley) A.; m. Lois Anna Grissel, Feb. 23, 1946; children: Katheryn, Harl III, Barbara, Jean, Kent. SB, MIT, 1947, ScD, 1951. Registered profl. engr., Mass. Asst. prof. soil mechanics MIT, 1951-57; vis. lectr. soil mechanics Harvard U., 1955-56; prin. Haley & Aldrich, Inc., Cambridge, Mass., 1957-92, pres., chmn., 1971-83, chmn., 1983-90; pres. Terra Ins., Ltd., Bermuda, 1981-84. Trustee MIT Corp., 1980-86. With USN, 1944-45. Fellow Am. Cons. Engrs. Coun.; mem. ASCE (hon.), NAE, Boston Soc. Civil Engrs. (pres. 1968-69), MIT Alumni Assn. (pres. 1980-81). Avocations: tennis, travel, genealogy. Home: 91 Rollingwood Ln Concord MA 01742-4301

ALDRICH, JOHN HERBERT, political science educator; b. Pitts., Sept. 24, 1947; s. Herbert Canon and Ruth Eleanor (Taggart) A.; m. Cynthia Kay Aldrich, June 13, 1970; 1 child, David Shawn. B.A., Allegheny Coll., 1969; M.A., U. Rochester, 1971, Ph.D., 1975. Asst. prof. polit. sci. Mich. State U., East Lansing, 1974-78, assoc. prof., 1978-81; assoc. prof. polit. sci. U. Minn., Mpls., 1981-83, prof., 1983-87; prof. Duke U., Durham, N.C., 1987—, chmn. dept. polit. sci., 1992-96, 99—, Pfizer-Pratt univ. prof., 1997—; vis. prof. Harvard U., 1996-97. Co-author: Change and Continuity in the 1980 Elections, 1982, rev. edit., 1983, Change and Continuity in the 1984 Elections, 1986, rev. edit., 1987, Change and Continuity in the 1988 elections, 1990, rev. edit., 1991, Change and Continuity in the 1992 Elections, 1994, rev. edit., 1995, Change and Continuing in the 1996 Elections, 1997, Change and Continuity in the 1996 and 1998 Elections, 1999; author: Before the Convention, 1980, Why Parties?, 1995; co-editor: Am. Jour. Polit. Sci., 1985-87; contbr. articles to profl. jours. Served with U.S. Army, 1970-72, Vietnam. Ctr. for Advanced Study in Behavioral Scis. fellow, 1989-90; NSF rsch. grantee, 1977-79, 81-87; NEH teaching grantee, 1977-79. Mem. Am. Polit. Sci. Assn. (sec. 1993-94, Eulau prize 1990, Kammerer prize 1996, CQ Press award 1996), So. Polit. Sci. Assn. (rec. sec. 1992-93, v.p. 1995-96, pres. 1998-99, Pi Sigma Alpha award 1997). Office: Duke U Dept Polit Sci Durham NC 27708

ALDRICH, MICHAEL RAY, library curator, health educator; b. Vermillion, S.D., Feb. 7, 1942; s. Ray J. and Lucile W. (Hamm) A.; AB, Princeton, 1964; MA, U. S.D., 1965; PhD, SUNY, 1970; m. Michelle Cauble, Dec. 26, 1977. Fulbright tutor Govt. Arts and Commerce Coll., Indore, Madhya Pradesh, India, 1965-66; founder Lemar Internat., 1966-71; mem. faculty Sch. Critical Studies, Calif. Inst. Arts, Valencia, 1970-72; workshop leader Esalen Inst., San Francisco, 1972; co-founder AMORPHIA, Inc., The Cannabis Coop., Mill Valley, Calif., 1969-74; curator Fitz Hugh Ludlow Meml. Libr., San Francisco, 1974—. Freelance writer, photographer, lectr., cons. on drug rsch., and sociolegal reform specializing in drug laws and history to various colls., drug confs., publishers, svc. groups; cons. Commn. of Inquiry into Non-Med. Use of Drugs, Ottawa, Ont., 1973; rsch. aide, select com. on control marijuana Calif. Senate, 1974. Bd. dirs. Ethno-Pharmacology Soc., 1976-83, Nat. Assn. Ethnography & Social Policy, 1997—, Exotic Dancers Alliance, 1997—, Calif. Helping Alleviate Med. Problems, 1997—. Calif. Marijuana Initiative, 1971-74; mem. nat. adv. bd. Nat. Orgn. for Reform of Marijuana Laws, 1976-86; mem. Princeton working group Future of Drug Policy, 1990-93; asst. dir. Nat. Inst. on Drug Abuse AIDS Project Menu, Youth Environment Study, San Francisco, 1987-88; project adminstr. YES Tng. Ctr., 1989, program coord. Calif. AIDS Intervention Tng. Ctr. Inst. for Cmty. Health Outreach, 1990—. Author: The Dope Chronicles 1850-1950, 1979, Coricancha, The Golden Enclosure, 1983; co-author: High Times Ency. of Recreational Drugs, 1978, Fiscal Costs of California Marijuana Law Enforcement, 1986, YES Tng. Manual, 1989, Methods of Estimating Needle Users at Risk for AIDS, 1990; editor: Marijuana Review, 1968-74, Ludlow Library Newsletter, 1974-81; contbg. author: Cocaine Handbook, 1981, 2d edit., 1987, Cannabis in Medical Practice, 1997; mem. editorial rev. bd. Jour. Psychoactive Drugs, 1981—, marijuana theme issue editor, 1988; research photographer Life mag., 1984; contbg. editor High Times, 1979-85; contbr. articles to profl. publs. Office: PO Box 640346 San Francisco CA 94164-0346

ALDRICH, PATRICIA ANNE RICHARDSON, retired magazine editor; b. St. Paul, Apr. 6, 1926; d. James Calvin and Anna Catherine (Eskra) Richardson; m. Edwin Chauncey Aldrich, July 31, 1948; 1 son, Mason Calvin. Student, Stout Inst., 1944-45; BS in Journalism; scholar, Northwestern U., 1948. Editor Child's World News, The Child's World, Inc., Chgo., 1952-57; assoc. editor Home Life mag. Advt. Div., Inc., Chgo., 1957-71, editor, 1971-90, ret., 1990; pres. Aldrich Enterprises, Inc., Chgo. Mem. steering com., publicity chmn. Evanston Urban League, 1961-64. Democrat.

ALDRICH, RICHARD JOHN, agronomist, educator; b. Fairgrove, Mich., Apr. 16, 1925; s. George and Eva Ann (Misner) A.; m. June Ellen Ellison, Apr. 5, 1943; children: Judith Allman, Sharon, Jeffrey. B.S., Mich. State U., 1948; Ph.D., Ohio State U., 1950. Agronomist U.S. Dept. Agr., Rutgers U., New Brunswick, N.J., 1950-57; asst. dir. Agr. Exptl. Sta., Mich. State U., East Lansing, 1957-64; assoc. dir., dean agr. exptl. sta. U. Mo., Columbia, 1964-76; adminstr. CSRS, U.S. Dept. Agr., Washington, 1976-78; prof. agronomy U. Mo., Columbia, 1978-81; research agronomist, prof. SEA-ARS, Dept. Agr.-U. Mo., 1981-87, ret., 1987; cons. OTA, U.S. Congress, 1979, The Standard Oil Co., 1983; mem. adv. com. Fed. Assistance Rev., 1970-71; pres. Agr. Research Inst., 1974-75. Author: Weed Crop Ecology, 1983; co-author: Principles in Weed Management, rev. edit., 1997; editor: Weed Sci. Jour., 1989-94; contbr. articles to profl. jours. Served to 1st lt. USAAF, 1943-46. Fellow AAAS, Weed Sci. Soc. Am.; mem. Am. Soc. Agronomy (dir. 1949-50), Agrl. Research Inst. (pres. 1974-75), Nat. Assn. State Univs. and Land Grant Colls. Home: PO Box 236 Marcell MN 56657-0236 also: 2663 S Fade Dr Green Valley AZ 85614-1151

ALDRICH, RICHARD KINGSLEY, lawyer; b. Denver, Dec. 31, 1943; s. Harold Eugene and Mary Frances (Kingsley) A.; m. Katherine Ann Kirwan, Sept. 26, 1970; children: Amy Marie Aldrich McAffee, Lori Ann Aldrich Selwyn, Sara Kathleen. Student, Tex. Tech. U., 1962-64; BA in History, U. Mont., 1966, JD, 1969. Bar: Mont. 1969, U.S. Dist. Ct. Mont. 1969. Staff atty. Office of Field Solicitor, Dept. of Interior, Billings, Mont., 1969-85, field solicitor, supervising atty., 1985—. Bd. dirs. Billings Pub. Edn. Found., 1992-97, Mont. State U. Parent Assn., Bozeman, 1993-96, Billings Sr. Bronc Booster Club; bd. dirs., pres. Billings Sr. High Parent Adv., 1991-95. Recipient cert. of appreciation, U.S. Dept. Justice, Nat. Park Svc. and U.S. Fish and Wildlife Svc., 1994, 96, Dept. of Interior Merit Svc. award 1998. Mem. ABA (spkr. panel presentation 1997), Mont. State Bar, Phi Delta Phi, Sigma Nu. Avocations: long distance running, skiing, fly fishing, hiking, reading. Office: Dept of Interior Office of Field Solicitor 316 N 26th St Ste 3005 Billings MT 59101-1362

ALDRICH, RICHARD ORTH, lawyer; b. Cambridge, Mass., Feb. 13, 1921; s. Harold Jere and Hazel M. (Orth) A.; m. Lois Anne McKenney, Oct. 16, 1946; children: Hope A., Richard H., Caleb F. B.S., Harvard U., 1942, LL.B., 1948; grad., Advanced Mgmt. Program, 1967. Bar: Mass. 1948. Assoc. Tyler & Reynolds, Boston, 1948-55; asst. counsel John Hancock, Boston, 1955-59; assoc. counsel John Hancock, 1959-66, counsel, 1966—, v.p., 1970-84; of counsel Hale & Dorr, Boston, 1984-85. Mem. Wellesley (Mass.) Town Meeting, 1955-82; mem. Wellesley Bd. Appeal, 1955-74, chmn., 1965-74. Served with USN, 1942-46. Mem. ABA, Mass. Bar Assn., Boston Bar Assn., Assn. Life Ins. Counsel. Republican. Roman Catholic. Clubs: Univ. (Boston); Wellesley Country. Home and Office: 26 Lathrop Rd Wellesley MA 02482-7012

ALDRICH, ROBERT ADAMS, agricultural engineer; b. Veteran Twp., N.Y., Apr. 25, 1924; s. Luman Woodbridge and Mabel Hastings (Gibbs) A.; m. Roberta Ann Bowlby, Aug. 27, 1946; children—Susan Carol, Gail Jessica, Kathleen Lois, Margaret Louise. B.S. in Agrl. Engring, Wash. State U., 1950, M.S., 1952; Ph.D., Mich. State U., 1958. Instr., then asso. prof. agrl. engring. Wash. State U., 1951-58; asso. prof. U. Ky., 1958-59, Mich. State U., 1959-62; asso. prof., then prof. Pa. State U., 1962-79; prof. agrl. engring., head dept. U. Conn., Storrs, 1979-88, prof. dept. nat. rsch., mgmt. and engring., 1988-89, ret., 1989; prin. Aldrich Engring., Mansfield Center, Conn., 1989—. Author papers in field. Served with C.E. AUS, 1942-46. Mem. Am. Soc. Agrl. Engrs., Nat. Soc. Profl. Engrs. Home: 295 Wormwood Hill Rd Mansfield Center CT 06250-1033

ALDRICH, STEPHEN CHARLES, lawyer, judge; b. Mpls., Oct. 28, 1941; s. George Francis and Marjorie Belle (Shimel) A.; m. Myrna Sumption, Sept. 6, 1964; children: Jeffrey Stephen, David George. BA, Grinnell Coll., 1963; JD, U. Minn., 1971. Bar: Minn 1972, U.S. Dist. Ct. Minn. 1975. Staff asst. to Hon. Donald M. Fraser U.S. Congress, Washington, 1965; budget examiner U.S. Office of Mgmt. and Budget, Washington, 1965-67; admissions counselor Grinnell (Iowa) Coll., 1967-68; law clk. to Hon. Philip Neville U.S. Dist. Ct. Minn., Mpls., 1971-72; asst. senate counsel State of Minn., St. Paul, 1972-73; asst. city atty. City of St. Paul, 1973-75; sole practice Mpls., 1975-97; dist. judge Hennepin County, 1997—; mem. Supreme Ct. Bd. on Continuing Legal Edn., St. Paul, 1985-92. Contbr. articles to profl. jours. Mem. City Charter Commn., Mpls., 1972-80; sec., bd. dirs. Powderhorn Devel. Corp. Mpls., 1975-80. Fellow Am. Acad. Matrimonial Lawyers; mem. Hennepin County Bar Assn. (chmn. family law sect. 1985-86, mem. ethics com. 1980-85, 89-96). Mem. United Ch. Christ. Office: Dist Ct C1200 Govt Ctr Minneapolis MN 55497

ALDRICH, THOMAS ALBERT, former brewing executive, consultant; b. Rosebud, Tex., Nov. 30, 1923; s. John Albert and Georgia Opal (Hilliard) A.; m. Virginia Elaine Peterson, Mar. 1, 1944; children: Sharon Aldrich Lingis, Pamela Aldrich Williams, Thomas Charles. Student, Tex. A&M U., 1942-43, U. Chgo., 1943-44; BA in Math., George Washington U., 1961, MS in Bus. Adminstrn., 1968; student, Air War Coll., 1960-61. Commd. 2d lt. USAF, 1944, advanced through grades to maj. gen., 1974, pilot, meteorologist, 1943-57; dep. dir. air operations Air Weather Service, Washington, 1957-60; comdr. 57th Weather Reconnaissance Squadron, Melbourne, Australia, 1962-65; chief mil. employment div. Air Command and Staff Coll., 1965-68; dir. war plans Hdqrs. Mil. Airlift Command, Scott AFB, Ill., 1968-69; comdr. 9th Weather Reconnaissance Wing, McClellan AFB, Calif., 1969-70; vice comdr. USAF Air Weather Service, Scott AFB, Ill., 1970-71, comdr., 1973-74; comdr. U.S. Forces Azores, Portugal, 1971-73; dep. chief of staff plans Hdqrs. Mil. Airlift Command, 1974-75; comdr. 22d Air Force, Travis AFB, Calif., 1975-78; ret., 1978; v.p., corp. rep. Anheuser-Busch Cos., Inc., Sacramento, 1978-94, ret., 1994. Decorated D.S.M., Legion of Merit with oak leaf cluster, Meritorious Service medal. Mem. Nat. Honor Soc., Brewers Inst., Calif. Mfrs. Assn. (bd. dirs.), Calif. C. of C. (bd. dirs.), Air Force Acad. Falcon Found. (bd. dirs.), No. Calif. Ret. Officers Cmty. (vice chmn.), Phi Theta Kappa. Republican. Presbyterian. Home: 659 Lake Wilhaggin Dr Sacramento CA 95864-7226

ALDRICH, THOMAS KNIGHT, physician, scientist; b. Mpls., Sept. 11, 1950; s. C. Knight and Julie H. (Murphy) A.; m. Susan Yelsey, Sept. 16, 1972; children: Katie R., Drew K. BA, Swarthmore Coll., 1972; MD, U. Minn., 1975. Internship and residency Dept. Medicine U. Calif., Irvine, 1975-78; fellow pulmonary/allergy divsn. dept. medicine U. Va., Charlottesville, 1978-80; postdoctoral fellow in physiology U. Pa. Sch. Medicine, Phila., 1980-82; asst. prof. medicine Albert Einstein Coll. Medicine, Bronx, N.Y., 1982-87, assoc. prof. medicine, 1987-93, prof. medicine, 1993—, dir. pulmonary tng. program, 1992—; dir. Unified Pulmonary Med. Disvn. Albert Einstein Coll. Medicine and Montefiore Med. Ctr., Bronx, N.Y. Recipient J. Burns Amberson award N.Y. Lung Assn., 1983, Edward Livingston Trudeau scholar Am. Lung Assn., 1986. Mem. APA, Am. Coll. Chest Physicians, Am. Thoracic Soc., Am. Fedn. for Clin. Rsch. Office: Pulmonary Medicine Div Montefiore Med Ctr 111 E 210th St Bronx NY 10467-2401

ALDRIDGE, ADRIENNE YINGLING, accountant, business analyst; b. Hershey, Pa., June 10, 1959; d. Richard Terry Yingling and Dolores Jean (Ott) Brown. BA in Acctg. summa cum laude, N.C. State U., 1989. CPA, FLMI. Asst. mgr. Fast Fare, Raleigh, 1979-80; statis. analyst S.P.A.R., Elmsford, N.Y., 1980-81; relocation dir., sales assoc. Realty World, Cary, N.C., 1981-83; product mgr. Southeastern Electronics, Raleigh, 1983-84; results acct. No. Telecom, Rsch. Triangle Park, N.C., 1984-88; sr. auditor Deloitte & Touche, 1989-93; group contr. SPAR Mktg., Bloomington, Minn., 1994; pvt. practice, 1995; acctg. mgr. U. N.C. Physicians & Assocs., Chapel Hill, 1996-97, Carolina Power & Light, Raleigh, N.C., 1998—. Mem. AICPA, NCACPA, Phi Kappa Phi, Omicron Delta Epsilon. Avocations: photography, painting, physical fitness, travel, music. Home: 1204 Benoit Pl Apex NC 27502-4047 Office: PO Box 1551 CPB 16B2 411 Fayetteville St Raleigh NC 27602

ALDRIDGE, ALFRED OWEN, English language educator; b. Buffalo, Dec. 16, 1915; s. Albert and Jane (Ette) A.; m. Mary Hennen Dellinger, May 18, 1941 (div. 1956); 1 dau., Cecily (Mrs. John Ward); m. Adriana Garcia Davila, June 7, 1963 (div. 1988). B.S. in Edn, Ind. U., 1937; M.A., U. Ga., 1938; Ph.D., Duke U., 1942; D.U.P., U. Paris, France, 1955. Prof. comparative lit. U. Buffalo, 1942-47, U. Md., 1947-67; prof. comparative lit. U. Ill., 1967-86, prof. emeritus, 1986—; Will and Ariel Durant chair St. Peter's Coll., Jersey City, 1986-87; prof. comp. lit. Pa. State U., 1987-88; Fulbright prof., France, 1953, Korea, 1988; Smith-Mundt prof., Brazil, 1957; vis. prof. Nihon U., Japan, 1976, 82, Kuwait U., 1983, Nat. Cheng Chi U., Taiwan, 1989-90, Nat. Tsing Hua U., Taiwan, 1991. Author: Franklin and His French Contemporaries, 1957, Man of Reason: Life of Thomas Paine, 1959, Jonathan Edwards, 1964, Benjamin Franklin: Philosopher and Man, 1965, Benjamin Franklin and Nature's God, 1967, Comparative Literature: Matter and Method, 1969, The Ibero-American Enlightenment, 1971, Voltaire and the Century of Light, 1975, Hikaku Bungaku: Comparative Literature East and West, 1979, Early American Literature: A Comparatist Approach, 1982, Thomas Paine's American Ideology, 1984, Fiction in Japan and the West, 1985, The Reemergence of World Literature, 1986, The Dragon and the Eagle: China in the American Enlightenment, 1993; editor Jour. Comparative Lit. Studies, 1963—; adv. editor: Tamkang Rev., 18th Century: Theory and Interpretation, Modern Age. NEH fellow 1973-74. Mem. Am. Comparative Lit. Assn. (adv. bd. 1965-71, 74-77, v.p. 1977-80, pres. 1980-83), Internat. Comparative Lit. Assn. (adv. bd. 1970-78), Am. Soc. 18th Century Studies (adv. bd. 1968-75). Home: 101 E Chalmers St Champaign IL 61820-6001 Office: U Ill Modern Lang Bldg Urbana IL 61801

ALDRIDGE, CHARLES DOUGLAS, veterinarian; b. Ardmore, Okla., Nov. 17, 1958; s. Charles Stanton and Mary Ruth (Walcott) A.; m. Marsha Rhenea Lavers, July 24, 1982; children: Kaitlin Annaliese, Chelsea Lizanne, Ethan Douglas, Collin Drake. BS, Okla. State U., 1981, DVM, 1987. Lic. vet., Okla. Assoc. vet. Westwood Vet. Hosp., Ardmore, Okla., 1987-89; pres., vet. Westwood Hosp. of Ardmore, 1989—. Bd. dirs. Ardmore Animal Control Bd., 1994, Ardmore Animal Care, Inc., 1994-97, Ardmore Animal Care Trust Authority, 1994-97. Named Young Veterinarian of Yr. Okla. Vet. Med. Assn., 1998. Mem. Elks. Avocations: bicycling, golf, hunting. Home: 921 Q St SW Ardmore OK 73401-3520 Office: Westwood Vet Hosp 3905 W Broadway St Ardmore OK 73401-9693

ALDRIDGE, CHARLES RAY, brokerage house executive, trade director; b. Jefferson City, Mo., July 23, 1946; s. Ray and Helen Frances (Fowler) A.; m. Jeannine Frances Holtmeier, May 11, 1974; children: Kimberly Rae, Steven Charles. BSBA in Fin., U. Mo., 1969, MA in Polit. Sci., 1973. Mktg. specialist Mo. Dept. Agr., Jefferson City, 1973-74; commodities broker Clayton Brokerage Co. St. Louis Inc., 1974-82; v.p. Stock Index Futures Co. Inc., St. Louis, 1982-87, pres., 1987-90; v.p., dir. trading Alvery Bartlett Brokerage Co., St. Louis, 1982-87, pres., 1987-90; v.p. Mark Twain Brokerage Svcs., Inc., St. Louis, 1990-97, Mercantile Investment Svcs. Inc., St. Louis, 1997—; cons. dir. Lehman Venture Capital, N.Y.C., 1984-89. Contbr. articles to profl. jours. Served with U.S. Army, 1969-71, Vietnam. Decorated Bronze Star. Mem. Phi Delta Theta (pres. Alumni Club 1984-85). Republican. Avocations: golf, tennis, racquetball, basketball. Home: 12548 Clark Manor Cir Creve Coeur MO 63141-6379 Office: Mercantile Investment Svcs 12935 N Forty Dr Saint Louis MO 63141

ALDRIDGE, DAVID, sports announcer; b. Washington, Feb. 10, 1965. BA in Journalism, Am. U., 1987, BA in History, 1987. Sports reporter Washington Post, 1987-96; NBA reporter ESPN, 1996—; reporter ESPN News, 1999—, ESPN II Night, 1999—. Office: c/o ESPN ESPN Plaza Bristol CT 06010*

ALDRIDGE, DONALD O'NEAL, military officer; b. Solo, Mo., July 22, 1932. BA in History, U. Nebr.-Omaha, 1974; postgrad. Creighton U., 1975. Commd. 2d lt. U.S. Air Force, 1958, advanced through grades to lt. gen., 1988; asst. dir. plans U.S. Air Force, Washington, 1978-79; spl. asst. to dir. Joint Chiefs of Staff, Washington, 1979-80; dep. dir. Def. Mapping Agy., Washington, 1980-81; dep. U.S. rep. NATO Mil. Com., Brussels, Belgium, 1981-83; rep. Joint Chiefs of Staff, Geneva, Switzerland, 1983-86; comdr. 1st Strat. Aerospace div. Vandenberg AFB, Calif., 1986-88; vice-CINC Strategic Air Command, Offutt AFB, Nebr., 1988-91; mgmt. cons. Sacramento, Calif., 1991—; chmn. bd. Octus, Inc., 1995-98, Ceracon, Inc., 1996—, dir., Omaha Ops., Marconi Integrated Sys. Office: Aldridge Assocs 159 Orange Blossom Cir Folsom CA 95630-8117 Office: Marconi Integrated Sys 1620 Wilshire Dr Bellevue NE 68005

ALDRIDGE, GEOFFREY, security consultant; b. Lumberton, N.C., Aug. 13, 1942; s. James W. and Vonnie May Aldridge; m. Pamella Gayle Carter, Mar. 24, 1973. AAS, Wake Tech. Coll., Raleigh, N.C., 1977; BA in Criminal Justice and Police Sci., N.C. U., 1988. Capt. Durham (N.C.) County, 1979-82; safety dir. U. N.C. Hosps., Chapel Hill, 1982-94; pres. Security Assessments Internat., Durham, 1994—; assisted more than 400 healthcare facilities throughout the U.S. with their birthing ctr. security; cons. nat. media and law enforcement on infant abduction issues; appeared on ABC 20/20, PM mag.; keynote spkr. for nat. and internat. healthcare orgns.; presenter numerous workshops for state affiliates of Am. Hosp. Assn. throughout the U.S.; provider collaborative assistance for clients in Eng., Ireland, and Australia; nat. expert in the field of healthcare security; tech. advisor Nat. Ctr. for Missing and Exploited Children; authority on infant abduction prevention; expert on violence in the healthcare setting and emergency dept. security; mem. child exploitation subcom. Eastern Dist. N.C., U.S. Dept. Justice, 1990. Contbr. articles to profl. jours. including Security Mgmt., Access Control & Security Sys. Integration, Jour. Healthcare Protection Mgmt., Security Mgmt. Mem. Internat. Narcotic Enforcement Officers Assn., Nat. Assn. Drug Diversion Investigators, Assn. Soc. for Indsl. Security (certr. protection profl., CPP program chmn. N.C. Rsch. Triangle Park chpt. nat. standing com. on child abduction 1989), Internat. Assn. Hosp. Security and Safety, N.C. Safety Security Healthcare Coun. (pres. 1986-88), Southeastern Safety Security Healthcare Coun. (bd. dirs. 1989—). Republican. Baptist. Avocations: photography, amateur radio. Office: Security Assessments Internat 906 W Maynard Ave Durham NC 27704-3030

ALDRIDGE, JOHN, lawyer; b. Durham, N.C., Jan. 31, 1943. BA, Duke U., 1965; JD with honors, U. N.C., 1968. Bar: Ga. 1968, D.C. 1969. Mem. Long, Aldridge & Norman, Atlanta. Assoc. editor N.C. Law Rev., 1967-68. Mem. ABA, State Bar Ga., D.C. Bar, Atlanta Bar Assn., Lawyers Club Atlanta, Order of Coif. Office: Long Aldridge Norman LLP One Peachtree Ctr 303 Peachtree St NE Ste 5300 Atlanta GA 30308-3251*

ALDRIDGE, JOHN WATSON, English language educator, author; b. Sioux City, Iowa, Sept. 26, 1922; s. Walter Copher and Nell (Watson) A.; m. Leslie Felker, Dec. 10, 1954 (div. June 1968); 1 son, Geoffrey; children by previous marriages: Henry, Stephen, Leslie, Jeremy; m. Alexandra Bertash, July 13, 1968 (div. Dec. 1982); m. Patricia McGuire Eby, July 16, 1983. Student, U. Chattanooga, 1940-43; fellow, Breadloaf Sch. English, summer 1942; B.A., U. Calif.-Berkeley, 1947. Lectr. English U. Vt., 1948-50, asst. prof., 1950-53, 54-55; lectr. Christian Gauss Seminars Criticism, Princeton, N.J., 1953-54; mem. lit. faculty Sarah Lawrence Coll., also New Sch. Social Research, 1957; prof. English Queens Coll., 1957; Berg prof. English NYU, 1958; Fulbright lectr. U. Munich, Fed. Republic of Germany, 1958-59; writer-in-residence Hollins Coll., 1960-62; Fulbright lectr. U. Copenhagen, Denmark, 1962-63; prof. English U. Mich., 1964-91, prof. emeritus, 1991; book critic N.Y. Herald Tribune Book Week, 1965-66, Saturday Review, 1970-79; staff Bread Loaf Writers Conf., 1966-69; chief regional judge Book-of-the Month Writing Fellowship Program, 1966-67; spl. adviser for Am. studies U.S. Embassy, Germany, 1972-73; spl. adviser for Authors Am. Sta. WETA, 1990—; book commentator McNeil/Lehrer News Hour, 1983-84. Author: After the Lost Generation, 1951, Critiques and Essays on Modern Fiction, 1952, In Search of Heresy, 1956, The Party at Cranton, 1960, Time to Murder and Create, 1966, In the Country of the Young, 1970, The Devil in the Fire, 1972, The American Novel and the Way We Live Now, 1983, Talents and Technicians, 1992, Classics and Contemporaries, 1992; also articles.; editor: Selected Stories by P.G. Wodehouse, 1958. Served with AUS, 1943-45, ETO. Decorated Bronze Star; Rockefeller Humanities fellow, 1976-77. Mem. Authors Guild and League of Am., MLA, Nat. Book Critics Circle, P.E.N. Home: 1050 Wall St Apt 4C Ann Arbor MI 48105-1981

ALDRIDGE, KENNETH WILLIAM, physician; b. Birmingham, Ala., June 6, 1955; s. Carlton William Jr. and Marie (Hinote) A.; m. Julie Suzanne Dukes, May 1, 1982; children: Callie Suzanne, Caroline Frances, Kenneth William, Jr. BS with honors, U. Ala., 1977, MD cum laude, 1981. Diplomate Am. Bd. Urology. Intern in surgery Med. U. of S.C., Charleston, 1981-82, resident in surgery, 1982-83; resident in urology U. Ala., Birmingham, 1983-86; ptnr. Urology Assocs. of Tuscaloosa, Ala., 1986—; chief of staff West Ala. Hosp., Tuscaloosa, 1992—; clin. asst. prof. surgery and urology Univ. Ala. Coll. Community Health Scis. Fellow ACS; mem. AMA, Med. Assn. Ala. (v.p. 1997—), Tuscaloosa County Med. Soc. (sec.-treas. 1988-89, pres. 1992). Office: Urology Assocs Tuscaloosa 701 University Blvd E Ste 908 Tuscaloosa AL 35401-7423

ALDRIDGE, MELVIN DAYNE, electrical engineering educator; b. Crab Orchard, W.Va., July 20, 1941; s. William Bert and Gladys Revelle A.; m. Nancy L. Dickinson, June 6, 1963; children: Kenrick Lee, Randal Jay. BSEE with high honors, W.Va. U., 1963; MEE, U. Va., 1965, D of Elec. Engring., 1968. Registered profl. engr., W.Va. Electronic engr. NASA, 1963-68; from asst. prof. to assoc. prof. elec. engring. W.Va. U., Morgantown, 1968-76, prof., 1976-84; dir. Energy Rsch. Ctr., 1978-84; asst. dean for rsch. Auburn (Ala.) U., 1984-87, dir. engring. expt. sta., 1984-89, prof. elec. engring., 1984—, acting dean coll. engring., 1987-88, assoc. dean for rsch., 1988-90, assoc. dean for cross-disciplinary programs, 1989—, dir. ctr. for tech. mgmt., 1989—; officer Engring. Accreditation Commn., chmn.; cons. tp pvt. and govtl. orgns. Contbr. articles to profl. publs. Thomas Walter Eminent scholar Auburn U., 1994—; recipient Rufus A. West award, 1963; named Outstanding Young Engr. W.Va., 1977-78. Fellow IEEE (sr.), ASEE; mem. Indsl. Applications Soc. of IEEE (officer). Baptist. Home: 170 Holly Rdg Dadeville AL 36853-5603 Office: Auburn U Tech Mgmt Tiger Dr Auburn AL 36849

ALDRIDGE, SANDRA, civic volunteer; b. Iowa, Apr. 22, 1939; d. Maurice D. and Maureen M. (Bennett) Anderson; m. Guy E. Seymour, Jan. 8, 1960 (div. Oct. 1966); m. Victor E. Aldridge, Jr., Nov. 11, 1970 (dec. May 1995); 1 child, Victor E. III. Student, Millikin U., Decatur, Ill., 1957-58. Pres. Crawford Sch. PTA, 1976-78, Terre Haute Lawyers Aux., 1979; pres., dir. Wabash Valley Assn. for Gifted and Talented Children, 1981-83, Vigo County Task Force for Alcohol and Drug Abuse, 1983-84; treas., dir. Union Hosp. Svc. League; bd. dirs. YWCA of Terre Haute, Inc., 1987-89; v.p., fin. chair, mem. exec. coun. Wabash Valley coun. Boy Scouts Am., Inc.; mem. Vigo County Tax Adjustment Bd., 1986-88; mem. Class IX Leadership Terre Haute, 1985; bd. trustees Vigo County Sch. Corp., Terre Haute, 1985-97, v.p., 1992-93, 96; active Children's Theatre, United Way of Wabash Valley. Mem. Ind. Assn. Gifted Children, Swope Art Gallery, Vigo County Hist. Soc., Women's Dept. Club, Arts Illiana, Elks Women's Golf League. Democrat. Episcopalian. Home: 2929 Winthrop Rd Terre Haute IN 47802-3443

ALDROW-LIPUT, PRISCILLA R., elementary education educator; b. Kingston, Pa., Apr. 10, 1951; d. Thomas Edward and Martha Mae (Hadsall) Reese; children: Colin Michael, Justin John; m. Willard C. Aldrow. BS, Bloomsburg State Coll., 1973; student, Pa. State U., Wilkes-Barre. Cert. instructional II. Tchr. grade 5 Dallas (Pa.) Sch. Dist. Mem. NEA, Pa. State Edn. Assn., Dallas Edn. Assn. Home: PO Box 99 Sweet Valley PA 18656-0099

ALDY, RON, women's basketball coach; b. Jackson, Miss., Nov. 9, 1946; m. Wanda Edwards; children: Ronald Ray Jr., Brittany Ann. B.Phys. Edn., U. Miss., 1969. Head coach Chamberlain Hunt Acad., 1969-71, Grenada Kirk Acad., 1972-88, Holmes C.C., 1988-92; assoc. head coach U. Fla., Gainesville, 1992-97; head coach women's basketball U. Miss., University, 1997—. Office: Univ of Mississippi Tad Smith Coliseum University MS 38677*

ALEA, JORGE ANTONIO, physician; came to U.S., 1949; m. Barbara Chandler; children: Craig, Karen. BS in Chemistry, U. Ga., 1953; MD, Med. Coll. Ga., 1957. Diplomate Am. Bd. Internal Medicine, Am. Bd. Gastroenterology, Nat. Bd. Med. Examiners. Staff physician State Hosp., Raleigh, N.C., 1957-58; intern City Meml. Hosp., Winston-Salem, N.C., 1958-59; resident in internal medicine Henry Ford Hosp., Detroit, 1959-62; resident VA Hosp.- Med. Coll. VA, Richmond, Va., 1962-63; chief of gastroenterology VA Hosp., Buffalo, N.Y., 1963-69; asst. prof. medicine SUNY, Buffalo, 1963-69; chief med. svc. and charter mem. Doctor's Hosp., Lake Worth, Fla.; mem. staff JFK Med. Ctr., Lake Worth, Fla., 1969—. Contbr. articles to profl. jours. Deacon First Bapt. Ch., West Palm Beach, Fla. Capt. USAR. Fellow ACP, Am. Coll. Gastroenterology; mem. Am. Gastroenterologic Soc., Am. Soc. Gastrointestinal Endoscopy. Avocation: golf. Office: 1840 Forest Hill Blvd West Palm Beach FL 33406-6063

ALEGI, PETER CLAUDE, lawyer; b. New Haven, July 26, 1935; s. Claude D. and Margaret (Lettieri) A.; children from previous marriage: Gregory, Daniel, Peter; m. Lynda M. Martin. B.A. cum laude, Yale U., 1956, LL.B., 1959; postgrad. Fulbright scholar, U. Rome, Italy, 1959-60. Bar: Conn. 1959, R.I. 1962, Ill. 1965, U.S. Supreme Ct. 1965. Assoc. Hinckley, Allen, Salisbury Parsons, Providence, R.I., 1961-64, Baker & McKenzie, Chgo., 1964-65; ptnr. Milan & Rome, 1966-87; prin. Alegi & Assocs., Rome, 1987—; vis. lectr. Temple U. Law Sch., Phila., 1980-81; Yale U. Law Sch., New Haven, 1981—; bd. regents Marymount Sch., Rome, 1992-98; provost Am. U. Rome, 1997—; bd. trustees St. Thomas More Corp., Yale U. Author: Italian Income Taxation, 1988, 2d edit., 1994; contbr. articles to profl. jours. Chmn. Democrats Abroad-Italy, 1976-87, Democrats Abroad-Worldwide, 1991-95; mem. Dem. Nat. Com., 1984-95,96—, commr. Fulbright Commn., Rome, 1979-90; del. Dem. Nat. Convs., 1988, 92, 96; Rome com. U.S. C. of C. for Italy, 1994-96. Mem. ABA, Yale Law Alumni Assn. (exec. com. 1985-92, treas. 1991-92),bd. dir. Centro Studi Americani, Italian Assn. Tax Advisors, Internat. Bar Assn., Internat. Fiscal Assn. Roman Catholic. Club: Tennis Parioli (Rome). Office: Alegi & Assocs, Via Venti Settembre 1, 00187 Rome Italy

ALEKSANDRAS, DELORIS NILES, retired nursing educator; b. Odell, Ill., Sept. 1, 1912; d. Arthur and Edna Louise (Cory) Niles; m. Alphonse B. Aleksandras, Dec. 26, 1959. Diploma, Augustana Hosp. Sch. Nursing, Chgo., 1951; student, Loyola U., Chgo., 1956; BS Nursing Edn., Columbia U., 1958, MA, 1959. Instr. BS program Tchrs. Coll., Columbia U., N.Y.C.; instr. AD program Elgin (Ill.) Community Coll., Amundsen-Mayfair City Coll., Chgo.; instr. continuing edn. Coll. Lake County, Grayslake, Ill. Mem. ANA (conf. del., chmn., mem. various coms.), Nat. League for Nursing, Ill. Nurses Assn. (bd. dirs.), Columbia U. Tchrs. Coll. Alumni Assn., Kappa Delta Pi, Pi Lambda Theta. Home: 201 E Wilmette Ave Palatine IL 60067-7248

ALEKSANDROV, LEONID NAUMOVITSH, physicist, educator, researcher; b. Dnepropetrovsk, USSR, Sept. 27, 1923; s. Naum Lvovitsh and Vera Markovna A.; m. Julia Makarovna Melnik, Aug. 19, 1953; children: Svetlana, Andrej. Degree, U. Dnepropetrovsk, 1950; candidate sci., Sci. Coun., Dnepropetrovsk, 1954; DSc, Sci. Coun., Moscow, 1964. Head of chair solid state physics U. Saransk, USSR, 1953-65, prof., 1965; head rsch. lab. Inst. Light Sources, Saransk, 1958-65; head thin film rsch. lab. Inst. Semiconductor Physics, Acad. Sci., Novosibirsk, USSR, 1965-77; chief scientist Inst. Semiconductor Phsyics, Acad. Sci., Novosibirsk, Russia, 1977—; prof. microelectronics Electrotech. Inst.-Tech. U., Novosibirsk, 1968—; merited sci. and engring. worker of Russia, 1983—; prof., cons. U. Saransk, 1965-90, UNESCO, U. Habana, Cuba, 1975-76; guest prof. physics U. Vienna, Austria, 1991, Tech. U. Chemnitz, Germany, 1980, 81, 94. Author: Transition region in Epitaxial Semiconductor Films, 1978 (Acad. Sci. award 1979), Growth of Crystalline Semiconductor Materials on Crystal Surfaces, 1984, Crystallization and Regrowth of Semiconductor Films, 1986 (Branch Acad. award 1986), 10 other books; mem. edit. bd. Thin Solid Films, Physica Status Solidi; patentee in field; contbr. articles to profl. jours., chpts. to books. Mem. Dep. Soviet Coun. of Region, Novosibirsk, 1969-73; mem. Coun. of Vets., Novosibirsk, 1987—; mem. Znanja, Novosibirsk, 1950-91, 11 Govt. awards. Lt. Soviet Army, 1943-45. Recipient prize for thin film rsch. Siberian Acad., 1982, Gold Medal and State award for laser epitaxy works USSR Govt., 1988, 20th Century Achievement award Cambridge IBC, 1996. Mem. Munich Bundes Republik Deutschland Exhbn., Scis. Com. Electronics (medal 1989), N.Y. Acad. Scis., E-MRS (Strasbourg). Avocations: photography, philately, touring, radio, light athletics. Home: Vojevodskogo 5 w 2, 630090 Novosibirsk Russia Office: Acad Sci Russia, Inst Semiconductor Physics, 630090 Novosibirsk Russia

ALEKSICH-AKEY, SUE, Republican party chairman. Chmn. Mont. State Rep. Party, 1994—. Office: 1419B Helena Ave Helena MT 59601-3024*

ALEMÁN, MARTHANNE PAYNE, environmental planner, consultant; b. Houston, Dec. 3, 1938; d. Charles Franklin and Evelyn Inez (Dudley) Payne; m. Samuel Garza Alemán, July 5, 1968. BS in Landscape Arch. magna cum laude, Tex. A&M U., 1988; MS in Interdisciplinary Studies, Tex. Tech. U., 1989; PhD in Urban and Regional Sci., Tex. A&M U., 1995. Engring. aide City of Austin, 1966-69, Bryan-Curington Engrs., Austin, 1969-72; entrepreneur Rio Verde Farm, San Benito, Tex., 1972-83; rsch. asst. Tex. Tech. U., Lubbock, 1988-91, Tex. A&M U., College Station, 1993-94; cons. Rio Verde Land & Investment, Calvert, Tex., 1995—; sec./treas., bd. dirs. Tex. Avocado Growers Assn., Weslaco, 1979-83. *Planned a 4,384 acre community for the Lower Rio Grande Valley of Texas for a major research university. Analyzed soil types as determinants for allocation of land use for a multiplicity of human activities while preserving Class I and II agricultural farmland. Resolved problem of urban encroachment through a plan permitting development for human use while preserving limited farmland. Authored a 650 page reference work researching and analyzing the multiple causes of global problem of desertificcation. Originated system to guide decision making processes for land planners, policy makers, and educators through reevaluation of established procedures.* Author: Soil Salinity in the Texas Lower Rio Grande Valley: Cause for Concern, 1987, Export-Driven Development of Soil and Water Resources: Barrier to Sustainable Development and Inducement to Desertification, 1995. Mem. and active participant Robbertson County Hist. Commn., Calvert, 1980-83. Smithsonian Instn. intern, Washington, 1987, Presdl. scholar U.S. Fed. Register, 1993; recipient Nat. Collegiate Archtl. and Design award, U.S. Achievement Acad., Lexington, Ky., 1989. Mem. Am. Planning Assn., Soil and Water Conservation Soc. of Am. (vol. Heart of Tex. chpt., Waco, Tex.). Avocations: breeding, showing, and training collies. Office: Rio Verde Land and Investment 201 Browning Calvert TX 77837

ALEMAN, MINDY R., advertising and public relations consultant, marketing and development executive, newspaper columnist, freelance writer; b. Nov. 23, 1950; d. Lionel and Jocelyn (cohen) Luskin; m. Gary Aleman, Aug. 27, 1983. BA, U. Akron, 1972, MA, 1975. Instr. speech U. Akron, 1973-83; car salesperson Dave Towell Cadillac, Akron, 1977-79, mgr. fin. and ins., 1979; account exec., pub. rels. dir. Loos, Edwards & Sexauer, Akron, 1980-82; mktg. svcs. coord. Century Products, Stow, Ohio, 1982-83; mgr. advt., pub. rels. Cemtury Products, Gerber Furniture Group, Stow, 1983-86, Macedonia, Ohio, 1986-89; dir. rsch. and promotion Akron Beacon Jour., 1989-95; owner Mindy Aleman Mktg. & Promotion Showbiz and Speak-On Workshop, 1995-96; mktg./promotion mgr. John S. Knight Ctr. and Akron/Summit Conv. and Bus. Bur., 1997-99; mktg. and devel. dir. Kent (Ohio) State U. Mus., 1999—; instr. comm. U. Akron, 1975-95, part-time faculty mem., 1975-96, instr. com. and advt., 1973-82, 95—; instr. Walsh U., 1996—. Playwright Danny's Choice, 1972; weekly columnist Ready or Not Sunday beacon Mag., 1991-95. Mem. Internat. Newspaper Mktg. Assn. (various awards 1989-93), Am. Mktg. Assn., Newspaper Assn. Am., Pub. Rels. Soc. Am. (accredited), Akron Advt. Club (various awards 1983-98), Cleve. Advt. Assn., Women's Network. E-mail: mktpro@ss-net.com. Office: KSU Mus PO Box 5190 Kent OH 44242-0001

ALENIKOFF, FRANCES, choreographer, performer, writer, dancer, artist; b. N.Y.C., Aug. 20, 1920; d. Clement Jack Lipman and Ruth (Alder) Taylor; m. Martin Freedman, 1936 (div. 1973); children: Francesca Rheannon. BA, Bklyn. Coll., 1940. founding mem. Dance Theatre Workshop, N.Y., 1968—. Soloist and company at colls., univs., theaters, in festivals and community ctrs. in U.S. and abroad, 1959-93; soloist in films including Frekoba, 1969, Alenka, 1968, Episodes On The Edge, 1973, Shaping Things, 1978; soloist at Lincoln Ctr.. 1985; choreographer for Zaide, 1956, L'Histoire Du Soldat, 1957, Josephine Baker Show On Broadway, 1964, Joan and the Devil, 1978; performer Dream Play, 1970, Oddfellows Players, 1991—; participant in various art festival, 1966-86; dir. Eden's Expressway, 1975—; dance critic Dance News, 1970-82; staff writer Craft Horizons Mag., 1971-74; actress in Witness, Blood Summer Rituals, 1994; dancer St. Mark's Dancespace, 1996, Frederick Loewe Theater, 1996, Dance Theatre Workshop, 1996, Soho Arts Festival, 1996, 97, Judson Ch., N.Y.C., 1997, Downtown Arts Festival, 1998; contbr. articles to profl. jours. Recipient Grant N.Y. State Coun. on the Arts, 1972-80, NEA, 1973-74, N.Y. City Cultural Coun., 1978, Meet the Composer, 1980, N.J. State Coun. on the Arts, 1972, Cine Internat. Golden Eagle award, 1978; named Pick of Yr. for Best in Dance, Village Voice, 1997. Mem. Dancers Over Forty. Home: 537 Broadway New York NY 10012-3930

ALENIKOV, VLADIMIR, motion picture director and writer; b. Leningard, Russia, Aug. 7, 1948; came to U.S., 1990; s. Michael and Stella (Alenikova) Volkenshtein; 1 child, Philip; m. Tamara Karpovitch; 1 child, Anastassia. Student, Leningrad State U., 1965-67, Leningrad Inst. Theatre, 1967-69, Moscow State U., 1969-72. Tchr. Russian lit. and french, dep. prin. Secondary Sch. 2, Moscow, 1969-72; dir. Gorky Film Studios, Moscow, 1974-78, 88-89, Odessa Film Studio, 1982-84; dir. music Ekran TV Studio, Moscow, 1979-81, dir., 1985-87; dir., pres. Aquilon Co., Moscow, 1989—; dir., owner Destiny Films, L.A., 1992—; lectr. at film showing; mem. 1st Soviet del. of cinematographers, Cyprus, Greece. Author: The White Page, 1972, The Mysteries of a Women's Heart, 1975, also articles, poems and short stories; Dir. and writer of feature films: The Garden, 1973, The Composer Comitas, 1974, The Room of Laughter, 1975, What a Mess, 1976, There Lived a Piano-Tuner, 1979, The Adventures of Petrov and Vasechkin, Ordinary and Extraordinary, 1982, The Hooligan, 1983, The Knight, 1983, Unique, 1986, Valuable Friends, 1987, The Drayman and the King, 1989, The Time of Darkness, 1991, The Awakening, 1991, Monique, 1993; Dir. and writer of stage plays: The Locals, 1976, The Adventures of d'Artagnan, 1986, (with David Wolcomb), Peace Child, 1985, The Hooligan is Coming, 1986, The Tale of the Warrior, 1987, The Tower, 1988, White Mercedes, 1992; Screen plays include: August Weather Forecast, 1984, A Night Story, 1985, To Kill and be Alive, 1990, The Incredible Adventures of Ricky Plim, 1992, Without Past, 1993, War of Princess, 1993. Pres. Russian-Am. Art Ctr., L.A., 1992—. Recipient 1st prize for best TV film 22d Internat. Festival Children and Youth Films Gijon Spain 1984, award for best film dir.'s debut Internat. Festival TV Films Montreux Switzerland 1979, Danube prize 8th Internat. Festival Childrens' TV Films Bratislava Czechoslovakia 1985, Grand Prix Soviet Nat. Festival Youth-83 1983, Grand Prix First Moscow Film Festival of Children's Scetches 1987, prize for funniest movie 10th Internat. Festival Children's Films Moscow 1987, AFI Film Internat. Festival award L.A. 1990, Jerusalem Film Festival award 1990, Toronto Festival of Festivals diploma 1990, Moscow Internat. Film Festival award 1991; also others. Mem. Russian Film Makers, Russian Guild Scriptwriters, Russian Guild Dir., Moscow Guild Diirs., L.A. Press Club. Jewish. Avocations: reading, writing. Home and Office: 19030 Hamlin St #8 Reseda CA 91335-5905

ALENIUS, JOHN TODD, insurance executive; b. Denver, Sept. 27, 1938; s. Robert and Elizabeth Frances (Todd) A.; m. Sandra Lee Mally, June 30, 1962; children: Constance, Mark, Patricia, William. BBA, Regis. Coll., 1961; postgrad., Havard U., 1971; MA in Mgmt., Webster Coll., 1979. Commd. USAF, 1962, advanced through grades to col.; personnel mgr. USAF, Vietnam, 1966-67, Colorado Springs, Colo., 1962-67; systems mgr. USAF, San Antonio, 1971-75; with exchange duty Canadian Armed Forces, Ottawa, Ont., Can., 1975-77; various system mgmt. positions USAF, San Antonio, 1977-83; dir. logistic mgmt. systems USAF, Sacramento, 1983-85; v.p. info. systems Vision Service Plan, Sacramento, 1985-88, exec. v.p. ops., 1988-98, exec. v.p., 1998—. Mem. Soc. Info. Mgmt., Am. Mgmt. Assn. Republican. Roman Catholic. Avocations: fishing, golf. Office: California Vision Service Inc 3333 Quality Dr Rancho Cordova CA 95670-7985

ALEPIAN, TARO, engineering and construction executive; b. Nicosia, Cyprus, Sept. 28, 1945; arrived in Can., 1963; s. Melcon and Anahid (Melikian) A.; m. Anahid Manoukian, July 14, 1968; children: Ronald, Norma,

Alida. BE with honors, McGill U., Montreal, Que., Can., 1967; postgrad., Harvard U., 1994. Cert. engr., Que., Alta. Process engr. Shell Can. Ltd., Montreal, 1967-72, project mgr., 1972-73; sr. analyst Shell Can. Ltd., Toronto, Ont., Can., 1973-74; dir. mktg. SNC Inc., Montreal, 1974-77, v.p. mktg., 1977-79, sr. v.p., 1979-88, sr. group v.p., 1988-91; group pres. indsl. SNC-Lavalin Inc., Montreal, 1991-94, exec. v.p., office of pres., 1995—; bd. dirs. several subs. SNC-Lavalin Inc., Montreal. Mem. St. James's Club. Mem. Christian Orthodox Ch. Avocations: charitable and cultural organizations, tennis, squash. E-mail: alept@snc-lavalin.com. Office: SNC-Lavalin Inc, SNC-Lavalin Group Inc, 455 Rene-Levesque Blvd W, Montreal, PQ Canada H2Z 1Z3

ALEPRA, SHERRY JO, elementary school educator; b. Litchfield, Ill., July 17, 1948; d. Harry Forsyth and Agnes Finney Campbell. BS, So. Ill. U., 1970, MS, 1981. Cert. tchr., Ill. Tchr. Gillespie (Ill.) Unit Dist. 7, 1971—; EMT Gillespie/Benld Area Ambulance, 1990—; homebound tchr. Gillespie H.S.; tchr. Safe Sch., Carlinville, Ill., summer, 1998. Contbr. articles to profl. jours. Mem. sports boosters club Gillespie H.S., 1988-93; vol. Baskets for Needy, Gillespie; donation chmn. Am. Cancer Soc., 1989; mem. Sts. Simon and Jude Ch. Altar Soc. Grantee Partnership for Ednl. Excellence, St. Louis Sci. Ctr., 1989. Roman Catholic. Avocations: tutoring, gardening, fishing, reading, writing. E-mail: salepra@ctnet.net. Home: 710 W Plum Gillespie IL 62033

ALES, BEVERLY GLORIA RUSHING, artist; b. Laplace, La.; d. William Pinckney and Clementine Marie (Madere) Rushing; m. Warren Vincent Ales, Dec. 29, 1946 (dec. June 1991); children: Merrick Vance Patrick, Sheryl Ann (dec.), Lori Patrice. BA, Felt & Tarrant, New Orleans; student, La Stae U., U. New Orleans. Civil svc. clerk Am. Agrl., Baton Rouge, U.S. Naval Depot, New Orleans; office mgr. Nat. Auto Assn., New Orleans; cosmetician Labiche's Inc., New Orleans; art gallery owner, mgr. Gallery Toulouse, New Orleans, Village D'Artiste, Metairie, La.; pvt. practice Metairie; past pres. Metairie Art Guild, Le Petit Art Guild, New Orleans, New Orleans Art Assn.; art tchr. East Jefferson H.S., T.H. Harris Mid. Sch., Magnolia Spl. Sch. Author poetry. Mem. Rep. Nat. Com., Rep. Pres. Trus; bd. dirs. Rep. Women's Club in Jefferson Parish; past pres. La Soc. De Femme, Metarie. Recipient Great Lady award East Jefferson Hosp. Aux., Legion of Merit award. Mem. Nat. Mus. Women in Arts (charter), Nat. Authors Registry, Internat. Soc. Poets (bd. dirs.), Workers of Magnolia Spl. Sch. (pres.), New Orleans Garden Soc., Heart Ambassadors (v.p.). Roman Catholic. Home: 1149 Melody Dr Metairie LA 70002-1924 Address: 1500 Melody Dr Metairie LA 70002-1924

ALESHIRE, RICHARD JOE, banker; b. Anthony, Kans., Feb. 18, 1947; s. Robert Allen and Alma Evelyn (Chesnut) A.; m. Janet Jean Bohrer, Apr. 30, 1977; children: Jeff Allen, Jennifer Anne. BS in Edn., Emporia (Kans.) State U., 1970. Tchr., coach Las Cruces (N.Mex.) High Sch., 1970-72; tennis tchr. Tennis Club of Albuquerque, 1972; loan officer Capitol Fed. Savs. and Loan, Overland Park, Kans., 1973-78; exec. v.p. D.L. Mayor Realtors, Overland Park, 1978-79; sr. v.p., area mgr. Capitol Fed. Savs. and Loan, Wichita, 1979-97; exec. v.p. retail ops. Capitol Fed. Savs., Topeka, 1997—. Campaign chmn. United Way of Plains, Wichita, Kans., 1988, chmn. bd., 1990-91; bd. dirs. St. Joseph Med. Ctr., 1991—, vice chmn., 1993-94, chmn. 1995; chmn. Via Christi Health Sys., 1996-97; v. chmn. Govt. Rels. Topeka C. of C., 1999; bd. dirs. Topeka United Way, 1999. Mem. Wichita Real Estate Industry Coun. (chmn. 1988—), Wichita Area C. of C. (bd. dirs. 1993-97, vice chmn. membership 1994, 96, first vice chmn. bd. 1997), Rotary (v.p. East Wichita 1990-91, pres. 1991-92). Republican. Avocations: golf, tennis, weight lifting, reading. Home: 3900 SW Clarion Pl Topeka KS 66610 Office: 700 S Kansas Ave Topeka KS 66603-3809

ALESIA, JAMES H(ENRY), judge; b. Chgo., July 16, 1934; m. Kathryn P. Gibbons, July 8, 1961; children:Brian J., Daniel J. BS Loyola U., 1956; LLB, IIT, Chgo., 1960. Grad. Nat. Jud. Coll., U. Nev.-Reno, 1976. Bar: Ill. 1960, Minn. 1970. Police officer City of Chgo., 1957-60; with Law Office Anthony Scariano, Chicago Heights, Ill., 1960-61; assoc. Pretzel & Stouffer, Chgo., 1961-63; asst. gen. counsel Chgo. & North Western Transp. Co., Chgo., 1963-70; assoc. Rerat Law, Mpls., 1970-71; asst. U.S. atty. No. dist. Ill., Chgo., 1971-73, trial counsel Chessie System, Chgo., 1973; U.S. adminstrv. law judge, 1973-82; ptnr. Reuben & Proctor (firm merged with Isham, Lincoln & Beale), Chgo., 1982-87; judge U.S. Dist., No. Ill., 1987—; faculty Nat. Jud. Coll., U. Nev.-Reno, 1979-80. Mem. Fed. Bar Assn., Justinian Soc. Lawyers, Celtic Legal Soc. Republican. Roman Catholic. Office: US Dist Ct 219 S Dearborn St Chicago IL 60604-1702

ALESSANDRONI, VENAN JOSEPH, lawyer; b. N.Y.C., Mar. 1, 1915; s. Anthony P. and Andromeda (Rossini) A.; m. Alice Shaughnessy, Feb. 2, 1949 (dec. June 1973); m. Adelle Lincoln, Mar. 10, 1974. A.B., Columbia U., 1937, J.D., 1939. Bar: N.Y. 1941, also, Supreme Ct. of Korea 1946. Announcer CBS Artists Service, Inc., 1940; U.S. atty. Bd. Econ. Warfare, 1942; mem. U.S. Fgn. Econ. Adminstrn. Mission, Belgian Congo, 1943; sr. partner Wormser, Kiely, Alessandroni, Hyde & McCann (and predecessor firm), 1959—; Legal officer Mil. Govt. Korea, 1945-46; legal adviser to provincial gov. Kyunggi-Do, Korea, 1946; chief provost judge, City of Seoul, 1946; adj. prof., law sch. U. Miami, 1974—; lectr. various tax insts., univs., profl. assns. Author: The Executor, 1963, Applied Estate Planning, 1963, also articles.; Departmental editor: Jour. Taxation, 1955-56. Recipient U.S. Army Commendation award, 1946; regional award N.Y. Times, 1932; Curtis medal Columbia, 1936. Home: Eggleston Ln Old Greenwich CT 06870 Office: Wormser Kiely Galef & Jacobs 711 3rd Ave New York NY 10017-4014

ALESSI, GEORGE ANTHONY, financial advisor, consultant; b. N.Y.C., May 30, 1926; s. Anthony and Anna Cecilia (Li Greci) A.; m. Madeline Costanza, Nov. 21, 1953; 1 child, Anthony. BBA in Indsl. Mgmt., CCNY, 1949; cert. in elec. engring., Oreg. State U., 1945, MBA, 1952; cert., Ohio State U., 1960. Cert. profl. contract mgr., Washington. Employment interviewer City of N.Y. Dept. Social Svcs., 1949-52; various mgmt. and exec. positions U.S. Govt. Dept. of Def., 1952-86; cons., fin. advisor Galessi Enterprises, Yonkers, N.Y., 1986—. Mem. Archdiocesan Pastoral Coun., N.Y., 1985-91; chmn. Vicariate of N.E. Bronx, N.Y., 1983-91; cooperator Opus Dei, 1990—; mem. Cath. League for Religious and Civil Rights; bd. dirs. Lawrence Hosp. Aux., 1996—. Decorated Knight of the Holy Sepulchre, Pope John Paul II, 1984; recipient Disting. Svc. award Archdiocesan Union of Holy Name, 1985, Insignus Jesuit Community at Loyola Retreat House, Morristown, N.J., 1966. Fellow Profl. Contracts Mgmt. Assn. (cert. 1976), Cardinal Spellman Retreat League (pres. Riverdale, N.Y. 1980-82), Archdiocesan Union of Holy Name Soc. (pres. 1977-79), Male Glee Club Yonkers (v.p. 1986-87), Serra Internat. (dist. gov. 1989-92, pres. 1996—), Congregation of the Passion (assoc.). Republican. Roman Catholic. Home and Office: 10 Massitoa Rd Yonkers NY 10710-5016

ALEWINE, JAMES WILLIAM, financial executive; b. Williamston, S.C., Apr. 26, 1930; s. David Andrew and Ruby Mae (Moore) A.; children: David, Susan. BA, Carolina Sch. Commerce, 1961. Cert. internal auditor, S.C. With Daniel Internat. Corp., Greenville, S.C., 1947-92, mgr. internal audit, 1970-72, mgr. M & M divsn., 1972-73; fin. adminstr. Daniel Internat. Corp., Jenkinsville, S.C., 1973-77; mgr. acctg. M-E-T Group Daniel Internat. Corp., Greenville, S.C., 1977-78, asst. treas., 1978-92. With USN, 1952-55, maj. S.C. State Guard, 1993—. Mem. Inst. Internal Auditors (pres. Palmetto chpt. 1975-76), Masons (past grand high priest, knight York grand cross of honour, 32d degree), Scottish Rite, Elks. Baptist. Home: 2 Broad St Williamston SC 29697-1808

ALEX, JOANNE DEFILIPP, educator Montesorri school; m. Joseph Alex; children: Jessica, Joel, Julianna. BA in Art and Edn., Colby Coll., 1976; grad., Montessori Methods, 1979; postgrad in Edn., U. Maine, 1995—. Tchr., kindergarten, Montessori schs. Various Cities, 1979-83; founder, tchr. Montessori Sch., Stillwater, Maine, 1983—; AMS Monetessori intern supr.; presenter numerous workshops and confs.; trained facilitator of Systematic Tng. for Effective Parenting; instr. parenting courses; ednl. cons.; facilitator Project Learning Tree, Project Wild, Project Aquatic, Project Wet workshops; coord 1st Maine Tchrs. Forum, 1998. Selected to attend Nat. Geographic Soc. Summer Inst.; named Outstanding Environ. Educator of Yr. (nat.), Am. Tree Found., 1994, Tchr. of Yr., Maine Audubon Soc., 1995, Maine Tchr. of Yr., 1998; recipient award for outstanding contbns. to child-care in Maine. Mem. Am. Montessori Soc. (tchr.), N. Am. Montessori Tchrs. Assn., Ea. Maine Assn. for Edn. of Young Children, Maine Montessori Assn. (treas.). Avocations: biking, hiking, wild flowers, children's books, children's resources. Office: Stillwater Montessori Sch 775 Stillwater Ave Old Town ME 04468

ALEXAKOS, FRANCES MARIE, business owner, psychology educator, researcher, producer, editor; b. Fitchburg, Mass., Dec. 29, 1947; d. Samuel Rosario and Mary (Cucchiara) Sciabarrasi; m. Haritos Kyniacou Agadakos, June 5, 1972 (dec. Feb. 1987); m. Demetrios P. Alexakos, June 5, 1988; children: Katerina, Demetra, Artemis, Alexis. BA in Psychology, U. Mass., 1970; MA in Psychology, Assumption Coll., 1972; BA in Studio Art, U. R.I., 1994; cert. in humanities, Salve Regina U., 1996, postgrad., 1995—. Social worker, Mass.; psychologist, Mass.; cert. tchr., R.I.; cert. sch. counselor, R.I. Social worker St. Vincent's Hosp., Worcester, Mass., 1970-72; sr. med. social worker Roger William Hosp., Providence, 1972-78; pres. Richeys of Wakefield, R.I., 1978—; prof. psychology Johnson & Wales U., Providence, 1991-94, C.C. R.I., Warwick, 1994-96; dir. mktg. Oak Internat. Academies, Guadelahara, Mex., 1996-97; dir., R.I. health care reform Kaiser Health, Providence, 1993-95; mem. vis. faculty summer ethics inst. Dartmouth Coll., 1998. Editor, Mediterranean bur. chief Slugfest lit. mag., 1997—; author: Medicine and Health, 1999, Rhode Island Physicians' Attitudes Toward Genetic Testing and Breast Cancer; cable TV producer Cox & TCI: Genetiots & Society. Mem. Zoning Bd. of Rev., Narragansett, R.I., 1976-78, South Kingston, R.I., 1976-78; sch. counselor, Westerly, R.I., 1998—; mem. R.I. Genetics Task Force, 1999—; genetics trainer March of Dimes, 1998-99. Recipient scholarship Daus. of Penelope, 1994; NIH grantee, 1998. Mem. LWV (bd. dirs., R.I. state coord. health care reform, R.I. state treas.), Assn. Practical and Profl. Ethics, Rotary (scholarship com. 1997), Wakefield C. of C. (bd. dirs., Bus. Person of Yr. 1987, Leadership R.I. award 1995), Golden Key Honor Soc. Greek Orthodox. Avocations: tennis, art, computers, research.

ALEXANDER, ANDREW JAMES, commercial lender; b. Bellaire, Ohio, Aug. 3, 1969; s. Daniel Richard Alexander. BSBA, Ohio State U., 1991; MBA, U. Pitts., 1999. Sales assoc. Prudential Securities, Wheeling, W.Va., 1992-93; controller 5B's Inc., Zanesville, Ohio, 1993-96; sr. fin. analyst PNC Bank, Pitts., 1996-97; relationship mgr. corp. banking Nat. City Bank, Pitts., 1997—; MIS cons., Pitts. Republican. Roman Catholic. Avocations: golf, tennis, reading novels. Home: 374 Newburn Dr Pittsburgh PA 15216 Office: 1000 Gamma Dr Pittsburgh PA 15238-2929

ALEXANDER, ANDREW LAMAR (LAMAR ALEXANDER), lawyer, former secretary of education, former governor; b. Maryville, Tenn., July 3, 1940; s. Andrew Lamar and Genevra Floreine (Rankin) A.; m. Leslee Kathryn Buhler, Jan. 4, 1969; children: Andrew, Leslee, Kathryn, Will. B.A., Vanderbilt U., 1962; J.D., NYU, 1965. Bar: Tenn. 1965. Law clk. to Hon. John Wisdom U.S. Ct. Appeals (5th cir.), New Orleans; assoc. Fowler, Rountree, Fowler & Robertson, Knoxville, 1965; legis. asst. to Senator Howard Baker, 1967-68; exec. asst. to Bryce Harlow, White House Congl. Liaison Office, 1969-70; ptnr. Dearborn and Ewing, Nashville, 1970-76; gov. State of Tenn., Nashville, 1979-87; chmn. Leadership Inst. Belmont Coll., Nashville, 1987-88; pres. U. Tenn., 1988-91; sec. Dept. Edn., Washington, 1991-93; counsel Baker, Donelson, Bearman & Caldwell, Nashville, 1993-98; mem. Pres.'s Task Force on Federalism; chmn. Nat. Govs. Assn., 1985-86, Pres.'s Commn. on Ams. Outdoors, 1985-87; co-director Empower Am., 1994-95. Author: Steps Along the Way, 1986, Six Months Off, 1988, We Know What To Do, 1995; co-editor: The New Promise of American Life, 1995. Mgr. Winfield Dunn for Gov. Campaign, 1970, chief transition, 1970-71; Rep. nominee for Gov. of Tenn., 1974; chmn. Rep. Exch. Satellite Network, 1993-95; Rep. Presdl. candidate, 1995-96. Recipient Nat. Disting. Svc. to Edn. award Burger King, 1988, James B. Conant award Edn. Commn. of the States, 1988, Disting. State Leadership award Am. Assn. State Colls. and Univs., 1989, Teddy Roosevelt award Nat. Coll. Athletic Assn., 1993, honored as Silver Anniversary scholar-athlete, 1987; NYU Law Sch. Root-Tilden scholar. Fellow (sr.) Hudson Inst.; mem. Phi Beta Kappa. Republican. Presbyterian. *

ALEXANDER, ANTHONY J., electric power industry executive. BS, U. Akron, 1972, JD, 1975. Bar: Ohio 1976. Sr. tax acct. Ohio Edison Co., Akron, 1972-76, atty., 1976-83, sr. atty., 1984-87, assoc. gen. counsel, 1987-89, v.p., gen. counsel, 1898-91, sr. v.p., gen. counsel, 1991—. Office: FirstEnergy Corp Fl 18th 76 S Main St Fl 18th Akron OH 44308-1812*

ALEXANDER, ARTHUR JACOB, economist; b. Carbondale, Pa., Oct. 6, 1936; s. Howard R. and Sylvia (Eisner) A.; m. Elaine Averich, Aug. 25, 1963; children: Sarah, Jonathan. BS, Mass. Inst. Tech., 1958; MSc, London Sch. Econs., 1966; PhD, Johns Hopkins U., 1969. Sys. analyst IBM, Poughkeepsie, N.Y., 1960-63; rsch. economist Rand Corp., Santa Monica, Calif., 1968-90; pres. Japan Econ. Inst., Washington, 1990—; vis. prof. UCLA, 1988-90, Johns Hopkins U., 1994-97, George Mason U., 1998—; mem. U.S. Army Sci. Bd., Washington, 1978-82; rsch. assoc. Internat. Inst. Strategic Studies, London, 1976-77. With U.S. Army, 1959-60. Mem. Internat. Inst. Strategic Studies. Avocations: photographica collections, running. Office: Japan Econ Inst 1000 Connecticut Ave NW Washington DC 20036-5302

ALEXANDER, BARBARA LEAH SHAPIRO, clinical social worker; b. St. Louis, May 6, 1943; d. Harold Albert and Dorothy Miriam (Leifer) Shapiro; m. Richard E. Alexander. B in Music Edn., Washington U., St. Louis, 1964; postgrad., U. Ill., 1964-66; MSW, Smith Coll., 1970; postgrad., Inst. Psychoanalysis, Chgo., 1971-73, grad., child therapy program, 1976-80; cert. therapist Sex Dysfunction Clinic, Loyola U., Chgo., 1975. Diplomate in Clin. Social Work. Rsch. asst., NIMH grantee Smith Coll., 1968-70; probation officer Juvenile Ct. Cook County, Chgo., 1966-68, 70; therapist Madden Mental Health Ctr., Hines, Ill., 1970-72; supr., therapist, field instr. U. Chgo., U. Ill. Grad. Schs. Social Work; therapist Pritzker Children's Hosp., Chgo., 1972-82; therapist, cons., also pvt. practice, 1973—; pres. On Good Authority, 1992—; intern Divorce Conciliation Svc., Circuit Ct. Cook County, 1976-77. Contbr. articles to profl. jours. Bd. dirs., Grant Park Concerts Soc.; sec. Art Resources in Teaching. Recipient Sterling Achievement award Mu Phi Epsilon, 1964. Mem. Nat. Fed. Soc. for Clin. Social Work (chmn. 20th ann. conf., exec. bd.), Ill. Soc. Clin. Social Work (pres. 1986-90, bd. dirs., chmn. svcs. to mems. com., dir. pvt. practitioners' referral service), Assn. Child Psychotherapists, Amateur Chamber Music Players Assn., Jewish Geneal. Soc., Smith Coll. Alumni Assn. (bd. dirs., v.p. 1992-94). Home and Office: 6 Horizon Ln Galena IL 61036-9258

ALEXANDER, BARBARA TOLL, investment banker; b. Little Rock, Dec. 18, 1948; d. Lawrence Jesser and Geraldine Best (Proctor) Toll; m. Lawrence Allen Alexander, Jan. 25, 1969 (div. 1980); m. Thomas Beveridge Stiles, II, Mar. 7, 1981; stepchildren: Thomas B. Stiles III, Jonathan E. Stiles. BS, U. Ark., 1969, MS, 1970. Asst. v.p. Wachovia Bank & Trust Co., Winston-Salem, N.C., 1972-77; security analyst Investors Diversified Services, Mpls., 1977-78; 1st v.p. Smith Barney Inc., N.Y.C., 1978-84; mng. dir. Salomon Bros., N.Y.C., 1984-91, Dillon Read & Co., 1992-97, Warburg Dillon Read, 1997—; former chmn. policy adv. bd. Joint Ctr. for Housing Studies of Harvard U., mem. exec. com.; mem. N.Y. adv. bd. Enterprise Found; bd. dir. Covenant House; mem. exec. com. Covenant House. Presbyterian. Home: 87 Monarch Bay Dr Monarch Beach CA 92629 Address: Warburg Dillon Read 299 Park Ave Fl 36 New York NY 10171-0002

ALEXANDER, BRAD L., legislative staff member; b. Commerce, Ga., May 7, 1974. BA, Barry Coll., 1995. Dist. comm. dir. Office of Rep. Bob Barr, Marietta, Ga., 1996-98; comm. dir. Office of Rep. Bob Barr, Marietta, 1998—. Mem. Rep. Comm. Assn. Office: Office US Rep Bob Barr 1207 Longworth House Bldg Washington DC 20515-1007*

ALEXANDER, BRUCE DONALD, real estate executive, educator; b. Hartford, Conn., May 11, 1943. BA, Yale U., 1965, MA (hon.), 1998; JD, Duke U., 1968. With Rouse Co., Balt., 1969-96, sr. v.p., dir. comml. devel. divsn., 1978-93, sr. v.p., dir. new bus., 1993-96; dir. Balt. Equitable Ins., 1987-89, Enterprise Social Investment Corp., 1995—, Balt. Devel. Corp., 1996-98, R.W.D. Techs., Inc., 1997—; v.p., dir. New Haven and State Affairs Yale U., New Haven, 1998—, adj. prof. real estate, Yale Sch. Mgmt., 1998—. Trustee Goucher Coll., Balt., 1984—, chmn., 1991-96; trustee Columbia (Md.) Found., 1981-86, pres., 1983-85; trustee Balt. Ednl. Scholarship Trust, 1990-93; co-chair eastern region Yale U. Campaign, 1991-97; bd. dirs. Balt. Symphony Orch., 1986-91. Recipient John Franklin Goucher medal. Office: Yale Univ 433 Temple St New Haven CT 06511-6803

ALEXANDER, BURT EDWARD, management executive; b. Warren, Pa., June 21, 1946; s. Robert Henry and Margaret (Beckenbach) A.; m. Patricia Alene Wolfe, Mar. 15, 1969 (div.); 1 child, Jeffrey Robert; m. Lida Frances Greene, May 29, 1971 (separated); children: William Andrew, Christopher Edward. BS in Phys. Edn., W.Va. Wesleyan Coll., 1968; MA in Human Resource Mgmt., Pepperdine U., 1981; postgrad., Va. Poly. Inst. and State U., 1983-84. Mgmt. cons. Achievements in Mgmt., Unltd., Knoxville, Tenn., 1989-90; quality improvement cons. QualPro, Knoxville, 1990-97; v.p. orgn. effectiveness Beaulieu of Am., Dalton, Ga., 1997—. Pres. San Onofre PTO, Camp Pendleton, Calif., 1979-81; chmn. San Onofre Parents Action Com., Camp Pendleton, 1980-82; mem. U.S. English, Inc., Washington, 1986—; mem. Fedn. for Am. Immigration Reform, Washington, 1986—; bd. dirs. Setenga chpt. Nat. Multiple Sclerosis Soc., 1994-96; vice-chmn. bd. advisors Ctr. Internat. Standards and Quality, Ga. Inst. Tech. Lt. col. USMC, 1968-89. Mem. Am. Soc. Quality, Ret. Officers Assn. Republican. Methodist. Avocations: home improvement, theater, motivational speaking. Office: Beaulieu of Am 1502 Coronet Dr Dalton GA 30720-2664

ALEXANDER, C. ALEX, physician; b. Kerala, India, Mar. 1, 1935; s. Chandy and Sarah (Yohannan) A.; came to U.S., 1962, naturalized, 1974; m. Sudha Trivedi, July 1, 1982. M.D., U. Madras (India), 1958; M.P.H., Johns Hopkins U., 1964, D.P.H., 1966. Diplomate Am. Bd. Preventive Medicine, Intern, Muhlenberg Hosp., Plainfield, N.J., 1962-63; resident in preventive medicine Johns Hopkins U., Balt., 1964-66, asst. to assoc. prof. public health adminstrn., 1966-72; dir. med. affairs Provident Hosp., Balt., 1971-73; assoc. prof. social and preventive medicine Med. Sch., U. Md., Balt., 1972-75; chief of staff VA Med. Ctr., Dayton, Ohio, 1975-83, VA Med. Ctr., Castle Point, N.Y., 1983-90; chief of staff VA Med. Ctr., Ft. Howard, Md., 1990-95; dir. John J. Pershing VA Med. Ctr., Poplar Bluff, Mo., 1995-96; chief med. officer Vets. Integrated Svc., Network #6, Durham, N.C., 1996—; clin. prof. community medicine Wright State U., Dayton, 1975-83, asst. dean Sch. of Medicine, 1975-76; clin. prof. community medicine N.Y. Med. Coll., 1984-90, health svcs. adminstrn. uniformed svcs. U. Health Sci., Bethesda, Md., 1990-95; cons. WHO, 1969, USPHS, 1967-75. Col. M.C., U.S. Army Res. Recipient Disting. Service award Community Health Council Md., 1974; Leadership award VA, 1979; decorated meritorious svc. medal U.S. Army, 1991. Fellow Am. Coll. Preventive Medicine, Am. Public Health Assn., Am. Coll. International Physicians (pres. 1978-79, 90-91), Am. Coll. Healthcare Execs.; mem. Am. Legion. Syrian Orthodox. Office: Dept Vet Affairs Vets Integrated Svc # 1402 300 W Morgan St Durham NC 27701-2162

ALEXANDER, CARL ALBERT, ceramic engineer, educator; b. Chillicothe, Ohio, Nov. 22, 1928; s. Carl B. and Helen E. Alexander; m. Dolores J. Hertenstein, Sept. 4, 1954; children: Carla C., David A. B.S., Ohio U., 1953, M.S., 1956; Ph.D., Ohio State U., 1961. Mem. staff Battelle Columbus Labs., 1956—, research leader, 1974—, mgr. physico-chem. systems, 1976—; mem. faculty Ohio State U., 1963—, prof. ceramic and nuclear engring., 1977—; sr. research leader, chmn. tech. council of Biol. and Chem. Scis. Directorate, 1987—, chief scientist, 1987; prof. materials sci. and engring, 1988—;. Author; patentee in field. Served to lt. (j.g.) USNR, 1951-54. Recipient Merit award NASA, 1971, IR-100 award, 1987, R&D-100 award, 1988; citations Dept. Energy, citations AEC, citations ERDA. Mem. Am. Soc. Mass Spectrometry, Keramos, Sigma Xi. Home: 4249 Haughn Rd Grove City OH 43123-3216 Office: 505 King Ave Columbus OH 43201-2696

ALEXANDER, CECIL ABRAHAM, college official, architect, consultant; b. Atlanta, Mar. 14, 1918; s. Cecil Abraham and Julia (Moses) A.; m. Hermione Weil, Jan. 20, 1943 (dec. 1983); children: Therese, Judith, Douglas; m. Helen Eisemann, 1985. Student, Ga. Inst. Tech., 1936; A.B., Yale, 1940; student, Mass. Inst. Tech., 1941; M. Arch., Harvard, 1947. Partner Alexander & Rothschild (architects), Atlanta, 1949-58; chmn. bd. Finch, Alexander, Barnes, Rothschild & Paschal, Architects and Engrs., Inc., Atlanta, 1958-86; archtl. cons. Atlanta, 1986-90; coord. continuing edn. Ga. Inst. Tech. Coll. Architecture, Atlanta, 1994-96; prin.-in-charge Leo A. Daley Archtl. Engrs., Atlanta, 1996-97; ptnr. Alexander-Weiner Architects, Atlanta, 1997—; coord.; chmn. bd. A.S.D. Inc., interior design svc.; dir. Atlanta office Leo A. Daly Archtl. Engring. Internat.; chmn. Atlanta Citizens Adv. Com. Urban Renewal, 1958-60; vice chmn. Atlanta Met. Planning Commn., 1962—; past chmn. Ga. Fgn. Trade Zone Corp. Prin. works include Ga. Power Bldg., Atlanta, 1st Nat. Bank, Atlanta, Cin. Riverfront Stadium, Coca-Cola Internat. Hdqs., Sci. Atlanta Hdqs., U.S. Pavilion Expo '82, So. Bell. Hdqs. Past vice chmn. Community Coun., Atlanta, Ga.; mem. Mayor's Adv. Com. Race Relations, Nat. Citizens Com. Community Rels.; chmn. Atlanta chpt. Am. Jewish Com., 1963; chmn. housing resources com. City of Atlanta; past chmn. com. Yale Sch. Architecture; pres., founder Resurgens Atlanta; past v.p. Atlanta Symphony Orch.; Mem. Yale Nat. Alumni Bd., 1963; bd. dirs. Atlanta U.; bd. dirs., Clark Atlanta U.; past bd. dirs. Marist High Sch., Atlanta; chmn. Com. to Combat Drugged and Drunken Driving; past pres. Atlanta's Clifton Corridor Biomed. Rsch. Com. Served to lt. col. USMCR, World War II. Decorated Air medal, D.F.C.; (2) Recipient Brotherhood award NCCJ, 1973; Archdiocesan medal of St. Paul, 1980, Yale medal, 1980. Fellow AIA (pres. Ga. 1957, Ivan Allen award); mem. Atlanta C. of C. (dir.). Home: 2677 Rivers Rd NW Atlanta GA 30305-3549

ALEXANDER, CHRISTINA ANAMARIA, translator, performing company executive; b. Bucuresti, Romania, June 30; naturalized U.S. citizen, 1975.; d. Peter Vladimir and Maria Nicolae (Suciu) A. BA, Old Dominion U., 1990, MA, 1992; PhD in Religion (hon.), Pacific Universal Life Ch., 1996. Translator, interpreter Word for Word, Inc., Norfolk, Va., 1990—; exec. dir. KultureKastle, Virginia Beach, Va., 1996—; instr. lang. Prague (Czech Republic) Lang. Sch., 1990-91; adj. faculty Old Dominion U., Norfolk, 1993; cons. pub. rels. High Frequency Wavelengths, N.Y.C., 1995-96; cons. V.A.C.A., Richmond, Va., 1995-96. Performing artist MARA Agy., Vienna, Austria, 1994, Joy Fund Theater, Norfolk, 1996-97, Boys and Girls Club, Inc., Newport News, Va., 1997, M.E. Cox Ctr., Virginia Beach, 1997, Waterfront Arts Festival, Virginia Beach, 1997, Cox Comm., 1997; creator, dancer, choreographer Secret of the Lost Treasure, 1997 (award 1997); dancer Mantra, 1997; performing artist Mara Agy., Vienna. Named Ms. Petite Va. Beach, 1996. Mem. Hampton Roads Cultural Alliance. Avocations: skiing, traveling, costume design, nutrition. Office: Ste 125 5649 Princess Anne Rd Virginia Beach VA 23462-6119

ALEXANDER, CLIFFORD JOSEPH, lawyer; b. New Orleans, Oct. 2, 1943; s. Charles Ernest and Lois Primus (Boley) A.; m. Elizabeth McAnany, June 11, 1966; children: Brian, Heather, Rachel. A.B. Rockhurst Coll. 1966, J.D. Georgetown U. 1969. Bar: Mass. 1970, D.C. 1977. Mem. staff SEC, Washington, 1967-70; assoc. Gaston Snow & Ely Bartlett, Boston, 1970-75; mem. staff U.S. Senate Banking Com., Washington, 1975-77; mem. Kirkpatrick & Lockhart LLP (formerly Kirkpatrick, Lockhart, Hill, Christopher & Phillips, and predecessor), Washington, 1977—. Editor: Money Managers Compliance Manual, The Investment Lawyer. Mem. ABA (corp., banking and bus. law sect.), Boston Bar Assn., Fed. Bar Assn. (securities and banking law sects.). Home: 8721 Bluedale St Alexandria VA 22308-2307 Office: Kirkpatrick & Lockhart 1800 Massachusetts Ave NW Fl 2 Washington DC 20036-1800

ALEXANDER, DAWN ALICIA, public relations executive; b. Washington, Dec. 13, 1955; d. Kenneth Sandy and Vashti (Tansil) A. Student, New Eng. Conservatory Music, Boston, 1973-75, Howard U., 1975-77. Asst. pres. sec. U.S. Senator Gary Hart, Washington, 1976-85; press sec. Oliver Pudge Henkel campaign mgr. Gary Hart for Pres., Dem. Nat. Conv., San Francisco, 1984; regional press desk coord. Mondale-Ferraro campaign, Washington, 1984; dep. press sec. Gary Hart for Pres., Denver, 1987; exec. asst., press sec. Hon. Charlene D. Jarvis, nat. co-chair Clinton-Gore Campaign, Washington, 1985—; dep. press sec. 1992 Presdl. Inaugural Com., Washington, 1993; asst. pres. sec. The White House, Washington, 1993-95; v.p. Burson-Marsteller, Washington, 1995-96, sr. v.p., dir., 1996—. Vice pres., pres.-elect Bright Beginnings, 1999—. Mem. D.C. C. of C. (bd. dirs., chair comm. com. 1998). Office: Burson-Marsteller 1801 K St NW Washington DC 20006-1301

ALEXANDER, DEAN, museum director. Supt. Kalaupapa (Hawaii) Nat. Hist. Park. Office: Kalaupapa Nat Hist Park 7 Puahi St PO Box 2222 Kalaupapa HI 96742-2222

ALEXANDER, DON, state official; m. Anita Alexander; children: Greg, Chris. Ed., Ark. State U., Jonesboro. With Ark. State Plant Bd., 1973—, mgr. comml. pest control sect., dir. plant industry divsn., dir., 1995—; mem. Ark. Fire Ant Adv. Bd., So. Plant Bd., Nat. Plant Bd. Mem. Bryant (Ark.) City Coun. Mem. Soc. for Regulatory Protection, Optimists Internat. Office: Ark State Plant Bd 1 Natural Resources Dr Little Rock AR 72205

ALEXANDER, DONALD CRICHTON, lawyer; b. Pine Bluff, Ark., May 22, 1921; s. William Crichton and Ella Temple (Fox) A.; m. Margaret Louise Savage, Oct. 9, 1946; children: Robert C., James M. BA with honors, Yale U., 1942; LLB magna cum laude, Harvard U., 1948; LLD (hon.), St. Thomas Inst., 1975, Capital U., 1989. Bar: D.C. 1949, Ohio 1954, N.Y. 1978. Assoc. Covington & Burling, Washington, 1948-54, Taft, Stettinius & Hollister, Cin., 1954-56; ptnr. Taft, Stettinius & Hollister, 1956-66, Dinsmore, Shohl, Coates & Deupree, Cin., 1966-73; commr. IRS, 1973-77; mem. Commn. on Fed. Paperwork, 1975-77; ptnr. Olwine, Connelly, Chase, O'Donnell & Weyher, N.Y.C., Washington, 1977-79, Morgan, Lewis & Bockius, N.Y.C. and Washington, 1979-85, Cadwalader, Wickersham & Taft, Washington, 1985-93, Akin, Gump, Strauss, Hauer & Feld, Washington, 1993—; mem. adv. bd. NYU Tax Inst., 1969-73, 77-87, Tax Mgmt., Inc., 1968-73, 77—; mem. adv. Treas. Dept., 1970-72; mem. adv. group to commr. IRS, 1969-70, chmn. exempt orgns. adv. group, 1987-89; mem. adv. bd. Mertens, 1986—, Maxwell Macmillan fed. Taxes 2d, 1989-92; commr. Martin Luther King, Jr. Fed. Holiday Commn., 1993-96. Author: The Arkansas Plantation, 1943; contbr. more than 40 articles on fed. taxation. Co-chmn. bd. advisors NYU/IRS Continuing Profl. Edn. Program, 1982-85; dir. Treasury Hist. Assn., 1996—. Served to capt. AUS, 1942-45. Decorated Silver Star, Bronze Star. Mem. ABA (vice chmn. taxation sect. 1967-68), Am. Law Inst. (tax adv. group), U.S. C. of C. (taxation com. 1971-91, bd. dirs. 1984-89, health and employee benefit com. 1989-94, regulatory affairs com. 1993—), Chevy Chase Club (Md.), Met. Club, Nantucket Yacht Club (Mass.), Mill Reef Club (Antigua, B.W.I.), Yale Club N.Y. Home: 2801 New Mexico Ave NW Washington DC 20007-3921 Office: Akin Gump Strauss Hauer & Feld Ste 400 1333 New Hampshire Ave NW Washington DC 20036-1564

ALEXANDER, DRURY BLAKELEY, architectural educator; b. Paris, Tex., Feb. 4, 1924; s. Drury Blakeley and Katherine (Stone) A. B.Arch., U. Tex., 1950, B.S. in Art, 1951; M.A., Columbia U., 1953. Instr. Kans. State U., Manhattan, 1953-55; asst. prof. architecture U. Tex., Austin, 1955-60, assoc. prof. architecture, 1960-67, prof. architecture, 1967-84, Meadows Found. prof. Architecture, 1984-94, emeritus prof., 1994—. Author: Texas Homes of the 19th Century, 1966; Sources of Classicism, 1978. Chmn., Historic Landmark Commn., Austin, 1975-85. Served with U.S. Army, 1943-46, ETO. Recipient Disting. Svc. award City of Austin, 1976, Svc. award for Hist. Preservation, Heritage Soc. of Austin, 1976, Tex. Hist. Preservation award Tex. Hist. Commn., 1986, Nat. Preservation Honor award Nat. Trust for Hist. Preservation, 1991, Tex. Soc. Architects Disting. Achievement award in Archtl. Edn., 1994, Disting. Prof. award Assn. Collegiate Schs of Arch., 1995; named Eugene McDermott Lectr., U. Tex., 1983-85; Alexander Archtl. Archive named in his honor U. Tex. Mem. Soc. Archtl. Historians (bd. dirs. 1979-82), Assn. Preservation Technologists, Victorian Soc. Am. Democrat. Presbyterian. Avocations: Book collecting; travel. Home: 811 E 38th St Austin TX 78705-1809 Office: Sch Architecture U Tex Austin TX 78712

ALEXANDER, DUANE FREDERICK, pediatrician, research administrator; b. Balt., Aug. 11, 1940; s. Fred Lucas and Christiana H. (Showacre) A.; m. Marianne Ellis, June 23, 1963; children: Keith Duane, Kristin Marianne. B.S., Pa. State U., 1962; M.D., Johns Hopkins U., 1966. Diplomate: Am. Bd. Pediatrics. Intern Johns Hopkins Hosp., Balt., 1966-67, resident, 1967-68, fellow, 1970-71; commd. officer USPHS, 1968—, now rear adm.; clin. assoc. Nat. Inst. Child Health and Human Devel., NIH, Bethesda, Md., 1968-70, asst. to sci. dir., 1971-74, asst. to dir., 1978-82, dep. dir., 1982-86, dir., 1986—; staff pediatrician Nat. Commn. for Protection of Human Subjects of Research, 1974-78. Contbr. articles to profl. jours. Recipient Commendation medal USPHS, 1970, Meritorious Svc. medal USPHS, 1985, Spl. Recognition medal USPHS, 1985, Surgeon Gen.'s Exemplary Svc. medal, 1990, Irving B. Harris Lectureship award Soc. Behavioral Pediatrics, 1991, Pub. Svc. award Am. Coll. Ob-Gyn., 1992, Surgeon Gen.'s Medallion, 1993, Disting. Pub. Svc. award Am. Acad. Phys. Medicine and Rehab., 1993, Presdl. Citation, APA, 1992; Sec.'s Disting. Svc. award HHS, 1997, 98; alumni fellow Pa. State U. Alumni Assn, 1993. Fellow Am. Acad. Pediatrics, Soc. Devel. Pediatrics, Am. Pediatric Soc., Assn. for Retarded Citizens. Methodist. Office: Nat Inst Child Health-Human Devel Bldg 31 Rm 2A03 31 Center Dr MSC 2425 Bethesda MD 20892-2425

ALEXANDER, EBEN, JR., neurological surgeon; b. Knoxville, Tenn., Sept. 14, 1913; s. Eben and Elizabeth (MacMath) A.; m. Elizabeth West, Oct. 8, 1942; children: Jean Alexander, Eben III, Elizabeth MacMath, Phyllis Slye. AB, U. N.C., 1935; MD cum laude, Harvard U., 1939. Diplomate: Am. Bd. Neurol. Surgery. Intern Peter Bent Brigham Hosp., Boston, 1939-41, resident in neurosurgery, 1947-48, jr. assoc. neurosurgery, 1946-47; intern The Children's Hosp., Boston, 1939-41, resident in neurosurgery, 1941-42, 47-48, also neurosurg. fellow; surg. fellow Harvard U. Med. Sch., Cambridge, Mass., asst. in surgery, 1947-48; resident in neurosurgery Toronto (Can.) Gen. Hosp., 1948-49; mem. faculty Bowman Gray Sch. Medicine, Wake Forest U., Winston-Salem, N.C., 1949—, prof. neurosurgery, 1954—, head sect. neurosurgery, 1949-78, chmn. com. on ethics, mem. joint adminstrv. bd. with N.C. Bapt. Hosp., 1972-78; chief profl. services N.C. Bapt. Hosp., Wake Forest U., 1953-73, mem. staff, 1949—; bd. sci. counselors Nat. Inst. Neurol. Disease and Blindness, 1961-64, mem. program project com., 1967-71, mem. neurol. sci. research com., 1962-66; adv. com. Clin. Neurol. Info. Ctr., 1972—; mem. brain tumor study group Nat. Cancer Inst., 1968-81; past pres. United Med. Research Found., N.C.; mem. Nat. Bd. Med. Examiners, 1980-87, liaison com. med. edn., 1981-85; mem. N.C. Bd. Med. Examiners, 1984-87, chmn., 1988—. Author numerous articles in field.; mem. editorial bd.: Jour. Neurosurgery, 1961-70, editorial bd., chmn. 1969-70; editor: Surg. Neurology, 1986-93. Pres. Harvard U. Med. Sch. Class 1939. Served to maj. M.C., AUS, 1942-46. Decorated Bronze Star. Fellow ACS (v.p. 1976-77); mem. AAAS, Am. Acad. Neurol. Surgeons (sec.-treas. 1953-57, v.p. 1962-63, pres. 1980-81), Am. Surg. Assn., Harvey Cushing Soc. (pres. 1966), AMA (chmn. sect. coun. neurosurgery 1969-74, del. intersplty. adv. bd. 1971-81, adv. bd. 1976-78, chmn. 1979-80, mem. coun. on med. edn. 1978-86, Disting. Svc. award 1989), Am. Assn. Neurol. Surgeons (Soc. of Neurol. Surgeons award, Disting. Svc. award, 1990), Harvard Med. Alumni Assn. (pres. 1980-81), N.C. Surg. Assn., Mass., Forsyth County, N.C. med. socs., Neurosurg. Soc. Am., Congress Neurol. Surgeons (honored guest), Neurosurg. Travel Club, N.C., So. neurosurg. socs., Soc. Neurol. Surgery (pres. 1972-73, historian 1984—), Deutsche Gesselschaft für Neurochirurgie (corr.), Torch Club, Old Town Club, Forsyth Assembly Club (pres. Winston-Salem 1977), Rotary (past pres. Winston-Salem 1977), Alpha Omega Alpha, Nu Sigma Nu, Sigma Alpha Epsilon. Methodist. Home: 767 Arbor Rd Winston Salem NC 27104-2209 Office: Wake Forest U Bowman Gray Sch Medicine Med Ctr Blvd Winston Salem NC 27157-1002

ALEXANDER, EDWARD RUSSELL, retired disease research administrator, educator; b. Chgo., June 15, 1928; s. Russell Green and Ethelyn Satterlee (Abel) A. PhB, U. Chgo., 1948, BS, 1950, MD, 1953. Intern Cin. Gen. Hosp.; chief surveillance sect. Communicable Disease Center, Atlanta, 1955-57, 59-60; resident, instr. dept. pediatrics U. Chgo., 1954-55, 57-59; asst. prof. dept. preventive medicine and dept. pediatrics U. Wash., Seattle, 1961-65; asso. prof. U. Wash., 1965-69, prof., 1969-79; chmn. dept. epidemiology U. Wash. (Sch. Pub. Health), 1970-75; prof. dept. pediatrics U. Ariz., Tucson, 1979-83; dir. rsch. br., venereal diseases control div. Ctrs. for Disease Control, Atlanta, 1983-89, asst. dir. sci. sexually transmitted diseases div., 1989; chief of epidemiology Seattle King County Dept. Pub. Health, Seattle, 1990-98; prof. dept. epidemiology U. Wash. Sch. Pub. Health, Seattle, 1990-98, prof. emeritus, 1998—. Contbr. articles to profl. jours. Markle scholar, 1962-67. Mem. Am. Acad. Pediatrics, Am. Pediatric Soc., Am. Pub. Health Assn. (Abraham Lilienfeld award 1988), Assn. Tchrs. Preventive Medicine, Am. Epidemiol. Soc. (pres. 1986-87), Soc. Epidemiol. Research, Internat. Epidemiol. Soc., Am. Venereal Disease Assn. (Thomas Parran award 1984, pres. 1985-87).

ALEXANDER, ELLIN DRIBBEN, financial marketing company executive; b. Albany, N.Y., July 20, 1955; d. Irving S. and Helen (Meyer) Dribben; m. Richard D. Alexander, May 18, 1984; children: Evan R., Elisabeth D., Hannah Claire. BA, St. Lawrence U., 1977; postgrad., Boston U., 1978—. Asst. dir. devel. Northea. Assn of the Blind, Albany, 1979-80; mktg. rep. Newkirk, Albany, 1980-85, asst. v.p., 1985—, mgr. trust info. and comm. sys., 1990-98, product mgr. will files and direct mail programs, 1998—; bd. dirs. Albany Dist. Postal Customer Coun. Fundraiser Am. Cancer Soc., Albany, 1988-92; bd. dirs. Arbor House, Albany, 1980-88; bd. dirs. ARC N.E. N.Y., 1992—, chairperson bd. dirs., 1995-97; mem. N.Y. State Svc. Coun., ARC, 1997—; campaign divsn. chmn. United Way of N.E. N.Y., bd. dirs., 1990-95. Mem. N.Y. State Realtors Assn., Albany County Bd. Realtors, Jr. League Albany (bd. dirs. 1980-81, 83, 86, 88, 90-95), Phi Beta Kappa, Omega Delta Kappa. Roman Catholic. Avocations: gardening, theatre, volunteer work. Office: Newkirk 15 Corporate Cir Albany NY 12203-5177

ALEXANDER, EUGENE MORTON, electronics engineer; b. Phila., Aug. 15, 1926; s. Morris and Jennie Alexander; m. Marcia Geer, Dec. 18, 1949; children: Susan, Amy. Student Swarthmore Coll., 1944-45. BSEE, U. Pa., 1949, MSEE, 1961. Electronic engr. Philco Corp., Phila., 1949-54; with RCA Corp., 1955-87, mgr. communications systems design, Camden and Paramus, N.J., Tucson, Ariz., 1961-65, mgr. med. electronic design, Camden and Nutley, N.J., 1966-68, mgr. communication and electronic mail systems design, Camden, 1969-79, mgr. electronic computer-originated mail project for U.S. Postal Svc., Camden, 1980-84, mgr. robotic vision and adaptive robotics programs, RCA Advanced Tech. Labs., Moorestown, N.J., 1984-87; mgr. technical program mgmt. GE/RCA Advanced Tech Labs, Moorestown; ind. cons. in tech. mgmt., 1988—. Ensign USNR, 1944-46. Recipient Engring. Achievement award Philco Corp., 1953. Mem. IEEE (sr.). Home and Office: 309 Cranford Rd Cherry Hill NJ 08003-3147

ALEXANDER, F. WILEY, columnist; b. Trinity, Tex., Aug. 25, 1935; s. Joe and Mary Sue (Gregory) A.; m. Norma F. McSpadden, June 17, 1956; children: Karen Sue, Susan Kay, Kristy Marie. BA, Okla. Bapt. U., 1962. Country music columnist Ft. Worth Star-Telegram, Houston Post, San Antonio Express News; country music reporter Country Weekly Mag., Nashville. Vol. spokesperson Door for the Disabled, San Antonio, 1994. Wiley award named in his honor San Antonio chpt. Tex. Music Assn., 1997; named to Tex. Music Hall of Fame. Home: 2803 Hitching Post St San Antonio TX 78217-5847 Office: San Antonio Express News Ave E at Houston San Antonio TX 78297

ALEXANDER, FRANK, publisher, editor; b. San Diego, Feb. 20, 1943. BA, Utah State Coll., 1965; MA, Stanford Univ., 1967. Publ., editor Front Row Experience, Byron, Calif., 1974—. Office: Front Row Experience 540 Discovery Bay Blvd Byron CA 94514-9454*

ALEXANDER, FRED CALVIN, JR., lawyer; b. Abingdon, Va., Nov. 4, 1931; s. Fred C. and Mary F. (White) A.; m. Betsy Jones, May 17, 1957 (div.); children—Mitchell, Mary, Marjorie, Margaret; m. Janet Lee Hammond, Jan. 2, 1982. Student, Davidson Coll., 1950-52; BA, U. Va., 1954, LLB, 1959. Bar: Va. 1959, U.S. Dist. Ct. (ea. dist.) Va. 1959, U.S. Ct. Appeals (4th cir.) 1960. Assoc. Boothe, Prichard & Dudley, Alexandria, Va., 1959-64; ptnr. McGuire, Woods, Battle & Boothe LLP and predecessor firms, Alexandria, Va., 1964-97; ret. McGuire, Woods, Battle & Boothe LLP and predecessor firms, McLean, Va., 1997; mem. jud. conf. U.S. Ct. Appeals (4th cir.), 1964—; lectr. legal edn. Va. State Bar, 1970, 75-77, 89; chmn. adv. com. rules of ct. Supreme Ct. of Va., 1984-98; bd. dirs. Thomas Rutherford, Inc. Past bd. dirs. counsel to Alexandria Hosp., St. Stephens Sch. 1st lt. U.S. Army, 1954-56. Fellow Am. Coll. Trial Lawyers (chmn. Va. com. 1994-96), Va. Law Found.; mem. Alexandria Bar Assn. (pres. 1969-70), Va. Bar Assn. (chmn. civil litigation sect. 1989-92), Va. Assn. Def. Attys., Va. Trial Lawyers Assn., Nat. Assn. R.R. Trial Counsel, Def. Rsch. Inst. (chmn. railroad law com. 1989-92), Belle Haven Country Club (bd. dirs. 1997—), Wyndemere Country Club. Episcopalian. Home: 1313 Gatewood Dr Alexandria VA 22307-2033 Office: McGuire Woods Battle & Boothe LLP 1750 Tyson Blvd McLean VA 22102*

ALEXANDER, GARY R., lawyer, state legislator, lobbyist; b. Washington, Nov. 16, 1942; s. Orville I. and Ann C. (Zalkind) A.; m. Carole R. Coburn, Dec. 23, 1967; children: Jennifer Paige, Cory Brooke. BA, U. Va., 1964; LLB, George Washington U., 1967. Pvt. practice Washington, Md. and Va., 1967-69; ptnr. Giordano, Alexander, Haas, Mahoney & Bush, Oxen Hill, Md., 1970-78, Haas & Alexander, Md., 1978-82; prin. ptnr. Alexander & Cleaver, P.A., Ft. Washington, Md., 1982—; bd. dirs., chmn. Prince George County bar legis. com., 1972-79. Del. Md. Ho. of Dels., 1983-94, spkr. pro tem, 1993-94; chmn. Dem. Cen. Com., Prince George County, 1978-86; people's counsel Md. Pub. Svc. Commn., 1974-78; apptd. Gov.'s Task Force to Study Gambling, Md., 1993; mem. taxation com. Md. C. of C., 1995; bd. dirs. U. Md. Found. Recipient Outstanding Svc. award Md. Senate, 1976, Outstanding Svc. citation, 1976, Pub. Svc. cert. Prince George County Exec. and County Coun., 1976, Local Employer of Yr. award Bus. and Profl. Woman's Club, 1993, Outstanding Atty. award Washington mag., 1997. Mem. ABA (chmn. automobile law com. 1975-77, chmn. automobile ins. legis. com. 1977-80), Nat. Conf. State Legislatures, Md. Bar Assn. (chmn. fed. laws com. 1973-79), D.C. Bar Assn., Va. Bar Assn., Md. Govt. Rels. Assn. Jewish. Avocations: history, gardening, golf. Office: Alexander & Cleaver PA 11414 Livingston Rd Fort Washington MD 20744-5145 also: Alexander & Cleaver PA 54 State Cir Annapolis MD 21401-1906

ALEXANDER, GEORGE JONATHON, law educator, former dean; b. Berlin, Germany, Mar. 8, 1931; s. Walter and Sylvia (Grill) A.; m. Katharine Violet Sziklai, Sept. 6, 1958; children: Susan Katina, George Jonathon II. AB with maj. honors, U. Pa., 1953, JD cum laude, 1959; LLM, Yale U., 1965, JSD, 1969. Bar: Ill. 1960, N.Y. 1961, Calif. 1974. Instr. law, Bigelow fellow U. Chgo., 1959-60; instr. internat. relations Naval Res. Officers Sch., Forrest Park, Ill., 1959-60; prof. law Syracuse U. Coll. Law, 1960-70, assoc. dean, 1968-69; prof. law U. Santa Clara (Calif.) Law Sch., 1970—, disting. univ. prof., 1994-95, Elizabeth H. and John A. Sutro prof. law, 1995—, pres. faculty senate, 1996-97, dean, 1970-85, dir. Inst. Internat. and Comparative Law, 1986—, dir. grad. programs, 1997—; dir. summer programs at Oxford, Geneva, Strasbourg, Budapest, Tokyo, Hong Kong, Beijing, Ho Chi Minh City, Singapore, Bangkok, Kuala Lumpur, Seoul, Munich; vis. prof. law U. So. Calif., 1963; vis. scholar Stanford (Calif.) U. Law Sch., 1985-86, 92; cons. in field. Author: Civil Rights, U.S.A., Public Schools, 1963, Honesty and Competition, 1967, Jury Instructing on Medical Issues, 1966, Cases and Materials on Space Law, 1971, The Aged and the Need for Surrogate Management, 1972, Commercial Torts, 1973, 2d edit. 1988, U.S. Antitrust Laws, 1980, Writing A Living Will: Using a Durable Power of Attorney, 1988, (with Scheflin) Law and Mental Disabilities, 1998; author, editor: International Perspectives on Aging, 1992; also articles, chpts. in books, one film. Dir. Domestic and Internat. Bus. Problems Honors Clinic, Syracuse U., 1966-69, Regulations in Space Project, 1968-70; ednl. cons. Comptroller Gen. U.S., 1977—; mem. Nat. Sr. Citizens Law Ctr., 1983-89, pres., 1986-90; co-founder Am. Assn. Abolition Involuntary Mental Hospitalization, 1970, dir., 1970-83. With USN, 1953-56. U.S. Navy scholar U. Pa., 1949-52; Law Bds. scholar, 1956-59; Sterling fellow Yale, 1964-65; recipient Ralph E. Kharas Civil Liberties award, 1970, Owens award as Alumnus of Yr., 1984, Disting. prof. Santa Clara Univ. Faculty Senate, 1994-95. Mem. Internat. Acad. Law Mental Health (mem. sci. com. 1997—), Calif. Bar Assn. (first chmn. com. legal problems of aging), Assn. Am. Law Schs., Soc. Am. Law Tchrs. (dir., pres. 1979), AAUP (chpt. pres. 1962), N.Y. Civil Liberties Union (chpt. pres. 1965, dir., v.p. 1966-70), Am. Acad. Polit. and Social Sci., Order of Coif, Justinian Honor Soc., Phi Alpha Delta (chpt. faculty adviser 1967-70). Home: 11600 Summit Wood Ct Los Altos CA 94022-4500 Office: U Santa Clara Sch Law Santa Clara CA 95053 *I think a primary purpose of law is the protection of individual rights. That requires disproportionate attention to the interests of groups not in the mainstream of our society.*

ALEXANDER, GERRY L., state supreme court justice; b. Aberdeen, Wash., Apr. 28, 1936. BA, U. Wash., 1958, JD, 1964. Bar: Wash. 1964. Pvt. practice Olympia, Wash., 1964-73; judge Wash. Superior Ct., Olympia, 1973-85, Wash. Ct. Appeals Divsn. II, Olympia, 1985-95; justice Wash. Supreme Ct., Olympia, 1995—. Lt. U.S. Army, 1958-61. Mem. ABA, Am. Judges Assn., Wash. State Bar Assn., Thurston-Mason County Assn. (pres. 1973), Puget Sound Inn of Ct. (pres. 1996). Office: Temple of Justice PO Box 40929 Olympia WA 98504-0929

ALEXANDER, HAROLD CAMPBELL, insurance consultant; b. Houston, Dec. 11, 1920; s. Henry Campbell and Essie Mae (Gilbert) A.; m. Dorothy Emma Schraub, Aug. 21, 1925; children: Linda Carol, Beverly Lynn Whitworth, Daniel James Alexander, William Campbell. BS, Miss. State U., 1938-42; postgrad., South Tex. Sch. Law, 1954-56, Harvard U., 1943, Navy Fin. and Supply Sch., 1942-43. Asst. div. credit mgr. Continental Emsco Co., Houston, 1953-56; gen. agt. and mgr. United Founders Life Ins. Co., 1956-69; mgr. Holt & Bridges Ins., Houston, 1960-69; owner, pres. Holt & Alexander Ins. Agy., Inc., Houston, 1969-85; ins. cons. Lawrence Ilfrey & Co., Houston, 1985—; adv. bd. dirs. NBC Bank. Pres. Meyerland Cmty. Improvement Assn., 1969. Served as lt. commdr. USN, 1942-46, 1950-52. Mem. Profl. Ins. Agts. Tex. (state bd. dirs. 1973-74), Soc. Cert. Ins. Counselors. Republican. Presbyterian. Club: Pine Forest Country, Club of Houston. Avocation: golf. Home and Office: 8727 Manhattan Dr Houston TX 77096-1318

ALEXANDER, HERBERT E., political scientist; b. Waterbury, Conn., Dec. 21, 1927; s. Nathan and Pearl (Shub) A.; m. Nancy Frances Greenfield, Dec. 5, 1953; children: Michael David, Andrew Steven, Kenneth Bruce. BA, U. N.C., 1949; MA, U. Conn., 1951; PhD, Yale U., 1958. Asso. dir. adminstrn. officer money in politics research project U. N.C. at Chapel Hill, 1954-55; instr. Princeton U., 1956-58; dir. Citizens' Rsch. Found., Princeton, 1958-78; dir. Citizens' Rsch. Found., L.A., 1978-98, dir. emeritus, 1998—; prof. polit. sci. U. So. Calif., 1978—, prof. emeritus, 1998—; exec. dir. Pres.'s Com. on Campaign Costs, Washington, 1961-62; cons. Pres. U.S., 1962-64, House Adminstrn. Com., 1966-67, Comptroller Gen. U.S. and Office Fed. Elections at GAO, 1972-73, Senate Select Com. on Presdl. Campaign Activities, 1973-74; vis. lectr. Princeton U., 1965, U. Pa., Phila., 1967-68, Yale U., 1977; cons. N.J. Election Law Enforcement Commn., 1973-78, 82, 86, N.Y. State Bd. Elections, 1974-76, Ill. Bd. Elections, 1974-75, Gov. of R.I., 1987, others. Author: Money in Politics, 1972, Financing the 1976 Election, 1979, Financing the 1980 Election, 1983, Financing Politics, 1976, 2d edit., 1980, 3d edit., 1984 4th edit., 1992, Campaign Money, 1976; (with Brian A. Haggerty) Financing the 1984 Election, 1987; editor: Studies in Money in Politics, vol. 1, 1965, vol. 2, 1970, vol. 3, 1974, Comparative Political Finance in the 1980s, 1989, (with Rei Shiratori) Comparative Political Finance Among the Democracies, 1994, (with Monica Bauer) Financing the 1988 Election, 1991, Reform and Reality: The Financing of State and Local Campaigns, 1991, (with Anthony Corrado) Financing the 1992 Election, 1995. Served with AUS, 1946-47. Mem. Am. Polit. Sci. Assn., Nat. Mcpl. League, Pi Sigma Alpha. Home: Unit 311 2900 N Leisure World Blvd Silver Spring MD 20906

ALEXANDER, JAMES GARTH, architect; b. Phila., Aug. 25, 1942; s. Nelson Eugene and Lenore Lillian (Hummel) A.; m. Suzanne Carolyn Salisbury, June 17, 1962 (div. Oct. 1968); children: Kimberly Alexander Shilland, Amy Alexander Swarts. BArch, Pa. State U., 1965; postgrad., Archtl. Assn., London, 1964. Arch. Anderson, Notter Assocs., Boston, 1969-72, assoc., 1972-77; prin. Anderson Notter Finegold Inc., Boston, 1977-83, Notter Finegold & Alexander Inc., Boston, 1983-92, Finegold Alexander & Assocs., Inc., Boston, 1992—; thesis advisor, guest lectr. Boston Archtl. Ctr., 1972—; guest design critic Harvard Grad. Sch. of Design, Cambridge, Mass., 1988, 90, 93. Prin. works include 303 Congress St., Boston, Old City Hall (Nat. honor award 1972), Boston, Market Sq. (Nat. honor award 1980), Newburyport, Mass., The Berkeley Bldg., Boston (Bldg. Mgrs. and Owners Assn. Bldg. of Yr. award 1990, Mass. Hist. Commn. award 1989), restoration of Nott Meml., Union Coll., (Nat. Trust Honor award), 1996. Dir. Hist. Mass., Inc., Boston, 1993—, Ellis Meml. Neighborhood Care Svcs., Boston, 1988—; v.p. Bostonian Soc., 1989—; mem. Boston Landmarks Commn., 1982-98. Recipient honor award for restoration of Immigration Mus., Ellis Island Nat. Endowment of the Arts, 1991, Nat. Trust for Hist. Preservation, 1991. Fellow AIA (Bacon medal for restoration of Ellis Island Nat. Mus. Immigration 1991); mem. Boston Soc. Archs. (bd. dirs. 1991-93), Nat. Trust for Hist. Preservation, Bldg. Owners and Mgrs. Assn. Avocations: tennis, swimming, skiing, restoration of historic homes. Home: 16 Gray St Boston MA 02116-6226 Office: Finegold Alexander & Assocs 77 N Washington St Boston MA 02114-1908

ALEXANDER, JAMES WESLEY, surgeon, educator; b. El Dorado, Kans., May 23, 1934; s. Rossiter Wells and Merle Lydia Alexander; m. Maureen L. Strohofer; children: Joseph, Judith, Elizabeth, Randolph, John Charles, Lori, Molly. Student, Tex. Technol. Coll., 1951-53; MD, U. Tex., 1957; ScD, U. Cin., 1958-64; postgrad., U. Minn., 1966-67. Diplomate Am. Bd. Surgery, Am. Bd. Thoracic Surgery; lic. physician, Ohio. Intern Cin. Gen. Hosp., 1957-58; resident U. Cin.-Cin. Gen. Hosp., 1958-64; mem. faculty Coll. Medicine, U. Cin., 1962-64, 66—, prof. surgery, 1975—, dir. transplantation div., dept. surgery, 1967—, dir. surg. immunology lab., 1967—; dir. research Shriners Burns Inst., 1979-90; practice medicine and surgery Cin., 1966—; mem. staff U. Cin. Hosp., Bethesda Hosp., Cin. Children's Hosp., Christ Hosp., Good Samaritan Hosp., Jewish Hosp.; mem. study sect. NIH, 1983-87, 89-93, chmn., 1990-93, ad hoc com., 1990-99. Author: (with R.A. Good) Fundamentals of Clinical Immunology, 1977; mem. editl. bd. Annals of Surgery, 1975—, Jour. Burn Care and Rehab., 1979—, Burns, Including Thermal Injury, 1985—, Graft, 1998, Jour. Parenteral and Enteral Nutrition, 1991—, Nutrition, 1991—, Transplantation Sci., 1991-94, Transplantation, 1994—, Jour. Trauma, 1998; contbr. more than 650 articles to profl. jours. Served as capt. M.C., U.S. Army, 1964-66. Mem. AAAS, Am. Assn. for Surgery of Trauma, Am. Assn. Immunologists, Am. Burn Assn. (pres. 1984-85), ACS, Am. Soc. Transplant Surgeons (sec. 1985-87, pres. elect 1987-88, pres. 1988-89), Am. Soc. Parenteral and Enteral Nutrition, Am. Surg. Assn., Assn. for Acad. Surgery, Central Surg. Assn., Cin. Acad. Medicine, Cin. Surg. Soc., Halsted Soc., Internat. Soc. Surgery, Colombian Coll. Surgeons (hon.), Peruvian Acad. Surgery (hon.), St. Paul Surg. Soc. (hon.), Ohio Med. Assn., Soc. Univ. Surgeons, Surg. Biology Club, Surg. Infection Soc. (sec. 1981-84, pres.-elect 1985-86, pres. 1986-87), Tranplantation Soc., Shock Soc., Mont Reid Surg. Soc., Alpha Omega Alpha, Alpha Chi, Alpha Epsilon Delta, Phi Eta Sigma. Home: 757 Riverwatch Dr Crescent Springs KY 41017-4480 Office: U Cin Coll Medicine 231 Bethesda Ave Cincinnati OH 45229-2827

ALEXANDER, JANE, federal agency administrator, actress, producer; b. Boston, Oct. 28, 1939; d. Thomas Bartlett and Ruth (Pearson) Quigley; m. Robert Alexander, July 23, 1962 (div. 1969); 1 child, Jason; m. Edwin Sherin, Mar. 29, 1975. Student, Sarah Lawrence Coll., 1957-59, U. Edinburgh, 1959-60; LHD, Wilson Coll., 1984; DFA (hon.), The Julliard Sch., 1994, N.C. Sch. Arts, 1994, N.C. Sch. Arts, 1994, U. Pa., 1995; PhD (hon.), U. Pa., 1995; DFA (hon.), The New Sch. Social Rsch., 1996; PhD (hon.), Duke U., 1996; LHD, The Coll. of Santa Fe, 1997; PhD, Sarah Lawrence Coll., 1998; DFA, Smith Coll., 1999. Ind. TV, film and theatrical actress, 1962—; chmn. Nat. Endowment for Arts, Washington, 1993-97; guest artist in residence Okla. Arts Inst., 1982, tchr. adult theatre workshop, 1984, 91, tchr. master class, 1990; bd. trustees Wildlife Conservation Soc., 1997—, Am. Bird Conservancy, 1995-98, The MacDowell Colony, 1997—. Author: (with Greta Jacobs) The Bluefish Cookbook, 5 edits., 1979-95, ; translator: (with Sam Engelstad) The Master Builder (Henrik Ibsen), 1978; appeared in prodns.: Charles Playhouse Boston, 1964-65, Arena Stage, Washington, 1965-68, 70—, Am. Shakespeare Festival; plays include Major Barbara, Mourning Becomes Electra, Merry Wives of Windsor, Stratford, Conn., summers 1971-72; Broadway prodns. include The Great White Hope, 1968-69 (Tony award 1969, Drama Desk award, Theatre World award), 6 Rms Riv Vu, 1972-73 (Tony nomination), Find Your Way Home, 1974 (Tony nomination), Hamlet, 1975, The Heiress, 1976, First Monday in October, 1978 (Tony nomination), Goodbye Fidel, 1980, Monday After the Miracle, 1982, Night of the Iguana, 1988, Shadowlands, 1990-91, The Visit, 1992 (Tony nomination), The Sisters Rosensweig, 1993 (Drama Desk award 1992-93, Tony award nomination, Obie award 1993), Honour (Tony nomination), 1998; also appeared in plays The Time of Your Life, Present Laughter, 1975, The Master Builder, 1977, Losing Time, 1980, Antony and Cleopatra, 1981, Hedda Gabler, 1981, Old Times, 1984, Approaching Zanzibar, 1989, Mystery of the Rose Bouquet, 1989; appeared in films The Great White Hope, 1970 (Acad. award nomination), A Gunfight, 1970, The

New Centurions, 1972, All the President's Men, 1976 (Acad. award nomination), The Betsy, 1978, Kramer vs. Kramer, 1979 (Acad. award nomination), Brubaker, 1980, Night Crossing, 1981, Testament, 1983 (Acad. award nomination), City Heat, 1984, Sweet Country, 1986, Square Dance, 1987, Glory, 1989, The Cider House Rules, 1999; appeared in TV films Welcome Home Johny Bristol, 1971, Miracle on 34th Street, 1973, Death Be Not Proud, 1974, This Was the West That Was, 1974, Eleanor and Franklin, 1976 (Emmy nomination), Eleanor and Franklin: The White House Years, 1977 (Emmy nomination, TV Critics Circle award), Lovey, 1977, A Question of Love, 1978, Playing for Time, 1980 (Emmy award 1980), Calamity Jane: The Diary of a Frontier Woman, 1981, Dear Liar, 1981, Kennedy's Children, 1981, In the Custody of Strangers, 1982, When She Says No, 1983, Mountainview, 1989, Daughter of the Streets, 1990, A Marriage: Georgia O'Keeffe and Alfred Stieglitz, 1991; appeared in TV spls. A Circle of Children, 1977, Blood and Orchids, 1986, Calamity Jane, 1984 (Emmy nomination), Malice in Wonderland, 1985 (Emmy nomination), In Love and War, 1987, Open Admissions, 1988, A Friendship in Vienna, 1988, Stay the Night, 1992. Recipient Achievement in Dramatic Arts award St. Botolph Club, 1979, Israel Cultural award, 1982, Western Heritage Wrangler award, 1985, Helen Caldicott Leadership award, 1984, Living Legacy award Women's Internat. Ctr., San Diego, 1988, Environ. Leadership award Eco-Expo, 1991, Muse award N.Y. Women in Film, 1993, Torch of Hope award, 1992, Lectureship award NIH, 1994, Houseman award The Acting Co., 1994, medal UCLA, 1994, Outer Critics Circle award Disting. Voice in Theatre, 1994, Helen Hayes award Am. Express Tribute, 1994, Women of Achievement award Anti-Defamation League, 1994, Margo Jones award, 1995, Mass. Soc. award, 1995, N.Am. Mont Blanc de la Culture award, 1995, Commonwealth award, 1995, Creative Coalition: Christopher Reeve award, 1998, Outstanding Leadership for Advancement in Arts, People for Am. Way, 1998, Lifetime Achievement award Americans for Arts and U.S. Conf. Mayors, 1999, Harry S. Truman award for pub. svc., Independence, Md., 1999; named to Theatre Hall of Fame, 1993. Mem. AFTRA, SAG, Actors Equity Assn., Acad. Motion Picture Arts and Scis., Actors Fund, Wildlife Conservation Soc. (bd. trustees 1997—). Office: William Morris Agy c/o Samuel Life 1325 Avenue of Americas New York NY 10019

ALEXANDER, JANICE HOEHNER, physician, educator; b. Detroit; d. Robert Paul and Leafy Edna (Phillips) Hoehner; m. Michael Alexander; children: Jason, Janelle Collins. BSN, Wayne State U., 1971, MD, 1979. Resident in family practice, emergency rm. Providence Hosp., Southfield, Mich., 1980-86; resident in ob-gyn. Saginaw (Mich.) Gen. Hosp., 1986-88; staff surgeon ob-gyn. Columbia and St. Joseph Hosps., Milw., 1988—; clin. instr. Mich. State U., Lansing, 1986-88, Med. Coll. Wis., Milw., 1988—; physician, tchr. Women's Med. Internat. People to People, Russia, Latvia, Lithuania, 1993. Instr. CPR ARC, Milw., 1991—. Fellow AAFP; mem. ACOG, AMA, AFS, SLS, MGynS, Milw. Med. Soc., Wis. Med. Soc. Avocations: musician, piano, flute, guitar, vocalist. Office: 2025 E Newport Ave Ste 129 Milwaukee WI 53211-2906*

ALEXANDER, JASON (JAY SCOTT GREENSPAN), actor; b. Newark, Sept. 23, 1959; s. Alexander and Ruth Minnie (Simon) Greenspan; m. Daena E. Title, May 31, 1982;1 child, Gabriel. Student, Boston U., 1977-80. N.Y.C. stage debut in Merrily We Roll along, Alvin Theatre, 1981; other theater appearances include America Kicks Up Its Heels, 1982, On Hold With Music, 1982, Fragments, 1982, Forbidden Broadway, 1983, The Rink, 1984, D, 1985, Personals, 1985-86 season, Broadway Bound, 1986-87 season, Jerome Robbins' Broadway, 1989 (Tony award for best performance by a leading actor in a musical), Accomplice, 1990, Light Up The Sky, 1990, Give 'Em Hell, Harry, 1993 (Drama-Loge award); film debut in The Burning, 1979; other film appearances include The Mosquito Coast, 1986, Brighton Beach Memoirs, 1986, Pretty Woman, 1989, Jacobs Ladder, 1989, White Palace, 1989, I Don't Buy Kisses Anymore, 1991, Coneheads, 1993, North, 1994, The Paper, 1994, Blankman, 1994; actor, dir. For Better or Worse, 1995, The Last Supper, 1995, Love! Valour! Compassion!, 1996, the Hunchback of Notre Dame, 1996, For Better or Worse, 1996, Dunston Checks In, 1996; TV films include Senior Trip, 1981, Rockabye, 1986, Favorite Son, 1988, Sexual Healing, 1993, Bye Bye Birdie, 1995, Cinderella, 1998, Denial, 1998, Love & Action in Chicago, 1998, Adventures of Rocky & Bullwinkle, 1999; TV series: E/R, 1984-85, Everything's Relative, 1987, Seinfeld, 1990— (Emmy nomination, Supporting Actor - Comedy, 1993, 94), Duckman (voice only), 1994—; guest appearances include Dream On, 1993 (Emmy nomination, Guest Actor - Comedy Series, 1994), Star Trek, Voyager, 1999. Office: William Morris Agy 151 S El Camino Dr Beverly Hills CA 90212-2775*

ALEXANDER, JASPER D., publishing executive; m.; 1 child. BA in English and history, Wake Forest U., 1966. Reporter Winston-Salem (N.C.) Jour., 1958-59; dir. info. Bowman Gray Sch. Medicine, Winston-Salem, 1960; from copy editor to asst. nat. editor Washington Post, 1967-74; exec. asst. to publ. N.Y.C., 1975-76; mng. editor San Diego Union, 1977-86; exec. editor Seattle Post-Intelligencer, 1986-93, editor, publ., 1993—; lectr. in field. Founding dir. Calif. Soc. Newspaper Editors; past chmn. journalism edn. com. Pacific N.W. Newspaper Assn.; trustee Corp. Coun. for the Arts; dir., vice chair TVW, 1999—. With USAF, 1965-65. Mem. Am. Soc. Newspaper Editors, Allied Daily Newspapers (bd. dirs.), Greater Seattle C. of C. (trustee), Wash. State Hist. Soc. (trustee). Office: Seattle Post Intelligencer 101 Elliott Ave W Seattle WA 98119-4295

ALEXANDER, JEFFREY CHARLES, sociology educator; b. Milw., May 30, 1947; s. Frederick Charles and Esther Lea (Schlossman) A.; m. Ruth Heidi Bloch (div. Feb. 1997); children: Aaron, Benjamin; m. Maria Pia Lara, Apr., 1997. BA, Harvard Coll., 1969; PhD, U. Calif., Berkeley, 1978. Lectr. U. Calif., Berkeley, 1974-76; asst. prof. UCLA, 1976-81, prof., 1981—; chair dept. sociology UCLA, 1989-92, dir. social sci. collegium, 1992-97; prof. U. Bordeaux, France, 1994; vis. prof. Inst. Advanced Studies, Vienna, Austria, 1995. Author: Theoretical Logic in Sociology, vols. I-IV, 1982-83, Twenty Lectures: Sociological Theory Since World War Two, 1987, Action and Its Environments: Towards a New Synthesis, 1988, Structure and Meaning: Relinking Classical Sociology, 1989, Teoria Sociologia E Mutamento Sociales, Un Analisi Multidemensionale della Modernita, 1990, Soziale Differenzierung und Kultureller Wandel Studien zur Neofunktionalistischen Gesellschafstheorie, 1993, Fin-de-Siecle Social Theory: Relativism, Reduction and the Problem of Reason, 1995, Neofunctionalism and After, 1998, (Japanese trans.) Neofunctionalism and Civil Society, 1996; editor: Neofunctionalism, 1985, Durkheimian Sociology: Cultural Studies, 1988, Real Civil Societies, 1997; co-editor: The Micro-Macro Link, 1987, Differentiation Theory and Social Change: Historical and Comparative Perspectives, 1990, Rethinking Progress: Movements, Forces and Ideas at the End of the Twentieth Century, 1990, Culture and Society: Contemporary Debates, 1990, Diversity and Its Discontents, 1999. Guggenheim fellow, 1979-80; Travel and Study fellow Ford Found., 1980; Princeton Inst. for Advanced Studies fellow, 1985-86; Swedish Colloquium for Advanced Study in the Social Scis., 1992, 96; Ctr. for Advanced Studies in the Behavioral Scis., 1998-99. Mem. Am. Sociol. Assn., Internat. Sociol. Assn. (founder, co-chair rsch. com. sociol. theory 1990-94), Sociol. Rsch. Assn. Democrat. Jewish. Avocations: photography, tennis, skiing. Home: 36 26th Pl Venice CA 90291 Office: U Calif Dept Sociology Los Angeles CA 90024

ALEXANDER, JOHN BRADFIELD, scientist, retired army officer; b. N.Y.C., Nov. 21, 1937; m. Victoria Lacas Alexander; children: Marc Bradfield, Joshua John. BGS in Sociology, U. Nebr., 1971; MA in Edn., Pepperdine U., 1975; PhD in Edn., Walden U., 1980; postgrad., UCLA, 1990, MIT, 1991, Harvard U., 1993; attended various milit. schs. Pvt. U.S. Army, 1956, advanced through grades to col., 1986; comdr. Army Spl. Forces Teams U.S. Army, Thailand, Vietnam, 1966-69; chief human resources divsn. U.S. Army, Ft. McPherson, Ga., 1977-79; inspector gen. Dept. of Army U.S. Army, Washington, 1980-82; chief human tech. Army Intelligence Command U.S. Army, Arlington, Va., 1982-83; mgr. tech. integration Army Materiel Command U.S. Army, Alexandria, Va., 1983-85; dir. advanced concepts U.S. Army Lab. Command U.S. Army, Adelphi, Md., 1985-88; ret. U.S. Army, 1988; mgr. nonlethal weapons def. tech. Los Alamos (N.Mex.) Nat. Lab., 1988-95 (ret.), mgr. anti-materiel tech. Def. Initiatives Office, 1988-91, program mgr. contingency missions tech. Conventional Def. Tech., 1991-92; dir. for sci. liaison Nat. Inst. for Discovery Sci., Las Vegas, Nev., 1995—; vis. scientist Los Alamos, 1995-96; panelist Nat. Inst. Justice, Washington, 1994; adj. prof. Grad. Sch. Union Inst., Cin., 1992-97; U.S. del. to NATO adv. group aerospace R&D, 1994-97; chmn. NonLethal Def. Conf. Johns Hopkins Applied Physics Lab., 1993, NonLethal Def. Conf. II, 1996, III, 1998; mem. tech. panel Advanced Weapons Conf., 1992, tech. opportunities in low intensity conflict panel LIC Tech. Conf., RAND Corp., 1992; cons. Office Sec. of Def., 1996—; spkr., presenter in field. Author: Future War: Non-Lethal Weapons 21st Century Warfare, 1999; co-author: The Warrior's Edge, 1990; contbr. numerous articles to profl. jours. Bd. dirs., past v.p. Children's Hospice Internat., Alexandria, 1982-96. Recipient Nat. Award for Volunteerism by Pres. Reagan, 1987, Aerospace Laureate award Aviation Week, 1993, 94, Weapons Program recognition of excellence, 1994; decorated numerous milit. awards; inducted into Laureate Hall of Fame U.S. Air and Space Mus., 1997. Mem. Soc. Sci. Exploration. Home: 9521 Grand Canal Dr Las Vegas NV 89117-0860

ALEXANDER, JOHN CHARLES, editor, writer; b. Lincoln, Nebr., Jan. 25, 1915; s. John Merriam Alexander and Helen (Abbott) Boggs; m. Ruth Edna McLane, Aug. 20, 1955. Student, U. Nebr., 1933-37, Chouinard Art Inst./Ben Bard Playhouse Sch., L.A., 1937-38, Pasadena Playhouse, 1939-42, UCLA, 1945-47. Aircraft assembler N. Am. aviation, Inglewood, Calif., 1941-42; engring. writer Lockheed-Vega Aircraft, Burbank, Calif., 1942-45; prodn. mgr/actor Gryphon Playhouse, Laguna Beach, Calif., 1947-49; asst. producer/writer Young & Rubicam/ABC, Hollywood, Calif., 1949-51; editor-in-chief Grand Cen. Aircraft, Tucson, 1952-53; sr. writer/editor various cos., Calif., 1953-60; sr. editor/writer, sec. Sci. Guidance Rsch. Coun. Stanford Rsch. Inst., U.S. Army Combat Devel. Command, Menlo Park, Calif., 1962-66; editor-in-chief Litton Sci. Support Lab. USACDC, Fort Ord, Calif., 1966-70; editorial dir./sec. The Nelson Co., Film and Video Prodn., Tarzana, Calif., 1971—; editorial cons., dir. Human Resources Rsch. Office, George Washington U., The Presidio, Monterey, Calif., 1960-62; book editor The Dryden Press, Hinsdale, Ill., 1971-72; book editor/adaptor Gen. Learning Press, Silver Burdette Co., Morristown, N.J., 1972-74; contbg. editor West Coast Writers Conspiracy mag., Hollywood, Calif., 1975-77; contbg. editor/book reviewer Santa Ynez Valley Times, Solvang, Calif., 1976-77; participant Santa Barbara Writers Conf., Montecito, Calif., 1974, 75. Author: (TV plays) Michael Has Company for Coffee, 1948, House on the Hill, 1958, (radio drama) The Couple Next Door, 1951; co-author nine films for U.S. Dept. Justice: Under the Law, Parts I and II, 1973; co-author 10 films for Walt Disney Ednl. Media Co.: Lessons in Learning, Parts I and II, 1978-81; author: (with others) The American West Anthology, 1971; editorial cons. Strangers in Their Land: CBI Bombardier, 1939-45, 1990-92. Recipient award for short story, Writer's Digest, 1960, 61, Gold award, The Festival of the Americas, Houston Internat. Film Festival, 1977. Mem. Nat. Cowboy Hall of Fam, Nat. Geog. Soc., Nat. Soc. Lit. and Arts, Soc. Tech. Writers and Pubs., Western Hist. Soc., Calif. Acad. Sci., Nat. Air and Space Mus., Smithsonian Instn., Woodrow Wilson Internat. Ctr. for Scholars, Aircraft Owners and Pilots Assn., Air Force Assn., U. Nebr.-Lincoln Alumni Assn., Stanford Rsch. Internat. Alumni Assn., Sigma Nu, Alpha Phi Omega. Avocations: scale model building, environmental/wildlife conservation, aviation, science, foreign affairs, intelligence. Home: 23123 Village 23 Camarillo CA 93012-7602

ALEXANDER, JOHN CHARLES, pharmaceutical company executive, physician; b. Perth Amboy, N.J., Dec. 28, 1943; s. Charles John and Agnes (Maloney) A.; m. Margaret Ann Kohler, July 19, 1969; children: Laurel, Jennifer, Anna. BS, St. Francis Coll., Loretto, Pa., 1965; MD, St. Louis U., 1970; MPH, Johns Hopkins U., 1972. Intern Barnes Hosp./Washington U., St. Louis, 1970-71; resident in gen. preventive medicine State of Va./Med. Coll. Va., Richmond, 1974-76; asst. clin. rsch. dir. Squibb Inst. Med. Rsch., Princeton, N.J., 1976-77, assoc. clin. rsch. dir., 1977-79, dir. clin. rsch., 1979-82, v.p. cardiovascular clin. rsch., 1982-86, sr. v.p. med. affairs, 1986-90; v.p. rsch. Bristol-Myers-Squibb Pharm. Rsch. Inst., Princeton, 1990-91; sr. v.p. med. rsch. Searle, Skokie, Ill., 1991-93, exec. v.p. med. rsch., 1993—; Mem. Ill. Sci. and Tech. Adv. Com. Patentee in field. Lt. comdr. USN, 1972-74. Mem. Drug Info. Assn. (v.p., bd. dirs.), Alpha Omega Alpha. Home: 1100 Pelham Rd Winnetka IL 60093-2016 Office: Searle 4901 Searle Pkwy Skokie IL 60077-2919

ALEXANDER, JOHN DAVID, JR., college administrator; b. Springfield, Tenn., Oct. 18, 1932; s. John David and Mary Agnes (McKinnon) A.; m. Catharine Coleman, Aug. 26, 1956; children: Catharine McKinnon, John David III, Julia Mary. BA, Southwestern at Memphis, 1953; student, Louisville Presbyn. Theol. Sem., 1953-54; DPhil (Rhodes Scholar), Oxford (Eng.) U., 1957; LLD, U. So. Calif., Occidental Coll., 1970, Centre Coll. of Ky., 1971, Pepperdine U., 1991, Albertson Coll. Idaho, 1992; LHD, Loyola Marymount U., 1983; LittD, Rhodes Coll., 1986, Pomona Coll., 1996. Assoc. prof. San Francisco Theol. Sem., 1957-65; pres. Southwestern at Memphis, 1965-69, Pomona Coll., Claremont, Calif., 1969-91; Am. sec. Rhodes Scholarship Trust, 1981-98; mem. commn. liberal learning Assn. Am. Colls., 1966-69, mem. commn. instl. affairs, 1971-74; mem. commn. colls. So. Assn. Colls. and Schs., 1966-69; mem. Nat. Commn. Acad. Tenure, 1971-72; dir. Am. Coun. on Edn., 1981-84, Nat. Assn. Ind. Colls. and Univs.; bd. dirs. Children's Hosp. L.A., chair Rsch. Inst., 1997—; trustee Tchrs. Inst. and Annuity Assn., 1970—, Woodrow Wilson Nat. Fellowship Found., 1978—, Seaver Inst., 1992—, Phi Beta Kappa Assocs., 1993—, Wenner-Gren Found. for Anthrop. Rsch., 1995—, Webb Schs. Calif., 1995—; bd. overseers Huntington Libr., 1991—. Editor: The American Oxonian, 1997—. Decorated Comdr. of the Order of Brit. Empire (hon.). Mem. Soc. Bib. Lit., Soc. Religion in Higher Edn., Phi Beta Kappa Alumni in So. Calif. (pres. 1974-76), Century Club, Calif. Club, Bohemian Club, Phi Beta Kappa, Omicron Delta Kappa, Sigma Nu. Office: Pomona Coll 333 N College Way Claremont CA 91711-4429

ALEXANDER, JOHN DEWEY, internist; b. Sacramento, Calif., Dec. 31, 1924; s. John Dewey and Ethel Laurine (Rivers) A.; m. Mary Louise McCormick, May 5, 1951. MD, U. Pa., 1949. Diplomate Am. Bd. Med. Examiners. Intern Phila. Gen. Hosp., 1949-51, fellow in infectious diseases, 1952-53; fellow in internal medicine Mayo Found., Rochester, Minn., 1953-56; pvt. practice medicine, 1956—; med. cons. TransAm.-Occidental Life Ins. Co., Phila., 1965-90. Capt. USAF, 1950-52. Fellow ACP. Home: 2507 Pine St Philadelphia PA 19103-6420

ALEXANDER, JOHN J., chemistry educator; b. Indpls., Apr. 13, 1940; s. John Gregory and Inez Helene (Snedaker) A. A.B. summa cum laude, Columbia U., 1962, M.A., 1963, Ph.D., 1967. Postdoctoral fellow Ohio State U., Columbus, 1967-69, research assoc., 1977-78; asst. prof. chemistry U. Cin., 1969-73, assoc. prof., 1973-79, prof., 1979—, dir. undergrad. studies in chemistry, 1998—, faculty fellow, 1972-74; vis. prof. Ohio State U., 1985-86, 94. Author: (with M.J. Steffel) Chemistry in the Laboratory, 1976, 2d edit., 1988, (with B.E. Douglas, D.H. McDaniel) Concepts and Models of Inorganic Chemistry, 1994, Problems for Inorganic Chemistry, 3d edit., 1994; column editor: Jour. Chem. Edn., 1976—; mem. editl. adv. team for chemistry Ency. Britannica, 1999—; contbr. chpts. to books, articles to profl. jours. Vestryman Calvary Episcopal Ch., 1999—. Woodrow Wilson fellow; NSF fellow Columbia U., 1963-65, faculty fellow, 1966; grantee NSF, Petroleum Rsch. Fund. Mem. Am. Chem. Soc. (past chmn., trustee), Phi Beta Kappa, Sigma Xi, Phi Lambda Upsilon. Democrat. Episcopalian. Home: 3446 Whitfield Ave Cincinnati OH 45220-1537 Office: U Cin Dept Chemistry Cincinnati OH 45221-0172

ALEXANDER, JOHN MACMILLAN, JR., chemistry educator; b. Columbia, Mo., Aug. 17, 1931; s. John Macmillan and Victoria (Holladay) A.; m. Betty Jo Linton, Aug. 1, 1953; children: Mary Jo, John Macmillan III, Frank Linton, James Holladay. BS, Davidson Coll., 1953; PhD, MIT, 1956. Research assoc. MIT, 1956-57; research chemist Lawrence Radiation Lab., Berkeley, Calif., 1957-63; assoc. prof. chemistry SUNY at Stony Brook, 1963-67, prof., 1968—, chmn. exec. com. faculty senate, 1969, chmn. dept. chemistry, 1970-72; AEC-ERDA, Dept. Energy researcher, 1964—; research collaborator Brookhaven Nat. Lab., 1964—; chmn. Gordon Research Conf. on Nuclear Chemistry, 1966; mem. exec. com. Berkeley Superhilac Accelerator, 1975-78, 85-87; vis. scientist Centre d'Etudes Nucléaires, Bordeaux, France, 1974; vis. prof. Centre d'Etudes Nucléaires de Bordeaux-Gradignan and Institut de Physique Nucléaire, Orsay, France, 1978; program adv. com. Tandem Van De Graaff Accelerator, Brookhaven Nat. Lab., 1977-83, Holifield Heavy Ion Research Facility, Oak Ridge Nat. Lab., 1986-87, SARA accelerator Institut des Sciences Nucléaires de Grenoble, France, 1988. Assoc. editor: Am. Chem. Soc. Monographs, 1968-69; contbr. articles to profl. jours. Recipient Great Amer. Home award Nat. Trust for Historic Preservation, 1993; Dupont teaching fellow, 1955-56, Sloan fellow, 1964-67, Guggenheim fellow Laboratoire de Chimie Nucléaire, Orsay, France, 1969-70. Fellow Am. Phys. Soc.; mem. Am. Chem. Soc. (chmn. divsn. nuclear chemistry and tech. 1988, vice chmn. 1987, nuclear chemistry award 1991), Phi Beta Kappa. Democrat. Achievements include research on radioactivity, high-energy nuclear reactions: fission, spallation and fragmentation; heavy ion reactions: elastic scattering, complete and incomplete fusion and reaction cross sections; energy thermalization mechanisms from low to relativistic energies; hot nuclei; energy and spin dissipation, evaporative deexcitation; fragmentation; emission lifetimes; nuclear equation of state; statistical and dynamical models. Home: 14 Highwood Rd East Setauket NY 11733-1512 Office: SUNY Dept Chemistry Stony Brook NY 11794-3400

ALEXANDER, JOHN THORNDIKE, historian, educator; b. Cooperstown, N.Y., Jan. 18, 1940; s. Edward Porter and Alice Wagner (Bolton) A.; m. Maria Kovalak Hreha, June 13, 1964; children—Michal Porter, Darya Ann. B.A., Wesleyan U., Middletown, Conn., 1961; cert. regional specialization Russian Inst., Ind. U., 1963, M.A., 1963, Ph.D., 1966. Asst. prof. U. Kans., Lawrence, 1966-70, assoc. prof., 1970-74, prof. history, 1974—; fellow Inter-Univ. Com. on Travel Grants, 1964-65, Internat. Research and Exchanges Bd., 1971, 75, 96. Author: Autocratic Politics, 1969, Emperor of the Cossacks, 1973, Bubonic Plague in Russia, 1980, Catherine the Great, 1989 (Byron Caldwell Smith award for best book by a Kans. author pub. in 1987-88); translator, editor: Platonov, Time of Troubles, 1970, Anisimov, Reforms of Peter the Great, 1993, Anisimov, Empress Elisabeth, 1995. Recipient Balfour Jeffrey Higuchi Endowment Rsch. Achievement award, 1992. Mem. Am. Hist. Assn., Am. Assn. for Advancement Slavic Studies, Brit. Study Group on 18th Century Russia. Democrat. Roman Catholic. Avocation: sports. Home: 2216 Orchard Ln Lawrence KS 66049-2706 Office: U Kans Dept History Lawrence KS 66045

ALEXANDER, JONATHAN, cardiologist, consultant; b. N.Y.C., Nov. 29, 1947; s. Josef and Hannah (Margolis) A.; m. Karen Deborah Einhorn, Aug. 8, 1971; children: Jessica Beth, Daniel Lewis, Benjamin Joel. BA, Harvard U., 1968; MD, Albert Einstein Coll. Medicine, 1973. MD. Intern, resident Yale-New Haven Hosp., 1973-76; fellow dept. cardiology Sch. Medicine Yale U., New Haven, 1976-78, asst. clin. prof. medicine, 1978-83, assoc. clin. prof., 1983-95, clin. prof., 1995—; attending physician Danbury (Conn.) Hosp., 1978—, West Haven (Conn.) Vets. Hosp., 1978—, New Milford (Conn.) Hosp., 1980; dir. cardiac rehab. unit and nuclear cardiology Danbury (Conn.) Hosp., 1978—. Recipient Samuel Kushlan award Yale-New Haven Hosp., 1974, Revlon award 11th Internat. Congress Chemotherapy, 1983. Fellow ACP, Am. Coll. Cardiology (gov. Conn. 1993-96), Conn. chpt. Am. Coll. Cardiology (pres. 1993-96), Conn. Hosp. Assn., Found. for Cmty. Health Care. Jewish.

ALEXANDER, JOSEPH KUNKLE, JR., physicist; b. Staunton, Va., Jan. 9, 1940; s. Joseph Kunkle and Charlotte (Harper) A.; m. Diana Lenore Titolo, Sept. 22, 1962; children: Kathryn, Stephen, David. BS in Physics, Coll. William and Mary, 1960, MA in Physics, 1962. Physicist Nat. Bur. Standards, 1960; research asst. Coll. William and Mary, Williamsburg, Va., 1960-62; physicist Goddard Space Flight Ctr., NASA, Greenbelt, Md., 1962-85, head planetary magnetospheres br., 1976-84; dep. chief scientist NASA, Washington, 1985-87, asst. assoc. adminstr. space sci. and applications, 1987-93; assoc. dir. space scis. Goddard Space Flight Ctr., NASA, Greenbelt, Md., 1993-94; dep. asst. adminstr. R&D EPA, Washington, 1994-98; dir. space studies bd. Nat. Acad. Scis. Nat. Rsch. Coun., Washington, 1998—; vis. scientist U. Colo., 1973-74; sr. policy analyst White House Office Sci. and Tech. Policy, Washington, 1984-85; assoc. chief Lab. Extraterrestrial Physics, 1985, acting dir. life scis. NASA, Washington, 1992-93; acting chief Lab. Extraterrestrial Physics, Goddard Space Flight Ctr., NASA, Greenbelt, Md., 1994. Contbr. articles to sci. and tech. jours. Mem. Am. Geophys. Union, Am. Astron. Soc., Internat. Astron. Union. Office: Nat Acad of Scis 2101 Constitution Ave NW Washington DC 20418-0007

ALEXANDER, JOYCE LONDON, judge. BA, Howard Univ., D.C.; JD, New Eng. Law Sch., 1972; LLD, Northeastern Univ., New Eng. Law Sch., Bridgewater State Coll. Staff atty. Greater Boston Legal Assistance Project, 1972-74; legal counsel Youth Activities Commn., Boston, 1974-76; gen. counsel Mass. Bd. of Higher Edn., 1976-79; magistrate judge U.S. Dist. Ct. (Mass. dist.), 1st circuit, Boston, 1979-96, chief magistrate judge, 1996—; asst. prof. Tufts Univ., 1974-75; legal editor WBZ-TV, Boston, 1978-79. Trustee Boys & Girls Club of Greater Boston. Recipient Martin Luther King Jr. Drum Major for Justice award So. Christian Leadership Conf., 1985, Raymond Pace Alexander award Nat. Bar Assn.; named Outstanding Young Leader of Mass. Boston Jaycees, 1980. Mem. Am. Judicature Soc., Nat. Bar Assn., Nat. Coun. of U.S. Magistrate, Mass. Black Judges Conf., Urban League of Ea. Mass. (co-founder, pres. emeritus), World Peace Through Law Conf., Orgn. of Black Airline Pilots. Office: John W McCormack Courthouse 90 Devonshire St Rm 932 Boston MA 02109-4501

ALEXANDER, JUDD HARRIS, retired paper company executive; b. Owatonna, Minn., Mar. 23, 1925; s. Mark Hastings and Veta Enola (Harris) A.; m. Theo Mary Paltzer, May 19, 1956; children: Morah Lee, Duncan McIndoe, Todd Stewart. B.A., Carleton Coll., 1949; postgrad. in bus, Harvard U., 1967. Co-founder Nu-Bilt Co., Owatonna; dir. Nu-Bilt Co., 1942-71; sec. in pres.'s office, salesman Marathon Corp., Rothschild, Wis., 1949-57; with Am. Can Co., Greenwich, Conn., 1957-82, v.p., gen. mgr. spl. products packaging, 1972-73, sr. v.p. group exec. packaging, 1974-75, sr. v.p. office of chmn., 1975-81, exec. v.p. paper sector, 1981-82; exec. v.p. James River Corp., Norwalk, Conn., 1982-89, ret., 1989; chmn. Paperboard Packaging Council, 1976-78, Can Mfrs. Inst., 1978-80, Solid Waste Coun. of Paper Industry, 1977-88; bd. dirs. encore Paper Co., Inc., 1992-95; adj. prof. environ. sci. SUNY, Syracuse, 1979-84. Author: In Defense of Garbage, 1993; contbr. articles to profl. and bus. jours., including Wall Street Jour., N.Y. Times, Industry Week. Trustee Carleton Coll., 1973—, Am. Shakespeare Theater, 1980-82; bd. dirs. New Eng. Legal Found., 1979-82, Norwalk (Conn.) Hosp., 1985-88, Ctr. for Advanced Studies U. Va., 1988—; chmn. bd. trustees Keep Am. Beautiful (bd. dirs. 1979-90), 1986-88. Decorated Bronze Star medal; Woodrow Wilson vis. fellow, 1975-82. Mem. Conn. Bus. Industry Assn. (bd. dirs. 1976-80, 85-89), Quechee Club, Isleworth Club. Republican. Congregationalist. Home: 3041 Ironwood Rd Carefree AZ 85377

ALEXANDER, JUDITH ELAINE, psychologist, consultant; b. Worcester, Mass., Nov. 30, 1948; d. Frank E. and Winnona V. (Tracy) A.; divorced; children: Kimberly, Jenniferlyn. BS, Worcester State Coll., 1981; MA, Assumption Coll., Worcester, 1986; PsyD, Antioch New Eng., Keane, N.H., 1991. Lic. psychologist. Dir. mental health Indian Health Svc., Ft. Thompson, S.D., 1992-95; cons. self employed, 1995—; adj. faculty Mt. Wachusett C.C., Gardner, Mass., 1996—, Western New Eng. Coll., 1996—. Contbr. articles to profl. jours. Mem. APA, NEA, Nat. Assn. Forensic Counselors, Mass. Tchrs. Assn. Home: 465 Oxford St N Auburn MA 01501-1939

ALEXANDER, KATHARINE VIOLET, lawyer; b. N.Y.C., Nov. 19, 1934; d. George Clifford and Violet (Jambor) Sziklai; m. George Jonathon Alexander, Sept. 6, 1958; children: Susan Katina, George J. II. Student, Smith Coll., Geneva, 1954-55; BA, Goucher Coll., 1956; JD, U. Pa., 1959; student specialized courses, U. Santa Clara, 1974-76. Bar: Calif. 1974, U.S. Dist. Ct. (no. dist.) Calif. 1974, U.S. Ct. Appeals (9th cir.) 1974; cert. criminal lawyer Calif. State Bar Bd. Legal Specialization. Research dir., adminstr. Am. Bar Found., Chgo., 1959-60; lectr. law San Jose (Calif.) State U., 1972-74; sr. atty. Santa Clara County, San Jose, 1974-97, ret., 1997. Editor: Mentally Disabled and the Law, 1961; contbg. author: The Aged and the Need for Surrogate Management, 1969-70, Jury Instructions on Medical Issues, 1965-67. Community rep. Office Econ. Opportunity Com., Syracuse, N.Y., 1969-70. Mem. AAUW, Food and Wine Inst., Calif. Bar Assn., Santa Clara County Bar Assn. (trustee 1981-82), Calif. Attys. for Criminal Justice (bd. govs. 1988-92), Jr. League, Anthropology and Stanford Museum of Arts. Presbyterian. Avocations: stock market, gourmet, traveling. Home and Office: 11600 Summit Wood Ct Los Altos Hills CA 94022

ALEXANDER, KENNETH LEWIS, editorial cartoonist; b. Gridley, Calif., June 16, 1924; s. Zareh and Rose (Affolter) A.; m. Dariel A. Hereford, July

15, 1949; children: Mark Kenneth, Stephen Scott, Peter Neil. Student, U. Calif. at Berkeley, 1942-43, Rutgers U., 1943-44, Calif. Coll. Arts and Crafts, 1946-47. Free-lance comml. artist, 1947-58; editor Pictorial Living mag., San Francisco Examiner, 1958-63; Sunday art dir., 1963-66, editorial cartoonist, 1966-84, syndicated Copley News Service, 1982-89; TV editorial cartoonist, Sta. KGO-TV, 1968-69; author: (with Andrew Curtin) A Gallery of Great Americans. Served with AUS, 1943-46. Mem. Nat. Cartoonists Soc., Soc. Am. Editorial Cartoonists, Am. Newspaper Guild, AFTRA, Kappa Alpha. Home: 1182 Glen Rd Lafayette CA 94549-3044 *As a relatively successful member of a profession whose sine qua non is the ability to come up with an endless supply of interesting, original ideas, I assign myself no credit whatever for having that ability. It is a God-given talent, and it is to Him I turn for the inspiration, the comfort, and the reassurance that He so generously and lovingly provides. And it is to Him I give my daily thanks.*

ALEXANDER, KENT B., lawyer; b. Atlanta, Nov. 7, 1958. BA in Polit. Sci. magna cum laude, Tufts U., 1980; JD, U. Va., 1983. Bar: Ga. 1983. Assoc. Long & Alridge, Atlanta, 1983-85; asst. U.S. atty. for no. dist. Ga., U.S. Dept. Justice, Atlanta, 1985-92, U.S. atty., 1994-97; of counsel, ptnr. King & Spalding, Atlanta, 1992-94, ptnr., 1997—. Co-founder Hands On Atlanta. Office: King & Spalding 191 Peachtree St SW Atlanta GA 30303-3637

ALEXANDER, LAMAR See ALEXANDER, ANDREW LAMAR

ALEXANDER, LESLIE LEE, professional sports team executive; b. N.Y.C., June 30, 1943. BS, NYU, 1964; JD, Western State Coll., 1977. Owner, pres. Houston Rockets, 1987—. Office: Houston Rockets Ste 400 2 Greenway Plz Houston TX 77046-3865*

ALEXANDER, LESLIE M., ambassador; b. Frankfurt, Germany, Nov. 9, 1948; s. Leslie M. and Ginette Chevalon Alexander; m. Deborah A. McCarthy, 1992; children: Margaret, Natalia. BA, U. Md., 1970; MS, Salve Regina U., 1986; MA, U.S. Naval War Coll., 1991. Officer U.S. Fgn. Svc., 1971—; various assignments in Washington and abroad, 1971—; prin. officer U.S. Consulate Porto, Alegre, Brazil, 1983-85; econ. coun. U.S. Embassy, Rome, 1986-89; dep. dir. Caribbean Affairs, U.S. Dept. State, 1989-91; dep. chief of mission Haiti, 1991-92; U.S. chargé d'affairs, 1992-93, U.S. amb. to Comoros & Mauritius, 1993-96, U.S. amb. to Ecuador, 1996—. Home: 200 S Bayshore Dr Miami FL 33133 Office: US Amb Ecuador US Embassy Quito APO AA 34039

ALEXANDER, LEWIS MCELWAIN, geographer, educator; b. Summit, N.J., June 15, 1921; s. Harry Louis and Laura (Stryker) A.; m. Jacqueline Peterson, Dec. 30, 1950; children: Louise Anne, Lance Stryker. A.B., Middlebury (Vt.) Coll., 1942; M.A., Clark U., 1948, Ph.D., 1949. Instr. geography Hunter Coll., 1949-50; asst. prof. geography Harpur Coll., State U. N.Y., 1950-57, asso. prof., 1957-60; prof. geography U. R.I., Kingston, 1960-80, 83-91, prof. emeritus, 1991—, chmn. dept., 1960-80; dir. marine affairs program U. R.I., 1968-80, dir. Ctr. for Ocean Mgmt. Studies, 1983-89; cons. State Dept., 1963-80; dir. Office of Geographer, 1980-83; exec. dir. Law of Sea Inst., 1965-73, mem. exec. bd., 1973-82, 85-91; mem. ocean affairs adv. com. Dept. State, 1973-80; dep. dir. Pres.'s Commn. on Marine Sci., Engring. and Resources, 1967-68; cons. Nat. Coun. for Marine Resources and Engring. Devel., 1969-70; mem. adv. com. on law of sea Interagy. Law of Sea Task Force, 1973-80; mem. ocean policy com., ocean affairs bd. NRC, 1973-76; maritime boundary cons. Govt. of Bahrain, 1998—. Author: World Political Patterns, 2d edit, 1963, Offshore Geography of Northwestern Europe, 2d edit, 1966, The Northeastern United States, 2d edit., 1976, Regional Cooperation in Marine Science, 1979, Navigational Restrictions within the New Los Context: Geographical Implications for the United States, 1986; mem. editorial bd. Ocean Devel. and Internat. Law Jour., 1973—, Ocean Mgmt., 1973-87, Marine Policy, 1976-98; editor: (with J. Charney) International Maritime Boundaries, 3d edit., 1998. Served with USAAF, 1942-46. Recipient Ann. award Sea Grant Assn., 1979, U. R.I. Acad. Achievement award, 1986; Office Naval Rsch. grantee, 1958, 62, 66, 76. Mem. Assn. Am. Geographers (Honors award 1980), Am. Geog. Soc., Am. Soc. Internat. Law, Marine Tech. Soc. Club: Cosmos. Home: 66 Beech Hill Rd Peace Dale RI 02879-2524 Office: U RI Washburn Hall Kingston RI 02881

ALEXANDER, LISA D., nursing administrator; b. Jonesville, La., Dec. 20, 1964; d. J.D. Jr. and Martha Rea (Ainsworth) A.; 1 child, Jessica Lee Boothe. Diploma, La. State U., Alexandria, 1986; BSN, Northwestern Stae U., Natchitoches, La., 1995. RN, La.; cert. BLS instr., ACLS instr. Staff nurse St. Frances Cabrini Hosp., Alexandria, 1987-89; charge nurse, staff nurse ICU Natchez (Miss.) Cmty. Hosp., 1989-91; staff surg. nurse Natchez Regional Med. Ctr., 1989-91; dir. edn. Natchez Cmty. Hosp., 1991-93, dir. quality mgmt., 1993-95; dir. clin. svcs. Four Rivers Home Care, Inc., Pineville, La., 1995—. Mem. AACCN, Nat. Assn. Healthcare Quality, Am. Heart Assn., Sigma Theta Tau. Baptist. Avocations: travel, horseback riding, basketball, swimming, skiing. Home: HC 86 Box 24A Harrisonburg LA 71340-9707

ALEXANDER, LLOYD CHUDLEY, author; b. Phila., Jan. 30, 1924; s. Alan Audley and Edna (Chudley) A.; m. Janine Denni, Jan. 8, 1946; 1 dau., Madeleine (Mrs. Zohair Khalil). Student, West Chester (Pa.) State Coll., 1942, Lafayette Coll., 1943, U. Paris, 1946. Free-lance writer and translator, 1946—, cartoonist, pianist, advt. writer, mag. editor, 1948—; author-in-residence Temple U., 1970. Author: And Let The Credit Go, 1955, My Five Tigers, 1956, Janine is French, 1958, August Bondi, 1958 (Isaac Siegel Meml. award 1959), My Love Affair with Music, 1960, Aaron Lopez, 1960, Time Cat, 1963, Fifty Years in the Doghouse, 1964, (with Dr. Louis J. Camuti) Park Avenue Vet, 1962, The Book of Three, 1964 (A.L.A. notable book 1964), The Black Cauldron, 1965 (A.L.A. notable book 1965), Coll and His White Pig, 1965, The Castle of Llyr, 1966 (A.L.A. notable book 1966), Taran Wanderer, 1967, The Truthful Harp, 1967, The High King, 1968 (Newbery medal 1969), The Marvelous Misadventures of Sebastian, 1970 (Nat. Book award 1971), The King's Fountain, 1971, The Four Donkeys, 1972, The Foundling, 1973 (A.L.A. notable book 1973), The Cat Who Wished to be a Man, 1973 (A.L.A. notable book), The Wizard in the Tree, 1975, The Town Cats, 1977 (ALA notable book 1977), The First Two Lives of Lukas-Kasha, 1978, Westmark, 1981 (Am. Book award 1982), The Kestrel, 1982, The Beggar Queen, 1984, The Illyrian Adventure, 1986, The El Dorado Adventure, 1987, The Drackenberg Adventure, 1988, The Jedera Adventure, 1989, The Philadelphia Adventure, 1990, The Remakable Journey of Prince Jen, 1991, The Fortune-tellers, 1992, The Arkadians, 1995, The House Gobbaleen, 1995, The Iron Ring, 1997, Gypsy Rizka, 1999; translator from French: (Paul Eluard) Selected Writings, 1950, (Jean-Paul Sartre) The Wall, 1951, Nausea, 1953, (Paul Vialar) The Sea Rose, 1951. Bd. dirs. Carpenter Lane Chamber Music Soc., Phila. Served with AUS, World War II. Recipient Golden Cat award, 1984, Regina medal, 1986, Carolyn W. Field medal, 1987, Otter award, 1993, Horn Book-Boston Globe award 1993. Mem. Authors League Am., P.E.N. Address: 1005 Drexel Ave Drexel Hill PA 19026-3306 also: E P Dutton Pub Co 375 Hudson St New York NY 10014-3658 also: Dell Pub Co 1540 Broadway New York NY 10036-4039

ALEXANDER, LYNN See MARGULIS, LYNN

ALEXANDER, MARCELLUS W., television station executive; b. Austin, Tex.. BS in Speech and Journalism, Southwest Tex. State U., 1973. From nat. sales mgr. to owner and COO WRIF Radio, Detroit, 1977-87; sta. mgr. KYW-TV, Phila., 1987-89, gen. mgr., 1989; v.p., gen. mgr. WJZ-TV, Balt., 1989-98, KYW-TV, Phila., 1998—. Mem. bd. dirs. Advtg. Assn. Balt.; mem. devel. com. Kennedy Krieger Inst.; mem. Balt. C. of C., Greater Balt. Coms. Econ. Devel. Counsel, Md. Bus. Roundtable for Edn.; mem. bd. trustees Balt. Mus. Art, Md. Citizens for the Arts, Inc. Named One of Balt's. "Power Elite" Warfields Bus. Record, 1994. Office: KYW-TV 101 S Independence Mall E Philadelphia PA 19106*

ALEXANDER, MARCELLUS W., JR., television station executive; b. Austin, Tex.. BS in Speech and Journalism, Southwest Tex. State U., 1973. From nat. sales mgr. to owner and COO WRIF Radio, Detroit, 1977-1987; sta. mgr. KYW-TV, Phila., 1987-89, gen. mgr., 1989; v.p., gen. mgr. WJZ-TV, Balt., 1989—. Mem. bd. dirs. Advtg. Assn. Balt.; mem. devel. com. Kennedy Krieger Inst.; mem. Balt. C. of C., Greater Balt. Coms. Econ. Devel. Counsel, Md. Bus. Roundtable for Edn.; mem. bd. trustees Balt. Mus. Art, Md. Citizens for the Arts, Inc. Named One of Balt's. "Power Elite" Warfields Bus. Record, 1994. Office: WJZ-TV ch 13 TV Hill Baltimore MD 21211*

ALEXANDER, MARJORIE ANNE, artist, hand papermaker, art consultant; b. Chgo., Apr. 16, 1928; d. Alexander and Nancy Rebecca (Cordrey) Roberts; m. Harold Harman Alexander, June 13, 1948; children: Jeffrey C., Cassandra J., Peter B., Timothy C., Patrick J. Student, Wilson Jr. Coll., 1945-47; MFA in Painting, U. Ill., 1968, MA in Art Edn., 1972. cert. tchr. K-12: Ill., Minn. Graphic artist Barry Martin Studio, Rumson, N.J., 1963-65; instr. painting, drawing U. YMCA, Champaign, Ill., 1968-72; teaching asst. U. Ill., Urbana, 1968-72, rsch. assoc., 1972-76; instr. art Champaign High Sch., 1973-75, Urbana High Sch., 1976-80, Concordia Acad., St. Paul, Minn., 1982-84, U. Minn., Mpls., 1984-87; design, housing and apparel artist in residence U. Minn., St. Paul, 1984-88; craft cons. and educator tech. assistance program USAID, OAS, U. Minn., Kingston, Jamaica, 1986—; design cons. J.A.M. Corp., Mpls., 1988—; tech. cons. OAS, Kingston, 1990-91, Blandin Found. grantee, Minn., 1989—; rsch. and product devel. agrl. unilization rsch. inst., 1992-95; tech. cons. Zabbaleen Paper Project, Assn. for the Protection of the Environment, Cairo, 1993—, St. Lucia Paper project Weyerhauser Found., 1994—, paper project YMCA, Jamaica, W.I., 1997—. Works have appeared in over 30 solo shows, 1960—, over 50 invitational shows nationally and internationally, 1985—; work chosen for inclusion 1996 Internat. Calendar Papierfabak Schfufelen Lenningen, Germany; represented in permanent collection Imadate, Fukui, Japan, U. Ill., U. Minn., So. Cross U., NSW, Australia, Montclair (N.J.) Art Mus., Am. U, Cairo, other univs. and colls. and corp. collections; co-author (book): Selected Papers, 1994, Handcrafted paper and Paper Products Made from Indigenous Plant Fibers, 1997; contbr. articles to profl. jours. Vestry mem. St. John's Episcopal Ch., Champaign, 1975-78, St. Matthew's Episcopal Ch., St. Paul, 1989—. Recipient Celebrity award Minn. State Fair, 1984, book First award 1986, Honorable mention 3rd Onn/Off Paper Nat., Wis., 1984; grantee Blandin Found. U. Minn., 1989-90, OAS, 1990-91, Agrl. Utilization Rsch. Inst. grantee, 1992-95, Weyerhauser Found., 1997. Mem. Nat. League Am. Penwomen (Minn. art chair 1990-94, state v.p. 1994-96), Internat. Assn. Hand Papermakers and Paper Artists, Friends of Dard Hunter Paper Mus. (com. chair 1990-95). Episcopalian. Avocations: swimming, cooking, theatre, travel. Home: Graybridge 3251 Fernwood St Arden Hills MN 55112

ALEXANDER, MARTHA SUE, librarian; b. Washington, June 8, 1945; d. Lyle Thomas and Helen (Goodwin) Alexander; m. David Henry Bowman, June 11, 1965 (div. 1982); 1 child, Elaine. B.A., U. Md., 1967; M.S. in Library Sci., Cath. U. Am., 1969. Librarian U. Md., College Park, 1969-72, head acquisitions, 1973-75; asst. univ. librarian George Washington U., Washington, 1975-78, assoc. univ. librarian, 1978-82; univ. librarian U. Louisville, 1983-90; dir. libraries U. Mo., Columbia, 1990—; chmn. bd. dirs. SOLINET (Southeastern Library Network), 1987-88. Coord. U. Louisville United Way, 1987; bd. dirs. Mo. Libr. Network Corp., 1990-96. Mem. ALA (chmn. poster sessions 1983-85, co-chmn. nat. conf. in Cin. 1989), Am. Assn. Higher Edn., Athletic Assn. U. Louisville (vice chmn., bd. dirs. 1989-90), D.C. Library Assn. (pres. 1981-82), Women Acad. Libr. Dirs. Exch. Network. Episcopalian. Home: 100 Mumford Dr Columbia MO 65203-0226 Office: Univ Mo Columbia-Ellis Libr Columbia MO 65201*

ALEXANDER, MARTIN, environmental toxicologist, consultant; b. Newark, Feb. 4, 1930; s. Meyer and Sarah (Rubinstein) A.; m. Renee Rafaela Wulf, Aug. 26, 1951; children: Miriam H., Stanley W. B.S., Rutgers U., 1951; M.S., U. Wis., 1953, Ph.D., 1955. Asst. prof. Cornell U., Ithaca, N.Y., from 1955, now L.H. Bailey prof; advisor agys. fed. govt., Washington, 1965—, UN agys., Kenya, France, Italy, 1963—; mem. coms. Nat. Acad. Sci., Washington, 1971—; cons. Author: Microbial Ecology, 1971, Introduction to Soil Microbiology, 1977, Biodegradation and Bioremediation, 1994; editor: Advances in Microbial Ecology, 5 vols., 1977-81. Recipient Indsl. Research 100 award, 1968, Fisher award Am. Soc. Microbiology, 1980, Superior Svc. award USDA, 1989. Fellow Am. Acad. Microbiology, AAAS, Internat. Inst. Biotechnology, Am. Soc. Agronomy (Soil Sci. award 1964). Home: 301 Winthrop Dr Ithaca NY 14850-1736 Office: Cornell U Bradfield Hall Ithaca NY 14853

ALEXANDER, MARY ELSIE, lawyer; b. Chgo., Nov. 16, 1947; d. Theron and Marie (Bailey) A.; m. Lyman Saunders Faulkner, Jr., Dec. 1, 1984; 1 child, Michelle. BA, U. Iowa, 1969; MPH, U. Calif.-Berkeley, 1975; JD, U. Santa Clara, 1982. Bar: Calif. 1982, U.S. Dist. Ct. (no. dist.) Calif. 1982, U.S. ct. Appeals (9th cir.) 1982. Rschr., U. Cin., 1969-74; dept. dir., sr. environ. health scientist Stanford Rsch. Inst., Menlo Park, Calif., 1975-80; cons. Alexander Assocs., Ambler, Pa., 1980-82; assoc. Caputo, Liccardo Rossi Sturges & McNeil, San Jose, Calif., 1982-84; assoc. Cartwright, Slobodin, Bokelman, et al, San Francisco, 1984-88, ptnr., 1988-96; ptnr. The Cartwright & Alexander Law Firm, 1996—. Com. mem. Cancer Soc., San Jose, 1983; elder Valley Presbyn. Ch., Portola Valley, 1987-90; active Am. Heart Assn., Santa Clara County. Named one of top 10 Trial Lawyers San Francisco Bay Area, San Francisco Chronicle, 1990. Nat. Inst. Occupl. Safety and Health scholar U. Calif., Berkeley, 1975. Mem. ABA, AAAS, ATLA (state del.), pres. 1996. Consumer Attys. Calif. (formerly Calif. Trial Lawyers Assn.) (PAC bd. 1989—, parliamentarian 1991, v.p. 1992, chair mem. com., editor Forum, pres. elect 1995), San Francisco Trial Lawyers Assn., Trial Lawyers for Pub. Justice, Calif. Women Lawyers, Am. Indsl. Hygiene Assn. (bd. dirs. 1979-81, treas. 1977-79), Santa Clara Trial Lawyers Assn. (bd. dirs. 1983-84). Democrat. Office: Cartwright & Alexander 222 Front St Ste 5 San Francisco CA 94111-4418

ALEXANDER, MARY K., electronics company executive; b. Oak Ridge, Tenn., Sept. 8, 1947; m. Steve L. Malone; 1 son, Joseph Andrew Melrose. BA, Ursinus Coll., 1969. Staff aide Congressman Orval Hansen (R.I.), Washington, 1969-71; spl. asst. Sen. Charles H. Percy, Washington, 1971-77; asst., cons. Am. Embassy, Damascus, Syria, 1977-80; staff asst. U.S. Senate Fin. Com. Trade Subcom., Washington, 1984-86; dir. trade policy Citizens for a Sound Economy, Washington, 1986-88; asst. gen. mgr. Panasonic Co., Washington, 1988—; legis. liason Assn. Am Fgn. Svc. Women, Washington, 1981-83. Author (newspaper commentator) Fgn. Trade Policy, 1986-88. Mem. Women in Internat. Trade (bd. dirs. 1990-92, pres. 1998-99). Avocations: hiking, travel. Office: Panasonic 1620 L St NW Ste 1150 Washington DC 20036

ALEXANDER, MARY L., historic site adminstrator; b. Beach Grove, Ind., Feb. 11, 1964. BA, Ind. U., 1986. Curator Angel Mounds State Hist. Site, Evansville, Ind., 1993—. Vol. U.S. Peace Corps, Gambia, 1989-92, UN, Belize, 1992-93. Office: Angel Mounds State Hist Site 8215 Pollack Ave Evansville IN 47715-6231*

ALEXANDER, MELVIN TAYLOR, quality assurance engineer, statistician; b. Greensboro, N.C., June 2, 1949; s. Melvin Taylor and Sabina Mae (Anglin) A.; m. Karen Gwendolyn Davenport, Aug. 22, 1973 (div. 1982); children: Asia Trinicia, Sabina, Melvin Taylor III; m. Lucia Antoinette Ward, Apr. 23, 1983. Student, Guilford Coll., 1967-70; BS in Math., N.C. A&T State U., 1972; MSPH in Biostats., U. N.C., 1979. Registered quality engr. Instr. math. N.C. A&T State U., Greensboro, 1975-77; grad. asst. biostatis. dept. U. N.C., Chapel Hill, 1977-79; rsch. assoc. Sch. Pub. Health, Chapel Hill, 1980-81, jr. statis. analyst, 1981-82; engring. staff asst. Westinghouse Electronic Systems Group, Balt., 1982-83, sr. engr., 1983-95; prin. quality analyst ARINC, Annapolis, Md., 1996-97; biostatistician GloboMax LLC, Hanover, Md., 1997—; cons. N.C. Dept. Adminstrn., Raleigh, 1979-80, S.C. Conf. Black Mayors, Gifford, 1980. Co-author: Managing Industrial Processes, 1984. USPHS grantee, 1977; U. N.C. Minority Student fellow, 1978. Mem. Am. Statis. Assn., Am. Soc. Quality (sec. Balt. sect. 1990-91, vice chmn. 1991-92, chmn. 1996, health care div., chair-elect 1999—), Internat. Soc. for Hybrid Microelectronics. Democrat. Presbyterian. Avocations: music; photography; computers.

ALEXANDER, MILES JORDAN, lawyer; b. Reading, Pa., Nov. 20, 1931; s. Abe Alexander and Sarah (Gold) Fidlow; m. Elaine Eve Barron, May 29, 1955; children: Kent, David, Michael, Paige. BA in Polit. Sci. with honors., Emory U., 1952; LLB cum laude, Harvard U., 1955. Bar: Ga. 1955, D.C. 1977. Assoc. Kilpatrick & Stockton, Atlanta, summers 1954-55; teaching fellow Harvard U., Cambridge, 1957-58; assoc. Kilpatrick Stockton LLP, Atlanta, 1958-63; chmn. Kilpatrick & Stockton LLP, Atlanta, 1996—; lectr. P.L.I., Internat. Trademark Assn., Am. Law Inst., ABA Internat. Franchise Assn., other seminars on trademarks and unfair competition, antitrust, franchising, dispute resolutions and litigation tactics; guest lectr. on trademark law NYU, U.Ga., Ga. State Law Sch., also bd. visitors; bd. visitors Emory U. Editor-in-chief: The Trademark Reporter, 1978-80; contbr. numerous articles to jours. in trademark field. Mem. City of Atlanta Ethics Bd., chmn., vice-chmn., 1980-92, Emory U. and Harvard Law Sch. Alumni Funds; legal counsel to Mayor Maynard Jackson, 1974-82, 89-93; chmn. City of Atlanta Lic. Rev. Bd., 1976-79; former pres. Am. Jewish Com.; mem. Friends of Morehouse Coll.; adv. bd. Family Outreach Ctr. Capt. USAF, 1955-57. Recipient Human Rels. award Anti-Defamation League, 1997. Fellow Am. Bar Found., Am. Coll. Trial Lawyers; mem. ABA, Internat. Trademark Assn. (counsel 1997—), Ga. Bar Assn., Ga. State Bar Assn. (former chmn. antitrust sect., advisor to legal counsel 1997—), Atlanta Bar Assn., Lawyers Club Atlanta, Internat. Trademark Assn. (lectr., bd. dirs. 1980-82, rev. commn. 1986, legal counsel 1987—), Am. Law Inst. (adv. com. restatement of law of unfair competition 1986-95), 191 Club (bd. dirs.), Atlanta City Club (chmn. bd.), Commerce Club, Standard Club, Old War Horse Lawyers Club , Phi Beta Kappa. Avocations: reading, sports. Office: Kilpatrick & Stockton LLP 1100 Peachtree St NE Ste 2800 Atlanta GA 30309-4501

ALEXANDER, NORMAN JAMES, investment consultant; b. Regina, Sask., Can., Feb. 9, 1909; s. Robert Merrillees and Catherine (Clarke) A. Former v.p. James Richardson & Sons, Ltd., Winnipeg, Man., Can.; mng. ptnr. Richardson Securities of Can.; investment cons. James Richardson & Sons. Mem. Vancouver Club, St. Charles Golf and Country Club, Manitoba Club, Squash Racquet Club. Home: 66 Wilton St, Winnipeg, MB Canada R3M 3C1 Office: 1220 Richardson Bldg, 1 Lombard Pl, Winnipeg, MB Canada R3B 0X3*

ALEXANDER, PATRICIA ROSS, administrative assistant; b. Blue Ridge, Ga., May 19, 1955; d. Ernest B. and Sara P. (Williams) Ross; m. Robert W. Alexander, Jr., June 24, 1978; children: Sarah E., Robert R. AA, Young Harris (Ga.) Coll., 1975; BA, North Ga. Coll., 1978, postgrad.; postgrad., Emory U. Fiber artist Morganton, Ga.; clk., postmaster relief U.S. Postal Svc., Mineral Bluff, Ga., 1987-96; adminstrv. asst. Indsl. Strength Art, Morganton. Contbr. articles to publs. Recipient cert. of Appreciation and Pride in Performance Gold medal, U.S. Postal Svc., 1992; grantee Ga. Coun. for Arts, 1984, NSF, 1979. Mem. NAPUS, So. Highlands Handicraft Guild, Ga. Mountain Crafts (bd. dirs. 1981-84), Copper Basin/Fannin C. of C., Blue Ridge Mountains Arts Assn. (v.p. 1979-80, coord. 1980-81, bd. dirs. 1993-96), Basket Weavers Guild Ga., Fannin County Heritage Found., Fannin County Tree League (bd. dirs. 1993-95), Ga. Pub. TV Leadership Cir. Baptist. Avocations: photography, fiber art, jewelry making. Home: PO Box 599 Morganton GA 30560-0599 Office: US Post Office Mineral Bluff GA 30559

ALEXANDER, PATRICK BYRON, zoological society executive; b. Texas City, Tex., May 11, 1950; s. Alvin Wesley and Mabel Bernice Alexander; m. Linda Graham, May 7, 1975. BA in Econs., George Mason Coll., U. Va., 1972. Publs. dir. George Mason U., Fairfax, Va., 1973-75, U. Okla. Health Scis. Ctr., Oklahoma City, 1975-78, Presbyn. Hosp. Inc., Oklahoma City, 1978-79; mng. dir. Okla. Symphony Orch., Oklahoma City, 1979-88; exec. dir. Allied Arts Found., 1988-92; exec. dir. Okla. Zool. Soc., 1992—. Bd. dirs. Ambassador's Concert Choir, Okla. Philharm. Found., Allied Arts Found., Okla. Philharm. Orch. English-Speaking Union Okla. Kerr Found. fellow, 1981; recipient Gov.'s award for Excellence in Arts, 1987, Okla. Fundraiser of Yr. award, 1991. Mem. Nat. Soc. Fund Raising Execs., Am. Zoo and Aquarium Assn., Rotary, Club 29, Econ. Club, Men's Dinner Club, Twin Hills Golf and Country Club. Home: 1515 Glenwood Ave Oklahoma City OK 73116-5206 Office: Okla Zool Soc Inc PO Box 18424 Oklahoma City OK 73154-0424

ALEXANDER, PETER HOUSTON, artist; b. Los Angeles, Feb. 27, 1939; s. Richard Henry and Marion Celeste (Pluard) A.; B.A., UCLA, 1965, M.F.A., 1968; m. Clytie Patricia Moore, June 8, 1964; children—Clytie Hope, Julia Pebrina. One-man shows: Nicholas Wilder Gallery, Los Angeles, 1970, Robert Elkon Gallery, N.Y.C., 1970, Art in Progress, Munich, Germany, 1973, U. Calif., Irvine, 1975, Calif. State U., Long Beach, 1976, Rico Mizuno, Los Angeles, 1980, James Corcoran, Los Angeles, 1981, Charles Cowles Gallery, N.Y.C., 1982, Arco Ctr., Los Angeles, 1983, Los Angeles Mcpl. Art Gallery, 1983, Cirrus Gallery, Los Angeles, 1983, Fuller Goldeen Gallery, San Francisco, 1984; group shows include: Seattle Art Mus., 1968, Mus. Modern Art, N.Y.C., 1969, 83, 84, Walker Art Center, Milw., 1969, Whitney Mus. Am. Art, N.Y.C., 1969, Mus. Contemporary Art, Chgo., 1970, Locksley/Shea Gallery, Los Angeles, 1971, Calif. State U., Long Beach, 1975, 78, San Francisco Mus. Modern Art, 1976, La Jolla (Calif.) Mus. Contemporary Art, 1981, Art Center Coll. Design, Pasadena, Calif., 1981, Bklyn. Mus., 1983; represented in permanent collections: Walker Art Center, Mpls., Mus. Modern Art, N.Y.C., La Jolla Art Mus., Vancouver (Can.) Mus. Art, Los Angeles County Mus. Art, Corcoran Gallery Art, Washington, Fort Worth Art Mus., San Francisco Mus. Modern Art, Bklyn. Mus., Newport Harbor Art Mus., Walker Art Center, Fogg Mus., Harvard U., others. Served with USMC, 1961-66. Nat. Endowment for Arts artist fellow, 1980.

ALEXANDER, RALPH WILLIAM, JR., physics educator; b. Phila., May 17, 1941; s. Ralph William and Gladys (Robin) A.; m. Janet Erdien Bradley, Sept. 4, 1965; children: Ralph III, Margaret. BA, Wesleyan U., Middletown, Conn., 1963; PhD, Cornell U., Ithaca, N.Y., 1968; postdoctoral study, U. of Freiburg, Fed. Republic Germany, 1968-70. From asst. to assoc. prof. physics U. Mo., Rolla, 1970-80, prof., 1980—, chmn. dept., 1983-92. Contbr. articles to profl. jours. Mem. Am. Phys. Soc., Assn. Am. Physics Tchrs. Office: U Mo Dept Physics Rolla MO 65409

ALEXANDER, RICHARD DALE, zoology educator; b. White Heath, Ill., Nov. 18, 1929; m. 1950; two children. BSc, Ill. State U., 1950; MSc, The Ohio State U., 1951, PhD in Entomology, 1956; LHD, Ill. State U. Rsch. assoc. Rockefeller Found., N.Y.C., 1956-57; from instr. to assoc. prof. U. Mich., Ann Arbor, 1957-69; curator Insects U. Mich. Mus. Zoology, Ann Arbor, 1957—, prof. Zoology, 1969—, Hubbell Dist. U. Prof. Evolutionary Biol., 1990—; J.S. Guggenheim fellow, 1968-69. Recipient Daniel Giraud Elliot medal, 1971; Newcomb Cleveland prize, AAAS, 1961. Mem. Fellow AAAS, Animal Behavior Soc., mem. Nat. Acad. Scis. Office: Mus Zool U Mich 1109 Geddes Ave Ann Arbor MI 48109-1079

ALEXANDER, ROBERT C., lawyer; b. Clarksville, Tenn., Aug. 7, 1947; s. Donald C. and Margaret S. Alexander; m. Rosalie Bailey, June 14, 1969. BA cum laude, Yale Coll., 1969; JD magna cum laude, Harvard U., 1972. Bar: Calif. 1972, D.C. 1973. Law clk. to Hon. Alfred T. Goodwin U.S. Ct. Appeals, 9th cir., San Francisco, 1972-73; shareholder Heller, Ehrman, White & McAuliffe, San Francisco, 1973-86, 88—; prin. Babcock & Brown, San Francisco, 1986-87; writer in field. Mem. ABA, State Bar Calif., D.C. Bar, Internat. Fiscal Assn., Equipment Leasing Assn. Office: Heller Ehrman White & McAuliffe 333 Bush St San Francisco CA 94104-2806

ALEXANDER, ROBERT EARL, university chancellor, educator; b. Kinston, N.C., Oct. 21, 1939; s. Joseph Culbreath and Pauline (Fussell) A.; m. Leslie Johnson, Mar. 11, 1971; children—Lara, Robert. B.A. in Polit. Sci., Duke U., 1962, M.Div., 1966; D. in Higher Edn., U. S.C., 1977. Ordained to ministry United Methodist Ch., 1967. Assoc. chaplain N.C. State U., Raleigh, 1965-66; assoc. chaplain U. S.C., Columbia, 1966-68, dir. vol. services, 1969-70, adminstrv. asst. to v.p. student affairs, 1970-71, dean student activities, 1971-75, dean students, asst. v.p. student affairs, 1975-78, assoc. prof., 1981-83, assoc. v.p. for 2-year campuses and continuing edn., 1978-83; chancellor U. S.C., Aiken, 1983—; chmn. systems rev. panel U. S.C., 1981-83; bd. dirs. Security Fed. Bank S.C. Contbr. articles to profl. jours. Nat. observer White House Conf. on Youth, Denver, 1971; bd. dirs. United Way, Aiken, S.C., Bus. Tech. Ctr. of N. Augusta, S.C., 1984-89, Strom Thurmond Found., Inc., Aiken, 1985—, now sec. Econ. Devel. Partnership, 1984—, sec., 1989—; mem. Commn. on Future S.C., 1987-89, Commn. on Future of Aiken County, 1987-89, chmn., 1989-90; trustee Hopeland Gardens, Aiken,

1984-88; mem. S.C. Coun. Econ. Edn., 1988-96; chmn. Peach Belt Athletic Conf., 1989-91; mem. regional adv. bd. SCANA, 1990—; mem. nat. adv. com. on Student Fin. Assistance, 1991-97, chair 1996-97; bd. trustees Aiken Regional Med. Ctrs., 1992—; vice chmn., chmn. exec. com. Savannah River Regional Diversification Initiative, 1993-96. Named Man of Yr., Greater Aiken C. of C., 1985; Kellog grantee, 1981; NEH grantee, 1982, 85—. Mem. S.C. Assn. Higher Continuing Edn. (pres. 1980-81, Outstanding Pres.'s award 1987), S.C. Assn. for Comty. Edn., Nat. Comty. Edn. Assn., Assn. Higher Continuing Edn., Nat. Entertainment and Campus Activities Assn. (bd. dirs. 1973-79), Inst. for Continuing Edn. Nat. Univ. Continuing Edn. Assn. (bd. dirs. 1981-83), S.C. Coun. Pub. Coll. and Univ. Pres. (chmn. 1996—), S.C. 2000 (bd. dirs. 1989-91), Greater Aiken C. of C. (pres. 1987), Am. Assn. State Colls. and Univs. (com. on sci. and tech. 1987-90, state rep. 1990-95, fins. in higher edn. 1991—, fed./state rels. com. 1984-94), Rotary (Aiken bd. dirs. 1984—, scholarship com. Internat. chpt. 1993—), Houndslake Country Club, Woodside Plantation Country Club, Green Boundary Country Club, Phi Delta Kappa, Alpha Kappa Psi, Gamma Beta Phi, Omicron Delta Kappa. Methodist. Avocations: woodworking; winemaking; reading. Office: Univ SC 471 University Pkwy Aiken SC 29801-6389*

ALEXANDER, ROBERT JACKSON, economist, educator; b. Canton, Ohio, Nov. 26, 1918; s. Ralph S. and Ruth (Jackson) A.; m. Joan O. Powell, Mar. 26, 1949; children: Anthony, Margaret. B.A., Columbia U., 1940; M.A., Columbia U., 1941; Ph.D., Columbia U., 1950. Asst. economist Bd. Econ. Warfare, 1942, Office Inter-Am. Affairs, 1945-46; mem. faculty Rutgers U., 1947—, prof. econs., 1961-89, prof. emeritus, 1989—; mem. Pres.-elect Kennedy's Latin Am. Task Force, 1960-61. Author 35 books including Juan Domingo Peron: A History, 1979, Romulo Betancourt and the Transformation of Venezuela, 1982, Bolivia: Past, Present and Future of Its Politics, 1982, Biographical Dictionary of Latin American and Caribbean Politics, 1988, Juscelino Kubitschek and the Development of Brazil, 1991, International Trotskyism 1929-85, 1991, The ABC Presidents, 1992, The Bolivarian Presidents, 1994, The Presidents of Central America, Mexico, Cuba and Hispaniola, 1995, Presidents, Prime Ministers and Governors of the English Speaking West Indies and Puerto Rico, 1997. Mem. nat. bd. League Indsl. Democracy, 1955—; mem. nat. exec. com. Socialist Party-Social Dem. Fedn., 1957-66; bd. dirs. Rand Sch. Social Sci., 1951-56; mem. exec. com. Open Door Student Exch., 1970-94. Decorated officer Order Condor of the Andes Bolivia. Mem. Am. Econ. Assn., Latin Am. Studies Assn., Mid. Atlantic Coun. Latin Am. Studies (v.p. 1986-87, pres. 1987-88), Coun. Fgn. Rels., Interam. Assn. Democracy and Freedom (chmn. N.Am. com. 1970-87), Phi Gamma Delta. Home: 944 River Rd Piscataway NJ 08854-5504 Office: Rutgers U Dept Econs New Brunswick NJ 08903 *I have sought to extend the bounds of knowledge through research and writing, and to pass on to my children and students not only what I have learned, but also, hopefully, some idea of how to behave in a civilized manner.*

ALEXANDER, ROBERT WAYNE, medical educator; b. Memphis, Mar. 19, 1941. AB, U. Miss., 1962; MS in Physiology, Emory U., 1967, PhD in Physiology, 1968; MD, Duke U., 1969. Diplomate Am. Bd. Internal Medicine, Am. Bd. Cardiovascular Disease. Intern in medicine Duke U., 1969-70, fellow in cardiology, 1974-76; resident in medicine U. Wash., 1970-71; asst. prof. medicine Harvard U., 1976-82, assoc. prof., 1982-88; assoc. phys. Brigham and Women's Hosp., Boston, 1982-88; asst. in medicine Beth Israel Hosp., Boston, 1982-88; chief of cardiology Emory U. Hosp., 1988—; dir. divsn. cardiology Emory U., 1988—, R. Bruce Logue prof. medicine, 1988—; staff assoc., sr. surgeon experimental therapeutics br. Nat. Heart and Lung Inst., Nat. Inst. Health, Bethsda, Md., 1971-74; vis. prof. Duke U. Med. Ctr., 1986, U. Tex. Southwestern Med. Ctr., Dallas, 1988, Mt. Sinai Med. Ctr., N.Y.C., 1990, Kobe U., Japan, 1992, Ohio State U., 1995; Pfizer vis. prof. U. Mich., 1993; Pfizer vis. prof. Allegheny Med. Sch., 1997; Simon Dack vis. prof. Mt. Sinai Med. Ctr., 1995. Mem. editl. bd. Jour. Clin. Investigation, 1992—, Circulation Rsch., Advances in Pharmacology, Advances in Hypertension, all 1989-93; co-editor The Heart, 8th edit., 1993, sr. editor, 9th edit., 1998; circulation-cons. editor Jour. Am. Coll. Cardiology, 1993—. Recipient Rsch. Career Devel. award, 1977-82; Pfizer traveling fellow Clin. Rsch. Inst. Montreal, 1983. Fellow AAAS, Am. Coll. Cardiology, Am. Heart Assn. (v.p. rsch. 1995, bd. dirs. 1995—); mem. AMA, Assn. Am. Physicians, Am. Soc. Clin. Investigation, High Blood Pressure Rsch. Coun. Australia (hon. life), Am. Fedn. Clin. Rsch., Am. Clin. and Climatological Soc., Assoc. Univ. Cardiologists (pres. 1998—). Home: 453 Argonne Dr NW Atlanta GA 30305-2842 Office: Emory U Sch of Medicine 1639 Pierce Dr Atlanta GA 30322

ALEXANDER, ROBERTA SUE, history educator; b. N.Y.C., Mar. 19, 1943; d. Bernard Milton and Dorothy (Linn) Cohn; m. John Kurt Alexander, 1966 (div. Sept. 1972); m. Ronald Burett Fost, May 7, 1977. BA, UCLA, 1964; MA, U. Chgo., 1966, PhD, 1974. Instr., Roosevelt U., Chgo., 1967-68; prof. U. Dayton, Ohio, 1969—; mem. editorial bd. Cin. Hist. Soc., 1973—. Author: North Carolina Faces the Freedmen: Race Relations During Presidential Reconstruction, 1985; chpt. in book. Recipient Summer stipend NEH, Washington, 1975, Teaching Exellence and Campus Leadership award Sears-Roebuck Found., 1990, Teaching Exellence in History award Ohio Acad. History, 1991; fellow in residence NEH, 1976-77, fellow Inst. for Legal Studies, NEH, 1982, summer research fellow U. Dayton, 1972, 74, 76, 80. Mem. Am. Hist. Assn., Orgn. Am. Historians, Am. Soc. Legal History, So. Hist. Assn., Mortar Board, Phi Beta Kappa, Phi Alpha Theta. Club: Am. Contract Bridge Assn. (life master 1983). Avocations: bridge; golf. Home: 7715 Legendary Ln West Chester OH 45069-4605 Office: U Dayton Dept History Dayton OH 45469-0310

ALEXANDER, ROY, public relations executive, editor, author; b. Asheville, N.C., Feb. 3, 1930; s. William Roy and Ruth (Upshaw) A. PhB, Northwestern U., 1954. Mng. editor Daily Northwestern, 1951-52; assoc. editor Food Retailing, 1951-55; dir. pub. relations Mid-States Corp., 1952-53; editor Splty. Salesman, 1953-56, Mobile Homes mag., 1953-54; account exec. Philip Lesly Co., 1956-58; sr. v.p. Philip Lesly Co. (N.Y.C. Office), 1958-62; pres. Alexander Co., N.Y.C., 1962-93, Taggart & Alexander, N.Y.C., 1993—; editor Mktg. Times, 1970—; mgr. N.Y. product publicity for Wurlitzer Co.; pub. relations counsel to Grad. Sch. Sales Mgmt. and Mktg., Lincoln Logs Ltd., The Maleck Group, Sturm Ruger & Co., Southport, Conn., Barter Advantage, Inc., Log Home Guide, Solar Additions, Inc., Hearthstone Homes, Dandridge, Tenn., Mantis Mfg. Co., Huntingdon Valley, Pa.; counselor Info. Industry Assn., Bethesda, Md., Environment Info., Ctr., N.Y.C., Flexmaster of Can., Toronto, Z-Flex, Manchester, N.H., Uni-Flex, Berlin, N.J., Danflex Hose Co., Charlotte, N.C., Sturm, Ruger & Co., Southport, Conn. Writer, exec. producer: (color motion picture) The Greening of Augusta; dir.: (pub. edn. program) Iron Mountain Stoneware, Classic Travel, N.Y.; creator: (pub. edn. program) W.Va. Coal Assn.; designer, creator (communications and promotion program) Singer Bus. Machines; dir. nationwide pub. edn. program Nat. Pest Control Assn.; author: Direct Salesman's Handbook, 1958, Mehdi: Story of Metlife's Top Salesman, 1977, Duke Medical Center's Ricer's Guide, 1984, Power Speech: Your Quickest Route to Success, 1986, Taking Your Company Public, 1990, Commonsense Time Management, 1992. Served with AUS, 1946-49; feature editor Armed Forces Press Service, 1948-49. Address: 333 E 34th St New York NY 10016-4977 *My guiding principles: (1) Do something even if it's wrong - percentages favor the activist. (2) Don't waste words or time; both are in finite supply. (3) All generalizations are false, including these. (4) Assume most people will fail their responsibilities and plan accordingly. (5) Anything worth doing is worth doing with quality. (6) Avoid all medication; solve health problem with diet and exercise. (7) Never forget: The market economy made it all possible.*

ALEXANDER, S. ALLAN, lawyer; b. Greenville, Miss., Aug. 25, 1951; d. Hugh Allan and Charlotte Joll (Jolley) A. BA, William Woods Coll., 1973; JD, U. Miss., Oxford, 1978. Bar: Miss. 1978. Law clk. to chief judge U.S. Dist. Ct., Greenville, 1978-80; assoc. Holcomb, Dunbar, Connell, Merkel, Tollison & Khayat, Oxford, 1980-82; ptnr. Tollison and Alexander, Oxford, 1982-90, Tollison Austin and Twiford, Oxford, 1990—; adj. prof. sch. law U. Miss., Oxford, 1989-90; sec. young lawyers sect. Miss. Bar, 1988-89; chair Miss. Bar Com. on Cts. in 21st Century, 1990-93; mem. Continuing Legal Edn. Commn., 1989-92. Editor-in-Chief Miss. Law Jour., 1977. Bd. dirs. Domestic Violence Project, Oxford, 1983-86, United Way, Lafayette County, Miss., 1986-87. Mem. ABA, Miss. Bar Assn., Assn. Trial Lawyers Am., Miss. Trial Lawyers Assn., Fed. Bar Assn., Miss. Bar Found., Nature Conservancy. Office: Tollison Austin & Twiford 103 N Lamar Blvd Oxford MS 38655-3701

ALEXANDER, SAMUEL RUDOLPH, retired concert manager, educational administrator; b. Goldsboro, N.C., Nov. 2, 1930; s. Samuel W. Alexander and Alice (Ezzell) Scott; m. Frances Baker, Sept. 7, 1952(div. Jan. 1977); children: Gregory, Martha, Steven, Christy; m. Jennie M. Parker, Aug. 10, 1980. BS, E. Carolina Coll., 1952, MA, 1953. Dist. scout exec. Boy Scouts Am., Wilson, N.C., 1956-62; asst. dean student affairs East Carolina Coll., Greenville, N.C., 1962-73; assoc. dean student affairs E. Carolina U., Greenville, N.C., 1973-87; asst. vice chancellor student life East Carolina U., Greenville, N.C., 1987-95. Chmn. Greenville/Pitt County Convention and Visitors Authority, 1987-97, Pitt County United Fund Budget Allocations Com., Greenville, 1972-74; cubmaster Boy Scouts Am., Greenville, 1963-66, 68-71, asst. scoutmaster, 1966-68, 71-74; chmn. bd. dirs. E. Carolina Village of YesterYear, Greenville, 1990-96. With U.S. Army, 1953-55. East Carolina U. Performing Arts Series named in his honor, 1995, Outstanding Alumni award, 1995. Mem. Assn. Colls., Univs. and Community Arts Adminstrs. (exec. bd. 1970-73, 77-80, chair numerous coms., instr. nat. workshops, confs. 1965-87, Fanny Taylor award 1982), Internat. Platform Assn. (Drew Pearson award 1974, bd. govs. 1975-76), Nat. Assn. Campus Activities (founder), So. Assn. Colls. and Schs. (mem. accrediting team 1970-74). Republican. Methodist. Avocations: photography, gardening. Home: 304 Eleanor St Greenville NC 27858-8616

ALEXANDER, SHANA, journalist, author, lecturer; b. N.Y.C., Oct. 6, 1925; d. Milton and Cecelia (Rubenstein) Ager; m. Robert Shulman, 1946 (div.); m. Stephen Alexander, 1951 (div.); 1 dau., Katherine (dec.). BA, Vassar Coll., 1945. With PM, 1944-46, Harper's Bazaar, 1946-47; with Flair, 1950; reporter Life mag., 1951-61, staff writer, 1961-64; writer twice monthly column The Feminine Eye, 1964-69; editor McCall's mag., N.Y.C., 1969-71; v.p. Norton Simon Communications, Inc., 1971-72; radio and TV commentator Spectrum CBS News, 1971-72; columnist, contbg. editor Newsweek, 1972-75; commentator CBS 60 Minutes, 1975-79; Bd. dirs. Am. Film Inst. Author: The Feminine Eye, 1970, Shana Alexander's State-by-State Guide to Women's Legal Rights, 1975, Talking Woman, 1976, Anyone's Daughter, 1979, Very Much a Lady: The Untold Story of Jean Harris and Dr. Herman Tarnower, 1983, Nutcracker: Money, Madness, Murder: A Family Album, 1985, The Pizza Connection, 1988, When She Was Bad: The Story of Bess, Nancy, Hortense and Sukhreet, 1989, Happy Days: My Mother, My Father, My Sister and Me, 1995. Recipient Sigma Delta Chi and U. So. Calif. Nat. Journalism award, 1965, Los Angeles Times Woman of Year award, 1967, Golden Pen award Am. Newspaper Womens Club, 1969, Front Page award Newswomen's Club N.Y., 1973, Matrix award N.Y. Women in Communications, 1973-74, Spirit of Achievement award Albert Einstein Coll. Med., 1976; Creative Arts award Nat. Women's div. Am. Jewish Congress. Office: Levine Thall Plotkin & Menin care Robert Levine 1740 Broadway Fl 22 New York NY 10019-4396*

ALEXANDER, STANLEY F., municipal agency administrator; b. Bronx, N.Y., July 23, 1937. Grad. high sch., Bronx, 1955. Ptnr. Alstan Trucking Corp., Bronx, 1961-87; dispatcher City of Yonkers (N.Y.), Dept. Pub. Works Action Ctr., 1988; inspector City of Yonkers, Office Consumer Protection, 1989-93; dir. licensing and consumer protection City of Yonkers, 1996—; records and archives Westchester County, 1993-96. Office: City of Yonkers Health Center Blvd 87 Nepperhan Ave Yonkers NY 10701-3818*

ALEXANDER, STEVEN, artist, educator; b. Stamford, Tex., Aug. 27, 1953; s. Thomas D. and Barbara J. Alexander; m. Laura Duerwald; children: Erin Marcelle, Ava Reed. BA, Austin Coll., 1975; MFA, Columbia U., 1977. Adj. prof. Austin (Tex.) C.C., 1989-93, U. Scranton, Pa., 1993-95; asst. prof. art Marywood U., Scranton, 1995—; studio resident P.S. 1 Contemporary Art Ctr., Long Island City, N.Y., 1978; vis. artist Studio Art Ctrs. Internat., Florence, Italy, 1999. Editor, designer exhbn. catalog: Rooms P.S. 1, 1976; curator, editor exhbn. catalog: The Poetic Object: Paintings of Rebecca Purdum, 1997; rep. by Gremillion and Co. Fine Art, Houston, exhibited in at Janus Gallery, Santa Fe, N. Mex., 1992, Takasaki (Japan) Art Ctr., 1994, painting Ctr., N.Y.C., 1996, Gremillion and Co. Fine Art, Houston, 1998. Chmn. Borough Planning Commn., Montrose, Pa., 1998—. Mem. Coll. Art Assn., Founds. in Art: Theory and Edn., Susquehanna Agrl. Soc. (v.p. 1998—). E-mail: salexander@ac.marywood.edu. Office: Marywood U Art Dept 2300 Adams Ave Scranton PA 18509

ALEXANDER, STEWART MURRAY (BUDDY ALEXANDER), golf coach; b. St. Petersburg, Fla., Feb. 20, 1953. BS in Recreation, Ga. So. U., 1975, MA in Ednl. Adminstrn., 1980. Tennis player, 1974-77; head coach Ga. So. U., 1977-80, La. State U., 1983-87, U. Fla., Gainesville, 1988—. Named All-Am., 1974, 75, Ea. Amateur Tennis Champion, 1977, U.S. Amateur Champion, 1986, World Cup Team, 1986, U.S. Walker Cup Team, 1987; inducted into Golf Coaches Hall Fame NJCAA, 1991; recipient Nat. Coach Yr. Golfweek mag., 1993. Office: U Fla Athletic Dept PO Box 14485 Gainesville FL 32604-2485*

ALEXANDER, THOMAS BENJAMIN, history educator; b. Nashville, July 23, 1918; s. Thomas Benjamin and Mary Christine (Sanders) A.; m. Elise Hadley Pritchett, June 16, 1941; children: Wynne Hadley Alexander Guy, Elaine Elliston Alexander Gates, Carol Pope. BA, Vanderbilt U., 1939, MA, 1940, PhD, 1947. From asst. prof. to assoc. prof. history Clemson U., S.C., 1946-49; prof., chmn. div. social scis. Ga. So. U., Statesboro, 1949-57; from assoc. prof. to prof. history U. Ala., Tuscaloosa, 1957-69; prof. history U. Mo., Columbia, 1969-88, Middlebush prof. history, 1979-82, prof. emeritus, 1988—, Sesquicentennial prof., 1990. Author: Political Reconstruction in Tennessee, 1950, Thomas A.R. Nelson of East Tennessee, 1956, Sectional Stress and Party Strength, 1836-1860, 1967, The Anatomy of the Confederate Congress, 1972 (Sydnor award 1973, Jefferson Davis award 1972). Served to lt. USNR, 1943-46, ETO. Fellow Guggenheim Found., 1955-56; grantee Social Sci. Research Council, 1947, 67-68; fellow Inst. So. History, 1968-69. Mem. AAUP, So. Hist. Assn. (pres. 1980), Am. Hist. Assn., Orgn. Am. Historians, Social Sci. History Assn. (pres. 1986), S.C. Hist. Assn. (pres. 1958). Home: 2606 Summit Rd Columbia MO 65203-1336 Office: U Mo Dept History Columbia MO 65211

ALEXANDER, VERA, dean, marine science educator; b. Budapest, Hungary, Oct. 26, 1932; came to U.S., 1950; d. Paul and Irene Alexander; div.; children: Graham Alexander Dugdale, Elizabeth Alexander. BA in Zoology, U. Wis., 1955, MS in Zoology, 1962; PhD in Marine Sci., U. Alaska, 1965; Doctor of Laws, Hokkaido U., Japan, 1999. From asst. prof. to assoc. prof. marine sci. U. Alaska, Fairbanks, 1965-74, prof., 1974—, dean Coll. Environ. Scis., 1977-78, 80-81, dir. Inst. Marine Sci., 1979-93, acting dean Sch. Fisheries and Ocean Scis., 1987-89, dean, 1989—; mem. adv. com. to ocean scis. divsn. NSF, 1980-84, chmn. adv. com., 1983-84; mem. com. to evaluate outer continental shelf environ. assessment program Minerals Mgmt. Svc., Bd. Environ. Sci. and Tech. NRC, 1987-91, mem. com. on geophys. and environ. Data, 1993-98; mem. adv. com. Office Health and Environ. Rsch., U.S. Dept. Energy, Washington, 1987-90; vice chmn. Arctic Ocean Scis. Bd., 1988-89; commr. U.S. Marine Mammal Commn., 1995—; U.S. del. to North Pacific Marine Sci. Orgn.; bd. dirs. Western Regional Aquaculture Ctr.; mem. sci. adv. bd. NOAA, 1998—, mem. ocean rsch. adv. panel; bd. govs. consortium for oceanographic rsch. and edn. Editor: Marine Biological Systems of the Far North (W.L. Rey), 1989. Sec. Fairbanks Light Opera Theatre Bd., 1987-88; chairwoman Rhodes Scholar Selection Com., Ak., 1986-95. Research grantee U. Alaska. Fellow AAAS, Arctic Inst. N.Am., Explorers Club (sec., treas. Alaska/Yukon chpt. 1987-89, 91—, pres. 1990-91); mem. Am. Soc. Limnology and Oceanography, Am. Geophys. Union, Oceanography Soc., Am. Fisheries Soc., Rotary. Avocations: classical piano, horsemanship. Home: PO Box 80650 Fairbanks AK 99708-0650 Office: U Alaska PO Box 707220 Fairbanks AK 99775

ALEXANDER, WILLIAM BROOKS, lawyer, former state senator; b. Boyle, Miss., Dec. 23, 1921; s. William Brooks and Vivien (Beaver) A.; m. Belle McDonald, Mar. 12, 1950; children—Brooks, Becky, John, Jason, Grace. Student, Miss. Coll., 1940-42; LL.B., U. Miss., 1948. Bar: Miss. 1948. Ptnr. firm Alexander, Johnston & Alexander, Cleveland, 1948—; mem. Miss. Senate, 1960-83, past pres. pro tem. Past pres. Miss. Heart Assn.; bd. dirs. Miss. Coll. Served with AUS, 1942-46; bd. dirs. Delta Council, Miss. Econ. Council. Mem. Miss. Bar Assn. (Outstanding Legislator), Bolivar County Bar Assn., Am. Legion, VFW (past dep. comdr.). Baptist. Club: Exchange. Lodge: Masons. Office: PO Box 1737 Cleveland MS 38732-1737

ALEXANDER, WILLIAM D., III, civil engineer, consultant, former army air force officer; b. Charlotte, N.C., June 20, 1911; s. William D. Jr. and Elizabeth G. A.; m. Louise Elizabeth York, Nov. 14, 1936 (dec. 1983); 1 child, William D. IV; m. Jean DeZonia Mahan, Nov. 30, 1985 (dec. 1988); m. Alice West Dorrier, Aug. 9, 1990. BS, Va. Mil. Inst., Lexington, 1934; CE, N.C. State U., Raleigh, 1953. Registered profl. civil engr. Commd. 2d lt. U.S. Army-Air Force, 1940, advanced through grades to col., ret., 1962; from v.p. to pres. SSV&K, N.Y.C., 1962-75; asst. gen. mgr. MARTA, Atlanta, 1975-79. Bd. dirs. Georgetown County Water and Sewer, S.C., 1982-87. Fellow ASCE, Soc. Am. Mil. Engrs.; mem. The Moles, Nat. Acad. Engrs., Phi Kappa Phi (N.C. State chpt.), Tau Beta Pi (Citadel chpt.). Home: 120 Lakes at Litchfield Pawleys Island SC 29585

ALEXANDER, WILLIAM HERBERT, business educator, former construction executive; b. Harrisburg, Pa., Apr. 17, 1941; s. Wallace Hale and Jeannette Kauffman (Hackenberger) A.; m. Marion Elizabeth Carey, Nov. 30, 1963; children: Charles, Elizabeth, Robert, Kathryn. B.S., U.S. Mil. Acad., 1963; M.B.A., U. Pitts., 1969; D of Pub. Svc. (hon.), Harrisburg Community Coll., 1992. Registered profl. engr., Pa. Commd. 2d lt. U.S. Army, 1963, advanced through grades to capt., 1968; platoon leader, co. comdr. Kitzingen, Germany, 1963-66; capt., co. comdr. Officer Candidate Regiment, Ft. Belvoir, Va., 1966-67; staff officer, engr. constrn. battalion Cu Chi, Vietnam, 1968; resigned, 1968; project mgr. H.B. Alexander & Son, Inc., Harrisburg, 1970-77; chmn. H.B. Alexander & Son, Inc., 1977-94; dir. Pa. Blue Shield, Mchts. & Businessmen's Mut. Ins. Co., 1977—; dir. family bus. programs Wharton Sch. U. Pa., 1988-94, mng. dir. Sol. C. Snider Entrepreneurial Ctr. Wharton Sch., 1994—; pres. Capital Region Econ. Devel. Corp., 1987-88; bd. dirs. Hershey Foods Corp., Hershey Trust Co. Bd. dirs. AAA Ctrl. Penn Auto Club (chmn. 1991-93); pres. Tri County United Way, 1979-80, Ams. for Competitive Enterprise System, 1981-82; bd. mgrs. Milton Hershey Sch.; chmn. Harrisburg C.C. Found. Decorated Bronze Star. Mem. ASCE, Pa. Soc. Profl. Engrs. (Engr. of Yr. in Central Pa. 1986), Harrisburg C. of C. (bd. dirs., chmn. 1982-83), Harrisburg Rotary (pres. 1981-82), Beta Gamma Sigma, Delta Mu Delta. Presbyterian (elder). Home: 16 Wagner St Hummelstown PA 17036-9113 Office: 406 Vance Hall 3733 Spruce St Philadelphia PA 19104-4108

ALEXANDER, WILLIAM OLIN, finance company executive; b. Lexington, Ky., Aug. 2, 1939; s. Elby Olin and Louise (Watson) A.; m. Yvonne Davis, Jan. 26, 1961; children: Keith Davis, Hope. B.S., U. Ky., 1961. C.P.A., Fla. Auditor Ring, Mahony & Arner (C.P.A.s), Miami, Fla., 1961-62; sr. auditor Ring, Mahony & Arner (C.P.A.s), 1964-66; v.p., treas. Seabird Industries, Miami, 1966-70; exec. v.p. Seabird Industries, 1970-73; controller Belcher Oil Co., Miami, 1973-75; treas. Belcher Oil Co., 1976-83; sr. v.p., treas. Mitchell Co., Mobile, Ala., 1983-85; pres. Alexander & Co., Inc., 1985—. Served to 1st lt. AUS, 1962-64. Mem. AICPA, Fla. Inst. CPAs, Porsche Club Am., Beta Alpha Psi, Delta Sigma Pi, Delta Tau Delta. Republican. Home: 10910 Juniperus Pl Tampa FL 33618-3818 Office: 14033 N Dale Mabry Hwy Tampa FL 33618-2401

ALEXANDER, WILLIAM POWELL, business advisor; b. Buffalo, June 16, 1934; s. James Nelson and Helen (Johnston) A.; m. Eunice Gail Elwood, May 8, 1981; 1 child from previous marriage, Christine Alexander Johnson. B.A., Gettysburg Coll., 1956; postgrad., Temple U., 1960-62. With Aetna Casualty & Surety Co., 1956-57; with RCA Corp., N.Y.C., 1960-86, asst. sec., 1968-73, sr. asst. sec., 1973-78, sec., 1978-86; also sec. NBC, Coronet Industries, RCA/Ariola, Hertz, Random House; sec. to office of chmn., asst. to chmn. Marine Midland Banks, Inc., 1987-88; adminstrv. dir. The Gt. Atlantic & Pacific Tea Co. Inc., 1988-89. Served to 1st lt. USAAF, 1957-59. Mem. Am. Soc. Corp. Secs., Phi Kappa Psi. Club: Cavalier Golf and Yacht (Virginia Beach, Va.). Home and Office: 1135 Crystal Dr Virginia Beach VA 23451-3855

ALEXANDRE, KRISTIN KUHNS, public relations executive, writer; b. Dayton, Ohio, July 15, 1948; d. James Edward and Faith (Colgan) Kuhns; m. DeWitt Loomis Alexandre, 1988; children: James Andrew, Cynthia Lenox Banks. BA, Sweet Briar, 1968. Editor C.I.T. Finance Corp., N.Y.C., 1970-73; newscaster Channel 5 News, N.Y.C., 1973-74, Channel 13 News, N.Y.C., 1974-75; editor Champion Internat., N.Y.C., 1975-76; copy editor House Beautiful, N.Y.C., 1975-76; pub. rels. officer Economic Devel. Adminstrn. Puerto Rico, N.Y.C., 1976-80; pres. Kristin Alexandre Pub. Rels., N.Y.C., 1980—; bd. dirs. Kuhns Investment Corp., Dayton; pres. Robert Kuhns, Inc., Dayton. Bd. trustees Friends Clarence Dillo Libr. Mem. New York Jr. League. Home: PO Box 367 Far Hills NJ 07931-0367

ALEXANDROV, SIMONA, artist, art educator, administrator; b. St. Petersburg, Russia, Apr. 5, 1964; d. Felix I. and Inna (Shapiro) A.; m. Roman Gavrilman, June 20, 1993 (div. Dec. 1998). MFA, Muchina Sch. Applied Arts, St. Petersburg, Russia, 1988, Cranbrook Acad. Art, Bloomfield Hills, Mich., 1991. Tchr., lectr. Pewabic Pottery Sch., Detroit, 1988-91; tchr. Paint Creek Ctr. for the Arts, Rochester, Mich., 1990-92; ceramic instr. Danforth Mus. Sch., Framingham, Mass., 1993-96; tchr. Mudflat Sch., Somerville, Mass., 1994-97; tchr., lectr. Radcliffe Coll. at Harvard U., Cambridge, Mass., 1996-97; tchr., exec. dir. Cera-Mix Fine Art Sch. Studio, Waltham, Mass., 1993—; vis. lectr. Mass. Coll. Art, Boston, 1996. Exhibited works in solo show at The Clay Studio Gallery, 1992; exhibited in group shows at Miami Expo, 1997, Shaw/Guido Gallery, 1996, 97, Joanne Rapp Gallery, 1997. Avocations: writing, travel, diving, philosophy. Office: Cera-Mix Fine Art Studio 621 Main St Waltham MA 02452

ALEXANDROV, VLADIMIR EUGENE, Russian literature educator; b. Germany, May 9, 1947; married; 2 children. BA in Geology magna cum laude, CUNY, 1968, MA in Geology, 1971; MA in Comparative Lit., U. Mass., Amherst, 1973, Princeton U., 1976; PhD, Princeton U., 1979. Instr. dept. geology CUNY, 1970-71; lectr. Slavic dept. Princeton (N.J.) U., 1978-79; asst. prof. Slavic dept. Harvard U., 1979-84, dir. undergraduate studies in Russian lit. and Soviet studies Slavic dept., 1979-86, assoc. dir. Slavic and East European Lang. and Area Ctr., 1980-86, assoc. prof. Slavic dept., 1984-86; assoc. prof. Slavic dept. Yale U., New Haven, Conn., 1986-90, dir. grad. studies Slavic dept., 1987, 89-91, dir. undergrad. studies Slavic dept., 1989, prof. Russian lit. Slavic dept., 1990—, chmn. Slavic dept., 1991-97; coord. Eastern European area Federally Funded Fgn. Lang. Area Studies Fellowships, Harvard U., 1980-86; vis. assoc. prof. Slavic dept. Yale U., 1985, coun. on Soviet and Easter European studies, 1986—, com. on fgn. lang. proficiency, 1987-88, Whiting and Traveling Lurcy fellowship com. grad sch., 1988-90, tenure appointments com. in humanitites, 1990-91, adv. com. divsn. humanities, 1990-91, mem. quorum joint bds. permanent officers grad. sch., 1990—, exec. com. grad sch., 1990-92, mem. prize tchg. fellowship com. Yale Coll., 1991; coord for fgn. participants Internat. Conf. on Vladimir Nabokov, Moscow, 1990; evaluator NEH Scholarly Grants Program, Harvard-Radcliffe Bunting Inst. Fellowship Program, NEH Program for Scholarly Transition; outside referee on appointments, promotion and tenure U. Calif., Davis, Bryn Mawr Coll., Middlebury coll., U. Wis., Madison, Stanford U., U. Kans., Pa. State U., Dartmouth Coll., Columbia U., Cornell U., U. Va., Brown U., U. Wash., Seattle; lectr., spkr., presenter in field. Author: Andrei Bely: The Major Symbolist Fiction, 1985, Nabokov's Otherworld, 1991; referee Slavic and East European Jour., Slavic Rev., Russian Rev., Mosaic, Nabokov Studies, UCLA Slavic Studies, Northwestern U. Press, Princeton U. Press, Doubleday, Garland Pub.; editor: The Garland Companion to Vladimir Nabokov; contbr. articles and book revs. to profl. publs. Fellow Am. Coun. Learned Socs., 1982, Travel grantee, 1984; Harvard Russian Rsch. Ctr. fellow, 1983-84; Ind. Study and Rsch. fellow NEH, 1986; Com. Faculty Rsch. Support grantee Harvard U., 1981-83, 83-85, 85-86; Travel grantee Internat. Rsch. and Exchs. Bd., 1992. Mem. Am. Assn. for Advancement Slavic Studies (com. on lang. tng. 1991-93), Modern Lang. Inst. Am., Russian-Am. Inst. (steering com. 1990—). Office: Yale Univ Slavic Dept PO Box 208236 New Haven CT 06520-8236*

ALEXANIAN, RAYMOND, hematologist; b. N.Y.C., June 8, 1932; s. Hagop and Eleeza (Bynderian) A.; m. Lois Abbott, Jan. 16, 1960; 1 dau., Jane. B.A. with highest honors, Dartmouth Coll., 1952; M.D., Harvard U., 1955. Diplomate: Am. Bd. Internal Medicine. Intern King County Hosp.,

Seattle, 1955-56; successively asst. resident in medicine, research fellow in hematology, instr. medicine U. Wash. Med. Sch., 1958-64; mem. faculty U. Tex. M.D. Anderson Hosp., Houston, 1964—; prof. medicine U. Tex. M.D. Anderson Hosp., 1975—. Contbr. numerous articles on myeloma and related disorders to med. jours. Served as capt. M.C. AUS, 1956-58. Mem. Am. Soc. Hematology, AMA, Tex. Med. Assn. (Waldenstrom award 1997). Home: 4082 Breakwood Dr Houston TX 77025-4033 Office: MD Anderson Hosp Dept Lymphoma-Myeloma 1515 Holcombe Blvd Houston TX 77030-4009

ALEXEFF, IGOR, physicist, electrical engineer, educator emeritus; b. Pitts., Jan. 5, 1931; s. Alexander and Tamara (Tchirkow) A.; m. Anne I. Fabina, Feb. 4, 1954; children: Alexander, Helen. BA with honors, Harvard U., 1952; MS, U. Wis., 1955, PhD, 1959. Registered profl. engr., Tenn. Research engr. Westinghouse Corp., Pitts., 1952-53; NSF postdoctoral fellow U. Zurich, Switzerland, 1959-60; group leader controlled thermonuclear fusion Oak Ridge Nat. Lab., 1960-71; prof. elec. engring. U. Tenn., 1971-96, prof. emeritus, 1996—; vis. prof. Inst. Plasma Physics, Nagoya, Japan, 1973, Phys. Rsch. Lab., Ahmedabad, India, 1975, physics dept. U. Natal, Durban, South Africa, 1976, U. Fed. Fluminense Niteroi, Brazil, 1978, Birla Inst. Tech., Ranchi, India, 1991; organizer Plasma Physics Workshop, U.S. and India, 1976; chmn. Gordon Rsch. Conf. on Plasma Physics, 1974; pres. So. Appalachian Sci. and Engring. Far, 1985-86. Co-author: High Power Microwave Sources, 1987; contbr. articles to profl. jours.; over 10 patents in field. Chancellor's rsch. scholar U. Tenn., 1984; recipient Advanced Tech. award Internat. Hall of Fame, 1989, 91, (with others) R&D 100 award R&D Mag., 1989, 91; named Most Outstanding Tchr. of Yr., U. Tenn. Elec. Engring. Dept., 1992. Fellow IEEE (assoc. editor Trans. on Plasma Sci., organizer 1st Internat. Conf. on Plasma Sci. 1974, former pres. Oak Ridge sect., Centennial medal 1987, Outstanding Engr. in S.E. award 1987), Am. Phys. Soc. (past sec.-treas. div. plasma physics); mem. Tenn. Inventors Assn. (founding pres., Inventor of Yr. award 1988), Nuclear and Plasma Scis. Soc. of IEEE (chmn. plasma sect. 1983-84, v.p. 1998, pres. 1999—, Shea award for outstanding svc.). Home: 2790 Turnpike Oak Ridge TN 37830 Office: U Tenn Ferris 315 Knoxville TN 37996-2100 also: 1907 Holston River Rd Knoxville TN 37914-6144

ALEXENBERG, MEL, artist, art educator; b. N.Y.C., Feb. 24, 1937; s. Abraham and Jeanne (Kahn) A.; m. Miriam Benjamin, Oct. 25, 1959; children: Iyrit, Ari, Ron, Moshe. BS, Queens Coll., CUNY, 1958; MS, Yeshiva U., 1959; EdD, NYU, 1969. Sci. tchr. N.Y.C. Pub. Schs., Queens, 1959-61; sci. supr. Manhasset (N.Y.) Pub. Schs., 1961-65; asst. prof. Adelphi U., L.I., N.Y., 1965-69; sr. lectr. Tel Aviv U., 1969-73; assoc. prof. Columbia U., N.Y.C., 1973-77; pres. Ramat Hanegev Coll., Yeroham, Israel, 1977-84; assoc. prof. Bar Ilan U., Ramat Gan, Israel, 1978-84; rsch. fellow MIT, Cambridge, Mass., 1984-88; chmn. dept. fine arts Pratt Inst., Bklyn., 1985-90; dean New World Sch. Arts, Miami, Fla., 1990—; chair. com. on design. edn. Israel Ministry Edn., 1983-84. Author: Light and Sight, 1969, A Semiotic Taxonomy of Contemporary Art Forms, 1976, Aesthetic Experience in Creative Process, 1981, Art with Computers: The Human Spirit and the Electronic Revolution, 1988, Miami in Ecological Perspective, 1994, Art Thrones and Legacy Scrolls, 1998; art editor Visual Computer: Internat. Jour. Computer Graphics; works include Lights Orot, 1987-89, Digitized Homage to Rembrandt, 1989-90, Four Corners of Am., 1995-96, Centers: Lebanon (Kansas) and Jerusalem (Israel), 1996, Memory-Aspiration Thrones, Intergenerational Pub. Art with Miriam Benjamin, 1997, Legacy Scrolls, 1998, Trees of Good Deeds & Wisdom, Synagogue Designed with Arch. K. Treister, 1999; represented in permanent collections Met. Mus. Art, N.Y.C., Mus. Modern Art, N.Y.C., Princeton (N.J.) Art Mus., Del. Art Mus., Wilmington, Phila. Mus. Art, Balt. Mus. Art, Tel Aviv Mus., Victoria and Albert Mus., London, Mus. Moderner Kunst, Vienna, Austria, Museo de Arte Contemporaneo, Caracas, Venezuela, Israel Mus., Jerusalem, Haags Gemeentemuseum, The Netherlands, Malmo (Sweden) Mus., High Mus. Art, Atlanta, Museo Nacional de Artes Plasticas Montevideo, Uruguay. Bd. trustees Torah Sch. for Environ. Studies, Mitzpeh Ramon, Israel. Recipient award for art direction Am. Film Festival, 1964; Founders Day award NYU, 1969; MIT rsch. fellow, 1984-88. Mem. Internat. Soc. Edn. Through Art, Nat. Art Edn. Assn., Israel Soc. Painters and Sculptors. Jewish. Office: New World Sch of Arts 300 NE 2nd Ave Miami FL 33132-2204

ALEY, SHELLEY B., composition and rhetoric educator; b. Kansas City, Mo., Dec. 28, 1951; d. William Levis and Gloria Jean (Shields) Sellers/Miller. BS in Edn., S.W. Mo. State U., 1981, MA, 1988; PhD, Tex. Christian U., 1994. High sch. tchr. Forsyth (Mo.) H.S., 1981-96; lectr. S.W. Mo. State U., Springfield, 1988-91; asst. prof. Cottey Coll., Nevada, Mo., 1993-99, James Madison U., Harrisonburg, Va., 1999—; English dept. adv. bd. S.W. Mo. State U., Springfield, 1993-99. Mem. MLA, Mo. Philological Assn., Am. Culture Assn., Coll. Composition & Comm. Office: Writing Program James Madison Univ Harrisonburg VA 22801

ALFANGE, DEAN, JR., political science educator; b. N.Y.C., May 6, 1930; s. Dean and Thalia (Perry) A.; m. Barbara Jean Vance, June 6, 1959. A.B., Hamilton Coll., 1950; M.A., U. Colo., 1960; Ph.D., Cornell U., 1967. Instr., then asst. prof. govt. Lafayette Coll., Easton, Pa., 1963-67; from asst. prof. to assoc. prof. polit. sci. U. Mass., Amherst, 1967-75; prof. U. Mass., 1975—; dean Faculty Social and Behavioral Scis., 1970-75, acting vice chancellor for acad. affairs, 1975-76, 83; vis. scholar Yale Law Sch., 1977-78, Stanford Law Sch., 1986, 92. Served to 1st lt. USAF, 1952-57. Home: 5 Montague Rd Leverett MA 01054-9725 Office: U Mass Dept Political Science Amherst MA 01003

ALFANO, CHARLES T., JR., lawyer; b. Hartford, Conn., Apr. 1, 1959. BA, Tufts U., 1981; JD, U. Louisville, 1984. Bar: Conn. 1984. Mem. ethics com. Town of Suffield (Conn.), 1985, mem. bd. fin., 1985-89, town atty., 1989-91, mem. econ. redevel. commn., 1991—; active charter revision commn. Town of Suffield. Bd. dirs. Suffield Vis. Nurse & Emergency Aid Assn. Mem. ABA, Assn. Trial Lawyers Am., Conn. Bar Assn., Conn. Trial Lawyers Assn., Hartford County Bar Assn., Phi Alpha Delta (marshall 1983-84). Office: c/o Alfano & Flynn 53 Mountain Rd Suffield CT 06078-2088

ALFANO, CHARLES THOMAS, SR., lawyer; b. Suffield, Conn., June 21, 1920; s. Dominick and Rosina (Dimartino) A.; m. Mary Ann Sinatro, Nov. 13, 1954; children: Diane Elizabeth, Andrea Rose, Charles Thomas Jr., Susan Marie. Student, Ill. Coll., 1939-40; B.A. cum laude, U. Conn., 1943; LL.B., J.D., U. Mich., 1948. Bar: Conn. 1948. Since practiced in Hartford; partner firm Alfano Halloran & Flynn; judge Town Ct. of Suffield, 1949-51, 55-59; mem. Conn. Senate, 1959-77, asst. majority leader, 1966, pres. pro tem, 1967-73, minority leader, 1973-75, v.p. pro tem, 1975-77; corp. counsel Town of Suffield, 1977-83; dir., chmn. bd. Suffield Savs. Bank; dir. Conn. Water Co. Bd. dirs. Conn. Pub. TV. Served with USNR, 1942-47, ETO. Mem. ABA, ATLA, Conn. Bar Assn., Hartford County Bar Assn., Conn. Trial Lawyers Assn. (bd. dirs.), Hartford Club, Mystic Yacht Club, Mason's Island Yacht Club, N.Y. Athletic Club, KC, Sigma Nu. Home: 50 Marbern Dr Suffield CT 06078-1533 Office: 89 Oak St Hartford CT 06106-1515 also: 53 Mountain Rd Suffield CT 06078-2041

ALFANO, EDWARD CHARLES, JR., elementary education educator; b. Bklyn., Mar. 20, 1945; s. Edward Charles and Victoria Helen (Fanti) A.; m. Mary Fien, Aug. 27, 1983; children: Elizabeth Anne, Christina Irene. BA in Philosophy, Cathedral Coll., 1967; postgrad., Bklyn. Coll., 1967-70; MS in Edn., L.I. U., 1972; postgrad. in Archaeology, Oxford (U.K.) U., 1973; postgrad. in Art, L.I. U., 1976; art studies, Bklyn. Mus., 1990. Cert. elem. tchr., N.Y. Tchr. English St. Mark Sch., Bklyn., 1968-69; tchr. pub. schs. Bklyn., 1969—; math. specialist Pub. Sch. 15, Bklyn., 1976-78; tchr. English as 2d lang. Pub. Sch. 169, Bklyn., 1985-86, tchr. art, 1986-94, tchr. sci., 1994-95, tchr. Engish, 1995-96, tchr. music movement/phys. edn. Early Childhood Learning Ctr, 1996—; del. United Fedn. Tchrs., Bklyn., 1977-78; faculty rep. policy consultation com. Pub. Sch. 169, 1979-92, dir. summer recreation program, 1989-97; presenter workshops and symposia; tchr. Murals in Park Project, Bklyn., 1990, Summer Literacy Program, 1998. Narrator video The Passion of Our Lord According to Saint John, 1993; contbr.poetry and articles to various publs. Pres. Friends of L.I. U. Libr., 1977-80; mem. vis. com. L.I. U., Bklyn., 1978-80; bd. dirs. Hispanic Young People's Alternatives, Bklyn., 1990-95; lector Good Shepherd Ch., Bklyn., parish coord. Sanctity of Life com., 1993—; mem. Bklyn. Diocesan Pastoral Team for Charismatic Renewal, 1995—. Recipient cmty. svc. award Cmty. Bd. 7, Bklyn., 1990, 91, Sanctity of Life Recognition award Roman Cath. Diocese of Bklyn., 1997, Pro-Life award Flatbush Coun. 497 KC, 1998. Mem. Cath. Tchrs. Assn. (Educator of Yr. award 1992), So. Poetry Assn., Charismatic Prayer Group, Sanctity of Life Com., L.I. U. Alumni Assn. Democrat. Avocations: poetry, art, swimming, music, dramatics. Office: Pub Sch 169 Early Childhood Learning Ctr 411 46th St Brooklyn NY 11220-1213

ALFANO, MICHAEL CHARLES, dental school dean; b. Newark, Aug. 8, 1947; s. Michael Ferdinand and Anne Marie (Barrington) A.; m. JoAnn Mary Coletta, Mar. 30, 1969; children: Michael Anthony, Kristin Lynn. Student, Rutgers U., 1965-67; DMD, U. Medicine and Dentistry of N.J., 1971; postgrad. in periodontics, Harvard U., 1971-74; PhD, MIT, 1975. Asst. prof. dentistry Fairleigh Dickinson U., Hackensack, N.J., 1974-77, assoc. prof., 1977-80, prof. with tenure, 1980-82, dir. Oral Health Research Ctr., 1977-82, asst. dean grad. affairs and research, 1981-82; v.p. dental research Block Drug Co., Inc., Jersey City, 1982-84, sr. v.p. R&D, 1987-98, bd. dirs., 1988-98, pres. dental products div., 1985-88, cons. office of chief exec., 1990-98; dean Coll. Dentistry NYU, 1998—, prof. basic scis. & periodontology Coll. Dentistry, 1998—; cons. Nat. Inst. Dental Rsch., Bethesda, Md., 1976-82; apptd. nat. adv. dental rsch. coun. NIH, Bethesda, 1994-98; apptd. vis. prof. Nat. Dairy Coun., Chgo., 1981; vis. sr. scientist Fairleigh Dickinson U., 1982-88; adj. prof. U. Medicine and Dentistry of N.J., Newark, 1985—; mem. sci. adv. coun. Office of Gov., State of N.J., 1981-84. Editor: Symposium on Nutrition, 1976; contbr. articles to profl. jours. and chpts. to books; patentee in field. Trustee Found. of U. Medicine and Dentistry of N.J., 1988-98; adv. bd. Columbia U. Sch. Dental and Oral Surgery, 1990-98; mem. program com. Am. Fund for Dental Health, 1991-93; bd. overseers Forsyth Dental Ctr., Boston, 1992—, U. Pa. Coll. Dental Medicine, 1992—; trustee Santa Fe Group, 1998—; founding dir. Friends of Nat. Inst. of Dental Rsch. Recipient Leadership citation Newark YMCA, 1966, Disting. Alumnus award U. Medicine and Dentistry of N.J., 1986, Harvard U. Sch. Dental Medicine, 1998; NIH research grantee, 1974-82; NIH postdoctoral fellow, 1971-74. Fellow Am. Coll. Dentists, Am. Coll. of Prosthodontists (hon. fellow); mem. ADA (cons., Nat. Achievement award 1978), Internat. Assn. for Dental Rsch., Am. Assn. for Dental Rsch. (pres. N.J. chpt. 1985), Am. Inst. Nutrition. Independent. Roman Catholic. Achievements include 6 patents, 1 patent pending; discovery of role of Vitamin C in mucous membrane barrier function. Home: 29 Washington Sq W New York NY 10011-9132 Office: NYU Coll Dentistry 345 E 24th St New York NY 10010-4086

ALFARO, FELIX BENJAMIN, physician; b. Managua, Nicaragua, Oct. 22, 1939; came to U.S., 1945, naturalized, 1962; s. Agustin Jose and Amanda Julieta (Barillas) A.; student (State scholar) U. San Francisco, 1958-59, 61-62; M.D., Creighton U., 1967; m. Carmen Heide Meyer, Aug. 14, 1965; children—Felix Benjamin, Mark. Clk., Pacific Gas & Electric Co., San Francisco, 1960-61; intern St. Mary's Hosp., San Francisco, 1967; resident Scenic Gen. Hosp., Modesto, Calif., 1970; practice family medicine, Watsonville, Calif., 1971—; active staff Watsonville Community Hosp., 1971—. Served to capt., M.C., U.S. Army, 1968-69. Lic. physician, Nebr., La., Calif. Diplomate Am. Bd. Family Practice. Fellow Am. Acad. Family Practice; mem. AMA, Calif. Med. Assn., Santa Cruz County Med. Soc., 38th Parrallel Med. Soc. of Korea, Nat Rifle Assn., VFW. Republican. Roman Catholic. Office: 30 Brennan St Watsonville CA 95076-4303

ALFERS, GERALD JUNIOR, retired banker; b. Axtell, Kans., Dec. 12, 1931; s. Joseph Gerald and Olive (Gates) A.; m. Barbara Ruth Small, Aug. 20, 1955; children: Jerilyn, Joseph, Jean, John, James, Jennifer, Jeffrey. Grad. certificate, Am. Inst. Banking, 1964; grad., Pacific Coast Banking Sch., 1967, Nat. Comml. Lending Grad. Sch., U. Okla., 1976. Cert. comml. lender. With Pacific Nat. Bank, Seattle, 1949-80, asst. v.p., 1961-63, v.p., cashier, 1963-72, v.p., mgr. Univ. br., 1972-74, v.p., regional mgr., 1974-76, sr. v.p., 1976-81; exec. v.p. First Interstate Bank of Wash., Seattle, 1981-91; chmn., chief exec. officer First Interstate Ins. Agy. of Wash., Seattle, 1986-91; area pres. First Interstate Bank of Wash., Tacoma, 1991-93; ret., 1993; instr. Seattle C.C., Shoreline C.C.; pres., dir. Seafair Fund, 1982-83. Bd. govs. YMCA, 1972-75, chmn., 1974-75; bd. dirs. Seafair, 1979-88, pres., 1981-82; trustee Seattle Youth Symphony Orch., 1984-87; bd. dirs. Am. Lung Assn., Wash., 1984-97, pres., 1992-94; sector chmn. United Way Pierce County; bd. dirs. Econ. Devel. Bd. Tacoma-Pierce County, 1991-94; mem. fin. coun. Cath. Archdiocese of Seattle, 1994—, chmn., 1997—; mem. pastoral coun. St. Michael's Parish, 1997—. Mem. Acad. Cert. Adminstrv. Mgrs., Am. Bankers Assn., (bank leadership coun. 1989-91, exec. com. retail banking divsn. 1991-94), Wash. Bankers Assn. (chmn. bank ops. com. 1967-72), bd. dirs. 1984-92, pres. 1989-90), Adminstrv. Mgmt. Soc. (bd. dirs. 1972-74), Clearing House Assn. Seattle (chmn. bank ops. com. 1969-72), Am. Inst. Banking (sec., bd. dirs. 1956-61, chmn. 1988-89), Indian Summer Golf & Country Club (pres. 1996-97), Wash. Athletic Club, Broadmoor Golf Club. Roman Catholic. Home: 6439 Troon Ln SE Olympia WA 98501-5172

ALFERS, STEPHEN DOUGLAS, lawyer; b. L.A., Dec. 26, 1945; s. Francis A. and Mary Martha (Wood) A. BA cum laude, U. Denver, 1968, MA in Econs., 1973; JD, U. Va., 1976. Bar: U.S. Dist. Ct. Colo. 1976, U.S. Ct. Appeals (10th cir.) 1980, U.S. Supreme Ct. 1980. Lawyer Sherman & Howard, Denver, 1976-79; ptnr. Davis, Graham & Stubbs, Denver, 1979-92, Morrison & Foerster, Denver, 1992-95; founder Alfers & Carver, LLC, 1996—. Contbr. articles to profl. jours. Lt. USN, 1969-73. Mem. ABA, Colo. Bar Assn., Colo. Mining Assn. (trustee), Rocky Mountain Mineral Law Found., Phi Beta Kappa. Avocations: fly fishing, geology. E-mail: salfers@alfers-carver.com. Office: Alfers & Carver LLC The Equitable Bldg 730 17th St Ste 340 Denver CO 80202-3513

ALFIDI, RALPH JOSEPH, radiologist, educator; b. Rome, Apr. 20, 1932; s. Luca and Angeline (Panella) A.; m. Rose Esther Senesac, Sept. 3, 1956 (div. 1991); children: Suzanne, Lisa, Christine, Katherine, Mary, John; m. Mariella Boller, Aug. 29, 1992. A.B., Ripon (Wis.) Coll., 1955; M.D., Marquette U., Milw., 1959. Intern Oakwood Hosp., Dearborn, Mich., 1959-60; resident, chief resident, A.C.S. fellow U. Va., 1960-63; practice medicine, specializing in radiology Cleve., 1965—; staff mem. Cleve. Clinic, 1965-78, head dept. hosp. radiology, 1968-78; dir. dept. radiology Univ. Hosps., Cleve., 1978-92; cons. VA Hosp., Cleve.; chmn. dept. radiology Case Western Res. U. Sch. Medicine, 1978-92; chmn. staff Cleve. Clinic Found., 1975-76; bd. dirs. Cuyahoga Savs. and Loan, Cleve. Author: Complications and Legal Implications of Special Procedures, 1972, Computed Tomography of the Human Body: An Atlas of Normal Anatomy, 1977; editor: Whole Body Computed Tomography, 1977; contbr. articles to radiology jours. Served to capt., M.C. U.S. Army Res., 1963-65. Picker Found. grantee, 1969-70; NRC grantee, 1969-70. Fellow Am. Coll. Radiology; mem. Radiol. Soc. N. Am., Am. Roentgen Ray Soc., Am. Heart Assn., Soc. Cardiovascular Radiology, Soc. Gastrointestinal Radiology, Soc. Computed Body Tomography (pres. 1977-78), Eastern Radiol. Soc., Ohio Radiol. Soc., Cleve. Radiol. Soc. (pres. 1976-77). Roman Catholic. Club: Kirtland Country. Home: 2074 Abington Rd Cleveland OH 44106-2602 Office: U Hosps Cleve Radiology Dept 2074 Abington Rd Cleveland OH 44106-2602

ALFIERI, JOHN CHARLES, JR., educational administrator; b. Passaic, N.J., Dec. 25, 1949; s. John C. and Anne (Zangara) A.; m. Theresa Meskis, Oct. 26, 1974; children: Christopher, Carlea. BA in Elem. Edn., William Paterson Coll., Wayne, N.J., 1971, MA in Edn., 1975, MA in Adminstrn., 1979. Tchr. grade 6 Bergenfield (N.J.) Bd. Edn., 1971-82, 90-91, math/sci. resource tchr., 1982-90, grade 7 writing lab/study skills tchr., 1991-95, adminstrv. intern, 1971-91, mem. tech. com., 1993—; dir. Bergenfield Cmty. Sch., 1991-95; prin. Lincoln Sch., 1995—. Coach soccer, basketball, track Saddle Brook (N.J.) Recreation, 1985-92; advancement chmn. Boy Scouts Am., Troop 213, Pack 222, Saddle Brook, 1985—; past pres. and co-founder Friends of Saddle Brook Libr., 1990—. Staff sgt. N.J. Army N.G., 1971-77. Named Tchr. of Yr., Bergenfield Optimist Club, 1992; A Plus for Tchrs. grantee Channel 9 TV, 1991. Mem. ASCD, Nat. Assn. Elem. Sch. Prins., N.J. Prins. and Suprs. Assn., Bergen County Elem. and Mid. Sch. Adminstrs. Assn., Saddle Brook Main Lions Club. Avocations: computers/technology, photography, sports. Office: Lincoln Sch 115 Highview Ave Bergenfield NJ 07621-3400

ALFONSO, ANTONIO ESCOLAR, surgeon; b. Manila, Nov. 25, 1943; came to U.S., 1968, naturalized, 1978; s. Ricardo Lagdameo and Marita (Escolar) Alfonso; m. Teresita Nazareno, Apr. 25, 1970; children: Margaretta, Roberto. A.B. cum laude, Ateneo U., 1963; M.D. cum laude, U. Philippines, 1968. Diplomate: Am. Bd. Surgery. Intern U. Philippines-Philippine Gen. Hosp., 1968; instr. surgery Temple U., Phila., 1968-72; sr. fellow surg. oncology Meml. Sloan-Kettering Cancer Ctr., N.Y.C., 1972-74; dir. head and neck surgery service SUNY Downstate Med. Ctr., Bklyn., 1974—, assoc. dir. div. surg. oncology, 1974—, asst. prof. surgery, 1974-77, assoc. prof., 1977-82, prof., 1982—, vice-chmn. dept. surgery, 1988—; chmn. dept. surgery Bklyn. Hosp., 1982-88; chmn. Dept. Surgery L.I. Coll. Hosp., 1988—; cons. head and neck surgery Bklyn. VA Hosp., 1974—. Author: Principles of Surgery Oncology; contbr. articles in med. to profl. jours., chpts. to med. books. Recipient research essay prize N.Y. Colon and Rectal Surg. Soc., 1973; grantee Am. Cancer Soc., 1978. Mem. ACS (bd. govs. Bklyn.-L.I. chpt., gov. 1998—), Assn. Acad. Surgeons, Am. Soc. Clin. Oncology, Am. Assn. Cancer Edn., Soc. Head and Neck Surgeons, N.Y. Surg. Soc. (treas. 1994, v.p. 1998, pres. 1999), Bklyn. Surg. Soc. (pres. 1986-87), N.Y. Cancer Soc. (v.p. 1986-87, pres.-elect 1987-88, pres. 1988-89), Soc. Surg. Oncology, N.Y. Head and Neck Soc. (sec. 1993-97, pres. 1998), N.Y. Soc. Colon and Rectal Surgeons, Triboro Dirs. of Surgery Assn. (pres. 1989—), Phi Kappa Phi. Roman Catholic. Home: 50 Olive Pl Flushing NY 11375-5938 Office: LI Coll Hosp Dept Surgery 340 Henry St Brooklyn NY 11201-5514

ALFONSO, ROBERT JOHN, university administrator; b. N.Y.C., Dec. 17, 1928; s. Robert Richard and Bertha Rose (Schmitt) A.; m. Martha Sue Ralston, June 9, 1956; children: Allison Denise, Robert John, Andrea Diane (dec.). B.A., Roberts Wesleyan Coll., 1952; postgrad., N.Y. U., 1952-53; Ph.D., Mich. State U., 1962. High sch. English tchr. Syracuse, N.Y., 1956-58, Billings, Mont., 1958-59; asst. to dean Coll. Edn., Mich. State U., 1959-60; asst. prof. edn. Queens Coll., N.Y.C., 1962-64; assoc. exec. sec. Assn. for Supervision and Curriculum Devel., 1964-67; assoc. prof. curriculum and supervision Coll. Edn., U. Ala., 1967-68; asst. dean instrn. and grad. studies, prof. Coll. Edn., Kent State U. (Ohio), 1968-71; dean Coll. Edn. and Grad. Sch. Edn., also prof., 1971-80, assoc. v.p., dean faculties, 1980-82; v.p. acad. affairs East Tenn. State U., Johnson City, 1984-94, v.p. emeritus, 1994—; vis. prof. U. Ga., 1982-83. Author: Instructional Supervision: A Behavior System, 1975, 2d edit., 1981; Asst. editor: Mich. Jour. Secondary Edn, 1959-62. Bd. dirs. Nat. Interagy. Council on Smoking and Health, 1964-67; Inter-Profl. Research Commn. on Pupil Personnel Services, 1965-68. Served to 1st lt. USMCR, 1953-56. Recipient Alumnus of Year award Roberts Wesleyan Coll., 1967. Mem. Assn. for Supervision and Curriculum Devel. (dir.), Am. Assn. Sch. Adminstrs., Nat. Council Tchrs. English (dir. 1965-68), Ohio Assn. for Supervision and Curriculum Devel. (pres.), Am. Ednl. Research Assn., Ohio Congress Sch. Adminstr. Orgns. (v.p.), Phi Delta Kappa, Kappa Delta Pi, Phi Kappa Phi. Methodist. Home: 104 Ridgemont Rd Johnson City TN 37601-3940 Office: East Tenn State U Dossett Hall Johnson City TN 37614

ALFONSO, ROBERTA JEAN, emergency room nurse; b. Lake County, Ohio. ADN, Lakeland Community Coll., Mentor, Ohio, 1982; BSN, Ursuline Coll., Pepper Pike, Ohio, 1989; MSN, Gannon U., 1994. RN, Ohio; cert. emergency room nurse, ACLS, trauma nurse care course provider, BLS instr., pediatric advanced life support provider. Nurse Lake Hosp. Systems, Painesville, Ohio, 1982—, emergency room nurse, 1987—. Recipient Isabell Sutch Nurse of Yr. award, 1995. Mem. Emergency Nurses Assn., Nat. League for Nursing, Am. Stroke Assn.

ALFORD, BOBBY RAY, physician, educator, university official; b. Dallas, May 30, 1932; s. Bryant J. and Edith M. (Garrett) A.; m. Othelia Jerry Dorn, Aug. 28, 1953; children: Bradley Keith, Raye Lynn, Alan Scott. AS, Tyler Jr. Coll., 1951; postgrad., U. Tex., 1951-52; MD, Baylor U., 1956. Diplomate Am. Bd. Otolaryngology (dir. 1972-90, pres. 1985-86, exec. v.p. 1986-90). Intern Jefferson Davis Hosp., Houston, 1956-57; resident Baylor U. Coll. Medicine Affiliated Hosps. Program, 1957-60; mem. faculty Baylor U. Coll. Medicine, 1962—, prof. otolaryngology, 1966—, chmn. dept., 1967-95, 96—, v.p. and dean acad. and clin. affairs, 1984-88, exec. v.p., dean medicine, 1988—, disting. service prof., 1985—, interim chmn. dept. surgery, 1993-94; pres., CEO BaylorMedCare, Houston, 1994-96; chmn., CEO Nat. Space Biomed. Rsch. Inst., 1997—; mem. rev. panel surgeon gen. on neurol. and sensory disease USPHS, 1965-67; cons. Nat. Inst. Neurol. Disease and Stroke, 1970-74; cons. to surgeon gen. U.S. Army, 1963-73; mem. nat. adv. coun. Neurol. and Communicative Disorders and Stroke, NIH, 1977-80, Deafness and Other Communicative Disorders, 1991-95; chmn. aerospace medicine adv. com. NASA, 1993-94, mem. nat. adv. coun., 1992-95, chmn. life microgravity scis. and applications adv. com., 1993-95. Author: Neurological Aspects of Auditory and Vestibular Disorders, 1964, Electrophysiologic Evaluation in Otolaryngology, 1997; Chief editor: A.M.A. Archives of Otolaryngology, 1970-79. Bd. dirs. Houston Acad. Medicine Tex. Med. Ctr. Libr., 1983-94. Recipient Herman Johnson award Baylor U. Coll. Medicine, 1956; spl. NIH fellow Johns Hopkins Hosp., 1961-62. Fellow ACS (bd. govs. 1977-82); mem. NAS Inst. Medicine, Am. Laryngol. Assn., Soc. Univ. Otolaryngologists-Head and Neck Surgeons (sec. 1965-69), Am. Otol. Soc., Assn. Acad. Dept. Otolaryngology-Head and Neck Surgery, Am. Laryngol., Rhinol. and Otol. Soc., Am. Soc. Head and Neck Surgery (councillor 1978-80) Am. Acad. Otolaryngology-Head and Neck Surgery (pres. 1981), Am. Coun. Otolaryngology-Head and Neck Surgery (pres. 1980-81), Am. Bronchoesophagological Assn., Soc. Head and Neck Surgeons, Acoustical Soc. Am., Collegium Oto-Rhino-Laryngologicum Amicitiae Sacrum, Johns Hopkins U. Soc. Scholars, Univ. Space Rsch. Assn. (bd. dirs. 1991-95), Tex. Corinthian Yacht Club (bd. dirs. 1978-80, 94-95), Doctor's Club (bd. govs. 1967-70, 91-93), Waterford Harbour Yacht Club, Lakewood Yacht Club, Alpha Omega Alpha. Office: Baylor Coll Medicine One Baylor Plz Houston TX 77030

ALFORD, DELTON LYNOL, religious organization executive. Dir. of music ministries Spiritsound Music Group Ch. of God, Cleve., Tenn., 1991; producer, writer, arranger Christian music. Office: Ch of God PO Box 2430 Cleveland TN 37320-2430*

ALFORD, JEFFREY WHITWAM, university administrator; b. Providence, R.I., Oct. 2, 1947; s. Kenneth William and Lucille (Whitwam) A.; m. Gail Alford, June 1973; children: Jared, Kenneth G.; m. Terry Alford, Apr. 6, 1984. BS in Journalism, U. Fla., 1969. Edn. writer Palm Beach Post, West Palm Beach, Fla., 1971-74; asst. city editor Ft. Lauderdale (Fla.) News, 1974-76; exec. editor U. Fla., Gainesville, 1976-79; assoc. dir. pub. info. Tex. A&M U., College Station, 1979-87; exec. dir. univ. rels. Ball State U., Muncie, Ind., 1987—; comm. cons. Taylor U., Upland, Ind., 1995. Contbr. articles to profl. jours. Elder Westminster Presbyn. Ch., Muncie, 1987—. Sgt. U.S. Army, 1969-71. Recipient William Hearst Prize for Editls. William R. Hearst Found., 1969, Fla. Sch. Bd. award United Tchrs. of Fla., 1974, Award of Excellence Internat. Assn. Bus. Communicators, 1993. Mem. Soc. of Profl. Journalists, Coun. for Advancement and Support of Edn. (Regional award for news writing 1986), Hoosier State Press Assn., Phi Gamma Delta. Presbyterian. Avocations: weight lifting, photography. Home: 4517 N Gishler Dr Muncie IN 47304-1232 Office: Ball State U University Relations Muncie IN 47306

ALFORD, JOAN FRANZ, entrepreneur; b. St. Louis, Sept. 16, 1940; d. Henry Reisch and Florence Mary (Shaughnessy) Franz; m. Charles Hebert Alford, Dec. 28, 1978; stepchildren: Terry, David, Paul. BS, St. Louis U., 1962; postgrad. Consortium of State U., Calif., 1975-77; MBA, Pepperdine U., 1987, postgrad., Fielding Inst., 1988-90. Head user svcs. Lawrence Berkeley Lab., Calif., 1977-78, head software support and devel. Computer Ctr., 1978-82, dep. head, 1980-81; regional site analyst mgr. Cray Rsch., Inc., Pleasanton, Calif., 1982-83; owner, pres. Innovative Leadership, Oakland, Calif., 1983-91; realtor, assoc. Mason-McDuffie Real Estate, Inc., 1991-96, Coldwell Banker, 1996—; bd. dirs. Oakland Multiple Listing Svc., 1994, 96—, treas., 1994, pres., 1997; co-chair computer user com. OAR, 1992-93, chair, 1993-94; bd. dirs. Oakland Assn. Realtors, 1995—, chair of bus. and tech., 1996, pres., 1998, Realtor of the Year Awd., 1998, bd. dirs., East Bay Regional Data, Inc., 1994-96, 1998, 99. Contbr. articles to profl. jours. Bd. dirs., sec. Vol. Ctrs. of Alameda County, 1985, chair nominating com., 1990-91, pres. bd. dirs., 1991—; campaign mem. Marge Gibson for County Supr., Oakland, 1984; pres. bd. dirs. Vol. Ctrs. Alameda City, 1991-92; mem.

Oakland Piedmont Rep. Orgn., Alameda County Apt. Owners Assn., 1982. Mem. Assn. Computing Machinery, Spl. Interest Group on Computer Pers. Rsch. (past chmn.), Nat. Assn. Realtors, Calif. Assn. Realtors (bus. and tech. com. 1997), Oakland Assn. Realtors, Internat. Platform Assn., Small Owners for Fair Treatment. Republican. Clubs: Claremont Pool and Tennis, Lakeview, San Francisco Opera Guild. Avocations: swimming, skiing, opera, horseback riding, gardening. Home: 2605 Beaconsfield Pl Piedmont CA 94611-2501 Office: Coldwell Banker 6137 La Salle Ave Oakland CA 94611-2801

ALFORD, JOYCE WRAY, educational administrator; b. Charlotte, N.C., Oct. 24, 1936; d. Howard Franklin and Grace Amelia (Smithdeal) Wray; m. James Donald Alford, June 29, 1957; children: Howard L., Lee Ashley. BS in Edn. cum laude, U. Fla., 1958, MEd, 1972. Secondary and jr. high sch. tchr. Volusia County Sch. Bd., Daytona Beach, Fla.; jr. high sch. tchr. Duval County Sch. Bd., Jacksonville, Fla., elem. sch. guidance dir.; mid. sch. guidance dir. Clay County Sch. Bd., Orange Park, Fla.; asst. prin. Clay County Sch. Bd., Orange Park; dir. student svcs. Clay County Sch. Bd., Green Cove Springs, Fla., 1979—; elected supervisory com. Ednl. Cmty. Credit Union, 1988—, chairperson supervisory com., 1993-97. Exec. bd. dirs. Children's Haven Inc., Clay County, 1984—; exec. chmn. Sch.-Cmty. Action Team Against Drugs and Violence, 1988—, adv. bd. Charter Hosp. of Jacksonville, 1990-95; first chairperson Clay County Juvenile Justice Coun., 1993-94. Recipient Supt.'s Appreciation award, 1987, Appreciation award Juvenile Justice Coun., 1994, Mitzi May Outstanding Leadership award Clay County Community, 1994; grantee Clay County Children's Commn. Mem. Nat. Assn. Pupil Svcs. Adminstrs. (exec. bd. 1988-92, presenter 1990, 94, treas. 1991), Fla. Assn. Instrnl. Sch. Adminstrs. (com.), Fla. Assn. Student Svcs. Adminstrs. (past pres., exec. bd. dirs. 1990—), Fla. Assn. Sch. Adminstrs. (statemem. com. 1989-91), Fla. Assn. Counseling and Devel., Tri County Guidance Assn. (past pres.), Clay County Guidance Assn. (past pres.), Phi Delta Kappa (past pres. Jacksonville chpt. 1983-85, temporary pres. 1985, mem. Fla. 1st Coast chpt. 1986-95).

ALFORD, MARGIE SEARCY, lawyer; b. Tuscaloosa, Ala., Dec. 20, 1949; d. Joseph Alexander and Margaret Tyler (Zehmer) Searcy; m. Andrew Ray Alford, Sept. 4, 1992. BS, U. Ala., 1967-69, 70-71; student, U. Ams., Mexico City, 1969, Emory U., Atlanta, 1970; JD, U. Ala., 1974. Bar: Ala. 1974; U.S. Dist. Ct. (no. dist.) Ala. 1975. Assoc. univ. counsel U. Ala., Tuscaloosa, 1974-75; pvt. practice Tuscaloosa, 1975-92, Birmingham, Ala., 1992—. Prin. author: A Guide to Toxic Torts, 4 vols., 1986; contbg. author: Matthew Bender's Drug Product Liability, 4 vols.; contbr. numerous articles to legal jours., freelance writer for numerous publs. Mem. Jefferson County Stormwater Adv. Com., Ala., 1996-98, Jefferson County Lead Poisoning Prevention Com., 1997. Named Most Outstanding Young Career Woman in Ala. Ala. Bus. and Profl. Women, 1986. Mem. ATLA (twice nat. chair environ. and toxic tort law sect., twice nat. chair of women trial lawyers caucus), Ala. Environ. Coun., Ala. Trial Lawyers Assn. Democrat. Presbyterian. Avocations: antiques, chow chow dog breeder, gardening. Fax: (205) 520-5083. E-mail: margialfor@aol.com. Office: Atty at Law PO Box 610781 Birmingham AL 35261-0781

ALFORD, NEILL HERBERT, JR., retired law educator; b. Greenville, S.C., July 13, 1919; s. Neill Herbert and Elizabeth (Robertson) A.; m. Elizabeth Talbot Smith, June 26, 1943; children: Neill Herbert III, Margaret Dudley, Eli Thomas Stackhouse. BA, The Citadel-Mil. Coll. S.C., 1940; LLB, U. Va., 1947; JSD, Yale U., 1966. Bar: Va. 1954. Mem. faculty law U. Va. Law Sch., Charlottesville, 1947-61, 62-90; Doherty Found. prof. U. Va. Law Sch., 1966-74, spl. cons. to pres. univ., legal adviser to rector and bd. dirs., 1972-74; Joseph Henry Lumpkin prof., dean Law Sch. U. Ga., Athens, 1974-76; Percy Brown Jr. prof. law U. Va., 1976-90; state reporter Supreme Ct. Va., 1977-84; counsel Woods, Rogers & Hazelgrove, Charlottesville, 1991-97; prof. chair internat. law Naval War Coll., 1961-62, cons. 1962-68; spl. counsel Va. Code Commn. 1954-57; dir. Va. Bankers Assn. Trust Sch., 1958-61; summer tchr. George Washington U., U. N.C.; chmn. bd. dirs. U. Va. Press, 1970-74, 87-89; prof. law emeritus U. Va., 1990—; Lehmann Disting. vis. prof. law Washington U., St. Louis, 1991; Hofstedler prof. Ohio State U. Law Sch., 1992; prof. Washington and Lee Law Sch., 1992. Author: Cases and Materials on Decedents Estates and Trusts, 8th edit, 1993, Modern Economic Warfare: Law and the Naval Participant, 1967; Contbr. articles to profl. jours. Comdr. civil affairs group U.S. Army Res., 1947-66. Lt. col. inf. AUS, 1941-46, ETO; col. inf. AUS; ret. 1968. Decorated Bronze Star, Combat Inf. badge.; Sterling fellow Yale U., 1950-51, Ford fellow U. Wis., 1958. Fellow Va. Law Found., Am. Bar Found.; mem. ABA, Selden Soc., Am. Soc. Legal History, Am. Judicature Soc., Am. Law Inst., Va. State Bar, Va. Bar Assn., Charlottesville Albemarle Bar Assn., Raven Soc., Colonnade Club, Order of Coif, Phi Alpha Delta, Omicron Delta Kappa. Home: 1868 Field Rd Charlottesville VA 22903-1619

ALFORD, PAUL LEGARE, college and religious foundation administrator; b. Tampa, Fla., Mar. 16, 1930; s. Louis Emerson and Mary (Alderman) A.; m. Grace Alford, Dec. 29, 1951; children: Rebecca Grace, Sharon Ann. Student, U. Fla., 1947; diploma, Nyack Coll., 1948-51; DD (hon.), Trinity Coll., 1964, Asbury Coll., 1978; LLD (hon.), Toccoa Falls Coll., 1976. Supt. Ind. Life, Columbus, Ga., 1951-53; founding pastor Christian & Missionary Alliance, Columbus, 1951-56; missionary Ecuador, 1956-60; dir. Spanish ministries Christian Missionary Alliance, Nyack, N.Y., 1960-70; dist. supt. Christian & Missionary Alliance, Orlando, Fla., 1970-79, v.p., 1976-86; pres. Toccoa Falls (Ga.) Coll., 1979—; chmn. DeLand (Fla.) Retirement Bd., 1970-79; bd. mgrs. Christian and Missionary Alliance, Colorado Springs, Colo., 1993-99; trustee Asbury Coll., Wilmore, Ky.; chmn. bd. dirs. Lake Swan Conf. Grounds, Melrose, Fla., Shell Point Village, Ft. Myers, Fla., Trans World Radio, 1995-99; del. Congress on Edn., 1971, 86. Mem. editorial bd. New King James Bible; producer daily radio broadcast, 1975—. Mem. leadership coun. Stephens County, Toccoa, 1982—; bd. dirs. Salvation Army, Toccoa, 1986-93; pres. Ga. Assn. Colleges and Univs., 1997-98. Served with USNR, 1947-54. Named to Hillsborough High Sch. Hall of Fame, Tampa, 1994. Mem. Am. Assn. Bible Colls. (bd. dirs. 1987-92), So. Assn. Colls. and Schs. (evaluation com.), Rotary. Republican. Avocations: golf, tennis. Home: 380 Carlyle Cir Toccoa Falls GA 30598 Office: Toccoa Falls Coll Chapel Dr Toccoa Falls GA 30598

ALFORD, PAULA N., federal agency administrator; b. Monterey, Calif., Nov. 18, 1952; d. Paul and Thelma Nuschke; m. James K. Alford; 1 child, Karen Louise. BA, Scripps Coll., 1974; MPA, George Washington U., 1978. Fed. rels. assoc. Adv. Commn. Intergovernmental Rels., 1979-81; dir. fed. legislation and regulations Nat. Assn. Towns and Twps., 1982-86; cons. hazardous materials transp. and environ. issues, 1986-88; dir. external affairs Monitored Retrievable Storage Rev. Commn., 1988-89, Nuclear Waste Tech. Rev. Bd., Arlington, Va. Author various publs. in field. Mem. Pi Alpha Alpha. Office: Nuclear Waste Tech Review Bd 2300 Clarendon Blvd Ste 1300 Arlington VA 22201-3351*

ALFORD, ROBERT ROSS, sociologist; b. Stockton, Calif., Apr. 18, 1928; s. Ellsworth and Grace (Ross) A.; m. Gloria Kramer, June 18, 1949 (div. 1987); children: Heidi, Jonathan, Elissa; m. Nayra Atiya, Dec. 1, 1989 (div. 1995). A.B., U. Calif., Berkeley, 1950, M.A., 1952, Ph.D., 1961. Lectr. sociology U. Calif., Berkeley, 1959-61; mem. faculty U. Wis., 1961-74, prof. sociology, 1966-74; assoc. dir. Survey Research Lab., 1961-63; vis. prof. govt. U. Essex, Eng., 1966-67; vis. fellow Netherlands Inst. Advanced Study, 1981-82; vis. prof. sociology Columbia U., 1970-71, 80-81, NYU, 1987-88; prof. sociology U. Calif.-Santa Cruz, 1974-88, chmn. bd. studies in sociology, 1974-76, dir. Interdisciplinary Grad. Program in Sociology, 1976-79, acad. adminstr. research unit in instl. analysis and social policy, 1982-88; Disting. prof. sociology CUNY Grad. Ctr., 1988—; exec. officer grad. program in sociology CUNY, 1988-92, 97-98. Author: Party and Society, 1963, Bureaucracy and Participation: Political Cultures in Four Wisconsin Cities, 1969, Health Care Politics, 1975, Powers of Theory, 1985, The Craft of Inquiry, 1998; editor: Stress and Contradiction in Advanced Capitalist Societies, 1975. Mem. Am. Sociol. Assn. (exec. coun. 1988-91, chair polit. sociology sect. 1993-95), Am. Polit. Sci. Assn. (Woodrow Wilson Found. award 1976). Office: CUNY Grad Ctr 365 5th Ave New York NY 10016

ALFORD, ROBERT WILFRID, JR., elementary school educator; b. Langley, Va., Nov. 8, 1955; s. Robert Wilfrid and Ella Ramona (Coker) A.; m. Cynthia Marie Avery, Dec. 23, 1978 (div. 1999); children: Deborah Louise, Phillip Glenn. BS, Appalachian State U., 1978. Cert. social sci. tchr. Tchr. Greenville Mid. Sch. (S.C.) County Sch. Dist., 1984—; cons. Student Svcs., Greenville, 1985-91. Scoutmaster Troop 749, 1989-93, troop 159 asst. scoutmaster, 1998—; deacon Fourth Presbyn. Ch. Named Boy Scouter of Yr., Reed Falls dist. Boy Scouts Am., 1994. Mem. Greenville County Edn. Assn. (bd. dirs. 1986-88, sec. 1988-89), S.C. Council Social Studies Tchrs., S.C. Council Middle Schs., S.C. Edn. Assn. (educator rights com. 1987-88), Kappa Delta Pi, Phi Alpha Theta, Alpha Phi Omega (pres. Tau Beta chpt. 1976-77). Democrat. Presbyterian. Avocations: camping, travel. Office: Greenville Mid Sch 339 Lownes Ave Greenville SC 29607

ALFORD, SANDRA ELAINE, university official; b. Steubenville, Ohio, Oct. 26, 1944; d. Island Lee and Katherine (Agee) Johnson; m. Roger Kent Alford, Aug. 17, 1968 (dec.); children: Deidre Shannon, Jarrett Anthony. BS in Edn., West Chester (Pa.) U., 1971; MS in Child Devel., U. Pitts., 1973, PhD in Higher Edn., 1982. Tchr. kindergarten Pitts. Bd. Edn., 1971-72; adj. asst. prof. dept. child devel. and child care U. Pitts., 1974-79, child devel. specialist Arsenal Family and Children's Ctr., 1974-75, 76-79; edn. specialist CETA child care Urban League, Pitts., 1975-76; rsch. asst. Ctr. for Urban Studies, Wayne State U., Detroit, 1980-82, rsch. assoc., 1982-85, dir. Project 350, 1985-90, dir. div. community edn., 1990—; assoc. dean for student svcs., 1991—; chmn. Met. Detroit Teen Conf., 1989-90. Editorial asst., reviewer Jour. Ednl. Opportunity, 1989-90. Recipient Provost Devel. award U. Pitts., 1976, Outstanding Female Faculty and Staff award Wayne State U., 1989, Presdl. Bonus award, 1990, '91, Spirit of Detroit award, Detroit City Coun., 1990,'91, Appreciation award Met. Detroit Teen Conf., 1990; grantee NIMH, 1972-75. Mem. Mid-Am. Assn. Ednl. Opportunity Program Pers. (regional bd. dirs. 1988-90, bd. dirs. Mich. chpt., pres. 1989-90, validation facilitator exemplary program 1988—, Distinctive Leadership award 1989). Democrat. Office: Wayne State U Coll Lifelong Learning 5700 Cass Ave Detroit MI 48202-3629

ALFORD, STEPHEN CLARK, communications executive, multi image programmer; b. Killeen, Tex., Apr. 6, 1954; s. Bill Tom and George Ann (Clark) A.; m. Claire Adele Deibert, Aug. 9, 1980; children: Christopher Clark, Kenneth James. BS in telecom., Oral Roberts U., 1976; MEd in Indsl. Tech., Temple U., 1977. Radio announcer Sta. KLEN AM/FM, Killeen, 1970-72; media specialist Oral Roberts Univ., Tulsa, Okla., 1974-77; media coord. Oral Roberts Univ., 1978-79; multi-image programmer Kimball Audio-Video, Inc., Dallas, 1978-82, dir. media svcs., 1982-84; owner Alford Media Svcs., Dallas, 1984-89; pres., prin. Alford Media Svcs., Inc., Dallas, 1989—, Alford Media Sales, Inc., Dallas, 1991-98. Mem. Nat. Fedn. Ind. Businessmen, North Dallas Chamber, Coppell Chamber, Dallas Convention Vistor's Bureau; lay leader Whites Chapel United Meth. Ch., Southlake, Tex., 1997—; bd. dirs. Students in Free Enterprise, Sonscape Ministries. Recipient Dallas 100 award CEO Inst., 1995, 96, 98, Texas Family Owned Bus. of Year, 1997. Mem. Assn. Multi-Media Internat. (Dallas/Fort Worth pres. 1988-93, Merit Awards for Programming, 1980-89), Internat. Comm. Industry Assn., Video Assn. Dallas (bd. dirs.). Protestant. Avocations: mission work, golf, travel. Home: 1213 Wood Creek Ln Southlake TX 76092-4833

ALFORD, STEVE, college basketball coach; b. New Castle, Ind., Nov. 23, 1964; m. Tanya Frost; children: Kory, Bryce, Kayla. B in Bus., Ind. U. Mem. gold-medal U.S. basketball team Olympic Games, L.A., 1984; professional basketball player Dallas Mavericks, Golden St. Warriors; head coach Manchester (Ind.) Coll., 1992-95; conf. title champions, 1994, 95; conf. title champions S.W. Mo. State U. Bears, 1995-99, reached NCAA Sweet 16, 1999; headcoach U. Ia. Hawkeyes, 1999—. Named Ind. Collegiate Conf. Coach of Yr., 1993, 94, 95. Office: c/o U Ia Athletic Dept 240 Carver-Hawkeye Arena Iowa City IA 52242-1020*

ALFRED, R. See BEATTY, ROBERT ALFRED

ALFRED, STEPHEN JAY, lawyer; b. N.Y.C., Aug. 15, 1934; s. George J. Alfred and Janet (Brenner) Miller; m. Nora Richman, June 24, 1956 (div. 1980); children: Deborah Susan, Lynda Beth, Bruce David, Julianne Richman; m. Lynne Belofsky Durchslag, Jan. 10, 1981 (div. 1992); m. Rita G. Hungate, Aug. 23, 1997. AB, Princeton U., 1956; JD, Harvard U., 1959. Bar: Ohio 1959. Assoc. Squire, Sanders & Dempsey, Cleve., 1959-69, ptnr., 1969-97; exec. dir. Common Cause/Ga., 1998—. Contbr. articles to profl. jours. Councilman City of Shaker Hts., Ohio, 1972-79, 81, mayor, 1984-91; trustee Citizens League of Cleve., 1976-83, trustee com. for Sandy Springs, Atlanta, 1998—; t rustee Beech Brook Children's Home, Orange, Ohio, 1968-84, pres., 1971-72, treas., 1979-81; pres. Lomond Assn., Shaker Hts., 1965-67. Mem. Cleve. Tax Inst. (gen. chmn. 1981), Harvard U. Law Sch. Assn. of Cleve. (pres. 1982). Democrat. Jewish.

ALFRED, SUELLEN, English education educator; b. May 2, 1941; d. Andrew and Freeda (Murray) A. BA, Carson-Newman Coll., 1963; MA, Ga. State U., 1969; EdD, U. Tenn., 1991. Cert. secondary English, gifted edn. Assoc. prof. curriculum and instrn. Tenn. Tech. U., Cookeville, 1990—. Co-author: Teaching Through Stories: Yours, Mine, and Theirs, 1998; editor Tenn. English Jour.; co-editor: Southern Voices in Every Direction, 1996; contbr. articles to profl. jours.; author poems. NEH fellow Vanderbilt U., 1984. Mem. ASCD, NEA, Nat. Coun. Tchrs. English, Internat. Reading Assn., Tenn. Edn. Assn. (comms. com. 1978-79), Tenn. Tech. U. Edn. Assn., Tenn. Coun. Tchrs. English (pres. 1993-94; Excellence in Tchg. of English award 1996). Home: East Lake Estates 3623 Bartlett Dr Cookeville TN 38506-7412 Office: Tenn Tech U PO Box 5042 Cookeville TN 38505

ALFREDO, JOSEPH ALBERT, landscape architect; b. Mt. Vernon, N.Y., Nov. 26, 1931; s. Albert Michael and Rose (Russo) A.; married, Dec. 27, 1957; 6 children. BS, Cornell U., 1953. Pres. A. Alfredo Nurseries, Inc., White Plains, N.Y., 1957-70, Servo Systems, Inc., Purchase, N.Y., 1970-78, Alfredo, Inc., White Plains, 1980-89, Associated Lands & Cons., Inc., Rye, N.Y., 1989—. Chmn. beautification com. Town of Harrison, N.Y., 1985-89, Boys Town of Italy. 1st lt. U.S. Army, 1953-55. Recipient Hon. Man of Yr. internat. award Boys Town Italy, 1998. Mem. Westchester Country Club (chmn. srs.), N.Y. Athletic Club, Boca Hotel & Resort Club, Boys Town Italy (chmn. 1990-97). Avocations: golf, stamp & coin collecting. Office: Alfredo Lands & Cons Inc PO Box 648 Purchase NY 10577-0648 also: 2921 S Ocean Blvd Apt 703 Highland Bch FL 33487-1802 also: 20 Carpenters Brook Rd Greenwich CT 06831-2547

ALFREY, LYDIA JEAN, musician educator; b. Kingsport, Tenn., July 16, 1954; d. Milburn Flay and Betty Jo (Sensabaugh) Brooks; m. Charles Leonard Alfrey, Oct. 2, 1987; children: Benjamin Daniel, Tyler Nathaniel, Ryan Daniel. BA, Anderson (Ind.) U., 1977. Music tchr. Huntington Sch., Ferriday, La., 1978-80; elem. tchr. Warner Christian Acad., Daytona Beach, Fla., 1982-83; pvt. practice Eustis, Fla., 1993—; prin. pianist First Bapt. Ch., Eustis, 1994—; adjudicator piano competitions Lake County Music Tchrs., Eustis, 1994-97; dir., coord. Summer Music Camps, Eustis, 1994, 95, 97; pianist jazz orch.; guest artist numerous recitals. Mem. Nat. Guild of Piano Tchrs., Music Tchrs. Nat. Assn. (publicity chairperson, Fla. chpt. rec. sec. 1994—), Pi Kappa Lambda, Kappa Delta Pi, Delta Omicron. Baptist. Avocations: floral arranging, interior designing, oil painting. Home: 1375 Old Mount Dora Rd Eustis FL 32726-7949

ALGEO, JOHN THOMAS, retired educator, association executive; b. St. Louis, Nov. 12, 1930; s. Thomas George and Julia Winifred (Wathen) A.; m. Adele Marie Silbereisen, Sept. 6, 1958; children: Thomas John, Catherine Marie. EdB cum laude, U. Miami, 1955; MA, U. Fla., 1957, PhD, 1960. Instr. Fla. State U., Tallahassee, 1959-61; from asst. to full prof. U. Fla., Gainesville, 1961-71, asst. dean grad. sch., 1969-71, dir. program in linguistics, 1969-71; prof. U. Ga., Athens, 1971-88, dir. program in linguistics, 1974-79, head dept. English, 1975-79, alumni found. disting. prof., 1988-94; nat. pres. Theosophical Soc. in Am., Wheaton, Ill., 1993—; accreditation cons. So. Assn. Colls. and Schs., Atlanta, 1967-90; cons. NEH, Washington, 1974-94; dir. Commn. on the English Lang., Nat. Coun. Tchrs. of English, Urbana, Ill., 1976-82; del. Am. Coun. Learned Socs., N.Y.C., 1984-87; cons. in lang. and lexicography Cambridge Univ. Press, N.Y.C., 1987-93; cons. in Am. usage Kenkyusha Ltd., Tokyo, 1991—; cons. Webster's New World Dictionary, 4th edit., Cleve., 1993-95. Author: Problems in the Origins and Development of the English Language, 1966, 4th edit., 1993, On Defining the Proper Name, 1973, Exercises in Contemporary English, 1974, Reincarnation Explored, 1987, Fifty Years "Among the New Words": A Dictionary of Neologisms, 1941-91, 1991, Eigo no kigen to hatatsu, 1991; co-author: English: An Introduction to Language, 1970, Spelling: Sound to Letter, 1971, The Origins and Development of the English Language, 1982, 4th edit., 1993, Elements of Literature, Sixth Course: Literature of Britain, 1989; editor: American Speech 1972-81, Thomas Pyles: Selected Essays on English Usage, 1979, Among the New Words, American Speech, 1987-97; assoc. editor: The Oxford Companion to the English Language, 1992; mem. editl. bd. Jour. of English Linguistics, 1970—, Internat. Jour. Lexicography, 1990—, World Englishes, 1996—, Names, 1997—, Language Problems Language Planning, 1997—. Sgt. U.S. Army, 1951-54, Korea. Fellow Guggenheim Found., London, 1986-87; Fulbright scholar U. Coll. London, Eng., 1986-87. Mem. Am. Dialect Soc. (pres. 1979), Am. Name Soc. (pres. 1984), Internat. Assn. Univ. Profs. English, Internat. Linguistic Assn., Internat. Order Co-Freemasonry, Internat. Phonetic Assn., Internat. Soc. Anglo-Saxonists, Linguistic Assn. of the U.S. and Can., Linguistic Soc. Am., Modern Lang. Assn. Am., Philological Soc., Southeastern Conf. on Linguistics (pres. 1970-71), Dictionary Soc. N.Am. (pres. 1995-97), Theosophical Soc. (nat. pres. 1993—). Democrat. Home: PO Box 80206 Athens GA 30608-0206 Office: Theosophical Soc Am PO Box 270 Wheaton IL 60189-0270

ALGER, CHADWICK FAIRFAX, political scientist, educator; b. Chambersburg, Pa., Oct. 9, 1924; s. Herbert and Thelma (Drawbaugh) A.; m. Elinor Reynolds, Aug. 28, 1948; children: Mark, Scott, Laura, Craig. BA, Ursinus Coll., 1949, LLD, 1979; MA, Johns Hopkins U., 1950; PhD, Princeton, 1958. Internat. relations specialist Dept. Navy, 1950-54; instr. Swarthmore Coll., 1957; faculty Northwestern U., Evanston, Ill., 1958-71, prof. polit. sci., 1966-71, dir. internat. relations program, 1967-71; Mershon prof. polit. sci. and pub. policy Ohio State U., 1971-95, emeritus prof., 1995—, dir. transnat. intellectual cooperation program, 1971-80, dir. world affairs program, Mershon Ctr., 1980-88, coord. working group on global rels. and peace studies, 1988-95, acting dir. univ. ctr. for internat. studies, 1990-91; vis. prof. UN affairs N.Y.U., 1962-63. Author: Internationalization from Local Areas: Beyond Interstate Relations, 1987, Perceiving, Understanding and Coping with World Relations in Everyday Life, 1993, The United Nations System: Potential for the Twenty-First Century, 1998; co-author: Simulation in International Relations, 1963, You and Your Community in the World, 1978, Conflicts and Crisis of International Order: New Tasks for Peace Research, 1985, A Just Peace Through Transformation: Cultural, Economic and Political Foundations for Change, 1988, The United Nations System: The Policies of Member States, 1995; contbr. articles to profl. jours. Mem. Trade Coun., State of Ohio, 1984-87. Served with USNR, 1943-46. Recipient Disting. Scholar award Internat. Soc. for Ednl., Cultural and Sci. Interchanges, 1980, Golden Apple award Am. Forum for Global Edn., 1993. Mem. Am. Polit. Sci. Assn. (coun. 1970-72), Internat. Polit. Sci. Assn., Internat. Studies Assn. (pres. 1978-79), Internat. Peace Rsch. Assn. (coun. 1971-77, sec.-gen. 1983-87), Midwest Conf. Polit. Scis. (recipient prize 1966), Consortium on Peace Rsch., Edn. and Devel. (exec. com. 1971-77, chmn. 1976-77), Hunger and Devel. Coalition of Cen. Ohio (bd. dirs. 1983-90), Columbus Coun. on World Affairs (bd. dirs. 1974-88), UN Assn. (pres. Columbus chpt. 1991-93). Home: 2674 Westmont Blvd Columbus OH 43221-3354 Office: Ohio State U Mershon Ctr 1501 Neil Ave Columbus OH 43201-2602

ALGIER, ANGELA JANE, newspaper editor; b. Providence, June 29, 1953; d. Mariano and Lillian (DiSanto) Rodrigues; m. David D. Spadola, June 10, 1972 (div. 1985); m. Bruce Gregory Algier, Sept. 7, 1985; 1 child, Alisha Lillian; st epchildren: Bruce Gregory Jr., Corinn M. BA in Journalism, U. R.I., 1976. Mgr. Spectrum India, Wakefield, R.I., 1974-76; modeling instr. Barbizon Sch., Providence, 1976-84; model various locations, 1976-90; reporter East Providence (R.I.) Post, 1979-81; reporter The Westerly (R.I.) Sun, 1981-83, sectional editor, 1983-94, city editor, 1994—. Leader Girl Scouts R.I., Westerly, 1995-97; sch. site coun. Bradford Sch., Westerly, 1994-96, Springbrook Sch., Westerly, 1995-97; softball coach Westerly Girls, 1996-97, 97-98, bd. dirs. 1999—. Recipient achievement award Boy Scouts Am., Westerly, 1994, award New Eng. Press Assn., 1998, award spot news New Eng. Newspaper Assn., 1998, spot news, news awards R.I. Press Assn., 1998. Avocations: softball, fitness instructor, body building, kickboxing instructor. Home: 29 Potter Hill Rd Westerly RI 02891-1135 Office: The Westerly Sun 56 Main St Westerly RI 02891-2155

ALGIERE, DENNIS LEE, state senator; b. Westerly, Rhode Island, July 30, 1960; s. Joseph L. and Ida R. (Vacca) A.; m. Leigh A. Williams, Nov. 7, 1992. BA, Providence Coll., 1982; MS, Northea. U., 1984; JD, So. New England Sch. Law, 1991. Town councilor Town of Westerly, R.I., 1990-92; mem. R.I. Senate, 1993—, minority leader, 1997—; v.p. Washington Trust Co.; bd. dirs. R.I. Econ. Devel. Corp. Chmn. Westerly Rep. Town Com., 1991-92; bd. dirs. Chorus of Westerly, 1990—, March of Dimes, R.I., ARC of R.I.; mem. adv. bd. Literacy Vols. Am., Westerly; mem. Coastal Resource Mgmt. Coun., R.I., 1993—; mem. bd. dirs. Westerly Hosp., R.I. Main St. Corp. Mem. Dante Soc., Lions, Westerly Hist. Soc. Republican. Roman Catholic. Home: 6 Elm St Westerly RI 02891-2126 Office: RI Senate State House Rm 120 Providence RI 02908

ALGRA, RONALD JAMES, dermatologist; b. Artesia, Calif., Feb. 23, 1949; s. Cornelius and Helena Joyce (De Boom) A.; m. Phyllis Ann Brandsma, July 31, 1970; children: Brian David, Stephanie Ann. BS in Chemistry, Calvin Coll., 1971; MD, Baylor Coll. Medicine, 1974; MBA, Pepperdine U., 1989. Diplomate Am. Bd. Dermatology. Intern Gen. Hosp. Ventura County, Ventura, Calif., 1974-75; resident in dermatology Baylor Coll. Medicine, Houston, 1975-78; pvt. practice Hawthorne, Calif., 1978-88; asst. med. dir. FHP, Inc., Fountain Valley, 1988-89, assoc. med. dir., 1990-91, med. dir., 1991-93, sr. med. dir., 1993, assoc. v.p. med. affairs, 1993-95; COO, horses, zebras & unicorns, Irvine, Calif., 1995-96; exec., med. dir. Providence Health Plans, Eugene, Oreg., 1996-98; med. dir. HealthCare Ptnrs. Ltd., Torrance, Calif., 1999—. Fellow Am. Acad. Dermatolgoy; mem. Am. Med. Informatics Assn., Am. Coll. Physician Execs., Alpha Omega Alpha. Republican. Mem. Christian Reformed Ch. Avocations: computers, photography, running, gardening, hiking. Office: Providence Health Plans 1500 Valley River Dr Ste 200 Eugene OR 97401-2163

ALHADEFF, DAVID ALBERT, economics educator; b. Seattle, Mar. 22, 1923; s. Albert David and Pearl (Taranto) A.; m. Charlotte Pechman, Aug. 1, 1948. B.A., U. Wash., 1944; M.A., Harvard U., 1948, Ph.D., 1950. Faculty U. Calif.-Berkeley, 1949-87, prof. bus. adminstrn., 1959-87, prof. emeritus, 1987—, assoc. dean Sch. Bus. Adminstrn.,, 1980-82, 85-86. Author: Monopoly and Competition in Banking, 1954, Competition and Controls in Banking, 1968, Microeconomics and Human Behavior, 1982; Contbr. articles to profl. jours., chpts. to books. Served with AUS, 1943-46. Recipient The Berkeley Citation U. Calif.-Berkeley, 1987. Mem. Am. Econ. Assn., Western Econ. Assn., Am. Fin. Assn. Home: 2101 Shoreline Dr Apt 456 Alameda CA 94501-6209 Office: Haas Sch Bus Berkeley CA 94720

ALHADEFF, JACK ABRAHAM, biochemist, educator; b. Vallejo, Calif., May 9, 1943. BA, U. Chgo., 1965; PhD in Biochemistry, U. Oreg., 1972. Fellow U. Calif., San Diego, 1972-74, asst. rsch. neuroscientist, 1974-75, from asst. prof. to assoc. prof., 1975-82; prof. biochemistry Lehigh U., 1982—. Recipient Rsch. Career Devel. award NIH, 1978. Mem. AAAS, Am. Chem. Soc., Biochem. Soc., Sigma Xi. Achievements include research in biochemical studies on glycoconjugate metabolism in normal and pathological (cancer, diabetes, cystic fibrosis) human tissues. Office: Lehigh U Inst Health Scis 111 Research Dr Bethlehem PA 18015-4732

AL-HAFEEZ, HUMZA, minister, editor; b. N.Y.C., Feb. 28, 1931; s. Asa Mose and Rose Mae (Danielson) Weir; children: Jacqueline, Yuhanna, Rasul, Bismillah, Habib, Wardi, Larry, Don, Mariama. Student, Food Trades Vocat. Sch., 1947-48. Patrolman N.Y.C. Police Dept., from 1959; chmn. Temple of Islam, Inc.; founder Nat. Soc. Afro-Am. Policemen Inc.; also past pres.; cons. community relations to chief insp. N.Y.C. Police Dept., to; U.S. Dept. Justice; investigator of corruption among N.Y.C. police officers Knapp Commn.; undercover narcotic officer, investigator Manhattan office Dist. Atty.; investigator Office of 1st Dep. Policy Commr.; undercover investigator U.S. Dept. Justice.; insp. N.Y. State Athletic Commn.; Lectr. Princeton U., Mich. State U., N.Y. State U., Pace Coll., Bklyn. Coll., U. Chgo., NYU, Satellite Acad., N.Y.C., Kinlock Mission for Blind, City N.Y.

Police Acad., Nassau Community Coll.; others. Appeared on radio and TV.; Editor-in-chief: Your Muhammad Speaks newspaper; author The Slanderer, 1987. Pastoral bd. Interfaith Hosp.; chaplain Frackville (Pa.) Correctional Facility, 1995—. Recipient Father of Yr. award Kinlock Freedom Found. for the Blind, 1973; Community Service award United Council of Chs., 1975; named Person of Yr. Nat. Assn. Black Policemen, 1982. Mem. Internat. Platform Assn. Mem. Nation of Islam; minister Muhammad's Temple of Islam, Bklyn. Home: 361 Clinton Ave Apt 12C Brooklyn NY 11238-1145 Office: 1211 Atlantic Ave Brooklyn NY 11216 *To expect all of the people to cooperate is something that should be given some thought. Change comes through the efforts of a person, or a small group of people, not all of the people. However, all of the people may benefit, or suffer, from the action of a person, or a small group. History will bear me witness.*

AL-HASHIMI, IBTISAM, oral scientist, educator; b. Karbala, Iraq; d. Hadi A. and Rabab H. Al-H. B Dental Sci., Sch. Dentistry, Baghdad, 1973; MS, SUNY, Buffalo, 1985, PhD, 1989. Diplomate in Oral Surgery. Registrar Sch. Dentistry, Baghdad, 1975-81; postdoctoral assoc. SUNY, Buffalo, 1984-88, asst. prof., 1988-89; asst. prof. U. Pacific, San Francisco, 1989-90; dir. stomatology lab. Baylor Coll. Dentistry, Dallas, 1991—, dir. salivery dysfunction clinic, 1992—; clin. asst. prof. surgery U. Tex. Southwestern Med. Ctr., Dallas, 1996—; adv. com. mem. SS Found. (we. N.Y. chpt.) Buffalo, 1985-89, Dallas-Ft. Worth chpt., 1992—; mem. med. adv. bd., organizer Sjogren's Multispecialty Referral Ctr., 1996; pres. Salivery Rsch. Group, Nat. Inst. Dental Rsch., 1999. Author: Proceeding of the Second Dows Symposium, 1987; contbr. articles to profl. jours. Mem. med. adv. bd. SS Found., 1995. Mem. AAAS, Am. Assn. Dental Schs., N.Y. Acad. Sci., Internat. Platform Assn., Internat. Assn. Dental Rsch., Libr. Congress Assn., Salivary Rsch. Group, Sigma Xi. Achievements include research on molecular mechanisms of salivary gland diseases, development of a laboratory test for the diagnosis of Sjogren's Syndrome using salivary protein electrophoresis; characterization of a major salivary enzyme inhibitor in the mouth; identification of the principal protein components that participate in the formation of the protective coat of the teeth of healthy subjects. Office: Baylor Coll Dentistry 3302 Gaston Ave Dallas TX 75246-2013

ALHO, SISTER BONNIE KATHLEEN, religion educator; b. Superior, Wis., Feb. 6, 1942; d. Jack Wayne and Agnes (Osman) A. BS in Elem. Edn., Mt. Senario Coll., Ladysmith, Wis., 1970; MRE, St. Thomas U., Houston, 1978. Joined Order Servants of Mary, Roman Cath. Ch., 1959. Kindergarten tchr. St. Domitilla's Sch., Hillside, Ill., 1961-62; 3rd grade tchr. Annunciata, Chgo., 1962-67; 2nd grade tchr. St. Rose of Lima Sch., St. Paul, 1967-71; 1st grade tchr. St. Joseph's Sch., Carteret, N.J., 1971-72; mem. staff Diocese of Superior, Cameron, Wis., 1972-81; dir. religious edn. Our Lady of Sorrows, Ladysmith, 1981-93; sabbatical Boston Coll., 1993-94; pastoral assocs. St. Joseph's Parish, Rice Lake, Wis., 1994—; mem. steering com. Wis. Dirs. of Religious Edn., State of Wis., 1979, bd. com. mem. 1987-90; bd. dirs. deacons com. Diocese of Superior, 1983-89, chair. Summit Bd., 1986-89, initiated Marriage Encounter; active in formation of retreat programs for teens; co-chair., treas. Area Clergy Assn., Ladysmith, 1991—. Bd. dirs., chair ch. rels. com. Barron County Habitat for Humanity. Recipient Outstanding Leadership in Catechetical Ministry award Diocese of Superior, Mt. Telemark, Wis., 1988, Spirit of Teens Encounter Christ award Diocese of Superior, 1999. Mem. Wis. Dirs. Religious Edn. (bd. dirs. 1987-98), Nat. Assn. Lay Ministers. Home: 334 N Wilson Ave Rice Lake WI 54868-1661 Office: St Joseph Parish 111 W Marshall St Rice Lake WI 54868-1648 *It has been said "For all that has been Thanks...For all that will be Yes." It is important to me to approach life in this way.*

ALI, MUHAMMAD (CASSIUS MARCELLUS CLAY), retired professional boxer; b. Louisville, Jan. 17, 1942; s. Marcellus and Odessa (Grady) Clay; m. Sonji (div. 1966); m. Kalilah Tolona (Belinda Boyd), Apr. 18, 1967 (div. 1977); 4 children; m. Veronica Porshe, June 19, 1977 (div.); 1 child; m. Yolanda Williams, Nov. 19, 1986; 1 child. Ed. pub. schs., Louisville. Appeared in movie The Greatest, 1977, TV movie Freedom Road; author: The Greatest: My Own Story, 1975. Mem. World Community Islam. Light heavyweight champion AAU, 1959, 60; light heavyweight champion Golden Gloves, 1959, heavyweight champion, 1960; light heavy weight champion Olympic Games, 1960, world heavyweight champion, 1964-67, 74-78, 78-79; lost to heavyweight champion Larry Holmes, 1980. Home: PO Box 160 Berrien Springs MI 49103-0160*

ALIBER, ROBERT Z., economist, educator; b. Keene, N.H., Sept. 19, 1930; s. Norman H. and Sophie (Becker) A.; m. Deborah Baltzly, Sept. 9, 1955; children: Jennifer, Rachel, Michael. BA, Williams Coll., 1952, Cambridge U., 1954; MA, Cambridge U., 1957; PhD, Yale U., 1962. Staff economist Commn. Money and Credit, N.Y.C., 1959-61; staff economist Com. on Econ. Devel., Washington, 1961-64; sr. econ. advisor AID, Dept. State, Washington, 1964-65; assoc. prof., then prof. internat. econs. and fin. U. Chgo., 1965—; vis. prof. Brandeis U., 1987-93, Houblon-Norman fellow, Bank of Eng., 1996. Author: The International Money Game, 1973, 76, 79, 83, 87, Exchange Risk and Corporate International Finance, 1978, Your Money and Your Life, 1982; co-author: Money, Banking, and the Economy, 1981, 84, 87, 90, 93, The Multinational Paradigm, 1993; editor: National Monetary Policies and the International Financial System, 1974, The Political Economy of Monetary Reform, 1976, The Reconstruction of International Monetary Arrangements, 1987, The Handbook of International Financial Management, 1989; co-editor Global Portfolios, 1991, Readings in International Business: A Decision Approach, 1993. With U.S. Army, 1954-56. Fulbright fellow, 1952-54. Mem. Am. Econs. Assn., Acad. Internat. Bus., Quadrangle Club, Williams Club of N.Y., Post Mills Soaring Club, Chgo. Gliding Club. Home: 5638 S Dorchester Ave Chicago IL 60637-1722 Office: 1101 E 58th St Chicago IL 60637-1511

ALICEA, LUIS RENE, professional baseball player; b. Santurce, P.R., July 29, 1965. Ed., Fla. State U. With St. Louis Orgn. Minor League Teams, 1989-91, St. Louis Cardinals, 1988, 91-94, 96; second baseman Boston Red Sox, 1995; with Anaheim Angels, 1997-98; infielder Tex. Rangers, 1998—. Named to Coll. All-Am. Team, The Sporting News, 1986. Office: Tex Rangers 1000 Ballpark Way Arlington TX 76011*

ALICH, JOHN ARTHUR, JR., manufacturing company executive; b. Cleve., Dec. 2, 1942; s. John Arthur and Jeanette Marie (Kusa) A.; m. Susan Jane Moras, May 8, 1965; children: Michelle Monet, Amy Catherine. BS in Engring., U.S. Naval Acad., 1964; MBA, U. Del., 1971. Sr. cons./dir. Stanford Rsch. Inst., Menlo Park, Calif., 1973-77; mgr. devel. Baker Hughes Inc./Envirotech Corp., Menlo Park, 1977-80; v.p. devel. Baker Hughes Inc./Eimco Mining Machinery Internat., Menlo Park, 1980-82; v.p. mktg. Baker Hughes Inc./Eimco Mining Machinery Internat., Salt Lake City, 1982-85; group v.p., gen. mgr. Baker Hughes Inc./Eimco Secoma, Lyon, France, 1985-87; exec. v.p. ops. Baker Hughes Inc./Eimco Jarvis Clark, Toronto, Can., 1987-88; pres. Baker Hughes Inc./Baker Hughes Mining Tools, Grand Prairie, Tex., 1988-92, Baker Hughes Inc/Envirotech Measurements and Controls, Austin, Tex., 1992-94, Thermo Instrument Controls Inc., Austin, 1994-95; bus. devel. dir. Thermo Instrument Sys. Inc., Austin, 1995-97; pres. Kevex Instruments, Valencia, Calif., 1998, Kevex Spectrace, Sunnyvale, Calif., 1999—. Bd. dirs. Serra H.S. Bd. Regents, San Mateo, Calif., 1975-77, Boys and Girls Club, Grand Prairie, 1988-92. Lt. USN, 1964-70. DuPont fellow U. Del., 1970-71. Mem. Soc. Mining Engrs., Inst. Soc. Am., Am. Nuclear Soc., Beta Gamma Sigma. Avocations: golf, running, squash, personal computers. Fax: 805-257-3392. Office: Kevex Spectrace 1275 Hammerwood Ave Sunnyvale CA 94089

ALIE, ALLEYN A., construction and engineering company executive; b. Boston, Jan. 22, 1952; s. Abed and Sara (Richard) A. BSCE, U. Mass., 1977; postgrad., U. Hartford, 1990, Harvard Grad. Sch. Design, 1992; CSS Adminstrn. Mgmt., Harvard U. Grad. Mgmt. Program, 1997. Registered profl. engr., Tex.; cert. constrn. mgr.; cert. in constrn. disputes. Structural engr. H.L. Gaddy & Assocs., Houston, 1977-80; project structural engr. W.P. Moore & Assocs., Houston, 1980-81; project engr. Bechtel Corp., Houston, 1981-82; project mgr. The Quantum Group, Houston, 1982-84; resident constrn. mgr. KRI Constructors Inc., Houston, 1984-86; v.p. project ops. C.R. Klewin, Inc., Norwich, Conn., 1986-93; constrn. resident engr. Bechtel Corp., Boston, 1993—. Fellow ASCE. Avocations: jogging, cycling, travel, reading/writing and teaching. Home: 79 Endicott St Westwood MA 02090-2113 Office: Bechtel Corp One South Sta Boston MA 02110

ALIEV, ELDAR, artistic director, choreographer, educator. Grad. with honors, Baku Choreographic Acad. Artistic dir. Ballet Internationale, Indpls., 1994—; former prin. ballet dancer with the Kirov Ballet, appearing in more than 30 countries; guest star with Bolshoi Ballet and the Australian Ballet; choreographer ballets 1001 Nights, 1995, The Nutcracker, 1996. Office: Ballet Internationale USA 502 N Capitol Ave Ste B Indianapolis IN 46204-1204*

ALIG, FRANK DOUGLAS STALNAKER, retired construction company executive; b. Indpls., Oct. 10, 1921; s. Clarence Schirmer and Marjory (Stalnaker) A.; m. Ann Bobbs, Oct. 22, 1949; children: Douglas, Helen, Barbara. Student, U. Mich., 1939-41; BS, Purdue U., 1948. Registered profl. engr., Ind. Project engr. Ind. State Hwy. Commn., Indpls., 1948; pres. Alig-Stark Constrn. Co., Inc., 1949-57, Frank S. Alig, Inc., 1957-97—; ret.; v.p., bd. dirs. Bo-Wit Products Corp., Edinburg, Ind.; CEO, bd. dirs. Home Land Investment Co., Inc. With AUS, 1943-46. Mem. Dramatic Club, Lambs Club. Republican. Presbyterian.

ALIKI (ALIKI LIACOURAS BRANDENBERG), author, illustrator children's books; b. Wildwood Crest, N.J., Sept. 3; d. James Peter and Stella (Lagakos) Liacouras; m. Franz Brandenberg, Mar. 15, 1957; children: Jason, Alexa Demetria. Grad., Mus. Coll. Art, 1951. Muralist, commercial artist Phila. and N.Y.C., 1951-56. Author, illustrator Story of William Tell, 1960, My Five Senses, 1962, My Hands, 1962, The Wish Workers, 1962, The Story of Johnny Appleseed (Jr. Lit. Guild, World of Reading Readers' Choice award Silver Burdett & Ginn 1989), George and the Cherry Tree, 1964, The Story of William Penn (Jr. Lit. Guild), A Weed is a Flower: The Life of George Washington Carver, 1965, Keep Your Mouth Closed, Dear (Omar's Book award 1986), Three Gold Pieces: A Greek Folk Tale (Boys' Clubs Am. Jr. Book award 1968), New Year's Day, 1967, (editor) Hush Little Baby: A Folk Lullaby, 1968, My Visit to the Dinosaurs, 1969, The Eggs: A Greek Folk Tale, 1969, Diogenes: The Story of the Greek Philosopher, 1969, Fossils Tell of Long Ago, 1972, June 7, 1972, The Long Lost Coelacanth and Other Living Fossils, 1973, Green Grass and White Milk, 1974, Go Tell Aunt Rhody, 1974, At Mary Bloom's (Am. Inst. Graphic Arts Children's Book Show, Jr. Lit. Guild), 1976, Children's Book Coun. for Children's Book Showcase), Corn Is Maize: The Gift of the Indians (Children's Sci. Book award N.Y. Acad. Scis.), The Many Lives of Benjamin Franklin, 1977, Wild and Woolly Mammoths, 1977, rev. edit., 1995, The Twelve Months, 1978, Mummies Made in Egypt (Silver Slate Pencil award Dutch Children's Book Coun., Garden State (N.J.) Children's Book award), The Two of Them, 1979, Digging Up Dinosaurs, 1981, We Are Best Friends, 1982, Use Your Head, Dear, 1983, A Medieval Feast, 1983, Feelings (Prix du Livre pour Enfants Geneva), Dinosaurs Are Different, 1985, How a Book Is Made, 1986, Jack and Jake, 1986, Overnight at Mary Bloom's, 1987, Dinosaur Bones, 1988, King's Day: Louis XIV of France, 1989, My Feet, 1990, Manners, 1990, Christmas Tree Memories, 1991, I'm Growing, 1992, Milk: From Cow to Carton, 1992, Communication, 1993, My Visit to the Aquarium, 1993, The Gods and Godesses of Olympus, 1994, Tabby, 1995, Best Friends Together Again, 1995, Hello, Good-Bye, 1996, Those Summers, 1996, My Visit to the Zoo, 1997; illustrator: Who Lives Here?, 1961, Cathy Is Company, 1961, Listening Walk, 1961, What's for Lunch, Charley?, 1961, What Can I Buy?, 1962, A Book to Begin On: Alaska, 1962, The Lazy Little Zulu, 1962, This Is the House Where Jack Lives, 1962, The Horse That Liked Sandwiches, 1962, Archmedes and His Wonderful Discoveries, 1962, Computers at Your Service, 1962, New Ways in Math, 1962, Television and How It Works, 1962, Electricity in Your Life, 1963, Mister Moonlight and Omar, 1963, That's Good, That's Bad, 1963, Bees and Beelines, 1964, More New Ways in Math, 1964, Sherlock on the Trail, 1964, Everything Has a Size, 1964, Everything Has a Shape, 1964, One Day It Rained Cats and Dogs, 1965, Five Dolls in a House, 1965, Is It Blue as a Butterfly?, 1965, Mother's Day, 1965, I Want to Read!, 1965, Is That A Happy Hippomatus?, 1966, Everything Has a Shape and Everything Has a Size, 1966, Five Dolls in the Snow, 1967, Five Dolls and the Monkey, 1967, Five Dolls and Their Friends, 1968, Five Dolls and the Duke, 1968, Mrs. Neverbody's Recipes, 1968, At Home: A Visit in Four Languages, 1968, Oh Lord, I Wish I Was a Buzzard, 1968, Birds at Night, 1968, Weighing and Balancing, 1970, On the Other Side of the River, 1972, Ears and Tails and Common Sense: More Stories from the Caribbean, 1974, Averages, 1975, Evolution, 1987; illustrator books by Franz Brandenberg: I Once Knew a Man, 1970, Fresh Cider and Pie, 1973, No School Today!, 1975, A Secret for Grandmother's Birthday, 1975, A Robber! A Robber!, 1976, I Wish I Was Sick, Too!, 1976, What Can You Make of It?, 1977, Nice New Neighbors, 1977, A Picnic, Hurrah!, 1978, Six New Students, 1978, Everyone Ready?, 1979, It's Not My Fault!, 1980, Leo and Emily, 1981, Leo and Emily's Big Idea, 1982, Aunt Nina and Her Nephews and Nieces, 1983, Aunt Nina's Visit, 1984, Leo and Emily and the Dragon, 1984, The Hit of the Party, 1985, Cock-a-Doodle-Doo, 1986, What's Wrong with a Van?, 1987, Aunt Nina, Good Night!, 1989; Marianthe's Story: Painted Words & Spoken Memories (Double Book), 1998, Painted Stories, 1998, William Shakespeare and the Globe, 1999; illustrator book by Alice Low: Mommy's Briefcase, 1995,. Recipient citation Drexel U. and Free Libr. Phila., 1991, recognition for outstanding contbns. in field lit. Pa. Sch. Libr. Assn., 1991. Avocations: gardening, theater, museums, travelling, reading. Office: Greenwillow Books 1350 Avenue Of The Americas New York NY 10019-4702

ALIMANESTIANU, CALIN, retired hotel consultant; b. Bucharest, Roumania, Dec. 29, 1925; came to U.S., 1953, naturalized, 1961; s. Virgil and Nineta (Leon) A.; m. Cecilia Ciocalteu, 1948 (div. 1953); m. Joan Carpenter, 1955 (div. 1957); m. Bettie Nicholas, 1959 (div. 1967); 1 child, Simone; m. Maria Elizabeth Texeira, 1984 (div. 1996). Ed. in, Rome. Mgmt. trainee Woodner Hotel, Washington, 1955, Bismarck Hotel, Chgo., 1957; asst. to gen. mgr. Oxford House, Chgo., 1958-60; gen. mgr. Holiday Inn, Newburgh, N.Y., Plainview, L.I., N.Y., 1960-67; v.p. operation, gen. mgr. Holiday Inn, N.Y.C., 1967-71; mng. dir. Dering Harbor Inn, Shelter Island, N.Y.; hotel cons., 1973-90; pres. Creative Hotel Cons. Internat., St. Petersburg Beach, Fla., 1977-88. Mem. GOP Heritage Groups (nationalties div.), Julio Maniu Am. Roumanian Relief Found. Mem. Royal Automobile Club Roumania. Mem. Eastern Orthodox Ch. Home: 4370 Community Dr Apt 216 West Palm Beach FL 33409-2978

ALIMARAS, GUS, lawyer; b. N.Y.C., Oct. 30, 1958; s. Nicholas Constantine and Libby (Keffas) A.; m. Constance N. Siomkos, May 15, 1983; children: Justin Christopher, Alyssa Nicole. BA, CUNY, 1979; JD, Hofstra U., 1982. Bar: N.Y. 1983, U.S. Dist. Ct. (ea. and so. dists.) N.Y. 1985, U.S. Ct. Internat. Trade 1985, U.S. Dist. Ct. (no. and we. dists.) N.Y. 1990, U.S. Supreme Ct. 1994. Assoc. John A. Sotirakis, Astoria, N.Y., 1983, George Kazazis, Astoria, 1983-87; ptnr. Kazazis & Alimaras, LLP, Astoria, 1987—; real estate continuing edn. instr. Queens Coll., CUNY, 1993-97; lectr. Nat. Bus. Inst. Mem. ABA, N.Y. State Bar Assn., Queens County Bar Assn., Long Island City Lawyers Club (pres. 1992-93), Ea. Orthodox Lawyers Assn., Phi Alpha Delta. Office: Kazazis & Alimaras LLP 36-12 34th Ave Ste 200 Long Island City NY 11106-1110

ALIN, ROBERT DAVID, lawyer; b. Mt. Vernon, N.Y., Oct. 10, 1952; s. Morris and Sylvia (Horowitz) A.; m. Arlene Susan Kerner, Feb. 14, 1988; children: Dustin, Lauren. BA in Math., U. Rochester, 1974; JD, NYU, 1977, LLM in Taxation, 1983. Bar: N.Y. Assoc. atty. Willkie Farr & Gallagher, N.Y.C., 1977-79, Halperin Shivitz Eisenberg Schneider & Greenawalt, N.Y.C., 1979-84, Berman Koerner Silberberg P.C., N.Y.C., 1984-86; sr. v.p., sec., gen. counsel The Pentegra Group, White Plains, N.Y., 1986—. Mem. ABA, N.Y. State Bar Assn., Web Network. Democrat. Jewish. Avocations: tennis, bridge, music. Home: 500 E 77th St New York NY 10162-0025 Office: The Pentegra Group 108 Corporate Park Dr White Plains NY 10604-3805

ALISKY, MARVIN HOWARD, political science educator; b. Kansas City, Mo., Mar. 12, 1923; s. Joseph and Bess June (Capp) A.; m. Beverly Kay, June 10, 1955; children: Sander Michael, Joseph. BA, U. Tex., 1946, MA, 1947, PhD, 1953; cert., Instituto Tecnologico, Monterey, Mex., 1951. News corr. S.W. and Latin Am. NBC, 1947-49, news corr. Midwest, 1954-56; news corr. NBC and Christian Sci. Monitor, Latin Am., 1957-72; asst. prof. Ind. U., 1953-57; assoc. prof. journalism and polit. sci. Ariz. State U., Tempe, 1957-60; prof. polit. sci. Ariz. State U., 1960—, founding chmn. dept. mass communication (now Sch. Journalism and Telecommunications), 1957-65, founding dir. Ctr. Latin Am. Studies, 1965-72; vis. fellow Princeton U., 1963-64, Hoover Inst., Stanford, 1978; Fulbright prof. Cath. U., Lima, Peru, 1958, U. Nicaragua, 1960; researcher U.S.-Mex. Interparliamentary Conf., Baja, Calif., 1965, Latin Am. Inst., Chinese Acad. Social Scis., Beijing, 1986, European Inst. Def. and Strategic Studies, London, 1985, Politics Inst., Copenhagan, Denmark, 1987, U. So. Calif., 1982—; U.S. del. UNESCO Conf., Quito, Ecuador, 1960; dir. Gov.'s Ariz.-Mex. Commn., 1975—; U.S. State Dept. lectr., Costa Rica, Peru, Argentina, Chile, 1983, 88; bd. dirs. Goldwater Inst. Pub. Policy Rsch., 1989—. Author: Governors of Mexico, 1965, Uruguay: Contemporary Survey, 1969, The Foreign Press, 1964, 70, Who's Who in Mexican Government, 1969, Political Forces in Latin America, 1970, Government in Nuevo Leon, 1971, Government in Sonora, 1971, Peruvian Political Perspective, 1975, Historical Dictionary of Peru, 1979, Historical Dictionary of Mexico, 1981, Latin American Media: Guidance and Censorship, 1981, Global Journalism, 1983; co-author: Political Systems of Latin America, 1970, Political Parties of the Americas, 1982, Yucatan: A World Apart, 1980, (with J.E. Katz) Arms Production in Developing Nations, 1984, Mexico: Country in Crisis, 1986, (with Phil Rosen) International Handbook of Broadcasting Systems, 1988, Dictionary Latin American Political Leaders, 1988, (with W.C. Soderlund) Mass Media and the Caribbean, 1990; columnist Thompson Corp. Newspapers in ariz., 1999—; contbr. numerous articles to profl. jours. and mags. Bd. dirs. Phoenix Com. on Fgn. Res., 1975—, Ariz. Acad. Town Hall, 1981, Tempe Pub. Libr., 1974-80; mem. U.S. Bd. Fgn. Scholarships Fulbright Commn. Bd., 1984—, Acad. Coun. Goldwater Inst. of Pub. Policy, 1989—. Ensign USNR, 1944-45. NSF grantee, 1984, Ariz. State U. rsch. grantee, 1962, 65, 70, Southwestern Studies Ctr. rsch. grantee, 1983, Latin Am. Rsch. in China grantee, 1986, World Media Rsch. in Soviet Union grantee, 1989, rsch. grantee, London, 1992, 94, Edinburgh, 1994, 97, 99, Vancouver, 1998. Fellow Hispahic Soc. Am.; mem. Am. Polit. Sci. Assn., Western Polit. Sci. Assn., Latin Am. Studies Assn., Pacific Coast Coun. Latin Am. Studies (bd. dirs.), Inter-Am. Press Assn., Inter-Am. Broadcasters Assn. (rsch. assoc.), Assocs. Liga de Municipios de Sonora, Friends of Mex. Art, Southwestern Polit. Sci. Assn. (chmn. 1976-77), Nat. Assn. Scholars, Soc. Profl. Journalists (life), Tempe Rep. Men's Club, Knights of Sq. Roundtable, Sigma Delta Chi. Home: 44 W Palmdale Dr Tempe AZ 85282-2139 Office: Ariz State U Dept Polit Sci Tempe AZ 85287-2001 *My life as an educator, writer, and journalist-broadcaster has enable me to share and exchange important and vital thought with friends, associates, and fellow Americans.*

ALITO, SAMUEL ANTHONY, JR., federal judge; b. Trenton, N.J., Apr. 1, 1950; s. Samuel A. and Rose (Fradusco) A.; m. Martha-Ann Bomgardner, 1985; children: Philip Samuel, Laura Claire. AB, Princeton U., 1972; JD, Yale U., 1975. Bar: N.J. 1975, N.Y. 1982, U.S. Dist. Ct. N.J. 1975, U.S. Ct. Appeals (3d cir.) 1977, U.S. Ct. Appeals (2d cir.) 1980, U.S. Ct. Appeals (D.C. cir.) 1987, U.S. Supreme Ct. 1979. Law clk. to judge U.S. Ct. Appeals (3d cir.), Newark, 1976-77; asst. U.S. atty. U.S. Atty.'s Office, Newark, 1977-81, U.S. atty., 1987-90; asst. to solicitor gen. Office of Solicitor Gen. Dept. Justice, Washington, 1981-85; dep. asst. atty. gen. Office of Legal Counsel Dept. Justice, Washington, 1985-87; judge U.S. Ct. Appeals for 3d Cir., Newark, 1990—. Office: US Courthouse PO Box 999 Newark NJ 07101-0999

ALJIAN, JAMES DONOVAN, investment company executive; b. Oakland, Calif., Nov. 5, 1932; s. George W. and Marguerite (Donovan) A.; m. Marjorie L. Townsend, Oct. 17, 1959; children: Mark Donovan, Mary Anne, Reed Townsend. B.S., U. Calif., Berkeley, 1955; M.B.A., Golden Gate U., 1965. Office mgr. Uniroyal Co., San Francisco, 1957-60; audit supr. Ernst & Ernst, San Francisco, 1960-65; sec.-treas. Tracy Investment Co., Las Vegas, 1965-73, Internat. Leisure Corp., Las Vegas, 1967-70; sr. v.p. fin. MGM, Culver City, Calif., 1973-79; pres. Tracinda Corp., Las Vegas, 1979-82; sr. v.p. fin. planning MGM/UA Entertainment Co., Culver City, Calif., 1982-85; exec. v.p., chief fin. officer, dir. Southwest Leasing Corp., Los Angeles, 1985-87, also bd. dirs.; with Tracinda Corp., Las Vegas, Nev., 1987—; mem. shareholder com. Daimler Chrysler AG; bd. dirs. MGM Grand, Inc., Metro-Goldwyn-Mayer, Inc. Served with AUS, 1955-57. Mem. Am. Inst. C.P.A.s, Calif. Soc. C.P.A.s, Acad. Motion Picture Arts and Scis.

ALKANA, RONALD LEE, neuropsychopharmacologist, psychobiologist; b. L.A., Oct. 17, 1945; s. Sam Alkana and Madelyn Jane Davis; m. Linda Anne Kelly, Sept. 12, 1970; children: Alexander Philippe Kelly, Lorna Jane Kelly. Student, UCLA, 1963-66; PharmD, U. So. Calif., 1970; PhD, U. Calif., Irvine, 1975. Resident asst. dir. divsn. neurochemistry U. Calif., Irvine, 1976; asst. prof. pharmacy/pharmacology U. So. Calif., L.A., 1976-82, assoc. prof. pharmacy/pharmacology and toxicology, 1982-89, prof. molecular pharmacology and toxicology, 1989—, asst. dean grad. affairs, 1995-98, asst. dean interdisciplinary programs Sch. Pharmacy, 1998—; asst. dean grad. affairs, 1995-98, asst. dean interdisciplinary programs Sch. Pharmacy U. So. Calif., 1998—. Editl. bd. Alcholism: Clinical and Experimental Research, 1989-94; assoc. editor, 1994-98; contbr. chpts. to books, articles to profl. jours. Recipient various scholarships and grants; named Outstanding Alumnus U. So. Calif. Sch. of Pharmacy, 1999. Mem. AAAS, Soc. Neurosci., Am. Soc. Pharmacology and Exptl. Therapeutics, Internat. Soc. Biomed. Research on Alcoholism, Research Soc. Alcoholism, Internat. Brain Rsch. Organization World Fedn. Neuroscientists, Soc. of Toxicology, Western Pharmacology Soc., QSAD (bd. dirs. 1998—), Sigma Xi, Phi Delta Chi (bd. dirs. Omicron alumni 1997—, Omicron chpt., Outstanding Alumnus of Yr. 1996, 99). Office: U So Calif Sch Pharmacy Dept Molecular Pharmacolgy Toxicology 1985 Zonal Ave Los Angeles CA 90033

ALKER, HAYWARD ROSE, political science educator; b. N.Y.C., Oct. 3, 1937; s. Hayward Rose and Dorothy (Fitzsimmons) A.; m. Judith Ann Tickner, June 3, 1961; children: Joan Christina, Heather Jane, Gwendolyn Ann. BS, MIT, 1959; MS, Yale U., PhD, 1963. Instr. to assoc. prof. polit. sci. Yale U., 1963-68; vis. prof. U. Mich., 1968, others; prof. polit. sci. MIT, 1968-95; John A. McCone prof. internat. rels. U. So. Calif., L.A., 1995—; Olaf Palme vis. prof. U. Stockholm, U. Uppsala, 1989; vis. prof., scholar Brown U., 1996, 97; chmn. Math. Social Scis. Bd., 1970-71. Author: Mathematics and Politics, 1965, (with others) World Handbook of Political and Social Indicators, 1966, (with Russett) World Politics in the General Assembly, 1966, (with Bloomfield and Choucri) Analyzing Global Interdependence, 1974, (with Hurwitz) Resolving Prisoner's Dilemmas, 1981, Rediscoveries and Reformations, 1996; mem. bd. editors Jour. Interdisciplinary History, 1969-71, Internat. Orgn., 1970-76, Quality and Quantity, 1974—, Internat. Studies Quar., 1980-89, Internat. Interactions, 1981-88. Congl. intern Office of Chester Bowles, 1960. Fellow Center for Advanced Studies in Behavioral Scis., Stanford, Calif., 1967-68. Mem. Am. Polit. Sci. Assn., Internat. Polit. Sci. Assn., Internat. Peace Rsch. Assn., Internat. Studies Assn. (v.p. 1990-91, pres. 1992-93), Internat. Social Sci. Coun. (exec. com. 1990-92, coord. conflict early warning sys. rsch. program 1992-99).

ALKIRE, JOHN D., lawyer, mediator, arbitrator; b. Seattle, Nov. 15, 1948; s. Durwood Lee and Dorys (Maryon) A.; m. Karen A. Heerensperger, May 6, 1994; children: Lauren M., Kevin G. Student, U. Calif., Berkeley, 1967-68; BA, Principia Coll., Elsah, Ill., 1970; JD, U. Wash., 1975. Bar: Wash. 1975, Washington 1977, U.S. Dist. Ct. (we. dist.) Wash., U.S. Ct. Appeals (4th, 9th and D.C. cirs.), U.S. Supreme Ct. Budget analyst Office Mgmt. and Budget, Seattle, 1970-72; law clk 9th cir. Honorable Eugene A. Wright, Seattle, 1975-76; assoc. Jones, Grey & Bayley, Seattle, 1976-77, Steptoe & Johnson, Washington, 1977-80; assoc. Perkins Coie, Seattle, 1980-85, ptnr., 1985—. Mem. ABA, Wash. State Bar Assn. Avocations: outdoor sports, major league baseball, music, volunteer mediation. Office: Perkins Coie 1201 3rd Ave Fl 40 Seattle WA 98101-3000

ALKON, ELLEN SKILLEN, physician; b. Los Angeles, Apr. 10, 1936; d. Emil Bogen and Jane (Skillen) Rost; m. Paul Kent Alkon, Aug. 30, 1957; children: Katherine Ellen, Cynthia Jane, Margaret Elaine. BA, Stanford U., 1955; MD, U. Chgo., 1961; MPH, U. Calif., Berkeley, 1968. Diplomate Nat. Bd. Med. Examiners, Am. Bd. Pediat., Am. Bd. Preventive Medicine in Pub. Health. Chief sch. health Anne Arundel County Health Dept., Annapolis, Md., 1970-71; practice medicine specializing in pediat. Mpls. Health Dept., 1971-73, dir. MCH, 1973-75, commr. health, 1975-80; chief preventive and pub. health Coastal Region of Los Angeles County Dept. Health Svcs., 1980-81; chief pub. health West Area Los Angeles County Dept. Health Svcs., 1981-85; acting med. dir. pub. health Los Angeles County Dept. Health, 1986-87, med. dir. pub. health, 1987-93, 98—; med. dir. Coastal Cluster Health Ctrs. L.A. County Dept. Pub. Health Svcs., 1993-96, CEO, 1996-98, med. dir., 1996-98; adj. prof. UCLA Sch. Pub. Health, 1981—; adminstr. vis. nurses svc., Mpls., 1975-80. Fellow Am. Coll. Preventive Medicine, Am. Acad. Pediatrics; mem. So. Calif. Pub. Health Assn. (pres. 1985-86), Minn. Pub. Health Assn. (pres. 1978-79), Am. Pub. Health Assn., Calif. Conf. Local Health Officers (pres. 1990-91), Delta Omega. Office: Comprehensive Health Ctr 1333 Chestnut Ave Long Beach CA 90813-2944

ALKON, PAUL KENT, English language educator. A.B., Harvard U., 1957; Ph.D. in English Lit., U. Chgo., 1962. Instr., asst. prof. English lit. U. Calif.-Berkeley, 1962-70; assoc. prof. U. Md., 1970-71; assoc. prof. English U. Minn., Mpls., 1971-73, prof., 1973-80; Leo S. Bing prof. English U. So. Calif., Los Angeles, 1980—; vis. prof. English, Ben Gurion U. of Negev, Israel, 1977-78. Author: Samuel Johnson and Moral Discipline, 1967, Defoe and Fictional Time, 1979, Origins of Futuristic Fiction, 1987, Science Fiction Before 1900, 1994. Mem. Am. Soc. 18th Century Studies (pres. 1989-90), Sociètè française d'Etude du 18ème Siècle, Internat. Churchill soc. Home: 17 Masongate Dr Palos Verdes Peninsula CA 90274-1560 Office: U So Calif Dept English Los Angeles CA 90089

ALKSNE, JOHN F., dean. Dean Sch. of Medicine U. Calif., La Jolla, 1995—. Office: U Calif San Diego Sch Medicine La Jolla CA 92093-0602 also: Univ Calif San Diego 9500 Gilman Dr La Jolla CA 92093-5003*

ALLABY, STANLEY REYNOLDS, clergyman; b. Providence, Dec. 28, 1931; s. Edwin T. and Hope (Swift) A.; m. Marion Arlene Johnson, Dec. 18, 1954; children—Norman R., Darlene R., Kimberly A., Stephen R. A.B., Gordon Coll., 1953; M.Div., Gordon Conwell Sem., 1956; D.D., Barrington (R.I.) Coll., 1977; D.Min., Westminster Theol. Sem., 1978. Ordained to ministry, 1956; pastor Black Rock Conglist. Ch., Fairfield, Conn., 1956-97; dir. Sudan Interior Mission, N.C., 1970—; chmn. bd. Sudan Interior Mission, 1985—, vice chmn. internat. bd. govs., 1985-90; vice chmn. Billy Graham New Haven Crusade, 1982; exec. com. Billy Graham Hartford Crusade, 1985; Ockenga lectr. Gordon-Conwell Sem., 1983; guest lectr. Tyndale Theol. Sem., Amsterdam, 1996; lectr. Bethel Seminary of the East, 1999—. Bd. dirs. United Neighbors for Self Devel., Bridgeport, Conn., 1963-64, Christian Freedom Found., 1960-70, Operation Hope, Fairfield, 1986-89; trustee Gordon Div. Sch., 1965-69. Recipient George Washington honor medal Freedoms Found., 1968, 69; Alumnus-of-Year award Gordon Coll., 1976. Mem. Gordon Coll. Alumni Assn. (past pres.), Nat. Assn. Evangelicals (dir. 1974-95, exec. com. 1980-82, nat. conv. coordinator 1981-82, (chmn. resolutions com. 1982-83), Bridgeport Pastors Assn. (past pres.), Greater Bridgeport Fellowship Evangelicals (past pres.). Home: 123 Lyon Rd Woodstock Valley CT 06282

ALLAIN, LOUIS, literature educator, scientific advisor; b. Brest, France, June 28, 1933; s. Louis and Louise (Nicolas) A.; m. Annie Luc, May 21, 1964; children: Andree-Lise, Juliette, Laurence, Alexandre. B Degree, Ecole Normale Superieure, Paris, 1958, Agregation, 1957; Doctorate, Sorbonne, Paris, 1979. Sch. tchr. Lycee Lakanal, Paris, 1961; asst. lectr. Sorbonne, 1961-63, sr. lectr., 1963-69; mng. lectr. Univ. Lille, 1969-81, prof., head dept. Slavic langs., 1981-98, prof emeritus, 1998—; contbr. Acad. Sci., Hungary, 1988, Russia, 1988, 90, 94, 96, Israel, 1994, Poland, 1995, 96, 97, 98, Montenegro, 1996, U. Houston, 1989, Cornell U., 1994, Columbia U., 1998, Dostoevsky Symposium, Cerisy-la-Salle, 1983, Ljubljana, 1989, Oslo, 1992, Kartause Gaming, 1995, N.Y. 1998, Gumilev Symposium I & II, Glasgow, 1986, St. Petersburg, 1996, Chekhov Symposium I & II, Badenweiler, 1985, 94, From Dissidence to Democracy, Paris, 1996., Jerusalem in Slavic cultures and religious traditions, 1996, others. Author: Dostoievski et Dieu, 1981, Dostoievski et l'Autre, 1984, Etiudy o russkoi literature, 1989, Dostoevsky i Bog, 1993, F.M. Dostoevsky: Poetika, mirooshchushchenie, bogoiskatel'stvo, 1996, Skvoz' prizmu vekov, 1998, Shtrikhi k portretu F.M. Dostoevskogo, 1998; editor: B. Poplavsky, I&II, 1993, N. Otsup, 1993-95, G. Adamovich, 1993, G. Ivanov, 1993, V. Vishnjak, 1993, V.V. Rozanov, (study), 1993, A. Remizov, 1994, N. Plevitskaya, 1994, N. Fedorova, 1994, V. Gippius, 1994, V. Zen'kovsky, 1994, I. Napelbaum, 1995, M. Voloshin (study), 1996, F. M. Dostoevsky: Poetika, mirooshchushchenie, bogoiskatel'stvo, 1996, Skvoz' Prizmu Vekov, 1998, Shtrikhi k portretu F.M. Dostoevskogo, 1998; co-editor: Jews and Slavs, vol. 2, 1994; contbr. articles to profl. jours. Lt. French Navy, 1958-61, France. Comdr. of Acad. Palms, French Ministry of Edn., 1990, medal City of Lille, 1994, Melanges offerts au Professeur Louis Allain, Lille, 1996. Mem. Alumni Ecole Normale Superieure, Intra-Marine/France, Internat. Dostoevsky Soc., Inst. Slavic Studies, Paris. Avocations: cooking, gardening. Home: Rue Jules Guesde 408, Villeneuve d'Ascq 59650, France Office: Charles de Gaulle Univ, BP 149, Villeneuve d'Ascq Cedex 59653, France

ALLAIRE, GLORIA KAUN, Italian language educator; b. Reedsburg, Wis., Feb. 20, 1954; d. Robert W. and Arlowene Marie (Wolter) Kaun. MusB with honors, U. Wis., 1976, MA in Italian, 1986, PhD, 1993. Italian lang. tutor and translator, 1984—; vis. lectr. in Italian lang. and lit. Univs. Mich. and Wis. Studies Abroad Program, Florence, Italy, 1987-88; grad. teaching asst. dept. French and Italian U. Wis., Madison, 1988-93, 84-87; vis. asst. prof. dept. modern langs. and linguistics Fla. State U., Tallahassee, 1993-94; vis. asst. prof. dept. modern langs. Ohio U., Athens, 1994—; vis. instr. dept. fgn. langs. and lits. Purdue U., West Lafayette, Ind., 1997—; Italian lang. coach Madison Opera, 1985-87. Author: Andrea da Barberino and the Language of Chivalry, 1997; contbr. articles to profl. jours. Officer, newsletter editor Madison Opera Buffs, 1980-87. Fulbright grantee, 1990-91, Am. Philosophy Soc. grantee, 1996; summer fellow UCLA Ctr. for Medieval and Renaissance Studies, 1994, NEH Summer Inst., 1995. Mem. MLA, Am. Assn. Tchrs. Italian, Am. Assn. for Italian Studies, Medieval Acad. Am., Lyrica Soc., Soc. Rencesvals, ACTFL. Avocations: bicycling, cats, equitation.

ALLAIRE, JOSEPH LEO, French educator; b. Detroit, Feb. 23, 1929; s. Leonel J. and Stella Marie (Latour) A.; m. Andrea Woodruf Jensen, June 19, 1974; 1 child, Joseph Arnold Leonel. AB, U. Detroit, 1952; MA, Wayne State U., 1957, PhD, 1966. Tchr. French U. Detroit High Sch., 1952-53; tchr. French, Latin, Spanish Detroit Pub. Schs., 1953-62; head fgn. lang. dept. Cody High Sch., Detroit Pub. Schs., 1962-67; asst. prof. to assoc. prof. French Fla. State U., Tallahassee, 1967—; adj. French, Wayne State U., 1962-67. Editor: Le Miroir de l'Ame Pecheresse, 1972; contbr. (bibliography) Critical Bibliography of French Literature: 16th Century, 1984. Mem. MLA, Am. Assn. Tchrs. French (pres. Fla. chpt. 1974-75), South Atlantic MLA (v.p. 1975, pres. 1976), Soc. Internat. des Seiziemiste, Renaissance Soc. of Am. Home: 1004 Shalimar Dr Tallahassee FL 32312-3019 Office: Fla State U Dept Modern Langs Tallahassee FL 32306-1540

ALLAIRE, PAUL ARTHUR, office equipment company executive; b. Worcester, Mass., July 21, 1938; s. Arthur E. Allaire and Elodie (LePrade) Murphy; m. Kathleen Buckley, Jan. 26, 1963; children: Brian, Christiana. BSEE, Worcester Poly. Inst., 60; MSIA, Carnegie-Mellon U., 1966. Fin. analyst Xerox Corp., Rochester, N.Y., 1966-70; dir. fin. analysis Rank Xerox Ltd., London, N.Y., 1970-73; dir. internat. ops. fin. Xerox Corp., Stamford, Conn., 1973-75; chief staff officer Rank Xerox Ltd., London, 1975-79, mng. dir., 1979-83; sr. v.p., chief staff officer Xerox Corp., Stamford, Conn., 1983-86, pres., 1986-91, chmn., 1991, chmn. bd., 1991—, also. chmn. exec. com., CEO, bd. dirs.; bd. dirs. Rank Xerox Ltd., Fuji Xerox Co., Ltd., Sara Lee Corp., J.P. Morgan, N.Y. City Ballet, Catalyst, SmithKline Beecham plc, Lucent Techs., The Ford Found.; mem. Coun. on Competitiveness; mem. bus. adv. coun., trustee Grad. Sch. Indsl. Sch. Indsl. Adminstrn. Trustee Worcester Poly. Inst. Mem. Coun. on Fgn. Rels. (bd. dirs.), Nat. Acad. Engring., Tau Beta Pi, Eta Kappa Nu. Democrat. Office: Xerox Corp PO Box 1600 800 Long Ridge Rd Stamford CT 06902-1288*

ALLAIS, MAURICE-FELIX, economist; b. Paris, May 31, 1911; s. Maurice and Louise (Caubet) A.; m. Jacqueline Bouteloup, Sept. 6, 1960; 1 child, Christine. Grad. 1st pl., Poly. Sch., Paris, 1933; grad., Nat. Higher Sch. Mines, Paris, 1936; D Eng, Faculty of Scis., Paris, 1949; D honoris causa, U. Groningen, The Netherlands, 1964, U. Mons, Belgium, 1992, Am U., Paris, 1992, U. Lisbonne, Portugal, 1993; diplome d'Honneur Hautes Etudes Commls., U. Paris, Paris, 1993. Engr. Dept. Mines and Quarries, 1937-43; dir. Bur. Documentation and Stats., 1943-48, Econ. and Social Rsch. Group, Paris, 1944-70; prof. econ. analysis Nat. Higher Sch. Mines, Paris, 1944-88; dir. Econ. Analysis Ctr., Paris, 1944—; prof. econ. theory Inst. Stats. U. Paris, 1947-58, dir. Ctr. Clement Juglar for Monetary Analysis, 1970-85; dir. rsch. Nat. Ctr. Sci. Rsch., Paris, 1954-79; prof. Grad. Inst. Internat. Studies, Geneva, 1967-70; disting. vis. scholar Thomas Jefferson, U. Va., Charlottesville, 1958-59; mem. energy commn. Econ. Coun., Paris, 1960-61; chmn. com. of experts for study of options in transport tariff policy EEC, Brussels, 1963-64. Author: A la Recherche d'une Discipline Economique, 1943, 2d edit. Traité d'Economic Pure, 1952, 3d edit., 1994, Abondance ou Misère, 1946, Economie et Intérêt, 1947, 2d edit., 1998, La Gestion des Houillères Nationalisées et la Théorie Economique, 1949, Les Fondements Comptables de la Macroéconomique, 1954, 2d edit., 1992, Fondements d'une Théorie positive des choix comportant un risque, 1955, Notes to French Academy of Sciences on the Anomalies in the Movements of the Paraconic Pendulum, 1957-58, Should the Law of Gravitation Be Reconsidered?, 1959, L'Europe Unie, Route de la Prospérité, 1959 , L'Algérie d'Evian, 1962, 2d edit. 1999, The Role of Capital in Economic Development, 1963, Reformulation de la Théorie Quantitative de la Monnaie, 1965, L'Impôt sur le Capital, 1966, Les Conditions de l'Efficacité dans l'Economie, 1967, Growth Without Inflation, 1968, Growth and Inflation, 1969, La Libéralisation des Relations Economiques Internationales, 1970, 2d edit., 1995, Les Théories de l'Equilibre Economique Général et de l'Efficacité Maximale, 1971, Inégalité et Civilisations, 1971, Inequality and Civilizations, 1973, L'Inflation Française et la Croissance, 1974, Inflation, Income Distribution and Indexation, 1976, L'Impôt sur le Capital et la Réforme Monétaire, 1977, 2d edit., 1988, Expected Utility Hypothesis and the Allais' Paradox, 1979, La Théorie Générale des Surplus, 1980, 2d edit., 1989, Frequency, Probability and Chance, 1982, Foundations of Utility and Risk Theory, 1983, Détermination de l'Utilité Cardinale suivant un modèle intrinsèque invariant, 1984, Credit Mechanism, 1984, The Empirical Approaches of the Hereditary and Relativistic Theory of the Demand for Money, 1986, The Concepts of Surplus and Loss and the Reformulation of the General Theory of Economic Equilibrium and Maximum Efficiency, 1986, The General Theory of Random Choices in Relation to the Invariant Cardinal Utility Function and the Specific Probability Function, 1986, The Equimarginal Principle: Meaning, Limits and Generalization, 1987, Les Conditions Monétaires d'une Economie de Marchés, 1987, My Life Philosophy, 1988, Autoportraits, 1989, Pour l'Indexation, 1990, Pour la Réforme de la Fiscalité, 1990, L'Europe face à son avenir-Que Faire?, 1991, De l'Europe des Douze à la Grande Europe, 1992, Erreurs et Impasses de la Construction Européenne, 1992, Cardinalism, 1994, Combats pour l'Europe 1994, L'anisotropie de l'espace, 1997, la crise mondiale d'aujourithui, 1999, L'umon Europeeune la Foudiobiation et le chóurage, 1999; also sci. papers on risk and utility theory; editorial bd. Polit. Econ. Rev., 1952—. Lt. arty., French Army, 1939-40. Named Laureate French Acad. Scis., 1933, French Acad. Moral and Polit. Scis., 1954, 59, 83, 84; recipient Lanchester prize Johns Hopkins U. and Operational Rsch. Soc. Am., 1958, Great Prize of Atlantic Community, 1959, Galabert prize French Astronautical Soc., 1959, Gravity Rsch. Found. prize, 1959, Grand Prix André Arnoux, 1968, Zerilli Marimo, 1984, Gold medal Soc. for Promotion of Nat. Industry, 1971, French Nat. Ctr. for Sci. Rsch., 1978, Prix Spl. Jury Dupuit-de Lesseps, 1987, Nobel prize in econ. scis., 1988, medal U. Paris-X, 1989, Gold medal City of Paris, 1989, Great Gold medal City of Nancy, 1990, Gold medal Etoile Civique, 1990, Amis de François Quesnay, 1994; decorated Officer of Palmes Académiques, 1949, Chevalier Nat. Economy Order, 1962, Comdr. Legion of Honor, 1989, Grand Officier Ordre Nat. du Mérite, 1998. Fellow Ops. Rsch. Soc. Am., Internat. Econometric Soc. (editorial bd. 1959-69), mem. NAS (assoc.), Nat. Acad. Scis., Morales et Politiques, Acad. Nat. dei Lincei (assoc.), French Assn. Econ. Sci. (chmn. 1972), Am. Econ. Assn. (hon.), Internat. Statis. Inst., Statis. Soc., Racing Club Paris. Avocations: history, theoretical and experimental physics. Home: 15 rue Des Gate-Ceps, 92210 Saint Cloud France Office: Econ Analysis Ctr, 60 Blvd Saint Michel, 75006 Paris France

ALLAM, MARK WHITTIER, veterinarian, former university administrator; b. Fernwood, Pa., Aug. 17, 1908; s. Clyde Macfarl and Helen (Hubbard) A.; m. Lila Josephine Griswold, Apr. 15, 1933; children: Shelley Lee, Maryjane Whittier. V.M.D., U. Pa., 1932. Diplomate Am. Coll. Vet. Surgeons (chmn. bd. 1966—). Gen. practice vet. medicine, 1932-45; instr. vet. surgery Sch. Vet. Medicine, U. Pa., 1943-45, asst. prof., 1945-48, assoc. prof., 1948-51, prof., 1951-77, prof. emeritus, 1977—, chmn. dept. surgery, 1951-55; research Harrison Dept. Surg. Research, Sch. Medicine, 1947-51, dean of faculty, 1952-73, asst. v.p. for health affairs, 1973-77; cons. Pan Am. San. Bur., WHO; mem. med. adv. bd. FDA, 1965-69, mem. vet. med. adv. bd., 1967-70; pres. Pa. Health Council, 1969-72; mem. expert panel on vet. edn. FAD-WHO, 1966—; pres. bd. edn. Media Borough Sch. Dist., 1941-60; pres. Media Civic Forum, 1964-67, Media Historic Preservations, 1977-80. Contbg. author: General Surgery, 1953; Author articles in field. Fellow Coll. Physicians Phila.; mem. AVMA (v.p. 1956, exec. bd. 1958-63), Phila. Soc. for Promoting Agr. (pres. 1974), Am. Vet. Medicine Alumni Assn. (pres. 1943), Pa. Keystone Vet. Med. Assn., Royal Coll. Vet. Surgeons (U.K., hon. assoc.), N.Y. Acad. Scis., Quaker City Farmers, Sigma Xi, Phi Zeta (nat. pres. 1948). Republican. Presbyterian. Home: Yale & Harvard Ave Swarthmore PA 19081 Office: New Bolton Ctr Kennett Square PA 19348*

ALLAMONG, BETTY D., academic administrator; b. Morgantown, W.Va., Apr. 8, 1935; d. Lonnie R. and Jessie R. (Hoffman) Davis; m. Joseph K. Allamong, Sept. 12, 1954; 1 child, John Bradley. BS, W.Va. U., 1961, MA, 1964, PhD, 1971; student, Inst. for Ednl. Mgmt. Harvard U., 1984. Instr. biology Morgantown High Sch., W.Va., 1961-67; instr. edn. W.Va. U., Morgantown, 1965-67, instr. biology, 1967-72; asst. to full prof. Ball State U., Muncie, Ind., 1972-87, assoc. dean, scis. and humanities, 1981-86, acting dean, scis. and humanities, 1986-87; provost and v.p. acad. affairs Bloomsburg U., Pa., 1987-92; mem. Ind. Corp. for Sci. & Tech., 1983-87. Co-author: Energy for Life, 1976; author numerous lab. manuals; contbr. articles to profl.jours. Mem. Ind. Corp. Sci. & Tech., 1983-87. Recipient Women of Achievement edn. award Women in Comms. Inc., Muncie, 1981. Fellow Ind. Acad. Sci. Home: 253 Pixler Hill Rd Morgantown WV 26508-9541

ALLAN, BARRY DAVID, research chemist, government official; b. Steubenville, Ohio, Jan. 20, 1935; s. John Young and Frances Lucy (Halbrunner) A.; m. Inge Elisabeth Bergeler, Aug. 5, 1961; children—Barbara Diane, Stephen Barry. B.S., Ariz. State U., 1956; M.S., U. Ala., 1964, Ph.D., 1968. Chemist White Sands Missile Range, N.M., 1956; aero. fuels research chemist Army Missile Command, Redstone Arsenal, Ala., 1958-62; research chemist-phys. Army Missile Command, Redstone Arsenal, 1962-98, research chemist, 1968-95; prof. J.C. Calhoun Coll., Decatur, Ala., 1969-73, Athens (Ala.) Coll., 1970-73, U. Ala., Huntsville, 1974-76; cons., 1996—; cons., 1965—; reviewer Nat. Sci. Found., 1973—. Publs. in field. Active Huntsville Civic Assn., 1961—. Served to capt. AUS, 1956-58. Recipient Army Research And Devel. Achievement award, 1962, Navy commendation, 1968, Army commendation, 1971, 72. Mem. Am. Chem. Soc. (treas. 1969-73, pres. 1974-76), Combustion Inst., Pasteur Soc., Assn. U.S. Army, N.Y. Acad. Scis., Joint Army, Navy, NASA, Air Force Propellant Characterization Group on Fluids and Materials, Sigma Xi, Gamma Sigma Epsilon, Theta Chi. Fax: 256-881-4101. Home: 7803 Michael Cir SW Huntsville AL 35802-2900 Office: Barry D Allan Cons 7803 Michael Cir SW Huntsville AL 35802-2900

ALLAN, CLAYTON PAUL, publishing executive; b. Kansas City, Mo., Nov. 6, 1967; s. William Paul Allan and Linda Lee Allan Huff; m. Kimberly Ann Robinson, Aug. 2, 1991; 1 child, Cooper Joshua. BBA, U. Mo., Kansas City, 1990. Sales mgr. ADT/Ever-Green, Grandview, Mo., 1990-92; v.p. Townsend Outlook Pub., Kansas City, Mo., 1992—. Avocations: fishing, hunting. Home: 4606 E 219th St Belton MO 64012 Office: Townsend Outlook Pub 20 E Gregory Kansas City MO 64114

ALLAN, COLIN JAMES, research and development manager; b. Winnipeg, Man., Can., May 6, 1943; s. James and Eileen (Shaw) A.; m. Lynn Margaret Tasker, Sept. 21, 1968; children: James, Jennifer, Robert. BSc in Math and Physics with honors, U. Man., Winnipeg, 1965, PhD in Nuclear Physics, 1970. Nat. Rsch. Coun. fellow U. Uppsala, Sweden, 1970-72; rsch. and devel. scientist reactor control br. Atomic Energy Can. Ltd. Rsch., Chalk River, Ont., Can., 1972-81, mgr. instrument devel. br., 1981-86, mgr. radiation engring. br., 1986-87; exec. asst. to pres. Atomic Energy Can. Ltd. Rsch., Ottawa, Ont., 1987-88; dir. planning reactor devel. divsn. Atomic Energy Can. Ltd. Rsch., Chalk River, 1988-90, acting dir. advanced reactor devel. divsn., 1990-91; v.p. environ. scis. and waste mgmt. Atomic Energy Can. Ltd. Rsch., Pinawa, Man., 1991-94, v.p. phys. and environ. scis., 1994-95; gen. mgr. phys. and environ. scis. Atomic Energy Can. Ltd., Pinawa, 1995-98, gen. mgr. sys. devel. and engring., 1998—; past mem. internat. radioactive waste mgmt. adv. com., sr. mem. waste safety standards adv. com. Internat. Atomic Energy Agy.; past mem. radioactive waste mgmt. com. Nuclear Energy Agy./Orgn. Econ. Cooperation And Devel.; mem. Internat. Nuclear Safety Adv. Group. Internat. Atomic Energy Agy., Can. Nuclear Soc., Can. Assn. Physicists. Office: Atomic Energy Can Ltd, Chalk River Labs, Chalk River, ON Canada K0J 1J0

ALLAN, JONATHAN DAVID, autograph dealer, pop culture historian; b. Grasmere, N.H., July 23, 1948; s. David Nisbet and Natalie Mary (Chandler) A.; m. Barbara Lauderbach, 1966 (div.); 1 child, Jonathan David II; m. Nancy Page, 1982. BA magna cum laude, U. N.H., 1972. Registered dealer. Bookseller, book buyer, columnist, book reviewer, freelance writer, 1972-81; co-owner, pres. Elmer's Nostalgia, Inc., Sanford, Maine, 1981—. Author: The Rock Trivia Book, 1976; columnist; mem. adv. bd. Autograph Collector Mag., 1986-92. N.H. chmn. Nat. Com. to Reopen the Rosenberg Case, 1973-77; vol. York County Shelters, Alfred, Maine, 1993—. Served with USNR, 1966-67. Mem. ACLU, NAACP, Universal Autograph Collectors Club (Outstanding Autograph Dealer award 1998), Am. Polit. Items Collectors, Maine People's Alliance, Planned Parenthood, People for the Am. Way, So. Poverty Law Ctr., Amnesty Internat., Wallace Found. for Study of So. Politics, McFarlane Clan Soc.Phi Beta Kappa. Mem. Socialist Party U.S.A. Avocations: collecting autographs and historical ephemera, painting, gardening, doing historical research. Email: jon@elmers.net. Home: 3 Putnam St Sanford ME 04073 Office: Elmer's Nostalgia Inc 3 Putnam St Sanford ME 04073

ALLAN, RALPH THOMAS MACKINNON, insurance company executive; b. Montreal, Feb. 17, 1942; s. Ralph Percival Hall and Margaret Hunter (Lawrie) A.; m. Suzanne Patricia Delaute, May 18, 1968; children: Alison and Margaret (twins). B in Commerce, Mount Allison U., Sackville, N.B., Can., 1963. With Sun Life Assurance Co. Can., Montreal, 1963-78; v.p. comml. lending Cen. Trust Co., Halifax, N.S., Can., 1979-80; v.p. London (Ont.) Life Ins. Co., 1981-86, sr. v.p. investments, 1986-89, exec. v.p. investments, 1989-97; exec. v.p. investments London Ins. Group, Inc., 1989-97; exec. v.p. corp. investments London Life, 1997—, London Ins. Group, Inc., 1997—, Great-West Life Assurance Co., 1997—; chmn., CEO London Reinsurance Group; bd. dirs., chmn. Toronto Coll. Park, London Guarantee Ins. Co., Lifestyle Retirement Cmtys. Ltd.,; pres. bd. dirs. London Life Fin. Corp., 1981, Lonvest Equities Ltd.; bd. dirs. Shin Fu Life Ins. Co., GWL Realty Advisors, London Fin. Ctr., Intrawest Corp., Trojan Techs., Inc, Lonlife Data Svcs. Ltd. Mem. investment com. London Community Found., 1982—, Lawson Found., 1994—; mem. adv. bd. St. Joseph's Health Ctr., London. Clubs: London, London Hunt and Country. Office: London Life Ins Co, 255 Dufferin Ave, London, ON Canada N6A 4K1

ALLAN, RICHMOND FREDERICK, lawyer; b. Billings, Mont., Apr. 22, 1930; s. Roy F. and Edith (Prater) A.; m. Dorothy Frost, Aug. 9, 1954; children: Richmond P., David F., Michael R. BA, U. Mont., 1954, JD, 1957; postgrad., London Sch. of Econs., 1957-58. Bar: Mont. 1957, U.S. Supreme Ct. 1961, D.C. 1965. Law clk. U.S. Ct. Appeals (9th cir.), San Francisco, 1958-59; ptnr. Kurth, Conner, Jones & Allan, Billings, 1959-61; chief asst. U.S. atty. U.S. Dept. of Justice, Billings, 1961-64; assoc. solicitor U.S. Dept. of Interior, Washington, 1965-67, dep. solicitor, 1968-69; ptnr. Weissbrodt & Weissbrodt, Washington, 1969-77, Casey, Lane & Mittendorf, Washington, 1977-78, Duncan, Weinberg, Miller & Pembroke, P.C., Washington, 1979—. Fulbright Commn. scholar, 1957. Mem. Fed. Bar Assn. (pres. Mont. chpt. 1963-65). Avocations: trap and skeet shooting. Office: Duncan Weinberg Genzer & Pembroke PC 1615 M St NW Ste 800 Washington DC 20036-3266

ALLAN, ROBERT MOFFAT, JR., corporate executive, educator; b. Detroit, Dec. 8, 1920; s. Robert M. and Jane (Christman) A.; m. Harriet Spicer, Nov. 28, 1942; children: Robert M. III, Scott, David, Marilee. BS, Stanford U., 1941; postgrad. Stanford Grad. Sch. Bus., 1941-42; MS, UCLA, 1943; postgrad. Loyola Law Sch., 1947-50. Economist research dept. Security First Nat. Bank, 1942; exec. Marine Ins., 1946-53; asst. to pres., work mgr. Zinsco Elec. Products, 1953-55, v.p., dir., 1956-59; asst. to pres. The Times-Mirror Corp., 1959-60, corp. v.p., 1961-64; pres., dir. Cyprus Mines Corp., 1964-67; pres. Litton Internat., 1967-69; pres. U.S. Naval Postgrad. Sch. Found., prof. internat. mgmt. 1969-85. Bd. dirs., advisor U.S. Naval Acad.; trustee Boys Republic, Pomona Grad. Sch., Claremont Grad. Sch., Del Monte Forest Homeowners; vis. prof. of internat. mgmt. grad. schs. of bus. MBA Stanford, Harvard, U. of Chgo., UCLA, USA and Internat. Inst. Fgn. Studies, Monterey; adv. trustee Monterey County Sheriff, 1982—. Capt. USAF, 1942-45. Recipient award Helms Athletic Found., 1947, 49, Navy Cross of Merit, 1976, Plaque of Merit USCG, 1990, Medal for Heroism, 1990; named Outstanding Businessman of Yr., L.A., Nat. Assn. Accts., 1966; elected to Sailing Hall of Fame, 1969; named Monterey Inst. Fgn. Studies trustee and sr. fellow, 1976. Mem. Mchts. and Mfrs. Assn. (dir.), Intercollegiate Yachting Assn. (regional dir. 1940-55), Phi Gamma Delta, Phi Delta Phi. Clubs: Newport Harbor Yacht (commodore 1962), Trans-Pacific Yacht, Carmel Valley Country. Home: 167 Del Mesa Carmel CA 93923

ALLAN, SARAH KATHERINE, Oriental studies educator; b. Atlanta, Feb. 20, 1945; d. Frederic and Elizabeth (Jones) Meyers; m. Nicol Allan, Sept. 28, 1963; B.A., UCLA, 1966; M.A., U. Calif.-Berkeley, 1969, Ph.D., 1974. Lectr. in Chinese, Sch. Oriental and African Studies, U. London, 1972—; founder, chmn. Early China Seminar, London, 1982-84, 1985—; mem. adv. bd. East Asian Civilizations, 1982—. Author: The Heir and the Sage, 1981; (with others) Oracle Bone Collections in Great Britain, 1985. Co-editor: Legend, Lore and Religion in China, 1979. Contbr. articles on Chinese legend, myth and religion to scholarly publs. Grantee Brit. Acad., 1982, 84; exchange scholar Brit. Acad.-Chinese Acad. Social Scis., Beijing, 1984. Mem. Brit. Assn. Chinese Studies, European Assn. Chinese Studies, Soc. Study Early China. Office: SOAS Malet St, London WC1E 7HP, England

ALLAN, WILLIAM GEORGE, painter, educator; b. Everett, Wash., Mar. 28, 1936. BFA, San Francisco Art Inst., 1958. Instr. painting U. Calif., Davis, 1965-67, Berkeley, 1969; prof. art Calif State U., Sacramento, 1968—. Exhibited in group shows at Carnegie Internat. Exhbn., Pitts., 1975, Continuing Surrealism, La. Jolla (Calif.) Mus. Art, 1971, Whitney Painting Ann., N.Y.C., 1972, 70th Ann. Exhbn. Art Inst. Chgo., 1972, Indpls. Mus. Art Exhbn., 1972, Whitney Mus. Am. Art, N.Y.C., 1973-74, Painting and Sculpture in Calif.: The Modern Era, San Francisco Mus. Modern Art, 1976, Chgo. Arts Club, 1978; represented in permanent collections at Dallas Mus. Art, San Francisco Mus. Art, Phila. Mus. Art, Whitney Mus. Am. Art, Mus. Modern Art, N.Y.C. Office: Calif State U Sacramento Dept Art 6000 J St Sacramento CA 95819-6106*

ALLAND, LAWRENCE MARTIN, pastoral counselor, marriage and family therapist; b. Ft. Worth, Sept. 29, 1931; s. Alvin Henry and Mary Estelle (Belew) A.; m. Rosemary Evans, Dec. 29, 1953; children: Mary Margaret, John Mark, James Michael, Timothy Kirk. BA, Tex. Christian U., 1953, MDiv, 1957, ThM, 1972; postgrad., Mich. State U., 1980-82. Lic. profl. counselor, Tex.; lic. marriage counselor, Mich., lic. marriage and family therapist, Tex.; ordained to ministry Christian Ch. (Disciples of Christ), 1957. Missionary tchr. United Christian Missionary Soc., Indpls., 1957-60; assoc. min. Country Club Christian Ch., Kansas City, Mo., 1960-63; resident in psychiatry and religion Menninger Found., Topeka, 1963-64; min. Highlands Christian Ch., Dallas, 1964-67; min. counseling Park Congl. Ch., Grand Rapids, Mich., 1967-71; exec. dir. Community Counseling Ministry, Grand Rapids, 1971-77; ptnr. Kooistra, Alland, Jansma and Elders, Grand Rapids, 1977-82; exec. dir. Samaritan Counseling Ctr., Ft. Worth, 1982-84; ptnr. Counseling and Consulting Assocs., Ft. Worth, 1984-95; ret., 1995; mem. adj. faculty Mich. State U. Med. Sch., Lansing, 1972-82, Brite Div. Sch., Tex. Christian U., Ft. Worth, 1985-94. Bd. dirs. Project Rehab. Drug Treatment Ctr., Grand Rapids, 1968-74; pres. bd. dirs. Grand Rapids Child Guidance Clinic, 1970-72; chmn. gen. bd. Univ. Christian Ch., Ft. Worth, 1990-92. Alumni scholar Tex. Christian U., 1953; fellow NIMH, 1963-64. Mem. Am. Assn. Pastoral Counselors (diplomate, pres. Midwest region 1977-79, nat. bd. govs. 1978-79), Am. Assn. Marriage and Family Therapy (clin.), Tarrant County Assn. Marriage and Family Therapy (pres. 1989-90). Democrat. Avocations: golf, reading, travel. Home: 4701 Shady Ridge Ct Fort Worth TX 76109-1803

ALLARD, A. WAYNE, senator, veterinarian; b. Dec. 12, 1943; m. Joan Malcolm, Mar. 23, 1967; children: Cheryl, Christie. DVM, Colo. State U., 1968. Veterinarian Allard Animal Hosp.; mem. Colo. State Senate, 1982-91; chmn. health, environment and instn. com., chmn. senate majority caucus; mem. 102nd-104th Congresses from 4th dist., Colo., 1991-96; mem. agrl. com., 1991-92, 93-94, 95-96, mem. small bus. com., 1991-92, mem. interior and insular affairs com., 1991-92, mem. com. on coms., 1991-92, 93-94, mem. budget com., 1993-94, 95-96, mem. natural resources com., 1993-94, 95-96, mem. joint com. on reorganization of Congress, 1993-94, 95-96, chmn. subcom. of agr. conservation, forest and water, 1995-96; senator 105th Congress, 1997—, mem. banking, urban affairs com., 1997—, environment and pub. works com., 1997—, intelligence select com., 1997—, Senate armed svcs. com., banking, housing and urban affairs com., select com. on intelligence; mem. select com. on intelligence, armed svcs. com., chmn. pers. subcom., banking, housing and urban affairs com., chmn. subcom. on housing and transp. 106th Congress; health officer, Loveland, Colo.; mem. regional adv. coun. on vet. medicine Western Interstate Commn. Higher Edn.; mem. Colo. Low-Level Radioactive Waste Adv. Com. Chmn. United Way; active 4-H Found. Mem. AVMA, Colo. Vet. Medicine Assn., Larimer County Vet. Medicine Assn. (past pres.), Bd. Vet. Practitioners (charter mem.), Am. Animal Hosp. Assn., Nat. Conf. State Legislatures (vice-chmn. human resources com. 1987—, healthcare cost containment com.), Loveland C. of C., Republican. Methodist. Home: PO Box 2405 Loveland CO 80539-2405 Office: US Senate 513 Hart Bldg Washington DC 20510

ALLARD, DAVID HENRY, judge; b. Snohomish, Wash., Jan. 10, 1929; s. Clayton Frederick and Ruth Elizabeth (Winston) A.; m. Elizabeth Ellen Burrill, Nov. 26, 1960; children: John M., Clayton Frederick II. A.B., Whitman Coll., 1951; LL.B., Duke U., 1956. Bar: Wash. 1957, U.S. Supreme Ct. 1965. Mem. staff ICC, Washington, 1958-67; adminstrv. law judge ICC, 1967-72, 73-80, Office Hearings and Appeals, Social Security Adminstrn., 1986—; chief adminstrv. law judge ICC, 1980-86; adminstrv. chief law judge HHS, Tucson, 1986-92; regional chief adminstrv. law judge SSA, Boston, 1992-97; adminstrv. law judge FTC, 1972-73; law reporter Presdl. Task Force on Career Advancement, 1967; mem. comml. panel Am. Arbitration Assn. law reporter Presdl. Task Force on Career Advancement, 1967; mem. comml. panel Am. Arbitration Assn.; spl. master U.S. Ct. Appeals (1st cir.), 1992. Served with AUS, 1951-53. Mem. ABA (Achievement award young lawyers sect. 1965), Fed. Bar Assn. (editor-in-chief jour. 1972, pres. 1974, chmn. edn. bd. 1976-82), Fed. Adminstrv. Law Judges Conf., Delta Tau Delta. Presbyterian. Home: 30 Parker Ridge Way Newburyport MA 01950-1959

ALLARD, DEAN CONRAD, historian, retired naval history center director; b. Kansas City, Mo., Oct. 19, 1933; s. Dean Conrad Sr. and Elizabeth Donaldson (Graves) A.; m. Constance Lynne Morgan, June 17, 1955; children: Scott, Hunt, Elizabeth. AB, Dartmouth Coll., 1955; MA, Georgetown U., 1959; PhD, George Washington U., 1967. Head Naval Operational Archives, Washington, 1958-82; sr. historian Naval Hist. Ctr., Washington, 1982-89; dir. naval history USN, Washington, 1989-95; adj. prof. George Washington U., 1979-89. Author: The United States Navy and the Vietnam Conflict, Vol. I, 1976, Spencer Fullerton Baird: A Study in the History of American Science, 1978; also articles on naval and maritime history; editor: U.S. Naval History Sources in the United States, 1979. Chmn. Hist. Commn., Arlington, Va., 1978-80; pres. Arlington Hist. Soc., 1974-75; mem. coun. Woodlawn Plantation, Fairfax, Va., 1976-84; mem. French-U.S. Sci. Com. on CSS, Ala., 1991-95. Lt. (j.g.) USN, 1955-58. Recipient Superior Civil Svc. award U.S. Govt., 1995, Samuel Eliot Morison award for Disting. Svc., USS Constn. Mus. Found., Boston, 1995. Fellow Inter-Univ. Seminar Armed Forces and Soc.; mem. N.Am. Soc. for Oceanic History (pres. 1985-89), Soc. for Mil. History (v.p. 1983-86), World War II Studies Assn. (bd. dirs.), U.S. Commn. Mil. History (pres. 1995—), Internat. Commn. Maritime History (mem. exec. coun. 1990—), Cosmos Club (Washington), Phi Beta Kappa. Avocations: gardening, hiking. Home: 2701 N Quincy St Arlington VA 22207-5046

ALLARD, JEAN, lawyer, urban planner; b. Trenton, Mo., Dec. 16, 1924; d. Ben J. and Marion (Watson) McGuire; 1 son, John Preston. AB, Culver-Stockton Coll., 1945, LLD (hon.), 1977; AM, Washington U., St. Louis, 1947; JD, U. Chgo., 1953; LLD (hon.), Elmhurst Coll., 1979. Bar: Ill. 1953, Ohio 1959. Counselor psychology dept. U. Chgo., 1948-51, rsch. assoc. Law Sch., 1953-58, asst. dean, 1956-58, v.p. for bus. and fin., 1972-75; assoc. firm Fuller, Harrington, Seney & Henry, Toledo, 1958-59, Lord, Bissell & Brook, Chgo., 1959-62; sec., gen. counsel Maremont Corp., Chgo., 1962-72; ptnr. Sonnenschein Nath & Rosenthal, Chgo., 1976-91, of counsel, 1991—; bd. dirs. Met. Planning Coun., 1991—, pres., 1991-96; bd. dirs. Castlerock Group, Inc. Trustee Culver-Stockton Coll., 1976—; dir. Metro Chgo. Info. Ctr. Mem. ABA, Am. Law Inst., The Chgo. Network, Internat. Women's Forum, Econ. Club, Comml. Club, Law Club of Chgo. Home: 5844 S Stony Island Ave Chicago IL 60637-2022 Office: Sonnenschein Nath & Rosenthal 8000 Sears Tower Chicago IL 60606

ALLARD, JUDITH LOUISE, secondary education educator; b. Rutland, Vt., Feb. 21, 1945; d. William Edward and Orilla Marion (Trombley) A. BA, U. Vt., 1967, MS, 1969. Tchr. math., sci. Edmunds Jr. H.S., Burlington, Vt., 1969-73; biology tchr. Edmunds Jr. H.S., Burlington, 1973-78, sci. dept. chair, 1975-78; biology tchr. Burlington (Vt.) H.S., 1978—; instr. environ. studies U. Vt., Burlington, 1988-89; adviser Nat. Honor Soc., 1986—. Co-author Favorite Labs of Outstanding Tchrs., 1991. Active Amnesty Internat., 1985—; mem. Discovery Mus., Essex Junction, Vt., 1986—, Lake Champlain Com., Burlington, 1987—; mem. Vt. Goals 2000 Panel, 1995—; state bd. dirs. Odyssey of the Mind, 1986—; mem. Vt. State Licensing Commn., 1995-96, Vt. Stds. Bd. for Profl. Educators, 1996—. Recipient Presdl. Sci. Tchg. award NSF, 1983, Tech. award Tandy, 1998; named Outstanding Vt. Educator, U. Vt., 1983, Outstanding Vt. Sci. Tchr., Sigma Xi Soc., 1984, Vt. Tchr. Yr., 1998; Tandy Tech. scholar, 1990; Genentech Access Excellence fellow, 1995, 96, Access Excellence Retro fellow, 1996. Mem. NEA (bd. dirs. Vt. chpt.), Vt. Sci. Tchrs. Assn. (bd. dirs. 1980-92, treas. 1985-92), Burlington Profl. Stds. Bd. (chair 1991—), Parents and Friends of Edn. (trustee), Nat. Assn. Biology Tchrs. (dir. Vt. Outstanding Biology Tchr. award program 1977—, Outstanding Biology Tchr. award 1975), Assn. Presdl. Awardees in Sci., Phi Delta Kappa. Roman Catholic. Avocations: needlework, fishing, music. Home: 221 Woodlawn Rd Burlington VT 05401-5722 Office: Burlington High Sch 52 Institute Rd Burlington VT 05401-2721

ALLARD, LINDA MARIE, fashion designer; b. Akron, Ohio, May 27, 1940; d. Carroll Preston and Zella Viola (Indoe) A. BFA, Kent State U., 1962, LHD (hon.), 1992. Dir. design Ellen Tracy, N.Y.C., 1962—; design critic Fashion Inst. Tech., N.Y.C.; vis. prof. Internat. Acad. Merchandising and Design, Chgo. Author: Absolutely Delicious cookbook, 1994. Bd. dirs. N. Y. adv. bd. Kent State U.; bd. dirs. Kent State U. Found. Bd. Recipient Dallas Fashion award Dallas Apparel Mart, 1986, 87, 94. Mem. Fashion Group Internat., Inc. (past bd. dirs.), Coun. Fashion Designers Am. Avocations: cooking, gardening, painting. Office: Ellen Tracy 575 7th Ave Fl 11 New York NY 10018-2095*

ALLARD, NICHOLAS W., lawyer; b. Suffern, N.Y., Oct. 4, 1952. BA with honors, Princeton U., 1974; MA, Oxford U., 1976; JD, Yale U., 1979. Bar: N.Y. 1981, D.C. 1981. Law clk. to chief U.S. dist. judge Robert F. Peckham San Francisco; law clk. to U.S. cir. judge Patricia M. Wald Washington; chair govt. rels. practice group Latham & Watkins; ptnr. Latham & Watkins, Washington; mem. minority staff counsel, prin. legal counsel to Sen. Edward Kennedy, Senate Com. on Judiciary, 1983-86; liaison Nat. Assn. State Attys. Gen.; adminstrv. asst., chief of staff to Sen. Patrick Moynihan, 1986-87; spkr. on health and comms. issues. Mem. editl. bd.; contbr. Spectrum, Pvt. Cable and Wireless Cable Mag., others; contbr. articles to profl. jours. Rhodes scholar Oxford U., 1976. Office: Latham & Watkins Ste 1300 1001 Pennsylvania Ave NW Washington DC 20004

ALLARD, ROBERT WAYNE, geneticist, educator; b. L.A., Sept. 3, 1919; s. Glenn A. and Alma A. (Roose) A.; m. Ann Catherine Wilson, June 16, 1944; children: Susan, Thomas, Jane, Gillian, Stacie. BS, U. Calif., Davis, 1941; PhD, U. Wis., 1946; ScD (hon.), U. Helsinki, 1996, U. Léon, 1997. From asst. to assoc. prof. U. Calif., Davis, 1946—, prof. genetics, 1955—. Author books; contbr. articles to profl. jours. Served to lt. USNR. Recipient Crop Sci. award Am. Soc. Agronomy, 1964, DeKalb Disting. Career award Crop Sci. Soc. Am., 1983; Guggenheim fellow, 1954, 60; Fulbright fellow, 1955. Mem. Nat. Acad. Scis., Am. Acad. Arts and Scis., Am. Soc. Naturalists (pres. 1974-75), Genetics Soc. Am. (pres. 1983-84), Am. Genetics Assn. (pres. 1989), Phi Beta Kappa, Sigma Xi, Alpha Gamma Rho, Alpha Zeta. Democrat. Unitarian. Home: PO Box 185 Bodega Bay CA 94923-0185

ALLARD, SCOTT MORGAN, cost, benefit analyst, information professional; b. Washington, Feb. 28, 1958; s. Dean C. and Constance M. (Morgan) A.; m. Arlene Bright-Allard, Apr. 26, 1997; 1 child, Charles Bright. BA in Econs., Duke U., 1980. Cert. cost estimate analyst. RF engr. Lohnes & Culver Consulting Engrs., Washington, 1979-83, Comms. Engring. Svcs., Arlington, Va., 1983-85; cost analyst Project Engring. Inc., Silver Springs, Md., 1985-87; cost/benefit analyst NCR Federal Inc., McLean, Va., 1987—. Contbr. articles to profl. jours. Pres. Bancroft Sch. & Civic League, Arlington, 1994-96; com. chair Arlington Civic Fedn., 1994-97; mem. Com. 100, Arlington, 1995—. Recipient Cert. Commendation U.S.M.C., Quantico, Va., 1995. Mem. Soc. Cost Estimating & Analysis. Office: Further Prodns Inc 518 N Lombardy St Arlington VA 22203-1027

ALLARD, WILLIAM KENNETH, mathematician; b. Lowell, Mass., Oct. 29, 1941; s. Frederic Pratt and Jeannette Edna (Perrault) A.; m. Priscilla Elaine May, Aug. 10, 1968; children: Felicia, Christopher. Sc.B., Villanova U., 1963; Ph.D. in Math, Brown U., 1968. Asst. prof. math. Princeton U., 1971-75; prof. math. Duke U., Durham, N.C., 1975—; chmn. dept. Duke U., 1985-86. Mng. editor: Duke Math. Jour. 1983-85. Alfred P. Sloan fellow, 1970-72. Mem. Am. Math. Soc. Home: PO Box 91275 Durham NC 27708-1275 Office: Duke U Dept Math Durham NC 27706

ALLARDICE, JOHN MCCARRELL, coatings manufacturing company executive; b. Balt., May 30, 1940; s. James Barclay and Rebecca Jane (McCarrell) A.; m. J. Ann Benjamin, May 30, 1962 (div. 1979); children: John McCarrell Jr., Scott, Julie; m. Susan Bryson Miller, Aug. 15, 1981; stepchildren: Shawn, Ben, Ted. Student, Washington and Jefferson Coll., 1958-6l; BS in Chemistry, U. Pitts., 1963. Salesman chem. div. PPG, Pitts., 1964; silicone div. GE, Waterford, N.Y., 1965; salesman Stauffer Chem. Co., Adrian, Mich., 1965-69; salesman, sales mgr. Fre Kote, Inc., Boca Raton, Fla., 1969-78; pres. Releasomers, Inc., Bradford Woods, Pa., 1978—. Patentee bladder lubricants. Republican. Mem. Unity Ch. Avocations: golf, tennis, acting, singing, old cars. Office: Releasomers Inc PO Box 82 Bradfordwoods PA 15015-0082

ALLAWAY, WILLIAM HARRIS, retired university official; b. Oak Park, Ill., Mar. 31, 1924; s. William Horsford and Helen Margaret (Harris) A.; m. Olivia Woodhull Foster, June 28, 1952; children: William Harris Jr., Ben Foster, Eve Olivia. BS, U. Ill., 1949; postgrad., U. Grenoble, France, 1950-51; MA, U. Ill., 1951; EdD, U. Denver, 1957. Traveling sec. World Student Svc. Fund, 1947-48; spl. asst. to chmn. U.S. Nat. Commn. for UNESCO, 1949; asst. to field dir. World U. Svc. attached to Internat. Refugee Orgn., Salzburg, Austria, 1951; field rep. Inst.of Internat. Edn., Chgo. and Denver, 1952-54; gen. sec. U. Kans. YMCA, 1954-57; asst. dean of men and dir. Wilbur Hall Stanford (Calif.) U., 1957-61; dir. edn. abroad program U. Calif., Santa Barbara, 1961-89, spl. asst. to chancellor, 1990-93; cons. and lectr. in field; mem. ednl. assoc. adv. com. Inst. Internat. Edn., 1984-87; mem. Pres.'s Coun. for Internat. Youth Exch., 1982-85; mem. U.S. Del. to conf. on ednl. exch. between U.S. and U.K., 1970, 1974. Co-chair Peace and Justice Com., Goleta Presbyn. Ch., chair steering com. PAX 2100; mem. Nuclear Age Peace Found., Santa Barbara, Internat. Peace Rsch. Assn., Yellow Springs, Ohio; mem. Coun. on Internat. Ednl. Exch., 1961—, chmn. bd. dirs. 1978-83; past bd. dirs., hon. trustee Am. Ctr. for Students and Artists, Paris; bd. advisors Hariri Found., 1987—; exec. sec. Internat. Com. for Study of Edn. Exch., 1970-95, exec. com. Inter-Univ. Ctr. Postgrad. Studies, Dubrovnik, 1988-96, bd. dirs., 1996—. With USAAF, 1943-46. Hon. DHC, U. Sussex, Eng., 1992; PhD h.c. U. Bergen, Norway, 1990; DHC, U. Bordeaux, France, 1988; Hon. Dr. of U. of Stirling, Scotland, 1981; recipient Scroll of Appreciation Leningrad State U., 1989, Award for Svc. to Internat. Ednl. Exch. Council on Internat. Ednl. Exch., 1989, Silver medal U. Lund, Sweden, 1990, Alumni Achievement award Coll. Liberal Arts and Sci. Alumni Assn. U. Ill., 1990, Gold Medal of Honor of the Complutense U. of Madrid, Spain, 1991. Mem. NAFSA Assn. Internat. Educators (hon. life mem.), Internat. Assn. Univs. (dep. mem., adminstrv. bd. 1995—, chair task force on internationalization of higher edn.), La Cumbre Golf and Country Club. Democrat. Presbyterian. Avocations: golf, skiing, choir, reading. Fax: (805) 687-5779. E-mail: boallaway@aol.com. Home: 724 Calle De Los Amigos Santa Barbara CA 93105-4439

ALLBEE, SANDRA MOLL, real estate broker; b. Reading, Pa., July 15, 1947; d. Charles Lewars and Isabel May (Ackerman) Frederici; m. Thomas J. Allbee, Oct. 18, 1975 (div. 1987). Exec. sec. Hamburg (Pa.) State Sch. and Hosp., 1965-73; regional mgr. Am. Bus. Service Corp., Newport Beach, Calif., 1973-78; v.p. T.A.S.A., Inc., Long Beach, Calif., 1978-86; realtor Very Important Properties, Inc., Rolling Hills Estates, Calif., 1986-90, Re/Max Palos Verdes Realty, Rolling Hills Estates, Calif., 1990—. Bd. dirs., v.p. Nat. Coun. on Alcoholism, Torrance, Calif., 1987-96; pres. Rollingwood Homeowners Assn., Rolling Hills Estates, Calif., 1985-92. Recipient 100% Club award. Mem. Palos Verdes Rep. Women's Club (bd. dirs. 1989-94). Office: Re/Max Palos Verdes Realty 4030 Palos Verdes Dr N Ste 104 Rolling Hills Estates CA 90274

ALLBRIGHT, KARAN ELIZABETH, psychologist, consultant; b. Oklahoma City, Okla., Jan. 28, 1948; d. Jack Gahnal and Irma Lolene (Keesee) A. BA, Oklahoma City U., 1970, MAT, 1972; PhD, U. So. Miss., 1981. Cert. sch. psychologist, psychometrist; lic. psychologist, Okla., Ark. Psychol. technician Donald J. Bertoch, Ph.D., Oklahoma City, 1973-76; asst. adminstr. Parents' Assistance Ctr., Oklahoma City, 1976-77; psychology intern Burwell Psycho-ednl. Ctr., Carrollton, Ga., 1980-81; staff psychologist Griffin Area Psychoednl. Ctr., Ga., 1981-85; clinic dir. Sequoyah County Guidance Clinic, Sallisaw, Okla., 1985-88; psychologist Baker Psychiatric Clinic, Ft. Smith, Ark., 1988-90; cons. Harbor View Mercy Hosp., 1988-90, Integris Bethany Med. Ctr., 1992—; pvt. practice, Oklahoma City, 1990—, Mercy Health Ctr., 1996—; lectr. various orgns.; bd. dirs. workshops. Mem. Task Force to Prevent Child Abuse, Fayette County, Ga., 1984-85, Task Force on Family Violence, Spalding County, Ga., 1983-85; cons. Family Alliance (Parents Anonymous) Sequoyah County, Okla., 1985-88; assoc. bd. dirs. Lyric Theatre. Named Outstanding Young Women in Am., 1980. Mem. APA, Southeastern Psychol. Assn., Nat. Assn. Sch. Psychologists (cert. sch. psychologist), Okla. Psychol. Assn., Nat. Register Health Svc. Providers in Psychology, Psi Chi, Delta Zeta (chpt. dir. 1970-72). Democrat. Presbyterian. Home: 3941 NW 44th St Oklahoma City OK 73112-2517 Office: Northwest Mental Health Assocs 3832 N Meridian Ave Oklahoma City OK 73112-2849

ALLBRITTON, JOE LEWIS, diversified holding company executive; b. D'Lo, Miss., Dec. 29, 1924; s. Lewis A. and Ada (Carpenter) A.; m. Barbara Jean Balfanz, Feb. 23, 1967; 1 son, Robert Lewis. LLB, Baylor U., 1949, LLD (hon.), 1964, JD, 1969; LHD, Calif. Pept. Coll., 1973. Bar: Tex. 1949. Dir. Perpetual Corp., Houston, 1958—; pres. Perpetual Corp., 1965-76, 78-81, chmn. bd., 1973—; bd. dirs. Pierce Nat. Life Ins. Co., L.A., chmn., 1958-82, 75-92; chmn. Allbrittoon Comms. Co., 1974-98, chmn. exec. com., 1998—chmn. Univ. Bancshares, Inc., Houston, 1975-97, Houston Fin. Svcs., Ltd., London, 1977—, Riggs Nat. Corp., Washington, 1981—, Riggs Bank, N.A., Washington, 1983—; dep. chmn. Riggs Bank Europe Ltd., London, 1986-92, chmn., 1992—; mem. Greater Washington Bd. Trade, 1983-88, 92—; trustee The Mitre Corp., Bedford, Mass., 1987-93. Trustee Fed. City Coun., Washington, 1975—, John F. Kennedy Ctr. for Performing Arts, Washington, 1985-90, Nat. Geog. Soc., 1986—, The Ronald Reagan Presdl. Found., L.A., 1990—, George Bush Presdl. Found., College Station, Tex., 1993—; bd. dirs. Nat. Fund for U.S. Bot. Garden, 1992-95, The Lyndon Baines Johnson Found., 1989—, Georgetown U., Washington, 1990-96. With USN, 1943-46. Mem. State Bar Tex., Assn. Res. City Bankers. Office: Perpetual Corp 808 17th St NW Washington DC 20006-3910

ALLCOCK, HARRY R., chemistry educator; b. Loughborough, Eng., Apr. 8, 1932; naturalized U.S. citizen; s. Claud Leonard and Nora (Clarke) A.; m. Noreen Raworth, Nov. 14, 1959. BSc, U. London, 1953, PhD, 1956. Cert. chemist. Postdoctoral fellow Purdue U., West Lafayette, Ind., 1956-58, Can. Nat. Rsch. Coun., Ottawa, Ont., 1958-60; rsch. scientist Cen. Rsch. Labs. Am. Cyanamid Co., Stamford, Conn., 1961-66; assoc. prof. chem. Pa. State U., University Park, 1966-70, prof. chem., 1970-85, Evan Pugh Prof. Chem., 1985—. Author: Heteroatom Ring Systems and Polymers, 1967, Phosphorus-Nitrogen Compounds, 1972; (with F.W. Lampe) Contemporary Polymer Chemistry, 1981, 2d edition, 1990; (with J.E. Mark and R.C. West) Inorganic Polymers, 1992; co-editor (with M. Zeldin & K.J. Wynne) Inorganic and Organometallic Polymers, 1988; (with P. Wisian-Neilson and K.J. Wynne) Inorganic and Organometallic Polymers II, 1994; editor: Inorganic Syntheses Vol. XXV, 1989; mem. editorial bds. jours. Phosphorus, 1973-77, Macromolecules, 1974-79, Chemical Revs., 1974-79, Biomaterials, 1980-82, Jour. of Polymer Sci., 1987—, Inorganic Chemistry, 1988-91, Chemistry of Materials, 1988—, Heteroatom Chemistry, 1988-93, Jour. Inorganic and Organometallic Polymers, 1990—. Guggenheim fellow 1986-87. Fellow Am. Inst. Chemists (Chem. Pioneer award 1989); mem. Am. Chem. Soc. (nat. award polymer chemistry 1984, nat. award chemistry of materials 1992, Herman Mark award polymer chemistry 1994), Royal Soc. Chemistry (various coms.), Corp. Inorganic Syntheses. Office: Pa State U Dept Chemistry 152 Davey Lab University Park PA 16802-6300

ALLCORN, TERRY ALAN, principal, educator; b. Springfield, Mo., Dec. 7, 1952; s. Calbert and Bonnie Lee (Taylor) A.; m. Rhonda Gay Martens, May 24, 1974; children: Eric Alan, Nathan Scott. ThG, Bapt. Bible Coll., 1974, BS, 1977; MA, S.W. Mo. State U., 1980. Assoc. pastor Prairie Garden Bapt. Ch., Houston, 1974-76; purchasing agt. Fed. Enterprises, Inc., Nixa, Mo., 1976-80; prin. Christian Schs. of Springfield, 1980-85, 89—; pastor Mt. Calvary Bapt. Ch., Richmond, Mo., 1985-89; tchr. Pisgah Christian Sch., Excelsior Springs, Mo., 1987-88, adminstr., 1988-89; prof. U.S. history Bapt. Bible Coll., Springfield, 1990—. Mem. Police Pers. Bd., Richmond, 1987-89; election judge Ray County, Richmond, 1985-89; dep. registrar Greene County Clk., Springfield, 1983-85, 89—; deacon Bapt. Temple, 1977-80. Mem. Mo. Assn. Christian Schs., Kansas City, 1984-85, 90—. Avocations: softball, golf. Home: PO Box 8464 Springfield MO 65801-8464 Office: Christian Schs Springfield 739 W Talmage St Springfield MO 65803-1117

ALLDAY, MARTIN LEWIS, lawyer; b. El Dorado, Ark., May 30, 1926; s. Martin L. Sr. and Bess (Kavanaugh) A.; m. Patricia Pryor, May 1, 1954; children: Katherine, Elizabeth, Martin III. JD, U. Tex., Austin, 1951. Bar: Tex. 1951. Examiner oil and gas div. R.R. Commn. of Tex., Austin, 1951-53; legal dept. Superior Oil Co., Midland, Tex., 1953-57, Houston, 1957-59; ptnr. Lynch, Chappell, Allday and Alsup, Midland, Austin & Dallas, 1959-89; past solicitor Dept. of Interior, Washington, 1989; chmn. Fed. Energy Regulatory Commn., Washington, 1989-93; of counsel Scott, Douglass and McConnico, Austin, Houston, Dallas, Tex., 1993—; bd. dirs. N.Am. Royalties, Inc. Past pres. Midland Jaycees, C. of C., Indsl. Found.; past trustee, gov. Midland Meml. Hosp.; bd. trustees Petroleum Mus. Hall of Fame; presiding officer Tex. State Cemetery Com. With Inf. U.S. Army, 1944-46. Decorated Purple Heart, Bronze Star. Mem. ABA, Tex. Bar Assn. (chmn. oil, gas and mineral sect. 1970), D.C. Bar Assn., Tex. Bar Found., Midland County Bar Assn. (prs. 1972-73), Midland Country Club (pres.), Petroleum Club (bd. dirs.). Republican. Episcopalian. Avocations: fishing, hunting, golf. Office: 600 Congress Ave Ste 1500 Austin TX 78701-3236

ALLDREDGE, LEROY ROMNEY, retired geophysicist; b. Mesa, Ariz., Feb. 6, 1917; s. Leo and Ida (Romney) A.; m. Larita Williams, Dec. 27, 1940; children—Carol, David Leroy, Joseph Leo, Gary Dean, Mark Evans, Janice, Luann. B.S., U. Ariz., 1939, M.S., 1940; M.Sc. in Engring, Harvard, 1953; Ph.D., U. Md., 1955. Instr. physics U. Ariz., 1940-41; fed. radio insp. FCC, Los Angeles, also Washington, 1941-44; radio engr. dept. terrestrial magnetism Carnegie Inst. of Washington, 1944-45; chief electricity and magnetism div. Naval Ordnance Lab., White Oak, Md., 1945-55; analyst operations research office Johns Hopkins, 1955-59; research geophysicist Coast and Geodetic Survey, Dept. Commerce, Washington, 1959-66; acting dir. Inst. Earth Scis., Environmental Sci. Services Adminstrn., Boulder, Colo., 1966; dir. Earth Scis. Labs., 1967-69, Earth Sci. Lab. Nat. Oceanographic and Atmospheric Adminstrn., 1969-73; research geophysicist U.S. Geol. Survey, 1973-88; gen. sec., dir. central bur. Internat. Assn. Geomagnetism and Aeronomy, 1963-75. Assoc. editor: Jour. Geophys. Research, 1966-69. Mem. Am. Geophys. Union (sect. on geomagnetism and aeronomy 1950-56, v.p. sect. 1956-59, pres. sect. 1959-61, chmn. Eastern meeting com. 1962-66), Sigma Xi, Phi Kappa Phi. Mem. Ch. of Jesus Christ of Latter-day Saints. Home and Office: 4475 Chippewa Dr Boulder CO 80303-3616 *Science and engineering are very precise. For a man to properly help with the orderly development in any area of science he must treat his data and report them with strict honesty. The same principle is even more valuable in ordinary daily contacts with his friends and acquaintances. A performance that includes half truths or deceit in any form will very likely lead to unhappiness.*

ALLEGRA, ANTONIA, editor, writer; b. San Francisco, Feb. 21, 1946; d. Carlo Louis and Antonette Delfina (Laiolo) Lastreto; m. John H. Griffin, Aug. 14, 1965 (div. Feb. 1983); children: John, Deanna, Paul; m. Donn L. Black, Apr. 14, 1996. Student, Harvard U., 1969-71, Santa Clara U., 1963-65; Culinary Degree, Ecole de Cuisine Gaston, LeNotre, Paris, 1978, Le Cordon Bleu, Paris, 1981. Food editor San Diego (Calif.) Tribune, 1982-88; dir. culinary programs Beringer Winery, St. Helena, Calif., 1988-91; co-host Wine Valley Radio, St. Helena, 1995—; dir. Symposium for Profl. Food Writers, 1989—; dir. adminstrn. and comm. liaison Culinary Inst. of Am., St. Helena, 1991-95; pres. Internat. Assn. of Culinary Profls., Louisville, 1997; editor-in-chief Appellation Mag., Napa, Calif., 1992-96; lectr./cooking demonstrator Seabourn/Radisson Cruises, 1975-93; judge various food competitions; panelist various food/wine confs.; speaker in field; writing coach, carrer coach. Author: (book) Napa Valley: The Ultimate Winery Guide, 1993; contbr. articles to profl. jours.; author introductions to books in field. Recipient award for Best New Regional Mag. (Appellation), Western Pub. Assn., L.A., 1994; named Woman of Distinction in the Culinary Professions, U. Calif. San Diego Cancer Ctr., 1987. Mem. Internat. Assn. of Culinary Profls. (v.p. 1996-97, pres. 1997-98), Internat. Women's Forum West, Assn. of Food Journalists (v.p. 1987), Napa Valley Culinary Alliance (pres. 1988-89), San Francisco Profl. Food Soc. (bd. dirs. 1989-90), Les Dames d'Escoffier Internat. (pres. San Francisco chpt. 1992), Napa Valley Wine Libr. Assn., Sonoma County Culinary Guild, Women for WineSense, Internat. Women's Forum, Sigma Delta Chi, others. Avocation: cooking. Office: Antonia Allegra & Assocs PO Box 663 Saint Helena CA 94574-0663

ALLEGRUCCI, DONALD LEE, state supreme court justice; b. Pittsburg, Kans., Sept. 19, 1936; s. Nello and Josephine Marie (Funaro) A.; m. Joyce Ann Thompson, Nov. 30, 1963; children: Scott David, Bowen Jay. AB, Pittsburg State U., 1959; JD, Washburn U., 1963. Bar: Kans. 1963. Asst. county atty. Butler County, El Dorado, Kans., 1963-67; state senator Kans. Legislature, Topeka, 1976-80; mem. Kans. Pub. Relations Bd., 1981-82; dist. judge Kans. 11th Jud. Dist., Pittsburg, 1982-87, adminstrv. judge, 1983-87; justice Kans. Supreme Ct., Topeka, 1987—; instr. Pittsburg State U., 1969-72; exec. dir. Mid-Kans. Community Action Program, Inc. Mem. Dem. State Com., 1974-80; candidate 5th Congl. Dist., 1978; past pres. Heart Assn.; bd. dirs. YMCA. Served with USAF, 1959-60. Mem. Kans. Bar Assn. Democrat. Office: Kansas Supreme Court 374 Kansas Judicial Ctr 301 SW 10th Ave Fl 3 Topeka KS 66612-1599

ALLEN, ALICE, communications and marketing executive; b. N.Y.C., May 31, 1943; d. C. Edmonds and Helen (McCreery) A.; 1 child, Helen. Student, Conn. Coll., 1961. Pres. Alice Allen, Inc., N.Y.C., 1970-83; sr. v.p. Robert Marston, N.Y.C., 1983-84, Cunningham & Walsh, N.Y.C., 1984-86, Carl Byoir (acquired by Hill & Knowlton), N.Y.C., 1986; sr. v.p., dir. comms. and corp. mktg. Hill & Knowlton, N.Y.C., 1986-88; pres., owner Allen Comms. Group, Inc., N.Y.C., 1988-95, Alice Allen Comms, 1995—. Bd. dirs. Family Dynamics, N.Y.C., 1976-78, Veritas, 1980-85; v.p. Jr. League, N.Y.C., 1975-76; Mem. adv. bd. Enterprise Found., 1992—. Mem. Pub. Rels. Soc. Am., Pub. Publicity Assn. (pres. 1969-71), Women's Media Group, Comm. Network. Office: Alice Allen Comms 320 E 72nd St New York NY 10021-4769

ALLEN, ANNA JEAN, chiropractor; b. Henderson, Ky., Apr. 6, 1955; d. Harold D. and Aiko (Nakashima) A. AS, U. Ky., 1973, BS, 1976; Dr.Chiropractic, Palmer U., 1980; postgrad., Pan Am. U., 1981, San

Antonio Coll., 1983. Health instr. Nautilus, Davenport, Iowa, 1978-80; dir. chiropractic Harlington, Tex., 1980-81, Handley Chiropractic, San Antonio, Tex., 1982-83, NE Chiropractic Ctr., El Paso, Tex., 1983-84, Viscount Chiropractic, El Paso, 1984—; bd. dirs. White Harvest Ministries. Mem. exec. com. Nat. Right to Life Com., 1986; active Found. for Chiropractic Edn. and Rsch., 1989-90, 90-91, 92-93; de. Rep. Nat. Congl. Com. Recipient El Paso Comty. Health Fair citation, 1989, Presdl. Cert. Appreciation, 1989, Congl. Cert. Appreciation, 1991, Comty. Leaders Am. award, others. Mem. NAFE, Am. Bus. Woman's Assn., Nat. Fedn. Ind. Bus., Chiropractic Orthopedist Assn., Christian Chiropractic Assn., Found. for Chiropractic Rsch., Found. for Chiropractic Rsch., Tex. Palmer Alumni Assn., Palmer Alumni Assn., Am. Chiropractic Assn., Tex. Chiropractic Assn.; bd. dir. Fellowship of Christian Athletics, El Paso ANS for Life. Avocations: scuba diving, weight lifting, running, bicycling, painting. Office: Viscount Chiropractic Health Ctr 8838 Viscount Blvd El Paso TX 79925-5822

ALLEN, ANNA MARIE, financial executive; b. Ft. Scott, Kans., Aug. 3, 1955; d. Harold Laverne and Dorothy Arlene Kirk; m. John Leroy Allen, Sept. 18, 1982. AA, Johnson County C.C., Overland Park, Kans., 1976; BSBA in Fin., Pittsburg (Kans.) State U., 1979; MBA in Internat. Bus., Ohio State U., 1995. CPA, Kans. Asst. teller supr. Kans. Nat. Bank & Trust, Prairie Village, 1975-77; bookkeeper Foodtown, Pittsburg, 1978-79; sr. v.p. tax GRA, Inc., Merriam, Kans., 1979-89; sr. cons. Grant Thornton, Wichita, Kans., 1989-91; mgr. fin. ops. Legent Corp., Columbus, Ohio, 1991-94; asst. treas. CompuServe Inc., Columbus, 1994-96; v.p. fin. North Am. Baking, Cin., 1997—. Com. bd. Kansas City (Mo.) Ballet Guild, 1985-89; past mem. Jr. League Kans. City, Columbus Jr. League; bd. dirs. Jr. League, Cin.; charter mem. Women's Resource Ctr., Johnson County bd. dirs., 1986-89. Mem. AICPA, AAUW (bd. dirs. Shawnee Mission, Kans chpt. 1979-89), Treasury Mgmt. Assn., Am. Legion Aux., Tri-Health Athletic Club, Phi Kappa Phi, Delta Mu Delta. Baptist. Avocations: running, tatting, the flute.

ALLEN, B. MARC, managed care executive; b. Balt.; s. Ralph A. and Frona B. A.; B.A., U. Balt., 1967, J.D., 1971; m. Judy E. Luray, Jan. 24, 1967; children—Lara Ann, Mason Luray. Mgr. med. affairs Md. Blue Cross, Balt., 1967-73; cons. Am. Health Systems, Boston, 1973-74; dir. field ops. Bay State PSRO, Boston, 1974-75; exec. dir. Essex Physicians' Rev. Orgn., South Orange, N.J., 1975; chmn., chief exec. officer Med. Rev. Corp., Randolph, N.J., MediChoice Provider Network, Randolph; cons. in field; guest lectr. health policy Rutgers U.; expert witness U.S. Senate Fin. Com., U.S. Select Com. on Aging. Active SSS, 1972-73, New Democratic Coalition, 1969-70; past-pres. Temple B'nai Or, Morristown, N.J. Mem. Nat. Health Lawyers Assn., Am. Med. Peer Rev., Inc. (chmn. task force on impact). Contbr. articles to profl. jours. Office: 1240 Sussex Tpke Randolph NJ 07869-2921

ALLEN, BEATRICE, music educator, pianist; b. N.Y.C., June 30, 1917; d. Samuel and Rose (Krell) Hyman; m. Eugene Murray Allen, Jan. 23, 1937; children: Marlene Allen Galzin, Julian Lewis. Student NYU, 1933-36; diploma (scholar), Inst. Musical Arts, N.Y.C., 1939, postgrad. (scholar), 1939-40; diploma (fellow, letter commendation), Juilliard Grad. Sch., N.Y.C., 1943; BA magna cum laude Cedar Crest Coll., 1980. Mem. faculty prep. div. Juilliard Sch. Music, 1957-69, Moravian Coll., 1967-68, Northampton County Area Community Coll., 1968-70, Manhattan Sch. Music, 1969-89; mem. founding faculty Community Music Sch., Allentown, Pa., 1982—; artist-in-residence, condr. Tchrs. Workshop, Antioch Coll., Yellow Springs, Ohio, 1966; Bach lectr., recitals various univs.; concert appearances Town Hall, N.Y.C., Chautauqua, N.Y., others. Winner N.J. Artists contest, 1936. Mem. Music Tchrs. Nat. Assn. (program chmn. Lehigh Valley chpt. 1981-82), Pa. Music Tchrs. Assn. Address: 2100 Main St Bethlehem PA 18017-3752

ALLEN, BELLE, management consulting firm executive, communications company executive; b. Chgo.; d. Isaac and Clara (Friedman) A. U. Chgo. Cert. conf. mgr. Internat. Inst. Conf. Planning and Mgmt., 1989. Report, spl. correspondent The Leader Newspapers, Chgo., Washington, 1960-64; Cons., v.p., treas., dir. William Karp Cons. Co. Inc., Chgo., 1961-79, chmn. bd., pres., treas., 1979—; pres. Belle Allen Comms., Chgo., 1961—; nat. corr. CCA Press, 1990—; v.p., treas., bd. dirs. Cultural Arts Survey Inc., Chgo., 1965-79; cons., bd. dirs. Am. Diversified Rsch. Corp., Chgo., 1967-70; v.p., sec., bd. dirs. Mgmt. Performance Systems Inc., 1976-77; cons. City Club Chgo., 1962-65, Ill. Commn. on Tech. Progress, 1965-67; hearing mem. Ill. Gov.'s Grievance Panel for State Employees, 1979—; hearing mem. grievance panel Ill. Dept. Transp., 1985—; mem. adv. governing bd. Ill. Coalition on Employment of Women, 1980-88; spl. program advisor President's Project Partnership, 1980-88; mem. consumer adv. coun. FRS, 1979-82; reporter CCA Press Svc., 1990—; panel mem. Free Press vs. Fair Trial Nat. Ctr. Freedom of Info. Studies Loyola U. Law Sch., 1993, mem. planning com. Freedom of Info. awards, 1993; conf. chair The Swedish Inst. Press Ethics: How to Handle, 1993. Editor: Operations Research and the Management of Mental Health Systems, 1968; contbr. articles to profl. jours. Mem. campaign staff Adlai E. Stevenson II, 1952, 56, John F. Kennedy, 1960; founding mem. women's bd. United Cerebral Palsy Assn., Chgo., 1954, bd. dirs., 1954-58; pres. Dem. Fedn. Ill., 1958-61; pres. conf. staff Eleanor Roosevelt, 1960; mem. Welfare Pub. Rels. Forum, 1960-61; bd. dirs., mem. exec. com., chmn. pub. rels. com. Regional Ballet Ensemble, Chgo., 1961-63; bd. dirs. Soc. Chgo. Strings, 1963-64; mem. Ind. Dem. Coalition, 1968-69; bd. dirs. Citizens for Polit. Change, 1969; campaign mgr. aldermanic election 42d ward Chgo. City Coun., 1969; mem. selection com. Robert Aragon Scholarship, 1991; planning com. mem. Hutchins Era reunion U. Chgo., 1995; mem. reunion planning com. U. Chgo., 1995. Recipient Outstanding Svc. award United Cerebral Palsy Assn., Chgo., 1954, 55, Chgo. Lighthouse for Blind, 1986, Spl. Comms. award The White House, 1961, cert. of appreciation Ill. Dept. Human Rights, 1985, Internat. Assn. Ofcl. Human Rights Agys., 1985; selected as reference source Am. Bicentennial Rsch. Inst. Libr. Human Resources, 1973; named Hon. Citizen, City of Alexandria, Va., 1985. Mem. AAAS, NOW, AAAU, Affirmative Action Assn. (bd. dirs. 1981-85, chmn. mem. and programs com. 1981-85, pres. 1983—), Chgo. Bar Assn. (pub. mem., jud. evaluation com.), Fashion Group (bd. dirs. 1981-83, chmn. Restrospective View of an Hist. Decade 1960-70, editor The Bull. 1981), Indsl. Rels. Rsch. Assn. (bd. dirs., chmn. pers. placement com. 1960-61), Sarah Siddons Soc., Soc. Pers. Adminstrs., Women's Equity Action League, Nat. Assn. Inter-Group Rels. Ofcls. (nat. conf. program 1959), Publicity Club Chgo. (chmn. inter-city rels. com. 1960-61, Disting. Svc. award 1968), Ill. C. of C. (cmty. rels. com., alt. mem. labor rels. com. 1971-74), Chgo. C. of C. and Industry (merit employment com. 1961-63), Internat. Press Club Chgo. (charter 1992—, bd. dirs. 1992—), Chgo. Press Club (chmn. women's activities 1969-71), U. Chgo. Club of Met. Chgo. (program com. 1993—, chair summer quarter programs 1994), Soc. Profl. Journalists (Chgo. Headline Club 1992—, regional conf. planning com. 1993, co-chair Peter Lisagor awards 1993, program com. 1992—), Assn. Women Journalists, Nat. Trust for Historic Preservation. Office: 111 E Chestnut St Ste 36G Chicago IL 60611-6013

ALLEN, BESSIE MALVINA, music educator, church organist; b. LaKemp, Okla., Oct. 14, 1918; d. Percy J. and Mary Allen (Hagler) Gheen; m. Edgar Charles Allen, Aug. 29, 1940 (dec. May 1981); children: Stanley Charles, Stephen Wayne. BA in English, Tex. Woman's U., 1939; MA in Music, W. Tex. State U., 1970. Cert. secondary edn. Tchr. English Balko (Okla.) High Sch. and Jr. High Sch., 1939-40; pvt. practice Phillips, Tex., 1950-85; tchr. music frank Phillips Coll., Borger, Tex., 1960-63, 65-73, 76-85; pvt. practice Borger, 1986—; organist First Bapt. Ch., Borger, 1947-65, Faith Covenant Ch.-Ind., Borger, 1970-81, First Christian Ch., Borger, 1981-82, Faith Covenant Ch., Borger, 1982—. Active Nat. Rep. Senatorial Com., Washington, 1988-91. Recipient Presdl. Order of Merit, Nat. Rep. Senatorial Com., 1991; McCulley Organ scholar, W. Tex. State U., Canyon, 1969. Mem. Music Tchrs. Nat. Assn., Tex. Fedn. Music Clubs, Amarillo Music Tchrs. Assn., Borger Music Club. Avocations: gardening, reading. Home and Office: 221 Inverness St Borger TX 79007-8215

ALLEN, BETTY (MRS. RITTEN EDWARD LEE, III), mezzo-soprano; b. Campbell, Ohio, Mar. 17, 1930; d. James Corr and Dora Catherine (Mitchell) A.; m. Ritten Edward Lee, III, Oct. 17, 1953; children: Anthony Edward, Juliana Catherine. Student, Wilberforce U., 1944-46; certificate, Hartford Sch. Music, 1953; pupil voice, Sarah Peck More, Zinka Milanov, Paul Ulanowsky, Carolina Segrera Holden; LHD (hon.), Wittenberg U., 1971; MusD (hon.), Union Coll., 1981; DFA (hon.), Adelphi U., 1990, Bklyn. Coll., 1991; LittD (hon.), Clark U., 1993; MusD (hon.), New Sch. Social Rsch., 1994. Faculty Phila. Mus. Acad., 1979, Manhattan Sch. Music, 1971, N.C. Sch. Arts, 1978-87; now faculty Harlem Sch. Arts; tchr. master classes Inst. Teatro Colon, 1985-86, Curtis Inst. Music, 1987—; exec. dir. Harlem Sch. Arts, 1979, now pres.; vis. faculty Sibelius Akademie, Helsinki, Finland, 1976; mem. adv. bd. music panel Amherst Coll.; mem. music panel N.Y. State Council of the Arts, Dept. State Office Cultural Presentations, Nat. Endowment Arts.; bd. dirs. Arts Alliance, Karl Weigl Found., Diller-Quaile Sch. Music, U.S. Com. for UNICEF, Manhattan Sch. Music, Theatre Devel. Fund, Children's Storefront; mem. adv. bd. Bloomingdale House of Music; bd. vis. artists Boston U.; bd. dirs., mem. exec. com. Carnegie Hall, Nat. Found. for Advancement in the Arts; bd. dirs. Chamber Music Soc. of Lincoln Ctr., N.Y.C. Housing Authority Orch., Independent Sch. Orch., N.Y.C. Opera CO., Joy in Singing, Arts & Bus. Coun.; mem. Mayor's adv. commn. Cultural Affairs. Appeared as soloist: Leonard Bernstein's Jeremiah Symphony, Tanglewood, 1951, Virgil Thomson's Four Saints in Three Acts, N.Y.C. and Paris, 1952, N.Y.C. Light Opera Co., 1954; recitalist, also soloist with major symphonies on tours including ANTA-State Dept. tours, Europe, N. Africa, Caribbean, Can., U.S., S.Am., Far East, 1954-, S.Am. tour, 1968, Bellas Artes Opera, Mexico City, 1970; recital debut, Town Hall, N.Y.C., 1958, ofcl. debuts, London, Berlin, 1958, formal opera debut, Teatro Colon, Buenos Aires, Argentina, 1964; U.S. opera debut San Francisco Opera, 1966; N.Y.C. opera debut, 1973, Mini-Met. debut, 1973; Broadway debut in Treemonisha, 1975; opened new civic theaters in San Jose, Calif., and Regina, Sask., Can., concert hall, Lyndon Baines Johnson Library, Austin, Tex., 1971; artist-in-residence, Phila. Opera Co.; appeared with Caramoor Music Festival, summer 1965, 71, Cin. May Festival, 1972, Santa Fe Opera, 1972, 75, Canadian Opera Co., Winnipeg, Man., 1972, 77, Washington Opera Co., 1971, Tanglewood Festival, 1951, 52, 53, 67, 74, Oslo, The Hague, Montreal, Kansas City, Houston and Santa Fe operas, 1975, Saratoga Festival, 1975, Casals Festival, 1967, 68, 69, 76, Helsinki Festival, 1976, Marlboro Festival, 1967-74, numerous radio and TV performances, U.S., Can., Mex., Eng., Germany, Scandinavia; rec. artist, London, Vox, Capitol, Odeon-Pathe, Decca, Deutsche Grammophon, Columbia Records, RCA Victor records; represented U.S. in Cultural Olympics, Mexico City, 1968. Recipient Marian Anderson award, 1953-54, Nat. Music League Mgmt. award, 1953, 52 St Am. Festival Duke Ellington Meml. award, 1989, Bowery award Bowery Bank, 1989, Harlem Sch. of the Arts award Harlem Sch. and Isaac Stern, 1990, Womans Day Celebration award St. Thomas Episcopal Ch., 1990, St. Thomas Ch. award St. Thomas Catholic Ch., 1990, Men's Day Celebration award St. Paul's Ch., 1990, Martell House of Segram award Avery Fisher Hall, 1990; named Best Singer of Season Critics' Circle, Argentina and Chile, 1959, Best Singer of Season Critics' Circle, Uruguay, 1961; Martha Baird Rockefeller Aid to Music grantee, 1953, 58; John Hay Whitney fellow, 1953-54; Ford Found. concert soloist grantee, 1963-64. Mem. NAACP, Urban League, Hartford Mus. Club (life), Am. Guild Mus. Artists, Actors Equity, AFTRA, Silvermine Guild Artists, Jeunesses Musicales, Gioventu Musicale, Student Sangverein Trondheim, Unitarian-Universalist Women's Fedn., Nat. Negro Musicians Assn. (life), Concert Artists Guild, Met. Opera Guild, Amherst Glee Club (hon. life), Union Coll. Glee Club (hon. life), Met. Mus. Art, Mus. Modern Art, Am. Mus. Natural History, Century Assn., Sigma Alpha Iota (hon.). Unitarian-Universalist. Clubs: Cosmopolitan, Second. Office: Harlem Sch of Arts 645 Saint Nicholas Ave New York NY 10030-1098 *To be able to combine childhood fantasies of self-expression, to travel and roam the world, to meet again and make new friends, to serve the demanding, yet fulfilling art of music - these are some of the wonderful joys of being a singer. I have been free to be me.*

ALLEN, BRENDA JOYCE, management consultant, editor-in-chief; b. Detroit, June 10, 1950; d. William Howard and Ottie Fay (Mills) A.; m. Robert Edward Arthur Lightbourne, Mar. 2 (div. Jan., 1980); 1 child, Shonja Diane; m. Thomas M. Kyle, May 19, 1984; children: Portia Lynne Allen Kyle, Tomantha Mercedes Allen Kyle. AB in Math., U. Calif., 1976; MS in Engring., George Washington U., D.C., 1981. Cert. profl. logistician, Soc. Logistics Engrs. Sci. data analyst Lawrence Berkeley Lab., Berkeley, Calif., 1972-76; lectr. Howard U., Washington, 1977-78; sr. fellow Logistics Mgmt. Inst., Washington; sr. logistics engr., sr. sys. analyst TASC, Reading, Mass., 1983-85; program logistics engr. ITT Defense Comm. Divsn., Nutley, N.J., 1985-87; adj. prof. Bergen C.C., Paramus, N.J., 1989-94; sr. cons. NCR, Berkeley Heights, N.J., 1994-97; cons. UN, World Bank, AT&T, Bankers Trust, Washington Global Mgmt. and N.Y.C., 1983-84. Editor in chief Global Digest mag., 1995—. Sec., bd. dirs., exec. Teaneck (N.J.) Jr. Soccer League, 1995—; mem. exec. bd. Working Parents Assn., Teaneck, 1995-96, Gifted and Talented Parents, Teaneck, 1995-96; mem. Lowell Sch. Quality Mgmt. Team, 1996-98. Mem. Calif. Scholarship Fedn. (life), N. Jersey Soc. Logistics Engrs., Nat. Assn. Self Employed, Delta Sigma Theta (local chpt. treas. 1972—, Montgomery County alumni treas. 1977-78, Golden Life 1975). Avocations: photography, piano, violin, clarinet, stained glass, renovations. Home: 585 Ramapo Rd Teaneck NJ 07666-1803 Office: BJ Assocs 585 Ramapo Rd Teaneck NJ 07666-1803

ALLEN, BRUCE JOHN, writer, activist; b. Buffalo, Apr. 16, 1960; s. John Edgar and Isabel Sarah (Nicholson) A.; m. Sarah Bragg Lindsley, Mar. 31, 1992; 1 child, John Edgar. BA in English lit. magna cum laude, U. Colo., 1985. Columnist Colo. Daily, Boulder, 1985; field mgr. Colo. Pub. Interest Rsch. Group, Boulder, 1985-86; editor Nat. Student News Svc., Boston, 1986-88; writer The New Paper, Providence, 1988-91; comm. dir. Save the Bay, Providence, 1990-92, Ctr. for Econ. Conversion, Mountain View, Calif., 1993-96; publs. cons. Calif. Abortion Rights Action League, San Francisco, 1993. Mem. Save El Dorado Mountain Campaign, Boulder, 1985; advisor People Against the CIA, Providence, 1989; co-founder Preserve the Presidio Campaign, San Francisco, 1994; bd. dirs. Calif. Peace Action, 1996—. Home: 560 Crestlake Dr San Francisco CA 94132-1325

ALLEN, BRUCE TEMPLETON, economics educator; b. Oak Park, Ill., Jan. 27, 1938; s. William Hendry and Harriet (Iverson) A.; m. Virginia Elizabeth Peterson, June 16, 1962; children: Elizabeth Rachel, Catherine Grace. AB, De Pauw U., 1960; MBA, U. Chgo., 1961; PhD, Cornell U., 1965. Asst. prof. econs. Mich. State U., East Lansing, 1965-75, assoc. prof., 1975-80, prof., 1980—. Mem. Am. Econ. Assn. Avocations: railroads. Office: Mich State U Dept Econs East Lansing MI 48824

ALLEN, CAROL LINNEA OSTROM, art educator; b. Phila., Apr. 23, 1936; d. Gustaf Adolph Ostrom and Anne Marie (Scheib) Heckman; m. David Wilford Allen Sr., Mar. 8, 1932; children: Jonathan Ostrom, David Wilford. BS in Art Edn. with honors, Kutztown U., 1958; MA in Art Edn., U. of the Arts, 1991. Cert. tchr., supr. art, English. Jr. H.S. art tchr. West York (Pa.) Sch. Dist., 1958-60; elem. art supr. Colonial Sch. Dist., Plymouth Meeting, Pa., 1960-62; substitute tchr., art tchr., English tchr. Phoenixville (Pa.) Area Sch. Dist., 1968—, art dept. head, yearbook advisor, 1991—, mem. strategic planning com., 1992-94; presenter at state and nat. art confs., 1986—. Exhibited in group shows at Nat. Art Edn. Assn. Electronic Gallery, 1989, 95. Mem. LWV, Valley Forge, 1992—. Mem. AAUW, NOW, Nat. Art Edn. Assn., Pa. Art Edn. Assn., Phoenixville Area Edn. Assn. (polit. action com. for edn. chair 1992—). Office: Phoenixville Area Sch Dist 1120 Gay St Phoenixville PA 19460-4417

ALLEN, CHARLES ETHELBERT, III, lawyer; b. Louisville, May 14, 1948; s. Charles Ethelbert and Elsie Kathryn (Liliequist) A. BA, Duke U., 1970; JD, U. Ky., 1977. Bar: Ky. 1977, U.S. Dist. Ct. (we. dist.) Ky. 1977, U.S. Dist. Ct. (ea. dist.) Ky. 1985, U.S. Ct. Appeals (6th cir.) 1985, U.S. Dist. Ct. (so. dist.) Ind. 1998. With Brown, Todd & Heyburn, Louisville, 1977—, ptnr., 1983—, vice chair labor & employment group, 1983—, assoc. coord., 1987-93. Dir. Louisville Regional Sci. Fair, 1994—, v.p., 1997—, judge, 1993—; dir. Internat. Sci. and Engring. Fair Ky., Inc., 1994-98, sec. 1995-98; vice chair ISEF 97, 1994-96, grand awards judge ISEF, 1995; dir. Ky. Sci. Fair Endowment, Inc., 1998—, sec., 1998—; presenter numerous programs, lectrs. astronomy, space sci., 1960—. 1st lt. USAF, 1971-74. Recipient Air Force Commendation medal, 1974; named to Waggener H.S. Hall of Fame, 1997. Mem. Am. Astronomical League (bd. dirs., v.p. 1994-98, pres. 1998—, chair Great Lakes Region, 1991-95, chair, founder Nat. Young Astronomer award 1991—), Louisville Astronomical Soc. (bd. dirs., pres. 1991-94, v.p. 1990-91, 95-96, 97-98, sec. 1994-95, 96-97), Beta Omega Sigma, Pi Sigma Alpha. Republican. Presbyterian. Avocations: astronomy, pub. edn. astronomy, sci. fair orgn., ski racing, mountain climbing. Home: 1007 Rollingwood Ln Goshen KY 40026-9523 Office: Brown Todd & Heyburn 3200 Aegon Ctr Louisville KY 40202-3363

ALLEN, CHARLES EUGENE, college administrator, agriculturist; b. Burley, Idaho, Jan. 25, 1939; s. Charles W. and Elsie P. (Fowler) A.; m. Connie J. Block, June 19, 1960; children: Kerry J., Tamara S. BS, U. Idaho, 1961; MS, U. Wis.-Madison, 1963, PhD, 1966. NSF postdoctoral fellow Sydney, Australia, 1966-67; asst. prof. of agr. U. Minn., St. Paul, 1967-69, assoc. prof., 1969-72, prof., 1972—, dean Coll. Agr., assoc. dir. agrl. expt. sta., 1984-88, acting v.p., 1988-90, v.p. agriculture, forestry and home econs., dir. Minn. Agr. Expt. Sta., 1990-95, provost profl. studies, dir. Minn. Agr. Expt. Sta., 1995-97, dir. global outreach, exec. dir. Internat. progs., 1997-98, exec. dir. internat. programs, 1998—; vis. prof. Pa. State U., 1978; cons. to industry; C. Glen King lectr. Wash. State U., 1981; Univ. lectr. U. Wyo., Laramie, 1984; adj. prof. Hassan II U., Rabat, Morocco, 1984. Contbr. numerous chpts. to books, articles to sci. jours. on growth and metabolism of muscle and adipose tissue, meat quality. Recipient Horace T. Morse-Amoco Found. award in undergrad. edn. U. Minn., 1984, Disting. Tchr. award U. Minn. Coll. Agr., 1984, Disting. Alumni award U. Idaho, 1989. Fellow AAAS, Inst. Food Tech.; mem. Am. Meat Sci. Assn. (dir. 1970-72; Research award 1980, Signal Service award, 1985), Am. Soc. Animal Sci. (Exceptional Research Achievement award 1972, Research award 1977), Sigma Xi. Avocations: bowling, photography, reading, outdoor sports, golf.

ALLEN, CHARLES MENGEL, federal judge; b. Louisville, Nov. 22, 1916; s. Arthur Dwight and Jane (Mengel) A.; m. Betty Anne Cardwell, June 25, 1949; children: Charles Dwight, Angela M. BA, Yale U., 1941; LLB, U. Louisville, 1943. Bar: Ky. 1944. Assoc. Doolin, Helm, Stites and Wood, 1944-45; pvt. practice Louisville, 1946-47; assoc. Farnsley, Hottell and Stephenson, 1947-53; pvt. practice, 1953-55; asst. U.S. atty. Western Dist. Ky., Dept. Justice, 1955-59; ptnr. Booth, Walker & Allen, Louisville, 1959-61; circuit judge Jefferson Cir. Ct., 4th Chancery Br. Jefferson County, 1961-71; dist. judge U.S. Dist. Ct. (we. dist.) Ky., Louisville, 1971-77, chief judge, 1977-85, sr. judge, 1985—. Named Outstanding Alumnus U. Louisville, 1984; recipient Brandeis award U. Louisville Law Sch., 1985, Thomas Hogan Meml. Found award Ky. Civil Liberties Union, 1986, Grauman award U. Louisville, 1986. Mem. ABA, Fed. Bar Assn., Ky. Bar Assn. (Judge of Yr. award 1996), Louisville Bar Assn., Nat. Ry. Hist. Soc. Avocations: tennis, trains, photography, bridge. Office: US Dist Ct 252 US Courthouse 601 W Broadway Ste 450 Louisville KY 40202-2249*

ALLEN, CHARLES NORMAN, television, film and video producer; b. Miami, July 13, 1944; s. Claude Braswell and Virginia Lucille (Gravitt) A.; m. Susan Carole Dorn, May 1, 1970; children: Jennifer, Brian. BS, U. Miami, 1967. V.p. Tel-Air Interests Inc., Miami, 1967-79; pres. Cinema East Corp., Miami, 1979—, World Studios Corp., Atlanta, 1987—, ADR Internat., Miami, 1991—; bd. dirs. World Studios Corp., ADR Internat. Representer prodns. U.S. internat. film events CINE-Washington, 1974, 75, 80, 81, 87, 88, 89, 92. Trustee Dade County Pub. Health Trust; commr. Biscayne Park, Fla., 1974-76; active Dade County Dem. Exec. Commn., 1976-80, Dade Dem. Treas., 1976-79; mem. Gov.'s Fla. Motion Picture and TV Adv. Coun., 1978-80. Mem. Am. Advt. Fed., South Fla. Film & Tape Producers Assn., Assn. Indep. Comml. Producers, Nat. Advt. Fraternity, Greater Miami Advt. Fed., Advt. Miami, Greater Miami C. of C., Sigma Chi Frat., Iron Arrow Honor Soc., Alpha Delta Sigma. Democrat. Methodist. Office: Cinema East Corp 5859 Biscayne Blvd Miami FL 33137-2690

ALLEN, CHARLES RAYMOND, television station executive. Gen. mgr. KAET-Ariz. State U., Tempe. Office: KAET Ariz State U Stauffer Hall B-Wing PO Box 871405 Tempe AZ 85287-1405*

ALLEN, CHARLES RICHARD, retired financial executive; b. Cleve., Mar. 10, 1926; s. Charles Ross and Jennie (Harmon) A.; m. Marion Elizabeth Taylor, Aug. 17, 1946; children: Kathleen Allen Templin, Jeanne Allen Duffy, Kenneth. Student, Occidental Coll., 1942-43; BS, UCLA, 1945. Acctg. supr. N.Am. Aviation, Inc., Los Angeles, 1946-55; div. controller TRW, Inc., Los Angeles, 1955-61, dir. fin., 1961-64; assoc. controller TRW, Inc., Cleve., 1964-66, controller, 1966-67, v.p., 1967-77, exec. v.p., 1977-86, chief fin. officer, 1967-86; advisor New Court Ptnrs., N.Y.C.; bd. dirs. Titan Corp., San Diego. Trustee Maritime Mus. San Diego; mem. San Diego World Affairs Coun. Served with USNR, 1943-46. Mem. Fin. Execs. Inst., Univ. Club, City Club of San Diego. Home: 1730 Avenida Del Mundo Coronado CA 92118-3021

ALLEN, CHARLES WILLIAM, mechanical engineering educator; b. Newbury, Eng., July 24, 1932; s. Isaac William and Emily (Butler) A.; m. Rita Joyce Pembroke, Dec. 28, 1957; children: Malcolm Charles, Verity Simone. B.S., U. London, 1957; M.S., Case Inst. Tech., 1962; Ph.D., U. Calif., Davis, 1966. Design engr. Lear Siegler, Cleve., 1957-62; group leader Aerojet Gen., Sacramento, 1962-63; assoc. engring. U. Calif., Davis, 1965-66; assoc. prof. Calif. State U., Chico, 1966-71; prof. engring. Calif. State U., 1971-88, prof. emeritus, 1988—, head mech. engring., 1976-79, 82-84; vis. fellow U. Leicester, Eng., 1974; vis. lectr., rschr. U. Guadalajara, Mex., 1986, guest prof., 1997. Contbr. articles to profl. jours. Fellow NASA, 1967, 68, 69. Mem. ASME. Home: 1691 Filbert Ave Chico CA 95926-1777 Office: Calif State U Dept Mech Engring Chico CA 95629

ALLEN, CHRISTOPHER C., publishing executive. V.p., pub. Cooking Light mag., Birmingham, Ala. Office: care Cooking Light PO Box 1748 2100 Lakeshore Dr Birmingham AL 35201*

ALLEN, CLARENCE RODERIC, geologist, educator; b. Palo Alto, Calif., Feb. 15, 1925; s. Hollis Partridge and Delight (Wright) A. BA, Reed Coll., 1949; MS, Cal. Inst Tech., 1951, PhD, 1954. Asst. prof. geology U. Minn., 1954-55; mem. faculty Calif. Inst. Tech., 1955—, prof. geology and geophysics, 1964-91, prof. emeritus, 1991—; interim dir. Seismological Lab., 1965-67, acting chmn. division of geological scis., 1967-68; Phi Beta Kappa Disting. lectr., 1978; chmn. cons. bd. earthquake analysis Calif. Dept. Water Resources, 1965-74; chmn. geol. hazards adv. com. for program Cal. Resources Agy., 1965-66; mem. earth scis. adv. panel NSF, 1965-68, chmn., 1967-68, mem. adv. com. environmental scis., 1970-72; mem. U.S. Geol. Survey adv. panel to Nat. Center Earthquake Research, Calif. Cal. Mining and Geology Bd., 1969-75, chmn., 1975; mem. task force on earthquake hazard reduction Office Sci. and Tech., 1970-71; mem. Can. Earthquake Prediction Evaluation Council, 1983-88; vice-chmn. Nat. Acad. Sci. Com. on Advanced Study in china, 1981-85; chmn. geology sect. Nat. Acad. Sci., 1982-85, Com. on Scholarly Communication with People's Republic China, 1984-89, chmn., 1987-89; mem. Nat. Acad. Sci. Commn. on Phys. Scis., Math. and Resources; mem. Pres.'s Nuclear Waste Tech. Rev. Bd., 1989-97. Served to 1st lt. USAAF, 1943-46. Recipient G.K. Gilbert award seismic geology Carnegie Instn., 1960. Fellow Am. Geophys. Union, Geol. Soc. Am. (counselor 1968-70, pres. 1973-74), Am. Acad. Arts Scis.; mem. Nat. Acad. Scis., Earthquake Engring. Research Inst. (bd. dirs. 1985-88), Seismological Soc. Am. (dir. 1970-76, pres. 1975-76, medal 1995), Nat. Acad. Engring., Phi Beta Kappa. Home: 1000 E California Blvd Apt 306 Pasadena CA 91106-4055 Office: Calif Inst Tech Dept Geology Pasadena CA 91125

ALLEN, CLAUDETTE A., educational administrator; b. Jan. 6, 1955. BA, U. V.I., 1978; MA, Ind. State U., 1985; EdS, Nova Southeastern U., 1995. Tchr. English, Charlotte Amalie H.S., St. Thomas, V.I., 1978-86; asst. prin. Bloomingdale H.S. and Brandon (Fla.) H.S., 1986-97, Armwood H.S., Seffner, Fla., 1997—; tchr. English Brandon H.S., Valrico, Fla., 1986-97, Bloomingdale H.S., Valrico, 1986-97; asst. prin. Armwood H.S., Saffner, Fla., 1997—. Tchr. trainer 1st Wesleyan Ch., St. Thomas, 1983-86; coord. 34th Street Ch. Sch., Tampa, Fla., 1993-96; chmn. sch. bd. Kings Kids Christian Acad., Tampa, 1994-96; tchr. coord. 34th St. Ch. Sch. Home: 1327 Larson Ln Tampa FL 33619-4807 Office: 12000 US Hwy 92 Seffner FL 33584-3418

ALLEN, CLAXTON EDMONDS, III, investment banker; b. N.Y.C., Aug. 27, 1944; s. C. Edmonds and Helen (McCreery) A. AB, Washington and Lee U., 1964, JD, 1967. Bar: N.Y. 1969. Assoc. Simpson Thacher & Bartlett, N.Y.C., 1967-70; assoc. gen. counsel GE Credit Corp., N.Y.C., 1970-71; investment banker Merrill Lynch, Pierce, Fenner & Smith, Inc.,

N.Y.C., 1971-72; pres. Gloucester Internat. Ltd., N.Y.C., 1972-82, Comanche Exploration Corp., N.Y.C., 1981-86, Compass Internat. Corp., N.Y.C., 1982—, Horizon Coal Corp., Mineral Res. Corp., N.Y.C., 1982-85, Compass Coal Corp., N.Y.C., 1986-91, Overseas & Fgn. Investors, Inc., N.Y.C., 1990—; bd. dirs. Purbrook Ltd., Cranwood Investments Ltd., L&H Internat. Ltd. Mem. Met. Club. Home: 405 E 54th St New York NY 10022-5123 Office: 123 E 54th St 8th Fl New York NY 10022

ALLEN, CLAYTON HAMILTON, physicist, acoustician; b. Whitinsville, Mass., June 2, 1918; s. Charles Aaron and Edith Gertrude (Peck) A.; m. Doris Elizabeth LeClaire, Dec. 7, 1981. BS in Physics, Worcester Poly. Inst., 1940; MS in Physics and Math., Pa. State U., 1942, PhD in Physics and Math., Phys.-Chemistry, 1950. Grad. asst. Pa. State U., 1940-42; grad. assoc. Pa. State U., State College, 1945-50; acoustical communications researcher Aircraft Radio Lab., Wright-Patterson AFB, Ohio, 1942-45; ultrasonic researcher Corning (N.Y.) Glass Works, 1950-54; cons. on noise control Bolt Beranek and Newman Inc., Cambridge, Mass., 1954-74; v.p. noise control Sci. Applications Inc., La Jolla, Calif., 1974-75; pres. The Clayton H. Allen Corp., Chebeague Island, Maine, 1975—; lectr. profl. confs. and meetings. Contbr. articles to Jour. Acoustical Soc. Am., Jr. Cellular and Comparative Physiology, Noise Control, Mech. Contractor, Heating, Piping and Air Conditioning, Am. Indsl. Hygiene Assn., Sound, chpts. to ref. books. Fellow Acoustical Soc. Am.; mem. AAAS, Am. Phys. Soc., Acad. Applied Sci., Innovation Group, Am. Foundrymen's Soc., Nat. Coun. Acoustical Cons., Mass. Coun. Acoustical Cons., Mass. Engrs. Coun., Inst. Noise Control Engring. (past mem. bd. dirs. and bd. examiners), Sigma Xi, Sigma Pi Sigma. Achievements include design of a megawatt acoustic facility for full scale aircraft body component sonic fatigue testing at Wright Patterson AFB, and noise control modifications for: submarines, spacecraft instrumentation, a Brit. gas cooled nuclear reactor, a number of multi-megawatt electric induction heater designs, indsl. plants, hosps., cmty. projects, and the like; 15 patents (some with others) include coverage of high frequency siren designs, apparatus for silencing vibrating machinery, method of fabricating miniature phonograph records, linear and nonlinear hearing protecting devices, and apparatus for alloying metal coatings; other patents pending; engaged in field of applied electronic and mechanical research, design and development. Office: 80 South Rd Chebeague Island ME 04017

ALLEN, CLIVE VICTOR, lawyer, communications company executive; b. Montreal, Que., Can., June 11, 1935; s. John Arthur and Norah (Barnett) A.; m. Barbara Mary Kantor, Feb. 22, 1964; children: Drew, Blair. B.A., McGill U., 1956, B.C.L., 1959. Bar: Que. 1960. Mem. firm Hackett, Mulvena, Drummond & Fiske, 1960-63, Fiske, Emery, Allen & Lauzon, 1964-66; v.p., sec. Allied Chem. Can. Ltd., 1966-74; sr. v.p., gen. counsel Northern Telecom Ltd., 1974-97, exec. v.p. law, 1998—; bd. dirs. Allendale Mut. Ins. Co.; mem. adv. bd. Can.-U.S. Law Inst. Mem. ABA, Can. Bar Assn., Bar of Que., Internat. Bar Assn., Assn. Can. Gen. Counsel, Montreal Badminton and Squash Club, St. James' Club (Montreal), Granite Club (Toronto). Home: 14 Pine Hill Rd, Toronto, ON Canada M4W 1P6 Office: Nortel Networks Corp, 8200 Dixie Rd Ste 100, Brampton, ON Canada L6T 5P6

ALLEN, DANNY EUGENE, writer, naturalist, activitist; b. St. Louis, June 28, 1964; s. Elmo and Rosie Lee (Dinkins) A. AA, St. Louis Coll., 1985; student, U. Mo., 1992. Animal caretaker Humane Soc., St. Louis, 1986-87, ASPCA, Columbia, Mo., 1992. Author: Bo Jon Littlehorse, 1996; contbr. poetry to Sparrowgrass Poetry. Activist World Wilflife Fund, Nat. Wildlife Found., Sierrra Club.

ALLEN, DAVID, government official; b. York, Maine, May 15, 1942; s. Pliny Arunah and Tillie (MacQuinn) A.; m. JoAnn Moeckly, 1968 (div. 1975); children: Torrie, Heather; m. Robin Lee Perry, Mar. 11, 1983; children: Rebecca, Patrick. BA, Lake Forest Coll., 1965; MA, U. Ariz., 1967, PhD, 1968. Asst. prof. dept. psychology S.D. State U., Brookings, 1968-71; rsch. psychologist CIA, Washington, 1971-78; chief rsch. br. CIA, 1978-85, dep. chief psychol. svcs. divsn., 1985-87; chief rsch. and info. systems divsn. CIA, Washington, 1987-90, trustee investment plan, 1988-92, investigator Office of Insp. Gen., 1990-92, chief info. systems Latin Am. divsn., 1992-95; chief electronic messaging divsn., program dir. Enterprise Messaging Svcs., Office of Comm. CIA, Washington, 1995-97; dir. program planning for Ctr. for Info. Sys. Mitretek Sys., Inc., 1998—. *After 26 years service at the CIA, he currently directs program plannning for the Center for Information Systems at Mitretek Systems, Inc.- a non-profit coporation providing systems engineering services in the public interest. An Intelligence Medal recipient, he continues service to the public as a senior Mitretek marketing director providing innovative technology solutions to consumer areas like public safety, health, transportation, environmental protection, information technology, telecommunications and law enforcement. A strategic thinker widely known for his creative approaches to solving intractable problems, he brings to private industry his broad experience as an intelligence officer, scientist and senior government manager.* Contbr. articles to profl. jours. Rsch. fellow USPHS, 1967-68; rsch. grantee NSF, 1970-71; recipient U.S. Govt. Career Intelligence medal, CIA, 1997. Republican. Avocations: choral singing, amateur radio, cosmology, mathematics, high technology. Home: 905 N Emerson St Arlington VA 22205-2562

ALLEN, DAVID CHARLES, computer science educator; b. Syracuse, N.Y., Jan. 15, 1944; s. Charles Robert and Jane Loretta (Doolittle) A.; m. Mary Ann Stanke, June 15, 1968 (div. Mar. 1994); children: Meredith Rae, Amelia Kathrine, Carl James; m. Barbara Ann Riis, Mar. 14, 1994. B.Tech. Edn., Nat. U., San Diego, 1983, MA in Human Behavior, 1984. Dir. retail sales Nat. U. Alumni Assn., 1981-83; audiovisual technician Grossmont Union H.S. Dist., La Mesa, Calif., 1983-84; spl. project instr. San Diego C.C., 1985-91; instr. computer tech. Coleman Coll., 1991-98, sr. instr. computer applications and networking, 1998—. Mem. Presdl. Task Force; mem. Congl. Adv. Com. on Vets. Benefits for congressmen 44th. With USN, 1961-81. Mem. DAV, VFW, Am. Legion, Vietnam Vets. Am., Fleet Reservation Assn., Nat. U. Student and Alumni Assn., Am. Tech. Edn. Assn., Beta Sigma Phi (hon.). Republican. Roman Catholic. Home: 3156 Lamar Ct Spring Valley CA 91977-2650 Office: Coleman Coll Computer Applications & Networking 7380 Parkway Dr La Mesa CA 91942-1532

ALLEN, DAVID HARLOW, business educator, logistician, consultant; b. Lynn, Mass., May 26, 1930; s. Donald H. and Miriam Ellsworth (Harlow) A.; m. Roberta Arlene Miller, July 15, 1952; children: Donald Bruce, Richard Leroy, William David. BS in Gen. Edn., U. Nebr., Omaha, 1967; MBA, N.Mex. Highlands U., 1978. Cert. profl. logistician, cost analyst. Enlisted USAF, 1948-55, commd. 2d lt., 1955, advanced through grades to lt. col., 1970; instr., planner, aircraft maintenance, staff, prodn. control officer, squadron comdr., wing asst. dep. comdr. maintenance SAC, 1948-74; dir. aircraft maintenance, dir. material Air Force Inspection and Safety Ctr., San Bernardino, Calif., 1969-72; dep. dir. logistics Air Force Test and Evaluation Ctr., Albuquerque, 1974-78; ret., 1978; sr. sys. analyst, space sys. project leader Arinc Rsch. Corp., 1978-84; airborne missile system dep. program mgr. for logistics, logistics project mgr. Ventura divsn. Northrop Corp., 1984-91; assoc. prof. West Coast U. Coll. Bus. and Mgmt., L.A., 1988-97; asst. dean West Coast U., L.A., 1988-90; com. chmn. So. Calif. Logistics Conf. and Workshop, 1989-93; program chmn. 29th Internat. Logistics Conf. and Tech. Exposition, 1994; v.p., mem. bd. govs., trustee Logistics Edn. Found., 1993-96. Contbr. articles to profl. jours. Active state and nat. Rep. orgns., 1978—; mem. Ventura County-Santa Barbara County Planning Com. for Nat. Engring. Week, 1990-98. Decorated Bronze Star. Mem. Soc. Logistics Engrs. (chmn. chpt. 1988-90, Pres.'s award for merit 1994), Logistics Edn. Found. (v.p., bd. trustees 1993-95, Pres.'s award for merit 1996), Soc. Cost Estimating and Analysis, Air Force Assn., Ret. Officers Assn., Am. Assn. Ret. Persons, Phi Kappa Phi. Avocations: racquetball, golf, swimming. Home and Office: 428 Moondance St Thousand Oaks CA 91360-1209

ALLEN, DAVID JAMES, lawyer; b. East Chicago, Ind.. BS, Ind. U., 1957, MA, 1959, JD, 1965. Bar: Ind. 1965, U.S. Dist. Ct. (so. dist.) Ind. 1965, U.S. Ct. Appeals 1965, U.S. Ct. Appeals (fed. and 7th cirs.) 1983, U.S. Tax Ct. 1965, U.S. Supreme Ct. 1965. Ptnr. Hagemier, Allen and Smith, Indpls., 1975—; adminstrv. asst. to Gov. of Ind. Matthew E. Welsh, 1961-65, 65-69; legis. counsel to Gov. of Ind. Roger D. Branigin, 1989-90, Ind. Gov. Bayh; spl. counsel to Gov. Frank O' Bannon State of Ind., 1997—; mem. Spl. Commn. on Ind. Exec. Reorgn., 1967-69; commr. Ind. Utility Regulatory Comm., 1970-75; mem. Ind. Law Enforcement Acad. Bd. and Adv. Coun., 1968-85; mem. Ind. State Police Bd., 1968—; commr. for revision Ind. Adminstrv. Adjudication Act, 1983-87; mem. Ind. Commn. to Recommend Changes in Ind. Legis. Process, 1990—; commr. Ind. Criminal Code Revision Study Commn.; nat. judge advocate Acacia Frat., 1980-86, 92—; chief counsel Ind. Ho. of Reps., 1975-76; spl. counsel Ind. Senate Majority, 1977-78; legis. counsel Ind. Ho. of Reps., Ind. Senate minority parties, 1979-89, Ind. Senate, 1990-97; adj. prof. pub. law Ind. U., Bloomington, 1976—. Author: New Governor In Indiana: Transition of Executive Power, 1965. Mem. ABA, Ind. State Bar Assn. (mem. adminstrv. law com. 1968-77, chmn. adminstrv. law com. 1973-76, mem. law sch. liaison com. 1977-78, criminal justice law exec. com. 1966-72), Indpls. Bar Assn. Office: 1170 Market Tower 10 W Market St Indianapolis IN 46204-2954

ALLEN, DAVID RUSSELL, lawyer; b. Oak Park, Ill., July 30, 1942; s. Paul C. and Lucille (Meyer) A.; m. Penny Grieb, Aug. 27, 1966; children—Todd, Travis. BA, Stanford U., 1964; JD, U. So. Calif., 1968. Bar: Calif. 1969. Ptnr. Atherton and Allen, San Diego and Chula Vista, Calif., 1969-81, Atherton, Allen, Mason, Cannon and Geerdes, San Diego, Calif., 1982-86, Atherton, Allen and Geerdes, Chula Vista, Calif., 1986-96, Atherton & Allen, Chula Vista, 1996—. Chmn. bd. trustees Comty. Congl. Ch., Chula Vista, 1981; trustee Chula Vista Comty. Hosp., 1981-94; com. chmn. Cub Scout Pack 885, San Diego County coun. Boy Scouts Am., 1981, com. chmn. Boy Scout Troop 885, 1983. Lt. USNR, 1964-65. Mem. Calif. Bar Assn. (cert. legal specialist probate, estate planning and trust law), San Diego Bar Assn. (chmn. estate planning, trust and probate law 1986), South Bay Bar Assn., Internat. Wine and Food Soc. (chmn. Chula Vista chpt. 1983), Am. Inn Ct. (William L. Todd Jr. chpt. master), Rotary (pres. Chula Vista chpt. 1976-77, gov. dist. 534, 1989-90). Republican. Address: 345 F St Ste 210 Chula Vista CA 91910-2634

ALLEN, DAVID WOODROFFE, computer scientist; b. Hampton, Iowa, Sept. 20, 1944; s. Edward DeWalt and Julia Woodroffe (Lamb) A.; m. Barbara Ann Schneider, Sept. 15, 1973. BA, Grinnell Coll., 1967; MS, U. Pitts., 1974. Assoc. engr. Westinghouse Electric Corp., Sharon, Pa., 1967-70, engr., 1970-79, sr. engr., 1979-84; sr. computer scientist Westinghouse Electric Corp., Pitts., 1984-90, prin. engr., 1990-94, fellow engr., 1994-96; dir., officer, sr. engr. Propulsor Tech. Inc., Pitts., 1996—. Contbr. articles to profl. jours. Recipient George Westinghouse Signature award of excellence, 1989, 92, George Westinghouse Innovation award, 1993. Mem. IEEE (sect. sec.-treas. 1981-82, referee tech. papers for Computer jour.), Assn. for Computing Machinery, Silicon Graphics Users Group We. Pa. (treas. 1991-94), Digital Equipment Computer Users Soc. Democrat. Achievements include research in current transformer transient performance, magnetic and electric field computation and analysis, computer-aided geometric design. Avocations: woodworking, gardening, reading. Home: 2637 Rossmoor Dr Pittsburgh PA 15241-2572 Office: Propulsor Technology Inc 811 State Route 51 S Large PA 15025-3663

ALLEN, DEBBIE, actress, dancer, director, choreographer; b. Houston, Jan. 16, 1950; d. Vivian Ayers; m. Win Wilford (div.); m. Norm Nixon; 2 children: Vivian, Norman, Jr. BA, Howard U. Appeared in Broadway musicals including Purlie, 1972, West Side Story (revival), Guys and Dolls, Raisin, Aint Misbehavin, Sweet Charity, 1986 (revival, Tony Award); appeared in (play) Sweet Charity, Los Angeles, 1985, choreographer Broadway prodn. Carrie, 1988; (TV spl.) Dancing in the Winds, 1985, (TV series) Fame, 1982-87 (3 Emmys for choreography), In the House, 1995; dir. TV series A Different World, 1988-92; dir. episodes TV series Family Ties; dir., producer films including The Fish That Saved Pittsburgh, 1979, Fame, 1980, Ragtime, 1981, JoJo Dancer, Your Life is Calling, 1986, Mona Must Die, 1994, Blank Check, 1994, Out-of-Sync, 1995, Everything's Jake, 1999, (TV movie) C Bear and Jamal (voice), 1996; star, dir., prod., co-writer, choreographer The Debbie Allen Special, ABC-TV, 1988; dir., choreographer Polly (mus. version Disney's Pollyanna), 1989; dir., appeared in CBS Stompin' at the Savoy, 1992; rec. album Special Look, MCA Records, 1989; dir. pilot and 1st episode NBC series The Fresh Prince of Bel Air, 1990; dir., choreographer NBC-Disney movie Polly II, 1990; choreographer of 63d Acad. Awards, 1991, 64th Acad. Awards, 1992, 65th Acad. Awards, 1993, 66th Acad. Awards, 1994. Mem. exec. com. dean's adv. bd. UCLA Sch. Theatre, Film and TV, 1993. Office: Lisa Kasteler Wolf-Kasteler 132 S Rodeo Dr Ste 300 Beverly Hills CA 90212-2414*

ALLEN, DELMAS JAMES, anatomist, educator, university administrator; b. Hartsville, S.C., Aug. 13, 1937; s. James Paul and Sara (Segars) A.; m. Sarah Bahous, July 5, 1958; children—Carolyn, James, Susan. B.S. in Biology, Am. U. of Beirut, Lebanon, 1965, M.S., 1967; postgrad., Med. Coll. Ga., 1968; cert. in Radiation Sci., Colo. State U., 1969; Ph.D., U. N.D., 1974; postgrad., Ga. State U. Teaching fellow dept. biology Am. U. Beirut, Lebanon, 1965-67; instr. dept. biology Clarke Coll., Dubuque, Iowa, 1968-69, asst. prof., 1969-72, chmn. dept. biology, 1969-72; grad. teaching fellow and research asst. U. N.D., Grand Forks, 1972-74; asst. prof. dept. anatomy U. South Ala., Mobile, 1974-75; asst. prof. dept. anatomy Med. Coll. Ohio, Toledo, 1975-77, assoc. prof. dept. anatomy, 1977-82, prof. dept. anatomy, 1982-86, asst. dean Grad. Sch., 1979-86; assoc. dean Coll. Health Scis. Ga. State U., Atlanta, 1986-88; pres. North Ga. Coll., Dahlonega, 1993-97; vis. prof. Brazil, 1980, Ryad U. Sch. Medicine, Saudi Arabia, 1981, U. Alta. Heritage Found., 1984, United Arab Emirates U. System, 1992. Co-author: Review of Neuroscience, 1980, 2d ed., 1988, Atlas of Human Anatomy, CT Scan and NMR, 1988; contbr. articles on neuroanatomy and electron microscopy to sci. jours.; editor: Three-Dimensional Microanatomy, 1981; contbr. chpts. in field to various textbooks. Recipient A. Rodger Denison award N.D. Acad. Sci., 1973; Ala. Heart Assn. grantee, 1974-75, Am. Cancer Soc. grantee, 1977, Am. Heart Assn. grantee, 1977-80; geriatrics-gerontology grantee, 1980-81; recipient Golden Apple award for Excellence in Teaching, Med. Coll. Ohio, 1977, 78, 79, 80, 82, 86; research award Brazilian Acad. Medicine, 1980, Northwestern Ohio Electron Microscopic Soc., 1980; Faculty Recognition award Med. Coll. Ohio, 1983. Fellow Ohio Acad. Sci. (membership chmn. med. sci. sect. 1977-78, v.p. med. sect. 1978-79); mem. Soc. for Neurosci., Am. Assn. Anatomists, So. Soc. Anatomists, Am. Soc. Cell Biology, Midwest Assn. Anatomists, Pan Am. Soc. Anatomy, N.Y. Acad. Scis., Am. Heart Assn., European Brain and Behavior Soc. (hon. mem.), Brit. Brain Research Assn. (hon. mem.), Sigma Xi (Thesis Excellence award 1967, Award of Merit 1974, pres. Med. Coll. Ohio club 1978-79), Rotary (pres. elect Dahlonega Club 1992—, Paul Harris fellow 1992), Phi Kappa Phi, Omicron Delta Kappa, Phi Eta Sigma. Home: 18827 E Ashley Pl Rowland Heights CA 91748-4870

ALLEN, DENSIL E., JR., agricultural studies educator. Prof. agriculture Ctrl. Mo. State U., Warrensburg. Fellow Nat. Assn. Colls. Tchrs. Agriculture, 1992. Office: Central Missouri State U Dept Agriculture Warrensburg MO 64093*

ALLEN, DIOGENES, clergyman, philosophy educator; b. Lexington, Ky., Oct. 17, 1932; m. Jane Mary Billing, Sept. 8, 1958; children: Mary, George, John, Timothy. B.A. with high distinction, U. Ky., 1954; postgrad., Princeton U., 1954-55; B.A. with honors, Oxford U., 1957, M.A., 1961; B.D., Yale U., 1959, Ph.D., 1965. Ordained to ministry Presbyterian Ch., 1959. Minister Windham Presbyn. Ch., N.H., 1958-61; asst. prof. York U., Toronto, Ont., Can., 1964-66, assoc. prof. philosophy, 1966-67; assoc. prof. Princeton Theol. Sem., N.J., 1967-74, prof., 1974—, Stuart prof. philosophy, 1981—. Author: The Reasonableness of Faith, 1968, Finding Our Father, 1974, reissued under title The Path to Perfect Love, 1992, Between Two Worlds, 1978, reissued under title Temptation, 1985, Traces of God, 1981, Three Outsiders: Pascal, Kierkegaard and S. Weil, 1983, Mechanical Explanations and Their Relation to the Ultimate Origin of the Universe According to Leibniz, 1983, Philosophy for Understanding Theology, 1985, Love, 1987, Christian Belief in a Postmodern World, 1989, Quest, 1990, Primary Reading in Philosophy for Understanding (with Eric Springsted), 1992, (with Eric Springsted) Nature, Spirit, Community: The Thought of Simone Weil, 1994, Spiritual Theology, 1997; editor: Theodicy (Leibniz), 1966. Rhodes scholar, 1955-57, 63-64, Pew Evang. scholar, 1991-92; fellow Rockefeller Found., 1962-64, Ctr. Theol. Inquiry, Princeton, 1985-88, 94-95, Adv. Bd. Ctr. Theol. Inquiry, 1988-94. Mem. Soc. Christian Philosophers (bd. dirs.), Am. Weil Soc. (bd. dirs.), Leibniz Gellschaft, N.J. Com. for the Humanities, Phi Beta Kappa. Home: 133 Cedar Ln Princeton NJ 08540-5310 Office: Princeton Theol Seminary Dept Philosophy Princeton NJ 08542 *In my life I have found there are many people who are glad to encourage and help another person in the pursuit of worthwhile tasks.*

ALLEN, DON LEE, dentistry educator; b. Burlington, N.C., Mar. 13, 1934; s. William Arthur and Gena (Davis) A.; m. Winifred Rouse, Aug. 2, 1958; children: Don Lee, Michael Denmark, Susan Winifred. Student, Elon Coll., 1952-55; DDS, U. N.C., 1959; MS in Periodontics, U. Mich., 1964. Instr. U. N.C. Sch. Dentistry, Chapel Hill, 1959-62; asst. prof. U. N.C. Sch. Dentistry, 1962-65, assoc. prof., 1965-69, prof., assoc. dean, 1969-70; prof., assoc. dean U. Fla. Coll. Dentistry, Gainesville, 1970-73; dean U. Fla. Coll. Dentistry, 1973-82; dean U. Tex. Dental Br. at Houston, 1982-92, William N. Finnegan prof. dental scis., 1985—, prof. Dept. Practice Mgmt., 1992—; univ. evaluation adminstr., 1993—; staff Shands Teaching Hosp., 1970-82; hon. prof. Tianjin Med. Coll., 1987; hon. lectr. Tokyo Dental Coll., 1986; nat. adv. coun. health profl. edn. HHS, 1978-82; commn. dental edn. and practice mem. Fedn. Dentaire Internat., 1981-87, vice-chmn., 1990, chmn. 1991-92; vice-chmn. Fedn. Dentaire Internat. Commn., 1991-97, chmn. sect. dental deans and educators, 1994-96; med. br. mem. Harris County (Tex.) Hosp. Dist., 1990-92; cons. USPHS, 1962-64, Coun. Dental Edn., 1970-78, 86-93, VA Hosp., Gainesville, 1970-82, commn. on dental accreditation appeal bd., 1995—; vis. prof. U. Stellenbosch, 1990, Kings Coll., London, 1993, U. Buenos Aires, 1996. Author: (with G. Hunter, W. McFall) Periodontics for the Dental Hygienist, 1968, 2d edit., 1974, 3d edit., 1980, 4th edit., 1987; contbg. editor: Gould Med. Dictionary. Active Y-Indian Guides, Chapel Hill, 1968-70, Gainesville, 1973-75; elder Presbyn. Ch., 1972-75, 78-82; mem. adminstrv. coun. Meth. Ch., 1990-94. Recipient Merit award Federation Dentaire Internationale, 1997, teaching award U. N.C. Class of 1966; named Disting. Alumnus, Elon Coll., 1985. Fellow Am. Coll. Dentists (chmn. Fla. sect. 1980-81), Internat. Coll. Dentists (pres. 1981-82, master 1986); mem. ADA (coun. dental edn., commn. on dental accreditation 1978-86, chmn. 1984-86), Am. Acad. Peridontology, Am. Assn. Dental Schs. (pres. 1982-83), Internat. Assn. Dental Rsch., So. Conf. Dental Deans and Examiners (pres. 1983-84), Pierre Fauchard Acad., Houston Forum, Omicron Kappa Upsilon. Office: U of Tex Health Scis Ctr School Of Dentistry Houston TX 77225

ALLEN, DONALD MERRIAM, editor, publisher; b. Muscatine, Iowa, Mar. 26, 1912; s. Paul Edward and Mildred Gertrude (Quinn) A. BA, U. Iowa, 1934, MA, 1935; postgrad., U. Wis., 1941-42, U. Calif., Berkeley, 1947-49. Editor Grove Press, N.Y.C., 1951-53, adv. editor, 1956-63; editor, pub. New Directions, N.Y.C., 1954, Criterion Books, N.Y.C., 1955; pres. Four Seasons Found., San Francisco, 1964—, Grey Fox Press, San Francisco, 1971—. Co-editor Evergreen Rev., 1956-60; editor: (anthology) The New American Poetry, 1960, (book) Frank O'Hara Collected Poems, 1971 (Nat. Book award 1971); translator (drama): Ionesco - 4 Plays, 1958. Lt. USN, 1942-47. Decorated Purple Heart, Bronze Star medal. Avocations: walking, reading.

ALLEN, DONALD VAIL, investment executive, writer, concert pianist; b. South Bend, Ind., Aug. 1, 1928; s. Frank Eugene and Vera Irene (Vail) A.; m. Betty Dunn, Nov. 17, 1956. BA magna cum laude, UCLA, 1972, MA, 1973, D (hon.), 1973. Pres., chmn. bd. dirs. Cambridge Investment Corp.; music editor and critic Times-Herald, Washington; music critic L.A. Times; lectr. George Washington U., Am. U., Washington, Pasadena City Coll. Transl. works of Ezra Pound from Italian into English; author of papers on the musical motifs in the writings of James Joyce and Stravinsky; mem. Steinway Roster of Concert Artists; specialist in works of Beethoven, Chopin, Debussy and Liszt; premiere performances of works of Paul Creston, Norman dello Joio, Ross Lee Finney, appearances in N.Y., L.A., Washington; represented by William Matthews Concert Agy., N.Y.C. Pres. Funds for Needy Children, 1974-76. Mem. Ctr. for Study of Presidency, Am. Mgmt. Assn., Internat. Platform Assn., Nat. Assn. Securities Dealers, Am. Guild Organists, Chamber Music Soc., Am. Mus. Natural History. Avocations: languages, music, travel, writing, stock market. Home: 670 W Via Rancho Pkwy Escondido CA 92029-7313

ALLEN, DOROTHEA, secondary education educator; b. Rockaway, N.J., Apr. 30, 1919; d. Harrison Engleman and Caroline (Tierney) A. AB, Montclair U., 1941, MA, 1949. Cert. secondary, sci., math. tchr., counselor, supr., prin., N.J. Tchr. sci. and math. Denville (N.J.) Jr. High Sch., 1942-46; tchr. sci. Boonton (N.J.) High Sch., 1946-94, supr. sci. dept., 1978-94; lab. technician Drew Chem. Corp., Boonton, 1942-47; tech. asst. Bell Telecom. Lab., Whippany, N.J., 1956; rsch. scientist Warner Lambert Rsch. Inst., Morris Plains, N.J., 1959-62; tchr. sci. enrichment Boonton Summer Sch., 1963-85; curriculum developer Morris County Vocat.-Tech. Sch., Denville, 1987; conf. program presenter, 1978, 85; project evaluator sci. fairs, N.J., 1970—; program evaluator Mid. States Assn., 1973, 79; facilitator Ptnrs. in Edn. Program; spkr., promoter Media Ctr. Open House; cons., reviewer Am. Biol. Tchr. mag., 1975—; com. mem. Sch. Articulation Program, Boonton Schs., 1991-94; spkr., resource person Career Confs.; media ctr. spkr. Meet the Author; sponsor Student Showcase of Excellence in Sci., 1990-94, faculty sponsor, mentor h.s. students, 1966-94; mentor Alt. Rt. Program Tchrs., N.J. Organizer Am. Dental Health Clinic, Boonton, 1968-72; mem. career com. N.J. divsn. Theobald Smith Soc., 1975-76; fundraiser Am. Hemophilia Found., Rockaway, N.J., 1985—, Am. Heart Assn., 1995—, Muscular Dystrophy Found., 1995—, Nat. Children's Cancer Soc., 1996—; cons. Cmty. Mid. Sch. Planning Com., Boonton, 1988-90; bd. advisors ABI Rsch., 1995—. Recipient Disting. Citizen's award Town of Rockaway, 1984, Gov.'s and Edn. award N.J. Dept. Edn., 1984, Morris County Tchr. of Yr. award, 1990, Presdl. award NSF, 1984, Cert. of Honor State of N.J., 1985, World Lifetime Achievement award, 1994, Internat. Order of Merit, 1994, Spotlight award Boonton Bd. Edn., 1980-86, Tchr. of Yr., 1984, 90, Women's Inner Circle of Achievement award, 1995; named outstanding Biology Tchr. Nat. Assn. Biology Tchrs., 1972, Outstanding Sci. Tchr. Rsch. Assn. N.Am., 1980, 86, Woman of Yr., 1993-98, Sci. Edn. Hall of Fame, 1994-98, Boonton H.S. Hall of Fame, 1996, 97, 98. Mem. NEA, NEA Ret., ASCD, NSTA, Morris County Ret. Educators Assn., Nat. Assn. Secondary Sch. Prins., Assn. Presdl. Award Winners in Sci. Tchg., N.J. Edn. Assn., N.J. Prins. and Suprs. Assn., N.J. Acad. Alliance for Math. and Sci., N.J. Dept. Edn. Exec. Acad., Morris Area Sci. Alliance. Avocations: reading, propagating plants, collecting gold coins. Home: 115 Jackson Ave Rockaway NJ 07866-3039

ALLEN, EDGAR BURNS, records management professional; b. L.A., Sept. 1, 1929; s. Harry James and Hela Ruth (Graham) A.; m. Eleanor Angela Gregory, July 24, 1960; children: Linda Marie, Lisa Ann. AA, L.A. City Coll., 1958; student, Calif. State U., L.A., 1958, 81; BS, UCLA, 1985. Supr. records ctr. L.A. Dept. Water and Power, 1958-67, records mgr., 1967-76; records mgmt. officer City of L.A., 1976-85; records mgmt. cons. L.A., 1985—; profl. creator records mgmt. systems, tax preparer, L.A., 1990—; established City Records Ctr. and City Archives. Chmn. Leimert Pk. Community Assn., L.A., 1972-75. Mem. Assn. Records Mgrs. and Adminstrs. (bd. dirs. 1975-76), Soc. Calif. Archivists, All Yr. Figure Skating Club (bd. dirs. 1970-79). Democrat. Roman Catholic. Avocations: bowling, walking, travel.

ALLEN, EDWARD LAWRENCE, JR., government relations executive, lobbyist; b. Alexandria, Va., Mar. 3, 1964; s. Edward Lawrence and Ann (Hoffman) A.; m. Laura Evelyn Swann, Apr. 23, 1988. BA, Emory U., 1986; postgrad., American U., 1986-87. Communications coord. Friends of Frank Wolf, McLean, Va., 1986; legis. asst. U.S. Rep. Alex McMillan, Washington, 1987-90; asst. dir. Nat. Assn. State Univs. and Land Grant Colls., Washington, 1990-91; exec. dir. Coalition for Govt. Procurement, Washington, 1991—. Editor: (newsletter) International Letter, 1990; contbr. articles to newsletters and profl. jours. Mem. Arlington County (Va.) Rep. Com., 1987-89; vice-chmn. Arlington County Young Reps., 1989. Mem. Washington Golf and Country Club. Republican. Roman Catholic. Avocations: golf, U.S. history, viticulture. Home: 3815 N Richmond St # A Arlington VA 22207-4571 Office: Coalition for Government Procurement 1990 M St NW Washington DC 20036-3404*

ALLEN, ELEANOR KATHLEEN (MISSY ALLEN), elementary education educator; b. Houston, Dec. 30, 1951; d. William Brunswick and Eleanor Julia (Blohm) Houston; m. Stephen Charles Allen, Dec. 27, 1973 (div. June 1997); children: Abigail Ashley, Andrew Stephen. BS in Elem. Edn., U. Tex., Austin, 1973. Cert. gifted/talented tchr., Tex. Elem. tchr. Arlington

(Tex.) Ind. Sch. Dist., 1973-78; non-profit agy. dir. Arlington Crisis Pregnancy Ctr., 1984-90; elem. tchr. Hurst-Euless-Bedford (Tex.) Ind. Sch. dist., 1990—; local, state and nat. conf. spkr., 1990—; mem. (performance group) A Tchr. Line, 1992-99; mem. dist. strategic planning com., 1994-95; team coord. Meadow Creek Elem. Sch., Bedford, 1994-99, Rockenbaugh Elem. Sch., Southlake, Tex., 1999—. Author, creator (staff handbook, mktg. folder) Non Profit Organization, 1984-90; contbr. rsch. articles to profl. jours. Inspirational/motivational spkr., Iowa and Tex., 1980-90; chair 1st Covenant Ch. Ladies Ministries, Iowa, 1980-82; mem. Tex. Band Boosters, 1991-97; founder, pres. Key Women Auxiliary, Iowa, 1980-83. Mem. PTA (parent edn. com.), Internat. Reading Assn., Assn. Tchrs. and Profl. Educators, Tex. Assn. Gifted/Talented, Hurst-Euless-Bedford Assn. Gifted/Talented. Avocations: reading, antiques, music, photography. Home: 2805D Meadow Park Dr Bedford TX 76021-4719 Office: Rockenbaugh Elem 301 Byron Nelson Pkwy Southlake TX 76092

ALLEN, ELIZABETH MARESCA, marketing and telecommunications executive; b. Red Bank, N.J., Jan. 4, 1958; d. Paul William Michael and Roberta Gertrude (Abbes) Maresca; m. David D. Allen; 1 son, Brandon D. Student, Brookdale Community Coll., 1976-77; A Bus. Adminstrn., Tidewater C.C., 1988; BA in Bus. Mgmt., Va. Wesleyan Coll., 1997. Systems analyst Methods Research Corp., Farmingdale, N.J., 1977-79; divsn. mgr. Abacus Comm. L.P., Virginia Beach, Va., 1979—, dir. telecomm. Bd. dirs. Arthritis Found., Norfolk, Va., 1986-90; v.p. Charlestowne Civic League, Virginia Beach, 1983-84, Plantation Lakes Homeowners Assn., Chesapeake, Va., 1992—; advisor Commonwealth Coll., Norfolk, 1984-91; del. Va. Rep. Conv., 1993—; mem. gov.'s coun. Republican Nat. Com., 1997; mem. South Norfolk Revitalization Commn., 1999—. Mem. Women's Network Hampton Roads (publicity chmn. 1988-91, chmn. publicity for Job Fair 1989), Hampton Roads C. of C. (com. chmn. 1985, 88), Williamsburg Area C. of C. (exhibit chmn. 1987). Republican. Roman Catholic. Avocations: tennis, Civil War history, collecting antiques, gardening. Office: Abacus Communications LP 4452 Corporation Ln Virginia Beach VA 23462-3173

ALLEN, ERIC ANDRE, professional football player; b. San Diego, Nov. 22, 1965. BA in Broadcasting, Ariz. State, 1988. Cornerback Phila. Eagles, 1988-95; with New Orleans Saints, 1994—. Played in Pro Bowl, 1989, 91, 92, 93.

ALLEN, FRANK CARROLL, retired banker; b. Hazlehurst, Miss., Nov. 10, 1913; s. Walter Scott and May (Ellis) A.; m. Clara Marnee Alford, June 23, 1937 (dec. Apr. 1988); children: Marnee Louise, Susan Carroll, Elizabeth Jane; m. Pattie Henry Hudson, Sept. 8, 1990; stepchildren: Robbie Hudson Jones, Joseph W. Hudson, Jr. A.A. with high honors, Copiah-Lincoln Jr. Coll., Wesson, Miss., 1933; student, Am. Inst. Banking, 1935, 36, 37, 47, 49. Bookkeeper, teller Georgetown Bank, Miss., 1933-34; cashier, dir. Georgetown Bank, 1937-41; bookkeeper Deposit Guaranty Bank & Trust Co., Jackson, Miss., 1934-37; bank examiner Miss., 1942-46; cashier, dir. Brookhaven Bank & Trust Co., Miss., 1947-49; pres., dir. Lawrence County Bank, Monticello, Miss., 1949-65; pres. Monticello Bank br. Deposit Guaranty Nat. Bank, 1966-78; chmn. adv. bd. Monticello/Newhebron Bank brs., 1966-84; adv. bd. Deposit Guaranty Nat. Bank of, Jackson, 1966-84, Deposit Guaranty Corp., 1966-84; chmn. bd. Ins. & Realty Underwriters, 1971-75, dir., 1961-76; Bd. dirs. Miss. Econ. Council, 1950-53; commr. Monticello Planning Bd., 1964-74; commr. banking and consumer fin. State of Miss., 1980; bd. dirs. S.W. Miss. Devel. Assn., 1960-72; Chmn. scholarship bd. Monticello Mfg. Co., 1960-72. Mem. exec. bd. Andrew Jackson council Boy Scouts Am., 1975-87. Served to 1st lt. AUS, 1942-46. Recipient Silver Beaver award Boy Scouts Am., 1986; named to Miss. Agrl. and Forestry Mus. Hall of Fame, Jackson, 1988. Mem. Am. Bankers Assn. (chmn. Miss. dist. 7 on U.S. Savs. Bonds 1952-84), Miss. Bankers Assn. (chmn bank mgmt. com. 1948-49, group v.p. 1948-49), Monticello C. of C. (pres. 1951-53, 60-61, dir. 1951-81, Graham award excellence 1989), Newcomen Soc. N.Am. Baptist (deacon 1953—, Sunday sch. supt. 1958-60). Club: Lion (life) (pres. Monticello 1954-55). Home and Office: PO Box 368 Monticello MS 39654-0368

ALLEN, F(RANK) C(LINTON), JR., lawyer, retired manufacturing executive; b. 1934. BSChE, Tulane U., 1955, JD, 1964. With McDermott, Inc., New Orleans, 1978—, mem. legal staff, 1978-80, asst. gen. counsel, 1980-87, v.p., sec. gen. counsel, 1987-93; v.p. risk mgmt. safety, health and environ. McDermott Internat. Inc., New Orleans, 1993-99, ret., 1999; with Jones, Walker Law Firm, New Orleans, 1999—. Office: McDermott Internat Inc 1450 Poydras St Fl 22 New Orleans LA 70112-6010

ALLEN, FREDERICK WARNER, federal agency executive; b. New Haven, Conn., May 26, 1947; s. Yorke and Elizabeth (Sizer) A.; m. Margaret A. Weekes, May 20, 1978; children: Abigail Weekes, Nathaniel Potts, Eloise Reina Russo. BA, Yale U., 1969; MBA, Harvard U., 1973. Vista vol. N.Y.C. Dept. Corrections, 1969-71; analyst Cost of Living Coun., Washington, 1973-74; exec. asst. Fed. Energy Adminstrn., Washington, 1974-76; asst. dir., exec. sec. U.S. Dept. Labor, Washington, 1976-78; various positions U.S. EPA, Washington, 1978—; dir. EPA Office Strategic Planning and Environ. Data Washington, 1992—. Contbr. numerous articles to profl. jours. Pres. Spring Valley Wesley Heights Citizens Assn. Washington, 1989-91; moderator Cleveland Park Congl. Ch., Washington, 1993-94, trustee, 1996—. Home: 3807 48th St NW Washington DC 20016-2301 Office: US EPA (2161) 401 M St SW Washington DC 20024-2610*

ALLEN, GARLAND EDWARD, biology educator, science historian; b. Louisville, Feb. 13, 1936; s. Garland Edward and Virginia (Blandford) A.; children: Tania Leigh, Carin Tove. AB, U. Louisville, 1957; AMT, Harvard U., 1958, AM, 1963, PhD, 1966. Programmer, announcer WFPL-WFPK, Louisville, 1956-58; tchr. Mt. Hermon (Mass.) Sch., 1958-61; Allston-Burr sr. tutor, instr. history of sci. Harvard, 1965-67; asst. prof. biology Washington U., St. Louis, 1967-72; assoc. prof. Washington U., 1972-80, prof., 1980—; cons. Ednl. Rsch. Corp., Cleve., 1967-85; commr. Commn. Undergrad. Edn. in Biol. Scis., 1967-70; mem. NSF Panel for Social Scis., 1968-71; trustee Marine Biol. Lab., Woods Hole, Mass., 1985-93; Sigma Xi nat. lectr., 1973-74, bicentennial lectr., 1974-77; Watkins vis. prof. Wichita State U., 1984; vis. prof. dept. history of sci. Harvard U., 1989-91, Sarton Award Lecture, AAAS, 1998. Author: Life Sciences in the Twentieth Century, 1975, 78, T.H. Morgan: The Man and His Science, 1978, (with J.J.W. Baker) Matter, Energy and Life, 1965, 70, 75, 81, The Study of Biology, 1967, 4th edit., 1982, Hypothesis, Prediction and Implication, 1969, The Process of Biology, 1970; co-editor Mendel Newsletter, 1989-92; mem. editl. bd. San José Studies, Jour. History of Biology, 1968-91, Folia Medeliana; co-editor Jour. History of Biology, 1998—. Fellow Charles Warren Ctr. for Studies in Am. History, Harvard U., 1981-82. Mem. AAAS (coun., sect. L exec. com. 1975, Sarton award lectr. 1998), Am. Assn. History of Medicine, History Sci. Soc. (chmn. Schumann Prize com. 1972, Pfizer prize com. 1977, 80, 91-94, HSS coun. 1994-96, vis. lectr. program 1985-87), Sigma Xi. Home: 2323 Whittemore Pl Saint Louis MO 63104-2531 Office: Washington U Biology Dept Saint Louis MO 63130

ALLEN, GARY WAYNE, career officer, dentist; b. Portland, Oreg., July 5, 1947; s. Rex Wayne and Elizabeth Bell (Talbot) A.; m. Susan Jean Clark, June 17, 1972; children: Leana Cristine, Chandra Michele. BS in Gen. Sci., U. Oreg., 1969, DMD in Dental Medicine, 1973; MS in Oral Biology, George Washington U., 1978. Diplomate Am. Bd. Oral Pathology, Am. Bd. Oral Medicine. Commd. 2d lt. U.S. Army, 1973, advanced through grades to col., 1987; gen. dentistry officer 769th Med. Detachment, Augsburg, Fed. Republic of Germany, 1973-76; student Army Med. Dept. Officer Advanced Course, Ft. Sam Houston, 1976-77; resident in oral pathology U.S. Army Inst. Dental Rsch., Walter Reed Med. Ctr., Washington, 1977-79; chief div. profl. devel. U.S. Army Inst. Dental Rsch., Washington, 1979-82; chief oral pathology and oral medicine svc. U.S. Army Dental Activity, Ft. Gordon, Ga., 1982-83; student U.S. Army Command and Gen. Staff Coll., Ft. Leavenworth, Kans., 1983-84; comdr. 257th Med. Detachment, 44th Med. Brigade, Ft. Bragg, N.C., 1984-86; sr. adminstrv. fellow Office of Asst. Surgeon Gen. for Dental Svcs., Falls Church, Va., 1986-87; chief grad. dental edn. br. Office Surgeon Gen., Falls Church, 1987-91; comdr. U.S. Army Dental Activity, Ft. Bragg, N.C., 1992-94; chief dental corps br. U.S. Total Army Pers. Command, Alexandria, Va., 1994-95, chief health svcs. divsn., 1995-97, comdr. North Atlantic Regional Dental Command, 1997—; cons. Surgeon Gen. in oral pathology, 1992-95; del. coun. deans Am. Assn. Dental Schs., 1988-91; mem. Dental Health Professions Scholarship Selection Bd., 1990; mem., rep. numerous dental confs.; clin. asst. prof. oral pathology and oral biology Med. Coll. Ga., 1982-83; asst. professorial lectr. George Washington U., 1979-82; dir. dental edn. U.S. Army Inst. Dental Rsch., 1979-81. Contbr. articles to profl. jours. Decorated Legion of Merit with oak leaf cluster, Meritorious Svc. medal with two oak leaf clusters, Army Achievement medal with three oak leaf clusters, Nat. Def. Svc. medal with bronze star, Expert Field Med. badge; recipient Surgeon Gen.'s Profl. Excellence award. Fellow Internat. Coll. Dentists, Am. Coll. Dentists, Am. Acad. Oral Pathology; mem. Am. Dental Assn., Oreg. Dental Assn., Am. Acad. Oral Pathology, Am. Acad. Oral Medicine, Am. Assn. Dental Schs., Am. Assn. Stomatologists, Pierre Fauchard Acad., Fed. Health Care Execs. Inst., Assn. Mil. Surgeons U.S., Army Med. Dept. Regiment, Assn. U.S. Army, Assn. Indsl. Coll. Armed Forces, Order of Mil. Med. Merit. Republican. Avocations: hiking, basketball, dental antiques and collectibles. Home: 5606 Glanmore Ct Fairfax VA 22032-3147*

ALLEN, GEORGE DESMOND, epidemiology nurse, surgical nurse; b. Trinidad and Tobago, July 24, 1952; s. George Nevielle and Ilene Gertrude Allen; m. Bernice Eileen Redman, Apr. 7, 1984; 1 child, Troy. BSN, CUNY, 1984; MS in Adminstrn., Cen. Mich. U., 1991; PhD in Pub. Adminstrn., Kensington U., 1998. RN, N.Y.; CNOR; cert. in infection control. Staff nurse operating rm. Kings County Hosp., Bklyn., 1979-85; staff nurse operating rm. Interfaith Med. Ctr., Bklyn., 1986, nurse epidemiologist, infection control coord., 1986-91; sr. nurse epidemiologist, dir. infection control program Univ. Hosp. Bklyn., 1991—; staff nurse oper. rm. per diem St. Lukes ROosevelt Hosp., N.Y.C., 1986-95, Meth. Hosp., Bklyn., 1989—. Mem. APHA, Assn. Oper. Rm. Nurses (bd. dirs. 1990-91, v.p. Bklyn. chpt. 1992-93, pres. 1994-96), Assn. Practitioners in Infection Control (v.p. 1999-2000), Nat. League Nursing, N.Y. State Nursing Assn. Democrat. Office: SUNY Univ Hosp Bklyn Box 37 Brooklyn NY 11203-0037

ALLEN, GEORGE FELIX, lawyer; b. Whittier, Calif., Mar. 8, 1952; s. George H. and Henrietta Lumbroso A.; m. Susan M. Brown; children: Tyler, Forrest, Brooke. BA cum laude in History, U. Va., 1974, JD, 1977. Mem. Va. Ho. of Dels., Richmond, 1983-91, 102d Congress from 7th Dist. Va., 1991-93; gov. State of Va., 1994-98; ptnr. McGuire Woods Battle & Boothe, LLP, Richmond, 1998—. Advisor Pres. Coun. Phys. Fitness and Sports, 1981-91; chmn. Chesapeake Bay Exec. Coun., 1995-96, So. Gov.'s Assn., 1996-97. Presbyterian. Office: McGuire Woods Battle & Boothe LLP One James Ctr 901 E Cary St Richmond VA 23219-4057*

ALLEN, GEORGE HOWARD, publishing management consultant; b. Boston, June 1, 1914; s. Albert Hacker and Myrtie A. (Lawton) A.; m. Virginia Russell, Sept. 7, 1940; children: Russell Lawton, Douglas Winslow (dec.). B.S., U. Mass., 1936, LL.D., 1967; M.B.A., Harvard U., 1938. Asst. to pres. Nat. Theatre Supply Co., N.Y.C., 1938-40; research mgr. Sta. WOR, 1941, asst. dir. promotion and research, 1942-43; radio cons. U.S. Treasury Dept., 1943-45; gen. mgr., sec. bd. Coop. Analysis of Broadcasting, N.Y.C., 1944-46; N.E. sales mgr. N.Y. Herald Tribune, 1946, promotion mgr., 1947-50; chmn. 20th Nat. Bus. Conf., Harvard, 1950; dir. sales promotion McCall's mag., 1950-57, asst. pub., gen. mgr., 1957-60; pub. Better Living mag., 1956; v.p. Mass Markets Publs., Inc., 1953-54, pres., 1954-55, dir., 1953-55; spl. asst. to pres. Meredith Pub. Co., N.Y.C., 1960-61; v.p. Meredith Pub. Co., 1961-66, bd. dirs., 1965-66; gen. mgr. mag. pub. div. Meredith Pub. Co., Des Moines, 1962-66; pub. Better Homes and Gardens, Successful Farming mags., 1964-66; chmn. bd. Nat. Plan Service, Chgo., 1965-66; pub., v.p. bd. dirs. Fawcett Publs., Inc., N.Y.C., 1966-72; exec. v.p., dir. Fawcett Publs., Inc., 1972-77; sr. v.p. mags. CBS Publs., 1977-84, sr. v.p., 1978-82, spl. interest group pub. (Audio, Road & Track, World Tennis, Am. Photographer, Cycle World), 1982—; pub. Woman's Day, 1966-80, Audio, Road & Track, World Tennis, Am. Photographers, Cycle World, 1982-84; cons. pub. mgmt., 1984—; mem. panel Pres.'s White House Conf. on Food and Nutrition, 1969; Bd. dirs. Internat. Exchange Program, Ann Arbor, chmn., 1978-79; bd. dirs. Advt. Council, 1969—; chmn. Intercorp. Communications Group; mem. council judges Advt. Hall of Fame, 1982. Author: Individual Initiative in Business; Contbr. articles profl. mags. Mem. Chancellor's Council U. Mass, 1982, mem. bus. adv. Council Sch. Mgmt., 1983. Recipient leadership award Am. Legion, 1932; Young Advt. Man of Year, 1956; Achievement Award Wash. Ad Club, 1956; Silver Anvil award Am. Pub. Relations Assn., 1957; Bill Ringer award Salt Lake City Ad Club, 1957; Pub. Relations News award, 1957; Iowa Mgmt. Man of Year, 1965; named Pub. of Year; also recipient Henry Johnson Fisher award of mag. industry, 1980; named to Pub. Hall of Fame, 1985. Mem. Am. Mktg. Assn. (pres. N.Y. 1946), NAM (dir. 1965-66), Mag. Pubs. Assn. (dir., sec. 1974-75, chmn. 1977, chmn. kelly awards com. 1980—), Advt. Fedn. Am. (dir. 1965-67), U.S. C. of C. (edn. com. 1964-66), Advt. Rsch. Found. (dir. 1965, sec.-treas. 1971, vice chmn. 1972, chmn. 1974-75), U. Mass. Alumni Assn. (v.p.), Harvard Bus. Sch. Assn. (pres. 1967), Pubs. Info. Bur. (dir. 1966, vice chmn. 1974), Harvard Alumni Assn. (dir. 1958-59), Sales Promotion Execs. Assn. (mem. nat. bd. 1958), Broadcast Pioneers), All Media Exec. Roundtable (chmn.), Pub. Rels. Soc. Am., Harvard Club (N.Y.C.), Sky Club (N.Y.C.), Congregationalist. Office: Cons to Pub Mgmt 281 Harbor House Dr Osprey FL 34229-9742 *Togetherness is still the glue that structures our society.*

ALLEN, GEORGE SEWELL, neurosurgery educator; b. St. Louis, Jan. 10, 1942; s. Mitchell Vincent and Cleo (Scott) A.; m. Shannon Hersey, May 30, 1982; children: Kathrine Long, Jennifer Savage, Elizabeth Scott. BA in Chemistry, Wesleyan U., 1963; MD, Washington U., St. Louis, 1967; PhD, U. Minn., 1975. Diplomate Am. Bd. Neurol. Surgeons. Intern Duke U., Durham, N.C., 1967-68; rsch. assoc. Nat. Inst. Neurol. Disease and Stroke, NIH, 1968-70; resident dept. neurol. surgery U. Minn., Mpls., 1970-75; asst. prof. neurol. surgery Johns Hopkins U. and Hosp., Balt., 1975-79, assoc. prof., 1979-83, prof., 1983-84; prof. neurol. surgery, chmn. dept. Vanderbilt U. Med. Ctr., Nashville, 1984—; mem. med. staff Vanderbilt U. Hosp., Met. Nashville Gen. Hosp., VA Hosp., Nashville, St. Thomas Hosp., Nashville, all 1984—; A.W. Rogers lectr. Milw. Acad. Medicine, 1988, J. Jay Keegan Meml. lectr. U. Nebr. Med. Ctr., Omaha, 1988, J. Cochran lectr. Med. Assn. Ala., Montgomery, 1988, A.B. Baker lectr. U. Minn., Mpls., 1988. Contbr. articles to profl. jours. Comdr. USPHS, 1968-70. Mem. ACS, Am. Assn. Neurol. Surgeons, Congress of Neurol. Surgeons, Brain Surgery Soc., Soc. Neurol. Surgeons, H. William Scott, Jr. Soc., Soc. Neurosurg. Anesthesia and Neurologic Supportive Care, Md. Club (Balt.). Office: Vanderbilt U Med Ctr N Dept Neurosurgery Rm T 4224 Nashville TN 37232-2380

ALLEN, GERALD CAMPBELL FORREST, management consulting company owner; b. Boston, Nov. 1, 1923; s. Charles Francis and Sarah Ann (Campbell) A.; m. Anne Elisabeth Conrad, May 23, 1944; children: Katherine Sarah Anne, Ethan William John Campbell, Elisabeth Amy Martha Joan. BA, MA, Harvard U., 1945-49; PhD, U. Chgo., 1952. Ency. editor Consol. Book Pub., Chgo., 1952-54; advt. exec. Chgo. Tribune, 1954-59; pres. Gerald Allen Co., Chgo., 1960-66; v.p. Klau-Van Pietersom-Dunlap, Inc., Milw., 1967-71; v.p., dir. Unidex Pub. Co., Inc., Milw., 1971-80; chmn., chief exec. officer Allen Mgmt. Group, Inc., Milw., 1980—; pres. Psychologists in Advt., Chgo., 1965; instr. mktg. and bus. adminstrn. U. Wis., 1967-68; v.p., dir. Benchmark Mfg. Co., Inc., Milw.; cons. Kellett Commn. on Higher Edn. Mem. ad hoc Low Income Energy Task Force, State of Wis.; mem. energy crisis planning com. City of Milw. Capt. royal arty. Brit. Army, 1944-45, ETO. Fellow Royal Hort. Soc.; mem. Am. Mktg. Assn., Am. Statis. Assn., AAAS, Am. Econ. Assn., N.Y. Acad. Scis., Harvard Club of Wis., Harvard Club of Chgo., Mensa. Republican. Home: 1500 Center St # 15 Kewaunee WI 54216-1735 Office: Allen Mgmt Group Inc 1508 Center St Kewaunee WI 54216-1777

ALLEN, GLENN T., manufacturing executive; b. Bastrop, Tex., May 28, 1974; s. Paul Jay Allen and Theresa Flores Allen Warren. Student, Keesler Tech. Coll., 1992, Riverside (La.) C.C., 1993, USAF Acad., 1992-94. Wafer fab technician Advanced Micro Devices, Austin, Tex., 1995—. With USAF, 1992-94. Democrat. Roman Catholic. Avocations: hiking, biking, weightlifting, rollerblading, traveling. E-mail: glenn.allen@amd.com. Office: Advanced Micro Devices 5204 E Ben White Blvd Austin TX

ALLEN, HEATH LEDWARD, lawyer; b. Harrisburg, Pa., June 24, 1927; s. Albert Leroy and Alice Lenore (von Keller) A.; m. Eleanor Ann Martin, June 18, 1949; children: Barbara J. Reich, Heath Ledward II, Melissa A. Smith, Martin R. AB, Princeton U., 1949; LLB, Yale U., 1952. Bar: Pa. 1952. Assoc. Hull, Leiby & Metzger, Harrisburg, 1952-55, ptnr., 1955-66; ptnr. Metzger, Hafer, Keefer, Thomas & Wood, Harrisburg, 1966-77, Keefer, Wood, Allen & Rahal, Harrisburg, 1977—; sec., bd. dirs. Arnold Industries, Inc., Lebanon, Pa., New Penn Motor Express, Inc.; bd. dirs. Tim-Bar Corp., Hanover, Pa., Rogele, Inc., Warden Asphalt Co., Harrisburg. Pres. Tri-County United Way, Harrisburg, 1960-61. Served with U.S. Army, 1946-47, Korea. Fellow Am. Coll. Trust and Estate Counsel; mem. ABA, Pa. Bar. Assn. (house of dels. 1961-64), Dauphin County Bar Assn. (pres. 1960-61). Republican. Presbyterian. Clubs: The Country of Harrisburg, Desert Mountain, Nantucket Golf. Avocations: golf, travel. Home: 321 N 28th St Camp Hill PA 17011-2837 Office: Keefer Wood Allen & Rahal 210 Walnut St PO Box 11963 Harrisburg PA 17108-1963

ALLEN, HEATHER LINDSEY, textile artist, art educator, writer; b. Concord, N.H., Feb. 1, 1963; d. Peter Herbert and Marion Lindsey (Butson) A. Cert. in lang. proficiency, Nanzan U., Nagoya, Japan, 1985; BFA, U. N.H., 1989; MFA, U. Mass., Dartmouth, 1992. Screenprinter N.H. Printwork, Greenland, 1989; color separator Roth Tec Engraving Corp., New Bedford, Mass., 1990; exhbn. tech. Childrens Mus., Dartmouth, Mass., 1990-91; emerging profl. artist residency Appalachian Ctr. for Crafts, Smithville, Tenn., 1993-95, workshop tchr., 1993-97; tchr. U. Mass., Darthmouth, 1991-93; workshop tchr. Quilt Surface Design Symposium, Columbus, Ohio, 1995-98, Arrowmont Sch. Art and Crafts, Gatlinburg, Tenn., 1996-97; tchr. Penland (N.C.) Sch. Crafts, 1997—; v.p. Highland Rim Tenn. Assn. Craft Artists, Smithville, 1993-95; contbg. artist Art in Embassies Prog., 1996-99. Author: Weaving Contemporary Rag Rugs, 1998; contbr. articles to craft mags. Big sister Big Brother Big Sister Prog., New Bedford, Mass., 1990-93. Recipient Spotlight '94 Handweavers Guild Am. award, Winston-Salem, N.C., Niche award Phila. Buyers Market, 1996; NEA Regional fellow So. Arts Fedn., Atlanta, 1995, artist fellow Tenn. Arts Commn., Nashville, 1995. Mem. Fiberarts Internat., Am. Craft Coun., Surface Design Assn., Textile Arts Ctr., Piedmont Craftsmen Inc., Studio Art Quilt Assn. Avocations: gardening, traveling, color. Home and Office: PO Box 7646 Asheville NC 28802-7646

ALLEN, HENRY WESLEY, biomedical researcher; b. Louisville, Oct. 16, 1927; s. John Turk and Irene Victoria (Slater) A.; m. Evelyn Chen, Dec. 29, 1968 (div. Dec. 1988); children: Lillian Chen, Rosaniline Chen, Dianne Chen. Student, U. Louisville, 1945-46, U. Chgo., 1946-47, U. So. Calif., 1960-61. Rschr. Loma Linda (Calif.) U., 1962-77, Am. Biologics, Chula Vista, Calif., 1977—. Author: International Protocols in Cancer Management, 1983, The Study of Reactive Oxygen Toxic Species and Their Metabolism, 1985, 2d edit., 1997, The Biochemistry of Live Cell Therapy, 1986; contbr. articles to Jour. of Theoretical Biology, Analytical Biochemistry, Nature, others. Achievements include patents in field. Office: Am Biologics 1180 Walnut Ave Chula Vista CA 91911-2622

ALLEN, HERBERT, investment banker; b. N.Y.C., Feb. 13, 1908; s. Charles and Francis (Mayer) A.; m. Kathleen Heffernan (dec.); children—Herbert Anthony, Susan Kathleen Allen; m. Ethel Strong. D.C.S. (hon.), Ithaca Coll. Ptnr. Allen & Co., N.Y.C., 1927—; dir. emeritus Irvine Co., Newport Beach, Calif. Trustee, v.p. Hackley Sch., Tarrytown, N.Y. Clubs: Deepdale Golf; Indian Creek Golf (Fla.); Mark's (London); Saratoga Golf and Polo; Bal Harbour Club. *Died Jan. 18, 1997.*

ALLEN, HERBERT ELLIS, environmental chemistry educator; b. Sharon, Pa., July 19, 1939; s. Jacob Samuel and Florence (Safier) A.; m. Deena Wilner, 1962 (dec. 1983); children: Francine Joy, Julie Michelle; m. Ronnie Magil, 1984. B.S. in Chemistry, U. Mich., 1962; M.S., Wayne State U., 1967; Ph.D., U. Mich., 1974. Chemist U.S. Bur. Comml. Fisheries, Ann Arbor, Mich., 1962-70; lectr. U. Mich., Ann Arbor, 1970-74; asst. prof. Ill. Inst. Tech., Chgo., 1974-76, assoc. prof., 1976-80, prof. environ. engring., 1980-83; dir. Environ. Studies Inst., Drexel U., Phila., also prof. chemistry, 1983-89; prof. civil engring. U. Del., Newark, 1990—; dir. Del. Waste Reduction Assistance Program, 1991-95; vis. prof. Water Rsch. Ctr., Medmenham, Eng., 1980-81, Nankai U., Tianjin, People's Republic of China, 1993—; cons. WHO, U.S. EPA. Editor: Nutrients in Natural Waters, 1972, Analysis and Effects of Metal Speciation, Applications to Water, Waste, Soil, 1988, Metals in Groundwater, 1993, Metal Speciation and Contamination of Soil, 1994, Metal Contaminated Aquatic Sediments, 1995, Metals in Surface Water, 1998. WHO fellow, 1981. Mem. Am. Chem. Soc. (chmn. div. environ. chemistry 1972-75), Water Environment Fedn., Soc. for Environ. Toxicology and Chemistry, Internat. Assn. on Water Quality. Home: 21 E Levering Mill Rd Bala Cynwyd PA 19004-2251 Office: Univ Delaware Dept Civil & Environ Engring Newark DE 19716

ALLEN, IVAN, JR., office products company owner; b. Atlanta, Mar. 15, 1911; s. Ivan and Irene (Beaumont) A.; m. Louise Richardson, Jan. 1, 1936; children: Inman, Beaumont. Grad., Georgia Inst. Tech., 1933; LL.D., Morris Brown Coll., Clark Coll., Atlanta U., La Grange Coll., Emory U., Davidson Coll.; D of Pub. Svc., Ga. Inst. Tech., 1996. With Ivan Allen Co., Atlanta, 1933—, pres., 1946-57, vice chmn. bd., 1957, chmn. bd., 1969-95, chmn. emeritus, 1995—; dir. Equitable Life Assurance Soc. Scout, scoutmaster, area pres., regional committeeman, mem. nat. exec. bd. Boy Scouts Am.; chmn. Greater Atlanta Community Chest, 1949; Lt. col. Gov.'s Staff, 1936; treas. Ga. State Hosp. Authority, 1936; sec. exec. dept. State Ga., 1945-46; mayor of Atlanta, 1961-69; Trustee Ga. Tech. Found. Served as maj. inf. AUS, World War II. Awarded Silver Beaver; awarded Silver Antelope, Silver Buffalo; Recipient Armin Maier award Atlanta Rotary Club, 1952. Mem. Ga. Tech. Alumni Assn. (pres. 1953-54), Atlanta C. of C. (pres. 1961), Nat. Stationery and Office Equipment Assn. (dist. gov. 1938-40, pres. 1955-56), Rotary, Sigma Alpha Epsilon. Home: 3700 Northside Dr NW Atlanta GA 30305-1035 Office: Ivan Allen Co 221 Peachtree Center Ave NE Atlanta GA 30303-1748

ALLEN, JAMES HENRY, magistrate; b. Memphis, May 10, 1935; s. Henry L. and Hazel V. A.; m. Charlene Anne Jayroe, July 29, 1961; children—James Henry, Elizabeth Hazel, Luanne Mae. A.B., Memphis State U., 1957; LL.B., Tulane U., 1960. Bar: La. 1960, Tenn. 1961, U.S. Dist. Ct. (we. dist.) Tenn. 1961, U.S. Ct. Appeals (6th cir.) 1973, U.S. Supreme Ct. 1969. Assoc. Tual, Allan, Keltner, and Lee, Memphis, 1960; assoc. Nelson, Norvell & Floyd, Memphis, 1961; claims adjuster State Farm Mut. Automobile Ins. Co., Memphis, 1961-65; adminstrv. asst. law clk. Bankruptcy Ct., Memphis, 1965-67; assoc. Charles G. Black, Memphis, 1967-69; asst. atty. gen. Shelby County (Tenn.), 1969-79; U.S. magistrate, Memphis, 1979—; lectr. on criminal law, recruit class Shelby County Sheriff's Dept., Memphis, 1976; lectr. on fed. rules civil procedure Continuing Legal Edn., Memphis, 1981. Served with USMCR, 1957-65. Tulane U. scholar, 1957-60. Mem. La. State Bar Assn., Memphis and Shelby County Bar Assn., Nat. Council U.S. Magistrates, Phi Alpha Delta. Baptist. Fax: 901-495-1384. Office: US Dist Ct 338 Federal Bldg 167 N Main St Memphis TN 38103-1816

ALLEN, JANE INGRAM, artist, educator; b. Delta, Ala., Sept. 23, 1940; d. John D. and Frances (Ligon) Ingram; m. Timothy S. Allen, Dec. 27, 1968; children: Christopher S., Jennifer J. BA, Ala. Coll., 1961; MEd, U. Fla., 1970. Cert. art tchr., N.Y., Calif. Tchr. English Jr. H.S., Ala., 1961-63; tchr. art secondary schs., Fla., Va., 1963-72; instr. art colls., Fla., Ga., Calif., 1972-88, SUNY, Morrisville, 1989-94, 98—; tchg. artist Arts in Edn. Inst., Utica, N.Y., 1995—; instr. art Cazenovia (N.Y.) Coll., 1992-94; artist in residence Duntog Found., Baguio City, The Philippines, 1996. One man shows include Percival Galleries, Des Moines, 1996, Arts Ctr., Old Forge, N.Y., 1996, 171 Cedar Arts Ctr., Corning, N.Y., 1995, Rome (N.Y.) Art and Cmty. Ctr., 1994, Kirkland Arts Ctr., Clinton, N.Y., 1994, CUNY, 1993, Ctrl. N.Y. Cmty. Arts Coun. Gallery, Utica, 1992, N.Y. Inst. Tech. Midge Karr Fine Arts Ctr. Gallery, Old Westbury, N.Y., 1992, Chenango County Coun. Arts Gallery, Norwich, N.Y., 1991, Herkimer (N.Y.) County C.C. Gallery, 1991; exhibited in group shows at Connemara Conservancy, Dallas, 1998, U. Minn., Mpls., 1998, Empire-Fulton Ferry State Park, Bklyn., 1995, Chesterwood Mus., Stockbridge, Mass., 1995, Utica Coll. Barrett Art Gallery, 1995, Gannett Gallery, 1995, SUNY Tech Utica-Rome, 1995, Wells Coll., 1995, Nassau C.C. Gallery, 1995, 94, U. Gallery, SUNY, Stony Brook, 1994, Mus. Art Munson Williams Proctor Inst., Utica, 1993, Deland (Fla.) Mus. Art, 1991; represented in permanent collections Corning Natural Gas Co., Corning Glass Credit Union, Fed. Res. Bank N.Y., ASCAP, U. Iowa Hosps., Townsend Engring, Des Moines, Allied Ins. Corp., Des Moines,

Abraham Joel C&A Gallery, N.Y., First Interstate Bank, Des Moines, Barnett Bank, West Palm Beach, Fla., DBA Sys., Inc., Melbourne, Fla., Motorola Corp., Delray Beach, Fla., La. State U., Alexandria. Mem. Coll. Art Assn., Women's Caucus for Art.

ALLEN, JANICE M., interior designer, nurse, office manager, actress, model; b. Evanston, Ill., May 29, 1953; d. Paul John and Claudia Stroman (White) Mandabach; m. George Whitaker Allen, Apr. 26, 1980. Student, Syracuse U., 1971-72; BSN, Tex. Christian U., 1976. Nurse oper. rm., circulating nurse oper. rm. Northwestern Meml. Hosp., Chgo., 1976-78; model, actress Chgo., 1978-86, 94—; nurse, office mgr. George W. Allen, MD, Chgo., 1986—. Mem. Carlton Club, Sand Creek Country Club. Republican. Methodist. Avocations: golf, downhill skiing, acting, international travel, salt water aquariums. Home: 1503 Sand Creek Dr Chesterton IN 46304-9373 Office: George W Allen MD 150 E Huron St Chicago IL 60611-2999

ALLEN, JAY PRESSON, writer, producer; b. Ft. Worth, Mar. 3, 1922; d. Albert Jeffry and Willie (Miller) Presson; m. Lewis Maitland Allen, Mar. 12, 1955; 1 child, Anna Brooke. Screenplays include Marnie, 1964, The Prime of Miss Jean Brodie, 1969, Cabaret, 1972 (Academy award nomination best adapted screenplay 1972), Travels with My Aunt, 1972, Funny Lady, 1975; playwright, dir.: Tru, 1989, The Big Love, 1991; playwright: The Prime of Miss Jean Brodie, 1966, Forty Carats, 1968, I and Albert, 1972, A Little Family Business, 1982; screenwriter, exec. prodr.: It's My Turn, 1980, Just Tell Me What You Want, 1980 (David DiDonatello award 1980), Prince of the City, 1981 (Academy award nomination best adapted screenplay 1981), Deathtrap, 1982; creator: (TV series) Family, 1976-80; creator, exec. prodr.: (TV series) Hothouse, 1988; author: (novels) Spring Riot, 1948, Just Tell Me What You Want, 1975. Recipient Humanitas award, 1976, Screenwriters' Guild awards (3), Lifetime achievement award, 1997. Mem. Writers Guild, Dramatists Guild, Acad. Motion Picture Arts and Scis. Office: Lewis Allen Prodns 1501 Broadway Ste 1614 New York NY 10036-5601*

ALLEN, JEFFREY MICHAEL, lawyer; b. Chgo., Dec. 13, 1948; s. Albert A. and Miriam (Feldman) A.; m. Anne Marie Guaraglia, Aug. 9, 1975; children: Jason M., Sara M. BA in Polit. Sci. with great distinction, U. Calif., Berkeley, 1970, JD, 1973. Bar: Calif. 1973, U.S. Dist. Ct. (no. and so. dists.) Calif. 1973, U.S. Ct. Appeals (9th cir.) 1973, U.S. Dist. Ct. (ea. dist.) Calif. 1974, U.S. Dist. Ct. (cen. dist.) Calif. 1977, U.S. Dist. Ct. (so. dist.) Calif., U.S. Supreme Ct.; lic. real estate broker. Prin. Graves & Allen, Oakland, Calif., 1973—; teaching asst. dept. polit. sci. U. Calif., Berkeley, 1970-73; lectr. St. Mary's Coll., Moraga, Calif., 1976-90; mem. faculty Oakland Coll. of Law, 1996-98; bd. dirs. Family Svcs. of the East Bay, 1987-92, 1st v.p., 1988, pres., 1988-91; mem. panel arbitrators Ala. County Superior Ct.; arbitrator comml. arbitration panel Am. Arbitration Assn. Mem. editorial bd. U. Calif. Law Rev., 1971-73, project editor, 1972-73; mem. Ecology Law Quar., 1971-72, editor-in-chief Tech. and Practice Guide, chmn. tech. com.; contbr. articles to profl. jours. Treas. Hillcrest Elem. Sch. PTA, 1984-86, pres., 1986-88; past mem. GATE adv. com., strategic planning com. on fin. and budget, dist. budget adv. com., instructional strategy counsel Oakland Unified Sch. Dist., 1986-91; mem. Oakland Met. Forum, 1987-91, Oakland Strategic Planning Com., 1988-90; mem. adv. com. St. Mary's Coll. Paralegal Prog.; bd. dirs. Montera Sports Complex, 1988-89; bd. dirs. Jack London Youth Soccer League, 1988-94; commr. Bay Oaks Youth Soccer, 1988-94; asst. dist. commr. dist. 4 Calif. Youth Soccer Assn., 1990-92, sec. 1993-96, bd. dirs. 1993—, also bd. dirs., pres. dist. 4 competitive league, 1990-93; sec., bd. dirs. Calif. Youth Soccer Assn., 1993-96, chmn. bd. dirs., 1996—; bd. dirs. Calif. Soccer Assn. North, 1996—; mem. U.S. Soccer database mktg. com., 1997—, U.S. Soccer Constl. Commn., 1997-98, U.S. Youth Soccer bylaws com., 1998—, U.S. Youth Soccer Region 4 Regional Coun., 1996—; chmn. U.S. Youth Soccer database mktg. com., 1998—. Mem. ABA (chmn. real property com. gen. practice sect. 1987-91, mem. programs com. 1991-93, chmn. subcom. on use of computers in real estate trans. 1985-86, adv. coord. 1993-96, sect. coun. 1994-98, mktg. bd. 1996—, chmn. tech. com. 1998—, editor Tech. and Practice Guide 1998—), Alameda County Bar Assn. (past vice chmn. com. continuing edn., exec. com. alternative dispute resolution programs, panel mediator, arbitrator), U.S. Soccer Assn. (database mktg. com., constl. commn.), Calif. Bar Assn., Calif. Scholarship Fedn., U.S. Soccer Fedn. (nat. C lic. coach and state referee, state referee instr. and state referee assessor), Calif. North Referee Assn. (referee adminstr. dist. 4 1992-96, state bd. dirs. 1996—), Soc. for Profls. in Dispute Resolution, Oakland C. of C., Rotary (bd. dirs. Oakland 1992-94). Avocations: reading, computers, photography, skiing, baseball, coaching and refereeing youth soccer. Office: Graves & Allen 436 14th St Ste 1400 Oakland CA 94612

ALLEN, JEFFREY RODGERS, lawyer; b. West Point, N.Y., Aug. 15, 1953; s. James R. and Kathryn (Lewis) A.; m. Cynthia Lynn Colyer, Aug. 10, 1975; children: Emily Rodgers, Elizabeth Colyer, Richard Byrd. BA in History, U. Va., 1975; JD, U. Richmond, 1978. Bar: Va. 1978, U.S. Ct. Mil. Appeals 1981, U.S. Ct. Appeals (4th cir.) 1982, U.S. Supreme Ct. 1982. Trial atty. Michie, Hamlett, Donato & Lowry, Charlottesville, Va., 1982-86; chief counsel Va. Dept. Mil. Affairs, Richmond, 1986—; atty., advisor U.S. Army Mobile Air Surg. Transport Team, Savannah, Ga., 1980-82; mem. steering com. X-Car Litigation Group, 1983-85; lectr., organizer Law Everyone Should Know series Piedmont (Va.) C.C., Charlottesville, 1984-86; trial atty., of counsel Thorsen, Marchant & Scher, L.L.P., Richmond, 1986-98; mem. legal adv. com. Va. Gov.'s Mil. Adv. Commn., 1987—, judge advocate adv. coun. N.G. Bur., 1993-96, TJAG Air N.G. judge advocate adv. coun., 1997—, recording sec. ST HQ Liason (East), mem. strategic planning com. Pres. Regency Woods Condominium Assn., Richmond, 1976-78, Ashcroft Neighborhood Assn., Charlottesville, 1983-86; treas. Va. N.G. Found., 1986—. Capt. U.S. Army, 1978-82, lt. col. JAGC, Va. Air N.G., 1982—. Mem. Assn. Trial Lawyers Am., Va. Trial Lawyers Assn., Richmond Bar Assn. Republican. Methodist. Avocations: jogging, mountain climbing, photography, fishing, swimming. Home: 2700 Cottage Cove Dr Richmond VA 23233-3318 Office: Va Dept Mil Affairs Bldg 316 Ft Pickett Blackstone VA 23824-6316

ALLEN, JERRY L., university dean, communication educator; b. Parma, Mo., Jan. 1, 1938; s. Alton and Bernice (Grissom) A.; m. Annitta L. Wagley, Oct. 16, 1955 (div. 1972); children: Tom, Deborah, Richard, Tracy; m. Betty L. Scott, Sept. 1, 1972; children: Leland, Ken, Cindi. BS in Edn., Southeast Mo. State U., 1959; MS in Edn., So. Ill. U., 1961, PhD in Speech Comm., 1978. Tchr. Fox H.S., Arnold, Mo., 1959-64, Lindberg H.S., St. Louis, 1964-65; asst. prof. speech St. Louis U., 1965-71; prof., chair dept. U. Bridgeport, Conn., 1973-90; prof., chair dept. U. New Haven, West Haven, Conn., 1990-95, acting dean, Sch. Bus., 1995-96, dean grad. studies, 1996—; comm. cons. Mo., 1965-71, Conn. 1973-97; adj. prof. U. Mo., 1969-70, So. Conn. State U., 1973-94; Albertus Magnus Coll., 1989. Contbg. author: Interpersonal Communication: A Laboratory Manual, 1980, Instructor's Manual for Interplay: The Process of Interpersonal Communication, 4th edit.; editor Comm. Rsch. Reports, 1996—; mem. editl bd. various jours., 1968—; contbr. articles to profl. jours. Littlefield Chair Rsch. grantee U. Bridgeport, 1985. Mem. Nat. Comm. Assn. (chair comm. apprehension com. 1986-87), World Comm. Assn. (bd. dirs. 1991—), Internat. Comm. Assn., Eastern Comm. Assn. (exec. sec. 1992-95, first v.p. 1997-98, pres. 1998—). Democrat. Avocations: photography. Home: 5053 Main St Stratford CT 06614-8803 Office: Univ New Haven 300 Orange Ave West Haven CT 06516-1999

ALLEN, JERRY WAYNE, organization executive; b. Cadiz, Ky., Jan. 6, 1948; s. Florice R. Kennie and C. Charlene (Lane) A.; m. Vickie Diane Allen, Mar. 10, 1980; children: Robert, Christopher. BS in Wildlife Biology, Murray State U., 1972, BS in Indsl. Arts, 1972, MS in Journalism, 1975. Founder, exec. Quail Unlimited Inc., Edgefield, S.C., 1981—. Researcher in field studies, 1970, 71. Pres. West Side Community Ctr., Edgefield, S.C., 1984-86; founder West Side Fire Dept., Edgefield, 1986-87. Mem. Am. Soc. Assn. Execs., Pub. Rels. Soc., Nat. Wild Turkey Federated, Water fowl USA. Avocations: hunting, woodworking. Home: RR 3 Box 29B Edgefield SC 29824-9304 Office: Quail Unlimited PO Box 610 Edgefield SC 29824-0610*

ALLEN, JESSE OWEN, III, management development and organizational behavior; b. Albany, Ga., Apr. 7, 1938; s. Jesse Owen Jr. and Erma Hazel (Pearson) A.; children by previous marriage: Charlotte Renee, Garrett Owen, Cheryl Hazel; m. Barbara Joanna Smith Ozment, May 23, 1987; 1 stepchild, Pamela Ozment Cartee. LLB, LaSalle Law Sch., 1967; AS, U. State N.Y., Albany, 1978, BS in History, Lit. and Bus., 1986; MA in Philosophy, Calif. State U., 1987; PhD in Organizational Behavior, The Union Grad. Sch., 1991; postgrad., Oxford U., England, 1997. Founder, pres. Specific Action Corp., Greensboro, N.C., 1971—; pres. Inst. for Christian Studies, Inc., Greensboro, N.C., 1987—; bd. dirs. ECA Internat.; pres. Worldwide Travel, Greensboro, N.C., 1994—; lectr., cons. in field internat. Author: (book, manual, course) Weatherization Production Control, 1978, Personal Profile Labs, 1980, Management Power: The Specific Action Way, 1985, Personality Power: The Specific Action Way, 1988, Master of Personal Excellence Program, 1994; contbr. articles to profl. jours., Specific Action Management System, 1996, Specific Action Personality System, 1996, Specific Action Team System, 1997; patentee Allen valve, 1967. Named to Hon. Order of Ky. Cols., Commonwealth of Ky., 1978, Hon. Adm. State of Nebr., 1978. Mem. Am. Soc. Tng. and Devel. (pres. 1976, Best Chpt. award 1976), Nat. Speakers Assn. (cert. speaking profl. 1988), Greensboro City Club, Inst. Mgmt. Cons. (cert. 1989). Republican. Home: 520 Lindley Rd Greensboro NC 27410-4933 Office: Specific Action Corp PO Box 19125 Greensboro NC 27419-9125

ALLEN, JOAN, actress; b. Rochelle, Ill., Aug. 20, 1956. Student, Ea. Ill. U., No. Ill. U. Founding mem. Steppenwolf Theatre Co., Chgo.; theater appearances include (debut) And A Nightingale Sang, N.Y.C. (Clarence Derwent award, Drama Desk award, Outer Critics Circle award 1984), Steppenwolf Theatre Co., also Hartford, 1983, The Marriage of Bette and Boo, N.Y. Shakespeare Festival, 1986, Burn This! (Tony awrd for Best Actress 1988) Mark Taper Forum, L.A., also N.Y.C., 1987, The Heidi Chronicles, N.Y.C., 1988, 89; film appearances include Compromising Positions, 1985, Peggy Sue Got Married, 1986, Manhunter, 1986, Tucker: The Man and His Dream, 1988, In Country, 1989, Ethan Frome, 1993, Searching for Bobbie Fischer, 1993, Josh and S.A.M., 1993, Nixon, 1995 (Acad. award nominee for best supporting actress 1996), Mad Love, 1995, The Crucible, 1996, Ice Storm, 1996, Face/Off, 1997, Pleasantville, 1998, Veronica Guerin, 1999, All the Rage, 1999; TV appearances include miniseries Evergreen, 1985, All My Sons, 1986, Am. Playhouse, PBS, 1987, Robert Frost, Voices and Visions, PBS, 1988, TV film The Room Upstairs, 1987, Without Warning: The James Brady Story, 1991, Say Goodnight, Gracie, PBS. Office: Internat Creative Mgmt care Brian Mann 8942 Wilshire Blvd Beverly Hills CA 90211-1934*

ALLEN, JOHN CARLTON, minister; b. Galveston, Tex., Dec. 7, 1943; s. F.A. and A.V. (Spiller) A.; m. Alice M. Geters, July 8, 1966; children: Renard D., John Carlton Jr., Joel C. BA, Bishop Coll., 1965; LLD (hon.), Guadalupe Coll., Union Bapt. Coll. Ordained to ministry Nat. Bapt. Conv. Am., 1961. Pastor St. Matthew Bapt. Ch., 1965-67, New Mt. Pleasant Bapt. Ch., San Antonio, 1967—; auditor Nat. Bapt. Conv. Am., 1986—, Missionary Bapt. Gen. Conv. Tex., 1975—. Mem. Bapt. Mins. Union San Antonio (pres. 1976-78). Office: Nat Baptist Conv Am 777 S R L Thornton Fwy Dallas TX 75203*

ALLEN, JOHN JAY, Spanish language educator; b. May 20, 1932. AB, Duke U., 1954; MA, Middlebury Coll., 1957; PhD, U. Wis., 1960. Prof. Spanish, U. Fla., Gainesville, 1960-83, U. Ky., Lexington, 1983—. E-mail: jjallen@kih.net. Home: 1153 Stirling Dr Danville KY 40422 Office: Spanish and Italian U Ky POT 1115 Lexington KY 40506-0027

ALLEN, JOHN LOGAN, geographer; b. Laramie, Wyo., Dec. 27, 1941; s. John Milton and Nancy Elizabeth (Logan) A.; m. Anne Evelyn Gilroy, Aug. 9, 1964; children: Traci Kathleen, Jennifer Lynne. BA (Gen. Motors Corp. scholar 1959-63), U. Wyo., 1963, MA, 1964; PhD (univ. grad. fellow 1964-67), Clark U., Worcester, Mass., 1969; PhD NSF postdoctoral fellow, 1970-71. Mem. faculty U. Conn., Storrs, 1967—, prof. geography, 1979—, head dept., 1976-94, dir. grad. program in geography, 1992—, mem. nat. exec. com. Faculty Athletic Rep. Assn., 1987-96; parliamentarian Faculty Athletic Rep. Assn., 1996—; non-resident fellow Ctr. Great Plains Studies; cons. in field. Author: Passage Through the Garden: Lewis and Clark and the Geographical Lore of the American Northwest, 1975, Jedediah Smith and the Mountain Men of the American West, 1991, Lewis and Clark and the Images of the American Northwest, 1991, Student Atlas of World Politics, 1991, 2d edit., 1993, 3d edit., 1997, Atlas of Economic Development, 1997, Atlas of Environmental Issues, 1997, Student Atlas of World Geography, 1998; editor: (ann. edits.) Environment, 1982—, Reshaping Traditions, 1994; mem. editl bd. Jour. Hist. Geography; project dir., gen. editor North American Exploration; A Comprehensive History, 3 vols., 1997; contbr. articles to profl. jours., chpts. to books. Pres. Mansfield (Conn.) Middle Sch. Assn., 1979-80; mem. Mansfield Conservation Commn.; vice chmn. Mansfield Zoning Bd. Appeals; mem. Mansfield Planning and Zoning Commn. Recipient Meritorious Achievement award Lewis and Clark Trail Heritage Found., 1976, Excellence in Teaching award U. Conn. Alumni Assn., 1987, Outstanding Contbn. award UCONN Club, 1993, Outstanding Alumnus award U. Wyo. Coll. Arts and Scis., 1999. Fellow Am. Geog. Assn., Royal Geog. Soc.; mem. Assn. Am. Geographers, Western History Assn., Soc. Historians Early Am. Republic, Soc. History Discovery (nat. councilor), AAAS, Phi Beta Kappa, Phi Kappa Phi, Omicron Delta Kappa. Democrat. Congregationalist. Clubs: Elks, Masons. Home: 21 Thomas Dr Storrs Mansfield CT 06268-1211 Office: U Conn U-148 Storrs Mansfield CT 06269-2148 *As a scientist and educator, I have tried to abide by the principle that learning is necessary for the public good and that academicians should make their skills and knowledge available to society at large. Service to others is as important an educational function as the more frequently recognized components of teaching and research.*

ALLEN, JOHN LYNDON, social studies educator; b. Boston, June 7, 1934; s. Lyndon Ball and Irene Butterfield (Roys) A.; children: Jennifer, Geoffrey, Jason Allen. BA, Northeastern U., 1957, MEd, 1966. Social studies tchr. jr. and h.s. Kennedy Jr. H.S., Randolph, Mass., 1965-71; social studies tchr. sr. h.s. Randolph (Mass.) H.S., 1971-94; supr. student tchrs. Bridgewater State Coll. Sch. Edn., 1996—. Mem. vestry Episcopal ch., Whitman, Mass., 1980-84, edn. adv. com., 1981-82, govt. study com., 1979-81, fin. com., 1986-87. Recipient Disting. Svc. cert. Mass. Tchrs. Assn., 1994, Plaque of Appreciation, Football Boosters Club, 1993. Mem. RAndolph Tchrs. Assn. (v.p. jr. h.s. 1967-70, v.p. sr. h.s. 1971-74, profl. policies com. 1974-76, bldg. rep. h.s. 1976-82), South Shore Coun. for Social Studies. Avocations: photography, fishing, hiking.

ALLEN, JOHN RYBOLT L., chemist, biochemist; b. Indpls., Sept. 14, 1926. BA, Ball State Tchrs. Coll., 1949; PhD in Biochemistry, U. Ill., 1954. Rsch. assoc. biochemistry Northwestern U., 1953-56; asst. prof. Coll. Med. Baylor U., 1956-59; sr. scientist Warner-Lambert Pharm. Co., N.J., 1959-60; rsch. assoc. Dental Sch. Wash. U., 1960-62; prof. chemistry, head. dept. Union Coll., Ky., 1962-64; clin. assoc. clin. chemistry U. Hosp. Case Western Reserve U., 1964-65; asst. prof. pathology and radiology coll. medicine Ohio State U., 1965-68; clin. chemist St. John's Mercy Hosp., St. Louis, 1968-69, Decatur Meml. Hosp., Ill., 1969-70, San Diego Inst. Pathology, 1970, San Bernardino County Hosp., 1970-75; instr. chemistry Phoenix Coll., 1975-80. Recipient G.K. Warren prize Nat. Acad. Scis., 1990, Penrose medal Geol. Soc. Am., 1996. Fellow AAAS, Am. Assn. Clin. Chemistry, Am. Chemistry Soc., Acad. Clin. Lab. Physicians & Scientists, Am. Inst. Chemistry. Achievements include research in quality control and methods, creating phosphokinase, vitamin E deficiency, lipid metabolism and structure. Home: 9627 N 32nd St Phoenix AZ 85028-4832

ALLEN, JOI LIN, government official; b. Jan. 13, 1969. BA, Weber State U., Ogden, Utah, 1989; MPA, U. Utah, 1995. Investigator U.S. Dept. Labor, Salt Lake City, 1988—, coord. edn. and outreach, 1995—. Mem. ASPA (chmn. spkr. com. Utah chpt. 1998—). E-mail: jallen@dal.dol-esa.gov. Office: US Dept Labor 10 W Broadway Ste 307 Salt Lake City UT 84101-2075

ALLEN, JOSE R., lawyer; b. Panama, Sept. 8, 1951; arrived in U.S., 1956; s. Joseph R. and Grace A. (Osborne) A.; m. Irvenia E. Waters, July 20, 1986; 1 child, Jeffrey Richard Allen. BA, Yale U., 1973; JD, Boston Coll., 1976. Bar: Mass. 1977, Calif. 1986. Asst. atty. gen. Mass. Atty. Gen. Office, Boston, 1976-79; trial atty. U.S. Dept. Justice, Washington, 1979-80, asst. sect. chief, 1980-82, sect. chief, 1982-85; of counsel Orrick, Herrington & Sutcliffe, San Francisco, 1985-88; ptnr. Skadden, Arps, Slate, Meagher & Flom LLP, San Francisco, 1988—; mem. adv. com. Practicing Law Inst., N.Y.C., 1992—. Bd. dirs. San Francisco Bay Area Lawyers' Com. Urban Affairs, 1990, Legal Aid Soc. San Francisco, 1993. Mem. ABA, Bar Assn. San Francisco, Charles Houston Bar Assn., State Bar Calif. (mem. environ. law sect.). Office: Skadden Arps Slate Meagher & Flom LLP Four Embarcadero Ctr San Francisco CA 94111*

ALLEN, JULIE MICHELLE, secondary education educator; b. Ann Arbor, Mich., Feb. 27, 1969; d. Herbert E. and Deena (Wilner) Allen. BA, DePaul U., Chgo., 1993. Cert. tchr., Ill. English tchr. Josephinum H.S., Chgo., 1993-94, Roosevelt H.S., Chgo., 1994—. Active Art Inst. Chgo., 1997-98, Hadassah, Chgo., 1998. Mem. TESOL, Nat. Coun. Tchrs. English. Avocations: cooking, sewing, reading, writing. Home: 515 W Barry Ave Apt 566 Chicago IL 60657-5462

ALLEN, KAREN JANE, actress; b. Carrollton, Ill., Oct. 5, 1951; d. Carroll Thompson and Patricia (Howell) A. Student, George Washington U., 1974-76. Mem. Washington Theatre Lab., 1973-77. Appeared in films The Whidjit-Maker, 1977, National Lampoon's Animal House, 1978, The Wanderers, 1979, Manhattan, 1979, A Small Circle of Friends, 1979, Cruising, 1979, Raiders of the Lost Ark, 1981, Shoot The Moon, 1981, Split Image, 1981, Aftermath, 1982, Strange Invaders, 1983, Until September, 1984, Starman, 1984, The End of the Line, 1986, Terminus, 1986, The Glass Menagerie, 1987, Backfire, 1987, Scrooged, 1988, Animal Behavior, 1989, Sweet Talker, 1991, Malcolm X, 1992, Secret Places of the Heart, Confidence, Exile, The Sandlot, 1993, King of the Hill, 1993, Ghost in the Machine, 1994, Til There Was You, 1996, Crocodile Tears, 1997, Wind River, 1998, Falling Sky, 1998, The Basket, 1999; TV films Lovey: A Circle of Children, Part II, 1978, East of Eden, 1980, Secret Weapon, 1990, Challenger, 1990, Rapture, 1993, Voyage, 1993, Kerry Ellison Story, 1996, All the Winters That Have Been, 1997, Wind River, 1998, Falling Sky; TV series Knots Landing, 1979, The Road Home, 1994, The Road Home, 1994; Broadway debut as Helen Keller in Monday After the Miracle, 1982; other stage appearances include Two For the Seesaw, 1981, Monday After The Miracle, Actors Studio (N.Y.C.), Kennedy Ctr. (Washington), (Theatre World award 1983), Tennessee Williams: A Celebration, Williamstown Theatre Festival, 1982, Extremities, West Side Arts Theatre, N.Y.C., 1983, The Glass Menagerie, Williamstown Theatre Festival, 1985, Longwharf Theatre, New Haven, Ct., 1986, The Miracle Worker, Roundabout Theatre, N.Y.C., 1987, Beautiful Bodies, The Whole Theatre, 1987, As You Like It, Mount Theatre, 1988, The Country Girl, Roundabout Theatre, N.Y.C., 1990-91. Mem. Screen Actors Guild, Actor's Equity Assn. Address: 17 Cronk Rd Monterey CA 01245*

ALLEN, KATHERINE SPICER, writer, former chemist; b. Plainfield, N.J., Apr. 29, 1919; d. Arthur Joseph and Linda Varner (Morrison) Spicer; m. Carl Holley Allen, Sept. 24, 1943; children: Carl Holley, Jr., David Randolph, Katherine Allen Fehn, Linda Ruth Allen Taylor. BA, U. Del., 1942. Libr. asst. State Libr., Dover, Del., summers 1936-41; typist U. Del., Newark, 1940-42; chemist Esso Rsch. Divsn., Bayway, Elizabeth, N.J., 1942-46; analyst Azoplate Corp., Murray Hill, N.J., 1963-67; enumerator U.S. Census Bur., Somerset County, N.J., 1980, 90; contbg. writer Bernardsville (N.J.) News, 1982—. Co-author: A History of the Presbyterian Church of Liberty Corner, 1837-1987, 1987, (booklet) Christian Education Goals and Objectives, 1991 (with others) Past and Present Lives of New Jersey Women, 1990. Mem. Bernards Twp. Local Assistance Bd., 1972-96, sec., 1974-89, chmn., 1990; mem. Bernards Twp. Mcpl. Alliance, 1992-96; mem. Somerset County Rep. Com., 1972-93; mem. personnel com. Mcpls. Com. Bernards Twp., 1990-93, mem. comm. com. am. Cancer Soc., 1990-94, vol. Reach to Recovery, 1985—, Somerset County coord. programs, 1987-89; ordained elder Presbyn. Ch. U.S.A., 1980; mem. justice for women com. Elizabeth Presbytery, 1988—, mem. comm. com., 1992—, commr. to Synod of N.E., 1991, 92-93, mem. media com. 1988-90, mem. nominating com. 1987-92, vice chairperson 1990-92, mem. search com. for assoc. exec. 1993; pres. Liberty Corner Presbyn. Ch. Women's Assn., 1973, 74, 84, ch. sch. tchr., 1952-81, ruling elder, 1980-82; mission chair United Presbyn. Ch., Plainfield, 1995-97; dir. Ch. Women United Somerset County, 1979-81; state chmn. Ecumenical Action, 1982-83; mem. Somerset County Breast Cancer Awareness Task Force, 1996-97—; mem. Plainfield Area Mission Group, 1998—. Named Somerset County Reach to Recovery Vol. of Yr., Am. Cancer Soc., 1991; recipient svc. pins. Mem. N.J. Press Women (various awards for articles written in Bernardsville News). Avocations: cooking, computers, travel, reading, crosswords. Home: 218 Lurline Dr Basking Ridge NJ 07920-2624

ALLEN, LARRY CHRISTOPHER, football player; b. L.A., Nov. 27, 1971; m. Janelle Allen; 1 child, Jayla. Student, Butte Jr. Coll., Sonoma State U. Tackle Dallas Cowboys, 1994—. Named to Sporting News NFL All-Pro Team, 1995, Pro Bowl, 1995, 96. Office: care Dallas Cowboys 1 Cowboys Pkwy Irving TX 75063-4945*

ALLEN, LAYMAN EDWARD, law educator, research scientist; b. Turtle Creek, Pa., June 9, 1927; s. Layman Grant and Viola Iris (Williams) A.; m. Christine R. Patmore, Mar. 29, 1950 (dec.); children: Layman G., Patricia R.; m. Emily C. Hall, Oct. 3, 1981 (div. 1992); children: Phyllip A. Hall, Kelly C. Hall; m. Leslie A. Olson, June 10, 1995. Student, Washington and Jefferson Coll., 1945-46; AB, Princeton U., 1951; MPub. Admnstrn., Harvard U., 1952; LLB, Yale U., 1956. Bar: Conn. 1956. Fellow Ctr. for Advanced Study in Behavioral Scis., 1961-62; sr. fellow Yale Law Sch., 1956-57, lectr., 1957-58, instr., 1958-59, asst. prof., 1959-63, assoc. prof., 1963-66; assoc. prof. law U. Mich. Law Sch., Ann Arbor, 1966-71, prof., 1971—; sr. rsch. scientist Mental Health Rsch. Inst., U. Mich., 1966—; cons. legal drafting Nat. Life Ins. Co., Mich. Blue Cross & Blue Shield (various law firms); mem. electronic data retrieval com. Am. Bar Assn.; ops. rsch. analyst McKinsey & Co.; orgn. and methods analyst Office of Sec. Air Force.; trustee Ctr. for Study of Responsive Law. Editor: Games and Simulations, Artificial Intelligence and Law Jour.; author: WFF 'N PROOF: The Game of Modern Logic, 1961, latest rev. edit., 1973, (with Robin B.S. Brooks, Patricia A. James) Automatic Retrieval of Legal Literature: Why and How, 1962, WFF: The Beginner's Game of Modern Logic, 1962, latest rev. edit., 1973, EQUATIONS: The Game of Creative Mathematics, 1963, latest rev. edit., 1973, (with Mary E. Caldwell) Reflections of the Communications Sciences and Law: The Jurimetrics Conference, 1965, (with J. Ross and P. Kugel) QUERIES 'N THEORIES: The Game of Science and Language, 1970, latest rev. edit., 1973, (with F. Goodman, D. Humphrey and J. Ross), ON-WORDS: The Game of Word Structures, 1971, rev. edit., 1973; contbr. articles to profl. jours.; co-author/designer: (with J. Ross and C. Stratton) DIG (Diagnostic Instrnl. Gaming) Math; (with C. Saxon) Normalizer Clear Legal Drafting Program, 1986, MINT System for Generating Dynamically Multiple-Interpretation Legal Decision-Assistance Systems, 1991, The Legal Argument Game of LEGAL RELATIONS, 1997. With USNR, 1945-46. Mem. ABA (coun. sect. sci. and tech.), AAAS, ACLU, Assn. Symbolic Logic, Nat. Coun. Tchrs. Math. Democrat. Unitarian. Home: 2114 Vinewood Blvd Ann Arbor MI 48104-2762 Office: U Mich Sch Law 625 S State St Ann Arbor MI 48109-1215

ALLEN, LEATRICE DELORICE, psychologist; b. Chgo., July 15, 1948; d. Burt and Mildred Floy (Taylor) Hawkins; m. Allen Moore, Jr., July 30, 1965 (div. Oct. 1975); children: Chandra, Valarie, Allen; m. Armstead Allen, May 11, 1978 (div. May 1987). AA in Bus. Edn., Olive Harvey Coll., Chgo., 1975; BA in Psychology cum laude, Chgo. State U., 1977; M.Clin. Psychology, Roosevelt U., 1980; MA in Health Care Adminstrn., Coll. St. Francis, Joliet, Ill., 1993. Lic. clin. profl. counselor. Clk., U.S. Post Office, Chgo., 1967-72; clin. therapist Bobby Wright Mental Health Ctr., Chgo., 1979-80; clin. therapist Community Mental Health Council, Chgo., 1980-83, assoc. dir., 1983—; cons. Edgewater Mental Health, Chgo., 1984—, Project Pride, Chgo., 1985—; victim services coordinator Community Mental Health Council, Chgo., 1986-87; mgr. youth family services Mile Square Health Ctr., Chgo., 1987-88; coord. Evang. Health Systems, Oakbrook, Ill., 1988-93; adminstr. Human Enrichment Devel. Assn., Hazel Crest, Ill., 1993-96; dir. Ada S. McKinley, Chgo., 1996—. Scholar Chgo. State U., 1976, Roosevelt U., 1978; fellow Menninger Found., 1985. Mem. Am. Profl. Soc. on Abuse of Children, Nat. Orgn. for Victim Assistance, Ill. Coalition Against Sexual Assault (del. 1985—), Soc. Traumatic Stress Studies (treatment innovations task force), Chgo. Sexual Assault Svcs. Network (vice-chair, bd. dirs.), Chgo.

Coun. Fgn. Rels. Avocations: aerobics, reading, theatre, dining, making and collecting dolls.

ALLEN, LEE HARRISON, industrial consultant, wholesale company executive; b. Cleve., Oct. 12, 1924; s. Horace Joseph and Eleanor Quayle (Malone) A.; m. Marieke Sellenraad, Sept. 18, 1954; children: Horace, Jan, Adrian, Carel, Eleanor. BEngring. in Metallurgy, Yale U., 1948. With Hickman, Williams & Co., Detroit, 1948—, metallurgist, 1951-70, divsn. mgr., 1970—, v.p., dir., 1971-76, pres., 1976-84, chmn. bd., chief exec. officer, 1984-89; chmn. bd., chief exec. officer Hickman, Williams Can., Inc., 1980-89; owner L.H. Allen & Sons, Frankenmuth, Mich., 1969—; chmn. bd. dirs. Mich. Shelf Distbrs. Inc., 1985—. Trustee Grosse Pinte Bd. Edn., 1968-76. Mem. Am. Arbitration Assn. (arbitrator), Country Club Detroit. Home and Office: 71 Moross Rd Grosse Pointe Farms MI 48236

ALLEN, LEE NORCROSS, historian, educator; b. Shawmut, Ala., Apr. 16, 1926; s. Leland Norcross and Dorothy (Whitaker) A.; m. Catherine Ann Bryant, Aug. 24, 1963; children—Leland Norcross, Leslie Catherine. B.S., Auburn U., 1948, M.S., 1949; Ph.D., U. Pa., 1955. From instr. to prof. history Ea. Bapt. Coll., St. Davids, Pa., 1952-61; prof. history Samford U., Birmingham, Ala., 1961—; grad. dean Samford U., 1965-86; dean Howard Coll. Arts and Scis., 1975-90. Author: (with Mrs. E.S. Bee) History of Ruhama, 1969, The First One Hundred Fifty Years: First Baptist Church of Montgomery, 1979, Born for Missions, 1984; Southside Baptist Church: A Centennial History, 1985, Woodlawn Baptist Church: The First Century, 1886-1986, 1986; (with Catherine B. Allen) Courage to Care, 1988; Expanding the Dream, Montgomery Baptist Hospital, 1988, Notable Past, Bright Future: First Baptist Church 1893-1993, 1993, Born for Missions, 16th Decade, 1993, Ralph W. Beeson: A Biography, 1994, Outward Focus: Mountain Brook Baptist Church, The First Fifty Years, 1994, The First 150 Years Supplement: 1980-1995, 1996, (with Catherine B. Allen) Christ Is Our Salvation: Paul Piper, 1998, (with Catherine B. Allen) The Boaz Heritage: A Centennial History, Boaz, Alabama, 1897-1997, 1998. Served with AUS, 1944-46. Recipient Commendation cert. Am. Assn. State and Local History, Thomas Jefferson award, 1995, disting. svc. award Ala. Baptist Hist. Commn., 1996; Auburn U. rsch. fellow, 1948-49; Harrison fellow U. Pa., 1949-52. Mem. Am. Hist. Assn., Am. Bapt. Hist. Assn., So. Bapt. Hist. Assn. (pres. 1987-88), So. Hist. Assn., Ala. Hist. Assn. (editor newsletter 1989—, pres. 1994-95), So. Bapt. Club, Rotary (pres. Shades Valley chpt. 1969-70), Omicron Delta Kappa, Phi Alpha Theta, Phi Kappa Phi, Pi Gamma Mu. Baptist. Home: 5025 Wendover Dr Birmingham AL 35223-1631

ALLEN, LEON ARTHUR, JR., lawyer; b. Springfield, Mass., July 15, 1933; s. Leon Arthur Sr. and Elsie (Shoemaker) A.; m. Patricia Mellion, June 23, 1961; 1 child, Christopher L. BEE, Cornell U., 1955; LLB, NYU, 1964. Bar: N.Y. 1964, U.S. Dist. Ct. (so. and ea. dists.) N.Y. 1965. Tech. editor McGraw Hill Pub. Co., N.Y.C., 1958-62; constrn. engr. Gilbert Assocs., N.Y.C., 1962-64; assoc. LeBoeuf, Lamb, Leiby & MacRae, N.Y.C., 1964-70; ptnr. LeBoeuf, Lamb, Leiby & MacRae (name changed to LeBoeuf, Lamb, Greene & MacRae), N.Y.C., 1971—. Served with U.S. Army, 1956-58. Mem. ABA, Assn. of Bar of City of N.Y. (chmn. adminstrv. law com. 1972-74). Clubs: Racquet & Tennis (N.Y.C.); Union (N.Y.C.), Tuxedo (Tuxedo Park, N.Y.). Home: 530 E 86th St New York NY 10028-7535 Office: LeBoeuf Lamb Greene MacRae 125 W 55th St New York NY 10019-5369

ALLEN, LEONARD BROWN, retired tax manager; b. Longmont, Colo., Sept. 5, 1932; s. Victor Brown and Anna Catherine (Cottrell) A.; m. Virginia Lee Harvey, May 27, 1960; children: Susan Ann, Denise Diane. BS, Colo. A&M Coll., 1954; MS, Colo. State U., 1967. CPA, Ill. Office mgr. Walco Distbg., Craig, Colo., 1962-65; teaching asst. Colo. State U., Ft. Collins, 1965-67; internal auditor Deere & Co., Moline, Ill., 1967-68, acct. consolidations dept., 1968-70, tax acct., 1970-73, mgr. state and local taxes, 1973-97; ret., 1997. Mem. stewardship and mission com. No. Assn. United Ch. of Christ, 1989-92, chmn., 1991-92. Capt. USAF, 1954-57, with USAFR, 1967. Mem. Ill. CPA Soc., Chgo. Tax Club (bd. dirs. 1986-88), Iowa Taxpayers Assn. (bd. dirs., chmn. 1991-93, mem. exec. com.), Taxpayers Fedn. Ill. (adv. com.), Wis. Mfrs. and Commerce Assn. (taxation com.), Ill. C. of C. (chmn. state and local tax com., tax com. 1991), Masons (master 1964-65). Republican. Mem. United Ch. of Christ. Home: 38 Crestview Dr Geneseo IL 61254-9514

ALLEN, LEW, JR., laboratory executive, former air force officer; b. Miami, Fla., Sept. 30, 1925; s. Lew and Zella (Holman) A.; m. Barbara Frink Hatch, Aug. 19, 1949; children: Barbara Allen Miller, Lew III, Marjorie Allen Dauster, Christie Allen Jameson, James Allen. BS, U.S. Mil. Acad., 1946; MS, U. Ill., 1952, PhD in Physics, 1954. Commd. 2d lt. USAAF, 1946; advanced through grades to gen. USAF, 1977, ret., 1982; physicist test div. AEC, Los Alamos, N.Mex., 1954-57; sci. advisor Air Force Spl. Weapons Lab., Kirtland, N.Mex., 1957-61; with office of spl. tech. Sec. of Def., Washington, 1961-65; from dir. spl. projects to dep. dir. adv. plans Air Force Space Program, 1965-72; dir. Nat. Security Agy., Ft. Meade, Md., 1973-77; comdr. Air Force Systems Command, 1977-78; vice chief of staff USAF, Washington, 1978, chief of staff, 1978-82; dir. Jet Propulsion Lab., Calif. Inst. Tech., Pasadena, Calif., 1982-90; chmn. bd. Draper Lab, Boston, 1991-95. Decorated Def. D.S.M. with two clusters, Air Force D.S.M. with one cluster, Nat. Intelligence D.S.M., NASA D.S.M., Legion of Merit with two oak leaf clusters; recipient Robert H. Goddard Astronautics award Am. Inst. Aeronautics and Astronautics, 1995. Fellow AIAA (hon.), Am. Phys. Soc.; mem. Am. Geophys. Union, Nat. Acad. Engring., Coun. on Fgn. Rels., Sigma Xi, Sunset Club (L.A.), Alfalfa Club (Washington). Republican. Episcopalian. Avocations: ballooning, rafting.

ALLEN, LINDA GRAVES, air medical transport company executive; b. Indpls., Oct. 8, 1959; d. Charles Edward and Barbara Jean (Antle) Graves; m. William Allen, Nov. 16, 1985; children: Clarke, Jordan. BSN, U. Mo., 1981, MHA, 1995. RN, Mo.; cert. emergency nurse, Mo.; cert. instr. trauma nurse, advanced burn life support, cert. provider pediatric advanced cardiac and trauma/pediatric advanced life support, cert. trauma nurse specialist, cert. emergency nurse, advanced cardiac life support. Staff nurse level IV St. John's Mercy Med. Ctr., St. Louis, 1981-92; trauma coord. Barnes Hosp., St. Louis, 1992-96; re-engring. cons. Barnes Jewish Hosp., St. Louis, 1996-97; managed care specialist BJC Health Sys., St. Louis, 1997; v.p. med. svcs. ARCH Air Med. Svcs., St. Louis, 1998—. Mem. AACN, Emergency Nurses Assn., Am. Trauma Soc., Am. Coll. Healthcare Execs., Soc. Trauma Nurses, Healthcare Fin. Mgmt. Assn. Office: ARCH Air Med Svcs 18500 Edison Ave Chesterfield MO 63005

ALLEN, LOUIS ALEXANDER, management consultant; b. Glace Bay, N.S., Oct. 8, 1917; s. Israel Nathan and Emma (Greenberg) A.; m. Ruth Graham, Aug. 24, 1946; children: Michael, Steven, Ace, Terry Allen Beck, Deborah Allen. BS cum laude, Wash. State U., 1941. Cert. mgmt. cons. Asst. to dean of men Wash. State U., Pullman, 1940-42; tng. supr. Aluminum Co. Am., Pitts., 1946-49; mgr. pers. adminstrn. Koppers Co. Inc., Pitts., 1949-53; dir. rsch. projects The Conf. Bd., N.Y.C., 1953-56; dir. orgnl. planning Booz, Allen & Hamilton, Chgo., 1956-58; pres., chmn. emeritus Louis Allen Assocs., Los Altos, Calif., 1958—; lectr. on bus. mgmt. Stanford U., U. Chgo., NYU, Japan, China, Australia, Africa and Europe. Author: Improving Staff and Line Relationships, 1956, Preparing the Company Organization Manual, 1957, Organization of Staff Functions, 1958, Management and Organization, 1958, The Management Profession, 1964, Professional Management: New Concepts and Proven Practices, 1973, Time before Morning: Art and Myth of the Australian Aborigines, 1975, Making Managerial Planning More Effective, 1982, The Allen Guide for Management Leaders, 1989, Common Vocabulary for Management Leaders, 1989, The Louis Allen Leader's Handbook, 1995, The New Leadership, 1996; (mus. catalog) Australian Aboriginal Art, 1972; translated into Japanese, German, French, Finnish, Swedish, Dutch, Spanish, Portuguese, Bahasa; contbr. numerous articles and monographs to profl. jours. on mgmt., primitive art; exhibitor primitive art major mus. worldwide, 1969—. Maj. USAF, 1942-55, PTO. Decorated Legion of Merit; recipient McKinsey award Acad. Mgmt. Mem. Inst. Mgmt. Cons. (sr. assoc., regional pres. 1985). Avocations: hiking, theater, opera, gardening. Office: Louis Allen Rsch PO Box 11 Palo Alto CA 94302-0011

ALLEN, LYLE WALLACE, lawyer; b. Chillicothe, Ill., June 17, 1924; s. Donald M. and Mary Ellen (McEvoy) A.; m. Helen Kolar, Aug. 16, 1947; children: Mary Elizabeth Watkins, Bryan James. Student, N.C. State Coll., 1943-44; B.S., Northwestern U., 1947; postgrad., Columbia Law Sch., 1947-48; J.D., U. Wis., 1950. Bar: Ill. 1950, Wis. 1950. Of counsel Heyl Royster Voelker & Allen, Peoria, Ill., 1951—. Served with 87th Inf. Div. U.S. Army, World War II. Decorated Purple Heart, Bronze star. Mem. ABA, Ill. State Bar Assn. (pres. 1972-73), Assn. of Ins. Attys. (pres. 1965-66), Venice Yacht Club, Wig and Pen Club (London). Democrat. Presbyterian. Office: 124 SW Adams St Ste 600 Peoria IL 61602-1320*

ALLEN, MARCUS, retired professional football player; b. San Diego, Mar. 26, 1960. Student, U. So. Calif. Running back with Los Angeles Raiders, NFL, El Segundo, Calif., 1982-92; with Kansas City Chiefs, NFL, 1993-97; nat. analyst, broadcaster CBS Sports, N.Y.C., 1998; co-host Marcus Allen Show KCTV 5, Kansas City, Mo., 1997-98; features/sideline reporter CBS Sports, 1999—; co-owner Pro Ball Beverage Corp.; v.p. Marcus Allen's Broadway Ford, Kansas City, Mo. Author: (with Carlton Stowers) Marcus: The Autobiography of Marcus Allen, 1997. Recipient Heisman Trophy Downtown Athletic Club of N.Y.C., 1981; named Coll. Football Player of Yr., Sporting News, 1981, The Sporting News NFL Rookie of Yr., 1982, Player of Yr., 1985; named to Sporting News Coll. All-Am. Team, 1981. Played in NFL championship game, 1984, Pro Bowl, 1983, 85, 86, 88; established NFL season record for most combined yards, 1985; holds NFL record for most consecutive games with 100 or more yards rushing (11), 1986. Office: Marcus Allen's Ford 3401 Broadway Kansas City MO 64111*

ALLEN, MARILYN MYERS POOL, theater director, video producer; b. Fresno, Calif., Nov. 2, 1934; d. Laurence B. and Asa (Griggs) Myers; m. Joseph Harold Pool, Dec. 28, 1955; children: Pamela Elizabeth, Victoria Anne, Catherine Marcia; m. Neal R. Allen, Apr. 1982. BA, Stanford U., 1955, postgrad., 1955-56; postgrad., U. Tex., 1957-60, West Tex. State U., summer 1962, 63, Odessa Coll., 1987-88. Pvt. tchr. drama, speech, acting, directing, speech correction Amarillo, Tex., 1960-82; pvt. tchr. drama, speech, acting, directing, speech Midland, Tex., 1982—; free-lance radio and TV actress; adj. prof. theatre Midland Coll., 1997-98, dir. Globe Theater, Odessa, 1998; asst. mng. dir. Amarillo Little Theatre, 1964-66, mng. dir., 1966-68; mng. dir. Horseshoe Players, touring profl. theater, 1969-73; actress, multi-media prodn. Palo Duro Canyon, 1971; dir. touring children's theatre, 1978-79; guest actress in Medea, Amarillo Coll., 1981; guest reciter Amarillo Symphony, 1972, Midland-Odessa Symphony, 19984. Pres. Tex. Non-Profit Theatres, 1972-74, 75-77, bd. dirs., 1988-91; 1st v.p. High Plains Ctr. for Performing Arts, 1969-73; adv. mem. dept. fine arts Amarillo Coll., 1980-82; adv. mem. Tex. Constnl. Revision Commn., 1973-75; mem. adv. coun. U. Tex. Coll. Fine Arts, 1969-72; cmty. adv. com. for women Amarillo Coll., 1975-79; conv. program com. Am. Theatre Assn., 1978, program participant, 1978-80, bd. dirs., 1980-83; bd. dirs. Amarillo Found. Health and Sci. Edn., 1976-82, program v.p., 1979-81; bd. dirs. Domestic Violence Coun., 1979-82, March of Dimes, 1979-81, Tex. Panhandle Heritage Found., 1964-82, Friends of Fine Arts, West Tex. State U. (now West Tex. A&M U.), 1980-82, Amarillo Pub. Libr., 1980-82, Amarillo Symphony, 1981-82; publicity chmn. Midland Cmty. Theatre, 1984-87, bd. govs., 1986-92, sec., 1987-88, v.p., 1988-92; bd. dirs. Globe of the Great S.W., Odessa; mem. Mus. of S.W., Midland Arts Assembly; bd. dirs. Midland County Rep. Women, Ways and Means Ch., 1991, 1st v.p., 1992, publicity chair, 1994; mem. Midland County Redistricting com., 1991; cultural exch. del. from Midland, Tex., to Dong Ying, China, 1993; Tex. UIL one act play adjudicator, 1974—. Recipient cert. of appreciation Woman of Yr., Amarillo Bus. and Profl. Women's Club, 1966, Best Actress award for Hedda Gabler role Amarillo Little Theatre, 1965, Best Dir. award for Rashomon, 1967, 1st Pl. award for video spl. Tex. Press Conf., 1988, 1st Pl. award for news Tex. Press Conf., 1989, Disting. Svc. award Tex. Non-Profit Theatres, 1992; named Amarillo Woman of Yr., Beta Sigma Phi, 1980, Broadcaster of the Yr., Rocky Mountain Press Conf., 1988, Hamhock of Yr., Midland Cmty. Theatre, 1992, Outstanding Svc. award Midland Arts Assembly, 1992; Travel fellow AAUW, 1973, 78. Fellow Am. Assn. Cmty. Theatre (dir. 1969-72, 82-84, v.p. planning and devel. 1985-87, co-chair AACT/Fest '95), Internat. Amateur Theatre Assn. 23d World Congress (del. Monaco 1997); mem. USTA (sr. women's team sect. winner 1993, 94), S.W. Theatre Conf. (dir. 1973-76, 82-84, exec. com. 1982-84, Disting. Svc. award 1985), Tex. Theatre Coun. (dir. 1974-78, exec. com., pres. 1975-76), AAUW (br. pres. 1973-75, state chmn. cultural interests 1975-77, 86-88, state program v.p. 1977-79, state bd. dirs. 1984-88, program v.p. Midland 1988-89), Episc. Ch. Women (program v.p. Midland 1988-89, outreach chair 1996, program v.p., pres.-elect 1997-98, pres. 1999—), DAR (chpt. chaplain 1971-75, historian 1975-77), C. of C. (fine arts coun.), U.S. Judo Assn., Symphony Guild, Amarillo Art Assn., Midland Symphony Guild (arrangements chmn. 1983-84), Act IX, Shakespeare As We Like It, Amarillo Law Wives Club (pres. 1976-77), Midland Law Wives, Hamhocks (v.p. 1985-86).

ALLEN, MARY LOUISE HOOK, secondary education educator; b. Ironwood, Mich., July 18, 1930; d. Frank Eugene and Elsie Clara (Schneider) Hook; m. Dale Sanson Allen, June 30, 1955; children: Jack Eugene, Bradley Arthur. BS in Phys. Edn. cum laude, U. Mich., 1951; MA in Phys. Edn., U. Minn., 1970, postgrad., 1987—. Life teaching cert., coaching lic., Minn. Secondary edn. tchr. New Trier Twp. High Sch., Winnetka, Ill., 1951-55, Richfield (Minn.) Sch. Dist., 1955-59; teaching assoc. U. Minn., Mpls., 1969-70; part-time lectr. U. Minn., 1985-86; tchr. Bloomington (Minn.) Sch. Dist., 1961-85; adj. prof. Concordia Coll., St. Paul, Minn., 1987-92; officiator U.S. Synchro Minn. Assn., Minn. State High Sch. League, Pan-Am. Trials Swimming Co-Chair, others; past officiating bd. chmn. North Shore (Winnetka) Basketball/Volleyball, Ill. State Basketball com., others. Co-author: Soccer/Speedball Rule Book - Creative Game, 1952; dir. Aqua Debs Synchronized swim shows, 1962-82. Mem. Atonement Luth. Ch., Bloomington, 1956—; worker Dem. Party, Bloomington, 1988—; dir. Synchronized Swimming Camp, 1980-87. Recipient numerous athletic awards, Minn. Pathfinder award Nat. Assn. Girls and Women in Sport, 1996, U. Mich. Kinesiology Alumni Achievement award, 1996. Mem. AAHPERD (mem. com. 1949—), Minn. Assn. Health, Phys. Edn., Recreation and Dance (sec. 1982-83, pres.-elect 1984, pres. 1985, past pres. 1986, conv. chmn. 1984, 86, student confs. 1988-92), Synchronized Swim Coaches Assn. (state chmn. 1980-82), Athletic Fedn. Coll. Women (chmn. nat. conv. 1951), Mortarboard, Phi Beta Kappa, Phi Kappa Phi, Pi Lambda Theta, also others. Avocations: athletics, camping, politics, gardening. Home: 10312 Wentworth Ave Bloomington MN 55420-5249

ALLEN, MARYON PITTMAN, former senator, journalist, lecturer, interior and clothing designer; b. Meridian, Miss., Nov. 30, 1925; d. John D. and Tellie (Chism) Pittman; m. Joshua Sanford Mullins, Jr., Oct. 17, 1946 (div. Jan. 1959); children: Joshua Sanford III, John Pittman, Maryon Foster; m. James Browning Allen, Aug. 7, 1964 (dec. June 1978). Student, U. Ala., 1944-47, Internat. Inst. Interior Design, 1970. Office mgr. for Dr. Alston Callahan, Birmingham, Ala., 1959-60; bus. mgr. psychiat. clinic U. Ala. Med. Center, Birmingham, 1960-61; life underwriter Protective Life Ins. Co., Birmingham, 1961-62; women's editor Sun Newspapers, Birmingham, 1962-64; v.p., ptnr. Pittman family cos., J.D. Pittman Partnership Co., J.D. Pittman Tractor Co., Emerald Valley Corp., Mountain Lake Farms, Inc., Birmingham; mem. U.S. Senate (succeeding late husband James B. Allen), 1978; dir. pub. rels. and advt. C.G. Sloan & Co. Auction House, Washington, 1981; feature writer Birmingham News, 1964; writer syndicated column Reflections of a News Hen, Washington, 1969-78; feature writer, columnist Maryon Allen's Washington, Washington Post, 1979-81; columnist McCall's Needlework Mag., 1993—; owner The Maryon Allen Co. Cliff House (Restoration/Design), Birmingham. Contbg. editor So. Accents Mag., 1976-78. Mem. Ladies of U.S. Senate unit ARC, Former Mems. of Congress, Ala. Hist. Commn., Blair House Fine Arts Commn.; charter mem. Birmingham Com. of 100 for Women; trustee Children's Fresh Air Farm; trustee, deacon, elder Ind. Presbyn. Ch., Birmingham; Democratic Presdl. elector, Ala., 1968. Recipient 1st place award for best original column Ala. Press Assn., 1962, 63, also various press state and nat. awards for typography, fashion writing, food pages, also several awards during Senate service; sponsor, U.S. Navy Nuclear submarine, U.S.S. Birmingham, S.S.N. 695, launched Newport News, Va., 1977, commissioned 1978. Mem. Nat. Press Club, 1925 F Street Club, 91st Congress Club, Congl. Club, Birmingham Country Club. Home: Cliff House 3215 Cliff Rd S Birmingham AL 35205-1405 *You have to believe in yourself, your talents and the premise that you were put here to contribute of yourself...not always to take.*

ALLEN, MATTHEW ARNOLD, physicist; b. Edinburgh, Scotland, Apr. 27, 1930; came to U.S., 1955; s. William Wolff and Clara (Bloch) A.; m. Marcia Harriet Katzman, Sept. 15, 1957; children: Bruce William, Peter Jonathan, David Michael. BSc in Physics, U. Edinburgh, 1951; PhD in Physics, Stanford U., 1959. Rsch. assoc. Hansen Labs., Stanford (Calif.) U., 1959-61; rsch. mgr. tube div. Microwave Assocs., Burlington, Mass., 1961-65; radio frequency group leader Stanford Linear Accelerator Ctr., 1965-82, head accelerator physics dept., 1982-84, head klystron microwave dept., 1984-90, asst. dir. for elec. and electronic systems, 1989-90, assoc. dir. lab., 1990—; cons. Microwave Assocs. Inc., 1965-71, Aerojet Gen., Azusa, Calif., 1959-62, Bechtel Corp., San Francisco, 1965-67; mem. tech. rev. com. Synchotron Radiation Rsch. Ctr., Taipei, Taiwan, 1985-98; chmn. U.S.A. Particle Accelerator Conf., 1991. Contbr. articles to profl. jours.; patentee in field. Commr. Environ. Planning Commn., Mountain View, Calif., 1971-74; councilman Mountain View City Coun., 1974-82; mayor City of Mountain View, 1977, 81; pres. Mountain View Community TV, 1989. Lt. British Army, 1953-55. Fellow IEEE, Am. Phys. Soc.; mem. IEEE Nuclear and Plasma Scis. Soc. (adminstrv. com. 1978-84, 98—), Dem. Club (bd. dirs. 1980-84), Sigma Xi. Democrat. Avocations: skiing, running, TV producing. Home: 325 Chatham Way Mountain View CA 94040-4471 Office: Stanford U Linear Accelerator Ctr Stanford CA 94309

ALLEN, MAURICE BARTELLE, JR., architect; b. Lansing, Mich., Mar. 20, 1926; s. Maurice Bartelle and Marguerite Rae (Stahl) A.; m. Nancy Elizabeth Huff, June 29, 1951; children—Robert (dec.), Katherine, David. Student, Western Mich. U., 1944, Notre Dame U., 1944-46; BArch, U. Mich., 1950. Registered profl. architect, Mich. Draftsman, designer Smith, Hinchman & Grylls (architects), Detroit, 1950-51; designer, asso. Eero Saarinen & Assos., Bloomfield Hills, Mich., 1951-61; v.p. design and planning TMP Assos. (architects, engrs. and planners), Bloomfield Hills, 1961-92; emeritus, 1993; design critic, lectr. Coll. Architecture and Urban Planning, U. Mich., 1958—. Prin. archtl. works include Gen. Motors Inst. campus devel. and bldgs, Flint, Mich., Mackinac and Manitou halls, Grand Valley State Coll, O'Dowd Hall, Oakland U, Prototype Regional Correctional Facilities, Mich. Dept. Corrections, Fine Arts Ctr. and Theater, Allied Scis. Bldg., Macomb Community Coll., Scheide Music Ctr., Coll. of Wooster, Towsley Ctr. Sch. of Music, U. Mich., Camelback Bible Ch., Paradise Valley, Ariz., Performing Arts Ctr. and Student Ctr., Lake Superior State U., Art Music Humanities Ctr., Wabash Coll., Univ. Community Ctr., Univ. Western Ont., Drama Theater and Arts Bldg., Concordia Coll., St. Paul. Active Detroit Area council Boy Scouts Am., 1969—; mem. environmental arts com. Mich. Council for Arts, 1970; vice chmn. Mich. Gov.'s Spl. Commn. on Architecture, 1971. Served with USNR, 1944-47. Recipient honor awards Detroit chpt. AIA, 1970-71, Gold medal, 1994, citation for design high rise structures Am. Iron and Steel Inst., 1971, citation of excellence Architecture for Justice Exhbn., 1982. Mem. Coll. of Fellows AIA (co-chair urban priorities Detroit chpt. 1995—), Mich. Soc. Architects (honor awards 1970-71), Sr. Men's Club Birmingham, Masons, Alpha Tau Omega. Republican. Episcopalian. Home and Office: 4325 Derry Rd Bloomfield Hills MI 48302-1835 Office: 1191 W Square Lake Rd Bloomfield Hills MI 48302-0374

ALLEN, MELISSA J., federal agency administrator. Asst. sec. for adminstrn. U.S. Dept. Transp., Washington, 1995—. Office: US Dept Transp Office of Adminstrn 400 7th St SW Washington DC 20590-0001*

ALLEN, MERLE MAESER, JR., lawyer; b. Prescott, Ariz., June 6, 1932; s. Merle Maeser and Centenna (Haymore) A.; m. Carol Beckstrand, Aug. 16, 1954; children: Leslie Ann, Shauna, Denise, Colette, Mark M., Brian T. BA, Brigham Young U., 1954; JD, U. Ariz., 1960. Bar: Ariz. 1960. With firm Moore & Romley, Phoenix, 1960-72; ptnr. Udall, Shumway, Blackhurst, Allen & Lyons, Mesa, Ariz., 1973-97; adj. faculty Brigham Young U. Hawaii Sch. Bus., 1997—. Author: Advertising Protection Through Copyright, 1960. Active membership drive Downtown Phoenix YMCA, 1963; bd. dirs. Mesa YMCA, 1974-77, Mesa Pub. Safety Found., 1976-87, Mesa Citrus Growers Assn., 1992-97; v.p., membership chmn. Mesa Fine Arts Assn., 1978-79; active Theodore Roosevelt coun. Boy Scouts Am., 1963-97. Pilot USAF, 1954-57. Recipient award for interest in and services to youth of community Boy Scouts Am., 1968, 87. Mem. State Bar Ariz. (com. on examinations 1982-89), Rotary (pres. Mesa West club 1975-76, dist. 550 sec. 1989-90). Mem. LDS Ch. (bishop 1967-71, 77-81). Home: Box 6088 55-550 Naniloa Loop Laie HI 96762-1264

ALLEN, MERRILL JAMES, marine biologist; b. Brady, Tex., July 16, 1945; s. Clarence Francis and Sara Barbara (Finlay) A. BA, U. Calif., Santa Barbara, 1967; MA, UCLA, 1970; PhD, U. Calif., San Diego, 1982. Cert. jr. coll. tchr., Calif. Asst. environ. specialist So. Calif. Coastal Water Rsch. Project, El Segundo, 1971-77; postdoctoral assoc. Nat. Rsch. Coun., Seattle, 1982-84; oceanographer Nat. Marine Fisheries Svc., Seattle, 1984-86; sr. scientist MBC Applied Environ. Scis., Costa Mesa, Calif., 1986-93; prin. scientist So. Calif. Coastal Water Rsch. Project, Long Beach and Westminster, Calif., 1993—; tech. adv. com. Santa Monica Bay Restoration Project, Monterey Park, Calif., 1989—; steering com. So. Calif. Bight Pilot Project, 1993-98, So. Calif. Bight 1998 Regional Marine Survey, 1998—; affiliate asst. prof. sch. fisheries U. Wash., Seattle, 1985-89; mem. sci. rev. panel for marine ecol. reserves rsch. program Calif. Sea Grant Coll., 1996-97; adj. prof. dept. biology Calif. State U., Long Beach, 1996—. Mem. AAAS, Am. Inst. Fisheries Rsch. Biologists (dir. So. Calif. dist. 1991-93), Am. Fisheries Soc., Am. Soc. Ichthyologists and Herpetologists. Achievements include development of most comprehensive atlas of marine fishes from Bering Sea to Mexico; description of state of contamination of Santa Monica Bay. Office: So Calif Coastal Water Rsch Project 7171 Fenwick Ln Westminster CA 92683-5218

ALLEN, MICHAEL G., management consultant. BSc, London U.; MA, Cambridge U. Mgmt. trainee English Electric-Marconi; ops. rsch. mgr. Richard Thomas & Baldwins; sr. assoc. McKinsey & Co., London and N.Y.C.; with GE, 1972-79, v.p. corp. strategy, 1974-79; pres., founding ptnr. Michael Allen Co., Westport, Conn., 1979—. Contbr. articles to profl. jours., chpts. to books. Office: Michael Allen Co 1 Gorham Island Westport CT 06880

ALLEN, MICHAEL JOHN BRIDGMAN, English educator; b. Lewes, Eng., Apr. 1, 1941; came to U.S., 1966; m. Elena Hirshberg; children: William, Benjamin. BA, Oxford (Eng.) U., 1964, MA, 1966, DLitt, 1987; PhD, U. Mich., 1970. Asst. prof. UCLA, 1970-74, assoc. prof., 1974-79, prof. English, 1979—, assoc. dir. Ctr. for Medieval and Renaissance Studies, 1978-88, dir., 1988-93; editor Renaissance Quar., 1993—; faculty rsch. lectr. UCLA, 1998. Author: Marsilio Ficino: The Philebus Commentary, 1975, Marsilio Ficino and the Phaedran Charioteer, 1981, The Platonism of Marsilio Ficino, 1984, Icastes: Marsilio Ficino's Interpretation of Plato's "Sophist," 1989, Nuptial Arithmetic, 1994, Plato's Third Eye: Studies in Marsilio Ficino's Metaphysics and Its Sources, 1995, Synoptic Art: Marsilio Ficino on the History of Platonic Interpretation, 1998; co-author: Sources and Analogues of Old English Poetry, 1976; co-editor: Shakespeare's Plays in Quarto, 1984, Sir Philip Sidney's Achievements, 1990, First Images of America, 1976. Recipient Eby award for disting. teaching UCLA, 1977; Guggenheim fellow, 1977; disting. vis. scholar Centre for Reformation and Renaissance Studies, U. Toronto, 1997. Office: UCLA 2225 Rolfe Hall 405 Hilgard Ave Los Angeles CA 90095-9000

ALLEN, MICHAEL W, management consultant; b. Sacramento, Calif., May 15, 1948; s. Edgar Wall and Beverly Mae (Messinger) A.; m. Cynthia Mull, Jan. 28, 1978; children: Taylor Anne, Colin Michael. BS, U. Calif., Berkeley, 1970, MBA, 1972. Info. systems analyst, internal cons. Pacific Gas & Electric Co., San Francisco, 1972-74; policy analyst Fed. Energy Adminstrn., Washington, 1974-75; ptnr., practice leader Temple, Barker & Sloane, Inc., Lexington, Mass., 1975-88; v.p., prin. Beacon Hill Fin. Corp., Boston, 1988-90; mng. dir., ptnr. Barrington-Wellesley Group, Inc., Wellesley, Mass., 1990—; speaker at confs. Contbr. articles to profl. jours. Avocations: motorcycling, windsurfing, woodworking. Office: Barrington-Wellesley Group 302 Grove St Wellesley MA 02482-7411

ALLEN, M(ILFORD) RAY, secondary education educator; b. Martin, Ky., July 7, 1941; s. Ralph Earl and Pauline (Hall) A.; m. Cherie Suzanne Davis, Aug. 5, 1973; children: Landon Ray, Jana Cherie, Amber Suzanne, Anmarie

Rosalee. BA in English, Phys. Edn., Morehead State U., 1963, MA in Secondary Edn., 1965; MFA in Theater Arts, UCLA, 1980. Coach baseball, basketball Lewis County H.S., Vanceburg, Ky., 1963-65; coach baseball, cross country Fraser (Mich.) H.S., 1965-67; coach baseball, basketball Marina H.S , Huntington Beach, Calif., 1967-75; tchr. Fountain Valley (Calif.) H.S., 1976-78; coach basketball, golf Alleghany County H.S., Covington, Va., 1978-83; tchr. Alleghany County H.S., Covington, 1985—; coach golf Clifton Middle Sch., Clifton Forge, Va., 1983-85. Editor: Teach Me to Plow, 1988, The Roads I Travel, 1990, Between the Thorns: Windcarver Songs of Appalachia, 1991, Appalachian Legacy, 1999, Beyond Star Bottom and Other Poems, 1999; sports editor Alleghany Highlander, 1981-85. Mem. adv. bd. Green River Writers, Louisville, 1990-97. Named to Morehead State U. Alumni Hall of Fame, 1991. Mem. Appalfolks Am. Assn. (founder, pres. 1985-99), Appalachian Writer Assn., Appalachian South Writers Coop. (founder), Order Ky. Cols. Democrat. Avocations: fishing, bowling, swimming, jogging, golf. Home: 720 Callie Mines Rd Clifton Forge VA 24422-3714 Office: Appalfolks Am Assn PO Box 613 510 Main St Clifton Forge VA 24422-1167

ALLEN, NANCY, musician, educator; b. N.Y.C.. BM, The Juilliard Sch., N.Y.C., MM; studied with, Marcel Grandjany. Mem. faculty The Juilliard Sch., 1985—; Toured as harp soloist U.S., in duo with flutist Ransom Wilson. Performed with English Chamber Orch., L.A. Chamber Orch., Mostly Mozart Festival; recorded for Angel, EMI, RCA, CRI; recordings include Ravel's Introduction and Allegro (Grammy nomination), A Celebration For Harp. Recipient First prize Internat. Harp Competition, Israel, 1973; Solo Recitalist grantee Nat. Endowment for Arts. Office: Emerson String Quartet care IMG Artists North America 22 E 71st St New York NY 10021-4911 also: care CEMA Distbn 21700 Oxnard St Ste 700 Woodland Hills CA 91367-3617 also: Columbia Artists Mgmt Inc Wilford Divsn 165 W 57th St New York NY 10019-2201*

ALLEN, NATALIE, cable news anchor. Postgrad., Memphis State U.; B in Radio, T.V. and film, U. So. Miss. News anchor, reporter Sta. WREG-TV, Memphis, 1985-88, Sta. WFTV-TV, Orlando, Fla., 1988-92; co-anchor CNN Today, Atlanta, 1992—. Recipient Emmy award for Spot News Reporting, 1989, Edward R. Murrow award, 1990. Office: c/o CNN 1 CNN Ctr PO Box 105366 Atlanta GA 30348-5366*

ALLEN, NEWTON PERKINS, lawyer; b. Memphis, Jan. 3, 1922; s. James Seddon and Sarah (Perkins) A.; m. Malinda Lobdell Nobles, Oct. 4, 1947 (dec. Nov. 1986); children: John Lobdell, Malinda Nobles, Newton Perkins, Cannon Fairfax; m. Malinda Lobdell Crutchfield, June 23, 1990. AB, Princeton, 1943; JD, U. Va., 1948. Bar: Tenn. 1947, N.C. 1990. Assoc. Armstrong, Allen, Prewitt, Gentry, Johnston & Holmes, Memphis, 1948, ptnr., 1950-95; assoc. Dann & Allen, 1996—. Contbr. articles to profl. jours. Mem. Chickasaw coun. Boy Scouts Am., 1958-60, exec. bd. mem., 1961-69; trustee LeBonheur Children's Hosp., Memphis, 1964-72, vice chmn. bd., 1965; mem. alumni coun. Princeton, 1954-64, 90-93; pres. bd. trustees St. Mary's Episcopal Sch., 1966-67, v.p., 1972-73; chmn. Greater Memphis Coun. on Crime and Delinquency, 1976-80; co-chmn. Memphis conf. Faith at Work, 1975, bd. dirs., 1976-79; bd. dirs. Memphis Orch. Soc., pres., 1979-81. Mem. ABA (editl. bd. sr. lawyers divsn. 1990, publs. com. chair 1993-95, coun. mem. 1994-95, chair travel and leisure com. 1995-96, vice chair 1996-97, chair-elect 1997-98, chair 1998—), Am. Coll. Trust and Estate Coun., Tenn. Bar Assn., Memphis Bar Assn., Tenn. Def. Lawyers Assn., N.C. Bar Assn., Princeton Alumni Assn. Memphis (pres. 1992), Memphis Lions (pres. 1956). Republican. Office: 6263 Poplar Ave Ste 1103 Memphis TN 38119-4724

ALLEN, NORMA ANN, librarian; b. Balt., Jan. 22, 1951; d. James Crawley and Thelma Agusta (Keaton) Ghee; children: Lamont Ricardo Ghee, Alissa S. Allen, Avery O. Allen. BA in Adminstrn. Mgmt., Sojourner Douglass Coll., Balt., 1987; postgrad. in instrl. tech., Towson State U. Instr. data processing PSI Inst., Balt., 1987-88; acquisition technician Social Security Adminstrn., Balt., 1987-89, reference librarian, 1989-91, acquisitions librarian, 1991—; instrnl. developer Computer Asst. Instrn., Towson U., 1995—; freelance floral designer/arranger, freelance instr. basic writing skills and computer literacy. Sec., bd. dirs. New Image Child Care Facility, Balt., 1992; instr. active reading literacy program Enoch Pratt Libr., Balt., 1992; instr. United Missionary Bapt. Conv., 1997. Multicultural scholar Towson U., 1995-96. Mem. ALA, Spl. Libraries Assn. Office: Social Security Adminstrn 6401 Security Blvd Rm 571 Baltimore MD 21235-0001

ALLEN, PAGE RANDOLPH, artist; b. St. Charles, Ill., Sept. 6, 1951; d. Thomas Eliot and Ann Page (Platt) A.; m. W. Scott Morris, June 19, 1970 (div. May 1977); m. Nathaniel Otis Owings, July 26, 1981; 1 child, Maya Jehan. Student, Princeton U., 1969-70; BA, Hampshire Coll., 1974; MA, No. Ill. U., 1980; postgrad., Santa Fe Inst. Fine Arts. One woman shows include ARC Gallery, Chgo., 1980, Raw Space/ARC Gallery, Chgo., 1981, Fine Arts Gallery, U. Mont., Missoula, 1983, U. Club Gallery, Chgo., 1984, Northcutt Gallery, Ea. Mont. Coll., Billings, 1986, Owings-Dewey Fine Art, Santa Fe, 1987, 88, 90, 91, 94, CAFE Gallery, Albuquerque, 1992, DeWeese Gallery of Contemporary Arts, Bozeman, Mont., 1994, Danforth Gallery, Livingston, Mont., 1994, Meredith Long & Co., Houston, 1996; exhibited in group shows at Arvada (Colo.) Ctr. Arts and Humanities, 1992, Meredith Long & Co., 1993, Albuquerque Mus., 1994, Nora Eccles Harrison Mus. Art, Logan, Utah, 1994; represented in permanent collections Albuquerque Mus. Art, Arvada Ctr. Arts and Humanities, Eiteljorg Mus. Am. Indian and Western Art, Indpls., Missoula Mus. Arts, Mus. Fine Arts, Mus. N.Mex., Santa Fe, Pepsi Cola/Frito Lay Corp., Dallas, Telecomm. France Corp., N.Y.C., Temple (Tex.) Ctr. Contemporary Art. NEA grantee, 1981, Ill. State Arts Coun. grantee, 1981; named Artist in Edn., Mont. Arts Coun., NEA, 1982-84. Democrat. Avocations: travel, walking, gardening, reading. Office: Page Allen Studio 1229 Bishops Lodge Rd Santa Fe NM 87501-1002

ALLEN, PAUL, computer executive, professional sports team owner. Student, Wash. State U. Co-founder Microsoft Corp., Redmond, Wash., 1975, exec. v.p., 1975-83; founder Asymetrix Corp., Bellevue, Wash., 1985—, Starwave Corp., Bellevue; founder, chmn. Intervas Rsch., Palo Alto, Calif.; CEO Vulcan Ventures, Bellevue, 1987—; owner, chmn. Seattle Seahawks; owner, chmn. bd. Portland (Oreg.) Trail Blazers, 1988—; bd. dirs. Egghead Discount Software, Microsoft Corp., Darwin Molecular, Inc.

ALLEN, PAUL ALFRED, lawyer, educator; b. New Canaan, Conn., Feb. 18, 1948; s. Alfred J. and Wilma T. (DeWaters) A. BA, Johns Hopkins U., 1970; JD, NYU, 1974; MBA, U. Colo., 1989. Bar: Md. 1974, D.C. 1978, Colo. 1984, Calif. 1992. Exec. dir. Md. Environ. Trust, Balt., 1974-75; assoc. Bergson, Borkland, Margolis & Adler, Washington, 1975-79, ptnr., 1980-82; gen. counsel Plus System, Inc., Denver, 1983-91; counsel Visa USA, Inc., San Francisco, 1991-92, exec. v.p., gen. counsel, 1992—; lectr. Grad. Sch. of Banking, Boulder, Colo., 1984-86, U. Denver Law Sch., 1985-90. Editor: How to Keep Your Company Out of Court, 1984; contbr. articles to profl. jours. Recipient Svc. award Supreme Ct. Colo. Mem. ABA, Calif. Bar Assn., Colo. Bar Assn., Am. Corp. Counsel Assn. Democrat. Office: Visa USA Inc PO Box 8999 San Francisco CA 94128-8999

ALLEN, PAUL HOWARD, financial institutions investor; b. Aldershot, Eng., Apr. 5, 1954; came to U.S., 1979; s. William and Frances Elva (Mason) A.; m. Sandra C. Allen, June 11, 1994; children: Emma Elizabeth, Mark William Philip, Caroline Victoria Frances, Edward Christopher James. BA in Jurisprudence, Oxford (Eng.) U., 1976; MA in Jurisprudence, Oxford U., 1988; MBA, Harvard U., 1981. Bar: solicitor Eng. and Wales 1977. Solicitor of Supreme Ct. London, Freshfields, Eng., 1977-79; lectr. law Exeter Coll. Oxford U., 1978-79; assoc. McKinsey and Co. Inc., London, 1981-84; assoc. McKinsey and Co. Inc., N.Y.C., 1984-87, ptnr., 1987-89; founder Aston Assocs., Greenwich, Conn., 1989—. Author: Reengineering The Bank, 1995, Creating the New Bank, 1996; contbr. articles to profl. publs. Cons. CARE, N.Y.C., 1987—. McKinnon scholar Magdalen Coll. Oxford U., 1976; Harkness Fellow Commonwealth Fund N.Y., 1979-81; Baker scholar Harvard U., 1981. Mem. Brit. Inst. Mgmt. Avocations: tennis, golf, running, theatre. Office: Aston Assocs 35 Mason St Greenwich CT 06830-5433

ALLEN, PHILIP MARK, arts and humanities educator, dean, writer; b. Phila., Mar. 11, 1932; m. Susan Davidson, Feb. 1, 1986; children: Catherine Stewart, Jameson Louis. BA with highest honors, Swarthmore Coll., 1953; PhD, Emory U., 1956. Fgn. svc. officer U.S. Dept. of State, Washington, Hamburg, Antananarivo, 1956-66; regional rep. African Am. Inst., Lagos, Nigeria, 1966-67, Abidjan, Ivory Coast, 1966-67; dir. R & D African Am. Inst., N.Y.C., 1968-70; from assoc. prof. to prof. Johnson (Vt.) State Coll., 1970-87; dean sch. arts and humanities Frostburg (Md.) State U., 1987—; cons., lectr. Raymond & Whitcomb Co., N.Y. and Africa, 1970-75. Author: The Western Indian Ocean, 1987, Madagascar: Conflicts of Authority, 1995; co-author: The Traveler's Africa, 1973; editor: Vermont and the Year 2000, 1976. Mem. planning commn. Danby, Vt., 1972-74; mem. com. Md. Info. Tech. Bd., 1995—; bd. dirs., mem. exec. com. Md. Citizens for the Arts, Balt., 1995—; founding bd. dirs. Cumberland (Md.) Theatre, 1987—. Fulbright lectr. U.S. Dept. State, Senegal, 1981-82, Algeria, 1985-86; travel to collections grantee NEH, France, 1985. Mem. Internat. Coun. Fine Arts Deans (com. chair). Avocations: theater, music, hosting public radio opera program. Office: Frostburg State U PAC 127 Frostburg MD 21532

ALLEN, RALPH DEAN, diversified company corporate executive; b. Stanhope, Iowa, July 3, 1941; s. Ralph Carlton and Arvella Ruth (Tade) A.; m. Joanne Johnson; children: June Ann, Lisa Renee, Jeffrey Carlton. BSBA, Drake U., 1964; postgrad., U. Rochester, N.Y.; Advanced Mgmt. Program, Duke U., 1989. With Eastman Kodak Co., 1964-80, dir. shareowner relations, 1976-80; dir. investor relations ITT Corp., N.Y.C., 1980-95; v.p. ITT Corp., 1981-95; v.p., dir. investor rels. ITT Industries, White Plains, N.Y., 1995—; guest lectr. Fordham U. Grad. Sch. Mem. Investor Rels. Assn. (pres. 1981-82), Nat. Inst. Investor Rels. (bd. dirs.), Fin. Analysts Fedn. Office: ITT Industries 4 W Red Oak Ln Ste 2 White Plains NY 10604-3617

ALLEN, RALPH GILMORE, dramatist, producer, drama educator; b. Phila., Jan. 7, 1934; s. Ralph Bergen and Sara Beddoe (Walker) A.; m. Harriet Phyllis Nichols, Aug. 24, 1957. BA summa cum laude, Amherst Coll., 1955, DHL (hon.), 1980; DFA, Yale U., 1960. From asst. prof. theatre and drama to assoc. prof. U. Pitts, 1960-68; prof., chmn. dept. drama U. Victoria, B.C., Can., 1968-72; chmn. dept., prof. theatre U. Tenn., Knoxville, 1972-80; prof. drama Queens Coll., N.Y.C., 1983—, prof. emeritus, 1999—; dir. Clarence Brown Theatre Co., Knoxville, 1972-77; theatre cons.; prodr. John F. Kennedy Ctr., Washington, 1980-83; dir. more than 40 prodns. Co-author: (with John Gassner) Theatre and Drama in the Making, 1965, rev. edit., 1992; playwright: (with Joshua Logan) Rip Van Winkle, 1976, The Tax Collector, 1977; (with David Campbell and Michael Valenti) Honky Tonk Nights, 1986, A Horse of a Different Color, 1989; dir: many plays including Everyman, 1972-75, The New Majestic Follies, 1977; author: (revue) Sugar Babies, 1979 (Tony award nomination 1980), Best Burlesque Sketches, 1994; editor Theatre Survey, 1965-69; translator: Imaginary Invalid (Moliere), 1991, The Servant of Two Masters (Goldoni), 1992, The Gardener's Dog (Lope de Vega), 1993, The Palace of the Dead (Lope de Vega), 1994; contbr. numerous articles to profl. jours. John Golden fellow, 1957-59, Guggenehim fellow, 1965, Charles E. Merrill fellow, 1961; named Artist of Yr., Phi Kappa Phi, 1983; recipient Award for Service to Arts Mayor of Phila., 1983, Award of Merit Am. Theatre Assn., 1983. Fellow ASCAP, Dramatists Guild, Am. Theatre Assn. (v.p. 1972); mem. Am. Soc. Theatre Rsch. (dir., exec. com. 1977-80), Theatre Can. (gov. 1970-71), Nat. Theatre Conf.

ALLEN, RANDY LEE, corporate executive; b. Ithaca, N.Y., June 24, 1946; d. Richard Hallstead and Mary Elizabeth (Howe) Hallstead Baker; m. John James Meehan, Apr. 24, 1983 (div. Aug. 1987); 1 child, Scott Hallstead. BA in Physics, Cornell U., 1968; postgrad., Syracuse U., 1968, Seattle U., 1973-74. Cert. mgmt. cons., cert. systems profl. Programmer IBM, Endicott, N.Y., 1968-69; product and industry mgr. Boeing Computer Svc., Seattle, 1969-74; dir. mktg. Androcor subs. Boeing Computer, Calumet City, Ill., 1974-76; ptnr. Touche Ross & Co., Newark, 1976-93; ptnr.-in-charge Mgmt. cons. Trade Office, N.Y.C., 1988-93; prin. Deloitte & Touche, N.Y.C., 1990-93; v.p., chief adminstr., info. officer Phillips-Van Heusen Corp., Bridgewater, N.J., 1993-96, prin., 1996—; trustee N.J. Inst. Tech., Newark, 1984-87, 96—, bd. overseers, 1988—, vice chmn. fin., 1991—, mem. adv. bd. computer info. scis. dept. Author: OCR-A Cost/Benefit Guide; Pos Trends in the '80s; Bottom Line Issues in Retailing; Pos Current Trends and Beyond, 1987; also articles. Regional fundraiser Cornell U., 1983—, vice chair, 1996, mem. Cornell Coun., 1989-93, 95—; mem. Pres.'s Coun. Cornell Women, 1989—, chair, 1991-93; bd. dirs. Chamber Music Am., 1989-93, RETEX, 1996—. Recipient Acad. Women Achievers award YWCA, 1984. Mem. Inst. Mgmt. Cons., Am. Mgmt. Assn., Am. Arbitration Assn., Exec. Women of N.J. (pres. 1979-81, bd. dirs. 1981-85, 93-94), Cornell Club, Basking Ridge Golf Club, Cornell U. Alumni Ambs. Avocations: skiing, tennis, stamp collecting, symphony, art. Office: Phillips Van Heusen Corp 1001 Frontier Rd Bridgewater NJ 08807-2902

ALLEN, RENEE, principal. Prin. Villa Duchesne Sch., St. Louis, 1988—. Recipient Blue Ribbon Sch. award U.S. Dept. Edn., 1990-91. Office: Villa Duchesne Oakhill Sch 801 S Spoede Rd Saint Louis MO 63131-2606*

ALLEN, REX WHITAKER, architect; b. San Francisco, Dec. 21, 1914; s. Lewis Whitaker and Maude Rex (Allen) A.; m. Elizabeth Johnson, Oct. 11, 1941 (div. 1949); children: Alexandra A., Frances Lambert (Mrs. Andrew Dunn); m. Ruth Batchelor, Apr. 1, 1949 (div. 1971); children: Mark B., Susan Moore (Mrs. Kofy Lechner); m. Bettie J. Crossfield, Nov. 6, 1971. A.B., Harvard U., 1936, M.Arch., 1939; student, Columbia U. Arch. Sch., 1936-37. With Research and Planning Assos., N.Y.C., 1939-42, Camloc Fastener Corp., N.Y.C., 1942-45, Isadore Rosenfield (architect), N.Y.C., 1945-48, Blanchard and Maher (architects), San Francisco, 1949-52; established pvt. practice San Francisco, 1953; pres. Rex Whitaker Allen & Assos., San Francisco, 1961-71, Archtl. Prodns., Inc., 1971-76; prin. Hugh Stubbins/Rex Allen Partnership, 1968, Rex Allen Partnership, 1971-76; pres. Rex Allen-Drever-Lechowski, Architects, 1976-85, Rex Allen/Mark Lechowski & Assocs., 1985-87; cons. architect, health facility planner, 1987—; mem. Calif. Bldg. Safety Bd., 1973-93. Author: (with Ilona von Karolyi) Hospital Planning Handbook, 1976; Contbr. articles to profl. jours.; prin. works include French Hosp, San Francisco, Mercy Hosp, Sacramento, Roseville (Calif.) Dist. Hosp, Highland Hosp, Oakland, St. Francis Hosp, San Francisco, Dominican Hosp, Santa Cruz, Alta Bates Hosp, Berkeley, Calif., Boston City Hosp, Out-Patient bldg. Woodland (Calif.) Meml. Hosp, Stanislaus Meml. Hosp, Modesto, Calif., Madera (Calif.) Community Hosp, Sacred Heart Hosp, Eugene, Oreg., St. Joseph Hosp, Mt. Clemens, Mich., Commonwealth Health Center, Saipan, Guam Meml. Hosp. and Nursing Facility. Chmn. Mill Valley Adv. Edn. Council, 1956; mem. Blue Ribbon com. Sonoma Valley Unified Sch. Dist., 1997—. Fellow AIA (v.p. No. Calif. chpt. 1964, bd. dirs. Calif. coun. 1955-56, 1962-64, nat. pres. 1969-70); hon. fellow Royal Archtl. Inst. Can.; mem. Constrn. Specification Inst. (pres. San Francisco 1961), San Francisco Zool. Soc. (bd. dirs. 1974-86, 88-95, exhibits com. 1988—, chmn. design stds. com. Assn. Western Hosps., chmn. arch. sect. 1957-58), Calif. Hosp. Assn., Am. Hosp. Assn., Internat. Hosp. Fedn., Am. Assn. Hosp. Planning (pres. 1971-72), Union Internat. des Architectes Pub. Health Work Group (dir. 1979-80), La Sociedad de Arquitectos Mexicanos (hon. mem.), Federaciñn Panamericana de Asociaciones de Arquitectos (v.p. 1980-84), San Francisco Planning and Urban Renewal Assn., San Francisco Mus. Modern Art, Mus. Soc., San Francisco Symphony Found., Sierra Club. Club: Harvard (N.Y.C. and San Francisco). Home and Office: 1070 Siesta Way Sonoma CA 95476-4401

ALLEN, RICHARD BLOSE, legal editor, lawyer; b. Aledo, Ill., May 10, 1919; s. James Albert and Claire (Smith) A.; m. Marion Treloar, Aug. 27, 1949; children: Penelope, Jennifer, Leslie Jean. BS, U. Ill., 1941, JD, 1947; LLD, Seton Hall U., 1977. Bar: Ill. 1947. Staff editor ABA Jour., 1947-48, 63-66, exec. editor, 1966-70, editor, 1970-83, publ., 1983-86; pvt. practice Aledo, 1949-57; gen. counsel Ill. State Bar Assn., 1957-63. Editor Sr. Lawyer, 1986-90, 94—; mng. editor Def. Counsel Jour., 1987—. Maj. Q.M.C., AUS, 1941-46. Mem. ABA (mem. ho. of dels. 1996-99), Ill. Bar Assn. (mem. assembly 1972-74), Chgo. Bar Assn., Am. Law Inst., Selden Soc., Scribes, Mich. Shores Club, Sigma Delta Chi, Kappa Tau Alpha, Phi Delta Phi, Alpha Tau Omega. Office: Def Counsel Jour 1 N Franklin St Ste 2400 Chicago IL 60606-3421

ALLEN, RICHARD CHESTER, retired lawyer, educator; b. Swampscott, Mass., Jan. 24, 1926; s. Chester George and Edith Lydia (Hickford) A.; (div.); children: Steven, Craig, Scott. A.B., Washington U., St. Louis, 1948; J.D., Washington U., 1950; LL.M., U. Mich., 1963. Bar: Mo. 1948, Kans. 1956, Minn. 1976. Assoc. Thompson, Mitchell, Thompson & Douglas, St. Louis, 1950-52; mem. gen. legal dept. Southwestern Bell Telephone Co., St. Louis, 1953-56; area counsel Southwestern Bell Telephone Co., Topeka, Kans., 1956-59; ptnr. Gray and Allen, Topeka, 1956-59; mem. faculties Washburn U. Sch. Law and Menninger Sch. Psychiatry, Topeka, 1959-63; prof. law George Washington U., 1963-76, founder, dir. Inst. Law, Psychiatry and Criminology, prof., chmn. dept. forensic sci.; prof. law, dean Hamline U., St. Paul, 1976-81; Fulbright prof., Swaziland, Africa, 1981-83; past cons. Pres.' Com. on Mental Retardation; past mem. Nat. Adv. Coun. on Correctional Manpower and Tng.; past chmn. commn. on mentally disabled and the cts., Minn. Supreme Ct.; broadcaster radio reading svc. WGCU, Ft. Myers, Fla., WUSF, Tampa, Fla. Author: Mental Health in America: The Years of Crisis, 1979, Readings in Law and Psychiatry, 1968, revised edit., 1975, Legal Rights of the Disabled and Disadvantaged, 1969, Mental Impairment and Legal Incompetency, 1968; columnist several newspapers. Past bd. dirs. Minn. CLU, ACLU of Fla., Mental Health Assn. Minn.; past mem. Human Rels. Rev. Bd., Lee County, Fla. Fulbright vis. prof., Swaziland, Africa, 1981. Fellow Am. Acad. Forensic Scis.; mem. ABA, Mo. Bar Assn., Kans. Bar Assn., Minn. Bar Assn. (past bd. govs.), Am. Arbitration Assn. (arbitrator), Amnesty Internat. (bd. dirs. S.W. Fla.). Democrat. Episcopalian. Home and Office: 35 Palmetto Dr Fort Myers FL 33908-3804

ALLEN, RICHARD GARRETT, health care and education consultant; b. St. Paul, July 8, 1923; s. John and Margaretta (Taggert) A.; m. Ida Elizabeth Vernon, July 5, 1944; children—Richard Garrett, Barbara Elizabeth, Julie Frances (dec.). B.S. cum laude, Trinity U., 1954; M.H.A., Baylor U., 1957; postgrad., Indsl. Coll. of Armed Forces, 1962, USAF Command and Staff Coll., 1962. Commd. 2d lt. Med. Service Corps U.S. Air Force, 1948, advanced through grades to maj., 1961; served in U.S., Pacific, Germany; ret., 1964; asst. adminstr. U. Ala. Hosp. and Clinics; dir. Ctr. for Hosp. Continuing Edn., Sch. for Health Services, U. Ala., Birmingham, 1965-68; dir. edn. New Eng. Hosp. Assembly, Inc., New Eng. Ctr. for Continuing Edn., U. N.H., Durham, 1968-74; dir. Office Health Care Edn., 1970-74; exec. v.p. Edn. and Research Found., San Francisco, 1974-77, Assn. West Hosps., 1974-77; v.p. health affairs M G & M Communications, Foster City, Calif.; pres. Calif. Coll. Podiatric Medicine; chief exec. officer Calif. Podiatry Hosp. and Outpatient Clinic, San Francisco, 1977-81; prof. health care adminstrn. St. Mary's Coll. of Calif., Moraga, 1982-85; cons. health care and edn., 1985—; owner Sleepy Hollow Books, 1985—; mem. Nat. Adv. Coun. on Vocat. Edn., 1969-71; also cons.; cons. Booz, Allen & Hamilton, Washington, Ops. Rsch., Inc., Silver Spring, Md., Republic of Korea Air Force Med. Svcs., Seoul, Bio-Dynamics, Inc., Cambridge, Mass., HEALTH-SAT—Appalachia Community Svcs. Network, Washington, 1980—. Pub.: Hosp. Forum, San Francisco, 1974-77; Contbr. articles to profl. jours. Decorated Air Force Commendation medal with oak leaf cluster. Fellow Am. Coll. Hosp. Adminstrs.; mem. Am. Soc. for Health Manpower Edn. and Tng., Am. Hosp. Assn., AAUP, Am. Soc. Hosp. Edn. and Tng. (pres. 1972), Am. Assn. Colls. Podiatric Medicine (pres. 1979-81), Sherlock Holmes Soc. London. Episcopalian. Lodge: Masons. Home and Office: 1455 Camino Peral Moraga CA 94556-2018 *Uncertainty is a fact of life; there is no progress free of the risk of change. Sharpen your sense of timing and know when it is time to let go and when to hang on. Trials and defeats are inevitable elements of the committed life; welcome these conflicts for it is your principles that are involved. Appreciate the past, but focus on today's tasks—while realizing that tomorrow will be nothing like you expect it to be. Cultivate a cheerful acceptance of your own mortality, and its attendant limitations and blessings.*

ALLEN, RICHARD STANLEY (DICK ALLEN), English language educator, author; b. Troy, N.Y., Aug. 8, 1939; s. Richard Sanders and Doris (Bishop) A.; m. Loretta Mary Negridge, Aug. 13, 1960; children: Richard Negridge, Tanya Angell. A.B., Syracuse U., N.Y., 1961; M.A., Brown U., 1963. Teaching assoc. Brown U., 1962-64; instr. English Wright State U., Dayton, Ohio, 1964-68; mem. faculty U. Bridgeport, (Conn.), 1968—, prof. English, 1976-79; Charles A. Dana prof. English U. Bridgeport, Conn., 1979—, also dir. creative writing. Author: Anon and Various Time Machine Poems, 1971 , Overnight in the Guest House of the Mystic, 1984, Regions with No Proper Names, 1975, Flight and Pursuit, 1987, Ode to the Cold War: Poems New and Selected, 1997; also poems, articles, revs.; editor, poetry editor: Mad River Rev., 1964-68; co-editor: Detective Fiction: Crime and Compromise, 1974, Looking Ahead: The Vision of Science Fiction, 1975; contbg. editor: Am. Poetry Rev.; book reviewer: Poetry, Hudson Rev., Am. Book Rev.; editor: Science Fiction: The Future, 1982, Crosscurrents Expansive Poetry: The New Formalism and the New Narrative, 1989. Recipient poetry prize Union Arts and Civic League, 1971, Disting. Tchg. award MLA-Assn. Depts. English, 1971, San Jose poetry prize, 1976, poetry prize Nassau Rev., 1995; Hart Crane Meml. poetry fellow, 1966, Robert Frost poetry fellow, 1972, Mellon rsch. fellow, 1981, poetry writing fellow Ingram Merrill Found., 1986; poetry writing grantee Nat. Endowment Arts, 1984. Mem. MLA, Associated Writers Programs, Poets and Writers, Nat. Assn. Scholars, PEN, Poetry Soc. Am. (Carolyn Davies Meml. Poetry award 1986), Modern Poetry Soc. Republican. Unitarian. Home: 74 Fern Cir Trumbull CT 06611-4910 Office: U Bridgeport Dept Liberal Arts UB Mail Room Bridgeport CT 06604-5692

ALLEN, RICHARD VINCENT, international business consultant, bank executive; b. Collingswood, N.J., Jan. 1, 1936; s. Charles Carroll and Magdalen (Buchman) A.; m. Patricia Ann Mason, Dec. 28,1957; children: Michael, Kristin, Mark, Karen, Kathryn, Kevin, Kimberly. B.A., U. Notre Dame, 1957, M.A., 1958; postgrad., U. Munich, W. Ger., 1958-61; hon. doctorate, Hanover Coll., Korea U. Instr. U. Md. Overseas Div., 1959-61; asst. prof. polit. sci. Ga. Inst. Tech., 1961-62; sr. staff mem. Center for Strategic and Internat. Studies, Georgetown U., 1962-66, Hoover Instn. on War, Revolution and Peace, Stanford U., 1966-69, Nat. Security Council, White House, 1969; dep. asst. to Pres. U.S., White House, 1971-72; pres. Potomac Internat. Corp., Washington, 1972-80; sr. fgn. policy and nat. security adv. to Ronald Reagan, 1978-80; asst. for nat. security affairs Pres. U.S., White House, 1981-82; pres. Richard V. Allen Co., Washington, 1982-90, chmn., 1991—; disting. fellow, chmn. Asian Studies Ctr. Heritage Found., 1982-98; sr. counselor for fgn. policy and nat. security Rep. Nat. Com., 1982-88; sr. fellow Hoover Instn., 1983—; vice chmn. Internat. Dem. Union, 1983-88; chmn. German-Am. Tricentennial Found., 1983; mem. Pres.'s Task Force on U.S. Govt. Internat. Broadcasting, 1991-92; mem. adv. bd. Cath. Campaign for Am., 1993—; mem. Rep. Congl. Policy Adv. Bd., 1998—. Author: Peace or Peaceful Coexistence, 1966, (with others) Communism and Democracy: Theory and Action, 1967; editor: (with David M. Abshire) National Security: Political, Military and Economic Strategies in the Decade Ahead, 1963, Yearbook on International Communist Affairs, 1969. Chmn. com. on intelligence Republican Nat. Com., 1977-80; trustee St. Francis Prep. Sch., Spring Grove, Pa.; fgn. policy coord. for Richard Nixon, 1968. Named Patriot of Yr. SAR, 1981; H.B. Earhart fellow Relm Found., 1958-61; decorated Order of Diplomatic Merit Republic of Korea, 1982, Knight Comdr.'s Cross Fed. Republic of Germany, 1983, Badge and Star of Order of Merit Fed. Republic of Germany, 1983, Order of Brilliant Star, Republic of China, 1986, Sovereign Mil. Order of Knights of Malta, 1987. Mem. Am. Polit. Sci. Assn., Coun. on Fgn. Rels., Intercollegiate Studies Inst. (trustee), Com. on Present Danger (dir. 1976-90), Univ. Club, Fed. City Club, Farmington Country Club (Charlottesville, Va.), Burning Tree Club (Bethesda, Md.), Met. Club, Robert Trent Jones Golf Club, Cordillera Club (Colo.). Office: 905 16th St NW Ste 400 Washington DC 20006-1703

ALLEN, ROBERT, wholesale distribution executive. CEO Core-Mark Internat, South San Francisco. Office: c/o Core-Mark Internat 395 Oyster Point Blvd Ste 415 South San Francisco CA 94080-1932*

ALLEN, ROBERT, communications company executive. Mng. ptnr. Modem Media, Saughtuck, Conn., 1989-96, pres., 1996—. Mem. Direct Mktg. Assn., Am. Assn. Advt. Agys. (CASIE com.). Office: Modem Media Poppe Tyson 230 East Ave Norwalk CT 06855*

ALLEN, ROBERT DEE, lawyer; b. Tulsa, Oct. 13, 1928; s. Harve and Olive Jean (Brown) A.; m. Mary Latimer Conner, May 18, 1957; children: Scott, Randy, Blake. BA, U. Okla., 1951, LLB, 1955, JD, 1970. Bar: Okla. 1955, Ill. 1979, U.S. Dist. Ct. (we., no. and ea. dists.) Okla. 1955, U.S. Dist.

Ct. (no. dist.) Ill. 1979, U.S. Ct. Appeals (10th cir.) 1956, U.S. Ct. Appeals (7th cir.) 1980, U.S. Supreme Ct. 1985. Assoc. Abernathy & Abernathy, Shawnee, Okla., 1955; law clk. to judge 10th U.S. Ct. Appeals, Denver, 1956; to judge Western Dist. Okla., 1956-57; asst. ins. commr., gen. counsel Okla. Ins. Dept., 1957-63; partner firm Quinlan, Allen & Batchelor, Oklahoma City, 1963-65, DeBois & Allen, 1965-66; counsel AT&T, Washington, 1966-67; gen. atty. Southwestern Bell Telephone Co., Okla., 1967-79; v.p., gen. counsel Ill. Bell Telephone Co., Chgo., 1979-83; sole practice law Chgo. and Oklahoma City, 1983—; mcpl. counselor Oklahoma City, 1984-89; of counsel Hartzog, Conger & Cason, 1983-90, Kimball, Wilson, Walker and Ferguson, 1990-93, Berry & Durland, 1993-94, Durland & Durland, 1994-96, White, Coffey, Galt & Fite, P.C., 1996-97, Phillips, McFall, McCaffrey, McVay & Murrah, P.C., 1997—; spl. counsel Okla. Mcpl. Power Authority, 1990-94, City of Altus, Okla., 1990—; mem. Gov.'s Ad Valorem Tax Structure and Sch. Fin. Commn., 1972; bd. dirs. Taxpayers Fedn. Ill., 1980-83; adv. bd. dirs. Southwestern Legal Found., 1985—; rsch. fellow Southwestern Legal Found., 1994—; adj. prof. ins. law Oklahoma City U. Coll. Law, 1985—, agy. and partnership law, U. Okla. Coll. Law, 1989—; Okla. State chmn. Nat. Inst. Mcpl. Law Officers, 1984-89; apptd. mem. Legis Task Force on Okla. Adminstrv. Code, 1987; founding mem. U. Okla. Assocs., 1980. Bd. dirs. Oklahoma County Legal Aid Soc., 1973—; trustee Oklahoma City Riverfront Redevel. Authority, 1997—. With U.S. Army, 1946-48, 1st lt., 51-53; lt. col. USAR. Fellow Am. Bar Found.; mem. ABA, Fed. Bar Assn. (v.p. Okla. Chpt. 1977—), Okla. Bar Assn., Okla. County Bar Assn., Chgo. Bar Assn., Am. Judicature Soc., Okla. Assn. Mcpl. Attys. (bd. dirs. 1984-89), Order of Coif, Phi Delta Phi, Sigma Phi Epsilon (dir.). Presbyterian. Clubs: Chicago, Oklahoma City Golf and Country, Sunset Ridge Country (Northfield, Ill.). Home: 8101 Glenwood Ave Oklahoma City OK 73114-1107

ALLEN, ROBERT EDWARD, JR., physician assistant; b. Omaha, Mar. 27, 1950; s. Robert Edward and Virginia (Connor) A.; m. Christine Ann Rahm, July 16, 1985; children: Sean Edward, Erin Christine. Student, Brooke Army Hosp., San Antonio, 1968-69, St. Anthony Ctrl. Hosp., Denver, 1984, 86. Cert. Nat. Bd. Orthopaedic Physician Assts.; cert. EMT, vocat. tchr., Colo.; lic. physician asst., Colo.; cert. BLS. Mem., patroller, instr. Nat. Ski Patrol, 1974-90; orthopaedic physician asst., orthopaedic technician Luth. Med. Ctr., Wheatridge, Colo., 1980-85, instr. EMT program, 1983-89; physician asst., mem. staff St. Joseph Hosp., Denver, 1985-87; physician asst. Denver Orthopedic Clinic and Inst. for Limb Preservation, 1987-96, Advanced Orthopedics Assoc., 1996—; part-time EMT, Golden, Colo., 1980-84; lectr. continuing med. edn. Colo. Emergency Med. Svcs. Sys., also nursing staffs; manuscript reviewer William and Wilkins, Balt., 1993—; splty. lectr. oncology Clinicians Rev., Clifton, N.J., 1993—; insvc. lectr. in field. Exec. prodr. instrnl. videos; contbr. articles to profl. publs.; designer saw blade for arthroscopic anterior crucial ligament reconstrn.; co-designer antibiotic bead maker. Vol. Toys for Tots, Denver, 1992—. With Spl. Forces, U.S. Army, 1968-71, Vietnam. Recipient 2nd place in best case study for alkaptonuria/ochrunosis Alvarez PA mag., 1997. Fellow Am. Soc. Orthopedic Physician Assts.; mem. Am. Acad. Physician Assts., NRA. Lutheran. Avocations: scuba diving, hunting, fishing, water and snow skiing. Home: 14650 E Floyd Ave Aurora CO 80014-3803 Office: Advanced Orthopedics Assocs 360 S Garfield St Ste 630 Denver CO 80209-3136 also: 4500 E 9th Ave Ste 150S Denver CO 80220-3932

ALLEN, ROBERT ENGLISH, business development executive, consultant; b. Mt. Pleasant, Tenn., Mar. 31, 1945; s. Robert English and Ruth Faye (Hill) A.; children: George Clayton, Paedra Thais. BS in Chemistry, U. Tenn., 1968; PhD in Chemistry, Iowa State U., 1974. Rsch. scientist Celanese Fibers Co., Charlotte, N.C., 1974-78; tech. mgr. Celanese Fibers Mktg. Co., Charlotte, 1978-82; mgr. new bus. devel. Celanese Fibers Ops. Co., Charlotte, 1982-85; dir. ops. Chardon Labs, Charlotte, 1985; pres., CEO, Allen Cons. Group Inc., Charlotte, 1985-90; mgr. bus. devel. separations divsn. Hoechst Celanese, Charlotte, 1990-94; dir. mktg. and bus. devel. Rexham Custom, Matthews, N.C., 1994-96; gen. mgr., COO FyPro, Inc., Charlotte, 1996-99; dir. mktg. bus. devel. Pioneer Eclipse Corp., Sparta, N.C., 1999—; cons. Jordan Constrn. Co., Charlotte, 1984-90, Oro Mfg. Co., Monroe, N.C., 1986-90; CEO, Allen-Marshall Inc., Charlotte, 1987-88; pres. Rosegate Internat. Inc., Charlotte, 1988-89; arbitrator N.Y. Stock Exch., 1993-94. Contbr. articles to profl. jours. Bd. dirs. Drug Edn. Ctr., 1992-94; bd. dirs. Jr. Achievement, Charlotte, 1986-97, mem. pub. rels. and strategic planning coms. 1986-93. Mem. Charlotte C. of C. (small bus. action coun. 1987-88, pub. affairs com. 1988-92), Execs. Club (v.p. 1987-88, pres. 1988-89), Tips Club (v.p. 1986-88), Phi Kappa Phi, Phi Lambda Upsilon, Alpha Chi Sigma. Republican. Avocations: guitar playing, golf, target shooting, economic education in secondary schools. Home: 16 Red Fox Trl Fort Mill SC 29715-9754 Office: Pioneer Eclipse Corp PO Box 909 1 Eclipse Rd Sparta NC 28675

ALLEN, ROBERT EUGENE BARTON, lawyer; b. Bloomington, Ind., Mar. 16, 1940; s. Robert Eugene Barton and Berth R. A.; m. Cecelia Ward Dooley, Sept. 23, 1960 (div. 1971); children: Victoria, Elizabeth, Robert, Charles, Suzanne, William; m. Judith Elaine Hecht, May 27, 1979 (div. 1984); m. Suzanne Nickolson, Nov. 18, 1995. BS, Columbia U., 1962; LLB, Harvard U., 1965. Bar: Ariz. 1965, U.S. Dist. Ct. Ariz. 1965, U.S. Tax Ct., 1965, U.S. Supreme Ct. 1970, U.S. Ct. Customs and Patent Appeals 1971, U.S. Dist. Ct. D.C. 1972, U.S. Ct. Appeals (9th cir.) 1974, U.S. Ct. Appeals (10th, and D.C. cirs.) 1984, U.S. Dist. Ct. N.Mex., U.S. Dist. Ct. (no. dist.) Calif., U.S. Dist. Ct. (no. dist.) Tex. 1991, U.S. Ct. Appeals (fed. cir.) 1992, U.S. Dist. Ct. (ea. dist.) Wis. 1995. Ptnr., dir. Allen & Price, Phoenix; spl. asst. atty. gen. Ariz. Ct. Appeals, 1978, judge pro-tem, 1984, 92, 99; Nat. pres. Young Dems. Clubs Am., 1971-73, mem. exec. com. Dem. Nat. Com., 1972-73, Ariz. Gov.'s Kitchen Cabinet working on a wide range of state projects, bd. dirs. Phoenix Bapt. Hosp., 1981-83, Phoenix and Valley of the Sun Conv. and Visitors Bur., United Cerebral Palsy Ariz., 1984-89, Planned Parenthood of Cen. and No. Ariz., 1984-90, Ariz. Aviation Futures Task Force, chmn. Ariz. Airport Devel. Criteria Subcom., mem. Apache Junction Airport Rev. Com., Am. rep. exec. bd. Atlantic Alliance of Young Polit. Leaders, 1973-77, 77-80, trustee Am. Counsel of Young Polit. Leaders, 1971-76, 81-85, mem. Am. delegations to Germany, 1971, 72, 76, 79, USSR, 1971, 76, 88, France, 1974, 79, Belgium, 1974, 77, Can., 1974, Eng., 1975, 79, Norway, 1975, Denmark, 1976, Yugoslavia and Hungary, 1985, Am. observer European Parlimentary elections, Eng., France, Germany, Belgium, 1979, Moscow Congrssional, Journalist delegation, 1989, NAFTA Trade Conf., Mexico City, 1993, Atlantic Assembly, Copenhagen, 1993, Internat. Coun. Ariz. Heart Inst. Found., 1998—, trustee Environ. Health Found., 1994-97, Friends of Walnut Canyon, 1994-97, Cordell Hull Found. for Internat. Edn., 1996—, spkr. seminars and profl. assns. *Founder of the law firm Allen & Price. Allen practices in the areas of intellectual property and technology, health care, patent and trade secret litigation, antitrust and securities litigation, and general business and personal counseling. The firm of Allen & Price has been the subject of newspaper and magazine articles emphasizing the firm's use of technology to provide prompt and timely business representation at lower cost than the traditional large law firms.* Contbr. articles on comml. litigation to profl. jours. Mem. ABA, Ariz. Bar Assn., Maricopa County Bar Assn., N.Mex. State Bar, D.C. Bar Assn., Am. Judicature Soc., Fed. Bar Assn., Am. Arbitration Assn., Phi Beta Kappa, Harvard Club. Democrat. Episcopalian (lay reader). Office: Allen & Price 2850 E Camelback Rd Phoenix AZ 85016-4311

ALLEN, ROBERTA, fiction and nonfiction writer, conceptual artist; b. N.Y.C., Oct. 6, 1945; d. Sol and Jeanette (Waldner) A. AAS, Fashion Inst. Tech., N.Y.C., 1964; postgrad., Inst. Bellas Artes, Mex. Lectr. Corcoran Sch. Art, Washington, 1975, Kutztown State Coll., 1979, C.W. Post Coll., 1979; instr. creative writing Parsons Sch. Design, N.Y.C., 1986; instr. The Writer's Voice, 1992-97, The New Sch., 1993-99, Dept. Continuing Edn., NYU, 1993-99; Tennessee Williams fellow, writer-in-residence U. of the South, Sewanee, Tenn., 1998, Columbia U. Sch. of the Arts, 1998-99. Author: Partially Trapped Lines, 1975, Pointless Arrows, 1976, Pointless Acts, 1977, Everything In The World There Is To Know Is Known By Somebody, But Not By the Same Knower, 1981, The Traveling Woman (fiction collection), 1986, (nouvella) The Daughter, 1992, Amazon Dream (travel memoir), 1993, Certain People (fiction collection) 1997, Fast Fiction, 1997, Writing Guide; one-woman shows include Galerie 845, Amsterdam, The Netherlands, 1967, John Weber Gallery, N.Y.C., 1974, 75, 77, 79, Inst. for Art and Urban Resources, N.Y.C., 1977, 80, Galerie Maier-Hahn, Dusseldorf, Germany, 1977, MTL Galerie, Brussels, 1978, C.W. Post Coll., Glenvale, N.Y., 1978, Galerie Walter Storms, Munich, 1981, Kunstforum, Stadt. Galerie in Lenbachhaus, Munich, 1981, Galleria Primo Piano, Rome, 1981, Perth Inst. Contemporary Arts, 1989. Fellow MacCowell Colony, 1971, 72, Ossabaw I. Project fellow, 1972, Yaddo fellow, 1983, 87, 93, Va. Ctr. for Creative Arts fellow, 1985, 94, Tennessee Williams fellow in creative writing U. of the South, 1998; grantee LINE, 1985, Creative Artists Pub. Svc., 1978-79. Home and Office: 5 W 16th St New York NY 10011-6307

ALLEN, RODNEY DESVIGNE, music educator; b. Dover, Del., June 7, 1957; s. Emmitt and Rocelia (Jones) A.; m. Belinda Price, June 2, 1984; children: (twins) Bartholomew Von, Timothy Lee. *Rodney D. Allen has two sons, Timothy Lee Allen and Bartholomew Von Allen, both born on July 20, 1994. Rodney D. Allen was adopted at birth and has found his birth family. He has four sisters: Lorraine Weeks, Loretta Rogers, Patricia Randall, and Sharon Lee.* BS, Ind. State U., 1979; MusM in violin, West Chester U., 1981. Cert. music tchr., Del., Ind., N.J. Violinist Terre Haute (Ind.) Symphony Orch., 1975-79; tchr. piano and violin theory Christina Cultural Arts Ctr., Wilmington, Del., 1980—; tchr. band and orch. Caravel Acad., Bear, Del., 1981-85; tchr. piano theory Jewish Community Ctr., Wilmington, Del., 1985-86; instr. Hartford Heights Elem. Sch., 1989-94, Brehmns Lune Elem. Sch., 1994-98, Furley Elem., Madison Square Elem. Sch., Balt. City Pub. Schs., 1998—; chmn. string dept. Chri' Cult' Arts Ctr., 1980-88, 1st violin John Hopkins Symphony Orch., 1988—; 2d trumpet, 287th Army Band, 1987—, St. Paul String Quartet, 1988—; testing supr. student tchrs. Morgan State, 1988—; Suzuki Cert. Violin, 1983. Served with Del. N.G., 1987—. Music scholar Wilmington Music Sch., 1973. Mem. Del. Music Tchrs. Assn., NAACP. Episcopalian. Avocation: table tennis. Home: 8294 Berryfield Dr Baltimore MD 21236-5510

ALLEN, RONALD JAY, law educator; b. Chgo., July 14, 1948; s. J. Matteson and Carolyn L. (Latchum) A.; m. Debra Jane Livingston, May 25, 1974 (div. 1982); children: Sarah, Adrienne; m. Julie O'Donnell, Sept. 2, 1984; children: Michael, Conor. BS, Marshall U., 1970; JD, U. Mich., 1973. Bar: Nebr. 1974, Iowa 1979, U.S. Ct. Appeals (8th cir.) 1980, U.S. Supreme Ct. 1981, Ill. 1986. Prof. law SUNY, Buffalo, 1974-79, U. Iowa, Iowa City, 1979-82, 83-84, Duke U., Durham, N.C., 1982-83; prof. law Northwestern U., Chgo., 1984—, John Henry Wigmore prof., 1992—; pres. faculty senate U. Iowa, 1980-81. Author: Constitutional Criminal Procedure, 1985, 91, 95, An Analytical Approach to Evidence, 1989, Evidence: Text, Cases and Problems, 1997, Arthritis of the Hip and Knee: The Active Person's Guide to Taking Charge, 1998; contbr. articles to profl. jours. Mem. ABA (rules com. criminal justice sect.), Am. Law Inst. Office: Northwestern U Sch Law 357 E Chicago Ave Chicago IL 60611-3059

ALLEN, RONALD JOHN, astrophysics educator, researcher; b. Prince Albert, Sask., Can., Nov. 12, 1940; s. Arthur and Lillian May (Brown) A.; m. Janice Ruth Nielsen, Jan. 7, 1967; children: Melanie Ruth, Matthew John, Stefan Ronald. BA in Physics with honors, U. Sask., 1962; PhD in Physics, MIT, 1967. Postdoctoral fellow NRC Can., Paris, 1967-68; rsch. assoc. Kapteyn Astron. Inst., U. Groningen, The Netherlands, 1969-70, rsch. supr., 1971, lectr. in radio astronomy, 1972-80, prof. radio astronomy, 1980-85, chmn., 1982-85; prof., head dept. astronomy U. Ill., Urbana, 1985-88; astronomer, head sci. computing divsn. Space Telescope Sci. Inst., Balt., 1989-95, head rsch. programs office, 1995—; vis. lectr. Cavendish Lab., Cambridge, Eng., 1971; mem. acad. council Ministry Edn. and Sci., The Netherlands, 1982-85; mem. vis. com. Nat. Radio Astronomy Obs., Charlottesville, Va., 1986-89; sr. scientist NATO, U.S., 1975-76; vis. prof. Kapteyn Astron. Inst., 1985-95; adjunct prof. Johns Hopkins U., 1991—. Co-editor: Image Processing in Astronomy, 1979, The Milky Way Galaxy, 1985, The Restoration of HST Images and Spectra, 1991; contbr. numerous articles to sci. jours. Fellow Inst. des Hautes Etudes Scientifiques, Bures-sur-Yvette, France, 1974. Mem. Internat. Astron. Union, Am. Astron. Soc., Internat. Radio Sci. Union. Office: Space Telescope Sci Inst 3700 San Martin Dr Baltimore MD 21218-2464

ALLEN, RONALD WESLEY, financial executive; b. Jacksonville, Fla., Sept. 7, 1948; s. John Wesley and Frances Alida (Hadler) A.; m. Bonnie June Smith, Aug. 31, 1968; children: Donna Laurie, Marguerite Theresa. Student, Tulane U., 1966-67; AA with high honors, Fla. Jr. Coll., Jacksonville, 1972; BA with honors, U. North Fla., 1974; MS, U. Fla., 1976. CFP Coll. Fin. Planning. Salesman, electronic technician J.W. Allen & Assocs., Inc., Jacksonville, 1971-74, exec. v.p., 1976-88, chief exec. officer, 1988—; pres. Steamchem Products, Inc., Gainesville, 1975, A&B Carpet Cleaning, Inc., Gainesville, Fla., 1974-75; chief exec. officer Allen Wholesale Supply div. J.W. Allen & Assocs., Inc., Jacksonville, 1979-88; regional v.p. Primerica Fin. Svcs., Jacksonville, 1989-97; dir., sec., treas. Madcem Inc., Jacksonville, 1985-87, Madcem of Fla., Inc., 1987-96; bd. dirs. Beaches Acad., Inc., Jacksonville, Crown Offshore Products, Inc., 1985-92, Forest Hills Meml. Park, Palm City, Fla., 1987-96, Forest Hills Funeral Home, Palm City, 1987-96, Crown Coast Mgmt. Inc., Jacksonville, 1983-94; gen. ptnr. First Coast Investments, Ltd., Jacksonville, 1984-92, J&R Products, Jacksonville, 1991-94; adj. faculty Nova Southeastern U., 1998—; prin. Bull and Bear Capital Advisers, Inc., 1998—. Vestry mem. Christ Ch., Ponte Verda Beach, Fla., 1988-91; v.p. exec. bd. Towers of Love, Inc., St. Augustine, Fla., 1984-95; vol. ann. fund Bolles Sch., Jacksonville, 1976—, Ronald McDonald Ho., Jacksonville, 1991; exec. bd. Living Waters Ministries, St. Augustine, Fla., 1991-93; lay min. Espiscopal Diocese of Fla., 1991—. Sgt. USAF, 1968-72. Mem. Jacksonville C. of C. (com. of 100, 1976-79, armed forces com. 1976-79), Northside Bus. Club, Beaches Bus. Assn. (bd. dirs. 1991-93), Alumni Coun. Bolles Sch., North Fla. Cruising Club (bd. dirs. 1979-86, Yachtsman of Yr. 1983), Navy Jacksonville Yacht Club, Performance Racing Handicap Circuit (bd. dirs. 1982-86, chmn. 1986, Yachtsman of Yr. 1983), Ponte Vedra Country Club, U. North Fla. Alumni Assn. Episcopalian. Avocations: sailing, yacht racing, music, lay ministry, motorcycling. Office: Corp Offices PO Box 3805 Jacksonville FL 32206-0805

ALLEN, ROSE LETITIA, special education educator; b. Dayton, Ohio, Oct. 10, 1960; d. Billie Wesley and Elisabeth Julia (Coler) Taylor; m. Randolph Eugene Allen, June 27, 1987; 1 child, Michelle Elisabeth. BSN, Wright State U., 1982; MS in Edn., U. Bridgeport, 1987. Cert. elem., K-12 handicapped edn., developmentally handicapped and specific LD tchr. Tchr. Hawaii Dept. of Edn., Honolulu, 1989-91; substitute tchr. Montgomery County Bd. Mental Retardation and Devel. Disabilities, Dayton, Ohio, 1993; tchr. Dayton Pub. Schs., 1994—; mem. Faculty Coun., Dayton, 1994-95. 2d lt. USAF, 1983-84. Mem. AAUW, Alpha Xi Delta. Home: 2421 Orange Ave Dayton OH 45439-2839

ALLEN, ROY VERL, life insurance company executive; b. Hyrum, Utah, Aug. 3, 1933; s. Winfrd A. and Sarah Ann (Nielsen) A.; m. Judith Green, Aug. 11, 1961; children: Ann Marie Allen Webb, Michael R., Blair J. BS, Utah State U., 1958. CLU, Chartered Fin. Cons. Mgr. employee benefits Thiokol Chem. Corp., Brigham City, Utah, 1959-61; employment interviewer Hercules, Salt Lake City, 1962-63; agy. mgr. Standard Ins. Co., Salt Lake City, 1963—. Maj. U.S. Army Res., 1962-79. Mem. CLUs (bd. mem. 1973-75), Estate Planning Coun. (bd. mem. 1979-81), Utah Gen. Agts. and Mgrs. (sec., v.p., pres. 1979-83), Utah Assn. Life Underwrtiers (pres. 1988-89), Exchange Club. Republican. Mormon. Avocations: fishing, hunting, basketball. Home: 2526 Olympus Dr Salt Lake City UT 84124-2916 Office: Standard Ins Co 525 3rd Ave Salt Lake City UT 84103-2973

ALLEN, RUSSELL G., lawyer; b. Ottumwa, Iowa, Nov. 7, 1946. BA, Grinnell Coll., 1968; JD, Stanford U., 1971. Bar: Calif. 1971. Ptnr. O'Melveny & Myers LLP, Newport Beach, Calif. Capt. JAGC, USAF, 1971-75. Fellow Am. Coll. Trust and Estate Counsel; mem. ABA (real property, probate and trust law and taxation sects.), Orange County Bar Assn. (estate planning, probate and trust sects.). E-mail: rallen@omm.com. Office: O'Melveny & Myers LLP Ste 1700 610 Newport Center Dr Newport Beach CA 92660-6429

ALLEN, SALLY LYMAN, biologist; b. N.Y.C., Aug. 3, 1926; d. Alexander Victor and Dorothy (Rogers) Lyman; 1 dau., Susan L. AB, Vassar Coll., 1946, PhD (John M. Prather fellow); PhD (USPHS fellow), U. Chgo., 1954. Research assoc. dept. zoology U. Mich., Ann Arbor, 1955-73, assoc. prof. botany, 1967-71, prof., 1971-75, prof. zoology, 1973-75, prof. biol. scis., 1975—, assoc. dean Coll. Lit., Sci. and the Arts, 1988-91; chmn. dept. cellular and molecular biology, div. biol. scis., 1975-77; vis. prof. genetics Ind. U., 1967; cons. Am. Type Culture Collection, 1975—. Mem. editorial bd. Jour. Protozoology, 1974-78, Devel. Genetics, 1990-92; assoc. editor: Genetics, 1973—; co-editor spl. issues Devel. Genetics, 1992; contbr. articles to profl. jours. Fellow AAAS; mem. Am. Inst. Biol. Sci., Genetics Soc. Am., Soc. Protozoologists, Am. Naturalists Soc. (v.p. 1978), Am. Soc. for Cell Biology (mem. council 1973-75), Phi Beta Kappa, Sigma Xi, Golden Key (hon.). Office: U Mich Dept Biology Ann Arbor MI 48109

ALLEN, SAM RAYMOND, organization development specialist; b. Cody, Wyo., Oct. 6, 1953; s. Robert Sam and Jerrine (Cross) A.; m. Melinda Jo Daniels, Oct. 23, 1979; children: Eric Samuel, Andrew William. BS, U. Wyo., 1976, MBA, 1986; postgrad., George Washington U., 1977-79, Hastings Coll., Nebr., 1972-74. Accredited pub. rels. cert. Teller Bank of Va., Rosslyn, Va., 1978-79; legis. asst. U.S. Senate/Alan K. Simpson, Washington, 1979-81; bus. mgr. Coors Brewing Co., Golden, Colo., 1986-87; vol. prog. mgr. Coors Brewing Co., 1987-90, tng. mgr., 1990-96; exec. dir. tng. svcs. Red Rocks Inst., Lakewood, Colo., 1996—. Editor V.I.C.E. Activity Guide newsletter, 1987-90. Bus. advisor Jr. Achievement, Denver, 1988-90; corp. mem. Assn. for Vol. Adminstrn., Boulder, 1987-90; elder Shepherd of the Hills Presbyn. Ch., 1986-89. Named Outstanding Corp. Coord., Adopt-A-School, Denver, 1987. Mem. ASTD, U. Wyo. Alumni Assn., Pub. Rels. Soc. Am., Rotary (community svc. dir. 1989), Alpha Kappa Psi. Republican. Presbyterian. Avocations: nature photography, public speaking, skiing. Home: 11636 W 74th Way Arvada CO 80005-3274 Office: Red Rocks Institute c/o Red Rocks Cmty College 13300 W 6th Ave Lakewood CO 80228-1213

ALLEN, SONNY, professional basketball coach. Student, Marshall U. Coach freshman team Marshall U., 1959-65; coach Old Dominion U., 1965-75, So. Meth. U., 1975-80, U. Nev., Reno, 1980-87, Santa Barbara Islanders, Las Vegas Silver Streaks; NBA scout Charlotte Hornets, 1990-94; NBA scout Dallas Mavericks, 1994-96, asst. coach, 1996-97; asst. coach Detroit Shock, 1997-98; head coach Sacramento Monarchs, 1998—. Named Coach of the Yr., AP and Nat. Assn. Basketball Coaches, 1975, Southwest Conf. coach of the Yr., 1976, big Sky Coach of the Yr. awards, 1984, 85, Coach of the Yr. , WNBA, 1990. Office: c/o Sacramento Monarchs One Sports Pkwy Sacramento CA 95834*

ALLEN, STEPHEN D(EAN), pathologist, microbiologist; b. Linton, Ind., Sept. 8, 1943; s. Wilburn and Betty (Moffett) A.; m. Vally C. Autrey, June 17, 1964; children: Christopher D., Amy C. BA, Ind. U., 1965, MA, 1967; MD, Ind. U., Indpls., 1970. Diplomate Am. Bd. Pathology; cert. in anatomic and clin. pathology and med. microbiology. Intern in pathology Vanderbilt U. Hosp., Nashville, 1970-71; resident in pathology Vanderbilt U. Hosp., 1971-74; clin. asst. prof. pathology Emory U., Atlanta, 1974-77; asst. prof. clin. pathology Ind. U., Indpls., 1977-79, asst. prof. pathology, 1979-81, assoc. prof. pathology, 1981-86, prof. pathology, 1986-92, prof. pathology and lab. medicine, 1992—, assoc. dir. div. clin. microbiology, dept. pathology, 1977—, dir. grad. progam pathology, 1986—, sr. assoc. chmn. dept. pathology, 1990-91, dir. divsn. clin. microbiology dept. pathology/lab. medicine, 1992—, assoc. chair dept. pathology and lab. medicine & dir. labs., 1996—; dir. disease control lab. divsn. Ind. State Dept. Health, Indpls., 1994—; mem. residency rev. com. for pathology Accreditation Coun. for Grad. Med. Edn., 1996—, mem. residency rev. com. for molecular genetic pathology. Co-author: Color Atlas of Diagnostic Microbiology, 5th edit. 1997, Introduction to Diagnostic Microbiology, 1994, Direct Smear Atlas, 1998; contbr. articles to profl. jours. With USPHS, 1974-77. Fellow Coll. Am. Pathologists, Am. Acad. Microbiology, Am. Soc. Clin. Pathologists (coun. mem. microbiology 1983-89), Infectious Diseases Soc. Am., Binford-Dammin Soc. Infectious Disease Pathologists, Soc. Sigma Xi; mem. Am. Bd. Pathology (trustee 1995—, chair microbiology test com.), Masons (32 deg.), Shriners. Avocations: music, electric bass and trumpet, fly-fishing. Office: Ind U Hosp Rm 4430 550 N University Blvd Indianapolis IN 46202-5283

ALLEN, STEPHEN VALENTINE PATRICK WILLIAM, television comedian, author, pianist, songwriter; b. N.Y.C., Dec. 26, 1921; s. Carroll and Isabelle (Donohue) A.; m. Dorothy Goodman, Aug. 23, 1943; children: Stephen, Brian, David; m. Jayne Meadows, July 31, 1954; 1 child, William Christopher. Student journalism, Drake U., 1941, State Tchrs. Coll., Ariz., 1942. Radio announcer Sta. KOY, Phoenix, 1942, Stas. KFAC and KMTR, Los Angeles, 1944; comedian MBS, 1945; entertainer CBS, 1948-50; wrote narration and appeared in movie: Down Memory Lane; also appeared in motion pictures Warning Shot, The Benny Goodman Story, Amazon Women on the Moon, Great Balls of Fire, The Player, after 1950; appeared in Broadway play The Pink Elephant, 1953; creator, host Tonight Show, NBC, 1953-57; host TV shows Steve Allen Show, NBC, 1956-60, WBC syndicate, 1961-64, I've Got A Secret, 1964-67, Laughback, 1976-77, Meeting of Minds, 1977-81; composer over 7,000 songs including Picnic, Impossible, This Could Be The Start; author 43 books including Fourteen for Tonight, 1955, Bop Fables, 1955, The Funny Men, 1956, Wry on the Rocks, 1956, The Girls on the Tenth Floor, 1958, The Question Man, 1959, Mark It and Strike It; autobiography, 1960, Not All of Your Laughter, Not All of Your Tears, 1962; Letter to a Conservative, 1965, The Ground is Our Table, 1966, Bigger Than A Breadbox, 1967, A Flash of Swallows, 1969, The Wake, 1972, Princess Snip-Snip, 1973, Curses!, 1973, Schmock-Schmock!, 1975, What To Say When It Rains, 1974, Meeting of Minds, 1978, Chopped Up Chinese, 1978, Ripoff, 1979, Explaining China, 1980, Funny People, 1981, The Talk Show Murders, 1982, More Funny People, 1982 Beloved Son: A Story of the Jesus Cults, 1982, More Funny People, 1982, How To Make a Speech, 1986, How To Be Funny, 1987, Murder on the Glitter Box, 1989, (with Bill Adler Jr.) The Passionate Nonsmoker's Bill of the Rights, 1989, Dumbth: And 81 Ways to Make Americans Smarter, 1989, The Public Hating, 1990, Murder in Manhattan, 1990, Steve Allen and The Bible: Religion and Morality, 1990, Murder in Vegas, 1991, Hi-Ho, Steverino! My Adventures in the Wonderful Wacky World of TV, 1992, How to be Funny, 1992, The Murder Game, 1993, More Steve Allen on the Bible, Religion & Morality, Book Two, 1993, Make 'Em Laugh, 1993, Reflections, 1994, Murder on the Atlantic, 1995, The Man Who Turned Back the Clock and Other Short Stories, 1995, The Bug and The Slug in The Rug, 1995, But Seriously..., 1996, Wake Up to Murder, 1996, Die Laughing, 1998, Dumbth: The Lost Art of Thinking, 1998, 100 Song Lyrics by Steve Allen, 1999. Recipient Grammy award for Gravy Waltz, 1964; named to TV Acad. Hall of Fame, 1986. Address: Ste B 15201 Burbank Blvd Van Nuys CA 91411-3532

ALLEN, STEVEN PAUL, microbiologist; b. Oak Park, Ill., Nov. 6, 1958; s. Paul Samuel and Rosemary (Bieber) A.; m. Wendy Dianne Gunia, Sept. 11, 1982; children: Samantha Rose, Matthew David, Timothy Bryan. BS, U. Ill., 1980, PhD, 1990; MS, Iowa State U., 1982. Rsch. asst. Iowa State U., Ames, 1980-82; rsch. specialist U. Ill., Chgo., 1982-85; rsch. asst. U. Ill., Urbana, 1985-90; postdoctoral assoc. Monsanto Corp. Rsch., St. Louis, 1990-93; tech. specialist metabolic bus. team Abbott Lab., Abbott Park, Ill., 1993-95, mgr. STD/hepatitis rare reagent validations for infectious disease and assay devel., 1995-98, sr. scientist monolconal antibody purification process devel, 1998—. Contbr. numerous articles to profl. jours. Mem. Am. Soc. for Microbiology, Inst. of Food Technologists (fellowship 1989-90, merit fellowship 1987), Phi Kappa Phi, Gamma Sigma Delta, Sigma Xi. Achievements include development of first intact-cell DNA transformation protocol for the bacterium Clostridium perfringens. Office: Abbott Labs 100 Abbott Park Rd Abbott Park IL 60064-3502

ALLEN, TERRY, artist; b. Wichita, Kans., May 7, 1943. BFA, Chouinard Art Inst., 1966. instr. drawing Chouinard Art Inst., L.A., 1968-69; assoc. prof. Calif. State U., Fresno, 1974-77, prof., 1978-79. Exhibitions include Joslyn Art Mus., Omaha, 1970, San Francisco Mus. Art, 1970, Chgo. Art Inst., 1975, Ft. Worth Art Mus., 1976, San Francisco Mus. Modern Art, 1978, São Paulo (Brazil) Biennial, 1985, Documenta 8, Kassal, West Germany, 1987, L.A. County Mus. Art, 1987, Kimbell Art Mus., Ft. Worth, 1991, Wexner Ctr. Visual Arts, Columbus, Ohio, 1992, Mus. Modern Art, Paris, 1982, others. Recipient Bessie award, 1986, Adaline Kent award, 1989; Guggenheim fellow, 1986, SArtists Residency fellow Wexner Ctr. Arts, 1992. Office: W Alameda RR 10 Box 88N Santa Fe NM 87501-9402*

ALLEN, TERRY DEVEREUX, urologist, educator; b. Dallas, Nov. 28, 1930; s. Lester E. and Gladys (McIver) A.; m. Carolyn Latham, June 26, 1955; children: Kevin, Kathleen, Cheryl, Robin. Student, Rice U., 1951; MD, Baylor Med. Sch., 1955. Diplomate Am. Bd. Urology. Intern Jefferson

Davis Hosp., Houston, 1955-56; attending physician Terrell (Tex.) State Hosp., 1958-59; resident surgery Parkland Meml. Hosp., Dallas, 1959-60, resident urology, 1960-63; pvt. practice Dallas Med./ Surg. Clinic, 1963-70; faculty Southwestern Med. Sch., Dallas, 1971—; mem., chair Residency Rev. Com., 1977-83; exec. com. mem. Am. Bd. Med. Specialties, 1992-94; trustee Am. Bd. Urology, 1985-91. Assoc. editor Jour. Urology, Balt., 1983-93; contbr. numerous articles to profl. jours., chpts. to books. Capt. USAF, 1956-58. Fellow Am. Coll. Surgeons (gov.), Am. Acad. Pediatrics (urology, pres. 1984-85); mem. Soc. Univ. Urologists (sec., pres. 1985-86), Soc. Pediatric Urology (sec.pres. 1977-79, 81-83), Am. Urol. Assn. (Edn. award 1985, Hugh Hampton Young 1990), Am. Assn. GU Surgeons. Avocations: sailing, fgn. langs. Home: 9829 Elmcrest Dr Dallas TX 75238-1831 Office: Children's Med Ctr Bank One Tower 14th Fl 6300 Harry Hines Blvd Dallas TX 75235-5259*

ALLEN, THOMAS, alderman; m. Janis Groya; children: Tommy, Sarah, Kevin, Claire. Grad. cum laude, Ill. Benedictine Coll. Adminstrv., legis. asst., worker in criminal justice City of Chgo., alderman 38th ward, 1993—; mem. Aviation Com., Budget and Govt. Ops. Com., Bldgs. Com., Rules and Ethics Com., Zoning Com., Transp. & Pub. Way Com.; with Chgo. City Coun. Mem. Sunshine Activity Ctr. for Mentally Handicapped. Mem. Portage Park C. of C. (bd. dirs.), Polish-Am. Police Assn., Irish Fellows Club. Democrat. Office: 5817 W Irving Park Rd Chicago IL 60634*

ALLEN, THOMAS B., writer; b. Bridgeport, Conn., Mar. 20, 1929; s. Walter L. and Catherine Elizabeth (Reilly) A.; m. Florence Elizabeth MacBride, June 5, 1950; children: Christopher, Constance, Roger. BA in Journalism, U. Bridgeport, 1956. Reporter, columnist Bridgeport (Conn.) Herald; feature writer N.Y. Daily News, 1956-63; mng. editor Trade divsn. Chilton Books, 1964-65; writer for book divsn. Nat. Geographic Soc., 1965-74. Author: War Games, 1987, The Blue and the Gray, 1992, Possessed, 1993, Offerings at the Wall, 1995, Animals of Africa, 1997, America From Space, 1998, The Shark Almanac, 1999, others; (with Norman Polmar) Rickover: Controversy and Genius, 1982, Merchants of Treason, 1988, World War II: America at War 1941-1945, 1991, Code-name: Downfall, 1995; Spy Book: The Encyclopedia of Espionage, 1996; (with William Cohen) Murder in the Senate, 1992; contbr. articles to Nat. Geographic, N.Y. Times Mag., Mil. History Quar., Washington Post, Washingtonian, Smithsonian, Popular Sci. Ann., A. History, others. Served with USN, 1951-53. Mem. Nat. Press Club. Democrat. Unitarian.

ALLEN, THOMAS DRAPER, lawyer; b. Detroit, June 25, 1926; s. Draper and Florence (Jones) A.; m. Joyce M. Johnson, July 18, 1953; children—Nancy A. Bowser, Robert D., Rebecca A. Hubbard. BS, Northwestern U., 1949; JD, U. Mich., 1952. Bar: Ill. 1952, U.S. Supreme Ct. 1971. Assoc. Kirkland & Ellis, Chgo., 1952-60, ptnr., 1961-67; ptnr. Wildman, Harrold, Allen & Dixon, Chgo., 1967—. Chmn. Community Caucus, Hinsdale, Ill., 1960-61; mem. Hinsdale Bd. Edn., 1965-71, pres., 1970-71; pres. West Suburban coun. Boy Scouts Am., 1980-82, mem. nat. exec. bd., 1986—, chmn. internat. com., 1995—, mem. world program com., 1983-93; moderator Union Ch., Hinsdale, 1983-84; trustee Chgo. Theol. Sem., 1988-97, chair, 1990-96, life trustee, 1997—. With USN, 1944-46. Recipient Silver Beaver award Boy Scouts Am., 1964, Silver Buffalo award, 1997, Bronze Wolf award World Scout Orgn., 1993. Fellow Am. Coll. Trial Lawyers (state chair 1984-85, chair internat. com. 1997—); mem. ABA, Ill. Bar Assn., Chgo. Bar Assn. (bd. of mgrs 1989-91), Law Club of Chgo., Legal Club of Chgo., Jaycees Internat. (senator, 1965), Internat. Bar Assn., Hinsdale Golf Club, Chgo. Athletic Club. Mem. United Ch. of Christ. Home: 505 N Lake Shore Dr Chicago IL 60611-3427 Office: Wildman Harrold Allen & Dixon 225 W Wacker Dr Chicago IL 60606-1224

ALLEN, THOMAS H., congressman, lawyer; b. Portland, Maine, Apr. 16, 1945; s. Charles and Genevieve A.; m. Diana Bell; children: Gwen, Kate. BA, Bowdoin Coll., 1967; BPhil, Oxford U., 1970; JD, Harvard U., 1971. Mem. Drummond, Woodsum, Plimpton and MacMahon, Maine, Portland (Maine) City Coun., 1989-95; mayor City of Portland, 1991-92; mem. 105th Congress from 1st Maine dist., 1996—; mem. Congressional Com. Govt. Reform and Oversight, 1997—, Nat. Security, 1997—. Dem. candidate for Gov., State of Maine, 1994, for U.S. House of Reps., 1st Dist., Maine, 1996; chair Clinton/Gore campaign, Maine, 1992; mem. Pres. Clinton's Agrl. Transition Team; bd. overseers Bowdoin Coll.; bd. dirs. Shalom House, United Way; chair Gov. Joseph Brennan Task Force on Foster Care for Children; pres. Portland Stage Co.; mem. exec. and legis. policy coms. Maine Mcpl. Assn. Rhodes scholar Oxford U. Mem. Phi Beta Kappa. Office: US Ho of Reps 1717 Longworth Hse Ofc Bldg Washington DC 20515 also: 234 Oxford St Portland ME 04101-3029*

ALLEN, THOMAS WESLEY, medical educator, dean; b. Chgo., Sept. 13, 1938; s. Thomas and Helen Irene (Spitler) A.; m. Annette Faye Power, June 23, 1962 (div. 1988); children: Roderick Nelson, Andrea Jane; m. Keith Mayo Capen, Oct. 16, 1988; 1 stepchild, Hilary Tate. BA, Ottawa (Kans.) U., 1960; DO, Midwestern U., Chgo., 1964; DHL (hon.), U. New Eng., Biddeford, Maine, 1989. Diplomate internal medicine with subspecialty in pulmonary medicine, Am. Osteo. Bd. Internal Medicine. Intern Met. Hosp., Grand Rapids, Mich., 1964-65; resident in internal medicine Hosps. Chgo. Coll. Osteo. Medicine, 1965-68; fellow in pulmonary medicine Northwestern U., 1969-70; from asst. to prof. medicine Chgo. Coll. Osteo. Medicine, 1968-87; pvt. practice Chgo., 1970-78; dean and v.p. acad. affairs and prof. medicine Midwestern U. Coll. Osteo. Medicine, Chgo., 1978-87; assoc. dean for acad. and clin. affars, prof. medicine U. Medicine and Dentistry of N.J. Coll. of Osteo. Medicine, 1987-91; provost, dean, prof. medicine Okla. State U. Coll. Osteo. Medicine, Tulsa, 1991—; mem. Nat. Adv. Coun. on Nat. Health Service Corps, Washington, 1994-97, Nat. Adv. Coun. on Health Professions Edn., Washington, 1986-90. Editor-in-chief Jour. Am. Osteo. Assn., 1987-98. Civic unit chair Tulsa Area United Way, 1995; trustee Village of Western Springs, Ill., 1981-85. Col. USAR, 1988—. Recipient Outstanding Achievement award Chgo. Coll. Osteo. Medicine Alumni Assn., 1993. Fellow Am. Coll. Osteo. Internists, Am. Coll. Chest Physicians; mem. Am. Osteo. Assn., Am. Assn. Colls. Osteo. Medicine, Am. Osteo. Acad. Sports Medicine, Am. Coll. Sports Medicine, Phi Kappa Phi. Episcopalian. Avocations: running, horseback riding. Home: 8911 S Florence Pl Tulsa OK 74137-3333 Office: Okla State Univ College Osteopathic Med 1111 W 17th St Tulsa OK 74107-1800

ALLEN, TIM (TIMOTHY ALLEN DICK), actor, comedian; b. Denver, June 13, 1953. Grad., Western Mich. U. Appeared in numerous Showtime spls.; actor: (TV series) Home Improvement, 1991-99 (Emmy award nomination, Lead actor - comedy 1993); (films) The Santa Clause, 1994; (voice) Toy Story, 1995, Meet Wally Sparks, 1997, Jungle2Jungle, 1997, For Richer or Poorer, 1997, Toy Story 2, 1999; (television specials) Men Are Pigs, 1990, Showtime Comedy Club All-Stars II, 1988; author: I'm Not Really Here, 1996, Don't Stand Too Close to a Naked Man, 1994, Jungle 2 Jungle, 1997. Recipient Golden Globe, 1995, Favorite Comedy Actor People's Choice award, 1995,97, 98, 99, TV Guide award 1999; nominated for Golden Globe awards 1993, 94, 96, 97, Blockbuster Entertainment award 1998. Office: c/o Wind Dancer Prods. Group Prod Bldg 3rd Flr Burbank CA 91521-2215*

ALLEN, TONI K., lawyer; b. N.Y.C., Aug. 6, 1940; d. Irving M. and Mary (Sackler) Schoolman; m. Robert W. Clark III, July 22, 1985. AB, Wellesley Coll., 1960; LLB, NYU, 1964. Bar: N.Y. 1964, D.C. 1972. Atty. Office of Irving M. Wall, Esquire, N.Y.C., 1964-68; gen. counsel, asst. to pres. Nat. Econ. Rsch. Assocs., N.Y.C., 1968-71; atty., advisor Postal Rate Commn., Washington, 1971-72; assoc. Wald, Harkrader & Ross, Washington, 1972-73, ptnr., 1974-85; ptnr. Piper & Marbury LLP, Washington, 1986-98, chmn. environ. dept., 1991-94, mem. policy and mgmt. com., 1992-94, ptnr. emeritus, 1999—. Trustee Levine Sch. Music, Washington, 1981—, pres., 1991-96; co-chair exec. bd. The Environmental Lawyer, 1994-96, Leadership Washington, 1996-97. Fellow Am. Bar Found.; mem. ABA (natural resources, energy and environ. law sect.), Order of Coif. Democrat. Avocations: sports, music. Office: Piper & Marbury LLP 5640 Bent Branch Rd Bethesda MD 20816

ALLEN, VERNA L., state commissioner. BA in Biol. Scis. summa cum laude, Calif. State U., Fresno, 1972, MA in Edn. Adminstrn., 1983. Advanced sci. tchr. Clovis (Calif.) Unified Sch. Dist., 1973-80; MESA ctr. dir. Calif. State U. Sch. Engring., Fresno, 1980-85; tutorial coord. San Jose (Calif.) State u., 1985-86; assoc. dir. U. N.C., Chapel Hill, 1986-89; statewide dir. Morgan State U., Balt., 1989-91; nat. assoc. dir. The Coll. Bd., N.Y.C., 1991-96; assoc. exec. dir. Ariz. Commn. for Postsecondary Edn., Phoenix, 1996-97, exec. dir., 1997—. Office: Ariz Commn Post-Secondary Edn 2020 N Central Ave Ste 275 Phoenix AZ 85004-4503

ALLEN, VICKI LYNETTE, physical education educator; b. Denver, Oct. 27, 1952; d. Donald Joseph and Jacqueline (Jones) Roth; m. Robert Craig Allen, Aug. 14, 1976; children: Jeffrey, Gregory, Stacy. BA magna cum laude, Calif. State U., Northridge, 1974; MEd summa cum laude, U. Nev., Las Vegas, 1987. Cert. tchr., Nev. Tchr. phys. edn., jr. varsity basketball coach Beverly Hills (Calif.) Unified Sch. Dist., 1975-78; tchr. secondary phys. edn. Clark County Sch. Dist., Las Vegas, 1978-89, elem. tchr. phys. edn., 1989-96, basketball coach, 1988-89; tchr. on spl. assignment in phys. edn. Clark County Sch. Dist., 1997—; adj. instr. U. Nev., Las Vegas, 1993-97; mem. phys. fitness task force Clark County Sch. Dist., 1990-91, integrated curriculum task force, 1992-93, task force on curriculum revision and assessment, 1996-97; mem. Nev. State Bd. Edn. team to write Stds. for Phys. Edn., 1999; mem. Nev. State Dept. Edn. com. to set stds. for phys. edn. tchr. licensure, 1993. Author phys. fitness and multicultural games publs.; mem. editl. bd. Teaching Elem. Phys. Edn., 1995-97. Coach Nev. State Youth Soccer Orgn., Las Vegas, 1988-91, Am. Youth Soccer Orgn., 1992; eucharistic min. St. Thomas More Cath. Ch., Las Vegas, 1991—; core leader for youth group, Las Vegas, 1994-95; mem. Nat. Charity League, 1998—. Named Nev. Elem. Phys. Educator of Yr., 1996-97; Jr. League Nev. grantee, 1991. Mem. NEA, AAHPERD, Nev. Alliance Health, Phys. Edn., Recreation and Dance (sec. 1995-96), So. Nev. Alliance for Health, Phys. Edn., Recreation and Dance (bd. mem. 1988—), Phi Kappa Phi. Avocations: camping, weight lifting, reading, crafts, hiking. Office: Whitney Elem Sch 5005 Keenan Ave Las Vegas NV 89122-7461

ALLEN, VICKY, sales and marketing professional; b. Springfield, Pa., May 27, 1957; d. James Joseph and Ann Marie (Cifone) Cattafesta; m. James Francis DeLeone, Aug. 11, 1979 (div. 1982); m. Dennis Ronald Allen, June 30, 1990; children: Amber, Austen. BBA in Computer Sci., Temple U., 1979. Quality assurance Burroughs Corp., Downingtown, Pa., 1977, software QA, 1978, systems analyst, 1979-81; program analyst Crocker Internal Systems, San Jose, Calif., 1981-83; sr. systems analyst Avantek, Inc., Santa Clara, Calif., 1983-84; product mktg. program specialist Micro Focus, Palo Alto, Calif., 1984-96; OEM sales account mgr. Netscape Comms. Corp., Mountain View, Calif., 1996—; programmer cons. Fin. Group, Palo Alto, 1985-86. Active Sierra Club. Mem. Phi Sigma Sigma (sec. 1978-79). Democrat. Roman Catholic. Avocations: music, hiking, biking, race walking. Office: Netscape 501 Middlefield Rd Palo Alto CA 94301-2124

ALLEN, W. WAYNE, oil industry executive; b. 1936. BS, Okla. State U., 1959, MME, 1969. With Phillips Petroleum Co., 1961-84, regional mgr. U.K., 1984-85, gen. mgr. exploration and prodn. western divsn., 1986-89, sr. v.p. exploration and prodn., 1989-91, pres., COO, 1991-94, chmn. bd., CEO, 1994—. Capt. U.S. Army, 1959-61. Office: Phillips Petroleum Co 18 Phillips Bldg Bartlesville OK 74004

ALLEN, WILLIAM CECIL, physician, educator; b. LaBelle, Mo., Sept. 8, 1919; s. William H. and Viola O. (Holt) A.; m. Madge Marie Gehardt, Dec. 25, 1943; children: William Walter, Linda Diane Allen Deardeuff, Robert Lee, Leah Denise Rogers. A.B., U. Nebr., 1947, M.D., 1951; M.P.H., Johns Hopkins U., 1960. Diplomate Am. Bd. Preventive Medicine. Intern Bishop Clarkson Meml. Hosp., Omaha, 1952; practice medicine specializing in family practice Glasgow, Mo., 1952-59; specializing in preventive medicine Columbia, Mo., 1960—; dir. sect. chronic diseases Mo. Div. Health, Jefferson City, 1960-65; asst. med. dir. U. Mo. Med. Ctr., 1965-75; assoc. coordinator Mo. Regional Med. Program, 1968-73, coordinator health programs, 1969—, clin. asst. prof. community health and med. practice, 1962-65, asst. prof. community health and med. practice, 1965-69, assoc. prof., 1969-75, prof., 1975-76, prof. dept. family and community medicine, 1976-87, prof. emeritus, 1987—; cons. Mo. Regional Med. Program, 1966-67, Norfolk Area Med. Sch. Authority, Va., 1965-66; governing body Area II Health Systems Agy., 1977-79, mem. coordinating com., 1977-79; founding dir. Mid-Mo. PSRO Corp., 1974-79, dir., 1976-84. Contbr. articles to profl. jours. Mem. Gov.'s Adv Council for Comprehensive Health Planning, 1970-73; trustee U. Mo. Med. Sch. Found., 1976—. Served with USMC, 1943-46. Fellow Am. Coll. Preventive Medicine, Am. Acad. Family Physicians (sci. program com. 1972-75, commn. on edn. 1975-80), Royal Soc. Health; mem. Mo. Acad. Family Physicians (dir. 1956-59, 76-82, alt. del. 1982-87, pres. 1985-86, chmn. bd. 1986-87), Mo. Med. Assn., Howard County Med. Soc. (pres. 1958-59), Boone County Med. Soc. (pres. 1974-75), Am. Diabetes Assn. (pres. 1978, dir. 1974-77), Mo. Diabetes Assn. (pres. 1972-73), Soc. Tchrs. Family Medicine, AMA, Mo. Public Health Assn., Am. Heart Assn. (program com. 1979-82), Am. Heart Assn. of Mo. (sec. 1980-81), Mo. Heart Assn. (sec. 1979-82, pres.-elect 1982-84, pres. 1984-86). Methodist. Office: U Mo M218 Medical Ctr Columbia MO 65203

ALLEN, WILLIAM HAYES, lawyer; b. Palo Alto, Calif., Oct. 19, 1926; s. Ben Shannon and Victoria Rose (French) A.; m. Joan Webster Emmett, July 16, 1950; children: Edwin Hayes, Neal French, William Kent. Student, Deep Springs Coll., 1942-44; BA with gt. distinction, Stanford U., 1948, LLB, 1956. Bar: D.C. 1958. Corr. AP, Fresno, Calif., 1948-49; newsman AP, Sacramento, 1950-53; law clk. to Chief Justice Earl Warren U.S. Supreme Ct., Washington, 1956-57; assoc. Covington & Burling, Washington, 1957-64, ptnr., 1964-92; ret., 1993—; acting. prof. Stanford U. Law Sch., 1979; adj. prof. Howard U. Law Sch., 1981-83; lectr. George Mason U. Law Sch., 1983-86; practitioner-in-residence Cornell U. Law Sch., 1992; vis. prof. Deep Springs Coll., 1996; chmn. jud. rev. com. Adminstrv. Conf. U.S., 1972-82, sr. conf. fellow, 1982-95; mem. steering com. Nat. Prison Project, 1975-93. Pres. Stanford Law Rev., vol. 8, 1955-56; contbr. articles to legal jours. Trustee Deep Springs Coll., 1984-92, chmn. bd. trustees, 1992; mem. Fair Housing Bd., Arlington County, Va., 1974-79. With U.S. Army, 1945-47. Mem. ABA (mem. coun. adminstrv. law sect. 1969-72, 79-81, chmn. 1982-83), D.C. Bar (chmn. legal ethics com. 1976-78), Am. Law Inst., Nat. Press Club, Am. Acad. of Appellate Practice, Order of Coif. Democrat. Mem. United Ch. of Christ. Office: Covington & Burling 1201 Pennsylvania Ave NW PO Box 7566 Washington DC 20044-7566

ALLEN, WILLIAM JERE, minister; b. Greenville, Miss., Apr. 23, 1934; s. Marion Goodman and Gradie Lee (Yates) A.; m. Lorena Faye Franklin, June 24, 1960; children: Lorena Lynn Brickson, Jennifer Dawn Moradi, William Jere Allen Jr. B of Bldg. Constrn., Auburn U., 1956; BDiv, So. Bapt. Theol. Sem., 1963; DMin, Union Theol. Sem., 1973. Ordained to ministry First Bapt. Ch., 1960. Pastor 45th Street Mission, Ashland, Ky., 1959-60, Rose Hill Bapt. Ch., Ashland, 1960-62, Colonial Ave. Bapt. Ch., Roanoke, Va., 1962-67, Bainbridge St. Bapt. Ch., Richmond, Va., 1967-71, Bainbridge Southampton Bapt. Ch., Richmond, 1972-75; cons., dir. spl. missions dept. Ala. Bapt. State Conv., Montgomery, 1975-79; assoc. then dir. met. mission dept. Home Mission Bd., So. Bapt. Conv., Atlanta, 1979-91; exec. dir., min. D.C. Bapt. Conv., Washington, 1992—; mega focus cities cons. Home Mission Bd., So. Bapt. Conv., Atlanta, 1982—; bd. trustees Bapt. Sr. Adult Ministries, Washington, 1993—. Co-author: Shaping a Future for Church in Changing Community, 1981, Church and Community Diagnostic Workbook, 1986; author: (with others) Shooting the Rapids: Efective Ministry in a Changing World, 1990, Faith and Social Ministry: Ten Christian Perspectives, 1990. Mem. Interfaith Conf., Washington, 1992—, Dem. Nat. Com., 1993—. Capt. USAF, 1956-62. Mem. Assn. of So. Bapt. Exec. Dirs., Regional Exec. Ministries Coun., Am. Bapt. Chs. (gen. exec. coun.), Faith Group Leaders of Washington. Avocations: jogging, reading, family travel, golf. Home: 3041 Chestnut St NW Washington DC 20015-1407 Office: DC Bapt Conv 1628 16th St NW Washington DC 20009-3099

ALLEN, WILLIAM L., editor. Editor Nat. Geog., Washington. Office: Nat Geog Soc 1145 17th St NW Washington DC 20036-4688*

ALLEN, WILLIAM MARION, III, retired graphic designer, artist; b. Ft. Worth, July 10, 1927; s. William Marion and Lucile Beasley Allen. Student, Southwestern U., 1944-45, Tex. Christian U., 1945-46; BFA, U. Tex., 1950; postgrad., UCLA, 1954; MFA, U. So. Calif., 1955. Art tchr. El Paso Pub. Schs., 1950-51; illustrator Ramo Wooldridge Corp., L.A., 1956-58, Space Tech. Labs., L.A., 1958-60; graphic design coord. The Aerospace Corp., L.A., 1960-89; ret., 1989. One-man shows include Comara Gallery, L.A., 1975, 76, Art Gallery-The Aerospace Corp., L.A., 1982; group shows include Long Beach Mus. Art, Calif. State Fair, Chico State Coll., Tex. Fine Arts Assn., Butler Inst. Am. Art, Youngstown, Ohio, Ft. Worth Art Assn., L.A. Art Assn., others. With U.S. Army, 1951-53, PTO. Recipient Cash award 18th Annual Artists Show, Ft. Worth, 1957, Purchase award 19th Annual Tex. State Fair, Dallas Mus. Art, 1957, Cash award 22nd Annual Local Artists Show, Ft. Worth, Award of Merit, Mus. N.Mex. Art Show, Santa Fe, 1959, Bertram M. Newhouse award 1st prize oil 27th Annual Local Artists Show, Ft. Worth, 1967, Third award contemporary So. Calif. Exbhn., Del Mar, Calif., 1967, Buza Cardoza Cash award 52nd Annual Calif. Nat. Watercolor Soc., 1972, Award of Merit, Templeton June Show, Ft. Worth, 1992, Award of Merit, 1996 Main St., 11th Annual Festival Exhbn., Ft. Worth, 1996, Cash award, Arches Paper award, Nat. Watercolor Soc. 77th Annual Exhbn., L.A., 1998, Cash award 7th Annual Soc. Watercolor Artists Membership Exhbn., Ft. Worth, 1998, Cash award 500X Gallery, Expo '98, Dallas, 1998, Cash award 8th Annual Juried Exhbn., Soc. Watercolor Artists, Ft. Worth, 1998, Cash award 18th Juried Exhbn., Soc. Watercolor Artists, Ft. Worth, 1999. Mem. Nat. Watercolor Soc., Soc. Watercolor Artists. Avocations: gardening, traveling. Home: 3754 Somerset Ln Fort Worth TX 76109

ALLEN, WILLIAM MERLE, university administrator, museum director; b. San Luis Obispo, Calif., Oct. 9, 1939; s. Lloyd Marion and Berwyn Rose (Palmer) A.; m. Janet Laurentine Clayton, June 11, 1963; children: Barbara, Gregory. BA in Chemistry, La Sierra Coll., 1961; PhD in Organic Chemistry, U. Md., 1967. From instr. to asst. prof. chemistry Andrews U., Berrien Springs, Mich., 1966-68; from asst. prof. to prof. chemistry Loma Linda U., Riverside, Calif., 1968-84; sr. v.p. acad. adminstrn. So. Coll. Seventh Day Aventists, Collegedale, Tenn., 1984-87; dean grad. sch. Loma Linda U., 1987-88; dir. ctr. lifelong learning La Sierra U., Riverside, 1988-98, dir. World Mus. Nat. History, 1988—, dir. devel., 1998—; chair chemistry dept. Loma Linda U., 1971-79, dir. divsn. natural sci., 1977-81; sec., trustee So. Coll. Seventh Day Adventists, 1984-87. Internet website developer. Trustee Smyrna Hosp., Atlanta, 1986-87. Republican. Avocations: gardening, racquetball, collecting autographed books. Office: La Sierra U World Museum Natural History 4700 Pierce St Riverside CA 92505-3332

ALLEN, WILLIAM RICHARD, retired economist; b. Eldorado, Ill., Apr. 3, 1924; s. Oliver Boyd and Justa Lee (Wingo) A.; m. Frances Lorraine Swoboda, Aug. 15, 1948; children: Janet Elizabeth, Sandra Lee. A.B., Cornell Coll., Iowa, 1948; Ph.D., Duke U., 1953. Faculty, Washington U., St. Louis, 1951-52; faculty UCLA, 1952—, prof., 1963-91, prof. emeritus, 1991—; vis. prof. Northwestern U., 1952, U. Wis., 1964, U. Mich., 1965, So. Ill. U., 1969, Tex. A&M, 1971-73; cons. Dept. Commerce, 1962; v.p. Found. Rsch. in Econs. and Edn., 1971-73; pres. Internat. Inst. Econ. Rsch., 1974-86; v.p. Inst. for Contemporary Studies, 1986-90; assoc. Reason Found., 1990-92; newspaper, mag. columnist; nationally syndicated radio commentator, 1979-92. Author: (with others) Foreign Trade and Finance, 1959, Essays in Economic Thought, 1960, University Economics, 3d edit., 1972, Exchange and Production, 3d edit., 1983, International Trade Theory, 1965, Midnight Economist, 1981, vol. 2, 1989, vol. 3, 1997; mem. adv. bd.: History of Polit. Economy, 1969-84, Social Sci. Quar., 1975—; contbr. articles to profl. jours. Served with USAAF, 1943-46. Social Sci. Research Council grantee, 1950-51, 62; Ford Found. grantee, 1958-59, 72-74; NSF grantee, 1965-66; Earhart Found. grantee, 1972, 74-75. Mem. Western Econ. Soc. (pres. 1970-71), So. Econ. Assn. (v.p. 1978-79), History of Econs. Soc. (v.p. 1974-75), Phi Beta Kappa. Home: 11809 Allaseba Dr Los Angeles CA 90066-1112

ALLEN, WILLIAM RILEY, lawyer; b. Coral Gables, Fla., Oct. 24, 1953; s. William George and Winnie (Woodall) A.; m. Mary Faith Ford, June 3, 1989. BA with honors, U. Cen. Fla., 1977; JD with honors, Fla. State U., 1981. Bar: Fla. 1982, U.S. Dist. Ct. (mid. dist.) Fla. 1982, U.S. Ct. Appeals (11th cir.) 1982, U.S. Ct. Appeals (4th cir.) 1988, U.S. Supreme Ct., 1992. With Pitts, Eubank & Ross, P.A., Orlando, 1981-85; prin. W. Riley Allen P.A., Orlando, 1985—. Author: Do Students Know Their Rights?, 1978, Bad Faith Litigation, 1984, Insurance Litigation in Florida, 1992. Recipient Am. Jurisprudence award in criminal law. Mem. ABA (tort and ins. practice com.), ATLA (sustaining, trial lawyer sect.), Fla. Bar Assn. (trial laywers sect.), Acad. Fla. Trial Lawyers (EAGLE, trial lawyers sect.), Orange County Bar Assn. (law and edn., lawyer advt. com., guardian ad litem coms. 1981—, award of excellence 1993, named Guardian Ad Litem of Yr. 1997), Def. Rsch. Inst., Am. Judicature Soc., Cen. Fla. Trial Lawyers (founding dir.), Phi Delta Phi. Republican. Anglican Catholic. Avocations: softball, water and snow skiing, basketball, tennis, running. Office: 228 Annie St Orlando FL 32806-1208

ALLEN, WILLIAM SHERIDAN, history educator; b. Evanston, Ill., Oct. 5, 1932; s. William S. and Rose (Brahm) A.; m. Karen Miller, Jan. 9, 1982; children: Caitilyn, Jefferson, Rebecca, Claire. AB, U. Mich., 1955; MA, U. Conn., 1956; PhD, U. Minn., 1962. Instr. history Bay City (Mich.) Jr. Coll., 1957-58; instr. humanities MIT, Cambridge, Mass., 1960-61; asst. prof. history U. Mo., Columbia, 1961-65, assoc. prof. history, 1966-67; assoc. prof. history Wayne State U., Detroit, 1967-70; prof. history SUNY, Buffalo, 1970—, chmn. history dept., 1987-90; vis. prof. U. Mich., Ann Arbor, 1967; cons. Time-Life Books, Alexandria, Va., 1988-89. Author: The Nazi Seizure of Power, 1984; editor, translator: The Infancy of Nazism, 1976; contbr. articles to profl. jours. V.p. Holocaust Resources Ctr., Buffalo, 1985-90; pres. Buffalo chpt. United Univ. Profs., 1978-81; publicity chmn. Buffalo Group Amnesty Internat., 1985-87; dir. Parkside Fed. Credit Union, Buffalo, 1986-87; organizer Socialist Party Am., Columbia, 1961-67,. Recipient SUNY Chancellor's award for excellence in teaching, 1976; fellow Alexander von Humboldt Found., 1965-66, NEH, 1979. Mem. Am. Hist. Assn., German Studies Assn., Am. Conf. Irish Studies, N.Y. State Assn. European Historians (pres. 1983-84), United Univ. Professions, Bison City Yacht Club (Buffalo). Avocations: sailing, gardening. Office: Dept History SUNY Buffalo 546 Park Hall Buffalo NY 14260

ALLEN, WILLIAM THOMAS, educator, lawyer, judge; b. Phila., July 17, 1944; s. E. William and Mary E. (Graef) A.; m. Ruth Horowitz, June 28, 1981. BS, N.Y.U., 1969; JD, U. Tex., 1972; LLD, Dickinson Law, 1990. Law clerk Hon. W.K. Stapleton, Wilmington, Del., 1972-74; assoc. Morris, Nichols, Arsht & Tunnell, Wilmington, Del., 1974-79, partner, 1979-85; chancellor Ct. Chancery, State of Del., Wilmington, Del., 1985-97; dir. Ctr. for Law and Bus. NYU, N.Y.C., 1997; of counsel Wachtell, Lipton, Rosen & Katz, N.Y.C., 1997—; bd. pardons, State of Del., 1985-97; Phelger vis. prof. Stanford Law Sch., 1991, 94; adj. prof. law U. Pa. Law Sch., 1990, 93-95; Raben lectr. Yale Law Sch., 1996. Trustee U. Del., Newark, 1997. Recipient Chief Justice award for Jud. Svc., Del. Supreme Ct., 1997. Mem. AICPA (chmn. independence stds. bd. 1997—), Del. Bar Assn. (1st state distinguished svc. award, 1997), Am. Law Inst., Tulane Corp. Law Inst. (exec. com., 1987-98), Calif. Securities Law Inst. (exec. com., 1991-98). Office: Stern Sch Bus 44 W 4th St New York NY 10012-1126 also: Sch of Law NYU 40 Washington Sq S New York NY 10012-1005

ALLEN, WOODY (ALLEN STEWART KONIGSBERG), actor, filmmaker, author; b. N.Y.C., Dec. 1, 1935; s. Martin and Nettie (Cherry) Konigsberg; m. Louise Lasser (div.); 1 child (with Mia Farrow), Satchel; adopted children: Moses, Dylan. Student, NYU, 1953, CCNY, 1953. Writer TV comedy for Sid Caesar, 1957, Art Carney, 1958-59, Herb Shriner, 1953; appeared in numerous nightclubs, TV shows, from 1961; author screenplay, also appeared in motion picture What's New Pussycat?, 1964-65; screenplay, dir., actor Take the Money and Run, 1969, Bananas, 1971, What's Up Tiger Lily?, 1966, Everything You Always Wanted to Know About Sex But Were Afraid to Ask, 1972, Sleeper, 1973, Love and Death, 1975, The Front, 1976, Manhattan (Brit. Acad. award 1979, N.Y. Film Critics award), Stardust Memories, 1980; writer, dir., prodr., actor films Annie Hall (N.Y. Film Critics Circle award for Best Dir. and Best Screenplay 1977, Acad. awards for best film, best direction, Nat. Soc. Film Critics Screenwriting award), Zelig, 1983, Broadway Danny Rose, 1984, Hannah and Her Sisters, 1986 (Acad. award for best screenplay, D.W. Griffith award for best dir. Nat. Bd. Rev. of Motion Pictures), Oedipus Wrecks, 1989, Mighty Aphrodite, 1995 (Acad. award nominee for best screenplay 1996), Everyone Says I Love You, 1996, Deconstructing Harry, 1997; writer, dir., narrator film Radio Days, 1987; screenplay, dir. films Interiors, 1978, Purple Rose of Cairo, 1985, A Midsummer Night's Sex Comedy, 1982, September, 1987, Another Woman, 1988, Crimes and Misdemeanors, 1989, Alice, 1990, Shadows and Fog, 1992, Husbands and Wives, 1992, Manhattan Murder Mystery, 1993, Bullets Over Broadway, 1994, Mighty Aphrodite, 1995; author play: Don't Drink the Water, 1966 (actor, dir. of TV movie, 1994), The Floating Lightbulb, 1981, (one act) Death Defying Acts, 1995; play, screenplay Play It Again, Sam, 1969, film, 1972; actor, film King Lear, 1988, Scenes From a Mall, 1990, Antz, 1998, Wild Man Blues, 1998, Stuck on You, 1998, Company Man, 1999; author: Getting Even, 1971, Without Feathers, 1975, Side Effects, 1980; contbr. numerous pieces to Playboy, New Yorker, other mags. Recipient Sylvania award, 1957; Spl. award Berlin Film Festival, 1975; nominated for Emmy award as TV writer, 1957. Democrat. Office: 930 5th Ave New York NY 10021-2651*

ALLENDER, JOHN ROLAND, lawyer; b. Boone, Iowa, Oct. 22, 1950; s. John S. and C. Corinne (Hayes) A.; m. Patti Allender; children: Susan A., Andrew J. BS, Iowa State U., 1972; JD, U. San Diego, 1975; LLM in Taxation, NYU, 1976. Bar: Calif. 1976, Tex. 1977, U.S. Ct. Claims 1977, U.S. Tax. Ct. 1977, U.S. Dist. Ct. (so. dist.) Tex. 1977. Assoc. Fulbright & Jaworski, Houston, 1976-83, ptnr., 1983—; mem. adv. commn. Tex. Bd. Legal Specialization, 1986—. Bd. dirs. Ronald McDonald House, Houston, 1990—. Mem. State Bar of Tex. (chmn. sect. taxation 1990), Houston Bar Assn. (chmn. sect. taxation 1979). Office: Fulbright & Jaworski 1301 Mckinney St Houston TX 77010-3031

ALLENSPACH, KEVIN RAY, sportswriter; b. Mpls., May 1, 1969; s. Jerry Ardon and Noreen Mavis (Dahmes) A.; m. Danell Rae Tatro, Oct. 25, 1997. BS, U. Minn., 1992. Sportswriter Brainerd Daily Dispatch, 1987-89, Minn. Daily, Mpls., 1987-92; asst. pub. rels. Minn. North Stars, Bloomington, 1990-91; sportswriter St. Paul Pioneer Press, 1990-95, St. Cloud (Minn.) Times, 1995—. Named Best Columnist, Minn. Newspaper Assn., 1996, Top 10 Columnist, AP Sports Editors, 1997. Mem. Soc. Profl. Journalists. Republican. Methodist. Avocations: collecting sports memorabilia, collecting works of authors Raymond Chandler, Dashiell Hammett and James Cain. E-mail: kevin@cloudnet.com. Home: 1812 8th Ave SE Saint Cloud MN 56304 Office: St Cloud Times 3000 7th St N Saint Cloud MN 56302

ALLENTUCK, MARCIA EPSTEIN, English language and art history educator; b. Manhattan, N.Y., June 8, 1928; m. 1949; 1 child. BA, NYU, 1948; PhD, Columbia U., 1964. Lectr. English Columbia U., N.Y.C., 1955-57, Hunter Coll., N.Y.C., 1957; from lectr. to prof. English CCNY, N.Y.C., 1959-88; prof. history of art Grad. Ctr. CUNY, N.Y.C., 1974-88, prof. emerita, 1988. Author: The Works of Henry Needler, 1961, Henry Fuseli: The Artist as Critic and Man of Letters, 1964, The Achievements of Isaac Bashevis Singer, 1969, John Graham's System and Dialectics of Art, 1971; contbr. articles to profl. jours. Morrison fellow AAUW, 1958-59, Howard fellow Brown U., 1966-67, Huntington Libr. fellow, 1968, 77, fellow Nat. Translation Ctr. U. Tex., 1968-69, Chapelbrook Found., 1970-72, Dumbarton Oaks Harvard U., 1972-73, sr. fellow NEH, 1973-74, vis. fellow Wolfson Coll. Oxford U., 1974—, fellow Brit. Acad. Newberry Libr., 1980, Murray rsch. fellow Radcliffe Coll., Harvard U., 1982, fellow Inst. Advanced Studies in the Humanities, Edinburgh (Scotland) U., 1984, rsch. fellow Swann Found., 1989—; vis. scholar Burrell Art Collection, Glasgow, Scotland, 1978, 88; Am. Philos. Soc. grantee, 1966-67. Fellow Royal Soc. Arts London; mem. MLA (del. assembly 1989—), Brit. Soc. Archtl. Historians, Milton Soc. Am., Augustan Reprint Soc. Archtl. Historians, Coll. Art Assn., Phi Beta Kappa. Home: 5 W 86th St Apt 12B New York NY 10024-3665

ALLER, JOHN COSMOS, diplomat; b. Oakland, Calif., Oct. 29, 1955; s. Curtis Cosmos and Mary Geneva (Aldridge) A.; m. Angels Lee, Oct. 30, 1982. BA, U. of the Pacific, 1979; MA, U. Wash., 1986, MPA, 1988. Tchg. cert., Calif. Vol. Peace Corps, Kapyong, Korea, 1979-81; instr. Korean Army, Seoul, 1982-83; prof. Kyunguee U., Seoul, 1988-91; VISA officer U.S. State Dept., Seoul and Bangkok, 1991-94; U.S. dep. rep. to ESCAP U.S. State Dept., Bangkok, 1995-96; Korea desk officer U.S. State Dept., Washington, 1996-98, labor officer, 1998—; adj. prof. U. Md., Seoul, 1988-91; sec.-treas. Korean Orgn. of Tchrs. of English as a Second Lang., Seoul, 1989-91; rep. Am. Fgn. Svc. Assn., Bangkok, 1995-96. Democrat. Roman Catholic. Avocations: running, hiking, reading, computers, music. Home: 6022 Katelyn Ct Alexandria VA 22310-4423

ALLER, LAWRENCE HUGH, astronomy educator, researcher; b. Tacoma, Wash., Sept. 24, 1913; s. Leslie E. and Lena Belle (Davis) A.; m. Rosalind Duncan Hall; children—Hugh Duncan, Raymond Donald, Gwendolyn Jean. AB, U. Calif. Berkeley, 1936; MA, Harvard U., 1938, PhD, 1943. Instr. physics Harvard U., Cambridge, Mass., 1942-43; research physicist radiation lab. U. Calif. Berkeley, 1943-45; asst. prof. astronomy Ind. U., Bloomington, 1945-48; assoc. prof. astronomy U. Mich., Ann Arbor, 1948-54, prof. astronomy, 1954-62; prof. astronomy UCLA, 1962-84, prof. emeritus, 1984—; vis. prof. U. Tasmania, Hobart, Australia, 1969, U. Queensland, Brisbane, Australia, 1977-78, Australian Nat. U., Canberra, 1960-61, U. Toronto, Ont., Can., 1961-62, U. Sydney, New South Wales, Australia, 1968; guest investigator radiophysics CSIRO, Epping, New South Wales, Australia, 1968, 69, 77; vis. lectr. Raman Inst., Bangalore, India, 1978, Sch. Advanced Studies, Trieste, Italy, 1981; guest investigator Mt. Wilson Obs., Pasadena, Calif., 1949-82. Author: Atmospheres of Sun and Stars, 1953, 2d edit., 1962; Stellar Interiors, Nuclear Transformations, 1954; Gaseous Nebulae, 1956; Abundances of Elements, 1961; Atoms, Stars and Nebulae, 1971, 3d edit., 1991, Physics of Thermal Gaseous Nebulae, 1984. Editor (with Dean B. McLaughlin) Stellar Structure and Evolution, 1965; (with Barbara Middlehurst) Interstellar Medium, 1967. NSF research fellow, 1968-69, 60-61. Mem. Am. Astron. Soc. (councillor 1953-56), Internat. Astron. Union (pres. stellar-spectroscopy group 1959-64), Astron. Soc. of Pacific (bd. dirs. 1974-77), Am. Acad. Arts and Scis., Nat. Acad. Scis. Mem. Soc. of Friends. Lodge: Masons. Avocations: travel; photography. Home: 18118 Kingsport Dr Malibu CA 90265-5634 Office: U Calif Astronomy Divsn Dept Physics and Astronomy Los Angeles CA 90095-1562

ALLER, WAYNE KENDALL, psychology educator, researcher, computer education company executive, property manager; b. Slyvia, Kans., Feb. 20, 1933; s. Alvin Ray and Florence Dorothy (Snowbarger) A.; m. Sharon Cecelia Forray, Aug. 21, 1962 (div.); children: Jay Ramzi, Joyce Amal; m. Sonia Y. Konialian, Apr. 8, 1969. B.A. in Physics, N.W. Nazarene Coll., Nampa, Idaho, 1955; M.S. in Psychology, U. Wash., 1960, Ph.D. in Psychology, 1964. Asst. prof. psychology Pacific Lutheran U., 1962-64; asst. prof., chmn. div. behavioral scis. Beirut Coll. for Women, 1964-67; assoc. prof. Mankato State Coll., Minn., 1967-68; assoc. prof. Ind. State U., Terre Haute, from 1968, prof., to 1985; pres. Learning Unlimited, 1983—, CompuLearn, 1983-87; adj. prof. psychology Calif. State U., Northridge, 1984—; sr. rsch. adv. Ctr. Ednl. R&D, Ministry Planning, Republic Lebanon, Beirut, 1974-75; sr. rsch. assoc. Ctr. Behavioral Rsch., Am. U. of Beirut, 1974-75; vis. scholar dept. psychology UCLA, 1982-83; cons. English as fgn. lang. Vietnamese Affairs Ctr., Terre Haute, 1976-78. Author: Readings and Experiments in General Psychology, 1970, rev. edit., 1971. Ford Found. grantee, 1974-75. Mem. Western Psychol. Assn., N.Y. Acad. Scis., Soc. for Computers in Psychology, Computer Users Speech and Hearing, Sigma Xi, Psi Chi, Sigma Phi Iota. Presbyterian. Club: Wabash Valley Apple Byters (pres. 1981-82) (Terre Haute). Home: 12045 Susan Dr Granada Hills CA 91344-2642

ALLERS, MARLENE ELAINE, legal administrator; b. Crosby, Minn., Dec. 29, 1931; d. Robert Prudent and Tressa Ida May (Hiller) Huard; m. Herbert Dodge Allers, Aug. 29, 1950 (dec. Aug. 1977); children: Melanie Lynn, Geoffrey Brian. B.S. in Math., U. Minn.-Mpls., 1966, BA in Acctg., 1968, MBA in Pers. and Fin. Mgmt., 1972. Bus. mgr., Earl Clinic, St. Paul, 1959-68, Lindquist & Vennum, Mpls., 1968-79, Stacker, Ravich & Simon, Mpls., 1979-82, Wagner, Johnston & Falconer, Ltd., Mpls., 1983-90; owner Minn. Express Process Servers, 1989—; lectr. Inst. of Continuing Legal Edn., Mpls., 1977. Recipient Outstanding Achievement award in Bus. Young Women's Christian Assn., Mpls., 1978. Mem. Minn. Legal Adminstrs. Assn., Mensa. Avocations: bridge, reading. Home: 608 Queen Ave S Minneapolis MN 55405-1968

ALLERTON, JOHN STEPHEN, association executive; b. N.Y.C., Dec. 22, 1926; s. Moses Alexander and Rebecca A.; m. Juanita Grace Lee, Nov. 9, 1956. B.A. in Indsl. Engring, N.Y. U., 1950; grad. Advanced Mgmt. Program, Harvard Bus. Sch., 1971. With Am. Automobile Assn., Falls Church, Va., 1955-90; dir. mktg. Am. Automobile Assn., 1957-62; CEO Automobile Club of Wash., Seattle, 1962-65; pres. Ohio Motorists Assn., 1965-78; exec. v.p., gen. mgr. Am. Automobile Assn., 1978-90; Bd. dirs. Salvation Army, Ohio, 1966-76, Am. Cancer Soc., 1966-70, Crawford Automotive-Aviation Mus., Cleve., 1973-78; Bd. govs. Found. Internat. Meetings. Served with U.S. Navy, 1944-46. Mem. Harvard Club, Rotary. Presbyterian.

ALLERTON, SAMUEL ELLSWORTH, biochemist; b. Three Rivers, Mich., Aug. 21, 1933; s. Sanford Ellsworth and Virginia Mary (Dickenson) A.; m. Theresa Mary Pawlak, Aug. 20, 1966; children: Adam Sanford, Eve Samantha. BA summa cum laude, Kalamazoo (Mich.) Coll., 1955; PhD, Harvard U., 1962. Teaching fellow Harvard U. Med. Sch., Boston, 1957-61; rsch. assoc. Rockefeller U., N.Y.C., 1961-65; asst. prof. U. So. Calif., L.A., 1965-69, assoc. prof., 1969—; cons. Woodroof Labs., Santa Ana, Calif., 1978-89. Contbr. articles to profl. jours. Bd. dirs. Huntington Beach (Calif.) Community Clinic, 1990-92. Named Outstanding Young Man of Am., Jaycee's, 1966. Mem. N.Y. Acad. Scis., Am. Coll. of Nutrition, Elks, Sigma Xi, Omicron Kappa Upsilon. Anglican. Achievements include rsch. on phys.-chem. characterization of proteins, tumor products, studies on absorption of copper. Office: Dentistry U So Calif University Park Mc # 0641 Los Angeles CA 90007

ALLERTON, WILLIAM, III, public relations executive; b. New Orleans, June 20, 1951; s. William Jr. and Marion (Helmstetter) A.; m. Constance Rose Driscoll, Dec. 18, 1971; children: Amy Elizabeth, Timothy Daniel, Sean Patrick, Colleen Rose. Student, U. New Orleans, 1969-73; fellow, Loyola U. Inst. Politics, 1980-81. Pres. Capitol Pub. Rels., 1978-86; chmn., CEO Capitol Comm., New Orleans, 1986—; with office presdl. advance White House, 1990-93; dir. Advertisers Legis. Action Council, Baton Rouge, 1985-86; bus. ptnr. Benjamin Franklin High Sch. New Orleans Pub. Schs., 1987—; bd. dirs. Inst. Politics Loyola U.; del. White House Conf. on Small Bus., Washington, 1995. Participant Met. Area Com. Tulane U., 1978; apptd. mem. nat. adv. com. U.S. SBA, 1989-93; mem. La. State Bd. Elem. and Secondary Edn. Non-Pub. Sch. Commn., 1986—, Nat. Coun. Trustees Freedoms Found. at Valley Forge, 1989—, La. Commn. on the Bicentennial of U.S. Constn., 1986-91; vice-chmn. Marine Corps Scholarship Fund Leatherneck Ball, 1986; vice chmn. 83d Anniversary Dinner of Navy League of U.S., 1987; mem. exec. com. Archbishops Cmty. Appeal, 1975-85; mem. U.S. adv. coun. SBA dist., La., 1973-76; mem. Mayor's Coun. Youth Opportunity, New Orleans, 1969-70; dist. chmn. New Orleans coun. Boy Scouts Am., 1992-93, mem. exec. bd., 1990—, chmn. centennial pledge of allegiance salute, 1992, coun. activities chmn., 1992—, mem. exec. com., 1992—, mem. nat. coun., 1994—, New Orleans coun. commr., 1995—; bd. dirs. La. State Mus., 1988-94; participant Columbia U. Am. Assembly, 1989; chmn. La. Com. George Washington Bicentennial, 1999; mem. La. State Mineral Bd., 1996—, La. State Tech. Adv. Com., 1997—. Recipient Addy award Am. Advt. Fedn., 1983, Tops award Dallas Advt. League, 1983, George Washington Honor medal Freedoms Found. at Valley Forge, 1989, Friends of Edn. award La. Fedn. Tchrs., 1989, Presdl. Recognition Office Nat. Svc., Points of Light Found., 1992, Silver Beaver award Boy Scouts Am., 1992; James E. West Fellowship award, 1994, Cathedral award Archdiocese of New Orleans Cath. Com. on Scouting, 1995. Mem. Am. Assn. Polit. Cons. (Media Excellence awards 1984, 86, 88, 98), So. Polit. Sci. Assn., Acad. Polit. Sci., Soc. for U.S. Constn., U.S. Capitol Hist. Soc., Ctr. for Study of the Presidency, Assn. Descendants Isaac Allerton Mayflower, Order of Arrow (Chilantakoba lodge). Office: Capitol Comm PO Box 791348 New Orleans LA 70179-1348

ALLES, RODNEY NEAL, SR., information management executive; b. Orleans, Nebr., Aug. 24, 1950; s. Neal Stanley and Evelyn Dorothy (Zelske) A.; m. Diana Kay Koenig, Nov. 25, 1978; children: Rodney Neal Jr., Jennifer E., Victoria E. BS in Indsl. Engring., U. Okla., 1973, MBA, 1977, PhD in Info. Systems, 1998. Asst. to the pres. Skytop Brewster Co., Inc., Houston, 1978-79, mgr. planning and mfg., 1979-83; v.p. adminstrn. Internat. Meter Co. Inc., Arkansas City, Kans., 1983-84, v.p., 1984-85; dir. info. mgmt. McAlester (Okla.) Army Ammunition Plant, 1987-96; chief info. sys. divsn. S.E. Regional Civilian Pers. Ops. Ctr., Ft. Benning, Ga., 1996—. Lt. USN, 1973-76. Mem. Am. Inst. Indsl. Engrs., Fed. Info. Processing Coun., Fed. Mgrs. Assn., U.S. Golf Assn., Okla. Golf Assn., Loyal Knight of Old Trusty, U. Okla. Alumni Assn. (alumni coun. Coll. Bus. Adminstrn.), Rotary Internat., McAlester Country Club, Omicron Delta Kappa, Tau Beta Pi, Sigma Tau, Alpha Pi Mu. Democrat. Lutheran. Avocation: golf. Office: SE Regional Civilian Pers Ops Ctr Attn: SFCP-SE-A Meloy Hall Bldg 6 Fort Benning GA 31905

ALLEY, EARL GIFFORD, chemist; b. Corsica, S.D., Dec. 10, 1935; married, 1962; 2 children. BS, Miss. State U., 1959, MS, 1961; PhD in Organic Chemistry, U. Ill., Urbana, 1968. Chemist Dow Chem. Co., 1967-69; dir. rsch. divsn. Miss. State Chem. Lab., 1970-91, state chemist, 1991—; prof. chem. chem. dept. Miss. State U.; cons. in field. Mem. AAAS, Am. Chem. Soc., Sigma Xi. Achievements include photochemistry and degradation of agricultural chemicals; involvement of charge transfer and adsorption in these processes; analyses of trace metals and organic materials. Home: 1064 Southgate Dr Starkville MS 39759-9436 Office: Box CR Mississippi State MS 39762*

ALLEY, FRANK R., federal judge. Apptd. bankruptcy judge U.S. Dist. Ct. Oreg., 1995. Fax: (541) 465-6898. Office: 151 W 7th Ave Ste 300 Eugene OR 97401-2676

ALLEY, KIRSTIE, actress; b. Wichita, Kans., Jan. 12, 1951; children: William True, Lillie. Student, U. Kans., Kans. State U. Actress: (stage prodns.) Cat on a Hot Tin Roof, Answers; (feature films) Star Trek II: The Wrath of Khan, 1982, Blind Date, 1984, Champions, 1984, Runaway, 1984, Summer School, 1987, Shoot to Kill, 1988, Look Who's Talking, 1989, Daddy's Home, 1989, One More Chance, 1990, Madhouse, 1990, Sibling Rivalry, 1990, Look Who's Talking Too, 1990, Look Who's Talking Now, 1993, Village of the Damned, 1995, It Takes Two, 1995, Sticks and Stones, 1996, Nevada, 1996, For Richer of Poorer, 1997 (People's Choice award 1997), Deconstructing Harry, 1997 (People's Choice award 1997), Toothless, 1997, Drop Dead Gorgeous, 1999, The Mao Game, 1999; (TV mini-series) North and South Book I, 1985, North and South, Book II, 1986, The Last Don, 1997; (TV movies) Sins of the Past, 1984, A Bunny's Tale, 1984, The Prince of Bel Air, 1985, Stark: Mirror Image, 1986, Infidelity, 1987, David's Mother, 1994 (Emmy award, Lead Actress - Special, 1994), Radiant City, 1996; (TV series) Masquerade, 1984-85, Cheers, 1987-1993 (Emmy award as Outstanding Lead Actress in a Comedy Series 1991), (TV miniseries) The Last Don, 1996, The Last Don Part II, 1998 (Emmy nomination); prodr., actress Veronica's Closet, 1997; tv appearances include The Match Game, The Love Boat, The Hitchhikder, The Roseanne Show; co-prodr.: Nevada, 1997. Spokesperson for Narcanon Drug Rehab.; founder Ch. of Scientology, Mission of Wichita. Recipient People's Choice award, 1998. *

ALLEY, WAYNE EDWARD, federal judge, retired army officer; b. Portland, Oreg., May 16, 1932; s. Leonard David and Hilda Myrtle (Blum) A.; m. Marie Winkelmann Dommer, Jan. 28, 1978; children: Elizabeth, David, John; stepchildren: Mark Dommer, Eric Dommer. A.B., Stanford U., 1952, J.D., 1957. Bar: Calif. 1957, Oreg. 1957, Okla. 1985. Ptnr. Williams & Alley, Portland, 1957-59; commd. officer JAGC, U.S. Army, advanced through grades to brig. gen., ret., 1981; dean Coll. Law, dir. Law Ctr. U. Okla., Norman, 1981-85; judge U.S. Dist. Ct. Western Dist. Okla., Oklahoma City, 1985—. Decorated D.S.M., Legion of Merit, Bronze Star. Mem. Fed. Bar Assn., Oreg. Bar Assn., Okla. Bar Assn., Order of Coif, Phi Beta Kappa. Office: US Dist Ct 3102 US Courthouse 200 NW 4th St Rm 1210 Oklahoma City OK 73102-3092

ALLIGOOD, ELIZABETH ANN HIERS, retired special education educator; b. W. Palm Beach, Fla., Dec. 7, 1931; d. Hubert Victor and Ethel Ruth (Palmer) Hiers; m. Jesse LeRoy Alligood, Aug. 24, 1952; children: Stephen Leon, Larry Lamar, Miriam Ruth, Julia Ann, Carol Beth. AA, Norman Coll., 1951; BS in Edn., Valdosta State, 1978; postgrad., Columbus Coll., 1987, 92. Cert. tchr., Ga. Resource educator Irwin County Bd. Edn., Ocilla, Ga., 1969-71; dir. Sunny Dale Tng. Ctr., Ocilla, Ga., 1971-78, Green Oaks Tng. Ctr., Moultrie, Ga., 1978-81; tchr. Calhoun County Bd. Edn., Edison, Ga., 1978; cons. Am. Heart Assn., Columbus, Ga., 1984-86; tchr. Thomas County Bd. Edn., Thomasville, Ga., 1987-89, Muscogee County Bd. Edn., Columbus, 1989-94, Colquitt County Bd. Edn., Moultrie, Ga., 1994-97; ret., 1997; founder Sunny Dale Tng. Ctr., 1969; mem. adv. bd. Columbus Specialized Preschool, 1985. Chairperson W. Ga. area Mental Health Adv. Coun., Columbus, 1986-87. Named to Honors Day, Sunny Dale Tng. Ctr., 1992. Mem. Civitan (treas. 1997—), Assn. Retarded Citizens Ga. (bd. dirs. at large 1977-78, state sec. 1980-81), Ga. Assn. Educators, Norman Coll. Alumni Assn. (editor Normanlite 1998—). Democrat. Baptist. Avocations: bowling, computers, writing.

ALLIGOOD, LOLA LURVEY, educator; b. Washington, N.C., Nov. 15, 1947; d. William David and Dicie Elizabeth Latham Lurvey; m. Charles Michael Alligood, Aug. 25, 1968; 1 child, elizabeth Anne. BS in Libr. Sci., East Carolina U., 1971, MLS, 1976. Libr. Rooe H.S., Greenville, N.C., 1970-71; media coord. John Small Elem. Sch., Washington, N.C., 1971—. Mem. planning bd. City of Washington, 1985—; chmn. Beaufort County Rep. Party, 1989-99; vice-chmn. GOP 1st Congl. Dist., 1997-99, sec., 1995-97, 99—; chmn. historic Bath (N.C.) Commn., 1993-97. Mem. NEA, N.C. Assn. Educators (rep.), N.C. Libr. Assn., Carriage Assn. Am., Friends Greater Bath, Delta Kappa Gamma. Mem. Christian Ch. Avocations: horses, horse drawn carriages, historic preservation. Home: 220 Simmons St Washington NC 27889 Office: John Small Elem Sch 820 N Bridge St Washington NC 27889

ALLIGOOD, MARY SALE, special education educator; b. Richmond, Va., Oct. 28, 1942; d. Charles Latané and Virginia Carter (Elmer) Sale; m. Frederick Marvin Alligood, Jr., June 12, 1965; children: Anne Hassell Alligood Tadlock, Frederick Carter. BA in Psychology, Mary Washington Coll., 1965; MEd in Spl. Edn./Learning Disabilities, Va. Commonwealth U., 1982. 2d grade tchr. West Columbia-Cayce Schs., Columbia, S.C., 1965-67; 3d/4th grade tchr. Riverside Sch., Richmond, Va., 1972-79; 1st/2d grade tchr. Steward Sch., Richmond, Va., 1979-83; learning disabilities tchr. Chesterfield County Schs., Richmond, Va., 1983-85; spl. edn. educator Powhatan (Va.) County Schs., 1985-96. Bd. dirs., sec., chair Redeemer Episcopal Day Sch., Midlothian, Va., 1992-97; mem., treas. Episcopal Ch. Women, Richmond, 1967—; mem. vestry Episcopal Ch. of Redeemer, Midlothian, 1975-78, 81-83, mem. search com., 1994, stewardship co-chair, 1996—. Mem. ASCD, Coun. for Learning Disabilities, Assn. for Children/Adults with Learning Disabilities, Powhatan County Edn. Assn. (pres. 1989-91), Delta Kappa Gamma (membership com., programs 1989-92, pres. 1996-98). Home: 2841 River Oaks Dr Midlothian VA 23113-2226

ALLIK, MICHAEL, diversified industry executive; b. N.Y.C., Aug. 28, 1935; s. Michael and Alma (Busch) A.; m. Deborah Dixon, Jan. 2, 1983; children—William Michael, Timothy John, Ryan Andrew, Lauren Alexandra. B.S., MIT, 1957; M.B.A., Harvard U., 1961. V.p. Kondu Corp., Erie, Pa., 1961-66; assoc. Booz, Allen & Hamilton, Cleve., 1966-69; gen. mgr. Textile Friction Group H.K. Porter, Pitts., 1969-71; gen. mgr. transformer div. Allis Chalmers, Pitts., 1971-75; exec. v.p. Mead Paper Group, Dayton, Ohio, 1975-78; sr. v.p. strategy and adminstrn. Mead Corp., Dayton, 1978-81; sr. v.p. fin. and adminstrn. Dart & Kraft, Inc., Northbrook, Ill., 1981-83, pres. Splty. Products Group, 1984-86; pres., chief oper. officer, dir. RTE Corp., Milw., 1986-89; pres. Premier Aluminum, Inc., Racine, Wis., 1989—; ptnr. Harvest Capital Mgmt., Inc., Vero Beach, Fla.; mem. coun. Grad. Sch. Bus., U. Chgo., 1985-92. Pres. bd. trustees Victory Theatre, Dayton, 1980-81; bd. dirs. Chgo. Hort. Soc., 1982-86, Milw. Repertory Theater, 1991-93. Served to 1st lt. C.E. U.S. Army, 1957-59. Mem. Wis. Taxpayers Alliance (bd. dirs. 1987). Club: Chgo. Economic. Home: 2260 Seaside St Vero Beach FL 32963-3131

ALLIN, BONNIE A., city official; b. Apr. 26, 1956; m. David Allin; 3 children. Student, U. Ariz.; BBA in Fin. cum laude, Corpus Christi (Tex.) State U. With Tucson Airport Authority, 1976-84; with Corpus Christi Internat. Airport, 1988—, dir. aviation, 1996—. Recipient Hometown Hero award Corpus Christi Conv. and Visitors Bur., 1993, Women in Careers award YWCA, 1997. Mem. Am. Assn. Airport Execs. (cert. accredited airport exec., bd. dirs., past pres. South Ctrl. chpt.), Corpus Christi Transp. Assn., Greater Corpus Christi Bus. Alliance (transp. com.), Rotary. Office: City of Corpus Christi Aviation Dept 1000 International Blvd Corpus Christi TX 78406-1809*

ALLINGER, NORMAN LOUIS, chemistry educator; b. Alameda, Calif., Apr. 6, 1928; s. Norman Clarke and Florence Helen (Young) A.; m. Irene Saez; children: Alan Louis, Ilene Suzanne, James Augustus, Maritza Ivonne Quinn, Vilma Ivelise Veveles, Aida Irene Quinones. BS, U. Calif., Berkeley, 1951; Ph.D., UCLA, 1954. Research fellow U. Calif. at Los Angeles, 1954-55, Harvard, 1955-56; asst. prof. chemistry Wayne State U., 1956-59, asso. prof., 1959-60, prof., 1960-69; prof. chemistry U. Ga., 1969—. Editor: Jour. Comp. Chemistry; contbr. articles to profl. jours. Served with AUS, 1946-48. Alfred P. Sloan fellow, 1959-63; Arthur C. Cope scholar, 1988. Mem. NAS, Am. Chem. Soc. (Herty medal Atlanta sect. 1988, James Flack Norris award 1989, ACS award for Chem. Pharm. Rsch. 1996), Chem. Soc. London. Office: U Ga Dept Chemistry CCMSD 2526 Athens GA 30602

ALLINGTON, RICHARD LLOYD, literacy studies educator; b. Grand Rapids, Mich., May 13, 1947; s. George C. and Eldona L. (Weller) A.; m. Susan Gordon, Apr. 6, 1969 (div. May 1979); children: Heidi, Tinker, Bo; m. Anne McGill-Franzen, Jan. 11, 1980; children: Maggie, Michael. BA, Western Mich. U., 1968, MS, 1969; PhD, Mich. State U., 1973. Tchr. Kenty City (Mich.) Pub. Schs., 1968-69; adminstr. fed. program Belding (Mich.) Area Pub. Schs., 1969-71; grad. rsch. asst. Mich. State U., East Lansing, 1971-73; from asst. to assoc. prof. SUNY, Albany, 1973-84, prof., 1984-99, chair dept. reading, 1982-89, 94-99; Irving and Rose Fien prof. elem. and spl. edn. U. Fla., Gainesville, 1999—; cons. Dept. Edn., Office Edn. Rsch. and Improvement, Nat. Assessment of Ednl. Progress, Office Spl. Edn. and Rehab., Nat. Faculty, numerous others; sr. rsch. scientist Nat. Ctr. Lit. Tchg., 1990-96; sr. rsch. scientist NRC on English Learning and Achievement, 1996—. Author: (children's books), Beginning to Learn About series, 1982; sr. author: (classroom reading series) Celebrate Reading, 1993; author: (with Patricia Cunningham) Classrooms that Work, 1993, Schools That Work, 1996; (with Sean Walmsley) No Quick Fix: Rethinking Literacy Programs in America's Elementary Schools, 1995; contbr. over 100 articles to profl. jours. Bd. dirs. Pierce Hall Daycare Ctr., SUNY, Albany, 1988-90. Rsch. grantee U.S. Dept. Edn., 1986, 88, 90. Fellow Nat. Conf. Rsch. in English (bd. dirs. 1992-95), Internat. Reading Assn. (bd. dirs. 1995-98, co-recipient with Anne McGill-Franzen the Albert Harris award 1990, named to Reading Hall of Fame 1995); mem. Nat. Reading Conf. (v.p. 1995, pres. 1996, bd. dirs. 1988-91), Am. Ednl. Rsch. Assn., N.Y. State Reading Assn. (Outstanding Reading Educator award 1992).

ALLINGTON, ROBERT WILLIAM, instrument company executive; b. Madison, Wis., Sept. 18, 1935; s. William B. and Norma Evelyn (Peterson) A.; m. Mary Lynn Kaylor, Sept. 4, 1976. BS, U. Nebr., 1959, MS, 1961, ScD (hon.), 1985. CEO, chmn. Isco, Inc., Lincoln, Nebr., 1961—. Inventor in field; contbr. numerous articles to profl. jours. Bd. dirs. League Human Dignity, Lincoln, 1981—, Nebr. Rsch. and Devel. Authority Lincoln, 1986-94, chmn., 1990-94; mem. Gov.'s Com. on Employment of the Handicapped, Lincoln, 1983; mem. Indsl. Adv. Bd., Dept. Chemistry, U. Nebr., 1988—; bd. dirs. Lincoln Cmty. Found. Inc., 1989-96; chmn. Nebr. EPSCOR Com., 1991—. Named Handicapped Nebraskan of the Yr., Gov. of Nebr., 1972, Outstanding Engring. Achievement Profl. Engrs., 1975, Nat. Small Bus. Person of the Yr., SBA, 1985, Exec. of the Yr., R&D Mag., 1991, U. of Nebr. Outstanding Alumnus, 1993, Entrepreneur of Yr. Nebr. Ctr. Entrepreneurship Lincoln Coll. Bus. Adminstrn. U. Nebr., 1998; recipient Disting. Svc. award Kiwanis, 1978, Support of Rsch. award Sigma Xi, 1986. Mem. Am. Chem. Soc., Am. Inst. Chemists, IEEE, Instrument Soc. Am., Nat. Soc. Profl. Engrs., Analytical and Life Sci. Sys. Assn. (bd. dirs. 1992-95), Univ. Club, The Club. Episcopalian. Avocation: sci. and tech. history. Office: Isco Inc 4700 Superior St Lincoln NE 68504-1398

ALLINSON, CARL, radiologist; b. New Haven, CT, Feb. 20, 1912; s. Jacob Samuel and Sophie Allinson; m. Roze Bernstene Rapaport, Nov. 11,

1986;children: Arthur, Robert, Nancy, Jeffrey. BS, Yale U., 1932; PhD in Biochemistry, Boston U., 1938; MD, U. Ark., Little Rock, 1945. Diplomate Am. Bd. Radiology. Radiologist Franklin Hosp., Benton, Ill., 1957-75; A.G. Holley State Hosp., Lantana, Fla., 1981—; instr. physiology U. Ark. Sch. Medicine, Little Rock, Ark., 1940-45; instr. biochemistry La. State U., New Orleans, 1939-40; Rschr. in field; contbr. articles to profl. jours. Avocations: playing violin, building violins.

ALLIO, ROBERT JOHN, management consultant, educator; b. N.Y.C., Sept. 1, 1931; s. Albert Joseph and Helen (Gerbereux) A.; m. Barbara Maria Littauer, Oct. 3, 1953; children: Mark, Paul, David, Michael. BMetE, Rensselaer Poly. Inst., 1952; MS, Ohio State U., 1954; PhD, Rensselaer Poly. Inst., 1957. Mgr. advanced materials Gen. Electric Co., Schenectady, 1957-60; sr. staff AEC, Washington, 1962; engring. mgr. atomic power div. Westinghouse Corp., Pitts., 1962-68; dir. corp. planning Babcock & Wilcox, N.Y., 1968-75; v.p. Can. Wire Co., Toronto, Ont., 1975-78; pres. Canstar Communications, Toronto, 1976-78; sr. staff mem. Arthur D. Little Co., Cambridge, Mass., 1978-79; dean Rensselaer Poly. Inst. Sch. Mgmt., Troy, N.Y., 1981-83; pres. Robert J. Allio and Assoc., Atlanta, 1979—; prof. mgmt. Babson Coll, Wellesley, Mass., 1979—; bd. dirs. TBS Funding Corp.; chmn. Trac Rac Inc., NICON, Inc., Atlanta. Author: Corporate Planning: Techniques and Applications, 1979, Corporate Planning, 1985, The Practical Strategist, 1988; editor: Planning Rev. Jour. Mem. Planning Forum (pres. 1976-77), Union League Club (N.Y.C.). Office: 125 Lincoln Ave Ste 213 Santa Fe NM 87501-2057

ALLIS, BARBARA A., physician; b. N.Y.C., Jan. 17, 1953; d. Anthony Arthur and Christine Grace A.; m. Gerald Cordani, May 11, 1993 (div. Oct. 1997); 1 child, Kathryn Jane. BA, Barnard Coll., 1974; MD, Med. Coll. Pa., 1983. Resident Mt. Sinai Med. Ctr., N.Y.C., 1984-88; neurologist North Shore Med. Group, Huntington, N.Y., 1988—; Co-chmn. credentials com. Huntington Hosp., 1995-97. Contbr. articles to profl. jours. Mt. Sinai Sch. Medicine fellow. Fellow Am. Acad. Neurology. Office: North Shore Med Group 325 Park Ave Huntington NY 11743

ALLISON, ADRIENNE AMELIA, voluntary organization administrator; b. Toronto, Ont., Can., Nov. 2, 1940; d. Harold Whitfield and Emmeline Amelia (Banister) Hedley; m. Stephen Vyvyan Allison, Jan. 2, 1960 (div. 1984); children: Mark Hedley, Myles Stephen, Alexander Andrew; m. Armin U. Kuder, Aug. 26, 1989. BA, George Washington U., 1978; MA, Georgetown U., 1980; MPA, Harvard U., 1986. Social sci. analyst AID, Washington, 1980-85, project mgr., 1986-89, presdl. com. on HIV epidemic, 1987-88; program dir. Centre for Devel. and Population Activities, 1988-91; v.p. Centre for Devel. and Population Activities, 1991-98; dir. maternal and neonatal health program Johns Hopkins Program in Reproductive Health, Balt., 1998—; adj. prof. George Washington U. Sch. Medicine, Johns Hopkins U. Sch. Hygiene and Pub. Health. Co-author: Vegetable Gardening in Bangladesh, 1975. Vestry mem. St. Albans Parish, Washington, 1988; co-chair Peace Commn. Diocese of Washington, 1999—. Mem. APHA, Population Assn. Am., Cosmos Club. Home: 8011 Glendale Rd Chevy Chase MD 20815

ALLISON, ANDREW MARVIN, church executive; b. Long Beach, Calif., May 21, 1949; s. Howard C. and Wilma A. (Franks) A.; m. Kathleen L. Anderson, May 28, 1971; children: Rebecca, Nathan, Joanna, Spencer, Jacob, Camilla. AA, Glendale (Ariz.) C.C., 1972; BA in History, Brigham Young U., 1974; PhD of Polit. Sci., Coral Ridge U., 1993. Cert. secondary tchr., Ariz., Utah. Adminstrv. staff, editor Brigham Young U., Provo, Utah, 1972-74; adminstrv. asst. LDS Ch., Salt Lake City, 1977-79; prin., tchr. LDS Seminaries, Ariz.,Utah, 1974-77, 79-80; assoc. editor, art dir. Bookcraft Publs., Salt Lake City, 1983-85; dir. rsch. and publs. Nat. Ctr. for Constl. Studies, Salt Lake City, 1980-83, 85-91; chmn., pres. Nat. Ctr. for Constl. Studies, West Jordan, Utah, 1991-95; product devel. editor Deseret Book Co., Salt Lake City, 1995-96; supr. confidential applications LDS Ch., Salt Lake City, 1996-99, mgr. confidential records, 1999—; adj. prof. polit. sci., George Wythe Coll., Cedar City, Utah, 1993—. Author: The Real Thomas Jefferson, 1982, The Real Benjamin Franklin, 1983, The Real George Washington, 1991; contbr. articles to profl. jours. Mem. Phi Kappa Phi.

ALLISON, ANNE MARIE, retired librarian; b. Oak Park, Ill., Oct. 3, 1931; d. Gerald Patrick and Anna Evelyn (Beam) Myers; m. James Dixon Alison, Aug. 28, 1954; children: Mark, Mary, Clare, Ruth, Edward. BA in French, St. Mary of the Woods Coll., 1951; postgrad., U. Fribourg, 1952-53; MLS, Rosary Coll., 1968. Asst. libr. Triton Coll., River Grove, Ill., 1967-68; asst. libr. tech. svcs. Moraine Valley Community Coll., Palos Hills, Ill., 1968-69; dir. learning resources, head libr. Coll. Lake County, Grayslake, Ill., 1969-71; asst. head catalog dept. Kent (Ohio) State U. Librs., 1971-73, head processing dept., 1973-79, asst. dir. libr. svcs., 1979-81; acting dir. Fla. Atlantic U. Libr., Boca Raton, 1980-81; asst. dir., head tech. svcs. Wayne State U. Librs., Detroit, 1981-83; dir. librs. U. Cen. Fla., Orlando, 1983-97, ret., 1997; past chair, bd. dirs. Fla. Extension Libr., Tampa; bd. dirs. Ctr. for Libr. Automation, Gainesville, Fla., Cen. Fla. Holocaust Meml. Resource Ctr., Orlando; adj. prof. Libr. and Info. Sci., U. S. Fla., Tampa. Editor: OCLC: A National Library Network, 1979; contbr. articles to profl. jours. Arbitrator alternative dispute resolution program Better Bus. Bur. Cen. Fla., Maitland, 1985—; active Friends Winter Park Pub. Libr., Friends of Orlando Pub. Libr. Recognized for Outstanding Leadership in Edn. Cen. Fla. Ednl. Consortium for Women, 1990. Mem. ALA (chair profl. ethics com.), Fla. Libr. Assn., Fla. Assn. Coll. and Rsch. Librs. (pres. bd. dirs.). Avocations: fruit farming, collecting china. Office: U Cen Fla PO Box 25000 Orlando FL 32816-0001

ALLISON, BEVERLY GRAY, seminary president, evangelism educator; b. La., May 7, 1924; s. John Richard Preston and Ora (Byram) A.; m. Voncille Cruse; children: Suzanne Grigsby, Charlotte Miller, Gray Maloy. BS, La. Polytech. Inst. (now La. Tech. U.), 1948; BD, New Orleans Bapt. Theol. Sem., 1952, ThD, 1954. Spl. agt. N.Y. Life Ins. co., Ruston, La., 1948-49; pastor New Prospect Bapt. Ch., Hilly, La., 1951-52, Sharon (La.) Bapt. Ch., 1951-52; assoc. pastor Temple Bapt. Ch., Ruston, La., 1952-54; pastor Southside Bapt. Mission, Ruston, 1953-54; asst. prof. church history New Orleans Bapt. Theol. Sem., 1954-56, assoc. prof. missions, 1955-60, prof. evangelism, 1964-66; evangelist Allison Evangelistic Assn., Ruston, 1960-72; assoc. dir. div. evangelism Home Mission Bd. So. Baptist Convention, 1966-67; pres. Mid-Am. Bapt. Theol. Sem., Memphis, 1972-97, pres. emeritus, 1997—, prof. evangelism, 1972—. Contbr. articles to profl. jours. With USAAF, 1943-45. Office: Mid-Am Bapt Theol Sem PO Box 381528 Germantown TN 38183-1498*

ALLISON, BROOKE HASTINGS, artist; b. N.Y.C., Feb. 12, 1940; s. Frederick Gay and Miriam Lorraine (Watkins) Hastings; m. John Borden Allison, Dec. 17, 1966 (dec. 1996); children: Brooke Allison Scannell, Jaime Joy; stepchildren: Jeffrey Clark, Jay Borden, Jerrianne Allison Anderson, Jane Sue. Student, Shimer Coll., 1957-58, Art Inst. Chgo., 1958-60, 81-82, Am. Acad. Art., 1960-61, Lake Forest Coll., 1961. Instr. Dunedin (Fla.) Fine Art Ctr., 1984-98. Exhibited in groups shows Tampa Mus. Art, 1997, Jacksonville (Fla.) Mus. Art, 1998, works featured in 200 Great Painting Ideas, 1998, Artist Mag., 1998. Pinella County Artists Resource grantee, 1999; recipient award Catharine L. Wolfe Exhbn., 1993-94, others. Mem. Pastel Soc. Am. (signature), Pastel Soc. of West Coast, Midwest Pastel Soc., Profl. Assn. Visual Artists (past. pres. 1992-94), Fla. Artist's Group, Catherine Lorillard Wolfe Art Club. Presbyterian. Avocations: reading, service work. Home: 1654 Mckay Ct Dunedin FL 34698-3529

ALLISON, CHRISTOPHER FITZSIMONS, bishop; b. Columbia, S.C., Mar. 5, 1927; s. James Richard and Susan Milliken (FitzSimons) A.; m. Martha Allston Parker, June 10, 1950. B.A., U. of South, 1949, D.D., 1978; M.Div., Va. Theol. Sem., 1952, D.D., 1981; D.Phil., Oxford U., 1956; D.D., Episcopal Theol. Sem. Ky., 1981. Asst. Trinity, Columbia, 1952-54; assoc. prof. ch. history U. of South, Sewanee, Tenn., 1956-67; prof. ch. history Va. Theol. Sem., Alexandria, 1967-75; rector Grace Ch., N.Y.C., 1975-80; bishop of S.C. Episcopal Ch., Charleston, S.C., 1980-90, ret., 1990. Author: Fear, Love & Worship, 1962, Rise of Moralism, 1966, Guilt, Anger & God, 1972, The Cruelty of Heresy: An Affirmation of Christian Orthodoxy, 1994. Served as sgt. U.S. Army, Italy, 1945-47. Home: 1081 Indigo Ave Georgetown SC 29440-2875

ALLISON, DAVID BRADLEY, psychologist; b. N.Y.C., Feb. 2, 1963; s. Ronald L. and Bernice C. (Goldschlager) A. BA in Psychology, Vassar Coll., 1985; MA in Clin. and Sch. Psychology, Hofstra U., 1987, PhD in Clin. and Sch. Psychology, 1990. Lic. clin. psychologist, N.Y.; cert. sch. psychologist, N.Y.; cert. instr. phys. intervention and restraint N.Y. State Office Mental Retardation and Devel. Disabilities. Behavior therapist Physician's Weight Loss Ctr., Hicksville, N.Y., 1985-86; child care worker Blueberry Treatment Ctr., Bklyn., 1985-86; psychiat. asst. St. Francis Hosp., Roslyn, N.Y., 1986-87; mental health asst. Mercy Hosp. Community Residence, Wantagh, N.Y., 1987-88; intern psychologist Farmingdale (N.Y.) Sch. Dist., 1987-88, Astor Child guidance Ctr., Bronx, N.Y., 1988-89; applied behavior specialist Plus Group Homes, Westbury, N.Y., 1988-90; postdoctoral fellow Johns Hopkins U. Sch. Medicine, Balt., 1990-91; psychologist Obesity Rsch. Ctr., Columbia U. Coll. Physicians and Surgeons, N.Y.C., 1991-94, asst. prof. med. psychology, 1994—; assoc. rsch. sci. N.Y. Obesity Rsch. Ctr. St. Luke's and Roosevelt Hosp. Ctr., N.Y.C., 1994—; mem. adj. faculty St. John's U., Queens, N.Y., 1990, 92—, Nassau C.C., Garden City, N.Y., 1990, Hofstra U., Hempstead, N.Y., 1990; mem. Obesity & Health Task Force on Weight Loss Abuse; mem. adv. bd. Betty Jane Rehab. Ctr. Ohio; cons. to NIH grant, Knoll Pharms., Corning HTA, Glaxo Pharms., Crossroads Sch. Child Devel., 1995—, FDA, 1996—, Rsch. Testing Labs., Inc., 1996; statis. cons. for doctoral students Hofstra U., Johns Hopkins U., Albert Einstein Coll. Medicine, Internat. Life Scis. Inst. and U.S. Dept. Agr., U.S. Dept. Justice, and numerous grants; mem. selection com. for TV entries for AAAS-Westinghouse Sci. Journalism 1990 awards; mem. nutritional adv. bd. Nabisco. Author: (with others) Parenteral Nutrition, vol. 1, 2 edit., 1993, Understanding Eating Disorders, 1994, Body Image, Eating Disorders, and Obesity: An Integrative Guide to Assessment and Treatment, 1996, Obesity Prevention: Theoretical and Methodological Issues, 1996; co-author and co-editor: Obesity Treatment: Establishing Goals, Improving Outcomes, and Reviewing the Research Agenda, 1995, Handbook of Methods for the Assessment of Eating Behaviors and Weight-Related Problems, 1995, Methods for the Design and analysis of Single-Case Research, 1997; reviewer Jour. Applied Behavior Analysis, 1991, 96, Children and Youth Svcs. Rev., 1991, Measurement and Evaluation in Counseling and Devel., 1992, Appetite, 1992, Jour. Cons. and Clin. Psychology, 1992, Psychol. Assessment, 1992, Internat. Jour. Obesity, 1992-97, Jour. Applied Physiology, 1994-96, Medicine and Sci. in Sports and Exercise, 1995, Am. Jour. Epidemiology, 1997, Psychol. Methods, 1997, and numerous others; contbr. articles and abstracts to profl. jours. Recipient Clin. Nutrition Fellows award Am. Soc. Clin. Nutrition, 1992, Award to Young Investigators, 1993, 95, Theodore Tjossom postdoctoral award, 1994, Bursary award Ciba Found., 1995, Neal Miller Early Career award Acad. Behavioral Medicine, 1996; grantee NIH, NATO, APA, Orgnl. Behavior Mgmt. Network, Nat. Inst. Diabetes, Digestive anad Kidney Diseases, Nat. Inst. Aging, 1995—, Ctrs. Disease Control and Prevention, 1996—, and numerous others. Mem. AAAS, APA (mem. divsn. 38, divsn. 5), Am. Psychol. Soc., Am. Assn. Applied and Preventive Psychology, Soc. Behavioral Medicine (Merit Citation 1992), N.Am. Assn. for Study Obesity (mem. coun. 1995—, nominations com. 1996—, publs. com. 1996—, chair orgn. com. 1996-97), European Assn. for Study Obesity, Soc. for Study Ingestive Behavior, Assn. for Advancement Behavior Therapy, Am. Statis. Assn. (mem. exec. bd. N.Y. chpt. 1995—), The Biometric Soc., Inst. Math. Stats., Classification Soc. N.Am., Am. Assn. Human Genetics, Math. Assn. Am., Am. Diabetes Assn., Assn. for Measurement and Evaluation in Couseling and Devel., N.Y. Acad. Sci. Achievements include research on methodology for genetic studies of twins and families, relative effectiveness and cost-effectiveness of coop., competitive and ind. monentary incentive systems for improving staff performance. Office: Columbia U Coll Phys & Surg Surgeons Obesity Rsch Ctr 1090 Amsterdam Ave Fl 14B New York NY 10025-1737*

ALLISON, DAVID C., state legislator; b. Pitts., July 8, 1924; m. Mary Elizabeth Allison; 3 children. BS, Rensselaer Poly., 1948, Wittenberg Coll., 1950. N.H. state rep. Dist. 7, Sullivan Dist. 10, 1994—; mem. com. and small bus. coms. N.H. Ho. of Reps., mem. judiciary and family law coms.; mem. Sullivan County Fin. Com., 1990-94, chmn., 1992-94; editor, writer; sec. Sullivan County Dem., 1992-94, chmn., 1994—; mem. exec. com. N.H. Dem. Party, 1994—. Assoc. editor Bus. Week, 1951-56; tech. editor Time, Inc., 1956-61; sr. editor Internat. Sci. & Tech., 1961-68. Bd. dirs. Conn Valley Home Care, 1994—. Address: RR 2 Box 889 Cornish NH 03745*

ALLISON, DIANNE J. HALL, insurance company official; b. Wadsworth, Ohio, June 9, 1936; d. Glenn Mackey and Dorothy Laverne (Broomall) Hall; widowed; children: Christine M. Gardner Fiocca, Jon R. Gardner; m. David L. Allison, May 8, 1998. *Great, great, great, great, great grandfather, Ebenezer Pardee, fought in the American Revolution. He was wounded at White Plains, NY in October 1776 and died. Dianne Allison is documenting her genealogy in order to join the DAR.* BA in Speech, Heidelberg Coll., Tiffin, Ohio, 1958. Receptionist Buckeye Union Ins. Co., Akron, Ohio, 1966-67; adjuster Liberty Mut. Ins. Co., Akron, 1967-69; claims liaison Ostrov Agy., Akron, 1969-70; underwriter Clark Agy., Wadsworth, 1971-72; adjuster Celina Group, Wadsworth, 1972-73, Nationwide, Canton, Ohio, 1973-77; asst. claim mgr. Motorist Mut. Ins. Co., Akron, 1977-87; claim rep. Ohio Casualty Ins. Co., San Diego, 1987-88; claims adminstr. Riser Foods, Inc. Risk Mgmt., Bedford Heights, Ohio, 1989-97; claims specialist Motorists Ins. Co., Uniontown, Ohio, 1998—. Mem. Ohio Hist. Soc., Friends of Gettysburg. Mem. Assn. for Preservation of Civil War Sites Inc., Ohio State Claims Assn., Akron Claims Assn. (pres. 1985). Avocations: Civil War history, genealogical research, reading, painting. Office: Motorists Ins Cos 3532 Massillon Rd Uniontown OH 44685-7859

ALLISON, DWIGHT LEONARD, JR., investor; b. Boston, Oct. 27, 1929; s. Dwight Leonard and Stella (DeGrasse) A.; m. Lyona G. Strohacker, June 19, 1954; children: Dwight Leonard III, Barbara Lynn, Laurie. AB, Dartmouth Coll., 1951, MBA, 1952; LLB, Harvard U., 1956; DCS (hon.), Suffolk U., 1989. Bar: Mass. 1956. Practiced in Boston, 1956-66; assoc. Goodwin, Procter & Hoar, 1956-64, ptnr., 1965-66; v.p., dir. Gardner Assocs., Inc., Boston, 1966-68; chmn. fin. com. C.H. Sprague & Son Co., 1968-69; chmn. bd. Sprague Assoc., Inc., Boston, 1969-71; gen. ptnr. Sprague & Co., 1971-80; pvt. investor, 1973-77; pres., chief exec. officer Boston Co., 1977-81, chmn. bd., 1981-83, vice chmn., 1983-86; pvt. investor, 1986—; bd. dirs. Avery Dennison Corp., Mellon Bank Corp., Mellon Bank, N.A. 1st lt. USAF, 1952-53. Office: 4015 Shelldrake Ln Boynton Beach FL 33436-5241 Address (summer): PO Box 430 Melvin Village NH 03850-0430

ALLISON, FRED, JR., physician, educator; b. Abingdon, Va., Sept. 8, 1922; s. Fred and Elizabeth Harriet (Kelly) A.; m. Clara Knox, Oct. 14, 1949; children: Rebecca Allison Parsley, Martha Allison Brown, Fred III, Robert Gardiner. B.S., Ala. Poly. Inst., 1944; M.D., Vanderbilt U., 1946. Diplomate: Am. Bd. Internal Medicine. Intern Vanderbilt Hosp., Nashville, 1946-47; resident Peter Bent Brigham Hosp., Boston, 1949-50; practice medicine specializing in internal medicine, 1946—; asst. prof. medicine Washington U., St. Louis, 1955; prof. medicine, head infectious disease dept. U. Miss., Jackson, 1955-68; vis. scientist Rockefeller U., N.Y.C., 1966-67; Edgar Hull prof. medicine, head dept. medicine La. State U., New Orleans, 1968-87; head La. State U. div. Charity Hosp., 1968-87; prof. medicine emeritus La. State U., 1987—; prof. medicine Vanderbilt U., Nashville, 1987-96, prof. medicine emeritus, 1996—, med. cons. Zerfoss Student Health Svc., 1996-98; clin. prof. medicine Meharry Med. Coll., Nashville, 1987; physician-in-chief Met. Nashville Gen. Hosp., 1987-93; chief, divsn. gen. internal medicine Vanderbilt U., 1993-96; ret., 1998. Served with U.S. Army, 1943-46, 47-49. Home: 418 Fairfax Ave Nashville TN 37212-4009

ALLISON, GEORGE BURGESS, systems analyst; b. Balt., Sept. 15, 1951; s. George Poole and Dorothy Ann Burgess; m. Christine Apple, June 2, 1973; children: Tracy Lee, John Burgess. BA, U. Del., Newark, 1973; JD, U. Mich., 1976. Bar: Del. 1976. Assoc. Tunnell & Raysor, Georgetown, Del., 1976-77; systems mgr. Advanced Computer Mgmt. Corp., Troy, Mich., 1977-79; cons. Coopers & Lybrand, Washington, 1979-83; systems engr. The Mitre Corp., McLean, Va., 1983—. Author: The Lawyers Guide to the Internet, 1995; editor Pub. Law Practice Mgmt., 1990-93, columnist, 1982—. Mem. ABA (tech. editor Law Practice Mgmt. 1986—, mem. editorial rev. bd. 1985—, chmn. hotline com., mem. products media bd. 1987-90, mem. sect. coun. 1989-93, chmn. internet bd. 1995—, publ. bd. 1993—), Del Bar Assn., Omicron Delta Epsilon, Omicron Delta Kappa. Home: 8301 Westchester Dr Vienna VA 22182-5217 Office: The Mitre Corp 1820 Dolley Madison Blvd Mc Lean VA 22102-3480

ALLISON, JAMES CLAYBROOKE, II, broadcasting executive; b. Washington, Ky., May 26, 1942; s. James Claybrooke and Mary Frances (Orme) A.; m. Rosa Lee Parr, Aug. 29, 1965; children: Frances Michelle, James Claybrooke III. BA in Radio-TV, U. Ky., 1964. Announcer Sta. WVLK, Lexington, Ky., 1962-64; news dir. Sta. WCMI, Ashland, 1964; news reporter Sta. WLAP, Lexington, 1965, announcer, copywriter, 1966-68, dir. ops., 1967, asst. gen. mgr., 1968-70, gen. mgr., 1970-86; news dir. Sta. WLEX-TV, Lexington, 1987-92, mgr. sta. rels., 1992—. V.p. Ky. chpt. Leukemia Soc., 1977-84, nat. trustee; bd. dirs. Big Bros./Big Sisters, Lexington, 1979-87, Central Ky. Youth Orch. Inc., United Way of Blue Grass, 1986-88; bd. dirs. Blue Grass coun. Boy Scouts Am., 1997—, exec. bd. 1997—. Mem. Sales and Mktg. Execs. Lexington (bd. dirs. 1978-85), Ky. Assn. Broadcasters (bd. dirs. 1978-82, Ky. Mike award 1986), Ky. Broadcasters Assn. (TV dir. 1987-89, pres. 1991), Radio-TV News Dirs. Assn., Lexington Advt. Club (pres. 1980-81) adv. bd. ret. sr. vol. program), Lafayette Club, Lexington Sports Club, Rotary (bd. dirs. 1988-89). Democrat. Avocations: tennis, photography, personal computers, fitness. Home: 3528 Colt Neck Ln Lexington KY 40502-3060 Office: Sta WLEX-TV 1065 Russell Cave Rd Lexington KY 40505-3409

ALLISON, JASON, professional hockey player; b. North York, Ont., Can., May 29, 1975; m. Christine Allison. Center Washington Capitals, 1993, Boston Bruins, 1995—. Office: Boston Bruins Fleet Ctr One Fleet Ctr Ste 250 Boston MA 02114-1303*

ALLISON, JOAN KELLY, music educator, pianist; b. Denison, Iowa, Jan. 25, 1935; d. Ivan Martin and Esther Cecelia (Newborg) K.; m. Guy Hendrick Allison, July 25, 1954 (div. Apr. 1973); children: David, Dana, Douglas, Diane. MusB, St. Louis Inst. of Music, 1955; MusM, So. Meth. U., 1976. Korrepetitor Corpus Christi (Tex.) Symphony, 1963-85; staff pianist Am. Inst. Mus. Studies, Graz, Austria, 1974-89; prof. Del Mar Coll., Corpus Christi, 1976—; adj. prof. Del Mar Coll., 1959-75, Corpus Christi State U., 1978-93, Tex. A&M U., Corpus Christi, 1993—; program dir. Corpus Christi Chamber Music Soc., 1986—; piano chmn. Corpus Christi Young Artists' Competition, 1987—; chmn. Del Mar Coll. Student Programs Com., 1986-88, 91-92, 94-95; chmn. radio com., S.Tex. Pub. Broadcasting Svc., Corpus Christi, 1987-88; asst. mus. dir. Little Theater, Corpus Christi, 1970-74; judge, Houston Symphony Auditions, 1988, S.C. Young Artist Competition, Columbia, 1990; freelance accompanist, 1955—, adjudicator, 1960—; v.p. united fac., Del Mar Coll., 1986-88; pianist with Del Mar Trio, 1965-95, Young Audiences, Inc., 1975-83; recital tours in U.S., Mex., Austria, 1954-88. Piano soloist, St. Louis Symphony, 1956, 57, Bach Festival Orch., St. Louis, 1955, Corpus Christi Symphony; recipient Artist Presentation award, Artist Presentation Soc., St. Louis, 1956; contbr. articles to profl. jours., including Internat. Piano Quar. Co-chmn. Mayor's Com. on Recycling, Corpus Christi, 1989-91; bd. dirs. Corpus Christi Symphony; adv. bd. Corpus Christi Concert Ballet; mem. steering com. cultural devel. plan City of Corpus Christi, 1995-96. Recipient Women in Careers award YWCA, 1985. Mem. Music Tchrs. Nat. Assn., Tex. Music Tchrs. Assn., Corpus Christi Music Tchrs. Assn., Liszt Soc. (contbr. to jour.). Avocations: foreign travel, water-skiing, hiking, acting in community theatre. Home: 4709 Curtis Clark Dr Corpus Christi TX 78411-4801 Office: Del Mar Coll Baldwin & Ayers Corpus Christi TX 78404

ALLISON, JOHN LANGSDALE, naval architect, marine engineer; b. Sutton Coldfield, Eng., Aug. 10, 1930; came to U.S., 1966; s. Herbert Mandall and Eva May (Langsdale) A.; m. Eunice Quick, Apr. 7, 1956; children: Christopher John, Nigel Mark, Katherine Sarah. BSc in Engring., U. Nottingham, Eng., 1954; postgrad., U. Nottingham; aero. engring. cert., Royal Naval Engring. Coll., Plymouth, Eng., 1955; profl. mgmt. cert., U. Aston, Birmingham, Eng., 1959. Chartered engr., Eng. Sr. rsch. engr. Birmingham Small Arms Co./Daimler Group Rsch., 1956-58; lectr. in engring. Bromsgrove Coll. of Further Edn., Worcestershire, Eng., 1958-66; sr. rsch. engr. Bell Aerospace Textron, Buffalo, 1966-71; chief engr. ship tech. Textron Marine Sys. Inc. divsn. Bell Aerospace Textron, New Orleans, 1971-87; chief engr. Band, Lavis & Assocs., Inc., Severna Park, Md., 1987—; student advisor George Washington U., Washington, 1991-92; cons. Outboard Motor Corp., Waukegan, Ill., 1994—; presenter, cons. Inst. for Maritime Dynamics and Meml. U., St. Johns, Nfld., Can., 1995; cons. Kvaerner Mandal (Norway) A.S., 1995—; advisor H.S. students Hi-Frontiers Ann. Competition. Author numerous tech. articles, conf. procs., papers in field. Sub-lt. Royal Navy, 1954-56. Recipient Maritech award U.S. Govt./Advanced Rsch. Projects Agy., 1995. Fellow Inst. Mech. Engrs (chartered), Royal Instn. Naval Architects; mem. Am. Soc. Naval Engrs., Soc. Naval Architects and Marine Engrs. (Vice Adm. Cochrane award 1993), Navy League, U.S. Naval Inst. Republican. Presbyterian. Achievements include patents for waterjet steering and reversal for large ships and heavy lift air cushion vehicle. Home: 792 Tremaine Way Severna Park MD 21146 Office: Band Lavis & Assoc Inc 900 Ritchie Hwy Severna Park MD 21146-4142

ALLISON, JOHN MCCOMB, retired aeronautical engineer; b. Guthrie, Okla., Nov. 27, 1901; s. John McComb and Mary Ann (Miller) A.; m. Dorothy Louise Olson, Nov. 15, 1931; children: John, Mary Ann, David. BSME, U. Ka., 1928. Design staff Stinson Tri-Motor Airliner, 1928-29; aeronautical engr. Akron, Macon rigid airships & nonrigids U.S. Naval Air Sta., Lakehurst, N.J., 1929-33; rsch. engr. Nat. Adv. Com. for Aeronautics (name change to NASA), Langley Field, Va., 1933-38; flight test engr. USN Test Sta., Anacostia, 1938-39; evaluator flight test performance of new Navy aircraft Anacostia, Washington, 1938-39; Bur. Aeronautics rep. various aircraft mfg. plants USNR, 1939-46; head new Navy aircraft and guided missiles test dept. U.S. Naval Air Missile Test Ctr., Pt. Mugu, Calif., 1946-50; engr. missile devel. Bur. Ordnance, Washington, 1950-57; head specifications Goodyear Aircraft Corp., Akron, 1957-59; proposal engr., guided missiles Rockwell Internat., Columbus, Ohio, 1959-69, ret., 1969; cons. light airplane constrn. Allison Airplane Co., North Miami, Fla., 1977-85; founder Langley Fed. Credit Union, 1936. Contbr. articles to profl. jours. Del. Nat. Rep. Planning Com., Washington, 1992. Capt. USN, 1939-46. Fellow AIAA (assoc.), Ox-5 Club. Immanuel Lutheran. Achievements include patent for a wrap around rocket to supply boost for another rocket engine or ram jet sustainer, thus shortening missile; a hybrid turbo rocket engine that can house solid booster propellant in its normal combustion chamger: patent disclosure for a retractable hydrofoil at the normal step position of a flying boat to improve take-off; private pilot, 1931—.

ALLISON, JOHN ROBERT, lawyer; b. San Antonio, Feb. 9, 1945; s. Lyle (stepfather) and Beatrice (Kaliner) Forehand; m. Rebecca M. Picard; 1 child, Katherine. BS, Stanford U., 1966; JD, U. Wash., 1969. Bar: Wash. 1969, D.C. 1973, Minn. 1994, U.S. Supreme Ct. 1973. Assoc. Garvey, Schubert & Barer, Seattle, 1969-73; ptnr., 1973-86; prin. Betts, Patterson & Mines, P.S., 1986-94; sr. counsel Minn. Mining & Mfg. Co., 1994—; lectr. bus. law Seattle U., 1970, U. Wash., 1970-73; judge pro tem, King County Superior Ct., 1983-94. Mem. ABA (vice chmn. toxic and hazardous substances and environ. law com. 1986-91, chair elect 1991-92, chair 1992-93), Minn. Bar Assn., Seattle-King County Bar Assn. (chmn. jud. evaln. polling com. 1982-83), Wash. State Bar Assn. (bd. bar examiners 1984-94), D.C. Bar Assn., Nat. Inst. Pollution Liability (co-chmn. 1988), Order of the Coif, Wash. Athletic (Seattle). Office: 3 M Ctr Saint Paul MN 55144-1000

ALLISON, JONATHAN, retired lawyer; b. Washington, Pa., Apr. 17, 1916; s. Albert Johnson and Etta (Tucker) A. *In 1774 James Allison, who was married to Mary Bradford, sister of James Bradford of the Whiskey Insurrection fame in 1894, settled in what is now Chartiers Township in Washington County, Pennsylvania. James' line of descendents is Thomas, Jonathan, Albert and Jonathan Allison, the subject of this biographical sketch. He is the fifth generation that has resided and prospered in Washington County. The family is now in the eighth generation.* BS, Washington and Jefferson Coll., 1937; JD, U. Pa., 1940; postgrad., Harvard Grad. Bus. Adminstrn., 1940-41. Bar: Pa. 1942. Pvt. practice Washington, 1946-95; ret., 1995. Maj. AUS, 1941-46. Mem. ABA, Pa. Bar Assn., Washington County Bar Assn., Duquesne Club (Pitts.), Southpointe Golf Club, St. Clair Country Club (Upper St. Clair). Republican. Presbyterian. Home: 20 Fairmont Ave Washington PA 15301-3509 Office: 438 Washington Trust Bldg Washington PA 15301

ALLISON, LAIRD BURL, business educator; b. St. Marys, W.Va., Nov. 7, 1917; s. Joseph Alexander and Opal Marie (Robinson) A.; m. Katherine

Louise Hunt, Nov. 25, 1943 (div. 1947); 1 child: William Lee; m. Genevieve Nora Elmore, Feb. 1, 1957 (dec. July 1994). BS in Personnel and Indsl. Relations magna cum laude, U. So. Calif., 1956; MBA, UCLA, 1958. Chief petty officer USN, 1936-51, PTO; asst. prof. to prof. mgmt. Calif. State U., L.A., 1956-83; asst. dean Calif. State U. Sch. Bus. and Econs., L.A., 1971-72, assoc. dean, 1973-83, emeritus prof. mgmt., 1983—; vis. asst. prof. mgmt. Calif. State U., Fullerton, 1970. Co-authored the Bachelors degree program in mgmt. sci. at Calif. State U., 1963. Mem. U.S. Naval Inst., Navy League U.S. Ford Found. fellow, 1960. Mem. Acad. Mgmt., Inst. Mgmt. Sci., Western Econs. Assn. Internat., World Future Soc., Am. Acad. Polit. Social Sci., Calif. State U. Assn. Emeriti Profs., Calif. State U. L.A. Emeriti Assn. (program v.p. 1986-87, v.p. adminstrn. 1987-88, pres. 1988-89, exec. com. 1990-91, treas. 1991—), Am. Assn. Individual Investors, Am. Assn. Ret. Persons, Ret. Pub. Employees Assn. Calif. (chpt. sec. 1984-88, v.p. 1989, pres. 1990-92), Am. Legion, Phi Kappa Phi, Beta Gamma Sigma, Alpha Kappa Psi. Avocations: history, travel, photography, hiking. Home: 2176 E Bellbrook St Covina CA 91724-2346 Office: Calif State U Dept Mgmt 5151 State University Dr Los Angeles CA 90032-4226

ALLISON, MARY MOON SOUTHWELL, community health nurse, nursing administrator; b. Ocala, Fla., Jan. 26, 1955; d. Elmer Lee Jr. and Patricia Ann (Moon) Southwell; m. Charles Richard Allison, June 12, 1976; children: Kelly Moon, Charles Richard Jr., Kevin Lee. ADN, Armstrong State Coll., 1976, BSN, 1980; M in Health Sci. Edn., U. Fla., 1987. Staff nurse Cumberland County Meml. Hosp., Fayetteville, N.C., 1977-78; staff/charge nurse surgery dept. Riverside Hosp., Jacksonville, Fla., 1980; staff/charge nurse ob-gyn. dept. Comanche County Meml. Hosp., Lawton, Okla., 1982-84; quality assurance mgr., edn. coord. Hosp. HomeCare, Albuquerque, 1987-91; dir. profl. svcs. Olsten Health Care, Las Vegas, Nev., 1991-95; dir. quality improvement Personal Touch Home Care, Washington, Va., 1995—. Mem. Sigma Theta Tau.

ALLISON, MICHAEL DAVID, space scientist, astronomy educator; b. Salem, Ill., Oct. 11, 1951; s. James M. and Claudine K. A.; m. Siri Wannamaker, Feb. 4, 1984; children: Hilary Kirstyn, Christopher Caleb. AB in Physics and English, Wittenberg U., 1973; SM in Physics, U. Chgo., 1976; PhD in Space Physics and Astronomy, Rice U., 1982. Resident rsch. assoc. Nat. Rsch. Coun. NASA/Goddard Inst for Space Studies, N.Y.C., 1981-83, space scientist, 1984—; guest lectr. Am. Mus. Natural History, Hayden Planetarium, N.Y.C., 1984-88, 94-97; mem. joint sci. working group for the NASA/ESA assessment study of the Cassini mission to Saturn and Titan, 1984-89; adj. prof. astronomy Columbia U., N.Y.C.- 1987—; co-investigator Huygens, Titan Doppler Wind Expt., U. Bonn., Germany, 1990—; rsch. assoc. Am. Mus. Dept. Astronomy, 1997-99. Co-editor: (conf. proceedings) The Jovian Atmospheres, 1986; contbr. articles to profl. jours. including Science, Icarus, Jour. of Atmospheric Scis., Geophys. Rsch. Letters. Participating scientist Mars Observer and Surveyor '98 Missions, NASA, 1992—. Mem. Am. Astron. Soc. (divsn. for planetary scis.), Am. Meteorol. Soc. Episcopalian. Achievements include research in planetary atmospheric dynamics and meteorology, application of potential vorticity homogenization to planetary zonal circulation studies, first identification of Saturn's polar hexagon as a planetary Rossby wave, inference of a probable super-solar abundance of water on Jupiter based on the diagnostic analysis of equatorial waves. Home: 29 Teller Ave Beacon NY 12508-3045 Office: NASA/Goddard Inst Space Studies 2880 Broadway New York NY 10025-7886

ALLISON, RALPH BREWSTER, psychiatrist; b. Manila, May 13, 1931; s. W. Theodore and Metta L. (Brewster) A.; m. Mary Burden, Jan. 1, 1957 (div. 1997); children: Ann Allison-Marsh, Amy Allison Maiman, Jill Aguiar, John Allison. BA, Occidental Coll., L.A., 1952; MD, UCLA, 1956. Diplomate Am. Coll. Forensic Examiners. Staff psychiatrist Santa Clara County Mental Health Svcs., Palo Alto, Calif., 1962-63; program chief Santa Cruz County Mental Health Svcs., Santa Cruz, Calif., 1964-67; pvt. practice Palo Alto & Santa Cruz, 1962-78; staff psychiatrist Yolo County Mental Health Svcs., Broderick, Calif., 1978-81; forensic psychiatrist Davis, Calif., 1978-81; sr. psychiatrist Calif. Men's Colony, San Luis Obispo, Calif., 1981-93, ret. annuitant psychiatrist, 1994-95; sec. UAPD, Oakland, Calif., 1988-93; pres. SEPA, Oakland, 1990-93; mem. Mental Health adv. bd., Santa Cruz, 1964-67. Co-author: Minds in Many Pieces, 1980; contbr. articles to profl. jours. Founder Suicide Prevention Svcs., Santa Cruz, 1968-74. Capt. USAF, 1957-59. Recipient Cornelia B. Wilbur award ISSD, Skokie, Ill., 1995. Fellow Am. Psychiatric Assn. (life); mem. Am. Anthropological Assn., Internat. Soc. for Study Dissociation (charter), Rotary. Avocations: writing, personel computers. Home: 2162 Mountain View Dr Los Osos CA 93402-3312

ALLISON, ROBERT ARTHUR, race car owner, retired professional stock car driver; b. Miami, Fla., Dec. 3, 1937; s. Edmond J. and Katherine F. (Patton) A.; m. Judith A. Bjorkman, Feb. 20, 1960; children: David, Bonnie, Clifford, Caralene. Ed. parochial schs., Miami. Stock car racer, 1955-88; with Grand Nat. Winston Cup div. Nat. Assn. Stock Car Auto Racing, 1965-88; pres. Bobby Allison Racing, Inc. Mem. Hueytown (Ala.) Indsl. Devel. Bd.; Active Boy Scouts Am. Named Driver of Yr. Martini & Rossi, 1972, Driver of Yr. Nat. Motor Sport Press Assn., Driver of Yr. Olsenite, 1983; named Most Popular Driver Motor Racing Network poll, 1971, 72, 73, 81, 82, 83, Ala. Pro Athlete of 1978 Ala. Sportswriters Assn.; named to Am. Auto Racing Writers and Broadcasters Assn. All Am. Team, 1978; named champion Winston Cup, 1983, Ala. Citizen of Yr., 1985; winner Winston 500 NASCAR event, 1986, Firecracker 400, 1987, Daytona 500, 1978, 82, 88. Mem. Nat. Assn. Stock Car Auto Racing (84 Winston cup wins 1961-82, Most Popular Driver in Winston Cup Grand Nat. Div. 1971, 72, 73, 81, 82). Roman Catholic. Club: Lions (Hueytown). Office: Bobby Allison Racing Inc 140 Church Ave Hueytown AL 35023-2409*

ALLISON, ROBERT CLYDE, business and computers consultant; b. Portland, Oreg., May 14, 1953; s. Harry Updike and Charlene Ann (Hare) A. BS, Portland State U., 1993. Owner Bob Allison Enterprises, Beaverton, Oreg., 1990—. Republican. Roman Catholic. Avocations: golf, flying, reading, audio/video/computer.

ALLISON, ROBERT HARRY, school counselor; b. Hazleton, Pa., Oct. 26, 1952; s. Harry John and Loretta Ida (Henry) A. m. Barbara Joyce Ent, Oct. 28, 1978; 1 child, Diane Amy. BS in Rehab. Edn., Pa. State U., 1974, principal's cert., 1992; MS in Counselor Edn., U. Scranton, 1976; supervisory cert., Shippensburg (Pa.) U., 1981. Work experience coord. Carbon County Area Vocat.-Tech. Sch., Jim Thorpe, Pa., 1974-75; rehab. counselor R.B. Nipon Assn., Phila., 1975-76; career svcs. coord. Sleighton Sch., Lima, Pa., 1976-77; sch. counselor West Perry Sch. Dist., Loysville, Pa., 1977-79; counselor/coord. Alternative Sch. Miffin County Sch. Dist., Lewistown, Pa., 1979-80; elem. counselor Jersey Shore (Pa.) Sch. Dist., 1980-82; mid. sch. counselor, spl. edn. liaison, career edn. coord. Brandywine Heights Sch. Dist., Topton, Pa., 1982-90, mid.-elem. counselor, 1990-93; sch.-to-work transition/elem. counselor Brandywine Heights Sch. Dist., Topton, 1994—; regional mgr. Primorica Fin. Svcs., 1985—. Bd. dirs. Weatherly Area Jaycees, 1974-75; asst. dist. commr. Boy Scouts Am., 1977-83, asst. dist. commr. for exploring, 1990-94, dist. com. mem. 1994-96. Mem. Am. Sch. Counselors Assn., Am. Vocat. Assn., Pa. Sch. Counselors Assn., Assn. for Career and Tech. Edn., Phi Kappa Phi. Lutheran. Home: 104 W Jackson St Fleetwood PA 19522-1706 Office: Brandywine Heights Sch Dist 200 W Weis St Topton PA 19562-1532

ALLISON, SANDY, genealogist, appraiser, political consultant; b. Newburg, Mo., June 30, 1950; d. Jimmy James and A. Colleen (Bricker) Arthur; m. Lynn Leonard Allison, Oct. 3, 1969 (div., 1998); children: Eric Lynn, Jason Wayne. AA, Columbia Coll., Rolla, Mo., 1995, BA, 1996, postgrad., 1996—; student, U. Mo., Rolla. Sec./bookkeeper Biederman Furniture Store, Rolla, 1969-72; bookkeeper/clk. Rolla Auction Co.; degree State Farm Ins., Rolla, 1995; demonstrator, salesperson Roth Distbn., St. Louis; home inspector Allison Assn., Rolla; owner/designer Allison Residential Contr., Rolla; owner/acct. Flowers Unltd. Inc., Rolla; appraiser Stoltz Appraisal Co., Rolla, 1985-91; med. placement cons. Assoc. Svcs., Rolla, 1991-92; pub. adminstr. Phelps County, Rolla, 1992—, dir. econ. devel., 1996—; field dir. Carnahan for Gov. Campaign, St. Louis, 1991-92; with Sumner County Econ. Devel., Wellington, Kans., 1998-99; dir. Higginsville (Mo.) Econ. Devel., 1999—. Author/editor: Allison Book, 1995; editor, chmn. com.: The Phelps County Missouri Heritage, 1991. Dem. Nat. committeewoman for State of Mo., 1992—; 8th Dist. pres. Dem. Party, 1990-95; bd. dirs. Connect Mo., 1993-94; v.p., pres., bd. dirs. PHelps County Univ. Ext., 1989-95; chairwoman Phelps County Dem. Party; v.p., membership chair Jeffersonian Women's Group; mem. solid waste commn. Meramec Regional Planning Commn.; mem. Mothers Against Drunk Drivers; dir. Sumner Cty. Econ. Devel., 1997-98; bd. mem. Sumner Cty. Geneology Soc. Named Dem. Outstanding Woman. Mem. Geneal. Soc. Mo. (pres., v.p., bd. dirs., State award 1992), Nat. Assn. Counties for Cmty. and Econ. Devel. (bd. dirs. 1992-93), Bus. and Profl. Women's Club (pres., legis. state chair 1991-94), Rolla Area C. of C., Phelps County Geneal. Soc. (founder, pres.), Toastmasters Internat., Nat. Assn. Real Estate Appraisers, Ind. Fee Appraisers Assn., Internat. Platform Assn., Alpha Sigma Alpha. Avocations: horseback riding, golf, gardening, reading, computers. E-mail: sandydallison@hotmail.com. Home and Office: 100 E 15th St Higginsville MO 64037

ALLISON, STEPHEN GALENDER, broadcast executive; b. Springfield, Mo., Dec. 11, 1952; s. Edgbert Allcorn and Naomi Louise (Chamless) A.; m. Linda Lavelle, June 6, 1974 (div. Dec. 1981); children: Julie Ann, Jennifer Erin; m. Tara Rae Foster, Aug. 20, 1986 (div. Aug. 1994). Cert. radio mktg. cons. Radio Advt. Bur. On-air personality Sta. WSBB, New Smyrna, Fla., 1971-72, Sta. WMFJ-AM-FM, Daytona Beach, Fla., 1972-75, Sta. KADI-FM, St. Louis, 1975-76, Sta. KAUM-FM, Houston, 1976-79, Sta. WKYS-FM, Washington, 1979-81; gen mgr. Sta. KSTM-FM, Phoenix, 1981-85; pres. Allison Broadcasting Co., Inc., Phoenix, 1985—, Allison Broadcast Group, Inc., Dallas, Del Mar, Calif., 1987—; owner Stas. KGRX-FM/KIKO, Phoenix, 1986-91, Sta. KDGE-FM, Dallas, 1989-94, WLVX-FM, Gainesville, Fla., 1994-95; mgr. talk/bus./ESPN programming ABC Radio Networks, Dallas, 1996-97; dir. Clear Channel Comms., Tampa, 1997-98; nat. dir. mktg. Metro Networks, Phoenix, 1998—; mktg. cons. St. Louis Post-Dispatch, 1975-76, Houston Chronicle, 1976-79, Washington Star, 1980-81; advt. cons. Celebrity Theatre, Phoenix, 1985-86; pres. JFM Branson (Mo.) Inc., 1993—; owner Doc Severinsen Theater. Bd. dirs. Desert-Mt. Foothills Assn., Scottsdale, Ariz., 1981-91, 98—, Alwun House Cultural Ctr., Phoenix, 1982—, Film in Ariz., Phoeniz, 1985-93, Ariz. Commn. on the Arts, Phoenix, 1986-89; active Nat. Rep. Congl. Com., 1988-93, No. Tex. Commn. Mem. Nat. Assn. Broadcasters, Ariz. Broadcasters Assn., Tex. Assn. Broadcasters, Phoenix Active 20-30 Club, Internat. Platform Assn., Las Colinas Sports Club, Pointe Royale Country Club, Preston Trails Country Club, The Heritage Club. Avocations: collecting classic cars, traveling, racquetball, golfing, boating. Home: # 102-225 6339 E Greenway Pkwy Scottsdale AZ 85254 Office: Metro Networks 14605 N Airport Dr Ste 330 Scottsdale AZ 85260-2491

ALLMAN, AVIS ASIYE, artist, poet, Turkish and Islamic culture educator; b. Phila., Dec. 27, 1954; d. William Berthold and Margo (Hutz) A. BFA in Painting, Windham Coll., 1975; MBA in Arts, SUNY, Binghamton, 1978; postgrad., Hunter Coll., 1983, NYU, 1987-88, 91-95. Devel. officer The Bklyn. Mus., 1977; program analyst N.Y. State Coun. Arts, N.Y.C., 1977-80, dir. spl. projects, 1980-81; dir. adminstrn. Mus. Broadcasting, N.Y.C., 1981; sr. fin. analyst CBS TV Network, N.Y.C., 1981-82; rsch. cons. Am. Coun. on Arts, N.Y.C., 1983-84; fin. analyst Cmty. Svc. Soc., N.Y.C., 1983-84; pres. Allman Fin. Svcs., Bklyn., 1985—; artist-in-residence (tiles) Canakkale Ceramics, Istanbul, Turkey, 1991-96, (carpets) Net Holding, Izmir, Turkey, 1989, (painter, poet) Zaman Newspaper, Ankara, Turkey, 1997; rsch. assoc. Georgetown U. Muslim-Christian Understanding, 1998-99. One-woman shows include Mus. Turkish/Islamic Arts, Istanbul, 1987, 90, 92, French Cultural Ctr., Izmir, 1992, Women's Libr., Istanbul, 1996, Mus. Calligraphy, Istanbul, 1996; exhibited in group shows at Müsiad/IBF Forum, Istanbul, 1997, Altinpark, Ankara, 1997; represented in permanent collections at Vatican, Mus. Turkish/Islamic Arts, Indpls. Mus. Art; author: Road to Democracy, 1997, Religious Freedom in Turkey, 1999. Sr. Rsch. Fulbright scholar U.S. Info. Agy, 1988-89; vis. scholar NYU, 1991-94; recipient Exhbn. grants U.S. Info. Svc., Ankara, 1987, Greek Consulate, Izmir, Turkey, 1992, Kale Group, Istanbul, 1992, 96, Glaxo Wellcome, Istanbul, 1996. Democrat. Muslim. Avocations: dancing, praying to God, Mediterrean Sea, walking. Studio: 113 S 22nd St Fl 2D Philadelphia PA 19103-4310 Office: Allman Fin Svcs 20 Henry St Apt 3G Brooklyn NY 11201-1348

ALLMAN, GREGG, musician; b. Nashville, Dec. 8, 1947; m. Cher Bono, (div.); 1 child. Co-founder: (bands) Hour Glass, Allman Bros. Band; albums include The Allman Bros. Band, 1969, Idlewild South, 1970, The Allman Bros. Band at Fillmore East, 1971, Eat a Peach, 1972, Brothers and Sisters, 1973, 94, Beginnings, 1973, Win, Lose of Draw, 1975, The Road Goes on Forever, 1975, Enlightened Rogues, 1979, Reach for the Sky, 1980, Bros. of the Road, 1981, Dreams, 1989, Live at Ludlow's Garage: 1970, 90, Seven Turns, 1990, A Decade of Hits: 1969-1979, 1991, Shades of Two Worlds, 1991, An Evening With..., 1992, Where It All Begins, 1994, Hell & High Water: The Best of the Arista Years, 1994, Brothers and Sisters, 1994, Back to Back: At Their Best, 1995; solo albums Laid Back, 1973, Playing up a Storm, 1977, I'm No Angel, 1987, Just Before Bullets Fly, 1988, Searching For Simplicity, 1997; film debut, Rush, 1991. Inducted Rock and Roll Hall of Fame as member of The Allman Brothers Band, 1995. Office: Fin Svcs Co 418 Foss St Healdsburg CA 95448

ALLMAN, MARGARET ANN LOWRANCE, counselor; b. Carmel, Calif., June 2, 1938; d. Edward Walton and Rhoda Elizabeth (Patton) Lowrance; m. Jackie Howard Hamilton, Dec. 21, 1959 (div. May 1976); children: John Scott, David Lee, Dennis Lynn; m. Jack Fredrick Allman, Dec. 22, 1977; stepchildren: John Frederick, James Paul, Jeffrey Lee. AA, Christian Coll., 1958; BA in Spanish, U. Mo., 1960, MEd, 1971, EdD, 1994. Tchr. Spanish Neosho (Mo.) H.S., 1961-62, asst. prin., 1974-77; florist Wallflower Shop and Greenhouse, Joplin, Mo., 1962-69; dean girls Joplin Sr. H.S., 1967-69; florist, bookkeeper Mueller's Garden Ctr., Columbia, Mo., 1969-71; instr. edn., asst. dean of students Columbia (Mo.) Coll., 1971-74; dir. guidance Am. Cmty. Sch., Buenos Aires, 1978-81; tchr. Spanish, psychology Ava (Mo.) H.S., 1982-84; tchr. Spanish, social studies McDonald County H.S., Anderson, Mo., 1984-88; counselor Mo. So. State Coll., Joplin, 1988—; mem. adv. bd. Adult Basic Edn., Joplin, 1992—; cons. Mo. So. State Coll., 1990—, mem. internat. task force, 1994-96; presenter Ctr. for Applications of Psychol. Type Internat. Conf., 1996. Recipient William D. Phillips Music award 1st Christian Ch., Columbia, 1956; named to Outstanding Young Women of Am., 1972. Mem. Mo. Sch. Counselor Assn., Southwest Mo. Sch. Counselor Assn. (sec. 1994-97, v.p. 1992-94, mem. governing bd., chmn. publs. and rsch. com. 1997—), Kappa Delta Pi, Phi Theta Kappa, Sigma Phi Gamma, Delta Eta Chi, Phi Sigma Iota (romance lang., pres 1959-60), Sigma Delta Pi. Avocations: music, photographer, sketch artist, needlecrafts, jewelry crafts. Home: 1214 Circle Dr Neosho MO 64850-1301 Office: Mo So State Coll 3950 Newman Rd Joplin MO 64801-1512

ALLMAN, MARGO HUTZ, sculptor, painter; b. N.Y.C., Feb. 23, 1933; d. Werner H. and Avis (Newcomb) Hutz; student Smith Coll., 1950-51, Moore Coll. Art, 1952-54, Hans Hofmann Sch. Art, 1953, U. Del., 1967-70; m. William B. Allman, Feb. 19, 1954; children—Avis Louise, David Drue. One-person shows include: Wallingford (Pa.) Art Center, 1964, Windham Coll., 1974, Bloomsburg State Coll., 1976, 77, Moore Coll. Art and Design, 1979, Marian Locks Gallery, Phila., 1984, McKinney Gallery West Chester U., Pa., 1994; group shows include: Phila. Art Alliance, 1954, Del. Art Museum, Wilmington, 1958 (Ann. Show Drawing prize), 65, 67, Print Club, Phila., 1959, U. Del., 1977, Del. State Arts Council, Wilmington, 1981, C. Grimaldis Gallery, Balt., 1983, Art in Form Gallery, Karlsruhe, W.Ger., Contemporary Women Artists of Phila., 1986-87, Del. Art Mus., 1993, Del. Ctr. Comtemporary Arts, 1995, Long Beach Isl. Found. Arts and Scis., Loveladies, N.J., 1995; Artist-in-Residency, Canakkale Seramik, Can., Turkey, 1995; represented in permanent collections, including: Del. Mus., Phila. Mus.; works include: Ferro Cement Sculpture, Tidewater Pub. Co., Centerville, Md., 1975, Crocheted Sculpture of Herculon, Hercules Inc., Wilmington, 1975. Bd. dirs. Robert Small Dance Co., N.Y.C., 1979-80. Recipient Mildred Boericke prize Print Club, Phila., 1958, Landscape prize Wilmington Trust Bank, 1969, Disting. Alumnae award Moore Coll. Art Design, 1998. Mem. Moore Coll. Art and Design Alumnae Assn., Del. Center Contemporary Arts, Del. Art Mus., Nat. Mus. Women in the Arts (charter mem.). Unitarian. Home: 202 State Rd West Grove PA 19390-8906

ALLMAN, MARK C., engineer, physicist; b. Rochester, Pa., Aug. 4, 1958; s. Crawford Marcus and Darl Terresa (Hazenstab) A.; m. Mary Beth Decker, Apr. 30, 1983 (div. 1987); m. Janice Kay Hempleman, Dec. 8, 1989. BSBA, Robert Morris Coll., 1980; MS in Phys. Sci., U. Houston Clear Lake, 1991. Programmer/analyst Transcomm Data Systems, Inc., Pitts., 1980-81; ind. cons. Pitts., 1981-82; programmer/analyst, cons. ComTech Systems, Inc., Columbus, Ohio, 1982-83; systems programmer, mgr., project leader DataCom, Inc., Columbus, 1983-86; systems engr. R&D Discovery Systems, Dublin, Ohio, 1986-88; systems analyst On-Line Computer Libr. Ctr., Dublin, 1988-89; engr., physicist Rockwell Space Ops. Co., Houston, 1989-95; sr. engr. McDonnell Douglas/Boeing, 1995-98; pvt. practice Allman Profl. Cons. Inc., 1998—; pvt. pilot, 1997—; mem. data collection team Allegheny Obs., U. Pitts., 1981-82; presenter at profl. confs. Author: Introduction to the C Programming Language, 1994; co-author: Modern Astrodynamics, 1996. Mem. campaign coun. Rep. Nat. Com., Washington, 1991—, Haw Rang Do Kung-Fu Martial Arts Team, 1991—. Mem. AIAA, AAAS, Am. Astron. Soc. (assoc.), Coun. Fgn. Rels., Wu Shu Kung Fu Fedn. (2d deg. black belt), Greater Houston Deming Alliance. Republican. Roman Catholic. Home and Office: 2912 Hamm Rd Pearland TX 77581-5550

ALLMAN, RICHARD MARK, physician, gerontologist; b. Columbus, Ohio, Feb. 23, 1955; m. Connie Lou Allman; children: Justin Mark, Philip Randolph. BA in Biology magna cum laude, W.Va. U., 1977, MD, 1980. Diplomate Am. Bd. Internal Medicine, Am. Bd. Geriat. Medicine, Nat. Bd. Med. Examiners. Intern W.Va. U. Sch. Medicine, 1980-81, resident in internal medicine, 1981-83; fellow in internal medicine Johns Hopkins U., Balt., 1983-85; asst. in medicine, staff physician Johns Hopkins U./Hosp., Balt., 1985-86; staff physician U. Ala. Hosp., VA Med. Ctr., Birmingham, 1986—; asst. prof. medicine U. Ala., Birmingham, 1986-90, assoc. prof. medicine, 1990-96, prof. medicine, 1996—, dir. Ctr. for Aging, 1992—, dir. Geriatric Edn. Ctr., 1993—; prin. clin. coord. Ala. Quality Assurance Found., Birmingham, 1995—; Chief geriat. sect. Birmingham VA Med. Ctr., 1990—; dir. divsn. gerontology/geriat. med. U. Ala., 1990—. Assoc. editor Am. Jour. Medicine, 1988-92; mem. editl. bd. Advances in Wound Care, 1989-97, Jour. Am. Geriat. Soc., 1994-97, Jour. Gerontology: Med. Sci., 1996—; ad hoc reviewer for jours.; contbr. articles to profl. jours. Recipient Lange Book award, 1977, Mosby Book award, 1978, others. Mem. ACP, Am. Geriat. Soc. (rsch. com. 1996—), Gerontol. Soc. Am., Assn. for Dirs. Geriat. Acad. Programs (nat. com. 1993—), Am. Fedn. for Med. Rsch. (nat. com. 1992-95, Henry Christian Meml. award 1993), Soc. for Gen. Internal Medicine, Am. Health Quality Assn., Nat. Pressure Ulcer Adv. Panel (bd. dirs. 1991-95), Southern Soc. for Clinical Investigation, Ala. Geron. Soc., Phi Beta Kappa, Alpha Omega Alpha. Office: U Ala Ctr for Aging 933 19th St S Ste 201 Birmingham AL 35205-3703

ALLMAN, WILLIAM BERTHOLD, musician, engineer, consultant; b. Phila., Feb. 16, 1927; s. Drue Nunez and Blanche (Oppenheimer) A.; m. Margo Hutz, Feb. 19, 1954; children: Avis Louise, David Drue. BSEE, Drexel U., 1949; MBA, U. Pa., 1951. Registered profl. engr., Pa. Contract engr. Atlantic Refining, Phila., 1951-55, E.I. DuPont de Nemours & Co., Inc., Wilmington, Del., 1955-58; constrn. engr. Niagra Falls, N.Y., 1958-59; cons. engr. Wilmington, 1959-82, Allman Assocs., West Grove, Pa., 1982—; owner, mgr. Allman Bldgs., Phila., 1965-87. Contbr. numerous articles on plastic pipe to profl. mags.; drummer, washboard player with Allman, Melton and Co. band; performed with various musicians including Lionel Hampton, Brownie McGhee, Mississippi Fred McDowell, Sonny Terry. Mem. Bi-racial com. City of Newark, Del., 1963-71, chmn. 1965, London Grove Township Mcpl. Authority, Chester County, Pa., 1985-89, chmn. 1986; Dem. committeeman, Del., 1964-71, chmn., 1968; candidate Mayor City of Newark, 1970; adv. coun. Neighborhood Svcs. Ctr., Oxford, Pa., 1989—. With USNR, 1945-46. ETO. Mem. Am. Assn. Individual Investors, Del. Ctr. Contemporary Arts, Del. Art Mus., Phila. Mus. Art, Nature Conservancy. Democrat. Unitarian. Avocations: painting, music, gardening, traveling, reading. Home and Office: 202 State Rd West Grove PA 19390-8906

ALLMAND, LINDA F(AITH), retired library director; b. Port Arthur, Tex., Jan. 31, 1937; d. Clifton James and Jewel Etoile (Smith) A. BA, North Tex. State U., 1960; MA, U. Denver, 1962. Clerical asst. Gates Meml. Libr., 1953-55; libr. asst. Houston Pub. Libr., 1955-58; children's libr. Denver Pub. Libr., 1960-63; children's coord. Anaheim Pub. Libr., Calif., 1963-65; br. mgr. Dallas Pub. Libr., 1965-71, chief br. svcs., 1971-81; dir. Ft. Worth Pub. Libr., 1981-98; instr. North Tex. State U., Denton, 1967—; instr. Dallas County C.C., 1981; bldg. cons. Dallas Pub. Libr., 1974-80, Hurst Pub. Libr., 1977-78, Jacksonville (Tex.) Pub. Libr., 1976-79, Carrollton Pub. Libr., 1979-81, Haltom (Tex.) City Pub. Libr., 1984, Iowa Park (Tex.) Pub. Libr., 1985, S.W. Regional Libr., Ft. Worth, 1987. Author: 1981-2000, Ft. Worth Public Library—Facilities and Long-Range Planning Study, 1982; contbr. chpts. to books, articles to profl. jours. Bd. dirs. City of Dallas Credit Union, 1973-81, Sr. Citizen's Ctrs., Inc., 1982; com. chmn. Goals for Dallas, 1967-69; mem. Forum Ft. Worth, 1983; mem. Edn. Info. Task Force, Downtown Fort Worth, Inc., 1992-93. Pilot Club of Port Arthur scholar, 1954, Libr. Binding Inst. scholar, 1958; recipient Disting. Alumnus award North Tex. State U., 1983, U. North Tex., 1998, Leadership Ft. Worth, 1982-83; named Tarrant County Newsmaker of the Yr., 1984, Outstanding Leader, Ft. Worth Star Telegram, 1989, Outstanding Woman of the Yr., Mayor's Commn. on Status of Women, 1989, North Tex. Pub. Adminstr. of the Yr., 1990. Mem. ALA, AAUP, AAUW (Tarrant County pres.-elect 1998, pres. 1999), Tex. Libr. Assn. (pres. pub. libr. divsn. 1980-81, chmn. planning com. 1982-84, pres.-elect 1985-86, pres. 1986-87, Libr. of Yr. award 1985, North Tex. Pub. Adminstr. of Yr. award 1990), Tarrant Regional Librs. Assn., Am. Mgmt. Assn., Dallas County Librs. Assn. (pres. 1968-69), Downtown Ft. Worth (mem. edn. info. task force 1992-93), Freedom to Read Found., Ft. Worth C. of C. (bd. dirs. 1993—), Rotary, Sister Cities, Inc., Ft. Worth Pub. Libr. Found. Home: 701 Timberview Ct N Fort Worth TX 76112-1715

ALLMENDINGER, BETTY LOU, retired bank employee; b. Aberdeen, S.D., July 4, 1931; d. Alvia E. Bain and Lydia Dobrick; m. Melvin E. Allmendinger, Mar. 2, 1951 (div. Sept. 1972); children: Terry Lee, Robin Dawn, Valerie Ann. GED, Washington H.S., Sioux Falls, S.D., 1981. Machine operator Fenn's Ice Cream, Sioux Falls, S.D., 1950-65; checker Prairie Market, Sioux Falls, 1967-79; Ramada Inn, Sioux Falls, 1980-86; sales rep. Avon, Sioux Falls, 1986-88; City Bank, Sioux Falls, 1988-96; ret., 1996. Pfc. U.S. Army, 1953-55. Mem. Am. Legion. Home: 2010 W Brookings St Sioux Falls SD 57104-1206

ALLMENDINGER, PAUL FLORIN, retired engineering association executive; b. Moline, Ill., Mar. 2, 1922; s. Andrew Louis A. and Nellie L. (Florin) Inman; m. Sara Jo Breazeale, Aug. 31, 1947; children: James, Glen, John. Student, Augustana Coll., Rock Island., Ill., 1940-41; B.S., U.S. Naval Acad., 1944. Dir. engring. Prestolite Co.-Eltra Corp., Toledo, Ohio, 1961-67; dir. engring. Power Tool div. Rockwell Internat., Pitts., 1967-68, v.p. engring. Power Tool div., 1968-77; v.p. tech. affairs Motor Vehicle Mfrs. Assn., Detroit, 1977-81; dep. exec. dir. ASME, N.Y.C., 1981-82, exec. dir., 1982-87. Treas., bd. dirs. Nat. Alliance for the Mentally Ill, 1998—. Served to lt (j.g.) USN, 1941-47. Fellow Inst. Mech. Engrs., ASME (Centennial award 1980); mem. Soc. Automotive Engrs. (bd. dirs. 1963-66), Am. Soc. Engring. Edn., Soc. Mfg. Engrs., Engrs. Council for Profl. Devel. (bd. dirs. 1973-80, pres. 1976-78, Grinter Disting. Service award 1986), Am. Nat. Standards Inst. (bd. dirs. 1977-82), Lake Keowee Assn. (bd. dirs. 1988-91, pres. 1990-91), Tau Beta Pi. Republican. Presbyterian. Clubs: University (Washington and N.Y.C.). Office: Am Soc Mech Engrs 345 E 47th St New York NY 10017-2330

ALLMON, MICHAEL BRYAN, financial consultant; b. Oceanside, Calif., July 14, 1951; s. William Bryan and Cecelia Audrey (Wright) A.; m. Monika Ann Arth, Sept. 15, 1979; children: Stefanie Michele, Danika Audrey. BBA, U. Tex., 1975; MBT, U. So. Calif., 1986. CPA, Calif. CPA Alexander Grant & Co., L.A., 1976-77, Laventhol & Horwath, CPAs, L.A., 1977-85; dir. tax, fin. planning svcs. Zusman, Cameron and Allmon, CPAs, 1985-88; CEO, dir. Essential Profl. Svcs., Inc., 1985-86; ptnr. Michael B. Allmon & Assocs. LLP, CPAs, Marina Del Rey, 1988—; pres. The MBA Group, Inc., Marina Del Rey, 1991—; trustee several pvt. trusts, 1995—; mem. exec. bd. dirs. estate and gift com. of taxation sect. State Bar Calif. Contbr. articles to profl. jours. Mem. AICPAs (fed. tax divsn.), Calif. Soc. CPAs (fin. planning com., v.p., bd. dirs. L.A. chpt. 1992—, statewide bd. dirs. 1995-97, chair estate planning com. 1993—), Am. Assn. Profl. Fin. Planners (L.A. chpt. pres.), Walnut Track Club (pres. team) (L.A.), Manhattan Beach (Calif.) Country Club. Office: 4720 Lincoln Blvd Ste 300 Marina Del Rey CA 90292

ALLNER, WALTER HEINZ, designer, painter, art director; b. Dessau, Germany, Jan. 2, 1909; came to U.S., 1949, naturalized, 1957; m. Colette Vasselon, Mar. 8, 1938 (div. June 1951); 1 son, Michel; m. Jane Booth Pope, Apr. 4, 1954; 1 son, Peter. Student, Bauhaus-Dessau, 1927-30. Designer Gesellschafts-und Wirtschafts-Museum, Vienna, Austria, 1929; asst. to typographer Piet Zwart, Wassenaar, Holland, 1930; editorial, painting, and advt. designer Paris, 1932-49; ptnr. Omnium Graphique, Paris, 1933-36; art dir. Formes, Editions d'Art Graphique et Photographique, Paris, 1933-36; Paris editor Swiss art mag. Graphis, 1945-48; founder, editor Internat. Poster Ann., 1948-52; co-dir. Editions Paralleles, Paris, 1948-51; mem. staff Fortune mag., N.Y.C., 1951-74, art dir., 1962-74; mem. faculty Parsons Sch. Design, N.Y.C., 1974-86; vis. critic, mem. Comite de Parrainage Ecole Superieure d'Arts Graphiques, Paris, 1979—; free-lance designer design cons. companies; lectr. in Australia, 1983. Designer posters for traffic safety campaign, Outdoor Advt. Assn. Am., 1959-60; exhibits, Salon des Surindependants, Paris, Salon des Réalités Nouvelles, Paris, numerous others, Germany, Austria, U.S., Eng., France, Holland, Switzerland, Latin Am., Japan.; Compiler, editor: A.M. Cassandre, Peintre d'Affiches, 1948; editor: Posters, 1952; corr. Signes mag., Paris, 1990-92; contbg. editor Design Jour., Seoul, Korea, 1990-92; author numerous articles on poster art. Recipient medal Bauhaus-Dessau German Acad. Architecture, 1979, The Bruno Biennale Hon. Membership, Spl. Prix of Jury for Investment in Devel. World Graphic Design, Alliance Graphique Internat. statuette for graphic design, 1998; named Laureate 4th Block, Kharkov, Ukraine, 1997. Mem. Alliance Graphique Internationale (internat. pres.), Am. Inst. Graphic Arts, Associazione Italiana Creativi Comunicazione Visiva (hon.). Home: 110 Riverside Dr New York NY 10024-3715 also: PO Box 167 Truro MA 02666-0167

ALLNUTT, ROBERT FREDERICK, management consultant, corporate director; b. Richmond, Va., June 15, 1935; s. Robert Carhart and Evelyn Rosalie (Brooks) A.; m. Jan Latven, July 17, 1938; children: Robert David, Thomas Frederick. B.S. in Indsl. Engring, Va. Poly. Inst., 1957; J.D. with distinction, George Washington U., 1960, LL.M., 1962. Bar: D.C. 1960, Va. 1960. Patent examiner U.S. Patent Office, 1957-60; with NASA, 1960-70, 78-83, asst. adminstr. legis. affairs, 1967-70, assoc. dep. adminstr., 1978-81, assoc. adminstr. external relations, dep. gen. counsel, 1981-83; legal counsel, corp. sec. U.S. Com. Energy Awareness, 1983-84; v.p. Communication Satellite Corp., 1984-85; exec. v.p. Pharm. Mfrs. Assn., 1985-95; sr. counselor APCO Assocs., Washington, 1995—; assoc. gen. counsel Commn. on Govt. Procurement, 1970-73; staff dir. com. aero. and space scis. U.S. Senate, 1973-75; dep. asst. adminstr. ERDA, 1975-78; lectr. law Am. U. Law Sch., 1964; bd. dirs. Cortex Pharms., Inc., Irvine, Calif., Cypros Pharms., Inc., Carlsbad, Calif., Penederm, Inc., F. Dohmen Co., Inc., Germantown, Wis. Trustee Air and Space Heritage Coun.; bd. dirs. Nat. Health Coun., 1987-98, Nat. Coun. on Aging, 1990-98; mem. Com. of 100, Va. Poly. Inst., 1991—; mem. program coun. of Internat. Ctr. for Sci. Lit., Chgo. Acad. Scis.; bd. dirs. Nat. Medals Sci. & Technology Found., 1997—, Partnership for Caring, 1998—. Recipient Superior Performance award U.S. Patent Office, 1959, Apollo Achievement award NASA, 1969, Meritorious Service medal ERDA, 1976, Exceptional Service medal NASA, 1981, Disting. Service medal NASA, 1983; named Meritorious Fed. Exec. with Presdl. Rank Office of Pres., 1981. Mem. Legal Aid Soc. D.C. (bd. dirs.), Nat. Space Soc. (bd. govs.), NASA Alumni League (v.p.), Edgemoor Tennis Club (Bethesda, Md.;pres. 1987-89), Order of Coif. Home: 5415 Moorland Ln Bethesda MD 20814-1335 Office: APCO Assocs 1615 L St NW Washington DC 20036-5610

ALLOWAY, ROBERT MALCOMBE, computer consulting executive; b. Cleve., Apr. 15, 1944; s. Robert Malcombe and May (Tingley) A.; divorced; children: Megan, Brook. BA, Brown U., 1967; MBA, Boston Coll., 1972; D in Bus. Adminstrn., Harvard U., 1975. Cert. data processor. Project mgr. Sealtest Foods, Rocky River, Ohio, 1968-70, First Nat. Stores, Summerville, Mass., 1970-72; research assoc. Boston Coll., Chestnut Hill, Mass., 1972-73; asst. prof. mgmt. sci. MIT, Cambridge, 1975-84; pres. Alloway Inc., Lexington, Mass., 1984-97; retired, 1997; prof. staff U.S. Ho. of Reps., 1997—; guest prof. Stockholm Sch. Econs., 1976-77; rsch. faculty Ctr. for Info. Systems Rsch., MIT, 1975-84. Contbr. articles to profl. jours. Pres. World Future Soc., Boston, 1973-75. Mem. Soc. for Mgmt. Info. (reviewer) 1983—). Avocations: sailing, skiing, tennis. Office: Alloway Inc Ste 1605 203 Yoakum Pkwy Alexandria VA 22304-3768

ALLRED, ALBERT LOUIS, chemistry educator; b. Mount Airy, N.C., Sept. 19, 1931; s. Caleb Haynes and Bessie (Brown) A.; m. Nancy Jean Willis, Aug. 30, 1958; children—Kevin Scott, Gregg Warren, Sarah Elaine. B.S. in Chemistry, U. N.C., 1953; A.M., Harvard, 1955, Ph.D., 1956. Chemist E.I. du Pont de Nemours Co., Wilmington, Del., 1952, 55, Mallinckrodt Chem. Works, St. Louis, 1954, Argonne (Ill.) Nat. Lab., 1958, 76; mem. faculty Northwestern U., 1956—, prof., 1969-91, prof. emeritus, 1991—, assoc. dean Coll. Arts and Scis., 1970-74, chmn. dept. chemistry, 1980-86, acting dean Coll. Arts and Scis., 1987-88, acting v.p. for rsch. and dean Grad. Sch., 1992, acting provost, 1995; vis. scholar Cambridge (Eng.) U., 1987. Alfred P. Sloan fellow, 1963-65; postdoctoral fellow U. Rome, Italy, 1967; hon. research assoc. Univ. Coll., London (Eng.), 1965. Mem. AAUP (pres. Northwestern U. 1968-69), , Am. Chem. Soc., Chem. Soc. (London), Coun. Chem. Rsch. (gov. bd. 1985-88), Rotary Internat., Phi Beta Kappa, Phi Lambda Upsilon, Sigma Xi, Alpha Chi Sigma. Home: 820 Milburn St Evanston IL 60201-2450

ALLRED, MICHAEL SYLVESTER, lawyer; b. Natchez, Miss., July 10, 1945; s. Samuel S. and Nina Kathryn (Worrell) A.; m. Gretchen Ann Gulmon, Jan. 20, 1970 (div. Oct. 1990); children: Jeffrey Balfour, Gordon Woods, Jennifer Allison; m. Patricia L. Duggar, Jan. 23, 1991. BA, Miss. State U., 1968; JD, U. Miss., 1970. Bar: Miss. 1970, U.S. Dist. Ct. (no. and so. dists.) Miss. 1970, U.S. Ct. Appeals (5th cir.) 1970, U.S. Supreme Ct. 1987. Clk. Miss. Supreme Ct., Jackson, 1970-71; assoc. Satterfield, Shell, Williams & Buford, Jackson, 1971-75; instr. Jackson Sch. Law, 1972-75; ptnr. Satterfield & Allred, Jackson, 1976-90, Thomas, Price, Alston, Jones & Davis, Jackson, 1990-92; Allred & Donaldson, 1992-96; gen. counsel Am. Pub. Life Ins. Co., Jackson, 1980-96 , Miss. Republican Party, 1978-93. articles editor Miss. Law Jour., 1969-70. Mem. exec. com. Nat. Young Rep. Fedn., 1968-70, state chmn. Miss. Young Rep. Fedn., 1968-72, mem. coun. legal advisers Rep. Nat. Com., 1982-96. Served to capt. F.A., U.S. Army Res., 1968-71. Fellow Am. Bar Found.; mem. ABA (standing com. on aero law 1977-83), Miss. State Bar, Am. Judicature Soc., Ind. Petroleum Assn. of Am., Aviation Ins. Assn., Mid-Continent Oil and Gas Assn., Hinds County Bar Assn., Jackson C. of C., Phi Delta Phi, Omicron Delta Kappa. Methodist.

ALLSHOUSE, MERLE FREDERICK, educational organization administrator; b. Pitts., Apr. 26, 1935; s. Merle Lawrence and Helen (Frederick) A.; m. Myrna Mansfield, Apr. 1, 1956; children: Frederick Scott, Kimberly Dawn. B.A. (Rector fellow), DePauw U., 1957; M.A. (Rockefeller Theol. fellow), Yale, 1959, Ph.D. (Rockefeller fellow 1959-61, Kent fellow 1961), 1965. Instr. philosophy Dickinson Coll., 1963-65, asst. prof., 1965-68, assoc. dean of coll., assoc. prof. philosophy, 1968-70; dean of coll., prof. philosophy Bloomfield (N.J.) Coll., 1970-71, pres., 1971-86; pres. Myron Stratton Home Found., Colorado Springs, Colo., 1986-88; prof. publ adminstr. Grad. Sch. Pub. Affairs, U. Colo., 1988; v.p. U. Colo. Found., 1989-94; exec. dir. Acad. Sr. Profls., Eckerd Coll., St. Petersburg, Fla., 1994—; Mem. N.J. Student Assistance Bd. Bd. dirs. Presbyn. Career and Counseling Ctr., N.J. Coll. Fund, Inc., Colo. Children's Campaign-The Goodwill of Colorado Springs, The Colorado Springs Symphony Orch., Coun. Ind. Colls., N.E. region Boy Scouts Am., Colorado Springs Symphony Orch., The Broadmoor Improvement Soc.; pres., Beth El Coll. Nursing, Goodwill of Colorado Springs; moderator Broadmoor Community Ch.; div. chmn. United Way; mem. Da Vinci Quartet; trustee Montclair Kimberley Acad.; pres. Presbyn. Coll. Union. HEW fellow, 1979-80. Mem. Metaphys. Soc. Am., Am. Philos. Assn., Am. Acad. Religion, Assn. Ind. Colls. and Univs. in N.J. (dir., chmn. bd.), Nat. Assn. Ind. Colls. and Univs. (chmn. secretariat 1983-86, bd. dirs.), Council Ind. Colls. (bd. dirs.), St. Petersburg Rotary. Home: College Landings 15 Crescent Pl S Saint Petersburg FL 33711-5118 Office: Acad Sr Prof Eckerd Coll 4200 54th Ave S Saint Petersburg FL 33711-4744

ALLSHOUSE, ROBERT HAROLD, history educator; b. Erie, Pa., Apr. 30, 1940; s. Harold and Anne Marie (Dranzek) A.; m. Marcia Catherine Windsor, Aug. 17, 1963; children: Lisa Catherine, Heather A. Kenny, Todd Anthony. BBA, Cleve. State U., 1963; MA, Case Western Res. U., 1965, PhD, 1967. Instr. Russian history Alliance Coll., Cambridge Springs, Pa., 1966-67; instr. Russian history Gannon U., Erie, 1967-70, asst. prof., 1970-77, assoc. prof., 1977-82, prof., 1982—, chmn. dept. history, 1981-89, grad. dir. social sci., 1977-96; sec., treas. Gt. Lakes Pen Sales, Inc., Erie, 1976-98; pres. Allegheny Internat. Devel. Inc., Erie, 1990—; sec., treas. Pennfoil Tech. Inc., Erie, 1993—; vis. prof. Latvian State U., Riga, 1991; mem. fgn. trade com. Erie Excellence Coun., 1992—. Author: Aleksander Izvolskii and Russian Foreign Policy, 1910-1914, 1977; editor: A Select Bibliography of Military History Since 1715, 1977, Photographs for the Tsar, 1980 (Photog. Soc. N.Y. Merit award 1980); gen. editor A Centennial History of the Erie Yacht Club, 1996. Mem. adv. bd. United Way, Erie, 1989—, Erie County Historic Preservation Bd., 1983—; pres. Erie Mus. Authority, 1985-87; bd. trustees Flagship Niagara League, 1998—, sec., 1999—. Recipient Cmty. Edn. award Erie Sch. Dist., 1986, All Russian State TV award Russian State TV Co., Moscow, 1991, cert. of honor Assn. Ind. Video Prodrs., Russia, 1991, cert. of leadership All Union Inst. TV/Radio Broadcasting, Moscow, 1991, cert. of appreciation SAR, 1992. Fellow Phi Alpha Theta, Pi Gamma Mu; mem. Internat. Order Blue Gavel, Erie C. of C., Rotary Internat., Erie Yacht Club (fleet capt. 1988-89, rear commodore 1989-90, vice commodore 1990-91, commodore 1991-92, svc. award 1992). Avocations: sailing, travel. Office: Gannon U Perry Sq Erie PA 16541

ALLUKIAN, MYRON, JR., government administrator, public health educator, dental educator; b. Cambridge, Mass., Jan. 6, 1939; s. Myron and Mary (Nahabedian) A.; m. Ruth Felice Losco, Oct. 11, 1975; children: Myron III, Kristin, Alison, Jason, Alexandra, Nathan. BS in Psychology, Tufts U., 1960; DDS, U. Pa., 1964; MPH, Harvard U., Boston, 1967. Chief dental health Bunker Hill Health Ctr., Mass. Gen. Hosp., Boston, 1969-77; dir. and asst. dep. commr. cmty. dental programs Boston Dept. Health and Hosps., 1970-96, dir. personal health svcs., 1991-93; dir. cmty. dental programs Boston Pub. Health Commn., 1996—; assoc. vis. dentist Boston City Hosp., 1970-96, Boston Med. Ctr., 1996—; lectr. Georgetown U. Sch. Dentistry, 1979-89, Tufts Sch. Dental Medicine, 1994—, U. Mass. Sch. Pub. Health, 1984-93, U. Minn. Sch. Pub. Health, 1981-92, Forsyth Sch. for Dental Hygienists, Boston, 1970—, Boston U. Dental Sch., 1977—, Mich. Sch. Pub. Health, Ann Arbor, 1980—; assoc. clin. prof. Sch. Dental Medicine, Harvard U., 1977—, lectr. Sch. Pub. Health, 1991—; regional cons. Job Corps, U.S. Dept. Labor, New Eng., 1973-98; corp. mem. Mass. Dental Svc. Corp., 1971-79; vis. prof. Columbia U. Sch. Dentistry, N.Y.C., 1991, mem., 1978-88; chmn., sec. Mass. Bd. Registration in Dentistry, 1980-86; mem. Am. Bd. Dental Pub. Health, treas., 1991-92, v.p., 1992-93, pres., 1993-94, diplomate, 1973—; adj. prof. Boston U. Sch. Pub. Health, 1997—. Mem. editl. adv. com. Nation's Health, 1991-92; mem. editorial bd. Am. Jour. Pub. Health, 1979-82, Jour. Pub. Health Dentistry, 1985-89; editorial cons. Jour. Pub. Health Policy, 1985—; contbr. over 100 articles and abstracts to profl. jours., chpts. to books. Chmn. U.S. Surgeon Gen.'s Work Group on Fluoridation and Dental Health, 1990, Prevention Objectives for The Nation, 1978-80; mem. healthy people 2010, oral health work group, 1997—, tobacco control work group U.S. Dept. Health and Human Svcs., 1998—; reviewer U.S. Surgeon Gen.'s report on oral health, 1998—; mem. nat. dental tobacco-free steering com. Nat. Cancer Inst., 1989—; corp. mem. Boston Young Men's Christian Union, 1974—; clin. dental dir. New England AIDS Edn. and Tng. Ctr., 1991—, Northeast Regional Bd. Dental Examiners, mem., 1978—, steering com., 1980-86; adv. com. Boston Health Care for The Homeless, 1992-96, Nat. Bd. Examiners in Optometry, examination com., 1992-97, chair pub. health/clin.- legal issues com., 1994-96, Harvard Sch. Pub. Health Alumni Assn. Coun., 1992—, pres.- elect 1993-95, pres., 1995-97, Mass. "Assist", 1991-93, chmn. Statewide Tobacco Control Planning Com., 1992, Pub. Health Mus. Mass., bd. dirs., 1992—, pres., 1993-94, cons. commn. dental accreditation Am. Dental Assn., 1996—; accreditation reviewer Coun. Edn. for Pub. Health, 1996—; bd. dirs. Urban Health Project, Harvard Med. Sch., 1996—. Lt. Dental Corps, USN, 1964-66, Vietnam, 3rd Marine Divsn. FMF, 1965. Recipient cert. of appreciation U.S. Dept. Labor, 1981, Community Svc. award Health Planning Coun. Greater Boston, 1986, Disting. Faculty award Harvard Sch. Dental Medicine, 1986, Disting. Alumni award, 1996, Alumni Merit award U. Pa. Dental Sch., 1987, Exemplary Svc. award USPHS, 1990, 97, Vision Svc. award Mass. Soc. Optometrists, 1992, Outstanding Achievement award Armenian-Am. Behavioral Sci. Assn., 1995, Kabakjian Sci. award Armenian Students Assn., 1999; postdoctoral rsch. fellow meritorious Harvard Sch. Dental Medicine, 1969. Fellow Royal Soc. Health (hon.), Internat. Coll. Dentists; mem. APHA (pres. 1989-90, John W. Knutson award 1998), Inst. Medicine of NAS (com. educating dentists for the future 1992-93), Am. Assn. Pub. Health Dentistry (pres. 1984-85, spl. merit award 1987), Mass. Pub. Health Assn. (pres. 1977-78, Disting. Svc. citation 1988), Mass. Health Coun. (pres. 1977-78, ann. award 1989), Armenian-Am. Dental Soc. (pres. 1982-84, trustee 1985—, founding mem. 1978), Harvard Alumni Assn. (bd. dirs. 1997—). Office: Community Dental Programs 1010 Massachusetts Ave Boston MA 0218-2600

ALLUMS, HENRIENE, elementary education educator; b. Jackson, Miss., July 30, 1945; d. Henry and Annie (Johnson) A. BA, Calif. State U., Long Beach, 1967; MA, U. San Francisco, 1978. Cert. elem., secondary tchr., Calif., ESL tchr., cross cultural, language and acad. devel. tchr. Tchr., grades 1-3 L.A. Unified Sch. Dist. Mem. Calif. Assn. bilingual Edn., Calig. Tchrs. English to Speakers of Other Langs., Internat. Reading Assn., Tchrs. English to Speakers of Other Langs. Home: 1522 E 123rd St Los Angeles CA 90059-2920

ALLUMS, JAMES A., retired cardiovascular surgeon; b. Kountze, Tex., Sept. 28, 1937; m. Elizabeth Dee Walton, June 24, 1961; children: Ann Elizabeth, Sarah Dee, Benjamin Walton. BA, U. Tex., 1959; MD, U. Tex. Med. Br., 1962. Diplomate Am. Bd. Med. Examiners, Am. Bd. Surgery, Am. Bd. Thoracic Surgery, Am. Bd. Gen. Vascular Surgery. Rotating intern Phila. Gen. Hosp., 1962-63; resident gen. surgery Med. Br. U. Tex., Galveston, 1963-66, 68-69; ptnr. Thoracic and Cardiovascular Surg. Assocs., Beaumont, Tex., 1971-97; clin. asst. prof. dept. thoracic and cardiovascular surgery U. Tex. Med. Br., Galveston, ret., 1997; active physician St. Elizabeth Hosp., chief of staff 1976-77, 87-88; active Beaumont, Bapt. Hosp. of S.E. Tex., Beaumont, Beaumont Regional Med. Ctr., Beaumont Regional Med. Ctr., Park Place Hosp.; courtesy staff St. Mary Hosp., Port Arthur, Mid Jefferson Hosp., Nederland, Tex.; cons. staff U. Tex. Med. Br. Hosp., Galveston; mem. cardiovascular com. Bapt. Hosp., 1991-93, 1996, physician, nurse ad hoc com., 1992; clin. asst. prof. Dept. of Surgery U. Tex. Med. Br. Hosp., 1993-94; OR com. St. Elizabeth Hosp., Beaumont, 1990-91, 93-94, cardiovascular quality assurance subcom., 1991-92, cardiovascular/coronary care com., 1990-91, 92-93, CCU quality assurance subcom. Contbr. articles to profl. jours. Capt. U.S. Army, 1966-68. Recipient J.C. Crager award Am. Heart Assn., 1992, Mr. East Tex. award Tyler County Dogwood Festival, 1993. Fellow ACS (gov. 1989-94, pres. South Tex. chpt. 1987), Am. Coll. of Angiology, Am. Coll. of Cardiology, Am. Coll. of Chest Physicians, Beaumont Acad. of Medicine; mem. AMA, Assn. of Am. Physicians and Surgeons, Bapt. Hosp. P.H.O., Beaumont Regional P.H.O., Jefferson County Med. Soc., Singleton Surg. Soc., Soc. of Thoracic Surgeons, So. Assn. for Vascular Surgery, So. Med. Assn., So. Thoracic Surg. Assn., St. Elizabeth Hosp. P.H.O., Tex. Med. Assn. (coun. on med. edn. 1985-92), Tex. Surg. Soc., Alumni Assn. of the U. of Tex. Med. Br. (pres. 1984-85)Phi Eta Sigma, Alpha Epsilon Delta.

ALM, ALVIN LEROY, retired technical services executive; b. Denver, Jan. 27, 1937; s. Emil and Minnie (Lentz) A.; m. Ronnie Marie Elwell, Sept. 10, 1979 (div.); 1 child, Jessica. BA, U. Denver, 1960; MPA, Syracuse U., 1961. Various positions U.S. Bur. Budget (name now Office Mgmt. and Budget), Washington, 1963-70; staff dir. Coun. on Environ. Quality, Washington, 1970-73; asst. adminstr. for planning and mgmt. EPA, Washington, 1973-77, dep. adminstr., 1983-85, chair com. on rsch. strategics Sci. Adv. Bd.; asst. sec. policy and evaluation U.S. Dept. Energy, Washington, 1977-79; dir. energy security program Harvard U., Cambridge, Mass., 1979-83; chief exec. officer, chmn. bd. Thermo Analytical, Waltham, Mass., 1985-87; pres., chief exec. officer Alliance Techs. Corp., Bedford, Mass., 1987-89; sr. v.p. for energy and environ. Sci. Applications Internat. Corp., San Diego, 1989-96, also bd. dirs.; asst. sec. environ. mgmt. Dept. Energy, Washington, 1996-98; exec. v.p. Columbus Group Energy and Environ. Consulting, 1998—; mem. sci. adv. bd. EPA. Recipient Arthur S. Fleming award, 1975. Mem. Nat. Acad. Pub. Adminstrn., Ctr. for Excellence in Govt., Ctr. for Hazardous Materials Rsch. (bd. dirs.).

ALM, STEVE, prosecutor; m. Haunani Ho; 1 child. MEd, U. Oreg., 1979; JD, U. Pacific, 1983. Editor West Pub. Co., 1983-85; dep. prosecuting atty. City and County of Honolulu, 1985-87, line-dep., then felony team supr., 1987-90, dir. dist. and family ct. divsn., 1990-94; U.S. atty. for Hawaii U.S. Dept. Justice, Honolulu, 1994—; adj. prof. Richardson Sch. Law U. Hawaii. Mem. ABA (mem. gov. com. on crime), Hawaii State Bar Assn. (ex-officio mem. domestic violence coordinating coun., v.p. criminal justice and corrections sect.). Office: US Dept Justice Box 50183 300 Ala Moana Blvd Rm 6-100 Honolulu HI 96850-0001*

AL-MARAYATI, ABID A., political science educator; b. Baghdad, Iraq, Oct. 14, 1931; came to U.S,. 1949; s. Amin Hussien and Badriah (Haj Ghazi) Al-M.; 1 child, Ghazi Daniel. BA, Bradley U., 1952, MA, 1954; PhD, NYU, 1959. Instr. U. Mass., Boston, 1960-62; assoc. prof. SUNY, Plattsburgh, 1962-64, Ariz. State U., Tempe, 1965-68; prof. emeritus U. Toledo, 1968—; vis. prof. Beijing Fgn. Studies U., spring 1991; lectr. Beijing U., Fudan U., Shanghai Inst. for Internat. Studies, Fgn. Affairs Coll.; guest lectr. univs. in Australia and New Zealand, summer 1990; commentator radio and TV programs in U.S. and abroad; liaison officer U.S. Com. for UN U.; panelist Mid. East Inst. Conf. on the Mid. East and the UN, 1965, Rocky Mountain Social Sci. Assn., 1968, Bowling Green U., 1969, Peace Sci. Soc., 1973, U. Houston, 1973; cons. com. on internat. rels. Group for Advancement of Psychiatry; chairperson, panelist numerous ann. meetings including Internat. Studies Assn., Duquesne History Foru, Comparative and Internat. Edn. Soc., Midwest Regional Meeting, Midwest Polit. Sci. Assn., Mid. East Studies Assn., Acad. Coun. on the UN Sys., 1976—; rschr., lectr. Soviet Acad. Scis. and Internat. Rsch. and Exch. Bd. under the U.S.-U.S.S.R. Ednl. Exch. Program, summer 1974. Author: A Diplomatic History of Modern Iraq, 1961, Middle Eastern Constitutions and Electoral Laws, 1968, The Middle East: Its Government and Politics, 1972; editor: International Relations of the Middle East and North Africa, 1985; contbr. articles to profl. jours. Mem. Dem. Orgn.; trustee Toledo Coun. World Affairs. Recipient Key to Golden Door City of Toledo, 1984; fellow Rockefeller Found., Ella Lyman Cabot Trust, Carl and Lilly Pforzheimer Found., U. Toledo, Am. Philos. Soc.; grantee NYU Rsch. Found., Ariz. State U., U. Toledo. Mem. NAACP, Assn. Student Edn., World Assn. Former UN Interns and Fellows (bd. dirs.), Popular Culture Assn., Midwest Internat. Studies Assn., Assn. for Advancement of Policy, Am. Cultural Assn., Inst. for Oriental Studies (Moscow and St. Petersburg), Arab Polit. Thought Forum (Jordan), Bus. Adminstrn. Assn., Gulf Ctr. for Strategic Studies (London), Inst. for Psychiatry and Fgn. Affairs, Group for Advancement of Psychiatry, Am. Polit. Sci. Assn., Internat. Studies Assn., Mid. East Studies Assn. N.Am., Mid. East Inst., Phi Kappa Phi. Muslim-Shi'ite. Avocations: swimming, walking, exercising, reading. Home: 2109 Terrace Vw W Toledo OH 43607-1066

ALMEIDA, JOSÉ AGUSTÍN, romance languages educator; b. Waco, Tex., Aug. 28, 1933; s. Jesse M. and Teodora (Mancillas) A.; m. Maritza Barros, Sept. 5, 1964; 1 son, José Rodolfo. BA, Baylor U., 1961; MA, U. Mo., 1964, PhD, 1967. Teaching asst. U. Mo., Columbia, 1961-66; instr. Baylor U., Waco, 1962-63; asst. prof. dept. Romance langs. U. N.C., Greensboro, 1966-77, assoc. prof., 1977—, chmn. Latin Am. studies, 1979-81; vis. prof. Elmira (N.Y.) Coll., summer 1967; asst. prof. Inst. in Mid. Am., summers 1968-69, Cali, Colombia, summer 1973; assoc. prof. study abroad program U. N.C.-Greensboro-Guilford Coll., Madrid, 1980, dir. grad. studies in Spanish, 1991-95; cons. verbal-active teaching method Hampton Inst., 1976, 77, U. N.C.-Charlotte, 1984; lectr. 1st Internat. Conf. Picaresque Lit., Madrid, 1976, 6th Conf. Internat. Assn. Hispanists, 1977, 1st Internat. Conf. on Lope de Vega, 1980. Author: (with Stephen C. Mohler and Robert R. Stinson) Descubrir y crear, 1976, 3d edit., 1986; La crítica literaria de Fernando de Herrera, 1976. With USAF, 1953-57. Nat. Endowment for Humanities fellow, 1970. Mem. MLA, Am. Assn. Tchrs. Spanish and Portuguese, Internat. Assn. Hispanists, Cervantes Soc. Am., Asociación de Cervantistas, Sigma Delta Pi (faculty sponsor 1989—). Democrat. Roman Catholic. Home: 1410 Valleymede Rd Greensboro NC 27410-3938

ALMEIDA, MICHAEL JAMES, philosophy educator; b. Fall River, Mass., Jan. 16, 1958; s. Gilbert and Philomena (Botelo) A.; m. Yvette Salazar. BA, Bridgewater State Coll., 1982; PhD, The Ohio State Univ., 1988. Vis. asst. prof. Univ. Memphis, Memphis, Tenn., 1988-89, Univ. Wis., Oshkosh, Wis., 1989-90; asst. prof. Univ. Tex., San Antonio, 1990-96, assoc. prof., 1996—. Contbr. articles to profl. jours. Mem. Am. Philosophical Assn., Internat. Philosophy Honor Soc., Southwestern Philosophical Soc., Soc. for Philosophy & Psychology, Southern Soc. Philosophy & Psychology, Phi Sigma Tau. Office: Univ Tex Dept Philosophy San Antonio TX 78249

ALMEIDA, ONÉSIMO TEOTÓNIO, foreign language educator; b. Pico da Pedra, S. Miguel, Azores, Portugal, Dec. 18, 1946; came to U.S., 1972; s. Manuel Francisco and Marcolina Estrela (Pereira) A.; m. Mary Tsangarakis, July 20, 1974 (div. Dec. 1991); 1 child, Tatyana; m. Leonor Isabel Goncalves Simas, Nov. 28, 1992; children: Fernando Pedro, Duarte Filipe. BA, Portuguese Cath. U., Lisbon, 1972; MA, Brown U., Providence, 1977, PhD, 1980. Asst. prof. Brown U., Providence, 1980-86, assoc. prof., 1986-91, prof., 1991—, chmn. dept. Portuguese Brazilian Studies, 1991—; prodr., moderator cultural program Whaling City Cable-TV, 1979—; vis. prof. U. Azores, Portugal, U. Calif., Santa Barbara, U. Mass., Dartmouth, New U., Lisbon, Portugal; lectr. throughout U.S.A. and many countries; dir. Gavea-Brown Publs., Providence, 1980—; exec. bd. Watson Inst. Internat. Studies, Providence, 1994—, R.I. Com. for Humanities, Providence, 1994—. Author: Ah! Monim Dum Corisco!, 1978, (Sapa) Teia Americana, 1983, Mensagem-Tent. de Reint., Derein, 1986, Que Nome é Esse o Nezimo?, 1994, Rio Atlantico, 1997, others; co-editor Gavea-Brown Jour., 1980—; contbr. articles to profl. jours; mem. bd. Portuguese Studies, Santa Barbara Portuguese Studies, Portuguese Literary and Cultural Studies, Veredas. Bd. mem. Portuguese-Am. Congress, Fall River, Mass., 1984-94, Family Svcs., Providence, 1982-86, Portuguese Youth Cultural Orgn., Fall River, 1976-88; bd. mem., v.p. Casa Dos Acores New Eng., East Providence, R.I., 1990-94. Recipient award of excellence Portuguese-U.S.A. C. of C., 1997; named officer Prince Henry Order Pres. of Portugal, Lisbon, 1997; libr. reading rm. named after him, P. Pedra Azores, Portugal, 1997. Mem. Am. Philos. Assn., Am. Assn. Tchrs. Spanish and Portuguese, Internat. Soc. Value Inquiry, Portuguese Writers Assn., Azorean Cultural Inst., Soc. for Study European Ideas. Home: 282 Rochambeau Ave Providence RI 02906-3514 Office: Brown U 159 George St Providence RI 02912-9041

ALMEIDA, RICHARD JOSEPH, finance company administrator; b. N.Y.C., Apr. 29, 1942; s. Caetano Escudero and Grace (Maya) A.; m. Jill Farris, Mar. 17, 1979; 1 child, Alexis Ferris. BA in Internat. Affairs, George Washington U., 1963; MA in Internat. Adminstrn., Syracuse U., 1965. Comml. and internat. banker Citibank, N.Y. and South Am., 1966; area head comml. and internat. banking Citicorp/Citibank, Chgo., 1976, L.A., 1978-84; dep. strategic planning Citicorp/Citibank, N.Y.C., 1984; head fin. inst. and investment banking Citicorp Investment Bank, N.Y.C., 1985-87; CFO Heller Fin., Inc., Chgo., 1987—, also bd. dirs.; chmn., CEO Heller Fin., Inc and Heller Internat., Inc., 1995—; bd. dirs. Fuji Bank & Trust, N.Y.C., Fuji Securities, Inc.,Chgo. Youth Programs. Trustee, treas. The Latin Sch. of Chgo. With USCG, 1966-72. Mem. Chgo. Club, The Casino. Roman Catholic. Office: Heller Fin Inc 500 W Monroe St Chicago IL 60661-3630*

ALMEN, LOWELL GORDON, church official; b. Grafton, N.D., Sept. 25, 1941; s. Paul Orville and Helen Eunice (Johnson) A.; m. Sally Arlyn Clark, Aug. 14, 1965; children: Paul Simon, Cassandra Gabrielle. BA, Concordia Coll., Moorhead, Minn., 1963; MDiv, Luther Theol. Sem., St. Paul, 1967; LittD (hon.), Capital U., 1981; DD (hon.), Carthage Coll., 1989, Concordia Coll., 1994. Ordained to ministry Luth. Ch., 1967. Pastor St. Peter's Luth. Ch., Dresser, Wis., 1967-69; asso. campus pastor, dir. communications Concordia Coll., Moorhead, Minn., 1969-74; mng. editor Luth. Standard ofcl. publ. Am. Luth. Ch., Mpls., 1974-78; editor Luth. Standard, 1979-87; sec., officer Evangelical Luth. Ch. Am., Chgo., 1987—. Author: Old Songs for a New Journey, 1990, One Great Cloud of Witnesses, 1997; author, co-editor: The Many Faces of Pastoral Ministry, 1989; editor: World Religions and Christian Mission, 1967, Our Neighbor's Faith, 1968. Recipient Disting. Alumnus award Concordia Coll., 1982; Bush Found. grantee, 1972. Office: Evang Luth Ch 8765 W Higgins Rd Chicago IL 60631-4101

ALMES, JUNE, retired education educator, librarian; b. Pitts., Feb. 14, 1934; d. Donald John Rowbottom and Marie Catherine (Linz) Douglas; widowed; children: Lawrence John, Douglas Alan. BS in Edn., Ind. U. of Pa., 1955; MLS, U. Pitts., 1969. Tchr. Shippensburg (Pa.) Area High Sch., 1964-68; assoc. prof. Lock Haven (Pa.) U., 1971-94; ret., 1990; instr. Changsha U. Electric Power, Hunan, China, 1989-90, 95. Trustee Ross Pub. Libr., Lock Haven, 1975-88, community story programs, 1973-86; tutor Clinton City Literacy Found., Lock Haven, 1979. Mem. Am. Assn. Sch. Librs., Pa. Assn. Sch. Librs., ACLU, Phi Kappa Phi, Phi Delta Kappa. Democrat. Avocations: playing bridge, reading, travel, literacy. Home: 228 Hillside Dr Lock Haven PA 17745-1733

ALMON, RENEAU PEARSON, state supreme court justice; b. Moulton, Ala., July 8, 1937; s. Nathaniel Lee and Mary (Johnson) A.; m. Deborah Pearson Preer, June 27, 1974; children by previous marriage: Jonathan, Jason, Nathaniel; 1 stepson: Tommy Preer. B.S., U. Ala., 1959; LL.B., Cumberland Sch. Law Samford U., 1964. Bar: Ala. 1964. Price analyst NASA; law clk. to justice Ala. Supreme Ct.; sole practice Moulton; judge 36th Jud. Circuit Ala., 1966-69, Ala. Ct. Criminal Appeals, 1969-75; justice Ala. Supreme Ct., Montgomery, 1974—. Served with U.S. Army. Named one of Outstanding Young Men in Am., 1971. Mem. ABA, Ala. Bar Assn., Lawrence County Bar Assn., Montgomery County Bar Assn., Kappa Alpha, Phi Alpha Delta, Omicron Delta Kappa. Methodist. Office: Ala Supreme Ct 300 Dexter Ave Montgomery AL 36104-3741*

ALMOND, CARL HERMAN, surgeon, physician, educator; b. Latour, Mo., Apr. 1, 1926; s. Hugh Herman and Sylvia (Morrison) A.; m. Nancy Ginn, June 18, 1964 (div. 1990); children: Carrie, Callie, Carl, Christopher. BS, Washington U., St. Louis, 1949, MD, 1953. Diplomate: Am. Bd. Surgery, Am. Bd. Thoracic Surgery. Rotating intern Los Angeles County Gen. Hosp., 1953-54; resident surgery U. Mich., Ann Arbor, 1954-56, jr. clin. instr. surgery, 1956-57, sr. clin. instr., 1957-58; fellow surg. pathology Barnes Hosp.-Washington U., St. Louis, 1956; sr. surg. resident in urology Baylor U. Affiliated Hosps., 1958-59; resident thoracic surgery U. So. Calif., Los Angeles, 1959, fellow thoracic surgery, 1962-63; staff surgeon Univ. Hosp., Columbia, Mo., 1959-78, dir. thoracic and cardiovascular surgery, 1968-77; dir. thoracic and cardiovascular surgery VA Hosp., Columbia; fellow Brompton Hosp., London, Eng., 1961; asst. prof. surgery U. Mo. Sch. Medicine, Columbia, 1959-64, assoc. prof., 1964-69, prof., chief thoracic and cardiovascular surgery, from 1969; prof. and chmn. dept. surgery Sch. Medicine, U. S.C., Columbia, 1978-85, dir. gen. surgery residency program, 1979-85, assoc. dean clin. research and devel., 1986-90; vis. prof. U. Geneva, Switzerland, 1972-73; Mem. med. adv. panel FAA, 1970-75; mem. U.S. Commn. on UNESCO, 1983. Contbr. articles to profl. jours. Served with USNR, 1944-52. Fellow A.C.S.; mem. AMA, Boone County Med. Soc., Columbia Med. Soc., S.C. Med. Assn., S.C. Thoracic Soc., Am. Assn. Med. Colls., Frederick H. Coller Surg. Soc., St. Louis Surg. Soc., Am. Coll. Cardiology, Am., S.C. heart assns., Am. Soc. Artificial Internal Organs, Soc. Med. Cons. to Armed Forces, Am. Coll. Chest Physicians, So. Thoracic Surg. Assn., Central Surg. Soc., Am. Assn. Thoracic Surgery, So. Surg. Assn., S.C. Surg. Soc., Chest Club, Soc. Surg. Chairmen, Marion S. DeWeese Surg. Soc., Southeastern Surg. Soc., So. Surg. Soc., Internat. Cardiovascular Soc., Soc. Thoracic Surgeons, Sigma Xi, Nu Sigma Nu, Sigma Chi. Home: 2831 Gervais St Columbia SC 29204-2329 Office: U SC Sch Medicine Dept Surgery Two Medical Park/Ste 300 Columbia SC 29203

ALMOND, DAVID RANDOLPH, lawyer, company executive; b. Richmond, Va., Mar. 8, 1940. BS, U. Va., 1962, LLB, 1967; postgrad. in Exec. Program, MIT, 1981. Assoc. Reid & Priest, N.Y.C., 1967-71; asst. gen. counsel Boise Cascade Corp., Idaho, 1971-77, assoc. gen. counsel and asst. sec., 1977-84; sr. v.p. Wilson Foods Corp., Oklahoma City, 1985-89; sr. v.p., gen. counsel, sec. Fleming Cos. Inc., Oklahoma City, 1989—. Fellow Am. Bar Found. (life); mem. ABA, Okla. Bar Assn., N.Y. State Bar Assn. Bar Assn. Office: Fleming Cos Inc 6301 Waterford Blvd Oklahoma City OK 73118-1198

ALMOND, GABRIEL ABRAHAM, political science educator; b. Rock Island, Ill., Jan. 12, 1911; s. David Moses and Lisa (Elson) A.; m. Maria Dorothea Kaufmann, Apr. 29, 1937; children: Richard J., Peter O., Susan J. PhB, U. Chgo., 1932, PhD, 1938. Fellow Social Sci. Research Council, 1935-36, 46; instr. polit. sci. Bklyn. Coll., 1939-42; with OWI, Washington, 1942-44, War Dept., ETO, 1945; research assoc. Yale U. Inst. Internat. Studies, 1947-49, assoc. prof. polit. sci., 1949-51, prof. polit. sci., 1959-63; assoc. prof. internat. affairs Princeton, 1951-54, prof., 1954-57, prof. politics, 1957-59; prof. polit. sci. Stanford, 1963-76, exec. head dept. polit. sci., 1964-68; prof. emeritus, 1976; cons. Air U., 1948, Dept. State, 1950, Office Naval Rsch., 1951, Rand Corp., 1954-55, sci. adv. bd. USAF, 1960-61; vis. prof. U. Tokyo, Japan, 1962, Kiev State U., USSR, 1989; Overseas fellow Churchill Coll. U. Cambridge, 1972-73; vis. fellow Australian Nat. U., 1983. Author: The American People and Foreign Policy, 1950, The Appeals of Communism, 1954, (with others) The Struggle for Democracy in Germany, 1949, The Politics of the Developing Areas, 1960, (with Sidney Verba) The Civic Culture, 1963, (with G. Bingham Powell) Comparative Politics, 1966, Political Development, 1970, (with others) Crisis, Choice and Change, 1973, Comparative Politics Today, 1974, 80, 84, 88, 92, 96, (with G. Bingham Powell) Comparative Politics: System, Process, Policy, 1978, (with Sidney Verba and others) The Civic Culture Revisited, 1980, (with others) Progress and its Discontents, 1982, A Discipline Divided, Schools and Sects in Political Science, 1990, Comparative Politics: A Theoretical Approach, 1996, (with G. Bingham Powell) Plutocracy and Politics in New York City, 1998, (with others) European Politics Today, 1999. Recipient Travel and Study award Ford Found., 1962-63; fellow Center for Advanced Study in the Behavioral Scis., 1956-57; sr. fellow Nat. Endowment for Humanities, 1972-73. Fellow Am. Acad. Arts and Scis.; mem. Nat. Acad. Scis., Am. Philos. Soc., Social Sci. Research Council (bd. dirs., chmn. com. comparative politics), Am. Polit. Sci. Assn. (pres. 1965-66, James Madison award 1981, Frank Goodnow award). Home: 4135 Old Trace Rd Palo Alto CA 94306-3728 Office: Stanford Univ Politic Sci Dept Stanford CA 94305

ALMOND, GILES KEVIN, accountant, financial planner; b. Albemarle, N.C., June 16, 1956; s. Horace David and Helen Ruth (Hauser) A.; m. Anita Elizabeth Lanier, Oct. 21, 1978; children: Cassandra, Kevin, Alice. BS in Acctg., U. N.C., Wilmington, 1978. CPA, N.C., S.C.; CFP; PFS. Revenue agt. IRS, Dothan, Ala., 1978-82; acct. Brittain, Almond & Simpson, P.A., Charlotte, N.C., 1982-87; sr. tax mgr. Nasekos, Ryan and Co. CPAs, Charlotte, 1987-90; pres. Matrix Fin. Mgmt. Cons., Charlotte, 1990—; mem. N.C. Bd. CPA Examiners, Raleigh, 1986-89; mem. steering com. Queens Coll. Estate Planners Day; chmn. ednl. needs analysis task force Internat. Bd. Standards and Practices for Cert. Fin. Planners, 1992-94. Mem. council Cen. Ch. God, Charlotte, 1986—. Fellow N.C. Assn. CPA; mem. AICPA, Nat. Assn. Personal Fin. Advisors, Fellowship Christian Fin. Advisors, Inst. CFPs, Charlotte Estate Planning Coun. Republican. Office: 930 East Blvd Charlotte NC 28203-5204

ALMOND, JOAN, retired chemist; b. Bklyn., May 19, 1934; d. Harry Christian Nintzel and Helen Pauline (Diviak) Levesen; m. Randall Leroy Field Sr., Nov. 15, 1952 (div. Feb. 1972); children: Randall Leroy Jr., Roland, Gary, Brian, Lorraine, Thomas; m. Bransford Wayne Almond, Dec. 9, 1986 (div. Apr. 1993). Grad. high sch., Bklyn. Sec. Fulton Savs. Bank, Bklyn., 1952-53; mgr. reprodn. Air Pre-heater Corp., Wellsville, N.Y., 1958; chemistry technician fibers div. Allied Chem., Hopewell, Va., 1963-76; chemistry technician Va. Power Co.-North Anna Power Sta., Mineral, 1976-86, assoc. instr., 1987-92, sr. chemistry technician, 1992-94, sr. chemistry technician shift leader, 1992-94; ret., 1994; craft shop owner Stuffed Stuff and Other Stuff, Bumpass, Va., 1994—. Recipient cert. of achievement Nat. Acad. for Nuclear Tng., 1988. Mem. Women of Moose (com. chmn. Moosehart Hopewell 1971). Roman Catholic.

ALMOND, LINCOLN, governor, lawyer; b. Central Falls, R.I., 1936. BS, U. R.I.; LLB, Boston U. Bar: R.I., 1962. Adminstr. Town of Lincoln, R.I., 1963-67; U.S. atty. R.I., Dept. Justice, Providence, 1967-78, 81-93; pvt. practice, 1967-69, 78-81; with Blackstone Valley Devel. Found., 1993-95; gov. State of R.I., Providence, 1995—. Office: Office of Gov 115 State House Providence RI 02903

ALMOND, PAUL, film director, producer, writer; b. Montreal, Que., Can., Apr. 26, 1931; s. Eric and Irene Clarice (Gray) A.; m. Joan Elkins, Sept. 11, 1976; 1 son, Matthew James. Student, McGill U., Montreal, 1948-49; B.A., Balliol Coll., Oxford, 1952, M.A., 1954. TV producer-dir. CBC, Toronto, also in Los Angeles, N.Y.C., London, 1954-67; pres. Quest Films, Montreal, 1967—. Writer, producer, dir.; feature films Isabel, 1968 (DGA nomination Best Feature Dir.), Act of the Heart, 1970 (Genie-Best Cand. Dir.), Journey, 1972, Ups and Downs, 1982, The Dance Goes On, 1991; dir. Captive Hearts, 1984; subject of book: (Janet Edsforth) Paul Almond, The Flame Within, 1973; pub. High Hopes, 1999. Recipient Spl. diploma of merit Prague for Seven Up, 1963; Genie as Best Can. TV drama dir., 1980. Mem. Dirs. Guild Am., Dirs. Guild Can. (hon. life), Royal Can. Acad. Arts. Anglican. Home: 54 Malibu Colony Malibu CA 90265-4637

ALMONY, ROBERT ALLEN, JR., librarian, businessman; b. Charleston, W.Va., Oct. 14, 1945; s. Robert Allen and Margaret Elizabeth A.; m. Carol A. Krzeminski, May 6, 1972; children—Robby, Michael, Chandra, Rachel. A.A., Grossmont Coll., 1965; B.A., San Diego State U., 1968; M.L.S., U. Calif.-Berkeley, 1977. Sr. div. clk. San Diego State U. Library, 1965-68; acct. Calif. Tchrs. Fin. Services, Orange County, 1968-70, v.p., gen. mgr., 1971-76; research asst. library sch. U. Calif.-Berkeley, 1976-77; reference librarian Oberlin Coll. Library, Ohio, 1977-79; asst. dir. libraries U. Mo., Columbia, 1980—; owner Almony & Assocs. Tax and Fin. Planning, Columbia, 1980—; distbr. USA Today, Columbia, 1984-88; guest lectr. libr. budgeting; cons. libr. copy svcs.; faculty coun. exec. bd., recorder Mo. U., 1994—, learning strategies tchr., 1986—, adj. faculty Libr. Sch., 1997—. Contbr. articles to profl. jours. Treas. Bahai's of Columbia, 1982-86, 95-97, sec., 1987-89, 93-95, 1998—, chmn., 1989-93; coach Columbia Youth Soccer League, 1981-92; cubmaster Boy Scouts Am., Columbia, 1983-85; asst. scoutmaster, 1985-91; hon. warrior Mic-O-Say, 1986—, treas. Mo. U. Soccer Boosters, 1996—. Mem. ALA, Mo. Libr. Assn. (treas. 1996-97,98—), Assn. Coll. and Rsch. Librs. (exec. com. 1983-86), Libr. Adminstrn. and Mgmt. Assn. (chmn. mem. 1991-93, Outstanding Svc. award 1994, B & F Officers Group Libr. Adminstrn. and Mgmt. (chmn. 1987-91), Nat. Commn. on Ednl. Stats. Integrated Post-Secondary Edn. Data Sys. Acad. Librs. (coord. for Mo. 1992—), Mo. Assn. Coll. and Rsch. Librs (vice chmn., chmn. 1982-84), Hickman Athletic Boosters (pres. 1991-94), Maplewood Barn Theater (bd. dirs. 1993—, sec., treas. 1998—), COE Coll. Parents (bd. dirs. 1993-95). Home: 301 Rothwell Dr Columbia MO 65203-0257 Office: U Mo 104 Ellis Libr Columbia MO 65201-5149 *Be of service to others in everything you do. Become a person of value to others.*

ALMQUIST, DON, illustrator, artist; b. Hartford, Conn., July 21, 1929; s. Nils Herbert and Jeannette Theresa (Perrow) A.; m. Kerstin Rigmor Jesslen, May 21, 1955; children—Kristina, Jan Christian. BFA, R.I. Sch. of Design, 1951. Staff artist Esquire, Inc., N.Y.C., 1951; creative dir. Ahlen & Akerlund, Stockholm, Sweden, 1963-66; adj. prof. Paier Coll. of Art, Hamden, Conn., 1979-84; graphic advisor U.S. Dept. of Fish and Wildlife, Washington, 1981-83. Illustrator: Christmas With Ed Sullivan, 1960, Doomed Road of Empire, 1962, What Did I See?, 1961, Loudmouse, 1962, (new illustrations) 1967, (new edit./illustrations) 1982, Spring is Like the Morning, 1964, Summer is a Very Busy Day, 1967, Dolls from Cheyenne, 1968, Some Animals Are Vary Small, 1968, When Grandmother was Young, 1970, When Great Grandmother was Young, 1971, Getting to Know New York State, 1971, Den Förtrollade Lådan, 1967, It Never Is Dark, 1967, Not Very Much of a House, 1967, Cathy Uncovers a Secret, 1969, Ginnie and the Mystery Light, 1973, Libby Shadows a Lady, 1974, Season at the Point, 1991, The Little Red Hen, 1991, Dragged Abroad, 1998; exhibited paintings and drawings in group and one-man shows New Castle (Del.) Arts Gallery, Ltd., 1991, Springfield Art Mus., 1993, Soc. Devel. en Arts Contemporains, Montreal, Que., Can., 1994; one-man shows include Askersund, Sweden, 1993, Miriam Schiell Fine Arts, Toronto, 1994, Gallery M2, Stockholm, 1995, Gallery Vattern Askersund, Sweden, 1996, Montchanin (Del.) Arts, 1996, New Castle Arts, 1998, Galleri Cafe Lucas, Stockholm, 1999; juried exhbns. include Miss. Watercolor Soc., Miss. Mus. Art, Hoyt Inst. Fine Arts, 1993, Nat. Art Show, New Castle, Pa., La. Art & Artists Guild and River Show, 1993, Aqueous '95 Show, Louisville (Grumbacher golf medal), Charlotte County Art Guild, Punta Gorda, 1997, 98, New Castle Hist. Soc., Kent. Watercolor Soc., 1997. Served as sgt. U.S. Army, 1951-53, Korea. Recipient numerous awards of merit Soc. of Illustrators, N.Y.C., 1953-84, Silver Medal, Phila. Art Dirs., 1955, Gold Medal, Milw. Art Dirs., 1963, numerous awards of merit N.Y. Art Dirs., N.Y.C. Episcopalian. Avocation: horticulture. E-Mail: ARTdonalmq@aol.com. Home and Office: 103 The Strand New Castle DE 19720-4827

ALMQUIST, DONALD JOHN, retired electronics company executive; b. Elwood, Ind., Aug. 30, 1933; s. Elliott John and Gladys Ione (Jones) A.; m. Charline Gail Mull, Dec. 17, 1955; children: Gregory John, Tracy Gail. B in Indsl. Engring., Gen. Motors Inst., 1955. Supr. Delco Remy div. Gen. Motors Co., Anderson, Ind., 1956-64, plant supt., 1964-69, planr mgr., 1969-72, asst. dir. personnel, 1972-74, mgr. mfg., 1974-78, gen. mgr. mfg., 1978-82, gen. mgr., 1982-84; gen. mgr. Delco Electronics div. Gen. Motors Corp., Kokomo, Ind., 1984-86; v.p., gen. mgr. Delco Electronics Corp., Kokomo, 1986-89, chmn., pres., chief exec. officer, 1989-93; exec. v.p. GM Hughes Electronics, 1989-93; bd. dirs. Aladdin Industries LLC, Nashville, Ind. Corp. for Sci. Tech., Indpls., Trinity Cons., Inc., Dallas, Ind. Bus. Modernization and Tech. Corp., Indpls., State Sci. and Tech. Inst., Columbus, Ohio. Bd. trustees Rose Hulman Inst. Tech., Terre Haute, Ind., 1984—; bd. dirs. St. Johns Med. Ctr., Anderson, 1982-84, Ind. Vocat. Tech. Coll., Kokomo, 1984-86, St. Joe Hosp., Kokomo, 1984-86. Mem. Ind. C. of C. (bd. dirs. 1984-93). Methodist. Lodge: Elks. Home: 7249 Lands End Cir Noblesville IN 46060-9416

ALMQUIST, THEODORE C., retired military officer; m. Jolayne B. Swenson; children: Peter, Andrew, Anna. BS, Gustavus Adolphus Coll., 1963; DDS, U. Iowa, 1966; MS, U. Tex., 1972. Dental intern USAF, Lackland AFB, 1966-67; gen. dentist, asst. base dental surgeon USAF, 1967, advanced through grades to asst. surgeon gen. for dental svcs., comdr. 89th med. group, 1995-98; ret., 1998; chmn. TRICARE, 1995—; del. ADA; assoc. prof. U. Tex. Health Scis. Ctr. at Houston Dental Br.; bd. regents adviser Uniformed Svcs. U. Health Scis.; adv. coun. U. Tex. Health Sci. Ctr., San Antonio. Decorations include Legion of Merit, Bronze Star, seven oak leaf clusters. Mem. Air Force Assn., Acad. Operative Dentistry (charter), Acad. Gen. Dentistry (charter), Assn. Mil. Surgeons U.S., Am. Assn. Dental Schs. (Air Force rep. dean's coun.), Psi Omega. Office: 89 MDG/CC 1050 W Perimeter Rd Andrews Air Force Base MD 20762-6601*

ALMY, EARLE VAUGHN, JR. (BUDDY ALMY), real estate executive; b. Fort Worth, July 29, 1930; s. Earle Vaughn and Minnye Ruth (Rounsaville) A.; m. Gorden Yetive McGowan, July 31, 1964 (div. 1967). BS in Animal Husbandry, Tex. Tech. U., 1952; postgrad., Am. Inst. Banking, 1956-62, cert., Realtors Inst., 1977. Cert. real estate brokerage mgr.; accredited land cons.; cert. real estate appraiser, Texas State Certified General Real Estate Appraiser. Credit analyst First Nat. Bank, Fort Worth, 1956-62; dir.finance and poultry feed sales Burrus Feed Mills, Saginaw, Tex., 1963-69; pres., mgr. Almy and Co., Hurst, Tex., 1970-79, Granbury, Tex., 1979—; v.p., dir. Northeast Tarrant County Bd. of Realtors, Hurst, 1972-74; pres. Almy and Co. Realtors, Weatherford, Tex., 1973-78; instr. appraisal of farms and ranches Weatherford Coll., 1986-89. Mem. Fort Worth Farm and Ranch Club; usher Acton United Meth. Ch.; pres. Rep. Club Hood County, 1991. With USAF, 1952-56. Sears Roebuck scholar, 1951. Mem. Nat. Assn. Realtors, Tex. Assn. Realtors, Granbury Assn. Realtors, Nat. Realtors Land Inst., Tex. Realtors Land Inst., Nat. Assn. Real Estate Appraisers (cert. real estate appraiser). Republican. Clubs: Pecan Plantation Country. Avocations: golf, hunting, fishing, boating, swimming. E-mail: almyco@cnews.com. Home: PO Box 129 Granbury TX 76048-0129

ALMY, THOMAS PATTISON, physician, educator; b. N.Y.C., Jan. 10, 1915; s. Don Robinson and Marie (Pattison) A.; m. Katharine Whitin Swift, Nov. 12, 1943; children: Susan, Anne (dec.), Christine. AB, Cornell U., 1935, MD, 1939; MA (hon.), Dartmouth Coll., 1970. Intern N.Y. Hosp., 1939-40, resident in internal medicine, 1940-43; from asst. prof. to prof. medicine Cornell U. Med. Coll., 1946-68; Nathan Smith prof. medicine, chmn. dept. Dartmouth Med. Sch., 1968-73, Third Century prof., 1973-85, prof. medicine and community medicine emeritus, 1985—; disting. physician VA, 1982-85; cons NIH, NRC, Am. Cancer Soc. Author articles in clin. physiology gastrointestinal disease and in med. edn. Recipient award of distinction Cornell U. Med. Coll. Alumni Assn., 1967. Master A.C.P. (bd. regents 1968-73); mem. Assn. Am. Physicians, Am. Gastroenterol. Assn. (pres. 1964, Julius Friedenwald medal 1976), Inst. Medicine NAS (sr. mem.). Home: 80 Lyme Rd Apt 222 Hanover NH 03755-1231

AL-OBAIDI, JABBAR A., communication educator, film producer; b. Baghdad, Iraq, July 1, 1950; came to U.S., 1996; s. Audah Allawi and Tanzeel K. Al-Obaidi; m. Wafaa Jafar Alhassan, Mar. 1, 1980; children: Sarah, Ghayath. BA in Stage Directing, Baghdad U., 1974; MAEd in Video and Film, Hartford U., 1979; PhD in Comm., U. Mich., 1983. Chair radio, TV and film dept. Baghdad U., 1984-91, from asst. prof. to assoc. prof., 1983-91; assoc. prof. Yarmouk U., Irbid, Jordan, 1991-92; prof. comm. Sana'a (Yemen) U., 1992-96; comm. trainer UNICEF, Sanay, Yemen, 1994-96; rsch. scholar U. Mich., Ann Arbor, 1997-98; prof. comm. studies dept. Bridgewater (Mass.) State Coll., 1998—; acad. advisor Emberical Rsch./Women Studies Ctr., Sana'a, 1993-96; mem. adv. bd. Ednl. TV, Baghdad, 1984-91; editl. advisor Alkalima Mag., Sana'a, 1993—; dir. Commonealth Politics TV Program, 1998; exec. prodr. Cabo Video in English, Inside BSC. Author: Introduction to Mass Media, 1989, Public Relations Programs, 1995, Communications Issues, 1994; writer dir. TV documentary One Step Forward, 1994; prodr., dir.: (documentary film) Women Voices: 1/2 Censored, 1997; contbr. articles to profl. jours. Ministry of Higher Edn. scholar, 1997; U. Mich. fellow, 1982. Mem. Internat. Orgn. Journalists, Assn. for Edn. and Mass. Comm., Nat. Comm. Assn. Avocations: travel, reading, music, social activities, theatre. Home: 70 Fox Hill Dr Bridgewater MA 02324-2336 Office: Bridgewater State Coll Comm Studies Dept Bridgewater MA 02325

ALOFF, MINDY, writer; b. Phila., Dec. 20, 1947; d. Jacob and Selma (Album) A.; m. Martin Steven Cohen, June 16, 1968; 1 child, Ariel Nikiya. *Father Jacob Aloff, BA Harvard 1934, is an electrical engineer who, for the past 50 years, has fought for the rights of the ratepayer on various state and federal regulatory issues in the fields of electrical power and insurance. Mother Selma Album Aloff, BS Temple 1934, has served as a model of a working mother. Her extensive professional career includes 25 years as a teacher at William Penn High School for Girls in Philadelphia. Among her many awards is a plaque from her 1971 stenography class: "The most wonderful and considerate person we have ever had the pleasure of knowing".* AB in English, Vassar Coll., 1969; MA in English, SUNY, Buffalo, 1972. Asst. prof. English U. Portland, Oreg., 1973-75; editor Encore Mag. of the Arts, Portland, 1977-80, Vassar Quar., Poughkeepsie, N.Y., 1980-88; free-lance writer Bklyn., 1988—; coord. Portland Poetry Festival, 1974-75. Author: (poems) Night Lights, 1979; author essays and revs. theatrical dancing and lit. for N.Y. Times Weekend, Book Rev. and Arts & Leisure, New Republic mag., Nation mag., Threepenny Rev., Dance mag., New Yorker mag., ann. Ency. Britannica, others. Recipient Whiting Writers award Mrs. Giles Whiting Found., N.Y.C., 1987; Woodrow Wilson Found. fellow, 1969, Woodburn fellow SUNY-Buffalo, 1972, Am. Dance Festival Dance Critics Inst. fellow, New London, Conn., 1977, John Simon Guggenheim Meml. Found. fellow, 1990. Mem. Nat. Book Critics Circle (bd. dirs. 1988-91), Phi Beta Kappa.

ALOIA, ROLAND CRAIG, scientist, administrator, educator; b. Newark, Dec. 21, 1943; s. Roland S. and Edna M. (Mahan) A. BS, St. Mary's Coll., 1965; PhD, U. Calif., Riverside, 1970. Postdoctoral fellow City of Hope, Duarte, Calif., 1971-75; research biologist U. Calif., Riverside, 1975-76; asst. prof. Sch. of Medicine Loma Linda (Calif.) U., 1976-79; assoc. prof. Loma Linda (Calif.) U., 1979-89, prof. anesthesiology and biochemistry, 1989—; chemist VA, Loma Linda, 1979-94, chief rsch. ops., 1994—; pres., chmn. Loma Linda VA for Rsch. and Edn., 1988-94, pres., CEO, 1994—. Editor: Membrane Fluidity in Biology, Vols. 1-4, 1983, 85; sr. editor: (series) Advanced in Membrane Fluidity vols. 1-3, 1988, vol. 4, 1989, vol. 5, 1991, vol. 6, 1992. Pres. Riverside chpt. Calif. Heart Assn., 1979-80, 1984-86, bd. dirs., exec. com. mem., 1973-86, v.p., 1984-86. Calif. Heart Assn. fellow, 1971-73. Mem. Am. Chem. Soc., N.Y. Acad. Scis., Soc. Cell Biology, Sigma Xi (pres. Loma Linda chpt. 1991-92, pres.-elect 1990-91). Avocations: flying, jogging, reading. Office: VA Med Ctr Rsch Svc 151 JL Pettis Loma Linda CA 92357

ALOISI, CAROL ANN, marketing executive; b. Plainfield, N.J., Nov. 29, 1953; d. Edward Charles and Evelyn Helen (Nowhark) Schaffernoth; m. Michael Francis Aloisi, Jan. 20, 1979. BA, Rutgers the State U., 1978; MBA, Rutgers the State U., Newark, 1991. Mgr. employment Bamberger's/Macy's, Newark, 1975-78; pers. adminstr. John Wiley & Sons., N.Y.C., 1978-79, corp. pers. mgr., 1979-81; mgr. pers. adminstrn. Ortho Diagnostic Sys., Inc., Raritan, N.J., 1981-82; mgr. employee rels. Ortho Diagnostic Sys., Inc., Raritan, 1982-83, dir. employee rels., 1984-85, nat. account exec., 1985-87, product mgr., 1987-89, dir. mktg., 1989-92; gen. mgr. Ortho Diagnostic Systems Inc., Raritan, 1992-93; pres. Career Mgmt. Cons., Inc., Bound Brook, N.J., 1994—. Recipient Tribute to Women in Industry award YWCA/TWIN of Cen. N.J., 1987. Mem. Tribute to Women in Industry, Internat. Assn. Career Mgmt. Profls. Avocations: tennis, birdwatching, biking. Office: Career Mgmt Cons Inc 20 W Maple Ave Bound Brook NJ 08805-1734

ALOISIO, MARIA THERESA, tax accountant; b. Chgo., July 11, 1960; d. Alfredo and Maria Rose (Altomari) Talarico. BS in Commerce, DePaul U., Chgo., 1982, MS in Taxation, 1988. CPA, Ill. Jr. tax acct. Harris Trust and Savs. Bank, Chgo., 1982-86, tax acct., 1986-87, sr. tax acct., 1988-89; tax supr. Aon Corp., Chgo., 1989-91; sr. tax. cons. Arthur Andersen & Co., Chgo., 1991-92, experienced sr. tax cons., 1992-94, asst. tax mgr., 1994-97, tax mgr., 1997—. Mem. AICPA, Ill. Soc. CPAs.

ALOMAR, ROBERTO VELAZQUEZ, professional baseball player; b. Ponce, P.R., Feb. 5, 1968. With San Diego Padres, 1988-90, Toronto Blue Jays, 1990-95, Balt. Orioles, 1996-98, Cleve. Indians, 1998—. Recipient Am. League Gold Glove award, 1991-94; named to All-Star team, 1990-96, Sporting News Am. League Silver Slugger Team, 1992, 96, All-Star Team, 1992. Office: Cleveland Orioles 2401 Ontario St Cleveland OH 44115*

ALOMAR, SANDY, JR. (SANTOS VELAZQUEZ ALOMAR), professional baseball player; b. Salinas, P.R., June 18, 1966. With San Diego Padres, 1988-89, Cleve. Indians, 1990—. Named Rookie of Yr. Baseball Writers' Assn. Am., 1990, Sporting News, 1990, named to Am. League All-Star team, 1990, 91; recipient Am. League Gold Glove award, 1990. Office: Cleve Indians Jacobs Field 2401 Ontario St Cleveland OH 44115-4003*

ALONSO, ANTONIO ENRIQUE, lawyer; b. Havana, Cuba, Aug. 31, 1924; came to U.S., 1959; s. Enrique and Inocencia (Avila) A.; m. Daisy Ojeda, July 20, 1949; children: Margarita, Antonio, Enrique, Jorge. JD, U. Habana, Cuba, 1946; PhD, U. Habana, 1952; student, U. Fla., 1974-76. Bar: Fla. 1976. Pub. defendant High Ct. Las Villas, Cuba, 1946-49; atty. Provincial Gov., Cuba, 1950-52; under sec. Treasury, Cuba, 1952-54; mem. House of Reps. Congress of Cuba, 1954-58; prof. U. Jose Marti, 1952-58, Inst. Soc. Action, 1964-65; prof. modern lang. Coll. St. Teresa, 1968; sole practice Miami, 1976—; adj. prof. St. Mary's Coll., Minn., summers, 1968-73. Author: (with others) Violation of Human Rights in Cuba, 1962, History of the Communist Party of Cuba, 1970; weekly columnist on real estate and law Diario Las Ams. newspaper; contbr. articles to profl. jours. Recipient Field Svc. Program award Nat. Assn. Student Affairs, 1973. Mem. AAUP, Am. Assn. Tchrs. Spanish and Portuguese, Fla. Bar Assn. Republican. Roman Catholic. Home: 1900 SW 12th Ave Miami FL 33129-2613 Office: 1699 Coral Way Ste 315 Miami FL 33145-2860

ALONSO, DIANE LINDWARM, cognitive psychologist; b. Washington, May 19, 1962; d. Joseph and Naomi Rose (Kotch) Lindwarm; m. W. Thomas Alonso Jr., May 31, 1993; children: Lisa Lindwarm Alonso, Johanna Lynn Alonso. BS in Computer Sci., U. Md., 1985, MS in Psychology, 1995, PhD in Psychology, 1998. Systems engr. IBM, San Jose,

Calif., 1983, Balt., 1984; computer programmer IBM, Gaithersburg, Md., 1985-88, systems engr., 1988-89; human factors engr. IBM, Shady Grove, Md., 1989-91; rsch. asst. Human-Computer Interaction Lab. U. Md., College Park, 1984-85, rsch. and tchg. asst., 1992-96, instr. psychology, 1997. Mem. Assn. Computing Machinery, Human Factors and Ergonomics Soc., Potomac chpt. Human Factors and Ergonomics Soc., Phi Kappa Phi. Avocations: music, dance, theater, tennis, aerobics. Home and Office: 3014 Cluster Pines Ct Ellicott City MD 21042-7619

ALONSO, MARIA CONCHITA, actress, singer; b. Cienfuegos, Cuba, June 29, 1957; d. Ricardo José and Conchita (Bustillo) Alonso. Appeared in films Moscow on the Hudson, 1984, A Fine Mess, 1986, Touch and Go, 1986, Extreme Prejudice, 1987, The Running Man, 1987, Colors, 1988, Vampire's Kiss, 1990, Predator II, 1990, Roosters, 1993, House of the Spirits, 1994, Caught, 1996, Caught, 1997, El Grito en el Cielo, 1997, Catherine's Grove, 1997, Acts of Betrayal, 1997, Knock out, 1998, Exposé, 1998; appeared in numerous Venezuelan films and soap operas; TV appearances include Blood Ties, 1986, One of the Boys, 1989, Sudden Terror: The Hijacking of School Bus # 17, 1996, La Limpia, Fx, Chicago Hope, The Gun, Acts of Betrayal, The Vaccine, Me Shayne; recording artist, albums include: Maria Conchita, 1984 (Grammy award nomination for Best Latin Artist 1985), O ella o yo, 1985. Named Miss World Teenager, 1971, Miss Venezuela, 1975. *

ALONZI, LORETO PETER, finance executive; b. Evanston, Ill., Sept. 16, 1951; s. Saverio Joseph and Sheila Helen (McEnery) A.; m. Mary Rose Sievers; children: Loreto Peter III, Christopher Patrick, Nicholas Daniel. BA magna cum laude, Loyola U., Chgo., 1973; MA in Econs., U. Iowa, 1976, PhD in Econs., 1979. Asst. prof. econs. Bowling Green (Ohio) State U., 1978-80, Loyola U., Chgo., 1980-86; v.p. Sora Loan Corp., Chgo., 1986-87, pres., chief operating officer, 1988-90; sr. mgr. market devel. Chgo. Bd. Trade, 1991—; bd. dirs. Sora Loan Corp.; speaker Chgo. Bd. Trade, 1982-87, Commodities Edn. Inst., Iowa, 1987-88; adj. prof. econs., Loyola U. Chgo., 1996—. Contbr. articles to profl. jours. Recipient Teaching Rsch. Fellowship U. Iowa, Iowa City, 1973-77; named Tchr. of Yr. Alpha Lambda Delta, Bowling Green, 1981, Kemper Faculty Scholar, Loyola U., 1985. Mem. Internat. Wine and Food Soc. of Chgo., Am. Econ. Assn., Midwest Fin. Assn. (instl. dir.), Nat. Futures Assn. (mem. ednl./testing adv. com. 1994-96), Ind. Fin. Assn. of Ill. (bd. dirs. 1987-90), Order of the Arrow Brotherhood, Beta Gamma Sigma, Omicron Delta Epsilon. Avocations: golf, scouting, oenology. Home: 431 Greenleaf Ave Wilmette IL 60091-1911 Office: Chgo Bd Trade Market and Product Devel Lasalle At Jackson Chicago IL 60604

ALONZO, MARTIN VINCENT, mining and aluminum company executive, investor, financial consultant; b. N.Y.C., Apr. 8, 1931; s. Mariano and Mary (Traina) A.; m. Sabina Gallucci, June 7, 1952; children: Martin Vincent, Marlene, Sabrina. BBA in Acctg. cum laude, Baruch Coll., CUNY, 1952, MBA in Fin. and Investments, 1971. CPA, N.Y. Acct. Eisner and Lubin CPAs, N.Y.C., 1952-57; treas., contr. Credit-Am. Corp., N.Y.C., 1957-60; asst. v.p. indsl. time sales, financing and leasing A.J. Armstrong Co., Inc., N.Y.C., 1960-65; treas., sec. So. Nitrogen Co., Savannah, Ga., 1965-67; asst. to v.p. fin. AMAX Inc., Greenwich, Conn., 1967-68, mgr. fin. planning, 1968-69, asst. contr., 1969, contr., 1970, v.p. and contr., 1973-78, sr. v.p. controls and adminstrn., 1978-80, sr. v.p. and pres. indsl. minerals div., 1981-82, exec. v.p. and pres. splty. and light metals ops., 1982-83, exec. v.p., chief fin. officer, 1983-87; pres. MVA Fin. Corp., 1987—; chmn., pres., CEO Chase Industries, Inc., 1990—; bd. dirs. Copper & Brass Fabricators Coun., Inc., Copper Devel. Assn.; pres.'s coun. MAPI, 1993; mem. INternat. Wrought Copper Coun., 1999. Bd. dirs. Greenwich Health Assn., 1978-90, Am. Found., 1993-95; active Greenwich Bd. Health, 1982-92, U.S. Nat. Com. Pacific Econ. Cooperation, 1993—. Mem. Nat. Assn. Accts. (chmn. mgmt. acctg. practices com. 1976-79), Conf. Bd., Coun. Fin. Execs., Fin. Adv. Coun. (exec. com. 1984-87), Extractive Industries Luncheon Group (chmn. 1978-79), Am. Mining Congress (chmn. acctg. com. 1980-82, mem. pension com. 1978-82), Internat. Magnesium Assn. (bd. dirs. 1983-84), AICPA, Fin. Execs. Inst., AIME, Phosphate Rock Export Assn. (dir. 1982-83), Mining Club N.Y.C. (dir.), Econ. Club N.Y., Westchester Country Club, Sky Club, Roundtable of Greenwich, Beta Alpha Psi, Beta Gamma Sigma, Am. Assn. Sovereign Mil. Order of Malta. Republican. Office: 300 Park Ave Fl 17 New York NY 10022-7402

ALOTTA, ROBERT IGNATIUS, historian, educator, writer; b. Feb. 26, 1937; s. Peter Philip and Jean (Sacchetti) A.; m. Alice J. Danley, Oct. 1, 1960; children: Peter Anthony, Amy Louise. BA, LaSalle Coll., Phila., 1959; MA, U. Pa., 1981; PhD, Temple U., 1984. With Triangle Publs., Phila., 1956-67, merchandising mgr. Inquirer divsn., 1959-63, mgr. customer svc. Inquirer-Daily News, 1963-66, new bus. coord. Daily News, 1966-67; mgr. spl. projects Penn Cen. Transp. Co., Phila., 1967-72; dir. pub. info. Phila. Housing Authority, 1972-81; asst. prof. comms. Grand Valley State Coll., Allendale, Mich., 1981-84; from asst. prof. comm. to assoc. prof. Miss. State U., 1984-92; pres. Alotta Ink, 1992—; prof., dean Sr. U., Ctr. Mil. Studies; dir. edn. and info. svcs. Rockingham County Sheriff's Office, 1996—; adj. assoc. prof. Blue Ridge C.C., 1999—. Exec. prodr.: (TV series) The Kids Show, 1985-86; scriptwriter: (radio series) A Philadelphia Moment, 1982, Past/Prolog, 1976, other radio, TV series, 1969—; host: (TV series) Perceptions of War, 1988-89; co-host TV series Midweek, 1989, (radio show) Midday; narrator: (radio series) A Minute of Your Time, 1977-78; host, prodr.: (radio show) Point of View, 1996-98; author: Street Names of Philadelphia, 1975, Stop the Evil, 1978, Old Names and New Places, 1979, A Look at the Vice President, 1981, Military Executions of the Union Army, 1861-1866, 1984, Civil War Justice, 1989, Mermaids, Monasteries Cherokees and Custer: The Story Behind Philadelphia's Street Names, 1990, Another Part of the Field: Philadelphia's Revolution, 1777-78, 1991, Signposts and Settlers: The History Behind the Place Names Beyond the Rockies, 1993; contbr. articles, book revs. to publs. Pres. Shackamaxon Soc., 1967—; mem. pres.'s coun. LaSalle Coll., 1976-81. With Security Agy., AUS, 1960-61. Recipient Freedom Found. at Valley Forge awards, 1970, 73, 74, 76, Legion of Honor award Chapel of 4 Chaplains, 1975, Colonial Dames, DAR awards, 1976, Americanism award County Detectives Assn. Pa., 1977, 17 Web site design awards. Mem. Am. Name Soc. (trustee 1982-84), Coun. on Am.'s Mil. Past (bd. dirs. 1984-88, 89-92), Mil. History Inst., Orgn. Am. Historians, Am. Hist. Assn., Cross Keys, Order of Sons of Italy (trustee 1983-84), Nat. Press Club (Washington), KC, Sigma Delta Chi (bd. dirs. Golden Triangle chpt. 1984-86), Tau Alpha Pi, Alpha Phi Omega. Home: 283 Newman Ave Harrisonburg VA 22801-4027

ALOU, FELIPE ROJAS, professional baseball manager; b. Santo Domingo, Dominican Republic, May 12, 1935. Player San Francisco Giants, 1958-62, Milw. Braves, 1964-65, Atlanta Braves, 1966-69, Oakland Athletics, 1970-71, N.Y. Yankees, 1971-73, Montreal Expos, 1973, Milw. Brewers, 1974; coach Montreal Expos, 1979-80, 84, mgr., 1992—. Named to Nat. League All-Star team Sporting News, 1966; named Nat. League Mgr. of Yr. Sporting News, 1994, Baseball Writers' Assn. Am., 1994. Office: Montreal Expos, 4549 Pierre-de-Coubertin Ave, Montreal, PQ Canada H1V 3N7*

ALOU, MOISES, professional baseball player; b. Atlanta, July 3, 1966; s. Felipe Alou. Outfielder Pitts. Pirates, 1986-90, Montreal Expos, 1990-96, Fla. Marlins, 1996-97, Houston Astros, 97-. Named to Nat. League All-Star Team, Sporting News, 1994, Nat. League Silver Slugger Team, Sporting News, 1994, Buck Canel award for Top L.Am. Player, 1994, Player of Yr., Montreal Expos, 1994. Office: Houston Astros PO Box 288 Houston TX 77001-0288*

ALPEN, EDWARD LEWIS, biophysicist, educator; b. San Francisco, May 14, 1922; s. Edward Lawrence and Margaret Catherine (Shipley) A.; m. Wynella June Dosh, Jan. 6, 1945; children: Angela Marie, Jeannette Elise. B.S., U. Calif., Berkeley, 1946, Ph.D., 1950. Br. chief, then dir. biol. and med. scis. Naval Radiol. Def. Lab., San Francisco, 1952-68; mgr. environ. and life scis. Battelle Meml. Inst., Richland, Wash., 1968-69, assoc. dir., then dir. Pacific N.W. div., 1969-75; dir. Donner Lab., U. Calif., Berkeley; also assoc. dir. Lawrence Berkeley Lab., 1975-87; prof. biophysics emeritus U. Calif., Berkeley, 1975—; prof. radiology emeritus U. Calif., San Francisco, 1976—; dir. study ctr. U. Calif., London, 1988-90; councillor, dir. Nat. Council Radiol. Protection, 1969-92; exec. v.p., tech. dir. Neutron Tech. Corp., Berkeley, 1990-93; mem. Gov. Wash. Council Econ. Devel., 1973-75; bd. dirs. Wash. Bd. Trade, 1973-76. Author books, papers, abstracts in field. Served to capt. USNR, 1942-46, 50-51. Recipient Navy Sci. medal, 1962, Disting. Service medal Dept. Def., 1963, Sustaining Members medal Assn. Mil. Surgeons, 1971; fellow Guggenheim Found., 1960-61; sr. fellow NSF, 1958-59. Fellow Calif. Acad. Scis.; mem. Bioelectromagnetics Soc. (pres. 1979-80), Radiation Rsch. Soc., Soc. Exptl. Biology and Medicine, Biophys. Soc., Brit. Inst. Radiology, Am. Philatelic Soc., Sigma Xi (nat. lectr. 1994-96). Episcopalian. Home: 1182 Miller Ave Berkeley CA 94708-1755

ALPER, HOWARD, chemistry educator; b. Montreal, Oct. 17, 1941; s. Max and Frema (Weinstein) A.; m. Anne Elizabeth Fairhurst, June 4, 1966; children: Lara, Ruth. BS, Sir George Williams U., Montreal, 1963; PhD, McGill U., 1967. From asst. prof. to assoc. prof. SUNY, Binghamton, 1968-74; assoc. prof. U. Ottawa, 1975-77, prof., 1977—; chmn. dept. chemistry U. Ottawa, 1982-85, 88-94, asst. v.p. rsch., 1995-96, v.p. rsch., 1997—. Editor 2 books on organometallic chemistry and catalysis; contbr. over 400 articles to profl. jours.; holder 33 patents. Recipient Alfred Bader award in organic chemistry, 1990, Commemorative medal for significant contbns. to Can., 125th Anniversary of Can., 1992, E.W.R. Steacie award for disting. contbns. to chemistry, Can. Soc. for Chemistry, 1993, Urgel-Archambault prize in phys. scis., math. and engring., 1996, Bell Can. Forum award, 1998; NATO postdoctoral fellow Princeton U., 1967-68, E.W.R. Steacie fellow Nat. Sci. Engring. Rsch. Coun. Can., 1980-82, Guggenheim fellow, 1985-86, Killam rsch. fellow Killam Found., 1986-88. Fellow Royal Soc. Can. (v.p. Acad. of Sci. 1995-98, chair partnership group for sci. and engring. 1995-99); mem. Natural Scis. and Engring. Rsch. Coun. Can. (group chmn. chemistry 1987-90), Am. Chem. Soc., Royal Soc. Chemistry (London), Chem. Inst. Can. (Alcan award 1980, Catalysis award 1984, CIC medal 1997), European Acad. Arts Sci. Humanities (titular mem.), Order of Can. (officer 1999). Jewish. Office: U Ottawa Dept Chemistry, 10 Marie Curie, Ottawa, ON Canada K1N 6N5

ALPER, JEROME MILTON, lawyer; b. N.Y.C., Aug. 26, 1914; s. David Samuel and Ethel (Gordon) A.; m. Janet Adrian Levy, Jan. 4, 1948 (dec.); children: Jonathan Louis (dec.), Alan Irwin, Andrew Michael; m. Muriel C. Pearl, (dec.) Jan. 17, 1981. B.A., U. Chattanooga, 1934; J.D., U. Chgo., 1937. Bar: Tenn., Ill., D.C. Practiced in Chattanooga, 1938; atty. SEC, 1939-50; ptnr. Alper, Schoene Horkan & Mann and successor firms, Washington, 1950-88, ret.; counsel Joint Transp. Commn. for Negotiation of Washington Met. Area Transit Regulation Compact and Washington Met. Area Transit Authority Compact, 1959-66; Counsel Gov.'s Steering Com. on Mass Transp. for Balt. Met. Area, 1967-69. Contbr. articles to profl. jours. Pres. Montgomery County Art Center, Inc.; chmn. bus. com. Folger Shakespeare Library, 1975-76; Trustee Urban Am., Inc., 1964-67, Am. Planning and Civic Assn., 1960-64. Served to lt. comdr. USNR, 1941-45, ETO, PTO. Mem. ABA, D.C., Tenn., Fed. Power bar assns., Bar Assn. of D.C., Am. Judicature Soc. Jewish (dir. temple 1954-58). Club: Nat. Democratic (Washington). Home: 7702 Rocton Ave Bethesda MD 20815-3916*

ALPER, MERLIN LIONEL, financial executive; b. Bklyn., May 25, 1932; s. James B. and Rose (Mellis) A.; m. Elaine R. Honig, Dec. 21, 1957; children: Jerome Eric, Alyssa Ellen. B.B.A., Adelphi U., 1955. C.P.A., N.Y. With Arthur Andersen & Co., N.Y.C., 1955-68; comml. audit mgr. Arthur Andersen & Co., 1963-68; dir. fin. controls ITT, N.Y.C., 1968-73; asst. comptr. ITT, 1973-93, corp. v.p., 1979; v.p., contr. ITT Europe, Inc., 1978-84; corp. v.p., comptr. ITT Telecom. Corp., 1984-85, also dir.; v.p., dep. contr. ITT Corp., N.Y.C., 1993-95; exec. v.p., CFO Madison Sq. Garden, N.Y.C., 1995-98; mng. dir. Ind. Coll. Fund N.Y., 1999—; mem. emerging issues task force of Fin. Acctg. Standards Bd., 1990-95. Served with Chem. Corps AUS, 1956-58. Named to Adelphi U. Alumni Acad. of Distinction, 1984. Mem. AICPA, N.Y. State Soc. CPAs, Nat. Assn. Accts. (dir. N.Y. chpt. 1965-66), Fin. Execs. Inst. (mem. corp. reporting com.).

ALPERIN, IRWIN EPHRAIM, clothing company executive; b. Scranton, Pa., Apr. 29, 1925; s. Louis I. and Bessie (Wickner) A.; m. Francine Leah Friedman, Dec. 5, 1948; children: Barbara Joy, Jane Leslie. Cert. Mech. Engring., Pa. State U., 1945; BS in Indsl. Engring., Lehigh U., 1947; DHL (hon.), U. Scranton, Pa., 1991. Mgmt. trainee Mayflower Mfg. Co., Scranton, 1947-49, sec., 1952-79, pres., 1980-91; with Triple A Trouser Mfg. Co., Inc., Scranton, 1952, v.p., treas., 1958-79, pres., 1980-91; with Gold Star Mfg. Co., Inc., Scranton, 1956, pres., 1956-91; sec. Astro Warehousing, Inc., Scranton, 1962-91; sec.-treas. Bondeal, Inc., Scranton, 1978-89, pres., 1989—; v.p. RCO, Inc., 1989-91; vice chmn. Montage, Inc., 1979-92; sec. Alperin, Inc., 1982-91, pres., 1991—; sec. All Star Industries, Inc., 1989-92, pres., 1993—; treas. Calvin Clothing Co. Inc., 1996—. Bd. dirs. Econ. Devel. Coun. N.E. Pa., Avoca, 1974-96, v.p., 1978-83; bd. dirs. ARC, Scranton, 1968-88, pres. spl. adv. bd., 1988—; bd. dirs. Jewish Home Ea. Pa., Scranton, 1970—, treas., 1981-97; pres. Elan Gardens, 1995—; bd. dirs. Jewish Cmty. Ctr., Scranton, 1971-86, now life mem.; bd. dirs. Pa. United Way, Harrisburg, 1973-78, Scranton Counseling Ctr., 1975-78, trustee, 1979-95; pres. Planning coun. Social Svcs. Lackawanna County, 1972-74, now life mem.; pres. Jewish Family Svc. of Lackawanna County, 1967-70, now life bd. mem.; v.p. United Way Lackawanna County, 1974-78, exec. com., 1978-86; pres. Alperin Found., Scranton, 1962-93; treas. Scranton-Lackawanna Jewish Fedn., 1973-75, life mem. bd. dirs.; trustee Amos Lodge Found., 1982—, v.p., 1989-91; trustee Found. Jewish Elderly, 1994—, v.p., 1985—; trustee Pocono N.E. Devel., 1983—, sec., 1986-95, pres., 1995-96; pres. Temple Hesed, 1969-71, life mem., bd. dirs., Scranton; mem. Lackawanna County Libr. Bd., 1983-85; treas. Lackawanna Regional Cultural Coun., 1988-91, bd. dirs. 1988-93; bd. dirs. Broadway Theatre League Lackawanna County, 1989—, vice chmn., 1994-99; bd. dirs. Masonic Temple Civic Ctr. Found., 1989-93; trustee U. Scranton, 1991-97. With C.E. AUS, 1944-46. Recipient Americanism award, 1982; named Man of Year, Jewish Community Ctr., 1973, Disting. Pennsylvanian, Phila. C. of C., 1982. Mem. Am. Inst. Indsl. Engrs. (sr.), Glen Oak Country Club (Clarks Summit, Pa.), Wave Oak Realty (Clarks Summit) (v.p. 1989-91), Masons, Shriners, Elks, B'nai B'rith (trustee, Man of Yr. 1982). Home: 1010 Victoria Ln Clarks Summit PA 18411-9248 *To know your god—know yourself.*

ALPERIN, RICHARD MARTIN, clinical social worker, psychoanalyst; b. Mt. Vernon, N.Y., Oct. 16, 1946; s. Israel and Sara A.; children: Heather Nicole, Alexander Scott. BBA, Western Mich. U., 1968; MSW, Fordham U., 1974; DSW, Columbia U., 1982; postdoctoral diploma in psychotherapy and psychoanalysis, Adelphi U., 1988. Cert. social worker, N.Y.; lic. clin. social worker, N.J.; diplomate Am. Bd. Examiners in Clin. Social Work. Cons. Mt. Vernon Youth Bd., 1972-76; adj. faculty Marymount Manhattan Coll., N.Y.C., 1974-76; psychotherapist Riverdale Mental Health Clinic, N.Y.C., 1974-77; psychol. counselor, psychotherapist Ctr. Counseling and Psychol. Svcs. Ramapo Coll. of N.J., 1976-81, adj. faculty, 1977-86, moderator evening forums, 1978, 80; counselor, psychotherapist Ctr. Counseling and Psychol. Svcs. SUNY, Purchase, 1981-82, 84-85, acting dir., 1982-84; clin. cons. Westside Ctr. for Family Svcs., N.Y.C., 1985-87; guest lectr. Cabrini Med. Ctr., 1979; pvt. practice psychotherapy and psychoanalysis Riverdale, N.Y., 1977—, Teaneck, N.J., 1980—, N.Y.C., 1984—; grand rounds dept. psychiatry, Brookdale Hosp. Med. Ctr., 1996; field instr. Sch. Social Work-Columbia U., 1983-85; adj. assoc. prof. Sch. Social Svc.-Fordham U., 1985—; adj. asst. prof. Grad. Sch. Social Work-NYU, 1989-91; mem. faculty, dean curriculum Rockland Inst. for Psychoanalysis and Psychotherapy, 1990-95; mem. faculty Advanced Inst. Analytic Psychotherapy, 1992-95, Object Rel. Inst. Psychoanalysis and Psychotherapy, 1992—, Psychoanalytic Psychotherapy Study Ctr., 1994—, N.J. Inst. for Tng. in Psychoanalysis, 1994—. Co-editor: The Impact of Managed Care on the Practice of Psychotherapy: Innovation, Implementation, and Controversy, 1996; contbr. articles to profl. jours.; rsch. on psychotherapy, suicide and provision of preventative svcs. Nat. Jewish Welfare Bd. fellow Fordham U., 1972-74. Trainee NIMH Columbia U., 1978. Mem. NASW, N.Y. State Soc. Clin. Social Work (chair com. on psychoanalysis 1991-96, Awarded diplomate 1997), Adelphi Soc. Psychoanalysis and Psychotherapy, Am. Group Psychotherapy Assn., Inc., Ea. Group Psychotherapy Soc., Acad. Cert. Social Workers (cert.), Nat. Fedn. Soc. Clin. Social Work, Nat. Membership Com. Psychoanalysis Clin. Social Work (chair N.Y.-N.J. area 1992-94, treas. 1991-93), Alliance for Universal Access to Psychotherapy (founder, membership chair, mem. steering com. 1994-96), Nat. Study Group on Social Work and Psychoanalysis, N.J. Coalition Mental Health Profls. and Consumers (mem. adv. bd.). Office: 175 Cedar Ln Teaneck NJ 07666-4315

ALPERN, ANDREW, lawyer, architect, architectural historian; b. N.Y.C., Nov. 1, 1938; s. Dwight K. and Grace M. (Michelman) A.; BArch., Columbia U., 1964; ScD (hon.), London Coll. Applied Sci., 1971; JD magna cum laude Benjamin N. Cardozo Sch. Law, 1992. Bar: N.Y. 1993, U.S. Dist. Ct. (so. and ea. dists.) N.Y. 1994; registered architect, N.Y., Calif., D.C.; cert. Nat. Coun. Archtl. Registration Bds. With Haines Lundberg Waehler, architects, N.Y.C., 1962-67; project dir. Saphier, Lerner, Schindler, Environetics, space planning and design, N.Y.C., 1968-72; v.p., dir. arch. Environ. R & D, Inc., Space Planning and Design, N.Y.C., 1972-75; dir. rsch. Corp. Planners and Coordinators, real estate cons. and brokers, N.Y.C., 1973-75; project mgr. Hellmuth, Obata & Kassabaum, P.C., architects, engrs. and planners, N.Y.C., 1977-78; mgr. real estate and facilities planning Pricewaterhouse Coopers LLP, N.Y.C., 1978-88; ind. cons. architect for real estate, hist. architecture, landmarking, rsch. and analysis, N.Y.C., 1988—; ind. cons. lawyer real estate, landmarking, constrn. law, gen. comml. and contract matters, 1993; spl. counsel Hughes Hubbard & Reed LLP, 1994—; lectr. City U. N.Y., Inst. Architecture and Urban Studies, Grolier Club, Mcpl. Art Soc. Mem. adv. bd. Inst. Applied Psychotherapy, 1969-72; mem. nat. panel arbitrators Am. Arbitration Assn., 1971-86. Recipient Presdl. Citation N.Y. State Assn. Architects, 1991. Recipient West Publishing Co. award for Acad. Excellence. Mem. AIA, Assn. Bar City N.Y. (construction law com. 1993-96), Soc. Archtl. Historians, Bklyn. Hist. Soc., N.Y. Hist. Soc., Mcpl. Art Soc., N.Y. State Assn. Architects,Real Estate bd. N.Y. (landmark buildings com., 1992—), Brownstone Revival Com., Friends of Cast Iron Architecture, Coffee House Club (N.Y.C.). Author: Apartments for the Affluent: A Historical Survey of Buildings in New York, 1975, Garret Ellis Winants: 1813-1890, 1976, Alpern's Architectural Aphorisms, 1979, Handbook of Specialty Elements in Architecture, 1981, Holdouts!, 1983, In the Manor Housed, 1982, Fifth Avenue, 1986, New York's Fabulous Luxury Apartments, 1987, Statutes of Repose and the Construction Industry: a Proposal for New York, 1991, Luxury Apartment Houses of Manhattan: an Illustrated History, 1993, Historic Manhattan Apartment Houses, 1996, New York's Architectural Holdouts, 1997, 101 Questions About Copyright Law, 1999; pub. F.M.R.A. (Edward Gorey), 1980; editor-in-chief: Legal Briefs for the Constrn. Industry, 1978-92; contbg. editor N.Y. Habitat, 1985-92; bd. advisors Professional Office Design mag., 1986-89; design awards com. Fifth Ave. Assn. N.Y., 1988—; selection jury for Hall of Fame of Real Estate Bd. of N.Y., 1988—.

ALPERN, LINDA LEE WEVODAU, health agency administrator; b. Harrisburg, Pa., July 16, 1949; d. William Irvin Wevodau and Maretia Christine (Mills) Staley; m. Neil Stephen Alpern, Apr. 12, 1985; 1 child, Philip Wevodau. BS in Edn., Shippensburg (Pa.) U., 1971. Unit program coord. Pa. Div. Am. Cancer Soc., Harrisburg, 1973-75, unit exec. dir., 1975-76, div. svc. dir., 1976-81; div. med. affairs dir. Pa. Div. Am. Cancer Soc., Hershey, 1981-83; div. crusade dir. Md. Div. Am. Cancer Soc., Balt., 1983-87, div. v.p. for field ops., 1988, div. dep., exec. v.p. ops., 1988-95, divsn. chief oper. officer, 1995-96; sr. v.p. field ops. Mid-Atlantic divsn. Am. Cancer Soc., Balt., 1997—. Bd. dirs., sec. Cmty. Assn.; treas., v.p., pres. PTA; trustee Balt. Hebrew-Congregation Day Sch. Democrat. Methodist. Avocations: photography, gardening, reading. Home: 4108 Colonial Rd Baltimore MD 21208-6042

ALPEROVITZ, GAR, author, educator; b. Racine, Wis., May 5, 1936; s. Julius and Emily (Bensman) A.; m. Sharon Sosnick, Aug. 29, 1976; children by previous marriage: Kari Fai, David Joseph. B.S. in History, U. Wis., 1958; M.A. in Econs, U. Cal. at Berkeley, 1960; Ph.D. in Polit. Economy, U. Cambridge, Eng., 1964. Congl. legis. asst., 1961-62; Senate legis. dir. U.S. Senate staff, 1964-65; spl. asst. Dept. State, 1965-66; fellow King's Coll., Cambridge (Eng.) U., 1964-68, Inst. Politics Harvard, 1965-68, Brookings Instn., 1966, Inst. Policy Studies, 1968-69, 89-99; co-dir. Cambridge (Mass.) Inst., 1968-71; dir. exploratory project econ. alternatives, 1973—; pres. Nat. Center Econ. and Security Alternatives, 1978—; guest prof. Notre Dame U., 1982-83; sr. rsch. scientist, dept. govt. and politics U. Md., College Park, 1993-96, Harrison rsch. prof. dept. govt. and politics, 1996-99, Lionel R. Bauman prof. polit. economy, 1999—. Author: Atomic Diplomacy: Hiroshima and Potsdam, 1965, rev., 1985, repub. 1994, Cold War Essays, 1970, Strategy and Program, 1973, Rebuilding America, 1984, American Economic Policy, 1985, The Decision to Use the Atomic Bomb, 1995; also articles. Home: 2317 Ashmead Pl NW Washington DC 20009-1413 Office: 2000 P St NW Ste 330 Washington DC 20036-6923 also: Univ Md 3140 Tydings Hall College Park MD 20742-8221

ALPERS, DAVID HERSHEL, physician, educator; b. Phila., May 9, 1935; s. Bernard Jacob and Lillian (Sher) A.; m. Melanie Goldman, Aug. 12, 1977; children: Ann, Ruth, Barbara. BA, Harvard U., 1956, MD, 1960. Intern Mass. Gen. Hosp., Boston, 1960-61, resident in internal medicine, 1961-62; instr. medicine Harvard U., 1965-67, assoc. in medicine, 1967-68, asst. prof., 1968-69; asst. prof. medicine Washington U., St. Louis, 1969-72, assoc. prof., 1972-73, prof., 1973—, William B. Kountz prof., 1997—, dir. gastrointestinal divsn., 1969-97. Author: (with others) Manual of Nutritional Therapeutics, 3rd edit., 1995; assoc. editor: Textbook of Gastroenterology, 3d edit., 1999, Physiology of the Gastrointestinal Tract, 3rd edit., 1994; assoc. editor Jour. Clin. Investigation, 1977-82; editor Am. Jour. Physiology, Gastrointestinal and Liver Physiology, 1991-97; contbr. articles and revs. to profl. jours., chpts. to books. With USPHS, 1962-64. Mem. Am. Soc. Clin. Investigation, Assn. Am. Physicians, Am. Gastroent. Assn. (pres. 1990-91, Friedenwald medal 1997), Am. Soc. Biochem. Molecular Biology (editl. bd. 1998—), Am. Fedn. Clin. Rsch., Am. Soc. Clin. Nutrition. Office: Washington U Med Sch Dept Internal Medicine PO Box 8124 Saint Louis MO 63156-8124

ALPERS, EDWARD ALTER, history educator; b. Phila., Apr. 23, 1941; s. Bernard Jacob and Lillian (Sher) A.; m. Anne Adele Dixon, June 14, 1963; children: Joel Dixon, Leila Sher. AB magna cum laude, Harvard U., 1963; PhD, U. London, 1966. Lectr. history Univ. Coll., Dares Salaam, Tanzania, 1966-68; from asst. prof. to prof. history UCLA, 1968—, dean divsn. honors Coll. Letters and Sci., 1985-87, dean honors and undergrad. programs, 1987-96. Author: Ivory and Slaves in East Central Africa, 1975; editor: Walter Rodney: Revolutionary and Scholar, 1982, (newsletter) Assn. Concerned Africa Scholars, 1983-85; contbg. editor: Comparative Studies of South Asia, Africa and the Middle East, 1997—; contbr. articles to scholarly jours. Fellow Ford Found., 1972-73, NEH, 1978-79, Fulbright Found., 1980; Conf. fellow Humanities Rsch. Ctr., Nat. Australia U., Canberra, 1998; Fundacao Calouste Gulbenkian grantee, Lisbon, Portugal, 1975. Mem. Am. Hist. Assn. (mem. com. Joan Kelly Meml. prize 1998—), Africa Studies Assn. (bd. dirs. 1985-88, v.p. 1992-93, pres. 1993-94), Assn. Concerned Africa Scholars (bd. dirs. 1983-93), Alliance for Undergrad. Edn. (UCLA rep. 1987-95, co-chair 1989-92), Hist. Abstracts (adv. bd. 1994—). Office: UCLA Dept History Los Angeles CA 90095-1473

ALPERS, JOHN HARDESTY, JR., financial planning executive, retired military officer; b. Richmond, Va., Sept. 7, 1939; s. John Hardesty and Laura Elizabeth (Gaylor) A.; m. Sharon Kay Kurrie, May 1, 1971; 1 child, John Hardesty III. BS, U. Colo., 1963; MBA, InterAm. U., 1969; postgrad., USAF Squadron Officers Sch., 1968-69, USAF Command and Staff Coll., 1976-78, USAF Air War Coll., 1978-79; CFP, Nat. Endowment for Fin. Edn., 1989; CFS, Inst. Cert. Fund Specialists, 1994. Registered investment adv. svc. exec. Commd. 2d lt. USAF, 1964; advanced through grades to lt. col., 1979; SAC B-52 navigator, select radar bombardier P.R., 1967-70; squadron weapon systems officer Ubon RTAFB, Thailand, 1970-71; radar strike officer Linebacker II strike plans officer, 1972; prisoner of war Hanoi, North Vietnam, 1972-73; asst. wing weapons officer Seymour-Johnson AFB, N.C., 1971-72; wing command post contr. Seymour-Johnson AFB, 1973-74; asst. prof. aerospace studies AFROTC U. Ariz., Tucson, 1974-78; asst. div. chief aviation sci. USAF Acad., Colorado Springs, 1978-79, spl. asst. to commandant, 1979-80; divsn. chief plans, policy and standardization/evaluation, 1980-83, ret., 1983; reg. rep. Waddell & Reed, Inc., 1986-90, Fin. Network Investment Corp., 1990-97; lectr., spkr. in field. POW/MIA Activist. With USCG, 1961-63. Decorated Legion of Merit, DFD (2), Bronze Star for Valor, Air Medal (9), Air Force Commendation medal (2), Purple Heart (2), Vietnamese Cross of Gallantry; recipient ceremonial sabre U.S. Air Force Acad. Cadet Corps., 1983. Mem. Air Force Assn., Ret. Officers Assn., U.S. Strategic Inst., Am. Def. Inst., Red River Valley Fighter Pilots Assn., Arnold Air Soc., Nam-POWS, Inc., Inst. CFPs, CFP Bd. Stds., Registry Fin. Planning Practitioners, Internat. Platform Assn., Pi Kappa Alpha. Republican. Home: 90 Baker Ln Erie CO 80516 Office: Gateway Fin

Strategies Inc 212 Wells St Ste B Erie CO 80516 Address: PO Box 957 Erie CO 80516-0957

ALPERT, ANN SHARON, insurance claims examiner; b. Indpls., Feb. 24, 1938; d. Oscar and Adele Alpert. BS in Edn., Ind. U., 1959. Tchr. Indpls. Pub. Schs., 1959-60; libr. George Fry & Assocs., Chgo., 1960-62, DeLeuw, Cather & Co., Chgo., 1962-65, Arthur Young & Co., CPAs, Chgo., 1965-74; statis. asst. Sargent & Lundy, Chgo., 1974-81, computer liaison agt., 1981-83, tech. editor, 1983-87; sales assoc. Jewelmaster, Inc., Chgo., 1987-88; claims processor Benefit Trust Life Ins. Co., 1988-90; claims examiner Ft. Dearborn Life Ins. Co., 1990-91, sr. claims examiner, 1991—. Fellow Life Mgmt. Inst. (assoc. customer svc.); mem. Chgo. Claims Assn.

ALPERT, CAROLINE EVELYN, nurse; b. Bklyn., June 18, 1926; d. Harry Noah and Anna Fanny (Walfish) Spalter; m. Meyer Alpert, Jan. 21, 1951; children: Robert, Linda, Mark, David, Steven. Diploma, Jewish Hosp. Bklyn., 1947; AAS in Human Services, Westchester Community Coll., 1988. RN, N.Y. Staff nurse Jewish Hosp. Bklyn., 1947-51, 53, Burbank Hosp., Fitchburg, Mass., 1952-53; radiation therapy staff nurse Roswell Park Meml. Inst., Buffalo, 1953-54; substitute sch. nurse Westchester County Schs., N.Y., 1974-85; sch. nurse Yonkers (N.Y.) Bd. Edn., 1985-96, ret., 1996; substitute sch. nurse Yonkers Schs., 1996—; nurse Westchester Summer Day Camp, Mamaroneck, N.Y., summers, 1976-86. Mem. Jewish Hosp. Bklyn. Alumni Assn. (life). Democrat. Avocations: knitting, sewing, photography, computers, reading. Home: 80 Avondale Rd Yonkers NY 10710-2021

ALPERT, DANIEL, television executive; b. Chgo., June 20, 1952; s. Herbert and Miriam Florence (Nemiroff) A.; m. Doreen Marie Podolski, Apr. 30, 1976; children: Hilary Marie, Neil Andrew. BA, Mich. State U., 1973, postgrad., 1974-76. News reporter, disk jockey Sta. WITL-AM-FM, Lansing, Mich., 1973; audio producer Instructional Media Ctr. Mich. State U., East Lansing, 1973-74; dir. pub. info. Sta. WKAR-TV, East Lansing, 1974-76; v.p., dir. pub. info. Sta. WTVS, Detroit, 1976-82, sr. v.p., acting gen. mgr., 1983, sr. v.p., asst. gen. mgr., 1983-96, sr. v.p. sta. mgr., 1996—. Contbr. articles on travel and sci. local newspapers. Trustee Karmanos Cancer Inst., Detroit, 1984—. Recipient Devel. award Corp. for Pub. Broadcasting, 1976, Promotion award Broadcast Promotion Assn., 1978, Pub. Broadcasting Svc., 1981, Govt. Rels. awards Nat. Assn. Pub. TV Stas., 1989, 96, ACE award Mich. Assn. Broadcasters, 1991. Mem. Nat. Acad. TV Arts and Scis. (gov. Detroit chpt. 1980-97), Mich. Assn. Broadcasters, Mich. Pub. Broadcasters (exec. com. 1995—). Office: Sta WTVS 7441 2nd Ave Detroit MI 48202-2701

ALPERT, DEDE WHITTLETON (DEDE ALPERT), state legislator; b. N.Y.C., Oct. 6, 1945; d. Harry Mark and Dorothy (Lehn) Whittleton; m. Michael Edward Alpert, Jan. 1, 1964; children: Lehn, Kristin, Alison. Student, Pomona Coll., 1963-65; LLD (hon.), Western Am. U., 1994. Mem. from 78th dist. Calif. State Assembly, Sacramento, 1990-96; mem. from 39th dist. Calif. Senate, Sacramento, 1997—; chairwoman Women's Legislators Caucus, Sacramento, 1993, Assembly Edn. Com., 1995, Senate Revenue and Taxation Com.; active Calif. Tourism Commn., Sacramento, 1990—, Calif. Libr. Allocations Bd., Sacramento, 1993—; com. mem. Edn. Standards and Teaching Training, Appropriations Subcom. on Fiscal Oversight, Joint Com. on Fisheries and Aquaculture, Pacific Fisheries Legis. Task Force, Calif. Commission on Status of Women. Author: Mammography Quality Assurance Act 1992, Assembly Bill 114 of 1993, Workplace Violence Safety Act, 1994, Battered Women's Protection Act, 1994, ABC, 1995, California Assessment Academic Achievement Act, 1995. Spl. advocate Voices for Children, San Diego, 1982-90; mem. bd. Solana Beach (Calif.) Sch. Bd., 1983-90, also pres.; pres. beach and county guild United Cerebral Palsy, San Diego, 1986. Recipient Legis. award Calif. Regional Occupation Program, 1991-92, Am. Acad. Pediats., 1991-92, San Diego Psychol. Assn., 1993-94, Commitment to Children award Calif. Assn. for Edn. of Young Children, 1991-92, Legis. Commendation award Nat. Assn. for Yr.-Round Edn., 1991-92, State Commn. on Status of Women, 1993-94, Friend of Public Edn. award Calif. Sch. Bds. Assn., 1997-98; named Friend of Yr., Children's PKU Network, 1991-92, Woman of Yr., Nat. Women's Polit. Caucus San Diego, 1991-92, Orgn. for Rehab. through Tng., 1993-94, High Tech Legislator of Yr., Am. Electronics Assn., 1991-92, 1993-94, 1997, Calif. Sch.-Age Consortium, 1993-94, Women of Distinction, Soropimists Internat. of La Jolla, 1993-94, Assemblymember of Yr., Calif. Assn. Edn. Young Children, 1993-94, Calif. Tourism Hall of Fame, 1997. Mem. Charter 100 of San Diego, Calif. Elected Women's Assn. for Edn. and Rsch. (pres. 1995-96). Democrat. Mem. Congregation Ch. Avocations: golf, reading. Office: State Capitol District 39 Sacramento CA 95814 also: 1557 Columbia St San Diego CA 92101-2934

ALPERT, HOLLIS, writer; b. Herkimer, N.Y., Sept. 24; s. Abram and Myra (Carroll) A.; m. Joan O'Leary (dec.). Student, New Sch. Social Research, 1947-49. Book reviewer Sat. Rev., N.Y. Times, others, 1947-59; film critic Sat. Review, after 1950, Woman's Day, 1953-60; assoc. fiction editor New Yorker, 1950-56; contbg. editor Woman's Day, 1956-69; mng. editor World Mag., after 1972, film editor, lively arts editor, after 1973; editor in chief Am. Film Mag., Washington, 1975-80; Algur Meadows Disting. vis. prof. So. Meth. U., 1982; freelance author, 1980—; Past dir. Edward MacDowell Assn.; vis. lectr. Yale U., 1972; film lectr Philharm. Ctr., Naples, Fla., 1995—. Author: The Summer Lovers, 1958, Some Other Time, 1960, The Dreams and the Dreamers, 1962, For Immediate Release, 1963, The Barrymores, 1964, The Claimant, 1968, The People Eaters, 1971, Smash, 1973, (under name Robert Carroll) A Disappearance, 1974, The Life and Times of Porgy and Bess, 1990, Broadway! 125 Years of Musical Theatre, 1991; editor: The Actors Life—Journals, Charlton Heston, 1978, Burton, 1986, Fellini, 1986; contbr. numerous short stories to mags. including Harper's Bazaar, The New Yorker. Served to 1st lt. AUS, 1942-46, ETO. Recipient Critic's award Screen Dirs.' Guild Am., 1957. Mem. Nat. Soc. Film Critics (chmn. 1972-73). Home: 130 San Rafael Ln Naples FL 34119-4652

ALPERT, JOEL JACOBS, medical educator, pediatrician; b. New Haven, May 9, 1930; s. Herman Harold and Alice (Jacobs) A.; m. Barbara Ellen Wasserstrom, July 13, 1957; children: Norman, Mark, Deborah. AB, Yale U., 1952; MD, Harvard U., 1956. Diplomate Am. Bd. Pediatrics. Intern in medicine Children's Hosp. Med. Ctr., Boston, 1956-57, jr. asst. resident in medicine, 1957-58, chief resident for ambulatory svcs., fellow in medicine, 1961-62, from asst. to sr. assoc., 1962-72; exch. registrar St. Mary's Hosp. Med. Sch., London, 1958-59; from instr. to assoc. prof. Med. Sch., Harvard U., Boston, 1962-72, lectr., 1972; pediatrician in chief Boston City Hosp., 1972-92; prof. pediatrics and pub. health Boston (Mass.) U. Sch. Medicine, 1972—, chmn. dept. pediatrics, 1972-93, also prof. sociomed. scis. and pub. health law, 1980—; Dozer vis. prof. Ben. Gurion Sch. Medicine, Beersheva, Israel, 1979; Raine Found. vis. prof. U. Western Australia, Perth, 1983; James and Jean Davis Prestige visitor U. Otago, Dunedin, New Zealand, 1995; cons. USPHS, 1972—, Children's Hosp., Boston, 1972; spl. cons. pres. N.Y.C. Health and Hosps. Corp., 1989; vis. prof. pediatrics Columbia Coll. Phys. and Surg., NYU Sch. Medicine; mem. med. adv. com. N.Y.C. Health and Hosps. Corp., 1989—. Author books, including: The Education of Physicians For Primary Care, 1974; also numerous papers. Mem. Town Meeting, Winchester, Mass., 1970-72; mem. exec. com. Mass. Com. for Children and Youth, Boston, 1975-82; chmn. adv. com. Mass. Poison Info. System, Boston, 1980-92; bd. dirs. Med. Found., Boston, 1992—; cons. Commonwealth Fund and MEM Assocs., 1996—. Capt. U.S. Army, 1959-61. Recipient lifetime achievement award Mass. Poison Info. System, 1992, Hon. Mention Pub. Health Svc. award Pew Found., 1999, Pew Found. award for Achievement in Primary Care Edn.; numerous grants, 1965—; spl. fellow Nat. Ctr. Health Svcs. Rsch., London, 1971. Fellow Am. Acad. Pediatrics (v.p. 1997-98, pres. 1998-99, Job Lewis Smith award 1992); mem. Inst. Medicine of NAS (mem. governing coun. 1993-95, mem. bd. families and children 1993-95, mem. task force on future of primary care 1994-96), Am. Pediatric Soc., Soc. Pediatric Rsch., Ambulatory Pediatric Assn. (pres. 1969, George Armstrong medal 1989), Mass. Assn. Pediat. Dept. Chmn. (chmn. 1976-78, 81-93), Yale Club, Harvard Club, Aescalapian Club, Lancet Club, St. Botolph Club, Alpha Omega Alpha. Jewish. Home: 224 Allandale Rd Apt B Chestnut Hill MA 02467-3287 Office: Boston U Sch Medicine Boston Med Ctr 91 E Concord St Boston MA 02118-2335

ALPERT, JOSEPH STEPHEN, physician, educator; b. New Haven, Feb. 1, 1942; s. Zelly Charles and Beatrice Ann (Kopsofsky) A.; m. Helle Mathiasen, Aug. 6, 1965; children: Eva Elisabeth, Niels David. BA magna cum laude, Yale U., 1963; MD cum laude, Harvard U., 1969. Diplomate Am. Bd. Internal Medicine (cardiovascular disease). Successively intern, resident in internal medicine, fellow in cardiovascular disease Peter Bent Brigham Hosp.-Harvard U. Med. Sch., Boston, 1969-74; dir. Samuel A. Levine cardiac unit, asst. prof. medicine Peter Bent Brigham Hosp.-Harvard U. Med. Sch., 1976-78; prof., dir. divsn. cardiovascular medicine U. Mass. Med. Sch., Worcester, 1978-92, vice-chm. dept. medicine, 1990—, Edward Budnitz prof. of cardiovascular medicine, 1988-92; Robert W. and Irene P. Flinn prof., chmn. dept. medicine U. Ariz., 1992—; cons. W. Roxbury VA Hosp., Boston, VA Med. Ctr., Tucson; sec., treas. med. staff U. Mass. Med. Ctr., 1979-81, pres. med. staff, 1981-82. Author: The Heart Attack Handbook, 1978, 2d edit., 1985, 3d edit., 1993, Cardiovascular Physiopathology, 1984; co-author: Manual of Coronary Care, 1977, 80, 84, 87, 93, Manual of Cardiovascular Diagnosis and Therapy, 1980, 84, 88, 96, Valvular Heart Disease, 1981, 87, Intensive Care Medicine, 1985, 2d edit., 1991, The Clinician's Companion, 1986, Modern Coronary Care, 1990, 2d edit., 1996, Diagnostic Atlas of the Heart, 1994, Cardiology for the Primary Care Physician, 1996, 2d edit., 1998, Primary Care of Native American Patients, 1999; assoc. editor: Jour. History of Medicine and Allied Scis., 1977-80; editl. cons. Little, Brown & Co., Appleton-Century Crofts; mem. editl. bd. Am. Jour. Cardiology, 1985—, Archives Internal Medicine, 1987—, Heart and Lung, 1987-90, Cardiology, 1985—, assoc. editor, 1987—, editor-in-chief, 1991—; mem. editl. bd. Geriatric Cardiovascular Medicine, 1988-89, Am. Jour. Noninvasive Cardiology, 1987-95, Am. Heart Jour., 1992-97, Internat. Jour. Cardiology, 1992—, European Heart Jour., 1995—; contbr. articles to profl. jours. Lt. comdr. USNR, 1974-76. Recipient Gold medal U. Copenhagen, 1968, Edward Rhodes Stitt award San Diego Naval Hosp., 1976, George W. Thorn award Peter Bent Bingham Hosp., 1977, Outstanding Tchr. award U. Mass. Med. Sch., 1981, 86, 87, 90, U. Ariz. Cardiology, 1995, 97-99; Fulbright scholar Copenhagen, 1963-64; USPHS-Mass. Heart Assn. fellow, 1971-72, NIH spl. rsch. fellow, 1972-73. Fellow ACP, Am. Coll. Cardiology (jour. editl. bd. mem. 1983-86, chmn. tng. dirs. com. 1991—, bd. trustees 1996-2001), Am. Coll. Chest Physicians (gov. for Mass. 1983-85); mem. AAAS, Am. Heart Assn. (fellow coun. clin. cardiology, vice chmn. 1991-92, chmn. 1993-95, exec. com. 1986—), Am. Assn. History of Medicine, Am. Fedn. Clin. Rsch., Assn. Univ. Cardiologists, New Eng. Cardiovascular Club, Assn. Profs. of Medicine, Danish Cardiology Assn. (hon.), Argentine Heart Assn. (fgn. corr.), Aesculapian Club, Phi Beta Kappa, Sigma Xi, Alpha Omega Alpha. Office: 1501 N Campbell Ave Tucson AZ 85724-0001 *I have lived my life following 3 rules: (1) maintain enthusiasm for living and learning; (2) love family and friends; and (3) work hard.*

ALPERT, MARK IRA, marketing educator; b. Duluth, Minn., Nov. 6, 1942; s. Isadore L. and Lillian Alpert; m. Judith Itzkovits, Sept. 3, 1967; 1 child, Nicole Deborah. BS, MIT, 1964; MBA, U. So. Calif., 1965, MS, 1967, D of Bus. Adminstrn., 1968. Asst. prof. mktg. Calif. State U., Long Beach, 1967-68; asst. prof. mktg. U. Tex., Austin, 1968-72, assoc. prof., 1972-76, prof., 1976—, La Quinta Motor Inns Centennial prof. bus., 1982-87, Foley's Federated prof. in retailing, 1987—; vis. prof. bus. U. Pitts., 1978; cons. Zenith Mgmt. Co., Duluth, 1980—. Author: Pricing Decisions, 1971; co-author: Managerial Analysis Marketing, 1970; also articles in profl. jours.; mem. editorial rev. bd. Jour. of Mktg., 1979—, Jour. of Retailing, 1979—, Jour. Mktg. Rsch., 1985-91, Jour. of Bus. Rsch., 1988—. Mem. exec. com. Congregation Agudas Achm, Austin, 1977, 78, bd. dirs., 1977-79, 85-88; bd. dirs. B'nai Brith Hillel, Austin, 1980-85. Mem. Am. Mktg. Assn. (track chmn. 1976, 87), Assn. for Consumer Research, Am. Psychol. Assn. Avocations: tennis, golf, water skiing, music. Home: 5956 Highland Hills Dr Austin TX 78731-4059 Office: Univ Tex Dept Mktg Cba 7 # 202 Austin TX 78712

ALPERT, MARTIN JEFFREY, chiropractic physician; b. N.Y.C., Apr. 22, 1951; s. Sheldon Lee and Beatrice (Ostrager) A.; m. Elyse Shelly Sherman, Dec. 26, 1976; children: Chad, Mitchell. BA, Syracuse U., 1972; D Chiropractic, N.Y. Chiropractic Coll., 1976; MS, U. Bridgeport, 1979. Diplomate Am. Bd. Disability Analysts, Am. Acad. Pain Mgmt., Am. Bd. Profl. Disability Cons. Pvt. practice, Yonkers, N.Y., 1977-84, Hollywood, Fla., 1985, Coconut Creek, Fla., 1987-92, Miami, Fla., 1992-95, Ft. Lauderdale, Fla., 1985—, Orlando, Fla., 1994—. Lt. col., SC, USAR, 1970-99. Fellow Am. Back Soc.; mem. Am. Chiropractic Assn., Internat. Chiropractors Assn., Am. Coll. Sports Medicine, Fla. Chiropractic Assn., N.Y. Acad. Scis., Am. Public Health Assn. Democrat. Avocations: jogging, chess, basketball, piano. Home: 11095 NW 14th St Coral Springs FL 33071-8214 Office: 3d Ave Chiropractic Ctr Inc 300 W Sunrise Blvd Ste 7 Fort Lauderdale FL 33311-6200

ALPERT, MICHAEL EDWARD, lawyer; b. Annapolis, Md., Nov. 13, 1942; s. Myron M. and Mary A. (Byrnes) A.; m. Deirdre Lehn Whittleton, Jan. 1, 1964; children: Lehn Patricia, Kristin Anne, Alison Daley. AB, Pomona Coll., 1965; JD, UCLA, 1969. Bar: Calif. 1970. Assoc. Gibson, Dunn & Crutcher, L.A., 1969-72, L.A. and San Diego, 1974-77; chief dep. commr. corps. State of Calif., 1972-74; ptnr. Gibson, Dunn & Crutcher, L.A. and San Diego, 1977-92, of counsel, 1992—. mem. editl. bd. UCLA Law Rev., 1967-69. Bd. dirs. Foodmaker, Inc., 1992—, San Diego Repertory Theatre, 1978-89, pres., 1988; mem. San Diego County Juvenile Justice Commn., 1993-97, vice-chmn., 1995, chmn., 1996, Calif. Little Hoover Commn., 1994—, vice chmn., 1995—; bd. dirs. San Diego chpt. Assn. Corp. Growth, 1987-89; mem. exec. bd. Calif. State Dem. Party. Mem. State Bar Calif., San Diego County Bar Assn., San Diego Corp. Fin. Coun. (chmn. 1982-83), Order of Coif, Lomas Santa Fe Country Club (San Diego), Phi Sigma Alpha. Office: Gibson Dunn & Crutcher 401 W A St San Diego CA 92101-7901*

ALPERT, NORMAN, chemical company executive; b. Phila., May 5, 1921; s. Barnet and Celia A.; m. Adeline Edna Gushman, Apr. 9, 1948; children: Rosalind Alice, Barbara Naomi. A.B. in Chemistry, Temple U., 1942, M.A., 1947; Ph.D. (AEC research fellow 1948-49), Purdue U., 1949. Devel. engr. Publicker Industries, Phila., 1942-45; group head Texaco, Inc., Beacon, N.Y., 1949-59; div. mgr. Exxon Research, Linden, N.J., 1959-79; v.p., dir. research Hooker Chem. Co., Grand Island, N.Y., 1979-82; v.p. spl. environ. projects Occidental Chem. Corp., Niagara Falls, N.Y., 1982-84, v.p. corp. environ. affairs, 1984-86; environmental cons. Author. Mgr. Career Explorer Post local Boy Scouts Am., 1981. Mem. Am. Chem. Soc., Soc. Automotive Engrs., Niagara Frontier Assn. Research and Devel. Dirs. Patentee in field. Home: 4060 Lower River Rd Youngstown NY 14174-9739

ALPERT, WARREN, oil company executive, philanthropist; b. Chelsea, Mass., Dec. 2, 1920; s. Goodman and Tena (Horowitz) A. BS, Boston U., 1942; MBA, Harvard U., 1947; DBA (hon.), Bryant Coll. Mgmt. trainee Standard Oil Co. of Calif., 1947-48; financial specialist The Calif. Oil Co., 1948-52; pres. Warren Petroleum Co., 1952-54; now chmn. bd.; founder, pres., chmn. bd. Warren Equities, Inc., from 1954; chmn. emeritus Ritz Tower Hotel, 1995—; chmn. bd. Kenyon Oil Co., Inc., Mid-Valley Petroleum Corp., Puritan Oil Co., Inc., Drake Petroleum Co., Inc.; mem. of U.S. Com. for UN, 1958; exec. com. Small Bus. Adminstrn., 1958; adminstr. for adminstrn. U.S. AID, 1962; former trustee, mem. exec. com. Boston U.; trustee Emerson Coll.; former v.p. Petroleum Mktg. Edn. Found.; bd. dirs. Assocs. of Harvard Bus. Sch., Mass. Life; mem. com. for resource and devel. Harvard Med. Sch., bd. fellows. Bd. dirs. World Coun. Synagogues; bd. overseers Albert Einstein Med. Sch.; founder Warren Alpert Found.; bd. fellows Harvard Med. Sch.; former trustee Boston U., Emerson Coll. Andrew Wellington Cordier fellow Sch. Internat. Affairs, Columbia U.; Harvard Med. Sch. Rsch. Ctr. Bldg. named in his honor, 1993. Mem. Am. Petroleum Inst. (dir. mktg. divsn.), Harvard Bus. Sch. Club (exec. com., dir., bd. govs., pres. 1960-61), Am. Petroleum Industry 25 Year Club, Young Presidents Orgn. (past dir.), Harvard Club (N.Y.C., mem. house com.), Marco Polo Club, Met. Club, University Club. Office: Warren Equities Inc 375 Park Ave Ste 2502 New York NY 10022*

ALPERT, WILLIAM HAROLD, artist; b. N.Y.C., Dec. 21, 1934; s. Jacob Joseph and Fannie (Leff) Alperovicz. BA, UCLA, 1963, MA, 1965. adj. prof. painting Cooper Union Sch. Art, N.Y.C., 1979-82; adj. instr. drawing Parsons Sch. Design, N.Y.C., 1981-82, Pratt Inst. Summer Program, 1981; instr. painting, drawing and watercolor Sch. Visual Arts, 1989—. Exhbns. include Constructs Orgn. Ind. Artists, Bleecker Renaissance, N.Y., 1978, Orgn. Ind. Artists Postcard Show, Bologna Art Fair, Italy, 1978, Indpls. Mus. Art, 1978, Albright-Knox Mus., 1978, Joe & Emily Lowe Art Gallery, Syracuse U., 1980, W. Paterson Collection of N.J., 1981, Coll. Charleston (S.C.), 1987, 89, The N.Y. Bot. Garden, Bronx, 1993; pub. collections include Power Gallery Contemporary Art, Sydney, Australia; contbr. to N.Y. Art Yearbook, 1975-76. Avocations: pharmacy, photography, travel. Home: 64 Grand St # 5 New York NY 10013-2267

ALPERT-GILLIS, LINDA JAYNE, clinical psychologist; b. Quincy, Mass., Nov. 12, 1959; d. Edwin and Joyce Eleanor (Zucker) Alpert; m. Stephen Michael Gillis, June 2, 1985; children: Sarah Elizabeth, Michael David, Andrew James. ScB magna cum laude, Brown U., 1982; MA, U. Rochester, 1985, PhD, 1987. Lic. psychology, N.Y. Clin. assoc. psychology U. Rochester (N.Y) Dept. Psychology Ctr. for Community Study, 1986-87; sr. instr. psychiatry U. Rochester Sch. Medicine & Dentistry, 1987-88, asst. prof. psychiatry and pediatrics, 1988-94, dir. child and adolescent psychology tng. program, 1992—, assoc. prof. psychiatry and pediatrics, 1994—; dir. Child and Adolescent Psychiatry Clinic Strong Meml. Hosp., 1996—; asst. dir. children of divorce intervention program U. Rochester, 1986-89; cons. single-parent family project Western Monroe Mental Health Ctr., 1984-86, Noyes Meml. Hosp., Dansville, N.Y., 1988-94; investigator children and families affected by divorce, children and families affected by critical illness. Contbr. articles to profl. jours.; co-author (curricula) Interventions for Children of Divorce, various children's books. Mem. Am. Psychol. Assn., N.Y. State Psychol. Assn., Genesee Valley Psychol. Assn., Soc. Pediat. Psychology, Phi Beta Kappa, Sigma Xi. Office: U Rochester Med Ctr 300 Crittenden Blvd Rochester NY 14642-0001

ALPHER, RALPH ASHER, physicist; b. Washington, Feb. 3, 1921; s. Samuel and Rose (Maleson) A.; m. Louise Ellen Simons, Jan. 28, 1942; children: Harriet Alpher Lebetkin, Victor. B.S. George Washington U, 1943, M.S., 1945, Ph.D., 1948; ScD Honoris Causa, Union Coll., 1992, Renssalaer Poly. Inst., 1993. Physicist Bur. Ordnance and Naval Ordnance Lab., U.S. Navy, Washington, 1940-44, Applied Physics Lab., Johns Hopkins U., Silver Spring, Md., 1944-55, Gen. Electric Research and Devel. Ctr., Schenectady, 1955-86; disting. research prof. of physics Union Coll., Schenectady, 1986—; adj. prof. aero. engring. Rensselaer Poly. Inst., 1958-63, adj. prof. physics, 1986-92. Contbr. articles to books and profl. jours. in fields astrophysics, cosmology, physics of fluids. Bd. dirs. Mohawk-Hudson Council for Ednl. TV, 1974-80, 82-87, chmn., 1978-80, 86-87; bd. dirs. Dudley Obs., Union U., Albany, N.Y., 1968-72, 80-86, v.p. 1983-86, adminstr., disting. sr. scientist, 1987—. Recipient Magellanic Premium Am. Philos. Soc., 1975, Georges Vanderlinden prize Belgian Royal Acad. Scis., Letters and Fine Arts, 1975, John Price Wetherill medal Franklin Inst., 1980, Phys. and Math. Scis. prize N.Y. Acad. Scis., 1981, Disting. Alumnus award George Washington U., 1987, Henry Draper medal NAS, 1993. Fellow Am. Phys. Soc. (councillor-at-large 1979-82, exec. com. 1980-81), AAAS (sect. B physics steering com. 1982-86), Am. Acad. Arts & Scis.; mem. Fedn. Am. Scientists, Am. Astron. Soc., Internat. Astron Union, Sigma Xi. Club: Internat. Torch. Home: 2159 Orchard Park Dr Niskayuna NY 12309-2218 Office: Union Coll Dept Physics Schenectady NY 12308

ALPHER, VICTOR SETH, retired clinical psychologist, consultant,; b. Washington, Oct. 20, 1954; s. Ralph Asher and Louise Ellen (Simons) A. BA, U. Pa., 1976; PhD, Vanderbilt U., 1985. Diplomate in clin. psychology Am. Bd. Profl. Psychology. Grad. fellow Vanderbilt U., Nashville, 1981-85; asst. prof. U. Tex. Health Sci. Ctr., Houston, 1986-88, clin. asst. prof., 1989-96; ret., 1996; cons. Rsch. Inst. on Addictions, Buffalo, 1990—, Meml. Geriatric Evaluation and Resource Ctr., Houston, 1991-95; bd. cons. Fla. Inst. Psychology, 1994—. Cons. reviewer Jour. Cons. and Clin. Psychology, 1996; contbr. articles to profl. jours., including Jour. Cons. and Clin. Psychology, Jour. Personality Assessment, Jour. Psychopathology and Behavioral Assessment, Psychotherapy, and Jour. Applied Physiology. Fellow Acad. Clin. Psychology; mem. Sigma Xi.

ALPIAR, HAL, management and marketing consultant, author; b. New Rochelle, N.Y., Apr. 29, 1941; s. Harold Peter and Vernetta (Roth) A.; divorced, 1972; children: Haley Alpiar Murphy, Christopher Kennedy and Melissa Monica (twins); m. Kathleen Ann Marshall, Oct. 10, 1987. BBA, Iona Coll., 1964; MBA, L.I. U., 1965; cert., Inst. Advanced Advt. Studies, 1971, New Sch. for Entrepreneurs, 1979. Account exec. Young & Rubicam, Inc., N.Y.C., 1965-68, Foote, Cone, Belding, Inc., N.Y.C., 1968; account supr. Lake Spiro Shurman, Inc., Memphis, 1968-69; mktg. and new bus. dir. Friedlich, Fearon, Strohmeier, Inc., N.Y.C., 1969-71; account supr. Wells, Rich, Greene, Inc., N.Y.C., 1971-73; mktg. and promotion mgr. Guidance Assocs. divsn. Harcourt, Brace Jovanovich, Inc., Pleasantville, N.Y., 1973-74; dir. coop. edn., asst. prof. bus. Ocean County Coll., Toms River, N.J., 1974-79; exec. dir. Mgmt. Tng. Ctr., Point Pleasant Beach, N.J., 1979-82; pres., chief exec. officer A&B Businessworks, Inc., Brick, N.J., 1982—; cons. health professions; founding exec. dir. Pa. Heart Inst., Bethlehem, 1995-96; adj. prof. bus. Pace U., 1971-73, Georgian Ct. Coll., 1980-83; pub. rels. dir. Pharm. Soc. State N.Y., 1970-72; trustee, bus. cons. Ocean County First Aid Acad., Toms River, 1979-81; two fed. appointments to region II adv. coun. SBA, 1987-91; appointee Nat. Com. for Quality Health Care, Washington, 1998, 99. Author: Doctor Business, 1994, Doctor Shopping, 1996 (Nat. Health Info. award 1997); author, editor: Job Hunter, 1971; author, producer, host 700 daily radio seminars for bus. and profl. practice mgmt.; designer, presenter: 2000 mgmt. skill devel. seminars and workshops; editor-in-chief Bus. Talk Mag., 1988; contbg. editor (cassette newsletter) M.D. Memo; columnist Healthcare Marketer's Exec. Briefing (nat. newsletter), 1998—. Avocations: swimming, landscaping, writing, reading, music. Office: Businessworks Inc Seawood Harbor PO Box 4211 Brick NJ 08723-1411

AL-QADI, IMAD LUTFI, civil engineering educator, researcher; b. Nablus, Palestine, Feb. 5, 1962; came to U.S., 1985; s. Lutfi A. and Fatemah (Abdulmajeed) M.; m. Muna M. Atout, Dec. 24, 1987; children: Dana I., Nora I., Kareem. BSCE, Yarmouk U., Irbid, Jordan, 1984; M in Engring., Pa. State U., 1986, PhD, 1990. Registered profl. engr., Pa., Va. Project engr. Nablus, 1984-85; instr., rsch. engr. Pa. State U., University Park, 1988-90; asst. prof. Va. Tech. U., Blacksburg, 1990-94, assoc. prof., coord. materials divsn., 1994-98, prof., 1998—; cons. AMACO, Atlanta, 1992, Charles Barger & Son, Inc., Lexington, Va., 1992—, numerous others; mem. Va. Bituminous Adv. Rsch. Com., Charlottesville, Va., Va. Transp. Tech. Transfer Ctr., mem. over 15 other tech. coms.; founding mem. Va. Tech. Ctr. Infrastructure Assessment and Mgmt.; presider several internat. confs. and sessions. Contbr. more than 140 articles to profl. jours. including Transp. Engring./ASCE, IEEE Trans. of Geosci. and Remote Sensing, Jour. Sci. and Engring. Corrosion/NACE, ASTM, SHRP/NRC. Recipient young investigator award NSF, 1994, STS award Edinborough U., 1993; grantee NSF, 1992, Ctr. Innovative Tech., 1992—, Ctr. Adhesive & Sealant Sci., 1991—, others. Mem. ASCE, ASTM, Transp. Rsch. Bd., Am. Soc. Engring. Edn., Assn. of Asphalt Paving Technologists (chmn. TRB com. on geosynthetics in pavements). Achievements include development of a dynamic triaxial apparatus to simulate stopping mechanism of arrester beds, of a new dynamic normal/shear testing technique to evaluate sealants, of a methodology to evaluate membranes used on bridge decks, of different techniques to abate steel corrosion in reinforced concrete; pioneering use of electromagnetic waves in hot-mix asphalt and concrete; application of geosynthetics in pavements and bridges.

AL-QUDSI, HASSAN SHABAN, engineer, project manager; b. Beirut, Mar. 12, 1958; s. Shaban H. and Samia M. (Najjar) Al-Q.; m. Hayat F. Al-Qutub, Feb. 10, 1988; children: Dalal, Mahmoud, Omar, Ali, Abdallah. BS in Engring., U. Calif., Davis, 1979; postgrad., Newport U. Registered profl. engr., Calif. Structural engr. Pace, Kuwait City, Kuwait, 1979-81; cons. II Nutech Engr., San Jose, Calif., 1981-83; resident engr. KEO, Kuwait City, 1983-89; project mgr. KNRS, Kuwait City, 1989-90; prin. River City Balsam, Calif., 1990-93; sr. project mgr. Baker Mellon Stuart, Pitts., 1993—; head engring. group ICCI, Chgo., 1995—. Pres. ICCI, 1997-99; bd. dirs., exec. com. Coll. Prep. Sch. Am., 1997—. Mem. ASCE (assoc.), Internat. Conf. of Bldg. Ofcls. (profl. mem.). Republican. Muslim. Home: 1011 Childs St Wheaton IL 60187-4814 Office: Baker Mellon Stuart 410 Rouser Rd Coraopolis PA 15108-2722

ALSAKER, ROBERT JOHN, information systems specialist; b. Los Angeles, June 15, 1945; s. Lauris Ronald and Hazel Mildred (Danz) A.; m. Cynthia Ann Gillesvog, Feb. 25, 1984; children: Troy R., Erik G., Karlee A. AA, Fullerton (Calif.) Jr. Coll., 1966; BS, Moorhead (Minn.) State Coll., 1970. Project mgr. Jet Propulsion Lab., Pasadena, Calif., 1970-80; mgr. mgmt. info. systems Kroy Inc., Scottsdale, Ariz., 1980-85; adminstr. City of Pasadena, 1985-86; mgr. tech. cons. U.S. West Info. Systems, Phoenix, 1986-88; v.p. MIS ACB Cos., Phoenix, 1988-95; dir. MIS Midwest Pub., Inc., Phoenix, 1995-97; v.p. MIS Santa Fe Natural Tobacco Co., 1997—. Served in U.S. Army, 1968-69, Vietnam. Republican. Lutheran. Office: 1368 Cerrillos Rd Santa Fe NM 87505-3507

ALSAPIEDI, CONSUELO VERONICA, psychoanalytic psychotherapist, consultant; b. N.Y.C., Nov. 9, 1927; d. Vernon Joseph Karram and Constance Agatha Taylor; m. John Romeo Alsapiedi, May 12, 1951; children: John Rino, Sharon Anne. BA, Seton Hill Coll., 1949; MSW, Fordham U., 1972; D Social Work, Psychoanalytic Inst. for Clin.Social Workers, N.Y.C., 1985. Lic. and cert. social worker, N.Y.; cert. alcoholism counselor, substance abuse counselor; bd. cert. diplomate. Case aide II, Cath. Charities, Bklyn., 1949-51, clin. social worker, 1963-70, clin. social worker rep. in Family Ct., 1965-70; inpatient and outpatient psychiat. social worker Office Mental Health, Queens Village, N.Y., 1972-95; pvt. practice psychoanalytic psychotherapy, N.Y.C., 1975-89, Forest Hills, N.Y., 1989—; ednl. lectr.; condr. workshops; mem. art adv. bd. Queens Ind. Living Ctr., Jamaica., N.Y., 1996—, vol., 1996, bd. dirs., 1998—. Vol. Nat. Mental Health Assn., Catskill, N.Y., 1994. Mem. N.Y. State Soc. for Clin. Social Work Psychotherapy (diplomate, sec.-rec. sec. 1979-82, membership chmn. 1990—, pres. Queens chpt. 1986-88, sec. 1992—), Brain Injury Assn., Menninger Soc. Roman Catholic. Avocations: piano, music, ballet and stage performances, art appreciation. Office: 71-36 110th St Ste 1K Forest Hills NY 11375-4838

ALSBERG, DIETRICH ANSELM, electrical engineer; b. Kassel, Germany, June 5, 1917; came to U.S., 1939, naturalized, 1943; s. Adolf and Elisabeth (Hofmann) A.; m. Glenna Rose Le Baron, Nov. 6, 1942; children: Peter Allyn, Ronald Ashley, Terry Wayne, David James (dec.). B.S. in E.E, Tech. U., Stuttgart, 1938; postgrad., Case Sch. Applied Sci., Cleve., 1939-40. Engr. Wright Tool and Forge Co., Barberton, Ohio, 1940-41, Bridgwater Machine Co., Akron, Ohio, 1941-43; with Bell Labs., Holmdel, Murray Hill, Whippany (N.J.) and N.Y., 1945-82; head various depts. Bell Labs., 1965-82. Contbr. articles to profl. jours. and books. Mem. Berkeley Heights (N.J.) Bd. Edn., 1955-58; chmn. Environ. Commn., Berkeley Heights, 1971-76; various office positions local Meth. Ch. With U.S. Army, ETO, 1943-45. Fellow IEEE (life).; mem. Electromagnetics Acad. Methodist. Patentee in field of communications, electromagnetic waves, missile and space guidance and civil engineering. Home: 8545 Carmel Valley Rd Carmel CA 93923-9556

ALSCHULER, JOHN HAAS, architect; b. Chgo., Sept. 19, 1918; s. Alfred Samuel and Rose (Haas) A.; m. Betty Marie Rogers, Sept. 14, 1942 (div. Apr. 1963); children: Jeannie Reed, John Jr., Liora; m. Madge Friedman, Apr. 30, 1965. BArch, MIT, 1943. Lic. architect, Ill, NCARB. Draftsman Perkins & Will, Chgo., 1947-48; ptnr. Friedman, Alschuler & Sincere, Chgo., 1948-62; pvt. practice Chgo., 1963—; arbitrator Am. Arbitration Assn., Chgo., 1980—. Chmn. code drafting com. sch. safety Ill. Supt. Pub. Instrn., Springfield, 1963-70. Lt. USN, 1943-46. Mem. AIA. Home and Office: 538 W Dickens Ave Chicago IL 60614-4521

ALSCHULER, SAM, retired lawyer; b. Aurora, Ill., June 16, 1913; s. Benjamin P. and Lillian (Reinheimer) A.; m. Winifred King, Feb. 8, 1939 (dec. Dec. 1998); children: Albert W., Therese Alschuler Hale. AB, U. Wis., 1933; JD, U. Chgo., 1935. Bar: Ill. 1935, U.S. Supreme Ct. 1953. Pvt. practice Aurora, 1935; ptnr. Alschuler & Funkey, 1935-84, counsel, 1984-96; ret.; bd. dirs. Weslin Properties, Inc., 1982-93. Mem. Aurora Spl. Svc. Area Com., 1976; pres. bd. dirs. United Cmty. Svc., Aurora, 1959-68; chmn. United Fund Gen. Campaign, 1966; mem. Citizens Cmty. Survey Com., 1964; vice chmn., dir. Kane County Coun. for Equal Opportunity, 1966-69; corp. counsel City of Aurora, 1961-65; pres., trustee Ill. Assn. for the Crippled, 1948-63, pres., 1963; governing mem. Copley Meml. Hosp., Rush-Copley Meml. Ctr., 1942; past pres., hon. bd. dirs. Rehab. Ctr. for So. Kane, Kendall and DeKalb Counties. With AUS, 1944-45. Recipient Copley Caring award Copley Healthcare Found., 1991. Mem. ABA, Ill. Bar Assn., Kane County Bar Assn. (Community Svc. award 1993), Am. Judicature Soc., Greater Aurora C. of C. (pres. 1953-55, dir.), Elks, Moose, Rotary, Sigma Delta Chi, Zeta Beta Tau. Democrat. Home: 119 S Buell Ave Aurora IL 60506-4603

ALSEN, EBERHARD, educator; b. Nuremberg, Germany, Oct. 26, 1939; came to U.S., 1962; s. Karl and Gertrud Alsen; married; children: Emilia, Louisa. MA, Ind. U., 1965, PhD, 1967. Teaching asst. Ind. U., Bloomington, 1963-65; asst. prof. U. Minn., Mpls., 1966-69; assoc. prof., prof. SUNY, Cortland, N.Y., 1969—; Fulbright prof. U. Tubingen, Germany, 1975-76, 81-82; C4 prof. U. Trier, Germany, 1993-95. Author: Salinger's Glass Stories as a Composite Novel, 1983, American Short Stories on Film: Bartleby, 1986, Romantic Postmodernism in American Fiction, 1996. Travel grantee Fulbright Commn., Washington, 1993-95. Avocation: sailboat racing. Home: 12 Le Roy Ave Myers NY 14882 Office: SUNY Dept English Cortland NY 13045

ALSENTZER, WILLIAM JAMES, JR., lawyer; b. Ravenna, Ohio, Mar. 15, 1942; s. William J. Alsentzer and Vivian (Guy) Soash; children: Lesley Joan, Michelle Guy. AB, Duke U., 1964, JD, 1966. Bar: Del. 1966, U.S. Dist. Ct. Del. 1967, Ariz. 1980, U.S. Dist. Ct. Ariz. 1980. Assoc. Wilson & Lynam, Wilmington, Del., 1967-70; ptnr. Bayard, Brill & Handelman, Wilmington, 1970-79; v.p., gen. counsel Bapt. Hosps. and Health Systems, Phoenix, 1979—, now exec. v.p., gen. counsel. Mem. ABA, Maricopa County Bar Assn., Am. Health Lawyers Assn., Fedn. Ins. and Corp. Counsel. Office: Bapt Hosps and Health Systems 2224 W Northern Ave Ste 300D Phoenix AZ 85021-4928

ALSOBROOK, HENRY BERNIS, JR., lawyer; b. New Orleans, Nov. 9, 1930; s. Henry Bernis and Ethel (Smith A.; children: Eugenie Wilson, John Gleason, Emily Woodward. B.A., Tulane U., 1952, J.D., 1957. Bar: La. 1957. Since practiced in New Orleans; sr. partner firm Adams & Reese; past mem. faculty Tulane U. Law Sch.; bd. dirs. Def. Research Inst., 1978-81, 85-88, chmn. med.-legal com., 1967-72; lectr. in field. Author articles in field; mem. editorial bds. legal jours. Chmn. dean's coun. Tulane U., 1983-88; elder St. Charles Ave. Presbyn. Ch., New Orleans; 1st pres. Les Compagnons du Barreau de La Louisiane, 1985—; treas., bd. dirs. La. State Mus.; bd. dirs. New Orleans Symphony Soc., New Orleans Opera.; mem. La. Gov.'s Commn. on Med. Malpractice, 1989—; mem. Audubon Inst. Aquarium Capital Campaign Commn. With USNR, 1953. Fellow Am. Bar Found., Am. Coll. Trial Lawyers; mem. ABA (past chmn. standing com. commerce, ho. of dels. 1984-89), La. Bar Assn. (pres. 1982-83), New Orleans Bar Assn., Internat. Assn. Def. Counsel (exec. com. 1982-88, pres. 1986-87), Fedn. Ins. Counsel, New Orleans Assn. Def. Counsel, La. Assn. Def. Counsel (gov. 1965), La. Law Inst. (council 1984-89), Soc. Med. Assn. Counsel (charter), Soc. Hosp. Attys. (charter), AMA (hon.). Clubs: New Orleans Country, La, Avoca Duck, Lakeshore, Pickwick. Office: Adams & Reese 4500 One Shell Sq New Orleans LA 70139-4501

ALSOP, DONALD DOUGLAS, federal judge; b. Duluth, Minn., Aug. 28, 1927; s. Robert Alvin and Mathilda (Aaseng) A.; m. Jean Lois Tweeten, Aug. 16, 1952; children: David, Marcia, Robert. BS, U. Minn., 1950, LLB, 1952. Bar: Minn. 1952. Pvt. practice New Ulm, Minn.; ptnr. Gislason, Alsop, Dosland & Hunter, 1954-75; judge U.S. Dist. Ct. Minn., St. Paul, 1975—, chief dist. judge, 1985-92, sr. dist. judge, 1992—; mem. 8th cir. jud. coun., 1987-92, Jud. Conf. Com. to Implement Criminal Justice Act, 1979-87; mem. exec. com. Nat. Conf. Fed. Trial Judges, 1990-94. Chmn. Brown County (Minn.) Republican Com., 1960-64, 2d Congl. Dist. Rep. Com., 1968-72, Brown County chpt. ARC, 1968-74. Served with AUS, 1945-46. Mem. 8th Cir. Dist. Judges Assn. (pres. 1982-84), New Ulm C. of C. (pres. 1974-75), Order of Coif. Office: US Dist Ct 754 Fed Bldg 316 Robert St N Saint Paul MN 55101-1495

ALSOP, STEWART, communications executive. Ptnr. New Enterprise Assocs., Menlo Park, Calif., 1996—; former exec. editor Inc. mag.; former exec. v.p. InfoWorld Pub. Co., former editor in chief; founder P.C. Letter; columnist Fortune Mag. Office: New Enterprise Assocs 2490 Sand Hill Rd Menlo Park CA 94025-6940*

ALSPACH, PHILIP HALLIDAY, manufacturing company executive; b. Buffalo, Apr. 19, 1923; s. Walter L. and Jean E. (Halliday) A.; m. Jean Edwards, Dec. 20, 1947 (dec.); children: Philip Clough, Bruce Edwards, David Christopher; m. Loretta M. Hildebrand, Aug. 1982. BME, Tulane U., 1944. Registered profl. engr., Mass., Wis., La. With Gen. Electric Co., 1945-64, mgr. indsl. electronics div. planning, 1961-64; v.p., gen. mgr. constrn. machinery div. Allis Chalmers Mfg. Co., Milw., 1964-68; exec. v.p., dir., mem. exec. com. Jeffrey Galion, Inc., 1968-69; v.p. I.T.E. Imperial Corp., Springhouse, Pa., 1969-75; pres. E.W. Bliss div. Gulf & Western Mfg. Co., Southfield, Mich., 1975-79; group v.p. Katy Industries, Inc., Elgin, Ill., 1979-85; pres. Intercon Inc., Irvine, Calif., 1985—, also bd. dirs.; pres. Intercon Publ., Irvine, 1991—; bd. dirs. Fortifiber Corp.; advbd. Diamond Stainless, Inc., United Green Mark, Inc., McFarlands Foods, Inc. Author: Swiss-Bernese Oberland, 1992; papers in field. Mem. pres.'s coun. Tulane U., 1982-90. Mem. IEEE, Soc. Automotive Engrs. (sr.), Soc. Mfg. Engrs., Internat. Forum Corp. Dirs., Inst. Dirs. (U.K.), Am. Mgmt. Assn., Chaine des Rotisseurs (officier). Home: 23 Alejo Irvine CA 92612-2913 Office: Intercon Inc 2500 Michelson Dr Ste 465 Irvine CA 92612-1545

ALSPAUGH, DALE WILLIAM, university administrator, aeronautics and astronautics educator; b. Dayton, Ohio, May 25, 1932; m. Marlowe Anne Alspaugh; 4 children. ME, U. Cin., 1955; MS in Engring. Scis., Purdue U., 1958, PhD in Engring. Scis., 1965. Profl. engr., Ohio. Project engr. GMC Frigidaire div., 1955-56, 59; instr. sch. aeronautics and astronautics & engring. Purdue U., West Lafayette, Ind., 1957-58, 59-64, asst. prof., 1964-68, assoc. prof., 1968-81; vice chancellor for acad. svcs., prof. Purdue U. North Cen. campus, Westville, Ind., 1981-82, acting chancellor, prof., 1982-84; chancellor, prof. aeronautics and astronautics Purdue U. North Cen. campus, Westville, 1984—; mem. numerous coms. Purdue U.; cons. Midwest Applied Sci. Corp., West Lafayette, 1959-66, Roper Corp., West Lafayette, 1972-73, Switzer div. Wallace Murray Corp., Indpls., 1972-73, Los Alamos (N.Mex.) Scientific Lab., 1977, U.S. Army MICOM, Huntsville, Ala., 1978-82, Campbell & Pryor Cons. Corp., Michigan City, Ind., 1984-86, Colsa, Inc., Huntsville, 1988; reviewer Applied Mechs. Rev., J. Franklin Inst., ASME Jour. Heat Transfer, Internat. Jour. Engring. Sci., also NSF rsch. proposals, various books; bd. dirs. Meml. Hosp. Michigan City, 1st Citizens Bank of Michigan City, Horizon Bancorp. Contbr. articles to profl. jours.; also numerous reports, papers, seminars. Mem. West Lafayette Bd. Sch. trustees, 1976-81, sec., 1976-77, v.p. 1977-78, pres. 1978-79; mem. West Lafayette Park & Recreation Bd., 1976-81, treas. 1979-80; mem. West Lafayette Sch. Bd. Negotiating Team, 1977-78, chief negotiator, 1978; mem. West Lafeyett Sch. Supt. screening Com., 1980-81; mem. West Lafayette Community Sch. Coun., 1970-73, pres., 1973; pres. Burtsfield PTA, 1970-71; supt. Covenant Presbyn. Ch. Sch., 1969-74; mem. West Lafayette Little League Bd., 1969-72; bd. dirs. N.W. Ind. Forum, 1983—, mem. subcom. on strategic planning, 1983-85, N.W. Ind. ednl. pub. TV consortium, 1984, subcom. on legis. affairs, 1985—, subcom. on hazardous materials, 1986-87, ednl. consortium, 1988—; mem. Barker Commn., 1986—; bd. dirs. Friends of Barker; mem. City of Valparaiso Ethics Commn., 1995—. Recipient grants NASA, Purdue Rsch. Found., Fund for Instructional Devel. & Innovative Teaching, Fund for Alternatives in Engring. Edn., U.S. Army MICOM. Mem. AIAA (coun. Cen. Ind. sect. 1969-71), Am. Soc. Engring. Edn. (space engring. com. 1970-78), Greater Valparaiso C. of C. (bd. dirs. 1985-90, chmn. div. on local & govtl. affairs 1987-88), Rotary. Office: Purdue U N Cen Campus Office of the Chancellor 1401 S Us Highway 421 Westville IN 46391-9542

ALSTADT, DONALD MARTIN, business executive; b. Erie, Pa., July 29, 1921; s. Rheinhold L. and Jean M. Alstadt; m. Judith Carlow, Nov. 23, 1984; 1 child, Karen. B.S., U. Pitts., 1947; Sc.D. (hon.), Thiel Coll., 1980. With Lord Corp., Erie, 1961—; v.p., gen. mgr. Lord Corp., 1964-66, exec. v.p., 1966-68, pres., 1968-75, also chmn. bd., chief exec. officer, 1982-91, now chmn. bd., 1993—; cons. Carborundum Co., Transistor Products Co. of Boston, 1952-56; dir. Keithley Instruments Inc.; cons. Lincoln Project, 1952-53, NSF, 1980—; guest lectr. Internat. Inst. Mgmt. Sci. Ctr., Berlin, 1979; vis. scientist MIT, 1986. Contbr. articles to profl. jours. Chmn. bd. overseers Franklin Pierce Law Ctr., 1981—; mem. adv. bd. Ctr. for Advanced Engring. Study, MIT, 1981—; mem. Pa. Sci. and Engring. Found., 1980—; bd. advisors Case Western Res. Sch. Mgmt., Cleve., 1970—; bd. visitors U. Pitts. Grad. Sch. Bus., 1972—; trustee Poly. Inst. N.Y., Bklyn., 1973—, Kolff Found., Cleve., 1974—, Hamot Med. Center, Erie, Pa., 1973-78, Rose Poly. Inst., 1976-79; mem. adv. bd. Mellon Inst. Research; met. chmn. Nat. Alliance of Businessmen, 1969; mem. president's council Tulane U., 1976—; mem. vis. com. Sch. Engring., M.I.T., 1980—, Sch. Engring., Duke U., 1980—; mem. policy com. Pa. Bus. Council, 1979—; dir., pres. Lord Found. of N.C., Lord Fond. of Calif., Lord Found. of Mass., Lord Found. of Pa., Lord Found. of Ohio. Recipient Medal of Merit Edinboro State Coll., 1979; Univ. medal Pa. State U., 1981; Disting. Service award Sch. Engring. Duke U., 1985, Adhesives and Sealant Council, 1985; named Hon. Football Coach, U. So. Calif. Fellow Am. Inst. Chemists; mem. Am. Phys. Soc., Am. Chem. Soc., Faraday Soc. of Eng., Electrochem. Soc., Chemists Club N.Y., N.Y. Acad. Scis., Inst. Mgmt. Sci., Am. Security Council, Swedish Royal Acad. Engring. Sci. (guest lectr. 1984), Acad. Applied Sci. Republican. Presbyterian. Avocation: fishing. Office: Lord Corp PO Box 8012 11 Lord Dr Cary NC 27512-8012

ALSTADT, LYNN JEFFERY, lawyer; b. Erie, Pa., Dec. 27, 1951; s. Willis Harry and Norma Margaret (Linn) A.; m. Nancy Ann Welz, Apr. 16, 1977. BS, U. Pitts., 1973, BA, 1973, JD, 1976. Bar: Pa. 1976, U.S. Dist. Ct. (we. dist.) Pa. 1976, U.S. Patent and Trademark Office 1979, U.S. Ct. Appeals (3d cir.) 1980, U.S. Ct. Appeals (6th and Fed. cirs.) 1983, U.S. Supreme Ct. 1982, U.S. Ct. Internat. Trade 1983. Assoc. Blenko, Buell, Ziesenheim & Beck, Pitts., 1976-79; ptnr. Buell, Blenko, Ziesenheim & Beck, Pitts., 1979-84, Buell, Ziesenheim, Beck & Alstadt, Pitts., 1984-88; ptnr. Buchanan Ingersoll, Pitts., 1988—; adj. prof. U. Pitts. Sch. Law, 1988—, Duquesne U. Sch. Law, 1995—; dir. Internat. Congress on Tech., Pitts., 1983-84. Contbr. articles to legal jours. Treas. Moon Twp. Planning Agy., 1984; mem. Moon Twp. Vol. Fire Dept., 1981—. Recipient Samuel G. Wagner prize U. Pitts. Law Sch., 1976. Mem. ABA, Pa. Bar Assn., Allegheny County Bar Assn., Pitts. Intellectual Property Law Assn. (chmn. pub. rels. 1982-83, treas. 1993, chmn. ethics grievences and membership coms. 1994-95), Rivers Club, Phi Alpha Delta. Republican. Home: 102 Greenlea Dr Moon Township PA 15108-2610

ALSTAT, GEORGE ROGER, special education educator; b. Murphysboro, Ill., Aug. 20, 1941; s. George Lewis and Vernice C. Alstat; m. Carol Ann Sikora, Sept. 11, 1971 (div. Mar. 1982); children: Joseph Todd, George Ryan; m. Deborah Lynn Dame, June 19, 1986 (dec. June 1991); 1 child, Jessica Danielle. BS, So. Ill. U., Carbondale, 1971; MS, So. Ill. U., Edwardsville, 1974. Cert. tchr. and supervision in learning disabilities, emotional, social and educable mental handicapped, adminstrv. endorsement, Ill. Tchr. spl. edn. Centralia (Ill.) City Schs., 1974-78; supr. spl. edn. Franklin-Jefferson County Spl. Edn. Dist., Benton, Ill., 1978-83; direct salesman investment firm, Fairview Heights, Ill., 1983-86; owner So. Ill. Mktg., Benton, 1986-91; subsitute tchr. Murphysboro Sch. Dist., Ill., 1991-93; tchr. spl. edn. Nokomis (Ill.) Elem. Sch., 1993-94, East Richland Cmty. Unit Sch. Dist. 1, Olney, Ill., 1994-95; spl. edn. tchr. Chester Grade Sch., Ill., 1995-96. Avocations: bicycling, fishing, travel.

ALSTED, PETER, lawyer; b. Copenhagen, Jan. 13, 1934; s. Gunnar Alsted and Gerda (Salomonsen) Gudme; m. Alette Arntz, 1963 (div. 1981); children: Charlotte Solovej, Gregers, Michala; m. Lissi Hansen Rosendal, Oct. 21, 1982. Candidatus Juris, U. Copenhagen, 1958. Bar: Denmark, 1962. Sole practitioner law Copenhagen, 1964—; chmn., bd. dirs. charitable founds., corps. and profl. socs.; sec.-gen. Danish Ins. Brokers Assn., 1980-89. Co-author: Handbook on European Community Company Law, 1997; author articles in field. Mem. Union Internationale des Avocats (corr.), SAME (nat. bd. dirs.), Danish Bar Assn., Internat. Tax Planning Assn. Home: 13 Vilvordeparken, Charlottenlund 2920, Denmark Office: Advokaterne Ret & Raad, 90 Vester Voldgade, Copenhagen 1552, Denmark

ALSTON, ALYCE, publisher. Pub. YM/Young & Modern/Gruner & Jahr, USA Pub., N.Y.C. Office: YM/Young & Modern Gruner & Jahr USA Pub 375 Lexington Ave Fl 8 New York NY 10017-5514*

ALSTON, WILLIAM PAYNE, philosophy educator; b. Shreveport, La., Nov. 29, 1921; s. William Payne and Eunice (Schoolfield) A.; m. Mary Frances Collins, Aug. 15, 1943 (div.); 1 dau., Frances Ellen; m. Valerie Tibbetts Barnes, July 3, 1963. B.M., Centenary Coll., 1942; Ph.D., U. Chgo., 1951; LHD (honoris causa), Ch. Div. Sch. Pacific, 1988. Instr. philosophy U. Mich., 1949-52, asst. prof., then asso. prof., 1952-61, prof., 1961-71, acting chmn. dept., 1961-64; prof. philosophy Rutgers U., 1971-76, U. Ill., Champaign, 1976-80; chmn. dept. U. Ill., 1977-80; prof. philosophy Syracuse (N.Y.) U., 1980-99; vis. asst. prof. UCLA, 1952-53; Austin Fagothey vis. prof. philosophy Santa Clara U., 1991; vis. lectr. Harvard U., 1955-56; fellow Ctr. for Advanced Study in the Behavioral Scis., 1965-66; dir. summer seminars for coll. tchrs. NEH, 1978-79, NEH Summer Inst. in Philosophy of Religion, 1986, NEH Fellowship for Univ. Tchrs., 1988-89, Vatican Obs. Project on Divine Action in the Light of Contemporary Sci., Symposium of Chinese-Am. Philosophy and Religious Studies, 1994; Calvin Coll. Sumer Seminar in Christian Scholarship, 1999. Author: Religious Belief and Philosophical Thought, 1963, (with G. Nakhnikian) Readings in Twentieth Century Philosophy, 1963, Philosophy of Language, 1964, (with R.B. Brandt) The Problems of Philosophy: Introductory Readings, 1967, 3d edit., 1978; Divine Nature and Human Language, 1989, Epistemic Justification, 1989, Perceiving God, 1991, The Reliability of Sense Perception, 1993, A Realist Conception of Truth, 1996; editor: Philos. Rsch. Archives, 1974-77, Faith and Philosophy, 1982-90, Cornell Studies in Philosophy of Religion, 1987—; contbr. articles to profl. jours., chpts. in books. Served with AUS, 1942-46. Recipient Chancellor's Exceptional Acad. Achievement award Syracuse U., 1990. Mem. Am. Acad. Arts and Scis., Am. Philos. Assn. (pres. Western div. 1978-79), Soc. Christian Philosophers (pres. 1978-81), Scholarly Engagement Anglican Doctrine. Home: 4 Bittersweet Ln Fayetteville NY 13066-1702 Office: Syracuse U Dept Philosophy Syracuse NY 13244

ALSTOTT, MICHAEL JOSEPH (MIKE ALSTOTT), professional football player; b. Joliet, Ill., Dec. 21, 1973. Purdue U. Fullback Tampa Bay Buccaneers, 1996—. Office: Tampa Bay Buccaneers 1 Buccaneer Pl Tampa FL 33607*

ALSTROM, SVEN ERIK, architect; b. Emporia, Kans., July 27, 1951; s. William E. and Willa M. (Russell) A.; m. Lynn M. Mathews, June 22, 1974 (div. June 1983). B. in Gen. Studies, U. Kans., 1975; postgrad., U. Denver, 1984. Registered arch., Calif., Colo., Kans., Mo., N.Mex., Ariz., Tex. (non-active); cert. Nat. Coun. Archtl. Registration Bds. Arch. PGAV Archs., Kansas City, Mo., 1972-74, Horner Blessing, Kansas City, 1977-79, MSFS Archs., Kansas City, 1979-80, Urban Design, Denver, 1981-82, Dominck Assocs., Denver, 1983-84; with C. Welton Anderson & Assocs., Aspen, Colo., 1989-90; pvt. practice Alstrom Group, Aspen, 1990-99; arch. Alstrom Bernstein Archs., 1999—. Mem. AIA (Colo.). Mem. Zen-Presbyn. Ch. Home: PO Box 551 Aspen CO 81612-0551 Office: Alstrom Group PC 121 S Galena St Ste B Aspen CO 81611-1960

ALSUP, WILLIAM, lawyer; b. June 27, 1945. BS, Miss. State U., 1967; MPP, Kennedy Sch. Govt., 1971; JD, Harvard U., 1971. Bar: Miss. 1972, Calif. 1973. Law clk. to Hon. William O. Douglas U.S. Supreme Ct., 1971-72; mem. Morrison & Foerster, San Francisco, 1972—; asst. to solicitor gen. U.S. Dept. Justice, 1978-80; mem. Morrison & Foerster, San Francisco; law del. 9th Cir. Jud. Coun., 1993-96. Mem. Am. Coll. Trial Lawyers. Office: Morrison & Foerster 425 Market St Ste 3100 San Francisco CA 94105-2482*

ALT, BETTY L., sociology educator; b. Walsenburg, Colo., Nov. 12, 1931; d. Cecil R. and Mary M. (Giordano) Sowers; m. William E. Alt, June 19, 1960; 1 child, Eden Jeanette Alt Murrie. BA, Colo. Coll., 1960; MA, NE Mo. State U., 1968. Instr. sociology Indian Hills Community Coll., Centerville, Iowa, 1965-70; dept. chmn. Middlesex Community Coll., Bedford, Mass., 1971-75; instr. sociology Auburn U., Montgomery, 1975-76; div. chmn. Tidewater Community Coll., Virginia Beach, Va., 1976-80; program coord. Pikes Peak Community Coll., Woomera, Australia, 1980-83; instr. sociology Hawaii Pacific Coll., Honolulu, 1983-86, U. Md., Okinawa, Japan, 1987-88, Christopher Newport Coll., Newport News, Va., 1988-89, U. Colo., Colorado Springs, 1989-96, U. So. Colo., Pueblo, 1992—. Co-author: Uncle Sam's Brides, 1990, Campfollowing: A History of the Military Wife, 1991, Weeping Violins: The Gypsy Tragedy in Europe, 1996, Slaughter in Cell House 3, 1997. Mem. League Women Voters. Mem. AAUW, Pen Women, N.E. Mo. State U. Alumni Assn. (bd. dirs. 1993-97). Home: 2460 N Interstate 25 Pueblo CO 81008-9614 Office: U So Colo 2200 Bonforte Blvd Pueblo CO 81001-4901

ALT, FREDERICK W., geneticist, pediatrician. BS, Brandeis U., 1971; PhD in Biological Scis., Stanford U., 1977. Resident fellow MIT, Cambridge, Mass., 1977-82; from asst. prof. to prof. in Biochemistry Columbia U., N.Y.C., 1982-91; prof. Microbiology Columbia U., 1986-91; prof. in Genetics and Pediatrics Harvard Med. Sch., Boston, 1991—; investigator Howard Hughes Med. Inst. Children's Hosp., Boston, 1991—; sr. investigator Ctr. Blood Rsch., 1991—, Charles A. Janeway prof. Genetics and Pediatrics, 1991—. Contbr. articles to profl. jours. Recipient Stephen J. Fox. Meml. award, Stanford U., 1973, Irma T. Hirschl Career Scientist award, 1983, Searle Scholars award, 1983, Mallinckrodt Schoolar, 1984. Mem. Nat. Acad. Scis. (pres., 1994), Am. Acad. Microbiol. (pres., 1994), AAAS (pres., 1994). Office: Howard Hughes Med Inst Childrens Hosp 300 Longwood Ave Boston MA 02115-5724*

ALT, JAMES EDWARD, political science educator; b. N.Y.C., Aug. 16, 1946; s. Franz Leopold and Alice (Modern) A.; m. Elaine Fiore, June 26, 1968; children—Rachel, Adam. AB, Columbia U., 1968; MSc in Econs., London Sch. Econs., 1970; PhD, Essex U., Eng., 1978. Lectr. U. Essex, Wivenhoe Park, Eng., 1971-79; assoc. prof. Washington U., St. Louis, 1978-82, prof., 1982-86; prof. Harvard U., Cambridge, Mass., 1986—; dir. Ctr. for Basic Rsch. in Social Sci., 1998—. Author: Politics of Economic Decline, 1979, (with K. Chrystal) Political Economics, 1983; editor: (with K. Shepsle) Perspectives on Positive Political Economy, 1990; contbr. articles to profl. jours. Rsch. grantee NSF, 1980, 85, 91, 93; Guggenheim fellow, 1997-98. Mem. Brit. Politics Group (pres. 1983-85), Am. Polit. Sci. Assn. (coun. 1996-97), Midwest Polit. Sci. Assn. (exec. coun. 1985-88). Office: Harvard U Dept Govt Cambridge MA 02138

ALTABE, JOAN AUGUSTA BERG, artist, writer, art and architecture critic; b. N.Y.C., Apr. 27, 1935; d. Harold and Evelyn (Cooperman) Berg; m. David F. Altabe, Sept. 28, 1958; children: Richard Jonathan, Madeline Nissa. Studied with Robert Motherwell; BA, Hunter Coll., 1956, postgrad., 1956-57. Tchr. fine art N.Y.C. secondary schs., 1957-72; vol. sculpture tchr. N.Y. Lighthouse For Blind, 1950-53; curator Bicentennial exhibit Long Beach (N.Y.) Mus. Art, 1975-76. Artist and muralist, 1982—; prin. work includes 6 stained glass window murals N.Y. Synagogue, 1973, heraldic deisgn Smithsonian Instn. Bicentennial Travelling Exhibit, 1976-78; represented in permanent collection at Santa Barbara (Calif.) Mus.; book reviewer: Leonardo, Pergamon Press, Eng., 1980-94; feature writer Art Press, Paris, 1992; art writer Art & Antiques mag., 1998, 99; art and architecture critic, feature writer Sarasota Herald Tribune, 1986—; book reviewer Western Humanities Rev., N.Y. Times; contbr. articles and illustrations to profl. jours. Recipient citation for excellence in journalism criticism Soc. Profl. Journalists, 1990, 95, 96, Fla. Press award, 1990, 91, 96, Chmn. award N.Y. Times, 1997, Criticism award Fla. Soc. Newspaper Editors, 1998, 99. Mem. Soc. Profl. Journalists (award in criticism 1995, 96, 97, 99, Tampa Bay chpt.), Fla. Soc. Newspaper Editors (columns and criticism 1997, criticism award 1996, Sunshine State award 1999). Home: 604 Avenida De Mayo Sarasota FL 34242-1502 *To transcend my life through painting, teaching or publishing, with loyalty to my individual spirit and dedication to communication.*

ALTAN, TAYLAN, engineering educator, mechanical engineer, consultant; b. Trabzon, Turkey, Feb. 12, 1938; came to U.S., 1962; s. Seref and Sadife (Baysal) Kadioglu; m. Susan Borah, July 18, 1964; children—Peri Michele, Aylin Elisabeth. Diploma in engring., Tech. U., Hannover, Fed. Republic Germany, 1962; M.S. in Mech. Engring., U. Calif.-Berkeley, 1964, Ph.D. in

Mech. Engring., 1966. Research engr. DuPont Co., Wilmington, Del., 1966-68; research scientist Battelle Columbus Labs, Ohio, 1968-72, research fellow, 1972-75, sr. research leader, 1975-86; prof. mech. engring., dir. engring. rsch. ctr. Ohio State U., Columbus, 1985—; chmn. sci. com. N.Am. Mfg. Rsch. Inst. Soc. Mfg. Engrs., Detroit, 1982-86, pres., 1987; dir. Ctr. for Net Shape Mfg. Co-author: Forging Equipment, 1973, Metal Forming, 1983, Metal Forming and the Finite Element Method, 1989; assoc. editor Jour. Materials Processing Tech., Eng., 1978—; contbr. over 150 tech. articles to profl. jours. Fellow Am. Soc. Metals (chmn. forging com. 1978-87), Soc. Mfg. Engrs. (Gold medal 1985), ASME. Avocations: languages, travel. Office: Ohio State U 210 Baker Bldg 1971 Neil Ave Columbus OH 43210-1210

ALTBACH, PHILIP, higher education director, educator; b. Chgo., May 3, 1941; s. Milton and Josephine (Huebsch) A.; m. Edith Hoshino, June 16, 1962; children: Eric, Frederick Gabriel. BA, U. Chgo., 1962, MA, 1964, PhD, 1966. Lectr. Harvard U., Cambridge, Mass., 1967-68; from asst. prof. to assoc. prof. U. Wis., Madison, 1968-75; prof., chmn. dept. ednl. orgn., adminstrn. and policy SUNY, Buffalo, 1976-80, 86-92, dir. Comparative Edn. Ctr., 1978-94; prof. sch. edn. Boston Coll., 1994—, dir. Ctr. Internat. Higher Edn., 1995—, J. Donald Monan SJ prof. higher edn., 1996—; Fulbright rsch. prof. U. Bombay, 1968; cons. Regional Inst. Higher Edn., Singapore, 1979, 81, 82, Carnegie Found. Advancement Tchg., 1990-94, Rockefeller Found., 1991—; vis. prof. Moscow State U., 1981, Stanford U., 1989; Fulbirght cons. U. Singapore, 1982; sr. assoc. Carnegie Found. Advancement Tchg., 1992-96; sec.-gen. Bellagio Publ. Network, 1992-98; guest prof. Peking U. Author: Student Politics in America, 1975, rev. edit., 1997, Comparative Higher Education, 1979, Higher Education in Third World, 1982, Knowledge Context, 1987, International Higher Education: An Encyclopedia, 1991, publishing and Development in the Third World, 1994, Higher Education in the 21st Century, 1999, 30 additional books; editor Comparative Edn. Rev., 1979-89, Review of Higher Edn., 1996—, Ednl. Policy, Parkside News, 1981-88, Bellagio Pub. Network Newsletter, 1991-97; exec. editor Internat. Jour. Edn. Devel., 1989-94; adv. editor SUNY Press; contbr. articles to profl. jours. Mem. capital budget rev. com. City of Buffalo, 1980. Grantee NEH, 1976, Exxon Edn. Foun., 1982, 84, NSF, 1987, Rockefeller Found., 1993, 94, 95. Mem. Comparative Edn. Soc. (editor jour. 1980-89), Assn. Study Higher Edn. (editor jour. 1996—). Office: Boston Coll 207 Campion Hall Chestnut Hill MA 02467

ALTEKRUSE, JOAN MORRISSEY, retired preventive medicine educator; b. Cohoes, N.Y., Nov. 15, 1928; d. William T. Dee and Agnes Kay (Fitzgerald) Morrissey; m. Ernest B. Altekruse, Dec. 17, 1950; children—Philip, Clifford, Lisa, Janice, Charles, Sean, Lowell, Patrick, E. Caitlin. AB, Vassar Coll., N.Y., 1949; MD, Stanford U., Calif., 1960; MPH, Harvard U., Cambridge, 1965; DPH, U. Calif., Berkeley, 1973. Cons., program dir. Calif. State Health Dept., 1966-69; mem. faculty U. Heidelberg, Germany, 1970-72; med. dir. regional office Fla. State Health Dept., 1972-75; prof., dir. health adminstrn. Sch. Pub. Health, U. S.C., Columbia, 1975-77; prof. preventive medicine Univ. S.C. Sch. of Medicine, Columbia, 1975-94, chmn. dept., 1979-89, disting. prof. emerita, 1994—; fellow, assoc. dir. Irish Peace Inst., U. Limerick, Ireland, 1990—; vis. scholar Ctr. for Rsch. in Disease Prevention, Stanford U., 1992; women in medicine liaison officer Assn. Am. Med. Colls., 1980-94; mem. editl. bd. Aspen Publs. Mem. editorial bd. Family and Community Health Jour., Jour. Community Health; editorial adv. bd. VA Practitioner. Pres. Harvard Sch. Pub. Health Alumni Coun., 1999—; sr. docent chair, vol. bd. mem. Hunter Mus. Am. Art, Chattanooga. Lt. USMC, 1949-51; sr. surgeon USPHS, 1960-64. Recipient Adminstrn. award Women in Higher Edn., 1989, Achievement award S.C. Commn. on Women, 1990, Ann. award, 1991, Life Achievement award Emma Willard Sch., 1996; WHO travel fellow, Eng., 1974; grantee NIH, NCI, Ctr. for Disease Control, pvt. founds; recipient Alumni award of merit Harvard Sch. Pub. Health, 1997. Fellow Am. Coll. Preventive Medicine, Assn. Tchrs. Preventive Medicine (pres. 1986, Spl. Recognition award 1995), Am. Pub. Health Assn. (mem. emerita); mem. Am. Bd. Preventive Medicine (trustee 1984-93), Am. Bd. Med. Specialities (del. 1990-93), Am. Heart Assn. (S.C. affiliate pres. 1986, agenda planning com. 1987-89, women and minorities leadership com. 1989-92, Lifetime Achievement award 1992), Nat. Bd. Med. Examiners (comprehensive test com. 1986-92), Am. Womens Med. Assn. Democrat. Catholic.

ALTENBERGER, WILLIAM V., federal judge; b. 1935. BS, U. Ill., 1957, LLB, 1963. Atty. Kavanagh, Scully, Sudow, White and Frederick, P.C., 1964-85; chief bankruptcy judge U.S. Bankruptcy Ct. (ctrl. dist.) Ill., 1985—. 1st lt. USAF, 1957-60. Office: US Bankruptcy Ct 131 Federal Bldg 100 NE Monroe St Peoria IL 61602-1003

ALTENBURG, JOHN D., JR., career officer; b. June 10, 1966. Commd. U.S. Army, advanced through grades to maj. gen., 1997. Office: 2200 Army Pentagon Washington DC 20310-2200

ALTENBURGER, KARL MARION, allergist, immunologist; b. Coral Gables, Fla., Nov. 13, 1949; s. Karl and Carol Altenburger; m. Carol Bauer, May 25, 1974; children: Laura Alyson, Ashley Carolyn, Elizabeth Ann, Allison Nicole. BA in Zoology, U. South Fla., 1971, MD, 1974. Diplomate Am. Bd. Pediatrics, Am. Bd. Allergy and Immunology, Nat. Bd. Med. Examiners. Intern in pediatrics U. Colo. Med. Ctr., Denver, 1975-76, resident, 1976-78, fellow in allergy and immunology, 1978-81; fellow in allergy and immunology Nat. Jewish Hosp. and Rsch. Ctr.-Nat. Asthma Ctr., Denver, 1978-81; pvt. practice, Ocala, Fla., 1981—; instr. dept. pediatrics U. Colo. Sch. Medicine, 1980-81; bd. dirs. Fla. Med. Polit. Action Com., 1991—, pres., 1998—. Contbr. articles to med. jours. Trustee Am. Lung Assn. Ctrl. Fla., 1985-93. Fellow Am. Acad. Allergy, Asthma and Immunology, Am. Coll. Allergy Asthma and Immunology, Am. Acad. Pediatrics; mem. AMA, Southeastern Allergy Assn., Am. Assn. for History Medicine, Fla. Med. Assn. (Marion County del. 1990—), Fla. Allergy Asthma and Immunology Soc. (exec. com. 1990-96, pres. 1993-94), Marion County Med. Soc. (bd. dirs. 1983-88, pres. 1985-86, editor Bull. 1986-89), U. South Fla. Coll. Medicine Alumni Assn. (pres. 1983-87), Alpha Omega Alpha. Roman Catholic. Avocations: faith, family, friends. Office: 1800 SE 17th St Ste 300 Ocala FL 34471-4173

ALTENHOFEN, JANE ELLEN, federal agency administrator, auditor; b. Seneca, Kans., Sept. 4, 1952; d. Justin Leo and Marva Mae (Sextro) A.; m. John Dean Arnette, Sept. 12, 1975 (div. Mar. 1978). BBA cum laude, Wichita (Kans.) State U., 1973; MPA, Am. U., 1982; cert., Inst. Internal Auditors, 1986. Cert. internal auditor, cert. fraud examiner, cert. govt. fin. mgr. Auditor U.S. Gen. Acctg. Office, Kansas City, Kans., 1974-76, Honolulu, 1976-80, Washington, 1980-84; auditor Fed. Emergency Mgmt. Agy., Washington, 1984-89; insp. gen. U.S. Internat. Trade Commn., Washington, 1989-99, Nat. Labor Rels. Bd., Washington, 1999—. Mem. Adopt a Grandparent Program, Wichita, 1973; vol. reading course work to blind students, Wichita, 1973; vol. Vis. Nurse Assn., Washington, 1986—; host, traveler, Wash. area rep. SERVAS, 1987—; commr. Adv. Neighborhood Commn., Washington, 1986-89; troop leader Girl Scouts U.S., Washington, 1983-85; foster home Washington Humane Soc., 1994—. Mem. Inst. Internal Auditors, Nat. Intergovtl. Audit Forum, Assn. Govt. Accounts, Nat. Assn. Cert. Fraud Examiners, Phi Kappa Phi, Pi Alpha Pi. Home: 507 2nd St SE Washington DC 20003-1928 Office: Nat Labor Rels Bd Rm 9820 1099 14th St NW Washington DC 20570

ALTER, ANDREW WILLIAM, lawyer. BS, Yale Coll., 1983; JD, Harvard U., 1986. Assoc. Cravath, Swaine & Moore, 1986-89, Breed, Abbott & Morgan, 1989-90; dir. in counsel Salomon Brothers Inc., N.Y.C., 1990—. Office: Salomon-Smith Barney Inc 388 Greenwich St New York NY 10013-1102*

ALTER, DAVID, lawyer; b. Izka, Czechoslovakia, Oct. 31, 1923; came to U.S., 1929; s. Morris and Bertha Alter; m. Deborah King; children—Lisa, Amy. B.S., CCNY, 1947; LL.B., Harvard U., 1950. Bar: N.Y. 1950, U.S. Dist. Ct. (so. dist.) N.Y. 1953, U.S. Ct. Appeals (2d cir.) 1953, U.S. Dist. Ct. Conn. 1954, U.S. Ct. Appeals (4th cir.) 1957, U.S. Supreme Ct. 1962. Ptnr. Shea & Gould, N.Y.C., 1979-89, Squadron, Ellenoff, Plesent & Lehrer, N.Y.C., 1989-99; nat. counsel Screen Actors Guild, N.Y.C., 1998—; counsel Screen Actors Guild, 1966—; trustee, mem. Fin. Com., Screen Actors Guild-Producers Pension & Health Plans, 1966-87, counsel 1987—. Pres. Hamlet of Seaview, Fire Island, N.Y., 1975-81; bd. dirs. Astoria Motion Picture and TV Ctr. Found., 1980-82, Am. Mus. of the Moving Image, 1983-86. Served with USAF, 1943-46. Mem. ABA, Assn. of Bar of City of N.Y., N.Y. State Bar Assn. Club: Harvard (N.Y.C.). Home: 40 5th Ave New York NY 10011-8843 Office: Screen Actors Guild 1515 Broadway New York NY 10036

ALTER, EDWARD T., state treasurer; b. Glen Ridge, N.J., July 26, 1941; s. E. Irving and Norma (Fisher) A.; m. Patricia R. Olsen, 1975; children: Christina Lyn, Ashly Ann, Darci Lee. B.A., U. Utah., 1966; M.B.A., U. Utah, 1967. C.P.A., Calif., Utah. Sr. acct. Touche Ross & Co., Los Angeles, 1967-72; asst. treas. U. Utah, Salt Lake City, 1972-80; treas. State of Utah, Salt Lake City, 1981—; pres. Nat. Assn. State Treas., 1987-88. Bd. dirs. Utah Housing Fin. Agy., Utah State Retirement Bd., pres., 1984-93; mem. Utah State Rep. Cen. Com., 1981—, Anthony Com. on Pub. Fin., 1988-92. Sgt. USAR, 1958-66. Named to All-pro Govt. Team, City and State Mag., 1988; recipient Jesse M. Uhruh Award for Svc. to State Treas.', 1989. Mem. Am. Inst. CPAs, Nat. Assn. State Treas. (past sr. v.p., pres. 1987), Delta Sigma Pi, Delta Phi Kappa. Club: Utah Bond (pres. 1981-82). Office: State Capitol 215 State Capitol Building Salt Lake City UT 84114-1202

ALTER, ELEANOR BREITEL, lawyer; b. N.Y.C., Nov. 10, 1938; d. Charles David and Jeanne (Hollander) Breitel; children: Richard B. Zabel, David B. Zabel. BA with honors, U. Mich., 1960; postgrad., Harvard U., 1960-61; LLB, Columbia U., 1964. Bar: N.Y. 1965. Atty., office of gen. counsel, ins. dept. State of N.Y., 1964-66; assoc. Miller & Carlson, N.Y.C., 1966-68, Marshall, Bratter, Greene, Allison & Tucker, N.Y.C., 1968-74; mem. firm Marshall, Bratter, Greene, Allison & Tucker, 1974-82, Rosenman & Colin, 1982-97, Kasowitz, Benson, Torres & Friedman, N.Y.C., 1997—; fellow U. Chgo. Law Sch., 1988; adj. prof. law NYU Sch. Law, 1983-87; vis. prof. law U. Chgo., 1990-91, 93; lectr. in field. Editorial bd.: N.Y. Law Jour. Contbr. articles to profl. jours. Trustee Lawyers' Fund for Client Protection of the State of N.Y., 1983—, chmn., 1985—; bd. visitors U. Chgo. Law Sch., 1984-87. Mem. Am. Law Inst., Am. Coll. Family Trial Lawyers, N.Y. State Bar Assn., Assn. of Bar of City of N.Y. (libr. com. 1978-80, com. on matrimonial law 1977-81, 87-88, judiciary com. 1981-84, 94, 95, 96, exec. com. 1988-92), Am. Acad. Matrimonial Lawyers. Office: Kasowitz Benson Et Al 1301 Avenue Of The Americas New York NY 10019-6022

ALTER, JONATHAN HAMMERMAN, journalist; b. Chgo., Oct. 6, 1957; s. James M. and Joanne (Hammerman) A.; m. Emily Lazar, Oct. 18, 1986; children: Charlotte Helen, Thomas Beck, Molly Cecelia. AB in History cum laude, Harvard U., 1979. Mem. staff speech writing office The White House, 1978; editor The Washington Monthly, 1981-82; sr. editor, columnist, media critic Newsweek, N.Y.C., 1983—; on-air analyst, corr. NBC News, 1996—; Ferris vis. prof. Princeton U., 1997. Co-author: Selecting A President, 1980; editor: (with Charles Peters) Inside the System. 5th edit., 1984. Recipient Gerald Loeb award 1987, Lowell Mellett award for Improving Journalism, 1987; fellow U.S.-Japan Leadership program, 1992-93; named 1 of Top 10 Media Critics in U.S., Columbia U., 1991. Office: care Newsweek Magazine 251 W 57th St New York NY 10019-1802

ALTER, MILTON, neurologist, educator; b. Buffalo, Nov. 11, 1929; s. Samuel and rose (Schaffer) A.; m. Reina Rolnick, Aug. 31, 1952; children: David S., Daniel M., Michael A., Naomi T., Joel A. BA, U. Buffalo, 1951, MD, 1955; PhD, U. Minn., 1966. Diplomate Am. Bd. Psychiatry and Neurology. Intern U. Minn., Mpls., 1955-56; sr. surgeon USPHS, Bethesda, Md., 1956-62; fellow Med. Coll. S.C., Charleston, 1956-57, Dalhousi U., Halifax, N.S., Can., 1957, Columbia U. Coll. Physicians and Surgeons, N.Y.C., 1957-58, Hebrew U., Jerusalem, 1960-62; mem. faculty, chief neurology svc. U. Minn., Mpls., 1962-76, Mpls. VA Hosp., 1967-76; chmn. dept. neurology Temple U., Phila., 1976-87; prof. neurology, dir. residency tng. Med. Coll. Pa., Phila., 1989-91; clin. prof. neurology Allegheny U., 1995; mem. sci. adv. bd. Nat. Multiple Sclerosis Soc., N.Y.c., Dystonia Med. Rsch. Found., Alzheimer Disease assn.; peer reviewer Epidemiology and Disease Control 1 and 2, NIH, Bethesda, Md. Guest editor numerous profl. jours.; editor-in-chief Neuroepidemiology, 1989-86, editor emeritus, 1997; contbr. numerous articles to med. jours., chpts. to books. Capt. USPHS; res., 1962. NIH grantee. Mem. AMA, Am. Acad. Neurology, Am. Neurol. assn., Assn. Rsch. Nervous and Mental Diseases, Am. Epidemiology Soc., World Fedn. of Neurol. (chair rsch. group in epidemiology 1998). Democrat. Jewish. Home: 236 Indian Creek Rd Wynnewood PA 19096-3404 also: Lankenace Med Rsch Ctr 100 E Lancaster Ave Wynnewood PA 19096-3450

ALTER, NELSON TOBIAS, jewelry retailer and wholesaler; b. San Antonio, July 14, 1926; s. William and Celia (Tobias) A.; m. Shirley Ann Jacobs, June 12, 1949; children: Dennis Ira, Keith Alan, Brian Reid, Wendy Ilene. BBA in Acctg., U. Tex., 1948, JD, 1950. Mgr. 9 coin-operated washeterias, 1960-67; mgr. Sta. KOGT radio, Orange, Tex., 1950-65; ptnr. Calder Properties, 1977—; mng. ptnr. Crow Road Devel. Co., Beaumont, Tex., 1976-77, Normandy Townhomes, Beaumont, 1978—, Griffing Devel. Co., Beaumont, 1978—, Griffing Realty Joint Venture, Beaumont, 1983—; comptroller Gem Jewelry Co., Beaumont, 1950-58; pres. Gem Jewelry Co. of Beaumont, Inc., 1958—, chmn. of bd., 1991—; mng. ptnr. Gem Distbg. Co. Wholesale Jewelry, Beaumont, 1958—; also pres., chmn. of bd. Gem Jewelry Co. of Port Artur, Inc., 1991—, Gem Jewelry C. of Orange, Inc., 1991—, Gem. Jewelry C. of Alexandria (La.), Inc., 1991—, Gem. Jewelry C. of Rapides (La.) Inc., 1991, Gem Jewelry Distbg. Co. Inc., 1991—; U.S. rep. Tex. region Habsbourg-Feldman Fine Art Auctioneers, Geneva, 1986, 87, 88, 89; real estate developer Normandy Townhomes, Griffing Devel. Co., Joint Venture, Griffing Realty Joint Venture, Partner Calder Properties. Past pres. Downtown Beaumont Unltd.; co-chmn. Beaumont Urban Renewal; drive chmn. United Jewish Appeal, Beaumont, 1954, 67; v.p. Temple Emanuel, 1974-75, pres., 1981; mem. Beaumont Heritage Soc., Beaumont Music Commn., Beaumont Symphony Soc., Am. Cancer Soc.; co-founder, mem. BBB S.E. Tex.; bd. dirs. A.W. Schlesinger Geriatric Ctr., 1996-98. Mem. Tex. Retail Jewelers Assn. (v.p. 1974-75), Jefferson County Bar Assn., Tex. Bar Assn., Edna Gladney Aux., Beaumont Jewish Fedn., Buckner Benevolences, Tower Club, Masons, B'nai Brith, Phi Eta Sigma, Beta Gamma Sigma, Phi Alpha Delta, Sigma Alpah Mu. Jewish. Avocations: art collecting, swimming, golf. Office: Gem Jewelry Co 795 N 11th St Beaumont TX 77702-1547

ALTER, ROBERT A., hotel executive. BS in Hotel Adminstrn., Cornell U. Chmn., CEO Sunstone Hotel Investors, Inc., 1995—; chmn. Sunstone Hotel Properties, Inc., Sunstone Hotel Mgmt., Inc.; operator Sunstone Hotels. Office: Sunstone Hotel Mgmt Inc PO Box 4240 San Clemente CA 92672-4240

ALTER, ROBERT B., comparative literature educator and critic; b. N.Y.C., Apr. 2, 1935; s. Harry and Tillie (Zimmmerman) A.; m. Judith Berkenbilt, June 4, 1961 (div. 1973); children: Miriam, Dan; m. Carol Cosman, June 17, 1973; children: Gabriel, Micha. BA, Columbia U., 1957; MA, Harvard U., 1958, PhD, 1962; LHD (hon.), Hebrew Union Coll., 1985. Instr., then asst. prof. English Columbia U., 1962-66; mem. faculty U. Calif.-Berkeley, 1967—, prof. Hebrew and comparative lit., 1969—, chmn. dept. comparative lit., 1970-73, 88-89, class of 1937 prof., 1989—; columnist Commentary mag., 1965-73, contbg. editor, 1973-86. Author: Rogue's Progress: Studies in the Picaresque Novel, 1964, Fielding and the Nature of the Novel, 1968, After the Tradition, 1969, Partial Magic: The Novel as a Self-Conscious Genre, 1975, Defenses of the Immagination, 1977, A Lion for Love, 1979, The Art of Biblical Narrative, 1981, Motives for Fiction, 1984, The Art of Biblical Poetry, 1985; co-editor: The Literary Guide to the Bible, 1987, The Invention of Hebrew Prose, 1988, The Pleasures of Reading in an Ideological Age, 1989, Necessary Angels, 1991, The World of Biblical Literature, 1992, Hebrew and Modernity, 1994, Genesis: Translation and Commentary, 1996; contbg. editor: Tri Quarterly mag., 1975—. Recipient essay prize English Inst., 1965, Nat. Jewish Book award for Jewish thought, 1982, Present Tense award for Jewish thought, 1986, Bay Area Book Reviewers Transl. award, 1997; Guggenheim fellow, 1966-67, 78-79, sr. fellow NEH, 1972-73, fellow Inst. for Advanced Studies, Jerusalem, 1982-83; scholar Nat. Found. for Jewish Culture, 1995. Fellow Am. Acad. Arts and Scis.; mem. Am. Comparative Lit. Assn., Council of Scholars of Library of Congress, Assn. Lit. Scholars and Critics (pres. 1996-97). Jewish. Home: 1475 Le Roy Ave Berkeley CA 94708-1911 Office: U of Calif Dept of Comp Lit 4408 Dwinelle Hall Berkeley CA 94720-2510

ALTER, SHIRLEY JACOBS, jewelry store owner; b. Beaumont, Tex., June 23, 1929; d. Morris Louis and Helen (Dow) Jacobs; m. Nelson Tobias Alter, June 12, 1949; children: Dennis, Keith, Brian, Wendy. Student, U. Tex., Austin, 1950. Owner Gem Jewelry Co., Beaumont, 1950—. Pres. Nat. Coun. Jewish Women, Beaumont, 1965, 66, Sisterhood of Temple Emanuel, Beaumont, 1967, 68, Buckner Bapt. Benevolence Aux., Beaumont, 1970-72; bd. dirs. Temple Emmanuel, pres. elect, 1994-96, pres. 1996-98; active Beaumont Music Commn., 1990; founder Beaumont Reach to Recovery, 1973; active BMW Drive for the Cure of breast cancer, 1997. Named Hero, Susan Komen Found., 1997. Democrat. Office: Gem Jewelry Co 795 N 11th St Beaumont TX 77702-1547

ALTERMAN, BARRY, performing company executive; b. N.Y.C.. Student, SUNY, Brockport, Neighborhodd Playhouse Sch. Theatre. Journalist The Berkeley Barb, The Guardian, San Francisco, 1974-79; trial investigator Lipsig, Sullivan, and Liapakis, N.Y.C., 1980-84; gen. dir. Mark Morris Dance Group, N.Y.C., 1984—. Office: Mark Morris Dance Group 225 Lafayette St Rm 504 New York NY 10012-4087*

ALTERMAN, IRWIN MICHAEL, lawyer; b. Vineland, N.J., Mar. 4, 1941; s. Joseph and Rose A.; m. Susan Simon, Aug. 6, 1972 (dec. Apr. 1997); 1 son, Owen. AB, Princeton U., 1962; LLB, Columbia U., 1965. Bar: N.Y. 1966, Mich. 1967. Law clk. to chief judge Theodore Levin U.S. Dist. Ct. (ea. dist.) Mich., 1965-67; assoc. Kaye, Scholer, Fierman, Hays & Handler, N.Y.C., 1967-70, Hyman, Gurwin, Nachman, Friedman & Winkelman, Southfield, Mich., 1970-74; ptnr. Hyman, Gurwin, Nachman, Friedman & Winkelman, 1974-88, Kaufman and Payton, Farmington Hills, Mich., 1988-89, Kemp, Klein, Umphrey & Endelman, Troy, Mich., 1989—. Author: Plain and Accurate Style in Court Papers, 1987; founding editor Mich. Antitrust, 1975-92; editor Mich. Antitrust Digest 2nd edit., 1998; contbr. articles to profl. jours. Bd. gov. Jewish Fedn. Detroit, 1990—; mem. nat. young leadership cabinet United Jewish Appeal, 1978-79, mem. nat. exec. com., 1980; past pres. Adat Shalom Synagogue, Farmington Hills, Mich. Mem. ABA, Am. Law Inst., Assn. of Bar of City of N.Y., State Bar Mich. (past chmn. com. on plain English, past chmn. antitrust sect.), Detroit Bar Assn., Princeton Club (past pres. Mich.). Office: Kemp Klein Umphrey & Endelman 201 W Big Beaver Rd Ste 600 Troy MI 48084-4136

ALTERSITZ, JANET KINAHAN, principal; b. Orange, N.J., May 19, 1951; d. Patrick Joseph and Ida (Ciamillio) K.; 1 child, Jacob. AA, County Coll. Morris, 1971; BA, Glassboro State Coll., 1973; MEd, Ariz. State U., 1980. Educator Washington (N.J.) Twp. Mid. Sch., 1974-77, Deer Valley Sch. Dist., Phoenix, 1977-82; asst. prin. Desert Sky Mid. Sch., Glendale, Ariz., 1983-86, prin., 1986—; cons. and presenter in field. Mem. ASCD, NAASP (mid. level rep. 1993—), Nat. Mid. Sch. Assn., Western Regional Mid. Level. Assn. (program chmn. 1992), Ariz. Sch. Adminstrs. (sec., treas. 1989-90, pres. 1990-91), Cen. Ariz. Mid. Level. Assn. (bd. dirs. 1989—, exec. dir. 1994—), P.O.K. Democrat. Roman Catholic. Home: 4642 W Villa Rita Dr Glendale AZ 85308-1520 Office: Desert Sky Mid Sch 5130 W Grovers Ave Glendale AZ 85308-1300

ALTFEST, LEWIS JAY, financial and investment advisor; b. N.Y.C., Oct. 14, 1940; s. Sam and Ruth (Zwang) A.; m. Karen Caplan, Dec. 25, 1966; children: Ellen Wendy, Andrew Gamer. BBA with honors, CCNY, 1962; MBA, NYU, 1970; PhD, CUNY, 1978. CPA, N.Y.; chartered fin. analyst; cert. fin. planner, personal fin. specialist. Sr. investment analyst Wertheim and Co., N.Y.C., 1969-75, Lehman Bros., N.Y.C., 1975-76; dir. research, gen. ptnr. Lord Abbett and Co., N.Y.C., 1976-82; pres. L.J. Altfest and Co., Inc., N.Y.C., 1982—; assoc. prof. fin. Pace U. Grad. Sch. Bus., N.Y.C., 1984—; dir. fin. planning and investments program New Sch. for Social Rsch., N.Y.C., 1988—; arbitrator Nat. Assn. Securities Dealers, Am. Arbitration Assn.; bd. dirs. Consumer Fin. Edn. Found. Author: (with others) Introduction to Business, 1978, Capital Budgeting Handbook, 1986; author: Lew Altfest Answers Almost All Your Questions About Money, 1992, revised edit., 1994; contbr. articles to profl. jours. Pres. 240 E. 79th Coop. Bd., N.Y.C., 1983-86; bd. dirs. Consumer Fin. Edn. Found., 1993-97. With U.S. Army, 1962-63. Named one of best fin. planners in U.S. Money Mag., 1987, one of best fin. advisors Worth Mag., 1996, 97, 98, one of best advisers for physicians, Med. Econs., 1998; recipient Disting. Alumni award Ph.D. Alumni Assn. CUNY, 1992. Mem. Nat. Assn. Personal Fin. Advisors (bd. dirs. 1985-89, Outstanding Leadership award 1989), AICPA, Internat. Assn. for Fin. Planning (bd. dirs. N.Y. chpt. 1987-93), Inst. Chartered Fin. Analysts, Am. Fin. Assn., Fin. Analysts Fedn., Fin. Mgmt. Assn., N.Y. Soc. Security Analysts, Registry Fin. Planning Practitioners, CCNY Bus. Alumni Assn. (bd. dirs. 1983-87), Acad. of Fin. Svcs. Office: L J Altfest & Co Inc 116 John St Rm 1120 New York NY 10038-3301

ALTHAUS, DAVID STEVEN, chemicals executive, controller; b. Massilon, Ohio, Dec. 25, 1945; s. James Horace and Mary Jane (Horan) A.; m. Joan Elizabeth Wrenn, Aug. 4, 1973; children: D. Steven Jr., Matthew, Beth Anne; foster children: James, Elise. BA, Miami U., Oxford, Ohio, 1967; cert., Def. Lang. Inst., Monterey, Calif., 1969; MBA, Miami U., Oxford, Ohio, 1976. CPA, N.C., Ohio. Internal auditor Harris Corp., Cleve., 1976-77; sr. staff acct. Harris Corp., Rochester, N.Y., 1977-78; acctg. supr. Imperial Group Ltd., Wilson, N.C., 1978-80; dir. planning Am. Mortgage Ins. Cos., Raleigh, N.C., 1980-83; asst. v.p., budget mgr. Gen. Electric Mortgage Ins. Cos., Raleigh, 1983-84; contr., asst. treas. Chem. Industry Inst. Toxicology, Research Triangle Park, N.C., 1984—, mgr. human resources, 1984-90, asst. sec., 1989—. Cubmaster Boy Scouts Am., 1986-90, asst. scoutmaster, 1990—. Capt. USMC, 1968-74, Vietnam. Decorated Cross of Galantry, Rep. of Vietnam, Da Nang, 1970. Mem. AICPA, Inst. Mgmt. Accts., Am. Compensation Assn., Contr.'s Coun., Soc. for Human Resources Mgmt. Baptist. Office: Chem Industry Inst Toxicology PO Box 12137 Durham NC 27709-2137

ALTHAVER, LAMBERT EWING, manufacturing company executive; b. Kansas City, Mo., May 18, 1931; s. Edward William and Dorothy Lambert (Ewing) A.; m. Holly Elizabeth Walpole, Feb. 28, 1953; children: Brian, Lauren. BA, Principia Coll, 1952. Account exec. Walbro Corp., Cass City, Mich., 1954-58, asst. to pres., 1958-65, v.p. fin., 1965-70, exec. v.p., 1970-77, pres., chief ops. officer, 1977-82, pres., chief exec. officer, 1982-87, chmn., pres., CEO, 1987-96, also bd. dirs., chmn., CEO, 1996-98; chmn. emeritus Walbro Corp., Cass City, 1998—. Councilman Village of Cass City, 1963-65, pres., 1965-84, 87—; mem. Tuscola County Planning Commn., Caro, Mich., 1966-94; chmn. Cass City Econ. Devel. Corp., 1983-96, Tuscola area Airport Authority, 1994—; bd. dirs. Tuscola County Econ. Devel. Corp., 1985—; vice chmn., sec., dir. Artrain, Inc., 1975-96, chmn., 1996—; v.p., bd. dirs. Lake Huron area Boy Scouts Am., 1988-94; co-founder, v.p. Village Bach Festival, 1979—; trustee Jordan Coll., 1990-95; mem. Mich Jobs Commn., 1996-99; trustee Hills & Dales Hosp., Cass City, 1998—; dir. Am. Bus. Conf., Washington, 1998—; dir. Mich. Mcpl. League Found., Ann Arbor, 1999—. With U.S. Army, 1952-54. Recipient Silver Beaver award Boy Scouts Am., 1995, Disting. Eagle Scout award, 1989; named Citizen of Yr. Cass City C. of C., 1978; Paul Harris fellow Rotary Internat., Evanston, Ill., 1979, 94; named Outstanding Bus. Leader, Northwood U., 1997. Mem. Mich. C. of C. (bd. dirs. 1986-92), Detroit Athletic Club, Rotary Club of Cass City. Avocation: golf. Office: Walbro Corp 6242 Garfield Ave Cass City MI 48726-1325

ALTHEIDE, PHYLLIS SAGE, computer scientist, software engineer; b. St. Louis, Apr. 13, 1963; d. Paul D. and Alvera Sage; m. Richard W. Altheide, Aug. 1984 (div. June 1999); children: Martha Elizabeth, Paul William. BS in Computer Sci., U. Mo., Rolla, 1985, MS in Computer Sci., 1992. GS-12 computer scientist U.S. Geol. Survey, Rolla, 1988-95, GS-13 computer scientist, 1996-98, GS-13 supervisory computer specialist software engring sect. rsch. tech. and application br., 1998—; lead developer Spatial Data Transfer Standard Task Force, Rolla, 1990-95; presenter workshops Australia, 1995, New Zealand, 1995, Malaysia, 1997; technical expert ISO working group on geospatial stds., 1998—. Author: (with others) GIS Data Conversion: Strategies, Techniques, Management, 1998. Recipient Superior Svc. Honor award Dept. of Interior, 1997. Mem. IEEE Computer Soc. Lutheran. Avocations: photography, travel, walking.

ALTHOFF, J(AMES) L., construction company executive; b. McHenry, Ill., June 9, 1928; s. William H. and Eleanor M. (Smith) A.; m. Joan E. Andreen, June 18, 1949; children: Tim, Betsy, Kate, Tod, Patti, Jim Jr., Karyn. G-rad., McHenry (Ill.) High Sch., 1947. Owner, pres. Althoff Gas Svc., McHenry, 1949-60, Fox Valley Propane, 1952-60, No. Equip. Corp., McHenry, 1958-72; CEO Althoff Industries, Crystal Lake, Ill., 1961—, Althoff & Assocs., McHenry, 1962—, Brookside Indsl., McHenry, 1991—; trustee Plumbers Welfare Fund, Chgo., 1972—; dir. McHenry Bank. Pres. McHenry High Sch. Bd. Edn., 1967-79, Fire Protection Dist., McHenry, 1964-92; chmn. bd. govs. Ill. Univs., 1980-91; commr. Ill. State Lottery, 1991—. Recipient award for outstanding leadership Chgo. State U., 1986, Leadership award No. Med. Ctr., McHenry, 1984, Ea. Ill. U., 1987. Mem. Contrs. Assn. No. Ill. (pres. 1969-72), Bradley Dads' Assn., Kiwanis. Home: 508 N Green St Mc Henry IL 60050-5684 Office: Althoff Industries 8001 S State Route 31 Crystal Lake IL 60014-8184

ALTIER, WILLIAM JOHN, management consultant; b. Drexel Hill, Pa., July 22, 1935; s. William John and Gertrude (Soule) A.; m. Mileen Rishel Bower, June 21, 1958; children: William Clark, Dwight Douglas. BA, Lafayette Coll., 1958; MBA, Pa. State U., 1962. Assoc. Kepner-Tregoe Inc., Princeton, N.J., 1964-68, Applied Synergetics Ctr., Waltham, Mass., 1968-69; dir. mktg. Comstock & Wescott Inc., Cambridge, Mass., 1969-70; gen. mgr. divsn. Princeton Rsch. Press, 1970-75, sr. assoc., 1975-76; pres. Princeton Assocs. Inc., Buckingham, Pa., 1976—; grad. asst. Dale Carnegie Courses; lectr. Assn. for Media-Based Continuing Edn. for Engrs.; guest lectr. Grad. Sch. Mgmt., New Sch. for Social Rsch., Wharton Sch., U. Pa., Pa. State U.; bd. dirs., vice chmn. Inst. Mgmt. Cons., also exec. editor IMC Newsletter. Author: The Thinking Manager's Toolbox, 1999; editor, pub. The PA Perspective; abstractor Jour. Product Innovation Mgmt.; mem. editl. rev. bd. Jour. Managerial Issues; contbg. author: Management Consulting, 3d edit., 1996, The Art of M&A Integration: A Guide to Merging Resources, Processes, and Responsibilities, 1997; contbr. articles to profl. jours.; patentee in field. Co-chmn. indls. divns. United Cmty. Fund, Carlisle, Pa., 1963; elder Doylestown Presbyn. Ch.; exec. v.p. Bucks County br. ARC, also mem. planning com. Southeastern Pa. chpt.; vol. worker civic orgns. Fellow Inst. Mgmt. Cons. (cert.); mem. Acad. Mgmt., Am. Chem. Soc., Am. Vacuum Soc., Armed Forces Comm. and Electronics Assn., Am. Mgmt. Assn., Product Devel. and Mgmt. Assn. (v.p.), Indsl. Mgmt. Club, Inst. Mgmt. Cons. (participative process cons. spl. interest group), Am. Arbitration Assn. (panel arbitrators), U. So. Calif. Ctr. for Futures Rsch., Assn. Mng. Cons. (trustee, editor newslette UPDATE II), Union League Phila., Mensa, Ctrl. Bucks C. of C., Tech. Coun. Greater Phila., Pa. Innovation Network, World Affairs Coun. Phila., Am. Creativity Assn., Exch. Club (bd. control 1960-64), 1000 Club, Kappa Sigma Alumni Corp. (chpt. pres.). Home: PO Box 820 Buckingham PA 18912-0820 Office: PO Box 820 Buckingham PA 18912-0820

ALTIERI, PETER LOUIS, lawyer; b. Norwalk, Conn., Dec. 7, 1955; s. John L. and Eileen Mary (Rudden) A.; m. Sandra Shelton White, Sept. 3, 1983; children: Brianna Burr, John Shelton. AB, Georgetown U., 1977; JD, Fordham Sch. Law, 1980. Bar: N.Y. 1981, U.S. Dist. Ct. (so. dist., ea. dist.) N.Y. 1981, U.S. Dist. Ct. (no. dist. and we. dist.) N.Y. 1983, U.S. Dist. Ct. Conn. 1983, U.S. Supreme Ct. 1984, U.S. Ct. Appeals (2d. cir.) 1986, Conn. 1987. Law clk. to judge U.S. Dist. Ct., 1978; intern U.S. Attys. Office, N.Y.C., 1978; assoc. Law Firm Malcolm A. Hoffmann, N.Y.C., 1980-87; ptnr. Epstein, Becker & Green, N.Y.C., 1987—. Mem. ABA, Conn. Bar Assn. (exec. com. antitrust sect. 1988—), Assn. Bar City N.Y. (com. uniform state laws 1985-88, com. on inter-Am. affairs 1997—), The Patterson Club Conn., Union League Club N.Y.C. Home: 140 Burr St Fairfield CT 06430-7105 Office: Epstein Becker & Green 250 Park Ave Ste 1201 New York NY 10177-0001

ALTMAN, ADELE ROSENHAIN, radiologist; b. Tel Aviv, Israel, June 4, 1924; came to U.S., 1933, naturalized, 1939; d. Bruno and Salla (Silberzweig) Rosenhain; m. Emmett Altman, Sept. 3, 1944; children: Brian R., Alan L., Karen D. Diplomate Am. Bd. Radiology. Intern Queens Gen. Hosp., N.Y.C., 1949-51; resident Hosp. for Joint Diseases, N.Y.C., 1951-52, Roosevelt Hosp., N.Y.C., 1955-57; clin. instr. radiology Downstate Med. Ctr., SUNY, Bklyn., 1957-61; asst. prof. radiology N.Y. Med. Coll., N.Y.C., 1961-65, assoc. prof., 1965-68; assoc. prof. radiology U. Okla. Health Sci. Ctr., Oklahoma City, 1968-78; assoc. prof. dept. radiology U. N.Mex. Sch. Medicine, Albuquerque, 1978-85. Author: Radiology of the Respiratory System: A Basic Review, 1978; contbr. articles to profl. jours. Fellow Am. Coll. Angiology, N.Y. Acad. Medicine; mem. Am. Coll. Radiologist, Am. Roentgen Ray Soc., Assn. Univ. Radiologists, Radiol. Soc. N.Am., B'nai B'rith Anti-Defamation League (bd. dirs. N.Mex. state bd.), Hadassah Club.

ALTMAN, ARNOLD DAVID, business executive; b. South Bend, Ind., Dec. 10, 1917; s. David and Goldie (Mooren) A.; children: Daniel Blair, Jonathan Estes. BSEE, U. Notre Dame, 1941. With Newman and Altman, Inc., South Bend, 1946-64; pres. Avanti Motor Corp., South Bend, 1976-82, Nat. Inventory Res., Inc., South Bend, 1980—; pres., CEO Rosenstein & Co., South Bend, 1985—. Lt. USN, 1942-46. Democrat. Jewish. Home: 1527 E Colfax Ave South Bend IN 46617-2601 Office: PO Box 4584 South Bend IN 46634-4584

ALTMAN, BRIAN DAVID, pediatric ophthalmologist; b. Temple, Tex., Feb. 29, 1944; s. Harold and Alice A. BA, Adelphi U., 1965; MD, Yale Med. Sch., 1969. Diplomate Am. Bd. Pediatrics, Am. Bd. Opthalmologists. Pediatric ophthalmologist pvt. practice, Huntington Valley, Pa., 1976-98, Plymouth, Pa., 1976-98, Ocean City, N.J., 1992—, Cape May Courthouse, 1992—; cons. in pediatric ophthalomogy several hosps. in Pa. and N.J., 1977—. Co-author: (with others) Medications in Pediatric Ophthalmology, 1975. Lt. cmmdr. USPHS, 1970-72. Fellow Am. Acad. Opthalmology, Am. Acad. Pediatrics, Am. Assn. Pediatric Ophthalmologists. Home and Office: 1300 Asbury Ave Ocean City NJ 08226-3279 also Office: 900 Rt 95 S Cape May Courthouse NJ 08210

ALTMAN, DREW E., foundation executive; b. Boston, Mar. 21, 1951; s. George and Harriet A.; m. Pamela Koch; children: Daniel, Jessica. BA magna cum laude, Brandeis U., 1973; MA, Brown U., 1974; PhD in Polit. Sci., MIT, 1983. Postdoctoral fellow, rsch. assoc. Harvard U. Sch. Pub. Health, Boston, 1975-76, 78-80; prin. rsch. assoc. Codman Rsch. Group, Boston, 1976-80; spl. asst. office of adminstr. Health Care Fin. Adminstrn. Dept. HHS, Washington, 1979-81; v.p. Robert Wood Johnson Found., Princeton, N.J., 1981-86; commr. N.J. Dept. Human Svcs., Trenton, 1986-89; program dir. health and human svcs. The Pew Charitable Trusts, Phila., 1989-90; pres., CEO Henry J. Kaiser Family Found., Menlo Park, Calif., 1990—. Contbr. articles to profl. jours. Mem. Inst. of Medicine, Nat. Acad. of Soc. Ins., Assn. for Health Svcs. Rsch. Office: Henry J Kaiser Family Found 2400 Sand Hill Rd Menlo Park CA 94025-6941*

ALTMAN, EDITH G., sculptor; b. Altenberg, Germany, May 23, 1931; arrived in U.S., 1939; BA, Wayne State U., 1949; student, Marygrove Coll., 1956-57. Instr. visual arts and printing project U. Omaha, 1984; asst. prof. painting, grad. advisor U. Chgo., 1984-85; vis. asst. prof. painting Sch. Art Inst. Chgo., 1985-86; lectr. painting U. Ill., Columbia Coll., Oakton C.C., Chgo. One-woman shows include NAME Gallery, 1987, Spertus Mus. Gallery Contemporary Art, 1988, Rockford Art Mus., 1989, State of Ill. Mus. Gallery, Chgo., 1992, Loyola U. Fine Arts Gallery, 1993, Peace Mus., Chgo., 1993, Mitchell Mus., Ill., 1995, Minn. Mus. Am. Art, 1995, others; exhibited in group shows Art Inst. Chgo., 1975, 79, 81, 85, Mus. Contemporary Art, Chgo., 1976, 81, 83, 97, Acad. Kunst, Berlin, 1987, Barbican Ctr., London, 1990; represented in permanent collections Standard Oil Co., Mus. Contemporary Art, Chgo., 1997, State of Ill., Yale U. Mus., Holocaust Mus., Peace Mus.; contbr. articles to profl. jours., newspapers. Individual Artist fellow Ill. Arts. Coun., 1984, 94; Individual Artist Fellow grantee NEA, 1990-91, Art Matters fellow, 1994. Mem. Chgo. Artist Coalition (founding mem., mem. com. artists rights, 1988). Address: 811 W 16th St Chicago IL 60608-2222

ALTMAN, HAROLD, artist educator; b. N.Y.C., Apr. 20, 1924. Student, Art Students League, 1941-42, Cooper Union, 1941-47, New Sch. Social Rsch., 1947-49, Acad. Grande Chaumiere, Paris, 1949-52, Black Mountain Coll., N.C. asst. prof. art N.Y. State Coll. Ceramics, Alfred U., 1952-54, U. N.C., Greensboro, 1954-56, U. Wis.-Milw., 1956-62; prof. art Pa. State U., 1962-76. Exhbns. include Mus. Modern Art, Met. Mus. Art & Whitney Mus. Art, N.Y., Art Inst., Chgo., Nat. Gallery Art, Washington; commns. include Entire print ed. Mus. Modern Art, 1960, Soc. Am. Graphic Artists, 1962, Hilton Rockfeller Hotel, 1963, Jewish Mus., N.Y., 1964; one-man shows include Martha Jackson Gallery, N.Y., 1958, Art Inst., Chgo., 1960, San Francisco Mus. Art, 1961, Sagot Le Garrec Gallery, Paris, 1968, 74, State Gallery Fine Arts, Istanbul, Turkey, 1975, among others; represented in permanent collections Boston Mus. Fine Arts, L.A. County Mus., Mus. Modern Art, N.Y.C., Whitney Mus., Bklyn. Mus., Met. Mus. Art, Milw. Art Ctr., Minn. Mus. Art, Nat. Gallery of Art, Phila. Mus. Art, San Francisco Mus. Art, Smithsonian Inst., Walker Art Ctr., Art Inst. Chgo., Cin. Mus. Art, Cleve. Mus. Art, Detroit Inst. Fine Arts, San Diego Mus. Art, Albright Knox Art Gallery, Des Moines Art Ctr., Newart Art Mus., Butler Inst. Am. Art, Ga. Mus. Art, Calif. Palace of Legion of Honor, Okla. Art Ctr., N.C. Mus. Art, Wadsworth Atheneum, Phoenix Art Ctr., Norfolk Mus., Peoria Art Ctr., Princeton U. Mus. Art, Yale U. Mus. Art, Fogg Mus. Art, Harvard U., Honolulu Acad. Art, N.Y. Pub. Libr., Libr. Congress, Pa. Acad. Art, Memphis Brooks Mus. Art, Kranner Art Mus., Decordova and Dana Mus., Univs. of Mass., Colo., Ky., Maine, Minn., Va. Wis., N.D., Nebr., Wake Forest, Ohio State, Pa. State, NYU, High Mus. Art, Atlanta, Rochester Meml. Art Gallery, Philbrook Mus. Art, Tulsa, Kalamazoo Inst. Art, Anchorage Mus. Art, Boston Pub. Libr., Victoria and Albert Mus., London, Stedellkj Mus., Amsterdam, Kunst Mus., Basel, Royal Mus. Fine Arts, Copenhagen, Bibliotheque Nat., Paris, Bibliotheque Royale, Belgium, Art Gallery Ont., Malmo Mus., Sweden, Mus. Modern Art Haifa, Israel, Mus. U. Glasgow, Scotland, Mus. Carnavalet, Paris, Art Gallery Greater Victoria, Escuela De Artes Plasticas, Mexico City. Guggenheim fellow, 1960-62, Fulbright Hayes Sr. Rsch. fellow, 1964-65, Tamarind Lithography fellow; recipient Nat. Inst. Arts & Letters award, 1963, Silver medal City of Paris; grantee Nat. Endowment for the Arts. Mem. Societe des Peintres, Graveurs, Francais, Nat. Acad. Design. Office: Multiple Impressions 128 Spring St New York NY 10012-3810 also: PO Box 777 729 Berry St Lemont PA 16851

ALTMAN, IRWIN, psychology educator. BA, NYU, 1951; MA, U. Md., 1954, PhD, 1957. Asst. prof. psychology Am. U., Washington, 1957-58, sr. rsch. scientist, assoc. prof., 1960-62, adj. prof., 1962-69; rsch. scientist in human scis. Arlington, Va., 1958-60; rsch. psychologist Naval Med. Rsch. Inst., Bethesda, Md., 1962-69; adj. prof. U. Md., 1968-69; prof. U. Utah, Salt Lake City, 1969-79, chmn. dept. psychology, 1969-76, dean Coll. Social and Behavioral Sci., 1979-83, v.p. for acad. affairs, 1983-87, disting. prof., 1987—. Author: (with J.E. McGrath) Small Groups, 1966, (with D.A. Taylor) Social Penetration, 1973, Environment and Social Behavior, 1975; (with M. Chemers) Culture and Environment, 1980; (with J. Wohlwill) Human Behavior and Environment: Vol. I, 1976, Vol. II, 1977, Vol. III, 1978, Vol. IV, 1980, Vol. V, 1981, Vol. VI, 1983, Vol. VII, 1984, (with C. Werner) Vol. VIII, 1985, (with A. Wandersman) Vol. IX, 1987, (with E. Zube) Vol. X, 1989, (with K. Christensen) Vol. XI, 1990, (with S. Low) Vol. XII, 1992, (with A. Churchman) Women and the Environment, Vol. XIII, 1994; (with D. Stokols) Handbook of Environmental Psychology, Vols I and II, 1987; (with J. Ginat) Polygamous Families in Contemporary Society, 1996; mem. editl. bds.: Small Groups, 1970-79, Man-Environment Systems, 1969-73, Jour. Applied Social Psychology, 1973-85, Sociometry, 1973-76, Environment and Behavior, 1975, Jour. Personality and Social Psychology, 1974-83, Contemporary Psychology, 1975-86, Environ. Psychology and Nonverbal Behavior, Psychology, 1976-90, Am. Jour. Cmty. Psychology, 1978-81, Population and Environment, 1979, Jour. Environ. Psychology, 1982, Computers and Human Behavior, 1985, Internat. Jour. Applied Social Psychology, 1984, Communication Monographs, 1992-95; assoc. editor Am. Jour. Cmty. Psychology, 1988-92; co-editor Jour. Environ. Psychology, 1990-98; contbr. articles to profl. jours. 1st lt. Adj. Gen. Corps, AUS, 1954-56. Mem. APA (pres. divsn. population and environment), AAAS, Soc. Exptl. Social Psychology, Soc. Psychol. Study of Social Issues, Soc. Personality and Social Psychology (pres.), Environ. Design Rsch. Assn., Am. Psychol. Soc.

ALTMAN, JOSEPH, author, neuroscientist; b. Budapest, Hungary, Oct. 7, 1925; came to U.S., 1955, naturalized, 1979; s. Samuel and Honor (Teitelbaum) A.; m. Shirley Ann Bayer, Dec. 8, 1973; 1 child, Magda. Ph.D., NYU, 1959. Asst. prof. NYU, N.Y.C., 1961; assoc. prof. MIT, Cambridge, 1962-68; mem. faculty Purdue U., West Lafayette, Ind., 1968-95, prof. biol. sci., 1968. Contbr. articles to profl. jours.; author: Atlas of Prenatal Rat Brain Development, 1995, Development of the Cerebellar System in Relation to its Evolution, Structure, and Functions, 1997, (with Shirley A. Bayer) Neocortical Development, 1991. NSF grantee, 1975-90; NIH grantee, 1962-88. Home and Office: 7715 W 88th St Indianapolis IN 46278-1164

ALTMAN, LAWRENCE GENE, biologist; b. July 4, 1952; s. Mark Eugene and Roberta Mercedes (Baron) A. BA in Biology, Fordham U., 1972, MS, 1974, PhD, 1982. Rsch. biologist VA, West Haven, Conn., 1982-85; asst. prof. divsn. sci. and math. Fordham U., N.Y.C., 1986-87; postdoctoral assoc. in pathology Yale U. Med. Sch., New Haven, 1982-85; cons. Coll. New Rochelle, N.Y., 1980-81, Polyscis., Inc., Warrington, Pa., 1985-89, Columbia U. Coll. Physicians and Surgeons Dept. Microbiol., N.Y.C., 1986-88; curriculum cons. Sacred Heart U., Fairfield, Conn., 1990-91; asst. prof. biology Western Conn. State U., Danbury, 1992-93, 94-95, 98, CUNY, 1998—; mem. part-time faculty Fordham U., N.Y.C., Western Conn. State U., Danbury, 1990-91, 96-98; pres. Cider Mill Pond Assn., Greenwich, Conn., 1994-96. Contbr. articles to profl. jours. Recipient Most Valuable Staff Mem. Faculty award Dowling Coll., 1975, Outstanding Performance award West Haven VA Med. Ctr., 1983; Fordham U. fellow, 1975-77. Mem. AAAS, Am. Soc. for Cell Biology, Electron Microscopy Soc. Am., Conn. Electron Microscopy Soc., Sigma Xi. Avocations: theater, traveling, educational technology. Home: 304 Lansdowne Westport CT 06880-5649

ALTMAN, LAWRENCE KIMBALL, physician, journalist; b. Quincy, Mass., June 19, 1937; s. William S. and Esther (Kimball) A. A.B. cum laude, Harvard U., 1958; M.D., Tufts U., 1962. Diplomate: Am. Vet. Epidemiology Soc. Intern Mt. Zion Hosp., San Francisco, 1962-63; USPHS epidemic intelligence service officer Centers for Disease Control, Atlanta, 1963-66; med. resident, fellow U. Wash. Hosp., Seattle, 1966-69; med. corr., columnist The Doctors World N.Y. Times, 1969—; clin. assoc. prof. medicine NYU, 1970—; vis. physician Serafimer Hosp., Karolinska Inst., Stockholm, Sweden, 1973; vis. scientist U. Wash., 1971; Chancellor's Disting. Lecture for Pub. Understanding of Sci., U. Calif., San Francisco, 1989. Author: Science of The Times, 1981, Who Goes First? The Story of Self-Experimentation in Medicine, 1987; contbr. chpts. to books, articles to profl. jours.; Ency. Brittanica, 1979, Grolier Ency., 1972-87. Recipient Howard W. Blakeslee award Am. Heart Assn., 1982, 83, 94, Claude Bernard award Nat. Soc. Med. Rsch., 1971, 74; Walter C. Alvarez award Am. Med. Writers Assn., 1980, Vincent Downing award 1988; journalism award Am. Acad. Pediat., 1982, pub. svc. award Nat. Kidney Found., George Polk award, 1986, journalism award Coll. Am. Pathologists, 1985, Med. Media Excellence award Friends Nat. Libr. Medicine, 1993. Master ACP, Am. Coll. Epidemiology, N.Y. Acad. Medicine; mem. Inst. Medicine/Nat. Acad. Scis., Am. Soc. Tropical Medicine and Hygiene, Soc. for Epidemiol., Am. Bd. Med. Spltys. (pub. 1986-88), Century Club (N.Y.C.), Harvard Club (N.Y.C. and Boston). Home: 140 W End Ave New York NY 10023-6131 Office: New York Times 229 W 43rd St New York NY 10036-3959

ALTMAN, LEO SIDNEY, lawyer; b. Denver, May 6, 1911; s. Simon and Gisela (Marmorstein) A.; m. Helen Kimball, Aug. 30, 1949. JD, U. Colo., 1935. Bar: Colo. 1935. Ptnr. Koperlik & Altman, Pueblo, Colo., 1935-56, Preston & Altman, Pueblo, 1956-64, Preston, Altman & Parlapiano, Pueblo, 1964-80, Preston, Altman, Parlapiano, Keilbach & Lytle, Pueblo, 1981-94, Altman, Keilbach, Lytle & Parlapiano, 1994-96, Altman, Keilbach, lytle, Parlapiano & Ware, 1996—; mcpl. ct. judge, Pueblo, 1942-50; U.S. commr., Pueblo, 1937-41. V.p. Pueblo Met. Mus. Bd., 1970-76; mem. Pueblo Civic Symphony Bd., 1968-69; bd. dirs. Pueblo chpt. ARC, 1959-72, chmn. 1961, resolutions com. nat. ARC, 1963, mem. Western Area adv. counsel ARC, 1970-73; pres. Temple Emanuel Congregation, 1952; pres. Allied Jewish Coun. of Pueblo, 1946-47; pres. Family Service Soc., 1951-52; comdr. Pueblo Post 2 Am Legion, 1946, Dist. 8. Colo., 1948. Served to lt. col. U.S. Army, 1942-46; Res., 1946-66. Fellow Am. Coll. Trust and Estate Counsel; mem. ABA, Colo. Bar Assn. (bd. govs. 1953-56, v.p. 1956), Pueblo County Bar Assn. (pres. 1952, chmn. grievance com. 1956-61), Colo. State Bd. Law Examiners (law com. 1964-68), Pi Lambda Phi. Republican. Jewish. Clubs: Pueblo Knife and Fork (pres. 1946-47), Pueblo Monday Evening (pres. 1966-67). Lodges: Masons (32 deg.), Shriners, B'nai B'rith (pres. Pueblo 1940, pres. tri-state 1942). Home: 1111 Bonforte Blvd Apt 810 Pueblo CO 81001-1830 Office: Altman Keilbach Lytle Parlapiano & Ware 229 Colorado Ave Pueblo CO 81004-2003

ALTMAN, LESLIE JOAN, secondary school educator; b. Cambridge, Mass., May 11, 1943; d. Sidney Arnold and Irene Marie (Sullivan) Wolbarst; children: Christopher Matthew, Timothy Alexander. AB, Smith Coll., 1964; MA, NYU, 1967; PhD, Boston Coll., 1973; M in Counseling, Ariz. State U., 1981. Tchr. Emerson Sch., Bolton, Mass., 1964-65, 86-87, Needham (Mass.) H.S., 1965-66, 67-69; lectr. Ariz. State U., Tempe, 1974-77, Southampton (Eng.) U., 1978; sch. counselor Frank Sch., Guadalupe, Ariz., 1981-86; tchr. English lang. and lit., dir. of lower grades St. Sebastian's Country Day Sch., Needham, 1987-93; tchr. English, dir. mentoring program Hawken Sch., Gates Mills, Ohio, 1993—; presenter numerous workshops; cons. English dept. Winsor Sch., 1991; mem. mid-career task force Ohio Assn. Ind. Schs. Contbr. articles to profl. jours. Vol. Habitat for Humanity, 1996—, Free Clin., Cleve., 1996—. Fulbright-Hays scholar, Africa, 1991, India, 1998; grantee NEH, 1989, 92; fellow Coun. for Basic Edn., summer 1990. Mem. Cleve. Counsel on World Affairs, New Eng. Assn. Tchrs. English (exec. bd. 1990-93, chmn. multicultural com.), Ohio Assn. Ind. Schs. (mem. profl. svcs. com.). Avocations: gardening, cooking, traveling. Office: Hawken Sch PO Box 8002 Gates Mills OH 44040-8002

ALTMAN, ROBERT ALLEN, educational assessment executive; b. Petersburg, Va., Mar. 30, 1943; s. Julian Allen and Katharine (Goldschmidt) A.; m. Jane Carol Rotman, June 13, 1965; children: Jennifer, John. AB, Harvard U., 1964; MA, Columbia U., 1965, PhD, 1969; JD (hon.), Montclair (N.J.) State U., 1995. Exec. sec. univ. task force on open admissions CUNY, 1965-69; dir. spl. higher edn. programs Western Interstate Commn. for Higher Edn., Boulder, Colo., 1969-72; exec. dir. Assn. Upper Level Colls. and Univs., Princeton, N.J., 1970-78; with Ednl. Testing Svc., Princeton, 1972-80, v.p., 1980-95; pres. Internat. Assessment Assocs., Princeton, 1995—; vis. scholar Montclair State U., 1995-96; cons. over 20 colls., univs., state bds. higher edn., State Edn. Commn., Beijing, 1995—; ednl. evaluation cons. World Bank, 1996—. Author: The Upper Division College, 1970; editor 3 books; contbr. articles, rsch. reports to profl. jours. Bd. dirs. Princeton Adult Sch., 1985-89; mem. Gov.'s Adv. Panel on Higher Edn. Restructuring, 1993; mem. N.J. State Bd. of Higher Edn., 1993-94; mem. N.J. State Coll. Governing Bds. Assn., 1989-94, chair, 1993-94; trustee Montclair State U., 1985-95, chair, 1989-95; mem. Gale Fund Rsch. Panel, Assn. Governing Bds., Washington, 1993-96; mem. Mercer Vicinage Com. on Minority Affairs, 1995-97, vice chair, 1996-97; trustee Mercer County C.C., 1980-84, chair, 1983-84; mem. N.J. Coun. County Colls., 1981-84. Home and Office: Internat Assessment Assocs 536 Cherry Valley Rd Princeton NJ 08540-7681

ALTMAN, ROBERT B., film director, writer, producer; b. Kansas City, Mo., Feb. 20, 1925; m. Kathryn Altman; children: Robert, Matthew; children by previous marriage: Michael, Stephen, Christine. Student, U. Mo., 3 years. Owner Sandcastle 5 Prodns. Writer, prodr., dir.: (TV) Kraft Theatre; writer, prodr., dir.: (TV pilot) The Long Hot Summer; co-prodr.: (film) The James Dean Story, 1957; dir.: (films) The Delinquents, 1957, Countdown, 1968, That Cold Day in the Park, 1969, M*A*S*H, 1970 (Grand Prix award Cannes Film Festival 1970, Best Film, Nat. Soc. Film Critics 1970), Popeye, 1980, Come Back to the 5 & Dime, Jimmy Dean, Jimmy Dean, 1982, Streamers, 1983, Beyond Therapy, 1987, The Gingerbread Man, 1997, (TV series) Gun, 1997; producer: The Late Show, 1977, Welcome to L.A., 1977, Rich Kids, 1979, Remember My Name, 1979, Mrs. Parker and the Vicious Circle, 1994; prodr. and dir.: A Wedding, 1978, Quintet, 1979, A Perfect Couple, 1979, Secret Honor, 1985, The Player, 1992 (Best Dir. citation Cannes Film Festival, 1992), After Glow, 1997; prodr., dir., screenwriter: Three Women, 1977, Health, 1979; dir., screenwriter: Brewster McCloud, 1970, McCabe and Mrs. Miller, 1971, Images, 1972, The Long Goodbye, 1973, Thieves Like Us, 1974, California Split, 1974, Buffalo Bill and the Indians, 1976, Fool for Love, 1985, Short Cuts, 1993 (Best Dir. Acad. award nominee 1993), Ready to Wear (Prêt-à-Porter), 1994, Kansas City, 1996; dir. for stage: (Broadway) Come Back to the 5 & Dime, Jimmy Dean, Jimmy Dean, 1982, (Lyric Opera of Chgo.) McTeague, 1993; prodr., dir.: (TV) The Laundromat, 1984, The Dumb Waiter, 1987, The Room, 1987, Caine Mutiny Court Martial, 1987, Tanner '88, 1988; dir. film Vincent and Theo, 1990; producer, dir. Nashville, 1976; actor: (TV movie) Frank Capra's American Dream, 1997. Served with AUS, 1943-47. Mem. Dirs. Guild Am. Office: Sandcastle 5 Prodns 502 Park Ave Ste 15G New York NY 10022-1108 also: ICM 8942 Wilshire Blvd Beverly Hills CA 90211-1934

ALTMAN, ROY PETER, pediatric surgeon; b. N.Y.C., Apr. 13, 1934; s. Charles and Sue (Solomon) A.; m. Hanna Diamond, Aug. 22, 1964; children: James David, Robert Ross. AB, Colgate U., 1955; MS, U. Rochester, 1958; MD, N.Y. Med. Coll., 1961. Diplomate Am. Bd. Surgery, Am. Bd. Thoracic Surgery, Am. Bd. Pediatric Surgery. Intern Mount Sinai Hosp., N.Y.C., 1961-62; surg. resident Tufts-New Eng. Med. Ctr, Boston, 1962-66, chief resident, 1966-67; postdoctoral fellow NIH, Dept. Surgery Tufts-New Eng. Med. Ct., 1964-65; chief resident in thoracic surgery Washington U. Hosp., Washington, 1967-689; chief resident in pediatric surgery Children's Hosp. Nat. Med. Ctr., Washington, 1967-69; spl. fellow clin./rsch. surgery (transplantation) U. Colo. Health Scis. Ctr., Denver, 1974; Rudolph N. Schullinger prof. surgery in surgery and pediatrics Coll. Physicians and Surgeons, Columbia U., N.Y.C., 1980—; dir. pediatric surgery, surgeon in chief Babies and Children's Hosp., Columbia-Presbyn. Med. Ctr., N.Y.C.; sr. v.p. med. affairs, physician in chief Children's Health Network N.Y., Presbyn. Hosp.; physician-in-chief Children's Healthcare Network, 1998; prof. surgery and child health George Washington Sch. Medicine, 1977-80; sr. attending surgeon Children's Hosp., Nat. Med. Ctr., Washington, 1973-80, dir. surg. rsch., 1975-80, surg. dir. clin. rsch. ctr., 1975-80, dir. organ transplantation, 1975-80; cons. surgeon Walter Reed Army Hosp., 1974-80, Dewitt Army Hosp., Ft. Belvoir, Va., 1973-80, The Hosp. for Sick Children, Washington, 1974-80; asst. prof.surgery and child health George Washington U. Sch. Medicine, 1970-73, Tufts U. Sch. Medicine,. Editl. cons. Pediat. Surgery Internat., 1985—; editl. adv. bd. Surgery Ann., 1986—, Surgery, 1992—, Jour. Pediat. Surgery, 1996; cons. editor Pediat. Surgery Sect. Microsurgery, 1986—. Bd. dirs. Ronald McDonald House and Found. Children's Oncology Soc., N.Y. C.V. Mosby Scholar, N.Y. Med. Coll., 1961. Fellow ACS, Am. Acad. Pediatrics; mem. Am. Surg. Assn., Soc. Univ. Surgeons, Internat. Coll. Surgery, Am. Pediat. Surg. Assn. (gov. 1996), Alpha Omega Alpha. Avocations: skiing, golf, tennis, music. Home: 15 W 81st St New York NY 10024-6022 Office: Babies Hosp Columbia-Presbyn Med Ctr 3959 Broadway # 204 New York NY 10032-1537

ALTMAN, SIDNEY, biology educator; b. Montreal, Que., Can., May 7, 1939. BS, MIT, 1960; PhD in Biophys., U. Colo., 1967; DSc (hon.), McGill U., Montreal, 1991, York U., U. Colo., U. Montreal, U. B.C. Teaching asst. Columbia U., 1960-62; Damon Runyon Meml. Fund cancer rsch. fellow in molecular biology Harvard U., 1967-69; Anna Fuller Fund fellow, then Med. Rsch. Coun. fellow Med. Rsch. Coun. Lab. Molecular Biology, 1969-71; from asst. to assoc. prof. Yale U., New Haven, 1971-80, prof. biology, 1980—, Sterling prof. biology, 1990—, prof. chemistry, 1994—, chmn. dept., 1983-85; dean Yale Coll., 1985-90; tutor Radcliffe Coll., 1968-69; researcher effects of acridines on T4 DNA replication, mutants, precursors of tRNA processing by catalytic RNA and ribonuclease function. Author: Transfer RNA, 1978. Recipient Nobel Prize in Chemistry, 1989. Fellow AAAS; mem. Am. Soc. Biol. Chemists, Genetics Soc. Am., Nat. Acad. Scis., Am. Philos. Soc. (Rosenstiel award 1989). Office: Yale U Dept Biology Kline Biology Tower PO Box 208103 New Haven CT 06520-8103*

ALTMAN, WILLIAM KEAN, lawyer; b. San Antonio, Feb. 18, 1944; s. Marion K. and Ruth (Nunnelee) A.; m. Doris E. Johnson, May 29, 1964; children: Brian, Brad, Blake. BBA, Tex. A&M U., 1965, MBA, 1967; JD, U. Tex., 1979. Bar: Tex. 1970, Okla. 1993, U.S. Dist. Ct. (no. and ea. dists.) Tex., U.S. Ct. Appeals (5th and 11th cirs.), U.S. Supreme Ct. Pres. Altman & Nix, Wichita Falls, Tex., 1970—. Mem. Wichita Falls City Coun., 1998—; bd. dirs. Beacon Ins. Group, 1997—. Mem. ABA, Tex. Bar Assn., Assn. Trial Lawyers Am. (life) (bd. of govs. 1980-83, active coms. and sects.), Tex. Trial Lawyers Assn. (assoc. bd. dirs. 1977-78, bd. dirs. 1978—, active various coms. and sect.). Democrat. Baptist. Office: PO Box 500 Wichita Falls TX 76307-0500

ALTMANN, STUART ALLEN, biologist, educator; b. St. Louis, June 8, 1930; s. Maurice Walter and Deborah (Freedman) A.; m. Jeanne Glaser, June 19, 1959; children—Michael Alexander, Rachel Ann. B.A. in Zoology, UCLA, 1953, M.A., 1954; Ph.D. in Biology, Harvard U., 1960. Asst. prof. zoology U. Alta., Can., 1960-65, assoc. prof., 1965; sociobiologist Yerkes Regional Primate Research Ctr., 1965-70; prof. anatomy U. Chgo., 1970-80, prof. biology, 1970-88, prof. ecology and evolution, 1988-95, prof. emeritus, 1995—; lectr., prof. ecology and evolutionary biology Princeton (N.J.) U., 1998—; hon. research assoc. Haile Sellaissie I U., Ethiopia, 1971; mem. exptl. psychology sci. adv. panel NIMH, 1969-73, primate conservation com. Nat. Acad. Scis.-NRC, 1970-72; grant reviewer NSF, NIH, NIMH, Spencer Found., Nat. Geog. Soc., Smithsonian Instn., others. Mem. editorial bd. Behavioral Ecology and Sociobiology, 1976-79, Am. Naturalist, 1977-79, Animal Behavior, 1978-79, Ethology, Ecology and Evolution, 1989—; mem. bd. editorial commentators The Behavioral and Brain Scis., 1977-82. Fellow AAAS, Am. Acad. Arts and Scis., Animal Behavior Soc. (pres. 1977, exec. com. 1975-78); mem. Am. Soc. Primatologists (chmn. founding membership com. 1976-77), Internat. Ethological Council (del. 1983-90). Avocations: making pottery, orchard farming. Office: Princeton U Dept Ecology-Evol Biology Princeton NJ 08544-1003

ALTON, BRUCE TAYLOR, educational consultant; b. Cleve., Apr. 11, 1939; s. Ralph Taylor and Marian Bannon (Black) A.; m. Christie Lichliter, Aug. 25, 1962; 1 son, James. B.A., Ohio Wesleyan U., 1961; M.A., Mich. State U., 1962; Ph.D., Ohio State U., 1971. Asst. dean men Ohio Wesleyan U., Delaware, 1965-69; dean students Rocky Mountain Coll., Billings, Mont., 1971-74; acting pres. Rocky Mountain Coll., 1974-75, pres., 1975-86, asst. prof. psychology, 1971-80, assoc. prof., 1980-86; sr. assoc. Presdl. Search Consultation Service, Assn. Governing Bds. of Univs. and Colls., Washington, 1986-88; sr. assoc., dir. Acad. Search Consultation Service, Washington, 1988-91, sr. prin., dir., 1991-98, sr. cons., dir., 1998—. Trustee, vice chmn. Billings Deaconess Hosp., 1976-82; chmn. bd. Western Ind. Coll. Found., 1983-84; mem. United Ch. Bd. for Homeland Ministries, 1982-87; mem. Council of Higher Edn., United Ch. Christ, 1974-86. Served with USAF, 1962-65. Mem. Mont. Ind. Coll. Assn. (founding pres. 1975-78), Phi Delta Kappa, Theta Alpha Phi., Pi Kappa Delta, Delta Tau Delta. Methodist. Home: 9285 Bailey Ln Fairfax VA 22031-1929 Office: Acad Search Consultation Svc 1818 R St NW Washington DC 20009-1604

ALTOSE, MURRAY DAVID, physician; b. Winnipeg, Man., Can., Oct. 1, 1941; came to U.S., 1969; m. Connie Jean Tesmer, Jan. 14, 1973; children: Michael Dov, Aaron Judah, Benjamin Isaac. BSc, MD, U. Man., 1965. Diplomate Am. Bd. Internal medicine, Am. Bd. Pulmonary Disease. Rotating intern Winnipeg Gen. Hosp., 1965-66, asst. resident in medicine, 1966-67, resident in critical care medicine, 1968-69; asst. resident medicine Cleve. Met. Gen. Hosp., 1969-70, resident-in-charge pulmonary disease sect., 1970-71, chief pulmonary divsn. dept. medicine, 1977-88, assoc. dir. dept. medicine, 1981-88; fellow pulmonary disease sect. Hosp. U. Pa., Phila., 1971-73, co-dir. respiratory ICU, 1973-74; dir. diagnostic svcs. Hosp. U. Pa., 1973-77; assoc. in medicine U. Pa. Sch. Medicine, Phila., 1973, asst. prof. medicine, 1973-77; assoc. prof. medicine Case Western Res. U. Sch. Medicine, Cleve., 1977-84, prof. medicine, 1984—; chief of staff Dept. Vets. Affairs Med. Ctr., Cleve., 1988—; assoc. dean Vets. Hosp. Affairs, 1988—; attending physician pulmonary in-patient svc. med. ICU and Pulmonary Cons. Svc. Cleve. Met. Gen. Hosp., 1977-78, med. dir. respiratory therapy dept., 1977-88, dir. respiratory ICU, 1977-81, attending physician med. ICU Univ. Hosps., Cleve., 1978—; mem. med. rsch. svc. rev. bd. for respiration VA, 1986-89; spl. reviewer NIH Clin. Sci., 1985, 88; cons. spl. emphasis panel NIH Nat. Heart, Lung and Blood Inst., 1996; temp. mem. NIH Respiratory and Applied Physiology Study Sect., 1996; attending physician respiratory ICU VA Med. Ctr., Cleve., 1988—, attending physician med. svc., 1988; lectr. in field. Mem. editl. bd. Jour. Applied Physiology, 1984-93, editl. referee, 1980—; contbr. articles to profl. publs., chpts. to books, abstracts. Trustee Northeast Ohio affiliate Am. Heart Assn., 1993-98, mem. rsch. allocation com., 1989-93. Mem. Am. Fedn. Clin. Rsch. (mem. program 1982, steering com. sect. on respiratory pathophysiology 1981-82, chmn. sect. 1982-84, mem. program and awards coms. ann. sci. assembly 1985), Am. Thoracic Soc. (program com. sci. assembly on respiratory structure and function 1989-90), Ohio Thoracic Soc., Am. Coll. Chest Physicians (program com., awards com. ann. sci. assembly 1985), Am. Physiol. Soc., Am. Coll. Physician Execs., Am. Heart Assn., Nat. Assn. VA Chiefs of Staff (pres. elect 1996, pres. 1997-98). Office: Cleve VA Med Ctr 10701 East Blvd Cleveland OH 44106-1702

ALTROCK, RICHARD CHARLES, astrophysicist; b. Omaha, Dec. 20, 1940; s. Raymond John and Ada Ann (Baumann) A.; m. Janice Carol Reed, Mar. 23, 1963 (div. 1977); children: Craig Edward and Christopher Raymond (twins); m. Sally K. Neidig, Mar. 10, 1979; children: Kristin Ann, Krystal Sara. BS in Physics and Math., U. Nebr., 1962; PhD in Astro-Geophysics, U. Colo., 1968. Air Force cert. aquisition profl. Rsch. asst. U. Nebr., Lincoln, 1959-61; teaching asst. U. Nebr., 1962; mathematician U.S. Army Engrs., Omaha, 1962; grad. asst. High Altitude Obs., Boulder, Colo., 1963-67; astrophysicist Air Force Rsch. Lab., Nat. Solar Obs., Sunspot, N.Mex., 1967—, work unit mgr., 1976—; project mgr. Coronal Synoptic Program, 1976—; project scientist Solar Mass Ejection Imager Space Expt., USAF, 1986-91, co-investigator, 1991—; guest investigator NASA Solar Maximum Mission, 1984-86; vis. research fellow U. Sydney, Australia, 1971-72. Editor: Solar and Stellar Coronal Structure and Dynamics, 1988; contbr. articles to profl. jours.; speaker in the field. Bd. govs. N.Mex. Civil Liberties Union, 1974-76. Recipient Sustained Superior Performance awards USAF, 1986-96, Quar. Sci. and Engring. Tech. Achievement award Air Force Systems Command, 1987; Woodrow Wilson fellow, 1962-63, High Altitude Obs. fellow, 1962-63; mem. Air Force Office of Sci. Rsch. Star Team, 1992—. Fellow AAAS; mem. Internat. Astron. Union, Am. Astron. Soc., Am. Geophys. Union, ACLU, Sigma Xi, Pi Mu Epsilon, Phi Beta Kappa, Delta Phi Alpha, Phi Gamma Delta. Achievements include co-discovery of the bimodal nature of solar rotation in Fe XIV data, which varies from strongly-differential to rigid over a solar cycle; that CaXV emission in the solar corona is not isolated in hot knots, but is ubiquitous over large energetic chromospheric active regions; of the first evidence of possible wave signature in the variation of spectral line intensity over the lifetime of a granule; first ground-based, two-dimensional photoelectric observation of a transient in the emission-line corona; proof (with other) that ground-based observations of the solar corona could be effectively used to predict recurrent geomagnetic disturbances; demonstration that emission maxima in the corona follow an unbroken progression from the poles to the equator over approximately 18 years, thus implying the existence of overlapping solar activity cycles, (with other) of the existence of convective overshoot phenomenon in the solar atmosphere, (with other) of the lack of solar pole-equator temperature differences in the photosphere and low chromosphere that could explain solar oblateness signals; invention of a new method for obtaining source functions from solar equivalent-width data for weak photospheric lines; research on solar granulation and solar corona. Home: PO Box 645 Cloudcroft NM 88317-0645 Office: Nat Solar Obs Sunspot NM 88349

ALTSCHAEFFL, ADOLPH GEORGE, civil engineering educator; b. Passaic, N.J., July 20, 1930; s. Ludwig and Crescenz (Liebl) A.; m. Martha Anne Filiatreau, Aug. 6, 1966. B.S.C.E., Purdue U., 1952, M.S.C.E., 1955, Ph.D., 1960. Instr. civil engring. Purdue U., West Lafayette, Ind., 1952-60, asst. prof. civil engring., 1960-64, assoc. prof., 1964-74, prof., 1974—, asst. head dept., 1983-91, head geotech. engring., 1994—; with Waterways Expt. Sta., C.E., Vicksburg, Miss., 1955, U.S. Geol. Survey, Indpls., 1956; cons. civil engring. with various architect and contractor firms. Contbr. articles to profl. jours. Served with USAR, 1950-61. Mem. Am. Soc. Engring. Edn., ASCE, Nat. Soc. Profl. Engrs. Office: Purdue U Civil Engring Bldg West Lafayette IN 47907

ALTSCHUL, ALFRED SAMUEL, airline executive; b. Chgo., Oct. 16, 1939; s. Herman and Lillian (Ginsburg) A.; m. Lynn Silverman, Sept. 8, 1968; children: Howard, Steven, Mark. B.S., U. Wis., 1961; M.B.A., U. Chgo., 1963. C.P.A., Ill. With G.A.T.X. Corp., Chgo., 1965-69; asst. treas. G.A.T.X. Corp., 1967-70, treas., 1970-81; v.p. fin., chief fin. officer Midway Airlines, Chgo., 1981-90, sr. v.p., chief fin. officer, 1990-92; CFO Sage Enterprises, Des Plaines, Ill., 1993-95; exec. v.p., CFO A. Epstein and Sons Internat., 1995-96; v.p., CFO Amtrak, 1996—; lectr. in field. Trustee Mt. Sinai Med. Ctr., Chgo.; Served with AUS, 1963-69. Mem. AICPA, Fin. Execs. Inst., Alpha Epsilon Pi. Jewish. Club: Standard (Chgo.). Home: 2111 Wisconsin Ave NW Apt Ph3 Washington DC 20007-2268

ALTSCHUL, ARTHUR GOODHART, investment banker; b. N.Y.C., Apr. 6, 1920; s. Frank and Helen (Goodhart) A.; m. Patricia Madelyn Dey; children from previous marriages: Stephen Frank, Charles, Arthur G. Jr., Emily Helen, Serena von Reis; 1 step-son, Whitney Sudler Smith. Grad., Deerfield Acad., 1939; A.B., Yale, 1943. Ltd. ptnr. The Goldman Sachs Group, L.P., N.Y.C., 1977—, 1977—; chmn. bd. Gen. Am. Investors Co., Inc., 1961-95 (chmn. emeritus 1995—); mem. distbn. com. N.Y. Community Trust. Trustee Am. Assembly; former chmn. bd. trustees Barnard Coll.; mem. governing bd. Yale U. Art Gallery, 1987-96. 1st lt. USMCR, 1943-45. Mem. Council Fgn. Relations. Office: The Goldman Sachs Group LP 85 Broad St New York NY 10004-2434

ALTSCHULER, SAMUEL, electronics company executive; b. N.Y.C., Aug. 13, 1927; s. Samuel and Sylvia (Sussman) A.; m. Nancy Treulich, Nov. 15, 1958; children: Jeffrey, Lisa, James, Jonathen, Pamela. BSEE, U. Conn., 1950; MBA, Northeastern U., 1958. Jr. engr. New London (Conn.) Instrument Co., 1950-51; engr. Western Electric, North Andover, Mass., 1951-56; sr. engr. Honeywell, Boston, 1956-58; chief quality control engr. L.F.E., Boston, 1958-59; v.p. mfg. Adage, Boston, 1959-70; founder, chmn., pres. Altron Inc., mfrs. printed cir. bds., backplanes, Wilmington, Mass., 1970—; bd. dirs. Massbank, Reading, Mass.; mem. engring. adv. bd. U. Conn., Storrs, 1990-94. Mem. corp. Northeastern U., Boston, 1993—; former mem. corp. Wentworth Inst., Boston. Recipient Disting. Engring. Alumni award U. Conn., 1993. Mem. Inst. for Interconnecting and Packaging Electronic Circuits (pres. 1992-94, Disting. Svc. award 1994), Eta Kappa Nu. Office: Altron Inc One Jewel Dr Wilmington MA 01887*

ALTSHULER, ALAN ANTHONY, political scientist; b. Bklyn., Mar. 9, 1936; s. Leonard M. and Janet A. (Sonnenstrahl) A.; m. Julie C. Maller, June 15, 1958; children: Jennifer, David. BA, Cornell U., 1957; MA, U. Chgo., 1959, PhD, 1961. Instr. Swarthmore Coll., 1960-61; Smith-Mundt vis. asst. prof. Makerere (Uganda) Coll., 1961-62; asst. prof. Cornell U., 1962-66; assoc. prof. MIT, 1966-69, prof. polit. sci. and urban studies and planning, 1969-71, 1975-83, chmn. dept. polit. sci., 1977-82; dean Grad. Sch. Pub. Adminstrn. NYU, 1983-88, dir. Urban Research Ctr., 1986-87; prof. urban policy and planning Kennedy Sch. Govt. and Grad. Sch. Design Harvard U., 1988—; dir. Taubman Ctr. State and Local Govt. Harvard U., 1988—, acad. dean Kennedy Sch. Govt., 1993-95; sec. transp. and constrn. Commonwealth Mass., 1971-75; dir. Boston Transp. Planning Rev. (part-time), 1970-71. Author: The City Planning Process: A Political Analysis, 1965, Community Control: The Black Demand for Participation in Large American Cities, 1970, The Urban Transportation System: Politics and Policy Innovation, 1979; co-author: The Future of the Automobile, 1984, Regulation for Revenue: The Political Economy of Land Development Exactions, 1993; editor: Current Issues in Transportation Policy, 1979; co-editor: The Politics of the Federal Bureaucracy, 1977, Innovation in American Government, 1997; contbr. articles to profl. jours. Mem. Nat. Acad. Pub. Adminstrn., Am. Polit. Sci. Assn., Am. Acad. Arts and Scis. Jewish.

ALTSHULER, DAVID T., software company executive. BA in Polit. Economy, Williams Coll., Williamstown, Mass., 1984; MBA, U. Pa., 1993. Rsch. and tchg. asst. Williams Coll., Williamstown, 1984-85; systems analyst Computer Solutions, Denver, 1985-87; dir. info. svcs. Internat. Investors, 1987-90; v.p. rsch. and devel. Apollo Adv. Group, N.Y.C., 1990-91; exec. dir., vice-chmn., dir., mem. fin. com. Telecomm. Coop. Networks, Cambridge, Mass., 1995-97; pres. Mut. Analytics Corp., Phila., 1991-98; adj. faculty fin., assoc. acad. dir. Pension Funds and Money Mgmt., Aresty Inst., Wharton Sch., U. Pa., Phila., 1993—, mem. adj. faculty law, 1995—. Mem. Coun. on Fgn. Rels., N.Y.C., 1996—; mem. fin. com., trustee The John Merck Fund, Boston, 1994—; exec. dir. TCN. Home: 15 Fayerweather St Cambridge MA 02138-3329

ALTSHULER, KENNETH Z., psychiatrist; b. Paterson, N.J., Apr. 11, 1929; s. Jacob and Altie (Freedman) A.; m. Gloria Seigel, June 14, 1952 (div. 1981); children: Steven, Lori, Dara; m. Ruth Collins Sharp, Dec. 5, 1987. BA, Cornell U., 1948; MD, U. Buffalo, 1952; DSc (hon.), Gallaudet Coll., 1972. Intern Kings County Hosp., Bklyn., 1952-53; resident N.Y. State Psychiat. Inst., N.Y.C., 1955-58; asst. in psychiatry Columbia U., 1958-59, instr., 1959-63, research assoc., 1963-67, asst. clin. prof., 1967-71, assoc. clin. prof., 1971-75, prof., 1975-77; tng. analyst Columbia U. Psychoanalytic Clinic for Tng. and Research, 1969-77; project dir. Essential Aspects of Deafness, 1972-76, Trauma and Sleep Physiology, 1975-77; Stanton Sharp prof., chmn. psychiatry U. Tex.-Southwestern Med. Sch., Dallas, 1977—; tng. analyst New Orleans Psychoanalytic Inst., 1979-86, Dallas Psychoanalytic Inst., Tex., 1986—; chief of deafness unit Rockland State Hosp., Orangeburg, N.Y., 1966-77; cons. to NIH; dir. Am. Bd. Psychiatry and Neurology, 1990—, pres., 1996; mem. Nat. Bd. Med. Examiners, 1986-89, chmn. Part II psychiatry com., 1988-89. Co-author: Managing Sleep Complaints, 1982; co-editor: Family and Mental Health Problems in a Deaf Population, 1963, Comprehensive Mental Health Services for the Deaf, 1966, Psychiatry and the Deaf, 1968, Expanded Mental Health Care for the Deaf, 1970, Depression: Mechanisms, Diagnosis and Treatment, 1986; others.; Contbr. articles to profl. jours. Mem. governing bd. Tex. Sch. for the Deaf, 1986-90. Served with USNR, 1953-55. Recipient Wilson award in genetics and preventive medicine, 1961, Disting. Community Service award Dallas County Mental Health Assn., 1986, Prism award, 1992, Disting. Alumnus award, SUNY, Buffalo, 1993, 1st Trailblazer award named in his honor, Dallas County Mental Health and Retardation Ctr., 1996, Tex. Star award for Outstanding Cmty. Svc. Tex. Mental Health Assn., 1997; named Outstanding Psychiatrist, Tex. Soc. Psychiat. Physicians, 1996, alumnus of the decade Columbia U., 1996; Kenneth Z. Altshuler clinic named in his honor by the Dallas County Mental Health and Mental Retardation Ctr., 1997. Fellow Am. Psychiat. Assn. (cert. of achievement bd. hosp. psychiatry, cert. of significant achievement for deafness program, N.Y. State, 1976, for Mental Health Connections program, 1995), Am. Coll. Psychiatrists, Am. Coll. Psychoanalysts; mem. AAAS, AMA, Am. Psychoanalytic Assn., Assn. for Psychoanalytic Medicine (Merit award 1965), Tex. Med. Soc., Dallas County Med. Soc., Am. Psychopathol. Assn., Assn. Dirs. Med. Student Edn. in Psychiatry (founder, v.p. 1976-77), Am. Assn. Chmn. Depts. Psychiatry (pres. 1990-91), So. Assn. Rsch. Psychiatry (pres.-elect 1992-93, pres. 1993-94).

ALTSTOCK, MARSHA MARIE, pediatrics nurse; b. Toledo, Feb. 8, 1955; d. Jack Stanley and Cecelia Jean Kirkland; m. Robert Randolph Altstock, May 13, 1978; children: matthew, Danielle. BS in Nursing, U. Portland, Oreg., 1978. Cert. pediatric nurse. Pediatric and obstectic charge nurse Cary Med. Ctr., Caribou, Maine, 1978-80; pediatric charge nurse Sutter Meml. Med. Ctr., Sacramento, 1980-83; charge nurse pediatrics Hendrick Med. Ctr., Abilene, Tex., 1986-90, pediatric and PICU nurse mgr., 1990-94, ednl. cons., 1994—; pediatric nurse provider Tex. Dept. Human Svcs., Austin, Tex., 1992—; Tex. medicare provider Nat. Heritage Ins. Co., Austin, Tex., 1993—; pediatric ednl. cons. Gamma Assocs., Carlsbad, Calif., 1994—; bd. dirs. The House That Kerry Built, Abilene; pediatric cons. Hendrick Med. Ctr., Abilene, 1994-95, Pediatric Svcs. Am., 1995—; v.p. Gamma Assocs., Carlsbad, Calif., 1994—. Reviewer:(book) Pediatric Critical Care, 1993. Dist. recorder Boy Scouts of Am., Abilene, 1993; svc. mgr. Girl Scouts Am., 1994-. Fellow Nat. Assn. Pediatric Nurses and Practioners; mem. Soc. Pediatric Nurses. Avocations: crafts, reading, camping.

ALTURA, BELLA T., physiologist, educator; b. Solingen, Germany; came to U.S., 1948; d. Sol and Rosa (Brandstetter) Tabak; m. Burton M. Altura, Dec. 27, 1961; 1 child, Rachel Allison. BA, Hunter Coll., 1953; MA, CUNY, 1962, PhD, 1968. Instr. exptl. anesthesiology Albert Einstein Coll. Medicine, Bronx, 1970-74; asst. prof. physiology SUNY Health Sci Ctr., Bklyn., 1974-82, assoc. prof. physiology, 1982-97, rsch. prof. physiology, 1997—, rsch. prof. pharmacology, 1998—; vis. prof. Beijing Coll. of Traditional Chinese Medicine, 1988, Jiangxi (China) Med. Coll., 1988, Tokyo U. Med. Sch., 1993, U. Brussels Esramé Hosp., 1995, Humboldt U.-Charité Hosp., 1995, Kagoshima U., Japan, 1995, U. Birmingham, U.K., 1996, Self Med. Def. Coll. Japan, 1996, Nat. Def. Med. Sch., Japan, 1996, Albert Szent Gyorgi Med. U., Szeged, Hungary, 1997; mem. Nat. Coun. on Magnesium and Cardiovascular Disease, 1991—; cons. NOVA Biomedical, 1989—; Niche pharm. cons. Protina GmbH, Munich, 1992-96, Otsuka Pharm. Co., Japan, 1995-97; co-prin. investigator NIH, Nat. Heart, Lung and Blood Inst., NIMH, Nat. Inst. on Alcoholism and Alcohol Abuse. Contbr. over 500 articles to profl. jours. Fellowship NASA, 1966-67, CUNY, 1968; co-recipient Gold-Silver medal French Nat. Acad. Medicine, 1984, Silver medal Mayor of Paris, 1984. Mem. Am. Physiol. Soc., Am. Soc. Pharmacology and Exptl. Therapeutics, Am. Soc. for Magnesium Rsch. (founder, treas. 1984—), Hungarian Soc. Electrochemistry (hon. co-pres. 1995—), Nat. Heart, Lung and Blood Inst., Nat. Inst. on Alcohol Abuse and Alcoholism, Phi Beta Kappa, Sigma Xi. Achievements include first measurement ionized magnesium with ion selective electrode in blood, serum and plasma in health and disease states; demonstration that substances of abuse can cause cerebrovasospasm and stroke. Office: SUNY Health Sci Ctr Box 31 450 Clarkson Ave Brooklyn NY 11203-2056

ALTURA, BURTON MYRON, physiologist, educator; b. N.Y.C., Apr. 9, 1936; s. Barney and Frances (Dorfman) A.; m. Bella Tabak, Dec. 27, 1961; 1 child, Rachel Allison. BA, Hofstra U., 1957; MS, NYU, 1961, PhD (USPHS fellow), 1964. Diplomate Am. Bd. Forensic Med., Am. Coll. Forensic Medicine, Am. Bd. Forensic Examiners. Teaching fellow in biology NYU, N.Y.C., 1960-61, instr. exptl. anesthesiology Sch. Medicine, 1964-65, asst. prof. Sch. Medicine, 1965-66; rsch. fellow Bronx Mcpl. Hosp. Center, 1967-76; asst. prof. physiology and anesthesiology Albert Einstein Coll. Medicine, N.Y.C., 1967-70, assoc. prof., 1970-74, vis. prof., 1974-78; prof. physiology SUNY Health Sci Ctr., Bklyn., 1974—, prof. medicine, 1992—; mem. Ctr. Cardiovascular and Muscle Rsch., 1995—; rsch. fellow Bronx Mcpl. Hosp. Center, 1967-76; prof. pharmacology SUNY Health Sci. Ctr., Bklyn., 1998—; mem. spl. study sect. on toxicology Nat. Inst. Environ. Health Scis., 1977-78; mem. Alcohol Biomed. Rsch. Rev. Com., Nat. Inst. Alcohol Abuse and Alcoholism, 1978-83, member, panel CNF bd. Inst. Med., NAS, 1996-97. A Food bd. FTC; adj. prof. biology Queens Coll., CUNY, 1983-84; cons. NSF, VA Grants Rev. Commn., Nat. Heart, Lung and Blood Inst., CUNY, Miles Inst., Nat. Inst. Drug Abuse, FDA, USDA, Merck, Sharpe and Dohme, Millipore Corp., Internat. Ctr. Disabled, Upjohn Co., Bayer AG, Ciba-Geigy, Zyma SA, Genentech, Nova Biomed., Parke, Davis & Co., Chem. Def. Unit, Brit. Govt., Schering-Key Corp., Sterling Drug Co., Searle Pharm. Co., Niche Pharm. Inc., Chem. Def. Establishment, U.K., Am. Speech and Hearing Assn., Protina GmbH, Otsuka Pharm. Co., Japan, Swiss Fed. Inst. Tech., Switzerland, Roberts Pharmaceuticals; hon. pres. Internat. Symposium on Interactions of Magnesium and Potassium on Cardiac and Vascular Muscle, Montbazon, France, 1984; hon. pres., hon. lectr. Hungarian Soc. Electrochemistry, Budapest, 1995; organizer, condr. symposia; organizer workshop Nat. Inst. Alcohol Abuse and Alcoholism, 1992; condr., chmn. Gordon Rsch. Conf. on Magnesium in Biochem. Processes and Medicine, 1984; chmn., organizer First Internat. Workshop Unique Magnesium Sensitive Ion Selective Electrodes, Orlando, Fla., 1993, Second Internat. Workshop Unique Magnesium Sensitive Ion Selective Electrodes, Crete, Greece, 1997; chmn. symposium Am. Soc. Nephrology, 1993; v.p. Fourth Internat. Symposium on Magnesium, Blacksburg, 1985; organizer Second Internat. Workshop Unique Magnesium Sensitive Ion Selective Electrodes, Crete, Greece, 1997; judge Am. Inst. Sci. and Tech., 1984, 85, 86, 88, 89, 90, 91, 93, Jr. Acad. N.Y. Acad. of Scis., 1987, 89, 90; mem. adv. council Nat. Found. for Addictive Drugs, 1986—; vis. prof. Yamaguchi U., Japan, 1988, 93, Beijing Coll. Traditional Chinese Medicine, People's Republic of China, 1988, Jiangxi Med. Coll., 1988, Beijing Med. U., 1988, Mass. Gen. Hosp., Harvard U. Med. Sch., 1989, U. Tokyo, 1993, Kokura Meml. Hosp. Kiyushi U. Japan, 1993, Yamaguchi U. Hosp., Japan, 1993, Tokyo U., 1993, Kyoto U. Sch. Medicine, 1993, Kumamoto U. Sch. Medicine, 1993, , U. Copenhagen-Herlev Hosp., 1994, U. Florence (Italy), 1994, U. Brussels-Erasmé Hosp., 1995, Humboldt U.-Charité Hosp., Berlin, 1995, U. Homburg-Saarland, 1995, U. Birmingham, U.K., 1996, U. Cin. Med. Ctr., 1996, Self-Med. Def. Med. Coll., Japan, 1996, Am. Coll. Advancement Medicine, 1996, Albert Szent Gyorgyi Med. Univ., Szeged, Hungary, 1997; vis. prof. Univ. California-Riverside, 1998; Florida Atlantic Univ., 1998; hon. prof. Yamaguchi U. Hosp., Japan, 1988; mentor Aaron Diamond fellowships, 1990-98; vis. prof., hon. lectr. Inst. for Water, Soil, and Air Hygiene, Fed Health Inst., Berlin, 1991; vis. prof., hon. lectr. Max Planck Inst., Dortmund, Germany, 1992, 94, Yamonouchi Co. Ltd., Japan, 1993, Searle Co., Japan, 1993, Otsuka Pharm. Co., Japan, 1995; mem. working group convened by Congressman Durbin III, 1991; mem. Nat. Coun. on Magnesium and Cardiovasc. Disease, 1991—; keynote spkr. Internat. Symposium Blood, Gas and Electrolytes, Linköping (Sweden), 1994, 15th Ann. Magnesium Symposium, Kagoshima, Japan, 1995, Nat. Dairy Coun. of Japan, 1996, Great Lakes Coll. of Medicine, 1997, keynote spkr., 1st Internatl. Symp. Cardiovasc. Med., Surg. and Biomechanics (Wash. DC), 1997, U. Oulu-32d Scandinavian Neurol. Congress Finland, 1998. Author: Microcirculation, 3 vols., 1977-80, Vascular Endothelium and Basement Membranes, 1980, Pathophysiology of the Reticuloendothelial System, 1981, Ionic Regulation of the Microcirculation, 1982; Handbook of Shock and Trauma, Vol. 1: Basic Science, 1983, Magnesium and the Cardiovascular System, 1985, Cardiovascular Actions of Anesthetic Agents and Drugs Used in Anesthesia, vol.,1986, vol. II, 1987, Magnesium, Stress and the Cardiovascular System, 1986, Magnesium in Biochemical Processes and Medicine, 1987, Magnesium in Clinical Medicine and Therapeutics, 1992, Unique Magnesium-Sensitive Ion Selective Electrodes, 1994; editor in chief: Physiology and Patho-physiology Series, 1976-81, Microcirculation, 1980-84, Magnesium: Exptl. and Clin. Research, 1981-89, Microcirculation, Endothelium and Lymphatics, 1984—, Magnesium and Trace Elements, 1990—; mem. editorial bd.: Jour. Circulatory Shock, 1973-85, Advances in Microcirculation, 1976-92, Jour. Cardiovascular Pharmacology, 1977-84, Prostaglandins, Leukotrienes and Fatty Acids, 1978—, Substance and Alcohol Actions/Misuse, 1979-84, Alcoholism: Clin. and Exptl. Research, 1982-87; assoc. editor: Jour. of Artery, 1974—; assoc. editor: Microvascular Research, 1978-85, Agents and Actions, 1981-88, Biogenic Amines, 1985-88, Jour. Am. Coll. Nutrition, 1982-94, Frontiers in Biocsci., 1996—, Internat. Jour. Cardiovasc. Medicine, Surgery and Biomechanics, 1997—; contbr. over 800 articles to profl. jours. Recipient Rsch. Career Devel. award USPHS, 1968-72, Silver medal for furthering French-U.S. sci. rels. Mayor of Paris, 1984, Medaille Vermeille, French Nat. Acad. Medicine, 1984, Travel awards NIH, 1968, Am. Soc. Pharm. and Exptl. Therapeutics, 1969; grantee NIH, 1968—, NIMH, 1974-78, Nat. Heart Lung Blood Inst., 1974-86, Nat. Inst. Drug Abuse, 1979-83, Nat. Inst. Alcohol Abuse and Alcoholism, 1990—. Fellow AAAS, Internat. Coll. Angiology, Am. Coll. Angiology, Am. Inst. Chemists, Am. Heart Assn. (mem. coun. on stroke 1973—, coun. basic sci. 1969—, coun. on thrombosis 1971—, coun. on circulation 1978—, coun. on high blood pressure 1978—, coun. on cardiopulmonary circulation, 1987—, cardiovasc. A study sect. 1978-81, coun. on arteriosclerosis, thrombosis, and vascular biology 1997—), Am. Coll. Nutrition, Am. Physiol. Soc. (mem. circulation group 1971—, pub. info. com. 1980-84, symposium organizer), Am. Coll. Forensic Examiners (life), Internat. Biog. Assn., Assn. Clin. Scientists; mem. AAUP, Biophysical Soc., Soc. for Magnetic Resonance, Am. Soc. Investigative Pathology, Am. Bd. Forensic Examiners (life fellow), Microcirculatory Soc. (past mem. exec. coun., mem. nominating com. 1973-74), Soc. Exptl. Biology and Medicine (editl. bd. 1976-83), Am. Assn. for Clin. Chemistry (hon. lectr. 1989, 92, 94), Am. Pub. Health Assn., Am. Chem. Soc. (divsn. medicinal chemistry, divsn. analytical chemistry), Am. Soc. Pharm. and Exptl. Therapeutics (symposium organizer), Endocrine Soc., Harvey Soc., Am. Coll. Toxicology, Rsch. Soc. on Alcoholism (organizer several symposia), Soc. for Critical Care Medicine, Am. Thoracic Soc., Soc. for Neurosci., Shock Soc. (founder, hon. lectr.), Am. Fedn. Clin. Rsch., Microscopy Soc. Am., European Conf. Microcirculation (symposium organizer, hon. lectr.), Neurotrauma Soc., Internat. Anesthesia Rsch. Soc., Fedn. Am. Soc. Exptl. Biology (pub. info. com. 1981-86), Am. Inst. Nutrition (organizer mini-symposium), Am. Soc. Microbiology, Internat. Soc. Thrombosis and Haemostasis, Internat. Soc. Biomed. Rsch. on Alcoholism (founding mem.), Biomed. Optics Soc., Internat. Soc. Biorheology, Soc. Leukocyte Biology, Soc. Environ. Geochemistry and Health, Soc. Neurosci., Soc. Cardiovasc. Pathology, Reticuloendothelial Soc. (hon. lectr.), Internat. Soc. Exposure Analysis, Soc. of Parenteral and Enteral Nutrition, Soc. Nutrition Edn., Soc. Scholarly Pub., Internat. Platform Assn., Am. Assn. Lab. Animal Sci., Am. Microscopical Soc., Am. Soc. Zoologists, The Oxygen Soc., Am. Soc. Cell Biology, Am. Soc. Bone and Mineral Rsch., Am. Soc. Magnesium Rsch. (founder, pres., exec. dir. 1984—, symposium, workshop, organizer), N.Y. Acad. Scis., Am. Pub. Health Assn., N.Y. Heart Assn., N.Y. Soc. Electron Microscopy, Coun. Biology Editors, Internat. Anesthesia Soc., Internat. Soc. for Hypertension, Am. Soc. Hypertension (founding mem.), Am. Assn. Pharm. Scis., Nat. Coun. for Magnesium and Cardiovasc. Disease, Am. Med. Writers Assn., Internat. Soc. Police Surgeons, Sigma Xi. Office: 450 Clarkson Ave Brooklyn NY 11203-2056

ALUMBAUGH, JOANN MCCALLA, magazine editor; b. Ann Arbor, Mich., Sept. 16, 1952; d. William Samuel and Jean Arliss (Guy) McCalla; m. Lyle Ray Alumbaugh, Apr. 30, 1974; children: Brent William, Brandon Jess, Brooke Louise. BA, Ea. Mich. U., 1974. Cert. elem. tch., Mich. Assoc. editor Chester White Swine Record Assn., Rochester, Ind., 1974-77; prodn. editor United Duroc Swine Registry, Peoria, Ill., 1977-79; dir., pres. Nat. Assn. Swine Records, Macomb, Ill., 1979-82; free-lance writer, artist Ill. and Nat. Specific Pathogen Free Assn., Ind. producers, Good Hope, Emden, Ill., 1982-85; editor The Hog Producer, Farm Progress Publs., Urbandale, Iowa, 1985—; coord. Master Farm Homemaker Program, Pub. div. Rural Press Ltd., Urbandale, 1985—, Family Living Program, Farm Progress Show, 1985—; mem. U.S. Agrl. Export Devel. Coun., Washington, 1979-82, apptd. mem. Blue Ribbon Com. on Agr., 1980-81. Contbr. numerous articles to profl. jours. Precinct chmn. Rep. Party, Linden, Iowa, 1988; mem. Keep Improving Dist. Schs., Panora, Iowa, 1990-91; v.p. Sunday sch. com. Sunset Circle, United Meth. Ch., Linden, 1990-91; pres. PTA, Panorama Schs., Panora, 1993-94; coach Odyssey of Mind Program World Competition, 1994—. Mem. Am. Agrl. Editors Assn. (chmn. dist. svc. com. 1991, co-chmn. Info-Expo com., co-chmn. comm. clinic, master writer 1997, chmn. comms. clinic, pres.-elect 1998, pres. 1999, World of Difference award 1995), U.S. Animal Health Assn., Iowa Pork Producers Assn. (legis. com. 1990-95, hon. master pork producer), Nat. Pork Producers Coun., McDonough County and Ill. Porkettes (county pres. 1978-79, Belleringer award 1979), Guthrie County Pork Prodrs., Iowa Master Farm Homemakers, Internat. Platform Assn. Avocations: reading, painting, flower gardening. Home: 2644 Amarillo Ave Linden IA 50146-8029 Office: Farm Progress Publs/ Wallaces Farmer 6200 Aurora Ave Ste 609E Urbandale IA 50322-2863

ALURI, RAO, book publisher; b. Moparru, India, Sept. 1, 1941; s. Narayana Rao and Raghavamma (Vadlamudi) A.; m. Mary L. Reichel, Jan. 6, 1977; 1 child, Krishna P. BSc, A.M.A.L. Coll., Anakapalle, India, 1963; MSc, U. Western Ontario, Can., 1971, MLS, 1972; PhD in Higher Edn. & Libr. Sci., SUNY at Buffalo, 1981. Ref. libr. U. Nebr., Omaha, 1973-76; asst. prof. Emory U., Atlanta, 1980-86; mgr. libr. Burr-Brown Corp., Tucson, 1987-92; pub., pres. Parkway Pubs., Inc., Boone, N.C., 1992—. Co-compiler: (book) U.S. Gov. Sci. and Technical Periodicals, 1976; co-author: (book) U.S. Govt. Scientific & Technical Resources, 1983, Subject Analysis in Online Catalogs, 1991; co-editor: (book) Expert Systems in Libraries, 1992. Sec. Rotary Club of Boone, 1994-95, pres.-elect, 1995-96, pres., 1996-97; bd. dirs. WAMY, Inc., Boone, 1997—; bd. dirs. High Country United Way, 1999—. Mem. ALA. Democrat. Hindu. Home: 421 Fairfield Ln Blowing Rock NC 28605-9755 Office: Parkway Publishers Inc PO Box 3678 Boone NC 28607

ALVARADO, LINDA G., construction company executive. Doctorate (hon.), Dowling Coll. Pres. Alvarado Constrn., Inc., Denver, 1976—; owner Colorado Rockies franchise; corp. dir. Pitney Bowes, Cyprus Amax Minerals co., Englehard Corp. Chmn. bd. dirs. Denver Hispanic C. of C.; dir. Nat. Hispanic Scholarship Fund; commrs. White House Initiative for Hispanic Excellence in Edn. Named Revlon Bus. Woman of Yr., 1996, Bus. Woman of Yr., U.S. Hispanic C. of C., 1996, 100 Most Influential Hispanics in Am., Hispanic Bus. Mag., others; recipient Nat. Minority Supplier Devel. Coun. Leadership award, 1996, Saral Lee Corp. Frontrunner award, others. Office: Alvarado Construction 1266 Santa Fe Dr Denver CO 80204-3546*

ALVARADO, LUIS MANUEL, physician; b. Managua, Nicaragua, Nov. 2, 1959; came to U.S., 1979; s. Eddy F. Alvarado and Paz Elvira Merlo; m. Elizabeth Ann Silva, Sept. 6, 1979; children: Luis Eddy, Lizette Christina. MD, Ctrl. East U., Dominican Republic, 1990; postgrad., Seton Hall U., 1994, Tulane U., 1995. Diplomate Am. Bd. Internal Medicine. Intern in internal medicine, 1994, resident in clin. pharmacology, 1995; with Tenet Physician Group, Franklinton, La., 1995-98. Mem. AMA, ACP, LAMPAC, SAM. Republican. Roman Catholic. Avocations: music, computers. Fax: 504-839-6230. E-mail: zodiac@communique.net. Office: TENET Physician Group 21012 Hwy 16 Franklinton LA 70438

ALVARADO, RICARDO RAPHAEL, retired corporate executive, lawyer; b. Mar. 29, 1927; s. Alfonso and Beatrice Alvarado; m. Rita Logue, Feb. 14, 1948; children: Donna, Bonita, Ricardo R. (dec.), Rita, Susan, Peter, Christina. BS, U.S. Merchant Marine Acad., 1948; JD, Am. U., 1953; LLM, Georgetown U., 1963; MA, George Washington U., 1976. Bar: Va. 1953. Commd. 2d lt. USAF, 1951, advanced through grades to col., 1969; dep. dir. Congl. liaison Office Sec. of Def., 1970-72; mgr. govt. rels. Lockheed Corp., Washington, 1972-73, corp. dir. govt. affairs, 1973-82; corp. v.p. The Signal Cos., Washington, 1982-85, Allied-Signal Inc., 1985-90. Decorated Legion of Merit with cluster. Mem. Air Force Assn. (life), Bus.-Govt. Rels. Coun., Washington Indsl. Round Table, Army Navy Club (bd. dirs. 1975-76), City Club (Washington), Army Navy Country Club (Arlington, Va.), Lighthouse Point Club (Lighthouse Point, Fla.). Home: 533 SW 15th Rd Boca Raton FL 33432-7214

ALVARADO, SANDRA EDGA, nurse practitioner, psychotherapist; b. Adjuntas, P.R., Dec. 3, 1952; d. Pedro Antonio Alvarado and Julia (Altoro) Gonzalez; m. Samuel Soto, Dec. 23, 1985; children: Jeremy Michael, Jonathan Matthew. BSN cum laude, City Coll., N.Y.C., 1973; MSN, Columbia U., N.Y.C., 1976; cert. psychoanalytic psychotherapy, Washington Sq. Inst., N.Y.C., 1980, cert. group psychotherapy, 1985; adv. cert. Practitioner Psychiatry, Columbia U., 1998. Cert. clin. specialist adult psychiat. nurse; cert. group psychotherapist. Staff nurse Met. Hosp., N.Y.C., 1973-77, head nurse, 1977-79; staff therapist psychotherapy dept. Washington Sq. Inst., N.Y.C., 1980-87, staff therapist group dept., 1984-88; nurse clinician Mt. Sinai Hosp., N.Y.C., 1979—. Vol. med. support team N.Y.C. (N.Y.) Marathon, 1985. Recipient Regents Nursing Scholarship award N.Y. State, N.Y.C., 1970-73, Fellowship award NIMH, 1974-75. Mem. ANA, Am. Group Psychotherapy Assn., Ea. Group Psychotherapy Soc., N.Y. State Nurses Assn., Phi Beta Kappa (award 1970). Roman Catholic. Avocations: camping, biking, photography. Office: Mt Sinai Hosp 1 Gustave L Levy Pl Fl 12 New York NY 10029-6574

ALVAREZ, AIDA, federal agency administrator; b. Aguadilla, P.R.. BA cum laude, Harvard U., 1971; LLD (hon.), Iona Coll., 1985. News reporter, anchor Metromedia TV, N.Y.C.; reporter N.Y. Post, N.Y.C.; mem. N.Y.C. Charter Revision Commn.; v.p. N.Y.C. Health and Hosps. Corp.; investment banker 1st Boston Corp., N.Y.C., San Francisco, 1986-93; dir. Office Fed. Housing Enterprise Oversight, Washington, 1993-97; adminstr. Small Bus. Adminstrn., 1997—. Former mem. bd. dirs. Nat. Hispanic Leadership Agenda, N.Y. Cmty. Trust, Nat. civic League; former chmn. bd. Mcpl. Assistance Corp./Victim Svcs. Agy., N.Y.C.; N.Y. State chmn. Gore Presdl. Campaign, 1988; nat. co-chmn. women's com. Clinton Presdl. Campaign, 1992; mem. President's Econ. Transition Team, 1992. Recipient Front Page award, award for excellence AP, 1982, Emmy nomination for reporting guerrilla activities in El Salvador. Office: Small Bus Adminstrn Office Adminstr 409 3rd St SW Washington DC 20041

ALVAREZ, BARRY, university football coach; b. Burgettstown, Pa., Dec. 30, 1946; m. Cindy Alvarez; children: Dawn Alvarez Ferguson, Stacy, Chad. BS, U. Nebr., 1969, MA, 1971. Asst. coach football Lincoln (Nebr.) N.E. H.S., 1971-74; head coach football Lexington (Nebr.) H.S., 1974-75, Mason City (Iowa) H.S., 1976-78; asst. coach (linebackers) U. Iowa, Iowa City, 1979-86; asst. coach football Notre Dame (Ind.) U., 1987, defensive coord., 1988, asst. head coach, 1989; head coach U. Wis., Madison, 1990—. *

ALVAREZ, FRANK, radio station executive. Pres., gen. mgr., promotions dir. CIRV-FM, Toronto, Ont., Canada. Office: CIRV-FM, 1087 Dundas St W, Toronto, ON Canada M6J 1W9*

ALVAREZ, JOSE FLORENCIO, food products executive, mechanical engineer; b. Camagüey, Cuba, June 25, 1948; came to U.S. 1962; s. Orlando L. and Angela (Portilla) A.; m. Patricia V. Suarez, Aug. 7, 1971; children: Andres, Carlos, Nicolas, Patrick. BSME, La. State U., 1972, MBA in Fin., 1980. Registered profl. engr., Fla. Applications engr. Ingersoll Rand, Phillipsberg, N.J., 1972-73; project engr. IPS Engrs., Baton Rouge, 1973-77; sr. mech. engr. Kaiser Aluminum and Chems., Gramercy, La., 1977-80; project mgr. Georgia-Pacific, Plaquemine, La., 1980-81; v.p., gen. mgr. Atlantic Sugar Assn., Belle Glade, Fla., 1981-89; v.p. planning and plant ops. Sugar Cane Grower Coop of Fla., 1989—; bd. dirs. Fla. Molasses Exch., Inc., Refined Sugar Inc., Yonkers, N.Y.; v.p., gen. mgr. Atlantic Sugar Assn., 1981-89. Mem. adv. bd. Palm Beach County St. Luke Sch., 1996—. Recipient George Samuels award Inter-Am. Sugar Cane Seminar, 1987. Mem. Am. Soc. Sugar Cane Tech. (exec. com. 1982-87, pres. 1986), ASME, Fla. Sugar Cane League (environ. quality com. 1983-89). Republican. Roman Catholic. Avocations: music, golf, camping, computers. Office: Sugar Cane Growers Coop Fla Airport Rd PO Box 666 Belle Glade FL 33430-0666

ALVAREZ, MARIANNE, artist, photographer, educator; b. Miami, Nov. 27, 1930; d. Walter Knox and Irma Margaret (Rempe) Payne; m. Jack Alvarez, Dec. 19, 1969. B in Art Edn., U. Fla., 1959; MA, U. South Fla., 1967. Adminstrv. sec. Walter Reed Army Med. Ctr., Washington, 1952-58; art tchr. Sligh Jr. H.S., Tampa, 1959-60, Tyrone Jr. H.S., St. Petersburg, 1960-61, Dunedin (Fla.)-Highland Jr. H.S., 1961-66; media specialist Volusia County Secondary Schs., Daytona Beach, Fla., 1967-90. Exhibited in solo show at The Capitol, Tallahassee, 1997; group shows include Carnegie Mus. Natural History, Pitts., 1992, 94, 96, Cork Gallery, Lincoln Ctr., N.Y.C., 1994, U. Mobile, Ala., 1995, Charles Sumner Sch. Mus., Washington, 1995, Mobile Mus. Art, 1996, Walter Greer Gallery, Hilton Head, S.C., 1997, Ctrl. Arts Collective, Tucson, 1998, S.E. Mus. Photography, Daytona Beach, Fla., 1999, Harris House, New Smyrna Beach, Fla., 1999; represented in permanent collections of Fla. State Capitol, also pvt. collections. Recipient Grumbacher Gold Medallion award, 1995, numerous other awards for art. Mem. Nat. League Am. Pen Women, Delta Kappa Gamma Soc. Internat. Democrat. Roman Catholic. Home: 2727 N Atlantic Ave Apt 611 Daytona Beach FL 32118-3047

ALVAREZ, PABLO, aeronautical and aerospace engineer; b. Valle de Lago, Spain, June 8, 1963; came to U.S., 1991; s. Aurelio and Maria Luisa Alvarez. BS in Aeronautical Engring., Poly. U. Madrid, 1989; MS in Aerospace Engring. with honors, Wichita State U., 1995. Stress engr. Casa, Madrid, 1989-90; nuclear engr. Asociacion Nuclear Asco, Tarragona, Spain, 1990-91; rsch. asst. Wichita State U., 1992-93; design engr. Raytheon Aircraft Co., Wichita, 1993-95, stress engr., 1995—. Vol. Big Bros. and Big Sisters, Wichita, 1997. Mem. AIAA, Phi Kappa Phi. Roman Catholic. Avocations: aircraft modeling, drawing, oil painting, hiking. E-mail: pablo@feist.com. Home: PO Box 780223 Wichita KS 67278-0223 Office: Raytheon Aircraft Co 9709 E Central Ave Wichita KS 67206-2599

ALVAREZ, PETER, JR., police chief; b. Corpus Christi, Tex., Oct. 4, 1941. BA, Tex. A&M U. Patrolman Corpus Christi Police Dept., 1967-71, sgt., 1971-74, lt., 1974-78, capt., 1978-88, comdr., 1988-93, asst. chief, 1993-96, chief of police, 1996—. Office: Corpus Christi Police Dept 321 John Sartain St Rm 525 Corpus Christi TX 78401-2511*

ALVAREZ, RAUL ALBERTO, internist; b. Holguin, Cuba, Aug. 7, 1956; came to U.S., 1967; s. Raul and Esperanza (Sedano) Alvarez; m. Maria Jose Sanjuan, Oct. 4, 1983; children: Raul Eduardo, Jessica Maria. MD, Cadiz Faculty Medicine, Spain, 1983. Diplomate Am. Bd. Internal Medicine. Resident in internal medicine St. Luke's Hosp., St. Louis, 1984-87; dir. emergency rm. svcs. Comprehensive Am. Care-HMO, Miami, Fla., 1987-88; primary care physician Greater Miami Med. Ctrs., North Miami Beach, Fla., 1991-94, Gratigny Cmty. Med. Ctr., North Miami Beach, 1995—, Biscayne Pk. Med. Ctr., Miami, 1998—; active med. staff Aventura Hosp. and Med. Ctr., 1991—, North Shore Hosp., Miami, 1994—, Parkway Regional Med. Ctr., Miami, 1991—; first, second yr. med. student mentor Nova Southeastern U., U. Miami; clin. asst. prof. U. Nova Southeastern U. Fellow ACP (assoc.); mem. AMA (Physician Recognition award 1990, 93), Am. Soc. Internal Medicine. Republican. Roman Catholic. Avocations: gardening, reading. Home: 8861 NW 151st St Miami Lakes FL 33018-1319 Office: Biscayne Park Med Ctr Miami FL 33161

ÁLVAREZ, RODOLFO, sociology educator, consultant; b. San Antonio, Oct. 23, 1936; s. Ramon and Laura (Lobo) A.; m. Edna Rosemary Simons, June 25, 1960 (div. 1984); children: Anica, Amira. *Daughter Anica Álvarez Nishio, BA Yale 1988, and her husband, Yoshi Nishio, BA and MA Oxford 1987, MFA University of California Los Angeles 1992, expect their first child March 1999. They reside in London (Kensington), England where Anica commissions and edits non-fiction books and Yoshi is an international investment consultant. Daughter Amira Álvarez, BA University of California Berkeley 1992, resides in Berkeley, California where she is a corporate relocations consultant to major business corporations.* BA, San Francisco State U., 1961; cert. European Studies, Inst. Am. Univs., Aix-en-Provence, France, 1960; MA, U. Wash., 1964, PhD, 1966. Teaching fellow U. Wash., Seattle, 1963-64; asst. prof. Yale U., New Haven, 1966-72; assoc. prof. sociology UCLA, 1972-80, prof., 1980—, dir. Chicano Studies Rsch. Ctr., 1972-74, chair undergrad. coun., 1995-97; vis. lectr. Wesleyan U., Middletown, Conn., 1970; founding dir. Spanish Speaking Mental Health Research Ctr., 1973-75. Author: Discrimination in Organizations: Using Social Indicators to Manage Social Change, 1979; Racism, Elitism, Professionalism: Barriers to Community Mental Health, 1976; mem. editorial bd. Social Sci. Quar., 1971-86. Pres. ACLU So. Calif., 1980, 81, sec., treas. 1999, Westwood Dem. Club, Calif., 1977-78; trustee Inst. for Am. Univs., Aix-en-Provence, France, 1968—; bd. dirs. Mex. Am. Legal Def. and Ednl. Fund, 1975-79, 88-92; mem. adv. commn. on housing 1984 Olympic Organizing Com., 1982-84; chmn. bd. dirs. Narcotics Prevention Assn., L.A., 1974-77; mem. bilingual adv. com. Children's TV Workshop, N.Y.C., 1979-82; candidate rep. Nat. Dem. Platform Com., Washington, 1976; alt. del. Nat. Dem. Conv., N.Y.C., 1976; bd. dirs. Univ. Credit Union, 1985-92, chmn. strategic plan com., 1987-92. Sgt. USMC, 1954-57. Pres. Mgmt. fellow U. Calif., 1994-95; recipient citation meritorious service for devel. Nat. Fed. Offenders Rehab. and Rsch. Program, State of Wash., 1967. Mem. Internat. Sociol. Honor Soc. (pres. 1976-79), Am. Sociol. Assn. (mem. coun. 1982-85, chairperson sect. racial and ethnic minorities 1989-90, assoc. editor Am. Sociol. Rev. 1989-91, chairperson sect. on sociol. practice 1990-91), Soc. Study of Social Problems (bd. dirs. 1982-87, pres. 1985-86), Pacific Sociol. Assn. (mem. coun. 1979-83, 87-89, v.p. 1991-93, pres. 1996-97), Marines Meml. Club, Rotary. Office: UCLA Dept Sociology 405 Hilgard Ave Los Angeles CA 90095-1551

ALVAREZ, SCOTT G., federal official. AB, Princeton U., 1977; JD cum laude, Georgetown U., 1981. Assoc. gen. counsel Fed. Res. Sys., Washington. Office: Fed Res Sys Bd Mems Office 20th & C Sts NW Washington DC 20551

ALVAREZ, THOMAS, film/video producer, director, theater director, arts consultant; b. Ft. Wayne, Ind., Jan. 1, 1948; s. Raul and Felicitas (Vargas) A. Student, Ind.-Purdue U., 1965-69. Producer, dir. McGraw-Hill Broadcasting Co. Inc./WRTV Channel 6, Indpls., 1973-88; pres. The Alvarez Group Inc., Indpls., 1988-98; mng. dir. Edyvean Repertory Theatre, 1998-99; freelance journalist Indpls. Star, Indpls. Monthly, Nuvo, Arts Inc., Ind. Bus. Mag., Indpls. New Times; bd. dirs. Dance Kaleidoscope, 1991-93; arts reporter Across Ind., WFYI-Channel 20, 1991-93, mem. adv. coun.; mem. cmty. adv. coun. Sta. WRTV, 1993-96, Sta. WFYI-FM, 1991-93; adj. faculty dept. journalism Ind. U., Indpls., 1995-96, 96-97. Prodr., dir. (documentaries) A Portrait of La Gente, 1975, Dave Baker: A Medley, 1976, Concord Today, 1977, Nine Leaves on a Sprig: The Story of Madame C.J. Walker, 1977, Domestic Violence, 1977, 500 Miles: Yesterday and Today, 1979, Tuckaway, 1982, Under the Influence, 1983, Rag to Bop: A Memoir of Indianapolis Jazz, 1984, A Woman's Story, 1985, Indiana State Museum: Living the Legend, 1986, Indiana Repertory Theatre: The First Fifteen Years, 1986, Solid Gold Years, 1987; prod. James Dean & Me: Nineteenth Star, 1995 (Telly award 1997, Emmy award 1997), The Rythm Makers: A Chronicle of Indiana Jazz, 1996. Bd. dirs. Phoenix Theatre, Indpls., 1982-85, First Step Inc.,1 988-90, Ind. Film Soc., 1988-90, ARC, 1989, United Way Cen. Ind., Greater Indpls. Coun. on Alcoholism, 1993; founder, chair Festival of New Can. Cinema, 1988, 89; mem. Ind. Cares, Inc., 1991-93; active Indpls. Men's Chorus; bd. dirs. Damien Ctr., 1996-98; mem. adv. com. Arts. Coun. Indpls., 1996. Recipient Casper award Community Svcs. Coun. Indpls., 1974, CEBA award of merit Advt. and Comm. to Black Communities Inc., 1981, Nat. Coun. on Family Rels. award, 1984, Arti award, 1991, Minority Bus. and Profl. Achievers award 1999; fellow media arts, Ind. Arts Commn. Avocations: travelling, cinema, running, gardening, photography. Home: 316 N East St Indianapolis IN 46202-3611

ALVAREZ, WALTER, geology educator; b. Berkeley, Calif., Oct. 3, 1940; s. Luis Walter and Geraldine (Smithwick) A.; m. Mildred Gearhart Millner, May 8, 1965. B.A., Carleton Coll., 1962; Ph.D., Princton U., 1967. Geologist Am. Overseas Petroleum Ltd., The Hague, Netherlands, 1967-68; geologist Am. Overseas Petroleum Ltd., Tripoli, Libya, 1968-70; NATO postdoctoral fellow Brit. Sch. Archaeology, Rome, 1970-71; research assoc. Lamont-Doherty Geol., Obs., Columbia U., Palisades, N.Y., 1971-77; from asst. prof. to prof. geology and geophysics U. Calif., Berkeley, 1977—. Contbr. numerous articles to profl. publs. Mem. NAS. Office: U Calif Dept Geology & Geoph 301 McCone Hall Berkeley CA 94720-4768*

ALVAREZ-BABIN, CARMEN MARIA, writer, retired educator; b. San José, Costa Rica, Sept. 20, 1917; came to U.S., 1926; d. Felix Pedriquez Alvarez and Agripina de la Vega Rodriguez; m. Ralph Dennis Babin, Dec. 18, 1950 (div. Sept. 1968). BA, City Coll. N.Y., 1973. Tchr. N.Y.C. Bd. Edn., N.Y. State Bd. Prisons, 1973-85. Author poems. Campaign canvasser Dem. Party, La., N.Y.C., 1946—. Recipient U.S. Citizenship Attainment Honors, U.S. Dept. State, 1945. Mem. AAUW, Internat. Soc. Poets (Merit award 1993), Nat. Mus. Women in Arts (charter mem.). Democrat. Roman Catholic. Avocations: print and electronic media critic, reading, writing. Home: 99 Fort Washington Ave New York NY 10032

ALVARIÑO DE LEIRA, ANGELES (ANGELES ALVARIÑO), biologist, oceanographer; b. El Ferrol, Spain, Oct. 3, 1916; came to U.S., 1958, naturalized, 1966; d. Antonio Alvariño-Grimaldos and Carmen Gonzalez Diaz-Saavedra; m. Eugenio Leira-Manso, Mar. 16, 1940; 1 child, Angeles. BS in Letters summa cum laude, U. Santiago de Compostela (Spain), 1933; M. Natural Scis., U. Madrid, 1941, cert. Doctorate, 1951, DSc summa cum laude, 1967. Cert. biologist-oceanographer, Spanish Inst. Oceanography, 1952. Prof. biology Coll. El Ferrol, Spain, 1941-48; fishery rsch. biologist dept. Sea Fisheries Spain, 1948-52; histologist Superior Coun. Sci. Rsch., 1948-52; biologist, oceanographer Spanish Inst. Oceanography, 1950-57; biologist Scripps Inst. Oceanography, U. Calif.-LaJolla, 1958-69; fishery rsch. biologist Nat. Marine Fisheries Svc. S.W. Fisheries Sci. Ctr., NOAA, U.S. Dept. Commerce, La Jolla, 1970-87; emeritus scientist Nat. Marine Fisheries Svc. S.W. Fisheries Ctr., NOAA, U.S. Dept. Commerce, La Jolla, 1987—; assoc. prof. U. Nat. Autonomous Mexico, 1976, San Diego State U., 1979-82; assoc. prof. U. San Diego, 1982—, rsch. assoc., 1982—; vis. prof. Poly. Tech. Mexico, 1982—, U. Parana, Brazil, 1982. Contbr. more than 100 sci. articles to profl. books and jours., chpts. to sci. books; discovered 22 new species and the indicator species for various oceanic regions, ocean dynamics, and the study of the biotic environment of fish spawning grounds. Brit. Coun. fellow, 1953-54, Fulbright fellow, 1956-57; NSF grantee, 1961-69, U.S. Office Navy grantee, 1958-69, Calif. Coop. Oceanic Fishery Investigations grantee, 1958-69, UNESCO grantee, 1979; recipient Great Silver Medal of Galicia, Spain, presented by King Juan Carlos and Queen Sofia of Spain, 1993. Fellow Am. Inst. Fishery Rsch. Biologists, San Diego Soc. Natural History; mem. Assn. Natural History Soc., Biol. Soc. Washington, Hispano-Am. Assn. Researchers on Marine Scis. Home: 7535 Cabrillo Ave La Jolla CA 92037-5206 Office: Nat Marine Fisheries Svc SW Fisheries Sci Ctr PO Box 271 La Jolla CA 92038-0271

ALVERSON, WILLIAM H., lawyer; b. Rockford, Ill., July 23, 1933. A.B., Princeton U., 1955; LL.B., U. Wis., 1960. Bar: Wis. 1960. Mem. firm Godfrey & Kahn. Pres. Milw. Profl. Sports and Services, 1972-76; chmn. Houston Rockets basketball team, 1977-79; chmn. bd. govs. Nat. Basketball Assn., 1975-76. Mem. Milw., Am. bar assns., State Bar Wis., Phi Delta Phi. Office: 780 N Water St Milwaukee WI 53202-3512*

ALVES, CONSTANCE DILLENGER, special education educator; b. Richmond, Va., Sept. 17, 1956; d. George Stuart and Betty Jane (Westwood) Dillenger; m. Bruce Alves, June 28, 1980; 1 child, Caitlin. BA in Speech, Audiology, Mary Washington Coll., 1978; MEd in Deaf Edn., U. Va., 1980; postgrad., Gallaudet U., 1980. Cert. tchr., Va. Tchr. of hearing-impaired students Danville (Va.) Pub. Schs., 1980-90, Henrico County Schs., Richmond, Va., 1990—; adj. faculty Danville Community Coll., 1980-89; adj. faculty interpreter's program J. Sargeant Reynolds, Richmond, 1990—; interpreter for deaf Va. Dept. Deaf and Hard of Hearing, Richmond, 1988—; chmn. Together for the Hearing Impaired, Danville, 1981, 82, 86-87; mem. Danville Local Adv. Com., 1984-86; chmn. Com. for Devising Evaluation Criteria for Teaching Hearing Impaired, Danville, 1984; cons., hearing-impaired specialist Pittsylvania County Schs., Chatham, Va., 1980—. Awarded Career Ladder Status Mark of Excellence in Teaching Danville Pub. Schs. Evaluation Com., 1987-90. Mem. NEA, Va. Edn. Assn., Va. Registry Interpreters for Deaf, Nat. Coun. on Edn. of Deaf (cert.). Home: 9612 Fireside Dr Glen Allen VA 23060-6281

ALVES, ROBERT MARK, priest; b. Phila., Sept. 7, 1958; s. James Thomason and Louella (Rice) A.; m. Polly Dulaney Barclay, Nov. 26, 1983; children: Mary Kathryn, James Barclay. BA in Econs., U. of the South, Sewanee, Tenn., 1981; MDiv, Va. Theol. Sem., Alexandria, 1989. Ordained priest Episcopal Ch., 1990. Asst. rector St. John's Episcopal Ch., Fayetteville, N.C., 1989-93; rector All Sts.' Episcopal Ch., Roanoke Rapids, N.C., 1993—. Mem. Fayetteville Urban Ministry Bd., 1990-93; chair Youth Commn., Kinston, N.C., 1991-93; v.p. Ptnrs.: Today & Tomorrow, Roanoke Rapids, 1994—; chair State of the Ch. Com., Raleigh, N.C., 1995-96; pres. Habitat for Humanity Halifax and Northampton County, Roanoke Rapids, 1995-97; mem. Diocesan Coun., Raleigh, 1996-99, standing com., 1999—; moderator Halifax (N.C.) Libr. Quiz Bowl, 1997-98. Mem. N.C. Episcopal Clergy Assn., Roanoke Rapids Clergy Assn. (pres. 1996-97), Chi Psi (treas. 1980-81), Newcomen Soc., Va. Hist. Soc. Avocations: U.S. history, book collecting, outdoor sports. Office: All Sts Episcopal Ch 635 Hamilton St Roanoke Rapids NC 27870-2703

ALVEY, DAVID LYNN, advertising executive, artist, curator, poet; b. Ft. Worth, Tex., Sept. 19, 1956; s. Lafayette Durham and Frances Ann (Hillburn) A.; m. Marsha Rose Smith, June 3, 1977 (div. Mar. 1991); children: David Zachary, Rodger Drew, Chad Lucas; m. Carolyn Ruth Bennett, Oct. 16, 1993; 1 child, Nicholas Wade. Copywriter Weekley & Assocs., Ft. Worth, 1983-85; broadcast prodr. Weekley-Champney, Dallas, 1985-89; v.p., creative dir. Champney & Assocs., Dallas, 1989-92; founder, owner Aardvark Studios, Dallas, 1992—; owner Aardvark Studios & Gallery, 1994-98; performer ArtNow, Washington, 1997; featured poet McKinney Ave. Contemporary, Dallas, 1997, Deep Ellum Art Fest, Dallas, 1998, 99; lectr. in field. Author: Aard Times, 1997, Aard Labor, 1998; editor: Art's Alive, 1997, Kids Talk, 1998; contbr. poetry to mags.; curator exhibns., 1995—. Mem. Tex. Poetry Project, 1997-98, Garland Visual Arts Com., 1994-98; juror PTA Reflections contest, Garland, Tex., 1995-97; co-founder Aardvark Studios Celebrity Garage Sale benefiting Leukemia Soc., 1995-99. With USN, 1978-82. Recipient citation Tex. Visual Artists Assn., 1994-96; Telly award, 1988, Gold Addy, Dallas Advt. League, 1992. Mem. Garland Artists Group (founder, facilitator), Dallas Artists Rschg. and Exhibiting. Avocations: art, photography, poetry, gardening, travel. E-mail: aard1vark@aol.com. Office: Aardvark Studios PO Box 542913 Dallas TX 75354-2913

ALVI, KHISAL AHMED, chemist; b. Karachi, Pakistan, Mar. 15, 1958; came to U.S., 1989; s. Wisal Ahmed Alvi and Abida Begum; m. Tanvir Sultana, July 4, 1989; children: Rida, Rohail. BS with honors, U. Karachi, 1981, MS, 1983, PhD, 1987. Rsch. asst. U. Southhampton, Eng., 1988-89; rsch. fellow U. Calif., Santa Cruz, 1989-91, sr. rsch. fellow, 1991-92; sr. scientist MDS-PANLABS, Inc., Bothell, Wash., 1993-99, TheTagen Inc., Bothell, Wash., 1999—; presenter in field. Contbr. articles to profl. jours. Spl. predoctoral scholar U. Grant Commn. Pakistan, 1986, postdoctoral scholar U. Calif. Cancer Rsch. Coordinating Com., 1989. Mem. AAAS, Am. Chem. Soc., Am. Soc. Pharmocognosy, Soc. Indsl. Microbiology, N.Y. Acad. Scis. Office: The Tagen 11804 N Creek Pkwy S Bothell WA 98011-8801

ALVIGGI, CHRISTOPHER, insurance broker; b. Newark, Feb. 23, 1964; s. S. Robert and Diana M. (Scassena) A.; m. Linda A. Alviggi, Oct. 13, 1995; 1 child, Alexis M. BBA, Coll. Ins., N.Y.C., 1991, MBA, 1995. Cert. assoc. in risk mgmt. Account rep. Am. Risk Svcs., N.Y.C., 1996—. Mem. Coll. Ins. Alumni Assn. (bd. dirs. 1993—), Italian Am. Police Officers Assn. (assoc.). Republican. Roman Catholic. Avocations: finance. Office: Am Risk Svcs 2 World Trade Ctr New York NY 10048-0203

ALVINE, ROBERT, industrialist, entrepreneur, international business leader; b. Newark, Aug. 25, 1938; s. James C. and Marie Alvine; m. Diane C. Marzulli, May 6, 1961 (div. 1995); children: Robert James, Laurie Anne. BS, Rutgers U., 1960; postgrad., Syracuse U., 1968-69; grad. PMD, Harvard Bus. Sch., 1972. With Celanese Corp., 1960-77; bus. mgr. nylon products Celanese Plastics Co., Newark, 1967-69, bus. mgr. polyolefin products, 1969-72; dir. mktg. and ops. Celanese Piping Systems and Fabricated Products Co., Hilliard, Ohio, 1972-75; v.p., gen. mgr. comml. Celanese Polymer Spltys. Co., Louisville, 1975-77, Uniroyal Inc., 1977-87; v.p., dir. strategy planning and bus. devel. Uniroyal-Chem., Naugatuck, Conn., 1977; v.p. corp. planning and devel. Uniroyal Inc., Middlebury, Conn., 1978; v.p., gen. mgr. Uniroyal Tire Co., 1979-80; pres. Uniroyal Merchandising Co., 1979-84; pres., CEO, Uniroyal Devel. Co., 1980-82; CEO, COO, group v.p. Uniroyal Engineered Products & Svcs., Worldwide, 1982-87; pres. Uniroyal Plastics Co., Uniroyal Footware Columbia, Uniroyal Power Transmission Co., Uniroyal Indsl. Products Cos., 1982-87; also corp. sr. v.p., corp. worldwide officer responsible for mergers and acquisitions and corp. strategic planning Uniroyal, Inc., 1979-87, and sr. corp. officer and major prin. and team leader in mgmt. leverage buy-out of Uniroyal, Inc., 1985; founder, chmn., CEO I-Ten Mgmt. Corp., Woodbridge, Conn., 1987—; founder, chmn., CEO, I-Ten Capital Corp., Woodbridge, 1987, Aim Capital Group, Woodbridge, 1987—; chmn., CEO, prin. shareholder Charter Power Sys. (now C&D Techs. Inc.), Blue Bell, Pa., 1988-94; entrepreneur, prin. Charterhouse Group Internat., Inc., N.Y.C., 1988-95; vice chmn., CEO, major shareholder AP Parts Mfg. Co., Toledo, 1989-93; prin., dir. Internat. Automobile Products Holdings Corp., N.Y.C., 1993-95; prin. Uniroyal Holdings, Waterbury, Conn., 1985—; trustee Uniroyal Liquidating Trust; bd. dirs. Jackson Rsch. Sys., E.D.O. Corp., N.Y.; chmn. compensation com., strategic com., exec. com., Jackson Labs., Bar Harbor, Maine, mem. capital campaign, rsch. resources and philantropy coms.; mem. adv. bd. Polaris Fund, N.Y.C., 1996—; mem. bd. govs. U. New Haven, 1998, mem. chair audit com., exec. com.; chmn. Henry Lee Inst. Forensic Scis.; mem. bd. Tax Rsch. Resources. Mem. Rep. Presdl. Task Force, Pres.'s Roundtable, Citizens Against Govt. Waste, Presdl. Legion of Merit; bd. dirs., trustee Nat. Theater of the Deaf, Chester, Conn., 1994—, chmn. bd. dirs., 1995—, Wildlife Conservation Soc., N.Y., trustee, Long Wharf Theatre, New Haven, mem. fin. com., chmn. bus. devel. com., strategy com., trustee; mem. adv. bd. Arts Scis. Coun., Rutgers U., N.J.; mem. Navy War Coll. Found.; mem. sch. bus. adv. bd. U. New Haven. With U.S. Army, 1962-68. Recipient numerous citations and recognitions including Disting. Bus. Achievement and Svcs. to the Nations award, Presdl. Legion Merit, Honor grad. Southeastern Signal Sch., 1962, Proclamation for Supreme Achievement Within the Internat. Cmty.; named Ky. Col., Gov. Ky., 1976. Mem. Nat. Assn. Corp. Dirs., Pres.'s Assn., Nat. Adv. Coun., Assn. Goverining Bds. of Univs. and Colls., Am. Inst. Mgmt., Internat. Bus. Coun., World Affairs Coun.-Conn., Nat. Planning Inst., Nat. Assn. Corp. Growth, Rubber Mfrs. Assn., Battery Coun. Internat., Newcomen Soc. Am. (Conn. com.), Soc. Plastics Industry (sr., past dir.), Soc. Plastics Engrs. (past dir.), Mfg. Chemists Assn., Societe de Chemie Industriale, Nat. Paint and Coatings Assn., Coun. of Ams., Nat. Maritime Hist. Soc., Nat. Trust for Hist. Preservation, New Haven Colony Hist. Soc., Columbus House, Rutgers Alumni Assn., Harvard Bus. Sch. Alumni Assn., Harvard Bus. Sch. Club Greater N.Y. (honor roll mem.), So. Conn., Ellis Island Found. (charter), U.S. Navy Meml. Found., WWII Meml. Found. (charter), Oaklane Country Club, Renaissance Club, Am. Legion, Commanders Club, Chi Phi. Mem. Ch. of Christ. Email: ialv@aol.com. Home: 55 N Racebrook Rd Woodbridge CT 06525-1407

ALVORD, JOEL BARNES, retired bank executive; b. Manchester, Conn., Nov. 29, 1938; s. Martin Earl and Elizabeth (Barnes) A.; m. Anne Stilson, June 23, 1962; children: Sarah, Seth. A.B., Dartmouth Coll., 1960, M.B.A., 1961. With Hartford Nat. Corp., Conn., 1963—; exec. v.p. investments and exec. v.p. Hartford Nat. Corp., 1976-78, pres., 1978-88, chief exec. officer, 1986-88, chmn., 1988—, also bd. dirs.; chmn. Conn. Nat. Bank subs. Shawmut Nat. Corp., 1986—; chmn., chief exec. officer Shawmut Nat. Corp., 1988-95; chmn. Fleet Fin. Group, Boston, 1995-98, chmn. exec. com., 1998—; dir. Hartford Steam Boiler Inspection and Ins. Co. Bd. dirs. Inst. of Living, Hartford; dir. Jobs for Mass.; active Mass. Bus. Roundtable, Mus. Fine Arts, Boston, the Backers Roundtable the Wadsworth Atheneum Hartford, Wang Ctr. for the Performing Arts, Boston. Congregationalist. *

ALVORD, W. GREGORY, statistician; b. Apr. 2, 1947; s. William Henry and Juanita A.; m. Mary Ann Karapetian, June 4, 1976; children: Bryce Kevin, Scott Alexander, Justin Keith. BS in Psychology, U. Md., 1969, MA in Comm., 1974, PhD in Measurement and Stats., 1983. Coll. lectr. U. Md., 1988-91; cons. stats. Nat. Cancer Inst./Frederick Cancer Rsch. and Devel. Ctr., 1985-88, dir. statis. svc., 1989—; cons. Rsch. Applications, Inc. and Washington Met. Area Transit Authority, 1981-85. Contbr. articles/essays to profl. jours., and publs. Mem. Am. Statis. Assn., Biometric Soc., Math. Assn. Am., Claymont Soc. Continuous Edn., MENSA, Robin Hood Swim, Tennis and Dive Club, U.S. Diving, Phi Kappa Phi. Office: Nat Cancer Inst/ Frederick Cancer R&D Ctr PO Box B Frederick MD 21702-1124

ALWAN, ABEER, electrical engineering educator; b. Baghdad, Iraq, Feb. 26, 1959; came to U.S., 1981; d. Abdul-Hussain Alwan Shlash and Amina Wahab Mashta. BSEE, Northeastern U., 1983; SMEE, MIT, 1986, EE, 1987, PhD in Elec. Engring., 1992. Intern Concord Data Systems, Waltham, Mass., 1982-83; rsch. asst., teaching asst. dept. elec. engring. MIT, Cambridge, Mass., 1982-92; asst. prof. dept. elec. engring. UCLA, 1992—; cons. Digital Equipment Corp., Waltham, 1990. Contbr. articles to profl. publs. Named one of Outstanding Young Women Am.; recipient Rsch. awards NSF, NIH and Okawa Found. Mem. IEEE, Acoustical Soc. Am., N.Y. Acad. Scis., Sigma Xi, Tau Beta Pi. Office: UCLA Dept Electrical Engring 405 Hilgard Ave Los Angeles CA 90095-9000

ALWARD, RUTH ROSENDALL, nursing consultant; d. Henry Rosendall and Freda Jonkman; m. Samuel Alward, Jan. 17, 1976. RN, Butterworth Hosp. Sch. Nursing, Grand Rapids, Mich.; BSN summa cum laude, Hunter Coll./CUNY, N.Y., 1980; MA, Columbia U., 1982, EdM, 1983, EdD, 1986. Sr. clin. nurse Wadsworth VA Hosp., L.A., 1966-68; exec. dir. nursing Care Corp, Grand Rapids, Mich., 1968-71; nursing cons. Humana Inc., Louisville, 1972-76; asst. prof., dir. nursing adminstrn. grad. prog. Hunter Coll., CUNY, N.Y.C., 1986-90; pres. Nurse Exec. Assocs., Inc., Washington, 1990—; series editor Delmar Pubs. Inc., Albany, 1993-96. Co-author: The Nurse's Shift Work Handbook, 1993, The Nurse's Guide to Marketing, 1991; contbr. articles to profl. jours.; mem. editorial adv. bd. Jour. of Nursing Adminstrn. Mem. Va Nurses Assn. (chair fin. com.), Nat. League Nursing (treas. D.C. chpt.), Coun. on Grad. Edn. for Adminstrn. in Nursing, Am. Orgn. Nurse Execs., Sigma Theta Tau. Home and Office: 2011 N St NW Washington DC 20036-2301

ALYWAHBY, NANCY, geriatric and adult nurse practitioner. Diploma, Kings County Hosp., Bklyn., 1975; BSN, L.I. U., 1978; MSN, Hunter-Bellevue Sch. Nursing, N.Y.C., 1985. RN, N.Y.; ANA cert. specialist GNP, adult nurse practitioner VA Domiciliary Program for Homeless Vet. Geriatric nurse practitioner VA Extended Care Ctr., St. Albans, N.Y., 1984—. Author: Rehabilitation Nursing Principles for Teaching for Individual Learning of Older Adults, 1989. Mem. Coalition Nurse Practitioners. Home: 1714 Rockaway Pky Brooklyn NY 11236-4824

AL-ZUBAIDI, AMER AZIZ, physicist, educator; b. Najaf, Iraq, June 10, 1945; came to U.S., 1974; s. Aziz Allawi and Shahai Ali (Al Fortousi) A.; m. Haifa M. Al-Zubaidi, Aug. 24, 1972; children: Samer, Akrum. BS in Physics, U. Baghdad, Iraq, 1966; MS in Physics, Pa. State U., 1976, postgrad., 1977, 81; postgrad., Va. Poly. Inst. and State U., 1977-82. bd. dirs. KCIK. High sch. tchr. Inst. for Tchrs., Riyadh, Suadi Arabia, 1966-68; high sch. tchr. physics, math., and related scis. Saudi Ministry of Edn., Riyadh, 1966-68; high sch. tchr. physics, math., mem. phys. lab. supplies and equipments com. Agrl. Vocat. Sch., Iraqi Ministry Edn., Baghdad, 1968-74; grad. teaching asst. Va. Poly. Inst. and State U., Blacksburg, 1976-82, rsch. sci. nuclear physics, 1982—; owner Al's Internat. Editor-in-chief Al-Kufa, 1994. Chmn. bd. dirs. Kufa Ctr. of Islamic Knowledge, editor-in-chief newsletter. Mem. Union of Concerned Scientists, Sigma Xi, Sigma Pi Sigma. Home: 2319 10th St NW Roanoke VA 24012-3929

AMABILE, JOHN LOUIS, lawyer; b. N.Y.C., Oct. 13, 1934; s. John A. and Rose (Singer) A.; m. Christina M. Leary, Nov. 23, 1963; children: Tracy Ann, John Christopher. BS cum laude, Coll. Holy Cross, 1956; LLB, St. John's Sch. Law, 1959. Bar: N.Y. 1959, U.S. Dist. Ct. (so. and ea. dists.) N.Y. 1961, U.S. Supreme Ct. 1964, U.S. Ct. Claims 1964, U.S. Ct. Appeals (2d cir.) 1970, U.S. Tax Ct. 1984, U.S. Ct. Appeals (9th cir.) 1984. Assoc. Law Office of Allen Taylor, N.Y.C., 1959-62; assoc. Schwartz & Frohlich, N.Y.C., 1963-69, ptnr., 1969; ptnr. Summit, Solomon & Feldesman (and predecessor firms), N.Y.C., 1971-93, Putney, Twombly Hall & Hirson, N.Y.C., 1993—; faculty mem. ann. seminar Practising Law Inst., 1987-91; mediator so. dist. U.S. Dist. Ct. N.Y., comml. divsn. Supreme Ct., N.Y.; arbitrator ea. dist. U.S. Dist. Ct., Bklyn.; panel chair appellate divsn. Disciplinary Com., 1980-85, 87-92; lectr. in field. Author: Responses to Complaints: Commercial Litigation in New York State Courts, 1995, Warranties: Business and Commercial Litigation in Federal Courts, 1998; editor St. John Law Rev. 1958-59. Regional commr. Am. Youth Soccer Orgn., Chappaqua, N.Y., 1975-84; mem. New Castle Recreation and Parks Commn., 1984-90, chairperson, 1987-89. Mem. ABA, N.Y. State Bar Assn., Assn. Bar City N.Y. (mem. com. on state legis. 1971-74, chair 1975-78, com. on grievances 1979-80, com. on women in cts. 1988-94, com. on judiciary 1989-92, interim mem. 1992, 93, 94, 96, 97, 98, 99, chair com. on gender bias in fed. cts. 1991-93, coun. judicial adminstrn. 1996—, com. on symposium 1997—, chair 1998—), Fed. Bar Coun., Practising Law Inst. (chair winning strategies for depositions in corp. litigation 1991-92, co-chair seminars on art of taking and defending depositions in corp. litigation 1982-85). Democrat. Roman Catholic. Home: 73 Westorchard Rd Chappaqua NY 10514-1003 Office: Putney Twombly Hall & Hirson 521 5th Ave New York NY 10175

AMACHER, RICHARD EARL, literature educator; b. Ridgway, Pa., Dec. 13, 1917; s. Albert and Emma (Luchs) A.; m. Cordelia Anne Ward, Aug. 26, 1953; 1 child, Alice Marie. A.B., Ohio U., 1939; postgrad., U. Chgo., 1939-42; Ph.D., U. Pitts., 1947. Instr. English Yale U., New Haven, 1944-45; instr. Rutgers U., New Brunswick, N.J., 1945-47; asst. prof. Rutgers U., 1947-53, lectr., 1953-54; chmn. English dept. Henderson State Tchrs. Coll., Arkadelphia, Ark., 1954-57; asso. prof. English Auburn (Ala.) U., 1957-65, prof., 1965-78, Hargis prof. Am. Lit., 1978-84, prof. emeritus, 1984—; Fulbright prof., Würzburg, Fed. Republic Germany, 1961-62, Konstanz, W. Ger., 1969-70. Author: Franklin's Wit and Folly, 1953, Practical Criticism, 1956, Benjamin Franklin, 1962, Edward Albee, 1969, rev. edit., 1982, (with Margaret Rule) Edward Albee at Home and Abroad, 1973, (with Victor Lange) New Perspectives in German Literary Criticism, 1979, American Political Writers, 1588-1800, 1979; editor: (with G. Polhemus) J.G. Baldwin's The Flush Times of California, 1966. Chmn. Auburn Chamber Music Soc., 1980-82, 85-86, 88-89; elder Presbyterian Ch. Am. Coun. Learned Socs. grantee, 1972. Mem. Am. Studies Assn. (pres. southeastern sec. 1977-79), Société Historique d'Auteuil et de Passy, Nat. Soc. Lit. and Arts. Democrat. Home: 515 Auburn Dr Auburn AL 36830-5547 Office: Auburn Univ English Dept Auburn AL 36849

AMADEI, DEBORAH LISA, librarian; b. Jersey City, June 13, 1952; d. Joseph and Thelma (Pugach) Irgon; m. Albert E. Amadei, July 19, 1987. BA, Northeastern U., 1975; MS, Pratt Inst., 1985. Cert. profl. librarian. Tech. libr. asst. Tracor Jitco, Dover, N.J., 1977-84, lead tech. libr. asst., 1984-85; sr. libr. East Orange (N.J.) Pub. Libr., 1986—. Mem. ALA, N.J. Libr. Assn., Toastmasters (ednl. v.p. Essex County, N.J. chpt. 1990-91, pres. 1992-93). Avocations: writing, hiking, movies. Office: East Orange Pub Libr 21 S Arlington Ave East Orange NJ 07018-3804

AMADIO-BACKOWSKI, THERESE MARIE, small business owner; b. Cleve., May 10, 1949; d. Henry Joseph and Therese Eleanor (Nicoll) Backowski; m. Alex Villena (div. 1974); m. Blase S. Amadio (div. 1986); children: Elizabeth Angelique, Charles Aaron, Angelo Benjamin, Margaret Eleanor, Jessica MariRose. Diploma, Erasmus Hall. Lic. vet. technician Ohio State Vet. Bd. Vet. technician Animal Med. Clinic, Dublin, Ohio, 1974-78; acct. Credit Bur. Svcs., Mansfield, Ohio, 1980-82; pres. Park Ave. Pets Inc., Mansfield, 1982—; grooming judge Groom Expo West, Burbank, Calif., 1992; tchr. dog obedience Madison H.S. Adult Edn., Mansfield, 1984-94; animal trainer for film Shawshank Redemption, Castle Rock Pictures, 1994; spkr. in field. Mem. bd. advisors Madison Adult Edn. Divorced Homemakers to Work Program, 1985-91, Richland County 4-H, Mansfield, 1991-97; mem. block grant com. HUD, Mansfield, 1982-85, chmn., 1984-85; pres. Poplar St. Neighborhood Assn., Mansfield; leader Heritage Trail coun. Girl Scouts U.S., Mansfield, 1981-85. Named Employer of Yr. Mansfield City Schs., 1987-88. Mem. NAFE, Nat. Dog Groomers Assn., Richland County Kennel Club. Republican. Roman Catholic. Avocations: horseback riding, fishing, reading, swimming. Home: 142 Poplar St PO Box 5289 Mansfield OH 44901-5289 Office: Park Ave Pets Inc 166 Park Ave W Mansfield OH 44902-1637

AMADO, HONEY KESSLER, lawyer; b. Bklyn., July 20, 1949; d. Bernard and Mildred Kessler; m. Ralph Albert Amado, Oct. 24, 1976; children: Jessica Reina, Micah Solomon, Gabrielle Beth. BA in Polit. Sci., Calif. State Coll., Long Beach, 1971; JD, Western State U., Fullerton, Calif., 1976. Bar: Calif. 1977, U.S. Dist. Ct. (ctrl. dist.) Calif. 1981, U.S. Ct. Appeals (9th cir.) 1981, U.S. Supreme Ct. 1994. Assoc. Law Offices of Jack M. Lasky, Beverly Hills, Calif., 1977-78; pvt. practice Beverly Hills, Calif., 1978—; lectr. in field. Contbr. articles to profl. jours.; mem. editl. bd. L.A. Lawyer mag., 1996—, articles coord., 1999—. Mem. Com. Concerned Lawyers for Soviet Jewry, 1979-90; nat. v.p. Jewish Nat. Fund, 1995-97; bd. dirs. Jewish Nat. Fund L.A., 1990—; sec. L.A. region, bd. dirs., 1991-94, Am. Jewish Congress, Jewish Feminist Ctr., 1992-99, co-chair steering com., 1994-96; mem. Commn. on Soviet Jewry of Jewish Fedn. Coun. Greater L.A., 1977-83, chmn., 1979-81, commn. on edn., 1982-83, cmty. rels. com., 1979-83. Mem. Calif. Women Lawyers (bd. govs. 1988-90, 1st v.p. 1989-90, jud. evaluations co-chair 1988-90), San Fernando Valley Bar Assn. (family law mediators and arbitrators planel 1983-94, judge pro-tem panel 1987-94), Beverly Hills Bar Assn. (family law mediators panel 1985-94), L.A. County Bar Assn. (family law sect., appellate cts. com. 1987—, chmn. subcom. to examine reorgn. Calif. Supreme Ct. 1990-94, judge pro tem panel 1985-95, appellate jud. evaluations com. 1989—, editl. bd. L.A. Lawyer mag. 1996—, articles coord. 1999—, dist. 2 settlement program 1996—), Calif. State Bar, Calif. Ct. Appeal. Democrat. Jewish. Office: 261 S Wetherly Dr Beverly Hills CA 90211-2515

AMADO, RALPH DAVID, physics educator; b. Los Angeles, Nov. 23, 1932; s. Richard Joseph and Suzanne (Nahoum) A.; children—Richard Lewis, David Philip. BA, Stanford U., 1954; PhD (Rhodes scholar), Oxford U., 1957. Rsch. assoc. U. Pa., 1957-59, asst. prof., 1959-62, assoc. prof., 1962-65, prof. physics, 1965—, vice provost for rsch., 1995—; Cons. Arms Control and Disarmament Agy., 1962-65, Los Alamos Sci. Lab., 1965—. Fellow Am. Phys. Soc., AAAS. Home: 509 Latmer Rd Merion Station PA 19066-1811

AMAN, ALFRED CHARLES, JR., dean; b. Rochester, N.Y., July 7, 1945; s. Alfred Charles, Sr. and Jeannette Mary (Czebatul) A.; m. Carol Jane Greenhouse, Sept. 23, 1976. AB, U. Rochester, 1967; JD, U. Chgo., 1970. Bar: D.C. 1971, Ga. 1972, N.Y. 1980. Law clk. U.S. Ct. Appeals, Atlanta, 1970-72; assoc. Sutherland, Asbill & Brennan, Atlanta, 1972-75, Washington, 1975-77; assoc. prof. Sch. Law, Cornell U., Ithaca, N.Y., 1977-82, prof. law, 1983-91, exec. dir. Internat. Legal Studies Program, 1988-90; prof. law, dean Sch. Law, Ind. U., Bloomington, 1991-99, dean, Roscoe C. O'Byrne chair in law, 1999—; cons. U.S. Adminstrv. Conf., Washington, 1978-80, 86—; trustee U. Rochester, 1980—; vis. fellow Wolfson Coll., Cambridge U., 1983-84, 90-91. Author: Energy and Natural Resources, 1983, Administrative Law in a Global Era, 1992, Administrative Law Treatise, 1992. Chmn. Ithaca Bd. Zoning Appeals, 1980-82. Mem. ABA, Am. Assn. Law Schs., D.C. Bar Assn., Ga. Bar Assn., N.Y. State Bar Assn., Phi Beta Kappa. Democrat. Avocations: music; jazz drumming; piano; composition and arranging. Home: 3703 Chaudion Ct Bloomington IN 47401-4465 Office: Ind U Sch Law Third St and Indiana Ave Bloomington IN 47405*

AMAN, GEORGE MATTHIAS, III, lawyer; b. Wayne, Pa., Mar. 2, 1930; s. George Matthias and Emily (Kalbach) A.; m. Ellen McMillan, June 20, 1959; children: James E., Catherine E., Peter T. A.B., Princeton U., 1952; LL.B., Harvard U., 1957. Bar: Pa. 1958. Assoc. Townsend Elliot & Munson, Phila., 1960-65; ptnr. Morgan Lewis & Bockius, Phila., 1965-93; of counsel High, Swartz, Roberts & Seidel, Norristown, Pa., 1993—. Commr. Radnor Twp., Pa., 1976-80, 86-92, planning commr., 1981-86; pres. bd. trustees Wayne Presbyn. Ch., Pa., 1981-84. Served to 1st lt. U.S. Army, 1952-54. Mem. ABA, Pa. Mcpl. Authorities Assn., Phila. Regional Mcpl. Fin. Officers Assn. (dir. 1983-87). Republican. Clubs: Merion Cricket (Haverford, Pa.); Princeton (Phila.) (dir 1977-79, treas. 1985-86). Home: 246 Upland Way Wayne PA 19087-4859 Office: High Swartz Roberts Seidel 40 E Airy St Norristown PA 19401-4803

AMAN, MOHAMMED MOHAMMED, university dean, library and information science educator; b. Alexandria, Egypt, Jan. 3, 1940; came to U.S., 1963, naturalized, 1975; s. Mohammed Aman and Fathia Ali (al-Maghrabi) Mohammed; m. Mary Jo Parker, Sept. 15, 1972; 1 son, David. BA, Cairo U., 1961; MS, Columbia U., 1965; PhD, U. Pitts., 1968. Librarian Egyptian Nat. Libr., 1961-63, Duquesne U., Pitts., 1966-68; asst. prof. libr. sci. Pratt Inst., N.Y.C., 1968-69; from asst. prof. to assoc. prof. St. John's U., Jamaica, N.Y., 1969-73; prof., dir. divsn. libr. and info. sci. St. John's U., 1973-76; prof. libr. sci., dean Palmer Grad. Libr. Sch., C.W. Post Ctr., L.I. U., 1976-79; prof., dean Sch. Libr. and Info. Sci., U. Wis., Milw., 1979—; cons. UNESCO, U.S., AID and UNIDO; USIA acad. specialist, Germany, 1989; Fulbright lectr. Cairo U., 1990-91; USIA-sponsored lectr. Mohamed V. Univ., Rabat, Morocco, 1997. Author: Librarianship and the Third World, 1976, Cataloging and Classifications of Non-Western Library Material: Issues, Trends and Practices, 1980, Arab Serials and Periodicals: A Subject Bibliography, 1979, Online Access to Databases, 1983, On Developing Computer-Based Library Systems (Arabic), 1984, Information Services (Arabic), 1985, Trends in Urban Library Management, 1989, The Bibliotheca Alexandrina: A Link in the Chain of Cultural Continuity, 1991, Information Technology Use in Libraries (Arabic), 1998; editor: Digest of Middle East Studies. Chmn. Black Faculty Coun., U. Wis., Milw.; mktg. com. Milw. Art Mus. Recipient Outstanding Achievement award Egyptian Libr. Assn., 1997. Mem. NAACP, ALA (chmn. internat. rels. com. 1984-86, John Ames Humphry/Forest Press Outstanding Contbn. award 1989, standing com. on libr. edn., internat. subcom. 1990-91, chmn. 1991-93, internat. rels. Round Table 1993-94, leadership award black caucus 1994, excelence award black caucus 1995), Assn. Libr. and Sci. (Svc. award 1988), Am. Soc. for Info. Sci. (chmn. spl. interest group in internat. info. issues, internat. rels. com.), Arab/Jewish Dialogue, Egyption-Am. Scholars Assn., Assn. for Libr. and Info. Sci. Edn. (chmn. internat. rels. com. 1983-85), Wis. Libr. Assn. (Svc. award 1992, P.N. Kaula Internat. award and medal 1996, Wis. Libr. of Yr. 1998), Libr. Svcs. and Constrn. Act. (adv. com. 1986-89), Internat. Archtl. Jury for Bibliotheca Alexandrina, Internat. Fedn. Libr. Assns. and Insts. (sec. on edn. and tng. 1983-92), The Gamaliel Chair (bd. dirs. 1995-97), Leaders Forum (bd. dirs. 1995—), America's Black Holocaust Mus. (bd. dirs. 1999—), Islamic Social Family Svcs. (bd. dirs. 1999—). Democrat. Moslem. Office: U Wis-Milw Sch Libr & Info Sci PO Box 413 Milwaukee WI 53201-0413

AMAN, REINHOLD ALBERT, philologist, publisher; b. Fuerstenzell, Bavaria, Apr. 8, 1936; came to U.S., 1959, naturalized, 1963; s. Ludwig and Anna Margarete (Waindinger) A.; m. Shirley Ann Beischel, Apr. 9, 1960 (div. 1990); 1 child, Susan. Student, Chem. Engring. Inst., Augsburg, Germany, 1953-54; B.S. with high honors, U. Wis., 1965; Ph.D., U. Tex., 1968. Chem. engr. Munich and Frankfurt, Ger., 1954-57; petroleum chemist Shell Oil Co., Montreal, Que., Can., 1957-59; chem. analyst A. O. Smith Corp., Milw., 1959-62; prof. German U. Wis., Milw., 1968-74; editor, pub. Maledicta Jour., Maledicta Press Publs., Santa Rosa, Calif., 1976—; pres. Maledicta Press, Santa Rosa, 1976—; dir. Internat. Maledicta Archives, Santa Rosa, 1975—. Author: Der Kampf in Wolframs Parzival, 1968, Bayrisch-oesterreichisches Schimpfwoerterbuch, 1973, 86, 96, Talking Dirty, 1993, Opus Maledictorum, 1996, Hillary Clinton's Pen Pal, 1996; gen. editor Mammoth Cod (Mark Twain), 1976, Dictionary of International Slurs (A. Roback), 1979, Graffiti (A. Read), 1977; editor Maledicta: The Internat. Jour. Verbal Aggression, 1977—, Maledicta Monitor, 1990-92; contbr. articles to profl. jours. U. Wis. scholar, 1963-65; U. Wis. research grantee, 1973, 74; NDEA Title IV fellow, 1965-68. Mem. Internat. Maledicta Soc. (pres.), Am. Dialect Soc., Am. Name Soc., Dictionary Soc. N.Am. Home and Office: PO Box 14123 Santa Rosa CA 95402-6123

AMANCIO, RUTH CARSON, safety professional; b. Honolulu, Nov. 13, 1956; d. Caliupe Carson and Julia (Donios) A.; m. Rodney Mitsuo Kaneshiro, June 8, 1980 (div. June 1992); children: Alane Kapeka, Jolie Mikala. AS, U. Hawaii, 1976, student, 1992—. Sales supr. Affirmed Med. Svc., Honolulu, 1982-96; safety adminstr. Albert C. Kobayashi Inc., Waipahu, Hawaii, 1996—; safety mgr., cons. OSHCON Inc., Honolulu, 1998—; trainer ARC, Honolulu, 1994-96; rec. sec. Non-Traditional Employment Task Force, 1996—. Mem. Vets. of Safety (scholar 1996), Am. Soc. Safety Engrs. (scholar 1992-95), Gen. Contractors Assn., Phi Theta Kappa (2d v.p. 1992-96). Avocations: sewing, music, dancing, aerobic weight training, reading.

AMANN, CHARLES ALBERT, mechanical engineer; b. Thief River Falls, Minn., Apr. 21, 1926; s. Charles Alois and Bertha Ann (Oetting) A.; m. Marilynn Ann Reis, Aug. 26, 1950; children: Richard, Barbara, Nancy, Julie. BS, U. Minn., 1946, MSME, 1948. Instr. U. Minn., Mpls., 1946-49; rsch. engr. Gen. Motors Rsch. Labs., Detroit, 1949-54; supervisory rsch. engr. Gen. Motors Rsch. Labs., Warren, Mich., 1954-71, asst. dept. head, 1971-73, dept. head, 1973-89, rsch. fellow, 1989-91; prin. engr. KAB Engring., 1991—; adv. com. mem. Gas Rsch. Inst., 1992-98, Oak Ridge Nat. Lab., 1996—, Litex, Inc., 1998—; guest lectr. Mich. State U., 1982—; invited lectr. Inst. for Advanced Engring., Seoul, 1994. Author: (with others) Automotive Engine Alternatives, 1986, Advanced Diesel Engineering and Operations, 1988; co-editor: Combustion Modeling in Reciprocating Engines, 1980; patentee in engine and transp. fields. Lt. (j.g.) USNR, 1944-46. Recipient James Clayton prize Inst. Mech. Engrs., 1975, Outstanding Achievement award U. Minn., 1991. Fellow Soc. Automotive Engrs. (Arch T. Colwell merit award, 1972, 84, Disting. Spkr. award 1981, 91); mem. NAE, ASME (Richard S. Woodbury award 1989, Soichiro Honda lectr. 1992, Spkr. award Internal Combustion Engine Divsn. 1997), Sigma Xi, Tau Omega, Tau Beta Pi. Presbyterian. Avocation: music.

AMAR, AKHIL REED, law educator; b. Ann Arbor, Mich., Sept. 6, 1958; s. Arjan D. and Kamla (Chabra) A.; m. Vinita Parkash, Sept. 3, 1989. BA summa cum laude, Yale U., 1980, JD, 1984; LLD (hon.), Suffolk U., 1997. From asst. prof. to assoc. prof. Yale Law Sch., New Haven, Conn., 1985-90, prof. law, 1990-93, Southmayd prof. law, 1993—; Samuel Rubin vis. prof. law Columbia Law Sch., N.Y.C., 1993. Author: The Constitution and Criminal Procedure, 1997, The Bill of Rights, 1998; co-author: For the People, 1998. Recipient Paul M. Bator award Federalist Soc., 1993; named 36th Ann. Coen lectr. U. Colo., 1992, Dillard lectr. U. Va., 1994, 7th ann. Barrett lectr. U. Calif., Davis, 1994, 57th Cleveland-Marshall lectr., 1994, Rutgers-Camden U., 1995, Suffolk U., 1996, Tuft lectr. U. Cin., 1998, Seegers lectr. Valparasio, 1998; DePaul Coll. Law Disting. scholar, 1991. Mem. United Ch. of Christ.

AMARA, LUCINE, opera and concert singer; b. Hartford, Conn., Mar. 1, 1925; d. George and Adrine (Kazanjian) Armaganian; married, Jan. 7, 1961 (div. June 1964). Student, Music Acad. of West, 1947, U. So. Calif., 1949-50. Artistic dir. N.J. Assn. Verismo Opera, Ft. Lee, Hackensack, N.J.; tchr. master classes, U.S., Mex. Appeared at Hollywood Bowl, 1948, soloist, San Francisco Symphony, 1949-50; career includes over 1000 operatic performances; with Met. Opera, N.Y.C., from 1950, sang 800 performances, 9 new prodns., 5 opening nights, 57 radio broadcasts, 4 telecasts including appeared on Met. Opera: In Performance, 1982, 83, 84, 85, 86, 87, 88, 90, 91; recorded Pagliacci, 1951, 60; singer with New Orleans, Hartford, Pitts., Central City operas, 1952-54, appeared Glyndebourne Opera, 1954, 55, 57, 58, Edinburgh Festival, 1954, singer, Aida, Terme Di Caracalla, Rome, 1954, also Stockholm Opera, N.Y. Philharm., St. Louis Civic Light Opera, 1955-56; has appeared in leading or title roles in several operas including: Tosca,

Aida, Amelia in Un Ballo in Maschera, Turandot, Riverside Opera Assn., 1986, others; appeared with St. Petersburg (Fla.) Opera, Venezuela Philharm. Orch., 1988, 93; opera and concert tour, USSR, 1965, 91, Manila, 1968, Paris, Mex., 1966, Hong Kong and China, 1983, Yugoslavia, 1988; rec. artist, Columbia, RCA, Victor, Angel records, Met. Opera Record Club; albums include: Beethoven's Symphony No. 9, Leon Cavallo, I Pagliacci, La Bohème, Verdi's Requiem. Recipient 1st prize Atwater-Kent Radio Auditions, 1948; inducted to Acad. Vocal Arts Hall Fame, 1989. Mem. N.J. Assn. Verismo Opera Assn. (artistic dir.). Office: Met Opera New York NY 10023-3659 *My life has been filled with new experiences. I have been most fortunate to have achieved a career that has introduced me to so many wonderful people. Some have become close friends; others, because of time and distance, have become warm acquaintances. I am humbly grateful for all God's blessings.*

AMAREL, SAUL, computer scientist, educator; b. Thessaloniki, Greece, Feb. 16, 1928; came to U.S., 1957, naturalized, 1962; s. Albert and Sol (Pelossof) Amario; m. Marianne Kroh, Dec. 20, 1953; children: Dan, David; m. Irene Rosenberg, Oct. 13, 1990. B.Sc., Israel Inst. Tech., Haifa, 1948, Ingenieur EE, 1949; M.S., Columbia, 1953, D.Eng. Sci, 1955. Sci. dep. Israel Ministry Def., 1948-52, project leader control and computer systems, 1955-57; research engr. Electronic Research Lab., Columbia, 1953-55; head computer theory research RCA Labs., Princeton, N.J., 1957-69; prof. computer sci. Rutgers U., New Brunswick, N.J., 1969-87, Alan M. Turing prof. computer sci., 1987—, chmn. dept. computer sci., 1969-84, dir. Lab. Computer Sci. Research, 1977-84, dir. Rutgers Research Resource in Computers in Medicine, 1971-83; dir. info. processing tech. office Def. Advanced Research Projects Agy., 1985-86, dir. Info. Sci. and Tech. Office, 1986-87; vis. prof. computer sci. Carnegie Mellon U., 1966, vis. sr. research scientist, spring 1985; vis. scholar Stanford U., 1979; vis. research fellow SRI Internat., spring 1983; dir. Hypercomputing & Design project Rutgers U., 1993—; mem. chmn./biol. info. handling rev. com. NIH, 1971-75; mem. info. sci. adv. com. N.J. Dept. Higher Edn., 1973-76; mem. exec. and adv. coms. SUMEX-AIM, 1974-90; trustee Internat. Joint Confs. Artificial Intelligence, 1981-89, gen. chmn., 1983; mem. nat. adv. com. Bionet, 1984-87; bd. dirs. N.J. Ednl. Computer Network, 1975-80; chair Fed. Coordinating Coun. for Sci. Engring. and Tech. of Office of Sci. and Tech. Policy Subcom. on Computer R&D, 1986-87; advanced tech. adv. com. NASA, 1987-90; mem. Info. Sci. and tech. Study Group, Inst. Def. Analyses, 1987-95, com. on scis. and arts, computer and cognitive cluster Franklin Inst., 1991-95. Mem. editl. bd. Artificial Intelligence, Internat. Jour., 1969-96, Jour. Computer Langs., 1974-85, Machine Learning Jour., 1984-94, Ency. Artificial Intelligence, 1983—, Symbolic Computation book series, 1984—; contbr. articles to sci. jours. Trustee Ramapo Coll., N.J., 1969-73, Charles Babbage Found., 1995—, bd. dirs., 1996—. Fellow IEEE, AAAS, Am. Assn. Artificial Intelligence (founding, exec. coun. 1982-86); mem. Soc. Indsl. and Applied Math., Assn. Computing Machinery, Sigma Xi. Home: 24 James Ct Princeton NJ 08540-2623 Office: Rutgers U Hill Ctr Busch Campus Dept Computer Sci New Brunswick NJ 08903

AMARI, JANE, editor; b. Phila.. BS in Comm., U. Ill.; MBA, Calif. State U. Staff mgr. Times Mirror, Knight Ridder, St. Petersburg Times; mng. editor Daily News, L.A., Rockford (Ill.) Register Star; mng. editor Kansas City Star, sr. v.p.; exec. editor The News Jour, New Castle, Del., 1997—; instr. journalism U. So. Calif., UCLA, U. Kans., U. Mo. Office: The News Jour 950 W Basin Rd New Castle DE 19720

AMARILIOS, JOHN ALEXANDER, lawyer, real estate consultant; b. Jamaica, N.Y., Apr. 18, 1958; s. Alexander Arthur and Amalia (Tomazinou) A. BS, LeHigh U., 1980, MBA, 1981; JD, U. Bridgeport, 1987. Bar: Conn., 1987, U.S. Dist. Ct., Conn. 1987. Ops. mgr. Bavarian Precision Products, New Canaan, Conn., 1981-84; import mgr. Omega Svc. Parts Corp., New Canaan, 1984-85; cons. Union Carbide Corp., Danbury, Conn., 1985-88; assoc. Tate, Capasse, Johnson, Westport, Conn., 1988, Lev, Spalter Berlin & Certilman PC, Rowayton, Conn., 1988-90; pvt. practice Stamford, Conn., 1991—; real estate cons. Union Carbide Corp., Danbury, Conn., 1985-88, Praxair Inc., Danbury Conn., 1993—. Vol. counsel Am. Radio Relay League, Newington, Conn., 1988—; past pres. Stamford chpt. Order of AHEPA. Mem. ABA, Conn. Bar Assn., Market Technicians Assn., Stamford Amateur Radio Assn., US Power Squadrons (past comdr. Darien chpt.),Iv anhoe Lodge (past master), 107 (Darien, Conn.). Avocations: sailing, amateur radio, electronics, horticulture. Home: PO Box 28 New Canaan CT 06840-0028 Office: 31 Parker Ave Stamford CT 06906-1713

AMATO, ANTHONY J., director state aviation department; b. Phila., Jan. 18, 1937. AA, U. Md., 1964. Enlisted U.S. Army, 1953, rose through ranks to 1st sgt., resigned, 1978; svc. contractor U.S. Govt., 1980-86; flight instr. pvt. practice, Cheswold, Del., 1987-93; dir. aviation dept. transp. State of Del., Dover, 1993—. Mem. Nat. Assn. Aviation Officials, Nat. Bus. Assn., Inc. Office: Del Dept Transp Office Aeronautics PO Box 778 Dover DE 19903

AMATO, CAMILLE JEAN, manufacturing executive; b. N.Y.C., Aug. 6, 1942; d. William and Mary Carmela (Lombardi) Tuorto; m. Thomas Amato, June 1, 1963; children: Dawn, Thomas. Assoc. Sci., SUNY, Albany, 1981, BS, 1983; BS, Empire State Coll., 1983, MBus and Policy, 1986. Lic. realtor, N.Y. Controller, owner Island Marine Inc., Bellmore, N.Y., 1977-93; account mgr. L.I. Luth. Assn., Brookville, N.Y., 1983-84, Borden Inc. Chem., Glen Cove, N.Y., 1984-85; real estate agt. N. of 25A R.E. Inc., Locust Valley, N.Y., 1986—; owner, pres. Penn Yan (N.Y.) Marine Mfg. Inc., 1986—; pres., owner Camille Properties, Inc., Penn Yan, 1986—; pres. Pendragon Co., 1991—; cons. in field. Cons. sub-com. edn. and safety N.Y. State Senate, 1976-77; exec. trustee Penn Yan Boat Mus., 1990—. Mem. NAFE. Roman Catholic. Avocation: classical piano. Home: Woodstock Manor Muttontown Oyster Bay NY 11771

AMATO, ISABELLA ANTONIA, real estate executive; b. Noto, Italy, July 17, 1942; d. Raimondo and Giuseppa (Pinna) Sesta; m. Vincent Amato; children: Alice, Claudine. Acctg. diploma, Inst. Tech. and Commerce, 1962. Cert. Comml. Investment Mgr., Comml. Investment Inst., Specialist Real Estate Securities, Real Estate Securities and Syndication Inst. V.p., dir. Thomas F. Seay & Assocs., Chgo., 1977-81; treas. Seay & Thomas Inc., Chgo., 1979-81; CFO Group One Investments, Chgo., 1981—; exec. v.p., registered prin. First Group Securities, Ltd., Chgo., 1983-95, pres., 1995—. Vol. translator Altrusa Lang. Bank, Chgo., 1980-86; v.p. Jr. Woman Club, Elk Grove Village, Ill., 1977; chairperson Atty. Exec. Forum, Chgo., 1985. Mem. Nat. Assn. Securities Dealers (prin.), Nat. Assn. Realtors, Chgo. Real Estate Bd., Real Estate Fin. Forum, Altrusa Profl. Woman (treas. Chgo. club 1984-85). Office: Group One Investments 77 W Washington St Ste 1005 Chicago IL 60602-2805

AMATO, VINCENT VITO, business executive; b. Bklyn., Oct. 14, 1929; s. Anthony and Josephine (Maniscalco) A.; m. Marie Dioguardi, Apr. 24, 1955; children—Stephanie, Janine, Anthony, Christopher. B.B.A., CCNY, 1951, M.B.A., 1958. Liaison to div. contr. Allied Chem. Corp., N.Y.C., 1951-59; acctg. systems rep. Olivetti-Underwood, N.Y.C., 1958-61; v.p. planning, contr., acquisitions exec. Ingredient Tech. SuCrest Corp., N.Y.C., 1961-72, v.p. planning, treas., 1972-73, pres. splty. products, 1973-78; pres., owner Market Makers Inc., Woodbridge, N.J., 1978-97; owner Automated Computer Engring. Inc., Woodbridge, N.J., 1991-97; adj. asst. prof. NYU; presenter seminars Am. Mgmt. Assn.; mem. food sci. adv. bd. Rutgers U., 1988—, also adv. bd. Cook Coll. Rutgers U. Pres. Lakeridges Civic Assn. Mem. Fin. Execs. Inst., Assn. for Corp. Growth, Am. Mgmt. Assn. (tech. adviser). Home and Office: Vincent V Amato Mktg Consulting 7 Alder Ct Matawan NJ 07747-3717

AMATOS, BARBARA HANSEN, accounting executive; b. Toledo, Aug. 30, 1944; d. John Richard and Irene Emily (Greunke) Hansen; m. James David Mokren, Sept. 12, 1964 (div. Feb. 1974); children: Frederic Hansen Mokren, Jennifer Joy Mokren; m. David Michael Amatos, Dec. 27, 1975; 1 stepchild, Anthony Steven. Student, Capital U., 1962-64, Cen. Mich. U., 1965-66; BBA, Franklin U., 1979. CPA, Ohio; cert. fraud examiner, cert. govt. fin. mgr. Account clk. Buckeye Mart, Columbus, Ohio, 1971-73, SCOA Industries Inc., Columbus, 1973-75; payroll mgr. City of Columbus Auditor's Office, 1975-86; mgmt. adv. cons. State of Ohio Auditor's Office, Columbus, 1986-87, acctg. mgr., 1987-95; fiscal officer I Ohio Dept. Human Svcs., Columbus, 1995—; ptnr. McGuiness Amatos Properties. Mem. Assn. Govt. Accts. (regional v.p. 1996—, pres. 1993-94, exec. com. 1989-90, emerging issues task force), Nat. Assn. Human Svcs. Fin. Officers. Office: Ohio Dept Human Svcs 30 E Broad St Columbus OH 43215-3414

AMAVISCA, EDWARD DEAN, electrical engineer; b. Yuma, Ariz., Aug. 12, 1965; s. Robert Manuel and Anna-Teresa (Mendoza) A.; m. Jamie Sue Felkins, July 7, 1995; stepchildren: Candice Cruz, Jesse Cruz. BSEE, U. Ariz., 1988, MS, 1991. Rsch. engr. asst. Allied Signal Aerospace, Phoenix, 1984-90; elec. engr. II Ariz. Pub. Svc. Co., Phoenix, 1992-99; computer engr. Info. Tech., 1997—. Mem. Soc. Hispanic Profl. Engrs. Republican. Roman Catholic. Avocations: running, swimming, hiking, skiing, music. Home: 20275 N 51st Dr Glendale AZ 85308-9319 Office: Ariz Pub Svc Co PO Box 52034 Phoenix AZ 85072-2034

AMBACH, DWIGHT RUSSELL, retired foreign service officer; b. Highland Park, Ill., Jan. 9, 1931; s. Russell William and Ethel (Repass) A.; m. Betsy Hunter, Aug. 27, 1955; children: Hunter MacKay, Nancy Cole, James Gordon. A.B., Brown U., 1952; M.A., Fletcher Sch., 1953; postgrad., MIT, 1963-64. Dep. dir. Office Regional Econ. Policy, Bur. Inter-Am. Affairs Dept. State, Washington, 1971-74; exec. asst. to chmn. Export-Import Bank, Washington, 1974-76, 84-86; counselor for econ. and comml. affairs Am. Embassy, Vienna, Austria, 1976-80; dean Fgn. Service Inst., Washington, 1980-84; office dir. Bur. Adminstrn. and Info. Services, 1986-88; cons., 1988-96; mem. Fgn. Svc. Res. Corps, 1993-96. Pres. Montgomery County chpt. Md. Mcpl. League. Recipient Superior Honor award Dept. State, 1973; Disting. Service award Export-Import Bank, 1985. Mem. Am. Fgn. Service Assn., Am. Econ. Assn., Phi Beta Kappa. Home: Aldendale PO Box 26 Susan VA 23163-0026

AMBACH, GORDON MAC KAY, educational association executive; b. Providence, Nov. 10, 1934; s. Russell W. and Ethel (Repass) A.; m. Lucy DeWitt Emory, Mar. 9, 1963; children: Kenneth Emory, Alison Repass, Douglas Mac Kay. BA, Yale U., 1956; MA, Harvard U. Grad. Sch. Edn., 1957, cert. advanced study, 1966. Tchr. social studies 7th and 8th grades East Williston Sch. Dist., L.I., N.Y., 1958-61; asst. program planning officer U.S. Office Edn., Washington, 1961-62, asst. legis. specialist, 1962-63, exec. sec. Higher Edn. Facilities Act Task Force, 1963-64; adminstrv. asst. to mem. Boston Sch. Com., 1964-65; staff seminar mgr., mem. staff Harvard U. Grad. Sch. Edn., Cambridge, Mass., 1966-67; spl. asst. to commr. for long range planning N.Y. State Edn. Dept., Albany, 1967-69, asst. commr. for long range planning, 1969-70, exec. dep. commr., 1970-77; commr. edn. and pres. U. State N.Y., Albany, 1977-87; exec. dir. Coun. Chief State Sch. Officers, Washington, 1987—; del., chmn. resolutions com. The White House Conf. on Librs. and Info. Scis., 1991; mem. Nat. Coun. on Edn. Standards and Testing; chmn. nat. adv. panel Ctr. Student Testing, Evaluation and Standards, Rsch. Ctr. on Learning Techs.; mem. adv. com. Getty Edn. Inst. for Arts; mem. Nat. Bd. Internat. Comparative Studies in Edn., U.S. rep. to Internat. Assn. for Evaluation of Edn. Achievement, mem. standing com. With USAR, 1957-63. Mem. Acad. Polit. Scis., Am. Assn. Sch. Adminstrs., World Standing Commns., PEW Forum on Edn. Reform, Phi Delta Kappa. Office: Coun Chief State Sch Officers One Massachusetts Ave NW Ste 700 Washington DC 20001

AMBARUCH, ARTHUR H., engineer; b. Feb. 12, 1963. BA, Union Coll., 1985; MEng., Cornell U., 1986; MBA, U. Mich., 1990. Supr. bus./cycle planning Ford Motor Co., Dearborn, Mich., 1995-97, engring. launch leader, 1998—. Office: 579 Glenmoore Ann Arbor MI 48103

AMBER, DOUGLAS GEORGE, lawyer; b. East Chicago, Ind., Apr. 15, 1956; s. George and Margaret (Watson) A. BA in Polit. Sci., Ind. U., 1978; JD, U. Miami, 1985. Bar: Fla. 1985, US. Ct. Claims 1986, U.S. Ct. Internat. Trade 1986, U.S. Tax Ct. 1986, U.S. Ct. Appeals (11th cir.) 1986, U.S. Dist. Ct. (mid. and so. dists.) Fla. 1987, U.S. Ct. Mil. Appeals 1987, U.S. Ct. Appeals (fed. cir.) 1987, Ind. 1988, U.S. Dist. Ct. (no. and so. dists.) Ind. 1988, U.S. Ct. Appeals (7th cir.) 1989, U.S. Supreme Ct. 1989. Dep. prosecutor 31st Jud. Cir. Ind., Crown Point, 1988-93; pvt. practice Munster, 1993—; adj. prof. polit. sci. Purdue U., 1997—. Mem. exec. bd. dirs. Calumet coun. Boy Scouts Am., 1994-96. Mem. ABA, Acad. Legal Studies in Bus., Nat. Dist. Attys. Assn., South Lake County Bar Assn., Ind. State Bar Assn., Lake County Bar Assn. (bd. dirs. 1990-96), Ind. Trial Lawyers Assn., Audio Engring. Soc., Soc. Audio Cons. (cert. video and audio cons.), Mensa, Delta Theta Phi. Avocations: bicycling, weight training. E-mail: amber@axp.calumet.Purdue.edu. Office: Amber & Golding Attorneys at Law 9250 Columbia Ave Ste 2E Munster IN 46321-3530

AMBERG, THOMAS L., public relations executive; b. Glen Cove, N.Y., Apr. 13, 1948; s. Richard Hiller Amberg and Janet Law Volkman; m. Tauna Urban, June 19, 1971 (div. Jan. 1980); children: Edward, Robert; m. Kathy Stewart, Oct. 9, 1982; 1 child, Thomas Jr. BA, Colgate U., 1971; MBA, U. Mo., St. Louis, 1980. Reporter, editor St. Louis Globe-Democrat, 1971-83; pres., coo Aaron D. Cushman and Assocs., Chgo., 1991—. Mem. adv. bd. Salvation Army, St. Louis, 1986-91, Chgo., 1992—; bd. dirs. Wishing Well Found., St. Louis, 1985-91, Hope Ctr., St. Louis, 1985-91; bd. trustees St. Patrick's Sch., Chgo., 1994—. Recipient Disting. Achievement award Inland Daily Press Assn., 1978, 82, Frank Kelly Meml. award, 1980, Gavel award ABA, 1983, Unity awards in Media Lincoln U., 1984. Mem. Mental Health Assn. St. Louis (pres. 1987-88), Pub. Relations Soc. Am., Press. Club Met. St. Louis (pres. 1981-83), Internat. Assn. Bus. Communicators, Soc. Am. Writers. Presbyterian. Home: 1783 Bowling Green Dr Lake Forest IL 60045-3559 Office: Aaron D Cushman & Assocs Inc 35 E Wacker Dr Ste 850 Chicago IL 60601-2122*

AMBLER, BRUCE MELVILLE, energy company executive; b. Phila., Apr. 12, 1939; s. Charles Melville Jr. and Elizabeth (Moxey) A.; m. Margaret Ogilby, June 16, 1961; children: Sharon D. Ambler Brosnan, Constance R. Ambler Tjarksen, Bruce M. Jr. BSChemE, Yale U., 1961; MBA, U. Pa., 1963. Mktg. mgr. Process Equipment, 1964-68; gen. mgr. Indsl. Chemicals, 1968-70, gen. mgr. Japan, 1970-72; gen. mgr. bus. areas Process Systems Group, 1972-75; joint mng. dir. Air Products Ltd., 1975-79; v.p. Internat. Air Products & Chemicals., 1979-80; sr. v.p. Catalytic Inc., 1980-86; v.p. Constellation Holdings Inc., Balt., 1986-87; pres. Constellation Energy Inc., Balt., 1987-89; pres., chief exec. officer Constellation Holdings Inc., Balt., 1989—, also bd. dirs.; bd. dirs., chmn. bd., CEO Constellation Power Inc., Constellation Real Estate Group Inc., Constellation Investments Inc., Constellation Oper. Svcs. Inc., Constellation Real Estate, Inc., Constellation Properties, Inc., Constellation Health Svcs. Inc., Constellation Sr. Svcs., Inc., CPI Ch. St. Inc.; bd. dirs. Constellation Realty Mgmt., LLC, Triad Investors Corp., chmn. audit com. Trustee The Walters Art Gallery, mem. com. on trustees, fin. com., mem. Walters 2000 com.; trustee Alcohol Beverage Med. Rsch. Found., mem. exec. com.; trustee Md. Sci. Ctr., chmn. fin. com.; bd. dirs. Greater Balt. Med. Ctr. Healthcare Inc., treas., chmn. fin./investment com., mem. compensation com, mem. bd. devel. com., strategic options task force. Mem. Merion Golf Club, Phila. Country Club, Pine Valley Golf Club, Center Club (membership com.), Green Spring Valley Hunt Club, Caves Valley Club Inc. Office: Constellation Holdings Inc 250 W Pratt St Ste 2300 Baltimore MD 21201-2437 also: Baltimore Gas & Electric Co PO Box 1475 Baltimore MD 21203-1475

AMBORSKI, LEONARD EDWARD, chemist; b. Buffalo, Aug. 23, 1921; s. Nicholas Leon and Angeline (Laskowska) A.; m. Irene Kazmierczak, Oct. 3, 1944; children: Donna Marie, David Paul. BS, Canisius Coll., 1943; MA, SUNY, Buffalo, 1949, PhD, 1951. Cert. indsl. hygienist Am. Bd. Indsl. Hygiene; cert. EPA instr. in lead abatement and hazardous materials worker tng. Instr. physics Canisius Coll., 1943-44; physicist Carnegie Mellon Inst., Washington, 1944-45; with E.I. DuPont de Nemours & Co., Buffalo, 1945-90, staff scientist, 1973-90, environ. health cons., 1973-90; cons. in environ. health, 1990—; rsch. assoc. Toxicoloty Rsch. Ctr., SUNY, Buffalo. Patentee in field. Bd. dirs. Am. Lung Assn. of N.Y. State, Buffalo, 1985—; chmn. Tonawanda (N.Y.) Citizen Pre-Treatment Program, 1985-86, Tonawanda Hazardous Materials Adv. Com., Buffalo, 1985-88; chmn. local emergency planning comm. Buffalo and Erie County, N.Y., 1988—; mem. citizens adv. com. Remedial Action Plan for Niagara River. Recipient Indsl. and Hazardous Waste award N.Y. State Water Pollution Control Assn., 1989. Mem. Air Pollution Control Assn. (chmn. 1983-84, Svc. award 1984), Am. Chem. Soc., Am. Indsl. Hygiene Assn., Am. Bd. Indsl. Hygiene, Am. Pub. Health Assn., Am. Soc. Safety Engrs., Water Pollution Control Fedn. Republican. Roman Catholic. Avocations: photography, swimming, cycling. Home: 62 Wedgewood Dr Buffalo NY 14221-1469

AMBROSE, ASHLEY AVERY, football player; b. New Orleans, Sept. 17, 1970. Student, Mississippi Valley State U. Cornerback Indpls. Colts, 1992-95, Cin. Bengals, 1996-99, New Orleans Saints, 1999—. Named to Pro Bowl, 1996. Office: c/o New Orleans Saints 5800 Airline Dr Metairie LA 70003*

AMBROSE, CHARLES STUART, sales executive; b. Jacksonville, NC, Nov. 28, 1951; s. Samuel Sheridan and Elizabeth (Stansbury) A. BBA, Emory U., 1974. Asst. mgr. Fifth Quarter Restaurant Shoney's, Birmingham, Ala., 1975; asst. chemist Mackay Paint Co., Birmingham, 1975-76; salesman, sales mgr. Francis & Lusky Co., Nashville, 1976-85; pres. SST Sales Co., Inc., Nashville, 1982—. Republican. Presbyterian. Home: 226 Waterview Dr Hendersonville TN 37075-5662 Office: SST Sales Co Inc 226 Waterview Dr Hendersonville TN 37075-5662

AMBROSE, DANIEL MICHAEL, publishing executive; b. Salem, Oreg., Nov. 1, 1955; s. Franklin Burnell and Jean Marie (Crakes) A.; m. Cynthia Barbara Friedman, Mar. 26, 1983; children: Robert Grant, Michael Bruce. BS in Polit. Sci., Lewis and Clark Coll., 1977. Mktg. mgr. Washington Monthly, 1978-79; advt. promotion mgr. Am. Film Mag., Washington, 1979-80, advt. mgr., 1980-81, advt. dir., 1981-83; advt. dir. Backpacker Mag., N.Y.C., 1983-84; advt. salesman House Beautiful, Hearst Mag., N.Y.C., 1984-85; corp. advt. dir. mag. div. Hearst Pub. Corp., N.Y.C., 1985-87; pub. Fathers Mag., N.Y.C., 1987-89; advt. dir. Cahners Pub. Co., N.Y.C., 1989-92; pub. Child Mag. Network Women's Mag. div. N.Y. Times Co., N.Y.C., 1992-94; mng. dir. ambro.com., N.Y.C., 1994—, DeSilva & Phillips Media Investment Bankers, N.Y.C., 1998—; interactive media cons., investments and sales, N.Y.C., 1994—. Contbr. articles on mag. mgmt. to Folio mag. Avocation: collecting books on publishing, skiing, tennis. Home: 3810 Vine Maple Dr Eugene OR 97405

AMBROSE, DONETTA W., federal judge; b. 1945. BA, Duquesne U., 1967, JD cum laude, 1970. Law clerk to Hon. Louis L. Manderino Commonwealth Ct. Pa., 1970-71, Supreme Ct. Pa., 1972; asst. atty. gen. Pa. Dept. Justice, 1972-74; pvt. practice atty. Ambrose & Ambrose, Kensington, Pa., 1974-81; asst. dist. atty. Westmoreland County, Pa., 1977-81; judge Ct. Common Pleas Westmoreland County, 1982-93, U.S. Dist. Ct. (we. dist.) Pa., Pitts., 1994—; resident advisor Duquesne U., 1967-70. Scholar Pa. Conf. State Trial Judges, 1992, State Justice Inst., 1993. Mem. ABA, Nat. Assn. Women Judges, Am. Judicature Soc., Pa. Bar Assn., Women's Bar Assn. Western Pa., Pa. Conf. State Trial Judges (sec. 1992-93), Westmoreland County Bar Assn., Italian Sons and Daus. Am., William Penn Fraternal Assn., New Kensington Women's Club, Delta Kappa Gamma. Office: 911 US Courthouse Office & Courthouse 700 Grant St Pittsburgh PA 15219*

AMBROSE, JAMES RICHARD, consultant, retired government official; b. Bangor, Maine, Aug. 16, 1922; s. James and Helen A.; m. Diane Ruth Johnson, Nov. 11, 1981; children by previous marriage: James, David, Gregory, Jeffery. Degree in engring. physics, U. Maine, 1943; postgrad., Georgetown U., Cath. U., U. Md. Staff Naval Research Lab., Washington, to 1955; with Lockheed Corp., 1955; v.p. Ford Aerospace and Communication Corp., to 1979; undersec. U.S. Army, 1981-88, acquisitions sec., 1987-88, ret., 1988; cons., 1989—. Recipient Disting. Engring. and Sci. award U. Maine, 1983, Disting. Pub. Svc. medal Dept. Defense, 1988. Mem. Am. Phys. Soc.

AMBROSE, JUDITH ANN, designer; b. San Jose, Calif., Oct. 22, 1940; d. Howard Linse and Beula May (Russell) Shannon; m James Paul Ambrose Sr., Apr. 17, 1965; children: Sheryl Ann Beckey, James Paul Jr. BS, Salem Coll., Winston-Salem, N.C., 1962; postgrad., Purdue U., 1963-64. Lic. home econ. tchr., Fla., N.C. Home econs. tchr. Broward County, Ft. Lauderdale, Fla., 1962-67; owner Decorative Accents, Ft. Lauderdale, 1984—; wedding coord. Christ Ch. United Meth., Ft. Lauderdale, 1990—; home econs. curriculum dir. Broward County Schs., Ft. Lauderdale, 1965, 66; pres. Parent Tchr. Fellowship, Westminster Acad., 1982-83. Bd. dirs. Jack & Jill Nursery Sch., Ft. Lauderdale, 1974—; bd. dirs. Children's Diagnostic and Treatment Ctr., Ft. Lauderdale, 1996—, mem. Resource Group, 1997—; founder Friends of Jack and Jill Nursery, Ft. Lauderdale; organizer shoe fund for children in cmty. Christ Meth. Ch., 1992—. Recipient Outstanding Cmty. Svc. award Jr. League of Ft. Lauderdale, 1989, Golden Rule award J.C. Penney, Ft. Lauderdale, 1995. Mem. AAUW, Charity Guild (publicity chmn. 1993-96, '92 and '97 chmn. fall function, pres. 1998-99), Coral Ridge Jr. Women's Club (hon.; past pres., Clubwoman of Yr. 1975-76). Republican. Methodist. Avocations: growing orchids, volunteer work. Home: 4720 NE 25th Ave Fort Lauderdale FL 33308-4811

AMBROSE, MYLES JOSEPH, lawyer; b. N.Y.C., July 21, 1926; s Arthur P.. and Ann (Campbell) A.; m. Elaine Miller, June 26, 1948 (dec. Sept. 1975); children: Myles Joseph, Kathleen Anne, Kevin Arthur, Elise Mary, Nora Jeanne, Christopher Miller; m. Lorraine Genovese, June 3, 1994. Grad., New Hampton Sch., N.H., 1944; BBA, Manhattan Coll., 1948, LLD (hon.), 1972; JD, N.Y. Law Sch., 1952. Bar: N.Y. 1952, U.S. Supreme Ct. 1969, D.C. 1973, U.S. Ct. Appeals (fed. cir.) 1970, U.S. Ct. Internat. Trade 1970, D.C. Ct. Appeals 1973. Pers. mgr. Devenco, Inc., 1948-49, 51-54; adminstrv. asst. U.S. atty. So. dist., N.Y., 1954-57; instr. econs. and indsl. rels. Manhattan Coll., 1955-57; asst. to sec. U.S. Treasury, 1957-60; exec. dir. Waterfront Commn. of N.Y. Harbor, 1960-63; pvt. practice law N.Y.C., 1963-69; chief counsel N.Y. State Joint Legislative Com. for Study Alcoholic Beverage Control Law, 1963-65; U.S. commr. customs Washington, 1969-72, spl. cons. to Pres., spl. asst. atty. gen., 1972-73; ptnr. Spear & Hill, 1973-75, Ambrose & Casselman, P.C., 1975-79, O'Connor & Hannan, Washington, 1980-88; ptnr. Ross and Hardies, Washington, 1988-98, of counsel, 1990-97; of counsel Arter & Hadden, Washington, 1998—; U.S. observer 13th session UN Commn. on Narcotics, Geneva, Switzerland, 1958; chmn. U.S. del. 27th Gen. Assembly, Internat. Criminal Police Orgn., London, 1958, 28th Extraordinary Gen. Assembly, Paris, 1959; U.S. observer 29th Gen. Assembly, Washington, 1960; mem. U.S. del., Mexico City, 1969, Brussels, 1970, Ottawa, 1971, Frankfurt, 1972; chmn. U.S.-Mexico Conf. on Narcotics, Washington, 1960, mem. confs., Washington and; Mexico City, 1969, 70, 71, 72; chmn. U.S.-Canadian-Mexican Conf. on Customs Procedures, San Clemente, Calif., 1970; chmn. U.S. del. Customs Cooperation Coun., Brussels, 1970; chmn., Vienna, 1971, U.S.-European Customs Conf. Narcotics, Paris and; Vienna, 1971; organized drug enforcement DEA, 1973; hon. consul Principality of Monaco, Washington, 1973-98; mem. adv. com. on customs comml. ops. U.S. Treasury Dept., 1988-91. Author: Primer on Customs Law. Bd. dirs. U. Coll. of Dublin-Grad. Bus. Sch., 1996—, Daytop Village; vice chmn. Reagan-Bush Inaugural Com., 1980. Decorated Chevalier Ordre Grimaldi, 1999; recipient Presdl. Mgmt. Improvement certificate Pres. Nixon, 1970, Sec. Treasury Exceptional Service award, 1970; decorated knight comdr. Order Merit Italian Republic; recipient Distinguished Alumnus award N.Y. Law Sch., 1973, Alumni award for pub. service Manhattan Coll., 1972. Fellow Am. Bar Found.; mem. ABA (past chmn. standing com. on customs law), Friendly Sons of St. Patrick, Alpha Sigma Beta, Phi Alpha Delta (hon.). Republican. Roman Catholic. Clubs: Metropolitan (N.Y.C.); University (Washington). Home: 19385 Cypress Ridge Ter Lansdowne VA 20176 Office: Arter & Hadden 1801 K St NW Washington DC 20006

AMBROSE, SAMUEL SHERIDAN, JR., urologist; b. Jacksonville, N.C., Oct. 2, 1923; s. Samuel Sheridan and Beatrice (Collins) A.; m. Betty Stuart Stansbury, Oct. 7, 1950; children: Charles Stuart, Ann Collins, Samuel Bruce. AB in Chemistry, Duke U., 1943, MD, 1947. Diplomate: Am. Bd. Urology, Nat. Bd. Med. Examiners. Intern in surgery, then asst. resident in urology Duke U. Hosp., 1947-50, resident in urology, 1953; instr. physiology Duke U. Med. Sch., 1947, instr. urology, 1953; mem. faculty Emory U. Med. Sch., 1954—, prof. urology, 1972-92, prof. urology surgery emeritus, 1992—, chmn. div. urology, 1985-89; mem. staff Emory U. Hosp., 1972-92, chief urology, 1972-91; pvt. practice medicine specializing in urology Atlanta, 1954-71; mem. staff Piedmont Hosp., 1954-72, chief urology, 1960; mem. staff Grady Meml. Hosp., 1954-92, Henrietta Egleston Hosp. for Children, 1956-92; retired, 1992. Contbr. numerous articles to med. jours. Served as officer M.C. USNR, 1950-52. Fellow Royal Soc. Medicine; mem. AMA,

ACS, Am. Urol. Assn. (hon. mem. S.E. chpt., pres. Southeastern sect. 1974-75, chmn. nat. sci. exhibits com. 1974-83, mem. exec. com. 1983-90, Disting. Svc. award 1990, Gold Cane award 1995, hon. mem. 1996—), Soc. Pediatric Urology (pres. 1971-72), Am. Assn. Clin. Urologists, Am. Acad. Pediat., Am. Assn. Genito-Urinary Surgeons, Soc. Internat. D'Urologie, Pan-Pacific Surg. Assn., Med. Assn. Ga., Ga. Urol. Assn. (pres. 1967), So. Med. Soc. (chmn. urology sect. 1970-71), Fulton County Med. Soc., Atlanta Clin. Soc. (v.p. 1964), Soc. Univ. Urologists, Piedmont Driving Club, Cherokee Town and Country Club (pres. 1968-69), Univ. Yacht Club (commodore 1973), Homosassa Fishing Club (v.p. 1980-81, 92-94). Presbyterian. Home: 1014 Nawench Dr NW Atlanta GA 30327-1340

AMBROSE, THOMAS CLEARY, communications executive; b. Kalispell, Mont., Mar. 6, 1932; s. William Patrick and Anne Marie (Cleary) A.; m. Joyce Leona Demco, Aug. 13, 1960; children: Thomas Neal, John Alan, Bridget Sharon. BA in Journalism, U. Mont., 1952. Editor Choteau (Mont.) Acantha, 1952; reporter Daily Chronicle, Spokane, Wash., 1954-57, bus. editor, 1957-64; rep., mgr. media rels. Weyerhaeuser Co., Tacoma, 1964-74, dir. external communications, 1974-91; prin. Ambrose & Assocs., Seattle and Sun Valley, 1991—. Author, editor: Where The Future Grows, 1989. Pres. Spokane Editorial Soc., 1963-64, Spokane Press Club, 1959-60; dir. Federal Way C. of C., 1968-71, Ketchum/Sun Valley Hist. Soc., 1995-96. 1st lt. U.S. Army, 1952-54, Korea.

AMBROSE, TOMMY W., chemical engineer, executive; b. Jerome, Idaho, Oct. 14, 1926; s. Fines M. and Avice (Barnes) A.; m. Shirley Ann Ball, June 23, 1951; children: Leslie Ann, Julie Lynn, Pamela Lee. *Daughter Leslie, born 1956, married Howard Miller and have two children, Shira and Joshua. She has a B.A. cum laude from Princeton, 1980. She works as a software engineer and human factors specialist. She is currently with IDX Systems, Seattle. Daughter Julie, born 1958, married Kirke Byers in 1998. She has a B.M. from the Oberlin Conservatory of Music, 1980. She also has a MBA Arts Administration, Golden Gate University, 1994. She was Principal Harp of the Chattanooga Symphony, 1981-91. She is currently the Christensen Society Manager for the San Francisco Ballet. Daughter Pamela, born 1960, married Timothy McFarland in 1994. She studied at the New England Conservatory of Music and the Longy School of Music, BM 1983. Masters, Cello Performance, Boston University, 1993. She is a performer and teacher in the Boston area.* B.S., U. Idaho, 1950, M.S., 1951, Ph.D. (hon.), 1981; Ph.D., Oreg. State U., 1957. Registered profl. engr., Wash., Ohio, Idaho. Engr. GE, Richland, Wash., 1951-54, 57-60; supr. reactor fuels GE, 1960-63, mgr. process and reactor devel., 1963-65, mgr. rsch. and engring., 1965; mgr. for rsch. and engring. Douglas United Nuclear Co., Richland, 1969-71; asst. dir. Battelle Seattle Rsch. Ctr., 1969-71, exec. dir., 1971-75; dir. Battelle Pacific N.W. Labs., Richland, 1975-79; corp. dir. multicomponent ops. Battelle Meml. Inst., Columbus, Ohio, 1979-88, dir. Battelle Edn. and Tng. Bus., 1988-90; v.p. Battelle Meml. Inst., 1975-90; liaison officer Lawrence Livermore (Calif.) Nat. Lab., 1990-91; spl. asst. lab. affairs U. Calif., Oakland, 1992-96. Mem. adv. bd. Coll. Engring., U. Idaho, Moscow, 1974-83, 85-91, chmn. adv. bd., 1988-91; mem. vis. com. Coll. Engring., U. Wash., 1974-83; mem. gov.'s adv. coun. Dept. Commerce and Econ. Devel., 1975-79; mem. Wash. State Coun. Postsecondary Edn., 1977-79; chmn. bd. trustees Columbia Basin Coll., 1967-69; bd. dirs. N.W.Coll., U. Assn. for Sci., 1976-79; v.p., trustee, mem. exec. com. Pacific Sci. Ctr. Found.; trustee, mem. exec. com. Columbus Symphony Orch., 1980-84; trustee Ohio Wesleyan U., 1987-91. Fellow AICE (chmn. comms. com. mgmt. divsn. 1981-87, program evaluator and mem. Accreditation Bd. for Engring. and Tech. engring. accreditation commn. 1989-96); mem. Am. Nuclear Soc., Ohio Acad. Sci., Sigma Xi, Pi Lambda Upsilon. Methodist. Home: 2500 E Spider Creek Rd Inkom ID 83245-1740

AMBROSE, WILLIAM WRIGHT, JR., college dean, accounting educator, tax researcher; b. Norfolk, Va., Oct. 13, 1947; s. William Wright and Charlotte Gertrude (Williamson) A.; m. Marcelia A. Conerly, Aug. 7, 1971 (div. Dec. 1986); children: William Wright III, Xandrea M., Mark S.; m. Jacqueline D. Woodard, Dec. 28. 1998. BSBA, Norfolk State U., 1974; MBA, Pepperdine U., 1982, postgrad. Enrolled agt. IRS; lic. ins. broker, notary pub., cmty. coll. teaching credential, Calif.; cert. tax profl. Quality assurance mgr. mfg. Corning (N.Y.) Glass Co., 1974-78; contr., plant mgr. Phillip Morris, Auburn, N.Y., 1978-79; sr. exec. mgr. Kerr Glass Corp., L.A., 1979-84; instr. Nat. Edn. Corp., Anaheim, Calif., 1985-87; assoc. prof., chmn. dept. acctg. and bus. DeVry Inst. Tech., Univ. Ctr., Pomona, Calif., 1987—; entrepreneur dba The Tax Inst., 1990; cons. Protrans, Santa Ana, Calif., 1985—, Castillo Electronics, Los Alamitos, Calif., 1986, Heriberto Constrn., Santa Ana, 1985—. Co-patentee polarized contaminate viewer. Sgt. Army Security Agy., U.S. Army, 1967-71, Vietnam. Mem. AAUP, Am. Assn. Higher Edn., Nat. Assn. Acad. Affairs Adminstrs., Nat. Assn. Accts., Nat. Bus. Edn. Assn., Am. Acctg. Assn., Am. Mgmt. Assn., Am. Prodn. and Inventory Control Soc., Nat. Soc. Tax Profls., Nat. Soc. Pub. Accts., Phi Beta Lambda, Sigma Beta Delta. Avocations: computer programming, golf, writing, investing. E-Mail: wambrose@admin.pom.devry.edu. Home: 795 S Pampas Ave Rialto CA 92376-2102 Office: DeVry Inst Tech 901 Corporate Center Dr Pomona CA 91768-2642

AMBROSINO, RALPH THOMAS, JR., retired telecommunications executive; b. Gloversville, N.Y., Aug. 5, 1940; s. Ralph Thomas and Mary Agnes (Peters) A.; m. Roberta Joy Goldman, Nov. 1, 1970; children: Robin, Jill. BS in Acctg., U. Buffalo, 1961. With Gen. Telephone Co., 1968-74; gen. comml. mgr. Upstate N.Y., Johnstown, 1968-70, gen. service office mgr., 1970-74; regulatory matters mgr. GTE Service Corp., Stamford, Conn., 1974-76, revenues and earnings mgr., 1976-78; dir. regulatory affairs Gen. Telephone Co. of Calif., Santa Monica, 1979-81; dir. regulatory matters GTE Service Corp., Stamford, 1981-84, asst. v.p. investor relations, 1984-87, asst. v.p. external affairs, 1987. Mem. Investor Relations Assn. Home: 324 Sunnieholme Dr Fairfield CT 06430-6693

AMBROSIO, DEBORAH ANN, critical care nurse; b. N.Y., Aug. 21, 1959; d. Raphael J. and Lydia C. (Roman) A.; m. Bruce R. Mawhirter, Oct. 2, 1983. BSN, Adelphi U., 1981, MS, 1996. RN, N.Y. Primary nurse med./surg. unit St. Francis Hosp., Roslyn, N.Y., 1981-83, primary nurse RICU, 1983-86; asst. coord. nursing care L.I. Vascular Ctr., Roslyn, 1986-88, coord. nursing care, 1988-94, clin. nurse specialist, 1994-97; performance improvement coord. nursing South Nassau Cmtys. Hosp., Oceanside, N.Y., 1996—; adj. faculty mem. Sch. Nursing Adelphi U., 1994—. Contbr. to profl. jours. and newletters. Mem. AACCN, Am. Heart Assn. (cert. instr. CPR), N.Y. State Nurses Assn., Am. Coll. Nutrition, Soc. Peripheral Vascular Nursing, Soc. Non-Invasive Vascular Tech., Sigma Theta Tau (pres.-elect 1998-99, Alpha Omega chpt., exec. com., com. scholarship fund raising, corr. sec.).

AMBROZIC, ALOYSIUS MATTHEW (HIS EMINENCE ALOYSIUS CARDINAL AMBROZIO), cardinal archbishop; b. Gabrje, Slovenia, Jan. 27, 1930; s. Aloysius and Helen (Pecar) A. Student, St. Augustine Sem., 1955; S.T.L., U. San Tommaso, Rome, 1958, Sacrae Scripturae Licentiatus, Biblicum, Rome, 1960; Th.D., U. Wurzburg, 1970. Ordained priest Roman Cath. Ch., 1955. Ordained aux. bishop of Roman Cath. Ch., Toronto, 1976; appointed coadjutor archbishop of Toronto, 1986, archbishop of Toronto, 1990—, created cardinal, 1998; parish work Port Colborne, Ont., Can., 1955-56; faculty St. Augustines Sem., Scarborough, Ont., Can., 1956-76, dean studies, 1971-76; prof. N.T. exegesis Toronto Sch. Theology, 1970-76; apptd. to Pontifical Coun. for Pastoral Care of Migrants and Itinerant People, 1990, Vatican Congregation for Clergy, 1991, Pontifical Coun. for Culture, 1993, Vatican Congregation for Divine Worship and Discipline of Sacraments, 1999; rep. Synod on the Formation of Priests, Rome, 1990, Synod on Religious Life, Rome, 1994. Author: The Hidden Kingdom: A Redaction-Critical Study of the References to the Kingdom of God in Mark's Gospel, 1972, Remarks on the Canadian Catechism, 1974; columnist The Cath. Register.

AMBRUS, CLARA MARIA, physician; b. Rome, Dec. 28, 1924; came to U.S., 1949, naturalized, 1955; d. Anthony and Charlotte (Schneider) Bayer; m. Julian Lawrence Ambrus, Feb. 17, 1945; children: Madeline Ambrus Lillie, Peter, Julian, Linda Ambrus-Broenniman, Steven, Katherine Ambrus-Cheney, Charles. Student, U. Budapest (Hungary), 1943-47; MD, U. Zurich, Switzerland, 1949; postgrad., U. Paris, 1949; PhD, Jefferson Med. Coll., 1955. Diplomate: Am. Bd. Clin. Chemists. Research asst. Inst. Histology, Embryology and Biology U. Budapest, 1943-45; demonstrator in pharmacology U. Budapest Med. Sch., 1946-47; asst. dept. pharmacology U. Zurich Med. Sch., 1947-49; asst. dept. therapeutic chemistry and virology Inst. Pasteur, Paris, 1949; asst. prof. pharmacology Phila. Coll. Pharmacy and Sci., 1950-52, asso. prof., 1952-55; research asso. Roswell Park Meml. Inst., Buffalo, 1955-58; sr. cancer research scientist Roswell Park Meml. Inst., 1958-64, asso. scientist, 1964-69, prin. cancer research scientist, 1969-85; prof. pharmacology State U. N.Y.; prof. pharmacology Buffalo Med. and Grad. Schs., 1955—, asso. prof. pediatrics, 1955-76, prof. pediatrics, 1976, research prof. ob-gyn, 1983—; chmn., founder, chief of R&D Hemex Inc., 1984—. Contbr. articles to med. and sci. jours. Trustee Nichols Sch., Buffalo, Community Music Sch. Named Outstanding Woman of Western N.Y. Community Adv. Council, SUNY, Buffalo, 1980, Lady Comdr. of the Equestrian Order of the Holy Sepulchre of Jerusalem, 1991, comdr., 1996; recipient George F. Koepf, MD award Hauptman-Woodward Med. Rsch. Inst., Buffalo, 1997. Fellow Am. Coll. Physicians, Internat. Soc. Hematology; mem. Am. Soc. Pharmacology and Exptl. The rapeutics, Am. Soc. Cancer Rsch., Am. Fedn. Clin. Rsch., Am. Physiol. Soc., Am. Soc. Hematology, Buffalo Acad. Medicine, Am. Med. Women's Assn., Clarksburg Country Club, Saturn Club, Garrett Club, Sigma Xi. Home: 143 Windsor Ave Buffalo NY 14209-1020 also: West Hill Farm Boston NY 14025 Office: Buffalo Gen Hosp 100 High St Buffalo NY 14203-1154

AMBRUS, JULIAN L., physician, medical educator; b. Budapest, Hungary, Nov. 29, 1924; came to U.S., 1949, naturalized, 1955; s. Alexander and Elizabeth Ambrus; m. Clara M. Bayer, Feb. 18, 1945; children: Madeline (Mrs. David Lillie), Peter, Julian, Linda (Mrs. Edward Broenniman), Steven, Katherine (Mrs. Thomas Cheney), Charles. Student. U. Budapest, 1942-47; MD., U. Zurich, 1949; postgrad., Sorbonne, 1949-50; PhD in Med. Sci, Jefferson Med. Coll., 1954; ScD (hon.), Niagara U., 1984. Diplomate: Am. Bd. Clin. Chemistry, Am. Acad. Pain Mgmt. Research asst., instr. histology U. Budapest, 1943-45, demonstrator pharmacology, 1946-47; asst. pharmacology U. Zurich, 1947-49; asst. dept. therapeutic chemistry, virology and tropical medicine Inst. Pasteur, Paris, 1949; asst. prof., asso. prof., prof. Phila. Coll. Pharmacology and Sci., 1950-55; prin. cancer research scientist Roswell Park Meml. Inst. and Hosp., 1955-65, asst. to the dir., 1961-65; dir. Springville Labs., 1965-75, dir. cancer research, head dept. pathophysiology, 1975-89, mem. dept. medicine, 1989-92; asst. prof. pharmacology U. Buffalo Med. Sch., 1955-61, asso. prof. pharmacology, 1961-65, prof., 1965-72; chmn. Roswell Park div. exec. com. Grad. Sch., 1955-65; assoc. in internal medicine SUNY, Buffalo, 1961-64, asst. prof. internal medicine, 1964-66, prof. biochem. pharmacology, 1964-80, assoc. prof. internal medicine, 1966-71, prof., 1971—; prof., chmn. dept. exptl. pathology Grad. Sch., 1972-92; prof. emeritus, 1992—; attending physician Roswell Park Meml. Cancer Hosp., 1955-92, prof. emeritus Roswell Park Cancer Inst., 1992—; attending physician Buffalo Gen. Hosp., Erie County Med. Ctr., Children's Hosp. Buffalo, 1983—; cons. Millard Fillmore Hosp., Sisters of Charity Hosp., Buffalo, 1983—; dir. Instnl. Cancer Tng. Program, USPHS, 1956-65; mem. com. Thrombolytic agts. USPHS-NIH, 1960-66; cons. adv. com. on thrombosis AMA Coun. Drugs; Blood Coagulation Components, Protein Found., Cambridge, Mass.; Bur. Drugs FDA, WHO, Geneva; commr. Lake Erie chpt. U.S. Pony Clubs, mem. intercollegiate polo com. Editor-in-chief: Revs. of Hematology Jour. Medicine; contbr. articles to profl. jours. Trustee Calasanctius Prep. Sch. for Acad. Gifted, 1964-92. Decorated Order of Alexander the Great (France), knight comdr. Equestrian Order Holy Sepulcher of Jerusalem; recipient first prize med. student paper Hungarian Med. Sch., 1947, 1st prize surgery U. Budapest, 1947, Nelson lectureship and medal U. Calif. Davis, 1972, George F. Koepf award in biomed. rsch. Hauptman-Woodward Med. Rsch. Inst., 1997, Heart and Hand award EUA, 1997, Louis A. and Ruth Siegel award SUNY Buffalo Sch. Medicine, 1997; named Disting. Alumnus Thomas Jefferson U., 1990. Fellow ACP, AAAS, Am. Coll. Nuclear Physicians, Am. Coll. Angiology, Royal Soc. Medicine, Am. Coll. Pharmacology and Chemotherapy, Coun. on Clin. Cardiology, Am. Heart Assn., Internat. Coll. Angiology, Am. Geriat. Soc., N.Y. Acad. Sci., Internat. Soc. Hematology; mem. NAS (fgn. mem. Hungary), Am. Soc. Hematology, Am. Soc. Pathologists, Am. Soc. Nuclear Medicine, Am. Soc. Pharmacology and Exptl. Therapeutics, Am. Soc. Physiology, Am. Assn. Cancer Rsch., Am. Soc. Clin. Oncology, Fedn. Clin. Rsch., Soc. Exptl. Biology and Medicine, Assn. Am. Med. Colls., Cath. Physicians Guild (pres. 1985-86, 93-96), Sigma Xi, Rho Chi, Physiol. Soc. Phila., Radiation Rsch. Soc., Buffalo Zool. Soc. (chmn. Sci. Coun. 1965-66), Buffalo Acad. Medicine (pres. 1976-77). Home: 143 Windsor Ave Buffalo NY 14209-1020 also: West Hill Farm Emmerling Rd Boston NY 14025 Office: Buffalo Gen Hosp SUNY/B 100 High St Buffalo NY 14203-1154

AMBRUS, LORNA, medical, surgical and geriatrics nurse; b. Phila., June 17, 1956; d. Walter C. and Joan B. (Watts) Beilfuss; 1 child, Victoria Ambrus. LPN, Upper Bucks Vo-Tech., Perkasie, Pa., 1976; diploma, Gwynedd Mercy Coll., Gwynedd Valley, Pa., 1989. RN. Nurse Doylestown (Pa.), Doylestown Hosp., Sellersville, Pa., Quality Care, Allentown, Pa., Comprehensive Home Care, Doylestown, Pa., Doylestown Manor. Home: 118 Jefferson Ct Quakertown PA 18951-1417

AMCHIN, ROBERT A., music educator. MusM in Music Edn. and Applied Music, New Eng. Conservatory of Music, 1981; cert., Orff Inst., Salzburg, Austria, 1981; PhD in Music and Music Edn., U. Mich., 1995. Music specialist Spring (Tex.) Ind. Sch. Dist., 1982-88; tchg. asst. U. Mich., Ann Arbor, 1988-91; temp. lectr. Ea. Mich. U., Ypsilanti, 1991; assoc. prof. music Mansfield (Pa.) U., 1992—; guest instr. Orff Cert. program, U. Cin., summer 1995, James Madison U., 1997—, U. Houston, spring/summer 1988, Mansfield U. Pa.; instr. percussion undergrad., New Eng. Conservatory of Music, Boston, spring 1981; tchr. The Am. Sch., Berchtesgarden, Germany, fall 1981; instr. music Freetown-Lakeville Pub. Schs., Freetown, Mass., winter 1982. Contbr. articles to profl. jours., chpts. to books. Active Congregation Shomray Hadath, Jewish Cmty. Ctr. of Chemung County; bd. dirs. program com. PTA, 1994-96. Mem. ASCD, Coll. Music Soc., Music Educators Nat. Conf., Music Educators Rsch. Coun., N.Y. State Suprs. Music Assn., Pa. Music Educators Assn., Soc. for Gen. Music, Soc. for Rsch. in Music Edn., Tchr. Edn. Coun., Am. Orff-Schulwerk Assn., Tex. Gulf Coast Orff-Schulwerk Assn. (life, 1st v.p. 1985-86, pres. 1986-87), Twin Tiers Orff Schulwerk Assn. (pres. 1998-99), Phi Delta Kappa, Kappa Kappa Psi. Home: 1160 W Church St Elmira NY 14905-2053

AMDAHL, BYRDELLE JOHN, business consulting executive; b. Ossian, Iowa, June 5, 1934; s. John G. and Mae (Vikse) A.; m. Agnes Nestegard, June 17, 1955 (div. May 1981); children: Gary, Mark; m. Gwen Nelson Clark, June 11, 1983. Student, Luther Coll., Decorah, Iowa, 1952-54; BBA, U. Minn., 1958, postgrad., 1971. CPA, Minn. Auditor Dept. Agr., Mpls., 1958, Ernst & Ernst, Mpls., 1958-64; exec. Cornelius Co., Mpls., 1964-74, v.p. fin., 1969-72, v.p. finance and adminstrn., 1972-73, exec. v.p., 1973-74, dir., 1971-74; exec. v.p. fin. and adminstrn., chief fin. officer Medtronic Inc., Mpls., 1974-77, exec. v.p. diversified ops., 1977-81; chmn., chief exec. officer, dir. Bionexus, Inc., 1981-87; v.p. Glaxo Latin Am. Inc., 1987-90, exec. v.p., regional dir., 1988-90; pres., chief oper. officer Orthomet, Inc., Mpls., 1990-92; pres., CEO AAMDAC Inc., Mpls., 1992-95; pres., prin. Global Bus. Ptnrs., Inc., Mpls., 1995—; pres., CEO InterAct Security Corp., St. Paul, 1995-98. Bd. dirs. Luth. Youth Encounter, 1968-75, Luth. Youth Encounter Found., 1990-96, Coun. for Entrepreneurial Devel. of N.C. Served with AUS, 1954-56. Mem. Decathlon Club, Alpha Kappa Psi.

AMDAHL, DOUGLAS KENNETH, retired state supreme court justice; b. Mabel, Minn., Jan. 23, 1919. B.B.A., U. Minn., 1945; J.D. summa cum laude, William Mitchell Coll. Law, 1951, L.L.D. (hon.), 1987. Bar: Minn. 1951, Fed. Dist. Ct. 1952. Ptnr. Amdahl & Scott, Mpls., 1951-55; asst. county atty. Hennepin County, Minn., 1955-61; judge Mcpl. Ct., Mpls., 1961-62, Dist. Ct. 4th Dist., Minn., 1962-80; chief judge Dist. Ct. 4th Dist., 1973-75; assoc. justice Minn. Supreme Ct., 1980-81, chief justice, 1981-89; of counsel Rider, Bennett, Egan & Arundel, Mpls., 1989—; asst. registrar, then registrar Mpls. Coll. Law, 1951-65; moot ct. instr. U. Minn.; faculty mem. and advisor Nat. Coll. State Judiciary; mem. Nat. Bd. Trial Advocacy; chmn. Nat. Ctr. for State Cts. Delay Reduction Adv. Com., 1986-88, Nat. Ctr. for State Cts. Coordinating Coun. on Life-Sustaining Decisionmaking by the Cts., 1989-93. Mem. ABA (chmn. com. on stds. of jud. adminstrn. 1987-96), Minn. Bar Assn., Hennepin County Bar Assn., Internat. Acad. Trial Judges, State Dist. Ct. Judges Assn. (pres. 1976-77), Conf. of Chief Judges (bd. dirs. 1987-88), Delta Theta Phi (assoc. justice supreme ct.). Home: 2322 W 53rd St Minneapolis MN 55410-2501

AMDAHL, GENE MYRON, computer company executive; b. Flandreau, S.D., Nov. 16, 1922; s. Anton E. and Inga (Brendsel) A.; m. Marian Quissell, June 23, 1946; children: Carlton Gene, Beth Delaine, Andrea Leigh. BSEE, S.D. State U., 1948, DEng (hon.), 1974; PhD, U. Wis., 1952, DSc (hon.), 1979; D.Sc. (hon.), Luther Coll., 1980, Augustana Coll., 1984. Project mgr. IBM Corp., Poughkeepsie, N.Y., 1952-55; group head Ramo-Wooldridge Corp., L.A., 1956; mgr. systems design Aeronutronics, L.A., 1956-60; mgr. systems design advanced data processing systems IBM Corp., N.Y.C., Los Gatos, Calif., Menlo Park, Calif., 1960-70; founder, chmn. Amdahl Corp., Sunnyvale, Calif., 1970-80; founder, chief exec. officer Trilogy Systems Corp., Cupertino, Calif., 1980-87; chmn. bd. Elxsi (name changed from Trilogy Systems Corp.), San Jose, Calif., 1987-89; founder, pres., CEO Andor International Ltd., Cupertino, 1987-94, also bd. dirs.; founder, chmn. Comml. Data Servers, Mountain View, Calif., 1994-98, ret., 1998. Patentee in field. With USN, 1942-44. Recipient Disting. Alumnus award S.D. State U., 1973, Centennial Alumnus award, 1987; Man of Yr. award Data Processing Mgmt. Assn., 1976, Disting. Svc. citation U. Wis., 1976, Michelson-Morley award Case Western Res. U., 1977; Harry Goode Meml. award for outstanding contbns. to design and manufacture of large, high-performance computers Am. Fedn. Info. Processing Socs., 1983, Eckert-Mauchly award 1987; Good Samaritan award City Team Ministries, San Jose, 1991, Man of Yr. Achievement award Computer Weekly mag., 1991; named to Info. Processing Hall of Fame, 1985; named One of 1000 Makers of 20th Century, London Times, 1991; laureate Jr. Achievement Bus. Hall of Fame, 1995; recipient Legend award Computer and Comm. Industry Assn., 1995; IBM fellow, 1965. Fellow IEEE, Brit. Computer Soc. (disting.), Computer Mus.; mem. Nat. Acad. Engring. IEEE (profl. group W.W. McDowell award 1976), Quadrato della Radio, Pontecchio Marcon. Presbyterian. Home: 165 Patricia Dr Atherton CA 94027-3922

AMDUR, JUDITH DEVORAH, artist, cook; b. Mpls., Sept. 18, 1948; d. Elias Joshua Amdur and Rosalyn Bassis Baker; m. Gary Dennis Jackson, May 26, 1985. BFA, Mpls. Coll. Art and Design, 1974; student, Sch. Painting and Sculpture, Skowhegan, Maine, 1973; MFA, Boston U., 1976. Exhibited in shows at Downey (Calif.) Mus. Art, 1996, LA. Mcpl. Art Gallery, 1996, San Bernardino (Calif.) County Mus., 1997, Armory Ctr. for the Arts, Pasadena, Calif., 1997; solo show at Las Vegas City Cultural Ctr., Las Vegas. Home: 2107 Camorilla Dr Los Angeles CA 90065-3401

AMDUR, MARTIN BENNETT, lawyer; b. N.Y.C., Aug. 19, 1942; s. Charles and Helen (Freedman) A.; m. Shirley Bell, May 25, 1975; children—Richard J., Stephen B. A.B., Cornell U., 1964; LL.B., Yale U., 1967; LL.M. in Taxation, NYU, 1968. Bar: N.Y. 1968, U.S. Tax Ct. 1970, U.S. Dist. Ct. (so. and ea. dists.) N.Y. 1971. With Weil, Gotshal & Manges LLP, N.Y.C., 1968—, ptnr., 1975—. Mem. ABA (sect. on taxation), N.Y. State Bar Assn. (taxation sect.), Assn. of Bar of City of N.Y., Am. Coll. Tax Counsel. Home: 17 Willow Ln Scarsdale NY 10583-3411 Office: Weil Gotshal & Manges LLP 767 5th Ave New York NY 10153

AMDURSKY, SAUL JACK, library director; b. Rochester, N.Y., Aug. 11, 1945; s. Harry S. and Eva (Forman) A.; m. Marion Susan Arndt, May 30, 1969; 1 child, Jacob Arthur. BA, St. John Fisher Coll., 1969; MSLS, U. Ky., 1971. Asst. mgr. Lincoln First Banks, Rochester, 1966-70; supervising libr. Prince William County Pub. Libr., Manassas, Va., 1971-75; dir. Albion (Mich.) Pub. Libr., 1975-79; adminstr. Racine (Wis.) County Libr. Sys., 1979-82; libr. dir. Bloomington (Ill.) Pub. Libr., 1982-87, Kalamazoo (Mich.) Pub. Libr., 1987—; interim part-time adminstr. Woodlands Libr. Coop., Albion, 1978-79; instr. Ill. State U., Normal, 1984. Contbr. articles to Libr. Jour., Ill. Librs., Va. Libr., book revs. to Libr. Jour., Sch. Libr. Jour., Am. Reference Books Ann. Mem. ALA, Mich. Libr. Assn. (pub. policy com.), Ill. Libr. Assn. (legis. com.), Pi Gamma Mu (lifetime). Office: Kalamazoo Pub Libr 315 S Rose St Kalamazoo MI 49007-5201

AMEDU, DAVIS JIMOH, industrial engineer; b. Benin City, Nigeria, Nov. 22, 1955; came to U.S., 1976; s. Okosun Onoabhagbe and Agnes Isimeme (Abhulimen) A.; m. Dorothy Grant, July 22, 1979; children: Aziz, Amina, Deaundrea, Dianna, Davis II. ASEE, Auchi Polytech., 1973; BS in Indsl. Engring., Jackson State U., 1979; MS in Indsl. Engring., Ea. Mich. U., 1980. Cert. plant engr., mfg. engr., chem. engr. London. Electrician Nigerian Ports Authority, Lagos, 1970-72; divsn. mgr. Bendel Rural Electricity Bd., Benin City, 1972-74; elec. engr. Nigerian Nat. Petroleum Co., Lagos, 1974-76; prodn. mgr. Delta Steel Co., Warri, Nigeria, 1981-84; elec. engr. Belya & Co., Jersey City, 1984-86; ops. mgr. Merck & Co., Rahway, N.J., 1986—. Mem. AIChE, ASHRAE, Am. Inst. Plant Engrs., Am. Inst. Indsl. Engrs. Baptist. Avocations: tennis, soccer, computers, travel. Home: 311 Fisher Ave Neptune NJ 07753-4630

AMEMIYA, TAKESHI, economist, statistician; b. Tokyo, Mar. 29, 1935; s. Kenji and Shizuko A.; m. Yoshiko Miyaki, May 5, 1969; children: Naoko, Kentaro. B.A., Internat. Christian U., 1958; M.A. in Econs., Am. U., 1961; Ph.D., Johns Hopkins U., 1964. Mem. faculty Stanford U., (Calif.), 1964-66, 68—, prof. econs., 1974-86, Edward Ames Edmonds prof. econs., 1986—; lectr. Inst. Econ. Research, Hitotsubashi U., Tokyo, 1966-68; cons. Author books and articles; mem. editl. bd. profl. jours. Recipient U.S. Sr. Scientist award Alexander von Humboldt Found., Fed. Republic Germany, 1988; Ford Found. fellow, 1963; Guggenheim fellow, 1975; NSF grantee; fellow Japan Soc. for Promotion of Sci., 1989. Fellow Econometric Soc., Am. Acad. Arts and Scis., Am. Statis. Assn.; mem. Internat. Statis. Inst., Am. Econ. Assn., Inst. Math. Stats., Phi Beta Kappa. Home: 923 Casanueva Pl Stanford CA 94305-1001 Office: Stanford Univ Dept of Econs Stanford CA 94305

AMEN, ROBERT ANTHONY, investor and corporate relations consultant; b. N.Y.C., June 7, 1937; s. Louis Joseph and Angela Amen; children: Brian, Allison. BA, CCNY, 1961. V.p. mktg. and communications Combustion Engring., Inc., Stamford, Conn., 1969-75; v.p. corp. relations Gulf and Western Inc., N.Y.C., 1975-77, Norton Simon Inc., N.Y.C., 1977-78; mng. dir. D.F. King & Co., Inc., N.Y.C., 1978-80; pres. Amen & Assocs., A Ketchum Comm. Company, Greenwich, Conn., 1980—; pres., CEO Ketchum Corp. Rels., 1995-97; ptnr., dir. Global Corp. Practice. Mem. Nat. Investor Relations Inst. (chmn., chief exec. officer 1988, pres. Fairfield/West chpt. 1990—), Internat. Soc. Fin. Analysts, N.Y. Soc. Security Analysts. Home: 337 North St Greenwich CT 06830-3901 Office: Amen & Assocs Inc Ketchum 55 Railroad Ave Greenwich CT 06830-6378 also: 292 Madison Ave New York NY 10017-6307

AMEND, WILLIAM JOHN CONRAD, JR., physician, educator; b. Wilmington, Del., Sept. 17, 1941; s. William John Conrad and Catherine (Broad) A.; m. Constance Roberts, Feb. 3, 1962; children—William, Richard, Nicole, Mark. B.A., Amherst Coll., 1963; M.D., Cornell U., 1967. Diplomate Am. Bd. Internal Medicine. Asst. clin. prof. U. Calif. Med. Ctr., San Francisco, 1974-76; assoc. clin. prof. U. Calif. Med. Ctr., 1977-82, prof. clin. medicine and surgery, 1982—; physician Falmouth Med. Assocs., Mass. Contbr. articles to med. jours. Chmn. med. adv. com. No. Calif. Kidney Found., 1987-88; mem. stewardship com. 1st Presbyn. Ch., Burlingame, Calif., 1983, 84, elder, 1982-85, 93-96. Maj. U.S. Army, 1969-71. Simpson fellow, 1963; recipient Gift of Life award No. Calif. Kidney Found., 1994. Fellow ACP; mem. Amherst Coll. Alumni Fund (class agt. 1973-83). Republican. Avocations: golf; gardening; hiking. Home: 2860 Summit Dr Burlingame CA 94010-6257 Office: U Calif Med Ctr 3D and Parnassus San Francisco CA 94143

AMENDOLA, SAL JOHN, artist, educator, writer; b. Fiumefreddo, Calabria, Italy, Mar. 8, 1948; came to U.S., 1948; s. Joseph and Mary (Amendola) A. Grad., Erasmus Hall H.S., Bklyn.; 3-yr. cert., Sch. Visual Arts, N.Y.C., 1966-69. Illustator, writer DC Comics, Archie Comics, Marvel, N.Y.C., 1969-86; asst. editor, prodn. DC Comics, N.Y.C., 1970; talent coord., editor DC Comics, Warner Communications, N.Y.C., 1983-86; illustration instr. Sch. Visual Arts, Fashion Inst., N.Y.C., 1974—; founder SRV plus 1, 1990; lectr., cons., instr. seminars at librs., mus., schs., U.S., Can., 1983-86; freelance illustrator, 1987—. Writer, illustrator: (comic book) Batman Night of the Stalker, 1972 (Best Story Nominee 1973); editor: (comic books) Elvira Mistress of the Dark, Talent Showcase, 1984-86; co-artist: (movie adaptation) Superman III, 1983, (comic book) Star Trek, 1984; author, artist: (book) Perspective for Artists, 1984, (book) Other Intelligences/A Sociopolitical View, 1990; artist: (comic book) Archie, 1987 (Best

Artist nominee 1988); designer toys and games; book illustrator, designer, illustrator book jackets. Mem. Nat. Cartoonist Soc. (profl. com. 1987), Soc. Illustrators. Liberal Democrat. Avocations: science, politics, foreign languages. Home: 1028 67th St Brooklyn NY 11219-5923

AMENT, RICHARD RAND, psychologist; b. Merrill, Wis., Aug. 5, 1950; s. Jacob John and Edith Jean (Selner) A.; m. Mary Elizabeth Beau, Aug. 5, 1978; children: Adrianne Beth, Jacob John II, Breanne Beau. BS, U. Wis., Eau Claire, 1972; MSEd, U. Wis., Stout of Menominee, 1974. Sch. psychologist Wausau (Wis.) Sch. Dist., 1974—; mem. profl. adv. bd. Children with Attention Deficit Disorders North Ctrl. Wis., 1991-92. V.p. Montessori Presch., Inc., Wausau, 1986, pres., 1987, 93-95; bd. dirs., 1992-94; treas. Marathon County Reps., Wausau, 1977—; campaign mgr. Kasten for Assembly, Wausau, 1982; Marathon County chmn. Gov. Thompson for Wis. campaign, 1990, 94; county chmn. Bush for Pres. campaign, 1992; mem. St. Michael's Cath. Ch., 1991-92; county coord. Vannes for Congress, 1992; bd. dirs. Citizens for Neighborhood Schs., 1991-94; parent adv. bd. Horace Mann Mid. Sch., 1994-95; treas. Friends of Judge Howard campaign, 1996—, Jacobson for Assembly campaign, 1996-98. Mem. Wis. Sch. Psychologists Assn. (mem. exec. bd. 1983-85), Sch. Psychologists of Wis.'s North (v.p. 1976-77, 81-82, pres. 1983-85). Avocations: golf, fishing, hunting, tennis. Home: 1800 Forest Valley Rd Wausau WI 54403-2038 Office: Wausau Pub Schs 415 Seymour St Wausau WI 54403-6267

AMERAULT, JAMES F., military officer; b. Somerville, Mass., Oct. 8, 1943; s. Alfred J. and Evelyn (Swimm); m. Cathryn Ann Corwin, Dec. 1, 1979; children: Nancy, Clay, Matthew, Alan, Lindsay. BS in Naval Engring., U.S. Naval Acad., 1965; MS in Ops. Rsch., Naval Postgrad. Sch., Monterey, Calif., 1972; MA in Fgn. Affairs and Arabic, U. Utah, 1976. Commd. ensign USN, 1965, advanced through grades to vice adm., 1998; gunnery officer, 1st It. Massey; officer in charge Patrol Craft Fast 52; engring. officer Taylor and Benner; exec. officer Dupont and Sierra; commissioning commdg. officer Nicholas; commdg. officer Samuel Gompers; staff combat info. ctr. officer for comdr. Cruiser Destroyer Group Two; comdr. Destroyer Squadron Six; dep./acting dir. Program Resource Appraisal Divsn.; exec. asst. to dir. surface warfare divsn. Office of Chief of Naval Ops.; dir. ops. divsn., office of budget and reports Office of Navy Comptr.; cmdr. Western Hemisphere group Mayport, Fla., 1997—; dir. fiscal mgmt., dep. chief naval ops. (logistics) USN, Washington, 1997—. Decorated Legion of Merit, Bronze Star with V device, Navy Commendation medal, Meritorious Svc. medal, Joint Svc. Commendation medal; Fed. Exec. fellow Rand Corp., 1987. Mem. Soc. Naval Engrs., Soc. Mil. Comptrs., U.S. Naval Inst., Mil. Ops. Rsch. Soc. (bd. dirs. 1988-90), Surface Navy Assn. (bd. dirs. 1994—), N.Y. Yacht Club. Avocations: running, sailboat racing. Home: 5203 Glen Meadow Rd Centreville VA 20120-1355

AMERINE, WENDY L., community health and gerontology nurse; b. Paso Robles, Calif., May 11, 1951; d. Lyndon E. and Mariann (Michels) Yearwood; m. Lee B. Amerine, May 2, 1981; 1 child, Michael. AA in Nursing, Bakersfield Coll., 1972. RN, Calif.; cert. gerontol. nurse. Office nurse Bakersfield (Calif.) Family Med. Clinic; evening supr. Parkview Real SNF, Bakersfield; home health nurse and supr. Med. Pers. Pool, Bakersfield; office nurse Helper Med., Bakersfield. Vol. cancer screening unit Community Health Faire; vol. mobile blood pressure screening unit Am. Heart Assn. Named Employee of Month, Med. Pers. Pool, 1984. Mem. Calif. Nurses Assn., Kern RN Soc. Home: 718 Greenwood Dr Bakersfield CA 93306-5926

AMERINGER, CHARLES D., history educator; b. Milw., Sept. 19, 1926; s. Carl and Pearl (Nelson) A.; m. Jean Stewart McNicol; children—Carl, William. B.A., U. Wis., Madison, 1949; M.A., Fletcher Sch. Law and Diplomacy, Medford, Mass., 1951, Ph.D., 1958. Asst. prof. history Bowling Green State U., Ohio, 1959-64; assoc. prof. history Pa. State U., University Park, 1964-74, prof. history, 1974-95; prof. history emeritus, 1995—; head dept. history Pa. State U., University Park, 1985-90. Author: The Democratic Left in Exile: The Antidictatorial Struggle in the Caribbean, 1945-59, 1974, Don Pepe: A Political Biography of Jose Figueres of Costa Rica, 1979, Democracy in Costa Rica, 1982, U.S. Foreign Intelligence: The Secret Side of American History, 1990, The Caribbean Legion: Patriots, Politicians, Soldiers of Fortune, 1996; editor: Political Parties of the Americas, 1980s to 1990s: Canada, Latin America and the West Indies, 1992. Capt. USAFR, 1951-69. Mem. Conf. Latin Am. History, Middle Atlantic Coun. Latin Am. Studies, Phi Beta Kappa. Office: Pa State U Dept History 108 Weaver Bldg University Park PA 16802-5500

AMERO, JANE ADAMS, state legislator; b. Rumford, Maine, Aug. 6, 1941; d. William Anthony and Evangeline Jean (McInnis) Adams; m. Gerald M. Amero, Sept. 4, 1961; children: Scott Martin, Brett Douglas, Melanie Jane. BA, Cornell U., 1963. Tchr. South Portland (Maine) Sch. Dist., 1965-67; mem. Cape Elizabeth (Maine) Sch. Bd., 1975-81; mem. Maine Bd. Edn., Augusta, 1987-92, chmn., 1989-92; mem. Maine Senate, Augusta, 1992—; mem. edn. com. & reappt. com. Maine Senate, 1992-94; asst. majority leader, chmn. legis. coun., state and local govt. com., 1994-96, Maine Senate, minority leader legis. coun., 1996—; mem. Maine Coalition for Excellence in Edn., 1990—, Commn. to Evaluate Tech. Coll. System, Augusta, 1990-91, 3 sch. funding task forces, Augusta, 1987, 88, 90-91. Mem. coun. Town of Cape Elizabeth, 1983-92, chmn., 1987; mem., pres. Catherine Morrill Day Nursery, Portland, 1981-87; mem. Commn. on Restructuring State Govt., Augusta, 1991; corporator Maine Med. Ctr., Portland, 1989—; active Vol. Lawyers Project, Portland, 1984-90; mem. Ptnrs. for Progress in Portland Leadership Initiative, 1990-94; bd. dirs. Portland Regional Opportunity Program, 1997—, Vis. Nurses Assn./Hospice, 1993—, Ronald McDonald House, Portland, 1995—. Recipient Svc. Above Self award Rotary Clubs, Cape Elizabeth, South Portland, 1991; named Regional Citizen of Yr. in Greater Portland Area, Greater Portland Coun. Govts., 1993, Art Adv. of the Yr. Maine Art Edn. Assn., 1998. Mem. Nat. Assn. State Bds. of Edn. (mem. nat. study com. on parent and cmty. invilvement in schs. 1989, Disting. Svc. award 1993), LWV (Emily Farley award Portland chpt. 1989), Phi Beta Kappa, Phi Kappa Phi. Republican. Avocations: golf, swimming, political campaigns, reading, family activities. Home: 444 Old Ocean House Rd Cape Elizabeth ME 04107-2625 Office: Maine State Senate State Capitol Augusta ME 04330

AMES, ADELBERT, III, neurophysiologist, educator; b. Boston, Feb. 25, 1921. MD, Harvard U., 1945. Intern, then resident in internal medicine Presbyn. Hosp., 1945-52; rsch. assoc. Med. Sch. Harvard U., Boston, 1955-69, prof. physiology, dept. surgery, 1969-91, Charles Anthony Pappas prof. neurosci. Med. Sch., 1983-91, prof. emeritus, 1991—; neurophysiologist in neurosurgery Mass. Gen. Hosp., Boston, 1983—. Recipient Rsch. Scientist award NIMH, 1968-80. Mem. Am. Physiol. Soc., Am. Soc. Neurochemistry, Soc. Neurosci., Internat. Soc. Neurochemistry. Home: RR 4 Box 475 Brattleboro VT 05301-9625

AMES, BRUCE N(ATHAN), biochemist, molecular biologist; b. N.Y.C., Dec. 16, 1928; s. Maurice U. and Dorothy (Andres) A.; m. Giovanna Ferro-Luzzi, Aug. 26, 1960; children: Sofia, Matteo. BA, Cornell U., 1950; PhD, Calif. Inst. Tech., 1953. Chief sect. NIH, Bethesda, Md., 1962-67; prof. biochemistry and molecular biology U. Calif., Berkeley, 1968—, chmn. biochemistry dept., 1983-89; mem. Nat. Cancer Adv. Bd., 1976-82. Research, publs. on bacterial molecular biology, histidine biosynthesis and its control, aging, mutagenesis, detection of environ. mutagens and carcinogens, genetic toxicology, oxygen radicals and disease. Recipient Flemming award, 1966, Rosenstiel award, 1976, Felix Wankel award, 1978, John Scott medal, 1979, Corson medal, 1980, Mott prize GM Cancer Rsch. Found., 1983, Gairdner award, 1983, Tyler prize for environ. achievement, 1985, gold medal Am. Inst. Chemists, 1991, Glenn Found. Gerontology award, 1992, Roentgen prize Nat. Acad. Lincei, 1993, Lovelace award for excellence in environ. health rsch., 1995, Honda prize/Achievement in Excellence award Ctr. for Excellence in Edn., Messel medal, 1996, Japan prize, 1997, Kehoe award, 1997, Joseph Priestly award Dickinson Coll., 1998, The Nat. Medal of Sci., 1998, Medal City of Paris, 1998. Fellow Acad. Toxicol. Scis., Am. Acad. Microbiology, Gerontol. Soc. Am.; mem. NAS, Am. Soc. Biol. Chemists, Am. Soc. Microbiology (N.B. lectr. 1980), Environ. Mutagen Soc. (award 1977), Genetics Soc., Am. Assn. Cancer Rsch., Soc. Toxicology, Am. Chem. Soc. (Eli Lilly award 1964, Gustavus John Esselen award 1992), Royal Swedish Acad. Scis., Am. Acad. Arts and Scis. Home: 1324 Spruce St Berkeley CA 94709-1435 Office: U Calif 401 Barker Hall Berkeley CA 94720-3203

AMES, DONALD PAUL, retired aerospace company executive, researcher; b. Brandon, Manitoba, Can., Sept. 13, 1922; came to U.S., 1932; s. Paul and Della Johanna (Hebel) A.; m. Doris Elizabeth Ubbelohde, Dec. 30, 1949; children: Elizabeth Carol Ames Herbert, Barbara Louise Ames Jones. BS in Chemistry, U. Wis., 1944, PhD in Phys. Chemistry, 1949; LLD (hon.), U. Mo., St. Louis, 1978. AEC postdoctoral fellow, 1949-50; staff chemist Los Alamos Sci. Lab., 1950-52; asst. prof. physical chemistry U. Ky., Lexington, 1952-54; staff chemist DuPont Co., Aiken, S.C., 1954-56; sr. rsch. chemist, scientist/fellow Monsanto, St. Louis, 1956-61; from scientist to sr. scientist rsch. div. McDonnell Aircraft Co., St. Louis, 1961-68; from dep. dir. rsch. to dir. rsch. McDonnell Douglas Rsch. Labs., St. Louis, 1968-71, dir., 1971-76, staff v.p., 1976-86, staff v.p., gen. mgr., disting. fellow, 1986-89, cons., 1989—; pres. Fluotech Inc., 1991—; adj. prof. physics U. Mo., St. Louis, 1989—, Washington U., St. Louis, 1989-99; mem. vis. com. dept. mech. engring. Lehigh U., 1984-90; mem. adv. bd. Coll. Engring., U. Ill., Urbana, 1986-89; mem. spl. com. U. Chgo. 7 GeV Synchrotron Light Source, 1984-89; adv. com. U. Mo. Rsch. Reactor, Columbia, 1985-92; mem. indsl. adv. coun. dept. chemistry U. Mo., St. Louis, 1985-95; mem. subcom. on materials sci. and engring. needs and opportunities in aerospace industry NAS, 1985-86; bd. dirs. St. Louis Tech. Ctr., 1983-95; participant Manhattan Project U.S. Army, 1944-46. Contbr. articles to profl. jours.; patentee in field. With U.S. Army, 1944-46. Recipient Civic award St. Louis sect. AIAA, 1985; Wis. Alumni Rsch. fellow, 1946-48, AEC fellow, 1948-49, Monsanto fellow, 1959-61, McDonnell Douglas Disting. fellow, 1986-89. Mem. Am. Phys. Soc., Am. Chem. Soc., Soc. Engring Sci., Combustion Inst., Mo. Acad. Sci., Phi Beta Kappa, Sigma Xi, Phi Eta Sigma, Phi Kappa Phi, Phi Lambda Upsilon, Gamma Alpha, Alpha Chi Sigma.

AMES, FRANK ANTHONY, percussionist, film producer; b. Wheeling, W.Va., Oct. 12, 1942; s. Louis Higgins and Camille (O'Brien) A.; m. Susan Whalley, June 14, 1966 (div. 1971); 1 child, Kristan; m. Annette Ruth Beck, 1980; 1 child, Angharad Elisabeth. MusB, Eastman Sch. Music, Rochester, N.Y., 1964; MFA, Carnegie Mellon U., 1966. Percussionist Pitts. Symphony, 1964-66, Balt. Symphony, 1966-68; prin. percussionist Nat. Symphony, Washington, 1968—; exec. dir. 20th Century Consort, Washington, 1975-83, Millennium Inc., Washington, 1979—; pres. Potomac Prodns., Washington, 1982—; ind. film producer Washington, 1982—. Producer, performer various recs., producer (film) Music of the 12th Century, 1986 (1st prize Houston Film Frestival 1986), (music) Arrangements for children's musical Red Shoes, 1993, showcased in Arlington, Va., 1993, Wheeling, W.Va., 1994; author: (script) Petrushka, 1987. Founder, dir. Nat. Symphony outreach program In Your Neighborhood, 1992-94. Recipient Mayor's Achievement award, Washington, 1982. Mem. Chamber Music Am., Cosmos Club Washington. Avocations: sailing, squash. Home and Office: 1235 Potomac St NW Washington DC 20007-3230

AMES, GEORGE JOSEPH, investment banker; b. N.Y.C., May 14, 1917; s. George Stanley and Catherine (Diercks) A.; m. Marion Patterson, July 19, 1941 (dec. Aug. 1992); children: Ruth Ames Solie, Joan Ames Berkowitz, Margery, Dorothy Ames Cummings; m. Bess R. Sammons, Feb. 12, 1994. A.B., Columbia U., 1937; J.D., Fordham Sch. Law, 1942. Bar: N.Y. 1942. With firm Lazard Freres & Co., N.Y.C., 1937-42, 46; gen. ptnr. Lazard Freres & Co., 1957-87, ltd. ptnr., 1888-95; ltd.mng. dir. Lazard Freres & Co., L.L.C., 1995—; chmn. emeritus bd. dirs. Louis August Jonas Found. Trustee N.Y. Med. Coll.; bd. dirs. Lila Acheson and DeWitt Wallace Fund for the Hudson Highlands; trustee Hartley House. Lt. USNR, 1942-46. Mem. ABA, Assn. Bar City N.Y. Clubs: Westchester Country (Rye, N.Y.), Am. Yacht (Rye, N.Y.), Metropolitan (N.Y.C.). Home: 28 Norman Dr Rye NY 10580-2250 Office: Lazard Freres & Co LLC 30 Rockefeller Plz Fl 59 New York NY 10112-5900

AMES, GEORGE RONALD, insurance executive; b. Washington, Dec. 9, 1939; s. George Franklin and Elizabeth L. (Martin) A.; m. Cherie Ann Cernik, Feb. 14, 1983; 1 child, Christopher Ronald; children by previous marriage: Jennifer Ann, Elizabeth Louise. BS in Aerospace Engring. with honors, U. Md., 1969; MS in Indsl. Adminstrn., Purdue U., 1970. With Arthur Andersen & co., Chgo., 1970-72, Omaha, 1972-76; mgmt. cons. specializing in mgmt. info. sys.; exec. v.p. computer data svcs. Mut. of Omaha and Untied of Omaha ins. cos., 1967-87, exec. v.p., dir. agy. ops., 1987-95, exec. v.p. acquisitions and info. svcs., 1995-97, exec. v.p. info. svcs. and small group, exec. officer, 1997—; bd. dirs. Mut. of Omaha Mktg. Corps., 1996—; CEO, bd. dirs. Innowave, Inc. Bd. dirs. Iowa Great Lakes Maritime Mus. Served to sgt. USAF, 1962-67. Mem. Tau Beta Pi (nat. officer 1969-77), Sigma Gamma Tau, Phi Kappa Phi, Omicron Delta Kappa. Home: 16609 Hilo Cir Papillion NE 68046-5602 Office: Mut of Omaha Ins Co Mut Omaha Plz Omaha NE 68175*

AMES, JAMES BARR, lawyer; b. Wayland, Mass., Apr. 20, 1911; s. Richard and Dorothy (Abbott) A.; m. Mary Ogden Adams, June 14, 1941 (dec. 1967); children: Elizabeth Bigelow (dec.), Richard, Charles Cabell; m. Suzannah Ayer Parker, Oct. 10, 1969. AB magna cum laude, Harvard U., 1932, JD cum laude, 1936. Bar: Mass. 1936. Assoc. Ropes & Gray, Boston, 1936-41, ptnr., 1947-83; of counsel Ropes & Gray, 1983—; bd. dirs. Fiduciary Trust Co., Boston, 1954-87, Air Asia Co., Ltd., 1957-74, Mass. Hosp. Life Ins. Co., 1962-82, Keystone Custodian Funds, Inc., 1982-83, Ivest, Inc., 1967-73. Author: Boston: A City Upon a Hill, 1980; co-author: How to Live and Die with Massachusetts Probate, 1982. Pres. Hosp. Planning for Greater Boston Inc., 1965-71, Mt. Auburn Hosp., Cambridge, 1953-59, Boston Athenaeum, 1971-83, Mass. Hist. Soc., 1975-78; hon. trustee Boston Athenaeum; hon. trustee, past treas. Mus. Fine Arts; chmn. Animal Rescue League Boston, 1958-70, Greater Boston Charitable Trust, 1970-73; trustee Buckingham Sch., Cambridge, 1959-62, Cambridge Savs. Bank, 1955-85. Lt. to col. USAF, 1942-45. Decorated Legion of Merit, Bronze Star with oak leaf cluster; recipient J.F. Kennedy medal for svc. to Am. history Mass. Hist. Soc., 1995. Fellow Am. Bar Found., Am. Coll. Trust and Estate Counsel (past state chmn.); mem. ABA, Am. Law Inst., Boston Bar Assn. (past chmn. probate com.), Cambridge Bar Assn. (past pres.), Somerset Club, Tavern Club, Phi Beta Kappa (past pres. Harvard chpt.). Unitarian. Office: Ropes & Gray 1 International Pl Boston MA 02110-2602

AMES, RICHARD POLLARD, physician, educator, lecturer; b. Northampton, Mass., Aug. 4, 1932; s. Harold Leslie and Effie Melissa (Crowley) A.; m. Janet Ann Shaw, Oct. 7, 1961; children: Patricia Jean, Brian Shaw. BA cum laude, Williams Coll., 1954; MD, Columbia U., 1958. Diplomate Am. Bd. Internal Medicine, Am. Bd. Nephrology, Am. Bd. Med. Oncology, Am. Bd. Hematology. Intern Boston City Hosp., 1958-59, resident, 1959-61; fellow N.Y. Heart Assn. Presbyn. Hosp., N.Y.C., 1961-63; clin. assoc. Nat. Cancer Inst., Bethesda, Md., 1963-65; investigator Nat. Inst. Arthritis Metab., Paris, 1965-66, Whitehall Found., N.Y.C., 1967-70; nephrologist St. Luke's Roosevelt Hosp., N.Y.C., 1970—, chief hypertension clinic, 1973-94, dir. phys. diagnosis, 1981-94, assoc. dir. nephrology, 1990-93; chief nephrology St. Clare's Hosp., N.Y.C., 1998—; dir. hypertension Am. Health Found., N.Y.C., 1972-82; clin. prof. Columbia U., N.Y.C., 1989—. Contributing author: Topics in Hypertension, 1980, Frontiers in Hypertension Res., 1981, Clinical Cardiovascular Therapeutics, 1989, Hypertension, 1995, Messerli's Cardiovascular Drug Therapy, 1996; co-editor: Medical Symposium Drugs, 1988. Asst. surgeon USPHS, 1963-65. Fellow ACP, AHA (mem. Coun. For High Blood Pressure Rsch.); mem. Phi Beta Kappa. Office: 16 E 90th St New York NY 10128-1332

AMES, ROBERT SAN, retired manufacturing company executive; b. N.Y.C., Jan. 23, 1919; s. Leonard and Felicia (San) A.; m. Margaret Grossman, Oct. 14, 1945; children: Linda (Mrs. K.J. Cassady), David, Elizabeth. B.A., Columbia U., 1940, B.S. in Mech. Engring., 1941; M.S. in Mech. Engring., 1942; M.S. in Indsl. Mgmt. (Sloan fellow), Mass. Inst. Tech., 1954. With Goodyear Aircraft Corp., Akron, Ohio, 1942-60; v.p. Aeroprojects, Inc., West Chester, Pa., 1960-62; mgr. planning RCA Def. Elec. Products, Camden, N.J., 1962-64; v.p. mfg. Bell Aerospace Co., Buffalo, 1964-68; group v.p. Textron, Inc., Providence, 1968-71; sr. v.p. ops. Textron, Inc., 1971-79, mem. adminstrv. and investment coms., exec. v.p.-aerospace, 1979-84; ind. gen. ptnr. Westford Venture Ptnrs., I, L.P.; pres., bd. dirs. Am. Rsch. and Devel. Corp., Boston, 1972-73; bd. dirs., individual gen. ptnr., Westford Tech. Ventures. Bd. dirs. Providence Athenaeum, 1972-75; bd. dirs. Lincoln Sch. Mem. Nat. Security Indsl. Assn. (chmn. bd. dirs. 1982), Aerospace Industries Assn. (chmn. bd. govs. 1983). Home: 626 Angell St Providence RI 02906-5533 Office: Rm 128 C One Richmond Sq Providence RI 02906

AMES, STEVEN REEDE, financial planner; b. Washington, Aug. 15, 1951; s. Reede Maughan and Mary (Soderberg) A.; m. Marsha M. Ames, Sept. 1994. BS in Bus. Adminstrn., U. Md., 1973; MPA, Am. U., 1976; MS, Coll. Fin. Planning, 1994. Cert. fin. planner; registered investment advisor; enrolled agt. IRS. Specialist bus. financing Gov.'s Office State Del., Dover, 1978-83; exec. v.p. Econ. and Bus. Devel. Corp. Montgomery County, Rockville, Md., 1983-85; owner, operator Scarborough Ames and Assocs., Annapolis, Md., 1986-92; owner Ames Fee-Only Fin. Planning, Annapolis, 1993—; instr. Anne Arundel Community Coll., Annapolis, 1987—; bd. arbitrators Nat. Assn. Securities Dealers. Bd. dirs. Annapolis Boys and Girls Club, Md. Hall for Creative Arts; mem. charitable gift planning adv. com. Anne Arundel Med. Ctr. Named among top 200 fin. advisors Worth Mag., 1996, 97, 98. Mem. Nat. Assn. Personal Fin. Advisors (regional pres., bd. dirs., pub. rels. com.), Nat. Assn. Securities Dealers (bd. arbitrators 1996—), Annapolis C. of C. (Mem. of Yr. 1990), Md. Soc. Accts., Kiwanis (bd. dirs. Annapolis club 1986-97, pres. 1989-90), Greater Annapolis C. of C. (bd. dirs.). Avocations: sports, travel, financial reading.

AMES, WILLIAM FRANCIS, mathematician, educator; b. Brandon, Man., Can., Dec. 8, 1926; s. Paul Main and Della Johanna (Hebel) A.; m. Theresa Danielson, May 29, 1951; children: Karen Anne, Susan Lynn, Pamela Margaret. M.S., U. Wis., 1950. Instr. U. Wis., Racine, 1953-55; sr. engr. DuPont Co., Wilmington, Del., 1955-59; prof. U. Del., Newark, 1959-67, U. Iowa, Iowa City, 1967-75, Ga. Inst. Tech., Atlanta, 1975—; Regents prof. Ga. Inst. Tech., 1980-91, prof. emeritus, 1991—, dir., 1981-87; research prof. U. Ga., Athens, 1977-79; cons. in field. Author: Nonlinear Partial Differential Equations in Engineering, Vol. I, 1965, Vol. II, 1972, Nonlinear Ordinary Differential Equations in Transport Processes, 1968, Numerical Methods for Partial Differential Equations, 1970, 77, 92, Nonlinear Boundary Value Problems in Science and Engineering, 1989; book and jour. editor for Academic Press; editor 9 books.; contbr. articles to profl. jours. Served with USNR, 1944-46, 51-52. NSF faculty fellow, 1963-64, NATO sr. fellow, 1972-73; grantee, 1964-67, 76-79, 79-81, 83-85, 89-91, 92-95, NBS grantee, 1967-71, USPHS grantee, 1961-63, EPA grantee, 1978-81, U.S. Army grantee, 1968-75, 81-87; Humboldt sr. scientist, 1974-75. Home: 125 Tamarisk Dr NE Atlanta GA 30342-1421 Office: Ga Inst Tech Sch Math Atlanta GA 30332

AMESTOY, JEFFREY LEE, state supreme court chief justice; b. Rutland, Vt., July 24, 1946; s. William Joseph and Diana (Wood) A.; m. Susan Claire Lonergan, May 24, 1980; children: Katherine Leigh, Christina Elizabeth, Nancy Claire. BA, Hobart Coll., 1968; JD, U. Calif., San Francisco, 1972; MPA, Harvard U., 1982; D of Pub. Adminstrn. (hon.), Norwich U., 1994. Bar: Vt. 1973, U.S. Dist. Ct. Vt. 1973. Assoc. Mahady & Klevana, Windsor, Vt., 1973-74; legal counsel Gov.'s Justice Commn., Montpelier, Vt., 1974-77; asst. atty. gen., chief of Medicaid fraud div. State of Vt., Montpelier, 1978-81, commr. labor and industry, 1982-84, atty. gen., 1985-97; chief justice Supreme Ct. Vt., 1997—; pres. Nat. Assn. of Attys. Gen., 1992-98. Trustee Thomas Waterman Wood Gallery, Montpelier, 1986-92. With USAR, 1968-74. Mem. Vt. Bar Assn., Kennedy Sch. Govt. Harvard U. Alumni Exec. Coun., Conf. Chief Justices. Republican. Congregationalist. Home: RR 1 Box 9760 Waterbury Center VT 05677-9750

AMETER, BRENDA K., English educator; b. Lawrenceville, Ill., Nov. 1, 1941; d. Gail Irving and Freda May (Simmons) Lappin; m. Malcolm Lee Ameter, June 15, 1963; 1 child, Christopher Ryan. BA, U. Ill., 1964; MA, Ind. State U., 1970; PhD, Ind. U., 1982. Instr. Vincennes (Ind.) U., 1965-66, Lincoln Trail Coll., Robinson, Ill., 1970-71; lectr. Ind. State U., Terre Haute, 1985-90; assoc. prof. English Troy State U., Dothan, Ala., 1991—, advisor creative writing club, 1991—, Sigma Delta Tau advisor, 1996—. Contbr. articles to profl. jours. Mem. S.E. Ala. Regional Arts Alliance, Dothan 1994-97, Ala. Writers Forum, Montgomery, 1995-97; pres. Houston Arts and Humanities, Dothan, 1995-96, mem., 1991-97. Recipient Tri-State Tchr. award Sta. WTVY-TV 4, 1996; Fulbright scholar St. Petersburg Russia, 2000. Mem. MLA, East Ctrl. Writing Ctr. Assn. (pres. 1990-91), Johnson Soc. London, Am. Soc. Eighteenth-Century Studies, Nat. Writing Ctr. (exec. bd. dirs. 1991-92), S.E. Soc. Am. Eighteenth-Century Studies. Baptist. Avocations: sailing, scuba diving. Office: Troy State U Dothan PO Box 8368 Dothan AL 36304-0368

AMEXO, KWAKU, internist; b. Accra, Ghana, Nov. 6, 1957; came to U.S., 1992; MD, Vinnitsa Med. Inst., 1987. Diplomate Am. Bd. Internal Medicine. Intern Brookdale Med. Ctr., Bklyn., 1992-93; resident Presbyn. Med. Ctr., Phila., 1993-95, asst. clin. instr., 1993-95; fellow Temple U. Hosp., Phila., 1995-96, clin. instr., 1995-96; pvt. practice Phila., 1997—; with Pa. Hosp., Phila., Mercy Hosp. of Phila. Mem. ACP, AMA. Office: 930 Washington Ave Philadelphia PA 19147-3840 also: 5501 Woodland Ave Philadelphia PA 19143-5607

AMEY, RAE, television and video developer, producer; b. Shreveport, La., Sept. 26, 1947; d. Bruce Harold and Genevieve (Amey) Gentry; m. John E. Scarborough, Dec. 18, 1971 (div. Nov. 1979). Student, La. State U., 1968-70, U. Houston, 1972-74; BA in Liberal Arts, Antioch U., 1985; grad., U. So. Calif., 1988—. Freelance photographer Calif., 1973—; adminstrn. coord. Y.E.S. Inc., Sta. KCET-TV, L.A., 1980-83; freelande ednl. TV writer, cons. L.A., 1983-84; asst. to pres. prodn. So. Calif. Consortium, Cypress, 1984, project mgr., dir. devel., project dir. The Human Condition, 1985-87; v.p. devel. and outreach The California Channel, L.A., 1990-92, project dir., 1991, 92; pres. Video Nexus, L.A., 1987—. Editor TV guide book, 1985; photography exhbns. include: Contemporary Art Mus., Houston, 1973, Galveston (Tex.) Arts Ctr., 1975, Cameravision Gallery, L.A.,1980, Aloft, Pasadena, 1989. Co-founder Harbor Arts Alliance; mem., bd. dirs. African Am. Arts Coun.; founder, chair, bd. dirs. CIVICS: a video project for cmty. edn. and conversation, 1993—; advisor Congress on Racial Equality; sr. advisor Creating a Civil Soc. in L.A., 1997—. Ellen Torgenson Shaw scholar Annenberg Sch. Communications, U. So. Calif., 1989. Mem. Women in Communications (bd. dirs., v.p. campus svcs. 1987-88, exec. v.p. 1988-89, bd. dirs. scholarship and edn. fund L.A. chpt.). Democrat. Avocation: photography. Home and Office: 255 S Grand Ave Apt 1914 Los Angeles CA 90012-3096

AMEZCUA, CHARLIE ANTHONY, social science counselor, educator; b. Los Angeles, Sept. 1, 1928; s. Carlos and Inez (Nunez) A.; B.A., UCLA, 1958; M.S., Calif. State U., Los Angeles, 1961; m. Kathleen Joyce Greene, Mar. 7, 1964; children—Colleen Alvita, Charles Anthony. Student psychologist Rancho Los Amigos Hosp., Downey, Calif., 1959-60; instr. in psychology East Los Angeles Coll., 1962-72, asst. prof. counseling, 1972-74, assoc. prof. counseling, 1974—, prof. psychology, 1980—, spl. edn. counselor, 1981—, coordinator vet. affairs, 1972—; personnel asst. Los Angeles City Sch. Dist., 1963-64; counselor Youth Tng. and Employment Project, Los Angeles, 1965-66, counseling supr., 1966, project dir., 1966-67; counseling psychologist VA, Los Angeles, 1967-70; dir. Head Start, Los Angeles County Econ. and Youth Opportunities Agy., 1970-71; bd. dirs. Tng. and Research Found., Child and Family Resources Centers; lectr. counselor edn. Calif. State U., Los Angeles; guest lectr. John F. Kennedy U., 1987—. Mem. Calif. Gov.'s Adv. Com. on Children and Youth, 1966-67; judge blue ribbon panel Nat. Acad. TV Arts and Scis., 1966-76. Served with USN, 1948-52; Korea; cert. community coll. counselor, supr.-adminstrn., jr. coll. teaching in psychology. Mem. Am. Psychol. Assn., Calif. State Psychol. Assn., Calif. Assn. Post-Secondary Educators of the Disabled, Western Psychol. Assn. Democrat. Home: 8348 Fable Ave Canoga Park CA 91304-3036 Office: East Los Angeles Coll 1301 Brooklyn Ave Monterey Park CA 91754-6001

AMHOWITZ, HARRIS J., lawyer, educator; b. N.Y.C., Mar. 19, 1934; s. Samuel and Ruth Amhowitz; m. Melanie Leigh Gale; children: Jennifer Ann, Joshua Seth. AB, Brown U., 1955; LLB, Harvard U., 1961. Bar: N.Y. 1961, U.S. Supreme Ct. 1967. Law clk. to judge U.S. Dist. Ct. N.Y., 1961-63; assoc. Hughes Hubbard & Reed, N.Y.C., 1963-69; gen. counsel Coopers & Lybrand, N.Y.C., 1970-96, dep. chmn., 1991-95, mem. internat. exec. com., 1991-95; of counsel Hughes Hubbard & Reed, 1996—; bd. dirs. ML (Bermuda) Ltd.; adj. prof. NYU Sch. Law, 1975-83; receiver, spl. master

U.S. Dist. Ct., 1963-70; pres. bd. dirs. Prosher Group, Ltd., 1970-71; trustee Citizens Budget Commn., Inc., 1983-97. Mem. Assn. Bar City N.Y. (spl. com. on lawyers' role in securities transactions 1975-77, com. profl. and jud. ethics 1983-86, com. profl. discipline 1987-91), Harmonie Club. Home: 12600 E Fort Lowell Rd Tucson AZ 85749-9614 Office: Hughes Hubbard & Reed One Battery Park Plz New York NY 10004

AMICHETTI, DENNIS JOSEPH, advertising executive; b. Phila., Apr. 24, 1946; s. Frank and Margret H. (Ziegler) A.; m. Elizabeth Keefe, June 27, 1970; children: Christine, Karen. BS, Drexel U., 1969, MBA, 1973. Mfg. engr. Gen. Electric Co., Phila., 1969-70; mgr. mktg. devel. ESB, Inc., Phila., 1970-74; asst. v.p., dir. mktg. Phila. Sav. Fund Soc., 1974-78; v.p. SE Nat. Bank, Malvern, Pa., 1978-79; sr. v.p. Mel Richman Inc., Bala Cynwyd, Pa., 1979-83; v.p. Beneficial Corp., Wilmington, Del., 1983-86; pres. Amichetti, Lewis & Assocs., Exton and Wayne, Pa., 1987—. Planning commn. East Goshen Twp., Pa., 1977-83. Recipient Gold Effie award for fin. advt. Mem. Am. Mktg. Assn., Acad. for Health Services Mktg., Direct Mktg. Assn., Beta Gamma Sigma. Republican. Roman Catholic. Avocations: music, theater, golf. Home: 814 Wetherill Ln Wayne PA 19087-2072 Office: Amichetti Lewis & Assocs Inc 300 N Pottstown Pike Ste 120 Exton PA 19341-2235

AMICK, STEVEN HAMMOND, senator, lawyer; b. Ithaca, N.Y., May 13, 1947; s. Arthur Hammond and Marolyn Dee (Hollingshead) A.; m. Helen Louise Masten, Aug. 9, 1969. BA, Washington Coll., 1969; JD, Dickinson Sch. of Law, 1972. Bar: Del. 1972, U.S. Dist. Ct. Del. 1973. Assoc. Daley & Lewis, Wilmington, Del., 1972-74; atty. E.I. Dupont De Nemours and Co., Wilmington, 1974-85, counsel, 1986-96; mem. Del. Ho. of Reps., Newark, 1986-94; mem. Del. Senate, Newark, 1994—, minority leader, 1998—; counsel Cooch & Taylor, Newark, 1996—. Pres. Com. of 39, Wilmington, 1978, Civic League for New Castle County, Wilmington, 1984-86. Mem. Del. Bar Assn. Republican. Presbyterian. Avocation: antique cars. Home: 449 W Chestnut Hill Rd Newark DE 19713-1132 Office: Cooch & Taylor 51 E Main St Ste 1 Newark DE 19711-4695

AMICK, WILLIAM WALKER, golf course architect; b. Scipio, Ind., June 16, 1932; s. George Ellsworth Sr. and Myrtle (Walker) A.; m. Sara Dell Rogers, Apr. 6, 1957; 1 child, David Walker. BA, Ohio Wesleyan U., 1954. Registered landscape architect, Fla. Golf course architectural asst. William H. Diddle, GCA, Carmel, Ind., 1954-55, Charles Adams, GCA, Atlanta, 1957-58; golf course architect Daytona Beach, Fla., 1959—. Capt. USAF, 1955-57. Mem. Am. Soc. of Golf Course Architects (treas., v.p., pres. 1975-77). Avocations: low handicap golf. Office: PO Box 1984 Daytona Beach FL 32115-1984

AMIDON, ROGER LYMAN, health administration educator; b. Burlington, Vt., Apr. 8, 1938; s. Ellsworth L. and Mae (Liddle) A.; m. JoAnn Reiland, Aug. 1, 1968. BA, U. Vt., 1960; MA, U. Iowa, 1965, PhD (USPHS trainee), 1968. Asst. prof. hosp. and health adminstrn. U. Iowa, 1968-73, asso. prof., 1973-77; prof., chmn. dept. health adminstrn. U. Okla., 1977-81; prof., chmn. dept. health adminstrn. U. S.C., 1981-88, on sabbatical, 1988-89, prof., grad. dir., 1989—; exec. sec. Nat. Ctr. Health Svcs. Rsch., 1975-76; dir. Am. Indian Grad. Program in Health Adminstrn., U. Okla., 1977-81; cons. China Med. Coll. Hosp., 1999—. Contbr. articles to profl. jours. Chair S.C. Ctr. for Gerontology, 1999-01. Served with M.S.C. U.S. Army, 1961-62. Mem. APHA, Am. Coll. Health Care Adminstrs., Am. Coll. Healthcare Execs., Am. Hosp. Assn. (life), Inst. Society, Ethics and Life Scis., Nat. Assn. Bd. Examiners Long Term Care Adminstrs. Home: 234 Saluda Ave Columbia SC 29205-3031 Office: U SC Sch Pub Health Dept Health Adminstrn Columbia SC 29208

AMIEL, JON, film director; b. London, May 20, 1948. Motion picture dir., prodr. Prodr. film Simply Irresistible, 1999; dir. films Queen of Hearts, 1989, Tune in Tomorrow, 1990, Sommersby, 1993, Copycat, 1995, The Man Who Knew Too Little, 1997, Entrapment, 1999; T.V. mini-series The Singing Detective, 1986. Office: c/o DGA 7920 Sunset Blvd Los Angeles CA 90046*

AMIN, MOHAMMAD, urology educator; b. Sargodha, Pakistan, Jan. 1, 1942; came to U.S., 1964; s. Mohammad and Gulzar (Begum) Nawaz; m. Elizabeth Anne Howarth, May 25, 1973; children: Daniel, Omar. MB, BS, King Edward U., Lahore, Pakistan, 1963. Diplomate Am. Bd. of Urology. Intern Muhlenberg Hosp., Plainfield, N.J., 1964-65; resident in surgery Norton Hosp., Louisville, 1965-66; asst. prof. urology U. Louisville, 1971-74, assoc. prof., 1974-80, prof. urology, 1980—, resident in urology, 1966-69; med. officer Social Security, Pakistan, 1969-70; house officer urology Southmede Hosp., Bristol, Eng., 1970-71. Contbr. articles and book chpts. to profl. jours. Recipient Health Advancement award Nat. Kidney Found., 1981. Fellow ACS; mem. Am. Urol. Assn. Societe Internatioale D'Urologie, Univ. Club. Democrat. Islamic. Office: 210 E Gray St Ste 1000 Louisville KY 40202-3906

AMIN, SHAMIMA, library and media services director, university professor; b. Sylhet, Bangladesh, Feb. 12, 1963; came to U.S., 1987; d. Ruhul Amin and Kohinoor Begum; m. Mohammad A. Bhuiyan, Aug. 28, 1986; 1 child, Avi Bhuiyan. Student, U. Fla., 1984-85; BA in English Lit. with honors, U. Dhaka, Bangladesh, 1985; M in Am. Lit., U. Dhaka, 1986; M in Libr. and Info. Sci., Clark Atlanta U., 1988. Libr. prin. assoc. Atlanta Fulton Pub. Libr., 1987-89; monograph cataloger U. Fla., Gainesville, 1989-92, instr. univ. libr., 1992-93; head tech. svcs. Savannah (Ga.) State U., 1993-96, interim dir. libr., 1996-97, dir. libr. and media, 1997—; spkr. Rotary, Savannah, 1997. Editor Libr.-Info World, 1996—. Grad. Leadership Ga., Atlanta, 1996; bd. dirs. Better Bus. Bur., Savannah, 1997; judge lang. competition ARC, Savannah, 1994-95. Mem. ALA (chair minorities recruitment 1998—, chair 3M Grant 1996, chair orientation 1994, judge award com. 1992-94). Home: 1 Captain Ferguson Ln Savannah GA 31411-1703 Office: Savannah State U Libr PO Box 20394 Savannah GA 31404-9705

AMINI, AMIR ARSHAM, biomedical engineering researcher, educator; b. Mar. 28, 1965; came to U.S., 1979; s. Ahmad and Khadijeh R. (Rahat) A. BS, U. Mass., 1983; MSE, U. Mich., 1984, PhD, 1990. Rschr. Yale U., New Haven, 1990-92, asst. prof., 1992-96; asst. prof. Washington U., St. Louis, 1996—. Contbr. articles to profl. jours. Grantee Whitaker Found., 1993—, NSF, 1995—, NIH, 1998—. Mem. IEEE (sr., program com. and organizing com. 1994—), Soc. Indsl. & Applied Math. Avocations: basketball, soccer, classical music. Home: PO Box 24216 Saint Louis MO 63130-0216

AMIRANA, M. T., surgeon; b. Bhanvad, India, Jan. 7, 1930; came to U.S., 1958; s. Tayob Amirana and Noorbai Abba; m. Annelene J. Vogt, July 30, 1959; children: Ebrahim, Omar, Jasmine. BS, Khalsa Coll., Bombay, 1953; MD, U. Heidelberg, Fed. Republic Germany, 1958. Instr. thoracic and cardiovascular surgery Albert Einstein Sch. Medicine, N.Y.C., 1966-67; pres. Rens County Med. Soc., Troy, N.Y., 1975-76; chmn. dept. surger Leonard Hosp., Troy, 1972-74, St. Mary's Hosp., Troy, 1981-83; pvt. practice, 1983—; adj. rsch. assoc. prof. Rensselaer Poly. Inst., Troy, 1968-74. Active Rens. County Med. Soc., Troy, 1967. Fellow Am. Coll. Surgeons, Am. Coll. Thoracic Surgeons; mem. N.Y. State Med. Soc. Home and Office: 230 Star Cluster Cir Las Vegas NV 89128-3950

AMIRI, AFSANEH, computer professional; b. Tehran, Iran, Nov. 19, 1962; came to U.S., 1984; parents Manouchehr and Parvin (Zand) A. BS, Ea. Mich. U., 1988; postgrad., George Mason U., 1988—. Teaching asst. different high schs., Tehran, 1980-84; grader, then computer cons. Ea. Mich. U., Ypsilanti, 1984-88; teaching asst. George Mason U., Fairfax, Va., 1988-89; mem. staff JMC Fin. Svc., Chantilly, Va., 1989—; acctg. cons. ASSAL market, Vienna, Va., 1989; sales mgr. P.C. Concepts, Arlington, Va., 1990-91; gen. mgr. PC Concepts, Arlington, 1991—; Return Merchandise Authorization gen. mgr. 5 cos. Advanced Computer Concepts, 1963-96; bus. mgr. security sys. Radian Inc., 1996—. Avocations: ice skating, music, dance, drawing, cooking. Home: 307 S Yoakum Pkwy Apt 1717 Alexandria VA 22304-4045

AMIRIKIA, HASSAN, obstetrician, gynecologist; b. Tehran, Iran, Dec. 10, 1937; came to U.S., 1966; d. Ahmad and Showkat (Asgari) Cheftsaz; m. Mino Vassigh Amirikia, Apr. 4, 1964; children: Arezo, Omid. MD, Tehran U., 1964. Cert. Am. Bd. Ob-Gyn. Intern Cook County Hosp., Chgo., 1966-67; resident Wayne State U., Detroit, 1967-71, fellow, 1971-72; practice reproductive endocrine specializing in infertility Detroit, 1972—; asst. prof. Wayne State U., Detroit, 1972—; dir. ob-gyn. tng. dept. family medicine Wayne State U., Detroit, Mich., 1979—; dir. infertility and reproductive endocrinology St. Joseph's Hosp., Pontiac, Mich., 1990-93; chief staff Detroit Med. Ctr., 1993—, pres. med. staff, 1997—; chief staff Hutzel Hosp., 1996—; researcher effects of androgens on the ovary; pres. med. staff Detroit Med. Ctr., 1998—; del. to AMA, 1996.. Contbr. articles to profl. jours. Fellow ACS, Am. Coll. Ob-Gyn (Mich. sect.), Royal Coll. Physicians and Surgeons, Wayne County Med. Soc. (pres. 1995-96), Mich. State Med. Soc. (bd. dirs. 1996—); mem. Mich. State Med. Soc. (bd. dirs. 1996—). Home: 1435 Lone Pine Rd Bloomfield Hills MI 48302-2632 Office: 4727 Saint Antoine St Detroit MI 48201-1423 also: 29877 Telegraph Rd Southfield MI 48034-1332

AMIS, SUZY, actress; b. Oklahoma City, Okla., Jan. 5, 1962. film appearances include: Fandango, 1985, The Big Town, 1987, Plain Clothes, 1988, Rocket Gibraltar, 1988, Twister, 1989, Where the Heart Is, 1990, The Ballad of Little Jo, 1993, Rich in Love, 1993, Watch It, 1993, Two Small Bodies, 1993, Blown Away, 1994, The Usual Suspects, 1995, One Good Time, 1995, Nadja, 1995, Last Stand at Saber River, 1996, 97, Titanic, 1996, Firestorm, 1996, Cadillac ranch, 1996, One Good Turn, 1996, Firestorm, 1998, (TV films) The Ex, 1996, The Beneficiary, 1997, Last Stand at Saber River, 1997, Dead by Midnight, 1997; stage appearances: Fresh Horses, 1986 (Theatre World award), Hurly Burly, 1989. Office: c/o ICM care Resa Shapiro 8942 Wilshire Blvd Beverly Hills CA 90211-1934*

AMITIN, MARK HALL, cultural organization administrator, educator, writer; b. N.Y.C., July 26, 1947; s. Ernest Jonah and Gladys Iris (Epstein) A. Diploma of profound studies, U. Paris, France, 1976, PhD, 1978. Gen. mgr. Radical Theatre Repertory, N.Y.C., 1968-69; exec. dir. Universal Movement Theatre, N.Y.C., 1971-76; coord. of troupes World Theatre Festival, Nancy, France, 1976-77; exec. dir. World of Culture, N.Y.C., 1982—; lectr. univs., insts., festivals worldwide, 1971—; producer, Albee Directs Albee, 1978-79; cons. Am. Theatre Assn., Washington, 1970-79; adjuticator Am. Coll. Theatre Festivals, Washington, 1981—; negotiator, U.S.-China Theatre Exch., Beijing, China, 1984; tchr., lectr. Shanghai and Beijing Drama Insts., 1983-85, U.S. Embassy and Consultate, Israel, Tel Aviv U., Hebrew U., Tel Aviv Tchrs. Coll., 1995, Beit Hageffen, Haifa, 1997; mem. faculty New Sch. Social Rsch.; lectr. Yale U., Columbia U., NYU, Wellesley U., Brown U., Brigham Young U., Notre Dame U., Drew U., Cornell U., Carnegie Mellon U., Drake U., Hampshire U., numerous others. Appeared in (films) L'Histoires D'Amerique, 1988, Alexa, 1988, In The Soup, 1991; (TV) The Equalizer, 1989; dir., author (play) Cafe Vulgaris, 1981, Seduction, 1999; co-author (film documentary) Signals through the Flames, 1984; co-dir., co-author (TV) The Eyes of a Friend, 1985; cultural and arts contbg. editor Hamptons Mag., 1991-93; film critic Chelsea-Clinton News, The Westsider; contbg. writer The Village Voice; arts and culture writer N.Y. Black Book, 1997—; dir. plays The Dispossessed, Gaza, 1997. mem. Nat. Conf. of Profl. Mgrs., Screen Actors Guild, Assn. for Theatre in High er Edn. Avocations: horseback riding, sailing, swimming, poetry, drawing. Home: 463 West St Apt A509 New York NY 10014-2033

AMLIN, GARY W., finance administrator; b. Springfield, Ohio, Mar. 24, 1944; m. Ann E. Otto. BA in Acctg., Georgetown Coll., 1965; MBA, Xavier U., 1973. CPA; cert. cost analyst. Dir. acctg. policy and systems divsn. Def. Fin. and Acctg. Svc., Washington, 1985-88, dep. fin. policy and banking, 1988-91; dep. asst. sec. Air Force Acctg., Fin. and Banking, Office of Asst. Sec. of Air Force, Washington, 1988-91; dep. dir. fin. Def. Fin. and Acctg. Svc., Washington, 1991-93, dep. dir., 1993-97, dir., 1997—. Mem. AICPA, Am. Soc. Mil. Comptrs., Assn. Govt. Accts., Sr. Exec. Assn. Office: Dept of Def Comptr Def Fin and Acctg 1931 Jeff Davis Hwy Arlington VA 22202-3517

AMLING, FREDERICK, economist, educator, investment manager; b. Cleve., Dec. 23, 1926; s. Gustav and Elsie (Fischer) A.; m. Gwendolyn Stewart, Feb. 17, 1951; children: Jeffrey, Scott, Terrance. B.A., Baldwin Wallace Coll., 1948; M.B.A., Miami U., Oxford, Ohio, 1949; Ph.D., U. Pa., 1957. Instr. U. Maine, 1948-50; instr. U. Pa., 1950- 52, U. Conn., 1952-55; prof. finance and investment chmn. dept. Miami U., Oxford, 1955-66; prof. finance U. R.I., Kingston, 1966-69; dean Coll. Bus. Adminstrn., 1966-69; prof. fin. Grad. Sch. Bus. and Pub. Mgmt. George Washington U.; pres. Frederick Amling & Assocs., computer models, Amling & Co. Investments; cons. fin. and investment, 1959—; cons. Riggs Nat. Bank, 1970-90, Am. Psychiat. Assn., 1975-91; bd. dirs. Torray Fund, Bethesda, Md.; bd. advisers Rsch. Ctr. Credito Emiliano, Milan, 1991-93. Author: Plaid on Investments, 1983, Dow Jones Irwin Guide to Personal Financial Planning and Personal Financial Management, 1986, Investments: An Introduction to Analysis and Management, rev. edit., 1993, (with Bill Droms) Investment Fundamentals, 1994, also videotapes; editor, contbr. articles on fin. to profl. jours., newspapers, and mags. Chmn. local Cancer Crusade, 1964; trustee Georgetown Presbyn. Ch., 1977-79. Served with USNR, World War II, lt. (j.g.) USNR, 1955. Recipient Alumni Merit award Baldwin Wallace Coll., 1973, Alumni award sch. bus. and pub. mgmt. George Washington U., 1982. Mem. Washington Soc. Financial Analysts (treas.), Financial Mgmt. Assn., Am. Finance Assn. (membership chmn. 1973-90), Eastern Finance Assn. (v.p. 1979), Beta Gamma Sigma (pres. George Washington U. chpt. 1985), Delta Sigma Pi, Lambda Chi Alpha. Presbyterian (elder 1962—). Clubs: University (Miami U., Oxford) (pres. 1964); Turks Head (Providence); George Washington Univ, Cosmos, Congl. Country, Colett, Poinciana. Home: 7312 Masters Dr Potomac MD 20854-3851 also: 17 New Salt Rd Ocean Park ME 04063 also: 3555 S Ocean Blvd Apt 312 Palm Beach FL 33480-5765 Office: George Washington U Dept Fin 2023 G St NW # 540 Washington DC 20006-4205 *To work for family and society with God's help.*

AMM, SOPHIA JADWIGA, artist, educator; b. Czestochowa, Poland, June 13, 1932; arrived in Can., 1948; came to U.S., 1987.; d. Romuald Witold and Jadwiga Wactawa (Kotowska) Sulatycki; m. Bruce Campbell Amm, Aug. 5, 1961; children: Alicia, Alexander, Christopher, Bruce Jr., Gregory. Diploma in nursing, Ont. Hosp., 1953; cert. in pub. health nursing, U. Toronto, Ont., Can., 1960; BFA with honors, York U., 1980; postgrad., Norwich U. RN, 1953. Pvt. duty nurse Allied Registry, Toronto, Ont., Can., 1954-56; asst. head nurse Reddy Meml. Hosp., Mont., Que., Can., 1957-59; pub. health nurse Dist. of Sudbury, Ont., Can., 1960-62; pvt. duty nurse Gen. Hosp., Millinocket, Maine, 1962-66; counselor to new immigrants Ont. Welcome House, Toronto, 1982; vis. nurse St. Elizabeth Vis. Nurses Assn., Toronto, 1983-87; artist, tchr. YMCA, Appleton, Wis., 1994—; vol. art tchr. children with devel. disabilities, Appleton, 1988-89, disabled srs. Colony Oaks Nursing Home, Appleton, 1988-91; condr. art workshops Very Spl. Arts Wis. festivals, state and regional, 1989, 90, 92; art rental and sales Art Gallery of Hamilton, 1985—. One person show Bergstrom Mahler Mus., Neenah, Wis., 1991; exhibited in group shows at Harbourfront Exhbn. Gallery, Toronto, 1978, Simpson's Art Gallery, Toronto, 1984, City Hall, Toronto, 1984, Ukrainian Art Found., Toronto, 1984, Art Gallery of Hamilton, Can., 1985-86, Pastel Soc. Can., Ottawa (nat. juried show), 1985, IDA Gallery, York U., Toronto, 1980-81, 86, Carnegie Gallery, Dundas, Can., 1986, Calumet Coll., York U., 1981, 84, Gallery 68, Burlington, Can., 1986, Charles A. Wustum Mus. Fine Arts, Racine, Wis., 1990-91, 94, Gallery Ten, Rockford, Ill., 1992, 94-95 (3d Pl. award 1992), New Vision Gallery, Marshfield, Wis., 1992, Neville Pub. Mus., Green Bay, Wis., 1987-89, 92, 94-96, 97, Lakeland Coll., Wis., 1994, U. Wis. Gallery, Madison, 1992, 94, Consilium Pl., Scarborough, Can., 1987, 89, 92-93, Del Bello Gallery, Toronto (internat. show), 1986-93, Butler Inst. Am. Art, Youngstown, Ohio, 1993, Alverno Coll., Milw., 1994, 97, Ariz. State U., 1995, Bergstrom Mahler Mus., 1995-96 (1st pl. award 1995, 3rd pl. award 1996, 97), Appleton Art Ctr., 1995, 96, Ctr. for Visual Arts, Wausau, Wis., 1996, Marian Coll. Art, Fond du Lac, Wis., 1996, Anderson Art Ctr., Kenosha, Wis., 1997, The Stage Gallery, Merrick, N.Y., (nat. juried show), 1997, 98, Norwich U. Vernon Coll. Gallery, Montpelier, Vt., 1998, 99. Vol. art tchr. People With Cancer, Appleton, Wis., 1997. Recipient Award of Excellence, North York (Can.) Arts Coun., 1982, 86, Best in Show Etobicoke (Can.) Arts Coun., 1982, 87; project grantee (2) Very Spl. Arts Wis., 1989. Mem. Nat. Mus. Women in Arts, Arts, Scarborough, Wis. Women in the Arts, Wis. Painters and Sculptors. Roman Catholic. Avocations: golf, gardening. Home: 1109 N Briarcliff Dr Appleton WI 54915-2848

AMMACCAPANE, DANIELLE, professional golfer; b. Babylon, NY, Nov. 27, 1965. Winner Standard Register PING, 1991; 2nd ranked woman LPGA Tour, 1992; winner Centel Classic, 1992, Lady Keystone Open, 1992, 1st Bank Presents the Edina Realty Classic, 1997. Office: LPGA 100 International Golf Dr Daytona Beach FL 32124-1092*

AMMAN, E(LIZABETH) JEAN, university official; b. Hoyleton, Ill., July 13, 1941; d. James Kerr and Marie Fern (Schnake) White; m. Douglas Dorrance Amman, Aug. 12, 1962; children: Mark, Kirk, Jill, Drew, Gwen. BA in English, Ill. Wesleyan U., 1963; MA in English, U. Cin., 1975. Cert. tchr., Ill. Tchr. lang. arts John Greer Jr. High Sch., Hoopeston, Ill., 1963-64, Pleasant Hill Sch., East Peoria, Ill., 1966-67; tchr. English, chmn. Am. studies Anderson Sr. High Sch., Cin., 1967-69; instr. English, No. Mich. U., Marquette, 1976-82; instr. English, Ball State U., Muncie, Ind., 1982-86, adminstrv. intern, 1983-84, asst. to chmn. dept., 1984-86, adminstrv. asst., 1986, asst. to provost, coord. provost's lecture series, 1986—, exec. sec. student and campus life coun., 1986—. Editor: Provost's Lecture Series: Perspectives on Culture and Society, Vol. I, 1988, Vol. II, 1991, The Associator, 1983-86. Mem. choir College Ave. Meth. Ch., Muncie, 1989—; fundraiser Delaware County Coalition for Literacy, 1989, 90; flutist Muncie Westminster Festival Orch., 1989—, Am.'s Hometown Band, 1991—, Baroque Consort, 1998—. Recipient recognition Black Student Assn., Ball State U., 1988, cert. of svc. for minority student devel., 1990, 91, 92. Mem. AAUW (pres. Muncie br. 1997-98, Ind. dir. programs 1999—), Ind. Coll. English Assn. (editor 1983-85, exec. bd. 1983-86), P.E.O. (pres. Muncie 1985-87), Sigma Alpha Iota (v.p. 1994-97, pres. 1999—, Sword of Honor 1995), Kappa Delta (Ind. Kappa Delta of Yr. 1994, advisor 1992-95, collegiate province pres. 1995-98), Phi Kappa Phi. Democrat. Avocations: travel, reading, music. Home: 4305 Castleton Ct Muncie IN 47304-2476 Office: Ball State U 2000 W University Ave Muncie IN 47306-0002

AMMANN, JEAN-CHRISTOPHE, art director; b. Berlin, Jan. 14, 1939. PhD, U. Fribourg, Switzerland, 1966. Asst. Kunsthalle Bern, Switzerland, 1967-68; dir. Kunstmuseum, Lucerne, Switzerland, 1968-77, Kunsthalle, Basle, Switzerland, 1978-88; dir. Mus. für Moderne Kunst, Frankfurt, Germany, 1989—, prof., 1998—; commr. German Pavillion of Biennial of Venice, Italy, 1995; lectr. U. Frankfurt/M. and Giessen, 1992—. Author: Rèmy Zaugg—Discussion with Jean-Christophe Ammann, 1994, (with Harald Szeemann) Von Hodler zur Antiform, 1968, Louis Moilliet: Das Gesamtwerk, 1972, Bewegung im Kopf. Vom Umgang mit der Kunst, 1993, Kulturfinanzierung, 1995, Annäherung. Über die Notwendigkeit von Kunst, 1996, Remy Zaugg-Conversation with Jean Christophe Ammann, French edit., 1990, German edit., 1994, Das Glück Zu Sehen, 1998; co-organizer of documenta 5, Kassel, 1972. Office: Museum für Moderne Kunst, Domstrasse 10, 60311 Frankfurt Germany

AMMANN, LILLIAN ANN NICHOLSON, writer, health products distributor; b. Pearsall, Tex., June 20, 1946; d. Harvey Franklin and Annie Laura (Matthews) Nicholson; m. Jack Jordan Ammann Jr., May 31, 1967; 1 child, William Erik. BA magna cum laude, Southwestern U., 1968. Mgr. inventory Kelly AFB, San Antonio, 1967-70; employment counselor Tex. Employment Commn., San Antonio, 1970-75; owner, operator Lillie's Lovely Little Gardens, San Antonio, 1975-77; owner, operator Lillie's Interior Landscapes, San Antonio, 1980-82, pres., 1983-96; sec. Jack Ammann Inc., 1983-87; pres. Lillie's & Sherry's Plants & Pottery, San Antonio, 1977-80; ind. distbr., diamond dir. Rexall Showcase Internat., 1996—. Author: Lillie's Lovely Little Gardening Book, 1976, Look Beyond Tomorrow: The Carola Spencer Story, 1998; editor: A Bouquet of Recipes from the Diocese of the Southwest, Anglican Church in America, 1998. Vol. All Saints Anglican Ch., Caring Connections San Antonio, Friends Carola, v.p., bd. em. Mem. Women in Bus. (past pres.), Tex. State Naturopathic Med. Assn. (sec. San Antonio chpt.), San Antonio Romance Authors (past pres.), San Antonio Writers Guild, Alamo City Rep. Women's Club, Romance Writers Am. Fax: (210)344-1958; e-mail: LilleA@aol.com. Home and Office: 603 Mauze Dr San Antonio TX 78216-3711

AMMAR, RAYMOND GEORGE, physicist, educator; b. Kingston, Jamaica, July 15, 1932; came to U.S., 1961, naturalized, 1965; s. Elias George and Nellie (Khaleel) A.; m. Carroll Ikerd, June 17, 1961; children: Elizabeth, Robert (dec.), David. AB, Harvard U., 1953; PhD, U. Chgo., 1959. Research assoc. Enrico Fermi Inst., U. Chgo., 1959-60; asst. prof. physics Northwestern U., Evanston, Ill., 1960-64; assoc. prof. Northwestern U., 1964-69; prof. physics U. Kans., Lawrence, 1969—; chmn. dept. physics and astronomy U. Kans., 1989—; (on sabbatical leave Fermilab and Deutsches Elektronen Synchrotron, 1984-85); cons. Argonne (Ill) Nat. Lab., 1965-69, vis. scientist, 1971-72; vis. scientist Fermilab, Batavia, Ill., summers 1976-81, Deutsches Elektronen Synchrotron, Hamburg, Germany, summers 1982-88, lab. of nuclear studies Cornell U., summers 1989-98; project dir. NSF grant for rsch. in high energy physics, 1962—. Contbr. articles to sci. jours. Fellow Am. Phys. Soc.; mem. AAUP. Home: 1651 Hillcrest Rd Lawrence KS 66044-4525 Office: U Kans Dept Physics and Astronomy Lawrence KS 66045

AMMARELL, JOHN SAMUEL, retired college president, former security services executive; b. nr. Reading, Pa., Mar. 21, 1920; s. John Samuel and Marie (Rothermel) A.; m. Florence Rebecca Althouse, June 27, 1942; children—John David, Robert Lynn. AB, Muhlenberg Coll., 1941, LLD (hon.), 1986; postgrad., George Washington U., 1942-43. Spl. agt., asst. chief liaison FBI, Washington, 1942-55; assoc. Gt. Am. Tchrs. Agy., Allentown, Pa., 1955-56; mgr. pers., dir. security Air Products & Chems., Inc., Trexlertown, Pa., 1956-58; chmn. exec. com., dir., exec. v.p. Wackenhut Corp., Coral Gables, Fla., 1958-83, chmn. exec. com., dir., sr. cons., 1983-94, sr. cons., 1994—; dir. Wackenhut Svcs. Inc., 1960-83, Wackenhut Internat. Inc., 1976-83, Stellar Systems, 1979-83; interim pres. Newberry Coll., S.C., 1984-85, pres., 1985-86; bd. dirs. Assoc. Industries Fla., 1966—, sec., 1968-69, treas., 1969-70, v.p., 1970-73, pres., 1973-74, chmn., 1974-75. Bd. dirs. Greater Miami Citizens Crime Commn., 1975-84, pres., 1979-80; trustee Newberry Coll., 1970-73, 74-85. Recipient Alumni Achievement award Muhlenberg Coll., 1971; named Community Leader Am., 1970-78. Mem. Soc. Former Spl. Agts. FBI (pres. Pan Am. chpt. 1967-68, treas. Indian River chpt. 1992-99m pres. 1999—), Com. Nat. Security Cos. (chmn. 1975-77), Am. Soc. Ind. Security (chmn. pvt. security svcs. coun. 1976-79), Lambda Chi Alpha, Omicron Delta Kappa, Phi Alpha Theta. Lutheran. Home: 2943 SW Brighton Way Palm City FL 34990-6083 *Work hard and strive to do your best at all times. Be a supportive and positive influence in all you do. Exhibit honesty, loyalty and integrity in your work and service to others. Recognize success is achieved by appreciating the support of others who work with you and treating people as you would want to be treated.*

AMMER, BONNIE, publisher; b. Toledo, Ohio, July 24, 1947. BS, Ohio State Univ., 1969. Head mktg. adult trade and ref. divsns. Macmillan, 1985-94; pres.,publ. Fodor's Travel Publ., Inc., N.Y.C., 1996—. Office: Fodor's Travel Publs Inc 201 E 50th St New York NY 10022-7703*

AMMER, WILLIAM, retired judge; b. Circleville, Ohio, May 21, 1919; s. Moses S. and Mary (Schallas) A. BS in Bus. Adminstrn., Ohio State U., 1941, JD, 1946. Bar: Ohio 1947. Atty., examiner Ohio Indsl. Commn., Columbus, 1947-51; assty. atty. gen. State of Ohio, Columbus, 1951-52; pvt. practice Circleville, 1953-57; pros. atty. Picaway County, Circleville, 1953-57, common pleas judge, 1957-95; ret., 1995; judge by assignment Supreme Ct. Ohio, 1995—; asst. city solicitor Circleville, 1955-57. Past. pres. Pickaway County ARC, Am. Cancer Soc. Served with inf., AUS, 1942-46. Mem. ABA, Ohio Bar Assn. (chmn. criminal law com. 1964-67), Pickaway County Bar Assn. (pres. 1955-56), Ohio Common Pleas Judges Assn. (pres. 1968), Masons, K.T., Shriners, Kiwanis (Ohio dist. chmn., past lt. gov.). Methodist. Home: PO Box 87 Circleville OH 43113-0087 Office: 113 1/2 South Court St PO Box 87 Circleville OH 43113-0087

AMMERAAL, BRENDA FERNE, secondary school educator; b. Grand Rapids, Mich., Mar. 20, 1943; d. Donald and Jean (Longstreet) Bysterveld; m. Robert Neal Ammeraal, June 14, 1966; children: Audrey Jeanne, Bret Alan, Julia Marie Ammeraal Adamski. BA, Calvin Coll., Grand Rapids, 1963; MA in Latin, U. Mich., 1965; MA in English, U. Chgo., 1978; MA in Ednl. Adminstrn., Governor's State U., 1997. Tchr. Rehoboth (N.Mex.) Mission Sch., 1963-64, Timothy Christian H.S., Elmhurst, Ill., 1965-66, Trinity Luth. Sch., Tinley Park, Ill., 1966-67, Marist H.S., Chgo., 1981—;

adj. prof. Trinity Christian Coll., Palos Heights, Ill., 1984-85, Moraine Valley C.C., Palos Hills, 1983—; essay grader Advanced Placement Exams, Princeton, N.J., 1988-95, summer workshop leader, Leelanau, Mich., 1992—, Ind. State U., 1994-97; midwest cons. Coll. Bd., 1991-98; contest judge Ill. Critical Thinking Essay Contest, Champaign, Ill., 1989. Contbr. articles to profl. jours.; editor Outlook, The Messenger. Mem. Friends of Worth Libr., 1967—; Sunday sch. tchr. Evergreen Park Christian Ref. Ch., 1968-70, Sunday sch. supt., 1970-71; vacation Bible sch. storyteller Orland Park Christian Reformed Ch. NEH grantee, 1985, 89, 91, 92, U. Chgo. Tuition grantee, 1978. Mem. Nat. Coun. Tchrs. English, Ill. Women in Adminstrn., Mensa, Phi Delta Kappa (program chmn. 1997—). Avocations: reading, gardening, computing, crossword puzzles.

AMMERAAL, ROBERT NEAL, biochemist; b. Grand Rapids, Mich., Oct. 11, 1936; s. Cornelius and Janet (Kolenbrander) A.; m. Brenda Ferne Bysterveld, June 14, 1966; children: Audrey Jeanne, Bret Alan, Julia Marie Adamski. BA, Calvin Coll., 1958; PhD, Wayne State U., 1963. Rsch. assoc. U. Chgo., 1962-65; asst. prof. biochemistry U. Ill., Chgo., 1965-67; asst. prof. Trinity Christian Coll., Palos Heights, Ill., 1967-69; rsch. project leader Am. Maize-Products Co., Hammond, Ind., 1969-96. Inventor in field; contbr. articles to profl. jours. and books. Lay preacher Orland Park (Ill.) Christian Reformed Ch.; lay pastor Calvary Reformed Ch., Orland Park, 1990-97. Fellow USPHS, 1963-65; cited for one of Top Ten Med. Discoveries by Time mag., 1966. Republican. Mem. Reformed Ch. Am. Avocations: molecular modeling, producing computer animation and graphics for video, electronic construction. Home: 11661 S Nagle Ave Worth IL 60482-2311

AMMERMAN, ROBERT RAY, philosopher, educator; b. Buffalo, Sept. 5, 1927; s. John Raymond and Frances Mura (Pettit) A.; 1 son, Robert Thompson. A.B. with highest honors, Swarthmore Coll., 1952; M.A., Brown U., 1954, Ph.D., 1956. Mem. faculty dept. philosophy U. Wis., Madison, 1956—; prof. U. Wis., 1967-89, prof. emeritus, 1989—; vis. researcher U. London, 1965. Author: (with M.G. Singer) Introductory Readings in Philosophy, 1962, Classics of Analytic Philosophy, 1965. Served with U.S. Army, 1945-48. Mem. Phi Beta Kappa. Home: 3038 Eastland Blvd Apt 202F Clearwater FL 33761-4121 Office: U Wis Dept Philosophy Madison WI 53706

AMMIANO, TOM, county and municipal official; life ptnr.; 1 child. BA in Communication Arts, Seton Hall U., 1963; MA in Spl. Edn., San Francisco State U., 1965. Stand-up comic, 1981—; tchr. disabled students program City Coll. San Francisco, 1991—, instr. AIDS peer edn., 1992—; San Francisco city supr. San Francisco Bd. Supt., 1994-98, pres. bd. suprs., 1998—; community resource tchr. AIDS spl. edn. project San Francisco Unified Sch. Dist.; classroom tchr. educable mentally retarded; tchr. of English in Vietnam; with Camp Easter Seal and Rec. Ctr. for the Handicapped, San Francisco. active Mission Coalition, Ethnic Minority Coalition, Bay Area Gay Liberation; organizer demonstrations resp. for including sexual orientation in tchr. hiring; founder Gay Tchrs. Coalition, Gay Lesbian Speakers Bur. in Schs.; mem. community group Project Ten; mem. San Francisco Bd. Edn., 1990—, pres. 1993, v.p. 1991; elected to San. Francisco Bd. Supt., 1994—. Office: San Francisco Bd Suprs City Hall 1 Dr Carlton B Goodlett Pl San Francisco CA 94102-4603*

AMMIRATI, RALPH, advertising agency executive. Student, Pratt Inst. With Carl Ally, from 1966; chmn., dir. Ammirati & Puris Inc., N.Y.C., 1973-96; adv. to chmn. worldwide Ammirati Puris Lintas, N.Y.C., 1996—. Served U.S. Marines. Office: Ammirati Puris Lintas 1 Dag Hammarskjold Plz New York NY 10017-2201*

AMMIRATO, VINCENT ANTHONY, lawyer; b. Somerville, N.J., Dec. 6, 1942; s. Vincent Salvatore and Elizabeth L. (Masiello) A.; m. Anna Maria Cook, June 19, 1965 (div. Apr. 1994); children: Lisa Maria, Vincent Salvatore II. BA, Long Beach (Calif.) State U., 1968; JD, U. San Diego, 1971. Bar: Calif. 1971, U.S. Supreme Ct. Atty. Buck, Ammirato, and Rutter, Long Beach, 1972-73, 73-88; dep. prosecutor Long Beach Prosecutor, 1973; atty. Burns, Ammirato, Palumbo, Milam & Baronian, Pasadena, Calif., 1989-99; Ammirato & Palumbo, LLP, 1999—. V.p. Shadow Park Home Owners Assn., Cerritos, Calif., 1978-83; mem. adv. coun. John Crowley for City Coun., Cerritos, 1988; advisor YMCA, Sacramento, 1993—; bd. dirs., pres. Cerritos-Artesia Little League, 1986-89. With U.S. Army, 1966-68, Germany. Mem. Am. Bd. Trial Advocates, Long Beach Bar Assn., Long Beach C. of C., Los Angeles County Bar Assn., Italian/Am. Lawyers of L.A., Forty-Niner Athletic Assn. Avocations: golf, racquetball, swimming. Fax: 626-432-5182. Home: 2361 Eastgate Pl Glendale CA 91208 Office: Ammirato & Palumbo LLP 65 N Raymond Ave Pasadena CA 91103-3947

AMMON, HARRY, history educator; b. Waterbury, Conn., Sept. 4, 1917; s. Grover and Lena Mary (Pyne) A. B.S., Georgetown U., 1939, M.A., 1940; Ph.D., U. Va., 1948. Editor Md. Hist. Mag., Balt., 1948-50; asst. prof. So. Ill. U., Carbondale, 1950-57, assoc. prof., 1957-66, prof. history, 1967—; prof. emeritus So. Ill. U., 1984—, chmn. dept., 1977-1983; Fulbright lectr. U. Vienna, Austria, 1954-55, Seoul Nat. U., Korea, 1984-85; vis. prof. U. Va., Charlottesville, 1968-69; guest lectr. Northeast Normal and Liaoning Univs., People's Republic of China, 1986, 88. Author: James Monroe: The Quest for National Identity, 1971, new edit. 1990, The Genet Mission, 1973, James Monroe A Bibliography, 1991. Mem. Phi Beta Kappa. Home: 401 S Orchard Dr Carbondale IL 62901-2340 Office: So Ill U History Dept Carbondale IL 62901

AMMON, JOHN RICHARD, anesthesiologist; b. N.Y.C., 1948. MD, U. Pa., 1974. Cert. in anesthesiology. Intern Crozer Chester Med. Ctr., 1974-75; resident in anesthesiology Mass. Gen. Hosp., Boston, 1975-77; fellow in cardiac anesthesiology Stanford (Calif.) Med. Ctr., 1977-78; dir., v.p. Am. Bd. Anesthesiology, Phoenix, 1988; pvt. practice Valley Anesthesiology Ltd., Phoenix. Mem. Am. Soc. Anesthesiology, Alpha Omega Alpha. Also: Am. Bd. Anesthesiology The Summit - Ste 510 4101 Lake Boone Trail Raleigh NC 27607-5506*

AMMON, R. THEODORE, food products executive; b. 1950. Assoc. Kohlberg Kravis Roberts & Co., 1984—; v.p. RJR Nabisco Inc., Atlanta, 1989—; now CEO Big Flower Press, N.Y.C., chmn. bd. *

AMMONS, ARCHIE RANDOLPH, poet, English educator; b. Whiteville, N.C., Feb. 18, 1926; s. Willie M. and Lucy Della (McKee) A.; m. Phyllis Plumbo, Nov. 26, 1949; 1 child, John Randolph. BS, Wake Forest Coll., 1949; student, U. Calif.-Berkeley, 1951-52; LittD, Wake Forest U., 1972, U. N.C.-Chapel Hill, 1973. Prin., Hatteras (N.C.) Elem. Sch., 1949-50; exec. v.p. Friedrich & Dimmock, Inc. (biol. glassware mfr.), Millville, N.J., 1952-61; asst. prof. English, Cornell U., 1964-68, asso. prof., 1968-71, prof., 1971—, Goldwin Smith prof. poetry, 1973—. Author: Ommateum with Doxology, 1955, Expressions of Sea Level, 1964, Corsons Inlet, 1965, Tape for the Turn of the Year, 1965, Northfield Poems, 1966, Selected Poems, 1968, Uplands, 1970, Briefings, 1971, Collected Poems, 1951-1971, 1972 (Nat. Book award poetry 1973), Sphere: The Form of a Motion, 1974, Diversifications, 1975, The Selected Poems: 1951-1977, 1977, The Snow Poems, 1977, For Doyle Fosso, 1977, Highgate Road, 1977, Breaking Out, 1978, Six-Piece Suite, 1978, Selected Longer Poems, 1980, Changing Things, 1981, A Coast of Trees, 1981 (Nat. Book Critics Circle award 1982, Am. Book award nominee 1982), Worldly Hopes, 1982, Lake Effect Country, 1983, Sumerian Vistas, 1987, The Really Short Poems of A.R. Ammons, 1991, Garbage, 1993 (Nat. Book award for poetry 1993); poetry editor: Nation, 1963. Served with USNR, 1944-46. Guggenheim fellow, 1966, Traveling fellow Am. Acad. Arts and Letters, 1967, MacArthur Prize fellow, 1981-86; Bread Loaf Writers Conf. scholar, 1961; recipient Levinson prize Poetry mag., 1970, Bollingen prize in poetry, 1974-75, N.C. Lit. award, 1986, Nat. Inst. Arts and Letters award, Frost Silver medal Poetry Soc. Am., 1994. Fellow Am. Acad. Arts and Scis., Fellowship of So. Writers; mem. Inst. of Arts and Letters. Office: Cornell Univ Dept English 252 Goldwin Smith Hall Ithaca NY 14853-3201*

AMMONS, BARBARA ELLEN, gerontological, oncological, medical/surgical nurse; b. Cleve., May 10, 1937; d. Joseph A. and Emily (Chaney) Taylor; m. H.F. Ammons, Sept. 7, 1963; children: William, Caroline. AD, Cuyahoga C.C., Cleve., 1979; BS in Profl. Arts, St. Joseph's Coll. Maine, 1998. RN, Ohio., cert. gerontological, med./surg. nurse. Office mgr., surg. nurse Dr. F.J. Regal, Cleve.; sr. receptionist Cleve. Clinic Found.; med./surg. nurse mgr. Community Hosp. of Bedford (Ohio); long term care dir. nursing Walton Manor; mem. The Multi Care Corp., Cleve. ARC CPR instr.; mem. bd. elections Cuyahoga County Ohio. Mem. ANA, NAFE, Nat. Nurses Assn., Ohio Cleve. League Nursing, Tri-C Alumni Assn.

AMOAKO, JAMES KWAKU, transportation services executive, financial analyst; b. Nkwatia, Ghana, Dec. 4, 1951; came to U.S., 1970; s. Kwame and Amma (Nyame) A.; m. Rose Tiokor; children: James Jr., Nicole, Jennifer. AS, Cosumnes River Coll., 1977; BS, Calif. State U., Sacramento, 1978; MBA, Golden Gate U., 1979; PhD, LaSalle U., 1997. Bank examiner Calif. State Banking Dept., San Francisco, 1979-80; fin. analyst Artec International Corp., Mountain View, Calif., 1980-83; cost acct. Sun Microsystems, Mountain View, Calif., 1983-88; pres., CEO Alpha Transp. Corp., Phoenix, Ariz., 1988—. Recipient Svc. award Am. Field Svc., 1970. Home: 8826 W Encanto Blvd Phoenix AZ 85037-3619 Office: Alpha Transp Corp 4024 S 16th St Phoenix AZ 85040-1315

AMOLSCH, ARTHUR LEWIS, publishing executive; b. L.A., Nov. 28, 1939; s. Arthur Bruce Amolsch and Mildred Lee (Guyott) Fry; m. Judith Ann Marolda, Aug. 27, 1963 (div. 1982); children: Christopher Bryan, Kira Leigh; m. Imelda Marie Moore Madden, Mar. 27, 1983. BS, Ea. Mich. U., 1963. Tchr. Edmondson Jr. High Sch., Ypsilanti, Mich., 1963-66; fgn. svc. officer Dept. State, Washington, 1971-72; head speech writer Com. for Reelection of the Pres., Washington, 1972; dep. dir., press rels. Presdl. Inaugural Com., Washington, 1973; dir. pub. info. FTC, Washington, 1973-76; pres., pub. Washington Regulatory Reporting Assoc., Washington, 1976—. Capt. USAF, 1967-71. Republican. Home: PO Box 356 Basye VA 22810-0356 Office: Washington Regulatory Reporting Assocs 601 Pennsylvania Ave NW Ste 900 Washington DC 20004-2601

AMON, CAROL BAGLEY, federal judge; b. 1946. BS, Coll. William and Mary, 1968; JD, U. Va., 1971. Bar: Va. 1971, D.C. 1972, N.Y. 1980. Staff atty. Communications Satellite Corp., Washington, 1971-73; trial atty. U.S. Dept. Justice, Washington, 1973-74; asst. U.S. atty. Ea. Dist. N.Y., 1974-86, U.S. magistrate, 1986-90, dist. ct. judge, 1990—. Recipient John Marshall award U.S. Dept. Justice, 1983. Mem. ABA, Assn. of Bar of City of N.Y., Va. State Bar Assn., D.C. Bar Assn. Office: US District Court 225 Cadman Plz E Brooklyn NY 11201-1818*

AMON, CHERYL ANN ATTRIDGE, elementary education educator; b. Wellsville, N.Y., Aug. 17, 1946; d. David Harrison and Shirley Louise (Ackerman) Attridge; 1 child, Amanda Cheryl. BS in Edn., Slippery Rock U., 1969, MEd, 1972, MA, 1981. Cert. elem., secondary tchr., reading specialist, Pa. Tchr. Slippery Rock (Pa.) Area Schs., 1969, Franklin (Pa.) Area Sch. Dist., 1969—; internet forum mgr. and IRC adminstr., 1997—. Mem. NEA, Pa. State Edn. Assn., Franklin Area Edn. Assn., Kappa Delta Pi, Lambda Epsilon Delta, Alpha Omicron Pi. Episcopalian. Avocations: music, reading, poetry, writing. Home: 186 Cranberry Rd Lot 3 Grove City PA 16127-4654 Office: Victory Elem Sch RR 1 Harrisville PA 16038-9801

AMON, WILLIAM FREDERICK, JR., biotechnology company executive; b. Chelsea, Mass., Jan. 11, 1922; s. William Frederick and Esther H. (Rautenberg) A.; m. Barbara Marie Erlandson, Aug. 2, 1944; children—William Frederick III, Janet B., Carol J., Robert J. B.S. Ch.E., Northeastern U., 1943. Vice pres. new bus. ventures Borden Chem., N.Y.C., 1968-72; pres., chief exec. officer Electrospin Inc., Columbus, Ohio, 1972-76; v.p. Story Chem. Co., Muskegon, Mich., 1975-76, Cetus Corp., Emeryville, Calif., 1976-87; ret., cons. Danville, Calif., 1987—. Mem. Comml. Devel. Assn., Am. Chem. Soc., Soc. Indsl. Microbiology. Lutheran. Holder numerous patents. Home and Office: 831 Matadera Cir Danville CA 94526-1836

AMONTE, ANTHONY LEWIS, professional hockey player; b. Weymouth, Mass., Aug. 2, 1970. Student, Boston U. Profl. hockey player N.Y. Rangers, 1988-94, Chgo. Blackhawks, 1994—. Named to Hockey East All-Rookie Team, 1989-90, NCAA All-Tournament Team, 1990-91, Hockey East All-Star 2d Team, 1990-91, NHL All-Star Rookie Team, 1991-92, NHL Rookie of the Yr., 1991-92. Office: Chgo Blackhawks 1901 W Madison St Chicago IL 60612-2459*

AMOR, JAMES MICHAEL, dentist, actor; b. Bklyn., Apr. 10, 1959; s. James and Louisa (Piñeiro) A.; m. Patricia Elvira Mancuso, Sept. 25, 1988; children: William Anthony, James Patrick. BS in Biology, Fairleigh Dickinson U., 1980, DMD, 1984. Lic. dentist, N.Y., N.J., Pa. Staff dentist Internat. Longshoremen's Assn. - N.Y. Shipping Authority, Hoboken, N.J., 1985-87, AFL-CIO Teamsters Union Local Dental Facility, Elmsford, N.Y., 1989-90; clin. assoc. Office of Thomas Doran, DDS, Huntington, N.Y., 1985-90; ptnr. Wolfe-Amor Dental Svcs., New Holland, Pa., 1990-95; owner New Design Dental Assocs., New Holland, 1995—; assoc. prof. Sch. Dentistry Fairleigh Dickinson U., Hackensack, N.J., 1985-89; dental cons. Ephrata (Pa.) Manor Nursing Home - U.C.C. Homes, 1992-95, Zerbe Sisters Nursing Home, Narvon, Pa., 1990-95, Luther Acres Nursing Home-Luth. Homes, Lititz, Pa., 1991-95. Mem. cast in Nutcracker, Fulton Opera House, Lancaster, Pa., 1997, 98, Pa. Renaissance Faire, 1998. Mem. ADA, Lancaster County Dental Soc. (mem. comprehensive cmty. care com. 1992-95), Acad. Gen. Dentistry, Hispanic Dental Assn., Kiwanis, Psi Omega. Roman Catholic. Avocations: classic cars, heraldry, Arthurian legend, photography, computers. Home: PO Box 6 New Holland PA 17557-0006 Office: New Design Dental Assocs 121 E Main St New Holland PA 17557-1227

AMOR, SIMEON, JR., photographer; b. Lahaina, Hawaii, Apr. 24, 1924; s. Simeon and Victoria Amor. Grad. high sch., Hilo, Hawaii. Post commdr. Engrs. Post #22, Am. Legion, Honolulu, 1952-53; approp. acct. Hawaii Air Nat. Guard, Honolulu, 1953-64; prodn. control supr. Svc. Bur. Corp., Honolulu, 1964-73; prodn. control computer ops. Bank of Hawaii, Honolulu, 1973-86; owner, propreitor Image Engring., Honolulu, 1986—; historian VFW Dept. Hawaii, Honolulu, 1987-90, 96-97, First Filipino Infantry Regiment Hawaii Connection; treas. DAV Dept. Hawaii, Honolulu. Tech. advisor: (film documentary) Untold Triumph, Saga of the American Filipino Soldier. Cpl. U.S. Infantry, 1943-46, master sgt. USNG, 1952-64. Recipient Disting. Svc. award Nat. Disabled Am. Vet., 1992-94, Oahu chpt. Disabled Am. Vet., 1992-94. Mem. Am. Photographer's Internat., VFW. Home: 1634 Kino St Honolulu HI 96819-2651

AMORE, MICHAEL JOSEPH, financial and administrative executive; b. N.Y.C., Dec. 13, 1947; s. Leonard Ralph and Bianca (Vettori) A.; BS, St. John's U., 1969; MBA, Hofstra U., 1983; m. Arlene Frances Fasullo, Sept. 19, 1970. Asst. controller Olympus Corp., Lake Success, N.Y., 1979-80, controller, 1980-83, dir. fin., 1984-94, dir. adminstrv. and tech. svc., 1994-95; CFO Interiors, Inc., Mt. Vernon, N.Y., 1995-97; chief acctg. officer Graham-Field Health Products, Inc., Hauppauge, N.Y., 1997; CPA, N.Y. Mem. Am. Inst. CPAs, N.Y. Soc. CPAs (fin. execs. in industry com. 1994-95). Home: 149 Cornell Dr Commack NY 11725-2526 Office: Graham-Field Health Products Inc 400 Rabro Dr Hauppauge NY 11788-4258

AMORELLO, MATTHEW JOHN, state senator; b. Worcester, Mass., Mar. 15, 1958; s. Edward Vincent and Eunice Colleen (Byrnes) A. BA, Assumption Coll., 1980; MPA, Am. U., 1983; JD, Suffolk Law Sch., 1990. Budget analyst U.S. EPA, Washington, 1983-86; program analyst U.S. EPA, Boston, 1986-87; state senator State of Mass., Boston, 1990-98; with Hwy. Commn., Boston, 1999—. Sec., commr. Blackstone River Valley Nat. Heritage Corridor, Woonsocket, R.I., 1991—; chmn. Ctrl. Mass. Legis. Caucus, 1992-93, Rep. Senate Caucus, Boston, 1992-94, Grafton (Mass.) GOP Com., 1990—. Named Outstanding Young Leader Worcester Jaycees, 1992, Legislator of Yr. Worcester County Bar Assn., 1993. Republican. Office: Hwy Commn Office 10 Park Plaza Rm 3510 Boston MA 02116*

AMORIM, CELSO LUIZ NUNES, government official. Student, Rio-Branco Inst., Diplomatic Acad. Vienna, London Sch. Econs. Amb. UN, Geneva, 1991-93; min. Ministry Fgn. Affairs, Brasilia, Brazil, 1993-94; permanent rep. Brazil UN, N.Y.C., 1995-99, Geneva, 1999—; spl. asst. to Ministry Sci. & Tech.; asst. prof. dept. polit. sci. and internat. rels. U. Brasilia, permanent mem. dept. internat. affairs Inst. Advanced Studies. Contbr. articles to profl. jours. Ofice: Permanent Mission Brazil/UN, 1218 Grand Sacconex, Geneva Switzerland*

AMOROSI, TERESA, artist; b. Gioiosa Ionica, Reggio Calabria, Italy, Nov. 17, 1932; d. Natale and Marianna (Quartiere) Fazzolare; m. Nicholas A. Amorosi, Apr. 22, 1956 (dec. 1988); children: Thomas, Elizabeth, Joseph. *Mrs. Amorosi's husband, Nicholas A., was a scientific illustrator at The Museum of Natural History in New York City after receiving his BFA from Pratt Institute. His works are in many collections including the Kerlan Collection for Children's Literature. Her son Thomas, a doctor of anthropology, is a graduate of Hunter College in New York City. Her son Joseph, doctor of engineering, received his degree from Columbia University also in New York City. Daughter Elizabeth A. Rosiello is an artist and received her degree from the School of Visual Art in New York City.* BA, Pratt Inst., 1956. Art dir. Norcross Greeting Card Co., 1950-57; artist Charmcraft Greetings, 1957-62, Manhattan Greeting Card Co., 1978-89, Magic Moments Greeting Card Co., 1989—, Sunshine Artists, 1990—, Bernard Picture Co., 1986-87, Art Resources Internat., Ltd., 1988-90; publ. Bernard Picture Co., 1988-90, Resources Internat. Ltd., 1988-90. Illustrator: International Mother's Book, 1980. Recipient awards Washington Square Outdoor Art Show, N.Y.C., 1976, 82, 85. Mem. Tri-County Artists L.I. (treas. 1994), Fortnightly of Rockville Ctr., (art dir. 1996). Roman Catholic. Office: Intaglio Dimension 93 Mill River Ave Lynbrook NY 11563-3810

AMOROSO, FRANK, retired communication system engineer, consultant; b. Providence, July 31, 1935; s. Michele and Angela Maria Barbara (D'Uva) A. BSEE, MSEE, MIT, 1958; postgrad., Purdue U., 1958-60, U. Turin, Italy, 1964-65. Registered profl. engr., Calif. Instr. elec. engring. Purdue U., West Lafayette, Ind., 1958-60; rsch. engr. Melpar Inc., Roxbury, Mass., 1959, MIT Instrumentation Lab., Cambridge, Mass., 1960, Litton Sys. Advanced Devel. Lab., Waltham, Mass., 1960-61; engr. Melpar Applied Sci. Divsn., Watertown, Mass., 1961; mem. tech. staff RCA Labs. David Sarnoff Rsch. Ctr., Princeton, N.J., 1962-64, Mitre Corp., Bedford, Mass., 1966-67; sr. applied mathematician Collins Radio Co., Newport Beach, 1967-68; comm. sys. engr. N.Am. Rockwell Corp., El Segundo, Calif., 1968-71, Northrop Electronics Divsn., Palos Verdes Peninsula, 1971-72; comm. sys. engr., sr. staff engr. Hughes Aircraft Co., Fullerton, 1972-89; ret., 1989, cons., developer, presenter ednl. seminars, 1989—; cons. Lincom, Inc., L.A., 1994-96; cons. client Sklar Comm. Engring., 1996-97; instr. continuing engring. edn. program George Washington U., San Diego, 1993; instr. ext. short courses UCLA, 1987-89, 98—. 1st lt. U.S. Signal Corps, 1961-62. Recipient Outstanding Achievement award RCA Labs., 1964; grad. study scholar Italian Govt., 1964-66. Mem. IEEE (sr. mem., session organizer, chmn. conf. on mil. com., presenter). Achievements include patents in field. Avocations: scuba diving, free lance writing. Home and Office: Digital Data Modulation Studies 271 W Alton Ave Apt D Santa Ana CA 92707-4171

AMOS, BETTY GILES, restaurant company executive, accountant; b. Lebanon, Mo., July 18, 1941; d. Clarence Edgar and Clara Mae (Gann) Giles; m. E.L. Amos, Sept. 18, 1959 (div. Oct. 1965); 1 child, Jeffrey Lee; m. Thomas R. Righetti, Jan. 2, 1983. BBA magna cum laude, U. Miami, Coral Gables, Fla., 1973, MBA, 1976; D of Bus. Adminstrn. honoris causa, Johnson & Wales U., 1990. CPA, Fla. Sec. City of Lebanon, 1959-63; dept. head Empire Gas Co., Lebanon, 1963-68; fin. analyst asst. Biscayne Assocs., Ltd., Miami, Fla., 1968-73; investment mgr. Universal Restaurants Inc., Miami, 1973-77; pvt. practice accountant, investment mgr. Miami, 1977-83; pres. The Abkey Cos., Miami, 1983—; founder, Mega Bank, Miami, 1983-94; adv. com. Fuddruckers, Inc., Boston. Trustee Miami Project, 1986-89, United Fund of Dade County, 1992—; pres. Humane Soc. Greater Miami, 1994—, bd. dirs., 1993—; mem. pres. coun. U. Miami, 1994—, mem. founder's soc., 1994—, bd. trustees, 1997—. Recipient Philip J. Romano Founders award, 1988. Mem. AICPA, Fla. Inst. CPAs, Am. Women's Soc. CPAs, Coconut Grove C. of C. (trustee 1988—), Nat. Assn. Women Bus. Owners (Outstanding Woman Bus. award 1993), U. Miami Alumni Assn. (nat. pres. 1999—). Republican. Roman Catholic. Avocations: snow skiing, water skiing, scuba diving, tennis, windsurfing. Home: 13724 SW 92nd Ct Miami FL 33176-6858 Office: The Abkey Cos 3444 48 Main Hwy 3d Floor PO Box 330927 Miami FL 33233-0927

AMOS, DANIEL PAUL, insurance executive; b. Pensacola, Fla., Aug. 13, 1951; s. Paul Shelby and Mary Jean (Roberts) A.; m. Mary Shannon Landing, Sept. 12, 1972; children—Paul Shelby, Lauren Alyse. B.S. in Risk and Ins. Mgmt., U. Ga., 1973. Co-state mgr. Am. Family Life Assurance Co., Columbus, Ga., 1973-78, state mgr., 1978-83, pres., 1983-96; now also dep. chief exec. officer Am. Family Corp., Columbus, Ga., 1996; vice chmn., pres., CEO AFLAC Inc., Columbus, Ga., 1996—; dir. Columbus Bank & Trust Co. Methodist. Avocation: bridge. Office: Am Family Life Assurance 1932 Wynnton Rd Columbus GA 31999-0001*

AMOS, DENNIS B., immunologist; b. Bromley, Eng., Apr. 16, 1923; s. Benjamin and Vera (Oliver) A.; m. Solange M. Labesse, Aug. 25, 1949 (dec. 1980); children: Susan V., Martin D., Christopher I., Nigel P., Irene C.; m. Kay B. Veale, Mar. 9, 1984. MBBS, Guy's Hosp., London, 1951, MD, 1963. House officer Guy's Hosp., London, 1951-52, rsch. pathologist, 1952-55; prin. cancer rsch. scientist Roswell Park Inst., Buffalo, 1955-62; prof. immunology, exptl. surgery Duke U., Durham, N.C., 1962-93, prof. emeritus, 1993—; cons. NIH, Bethesda, Md., 1957—. Mem. Nat. Acad. Scis., Inst. of Medicine. Office: Duke Med Ctr PO Box 3010 Durham NC 27715-3010

AMOS, HAROLD, retired biomedical researcher, educator; b. Pennsauken, N.J., Sept. 7, 1918. BS, Springfield Coll., 1941, PhD in Bacteriology, 1952. Rsch. fellow Harvard Med. Sch., 1953-55; instr. bacteriology Springfield Coll., Boston, 1947-48; from assoc. to asst. prof. to assoc. prof. Harvard Med. Sch., Boston, 1955-70, prof. microbiology and molecular genetics, 1970—; chmn. dept. microbiology Harvard Med. Sch., 1965-77, prof. emeritus, 1988—; Fulbright rsch. fellow Pasteur Inst., France, 1951-53; rsch. fellow Harvard Med. Sch., 1953-55; USPHS fellow, 1952-54, sr. rsch. fellow, 1958; mem. Nat. Cancer Adv. Bd., 1972-83; trustee Josiah Macy Found., 1973—. Recipient Fulbright Rsch. fellow, 1951-53, Pub. Welfare medal NAS, 1995. Mem. Inst. Medicine-NAS, Am. Soc. Biol. Chemists, Tissue Culture Assn., Am. Soc. Microbiology. Office: Harvard Med Sch Dept Microbiol & Molec Gen 200 Longwood Ave Boston MA 02115-5701

AMOS, JAMES LYSLE, photographer; b. Kalamazoo, Jan. 25, 1929; s. George Elsworth and Lois Hazel (Noffsinger) A.; m. Martha Imogene Holbrook, Sept. 1975. Student, U. Idaho, 1947-49; A.A.S., Rochester Inst. Tech., 1951. Trainee Eastman Kodak Co. (various locations), 1951-53; salesman Eastman Kodak Co., Des Moines, 1956; tech. sales rep. Eastman Kodak Co., Balt., 1957-67. Free lance photographer, 1967-69, 93—; staff photographer Nat. Geog. Soc., Washington, 1969-89, contract photographer, 1989-93; prin. photographer books on Hawaii and America's Inland Waterway. Served with AUS, 1953-55. Named Mag. Photographer of Yr., Nat. Press Photographers Assn., 1969, 70. Mem. White House News Photographers Assn., Profl. Photographers of Am., N.Am. Nature Photography Assn. Home: PO Box 118 Centreville MD 21617-0118 *To achieve success we must love what we are doing, be willing to take risks and trust our instincts.*

AMOS, JANICE RAE, automotive executive; b. Fairmont, W.Va., June 18, 1953; d. Albert Clyde and Frances (Lang) A.; m. David Lynn Schoewe. BME, Gen. Motors Inst., Flint, Mich., 1976; MBA, Case Western Res. U., 1981; Exec. MBA Program, Ind. U., 1994. Mech. engr. NDH div. GM, Sandusky, Ohio, 1976-78, maint. supr., 1978-82, div. buyer capital equipment, 1982-84; purchasing agt. Hydra-Matic div. GM, Ypsilanti, Mich., Toledo, 1984-87; supt. reliability Hydra-Matic div. GM, 1987-89; supt. mfg. Powertrain div. GM, 1989-91, bus. team mgr., 1991-94; area mgr. Delphi Chassis - Delphi Automotive, 1994-96; ops. mgr. Delphi Chassis - Delphi Automotive, Sandusky, Ohio, 1996—. Mem. Nat. Trust Hist. Preservation, Washington, 1988, YWCA Twin Forum, Toledo, 1986. Mem. Order Ky. Colonels. Republican. Presbyterian. Avocations: travel, collecting antiques, historic home preservation. Office: Delphi Chassis Systems 2509 Hayes Ave Sandusky OH 44870-5359

AMOS, JOHN, actor, producer, director; b. Newark, Dec. 27, 1941; s. John A. and Annabelle P. Amos; children: K.C., Shannon Patrice. Student, Colo.

State U., Long Beach City Coll. Creator, prodr., dir. Step and One Half Prodns., Califon, N.J.; former profl. football player Am., Can. and Continental Leagues. Actor: (Broadway debut) Tough to Get Help, Royale Theatre, (stage prodns.) Norman, is that You?, 1971, The Emperor Jones, 1979, Master Harold...and the Boys, 1983, Split Second, 1985, (feature films) Vanishing Point, 1971, The World's Greatest Athlete, 1973, Let's Do it Again, 1975, The Beastmaster, 1983, Dance of the Dwarfs, 1983, American Flyers, 1984, Coming to America, 1988, Lock Up, 1989, Diehard 2, 1990, Ricochet, 1991, Two Evil Eyes (The Black Cat), 1991, MAC, 1993, Hologram Man, 1995, (TV mini-series) Roots, 1977, (Emmy award nomination 1977), (TV movies) The President's Plane is Missing, 1971, Willa, 1979; regular: (TV series) Mary Tyler Moore Show, 1970-73, The Funny Side, 1971, Maude, 1973-74, Good Times, 1974-79, Hunter, 1984, 704 Hauser, 1994, South by Southwest, 704 Houser, 1994; guest star: (TV shows) The Tonight Show, The Merv Griffin Show, The Mike Douglas Show; dir.: (stage prodns.) And Miss Reardon Drinks a Little, Bahamian Repertory Co., Twelve Angry Men, Bahamian Repertory Co.; one man stage shows include Halleys, Comet, 1990—; producer, dir., writer (feature film) Grambling Takes it All Back Home. Social worker Vera Inst. Justice, N.Y.C. Mem. Screen Actors Guild, AFTRA, Young Men's Christian Assn. Avocations: scuba-diving, horseback riding, flying. Office: Abrams Artists & Assocs Inc 9200 W Sunset Blvd Ste 625 Los Angeles CA 90069-3508 Address: Step and One Half Prodns PO Box 587 Califon NJ 07830-0587*

AMOS, PAUL SHELBY, insurance company executive; b. Enterprise, Ala., Apr. 23, 1926; s. John Shelby and Mary Helen (Mullins) A.; m. Mary Jean Roberts, Oct. 24, 1948; 1 child, Daniel P. Co-founder, v.p. Am. Family Life Assurance Co., Columbus, Ga., 1956-64; state mgr. Ala. Am. Family Life Assurance Co. (W.Fla.), Columbus, Ga., 1964-74; 1st v.p., dir. mktg. Am. Family Life Assurance Co., Columbus, Ga., 1974-78, pres., 1978-83; vice chmn. Am Family Life Assurance Co., Columbus, Ga., 1983-90, chmn., 1990—; pres. Am. Family Corp., Columbus, 1981-83, vice chmn., 1983-90; chmn. AFLAC, Columbus, 1990—; owner Ben Franklin Stores, Milton, Fla., 1946-66; ptnr., v.p. Service Oil Co., Milton, 1958-66; pres., chmn. First Fed. Savs. & Loan, Milton, 1957-74. Trustee Asbury Theol. Sem. With USCGR, 1944-46, PTO. Mem. Columbus C. of C. Republican. Methodist. Club: Country of Columbus; Big Eddy. Home: 939 Overlook Dr Columbus GA 31906-3028 Office: AFLAC 1932 Wynnton Rd Columbus GA 31999-0002*

AMOS, WALLY, entrepreneur; b. Tallahassee, Fla., July 1, 1936; s. Wallace Sr. and Ruby Amos; m. Maria LaForey (div.); children: Michael, Gregory; m. Shirlee Ellis (div.); 1 child, Shawn; m. Christine Amos, 1979; 1 child, Sarah. Stockroom clk. Saks Fifth Ave., N.Y.C., 1957-58, stockroom supr., 1958-61; mail room clk. William Morris Agy., N.Y.C., 1961, sec., 1961-62, asst. agt., 1962; talent agt., 1962-67; ind personal mgr. L.A., 1967-75; founder Famous Amos Chocolate Chip Cookie Corp., Hollywood, Calif., 1975-89, Wally Amos Presents: Chip and Cookie, 1991-92, UNCLE Noname Cookie Co., 1992—. Author: The Famous Amos Story: The Face That Launched a Thousand Chips, 1983, The Power In You: Ten Secret Ingredients for Inner Strength, 1988, Mau with No Name: Turn Lemons Into Lemonade, 1994. Nat. spokesman Literacy Vols. of Am., 1979. With USAF, 1953-57. Recipient Pres.' award for Entrepreneurial Excellence, 1986, Horatio Alger award 1987, Nat. Literacy Honors award 1990. Home and Office: UNCLE Noname Cookie Co PO Box 897 Kailua HI 96734*

AMOS-GANTHER, LINDA, poet; b. York, Pa., Sept. 13, 1950; d. Herbert and Gloria (Stell) Gardner; m. Ralph Amos, Aug. 30, 1978 (dec.); 4 children; m. George William Ganther, Apr. 17, 1994. AS, York Coll. Pa., 1980, BA, 1984. Author: From A-to-Z, 1992, The Pieces of my Life, 1994, Carousel, 1998, A Garden of New Beginnings, 1997, Spring Greetings, 1998. Local parent rep. Head Start Parents Group, York, 1982-88, state parent rep. Pa., 1984-88, nat. parent rep., 1988; mem. steering com. Old York St Fair, 1999, Week of the Young Child, 1998-99; active Leadership York, 1985. Mem. Poetry Soc. Tex., Poets East Tex. Presbyterian. Avocations: traditional hand quilting, organic gardening. Office: The Wordwrite Shoppe RR 2 Box CL Murchison TX 75778-9802

AMOSS, W. JAMES, JR., shipping company executive; b. 1924; married. BBA, Tulane U., 1947. With Lykes Bros. Steamship Co. Inc., New Orleans, 1947-93, v.p. traffic, 1963-70, exec. v.p., 1970-73, pres., 1973-86, chief exec. officer, dir., 1981—, chmn., 1986-93; chmn. Interocean Steamship Corp, Tampa, Fla., 1986-93; pres. Marine Logistics, Inc., New Orleans, 1993—; dir. Hibernia Nat. Bank, 1973-95. With USN, 1942-46, 50-52. Office: Marine Logistics Inc 2 Canal St New Orleans LA 70130-1408

AMOSS, WALTER JAMES, III, editor; b. New Orleans, Oct. 22, 1947; s. Walter James Jr. and Berthe Lathrop (Marks) A.; m. Nancy Brooks Monroe, Apr. 5, 1975; children: Adam Brooks, Sophia Philomene. BA magna cum laude, Yale U., 1969. Reporter The States-Item, New Orleans, 1974-79; reporter The Times-Picayune, New Orleans, 1980-82, city editor, 1982-83, met. editor, 1983-88, assoc. editor, 1988-90, editor, 1990—; bd. vis. La State U. Manship Sch. Mass. Comms.; trustee Trinity Episcopal Sch. Mem. La. Com. of Selection for Rhodes Scholarships, 1982—. Rhodes scholar Oxford (Eng.) U., 1970-71; Journalistes en Europe grantee, 1979-80. Mem. Am. Soc. Newspaper Editors, AP Mng. Editors, Phi Beta Kappa. Roman Catholic. Office: The Times-Picayune 3800 Howard Ave New Orleans LA 70125-1429

AMPARADO, KEITH D., communications company executive; b. Bklyn., Oct. 5, 1952; m. Arcadeo and Sadie J. (Browne) A. BS, SUNY, Empire State Coll. Supr. data processing Franklin Nat. Bank/European Am. Bank, 1974-78; mgr. Ctr. for Computing Activity Columbia U., N.Y.C., 1978-80; systems analyst Morgan Guaranty Trust Co., 1980-81; programmer, analyst Europen Am. Bank, 1981-83; sr. tech editor Mfrs. Hanover Trust, 1983-85; founder, pres. KDA Comm, Bklyn., 1985—; cons. Siloam Presbyn. Ch., Bklyn., 1988—. Mem. Soc. for Tech. Communication (sr.), Am. Mgmt. Assn., Am. Mktg. Assn., Mktg. Rsch. Assn., Nat. Assn. Desktop Pubs., Qualitative Rsch. Cons. Assn., Internat. Assn. of Bus. Communicators.

AMPOLA, MARY G., pediatrician, geneticist; b. Syracuse, N.Y., Nov. 2, 1934; d. Mariangelo and Filomena (Albanese) Giambattista; m. Vincent G. Ampola, Aug. 7, 1966; children: Leanna, David. BA cum laude, Syracuse U., 1956; MD, SUNY, Syracuse, 1960. Diplomate Am. Bd. Pediatrics. Intern George Washington Univ. Hosp., Washington, 1960-61; pediatric resident Children's Nat. Med. Ctr., Washington, 1961-63, chief resident in pediatrics, 1963-64; genetics fellow Children's Hosp. Med. Ctr., Boston, 1964-66; metabolic diseases fellow Mass. Gen. Hosp., Boston, 1966-67; cytogeneticist New Eng. Med. Ctr., Boston, 1967-69, dir. pediatric amino acid lab., 1969—, pediatrician, 1969—, acting chief clin. genetics divsn. dept. pediatrics, 1989-96, chief divsn. metabolism, dept. pediatrics, 1996—; from asst. to assoc. prof. pediatrics New Eng. Med. Ctr./Tufts U. Sch. Medicine, Boston, 1967-92, prof., 1992—; chmn. PL-1 selection com. dept. pediatrics New Eng. Med. Ctr., 1975—, chmn. residency com., 1981-87, mem. residency com. 1987—, bd. dirs. Ctr. Children Spl. Needs, 1987—, mem. hosp. quality assurance com., 1982-92; mem. curriculum com., 1981-84; chmn. evaluation and promotions com. Tufts U. Sch. Medicine, 1998—. Editor: Early Detection and Management of Inborn Errors, 1976; author: Metabolic Diseases in Pediatric Practice, 1982; contbr. chpts. to books and articles to profl. jours. Named Alumna of Yr., SUNY Coll. Medicine, 1980. Fellow Am. Acad. Pediatrics (sect. genetics); mem. Am. Soc. Human Genetics, New Eng. Pediatric Soc. (sec.-treas. 1993—), Soc. Inherited Metabolic Disorders, Soc. Study Inborn Errors Metabolism, Phi Beta Kappa. Republican. Office: New Eng Med Ctr 750 Washington St Boston MA 02111-1526

AMPONSAH, WILLIAM APPIAH, international economics educator; b. Accra, Ghana, Oct. 31, 1958; s. Benjamin Appiah and Agnes (Dentah) A.; m. Valentina J. Ababio, Oct. 5, 1993; children: William Benjamin, Daniel Appiah K. BS, Berea (Ky.) Coll., 1984; MS, U. Ky., 1986; PhD, Ohio State U., 1991. Asst. prof. N.C. AT&T State U., Greensboro, 1991-95, assoc. prof., 1996—, dir. internat. trade ctr., 1998—. Author: (with others) Sustainability in Agriculture and Rural Development, 1998, Issues in Agricultural Development, 1992; co-editor: Trade Policy and Competition, 1998; contbr. articles to profl. jours. Pres. coun. mem. Good News Jail and Prison Ministry, Greensboro, 1998—; bd. dirs. Greensboro Cerebral Palsy, 1997—. Nat. rsch. initiative grant U.S. Dept. Agrl., 1997. Mem. Internat. Assn. of Agrl. Economists, Internat. Agrl. Trade Rsch. Consortium, Am. Agrl. Econs. Assn. (co-editor), So. Assn. of Agrl. Econs., Kiwanis Club Internat. (chairperson internat. rels. 1996—), Gamma Sigma Delta, Delta Tau Alpha. Methodist. Avocations: reading, tennis, soccer. E-mail: williama@ncat.edu. Home: 5 Thames Ct Greensboro NC 27411 Office: Internat Trade Ctr NC AT&T State U 1601 E Market St Greensboro NC 27411

AMRAM, DAVID WERNER, composer, conductor, musician; b. Phila., Nov. 17, 1930; s. Philip and Emilie (Weyl) A.; m. Loralee Ecobelli, Jan. 7, 1979; children: Alana, Adira, Adam. Student, Oberlin Conservatory Music, 1948-49, Manhattan Sch. Music, 1955-56; BA in European History, George Washington U., 1952; LLD, Moravian Coll., Bethlehem, Pa., 1979; studied composition with Vittorio Giannini, N.Y.C., studied horn with Gunther Schuller, 1956; MusD (hon.), Muhlenberg Coll., 1988, U. Hartford, 1989; DMus (hon.), St. Lawrence U., 1994. Head Free Schooltime Concert Series, Bklyn. Philharmonic Orch., 1971—; Leo Block chair for the Arts & Humanities, U. Denver. Condr., soloist with 14 orchs. annually including Montreal Symphony, Toronto Symphony, Milw. Symphony, Indpls. Symphony, Grant Park Orch., Nat. Jewish Arts. Festival; 1st composer-in-residence, N.Y. Philharmonic Orch., 1966-67; composer incidental music for prodns., N.Y. Shakespeare Festival, 1956-67, Broadway plays, 1958—, films include The Manchurian Candidate, Splendor in the Grass, others, 1957—, also TV (collaboration with Jack Kerouac and Allen Ginsberg); compositions for orch. include Ode to Lord Buckley for saxophone and orch., Violin Concerto, numerous others; commd. composer A Little Rebellion: Thomas Jefferson for narrator/wood-wind guintel, strings and percussion for Libr. Congress, 1995, Kokopelli, 1997; operas include The Final Ingredient, 12th Night, 1996; recording artist, conductor, composer, multi-instrumentalist Newport Classic Records, 1989, Premiere Records; works performed by Phila. Orch., N.Y. Philharmonic, other maj. orchs.; plays French horn, piano, guitar, numerous flutes and whistles; combines symphony, jazz and folk music with audience participation; recs. include Recordings of Symphonic Works, 1993, 94, 95, The Holocaust Open The Final Ingredient, 1996, The Manchurian Candidate, 1997; author: (autobiography) Vibrations: Adventures and Musical Times of David Amram, 1968, music dir. Internat. Jewish Arts Festival, 1992, 94, conducting mem. Met. Opera Orch., music dir. Aaron Copland Festival, 1992, 94; composed music for films: Splendor in the Grass, The Manchurian Candidate, The Arrangement, The Young Savages; guest soloist nat. TV with Dizzy Gillespie and Willie Nelson, 1987. Served with AUS, 1952-54. Recipient Obie award for compositions for Phoenix Theater and N.Y. Shakespeare Festival, 1959; named One of 20 Most Performed Composers of Concert Music in U.S., BMI: Many Worlds of Music. Subject of: 1-hour Nat. Ednl. TV Documentary The World of David Amram, 1969, David Amram and Friends, 1979, PBS Soundstage, a collection of papers at Mugar Library Boston Univ. Address: New World Music Artists 928 Peekskill Hollow Rd Putnam Valley NY 10579-1705

AMRHEIN, JOHN KILIAN, retired dean; b. Pitts., Sept. 20, 1938; s. Joseph Reinhold and Grace Rose (Babcox) A.; m. Elaine Marie Barnes, Apr. 4, 1970; children: Karl, Timothy. BA, Duquesne U., 1961; MLS, U. Pitts., 1963; MA, Pa. State U., 1967. Periodicals libr. Pa. State U., University Park, 1963-65, asst. libr. br. campuses, 1965-66, grad. asst., 1966-67; circulation libr. Kent (Ohio) State U., 1967-71; libr. dir. Kutztown (Pa.) U., 1971-84; dean libr. svcs. Calif. State U.-Stanislaus, Turlock, 1984-98; ret. Author revs. and book chpts. Home: 2181 Carlton Dr Turlock CA 95382-2116

AMSDEN, TED THOMAS, lawyer; b. Cleve., Dec. 11, 1950; s. Richard Thomas and Mary Agnes (Hendricks) A.; m. Ruth Anna Rydstedt, May 1, 1982; children: Jennifer Rydstedt, Matthew Lars, Alexis Linnea. BA, Wayne State U., 1972; JD, Harvard U., 1975. Bar: Mich. 1975, U.S. Dist. Ct. (ea. dist.) Mich. 1975, U.S. Ct. Appeals (6th cir.) 1975, U.S. Supreme Ct. 1979. From assoc. to ptnr. Dykema Gossett PLLC and predecessor firm, Detroit, 1975—. Chmn. Baha'i Justice Soc., 1986-88, corr. sec., 1988-92, bd. dirs., 1986-93, 95—; bd. dirs. Internat. Inst., Detroit, 1989-97, 99—, v.p. legal affairs, 1991-94, v.p., 1994-95, pres.-elect 1995-96, pres., 1996-97, co-chair Ethnic Summit '96; bd. dirs. Racial Justice Ctr., Grosse Pointe, Mich., 1992-94, Greater Detroit Interfaith Roundtable, 1994—, bd. dirs. Model of Racial Unity, Inc., 1995-97, treas., 1997—, chmn., 1998—, vice chmn.; mem. Mich. Bar Rep. Assembly, 1988-94. Recipient Detroit Principles award of Race Relations Coun. of Metropolitan Detroit, 1993, Spirit of Detroit award City of Detroit Common Coun., 1996, 97. Mem. ABA, Mich. Bar Assn., Wolverine Bar Assn., Detroit Bar Assn., Detroit Bar Assn. Found. (bd. dirs. 1992-98, sec., 1993-95, pres. 1995-97), Macomb County Bar Assn., Assn. Def. Counsel, Civic Searchlight (Macomb County steering com., jud. com. 1990-91, Wayne County jud. com. 1992-95). Home: 987 Lake Shore Rd Grosse Pointe MI 48236-1171 Office: Dykema Gossett 400 Renaissance Ctr Ste 3800 Detroit MI 48243-1603

AMSLER, KAREN MARIE, medical technologist, scientist; b. Duluth, Minn., May 10, 1960; d. Fred Ritts and Ilene Lucille (App) A.; m. Craig Alan Steensma, Aug. 31, 1986 (div. Mar. 1995). BA in Biology, Hollins (Va.) Coll., 1982; MS in Microbiology, Immunology, Thomas Jefferson U., 1996. Med. technologist Am. Med. Labs., Fairfax, Va., 1985-86, Bancroft Med. Lab., Wilmington, Del., 1986-89; rsch. technologist U. Pa. Sch. Vet. Medicine, Kennet Square, 1989-90; med. technologist Crozer-Chester Med. Ctr., Upland, Pa., 1991-93, Christiana Care Health System, Newark, Del., 1991-98, Smith Kline Beecham Clin. Labs., Norristown, Pa., 1993, Children's Hosp. Phila., 1994-96; staff scientist DuPont Pharm. Co., Wilmington, 1998—. Mem. DAR, Am. Soc. Clin. Pathologists (cert.), Am. Soc. Microbiology. Avocations: horseback riding, skiing, hiking, gardening. Home: 4749 Weatherhill Dr Wilmington DE 19808-1939 Office: DuPont Pharm Co Exptl Sta E400/3434 PO Box 80400 Wilmington DE 19880-0400

AMSPOKER, JAMES MACK, retired gas company executive; b. East Liberty, Ohio, July 28, 1926; s. Charley Mack and Blanche (Richardson) A.; m. Anne M. Guido, Dec. 2, 1955; children: Charley M., Stephanie. B.M.E., Ohio State U., 1948. With Columbia Engring. Corp., Columbus, Ohio, 1948-50, Columbia Gas System Service Corp., N.Y.C., 1950-53; gen. engr. Ohio Fuel Gas Co., Columbus, 1953-63; supervisory engr. Columbia Gas of Ohio, Columbus, 1963-67; chief engr. Columbia Gas of Ohio, 1967, v.p., 1967-70, sr. v.p., dir., 1970-73; sr. v.p., dir. Columbia Gas Transmission Corp., Charleston, W.Va., 1973-88. Served with USNR, 1944-46. Mem. Ohio State U. Com. for Tomorrow, Ohio Order of Engrs., Pinewild Country Club, Mason. Home: PO Box 5669 Pinehurst NC 28374-5669

AMSTADTER, LAURENCE, retired architect; b. Chgo., Apr. 9, 1922; s. Frank J. and Irene B. (Black) A.; m. Erma Jacqueline Kallen, Mar. 8, 1948; children: John Kallen, Marc Robert. BA in Architecture, Chgo. Tech. Coll., 1948; postgrad., Northwestern U., Evanston, Ill., 1948-49. Registered architect, Ill., 35 other states. Architect Ford Bacon & Davis Inc., Chgo., 1949-50, Skidmore Owings & Merrill, Chgo., 1950-51, Sidney Morris & Assocs., Chgo., 1951-52, Chgo. Housing Authority, 1952-53; sr. v.p. A. Epstein and Sons Inc., Chgo., 1953-87; cons., 1987—. Mem. Exec. Svc. Corps of Chgo. With Air Corps, U.S. Army, 1941-45, ETO. Mem. AIA (corp.), Svc. Corps Ret. Execs., Soc. Am. Registered Architects, Chgo. Com. on High Rise Bldgs. Democrat. Home: 1633 Cambridge Ave Flossmoor IL 60422-2127 Office: Amstadter Architects 200 W Superior St Chicago IL 60610-3553

AMSTER, LINDA EVELYN, newspaper executive, consultant; b. N.Y.C., May 21, 1938; d. Abraham and Belle Shirley (Levine) Meyerson; m. Robert L. Amster, Feb. 18, 1961 (dec. Feb. 1974). B.A., U. Mich., 1960; M.L.S., Columbia U., 1968. Tchr. English Stamford High Sch., Conn., 1961-63; research librarian The Detroit News, 1965-67; research librarian The N.Y. Times, N.Y.C., 1967-69, supr. news research, 1969-74, news research mgr., 1974—; bd. dirs. Council for Career Planning, N.Y.C., 1982—. Editor: The New York Times Passover Cookbook, 1999; contbr. articles to books, N.Y. Times and other publs. Mem. adv. com. N.Y.C. 100 Greater N.Y. Centennial Celebration. Mem. Spl. libraries Assn. Club: Coffee House. Home: 336 Central Park W New York NY 10025-7111 Office: The NY Times 229 W 43rd St New York NY 10036-3959

AMSTERDAM, ANTHONY GUY, law educator; b. Phila., Sept. 12, 1935; s. Gustave G. and Valla (Abel) A.; m. Lois P. Sheinfeld, Aug. 29, 1968. AB, Haverford Coll., 1957; LLB, U. Pa., 1960; LLD (hon.), John Jay Coll. Criminal Justice, 1987, Haverford Coll., 1993. Bar: D.C. 1960. Law clk. to U.S. Supreme Ct. Justice Felix Frankfurter, 1960-61; asst. U.S. atty., 1961-62; prof. law U. Pa., 1962-69; prof. law Stanford U., 1969-81, Montgomery prof. clin. legal edn., 1980-81; prof. law, dir. clin. programs and trial advocacy NYU, 1981—; cons. litigating atty. numerous civil rights groups; cons. govt. commns.; mem. Commn. to Study Disturbances at Columbia, 1968; trustee Death Penalty Info. Ctr., Lawyers Constl. Def. Com., NAACP Legal Def. Fund, Nat. Coalition to abolish the Death Penalty, So. Poverty Law Ctr., Brennan Ctr. for Justice; mem. Calif. Fed. Jud. Selection Com., 1976-80; mem. coord. coun. on lawyer competence Conf. of Chief Justices; gen. counsel N.Y. Civil Liberties Union; adv. counsel Civil Liberties Union No. Calif.; mem. ABA task force. Author: The Defensive Transfer of Civil Rights Litigation From State to Federal Courts, 1964, Trial Manual for Defense of Criminal Cases, 5th edit., 1989, (with Hertz and Guggenheim) Trial Manual for Defense Attornys in Juvenile Court, 1991; editor-in-chief: U. Pa. Law Rev., 1959-60; contbr. articles to profl. jours. Named Outstanding Young Man of Year Phila. and Pa. Jaycees, 1967; recipient First Disting. Service award U. Pa. Law Sch., 1968; Haverford award Haverford Coll., 1970; Arthur V. Briesen award Nat. Legal Aid and Defender Assn., 1972, 76; named Lawyer of Year Calif. Trial Lawyers Assn., 1973; recipient 1st Earl Warren Civil Liberties award No. Calif. chpt. ACLU, 1973, Citizen of Merit award Sun Reporter, 1974, Walter J. Gores award Stanford U., 1977, William O. Douglas award Pub. Counsel, 1977, 2d ann. award Calif. Attys. Criminal Justice, 1978, award for enhancement human dignity Durfee Found., 1982, Francis Rawle award ALI-ABA, 1984, 3d ann. Civil Liberties award Pa. ACLU, 1985, clinical legal edn. award AALS Sect. on Clinical Legal Edn., 1986, August Vollmer award Am. Soc. Criminology, 1986, Disting. Tchr. award NYU, 1988, award N.Y. Criminal Bar Assn., 1989, Tchg. Achievement award Soc. Am. Law Tchrs., 1999; named MacArthur fellow, 1989. Fellow Am. Acad. Arts and Scis. Home: 68 Middle Line Hwy Southampton NY 11968-1645 Office: NYU Sch Law 249 Sullivan St New York NY 10012-1079

AMSTERDAM, DAVID ERIK, school psychologist; b. Bronx, N.Y., June 27, 1962; s. Bernard Sidney and Ruth Marlene (Zapolsky) A. BA in Psychology, St. John's U., 1984, MS in Sch. Psychology, 1987. Cert. sch. psychologist, N.Y. Sch. psychology intern Herricks (N.Y.) Pub. Sch., 1986-87; sch. psychologist The Shield Inst., Flushing, N.Y., 1987—. Author: The Miracle of Elcarim, 1996. Mem. Nat. Assn. of Sch. Psychologists, N.Y. Assn. of Sch. Psychologists, N.Y. Road Runners Club, Broadway Ulta Soc. Jewish. Avocations: running, writing, inventing products. Home: 19014 37th Ave Flushing NY 11358-2401 Office: The Shield Inst 14461 Roosevelt Ave Flushing NY 11354-6252

AMSTERDAM, JAY D., psychiatrist, educator; b. Phila., Feb. 10, 1949. BA, Syracuse U., 1970; MD, Jefferson Med. Coll., 1974. Diplomate Am. Bd. Med. Examiners, Am. Bd. Psychiatry and Neurology; lic. physician, Pa., N.J. Intern in ob-gyn. Upstate Med. Ctr., Syracuse, N.Y., 1974; resident in psychiatry Thomas Jefferson U. Hosp., Phila., 1974-77, chief resident in psychiatry, 1976-77; sr. resident psychiat. rsch. svc. depression rsch. unit VA Med. Ctr., Phila., 1977-78; NIMH postdoctoral fellow in neuropsychopharmacology VA Med. Ctr./U. Pa. Hosp., Phila., 1978-79; asst. prof. psychiatry Thomas Jefferson U., Phila., 1978-83, adj. assoc. prof. psychiatry, 1983-88; dir. depression rsch. unit U. Pa. Hosp., Phila., 1979—; asst. prof. psychiatry U. Pa., Phila., 1979-86, assoc. prof. psychiatry, 1986-92, prof., 1992—; mem. instl. review bd. com. on studies involving human beings U. Pa., 1983—, human rsch. ethics group project informed consent, 1996, mem. sch. adminstrn. coun., 1996-97, faculty senate exec. com., 1987-88, univ. coun.,1987-88, undergrad. admissions and fin. aid, 1987-90, univ. facilities com., 1988-89, student affairs com., 1989-91, univ. disability bd., 1990-93; mem. student-faculty interaction com. U. Pa. Hosp. and Med. Sch., 1987-89, continuing med. edn. lecture series, 1986—, ad hoc com. on organ transplantation, 1988, pharmacy and therapeutics com., 1989-93, investigational drug task force, 1991-92, mem. clin. svcs. steering com., 1985-86, residency tng. com., 1985-86, rsch. com., 1985-90, Sachar Rsch. Award com., 1985—, faculty grievance com., 1996—; adj. assoc. prof. Wistar Inst. Anatomy, Phila., 1988—; mem. program planning com. IV World Congress Biol. Psychiatry, Phila., 1984-85; sci. adv. com. 2nd Internat. Conf. on Viruses, Immunity and Mental Health, Montreal, Que., Can., 1988; program dir. organizing com. 1st Internat. Conf. on Refractory Depression, Phila., 1988; mem. organizing com. 2nd Internat. Conf. on refractory Depression, Amsterdam, 1990-92; program organizer and dir. 3rd Internat. Conf. on Refractory Depression, 1992, Napa Valley, Calif., 1995; mem. Internat. Consensus Conf. to Define Refractory Depression, 1996—; vis. prof. Med. Acad. Sci., Poznan, Poland, 1996; prin. or co-investigator 60 industry sponsored drug trials. Editor (textbooks): Pharmacology of Depression: Applications for the Outpatient Practitioner, 1990, Refractory Depression, 1991 (with J. Mendels) Psychobiology of Affective Disorders, 1980, (with W. Nolan, J. Zohar S. Roose) Refractory Depression, 1994, (with M. Hornig-Rohan) Refractory Depression: Psychiatric Clinics of North America, 1996; assoc. editor Jour. Affective Disorders, 1986—; asst. editor Psychosomatics, 1987-96; referee Archives Gen. Psychiatry, Am. Jour. Psychiatry, Biol. Psychiatry, Jour. Clin. Psychopharmacology, Jour. Neuropsychiatry and Clin. Neuroscience, Psychoneuroendocrinology, Psychiatry Rsch., Psychosomatics, Psychosomatic Medicine, Psychobiology; asst. editor Psychiat. Annals, 1995—; assoc. editor Depression, 1995—; contbr. over 160 articles to med. and sci. jours., over 375 presentations, abstracts, and invited papers in field. Grantee NIMH, 1980-81, 1980-85, 89-94, 96—, Jack Warsaw Fund, 1984—; Biomedical Rsch. Support grantee NIH, 1989-90, Stanley Rsch. Found., 1995—. Fellow Am. Psychiat. Assn. (advisor mood disorders work group for DSM-IV 1989—, Marie H. Eldredge award 1986), Am. Bd. Med. Psychotherapists; mem. World Psychiat. Assn. (sect. on affective disorders 1995—), Am. Fedn. for Clin. Rsch., Am. Assn. History Medicine, Internat. Soc. Psychoneuroendocrinology, Internat. Soc. for Investigation of Stress, Soc. Biol. Psychiatry (membership com. 1988-91), Pa. Psychiat. Soc., Phila. Psychiat. Soc. (exec. coun. 1985—, chair clin. rsch. resource com. 1989—). Home: PO Box 1931 Cherry Hill NJ 08034-0128

AMSTERDAM, MARK LEMLE, lawyer; b. N.Y.C., June 10, 1944; s. Leonard M. and Erica (Lemle) A.; children: Lauren, Matthew. AB Columbia U., 1966, JD cum laude, 1969. Bar: N.Y. 1969, U.S. Dist. Ct. (so. ea., no. dists.) N.Y. 1972, U.S. Dist. Ct. (no. dist.) Tex., U.S. Supreme Ct. 1973. Assoc. Fried, Frank, Harris, N.Y.C., 1969-70; staff atty. Ctr. for Constl. Rights, N.Y.C., 1970-75; sole practice law, N.Y.C., 1975-76, 81—; ptnr. Rubin Hanley & Amsterdam, 1976-79, Katz Amsterdam & Weinstein, N.Y.C., 1980, Amsterdam and Lewinter, 1990—; instr. N.Y. Law Sch., 1982-83. Contbr. articles to legal jours. Mem. Gardeners Bay Country Club, Columbia. Home: 1220 Park Ave New York NY 10128-1733 Office: 9 E 40th St New York NY 10016-0402

AMSTUTZ, DANIEL GORDON, international trade association administrator, former grain dealer, government and intergovernment official; b. Cleve., Nov. 8, 1932; s. Gordon M. and Elizabeth (Kiss) A. B.S., Ohio State U., 1954. Trainee Cargill, Inc., Mpls., 1954-55; grain mcht. Tradax Can., Ltd., Montreal, Que., Can., 1955-56, Tradax Geneva, S.A., Geneva, 1956-57; mgr. Deutsche Tradax Gmbh, Hamburg, Germany, 1957-58; grain mcht. Cargill, Inc., Fort Worth, 1959, sr. grain merchant, Mpls., 1960-72; pres. Cargill Investor Services, Inc., Chgo., 1973-78; ptnr. Goldman, Sachs & Co., N.Y.C., 1978-82; undersec. for internat. affairs and commodity programs Dept. Agr., Washington, 1983-87; pres. Commodity Credit Corp., Washington, 1983-87; ambassador, chief trade negotiator for agr. USDA, Washington, 1987-89; exec. dir. Internat. Wheat Coun., London, 1992-95; pres./CEO North Am. Export Grain Assn., Inc., Washington, 1995—; mem. U.S. Agrl. Policy Adv. Com., 1998—; mem. com. agri-bus. U.S.-Russian Joint Commn. on Econ. and Tech. Coop., 1996—. Mem. U.S. Feed Grains Council (dir. 1967-72), Nat. Grain and Feed Assn. (dir. 1973-82), Ohio State U. Alumni Assn. (v.p. 1989, co-chair fund-raising campaign 1990—), dir. Ohio State U. Found., 1998—. Republican. *Perseverance pays; keep trying and trying and never stop believing in yourself.*

AMSTUTZ, HAROLD EMERSON, veterinarian, educator; b. Barrs Mill, Ohio, June 21, 1919; s. Nelson David and Viola Emma (Schnitzer) A.; m. Mabelle Josephine Bower, June 26, 1949; children: Suzanne Marie, Cynthia Lou, Patricia Lynn, David Bruce. BS in Agr, Ohio State U., 1942, DVM, 1945. Diplomate Am. Coll. Vet. Internal Medicine (pres. 1972-73, chmn. bd. regents 1973-74); hon. diplomate Am. Coll. Theriogenology. Pvt. practice vet. medicine Orrville, Ohio, 1946-47; instr. vet. medicine Ohio State U., 1947-52, asst. prof., 1952-54, asso. prof., 1954-56, prof., 1957-61, prof., head dept. vet. medicine, 1956-61; head dept. vet. clinics Purdue U., West Lafayette, Ind., 1961-75; prof. large animal clinics Purdue U., 1975-89, prof.

emeritus, 1989—. Editor: Bovine Medicine and Surgery Book, 1979; contbg. editor: Modern Veterinary Practice, 1979-84; mem. editorial bd. The Merck Vet. Manual, 6th, 7th and 8th edits.; contbr. to books on diseases of large domestic animals. Mem. exec. bd. Ind.-Ky. synod Luth. Ch. Am., 1986-88; pres. World Assn. for Buiatrics, 1972-84. Served with U.S. Army, 1945-46. Recipient Borden award for outstanding research in diseases of dairy cattle, 1978; named Disting. Alumnus Ohio State U. Coll. Vet. Medicine, 1974; recipient Alumni Faculty award Sch. Vet. Medicine, Purdue U., 1989, Sagamore of the Wabash Ind. Gov., 1990, Ark. Traveler award Ark. Gov., 1969, Gustav Rosenberger Meml. award Dutch Veterinary Assn., 1992, Alumni Recognition award Vet. Medicine Alumni Soc. Ohio State U., 1998. Mem. AVMA (12th Internat. Congress prize for contributing to internat. understanding of vet. medicine 1995), Am. Assn. Vet. Clinicians (pres. 1972), Am. Assn. Bovine Practitioners (exec. sec. 1971-89, exec. v.p. 1989-93, hon. mem. 1993), World Assn. Buiatrics (pres. 1972-84), Am. Coll. of Theriogenologists (hon. diplomate 1993), Sigma Xi, Phi Zeta, Gamma Sigma Delta (award of merit), Omega Tau Sigma (nat. Gamma award). Republican. Office: Purdue Univ Dept Veterinary Sci West Lafayette IN 47907

AMUNDSON, ROBERT A., state supreme court justice; m. Katherine Amundson; children: Beth, Amy. BBA, Augustana Coll., 1961; JD, U. S.D., 1964. Asst. atty. gen. Atty. Gen's. Office, 1965-69; mem. firm Belle Fourche and Lead, 1970-89; cir. judge 2d Jud. Cir., 1989-91; justice Supreme Ct. of S.D., Vermillion, 1991—. Office: Supreme Court of South Dakota State Capitol Bldg 500 E Capitol Ave Pierre SD 57501-5070*

AMY, JONATHAN WEEKES, scientist, educator; b. Delaware, Ohio, Mar. 3, 1923; s. Ernest Francis and Theresa Louise (Say) A.; m. Ruthanna Borden, Dec. 20, 1947; children—Joseph Wilbur, James Borden, Theresa. B.A., Ohio Wesleyan U., 1948; M.S., Purdue U., 1950, Ph.D., 1955. Research assoc. dept. chemistry Purdue U., West Lafayette, Ind., 1954-60, assoc. prof., 1960-70, prof., 1970—, assoc. dir. labs., 1960—, dir. instrumentation, 1970-84, emeritus, 1988; cons. chem. instrumentation; sec.-treas. Technometrics, Inc., 1968—; mem. adv. panels AAAS, Assn. Am. Univs., NSF, Am. Chem. Soc.; vis. scholar Stanford U., 1992. Assoc. editor Ind. Chem. News; patentee elec. measuring equipment and chem. instrumentation. Pres. Wabash Twp. Vol. Fire Dept., 1970-86. Served with U.S. Maritime Service, 1943-46. Recipient George award Lafayette Jour. and Courier, 1978. Mem. Am. Chem. Soc. (Chem. Instrumentation award), AAAS, Sigma Xi, Sigma Chi. Episcopalian. Home: 357 Overlook Dr West Lafayette IN 47906-1249 Office: Purdue U Dept Chemistry West Lafayette IN 47907

AMY, MICHAËL JACQUES, art historian, educator, art critic; b. Antwerp, Belgium, Sept. 26, 1964; s. Jean-Jacques and Marie-Claire (Nuyens) A. BA, Vrije U., Brussels, 1986; MA, NYU, 1989, PhD, 1997. Asst. to curator Mus. Contemporary Art, Ghent, Belgium, 1986-87; rsch. asst. Coe Kerr Gallery, N.Y.C., 1988-91; adj. prof. Montclair (N.J.) State U., 1996-97, CUNY, 1997—, Manhattanville Coll., Purchase, N.Y., 1997, NYU, 1997—, The Copper Union, 1999—; sec. Mnemosyne, Antwerp, Belgium, 1995—; lectr. in field.; art critic Art and Culture, Brussels, 1997—, Art in Am., N.Y.C., 1997—. Contbr. articles to profl. jours. Samuel H. Kress Found. fellow, 1994-95; recipient fellow Belgian Am. Ednl. Found., 1987-88, award Inst. Fine Arts fellow, 1988-89, 90-94, Bernard Berenson fellow, 1993-94. Mem. Internat. Assn. Art Critics, Renaissance Soc. Am., Coll. Art Assn. Avocations: interest in literature, music, politics and philosophy. Home: 485 Rugby Rd Brooklyn NY 11226-6505

AMY, PATRICIA ELEEN, psychologist; b. Phila., June 13, 1964; d. Norman Crozier and Patricia Marie (Trainer) C. BS, Western Mich. U., 1987, MA, 1989. Intern, therapist Dailey Life Ctr., Flint, Mich., 1989-90; therapist Family & Personal Stress Clinic, Flint, 1990-97, Genessee County Community Mental Health, 1991—; supr. Family & Personal Stress Clinic, Flint; tchr. Dept. Social Svcs., Flint., 1990. Vol. Compassionate Care, Fenton, Mich., 1989. Mem. Am. Psychol. Assn. Mich. Women Psychologists. Avocations: photography, reading, cross stitch, arts and crafts. Home: 935 Huron St Flint MI 48507-2554 Office: Community Mental Health 1102 Mackin Rd Flint MI 48502-1316

AMYLON, MICHAEL DAVID, physician, educator; b. Providence, Apr. 30, 1950; s. Sidney Robert and Mary Elisabeth (Alexander) A. AB, Brown U., 1972; MD, Stanford U., 1976. Diplomate sub-bd. hematology/oncology Am. Bd. Pediatrics. Resident physician Stanford (Calif.) U. Hosp., 1976-79; post-doctoral scholar Stanford U., 1979-81, acting asst. prof., 1981-82, asst. prof. pediat., 1982-89, assoc. prof. pediat., 1989—; clin. assoc. prof. pediat. U. Calif., San Francisco, 1998—; dir. marrow transplant svc. Children's Hosp. at Stanford, Palo Alto, Calif., 1986—; coord. nat. rsch. clin. trials in treatment pediatric leukemia and lymphoma Pediatric Oncology Group, St. Louis, Chgo., 1986—. Contbr. articles to profl. jours. Bd. dirs. Touchstone Support Network, Palo Alto, 1982-98, Robert J. Sturhahn Found., Novato, Calif., 1986-93, Okizu Found., Novato, 1993—, Parents Helping Parents, 1998—; med. dir. No. Calif. Oncology Camp, Nevada City, 1986—. Recipient For Those Who Care award Sta. KRON, 1990, "Ronnie" award Ronald McDonald House, 1992-93, Koshland prize Peninsula Cmty. Found., 1995, J.C. Penney Golden Rule award, 1996. Mem. Am. Acad. Pediatrics, Am. Soc. Clin. Oncology, Am. Soc. Hematology, Am. Soc. Pediatric Hematology/Oncology, Am. Soc. Blood and Marrow Transplantation. Office: Packard Children's Hosp 725 Welch Rd Palo Alto CA 94304-1601

ANACKER, EDWARD WILLIAM, retired chemistry educator; b. Chgo., June 2, 1921; s. Edward Frederick and Nellie Adelaide (Adolfs) A.; m. Stella Evelyn Lillo, Jan. 16, 1945; children: Steven Edward, David Carlyle, Eric Roland, John William. BS, Mont. State Coll., 1943; PhD, Cornell U., 1949. Instr. Mont. State Coll., Bozeman, 1949-52, asst. prof., 1952-58, assoc. prof., 1958-63, prof. chemistry, 1963-91, prof. emeritus, 1991—, head chemistry dept., 1972-77; summer participant Oak Ridge (Tenn.) Inst. Nuclear Studies, summer 1957; vis. prof. NSF Sci. Faculty Fellowship, U. Oreg., Eugene, 1964-65. Contbr. articles to profl. jours. Ensign USN, 1944-46, PTO. Named one of 100 Soc. Centennial Alumni, Mont. State U., Bozeman, 1993; grantee Rsch. Corp., 1950-56, Petroleum Rsch. Fund, 1957-60, Bur. of Reclamation, 1961-66, NSF, 1960-72, Mont. State U., 1981. Mem. Am. Chem. Soc. (chmn. Mont. sect. 1952-53, 67-68, 98-99), Mont. Acad. Scis. (pres. 1959-60), Sigma Xi (pres. Mont. chpt. 1973-74, faculty rsch. award 1967), Phi Kappa Phi, Alpha Chi Sigma. Lutheran. Avocations: running, hiking, bicycle racing. Office: Montana State U Bozeman MT 59717

ANAGNOST, DINO, artistic director. Music dir., condr. Little Orch. Soc. N.Y., 1979—. Office: Little Orch Soc care Andel Mgmt Assocs 330 W 42nd St Fl 12 New York NY 10036-7211*

ANANA-LIND, ELENITA M., critical care and medical/surgical nurse; b. The Philippines, Mar. 21, 1951; d. Epifanio G. and Felicitas (Mumar) Anana; m. Allan S. Lind, May 23, 1987; 1 child, Brittney R. ADN, Divine Word Coll., Tagbilaran, The Philippines, 1969; diploma, Bohol Provincial Hosp. Sch., Tagbilaran, 1972. RN, The Philippines, Ark., N.Y. Charge nurse Perpetual Succour Hosp., Cebu, The Philippines, 1972-74; team leader Bapt. Med. Ctr., Little Rock, 1975-77; nursing care coord. med.-surg. ICU and CCU Little Nech Cmty. Hosp. (formerly Deepdale Gen. Hosp.), N.Y.C., 1977-97; mem. staff critical care unit N.Y. Hosp. Med. Ctr. Queens, N.Y.C., 1997—. Mem. AACCN, Am. Heart Assn. Home: 336 Barwick Blvd Mineola NY 11501-2106

ANAND, SURESH CHANDRA, physician; b. Mathura, India, Sept. 13, 1931; came to U.S., 1957, naturalized, 1971; s. Satchit and Sumaran (Bai) A. m. Wiltrud, Jan. 29, 1966; children: Miriam, Michael. MB, BS, King George's Coll., U. Lucknow (India), 1954; MS in Medicine, U. Colo., 1962. Diplomate Am. Bd. Allergy and Immunology. Fellow pulmonary diseases Nat. Jewish Hosp., Denver, 1957-58, resident in chest medicine, 1958-59, chief resident allergy-asthma, 1960-62; intern Mt. Sinai Hosp., Toronto, Ont., Can., 1962-63, resident in medicine, 1963-64, chief resident, 1964-65, demonstrator clin. technique, 1963-64, U. Toronto fellow in medicine, 1964-65; rsch. assoc. asthma-allergy Nat. Jewish Hosp., Denver, 1967-69; clin. instr. medicine U. Colo., Denver, 1967-69; internist Ft. Logan Mental Health Ctr., Denver, 1968-69; pres. Allergy Assocs. & Lab., Ltd., Phoenix, 1974—; mem. staff Phoenix Bapt. Hosp., chmn. med. records com., 1987; mem. staff St. Joseph's Hosp., St. Luke's Hosp., Human Hosp., John C. Lincoln Hosp., Good Samaritan Hosp., Phoenix Children's Hosp., Tempe St. Luke Hosp., Desert Samaritan Hosp., Mesa Luth. Hosp., Scottsdale Meml. Hosp., Phoenix Meml. Hosp., Chandler (Ariz.) Regional Hosp., Valley Luth. Hosp., Mesa, Ariz.; pres. NJH Fed. Credit Union, 1967-68. Contbr. articles to profl. jours. Mem. Camelback Hosp. Mental Health Ctr. Citizens Adv. Bd., Scottsdale, Ariz., 1974-80; mem. Phoenix Symphony Coun., 1973-90; mem. Ariz. Opera Co., Boyce Thmpson Southwestern Arboretum; mem. Ariz. Hist. Soc., Phoenix Arts. Mus., Smithsonian Inst. Fellow ACP, Am. Coll. Chest Physicians (crit. care com.), Am. Acad. Allergy, Am. Assn. Cert. Allergists, Am. Coll. Allergy and Immunology (aerobiology com., internat. com., pub. edn. com. 1991-94); mem. AAAS, AMA, Internat. Assn. Allergy and Clin. Immunology, Ariz. Med. Assn., Ariz. Allergy Soc. (v.p. 1988-90, pres. 1990-91), Maricopa County Med. Soc. (del. ariz. Med. Assn., bd. dirs. 1996-98, exec. com. 1996-98), West Coast Soc. Allergy and Immunology, Greater Phoenix Allergy Soc. (v.p. 1984-86, pres. 1986-88, med. adv. team sports medicine Ariz. State U.), Phoenix Zoo, N.Y. Acad. Scis., World Med. Assn., Internat. Assn. Asthmology, Assn. Care of Asthma, Ariz. Thoracic Soc., Nat. Geog. Soc., Ariz. Wild Life Assn., Village Tennis Club. Office: 1006 E Guadalupe Rd Tempe AZ 85283-3044 also: 6553 E Baywood Ave Ste 201 Mesa AZ 85206-1754 also: 7331 E Osborn Dr Ste 340 Scottsdale AZ 85251-6422

ANANDAN, MUNISAMY, physicist; b. Perampattu, T.Nadu, India, July 1, 1939; came to U.S. 1987; s. Ramasamy Munisamy and Sali; m. Visalakshi Anandan, May 10, 1968; children: Sharadamani, Yesheswini. M.Tech., Indian Inst. Tech., Bombay, 1967; PhD, Indian Inst. Sci., Bangalore, 1979. Devel. engr. Bharat Electronics Ltd., Bangalore, 1967-69, sr. devel. engr., 1969-74, dep. mgr. devel., 1974-79, mgr. display devices, 1979-87; vis. scientist Bell Communications Rsch., Red Bank, N.J., 1987-88; rsch. scientist Thomas Electronics, Inc., Wayne, N.J., 1988-93; rsch. scientist R&D Lab. Matsushita Electric Works, 1993-96; sr. display scientist FED Corp., Hopewell Junction, N.Y., 1996-98, dir. process devel., 1998—. Guest editor Jour. of Soc. for Info. Display; contbr. articles to profl. jours. Recipient R & D Excellence 1st prize Electronic Components Industries Assn., India, 1985, R & D 100 award R & D Mag., 1992. Mem. IEEE (sr.), Soc. for Info. Display (Mid-Atlantic chpt. chmn. 1993, 98, mem. program subcom. internat. symposium 1996, 97, 98, 99). Achievements include patents for Thick Film Integrated Flat Fluorescent Lamp, Coplanar Electrode Electric Gas-Discharge Device (India), Method of Manufacturing True Analogue Multi-column Bar-Graph Liquid Crystal Display (India), An Efficient Large Area Flat Fluorescent Lamp; research for self-aligned process for the preparation of suspended electrodes for a single substrate AC color plasma display; substantially flat compac fluorescent lamp and method of manufacturing thereof; inter-channel discharge suppression in compact fluorescent flat lamp; integrally moulded flat compact flourescent lamp; variable color flourescent lamp; flashguard protection for field emission displays, corrugated substrate design for large area field emission displays. Office: FED Corp 1580 State Route 52 Hopewell Junction NY 12533-6526

ANANDARAJAH, ANNALINGAM, civil engineer, educator; b. Jaffna, Sri Lanka, Aug. 10, 1953; s. Kanagasabai and Ratnammah (Mylvaganam) Annalingam; married, July 8, 1983; children: Vinod, Nivay. BSc in Civil Engring., U. Sri Lanka, Peradeniya, 1977; MSc in Civil Engring., U. Calif., Davis, 1980, PhD in Civil Engring., 1982. Asst. prof. S.D. Sch. Mine and Tech., Rapid City, 1982-84; asst. prof. Johns Hopkins U., Balt., 1984-91, assoc. prof., 1991-95, prof. engring., 1995—; rsch. assoc. engring. and svc. ctr. USAF, Panama City, Fla., 1984; asst. engr. Ctrl. Engring. Cons. Bur., Colombo, Sri Lanka, 1977. Contbr. numerous articles to profl. jours. Grantee NSF, 1985, 86, 91, 92, 97, Air Force Office Sci. Rsch., 1993. Mem. ASCE. Avocations: running, traveling. Home: 13719 Killarney Ct Phoenix MD 21131-1613 Office: Johns Hopkins U Dept Civil Engring 3400 N Charles St Baltimore MD 21218-2680

ANANIA, WILLIAM CHRISTIAN, podiatrist; b. Long Branch, N.J., May 11, 1958; s. Joseph John and Marie (Forgione) A.; m. Pamela Capone, Dec. 18, 1982; 1 child, William Christian Jr. BS in Biology, Villanova U., 1980; D of Podiatric Medicine, Ohio Coll. Podiatric Medicine, 1984. Diplomate Am. Acad. Pain Mgmt., Nat. Bd. Podiatry Examiners; diplomate in podiatric surgery and medicine, Am. Podiatric Med. Specialties Bd. Resident James C. Giuffré Med. Ctr., Phila., 1984-86; pvt. practice Middletown, N.J., 1986—; cons. Fern Med., Boston, 1991. Chmn. editorial review bd. The Contemporary Podiatric Physician; assoc. editor: Jour. Current Podiatric Medicine, 1986-89; contbr. numerous articles to profl. jours. Treas. Middletown Township Housing Corp., 1994. Named Dr. of the Month Jour. Current Podiatric Medicine, 1986. Fellow Am. Soc. Podiatric Medicine, Am. Soc. Podiatric Dermatology, Nat. Soc. Conscious Sedation (med. advisor 1989—); mem. Am. Podiatric Med. Assn., Middletown Area C. of C. (bd. dirs. 19888-90, 2d v.p. 1990-91, pres. 1993), Middletown Bus. Assn. (pres. 1997). Avocations: Civil War reenactor, medical and military antique collectibles. Home and Office: PO Box 673 112 Tindall Rd Middletown NJ 07748-2337

ANANIAN, MICHAEL FRED, artist; b. Haverhill, Mass., Sept. 10, 1964; s. M. Michael and Janice E. Ananian. BFA, R.I. Sch. Design, 1987; MFA, Yale U., 1990. Norfolk tchg. fellow Yale U., New Haven, 1989; lectr. drawing Washington U., St. Louis, 1992-93, Fontbonne Coll., St. Louis, 1993-94; asst. prof. painting U. N.C., Greensboro, 1994—. One-man shows include First Street Gallery, 1995, Second Street Gallery, 1996, Lyons Wier Gallery, Chgo., 1998, Hollins Coll., Roanoke, Va., 1998, Peninsula Fine Arts Ctr., Newport News, Va., 1999; group exhbns. include Am. Acad. and Inst. Arts and Letters, 1994, NAD, 1996 (John Koch award), 98, St. Mary's (Md.) Coll., Hackett/Freedman Gallery, San Francisco. Home and Office: U NCG Art Dept 162 McIver Bldg 1000 Spring Garden St Greensboro NC 27412

ANANTHA NARAYANAN, VENKATARAMAN, physics educator; b. Madras City, Madras, India, Oct. 22, 1936; came to U.S., 1963; s. Subramanya Venkataraman and Venkataraman Valambal; m. Srinivasan Jayalakshmi, Aug. 27, 1967; 1 child, Radha Narayanan. BSc. with hons., Annamalai U., Annamalainagar, Madras, India, 1957, MSc, 1958; PhD, Indian Inst. Sci, 1962. Vis. fellow Mellon Inst., Pitts., 1963; Welch postdoctoral fellow Tex. A&M U., College Sta., Tex., 1964; prof. physics Savannah (Ga.) State U., 1965—; summer rsch. fellow Pitts. Energy Tech. Ctr., 1985, 86, 88, Oakridge (Tenn.) Nat. Lab., 1987, 89-94, 96-98. Contbr. more than 65 articles to profl. jours. including Jour. Chem. Edn., Physics Tchr., Physics Edn. and others. Recipient fellowship Mellon Inst., Pitts., summer rsch. awards Tex. A&M, Coll. Sta., 1964, Pitts. Energy Tech. Ctr., 1985, 86, 88, Oak Ridge Nat. Lab., 1987, 89-94, 96-98. Mem. AAUP, Am. Assn. Physics Tchrs., Indian Inst. Sci. Alumni Assn., Ga. Acad. Scis. Avocations: computer programming, developing low cost physics experiments. E-mail: ananthan@tigerpaw.ssu.peachnet.edu. Fax: 912-927-9330. Office: Savannah State U Rm 212 GD Bldg N Tompkins St Savannah GA 31404

ANAPLE, ELSIE MAE, medical, surgical and geriatrics nurse; b. Urbana, Ohio, Apr. 22, 1932; d. Marion N. and Mae Irene (Newell) Bodey; div.; children: Glenn, Gretchen, Gloria, Giselle, Gregory, Gordon, Gary. BSN, Ohio State U., 1955. Cert. med.-surg. nurse. Night supr. Shriner's Burn Inst., Cin., 1971-73; clin. instr. med.-surg. Deaconess Hosp. Sch. Nursing, Cin., 1973-75; staff nurse Good Samaritan Hosp., Cin., 1960-92; clin. nurse, staff nurse Univ. Hosp.-U. Cin., 1984-95, asst. head nurse med. unit, 1992; ret., 1995; part-time nurse Mercy Hosp., Fairfield, Ohio, 1980—, Drake Rehab. Ctr., Cin., 1995-97. Active Cin. chpt. ARC, Our Lady of Rosary Ch. Mem. ANA, Ohio Nurses Assn., S.W. Ohio Dist. Nurses Assn.

ANARDE, RUSSELL J., career officer. BA in Bus. Adminstrn.. Wash. State U., 1973, disting. grad. Air Force Res. Officer Tng. Corps, 1973; student missile combat crew tng., Sheppard AFB, Tex., 1974; student initial qualification tng., Vandenberg AFB, Calif., 1974; MBA, U. Utah, 1977; MS in Logistics Mgmt., Air Force Inst. Tech., 1979; disting. grad., Squadron Officer Sch., 1981, Air Command and Staff Coll., 1984; student, Indsl. Coll. Armed Forces, 1989; student program for execs., Carnegie-Mellon U., 1996. Commd. 2d lt. USAF, 1973, advanced through grades to brig. gen., 1998; stationed at Little Rock AFB, 1974-79; various positions 341st Strategic Missile Wing, Malmstrom AFB, Mont., 1979-83; chief missile officer assignments, directorate assignments Hdqs. Strategic Air Command, Offutt AFB, Nebr., 1984-86; comdr. 741st Strategic Missile Squadron, Minot AFB, N.D., 1986-88; various positions Hdqs. U.S. European Command, Stuttgart-Vaihingen City, Germany, 1989-92; comdr. 351st Ops. Group, Whiteman AFB, Mo., 1992-93; head space and missile transition team Hdqs. Air Force Space Command, Peterson AFB, Colo., 1993, chief missile sys. requirements div., 1993-94, directorate requirements, 1993-94; comdr. 21st Ops. Group, Peterson AFB, Colo., 1994-95; dep. dir. operational requirements Dep. Chief Staff Plans and Ops., Hdqs. USAF, Pentagon, Washington, 1995-96; comdr. 91st Space Wing, Minot AFB, N.D., 1996-98; dep. dir. ops. Nat. Mil. Command Ctr., Joint Staff, Washington, 1998—. Decorated Legion of Merit. Office: NMCC OT-2 1 Joint Staff Pentagon Washington DC 20318-0001

ANAS, JULIANNE KAY, retired administrative laboratory director; b. Detroit, Oct. 31, 1941; d. Theodore John and Lorraine (Comment) Knechtges; m. Donald Cartwright, Jan. 25, 1965 (div. June 1968); m. Daniel James Anas, Jan. 6, 1979. BS, Ea. Mich. U., 1969; MA, Cen. Mich. U., 1978. Cert. specialist in chemistry and med. tech. Am Soc. Clin. Pathologists. Med. technologist W.A. Foote Hosp., Jackson, Mich., 1962-63; med. technologist PCHA Annapolis Hosp., Wayne, Mich., 1964-65, supr. spl. chemistry and nuclear medicine, 1969-71; med. technologist Herrick Hosp., Tecumseh, Mich., 1965, Emma L. Bixby Hosp., Adrian, Mich., 1965-68; asst. clin. chemist Peoples Community Hosp. Authority, Wayne, 1971-81; adminstrv. lab. dir. Metro Med. Group Health Alliance Plan Henry Ford Health System, Detroit, 1981-96; ret., 1996; lab. adv. coun. Highland Pk. Cmty. Coll., 1994-96; adv. panel Medicalab Observor mag., 1988-96. Contbr. articles to profl. publs. Mem. Am. Soc. Med. Tech. (bd. dirs. Mich. sect. 1972-73, pres. Detroit sect. 1972), Hosp. Lab. Mgrs. Assn. (membership chmn. 1984, 85, 90), Detroit Soc. Med. Technologists (Med. Technologist of Yr. 1975), Am. Assn. Clin. Chemists (nominations chair Mich. sect. 1992), Founders Art Inst. Republican. Avocations: boating, gardening, art, reading. Home: 6369 Mabley Hill Rd Fenton MI 48430-9405

ANASTASI, RICHARD JOSEPH, computer software consultant; b. N.Y.C., Aug. 30, 1951; s. Alfred J. and Mary T. (Lo Cicero) A. Student, Boston Coll., 1973, U. Pa., 1975. Staff cons. Arthur Andersen & Co., N.Y.C., 1975-76; customer svc. rep. Compu Serve, West Caldwell, N.J., 1976-77, Turnkey Systems Internat., Norwalk, Conn., 1977-79; tech. svcs. rep. Applied Data Rsch., Paramus, N.J., 1980-84, regional tech. mgr., 1985-86; mgr. tactical svcs. Applied Data Rsch., Princeton, N.J., 1986-88; tech. dir. Computer Assocs. Internat., Irving, Tex., 1988-91, product cons., 1991-93; mgr. tech. resources Integris, Phoenix, 1993; pres., CEO, InfoVantage, Dallas, 1993-94; sr. product specialist Open Vision Techs., Inc. (merger Veritas Software, Inc.), Dallas, Tex., 1994—, sr. systems engr., 1994-97; sr. systems engr. Open Vision Techs., Inc. (merger with VERITAS Software), Dallas, 1997—. Roman Catholic. Home: 302 Old York Rd Irving TX 75063-4246 Office: 222 Las Colinas Blvd W Ste 1650 Irving TX 75039-5436

ANASTASI, WILLIAM JOSEPH, artist; b. Phila., Aug. 11, 1933; s. Joseph Anthony and Jeanette (Corona) A.; m. Irene Irardi, Aug. 15, 1951 (div. 1964); children: William, Lawrence, Jean. Student U. Pa., 1953-61. Tchr. painting Sch. Visual Arts, N.Y.C., 1971-86; co-artistic advisor Merce Cunningham Dance Co., N.Y.C., 1984—. Presenter in field. Exhibited in one-man shows Dwan Gallery, N.Y.C., 1966, 67, 70, Witherspoon Gallery, U. N.C., Greensboro, 1965, Washington Sq. Gallery, N.Y.C., 1964, PS 1 Mus., L.I., N.Y., 1977, Hetzler and Keller Gallery, Stuttgart, Germany, 1979, Whitney Mus. Am. Art, N.Y.C., 1979, 81, Kunstmuseum Dusseldorf, Fed. Republic Germany, 1979, Bess Culter Gallery, N.Y.C., 1987, 88, The New Mus., N.Y.C., 1987, Stalke Gallery, Copenhagen, Denmark, 1988, 96, Scott Hanson Gallery, 1989, Ball State U., Munice, Ind., 1990, Sandra Gering Gallery, N.Y.C., 1991, 93-95, Krister Fahl Gallery, Stockholm, 1994, The Sorbonne, Paris, 1994, Rosenbach Mus. & Libr., Phila., 1995, Brown U., Providence, R.I., 1995, Pier Gallery, Orkney, Stromness, Scotland, 1995, Moore Coll. Art and Design, Phila., 1995, Anders Tornberg Gallery, Lund, Sweden, 1996, Hubert Winter Gallery, Vienna 1997, Sophia Ungers Gallery, Cologne, Germany, 1998, The Mus. of Judaica, Phila., 1998, Stalke Gallery, Copenhagen, 1999, Specta Gallery, Copenhagen, 1999, Tatunz Gallery, N.Y.C., 1999, Galerij S65, Aalst, Belgium, 1999, Mus. Contemporary Art, L.A., 1999; represented in permanent collections Neuberger Mus., Purchase, N.Y., Met. Mus. Art., N.Y.C., Bklyn. Mus. Art, Phila. Mus. Art, Phoenix Mus. Art, Ga. Mus. Art, Walker Art Ctr., The Getty Ctr., Santa Monica, Calif., The Mus. Contemporary Art, L.A., Des Moines Art Ctr., Mus. Modern Art, N.Y.C., Art Inst. of Chgo., Nat. Gallery Art, Washington, Fogg Art Mus., Harvard Univ. Art Muss., Cambridge, Mass., Contemporary Mus., Honolulu, Musee Moderne, Stockholm, Sweden, Whitney Mus. Am. Art, Denver Art Mus., Chrysler Mus., Norfolk, Va., J.B. Speed Art Mus., Louisville, Ky., Jewish Mus., N.Y.C., Statensmuseum for Kunst, Copenhagen, Rooseum, Ctr. Contemporary Art, Malmo, Sweden, Guggenheim Mus., N.Y., Ark. Art Ctr., Oklahoma City Art Mus., Milw. Art Mus., Contemporary Arts Mus., Houston. Artist (book) Me Innerman Monophone,Duchamp on the Jarry Rd, Artforum, 1991; Jarry in Joyce, Jarry in Duchamp, Jarry in Cage, (book), 1998, (Edgewise Press, NY); Jarry, Joyce, Duchamp and Cage, 1993; (with Michael Seidel) Jarry in Joyce; contbr. articles to profl. jours.

ANASTASIA, DAVID JON, state legislator; b. Olean, N.Y., July 6, 1964; s. Ralph John and Marie Elaine (De Mark) A. AS in Bus. Adminstrn., Jamestown C.C., Olean, 1990. Loss prevention supr. AM&A/The Bon-Ton, Olean, 1987-95; laborer Cooper Power Sys., Olean, 1995—. Councilman City of Olean, 1986-95; legislator Dist. 10 Cattaraugus County, Olean, 1996—. Mem. Cattaraugus County Dem. Com. (exec.), City of Olean Dem. Com., Christopher Columbus Lodge, St. Stephen's Club, Pulaski Club, KC. Roman Catholic. Home: 1209 Maple St Olean NY 14760-1264 Office: Cattaraugus County Ctr 303 Court St Little Valley NY 14755-1028

ANASTOLE, DOROTHY JEAN, retired electronics company executive; b. Akron, Ohio, Mar. 26, 1932; d. Helen (Sagedy) Dice; children: Kally, Dennis, Christopher. Student, De Anza Jr. Coll., Cupertino, Calif., 1969. Various secretarial positions in mfg., 1969-75; office mgr. Sci. Devices Co., Mountain View, Calif., 1975-76; exec. adminstrv. sec. corp. office Cezar Industries, Palo Alto, Calif., 1976-77; office and pers. mgr. AM Bruning Co., Mountain View, 1977-81; dir. employee rels. Consol. Micrographics, Mountain View, 1981-83; pers. mgmt. cons., 1983-84; mgr. adminstrn./employee rels. Mitsubishi Electronics Am., Inc., Sunnyvale, Calif., 1984-89, sr. mgr., 1989-91, corp.-nat. v.p., 1991-96, ret., 1996; nat. adv. Field Philanthropy, 1992-96. Bd. dirs. Agnew State Hosp., San Jose, Calif., 1966-72, div. chmn. program mentally retarded, 1966-72, staff tutor, 1966-72; bd. dirs. Project Hired, Sunnyvale, 1991-93; bd. advisors The Senior Staff, 1994-96. Recipient Svc. award Agnew State Hosp., 1972.

ANATOL, KARL W. E., provost. BA in Speech and English, Andrews U.; MA in Interpersonal Communication, Purdue U.; PhD in Speech Communications, U. So. Calif. Dean of students Caribbean Union Coll., Trinidad, 1956-60; teaching asst. Purdue U., Lafayette, Ind., 1966-69; asst. prof. Calif. State U., Long Beach, 1969-73, assoc. prof., 1975-80, assoc. dean instrnl. support, 1978-82, acting dean sch. humanities, 1982-83, dean sch. humanities, 1983-89, acting dean sch. bus., 1988—, acting provost, 1989-90, provost, 1990—, sr. v.p. acad. affairs, 1989—; chmn. speech communications Calif. State U., Long Beach, 1977-78, acting exec. dir. libr. & learning resources, 1983-84, mem. univ. extension svcs. adv. bd.; program producer Radio Sta. WBAA Purdue U., 1969; staff assoc. Gen. Motors Inst., Mich., 1973; mem. City of Long Beach Spl. Task Force on Ednl. Redevel.; mem. adv. bd. Global Edn. Program in So. Calif.; mem. bd. advisors Am. Inst. Fgn. Study; mem. ednl. cons. team Weyerhauser Corp. Author: Fundamental Concepts in Human communication, The Process of Group Communication, Strategies for Persuasive Communication, Organizational Communication: Behavioral Perspectives, Public Communication, The Process of Group Communication, Organizational Communication: Behavioral Perspectives, Effective Oral Communication for Business and Professions, Oral Communication in Business and the Professions; contbr. articles to profl. jours. Chmn. allocations com. United Way; nat. exec. dir. Phi Beta Delta. Office: Calif State Univ 1250 Bellflower Blvd Long Beach CA 90840-0001*

ANAWALT, PATRICIA RIEFF, anthropologist; b. Ripon, Calif., Mar. 10, 1924; d. Edmund Lee and Anita Esto (Capps) Rieff; m. Richard Lee Anawalt, June 8, 1945; children: David, Katherine Anawalt Arnoldi, Harmon Fred. BA in Anthropology, UCLA, 1957, MA in Anthropology,

1971, PhD in Anthropology, 1975. Cons. curator costumes and textiles Mus. Cultural History UCLA, 1975-90, dir. Ctr. for Study Regional Dress, Fowler Mus. Cultural History, 1990—; trustee S.W. Mus., L.A., 1978-92; rsch. assoc. The San Diego Mus. Man, 1980—, UCLA Inst. Archaeology, 1994—; trustee Archaeol. Inst. Am., U.S., Can., 1983-95, 98—; traveling lectr., 1975-86, 94—, Pres.'s Lectureship, 1993-94, Charles E. Norton lectureship, 1996-97; cons. Nat. Geog. Soc., 1980-82, Denver Mus. Natural History, 1992-93; apptd. by U.S. Pres. to Cultural Property Adv. Com., Washington, 1984-93; fieldwork Guatemala, 1961, 70, 72, Spain, 1975, Sierra Norte de Puebla, Mex., 1983, 85, 88, 89, 91. Author: Indian Clothing Before Cortés: Mesoamerican Costumes from the Codices, 1981, paperback edit., 1990; co-author: The Codex Mendoza, 4 vols., 1992 (winner Archaeol. Inst. Am. 1994 James Wiseman Book award), The Essential Codex Mendoza, 1996; mem. editl. bd.: Ancient Mesoamerica, 1999; contbr. articles to profl. jours. Adv. com Textile Mus., Washington, 1983-87. Grantee NEH, 1990, 96, J. Paul Getty Found. 1990, Nat. Geog. Soc., 1983, 85, 88, 89, 91, Ahmanson Found., 1996; Guggenheim fellow, 1988. Fellow Am. Anthrop. Assn.; mem. Centre Internat. D'Etude Des Textiles Anciens, Am. Ethnol. Soc., Soc. Am. Archaeology, Soc. Women Geographers (Outstanding Achievement award 1993), Textile Soc. Am. (bd. dirs. 1992-96, co-coord. 1994 biennial symposium). Avocations: ballet, reading, hiking. Office: Fowler Mus Cultural History Ctr Study of Regional Dress Los Angeles CA 90095-1549

ANAYA, RICHARD ALFRED, JR., accountant, investment banker; b. N.Y.C., Dec. 19, 1932; s. Ricardo Martinez and Clara (Chamarro) A.; m. Ninette Calandra, Sept. 8, 1957; children: Suzanne, Richard J. BBA, CCNY, 1958. CPA, N.Y. Tax acct. C.I.T. Fin. Corp., N.Y.C., 1964-67; asst. treas. Mut. Broadcasting System, Inc., N.Y.C., 1967-72; treas. Host Internat., Inc., Santa Monica, Calif., 1972-85; dir. fin. Windsor Fin. Corp, Encino, Calif., 1985; ind. cons. mergers and acquisitions A&I Investments, Inc, Century City, Calif., 1986-87, Anaya Assocs., Century City, Calif., 1987-90; CPA cons. mergers and acquisitions Anaya Assocs., Woodlands Hills, Calif., 1990—; founder retail store chain, Clear Connect Comms., LLC, 1995. Served with U.S. Navy, 1952-54. Mem. AICPA, Calif. State Soc. CPAs, N.Y. State Soc. CPAs. Roman Catholic. Office: Anaya Assocs 21550 Oxnard St Ste 960 Woodland Hills CA 91367-7145

ANAYA, RUDOLFO, educator, writer; b. Pastura, N.Mex., Oct. 30, 1937; s. Martin and Rafaelita (Mares) A.; m. Patricia Lawless, July 23, 1966. BA, U. N.Mex., Albuquerque, 1963, MA, 1968; PhD (hon.), U. Albuquerque, 1982; PhD, Mary Crest Coll., 1984; LLD (hon.), U. N.Mex., 1996. Prof. U. N.Mex., Albuquerque, 1974—. Author: (novels) Bless Me Ultima, 1972 (Primo Quinto sol) Heart of Aztlan, 1976, Tortuga, 1979 (Before Columbus Found. award), Albuquerque, 1992, Zia Summer, 1995, The Farolitos of Christmas, 1995, Jalamanta, 1996, Rio Grande Fall, 1996, (children's picture book) Maya's Children, 1997, Shaman Winter, 1999. NEA fellow. Home: 5324 Canada Vista Pl NW Albuquerque NM 87120-2412 Office: U NMex English Dept Albuquerque NM 87131

ANBAR, MICHAEL, biophysics educator; b. Danzig, June 29, 1927; came to U.S., 1967, naturalized, 1973; s. Joshua and Chava A.; m. Ada Komet, Aug. 11, 1953; children: Ran D., Ariel D. MSc, Hebrew U., Jerusalem, 1950, PhD, 1953. Instr. chemistry U. Chgo., 1953-55; sr. scientist Weizmann Inst. Sci., 1955-67; prof. Frienberg Grad. Sch., Rehovoth, Israel, 1960-67; sr. rsch. assoc. NASA Ames Rsch. Ctr., 1967-68; dir. phys. sci. SRI Internat., Menlo Park, Calif., 1968-72; dir. mass spectrometry research ctr. SRI Internat., 1972-77; prof. biophysical sci., chmn. dept. Sch. Medicine, SUNY, Buffalo, 1977-90, Faculty prof., dir. Interdeptl. Clin. Biophysics Group, 1990—, exec. dir. Health Instrument and Device Inst., 1983-85; assoc. dean applied research Sch. Medicine, SUNY, 1983-85; v.p. R & D AMARA Inc, Amherst, N.Y., 1992—; rsch. prof. surgery Sch. Medicine, SUNY, 1998—. Author: The Hydrated Electron, 1970, The Machine of the Bedside: Strategies for Using Technology in Parient Care, 1984, Clinical Biophysics, 1985, Computers in Medicine, 1986, Quantitative Dynamic Telethermometry in Medical Diagnosis and Management, 1994; editor-in-chief: Thermology, 1993; contbr. articles to profl. jours. With Israeli Air Force, 1947-49. Grantee in field. Mem. IEEE, AAAS, IEEE Computer Soc., IEEE Engring. in Biology and Medicine Soc., Assn. Am. Med. Colls., Am. Inst. Physics, Am. Chem. Soc., Am. Inst. Ultrasound in Medicine, Am. Assn. Clin. Chemistry, Am. Assn. Dental Rsch., Am. Assn. Mass Spectrometry, Am. Acad. Thermology, Am. Assn. Med. Systems Informatics, N.Y. Acad. Scis., Internat. Assn. Dental Rsch., Radiation Rsch. Soc., Internat. Med. Informatics Assn., Isternat. Soc. Optical Engring. Office: SUNY 118 Cary Hall Buffalo NY 14214-3023 *Any scientist should first try to understand Nature and then to utilize knowledge for the betterment of the quality of life. Even a single modest contribution to medicine can help thousands, making it a worthwhile cause for any scientist. My research and teaching focus, therefore, is on the application of the physical sciences to medicine.*

ANBINDER, PAUL, publishing executive; b. Bklyn., Apr. 19, 1940; s. Tulea Herzel and Gussie (Dandeshane) A.; m. Helen Rabinowitz, Feb. 16, 1964; children: Mark Harris, Jeffrey Todd. BA, Cornell U., 1960; postgrad., Columbia U., 1960-61. Editor Dover Publs., N.Y.C., 1961-64; editor-in-chief Shorewood Pubs., N.Y.C., 1964-69; with Harry N. Abrams, Inc., N.Y.C., 1969-71, sr. v.p., 1972-73, pres., 1974-75; v.p., editor trade paperbacks Ballantine Books, N.Y.C., 1975-78; dir. spl. projects Random House/Alfred A. Knopf, N.Y.C., 1975-78; pres., pub. Hudson Hills Press, N.Y.C., 1978—. Bd. dirs. Friends of the Neuberger Mus. of Art, Purchase, N.Y., 1986-96. Mem. Assn. Am. Pubs. (bd. dirs. N.Y.C. and Washington chpts. 1987-91), Century Assn. Democrat. Jewish. Avocations: opera, collecting art. Office: Hudson Hills Press Inc 122 E 25th St Fl 5 New York NY 10010-2936

ANCELL, ROBERT MANNING, leadership organization executive; b. Phoenix, Oct. 16, 1942; s. Robert Manning and Alice (Lovett) A.; m. Janet Claire Neuber, Dec. 21, 1966 (div. Oct. 1984); children: Kevin Robert, Kristin Deann; m. Christine M. Miller, Mar. 30, 1995. BA, U. N.Mex., 1971. Lic. pvt. pilot. Reporter KOB Radio and TV, Albuquerque, 1966-72; sr. sales rep. Xerox Corp., Albuquerque, 1972-78; pub. Colo. Bus. mag., Denver, 1978-83; publ. mgr. Denver Bus. mag., 1983-84; pub. Endless Vacation mag., Indpls., 1985-88; mktg. mgr. World Pub. Co., Evanston, Ill., 1989-92; writer, 1962—; founder, exec. dir. Soc. for 4-Star Leadership, Alexandria, Va., 1998—; cons. Cowles Mags., Harrisburg, Pa., 1994-95, Exec. Books, Mechanicsburg, Pa., 1996-98. Author: The Biographical Dictionary of World War II Generals and Flag Officers, 1997; co-author: Who Will Lead?, 1996, Four-Star Leadership for Leaders, 1997, Vol. I and II, 1999. Lt. comdr. USNR, 1971-93. Recipient 1st pl. TV Documentary award N.Mex. Broadcasters Assn., Albuquerque, 1968, UPI, Albuquerque, 1968. Mem. Naval Order of U.S. (v.p. pub. affairs 1997—), Soc. for Mil. History, U.S. Naval Inst., Ret. Officers Assn., Assn. of U.S. Army, Air Force Assn., Am. Soc. Assn. Execs., Am. Turkish Soc., The Authors Guild, Inc., Am. Soc. Journalists and Authors, Christian Businessmen's Com., Surface Navy Assn., USN Pub. Affairs Alumni Assn. Republican. Presbyterian. Avocations: flying, photography, outdoors activities. E-mail: imancelljr@aol.com. Home: 7406 Salford Ct Alexandria VA 22315-4728 Office: Soc for 4-Star Leadership Ste 139 7011 A Manchester Blvd Alexandria VA 22310

ANCES, I. G(EORGE), obstetrician, gynecologist, educator; b. Balt., July 3, 1935; s. Harry and Fanny A.; m. Marlene Roth, Oct. 23, 1966; 1 son, Beau Mark. B.S., U. Md., 1956, M.D., 1959. Diplomate: Am. Bd. Obstetrics and Gynecology. Intern Ohio State U. Hosp., 1959-60; resident in obstetrics and gynecology Univ. Hosp., Balt., 1960-61, 63-65; mem. faculty U. Md. Med. Sch., Balt., 1966—; prof. obstetrics and gynecology U. Md. Med. Sch., 1975-83, dir. labs. obstetrics and gynecol. research and clin. labs., 1967-83, dir. div. adolescent obstetrics and gynecology and family planning, 1981-83;; prof. ob-gyn. Rutgers U. Sch. Medicine,, Camden,, N.J.,, 1983—; chmn. dept., 1983—. Contbr. chpts. to books, articles to profl. jours. Capt. sustaining fund drive Balt. Symphony Orch., Opera Co. Phila.; med. adv. com. Fire Dept. Balt. City. Served with USAF, 1961-63. Recipient of the Outstanding, Teaching, and Edn., award, Robert-Wood Johnson Sch. of Med-Cooper Hosp, 1989, 92, 96, Nat. Fac. award for Excellence in Resident Edn., 1996. Fellow Am. Coll. Obstetrics and Gynecology; mem. Endocrine Soc., Soc. Gynecol. Investigation, Soc. Study Reprodn. (charter), Internat. Soc. Rsch. in Biology Reprodn. (charter), Md. Obstetrics and Gynecol. Soc. (sec. 1978-81, dir. 1979—), Med. and Chirurgical Soc. Md., Soc. Adolescent Medicine, Douglas Obstet. and Gynecol. Soc. (pres. 1984—), N.J. State Med. Soc. (chmn. neo-natal coop. So. Jersey 1986—), Phila. Ob-Gyn. Soc., English Speaking Union, Cooper Found., N.J. Conservation Coun., Harbour League Club, Sigma Xi. Clubs: Maryland, Towson Golf and Country. Home: 1 Lane Of Acres Haddonfield NJ 08033-3504 Office: Rutgers U Sch Medicine Dept Ob-Gyn 3 Cooper Plz Camden NJ 08103-1438

ANCHETA, CAESAR PAUL, software developer; b. Manila, June 1, 1947; s. Carlos Fortunato and Rosalinda (Huliganga) A.; m. Ruth Segalman, June 1, 1969; children: Rebecca E., Amy L. BS in Physics, U. Tex., 1969; MS in Physics, UCLA, 1971. Mem. tech. staff Hughes Aircraft Co., Culver City, Calif., 1969-78; sr. staff engr. Fairchild Camera and Instrument, Simi Valley, Calif., 1978-82; software engr. Internat. Remote Imaging Systems, Chatsworth, Calif., 1982-84, Teradyne, Inc., Woodland Hills, Calif., 1984-86; sr. scientist Internat. Remote Imaging Systems, Chatsworth, 1986-88; rsch. scientist Teledyne Industries, Northridge, Calif., 1988-89; sr. systems engr. Hughes Aircraft Co., Long Beach, Calif., 1989-90; sr. software engr. GE, Milw., 1990-94; software devel. A&B Software, Brookfield, Wis., 1994—. Author: (publs.) Proceedings of the Society of Photo Optical Instrumentation Engineers, 1978, Proceedings of the International Test Conference, 1981. Mem. The Elfun Soc., Milw., 1992. Named New Elfun of Yr., Milw. chpt. The Elfun Soc., 1993; Hughes fellow Hughes Aircraft Co., 1969-71; Stevens scholar U. Tex., El Paso, 1965-68. Mem. AAAS. Achievements include patent pending (with Arthur F. Griffin) on Rectilinear Object Matcher; development of white blood cell recognition machine vision project, pap smear scanning machine vision project.

ANCHLIA, THAN MAL, wholesale distribution executive; b. Bikaner, Rajasthan, India, Oct. 18, 1918; s. Deokaran and Goura (Nahta) A.; m. Jethi Dey Sethia, Feb. 22, 1938; children: Kanchan, Chandra, Ratna. B in Commerce, St. Xavier Coll., Calcutta, India, 1938. Exec. dir. IMC, N.Y.C., 1975-90. Author: New Dictionary System, 1988. Mem. Rep. Task Force, Washington, 1979-80. Mem. Jain. Avocations: poetry, lyrics. Office: IMC PO Box 20028 New York NY 10017-0001

ANCIER, GARTH RICHARD, television broadcast executive; b. Perth Amboy, N.J., Sept. 3, 1957; s. Sherman and Jean A. BA, Princeton U., 1979. Exec. producer syndicated program Am. Focus, 1975-79; v.p. comedy programs NBC Entertainment, N.Y.C. and Burbank, Calif., 1979-86; pres. entertainment Fox TV Network, L.A., 1986-89; pres. network TV Walt Disney Studios, Burbank, 1989-90; corp. officer, producer Fox, Inc., L.A., 1991-92; pres. The WB TV Network, 1994-99, NBC Entertainment, Burbank, Calif., 1999—; TV cons. Dem. Nat. Com., Washington, 1991-92; trustee Nat. Coun. Families and TV, 1991—; creator, exec. producer (TV show) Ricki Lake, The Garth Ancier Co., 1992-97, exec. cons., 1997—. Mem. Hollywood TV & Radio Soc. (trustee 1996—). Democrat. Office: NBC Entertainment 3000 W Alameda Blvd Burbank CA 91523

ANCKER-JOHNSON, BETSY, physicist, engineer, retired automotive company executive; b. St. Louis, Apr. 29, 1927; d. Clinton James and Fern (Lalan) Ancker; m. Harold Hunt Johnson, Mar. 15, 1958; children: Ruth P. Johnson, David H. Johnson, Paul A. Johnson, Marti H. Johnson. B.A. in Physics with high honors (Pendleton scholar), Wellesley Coll., 1949; Ph.D. magna cum laude, U. Tuebingen, Germany, 1953; D.Sc. (hon.), Poly. Inst. N.Y., 1979, Trinity Coll., 1981, U. So. Calif., 1984, Alverno Coll., 1984; LL.D. (hon.), Bates Coll., 1980. Instr., jr. research physicist U. Calif., Berkeley, 1953-54; physicist Sylvania Microwave Physics Lab., 1956-58; mem. tech. staff RCA Labs., 1958-61; research specialist Boeing Co., 1961-70, exec., 1970-73; asst. sec. U.S. Dept. Commerce for Sci. and Tech., 1973-77; dir. phys. research Argonne Nat. Lab., Ill., 1977-79; v.p. environ. activities staff GM, Warren, Mich., 1979-92; affiliate prof. elec. engring. U. Wash., 1961-73; mem. Energy Rsch. Adv. Bd., 1983-87, adv. com. on inertial confinement fusion Dept. Energy, 1992-94, U.S. Safety Rev. Panel NSF, 1987-88; cons. Inland Steel Inc., 1991-96; bd. dirs. Enterprise Devel. Internat., 1993—, WaveBand, Inc., 1996—; mem. adv. com. Rowan Sch. Engring., 1993-96; Regents vis. prof. U. Calif., Berkeley, 1988-89. Author of 70 sci. papers; patentee in field. Mem. staff Inter-Varsity Christian Fellowship, 1954-56; mem. vis. com. elec. and computer divsn. MIT, U.S. Dept. Def. Sci. Bd.; mem. adv. bd. Stanford U. Sch. Engring., Fla. State U., Fla. A&M U., Congl. Caucus for Sci. and Tech.; trustee Wellesley Coll., 1971-77; chair bd. dirs. World Environ. Ctr., 1988-93, dir., 1988-99; founding trustee Johnson Scholarship Found., 1991—; founding dir. Work Place Influence, 1997—. AAUW fellow, 1950-51; Horton Hollowell fellow, 1951-52; NSF grantee, 1967-72; recipient Chmn's. award Am. Assn. Engring. Socs., 1986. Fellow AAAS, IEEE, Am. Phys. Soc. (councillor-at-large 1973-76); mem. NRC (bd. engring. edn. 1991-95, com. on women in sci. and engring. 1990-96, office sci. and engring. pers. adv. com. 1993-96), Nat. Acad. Engring. (councillor 1995—), Air Pollution Control Assn., Soc. Automotive Engrs. (bd. dirs. 1979-81), Phi Beta Kappa, Sigma Xi. Home: 3502 Mount Bonnell Rd Austin TX 78731-5829

ANCONA, FRANCESCO ARISTIDE, humanities and mythology educator, writer; b. N.Y.C., Mar. 5, 1947; s. Louis Joseph and Lena (Chiorazzi) A.; m. Janet Lee Simons, Apr. 7, 1979. BA in American Studies, Ramapo State Coll., 1974; MA in English, Montclair State U., 1977; ArtsD, St. John's U., 1983. Cert. tchr., N.J., cert. supr., N.J. Adj. prof. English various colleges, N.J., 1979-1983; instr. English Middlesex County Coll., Edison, N.J., 1980-84; asst. prof. English County Coll. Morris, Randolph, N.J., 1986-90; adj. prof. Mythology and English Upsala Coll., 1991-92; prof. mythology, humanities, and English Sussex County C.C., Newton, N.J., 1992—, coord. honors program, 1992—, subject coord. English, humanities, philosophy, and religion, 1996—; dir. corp. communications Walters Personnel, Paramus, N.J., 1990-92; treas. Sussex County C.C. Faculty Fedn., 1994—, v.p. 1998—. Author: Writing the Absence of the Father, 1986, Myth: Matter of Mind? 1994, Crisis in America: Father Absence, 1998; assoc. editor Jour. Evolutionary Psychology, 1992—; contbr. articles to profl. jours. Com. mem. Sussex County Arts and Heritage Coun., 1994; Rep. committeeman, Wood-Ridge, N.J., 1980-82; mem. N.J. Coun. for the Humanities; mem. Spkr.'s Bur. With U.S. Army, 1966-68. Fellow St. John's U., 1980-83; assistantship Montclair State U., 1975; N.J. scholar. Mem. MLA, N.J. Coll. English Assn. (trustee), Nat. Coun. Honors Coords., Inst. Evolutionary Psychology, Inst. Psychol. Study of the Arts, Joseph Campbell Archives and Libr. Ctr., Mensa, Skylands Writers and Artists Assn., Assn. Lit. Scholars and Critics. Avocations: reading, physical fitness. Home: 21 Cardinal Ln Newton NJ 07860-1476 Office: Sussex County C C College Hill Newton NJ 07860

ANCONA, GEORGE E., photographer, film producer, author; b. N.Y.C., Dec. 4, 1929; s. Ephraim Jose and Emma Graziana (Diaz) A.; m. Helga Von Sydow, July 20, 1968; children: Lisa, Gina, Tomas, Isabel, Marina, Pablo. Student, Academia de San Carlos, Mexico, 1949, Art Students League, 1950, Cooper Union Sch. Design, 1950. Art dir. Esquire Inc., N.Y.C., 1951-53, Seventeen mag., N.Y.C., 1953-54, Grey Advt. Agy., N.Y.C., 1954-58, Daniel & Charles Advt. Agy., N.Y.C., 1958-60; free lance photographer, film producer N.Y.C., 1960—; lectr. graphic design, photography Rockland Community Coll., 1973—, Parsons Sch. Design, 1974—, Sch. Visual Arts, 1978—. Author: Handtalk, 1974, Monsters on Wheels, 1974, What Do You Do?, 1976, I Feel, 1977, Growing Older, 1978, It's A Baby!, 1979, Dancing Is, 1981, Bananas, from Manolo to Margie, Team Work, 1983, Monster Movers, Sheepdog, Helping Out, Freighters, 1985, Handtalk Birthday, 1986 (N.Y. Times 10 Best Illustrated Children's Books of Yr.), Turtle Watch, 1987, Handtalk Zoo, 1989, Riverkeeper, 1990, Handtalk School, 1991, The Aquarium Book, 1991, Man and Mustang, 1992, Pow Wow, 1992, My Camera, 1992, Pablo Remembers, 1993, The Pinatamaker, 1994, The Golden Lion Tamarin Comes Home, 1994, Fiesta U.S.A., 1995, Cutters, Carvers & the Cathedral, 1995, Earth Daughter, 1995, Mayeros, 1997, Fiesta Fireworks, 1998, Barrio, 1998, Let's Dance, 1998, Charro, The Mexican Cowboy, 1999, Carnaval, 1999. *Curiosity is the biggest element in my work. Watching people and making contact through my photographs have given me a sense of myself. My work keeps me in touch with the world around me. Whether a person bakes, builds, sings or drives, people reach one another in their own way. Mine is taking pictures. Reaching out to others ... I think that's what living is all about.*

ANCONA, HENRY, software company executive; b. Cairo, Egypt, June 24, 1944; came to U.S., 1963; m. Deborah Gladstein, July 20, 1986; children: Marisa, Anna, Laura, Alberto. BS, MIT, 1967, MS, 1968; MBA, Harvard U., 1972. V.p. Digital Equipment, Maynard, Mass., 1972-94; exec. v.p. Polaroid, Cambridge, Mass., 1994-98; pres, CEO Bullsoft, Billerica, Mass., 1998—. Mem. Eta Kappa Nu, Tau Beta Pi, Sigma Xi. Office: Bullsoft 300 Concord Ave Cambridge MA 02138-1208

ANDARY, THOMAS JOSEPH, biochemist; b. Sault Sainte Marie, Mich., Oct. 8, 1942; s. Joseph Boula and Marion (Schwifetti) A. BS, No. Mich. U., 1966, MA, 1968; PhD, Wayne State U., 1974. Instr. biology No. Mich. U., Marquette, 1967-69; rsch. assoc. physiology Wayne State U., Detroit, 1973-76; sr. rsch. scientist, mgr. coagulation research Hyland Labs., Costa Mesa, Calif., 1976-83; dir. quality control Hyland Therapeutics, Glendale, Calif., 1983-90; dir. quality assurance and regulatory affairs Baxter/Hyland Div., Glendale, 1990-91; v.p. quality assurance and regulatory affairs, 1991—, responsible head, 1993-96; cons. in regulatory affairs/quality assurance to biopharmaceutical industry, 1996—; lectr. in field. Mem. Parenteral Drug Assn. NDEA fellow, 1969-72. Mem. Am. Chem. Soc., N.Y. Acad. Sci., Internat. Assn. Biol. Standardization, Drug Info. Assn., Sigma Xi (Rsch. award 1973). Roman Catholic. Contbr. over 25 articles to profl. publs. Home and Office: 531 N Canyon Blvd Monrovia CA 91016-1707

ANDE, JAN LEE, educator, poet; b. Tacoma, Apr. 3, 1948; d. Dale Eaton and Barbara Sumner Dow; m. James Anthony, Feb. 10, 1992; 1 child, Nicholas Dale. BA in Social Sci., St. Mary's Coll., 1972; MA in Asian Studies, Calif. Inst. Integral Studies, 1975; PhD in History of Consciousness, Union Grad. Sch., 1996. Prof. Union Inst. Coll. Undergrad. Studies, San Diego, 1993—, Ctr. Distance Learning, 1994—. Author of poems. Finalist Pablo Neruda prize Nimrod Internat. Jour., 1997. Mem. Acad. Am. Poets, Assn. Writing Programs, Poets and Writers. Home: 8633F Via Mallorca La Jolla CA 92037-2599

ANDELSON, ROBERT VERNON, social philosopher, educator; b. Los Angeles, Feb. 19, 1931; s. Abraham and Ada (Markson) A.; m. Bonny Orange Johnson, June 7, 1964. A.A., Los Angeles City Coll., 1950; A.B. equivalent, U. Chgo., 1952; A.M., U. So. Calif., 1954, Ph.D., 1960. Exec. dir. Henry George Sch. Social Sci., San Diego Extension, Calif., 1959-62; instr. philosophy and religion Northland Coll., Wis., 1962-63; asst. prof. govt. and philosophy Northwestern State U., La., 1963-65; mem. faculty Auburn (Ala.) U., 1965—; prof. philosophy Auburn U., 1973-92, prof. emeritus, 1992—, mem. grad. faculty, 1969-92; mem., dir. Robert Schalkenbach Found., 1986—, v.p., 1998—; v.p. Internat. Union Land Value Taxation and Free Trade, 1986-88, pres., 1997—; inaugural lectr. philosophy lecture series U. Ala. at Birmingham, 1975; mem. adj. faculty Ludwig von Mises Inst., 1983—; ordained to ministry Congregational Ch., 1959; reviewer instl. grant applications NEH, 1987; fac. assoc. Lincoln Inst. Land Policy, 1993—. Author: Imputed Rights: An Essay in Christian Social Theory, 1971; editor, co-author: Critics of Henry George, 1979, Commons Without Tragedy, 1991, Land-Value Taxation Around the World, 2d edit., 1997; joint author (with J.M. Dawsey) From Wasteland to Promised Land: Liberation Theology for a Post-Marxist World, 1992; mem. editl. bd. Am. Jour. Econs. and Sociology, 1969—, chmn. selection com. for editor-in-chief 1996; mem. editl. bd. The Personalist, 1975-80; contbr. articles to scholarly jours. Asst. sgt. at arms Republican Nat. Conv., 1952; mem. Lee County Rep. Exec. Com., 1967-79; trustee Henry George Found. Am., 1971-75, mem. adv. commn., 1975—. Recipient Rsch. awards Found. Social Rsch., 1959, Relm Found., 1967, 2 George Washington Honor medals Freedom Found., 1970, 72; Disting. rsch. fellow Am. Inst. for Econ. Rsch., 1993—. Mem. So. Soc. Philosophy and Psychology, Ala. Philos. Soc. (pres. 1968-69, 78-79). Home: 534 Cary Dr Auburn AL 36830-2502 Office: Auburn U Dept Philosophy Auburn AL 36849

ANDEREGG, KAREN KLOK, management and marketing consultant; b. Council Bluffs, Iowa; d. George J. and Hazel E. Klok; m. George F. Anderegg, Jr., Aug. 27, 1970 (div. Dec. 1993); m. William Drake Rutherford, Jan. 2, 1994. B.A., Stanford U., 1963. Copywriter Vogue mag., N.Y.C., 1963-72; copy editor Mademoiselle mag., N.Y.C., 1972-77, mng. editor, 1977-80; asso. editor Vogue Mag., N.Y.C., 1980-85; editor-in-chief Elle mag, N.Y.C., 1985-87; pres. Clinique USA, 1987-92; mktg. cons. N.Y.C. and Portland, Oreg., 1993—. Bd. dirs. The Coast Airlines, Concordia U. Mem. Cosmetics Exec. Women, Fashion Group Internat. Office: 6978 SW Foxfield Ct Portland OR 97225-6054

ANDERER, JOSEPH HENRY, textile company executive; b. Phila., Oct. 12, 1924; s. Joseph L. and Catherine (Fleck) A.; m. E. T'Lene Brinson, Apr. 4, 1948; children: Joseph D., Mark H., Nancy T. B.M.E., Ga. Inst. Tech., 1947, B.I.E., 1948. Chem. engr. Atlantic Richfield Corp., 1947-55; asst. prof. mech. engring. Drexel Inst., Phila., 1949-56; fiber rsch. mgr., textile devel. lab. mgr. Am. Viscose Corp., 1955-62; with Celanese Corp., 1962-69, exec. v.p. textile mktg., 1967-68; pres. cosmetic and fragrance div., also dir. Revlon, N.Y.C., 1969-71; pres., chief operating officer dir. M. Lowenstein, 1972-77; dir. Aloe Creme Labs., Ft. Lauderdale, Fla., 1974-78, Fairfax Mills, N.Y.C., 1977-78; chmn. bd., chief exec. officer Warren Corp., Stafford Springs, Conn., 1978-89, Grendel Corp., Greenwood, S.C., 1979-88; v.p., dir. Trivest Corp., Sarasota, Fla., 1989-92; trustee Lincoln Savs. Bank, N.Y.C., 1973-86, N.Y. Ocean Sci. Lab., Montauk, 1973-80, Mus. Am. Textile History, 1986-93; bd. dirs. U.S. Shoe Corp., Cin., 1980-95, Cleyn & Tinker Ltd., St. Laurent, Que., Can., 1990-94, Soundwaters, Stamford, Conn., 1990-93, Gen. Clutch Corp., Stamford, 1991-95, Storage Sol'ns, Inc., Stamford, 1993-95; chmn. nat. adv. bd. Ga. Inst. Tech., 1976-82; chmn. Emergency Med. Svcs., New Canaan, Conn., 1991-94. Asst. dist. mgr. SBA, Score, Conn., 1992-93, dist. mgr., 1993-94. Served to lt. USMCR, 1943-47. Named to Hall of Fame Ga. Tech. Coll. of Engring., 1997. Mem. Wool Mfg. Council (exec. com.), No. Textile Assn. (dir., v.p. 1986-88, chmn. 1988-90), Lugano Condominium Assn. (pres. 1997-98), N.Y. Yacht Club, Stamford Yacht Club (dir., comdr.), N.Am. Sta of Royal Scandinavian Yacht Clubs, Tau Beta Pi, Pi Tau Sigma. Methodist. Patentee fiber technology.

ANDERHALTER, OLIVER FRANK, educational organization executive; b. Trenton, Ill., Feb. 14, 1922; s. Oliver Valentine and Catherine (Vollet) A.; m. Elizabeth Fritz, Apr. 30, 1945; children: Sharon, Stephen, Dennis. B.Ed., Eastern Ill. State Tchrs. Coll., 1943, Ped.D. (hon.), 1956; A.M., St. Louis U., 1947, Ph.D., 1949. Mem. faculty St. Louis U., 1947—, prof. edn., 1957—; dir. Bur. Instl. Research, 1949-65, 1949-65; dir. Univ. Computer Center, 1961-69, chmn. research methodology dept., 1968-76; v.p. Scholastic Testing Service, Chgo., 1951-89; pres. Scholastic Testing Svc., Chgo. and St. Louis, 1989—; Chmn. finance com. Greater St. Louis Campfire Girls Orgn., 1958-59. Author, editor standardized tests. Served as pilot USNR, 1943-46. Mem. Am. Ednl. Research Assn., Nat. Council Measurement, Am. Statis. Assn., N.E.A. Home: 12756 Whispering Hills Ln Saint Louis MO 63146-4449 Office: Scholastic Testing Svc 4320 Green Ash Dr Earth City MO 63045-1208

ANDERS, ALLISON, film director, screenwriter; b. Ashland, Ky., Nov. 16, 1954. Co.-dir.: (film) Border Radio, 1982 (Best First Film award UCLA); writer, dir.: (feature films) Gas, Food, Lodging, 1992 (Best New Dir. award N.Y. Film Critics Circle 1992), Mi Vida Loca, 1994, Four Rooms (segment "The Missing Ingredient"),1995; dir: Grace of My Heart, 1996. MacArthur fellow, 1995. Office: UTA 9560 Wilshire Blvd Fl 5 Beverly Hills CA 90212-2401 also: care Joel Milner 10100 Santa Monica Blvd Ste 700 Los Angeles CA 90067-4100*

ANDERS, BRENDA MICHELLE, communications professional; b. Washington, July 9, 1971; d. Stephen R. and Mary (Phillips) A. BA, Smith Coll., 1993. Mem. advance staff Clinton/Gore '92, Little Rock, 1992; confidential asst. Sec. U.S. Dept. Edn., Washington, 1993-94; dir. scheduling and advance Alan Wheat for U.S. Senate, Kansas City, Mo., 1994; splty. press coord. The White House, Washington, 1995-96; press sec. to Tipper Gore Clinton/Gore '96, Washington, 1996; radio and spl. projects coord. The White House, Washington, dir. TV prodn., 1998—. Democrat.

ANDERS, CLAUDIA DEE, occupational therapist; b. Buffalo, May 2, 1951; d. Walter Gregory and Helen (Cedizlo) A.; (div. 1983); 1 child, Andrew T. Kiko. BS in Occupational Therapy (high honors), Va. Commonwealth U., 1973; postgrad., Ashland (Ohio) Coll., 1984, Walsh (Ohio) Coll., 1985, Kent (Ohio) State U., 1988, 89, Colo. State U., 1991, 92. Lic. occupational therapist, Ohio; bd. cert. pediatric occupational therapist, total body modification practicitioner. With Children's Rehab. Ctr., Warren, Ohio, 1974-76; mem. transdisciplinary team Goodwill Rehab. Ctr., Canton, Ohio, 1976-78;

pvt. practice, 1978-83; with Timken Mercy Med. Ctr., Canton, 1978-83; occupational therapist adult tng. team Stark County Bd. Mental Retardation, Canton, 1983-85; developer occupational therapy svcs. Stark County Local Schs., 1985-87; occupational therapist Lakewood (Ohio) City Schs., 1987-91; occupl. therapist, cons. Rehab Svcs. Inc., Seven Hills, Ohio, 1991-97; pvt. practice pediatric occupl. therapy and rehab. svcs. Berea, Ohio, 1991—; pediatric occupl. therapist Phys. Therapy Svcs., 1997-99; owner Eagle Seminars and Therapy, 1998; seminar presenter State of Ohio Occupl. Therapy Conf., 1995; presenter all day workshop, Toledo, 1996; dir. rehab. Northwestern Care Ctr., Berea. Vol. Nat. Park Svc., Cleve. Metroparks; sec. Rocky River Trailsiders, 1993-95. A. D. Williams scholar Va. Commonwealth U., 1972, 73. Mem. Am. Occupational Therapy Assn., Ohio Occupational Therapy Assn., Coun. for Exceptional Children, NDT, Inc. Avocations: gardening, bird watching, hiking, sewing, needlecraft. Home: 237 Kraft St Berea OH 44017-1448 Office: Eagle Selminars and Therapy PO Box 1520 Cleveland OH 44181-0520

ANDERS, EDWARD, chemist, educator; b. Libau, Latvia, June 21, 1926; came to U.S., 1949, naturalized, 1955; s. Adolph and Erica (Leventals) Alperovitch; m. Joan Elizabeth Fleming, Nov. 12, 1955; children: George Charles, Nanci Elizabeth. Student, U. Munich, Germany, 1946-49; AM, Columbia U., 1951, PhD, 1954. Instr. U. Ill., 1954-55; mem. faculty U. Chgo., 1955—, prof. chemistry, 1962-73, Horace B. Horton prof. chemistry, 1973-91, Horace B. Horton prof. emeritus, 1991—; vis. prof. Calif. Inst. Tech., 1960, U. Berne, Switzerland, 1963-64, 70, 78, 80, 83, 87, 89-90; research asso. Field Mus. Natural History, Chgo., 1968-91; resident research asso. NASA, 1961; cons. NASA, 1961-69, mem. lunar sample analysis planning team, 1967-69. Assoc. editor: Geochimica et Cosmochimica Acta, 1966-73, Icarus, 1970-91, Earth, Moon and Planets, 1974-91; contbr. articles to profl. jours. Recipient Univ. medal for excellence Columbia U., 1966; Quantrell award for excellence in undergrad. tchg. U. Chgo., 1973; NASA medal for exceptional sci. achievement, 1973; Guggenheim fellow, 1973-74; Fairchild disting. scholar Calif. Inst. Tech., 1992-93. Fellow AAAS (Newcomb Cleveland prize 1959), NAS (J. Lawrence Smith medal 1971), Meteoritical Soc. (v.p. 1968-72, 89-90, pres. 1991-92, Leonard medal 1974), Am. Acad. Arts and Sci., Am. Geophys. Union (Harry H. Hess medal 1995); mem. Am. Astron. Soc. (chmn. divsn. planetary scis. 1971-72, Kuiper prize 1991), Internat. Astron. Union (pres. com. on moon 1976-79), Geochem. Soc. (hon., v.p. 1987-88, Goldschmidt medal 1990), Acad. Creative Endeavors (fgn. mem.); assoc. Royal Astron. Soc. Achievements include research on the origin, age, composition of meteorites and lunar rocks, interstellar grains in meteorites, origin moon and planets. Home: Hintere Engehaldenstr 12, 3004 Bern Switzerland

ANDERS, GEORGE CHARLES, journalist, author; b. Chgo., Nov. 12, 1957; s. Edward and Joan Elizabeth (Fleming) A.; m. Elizabeth Anne Corcoran, Aug. 27, 1988. BA in Econs., Stanford U., 1978. Nat. copyreader Wall St. Jour., N.Y.C., 1978-81, Heard on the Street columnist, 1981-82, London bur. chief European edit., 1982-85, news editor, 1985-88, sr. spl. writer, 1988—; contbg. editor SmartMoney mag., N.Y.C., 1992-95. Author: Merchants of Debt, 1992, Health Against Wealth, 1996. Recipient Janus award Am. Mortgage Bankers Assn., 1987; shared in Pulitzer Prize for nat. reporting, 1997. Office: Wall St Jour 201 California St Ste 1350 San Francisco CA 94111-5015

ANDERS, JERROLD P., lawyer; b. Wilkes-Barre, Pa., Sept. 21, 1953; m. Joan Anders, June 28, 1975; children: Jessica, Douglas. AB magna cum laude, Franklin & Marshall Coll., 1975; JD cum laude, U. Pitts., 1978. Jud. law clk. to Hon. Martin J. Coyne Lehigh County Ct. of Common Pleas, 1978-79; ptnr. White and Williams, LLP, Phila., 1979—. Mem. Phi Beta Kappa, Order of Coif. Office: White and Williams LLP 1 Liberty Pl 1650 Market St Ste 1800 Philadelphia PA 19103-7304

ANDERS, WILLIAM ALISON, aerospace and defense manufacturing executive; b. Hong Kong, Oct. 17, 1933; s. Arthur Ferdinand and Muriel Florence (Adams) A.; m. Valerie Elizabeth Hoard, June 26, 1955; children: Alan Frank, Glen Thomas, Gayle Alison, Gregory Michael, Eric William, Diana Elizabeth. BS, U.S. Naval Acad., Annapolis, 1955; MS in Nuclear Engring., U.S. Inst. Tech., Wright-Patterson AFB, 1962. Commnd. 2d lt. U.S. Air Force, 1955, pilot, engr., 1955-69; astronaut NASA-Johnson Space Ctr., Houston, 1963-69, Apollo 8, 1st lunar flight, 1968; exec. sec. Nat. Aero. and Space Council, Washington, 1963-72; commr. AEC, Washington, 1973-74; chmn. Nuclear Regulatory Commn., Washington, 1975-76; U.S. Ambassador to Norway, 1976-77; v.p., gen. mgr. nuclear energy products div. Gen. Electric Co., 1977-80; v.p., gen. mgr. aircraft equipment div. Gen. Electric Co., DeWitt, N.Y., 1980-84; sr. exec., v.p. ops. Textron Inc., Providence, R.I., 1984-89; vice chmn. Gen. Dynamics, St. Louis, 1990-91; chmn., CEO Gen. Dynamics, 1991-93; chmn. bd. dirs. N000, 1993-94; pres. Apogee Group. Trustee Battell Meml. Inst., Reno Air Races Unltd. Class, 1997-98. Maj. gen. USAFR, 1983-88. Decorated various mil. awards; recipient Wright, Collier, Goddard and Arnold flight awards; co-holder several world flight records. Mem. Soc. Exptl. Test Pilots, Nat. Acad. Engring., Tau Beta Pi. Office: Apogee Group PO Box 1630 Eastsound WA 98245-1630

ANDERSEN, BURTON ROBERT, physician, educator; b. Chgo., Aug. 27, 1932; s. Burton R. and Alice C. (Mara) A.; m. Susan Berg; children: Ellen C., Julia A., Brian E., Jennifer Berg. Student, Northwestern U., 1950-51; BS, U. Ill., Urbana, 1953; MS, U. Ill., Chgo., 1957; MD, U. Ill., 1957. Intern Mpls. Gen. Hosp., 1957-58; resident and fellow U. Ill. Hosp., 1958-61; clin. assoc. NIH, Bethesda, Md., 1961-64; asst. prof. U. Rochester, N.Y., 1964-67; assoc. prof. Northwestern U., 1967-70; prof. medicine and microbiology U. Ill., Chgo., 1970—, chief infectious diseases, 1986—; chief infectious diseases West Side VA Med. Ctr., 1970-90. Contbr. sci. research articles to profl. jours. Served as sr. surgeon USPHS, 1961-63. Fellow ACP; mem. Am. Assn. Immunologists, Am. Soc. for Clin. Investigation, Central Soc. for Clin. Research. Office: U Ill Sect Infectious Diseases 808 S Wood St Chicago IL 60612-7300

ANDERSEN, ELMER LEE, manufacturing and publishing executive, former governor of Minnesota; b. Chgo., June 17, 1909; s. Arne and Jennie (Johnson) A.; m. Eleanor Johnson, 1932; children: Anthony L., Julian L., Emily E. BBA, U. Minn., 1931; LLD (hon.), Macalester College, St. Paul, 1965; LHD, Carleton Coll., 1972; D of Mgmt. (hon.), U. Minn., 1984. With H.B. Fuller Co. (mfrs. indsl. adhesives), 1934—, sales mgr., 1937-41, pres., 1941-61, 63-71, chmn., 1961-63, 71-92, chief exec. officer, 1971-74, chmn. bd., 1974-92, bd. dirs., 1992—; dir. Davis Consol. Industries, Sydney, Australia, Prenor Group Ltd., Montreal, Que., 1972-76, Geo. A. Hormel & Co., Austin, 1971-75, First Trust Co., St. Paul, 1969-74; mem. Minn. Senate, 1949-58; gov. of Minn., 1961-63; pub. Princeton (Minn.) Union Eagle, 1976—, Sun Newspapers, 1978-84; chmn. bd. ECM Publishers, Princeton, Minn., 1987—. Campaign chmn. St. Paul Community Chest, 1959—; exec. com. Boy Scouts Am.; mem. Nat. Parks Centennial Commn., 1971, Gov.'s Voyageurs Nat. Park Adv. Commn., Select Com. on Minn. Jud. System; chmn. Minn. Constl. Study Commn.; Bd. dirs., pres. Child Welfare League Am., 1965-67; past pres. St. Paul Gallery and Sch. of Art; past trustee Augsburg Coll., Mpls.; pres. Charles A. Lindbergh Meml. Fund, 1978-88, chmn. 1986-88; regent U. Minn., 1967-75; chmn. bd., 1971-75; chmn. Bush Found., St. Paul; bd. dirs. Council on Founds., N.Y.C; chmn. U. Minn. Found.; chmn. bd. Alliss Found., 1982-88; mem. exec. council Minn. Hist. Soc. Decorated Order of Lion Finland; recipient Outstanding Achievement award U. Minn., 1959, award of merit Izaak Walton League, Silver Beaver award, Silver Antelope award Boy Scouts Am., Conservation award Mpls. C. of C., Taconite award Minn. chpt. Am. Inst. Mining Engrs., 1976, Nat. Phi Kappa Phi award U. Minn., 1977, Minn. Bus. Hall Fame award, 1977, Greatest Living St. Paulite award St. Paul C. of C., 1980, award Adhesive and Sealant Council, 1980, David Preus Leadership award, 1993, others. Fellow Morgan Library (N.Y.C); Mem. Adhesive Mfrs. Assn. Am. (past pres.), Voyageurs Nat. Park Assn. (past pres.), Minn. Hist. Soc. (exec. com., pres. 1966-70), Am. Antiquarian Soc. Republican. Lutheran. Clubs: Rotary (St. Paul) (past pres. St. Paul, past dist. gov.), Grolier, Univ. (N.Y.C.); Rowfant Club Cleve.; St. Paul Gavel (past pres.). Home and Office: 1483 Bussard Ct Saint Paul MN 55112-3628

ANDERSEN, HANS CHRISTIAN, chemistry educator; b. Bklyn., Sept. 25, 1941; m. June Jenny, June 17, 1967; children: Hans Christian, Albert William. SB, MIT, 1962, PhD, 1966. Jr. fellow Soc. Fellows Harvard U., Cambridge, 1965-68; asst. prof. chemistry Stanford U., Calif., 1968-74, assoc. prof., 1974-80, prof., 1980—, assoc. dean Sch. Humanities and Scis., 1996-99; vis. prof. chemistry Columbia U., N.Y.C., 1981-82; co-dir. Stanford Ctr. for Materials Rsch., 1988-89, dep. dir., 1989-95; mem. allocation com. San Diego Supercomputer Ctr., 1986-89, chmn., 1988-89; vice-chmn. Gordon Rsch. Conf. on Physics and Chemistry of Liquids, 1989, chmn. 1991. Mem. editl. com. Ann. Rev. of Phys. Chemistry, 1983-87; mem. editl. bd. Jour. Chem. Physics, 1984-86, Chem. Physics, 1986-96; mem. adv. bd. Jour. Phys. Chemistry, 1987-92. Sloan fellow, 1972-74, Guggenheim fellow, 1976-77. Fellow AAAS, Am. Acad. Arts and Scis., Am. Phys. Soc.; mem. NAS, Am. Chem. Soc. (chmn. phys. chemistry divsn. 1986, Joel Henry Hildebrand award 1988). Office: Stanford U Dept Chemistry Stanford CA 94305-5080*

ANDERSEN, HAROLD WAYNE, contributing editor, newspaper executive; b. Omaha, July 30, 1923; s. Andrew B. and Grace (Russell) A.; m. Marian Louise Battey, Apr. 19, 1952; children: David, Nancy. BS in Edn., U. Nebr., Lincoln, 1945; DHL (hon.), U. Nebr., Omaha, 1975; LHD (hon.), Dana Coll., 1983, Doane Coll., 1984; LLD (hon.), Creighton U., 1986; D of Internat. Communications, Bellevue Coll., 1986. Reporter Lincoln (Nebr.) Star, 1945-46; with Omaha World-Herald, 1946—, dir., 1964-95, pres., 1966-85, also bd. dirs., chmn. bd. dirs., pub., 1985-89, dir., 1964-95; dir. Raleigh (N.C.) News & Observer, 1976-94, Newspaper Advt. Bur., 1974-90; chmn. World Press Freedom Com., 1980-96; past chmn. Fed. Res. Bank, Kansas City (Mo.), 1977-79; bd. dirs. infoUSA Inc., Williams Cos., 1988-96. Past pres. United Arts/Omaha; past bd. govs. Ak-Sar-Ben; past chmn. U. Nebr. Found., past pres. Jr. Achievement Omaha; chmn. Nebr. Game and Pks. Found.; past sr. v.p. North Ctrl. Flyway, Ducks Unltd.; bd. dirs. Bellevue Coll. Found.; past bd. dirs. Creighton U.; past trustee Nebr. Nature Conservancy. Recipient Disting. Journalist award U. Nebr. chpt. Kappa Tau Alpha, 1972, Americanism citation Henry Monsky lodge B'nai B'rith, 1972, Nebr. Builder award U. Nebr., Lincoln, 1976, Nat. Soc. Pks. Resources award, 1984, Comm. award Nat. Assn. Resource Dists., 1987, Casey award Inland Press Assn., 1989, Disting. Nebraskan award Nebr. Soc. Washington, 1989, Philanthropy Leadership award Heartland chpt. ARC, 1992, Humanitarian award NCCJ, 1993; named Omaha Health Citizen of Yr., 1986, Citizen of Yr., United Way of Midlands, 1987, Air Force Assn., 1990; named to Nebr. Newspaper Hall of Fame, 1988; inductee Omaha Bus. Hall of Fame, 1997. Mem. Newspaper Assn. of Am. (past chmn., dir.), Internat. Fedn. Newspapers Pubs. (past pres.), Nebr. Press Assn. (Master Editor-Pub. award 1979), Coun. Fgn. Rels., Omaha C. of C. (bd. dirs., chmn. 1987-88), Phi Beta Kappa, Phi Gamma Delta. Republican. Presbyterian. Home: 6545 Prairie Ave Omaha NE 68132-2747 Office: infoUSA 5711 S 86th Cir Omaha NE 68127-4146

ANDERSEN, JAMES A., retired state supreme court justice; b. Auburn, Wash., Sept. 21, 1924; s. James A. and Margaret Cecelia (Norgaard) A.; m. Billiette B. Andersen; children: James Blair, Tia Louise. BA, U. Wash., 1949, JD, 1951. Bar: Wash. 1952, U.S. Dist. Ct. (we. dist.) Wash. 1957, U.S. Ct. Appeals 1957. Dep. pros. atty. King County, Seattle, 1953-57; assoc. Lycette, Diamond & Sylvester, Seattle, 1957-61; ptnr. Clinton, Andersen, Fleck & Glein, Seattle, 1961-75; judge Wash. State Ct. of Appeals, Seattle, 1975-84; justice Wash. State Supreme Ct., Olympia, 1984-92, chief justice, 1992-95; ret., 1995. Mem. Wash. State Ho. of Reps., 1958-67, Wash. State Senate, 1967-72. Served with U.S. Army, 1943-45, ETO. Decorated Purple Heart; recipient Disting. Alumnus award U. Wash. Sch. of Law, 1995. Mem. ABA, Wash. State Bar Assn., Am. Judicature Soc. Home: 3008 98th Ave NE Bellevue WA 98004-1817

ANDERSEN, KENNETH BENJAMIN, retired association executive; b. Jamestown, N.Y., Apr. 6, 1905; s. Benjamin Gaylord and Esther Lydia (Nelson) A.; m. Mildred Mary Cederquist, June 1, 1935; children: Richard Tyler, Mary Gaylord, Kendal Elizabeth. B.S., Dartmouth, 1927; grad. student, N.Y.U., 1930-31. Budget supr., mgr. cost estimating dept. Dahlstrom Metallic Door Co., Jamestown, N.Y., 1927-30, 33-34; sec. Am. Management Assn., N.Y.C., 1930-33; asst. to pres. Am. Management Assn., 1939-41; asst. sec. Rubber Mfrs. Assn., 1934; adminstrv. asst. Office of Sec. Dept. Commerce, Washington, 1935-39; adminstrv. sec. Nat. Elec. Mfrs. Assn., N.Y.C., 1941-46; asst. to pres. Sci. Apparatus Makers Assn., 1947-48, exec. v.p., 1948-67; pres. Assn. Mem. Svcs., Inc., Chgo., 1967-87, ret., 1987. Assoc. editor: Handbook of Business Administration, 1931; contbg. author: Association Management, 1958. Mem. Winnetka Planning Commn., 1966-71; chmn. Winnetka Caucus Com., 1964-65, 70—; mem. St. James Cathedral Com., Chgo.; Pres. bd. mgrs. Nat. Inst., Mich. State U., 1956-57; regent Inst. Orgn. Mgmt. Mem. Trade Assn. Execs. Forum Chgo. (pres. 1954-55), Am. Soc. Assn. Execs. (pres. 1958), Nat. Indsl. Council (chmn. 1950), Phi Beta Kappa, Zeta Psi. Episcopalian. Home: 607 Oak St Winnetka IL 60093-2631

ANDERSEN, K(ENT) TUCKER, investment executive; b. Manchester, Conn., June 5, 1942; s. Alfred Hans and Dorothy Emily (Ray) A.; m. Karen Ann Kirchofer, Oct. 11, 1963; children: Heather Michele, Kristen Eileen. Student, Phillips Exeter Acad., N.H., 1957-59; BA, Wesleyan U., 1963. Chartered fin. analyst. Actuarial student Travelers Ins. Co., Hartford, Conn., 1963-66; security analyst Smith Barney & Co., N.Y.C., 1968-69; ptnr. Rudman Assocs., N.Y.C., 1969-72; ptnr. Cumberland Assocs. LLC, N.Y.C., 1972—, mng. ptnr., 1982-96, chief investment strategists, 1997—. Bd. dirs. Cato Inst., Washington, 1987—, exec. com., 1992—; trustee YWCA of Montclair, North Essex, N.J., 1980—, 1st United Meth. Ch., Montclair, 1976-94, Martin Luther King Scholarship Fund Montclair, 1989-94, Phillips Exeter Acad., 1989—, chmn. investment com., 1992—, bd. v.p. and chmn. exec. com., 1993—, admissions rep. N.J. area, 1983-93; exec. com. GOPAC, 1993—, bd. dirs., 1995—. With USPHS, 1966-68. Recipient Disting. Alumnus award Wesleyan U., 1988. Mem. Soc. Actuaries, N.Y. Soc. Security Analysts, Inst. Chartered Fin. Analysts, Polit. Club for Growth (mem. exec. com. 1984-94), Kappa Nu Kappa (pres. 1963). Republican. Avocation: N.Y.C. marathons. Office: Cumberland Assocs Rm 3803 1114 Avenue Of The Americas New York NY 10036-7703

ANDERSEN, KRISTI JEAN, political scientist; b. Omaha, Sept. 23, 1947; d. Robert Keith and Jean ELizabeth (Swarr) A.; m. Stuart John Thorson, Apr. 7, 1979; children: Emily Andersen Thorson, Daniel Andersen Thorson. BA, Smith Coll., 1969; PhD, U. Chgo., 1976. Assoc. study dir. Nat. Opinion Rsch. Ctr., Chgo., 1973-75; asst. prof. Ohio State U., Columbus, 1975-79, assoc. prof., 1979-84; assoc. prof. Syracuse (N.Y.) U., 1984-96, prof., chair, 1996—. Author: Creation of a Democratic Majority 1928-1936, 1979, After Suffrage: Women in Partisan and Electoral Politics Before the New Deal, 1996. Home: 11 Rippleton St Cazenovia NY 13035-9601 Office: Syracuse U Dept Polit Sci Syracuse NY 13244

ANDERSEN, KURT BYARS, writer; b. Omaha, Aug. 22, 1954; s. Robert and Jean (Swarr) A.; m. Anne Kreamer, May 9, 1981; children: Katherine, Lucy. AB magna cum laude, Harvard U., 1976. Writer NBC-TV, N.Y.C., 1976-80; writer Time Mag., N.Y.C., 1981-84, arch. critic, 1984-93; columnist, 1993-94; co-founder, co-editor Spy Mag., N.Y.C., 1986-93; editor-in-chief New York Mag., N.Y.C., 1994-96; columnist The New Yorker, N.Y.C., 1996—. Author: The Real Thing, 1980, Turn of the Century, 1999; co-author: Tools of Power, 1980, (off-Broadway revue and book) Loose Lips, 1994-95, 98; exec. prodr. TV pilots After Hours, 1987, Zero Hour, 1991, Pranks, 1992; exec. prodr., co-writer TV spl. How To Be Famous, 1990, The Hit List, 1992; host (TV spl.) Comedy Spotlight, 1996. Recipient journalism award ABA, 1983, Page One award Newspaper Guild N.Y., 1984. Office: New Yorker Mag 20 W 43rd St New York NY 10036-7400

ANDERSEN, LAIRD BRYCE, retired university administrator; b. Madison, S.D., Sept. 16, 1928; s. Andrew Christopher and Alyce (Farrington) A.; m. Joan Roberta Westwood, Nov. 23, 1961; children—Christopher Frederick, Elizabeth Virginia. B.S., U. Minn., 1950, M.S., 1951, M.A., 1961; Ph.D., U. Ill., 1954. Registered profl. engr., Mass., N.J. Asst. prof. Lehigh U., 1954-59; assoc. prof. Rice U., 1959-60, U. Nebr., 1961-63; prof., assoc. dean engring. N.J. Inst. Tech., 1963-66, dean engring., 1966-75, dean acad. affairs, 1972-74, v.p. acad. affairs, 1974-75, prof. chem. engring., 1975-80; dean Coll. Engring. U. Mass. Dartmouth, North Dartmouth, 1980-93, interim provost, 1993-94. Co-author: Principles of Unit Operations, 1960, 2d edit., 1980, Introduction to Chemical Engineering, 1960. Mem. Am. Soc. Engring. Edn. (chmn. chem. engring. div. 1967), Am. Inst. Chem. Engrs., Sigma Xi, Phi Lambda Upsilon, Tau Beta Pi, Alpha Chi Sigma, Triangle. Home: 28 Holly Ln Mattapoisett MA 02739-2110

ANDERSEN, LEONARD CHRISTIAN, former state legislator, real estate investor; b. Waukegan, Ill., May 30, 1911; s. Lauritz Frederick and Meta Marie (Jacobsen) A.; m. Charlotte O. Ritland, June 30, 1937; children: Karen Schneider, Paul R., Charlene Olsson, Mark Luther. BA, Huron (S.D.) Coll., 1933; MA, U. S.D., 1937. Tchr. Onida (S.D.) H.S., 1934-35; dir. bus. tng. Waldorf Coll., Forest City, Iowa, 1935-39; ins. salesman, 1939-41; tchrs. econs., current history Morningside Coll., Sioux City, Iowa, 1941-43; engaged in ins. and real estate Sioux City, 1943-76; mem. Iowa Ho. of Reps. from Woodbury County, 1961-64, 66-71; mem. Iowa Senate from 26th Dist., 1972-76, chmn. rules and adminstrn. com. Former mem. Iowa Commn. on Aging; former mem. investment adv. bd. IPERS; former mem. cen. com. Woodbury County Reps., del. county, dist. and state convs.; former mem. Simpco Projects Rev. Com.; former pres., chmn. bd. Siouxland Rental Assn.; past mem. Sioux City Housing Appeals Bd., Siouxland Council on Alcoholism; bd. regents Augustana Coll., Sioux Falls, S.D., 12 yrs., now mem. Augustana Fellows; mem. Vision 20-20 com., Sioux City; past chmn. Morningside Luth. Ch.; active Rep. Party Campaign, 1996; del. to state, dist. and county Rep. convs., Iowa, 1998; bd. dirs. Human Rights Commn., Sioux City, 1997—; del. to Evang. Luth. Ch. Dist. Conv., 1996, 97, 98. Mem. UN Assn. (past pres. Siouxland chpt.), Masons, Lions. Home and Office: 2525 Nebraska St Apt 113 Sioux City IA 51104-3508

ANDERSEN, LUBA, electrologist, electropigmentologist; b. Germany, Mar. 29, 1945; came to U.S., 1955; d. Osyp and Justyna (Drozd) Nahorniak; m. Roger A. Andersen, Dec. 9, 1989. A in Bus. and Acctg., DePaul U., 1977; BS in Commerce and Social Studies, LaSalle U., 1978; postgrad., U. Mich., 1984; cert., Ariz. Inst. Electrolysis, 1993. Cert. profl. electrologist, clin. electropigmentologist. From analyst to contr. Fed. Home Loan Bank, Chgo., 1965-83, v.p., contr., 1985-92; owner The Electrolysis Connection, Tucson, 1993—. Mem. NAFE, Am. Soc. Women Accts. (chair bylaws com. 1981), Am. Electrology Assn., Electrologists Assn. Ariz., Internat. Guild Profl. Electrologists, Inc., Fin. Mgrs. Soc., Soc. Cosmetic Profls., Assn. Clin. Electropigmentologists. Republican. Roman Catholic. Avocation: creating tapestries. Office: Electrolysis Connection 3131 N Country Club Rd Ste 110 Tucson AZ 85716-1637

ANDERSEN, MARIANNE SINGER, clinical psychologist; b. Baden nr. Vienna, Austria; came to U.S., 1940; naturalized, 1946; d. Richard L. and Jolanthe (Garda) Singer; 1 child, Richard Esten. BA, CUNY, 1950, MA, 1974; PhD, Fla. Inst. Tech., 1980. Rsch. assoc. Inst. for Rsch. in Hypnosis, N.Y.C., 1974-76, fellow in clin. hypnosis, 1976, dir. seminars, 1978-82, dir. edn., 1982—; psychotherapist specializing in hypnotherapy Morton Prince Ctr. for Hypnotherapy, dir. clin. svcs., 1981-82; dir. adminstrn. Internat. Grad. U., N.Y.C., 1974-77; pvt. practice psychotherapy, 1977—; adminstrv. coordinator Internat. Grad. Sch. Behavior Sci., Fla. Inst. Tech., 1978; co-dir. The Melbourne Group, 1983—; clin. instr. hypnotherapy Mt. Sinai Sch. Medicine, N.Y.C., 1996—; lectr. hypnosis and hypnotherapy to mental and phys. health profls., 1977—. Author: (with Louis Savary) Passages: A Guide for Pilgrims of the Mind, 1972; rsch. on treatment of obesity with hypnotherapy; book editor specializing in psychology and psychiatry including W.W. Norton Co., Sterling Pub. Co., E.P. Dutton Co., 1950-71. Fellow Soc. for Clin. and Exptl. Hypnosis; mem. APA, Internat. Soc. Clin. and Exptl. Hypnosis. Home: 60 W 57th St New York NY 10019-3909

ANDERSEN, NIELS HJORTH, chemistry educator, biophysics researcher, consultant; b. Copenhagen, Denmark, Oct. 9, 1943; came to U.S. 1949; s. Orla and Inger (Larsen) A.; m. Sidnee Lee (div. 1986); children: Marin Christine, Beth Arkady; m. Susan Howell, July 21, 1987. BA, U. Minn., 1963; PhD, Northwestern U., 1967. Rsch. assoc and fellow Harvard U., Cambridge, Mass., 1966-68; asst. prof. U. Wash., Seattle, 1968-72, assoc. prof., 1972-76, prof., 1976—; prin. scientist ALZA Corp., Palo Alto, Calif., 1970-75; cons. Genetic Systems, Seattle, 1984-86, Bristol-Myer Squibb, Princeton, N.J., 1984-95, Amylin Pharmaceutics, San Diego, 1992—. Contbr. articles to profl. jours. Pres. Friends of Northshore, Bothell, Wash., 1980-86. Recipient Teacher-Scholar award Dreyfus Found., 1974-79, Career Devel. award NIH, 1975-80. Mem. AAAS, Am. Chem. Soc., Am. Peptide Soc., Protein Soc. Democrat. Avocations: contemporary folk music and swing, dulcimer playing. Office: U Wash Dept Chemistry PO Box 351700 Seattle WA 98195-1700

ANDERSEN, RICHARD ESTEN, lawyer; b. N.Y.C., Oct. 26, 1957; s. Arnold and Marianne (Singer) A.; m. Patricia Anne Woods, May 9, 1987; children: Benjamin Singer, David Woods. BA, Columbia U., 1978, JD, 1981; LLM, NYU, 1987. Bar: N.Y. 1982, U.S. Tax Ct. 1982. Ptnr. Jones, Day, Reavis & Pogue, N.Y.C.; mem. bd. advisors Jour. Internat. Taxation, Tax Mgmt. Inc., World Trade Exec. Inc. Author: Foreign Tax Credits, 1996, U.S. Income Tax Withholding (Fgn. Persons), 1997. Mem. ABA, N.Y. State Bar Assn., Internat. Tax Inst., Internat. Fiscal Assn., Internat. Tax Assn. (mem. N.Y. exec. com.). Office: Jones Day Reavis & Pogue 599 Lexington Ave New York NY 10022-6030

ANDERSEN, ROBERT, health products/business executive; b. Bklyn., Oct. 9, 1937; s. Ingulf Bertel Andersen and Helen Jane Akin (McDowell) Miller; m. Elaine Marie Wood, June 13, 1958; children: Susan Marie, Robert Alan, Dori Ann. Grad. h.s., La Mesa, Calif. Area sales mgr. Golden Arrow Dairy, San Diego, 1958-66; retail sales mgr. Hollandia Dairy, San Marcos, Calif., 1966-69; pres. Health Best Inc., San Marcos, 1969-98; founding ptnr. Escondido Mills, San Marcos, 1980—; owner, operator Andersen Trading Co., Valley Center, Calif., 1984—; ptnr. Earth Products, Valley Center, 1989—; founding ptnr. Elaina's Snacks, San Marcos, 1991-94; owner, operator Andersen Gallery, Valley Center, 1992-98; pres. Gisé LLC, 1997—. Bd. dirs. Russian Art Guild, San Diego, 1992-96; exec. v.p. Kamut Assn. N.Am., San Marcos, 1990-97, pres., 1997—. Republican. Avocation: poetry. Home: 30126 Castlecrest Dr Valley Center CA 92082-4923 Office: Health Best 295 Distribution St San Marcos CA 92069-4359

ANDERSEN, ROBERT ALLEN, retired government official; b. Denver, Aug. 27, 1936; s. Emmett Christian and Margaret Irene (Maupin) A.; m. Jane Eng (dec.), May 13, 1967. AB in Polit Sci., U. S.C., 1958, MA in Polit Sci., 1961; postgrad. in law, U. Colo., 1958-59; PhD in Internat. Relations, Am. U., 1973. Area coordinator for econ. devel. Area Redevel. Adminstrn., Commerce Dept., 1962-64; acting dir. urban projects div., program officer, chief Project Adminstrn. VISTA (OEO), Washington, 1964-66; implementation programming, planning and budgeting system Office Program Planning and Evaluation, Office Edn., 1966-67; staff asst. to dep. postmaster gen. Postal Service, 1967-72, sr. planning officer, 1972-74; dir. evaluation Immigration and Naturalization Service, Washington, 1974-86, dir. Office of Program Inpection, 1986-88; dir. mgmt., planning and review Office Inspector Gen., Dept. Justice, Washington, 1988-90, dir. quality assurance rev., 1990-97; ret., 1997. Past pres. bd. dirs. D.C. Assn. Retarded Citizens; past. sec. The Arc. Episcopalian. Home: 5701 Nebraska Ave NW Washington DC 20015-1221

ANDERSEN, RONALD MAX, health services educator, researcher; b. Omaha, 1939; s. Max Adolph and Evangeline Dorothy (Wobbe) A.; m. Diane Borella, June 19, 1965; 1 dau., Rachel. BS, U. Santa Clara, 1960; MS, Purdue U., 1962, PhD, 1968. Research assoc. Purdue U., West Lafayette, Ind., 1962-63; assoc. study dir. Nat. Opinion Research Ctr., Chgo., 1963-66; research assoc. U. Chgo., 1963-77, assoc. prof., then prof. Grad. Sch. Bus., 1974-90, dir. Program in Health Adminstrn. and Ctr. for Health Adminstrn. Studies, 1980-90; Wasserman prof. dept. health svcs. and sociology UCLA, 1991—, chair dept. health svcs., 1993-96; chmn. editl. bd. Health Adminstrn. Press, Chgo., 1980-83, 88—, Med. Care Rsch. & Rev., 1994—; mem. coms. Agy. for Health Care Policy and Rsch., Rockville, Md., 1970—. Author: A Decade of Health Services, 1967, Two Decades of Health Service, 1976, Total Survey Error, 1979, Health Services in the U.S., 1980, Ambulatory Care and Insurance Coverage in an Era of Constraint, 1987, Training Physicians, 1994, Changing the U.S. Health Care System, 1996. NIH fellow, 1960-62; grantee Robert Wood Johnson Found., 1983, Kaiser Family Found., 1983, Agy. for Health Care Policy and Rsch., 1982, WHO, 1990. Mem. APHA, Am. Sociol. Assn. (chmn. med. sociology sect. 1980-81, Disting. Med. Sociologist 1994), Nat. Acad. Scis., Nat. Inst. Medicine, Assn. for Health Services Rsch. (dir. 1981-83), Assoc. Univ. Program in Health Adminstrn. (Baxter Allegiance prize 1999), Assn. for Health Svcs. Rsch. (Disting. Career awrd 1996). Roman Catholic. Home: 10724 Wilshire Blvd Apt

312 Los Angeles CA 90024-4453 Office: UCLA Sch Pub Health Los Angeles CA 90024

ANDERSEN, THEODORE SELMER, engineering manager; b. N.Y.C., Dec. 4, 1944; s. Selmer and Irene Frances (McManus) A.; m. Elva Glenna Layden, June 19, 1965; children: Elva Irene, Theodore Christian, Caroline Elizabeth. BChemE, Cooper Union, 1965; MSChemE, U. Pitts., 1968, PhDChemE, 1971, MBA, 1977. Registered profl. engr., Pa. From engr. to mgr. compensation, evaluation and tng. Bettis Atomic Power Lab. Westinghouse, West Mifflin, Pa., 1965-77; mgr. emerging systems programs Advanced Energy Systems Div Westinghouse, Waltz Mill, Pa., 1978-84, mgr. energy program, 1985-86, mgr. stragetic program mktg., 1987-88; dep. dir. AP600 Program Nuclear and Advanced Tech. Div. Westinghouse Elec., Pitts., 1989-94; mgr. bus. devel. BECO Engring. Co., Oakmont, Pa., 1995-96; chief process engr. ChemTech Consultants, Inc., Bridgeville, Pa., 1996—. Mem. AIChE, Am. Chem. Soc., Am. Wind Energy Assn. (pres. 1981-84), Am. Nuclear Soc. Republican. Methodist. Home: 5170 Caste Dr Pittsburgh PA 15236-1646 Office: ChemTech Consultants Inc 1370 Washington Pike Bridgeville PA 15017-2839

ANDERSEN, TORBEN BRENDER, optical researcher, astronomer, software engineer; b. Naestved, Denmark, May 17, 1954; came to U.S., 1983; U.S. citizen, 1994; s. Bjarne and Anna Margrethe (Brender) A.; m. Alice Louise Palmer, Nov. 3, 1990; children: Iris, Erik. PhD, Copenhagen U., Denmark, 1979. Rsch. fellow Copenhagen U., 1980-82, sr. rsch. fellow, 1982-85; optical cons. Nordic Optical Telescope Assn., Roskilde, Denmark, 1985; optical systems analyst Telos Corp., Santa Clara, Calif., 1985-88; rsch. scientist Lockheed Martin Missiles and Space, Palo Alto, Calif., 1988-93, staff scientist, 1993-95, sr. staff scientist, 1995-96; staff software engr. Lockheed Martin Missiles and Space, 1996—; vis. scholar Optical Scis. Ctr., U. Ariz., Tucson, 1983-85. Editor: Astronomical Papers Dedicated to Bengt Strömgren, 1978; contbr. articles to Jour. Quantitative Spectroscopy Radiation Transfer, Applied Optics, Astronomische Nachrichten. Mem. Optical Soc. Am., Internat. Astron. Union, Soc. Photo-Optical Instrumentation Engrs. Achievements include development of method for computing optical aberration coefficients to arbitrarily high orders; discovery of set of differential equations for the Voigt function; contributing to optical design software. Office: Lockheed Martin Advanced Tech Ctr O/H1-52 3251 Hanover St B/201 Palo Alto CA 94304-1121

ANDERSEN, WAYNE R., federal judge; b. Chgo., July 30, 1945; m. Sheila M. O'Brien, Jan. 5, 1991; children: Susan, David, Kristine, Mary, Maureen, Noreen. BA with honors, Harvard Coll., 1967; JD, U. Ill., 1970. Adminstrv. asst. Henry J. Hyde, majority leader Ill. House Reps., 1970-72; assoc. Burditt & Calkins, Chgo., 1972-76, ptnr., 1977-80; dep. sec. state Ill., 1981-84; judge Cir. Ct. Cook County, 1984-91; supr. judge traffic divsn. First Municipal Dist., 1989-91; dist. judge No. U.S. Courthouse, Ill., 1991—; dir. Rehab. Inst. Chgo.; interviewer schs. com. Harvard Club Chgo. Contbr. articles to profl. jours. Pres., dir., precinct capt. Maine Township Regular Rep. Orgn.; alt. del. Rep. Nat. Conv., Sixth Congrl. Dist. Ill., 1984; Rep. candidate for treas. Cook County, 1974. Mem. Ill. Judges Assn., Chgo. Bar Assn., Fed. Judges Assn. Office: US Courthouse 1486 Dirksen Bldg 219 S Dearborn St Chicago IL 60604-1702*

ANDERSLAND, ORLANDO BALDWIN, civil engineering educator; b. Albert Lea, Minn., Aug. 15, 1929; s. Ole Larsen and Brita Kristine (Okland) A.; m. Phyllis Elaine Burgess, Aug. 15, 1958; children: Mark, John, Ruth. BCE, U. Minn., 1952; MSCE, Purdue U., 1956, PhD, 1960. Registered profl. engr., Minn., Mich. Staff engr. NAS, Am. Assn. State Hwy. Ofcls. Road Test, Ottawa, Ill., 1956-57; rsch. engr. Purdue U., West Lafayette, Ind., 1957-59; mem. faculty Mich. State U., East Lansing, 1960—, prof. civil engring., 1968—, prof. emeritus, 1994—. Co-author: Geotechnical Software for the IBM, PC, 1987, Geotechnical Engineering and Soil Testing, 1992, An Introduction to Frozen Ground Engineering, 1994; co-editor: Geotechnical Engineering for Cold Regions, 1978; contbr. chpt. Ground Engineer's Handbook, 1987; contbr. articles to profl. jours.; patentee in field. 1st lt. C.E., U.S. Army, 1952-55. Decorated Nat. Def. Svc. medal; UN Svc. medal; Korean Svc. medal; recipient Best Paper award Assn. Asphalt Paving Technologists, 1956; postdoctoral fellow Norwegian Geotech. Inst., 1966; grantee NSF, EPA. Fellow ASCE (best paper award Cold Regions Engring. Jour. 1991); mem. ASTM (sr.), Internat. Soc. Soil Mechanics and Found. Engring., Am. Soc. Engring. Edn. (life), Sigma Xi, Chi Epsilon, Tau Beta Pi. Lutheran. Home: 901 Woodingham Dr East Lansing MI 48823-1855 Office: Dept Civil/Environ Engring Mich State U East Lansing MI 48824

ANDERSON, ALAN MARSHALL, lawyer; b. Postville, Iowa, Oct. 23, 1955; s. Hilbert Emil and Wilma Althea (Zummack) A.; m. Ann Marie Luken, Aug. 9, 1980. BA magna cum laude, Coe Coll., 1974-78; MBA with distinction, Cornell U., 1981, JD magna cum laude, 1982; cert. internat. comml. and bus. law, U. Pacific, 1988. Bar: Minn. 1983, U.S. Dist. Ct. Minn. 1983, U.S. Ct. Appeals (4th and 8th cirs.) 1983, U.S. Ct. Appeals (10th cir.) 1985, U.S. Ct. Appeals (fed. cir.) 1987, U.S. Supreme Ct. 1990, U.S. Ct. Appeals (7th cir.) 1992. Law clk. to cir. judge U.S. Ct. Appeals (4th cir.), Richmond, Va., 1982-83; assoc., then ptnr. Faegre & Benson, Mpls., 1983-90; ptnr. Robins, Kaplan, Miller & Ciresi, Mpls., 1990-92; shareholder Larkin, Hoffman, Daly & Lindgren, Mpls., 1992—. Contbr. articles to law revs. Mem. alumni coun. Coe Coll., 1998—. Recipient Chatman Labor Law Prize Cornell Law Sch. Faculty, 1982. Mem. ABA, Minn. Bar Assn. (cert. civil trial specialist), Am. Intellectual Property Law Assn., Fed. Cir. Bar Assn., Coe Coll. Alumni Coun., Nat. Assn. Securities Dealers (nat. bd. arbitrators 1990—), Am. Arbitration Assn. (panel of arbitrators 1993—), U.S. Judo Assn. (life mem., nat. bd. legal advisors 1989-94, Silver award), Order of Coif, Phi Beta Kappa, Phi Kappa Phi. Republican. Lutheran. Avocation: judo. Office: Larkin Hoffman Daly & Lindgren 7900 Xerxes Ave S Ste 1500 Minneapolis MN 55431-1128

ANDERSON, ALAN REINOLD, real estate executive, communications consultant; b. Danbury, Conn., Nov. 14, 1949; s. Charles Reinold and Lila Mae (Truesdale) A.; children: Sherry, Erick. AA, U.S. Naval Acad., 1971; BBA, Western Conn. State U., 1975, postgrad., 1977-82; postgrad., Boeing 727 Flight Engr. Sch., Aviation Tng. Ctr., 1979, Lockheed P-3 Orion Schs., Naval Counterinsurgency Sch., Spl. Warfare Sch. Competitor modified and grand nat. divsns. NASCAR, 1971-79; researcher, clk. Law Offices of Gemza & Daly, Danbury, Conn., 1972-77; prin. Anderson-Ricards & Co., Danbury, 1981-86, A.R. Anderson & Co., Danbury, Conn., 1977—. Conn. liaison Courageous Challenge 1987 America's Cup, 1985-87; town coord. steering and fin. com. Bush/Quayle 88, 1992; mem. George Bush for Pres. Adv. Com. in Conn.; alt. Conn., Rep. Nat. Conv., New Orleans, 1988; town coord. Weicker Gov., Conn., 1991; vice chmn. Environ. Impact Commn., Danbury, 1985-88; co-chmn. Stamford (Conn.) Dinner Com. Bush for Pres., 1987; del. GOP State Conv., 1982; ward chmn. Town Com., 1978-84; asst. football coach Immaculate H.S., 1988; town coord. Prescot Bush for U.S. Senate; town and state coord. Labriola for Gov., 1982, 86; rep. Presdl. Legion Merit; active Rep. Presdl. Task Force, Am. Bicentennial Presdl. Inaugural Ball, Washington, 1989; advisor Forbes for Pres., 1996; sponsor U.S. Navy Meml., Washington; charter mem. U.S. Holocaust Meml. Mus. With USN, 1967-73, Vietnam. Decorated Air medals, DFC, Navy Commendation with Combat V, Vietnam Gallantry Cross, Vietnam Campaign with Silver Star, Navy Unit citation, Meritorious Unit citation. Mem. Assn. Naval Aviation (life), Tailhook Assn. (life), Naval Helicopter Assn., Nat. Sporting Clays Assn., Am. Scandinavian Found., U.S. Golf Assn., U.S. Naval Acad. Athletic Assn. (commodore, life), Mobile Riverine Force Assn. Vietnam, Orvis Sandanona Sporting Clays, Milford Yacht Club, U.S. Sailing Assn., Yale Club (Greater Danbury), N.Y. Sports Clubs. Congregationalist. Avocations: yacht racing, autoracing, weight training, football, golf. Home: 60 Miry Brook Rd Danbury CT 06810-7411

ANDERSON, ALBERT SYDNEY, III, lawyer; b. Atlanta, July 7, 1940; s. Albert S. Jr. and Constance S. (Spalding) A.; children: Judith, William. BA in Math., Emory U., 1962; MS in Physics, Stanford (Calif.) U., 1964, PhD in Physics, 1968, JD, 1977. Bar: Ga. 1978, U.S. Patent and Trademark Office 1980, U.S. Supreme Ct. 1981. Assoc. Stokes & Shapiro, Atlanta, 1978-81, Kutak, Rock & Huie, Atlanta, 1981-84; ptnr. Jones & Askew, Atlanta, 1984-96; pvt. practice Norcross, Ga., 1996—; asst. atty. gen. State of Ga., Atlanta, 1984-88. Elder Trinity Presbyn. Ch., Atlanta, 1978-81; chmn. bd. trustees Trinity Sch., Atlanta, 1971-74. Mem. Am. Phys. Soc. Avocations: golf, hiking, music. Office: Patent Law Offices 35 Technology Pkwy S Ste 170 Norcross GA 30092-2928

ANDERSON, ALDEN ALVIN, music educator; b. Ada, Minn., Sept. 2, 1947; s. Alvin Arthur and Dagmar Alphilde (Saker) A.; m. Gloria Jean Brown, Dec. 17, 1977 (div. Apr. 10, 1984); 1 child, Maren Elizabeth. BA, Concordia Coll., 1969; postgrad., U. Minn., 1986, U. N.D., 1977, N.D. State U., 1984—, Bemidji State U., 1984. Cert. music, history and geography tchr., Minn. Vocal music tchr. Barnesville (Minn.) Pub. High Sch. Dist. 142, 1970-72, Gary (Minn.) Pub. Sch. Dist. 523, 1972-95, Norman County East Ind. Sch. Dist. # 2215, Gary, 1995-97; part time tchr. Little Falls Cmty. Ind. Sch. Dist., 1997-98, St. Cloud Ind. Sch. Dist., 1997. Clk. City of Gary, 1973-78; pres. Gary Luth. Ch., 1974-76; pres. Dist. 30 Music Educators, Minn., 1976-77, 89, 91-92. Mem. Am. Choral Dirs. Assn. (Fargo-Moorhead Master Chorale 1986—), Minn. Edn. AsMinn. Music Educators Assn. (bd. dirs. 1988-90), Minn. Elem. Music Educators (bd. dirs. 1990-92), Valdres Samband. Democrat. Avocations: photography, geneology. Home: 315 Third Ave E RR 1 Box 16 Gary MN 56545-9700

ANDERSON, ALFRED OLIVER, mathematician, consultant; b. Marmon, N.D., May 18, 1928; s. Frederick Gustav and Minnie Petrine (Jensen) A. BS, Oreg. State U., 1953. Systems programmer U.S. Army Ballistics Research Lab., Aberdeen (Md.) Proving Ground, 1953-83; cons. Aberdeen, 1983—; investment specialist, Liberty, Maine, 1983—. Mem. Mensa, Pi Mu Epsilon. Democrat. Lutheran. Avocations: wood working, investment analysis. Home and Office: RR 1 Box 1041 Liberty ME 04949-9716

ANDERSON, ALLAN, architectural firm executive. BArch cum laude, Carnegie-Mellon U., 1957; MArch, MIT, 1960. Cert. Nat. Coun. Archtl. Registration Bd.; lic. arch., N.Y., Conn., Mass., Pa., Vt., N.H., Fla., R.I., N.J., D.C. With Paul Schweikher, Architect, Pitts., 1957-58, Lawrence and Anthony Wolf, Architects, Pitts., 1958-59, Ulrich Franzen and Assocs., N.Y., 1960-72; pvt. practice, 1972—; ptnr. Anderson La Rocca Anderson Haynes Archs., 1978—; tchr., lectr. MIT, 1959, Boston Archtl. Ctr., 1960, Pratt Inst., 1962, Cornell U., 1963, McGill U., 1969-76; architect-in-residence White Plains Schs., 1976-82, Bedford, 1979-80, New Rochelle, 1981-82, others; mem. archtl. adv. com. Bd. Edn., Rye, N.Y. Prin. works include Milton Sch. (Honor awards Westchester and N.Y. State chpts. AIA 1977), Microsociety Sch. (Citation Am. Assn. Sch. Bus. Ofcls. 1991, 1st Honor award AIA 1992, Citation Nat. Sch. Bds. Assn. 1993), Rye Mid. Sch. (1st Honor award AIA 1993, Hist. Preservation award City of Rye 1993). Mem. Landmarks Commn., Rye; mem. Arts Gen. Edn. Adv. Coun., City of White Plains, N.Y.; mem. Planning Adv. Com., Rye; bd. dirs. Rye Art Ctr., Rye Performing Arts Coun., Westchester Preservation League. Recipient Hist. Preservation award Rye Mid. Sch., N.Y. Preservation League, 1966, Award for Excellence in Design, N.Y. State Assn. Architects, 1972, Award for Archtl. Excellence, Archtl. Record, 1972, 1st Honor award AIA, House & Home and Am. Home, 1972, Design Excellence award for New Fairfield Mid. Sch., Nat. Sch. Bds. Assn., 1996, Bldg. Design award Pub. Sch. Dist. 15, N.Y.C., Queens County, 1994. Mem. AIA (regional coord. learning by design, mem. environ. edn. com., dir. Westchester-Mid Hudson chpt., 1st Honor award Westchester chpt. 1973, Honor award 1977, Ednl. Program Achievement award N.Y. State chpt. 1978, First Honor award for New Fairfield Mid. Sch. 1996), Coun. Ednl. Facilities Planner Internat. Office: Anderson La Rocca Anderson Haynes Arch 22 Purchase St Rye NY 10580-3003*

ANDERSON, ALLAN CROSBY, hospital executive; b. Jamestown, N.Y., Sept. 18, 1932; s. Emmons E. and Gertrude (Sweet) A.; m. Pauline Culver, June 24, 1956; children: Todd Culver, Emily Ann. BS, Syracuse U., 1954; MHA, U. Minn., 1956. Asst. adminstr. Highland Hosp., Rochester, N.Y., 1959-62, adminstr., 1965-68; asst. dir. Presbyn. Hosp., Phila., 1962-65; exec. dir. Strong Meml. Hosp., U. Rochester, 1968-79; pres. Lenox Hill Hosp., N.Y.C., 1979-89; v.p., COO Milton S. Hershey Med. Ctr., dir. Univ. Hosps. Pa. State U., Hershey, 1990-96; asst. prof. health services U. Rochester Sch. Medicine and Dentistry.; mem. exec. com. Sub-Regional Adminstrs. Group, Adminstrs. Conf., Sub-Regional Exec. Conf.; chmn. bd. dirs. Rochester Regional Hosp. Assn., vice chmn. hosp. planning group; chmn. pub. rels. com., bd. dirs. Rochester Hosp. Svc. Corp.; dir. Univ. Hosp. Consortium, 1990-96, mem. exec. com., 1994-96; mem. Accreditation Coun. for Grad. MEd. Edn., 1990-96, treas., 1992-94, mem. exec. com., 1992-96, chmn., 1995; bd. dirs. Capital Blue Cross, 1993-95, United Way of the Capital Region, 1993-98, mem. exec. com., 1995-98. Mem. blood program com. Rochester-Monroe County chpt. A.R.C.; mem. med. adv. com. Planned Parenthood of Rochester and Monroe County.; Bd. dirs. Rochester Presbyn. Home, 1967-70, Home Care Assn. Rochester and Monroe County, Health Council Monroe County. Served to 1st lt., Med. Service Corps USAF, 1957-59. Mem. Am. Coll. Health Care Execs., Assn. Am. Med. Colls. (assembly) Hosp. Assn. N.Y. State (dir., regional orgns. com., govt. rels. com., trustee 1980-84), Greater N.Y. Hosp. Assn. (gov. 1980-89, treas. 1982, sec. 1983, vice chmn. 1984, 85, 86, chmn. 1987, chmn. fiscal policy com. 1982-83, chmn. ambulatory care comm. 1980), Am. Hosp. Assn. (regional adv. bd. 1986-89, regional policy bd. 1992-95, trustee 1985-89, exec. com. 1987-89), League Vol. Hosps. (chmn.-elect 1983-86, chmn. 1986-88). Presbyterian (ruling elder). Home: 1011 W Areba Ave Hershey PA 17033-2204

ANDERSON, ALLAN CURTIS, pharmaceuticals researcher; b. Miles City, Mont., Mar. 6, 1955; m. Natalie R. Cramer, Jan. 15, 1976; children: Brandie N., Jessica L. AA in Med. Sci., Miles C.C., Miles City, 1989; BS in Pharmacy, U. Mont., 1992; PharmD, SUNY, Buffalo, 1994. Photo lithography engr. Intel, Aloha, Oreg., 1978-80; engr. Crowley Maritime, Seattle, 1981-86; rsch. assoc. U. Mont., Missoula, 1989-92; forensic toxicology technician Mont. Dept. Justice, Missoula, 1991-92; clin. rschr. Clin. Phamacokinetics Lab., Buffalo, 1992-94; program dir. gastrointestinal rsch. Clin. Phamacokinetics Lab., 1995—; pharmacist Good Samaritan Pharmacy, New Brighton, Minn., 1994-95; postdoctoral fellow U. Minn., Mpls., 1995; dir. R & D Dynamic Concepts, Tonawanda, N.Y., 1995—; dir. clin. rsch. Gastrotarget Corp., Tonawanda, 1995—. Contbr. articles to profl. jours. Recipient Rsch. award Upjohn Pharmacy, 1991. Mem. Am. Coll. Clin. Pharmacy, Am. Soc. Health Sys. Pharmacists, Biomed. Engring. Soc., Am. Coll. Clin. Pharmacy, Am. Soc. Health System Pharmacists, Kappa Psi, Sigma Xi. Achievements include patents pending for novel med. devices, devel. of comml. applications of mil. tech., devel. of mfg. sys. for Intel Corp. Office: Tex Tech Univ Health Sci Ctr Sch Pharmacy 1300 Coulter Dr Rm 206 Amarillo TX 79106-1712

ANDERSON, ANDREW HERBERT, retired army officer; b. Bklyn., Sept. 8, 1928; s. Hjalmar and Anna (Rantanen) Andreason; m. Ellen Lee Miller, Sept. 1, 1956; children—James Andrew, Glenn Robert, Steven Michael. BS in History, Park Coll., 1963; MS in Pers. Adminstrn., George Washington U., 1968. Commd. in N.G., 1951; entered active duty as 1st lt. U.S. Army, 1954, advanced through grades to maj. gen., 1981—; troop comdr. Ft. Benning, Ga., 1958-60; served in Korea, 1964; mem. army staff Washington, 1965-67; bn. comdr. Vietnam, 1968, Federal Republic Germany, 1970-71; comdr. Support Command 1st Armored Div., Federal Republic Germany, 1973-74; chief of staff 1st Armored Div., 1975-76; dep. comdr. Tank-Automotive Materiel Readiness Command, Warren, Mich., 1977-79; comdr. U.S. Army Tank Automotive Research/Devel. Command, Warren, 1979-80; dep. insp. gen. Washington, 1980-81; dep. comdr. VII Corps, Fed. Republic Germany, 1981-84; comdr. Test and Evaluation Command, Aberdeen Proving Ground, Md., 1984-86; ret., 1986. Vice-pres. Talbot County Coun., 1990-98. Decorated D.S.M., Silver Star, Legion of Merit with 2 oak leaf clusters, D.F.C., Bronze Star with 3 oak leaf clusters and V device, Air medal with 7 oak leave clusters and V device, Army Commendation medal with 3 oak leaf clusters and V device, Purple Heart, George Washington honor medal for individual achievement freedoms found. at Valley Forge, 1991, Md. Veteran of the Yr., 1992, N.Y. State Conspicuous Svc. cross, N.Y. State Meritorious Svc. medal; German Armed Forces honor Cross in Gold. Mem. VFW, DAV, Md. Vets. Home Commn., Assn. U.S. Army, Armor Assn., Am. Legion, Amvets, Order Purple Heart, Masons (32d degree), Shriners. Republican. Home: 29995 Bolingbroke Ln Trappe MD 21673-1522

ANDERSON, ANNELISE GRAEBNER, economist; b. Oklahoma City, Nov. 19, 1938; d. Elmer and Dorothy (Zilisch) Graebner; m. Martin Anderson, Sept. 25, 1965. B.A., Wellesley Coll., 1960; M.A., Columbia U., 1965, Ph.D., 1974. Assoc. editor McKinsey and Co., Inc., 1963-65; researcher Nixon Campaign Staff, 1968-69; project mgr. Dept. Justice, 1970-71; from asst. prof. bus. adminstrn. to assoc. prof. Calif. State U.-Hayward, 1975-80; sr. policy adviser Reagan Presdl. campaign and transition, Washington, 1980; assoc. dir. econs. and govt. Office Mgmt. and Budget, Washington, 1981-83; sr. rsch. fellow Hoover Instn., Stanford U., Calif., 1983—, assoc. dir., 1989-90; mem. Nat. Sci. Bd., 1985-90; Office: Stanford U Hoover Institution Stanford CA 94305

ANDERSON, ARTHUR ALLAN, management consultant; b. Grand Rapids, Mich., Apr. 16, 1939; s. Alvin Alexander and Mildred Jane (Grice) A. AB in History, ScB in Chemistry, Brown U., 1962; LLB, Yale U., 1965. Bar: N.Y. 1966. Assoc. Fish & Neave, N.Y.C., 1965-69; co-founder, pres. Source Securities Corp., 1970-72; gen. counsel Teleprompter Corp., N.Y.C., 1973-74; ptnr. Anderson & Rubin, N.Y.C., 1975-82, Choate, Moore, Hahn & McGarry, N.Y.C., 1982-85; sole practice N.Y.C., 1985-87; prin. Morgan, Anderson & Co., N.Y.C., 1987-98; prin. Morgan Anderson Consulting, N.Y.C., 1998—, also bd. dirs.; bd. dirs. Woodstock Artists' Assn., Woodstock Guild. Mem. Nat. Arts Club. Home: Moonhaw Rd West Shokan NY 12494 Office: 136 W 24th St New York NY 10011-1908

ANDERSON, ARTHUR G., JR., chemistry educator; b. Sioux City, Iowa, July 1, 1918; s. Arthur G. and Lois (Mueller) A.; m. Sue Rinker, Sept. 16, 1944; children—Lynn, Joyce, Beth. A.B., U. Ill., 1940; M.Sc., U. Mich., 1942, Ph.D., 1944. Chemist Manhattan Project, Tenn. Eastman Corp., Oak Ridge, 1944-45; mem. faculty U. Wash., Seattle, 1946-88, assoc. prof. chemistry, 1952-57, prof., 1957-88, assoc. chmn., 1979-88, prof. emeritus, 1988—; Rsch. fellow U. Ill., 1946; NSF sr. postdoctoral fellow Heidelberg U., 1960-61; Vis. prof. Australian Nat. U., Canberra, 1966. Contbr. articles to profl. jours. Recipient Petroleum Research Fund Internat. award, 1966. Fellow N.Y. Acad. Scis., Am. Inst. Chemists, Chem. Soc. London; mem. Sigma Xi, Phi Beta Kappa, Phi Kappa Phi, Phi Lambda Upsilon. Research in synthesis and properties of nonbenzenoid aromatic, heterocyclic compounds. Home: 7035 53rd Ave NE Seattle WA 98115-6207

ANDERSON, ARTHUR GEORGE, laboratory director, former computer company executive, consultant; b. Evanston, Ill., Nov. 22, 1926; s. Arthur G. and Margaret (Bree) A.; m. Eliza Chavez Heninger, 1975; children: Joseph S., Robin R., Jennifer M. B.S., U. San Francisco, 1947-49; M.S., Northwestern U., 1951; Ph.D., NYU, 1958. With IBM Corp., 1951-84, head numerous engring. and managerial positions, 1951-65; staff dir. corporate tech. com. IBM Corp., Armonk, N.Y., 1965-67; dir. research IBM Corp., Yorktown, N.Y., 1967-69; v.p., dir. research IBM Corp., Yorktown, 1969-70; dir. tech. assessment IBM Corp., 1971-72; pres. Gen. Products div. IBM Corp., San Jose, Calif., 1972-79, 82-83; v.p., group exec. Data Products group IBM Corp., White Plains, N.Y., 1979-81; ret., 1984—; dir. Compression Labs Inc., 1984—; chmn. bd. dirs. Compression Labs., 1996-97; bd. dirs. VTEL. Served with USNR, 1944-46. Fellow Am. Phys. Soc. (Pake award 1984), IEEE; mem. AAAS, Nat. Acad. Engring. Patentee in field of storage techniques and digital circuitry. Home: 1360 White Spar Rd Prescott AZ 86303-7270*

ANDERSON, ARTHUR LEE, sculptor, writer; b. Washington, Nov. 28, 1952; s. Kenneth Arthur and Marjorie Ruth (Anderson) A.; m. Marion Mann, Oct. 18, 1981 (div. Nov. 1987); 1 child, Tanya Leah. Grad., Gemological Inst. Am., Santa Monica, Calif., 1986. Importer Washington, 1971-75; contractor New Orleans, 1976-80; deckhand Chotin Shipping Co., New Orleans, 1980-81; gem cutter, sculptor Speira Gems, Ashland, Oreg., 1984—; vol. spkr. on gemstone-related topics, pub. schs., Ashland, 1990—; bd. mem. Gemartists N.Am., 1996; judge Am. Gem Trading Assn. cutting edge competition, 1996. Editor Gemartists N.Am. Newsletter, 1995, 96; contbr. tech. articles to Gems and Gemology, Lapidary Jour. Recipient 1st pl. for creative gem cut Am. Gem Trade Assn., 1992, 1st pl. for objet d'art, 1993, 2d pl. fancy gem cut, 1994, 3d pl. pairs and suites, 1994, 1st pl. pairs and suites, 1995, 1st pl. German award for precious stones and jewelry, 1997, 1st pl. faceting, 1998, others. Libertarian. Avocations: music (guitar), Writing. E-mail: zlift@aol.com. Home: Speira Gems 680 Alton Alston Rd Pittsboro NC 27312 Office: Speira Gems PO Box 976 Carrboro NC 27510-0976

ANDERSON, ARTHUR N., retired utility company executive; b. N.Y.C., Jan. 18, 1912; s. Nels and Mathilda (Sandlund) A.; m. Marion A. Olson, Aug. 8, 1937; children: Marian Elaine, Nils A. B.S. in Mech. Engring, N.Y.U., 1933. With Consol. Edison Co. of N.Y., Inc., 1933-50, 54-73, various engring. and supervisory positions, gas and electric prodn. depts., engring. and constrn. depts., v.p. constrn., 1961-73; sec., treas. Assoc. Edison Illuminating Cos., N.Y.C., 1973-90; power engr. indsl. devel. atomic energy AEC, 1950-52; with Atomic Power Devel. Assos., Detroit, 1952-54. Mem. Soc. Gas Lighting N.Y.C. Home: 7 Elm Sea Ln Manhasset NY 11030-1008

ANDERSON, ARTHUR OSMUND, pathologist, immunologist, army officer; b. N.Y.C., Mar. 12, 1945; s. Arthur Edmund and Florence Ranveig (Osmundsen) A.; m. Julane Kay Pynn, Oct. 4, 1969; 1 child, Phoebe MacDonald Anderson. BS, Wagner Coll., 1966; MD, U. Md., 1970. Diplomate Am. Bd. Pathology. Intern in pathology Johns Hopkins Hosp., Balt., 1970-71, fellow in exptl. pathology, 1970-74, resident in pathology, 1971-73; commd. 2d lt. U.S. Army, 1974, advanced through grades to col., 1988; asst. prof. biology and pathology U. Pa., Phila., 1980-83; prin. investigator pathology div. U.S. Army Med. Rsch. Inst. Infectious Diseases, Ft. Detrick, Md., 1974-80, chief respiratory immunity, 1983—, chmn. human investigational rev. bd., 1976-80, 84—. Contbr. numerous articles to profl. jours., chpts. to immunology text books. Decorated Meritorious Svc. medal; N.Y. State Regents scholar, 1962-66. Mem. Found. for Advanced Edn. in Scis., Am. Assn. Immunologists, Am. Assn. Pathologists, Kiwanis (pres. Frederick 1988-89), Beta Beta Beta, Omicron Delta Kappa. Republican. Achievements include first documented role of endothelium in immunity; first showed evidence in vivo that lymphocytes adhered to endothelial cells in lymph nodes, first showed that adjuvants could enhance mucosal secretion of IgA. Office: US Army Med Rsch Inst Infectious Diseases Fort Detrick Frederick MD 21702

ANDERSON, ARTHUR RODNEY, secondary education educator; b. Oak Park, Ill., Feb. 14, 1930; s. Arthur J. and Hilda Marie (Fauske) A.; m. Marjorie Raglin, June 23, 1965. BS, So. Ill. U., 1981, MS, 1983, cert. adminstrn., 1988. Carpenter, Wade Constrn. Co., Itasca, Ill., 1962-72, foreman, 1962-65, supt., 1965-72; tchr. bldg. trades Lockport (Ill.) Twp. High Sch., 1972-92, developer vocat. bldg. trades course; lectr. secondary edn. workshops, 1968—; tchr. vocat. edn. workshop, Krasnoyarsk, Siberia, 1992. Pres., bd. dirs. Guardian Angel Exch. Club Ctr. for Prevention of Child Abuse. Recipient Outstanding Service award James McKinnon Smith chpt. Nat. Honor Soc., 1975; citation for outstanding contbn. to vocat. edn. studies So. Ill. U., 1981. Mem. Am. Vocat. Assn., Ill. Vocat. Assn., Ill. Indsl. Edn. Assn. (pres. Roundtable 4, 1983-84), United Brotherhood of Carpenters and Joiners (pres. local 558, Elmhurst, Ill. 1967-76), Iota Lambda Sigma, Sons of Norway, Nat. Exchange Club (sec., bd. dirs. Lockport, Ill. chpt., adv. coun. 1991-92). Methodist. Home: 15711 Liberty Ct Orland Park IL 60462-4557

ANDERSON, AUSTIN GILMAN, economics research company consultant; b. Mpls.; s. Clifford Hawkins and Katharine (Irving) A.; m. Marilyn Wheeler, Mar. 17, 1968; children: Guy, Alisa, Michael, Emily. BS, Stanford U., 1964, MBA, 1966. Systems analyst Jet Propulsion Lab., Pasadena, Calif., 1966-68; assoc. Econs. Rsch. Assoc., L.A., 1968-72, sr. v.p., 1977-88, pres., chief exec. officer, 1988—; dir. rsch. Property Rsch. Corp., L.A., 1972-73; prin. Levander, Partridge & Anderson, Beverly Hills, Calif., 1973-77; instr. Grad. Sch. Mgmt. UCLA, 1989, extension, 1987; bd. dirs. Crown Iron Works Co., Mpls., 1983—; mem. bd. counselors Sch. Urban and Regional Planning U. So. Calif., L.A., 1984-95; mem. bd. trustees Real Estate Investment Trust of Calif., 1994—. Mem. Urban Land Inst. Avocations: sculpting, golf. Home: 328 17th St Manhattan Beach CA 90266-4636 Office: Econs Rsch Assocs Ste 1500 10990 Wilshire Blvd Los Angeles CA 90024-3913

ANDERSON, AUSTIN GOTHARD, university administrator, lawyer; b. Calumet, Minn., June 30, 1931; s. Hugo Gothard and Turna Marie (Johnson) A.; m. Catherine Antoinette Spellacy, Jan. 2, 1954; children: Todd, Susan, Timothy, Linda, Mark. BA, U. Minn., 1954, JD, 1958. Bar: Minn.

1958, Ill. 1962, Mich. 1974. Assoc. Spellacy, Spellacy, Lano & Anderson, Marble, Minn, 1958-62; dir. Ill. Inst. Continuing Legal Edn., Springfield, 1962-64; dir. dept. continuing legal edn. U. Minn., Mpls., 1964-70, assoc. dean gen. extension div., 1968-70; ptnr. Dorsey, Marquart, Windhorst, West & Halladay, Mpls., 1970-73; assoc. dir. Nat. Ctr. State Cts., St. Paul, 1973-74; dir. Inst. Continuing Legal Edn. U. Mich., Ann Arbor, 1973-92; dir. Inst. on Law Firm Mgmt., 1992-95; prin. AndersonBoyer Group, Ann Arbor; pres. Network of Leading Law Firms, 1995—; adj. faculty U. Minn., 1974, Wayne State U., 1974-75; mem. adv. bd. Ctr. for Law Firm Mgmt. Nottingham Trent U., Eng.; draftsman ABA Guidelines for Approval of Legal Asst. Programs, 1973, Model Guidelines for Minimum Continuing Legal Edn., 1988; vice chair law practice mgmt. sect. State Bar Mich., 1997—; cons. in field. Co-editor, contbg. author: Lawyer's Handbook, 1975, co-editor 3d edit., 1992; author: A Plan for Lawyer Development, 1986, Marketing Your Practice: A Practical Guide to Client Development, 1986; cons. editor, contbg. author: Webster's Legal Secretaries Handbook, 1981; cons. editor Merriam Webster's Legal Secretarial Handbook, 2d edit., 1996; contbr. chpt. to book and articles to profl. jours. Chmn. City of Bloomington Park and Recreation Adv. Commn., Minn., 1970-72; chmn. Ann Arbor Citizens Recreation Adv. Com., 1981-89, Ann Arbor Parks Adv. Com., 1983-92, chair, 1991-92; rep. Class of '58 U. Minn. Law Sch., 1996—. Recipient Excellence award CLE sect. Assn. of Am. Law Schs., 1992. Fellow Am. Bar Found., State Bar Mich. Found.; mem. ABA (vice chmn. continuing legal edn. com. sect. legal edn. and admission to bar 1988-93, standing com. continuing edn. of bar 1984-90, chmn. law practice mgmt. sect. 1981-82, AII-ABA com. on continuing profl. edn. 1993-96, sec. Coll. of Law Practice Mgmt. 1993-97, ho. of dels. 1993—, commn. on lawyer advt. 1994-97, futures com.), Internat. Bar Assn., Mich. Bar Assn., State Bar of Mich. (vice chair law practice mgmt. sect.), Ill. Bar Assn., Minn. Bar Assn., Assn. Continuing Legal Edn. Adminstrs., Assn. Legal Adminstrs. (pres. 1969-70), Ann Arbor Golf and Outing Club. Home: 3617 Larchmont Dr Ann Arbor MI 48105-2855 Office: AndersonBoyer Group 3157 Packard St Ste C Ann Arbor MI 48108-1900

ANDERSON, BARBARA GRAHAM, philanthropic resources development consultant; b. Detroit, Dec. 2, 1934; d. Neill Edwin and Elizabeth (Blackwood) Graham; m. Donald L. Wells, Jan. 31, 1960 (div. Apr. 1976); m. K. Bruce Anderson, Apr. 1, 1978. AB in Speech/Comms., Fla. State U., Tallahassee, 1956. Dir. devel. Adoption Svc. of Westchester, White Plains, N.Y., 1966-68; founder, devel. chair The Art Barn, Greenwich, Conn., 1966-69; assoc. dir. for corp. appeals and maj. individual gifts Nat. Staff/YWCA, N.Y.C., 1969-70; project dir. Nat. Clearinghouse for Alcohol Info., Gaithersburg, Md., 1974-76; sr. assoc. The Oram Group, Inc., N.Y.C., 1973-74, 76-78, 86-88; counseling and profl. svcs. various clients in, San Francisco, 1978-86; with Coviello and Assocs., Chevy Chase, Md., 1988-94, 97—, Joyaux Assocs., R.I., 1994—; organizer workshops and seminars for orgns. including The Fund Raising Sch., 1982-86, The Found. Ctr., Washington, 1991-93, Bush Ctr., Yale U., 1997. Housing Authority commr. Town of Chatham, Mass., 1995-97. Mem. Nat. Soc. Fund Raising Execs. (cert. fund raising exec., bd. dirs. San Francisco 1980-86, bd. dirs., officer Greater Washington chpt. 1988-92, mem. nat. cert. bd. 1983-90). Democrat. Episcopalian. Home and Office: 2100 Walnut St Apt 11-K Philadelphia PA 19103

ANDERSON, BARBARA MCCOMAS, lawyer; b. Ft. Belvoir, Va., Dec. 18, 1950; d. Ben C. Jr. and Elsa A. (Hild) McComas; m. Roy Ryden Anderson Jr., Dec. 11, 1982; 1 child, Ryden McComas Anderson. BA, Trinity U., San Antonio, 1972; JD, U. Tex., 1978. Bar: Tex. 1978; cert. in estate planning and probate Tex. Bd. Legal Specialization. From assoc. to ptnr. Locke Purnell Rain Harrell, Dallas, 1978-97; of counsel Law Office of Barbara McComas Anderson, Dallas, 1997—, Locke Liddell & Sapp, LLP, Dallas, 1998—. Bd. dirs. Dallas Estate Planning Coun., 1986-87. Fellow Am. Coll. Trusts and Estates Counsel, Tex. Bar Found., Coll. of State Bar of Tex.; mem. Tex. Bar Assn. (coun. of real property, probate and trust law sect.), Dallas Bar Assn. (chmn. probate, trusts and estates sect. 1987-88), Tex. Acad. Probate and Trust Lawyers (charter). Avocations: reading, child rearing, gardening. Office: PO Box 181147 Dallas TX 75218-8147

ANDERSON, BERNARD E., economist; b. Phila.; s. William and Dorothy (Gideon) A.; m. Verdia D. Wilson; children: Melinda D., Bernard E. II. BA with highest honors, Livingstone Coll., 1959; MA, Mich. State U., 1961; PhD, U. Pa., 1969; LHD (hon.), Shaw U., 1984, Livingstone Coll., 1995. Economist U.S. Bur. Labor Stats., Washington, 1963-65; successively asst. prof., assoc. prof., prof. Wharton Sch. U. Pa., Phila., 1969-79; dir. social sci. The Rockefeller Found., N.Y.C., 1979-86; vis. fellow Woodrow Wilson Sch., Princeton U., N.J., 1985; mng. ptnr. The Urban Affairs Partnership, Phila., 1987-91; pres. The Anderson Group, Phila., 1991-93; asst. sec. U.S. Dept. Labor, 1994—; chmn. Pa. Intergovernmental Cooperation Authority, Phila., 1991-93; vice chmn., bd. dirs. Manpower Demostration Rsch. Co., N.Y.C., Pa. Econ. Devel. Partnership, Harrisburg, Provident Mut. Life Ins. Co. Author: Youth Employment and Public Policy, 1980; co-author: Black Managers in American Business, 1978, Impact of Government Training and Employment Programs, 1975, Managing Growth in American Business, 1978, Soul in Management, 1996; mem. editorial bd. Rev. Black Polit. Economy, 1977-89. Trustee Livingstone Coll., Salisbury, N.C., 1980—; chmn. bd. trustees Lincoln U., Oxford, pa., 1987-93; mem. Pres.'s Commn. on Employment Stats., Washington, 1979; mem. Nat. Commn. Jobs and Small Bus., Washington, 1986; bd. dirs. Com. Fgn. Rels., Phila., 1983—. With U.S. Army, 1961-63. Recipient Disting. Educator award Citizens for Urbanism, Phila., 1987, Community Svc. award Delaware Valley Housing Assn., 1989, Disting. Svc. award A. Philip Randolph Inst., 1990, Bayard Rustin Humanitarian award A. Philip Randolph Inst., 1996. Mem. Am. Econ. Assn., Indsl. Rels. Rsch. Assn. (mem. exec. com. 1979-82), Nat. Econ. Assn. (pres. 1982), Union League, U. Pa. Faculty Club, Princeton Club. Democrat. A.M.E. Zion.

ANDERSON, BERNARD JOSEPH, social studies educator; b. Reno, May 15, 1942; s. Bernard and Bridget T. Anderson; m. Clyda J. Hooper, Aug. 5, 1967; children: Cairn L., Natha Clyde. BS in Edn., U. Nev., 1970. Tchr. social studies Washoe County Sch. Dist., Reno, 1972—. Co-chair Sparks (Nev.) Charter Com., 1980-90; mem. Nev. State Legis. Com., Carson City, 1990—. Mem. NEA (bd. dirs.), KC (Grand Knight), Nev. State Edn. Assn. (bd. dirs.), Washoe County Tchr. Assn. (bd. dirs.). Democrat. Roman Catholic. Address: State Capitol Members of the Assembly District 31 Carson City NV 89710

ANDERSON, BETH ELLEN, English literature and composition educator; b. South Weymouth, Mass., May 30, 1941; d. Allison Webster and Madeline Lois (Wilcox) Stone; m. Panagiotis A. Argentinis, June 20, 1963 (div. 1967); 1 child, Christopher A. BA, U. Mass., 1963; MEd, Cambridge U., 1994. Cert. English, French tchr. English tchr. Whitman (Mass.) Hanson Regional H.S., 1965-85, advanced placement English tchr., 1985—. Recipient Presdl. Citation Pres. George Bush, 1989, Golden Apple award Quincy Patriot Ledger, 1991; named Top 72 Educators in New Eng. 21st Century Newspaper, 1992. Mem. NEA, Mass. Tchrs. Assn., Nat. Coun. Tchrs. of English, Soc. of Mayflower Descendants. Republican. Home: 68 Beaver Ln Abington MA 02351-1226 Office: Whitman Hanson HS Franklin St Whitman MA 02382

ANDERSON, BEVERLY JACQUES, academic administrator; b. New Orleans, Sept. 10, 1943; d. Alvin Joseph and Dorothy Ann (Angelety) Jacques; m. Ronald Lee Anderson, Sept. 6, 1967; children: Montina Jacquel, Monique Janee, Montez Jacques. BS cum laude, Dillard U., 1965; MS, Howard U., 1967; PhD, Cath. U. Am., 1978. Instr. math. Howard U., Washington, 1967-69; from instr. to prof. U. D.C., Washington, 1969-94, dean coll. arts & scis., 1994-97, provost, v.p. for acad. affairs, 1997—; instr. math. upward bound program Dillard U., Howard U., and Coll. of V.I., summers 1965-69; dir. minority affairs NRC, Washington, 1988-92; dir. instl. self-study U. D.C., Washington, 1992-94; bd. dirs. Prince Georges C.C., 1993—, chmn. 1996-97; presenter in field. Columnist Prince Georges News, 1991-95; contbr. articles to profl. jours. Bd. dirs., treas. Greater S.E. Healthcare Sys. Found., Washington, 1994—; bd. dirs. Ft. Washington Hosp., 1988—, chair, 1994-98; bd. dirs. YMCA, Metro. Washington, 1992-95; chair FDA Adv. Com., Washington, 1989-94. Grantee Office Naval Rsch., NASA, Office Post Secondary Edn., Nat. Security Agy.; recipient White House Initiative Faculty award, 1988, Outstanding Cmty. Svc. award Washington View Mag., 1990, Citation, Assn. Women in Math., 1991, Cmty. Svc. award Greater S.E. Healthcare Sys., 1993, Faculty Rsch. award NAFEO, 1993, Stewardship award United Negro Coll. Fund, 1996; named Outstanding Alumni, Howard U., 1997. Mem. Pi Mu Epsilon, Beta Kappa Chi, Phi Delta Kappa. Democrat. Roman Catholic. Avocation: travel. Home: 705 Muirfield Cir Fort Washington MD 20744-7021 Office: Univ DC 4200 Connecticut Ave NW Washington DC 20008-1175

ANDERSON, BOB, state legislator, business executive; b. Wadena, Minn., Jan. 16, 1932; s. Alfred Emmanuel and Frances Agnes (Hassler) A.; m. Janet Lynn Hemquist, Aug. 3, 1967. BBA, U. Miami, 1959; student, U.S. Army War Coll., 1996. Owner small business, Minn., 1954-96; mem. Minn. Ho. of Reps., 1976-96; mem. steering com. House DFL Caucus, 1993-94; mem. ways and means com., 1993-96, chair human svcs. fin. divsn., 1985-86, chair health and housing fin. divsn., 1993-94, chair health and human svcs. com., 1995-96; chair NCSL com. Agrl., 1985; vice chair, sec., mem. exec. com. Legis. Commn. on Waste Mgmt., 1980-96; dir. NCSL Found. for State Legislatures, 1987-93; legis. cons., 1997—; past pres. Viking-Land USA; bd. dirs. West Ctrl. Minn. EMS, Inc., 1999—. Past pres. Otter Tail Lake Property Owners Assn.; mem. Fergus Falls N.G. Citizens Com.; bd. dirs. West Ctrl. Minn. EMS, Inc. With U.S. Army, 1952-54. Decorated D.S.M. Named Hon. Citizen, City of Winnipeg, Chief Author Glendalough State Pk., Fergus Falls Vets. Home, Prairie Wetlands Environ. Learning Ctr.; recipient Highroad Explorer award, Hon. Viking award, Svc. award Minn. Assn. Rehab. Facilities, West Cen. Emergency Med. Corp, Minn. Ambulance Assn., Nat. Fedn. Ind. Bus., Minn. Head Start Assn., Econ. Justice award MNCAP, Ctrs. For Ind. Living, Minn. Community Action award, Pub. Ofcl. Yr. award Minn. Nurses Assn., 1994, Food First Coalition award, 1995. Mem. Nat. Conf. State Legislatures (exec. com. 1986-88, commerce, labor and regulation com. 1991-94), Minn. Meat Processors Assn. (past pres.), Otter Tail County Hist. Soc., Am. Legion, VFW (Ladies Aux. Vet. of Yr. award 1994), Minn. Outdoor Heritage Caucus, Fergus Falls Fish and Game Club, Millerville Sportsmen Club, Evansville Sportsmen Club, Ottertail Rod and Gun Club, Knob Hill Sportsmen, Sons of Norway, Elks, Masons, Shriners. Democrat. Home: PO Box 28 Ottertail MN 56571-0028

ANDERSON, BRADY KEVIN, professional baseball player; b. Silver Spring, Md., Jan. 18, 1964. Student, U. Calif., Irvine. Center field Boston red Sox, 1985-88, Balt. Orioles, 1988—. Office: c/o Baltimore Orioles Oriole Park at Camden Yards 333 W Camden St Baltimore MD 21201-2435

ANDERSON, BRIAN KEITH, editor; b. Ely, Minn., Apr. 2, 1964; s. William Andrew Anderson and Caroline Marie (Klobuchar) Olson; m. Terri Hamre, Aug. 26, 1995. AA, Vermilion C.C., 1984; BS, Bemidji State U., 1988. Reporter, PD mgr. The Cir. Newspaper, Mpls., 1988-90; city editor Hibbinc (Minn.) Daily Tribune, 1990-93; reporter, dist. mgr. Duluth (Minn.) News Tribune, 1994-96; editor, asst. gen. mgr. Chisholm (Minn.) Tribunal Press, 1996—. Vol. United Way; mem. Focus 2000. Recipient Best Sportswriter award Native Am. Press Assn., 1989. Democrat. Lutheran. Avocations: reading, volunteering, sports. Home: 3505 3rd Ave W Hibbinc MN 55746 Office: Chisholm Tribune Press 216 W Lake St Chisholm MN 55719

ANDERSON, BRIAN LYNN, urologist; b. Jan. 9, 1957; m. Lori Anderson; children: Robert, Robby, Susan. BS in Biochemistry and Biophysics, Oreg. State U.; grad. med. sch., Oreg. Health Scis. U., 1983. Diplomat Am. Bd. Urology. Intern Oreg. Health Scis. U., 1983-84, resident in gen. surgery, 1984-85, resident in urology, 1985-89. AFS Exch. student to Brazil, 1974. Mem. Wash. Med. Assn., Wash. Urol. Assn., N.W. Urol. Soc., Am. Urol. Assn. Office: 125 3rd St NE Ste 401 Auburn WA 98002

ANDERSON, BRUCE JAMES, electrical engineer, consultant; b. Springfield, Mass., Oct. 16, 1962; s. Bruce James and Frances (Cirillo) A.; m. Susan Patricia Bauer, Apr. 28, 1990. BSEE, Western New Eng. Coll., 1984. Sr. engr. Lockheed, Plainfield, N.J., 1984-90; dir. consumer systems Sarnoff Corp., Princeton, N.J., 1990—. Patentee in field. Mem. IEEE, Assn. of Computng Machines. Achievements include co-design of Grand Alliance High Definition TV Sys. Office: Sarnoff Corp 201 Washington Rd Princeton NJ 08540-6449

ANDERSON, BRUCE JOHN, foundation administrator; b. Waterbury, Conn., Mar. 9, 1943; s. George E. and Mary M. (Taylor) A.; m. Ann Marie Heath, July 8, 1967; children: Christopher, Carrie, Mark. BS, Ctrl. Conn. State, 1965, MS, 1967; CAGS, Fairfield U., 1969; EdD, U. Va., 1971. Tchr. Southington (Conn.) Sch., 1965-68; instr. Ctrl. Conn. State U., New Britain, Conn., 1968-69; jr. instr. U. Va., Charlottesville, 1969-71; assoc. prof. Old Dominion U., Norfolk, Va., 1971-80, prof., chair dept., 1981-83; v.p. Danforth Found., St. Louis, 1983-91, pres., 1991—; bd. dirs. St. Louis Regional Edn. Partnership; mem. adv. bd. Mo. Gov. Edn. Panel, Jefferson City, Mo. Co-editor: Democratic Leadership: Changing Context of Administrative Preparation, 1993. Bd. dirs. Met. Assn. Philanthropy, St. Louis, 1990—; mem. adv. bd. St. Louis Zoo, 1989—; mem. parish coun. St. Clares Roman Cath. Ch., St. Louis, 1991—. Office: Danforth Foundation 211 N Broadway # 2390 Saint Louis MO 63102-2733*

ANDERSON, BUIST MURFEE, lawyer; b. Marion, Ala., Nov. 17, 1904; s. Edward Buist and Mary Agnes (Murfee) A.; m. Dorothy Mary Crawford, Feb. 27, 1932; children: Mary Jeanne Anderson Jones, David Crawford, Dudley Buist. B.S., U. Va., 1924; LL.B., Yale U., 1929. Bar: Ala. 1928, Conn. 1930, U.S. Supreme Ct. 1937. Statistician, U.S. Dept. Agr., 1924-27; atty. Conn. Gen. Life Ins. Co., 1929-39, counsel, 1939-69, v.p., 1949-69; with firm Murtha, Cullina, Richter & Pinney, Hartford, 1969-82; dir. Colonial Life & Accident Ins. Co., 1972-90. Editor: Legal Notes, Transactions (Soc. Actuaries), 1941-64, Vance on Insurance, 3d edit., 1951, Anderson on Life Insurance, 1991. Mem. Am. Arbitration Assn., ABA, Assn. Life Ins. Counsel (pres. 1959-60), Am. Life Conv. (chmn. legal sect. 1948). Baptist. Home: 37 Prattling Pond Rd Farmington CT 06032-1803

ANDERSON, CARL ALBERT, academic administrator, lawyer; b. Torrington, Conn., Feb. 27, 1951; s. Carl August and Louise Joanna (Giorcelli) A.; m. Dorian Jean Lounsbury Anderson, Aug. 19, 1972; children: Carl, Matthew, Teresa, Katherine, Clare. BA in Philosophy, Seattle U., 1972; JD, U. Denver, 1975. Bar: D.C. V.p. John Paul II Inst. for Studies on Marriage and Family, Washington, Ind., 1987-99, New Haven, 1999—; dir., bd. dirs. Fellowship of Cath. Scholars, Notre Dame, Ind., 1992-97; legis. asst. U.S. Senate, Washington, 1976-81; counsellor to the Undersec. U.S. Dept. Health and Human Svcs., Washington, 1981-83; staff mem. White House Office of Policy Devel., Washington, 1983-85; spl. asst. to the Pres., 1985-87; acting dir. White House Office of Pub. Liaison, 1987; commr. U.S. Commn. on Civil Rights, Washington, 1990—. Contbr. articles to profl. jours. Transition Team Mem. Office of the Pres.-Elect, Washington, 1980, 88. Recipient Thomas Linacre award Nat. Fedn. Cath. Physicians' Guilds, 1992; Knight of the Equestrian Order of the Holy Sepulchre of Jerusalem. Mem. D.C. Bar Assn., KC (v.p. pub. policy 1987-97, state dep. for D.C. 1995-97, asst. supreme sssec. 1997—). Roman Catholic. Address: KC Columbus Plz New Haven CT 06507-3326*

ANDERSON, CAROL LEE, communications executive; b. Sharon, Pa., Nov. 5, 1943; d. James W. and Charlene Helen (Lang) Thomas; m. Duane A. Anderson, Dec. 16, 1978; children: Mark Powell, Steve Anderson. Student, Youngstown (Ohio) State U., 1961, Pa. State U., Sharon, 1964. Field mgr. Welcome Wagon Internat., Memphis, 1975-78; dir. Merrill Chase Gallery, Naperville, Ill., 1978-80; br. mgr. CONTEL/Executone, Burr Ridge, Ill., 1980-84; major mkt. account exec. Ill. Bell Comm., Westbrook, 1984-90; strategic account exec. govt. accounts Ameritech Custom Bus., Westbrook, Ill., 1990-93, sales mgr. fed., mil. and civilian, 1993-97; regional dir. govt. and edn. Ameritech Custom Bus., Westbrook, 1997-98; dir. bus. sales Ameritech Gen. Bus., 1998—. Mem. Internat. Orgn. Women in Telecommunications, Delta Chi Epsilon. Home: 213 Pfaff Dr Frankfort IL 60423-1624 Office: Ameritech Enhanced Bus Two Westbrook Corp Westchester IL 60154

ANDERSON, CAROLE ANN, nursing educator; b. Chgo., Feb. 21, 1938; d. Robert and Marian (Harrity) Irving; m. Clark Anderson, Feb. 14, 1973; 1 child, Julie. Diploma, St. Francis Hosp., 1958; BS, U. Colo., 1962, MS, 1963, PhD, 1977. Group psychotherapist Dept. Vocat. Rehab., Denver, 1963-72; psychotherapist Prof. Psychiatry and Guidance Clinic, Denver, 1970-71; asst. prof., chmn. nursing sch. U. Colo., Denver, 1971-75; therapist, coordinator The Genessee Mental Health, Rochester, N.Y., 1977-78; assoc. dean U. Rochester, N.Y., 1978-86; dean, prof. Coll. Nursing Ohio State U., Columbus, 1986—; lectr. nursing sch. U. Colo., Denver, 1970-71; prin. investigator biomed. rsch. support grant, 1986-93, clin. rsch. facilitation grant, 1981-82; program dir. profl. nurse traineeship, 1978-86, advanced nurse tng. grant, 1982-85. Author: (with others) Women as Victims, 1986, Violence Toward Women, 1982, Substance Abuse of Women, 1982; editor Nursing Outlook, 1993—. Pres., bd. dirs. Health Assn., Rochester, 1984-86; mem. north sub area council Finger Lakes Health Systems Agy., 1983-86, longrange planning com., 1981-82; mem. Columbus Bd. Health; dir. Netcare Mental Health Ctr. Am. Acad. Nursing fellow. Mem. ANA, Am. Sociol. Assn., Ohio Nurses Assn., Am. Assn. Colls. Nursing (bd. dirs. 1992-94, pres.-elect 1994-96, pres. 1996-98), Sigma Theta Tau. Home: 406 W 6th Ave Columbus OH 43201-3137 Office: The Ohio State Univ Coll Nursing 1585 Neil Ave Columbus OH 43210-1216

ANDERSON, CAROLYN HARVEY, retired pediatrician; b. Little Rock, Jan. 16, 1940; d. Vernon Turner and Pearle Irene (Eden) Harvey; children: Catherine, Carl-James, Kenneth. MD, U. Ark., 1965. Diplomate Am. Bd. Pediat. Physician Pediat. Rheumatology, Pitts., 1972-93; ret., 1993. Assoc. prodr. Shake Rattle and Roar, 1996. Commr. O'Hara (Pa.) Township, 1995-98. Mem. AMA, Am. Acad. Pediatrics, Am. Rheumatology Assn. Presbyterian. Avocations: skiing, tennis, golf.

ANDERSON, CATHERINE M., consulting company executive; b. N.Y.C., Feb. 28, 1937; d. Edward Charles and Elizabeth (O'Shea) McElligott; m. Robert Brown Anderson, June 22, 1963; children: Mark Robert, Jennifer Elizabeth. BA, Rutgers U., 1959, MA, 1960. Staff asst. to pres. Chatham Coll., Pitts., 1960-61; instr. urban studies ctr. Rutgers U., New Brunswick, N.J., 1961-63; prin. urban renewal coord. City of Cleve., Cleve., 1963-64; regional admisions counselor Am. Inst. Fgn. Study, Pitts., 1964-74; chief planner, mgr. emergency ops. ctr. Allegheny County Govt., Pitts., 1975-79; dir. accreditation svcs. Energy Cons., Inc., Pitts., 1981-83; pub. involvement cons. Pitts., 1983—. Contbr. articles to profl. jours. Committeewoman Mt. Lebanon (Pa.) Mcpl. Dem. Com., 1970-85; active United Way Allegheny County, Pitts., mem. rev. com., 1980—, chmn. rev. com., 1986-89; bd. dirs. Mt. Lebanon Nature Conservancy, v.p., 1985-88, pres., 1988-92; bd. dirs. Conservation Cons. Inc., v.p., 1983-92, pres., 1992-95; bd. dirs. Pitts. chpt. Women's Transp. Seminar, v.p., 1992-94, pres. 1994-95; bd. dirs. Exec. Women's Coun. Greater Pitts., v.p., 1986-88; bd. dirs. Carnegie-Mellon U. Art Gallery, 1986-89, USC Citizens for Land Stewardship, 1997—. Recipient Robert L. Wells award Mt. Lebanon Nature Conservancy, 1991, Outstanding Svc. award Exec. Women's Coun., 1988; Eagleton Inst. Politics grad. fellow Rutgers U., 1960. Mem. Am. Soc. Hwy Engrs. (sr. mem., bd. dirs. Pitts. chpt. 1998—), Exec. Women's Coun. (charter mem., v.p., 1987-88, Outstanding Svc. award 1988), Women's Transp. Seminar (v.p. 1992-94, pres. 94-95, nat. bd. dirs. com. co-chair), Women's Press Club Pitts. Home and Office: 2061 Outlook Dr Upper Saint Clair PA 15241-2223

ANDERSON, CHARLES ARTHUR, former research institute administrator; b. Columbus, Ohio, Nov. 14, 1917; s. Arthur E. and Huldah (Peterson) A.; m. Elizabeth Rushforth, Oct. 27, 1942; children: Peter C., Stephen E., Julia E. AB, U. Calif. at Berkeley, 1938; MBA, Grad. Sch. Bus. Adminstrn., Harvard U., 1940; LHD, Colby Coll., 1975. Asst. prof. Grad. Sch. Bus. Adminstrn., Harvard U., Boston, 1945-48; v.p. Magna Power Tool Corp., Menlo Park, Calif., 1948-58; prof., asso. dean Stanford Grad. Sch. Bus., 1959-61; v.p. Kern County Land Co., San Francisco, 1961-64; pres. Walker Mfg. Co., Racine, Wis., 1964-66, J.I. Case Co., Racine, 1966-68; pres., chief exec. officer SRI Internat., Menlo Park, 1968-79, also dir.; bd. dirs. KRI Internat., Japan, Eaton Corp., Conoco, Owens-Corning Fiberglas, NCR, Boise Cascade, Saga; mem. adv. council Bus. Sch., Stanford, 1966-72, 74-79; mem. industry adv. council Dept. Def., 1971-73. Author (with Anthony) The New Corporate Director. Mem. Menlo Park Planning Commn. and City Coun., 1955-61, Govs. Commn. on Reorgn. Wis. State Govt., 1965-67; bd. dirs. Calif. State C. of C., 1972-77, Internat. House, U. Calif., Berkeley, 1979-90; bd. dirs. Lucile Salter Packard Children's Hosp., Stanford, 1979—, chmn., 1992-94. With USNR, 1941-45. Recipient Exceptional Service award USAF, 1965. Mem. Palo Alto Club, Pacific-Union Club, Menlo Country Club. Presbyterian. Office: 555 Byron St Apt 207 Palo Alto CA 94301-2037

ANDERSON, CHARLES HILL, lawyer; b. Chattanooga, June 16, 1930; s. Ray N. and Lois M. (Entrekin) A.; div.; children: Eric S., Alicia L., Burton H.; m. Shirley Roach, May 17, 1996. JD, U. Tenn., 1953. Bar: Tenn. 1953, U.S. Dist. Ct. Tenn. 1953, U.S. Ct. Appeals (6th cir.) 1956, U.S. Supreme Ct. 1956, U.S. Ct. Mil. 1964. Pvt. practice Chattanooga, 1953-59; assoc. gen. counsel Life & Casualty Ins. Co. Tenn., Nashville, 1960-69; dist. atty. U.S. Dept. Justice, Nashville, 1969-77; pvt. practice Nashville, 1977-79, 87—; asst. adj. gen. State of Tenn., Nashville, 1979-87. Mem. U.S. Atty. Gen. Adv. Com., Washington, 1973-77; del. Tenn. Constl. Conv., Nashville, 1965-66; chmn. Met. Bd. Equalization, 1998—; dir. Nashville Pub. TV Coun., 1994-99; chmn. Met. Bd. of Equalization, 1998—. Brig. gen. USAR, ret., 1987. Mem. ABA, Tenn. Bar Assn., Nashville Bar Assn., Fed. Bar Assn. (pres. Nashville chpt. 1972), Am. Arbitration Assn. (arbitrator), Assn. Life Ins. Counsel, Nat. Fedn. Ind. Bus., Cumberland Club (pres. 1981-82), The Federalist Soc. Presbyterian. Home: 221 Diane Dr Madison TN 37115-2565 Office: BNA Corp Ctr Bldg 200 404 BNA Dr Ste 304 Nashville TN 37217

ANDERSON, CHARLES LEE ROYAL, retired academic administrator; b. Balt., Jan. 7, 1929; s. Charles Rose and Mabel Folsom (Hobbs) A.; m. Jessie Ann Rincicotti, July 16, 1955 (div. Feb. 1994); children: John Hobbs, Heather Anne. BA in English, Princeton U., 1951; MS in Pub. Adminstrn., George Washington U., 1964. Ship capt., planning and pers. mgmt. specialist U.S. Navy, Norfolk, Va., 1951-73; police procedures analyst Norfolk Police Dept., 1973-76; sr. cons. Westinghouse Justice Inst., Arlington, Va., 1976-77; indsl., comml., instnl. energy conservation program mgr. N.H. Gov.'s Coun. on Energy, Concord, 1977-79; dir. N.H. Correctional Industries, Concord, 1980-86; staff asst. to assoc. v.p. acad. affairs Fitchburg (Mass.) State Coll., 1986-97; faculty U.S. Armed Forces Staff Coll., Norfolk, Va., 1967-68; sr. adj. prof. Golden Gate U., 1974-88; adj. faculty Rivier Coll., Nashua, N.H., 1979-80. Served to cmdr. U.S. Navy, 1951-73, ret. 1997. Mem. Ret. Officers Assn. (past pres. N.H. chpt.), Am. Soc. Pub. Adminstrn. (past sec. sect. on criminal justice adminstrn.), Mass. Arms Collectors (past pres., dir.), Souhegan Comty. Nursing Assn. (past pres.), Ctrl. Mass. Mfg. Partnership (bd. dirs.), The Army and Navy Club (Washington). Republican. Episcopal. Avocations: U.S. military edged weapons, U.S. history, early American antiques.

ANDERSON, CHARLES S., college president, clergyman; b. Madison, Wis., Mar. 4, 1930; s. Sam C. and Guro (Lundeen) A.; m. Catherine Mary Gregerson, Dec. 23, 1951; children—Eric, Kristin. BA, St. Olaf Coll., 1951; MA, U. Wis.-Madison, 1954; BD, Luther Sem., St. Paul, 1957; PhD, Union Sem., N.Y.C., 1962. Ordained to ministry Lutheran Ch., 1957. Pastor various parishes N.Y.C., Wis., 1955-61; prof. Luther Sem., St. Paul, 1961-76; acad. dean Augsburg Coll., Mpls., 1976-80, pres., 1980-98, ret., 1998. Author: Faith and Freedom, 1967; Reformation Then and Now, 1968; Augsburg Historical Atlas, 1977. Chmn. Minn. Pvt. Coll. Coun., Minn. Pvt. Coll. Fund; trustee Interstate Cmty. Found., Phoenix. Capt. USMC, 1951-54. Fellow Rockefeller Found., 1959-61, Bush Found., 1973. Mem. Ch. History Soc., Ebenezer Soc. (bd. dirs.), Soc. for Reformation Rsch., Renaissance Soc., Am. Assn. Higher Edn., Phi Beta Kappa. Clubs: Minneapolis, Torsk. Lodge: Rotary. Avocations: reading, outdoor sports. Home: 1377 Grantham St Saint Paul MN 55108-1418*

ANDERSON, CHESTER GRANT, English educator; b. River Falls, Wis., Dec. 8, 1923; s. C.A. Chester and Inga Amelia (Grant) A.; m. Carole Nygard, Apr. 23, 1945; children: Stephen, Mark, Jonathan. Student, St. Olaf Coll., 1941-43; MA, U. Chgo., 1948; PhD, Columbia U., 1962. Asst. prof. English Creighton U., Omaha, 1948-50; asst. prof. Creighton U., 1954-57, Fordham U., N.Y.C., 1951-52; dir. State Soc. Services, AICPAs, 1952-54; assoc. prof. Western Conn. State U., 1957-63; asst. prof. Columbia U., 1963-68; prof. English U. Minn., Mpls., 1963-96, prof. emeritus, 1996—; Fulbright prof. Helsinki (Finland) U., 1963-64; Semester-at-Sea prof., 1987; W.B. Yeats Internat. Summer Sch. prof., Sligo, Ireland, 1987; vis. prof. Odense U., Denmark, 1977-78, Curtin U., Australia, 1989. Author: James Joyce and

His World, 1967, translation in Portugese and Italian, 1989, Spanish, 1990, Critical Edit. of James Joyce's A Portrait of the Artist, 1968, corrected 1992, Growing Up in Minnesota, 1976. Ensign AC, USNR, 1943-45. Mem. MLA, MLA Helsinki, Acad. Am. Poets, James Joyce Found. Home: 660 S Sand Lake Ct Mount Dora FL 32757 Office: U Minn Dept English Lind Hall 207 Church St SE Minneapolis MN 55455-0134

ANDERSON, CHRISTINE MARLENE, software engineer; b. Washington, D.C., Nov. 19, 1947; 2 children. BS in Math., U. Md., 1969. Mathematician Naval Oceanographic Office, Suitland, Md., 1969-71; sr. analyst, fgn. tech. divsn. Planning Rsch. Corp., Ohio, 1971-72; computer scientist USAF Avionics Lab., Wright-Patterson Air Force Base, Dayton, Ohio, 1971-74; sr. analyst USAF C3 Ctr., Cheyenne Mountain, Colorado Springs, Colo., 1974-76; chief computer tech. section USAF Wright Lab./ Armament Directorate, Eglin Air Force Base, Fla., 1982-92; ADA 9X project mgr. Office Sec. Defense, 1987-94; chief software tech. br. Phillips Lab., Kirtland Air Force Base, N.Mex., 1992-93, chief, space soperations and simulation divsn.oftware rsch. ctr., 1993-96, dir. space and missiles tech. directorate, 1996, mem. sr. exec. svcs., dir. space vehicles directorate, 1996—; co-chmn. on Ada computer programming lang. Am. Nat. Standards Inst., 1989—; editor Ada standard Internat. Standards Orgn., 1991—. Co-author: Aerospace Software Engineering, 1991; contbr. articles to profl. jours. Recipient Engr. of the Year USAF Armament Lab., 1989, Software Engring. award Am. Inst. Aeronautics, 1991, Program Mgr. of the Year award USAF Armament Lab., 1992, Sec. of Defense medal for Meritorious Civilian Svc., 1996. Fellow AIAA (chair software systems tech. com. 1987-89, bd. dirs. 1989—, Aerospace Software Engring. award 1991). Office: Air Force Rsch Lab AFRL/VS Kirtland AFB NM 87117*

ANDERSON, CHRISTOPHER JAMES, lawyer; b. Chgo., Nov. 26, 1950; s. James M. and Margaret E. (Anderson) A.; m. Lyn R. Buckley, Jan. 3, 1976; children: Vaughn Buckley, Weston Buckley. BA, Grinnell Coll., 1972; JD with highest distinction, U. Iowa, 1975. Bar: Mo. 1975. From assoc. to ptnr. Armstrong Teasdale LLP, Kansas City, Mo., 1975—. Mem. ABA, Mo. Bar Assn., Kans. City Bar Assn., Lawyers Assn. Kansas City, Estate Planning Soc. Office: Armstrong Teasdale Et Al 2345 Grand Blvd Ste 2000 Kansas City MO 64108-2617

ANDERSON, CLAUDIA W., oncology nurse; b. Hamilton, Ohio, Mar. 13, 1952; d. Gilbert Faye and Donna Jane Wolfe; m. Patrick Anderson, Sept. 1, 1991; children: William Marc Bowers, Matthew David Bowers. BSN, Ohio State U., 1974. Cert. hospice/palliative care nurse. Office nurse Family Practice, Richmond; asst. head nurse Reid Hosp., Richmond, Ind.; oncology nurse Reid Hosp., Richmond, hospice home care coord., head nurse oncology/acute med.; Mem. AIDS Task Force, Richmond; bd. mem. Mending Hearts, Richmond. Active Something Good Triple Essemble, Eaton, Ohio, First Presbyn. Ch., Eaton. Home: 6962 US 40 W New Paris OH 45347 Office: Reid Hosp 1401 Chester Blvd Richmond IN 47374

ANDERSON, CLIFFTON, science educator; b. French Camp, Calif., Sept. 5, 1961; s. Horace and Mamie Anderson; m. Melody R.M. Creer. BS in Biology, Pacific Union Coll., Angwin, Calif., 1991. Sci. tchr. Bakersfield (Calif) Adventist Acad., 1991—; asst. prin. Bakersfield Adventist Acad. Facilitator Boys to Men, Bakersfield, 1992—. With U.S. Army, 1979-82. Avocations: piano, gardening, construction. Home: 813 Greenwood Dr Bakersfield CA 93306-5927 Office: Bakersfield Adventist Acad 3333 Bernard St Bakersfield CA 93306-3005

ANDERSON, CLIFTON EINAR, writer, communications consultant; b. Frederic, Wis., Dec. 17, 1923; s. Andrew John and Ida Louise (Johnson) A.; m. Phyllis Mary Nolan, Oct. 5, 1943; children: Kristine, Craig. BS, U. Wis., 1947; MA, U. Calif., Berkeley, 1954. News editor Chgo. Daily Drover's Jour., 1943-45; asst. editor The Progressive, Madison, Wis., 1946-47; dir. publs. Am. Press, Beirut, 1948-53; mgr. rural programs Houston C. of C., 1957-62; faculty Tex. A&M U., College Station, 1962-65; rsch. fellow U. Tex., Austin, 1965-68; faculty Southwestern Okla. U., Weatherford, 1968-72; extension editor U. Idaho, Moscow, 1972-97, prof. emeritus, 1997—; speaker John Macmurray Centennial Conf. Marquette U., 1991; speaker Nat. Conf. on Peacemaking and Conflict Resolution, 1993, moderator the UN at 50 seminar, 1995; moderator Korea Today and Tomorrow Symposium Wash. State U., 1995. Editor: The Horse Interlude, 1976; author: History of the College of Agriculture at the University of Idaho, 1998, (with others) Ways Out: The Book of Changes for Peace, 1988, The Future: Opportunity Not Destiny, 1989, The Years Ahead: Perils, Problems and Promises, 1993, Eating Agendas: Food and Nutrition as Social Problems, 1995, Futurevision: Ideas, Insights, and Strategies, 1996; contbr. articles to profl. jours. and mags. Treas. Moscow Sister City Assn., 1986—; founding mem. Coalition for C.Am., Moscow, 1986; chmn. U. Idaho Affirmative Action Com., 1990; mem. coun. on home and cmty. care Area Agy. on Aging, 1995; writer campaign staff Senator R.M. La Follette, Jr., Madison, Wis., 1946; on senatorial campaign staff of Hubert H. Humphrey, Mpls., 1948; chmn. Borah Found. for Outlawry of War, U. Idaho, 1986-87, chmn. Borah Symposium, 1986-87. Recipient Rsch. award Fund for Adult Edn., 1954-55, U.S. Office Edn., 1965-68, 1st prize in newswriting competition Assn. Am. Agrl. Coll. Editors, 1976, merit award Agrl. Rels. Coun., 1995, Nat. Svc. award Washington Times Found., 1996. Fellow Martin Inst. Peace Studies and Conflict Resolution; mem. World Future Soc. (speaker 6th gen. assembly 1989, 7th gen. assembly 1993), Agr., Food and Social Values Soc., Assn. for Humanistic Psychology, Assn. for Religion and Intellectual Life, Profs. World Peace Acad., Internat. Forum on Globalization, World Constn. and Parliament Assn. Democrat. Avocations: gardening, photography, writing poetry. Home: 234 N Washington St Moscow ID 83843-2757 Office: U Idaho Agrl Communications Ctr Moscow ID 83844-2332

ANDERSON, CLYDE BAILEY, musician, educator; b. Mpls., Dec. 23, 1934; s. Arthur William and Florence Pearl (Bailey) A.; m. Judith Dawn Johansen, Sept. 17, 1977. BS, U. Minn., 1957, MA, 1967, profl. cert. in tng. and devel., 1984. Cert. tchr., Minn. Tchr. music Hopkins (Minn.) Pub. Schs., 1967-85, Mpls. Pub. Schs., 1989-96; profl. musician Mpls., 1953—; cons. Minn. Dept. Transp., 1988. Bd. dirs. Local Home Owners' Assn., Maple Grove, Minn., 1979-85. With U.S. Army, 1958-59. Mem. Music Educators Nat. Conf., Minn. Music Educators Assn., Am. String Tchrs. Assn., Am. Fedn. Musicians, Am. Fedn. Tchrs., Twin Cities Musicians Union (ofcl. 1978-85, 87—), Am. Legion, Evergreen Club, Phi Mu Alpha Sinfonia. Democrat. Avocations: fishing, collecting, sailing, cooking. Home: 343 W Eagle Lake Dr Maple Grove MN 55369-5552 Office: Twin Cities Musicians Union 1399 Eustis St Ste 202 Saint Paul MN 55108-1546

ANDERSON, DALE ARDEN, aerospace engineer, educator; b. Alta, Iowa, Aug. 11, 1936; s. Everett and Inez Birdene (Burwell) A.; m. Marleen Marie Ankerson, June 15, 1958; children: Gregory Dale, Lisa Dawn. B.A. in Aerospace Engring., St. Louis U., 1957; M.S., Iowa State U., 1959, Ph.D., 1964. Registered profl. engr., Iowa. Flight test engr. Douglas Aircraft, Santa Monica, Calif., 1958-60; aerodynamicist Boeing Co., Wichita, Kans., 1959-60; mem. tech. staff Aerospace Corp., San Bernardino, Calif., 1964-65; prof. aerospace engring. Iowa State U., Ames, 1965-84, dir. Computational Fluid Dynamics Inst., 1980-84; prof. aerospace engring., dir. Computational Fluid Dynamics Ctr. U. Tex.-Arlington, 1984-96; pres. MDA Engring. Inc., Arlington, Tex., 1987-96; assoc. dean Coll. of Engring. U. Tex., Arlington, 1996-97, v.p., dean grad. studies, 1997—; cons. Gen. Dynamics, Fort Worth, 1984-96, Union Carbide, Chgo., Hartford, Conn., Centerville, Iowa, 1977-89, Lockheed Rsch. Lab., Palo Alto, Calif., 1984, Rockwell Internat., Thousand Oaks, Calif., 1982-91, Brit. Petroleum, Houston, 1988-94, Lockheed-Martin, Fort Worth, 1996—. Author: Computational Fluid Mechanics and Heat Transfer, 1984; contbr. articles to profl. jours. Grantee NASA, Dept. Def., various indsl. firms, 1964—. Fellow AIAA (assoc.); mem. Sigma Xi. Presbyterian. Office: U Tex Aerospace Engring Dept Box 19018 Arlington TX 76019

ANDERSON, DALE C., state agency professional, travel consultant; b. Grinnell, Iowa, Sept. 13, 1953; s. Clifford Simon and Wilma Grace (Grunhaupt) A. AAS in Indsl. Mktg., Des Moines Area C.C., Ankeny, Iowa, 1973; BA in Comm. and Theatre, Cen. Coll., 1978. Asst. buyer Ardan Wholesaler, Des Moines, 1979; office mgr. Moingona Girl Scout Coun., Des Moines, 1979-82, dir. adminstrv. svcs., 1982-88, property/purchasing dir., 1988-96; travel cons. Al Travel, Des Moines, 1989-90, First Tours, Des Moines, 1990-95; clk. typist Iowa State Dept. Transp., Des Moines, 1996-97; acctg. clk. II Iowa Dept. Revenue and Fin., Des Moines, 1997-98; acct./ auditor 1 Iowa Dept. Corrections, Des Moines, 1998—; camp visitor for camp accreditation State of Iowa, 1990—. Campaign co-chmn. Kellogg (Iowa) Community Chest, 1983-85, pub. rels. chmn., 1982; leader local club Jasper County 4-H, Kellogg, 1971-76, state leadership conf. del., 1971, nat. citizenship del., Washington, 1971, instr. county officers tng. sch. Jasper County, 1970-71, Jasper County v.p., 1970, state conv. del., Ames, Iowa, 1970, state counselor Des Moines Area 4-H, Madrid, Iowa, 1970; local club pres. Kellogg Club 4-H, 1970-71. Recipient State Leadership award Jasper County 4-H, 1970, named Outstanding 4-H'er of Yr., 1971; named Kellogg's Outstanding Citizen, 1983. Mem. Am. Camping Assn. (stds. chair for camp accreditation Iowa chpt. 1992-95, state of Iowa sec. 1996), Am. Camping Assn. (mem. stds. camp accreditation com. Iowa chpt. 1996—), Iowa State Grange (lectr. 1983-85, 91-93, state youth com. 1981-82, Iowa state youth rep. 1976), Richland Grange (state del. 1980, 83, sec. 1980-84, steward 1970-73, 77-79, overseer 1973-77, youth chmn. 1973, 75-76). United Methodist. Avocations: collecting horse figures, ping pong, gardening, community service work, travel. Office: 686 Highway 224 S Kellogg IA 50135-8579

ANDERSON, DAMON ERNEST, lawyer; b. Minot, N.D., June 20, 1946; s. Melvin Ernest and Maxine I. (Spaulding) A.; m. Julie Kay Severson, Oct. 23, 1982; children: Joshua Daniel, Philip Kyle. BA, Dickinson State U., 1968; JD, U. N.D., 1974. Bar: N.D. 1974, Minn. 1981, U.S. Dist. Ct. N.D. 1974, U.S. Ct. Appeals (8th cir.) 1980, U.S. Supreme Ct. 1980. Pvt. practice Kessler and Anderson, Grand Forks, N.D., 1974-78, Grand Forks, N.D., 1978-98; asst. state's atty. Grand Forks County, N.D., 1978—. Past mem. divsnl. comdr. adv. coun. Salvation Army, Mpls., mem. Salvation Army local adv. bd., Grand Forks. Sgt. U.S. Army, 1968-70. Mem. Am. Legion, Masons. Lutheran. Office: 201 S 4th St Grand Forks ND 58201-4788

ANDERSON, DARRELL EDWARD, psychologist, educator; b. Coleridge, Nebr., May 2, 1932; s. Roy Blenton and Ruby Grace (Cisney) A.; m. Violeta Salazar, Sept. 3, 1951; children: Robert, James, Timothy. AB, York Coll., 1953; PhD, U. Nebr., 1958. Counselor, asst. prof. U. Nebr., Lincoln, 1957-59; asst. prof. psychology Wittenberg U., Springfield, Ohio, 1959-61; chief psychologist Weld County Mental Health Ctr., Greeley, Colo., 1961-62; asst. prof. U. No. Colo., Greeley, 1962-66, assoc. prof., 1966-70, prof., 1970-77, chmn. dept. psychology, 1972-77; prof. counselor edn. U. N.Mex., Albuquerque, 1977-87, chmn. dept., 1977-85, prof. counseling and family studies, 1987-92, prof. emeritus, 1992—; cons. psychologist Dulce (N.Mex.) Pub. Schs., 1984-85. Contbr. articles to profl. jours. Mem. APA, N.Mex. Psychol. Assn. Democrat. Methodist. Avocation: golf. Home: 4071 E Hinsdale Cir Littleton CO 80122-2277

ANDERSON, DARYL, actor; b. Seattle; s. Donald Anderson and Shirley Anderson Gallagher; m. Kathy Connell, July 28, 1984. B.F.A., U. Wash., Seattle, 1975. Actor: (TV series) Lou Grant, 1977-82, Hollywood Wives, 1985; actor (TV shows) The Phoenix, 1981, The People Across the Lake, 1988, Everybody's Baby: The Rescue of Jessica McClure, 1989, A Girl of the Limberlost, 1990, The Hit Man, 1991, Stranger in My Home, 1997; appearances in films include Butch and Sundance: The Early Days, 1979, The Monster Squad, 1987, Satan's Princess, 1990, The Break, 1995; TV appearances include T.J. Hooker, 1982, Whiz Kids, 1983, The A-Team, 1983, Melrose Place, 1992. Recipient Vet.'s Employment award Dept. Labor, 1979. Mem. SAG (nat. dir. 1980—, 9th nat. v.p. 1987-88, 3d nat. v.p. 1989-91, 95-97, trustee pension and health plans 1994—, Screen Actors Guild Awards (prodr. 1994—). Democrat. Office: care SAG 5757 Wilshire Blvd Los Angeles CA 90036-3635*

ANDERSON, DAVID, Canadian government official; b. Victoria, B.C., Can., 1937; m. Sandra Anderson; children: James, Zoe. Student, Victoria Coll.; student econs. and law, U. B.C.; student Inst. Oriental Studies, U. Hong Kong. With Dept. External Affairs; M.P. for Esquimalt Saanich Ho. of Commons, Ottawa, 1968-72; founder, former chmn. spl. com. on environment pollution Ho. of Commons, elected leader Liberal Party B.C., 1972, M.P. for Victoria, 1993—; min. of nat. revenue Ho. of Commons, Ottawa, Ont., 1993-96; mem. Legis. Assembly for Victoria, 1972; of counsel B.C. Wildlife Fedn., 1975-78; tchr. law Sch. Pub. Adminstrn. U. Victoria, 1978-84; mem. Immigration Appeal Bd., 1984-89; spl. advisor to premier on tanker traffic Govt. of B.C., 1989; commr. Commn. Inquiry into Fraser Valley Petroleum Exploration, 1990; min. nat. revenue Canada, 1993-96, min. of transport, 1996-97, min. of fisheries & oceans, 1997—; cons. Environment Can., 1975-78, 89-93. Mem. silver-medal rowing crews Rome Olympic and Chgo. Pan Am. Games. Named One of 125 Victorians Who Have Made a Difference, 1992. Mem. U. B.C. Alumni Assn. (75th Alumni of Distinction award 1990). Office: Fisheries & Oceans Can, 200 Kent St F 115, Ottawa, ON Canada K1A 0E6

ANDERSON, DAVID ALBERT, lawyer; b. Chgo., Aug. 14, 1941; s. Carl Roy and Mary Frances (Stoker) A.; m. Deborah Jo Kopp, Sept. 19, 1982; children: Jordan Christopher, Erik William, Wesley David. BS, Purdue U., 1963; JD, George Washington U., 1967. Bar: Ill. 1967, U.S. Supreme Ct. 1974, U.S. Ct. Appeals (fed. cir.) 1982. Trial atty. Brinks Hofer Gilson & Lione, Chgo., 1967—; adj. prof. law DePaul U., Chgo., 1972-86; dir. No. Ill. Flight Ctr., Lake-in-the-Hills, Ill., 1982-94. Editor-in-Chief: CBA Record (periodical), 1990-91. Mem. ABA, Am. Intellectual Property Law Assn., Intellectual Property Law Assn. Chgo., Licensing Execs. Soc., Christian Legal Soc., Law Club Chgo. Avocation: private pilot. Office: Brinks Hofer Gilson & Lione Ste 3600 455 N Cityfront Plaza Dr Chicago IL 60611-5599

ANDERSON, DAVID ARNOLD, law educator; b. 1939. AB, Harvard U., 1962; JD, U. Tex., 1971. Bar: Tex. 1972. Reporter, bur. chief United Press Internat., Austin, Tex., 1963-69; chief counsel Tex. Civil Jud. Coun., Austin, 1972; asst. prof. law U. Tex., Austin, 1972-75, prof., 1975-78, Thompson and Knight Centennial prof., 1987—; vis. Lee prof. William and Mary U., 1983, Queen Mary Coll. U. London, 1988, 92; vis. scholar Trinity Coll. Cambridge U., 1988. Fellow Gannett Ctr. Media Studies. Mem. Assn. Am. Law Schs. (mass communications law sect.), Order of Coif, Phi Delta Phi. Office: U Tex Sch Law 727 Dean Keeton St Austin TX 78705-3224

ANDERSON, DAVID BOWEN, lawyer; b. Seattle, Sept. 19, 1948; s. Gordon Browne and Elizabeth Josephine (Bowen) A.; m. Laura Ann Jorgensen, May 23, 1975; children: Elizabeth Christine, Christina Louise. BA with great distinction, Stanford U., 1970; JD, U. Mich., 1974; MBA, Western Wash. U., 1982. Bar: Wash. 1974, U.S. Dist. Ct. (we. dist.) Wash. 1974. Assoc. Bogle & Gates, Seattle, 1974-77; ptnr. Anderson , Connell & Murphy, Bellingham, Wash., 1977—; pres. San Juan Tug & Barge Co., 1979-85; arbitrator Whatcom County, Am. Arbitration Assn.; instr. Pacific N.W. Admiralty Law Inst., Seattle, 1983, Nat. Fishery Law Symposium, Seattle, 1984; lectr. constnl. law Western Wash. U., 1996; mediator U.S. Dist. Ct. (we. dist.) Wash. Mem. adv. com. Bellingham Sch. Bd., 1981-82, Bellingham Vocat. Tech. Inst., 1986; mem. Bellingham Pub. Sch. Found. Bd., 1992, pres., 1992-93. Mem. ATLA, ABA, Wash. State Bar Assn. (spl. dist. counsel, rules of profl. practice com.), Whatcom County Bar Assn. (pres. 1986), Maritime Law Assn. U.S. (proctor), Wash. Atheltic Club (Seattle), Bellingham Rotary Club (chmn. internat. svc. com.), Bellingham Golf and Country Club, Phi Beta Kappa. Presbyterian. Home: 500 16th St Bellingham WA 98225-6315 Office: Anderson & Connell 1501 Eldridge Ave Bellingham WA 98225-2801

ANDERSON, DAVID DANIEL, retired humanities educator, writer, editor; b. Lorain, Ohio, June 8, 1924; s. David and Nora Marie (Foster) A.; m. Patricia Ann Rittenhour, Feb. 1, 1953. B.S., Bowling Green State U., 1951, M.A., 1952; Ph.D., Mich. State U., 1960; D. Litt., Wittenberg U., 1986. From instr. to prof. dept. Am. thought and lang. to univ. disting. prof. Mich. State U., East Lansing, 1957-90; lectr. Am. Mus., Bath, Eng., 1980; editor U. Coll. Quar., 1971-80; Fulbright prof. U. Karachi, Pakistan, 1963-64; Am. del. to Internat. Fedn. Modern Langs. and Lit., 1969-93, Internat. Congress Orientalists, 1971-79, European Am. Studies Assn., 1994. Author: Sherwood Anderson, 1968 (Book Manuscript award 1961), Louis Bromfield, 1964, Critical Studies in American Literature, 1964, Sherwood Anderson's Winesburg, Ohio, 1967, Brand Whitlock, 1968, Abraham Lincoln, 1970, Suggestions for the Instructor, 1971, Robert Ingersoll, 1972, Woodrow Wilison, 1978, Ignatius Donnelly, 1980, William Jennings Bryan, 1981, Route two, Titus, Ohio, 1993, The Path in the Shadow, 1998; editor: The Black Experience, 1969, The Literary Works of Abraham Llincoln, 1970, Sunshine and Smoke: American Writers and the American Environment, 1971, (with others) The Dark and Tangled Path, 1971, Mid America, 1974, 2d edit., 1975, 3d edit., 1976, 4th edit., 1981, 9th edit., 1982, 10th edit., 1983, 11th edit., 1984, 12th edit., 1985, 13th edit., 1986, 14th edit., 1987, 15th edit., 1988, 16th edit., 1989, 17th edit., 1990, 18th edit., 1991, 19th edit., 1992, 20th edit., 1993, 21st edit., 1994, 22d edit., 1995, 23d edit., 1996, 24th edit., 1997, 25th edit., 1998, Sherwood Anderson: Dimensions of His Literary Art, 1976, Sherwood Anderson: The Writer at His Craft, 1979, Critical Essays on Sherwood Anderson, 1981, Michigan: A State Anthology, 1983, Myth, Memory and the American Earth: the Durability of Raintree County, 1998; editor Midwestern Miscellany, 1974—; also numerous articles, essays, short stories, poems. Served with USN, 1942-45; with AUS, 1952-53. Decorated Silver Star, Purple Heart; recipient Disting. Alumnus award Bowling Green State U., 1976, Disting. Faculty award Mich. State U., 1974, Disting. Faculty award Mich. Assn. Governing Bds., 1988, Disting Research award Mich. State U., 1988. Mem. ASA, AAUP, MLA, Popular Culture Assn., Soc. Study Midwestern Lit. (founder, exec. sec., Disting. Service award 1982), Assn. Gen. and Liberal Edn. Am. Assn. Advancement Humanities, Internat. Assn. U. Profs. English, Univ. Club. Home: 6555 Lansdown Dr Dimondale MI 48821-9428 Office: Mich State U Dept Am Thought and Lang East Lansing MI 48824

ANDERSON, DAVID E., zoological park administrator. Student, Pfeiffer Coll., 1964-65; BS in Zoology/Psychology, Duke U., 1972, postgrad., 1973. Colony supervisor Primate Ctr. Duke U., Durham, N.C., 1972-77, asst. dir. Primate Ctr., 1977-78; curator of mammals San Francisco Zool. Gardens, 1978-81, gen. curator, 1981-87, assoc. dir., gen. curator, 1987-90, dir., 1990—; tech. advisor Nature Conservancy La., 1987-90; animal tech. cons., mem. advisement com. La. State U.; mem. animal care com. Tulane U.; chmn. steering com. Madagascar Fauna Captive Propagation Group. Revs. editor Zoo Biology, 1982-88; contbr. articles to profl. publs. With USMC, 1965-69, Vietnam. Mem. Am. Assn. Zool. Parks and Aquariums (grad. mgmt. sch. 1982, ethics com., long range planning com., accreditation com., program chmn. Nat. Conf. 1981, others), Internat. Union Dirs. Zool. Gardens (captive breeding specialist group). Office: San Francisco Zool Gardens 1 Zoo Rd San Francisco CA 94132-1098

ANDERSON, DAVID GASKILL, JR., Spanish language educator; b. Tarboro, N.C., Feb. 21, 1945; s. David G. Sr. and Lucile (Gammon) A.; m. Jonetta Gentemann, Jan. 29, 1968; children: Allene Q., David III, James H., John G. AB, U. N.C., 1967; MA, Vanderbilt U., 1974, PhD, 1985. Instr. of langs. Union U., Tenn., 1975-76; from instr. Spanish to asst. prof. Ouachita Bapt. U., Ark., 1976-85; asst. prof. fgn. langs. N.E. La. U., 1985-87; asst. prof. Spanish, John Carroll U., Cleve., 1987-93, assoc. prof., 1993—, acting chmn. dept. classical and modern langs., 1996, chmn., 1997—, George Grauel faculty fellow rsch. sabbatical, spring 1997; tchg. fellow Vanderbilt U., 1983-84, NEH summer seminar on poetry, 1990; presenter in field. Author: On Elevating the Commonplace: A Structuralist Analysis of The Odas of Pablo Neruda, 1987; contbr. articles to profl. jours. vol. ESL Peace Corps, Colombia, 1968-70. Named Outstanding Young Men of Am., 1979. Mem. Am. Assn. U. Suprs. and Coords. Fgn. Lang. Programs, Am. Assn. Tchrs. Spanish and Portuguese, Modern Lang. Assn., Cleve. Diocesan Fgn. Lang. Assn. (bd. mem. 1988-93), Cleve. Assn., Phi Beta Kappa. Democrat. Home: 2573 Dysart Rd Cleveland OH 44118-4446 Office: John Carroll Univ Spanish Dept Cleveland OH 44118

ANDERSON, DAVID LAWRENCE, lawyer; b. Balt., Oct. 29, 1948; s. Robert L. and Ruth (Hahn) A. BS, Towson U., 1970; JD, U. Md., 1973. Bar: Md. 1973, U.S. Dist. Ct. Md. 1976, D.C. 1979, U.S. Dist. Ct. D.C. 1979, U.S. Ct. Appeals (D.C. cir.) 1976. Asst. revisor Gov.'s Commn. to Revise Md. Annotated Code, Annapolis, Md., 1973-74; counsel Gov.'s Task Force on Campaign Financing, Annapolis, Md., 1974-75; atty. Fed. Election Commn., Washington, 1975-77, Federal Energy Adminstrn., Washington, 1977; asst. chief counsel, trial atty. U.S. Dept. Energy, Washington, 1977-85; sr. trial atty., leader litigation team environ. enforcement sect., environment and natural resources div. U.S. Dept. Justice, Washington, 1986-90; lead counsel for Love Canal, Rocky Mountain Arsenal and New Bedford Harbor Superfund cases; sr. assoc. Shea & Gould, Washington, 1990-91, Arent Fox Kintner Plotkin & Kahn, Washington, 1992-93; ptnr. O'Connor & Hannan, Washington, 1993-95; mgr. regulatory and legis. svcs. group Waste Policy Inst., Arlington, 1995-99; mgr. regulatory, internat. and legis. svcs. Parsons Engring. Sci., Inc., Fairfax, Va., 1999—; adj. prof. polit. sci. Towson State U., 1971-73; adj. prof. legal rsch. and writing Am. U., 1985-87, 93-94. Recipient Outstanding Performance award Dept. Energy, 1981, medal and award Dept. Energy, 1983, spl. commendation Dept. Justice, 1989. Mem. ABA (natural resources sect., internat. sect.), D.C. Bar Assn., Nat. Def. Indsl. Assn., Soc. of Am. Mil. Engrs., Environ. Law Inst. (assoc.), Nature Conservancy. Email: davidúlúanderson@parsons.com. Home: 3440 S Utah St Arlington VA 22206-1921 Office: Parsons Engineering Science Inc 10521 Rosehaven St Fairfax VA 22030

ANDERSON, DAVID MARTIN, environmental health engineer; b. Boston, July 19, 1930; s. Martin Jens and Dorothy (Finnin) A.; grad. Boston Latin Sch., 1948; BS, Northeastern U., 1953; SM, Harvard U., 1955, PhD, 1958; m. Marjorie Gilbert, July 19, 1958; children: David, Michael, Anne, Stephen. Research fellow Harvard Sch. Pub. Health, 1953-58; pub. health engr. USPHS, Cin., 1958-60; indsl. health engr. Bethlehem Steel Corp. (Pa.), 1960-67; asst. mgr. environ. quality control, 1967-71, mgr., 1971-80, corp. dir. environ. affairs, 1980-84, dir. environ. and govtl. affairs, 1984-87, gen. mgr. environ. affairs, 1987-94, cons. environ. health, 1994—; vis. lectr. Pa. State U., 1966-71; vis. lectr. Harvard U., 1969-81; chmn. coun. tech. advisers Pa. Dept. Health, 1964-70, N.Y. Dept. Environ. Conservation, 1974-75; co-chmn. OSHA/Am. Iron and Steel Industry Task Force on coke oven emission standards, 1975-76; mem. Pa. Gov.'s Task Force on Occupational Health and Safety, 1975-76; mem. com. on biol. effects of atmospheric pollutants Nat. Acad. Scis., 1971-74; mem. nat. air quality criteria adv. com. EPA, 1971-76; mem. Sec. Health, Edn. and Welfare Coal Mine Health Research Adv. Council, 1972-76; mem. U.S. Dept. Commerce Adv. Com. on Indsl. Innovation, 1978-79, mem. adv. com., Ctr. for Risk Analysis Harvard U., 1989-94; mem. negotiated rulemaking com. U.S. EPA, 1992-93. Registered profl. engr., Pa. Diplomate Am. Acad. Environ. Engrs. Mem. Am. Iron and Steel Inst. (com. on environ. 1971-94, chmn. 1978-80, 87-89), Internat. Iron and Steel Inst. (com. on environ. 1980-94), Am. Chem. Soc., Am. Indsl. Hygiene Assn. (dir. 1968-71), Air and Waste Mgmt. Assn. (dir. 1971-74), Sigma Xi, Delta Omega. Contbr. articles to profl. jours. Research, patentee air cleaning tech. Home and Office: 1037 Westgate Cir Bethlehem PA 18017-3637

ANDERSON, DAVID POOLE, sportswriter; b. Troy, N.Y., May 6, 1929; s. Robert P. and Josephine (David) A.; m. Maureen Ann Young, Oct. 24, 1953; children: Stephen, Mark, Mary Jo, Jean Marie. BA, Holy Cross Coll., 1951. Sports writer Bklyn. Eagle, 1951-55, New York Jour.-Am., 1955-66, New York Times, 1966—. Author: Countdown to Super Bowl, 1969; (with Ray Robinson) Sugar Ray, 1970; (with Larry Csonka and Jim Kiick) Always On The Run, 1973; Pancho Gonzalez, 1974; (with Frank Robinson) Frank: The First Year, 1976, Sports Of Our Times, 1979; The Yankees, 1979; (with John Madden) Hey, Wait a Minute, I Wrote a Book, 1984, The Story of Football, 1985, One Knee Equals Two Feet, 1986, One Size Doesn't Fit All, 1988, The Story of Basketball, 1988, In The Corner, 1991, Pennant Races, 1994, The Story of the Olympics, 1996, All Madden, 1996, The Story of Golf, 1998; editor: The Red Smith Reader, 1981. Recipient Pulitzer prize for disting. commentary, 1981, Red Smith award, 1994; inducted into Nat. Sportscasters and Sportswriters Assn. Hall of Fame, 1990, N.Y. Sports Mus. and Hall of Fame, 1991. Office: NY Times 229 W 43rd St New York NY 10036-3959

ANDERSON, DAVID PREWITT, retired university dean; b. Twin Falls, Idaho, Sept. 14, 1934; m. Janice Gale Schmied, Dec. 21, 1962; children: Kathryn Lynn, Christopher Kyle. Student, U. Idaho, 1952-54; BS, Wash. State U., 1959, DVM, 1961; MS, U. Wis., 1964, PhD, 1965. NIH trainee U. Wis., 1961-62, asst. prof. vet. sci., asst. dir. biotron, 1965-69; prof. med. microbiology, dir. Poultry Disease Research Center, U. Ga., 1969-71, asso. dean research and grad. affairs Coll. Vet. Medicine, 1971-73, dean, 1975-96; retired, 1996; animal health com. NAS, 1977-80; animal health sci. rsch. adv. bd. USDA, 1978-85, nat. adv. com. on meat and poultry inspection, 1990-92;

adv. com. Ctr. for Vet. Medicine/FDA, 1984-88; tech. analysis group Food Safety Inspection Svc./USDA, 1994-95. Editor Avian Diseases, 1973-93. Mem. AVMA, Am. Coll. Vet. Microbiologists (diplomate), Am. Coll. Poultry Vets. (diplomate), Am. Assn. Avian Pathologists (pres. 1988-89), Nat. Acads. Practice. Home: 190 Harris St Winterville GA 30683-1549

ANDERSON, DAVID TREVOR, law educator; b. Winnipeg, Man., Can., Oct. 25, 1938; s. David and Mary (Irwin) A. BA, U. Man., 1959; BA in Jurisprudence, U. Oxford (Eng.), 1961, B in Civil Law, 1962. Asst. prof. law U. Alta., Edmonton, Can., 1962-66, assoc. prof., 1966-69, prof., 1969-71; prof. law U. Man., Winnipeg, 1971—, assoc. dean faculty of law, 1972-77, dean, 1984-89; bd. dirs. Alta. Inst. Law Rsch. and Reform, Edmonton, 1968-71; mem. Man. Law Reform Commn., Winnipeg, 1981-84, Man. Pub. Utilities Bd., 1988—. Named Queen's Counsel, Province of Man., 1985; Rhodes scholar, 1959. Mem. Law Soc. Man. (dir. edn. 1977-80, bencher 1984-89), Can. Bar Assn. Conservative. Presbyterian. Office: U Man Faculty of Law, Robson Hall, Winnipeg, MB Canada R3T 2N2

ANDERSON, DAVID TURPEAU, government official, judge; b. Cin., Aug. 9, 1942; s. Randall Hudson and Florida (Turpeau) A.; children: David Malcolm, Daniel Michel. B.S., U. Cin., 1963; J.D., George Washington U., 1972. Staff aide U.S. Congressman Robert Taft, Jr., Washington, 1967-69; asst. congl. relations U.S. HUD, Washington, 1970; asst. for legislation Am. Hosp. Assn., Washington, 1971-73; assoc. Stanley, Durham & Johnson, Phila., 1973-74; asst. city solicitor Office City Solicitor, Phila., 1974-81; chmn. Bd. Contract Appeals, HUD, Washington, 1981—. Mem. InterAm. Bar Assn., Nat. Bar Assn., Phila. Bar Assn., Sr. Execs. Assn., BCA Judges Assn. Club: Nat. Press. Home: PO Box 27552 Washington DC 20038-7552 Office: HUD Bd Contract Appeals 451 7th St SW Rm 2131 Washington DC 20410-0001

ANDERSON, DAVIN CHARLES, business representative, labor consultant; b. Mpls., July 26, 1955; s. Roland Lawrence Anderson and Merlyne (Aldrich) Bissell; m. Diane Elmshauser, Aug. 14, 1982; children: Kiersten Janel, Matilda Rae. Student, St. Cloud State U., Minn., 1973-76; BS, U. Minn., 1979. Technician Northwest Cinema, Mpls., 1976-78, Mann Cinemas, Mpls., 1978-81, Gen. Cinema Corp., Mpls., 1981—; account exec. Van Clemens & Co., Mpls., 1987—; sec. Assn. Entertainment Industries Unions, St. Paul, 1987—. Mem. AFL-CIO (del.), Internat Alliance Theatrical and Stage Employees (bus. rep. Local 219 1986—), Nat. Assn. Investors Clubs, Trades and Labor Council (del.), Cen. Labor Union Council (del.), Toastmasters. Lutheran. Avocations: fishing, boating, skiing, hiking, flying. Home: 9941 Olive St NW Minneapolis MN 55433-5126

ANDERSON, DEAN WILLIAM, educational administrator; b. Mpls., Aug. 28, 1946; s. Edward Marvin and Mabel (Gilland) A.; m. Elaine Heumann Gurian; children: Erik Wheeler, Matthew Edward. B.A., Macalester Coll., 1968; M.A., U. Calif.-Berkeley, 1970. Examiner Office Mgmt. and Budget, Washington, 1970-73; adminstrv. officer Smithsonian Instn., Washington, 1973-84, asst. sec. history and art, 1984-85, under sec., 1985-90; dep. dir. mgmt. and planning Woodrow Wilson Ctr., Washington, 1990-97, acting dir., 1997-99. Trustee Interlochen Ctr. for Arts. Recipient Robert Brooks award Smithsonian Instn., 1983; Minn. SPAN Assn. scholar, Israel, 1967; MacPherson Found. scholar, Mpls., 1967. Mem. Interlochen Alumni Orgn. (pres. 1994-98, nat. bd. dirs.), Phi Beta Kappa, Pi Sigma Alpha. Avocation: golf. Office: Woodrow Wilson Ctr 1300 Pennsylvania Ave NW Washington DC 20004-3002

ANDERSON, DENICE ANNA, editor; b. Detroit, Nov. 11, 1947; d. Carl Magnus and Geraldine Elizabeth (Willer) A. BA in Journalism, Mich. State U., 1970. Copy editor/reporter The State News, East Lansing, Mich., 1965-70; reporter/copy editor/photographer The Tecumseh (Mich.) Herald, 1966-68; copy editor/entertainment editor The State Jour., Lansing, Mich., 1970-76; freelance writer State Jour./Lansing Mag., 1977-79; freelance corr. Collier's Year Book, N.Y.C., 1977-79; copy editor, proofreader Booz, Allen & Hamilton, N.Y.C., 1980-81, Rogers & Wells, N.Y.C., 1981-83, Advanced Therapeutics Comm., N.Y.C., 1983-84; freelance editor, N.Y.C., Santa Fe, Clinton, Mich., 1984—. Contbr. articles to profl. jours. Bd. dirs., sec. March of Dimes, Lansing, 1972-76; vol./writer Polio Info. Ctr., N.Y.C., 1984-88; vol. Vol. Involvement Svcs., Santa Fe, N.M., 1989. Mem. Editorial Freelancers Assn. Lutheran. Home: 210 E Church St Rte 4 Clinton MI 49236

ANDERSON, DON LYNN, geophysicist, educator; b. Frederick, Md., Mar. 5, 1933; s. Richard Andrew and Minola (Phares) A.; m. Nancy Lois Ruth, Sept. 15, 1956; children: Lynn Ellen, Lee Weston. B.S., Rensselaer Poly. Inst., 1955; M.S., Calif. Inst. Tech., 1959, Ph.D., 1962. With Chevron Oil Co., Mont., Wyo., Calif., 1955-56; with Air Force Cambridge Research Center, Boston, 1956-58, Arctic Inst. N.Am., Boston, 1958; mem. faculty Calif. Inst. Tech., Pasadena, 1962—, assoc. prof. geophysics, 1964-68, prof., 1968—, dir. seismol. lab., 1967-89, Eleanor and John R. McMillan prof. of geophysics, 1990—; prin. investigator Viking Mars Seismic Expt.; mem. various coms. NASA; chmn. geophysics rsch. forum NAS, chmn. Arthur L. Day award com. NSF, Geosci. adv. com., 1994, adv. bd. for Sch. of Earth Scis., Stanford U., chmn. 1995); also mem. adv. com. Purdue U., U. Chgo., U. Tex., Stanford U., U. Calif. Berkeley, Carnegie Instn., Washington, U. Paris, Yale U., Rice U., chmn. 1996), Consortium for High Pressure Rsch. U. Calif.-Riverside, geosci. adv. com. NSF; co-founder Inc. Rsch. insts. for Seismology. Assoc. editor Jour. Geophys. Rsch., 1965-67, Tectonophysics, 1974-77; editor Physics of the Earth and Planetary Interiors, 1984-94. Recipient Exceptional Sci. Achievement award NASA, 1977; Sloan Found. fellow, 1965-67; Emil Wiechert Medal German Geophys. Soc., 1986, Craford prize Royal Swedish Acad. of Scis. 1998, Nat. medal of Sci., 1998; Guggenheim fellowship, 1998. Fellow AAAS, Am. Geophys. Union (James B. Macelwane award, 1966, pres. tectonophysics sect. 1971-72, chmn. Macelwane award com. 1975, mem. Bowie medal com. 1985, chair 1994, pres.-elect 1986-88, pres. 1988-90, Bowie medal 1990), Geol. Soc. Am. (assoc. editor bull. 1971—, Arthur L. Day medal 1987, mem. Penrose medal com. 1989, Arthur L. Day medal com. 1989-90, long range planning com. 1990—); mem. NAS (chmn. seismology com. 1975, chmn. Geophysics Research Forum 1984-86), Am. Philos. Soc., Royal Astron. Soc. (Gold medal 1988), Seismol. Soc. Am., Sigma Xi. Home: 669 Alameda St Altadena CA 91001-3001 Office: Calif Inst Tech Seismol Lab 252-21 Pasadena CA 91125

ANDERSON, DONALD BERNARD, oil company executive; b. Chgo., Apr. 6, 1919; s. Hugo August and Hilda (Nelson) A.; m. Patricia Gaylord, 1945 (dec. 1978); m. Sarah Midgette, 1980. BS in Mech. Engring, Purdue U., 1942. Vice pres. Hondo Oil & Gas Co. (formerly Malco Refineries, Inc.), Roswell, N.Mex.; vice pres. Hondo Oil & Gas Co. and subs. corps., Roswell, N.Mex., 1946-63; pres. Anderson Oil Co., Roswell, 1963—; pres. Cotter Corp., 1966-70, chmn. bd., 1966-74; founder, pres. Anderson Drilling Co., Denver, 1974—; pres., chmn. bd. Anderson Drilling Co., 1977—. Curator fine arts, mem. acquisitions com. Roswell Mus. and Art Center, 1949-56, trustee, 1956-85, pres. bd., 1960-85, 87—, trustee, pres. 1987-90; bd. dirs. Sch. Am. Rsch., Santa Fe, chmn. bd., 1985-88, bd. dirs. 1989—; bd. dirs. Jargon Soc., Penland, N.C.; regent Ea. N.Mex. U., 1966-72; commr. Smithsonian Instn., Nat. Mus. Am. Art, 1980-88. Lt. USNR, 1942-46. Office: PO Box 1 Roswell NM 88202-0001

ANDERSON, DONALD GORDON MARCUS, mathematics educator; b. Sarnia, Ont., Can., Jan. 4, 1937; s. Gordon Lincoln and Jean Merritt (McNaughton) A. B.S., U. Western Ont., 1959; A.M., Harvard, 1960, Ph.D., 1963. Lectr., research fellow Harvard, 1963-65, asst. prof. applied math., 1965-69, Gordon McKay prof. applied math., 1969—. Mem. AAAS, Soc. for Indsl. and Applied Math. Office: Maxwell Dworkin Lab 33 Oxford St Cambridge MA 02138-1903

ANDERSON, DONALD KEITH, chemical engineering educator; b. Iron Mountain, Mich., July 15, 1931; s. Milton Eugene and Edna Olive (Van Court) A.; m. Gina Dale Garrett, July 12, 1957; children: Shannon Elizabeth, Amanda Juliette. BSChemE, U. Ill., 1956; MSChemE, U. Wash., 1958, PhD in Chem. Engring., 1960. Registered profl. engr., Mich. Asst. prof. Mich. State U., East Lansing, 1960-64, assoc. prof., 1964-69, prof., 1969-77, prof., chairperson, 1977-95, Johansen-Crosby prof., 1996-98, prof. emeritus, 1998—; mem. Hazardous Waste Facility Siting Bd., State of Mich., Lansing, 1980—; bd. dirs. Accreditation Bd. for Engring. and Tech., Balt., 1992—. Mem. AIChE (edn. and accreditation com. 1960-95), Am. Chem. Soc., Am. Soc. for Engring. Edn. (chair chem. engring. divsn. 1971-72). Avocation: furniture making. Home: 1326 Ironwood Dr Williamston MI 48895-9186 Office: Mich State Univ Dept Chem Engring 1261 Engring Bldg East Lansing MI 48824

ANDERSON, DONALD KENNEDY, JR., English educator; b. Evanston, Ill., Mar. 18, 1922; s. Donald Kennedy and Kathryn Marie (Shields) A.; m. Kathleen Elizabeth Hughes, Sept. 11, 1949; children: David J., Lawrence W. A.B., Yale U., 1943; M.A., Northwestern U., 1947; Ph.D., Duke U., 1957. Instr. Geneva Coll., Beaver Falls, Pa., 1947-49; from instr. to asst. prof. Rose Poly. Inst., Terre Haute, Ind., 1952-58; asst. prof., assoc. prof. Butler U., Indpls., 1958-65; assoc. prof. U. Mo., Columbia, 1965-67, prof. dept. English, 1967-92; prof. emeritus U. Mo., Columbia, 1992—; assoc. dean Grad. Sch. U. Mo., Columbia, 1970-74. Author: John Ford, 1972; editor: John Ford's Perkin Warbeck, 1965, John Ford's The Broken Heart, 1968, Concord in Discord, The Plays of John Ford, 1586-1986, 1987. Served to lt. (j.g.) USNR, 1943-46. Folger fellow, 1965; U. Mo. Summer Research fellow, 1966, 68, 76, 79, 84. Mem. MLA (midwest regional del. 1972-75), AAUP (sec.-treas. 1962-63). Democrat. Methodist. Home: 1309 Ridge Rd Columbia MO 65203-2323 Office: U Mo Dept English Columbia MO 65211

ANDERSON, DONALD LLOYD, weapon systems consultant; b. Stoughton, Wis., Sept. 19, 1921; s. Carl Gustave and Bessie (Cook) A.; m. Augusta Neidermeier, Sept. 10, 1948; children: Anita Briggs, Cathrine Krakower, Christine Robertson. Student, U. Niagara, Niagara Falls, N.Y., 1960, U. Md., Sembach, Germany, 1963-64, City Coll., Riverside, Calif. Commd. USAF, 1940, advanced through grades to chief master sgt., 1963, supply supt., 1940-71; weapon systems specialist Dynalectron Corp., Norco, Calif., 1971-88, VSE Corona (Calif.), Inc., 1988-89; weapon systems specialist Dyncorp, Norco, Calif., 1989-92, cons., 1992—; tutor Myra Linn Sch., Riverside, Calif., 1991—. Author: (tng. manual) Standard Missile Data Processing Manual, 1989, 92. Vol. info. specialist Parkview Hosp., Riverside, 1992-96; staff mem., vol. NCO Acad., March AFB, Calif., 1991-94; vol. Citizens Patrol, Riverside Police Dept. Decorated Bronze Star medal, Meritorious Svc. medal, USAF Commendation medal, Vietnam Gallantry Cross with gold palm. Mem. DAV, VFW, NCOAC (life), Bombard Soc., Phoenix Club.

ANDERSON, DONALD MEREDITH, bank executive; b. Milan, Minn., Feb. 19, 1928; s. Meredith A. and Lydia (Helseth) A.; m. Christine Skorupa; 1 child, Karen. Student, St. Olaf Coll., Northfield, Minn., 1946-48; B.A., U. Minn., 1948-50; M.B.A., Harvard U., 1952; postgrad. Grad. Banking Sch., U. Wis.-Madison, 1965-67. Factory rep. Congoleum-Nairn, Inc., 1953-56; stockbroker J.M. Dain & Co., Mpls., 1956-58; v.p. comml. lending and corr. banking Northwestern Nat. Bank of Mpls., 1958-69; v.p. lending Santa Barbara Nat. Bank, Calif., 1969-71; pres. Santa Barbara Bank & Trust, 1971-89, chmn., 1989—; dir. Gen. Telephone Calif., 1976—, mem. audit com., 1982—; mem. regional adv. com. Comptroller of Currency, 1975-76. Bd. dirs. Blue Cross So. Calif., 1981—; bd. dirs. Mission council Boy Scouts Am., 1977—, v.p. 1977-80, pres. 1985; bd. dirs. Goleta Valley Hosp., 1978—, pres., 1979-80; mem. Industry Edn. Council, 1975—, chmn., 1984—; trustee U. Calif.-Santa Barbara, 1984—; mem. comdr.'s adv. bd. Vandenberg AFB, 1978—; mem. adv. bd. Vis. Nurses Assn., 1983—; past pres. bd. dirs. Trinity Lutheran Ch., United Way; bd. dirs. Santa Barbara Zoo, 1985—. Served to 1st lt. USAF, 1952-53. Mem. Calif. Bankers Assn. (dir. 1982—, chair comml. lending com. 1977), Santa Barbara C. of C. (v.p. 1979, dir. 1972, 78—, Western Ind. Bankers Assn. (pres. 1985, sec. 1983, dir. 1981—), Am. Bankers Assn. (bank investments com. 1976-79). Republican. Home: 485 Via Hierba Santa Barbara CA 93110-2214 Office: Santa Barbara Bank & Trust 1021 Anacapa St Santa Barbara CA 93101-2102

ANDERSON, DONALD MORGAN, entomologist; b. Washington, Dec. 27, 1930; s. John Kenneth and Alice Cornelia (Morgan) A. B.A., Miami U., Oxford, Ohio, 1953; Ph.D., Cornell U.l, 1958. Grad. teaching asst. Cornell U., 1954-57; asst. prof. sci. SUNY-Buffalo, 1959-60, rsch. fellow, 1960; rsch. entomologist Dept. Agrl., Washington, 1960-90, rsch. collaborator, 1990—; rsch. assoc. Buffalo Mus. Sci., 1972—, Smithsonian Instn., 1978—. Contbr. articles to profl. jours., chpts to books. Sigma Xi grantee, 1959. Mem. Entomol. Soc. Washington (corr. sec. 1963-65, pres. 1985), Entomol. Soc. Am., Coleopterists Soc., Am. Inst. Biol. Sci., St. Andrews Soc. Washington, Clan Anderson Soc. (editor 1979-84, treas. 1985-90, pres. 1990-92), Sigma Xi, Phi Kappa Phi. Home: 1900 Lyttonsville Rd Apt 804 Silver Spring MD 20910-2270 Office: Nat Mus Natural History Dept Agr Systematic Entomology Lab Washington DC 20560

ANDERSON, DONNA ELAINE, elementary and secondary school educator; b. Lone Wolf, Okla., Mar. 26, 1935; d. William Herbert and Lois Alta (Montgomery) Tolleson; m. Frank D. Anderson, Sept. 3, 1955; 1 child, Valerie Elaine. BA cum laude, U. North Tex., 1957, MEd, 1960. Cert. edn. diagnostician, elem. tchr., bus. tchr.; registered profl. ednl. diagnostician. Tchr. White Deer (Tex.) Ind. Sch. Dist., 1957-62; tchr. Pampa (Tex.) Ind. Sch. Dist., 1962-70, ednl. diagnostician, 1973—. Missionette dir. First Assembly God Ch., Pampa, 1973—; mem. Pampa Fine Arts Assn., 1978—, Community Concert Assn., Pampa, 1965—. Mem. NEA (life), Tex. Ednl. Diagnosticians Assn., Tex. State Tchrs. Assn. (life), Ednl. Diagnosticians Golden Spread, Coun. Exceptional Children, Knife and Fork Club, Delta Kappa Gamma. Democrat. Mem. Assemby of God Ch. Avocations: photography, piano. Office: Pampa HS 111 E Harvester Ave Pampa TX 79065-4401

ANDERSON, DONNA KAY, musicologist, educator; b. Underwood, N.D., Feb. 16, 1935; d. Freedolph E. and Olga (Mayer) A. Ph.D., Ind. U., 1966. Instr. piano MacPhail Sch. Music, 1956-59, Summit Sch., 1959-61; asst. prof. music history SUNY, Cortland, 1967-70, assoc. prof., 1970-78, prof., 1978—, chmn. dept. music, 1985-92, 95-97, faculty rsch. fellow, 1967-69, prof. emerita, 1997—. Author: Charles T. Griffes: Annotated Bibliography, Discography, 1977, The Works of Charles T. Griffes: A Descriptive Catalogue, 1983, Charles T. Griffes: A Life in Music, 1993; editor: Three Preludes for Piano, 1967, Four Impressions, 1970, Legend for Piano, 1972, De Profundis, 1978, Song of the Dagger, 1983, Seven English Songs, 1986, Rhapsody, 1992, The Pleasure Dome of Kubla Khan, 1993, The War-Song of the Vikings, 1995, Hampelas, 1995, Kinanti, 1995, Djakoan, 1995, Pieces for Children, 1995; editor, translator: Four German Songs, 1970, Nachtlied, 1983, Six German Songs, 1986, Three German Songs, 1995, A Winter Landscape, 1996. Recipient N.Y. State/United U. Professions Excellence award, 1991; summer grantee, 1972. Mem. Am. Musicol. Soc., Coll. Music Soc., Sonneck Soc., Music Library Assn., Tri-M, Mu Phi Epsilon, Pi Kappa Lambda, Alpha Psi Omega, Phi Kappa Phi. Office: SUNY 262 Music Cortland NY 13045

ANDERSON, DOUGLAS E., neurosurgeon; b. Ft. Monmouth, N.J., Sept. 2, 1952; m. Ann Leuking; children: Joseph, Ellie, David, Kjersten. MD, Chgo. Med. Sch., 1977. Diplomate Am. Bd. Neurosurgery. Neurosurgeon Loyola U. Med. Ctr., Maywood, Ill., 1983—; chief neurosurgery Hines (Ill.) VA Hosp., 1989—. Baritone Music of the Baroque, Chgo.; bd. elem. edn. Grace Luth. Ch. Sch., River Forest, Ill. Avocations: singing, boating, skiing. Office: Loyola U Med Ctr 2160 S 1st Ave Maywood IL 60513

ANDERSON, DOUGLAS RICHARD, ophthalmologist, educator, scientist, researcher; b. Memphis, Apr. 7, 1938; s. William Arnold Douglas and Hariott Isabel (Gates) A.; m. Wirtley Anne Raine, Nov. 28, 1964; children: John Douglas, Wendy Anne, Michael Allen Scott. AB magna cum laude, U. Miami, Coral Gables, Fla., 1958; MD, Washington U., St. Louis, 1962. Diplomate Am. Bd. Ophthalmology (bd. dirs. 1988-95). Rotating intern U. Hosp. Cleve., 1962-63; staff assoc. Nat. Cancer Inst., Bethesda, Md., 1963-65; resident in ophthalmology U. Calif. Med. Ctr., San Francisco, 1965-68; rsch. fellow Howe lab. Mass. Eye and Ear Infirmary, Boston, 1968-69; asst. prof. U. Miami (Fla.) Sch. Medicine, 1969-75, assoc. prof., 1975-82, prof., 1982—; mem. nat. eye adv. coun. NIH, Bethesda, 1982-86, visual sci. study sect. A, 1972-76, chmn., 1975-76; bd. govs. Anne Bates Leach Eye Hosp., Miami, 1987-93, 98—, outpatient med. dir., 1993-95. Author: Testing the Field of Vision, 1982, Perimetry With and Without Automation, 1987, Automated Static Perimetry, 1992, 2d edit., 1999; contbr. over 200 sci. articles and book chpts.; co-editor: Discussions on Glaucoma, 1977, Automatic Perimetry in Glaucoma, 1985, Encounters in Glaucoma Research I: Receptors, 1994, Optic Nerve in Glaucoma, 1995, How to Ascertain Progression and Outcome, 1996; assoc. editor Am. Jour. Ophthalmology, Chgo., 1973-90. Mem., active med. staff Anne Bates Leach Eye Hosp., v.p., 1983-84, pres., 1984-86. Surgeon USPHS, 1963-65. Recipient William and Mary Greve Internat. Scholars award Rsch. to Prevent Blindness, Inc., 1978, Sr. Sci. Investigator award, 1986, 93, Recognition award Alcon Rsch. Inst., Ft. Worth, 1986; rsch. grantee Nat. Eye Inst., 1969-91, 93-97, Am. Health Assistance Found., 1978-95, Glaucoma Rsch. Found., 1993-94. Fellow Am. Acad. Ophthalmology (councillor 1984-86, Gold medal 1972, Honor awards 1978, 83, Sr. Honor award 1992); mem. Am. Glaucoma Soc. (v.p. 1988-90, pres. 1990-92), Assn. for Rsch. in Vision and Ophthalmology (trustee 1983-88, pres. 1987, Mildred Weisenfeld award 1997), Am. Ophthal. Soc., Internat. Perimetric Soc. Fax: (305) 326-6306. Home: 11880 SW 63rd Ave Miami FL 33156-4802 Office: Bascom Palmer Eye Inst PO Box 016880 900 NW 17th St Miami FL 33101-6880

ANDERSON, DUWAYNE MARLO, earth and polar scientist, university administrator; b. Lehi, Utah, Sept. 9, 1927; s. Duwayne LeRoy and Fern Francell (Fagan) A.; m. June B. Hodgin, Apr. 2, 1980; children: Lynna Nadine, Christopher Kent, Lesleigh Leigh, Valerie Lynn, Susan Leslie, Nancy Lee. B.S., Brigham Young U., 1954; Ph.D. (Purdue Research Found. fellow), Purdue U., 1958. Prof. soil physics U. Ariz., Tucson, 1958-63; rsch. scientist, chief earth scis. br. (Cold Regions Research and Engring. Lab.), Hanover, N.H., 1963-76; chief scientist divsn. polar programs NSF, Washington, 1976-78; mem. Viking sci. team NASA, 1969-76; dean faculty natural scis. and math. SUNY Buffalo, 1978-84; assoc. provost for rsch. and grad. studies Tex. A&M U., College Station, 1984-92, prof. Coll. Geoscis., 1992-97; ret., 1997; also councilor Tex. A&M Rsch. Found., 1984-93; Pegrum lectr. SUNY, 1980; v.p. Assn. Tex. Grad. Schs., 1990-91, pres., 1991-92; cons. NASA, 1964, NSF, 1979-81, U.S. Army Cold Regions Rsch. and Engring. Lab., Hanover, N.H.; sr. U.S. rep., Antarctica, 1976, 77; bd. dirs., exec. com. Houston Area Rsch. Ctr., 1984-89; vis. prof., lectr., cons. numerous univs. Editor: (with O.B. Andersland) Geotechnical Engineering for Cold Regions, 1978; cons. editor Soil Sci, 1965—, Cold Regions Sci. and Tech., 1978-82; contbr. numerous sci. and tech. articles to profl. jours. Bd. dirs. Ford K. Sayre Meml. Ski Coun., Hanover, 1969-71; bd. dirs. Grafton County Fish and Game Assn., 1965-76, pres., 1968-70; bd. dirs. Hanover Conservation Coun., 1970-76, v.p., 1970-73. Served in USAF, 1946-49. Recipient Sci. Achievement award Cold Regions Research and Engring. Lab., 1968; co-recipient Newcomb Cleveland award AAAS, 1976; Sec. of Army Research fellow, 1966. Fellow Geol. Soc. Am., Am. Soc. Agronomy, Soil Soc. Am.; mem. AAAS, Internat. Glaciological Soc., Am. Polar Soc., Am. Geophys. Union (spl. task force on cold regions hydrology 1974-84), Soil Sci. Soc. Am., Niagara Frontier Assn. R&D Dirs. (pres. 1983-84), Licensing Execs. Soc., NASA Teams (Viking, Skylab and Planetary Geology and Geophys. Working Group), Comet Rendevous/Asteroid Flyby Mission Team, Arctic Rsch. Consortium U.S., Sigma Xi, Sigma Gamma Epsilon, Phi Kappa Phi. Home: PO Box 468 Hamilton WA 98255

ANDERSON, E. KARL, lawyer; b. Huntington, W. Va., Mar. 30, 1931; s. Earle Karl and Helen Emrie (Johnson) A.; m. Mary Elizabeth Williams, Nov. 13, 1953; children—Sharon Elizabeth, Charles Wesley. B.B.A., So. Methodist U., 1953, LL.B., 1960. Bar: Tex. 1960, U.S. Dist. Ct. (no. dist.) Tex. 1963, U.S. Supreme Ct. 1971. Field supr. Travelers Ins. Co., Dallas, 1956-57; claim mgr. Allstate Ins. Co., Dallas, 1958-62; practiced in Dallas, 1963—; pntr. Lastelick, Anderson and Arneson, Dallas, 1968—. 1st lt. USAF, 1954-56. Mem. Am. Bar Assn., Dallas Assn. Trial Lawyers (dir. 1964-65, 74-75), Tex. Trial Lawyers Assn., Assn. Trial Lawyers Am., Dallas Country Club, Delta Theta Phi, Sigma Iota Epsilon, Sigma Alpha Epsilon. Presbyterian. Home: 3111 Drexel Dr Dallas TX 75205-2910 Office: 1st Tex Bank Bldg PO Box 59105 Dallas TX 75229-1105

ANDERSON, EDGAR RATCLIFFE, JR., career officer, hospital administrator, physician; b. Baton Rouge, Mar. 13, 1940; m. Sandra Caston; children: Melisa, Edward, Mark. MD, La. State U., 1964; grad., Industrial Coll. Armed Forces, 1972, Air War Coll., 1982. Diplomate Am. Bd. Family Practice, Am. Bd. Dermatology, Am. Bd. Aerospace Medicine. Commd. 2d lt. USAF, 1965, advanced through grades to maj. gen., 1990; flight surgeon 464th Troop Carrier Wing USAF, Pope AFB, N.C., 1965-68; chief aerospace medicine 33d Tactical Fighter Wing USAF, Eglin AFB, Fla., 1968-69; undergrad. pilot tng. USAF, Williams AFB, Ariz., 1969-71; completed F-4 combat crew tng. USAF, MacDill AFB, Fla., 1971; aircraft comdr. 336th Tactical Fighter Squadron USAF, Seymour Johnson AFB, N.C., 1971; asst. ops. officer USAF, Ubon Royal Thai AFB; chief aeromed. svcs. USAF Regional Hosp. USAF, MacDill AFB, 1973-75; comdr. USAF Hosp. USAF, Seymour Johnson AFB, 1975-77; staff dermatologist USAF Med. Ctr. USAF, Keesler AFB, Miss., 1980-81; chief flight test ops. USAF-RAF exchange program USAF, Royal Air Force Station, Farnborough, Eng., 1981-83; comdr. USAF Regional Hosp. USAF, Langley AFB, Va., 1983-84; dir. profl. svcs. Office of Command Surgeon Tactical Air Command USAF, Langley AFB, 1984; command surgeon HQ Pacific Air Forces USAF, Hickam AFB, Hawaii, 1984-86; command surgeon SAC USAF, Offutt AFB, Nebr., 1986-90; comdr. Wilford Hall USAF Med. Ctr. USAF, Lackland AFB, Tex., 1990; surgeon general USAF, Washington, ret., 1996; CEO Truman Health Sys., Kansas City, Mo., 1996-98; exec. v.p. AMA, Chgo., 1998—; dean, prof. Sch. Med. U. Mo., Kansas City, 1996-98. Decorated D.S.M., Legion of Merit with oak leaf cluster, D.F.C. with oak leaf cluster, Meritorious Svc. Medal with two oak leaf clusters, Air medal with nine oak leaf cluster, Air Force Commendation Medal. Office: AMA 515 N State St Chicago IL 60610-4325*

ANDERSON, EDWARD G., III, army officer; b. Nov. 18, 1943; m. Ann Anderson; children: Ed IV, Lisa, Scott. Grad., U.S. Mil. Acad.; MS in Aero. Engring., Ga. Inst. Tech.; MA in Nat. Security and Strategic Study, Naval War Coll. Commd. 2d lt. U.S. Army, advanced through grades to lt. gen.; comdr. 6-80th Field Arty. U.S. Army, Korea; battery comdr. 2-12th Field Arty. U.S. Army, Vietnam; comdr. 1-18th Field Arty. U.S. Army, Augsburg, Germany, 1982-84, comdr. 117th Field Arty. Brigade, 1987-88; with Office of Dep. Chief of Staff R&D and Acquition Pentagon, Washington, dir. firepower Office of Dep. Chief of Staff; dir. combat devel. U.S. Army Field Arty. Ctr., Ft. Sill; asst. divsn. comdr. 1st Armored divsn. U.S. Army, Germany, 1991-92; dep. comdg. gen. for combat devel. U.S. Army Combined Arms Command, Ft. Leavenworth, Kans., 1992-94; asst. dep. chief of staff of ops. and plans Dept. of Army Hdqrs., 1994-96; comdr. U.S. Army Space and Missile Def. Command, Arlington, Va., 1996-98; dir. strategic plans and policy Joint Staff, Washington, 1998—. Decorated DSM, Legion of Merit with oak leaf cluster, Bronze Star with V device. Office: 51011 Joint Staff Pentagon Washington DC 20318-5101

ANDERSON, EDWARD RILEY, state supreme court chief justice; b. Chattanooga, TN, Aug. 10, 1932. BS, U. Tenn., 1955, JD, 1957. Bar: Tenn. 1958, U.S. Dist. Ct. (ea. dist.) Tenn. 1965, U.S. Ct. Appeals (4th cir.) 1985, U.S. Ct. Appeals (6th cir.), U.S. Supreme Ct. 1988. Assoc. Joyce & Wilson, Oak Ridge, Tenn., 1957-61; ptnr. Joyce, Anderson & Meredith, Oak Ridge, 1961-87; judge Tenn. Ct. Appeals, Knoxville, 1987-90; justice Tenn. Supreme Ct., Knoxville, 1990—, now chief justice; mem. Tenn. Jud. Conf., 1987—; chmn. Tenn. Jud. Coun., 1990—, Select Senate/House Com. on Ct. Automation, 1990—. Past commr. Oak Ridge City Charter. Fellow Am. Bar Found., Tenn. Bar Found.; mem. ABA, Am. Bd. Trial Advocates (pres. Tenn. chpt. 1987-88), Tenn. Bar Assn., Anderson County Bar Assn. (pres. 1961), Tenn. Def. Lawyers Assn. (pres. 1980-81), Am. Inns of Ct. (pres. Tenn. chpt. 1988-90). Avocations: reading, tennis. Office: Tenn Supreme Ct Supreme Court Bldg 719 Locust St Knoxville TN 37902

ANDERSON, EDWARD VIRGIL, lawyer; b. San Francisco, Oct. 17, 1953; s. Virgil P and Edna Pauline (Pedersen) A.; m. Kathleen Helen Dunbar, Sept. 3, 1983; children: Elizabeth D., Hilary J. AB in Econs., Stanford U., 1975, JD, 1978. Bar: Calif. 1978. Assoc. Pillsbury Madison & Sutro, San Francisco, 1978—, ptnr., 1987-94; mng. ptnr., mem. firm mgmt. com. Skjerven Morrill MacPherson Franklin and Friel, San Jose, Calif., 1994—. Editor IP Litigator, 1995—; mem. bd. editors Antitrust Law Devel., 1983-86. Trustee Lick-Wilmerding H.S., San Francisco, 1980—, pres.; trustee Santa Clara Law Found., 1995—, Hamlin Sch. for Girls, San Francisco, 1998—. Mem. ABA, Calif. Bar Assn., San Francisco Bar Assn., Santa Clara Bar Assn. (counsel), City Club San Francisco, Stanford Golf Club, Phi Beta

Kappa. Republican. Episcopal. Home: 330 Santa Clara Ave San Francisco CA 94127-2035 Office: Skjerven Morrill MacPherson Franklin and Friel 25 Metro Dr Ste 700 San Jose CA 95110-1349

ANDERSON, EDWYNA GOODWIN, lawyer; b. Tulsa, Feb. 11, 1930; d. Edward Lawrence and Jeanne (Osby) Goodwin; children: Kathie Dones-Carson, Jenni Robertson Dones. BA, Fisk U., 1950; JD, Detroit Coll. Law, 1974; AA degree (hon.), C.S. Mott C.C., Flint, Mich., 1980. Bar: Mich. 1974, U.S. Dist. Ct. (ea. dist.) Mich. 1976, Pa. 1989. Mng. editor, v.p. Okla. Eagle Pub. Co., Tulsa, 1951-53; social dir. and counselor Hurley (Mich.) Sch. Nursing, 1956-62; news reporter and feature writer The Flint Jour., 1963-65; asst. pros. attorney Consumer Protection and Econ. Crime Divsn., 1974-78; chief Consumer Protection and Econ. Crime div. Genesee County Pros. Atty.'s Office, 1978-80; pub. svc. commr. Mich. Pub. Svc. Commn., 1980-88; gen. counsel Duquesne Light Co., Pitts., 1988-94, spl. counsel to the pres., CEO, chmn., 1994-95, ret., 1995. Bd. dirs. Allegheny County chpt. ARC, Family Health Coun., Health Rsch. and Svcs. Found., Am. Corp. Counsel Assn., YWCA, others; prodr., director, writer numerous variety and dramatic prodns. in cmty. theater; active in cmty. edn. with chs. and orgns.; bd. dirs. ONEOK, Inc. Recipient achievement award ESOM,, Sojourner Truth award Negro Bus. and Profl. Women's Clubs, Flint, 1979, Outstanding contbn. award in law, Outstanding Community Achievement award 1978, Humanitarian award Flint New Human Rels. Commn., 1982, Outstanding Svc. award Concerned Pastors for Social Action, Flint, 1983, award Mich. conf. bd. Women's Missionary Soc., Quinn Chapel African Meth. Episcopal Ch., 1975; inducted to Booker T. Washington H.S. Hall of Fame, Tulsa, 1997. Mem. ABA, Mich. Bar Assn., Allegheny County Bar Assn., Pa. Bar Assn., Am. Corp. Counsel Assn., Exec. Women's Coun., Pitts. Urban League, Flint Women's Forum YMCA, Women in State Govt., Nat. Dist. Attys. Assn., Am. Assn. U. Women, Nat. League for Nursing, Mich. League for Nursing, Citizen's Ady. Bd., Flint Bd. Edn., Prosecuting Attys. Assn. of Mich., Genesee County Mental Health Soc., Mich. Heart Assn. (ea. dist.), Vis. Nurse Assn. Home: One Trimont Ln # 420B Pittsburgh PA 15211-1254*

ANDERSON, ELLIS BERNARD, retired lawyer, pharmaceutical company executive; b. Michigan City, Ind., Aug. 30, 1926; s. A.B. and Esther (Nicholson) A.; m. Adrienne Scotchbrook, Aug. 6, 1955 (dec. Aug. 1991); children: Rebecca J., Katherine V.; m. Jermain Johnson Andrews, May 22, 1993. AB cum laude, Ind. U., 1949, JD, 1952; grad., Advanced Mgmt. Program, Harvard U., 1970. Bar: Ind. 1952. Ptnr. Butt, Bowers & Anderson, Evansville, Ind., 1952-60; with Baxter Labs. Inc., Morton Grove, Ill., 1961-65; sr. v.p., gen. counsel, dir., mem. exec. com. Hoffmann-La Roche Inc., Nutley, N.J., 1965-88. With AUS, World War II. Mem. Nassau Club, Bay Head Yacht Club, Springdale Golf Club, Phi Beta Kappa. Home: 52 Elm Rd Princeton NJ 08540-2502

ANDERSON, ELSIE MINERS, mathematics educator; b. Harare, Zimbabwe, July 4, 1931; came to U.S., 1961; d. William James and Winifred Ethel (Lowe) Miners; m. Larry Vance Anderson, Dec. 22, 1961; children: Winifred Jean Whitmore, Margaret Elizabeth Daly. BS, Rhodes U., Grahamstown, South Africa, 1951, EdD, 1952; MLS, East Tex. State U., 1966. Tchr. geography and math. Govt. Cen. African Fedn., Salisbury, 1953-61; tchr. math. Desdemona (Tex.) Ind. Sch. Dist., 1962-64; head libr. Holding Inst., Laredo, Tex., 1971-72; instr. math. Western Tex. Coll., Snyder, 1973-74, prof. math., 1974-97; exchange tchr. in geography Mill Hill, North London, Eng., 1957. Active Girl Scouts U.S., Abilene, Tex., 1972—. Recipient Theater Patron award Western Tex. Coll. Drama Dept., Snyder, 1986. Mem. Order Eastern Star. Baptist. Avocations: stamp collecting, swimming, racquetball, travel, attending drama productions. Home: 600 29th St Snyder TX 79549-3614

ANDERSON, ERIC ANTHONY, city manager; b. New Orleans, June 2, 1946; s. Eric Albert and Edna (Barrie) A.; m. Linda Jane Briefstein, June 22, 1967; children: Eric Scott, Stacy Alissa. BA, Syracuse U., 1967; MPA, SUNY, Albany, 1968; MA, Maxwell Sch., Syracuse U., 1970, Harvard U., 1994. Adminstrv. intern City of Phoenix, 1970-71; asst. dir. Rsch. and Devel. Ctr., Internat. City Mgmt. Assn., Washington, 1971-73; asst. town mgr. Town of Windsor (Conn.), 1973-78; town mgr. Munster (Ind.), 1978-83; city mgr. Eau Claire (Wis.), 1984-91, Evanston, Ill., 1991-95, Des Moines, 1995—. Bd. mgrs. Windsor-Bloomfield YMCA, 1976-78; adv. coun. Urban League N.W. Ind., 1979. NEH fellow, 1977. Fellow Nat. Acad. Pub. Adminstrn.; mem. Ind. Mcpl. Mgmt. Assn. (pres. 1979-80), Conn. City Mgmt. Assn. (treas. 1977-78), Internat. City Mgmt. Assn. (v.p. midwest 1987-89, trustee retirement corp. 1989-92), Nat. League of Cities (community and econ. devel. policy com. 1984-91), League of Wis. Municipalities (com. on fin. and taxation 1984-90, bd. dirs. 1991), N.W. Mcpl. Conf. (exec. bd. 1991-92). Home: 3309 Wolcott Ave Des Moines IA 50321-1949 Office: Office of the City Manager City Hall 400 E 1st St Des Moines IA 50309-1809

ANDERSON, ERIC DAVID, electrical engineer; b. LaCrosse, Wis., July 11, 1957; s. Olaf Adrian and Barbara Ann Anderson; m. Cheryl Lynn Queenan, Oct. 3, 1981; children: Leif Eric, Bjorn David, Kjirsten Lynn. BSEE, U. Minn., 1979. Devel. engr. Honeywell, Inc., Mpls., 1980-83; software engr. Astrocom Corp., St. Paul, 1983-86; project mgr. Applied Spectrum Techs., Mpls., 1986-87; sr. software engr. Micro Display Systems, Inc., Hastings, Minn., 1987-88, dir. engring., 1988-89; software engr. Control Systems, Inc., Roseville, Minn., 1990-91, PC Tech, Inc., Lake City, Minn., 1991; design engr. Tech. Group, Inc., Neenah, Wis., 1991-93; software engr. PC Tech, Inc., 1993-96; dir. engring. Micron Elecs., Inc., Mpls., 1996-98; pres., founder Andar Engring., Inc., North Hudson, Wis., 1998—. Inventor in field. Pres. North Hudson Pepper Festival, 1987-90, village trustee, 1985-89; Scoutmaster Boy Scouts Am., North Hudson, 1997—; chmn. St. Croix Emergency Med. Svcs. Commn., Hudson, 1990-91. Mem. Jaycees. Lutheran. Avocations: hunting, fishing, camping, chess. E-mail: eanders@spacestar.net.

ANDERSON, ERIC SCOTT, lawyer; b. Grand Forks, N.D., Aug. 26, 1949; s. Lyle William and Norma Sylvia (Lundeby) A.; children: Peter Scott, Nathan William. BSCE, U. Wis., 1971, JD, 1977. Bar: Wis. 1977, Minn. 1977, U.S. Dist. Ct. (we. dist.) Wis. 1977, U.S. Dist. Ct. Minn. 1978. Assoc. Fredrikson & Byron, P.A., Mpls., 1977-83, shareholder, 1983—. Mem. Wis. Bar Assn., Minn. Bar Assn., Hennepin County Bar Assn., Phi Eta Sigma, Tau Beta Pi, Phi Kappa Phi, Order of Coif. Avocations: golf, running, music. Office: Fredrikson & Byron PA 900 2nd Ave S Ste 1100 Minneapolis MN 55402-3328

ANDERSON, ERIC SEVERIN, lawyer; b. N.Y.C., Dec. 16, 1943; s. Edward Severin and Dorothy Elvira (Ekbloom) A. BA in History summa cum laude, St. Mary's U., San Antonio, 1968; JD cum laude, Harvard U., 1971. Bar: Tex. 1971. From assoc. to ptnr. Fulbright & Jaworski, L.L.P., Houston, 1971—. Served with USAF, 1961-65. Mem. ABA, State Bar Tex., Houston Bar Assn. Democrat. Clubs: Houston Ctr., Houston City. Avocations: classical music, theater, sports. Home: 14 E Greenway Plz Unit 21-o Houston TX 77046-1406 Office: Fulbright & Jaworski LLP 1301 Mckinney St Houston TX 77010-3031

ANDERSON, ERIL W.L., web designer; b. Golden Valley, Minn., Apr. 23, 1968; s. Warren Ludwig and Lorraine Adele (Bosch) A.; m. Kimberly Joy Anderson, Oct. 23, 1993. Cert. Entrepreneurship, Chippewa Valley Tech. Coll., Menomonie, Wis., 1989; BA in Bus. Mgmt., U. San Moritz, London, 1999. Leasee, mgr. Dairy Queen, 1982-95, 98-99; pres. E. Warren Comms., Golden Valley, Minn., 1982-97; materials coord. Cardinal Stritch U., Edina, Minn., 1995-97; pres. KingdomBooks, Burnsville, Minn., 1992-99; web designer The QuikPages, Mpls., 1998—. Recipient Agape Gold Award of Webpage Excellence, 1998, Nat. Leadership and Svc. award U.S. Achievement Acad., 1986. Mem. HTML Writers Guild, 1999. Mem. Internat. Ch. Christ. Avocations: photography, bonsai, collecting pepsi memorabilia. Home E-mail address: ewla@bigfoot.com. Office E-mail Address: KingdomBooks@Disciples.com. Home: 14462 Portland Ave S Burnsville MN 55337 Office: KingdomBooks 14462 Portland Ave S Burnsville MN 55337

ANDERSON, EUGENE HAROLD, retired architect, sculptor; b. Chgo., Oct. 12, 1931; s. Harold Ingamar and Helen Elizabeth (Lund) A.; m. Elizabeth Eugenia Redd (dec. 1981); children: Devora Eugenia Anderson Peterson, Britta Eugenia Anderson Tinney. BArch, U. Ill., 1958. Registered arch., Ill., Iowa. Draftsman Ambrose Richardson & Assocs., Champaign, Ill., 1956-57; constrn. inspector U. Ill. Archtl. Office, Champaign, 1958-60; design arch. Stanley Internat., Monrovia, Liberia, 1960-61; chief design arch. Stanley Internat., Muscatine, Iowa, 1961-63; arch. Clark-Altay & Assocs., Urbana, Ill., 1964-65; assoc. univ. arch. U. Iowa, Iowa City, 1965-72; dir. hosp. archs. office U. Iowa Hosps. & Clinics, Iowa City, 1972-89; ret. U. Iowa Hosps. & Clinics, 1989; sculptor, 1990—. Assoc. design arch. exec. mansion Republic of Liberia, 1960; design arch. Nat. Customs Ctr. Republic of Bolivia, 1963; sculptor family group series, Coe Coll., Cedar Rapids, Ia., 1995. With U.S. Army, 1953-55. Mem. AIA, Arts Iowa City (bd. dirs. 1997-99). Unitarian. Avocation: internat. travel. Home: 1014 Wylde Green Rd Iowa City IA 52246-4829

ANDERSON, EUGENE ROBERT, lawyer; b. Portland, Oreg., Oct. 24, 1927; s. Andrew E. and Ruth Beatrice (White) A.; m. Jenny Morgenthau, Nov. 8, 1986: children—Matthew, Martin. BS, UCLA, 1949; postgrad., Oreg. State Coll., 1945; JD, Harvard U., 1952; LLM, NYU, 1960. Bar: N.Y. bar 1953, Mass., So. and Eastern dists. N.Y., Second Circuit, D.C. Circuit, U.S. Ct. Claims, U.S. Supreme Ct. bars 1953. Asso. firm Chadbourne & Parke, N.Y.C., 1953-61; partner Chadbourne & Parke, 1965-69; asst. U.S. atty. So. Dist. N.Y., Foley Square, 1961-65; chief civil div. So. Dist. N.Y., 1963-65; ptnr. firm Anderson Kill & Olick, P.C., N.Y.C., 1969—; asst. dist. atty. N.Y. County, 1977; dir. Fortune Brands, Inc., Greenwich, Conn.; Spl. hearing officer U.S. Dept. Justice, 1965-68; arbitrator Am. Arbitration Assn., 1965—, Small Claims Ct., 1970-76; mem. com. on trial practice and technique Second Circuit, 1967-73. Mem. N.Y.C. Mayor's Bus. Adv. Com., Mayor's Task Force Auto. Ins. Served with AUS, 1945-46. Mem. ABA, Fed. Bar Assn., Assn. Bar City N.Y., Police Athletic League (dir., gen. counsel). E-mail: eanderson@andersonkill.com. Office: Anderson Kill & Olick PC 1251 Avenue of the Americas Fl C New York NY 10020-1182

ANDERSON, FLETCHER NEAL, chemical executive; b. Kansas City, Mo., Nov. 5, 1930; s. Chester Gustav and Astrid Cecilia (Crone) A.; m. Marilyn Lucille Henke; children: Karl C., Keith F., Susan L. BSChemE, U. Mo., 1951; MSChemE, Washington U., St. Louis, 1956; grad. exec. program, Stanford U., 1972. Registered profl. engr., Mo., Pa. With Mallinckrodt, Inc., St. Louis, 1951-81, group v.p. food, drug and cosmetic chems. group, 1974-76, group v.p. chem. group, 1976-78, sr. v.p. chem. group, 1978-81, also dir.; pres., dir. Chomerics, Inc., Woburn, Mass., 1981-85; pres., chief exec. officer, dir. Chemtech Industries, St. Louis, 1986-89; interim pres., CEO Brulin Corp., Indpls., 1990, bd. dirs., 1990-93; exec. v.p., COO, dir. F&C Internat., Cin., 1992-93, pres., CEO, 1993, also bd. dirs.; bd. dirs. Cytogen Corp., Princeton, N.J., 1987-95, Sepracor Inc., Malborough, Mass., 1993-95; chmn. bd. Med. Materials, Inc., Camarillo, Calif., 1992-93; mem. adv. coun. U. Mo. Engring. Sch. Columbia, 1978-89. Mem. Florissant (Mo.) Charter Commn., 1961-63. Recipient Disting. Service to Engring. award U. Mo., Columbia, 1978. Mem. Am. Inst. Chem. Engrs., Algonquin Golf Club. Lutheran. E-mail: marand@earthlink.net.

ANDERSON, FRANCES SWEM, nuclear medical technologist; b. Grand Rapids, Mich., Nov. 27, 1913; d. Frank Oscar and Carrie (Strang) Swem; m. Clarence A.F. Anderson, Apr. 9, 1934; children: Robert Curtis, Clarelyn Christine (Mrs. Roger L. Schmelling), Stanley Herbert. Student, Muskegon Sch. Bus., 1959-60; cert., Muskegon Community Coll., 1964; cert. adult edn. computer course, Fruitport Cmty. Schs., 1992. Registered nuclear med. technologist Am. Registry Radiol. Technologists. X-ray file clk., film librarian Hackley Hosp., Muskegon, Mich., 1957-59, radioisotope technologist and sec., 1959-65; nuclear med. technologist Butler Meml. Hosp., Muskegon Heights, Mich., 1966-70; nuclear med. technologist Mercy Hosp., Muskegon, 1970-79, ret., 1979. Mem. Muskegon Civic A Capella choir, 1932-39; mem. Mother-Tchr. Singers, PTA, Muskegon, 1941-48, treas. 1944-48; with Muskegon Civic Opera Assn., 1950-51; office vol. Alive '88 Crusade; mem. com. for 60th H.S. Class Reunion; mem. Sr. Harvest Day Com., Muskegon County, 1995; active Forest Park Covenant Ch., mem. choir, 1953-79, 83—, choir pres. 1992, 93, choir sec. 1963-69, Sunday Sch. tchr. 1954-75, supt. Sunday Sch., 1975-78, sec., treas. 1981-86, sec. 1991, 92, 93, mem. support team, sec. 1993, chmn. master planning coun., 1982; coord. centennial com. to 1981, ch. sec. 1982-84, 87, 91, 95-96, registrar vacation Bible sch. 1988, 89, 90, 91, treas., 1995, 96; co-chmn. Jackson Hill Old Timer's Reunion, 1982, 83, 85. Mem. Am. Registry Radiologic Technologists, Soc. Nuclear Medicine (cert. nuclear medicine technologist), Omni Fitness Club. Home: 5757 Sternberg Rd Fruitport MI 49415-9740

ANDERSON, FRANCILE MARY, secondary education educator; b. Poland, Ind., Nov. 10, 1926; d. Matthew Henry and Dmma Alvina (Dettinger) Worthman; m. Robert Charles Anderson, Aug. 23, 1953; children: Sally Quick, Sue Wilkinson, Robert Charles, Russell. BA, U. Mich., 1948. Tchr. Pontiac (Mich.) Sch. Dist., 1948-54; co-organizer Mich. Law Related Edn. Conf., Lansing, 1978; mem. exec. bd. North Ctrl. Assn. Commn. on Schs., Tempe, Ariz., 1996—. Trustee North Oakland Med. Ctrs., Pontiac, 1994—; campaign chair United Way of Oakland County, 1995. Recipient Disting. Svc. award Mich. Assn. Secondary Sch. Prins., 1987; named to Mich. Edn. Hall of Fame, 1990. Mem. Oakland County Hosp. Assn. (pres.), Oakland County Bar Law Libr. Found., North Ctrl. Assn. Mich., North Oakland Med. Ctrs. Found. (pres.), Delta Kappa Gamma. Republican. Presbyterian. Home: 2570 Silverside Dr Waterford MI 48328-1760

ANDERSON, FRANK J., JR., career officer. BA in Bus. Mgmt. and Econ., Chapman Coll., 1972; student, Office Tng. Sch., Lackland AFB, Tex., 1973, Squadron Officer Sch., 1975; M in Mgmt., Ctrl. Mich. U., 1982; student, Air Command and Staff Coll., 1984, Def. Sys. Mgmt. Coll., 1987, Indsl. Coll. Armed Forces, 1992. Cert. lead assessor ISO 9000 quality sys., total quality mgmt. facilitator, program mgmt. level III, contracting level III. Commd. 2d lt. USAF, 1973, advanced through grades to brig. gen., 1997; base contracting officer, chief constrn. br. Washington Area Contracting Ctr., Andrews AFB, Md., 1973-76, chief specialized contracting br., 1973-76; with Edn. With Industry Program Boeing Co., Phila., 1976-77; chief subcontractor mgmt. div. then dep. chief contract adminstrn. divsn. GE Air Force Plant Rep. Office, Phila., 1977-79; stationed at Andrews AFB, Md., 1979-83, 89-91; comdr. Air Force Plant Rep. Office Rockwell Internat., Columbus, Ohio, 1984-87; dir. contracting Electronic Combat and Reconnaissance Sys. Program Office, Wright-Patterson AFB, Ohio, 1987-89; sys. program dir. Sys. Program Office Aero. Sys. Ctr., Eglin AFB, Fla., 1992-94, dir. Weapons, Air Base and Range Product Support Office, 1994-95, mgr. armament product group, 1995-96; dir. contracting Aero. Sys. Ctr., Wright-Patterson AFB, 1996-97; dep. asst. sec. contracting Office Asst. Sec. Acquisition, adv. gen. Air Force Competition Hdqs. USAF, Pentagon, Washington, 1997—. Decorated Legion of Merit. Recipient Air Force Professionalism in Contracting award, 1988; named Career Broadening Personnel Officer of Yr., Air Force Sys. Command, 1980, Co. Grade Officer of Yr., Air Force Sys. Command, 1982. Office: SAF/AQC 1060 Air Force Pentagon Washington DC 20330-1060

ANDERSON, FRED RICHARD, minister; b. San Bernardino, Calif., Dec. 27, 1941; s. Elmer Duffield and Gladys Lucile (Lawlace) A.; m. Questa Lucile Donnelly, Sept. 4, 1965; children: Larra Anne, Rebecca Lucile; 1 foster child, James Gordon Cushman. BM in Voice, U. Redlands, 1963; MDiv, Princeton Theol. Sem., 1973, D in Ministry, 1981. Pastor Pompton Valley Presbyn. Ch., Pompton Plains, N.J., 1973-78; sr. pastor Pine St. Church, Harrisburg, Pa., 1978-92, Madison Ave. Presbyn. Ch., N.Y.C., 1992—; bd. dirs. Liturgical Conf., 1990-94; bd. trustees Princeton Theol. Sem., 1992—; chair edn. bd. Reformed Liturgy and Music, 1983-89. Author: Singing Psalms of Joy & Praise, 1986, The Presbyterian Hymnal, 1990; assoc. editor: Book of Common Worship, 1993; contbr. articles to profl. jours.; opera, concert singer, 1963-64. Trustee Harrisburg Hosp., 1990-92, Chilton Meml. Hosp., Pompton Plains, 1976-78; pres. Pequennock (N.J.) Sr. City Housing, 1974-78; v.p. YMCA, Harrisburg, 1987-92, v.p., 1987-92. Capt. USAF, 1964-69. Recipient Fine Arts award Bank Am., 1959. Mem. Appeal Conscience Found. (assoc.), N.Am. Acad. Liturgy, Presbyn. Assn. Musicians, Union League Club (N.Y.C.), The Pilgrims. Avocations: jogging, boating, fishing, hymntext writing. Office: Madison Ave Presbyn Ch 921 Madison Ave New York NY 10021-3508

ANDERSON, FREDERICK RANDOLPH, JR., lawyer, law educator; b. Rutherfordton, N.C., June 28, 1941; s. Frederick Randolph and Ophelia (Meeler) A.; m. Barbara Alison Rose, Nov., 1991; 1 child, Molly Elizabeth. BA with highest honors, U. N.C., 1963; BA in Jurisprudence, Oxford (Eng.) U., 1965; JD, Harvard U., 1968. Bar: D.C. 1969, U.S. Supreme Ct. 1980, U.S. Ct. Appeals (D.C. cir.) 1995. Teaching fellow Harvard U., Cambridge, Mass.; editor in chief Environ. Law Reporter, Washington, 1970-73; exec. dir. Environ. Law Inst., Washington, 1973-78, pres., 1978-80, bd. dirs., 1980-86, 88-92, adv. coun., 1992—; prof. law U. Utah Coll. Law, Salt Lake City, 1980-85; dean Washington Coll. Law Am. U., 1985-88, Ann Loeb Bronfman Prof. Law, 1988-91; mem. firm Cadwalader, Wickersham & Taft, Washington, 1991-93, ptnr., 1993—, chmn. environ. law practice group, 1998—; mem. congl. study of common law relief for hazardous waste injuries, 1980-82; mem. Adminstrv. Conf. U.S., 1978-80, cons., 1983-84, 89-91; chmn. adv. working group on environ. sanctions U.S. Sentencing Commn., 1992-94. Author: NEPA in the Courts, 1973, Environmental Improvement Through Economic Incentives, 1978, Environmental Protection: Law and Policy, 1984, 2d edit., 1990, 3d edit., 1999; contbg. author: Federal Environmental Law, 1974, Occupational and Environmental Health, 1982, The Southwest under Stress, 1981. Chmn. bd. dirs. Ctr. for Internat. Environ. Law, 1993—; v.p. Western Network, 1986-89; mem. Harvard Group on Risk Mgmt. Reform, 1994-96; bd. dirs. René Dubos Ctr., 1994—. Morehead scholar, Nat. Merit scholar U. N.C., Marshall scholar Oxford U. Mem. ABA (chmn. standing com. on environ. law 1980-82, chmn. commn. on inter-Am. affairs 1986-88), NAS (mem. Comm. on Life Scis. 1995—, mem. bd. environ. studies and toxicology 1988-94, Am. Law Inst., Ctr. for the Cmty. Interest (co-chmn. bd. 1990-94), Cosmos Club. Office: Cadwalader Wickersham & Taft Ste 700 1333 New Hampshire Ave NW Washington DC 20036-1574

ANDERSON, GARRY MICHAEL, diagnostic radiologist; b. Houston, May 17, 1955; s. Dan Luther and Marcella Marie (Hanel) A. BS in Biology, Tarleton State U., Stephenville, Tex., 1977; BS in Medicine, Tex. A&M U., 1979, MD, 1981. Diplomate Nat. Bd. Med. Examiners, Am. Bd. Radiology. Intern in pathology Scott & White Hosp., Temple, Tex., 1981-82, resident in diagnostic radiology, 1982-86; fellow in imaging UCLA Ctr. of the Health Scis., 1986-87, asst. attending clin. prof., 1987-88; diagnostic radiologist Long Beach (Calif.) Cmty. Hosp., 1987—. Mem. Second Decade Coun., Am. Film Inst., L.A., 1993—. Named Outstanding Young Alumnus, Tarleton State U., 1991. Mem. Am. Coll. Radiology, Radiol. Soc. N.Am. Roman Catholic. Avocation: tennis. Home: 1813 Termino Ave Apt 8401 Long Beach CA 90815-2674 Office: Cmty Radiology Med Group 1703 Termino Ave Ste 107A Long Beach CA 90804-2126

ANDERSON, GARY ALLAN, professional football player; b. Parys, South Africa, July 16, 1959; naturalized, 1985; married; 2 children. BS, Syracuse U., 1982. Mem. Buffalo Bills Football Team, 1982; placekicker Pitts. Steelers Football Team, 1982-94, Phila. Eagles, 1995-96, San Francisco 49ers, 1997-98, Minn. Vikings, 1998—. Named to NFL All Rookey Team, 1982, NFL Pro Bowl, 1983, 85, 93, Offensive rookei of Yr., Dapper Dan Club, 1983, Placekicker of Yr., NFL Alumni, 1983, Leading Scorer, Am. Football League, 1983, 84, 85; recipient MacKey Leading Scorer award, 1985, 86. Avocations: fly fishing, golf. Office: Minn Vikings 9520 Viking Dr Eden Prairie MN 55344

ANDERSON, GARY WILLIAM, physician; b. Summit, N.J., Nov. 10, 1951; divorced; 1 child, Eric William George. BA, Seton Hall U., 1974; MA in Psychology, Fairleigh Dickinson U., 1977; MD, Autonomous U. Guadalajara, Mex., 1983. Intern Rutgers Med. Sch., New Brunswick, N.J., 1984; resident St. Joseph's Med. Ctr., Paterson, N.J., 1985; med. dir. Sandoz Rsch. Inst., East Hanover, N.J., 1985-96; global dept. exec. dir. clin. safety dept. Novartis Pharms., East Hanover, 1996—. Vol. med. dir., bd. trustees, exec. com. Sussex County (N.J.) Domestic Abuse Program, 1986-98. Mem. AMA, Am. Med. Writers Assn., Nat. Honor Soc. Psychology, Am. Acad. Family Physicians, N.J. Acad. Medicine. Republican. Office: Novartis Pharma RR 10 East Hanover NJ 07936

ANDERSON, GAVIN, public relations consultant; b. Melbourne, Victoria, Australia, Sept. 12, 1945; came to U.S., 1974; s. George and Dulcie (Busch) A.; m. Valia Olita Beldaus, Sept. 7, 1972; children: Tegwyn, Kylie, George. Student, Monash U., Melbourne, 1965-66. Mgr. Sydney area Pan Pub. Rels., Sydney, Australia, 1968-69; dir. Europe region Hill and Knowlton Inc., London, Eng., 1970-74; sr. v.p. internat. Hill and Knowlton Inc., N.Y.C., 1974-81; chmn., CEO Gavin Anderson & Co., N.Y.C., 1981—. Mem. Am. Australian Assn. (bd. dirs. 1986—), Internat. Pub. Rels. Assn., Econs. Club of N.Y. Office: Gavin Anderson & Co Inc 1633 Broadway New York NY 10019-6708

ANDERSON, GEOFFREY ALLEN, retired lawyer; b. Chgo., Aug. 3, 1947; s. Roger Allen and Ruth (Teninga) A. BA cum laude, Yale U., 1969; JD, Columbia U., 1972. Bar: Ill. 1972. Assoc. Isham, Lincoln & Beale, Chgo., 1972-79, ptnr., 1980-81; ptnr. Reuben & Proctor, Chgo., 1981-85; dep. gen. counsel Tribune Co., Chgo., 1985-92; gen. counsel Chgo. Cubs, 1986-90, corp. counsel, 1991-92; v.p. Timber Trails Country Club, Inc., 1992—. Elder Fourth Presbyn. Ch., Chgo., chmn. worship and music com., 1990-92, trustee, 1992-95, 99—, v.p., 1993-94; bd. dirs. The James Chorale, Chgo., 1993-96, chmn. program com., 1994-96. Recipient Citizenship award Am. Legion, 1965. Mem. Chgo. Bar Assn. (chmn. entertainment com. 1981-82, Best Performance award 1977), Yale Club (N.Y.C.), Phi Delta Phi.

ANDERSON, GEORGE See **WEISSMAN, JACK**

ANDERSON, GEORGE HARDING, broadcasting company executive; b. Buffalo, Mar. 6, 1931; s. Gordon and Adeline (Harding) A.; m. Sandra Bradley, Aug. 24, 1957 (div. 1972); 1 child, Geoffrey Bradley; m. Barbara Rich Tisdale, Jan. 18, 1974. BA, Harvard U., 1954. With First Nat. Bank Boston, 1955-58, Randolph Assos., Wellesley, Mass., 1959-61; pres. Precision Products Co. Inc., Waltham, Mass., 1961-64; sales mgr. WBZ-TV, Boston, 1964-66; office mgr. Blair Radio, Boston, 1966-67; sales mgr. WHDH-TV, Boston, 1967-68; exec. v.p., dir. Guy Gannett Broadcasting Services, Sta. WGAN-AM-FM-TV, Portland, Maine, Sta. WHYN-AM-FM-TV, Springfield, Mass., Sta. WINZ-AM-FM, Miami, Fla., 1968-78; pres. Sta. KENS-TV, San Antonio, 1980-84; pres., chief operating officer Harte-Hanks TV Group, 1981-84; corp. v.p. Harte-Hanks Communications, 1981-84; pres. Broadcast div. Diversified Communications, 1985-91, ret., 1991; dir. WTLV, Jacksonville, Fla., 1978-84, Maine Nat. Bank, Southworth Machine Co. Pres. Maine Audubon Soc., 1971, Portland Soc. Natural History, 1971; maj. Portland United Fund Dr., 1971, advance gifts chmn., 1972; co-chmn. fund dr. Edward Waters Coll., 1979; bd. dirs. Maine Cancer Soc., Jacksonville United Way, 1979—, San Antonio Red Cross, 1981—, vice chmn., 1983—, S.W. Tex. Blood Bank; bd. dirs. Camden Conf., 1993—; campaign chmn. N.E. Health Capital Campaign; N.E. Health Bd. Trustees, 1994-98; pres. trustees Camden Health Care Ctr., 1993-94, Camden Conf., 1994. Mem. Harvard Varsity Club, Owl Club, Camden Yacht Club, Megunticook Golf Club. Address: 104 Chestnut St Camden ME 04843-2229

ANDERSON, GEORGE HUGO, chemical engineer; b. Binghamton, N.Y., Oct. 12, 1946; s. Otto Hugo and Marie Alma (Yerkes) A.; m. Carilon D. Cain, Sept. 8, 1973; children: Michelle Lynn Anderson Wolf, Tiffany Beth, Jeffrey Scott, Matthew Christopher. BS in Biomed. Engring., Rensselaer Poly. Inst., 1968, M in Biomed. Engring., 1969; PhD of Chem. Engring., Rice U., 1977. Rsch. engr., coal liquification Exxon Rsch. & Engring., Baytown, Tex., 1977-80, sr. staff engr. synfuels, 1980-83; sect. head, planning Exxon Rsch. & Engring., Florham Pk., N.J., 1983-85; corp. tech. advisor Exxon Rsch. & Engring., Annandale, N.J., 1985-88; sect. head fuels processing devel. Exxon Rsch. & Engring., Baton Rouge, 1988-91, quality coord., 1990-91, catalyst coord., 1992—. Contbr. articles to profl. jours.; patent in field. Mem. bd. dirs. Sageglen Cmty. Assn., Houston, 1978-80; bd. mem. Parsippany (N.J.) Christian Sch., 1988. Sgt. USAF, 1970-73. Recipient 2 Internal Tech. Excellence awards Exxon Corp., 1982, Exxon Rsch. and Engring., 1993. Mem. AIChE, Sigma Xi. Baptist. Achievements include discovery of effects of shear stress on human blood platelet functions in clotting; invention of bottoms recycle process scheme for Exxon Coal Liquification process; devel. of kinetic model for coal liquification; coordination of devel. and commercialization of 6 catalysts covering reforming, fuels/lubes H/T and FCC process areas. Avocations: golf, basketball, reading, teaching Sun. sch., ch. deacon. Home: 19164 Hickory Bay Ct Baton Rouge LA

70817-1823 Office: Exxon Rsch & Devel Labs PO Box 2226 Baton Rouge LA 70821-2226

ANDERSON, GEORGE KENNETH, physician, foundation executive, retired air force officer; b. Providence, Feb. 17, 1946; s. George Raymond and Mildred (Caster) A.; m. Kimberly Kay Baker, May 18, 1968; children: George D., Ginger K. MD, U. Mich., 1971; MPH, Tulane U., 1973; postgrad., Nat. War Coll., Ft. McNair, Va., 1982-83. Diplomate Am. Bd. Preventive Medicine (chmn. 1991-95), Am. Bd. Med. Mgmt. (bd. dirs.). Intern Wilford Hall USAF Med Ctr., 1971-72; resident USAF Sch. Aerospace Medicine, 1973-75; commd. 2d lt. USAF, 1967, advanced through grades to maj. gen., 1993; comdr. USAF Hosp., Kunsan, Republic of Korea, 1975-76, 86th Tactical Hosp., Germany, 1976-79; mem. faculty USAF Sch. Aerospace Medicine, Brooks AFB, Tex., 1979-82; div. chief Office Surgeon Gen., Bolling AFB, Md., 1983-85, dep. dir., 1985-87; command surgeon Air Force Systems Command, Andrews AFB, Md., 1987-88; dir. med. inspection Air Force ISC, Norton AFB, Calif., 1988-90; comdr. Human Systems Ctr., Brooks AFB, 1990-94; dep. asst. sec. def. Health Svcs. Ops. and Readiness, Washington, D.C., 1994; ret. USAF, 1996; pres., CEO Koop Found. Inc., Rockville, Md., 1997-98; exec. v.p. Oceania Corp., Falls Church, Va., 1998—. Decorated Legion of Merit, Disting. Svc. medal; Koop Found. fellow. Fellow Am. Coll. Preventive Medicine (pres.), Am. Coll. Physician Execs., Aerospace Med. Assn. (Julian Ward award 1975); mem. AMA, Air Force Assn. (life). Office: Oceania 5203 Leesburg Pike Ste 900 Falls Church VA 22041-3468

ANDERSON, GEORGE ROSS, JR., federal judge; b. Anderson, S.C., Jan. 29, 1929; s. George Ross and Eva Mae (Pooler) A.; m. Dorothy M. Downie, Dec. 2, 1951; 1 son, G. Ross. B.Comml. Sci., Southeastern U., 1949; postgrad., George Washington U., 1949-51; LL.B., U. S.C., 1954, LLD (hon.), 1984; LLD (hon.), Anderson Coll., 1998. Bar: S.C. 1954. Mem. identification div. FBI, Washington, 1945-47; clk. to U.S. Senator Olin D. Johnston, Washington, 1947-51, Columbia, S.C., 1953-54; individual practice law Anderson, S.C., 1954-79; U.S. dist. judge Dist. Ct. of S.C., Anderson, 1980—. Asst. editor: U. S.C. Law Rev. 1953-54. Bd. dirs. Salvation Army, 1968, YMCA, 1968-79, Anderson Youth Assn., 1978-80. Served with USAF, 1951-52. Recipient War Horse award So. Trial Lawyers Assn., 1990. Fellow Internat. Acad. Trial Lawyers (dir. 1979-81), Internat. Soc. Barristers; mem. S.C. Bar Assn. (dir. 1977-80, past cir. v.p.), Assn. Trial Lawyers Am. (bd. govs. 1969-71), S.C. Trial Lawyers Assn. (v.p. 1970-71, pres. 1971-72, Outstanding Trial Judge of Yr. 1984), hon. doctor of Laws, U. SC, 1984, bd. dirs.,Federal Judges Assn., 1993-97. Democrat. Baptist. Office: US Dist Ct PO Box 2147 Anderson SC 29622-2147*

ANDERSON, GERALD DWIGHT, history educator; b. Dale, Minn., Nov. 18, 1944; s. Wilferd Dean and Violet Caria-Maria (Heigg) A.; m. Rhonda Waldahl, July 8, 1967 (div. May 1975); 1 child, Carmen Nell; m. Barbara Ann Thill, May 13, 1978; children: Karl August, Paul Martin. BA, Concordia Coll., Moorhead, Minn., 1965; MA, N.D. State U., 1966; PhD, U. Iowa, 1973. Asst. prof. history Waldorf Coll., Forest City, Iowa, 1966-70, Drake U., Des Moines, 1973, Iowa Wesleyan Coll., Mt. Pleasant, 1974; instr. Austin (Minn.) C.C., 1974-75; rschr. Minn. State Senate, St. Paul, 1976-79; asst. prof. Luther Coll., Decorah, Iowa, 1979-85; assoc. prof. history N.D. State U., Fargo, 1985—; cons. history textbooks Harper Collins, N.Y.C., 1988-97, West Pub., St. Paul, 1988-97; cons. various hist. socs. Author: Fascists, Communists, The National Government, 1983, The Uffda trial, 1994, The Western Perspective Study Guide, Vols. I and II, 1994. Precinct chair Moorhead DFL Party, 1986-97; v.p. Gooseberry Park Players, Moorhead, 1994-97. Named Outstanding Tchr., N.D. State U., 1992; Fulbright scholar U.S. State Dept., 1991, Internat. Seminar scholar Coun. for Internat. Edn., Moscow, 1994, Berlin, 1996, Budapest, 1999. Lutheran. Avocations: reading and writing detective fiction, Scandinavian ethnic studies. Home: 1320 5th St S Moorhead MN 56560-3420 Office: North Dakota State Univ Minard Hall 412H Fargo ND 58105

ANDERSON, GERALD EDWIN, utilities executive; b. Boston, Apr. 9, 1931; s. Clarence Gustav and Lela Pauline (Kelley) A.; m. Mary Elizabeth Iverson, May 21, 1955; children: Todd K., Timothy J., Kristin E. A.A., Worthington (Minn.) Jr. Coll., 1950; B.B.A., U. Minn., 1952. C.P.A., Minn. Staff accountant, audit mgr. Arthur Andersen & Co., Mpls., 1953-65; asst. comptroller Commonwealth Energy System (formerly New Eng. Gas & Electric Assn.), Cambridge, Mass., 1966, system comptroller, 1967-71, v.p., comptroller, 1971-72, treas. parent co., financial v.p. system, 1972-74, pres., 1974-91, chief exec. officer, 1975-91; ret., 1992; trustee parent co., 1974-91; also dir. operating subs. Commonwealth Energy Sys., 1972-91, Liberty Mutual Ins. Co., Liberty Mutual Fire Ins. Co., Liberty Life Assurance Co. of Boston, 1984-95, Liberty Fin. Cos., Inc. Vice chmn. United Ways Ea. New Eng., 1986; mem. town fin. com., Carlisle, Mass., 1968-73, chmn., 1972-73; dir. Swedish Coun. Am., 1987—; mem. Corp. of Mass. Gen. Hosp., 1988-95. 1st lt. USAF, 1952-53. Mem. AICPA, Minn. Soc. CPAs, Fin. Execs. Inst., Oyster Harbors Club, The Lakes Country Club, Somerset Club, Comml. Club of Boston, Beta Alpha Psi, Beta Gamma Sigma. Episcopalian. Home: 75 Hornbeam Ln Centerville MA 02632-3521 also: 245 Wild Horse Dr Palm Desert CA 92211

ANDERSON, GERALD LESLIE, financial executive; b. Washington, May 24, 1940; s. Paul Hash and Edith (Hathaway) A.; m. Margaret Marie Curley, June 8, 1974; children: Paul Charles, Laura Marie. B.S. in Indsl. Mgmt., Carnegie Mellon U., 1961, M.S. in Indsl. Adminstrn., 1962. Econ. analyst Sun Oil Co., Phila., 1962-66; asst. treas. Selas Corp. Am., Dresher, Pa., 1966-74; treas. Midrex Corp., Charlotte, N.C., 1974-76; v.p., treas. Georgetown Industries, Inc., Charlotte, 1976-85; v.p. fin., chief fin. officer Georgetown Industries, Inc., 1985-95; prin. Anderson Investments, Charlotte, N.C., 1995—. Active Ch. at Charlotte. Mem. Fin. Execs. Inst., Assn. for Corp. Growth, Carmel Country Club, Delta Tau Delta. Republican. Evangelical. Home and Office: 4519 N Parview Dr Charlotte NC 28226-3450

ANDERSON, GERALD VERNE, retired aerospace company executive; b. Long Beach, Calif., Oct. 25, 1931; s. Gordon Valentine and Aletha Marian (Parkins) A.; m. Judith B. Marx, May 14, 1992; children by previous marriage: Lori Jean Anderson Fronk, Gregory Verne, David Harman, Lynn Elaine Anderson Lee (dec.), Brian Earl, Michael Gordon. AA, Long Beach City Coll., 1952; BS, U. Calif., Berkeley, 1958. Registered profl. engr., Calif. Tech. specialist N. Am. Aviation Co., L.A., 1958-65; tech. specialist McDonnell Douglas Astronautics, Huntington Beach, Calif., 1965-84; mgr. McDonnell Douglas Astronautics, Huntington Beach, 1984-87; sr. mgr. McDonnell Douglas Aerospace, Huntington Beach, 1987-94; cons. Mitsubishi Heavy Industries, Nagoya, Japan, 1972-73, Aeritalia, Turin, Italy, 1975-76. Patentee portable vacuum chamber, electron beam welding device. Mem. Westminster (Calif.) Planning Com., 1974, Huntington Beach Citizens Adv. Com., 1975, Westminster Bicentennial Com., 1976, L.A. Classical Ballet Guild, 1992—. Mem. Soc. Mfg. Engrs., Soc. Automotive Engrs., Aerospace Industries Assn., AIAA. Republican. Avocations: photography, skiing, backpacking, snorkeling. Home: 3452 Falcon Ave Long Beach CA 90807-4814

ANDERSON, GERARD FENTON, economist, university program administrator; b. Mariemont, Ohio, June 24, 1951; s. Harry C. and Dorothy C. (Fenton) A.; m. Judith Rae Peres; 1 child, Anna. BA in Econs., Haverford Coll., 1973; PhD in Pub. Policy, U. Pa., 1978. Spl. asst. Cost of Living Coun. Exec. Office of the Pres., Washington, 1972; research analyst Fed. Reserve Bank, Washington, 1973-74; prin. investigator Phila. Health Mgmt. Corp., 1974-78; economist Office of the Sec. HHS, Washington, 1978-83; assoc. dir. Ctr. for Hosp. Fin. and Mgmt. Johns Hopkins U., Balt., 1983-87, dir., 1987—; co-dir. Johns Hopkins Program for Med. Tech. and Practice Assessment, Balt., 1986-94, 1994—; cons. Blue Cross Greater Phila., 1978, World Bank, Washington, 1988; adj. prof. Grad. Sch. Pub. Adminstrn. Am. U., Washington, 1978-82; presenter to Congl. coms. over 30 times. Author: Health Care Cost Containment, 1990, Providing Hospital Services, 1989; contbr. over 120 articles to profl. jours. Fellow U. Pa., Phila., 1978. Mem. Am. Econ. Assn., Am. Pub. Health Assn., Assn. for Health Svcs. Rsch., Phi Beta Kappa, Delta Omega. Democrat. Mem. Soc. of Friends. Home: 8022 Glendale Rd Chevy Chase MD 20815-5903 Office: Johns Hopkins U 624 N Broadway # 300 Baltimore MD 21205-1900

ANDERSON, GILLIAN, actress; b. Chgo., Aug. 9, 1968; d. Edward and Rosemary A.; m. Errol Clyde Klotz, Jan. 1, 1994; 1 child, Piper. BFA, DePaul U., 1990; grad., Goodman Theatre Sch., Chgo. Appeared on TV as Dana Scully in X-Files, 1993—; stage appearance in Absent Friends, Manhattan Theatre Club, 1991 (Theatre World award 1991), The Philanthropist, Along Wharf Theater, 1992; appeared in films Chicago Cab, 1995, X-Files the Movie, 1998. Recipient Golden Globe awards, 1995, 97, Screen Actors' Guild awards, 1996, 97, Emmy award, 1997; nominated for Best Actress in Drama Series, 1996. Office: X-Files Prodn Office Bldg 10, X-Files Prodn Office, Bldg 10 110-555 Brooks Ave, North Vancouver, BC Canada V7J 3S5 also: William Morris Agy 151 El Camino Dr Beverly Hills CA 90212*

ANDERSON, GLORIA BROWN, publishing executive. Reporter Associated Press, Madison, Wis., 1968-69, Sioux Falss, S.D., 1968-69; reporter, mag. editor The Cinn. Enquirer, 1970-74; sunday and features editor The Charlotte Observer, 1975-76; mng. editor Knight News Wire, Detroit, 1977, Washington, 1977; mng. editor The Miami (Fal.) News, 1978-81; founding editor, co-pub. Miami Today, 1982-87; editor, pub. The Kendall Gazette, Miami, 1988-91; editor Week in Review The N.Y. Times, N.Y.C., 1992; exec. editor The N.Y. Times Syndicate, N.Y.C., 1992-93; exec. editor, v.p. The N.Y. Times Syndication Sales Corp., N.Y.C., 1994-96, pres., 1997—; juror Pulitzer Prize, 1982, 83; adv. coun. Fla. Internat. U. Sch. Journalism, 1984—. mem. Performing Arts Ctr. Trust, Miami, 1990-91, long range planning com. United Way, 1987, Leadership Miami, 1981; bd. dirs. Hispanic Heritage Festival, Miami, 1981-88; founder, co-chmn. Kendall Awareness Week, 1989-92. Recipient Clarion award Women in Comm., 1976, Cmty. Headliner award, 1990; named Outstanding Citizen of Yr. South Miami and Kendall C. of C., 1989. Avocations: travel, latin american cultures, the arts, swimming, golf. Office: NY Time Syndicated Sales Corp 122 E 46th St Fl 14 New York NY 10017-2611*

ANDERSON, GORDON LOUIS, foundation administrator; b. St. Croix Falls, Wis., Nov. 16, 1947; s. Erwin Louis and Eunice Arlene (Johnson) A.; m. Mary Jane Evenson, July 1, 1982; children: Tamara, Jayna, Greta, Evan. BME, U. Minn., 1975; MDiv in Ethics, Union Theol. Sem., N.Y.C., 1980; MA in Religion, Claremont Grad. Sch., 1985, PhD Philosophy Religion, 1986. Engr. Gull Engring. Inc., Mpls., 1974-80, also bd. dirs.; owner, mgr. Aerograph Aerial Photography, Claremont, Calif., 1981-84; sec. gen., bd. dirs. Profs. World Peace Acad., N.Y.C., 1984-93; sec. gen. Profs. World Peace Acad., St. Paul, 1993—; sec., gen., bd. dirs. Internat. Cultural Found., Washington, 1986—; lectr. Unification Theol. Sem., Barrytown, N.Y., 1987-96, bd. dirs., 1988-96; lectr. 40 countries including Europe, Africa, Asia and South America. Assoc. editor Internat. Jour. on World Peace, 1985-94, editor, 1994—; editor: Morality and Religion in Liberal Democratic Societies, 1992, Worldwide State of the Family, 1995, The Family in Global Transition, 1997; contbr. articles and book revs. to profl. jours., chpts. to books. Mem. Citizens for Better N.J., 1986-92; bd. dirs. Paragon House Pubs., 1993—, exec. dir., 1996—; trustee U. Bridgeport, Conn., 1994—. With U.S. Army, 1969-72, Vietnam. Mem. World Future Soc., Am. Acad. Religion, Am. Polit. Sci. Assn., Internat. Studies Assn., Consortium on Peace Rsch. Mem. Unification Ch. Office: Profs World Peace Acad 2700 University Ave W Saint Paul MN 55114-1059 *Religion or culture has always defined manhood, womanhood, the relation to our neighbor, the government, the spiritual world and God. This has yet to take place in a normative way for the modern world.*

ANDERSON, GREG R., communications company executive; b. Virginia, Minn.; m. Linda Anderson; 4 children. Student, Bob Jones U., 1964-68. Staff announcer WRIO-FM, Cape May, N.J., 1969; various programming, sales and mgmt. positions various radio stas.; program mgr. WFBC-AM/FM, Greenville-Spartanburg, S.C., 1980-87, v.p. ops., multimedia radio divsn., 1987, exec. v.p., radio divsn., 1987-93; v.p., gen. mgr. Salem Comm. Corp., Irving, Tex., 1993-94, pres., Salem Nat., 1994-96; gen. mgr. KDFX Radio, Dallas, 1994—; mgr. WFBC-AM/FM, Greenville, 1980-87, KEEL/KITT-FM, Shreveport, La., 1980-87, WEZW-FM, Milw., 1980-87; overseer Salem Radio Network (SRN), SRN News, Morningstar Radio Network, and Salem Radio Reps. (SRR), Tex., 1994—. With USCG, 1969-73. Avocations: gardening, church and civic activities. Office: Salem Radio Networks 545 E John Carpenter Fwy Irving TX 75062-3973*

ANDERSON, GREGORY JOSEPH, botanical sciences educator; b. Chgo., Nov. 26, 1944. BS, St. Cloud State U., 1966; MS, Ind. U., 1968, PhD, 1971. Asst. prof. U. Nebr., Lincoln, 1971-73; asst. prof. U. Conn., Storrs, 1973-78, assoc. prof., 1978-84, prof. dept. ecology and evolutionary biology, 1984—, dept. head, 1990—, Disting. Alumni prof., 1997—; mem. and chair biology sect. Fulbright Panel, Washington, 1989-92. Contbr. articles to profl. jours. Trustee Joshua's Trust Land Conservation Trust, Mansfield, Conn., 1985—, vice chmn. 1986-89. NSF grantee, 1978-79, 82, 89-90, 90-92, 93-95, 95—. Mem. Soc. for Econ. Botany (sec. 1981-84, pres. 1986-87), Bot. Soc. Am. (sec. 1988-92, pres. 1992-93), Orgn. for Tropical Studies (sec. 1983-86), Soc. Study of Evolution, Am. Soc. Plant Taxonomy (mem. coun. 1988-91, pres. 1997), Am. Inst. Biol. Scis. (pres.-elect 1998). Office: U Conn Dept Ecology/Evol Biology 75 N Eagleville Rd 4-43 Storrs Mansfield CT 06269-3043*

ANDERSON, GREGORY MARTIN, medical company representative; b. Spokane, Wash., Mar. 3, 1959; s. Norman Clarence and Jean Marie (Huggar) A. BS, Ea. Wash. U., 1986, MS, 1988; M in Social Work, Walla Walla Coll., 1997. Med. rep. pharms. div. CIBA Geigy Corp., Yakima, Wash., 1989—; respiratory specialist Merch & Co., Inc., 1997—; registered counselor Washington State, 1997—; mem. adv. bd. Walk in the Wild Zoo, Spokane, 1986-88. Chpt. advisor Order of De Molay, Spokane, 1986; deacon 7th Day Adventist Ch. Ea. Wash. U. fellow, 1987, 88. Mem. Am. Inst. Biol. Sci., Eastern Wash. Lodge of Rsch., Manito Masons (jr. warden Spokane chpt. 1986), Sigma Xi. Home: 1321 n Stevenson Rd Liberty Lake WA 99019

ANDERSON, GREGORY SHANE, insurance executive; b. Mpls., Feb. 8, 1947; s. Donald Manfred and Inez Marie (Dickson) A.; m. Joyce Millicent Goetz, June 15, 1968; children: Kaarin Marie, Kirsten Elise, Todd Gregory, Kathryn Joy. BS, U. Minn., 1969. CLU. Spl. agt. Northwestern Mut. Life Ins. Co., St. Paul, 1970—. V.p. Tri-Lakes Improvement Assn., Lake Elmo, Minn., 1990, pres., 1991, 92. Named Man of the Yr., St. Paul Spl. Agts. Assn., 1984, 95-96, St. Paul Gen. Agts. and Mgrs., 1978, 91. Mem. Nat. Assn. Life Underwriters, Minn. Assn. Life Underwriters (pres. 1985-86), St. Paul Life Underwriters Assn. (pres. 1979-80), St. Paul CLU Soc. (pres. 1992-93), Million Dollar Round Table (Top of the Table 1993, 94), 25 Million Dollar Internat. Forum, 1996, Dellwood Hills Golf Club (pres. 1996). Republican. Lutheran. Avocations: golf, racquetball, tennis, biking. Home: 11 Spyglass Rd Dellwood MN 55110-1227 Office: Northwestern Mutual Life Court Internat Ste 455 S 2550 University Ave Saint Paul MN 55114-1052

ANDERSON, GUNNAR DONALD, artist; b. Berkeley, Calif., Mar. 3, 1927; s. Sven Gunnar and Margaret (Hultien) A.; m. Virginia Fletcher Bullock, Jan. 31, 1953; children: Greta, Karin, Paul. BFA, Art Ctr. Coll. of Design, Pasadena, Calif., 1951. Art dir. McCann ERickson, N.Y.C., 1951-53, Cunningham & Walsh, N.Y.C., 1953-55, Batten, Barton, Durstine & Osborne, San Francisco, 1955-63; artist Sonoma, Calif., 1963—. Artist: (children's book) Oscar Lincoln Busby Stokes, 1970; one man shows include U. Nebr., Lincoln, Frye Mus., Seattle, Conacher Galleries, San Francisco, Guildhall Galleries, Chgo., Meredith Long Galleries, Houston, Dalzell Hatfield Galleries, L.A., Lord and Taylor Art Galleries, N.Y.C., Rosicrution Mus., San Jose, Calif., Phillips Galleries, Dallas; exhibited in group shows at Ft. Worth Art Ctr., Palace of Fine Arts, San Francisco, De Saisset Gallery, Santa Clara, Calif. With USCG, 1945-46. Recipient Best in Fine Art award Soc. Art Ctr. Alumni, 1972. Mem. Soc. Western Artists (trustee 1993—, Best Figure or Portrait award 1971, 1st place award 1985, 90, 91, Grumbacher gold medallion 1986), Soaring Soc. Am., Bohemian Club. Avocations: soaring, wine making, aircraft model building. Home: 4583 Belmont Ct Sonoma CA 95476-8904

ANDERSON, HAROLD ALBERT, engineering and building executive; b. Beverly, Mass., Jan. 19, 1908; s. John Albert and Ann (Westerberg) A.; m. Grace Whittaker, Apr. 24, 1936; children—Harold Albert, Richard A. C.E., Tufts Coll., 1928. Registered profl. engr., numerous states. With Austin Co., Cleve., 1928-73; exec. v.p., gen. mgr. Austin Co., 1958-63, pres., 1963-73, also chief exec. officer, 1969-73, ret., 1973. Mem. ASCE, Nat. Soc. Profl. Engrs., Bay Head (N.J.) Yacht Club. Home: 974 Barnegat Ln Mantoloking NJ 08738-1710 Office: 3650 Mayfield Rd Cleveland OH 44121-1736

ANDERSON, HAROLD STERLING, retired adult education educator; b. Bethel, Conn., Sept. 24, 1928; s. Harold Julius and Mabelle Harriet (Nelson) A.; m. Margaretha Gall, Dec. 23, 1950; children: Steve (dec.), Dave Robert. BS, Mayville State Coll., 1951; MEd, Colo. State Coll., 1954, EdD, 1957. Instr. Ctrl. Wash. Coll., Ellensburg, 1954-55; assoc. prof. to prof. So. State Coll., Springfield, S.D., 1957-65; prof. Tchrs. Coll. Columbia U., N.Y.C., 1965-69; prof. Coll. Gt. Falls, Mont., 1969-94, dir. grad. studies, 1972-94, prof. emeritus, 1994—. Author: Primer of Planned Change, 1982, rev. edit., 1993; co-author: Thinking Skills Instruction, 1987. With U.S. Army, 1951-53. Recipient award Mont. Probation Officers Assn., 1980. Mem. NEA, AAUP, Phi Delta Kappa. Republican. Avocations: cowboy poetry, growing apples. Home: 44 US Highway 87 Belt MT 59412-8316

ANDERSON, HARRISON CLARKE, pathologist, educator, biomedical researcher; b. Louisville, Sept. 2, 1932; married, 1961. BA in Zoology, U. Louisville, 1954, MD, 1958. Diplomate Am. Bd. Pathology. Pathology intern Mass. Gen. Hosp., Boston, 1958-59; NIH rsch. trainee U. Louisville, Ky., 1959-60; resident in pathology Sloan Kettering Meml. Hosp, N.Y.C., 1960-62; postdoctoral fellow Sloan Kettering Inst., Rye, N.Y., 1962-63; from asst. prof., assoc. prof. to prof. pathology SUNY Downstate Med. Ctr., Bklyn., 1963-78; prof. pathology, chmn. dept. U. Kans. Med. Ctr., Kansas City, 1978-90, Harrington prof. orthopedic rsch., 1990—; mem. study sect. NIH, Bethesda, Md., 1977-81; chmn. Gordon Research Conf. on Bone, Meriden, N.H., 1981. Edit. bd. Am. Jour. Pathology, others, 1981—; contbr. articles to profl. jours. Recipient Biol. Mineralization Research award Internat. Assn. Dental Research, 1985, Sr. Faculty Research award U. Kans. Med. Ctr., 1986, Kappa Delta Orthopedic Rsch. award Orthopedic Rsch. Soc., 1982, Higuchi Biomed. Rsch. award U. Kansas, 1991; NIH rsch. fellow Strangeways Lab., Cambridge, Eng., 1971-72, NIH sr. rsch. fellow in cell biology Yale U., New Haven, , 1984-85; grantee NIH, 1967—. Mem. Am. Soc. Investigative Pathologists, Assn. Pathology Chmn. (pres. 1988-90), Am. Soc. Cell Biology, Am. Soc. Bone and Mineral Research, Orthopaedic Research Soc. Clubs: Am. Yacht (Rye); Carriage (Kansas City). Avocations: tennis, skiing, sailing. Office: U of Kansas Dept of Pathology 39th & Rainbow Kansas City KS 66160-7410

ANDERSON, HARRY FREDERICK, JR., architect; b. Chgo., Feb. 4, 1927; s. Harry Frederick and Sarah Matilda (Anderson) A.; m. Frances Annette Zeilstra, Jan. 27, 1951 (div. Jan. 1979); children: Scott H., Mark S., Robert R., Grant Alan; m. Elizabeth Jane Elden, Jan. 17, 1979 (dec. Apr. 1982); m. Joanell Vivian Mangan, Mar. 22, 1983. B.Arch., Ill. Inst. Tech., 1953. Chief draftsman Stade & Cooley, Chgo., 1953-55; ptnr. Stade, Dolan & Anderson, Chgo., 1955-65; project architect Perkins & Will Partnership, Chgo., 1965-67, ptnr., v.p., 1967-85, sr. v.p., 1973-74, exec. v.p., 1974-75, pres., chief exec. officer, 1975-85, chmn. bd., 1982-85; chmn., chief exec. officer Anderson, Mikos Architects Ltd., Oak Brook, Ill., 1985—; bd. dirs. Chgo. Bldg. Congress. Prin. works include Rockford (Ill.) Coll. Library, 1967, Sci. Bldg, 1968, Arts Complex, 1970, Women's Dormitory, 1969, Silver Cross Hosp, Joliet, Ill., 1971, Westlake Hosp, Melrose Park, Ill., 1970, Am. Soc. Clin. Pathologists bldg., Chgo., 1971, Ingalls Hosp, 1974, St. Mary of Nazareth Hosp, 1975, Childrens Meml. Hosp., Chgo., 1980, U. Chgo. Hosp, 1980, Northwestern Meml. Hosp., Chgo., 1987, Michael Reese Hosp., Chgo., 1987, Ctrl. Dupage Hosp., Winfield, Ill., 1998, Advocate Health Care Sys., Chgo., 1998. Chmn. adv. council Booth Meml. Hosp., Chgo., 1969-81; adv. bd. Chgo. Salvation Army, 1969-81. Served with USN, 1944-47. Fellow AIA; Mem. Internat. Hosp. Fedn., Am. Pub. Health Assn., Soc. Hosp. Planning and Mktg. Clubs: Park Ridge Country, Hinsdale Golf. Home: 721 W Walnut St Hinsdale IL 60521-3062 Office: Anderson Mikos Architects Ltd 1420 Kensington Rd Ste 306 Hinsdale IL 60523-2147

ANDERSON, HARVEY GREGG, pattern company executive; b. Chicopee Falls, Mass., July 12, 1953; s. Harvey Gustave and Joy Eileen Anderson; m. Sheri Marie Sander, Dec. 21, 1973; children: Denise Renee, Jeffrey Gregg, Christopher Harvey, Casey Lee. BS in Mfg., Western Mich. U., 1992. Layout technician Howmet Corp., Whitehall, Mich., 1973-75; gen. mgr. Anderson Candy, Inc., Salt Lake City, 1976-77; apprentice patternmaker Anderson Pattern, Inc., Muskegon Heights, Mich., 1977-81, journeyman patternmaker, 1981, prodn. mgr., 1981-85, tech. advancement mgr., 1986-88, 91-94, sales engr., 1989-91, mfg. strategist, 1994-97, mfg. mgr., 1998—; interim v.p. Modern Mold, Inc., Grand Rapids, Mich., 1988-89. Mem. adv. bd. Muskegon (Mich.) C.C., 1987—, Muskegon Schs., 1991—; mem. adv. coun. Muskegon Hts. Schs., 1991-93; mem. adv. com. Newaygo County Career-Tech. Ctr., 1994—. Recipient dist. citizen award Muskegon Community Coll., 1990, award of merit for vocat.-tech. edn., State of Mich., 1990. Mem. Soc. Mfg. Engrs. (sr.), Computer Automated Systems Assn. SME, Machine Tech. Assn. SME, Rapid Prototyping Assn. SME. Republican. Baptist. Avocations: scale models, motorsports, boating, water skiing, landscaping. Office: Anderson Pattern Inc 500 W Sherman Blvd Muskegon MI 49444-1315

ANDERSON, HERBERT HATFIELD, lawyer, farmer; b. Rainier, Oreg., Aug. 2, 1920; s. Odin A. and Mae (Hatfield) A.; m. Barbara Stuart Bastine, June 3, 1949; children—Linda, Catherine, Thomas, Amy, Elizabeth, Kenneth. B.A. in Bus. Adminstrn., U. Oreg., 1940; J.D., Yale U., 1949. Exec. trainee U.S. Steel Co., San Francisco, 1940-41; assoc. Spears, Lubersky, Campbell, Bledsoe, Anderson & Young, Portland, Oreg., 1949-54; ptnr. Spears, Lubersky, Bledsoe, Anderson, Young & Hilliard, 1954-90, Lane, Powell, Spears & Lubersky, Portland, 1990—; instr. law Lewis and Clark Coll., Portland, 1950-70. Mem. planning adv. com. Yamhill County, Oreg., 1974-82; bd. dirs. Emanuel Hosp., 1967—; bd. dirs. Flyfisher Found., 1972—, pres., 1972-84; bd. dirs. Multnomah Law Library, 1958—, sec. 1962-68, 77—, pres., 1964-74. Served to maj., parachute inf. U.S. Army, 1942-46, ETO. Fellow Am. Bar Found. (chmn. Oreg. chpt. 1988—); mem. ABA (chmn. governing com. forum on health law 1984-89, chmn. standing com. on jud. selection, tenure and compensation 1978-80, Lawyer's Conf., exec. com. 1980-94, chmn. 1989-90, judicial adminstrn. divsn. coun. 1978-94, sr. lawyer's divsn. coun. 1987-89), Am. Judicature Soc. (bd. dirs. 1981-85), Soc. Law and Medicine, Nat. Health Lawyers Assn., Am. Acad. Hosp. Attys., Oreg. Soc. Hosp. Attys. (pres. 1984-85), Multnomah Bar Found. (bd. dirs. 1955—, pres. 1959-64, 87—), Nat. Bankruptcy Conf. (conferee 1964—, exec. com. 1976-79, chmn. farmer insolvency com. 1985-88), Nat. Assn. R.R. Trial Counsel, Oreg. Bar Assn. (del. to ABA 1966-68), Multnomah Bar Assn. (pres. 1955), Western States Bar Conf. (pres. 1967), Oreg. Asian Pear Coun. (pres. 1989-91), Sigma Chi. Democrat. Lutheran. Clubs: Multnomah Athletic, Michelbook Country, Flyfishers Oreg. (pres. 1972), Willamette Amateur Field Trial (pres. 1968-72). Lodge: Masons. Home: River Meadow Farm 19289 SE Neck Rd Dayton OR 97114-7815 Office: Lane Powell Spears & Lubersky 520 SW Yamhill St Ste 800 Portland OR 97204-1383

ANDERSON, HERSCHEL VINCENT, librarian; b. Charlotte, N.C., Mar. 14, 1932; s. Paul Kemper and Lillian (Johnson) A. B.A., Duke U., 1954; M.S., Columbia U., 1959. Library asst. Bklyn. Public Library, 1954-59; asst. bookmobile librarian King County Public Library, Seattle, 1959-62; asst. librarian Longview (Wash.) Public Library, 1962-63; librarian N.C. Mus. Art, Raleigh, 1963-64; audio-visual cons. N.C. State Library, Raleigh, 1964-68; dir. Sandhill Regional Library, Rockingham, N.C., 1968-70; asso. state librarian Tenn. State Library and Archives, Nashville, 1970-72; unit dir. Colo. State Library, Denver, 1972-73; state librarian S.D. State Library, Pierre, 1973-80; dir. Mesa (Ariz.) Public Library, 1980—; dir. Bibliographical Ctr. for Rsch., Denver, 1974-80, v.p. 1977; mem. Western Coun. St. Librs., 1975-80, v.p., 1978, pres., 1979; mem. Ariz. LSCA Adv. Coun., 1981-84, pres., 1982-83; mem. Ariz. Libr. Devel. Coun., 1991-93, Ariz. State Libr. Adv. Coun., 1998—, chair, 1999—; mem. libr. technician tng. adv. com. Mesa C.C., 1982-85, mem. commn. for excellence, 1993—; chmn. Serials On-Line in Ariz. Consortia, 1985-86. Jr. warden St. Mark's Episcopal Ch., Mesa, 1985-87, vestryman, 1987-90, 95-98, sr. warden, 1996-98; del. ann. conv. Episcopal Diocese of Ariz., 1989-92, 94-98, mem. archives com., 1990-97, mem. Diocesan Coun. Episcopal, Diocese of Ariz., 1996-98; mem., treas. Maricopa County Libr. Coun., 1981—, pres., 1983, 93; mem. Valley Citizens League, 1991—; mem. Northeast Regional Parish steering com., 1994-98, chair Native Am. com., 1999—. With U.S. Army, 1955-57. Recipient

Emeritus Honors Ariz. Library Friends, 1987. Mem. ALA, S.D. Libr. Assn. (hon. life, Libr. of Yr. award 1977), Mountain Plains Libr. Assn. (pres. 1974, bd. dirs. 1974-77, 86-87, Intellectual Freedom award 1979), Ariz. Libr. Assn. (exe. com. 1986-87), Chief Officers of State Libr. Agys. (bd. dirs. 1974-76), Kiwanis (bd. dirs. Mesa 1981-86, v.p. 1983, pres. 1985-86), Phi Kappa Psi. Office: Mesa Pub Libr 64 E 1st St Mesa AZ 85201-6768

ANDERSON, HOLLY GEIS, women's health facility administrator, commentator, educator; b. Waukesha, Wis., Oct. 23, 1946; d. Henry H. and Hulda S. Geis; m. Richard Kent Anderson, June 6, 1969. BA, Azusa Pacific U., 1970. CEO Oak Tree Antiques, San Gabriel, Calif., 1975-82; pres., founder, CEO Premenstrual Syndrome Treatment Clinic, Arcadia, Calif., 1982—, Breast Healthcare Ctr., 1986-89, Hormonal Treatment Ctrs., Inc., Arcadia, 1992-94; lectr. radio and TV shows, L.A.; on-air radio personality Women's Clinic with Holly Anderson, 1990—. Author: What Every Woman Needs to Know About PMS (audio cassette), 1987, The PMS Treatment Program (video cassette), 1989, PMS Talk (audio cassette), 1989. Mem. NAFE, The Dalton Soc., Am. Hist. Soc. of Germans from Russia. Republican. Avocations: writing, genealogy, travel, hiking, boating. Office: PMS Treatment Clinic 150 N Santa Anita Ave Ste 755 Arcadia CA 91006-3148

ANDERSON, HOWARD PALMER, former state senator; b. Crystall Hill, Va., May 25, 1915; B.A., Coll. William and Mary, 1940; LL.B., U. Richmond, 1948; m. Mildred Graham Webb. Bar: Va. 1948 (dec.). Former FBI agt.; practice law, Halifax, Va., 1950—; mem. Va. Ho. of Dels., 1958-71, Va. State Senate, 1972-92. Trustee, Patrick Henry Meml. Found.; mem. Halifax County Sch. Bd., 1952-57. Served with USNR, World War II. Mem. Va. Bar Assn., Halifax County Bar Assn., U. Richmond Law Sch. Assn., Halifax County C. of C., Am. Legion, VFW, Va. Hist. Soc. Baptist. Clubs: Masons, Sportsman (Halifax). Office: PO Box 847 Halifax VA 24558-0847

ANDERSON, HUGH GEORGE, bishop; b. Los Angeles, Mar. 10, 1932; s. Reuben Leroy and Frances Sophia (Nielsen) A.; m. Synnøve Anna Hella, Nov. 3, 1956 (dec. Apr. 1982); children: Erik, Kristi; m. Jutta Ilse Fischer, July 2, 1983; children: Lars, Niels. AB, Yale U., 1953; BD, Luth. Theol. Sem., Phila., 1956, STM, 1958; MA, U. Pa., 1957, PhD, 1962; LittD, Lenoir Rhyne Coll., 1971; DD, Roanoke Coll., 1971, Wagner Coll., 1987, Gen. Theol. Sem., N.Y.C., 1996, Luther Coll., Decorah, Iowa, 1996; LHD, Newberry Coll., 1979, Columbia (S.C.) Coll., 1981. Ordained Lutheran minister. Tchg. fellow Luth. Theol. Sem., Phila., 1956-58; prof. ch. history Luth. Theol. So. Sem., Columbia, S.C., 1958-70, dir. grad. studies, pres., until 1982; pres. Luther Coll., Decorah, Iowa, 1982-95; presiding bishop Evang. Luth. Ch. Am., 1995—; chair Pub. House of the Evang. Luth. Ch. Am., 1987-93; co-chmn. U.S. Luth.-Roman Cath. Dialogue, 1979-90; mem. Commn. for a New Luth. Ch., 1982-86; v.p. Luth. World Fedn., 1996—. Author: Lutheranism in the Southeastern States, 1969, A Good Time to be the Church, 1997; co-author: Lutherans in North America, 1975; translator: I Believe (H. Thielicke), 1968, Historical Commentary on the Augsburg Confession (W. Maurer), 1986. Bd. dirs. Minn. Pub. Radio, St. Paul, 1983-91. Mem. Luth. World Fedn. (commn. on studies 1984-90). Avocations: astronomy, sailing. Home: PO Box 719 Prospect Heights IL 60070-0719 Office: Office of the Bishop ELCA 8765 W Higgins Rd Chicago IL 60631-4101

ANDERSON, ILSE JANELL, clinical geneticist; b. Elmhurst, Ill., May 3, 1959; d. Lowell Leonard and Avis Janell Anderson; m. Nicholas Thomas Potter, June 24, 1989; children: Nils Andrew, Anders Matthew. BS in Biology, Lehigh U., 1981; MD, N.Y. Med. Coll., 1985. Diplomate Nat. Bd. Med. Examiners, Am. Bd. Pediatrics, Am. Bd. Med. Genetics. Resident pediatrics U. Conn., Farmington, 1985-88, fellow human genetics, 1988-91; clin. geneticist Med. Ctr. U. Tenn., Knoxville, 1991—. Mem. Phi Beta Kappa. Office: Univ Tenn Med Ctr 1930 Alcoa Hwy Ste 435 Knoxville TN 37920-1520

ANDERSON, IRIS ANITA, retired secondary education educator; b. Forks, Wash., Aug. 18, 1930; d. James Adolphus and Alma Elizabeth (Haase) Gilbreath; m. Donald Rene Anderson, 1951; children: Karen Christine, Susan Adele, Gayle Lynne, Brian Dale. BA in Teaching, U. Wash., 1969; MA in English, Seattle U., 1972. Cert. English tchr., adminstr., Calif. Tchr. Issaquah (Wash.) Sr. High Sch., 1969-77, L.A. Sr. High Sch., 1977-79. Contbr. article to Skeptic mag. Nutrition vol. Santa Monica (Calif.) Hosp. Aux., Jules Stein Eye Inst., L.A.; mem. Desert Beautiful, Palm Springs Panhellenic; mem. Rancho Mirage Reps. W-Key activities scholar U. Wash. Mem. NEA, DAR (1st vice regent Cahuilla chpt.), AAUW (Anne Carpenter fellow 1998), LEV, Wash. Speech Assn., Nat. Thespians, Bob Hope Cultural Ctr., Palm Springs Press Women, Desert Music Guild, Coachella Valley Hist. Soc., Palm Desert Womens Club, Skeptics Soc., Calif. Ret. Tchrs. Assn., CPA Wives Club, Desert Celebrities, Rancho Mirage Womens Club, Round Table West, World Affairs Coun., Living Desert Wildlife and Bot. Preserve. Republican.

ANDERSON, IVAN VERNER, JR., newspaper publisher; b. Columbus, Ohio, Dec. 6, 1939; m. Josephine Blackwell; children: Thomas, Charlotte. BA, U. N.C., 1961; MBA, U. S.C., 1970. Sr. v.p. for loan adminstrn., regional mgr. Wachovia Bank and Trust Co., Winston-Salem, N.C., 1980-84; sr. v.p., regional exec. S.C. Nat. Bank, Charleston, 1984; exec. v.p. Evening Post Pub. Co., Charleston, 1984, pres., 1987—; asst. pub. The News and Courier, The Evening Post, Charleston, 1984; pub. The Post and Courier, 1987—. Bd. dirs. Trident United Way, S.C. Hist. Soc., Charleston Symphony Orch., Ashley Hall Sch., Enston Home, Ind. Colls. and Univs.; bd. visitors U. N.C., Chapel Hill; mem. city bd. Wachovia Bank S.C.; active U. S.C. Coll. Bus. Adminstrn. Bus. Partnership Found., Nature Conservancy. With USN, 1961-64. Mem. So. Newspaper Pub. Assn., Beta Gamma Sigma. Episcopalian. Avocations: golfing, hunting, fishing. Home: 133 Tradd St Charleston SC 29401-2419*

ANDERSON, J. TRENT, lawyer; b. Indpls., July 22, 1939; s. Robert C. and Charlotte M. (Pfeifer) A.; m. Judith J. Zimmerman, Sept. 8, 1962; children: Evan M., Molly K. BS, Purdue U., 1961; LLB, U. Va., 1964. Bar: Ill. 1965, Ind. 1965. Teaching asst. U. Cal. Law Sch., Berkeley, 1964-65; assoc. Mayer, Brown & Platt, Chgo., 1965-72, ptnr., 1972—; instr. Loyola U. Law Sch., Chgo., 1985. Mem. ABA, Law Club, Union League Club, Mich. Shores Club. Home: 3037 Iroquois Rd Wilmette IL 60091-1106 Office: Mayer Brown & Platt 190 S La Salle St Ste 3100 Chicago IL 60603-3441

ANDERSON, JACK OLAND, retired college official; b. Mich., Aug. 5, 1921; s. Seymour and Laura (Fox) A. Student, Ferris State Coll., 1940-41; B.S., Central Mich. U., 1948; M.A., U. Mich., 1950; Ed.D., Mich. State U., 1962. Tchr. pub. schs. Mich., 1949-59; instr. Mich. State U., 1959-62; dir. edn. Lansing (Mich.) Bus. Inst., 1962-65; exec. dir. Lockyear Bus. Coll., 1965-66; acad. dean Detroit Coll., 1966-69; pres. Bristol (Tenn.) Coll., 1969-83, chmn. bd. dirs., 1983-88; past chmn. Sullivan County Vocat. Adv. Com.; past vice chmn. region IV proprietary sch. coordinating coun. U.S. Dept. Edn.; past pres. Tenn. Bus. Coll. Assn., Southeastern Bus. Coll. Assn. Past mem. Sullivan County Bd. Equalization, Bristol Power Bd., Sullivan County Hist. Commn., Tenn. Pub. Svc. Coun., bd. adminstrn. 1st Bapt. Ch., Bristol, Appalachian Regional Commn. Health Systems Aging; past chmn. dist. 757, Rotary Found. Capt. U.S. Army, 1942-46. Paul Harris fellow Rotary, 1983. Mem. Rotary (Paul Harris fellow), B.P.O.E. Lodge (# 232). Home: 1101 Indian Hill Dr Bristol TN 37620-3554

ANDERSON, JACK ROY, health care company executive; b. Mansfield, Ohio, Feb. 14, 1925; s. Roy L. and Katherine (Munson) A.; m. Rose-Marie J. Garcia, June 24, 1950; children—Gail Ellen, Neil Robert, Barbara Ann. B.S., Miami U., Oxford, Ohio, 1947; M.S., Columbia U. Grad. Sch. Bus., 1949. Acctg. mgr. Time, Inc., N.Y.C., 1950-59; asst. to controller W.R. Grace & Co., N.Y.C., 1959-62; v.p., treas. Hartford Publs., Inc., N.Y.C., 1962-65; controller McCall Corp., N.Y.C., 1965-68; v.p. Reliance Group, Inc., N.Y.C., 1968-70; pres., dir. Hosp. Affiliates Internat., Inc., Nashville, 1970-76, chmn. bd., dir., 1977-81; chmn. INA Health Care Group, Dallas, 1978-81; pres. Manor Care, Inc., Silver Spring, Md., 1981-82, Calver Corp., Dallas, 1982—; adj. faculty Owen Grad. Sch. Mgmt., 1978-79; bd. dirs. FHP Internat. Corp., Horizon Mental Health Mgmt., Inc., United Dental Care, Inc. Author: The Road to Recovery, 1976. Vis. com. Vanderbilt Owen Grad. Sch. Mgmt., 1973-77; trustee Nat. Com. for Quality Health Care, 1979-87, vice chmn., 1979-82; mem. bus. adv. coun. Miami U., 1975-78, chmn., 1978. Lt. (j.g.) USNR, 1943-46. Mem. Columbia Bus. Assocs., Fin. Execs. Inst. (chmn. employee devefits com. 1980-82), The Blind Brook Club (Purchase, N.Y.), Desert Forest Golf Club (Carefree, Ariz.), Desert Mountain Country Club (Scottsdale, Ariz.), Greenwich (Conn.) Country Club, Hawk's Nest Golf Club (Vero Beach, Fla.), John's Island Club (Vero Beach), Preston Trail Gold Club (Dallas), Reform Club (London), Sky Club (N.Y.C.), Stanwich Club (Conn.), Sigma Chi, Beta Alpha Psi, Beta Gamma Sigma (hon.). Office: 16475 Dallas Parkway Addison TX 75001

ANDERSON, JAMAL SHARIF, professional football player; b. Woodland Hills, Calif., Sept. 30, 1972. Student, U. Utah. Running back Atlanta Falcons, 1994—; NFC conf. champions, 1998-99, lost Superbowl 33 to Denver Broncos, 1999. Office: c/o Atlanta Falcons 1 Falcon Pl Suwanee GA 30024*

ANDERSON, JAMES ARTHUR, humanities educator, academic director; b. Providence, Aug. 9, 1955; s. Arthur Charles and Ruth M. (Marshall) A.; m. Patricia A. Braza, Aug. 27, 1977 (div. 1998); children: Erik James, Nicholas Perry; m. Lynn Toney, June 5, 1999. BA, R.I. Coll., 1977, MA in English, 1987; PhD, U. R.I., 1992. Cert. fundraising exec. Assoc. editor R.I. Rev., Providence, 1981-84; instr. Johnson & Wales U., Providence, 1984-88; adj. prof. humanities Johnson & Wales U., 1988-93, devel. publs., rsch. coord., 1987-90, dir. rsch. and grants, 1990-93, asst. prof., 1993-95; prof., asst. dean Sch. of Arts and Scis., 1995—; presenter in field. Author: The Illustrated Bradbury: A Structuralist Reading of Bradbury's "The Illustrated Man", 1990, Out of the Shadows: A Structuralist Approach to Understanding the Fiction of H.P. Lovecraft, 1992; columnist, writer East Side Monthly, Province, 1984—; contbr. articles, poems to profl. jours. Coach Warwick (R.I.) Firefighters Soccer Club, 1990, 94; fundraiser Friends of H.P. Lovecraft, Brown U., Providence, 1990. Mem. MLA, Nat. Soc. Fund Raising Execs., Horror Writers Am., N.E. Tchrs. English, Internat. Assn. for the Fantastic in the Arts, Small Press Writers and Artists Orgn. (Gene Day award 1982), Island Fencing Club. Avocations: science fiction, baseball, fishing, fencing. Home: 1467 Warwick Ave Apt 20 Warwick RI 02888 Office: Johnson & Wales U 8 Abbott Park Pl Providence RI 02903-3775

ANDERSON, JAMES DONALD, mining company executive; b. Toledo, Oct. 31, 1935; s. Donald James and Erma Elizabeth (Dorfmeyer) A.; m. Norma Elvira Powers, Aug. 30, 1958; children: Scott David, Sharon Grace, Steven William. BS in Chemistry, Capital U., 1957; MS in Chemistry, Ohio U., 1957; MBA, St. Louis U., 1968; student, Stanford Exec. Program, 1979. Rsch. chemist rsch. and engring div. Monsanto, Dayton, Ohio, 1959-61; sr. rsch. chemist rsch. and devel. dept. Monsanto, St. Louis, 1961-68; asst. purchasing agt. Wm. G. Krummrich Plant Monsanto, Sauget, Ill., 1968; purchasing agt. Chemstrand Triangle Park Devel. Ctr. Monsanto, Durham, N.C., 1968-72; from raw materials mgr. to dir. corp. purchasing Monsanto, St. Louis, 1972-86; dir. purchasing and distbn. svcs. Monsanto Chem. Co., St. Louis, 1986-93; purchsing cons. J.D. Anderson and Assocs., Ballwin, Mo., 1993-94, 99—; dir. materials mgmt. Peabody Group, Mo., 1995-98. Patentee in field; contbr. chpts. to books and articles to profl. jours. Bd. dirs. Jr. Achievement, St. Louis, 1982—. Mem. AAIM Mgmt. Assn. (purchasing exec. roundtable 1986—), Nat. Assn. Purchasing Mgmt., Nat. Petroleum Refiners Assn. (bd. dirs. 1980—, Petrochem. com. chmn. 1988-89), Am. Chem. Soc., Soc. Chem. Industry. Phone/fax: 314-394-1305; e-mail: andersjd@swbell.net. Office: J D Anderson & Assocs 329 Hill Trl Ballwin MO 63011-2654

ANDERSON, JAMES DONALD, state official; b. Des Moines, Aug. 3, 1941; s. James Donald and Mildred L. (Smith) A.; m. Sharon Lee Pollitt, Aug. 18, 1962; children: James Denver, Jon Eric. BA, Drake U., 1976, MPA, 1979. Home office underwriter Ctrl. Life Assurance, Des Moines, 1963-69; ops. officer Valley Nat. Bank, Des Moines, 1969-76; fiscal and polity analyst Iowa Comptr.'s Office, Des Moines, 1976-86; divsn. adminstr. Iowa Dept. Mgmt., Des Moines, 1986—. Recipient Adult Scouters Key, Mid-Iowa coun. Boy Scouts Am., 1976; named hon. state trooper Iowa Hwy. Patrol, 1991. Mem. ASPA, Assn. Govt. Accts. (cert. govt. fin. mgr., pres. 1980), Nat. Geneal. Soc., Iowa Geneal. Soc., Meml. Hall Found., Pi Alpha Alpha. Avocations: Civil War research, genealogy. Home: 4011 Beaver Ave Des Moines IA 50310

ANDERSON, JAMES FRANCIS, lawyer; b. Glen Ridge, N.J., June 13, 1965. BA, Seton Hall U., 1987, JD, 1990. Bar: N.J. 1991, U.S. Supreme Ct. 1995. Pvt. practice Spring Lake, N.J., 1991—. Pro bono atty. Ocean-Monmouth Legal Svcs., Freehold, N.J., 1991—; mentor Manasquan (N.J.) H.S., 1994. Mem. ABA, Masons. Office: PO Box 144 Spring Lake NJ 07762-0144

ANDERSON, JAMES FREDERICK, clergyman; b. Elizabeth, N.J., Aug. 23, 1927; s. Fred and Hazel Minerva (Brown) A.; m. Bette Dillensnyder, Sept. 8, 1951; children: Judith (Mrs. Wayne Westbury) (dec.), James Frederick, Mark, Rebecca (Mrs. Patrick Williams). BA, Princeton U., 1948; BD, Princeton Theol. Sem., 1952; DD, Alma Coll., 1974. Ordained to ministry Presbyn. Ch., 1952; chaplain Hun Sch. for Boys, Princeton, 1953; instr. religion Lafayette Coll., Easton, Pa., 1954-55; pastor Presbyn. chs., Catasauqua, Pa., 1956-61, Narberth, Pa., 1961-66; pastor Second Presbyn. Ch., Richmond, Va., 1966-72; pastor Kirk in the Hills, Bloomfield Hills, Mich., 1972-94, pastor emeritus, 1994—; trustee emeritus Alma (Mich.) Coll. With USNR, 1945-46. Home: 12 Surf Ave Ocean Grove NJ 07756-1629

ANDERSON, JAMES GEORGE, sociologist, educator; b. Balt., July 24, 1936; s. Clair Sherrill and Kathryn Ann (Plovanich) A.; m. Marilyn Anderson, 1984; children: Robin Marie, James Brian, Melissa Lee, Derek Clair. B in Engring. Scis. in Chem. Engring, Johns Hopkins U., 1957, MSE in Ops. Rsch. and Indsl. Engring., 1959, MAT in Chemistry and Math., 1960, PhD in Edn. and Sociology, 1964. Adminstrv. asst. to dean Eve. Coll., Johns Hopkins U., 1964-65, dir. divsn. engring., 1965-66; rsch. prof. ednl. adminstrn. N.Mex. State U., 1966-70; mem. faculty Purdue U., 1970—, prof. sociology, 1974—; asst. dean for analytical studies Sch. Humanities, Social Sci. and Edn., 1975-78; assoc. dir. AIDS Rsch. Ctr., Purdue U., 1991—, co-dir. Rural Ctr. for AIDS/STD Prevention, 1993—; adj. prof. med. sociology grad. med. edn. program Meth. Hosp. Ind., 1991—; dir. Social Rsch. Inst., Purdue U., 1995-98; cons. in field. Author: Bureaucracy in Education, 1968; co-author: Use and Impact of Computers in Clinical Medicine, 1987, Simulation in Emergency Management and Engineering and Simulation in Health Care, 1991, Simulation in Health Care and Social Services, 1992, Simulation in the Health Sciences and Services, 1993, Simulation in the Health Sciences, 1994, Evaluating Health Care Information Systems: Methods and Applications, 1994, Health Sciences Physiological and Pharmacological Simulation Studies, 1995, Simulation in the Medical Sciences, 1996, Simulation in the Medical Sciences, 1997, Medical Scis. simulation Conf. Preceedings, 1998; guest editor spl. issue on simulation in health sci., Simulation, Apr. 1996, spl. issue on modeling epidemics, 1998, Health Scis. Simulation, 1999; contbr. chpts. to books, articles to profl. jours. Mem. Am. Assn. for Med. Systems and Informatics Del. to the Peoples Republic of China, 1985; mem., citizens amb. People to People Med. Informatics Del. to Hungary and Russia, 1993. USPHS grantee; recipient award for outstanding paper Am. Assn. Med. Sys. and Informatics, 1983, Gov.'s award for Outstanding Contbns. to State of Ind., 1987, T. Hale New Investigators award Assn. Am. Med. Colls., 1988, Wyeth-Ayerst/William Campbell Felch, M.D. award Alliance for Continuing Med. Edn., 1995, Am. Medal Info. Assn. Best Theoretical Paper award, 1997. Mem. AAUP, AAAS (rep. soc. for computer simulation biol. scis. sect. 1992—), Assn. for Computing Machinery, Am. Sociol. Assn., Am. Pub. Health Assn., Am. Ednl. Rsch. Assn. (treas. spl. interest group 1969-71), Am. Med. Informatics Assn. (internat. affairs com. 1993-96, sec. ethical, legal and social issues chair, 1997—, sci. program com. ann. conf. 1999), Soc. Computer Simulation (assoc. v.p. simulation in health care 1992—), Internat. Network for Social Network Analysis (chair life scis. 1997—), Internat. Soc. System Sci. in Health Care, Internat. Sociol. Assn., Social Sci. Computing Assn. (publ. com. 1991—). Office: Purdue U 1365 Winthrop St West Lafayette IN 47905

ANDERSON, JAMES GILBERT, chemistry educator. BS, physics, U Washington, Seattle, 1966; Ph.D., physics, astrogeophysics, U Colorado, Boulder, 1970. Prof. Harvard U., Cambridge, Mass., 1978—; now Philip S. Weld prof. atmospheric chemistry Harvard U., chmn. dept. chemistry and chem. biology. Recipient Am. Chem. Soc. award, 1989, Gustavus John Esselen award, 1993, Earth Day Internat. award UN, 1992, Arts and Scis. Disting. Alumnus Achievement award U. Wash., 1993, E.O. Lawrence award in environ. sci. and tech., 1993. Fellow Am. Geophysical Union, Am. Assn. for the Advancement of Sci., Am. Acad. of Arts and Sci.; mem. NAS (Arthur Lay prize and lectureship 1996). Achievements include research in stratospheric physics and chemistry central to the understanding of atmospheric ozone and the ozone hole above the Antarctic. Office: Harvard U Dept of Chem & Chem Biology 12 Oxford St Cambridge MA 02138-2902

ANDERSON, JAMES KEITH, retired magazine editor; b. Grand Junction, Colo., June 27, 1924; s. Arnold Plumer and Helen Catherine (Enright) A.; m. Doris Mae Johnson, Aug. 5, 1952; children: Catherine E., Charles E., William H. II. A.B., U. Mich., 1949. Reporter Jefferson City News and Tribune, Mo., 1949, Tampa Daily Times, Fla., 1949-51; editor Detroit Labor News, 1951-53; reporter Detroit News, 1953-68; editor VFW mag., Kansas City, Mo., 1968-89, West Mo. Spirit (Episcopal Diocese of West Mo.), 1989-91; ret., 1991; mem. adv. bd. Diocesan Sch. for Ministry. Served with USMCR, 1942-43, inf. AUS, 1943-45. Decorated Bronze Star, Purple Heart, Combat Inf. badge, Gold Cross of Merit Polish Govt. in Exile, Royal Yugoslav Commemorative War Cross, Latvian Pro Merito; recipient numerous awards for ethnic coverage. Mem. VFW, SAR, DAV, Ancient and Honorable Artillery Co. of Mass., Sons and Daus. 1st Settlers Newbury, Mass., Sigma Delta Chi, Sigma Tau Gamma. Home: 621 W 63rd St Kansas City MO 64113-1525

ANDERSON, JAMES LINWOOD, pharmaceutical sales official; b. Bangor, Maine, June 8, 1949; s. Linwood Lamont and Helena May (Armitage) A.; m. Susan Grace Hughey, Aug. 23, 1974 (div. Aug. 1994). BS in Biology and Premedicine, U. Maine, 1971, MS in Physiology, 1972. Narcotics officer Maine State Police/Drug Enforcement Agy., 1973-74; sales rep. Wallace Labs., 1974-76, Hoechst-Roussell, Somerville, N.J., 1976-84; pharm. sales rep. I Miles (Bayer) Pharms., New Haven, 1984-90, ter. sales specialist, 1990-91, hosp. sales specialist, 1991-93, pharm. sales rep. II, 1994—. Coord. pastoral affairs Calvary Bapt. Ch., Manchester, N.H., 1976-80. Mem. USCG Aux. (glotilla comdr. New Bedford, Mass. 1992-94, divsn. capt. S.E. Mass. 1994-96, rear commodore Mass. and R.I. 1996-97, vice commodore for Maine, N.H., Mass., R.I. and part of Vt. 1998-99), Order of DeMolay (master councilor 1965-66, state master councilor 1966-67, chevalier 1967—). Avocations: boating, gun collecting, color guard drill team. Home: 205 Stevenson St New Bedford MA 02745-3516

ANDERSON, JAMES MILTON, lawyer; b. Chgo., Dec. 29, 1941; s. Milton H. and Eunice (Carlson) A.; BA, Yale U., 1963; JD, Vanderbilt U., 1966; m. Marjorie Henry Caldwell, Jan. 22, 1966; children: James Milton Jr., Joseph H., Hilding F., Marjorie II. Bar: Ohio 1967; assoc. law firm Taft, Stettinius & Hollister, Cin., 1968-75, ptnr., 1975-77, 82-96, mem. exec. com., 1975-77, 91-96; pres. U.S. ops., dir. Xomox Corp., Cin., 1977-81; sec. Access Corp., 1984-96, dir., 1997—; asst. sec. Carlisle Cos., 1985-90; dir. Cin. Stock Exchange, 1978—, chmn. 1980-89; pres., CEO Children's Hosp. Med. Ctr., 1996—; bd. dirs. Am. Druggists Ins. Co, 1978-82, River City Ins. Ltd., 1991-95, Zollner Corp., 1988-91, Command System Inc., 1988—, Creative Waterworks, Inc., 1984-91, trustee, chmn. Monarch Found., 1988—. Mem. Indian Hill Coun., 1981-89, vice-mayor, 1985-87, mayor, 1987-89; mem. Hamilton County Airport Authority, 1980-85; trustee Children's Hosp. Med. Ctr., 1977—, chmn. bd. trustees, 1992-96, pres., CEO, 1996—; trustee The Children's Hosp. Found., 1990—, chmn. bd. trustees, 1990-93; trustee Cin. Ctr. for Devel. Disorders, 1969—, pres., 1974-80; trustee Dan Beard coun. Boy Scouts Am., 1982—, chmn., 1984-87, area pres. Ea. Cen. Region, 1989-91; trustee Cin. Mus. Natural History, 1984-87, Coll. of Mt. St. Joseph, 1990—, Joy Outdoor Edn. Ctr., 1984—, pres., 1991-93, chmn. 1993-95. Capt. AUS, 1966-68. Decorated Bronze Star with two oak leaf clusters; Air medal. Mem. ABA, Ohio Bar Assn., Cin. Bar Assn., Valve Mfrs. Assn., Young Presidents Orgn., Camargo Club, Queen City Club, Commonwealth Club, Yale Club of N.Y., Cin. Yale Club, Order of Coif. Avocation: sailing. Office: 1800 Star Bank Ctr 3333 Burnet Ave Cincinnati OH 45229-3039

ANDERSON, JAMES NOEL (JIM ANDERSON), recording engineer, producer; b. Butler, Pa., Dec. 23, 1951; s. Carl and Mary A.; children: Noel Chase, Graham Stuart. BS in Music Edn., Duquesne U., 1973, postgrad., 1973-74; postgrad., Eastman Sch. Music, 1976; postgrad. studies in Audio Engring., Sender Freis Berlin, 1978. Cert. elem. and secondary music edn. Audio engr. Sta. WDUQ-FM, Pitts., 1973-74, Nat. Pub. Radio, Washington, 1974-80; pres. James Anderson Audio, N.Y.C., 1980—; audio prodr. Jim Henson Prodns., 1987—; cons. Am. Pub. Radio, St. Paul, Minn. Pub. Radio, St. Paul, Carnegie Hall, N.Y.C. Co-producer (radio documentary) Segovia! (with Andres Segovia), 1983; rec. engr. (TV program) Segovia at the White House, 1980 (Emmy nomination 1981); (radio series) Taylor Made Piano/Billy Taylor, 1981 (Peabody award 1982), Riverwalk--LIve from the Landing, 1990 (CPB Silver Baton 1991); (album) Pepper Adams Live at Fat Tues., 1983 (Grammy nomination 1984), (album) James Moody Sweet & Lovely, 1989 (Grammy nomination 1990), (album) McCoy Tyner Big Band Uptown/Downtown, 1989 (Grammy nomination 1990), Phil Woods Quintet All Bird's Children (Grammy nomination 1992); (radio documentary) Sea Island Sketches; audio prodr. (TV) In Performance at the White House, 1992—, (album) Heard You Twice the First Time (Grammy Winner 1993), (album) Taylormade (Grammy Nominee 1993), (album) Desert Lady (Grammy Nominee 1994), (album) So Near, So Far (Double Grammy Winner 1994), (TV) Carnegie Hall Salutes the Jazz Masters (Emmy Nominee 1995), (album) Joe Henderson Big Band (Grammy award 1998), Jim Henson Prodns. (Muppets), 1987—. Recipient Peabody award U. Ga., N.Y.C., 1977, Gold Cindy award (radio documentary) Stock Car Racing, Info. Film Producers Am. N.Y.C., 1980, 1st pl. award Internat. Radio Festival, N.Y.C., 1982, Prix Futura award European Broadcasting Union, Berlin, 1986, Swing Jour. Best Sound and Best Album award Somethin' Else Records, Japan (V. Ralph Peterson Quintet), 1989, Silver Baton award Corp. for Pub. Broadcasting, 1991. Mem. audio Engring. Soc., Audio Inds. in Radio, Nat. Acad. Rec. Arts and Scis. Democrat. Lutheran. Avocations: tennis, steeplechasing, traveling, photography, world history. Home and Office: 12 Garfield Pl Brooklyn NY 11215

ANDERSON, JAMES RAYMOND, academic administrator; b. Pitts., Aug. 14, 1937; s. Arthur M. and Mildred N. (Nelson) A.; m. Lois Ann Constable, Aug. 14, 1937; children: Starr Beauchamp, Vicki Davidson. BA in Mgmt., Mich. State U., 1966; MS in Mgmt., Fla. State U., 1969, PhD in Econs., 1978. Enlisted USAF, 1955, advanced through grades to col.; exec. officer U.S. Logistics Group, Ankara, Turkey, 1969-71, 16th Air Force, Torrejon AB, Spain, 1971-73; assoc. prof. USAF Acad., Colorado Springs, Colo., 1973-75, 78-79; prof. econs. Air U., Maxwell AFB, Ala., 1979-83; comptroller Tactical Fighter Wing, Clark AB, Philippines, 1983-85; chief cost programs Hdqrs. USAF, 1985-87; ret.; chief cost programs Hdqrs. USAF Pentagon, Washington, 1985-87; dep. chancellor for coll. program Ctr. Tex. Coll., Killeen, Tex., 1987-88, chancellor, 1988—. Mem. Am. Econ. Assn., So. Econ. Assn., Am. Soc. Mil. Comptrollers, Ala. Stae U.'s Dean Adv. Coun., Killeen C. of C. (bd. dirs. 1989), Beta Gamma Sigma. Home: 5825 Greenforest Cir Killeen TX 76543-5552 Office: Cen Tex Coll Hwy 190 W PO Box 1800 Killeen TX 76540-1800*

ANDERSON, JAMES V., state agency administrator. BA in Journalism, U. Miss. Media reporter Memphis Bus. Jour., 1987-88; Southern press sec. Dukakis-Bentsen Com., 1988; staff writer Def. News, Washington, 1989; mil. legis. asst. U.S. Rep. Beverly Byron, Washington, 1989-90; prof. staff, exec. dir. Chesapeake Bay caucus Merchant Marine and Fisheries Com., Washington, 1990-91; dir. agriculture Miss. Dept. of Corrections, 1992-96; supt. Miss. State Penitentiary, Parchman, 1996-97; commr. of corrections Dept. Corrections State of Miss., Jackson, 1997—. Office: State of Miss Dept Corrections 723 North President Jackson MS 39202

ANDERSON, JAMES WINGO, physician; b. Hinton, W.Va., Aug. 6, 1936; s. Fred Wingo and Georgia Lee (Whittaker) A.; m. Gay Veree Gilbert, June 7, 1957; children: Katherine, Steven. BS, W.Va. U., 1957; MD, Northwestern U., 1961; MS, Mayo Clinic, 1965. Intern Presbyn. Med. Ctr., Denver; resident, fellow Mayo Clinic, Rochester, Minn.; asst. prof. medicine U. Calif., San Francisco, 1968-73; prof. medicine, chief clin. nutrition U. Ky. Coll. Medicine, Lexington, 1973-96; pres., founder HCF Nutrition Found., Lexington, 1979—. Author: Diabetes-A Practical Guide to HEalty Living, 1981, Dr.

Anderson's High Fiber Fitness Plan, 1994, Dr. Anderson;s Antioxident Antiaging, 1996. Trustee Georgetown (Ky.) Coll., 1988-96, chmn. bd. trustees, 1994-96. Capt. U.S. Army, 1965-68. Fellow Am. Coll. Physicians. Republican. Baptist. Home: 913 Taborlake Ct Lexington KY 40502-3032 Office: VA Med Ctr 2250 Leestown Rd Lexington KY 40511-1052

ANDERSON, JANE ELLSWORTH, secondary school educator; b. Chillicothe, Ohio, Mar. 30, 1943; d. Henry Branch and Beatrice Clara (Trainer) Ellsworth: m. George Leonard Anderson, Jr., Sept. 9, 1964; children: Doug, Jeff, Michele. BS in Edn., Ohio State U., 1983, MS in Edn., 1994. Cert. tchr. grades 7-12, Ohio. Long distance operator Ohio Bell Telephone Co., Dayton, 1962-64; real estate agt. Donna Vaughn Realtors, Dayton, 1965-67; sales rep., mgr. Tupperware Dayton Party Sales, 1972-74; tchr. Westerville (Ohio) City Schs., 1984—; advisor Westerville H.S. Yearbook, Golden Warrior, 1986 (1st pl. award), 1987 (1st pl. award). Sec., pres. etc. Englewood Hills Elem. Sch. PTA, Englewood, Ohio, 1971-76; youth dir. Unity Ch., Columbus, Ohio, 1978-80; phone counselor Bridge Counseling Ctr., Columbus, 1980-81; mem. Dem. Congl. Campaign Com. Mem. NEA, Ohio Edn. Assn., Westerville Edn. Assn., U.S. Holocaust Meml. Mus., So. Poverty Law Ctr., Emily's List. Avocations: writing, reading, biking. Office: Westerville City Schs 346 S Otterbein Ave Westerville OH 43081-2619

ANDERSON, JANICE LEE ATOR, secondary education mathematics educator; b. LaSalle, Ill., Aug. 8, 1948; d. Glen Bertran and Josephine Mary (Urichko) Ator; m. Gene Vernon Hook, July 20, 1968 (dec. 1974); m. Robert John Anderson, May 11, 1979 (div. 1983); 1 child, Karen Lynn. AA, Ill. Valley Community Coll., 1968; BS in Edn., Minot State Coll., 1970; MS in Edn., Ill. State U., 1997. Cert. tchr., Ill. Tchr. reading Tonica (Ill.) Elem. Sch., 1970-71; tchr. math., sci. Tonica Jr. High Sch., 1971-80, Tonica High Sch., 1980; tchr. math. Bradley (Ill.)-Bourbonnais Community High Sch., 1983—; coach math. team Bradley-Bourbonnais Community High Sch., 1983—. Mem. NEA, Ill. Edn. Assn., Bradley-Bourbonnais Edn. Assn. (sec. 1990-93, treas. 1993—), Women of Moose. Democrat. Roman Catholic. Avocations: coin collecting, stamp collecting, reading, tennis. Home: 904 Roosevelt Rd La Salle IL 61301-1405 Office: Bradley Bourbonnais Community High Sch 700 W North St Bradley IL 60915-1013

ANDERSON, JEFFREY LEE, physician, anesthesiologist, consultant; b. Fontana, Calif., Feb. 3, 1959; s. Earle R. and Joyce E. Anderson; m. Crystal G. Anderson, Dec. 18, 1987; children: Kimberly, Kristin. BS, USAF Acad., 1981; MD, Loma Linda U., 1985. Cert. in anesthesiology. Resident in anesthesiology Loma Linda (Calif.) U. Med. Ctr., 1985-89; chief anesthesiologist USAF Hosp., Mather AFB, Calif., 1989-93; staff anesthesiologist Mercy Hosp. of Folsom, Calif., 1990—, Mercy Gen. Hosp., Sacramento, 1992—, Mercy San Juan Hosp., Carmichael, Calif., 1997—; medicolegal cons. Med. Bd. Calif., Sacramento, 1995—; clin. faculty U. Calif. Davis Sch. Medicine, 1993-96; anesthesia cons. Blue Shield of Calif., 1998—. Co-author: (textbook) Manual of Postanesthesia Care, 1993. Instr., course dir. ACLS, Am. Heart Assn., Sacramento, 1992—; physician Mercy White Rock Free Clin., 1994—. Mem. AMA, Internat. Anesthesia Rsch. Soc., Am. Soc. Anesthesiologists, Calif. Soc. Anesthesiologists, C. of C. Office: 1650 Creekside Dr Folsom CA 95630-3400

ANDERSON, JEFFREY LYNN, stone company executive; b. Rochester, Minn., Dec. 3, 1955; s. Rolland Mayo and Lenora A. (Damann) A.; m. Renee Elizabeth Stanley, Apr. 22, 1977; children: Cimarron, Chelsea, William. Student, Brigham Young U., 1976-80, BS in Indsl. Edn., 1989; AA in Bus. Adminstrn., Rochester C.C., 1978; postgrad., Winona State U., 1980-86. With Rochester Granite Co., 1985-90, owner, 1990—, gen. mgr., 1985—; bus. teller, bookkeeper Marquette Bank, Rochester, 1974-76; mgr., owner Anderson Memls., Austin, Minn., 1979—; owner Rochester Granite Co., 1990—, Cemetery Meml. Sales & Svcs., Owatonna, Minn., 1991—; pres. Anderson Memls. Inc., Austin, 1993—; trustee Monument Industry Edn. Found., 1987—; owner Anderson's Rochester Crematory, 1994—, Bloedel Monument Co., New Ulm, Minn., 1996—, Fairmont Monument Co., 1997—; monument industry rep. Funeral Meml. Info. Coun., 1997—, pres. 1998. Designer, carver meml. art. Bishop LDS Ch. Mem. N.W. Monument Builders Assn. (pres. 1985-89), Monument Builders N.Am. (cert., v.p. 1990-92, pres. 1994, com. chmn. 1984-88, Archie L. Green award 1986, Grand prize expert divsn. 1987, Aspire award 1996, 98), Am. Inst. Commemorative Arts (bd. govs. 1996-98), Exch. Club. Republican. Avocations: woodworking, skiing, hunting, fishing. Home: 306 S Main St Austin MN 55912-4433 Office: Anderson Memls 106 4th St SW Austin MN 55912-3118 also: Rochester Granite Co 2843 S Broadway Rochester MN 55904-5517

ANDERSON, JERRY ALLEN, financial analyst; b. Ashland, Wis., Feb. 10, 1947; s. Elmer and Thelma Louise (Fallis) A.; m. Anne Marie Brown, June 7, 1975; 1 child, Kristen Marie. BBA, Temple U., 1969, MBA, 1975. Sr. investment officer Girard Bank, Phila., 1970-80; sr. investment analyst Sanford C. Bernstein, N.Y.C., 1980-83; dir. planning Sperry New Holland (Pa.), Inc., 1983-85, mgr. ops. analysis, 1985-87; fin. mgr. spl. markets Ford New Holland (Pa.), Inc., 1987-91; Mex. market mgr. Ford New Holland (Pa.) Inc., 1991-94; cons., 1994-96; v.p. investment rsch. Janney Montgomery Scott, 1996—; cons. in fin.; instr. sch. bus. Temple U., 1976-79, sch. bus. and govt. svcs., 1979-80. Recipient Cert. of Recognition Am. Mktg. Assn., 1968, 69, Outstanding Performance award Ford New Holland, 1987. Mem. Assn. for Investment Mgmt. and Rsch., Fin. Analysts of Phila., N.Y. Soc. Security Analysts, Model A Ford Club Am., Beta Gamma Sigma, Theta Chi. Avocations: Model A restoration, numismatics, fishing, scuba diving, hunting. Home: 544 Norwyck Dr Kng Of Prussa PA 19406-1583 Office: Janney Montgomery Scott Inc 1801 Market St Fl 9 Philadelphia PA 19103-1675

ANDERSON, JERRY MAYNARD, speech educator; b. Deronda, Wis., Sept. 16, 1933; s. Jens B. and Mamie P. (Hanson) A.; m. Betty Lou Schultz, Feb. 7, 1959; children: Gregory J., Timothy B. B.S., Wis. State U. at River Falls, 1958; M.S., No. Ill. U., 1959; Ph.D., Mich. State U., 1964. Instr. speech U. Maine, 1959-61; asst. prof. speech, dir. forensics Mich. State U., 1961-68; prof., chmn. dept. speech and dramatic arts Central Mich. U., Mt. Pleasant, 1968-72; vice provost Central Mich. U., 1972-73; v.p. acad. affairs Western Wash. U., 1973-75; vice chancellor, prof. speech U. Wis., Oshkosh, 1975-79; pres., prof. speech Ball State U., Muncie, Ind., 1979-81; sr. cons. Am. Assn. State Colls. and Univs., Washington, 1981-82; research adminstr. U. Wis., Stout, Menomonie, 1982-85; v.p. devel. Concordia Coll., Minn., 1985-88; prof. speech communication Concordia Coll., 1988-99. Author: Readings in Argumentation, 1968; also articles. Served with USN, 1952-54. Recipient 1st Sr. Disting. Professionalism award Central Mich. U., 1971; Research fellow Harry S Truman Found., 1965; fellow Am. Council on Edn. Acad. Adminstrn. Internship Program, 1971-72; Recipient Disting. Alumnus award Delta Sigma Rho-Tau Kappa Alpha, 1980; Sagamore of Wabash Public Service award Gov. of Ind., 1980. Mem. Ctrl. States Speech Assn. (pres. 1973, Outstanding Young Tchr. award 1966), Mich. Speech Assn. (pres. 1967-68), Am. Forensic Assn. (pres. 1972-74, Disting. Svc. award 1994), Midwest Forensic Assn. (pres. 1969-72), Speech Comm. Assn. (legis. coun. 1967, legis. assembly 1975), Kiwanis. Office: Speech Comm Concordia Coll Moorhead MN 56560 *During my adult years the aphorism attributed to the late Senator Robert M. laFollette, Sr., has guided my work with others: "Give the people the facts and freedom to discuss and all will go well."*

ANDERSON, JERRY WILLIAM, JR., technical and business consulting executive, educator; b. Stow, Mass., Jan. 14, 1926; s. Jerry William and Heda Charlotte (Petersen) A. ; m. Joan Hukill Balyeat, Sept. 13, 1947; children: Katheleen, Diane. BS in Physics, U. Cin., 1949, PhD in Econs., 1976; MBA, Xavier U., 1959. Rsch. and test project engr. Wright-Patterson AFB, Ohio, 1949-53; project engr., electronics div. AVCO Corp., Cin., 1953-70, program mgr., 1970-73; program dir. Cin. Electronics Corp., 1973-78; pres. Anderson Industries Unltd., 1978—; chmn. dept. mgmt. and mgmt. info. svcs. Xavier U., 1980-89, prof. mgmt., 1989-94, prof. emeritus, 1994—; lectr. No. Ky. U., 1977-78; tech. adviser Cin. Tech. Coll., 1971-80; co-founder, exec. v.p. Loving God "Complete Bible" Christian Ministries, 1988—. Contbr. articles on radar, lasers, infrared detection equipment, air pollution to govt. publs. and profl. jours.; author 3 books in field. Mem. Madeira (Ohio) City Planning Commn., 1962-80; founder, pres. Grassroots, Inc., 1964; active United Appeal, Heart Fund, Multiple Sclerosis Fund. With USNR, 1943-46. Named Man of Year, City of Madeira, 1964. Mem. MADD, Am. Mgmt. Assn., Assn. Energy Engrs. (charter), Internat. Acad. Mgmt. and Mktg., Nat. Right to Life, Assn. Cogeneration Engrs. (charter), Assn. Environ. Engrs. (charter), Am. Legion (past comdr.), Acad. Mgmt., Madeira Civic Assn. (past v.p.), Cin. Art Mus., Cin. Zoo, Colonial Williamsburg Found., Omicron Delta Epsilon. Republican. Home and Office: 7208 Sycamorehill Ln Cincinnati OH 45243-2101

ANDERSON, JIM, zoo director; b. Ft. Wayne, Ind., Jan. 8, 1957. BS, Purdue U., 1979; MS, Ind. U., 1992. Dir. Ft. Wayne (Ind.) Children's Zoo, 1994—. Office: Ft Wayne Childrens Zoo 3411 Sherman Blvd Fort Wayne IN 46808-1522*

ANDERSON, JOAN BALYEAT, religion educator, minister; b. Cin., Apr. 14, 1926; d. Hal Donal and Myrtle (Skinner) Hukill Balyeat; m. Jerry William Anderson, Jr., Sept. 13, 1947: children: Katheleen, Diane. AA, Stephens Coll., 1946. Ordained Christian minister, Ohio, 1988. Christian ch. bible tchr. Cin., 1944—, Christian counselor, advisor, 1964—; founder, pres., dir., ruling elder, and pastor Loving God "Complete Bible" Christian Ministries and First Ch., Cin., 1988—; daily and Sunday radio pastor, bible tchr. and preacher throughout east and midwest, 1988—. Coord., collector Heart Fund, T.B., 1948-90; civic assn. officer, rep. edn. com. to all Madeira Schs., 1960-62; co-founder, officer Grassroots, Inc., Cin., 1962-65; mem. U.S. Rep. Senatorial Adv. Com., Washington and Cin., 1987-88; mem. Rep. Senatorial Commn., Washington and Cin., 1996—; mem. Cin. Art Mus., 1972—, Cin. Zoo, 1974—, Colonial Williamsburg Found., 1979—, Nat. Right to Life, 1980—, MADD, 1985—, Heritage Found., 1996—, Am. Farmland Trust, 1998—, Am. Conservative Union, 1998—; lifelong activist for preservation of U.S. Constitution and Bill of Rights. Mem. Blue Book of Cin. Avocations: touring America by car. Home: 7208 Sycamorehill Ln Cincinnati OH 45243-2101 Office: Loving God Complete Bible Christian Ministries PO Box 43404 Cincinnati OH 45243-0404

ANDERSON, JOEL E., JR., university administrator; b. Newport, Ark., Jan. 20, 1942; s. Joel E. Sr. and Norris Hall Anderson; m. Ann Gaskill, Aug. 7, 1964; children: Lincoln Jay, Deverick John, Mitchell Reid. BA, Harding Coll., 1964; MA, Am. U., 1966; PhD, U. Mich., 1974. Instr. polit. sci. Harding Coll., 1966-67; from asst. to assoc. prof. U. Ark., Little Rock, 1971-81, prof., 1981—, dean grad. sch., 1977-84, vice chancellor, provost, 1984—, interim chancellor, 1993; pres. univ. assembly U. Ark., 1974-76; mem. vis. com. coll. bus. Abilene Christian U., 1994-97, chair, 1997; cons.-evaluator commn. instns. higher edn. North Ctrl. Assn. Colls. and Schs., 1994—; study dir. Plain Talk: The Future of Little Rock's Public Schools, 1997. Editor Ark. Polit. Sci. Rev., 1979-82. Charter mem. bd. trustees Kidney Found. Ark., 1975-79; mem. Pulaski County Bd. of Election Commrs., 1976-79; mem. bd. overseers Sta. KLRE-KUAR-FM, 1986-90; bd. dirs. Ark. 4-H Found., 1997—, Ark. Sci. and Tech. Authority, 1998—. Mem. Am. Assn. State Colls. and Univs. (mem. acad. affairs resource ctr. adv. com. 1994-98), Ark. Polit. Sci. Assn. (pres. 1975), Rotary, Alpha Chi, Phi Kappa Phi. Mem. Ch. of Christ. Office: U Ark Office of the Provost 2801 S University Ave Little Rock AR 72204-1099

ANDERSON, JOHN ALBERT, physician; b. Ashtabula, Ohio, Jan. 25, 1935; s. Albert Gunnard Anderson and Martha Anetta (Bieshline) White; m. Nicole Jeanne Anderson, July 10, 1963; children: Carole Beno, John-Marc, Christopher B. BS, U. Ill., 1958, MD, 1960. Diplomate Am. Bd. Pediat., Am. Bd. Allergy and Immunology. Intern U. Ill., 1960-61; resident in pediat. U. Ill., Chgo., 1961-62, U.S. Naval Hosp., Bethesda, Md., 1964-65; fellow in allergy and immunology Children's Hosp., Washington, 1967-69; mem. sr. staff Henry Ford Hosp., Detroit, 1969—, dir. pediat. allergy fellowship program, 1969-77, dir. allergy and immunology program, 1977—, head divsn. allergy and immunology, dept. pediatrics, 1977—, chmn. dept. pediatrics, 1982-90; clin. prof. pediat., U. Mich., Ann Arbor, 1985-94; prof. pediat. Case Western Res. U., Cleve., 1994—; dir. Am. Bd. Allergy and Immunology, 1990-96, sec., 1995-96. Contbr. more than 50 articles to profl. jours. Lt. comdr. USN, 1962-66. Fellow Am. Acad. Allergy and Immunology (pres. 1990-91), Am. Acad. Pediat. (chmn. allergy sect. 1979-82), Mich. Allergy Soc. (pres. 1978-79); mem. Asthma and Allergy Found. Am. (dir. 1992—, v.p. med. affairs 1992-95, v.p. rsch. 1995—), Coun. Med. Specialty Soc. (bd. dirs. 1992-94), Am. Bd. Med. Specialists, Sci. Advisors Internat. Life Scis. (allergy sect. 1990—), ACGME-RRC for Allergy and Immunology. Home: 16543 Winchester Dr Northville MI 48167-2349 Office: Henry Ford Hosp 1 Ford Pl Detroit MI 48202-3450

ANDERSON, JOHN BAYARD, lawyer, educator, former congressman; b. Rockford, Ill., Feb. 15, 1922; s. E. Albin and Mabel Edna (Ring) A.; m. Keke Machakos, Jan. 4, 1953; children: Eleanora, John Bayard, Diane, Karen, Susan Kimberly. A.B., U. Ill., 1942, JD, 1946; LLM, Harvard U., 1949; hon. doctorates, No. Ill. U., Wheaton Coll., Shimer Coll., Biola Coll., Geneva Coll., North Park Coll. and Theol. Sem., Houghton Coll., Trinity Coll., Rockford Coll. Bar: Ill. 1946. Practice law Rockford, 1946-52; with U.S. Fgn. Service, 1952-55; assigned West Berlin, 1952-55; mem. 87th-95th Congresses from 16th Dist. Ill., mem. rules com.; chmn. Ho. Republican Conf., 1969-79; ind. candidate for Pres. U.S., 1980; vis. prof. Stanford U., spring, 1981, Nova-Southeastern U. Ctr. for Study Law, 1987-99; vis. prof. polit. sci. Brandeis U., 1985, Oreg. State U., spring 1986, U. Mass., 1985—; vis. prof. law Washington Coll. Law Am. U., 1997—; lectr. polit. sci. Bryn Mawr Coll., spring 1985. Author: Between Two Worlds: A Congressman's Choice, 1970, Vision and Betrayal in America, 1976, The American Economy We Need, 1984, A Proper Institution: Guaranteeing Televised Presidential Debates, 1988; editor: Congress and Conscience, 1970. Ind. candidate for Pres. U.S., 1980. Mem. World Federalist Assn. (pres. 1992—), Ctr. for Voting and Democracy (pres. 1996—, co-chair nat. adv. bd. pub. campaign for campaign fin. reform 1997—), Coun. on Fgn. Rels., Phi Beta Kappa. Mem. Evang. Free Ch. (past trustee). Office: 3917 Massachusetts Ave NW Washington DC 20016-5104

ANDERSON, JOHN DAVID, architect; b. New Haven, Dec. 24, 1926; s. William Edward and Norma Vere (Carson) A.; m. Florence A. Van Dyke, Aug. 26, 1950; children—Robert Stewart, David Carson. A.B. cum laude, Harvard U., 1949, M.Arch., 1952. Draftsman John K. Monroe, Architect, Denver, 1952-54; draftsman, designer, assoc. Wheeler & Lewis, Architects, Denver, 1954-60; prin. John D. Anderson, Denver, 1960-64; ptnr. Anderson, Barker Rinker, Architects, Denver, 1965-69, A-B-R Partnership, Architects, Denver, 1970-75; prin., CEO Anderson Mason Dale P.C., Denver, 1975-96, sr. v.p., 1997—; vis. lectr. U. Colo., U. N.Mex., U. Nebr., U. Cape Town, Colo. State U., Plymouth Polytech., Eng.; chmn. Denver Bldg. Dept. Bd. Appeals, 1974-75; chmn. Colo. Gov.'s Task Force on Removal of Archtl. Barriers, 1972-74; vice chmn. Colo. Bd. Non-Residential Energy Conservation Stds., 1978-80. Prin. works include: Community Coll. Denver, North campus, Westminster, 1977, Solar Energy Rsch. Inst., Golden, 1980 (award winning solar heated structures). Served with USNR, 1944-46. Fellow AIA (pres. Colo. chpt. 1967, Western Mountain region dir. 1995-97, nat. v.p. 1999, Silver medal, 1984, Firm of Yr. award 1986 Western Mountain region); mem. Colo. Soc. Archs. (Arch. of Yr. award 1987, pres. 1971), Internat. Solar Energy Soc., Council Ednl. Facility Planners (internat. chmn. energy com. 1980). Republican. Congregationalist. Home: 57 S Rainbow Trail Golden CO 80401-8341 Office: Anderson Mason Dale PC 1615 17th St Denver CO 80202-1293

ANDERSON, JOHN DAVID, JR., aerospace engineer; b. Lancaster, Pa., Oct. 1, 1937; s. John David and Esther Pearl (Stoneback) A.; m. Sarah Allen West, Sept. 11, 1960; children: Katherine Josephine, Elizabeth Esther. B.Aero. Engring. with honors (Gen. Motors scholar, J. Hillis Meml. scholar), U. Fla., 1959; Ph.D. in Aero. Engring., Ohio State U. Chief hypersonics group Naval Ordnance Lab., White Oak, Md., 1966-73; prof., chmn. dept. aerospace engring. U. Md., College Park, 1973-99; prof. emeritus U. Md., College Park, 1999—; Charles Lindbergh prof. Nat. Air Space Mus. Smithsonian Instn., 1986-87; curator for aerodynamics Nat. Air Space Mus., Smithsonian Instn., 1998—. Author: Gasdynamic Lasers: An Introduction, 1976, Introduction to Flight: Its Engineering and History, 1978, 3d edit., 1989, Modern Compressible Flow: with Historical Perspective, 1982, 2d edit., 1990, Fundamentals of Aerodynamics, 1984, 2d edit., 1991, Hypersonic and High Temperature Gasynamics, 1989, Computational Fluid Dynamics, 1995; History of Aerodynamics, and Its Impact on Flying Machines, 1997, Aircraft Performance and Design, 1999; contbr. articles to profl. jours. Served with USAF, 1959-62. Named disting. scholar/tchr. U. Md., 1981-82; NSF fellow, NASA fellow Ohio State U., 1966; recipient Meritorious Civilian Service award Naval Ordnance Lab., 1972. Fellow Washington Acad. Scis. (Engring. Sci. award 1975), AIAA, Royal Aeronaut. Soc.; mem. Am. Soc. Engring. Edn., Am. Phys. Soc., Sigma Xi, Tau Beta Pi, Sigma Tau, Phi Kappa Phi, Phi Eta Sigma. Roman Catholic. Office: U Md Dept Aerospace Engring College Park MD 20742 *A prescription for success in professional life involves a proper balance of hard work, long hours, awareness and clear thinking, with a goal-oriented philosophy and outright love of one's profession. In addition, one must have the desire, abilities and opportunities to accomplish his goals.*

ANDERSON, JOHN EDWARD, mechanical engineering educator; b. Chgo., May 15, 1927; s. Claus Oscar and Ruth Melvina (Engstrom) A.; m. Cynthia Louise Howard, May 24, 1975; children: Candice, James, Stanley. BME, Iowa State U., 1949; MSME, U. Minn., 1955; PhD, MIT, 1962. Registered profl. engr., Minn., Ill. Aero. research scientist Nat. Adv. Com. for Aeros., Langley Field, Va., 1949-51; devel. engr. Honeywell, Inc., Mpls., 1951-53; research engr. Honeywell, Inc., 1953-55, prin. research engr., 1955-58, research project engr., 1954-58, sr. staff engr., 1958-62, mgr. space systems, 1963; mem. faculty U. Minn., Mpls., 1963-86; prof. mech. engring. U. Minn., 1971-86, Boston U., 1986-94; cons. Colo. Regional Transp. Dist., 1974-75, Raytheon Co., 1975-76, Mannesmann Demag, 1978-79, Arthr D. Little, Inc., 1981, Indpls. Transit Commn., 1979-81, Davy McKee Corp., 1984-85; founder, pres., CEO Taxi 2000 Corp. (formerly ATS Inc.), 1983—. Author: Magnetohydrodynamic Shock Waves, Magnetogasdynamics of Thermal Plasma, Transit Systems Theory; editor: Personal Rapid Transit II. With USN, 1945-46. Recipient Outstanding Inventor in Am. award Intellectual Property Owners Found., 1989; Convair fellow. NAS, 1967-68. Mem. AAAS, ASME, Union Concerned Scientists, Mensa, World Federalists Assn., Sierra Club. Unitarian. Home: 5164 Ranier Pass NE Minneapolis MN 55421-1338

ANDERSON, JOHN ERLING, chemical engineer; b. Quincy, Mass., Mar. 12, 1929; s. Victor Emanuel and Elin Helen (Nelson) A.; m. Karin Henrietta Thornberg, Feb. 3, 1951; children: Mark David, Lynn Karin, Kristin Leslie, Claire Martha. BSCE, MIT, 1950, DSc in Chem. Engring., 1955; MSCE, Ill. Inst. Tech., 1951. Sr. corp. fellow Praxair, Inc., Tarrytown, N.Y., 1954—; lect. chem. engring. dept. MIT, 1977; mem. adv. com. Solar Energy Rsch. Inst., Golden, Colo., 1985-87; mem. combustion program work group DOE Office of Indusl. Programs, Wash., 1986-88. Contbr. articles to profl. jours.; patentee in field. Recipient Personal Merit award Chem. Engring. mag., 1974, Kirkpatrick Chem. Engring. award Chem. Engring. mag., 1989; named Inventor of Yr., N.Y. Patent Assn., 1989. Mem. NAE, Combustion Inst., Am. Inst. Chem. Engrs., Am. Chem. Soc. Democrat. Mem. Unitarian Ch. Avocations: hiking, reading. Home: 476E Heritage Hills Dr Somers NY 10589-1920 Office: Praxair Inc Tarrytown Tech Ctr 777 Old Saw Mill River Rd Tarrytown NY 10591-6717

ANDERSON, JOHN FIRTH, church administrator, librarian; b. Saginaw, Mich., Oct. 5, 1928; s. Harlan Firth and Irene Martha (Bowser) A.; m. Patricia Ann Goble, June 18, 1950 (dec. Oct. 1995); children: Douglas Firth, Elizabeth Ann; m. Barbara Peterson Smith, May 18, 1996. B.A., Mich. State U., 1949; M.S. in L.S, U. Ill., 1950. Young people's librarian Enoch Pratt Free Library, Balt., 1950-52; with Balt. County Pub. Library, 1952-58, supr. adult work, 1955- 56, asst. county librarian, 1956-58; dir. Knoxville (Tenn.) Pub. Library System, 1958-62, Tucson Pub. Library, 1962-68, 73-82; city librarian San Francisco Pub. library, 1968-73; exec. presbyter, stated clk. Presbytery of Santa Barbara (Calif.), 1982-91; ret., 1991; interim exec. presbyter Presbytery de Cristo, 1993, stated clk., 1993—; mem. Presbyn. Churchwide Adminstrv. Coordinating Cabinet, 1987-89; cons. on library bldgs., devel. and mgmt. Contbr. articles to profl. publs. Bd. dirs. Amigos Bibliographic Council, 1977-81, vice-chmn., 1977-79, sec., 1980-81; mem. Ariz. Library Adv. Council, 1975-81; charter mem. Freedom to Read Found.; bd. dirs. Ariz. Theatre Co., 1978-82. Recipient Disting. Citizen award U. Ariz., 1981. Mem. ALA (mem. at large coun. 1961-65, 66-70, bd. dirs. pub. libr. assn. 1961-65, bd. dirs. libr. administrn. div. 1964-65, chmn. libr. orgn. and mgmt. sect. 1964-65, pres. libr. adminstrn. div. 1968-69), Calif. Libr. Assn. (coun. 1970-71), Southwestern Libr. Assn. (pres. 1976-78), Ariz. Libr. Assn. (pres. pub. librs. div. 1964-65, pres. 1967-68, Libr. of Year 1968, Rosenzweig award 1981), Ariz. Assn. County Librs. (pres. 1979-80), Ariz. China Coun. (pres. 1979-80), World Alliance Reformed Chs. (mem. Caribbean and N.Am. Area Coun. 1991-93, recording clk. 1992-93), Beta Phi Mu. Presbyterian (elder).

ANDERSON, JOHN FREDERICK, science administrator, entomologist, researcher; b. Fargo, N.D., Feb. 25, 1936; s. Oscar Frederick and Eleanor Birdee (Fiskum) A.; m. Marilynn Joy Robinson, June 30, 1958; children: Linda, John Jr., Kristin. BS, N.D. State U., 1957, MS, 1959; PhD, U. Ill., 1963. NSF postdoctoral fellow Dept. Entomology U. Ill., Urbana, 1963-64; asst. entomologist Conn. Agrl. Expt. Sta., New Haven, 1964-66, assoc. entomologist, 1966-69, chief entomologist, 1969-87, dir., 1987—; mem. Conn. Tree Examining Bd., New Haven, 1969-79; dir., pres. Conn. Tree Protective Assn., New Haven, 1976-84. Author: (with others) Biology of Sex, 1967, Diseases Transmitted from Animals to Man, 6th edit., 1975, Perspectives in Forest Entomology, 1976, Ecology and Environmental Management of Lyme Disease, 1993; editor: Perspectives in Forest Entomology, 1976; contbr. articles to profl. jours. 1st lt. Med. Svc. Corp. U.S. Army, 1959. Recipient award of Merit Conn. Tree Protective Assn., 1976, Bronze medal Fed. Garden Clubs Conn., 1981, Author Citation award Internat. Soc. Arboriculture, 1983, award of Merit Conn. Nurserymen's Assn., 1994. Mem. AAAS, Entomol. Soc. Am., Am. Mosquito Control Assn., Am. Soc. Microbiology, Am. Soc. Parasitologists, Am. Soc. Tropical Medicine and Hygiene, Soc. Invertebrate Pathology, Conn. Acad. Sci. and Engring., Phi Kappa Phi. Office: Conn Agrl Expt Sta 123 Huntington St PO Box 1106 New Haven CT 06504-1106

ANDERSON, JOHN GASTON, electrical engineer; b. Dante, Va., Aug. 21, 1922; s. Harvey Ellis and Lenora (Ingram) A.; m. Elizabeth Amelia Weller, Sept. 18, 1948 (dec. Mar. 1993); 1 son, David John; m. Avery Emma Weymouth, Sept. 24, 1994. B.S. with honors in Elec. Engring., Va. Poly. Inst., 1943. Registered profl. engr., Mass. With Gen. Electric Co., 1946-84; mgr. AC transmission studies Gen. Electric Co., Schenectady, 1972-74; mgr. high voltage lab. Gen. Electric Co., Pittsfield, Mass., 1974-80; cons. engr. transmission systems Gen. Electric Co., Schenectady, 1980-84; sr. cons. Power Techs., Inc., 1984-92; profl. cons. engr., 1992-95; cons., lectr. on high voltage and power transmission; mem. U.S. USSR Tech. Exch. for High Voltage Transmission. Co-author books in field; contbr. articles to profl. pubs.; editor: GE Transmission Mag., 1972-74. Active Boy Scouts Am., 1960-79. Served to capt. USAAF, 1943-45. Recipient Nat. prizes for papers Am. Inst. Elec. Engrs., 1957. Fellow IEEE (chmn. transmission and distbn. com. 1980-82, Centennial medal 1984, Halperin award 1991, Excellence Engring. medal 1997, Excellence in Power Distbn. Engring. award 1999); mem. NAE, Power Engring. Soc. (chmn. nat. pub. affairs subcom. 1979, chmn. tech. coun. 1982-85), Tau Beta Pi, Eta Kappa Nu, Phi Kappa Phi. Patentee in field.

ANDERSON, JOHN KERBY, writer, radio talk show host; b. Berkeley, Calif., Dec. 7, 1951; s. John Albert and Mary Lorraine (Allen) A.; m. Susanne Elise Pardey, Aug. 3, 1974; children: Amy, Jonathan, Catherine. BS, Oreg. State U., 1974; MFS, Yale U., 1976; MA, Georgetown U., 1981. Pres. Probe Ministries, Richardson, Tex., 1976—; host syndicated radio program Probe, 1983—; host The Kerby Anderson Show Salem Radio Network, 1995-96; host NewsTalk satellite radio talk show Criswell Radio Network, 1989-93; adj. prof. Dallas Theol. Sem., 1986—; guest host Point of View satellite radio talk show, USA Radio Network, Open Lane satellite radio talk show Moody Broadcasting Network. Author: Life, Death and Beyond, 1980, Genetic Engineering, 1982, Origin Science, 1987, Living Ethically in the 90s, 1990, Signs of Warning, Signs of Hope, 1994, Moral Dilemmas, 1998; contbg. author: Ency. Bibl. and Christian Ethics, 1987, Integrity of Heart, Skillfulness of Hands, 1994, Vital Contemporary Issues, 1994. Evangelical Christian. Avocations: writing, computers, basketball, tennis, fishing. Office: Probe 1900 Firman Dr Ste 100 Richardson TX 75081-6796

ANDERSON, JOHN LEONARD, chemical engineering educator; b. Wilmington, Del., Sept. 29, 1945; m. Patricia Siemen, June 8, 1968; children: Brian Christopher, Lauren Kathleen. B.Ch.E., U. Del., 1967; M.S., U. Ill., 1969, Ph.D., 1971. Asst. prof. chem. engring. Cornell U., Ithaca, N.Y., 1971-76;

assoc. prof. chem. engring. Carnegie-Mellon U., Pitts., 1976-79, prof., 1979—; dir. biomed. engring. Carnegie-Mellon U., 1980-85, head dept. chem. engring., 1983-94, dean coll. of engring., 1996—; Holts lectr. Johns Hopkins U., 1990; 5th ann. Berkeley lectr. chem. engring., 1989; Lacey lectr. Calif. Tech., 1998; vis. prof. MIT, 1982-83; vis. scholar Irish-Am. tech. exch. program dept. chem. engring. Univ. Coll. Dublin, 1983. Assoc. editor Advances in Chem. Engring., Indsl. and Engring. Chem. Research; contbr. articles to profl. jours. 1st lt. U.S. Army, 1972. Predoctoral fellow NIH, 1969-71, grantee, 1981—; Guggenheim fellow, 1982-83. Mem. NAE, AICE (symposium chmn. 1974—, Profl. Progress award, 1989); mem AAAS, Am. Chem. Soc. (symposium chmn. 1974—), Tau Beta Pi, Alpha Tau Omega. Office: Carnegie-Mellon U Dept Chem Engring Pittsburgh PA 15213

ANDERSON, JOHN MUELLER, retired philosophy educator; b. Cedar Rapids, Iowa, July 29, 1914; s. Arthur G. and Lois A. (Mueller) A.; m. Mary A. Gale, 1936 (dec.); m. Barbara C. Lax., 1970 (div.); m. Jean Sylvia Bixby, 1990. B.A., U. Ill., 1935, M.A. 1936; Ph.D., U. Calif. at Berkeley, 1939. Credit mgr. retail store Sears, Roebuck & Co., New Albany, Ind., 1939-41; research engr. Elgin Nat. Watch Co., Ill., 1941-42; chief spl. project Mpls.-Honeywell Co., 1942-43, asst. to chief engr., 1943-45; lectr. math. U. Minn., 1945-46; mem. faculty Pa. State U., 1946-80, prof. philosophy, 1951-68, Evan Pugh research prof. philosophy, 1968-80, prof. emeritus, 1980—; head dept., 1948-49, 52-55, 58-67, acting asst. dean for research, 1964, summer 1965; founder, 1st dir. Inst. Arts and Humanistic Studies, 1966-68; liberal arts editor Pa. State Studies; vis. lectr. U. Ill., summer 1965; guest prof. U. Otago, New Zealand, 1955, Free U. Berlin, Germany, 1961-62, U. Calif., Santa Cruz, 1979; cons. ops. research, computer design. Author: (with Anderson and Mandeville) Industrial Management, 1942, Calhoun Basic Documents, 1952, The Individual and the New World, 1955, (with H.W. Johnstone, Jr.) Natural Deduction, 1962, The Realm of Art, 1967, The Truth of Freedom, 1977; also articles; founding editor: Man and World, 1966—; editor: Dialogue Press, 1971—; translator: (with E.H. Freund) Heidegger: Discourse on Thinking, 1966. Mem. Am. Philos Assn., Western Pa. Philos. Assn., AAUP, Assn. Am. Studies, Assn. Symbolic Logic, Soc. Phenomenology and Existential Philosophy (exec. com. 1965-68), Am. Soc. for Aesthetics, Am. Math. Soc., Phi Beta Kappa, Sigma Xi, Pi Gamma Mu, Alpha Tau Omega. Patentee computers. Home: 120 Aspen Ln Huntingdon PA 16652-2739 Office: 240 Sparks Bldg University Park PA 16802-5201*

ANDERSON, JOHN MURRAY, operations executive, former university president; b. Toronto, Ont., Can., Sept. 3, 1926; s. Murray Alexander and Eleanor Montgomery (Valentine) A.; m. Eileen Anne McFaul, Nov. 3, 1951 (dec. Nov. 1983); children: Nancy, Susan, Peter, Katherine; m. Sylvia Richard, May 10, 1986. B.Sc.F., U. Toronto, 1951, Ph.D., 1958; LL.D., St. Thomas U., 1974, Dalhousie U., 1979; D.Ped., U. Maine, Orono, 1976. Asst. prof. U. N.B., Can., 1958-63; assoc. prof. Carleton U., 1963-67; dir. Fisheries Research Bd. Can. Biol. Sta., St. Andrews, N.B., 1967-72; dir. gen. Canadian Research and Devel., Fisheries and Marine Service, Dept. Environment, Ottawa, Ont., 1972-73; pres. U. N.B., 1973-79, J.M. Anderson Consultants Inc., 1980—; v.p. ops. Atlantic Salmon Fedn., 1984-96; pres., chmn. bd. dirs. Huntsman Marine Lab., St. Andrews, N.B., 1973-77, bd. dirs., 1985—, chmn. bd. dirs., 1995—; bd. govs. Rothesay (N.B.) Collegiate Sch., 1976, Kenya Tech. Tchrs. Coll., Nairobi, 1977-79; chmn. Assn. Atlantic Univs., 1978-79; v.p. Biol. Coun. Can., 1977-79; mem. Sci. Coun. of Can., 1988-92. Contbr. numerous articles on fish physiology to profl. jours. Bd. dirs. Internat. Atlantic Salmon Found., 1979-83, J.R. Bradfield Edn. Fund, Noranda, 1979-86, Aquaculture Assn., N.B., 1981—; pres., chmn. bd. trustees Sunbury Shores Arts and Nature Ctr., Inc., 1982-84; chmn. bd. trustees Mackenzie King Scholarship Trust, 1986—; trustee Nature Trust N.B., Inc., 1987-91; v.p. Atlantic Aquaculture Fair, 1993, pres., 1994; bd. dirs. St. Croix Estuary Program, 1990—. Fellow Royal Can. Geographic Soc.; mem. Inst. Can. Bankers (gov. 1974-79), Can. Soc. Zoologists (pres. 1973-74), Aquaculture Assn. Can. (pres. 1984-85), Assn. Univs. and Colls. Can. (dir. 1975-79, chmn. McCain Scholarship Group 1997—), Sigma Chi. Anglican. Office: Atlantic Salmon Fedn, Saint Andrews, NB Canada E0G 2X0

ANDERSON, JOHN QUENTIN, rail transportation executive; b. Portland, Oreg., July 30, 1951; s. Vernon G. and Loretta (Bezdek) A.; m. Wendy Sargent, June 23, 1973; children: Mark, Karen, Benjamin, Meredith. BS in Mech. Engring., Stanford U., 1973; MBA, Harvard U., 1977. Ptnr. McKinsey & Co., L.A., 1977-90; exec. v.p. Burlington No. R.R., Ft. Worth, 1990-95; sr. v.p. Burlington No. Santa Fe corp., Ft. Worth, 1995-96; exec. v.p. CSX Transp., Jacksonville, Fla., 1996—; fed. appointee Nat. Coal Coun., Washington, 1992-98; bd. dirs. N.Am. Electric Reliability Coun., 1999—. Dir. Joffrey Ballet, N.Y.C., L.A., 1987-90, Constl. Rights Found., L.A., 1988-90, Ft. Worth Ballet, 1994-96. Mem. Phi Beta Kappa. Office: CSXT 500 Water St Fl 1 Jacksonville FL 32202-4445

ANDERSON, JOHN RICHARD, entomologist, educator; b. Fargo, N.D., May 5, 1931; s. John Raymond and Mary Ann (Beaulieu) A.; m. Shereen V. Erickson, Mar. 26, 1955; children: Scott F., Lisa K., Steven F. BS, Utah State U., 1957; MS, U. Wis., 1958, PhD, 1960. Asst. prof. entomology U. Calif.-Berkeley, 1961-66, assoc. prof., 1967-70, prof., 1970-93, prof. emeritus, 1993—, assoc. dean research, 1979-85; trustee, past chmn. Alameda County (Calif.) Mosquito Abatement Dist., 1961-73, 79-93. Editoral bd.: Jour. Med. Entomology, 1968-72, Jour. Econ. Entomology, 1977-81, Thomas Say Found, 1968-72. Served with USN, 1950-54. Rsch. grantee; recipient Berkeley citation for Disting. Achievement, 1993. Fellow AAAS, Royal Entomol. Soc. (London); mem. Entomol. Soc. Am. (governing bd. 1987-90, C.W. Woodworth award Pacific br. 1988), Can. Entomol. Soc., Am. Mosquito Control Assn., Soc. Vector Ecologists, Nature Conservancy, Nat. Audubon Soc., Am. Mus. Natural History, Oreg. Nat. Resources Coun., Oreg. Nat. Desert Assn., High Desert Mus., Sierra Club. Home: 1283 NW Trenton Ave Bend OR 97701-1026 Office: Dept Insect Biology U Calif Berkeley CA 94720

ANDERSON, JOHN ROBERT, retired mathematics educator; b. Stromsburg, Nebr., Aug. 1, 1928; s. Norris Merton and Violet Charlotte (Stromberg) A.; m. Bertha Margery Nore, Aug. 27, 1950; children: Eric Jon, Mary Lynn. Student, Midland Coll., 1945-46; A.A., Luther Jr. Coll., 1949; B.S. (Regents scholar), U. Nebr., Lincoln, 1951, M.A. in Math, 1954; Ph.D., Purdue U., 1970. Tchr. math., coach Bloomfield (Nebr.) High Sch., 1951-52; control systems analyst, Allison div. Gen. Motors Corp., Indpls., 1954-60; prof. math. Depauw U., Greencastle, Ind., 1960, asst. dean, dir. grad. studies, 1973-76, dir. grad. studies, 1976-84, chmn. math. dept., 1984-90, prof. math., 1990-92, ret., 1992; resident dir. W. European studies program Depauw U., Fed. Republic Germany, France, 1975; resident dir. Mediterrenean Studies program Depauw U., 1982, 90; dir. NSF Coop. Coll. Sch., Sci. Inst., 1969-70; instr. NSF summer inst., 1972; instr. Challenge sci. and math. program U.S. Students in Europe, 1976, 77, 78, 80, 82; bd. dirs. Law Focused Edn., Indpls., 1975-77, Ind. Regional Math. Consortium, 1977-92. Bd. dirs. Luth. Brotherhood br. 8657, United Way Of Greencastle, Ind., 1992-98, treas., Putnam Co. Food Pantry, 1993-98; officer Peace Evangel. Luth. Ch., 1960—. Served with U.S. Army, 1946-48. Danforth Tchr. fellow, 1963-64; NSF sci. faculty fellow, 1964-65; Lilly Found. edn. grantee, summers 1961-63. Mem. Math. Assn. Am., Nat. Council Tchrs. Math., North Central Assn. (commr. 1974-78), Sigma Xi, Pi Mu Epsilon, Kappa Delta Pi, Beta Sigma Psi. Club: Rotary Internat. (sec. 1976-77, v.p. 1977-78, pres. 1978-79, 1998-99). Home: 1560 S Bloomington St Greencastle IN 46135-2212 *In working with people always keep in mind: "If I were in their place, is this the way I would like to be treated by someone in my position?".*

ANDERSON, JOHN ROBERT, psychology and computer science educator; b. Vancouver, B.C., Can., Aug. 27, 1947; came to U.S., 1968, naturalized, permanent resident 1974, citizen 1985.; s. John Leonard and Adeline (Langraff) A.; m. Lynne Marie Reder, Mar. 29, 1973; children—John Frank, Abraham Robert. B.A., U.B.C., 1968; Ph.D., Stanford U., 1972. Asst. prof. psychology Yale U., New Haven, 1972-73, prof., 1976-78; jr. fellow U. Mich., Ann Arbor, 1973-76; Walter Van Dyke Bingham prof. psychology and computer sci. Carnegie Mellon U., Pitts., 1978—. Author: Human Associative Memory, 1973, Language, Memory and Thought, 1976, Cognitive Psychology and Its Implications, 1980, Cognitive Skills and Their Acquisitions, 1981, The Architecture of Cognition, 1983, The Adaptive Character of Thought, 1990, Rules of the Mind, 1993, Learning and Memory: An Integrated Approach, 1995. Mem. Am. Psychol. Soc., Psychonomics Soc., Cognitive Sci. Soc. Office: Carnegie Mellon Univ Dept Psychology 342C Baker Hall Pittsburgh PA 15213*

ANDERSON, JOHN ROY, grouting engineer; b. Culberson, N.C., June 22, 1919; s. Oscar Garfield and Lula Adeline (Russell) A.; m. Rheba Ulma Nichols, Dec. 31, 1951 (dec. Oct. 1989); children: Richard Allen, John Steven, Mark Garfield. Student, Berea Coll., 1950. From clk. to field inspector, then constrn. engr. Govt. Agys., 1941-51; project engr., mgr. Intrusion Prepakt, Cleve., 1951-58, 64-65; regional mgr./project mgr. Lee Turzillo Contracting Co., Breaksville, Ohio, 1957-60; engr. foundations, ops. mgr. Harza Engring. Co., Chgo., 1960-61, 65-68, 1972-86; foundations engr. Tippetts Abbett McCarthy Stratton, N.Y.C., 1961-64, 68-72. Mem. ASCE. Baptist. Achievements include foundation engineering on dams, bridges, tunnels and high rise buildings throughout the world. Home and Office: 7770 Skipper Ln Tallahassee FL 32311-4530

ANDERSON, JOHN THOMAS, lawyer; b. Gary, Ind., July 13, 1930; s. Jack and Dorothy Genevieve (Gustafson) A.; m. Marvel Nancy Filkey, Aug. 15, 1953; children: Kirsten E. Teevens, Katherine L., Eric M. AB, DePauw U., 1952; LLB, Harvard U., 1955. Bar: Ind. 1955, Ill. 1956. Assoc. Lord, Bissell & Brook, Chgo., 1958-66, ptnr., 1966-95, of counsel, 1996—; bd. dirs. Phoenix Investment Ptnrs., Ltd. Trustee DePauw U., Greencastle, Ind., 1982—; chmn. bd. dirs. Joyce Found., Chgo., 1979—; bd. dirs. Gt. Lakes Protection Fund, 1993—. Lt. USNR, 1955-58. Methodist. Home: 2313 Cassia Ct Naples FL 34109-3370 Office: Lord Bissell & Brook Ste 3500 115 S La Salle St Chicago IL 60603-3801

ANDERSON, JOHN THOMAS, librarian, historian; b. Burlington, Iowa, Feb. 7, 1955; s. Alvin Jay and Margaret Ann (Thomas) A. BA, U. No. Iowa, 1976; MA, Coll. William and Mary, 1979; PhD, U. Va., 1982; M in Info. and Libr. Studies, U. Mich., 1987. Cert. postsecondary educator; cert. substitute tchr. Temp. asst. prof. history Chadron (Nebr.) State Coll., 1984; asst. libr. pub. svcs. Mid. Ga. Coll., Cochran, 1989-91; temp. reference libr. U. No. Iowa, Cedar Falls, 1991; reference libr. Palm Beach County Libr. Sys., Boca Raton, Fla., 1992; reference libr. Salve Regina U., Newport, R.I., 1992-93, catalog libr., 1993-94; media cataloger libr. Tex. A&M U., Commerce, 1997-98; libr. I, cataloger Abilene (Tex.) Pub. Libr., 1998—. *Anderson's Master's thesis in Early American History at the College of William and Mary, December 1979, was entitled: "A Political Biography of John Witherspoon from 1723 to 1776." His research director was Dr. John E. Selby, Professor of History. His doctoral dissertation in American Diplomatic History at the University of Virginia, May 1982, was entitled: "Senator Burton K. Wheeler and United States Foreign Relations." His dissertation director was Norman A. Graebner, Stettinius Professor of Modern American History. He is now seeking a publisher for a book completed in 1996, based on his dissertation, and tentatively titled "Liberal Isolationist: Senator Burton K. Wheeler of Montana and United States Foreign Relations."* Exhibits judge Nat. History Day Competition, Chadron, 1984. Philip Francis du Pont fellow Coll. William and Mary, 1976; Philip Francis du Pont fellow U. Va., 1977; Virginia Mason Davidge fellow U. Va., 1978, 79. Mem. ALA, Soc. Historians Am. Fgn. Rels., Phi Alpha Theta. Republican. Unitarian. Avocations: collecting postage stamps and first-edition books, public radio. Home: Apt 10-105 500 N Judge Ely Blvd Abilene TX 79601-6520 Office: Abilene Pub Libr 202 Cedar St Abilene TX 79601

ANDERSON, JOHN WILLIAM, protective services official; b. Balt., Apr. 5, 1947; s. William Allen and Lucille Angie (Branch) A.; m. Donna Anderson; children: Akeyo, Malaika, Imani Adia. AA in Criminal Justice, C.C. Balt., 1975; BS, Towson State Coll., 1978. Dep. sheriff Balt. City Sheriff's Office, 1972-81, lt. supervisory dep. sheriff, 1981-89, sheriff, 1989—; part-time instr. in law enforcement, Baltimore City C.C. Bd. dirs. Md. Youth Ranch, 1990-94, Franciscan Youth Adv., Balt., 1994. Sgt. USAF, 1966-70. Mem. Nat. Sheriff's Assn., Md. State Sheriff's Assn., Nat. Black Police Assn., Md. Chiefs of Police, Fraternal Order Police (lodge 22), Apollo Dem. Club, Stonewall Dem. Club, 46/26 Dem. Club, Am. Legion (Md. #285 chpt.), Elks. Baptist. Avocations: reading, collecting political memorabilia. Office: Balt City Sheriff's Office 100 N Calvert St Rm 114 Baltimore MD 21202-1709

ANDERSON, JOLENE SLOVER, small business owner, publishing executive, consultant; b. Tulare, Calif.; James P. Sr., and Helen B. (Walters) Slover; m. Douglas R. Anderson, June 14, 1975; 1 child by previous marriage, Sabrina Jo. Student, Victor Valley Coll., Riverside C.C. Model Connor Sch. Modeling, Fresno, Calif., 1955-65; actress M. Kosloff Studios, Hollywood, Calif., 1965; nat. sales mgr. Armed Services Publs., Hollywood, Calif., 1966-68; pres., dir. Sullivan Publs., Inc., Riverside, Calif., 1970-82; pres., chief exec. officer Heritage House Publs., Riverside, 1983-84; pres. Jolene S. Anderson Pub. Cons., Inc., Riverside, 1987—; bd. dirs. Riverside County Econ. Devel. Coun. Co-comdr. March AFB, Inland Empire Tourists and Conv.; mem. YWCA, City of Riverside Cultural Heritage Bd., Yr. 2000 Com., 1988, Riverside County Philharm. Bd., Temecula-Murrieta Econ. Devel. Corp.; mem. 101 Things to Do in Riverside com. Named Woman of Achievement YWCA, 1989, Humanitarian of Yr. Rotary, 1990. Mem. Riverside Downtown Assn., Sun City/Menifee Valley C. of C., Greater Riverside C. of C., Temecula Valley C. of C., Carson Valley C. of C., Soroptimists (Riverside chpt., Athena award). Office: PO Box 800 Riverside CA 92502-0800

ANDERSON, JON DAVID, lawyer; b. Wichita, Kans., Oct. 29, 1952; s. Charles Henry Anderson and Patricia (Vaughan) Ross; m. Leanne Winters, Dec. 20, 1973; children: Nicklas, Scott, Brandt, Chase, Barrett, Britten, Kieryn. BA, U. Wash., Seattle, 1974; JD, Brigham Young U., 1977. Bar: Calif. 1977. Assoc. Latham & Watkins, L.A., Newport Beach, Calif., 1977-84; ptnr. Latham & Watkins, Newport Beach, Costa Mesa, 1985—; mng. ptnr. Latham & Watkins, Costa Mesa, Calif., 1987-93. Bd. dirs. Orange County Coun., Boy Scouts Am. Mem. Calif. Bar Assn., Orange County Bar Assn., Marbella Country Club. Republican. Ch. of Jesus Christ of Latter-day Saints. Avocations: skiing, baseball, golf. Office: Latham & Watkins 650 Town Center Dr Ste 2000 Costa Mesa CA 92626-7135

ANDERSON, JON ERIC, lawyer; b. Jacksonville, N.C., Feb. 1, 1956; m. Lori Jean Schumacher, June 30, 1979; children: Andrew Jon, Elizabeth Ruth, Margaret Mary. BA, U. Wis., 1978; JD, Marquette U., 1981. Bar: Wis. 1981, U.S. Dist. Ct. (ea. and we. dists.) Wis. 1981, U.S. Ct. Appeals (7th cir.) 1996, U.S. Supreme Ct. 1988. Assoc. Mulcahy & Wherry, S.C., Milw., 1981-84; mng. atty. Mulcahy & Wherry, S.C., Sheboygan, Wis., 1984-87, Madison, 1987-90; shareholder Godfrey & Kahn, S.C., Madison, 1991—. Author: (with others) Comparable Worth-A Negotiator's Guide, 1985; contbg. author Pub. Sector Labor Rels., Wis., 1988. Thomas More Soc. scholar, 1979. Mem. ABA, Edn. Law Assn., Wis. Bar Assn. (bd. dirs. labor law sect. 1988-91), Blackhawk Country Club, Wis. Sch. Attys. Assn., Madison Club, Phi Delta Phi, Alpha Sigma Nu. Lutheran. Avocations: woodworking, music.

ANDERSON, JON MAC, lawyer; b. Rio Grande, Ohio, Jan. 10, 1937; s. Harry Rudolph and Carrie Viola (Magee) A.; m. Deborah Melton, June 1, 1961; children—Jon Gordon, Greta. AB, Ohio U., 1958; JD, Harvard Law Sch., 1961. Bar: Ohio 1961. Law clk. Hon. Kingsley A. Taft Ohio Supreme Ct., Columbus, 1961-62; assoc. Wright, Harlor, Morris & Arnold, Columbus, 1962-67, ptnr., 1968-76; ptnr. Porter, Wright, Morris & Arthur, Columbus, 1977—; adj. prof. law Ohio State U. Law Sch., Columbus, 1975-83; bar examiner State of Ohio, 1971-76, chmn., 1975-76; lectr. tax and estate planning insts.; bd. dirs. White Castle System, Inc., Columbus, ODC Enterprises, Inc. Trustee Berea Coll, Ky., 1976—, Pro Musica Chamber Orch., Columbus, 1980-98, Opera Columbus, 1985-88, 1st Congl. Ch., Columbus, 1979-83, Greater Columbus Arts Coun., 1989—; chmn., 1996-98; mem. adv. council The Textile Mus. Mem. ABA, Ohio State Bar Assn., Columbus Bar Assn., The Columbus Club, Rocky Fork Hunt and Country Club. Democrat. Avocations: music, art, textiles, literature, antique collections. Office: Porter Wright Morris & Arthur 41 S High St Ste 2800 Columbus OH 43215-6194

ANDERSON, JON STEPHEN, newswriter; b. Montreal, Que., Can., Mar. 13, 1936; came to U.S., 1963; s. William Howard and Dorothy Beatrice (Ryan) A.; m. Gail Rutherford, Feb. 20, 1960 (div. 1966); 1 child, Jon Gregory; m. Abra Prentice, Sept. 14, 1968 (div. 1976); children: Ashley Prentice, Abra Cantrill, Anthony Ryan. BA, Mt. Allison U., Sackville, Can., 1955; BCL, McGill U., Montreal, 1959; MAW, U. Iowa, 1991. Reporter Montreal Gazette, 1957-60; chief bur. Time Mag., Montreal, 1960-63; staff corr. Time Mag., Chgo., 1963-66; staff writer Chgo. Sun-Times, 1967-69; columnist Chgo. Daily News, 1969-72; pub. Chicagoan Mag., 1972-74; staff writer Chgo. Tribune, 1978—; writing instr. U. Iowa, 1989—. Contbr. articles to Readers Digest, 1977—, Chgo. Mag., 1977, Clothesline Rev., 1986. Gen. mgr. Second City Ctr. Pub. Arts, 1966-67; bd. dirs. Chgo. Internat. Film Festival, 1975-78. Recipient Stick o' Type award Newspaper Guild Am., 1969, Studs Turkel Journalism award, 1999. Mem. TV Critics Assn., Order Ky. Cols. Presbyterian. Home: 1447 W Birchwood Ave # 2 Chicago IL 60626-1806 Office: Chgo Tribune 435 N Michigan Ave Chicago IL 60611-4066

ANDERSON, JONPATRICK SCHUYLER, financial consultant, therapist, archivist; b. Chgo., July 20, 1951; s. Ralph Anderson and Helena Hilda (Robinson) Hardy; children: André, Mary, David. Attended, Cen. YMCA Cmty. Coll., Chgo., 1970, Lawrence Merrick Acad. Dramatic Arts, 1972-73, Cmty. Coll. Air Force, 1974, U. Md., 1975, Grossmont C.C., 1984; AA, L.A. Trade Tech. Coll., 1978; attended, Calif. State U., L.A., 1978-79; BA, UCLA, 1979; attended, San Diego Cmty. Coll. Dist., 1981, 89-92; DMin., Internat. Seminary Coll.; postgrad., Trinity Coll./U. Liverpool, SUNY, Albany, 1983, Govs. State U., 1985, San Diego State U., 1982-83; MRE, PhD, Internat. Sem. (in coop. with Unification Theol. Sem. N.Y.), 1989, DMin, 1994. Profl. life tchg. cert. Ariz. State C.C. Clerical supr. VA, L.A., 1976-80; fin. adminstr. Antioch Primitive Bapt. Ch., L.A., 1979-80; pres., exec. dir. All-Around Prodns., L.A., 1980-83; assoc. minister St. Stephen Ch., San Diego, Calif., 1983-87; stadium mgr. San Diego Jack Murphy Stadium, 1985-87; mgr. Horton Plaza Shopping Ctr., San Diego, 1985-86; exec. dir. Christ-Immanuel Ministerial Assn., San Diego, 1983—; acting supr. psychiatry dept. VA Mental Health Clinic, San Diego, 1991-96; intern in counseling and psychiatry U. Calif. San Diego Med. Ctr., 1992-93; supr. Enid Rockwell MD, 1992-94; tchr. K-12 City Schs. of Decatur, Ga., 1997—, Dekalb County Sch. Sys., Ga., 1998—; pvt. investigator Merit Protective Svcs., L.A., 1972-74; adminstrv. asst. Dept. Def., 1981; cons. pvt. practice mgmt., cons. comptr., San Diego, 1981-82; cons. writer All-Around Music divsn. Broadcast Music, Inc., San Diego, 1980—; instr. San Diego Community Coll. Dist., 1984; libr. asst. San Diego State U., 1982-83; chaplain of the Day U. Calif., San Diego, 1984-85; archives technician Nat. Archives & Records Adminstrn., Laguna Niguel, Calif., 1988; ind. assoc. Pre-paid Legal Svcs., San Diego, 1994—. Mem. Am. Freedom Coalition, Washington, 1988, Causa, USA, Washington, 1985-87; mem. Internat. Coun. of Cmty. Chs. With USMC, Vietnam, 1968-70; with U.S. Army, 1975-76; with USAF, 1974, 80-82; 2d lt. USAR, 1979-80. Grammy nominee NARAS, 1980; recipient Personal award former Pres. Ronald Reagan, L.A., 1988, Letter of Commendation from Duncan Hunter, U.S. Rep., 52nd Dist., Calif., 1994. Mem. NAACP (life), NARAS, AFTRA AGVA, Assn. MBA Execs. (Bus. award 1980), Assn. Christian Schs. Internat. (cert. tchg.-adminstrn./prin. K-12 1993—), UCLA Alumni Assn. (life, interviewing com. adv. and scholarship program 1988—, bd. dirs. scholarship chmn. 1991—), Res. Officers Assn. of U.S. (life), UCLA Black Alumni Assn. (life, bd. dirs., scholarship chmn.), N.G. Assn. Calif. (life), U. Calif.-San Diego Med. Ctr. Aux. (life), Nat. Conf. Ministry to Armed Forces, VFW (life), DAV (life), AMVETS, Am. Legion, Nat. Assn. Evangelicals, Urban League of L.A., Nat. Music Publishers Assn., Am. Guild Authors and Composers, UCLA Coll. Fine Arts Dean's Gold Medal Soc., San Francisco Theol. Sem.—Montgomery Soc., Am. Assn. Religious Counselors, UCLA Sch. of Theater, Film, and TV Alumni Assn. (life), N.Y. Acad. Sci. Democrat. Mem. Ch. of God. Avocations: reading, writing, gospel music, outdoor recreation, traveling. Office: PO Box 360424 Decatur GA 30036-0424

ANDERSON, JOSEPH ANDREW, JR., retired apparel company executive, retail consultant; b. Logan, Utah, Nov. 1, 1921; s. Joseph Andrew and Melicent H. (Willmore) A.; m. Gwen Elsie Smith, Sept. 29, 1954; children: Brian, Jodi, Paul, Bradley, Stacey, Jeffrey, Tiffani. BS, Utah State U., 1947; postgrad., Stanford U., 1949-50. With Zion's Coop. Mdse. Inst. Dept. Store, Salt Lake City, 1950-86, various positions, 1950-82, pres., chief exec. officer, 1982-84, vice chmn. bd., 1984-86, ret., 1986; chmn. bd. Mr. Mac Clothiers, Inc.; ret., 1988; retail cons., Salt Lake City, 1988-90; mem. consumer bd. Utah Dept. Commerce, 1985-92; bd. dirs. Zions 1st Nat. Bank, Salt Lake City. Chmn., bd. dirs. Salt Lake City, 1985-88, Westminster Coll. Found., Salt Lake City, 1985-86, Utah Opera Co., 1998—; bd. dirs. Westminster Coll. Bus. Sch., 1985—; trustee Westminster Coll., 1989-96, L.D.S. Hosp.-Deseret Found., 1987-88, Salt Lake Visitor Bur., 1987-89; corp. solicitation state chmn. Am. Cancer Soc. of Utah, 1989-90; pres., bd. dirs. AMICUS-Deseret Found., Salt Lake City, 1986-89; adv. bd. Sta. KSL-TV, 1985-88; mem. dean's adv. council Bus. Sch. Utah State U., 1982-89; mem. Utah Employer Support of the Guard and Res. Com. Area # 3, 1986-91; bd. dirs. Utah Youth Village, Salt Lake City, 1990-93, chmn., 1994-96; chmn. Fitness Inst. L.D.S. Hosp., Salt Lake City, 1991-93, bd. of fitness inst., 1994-97; chmn. Utah Youth Village, 1994-96. 1st lt. U.S. Army, 1943-46, ETO. Named Outstanding Boss of Yr. Salt Lake Nat. Bus. Women's Club, 1972; recipient Block "A" award, 1947, Outstanding Alumnus award Utah State U., 1984, Outstanding Svc. award L.D.S. Hosp. Desert Found., 1990. Mem. Utah Retail Merchants Assn. (dir., sec. 1983-87, bd. dirs. nat. assn. 1983-87), Execs. Assn. Salt Lake City (bd. dirs. 1990-91), Sons of Utah Pioneers (pres. 1976-77), Rotary. Republican. Mormon. Club: Alta (Salt Lake City). Lodge: Rotary, Lions (1st v.p. Salt Lake City club 1990-91, pres. 1991-92). Avocations: jogging, fishing, golf, tennis. Home: 4394 Adonis Dr Salt Lake City UT 84124-3433

ANDERSON, JOSEPH FLETCHER, JR., federal judge; b. 1949. BA, Clemson U., 1972; JD, U. S.C., 1975. Pvt. practice law Anderson, Anderson and Anderson, 1977-86; law clk. to presiding justice U.S. Ct. Appeals (4th cir.), 1975-76; mem. Ho. of Reps. 3d Congrl. Dist. S.C., 1980-86; judge U.S. Dist. Ct. S.C., Columbia, 1986—. Chmn. honor coun. U. S.C. Sch. Law, 1976-85, Edgefield Indsl. Devel. Corp., S.C., bd. dirs., 1978-86; mem. local adv. bd. First Citizens Bank and Trust Co., Trenton, S.C., 1983-86; chmn., vol. Edgefield County Re-election Campaign for Sen. Strom Thurmond, 1972, 84; chmn. Edgefield County Campaign for Congressman William Jennings Bryan Dorn for Dem. Nomination for Gov. of S.C.; bd. dirs. Edgefield County United Way, 1983-86; mem. exec. com. Coun. Boy Scouts Am., 1978-86. Named one of Three Outstanding Young Men of S.C., 1980. Mem. ABA, S.C. Bar Assn., S.C. Trial Lawyers Assn., S.C. Law Inst. Coun. Office: US Dist Ct PO Box 447 Columbia SC 29202-0447*

ANDERSON, JOSEPH NORMAN, executive consultant, former food company executive, former college president; b. Mpls., May 12, 1926; s. Joseph E. and Helen (Larson) A.; m. Ruth E. Anderson, Sept. 6, 1952; children: Peter, Timothy, Paul, Matthew, Robin, Kathryn, Charles. BBA with distinction, U. Minn., 1947. With Sears, Roebuck & Co., 1947-49, Gamble-Skogmo, Inc., 1950-64; v.p. fin., dir. Nat. Bellas Hess, Inc., 1964-67, pres., chief exec. officer, dir., 1967-69, chmn. bd., pres., chief exec. officer, 1969-75; pres. Jamestown (N.D.) Coll., 1975-83, Dakota Bake-n-Serv, Inc., 1979-86; exec. cons. Gladstone, Mo., 1986-90, Edwardsville, Ill., 1990—; Pres. Mchts. Rsch. Counc., 1961-62. With AUS, 1953-55. Mem. Phi Beta Kappa, Beta Gamma Sigma. Republican. Presbyterian.

ANDERSON, JUDITH HELENA, English language educator; b. Worcester, Mass., Apr. 21, 1940; d. Oscar William and Beatrice Marguerite (Beaudry) A.; m. E. Talbot Donaldson, May 18, 1971 (dec. Apr. 1987). AB magna cum laude, Radcliffe Coll., 1961; MA, Yale U., 1962, PhD, 1965. Instr. English Cornell U., Ithaca, N.Y., 1964-66, asst. prof. English, 1966-72; vis. lectr. Coll. Seminar Program, Yale U., New Haven, 1973; vis. asst. prof. English U. Mich., Ann Arbor, 1973-74; assoc. prof. Ind. U., Bloomington, 1974-79, prof., 1979—, dir. grad. studies, 1986-90, 93, mem. governing bd. univ. Inst. for Advanced Study, 1983-85, 86-88; chancellor's prof., 1999—; Morris W. Croll lectr. Gettysburg Coll., 1988, Kathleen Williams lectr., 1989, 95; dir. Folger Inst. Seminar, 1991. Author: The Growth of a Personal Voice, 1976, Biographical Truth, 1984, Words that Matter, 1996; editor: (with Elizabeth D. Kirk) Piers Plowman, 1990, (with Donald Cheney and David A. Richardson) Spenser's Life and the Subject of Biography, 1996; mem. editl. bd. Spenser Ency., 1979-90, Duquesne Studies in Lang. and Lit., 1976—, Spenser Studies, 1986—; mem. adv. bd. Textbase of Women Writers, Brown U., 1989—; contbr. articles on Renaissance lit. to profl. jours. Woodrow Wilson fellow, 1961-62, 63-64, NEH summer fellow and sr. rsch. fellow, 1979, 81-82, Dulin fellow Folger Libr., 1991; Huntington Libr. rsch.

grantee, 1978, 97, vis. fellow, 1985-86, Mayers Found. fellow, 1990-91, Nat. Humanities Ctr.; fellow, 1995-96; recipient Outstanding Scholar award Office of Women's Affairs Ind. U., 1996. Mem. MLA (mem. exec. com. Renaissance divsn. 1973-78, 86-90, del. to assembly 1991-93), AAUP, Spenser Soc. (pres. 1980, 88), Renaissance Soc. Am. (rep. for English to coun. 1991-93), Milton Soc., Shakespeare Assn., Phi Beta Kappa. Home: 2525 E 8th St Bloomington IN 47408-4214 Office: Ind U Dept English Bloomington IN 47405

ANDERSON, KARL PETER, controller; b. Mpls., June 17, 1960; s. James R. and Ardith E. (Larson) A.; m. Deborah L. Gerboth, June 5, 1993; children: Kaelyn Marie, Sarah Joy. Electroplater Minn. Plating Labs., Mpls., 1978-79; engring. tech. Minco Products, Fridley, Minn., 1981-82; shipping mgr. Fish Enterprises, Mpls., 1985-86; produce buyer Fish Enterprises, London, 1986-88; ops. mgr. Peaceful Family Products, Trimont, Minn., 1988-94, 95-96; owner Serenity Grove Woodworking, Fairmont, Minn., 1994-95; controller Overson Lumber Co., St. James, Minn., 1996—. Bd. dirs. Caring Pregnancy Ctr., Fairmont, 1995-97; treas. 2d Dist. Rep. Party, Minn., 1997-99; candidate Minn. Ho. of Reps., 1992; vol. fireman Odin (Minn.) Fire Dept., 1997—; chmn. Hosanna Free Luth. Ch., 1992-94, supt. Sunday sch., 1994-99. Republican. Avocations: woodworking, reading, Bible teaching.

ANDERSON, KARL RICHARD, aerospace engineer, consultant; b. Vinita, Okla., Sept. 27, 1917; s. Axel Richard and Hildred Audrey (Marshall) A.; B.S., Calif. Western U., 1964, M.A., 1966; Ph.D., U.S. Internat. U., 1970; m. Jane Shigeko Hiratsuka, June 20, 1953; 1 son, Karl Richard. Engr. personnel subsystems Atlas Missile Program, Gen. Dynamics, San Diego, 1960-63; design engr. Solar divsn. Internat. Harvester, San Diego, 1964-66, sr. design engr., 1967-69, project engr., 1970-74, product safety specialist, 1975-78; aerospace engring. cons., 1979-86; cons. engring., 1979—; lectr. Am. Indian Sci. and Engring. Soc. Served to maj. USAF, 1936-60. Recipient Spl. Commendation award San Diego County Bd. Supervisors, 1985, Spl. Commendation award San Diego City Council, 1985, Spl. Commendation award City of San Diego, 1994, Grace "Peter" Sargent award San Diego City Natural Park, 1994. Registered profl. engr., Calif. Home: 5886 Scripps St San Diego CA 92122-3212

ANDERSON, KATHLEEN GAY, consultant mediator, hearing officer, arbitrator; b. Cin., July 27, 1950; d. Harold B. and Trudi L. (Chambers) Briggs; m. J.R. Carr, July 4, 1988; 1 child, Jesse J. Anderson. Student, U. Cin., 1971-72, Antioch Coll., 1973-74; cert., Nat. Jud. Coll., U. Nev., Reno, 1987, Inst. Applied Law, 1987, Acad. Family Mediators, 1991. Cert. Am. Arbitration Assn. Comml. Arbitration Panel, Nat. Assn. Securities Dealers Arbitration and Mediation Panels, Lemmon Mediation Inst., Acad. Family Mediators, U.S. Postal Svc. Panel. Paralegal Lauer & Lauer, Santa Fe, 1976-79, Wilkinson, Cragun & Barker, Anchorage, 1981-82; employment law paralegal specialist Hughes, Thorsness, Gantz, Powell & Brundin, Anchorage, 1983-91; investigator, mediator Alaska State Commn. Human Rights, 1991; consultant mediator, arbitrator, trainer The Arbitration and Mediation Group, Anchorage, 1987—; hearing officer Municipality of Anchorage, 1993-99; State of Alaska, 1994—; mem. faculty nat. Jud. Coll., U. Nev., Reno, 1988-89; adj. prof. U. Alaska, Anchorage, 1985—, Alaska Pacific U., 1990-96, Chapman U., 1990; mem. Alaska Supreme Ct. Mediation Task Force, 1991-96; adv. com. Am. Arbitration Assn. for Alaska, 1995-99, ADR subcom. Supreme Ct. Civil Justice Reform task force, 1998-99; trainer mediation svcs. pvt. profit and nonprofit groups, pub. groups, U.S. mil., state and fed. govt.; arbitrator Anchorage Bd. Realtors, 1997—. Author, editor: Professional Responsibility Handbook for Legal Assistants and Paralegals, 1986; contbr. articles to profl. jours. Lectr. Alaska Bar Assn., NLRB, Bus. and Profl. Women, Coun. on Edn. and Mgmt., Small Bus. Devel. Coun., various employers and bus. groups. Mem. Am. Arbitration Assn. (cert. comml. arbitration panel 1996-99, U.S. Postal Svc. Mediation Panel 1999—, U.S. Forest Svc. 1999—), Soc. Profls. in Dispute Resolution, Acad. Family Mediators, Alaska Bar Assn. (assoc., alt. dispute resolution), Alaska Dispute Settlement Assn. (v.p. 1992-93, chair com. on credentialing and stds. of practice, pres. 1997-98). Avocations: jewelry design, antiques, gourmet cooking, rare bead collecting. Home: PO Box 100098 Anchorage AK 99510-0098 Office: PO Box 240783 Anchorage AK 99524-0783

ANDERSON, KATHRYN D., surgeon; b. Ashton-Under-Lyne, Lancashire, Eng., Mar. 14, 1939; came to U.S., 1961; m. French Anderson, June 24, 1961. BA, Cambridge (Eng.) U., 1961, MA, 1964; MD, Harvard U., 1964. Diplomate Am. Bd. Surgery with cert. in spl. competence in pediat. surgery. Intern in pediat. Children's Hosp., Boston, 1964-65; resident in surgery Georgetown U. Hosp., Washington, 1965-69, chief resident in surgery, 1969-70, attending surgeon, 1972-74; chief resident in pediat. surgery Children's Hosp., Washington, 1970-72, sr. attending surgeon, 1974-84; surgeon-in-chief Children's Hosp., L.A., 1992—; vice chmn. surgery George Washington U., Washington, 1984-92; prof. surgery U. So. Calif. Fellow ACS (sec. 1992—), Royal Coll. Surgeons (Eng.), Am. Acad. Pediatrics (sec. surg. sect. 1982-85, chmn. 1985-86), Am. Pediatric Surg. Assn. (sec. 1988-91); Am. Surg. Assn., Soc. Univ. Surgeons. Avocations: opera, yoga. Office: Childrens Hosp 4650 W Sunset Blvd Los Angeles CA 90027-6062

ANDERSON, KEITH, retired lawyer, retired banker; b. Phoenix, June 21, 1917; s. Carl and Helen (Fairchild) A.; m. Grace R. VanDenburg, 1941 (div. 1957); m. Catherine Huber, 1960; children: Fletcher F., Warren, Nicholas H. AB, Dartmouth Coll., 1939; LLB, Harvard U., 1942. Bar: N.Y. 1942, Ariz. 1946, Colo. 1950. Ret. lawyer. Mem. Univ. Club of Denver, Cactus Club. Democrat. *

ANDERSON, KENNETH JEFFERY, family financial planner, accountant, lawyer; b. Daytona Beach, Fla., May 7, 1954; s. Kenneth E. and Petronella G. (Jeffer) A.; m. Susan Wagner, Aug. 19, 1978; children: Melissa, Kiersten. BSBA, Valparaiso U., 1976, JD, 1979. CPA, Ill. Prof. staff, mgr. Arthur Andersen & Co., Chgo., 1979-84; mgr. Arthur Andersen & Co., L.A., 1984-90, ptnr., 1990—, dir. individual tax fin. svcs., western region; founding mem., mem. adv. bd. U. So. Calif. Family and Closely-Held Bus. Inst. Bd. govs., treas. Idyllwild (Calif.) Arts, 1990—; mem. L.A. Philanthropic Found., 1995; profl. adv. bd. Children's Bur., 1995; adv. bd. L.A. Philharmonic, 1996—; mem. assocs. bd. Chgo. Lung Assn., 1980-84; vol. Hospice of North Shore, Winnetka, Ill., 1981; bd. dirs. Boy Scouts Am. west. coun., 1998—. Mem. AICPA, Fla. Bar Assn., Ill. Bar Assn., Ill. CPA Soc., Calif. CPA Soc. (apptd. to state com. on personal fin. planning), Soc. CPA-Fin. Planners (bd. dirs. 1987-89), Sports Lawyers Assn., Calif. Club. Republican. Avocations: sports, sailing, music, golfing. Home: 28 Cinch Rd Bell Canyon CA 91307-1003 Office: Arthur Andersen & Co 633 W 5th St 26th Flr Los Angeles CA 90071-2005

ANDERSON, KENNETH NORMAN, retired magazine editor, author; b. Omaha, July 10, 1921; s. Duncan McDonald and Letitia Jane (Steed) A.; m. Lois Elaine Harmon, Jan. 12, 1945; children: Eric Stephen, Randi Laine, Jani Jill, Douglas Duncan. Student, U. Omaha, 1939-41, Oreg. State Coll., 1943-44, Stanford U., 1944-45, Northwestern U. Coll. Medicine, 1945-46, U. Chgo., 1958-60. With U.S. Army Fin. Office, Nebr. and Mont., 1941-42; engring. aid U.S. Army C.E., Omaha, 1946; news editor Radio Sta. KOIL, Omaha, 1946-47; bur. mgr. Internat. News Svc., Omaha, 1947-56, Kansas City, Mo., 1947-56; spl. features editor Better Homes and Garden mag., 1956-57; assoc. editor Popular Mechanics mag., 1957-59; editor Today's Health mag., pub. by AMA, Chgo., 1959-65, Holt, Rinehart & Winston, N.Y.C., 1965-70; exec. dir. Coffee Info. Inst., N.Y.C., 1970-81; pres. Pubs. Editorial Svcs., Inc., Katonah, N.Y., 1981-90, The Editorial Guild, Inc., Katonah, N.Y., 1981-90; lectr. mag. writing New Sch. Social Research, 1959, NYU, 1960, Omaha U., 1961, Rennselaer Poly. Inst., 1964; cons. med. editor Ferguson Pub. Co., 1971-76. Author: (with others) Lawyers' Medical Cyclopedia, 1962, The Family Physician, 1963, Today's Health Guide, 1965, Pictorial Medical Guide, 1967, Field and Stream Guide to Physical Fitness, 1969, New Concise Family Medical and Health Guide, 1971, Complete Illustrated Book of Better Health, 1973, The New Complete Medical and Health Ency., 4 vols., 1977, The Sterno Guide to the Outdoors, 1977, Eagle Claw Fish Cookbook, 1978, Guide to Weight Control and Fitness, 1978, Newsweek Ency. of Family Health, 1980, Urdang Dictionary of Current Medical Terms, 1981, Pocket Guide to Coffee and Teas, 1982, Bantam Medical Dictionary, 1982, Mosby's Medical and Nursing Dictionary, 1982, Longman's Dictionary of Psychology and Psychiatry, 1983; editor: Hudson Health Newsletter, 1982—, Orphan Drugs, 1983, Gourmet Guide to Fish and Shellfish, 1984, Prentice-Hall Dictionary of Nutrition and Health, 1984, U.S. Military Operations, 1945-84, 1984, Mosby's Medical Encyclopedia, 1985, The Language of Sex, 1986, Industrial Medicine Desk Reference, 1986, New Pediatric Guide to Drugs & Vitamins, 1987, Symptoms after 40, 1987, Signet/Mosby Medical Encyclopedia, 1987, Consumer Guide Illustrated Medical Dictionary, 1988, Sex A to Z, 1989, Mosby's Medical, Nursing and Allied Health Dictionary, 4th edit., 1994, New York Public Library Desk Reference, 1989, Mosby's Pocket Dictionary of Medicine, Nursing and Allied Health, 1990, 2d edit., 1994, History of U.S. Military Operations Since World War II, 1992, History of the U.S. Marines, 1992, Internat. Menu Speller, 1993, Internat. Dictionary of Food and Nutrition, 1993, Mosby's Medical, Nursing & Allied Health Dictionary, 4th edit., 1994 (Am. Jour. Nursing Book Yr. award 1994), 5th edit., 1998; Mosby's Pocket Medical Dictionary of Medicine, Nursing and Allied Health, 2d Edition, 1994, Wordsworth Dictionary of Sex, 1994, 3d edit. 1998; contbr. Grolier, Funk & Wagnalls Encys.; adv. editor Nutrition Today, 1965-75. Home and Office: 1278 Kingswood Blvd Mountain Home AR 72653-8083

ANDERSON, KENNETH PAUL, nephrologist, administrator; b. Council Bluffs, Iowa, June 17, 1952; s. Kenneth Paul and Kathleen Marie (Wyckoff) A.; m. Elizabeth Stephens, July 1, 1985; children: Jennifer, Cassie, Zach. BS with honors, U. Iowa, 1974; DO, Coll. Osteo. Medicine, Des Moines, 1978; MS, U. Wis., 1996; cert., Harvard U., 1993. Diplomate Am. Bd. Family Practice. Resident, chief resident Luth. Hosp.-U. Iowa, Des Moines, 1978-81, Norwalk (Conn.) Hosp.-Yale U., 1981-83; fellow in nephrology, clin. instr. U. So. Calif., L.A., 1983-85; med. dir. Mercy Hosp., Iowa Luth. Hosp., Des Moines, 1985-96; clin. instr. Coll. Osteo. Medicine, Des Moines, 1986-96; chief of staff Mercy Hosp. Med. Ctr., Des Moines, 1992-94; sec., bd. officers Iowa Luth. Hosp., Des Moines, 1989-90; chief med. officer Ptnrs. Nat. Health Plans, South Bend, Ind., 1996—; chmn., mem. ESRD Network # 12 of HCFA, Kansas City, 1984-95; pres., CEO Nephrology and Internal Medicine Specialists, Des Moines, 1985-96; med. dir. SecureCare of Iowa, Des Moines, 1992-96. Contbr. articles to profl. jours. Bd. dirs. Iowa State Bd. of Health, Des Moines, 1993-96; cons. Nat. Health Policy Adv. Team, Washington, 1989-94, Ind. Perinatal Task Force, 1997—. Fellow Am. Acad. Family Practice; mem. AMA, Am. Soc. Hypertension, Am. Coll. Physician Execs., Am. Soc. Nephrology, Iowa Osteo. Med. Assn. Democrat. Roman Catholic. Avocations: camping, blues music, fishing, biking, writing short stories. Home: 11034 Birch Lake Dr E Granger IN 46530-6013 Office: Ptnrs Nat Health Plans Ind 100 E Wayne St Ste 502 South Bend IN 46601-2354

ANDERSON, KENNETH WARD, investor, consultant; b. Evanston, Ill., Dec. 14, 1931; s. Sydney Cleminson and Grey (Simpson) A.; m. Jean Jensen, Mar. 21, 1953; children: Kenneth Ward, Richard Scott, Wendy Lynn. BSBA, Northwestern U., 1953; postgrad. in fin., UCLA, 1955-56, U. So. Calif., 1956-58. Asst. v.p. United Calif. Bank, L.A., 1956-63; v.p. fin., asst. sect. T.I.M.E.-DC, Lubbock, Tex., 1963-70; sr. v.p. fin. Campbell-Taggart, Dallas, 1970-80; sr. v.p., CFO Galveston-Houston Co., Houston, 1980-82; pres., CFO, dir. Cook Data Svcs., Dallas, 1983-85; pres., dir. Blockbuster Entertainment Corp., Dallas, 1985-87; pres., dir., chmn. bd. Amtech Credit Corp., Dallas, 1987-90; chmn. exec. com., dir. Amtech Corp., 1987-92; bd. dirs. Lake Area Health Ctr. Found., 1993—, Fossil, Inc., 1993—, Earful of Books, Inc., 1999—. Bd. dirs. Ch. at Horseshoe Bay Endowment Fund, 1996—; trustee Ch. at Horseshoe Bay, 1999—. With U.S. Army, 1953-55, Japan. Mem. Preston Trail Golf Club (Dallas), Horseshoe Bay Country Club. Republican. Methodist. Address: PO Box 8189 Horseshoe Bay TX 78657-8189

ANDERSON, KENT TAYLOR, lawyer; b. Salt Lake City, June 24, 1953; s. Neldon Leroy and Vera Minnie (Taylor) A.; m. Ellis Anderson (div. June 1979); m. Tara Dayle, Apr. 30, 1982; 1 child, Claire Marie. BA, U. Utah, 1975; JD, Georgetown U., 1978. Bar: Utah 1978, Calif. 1987. Assoc. Jones, Waldo, Holbrook & McDonough, Salt Lake City, 1978-83, ptnr., 1983-84; v.p., gen. counsel Am. Stores Properties, Inc., Salt Lake City, 1984-86; v.p., gen. counsel, asst. sec. Am. Stores Co., Salt Lake City, 1987—; sr. v.p., gen. counsel, sec. Alpha Beta Stores, Inc., Anaheim, Calif., 1986-89; exec. v.p., gen. counsel, asst. sec. Am. Stores Co., Salt Lake City, 1989-93, exec. v.p., 1993—; gen. mgr. Am. Stores Properties, Inc., Salt Lake City, 1993-95, COO strategy and devel., mem. exec. coun., 1995—; Mem. staff Georgetown Law Jour., 1976-78. Mem. Utah Bar Assn., Calif. Bar Assn., Phi Beta Kappa. Office: 1654 South Mohawk Way Salt Lake City UT 84108

ANDERSON, KERRII B., construction company executive; b. 1957. BS, Elon Coll., 1978; MBA, Duke U., 1987. With Peat, Marwick, Mitchell & Co., Greensboro, N.C., 1978-84, RJ Reynolds Corp., Winston-Salem, N.C., 1984-85, Key Co., Greensboro, N.C., 1985-87; sr. v.p., CFO, chmn. bd. M/I Schottenstein Homes Inc., Columbus, 1987—. Address: MI Schottenstein Homes 3 Easton Oval Columbus OH 43219-6012*

ANDERSON, KIMBALL RICHARD, lawyer; b. San Antonio, Aug. 20, 1952; s. Richard John and Martha (Bishop) A.; m. Karen Gatsis, Aug. 18, 1974; children: Alexis Katrina, Melissa Martha, Sophia Diane. BA, U. Ill., 1974, JD, 1977. Bar: Ill. 1977, U.S. Ct. Appeals (7th cir.) 1979, U.S. Supreme Ct. 1987; CPA, Ill. Assoc. Winston & Strawn, Chgo., 1977-84, ptnr., 1984—, mem. exec. com., 1994—; bd. dirs. Pub. Interest Law Initiative; Disting. Neutral, CPR Inst. for Dispute Resolution. Bd. dirs. Chgo. Lawyers Com. for Civil Rights Under Law, Inc. Named Person of Yr. 1996 Chgo. Lawyer. Fellow Am. Coll. Trial Lawyers; mem. ABA, Ill. Bar Assn., Chgo. Bar Assn. (bd. mgrs. 1990-92), Ill. CPA Soc. Home: 2045 N Seminary Ave Chicago IL 60614-4109 Office: Winston & Strawn 35 W Wacker Dr Ste 4200 Chicago IL 60601-1695

ANDERSON, KRISTINE JO, librarian; b. Aug. 1, 1945; d. Elvin Cornelius and Hilda Ellen A. MLS, U. Oreg., 1969; PhD in Comparative Lit., SUNY, Binghamton, 1983. Libr. Northeastern U., Boston, 1971-78; indexer MLA, N.Y.C., 1984-86; libr. N.Y.C. Pub. Libr., 1986-88; bibliographer for English and theatre Purdue U., W. Lafayette, Ind., 1988—. Contbr. articles to profl. jours. Mem. ALA, Soc. Utopian Studies, MLA. E-mail: kanderso@purdue.edu. Office: Humanities Soc Sci Edn Library Purdue U Stewart Ctr West Lafayette IN 47906

ANDERSON, KURT LEWIS, artist; b. Waterloo, Iowa, Mar. 2, 1958; s. Karl Clifton and Margaret (Stair) A.; m. Arlene Marie Dedini, Aug. 1, 1987. Student, U. Iowa, 1976-77, U. Minn., 1977-79, Atelier Lack Sch. of Fine Art, Mpls., 1977-80. Art instr. Silvermine Sch. Fine Art, New Canaan, Conn., 1984-86, Atelier LeSueur Sch. of Fine Art, Excelsior, Minn., 1987-88; owner Kurt Anderson Studio, St. Paul, 1987—. Author: Realistic Oil Painting Techniques, 1995; contbg. author: Realism in Revolution, 1985, The North Light Guide to Artist's Materials and Techniques, 1996, Fresh Flowers: The Best of American Floral Painting, 1997, The Best of American Portrait Painting, 1998; contbg. editor The Artist's Mag., 1990-95; editor: Classical Realism Quar., 1988-92; exhibited in group shows including Internat. Mus. of the Horse, 1997, 98, Foxhall Gallery, 1997, 98, Sutton Gallery, 1997, 98, Premier Gallery, 1995, The Minn. Mus. of Art, 1992-93, Mpls. Inst. of Arts, 1990-91, Heritage Art Gallery, 1985, 89, 92, Salmagundi Club, 1983, 84, 85, Meadows Mus., 1983; solo shows including Northwestern Gallery, 1996, 95, 94, 93. Recipient award Salmagundi Club, 1985, cert. Am. Portrait Soc., 1985; Stacey Found. scholar, 1983. Mem. Am. Soc. Classical Realism, Christians in the Visual Arts, St. Paul Art Collective. Office: Kurt Anderson Studio 275 4th St E Ste 750 Saint Paul MN 55101-1685

ANDERSON, LAUREL ALMA, nursing educator; b. Chgo., Dec. 5, 1952; d. Arthur J. and Lillian D. (Beling) A. BS, St. Xavier U., Chgo., 1974; MS, Loma Linda U., 1978; ND in Nursing Genetics, Rush U., Chgo., 1999. Staff nurse Christ Hosp., Oak Lawn, Ill., 1974-76, nursing supr., 1976-77; staff nurse Med. Staffing Svcs., Costa Mesa, Calif., 1977-78; mem. faculty Loma Linda (Calif.) U., 1979, Evangelical Sch. Nursing, Oak Lawn, Ill., 1979-88, St. Xavier U., Chgo., 1988-89, Ravenswood Hosp., Chgo., 1989-90, St. Xavier U., Chgo., 1990—; bd. dirs. Sertoma Centre, Inc., Alsip, Ill., 1981—; fellow U. Chgo., ELSI genetics faculty, asst. prof. Co-author: ILN Review Book, revised, 1994. Mem. ANA, Am. Soc. Human Genetics, Nat. League Nursing, Internat. Soc. Nurses in Genetics, Kiwanis, Sigma Theta Tau (Alpha Omicron chpt. faculty advisor 1998—). Avocations: crafts, bowling, cats, dogs, computers. Home: 10536 S Kolmar Ave Oak Lawn IL 60453-5216 Office: St Xavier U 3700 W 103rd St Chicago IL 60655-3105

ANDERSON, LAURENCE ALEXIS, lawyer; b. Willmar, Minn., July 20, 1940; s. Laurence Alexis and Ann Victoria (Carlson) A.; m. Elaine Mae Sather, Aug. 19, 1961; children: Jeanne Louise, Ross Laurence; m. Elizabeth J. McKie, Dec. 30, 1989; 1 child, Rachael McKie. BA in Polit. Sci. and Econs., Macalester Coll., 1962; JD, U. Minn., 1965; LLM in Taxation, William Mitchell Coll. of Law, 1994. Bar: Minn. 1965, U.S. Dist. Ct. Minn. 1965, U.S. Tax Ct. 1994. Assoc., Olson, Kief & Kalar, Bemidji, Minn., 1965-67; spl. asst. atty. gen. State of Minn., St. Paul, 1967-69; ptnr., dir., Crawford & Anderson, West St. Paul, Minn., 1969-84; mem., bd. dir. Bowman and London Ltd., 1984-89; mem., officer, bd. dirs. Jacobsen, Stromme & Harwood P.A., 1989-92, London, Anderson, Antolak & Hoeft, Ltd., Mpls., 1992—; bd. dirs., officer Legal Assistance of Dakota County (Minn.). Active Greater St. Paul United Way. Mem. ABA, Minn. State Bar Assn., Dakota County Bar Assn., Ramsey County Bar Assn., Hennepin County Bar Assn., West St. Paul C. of C., Southview Country Club, Optimists Club (West St. Paul). Republican. Office: 2250 One Financial Plz 120 S 6th St Minneapolis MN 55402-1803

ANDERSON, LAVERNE ERIC, lawyer; b. Rockford, Ill., Feb. 24, 1922; s. Eric J. and Alma M. (Johnson) A.; m. Lucille Hardy, Feb. 14, 1954. LLB, U. Ill., 1944, JD, 1946. Bar: Ill. 1947. Admitted to practice U.S. Treasury Dept., Fed. Ct.; pvt. practice law Rockford, 1947—, city atty., 1947-53; corp. counsel, 1953-57. Mem. Zion Devel. Corp.; mem. Zion Luth. Ch.; former chmn. Com. Interprofl. Cooperation. Mem. Ill. Bar Assn., Winnebago County Bar Assn., Broadway Bus. Assn., Masons, Shriners (rep. imperial coun., potentate Tebala Shrine Temple 1977), Royal Order Jesters, Phi Eta Sigma, Phi Beta Kappa, Phi Kappa Phi. Lutheran. Office: 724 Broadway Rockford IL 61104-4807

ANDERSON, LAWRENCE KEITH, electrical engineer; b. Toronto, Ont., Can., Oct. 2, 1935; came to U.S., 1957; s. Wallace Ray and Irene Margaret (Linn) A.; m. Katherine Florence Drechsler, Sept. 21, 1963; children—Susan Barbara, Robert Keith. B. in Engring. Physics, McGill U., 1957; PhDEE, Stanford U., 1962. With Bell Labs., 1961-85; dir. electronic components and Subsystems lab. Bell Labs., Allentown, Pa., 1981-85; v.p. component devel. Sandia Nat. Labs., Albuquerque, 1985-88; exec. dir. AT&T Bell Labs. Interconnection and Power Tech. Div., Parsippany, NJ, 1988-89; prof., dir. Alliance for Photonic Tech., Albuquerque, 1990-91; dir. Colo. Inst. Tech. Transfer and Implementation, U. Colo., Colorado Springs, 1991-95. Fellow IEEE (pres. Electron Devices Soc. 1976-77, dir. 1979-80), Engring. Mgmt. Soc. (bd. govs. 1999—). Home: 150 Whitetail Rd NE Albuquerque NM 87122-1921

ANDERSON, LEE STRATTON, newspaper publisher, editor; b. Trenton, Ky., Dec. 15, 1925; s. Herbert Love and Corinne (Kirkpatrick) A.; m. Elizabeth McDonald, June 10, 1950; children: Corinne Elizabeth Anderson Adams, Mary Stewart. AB, U. Chattanooga, 1948. Reporter Chattanooga Free Press, 1942-48, assoc. editor, 1948-58, editor, 1958—, pub., 1990-99; assoc. pub., editor Chattanooga Free Press and Chattanooga Times, 1999—. Author: Battles of Chickamauga and Chattanooga-1863, 1959, Israel: I Looked Over Jordan, 1996. Pres. Chattanooga Conv. and Visitor's Bur., 1958; chmn. Chattanooga chpt. ARC, 1968-70, United Way Campaign, 1979. With USAAF, World War II, maj. USAR. Recipient numerous awards for editls., lectrs. and civic svcs. Freedoms Found. Mem. Sigma Chi, Rotary (pres. Chattanooga 1964-65). Presbyterian (elder). Home: 220 N Crest Rd Chattanooga TN 37404-1018 Office: Chattanooga Free Press 400 E 11th St PO Box 1447 Chattanooga TN 37401-1447

ANDERSON, LEONE MARIE CASTELL, children's book author; b. L.A., Aug. 12, 1923; d. Carl Anton and Elsa Marie (Berggren) Castell; m. J. Eric Anderson, Aug. 17, 1946; children: Jon Scott, James Eric, Paul Lawrence. Student, Austin Acad. Music, Chgo., 1944-45, Highland Coll., Freeport, Ill., 1981, 89. Copywriter Russell Seeds Advt., Chgo., 1944-46; mem. staff, children's dept. Elmhurst (Ill.) Pub. Libr., 1969-74; owner Lee's Booklover's Shop, Stockton, Ill., 1979-90; children's book author Stockton, 1979—. Author: It's O.K. to Cry, 1979, Learning About Towers and Dungeons, 1982, The Wonderful Shrinking Shirt, 1983, My Friend Next Door, 1983, surprise at Muddy Creek, 1984, Christmas Handbook, 1984, the Good-By Day, 1987, My Own Grandpa, 1987, How Come You're So Shy?, 1987, Discovering Our Past, Vol. I, 1990, Vol. II, 1994, Humor Anthology, 1995, Why Leroy Smiled, 1997, Sean's War, 1998; Contbr. children's stories, poems and articles to Children's Playmate, The Friend, golden Mag., Jack and Jill, Jr. Scholastic, others; author newspaper columns and newsletters; theater performer in Chgo. area. Recipient 1st place for short story Highlights for Children, 1989, 1st place picture book award Fla. Freelance Writers, 1993. Mem. Soc. Children's Book Writers and Illustrators (No. Ill. networks com. rep. 1997—), Children's REading Table, Author's Guild. Avocations: music (piano accompaniment), drama. Home: 13115 E Chelsea Rd Stockton IL 61085-9726

ANDERSON, LINDA D., psychologist; b. Beaver Falls, Pa.; d. Addison S. and Elizabeth W. Anderson. BS in Elem. Edn., Ind. U. Pa., 1969, MEd in Elem. Edn., 1970, diploma in sch. psychology, 1973, postgrad., 1973-78, 87-93; diploma in supr. sch. psychol. svcs., Millersville U. Pa., 1978. Lic. psychologist; cert. sch. psychologist. Grad. asst. Ind. U. Pa., 1969-70; tchr. elem. edn. Ind. Area Sch. Dist., 1969-73; psychologist, case mgr. Lincoln Intermediate Unit # 12, New Oxford, Pa., 1973-74, 76-82; psychologist Camp Hill (Pa.) Sch. Dist., 1974-76; instr. Community Coll. Allegheny County, Pitts., 1982; psychologist D.T. Watson Rehab. Hosp., Leetsdale, Pa., 1982, Allegheny Intermediate Unit, Pitts., 1982, PACE Sch., Pitts., 1982-84; psychologist pre-sch. Westmoreland Intermediate Unit # 7, Greensburg, Pa., 1984—; writer presch. guidelines Pa. Dept. Edn., Harrisburg, 1990. Bd. dirs. presch. 1st Presbyn. Ch., Greensburg, 1989-91; past mother adviser, past worthy advisor Internat. Order of Rainbow for Girls. Mem. NEA, APA, Pa. Interagency Coordinating Coun. (Early Intervention Personnel Preparation Com. 1992-95), Pa. Psychol. Assn. (past pres. sch. divn., bd. dirs.), Nat. Assn. Sch. Psychologists, Assn. Sch. Psychologists Pa. (regional del., state bd. dirs. 1979-82, 88-90, recipient Pa. Outstanding Sch. Psychologist of the Yr. award 1991-92), Pa. State Edn. Assn., Lincoln I.U. Edn. Assn. (past treas.), Coun. Exceptional Children, Pa. Tourette Syndrome Assn. (sec./treas., bd. dirs. 1984-92), Little Beaver Hist. Soc. (life), Zelienople Hist. Soc. (life), Harmony Hist. Assn. (life)Mercer County Geneal. Soc., Beaver County Rsch. and Hist. Landmarks Found., Chem. Inquiry Network, HEAL Vets. of the Battle of the Bulge (assoc., life mem.), Western Pa. Geneol. Soc., Ind. Hist. and Geneal. Soc. (life), Nat. Cory Soc. (sec.), Butler County Hist. Soc., 99th Inf. Divsn. Checkerboard (assoc.), Kappa Delta Pi. Home: 204 N Shenandoah Dr Latrobe PA 15650-2550 Office: Westmoreland Intermediate Unit RD # 12 Box 205 Donohue Rd Greensburg PA 15601

ANDERSON, LLOYD LEE, animal science educator; b. Nevada, Iowa, Nov. 18, 1933; s. Clarence and Carrie G. (Sampson) A.; m. Janice G. Peterson, Sept. 7, 1958 (dec. Dec. 1966); m. JaNelle R. Hall, June 15, 1970; children: Marc C., James R. *The family cherished 20 years of love and loyal companionship with Cinnamon.* Student, Simpson Coll., 1951-52, Iowa State U., 1952-53; BS in Animal Husbandry, Iowa State U., 1957, PhD in Animal Reproduction, 1961. NIH postdoctoral fellow Iowa State U., Ames, 1961-62, asst. prof., 1961-65, assoc. prof., 1965-71, prof. animal sci., 1971—, Charles F. Curtiss Disting. prof. agr., 1992—; Lalor Found. fellow Sta. Recherches Physiologie Animale, Inst. Nat. Recherche Agronomique, Jouy-en-Josas, France, 1963-64; rschr. physiology of reprodn. and cen. nervous sys.-pituitary regulation of growth for increased prodn. efficiency of farm animals; mem. reproductive biology study sect. NIH, 1984-88, NIH Reviewers Res. (NRR), 1988-92; mem. peer rev. panel animal health spl. rsch. grants on beef and dairy cattle reproductive diseases USDA, 1986-88; Honor lectr. representing Iowa State U., Mid-Am. State Univs. Assn., 1989-90; mem. sustainable agrl. panel U.S. Dept. Agr., Agrl. Rsch. Svc., Nat. Program Staff to rev. rsch. projects, 1993; mem. referees panel for sponsored rsch. Kuwait U., 1998—; mem. Janice Peterson Anderson Excellence award and scholarship Coll. of Design, Iowa State U. Mem. editl. bd. Biology Reprodn., 1968-70, 86-90, Jour. Animal Sci., 1982-87, 98—, Animal Reprodn. Sci., 1978—, Inst. for Sci. Info. Atlas of Sci., 1987-90, Domestic

Animal Endocrinology, 1992-95, Endocrinology, 1993-97; contbr. articles to profl. jours. Mem. 4-H Club. With Constrn. Engrs., U.S. Army, 1953-55, Germany, Signal Corps USAR, 1955-61. USDA grantee, 1978—. Fellow AAAS, Am. Soc. Animal Sci. (hon. Animal Physiology and Endocrinology award 1988, Nat Pork Prodrs. Coun. Innovation award in basic rsch. 1993); mem. ACLU, NRA, VFW, Endocrine Soc., Am. Physiol. Soc., Iowa Physiol. Soc., Am. Assn. Anatomists, Soc. for Study of Reprodn., Soc. for Exptl. Biology and Medicine (mem. coun. 1980-83), Brit. Soc. for Study of Fertility, Soc. for Neurosci., Iowa Acad. Sci., Pituitary Soc., Am. Legion, Nat. Block and Bridle Club, Osborn Rsch. Club (chair 1994), Sigma Xi, Gamma Sigma Delta. Methodist. Home: 2812 Valley View Rd Ames IA 50014-4506 Office: Iowa State U Dept Animal Sci 2356 Kildee Hall Ames IA 50011

ANDERSON, LOIS D., nursing administrator, mental health nurse; b. Fulton, Mo., July 7, 1929; d. John Henry and Flossie Margaret (Myers) Dye; m. Morris B. Anderson, Nov. 4, 1947 (dec.); children: Sheila Sesti, John Anderson. AS, St. Louis Community Coll., Florissant, Mo., 1981. RN, Mo.; cert. mental health and psychiat. nurse. Head nurse Fulton State Hosp., quality assurance coord., retired 1991. Named hon. Red Cross Nurse, 1988. Mem. ANA, Mo. Nurses Assn., Profl. Nurses Assn. (treas.). Avocations: travel, reading, sewing.

ANDERSON, LONI KAYE, actress; b. St. Paul, Aug. 5, 1946; d. Klaydon Carl and Maxine Hazel (Kallin) A.; m. Ross Bickell (div.); 1 child, Deidra; m. Burton Leon Reynolds, Apr. 29, 1988 (div. 1994); 1 child, Quinton Anderson Reynolds. BA in Art and Drama, U. Minn., 1969. Appeared in numerous TV shows including WKRP in Cincinnati, 1978-82, Partners in Crime, 1984-85, Easy Street, 1986-87, Nurses, 1993-94, Three's Company, The Love Boat, The Bob Newhart Show, Three on a Date, (TV films) Jayne Mansfield: A Symbol of the 50's, 1980, Sizzle, 1981, Country Gold, 1982, My Mothers Secret Life, 1984, A Letter to Three Wives, 1985, Stranded, 1986, Necessity, 1987, A Whisper Kills, 1988, Too Good To Be True, 1988, Sorry Wrong Number, 1989, Coins in The Fountain, 1990, White Hot, 1991, The Price She Paid, 1992, Deadly Family Secrets, 1995, Melrose Place, 1996, Munchie Strikes Back, 1994, Gambler V: Playing for Keeps, 1994, (films) Stroker Ace, 1983; stage appearances Born Yesterday, Fiddler on the Roof, The Star Spangled Girl, Never Too Late, Any Wednesday, Can-Can, The Threepenny Opera, Munchie, 1992, Munchie Strikes Back, 1994, 3 Ninjas: High Noon at Mega Mountain, 1997, A Night at the Roxbury, 1998. Office: Media Four 2029 Century Park E Ste 3250 Los Angeles CA 90067-3018*

ANDERSON, LORRAINE, secondary education educator; b. Beulah, Miss., May 23, 1954; d. Milton and Catherine Anderson. BA, U. Ill., 1977, MA, 1981. Cert. tchr., Ill.; diploma in computer programming Control Data, 1978. Tchr. spl. edn. Martin Luther King H.S., Chgo. Pub. Schs., 1984-88, tchr. English, Chgo. H.S. Agrl. Scis., 1988—; judge Chgo. Metro History Fair, 1983-84; pension judge Chgo. Tchrs., 1995—; reader judge Chgo. Sci. Fair Symposium, Chgo., 1997-98. Truste, min.'s bd. dirs. Bethel House Prayer, United Holiness Ch. Am., Chgo., 1987—. Mem. Nat. Coun. Tchrs. English, Ill. Coun. Reading, Ill. Computing Educators, Secondary Reading League, Future Farmers Am. Alumni. Assn. Avocations: reading, singing in the community choir, writing poetry, travel. Office: Chgo HS Agrl Scis 3857 W 111th St Chicago IL 60655-4009

ANDERSON, LOUIE, comedian; b. Mpls.. Appeared in film Cloak & Dagger, 1984, Quick Silver, 1986, Ferris Bueller's Day Off, 1986, The Wrong Guys, 1988, Coming to America, 1988, Bebe's Kids, 1992, Mr. Wrong, 1996, (TV) Life with Louie (voice), 1995, The Louie Show, 1996; author: Dear Dad: Letters From an Adult Child, 1989; comedian: HBO Spl. Recipient Daytime Emmy, 1996. Office: ICM 8942 Wilshire Blvd Beverly Hills CA 90211-1934*

ANDERSON, LOUIS WILMER, JR., physicist, educator; b. Houston, Dec. 24, 1933; s. Louis Wilmer and Margaret Quarles (Brockett) A.; m. Marguerite Gillespie, Aug. 30; children—Margaret Mary, Louis Charles, Elizabeth Brockett. B.A., Rice U., 1956; A.M., Harvard U., 1957, Ph.D., 1960. Asst. prof. U. Wis.-Madison, 1960-63, assoc. prof., 1963-68, prof. physics, 1968-94, Julian E. Mack prof. physics, 1994—; cons. U. Calif.-Berkeley Lawrence Lab. Author 2 textbooks. Contbr. articles to profl. jours. Patentee type of N2 laser , collisional pumping source. Fellow U. Wis. Tchg. Acad.; co-recipient IEEE Particle Accelerator Conf. Tech. award for invention and devel. of optically pumped polarized H-Ion source, 1993. Fellow Am. Phys. Soc.; mem. Sigma Xi. Home: 1818 Chadbourne Ave Madison WI 53705-4045 Office: U Wis Dept Physics Madison WI 53706

ANDERSON, LOUISE STOUT, crime analyst; b. Wellsville, N.Y., Aug. 11, 1952; d. Carlton C. and Mary (Gasdik) Stout; m. Leonard M. Anderson, June 2, 1973. BA in German Lit., Polit. Sci., Mt. Holyoke Coll., 1974; MA in Polit. Sci., San Diego State U., 1977; MS Human Resources and Organizational Devel., 1994. Cert. C.C. tchr., Calif. Statistician Grossmont Coll., El Cajon, Calif., 1976-78; crime analyst San Diego Police Dept., 1978-80; crime analyst Career Criminal Apprehension Program, Marin County Sheriff's Office, San Rafael, Calif., 1980-83; crime analyst CCAP Unit, Sonoma County Sheriff's Office, Santa Rosa, Calif., 1983-85; mgr. mktg. svcs. Command Data Systems, Dublin, Calif., 1985-87, client svcs. mgr., 1988-92; contracts mgr. Tiburon Inc., 1992; mgr. field svcs. OCS Techs., 1992-95, v.p. nat. customers support, 1994-95; project mgr. IBM Global Svcs., 1995—; cons. Search Group Inc. for Automated Crime Analysis. Contbr. articles in field. Owner Acacia Assocs., public safety cons. and training orgn.; project mgmt. profl. Project Mgmt. Inst., 1994; bd. dirs. Mt. Holyoke Club So. Calif., 1996-98. Mem. Antioch Police Commn.; alumna recruiter Mt. Holyoke Club No. Calif., 1981-86.

ANDERSON, LYLE ARTHUR, manufacturing company executive; b. Jewell, Kans., Dec. 29, 1931; s. Arvid Herman and Clara Vera (Herman) A.; m. Harriet Virginia Robson, June 12, 1953; children—Brian, Karen, Eric. BS, U. Kans., 1953; MS, Butler U., 1961. C.P.A., Mo., Kans. Mgmt. trainee, internal auditor RCA, Camden, N.J. and Indpls., 1955-59; auditor Ernst & Ernst (C.P.A.'s), Kansas City, Mo., 1959-63; v.p. fin. and adminstrn., treas., dir. Affiliated Hosp. Products, Inc., St. Louis, 1963-71; sr. v.p. Sara Lee Corp., Deerfield, Ill., 1971-74; exec. v.p. fin. Consol. Foods Corp., Chgo., 1974-76; pres. Autotrol Corp., Crystal Lake, Ill. Bd. dirs. Crystal Lake Civic Ctr. Authority, Raue Ctr. for the Arts. With U.S. Army, 1953-55. Mem. Omicron Delta Kappa. Republican. Methodist. Home: 9804 Partridge Ln Crystal Lake IL 60014-6627 Office: 365 E Prairie St Crystal Lake IL 60014-4414

ANDERSON, MARGARET LAVINIA, history educator; b. Washington, Oct. 18, 1941; d. David and Margaret Lavinia (Anderson) A.; m. Charles Raff, Sept. 12, 1972; 1 dau., Sarah Elizabeth. B.A., Swarthmore Coll., 1963; Ph.D., Brown U., 1971. Asst. prof. history Swarthmore Coll. (Pa.), 1970-77, assoc. prof., 1977-84, prof., 1985—; mem. com. Ednl. Testing Service, Princeton, N.J., 1983-86. Author: Windthorst: A Political Biography, 1981; contbr. articles to profl. jours. Woodrow Wilson Found. fellow, 1963, 66-67; NDEA fellow Brown U., Providence, 1963-66, grantee, 1972; Humboldt Found. fellow, Bonn, W.Ger., 1974; Lang fellow Swarthmore Coll., 1981-82; Flack Faculty award for teaching, Swarthmore Coll., 1985; Mem. Am. Hist. Assn., Cath. Hist. Assn., German Studies Assn., Conf. Group on Cen. European History (bi-ann. prize for best articles 1984). Democrat. Episcopalian. Office: Swarthmore Coll Dept History Swarthmore PA 19081

ANDERSON, MARGARET TAYLER, real estate broker, career consultant; b. Castle Rock, Wash., May 1, 1918; d. George Lawrence and Frances Tressie (Huntington) Tayler; m. James Kress Anderson, Dec. 31, 1940; children: Bret Douglas, Blythe Rebecca Chase, Beth Lynn Murray, Burke Stuart. AB, Willamette U., 1939, MA, 1940; MA, Columbia U., 1967; profl. diploma, Columbia U., 1970; DHL (hon.), Dominican Coll. Blauvelt, 1991. Cert. English, social studies tchr., N.Y. Asst. travelling libr. Oreg. State Libr., Salem, 1940; chemist Reynolds Metals, Longview, Wash., 1941; electronic technician Sperry Gyroscope, Lake Success, N.Y., 1942-43; adminstrv. asst. New Sch. Social Rsch., N.Y.C., 1944-49; real estate broker Palisades, N.Y., 1952—; dir. Rockland County Guidance Ctr. Women, Nyack, N.Y., 1969-91; career counselor N.Y. State Dept. Adult and Continuing Edn., Albany, 1985-90; pres. Rockland County Bd. Realtors, 1968-69. Editor, co-author From Here to My Goal, 1979-80; co-author, co-editor N.Y. Adult Career Counseling Manual, 1988-91. Mem. com. Rockland County Dems., 1961—; co-chair Orangetown Dems., 1962-66; fundraiser Palisades Free Libr., 1960—; mem. alumni coun., devel., fundraising Columbia U. Tchrs. Coll., 1994—; bd. visitors Rockland State Hosp., Orangeburg, N.Y., 1956-63. Recipient Woman of Yr. award Bus. & Profl. Women, 1977, Disting. Alumni award Columbia U. Tchrs. Coll., 1992. Mem. NOW, LWV, AAUW (v.p. 1995-2000, Woman of Achievement award Rockland County sect. 1979), Nat. Assn. Women Edn. Avocations: horticulture, husbandry, handicrafts. Home and Office: 286 Route 9W Palisades NY 10964-1618

ANDERSON, MARILYN NELLE, elementary education educator, librarian, counselor; b. Las Animas, Colo., May 5, 1942; d. Mason Hadley Moore and Alice Carrie (Dwyer) Coates; m. George Robert Anderson, Sept. 4, 1974; children: Lisa Lynn, Edward Alan, Justin Patrick. BEd magna cum laude, Adams State Coll., 1962, postgrad., 1965; MEd, Ariz. State U., 1967; postgrad., Idaho State U., 1971, 86, Columbia Pacific U., 1991—. Cert. elem. tchr., K-12 sch. counselor. Tchr. Wendell (Idaho) Sch. Dist. 232, 1962-66, Union-Endicott (N.Y.) Sch. Dist., 1967-68; counselor, librarian West Yuma (Colo.) Sch. Dist., 1968-69; elem. sch. counselor Am. Falls (Idaho) Sch. Dist. 381, 1969-73; project dir. Gooding County (Idaho) Sr. Citizens Orgn., 1974-75; tchr. Castleford (Idaho) Sch. Dist. 417, 1982-92; placement specialist, referral counselor Idaho Child Care Program South Ctrl. Idaho Community Action Agy., Twin Falls, 1992—; mem. Castleford Schs. Merit Pay Devel. program, 1983-84, Accreditation Evaluation com., 1984-85, Math. Curriculum Devel. com., 1985-86. Leader Brownie Scouts, Endicott, 1967-68; chmn. fundraising com. Am. Falls Kindergarten, 1971-73. Recipient Leader's award Nat. 4-H Conservation Natural Resources Program, 1984. Mem. NEA, ASCD, Nat. Assn. Edn. Young Children, Assn. Childhood Edn. Internat., Idaho Edn. Assn., So. Idaho Assn. for Childhood Edn. Internat. (pres.), Idaho Coun. Internat. Reading Assn., Magic Valley Reading Assn., Support Unltd. Providers and Parents. Republican. Baptist. Avocations: reading, painting, writing short stories, photography. Home: 1675 BBH Wendell ID 83355-9801 Office: South Ctrl Idaho Community Action Agency Twin Falls ID 83301

ANDERSON, MARK BRIAN, psychologist; b. Enid, Okla., Mar. 3, 1965; s. Oran Gail and Mary Ellen (James) A.; m. Giorgia Anderson, Sept. 22, 1991; children: Jonathan Oran, Andrew Mark. BA in Psychology, Oakland U., Rochester, Mich., 1987; MA in Psychology, U. Detroit, 1990, PsyS, 1996; EdD, Indiana U. of Pa., 1998. Nat. cert. sch. psychologist, counselor. Mental health counselor Cottage and Bon Secours Hosps., Grosse Pointe, Mich., 1987-89; psychologist intern U. Detroit Psychology Clinic, 1989-90; psychologist Hazel Park (Mich.) Sch. Dist., 1990—; psychologist in pvt. practice Southfield, 1993—; pres. A-1-800-Therapist, Inc., Southfield, 1996—. Mem. APA., ACA, Mich. Psychol. Assn., Nat. Assn. Sch. Psychologists, Mich. Assn. Sch. Psychologists, Am. Mental Health Counselors Assn., Hazel Park Rotary (pres. 1996, 97). Greek Orthodox. Avocations: reading, running, music. Home: 32373 Nestlewood St Farmingtn Hls MI 48334-2739 Office: 26211 Central Park Blvd Ste 415 Southfield MI 48076-4159

ANDERSON, MARK EUGENE, specialized truck driver, safety inspector; b. Richland Center, Wis., Oct. 9, 1952; s. Harold Eugene and Laila Marie (Jacobson) A.; m. Marilyn Jones, June 22, 1972 (div. 1984); children: Michael, Kenneth, Thomas; m. Georgina Therese Scinta, Sept. 29, 1984. Grad., Mich. Ctr. for Design Driving, 1993, Mich. Ctr. Decision Driving. Enlisted U.S. Army, 1970, ret., 1977; mgr. Taco Bell, Farmington, N.Mex., 1977-78; truck driver Farmington Meat Processors, 1978-80, Nobel/Sysco, Albuquerque, 1980-89; specialized truck driver transuranic nuclear waste Dawn Enterprises Inc., Farmington, 1989-95, Steere Tank Lines, 1995, ABF Freight Sys. Inc., 1995—; truck driver, cert. safety inspector Comml. Vehicle Safety Alliance, Oreg., 1991; truck driver transp. safeguards div. U.S. Dept. Energy, Albuquerque, 1989. Mem. Mich. Truck Safety Commn., 1993. Named N.Mex. State Truck Driving Champion N.Mex. Motor Carriers, 1988, Grand Champion Truck Driving Championship, N.Mex. Motor Carriers, 1994. Avocations: classic cars, woodworking, motorcycling, home improvement. Home: 5201 Chuckwagon Trl NW Albuquerque NM 87120-2889 Office: Dawn Enterprises Inc PO Box 204 Farmington NM 87499-0204

ANDERSON, MARK ROBERT, data processing executive, biochemist; b. Oak Park, Ill., Aug. 11, 1951; s. Robert Hugo and Marilyn Pettee (Johnson) A.; m. Mary Jane Helsell, June 6, 1980; children: Berit Bracken, Evan Robert. BS, Stanford U., 1972; MS, Stanford U., Hopkins Marine Sta., 1973; postgrad., U. Brit. Columbia, Vancouver, 1973. Publisher Potlatch Press, Friday Harbor, Wash., 1974-77; assoc. prof. Western Wash. U., Bellingham, 1977, Harvard U., Boston, 1978; chief scientist Ocean Research & Edn. Soc., Boston, 1978; v.p. Moclips Cetological Soc., Friday Harbor, 1979-81; founder, exec. dir. The Whale Mus., Friday Harbor, 1979-81; pres. The Oikos Co., Friday Harbor, 1980—, San Juan Software, Friday Harbor, 1983-84; pres., bd. dirs. Island Tech. Inc., Friday Harbor, 1984—; founder, pres. Tech. Alliance Ptnrs., 1989—; bd. dirs. Worldesign, PreText, Inc., Wa. Software Assn.; bd. advisors HIT Lab., U. Wash., 1991—; founder, pres. Strategic News Svc. LLC, 1995—; founder WSA Investment Forum; CEO, bd. dirs. Carrier Wave, Inc., 1996—; program chair Online Advantage 96; founder, exec. dir. Orca Relief Citizens Alliance, 1998—; founder, mgr. The Resonance Fund, 1999—; bd. advisors Smarage, Inc., 1999—, E-CHRON, Stockholm, 1999—. Author: Nineteen Fathers, 1971, (software) The Agent's Advantage, 1983; producer TV film Survivors, 1980; editor, founder Jour. Cetus, 1981; discoverer Resonance Theory, 1981; columnist ABC News.com, 1998—. Founder San Juan Musicians Guild, 1974-78, Anti-Spray Coalition, 1977. Mem. Wash. Software Assn. (bd. dirs. 1988-90, chair pres.'s group 1989—). Avocations: theoretical physics, musical composition, skiing.

ANDERSON, MARK T., business developer, entrepreneur, financier; b. Provo, Utah, Jan. 28, 1953; s. Billy Joe and Norma (Tucker) A.; m. Aleca Alleman, May 5, 1976; children: John Tucker, Amy, Megan. BS in Econs. and Fin., Brigham Young U., 1984. Lic. pvt. and comml. pilot; cert. SCUBA dive master. Pres., dir. G.B. Mark T. Inc., Orem, Utah, 1975—, Mark Anderson & Assocs., Inc., Provo, 1979—, R&D Connections Inc., Salt Lake City, 1983-85; dir., exec. v.p. Kara Signature Chocolates Inc., Salt Lake City, 1985-88; mng. dir. Network Capital LTD., Salt Lake City, 1986-90; pres. Mark Anderson Mgmt. Co., 1988—; mng. dir. Network Fin. Group Inc., Salt Lake City, 1992—; exec. v.p. Viking Internat. Airlines, Inc. (DBA Eagle Airlines), Ft. Lauderdale, Fla., 1993-94, Viking Internat. Airlines (doing bus. as Eagle Airlines), Atlanta, 1993-94; wxec. v.p. Viking Internat. Airlines (doing bus. as Eagle Airlines), Las Vegas, 1993-94. Trustee, gen. mgr. Furresa's Trust Salt Lake City and L.A. Mem. Riverside Country Club (bd. dirs. 1997—, exec. com., sec. 1999—), Ridge Athletic Club, Kauai Marriott Beach Club (bd. dirs. 1998—), Elks. Republican. Mem. LDS Ch. Avocations: skiing, golf, tennis. Home: 4101 Timpview Dr Provo UT 84604-5130

ANDERSON, MARTIN CARL, economist; b. Lowell, Mass., Aug. 5, 1936; s. Ralph and Evelyn (Anderson) A.; m. Annelise Graebner, Sept. 25, 1965. AB summa cum laude, Dartmouth Coll., 1957, MS in Engring., MSBA; PhD in Indsl. Mgmt., MIT, 1962. Asst. to dean, instr. engring. Thayer Sch. Engring. Dartmouth Coll., Hanover, N.H., 1959; research fellow Joint Ctr. for Urban Studies MIT and Harvard U., Cambridge, 1961-62; asst. prof. fin. Grad. Sch. Bus. Columbia U., N.Y.C., 1962-65, assoc. prof. bus., 1965-68; sr. fellow Hoover Inst. on War, Revolution and Peace Stanford (Calif.) U., 1971—; spl. asst. to Pres. of U.S. The White House, 1969-70, spl. cons. for systems analysis, 1970-71, asst. for policy devel., 1981-82; mem. Pres.' Fgn. Intelligence Adv. Bd., 1982-85, Pres.' Econ. Policy Adv. Bd., 1982-88, Pres.' Gen. Adv. Com. on Arms Control and Disarmament, 1987-93; pub. interest dir. Fed. Home Loan Bank San Francisco, 1972-79; mem. Commn. on Crucial Choices for Ams., 1973-75, Def. Manpower Commn., 1975-76, Com. on the Present Danger, 1977—. Author: The Federal Bulldozer: A Critical Analysis of Urban Renewal, 1949-62, 1964, Conscription: A Select and Annotated Bibliography, 1976, Welfare: The Political Economy of Welfare Reform in the U.S., 1978, Registration and the Draft, 1982, The Military Draft, 1982, Revolution, 1988, Impostors in the Temple, 1992; columnist Scripps-Howard News Svc., 1993-94. Dir. research Nixon presdl. campaign, 1968; policy adviser Reagan presdl. campaign, 1976, 80; del. Rep. Nat. Conv., 1992-96; policy adviser Dole Presdl. Campaign, 1996; trustee Ronald Reagan Presdl. Found., 1985-92; mem. Calif. Gov.'s Coun. Econ. Advisors, 1993—, chmn. Congl. Policy Adv. Bd., 1998—. 2d lt. AUS, 1958-59. Mem. Am. Econ. Assn., Mont Pelerin Soc., Phi Beta Kappa. Club: Bohemian. Office: Stanford U Hoover Instn Stanford CA 94305-6010

ANDERSON, MARY JANE, public library director; b. Des Moines, Jan. 23, 1935; d. William Kenneth and Margaret Louise (Snider) McPherson; m. Charles Robert Anderson, Oct. 21, 1965 (div. Oct. 24, 1989); 1 child, Mary Margaret. BA in Edn., U. Fla., 1957; MLS, Fla. State U., 1963. Elem. sch. librarian Dade County Schs., Miami, Fla., 1957-61; children's/young adult librarian Santa Fe Regional Library, Gainesville, Fla., 1961-63; br. librarian Jacksonville (Fla.) Pub. Library, 1963-64, chief of children's services, 1964-66, head of circulation, 1966-67; pub. library cons. Fla. State Library, Tallahassee, 1967-70; dir. tech. processing St. Mary's Coll. of Md., St. Mary's City, 1970-72; coordinator children's services Balt. County Pub. Library, Towson, Md., 1972-73; exec. dir. young adult services div. ALA, Chgo., 1973-75, exec. dir. assn. for library service to children, 1973-82; pres. Answers Unltd., Inc., Deerfield, Ill., 1982-92; dir. Wilmington (Ill.) Pub. Libr., 1993-97; dir. media svcs. Newark (Ill.) County Sch. Dist., 1997-98; dir. Maud P. Palenske Pub. Libr., St. Joseph, Mich., 1998—; instr. and cons. in field; part-time faculty No. Ill. U., 1985-86, Nat. Coll. Edn., Evanston, Ill., 1989; head youth svcs. Waukegan (Ill.) Pub. Libr., 1988-93; mem. exec. com. U.S. sect. Internat. Bd. on Books for Young People, 1973-82; mem. adv. bd. Reading Rainbow, TV series, 1981-84; mem. sch. bd. Avoca Sch. Dist. 37, 1985-87; mem. ALSC Newbery Medal Com., 1991. Editor: Top of the News, 1971-73, Fla. State Library Newsletter, 1967-70, Nor'Easter (North Suburban Library System Newsletter), 1984-88; contbr. articles to profl. jours. Bd. dirs. Child Devel. Assocs. Consortium, 1975-83, Coalition for Children and Youth, 1978-80; mem. exec. bd. NSLS Youth Librs., 1991-93; mem. Episcopal Diocese Chgo. Diocesan Coun., 1988-94, standing com., 1994-97, dep. to gen. conv., 1997, mem. Bishop's search com. 1997-98, province V rep. 1998-99; mem. vestry St. Thomas' Episcopal Ch., Morris, Ill., 1996-98; mem. City of Wilmington Downtown Redevel. Commn., 1996-98. Mem. ALA (coun. 1992—, com. on orgn. 1999—), Mich. Libr. Assn., Rotary (sec.-treas. 1994-96, pres. 1996-97), Wilmington C. of C. (bd. dirs. 1996-97, sec. 1997), Beta Phi Mu, Sigma Kappa. Episcopalian. Office: 500 Market St Saint Joseph MI 49085-1368

ANDERSON, MARY THERESA, investment manager; b. Flushing, N.Y., Mar. 30, 1945; d. William John and Loretta (Lent) Donovan; m. Anders Franklin Anderson, Oct. 4, 1964; children: Krista J. Anderson Ross, A. Erik. BS magna cum laude, So. Oreg. State Coll., 1981; MBA, Fairleigh Dickinson U., 1996. Dir. sales and mktg. Riverside Conf. Ctr., Grants Pass, Oreg., 1981-82; sales mgr. Ashland (Oreg.) Hills Inn, 1982-84; fin. cons. Prudential Ins. Co., Portland, Oreg., 1984-87; investment counselor Vancouver (Wash.) Fed. Savs. Bank, 1987-89; fin. svcs. counselor United Brokerage Svcs. Inc., Lawrenceville, N.J., 1990; fin. svcs. assoc. United Jersey Bank, Hackensack, N.J., 1990-92, asst. v.p., mgr., 1992-93; cons. Pegnato Cons. Group Internat., Nutley, N.J., 1993-96; Anderson Fin. Svcs., 1997—. Vol. Josephine County Welfare Office, Grants Pass. Named Most Valuable Producer Mktg. One Inc., 1988. Mem. NAFE, Nat. Life Underwriters Assn.

ANDERSON, MAX ELLIOT, television and film production company executive; b. Nov. 3, 1946; s. Kenneth O. and Doris I. (Jones) A.; m. Claudia Lynd, Aug. 17, 1978; children: James Brightman, Sarah Lynd. BA in Psychology, Grace Coll., 1973. Advt. rep., cameraman Ken Anderson Films, Warsaw, Ind., 1969-78; prodr. Q Media Group, Rockford, Ill., 1978-83; pres. Philip Lasz Gallery, Warsaw, 1973—; pres., owner The Market Place, Rockford, 1986—; prodr., dir. Eagle Video, Rockford, 1986—; regional product distbr. Laney Honey, 1994—; founder MVP Prodns., 1998—; prodr., writer, dir. Tracy's Choices, 1997; prodr. promotional video W.A. Whitney (German, French, Italian, Mandarin transl.), 1996; prodr. corp. video programs W.A. Whitney, Roper Whitney, Barber Colman, Longview Fibre, 1995, 96, patient video promotion and orientation Swedish Am. Hosp., 1995-96, puppet video programs Woodward Gov.; nat. distbr. home video cassettes, 1985—; mktg. dir. Alley Oop Bowling Alley Ramp for People with Disabilities. Prodr.: (videos) Tracy's Choices, 1997 (Telly award 1998), Youth Haven, A Safe Place for Kids (Telly award 1999); prodr. nat. TV spots for True Value Hardware, 1985-96, 40th anniversary TV spots for Rockford Clin. (Raddy award 1992); assoc. prodr.: Gospel at the Symphony, 1979; cinematographer: (film) Pilgrims Progress (Best Cinematographer award Christian Film Distbrs. Assn. 1978). With U.S. Army, 1967-69. Recipient 1st pl. award Video Internat. Tech. Video Assn., 1989, award for Sunstrand sales video, 1991, award for Woodward Gov. corp. video, 1991, Raddy Award of Excellence, No. Ill. Advt. Coun., 1989-90, 1st pl. video award Hosp. Satellite Network, 1990, award Ill. Soc. for Healthcare Mktg. and Pub. Rels., 1998. Mem. Internat. Christian Video Assn., Am. Beekeeping Assn., Christian Booksellers Assn. Republican. Mem. Evang. Free Ch. Home and Office: 4112 Marsh Ave Rockford IL 61114-6142

ANDERSON, MAXWELL L., museum director; b. N.Y.C., May 1, 1956. AB, Dartmouth Coll., 1977; AM, Harvard U., 1978, PhD, 1981. Asst. curator Met. Mus., 1982-87; dir. Michael C. Carlos Mus., Atlanta, 1987-95, Art Gallery Ont., Toronto, Can., 1995-98, Whitney Mus. Am. Art, N.Y.C., 1998—; lectr. Roman art Princeton (N.J.) U., 1985; vis. prof. U. di Roma, 1987; adj. assoc. prof. Emory U., 1989—. Arranged exhbns. Treasures of the Holy Land, 1986, Roman Portraits in Context, 1988, Souls Grown Deep, 1996, Wired Mus., 1997. Mem. Am. Assn. Mus., Coll. Art Assn., Assn. Art Mus. Dirs. Office: Whitney Mus Am Art 945 Madison Ave New York NY 10021-2701

ANDERSON, MAYNARD CARLYLE, national and international security executive; b. Hesper, Iowa, Aug. 6, 1932; s. Carl Adolph and Mathilda Theodora (Wold) A. BA, Luther Coll., 1954. Mem. spl. ops. group Hqrs. Dept. of Navy, Washington, 1966-68; supervising agt. Naval Investigative Svc. Office Dept. of Navy, Guantanamo Bay, Cuba, 1968-69; asst. head internal security divsn. hqrs. Dept. of Navy, Washington, 1969-73, dir. spl. security and spl. activiites, 1973-78, dir. spl. security, 1978-79; dep. security policy Dept. of Def., Washington, 1979-82, dir. security plans and programs, 1982-88, asst. dep. under sec., 1988-93, acting dep. under sec. def., 1993-94; pres., mng. dir. Arcadia Group Worldwide, Inc., Fairfax, Va., 1994—; founder Arcadia Inst., Fairfax, 1997; prin. Strategic Trade Adv. Group, Inc., Washington, 1997—; dir. Nat. Intellectual Property Law Inst., Washington, 1994; chmn. policy com. Security Affairs Support Assn., Washington, 1988-94; former chmn. adv. com. Dept. of Def. Security Inst., Dept. of Def. Polygraph Inst., Def. Pers. Security Rsch. and Edn. Ctr.; chmn. Nat. Adv. Group/Security Countermeasures; hon. faculty mem. Def. Security Inst.; lectr. Sch. Criminal Justice, Coll. Social Sci., Mich. State U.; mem. rsch. task force Mich. State U.; lect. Luther Coll. Author/contbr.: Citizen Espionage: Studies in Trust and Betrayal, 1994; contbr. articles to profl. jours. Mem. pres. coun. Luther Coll., Decorah, Iowa, 1990—. Recipient Meritorious Exec. Presdl. Rank award, Washington, 1985, 92, Disting. Svc. award Luther Coll., Decorah, 1989, Donald B. Woodbridge award of excellence Nat. Classification Mgmt. Soc., Washington, 1990, Def. Disting. Svc. medal, 1992. Lutheran. Avocations: tennis,writing, lecturing, travel. Home: 205 S Yoakum Pky Apt 721 Alexandria VA 22304-3818 Office: Arcadia Group Worldwide Inc 11320 Random Hills Rd Ste 120 Fairfax VA 22030-6001 *Sometimes it seems that significant achievements have been realized by accident. Actually, they have resulted from taking advantage of opportunities.*

ANDERSON, BROTHER MEL, academic administrator; b. Oakland, Calif., Sept. 28, 1928. BA, St. Mary's Coll., Moraga, Calif., 1952; DLitt, St. Albert's Coll., 1976; LHD, Lewis U., 1979; DHL (hon.), U. San Francisco, 1994; D in Pedagogy (hon.), Manhattan Coll., 1994. Tchr. Sacred Heart High Sch., San Francisco, 1952-56; vice prin. La Salle High Sch., Pasadena, Calif., 1956-62; prin. San Joaquin Meml. High Sch., Fresno, Calif., 1962-64; prin., superior St Mary's High Sch., Residence Sch., Grammar Sch., Berkeley, Calif., 1964-69; pres. St. Mary's Coll. of Calif., Moraga, 1969-97; dir. spl. projects Diocese of Oakland, Calif., 1999—. Trustee St. Mary's Coll., Moraga., 1968-97. Recipient Alemany award Dominican Sch. of Theology and Philosophy, 1992, Papal Pro Ecclesia medal, 1994, Disting. Lasallian Educator award, 1997; named Alumnus of Yr., St. Mary's Coll., 1987; inductee Contra Costa County Hall of Fame, 1988, Anti-Defamation League's Torch of Liberty award, 1993; named Citizen of Yr. town of Moraga, 1994. Fellow Assn. Ind. Calif. Colls. and Univs. (sr.; exec. com. 1973—, chmn. 1988, 89); mem. Regional Assn. East Bay Colls. and Univs. (chmn. 1979-81, 90-91), Fratres Scholarum Christianarum. Democrat.

Roman Catholic. Lodge: Rotary Internat. Avocations: photography, woodworking, travel, drama, music. Office: Diocese of Oakland 2900 Lake Shore Ave Oakland CA 94610

ANDERSON, MELISSA EVA, small business owner; b. Grayson, Ky., Sept. 24, 1959; d. Thomas Erwin and Betty Jane (Mauk) Hall. Student, Araphoe Bus. Coll., Denver, 1976-78; BA, Morehead State U., 1979-84. Sales clk. Cases Hardware and Antiques, Olive Hill, Ky., 1970-72; waitress Los Gringitos, Morehead, Ky., 1975; tele-mktg. operator Citi-Corp Fin. Svcs., Denver, 1977-78; model, spokeswoman Ford Agy. NY, N.Y.C., 1979-81; counselor Christian Social Svcs., 1979-81; activities coord. Dept. Corrections, Denver, 1979; pres. ops. Dimensions Unltd. Inc., Denver, 1981-97; owner, pres. Dimensions Unltd. Inc., Huntington, W.Va., 1985-96, Unlimited Expressions, Olive Hill, Ky., 1996—; cons. Home Interior Designs, Inc., Denver, 1985-86; sec. Denver County Real Estate Commn., 1987-88; bd. dirs. Found. for Human Concerns, Morehead, Ky., 1987-90, Excalibur Fin. Svc., Olive Hill, Ky., Melissa E. Rose Inc., Internat. Mgmt. Specialists; cons. Ky. C. of C., Glasgow, 1988—; founder, pres. Unified Fortress Group, Inc., 1989, Gold Link Publs., 1991-92; contr. Alpha Mktg. Corp., 1992-95; owner Mystic Limousine, 1992—, Four Dragon Internat., Inc., 1997—. Author: Business Ethics 2nd Moral Values, 1987, Life After Death 2 Cultural Explorations, 1987, Business Marketing-Sales for the 90s, 1992, Secrets Through the Eyes of Stone, 1996 (autobiography). Spokesperson Nat. Rep. Group, Morehead, 1981; chairperson Tiffany's Gold Charity Soc., Denver 1986; sec. Bus. Devel. Soc., Las Vegas, 1987; charter sponsor NATO Culture Exch. in W.Va., NY, 1989; mem. Better Bus. Bur. of Ea. and Ctrl. Ky. Named Dutchess Hutt River Province, Australia, 1996. dem. NAFE, Am. Music Assn., Dunn V. Bradstree, Inc., Nat. Assn. Mchts., Encore Gold Purchasing Club, League Human Rights, Nat. Assn. European Bus. Cmtys., Met. Mus. Art, Smithsonian Instn., Citizens for a Better Govt. (chair), Country Music Assn. (Pres. award for Excellence, 1997), Platform Soc., NOW, Better Bus. Bur. Ky., U.S. C. of C. Avocations: painting, sculpting, reading, swimming, travelling. Office: Four Dragons Internat Inc PO Box 869 Olive Hill KY 41164-0869 also: Golden Link Publs PO Box 869 Olive Hill KY 41164-0869

ANDERSON, MICHAEL CURTIS, computer industry analyst; b. Belton, Tex., Nov. 19, 1953; s. Curtis Raymond Anderson and Joan Evelyn (Sievers) Bleuer; m. Debra Beth Shlaes, June 7, 1975; children: Sara Joyce, John Michael. BA cum laude, Augustana Coll., 1975; postgrad., U. Iowa, 1982—. Mgmt. sci. analyst Deere & Co., Moline, Ill., 1975-80, mgr. office automation, 1980-88; sr. planner office systems IBM, Roanoke, Tex., 1988-89, mgr. strategy and requirements, planning-office systems, 1989-90; program dir. office info. systems Gartner Group, Stamford, Conn., 1990-93; dir. mkt. rsch. & competitive analysis Ameritech, Chgo., 1993-94; v.p., rsch. dir. adv. techs. Gartner Group, Stamford, Conn., 1994—. Ill. State scholar, 1971, I.B. McGladrey Accountancy award McGladrey-Hendrickson, 1974. Avocations: tennis, golf, bicycling, fitness, coaching. Home: 2109 Reynolds Dr Colleyville TX 76034-5790 Office: Gartner Group 222 Las Colinas Blvd W Ste 640 Irving TX 75039-5423

ANDERSON, MICHAEL ROBERT, marketing representative; b. Mpls., Nov. 3, 1953; s. Arthur Robert Anderson and Patricia Roberta Carlson; divorced; children: Jenna Courtney, Evan Brendan. BSEE, U. Minn., 1976; MS in Sys. Mgmt., U. So. Calif., 1981. Microelectronics engr. Hughes Aircraft Co., Fullerton, Calif., 1977; mktg. rep. Hewlett Packard, Orange County, Calif., 1977-81; regional mgr. Group III Elec., Orange County, 1981-85; mktg. rep. Lisp Machines Inc., L.A., 1985-87, Sun Microsys., Inc., Orange, Calif., 1987-91; mktg.rep. Auspex Sys., Inc., Santa Clara, Calif., 1992-95, Raptor Systems, Waltham, Mass., 1995—. Active Big Brother, Big Bros. Inc., Orange, Calif., 1979-81. Fellow AAAS, Am. Assn. Artificial Intelligence, Planetary Soc. Avocations: reading, piano, family activities, bicycling, travel. Home: PO Box 5199 San Clemente CA 92674-5199 Office: Maxager Sys Inc Ste #200 302 N El Camino Real San Clemente CA 92672

ANDERSON, MICHAEL THOMAS, mathematics researcher, educator; b. Boulder, Colo., Nov. 17, 1950; s. Julian Thompson and Elinor Elizabeth (Uhl) A.; m. Myong Hu Kim, Aug. 15, 1986; 1 child, Steven. BA, U. Calif., Santa Barbara, 1975; MA, U. Calif., Berkeley, 1977, PhD, 1981. Rsch. instr. Rice U., Houston, 1981-84; from asst. to assoc. prof. Calif. Inst. Tech., Pasadena, 1984-88; assoc. prof. SUNY, Stony Brook, 1988-91, prof., 1991—; invited spkr. Internat. Congress Maths., Zurich, 1994. Assoc. editor Duke Math. Jour., 1991—; mem. editl. bd. Jour. Geometric and Functional Analysis, 1991—; contbr. articles to profl. jours. NSF grantee, 1981—; NSF postdoctoral fellow, 1984-86. Mem. Am. Math. Soc. (rsch. fellow 1990-91). Democrat. Office: SUNY Dept Math Stony Brook NY 11794

ANDERSON, MILADA FILKO, manufacturing company executive; b. Chgo., Nov. 17, 1922; d. John and Anna (Sianta) Filko; m. George Richard Anderson, Aug. 29, 1945 (div. July 1974); children: Mark (dec.), Renee, Teri. BS, Northwestern U., 1944, M in Mgmt., 1979. Tchr. history Evanston (Ill.) Township High Sch., 1946; tchr. social studies Mt. Prospect (Ill.) Jr. High Sch., 1947-48; dir. F&B Mfg. Co., Chgo., 1965—, pres., chmn. bd., 1972—. Mem. Northwestern U. Profl. Womens Assn., Nat. Assn. Investment Clubs, Zeta Tau Alpha. Republican. Lutheran. Avocations: opera, music, reading, investments, fishing. Office: F&B Mfg Co 5316 N 39th Ave Phoenix AZ 85063

ANDERSON, MILTON ANDREW, chemical executive; b. Fond du Lac, Wis., Oct. 22, 1927; s. Andrew Andreas and Bertha Victoria (Almquist) A.; m. Dorothy Mae Verke, Nov. 27, 1954; children: Edward, Victoria. BS, U. Wis., Madison, 1954; MS in Mgmt., Lake Forest Grad. Sch. Mgmt., 1980. Registered profl. engr., Calif. Specification engr. Johns-Manville, Waukegan, Ill., 1955-59; supr. Johns-Manville, Waukegan, 1959-64, chemist, 1964-70, devel. engr., 1970-73; supr. Abbott Labs., North Chicago, 1973-74, quality engr., 1974-77, cons., auditing., 1977-81, mgr. rsch. auditing good lab. practices/good clin. practices, 1981-92; pres. Rsch. Compliance Svcs. Ltd., Lake Villa, Ill., 1992—. Author: GLP Quality Audit Manual, 1987, 2d edit., 1991, GLP Essentials, 1995. Pres. Millburn Elem. Sch. Bd., 1971-73. Lt. naval aviator, 1948-52. Mem. Soc. Quality Assurance, Am. Soc.. for Quality Control (chmn. Northea. Ill. sect. 1980-82, sect. bd. dirs. 1982—). Republican. Home and Office: Rsch Compliance Svcs Ltd 19176 W Grass Lake Rd Lake Villa IL 60046-9242

ANDERSON, MOSES B., bishop; b. Selma, Ala., Sept. 9, 1928. Student, St. Michael's Coll., St. Edmunds Sem., U. Legon, Ghana. Ordained priest Roman Cath. Ch., 1958. Ordained aux. bisop Detroit; titular bishop of Vatarba, 1983. Office: Parish Office-Precious Blood 13305 Grove St Detroit MI 48235*

ANDERSON, NILS, JR., former government official, retired business executive, industrial historian; b. Plainfield, N.J., Jan. 28, 1914; s. Nils and Marguerite (Stephens) A.; m. Jean Derby Ferris, July 30, 1938. *His son Nils III, a Citadel graduate, international yachtsman, and infantry captain, died in the Vietnam War. His son Derby Ferris practices law in Southport, Connecticut, his son Stephen Massie is an employee of the City of Longmont, Colorado, and his son Ward Reynolds is a captain for U.S. Airways and a retired carrier pilot with the U.S. Navy Reserves. Both of his great grandfathers were boat captains and owners, William Rodney Massie on the Missouri River and Nils Anderson from Sweden to Baltic & European-Mediterranean ports.* Grad., Lawrenceville and Loomis Schs.; BA, Williams Coll., 1937; postgrad., Colo. Sch. Mines, George Washington U. Law Sch., Alexander Hamilton Inst. With Debevoise-Anderson Co., summers 1927-28; cadet engr. S.S. Iron Ranger Isthmian Steamship Co., summer 1930; cadet engr., chemist Koppers Co., Pitts., summers 1932-37; sales engr. Bakelite Corp., 1937-41; adv. chem. divsn., adminstr. War Prodn. Bd., 1941-45; adminstr. chief adhesives sect., govt. presiding officer Industry Adv. Com., 1942, adminstr. chief plastics br., 1944; v.p. Casein Co. Chem. divsn. Borden Co.; founder Alba S.A. Borden Co., Brazil, 1945-49; founder Casco, S.A. Borden Co., Argentina, 1945-49; pres. Debevoise-Anderson Co. Inc., 1950-60, chmn., CEO, 1965; pres. Fairfield Sales, 1950; organizer mining cos., P.R., Chile, Peru, Brazil, Angola, 1955-65, Cia Minera, Dominican Republic, C PorA, Dominican Republic; adv. chemical divsn. U.S. Dept. Agr. stockpile and shipping br., adhesive and plastic, textile, paper and pulp, plywood and furniture industry adv. coms., 1941-44; mem. 1st U.S. trade mission to Ea. Europe, 1965. *Nils Anderson, Sr. founded DeBevoise Anderson Co. (DACo) in 1905, exclusive sales agent for Coke for the Koppers Co., 1918-70. In early 1930s, sold large tonages of pig iron to Japan, became sole buying agent for pig iron for Great Britain and France shutting out sales to Japan. Nils Anderson, Jr. controlled DACo after his father's death. With the decline of the steel business in the 1970s and new technology, it was decided to dissolve DACo. However, Nils Anderson, Jr. pursued other business activities.* Author: North American Coke Today, Chemicals, Metals and Men; contbr. tech. articles on plastics and adhesives to profl. jours. and encyclopedias. Trustee, pres. U.S. Naval War Coll. Found., 1988-89; trustee Wakeman Meml. Assn. Southport, Conn.; past pres. Sasquanaug Assn., Southport; founder, past chmn. Southport Conservancy. Mem. ASME, Coke Oven Mgrs. Assn. (England), Am. Chem. Soc., Iron and Steel Engrs. Assn., Am. Coke and Coal Chemicals Inst. (hon.), Newcomen Soc. in N. Am., Gen. Soc. Colonial Wars, Soc. of War of 1812, Pilgrim Soc., Pa. Soc., Pequot Yacht Club (Southport), Fairfield (Conn.) Country Club, Univ. Club (N.Y.C.), Links Club (N.Y.C.), Alpha Delta Phi. Republican. Episcopalian. Avocations: golf, writing. *Don't deal with people about whose integrity and character there is question. It keeps your mind uneasy. It is better to lose the business-Alexander Brown.*

ANDERSON, ODIN WALDEMAR, sociologist, educator; b. Mpls., July 5, 1914; s. Edwin and Anna (Ormbreck) A.; m. Helen Hay, June 24, 1939; children: Kristin Alice, Thor Edwin. B.A., U. Wis., 1937, M.A., 1938; B.A. in L.S., U. Mich., 1940, Ph.D., 1948; Ph.D. (hon.), U. Uppsala, Sweden, 1977. Instr., U. Mich. Sch. Pub. Health, 1944-49; assoc. prof. dept. clin. preventive medicine, med. faculty U. Western Ont., London, 1949-52; research dir. Health Info. Found., N.Y.C., 1952-62, Health Info. Found., U. Chgo., 1962-64; research dir. Ctr. Health Adminstrn. Studies, 1964-66, assoc. dir., 1966-72, dir., 1972-80, assoc. prof. sociology, dept. sociology and Grad. Sch. Bus., 1962-64, prof., 1964-80, prof. emeritus, 1980—; prof. sociology U. Wis.-Madison, 1980—, prof. emeritus, 1995—; mem. rsch. com. Nat. Tb Assn., 1959-64, U.S. Nat. Com. Vital and Health Stats., 1959-63; vis. prof. Inst. Sociology and Polit. Sci. U. Trondheim, Norway, 1992. Author: (with Jacob J. Feldman) Family Medical Care and Voluntary Health Insurance, 1956, (with others) Family Medical Care and Health Insurance, 1963, (with Ronald Andersen) A Decade of Health Services: Social Survey Trends in Use and Expenditures, 1968, The Uneasy Equilibrium: Private and Public Financing of Health Services in the U.S., 1875-1965, 1968, Health Care: Can There Be Equity? The United States, Sweden, and England, 1972, The American Health Services, a Growth Enterprise Since 1875, 2nd edit., 1985, (with others) HMO Development: Patterns and Prospects, 1985, The Health Services Continuum in Democratic States: An Inquiry into Solvable Problems, 1989, Health Services as a Growth Enterprise in the United States Since 1875, 1990, The Evolution of Health Services Research: Personal Reflections on Applied Social Sciences, 1991; editor, translator: Sexual Customs in Rural Norway, 1993. Named Disting. Health Services Researcher, Assn. Health Services Research, 1985, One of Ten Most Admired Sr. Citizens Wis. for 1988 Wis. State Fair. Fellow Am. Sociol. Assn. (past chmn. sect. med. sociology, Disting. Med. Sociologist sect. med. sociology 1980), Am. Pub. Health Assn., Am. Coll. Hosp. Adminstrs. (hon.), AAAS, Assn. Health Svcs. Rsch.; mem. Inst. Medicine of Nat. Acad. Sci. Home: c/o Thor Anderson 1531 Sugar Grove Ct Saint Louis MO 63146-4406

ANDERSON, O(RVIL) ROGER, biology educator, marine biology and protozoology, researcher; b. East St. Louis, Ill., Aug. 4, 1937; s. Orvil Noel and Marie Elizabeth (Diekemper) A. BA, Washington U., St. Louis, 1959, MA, 1961, EdD, 1964. Asst. prof. sci. Columbia U. Tchrs. Coll., N.Y.C., 1964-67, assoc. prof., 1968-70, prof., 1971—; rsch. assoc. Lamont-Doherty Obs., Palisades, N.Y., 1965-70, sr. rsch. scientist, 1971—; faculty mem. at large Grad. Sch. Arts and Scis. Columbia U., N.Y.C., 1994—; vis. prof. Tübingen (Germany) U., 1979, 84, 86; vis. res. scientist Bermuda Biol. Station, 1970, 75, 76, 84, Bellairs Rsch. Inst., Barbados, 1972-85, 87-95, Caribbean Marine Biol. Inst., Curacao, 1980-82, Spanish Marine Biol. Inst., Tenerife, 1979, Freshwater Biol. Inst., Cumbria, Eng., 1994, Marine Biology Rsch. Inst., Isle of Cumbrae, Scotland, 1995-96; assoc. scientist in edn. Am. Mus. Natural History, N.Y.C., 1995-96. Author: Quantitative Analysis of Stucture in Teaching, 1971, Teaching Modern Ideas of Biology, 1972, The Experience of Science, 1976, Radiolaria, 1983, Protozoology: Ecology, Physiology, Life History, 1988, Modern Planktonic Foraminifera, 1989, Teaching and Learning of Biology in the United States; Second International Assessment of Biological Achievement, 1990; editor Jour. Rsch. in Sci. Teaching, 1970-75, Cytomechanics, 1987, The Biology of Foraminfera, 1991, Explore the World Using Protozoa, 1997; assoc. editor Jour. Protozoology, 1988—; mem. editorial bd. Marine Microbial Food Webs, 1987—; contbr. articles to profl. jours. Recipient Bermuda Biol. Sta. award for Marine Sci. Rsch., 1976, medal for Outstanding Rsch., Paleontol. Soc. Japan, 1999; NSF grantee, 1972—; Cocconeis andersonii species named in his honor for contbns. to symbiosis rsch., 1989. Fellow AAAS, Cushman Found. for Foraminiferal Rsch.; mem. NSTA (bd. dirs. 1976-77), Soc. Protozoologists (pres. 1994), Am. Soc. Limnology and Oceanography, Nat. Assn. for Rsch. in Sci. Tchg. (pres. 1976-77), Freshwater Biol. Assn. (U.K.), Black Rock Forest Consortium (exec. bd. dirs.), Sigma Xi (internat. com. 1992-96, sec. Kappa chpt. 1987-91, pres.-elect 1992-93, pres. 1993-95). Home: 501 W 120th St New York NY 10027-6622 Office: Columbia U Tchrs Coll 525 W 120th St New York NY 10027-6625

ANDERSON, OWEN RAYMOND, scientific and educational organization executive; b. Chestertown, Md., Aug. 27, 1919; s. Owen Raymond and Ida Frances (Jenkins) A.; m. Ida Lois Pritts, June 8, 1946; children: Penny Pritts, Jeri Alyce. B.A., Washington Coll., 1940. Tchr. Garrett County Bd. Edn., Kitzmiller, Md., 1940-41, 1946; with Nat. Geog. Soc., Washington, 1946—, div. supr., 1950, adminstrv. asst., 1952-61, asst. sec., 1961-66, assoc. sec., 1966-76, v.p., sec., 1976-80, exec. v.p., 1980-91, trustee, 1981-95, vice chmn. bd., 1984-95, trustee emeritus, 1995—. Served to capt. U.S. Army, 1941-46, 50-52, ETO, Korea. Decorated Bronze Star, Purple Heart, Combat Infantry badge; recipient Alumni Citation award Washington Coll., 1981. Mem. Am. Legion, Lambda Chi Alpha. Methodist. Club: Alfalfa. Home: Apt 111 5809 Nicholson Ln North Bethesda MD 20852

ANDERSON, PARKER LYNN, editorial columnist, playwright; b. Wickenburg, Ariz., Apr. 19, 1964; s. Harry Milton and Darla Raejean (Hangartner) A. Mem. prodn. com. Prescott (Ariz.) Fine Arts Assn., 1993-95, 98—, adv. mem., 1987—; columnist, theatre critic The Prescott News, 1995-96; with Cath. Social Svc. of Yavapai, 1983—; mem. adv. com. The Blue Rose Theatre Co., Prescott, 1994—; guest on talk shows Sta. KUSK-TV, 1991—. Author: (plays) The Startled Cowboys, 1991, Voices From the Past, 1995, The Sleeping Toad, 1997, Virgil Earp, 1998; freelance guest columnist and letters of comment in numerous Ariz. publs., 1990—; pub. Roasting Roderick. Home: PO Box 1285 Prescott AZ 86302-1285

ANDERSON, PAUL HOLDEN, state supreme court justice; b. May 14, 1943; m. Janice M.; children: Yovanna, Marina. BA cum laude, Macalester Coll., 1965; JD, U. Minn., 1968. Atty. Vols. in Svc. to Am., 1968-69; spl. asst. atty. gen. criminal divsn. dept. pub. safety Office Minn. Atty. Gen., 1970-71; assoc., then ptnr. LeVander, Gillen & Miller, South St. Paul, Minn., 1971-92; chief judge Minn. Ct. Appeals, 1992-94; assoc. justice Minn. Supreme Ct., 1994—. Deacon, ruling elder House of Hope Presbyn. Ch., St. Paul; mem. PER coms. Ind. Sch. Dist. # 199, 1982-84, mem. and chmn. cmty. svcs. adv. com., bd. dirs., chmn. bd. Mem. Dakota County Bar Assn. (bd. dirs., pres.), South St. Paul/Inver Grove Heights C. of C. (bd. dirs., mem. exec. com.). Avocations: tennis, gourmet cooking, bike riding. Office: Minn Supreme Court 425 Minnesota Judicial Ctr Saint Paul MN 55155-1500

ANDERSON, PAUL IRVING, management executive; b. Portland, Oreg., Mar. 23, 1935; s. William F. and Ruth M. (Sundquist) A.; m. Lorraine A. Franz, Nov. 21, 1959; children: Todd, Susan, Cheryl, Cynthia. B.S., Oreg. State U., 1956. Various positions in mktg., sales and engring. mgmt. 3M Co., St. Paul and Boston, 1956-74; gen. mgr. 3M Co., Brussels, Belgium, 1974-77; group bus. planning dir. 3M Co., St. Paul, 1977-79; sr. v.p., gen. mgr. Rayovac Corp., Madison, Wis., 1979-82; pres. Anderson Cons. Co., Madison, 1982-83; div. v.p. RCA Corp., Indpls., 1983-84; pres. Anderson & Assocs., La Costa, Calif., 1984-87; pres., CEO Electro-Imaging Advisors, Inc., La Jolla, Calif., 1987-93; CEO Strategic Catalysts Inc., La Jolla, Calif., 1993—. Mem. Am. Mgmt. Assn., Tau Beta Pi, Pi Tau Sigma, Sigma Tau. Republican. Presbyterian. Clubs: Columbia (Indpls.); Madison; Nakoma Golf (Madison). Home: 6418 Cayenne Ln Carlsbad CA 92009-4301

ANDERSON, PAUL MAURICE, electrical engineering educator, researcher, consultant; b. Des Moines, Jan. 22, 1926; s. Neil W. and Buena Vista (Thompson) A.; m. Virginia Ann Worswick, July 8, 1950; children: William, Mark, James, Thomas. B.S.E.E., Iowa State U., 1949, M.S.E.E., 1958, Ph.D. in Elec. Engring., 1961. Registered profl. elec. engr., Ariz., Calif., Iowa, Guam; registered control sys. engr., Calif. Elec. engr. Iowa Pub. Service Co., Sioux City, 1949-55; prof. elec. engring. Iowa State U., Ames, 1955-75; program mgr. Electric Power Research Inst., Palo Alto, Calif., 1975-78; pres., prin. engr. Power Math Assocs. Inc., Palo Alto, Tempe, Del Mar and San Diego, 1978—; prof. elec. engring. Ariz. State U., Tempe, 1980-84; Schweitzer vis. prof. elec. engring. Wash. State U., 1996-97. Author: Analysis of Faulted Power Systems, 1973, (with others) Power Control and Stability, 1977, (with others) Subsynchronous Resonance in Power Systems, 1990, (with others) Series Compensation of Power Systems, 1996, Power System Protection, 1999; cons. editor: Ency. Sci. and Tech., 1979-92; editor IEEE Press Series in Power Engring.; contbr. articles to profl. jours. NSF faculty fellow, 1960-61; recipient Faculty citation Iowa State U. Alumni Assn., 1973, Profl. Achievement citation Iowa State U., 1981. Fellow IEEE (life mem., chmn. Iowa sect. 1959-60), Conf. Internat. des Grands Reseaux Electriques, Sigma Xi, Phi Kappa Phi, Eta Kappa Nu, Pi Mu Epsilon. Republican. Home: 13335 Roxton Cir San Diego CA 92130-1841

ANDERSON, PAUL MILTON, steel company executive; b. Richland, Wash., Apr. 1, 1945; s. Paul Milton and Elfrieda (Blehm) A.; m. Kathleen Sue Kinzel, Feb. 25, 1984; children: Wendy Christine, Heather Colleen. BSME, U. Wash., 1967; MBA, Stanford U., 1969. Mgr. product planning Ford Motor Co., Dearborn, 1969-77; various positions Tex. Eastern Corp., Houston, 1977-85, v.p., 1985-87, sr. v.p., 1987-89; v.p. fin., chief fin. officer Inland Steel Industries, Chgo., 1990-91; exec. v.p. Panhandle Eastern Corp., 1991-94, pres., 1994—; pres. Panhandle Eastern Pipe Line Co., 1991—; pres., CEO Panenergy (named changed Duke Energy), Houston, 1991-97; pres., COO Duke Energy, 1997—. Mem. Interstate Natural Gas Assn. Am., Inst. Gas Tech.

ANDERSON, PAUL NATHANIEL, oncologist, educator; b. Omaha, May 30, 1937; s. Nels Paul E. and Doris Marie (Chesnut) A.; m. Dee Ann Hipps, June 27, 1965; children: Mary Kathleen, Anne Christen. BA, U. Colo., 1959, MD, 1963. Diplomate Am. Bd. Internal Medicine, Am. Bd. Med. Mgmt., Am. Bd. Med. Oncology. Intern Johns Hopkins Hosp., Balt., 1963-64, resident in internal medicine, 1964-65, fellow in oncology, 1970-72; rsch. assoc., staff assoc. NIH, Bethesda, Md., 1965-70; asst. prof. medicine, oncology Johns Hopkins U. Sch. Medicine, 1972-76; attending physician Balt. City Hosps., Johns Hopkins Hosp., 1972-76; dir. dept. med. oncology Penrose Cancer Hosp., Colorado Springs, Colo., 1976-86; clin. asst. prof. dept. medicine Colo. Sch. Medicine, 1976-90, clin. assoc. prof., 1990—; dir. Penrose Cancer Hosp., 1979-86, chief dept. medicine, 1985-86; founding dir. Cancer Ctr. of Colorado Springs, 1986-95, Pikes Peak Forum for Health Care Ethics, 1996—, Rocky Mountain Cancer Ctr., Colorado Springs, 1995—; med. dir. So. Colo. Cancer Program, 1979-86; pres., chmn. bd. dirs. Preferred Physicians, Inc., 1986-92; mem. Colo. Found. for Med. Care Health Stds. Com., 1985, sec., exec. com., 1990, bd. dirs., pres., 1992-93; mem., chmn. treatment com. Colo. Cancer Control and Rsch. Panel, 1980-83; prin. investigator Cancer Info. Svc. of Colo., 1981-87; pres., founder Timberline Med. Assocs., 1986-87, Oncology Mgmt. Network, Inc., 1985-95. Editor Advances in Cancer Control; editl. bd. Jour. Cancer Program Mgmt., 1987-92, Health Care Mgmt. Rev., 1988—; contbr. articles to med. jours. Mem. Colo. Gov.'s Rocky Flats Employee Health Assessment Group, 1983-84; mem. Gov.'s Breast Cancer Control Commn. Colo., 1984-89; founder, dir. So. Colo. AIDS project, 1986-91; mem. adv. bd. Colo. State Bd. Health Tumor Registry, 1984-87; chmn., bd. dirs. Preferred Physicians, Inc., 1986-92; bd. dirs. Share Devel. Co. of Colo. Share Health Plan of Colo., 1986-90, vice chmn., 1989-91; bd. dirs., chmn. Preferred Health Care, Inc., 1991-92; mem. health care stds. com., trustee colo. Found. for Med. Care (PRO); mem. nat. bd. med. dirs. Fox Chase Cancer Ctr. Network, Phila., 1987-89; mem. tech. expert panel Harvard Resource-Based Relative Value Scale Study for Hematology/Oncology, 1991-92. With USPHS, 1965-70. Mem. AMA (mem. practice parameters forum 1989-97, adv. com. to HCFA on uniform clin. data set), AAAS, Am. Coll. Forensic Examiners, Am. Soc. Clin. Oncology (chmn. subcom. on oncology clin. practice stds., mem. clin. practice com., rep. to AMA 1991—, mem. healthcare svcs. rsch. com., chmn. clin. guidelines subcom. 1993—), Am. Assn. Cancer Rsch., Am. Assn. Cancer Insts. (liaison mem. bd. trustees 1980-82), Am. Coll. Physician Execs., Am. Hospice Assn., Am. Soc. Internal Medicine, Nat. Cancer Inst. (com. for cmty. hosp. oncology program evaluation 1982-83), Colo. Soc. Internal Medicine, Assn. Cmty. Cancer Ctrs. (chmn. membership com. 1980, chmn. clin. rsch. com. 1983-85, sec. 1983-84, pres.-elect 1984-85, pres. 1986-87, trustee 1981-88), N.Y. Acad. Scis., Johns Hopkins Med. Soc., Colo. Med. Soc., Am. Mgmt. Assn., Am. Assn. Profl. Cons., Am. Soc. Quality, Am. Acad. Med. Dirs., Am. Coll. Physician Execs., El Paso County Med. Soc., Rocky Mountain Oncology Soc. (chmn. clin. practice com. 1989-94, pres.-elect 1990, pres. 1993-95), Acad. Hospice Physicians, Coalition for Cancer, Colorado Springs Clin. Club, Alpha Omega Alpha. Office: Rocky Mountain Cancer Ctr PO Box 7148 Colorado Springs CO 80933-7148 also: 32 Sanford Rd Colorado Springs CO 80906-4233

ANDERSON, PAUL THOMAS (PAUL THOMAS, IV), film director; b. Studio City, Calif., Jan. 1, 1970. Dir., writer: The Dirk Diggler Story, 1988, Cigarettes and Coffee, 1993, Sydney/Hard Eight, 1996 (Boston Soc. Film Critics award 1997, nominated Grand Spl. prize Deauville Film Festival, 1996, nominated Ind. Spirit awards, best 1st feature, best 1st screenplay, 1996); dir., writer, prodr.: Boogie Nights, 1997 (New Generation award L.A. Film Critics Assn., 1997, Metro Media award Toronto Internat. Film Festival, 1997, Boston Soc. Film Critics Best New Filmmaker award, 1997; nominated Oscar, best writing, screenplay written directly for screen, 1998, nominated Brit. Acad. award, best screenplay-original, 1998, nominated Five Continents award, European Film awards, 1997, nominated Golden Satellite awards, best dir. motion picture, best motion picture-drama, 1998, nominated Writers Guild Am. Screen award, best screenplay written directly for screen, 1997), Magnolia, 1999. Office: c/o DGA 7920 Sunset Blvd Los Angeles CA 90046*

ANDERSON, PAULA D.J., pharmacist; b. Yankton, S.D., Nov. 1, 1949; d. Ervin Marion and Ivy Lucille (Christiansen) A. BS in Biology, S.D. State U., Brookings, 1973; MEd, Northeastern Okla. U., Tahlequah, 1977; BS in Pharmacy, S.D. State U., Brookings, 1983; PharmD, U. Colo., 1998. Reg. pharmacist Tex., N.Mex., Colo., S.D., Iowa. Pharmacist, store mgr. Revco, Tex. and N.Mex., 1984-92; pharmacist immunizations AIDS, STD, HIV Dept. of Health, Santa Fe, N.Mex., 1993-95; dir. pharmacy Value Rx, Santa Fe, 1995-96; with Sacred Heart Hosp., Yankton, S.D., 1998, St. Luke Hosp., Sioux City, Iowa, 1999—; coord. HIV Pharmacy Bur. of HIV/STD/AIDS Dept. Health, N.Mex.; spkr., presenter in field. Pres. NOW, N.Mex., Nat. Breast Cancer Coalition. Mem. NAFE, Am. Pharmaceutical Assn., Am. Soc. Health System Pharmacist. Democrat. Home: 4143 Harrison Sioux City IA 51101

ANDERSON, PEER LAFOLLETTE, lawyer, petroleum corporation executive; b. Provo, Utah, 1944. JD, U. Okla., 1969; LLM, George Washington U., 1973. Now v.p., gen. counsel, sec. Citgo Petroleum Corp., Tulsa, 1986—. Office: Citgo Petroleum Corp PO Box 3758 Tulsa OK 74102-3758*

ANDERSON, PEGGY JOAN, English educator; b. Effingham, Ill., Aug. 2, 1955; d. Guy Earl and Helen Mary (Lemnah) Davidson; m. Roy Dean Anderson, June 23, 1990; children: Haley Elizabeth, Paige Elizabeth. BA, Ea. Ill. U., 1977. English tchr. Central H.S., Camp Point, Ill., 1977—. Mem. Nat. Coun. Tchrs. English, Ill. Assn. Tchrs. of English. Methodist. Avocations: reading, bicycling, travel. Home: 1515 Ohio St Quincy IL 62301-5029

ANDERSON, PEGGY REES, accountant; b. Casper, Wyo., Sept. 8, 1958; d. John William and Pauline Marie (Harris) Rees; m. Steven R. Anderson, May 26, 1984 (div. Sept. 1990). BS in Acctg. with honors, U. Wyo., 1980. CPA. Audit staff to sr. Price Waterhouse, Denver, 1980-84; asst. contr. to contr. Am. Investments Denver, 1984-88; cons. ADI Residential, Denver, 1988-89; contr., treas. Plante Properties, Inc., Denver, 1989-92; acctg. mgr. Woodward-Clyde Group, Inc., Denver, 1992-96; internat. fin. mgr. USWest, Inc., Denver, 1996-98; internat. acctg. mgr. Media One Group, Denver,

1998—. Diving scholar U. Wyo., 1976-78. Mem. Colo. Soc. CPAs. Roman Catholic. Avocations: skiing, swimming, aerobics, needlepoint, golf. Office: Media One Group 9785 S Maroon Cir Ste 210 Englewood CO 80112-5921

ANDERSON, PETER MACARTHUR, lawyer; b. New Castle, Ind., July 15, 1937; s. Earl Canute and Catherine Elizabeth (Schultz) A.; m. Ann Warren Gibson, Sept.1, 1962; children: David, Karen. AB, Dartmouth Coll., 1959; LLB, Stanford U., 1962. Bar: Calif. 1963, Wash. 1970. Assoc. O'Melveny & Myers, L.A., 1966-70; assoc. Bogle & Gates, Seattle, 1970-74, mem., 1974-99; ptnr. Preston Gates & Ellis, Seattle, 1999—; co-chmn. equal employment law com. ABA, 1983-86. Mem. Ecumenical. Commn. for Seattle Archdiocese, St. Petersburg-Seattle Sister Chs. Com. Capt. U.S. Army, 1963-65. Fellow Coll. Labor and Employment Lawyers; mem. Phi Beta Kappa. Roman Catholic. Home: 9200 SE 57th St Mercer Island WA 98040-5005 Office: Preston Gates & Ellis LLP 701 5th Ave Ste 5000 Seattle WA 98104-7078

ANDERSON, PHILIP SIDNEY, lawyer; b. Little Rock, May 9, 1935; s. Philip Sidney and Frances (Walt) A.; m. Rosemary Gill Wright, Sept. 26, 1959; children: Sidney Walt (Mrs. Geoffrey R.T. Kenyon), Philip Wright, Catherine Gill (Mrs. Jess L. Askew III). BA, U. Ark., 1959, LLB, 1959. Bar: Ark. 1960, U.S. Supreme Ct. 1966. Assoc. Wright, Lindsey & Jennings, Little Rock, 1960-65, ptnr., 1965-88; ptnr. Williams & Anderson, Little Rock, 1988—; lectr. Ark. Law Sch., 1963-66; mem. com. on jury instrns. Ark. Supreme Ct., 1962-97; mem. panel for the 8th cir. U.S. Cir. Judge Nominating Commn., 1978-79; mem. fed. adv. com. U.S. Ct. Appeals 8th cir., 1983-88, co-chmn., 1987-88; bd. dirs. Camden News Pub. Co., Little Rock Newspapers, Inc., Winburn Tile Mfg. Co. Co-author: Arkansas Model Jury Instructions, 1965, 74, 89. Pres. Friends of Little Rock Pub. Libr., 1968-69, Little Rock Unltd. Progress, Inc., 1973-74; trustee Cen. Ark. Libr. System, 1981-87, pres. 1984; trustee George W. Donaghey Found., 1976—, pres. 1979-80; trustee Southwestern Legal Found., 1996—. 2d lt. AUS, 1959-60. Fellow Am. Bar Found., Ark. Bar Found. (pres. 1973-74), ABA (chair ho. of dels. 1992-94, bd. govs. 1990-94, 97—, chair coalition for justice 1994-97, pres. 1998-99); mem. Ark. Bar Assn. (spl. award meritorious svc.), Am. Law Inst. (mem. coun. 1982—). Episcopalian. Home: 4716 Crestwood Dr Little Rock AR 72207-5436 Office: 2200 Stephens Bldg 111 Center St Little Rock AR 72201-4402

ANDERSON, PHILIP VERNON, retired pastor; b. Tanzania, Aug. 29, 1928; came to U.S., 1941; s. George N. and Annette L. (Elmquist) A.; m. Joan Audrey Carlson, Sept. 15, 1951; children: Christine Packwood, Karen, Carl, Janice, Erik. AB, Augustana Coll., Rock Island, Ill.; MDiv, Luth. Sch. Chgo., 1953; postgrad., U. Chgo., 1960-62. Ordained to ministry, Luth. Ch., 1953. Pastor Faith Luth. Ch., Syosset, N.Y., 1953-60; chaplain Augustana Hosp., Chgo., 1962-64; pastor Augustana Luth. Ch., Chgo., 1964-70; dir. pastoral care Augustana Hosp., Chgo., 1970-89; pastor Nazareth Luth. Ch., Hazel Crest, Ill., 1989-90; chaplain Hospice Care/Chicagoland, Homewood, Ill., 1990-91; pastor Bethesda Luth. Ch., Chgo., 1990-97; bereavement dir. VITAS—Innovative Hospice Care, Homewood, 1991-94; mgr. bereavement svcs. VITAS-Innovative Hospice Care, Chgo., 1994-98; instr. pastoral care Luth. Sch. Theology, Chgo., 1972-82; instr. field work McCormick Theol. Sem., Chgo., 1972-82. Avocation: pastoral counseling. Home: 5549 S Harper Ave Chicago IL 60637-1829

ANDERSON, PHILIP WARREN, physicist; b. Indpls., Dec. 13, 1923; s. Harry W. and Elsie (Osborne) A.; m. Joyce Gothwaite, July 31, 1947; 1 dau., Susan Osborne. BS, Harvard U., 1943, MA, 1947, PhD, 1949; DSc (hon.), U. Ill., 1979, Rutgers U., 1991, Ecole Normale Superieure, Paris, 1995, U. Sheffield, Eng., 1996. Mem. staff Naval Research Lab., 1943-45; mem. tech. staff Bell Telephone Labs., Murray Hill, N.J., 1949-84; chmn. theoretical physics dept. Bell Telephone Labs., 1959-60, asst. dir. phys. research lab., 1974-76, cons. dir., 1976-84; prof. theoretical physics Cambridge (Eng.) U., 1967-75, fellow Jesus Coll., 1969-75, hon. fellow, 1978-96; prof. physics Princeton (N.J.) U., 1975-96; prof. emeritus, 1996—; George Eastman prof. Oxford (Eng.) U., 1993-94; researcher in quantum theory, especially theoretical physics of solids, spectral line broadening, magnetism, superconductivity; Fulbright lectr. U. Tokyo, 1953-54; Loeb lectr. Harvard U., 1964; Overseas fellow Churchill Coll., Cambridge U., 1961-62; vice-chmn. sci. bd. Santa Fe Inst., 1990—. Author: Concepts in Solids, 1963, Basic Notions of Condensed Matter Physics, 1984, A Career in Theoretical Physics, 1994; The Theory of Superconductivity in High-Tc Cuprates, 1997. Chmn. bd. trustees Aspen Ctr. for Physics, 1982-87, Santa Fe Inst., 1987-97, 98—. Recipient Nobel prize, 1977, Guthrie medal Inst. Physics, 1978, Nat. Medal Sci., 1982, Centennial medal Harvard U., 1996, Bardeen prize Internat. Com. M2S-HTS Conf., 1997, Dannie Heinemann prize Göttingen Acad. Sci., 1975. Fellow AAAS, Am. Phys. Soc. (Buckley prize 1964), Am. Acad. Arts and Scis., Japan Acad., Indian Acad. Scis.; mem. NAS, Royal Soc., Accademia Lincei, Am. Philos. Soc., N.Y. Acad. Scis. (hon., life), Russian Acad. Scis.

ANDERSON, PHILLIP R., career officer; b. Sept. 11, 1948. Commd. U.S. Army, advanced through grades to maj. gen., 1997. Office: PO Box 80 Vicksburg MS 39181-0080

ANDERSON, POUL WILLIAM, author; b. Bristol, Pa., Nov. 25, 1926; M. Karen Kruse, Dec. 12, 1953; 1 child. BS in Physics, U. Minn., 1948. Works include: Brain Wave, 1954, Planet of No Return, 1956, War of the Wing-Men, 1958, Earthman Go Home!, 1960, Mayday Orbit, 1961, After Doomsday, 1962, Let the Spaceman Beware, 1963, Orbit Unlimited, 1963, Is There Life on Other Worlds, 1963, Time and Stars, 1964, The Stars Are Also Fine, 1964, Agent of the Terran Empire, 1965, The Trouble Twisters, 1966, the Horn of Time, 1968, Infinite Voyage: Man's Future in Space, 1969, Tau Zero, 1970, Brain Wave, 1970, Circus of Hells, 1970, Guardians of Time, 1970, Seven Conquests, 1970, Tales of the Flying Mountains, 1970, Operation Chaos, 1971, Byworlder, 1971, The Broken Sword, 1971, Hrolf Kraki's Saga, 1973, People of the Wind, 1973, Fire Time, 1974, the Many Worlds of Poul Anderson, 1975, Mirkheim, 1977, The Avatar, 1978, The Merman's Children, 1979, Orion Shall Rise, 1983, the Boat of a Million Years, 1989, Harvest of Stars, 1993, the Stars Are Also Fire, 1994, All One Universe, 1996, The Fleet of Stars, 1997, War of the Gods, 1998, Starfarers, 1998. Recipient Hugo award, 1961, 64, 68, 71, 73, 78, 82, Nebula award, 1971, 72, 81, Mythopoeic award, 1975, J.R.R. Tolkien Meml. award, 1978, SFWA Grand Master award, 1998. Mem. Sci. Fiction Writers Am. (pres. 1972-73), Baker St. Irregulars. Issue of Mag. Fantasy and Sci. dedicated to him, 1972. Home: 3 Las Palomas Orinda CA 94563-1915 Office: care Chichak Inc Lit Agy 1040 1st Ave New York NY 10022-2902

ANDERSON, RACHAEL KELLER, library administrator; b. N.Y.C., Jan. 15, 1938; d. Harry and Sarah Keller; m. Howard D. Goldwyn; children: Rebecca Anderson, Michael Goldwyn, Bryan Goldwyn, David Goldwyn. A.B., Barnard Coll., 1959; M.S., Columbia U., 1960. Librarian CCNY, 1960-62; librarian Mt. Sinai Med. Ctr., N.Y.C., 1964-73, dir. library, 1973-79; dir. Health Scis Libr. Columbia U., N.Y.C., 1979-91, acting v.p., univ. libr., 1982; dir. Ariz. Health Scis. Libr., U. Ariz., Tucson, 1991—; bd. dirs. Med. Libr. Ctr. of N.Y., N.Y.C., 1983-91; mem. biomed. libr. rev. com. Nat. Libr. Medicine, Bethesda, Md., 1984-88, chmn., 1987-88; mem. bd. regents Nat. Libr. Medicine, 1990-94, chmn., 1993-94; pres. Ariz. Health Info. Network, 1995. Contbr. articles to profl. jours. Mem. Med. Libr. Assn. (pres.-elect 1996-97, pres. 1997-98, bd. dirs. 1983-86), Assn. Acad. Health Scis. Libr. Dirs. (bd. dirs. 1983-86, pres. 1991-92). Office: Ariz Health Scis Libr 1501 N Campbell Ave Tucson AZ 85724-0001

ANDERSON, RAY C., carpet company executive; b. West Point, Ga., July 28, 1934. BS in Indsl. Engring. with highest honors, Ga. Inst. Tech., 1956. With Proctor & Gamble, Atlanta, 1956-58; engr. Callaway Mills, La Grange, Ga., 1959-68; with Deering Milliken, Inc., Atlanta, 1958-59; chmn. bd., CEO Interface, Inc., Atlanta, Ga., 1973—. Author: The Journey from There to Here - The Eco-Odyssey of a CEO, 1995, Face It, 1996. Mem. Pres. Coun. on Sustainable Devel. (appointed co-chair 1997—), Northside Methodist Ch., Atlanta. Named Internat. Businessman of Yr., Soc. Internat. Bus. Fellows, 1992, Ga. Conservancy Distinguished Conservationist, 1996; recipient Entrepreneur of Yr. award Southeast Region, Ernst & Young, 1996, Global Green USA Millennium award, 1996. Mem. Am. Archtl. Found. (bd. trustees), Acad. Distinguished Engring. Alumni Ga. Tech. (chmn. adv. bd. 1995-96), LaGrange Coll. (bd. trustees), U. Va. Sch. Architecture (adv. bd.), Bank South Corp. (bd. dirs 1991-96), NationsBank Corp. (bd. dirs.), Royal Ten Cate (bd. dirs.), Bus. Social Responsibility (bd. dirs.), Natural Step (bd. dirs.). Office: Interface Inc 2859 Paces Ferry Rd SE Ste 2000 Atlanta GA 30339-6216*

ANDERSON, RAYMOND QUINTUS, diversified company executive; b. Jamestown, N.Y., Nov. 27, 1930; s. Paul N. and Cecille (Ogren) A.; m. Sondra Rumsey, June 5, 1954; children: Heidi, Kristin, Gerrit, Mitchell, Tracy, Brooks. Grad., Phillips Acad., Andover, Mass., 1949; BS in Engring., Princeton U., 1953; postgrad., Sloane Sch., MIT, MIT. With Dahlstrom Corp., Jamestown, 1957-76, exec. v.p., 1965, pres., 1968-76; founder, pres. Aarque Steel Corp., Jamestown, 1976-78, Aarque Mgmt. Corp., Jamestown, 1978-96; founder, chmn. Aarque Cos., Jamestown, 1980-96, Aarque Capital Corp., 1996—; bd. dirs. Oneida Ltd., Bus. Coun. N.Y. State, Inc., Cold Metal Products Co., Inc., Aarque Steel Group, Kardex Sys., Inc.; trustee Northwestern Mut. Life Ins. Co. Patentee in field. Chmn. Jamestown United Fund drive, 1964, 74; bd. dirs. N.Y. State Dept. Environ. Conservation; dir. Oneida, Ltd.; trustee Roger Tory Peterson Inst., Chautauqua Found. Inc.; civilian aide to Sec. of the U.S. Army; mem. adv. bd. World Econ. Forum. Served with USNR, 1954-57. Mem. Mfrs. Assn. Jamestown Area (pres. 1967-68), Empire State C. of C. (pres. 1974-76), Royal Round Table of Swedish Coun. Am., U.S. Can. Trade Coun., U.S. Dept. Commerce Ind. Sector Adv. Com., Tau Beta Pi. Republican. Episcopalian. Clubs: Moon Brook Country (Jamestown); Sportsmen's (Chautaqua, N.Y.); Union League Met. (N.Y.C.). Office: Aarque Cos PO Box 310 111 W 2d St Jamestown NY 14702-0310

ANDERSON, REID BRYCE, ballet company artistic director; b. New Westminister, B.C., Can., Apr. 1, 1949; s. Warren Nels and Phyllis Jessie Bryce (Purser) A. Student dance, Dolores Kirkwood, Burnaby, B.C., Royal Ballet Sch., 1967, 68. Dancer Stuttgart (Fed. Republic Germany) Ballet, 1969-86, prin. dancer, 1975-86, ballet master, 1982-86; artistic dir. Ballet B.C., Vancouver, 1987-89, Nat. Ballet Can., Toronto, Ont., 1989—, Stuttgart Ballet, 1996—. Choreographer numerous works for performing cos. Decorated Order of Fed. Republic Germany, 1986; recipient 1995 John Cranko prize for svc. to Art of Classical Ballet and in particular teaching, coaching and maintaining the work of the late John Cranko around the world. Office: The Stuttgart Ballet, Obere Schlossgarten 6, 70173 Stuttgart Germany

ANDERSON, RICHARD CARL, geophysical exploration company executive; b. Pontiac, Mich., June 6, 1928; s. Earling Adolph and Blenda Maria (Johnson) A.; m. Georgia L. Carnahan, Aug. 14, 1949; children—Laurie Ann, Gary Carl, Curtis Murray, Denise Carla. B.S. in Mining Engring., N.Mex. Inst. Mining & Tech., 1950, M.S. in Geophysics, 1953. Engr. Allis Chalmers, Milw., 1949-51; geophysicist, v.p. Geophys. Service, Inc., Dallas, 1953-71; v.p., then exec. v.p. Digicon, Houston, 1971-75; sr. v.p., exec. v.p. Seismograph Service Corp., Tulsa, from 1975, pres., 1981-85; ret., 1985-88; pres. Fairfield Industries, Houston, 1988-91, vice chmn., chief exec. officer, 1991-93; ret., 1993; mem. Energy Advocates, Tulsa, 1981-93, coordinator, 1983, 86. Served with U.S. Army, 1946-47. Recipient Disting. Achievement award N.Mex. Inst. Mining and Tech., 1984. Mem. Soc. Exploration Geophysicists, Internat. Assn. Geophys. Contractors (hon. life mem., bd. dirs. 1977-85, 89-94, chmn. 1978-79). Home: 1111 Hermann Dr Apt 11F Houston TX 77004-6929

ANDERSON, RICHARD CHARLES, geology educator; b. Moline, Ill., Apr. 22, 1930; s. Edgar Oscar and Sarah Albertina (Olson) A.; m. Ethel Irene Cada, June 27, 1953; children: Eileen Ruth, Elizabeth Sarah, Penelope Cada. AB, Augustana Coll., Rock Island, Ill., 1952; SM, U. Chgo., 1953, PhD, 1955. Geologist Geophoto Svcs., Denver, 1955-57; from asst. prof. to prof. geology Augustana Coll., Rock Island, 1957-96; prof. emeritus, 1996—; rsch. affiliate Ill. State Geol. Survey, Champaign, 1959—. Editor: Earth Interpreters, 1992; author reports. Recipient Neil Miner award Nat. Assn. Geology Tchrs., 1992. Fellow Geol. Soc. Am. (sect. co-chair 1990). Lutheran. Home: 2012 24th St Rock Island IL 61201-4533 Office: Augustana Coll Dept Geology 639 38th St Rock Island IL 61201-2210

ANDERSON, RICHARD DEAN, actor; b. Mpls., Jan. 23, 1950; s. Stuart A. Student, St. Cloud State U., Ohio U. Stage appearance: Superman in the Bones; film appearances include Odd Jobs, 1986, Young Doctors In Love, 1982; TV Series: General Hospital, 1976-81, Seven Brides for Seven Brothers, 1982-83, Emerald Point, 1983-84, MacGyver, 1985-92, Legend, 1995, Stargate SG-1, 1997; TV films Today's FBI, 1981, Imaginary Heroes, 1986, Through the Eyes of a Killer, 1992, In the Eyes of A Stranger, 1992, MacGyver: Lost Treasure of Atlantis, 1994, Beyond Betrayal, 1994, Past the Bleachers, 1995, MacGyver: Trail to Doomsday, 1994; film Firehouse, 1997; TV miniseries: Pandora's Clock, 1996, Stargate SG-1, 1997; mem. rock band Ricky Dean and Dante; street mime, jester and juggler in L.A., former stage mgr Improvisation Theatre; writer, dir., actor Marineland; prodr. (films) MacGyver: Lost Treasure of Atlantis, 1994, MacGyver: Trail to Doomsday, 1994; TV guest appearances The Love Boat, 1977, The Facts of Life, 1979. Office: ICM 8942 Wilshire Blvd Beverly Hills CA 90211-1934*

ANDERSON, RICHARD EDMUND, city manager, management consultant; b. Ferndale, Mich., Dec. 23, 1938; s. Richard H. and Carolyn Jeanne (Figg) A.; m. Kay Clarke, Nov. 6, 1961 (div.); children: Pam, Mark, Linda; m. Linda Hawk Jenkins, Sept. 11, 1997. B.A., Mich. State U., 1962; postgrad. in advanced mgmt., Harvard U., 1979. Aide to mgr. City of St. Petersburg, Fla., 1962-64; adminstrv. asst. City of Ft. Lauderdale, Fla., 1964-67, dep. mgr., 1967-75, city mgr., 1975-80; v.p. Fla. Innovation Group, Tampa, 1980-81; pres. Integrated Systems Assocs., Inc., Ft. Lauderdale, 1981-90; city mgr. City of Florida City, Fla., 1990-94, City of Brooksville, Fla., 1995—. Contbr. articles to profl. jours. Mem. Internat. City Mgmt. Assn. Office: 201 Howell Ave Brooksville FL 34601-2041

ANDERSON, RICHARD ERNEST, agribusiness development executive, rancher; b. North Little Rock, Ark., Mar. 8, 1926; s. Victor Ernest and Lillian Josephine (Griffin) A.; m. Mary Ann Fitch, July 18, 1953; children: Vicki Lynn, Lucia Anita. BSCE, U. Ark., 1949; MSE, U. Mich., 1959. Registered profl. engr., Mich., Va., Tex., Mont. Commd. ensign USN, 1952, advanced through grades to capt., 1968, ret., 1974; v.p. Ocean Resources, Inc., Houston, 1974-77; mgr. maintenance and ops. Holmes & Narver, Inc., Orange, Calif., 1977-78; pres. No. Resources, Inc., Billings, Mont., 1978-81; v.p. Holmes & Narver, Inc., Orange, Calif., 1981-82; owner, operator Anderson Ranches, registered Arabian horses and comml. Murray Grey cows, Pony, Mont., 1982—; pres., dir. Carbon Resources Inc., Butte, Mont., 1983-88, Agri Resources, Inc., Butte, Mont., 1988-95, Anderson Holdings, Inc., Pony, Mont., 1995—. Trustee Lake Barcroft-Virginia Watershed Improvement Dist., 1973-74; pres. Lake Barcroft-Virginia Recreation Center, Inc., 1972-73. With USAAF, 1944-45. Decorated Silver Star, Legion of Merit with Combat V (2), Navy Marine Corps medal, Bronze Star with Combat V, Meritorious Service medal, Purple Heart; Anderson Peninsula in Antarctica named in his honor. Mem. ASCE, Soc. Am. Mil. Engrs. (Morrell medal 1965). Republican. Methodist. Office: Anderson Holdings Inc PO Box 266 Pony MT 59747-0266

ANDERSON, RICHARD LOUIS, electrical engineer; b. Mpls., Feb. 4, 1927; s. Ben Walter and Anna Elizabeth (Zitcowicz) A.; m. Claire Louise Petersen, Sept. 15, 1951; children: Gretchen, Betty Lise, Karl. B.S., U. Minn., 1950, M.S., 1952; Ph.D., Syracuse (N.Y.) U., 1960; D.Sc. (hon.), U. Sao Paulo, Brazil, 1969. Research asst. U. Minn., 1950-52; research engr. IBM Corp., Poughkeepsie, N.Y., 1952-60; from. instr. to prof. elec. and computing engring. Syracuse U., 1954-79; prof. elec. engring. U. Vt., Burlington, 1979-95, prof. emeritus elec. engring. and materials sci., 1995—; dir. materials sci. program U. Vt., 1981-91; Fulbright-Hayes prof. U. Madrid, 1960-61, U. Sao Paulo, 1967-69; cons. to govt. and industry; cons. UN Devel. Program, 1980-92, OAS, 1988, 91, 93. Author. Served with USNR, 1944-47. Recipient 1st Brazilian prize microelectronics, 1980; fellow Ford Found., 1967-69; grantee NSF, 1974-85, N.Y. State Sci. and Tech. Found., 1974-75, 77-78, Dept. Energy, 1979-83. Fellow IEEE; mem. AAUP, Am. Phys. Soc., Sigma Xi. Patentee in field. Home: 808 Wake Robin Dr Shelburne VT 05482-7582 Office: U Vt Elec Engring Dept Burlington VT 05405

ANDERSON, RICHARD MCLEMORE, internist; b. Gainesville, Fla., Mar. 3, 1930; s. Montgomery Drummond and Myrtle (McLemore) A.; m. Leewood Shaw, Mar. 21, 1959; children: Richard McLemore Jr., Bruce Dexter. BS, U. Fla., 1951; MD, Emory U., 1958. Diplomate Am. Bd. Internal Medicine. Chief of staff Alachua Gen. Hosp., Gainesville, Fla., 1973-75; internist Gainesville, Fla., 1962—; Chmn. of bd. Santa Fe Health Care, Gainesville, 1984-91; bd. dirs. Health Improvement Inc. (parent of AV Med. Inc.), AV Med. Inc., Santa Fe. Pres. Rotary Club of Gainesville, 1980-81. Capt. USAF, 1951-54. Mem. AMA, ACP, Alachua County Med. Soc. (v.p. 1972), Fla. Med. Assn. Presbyterian. Office: 106 SW 10th St Gainesville FL 32601-6201

ANDERSON, RICHARD NORMAN, actor, film producer; b. Long Branch, N.J., Aug. 8, 1926; s. Henry and Olga (Lurie) A.; m. Katherine Thalberg, Oct. 30, 1961 (div. Aug. 1973); children: Ashley, Brooke Dominique, Deva Justine. Grad. high sch., West Los Angeles, Calif. Actor Metro Goldwyn Mayer Studios, Culver City, Calif., 1950-56, 20th Century Fox Film Corp., Beverly Hills, Calif., 1961-62, 83-84, CBS, Hollywood, Calif., 1964-65, Quinn Martin Prodns., Hollywood, 1967-68, Universal/MCA, Universal City, Calif., 1973-78; pres. Richard Anderson Film Co., 1977—; TV spokesman Kiplinger Washington Letter, 1985—. Film actor, prin. films include Escape from Fort Bravo, Long Hot Summer, Paths of Glory, Compulsion, Tora, Tora, Tora, Scaramouche, The Magnificent Yankee, Seven Days in May, Wackiest Ship in the Army, Doctors Wives, Seconds, The Glass Shield, An American in Saigon, 1994; numerous TV appearances including Fall Guy, Whiz Kids, Fantasy Island, Love Boat, Condominium, The Immigrants, Big Valley, Gunsmoke, The Rifleman, Playhouse 90, The Eighty Yard Run; regular actor on Bus Stop, 1960, Perry Mason, 1961, Dan August, 1969, as Oscar Goldman in Six Million Dollar Man, 1972-77, Bionic Woman, 1974-77, Cover-Up, 1984; additional TV appearances include Perry Mason Returns, 1985, The A Team, 1986, Simon and Simon, 1986, Hardcastle and McCormick, 1986, Dynasty, 1986-87, Return of the Six Million Dollar Man and Bionic Woman, 1987, Stepford Children, 1987, Hoover Vs. Kennedys, 1987, Eminent Domain, 1987, Danger Bay, 1987, Kane and Abel, 1987, Return of the Six Million Dollar Man and the Bionic Woman II, 1988, (pilot series) The New Six Million Dollar Man/Bionic Woman, (2 hr. movie series) Bionics, 1990, Return of the Six Million Dollar Man and Bionic Woman, 1993, Alfred Hitchcock series, 1989, (miniseries) Lucky Chances, 1990, Killer Angels, 1993, Kung Fu: The Legend Continues, 1993, 94 (TV film) A Lake In The Woods, 1995; appeared on Broadway in The Highest Tree; appeared in summer stock, Lobero Theatre, Santa Barbara, Calif., Laguna Beach (Calif.) Playhouse. Served with AUS, 1944-46. Recipient Emmy nomination Acad. TV Arts and Scis., 1976, 77. Mem. ASAG, Acad. Motion Picture Arts and Scis., Actors Equity Assn., Friars Club, The Players. Avocations: biking, bird watching, history, traveling, tennis. Office: Lewis and Joffe Ste 520 10880 Wilshire Blvd Los Angeles CA 90024

ANDERSON, RICHARD PAUL, agricultural company executive; b. Toledo, Apr. 10, 1929; s. Harold and Margaret Mary (Meilink) A.; m. Frances Mildred Heilman, Nov. 28, 1953; children—Christopher, Daniel, James, Martha, Jennifer, Timothy. BS magna cum laude, Mich. State U., 1953. With The Andersons, Maumee, Ohio, 1946—, gen. ptnr., 1951—, gen. mgr., 1980-82, mng. ptnr., 1983—, pres., CEO, 1986-96, chmn., CEO, 1996-98, chmn., 1999—; bd. dirs. Chemfirst. Pres. Toledo Area council Boy Scouts Am., 1966-69; gen. chmn. Crusade of Mercy, Toledo, 1972; bd. dirs. Childrens Services, St. Luke's Hosp.; chmn. support council Ohio Agrl. Research and Devel. Ctr.; trustee U. Toledo Corp., 1985-98, chmn. bd. trustees, 1986—; bd. dirs. Pub. Broadcasting Found. NW Ohio, 1983—, chmn. bd. dirs., 1986-92. Served with AUS, 1954-56. Named Toledo Area Citizen of Yr. Toledo Bd. Realtors, 1974, Outstanding Lay Leader N.W. Ohio chpt. Nat. Assn. Social Workers, 1971; recipient Disting. Service award Ohio State U., 1986. Mem. Com. 100 (bd. dirs. exec. com. 1987-92). Republican. Roman Catholic. Club: Rotary (Toledo.) (pres. 1976-77). Home: 1833 S Holland Sylvania Rd Maumee OH 43537-1316 Office: The Andersons 480 W Dussel Dr Maumee OH 43537-1690

ANDERSON, RICHARD THEODORE, urban planner, association executive; b. Bklyn., Oct. 11, 1940; s. Charles Theodore and Lillian Elizabeth (Holmlin) A.; m. Anasta Frank, Oct. 3, 1970; children: Erik Theodore, Leslie Elisabeth. AB, Rutgers U., 1962; M of Regional planning, Cornell U., 1964; postgrad., NYU, 1964-67. Pres. Regional Plan Assn., N.Y.C., 1964-92; exec. dir. The Dallas Plan, N.Y.C., 1993-94; pres., CEO N.Y. Bldg. Congress, N.Y.C., 1994—; pres. N.Y. Bldg. Found., N.Y.C., 1998—; vic. asst. prof. dept. city & regional planning Pratt Inst., N.Y.C., 1979-92; chmn. Pres.' Coun. N.Y.C. Planning & Design Orgns., 1986-92. Bd. dirs. Water Resources Assn. Delaware River Basin, 1977-80, United Way, Pelham, N.Y., 1977-79; v.p., trustee Big Bros./Big Sisters, N.Y.C., 1969—, audrey Cohen Coll., 1998—; mem. coll.a dv. coun. Cornell U. Coll. Architecture, Art and Planning, 1984-94; mem. Village Planning Bd., Pelham, 1977-80; mem. Times Sq. Adv. Coun., N.Y.C., 1985-89; dir. Regional Alliance Small Contractors, 1994—; dir. ACE Mentorship Program, 1997—, Bklyn. Sports Found., 1998—; mem. Bus. Coun. N.Y. State, N.Y.C. Partnership; co-chmn. N.Y. chpt. Rebuild Am. Coalition. Recipient Ellis Island medal of honor, 1995; Vis. scholar NYU, 1992. Mem. Am. Inst. Cert. Planners, Am. Planning Assn. (dir. & treas. 1977-80, pres. 1980-81, Disting. Svc. award 1985), Am. Soc. Planning Ofcls. (bd. dirs. 1977-78), N.Y. Soc. Assn. Execs., Urban Land Inst. (full), N.Y. Acad. Scis., Met. Affairs Non-profit Corps, Ellis Island Medal of Hon. Soc., Rutgers Alumni Assn. (Loyal Son award 1989), N.Y.C. C. of C., Bklyn. C. of C. Lutheran. Home: 235 Monterey Ave Pelham NY 10803-2329 Office: NY Bldg Congress 44 W 28th St New York NY 10001-4212

ANDERSON, RICHARD VERNON, ecology educator, researcher; b. Julesburg, Colo., Sept. 9, 1946; s. Vernon Franklin and Charolett Iona (Jeppesen) A.; m. Arline June Rosentreter, Jan. 23, 1971; children: Rustle R., Michael C., Theodore F. Student, Chadron State Coll., 1964-66, Western State Coll., 1970; BS, No. Ill. U., 1974, MS, 1975; PhD, Colo. State U., 1978. Grad. teaching asst. No. Ill. U., DeKalb, 1974-75; grad. rsch. asst. Colo. State U., 1975-78, postdoctoral fellow Nat. Resource Ecology Lab., 1978-79; asst. prof. Western Ill. U., Macomb, 1979-82, assoc. prof., 1982-87, prof., dir. Kibbe Life Scis. Field Sta., 1987—; vis. asst. prof. inst. for. environ. studies Water Resources Ctr., U. Ill., 1980; mem. assoc. faculty Argonne Nat. Lab., 1985—; assoc. supportive scientist Ill. Natural History Survey, 1985—; proposal reviewer ecology, ecosystem studies, regulatory biology, divsn. internat. programs NSF, 1981—, mem. proposal panel for equipment and facilities grants, 1987; proposal reviewer U.S./Israel Binational Sci. Found., 1981-82, Natural Environ. Rsch. Coun., Eng., 1983-84; environ. cons. aquatic sect. Environ. Cons. and Planners, DeKalb, 1974; program chmn. Internat. Conf. on Ecological Integrity of Large Floodplain Rivers, 1994. Reviewer Natural Resource Ecology Lab., 1977-81, Jour. Nematology, 1977-81, Archives Environ. Contamination and Toxicology, 1978-81, Ecology, 1978-85, Argonne Nat. Lab., 1980—, Pedobiologia, 1982-87, Jour. Freshwater Ecology, 1982—, Freshwater Invertebrate Ecology, 1982—; contbr. over 250 sci. articles, reports, papers and abstracts; presenter papers in field. Grantee NSF, 1972, 73, 82, 83, 84, 85, (two grants), 86, (two grants), 87, 88, Western Ill. U., 1980, (two grants), 81, Upper Miss. River Basin Comm./U. Ill., 1980, Abbott Labs., 1981, Ill. Dept. Transp., 1981, 85, Ctrl. Ill. Light Co., 1981, 82, 83, 84, Nat. Fish and Wildlife Svc., 1983, Ill. Dept. Conservation, 1985, 87, 88, 89, 91, U.S. Fish and Wildlife Svc./Ill. Dept. Conservation, 1988, 89, 90, 91, Environ. Cons. and Planners, Inc., 1988, 89, 91, Booker Assocs., Inc., 1989, (two grants), Ill. Natural History Survey, 1989, Wetlands Rsch., Inc., 1989, 90, 91, 92, 95, USDA?U. Ill., 1991, 92, Hey and Assocs., Inc. Biotic Surveys, 1992, 83, 94, 95. Mem. Entomol. Soc. Am., N.Am. Benthological Soc. (program com. 1982-83, reviewer jour. 1990—), Ecol. Soc., Soc. Nematologists (ecology com. 1981-82, systematic resources com. 1981-82), Internat. Congress Ecologists, Ill. State Acad. Sci., Miss. River Rsch. Consortium (mem. exec. bd. 1981-82, v.p. bd. dirs. 1991-92, pres. bd. dirs. 1992-93), Internat. Conf. on Integrity of Large Floodplain River (program chmn. 1994), Xerces Soc., Sigma Xi (Rsch. of Yr. award 1984), Phi Kappa Phi. Achievements include research in invertebrate ecology, aquatic biology with an emphasis on large river ecosystems, aquatic invertebrates and freeliving nematodes, the effects of invertebrates on nutrient cycling. Home: 704 S Randolph St Macomb IL 61455-2966 Office: Western Ill U Dept Biol Scis Macomb IL 61455

ANDERSON, RICHARD W., federal judge. Apptd. magistrate judge U.S. Dist. Ct. Mont., 1991. Fax: (406) 247-7027. Office: 5405 Federal Bldg 316 N 26th St Billings MT 59101-1362

ANDERSON, ROBERT BARBER, architect; b. Summit, N.J., Apr. 17, 1944; s. Robert B. Anderson and Marion (Lent) Campbell; m. Dominique Elizabeth Astruc, June 2, 1972; children: Adriana, Joseph, Frederic. BArch, Clemson U., 1968; attended, Bklyn. Coll., 1971-72. Registered architect, Va. Ptnr. Anderson, Boyd & Assocs., Madison and Charlottesville, Va., 1976-78; prin. Kerns Group, Washington, 1979-82; v.p. The Benham Group East, Vienna, Va., 1982-85; pres. Anderson Pace, Inc. (named changed to Anderson O'Brien Archs.), Alexandria, Va., 1985-93, Heyward Boyd & Anderson, Charlottesville, Va., 1993—; Chmn. Archtl. Advisory Bd. Falls Church, Va., 1981-84. Cartoonist Zinc newspaper, Paris, 1971; illustrator Langman & Wordeman's Med. Ency., 1979; designed and built historic office bldg. at 1915 Eye Street, Washington, 1981. Recipient Design award Progressive Architecture mag., 1981, Masonry Inst. award, 1989, NAIOP Best Office Bldg. of Yr. award, 1989, Washington Met. Area Art Dirs. Club Best Corp. Brochure award, 1989. Mem. AIA (Design award 1982, D.C. chpt. Design award 1987, Northern Va. chpt. Design awards 1992, 94). Avocations: painting, pen and ink drawing, backcountry hiking, soccer, martial arts. Office: Heyward Boyd & Anderson 111 W High St Charlottesville VA 22902-5018

ANDERSON, R(OBERT) GREGG, real estate company executive; b. St. Joseph, Mo., Oct. 3, 1928; s. Clarence William and Marie Louise (Newman) A.; 1 child, Robert Gregg Jr. Student, U. Okla., 1948-49, U. Tulsa, 1950. Pres. Gregg Anderson Realty, San Diego, 1959-63; v.p. Trousdale Constrn. Co., L.A., 1963-67; pres. Amfac Properties div. Amfac, Inc., Honolulu, 1967-69; v.p. Amfac, Inc., Honolulu, 1967-69, sr. v.p., 1969-74; pres., chmn. bd. Accent Enterprises, Inc., Amfac Communities, Inc., Amfac Silverado Corp., Neilson Way Corp., 745 Fort St. Corp., Cen. Oahu Land Corp., L.A. Environ. Structures, Inc., 1969-74; chmn. bd. West Maui Properties, Inc., 1969-74; v.p. Silverado Country Club & Resort, Inc., 1969-74; pres. Gregg Anderson Realty & Devel., Inc., 1974—, Villa Pacific Bldg. Co., 1980—; gen. ptnr. Rancho Vista Devel. Co., Palmdale, Calif., 1980—; pres. Videocable, Inc., Palmdale, 1984-87; gen. ptnr. ProRep Assocs., 1991—. Bd. dirs. Antelope Valley Bd. Trade, 1991—; mem. exec. com. Gift Found. Antelope Valley Hosp. Med. Ctr., 1989-92. With USNR, 1950-54. Named Builder of Yr., Calif. Bldg. Industry Assn., 1998; inductee Calif. Bldg. Industry Hall of Fame, 1999. Mem. Bldg. Industry Assn. (bd. dirs. 1984-94), Rotary (hon.), Kiwanis (hon.). Republican. Avocations: tennis, golf, bowling. Office: Rancho Vista Devel Co Ste F 3011 Rancho Vista Blvd Palmdale CA 93551

ANDERSON, ROBERT HELMS, information scientist; b. Richmond, Calif., June 7, 1939; s. Oscar Nels and Elsie (Helms) A.; m. Lynn Shallenberger, Oct. 1965; children: Blythe, Kevin. B.A., U. Calif.-Berkeley, 1962; M.A., Harvard U., 1965, Ph.D., 1968. Head info. sci. dept. The Rand Corp., Santa Monica, Calif., 1976-79, dir. inst. for rsch. on interactive systems, 1985-88, exec. v.p. Interactive Systems Corp., Santa Monica, 1979-81, sr. info. sci., 1992—; pres. Robert H. Anderson and Assocs., Inc., Pacific Palisades, Calif., 1981-92; adj. assoc. prof. U. So. Calif., 1968-75. Contbr. articles to computer sci. jours. Served to 1st lt. U.S. Army, 1962-64. Mem. Assn. Computing Machinery, (nat. lectr. 1972-73), The Info. Soc. (editor in chief jour. 1991-95). Office: The Rand Corp 1700 Main St Santa Monica CA 90401-3297

ANDERSON, ROBERT HENRY, educator; b. Milw., July 28, 1918; s. Robert Dean and Eleanor (Weil) A.; m. Mary Jane Hopkins, July 19, 1941 (div. Jan. 1979); children: Dean Robert, Lynn Mary (Mrs. William D. Grant), Scott William, Carol Jane (Mrs. Herbert Gilmore); m. Karolyn J. Snyder, Jan. 24, 1979. BA, U. Wis., 1939, MA, 1942; PhD, U. Chgo., 1949; AM (hon.), Harvard U., 1959. Tchr. Oconomowoc, Wis., 1940-43; research asst. ednl. field service U. Chgo., 1946-47; prin. Roosevelt Sch., River Forest, Ill., 1947-49; supt. schs. dist. 163, Park Forest, Ill., 1949-54; mem. faculty Grad. Sch. Edn., Harvard U., 1954-73, prof. edn., 1962-73; prof., dean Coll. of Edn. Tex. Tech U., Lubbock, 1973-83, prof. and dean emeritus, 1983—; prof. edn. U. South Fla., 1984—; pres. Pedamorphosis, Inc., 1977—; lectr., cons. sch. orgn., adminstrn., staff devel. Author: Teaching in a World of Change, 1966, Education in Anticipation of Tomorrow, 1973, Opting for Openness, 1973; co-author: Managing Productive Schools, 1986, The Nongraded Elementary School, rev. edit., 1987, Clinical Supervision, 3d edit., 1993, Nongradedness, 1993; co-editor: As the Twig is Bent, 1971, Clinical Supervision Coaching, 1993; sr. editor: Current Trends in Education (pub. in Japanese), 1971; contbr. chpts. to books. With USNR, 1943-46. Mem. ASCD, Nat. Soc. Study Edn., Am. Assn. Sch. Adminstrs., Am. Ednl. Rsch. Assn., Phi Delta Kappa, Kappa Delta Pi (laureate chpt.). Episcopalian. Home: 13604 Waterfall Way Tampa FL 33624-6907 Office: PO Box 271669 Tampa FL 33688-1669

ANDERSON, ROBERT LANIER, III, federal judge; b. Macon, Ga., Nov. 12, 1936; s. Robert Lanier II and Helen A.; m. Nancy Briska, Aug. 18, 1962; children: Robert, William Hilliar, Browne McIntosh. AB magna cum laude, Yale U., 1958; LLB, Harvard U., 1961. Assoc. Anderson, Walkert, Reichert, Macon, Ga., 1963-79; Judge U.S. Ct. Appeals (11th cir.), 1979—. With USAR, 1058-61, capt. U.S. Army, 1961-63. Mem. ABA, Ga. Bar Assn., Macon Bar Assns., State Bar of Ga., Am. Judicature Soc. Office: US Ct Appeals PO Box 977 Macon GA 31202-0977*

ANDERSON, ROBERT MARSHALL, retired bishop; b. S.I., N.Y., Dec. 18, 1933; s. Arthur Harold and Hazel Schneider A.; m. Mary Artemis Evans, Aug. 24, 1960; children: Martha, Elizabeth, Catherine, Thomas. BA, Colgate U., 1955; STB, Berkeley Div. Sch., 1961, DD (hon.), 1977; DD (hon.), Seabury Western Sem., 1978, Yale U., 1977. Ordained priest Episcopal Ch. Curate St. John's Ch., Stamford, Conn., 1961-63, vicar, 1963-67, assoc. rector, 1968-72; priest in charge Middle Haddan, Conn., 1963-67, rector, 1967-68; dean St. Mark's Cathedral, Salt Lake City, 1972-78; bishop Episcopal Diocese of Minn., Mpls., 1978-93; interim recotr Church of the Holy Spirit, Lake Forest, Ill., 1994-95; asst. bishop Diocese of L.A., 1995-98. Served with U.S. Army. Danforth fellow, 1959-60. Mem. Berkeley Alumni Assn. (pres. 1972-76). Democrat. Clubs: Mpls, Minikahda. Home: 65 Atterideg Rd Lake Forest IL 60045 Office: Diocese of LA PO Box 512164 Los Angeles CA 90051-0164*

ANDERSON, ROBERT MONTE, lawyer; b. Logan, Utah, Feb. 19, 1938; s. E. LeRoy and Grace (Rasmussen) A.; m. Kathleen Hansen, Aug. 12, 1966; children: Jennifer, Katrina, Alexander. AB, Columbia Coll., 1960; LLB, U. Utah, 1963. Bar: Utah 1963, U.S. Cir. Ct. Appeals (10th cir.) 1967, U.S. Supreme Ct. 1976. Assoc., shareholder, v.p. Van Cott, Bagley, Cornwall & McCarthy, Salt Lake City, 1963-82; pres., shareholder Berman & Anderson, Salt Lake City, 1982-86; v.p., shareholder Hansen & Anderson, Salt Lake City, 1986-90; pres., shareholder Anderson & Watkins, Salt Lake City, 1990-95; pres. Anderson & Smith, Salt Lake City, 1995-97; lawyer, shareholder, pres. Van Cott, Bagley Cornwall & McCarthy, Salt Lake City, 1998—; bd. dirs., mem. exec. com. Anderson Lumber Co., Ogden, Utah. Trustee The Children's Ctr., Salt Lake City, 1973-77; pres. Utah Legal Svcs., Salt Lake City, 1979. Mem. ABA, Utah State Bar Assn. (cts. and judges com. 1991—), Alta Club, Cottonwood Club, Rotary. Avocations: tennis, skiing. Office: Van Cott Bagley Cornwall & McCarthy 50 S Main St Ste 1600 Salt Lake City UT 84144-0450

ANDERSON, ROBERT MORRIS, JR., electrical engineer; b. Crookston, Minn., Feb. 15, 1939; s. Robert Morris and Eleanor Elaine (Huotte) A.; m. Janice Ilene Pendell, Sept. 3, 1960; children—Erik Martin, Kristi Lynn. B.E.E., U. Mich., 1961, M.E.E., 1963, M.S. in Physics, 1965, Ph.D. in Elec. Engring, 1967. Asst. research engr. U. Mich., Ann Arbor, 1963-67; research engr. Conductron Corp., Ann Arbor, summer 1967; asst. prof. elec. engring. Purdue U., West Lafayette, Ind., 1967-71; assoc. prof. Purdue U., 1971-79, prof., 1979, engring. coordinator for continuing edn., 1973-79, Ball Bros. prof., 1976-79; mgr. engring. edn. and tng., corp. cons. services GE, Bridgeport, Conn., 1979-82, mgr. tech. edn. operation, corp. engring. and mfg., 1982-88; mgr. tech. edn., corp. mgmt. devel. Gen. Electric Co., Bridgeport, Conn., 1988-90; vice provost, dir. coop. extension Iowa State U., Ames, 1990-95, prof. elec. engring., 1990—. Author: multi-media learning package Fundamentals of Vacuum Technology, 1973, (with others) Divided Loyalties, 1980; contbr. (with others) articles to profl. jours. Named Best Tchr. Elec. Engring. Purdue U., 1974; recipient Dow Outstanding Young Faculty award, 1974. Fellow Am. Soc. Engring. Edn. (cert. of merit 1977, Joseph M. Biedenbach Disting. Svc. award 1986), IEEE (Meritorious Achievement award in continuing edn. activities 1987). Lutheran. Home: 3321 Kingman Rd Ames IA 50014-3942 Office: Iowa State U 303 Coover Hall Ames IA 50011-3060

ANDERSON, ROBERT ORVILLE, oil and gas company executive; b. Chgo., Apr. 13, 1917; s. Hugo A. and Hilda (Nelson) A.; m. Barbara Phelps, Aug. 25, 1939; children: Katherine, Julia, Maria, Robert Bruce, Barbara Burton, William Phelps, Beverley. B.A., U. Chgo., 1939. With Am. Mineral Spirits Co., Chgo., 1939-41; pres. Malco Refineries, Inc., Roswell, N.Mex., 1963-86; with Atlantic Richfield Co., Los Angeles, retired chmn. bd., chief exec. officer; mem. Com. Econ. Devel., Washington. Hon. chmn. Aspen Inst.; chmn. emeritus Lovelace Med. Found.; trustee Calif. Inst. Tech., U. Chgo. Mem. Nat. Petroleum Council, Am. Petroleum Inst. Clubs: Century (N.Y.C.); California (Los Angeles); Pacific-Union (San Francisco).

ANDERSON, ROBERT THEODORE, music educator, organist; b. Chgo., Oct. 5, 1934; s. Albert Theodore and Lillian Gertrude (Chalbeck) A. B.Sacred Music, Ill. Wesleyan U., 1955; M.Sacred Music, Union Theol. Sem., N.Y.C., 1957, D.Sacred Music, 1961. Mem. faculty So. Meth. U., 1960—, Univ. disting. prof. organ emeritus, 1972—, Meadows Found. disting. teaching prof., 1981-82; organ cons., lectr., tchr. master classes. Author articles; composer anthems. Fulbright grantee, 1957-59; named Distinguished Alumnus Ill. Wesleyan U., 1972. Mem. Am. Guild Organists, Internat. Bach Soc., Blue Key, Pi Kappa Lambda, Phi Mu Alpha, Phi Beta Phi. Methodist. Home: 6810 Stichter Ave Dallas TX 75230-5317 Office: So Meth U Meadows Sch of Arts Div Music PO Box 750356 Dallas TX 75275-0356

ANDERSON, ROBERT THOMAS, anthropologist, researcher, physician; b. Oakland, Calif., Dec. 27, 1926; s. Victor T. and Stella Irene (Hansen) A.; m. Barbara Gallatin Anderson, Aug. 20, 1956 (div. Aug. 20, 1972); children: Andrea, Robin, Scott; m. Edna May Steiner Mitchell, Oct. 10, 1973; children: Debby, Tom, Kris. BA in Anthropology with hons., U. Calif., 1949, MA in Anthropology, 1953, PhD in Anthropology, 1956; MD, U. Autonoma Ciudad Juarez, Mex., 1986; D of Chiropractic, Life Chiropractic Coll. West, 1982. Cert. physician, surgeon Mex.; cert. physician, surgeon Internat. Commn. Fgn. Med. Grads., U.S.; cert. radiology x-ray supr., oper., Calif.; lic. chiropractor, Calif. Asst. prof. anthropology U. Wash., Seattle, 1959-60; Asst. prof. anthropology U. Calif., Berkeley, 1960, assoc. prof., 1966-67, prof. anthropology, 1967; asst. prof. anthropology Mills Coll., Oakland, 1960-63, assoc. prof. anthropology, 1963-66, prof. anthropology, 1967—; dir. rsch. Life Chriropractic Coll. W., 1978-83, Am. Coll. Traditional Chinese Medicine, 1989-92; dir. manual medicine San Francisco Spine Inst. at Seton Med. Ctr., 1988-91; researcher in field; med. anthropologist, Mex., Nepal, Brazil. Author: Magic Science and Health: The Aims and Achievements of Medical Anthropology, 1996; co-editor: Conservative Care of Low Back Pain, 1991; assoc. editor: Newsletter of the Am. Back Soc., 1988-92; mem. editl. bd. Med. Anthropology, 1990-96, Yearbook of Transcultural Medicne Psychotherapy, 1991—; contbr. 8 chpts. to books, 44 articles to profl. jours. Served with USN, 1946-48. Decorated WWII Victory medal. E-mail: boba@mills.edu. Home: 2007 Manzanita Dr Oakland CA 94611-1148 Office: Mills Coll 5000 MacArthur Blvd Oakland CA 94613-1301

ANDERSON, ROBERT W., surgeon; b. Chgo., Aug. 7, 1937; m. Taimi T., Dec. 27, 1960; children: Michael, Jeffery, David. BS, Duke U., 1959; MD, Northwestern U. Med. Sch., 1964, M in Medicine, 1994. Diplomate Am. Bd. Surgery, Am. Bd. Thoracic Surgery. Intern Duke U. Med. Ctr., Durham, N.C., 1964-65, from asst. resident to chief resident in surgery, 1967-72, from asst. prof. to assoc. prof. surgery, 1972-77; prof. surgery U. Minn., Mpls., 1979-84; prof. surgery Northwestern U. Med. Sch., Chgo., 1984-94, prof. biomed. engring., 1985-94; prof. surgery Duke U. Med. Ctr., 1994—; vis. prof., lectr. in field. Capt. U.S. ARmy, 1965-67, Viet Nam. Fellow Am. Coll. Surgeons, Am. Coll. Cardiology; mem. AMA, Southeastern Cardiovasc. Soc., Soc. Univ. Surgeons, Soc. Thoracic Surgeons, Am. Surgical Assn., Am. Assn. Thoracic Surgery, Mpls. Surg. Soc., Twin Cardiovasc. Soc., Am. Heart Assn., Assn. Clin. Cardiac Surgeons, Chgo. Surg. Soc., Chgo. Med. Soc., So. Surg. Assn., N.C. Surg. Soc., Assn. Acad. Surgery, Med. Soc. N.C., Alpha Omega Alpha, Tau Beta Pi. Office: Duke U Med Ctr Dept Surgery Durham NC 27710

ANDERSON, ROBERT WOODRUFF, playwright, novelist, screenwriter; b. N.Y.C., Apr. 28, 1917; s. James Hewston and Myra Esther (Grigg) A.; m. Phyllis Stohl, June 24, 1940 (dec. 1956); m. Teresa Wright, Dec. 11, 1959 (div. 1978). AB magna cum laude, Harvard U., 1939, MA, 1940. Tchr. playwriting Am. Theatre Wing, 1946-50; writer for radio and TV, 1947-53, ind. playwright, author, screenwriter, 1951—; mem. Playwrights Co., 1953-60; faculty Salzburg Seminar in Am. Studies, 1968, Iowa Writers Workshop, 1976; past chmn. bd. overseer's com. to visit the performing arts Harvard U. Writer: Come Marching Home, produced N.Y.C., 1946, Love Revisited, produced Westport Country Playhouse, 1951, All Summer Long, Arena Stage, Washington, 1953, N.Y.C., 1954, Tea and Sympathy, N.Y.C., 1953, writer in residence, U. N.C., 1969; screenwriter (films) Tea and Sympathy, 1956, Until They Sail, 1957, The Nun's Story, 1959, The Sand Pebbles, 1966, (plays) Silent Night, Lonely Night, 1959, The Days Between, 1965, You Know I Can't Hear You When the Water's Running, 1967, I Never Sang for My Father, play, 1968, screenplay, 1970 (Writers Guild Am. award for best screenplay), Solitaire/Double Solitaire, 1971, Free and Clear, 1983, The Kissing Was Always the Best, 1985, The Last Act Is A Solo, 1989, (novels) After, 1973, Getting Up and Going Home, 1978, (TV drama) The Patricia Neal Story, 1979, (play) The Last Act Is A Solo (Ace award 1991), 1991, (TV drama) Absolute Strangers, 1991; co-editor: (six vol. set) Elements of Literature, 1988. Served to lt. USNR, 1942-46. Recipient 1st prize for Come Marching Home Army-Navy Playwriting Contest for servicemen overseas, 1945, William Inge Lifetime Achievement award 1985; named to Theater Hall of Fame, 1980; honoree Conn. Commn. on the Arts, 1992. Mem. Dramatists Guild Coun. (past pres.), New Dramatists Com. (past pres.), Harvard Club (N.Y.C.). Home and Office: 14 Sutton Pl S New York NY 10022-3071

ANDERSON, ROBERTA JOAN See MITCHELL, JONI

ANDERSON, ROBIN MARIE, secondary education educator; b. Blue Island, Ill., Apr. 18, 1965; d. Donald Albert Anderson and Rosemary (Campbell) King. BA in English, No. Ill. U., DeKalb, 1988; MEd, U. North Tex., Denton, 1997. Cert. tchr. secondary edn., English, reading, Tex. Tchr. English North Garland (Tex.) H.S., 1990-92, Lakeview Centennial H.S., Garland, 1992-93; tchr. reading Nimitz H.S., Irving, Tex., 1993-99; 8th grade reading tchr. Bowman Middle Sch., Plano, Tex., 1999—; mem. attendance policy violators com., mem. student vol. svc. hour com. Nimitz H.S. Chmn. adv. bd. Irving C.A.R.E.S., 1995; sponsor Cultural Awareness Soc., Irving, 1995-96, Jr. Historians, Irving, 1994—. Recipient High Spirited Citizen award Irving Conv. and Visitors Bur., 1996. Mem. ASCD, Internat. Reading Assn., Assn. Tex. Profl. Educators, Tex. Assn. for Improvement of Reading (conf. spkr. 1995). Democrat. Avocations: reading, music, environmental issues, aerobics, movies. Office: Bowman Middle Sch Jupiter Plano TX 75074

ANDERSON, ROGER E., bank executive; b. July 29, 1921. B.A., Northwestern U., 1942. With Continental Ill. Nat. Bank and Trust Co., Chgo., 1946-84, exec. v.p., 1968-71, vice chmn., 1971-73, chmn. bd., 1973-84; chmn. bd. Continental Ill. Corp., 1973-84. Served with USNR, 1942-46. Home: 40 Warrington Dr Lake Bluff IL 60044-1321

ANDERSON, ROGER GORDON, minister; b. Milw., Feb. 1, 1937; s. Arthur Gordon and Dorothy K. (Junger) A.; m. Margery V. Burleson; children: Jonathan P., Nancy L., Leslie J., Kristi A. BA, Grace Bible Coll., Grand Rapids, Mich., 1958; postgrad., Purdue U., U. Minn. Ordained to ministry Grace Gospel Fellowship, 1960. Pastor Grace Bible Ch., Lafayette, Ind., 1958-60, Preakness Bible Ch., Wayne, N.J., 1960-69, Bethesda Free Ch., Mpls., 1969-86, Grace Community Ch., Salinas, Calif., 1986-91; pres. Grace Gospel Fellowship, Grand Rapids, Mich., 1991—; pres. Evang. Ministers' Fellowship, Mpls., 1972-85; trainer Evangelism Explosion, Mpls., 1980-89. Bd. dirs. Goodwill Home and Rescue Mission, Newark, 1962-69; bd. dirs. Grace Bible Coll., Grand Rapids, 1975—, chmn. bd., 1984-91; bd. dirs. Grace Missions Inc., Grand Rapids, 1966-75; chaplain Police Dept., Mpls., 1975-80. Recipient Meritorious Svc. award City of Mpls., 1977. Mem. Grace Gospel Fellowship (bd. dirs. 1966-68). Republican. Office: Grace Gospel Fellowship 2125 Martindale Ave SW Grand Rapids MI 49509-1837 *Life is a constant series of choices, the best of which are always those made with God and His will as the central factor. All are spokes from that hub.**

ANDERSON, ROLPH ELY, marketing educator; b. Buchanan, Mich., Aug. 27, 1936; s. Eugene Jefferson and Susanna (James) A.; m. Sallie Durkee Warner; children: Rachel Elizabeth, Stuart James. BA, Mich. State U., 1958, MBA, 1964; Ph.D., U. Fla., 1971. Inventory mgr. Shell Oil Co., Detroit, 1958-59; contract adminstr. Westinghouse Elec. Corp., Pitts., 1962-63; mgr. new product devel. Quaker Oats Co., Chgo., 1964-67; prof., chmn. dept. bus. mgmt. Old Dominion U., Norfolk, Va., 1971-75; chmn. dept. mktg. Drexel U., Phila., 1975-97, Royal H. Gibson prof. bus. adminstrn., 1991—. Author: Professional Personal Selling, 1991, Essentials of Personal Selling: The New Professionalism, 1995; co-author: Introduction to Multivariate Data Analysis, 1974, Multivariate Data Analysis, 1979, 5th edit., 1998, Sales Management, 1983, Professional Sales Management, 3d edit., 1999; books transl. into fgn. langs., including Spanish and Czech. Mem. faculty adv. bd. U. Akron Fisher Inst. for Profl. Selling, 1998—. Served to capt. Supply Corps. USN (Ret.). Recipient award for best publ. article Mu Kappa Tau, 1988, Excellence in Reviewing award Personal Selling and Sales Management, 1996. Mem. S.E. Am. Inst. Decision Scis. (pres. 1977-78), Am. Inst. Decision Scis. (nat. coun. 1977-79), Am. Mktg. Assn. (internat. conf. co-chmn. 1978; v.p. programming Phila. chpt. 1984-85, bd. dirs. 1986-87, 92-93, sales interest group excellence in sales scholarship award 1998), Sales and Mktg. Execs. Internat., So. Mktg. Assn., Acad. Mktg. Sci. (sec. 1984-86), Naval Res. Assn., N.E. Am. Inst. Decision Scis. (bd. dirs. 1977-78), Res. Officers Assn., Beta Gamma Sigma. Office: Drexel Univ Coll Bus and Adminstrn Philadelphia PA 19104

ANDERSON, RON, advertising executive. Formerly exec. v.p., midwest creative dir., then pres. midwest Bozell & Jacobs (now Bozell Inc.), Mpls., until 1988; assoc. chief creative officer N.Y.C., 1987-88; vice-chmn., chief creative officer Bozell Inc., N.Y.C., 1988—; now vice chmn, exec creative dir Bozell, Kamstra, Minneapolis, MN. Office: Bozell Kamstra 100 N 6th St Ste 800A Minneapolis MN 55403-1515*

ANDERSON, RON JOE, hospital administrator, physician, educator; b. Chickasha, Okla., Sept. 6, 1946; s. Ted J. and Ruby (Harston) Anderson Benjamin; m. Sue Ann Blakely, Apr. 12, 1975; children: Sarah Elizabeth, Daniel Jerrod, John Charles. B.S. in Pharmacy, Southwest U. Okla., 1969; M.D., U. Okla., 1973. Diplomate Am. Bd. Internal Medicine, Am. Bd. Geriatrics. Intern U. Tex. Southwestern Med. Sch., Parkland Meml. Hosp., VA Hosp., Dallas, 1973-74, resident and chief resident in internal medicine, 1974-76; asst. prof. internal medicine U. Tex. Health Sci. Ctr., Dallas, 1976-81, asst. dean clin. affairs, 1979-82, prof. internal medicine, 1981—; med. dir. ambulatory-emergency services Dallas County Hosp. Dist., 1979-82, acting. med. dir., 1981-82, CEO, 1982—; chmn. Tex. Bd. Health, 1991-93; mem. task force on teaching hosps. Tex. Hosp. Assn., 1982—, task force on indigent health care, 1983-86; cons. on high blood pressure Am. Heart Assn., 1981-83; advisor Tex. Assn. Physician Assts.; chmn. Neighborhood Clinic Cooperating Com., Dallas, 1980-82; bd. dirs. Children's Oncology Services Tex., Dallas, 1982-86, Addison, Carrollton, Coppell, Farmers Branch chpt. Am. Heart Assn., 1978-80; mem. Tex. Gov.'s Task Force on Indigent Health Care, 1983-86, Tex. Health and Human Services Coordinating Council, 1983-86, Tex. Cancer Council, 1985-87, Spl. Task Force on Future of Long-Term Health Care for Tex., Mayor's Task Force on Internat. Devel., Dallas AIDS Planning Commn.; mem. Tex. Bd. Health, 1983—, chmn., 1983-87, 91—; mem. Dallas Council on Alcoholism and Drug Abuse, 1982, bd. dirs., 1982—, v.p., 1986, pres., 1987-88; mem. adv. com. program to improve maternal and infant care in South Robert Wood Johnson Found. Contbr. articles to profl. jours. Bd. dirs. Project Independence, Greater Dallas Ahead, 1985—, Kaiser Found. Health Plan Tex., 1991, Interfaith Housing Coalition; preceptor Dallas Ind. Sch. Dist. Talented and Gifted Program, 1977; mem. Dallas Commrs. Ct. Task Force on Mental Patients, 1979, Dallas Alliance, 1986—, Dallas Assembly, 1984—, Hogg Found. for Mental Health Commn. on Community Care of Mentally Ill, 1987—; adv. bd. Dallas Challenge, 19846; co-chmn. Tex. Response, 1985—; chmn. mission bd. 1st Bapt. Ch. of Oak Cliff, and others. Recipient Tex. Aging Leadership award, 1987, Community Service award Community and Migrant Health Ctrs. Tex., 1986, Tex. Leadership in Aging award Tex. 6th Annual Joint Conf. on Aging, 1987, Disting. Alumnus award S.W. U. Okla., 1987, James E. Peavy Meml. award Tex. Pub. Health Assn., 1988, Dallas Hist. Soc. award, Headliner award Dallas Press Club, Health Care Profl. of Yr. award Tex. Nurses Assn., 1990; named to Disting. Alumni Hall of Fame Southwestern Okla. State U., 1987. Fellow ACP; mem. AMA, Nat. Assn. Pub. Hosps. (bd. dirs., exec. com., chmn.-elect 1991, Safety Net awrd 1990), Nat. Pub. Health and Hosp. Inst. (bd. dirs., chmn. devel. com., chmn. 1991), Tex. Med. Assn., Dallas County Med. Soc., Am. Soc. Internat. Medicine, Soc. Gen. Internal Medicine, Dallas-Ft. Worth Hosp. Coun. (chmn.-elect 1991), Salesmanship Dallas Club. Democrat. Baptist. Office: Dallas County Hosp Dist Parkland Meml Hosp 5201 Harry Hines Blvd Dallas TX 75235-7708

ANDERSON, RONALD DELAINE, education educator; b. Poplar, Wis., Aug. 25, 1937; s. Leslie A. and Linnea A. (Bergsten) A.; m. Sandra Jean Wendt, June 1, 1963; children—Debra Jean, Timothy James, Nathan David. B.S., U. Wis., 1959, Ph.D., 1964. Asst. prof. edn. Kans. State U., Manhattan, 1964-65; mem. faculty U. Colo., Boulder, 1965—; prof. edn. U. Colo., 1971—, asso. dean edn., 1972-78; cons. to numerous ednl. agys. Co-author: Developing Children's Thinking Through Science, 1970, Issues of Curriculum Reform, 1994, Local Leadership for Science Education Reform, 1995, Portraits of Productive Schools, 1995, Study Curriculum Reform, 1996; contbr. articles to profl. jours. Program dir. Nat. Sci. Found., 1989-90. Fulbright scholar, 1986-87. Fellow AAAS (chair edn. sect. 1998-99); mem. Nat. Assn. Research Sci. Teaching (pres. 1975-76), Assn. Edn. Tchrs. in Sci. (pres. 1972-73), Nat. Sci. Tchrs. Assn., Phi Delta Kappa. Home: 300 W 4th Avenue Dr Broomfield CO 80020-1914 Office: Univ Colo Sch Edn Boulder CO 80309

ANDERSON, ROSS, columnist. Editorial writer, columnist The Seattle Times. Recipient Pulitzer Prize for nat. reporting, 1990. Office: The Seattle Times PO Box 70 Seattle WA 98111-0070*

ANDERSON, ROSS BARRETT, healthcare environmental services manager; b. Toronto, Ont., Can., Aug. 25, 1951; came to U.S., 1956; s. John Ross and Constance (Nielson) A.; m. Gladys Jeanette Vincent, Aug. 26, 1972; children: Christopher Matthew, John Ross II, Josiah Dan. Student, Boston U., 1970-73. Housekeeping supr. Parker Hill Med. Ctr., Roxbury, Mass., 1973-76; acct. mgr. Servicemaster Inc., 1973—; housekeeping mgr. Union Hosp., Lynn, Mass., 1976-77, Quincy (Mass.) City Hosp., 1977-78, St. Joseph's Hosp., Lowell, Mass., 1978-79; housekeeping mgr. Waltham Weston Hosp. and Med. Ctr., Waltham, Mass., 1979-86, support services mgr., 1986-90, dir. environ. svcs., 1991-93, chmn. customer svcs. bd., 1992; asst. dir. clin. engring. Good Samaritan Med. Ctr., Stoughton/Brockton, Mass., 1993-95; dir. environ. svcs. Harrington Meml. Hosp., Southbridge, Mass., 1995—. Mem. Boston Latin Sch. Assn., Scots Charitable Soc. Boston, Free Evang. Fellowship, Easton, Mass. Home: 133 Old Town Rd Ashford CT 06278-2020 Office: Harrington Meml Hosp 100 South St Ste 1 Southbridge MA 01550-4047

ANDERSON, ROY A., aerospace company executive; b. Ripon, Calif., Dec. 15, 1920; s. Carl Gustav and Esther Marie (Johnson) A.; m. Betty Leona Boehme, 1948; 4 children. Grad. Humphrey's Sch. Bus., Stanford U. Mgr. factory acctg. Westinghouse Electric Corp., 1952-56; mgr. acctg. and fin., dir. mgmt. controls Lockheed Missiles and Space Co., 1956-65; dir. finance Lockheed Ga. Co., 1965-68; asst. treas. Lockheed Aircraft Corp. (now Lockheed-Martin Corp.), 1968-69, v.p., controller, 1969-71, sr. v.p. finance, 1971-75, vice chmn. bd. dirs., chief fin. adminstrv. officer, 1975-77, chair, CEO, 1977-85, dir., chair exec. com., 1985-88, chair emeritus, 1991—; chair, CEO Weingart Found., 1994-98; chair Oversight Bd., State of Calif., 1997-98. Avocations: tennis, golf, gardening. Home: 4367 Shepherds Ln La Canada CA 91011 Office: Lockheed-Martin Corp 606 S Olive St Fl 23 Los Angeles CA 90014-1604

ANDERSON, ROY EVERETT, electrical engineering consultant; b. Batavia, Ill., Oct. 30, 1918; s. Elof and Nellie Amanda Anderson; m. Gladys Marie Nelson, Aug. 22, 1943; children: Paul V., David L., Barbara J. Anderson Wald, Dorothy M. Anderson Presser. BA in Physics, Augustana Coll., Rock Island, Ill., 1943; MSEE, Union Coll., Schenectady, 1952. Instr. physics Augustana Coll., 1943-44, 46-47; cons. engr. GE, Schenectady, 1947-83; co-founder, v.p. Mobile Satellite Corp., Malvern, Pa., 1983-88; owner, mgr., cons. Anderson Assocs., Glenville, N.Y., 1988—; pres. Rega Assocs., Inc., Glenville, 1993—; cons. Am. Mobile Satellite Corp., Washington, 1988-91; participant nat. and internat. regulatory and tech. orgns. leading to establishment generic mobile satellite svc. Contbr. over 125 articles to profl. jours.; patentee indsl. electronic measurement and quality control instruments, tone code ranging technique for position surveillance using satellites; developer Doppler radio direction finder. Trustee Dudley Obs., Schenectady, 1975-83, 90—, chmn. bd. trustees, 1980-83, 90. With USN, 1944-46. GE Coolidge fellow, 1970. Fellow IEEE, AAAS, Radio Club Am.; mem. AIAA, Inst. Navigation, Soc. Satellite Profls. Internat. Home and Office: PO Box 2531 Glenville NY 12325-0531

ANDERSON, RUDOLPH J., JR., lawyer; b. Bklyn., Apr. 15, 1924; s. Rudolph John and Nora (Cawley) A.; m. Helen O'Donnell, May 28, 1949; children: Mary Josephine Anderson Coughlin, Rudolph John III, Peter, Thomas, Michael, Rosemary, Christopher, Terrence. BS in Naval Sci., U. Notre Dame, 1945, BS in Chem. Engring., 1947; JD, Georgetown U., 1951. Bar: Va. 1950, D.C. 1955, N.J. 1963, Mo. 1985, Vt. 1989. Asst. to pres. Permacel div. Johnson & Johnson, 1955-60; assoc. gen. counsel, dir. patents Merck & Co., Inc., Rahway, N.J., 1960-83; gen. patent counsel Monsanto Co., St. Louis, 1984-87; of counsel Fitzpatrick, Cella, Harper & Scinto, N.Y.C., 1987-89. Former committeeman Scotch Plains Twp. Com., N.J. Served to lt. USNR, 1943-46, PTO. Mem. ABA (chmn. trademark and copyright law sect. 1984-85), Assn. Corp. Patent Counsel, Am. Intellectual Property Law Assn., Grand Harbour Golf Club. Roman Catholic. Avocation: golf. Home and Office: 5136 Saint Davids Dr Vero Beach FL 32967-7238

ANDERSON, RUTH G., education educator, consultant; b. Blue Eye, Mo., Apr. 14, 1929; d. Claude B. and Sylvia J. (Hudson) Gibson; m. Lev Z. Anderson, Aug. 14, 1948 (dec. June 1989); 1 child, Richard L. BS in Edn., Southwest Mo. State, 1951; MEd, U. Mo., 1962, EdD, 1974; postgrad., Ball State U., No. Ariz. U. Cert. elementary tchr., elementary prin., sch. supt. Tchr. S. Bee Creek Sch., Mincy, Mo., 1947-48, Blue Eye (Mo.) Schs., 1951-54; tchr. Waynesville (Mo.)-FLW Schs., 1955-58, 60-63, prin., 1963-65, asst. supt., 1965-71; tchr. Am. Dependent Schs., Kaisers Lautern, Frankfurt, Germany, 1958-60; from asst. to full prof. edn. Sch. of the Ozarks, Point Lookout, Mo., 1972—, chmn. edn. dept., 1980-90; prof. edn. Coll. of the Ozarks, Point Lookout, 1990—; ednl. cons., Blue Eye, 1974—; lectr. CHNN, Emmen, The Netherlands, 1994. Editor newsletter Alpha Psi News, 1990-92. Mem. NEA (life), ASCD, Internat. Reading Assn. (state pres.), Mo. State Tchrs. Assn. (state adviser student group 1992), Phi Delta Kappa, Delta Kappa Gamma, Kappa Kappa Iota (state pres. 1965-66). Avocations: reading, travel, sewing. Home: HC 1 Box 227 Blue Eye MO 65611-9615 Office: Coll of the Ozarks G 204 D Point Lookout MO 65726

ANDERSON, RUTH NATHAN, syndicated columnist, TV news host, writer, recording artist, lyricist; b. N.Y.C., Jan. 28; d. Solomon and Anna (Cornick) Gans; student N.Y. U., George Washington U., evenings 1952-56; m. Arthur Aksel Anderson, Jr., Sept. 11, 1971 (dec.); stepchildren—Jack Anderson, Barbara Anderson-Rouse, Terri Anderson-Sarli; m. T. William Fejer, Sept. 23, 1994. Newsletter editor Washington Post; chief med. writer, press officer Nat. Multiple Sclerosis Soc., N.Y.C.; feature editor Crusade for Freedom, Radio Free Europe, N.Y.C., 1955-58; editor jr. TV dept. TV Revue, N.Y.C.; feature-series reporter N.Am. Newspaper Alliance, Women's News Service, N.Y.C., 1961-79; writer, originator Doctor's Grapevine column Nat. Features Syndicate, Chgo., 1969-73; author-owner syndicated column VIP Med. Grapevin/ Celebrity Health News, Round Lake, Ill., 1973—; feature news corr. Waukegan (Ill.) News-Sun, 1977-82; writer, host Celebrity Health News, Cablenet TV, Chgo., 1985-89; feature writer Ind. News Alliance, Chgo.; Chgo. contbg. editor Music City Entertainer, Nashville, 1976—; writing projects dir. Comedy Hall of Fame, Chgo., 1989—; ethics writer Chgo. Journalist, 1998—; chief lyricist Anderson-Fejer Musicals, 1995—; tchr. journalism, creative writing, speech arts Fla. State Bd. Adult Edn., 1968-69; lectr. writing seminars for faculty U. Ill. at Chgo. Circle Campus, 1970-80. Trustee, v.p. bd. Round Lake Pub. Library, 1977-86; mem. Nat. Trust for Hist. Preservation; Right-to-Read vol. tutor jr. high schs., Round Lake, 1977-86; singer ARC entertainment com. Bedside Network, 1974-80; citizen amb. to South Africa with Creative Women of the Arts Del. under People-to-People Amb. Programs, 1999. Mem. Chgo. Women in Broadcasting, Nat. Acad. TV Arts & Scis., Am. Med. Writers Assn. (Beth Fonda award, 1984), Am. Mus. Women in the Arts (charter), Lake County Assn. Journalists, Nat. Assn. for Female Execs., Chgo. Unltd., Press Vets. Assn., Internat. Platform Assn., Future Physicians Am. (hon.), Soc. Profl. Journalists Headline Club, Nat. Acad. Recording Arts and Scis., Dramatists Guild mem. research bd. adv., The American Biographical Inst. Clubs: Chgo. Press, Chgo. Advt. author: Naked Brunch (poetry), 1996, How You Can Be a Part of Your United Nations, (booklet); contbr. articles to various mags. including Parents, Pageant, Mademoiselle, Science Digest, Reader's Digest, TV Guide, TV Radio Mirror, This Week, Am. Weekly, Am. Home, others; contbr. poems to (book) Nat. Libr. Poetry (Best Poems of 1995); features on U.S. presidents in archives of Hoover, Truman, Eisenhower, Kennedy and Johnson presdl. libraries. Recipient Golden Poet Trophy award Internat. Soc. Poets, 1990, Editor's Choice award Nat. Lib. of Poetry. Rec. artist mus. comedy songs, pop for Am. Sound label; author book and lyrics (musical play) Menage a Trois, 1997. Home: 161 Nasa Cir Round Lake IL 60073-2844

ANDERSON, SAMUEL DAVID, government affairs consultant; b. Vincennes, Ind., Dec. 20, 1947; s. Samuel Robert and Levenna Theodosia A.; m. Gayle Dolores Dunaway, Nov. 27, 1995. BA in Polit. Sci., Internat. Affairs, Fla. Internat. U., 1974; MA in Polit. Sci., U. Fla., 1977. Profl. staff mem. U.S. Congress (Senate and Ho. Reps.), Washington, 1973-74; liason officer office of Congl. and Intergovtl. affairs Dept. Energy, Washington, 1975-78; rep. Aerospace Corp., Washington, 1979-89; govt. affairs cons. pvt. practice, Washington, 1989—. Inventor: holds patent on swivel chair design, 1982; editor: Frank W. Draper Civil War Letter and Diaries, 1991; contbr. numerous articles to profl. jours. Bd. dirs. Advance Am. Found., 1991—. Republican. Episcopalian. Avocations: sailing, tennis, cross-country skiing. Home: 550 Park Ave Merritt Island FL 32953-6033 Office: 316 Independence Ave SE Washington DC 20003-1043

ANDERSON, SCOTT ROBBINS, hospital administrator; b. Fargo, N.D., Mar. 25, 1940. BA, U. N.D., 1962; M Health Adminstrn., U. Iowa, 1964. Adminstrn. res. St. Luke's Methodist Hosp., Veteran's Adminstrn. Med. Ctr., Cedar Rapids, Iowa City, 1963-64; adminstrv. asst. North Meml. Med. Ctr., Robbinsdale, Minn., 1964-65, asst. dir., 1965-69, adminstr., 1969-76, v.p., 1976-81, pres., 1981—; pres., ceo North Meml. Med. Ctr. (now North Meml. Health Care), Robbinsdale, Minn.; adj. prof. in field. Home: 2984 Pelican Point Cir Mound MN 55364-1954 Office: N Meml Health Care 3300 Oakdale Ave N Robbinsdale MN 55422-2926*

ANDERSON, SHALOR MARIA, medical/surgical and pediatrics nurse; b. Longview, Tex., May 24, 1958; d. Richard A. and Annie Laurie (Stoker) Lyons; m. Michael D. Anderson, Aug. 4, 1979; children: Daniel, Christopher. AS in Nursing, Kilgore (Tex.) Coll., 1978. RN, Tex.; cert. pediatric nurse; cert. in pediatric diabetic instrn., coronary care, neonatal life support; cert. PALS, CPR instr. Asst. clin. supr. Good Shepherd Med. Ctr., Longview, staff nurse, clin. supr. pediatrics and pediatric nurse pool staff nurse; office nurse for pediatrician Diagnostic Clinic, Longview; charge RN gen. pediat. Childrens Med. Ctr., Dallas, 1996-99, staff nurse ICU, 1999—; presenter in field.

ANDERSON, SPARKY (GEORGE LEE ANDERSON), broadcast analyst, former baseball team manager; b. Bridgewater, S.D., Feb. 22, 1934; m. Carol Valle; children: George Jr., Shirlee Trece, Albert William. Profl. baseball player Phila. Phillies, 1959; mgr. Cin. Reds, 1970-78, Detroit Tigers, 1979-95; broadcasting analyst Fox Sports, N.Y.C., 1996—; accouncer Anaheim (Calif.) Angels, 1997-98; Mgr. Nat. League All-Star Team, 1971, 73, 76, 77, Am. League All-Star Team 1985; mgr. World Series Championship Team, 1975-76, 84. Author: (with Dan Ewald) They Call Me Sparky, 1998. Founder Caring Athletes Team for Children's and Henry Ford Hosp. Named Nat. League Mgr. of Year, 1972; first baseball mgr. to achieve 100 wins in a season in both Nat. and Am. Leagues (Cincinnati Reds-1970, 75, 76; Detroit Tigers-1984); inducted into Cin. Reds Hall of Fame, Cin. chpt. Baseball Writers Assn., 1999. *

ANDERSON, STANFORD OWEN, architect, architectural historian, educator; b. Redwood Falls, Minn., Nov. 13, 1934; s. Carl Alfred and Dora Helena (Paulson) A. BA, U. Minn., 1957; MA in Arch., U. Calif., Berkeley, 1958, postgrad., 1958-59; PhD, Columbia U., 1968. Registered arch., Mass. Tchr. Archtl. Assn., London, 1962-63, 74-78; co-dir. research project Inst. for Architecture and Urban Studies, N.Y.C., 1970-72, fellow, 1971-81; asst. prof. history and architecture MIT, 1963-69, assoc. prof., 1969-72, prof., 1972—, head dept. architecture, 1991—; co-dir. archtl. transl. project Am. Acad. Arts and Scis., 1977-80; mem. adv. council Mcpl. Art Soc., City N.Y., 1972-78. Author: Muthesius: Style-Architecture and Building-Art, 1994, The Education of the Architect, 1997 (pub. in honor of Festschrift); editor: Planning for Diversity and Choice, 1969, On Streets, 1978. Mem. Boston Landmarks Commn., 1980-87, Massport Designer Selection Panel, 1993-97; bd. dirs. Boston Preservation Alliance, 1989-91, Batuz Found. USA, 1997—, Fulbright Assn., 1998—. Fulbright scholar, 1961-62; John Simon Guggenheim fellow, 1969-70; Graham Found. fellow, 1971; Am. Council Learned Socs. fellow, 1977-78. Mem. Assn. Collegiate Schs. Architecture, Brit. Soc. for Philosophy of Sci., Coll. Art Assn., Soc. Archtl. Historians (dir. 1969-72, 76-77), Boston Soc. Architects (bd. dirs. 1992—). Home: 63 Commercial Wharf Boston MA 02110-3814 Office: MIT Dept Architecture 77 Massachusetts Ave Cambridge MA 02139-4307

ANDERSON, STEFAN STOLEN, bank executive; b. Madison, Wis., Apr. 15, 1934; s. Theodore M. and Siri (Stolen) A.; m. Joan Timmermann, Sept. 19, 1959; children: Sharon Jill, Theodore Peter. AB magna cum laude, Harvard, 1956; MBA, U. Chgo., 1960; PhD (hon.), Ball State U., 1993. With Am. Nat. Bank & Trust Co. of Chgo., 1960-74, exec. v.p., 1969-74; exec. v.p., dir. 1st Mchts. Bank, Muncie, Ind., 1974, pres., 1979-98, chmn. bd. dirs., 1987—; pres., dir. First Mchts. Corp., Muncie, 1983-98, chmn. bd. dirs., 1987—; dir. Fed. Res. Bank of Chgo., 1991-97; past pres., dir. Del. Advancement Corp., 1991-95; bd. dirs. Maxon Corp. Past pres. Delaware County United Way, Muncie Symphony Orch.; trustee Roosevelt U., 1970-74, George Francis Ball Found., BMH Found., Ziegler Found.; pres. chair Ind. Nature Conservancy; past pres. Cmty. Found. of Muncie and Delaware County. Mem. Ind. State C. of C. (bd. dirs.), Minnetrista Cultural Found., Skyline Club (Indpls.), Rotary (past pres.), Phi Beta Kappa, Beta Gamma Sigma. Home: 2705 W Twickingham Dr Muncie IN 47304-1050 Office: 1st Mchts Bank 200 E Jackson St Muncie IN 47305-2800 *Say Yes to life. Daily affirming the privilege of living is a challenge worth going for. I can, without immodesty, applaud my successes because they are never mine alone.*

ANDERSON, STEPHEN FRANCIS, insurance company executive; b. Mattoon, Ill., Dec. 5, 1950; s. Francis J. and Juanita J. (Collings) A.; m. Mary Ann Pipek, Mar. 3, 1973; children: Matthew C., David S. BS in Bus, Ea. Ill. U., 1972. CLU; ChFC; CFP. Store mgr. Bush's IGA, Carrollton, Ill., 1972-76; agt. Country Co. Ins., Bloomington, Ill., 1976-80; agy. mgr. Country Co. Ins., Eureka, Ill., 1980-83, Woodstock, Ill., 1983-92; pres. Dreher Ins. Svcs., Oakbrook Terrace, Ill., 1992—; sr. v.p. Dreher & Assocs., Oakbrook Terrace, Ill., 1994—; pres. Agy. Mgrs. Conf. Ill., 1987—; mem. adv. panel Morningstar Internat., 1997—. Bd. dirs. Untied Way of McHenry County, Crystal Lake, 1988—, treas., 1989-90, pres. 1992; v.p. McHenry County 4-H Found., Woodstock, 1984—. Mem. Gen. Agts. Mgrs. Conf. (Career Devel. award 1988, Nat. Mgmt. award 1989-92), McHenry County Life Underwriters (pres. 1988—), Ill. Life Underwriters (Railsplitter bd. 1989-96), Chgo. Soc. CFPs (bd. dirs. 1993—, v.p. 1994—), Chgo. Soc. CLU/ChFC, Crystal Lake C. of C. (bd. dirs.), Rotary (bd. dirs. Woodstock chpt.). Republican. Avocations: computers, reading, gardening, U.S. presidential history, bicycling. Home: 2540 Pebble Creek Dr Lisle IL 60532-0802 Office: Dreher and Assocs 1 Oakbrook Ter Ste 708 Oakbrook Terrace IL 60181-4728

ANDERSON, STEPHEN HALE, federal judge; b. 1932; m. Shirlee G. Anderson. Student, Eastern Oreg. Coll. Edn., Brigham Young U.; LLB, U. Utah, 1960. Bar: Utah 1960, U.S. Claims Ct. 1963, U.S. Tax Ct. 1967, U.S. Ct. Appeals (10th cir.) 1970, U.S. Supreme Ct. 1971, U.S. Ct. Appeals (9th cir.) 1972, various U.S. Dist. Cts. Tchr. South H.S., Salt Lake City, 1956-57; trial atty. tax div. U.S. Dept. Justice, 1960-64; ptnr. Ray, Quinney & Nebeker, 1964-85; judge U.S. Ct. Appeals (10th cir.), Salt Lake City, 1985—; spl. counsel Salt Lake County Grand Jury, 1975; chmn. fed.-state jurisdiction com. Jud. Conf. U.S., 1995-98; mem. Nat. Jud. Coun. State and Fed. Cts., 1992-96; mem. ad hoc. com. on bankruptcy appellate panels 10th Cir. Jud. Coun., 1995-97; mem. various coms. U.S. Ct. Appeals (10th cir.). Editor-in-chief Utah Law Rev. Cpl. U.S. Army, 1953-55. Mem. Utah State Bar (pres. 1983-84, various offices), Salt Lake County Bar Assn. (pres. 1977-78), Am. Bar Found., Salt Lake Area C. of C. (bd. govs. 1984), U. Utah Coll. Law Alumni Assn. (trustee 1979-83, pres. 1982-83), Order of Coif. Office: US Ct Appeals 4201 Fed Bldg 125 S State St Salt Lake City UT 84138-1102

ANDERSON, STEPHEN MILLS, investment broker; b. Portland, Maine, Jan. 14, 1946; s. Stuart Mills and Elaine (Crommett) A.; BA, Ohio U., 1969; m. Mary Elizabeth Carter, Aug. 23, 1969; children: Melissa Carter, Hope Stuart. Dir. admissions, dir. devel., dir. alumni affairs Gould Acad., Bethel, Maine, 1973-76; investment broker Burbank & Co., Portland, Maine, 1976-82, office mgr., 1978-82; investment broker, office mgr., v.p. A.G. Edwards & Sons, Portland, 1982—, sr. v.p., 1996—; former pres. Stroudwater Corp.; mem. dirs. coun. A.G. Edwards and Sons. Bd. trustees Tilton Sch.; trustee Maine Med. Ctr., 1990, mem. corporators; bd. dirs. Brighton Med. Ctr. Found., 1992-96; chmn. Annual Fund Maine Med. Ctr. mem. adv. bd. Baxter State Park; chmn. adv. coun. The Capital Group, L.A. Mem. Nat. Assn. Registered Reps., Cumberland Club, Masons, Portland Country Club, Woodlands Club, Severance Lodge Club. Home: 6 Pinewood Ln Falmouth ME 04105-1155 Office: 2 Portland Sq Portland ME 04101-4088

ANDERSON, STEVEN HUNTER, media relations professional; b. Washington, Feb. 3, 1962; s. Alfred Joseph and Frances Helen (Harrison) Mendez; m. Nancy Louise Sowders, July 29, 1989. BA in Organizational Communications, James Madison U., 1985. Pub. affairs asst. Gannett Co., Inc., Arlington, Va., 1984-85, corp. writer, 1985-88; account exec. Jaffe Assocs., Washington, 1988; promotion ops. specialist USA Today, Arlington, 1988-89, pub. rels. coord., 1989-90, mgr. pub. rels., 1990-91, mgr. media rels., 1991-95, dir. media rels., 1995-98, dir comm., 1998—. Mem. Internat. Assn. Bus. Communicators. Republican. Roman Catholic. Avocations: golf, music, travel. Office: USA Today 1000 Wilson Blvd Ste 600 Arlington VA 22209-3905

ANDERSON, SUSAN ELAINE MOSSHAMER, education and organizational consultant; b. Detroit, Mar. 29, 1946; d. Edgar Lee and Reta (McDonough) Mosshamer; m. Thomas Scott Anderson Jr., Nov. 1, 1975; children: Elizabeth Erin, Kirk William. MusB with honors, Mich. State U., 1967; MEd with high honors, Wayne State U., 1982. Profl. singer (mezzo), pianist and organist, 1968—, sch. choral music dir. grades 7-12, 1968-77; instrnl. designer, orgnl. devel. cons. Myers-Briggs Adminstr., Ednl. Rschr., 1982—; pres. Orgl. Strategies Ltd., Bloomfield Hills, Mich., 1995—. Collaborating author: The Challenge of Living, 1983, Death and Dying, 1996; award-winning tng. programs for Ill. Dept. Employment Security and Ford/Lincoln-Mercury Dealerships. Vol. Roeper Sch., Bloomfield Hills, 1988-95, Cranbrook Schs., Bloomfield Hills, 1993—. Mem. ASCD, Problem-Based Learning Network, Assn. Psychol. Type, Mortar Board, Phi Kappa Phi. Avocations: skiing, reading, music.

ANDERSON, SUSAN STUEBING, business equipment company executive; b. Cin., Nov. 7, 1951; d. Edward Norman and Ruth Marcella Stuebing; m. Randall Anderson, 1988. BA, Western Ky. U., 1973, MA, 1975. Legis. aide U.S. Ho. of Reps., 1975-80; legis. cons. Harvard U., 1981; spl. asst. Nat. Telecommunications and Info. Adminstrn.-U.S. Dept. Commerce, Washington, 1981, dept. asst. sec., 1982-85, acting asst. sec. for communications and info., 1983; dir. Computer and Bus. Equipment Mfrs. Assn., Washington, 1985-86; mgr. govt. affairs Xerox Corp., Washington, 1987-92; mgr. investor svcs. Office of the Corp. Sec., Stamford, Conn., 1992—. Presbyterian. Office: Xerox Corp 800 Long Ridge Rd Stamford CT 06902-1288

ANDERSON, SYDNEY, biologist, museum curator; b. Topeka, Jan. 11, 1927; s. Robert Grant and Evelyn Fern (Hunt) A.; m. Ratia Justine Klusmire, Aug. 5, 1951; children: Evelyn Lee Anderson Wheelhouse, Charles Sydney, Laura Lynnette Anderson Dooley. Student, Baker U., 1944-49; BA, U. Kans., 1950, PhD, 1959. Asst. curator Mus. Natural History, instr. dept. zoology U. Kansas, Lawrence, 1955-59; asst. curator Am. Mus. Natural History, N.Y.C., 1960-64, assoc. curator, 1964-69, curator, 1969-92, curator emeritus, 1992—, chmn. dept. mammalogy, 1974-81; adj. prof. CUNY, 1969-91, NYU, 1973. Author: The Lives of Animals, 1966, Recent Mammals of the World, 1967, Readings in Mammalogy, 1970, Mammals of Chihuahua, 1972, Mammals of Bolivia, 1997; editor Mammalian Species, 1969-87, Recent Literature of Mammalogy, 1968-73. Trustee Closter Nature Ctr. Assn. Fellow AAAS; mem. Am. Soc. Mammalogists (dir., pres. 1974-76). Home: 98 Wainwright Ave Closter NJ 07624-2923 Office: Mus of Natural History Central Pk W at 79th St New York NY 10024

ANDERSON, TERRY MARLENE, civil engineer; b. Honolulu, Sept. 26, 1954; d. Stanley Dale and Anna Clara (Heigert) A.; m. Jack Willard Steinberg, Feb. 29, 1980 (div. May 1983). Student, U. San Diego, 1971-72, U. Calif., San Diego, 1972-74; BS in Biol. Scis., U. Calif., Davis, 1974, BS in Aquacultural Engrs., 1979; cert. in mgmt., U. Calif., 1991. Registered civil engr., Calif., Colo.; cert. grade 4 Water Treatment Plant Operator, Calif. Project mgr. John Carollo Engrs., Walnut Creek, Calif., 1979-85; assoc. civil engr. Grice Engring. Inc., Salinas, Calif., 1985; self-employed Durango, Colo., 1985-86; project engr. CWC-HDR, Inc., Cameron Park, Calif., 1987; sr. civil engr. El Dorado County Dept. Transp., Placerville, Calif., 1987-90; dep. dir. pub. works Medocino County Dept. Pub. Works, Ukiah, Calif., 1990-94; enging. divsn. mgr. pub. works Sonoma County, 1994-98, dist. engr., Lake County Spl. Dist.; owner TMA Engring., 1998—. Recipient Resolution of Appreciaiton, City Coun., City of Gonzales, 1983. Mem. Woman's Transp. Seminar, ASCE, WateReuse. Republican. Office: TMA Engring Dept Pub Works PO Box 215 Westport CA 95488

ANDERSON, THEODORE ROBERT, physicist; b. Lodi, Ohio, Jan. 30, 1949; s. Robert Anderson and LaVaughn (Mitchell) Gillotti. BS in Physics, Fla. State U., 1971; postgrad. in math. physics, U. Geneva, Switzerland, 1973, 75; MS in Physics, NYU, 1979, MS in Applied Sci., 1983, PhD in Physics, 1986. Nuclear engr. Gibbs & Hill Inc., N.Y.C., 1980-83; rsch. physicist elec. boat div. Gen. Dynamics, Groton, Conn., 1983-88; rsch. physicist Naval Underwater Systems Ctr., New London, Conn., 1988—; adj. prof. mech. engring., astronomy U. Conn., Storrs, Groton, 1983—; adj. prof. math. Mitchell Coll., New London Conn., 1985, U. Hartford, 1990—; adj. prof. mech. and aeronautical engring., mgmt. and mech. engring. U. Bridgeport, 1989—; adj. prof. mech. and aeronautical engring. Hunter Coll.; adj. prof. physics and astronomy CUNY, 1979-83; adj. prof. physics L.I. Univ., 1980-83; adj. prof. elec. and mech. engring. Rensselaer Poly. Inst., Hartford, 1986—; adj. prof. Sch. Bus. U. New Haven, 1989—, mech. engring., 1983—, elec. engring., 1983—; instr. Cooper Union Sch. Engring., N.Y.C., 1980. Rsch. in fluid dynamics, acoustics, atomic physics, and electromagnetic interference; numerous patents in field. Active Met. Opera Guild, N.Y.C., 1986—, Mus. Modern Art, N.Y.C., 1985—, Met. Mus. Art, N.Y.C., 1984—, Am. Mus. Natural History, N.Y.C., 1987—, N.Y. Shakespeare Festival, 1987—, N.Y. Zool. Soc., 1988—, Ea. Nat. Park and Monument Assn., 1990—. Recipient Spl. Achievement award USN, 1989, 90. Mem. IEEE, Electromagnetic Compatibility Soc., Nat. Geographic Soc., Nat. Parks and Conservation Assn., Am. Phys. Soc., Soc. Rheology, Nat. Parks and Conservation Assn., The Adirondack Coun., The Nature Conservancy, The Smithsonian Assocs., World Powerlifting Alliance, Amnesty Internat., Wilderness Soc., World Wildlife Fund, Sierra Club, Greenpeace. Achievements include research in fluid dynamics, plasma physics, acoustics and atomic physics, electromagnetic interference, nuclear engineering solar cells; holder several patents on plasma antenna. Home: 269 John Potter Rd West Greenwich RI 02817-2077

ANDERSON, THEODORE WILBUR, statistics educator; b. Mpls., June 5, 1918; s. Theodore Wilbur and Evelynn (Johnson) A.; m. Dorothy Fisher, July 8, 1950; children: Robert Lewis, Janet Lynn, Jeanne Elizabeth. BS with highest distinction, Northwestern U., 1939, DSc, 1989; MA, Princeton U., 1942, PhD, 1945; LittD, North Park U., 1988; PhD (honoris causa), U. Oslo, 1997. Asst. dept. math. Northwestern U., 1939-40; instr. math. Princeton U., 1941-43, rsch. assoc., 1943-45; rsch. assoc. Cowles Commn., U. Chgo., 1945-46; staff Columbia U., 1946-67, successively instr. math. stats., asst. prof., assoc. prof., 1946-56, prof., 1956-67, chmn. math. stats. dept., 1956-60, 64-65, acting chmn., 1950-51, 63; prof. stats. and econs. Stanford U., 1967-88, prof. stats. and econs. emeritus, 1988—; dir. project Office Naval Rsch., 1950-82; prin. investigator NSF project, 1969-92, Army Rsch. Office project, 1982-92; vis. prof. math. U. Moscow, 1968; vis. prof. stats. U. Paris, 1968; vis. prof. econs. NYU, 1983-84; acad. visitor math. Imperial Coll. Sci. and Tech., U. London, 1967-68, London Sch. Econs. and Polit. Sci., 1974-75, U. So. Calif., 1989; C.G. Khatri Meml. lectr. Pa. State U., 1992; rsch. visitor Tokyo Inst. Tech., 1977; sabbaticant IBM Systems Rsch. Inst., 1984; rsch. assoc. Naval Postgrad. Sch., 1986-87; cons. RAND Corp., 1949-66; mem. com. on basic rsch. adv. Office Ordnance Rsch., Nat. Acad. Scis.-NRC, 1955-58; mem. panel on applied math. adv. Nat. Bur. Standards, 1964-65; chmn. com. on stats. NRC, 1961-63; mem. exec. com. Conf. Bd. Math. Scis., 1963-64; mem. com. on support rsch. in math. scis. Nat Acad. Scis., 1965-68; mem. com. Pres.'s Statis. Socs., 1962-64; sci. dir. NATO Advanced Study Inst. on Discriminant Analysis and Its Applications, 1972. Author: An Introduction to Multivariate Statistical Analysis, 1958, 2nd edit., 1984, The Statistical Analysis of Time Series, 1971, (with Somesh Das Gupta and George P.H. Styan) A Bibliography of Multivariate Statistical Analysis, 1972, (with Stanley Sclove) Introductory Statistical Analysis, 1974, An Introduction to the Statistical Analysis of Data, 1986, (with Jeremy D. Finn) The New Statistical Analysis of Data, 1996; editor: (with Krishna B. Athreya and Donald L. Iglehart) Probability, Statistics and Mathematics: Papers in Honor of Samuel Karlin, 1989, (with Kai Tai Fang) Statistical Inference in Elliptically Contoured and Related Distributions, 1990, (with K.T. Fang and I. Olkin) Multivariate Analysis and Its Applications, 1994; editor Anns. of Math. Stats., 1950-52; assoc. editor jour. Time Series Analysis, 1980-88; mem. adv. bd. Econometric Theory, 1985—, Jour. Multivariate Analysis, 1988—; mem. editl. bd. Psychometrika, 1954-72. Recipient R.A. Fisher award Pres.'s Statis. Socs., 1985, Disting. Alumnus award North Park Coll. and Theol. Sem., 1987, Minnehaha Acad., 1992, Award of Merit Northwestern U. Alumni Assn., 1989; named Wesley C. Mitchell Vis. Prof. Columbia U., 1983-84; Guggenheim fellow, 1947-48, fellow Ctr. for Advanced Study in Behavioral Scis., 1957-58; vis. scholar, 1972-73, 80; Sherman Fairchild disting. scholar Calif. Inst. Tech., 1980; vis. disting. prof. Norwegian Coun. Sci. and Indsl. Rsch. U. Oslo; Abraham Wald Meml. lectr., 1982; S.S. Wilks lectr. Princeton U., 1983, P.C. Mahalanobis Meml. lectr., 1985, S.N. Roy Meml. lectr. Calcutta U., 1985, Allen T. Craig lectr. U. Iowa, 1991, C.G. Khatri Meml. lectr. Pa. State U., 1992, George Zyskind Meml. lectr. Iowa State U., 1995. Fellow AAAS (chmn. sect. 1990-91), Am. Statis. Assn. (v.p. 1971-73, Samuel S. Wilks Meml. medal 1988, R.A. Fisher lectr. 1985), Econometric Soc., Royal Statis. Soc., Inst. Math. Stats. (pres. 1963), Am. Acad. Arts and Scis.; mem. NAS, Am. Math. Soc., Internat. Statis. Insts., Internat. Chinese Stats. Assn., Psychometric Soc. (coun. dirs.), Bernouilli Soc. for Math. Stats. and Probability, Norwegian Acad. Sci. and Letters (fgn.), Phi Beta Kappa. Achievements include research in multivariate statistical analysis, time series analysis, and econometrics. Home: 746 Santa Ynez St Stanford CA 94305-8441 Office: Stanford U Dept Stats Stanford CA 94305-4065

ANDERSON, THOMAS CARYL, financial and administrative systems professional; b. St. Paul, Sept. 3, 1944; s. Willis Cecil and Mary Lou (Kaun) A.; m. Catherine Sophia Hofstede, Apr. 20, 1968; children: Nicole, Jennifer, Karilyn. BS, U. Minn., 1966, MS, 1970. Asst. prof. Northeastern U., Boston, 1971-74; lectr. SUNY-Albany, 1974-87, dir. grad. program Sch. Bus., 1976-81, dir. fin. and adminstrv. svcs., 1981-85, exec. officer adminstrn. and fin., 1985-87; dir. adminstrv. svcs. MGH Inst. Health Professions, Boston, 1987-90, v.p. adminstrn. and fin., 1990-93; v.p. fin. and adminstrn. Chatham Coll., Pitts., 1993-96; v.p. finance and adminstrn. Black Hills State U., Spearfish, S.D., 1996—; cons. various state govt. agys., Albany, 1978-87, Fund for Corp. Initiatives, N.Y.C., 1981—, GM, CPC Tarrytown, N.Y., 1988-89, U. Mass., Lowell, 1990-94, Wang Labs. Inc., Lowell, 1992-93,

Wayne State U., 1998—; asst. sec. MGH Inst. Bd. Trustees, Boston, 1987-93. Co-author: Elements of Organizational Behavior, 1972; contbr. articles to profl. publs. Mem. planning bd. Town of Hopedale, Mass., 1990-93, exec. com. Cen. Mass. Regional Planning Commn., 1990-93; treas. Black Hills State U. Found. Home: 1200 University St # 7559 Spearfish SD 57799-0001

ANDERSON, THOMAS DALE, retired geography educator, consultant, writer; b. Cleve., Sept. 23, 1929; s. Edward and Anna Marie (Schak) A.; m. Sylvia Jean Crum; children: Susan, Stefan, Kathryn. BA, Kent (Ohio) State U., 1953, MA, 1956; PhD, U. Nebr., 1966. From instr. to asst. prof. SUNY, Geneseo, 1959-64; prof. geography Bowling Green (Ohio) State U., 1965-97; prof. emeritus, 1997; summer instr. Kent State U., 1960, 61, 65, U. Va., Charlottesville, 1964, SUNY, Albany, 1966, Oreg. Coll. Edn., Monmouth, 1967; Fulbright lectr. Ctrl. U. of Venezuela, Caracas, 1974; summer lectr. Western Wash. U., Bellingham, 1985; vis. lectr. U. Mich., Ann Arbor, 1990; consulting geographer Ohio Blenders, Toledo, 1989-91. Author: Geopolitics of the Caribbean, 1984, (report) Environmental Analysis of Central Ohio, 1976; co-author: Geography as Human Ecology?, 1980. Mem. City Coun., Bowling Green, 1972-73, 87-95; mem. City Housing Commn., Bowling Green, 1969-72, chmn., 1979-86. 1st lt. U.S. Army Infantry, 1953-55, Korea. Grantee Whitehall Found., 1979, Hoover Instn., 1984. Mem. Assn. Am. Geographers, Am. Geog. Soc., Nat. Coun. for Geog. Edn., Pacific Sci. Assn., Conf. Latin Americanist Geographers, Sigma Xi. Democrat. Presbyterian. Avocations: travel, swimming, biking, reading. Home: 1103 Clark St Bowling Green OH 43402-3518

ANDERSON, THOMAS DUNAWAY, retired lawyer; b. Oklahoma City, Mar. 9, 1912; s. Frank Ervin and Burdine (Clayton) A.; m. Helen Sharp, Feb. 21, 1938; children: Helen Shaw, Lucille Streeter, John Sharp. Student, Rice Inst., 1930-31; LLB, Washington and Lee U., 1934; LLD (hon.), Lambuth Coll., 1967. Bar: Va. 1933, Tex. 1934. Assoc. Andrews & Kurth, 1934-41, 46-47; sr. v.p., trust officer Tex. Commerce Bank, Houston, 1947-51, 60-65; co-founder Tex. Fund, 1949; pres. Tex. Fund Mgmt. Co., Houston, 1952-60; ptnr. Anderson Brown & Jones, Houston, 1965-93; ret. Trustee emeritus Washington and Lee U.; past pres., chmn. Kelsey Seybold Found., Protestant Episcopal Ch. Coun., Diocese of Tex., Washington-on-Brazos State Park Assn., Mus. Fine Arts Houston, Houston Grand Opera; bd. dirs. Bayou Bend Gardens Endowment, Retina Rsch. Found., Harris County Hist. Commn., Winedale Adv. Coun., U. Tex.; Life Guard of Historic Mount Vernon, Va.; life mem., past pres. bd. visitors M.D. Anderson Cancer Ctr. First recipient Leon Jaworski award for vol. cmty. svc., 1988. Mem. ABA, Tex. Bar Assn., Philos. Soc. Tex., Bayou, Eagle Lake Rod and Gun Club, Houston Country Club, Petroleum Club of Houston, River Oaks Garden Club (hon.), SAR, Omicron Delta Kappa, Phi Delta Phi. Episcopalian. Office: River Oaks Bank Bldg 2001 Kirby Dr Ste 911 Houston TX 77019-6033

ANDERSON, THOMAS JEFFERSON, publisher, rancher, public speaker, syndicated columnist; b. Nashville, Nov. 7, 1910; s. William J. and Nancy Lucas (Joseph) A.; m. Carolyn Montague Jennings, Dec. 24, 1936; 1 child, Carolyn A. Porter. BA, Vanderbilt U., 1934; LLB (hon.), Bob Jones U., 1967. Securities salesman Gray-Shillinglaw & Co., Nashville, 1934-36; salesman Nunn-Schwab Securities Co., 1936-39; mgr. unlisted securities dept. J.C. Bradford Co., 1939-43; So. sales mgr. So. Agriculturist, Nashville, 1943-47; owner, pub. So. Farm Publs., 1947-71, Farm and Ranch mag., 1953-63, Am. Way Features (nat. newspaper syndicate), Straight Talk (weekly newsletter Anderson Enterprises); radio commentator, world traveler. Author: Straight Talk, 1967, Silence Is Not Golden It's Yellow, 1973. Vice presdl. candidate Am. Party, 1972, nat. chmn., 1976-78, presdl. nominee, 1976; mem. coun. John Birch Soc., 1959-76; nat. chmn. We-the-People, 1966-72. Lt. USN, 1943-46. Recipient Liberty awards Congress of Freedom, 1964—, Pub. Address award Freedoms Found. Valley Forge, 1959-60; named Man of Yr. God and Country Rally, 1966. Mem. Am. Agrl. Editors Assn. (pres. 1954), Phi Delta Theta (pres. Tenn. Alpha chpt. 1934, province pres. 1936-39), Omicron Delta Kappa. Baptist. Office: Jupiter Inlet Colony 128 Lighthouse Dr Jupiter FL 33469-3511 also: PO Box 1607 Blowing Rock NC 28605

ANDERSON, THOMAS JEFFERSON, JR., composer, educator; b. Coatesville, Pa., Aug. 17, 1928. BMus, W.Va. State Coll., 1950; MMusEd, Pa. State U., 1951; PhD, U. Iowa, 1958; D in Musical Arts (hon.), Coll. Holy Cross; D.Mus. (hon.), West Va. State Coll., 1989, Bridgewater State Coll., 1991, St. Augustine's Coll., 1996. Instr. W.Va. State Coll., 1955-56; prof. music, chmn. dept. Langston U., 1958-63; prof. Tenn. State U., 1963-69; vis. prof. Morehouse Coll., 1971-72; prof. music, chmn. dept. music Tufts U., Medford, Mass., 1972-80, Fletcher prof., 1978-90, Fletcher prof. emeritus, 1990—; scholar-in-residence The Rockefeller Found. Study and Conf. Ctr., Bellagio, Italy, 1984, 94; orchestrated 1st complete performance of opera Treemonisha by Scott Joplin, Atlanta, 1992. Author: (with others) Readings in Black American Music, 1971, Reflections on Afro-American Music, 1973, Canata, 1974, The Black Composer Speaks, 1978, Racial and Ethnic Directions in American Music, 1982, Black Music in our Culture, 1970; composer: Messages for orch., 1979, Spirituals for orch., jazz quartet, chorus children's choir, tenor and narrator, 1979, Vocalise for harp and violin, 1980, Soldier Boy, Soldier for opera, 1982, Jonestown for children's choir and piano, 1982, Call and Response for piano, 1982, Intermezzi for clarinet, alto sax and piano, 1983, Thomas Jefferson's Orbiting Minstrels and Contraband for multimedia, 1984, Sunstar for solo trumpet and cassette recorder, 1984, Bridging and Branching for flute and double bass, 1987, Chamber Concerto for Chamber Orch., 1988, Bahia, Bahia for orch., 1990, Broke Baroque for violin and piano, 1996, Huh! What Did you Say? for clarinet and string quartet, 1997, Whatever Happened to the Big Bands?, 1992, Walker for chamber opera, 1992, Spirit Songs for cello and piano, 1993, 7 Cabaret Songs for jazz singer, flute, viola, cello and piano, 1994, Grace for string quartet, 1994, Broke Baroque for violin and piano, 1996, Huh! for clarinet and string quartet, 1996, Shouts for oboe, violin, cello and piano, 1997, b Bop in 2 for alto saxophone, 1998, Aurelia, in memoriam for violin, 1999. Guggenheim fellow, 1988-89, fellow Nat. Humanities Ctr., 1996-97. Home: 111 Cameron Glen Dr Chapel Hill NC 27516-2333 Office: Tufts U Dept Music Medford MA 02155

ANDERSON, THOMAS PATRICK, mechanical engineer, educator; b. Chgo., Oct. 22, 1934; s. Clarence Kenneth and Anne (Moran) A.; m. Elizabeth Ann Toof, July 9, 1960; children—Patricia, James. B.S. in Mech. Engring., Northwestern U., 1956, M.S., 1958, Ph.D., 1961. Registered profl. engr., Ill., Iowa. Engr. Askania Regulator Co., Chgo., 1953-55; research engr. Cook Research Labs., Skokie, Ill., summer, 1956; rsch. engr. ARO Inc., Tullahoma, Tenn., summers 1958, 59; asst. prof., then assoc. prof. Northwestern U., 1960-66; prof. mech. engring. U. Iowa, 1966-75, chmn. dept., 1966-70; program mgr. Office Systems Integration and Analysis, NSF, 1974-75, program mgr. div. intergovtl. sci. and pub. tech., 1975-78, acting dir. indsl. program, 1976-78; dean Sch. Sci. and engring., So. Ill. U., Edwardsville, 1978-83; prof. Sch. Engring. So. Ill. U., 1978—; cons., assoc. dep. dir. interdeptl. energy study Office Sci. and Tech., 1963-65. Contbr. numerous articles to profl. jours. Named One of Ten Outstanding Young Men Chgo. Jr. Assn. Commerce and Industry, 1964. Fellow Iowa Acad. Sci.; mem. AAUP, Am. Geophys. Union, AIAA, Am. Phys. Soc., Am. Soc. Engring. Edn., ASME (Edward F. Obert award 1997), Inst. Indsl. Engrs., Ill. Acad. Sci., N.Y. Acad. Scis., Phi Kappa Phi, Sigma Xi.

ANDERSON, TIM, airport terminal executive. Dir. of airports Mpls. St. Paul Internat. Airport, 1996, dep. exec. dir. of ops., 1008—. Office: Mpls-St Paul Internat Airport 6040 28th Ave S Minneapolis MN 55450-2701*

ANDERSON, TIMOTHY CHRISTOPHER, consulting company executive; b. Hinsdale, Ill., Dec. 27, 1950; s. Paul Eugene and Mary Agnes (Donnell) A. BA in Polit. Sci. with honors, Boston Coll., 1973. Rsch. asst. to Rep. Thomas P. O'Neill U.S. Ho. Reps., Washington, 1973; ednl. cons. E.F. Shelly Co., Washington, 1973-74; exec. dir. Boston Zool. Soc., 1974-76, exec. dir., adminstr. Boston's two zoos, 1976-81; New Eng. regional v.p. Nat. Alliance Bus., Boston, 1981-83; pres. Dovetail Cons., 1983—, Boston Harbor Assocs., 1983-87; ecology coord. Hull (Mass.) Pub. Schs., 1992-93; dir. Hull Environment and Svc. Corps, 1992-94; bd. dirs. Ryan Communications, Boston, 1989-92; founder, CEO South Shore Charter Sch., 1994—, headmaster, 1994-97; spl. projects dir. South Shore Edn. Collaborative, 1993-94; pres. Nonprofit Properties, 1991-95; cons. NEH, 1977-78; dir. Blue Ice Internat., Washington, 1993—, trustee, chmn. bd. dirs. South Shore Charter Sch., 1994-95. Commr. Blue Hill Ave. Commn., 1977-80, mem., 1978-81; program com. Boston Cultural Edn. Collaborative, 1975-80; polit. cons. to Sen. Edward M. Kennedy, 1974; field coord. for Western Mass. Jimmy Carter's Primary Election Campaign, 1975-76; bd. dirs. Franklin Park Coalition, 1974-81; mem. coun., treas. Madison Park Community Sch., 1979-83; pres., trustee, v.p., treas. Mass. Cultural Alliance, 1980-92; mem. Gov.'s Pvt. Sector Initiative Task Force, 1982; mem. advocacy steering com. Mass. Coun. on Arts and Humanities, 1979-81; incorporator Boston Zool. Soc., 1982; trustee, v.p. Artists Found., 1982-86; trustee, Peddocks Island Trust, 1984-87; mem. Exec. Svc. Corps.; co-chmn. Ezra Merrill Seminar Series, 1985-86; treas. Save the Harbor/Save the Bay, 1986-87; chmn. Alliance for Boston Harbor Action, 1986-87; pres. W. Seavey Joyce S.J. Award Inc., 1988—; co-chmn. Artscoop, 1985-87; v.p. Mass. Youth Leadership Found., 1987-89; chmn. adminstrn. com. St. Mary of Assumption Parish, 1988-91; mng. dir. Hull (Mass.) Coun. for Bus. and Cultural Devel., 1988-98; mem. steering com. Bus. Vols. for Arts, Boston, 1989-90, Boston Coll. Fund Com., 1990-92; bd. dirs. Wellspring Multi-Svc. Ctr., 1989-90; chmn. pub. rels., mem. adv. coun. Boston Mgmt. Consortium, 1990-92 (Leadership award 1992), chmn. devel. com., 1991-92, chmn. pub. rels. com., 1990-91; mem. advocacy forum Alliance for Justice, Washington, 1990-95; chair adv. bd. Hull Environ. High Sch., 1990-93; fundraising chair Boston Children of War, 1990-92; mem. com. Boston Coll. Fund; bd. dirs. Project Overcoat, 1991-93; mem. Mayor's Customer Svc. Task Force, 1992; chair Hull Elder Access Coalition, 1992-94, Hull Ptnrs. in Edn., 1992-94; mem. comm. com. Quincy Community Action Programs, 1992; bd. dirs. South Coastal Regional Employment Bd., 1992-94; chair Friends of the Weir River Estuary, 1992-95; chair Hull Community Vans Com., 1993-94; co-chair S. Shore Advocates for Arts, Scis. and Humanities, 1992-93; mem. adv. bd. Quincy Coll. Water Treatment Program, 1992-98; cmty. svc. counsel Nat. Acad. Found., 1994-95; mem. adv. bd. Hull Lifesaving Mus., 1993-95; mem. bd. dirs. Mass. Pre-Engring. Program. 1995—; mem. bd. dirs. Very Special Arts, Mass., 1997—, chmn., 1998—. Recipient Community Svc. award Girl Scouts of Greater Boston, 1978, Leadership commendation award Nat. Alliance of Bus., 1983, Leadership award, Pres.'s award Mass. Cultural Alliance, 1986, Leadership award Franklin Park Coalition, 1987, John Ames award Boston Harbor Assocs., 1987, Leadership award Boston Mgmt. Consortium, 1992, Mayor's certificate of Recognition, 1992. Supts. Leadership award, 1992. Office: Dovetail Cons 936 Nantasket Ave Hull MA 02045-1453

ANDERSON, TIMOTHY J., chemical engineering educator. Prof., chmn. dept. chem. engring. U. Fla., Gainsville. Recipient Charles M.A. Stine award in Materials Engring. and Sci. Am. Inst. Chem. Engrs., 1994. Office: U Fla Chemical Engring Dept Gainesville FL 32611

ANDERSON, TIMOTHY R., investment banker; b. Chgo., Dec. 6, 1967; s. Donald R. Anderson and Linda Lee Ayers; m. Christine Marie Boyer, May 1, 1999. BSME, Purdue U., 1990; MBA, U. Chgo., 1996. Sr. engr. Boeing Co., Seattle, 1990-94; sr. cons. Deloitte & Touche, Chgo., 1995-97; assoc. Corp. Decisions, Boston, 1997-98; ptnr. Renaissance Homebuilders, Atlanta, 1997—; assoc. analyst Prudential Securities Inc., N.Y.C., 1999—. Avocations: sailing, rugby. E-mail: TimothyúR/Anderson@prusec.com. Home: One River Ct Jersey City NJ 07310 Office: Prudential Securities inc 1 New York Plz 17th Fl New York NY 10292

ANDERSON, URTON LIGGETT, accounting educator; b. Salem, Ohio, Dec. 10, 1951; s. Urton and Alice (Kenrich) A.; m. Deborah Mary Johnson, June 12, 1973; children: Bryony, Urton. BA in Greek and Philosophy magna cum laude, St. Olaf Coll., 1974; MA in Classics, U. Minn, 1977; PhD in Bus. Adminstrn., U. Minn., 1985. Cert. internal auditor. Instr. dept. acctg. U. Tex., Austin, 1984-85, asst. prof. dept. acctg., 1988-89, assoc. prof. dept. acctg., 1989-95, prof. dept. acctg., 1995—, assoc. dir. C. Aubrey Smith Ctr. for Auditing Edn. and Rsch., 1989-92, dir. C. Aubrey Smith Ctr. for Auditing Edn. and Rsch., 1992-93, acting dept. chair, 1996, assoc. dean ubdergrad. programs Coll. Bus., 1997—; Clark W. Thompson, Jr. professorship in acctg. edn. U. Tex., Austin, 1997. Author: Quality Assurance for Internal Auditing, 1983; co-editor Internal Auditing, 1990—; contbr. over 35 articles to profl and acad. jours. Rsch. fellow KPMG Peat Marwick Found., 1988-89, faculty fellow, 1990-92, Rsch. Opportunities in Auditing grantee, 1991, 94, Ernst & Young faculty fellow, 1988-93, Atlantic Richfield Centennial fellow in acctg., 1993-97. Mem. Inst. Internal Auditors Rsch. Found. (bd. rsch. advisors 1985-94, bd. regents 1994—). Office: U Tex Austin Dept Acctg CBA 4M 202 Austin TX 78712-1172

ANDERSON, VERNON RUSSELL, technology company executive, entrepreneur; b. San Francisco, July 3, 1931; s. Elmer Oran and Ethel Adelia (Carlson) A.; m. Lysbeth Warren, Dec. 27, 1953; children: Brenton, Lysanna, Dane. BS in Mech. Engring., Stanford U., 1953, MBA, 1957. Engineer Trane Co., LaCrosse, Wis., 1953-55; mgr. Sierra Electronics Corp., Menlo Park, Calif., 1957-59; co-founder, chief exec. officer VIDAR Corp., Mountain View, Calif., 1959-72; pvt. practice cons. Los Altos Hills, Calif., 1972-88; co-founder, chief exec. officer Collagen Corp., Palo Alto, Calif., 1975, Silicon Graphics Inc., Mountain view, 1982-84; vice-chmn. Axel Johnson Inc., Stamford, Conn., 1988-94; instr. Stanford (Calif.) U., 1968-72; chmn. Internat. Network Svcs., 1992—; chmn. adv. bd. Stanford Ctr. Econ. Policy Rsch., 1995—. Chmn. com. Resource Ctr. Women, Palo Alto, Calif., 1975-80; fin. chmn. Ed Zschau U.S. Senate, Silicon Valley, Calif., 1981-86; trustee Stanford U., 1985-90; bd. dirs. Camino Healthcare, 1995—. Recipient Disting. Svc. award Grad. Sch. Bus. Stanford U., 1986. Mem. Inst. Elec. Engrs., Swedish Acad. Sci. and Engring., Bohemian Club (San Francisco), Faculty Club Stanford U. Republican. Avocations: sea kayaking, aerobic sports, anthropology, world travel, birding.

ANDERSON, W. FRENCH, biochemist, physician; b. Tulsa, Dec. 31, 1936; married, 1961. AB, Harvard U., 1958, MD, 1963; MA, Cambridge U., 1960; LHD (hon.), U. Okla., 1992. Intern pediatric medicine Children's Hosp. Med. Ctr., Boston, 1963-64; rsch. assoc. lab. biochem. genetics Nat. Heart, Lung & Blood Inst., 1965-67, rsch. med. officer, 1967-68, head sect. human biochem., 1968-71, head sect. molecular hematology, 1971-73, chief molecular hematology br., 1973-92; prof. biochemistry and pediatrics, dir. gene therapy labs. U. So. Calif. Norris Cancer Ctr., 1992—; rsch. fellow bacteriology and immunology med. sch. Harvard U., 1964-65; prof. lectr. sch. medicine George Washington U., 1967-75; mem. faculty dept. genetics Grad. Program NIH, 1967-92, dept. medicine & physiology, 1981-92, chmn., 1984-92; mem. heart fellow bd. Nat. Heart & Lung Inst., 1968-70; mem. task force hemoglobinopathies Nat. Heart, Lung and Blood Inst. NIH, 1972, mem. nat. task group on Cooley's anemia, 1977-78, pres. assembly scientists, 1982, chmn. inter-inst. coord. com. on Cooley's anemia, 1972-77, mem. exec. com. bd. dirs. Found. Adv. Edu. in Sci., Inc., 1984-92, mem. working group human gene therapy recombinant DNA adv. com., 1984-86, mem. working group on viruses, 1985-86, hematology program dir. Lab. Molecular Hematology, 1985, mem. coord. com. human genome, 1988-92; chmn. interagy. coord. com. on Cooley's anemia HEW, 1975-77; mem. sr. exec. sci. svc. Dept. Health and Human Svc., 1980-92; cons. Pres. Commn. Study Ethical Problems Medicine & Biomed. Behavior Rsch., 1981-82, Human Gene Therapy Ctr. for Bioethics, Kennedy Inst. Ethics, Washington, 1982—; chmn. sci. adv. bd. Genetic Therapy Inc., Gaithersburg, Md., 1986-87, 92—; mem. sci. adv. bd. S/L Health Care Ventures, N.Y., 1986-88, 1993—; cons. human gene therapy St. Jude Childrens Rsch. Hosp., Memphis, 1990-92, U. Pitts., 1990-92; chmn. scientific adv. com. Children's Nat. Med. Ctr., Washington, 1990-92; lectr. Mider Lecture NIH, 1992, Timely Topics Lecture U.S. and Can. Acad. Pathology, 1992, Frontiers in Clin. Sci. Lecture Am. Fedn. Clin. Rsch., 1992, Myron Karon Meml. Lectureship Children's Hosp. L.A., 1992, Disting. Sci. Lecture Internat. and Am. Assns. Dental Rsch., 1993, Plenary Lecture 17th Internat. Congress of Genetics, 1993, Martin Meml. Lecture 79th Ann. Clin. Congress Am. Coll. Surgeons, 1993, Plenary Lecture Am. Acad. Pediatrics, 1993. Co-editor: Fifth Cooley's Anemia Symposium, 1985. Mem. med. resources coun. Cooley's Anemia Blood & Rsch. Found for Children, 1974-77; mem. adv. bd. Cooley's Anemia Found., Inc., 1977—; mem. sci. adv. com. Children's Hosp. Rsch. Found., Cin., 1985-88. Recipient Thomas B. Cooley award Sci. Achievement Cooley's Anemia Blood & Rsch. Found. for Children, 1977, Mary Ann Liebert Biotherapeutic award, 1991, Pres. Award lectr. Am. Thoracic Soc., 1991, Maude L. Menten award U. Pitts., 1991, Ralph R. Braund award U. Tenn., 1991, Presdl. Meritorious Exec. Rank award HHS, 1991, Fed. Lab. Consortium award for Excellence in Tech. Transfer, 1992, Disting. Svc. award Nat. Ctr. Infectious Diseases, 1993, Dr. Murray Thelin award Nat. Hemophilia Found., 1993, Drew award lectr., 1993, King Faisal ibn Abdul Aziz Internat. Prize for Medicine, 1994, NORD Leadership award Nat. Orgn. Rare Disorders, 1996; named BioPharm Person of Yr. Biopharm Mag. editl. adv. bd., 1994. Fellow AAAS; mem. Assn. Am. Physicians, Am. Soc. Clin. Investigators, Am. Soc. Hematology, Am. Soc. Human Genetics, Am. Soc. Biol. Chemistry, Am. Fedn. Clin. Rsch. Achievements include research in regulation of RNA and protein synthesis, hemoglobin biosynthesis, thalassemia and hemoglobinopathies, gene expression in mammalian cells, genetic engineering of mammalian cells, human gene therapy. Office: U So Calif Sch Medicine Norris Cancer Ctr 1441 Eastlake Ave Rm 6316 Los Angeles CA 90033-1048*

ANDERSON, WALTER DIXON, trade association management consultant; b. Elizabeth, N.J., July 22, 1932; s. Charles Michael and Hazel Mildred (Fieldstad) A. B.A., Emory U., 1954; M.A., U. Ga., 1958. State rep. Nat. Found. March of Dimes, Jacksonville, Fla., 1958-61; exec. sec. Fla. Turf-Grass Assn., Jacksonville, 1961-69; exec. dir. Irrigation Assn., Silver Spring, Md., 1969-80; exec. v.p. Irrigation Assn., 1980-85; exec. dir. Contractors Pump Bur., 1972-93; mng. dir. Resilient Floor Covering Inst., 1987-97, ret., 1997. Served with U.S. Army, 1954-56. Mem. ASTM, Am. Soc. Assn. Execs., Washington Soc. Assn. Execs., Sigma Delta Chi. Republican. Methodist. Home: 6700 Heatherford Ct Rockville MD 20855-1521

ANDERSON, WALTER HERMAN, magazine editor; b. Mt. Vernon, N.Y., Aug. 31, 1944; s. William Henry and Ethel Magdalena (Crolly) A.; m. Loretta Gritz, Sept. 9, 1967; children: Eric Christian, Melinda Christe. AA, Westchester Community Coll., 1970; BS summa cum laude, Mercy Coll., 1972; DHL (hon.), St. Ambrose U., 1988, Clemson U., 1990, Mercy Coll., 1989, U. of the Pacific, 1990. Reporter Reporter Dispatch, White Plains, N.Y., 1967-68, night city editor, 1968-69, editor, gen. mgr., 1975-77; police reporter Westchester Rockland Newspapers, White Plains, N.Y., 1969-70, help editor for action line, 1970-71, investigative reporter, 1971-72, mng. editor, 1973-74; editor, gen. mgr. Standard Star, New Rochelle, N.Y., 1974-75; sr. editor Parade mag., N.Y.C., 1977-78, mng. editor, 1978-80, editor, 1980—, editor-in-chief, 1994; guest lectr. Columbia U., NYU, U. Mass., U. of the Pacific; tchg. faculty New Sch. for Social Rsch., 1994—; adj. prof. psychology, sociology Westchester C.C., 1972-80. Author: Courage is a Three-Letter Word, 1986, The Greatest Risk of All, 1988, Read With Me, 1990, The Confidence Course, 1997; actor: Talkin' Stuff, a one-man show at Ford's Theatre, Washington, 1992. Chmn. bd. trustees Mercy Coll., Dobbs Ferry, N.Y., 1980-88; bd. dirs. St. Vincent's Hosp., 1975-80, N.Y. Vietnam Vets. Leadership Program Inc., 1984-89, Dropout Prevention Fund, 1987—, Nat. Ctr. for Family Literacy, 1990—, Very Spl. Arts, 1990—, Pub. Broadcasting Svc., 1990-98; nat. spokesman GED, 1985—; mem. Nat. Com. for Lit. Arts; bd. advisors Naval Postgrad. Sch., 1988—; mem. nat. adv. bd. Lit. Vols., 1990—; bd. trustees Phelps Stokes Fund; appointed to U.S. Commn. on Librs. and Info. Scis., Pres. Clinton, 1995—. With USMC, 1961-66. Recipient Frank Tripp Meml. award Gannett Group, 1971, Tree of Life award Jewish Nat. Fund, 1988, Spirit of Am. award, 1988, Napoleon Hill Gold award, 1989, Horatio Alger award, 1994, Literacy Vols. of Am. Stars in Literacy cert., 1990, others. Mem. Soc. Silurians, Sigma Delta Chi, Psi Chi. Club: Overseas Press. Office: Advance Publications Inc Parade 711 3rd Ave New York NY 10017-4014 *I hope a single driving desire remains with me always—that is, to encourage talented people. To share, even in the least of ways, in the growth of a creative talent is the highest goal of an editor, if his career is to matter at all.*

ANDERSON, WALTER LEE, environmental educator, artist, photographer; b. Mt. Vernon, Wash., Feb. 25, 1946; s. Arthur J. and Thelma E. Anderson; m. Rebecca M. Johnson, Feb. 3, 1968; children: Christopher Quill, Rowan Reed. BS with highest honors, Wash. State U., 1968; MS, U. Ariz., 1974; postgrad., U. Mich., 1976. Wildlife biologist, pub. use specialist U.S. Fish & Wildlife Svc., 1968, 70-72; co-dir. W. Butte Sanctuary Co., Colusa, Calif., 1976-78; founder, dir. Sutter Buttes Naturalists, Colusa, 1979-84; prof. environ. studies Prescott (Ariz.) Coll., 1991—; freelance artist, photographer, 1976—; internat. expedition guide Voyagers Internat., others, 1979—; cons. McCuen Properties, Sacramento, 1991—; lectr. Am. Orient Express, Seattle, 1996-98; dir. emeritus Mid. Mountain Found., Yuba City, Calif., 1998—. Author, illustrator: The Sutter Buttes: A Naturalist's View, 1983; illustrator: (book) Coexisting with Urban Wildlife, 1996; contbg. author, photographer: California's Wild Gardens, 1997. Merit badge counselor Boy Scouts Am., Wash., 1960-64, Ariz., 1995—; sec., bd. dirs. Ctrl. Ariz. Land Trust, Yavapai County, 1995-97; choir mem. 1st Congl. Ch., Prescott, 1996-98. Staff sgt. U.S. Army, 1968-70, Vietnam. Recipient Best in show award Nat. Wildlife Art Show, 1980; NSF fellow U. Ariz., U. Mich., 1973-75. Mem. Soc. Conservation Biology, Nat. Wildlife Fedn. (life), Am. Ornithologists' Union (life), Nat. Geographic Soc. (life), Nature Conservancy (bd. dirs. no. Calif. chpt. 1979-81), Ariz. Riparian Coun., Phi Beta Kappa, Phi Kappa Phi, Omicron Delta Kappa, Phi Eta Sigma. Avocations: hiking, singing. E-mail: aardvark@northlink.com. Home: 1964 Sherwood Dr Prescott AZ 86303 Office: Prescott Coll Environ Studies 220 Grove Ave Prescott AZ 86301

ANDERSON, WARREN, distribution company executive. BA in Polit. Sci., U. Mich., 1974, M in Journalism, 1977. CEO Anderson-DuBose Co., Cleve. Fax: (440) 248-6208. Office: Anderson-DuBose Co 6575 Davis Industrial Pkwy Cleveland OH 44139-3549

ANDERSON, WARREN MATTICE, lawyer; b. Bainbridge, N.Y., Oct. 16, 1915; s. Floyd E. and Edna (Mattice) A.; m. Eleanor C. Sanford, June 28, 1941 (dec.); children: Warren David, Lawrence, Richard, Thomas. BA, Colgate U., 1937; JD, Albany Law Sch., 1940, LLD (hon.), 1979; LLD (hon.), Hartwick Coll., 1976, Coll. of New Rochelle, 1979, Fordham U., 1980, Union Coll., 1981, Colgate U., 1982, Hamilton Coll., 1985, Clarkson U., 1987, St. Lawrence U., 1988, Elmira Coll., 1989, St. Francis Coll., 1991; LHD (hon.), Hofstra U., 1987. Bar: N.Y., 1940. Since practiced in Binghamton; asst. county atty. Broome County, N.Y., 1940-42; assoc. Hinman, Howard & Kattell LLP, 1949-52; ptnr. Hinman, Howard & Kattell, 1952—; mem. N.Y. State Senate, 1953-88, chmn. fin. com., 1966-72, pres. pro tem, majority leader, 1973-88. Del. Rep. Nat. Conv., 1972, 76, 80, 84, 88, mem. platform com., 1972; trustee Colgate U., 1964-70, Cornell U., 1973-88, Elmira Coll., 1989-95; vice chair bd. N.Y. State Hist. Assn.; mem. N.Y. State Commn. on Jud. Nominations; mem. Hartwick Coll. Coun.; mem. adv. com. Govt. Law Ctr., Albany Law Sch.; mem. bd. overseers Nelson A. Rockefeller Inst. Govt. With AUS, 1943-45, lt. JAGD, 1945-46. Recipient Alumni award Colgate U., 1972. Fellow Am. Bar Found.; mem. ABA, Broome County Bar Assn. Presbyterian. Clubs: Binghamton; Oteyokwa Lake (Hallstead, Pa.). Home: 34 Lathrop Ave Binghamton NY 13905-4343 Office: Hinman Howard & Kattell 700 Security Mut Bldg Binghamton NY 13902-5250

ANDERSON, WARREN RONALD, electrical engineering educator; b. Houston, July 31, 1914; s. Wallace Roy and Helen Adelia (Abrahamson) A.; m. Dantza Peinovich, May 28, 1945; children: Richard Godfrey, John Warren, Deborah Annete. *Son, Richard Godfrey, graduate of Dartmouth, 1968, earned MD from U. California, San Francisco, 1972 and is a radiologist in Visalia, California. He married Barbara Harris and have two daughters and a son. Son, John Warren, graduate of Colgate U., 1971, earned M.A. from U. New Hampshire and is the Dean of Admissions and Financial Aid, Kenyon College, Gambier, Ohio. He married Nancy Beronsky. They have one son. Daughter, Deborah Annete, graduate of U. California, San Diego, earned M.S. from U. Vermont, resides in Kennebunk, Maine with her son, daughter and husband, Dr. Robert Westcot, an opthamologist* AA, Bethel Coll., 1935; BS, U. Minn., 1939; BSEE, La. State U., 1944. Registered profl. engr., Calif. Design engr. Plant Engring. Agy., Phila., 1945-46; circuits engr. Automatic Electric, Chgo., 1946; prof. elec. engring. Calif. Polytech. State U., San Luis Obispo, Calif., 1946-76, head elec. engring. dept., 1976-79, prof. emeritus, 1979—; design engr. GE, Ft. Wayne, Ind., 1951; rsch. analyst Northup Aircraft, Hawthorne, Calif., 1952; sys. engr. Western Gear Corp., Lynwood, Calif., 1955; edn. cons. GE, Schenectady, 1956. Leader Boy Scouts Am., San Luis Obispo, 1958-64. With U.S. Army, 1942-45. Recipient Cert. of Appreciation, AIEE, 1963. Mem. IEEE, NSPE, Am. Soc. Engring. Edn., Calif. Soc. Profl. Engrs. (dir. 1949-55), Calif. State Employees Assn. (dir. 1955-59), Eta Kappa Nu. Democrat. Baptist. Home: 573 Jeffrey Dr San Luis Obispo CA 93405-1003 Office: Calif Poly State Univ Elec Engring Dept San Luis Obispo CA 93407

ANDERSON, WAYNE ARTHUR, electrical engineering educator; b. Jamestown, N.Y., May 20, 1938; s. Arthur Charles and Flora Mary (Funicello) A.; m. Marilyn Mae Anderson, July 28, 1964; children—Wayne P., Leslie M. B.A., SUNY-Buffalo, 1961, M.S., 1965, Ph.D., 1970. Research engr. Great Lakes Carbon, Niagara Falls, N.Y., 1961-65; instr. SUNY-Buffalo, 1965-70, prof. elec. engring., 1978—; prof. Rutgers U., New Brunswick, N.J., 1970-78; cons. Exxon, Linden, N.J., 1972-76, Amerace Corp., N.J., 1974-76; reviewer NSF, 1979—; dir., Ctr. for Electronic and Electro-Optic Materials, 1986-96, ECE dept. chmn. 1989-95. Contbr. more than 150 articles to profl. jours. Chmn. Internat. Students Com., 1983—; deacon 1st Baptist Ch., 1984-87, Westerly Rd. Ch., 1973-76. Grantee Solar Energy Research Inst., 1975-83, NSF, 1972-74, 80-83, 92-96, 97-99, Intelstat, 1980-84, ONR 1986-89. NYSERDA, 1991-95, Nat. Renewable Energy Lab., 1993-95, 98-99. Mem. IEEE (sr., bd. dirs. 1981-84), Materials Rsch. Soc., Am. Inst. Physics. Republican. Avocations: tennis; swimming; biking. Home: 39 Sleepy Hollow Ln Orchard Park NY 14127-4617 Office: SUNY Elec and Computer Engring 217C Bonner Hall Buffalo NY 14260-0108

ANDERSON, WAYNE CARL, public information officer, former corporate executive; b. Sheboygan, Wis., May 5, 1935; s. Chester Phillip and Mabel Mary (Edler) A.; m. Joan Dorothy Staranick, May 18, 1963; children: David Wayne, Steven Michael, Karen Colleen. BS in Bus. Adminstrn., Upsala Coll., 1977. Cert. arbitrator, mediator, Ariz. C.C. tchr. Dir. state govt. rels. Nabisco Brands Co., Parsippany, N.J., 1974-78; dir. fed. govt. rels. Nabisco Brands Co., Parsippany, 1978-79, dir. govt. rels., 1979-81, v.p. govt. rels., 1981-84, v.p. govt. and cmty. rels., 1984-87, v.p. pub. affairs, 1987; non-lawyer exec. Evans Kitchel & Jenckes, P.C., 1988-89; pres., CEO Ariz. C. of C., 1990-95; exec. v.p. Americare, 1996-98; guest lectr. in field. Editl. adv. bd. Pub. Affairs in Rev., 1980; contbr. articles to profl. jours. Mem. Roseland (N.J.) Planning Bd., 1978-79; mem. Roseland Citizens Adv. Com., 1977-78; pres. Grace Luth. Ch., Livingston, N.J., 1980-81, chmn. bd. elders, 1981-82; trustee State Govt. Rsch. and Edn. Found., 1981-82; mem. gov.'s adv. coun. on quality, 1991-95, gov.'s commn. econ. devel., 1991-95; mem. Ariz. Space Commn., 1992—, commr. emeritus, 1996; bd. dirs. Quality Alliance, 1992-95, Nat. Conf. Christians and Jews, Fiesta Bowl Com., Ariz. Econ. Forum, Ariz. Utility Investors; statewide com. chmn. Superbowl XXX, 1995-96; elder Redeemer Luth. Ch., Scottsdale, Ariz., 1997-98; chmn. adv. bd. NYU, Baruch Coll., U. N.Y.. Served with U.S. Army, 1958-60. Mem. Internat. Jaycees (senator 1989—), U.S. Jaycees (nat. dir. 1964-65), Pub. Affairs Coun. (exec. com. 1986, bd. dirs. 1988—), Nat. Fgn. Trade Coun. (dir. 1986), State Govt. Affairs Coun. (past pres. 1978-79), Ford's Theatre (bd. govs.), Acad. Polit. Sci., Pub. Affairs Profls. Ariz. (founder 1987—), World Affairs Coun. (pres. 1994-95), Thunderbird Am. Grad. Sch. Internat. Mgmt., Thunderbird Global Coun.

ANDERSON, WAYNE KEITH, dean; b. Pine Falls, Manitoba, Can., Apr. 4, 1941; s. Sigward Emmanuel and Verna Madelaine Anderson; m. Ellen Lorraine Robertson, Aug. 31, 1962; children: Brian Ross, Laura Elizabeth, Shari Lynn. BS in Pharmacy, U. Manitoba, 1962, MS, 1964; PhD, U. Wis., 1968. Asst. prof. to prof. medicinal chemistry Univ. at Buffalo (N.Y.), 1968-81, prof., medicinal chemistry, 1981—, prof., chemistry, 1993—, assoc. chmn., medicinal chemistry, 1994-95, dean Sch. Pharmacy, 1995—; peer reviewer Nat. Acad. Sci., Washington, 1995—, NIH, Washington, 1986-94, U.S. Army Med. Rsch., Washington, 1993-95, Nat. Cancer Inst., Washington, 1992—. Contbr. articles to profl. jours.; patentee in new anticancer drugs. Recipient Niagara Frontier Inventor of Yr., 1988; Drug Discovery grant Mitsubishi Kasei, 1988—; grantee NIH/Nat. Cancer Inst., 1971-95. Mem. Am. Assn. Coll. Pharmacy, Am. Chemical Soc. (medicinal chemistry divsn.), Am. Pharm. Assn., Pharmacists Soc. N.Y., Pharmacists Assn. Western N.Y. Avocations: genealogy, fishing, hockey, golf, travel. Office: Univ at Buffalo Sch Pharmacy 126 Cooke Hall Buffalo NY 14260-0109

ANDERSON, WILLIAM, retail company executive, business education educator; b. L.A., May 21, 1923; s. William Bert and Marie (Novotney) A.; m. Margaret Lillian Phillips, Aug. 16, 1951; children: Margaret Gwen, Deborah Kay, William Keven, Denise Marie. BA in Econs., UCLA, 1948, MEd, 1957. Cert. secondary tchr. (life), Calif. Tchr. bus. edn. Big Bear Lake (Calif.) High Sch., 1949-52, Ventura (Calif.) Unified Sch. Dist. Buena High Sch., 1952-89; chief exec. officer Day's Aircraft Inc., Santa Paula, Calif., 1967—; cons. micro computers Calif. State Dept. Edn., 1983-85; pres. "Dollars for Schollars", Ventura. Crew chief Olympic Games basketball stats., 1984, basketball stats. World Games for the Deaf, 1985, U.S. Olympic Festival, 1991; vol. Calif. Police Olympics, 1989. With USAAF, 1943-45, PTO. Mem. NEA (life), Calif. Bus. Edn. Assn. (pres. So. sect. 1959-60, state sec. 1960-61, hon. life 1991), Internat. Soc. Bus. Edn. (voting del. to Soc. Internat. pour l'Enseignement Comml., Western rep. 1988-89, apptd. historian 1991, 1st Medal for Outstanding Svc. 1997), Am. Aviation Hist. Soc., Calif. Assn. Work Experience Educators (life), Air Force Assn. (life), So. Calif. Badminton Assn. (past bd. dirs.), Phi Delta Kappa, Delta Pi Epsilon (hon. life). Democrat. Lutheran. Avocations: photography, aviation history, badminton, UCLA basketball stats. Home: 334 Manzanita Ave Ventura CA 93001-2227 Office: Day's Aircraft Co Inc PO Box 511 Santa Paula CA 93061-0511

ANDERSON, WILLIAM (ALBION), JR., investment banker; b. Paris, Ark., July 12, 1939; s. William A. and Maude (Rogers) A.; m. Patricia P. Puterbaugh, July 5, 1968; stepchildren—Charles L. Kuehn, Cynthia P. Robinson. B.S.B.A., U. Ark., 1961; M.B.A., Harvard U., 1963. With Blyth Eastman Dillon & Co., Inc., N.Y.C., 1963-75, exec. asst. to chief exec. officer, dir. planning, 1973-74; sr. v.p. Blyth Eastman Dillon & Co., Inc., 1974-75; sr. v.p., chief fin. officer ENSTAR Corp., Houston, 1975-84; pres. Farmers Oil Co., 1987-96; ltd. ptnr. Weller, Anderson, Cheneviere & Co., Ltd., Houston, 1988—; bd. dirs. Wing Corp.; mng. trustee J. G. Paterbaugh Trust. Mem. River Oaks Country Club (Houston), The Houston Club. Office: 811 Rusk St Ste 715 Houston TX 77002-2811

ANDERSON, WILLIAM BANKS, JR., ophthalmology educator; b. Durham, N.C., June 14, 1931; s. William Banks and Mildred Ursula (Everett) A.; m. Nancy Eldridge Walker, Sept. 17, 1960; children: Mary Banks, Mark Eldridge, Elizabeth Perry. A.B., Princeton U., 1952; M.D., Harvard U., 1956. Diplomate: Am. Bd. Ophthalmology (dir. 1986-92). Intern Duke U. Med. Ctr., Durham, N.C., 1956-57, resident, 1959-62, asst. prof. ophthalmology, 1962-67, assoc. prof. ophthalmology, 1967-76, prof. ophthalmology, 1976—, acting chmn., 1991-92; mem. profl. adv. com. N.C. Div. Services to the Blind, Raleigh, 1972-84. Chmn. bd. trustees Durham Acad., 1975-77. Served to capt. M.C. U.S. Army, 1957-59. Fellow ACS; mem. Am. Ophthalmol. Soc. (sec.-treas. 1989-98, v.p. 98—), Am. Acad. Ophthalmology (bd. dirs. 1986-89), Am. Bd. Ophthalmology (bd. dirs. 1986-93). Episcopalian. Home: 2401 Cranford Rd Durham NC 27706-2511 Office: Duke U Eye Ctr Erwin Rd Durham NC 27710

ANDERSON, WILLIAM CARL, association executive, environmental engineer, consultant; b. Vinton, Iowa, Sept. 24, 1943; s. Ivan D. and Lois B. (Schlotterback) A.; m. Elizabeth A. Dingman, Nov. 12, 1966; children: William Carl III, Erica Dawn. BSCE, Iowa State U., 1967. Registered profl. engr., N.Y., N.J., Pa., Iowa; diplomate Am. Acad. Environ. Engrs. Dir. environ. health Cayuga County Health Dept., Auburn, N.Y., 1969-73; owner Pickard & Anderson, Auburn, 1973—; trustee Am. Acad. Environ. Engrs., Annapolis, Md., 1982-85, exec. dir., 1985—. Editor: Environmental Engineer, 1985—. Gen. chmn. Cayuga County United Way, 1982, exec. com., 1982-84, bd. dirs., 1981-84; health and safety com. Cayuga County council Boy Scouts Am., 1969-83; parish council Sacred Heart Parish, 1981-82; bd. dirs. YMCA-WEIU Cayuga County, 1982-85. Served with USNR, 1967-69. Recipient Recognition award United Way, 1982; named Honorable Conceptor, Mich. Cons. Engrs. Council, 1983. Fellow ASCE (Outstanding Service award 1981, 86); mem. Am. Water Works Assn., Air Waste Mgmt. Assn., Assn. Environ. Engring. Profs., NSPE, N.Y. Soc. Profl. Engrs., N.Y. Water Pollution Control Assn. (Lewis Van Carpenter award 1974), Water Environment Fedn. (Philip F. Morgan medal 1973), Buick Club Am. (bd. dirs. 1996—), Chi Epsilon. Republican. Roman Catholic. Office: Am Acad Environ Engrs 130 Holiday Ct Ste 100 Annapolis MD 21401-7003

ANDERSON, WILLIAM CORNELIUS, III, lawyer; b. Haddonfield, N.J., Dec. 1, 1947; s. William Cornelius Jr. and Madelyn Anna (Penny) A.; m. Christine Joan Keck, June 20, 1970; children: William C. IV, Teresa, Stephen, Geoffrey, Thomas, Matthew. BA, Georgetown U., 1969; JD, Villanova U., 1975. Bar: Del. 1975, Ill. 1979. Atty. Morris, Nichols, Arsht & Tunnell, Wilmington, Del., 1975-77, Biggs & Battaglia, Wilmington, 1978; atty. Lord, Bissell & Brook, Chgo., 1979-85, ptnr., 1985—. Contbr. chpt. to book, articles to law jours. Capt. USAR, 1969-72. Fellow Am. Coll. Trial Lawyers; mem. ABA, Internat. Assn. Def. Counsel, Am. Acad. Healthcare Attys., Soc. Trial Attys., Union League Club of Chgo., North Shore Country Club, Kenilworth Club. Home: 717 Kent Rd Kenilworth IL 60043-1031 Office: Lord Bissell & Brook 115 S La Salle St Ste 3200 Chicago IL 60603-3972

ANDERSON, WILLIAM E., federal judge. Bankruptcy judge U.S. Dist. Ct. (we. dist.) Va., Lynchburg, 1980—. Fax: (804) 847-8401. Office: US Dist Ct (we dist) Va 1100 Main St Lynchburg VA 24504

ANDERSON, WILLIAM HENRY, psychobiologist, educator; b. Phila., Nov. 10, 1940; s. William Henry Schoen and Elizabeth Winifred (Laverty) A.; m. Catherine Sacchetti, Oct. 7, 1967 (dec. Sept. 1991); 1 child, Jennifer Ann Gist. B.S., MIT, 1962; M.A., U. Pa., 1967; M.D., Thomas Jefferson U., 1967; M.P.H., Harvard U., 1977. Diplomate: Am. Bd. Psychiatry and Neurology. Intern. Pa. Hosp., Phila., 1967-68; resident in psychiatry Mass. Gen. Hosp., Boston, 1968-71, assoc. psychiatrist dept. psychiatry, 1976-97, sr. psychiatrist, 1998—, dir. postgrad. edn., 1976-81; instr. psychiatry Harvard U., Boston, 1973-75, asst. prof., 1975-81, asst. clin. prof., 1981-82, lectr., 1982—; chmn. psychiatry St. Elizabeths Hosp., Boston, 1981-92; dir. clinical svcs. Augusta Mental Health Inst.; asst. attending psychiatrist Mclean Hosp., Belmont, Mass.; Cons. Scientists' Inst. Pub. Info.; mem. Carnegie Coun. Ethics and Internat. Affairs. Contbg. editor: The New Physician, 1977-79; editorial bd. Topics in Geriatrics, 1981-87, Jour. Geriatric Psychiatry and Neurology. Served to lt. comdr., M.C. USNR, 1971-73. Fellow Am. Psychiat. Assn., Human Biology coun.; mem. AAAS, Am. Acad. Clin. Psychiatrists, Internat. Soc. Polit. Psychology, Coun. on Fgn. Rels. (lectr. to coms.), Med. Assn. P.R. (hon.), Mass. Med. Soc., Soc. Ethnobiology, U.S. Naval Inst., Boston Athenaeum (proprietor), Harvard Club of Boston, Union Club, Sigma Xi. Office: 34 Coolidge Hill Rd Cambridge MA 02138-5527

ANDERSON, WILLIAM HOPPLE, lawyer; b. Cin., Feb. 28, 1926; s. Robert Waters and Anna (Hopple) A.; m. Jean Koop, Feb. 3, 1951; children: Susan Hopple, Nancy, Barbara, William Hopple Jr., Francie. Student, Carleton Coll., 1946; LL.B., U. Cin., 1952. Bar: Ohio bar 1952, U.S. Supreme Ct 1964. Mem. firm Becker, Loeb, & Becker, Cin., 1952-54; asst. pros. atty. Hamilton County, Ohio, 1953-57; ptnr. Graydon, Head & Ritchey, Cin., 1957—; judge Wyoming (Ohio) Mcpl. Ct., 1960-67. Mem. Ohio Ho. of Reps., 1967-69. With USMC, 1944-46. Mem. Cin. Bar Assn. Republican. Presbyterian. Home: 297 Mt Pleasant Ave Cincinnati OH 45215-4212 Office: 511 Walnut St Cincinnati OH 45202-3115

ANDERSON, WILLIAM R., botanist, educator, curator, director. BS Botany, Duke U., 1964; MS Systematic Botany, U. Mich., 1965, PhD, 1971. Assoc. curator N.Y. Botanical Garden, 1971-74; from asst. prof. to prof., dept. Biology U. Mich., 1974—, also assoc. curator, 1974-86, curator, 1986—, dir. Herbarium, 1986—; field work in Jamaica, 1963, 66, Hawaii, 1964, Mexico, 1965, 66, 68, 70, 81, 83, 88, 94, 95, 98, Costa Rica, 1969, 90, Brazil, 1972-76, 78, 82, 90, Argentina, 1982, 90, Venezuela, 1984, 96. Gen. editor numerous vols., chpts. in field; contbr. articles in field to profl. jours. Office: U of Mich Herbarium N University Building Ann Arbor MI 48109-1057

ANDERSON, WILLIAM ROBERT, career naval officer; b. Bakerville, Tenn., June 17, 1921; s. David Hensley and Mary (McKelvey) A.; m. Yvonne Etzel, June 10, 1943 (div. Apr. 1979); children: Michael David, William Robert; m. Patricia Walters, Dec. 26, 1980; children: Jane Hensley, Thomas McKelvey. Grad., Columbia Mil. Acad., 1939; BSEE, U.S. Naval Acad., 1942; DSc, Defiance Coll., 1958. Commd. ensign USN, 1942, advanced through grades to capt., 1960; assigned submarines Tarpon, Narwhal, Trutta and 11 Pacific combat patrols, World War II; postwar service submarine Trutta, Sarda; comdr. attack submarine USS Wahoo, Pearl Harbor, 1953-55; head tactical dept. Submarine Sch., 1955-56; staff naval reactors br. AEC, Washington, 1956-57; comdr. USS Nautilus, 1957-59; ret. USN, 1962; cons. to Pres. J.F. Kennedy, until 1963; mem. 89th-92d Congresses from 6th Tenn. Dist.; pvt. bus. exec., 1973—; co-founder Pub. Office Corp., database mgmt. firm. Author: Nautilus 90 North, 1959, First Under the North Pole, 1959, The Useful Atom, 1966; Contbr. articles to nat. mags. and profl. pubs. Decorated Bronze Star, Legion of Merit; recipient Stephen Decatur prize Navy League U.S., Distinguished Service award N.Y.C., Christopher Columbus Internat. Communications award Genoa, Italy; Elisha Kent Kane medalist Geog. Soc. Phila., 1959; Patron's medal Royal Geog. Soc., 1959; Leadership award Freedoms Found., 1960, Lowell Thomas award The Explorers Club, N.Y.C., 1997. Home: 10505 Miller Rd Oakton VA 22124-1709

ANDERSON, WILLIAM ROBERT, pathologist, educator; b. Kittanning, Pa., Jan. 26, 1929; s. John Dickson and Amelia Caroline (Haferland)A.; m. Lorna McLeod, June 15, 1951 (div. 1974); children: Caroline Elizabeth Anderson Fraser, Frederick Charles; m. Carol Jane (Gorder) Tammen, Nov. 1975. BA, U. Rochester, 1951; MD, U. Pa., 1958. Asst. pathologist Mount Sinai Hosp., Mpls., 1964-67; dir. anatomic pathology Hennepin County Med. Ctr., Mpls., 1967-84, chief of pathology, 1984-95; prof. pathology U. Minn. Sch. of Medicine, Mpls., 1975—; pathology cons. Hennepin County Med. Ctr., 1997—. Contbr. numerous articles to profl. pubs. Writer Habitat for Humanity, Twin Cities, 1995—; ch. coun. mem. Mt. Calvary Luth. Ch., Excelsior, Minn., 1996-99. Lt. (j.g.) USN, 1951-54. Fellow Coll. of Am. Pathologists; mem. Internat. Acad. of Pathologists, Soc. for Diagnostic Ultrastructural Pathology, Phi Beta Kappa, Sigma Xi. Lutheran. Avocations: history, travel, swimming, tennis. Home: 5725 Merry Ln Excelsior MN 55331-3310

ANDERSON, WILLIAM SCOVIL, classics educator; b. Brookline, Mass., Sept. 16, 1927; s. Edgar Weston and Katrina (Brewster) A.; m. Lorna Candee Bassette, June 12, 1954 (dec. Dec. 1977); children: Judith, Blythe, Heather, Meredith, Keith; m. Deirdre Burt, May 28, 1983. B.A., Yale U., 1950, Ph.D., 1954; A.B., Cambridge U., (Eng.), 1952; M.A., Cambridge U., 1955. Prix de Rome fellow Am. Acad. in Rome, 1954-55; instr. classics Yale U., 1955-59; resident in Rome, Morse fellow, 1959-60; mem. faculty U. Calif., Berkeley, 1960-94, prof. Latin and comparative lit., 1966-94, prof. charge Intercollegiate Ctr. Classical Studies, 1967-68, chmn. classics, 1970-73; rsch. prof. U. Melbourne, 1984; Robson lectr. Victoria Coll., Toronto, 1987; Blegen rsch. prof. Vassar Coll., 1989-90, vice chair comparative lit., 1990-93; vis. disting. prof. Fla. State U., spring 1995. Author: The Art of the Aeneid, 1969, Ovid, Metamorphoses, Critical Text, 1977, Essays on Roman Satire, 1982, Barbarian Play: Plautus' Roman Comedy, 1993, Ovid's Metamorphoses 1-5 Text and Commentary, 1997, Why Horace?, 1998. Served with AUS, 1946-48, Korea. NEH sr. fellow, 1973-74. Mem. Am. Philol. Assn. (pres. 1977), Danforth Assocs., Soc. Religion. Episcopalian. Office: Univ Calif Dept Classics Berkeley CA 94720

ANDERSON, WILLIAM THOMAS, art educator, artist; b. Mpls., Dec. 13, 1939; s. Bob and Evelyn Louise (Marsh) A.; m. Mary Kratzenstein, May 26, 1988; children: Susy, Chris, Brighton, Brandon. AA, El Camino Coll., Hawthorne, Calif., 1964; BA, Calif. State U., L.A., 1966, MA, 1967. Prof. art Humbolt State U., Arcata, Calif., 1967—, chmn. dept. art, 1985-90; chief reader advanced placement program studio art Ednl. Testing Svcs., Princeton, N.J., 1985-89. Search and rescue, disaster relief pilot Eureka (Calif.) Squadron 34, Calif. Wing CAP, 1990—. Office: Humbolt State U Art Dept Arcata CA 95521

ANDERSON, WYATT WHEATON, biology educator; b. New Orleans, Mar. 27, 1939; s. William Wyatt and Lottie (Johnson) A.; m. Margaret Ann Shugart, July 28, 1962; children: James Wyatt, Elizabeth Gail, Karen Lynn. BS, U. Ga., 1960, MS, 1962; PhD, Rockefeller U., 1967. Asst. prof. biology Yale U., New Haven, 1967-71, assoc. prof. biology, 1971-72; assoc. prof. zoology U. Ga., Athens, 1972-75, prof. zoology, 1975-80, prof. genetics, 1980-88, alumni found. disting. prof. genetics, 1988—, head genetics dept., 1980-87, dean Franklin Coll. Arts and Scis., 1992—; mem. panel population biology NSF, Washington, 1977-80. Contbr. articles to profl. jours. Served to capt. U.S. Army, 1967-69. Mem. NAS (chair population biology, evolution and ecology 1992—), Am. Genetic Assn. (pres. 1986-87), Am. Soc. Naturalists (pres. 1987), Soc. Study Evolution (v.p. 1981-82). Office: U Ga Office Dean Franklin Coll 310 New College Athens GA 30602-1732 also: U Ga Life Sci Bldg Dept Genetics Athens GA 30602*

ANDERSON, ZINA-DIANE, real estate executive; b. East Orange, N.J., Jan. 14, 1964; d. Sylvester Sr. Anderson and Barbara Ann (Anderson) Atlantic. Student, Essex County Coll., 1988. Counselor for homeless parents and children Isaiah House Shelter, East Orange, 1992-94; real estate adminstr. Anderson & Co., East Orange, 1994—; advocate Mental Health Assn., East Orange, 1992—. Candidate for county com., dist. #9 third ward Dem. Party, East Orange, 1996. Mem. NAFE (assoc.), Am. Mus. Natural History (assoc.), Smithsonian (assoc.). Baptist. Avocations: reading, writing, classical music. Office: Anderson & Co 111 Madonna Pl East Orange NJ 07018-2413

ANDERSON-SPIVY, ALEXANDRA, writer, editor; b. Boston, May 14, 1942; d. Henry and Marion Ruth (Thompson) Fuller; m. Samuel O.J. Spivy; children: Lafcadio, Genevieve, Oscar. BA, Sarah Lawrence Coll., 1961. Art editor Paris Rev., 1972-76, Village Voice, N.Y.C., 1973-76; features assoc. Vogue mag., N.Y.C., 1976-78; sr. editor Portfolio mag., N.Y.C., 1979-83; editor-in-chief Arts and Antiques mag., N.Y.C., 1983-85; exec. editor Am. Photographer, N.Y.C., 1985-87; arts editor Smart mag., N.Y.C., 1988-90; contbg. arts editor Esquire mag., N.Y.C., 1990-94; N.Y. editor The Argonaut, 1992-96; reviews editor The Art Jour., 1995—; editor-in-chief The Craftsman on CD-ROM, 1996—; projects editor Interactive Bur., 1996—; bd. dirs., mem. adv. bd. Franklin Furnace; bd. govs. Colby Coll. Art Mus.; profl. fellow Morgan Libr. Author: Anderson and Archer's SoHo: The Essential Guide to Art and Life in Lower Manhattan, 1979, Living With Art, 1988, Portraits of Olga, 1992, Keith Haring, Last Works, 1995, Gardens of Earthly Delight: The Art of Robert Kushner, 1997; mem. adv. bd. Rev. Mag., 1998—. Mem. exec. com. Mus. Modern Art, Contemporary Arts Coun. Recipient Art Critics' award NEA, 1978; Japan Found. travel grantee, 1976. Mem. Internat. Art Critics' Assn. (pres. Am. chpt. 1994-98).

ANDERSSON, ALLEN ARVID, computer scientist; b. Washington, Dec. 30, 1944; s. Arvid Ruben and Marie Elaine (Brandt) Anderson; m. Helen Kraus, Oct. 23, 1976; 1 child, Rachel Kraus. Grad., Phillips Acad., 1961; student, UCLA, 1966, Tufts U., 1968-69; BS in Mathematics, MIT, 1969, postgrad., 1970-74; postgrad., Harvard U., 1979. Restaurant proprietor Hyannis, Mass., 1961-64; assoc. prof. math. U. Nacional Autónoma de Honduras, Tegucigalpa, 1967; adj. prof. math. Facultad de Ingeniería, Comayagüela, Honduras, 1967; chmn. dept. math. Escuela Superior del Profesorado Francisco Morazán, Tegucigalpa, 1968; tchr. of English as 2d language Mary E. Curley Jr. High Sch., Boston, 1969; systems programmer John Hancock Mutual Life Ins. Co., Boston, 1969-70; computer scientist MIT Lab. for Nuclear Sci., Cambridge, 1970-76; mathematician Butler-Newton, Inc., Newton, Mass., 1977; software mgr. Atex, Inc., Bedford, Mass., 1978-80; pres. Software Decisions, Cambridge, 1980-81; founder, v.p. software devel., bd. dirs. Interleaf, Inc., Cambridge, 1981-83; dir. new products devel. Computer Consoles, Inc., Cambridge, 1984-86; founder, pres. Expert Image Systems, Inc., Somerville, Mass., 1986—; cons. on mgmt. of computer software devel., Academia de Ciencias, La Habana, Cuba, 1985, cons. on mktg. of computer software services, Instituto Nacional de Sistemas Automatizados y Técnicas de Computación, La Habana, 1985; bd. dirs. Expert Image Systems, Inc., Cambridge, 1986—. Contbr. articles on software devel.; creator of office pub. system for U.S. Supreme Ct., Interleaf desktop pub. system, pattern recognition software for bubble chamber physics research, internat. telephone network control system. Vol. U.S. Peace Corps, Tegucigalpa, 1966-68; counselor Boston Draft Resistance Group, Cambridge, 1969-70; cons. Cambridge Pub. Schs., 1979-80; cons. Cambridge Civic Assn., 1979; governing com., tchr. Centro Presente (orgn. for Cen. Am. refugees), 1983-84; campaign staff Mobilization for Survival, Cambridge, 1984. Home: 7501 Cayuga Ave Bethesda MD 20817-4821 Office: Expert Image Systems Inc 48 Baldwin Rd Tewksbury MA 01876-2406

ANDERSSON, CRAIG REMINGTON, retired chemical company executive; b. Winnipeg, Man., Can., June 16, 1937; came to U.S., 1937; s. Anders Einar and Doris (Pearson) A.; m. Dawn Marie Traver, June 13, 1959; children—Lee Erik, Karin Ingrid, Jon Kristien, Jenni Kate. B.S. in Chem. Engring., U. Minn., 1960; postgrad., U. Del., 1960-66. Researcher Sun Oil, 1960-67; v.p. ops. Custom Chems., Inc., 1967-68; Engr., supr. U.S. Steel Chems., Haverhill, Ohio, 1968-76; product mgr. U.S. Steel Chems., Pitts., 1976-80; gen. mgr. U.S. Steel Chems., Cin., 1980-82; v.p. U.S. Steel Chems., Pitts., 1982-85, pres., 1985-86; pres., chief operating officer Aristech Chem. Corp., Pitts., 1986-93; vice chmn. Aristech Chem. Co., Pitts., 1994-95; ret., 1995; cons.; bd. dirs. Albermarle Corp., RTI Internat. Metals, Inc., Duquesne U. Contbr. articles to profl. jours.; patentee in field. Mem. citizen's sponsoring com. Allegheny Conf. Cmty. Devel. Mem. AIChe, Alpha Chi Sigma. Lutheran. Avocations: golf; hunting; fishing; auto racing.

ANDERT, DAVID AUGUST, minister; b. Morris, Minn., Aug. 8, 1946; s. Audrew Bach and Bertha Clara (Huebner) A.; m. Anne Lee Graupner, July 31, 1982; children: Elizabeth, Katherine, Rebecca. Grad., Calif. Luth. Bible Sch., L.A., 1967; BA, U. Minn., 1970; MDiv, Luth. Northwestern Theol. Sem., St. Paul, 1974. Ordained to ministry, Evang. Luth. Ch. in Am., 1974. Assoc. pastor Normandale Luth. Ch., Edina, Minn., 1974-79; pastor Bethesda & Elim Luth. Chs., Carlton, Minn., 1979-88; sr. pastor Luth. Ch. of Good Shepherd, Duluth, Minn., 1988—; chmn., mem. ref. and counsel com. N.E. Minn. Synod, Duluth, 1987-91, consultation com., 1999—; mem. ch. coun. Evang. Luth. Ch. in Am., 1991-97; mem. NCCC-USA Gen. Assembly, 1996—. Mem. Minn. Coun. Chs. Office: Luth Ch Good Shepherd 45th Ave E & Colorado St Duluth MN 55804

ANDERT, JEFFREY NORMAN, clinical psychologist; b. Aberdeen, S.D., May 21, 1950; s. Norman Joseph and Irene Eleanor (Olson) A.; m. Diane Kay Dunham, May 29, 1971; Jason Ryan, Jonathan Erik, Justin Matthew. BA in Psychology, Augsburg Coll., 1971; MA in Psychology, Mankato (Minn.) State U., 1973; PhD in Psychology, U. So. Miss., 1976. Diplomate in Clin. Psychology Am. Bd. Profl. Psychology; lic. psychologist, Mich. Grad. asst. Mankato State U., Minn., 1972-73, U. So. Miss., Hattisburg, Miss., 1974-75; psychology intern Des Moines Child Guidance Ctr., Des Moines, 1975-76; clin. psychologist Battle Creek (Mich.) Child Guidance Clinic, 1976-80; pvt. practice Battle Creek, 1978—; pres., adminstrv. dir. Psychol. Cons. of Mich., P.C., Battle Creek, 1979—; administrv. dir. Chem. Dependency Resources, Battle Creek, 1982—; med. expert Office of Hearings and Appeals, Social Security Adminstrn., Lansing & Grand Rapids, Mich., 1986—. Contbr. articles to profl. jours. Trustee Lakeview Pub. Sch. Dist., Battle Creek, 1991—, pres. bd. trustees, 1995-97; adult leader Boy Scouts Am., Battle Creek, 1988-96. Disting. Svc. award, So. Cen. Mich. Substance Abuse Commn., Jackson, Mich., 1987. Fellow Acad. Clin. Psychology; mem. Am. Psychol. Assn., Mich. Psychol. Assn. (ethics com. 1997—), South Cen. Mich. Substance Abuse Program Dirs. Assn. (pres. 1986-87). Lutheran. Avocations: music, water sports, golf. E-mail: psychoconmi@aol.com. Home: 144 Waupakisco Bch Battle Creek MI 49015-3144 Office: Psychol Cons Mich PC 151 North Ave Battle Creek MI 49017-3467

ANDES, CHARLES LOVETT, direct marketing executive; b. Phila., Sept. 23, 1930; s. Charles Lovett and Gladys (Stead) A.; m. Dorothea Roberta Abbott, Aug. 25, 1961; children: Elizabeth, Susan, Karen, Page. Student, Swarthmore Coll., 1948-50; BA, Syracuse U., 1952. Pres. Adtech Industries, Phila., 1954-68; exec. v.p., dir. The Franklin Mint Corp., Franklin Ctr., Pa., 1969-73, pres., 1972-73, chmn. bd., CEO, 1973-85; chmn., CEO The Franklin Inst., Phila., 1985-91, chmn., 1991-93, chmn. emeritus, 1993—; pres., CEO Eastern Tech. Coun., 1991-95; chmn., CEO Interactive Mktg. Ventures, 1995-96; CEO Andes, Wickard, McClure, 1997—; chmn. The Andover Group, Plymouth Meeting, Pa., 1998—; ptnr. Tech. Leaders Venture Capital Fund; mem. Pa. Tech. Coun.; bd. dirs. Nat. Media Corp. Bd. dirs. Phila. Orch., Am. Music Theater Festival, Nat. Constn., Ctr., Penn Cancer Ctr., Pa. Acad. Fine Arts, Wistar Inst. Mem. Phila. Country Club, Union League, Merion Cricket Club, Johns Island (Fla.) Club. Presbyterian. Office: The McClure Group 600 W Germantown Pike Plymouth Meeting PA 19462-1046

ANDES, DERIEN ROMARIC, retired purchasing specialist; b. Cleve., Dec. 8, 1934; s. Ernest Lee and Dorothy Josephine (Martin) A.; m. Sheila Mary

Glynn, June 13, 1970; children: Kathleen, William, Christopher. BA, Cath. U. Am., 1957, postgrad., 1963-70. Travel counselor Am. Automobile Assn., Washington, N.C., 1955-65; rschr., writer, editor Am. Automobile Assn., Washington, 1965-71; pers. asst. N.J. Depts. Human Svcs. and Corrections, Trenton and Princeton, 1974-78; sr. pers. asst. The Richard Stockton Coll. N.J., Pomona, 1978-82, adminstrv. asst. to v.p., 1982-87, asst. buyer, 1987-99. Mem. Atlantic City Urban Area Transp. Coun., Atlantic County, N.J., 1982-92; candidate Pleasantville (N.J.) City Coun., 1986, Pleasantville Sch. Bd., 1981-83. With U.S. Army, 1958-60. Democrat. Roman Catholic. Avocations: choral singing, community theatre, genealogy. Home: 831 Linden Ave Pleasantville NJ 08232-1305

ANDES, LARRY DALE, minister; b. Warrenton, Va., June 7, 1947; s. William Christian and Hilda Elizabeth (Beach) A.; m. Bobbi E. Stephens, July 16, 1966; 1 child, Joshua Dale. BS in Pastoral Studies, North Ctrl. Bible Coll., 1970; student, U. Richmond, 1970, Bethel Theol. Sem., 1992. Ordained to ministry Assembly of God Ch., 1975, non-denominational, 1987. Assoc. pastor Calvary Assembly of God, Staunton, Va., 1971-72; youth min. Arlington (Va.) Assembly of God, 1972-75; assoc. pastor West End Assembly of God, Richmond, Va., 1975-76; founder, pres., festival dir. Fishnet Ministries Inc., Richmond, Front Royal, Va., 1976—; sr. pastor Fishnet Christian Ctr., Front Royal, 1992—. Named one of Outstanding Young Men of Am., 1984. Office: Fishnet Ministries Inc PO Box 1919 Front Royal VA 22630-1919

ANDES, PHOEBE CABOTAJE, women's health nurse, educator; b. Solano, Nueva Vizcaya, Philippines, Sept. 20, 1934; d. Adriano V. and Patricia Piggangay (Logan) Cabotaje; children: Edwin, Patricia. BSN, State U. of Philippines, 1956; student, NYU, 1959-61; MA, Columbia U., 1976. Exchange nurse Woman's Hosp.-St. Luke's, N.Y.C.; mem. faculty Far Eastern U., Manila; head nurse St. Elizabeth Hosp., Elizabeth, N.J.; assoc. prof. Middlesex County Coll., Edison, N.J., 1970-91; asst. prof. Passaic County C.C., Paterson, N.J., 1993-96; DON Valley Rest Nursing Home, 1996-98; spkr. in field. Mem. Coun. of Ministries, 1979-89, Wesley United Meth. Ch. Parebt Tchr. Student Assn. Adv. Coun., 1976-80; vol. homeless health fairs. Recipient Cmty. Leadership award Philippine-Am. Lions Club of N.Y., 1990, Outstanding Cmty. Leadership award Asian Am. Cultural Heritage Coun. of N.J., 1996; honored with a testimonial dinner dance for outstanding leadership Found. Philippine Am. Med. Soc. N.J., 1992; named grand marshall Philippine Independence Day Celebration, 1996. Mem. ANA, N.J. State Nurses Assn. (nurse of year 1988), Philippine Nurses Assn. Am. (founder, pres. 1982-84), Fedn. Philippine Socs. N.J. (pres. 1990-91), Asian Am. Polit. Coalition N.J. (pres. 1991-92), Found. Fedn. Philippine Socs. in N.J. (chairwoman 1993—), Philippine Nurses Assn. N.J. (founder, 1st pres.), U. of the Philippines Nursing Alumni Assn. of the East Coast (founding pres. 1988-92), U. of the Philippines Alumni Assn. of N.J. (pres. 1984-86), N.J. State Bd. Nursing, Sigma Theta Tau. Democrat.

ANDEWELT, ROGER B., federal judge; b. 1946. Judge U.S. Ct. of Federal Claims, Washington, 1987—. Office: US Ct of Federal Claims 717 Madison Pl NW Washington DC 20005-1011*

ANDOLINA, LAWRENCE J., lawyer; b. Rochester, N.Y., Apr. 27, 1948; s. Michael Carl and Nina (Formicola) A.; m. Sharon Jean Cemino, Sept. 22, 1973; children: Lindsay, Lauren. BA, Boston Coll., 1970; JD, Albany Law Sch., 1974. Bar: N.Y. 1975, U.S. Dist. Ct. (we. dist.) N.Y. 1976 (no. dist.) 1995, U.S. Ct. Appeals 1980 (2nd cir.). Asst. dist. atty. Monroe County (N.Y.) Dist. Atty. Office, Rochester, 1975-78; atty., assoc. Palmiere, Passero & Crimi, Rochester, 1978-80; atty., ptnr. Affronti, Jesserer, Andolina & Lamb, Rochester, 1980-85, Jesserer, Andolina & Lamb, 1985-87, Jesserer & Andolina, 1987, Harris, Beach & Wilcox, Rochester, 1988—. Mem. Nat. Assn. Crim. Def. Lawyers, New York State Assn. Crim. Def. Lawyers, Monroe County Bar Assn. (past pres. 1991-92). Office: Trevett Lenweaver & Salzer 16 E Main St Rochester NY 14614

ANDOLSEN, ALAN ANTHONY, management consultant; b. Cleve., Feb. 19, 1943; s. Lloyd Anthony and Helen Mae (Kozinski) A.; m. Barbara Hilkert, Jan. 20, 1968; children: Daniel, Ruth. AB magna cum laude, Borromeo Coll., 1964; MA, U. Dayton, 1967; postgrad., Vanderbilt U., 1967-69. Cert. mgmt. cons.; cert. records mgr. V.p. Bergamo East, Marcy, N.Y., 1969-71; dir. Met. Health Dept., Nashville, 1971-76; prin. Naremco Svc., Inc., N.Y.C., 1976-79, v.p., 1979-86, pres., 1986—; bd. dirs. Coun. of Cons. Orgns., N.Y.C., Assn. Mgmt. Cons. Firms. Editor: Management Consulting-A Model Course, 1989, 96; contbr. articles to profl. jours. Mem. Inst. Mgmt. Cons., Assn. Records Mgrs. and Adminstrs., Assn. Image and Info. Mgmt., Am. Mensa Ltd. Roman Catholic. Avocations: music, cycling, reading. Office: Naremco Svcs Inc 60 E 42nd St New York NY 10165-0006*

ANDORFER, DONALD JOSEPH, university president; b. Ft. Wayne, Ind., Dec. 31, 1937; s. Joseph and Cecil J. (Minich) A.; married Dec. 26, 1960; children: Susan, Joseph, Barbara. BS in Edn., Ball State U., 1960, MA in Edn., 1965; LLD (hon.), Tiffin U., 1989. Instr. Internat. Jr. Coll. Bus., Ft. Wayne, 1960-70, dean, dir., 1971-77; controller Ind. Inst. Tech., Ft. Wayne, 1978-81, v.p. fin., 1982-85, pres., 1985—. Mem. acad. com. Luth. Hosp. Bd., 1989-93; bd. dirs. Robert Morris Coll., Chgo., 1985—; bd. dirs. Ind. Pub. Broadcasting. Mem. Ind. Colls. Ind. (bd. dirs., chmn. 1994), Nat. Assn. Ind. Colls. and Univs., Nat. Assn. Ind. Athletics (nat. coun. pres. 1991-94), Ft. Wayne C. of C., Ind. Bus. Edn. Assn. (pres. 1980-81), Future Bus. Leaders Am. (bd. dirs. Outstanding Bus. Person for Ind. award 1981), Rotary (bd. dirs., v.p. 1994, pres.-elect 1995, pres. 1996, Paul Harris fellow 1998), Delta Pi Epsilon. Roman Catholic. Avocations: golf, fishing, spectator sports. Home: 15423 Connors Rd Fort Wayne IN 46819-9720 Office: Ind Inst of Tech Office of the President 1600 E Washington Blvd Fort Wayne IN 46803-1228

ANDORKA, FRANK HENRY, lawyer; b. Lorain, Ohio, July 25, 1946; s. Frank Henry and Sue (Parham) A.; m. M. Jean Deliman, Aug. 10, 1968; children: Frank Henry Jr., Claire E. AB, Ohio U., 1968; postgrad., Ind. U., 1968-69; JD, Cornell U., 1975. Bar: Ohio 1975, U.S. Dist. Ct. (no. dist.) Ohio 1975. From assoc. to ptnr. Baker & Hostetler, Cleve., 1975—. Author: A Practical Guide to Copyrights and Trademarks, 1989, What is a Copyright?, 1992. Served to 1st lt. U.S. Army, 1969-72. Mem. ABA (chmn. internat. copyright laws and treaties com. 1984-86, chmn. govt. rels. to copyright com. 1986-88, chmn. broadcasting, sound rec. and performing artists com. 1988-90, chmn. divsn. III copyrights 1990-92, chmn. divsn. IX publs. 1992-93), Ohio Bar Assn., Greater Cleve. Bar Assn. Avocations: bowling, tennis. Home: 31000 Clinton Dr Cleveland OH 44140-1500 Office: Baker & Hostetler 3200 Nat City Ctr 1900 E 9th St Cleveland OH 44114-3475

ANDRADE, EDNA, artist, art educator; b. Portsmouth, Va.; d. Thomas Judson and Ruth (Porter) Wright; m. C. Preston Andrade, Jr., July 12, 1941 (div. 1960). BFA, Pa. Acad. Fine Arts/U. Pa., 1937. Supr. art elem. schs. Norfolk, Va., 1938-39; instr. drawing and painting Newcomb Art Sch., Tulane U., 1939-41; lectr. U. N.Mex., 1971; prof. Phila. Coll. Art, 1959-72, 73-82, prof. emeritus, 1982—; prof. art Temple U., 1972-73; adj. prof. art Ariz. State U., 1986—; critic Pa. Acad. Fine Arts, 1988, 89. Artist, designer, OSS, 1942-44, free-lance designer, Washington, 1944-46, free-lance painter, designer, muralist, Phila. and, N.Y.C., 1946—, artist-in-residence, Hartford Sch. Art and Tamarind Inst., 1971, U. Sask., Can., 1977, U. Zulia, Maracaibo, Venezuela, 1980, Ariz. State U., Tempe, 1981, 83, Fabric Workshop, Phila., 1984, Hollins Coll., Va., 1985; vis. artist, Skidmore Coll., 1973, 74, one-woman shows, E. Hampton Gallery, N.Y.C., Peale Galleries Pa. Acad., Rutgers U., U. Hartford, Marian Locks Gallery, Phila., Hollins Coll., 1985; retrospective Pa. Acad. Fine Arts, 1993; group shows include AAAL, In This Acad., Pa. Acad. Fine Arts, Phila., William Penn Meml. Mus., Harrisburg, Three Centuries Am. Art, Phila. Collects Art Since 1940, Phila. Mus. Art, Bklyn. Mus., Ft. Worth Art Center, Des Moines Art Center, Philbrook Art Center, Tulsa, Contemporary Phila. Artists, 1990, Phila. Mus. Art, Artists Choose Artists, Inst. of Contemporary Art, Phila., 1991, others; represented in permanent collections, Phila. Mus. Art, Pa. Acad. Fine Arts, Print Club, Balt. Mus. Art, Addison Gallery Am. Art, McNay Art Inst., San Antonio, Montclair (N.J.) Art Mus., Nat. Collection Fine Arts, Library of Congress, USIA, Albright-Knox Art Gallery, Buffalo, Tamarind Collection, U. N.Mex. Mus., Woodmere Art Mus., Phila., Yale Art Gallery, Atlantic Richfield, Phila., Am. Telephone & Telegraph Co., Bell of Pa., Phila., Fed. Res. Bank, Phila., Price-Waterhouse, Phila., Edwin A. Ulrich Mus. Wichita State U., Pepsi-Cola, Leeway Found., Phila., Please Touch Mus., Phila. Mem. Mayor's Cultural Adv. Council, Phila., 1984-85. Recipient 1st and 2d Cresson European Traveling scholarships Pa. Acad., 1936, 37, Eyre medal Phila. Water Color Club, 1968, Mary Smith prize Pa. Acad. Fine Arts, 1968, Childe Hassam Meml. purchases AAAL, 1967, 68, Merit award Pa., 1971, Hazlett Meml. award in arts, 1980, Honor award Women's Caucus for Art, 1983, Hunt award visual arts Phila. Women's Way, 1984, Roland Gallimore Meml. award Interior Design Coun., Phila. Mayor's Arts and Culture award, 1991, Founders award Samuel S. Fleisher Art Meml., 1993. Mem. Fellowship of Pa. Acad. Fine Arts, Coll. Art Assn. (Disting. Tchr. of Art award 1996).

ANDRADE, JOSEPH J., III, counselor, educator; b. Salem, N.J., Apr. 17, 1957; s. Joseph T. Jr. and Clara B. (Stanton) A.; m. Katrina P. Andrade, May 21, 1957. BA, U. N.Mex., 1981; MS, Calif. State U., Sacramento, 1986. Lic. profl. clin. counselor, N.Mex.; nat. cert. counselor. Testing svcs. asst. Brookdale C.C., Lincroft, N.J., 1982-83; counseling intern Calif. State U., Sacramento, 1983-86; counselor Salisbury (Md.) State U., 1987-89, asst. dir., 1989-91; sr. counselor U. N.Mex., Albuquerque, 1992—; mem. steering com. Human Svcs. Collaborative, Albuquerque, 1994-96, chmn. suspension task force, 1995-96; mem. adv. bd. Highland H.S., Albuquerque, 1994-96, Van Buren Mid. Sch., Albuquerque, 1994-96; mem. faculty depts. comm., psychology, gen. studies, sociology and health sci. U. Phoenix, 1994—. Mem. ACA, Am. Coll. Counselors Assn., N.Mex. Counseling Assn., N.Mex. Mental Health Counselors Assn. Avocations: golf, tennis, literature, billiards, cooking. Office: U NMex Programs for Children 2600 Marble Ave NE Albuquerque NM 87106-2721

ANDRADE, MANUELA PESTANA, art educator; b. South Rogue, Portugal, Oct. 10, 1937; d. Silvestre and Eulalia (Bieira Da Luz) P.; m. Manuel Cristao, Jan. 11, 1956 (dec. May 1970); 1 child, Maria Pestana Goldstein; m. Antoni Pedro Rapazote (div. Feb. 1977); 1 child, Antonio Pedro; m. Virgil Sousa Andrade, July 15, 1986. BA, U. Porto, Portugal, 1978, 82, MA, 1980, 84. Tchr. Externato liceal de Moncao, Portugal, 1971-74, Ministry Edn., Portugal, 1971-87; dept. head Prep. Sch. Ermialindo, Portugal, 1981-82, 83-84, master tchr., 1984-85, 86; tchr. Portuguese United Edn. Sch., 1987—, ednl. dir., 1988—. *Manuela Pestana Andrade was born on Madeira Island. Her life has been dedicated to Poetry and the Plastic and Graphic Arts. She has Master's Degrees from the University of Oporto in Plastics Arts, in Painting and Sculpture, and in Design/Graphic Arts. She won a scholarship, during five years from the Calouste Gulbenkian Foundation in Portugal. She had received many awards and honorable mentions in literary and artistic competitions. Many of her works can be found in international and national museums and private collections in Portugal, Spain, Italy, France, Switzerland, Germany, England, Sweden, Denmark, Australia, Venezuela, South Korea, Japan, Brazil, Canada and the United States.* Author of poems; one-woman shows include Ctr. Internat. D'Art Contemporain, Paris, 1984, Funchal, Madeira, Portugal, 1984, Fall River (Mass.) Art Assn., 1988, Heritage Park, Fall River, 1988, Pilgrim Soc., Plymouth, Mass., 1989, Portuguese Am. Fedn. 25th Anniversary Festival, Bristol, R.I., 1990, Bentley Coll., Waltham, Mass., 1992, Portuguese Am. Women's Assn., Providence, 1998, Newport (R.I.) Art Mus., 1999; represented in permanent collections Nat. Kunsan U., South Korea, Calouste Gulbenkian Found., Portugal. Mem. Portuguese-Am. Bus. Assn., Portuguese-Am. Fedn., Nat. Soc. Fine Arts, Nat. Trust Historic Preservation, Casa da Madeira Norte, Portuguese Tchrs. Assn., Fall River Assn.,. Home: 27 Alfred St Fall River MA 02721

ANDRADE, WILLIAM THOMAS, professional golfer; b. Bristol, R.I., Jan. 25, 1964; m. Jody Andrade; children: Cameron James, Grace. BA in Sociology, Wake Forest U., 1987. Mem. Jr. World Cup Championship Team, 1981, World Amateur Championship Team, 1986, Walker Cup Championship Team, 1987; winner Kemper Open (PGA Tour), 1991, Buick Classic (PGA Tour), 1991, Bell Can. Open (PGA Tour), 1998; mem. PGA Tour Charity Team, THE TOUR Championship, 1999; co-host CVS Charity Classic, R.I., 1999. Co-organizer Billy Andrade/Brad Faxon Charities for Children, R.I. and Mass., 1991—. Office: c/o PGA Box 109601 100 Ave of Champions Palm Beach Gardens FL 33410*

ANDRAKO, JOHN, health sciences educator; b. Perth Amboy, N.J., Jan. 19, 1924; s. Charles and Helen (Turjanitsa) A.; m. Ruth Augusta Whitt, June 26, 1948 (dec. Oct. 19, 1973); children: John David, Diane Carol Shasky, Susan Elizabeth Heiligman; m. Wanda Jean Schutt Barth, Nov. 22, 1978. BS, Rutgers U., 1947, MS, 1949; PhD, U. N.C., 1953. Lic. pharmacist, Va. Teaching fellow in chemistry Rutgers U. Coll. Pharmacy, New Brunswick, N.J., 1947-49; instr. Sch. of Pharmacy U. N.C., Chapel Hill, 1949-53, asst. prof. Sch. of Pharmacy, 1953-55, assoc. prof. Sch. of Pharmacy, 1955-56; assoc. prof. Sch. of Pharmacy Med. Coll. of Va., Va. Commonwealth U., Richmond, 1956-62, prof. medicinal chemistry, 1962-91, asst. dean Sch. of Pharmacy, asst. v.p. for health scis., 1965-73, 73-75, asst. provost for acad. and profl. affairs, acad. planning, 1975-78, asst. v.p., assoc. v.p. for health scis., 1978-82, 82-92, interim v.p. for health scis., 1988-91; prof. emeritus Sch. Pharmacy, 1991; sr. advisor Inst. Structural Biology & Drug Discovery Va. Commonwealth U., 1996—. Contbr. articles to profl. jours. Sun. sch. tchr. St. Matthew's Episcopal Ch., 1960-69, mem. vestry 1963-67, 75-78). Recipient Ciba Teaching fellowship Rutgers U., 1947-49, Presdl. medallion Va. Commonwealth U., 1992; named Am. Found. for Pharm. Edn. Summer fellow U. N.C., 1949-50, vis. scientist Am. Assn. Colls. of Pharmacy and NSF, 1963-64; grantee NIH, 1962-66, 67-72, NIGMS, 1962-66, 67-72, Bur. of Health Manpower, 1979-82, 85-88, 88-91, Statewide Va. Health Edn. Ctr., 1990-91. Mem. Am. Pharm. Assn., Am. Pharm. Assn. Acad. Pharm. Scis., Am. Chem. Soc. (medicinal chemistry divsn.), Va. Pharm. Assn., Am. Assn. Colls. Pharmacy Coun. Faculties and Coun. Sects., Va. Orchid Soc. (pres. 1984-86, newsletter editor 1993-96), Rotary (med. svc. com. Richmond 1972-78, chmn. 1973-74), Rho Chi Soc., Sigma Xi, Alpha Sigma Chi, Kappa Psi Pharm. Frat. Episcopalian. Avocation: orchid culture. Home: 1970 Albion Rd Midlothian VA 23113-4147

ANDRASICK, JAMES STEPHEN, agribusiness company executive; b. Passaic, N.J., Mar. 27, 1944; s. Stephen Adam and Emily (Spolnik) A.; children: Christopher J., Gregory O.; m. Ginger Michael Simon, Feb. 22, 1997. BS, USCG Acad., 1965; MS, MIT, 1971. Commd. ensign USCG, 1965, advanced through grades to lt., 1968; assigned to Vietnam, 1967-68; resigned, 1969; sys. analyst Jamesbury Corp., 1970; corp. fin. and product devel. staffs Ford Motor Co., 1971-74; mgr. corp. devel. IU Internat. Corp., Phila., 1974-78; from v.p. planning, contr. to exec. v.p. C. Brewer & Co., Ltd., Honolulu, 1978-92, pres., 1992—, also bd. dirs.; chmn. bd., mng. gen. ptnr. ML Macadamia Orchards LP, 1986-88; chmn. bd. HCPC, Olokele Sugar Co., Hawaiian Sugar and Transp. Coop., 1993-96; chmn. Hawaiian Sugar Planters Assn., 1992-93; bd. dirs. Wailuku Agribus. Co. Bd. dirs. Aloha United Way, Honolulu, 1983-89; treas., bd. dirs. ARC, Hawaii, 1983-94, 96—, chmn., 1989-90; bd. dirs. Hawaii Employers Coun., 1992-98, chmn., 1995-98; trustee UH Found., 1988-94, vice chmn., 1992-93, chmn., 1993-94; trustee Hawaii Maritime Ctr., 1993-98; bd. dirs. Coast Guard Found., chmn., 1994. Office: C Brewer & Co Ltd PO Box 1826 Papaikou HI 96781-1826

ANDRASSY, TIMOTHY FRANCIS, trade association executive; b. Cleve., Feb. 13, 1948; s. Robert Steven and Matilda A.; m. Grace Elizabeth Wills, Jan. 3, 1970; children—Timothy Francis, Courtney, Alyson. BS, John Carroll U., Cleve., 1970. Assoc. producer, prodn. asst. Sta. WKBF-TV, Cleve., 1968-69; asst. dir. public rels. Thistledown Racing Club, North Randall, Ohio, 1969-70; dir. promotions and community rels. Thistledown Racing Club, 1976-77; asst. to pres. Gaffney Advt., Mentor, Ohio, 1970-71; stadium mgr., dir. broadcast ops. Cleve. Indians Profl. Baseball Club, 1971-74; mgr. communications Am. Soc. Metals, Metals Park, Ohio, 1974-76; exec. dir. Assn. Steel Distbrs., Cleve., 1977-81; v.p. Steel Svc. Ctr. Inst., Cleve., 1981-92; exec. dir. Steel Tube Inst. N.Am., Cleve., 1992—; mem. adv. coun. Cleve. Conv. Ctr. Dir. community rels. Geauga County Bi-Centennial Organizing Com., 1975-76. Mem. Am. Soc. Assn. Execs., Meeting Planners Internat., Greater Cleve. Growth Assn. (v.p. bd. dirs.), Greater Cleve. Soc. Assn. Execs., Downtown Euclid Assn., Walt Disney World Council of Advisors. Home: 8341 Twin Creek Ct Mentor OH 44060-8617 Office: 8500 Station St Ste 270 Mentor OH 44060-4970

ANDRAU, MAYA HEDDA, physical therapist; b. Digboi, Assam, India, Apr. 15, 1936; came to U.S., 1946; d. William Henry and Klara Irén Judit (Sima) Andrau; married, Sept. 1971 (div. July 1989); children: Francis Meher Traver, Darwin Meher Traver. BS in Phys. Therapy, Columbia U., 1958; MA in Social Anthropology, NYU, 1966. Lamaze cert. childbirth educator; lic. and registered phys. therapist. Phy. therapist Beekman-Downtown Hosp., N.Y.C., 1959-60; physiotherapist Stamford (Conn.) Hosp., 1963-64, Benedictine Hosp., Kingston, N.Y., 1966-69; pvt. practice in phys. therapy and lamaze Woodstock, N.Y., 1968-71; chief phy. therapist No. Duchess Hosp., Rhinebeck, N.Y., 1970-71; phy. therapist Waccamaw Pub. Health Dist., S.C. Dept. Health, Myrtle Beach, 1982-84; pain clinic specialist Pain Therapy Ctr. of Columbia (S.C.), Richland Meml. Hosp., 1986-87; phy. therapist Comprehensive Med. Rehab. Ctr., Conway, S.C., 1988-92; phys. therapist, instr. conditioning program Pawleys Island (S.C.) Wellness Inst., 1993; phys. therapist Total Care, Inc., N. Myrtle Beach, S.C., 1993-97; instr. phys. conditioning and therapeutic exercise courses, 1980-97; instr. conditioning program Health Focus Brief for TV, 1990; pvt. phys. therapist and instr. Conditioning-Wellness Program, UNCA (Coll. for Srs.), Asheville, N.C., 1998, Asheville-Buncombe Tech. C.C., 1999, Blue Ridge C.C., Flat Rock, N.C., 1999. Mem. Meher Spiritual Ctr., Inc., Alpha Kappa Delta. Follower of Avatar Meher Baba. Avocations: gardening, reading, swimming, handwork, singing.

ANDRE, CARL, sculptor; b. Quincy, Mass., Sept. 16, 1935; s. George Hans and Margaret Andre. Represented in public collections, Tate Gallery, London, Mus. Modern Art, N.Y.C., Rose Art Mus., Brandeis U., Columbus (Ohio) Gallery Fine Arts, Walker Art Center, Mpls., Milw. Art Center, La Jolla (Calif.) Mus. Contemporary Art, Dayton (Ohio) Art Inst., Albright-Knox Art Gallery, Buffalo, Monchengladbach Mus., Germany, Wallraf-Richartz Mus., Cologne, Haus Lange Mus., Krefeld, Germany, Kunstmus. Basel, Switzerland, Hessisches Landesmus., Darmstadt, Germany, Stedelijk Mus., Amsterdam, Van Abbe Mus., Eindhoven, Netherlands, Art Soc. Ghent, Belgium, Art Inst. Chgo., Los Angeles County Mus. Art, Musée Nat. d'Art Moderne, Paris, Carnegie Inst Mus. Art, Pitts., Musèo de Arte Moderno, Bogota, Colombia, Seattle Art Mus., High Mus. Art, Atlanta, Ohio State U. Gallery Fine Art, Bayerischen Staatsgemäldesammlungen, Munich, Kröller-Müller Mus., Otterlo, Netherlands, Detroit Inst. Arts, Guggenheim Mus., N.Y.C., City of Hartford, Conn., Mus. Boymans-van Beuningen, Rotterdam, Netherlands. Home: Cooper Sta PO Box 1001 New York NY 10276-1001 also: Paula Cooper 534 W 21st St New York NY 10011-2812 also: Konrad Fischer, Platanenstr 7, Düsseldorf 40233, Germany

ANDRE, L. AUMUND, management consultant; b. Marquette, Kans., Dec. 21, 1916; s. Anders and Lillian Amanda (Johnson) A.; m. Elsie Viola (Nelson), June 1, 1941 (dec. Feb. 1986); children: Carolyn Aleda, Denise Ardis; m. Phyllis Jean Richter-Russo, Sept. 17, 1988. BS, CUNY, 1939; postgrad., Columbia U., 1940-41, George Williams Coll., 1947. Youth program dir. various YMCAs, N.Y.C., Syracuse, Chgo., 1939-51; exec. dir. YMCA Met. Chgo., 1951-65; sr. v.p. Cen. YMCA Coll., Chgo., 1965-80; pvt. practice cons. Chgo., 1980-96; ret., 1997; instr. Sch. Edn. Syracuse (N.Y.) U., 1941-44; adj. prof. George William Coll., Chgo., 1948-55; lectr. Northwestern U., Evanston, Ill., 1978-80. Author: So Now You Are a Fund Raiser, 1977, Boys and Dogs Have Right of Way, 1987; author poetry; contbr. articles to profl. jours. Mem. county com. Am. Labor Party, Syracuse, 1943; chmn. Northwest Community Coun., 1954-56, Citizens Com. to Establish Triton Coll., River Grove, Ill., 1962-64; advisor Ill. Atty. Gen. Commn. to Study Fund Raising Laws and Enforcement., 1980. Named Father of Year Chgo. Area Father's Day Coun., 1962; recipient Svc. to Youth award, Lincolnland Assn. Profl Dirs. (YMCA), 1977. Mem. Nat. Soc. Fund Raising Execs. (officer , dir. 1968-79, Founder's award 1980). Democrat. Lutheran. Avocations: reading, music, traveling, writing poetry. Home and Office: 224 N Kenilworth Ave Oak Park IL 60302-2079

ANDRE, (KENNETH) MICHAEL, editor, publisher, writer; b. Halifax, N.S., Can., Aug. 31, 1946; s. Kenneth Bailey and Kathleen Mary (Warburton) A.; m. Erika Rothenberg, 1974 (div. 1983); m. Jane Adler (div. 1995); 1 child, Benjamin Eyton. BA, McGill U., 1968; MA, U. Chgo., 1969; PhD, Columbia U., 1973. Lectr. CCNY, N.Y.C., 1973, Baruch Coll., N.Y.C., 1974; editorial assoc. Art News, N.Y.C., 1973-77; treas. SoHo Baroque Opera Co., N.Y.C., 1980—; exec. dir. Unmuzzled Ox, N.Y.C., 1971—. Author: Experiments in Banal Living. Grantee Nat. Endowment Arts, Coordinating Coun. Lit. Mags., N.Y. State Coun. on Arts; grad. fellow Can. Coun. Fellow PEN; mem. MLA. Office: Unmuzzled Ox 105 Hudson St New York NY 10013-2331

ANDRE, MICHAEL PAUL, physicist, educator; b. Des Moines, Apr. 25, 1951; s. Paul Leo and Pauline (Vermie) A.; m. Janice Joan Hanecak, Mar. 12, 1988. BA, Cen. U. Iowa, 1972; postgrad., U. Ariz., 1972-73; MS, UCLA, 1975, PhD, 1980. Rsch. assoc. Inst. Atmospheric Physics, Tucson, Ariz., 1972-73; mem. tech. staff Hughes Aircraft Co., L.A., 1973-74; postgrad. researcher UCLA, 1974-77; cons. L.A., 1975-84; med. radiologic physicist LACO/UCLA Olive View, L.A., 1977-81; sr. radiation physicist Cedars-Sinai Med. Ctr., L.A., 1979-84; chief med. physicist Dept. Vet. Affairs, San Diego, 1981—; prof. radiology, chief divsn.Physics and Engring, sch. medicine U. Calif., La Jolla, 1981—; chief scientific officer Radco Corp., 1996—; qualified expert Calif. Radiol. Health Dept., Berkeley, 1979—; chmn. Nat. Physics Conf., San Diego, 1984-89. Editor: Physics and Biology of Radiology, 1988, Investigative Radiology, 1990—; guest editor: Internat. Jour. Imaging Sci. & Tech., 1997; contbr. articles to profl. jours. Mountain guide Sierra Club, L.A., 1977-80; dir. Ariz. PIRG, Tucson, 1973; mountain guide Am. Alpine Inst., Peru, 1987-90. Rsch. grantee U. Calif.-San Diego Found., 1989—, NIH,, Nat. Cancer Inst., 1986—, VA, 1989—, U.S. Army, 1994—. Mem. Am. Assn. Physicists in Medicine, Am. Inst. Ultrasound in Medicine, San Diego Radiol. Soc., Am. Inst. Physics, Soc. Photo-Optical Inst. Engrs. Avocation: Himalayan and Andean expeditions. Office: U Calif Dept Radiology 9114 La Jolla CA 92093

ANDRE, PAMELA Q. J., library director; b. Lewiston, Maine, Sept. 29, 1942; d. Charles Custer and Wilma (Hall) Quimby; m. Ronald E. Jensen, Dec. 26, 1966 (div. 1971); children: Stacy, Jaylyn; m. James Roch Andre, Mar. 3, 1973; 1 child, Brett. BA, U. N.H., 1964; MLS, U. Md., 1969. Computer programm U.S. Navy Dept., Washington, 1964-66; computer systems analyst Libr. Congress, Washington, 1968-81, asst. chief MARC editorial div., 1981-84; assoc. dir. for automation Nat. Agrl. Libr., USDA, Beltsville, Md., 1984-94, dir., 1994—; cons. UN FAO Hdqrs., Rome, 1989, Egyptian Nat. Agrl. Libr., Cairo, 1990. Mem. editorial bd. Libr. Hi Tech, 1989—, Internet Rsch.: Electronic Networking Applications and Policy, 1991—, Microcomputers for Information Management, 1993—; contbr. articles to jours. in field. Recipient Superior Svc. award USDA, 1990. Mem. ALA, IAALD. Office: US Dept Agriculture Nat Agrl Libr 10301 Baltimore Ave Beltsville MD 20705-2326*

ANDRE, RAE, writer, organizational behavior educator; b. Doylestown, Pa., Feb. 11, 1946; d. Thomas J. and Juanita (Birch A.; 1 child, Megan. BA cum laude, Cornell U., 1967; MA, UCLA, 1969; PhD, U. Mich., 1980. Project dir. UCLA/Am. Film Inst., 1967-69; account exec. and copywriter MCA, Inc., L.A., 1969-71; tchg. fellow U. Mich., Ann Arbor, 1975-78, lectr., 1978-79; asst. prof. GM Inst., Flint, Mich., 1979-82; prof. orgnl. behavior and theory Northeastern U., Boston, 1982—; cons. Internal Labor Office, U.s. Dept. Labor, GM Corp., New Eng. Telephone; visiting prof. U. Waikato, Hamilton, New Zealand, 1996, U. Pitts. Semester at Sea, 1996. Author: Homemakers, The Forgotten Workers, 1980 (Best Trade Book of Yr. award Chgo. Women in Pub. 1981), The 59 Second Employee: How to Stay One Second Ahead of Your One-Minute Manager, 1984, Positive Solitude, 1991; co-editor (with Peter J. Frost) Researchers Hooked on Teaching, 1996; contbr. over 40 articles to profl. jours. Former bd. dirs. Minerva Edn. Inst. Nat. Inst. Occupational Safety and Health. Top 200 nat. bestselling trade paperback 1983; Ford Found. Grant for continuing edn. of women, 1977. Mem. Acad. Mgmt., Authors Guild, Orgnl. Behavior Teaching Soc. (former bd. dirs.). Home: 36 Liberty Ave Lexington MA 02420-3445 Office: Northeastern U 360 Huntington Ave Boston MA 02115-5000 Address: 6611 SW Thistle Ter Palm City FL 34990-3852

ANDREA, JOYCE JOYCE See ROTHENBERG, JOYCE ANDREA

ANDREANO, RALPH LOUIS, economist, educator; b. Waterbury, Conn., Apr. 11, 1929; s. John and Loretta (Creasia) A.; m. Carol Jean Wessbecher, Sept. 5, 1955; children: Maria Carol, Nicholas George. A.B., Drury Coll., 1952; M.A., Washington U., St. Louis, 1955; M.A. Fulbright scholar, U. Oslo, Norway, 1952-53; Ph.D., Northwestern U., 1961. Instr. econs. Northwestern U., 1959-60; asst. prof. econs. Earlham Coll., 1961, asso. prof., chmn. dept., 1962-65; asst. prof. bus. adminstrn. Harvard Bus. Sch., 1961-62; Brookings Nat. Research prof., 1964-65; asso. prof. econs., dir. undergrad. program econs. U. Wis., 1965-67, prof., 1967—, dir. Health Econs. Research Ctr., 1969-87, chmn. dept. econs., 1980-83, dir. Ctr. for Devel.; emeritus prof. econs., 1994—; ofcl. del. Am. Econ. Assn. to Am. Council Learned Socs., 1964-70; adminstr. Div. Health State of Wis., 1976-78; economist WHO, Geneva, 1973-74. Author: (with H.F. Williamson and others) A History of American Petroleum Industry, 2 vols., 1959, 63, No Joy in Mudville: The Dilemma of Major League Baseball, 1965, Student Economists Handbook, 1967, (with B.A. Weisbrod and others) Disease and Economic Development, 1973, (with B.A. Weisbrod) American Health Policy, 1973; editor, author: New Views on American Economic Development, 1965; editor: Economic Impact of the Civil War, 1963, rev., 1967, The New Economic History: Papers on Methodology, 1971, (with J. Siegfried) Economics of Crime, 1981; editor, founder: Explorations in Entrepreneurial History, 2d series, 1963-71, Explorations in Economic History 1971-78; editor: Jour. Econ. History, 1974-75; sr. editor (econs.): Social Sci. and Medicine, 1983-87; contbr. articles to profl. jours. Ford Faculty Research fellow, 1968-69. Mem. Inst. Medicine of Nat. Acad. Scis. Home: 1815 Vilas Ave Madison WI 53711-2231

ANDREAS, DAVID LOWELL, banker; b. St. Paul, Minn., Mar. 1, 1949; s. Lowell Willard and Nadine B. (Hamilton) A.; m. Debra Kelley, June 20, 1985; 2 children. BA, U. Denver, 1971; MA, Mankato State U., 1976. Credit mgmt. trainee United Calif. Bank, Los Angeles, 1976-77; comml. loan officer Nat. City Bank of Mpls., 1977-80; from v.p., sr. vp., to chmn., chief exec. officer Nat. City Bancorp., Mpls., 1980—; chmn. ADAPA, Inc., Mpls., 1986-93; chmn. bd. Nat. City Bank, Mpls., 1991-94; pres., CEO Nat. City Bank, Mpls., 1994—. Mem. adv. bd. Mpls. Jr. League; mem. exec. com., dir. Children's Heart Link, 1988—, Minn. Ctr. Corp. Responsibility, Mankato U. Coll. Bus. Adv. Coun.; trustee Breck Sch., Golden Valley, Minn., 1997, Mpls. Coll. Art and Design. With U.S. Army, 1971-73. Mem. Mpls. Club. Avocations: skiing, running. Office: Nat City Bancorp 651 Nicollet Mall Minneapolis MN 55402-1636*

ANDREAS, DWAYNE ORVILLE, business executive; b. Worthington, Minn., Mar. 4, 1918; s. Reuben P. and Lydia (Stoltz) A.; m. Bertha Benedict, 1938 (div.); 1 dau., Sandra Ann Andreas McMurtie; m. Dorothy Inez Snyder, Dec. 21, 1947; children: TerryLynn, Michael D. Student, Wheaton (Ill.) Coll., 1935-36; hon. degree, Barry U. V.p., dir. Honeymead Products Co., Cedar Rapids, Iowa, 1936-46; chmn. bd., chief exec. officer Honeymead Products Co. (now Nat. City Bancorp.), Mankato, Minn., 1952-72; v.p. Cargill, Inc., Mpls., 1946-52; exec. v.p. Farmers Union Grain Terminal Assn., St. Paul, 1960-66; chmn. bd., chief exec. officer Archer-Daniels-Midland Co., Decatur, Ill., 1970-97, chmn. bd., 1997-98, chmn. emeritus, 1999—; bd. dirs. Hollinger Internat. Inc.; mem. Pres.'s Gen. Adv. Commn. of Fgn. Assistance Programs, 1965-68, Pres.'s Adv. Coun. on Mgmt. Improvement, 1969-73; chmn. Pres.'s Task Force on Internat. Pvt. Enterprise. Nat. bd. dirs. Boys' Club Am.; former chmn. U.S.-USSR Trade and Econ. Coun.; former chmn. Exec. Coun. on Fgn. Diplomats; former trustee Hoover Inst. on War, Revolution and Peace; former vice chmn. Woodrow Wilson Internat. Ctr. for Scholars; mem. Trilateral Commn.; chmn. Found. for Commemoration of the U.S. Constitution, 1986. Mem. Fgn. Policy Assn. N.Y. (dir.), Indian Creek Country Club (Miami Beach, Fla.), Blind Brook Country Club (Purchase, N.Y.), Links, Knickerbocker, Friars (N.Y.C.).

ANDREAS, GLENN ALLEN, JR., agricultural company executive; b. Cedar Rapids, Iowa, June 22, 1943; s. Glenn Allen and Vera Irene (Yates) A.; m. Toni Kay Hibma, June 19, 1964; children: Bronwyn Denise, Glenn Allen III, Shannon Tori. BA, Valparaiso U., 1965, JD, 1968. Bar: Colo. 1969. Atty. U.S. Treas. Dept., Denver, 1969-73; atty. Archer Daniels Midland Co., Decatur, Ill., 1973-75, asst. treas., 1975-86, treas., 1986—, v.p., chief fin. officer Europe, 1986-94, v.p., counsel to chief exec., 1994-96, mem. office of chief exec., 1996-97, pres., CEO, 1997-99, chmn., CEO, 1999—; bd. dirs. Nat. City Bancorp., Mpls., Oelmühle Hamburg A.G, Hamburg, Federal Republic of Germany. Mem. ABA, Colo. State Bar Assn., Decatur Bar Assn. Democrat. Clubs: Country of Decatur, Decatur. Avocation: golf. Office: Archer-Daniels-Midland Co 4666 E Faries Pkwy Decatur IL 62526-5666*

ANDREAS, WARREN DALE, lawyer; b. Clay Center, Nebr., Feb. 26, 1931; s. Leonard R. and Linda Helen (Ensz) A.; m. Arden Alanna Angst, Aug. 15, 1954 (dec. Nov. 1977); children: David Warren, Eric Alan, Alisyn Arden; m. Vera Colleen Andreas, July 14, 1984. BA, U. Kans., 1952, LLB, 1954, JD, 1968. Bar: Kans., U.S. Supreme Ct., U.S. Ct. Appeals (10th cir.), U.S. Dist. Ct. Kans. Ptnr. Andreas & Muret, LLP, Winfield, Kans., 1959-89, sr. ptnr., 1989-98; city atty. City of Winfield, 1978-98; former dep. county atty.; atty. Bd. Edn., Unified Sch. Dist. 465, Winfield, 1971-98. Contbr. articles to profl. jours. Lay leader, chmn. fin. com., chmn. bldg. com., chmn. coun. on ministries, chmn. pastor-parish rels. com. First United Meth. Ch.; past pres. bd. dirs. Winfield Cmty. Theater, also performer; bd. dirs. Winfield Recreation Commn., United Way, Cowley County ARC, Salvation Army, Meth. Youthville, Inc., Snyder Rsch. Found., Winfield Arts and Humanities Coun.; one of founding mems., past pres. bd. dirs. Cowley County Mental Health Assn. Fellow Kans. Bar Found.; mem. ABA, Kans. Bar Assn. (bd. govs, 1986-92, 94—, mem. title stds. com., awards com.), Cowley County Bar Assn. (past pres.), Kansas City Attys. Assn., Kans. Assn. Sch. Bds. (former mem. bd. govs.), Winfield C. of C. (bd. dirs.), Lions (past pres.), Rotary (bd. dirs.), Omicron Delta Kappa. Avocations: reading, travel, golf, tennis, theater. Office: Andreas and Muret LLP 303 State Bank Bldg Winfield KS 67156

ANDREASEN, CHARLES PETER, retired electronics executive; b. Bklyn., Mar. 18, 1930; s. Peter Kristian and Marie Paulene (Pedersen) A; m. Julia Kerekes, Nov. 27, 1952; 1 child; Jane Andreasen Della Grotta. Student in agrl. engring., Rutgers U., 1948-49; student in statis. quality control, Middlesex County Coll., 1970-71. Quality control engr. Gorn Aircraft Controls Co., Stamford, Conn., 1962-63; quality control supr. Lily-Tulip Cup Corp., Holmdel, N.J., 1963-70; corp. quality control lab. supr. Purolator Products Co., Rahway, N.J., 1970-73; mgr. quality control Scovill Mfg. Co., Waterbury, Conn., 1973-78; quality assurance mgr. All-State Legal Supply Co., Mountainside, N.J., 1979-81, Durex, Inc., Union, N.J., 1981-82; quality and reliability engr., asst. quality mgr. Triangle Microwave, Inc., East Hanover, N.J., 1982-92; ret., 1992. Mem. Bd. Edn., Edison, N.J., 1982-91; vol. Edison Twp. Domestic Violence Crisis Team, 1993-95; vol. video coord. Rutgers Coop. Ext. Svc.; vol. TV dir. Piscataway Cmty. TV Ctr. Channel 34, 1997—. Mem. Am. Soc. for Quality Control (met. section exec. bd. dirs.). Democrat. Roman Catholic. Lodge: Elks (audit chmn. 1970-78). Avocations: golf, swimming, photography, model railroading, fishing. Home: 24 Burchard St Edison NJ 08837

ANDREASEN, JAMES HALLIS, retired state supreme court judge; b. Mpls., May 16, 1931; s. John A. and Alice M. Andreasen; m. Janet Andreasen, June 25, 1961 (dec. July 1985); children: Jon A., Amy E., Steven J.; m. Marilyn McGuire, May 17, 1987. BS in Commerce, U. Iowa, 1953, JD, 1958. Bar: Iowa 1958. Pvt. practice law Algona, Iowa, 1958-75; with Algona City Coun., 1961-68; judge 3d Jud. Dist. Ct., 1975-87; judge Supreme Ct. Iowa, Des Moines, 1987-98, ret., sr. judge, 1998—. Lt. col. USAFR, 1954-75. Mem. ABA, Iowa State Bar Assn., Kossuth County Bar Assn. Republican. Methodist. Office: Kossuth County Courthouse St Capitol Bldg Algona IA 50511

ANDREASEN, NANCY COOVER, psychiatrist, educator, neuroscientist; d. John A. Sr. and Pauline G. Coover; children: Robin, Susan. BA summa cum laude, U. Nebr., 1958, PhD, 1963; MA, Radcliffe Coll., 1959; MD, U. Iowa, 1970. Instr. English Nebr. Wesleyan Coll., 1960-61, U. Nebr., Lincoln, 1962-63; asst. prof. English U. Iowa, Iowa City, 1963-66, resident, 1970-73, asst. prof. psychiatry, 1973-77, assoc. prof., 1977-81, Andrew H. Woods prof. psychiatry, 1981—, dir. Mental Health Clin. Rsch. Ctr., 1987—; sr. cons. Northwick Pk. Hosp., London, 1983; acad. visitor Maudsley Hosp., London, 1986. Author: The Broken Brain, 1984, Introductory Psychiatry Textbook, 1991; editor: Can Schizophrenia be Localized to the Brain?, 1986, Brain Imaging: Applications in Psychiatry, 1988; book forum editor: Am. Jour. Psychiatry, 1988—, dep. editor, 1989-93, editor, 1993—. Woodrow Wilson fellow, 1958-59, Fulbright fellow Oxford U., London, 1959-60. Fellow Royal Coll. Physicians Surgeons Can. (hon.), Am. Psychiat. Assn., Am. Coll. Neuropharmacologists; mem. Am. Psychopathol. Assn. (pres. 1989-90), Inst. of Medicine of NAS (coun. 1996—). Office: U Iowa Hosps & Clinics 200 Hawkins Dr Iowa City IA 52242-1009

ANDREASEN, NIELS-ERIK ALBINUS, religious educator; b. Asminderod, Denmark, May 14, 1941; came to U.S., 1963; s. Caleb A. and Erna E. (Pedersen) A.; m. Demetra Lougani, Sept. 5, 1965; 1 child, Michael. BA, Newbold Coll., England, 1963; MA, Andrews U., Mich., 1965, BD, 1966; PhD, Vanderbilt U., 1971. From asst. to assoc. prof. Pacific Union Coll., Calif., 1970-75; vis. lectr. Avondale Coll., Australia, 1975-77; prof., dean of religion Loma Linda (Calif.) U., 1977-90; pres. Walla Walla (Wash.) Coll., 1990-94, Andrews (Mich.) U., 1994—. Author: The Old Testament Sabbath, 1972, Rest and Redemption, 1978, The Christian Use of Time, 1978. Mem. Soc. Bibl. Lit. Seventh Day Adventist. Office: Andrews University Office of the President Berrien Springs MI 49104*

ANDREASEN, STEVEN W., lawyer; b. Salt Lake City, Sept. 17, 1948. BA, U. Utah, 1970, JD, 1974. Bar: Washington 1974. Mem. Davis Wright Tremaine, Seattle, 1974—. Comment Editor: Utah Law Review 1973-74. Mem. Seattle Estate Planning Coun., Order of Coif, Am. Coll. Trust and Estate Counsel. Office: Davis Wright Tremaine LLP 2600 Century Sq 1501 4th Ave Ste 2600 Seattle WA 98101-1688

ANDREASON, GEORGE EDWARD, university administrator; b. Seattle, July 4, 1932; s. Alfred M. Andreason and Alberta (Brewer) Andreason Thompson; B.S. in Bus. Adminstrn., Tex. Wesleyan U., Ft. Worth, 1960; M.P.A. (Ford. Found. scholar), Ind. U., 1966; Ph.D., Clayton U., St. Louis, 1979; m. Carolyn A. McKown, June 30, 1973; 1 son, Paul Edward. Program analyst U.S. Army, Washington, 1963-64; asst. chief mgmt. analysis div. FAA, Ft. Worth, 1964-67, chief mgmt. analysis div., Oklahoma City, 1968-70, exec. officer, 1970-71; mgmt. cons. Dept. Transpo., 1966-67; asst. dir. IRS, Denver, 1971-72, asst. regional commr. adminstrn., Dallas, 1972-74, dist. dir., Denver, 1974, asst. dir., St. Louis, 1974-76; dir. adminstrv. services McLennan Community Coll., Waco, Tex., 1976-77; v.p. bus. and adminstrn. U. Mary Hardin-Baylor, Belton, Tex., 1977-80, exec. v.p., 1980—; partner McGregor Assos., bus. and mgmt. cons., McGregor, Tex.; pres., CEO, A&A Consulting Co., 1989—. Served with USN, 1951-55. Recipient Career Edn. award FAA and Nat. Inst. Public Affairs, 1965. Fellow Nat. Inst. Public Affairs; mem. Am. Soc. Public Adminstrn., Personnel and Mgmt. Assn., Nat. Coll. and Univ. Bus. Officers, So. Assn. Coll. and Univ. Bus. Officers, Belton C. of C. Baptist. Clubs: Rotary (Belton); Masons (master McGregor 1977, Tex. dist. dep. grand master 1980) (McGregor and Ft. Worth). Home: PO Box 181 Mc Gregor TX 76657-0181 Office: U Mary Hardin-Baylor Sta Belton TX 76513

ANDREASON, JOHN CHRISTIAN, lawyer; b. Marysville, Calif., Nov. 18, 1924; s. John Christian and Sadie Louisa (Duus) A. B.A., J.D., Stanford U., 1958. Bar: Calif. 1958. With Aerojet-Gen. Corp., La Jolla, Calif., 1958-87, v.p., gen. counsel, 1980-87. Mem. ABA, Nat. Contract Mgmt. Assn., Am. Corp. Counsel Assn. Republican. Lodge: Masons. Home: PO Box 39 Plymouth CA 95669-0039

ANDREASON, SHARON LEE, sculptor; b. Lebanon, Oreg., Mar. 20, 1937; d. LeRoy and Galdys Edwina (Wells) A.; m. Raymond Locke Eller, Aug. 30, 1957 (div. 1981); 1 child, Jordan Lee; m. Stoddard Pintard Johnston, Dec. 21, 1985 (div. 1998). Performing artist Screen Extras Guild, Hollywood, Calif., 1962-70; profl. artist, Carmel, Calif., 1981—, Gaucin, Spain, 1998—. One-woman shows include Pacific Grove Art Ctr., 1984, Zantman Art Gallery, Carmel, 1989, Highlands Sculpture Gallery, Carmel, 1991, 92, 93, Galeria Brisamar, Marbella, Spain, 1993, Smith Cosby Gallery, Carmel, 1995, Silver Light Gallery, Carmel, 1996, 97, 98, 99, Marin-Price Galleries, 1997, Linnemann Gallery, Chgo., 1998, Galerie de Sculpture, Paris, 1999; group exhbns. include Monterey County (Calif.) Mus. Art, 1984, Gallery Mack, Seattle, 1993, Am. Acad. Equine Art, Ky. Horse Park, Lexington, 1993, 94, 95, Galeria Seris, Madrid, 1993, Galeries Kriesler, Madrid, 1994-95, Galeria Brisamar, Marbella, 1995, Galeria Sculpture, Paris, 1995, 96, 98, 99, Signature Gallery, Del Mar, Calif., 1995, Signature Gallery, San Diego, 1995, Galeria Iris Ryman, Marbella, 1996, Nova Galeria De Arte, Malaga, Spain, 1996, 97, 98, 99, Ky. Derby Mus., Louisville, 1996, 97-99, Klausner/Cooperage Gallery, Louisville, 1995-97, 98, 99, Perry House Gallery Competitives, Alexandria, 1997, Harpe Galeria, Galeria de Sculptures, Marbella, Spain, 1997, 98, 99, Gallery 444 Post, San Francisco, 1997, 98, 99, Reflections Gallery, Santa Fe, 1997, 98, 99, Linnemann Gallery, Chgo., 1997-98, Montecito (Calif.) Art and Frame Gallery, 1998, 99; most of her works are reproduced in bronze and sold for pvt. and pub. collections; represented in collections internationally. Pres., founder Horse Power Internat., Inc., 1989-97, Horse Power Sanctuaries, Inc., Horse Power Protection Projects, Inc., 1991-97; authored horse protection legislation Sacramento, 1993-94. Recipient Gwendolyn May award for outstanding achievement for individual humane contbn. Monterey County SPCA, Monterey, Calif., 1994, recipient, Legion of St. frances Awd., Internatl. Generic Horse Assn./Horse Aid, lifelong beneficience awd., 1999. Mem. Conv. on the Welfare and Protection of Animals in Transit (N.Am. Free Trade Agreement animal legis. group), Internat. Sculpture Ctr. Avocations: horse riding and related activities, ancient art and civilizations, travel. E-mail: andreasons@aol.com. Studios: PO Box 998 Carmel CA 93921-0998 also: Apartado 65 Gaucin, 29480 Malaga Spain

ANDREEN, AVIVA LOUISE, dentist, researcher, academic administrator, educator; b. Frankfurt, Fed. Republic of Germany, Jan. 6, 1952; (parents Am. citizens); d. Robert Benjamin Andreen and Margie Corinne (LaPointe) Marshall; m. Merrill R. Penn, Nov. 8, 1987 (div.); children: Robert Morton Salkin and Elizabeth Aliza Penn; Marc O'Dell, Feb. 19, 1999; stepchildren: Roy, Mary, Ralph. BA, NYU, 1975; DDS, NYU Coll. Dentistry, 1996; postgrad., Laser Inst. Am., 1980; AS, Westchester C.C., 1992. Cert. mobile laser operator, N.Y. Tchr. Kibbutz Regavim, D.N. Menasche, Israel, 1975-76; account rep. Traveler's Ins. Co., N.Y.C., 1976; spl. projects coordinator Sapan Engring. Co., N.Y.C., 1976-78; sec., treas. founder J. Sapan Holographic Studios, N.Y.C., 1979; owner, pres. Universal Media Cons., White Plains, N.Y., 1980-84; dir. edn., owner Am. Ctr. for Laser Edn., Bronx, N.Y., 1984-96; pres. Penn Laser Systems Inc., 1994-96; chief dental resident St. Barnabas Hosp., Bronx, N.Y., 1996-98; fellow in spl. patient care Helen Hayes Hosp., West Haverstraw, N.Y., 1998-99; lectr. Hudson River Mus., Yonkers, N.Y., 1986-87; producer laser light show, Andrus Planetarium; taught 1st laser safety course in Am. high sch., 1980; designed laser safety course for Westchester C.C., 1992. Curator Holography A New Dimension White Plains Mus. Gallery, Hudson River Mus., Yonkers, Troster Hall Sci. Mem. ADA, Acad. Gen. Dentistry, Alpha Omega. Avocations: reading, dental laser rsch., crochet, embroidery. Office: Helen Hayes Hosp Dental-Oral Surgery Dept Rt 9W West Haverstraw NY 10993

ANDREESSEN, MARC, communications company executive. BS in Computer Sci., U. Ill., 1993. Co-founder, v.p. tech. Netscape Comms. Corp., Mountain View, Calif., 1994-97, co-founder, exec. v.p., 1997—. Office: Netscape Comms Corp 501 E Middlefield Rd Mountain View CA 94043-4042*

ANDREOFF, CHRISTOPHER ANDON, lawyer; b. Detroit, July 15, 1947; s. Andon Anastas and Mildred Dimitry (Kolinoff) A.; m. Nancy Anne Krochmal, Jan. 12, 1980; children: Alison Brianne, Lauren Kathleen. BA, Wayne State U., 1969; postgrad. in law Washington U., St. Louis, 1969-70; JD, U. Detroit, 1972. Bar: Mich. 1972, U.S. Dist. Ct. (ea. dist.) Mich. 1972, U.S. Ct. Appeals (6th cir.) 1974, Fla. 1978, U.S. Supreme Ct. 1980. Legal intern Wayne County Prosecutor's Office, Detroit, 1970-72; law clk. Wayne County Cir. Ct., Detroit, 1972-73; asst. U.S. atty. U.S. Dept. Justice, Detroit, 1973-80, asst. chief Criminal Div., U.S. Atty.'s Office, 1977-80, spl. atty. Organized Crime and Racketeering sect. U.S. Dept. Justice, 1980-84, dep. chief Detroit Organized Crime Strike Force, 1982-85, mem. narcotics adv. com. U.S. Dept. Justice, 1979-80; ptnr. Evans & Luptak, Detroit, 1985-93, Jaffe, Raitt, Heuer & Weiss, Detroit, 1995—; lectr. U.S. Atty. Gen. Advocacy Inst., 1984. Recipient numerous spl. commendations FBI, U.S. Drug Enforcement Adminstrn., U.S. Dept. Justice, U.S. Atty. Gen. Mem. ABA, Fed. Bar Assn. (speaker trial advocate and criminal law sect. Detroit 1983—, bd. dirs. 1989-91, chmn. criminal law sect. 1990-91), Mich. Bar Assn., Fla. Bar Assn., Nat Assn. Criminal Def. Lawyers, Detroit Bar Assn. Greek Orthodox. Home: 4661 Rivers Edge Dr Troy MI 48098-4161 Office: Jaffe Raitt Heuer & Weiss One Woodward Ave Ste 2400 Detroit MI 48226

ANDREOLI, KATHLEEN GAINOR, nurse, educator, administrator; b. Albany, N.Y., Sept. 22, 1935; d. John Edward and Edmunda Elizabeth (Ringlemann) Gainor; children: Paula Kathleen, Thomas Anthony, Karen Marie. B.S.N., Georgetown U., 1957; M.S.N., Vanderbilt U., 1959; D.S.N., U. Ala., Birmingham, 1979. Staff nurse Albany Hosp. Med. Ctr., 1957; instr. St. Thomas Hosp. Sch. Nursing, Nashville, 1958-59, Georgetown U. Sch., Nursing, 1959-60, Duke U. Sch. Nursing, 1960-61, Bon Secours Hosp. Sch. Nursing, Balt., 1962-64; ednl. coordinator, physician asst. program, instr. coronary care unit nursing inservice edn. Duke U. Med. Ctr., Durham, N.C., 1965-70; ednl. dir. physician asst. program dept. medicine U. Ala. Med. Ctr., Birmingham, 1970-75; clin. assoc. prof. cardiovascular nursing Sch. Nursing U. Ala. Med. Ctr., 1970-77, asst. prof. nursing dept. medicine, 1971, assoc. prof., 1972—, assoc. prof. nursing Sch. Pub. and Allied Health, 1973—; assoc. dir. Family Nurse Practitioner Program, 1976, assoc. prof. community health nursing Grad. Program, 1977-79, assoc. prof. dept. pub. health, 1978-79; prof. nursing, spl. asst. to pres. for ednl. affairs U. Tex. Health Sci. Ctr., Houston, 1979-82, acting dean Sch. Allied Health Scis., 1981; v.p. for ednl. services, interdisciplinary edn., internat. programs U. Tex. Health Sci. Ctr., 1983-87; v.p. nursing affairs Rush-Presbyn.-St. Lukes's Med. Ctr., Dean Rush U. Coll. Nursing, Chgo., 1987—; mem. nat. adv. nursing coun. VHA, 1992; cons. in field. Author, editor: (with others) Comprehensive Cardiac Care, 1983; editor: Heart and Lung, Jour. of Total Care, 1971; contbr. articles to profl. jours. Mem. adv. bd. Robert Wood Johnson Clin. Nurse Sch. Program; mem. vis. com. Vanderbilt U. Sch. Nursing; mem. Leadership Ill., 1991; mem. nat. nursing adv. com. Voluntary Hosp. Am., 1991; mem. governing coun. Inst. for Hosp. Clin. Nursing Edn. Am. Hosp. Assn., 1993; bd. dirs. Ill. League for Nursing, 1994. Recipient Founder's award N.C. Heart Assn., 1970, Disting. Alumni award Vanderbilt U. Sch. Nursing, 1985, Leadership Tex. award, 1985, Disting. Alumni award U. Ala. Sch. Nursing, 1991. Fellow Am. Acad. Nursing; mem. ANA, ACNA, Am. Assn. Colls. Nursing (bd. dirs. 1998-2000), Inst. Medicine (mem. nat. rsch. coun. com. on health and adjustment of immigrant children and families 1996-99), Nat. League Nursing, Ala. Heart Assn., Coun. Family Nurse Practitioners and Clinicians, Am. Heart Assn. Coun. Cardiovascular Nursing, Nat. Nursing Adv. Coun. Hosps. of Am., Rotary One Club of Chgo., Sigma Theta Tau, Alpha Eta, Phi Kappa Phi. Roman Catholic. Home: 1212 S Lake Shore Dr Chicago IL 60605-2402 Office: Rush Presbyn-St Luke's Med Ctr 600 S Paulina St Ste 1080 Chicago IL 60612-3806

ANDREOPOULOS, GEORGE JOHN, history educator, lawyer, political science educator; b. Athens, May 20, 1953; s. Ioannis K. and Paraskevi A.; m. Giuliana Campanelli, Aug. 15, 1992; 1 child, Elena. BA, U. Chgo., 1976; LLB, U. Cambridge, Eng., 1977, PhD, 1986. Lawyer, Athens, 1984-86; post doctoral fellow Yale U., New Haven, 1986-88, assoc. dir. Orville Schell Ctr. for Internat. Human Rights, 1988-93, lectr., 1990-97; asst. prof. govt. John Jay Coll. Criminal Justice, CUNY, 1996—; asst. prof. govt. Grad. Sch. and Univ. Ctr. CUNY, 1998—. Author, editor: Genocide, 1994, The Aftermath of Defeat, 1994, The Laws of War, 1994, Human Rights Education for the Twenty-First Century, 1997; mem. editl. bd. Peace Bull., 1985-86, Human Rights Rev., 1999—. Mem. fundraising com. Habitat for Humanity, New Haven, Conn., 1989-91. With Greek Army, 1983-85. A.G. Leventis Found. fellow, 1986-87; grantee Conn. Humanities Coun. 1988, Ford Found., 1989-92, Marangopoulos Found., 1995, European Human Rights Found., 1996, Carnegie Corp. N.Y., 1997-98. Mem. Am. Hist. Assn., Am. Polit. Sci. Assn., Athens Bar Assn. Avocations: films, theater, literature, jogging, swimming. Office: Dept Govt John Jay Coll Criminal Justice CUNY New York NY 10019

ANDREOPOULOS, SPYROS GEORGE, writer; b. Athens, Greece, Feb. 12, 1929; came to U.S., 1953, naturalized, 1962; s. George S. and Anne (Levas) A.; m. Christiane Loesch Loriaux, June 6, 1958; 1 child, Sophie. AB, Wichita State U., 1957. Pub. info. specialist USIA, Salonica, Greece, 1951-53; asst. editorial page editor Wichita (Kans.) Beacon, 1955-59; asst. dir. info. svcs., editor The Menninger Quar., The Menninger Found., Topeka, 1959-63;; info. officer Stanford U. Med. Ctr., 1963-83; dir. comm., editor Stanford Medicine, 1983-93, dir. emeritus comm., editor emeritus, 1993—; editor Sun Valley Forum on Nat. Health, Inc. (Idaho), 1972-83, 85-95. Co-author, editor: Medical Cure and Medical Care, 1972, Primary Care: Where Medicine Fails, 1974, National Health Insurance: Can We Learn from Canada? 1975, Heart Beat, 1978, Health Care for an Aging Society, 1989; contbr. articles to newspapers and profl. jours. With Royal Hellenic Air Force, 1949-50. Mem. AAAS, Assn. Am. Med. Colls., Nat. Assn. Sci. Writers, Am. Med. Writers Assn., Am. Hosp. Assn., Am. Soc. Hosp. Mktg. and Pub. Rels., Coun. for Advancement and Support of Edn. Home: 1012 Vernier Pl Stanford CA 94305-1027

ANDREOS, GEORGE PHILLIP, lawyer; b. Chgo., Jan. 20, 1935; s. Nicholas and Harriet (MacKenzie) A.; m. Beverly Chadwell, Aug. 28, 1965; children: Leslie, Linda, Darin, Craig. BA, U. Ill., 1957; JD, Calif. Western Sch. Law, San Diego, 1964. Bar: Calif. (so. dist., 9th cir.), 1965. Dep. city atty. City of San Diego, 1965-66; sole practitioner San Diego, 1966—. Contbr. articles to profl. jours. Bd. dirs. For Parents' and Kids' Sake, Poway, Calif., 1984-92. Capt. USMC, 1957-60. Mem. San Diego County Bar Assn. (treas. 1989, v.p. 1990, pres. 1991), Calif. Trial Lawyers Assn. (bd. govs. 1979-83), San Diego Trial Lawyers Assn. (bd. dirs. 1977-82, pres. 1981), Outstanding Trial Lawyer 1982). Avocations: handball, hiking, avocado and grapefruit grower. E-Mail: GAndreos@aol.com. Office: 11405 W Bernardo Ct Ste 203 San Diego CA 92127-1639

ANDREOZZI, LOUIS JOSEPH, lawyer; b. N.J., 1959; m. Lisa Marie Clark, Apr. 12, 1987. BA, Rutgers U., 1981; JD, Seton Hall U., 1984. Bar: N.J. 1984. Asst. gen. counsel Gordon Pub., Inc., Randolph, N.J., 1984-93; dep. gen. counsel Elsevier U.S. Holdings, Morris Plains, N.J., 1985-93; v.p., sec., gen. counsel Reed Elsevier Med. Pub., Belle Mead, N.J., 1994-95; v.p., gen. counsel Lexis-Nexis, Miamisburg, Ohio, 1994-97; chief legal counsel Lexis-Nexis, 1997-98; COO Martindale-Hubbell, New Providence, 1996—, Marquis, NRP, New Providence, 1998—; vice-chmn. Reed Tech. and Info. Svcs., Inc., 1999—; pres., ceo Martindale-Hubbell, Marquis, NRP, New Providence, 1999—; mem. legal adv. bd. Lexis-Nexis, exec. bd. 1994—; mem. Friends of the Law Libr. of Congress; bd. dirs. Am. Assn. of Pub. Named to Dept. Distinction in Bus., Rutgers U., 1981, Nat. Honor Soc. in Econs. and Bus., 1981. Mem. ABA, N.J. Bar Assn., Internat. Bar Assn, Am Corp. Counsel Assn., N.J. Employment Law Assn. Roman Catholic.

ANDRES, REUBIN, gerontologist; b. Dallas, June 13, 1923; s. Harry and Ida Ray (Klejman) A.; m. Amelia Martin Cristol, Dec. 19, 1948; children: Julie, Clay, Laurence, Thomas. Student, So. Meth. U., 1939-41, Coll. Medicine Baylor U., 1941-43; MD, Southwestern Med. Coll., 1944. Diplomate Am. Bd. Internal Medicine. Intern Gallinger Mcpl. Hosp., Washington, 1945; resident VA Hosp., McKinney, Tex., 1947-50; from rsch. fellow to prof. dept. medicine Johns Hopkins U., 1950—; asst. chief medicine Balt. City Hosps., 1958-62; clin. dir. Nat. Inst. Aging, NIH, 1976—. Served with AUS, 1945-47. Recipient Superior Svc. award HEW, 1973, NIH Dirs. award, 1978, Award of Distinction Am. Fedn. Aging Rsch., 1986, Allied-Signal Achievement award in aging, 1986, Rsch. award Am. Aging Assn., 1989, Enrico Greppi prize Italian Soc. Gerontology, 1987, Rank prize in Nutrition, 1993. Fellow Am. Geriatrics Soc. (Henderson award 1986), Gerontol. Soc. Am. (Kleemeier award 1974, Freeman Lecture 1993); mem. Assn. Am. Physicians, Am. Physiol. Soc., Am. Soc. Clin. Investigation, Endocrine Soc., Am. Diabetes Assn. Home: 6010 Lake Manor Dr Baltimore MD 21210-1019 Office: Gerontology Rsch Ctr 4940 Eastern Ave Baltimore MD 21224-2735

ANDRES, RONALD PAUL, chemical engineer, educator; b. Chgo., Jan. 9, 1938; s. Harold William and Amanda Ann (Breuhaus) A.; m. Jean Mills Elwood, July 15, 1961; children: Douglas, Jennifer, Mark. BS, Northwestern U., 1959; PhD, Princeton U., 1962. Asst. prof. Princeton U., 1962-68, assoc. prof., 1968-76, prof. chem. engring., 1976-81; prof. chem. engring. Purdue U., West Lafayette, Ind., 1981—; head Sch. Chem. Engring. Purdue U.,

1981-87, Engring. Research prof., 1987—. Mem. AAAS, Am. Chem. Soc., Am. Inst. Chem. Engrs., Am. Phys. Soc., Materials Rsch. Soc., Sigma Xi, Tau Beta Pi, Pi Mu Epsilon, Phi Lambda Upsilon, Phi Eta Sigma. Office: Purdue U Sch Chem Engring West Lafayette IN 47907-1283

ANDRESEN, MALCOLM, lawyer; b. Medford, Wis., July 26, 1917; s. Thomas Whelen and Ethel (Malkson) A.; m. Ann Kimball, 1942 (div. 1968); children: Anthony M., Susan A. Bridges, Abbott K.; m. Barbara Brown, 1971 (div. 1976); m. Nigi Sato, 1979. BA, U. Wis., 1940, LLB, 1941. Bar: Wis. 1941, N.Y. 1946, U.S. Supreme Ct. 1958. Acct. J.D. Miller & Co., N.Y.C., 1946-47; jr. tax acct. Peat Marwick Mitchell & Co., N.Y.C., 1947-48; assoc. Davis Wagner Hallett & Russell, N.Y.C., 1948-52; tax counsel, then sr. tax counsel, sr. govt. rels. adviser Mobil Oil Corp., N.Y.C., 1952-70; dir. tax legal affairs Nat. Fgn. Trade Coun., N.Y.C., 1970-73; of counsel Delson & Gordon, N.Y.C., 1973-77, Whitman & Ransom, N.Y.C., 1977-86; pvt. practice N.Y.C., 1986—. Trustee, fin. v.p. Nat. Urban League, 1959-65; trustee, treas. Cathedral Ch. of St. John the Divine, N.Y.C., 1977-84. Capt. USMCR, 1942-46. Decorated Bronze Star medal. Mem. Assn. of Bar City of N.Y., Internat. Fiscal Assn. (coun. U.S.A. br. pres. 1971-72), Univ. Club (coun. mem. 1985-89, co-chair com. 1988). Democrat. Episcopalian. Home: 2 Lincoln Sq Apt 24D New York NY 10023-6218 Office: 675 3rd Ave Ste 3004 New York NY 10017-5704

ANDRESS, LUCRETIA ANN KING, health care executive; b. Durham, N.C., May 10, 1942; d. James Thomas and Gladys Virginia (Burgamy) King; m. Wayne Edward Andress, Aug. 26, 1961 (div. June 1979); children: Kevin Edward Andress, Jason Thomas Andress. BSBA, Tampa Coll., 1994. Br. mgr. Trust Co. Bank, Atlanta, 1974-81; dir. lending coord. Barnett Bank of Polk County, Fla., 1981-89; br. mgr. First Fla. Bank, Polk County, 1989-91; mktg. dir. Olsten Healthcare Svcs., Lakeland, Fla., 1991-93; field devel. rep. First Am. Home Care, Winter Haven, Fla., 1994—; bd. dir. Polk County Assn. for Handicapped Citizens, Inc., Lakeland, Olsten Healthcare, Lakeland. Bd. dirs. Am. Heart Assn., Lakeland, Ret. Sr. Vol. Program, Lakeland, Spouse Abuse Coun., Polk County, Resource Ctr. for Women, Polk County; mem. Polk Hardy Highland AIDS Svc. and Edn., client svcs. com.; mem. Polk County Aging Svcs., Polk County Cmty. Svcs. Coun., United Way of Ctrl. Fla., Sr. Orphans of Polk County; host task force Lakeland Ch., of Commerce. Recipient Membership award United Way of Ctrl. Fla., 1991. Mem. Sertoma, C. of C., Winter Haven C. of C. (amb.). Democrat. Episcopalian. Avocations: music, golf, camping. Home: 865 S Oakwood Loop Bartow FL 33830-7042

ANDRETTI, JOHN, professional race car driver; b. Bethlehem, Pa., Mar. 12, 1963; s. Aldo and Carolyn (Stofflet) A.; m. Nancy Ann Summers, Sept. 7, 1987; children: Jarett John, Olivia Elizabeth. BA in Bus. Mgmt., Moravian Coll. Vehicle maintenance Paul E. Smith Plumbing, 1977-78; gen. maintenance Firestone Tire & Rubber Co., 1978-81; sportsman stock cars, 1982, formula super vee, 1982, USAC midgets, 1983-85, 87-89, 93, sprint cars (USAC & CRA), 1983-87, IMSA GTP, 1986, 87, 89, 93, SCCA Can Am, 1984, IMSA showroom stock, 1986-87, CART Indy cars, 1987-94; chmn. bd. Andretti-Helmling Automotive Corp., 1991—; shareholder Andretti-Laird Racing, 1997, Andretti-Laird Helmling Mfg., 1997. Winner U.S. Auto Club Midget Championship, 1983, 24 Hours of Daytona, 1989, 1st Indy car win in Australia, 1991, USAC Championship Dirt Cars, 1985, Group A, 1988, Group C, 1988-89, NHRA Top Fuel Dragster, 1993, British F2, 1993, Land Speed Record, Subaru Legacy, 1993, Nascar Winston Cup, 1993-98, first Nascar Winston Cup pole position, 1995, first win Nascar Winston Cup, 1997, many others; only driver to compete in Indy 500 and World 600 in same day, 1994; named USAC Midget rookie of yr., 1983, Dorney Park rookie of yr., 1982. Roman Catholic. Office: c/o Petty Enterprises 311 Branson Mill Rd Randleman NC 28260

ANDRETTI, MARIO, race car driver; b. Montona, Italy, Feb. 28, 1940; came to U.S., 1955, naturalized, 1964; s. Alvise and Rina (Benvegnu) A.; m. Dee Ann Hoch, Nov. 25, 1961; children: Michael, Jeffrey, Barbra. Began racing career at age 19 Nazareth, Pa. Named Indy Car Nat. Champion, 1965, 66, 69, 84; Daytona 500 winner, 1967; three-time 12 Hrs. of Sebring winner, 1967, 70, 72; Indpls. 500 winner, 1969; three-time Indy 500 pole winner, 1966, 67, 87; USAC Nat. Dirt Track Champion, 1974; Formula One World Champion, 1978; Internat. Race of Champions titlist, 1979; Driver of the Yr., 1967, 78, 84; Driver of the Quarter Century, 1992; all-time leader in Indy Car Pole Positions won (67); all-time Indy Car lap leader (7,587); all-time record holder for Indy Car Starts (407); oldest race winner in recorded Indy car history (53 years 34 days, Phoenix, 1993); only driver to win Indy Car races in four decades; had 12 Forumla One victories and captured 18 Grand Prix pole positions.

ANDRETTI, MICHAEL MARIO, professional race car driver; b. Bethlehem, Pa., Oct. 5, 1962; s. Mario and Dee Ann (Hoch) A.; children: Marco, Marissa; m. Leslie E. Bergey, Dec. 24, 1997. Grad. high sch., Nazareth, Pa. Profl. race car driver Bertil Roos, 1980-81, Carl Haas Racing, Arciero Racing, GTC Racing, Garvin Brown Racing, 1982, Ralt Am., Preston Henn Racing, 1983, Kraco Racing, 1983-88, Alfa Romeo, Hendrick Motorsports, Conte Racing, 1987, Newman/Haas Racing, 1989-92, McLaren Internat. Ltd., 1993, Chip Ganassi Racing Teams, 1994, Newman/Haas Racing, 1995—; v.p. Andretti Enterprises Inc., Nazareth, 1986—, Andretti Devel. Co. Inc., Nazareth, 1987—, Andretti/Piazza Sports Cafes, Race Rock Theme Restaurants, Andretti Petroleum, Andretti Toyota. N.E. divsn. Formula Ford champion, 1981; Sports Car Club Am. Pro Rookie of Yr., 1982; Super Vee nat. champion, 1982; Formula Atlantic nat. champion, 1983; Indy 500 Co-Rookie of Yr., 1984; Indy Car nat. champion, 1991; Driver of Yr., 1991. Roman Catholic.

ANDREU-GARCIA, JOSE ANTONIO, territory supreme court chief justice. Chief justice Supreme Ct. of P.R. Office: Supreme Ct PR PO Box 9022392 San Juan PR 00902-2392

ANDREW, BRIAN J., information technology company executive. BS, Auckland U. CEO Triton Network Sys. Inc., Orlando, Fla., 1997—. Office: 8529 South Park Cir Orlando FL 32819

ANDREW, BRYAN HAYDN, astronomer; b. Glasgow, Scotland, Feb. 26, 1939; m. Moira Crawford, 1962; children: Susan, Heather. BS, Glasgow U., 1961; PhD in Radio Astronomy, Cambridge U., 1966. Asst. rsch. officer NRC Can., 1965-72, assoc. rsch. officer, 1972-79, sr. rsch. officer, 1979-84, chief program svc. br., 1984-86, dir. mgmt. svc. br., 1986-87, dir. Off. Natural Facil. Sci., asst. dir., 1987-90, dir. radio astronomy Herzberg Inst. Astrophysics, 1990-96; interim dir. gen. Inst. for Info. Tech., 1994-96; ret., 1996; vis. lectr. U. Toronto, 1974-76. Mem. Can. Astron. Soc. Achievements include research in molecules; extragalactic variables; planets; comets. Home: 6 Florette, Ottawa, ON Canada K1J 7L4

ANDREW, EDWARD RAYMOND, physicist; b. Boston, Eng., June 27, 1921; s. Edward Richard and Anne (Henderson) A.; m. Mary Farnham, 1948 (dec. 1965); children: Charmian Mary, Patricia Rosalind; m. Eunice Tinning, Aug. 1, 1972. BA, Cambridge U., Eng., 1942, MA, 1946, PhD, 1948, ScD, 1964; DSc (hon.), Turku U., Finland, 1980, U. Poznan, Poland, 1989, U. Leipzig, Fed. Republic Germany, 1990, U. Wales, 1998. Chartered physicist. Sci. officer Royal Radar Establishment, Malvern, Eng., 1942-45; Commonwealth fellow Harvard U., 1948-49; lectr. physics St. Andrews U., Scotland, 1949-54; prof. physics U. Wales, Bangor, 1954-64; Lancashire-Spencer Prof. Physics, U. Nottingham, Eng., 1964-83, dean faculty sci., 1975-78; grad. research prof. U. Fla., Gainesville, 1983—; fellow Christ's Coll., U. Cambridge, Eng., 1989, Clare Hall, U. Cambridge, Eng., 1996; pres. Groupement Ampere, Europe, 1974-80; chmn. Standing Conf. Profs. Physics, U.K., 1976-79. Author: Nuclear Magnetic Resonance, 1955, (with others) Clinical Magnetic Resonance, 1990; editor: Magnetic Resonance, 1974; joint editor Physics Reports, 1974-90, (book) High Magnetic Field Nuclear Magnetic Resonance, 1992; contbr. articles to profl. jours. Selby fellow Australian Acad. Sci.; Recipient Haddon prize Christ's Coll., Cambridge, 1942, Wellcome Found. medal Royal Soc., London, 1984. Fellow Am. Phys. Soc., Royal Soc., Royal Soc. Edinburgh, Inst. Physics, Internat. Soc. of Magnetic Resonance in Medicine; mem. European Phys. Soc. (coun. 1976-79), Soc. Magnetic Resonance in Medicine (charter, trustee 1983-91, editor-in-chief jour. 1983-91, Disting. Svc. medal 1991), British Biophys. Soc. (hon.), Internat. Soc. Magnetic Resonance (pres. 1984-87). Achievements include contributions to nuclear magnetic resonance, especially magic angle spinning and magnetic resonance imaging. Home: 4630 NW 12th Pl Gainesville FL 32605-4579 Office: Univ of Fla Dept Physics Gainesville FL 32611-8440

ANDREW, JOHN ALFRED, III, history educator; b. Boston, Jan. 16, 1943; s. John A. Andrew Jr. and Deborah Gould Marston; m. Roz Andrew, Sept. 3, 1945; children: John F., Lea W. BA in Govt., U. N.H., 1965, MA in History, 1967; PhD in History, U. Tex., Austin, 1973. Prof. history Franklin and Marshall Coll., Lancaster, Pa., 1973—. Author: Rebuilding the Christian Commonwealth, 1976, From Revivals to Removal, 1992, The Other Side of the Sixties, 1997, Lyndon Johnson and the Great Society, 1998. Chair City Dem. Party, Lancster, 1989-94. Mem. Orgn. Am. Historians, Soc. History Early Am. Republic, Am. Studies Assn., Pa. Hist. Assn. Democrat. Unitarian. Avocation: sports. Office: Franklin and Marshall Coll Dept History Lancaster PA 17604

ANDREW, JOHN HENRY, lawyer, retail corporation executive; b. Duluth, Minn., May 23, 1936; s. Frederick William and Florence Elizabeth (Phillips) A.; m. Floretta Claudette Townsend; children: Sean Townsend, Brett Townsend. B.A. cum laude with distinction, U. Minn., Duluth, 1958; J.D., Northwestern U., 1961. Bar: Ill. 1961, Calif. 1975, N.Y. 1980. Assoc., Pattishall, McAuliffe & Hofstetter, Chgo., 1961-71; sr. atty. J.C. Penney Co., Inc., N.Y.C., 1971-74, sr. counsel legis. and regional ops., Western regional counsel, L.A. and Buena Park, Calif., 1974-93, sr. govt. rels. counsel, Sacramento, Calif., 1993-97, chief counsel Govt. Rels, 1997. Contbr. articles to law revs. Chmn. pub. affairs com. Planned Parenthood Assn. of Chgo., 1970-71; mem. Calif. State Dem. Cen. Com., 1976-82. Mem. ABA, Ill. State Bar Assn. (chmn. internat. law sect. 1969-70), Calif. State Bar (com. on consumer fin. svcs. 1982-84, 90-93), Sacramento County Bar Assn., Royal Instn. Cornwall, Cornwall Family History Soc., Sullivan County (Pa.) Hist. Soc. (life), Sons of Union Vets. of the Civil War, Calif. C. of C. (regulatory, consumer and legal affairs com. 1974-86, mem. air and waste mgmt. com. 1994-97). Home: 11359 Mother Lode Cir Gold River CA 95670-3025

ANDREW, JOSEPH JERALD, lawyer, political party official; b. Indpls., Mar. 1, 1960; s. Jerald Lee Andrew and Sylvia (Huss) Hanselmann; m. Anne Slaughter, Sept. 9, 1989. BA, Yale U., 1982, JD, 1985. Bar: Ind., S.D., N.D., U.S. Ct. Appeals (7th cir.). Law clk to Judge Flaum U.S. Ct. Appeals (7th cir.), Chgo., 1985-86; assoc. Baker & Daniels, Indpls., 1986-89; chief dep. sec. of State of Ind., Indpls., 1989-91; with Bingham, Summers, Welsh & Spilman, Indpls., 1991-95, ptnr., 1992-95; chmn. Ind. Dem. Party, 1995-99; ptnr. Jamison Smith Pence, Indpls., 1997—; nat. chmn. Dem. Nat. Com., Washington, 1999—. Author: The Disciples, 1993; editor-in-chief Yale U., 1981-82. Glen Peters Legal scholar, 1983, 84, 85. Democrat. Office: Democratic National Committee 430 S Capitol St SE Washington DC 20003

ANDREW, KENNETH L., research physicist, physics educator; b. Wichita, Kans., June 14, 1919; s. I(saac) Ernest and Hulda (Cox) A.; m. Lois Renner, Sept. 1, 1940; children—Ralph K., Dale Ernest, Nancy Lee. A.B., Friends U., 1940; M.A., Johns Hopkins U., 1942; Ph.D., Purdue U., 1951. Head dept. physics Friends U., Wichita, 1942-56; chmn. dept. physics Dickinson Coll., Carlisle, Pa., 1956-57; assoc. prof. physics Purdue U., West Lafayette, Ind., 1957-68, prof. physics, 1968-89; prof. emeritus, 1989—; exchange prof. Lab. Aimé-Cotton, Orsay, France, 1968-69; cons. Los Alamos Nat. Lab., 1965-72, 77—, Argonne Nat. Lab. Ill., 1977-83; prin. investigator research grants in atomic emission spectroscopy NSF, 1958-83, research grants in atomic spectroscopy NASA, 1963-75, contracts in spectroscopy Office Naval Research, 1959-66; mem. com. on line spectra of elements NRC, 1961-73, chmn., 1966-68. Contbr. numerous articles to profl. jours. Recipient Disting. Alumnus award Friends U., 1971. Fellow Optical Soc. Am. (assoc. editor 1980-83); mem. European Group Atomic Spectroscopists, Am. Phys. Soc., Am. Assn. Physics Tchrs., Internat. Astron. Union, Sigma Xi. Home: 1637 May St Apt 1002 Wichita KS 67213-3503*

ANDREW, LUCIUS ARCHIBALD DAVID, III, corporate executive; b. Highland Park, Ill., Mar. 5, 1938; s. Lucius Archibald David Jr. and Victoria (Rollins) A.; m. Susan Ott, June 1, 1963 (div. 1973); children: Ashley W., L.A. David IV; m. Phoebe Haffner Kellogg, Dec. 21, 1974; children: Gaylord M., Charles H., Matthew K., Louise M. Kellogg. BS, U. Pa., 1962; MBA, NYU, 1965. Asst. treas. The Bank of N.Y., N.Y.C., 1962-68; instl. salesman Drexel, Harriman, Ripley, N.Y.C., 1968-70; v.p., br. mgr. Drexel, Firestone, Inc., Chgo., 1970-72; ptnr., br. mgr. Fahnestock & Co., Chgo., 1972-74; vice chmn. Viner's, Ltd., Sheffield, Eng., 1981-82; pres. N.E.A., Inc., 1975-85; chmn. exec. com. Cert. Mfg. Co., Shelton, Wash., 1975-85; bd. dirs. First Am. Bank, Chgo., 1965-91, chmn., 1982-91; dir. First Am. Bank Corp., 1985—, First Am. Data Corp., 1982—; chmn. FGI, Inc., Forest Grove, Oreg., 1985-86, Union St. Capital Corp., Seattle, Wash., 1986-87, Brudi Inc., Seattle, 1988-90. Trustee Brooks Sch.; past trustee Seattle Repertory Theatre; bd. dirs. The Found. for Lifetime Advocacy and Guardian Svcs., Swedish Med. Ctr. Found., chmn. Mem. The Brook, Racquet and Tennis (N.Y.C.); Racquet (Chgo.); Rainier, University, Golf, Tennis, (Seattle). Home: The Highlands Seattle WA 98177 Office: 200 1st Ave W Ste 400 Seattle WA 98119-4219*

ANDREWS, ALBERT O'BEIRNE, JR., lawyer; b. N.Y., Dec. 19, 1939; s. Albert O'Beirne and Frances (Hall) A.; m. Sharon R. Andrews, Aug. 10, 1963 (div. 1984); children: Laura, Albert; m. Lynn A. McEvers, July 30, 1993. BA, U. Mich., 1963; LLB, U. Minn., 1966. Bar: Minn. 1966, Wyo. 1990. Assoc. Wright & West, Mpls., 1966-70; ptnr. Wright, West, Diessner, Mpls., 1971-84; prin. Gray, Plant, Mooty, Mooty & Bennett, P.A., 1985—; lectr. U. Minn. Dept. Bus. Law, 1968-84; chmn. Bus. Law Dept. U. Minn., 1984—; vis. prof. Warsaw Sch. Econs., 1994, 96. Bd. dirs. Guthrie Theater, Mpls., 1969—, pres., chmn., 1976-79; bd. dirs. Minn. Pub. Radio, St. Paul, Greater Yellowstone Coalition, Bozeman, Mont., sec.-treas., 1987—; bd. dirs. Am. Rivers, Washington, 1994—, League of Conservative Voters, Washington, Minn. Gov. Commn. on Arts, 1975-76, Theatre Comm. Group, N.Y.C., 1973-78. Home: 1201 Yale Pl Minneapolis MN 55403-1901

ANDREWS, ARCHIE MOULTON, government official; b. Greenwich, Conn., July 29, 1919; s. Archie M. and Eleanor (Underwood) A.; m. Margaret Jane Jones, Mar. 3, 1944 (dec. Sept. 1977); children: Archie Moulton III, Peter Underwood, Duncan Trumbull; m. Nike Smith Middleton, Oct. 3, 1978 (dec. Mar. 1987); m. Dorothy Johnson Conley, Sept. 30, 1989. A.B., Princeton U., 1941. Exec. trainee W.R. Grace & Co., 1941-42; econ. analyst State Dept., 1942-43; U.S. rep. blacklist com. Ministry Econ. Warfare, Am. embassy, London, 1943-45; with Dictograph Products, Inc., Danbury, Conn., 1946-63; pres. Dictograph Products, Inc., 1962-63; also dir.; pres. Acousticon-Dictograph Co. Ltd., Can., 1963; dir. Acousticon-Dictograph Co. Ltd., 1958-63, Gen. Acoustics Ltd., Eng., 1950-63; dep. dir. Bur. Internat. Commerce, Dept. Commerce, 1964-69; dir. U.S. trade mission to N. Africa, 1966; comml. counsellor Am. embassy, London, 1970-75; dir. bus. services Office Internat. Affairs, HUD, Washington, 1976-77; dir. exporters service Office Export Adminstrn., Dept. Commerce, Washington, 1978-86; sr. policy analyst Office of Tech. and Policy Analysis, 1986-88, ret., 1988. Mem. SAR. Clubs: Princeton (Washington and N.Y.C.); Pilgrims; Diplomatic and Consular Officers Ret. Home: 326 Prospect Bay Dr W Grasonville MD 21638-1199

ANDREWS, BENNY, artist; b. Madison, Ga., Nov. 13, 1930; s. George Cleveland and Viola (Perryman) A.; m. Mary Ellen Jones Smith, Apr. 3, 1957; children: Christopher, Thomas Michael, Julia Rachael. Student, Ft. Valley State Coll., 1948-50, U. Chgo., 1956-58; BFA, Chgo. Art Inst., 1958. Instr. art New Sch. Social Research, N.Y.C., 1967-70, Queens Coll., N.Y.C., 1968—; vis. artist Calif. State Coll. at Hayward, 1969; vis. art critic Yale U., 1974. Author: Between the Lines, 1978; illustrator: Applachee Red (Raymond Andrews), 1978, Rosebell Lee Wildcat Tennessee (Raymond Andrews), 1980; contbr. articles on black art, culture to profl. jours.; asso. editor (art): Encore mag.; one man shows Kessler Gallery, Provincetown, Mass., 1960-70, Forum Gallery, N.Y.C., 1962-64-66, Henri Gallery, Alexandria, Va., 1963-64, Studio Mus., N.Y.C., 1970, ACA Gallery, N.Y.C., 1972, U. Md., 1972, Aronson-Midtown Gallery, Atlanta, 1973, Lerner-Heller Gallery, N.Y.C., 1979, 80, 81, Gallery of Sarasota, 1979, Savannah Coll. Art and Design, 1983, Sid Deutsch Gallery, N.Y.C., 1983, Merida Galleries, Louisville, 1984; exhibited in group shows at Detroit Inst., 1959, Phila. Acad. Art, 1960, Bklyn. Mus., 1963, Butler Inst. Am. Art, 1967, Mus. Modern Art, N.Y.C., 1968-71, High Mus., Atlanta, 1971, Wadsworth Atheneum, 1979, Art Inst. Chgo., 1979, Los Angeles County Mus. Art, 1982; represented in permanent collections Mus. Modern Art, N.Y.C., High Mus., Atlanta, African Mus., Washington, Norfolk Mus., Va., Butler Inst. Am. Art, Youngstown, Ohio, Chrysler Mus., Provincetown, Mass., La Jolla (Calif.) Mus., NYU, N.Y.C., Detroit Inst. Art, U. Kans. Art Mus., Lawrence, U. Wyo. Art Gallery, Laramie, Joslyn Mus. Art, Omaha, Bklyn. Mus., Joseph H. Hirschhorn Mus., Ohara Mus., Japan, Edwin A. Ulrich Mus., Wichita, Kans. Co-chmn. Black Emergency Cultural Coalition, 1969—; bd. dirs. Children's Art Carnival. Served with USAAF, 1950-54. John Hay Whitney fellow, 1965-67; Dorne Professionship U. Bridgeport, Conn., 1970; N.Y. Council Arts grantee, 1971; MacDowell Colony fellow, 1973-74; Nat. Endowment for Arts grantee, 1974. Office: 130 W 26th St New York NY 10001-6818 *My whole existence as a person and as an artist rests on how I relate to my principles. It is very important for me to keep those principles high, and in so doing, I hope to inspire others to do the same.**

ANDREWS, BILLY FRANKLIN, pediatrician, educator; b. Graham, N.C., Sept. 22, 1932; s. Dean Franklin and Arlee (Byers) A.; m. Faye Rich, Dec. 25, 1953; children: Ann Elizabeth Feigenbaum, Billy Franklin Jr., David Ashley. Student, Brevard (N.C.) Coll., 1950, Elon Coll., 1951; BS cum laude, Wake Forest Coll., 1953; MD, Duke U., 1957; prog. Chiefs of Clinical Services, Harvard Sch. Pub. Health, 1982. Diplomate Am. Bd. Pediatrics, 1963. Commd. 2nd lt. U.S. Army, 1956, advanced through grades to maj., 1962; intern Ft. Benning (Ga.) U.S. Army Hosp., 1957-58; resident in pediat. Walter Reed Gen. Hosp., Washington, 1958-60; with mil. med. and allied scis. course Walter Reed Army Inst. Rsch., Washington, 1960-61; chief pediat. svc. Rodriguez U.S. Army Hosp., Ft. Brooke, P.R., 1961-63; chief pediat. Tropical Med. Rsch. Lab., Ft. Brooke, P.R., 1963-64; res. U.S. Army, 1964; asst. prof. pediat. U. Louisville, 1964-66, dir. newborn svcs., 1964-75, assoc. prof., 1966-68, prof., 1968—, dept. chmn. Sch. Medicine, 1969-93, chmn. emeritus, 1993—, dir. Comprehensive Health Care Ctr. for High Risk Infants and Children, 1968-98; chief of staff Kosair Children's Hosp., Louisville, 1969-93; chief-of-staff emeritus Kosair Children's Hosp., 1993—; cons. div. maternal and child health Ky. Dept. Health, 1966—; lectr. Jour. Pediatrics Found., 1972; Staley Disting. Christian scholar Mary Baldwin Coll., Washington and Lee U., Sch. Medicine of U. Va., 1990; vis. scholar in med. history and ethics Green Coll., Oxford Univ. Oxford, Eng., 1993, vis. fellow, 1998. Author: Children's Bill of Rights, 1968; editor: Small-for-Date Infants, 1970, The Newborn, Pediatric Clinics of North America, 1977, Aphorisms, Tributes and Tenets of Billy F. Andrews: In Walls, M.E., 1986, Ideals and Inspiration (F.R. Andrews), 1993, Words to Live By (F.R. Andrews), 1993, A Statement on Transplantation and Organ Donors, 1994; contbr. numerous articles to profl. publs.; inventor, poet. Pres. Kornhauser Libr., Health Scis. Ctr., 1981-82, 90-91; mem., tchr., deacon, elder United Ch. of Christ. Recipient Helen B. Fraser award Norton-Children's Hosp., 1978, Award of Recognition, XVII Internat. Congress Pediat., Manila, 1983, Wisdom award of honor, eminent fellow The Wisdom Soc., 1991, The Billy F. Andrews, M.D. Endowed Chair in Pediat., U. Louisville, 1993, Winston Churchill medal of Wisdom Soc., Eminent Churchill Fellow of Wisdom Soc., 1993, Disting. Alumnus award Wake Forest U., 1983, The Billy F. Andrews, M.D. scholarship for pediat. U. Louisville Sch. Medicine, 1986, Festschrift to Billy F. Andrews, M.D., Jour. of Perinatology, 1995. Fellow ACP, Am. Acad. Pediat., Royal Soc. Medicine (London), Internat. Biog. Assn.; mem. AMA, Am. Pediat. Soc., Am. Osler Soc. (pres. 1996-97), Am. Soc. for Bioethics and Humanities, Soc. for Pediat. Rsch., So. Soc. Pediat. Rsch. (founding), Southeastern Perinatal Soc. (founding), Nat. Assn. Children's Hosps. and Related Instns. (founding), Ky. Med. Assn. (faculty Sci. Achievement award 1971, del. 1981-82, Ednl. Achievement award 1997), Jefferson County Med. Soc., Ky. Pediat. Soc., Louisville Pediat. Soc., U. Louisville Sch. Medicine Alumni Assn. (bd. govs. 1972-75), Univ. Pediatric Found. Inc. (pres. 1982-93), Internat. Assn. Bioethics, Order of Internat. Fellowship (Cambridge), Alpha Omega Alpha. Achievements include invention of infant oxygen hood, iontophoresis sweat induction apparatus, open infant warmer, infant blood warmer, diagnostic and treatment table with warmer and position changes, infant transport incubator, others. Office: Kosair Charities Pediat Ctr 571 S Floyd St Ste 449 Louisville KY 40202-3830 *Personal philosophy: "The level of civilization attained by any society will be determined by the attention it has paid to the welfare of its children." Also, "The responsibility of the physician is to prevent, to diagnose, to prognosticate, to treat when and if necessary, and always to keep foremost in mind 'Primum Non Nocere'".*

ANDREWS, BRYANT AYLESWORTH, software company executive; b. N.Y.C., Dec. 28, 1938; s. F. Emerson and Edith Severance Andrews; m. Elisabeth Power, July 5, 1974; children: Christopher, Suzanne. BA in English, Cornell U., 1962. Engring. writer Pratt & Whitney Aircraft, East Hartford, Conn., 1962-79, supr. engring. writers, 1979-83, mgr. system devel., office automation, 1983-85; pres., co-founder Integrated Custom Software, Inc., Glastonbury, Conn., 1985—. Author: (software) System Minder, Formsprint. Chmn. Columbia Fin. Bd., 1979-87; mem., chmn. Columbia Planning and Zoning, 1971-77, Windham Regional Planning Agy., Willimantic, Conn., 1971-75. Republican. Congregationalist. Avocation: private pilot. E-mail: icsandr@ibm.net. Home: 99 Route 87 Columbia CT 06237 Office: Integrated Custom Software Inc 12 National Dr Glastonbury CT 06033

ANDREWS, CAROL, primary education educator; b. Galveston, Tex., Apr. 21, 1945; d. Herbert and Amy Elsie (Johnson) Gumaer; m. Harlan Andrews, Dec. 30, 1968; children: Monique, Brad. BA in English with distinction, San Jose State U., 1970. Cert. multiple subject cred., Calif. Tchr. spl. edn. Moreland Sch. Dist., San Jose, Calif.; mid. sch. tchr. English, South Valley Carden Sch., San Jose, Calif., 1986—; history and K-8 ednl. cons. Docent Ainsley House Outreach Program. Recipient Francis Lanyon Meml. award. Mem. Campbell Hist. Soc.

ANDREWS, CHARLES, wholesale distribution executive. CEO, pres. Sunbelt Beverage, Lutherville, Md., 1997—. Office: Sunbelt Beverage 2164 N Batavia St Orange CA 92865-3104*

ANDREWS, CHARLES ROLLAND, library administrator; b. Scranton, Pa., July 5, 1930; s. Edgar W. and Margaret (Machenry) A.; m. Harriet Williams, Dec. 27, 1954 (dec. 1985); m. Dorothy Kramer, Dec. 10, 1988. BS in Edn., Bloomsburg U., 1954; MA in English Lit., U. Okla., 1959; MS in Lib. Sci., Case Western Res. U., 1964, PhD, 1967. Head reference dept. Cleve. Pub. Library, 1966-68; head reference dept. Case Western Res. Univ. Libraries, Cleve., 1968-69, librarian Freiberger Library, 1969-72, asst. dir. pub. services, 1972-74; univ. librarian Southeastern Mass. Univ. Library, North Dartmouth, 1974-76; dean library services Hofstra U. Library, Hempstead, N.Y., 1976-96, prof. emeritus, 1997—; lectr. Hofstra U. Coll. Continuing Edn., 1997—. Editor: Reference Books for Small and Medium-Sized Libraries, 1973; contbr. articles, revs. to profl. jours. Bd. trustees Unitarian Universalist Congregation, Garden City, N.Y., 1998—, chair art exhibits com., 1999—. Mem. ALA, Assn. Coll. and Rsch. Librs., Archons of Colophon, L.I. Libr. Resources Coun. (chair regional automation com. 1986-92, bd. trustees 1990-94), Am. Express (sr. adv. bd. mem. 1998-99). Democrat. Avocations: calligraphy, word processing, graphics. Home and Office: 305 Hillside Ave Bellmore NY 11710-3519

ANDREWS, CHRISTINE MARIE, graphic designer; b. Dayton, Ohio, Dec. 17, 1974; d. John Theodore and Kathryn Elizabeth Andrews. BA in Comm., Va. Tech. U., 1997; MA in Graphic Design, Savannah Coll. Art & Design, 1999. Prodn. mgr. Collegiate Times, Blacksburg, Va., 1995-97; sr. graphic designer Creative Loafing, Savannah, Ga., 1997—. mem. Soc. News Design. Republican. Roman Catholic. Avocations: photography, sports. E-mail: metexan@prodigy.net. Home: Apt 306 101 W Oglethorpe Ave Savannah GA 31401 Office: Creative Loafing Ste 5 1800 E Victory Dr Savannah GA 31401

ANDREWS, CLAUDE LEONARD, psychotherapist; b. Halifax County, N.C., Jan. 13, 1943; s. Leland Waverly and Annie Grey (Hyde) A.; m. Carol Gladys Cooper, June 10, 1967 (wid. Nov. 1986). BA, St. Andrews Coll., 1965; MDiv, Princeton (N.J.) Theol. Sch., 1969; MEd, U. Ga., 1972, ABD, 1974. Lic. psychol. assoc., N.C.; lic. marriage and family therapist, N.C., profl. counselor, N.C.; ordained to ministry Presbyn. Ch. Intern/chaplain

U.N.C., Chapel Hill, 1967-68; intern/clin. chaplain Milledgeville (Ga.) State Hosp., 1970-71; minister Lavonia (Ga.) Presbyn. Ch., 1971-74; marital therapist U. Ga., Athens, 1971-73, teaching intern, 1972-74; psychologist Edgecombe-Nash Mental Health Ctr., Rocky Mount, N.C., 1974-76; dir., psychologist Tarboro (N.C.) Unit Mental Health Ctr., 1976-77; pvt. practice Creative Living Assocs., Tarboro, 1977—; cons. Albemarle Presbytery, Greenville, N.C., 1975-87, Presbytery of New Hope, Rocy Mount, 1987—, Tarboro Police Dept., 1987—, Edgecombe Sheriff's Dept., Tarboro, 1987—, Critical Incident Stress Debriefing Team, Ctrl. Carolina Team, 1987—, Elm City E.M.S., Stoney Creek E.M.S.; part-time instr. E.M.S. law enforcement; cons. in mental health and psychology for N.E.E.D., Head Start. Min. Fountain (N.C.) Presbyn. Ch., 1991—; bd. dirs. N.C. Symphony. Mem. Am. Assn. Marriage and Family Therapists (clin. mem.), Rotary (bd. dirs., sec., v.p., pres.). Avocations: martial arts, electronics, sailing, salt water fishing. Home: 309 E Saint John St Tarboro NC 27886-4413 Office: Creative Living Assocs 309 E Saint John St Tarboro NC 27886-4413

ANDREWS, DAVID RALPH, lawyer; b. Oakland, Calif., Jan. 4, 1942; s. David and Mattie (Speeks) A.; m. Rozan McCurdy, July 1, 1962; children: David, Linda. BA, U. Calif., Berkeley, 1968; JD, U. Calif., 1971. Bar: Calif. 1971, D.C. 1986, U.S. Dist. Ct. (no. dist.) Calif. 1971, U.S. Dist. Ct. Hawaii 1991, U.S. Supreme Ct. 1980. Rsch. asst. U. Calif., Berkeley, 1969-71; assoc. McCutchen, Doyle, Brown & Enersen, San Francisco, 1971-75; regional counsel Reg. IX U.S. EPA, San Francisco, 1975-77; legal counsel and spl. asst. for policy U.S. EPA, Washington, 1977-79; dep. gen. counsel Dept. Health and Human Svcs., Washington, 1980-81; ptnr. McCutchen, Doyle, Brown & Enersen, San Francisco, 1981-97, chmn., 1991-95; legal adviser U.S. Dept. State, Washington, 1997—; co-chmn. San Francisco Lawyers' Com. Urban Affairs, 1989-91, ROC Econ. Coun., Ill., 1989-97; steering com. NAACP Legal Def. Fund, Calif., 1989-97. Contbr. articles to profl. jours. Trustee San Francisco Mus. of Modern Art, 1988-97; bd. trustees Golden Gate Nat. Park Assn., 1992-95, Marin Cmty. Found., 1996-97; mem. U.S. Agy. for Internat. Devel. Energy Tng. Program Adv. Com. of the Inst. Internat. Edn. Fellow Max Planck Inst. of Pub. Internat. Law, Heidelberg, Fed. Republic of Germany, 1974; recipient Outstanding Svc. award U.S. EPA, Washington, 1980, Sec.'s Spl. Citation Dept. Health and Human Svcs., Washington, 1981. Mem. ABA (natural resources sect.), Calif. Bar Assn. (vice chair, co-chair subcom. on environ. legis.), San Francisco Bar Assn. Avocations: photography, tennis, running. *

ANDREWS, DAVID SCOTT, thoracic and cardiovascular surgeon; b. Canton, Ohio, Feb. 23, 1950; s. Eugene and Thelma Mae Andrews; m. Julia Ann Jones, June 21, 1975; chidlren: Kelly, Collin, Meredith. BS, U. Notre Dame, 1972; MD, Ohio State U., 1975. Diplomate Am. Bd. Thoracic Surgery. Resident in gen. surgery Mt. Carmel Med. Ctr., Columbus, Ohio, 1976-79; resident in thoracic and cardiovascular surgery Ohio State U. Med. Ctr., Columbus, 1979-81; mem. group practice Kaiser Med., Fontana, Calif., 1981-82; fellow in cardiac surgery Cleve. Clinic Found., 1982-83; pvt. practice Charlotte, N.C., 1983—; mem. staff Presbyn. Hosp., chief dept. dept. thoracic and cardiovascular surgery, 1993—; mem. staff Mercy Hosp.; surgeon Hawthorne Cardiovascular Surgery, Charlotte, 1989—. Fellow ACS, Am. Coll. Cardiology; mem. Soc. Thoracic Surgery, Soo. Thoracic Surg. Assn. Republican. Roman Catholic. Avocations: golf, travel. Office: 301 Hawthorne Ln Charlotte NC 28226

ANDREWS, DENNIS, customer service professional. Customer svc. rep. Cargill, Wayzata, Minn. Office: Cargill 15407 Mcginty Rd W Wayzata MN 55391-2399

ANDREWS, DIANE RANDALL, nursing administrator, critical care nurse; b. Clinton, Iowa, Dec. 30, 1953; d. Eugene E. and Carol Lee (Walker) Randall; m. Thomas Wescott Andrews, Oct. 2, 1982; children: Christine, Charles. BSN, U. Iowa, 1976; MS, U. Ill., Chgo., 1981. RN, Fla., Ill. Unit leader/instr. Rush Presbyn. St. Lukes Med. Ctr., Chgo., 1976-84; cons. Longwood, Fla., 1990—; trustee, mem. nursing adv. com. Fla. Hosp. Coll. of Health Scis., 1993—; mem. women's ctr. adv. com. Fla. Hosp., 1992—; chair endowment oversight com. Fla. Hosp./Univ. of Ctrl. Fla., 1996—; chair founding bd. Fla. Hosp. Coll. Health Scis. Found., 1997—. Author: After Anesthesia; former editor jour. Kaleidoscope; former contbg. editor Jour. of the Fla. Med. Assn.; contbr. articles to profl. publs. Bd. dirs. Orange County Med. Soc. Alliance, Fla. Hosp. Golden Cir. of Friends, Fla. Hosp. Found., Fla. Med. Assn. Alliance, Jewish Family Svcs., Walt Disney Meml. Cancer Inst. State of Iowa scholar. Mem. Am. Soc. Post Anesthesia Nursing, Sigma Theta Tau. Home and Office: 1821 Alaqua Dr Longwood FL 32779-3105

ANDREWS, EARL, JR., commissioner, state and local; b. Queens, N.Y.. BA in Polit. Sci. and Bus., Morehouse Coll. Data processing sales rep. IBM Corp.; investment banker Shearson Hammill; ptnr. First Harlem Securities Corp.; v.p. First Boston Bank; mgr. Bear Stearns; mng. dir. WR Lazard and Co.; pres. Tax Comm. City of N.Y., 1994-96, commr. Dept. Bus. Svcs., 1996-98; vice chmn. N.Y.C. Housing Authority, 1998—. Fax: 212/618-8989. Office: NYC Housing Authority 250 Broadway New York NY 10007*

ANDREWS, EDSON JAMES, JR., radiologist; b. Tallahassee, Fla., Apr. 30, 1940; s. Edson James and Lola Irene (French) A.; m. Winifred Lynn Keller, Nov. 22, 1961; children: Michael Scott, James Brian. BA, U. Colo., 1962; MD, U. Fla., 1966. Diplomate Am. Bd. Radiology. Intern Charlotte (N.C.) Meml. Hosp., 1966-67; resident in radiology Barnes Hosp. of Washington U., Mallinckrodt Inst. Radiology, St. Louis, 1969-71; NIH postdoctoral fellow in cardiovascular radiology U. Fla., Gainesville, 1971-72; ptnr. Gadsden (Ala.) Radiology Assocs., 1972-77; staff radiologist West Fla. Hosp. Med. Ctr. Clinic, Pensacola, 1977—, co-chair dept. nuclear cardiology, 1979—, chief nuclear medicine, 1982—, chmn. dept. radiology, 1993-95; bd. dirs. Med. Edn. and Rsch. Found. West Fla.; adj. assoc. prof. U. Fla. Coll. Med., 1985-90; assoc. clin. prof. radiology U. South Ala., 1993—. Co-editor: (text) Color Atlas of First Pass Functional Imaging of the Heart, 1985; contbr. articles to profl. jours. Served with USPHS, 1967-69. Fellow Am. Coll. Radiology (councilor 1994—), fell. Am. Coll. Cardiology; mem. Am. Soc. Nuclear Cardiology (founding mem.), Soc. Nuclear Medicine, Radiol. Soc. N.Am., Am. Roentgen Ray Soc, v.p. Fla. Radiol. Soc., 1997-98. Republican. Home: 8925 Scenic Hills Dr Pensacola FL 32514-5650 Office: 8333 N Davis Hwy Pensacola FL 32514-6050

ANDREWS, EDWARD L., career officer; b. Sept. 9, 1944. Commd. U.S. Army, advanced through grades to maj. gen., 1996; with U.S. Army Test and Evaluation Command. Office: US Army Test and Evaluation Command Aberdeen Proving Ground MD 21005

ANDREWS, FRANK LEWIS, lawyer; b. Rhinebeck, N.Y., June 8, 1950; s. William Fisher and Merna Louise (Lewis) A.; m. Barbara Della Chapman, Aug. 30, 1980; children: William Chapman, S. Ross Chapman. Student, U. Vienna, Austria, 1971; BS magna cum laude, Mich. State U., 1973; JD cum laude, Harvard U., 1976. Bar: Mich. 1976. Sr. prin. Miller, Canfield, Paddock & Stone PLC, Detroit, Bloomfield Hills, Mich., 1983—, co-chmn. environ. law group, 1987—; speaker on corp. law, environ., hazardous materials, and corp. compliance to various bus. and bar assns.; course dir. and speaker on multiple environ. law programs Nat. Assn. Corp. Real Estate Execs., Inst. for Continuing Legal Edn., Continuing Legal Edn. Internat., Cambridge Inst., 1982—. Mem. legal subcom. Alexander Graham Bell Assn. for Deaf, Washington, 1989—; gen. counsel Mich. Host Com. for World Cup Soccer, 1994, 92-94. Mem. ABA (chmn. environ. legis. subcom. bus. law sect. 1993—). Avocations: skiing, sailing. Office: Miller Canfield Paddock & Stone 1400 N Woodward Ave Bloomfield Hills MI 48304-2854

ANDREWS, FRED CHARLES, mathematics educator; b. Aylesbury, Sask., Can., July 13, 1924; s. Henry Marmaduke and Margaret (Van de Bogart) A.; m. Joyce Davenny, Apr. 5, 1944; children—Linda (Mrs. Pierre Dunn), David W., Gail E.(Mrs. Gregory Crandell). BS in Math, U. Wash., 1946, MS in Math. Statistics, 1948; PhD, U. Calif., Berkeley, 1953; PhD (hon.), U. Tampere, Finland, 1985. Research asso. Applied Math. and Statistics Lab., Stanford, 1952-54; asst. prof. math., asso. statistician U. Nebr., 1954-57; asso. prof. math. U. Oreg., 1957-66; dir. U. Oreg. (Statistics Lab. and Computing Center), 1960-69, prof. math., 1966-89, prof. emeritus math., 1989—, head dept. math., 1973-80; Vis. statistician Math Centrum, Amsterdam, The Netherlands, 1963-64; Fulbright-Hays sr. lectr. U. Tampere, Finland, 1969-70; Fulbright-Hays sr. lectr. Univ. Coll., Cork, Ireland, 1976-77; Fulbright sr. lectr. U. Jordan, Amman, 1983-84. Contbr. articles to profl. jours. Pres. Met.-Civic Club, Eugene-Springfield, 1967-68; Trustee Oreg. Grad. Center, 1967-77. Served to lt. (j.g.) USNR, 1943-46. Fellow AAAS; mem. Sigma Xi. Office: U Oreg Dept Math Eugene OR 97403

ANDREWS, FREDERICK FRANCK, newspaper editor; b. Roanoke, Va., Apr. 20, 1938; s. Thomas Whiting and Frances Powers (Franck) A.; m. Carol Ann Corder, May 7, 1962 (div. 1975); 1 child: Frederick Ethan; m. Jane Gribbin, Jan. 2, 1977, 1 child, Luke Allan. AB, Duke U., 1960; MA, Princeton U., 1965. Advt. copywriter Union Carbide Corp., N.Y.C., 1962-63; rsch. dir. Fair Campaign Practices Com., N.Y.C., 1963-65; reporter Wall St. Jour., N.Y.C., 1968-76; stringer Time-Life news svc. N.Y. Times, Taipei, 1966-68; reporter N.Y. Times, N.Y.C., 1976-77, dep. bus.-fin. editor, 1977-85, bus.-fin. editor, 1985-92, asst. to mng. editor, 1992, deputy met. editor, 1993-94, sr. editor for devel., 1994—. Office: NY Times 229 W 43rd St New York NY 10036-3959

ANDREWS, GEORGE EYRE, mathematics educator; b. Salem, Oreg., Dec. 4, 1938; s. Raymond Leslie and Rovena Pearl (Eyre) A.; m. Joy Margaret Brown, Sept. 2, 1960; children: Amy Beth, Katherine Yvonne, Derek George. BS, Oreg. State U., 1960, MA, 1960; postgrad., Cambridge (Eng.) U., 1960-61; PhD, U. Pa., 1964. Asst. prof. math. Pa. State U., University Park, 1964-67, assoc. prof., 1967-70, prof., 1970-81, Evan Pugh prof. math., 1981—; math. dept. head, 1980-82, 95-97; Hedrick lectr. Math. Assn. Am., 1980, J.S. Frame lectr., 1993; adj. prof. U. Waterloo, Ont., Can., 1982-92, regional conf. lectr., NSF-Conf. Bd. Math. Scis., 1985. Author: Number Theory, 1971, Theory of Partitions, 1976, Partitions: Yesterday and Today, 1979, q-Series, 1986; editor: Collected Papers of P.A. MacMahon, Vol. I, 1978, Vol. II, 1986, Ramanujan Revisited, 1988, The Rademacher Legacy to Mathematics, 1994. Recipient Disting. Univ. Teaching award Allegheny mountain sect. Math. Assn. Am., 1993, Dottore ad Honorem in Fisica U. Parma, 1998; Guggenheim fellow, 1982-83; elected mem. Am. Acad. Arts and Scis., 1997. Republican. Avocation: piano. Home: RR 2 Box 133 Centre Hall PA 16828-9763 Office: Pa State U Dept Math 410 Mcallister Bldg University Park PA 16802-6404

ANDREWS, GERALD BRUCE, retired textile executive; b. Valley, Ala., Sept. 17, 1937; s. Bruce and Sara Andrews; m. Claire Smith; children: Gerald Bruce Jr., Benjamin G., Suzanne Andrews Smith. Diploma in textile mfg., Auburn U., 1956; BS in Mgmt. and Indsl. Engring., Auburn U., 1958; postgrad., Harvard U., 1979. Various positions WestPoint Pepperell, Inc., 1954-67, mgr. Opelika (Ala.) Mill, 1967-68; gen. mgr. no. ops. WestPoint Pepperell, Inc., Biddeford, Maine, 1968-70; dir. indsl. engring. WestPoint Pepperell, Inc., West Point, Ga., 1970-72; gen. mgr. towels ops. WestPoint Pepperell, Inc., Valley, 1972-74, v.p. mfg., 1974-80; sr. v.p. merchandising and mktg. WestPoint Pepperell, Inc., N.Y.C., 1980-87; pres. Stores div. N000, West Point, 1987-92; exec. v.p. merchandising WestPoint Pepperell, Inc., N.Y.C., 1992—; pres., COO Johnston Industries Inc., N.Y.C., 1992—; pres., CEO Johnston Industries Inc., Columbus, Ga., 1995-97, ret., 1997; chmn. com. to evaluate Sch. Textile Engring., Auburn (Ala.) U., alsos lay speaker Guest Speakers Bur.; mem. president's adv. com. So. Union Coll.; chmn. Westpoint Pepperell Polit. Action Com., West Point; bd. dirs. Ala. Textile Edn. Found., Johnston Industries Inc., Tapistron Internat., Tech. Textiles U.S.A.; instr. textile mfg. and indsl. engring. Pres. bd. trustees Lanier Meml. Hosp., Valley; chmn. Chattahoochee Valley Health Care Found., Valley; mem. Ala. Gov.'s Adv. Coun., Montgomery; trustee Christian City, Atlanta. Named Citizen of Yr., Valley-Lanett C. of C.; recipient President's award Geo. H. Lanier Coun. Boy Scouts Am.; inducted Engring. Hall of Fame, 1995. Mem. Am. Inst. Indsl. Engrs., Am. Textile Mfg. Assn. (dir. 1995, textile leader of yr. in Am. 1995), Ala. Textile Mfg. Assn. (pres.), Harvard Bus. Sch. Assn., Spring Wood Athletic Club (pres.), Rotary (pres. West Point), Harvard Club (N.Y.C.). Avocations: travel, golf, reading, architecture, painting. Home: 204 N 18th St Lanett AL 36863-6436 Office: Johnston Industries Inc 105 13th St Columbus GA 31901-2101

ANDREWS, GORDON CLARK, lawyer; b. Boston, Mar. 25, 1941; s. Loring Beal and Flora Spencer (Hinckley) A.; m. Deborah M. Devere, July 9, 1966; children: Christine Leigh, Cynthia Lyn, Carey Loring. BA, Dartmouth Coll., 1963; JD, NYU, 1969. Bar: N.Y. State bar 1970, Conn. bar 1971. Assoc. Morgan Lewis & Bockius (and predecessor), N.Y.C., 1969-72; asst. sec., asst. gen. counsel Howmet Corp., Greenwich, Conn., 1973-75; sec., asst. gen. counsel Beker Industries Corp., Greenwich, 1976—, v.p., 1978-81; gen. counsel M&T Chems., Inc., Woodbridge, N.J., 1982-86; v.p. law dept. M&T Chems., Inc., Woodbridge, 1986-90, sec., 1987-90; v.p., sec. Atochem Inc., Glen Rock, N.J., 1987—; gen. counsel, sec. ESSROC Corp., Bath, Pa., 1990—, sr. v.p., 1993—; ptnr. Epstein, Becker & Green, N.Y.C., 1995—; bd. dirs. San Juan Cement Co., Inc., Essroc Cement Corp., Inc.; mem. exec. com., sec./treas. Cement Kiln Recycling Coalition. Lt. USNR, 1963-69. Recipient Am. Law award, 1969. Mem. ABA, N.Y. State Bar Assn., Conn. Bar Assn., Am. Soc. Corp. Secs., Westchester-Fairfield Corp. Counsel Assn., Greenwich Country Club. Republican. Home: 46 Club Rd Riverside CT 06878-2034 Office: Epstein Becker & Green 250 Park Ave Ste 1201 New York NY 10177-0001

ANDREWS, GROVER JENE, adult education educator, administrator; b. Batesville, Ark., June 1, 1930; s. Grover Jones and Ruth Burlie (Ruble) A. BA, Vanderbilt U., 1963, MA, 1964; EdD, N.C. State U., 1972. Dir. univ. rels. Baylor U., Waco, Tex., 1955-61; asst. to pres. Peabody Coll. Vanderbilt U., Nashville, 1961-64; asst. prof. English, asst. acad. dean U. Ark., Little Rock, 1964-66; dir. of devel. Meredith Coll., Raleigh, N.C., 1966-67; asst. to dean of extension N.C. State U., Raleigh, 1967-68, assoc. vice chancellor for extension, assoc. prof. adult edn, 1979-89; assoc. exec. dir. commn. on colls. So. Assn. Colls. and Schs., Atlanta, 1968-79; assoc. dir. for instrn. U. Ga. Ctr. for Continuing Edn., 1989—, sr. pub. svc. assoc., chair sr. pub. svc. faculty, 1989—, adj. assoc. prof. adult edn., 1989—, asst. v.p. pub. svc. and outreach, 1998—, interim dir., 1998—; bd. dirs. Am. Tech. Inst., Memphis, 1985-98; trustee Coun. for Adult and Exptl. Learning, Chgo., 1985-91; dir. rsch. Internat. Assn. for Continuing Edn. and Tng., Washington, 1987-92, pres., 1992-96. Member Raleigh Lions, 1967-68, 79-89; chair Christmas pageant Waco Jaycees, 1956-60; patron Atlanta Arts Ctr., 1968-79. With USN, 1948-50. Named Educator of the Yr., Fedn. of Women's Clubs, 1966; recipient Nat. Leadership award Assn. for Continuing Higher Edn., 1984, Gruman award N.C. Adult Edn. Assn., 1985, Pinnacle award for outstanding leadership Internat. Assn. for Continuing Edn. and Tng., 1996; named to Internat. Hall of Fame for Adult and Continuing Edn., 1996; Grover J. Andrews Rsch. Endowment established by Internat. Assn., for Continuing Edn. and Tng., 1996. Mem. Nat. Univ. Continuing Edn. Assn. (chair elect rsch. divsn. 1996-97, chair rsch. divsn. 1998-99, Julius M. Nolte award 1995, chair rsch. divsn. 1997-98), Ga. Adult Edn. Assn., So. Assn. Colls. and Schs. (chair accrediting coms. 1980—), Phi Delta Kappa, Sigma Tau Delta, Pi Kappa Alpha. Democrat. Baptist. Avocations: gardening, arts, antiques. Fax: (700) 542-1991. E-mail: andrewsg@gactr.uga.edu. Home: 243 Ashbrook Dr Athens GA 30605-3956 Office: U Ga Ctr for Continuing Edn Athens GA 30602

ANDREWS, HOLDT, investment banker; b. N.Y.C., May 2, 1946; s. William Lloyd and Edna (Faulconer) A.; m. Nina Lawrence, Sept. 16, 1982; 1 child, Kelli. BS, U. Fla., 1968; MBA, Fla. Atlantic U., 1971. Asst. to v.p. mktg. Eltra Corp., Wilmington, Mass., 1972-74; v.p. Bank of Am., N.Y.C., 1974-81; group v.p. Amrobank, N.Y.C., 1981-84; exec. v.p. CenTrust Savs. Bank, Miami, Fla., 1984, KMC Group, Miami, 1985-86; sr. mng. dir. J.W. Charles Capital Corp.-Bush Securities, Boca Raton, Fla., 1986-89; v.p. corp. fin. dept. Internationale Nederlanden Bank N.V., N.Y.C., 1989-94; sr. v.p. S.N. Phelps and Co., Greenwich, Conn., 1994; chief oper. officer VHC, Ltd., West Palm Beach, Fla., 1994—; mem. adv. bd. Tucker State Bank, Jacksonville, Fla., 1987-88; bd. dirs. Qilu-Maul, Shandong, Peoples Republic China. 1st lt. U.S. Army, 1968-70. Mem. Blue Key. Avocations: tennis, sailing, skiing. Office: VHC Ltd 50 Cocoanut Row Ste 119 Palm Beach FL 33480-4026

ANDREWS, J. DAVID, lawyer; b. Decatur, Ill., July 5, 1933; s. Jesse D. and Louise Glenna (Mason) A.; m. Helen Virginia Migely, July 12, 1958; children: Virginia, Robert, Michael, Betsy. BA magna cum laude, U. Ill., 1955, JD with honors, 1960. Bar: Wash. 1961. Ptnr. Perkins Coie, Seattle, 1960-96, counsel, 1997—; bd. dirs., v.p. Am. Bar Ins. Plans Cons., Inc., 1991—, also bd. dirs.; pres. Wash. Law Fund, 1992—; bd. dirs. Cornish Inst., Seattle, 1977-83, pres. 1981-83; bd. dirs. Am. Bar Endowment, 1981-94, pres. 1985-87; bd. visitors U. Puget Sound Law Sch., 1976-94; trustee AEF Pension Fund, 1975-79. Contbr. articles to profl. jours. Bd. dirs. Leukemia Soc. Wash., 1984—, pres. 1985-91; nat. bd. dirs. Leukemia Soc. Am., 1992-96. Capt. USAF, 1955-57. Fellow Am. Bar Found. (bd. dirs., former treas.), Am. Coll. Trial Lawyers; mem. ABA (ho. of dels. 1967-69, 75—, asst. treas. 1972-74, treas. 1975-79, bd. govs. 1975-79, bd. dirs. Am. Bar Found., fed. judiciary standing com. 1985-90), Wash. Bar Assn. (chmn. pub. rels. com. 1971-73), Seattle-King County Bar Assn., Am. Judicature Soc. (bd. dirs. 1985-89), Phi Beta Kappa, Phi Kappa Phi, Phi Eta Sigma. Home: 9413 SW Quartermaster Dr Vashon WA 98070-7081 Office: Perkins Coie 1201 3rd Ave Ste 4000 Seattle WA 98101-3099

ANDREWS, JAMES E., career officer; m. Margaret Andrews; 1 child, Cliff. BS, Air Force Acad., 1970; MA, La. Tech. U., 1975; cert., Squadron Officer Sch., 1975, Armed Forces Staff Coll., 1981, Air War Coll., 1990. Commd. 2d lt. USAF, 1970, advanced through grades to maj. gen., 1998; pilot, instr. pilot, standardization and evaluation pilot 913th Air Refueling Squadron, 2d Bombardment Wing, Barksdale AFB, La., 1971-77; instr., mil. tng. divsn., chief cadet ops., comdt. cadets U.S. Air Force Acad., Colorado Springs, 1977-80; flight comdr., asst. ops. officer 911th Air Refueling Squadron, Seymour Johnson AFB, N.C., 1981-82; staff officer NATO War Plans Divsn. Hdqs. Allied Forces No. Europe, Oslo, 1982-84; squadron comdr. 70th Air Refueling Squadron, Grissom AFB, Ind., 1984-86; from dep. combat support group comdr. to asst. comdr. ops. 416th Bombardment Wing, Griffis AFB, N.Y., 1986-88; dep. comdr. ops. 305th Air Refueling Wing, Grissom AFB, Ind., 1988-89; from vice comdr. to comdr. 6th Strategic Reconnaissance Wing, Eielson AFB, Alaska, 1990-92; comdr. 380th Air Refueling Wing, Plattsburgh AFB, N.Y., 1992-93, 319th Air Refueling Wing, Grand Forks AFB, N.D., 1993-95; insp. gen. Hdqs. Air Mobility Command, Scott AFB, Ill., 1995-97; dep. asst. sec. of def. for res. affairs Readiness, Tng. and Moblsn., Washington, 1997—. Office: DASD RA (RT&M) 515 Defense Pentagon Rm 2E Washington DC 20301-1500

ANDREWS, JEAN, artist, writer; b. Kingsville, Tex., Dec. 23, 1923; d. Herbert and Katharine Keith (Smith) A.; divorced; children: Robert Fleming Wasson Jr., Jean Andrews Wasson (dec.). BS in Home Economics, U. Tex., 1944; MS in Edn., Tex. A & I Univ., 1966; PhD in Fine Arts, U. North Tex., 1976. Cert. home economist. Artist, writer Austin, Tex.; vis. scholar dept. botany U. Tex., Austin, also hon. mem. adv. coun. Coll. Natural Sci., mem. exec. com., 1986-97, chmn. botany dept. vis. com.; presenter to seminars and confs. in field. Author: Sea Shells of the Texas Coast, 1971, Shells and Shores of Texas, 1977, Texas Shells: A Field Guide, 1981, Peppers: The Domesticated Capsicums, 1984, rev. edit., 1995, 96, The Texas Bluebonnet, 1985, rev. edit., 1993, An American Wildflower: Florilegium, 1992, Texas Monthly Field Guide to Shells of the Texas Coast, 1992, Red Hot Peppers, 1993, Texas Monthly Field Guide to the Shells of the Florida Coast, 1994, The Peppers Lady's Pocket Pepper Primer, 1998, The Pepper Trail, 1999; also articles; one-woman shows include RGK Found. Gallery, Austin, 1993; numerous others. Nat. adv. bd. Leadership Am., 1988-95; trustee Laguna Gloria Art Mus., 1985-91, Nat. Wildflower Rsch. Ctr., 1987-94, adv. coun. 1995—; past trustee Art Mus. of S. Tex.; past bd. dirs. Planned Parenthood; mem. Austin Symphony Soc., Friends of Huntington Gallery/Univ. Tex., others. Recipient Disting. Alumna award U.North Tex., 1991, Hall of Honor award U. Tex. Coll. Natural Sci., 1991, Disting. Alumna award U. Tex. Austin, 1997; endowments include Jean Andrews vis. professorship in human nutrition U. Tex., vis. professorship in tropical and econ. botany, endowed scholar Tex. Found. for Women's Resources, also others; named Tex. Inst. Letters. Mem. DAR, Am. Malacol. Union, Tex. Pepper Found. (life), Tex. State Tchrs. Assn. (life), U. Tex. Alumni Assn. (life), U. North Tex. Alumni Assn. (life), Colonial Dames of 17th Century, Nat. Soc. Ams. of Royal Descent, Nat. Soc. Colonial Dames in Am., Nat. Soc. Magna Charta Dames, Daus. of Cin., Huguenot Soc., Order of Descendants of Ancient Planters, Daus. of the Confederacy, Descendents of Ancient Planters, Jamestowne Soc., Descendants of Colonial Govs.

ANDREWS, JOHN FRANK, editor, author, educator; b. Carlsbad, N.Mex., Nov. 2, 1942; s. Frank Randolph and Mary Lucille (Wimberley) A.; m. Vicky Roberta Anderson, Aug. 20, 1966 (div. 1983); children: Eric John, Lisa Gail; m. Janet Ann Denton, Oct. 15, 1994. AB, Princeton U., 1965; MAT, Harvard U., 1966; PhD, Vanderbilt U., 1971. Instr. English U. Tenn., Nashville, 1969-70; asst. prof. Fla. State U., Tallahassee, 1970-74, dir. grad. studies in English, 1973-74; dir. acad. programs Folger Shakespeare Library, Washington, 1974-84; chmn. Folger Inst., Washington, 1974-84; exec. editor Folger Books, Washington, 1974-84; dep. dir. div. edn. programs NEH, Washington, 1984-88; editor The Guild Shakespeare, 1988-92; pres. The Shakespeare Guild, 1992—; editor The Everyman Shakespeare, 1993—; cons. Time-Life TV, WNET/Thirteen, Corp. for Pub. Broadcasting, Pub. Broadcasting Svc., Nat. Pub. Radio, U.S. Dept. Edn., others; chmn. Nat. Adv. Panel for the Shakespeare Plays, 1979-85; core advisor The Shakespeare Hour, 1985-86; mem. adv. bd. Theatre for a New Audience, Humanities Coun. of Washington, Ctr. for Polit. and Strategic Studies, Ctr. for Renaissance and Baroque Studies, U. Md., others; cons. Shakespeare: The Globe and the World, touring exhbn., 1978-81; adminstr program grants NEH, Andrew W. Mellon Found., Exxon Corp., Met. Life, Surdna Found., others. Asst. editor: Shakespeare Studies, 1972-74; editor: Shakespeare Quar., 1974-85; editor-in-chief, contbr.: William Shakespeare: His World, His Work, His Influence, 1985; contbr. numerous articles to mags. and scholarly jours. Recipient rsch. awards Folger Shakespeare Libr., Fla. State U., NEH. Mem. AAUP (sec. chpt. 1972-74), Modern Lang. Assn., Milton Soc. Am., Nat. Council of Tchrs. of English, Renaissance Soc. Am. (mem. council 1975-84), Internat. Shakespeare Conf., Shakespeare Assn. Am. (trustee 1979-82), The Lit. Soc. Club: Cosmos. Home and Office: 2141 Wyoming Ave NW Apt 41 Washington DC 20008-3916

ANDREWS, JOHN FRANK, civil and environmental engineering educator; b. Cave City, Ark., July 10, 1930; s. Frank Ferd and Ruth Lanell (Puckett) A.; m. Margery Ann Hall, June 21, 1952; children: John Patrick, Carol Ann, Laurie Lanell. BS in Civil Engring., U. Ark., 1951, MS, 1953; PhD, U. Calif., Berkeley, 1964. Registered profl. engr., Ark. Instr. civil engring. U. Ark., 1953-55, asst. prof., 1955-59, assoc. prof., 1959-60; project engr. U. Calif. at Berkeley, 1962-63; assoc. prof., assoc. dir. water resources engring. program Clemson U., 1963-66, prof., dir. environmental systems engring., 1966-68, prof., dept head, 1968-74; prof. civil and environmental engring. U. Houston, 1975-81; prof. environ. sci. and engring. Rice U., 1981-91, prof. emeritus, 1991, ret., 1991; vis. prof. McMaster U., Can., Kyoto U., Japan, 1988; vis. rschr. Water Pollution Rsch. Lab., Eng., 1970; hon. prof. Harbin Inst. Archtl. and Civil Engring., People's Republic of China, 1990; cons. water pollution control Engring.-Sci., Inc., Los Angeles, Phila., Chgo., Mpls.; cons. U.S. Army, Bacardi Distilleries, Pan Am. Health Orgn., UN Devel. Program, Greeley & Hansen Engrs., Shell Devel. Co., Weyerhauser Co., Woodlands Devel. Co. Gulf Coast Waste Disposal Authority, Met. Sanitary Dist. Greater Chgo., others. Research, publs. in field. NSF grantee. Mem. ASCE, AIChE, Am. Chem. Soc., Am. Water Works Assn., Water Environ. Fedn. (Harrison Prescott Eddy award 1975), Internat. Assn. Water Quality (U.S. editor Water Research 1974-84, vice chmn. Vienna conf. 1971, 75, 79, 83, program chmn. London conf. 1973, Stockholm conf. 1977 Munich conf. 1981, Houston conf. 1985, Kyoto conf. 1990, hon. mem. 1986), Am. Soc. Engring. Edn., Assn. Environ. Engring. Profs. (dir. 1967-70, chmn. workshops 1968-70, chmn. nat. conf. 1977, v.p. 1984-85, pres. 1985-86), Sigma Xi, Tau Beta Pi, Phi Kappa Phi. Methodist. Home: 1719 E Rayview Dr Fayetteville AR 72703-2625

ANDREWS, JOHN HOBART MCLEAN, education educator; b. Kamloops, B.C., Can., May 15, 1926; s. John Ernest and Cynthia Maria (Robinson) A.; m. Doris Deborah Payne, Aug. 28, 1948; children: William John, Donald Wilfrid, Jeffrey Peter, Lorraine Doris. B.A. with honours in Physics, U. B.C., 1947, M.A. in Edn, 1954; Ph.D. in Ednl. Adminstrn, U. Chgo., 1957. Tchr., prin. B.C. schs., 1950-55; prof. edn. U. Alta., 1957-65; prof., chmn. ednl. adminstrn., asst. dir. Ont. Inst. for Studies in Edn., 1965-73; dean of edn. U. B.C., Vancouver, 1973-79; prof. ednl. adminstrn. U. B.C., 1979-88, dean emeritus, 1988—. Author articles on leadership, orgn. theory, and tchr. edn. Home: 703-1835 Morton Ave, Vancouver, BC Canada V6G 1V3

ANDREWS, JULIE, actress, singer; b. Walton-on-Thames, Eng., Oct. 1, 1935; d. Edward C. and Barbara Wells; m. Tony Walton, May 10, 1959 (div.); 1 dau., Emma; m. Blake Edwards, 1969. Studied with pvt. tutors, studied voice with Mme. Stiles-Allen. Debut as singer, Hippodrome, London, 1947; appeared in pantomime Cinderella, London, 1953; appearences include (Broadway prodns.) The Boy Friend, N.Y.C., 1954, My Fair Lady, 1956-60 (N.Y. Drama Critics award 1956), Camelot, 1960-62, Putting It Together, 1993, Victor/Victoria, 1995 (Tony award nominee Best Actress in a Musical); films include Mary Poppins, 1964 (Acad. award for Best Actress 1964), The Americanization of Emily, 1964, Torn Curtain, 1966, The Sound of Music, 1966, Hawaii, 1966, Thoroughly Modern Millie, 1967, Star!, 1968, Darling Lili, 1970, The Tamarind Seed, 1973, 10, 1979, Little Miss Marker, 1980, S.O.B, 1981, Victor/Victoria, 1982, The Man Who Loved Women, 1983, That's Life!, 1986, Duet For One, 1986, A Fine Romance, 1992; TV debut in High Tor, 1956; star TV series The Julie Andrews Hour, 1972-73 (Emmy award for Best Variety Series), Julie, 1992; also spls.; TV movies include Our Sons, 1991; author: (as Julie Edwards): Mandy, 1971, The Last of the Really Great Whangdoodles, 1974; recs.: The King and I, 1992. Recipient Golden Globe award Hollywood Fgn. Press Assn., 1964, 65; named World Film Favorite (female), 1967.

ANDREWS, KATHLEEN W., book publishing executive; widow; 2 children. BS, Notre Dame Coll., 1959; MS, U. Notre Dame, 1962; LHD (hon.), U. Portland, 1994, Spring Hill Coll. Vice chmn., CEO Andrews and McMeel Publishing, Kansas City. Bd. trustees Ctr. Mgmt. Assistance, 1988-93, U. Mo., Kansas City, 1989-92, Avila Coll., 1986—, Spring Hill Coll., 1990-98, Assn. of Governing Bds. of Univs. and Colls., 1998—, Notre Dame Colls., 1998—; bd. dirs. NCCJ, 1992—; trustee and fellow U. Notre Dame, 1993—; active Christmas in Oct., 1985—, Catholic Charities, 1989—; co-founder James F. Andrews Scholarship Fund, U. Notre Dame, 1981—. Mem. Am. Booksellers Assn., Newspaper Cartoonists Soc., Newspaper Features Coun., Malta Fed. Assn. (dame). Home: 433 Ward Pky Apt 3 Kansas City MO 64112-2128 Office: Andrews & McMeel 4520 Main St Kansas City MO 64111-1816*

ANDREWS, KENNETH RICHMOND, business administration educator; b. New London, Conn., May 24, 1916; s. William John and Myrtle (Richmond) A.; m. Edith May Platt, Apr. 29, 1945 (div. 1969); children: Kenneth Richmond, Carolyn; m. Carolyn Erskine Hall, Feb. 14, 1970. A.B., Wesleyan U., 1936, M.A., 1937; Ph.D., U. Ill., 1948; M.A. (hon.), Harvard U., 1957. Tchr. English U. Ill., 1937-41; instr. bus. adminstrn. Harvard Grad. Sch. Bus. Adminstrn., 1946-47, asst. prof., 1947-52, assoc. prof., 1952-57, prof., 1957-65, Donald K. David prof. bus. adminstrn., 1965-86, emeritus, 1986—, faculty chmn. Advanced Mgmt. Program, 1967-70, master Leverett House, 1971-81, chmn. gen. mgmt. faculty, 1981-83; cons. on mgmt. devel. and policy problems; dir. Xerox Corp. and other cos., 1972-86. Author: Nook Farm, 1950, (with others) Problems of General Management, 1962, Business Policy Text and Cases, 1965, rev. edit., 1969, 73, 77, 79, 87, 90, The Effectiveness of University Executive Development Programs, 1966, The Concept of Corporate Strategy, 1971, rev. edit., 1980, 3d edit., 1987; editor: The Case Method of Teaching Human Relations and Administration, 1953; chmn. editorial bd.: Harvard Bus. Rev, 1972-79; editor in chief, 1979-85. Trustee Wesleyan U., 1955-72. Served from pvt. F.A. to maj. USAAF, 1941-46. Recipient Harvard medal, 1986. Disting. Alumnus award, Wesleyan U., 1986, Disting. Svc. award, Harvard Bus. Sch., 1990; Wesleyan U. scholar, 1967. Mem. Phi Beta Kappa. Office: Soldiers Field Boston MA 02163

ANDREWS, LAUREEN E., foundation administrator; b. Seneca Falls, N.Y., July 28, 1954; d. Lawrence J. and Anita A.; m. Craig T. Scherer, Oct. 4, 1983; children: Casey Alena, Lindsey Adele. BA, George Washington U., 1976; MA in Law and Diplomacy, Fletcher Sch. Law and Diplomacy, Mass., 1978. Lobbyist, editor League of Women Votersof the U.S.A., Washington, 1978-80; dir. internat. rels. League of Women Voters Edn. Fund, Washington, 1980-85; dep. dir. def. budget project Ctr. Budget & Policy Priorities, Washington, 1985—; dep. dir. Ctr. for Stategic & Budgetary Assessments, Washington. Editor: (legis. newsletter) Report from the Hill, 1978-80. Mem. Phi Beta Kappa. Office: Ctr for Strategic & Budgetary Assessments 1730 Rhode Island Ave NW Washington DC 20036-3101*

ANDREWS, LAVONE DICKENSHEETS, architect; b. Beaumont, Tex., Sept. 18, 1912; d. Charles and Lavone (Lowman) Dickensheets; m. Mark Edwin Andrews, July 23, 1948; 1 son, Mark Edwin III. Student, Miss Hamlin's Sch., San Francisco, Marlborough Sch., L.A.; AB, Rice Inst., 1933, BS in Architecture, 1934. Assoc. with outstanding architects in Southwest, 1934-37; opened own office Houston, 1937-41; architect firm Anderson, Clayton & Co. (cotton firm), 1941-51; v.p. Ancon Oil & Gas, 1957-94; v.p. Ancon Oil & Gas, Inc., 1957-94, pres., 1992-94. Also pvt. work, museum in, Washington, Naval Hist. Found. & Health Center, schs. for City of Houston. Trustee Mus. Fine Arts in Houston; mem. YWCA World Service Council. Selected as 3d of the 10 outstanding women architects in Am. Archtl. Record, 1947. Fellow AIA, Royal Inst. Architects Ireland; mem. Pallas Athene Lit. Soc. of Rice Inst., Colony Club (N.Y.C.), Houston Club, River Oaks Country Club, Garden of Houston Club, Bayou Club, Garden of Am. Club. Episcopalian. Home: 2121 Kirby Dr Apt 109 Houston TX 77019-6067 Office: #109 2121 Kirby Dr Houston TX 77019

ANDREWS, LEWIS DAVIS, JR., trade association executive; b. Bridgeport, Conn., Mar. 17, 1946; s. Lewis Davis and Beatrice (Hawley) A.; m. Christina Kane, Nov. 14, 1970; children: Mary Wakeley, William Bradford. BA, Drew U., 1968. Aide to Congressman T.J. Meskill U.S. Congress, Washington, 1968-70; exec. dir. Conn. Republican, Hartford, 1971-73; dep. commn. commerce, dir. Conn. Devel. Authority, Hartford, 1973-74; v.p. Nat. Oil Jobbers Coun., Washington, 1975-77, Smith & Harroff, Washington, 1977-80; pres. The Glass Packaging Inst., Washington, 1980—. Coord. primary states Connolly for Pres., 1979-80; chair bd. trustees Drew U., Madison, N.J., 1997; dir. Young Republic Nat. Fedn., Washington, 1969. Mem. The City Tavern Club (pres. 1992-95), The Met. Club, Belle Haven C.C., Edgartown Yacht Club, Chappaquiddick Beach Club (v.p. 1996-97). Republican. Episcopalian. Avocations: golf, tennis, fishing. Office: The Glass Packaging Inst 1627 K St NW Washington DC 20006-1702

ANDREWS, MARK JOSEPH, lawyer; b. Chgo., July 27, 1944; s. Mark Lewis and Elizabeth (Glendening) A.; m. Martha Jo Shipman, Nov. 29, 1969(separated 1997); children: Eliza, Jonathan. AB, Harvard Coll., 1966; JD, Harvard U., 1969. Bar: U.S. Dist. Ct. D.C. 1970, U.S. Ct. Appeals (D.C. cir.) 1970, U.S. Ct. Appeals (5th and 11th cirs.) 1981, U.S. Ct. Fed. Claims 1983, U.S. Supreme Ct. 1990. From assoc. to ptnr. Verner, Liipfert, Bernhard, McPherson & Hand, Washington, 1969-91; ptnr. Barnes & Thornburg, Washington, 1991—; co-chmn. federal govt. sponsored task force on regulatory aspects of transp. ins. crisis, 1986-87. Contbr. articles to profl. jours. Pres. Amadeus Concerts (formerly Gt. Falls (Va.) Concert Series), 1985-87, bd. dirs., 1984—. Mem. Transp. Lawyers Assn. (Disting. Svc. 1985, exec. com. 1986—, pres. 1992-93), Assn. Transp. Law, Logistics and Policy, Can. Transport Lawyers Assn., Conf. Claims Counsel. Avocations: photography, hiking, collecting native Am. artifacts, music. Office: Barnes & Thornburg 1401 I St NW Ste 500 Washington DC 20005-6558

ANDREWS, MASON COOKE, mayor, obstetrician, gynecologist, educator; b. Norfolk, Va., Apr. 20, 1919; s. Charles James and Jean (Cooke) A.; m. Sabine Goodman, Sept. 24, 1949; c.Jean, Mason. B.A., Princeton U., 1940; M.D., Johns Hopkins U., 1943; Doctor of Laws (hon.), Eastern Virginia Med. School, 1987. Diplomate: Am. Bd. Ob-Gyn. Intern ob-gyn Johns Hopkins U., Balt., 1944, resident ob-gyn, 1946-50; pvt. practice ob-gyn Norfolk, Va., 1950-70; lectr. Johns Hopkins U. Sch. Medicine, Balt., 1971-72; prof. ob-gyn. Eastern Va. Med. Sch., Norfolk, 1974—, chmn. dept. ob-gyn., 1974-90; mayor City of Norfolk, 1992-94; bd. dirs. First Va. Bank of Tidewater, Chesapeake and Potomac Telephone Co.; mem., dir. Norfolk City Planning Commn., 1963-65, twice chmn., commr., exec. com. mem. Hampton Rds. Planning Dist. Commn., pres. (1971) Planning Coun. of United Communities, Norfolk City Coun., 1974—; chmn. Ea. Va. Med. Authority, 1964-70; pres. Am. Assn. Obstetricians Found., 1986-89. *As councilman, and subsequently Mayor, he lead in organizing government, citizen leadership and consultants to make, adopt, and implement plans for a downtown renaissance in Norfolk. He led the establishment of the Eastern Virginia Medical School, serving as founding chairman of the authority which organized and operates the school. As founding chairman of the Department of Obstetrics and Gynecology, he built a department which is recognized internationally for contributions to the knowledge of reproductive medicine including the first in vitro fertilization program in the United States.* Contbr. (numerous articles to sci. jours.). Councilman City of Norfolk, 1974—, vice mayor, 1978-82, mayor, 1992-94. Recipient First Citizen citation Norfolk Cosmopolitan Club, 1968, Norfolk citation for outstanding svc., 1964, award for cmty. svc. Med. Soc. Va., AMA, Nat. Brotherhood award Norfolk Conf. Christians and Jews. Fellow Am. Gynecol. and Obstet. Soc. (v.p. 1982-83, pres. 1992-93); mem. South Atlantic Assn. (pres. 1972), Va. Obstet. and Gynecol. Soc. (pres. 1975), Norfolk Acad. Medicine (pres. 1961), Johns Hopkins Soc. Scholars, Harbor Club, Norfolk Yacht and Country Club. Presbyterian. Home: 1011 N Shore Rd Norfolk VA 23505-3119 Office: Eastern Va Med Sch Dept Ob-Gyn 601 Colley Ave Norfolk VA 23507-1627

ANDREWS, MELINDA WILSON, human development researcher; b. N.Y.C., Aug. 12, 1956; d. William Maurice and Natalie Maxine (Amos) Wilson; m. James Robert Andrews, Dec. 3, 1977; children: Christopher Wilson Andrews, William James Andrews. BBA in Mgmt./Mktg., Abilene (Tex.) Christian U., 1977; MS in Human Devel., U. Tex., Dallas, 1988, postgrad., 1994—. Logics adminstr. Texas Instruments, Dallas, 1977-79, contract adminstr., 1979-81, 82-83; grocery mgr., co-asst. store dir. Tom Thumb, Dallas, 1981-82; teaching asst. U. Tex. at Dallas, Richardson, Tex., 1988-91; rsch. asst. U. Tex. at Dallas, 1991—; presenter in field. Contbr. articles to profl. jours. Mem. Richardson Symphony Orch., 1977-79, Canyon Creek Elem. PTA, 5th v.p., 1994-95, libr. rep., 1992-94; treas. exec. bd. Creative Presch. Coop., 1998-99, sec. ex. bd. 1999—. Mem. Soc. for Rsch. in Child Devel. (co-author paper-poster session 1991, 93 confs.), Southwest Soc. for Rsch. in Child Devel., Psi Chi. Mem. Ch. of Christ. Avocations: music, animals, carpentry. Home and Office: 2109 Flat Creek Dr Richardson TX 75080-2331

ANDREWS, NEIL CORBLY, surgeon; b. Mar. 31, 1916. BA, U. Oreg., 1939, MD, 1943; MSc, Ohio State U., 1950. Prof. surgery Ohio State U., Columbus, 1967-70; prof. surgery U. Calif., Davis, 1970-86, prof. emeritus surgery, 1986—. Home and Office: Box 3007 El Macero CA 95618

ANDREWS, OAKLEY V., lawyer; b. Cleve., Apr. 15, 1940. BA, Yale U., 1962; JD, Western Reserve U., 1965. Bar: Ohio 1965, U.S. Tax Ct. 1968, U.S. Dist. Ct. (no. dist.) Ohio 1968, U.S. Ct. Appeals (6th cir.) 1968. Ptnr. Baker & Hostetler, LLP, Cleve. Fellow Am. Coll. Trust and Estate Coun.; mem. Ohio State Bar Assn., Estate Planning Coun. Cleve. (pres. 1982-83), Cleve. Bar Assn. (chmn. Estate Planning, Probate and Trust law sect. 1984-85), Phi Delta Phi. Office: Baker & Hostetler LLP 3200 Nat City Ct 1900 E 9th St Ste 3200 Cleveland OH 44114-3475

ANDREWS, RALPH HERRICK, television producer; b. Chgo., Dec. 17, 1927; s. Henry Karl and Sylvia Angelica (Lorenzen Barth; m. Margaret Ann Belt, Feb. 5, 1951 (div. 1977); m. Aleksandra Vaz vel Wezykowska, June 1, 1986; children: William, Herrick, Phyllis, Patrice, Peter, James, Jakub, Matthew. Announcer, disc jockey, salesman radio stas. WSAM and WKNX, Saginaw, Mich.; page NBC, Hollywood; with Don Fedderson Prodns., Ralph Edwards Prodns.; dir. live programming Desilu; prin. Ralph Andrews Prodns.; co-founder, bd. dirs. Entertainment Industries Coun. Producer: Divorce Hearing, By the Numbers, Zoom, Show Me, You Don't Say, I'll Bet, Wedding Party, The Family Game, It Takes Two, It's Your Bet, Liars Club, The Mickie Finn Show, Celebrity Sweepstakes, 50 Grand Slam, Lingo, (movies) Silent Treatment, Skyjacked; producer, host: Lie Detector; host, writer (website) The TroubleMaker www.the-troublemaker.com. Cand. for Congress, 1972; nat. dir. edn. and tng. Rep. Nat. Com., Washington, 1972 (Presidential commendation). Republican. Roman Catholic. Avocations: skiing, flying, skating, running, sailing. Home and Office: 5021 Dantes View Dr Agoura Hills CA 91301

ANDREWS, RICHARD NIGEL LYON, environmental policy educator, environmental studies administrator; b. Newport, R.I., Dec. 6, 1944; s. Nigel Lyon and Constance Doane (Young) A.; m. Hannah Page Wheeler, June 7, 1969; children: Sarah Huntington, Christopher Page Monteith. AB, Yale U., 1966; M in Regional Planning, U. N.C., 1970, PhD, 1972. Vol. U.S. Peace Corps, Bharatpur, Nepal, 1966-68; budget examiner U.S. Office of Mgmt. and Budget, Washington, 1970-72; prof. U. Mich., Ann Arbor, 1972-81; prof. environ. policy U. N.C., Chapel Hill, 1981—, dir. U. N.C. Inst. Environ. Studies, 1981-91, dir. environ. mgmt. and policy program, 1990-94, mem. exec. com. faculty coun., 1994-97, chair of faculty, 1997—; cons. NSF, Washington, 1982-85, AID, Yaounde, Cameroon, 1983; mem. N.C. Natural Heritage Adv. Com., Raleigh, 1982-87; sr. staff mem. Commn. on Future of N.C., Raleigh, 1982-84; mem. Bd. Environ. Studies and Toxology, NAS, 1986-88; chmn. study com. on opportunities in applied environ. R&D, NAS, 1988-90; mem. risk reduction subcom. Sci. Adv. Bd., EPA, 1989-90, AID, Czech and Slovak Republics, 1991-94; mem. adv. com. Pew Conservation Scholars Program, 1991-94; mem. adv. com. EPA Decisionmaking, Nat. Acad. of Pub. Adminstrn., 1994-95; chmn. adv. panel new approach to environ. regulation Office Tech. Assessment U.S. Congress, Washington, 1993-95. Author: Environmental Policy and Administrative Change, 1976, Managing the Environment, Managing Ourselves: A History of American Environmental Policy, 1999; editor: Land in America, 1979, Environmental Change and Public Health-The Next Fifty Years, 1990; contbr. articles to profl. jours. Mem. vestry Episcopalian Ch., Chapel Hill, 1986-89. Resources for the Future Inc. fellow, 1971-72, Rockefeller Found. fellow, 1977-78, Fulbright fellow Vienna U. Econs., 1990, Salzburg Seminar faculty fellow, 1990, fellow Nat. Acad. of Pub. Adminstrn., 1996. Fellow AAAS (nominating com. sect. on societal impacts of sci. and engring. 1987-90, chair 1989-90, ann. meeting program com. 1988-90, chmn.-elect 1995-96, chmn. 1996-97, com. on sci. engring. and pub. policy 1997—); mem. Assn. Pub. Policy and Mgmt. Rsch., Golden Key, Sigma Xi, Delta Omega. Democrat. Avocations: tennis, sailing, camping, photography. Office: U NC Dept Environ Sci and Engring Cb7400 Rosenau Hall Chapel Hill NC 27599

ANDREWS, RICHARD OTIS, museum director; b. L.A., Nov. 8, 1949; s. Robert and Theodora (Hammond) A.; m. Colleen Chartier, Jan. 3, 1976; 1 child, Bryce. BA, Occidental Coll., L.A., 1971; BFA, U. Wash., 1973, MFA, 1975. Project mgr. Art in Pub. Places, Seattle Arts Commn., 1978-80, coord., 1980-84; dir. visual arts program Nat. Endowment for Arts, Washington, D.C., 1985-87; dir. Henry Art Gallery, U. Wash., Seattle, 1987—; co-curator Art Into Life: Russian Constructivism 1914-1932; cons. pub. art program devel., 1982-84; bd. trustees Assn. Art Mus. Dirs., 1997—. Author: Insights/On Sites, 1984, James Turrell: Sensing Space, 1992; editor Artwork/Network, 1984; contbg. editor Going Public, 1988. Office: U Wash Henry Art Gallery PO Box 351410 Seattle WA 98195-1410

ANDREWS, RICHARD VINCENT, physiologist, educator; b. Arapahoe, Nebr., Jan. 9, 1932; s. Wilber Vincent and Fern (Clawson) A.; m. Elizabeth Williams, June 1, 1954 (dec. Dec. 1994); children: Thomas, William, Robert, Catherine, James, John; m. Wyama Upward, Oct. 18, 1997. BS, Creighton U., 1958, MS, 1959; PhD, U. Iowa, 1963. Instr. biology Creighton U., Omaha, 1958-60; instr. physiology U. Iowa, 1960-63; asst. prof. Creighton U., Omaha, 1963-65, assoc. prof., 1965-68, prof. physiology, 1968-97, asst. med. dean, 1972-75, dean grad. studies, 1975-85, dean emeritus, 1995—, prof. emeritus, 1997—; vis. prof. Naval Arctic Rsch. Lab., 1963-72, U. B.C., 1985-86, U. Tasmania, 1993-94; cons. VA, NSF, NRC, ARS; plenary speaker USSR Symposium on Environment, 1970, Internat. Soc. Biomet., 1972. Contbr. articles to profl. jours. Served with M.C. U.S. Army, 1951-54. NSF fellow, 1962-63; NSF-NIH-ONR-AINA grantee, 1963—. Fellow Explorers Club, Arctic Inst. N.Am.; mem. Am. Physiol. Soc., Am. Mammal Soc., Endocrine Soc., Soc. Exptl. Biology and Medicine, Internat. Soc. for Biometeorology, Sigma Xi.

ANDREWS, ROBERT E., congressman; b. Bellmar, N.J., Aug. 4, 1957; m. Camille Spinello, Nov., 1993. BA summa cum laude, Bucknell U., 1979; JD magna cum laude, Cornell U., 1982. Bar: N.J. 1982. Assoc. Archer & Greiner, Haddonfield, N.J., 1982-84, Charles J. Clarke & Assocs., Haddonfield, 1984-85, Kenney & Kearney, Cherry Hill, N.J., 1985-88; mem. Camden County (N.J.) Bd. Chosen Freeholders, 1987-90, freeholder dir., 1988-90; mem. 101st-105th Congresses from 1st N.J. dist., Washington, D.C., 1990—; mem. edn. and workforce com., internat. rels. com. Contbr. articles to law jours. Bd. dirs. Camden County March of Dimes; mem. Task Force on Govt. Waste. Mem. Phi Beta Kappa. Democrat. Episcopalian. Avocation: jogging. Office: US House of Reps 2439 Rayburn Bldg Washington DC 20515-3001*

ANDREWS, ROBERT LEE, clergyman, architect; b. Chgo., July 10, 1946; m. Judith Ann Baker, Nov. 1, 1969; children: Toi N., Tre D., Tamu D. BArch, U. Ill., 1974; MArch and Urban Planning, Princeton U., 1976. Lic. architect, Ill., Ind. Draftsman Holabird & Root, Chgo., 1966-69, Heard & Assocs., Ltd., Chgo., 1969-71; village adminstr. Village of Robbins, Ill., 1976-80; chief constrn. adminstrn. Wendell Campbell & Assocs., Chgo., 1980-86; asst. dir. Bur. Architecture Chgo. Bd. Edn., 1986-89; pres. Andrews Architecture, Ltd., Chgo., 1990—. Pastor African Meth. Episcopal Ch., 1989—. Recipient svc. award Village of Robbins, 1980, fellowship Princeton U., 1974, 75. Mem. AIA, Nat. Orgn. Minority Architects (pres. 1983-85, svc. award 1985), Nat. Coun. Archtl. Registration Bds. Office: Andrews Architecture Ltd 10 W 35th St 16th Fl Chicago IL 60616-3703

ANDREWS, ROWENA, public relations executive; b. Chattanooga, Dec. 31, 1944; d. Mose Porter and Waudie Tarvin; married, 1966 (div. 1971); 1 child, Elizabeth Paige Andrews. BA in Journalism, U. Ga., 1974. Info. specialist NASA-Cosmic, Athens, Ga., 1967-74; pub. rels. and photography freelancer Chattanooga, 1974-76; comm. specialist Providence Life Ins., Chattanooga, 1976-78; dir. pub. info. Aid United Givers, L.A., 1978-80; corp. comm. mgr. Informatics Gen. Corp., Woodland Hills, Calif., 1980-81; dir. pub. rels. Candle Corp., L.A., 1981-83; pub. rels. cons. Andrews Pub. Rels., L.A., 1983-94, Moreland, Ga., 1994—. Avocations: horseback riding, making pottery, photography. Home and Office: Andrews PR PO Box 405 Moreland GA 30259-0405*

ANDREWS, SALLY MAY, healthcare administrator; b. Westfield, Mass., Feb. 29, 1956; d. Roger N. and Dorothy M. (Goodhind) A. Student, U. Conn., 1974-76; BA, Simmons Coll., Boston, 1978; MBA, Boston U., 1986. Payroll clk. Children's Hosp., Boston, 1978-79, asst. payroll supr., 1979-81, staff analyst dept. medicine, 1981-83, asst. adminstr. dept. medicine, 1983-86, adminstr. dept. medicine, 1986-97, vice chair adminstrn. and strategic planning dept. medicine, 1998—. Bd. overseers Lasell Coll., Newton, Mass. Mem. Am. Mgmt. Assn., Adminstrs. of Internal Medicine, Assn. Adminstrs. in Acad. Pediatrics (pres. 1996-97). Congregationalist. Office: Children's Hosp Dept Medicine 300 Longwood Ave Boston MA 02115-5737

ANDREWS, SUE E., park director; b. River Vale, N.J., Feb. 24, 1960. BA, East Straudsburg Coll., 1982. With Lowell (Mass.) Nat. Park, 1987-95; site mgr. Roger Williams Nat. Meml., Providence, 1995—. Office: 282 N Main St Providence RI 02903-1240*

ANDREWS, THEODORA ANNE, retired librarian, educator; b. Carroll County, Ind., Oct. 14, 1921; d. Harry Floyd and Margaret Grace (Walter) Ulrey; B.S. with distinction, Purdue U., 1953; M.S., U. Ill., 1955; m. Robert William Andrews, July 18, 1940 (div. 1946); 1 son, Martin Harry. Asst. reference libr. Purdue U., West Lafayette, Ind., 1955-56, pharmacy libr. , instr., 1956-60, pharmacy libr., asst. prof., 1960-65, pharmacy libr. an, assoc. prof. libr. sci., 1965-71, prof. libr. sci., pharmacy libr., 1971-79, prof. libr. sci., pharmacy, nursing and health scis. libr., 1979-90, prof. libr. sci., spl. bibliographer, 1991-92, prof. emerita of libr. sci., 1992—. Mem. Purdue Women's Caucus, 1973—, v.p., 1975-76, pres., 1976-77; mem. Internat. Women's Yr. Regional Planning Com., 1977; del. Ind. Gov.'s Conf. Librs. and Info. Svcs., 1978. U. Ill. grad. fellow, 1954-55. Mem. Spl. Libr. Assn. (John H. Moriarty award Ind. chpt. 1972), ALA, Med. Libr. Assn., AAUP, Am. Assn. Colls. Pharmacy, Kappa Delta Pi, Delta Rho Kappa. Baptist. Author: A Bibliography of the Socioeconomic Aspects of Medicine, 1975; A Bibliography of Drug Abuse Including Alcohol and Tobacco, 1977; A Bibliography of Drug Abuse, Supplement 1977-1980, 1981; Bibliography on Herbs, Herbal Remedies and Natural Foods, 1982; Substance Abuse Materials for School Libraries, an Annotated Bibliography, 1985; Guide to the Literature of Pharmacy and the Pharmaceutical Sciences, 1986; sect. editor Advances in Alcohol and Substance Abuse, 1981-92; contbr. articles to profl. jours. Office: Purdue U Sch Pharmacy West Lafayette IN 47907

ANDREWS, TIMOTHY WILLIAM, public relations executive; b. Bridgeport, Conn., Mar. 14, 1964; s. William Roy and Alice Frances (Arnett) A.; m. Sandra Lee Ellis, June 4, 1994; children: Jeremy, Benjamin. Student, Am. Inst. for Fgn. Study, Florence, Italy, 1985, Cambridge U., Eng., 1986; BA cum laude, U. N.H., 1986. Lic. marine radio telephone operator, FCC. Intern MacNeil, Lehrer News Hour, Washington, 1987; internat. radio broadcaster Voice of Am., Washington, 1987-90; producer, editor NBC Radio, Washington, 1990-92; asst. mng. editor Standard News Network, Washington, 1992-94; media dir., chief press officer Greenpeace, Washington, 1994-97; dir. pub. rels. Colonial Williamsburg (Va.) Found., 1997—; speaker, adviser Columbia U. Journalism Seminar, N.Y.C., 1994; chmn. Colonial Williamsburg (Va.) Tricentennial Com., 1992—. Mem. Pub. Rels. Soc. Am., Radio TV News Dirs. Assn., Soc. Profl. Journalists, Strathmore's Who's Who, Mortar Bd., Pi Gamma Mu, Sigma Alpha Epsilon. Avocations: skiing, scuba diving, roller blading, mountain biking. E-mail: andrews@cwf.org. Office: Colonial Williamsburg Found PO Box 1776 Williamsburg VA 23187-1776

ANDREWS, WILLIAM COOKE, physician; b. Norfolk, Va., June 7, 1924; s. Charles James and Jean Curry (Cooke) A.; m. Elizabeth Wight Kyle, Nov. 10, 1951; children—Elizabeth Randolph, William Cooke, Jr., Susan Carrington. A.A., Princeton U., 1946; M.D., Johns Hopkins U., 1947. Diplomate Am. Bd. Obstetrics and Gynecology. Intern N.Y. Hosp., 1947, resident in obstetrics and gynecology, 1948-50, 52-53; practice medicine specializing in obstetrics and gynecology Norfolk, Va., 1953-95; asst. in obstetrics and gynecology Cornell U. Med. Sch., 1948-50, 52-53; mem. attending staff Med. Ctr. Hosp.; prof. ob-gyn. Ea. Va. Med. Sch., Norfolk, 1975-95, prof. emeritus, 1995—, pres. faculty senate, 1976-77; mem. fertility and maternal health drug adv. com. FDA, 1979-83, chmn., 1982-83, cons., 1983-87; mem. sci. adv. bd. Alan Guttmacher Inst., 1992-94; co-chair women's health measurement adv. panel Nat. Com. Quality Assurance, 1996—. Contbr. articles in field to profl. jours. Chmn. Norfolk Bicentennial Commn., 1969-71; mem. Community Facilities Commn., 1971-73, chmn., 1973-79; bd. dirs. Va. League for Planned Parenthood, 1966-68; pres. Norfolk chpt. Planned Parenthood, 1966-68; bd. govs. The Jacobs Inst. Women's Health, 1997—. With M.C., USN, 1950-52. Named Hon. Officer of the Most Excellent Order of the Brit. Empire, Queen Elizabeth II, 1967; presented Order of Andres Bello, Pres. Carlos Andres Perez of Venezuela, 1992. Fellow Am. Coll. Obstetricians and Gynecologists (vice chmn. dist. IV 1985-88, chmn. 1988-91, v.p. 1992-93, pres.-elect 1993, pres. 1994-95, exec. bd. 1988-96), Am. Assn. Obstetricians and Gynecologists, Am. Gynecol. and Obstet. Soc., Royal Coll. Obstetricians and Gynecologists (hon.); mem. AMA, Am. Fertility Soc. (bd. dirs. 1970-73, pres. 1977, med. dir. 1986-88, exec. dir. 1988-92), Med. Soc. Va., Norfolk Acad. Medicine, Va. Tidewater Obstetricians and Gynecologists Soc., Continental Gynecol. Soc., South Atlantic Assn. Obs.-Gyns., Norfolk C. of C. (chmn. armed forces com. 1966-68, v.p. 1968-69, pres. 1970), Internat. Fedn. Fertility Socs. (asst. treas. 1974-80, pres. 1983-86, chmn. sci. program com. 1986-89, exec. com. 1974-92), Navy League U.S. (pres. Hampton Roads coun. 1968-70, nat. dir. 1970-74), English Speaking Union U.S. (pres. Norfolk-Portsmouth br. 1964-66), Planned Parenthood Fedn. Am. (cons. nat. med. com. 1975-85, chmn. 1981-83), Norfolk Yacht and Country Club (commodore 1966). Presbyterian. Home and Office: 929 Graydon Ave Norfolk VA 23507-1207

ANDREWS, WILLIAM DOREY, lawyer, educator; b. N.Y.C., Feb. 25, 1931; s. Sidney Warren and Margaret (Dorey) A.; A.B., Amherst Coll., 1952, LL.D., 1977; LL.B., Harvard U., 1955; m. Shirley May Herrman, Dec. 26, 1953; children: Helen Estelle Andrews Noble, Roy Herrman, John Frederick, Margaret Dorey Andrews Davenport, Susan Louise, Carol Mary Andrews Reid. Bar: Mass. 1959. Practice in Boston, 1959-63; assoc. Ropes & Gray, 1959-63; lectr. Harvard Law Sch., Cambridge, Mass., 1961-63, asst. prof., 1963-65, prof., 1965—, Eli Goldston prof. law, 1986— ; cons. Sullivan & Worcester, 1964—; assoc. reporter for accessions tax proposal Am. Law Inst. Fed. Estate and Gift Tax Project; gen. reporter for subchpt. C, Am. Law Inst. Fed. Income Tax Project, 1974-82, 86-93; cons. U.S. Treasury Dept., 1965-68. Mem. Zoning Bd. Appeals, Concord, 1966-73. Served to lt.

USNR, 1955-58. Mem. Am. Law Inst., Am. Bar Assn. Office: Harvard U Law Sch 1545 Massachusetts Ave Cambridge MA 02138

ANDREWS, WILLIAM EUGENE, construction products manufacturing executive; b. Augusta, Ga., May 9, 1943; s. William D. and Mildred (Aldridge) A.; m. Marilynn Knox, Mar. 21, 1975. BS, Miss. State U., State College, 1964, MBA, 1980. CPA, Miss. Auditor Coopers & Lybrand, Birmingham, Ala., 1964-69; div. contr. Ceco Bldg. div. Ceco Corp., Columbus, Miss., 1969-81; controller The Ceco Corp., Oak Brook, Ill., 1981-86, v.p., contr., 1986-89; contr. Windsor Door div. United Dominion Industries, Little Rock, 1989-92; sr. v.p., CFO, VARCO Pruden bldgs.-bldg. products segment United Dominion Industries, Memphis, 1992-97; sr. v.p., CFO adminstrn. and strategic programs VP Buildings, Inc., Memphis, 1997—. Named One of Outstanding Young Leaders, State Miss. Econ. Council, 1974. Mem. AICPA, Miss. Soc. CPA's. Republican. Presbyterian. Avocation: golf. Office: 3200 Players Club Cir Memphis TN 38125-8843

ANDREWS, WILLIAM FREDERICK, manufacturing executive; b. Easton, Pa., Oct. 7, 1931; s. William Frederick and Lydia Nielson (Cross) A.; m. Carol Beaman, Feb. 8, 1962; children: William Frederick III, Whitney, Carter, Clayton, Sloane. BS, U. Md., 1953; MBA, Seton Hall U., 1961. Product mgr. Scovill Mfg. Co., Waterbury, Conn., 1965-68; v.p., gen. mgr. Scovill Mfg. Co., Raleigh, N.C., 1968-73; group v.p. Scovill Mfg. Co., Nashville, 1973-79; pres. Scovill Mfg. Co., Waterbury, 1979-81; chmn., pres., chief exec. Scovill Mfg. Co., 1981-86; chmn., pres., CEO Singer Sewing Machine Co., 1986-89; pres. Massey Investment Co., 1989-90; pres., chief exec. officer UNR Industries Inc., 1990-92; CEO, chmn. bd. Amdura Corp., Conn., 1992-94; chmn. bd. Utica Corp., Utica, N.Y., 1992-94, Scovill Fasteners, Nashville, 1995—, Northwestern Steel and Wire Co., Nashville, 1998—; bd. dirs. Northwestern Steel & Wire Co., So. New Eng. Tel. Co., Corrections Corp., Navistar Internat. Co., Johnson Controls, Katy Industries, Black Box, Inc., Dayton Superior Corp. Capt. USAF, 1953-56. Recipient Silver Beaver award Boys Scouts Am., 1979, Significant Sig award Sigma Chi, 1992. Mem. Bellemeade Country Club (Nashville), Highfield Country Club, Waterbury (Conn.) Country Club, Chgo. Club, Univ. Club (N.Y.C.). Republican. Episcopalian.

ANDREWS REEVES, DONNA, golfer; b. Lynchburg, VA, Apr. 12, 1967; d. James Barclay and Helen Louise (Munsey) Andrews; m. John A. Reeves, Nov. 13, 1993. BBA, U. N.C., 1989. Qualified golfer LPGA Tour, Fla., 1990; winner Ping-Cellular One Golf Tounament, Portland, Oreg., 1993, Ping-Welch's Golf Tournament, Tucson, Ariz., 1994, Dinah Shore Major Golf Tournament, Palm Springs, Calif., 1994, Longs Drugs Challenge, Lincoln, CA, 1998. Office: LPGA 100 International Golf Dr Daytona Beach FL 32124-1092*

ANDREWS-WORTHY, ROSALIND, foundation consultant; b. Detroit, Oct. 2, 1959; m. Herman Worthy, 1993. Diploma, Alliance Francaise, 1985; student, Am. U. Paris, 1983-85, U. London, 1986. Contbg. journalist Khaleej Times, Dubai, United Arab Emirates, Paris, 1981-83; instr. French Nataki Mid. Sch., Detroit, 1988-91, U. Detroit, 1988-91; program asst. Wayne State U., Detroit, 1991-95; cons. W.K. Kellogg Found., Detroit, 1996—. Author: Claiming Our Inheritance, 1993, (children's book) Française Facilement, 1992; asst. editor: Words of Inspiration, 1997. V.p. Steppin'Out AIDS Fundraiser, Royal Oak, Mich., 1995—; cons. REACH Project, Detroit, 1996. Wayne State U. scholar, 1997. Mem. Smithsonian Inst., Habitat for Humanity. Avocations: collecting traditional African jewelry, research of rites of passage rituals. Home: 20177 Stratford Rd Detroit MI 48221-1317

ANDRIANO-MOORE, RICHARD GRAF, naval officer; b. Petaluma, Calif., May 25, 1932; s. Norvel Moore and Thelma Elizabeth (Cook) Koch-Andriano Atkins; m. Janice Lynn Hironaka, Jan. 10, 1976 (div. Feb. 1990); children: Erika Lynn, Stephen Albert. BA, San Jose State U., 1956; MBA, Pepperdine U., 1977; B in Metaphysical Sci., U. Metaphysics, 1993. Commd. ens. USN, 1957, advanced through grades to comdr.; 1st lt., and gunnery officer U.S.S. Jefferson Count LST1068, 1957-60; 7th grade tchr. Oasis Sch., Riverside County, Calif., 1960-63; pers. and legal officer U.S.S. Maury AGS-16, 1963-65; commdg. officer Naval & Marine Corps reserve Training Ctrl., Port Arthur, Tex., 1965-68; ops. officer U.S.S. Muliphen LKA 64, 1968-69; ASW & surface program officer 11th Naval Dist., San Diego, 1970-74; commdg. officer Naval Reserve Ctrl., Hunters Point, Calif., 1974-75, Army, Navy & Marine Corps Reserve Ctr, San Bruno, Calif., 1975-79; dir. of adminstrn. Nat. Com. for Employer, Washington, 1979-82; comdr., regional recruiting coord. for 10 western states, Alameda, Calif., 1982-84; chief of staff N.R. Readiness comdr., Treasure Island, Calif., 1984-85; tchr. Shoreline Unified Sch. Dist., Tomales, Calif., 1985-92, 94-99. Editor-in-chief: California Compatriot, 1976-80. Insp. Precinct Bd., Petaluma, Calif., 1987-90; scoutmaster Boy Scouts Am., 1989-92, dist. exec., 1992-94. Decorated Defense Meritorious Svc. medal Sec. of Def., Washington, 1982; recipient Ancestral Coat of Arms of the Counts of Andriano, Wappenrolle, Austria, 1985, Rome, Italy, 1994, Disting. Alumni award San Jose State U., 1991; knighted Order St. John of Jerusalem Knights Hospitaller, 1991. Mem. The Augustan Soc. Inc. (v.p. 1990-93, bd. dirs. 1995-99), Calif. Soc. SAR (state pres. 1986-87, San Francisco chpt. pres. 1976-77, Silver Good Citizenship medal 1978, Patriot medal 1985, Meritorious Svc. medal 1987, oak leaf cluster 1996), Mil. Order of Loyal Legion of U.S. (Calif. comdr. 1982-88), Naval Order U.S. Avocations: reading, hiking, biking, traveling, abstract artist. Office: 1253 Bertha Ln Santa Rosa CA 95405-7003

ANDRINGA, PATRICIA PERKINS, fundraiser, consultant; b. Apr. 9, 1944. BA in Polit. Sci. cum laude, Mt. Holyoke Coll., 1966. Rsch. asst. Office Planning & Sys. Analysis U.S. Office Postmaster Gen., Washington, 1966-68; writer, editor U. Wis., Wausau, 1968-69; cons., facilitator Washington, 1992—; bd. cons. Riggs Bank N.A., Washington, 1996—. Founder, pub. Potomac Pages Mag., 1984-85; editor Wickette mag., 1978-81. Bd. dirs. Boys & Girls Clubs Greater Washington, 1984—, chmn. bd. dirs. 1986-89; trustee Holton-Arms Sch., 1988-97, emeritus 1997—; founder, pres. The Washington Joffrey Bd., Washington, 1993-96; v.p. Adas Israel Synagogue, Washington, 1991-93; women's leadership round table mem. D.C. Commn. for Women; bd. dirs. Nat. Symphony Orch., 1980—, The Joffrey Ballet Chgo., 1993—, Children's Hosp., Washington, 1998—; mem. Leadership Washington, 1996—, bd. dirs. 1998—; chmn. Res. Devel. Com. Recipient Svc. Youth award Boys & Girls Clubs Am., 1994, medallion award, 1991, Silver medallion award, 1998, Vol. Fundraiser Yr. Nat. Soc. Fundraising Execs., 1992. Mem. Jr. League Washington (bd. dirs. 1983-85, v.p., Spirit Volunteerism award 1988). Avocations: travel, tennis, swimming, performing and visual arts, reading.

ANDRIOLE, STEPHEN JOHN, information systems executive; b. Phila., Oct. 22, 1949; s. Frank Richard and Grace Marie A.; m. Denise Marie De Felice, Aug. 7, 1971. BA magna cum laude, LaSalle Coll., 1971; MA, U. Md., 1973, PhD, 1974. NDEA research fellow U. Md., 1971-74, instr., 1974, asst. prof., 1975; research analyst Decisions and Designs, Inc., McLean, Va., 1975-76, project dir., 1975-76; program mgr. Def. Advanced Research Projects Agy., Dept. Def., Arlington, Va., 1977-78; dir. Cybernetics Tech. Office, 1977-79; pres. Internat. Info. Systems, Inc., 1979—; prof. info. tech. George Mason U., Fairfax, Va., 1986-90, chmn. dept. info. systems and systems engrng., 1987-89; prof. info. studies Drexel U., 1990—; chief technology officer Cigna Corp., 1995—; sr. tech. officer Safeguard Scientifics, Inc., 1998—; prin. TL Ventures, 1998—; participant profl. panels and seminars. Author or co-author 28 books on systems design and analytical methods; contbr. articles to profl. publs.; reviewer Automatica, 1983—, Large Scale Systems, 1983—, mem. editorial bd., 1975—. Mem. IEEE Systems, Man Cybernetics Soc., Armed Forces Communications and Electronics Assn., Am. Assn. Artificial Intelligence. Roman Catholic. *Tenacity is the real secret of "success."*

ANDRISANI, JOHN ANTHONY, editor, author, golf consultant; b. Bayshore, N.Y., Sept. 24, 1949; s. Pat and Gwendoline Mary (Rose) A. Student, SUNY, Stony Brook, 1968-71. Instr. golf in country club N.Y., 1971-78; freelance writer golf mags., 1977—; asst. editor Golf Illustrated mag., London, 1980-82; sr. editor instrn. Golf mag., N.Y.C., 1982-98. Co-author: (with Sandy Lyle) Learning Golf: The Lyle Way, 1986, (with Seve Ballesteros) Natural Golf, 1987 (Book of Month Club 1987), (with Chi Chi Rodriguez) 101 Supershots, 1990, (with Robin McMillan) The Golf Doctor, 1990 (Brentanos bestseller 1990), (with Mike Dunaway) Hit It Hard!, 1991, (with Phil Ritson) Golf Your Way, 1992, (with John Daly) Grip It, and Rip It!, 1992, (with Fred Couples) Total Shotmaking, 1994, (with Craig Stadler) I Am The Walrus, 1995, (with Claude "Butch" Harmon Jr.), The Four Cornerstones of Winning Golf, 1996, (with Jim McLean) The X-Factor Swing, 1996, The Tiger Woods Way, 1997, The Short Game Magic of Tiger Woods, 1998, (with Mark Russell) Golf Rules Plain and Simple, 1999; contbr. articles to jours. and mags. Mem. Golf Writer's Assn. (assn. champion 1985), Ballybunion Golf Club (life, Ireland).

ANDRISANI, PAUL, business educator, management consultant; b. Wilmington, Del., Oct. 19, 1946; s. Paul and Mary (Tavani) A.; m. Barbara Lee Frank, Nov. 23, 1968; children: Nathan, Damian, Danielle. BS, U. Del., 1968, MBA, 1970; PhD, Ohio State U., 1973, postgrad., 1973-74. Sr. rsch. assoc. Ctr. for Human Resource Rsch. Ohio State U., Columbus, 1973-74, vis. rsch. assoc., 1979; asst. prof. Sch. Bus., Temple U., Phila., 1974-76, assoc. prof., 1977-83, prof., 1983—; dir. Bur. Econ. Rsch., Phila., 1977-78, Ctr. for Labor and Human Resource Studies, Phila., 1985—; co-dir. Privatization Rsch. Ctr., Phila., 1997—, assoc. dean, 1989-91, chmn. dept. mgmt., 1993-95; pres. Paul J. Andrisani Mgmt. Cons. Svcs., Wilmington, Del., 1974—, St. Anthony's Edn. Fund, 1986—; pres. West End Neighborhood House Social Svc. Agy., 1995-97; cons. Price Waterhouse, U.S. EEOC, UPS, U.S. Army Recruiting Command, Acme Markets, CBS, Coca-Cola, City of Tucson, City of Phila., Chevron, Chrysler, Olsten, La. Power and Light, La. Land and Exploration, PanAm, Smith Kline, Carpenter Tech., The Aerospace Corp. of Am., Boeing Co., Dynalectron Corp., Lukens Steel, Nordstrom, Phila. Police Dept., Shoney's Inc., Martin Marietta, CIGNA, Airline Pilots Assn., Traveler's Ins., Suffolk County Police Dept.; Internat. Comms. Agy., N.Y. Times, U.S. Steel, Readers Digest, K-Mart, Wal-Mart, Russell Sage Found., United Food and Comml. Workers Union; lectr. Internat. Comms. Agy., Japan and Portugal, Brandeis U., Pa. State U., Columbia U., William and Mary Coll., U. So. Calif., Nat. Employment Law Inst., San Francisco and Washington. Author: Work Attitudes and Labor Market Experience, 1978, Pre-Retirement Years, vol. III, 1973, vol. IV, 1974, Career Thresholds, 1975; mem. editl. bd. Jour. Econs. and Bus., 1979-83; reviewer U. Mich. Press, Ohio State U. Press, Temple U. Press and various scholarly jours.; contbr. over 40 papers to profl. jours. and socs. Del. Econ. and Fin. Adv. Com., New Orleans Pub. Svc. Inc., Disability and Pension Rev. Com., Rockwell Internat., ARCO, Nationwide Ins., ICI Ams., DuPont, Witco Chem., Westinghouse, GTE, Inco, Gould Electronics, Olsten's, Chrysler, Dollar Bank, Rhone-Poulene Rorer, Ohio Edison, Delmarya Power, LaSalle Univ., gov. agys., others; del. Temple U. Law Sch. Bd. Visitors, 1996—. With U.S. Army, 1972-73. Recipient Wilmington Man of Yr. award, 1995, West End Neighborhood House Leadership award, 1997, Prof. of the Yr. award Temple U. Chpt. Soc. for Advancement of Mgmt., 1997, awards for vol. svc.; Salzburg fellow, Roosevelt Youth Policy fellow; grantee U.S. Dept. Labor, 1974-77, Nat. Commn. for Employment Policy, 1979-83, Adminstrn. on Aging, 1981-82, Social Sci. Rsch. Coun., 1982, U.S. Dept. Army, 1986, Human Resource Rsch. Orgn., 1989-90. Mem. Am. Econs. Assn., Indsl. Rels. Rsch. Assn., Acad. of Mgmt., Soc. Labor Economists, Strategic Mgmt. Soc. Office: Temple U Sch Bus & Mgmt Speakman Hall Rm 366 Philadelphia PA 19122

ANDRIST, DEBRA DIANE, Spanish language educator; b. Goodland, Kans., Nov. 14, 1950; d. Bill Lee and Gerre Danleia (Ingamells) A.; m. A.L. Freeman, Jr., Aug. 26, 1989. BA, Ft. Hays Kans. State U., 1972; MA, U. Utah, 1979; PhD, SUNY, Buffalo, 1985. Instr. Spanish Grosse Pointe (Mich.) Pub. Schs., 1972-73, Westside Pub. Schs., Omaha, 1975-77; teaching asst. U. Utah, Salt Lake City, 1977-79, SUNY, Buffalo, 1979-82; assoc. prof. Spanish Baylor U., Waco, Tex., 1982—; evening Spanish instr. Maryvale Pub. Adult Sch., Cheektowaga, N.Y., 1981-82; instr. Spanish, Lorena (Tex.) Meth. Pre-Sch., 1985-87, Lakewood Bapt. Pre-Sch., waco, 1985-87; book reviewer D.C. Heath, Heinle & Heinle, Holt, Rinehart and Winston, Prentice Hall, Houghton Mifflin, Arte Publico Press, HarperCollins, W.B. Saunders; owner/operator Panache. Author: Deceit Plus desire Equals Violence, 1989, Charlemos un poco, 3d edit., 1994, Ahora leamos, 3d edit., 1994; contbr. numerous articles to profl. jours. Bd. dirs. Ctrl. Tex. Women's Alliance, 1993, pres., 1994; mem. Historic Waco Found., 1992—; vol. Am. Heart Assn.; mem. Dallas Mus. Art, 1982—, Ft. Worth Mus. Art, 1984—, Kimball Mus., Ft. Worth, 1982—, Waco Art Ctr., 1982—, Tex. Arts Coun. Assn., exhbn. hostess, 1992; sec.-treas. Mackey Ranch Property Owners Assn., Eddy, Tex., 1987-88, pres., 1988-89; bilingual teaching vol. Utah Shriners Hosp., Salt Lake City, 1977-79; vol. Omaha Ballet, 1975-77, Joslyn Art Mus., Omaha, 1975-77, others. Named Multicultural Campus Community Creator of the Yr., Baylor U. Multicultural Alliance, 1992-93; grantee Grad. Student Assn. of SUNY-Buffalo, 1981, Baylor U., summer 1988, 89, Pan Am. U., 1991; Mellon fellow, 1989. Mem. AAUP (Tex. rep.-at-large 1992—, pres. 1992-93), MLA (South Ctrl. chpt. sec. 1989, 92, pres. 1990, 93, Women's Caucus sect. sec. 1991, pres. 1992, Spanish Am. lit. sect. sec. 1993, pres. 1994), Rocky Mountain MLA, Midwest MLA, Am. Assn. Tchrs. Spanish and Portuguese, Internat. Imagery Assn., Women's Studies assn., Medieval Feminist Scholars, L.Am. Studies Assn., Instituto Literario y Cultural Hispanico, S.W. Coun. L.Am. Studies, Feministas unidas, Asociacion de literatura femenina, PEO. Avocations: art history, skiing, reading, antiques. Office: Baylor Univ PO Box 97393 Waco TX 76798-7393

ANDRULIS, DENNIS P., health policy analyst executive, researcher; b. N.Y.C., Dec. 4, 1947; s. Peter Joseph and Irene (Richter) A. BS, Fordham U., 1969; PhD, U. Tex., 1973; MPH, U. N.C., 1976. Rsch. assoc. Office of Tech. Assessment, Washington, 1976-78; sr. rsch. assoc. Inst. Medicine Nat. Acad. Scis., Washington, 1978-79; sr. analyst HHS, Washington, 1979-82; dir. rsch. Nat. Assn. Pub. Hosps., Washington, 1982-88; v.p. Nat. Pub. Health and Hosps. Inst., Washington, 1988-89, pres., 1989-97; dir. Office of Urban Populations N.Y. Acad. Medicine, 1998—; adj. assoc. prof. George Washington U., Washington, 1988—; sr. lectr. Columbia U., N.Y.C., 1990—; mem. adv. group Opening Doors, 1992—. Author: Crisis at the Frontline, 1989, Managed Care and the Inner City, 1999, The Social and Health Landscape of Urban and Suburban America, 1999; contbg. editor Am. Jour. Medicine, 1992—; reviewer Jour. AMA, 1989—. Bd. dirs. Am. Internat. Health Alliance, Washington, 1992—, Hosp. for Sick Children, Washington, 1989-95. Grantee Robert Wood Johnson Found., Washington, 1992—; fellow USPHS, 1973, U.S. Govt., 1987-97. Mem. Am. Pub. Health Assn. Avocations: culinary arts, wine collecting, basketball. Home: 1436 Q St NW Washington DC 20009-3808 Office: NY Acad Medicine 1215 5th Ave New York NY 10029-5209

ANDRUS, CECIL DALE, academic administrator; b. Hood River, Oreg., Aug. 25, 1931; s. Hal Stephen and Dorothy (Johnson) A.; m. Carol Mae May, Aug. 27, 1933; children: Tana Lee, Tracy Sue, Kelly Kay. Student, Oreg. State U., 1948-49; LLD (hon.), Gonzaga U., U. Idaho, U. N.Mex., Coll. Idaho, Idaho State U., Whitman Coll. State gen. mgr. Paul Revere Life Ins. Co., 1969-70; gov. State of Idaho, 1971-77, 87-95; sec. of interior, 1977-81; chmn. Andrus Ctr. for Pub. Policy, Boise (Idaho) State U., 1995—; bd. dirs. KeyCorp., Albertson's, Inc., Coeur d'Alene Mines; mem. Idaho Senate, 1961-66, 69-70; mem. exec. com. Nat. Gov.'s Conf., 1971-72, chmn., 1976; chmn. Fedn. Rocky Mountain States, 1971-72. Chmn. bd. trustees Coll. of Idaho, 1985-89; bd. dirs. Sch. Forestry, Duke U. With USN, 1951-55. Recipient Disting. Citizen award Oreg. State U., 1980, Collier County Conservancy medal, 1979, Ansel Adams award Wilderness Soc., 1985, Audubon medal, 1985, Statesman of the Yr. award Idaho State U., 1990, Torch of Liberty award B'nai B'rith, 1991; named Conservationist of Yr. Nat. Wildlife Fedn., 1980, Idaho Wildlife Fedn., 1972, Man of Yr., VFW, 1959. Mem. VFW, Idaho Taxpayers Assn. (bd. dirs. 1964-66). Democrat. Office: Boise State U Andrus Ctr Pub Policy 1910 University Dr Boise ID 83725-0399

ANDRUS, ROGER DOUGLAS, lawyer; b. Floral Park, N.Y., Dec. 3, 1945; s. Winfield and Julia Margaret (Arduino) A.; m. Stephanie Andrus, Jan. 20, 1969 (div. 1983); children: Justin, Sarah; m. Patricia Ann McDonough, Oct. 4, 1986; children: Michael, David, Molly. AB cum laude, Wagner Coll., 1966; JD, NYU, 1969. Bar: N.Y. 1970, U.S. Dist. Ct. (ea. and so. dists.) 1975, U.S. Ct. Appeals 2d cir.) 1975. Assoc. Cahill Gordon & Reindel, N.Y.C., 1970-78, ptnr., 1978—. Mem. N.Y. State Bar Assn., Canoe Brook Country Club, Down Town Assn., Omicron Delta Kappa. Office: Cahill Gordon & Reindel 80 Pine St Fl 17 New York NY 10005-1790

ANDRUZZI, ELLEN ADAMSON, nurse, marital and family therapist; b. Colon, Panama, Dec. 15, 1917; d. Charles and Annie Isabel (Grinder) Adamson; m. Francis Victor Andruzzi, May 28, 1941; children: Barbara F., Francis C., Judith E., Antonette T., John J. BS in pub. health nursing, Cath. U. Am., 1947; MS in Nursing, 1951. Cert. clin. specialist. Psychiat. nurse pub. health nurse Washington Health Dept., 1942-44; instr. psychiat. nursing St. Elizabeth's Hosp., Washington, 1948-57; dir. nursing Glenn Dale Hosp., Md., 1961-67; chief mental health nurse dept. human resources Govt., D.C., 1967-73; cons. NIMH,HHS, Rockville, Md., 1973-81; marital and family therapist TA Assocs., Camp Springs, Md., 1973-94; assoc. GWITA, Rockville, 1975-79; instr. Charles County C.C., LaPlata, Md., 1976-78, Prince George Community Coll., Laargo, Md., 1973-81; assoc. Ctr for Study of Human Systems, Chevy Chase, Md., 1976-94; pvt. practice psychotherapist, nurse; Chmn. plan devel. com. So. Md Health Systems Agy., Clinto, 1984-89, (sec. governing body, 1978-80), Mental Health Adv. Com. Price George County, Cheverly, Md., 1983-85; mem. Blue Ribbon Commn. on Health, Prince George's County, 1991-92; Commn. Health, Prince George's County, 1992-94, health com. and voter reporter LWV, edn. com., Manatee County, LWV Manatee County (treasurer and bd. dirs., 1999—). Author: chpts. in books. Co-capt. Price Georgians for Glendening, Prince George County, Md., 1985-86; outreach vol. Manatee Widowed Persons Svc., 1996—I rsvp vol. Oneco Elem. Sch. Recient Disting. Nurse award St. Elizabeths Hos., 1985, Paula Hamburer Vol. award Mental Health Assn. Md., 1985; recognition of Service award Md. Nurses Assn., 1983, Prince Georgian of the Yr. award, 1994, vol. award Prince George's County, 1995; Fellow Am. Acad. ursing, Am. Orthropsychiat. Assn. Mem. Internat. Transactional Analysis Assn (clin.), Am. Nurses Assn., World Fedn. for Mental Health, Nat. Mental Health Assn. (v.p. 1984-87, bd. dirs. 1982-87), Mental Health Assn. Prince George County (pres. 1974-79, 87-88, Vol. of Yr. award 1993), Sigma theta Tau (Kappa chpt., Excellence in Nursing award 1984). Democrat. Roman Catholic.

ANDRYSIAK, FRANK LOUIS, videographer; b. Balt., Sept. 6, 1934; s. Francis Thomas and Clara (Weber) A.; m. Janice Rosa Hunt, Nov. 22, 1958; children: Alan, Karen, Jean. BS in bus. adminstrn., Loyola Coll., 1956; grad. U.S. Army Comman, Gen. Staff Coll., 1971; grad., Indsl. Coll. Armed Forces, 1973, U.S. Air War Coll., 1976. Cert. U.S. Customs tech. evaluation specialist. Control buyer Montgomery Ward, Balt., 1958-63; U.S. customs svc. Dept. Treasury, Washington, 1963-93; pres. All Occasions Video, Crofton, Md., 1993—; EEO adv. com. U.S. Customs Svc., Washington, 1990-93. Editor various family and wedding photo collages, wedding video montages (selected for showing on tv show "Here Comes the Bride-There Goes the Groom", Feb., 1996). Col. USAR, 1956-85. Mem. Wedding & Event Videographers' Assn. (WEVA), K of C. Independent. Roman Catholic. Avocations: indoor and outdoor model railroading. Home and Office: 1572 Farlow Ave Crofton MD 21114-1536

ANDRZEJAK, MICHAEL RICHARD, insurance agent; b. Royal Oak, Mich., Mar. 20, 1962; s. Francis Jacob and Jean Ann (Lewandowski) A.; m. Yvonne L. Macks, May 23, 1992 (div. Mar. 1995). Student, Cen. Mich. U., 1980-85. Assoc. agt. State Farm Ins., Madison Heights, Mich., 1992-97; agt., owner Farmers Ins. Group of Cos., Royal Oak, 1997—. City commr. City of Royal Oak, 1995—, mayor pro tem., 1997—; bd. trustees Royal Oak Pub. Libr., 1993—; bd. dirs. Boys and Girls Club of South Oakland County, 1995—; exec. bd. dirs. Oakland County Reps., 1996—. Republican. Roman Catholic. Home: 1912 Guthrie Ave Royal Oak MI 48067-3586

ANDRZEJEWSKI, CHESTER, JR., immunologist, research scientist; b. Bridgeport, Conn., Mar. 20, 1953; s. Chester Sr. and Helen (Sholomicky) A.; m. Kathleen Marie O'Connor, Aug. 7, 1976; children: Nicholas Chester, Michael Yuri, Danielle Natalya. ScB, Brown U., 1975; PhD, Tufts U., 1981, MD, 1984. Diplomate Am. Bd. Pathology, Nat. Bd. Med. Examiners. Resident, fellow Hosp. U. Pa., Phila., 1984-88; staff pathologist Wilford Hall USAF Med. Ctr., Lackland AFB, Tex., 1988-92; med. dir., transfusion medicine and clin. immunology Wilford Hall USAF Med Ctr., Lackland AFB, 1989-92; chief divsn. Baystate Reference Labs. Baystate Med. Ctr., Springfield, Mass., 1994-97; asst. prof. pathology Tufts U., Boston, 1993—; med. dir. sys. transfusion medicine svcs. Baystate Health Sys., Springfield, 1996—; adj. prof. dept. vet. and animal scis. U. Mass., Amherst, 1997—; clin. prof. medicine, physician asst. dept. Springfield Coll., 1997—; med. dir. Sys. Transfusion Medicine Svcs. Baystate Med. Ctr., Springfield, Mass., 1992—. Contbr. articles to profl. jours. Sub-deacon Orthodox Ch. Am., 1977; mem. med. adv. com. N.E. region ARC Blood Svcs., 1993—, chmn. 1998—, transfusion practices com., 1994—, Am. Assn. Blood Banks Accreditation program com./hematopoietic progenitor cell program unit, 1998—, Mass. Med. Soc. com. pub. health, 1998—; adv. panelist on Mass. Peer Review Orgn., 1995—. Scholar Nat. Blood Found., 1996; recipient Rsch. Fellowship award Mass. Lupus Found., 1979, Internat. Disting. Dissertation award Coun. Grad. Students in U.S. and Univ. Microfilms, 1981, Excellence Rsch. award Roche Labs., 1987, award Nat. Blood Found., 1987; Collaborative Biomedical Rsch. Program grantee Baystate/U. Mass., 1999. Mem. Am. Assn. Clin. Pathologists, Am. Assn. Blood Banks (mem. accreditation program com./mematopoietic progenitor cell program unit 1998—), Mass. Soc. Pathologists (exec. com.), Clin. Immunology Soc., Coll. Am. Pathologists, Am. Soc. Apheresis, Assn. Med. Lab., Internat. Cord Blood Soc. (founding, charter), Mass. Med. Soc. (mem. com. pub. health 1998—). Mem. Orthodox Ch. Am. Achievements include discovery of the first hybridoma monoclonal anti-DNA autoantibodies from a murine SLE model, the first anti-idiotypes to such antibodies;demonstration of the immunochemical and genetic relatedness of these autoantibodies; production of the first human warm reacting anti-red blood cell monoclonal autoantibodies using viral transformation techniques; described the first studies examining heterogeneity of human anti-erythrocyte autoantibodies using isoelectric focusing electrophoresis methods. Home: 19 Eaglebrook Dr Somers CT 06071-1754 Office: Baystate Med Ctr Dept Pathology Springfield MA 01199

ANDRZEJEWSKI, DARRYL LEE, clergyman; b. Detroit, Oct. 13, 1966; s. Norbert Leo and Marion Rose (Christy) A.; m. Kristen Margaret Alexander, July 23, 1988; children: Joshua Aaron, Jakob Alexander, Nicolas Jonah, Rachel Moriah. BA, Concordia Coll., Ann Arbor, Mich., 1989; MDiv, Concordia Theol. Sem., Ft. Wayne, Ind., 1993. Ordained to ministry Luth. Ch. (Mo. Synod), 1993. Assoc. pastor St. Thomas Luth. Ch., Eastpointe, Mich., 1993—; S.E. Mich. pastoral rep. Luth. Youth Ministry, Ann Arbor, 1994—. Avocation: coaching and participating in sports. Office: St Thomas Luth Ch 23801 Kelly Rd Eastpointe MI 48021-3499*

ANESI, MICHAEL RICHARD, restaurant executive; b. Auburn, Ala., Nov. 19, 1946; s. Richard Albeno and Elizabeth (Crane) A. AA, BA, Jordan Coll., Cedar Springs, Mich., 1981; student, U.S. Acad. Pvt. Investigation, Beverly Hills, Calif., 1995-96. Security and maint. worker Jordan Coll., Cedar Springs, Mich., 1981-86; custodian Camp Wonderland, Camp Lake, Wis., 1987, First Congl. Ch., Portland, Mich., 1987-96; porter Portland Burger King, 1997—. Mem. Nat. Model RR Assn., Nat. Fedn. Ind. Bus. Methodist. Avocations: fishing, biking, model railroading, dancing. Home: 423 Smith St Portland MI 48875-1850

ANFINSON, THOMAS ELMER, government financial administrator; b. Stockton, Calif., Aug. 16, 1941; s. Elmer and Elizabeth (Killebrew) A.; m. Lawrene Nixon, July 27, 1970; children: Kathleen, Rebecca, Thomas Edward. BS, U. So. Calif., 1964. CPA, Calif., Va. With Price Waterhouse, 1964-70; tax mgr. Toyota Motor Sales, USA, 1971-72; acct. Renegotiation Bd., L.A., 1972-76; pres. Anfinson Accountancy Corp., Newport Beach, Calif., 1976-81; exec. asst. to gen. mgr. New Cmty. Devel. Corp. HUD, Washington, 1981-83, spl. asst. to asst. sec. for pub. housing, 1985; dep. treas. Reagan-Bush 84 Presdl. Re-election Campaign, 1983-85; spl. asst. to asst. sec. for employment and tng. U.S. Dept. Labor, 1985-86; spl. asst. to dep. adminstr. Health Care Fin. Adminstrn., HHS, 1986; chmn. fed. prevailing rate adv. com. U.S. Office Pers. Mgmt., 1986-89; dep. under sec. for mgmt., chief fin. officer U.S. Dept. Edn., 1989-91; exec. dir. U.S. Savs. Bonds divsn. Dept. Treasury, 1991-93; pres. U.S. Savs. Bonds Found., Great Falls, Va., 1993; assoc. adminstr. fin., dir. fin. U.S. Ho. Reps., Washington, 1995-97, fin. adminstr., 1997—. Bd. dirs. U.S. Savs. Bonds Found., 1993—. Staff sgt. USAFR, 1965-70. Mem. AICPA, D.C. Inst. CPAs, Assn. Govt. Accts. (cert. govt. fin. mgr.), Fed. exec. Inst. Alumni Assn., U. So. Calif. Alumni Assn. Republican. Avocations: gardening, camping, travel. Home:

PO Box 817 Great Falls VA 22066-0817 Office: US House Reps Washington DC 20515

ANG, HOOI HOON, pharmaceutical educator; b. Ipoh, Perak, Malaysia, Jan. 11, 1964; d. Sim Teong Ang and Suet Pheng Yee. B Pharm. with honors, U. Sci. Malaysia, Georgetown, 1988, PhD, 1993. Registered pharmacist, Malaysia. Quality control mgr. pvt. firm, Ipoh, Malaysia, 1992-93; lectr. U. Sci. Malaysia, Georgetown, 1994—; doctoral fellow PHP Inst. of Asia, Tokyo, 1995; vis. prof. ASAIHL, Bangkok, 1996; presenter papers in field; invited spkr. and lectr. in field. Mem. editl. bd.: Malaysian Jour. of Pharmacy and Therapeutics, 1997—; contbr. numerous articles to profl. jours. Active numerous civic/polit. projects including steering com. ISO 9000/IEC Guide, Sch. Pharm. Scis., U. Sci. Malaysia, 1997—, coord. seminar, 1996—, other coms.; assoc. mem. Women Crisis Ctr., Penang, Malaysia, 1990-92; others. Recipient fellowships Third World Acad. of Sci., Trieste, Italy, 1997, UNESCO Yung Scientist award, Jakarta, Indonesia, 1997, Malaysian Young Scientist award Ministry of Sci. Tech. and Environment, Kuala Lumpur, 1997, Assn. of Southeast Asia Inst. of Higher Learning, Nat. U. Singapore, 1996, Gold medal-doctoral fellow PHP Inst. of Asia, Japan, 1995, Young Rschr.'s award Malaysian Soc. of Parasitology and Tropical Medicine, Inst. for Med. Rsch., Kuala Lumpur, Malaysia, 1995, Spl. award for Med. Scis., Irania Rsch. Orgn. of Sci. and Te., Tehran, 1995, others; rsch. grantee in field. Fellow PHP Inst. of Asia; mem. Malaysian Pharm. Soc., Malaysian Soc. Parasitology and Tropical Medicine, Malaysian Microbiology Soc., Japanese Soc. Parasitology, Korean Soc. Parasitology, Malaysian Pham. Soc.-Penang (vice-chmn. 1994-95, hon. sec. 1995—), Third World Acad. of Sci./Italy, Malaysian Natural Product Soc., Malaysian Tech. Forum, Malaysian Invention and Design Soc. Office: Sch Pharm Scis, U of Sci Malaysia, 11800 Penang Malaysia

ANGEL, ALLEN ROBERT, mathematics educator, author, consultant; b. N.Y.C., Oct. 13, 1942; s. Isaac and Sylvia (Budnick) A.; m. Kathryn Mary Pollinger, Feb. 14, 1966; children: Robert Allen, Steven Scott. AAS in Electrical Tech., N.Y.C. Community Coll., 1962; BS in Physics, SUNY, New Paltz, 1965; MS in Math., SUNY, 1967; postgrad., Rutgers U., 1969. Tchr. physics Rhineback (N.Y.) Cen. Sch., 1965-66; instr. physics, math. Sullivan County Community Coll., Loch Sheldrake, N.Y., 1967-70; prof. math. Monroe Community Coll., Rochester, N.Y., 1970—; chmn. math./computer sci. Monroe Community Coll., Rochester, 1988—; asst. dir. nat. sci. found., math. summer insts. Rutgers U., New Brunswick, N.J., 1970-72; cons. reviewer various pub. cos. including Prentice-Hall Pub. Co., Englewood Cliffs, N.J., 1983—, Addison-Wesley Pub. Co., Reading, Mass., 1978—; bd. dirs. Am. Math. Assn. Two Yr. Colls. Found. Author: (textbooks) A Survey of Mathematics with Applications, 5th edit., 1997, Elementary Algebra-A Practical Approach, 1985, Intermediate Algebra-A Practical Approach, 1986, Elementary Algebra for College Students, 4 edit., 1996, Intermediate Algebra for College Students, 4th edit., 1996, Algebra for College Students, 1988. Recipient Excellence in Tchg. award Nat. Inst. for Staff and Organizational Devel., 1991. Mem. Am. Math. Assn. of Two Yr. Colls. (v.p. 1985—, chmn. conv. 1984, bd. dirs., Pres.'s award), N.Y. State Math. Assn. of Two Yr. Colls. (pres. 1978-80, chmn. summer inst. 1976-78, Outstanding Contributions award), Math. Assn. of Am., Nat. Council of Tchrs. of Math., Assn. Math. Tchrs. of N.Y. State, New England Math. Assn. of Two Yr. Colls., Nat. Inst. Staff & Organizational Devel. (Excellence award 1991, 92). Avocations: camping, travel, investing. Home: 4036 Wellington Pkwy Palm Harbor FL 34685-1174 Office: Monroe Community Coll 1000 E Henrietta Rd Rochester NY 14623-5701

ANGEL, ARMANDO CARLOS, rheumatologist, internist; b. Las Vegas, N.Mex., Mar. 25, 1940; s. Edmundo Clemente and Pauline Teresa (Flores) Sanchez A.; m. Judith Lee Weedin, Aug. 5, 1961; children: Stephanie, Renee. BA, San Jose State U., 1963; MS, U. Ariz., 1970, PhD, 1971, MD, 1977. Diplomate Am. Bd. Internal Medicine, Am. Bd. Rheumatology. Chemist Tracerlab, Inc., Richmond, Calif., 1963-67; prof. chemistry Pima Coll., Tucson, 1971-74; intern U. N.Mex., Albuquerque, 1977-78, resident, 1978-80; resident VA Hosp., Lovelace Med. Ctr., 1978-80; pvt. practice rheumatology and internal medicine, Las Cruces, N.Mex., 1980-88, El Paso, Tex., 1990—; dir. pain program Rio Vista Rehab. Hosp., 1992; med. dir. Ctr. for Rehab. and Evaluation, 1992—; chief of staff Rio Vista Rehab. Hosp., 1997—; with Estrella Cons. Group, 1999—; cons. minority biomed. sci. project NIH, Washington, 1970-74, Ednl. Assocs., Tucson, 1971-74. Author: Llevve Tlaloc No. 2, 1973. Treas. Nat. Chicago Health Orgn., L.A., 1974-75; v.p. Mexican-Am. Educators, Tucson, 1973-74; pres. N.Mex. affiliate Am. Diabetes Assn., Albuquerque, 1983-85. Fellow U. Ariz., 1988-90. Fellow Am. Coll. Rheumatology; mem. AMA, ACP, Am. Diabetes Assn., Am. Assn. Internal Medicine, Tex. Med. Soc., El Paso County Med. Soc., Dona Ana County Med. Soc. (pres. 1983), Alpha Chi Sigma.

ANGEL, ARTHUR RONALD, lawyer, consultant; b. Long Beach, Calif., May 10, 1948; s. Morris and Betty Estelle (Unger) A.; 1 child, Jamie Kathryn. BA, U. Calif.-Berkeley, 1969; JD, Harvard U., 1972. Bar: Mass. 1972, D.C. 1975, Okla. 1979, U.S. Ct. Appeals (10th cir.) 1979, U.S. Dist. Ct. (we. dist.) Okla. 1980, U.S. Dist. Ct. (no. dist.) Okla. 1981, U.S. Supreme Ct. 1983. Atty. FTC, Washington, 1972-78; pvt. practice, Oklahoma City, 1978-87; ptnr., Angel & Ikard, Oklahoma City, 1987-93, of counsel Abel, Musser Sokolosky & Assoc., 1994—; mem. adv. panel on cardiovascular devices, Washington, 1979-82; cons. FTC, 1978-79. Recipient Meritorious Service award FTC, Washington, 1978. Fellow Inst. Law and Social Scis.; mem. Am. Arbitration Assn., Assn. Trial Lawyers Am., Okla. Trial Lawyers Assn., Okla. Bar Assn., D.C. Bar Assn., Mass. Bar Assn. Democrat. Jewish. Home: 1600 Westchester Dr Oklahoma City OK 73120-1310 Office: Abel Musser Sokolosky & Assocs 211 N Robinson Ave Ste 600 Oklahoma City OK 73102-7100

ANGEL, AUBIE, physician, academic administrator; b. Winnipeg, Man., Can., Aug. 28, 1935; s. Benjamin and Minnie (Kaplan) A.; m. Esther-Rose Newhouse; children: Jennifer, Jonathan, Suzanne, Steven, Michael. BSc in Medicine, U. Man., 1959, MD, 1959; MSc, McGill U., 1963. Speciality resident in diabetes and endocrinology Montreal Gen. Hosp., 1961-62; postgrad. dept. exptl. medicine McGill U., 1962-63; asst. resident in medicine Royal Victoria Hosp., Montreal, 1963-64; asst. prof. pathology McGill U., Montreal, Que., Can., 1965-68; staff physician Royal Victoria Hosp., Montreal, 1965-68; sr. physician and staff endocrinologist Toronto Gen. Hosp., 1968-90; asst. prof. medicine U. Toronto, Ont., Can., 1968-72, assoc. prof., 1972-81, prof. medicine, 1981-90, dir. Inst. Med. Sci., 1983-90; prof., head dept. medicine U. Man., 1991-95; physician in chief Health Sci. Ctr., Winnipeg, Man., 1991-95; vis. scientist U. Calif., San Diego, 1977-78, Hammerstein Hosp., London, 1978; founding pres. Diabetes Rsch. and Treatment Ctr., Winnipeg, 1991—; founding pres., chmn. bd. dirs. Alumni and Friends of MRC, 1994—; scholar-in-residence MRC, Can., 1996; pres. 7th Internat. Congress on Obesity, 1994; co-chair Internat. Conf. on Diabetes and Cardiovascular Disease, 1999. Editor: (with C.H. Hollenberg and D.A.K. Roncari) The Adipocyte and Obesity: Cellular and Molecular Mechanisms, 1983, (with J. Frohlich) Lipoprotein Deficiency Syndromes: Advances in Experimental Medicine and Biology, 1986, (with N. Sakamoto and N. Hotta) New Directions in Research and Clinical Works for Obesity and Diabetes Mellitus, 1991, (with H. Anderson, C. Bouchard, D. Lau, L. Leiter, R. Mendelson) Progess in Obesity Research, 1996. Project dir. Can. Internat. Devel. Agy., Toronto and Costa Rica, 1987-94. Recipient Outstanding Svc. award Heart and Stroke Found. Ont., 1985; U. Toronto Med. Rsch. Coun. scholar, 1965-71; Trinity Coll., Toronto, fellow, 1989—. Fellow Royal Coll. Physicians and Surgeons Costa Rica (hon.), N.Am. Assn. Study Obesity (pres. 1986-87), Can. Soc. Clin. Investigation (councillor 1977-80), Am. Soc. Clin. Investigation, Can. Inst. Acad. Medicine (founding pres. 1990-92), Internat. Assn. Study Obesity (bd. govs. 1986—), Juvenile Diabetes Found. Internat. (hon. bd. dirs. 1987-90), Obesity Canada (founding bd. dirs. 1999—). E-mail: aangel@hsc.mb.ca. Office: U Man Dept Internal Med, 820 Sherbrook St Rm GB-409, Winnipeg, MB Canada R3A 1R9

ANGEL, DENNIS, lawyer; b. Bklyn., Feb. 14, 1947; s. Morris and Rosalyn (Sobiloff) A.; m. Linda Marlene Lobel, May 15, 1977; children: Stephanie Lee, Michele Bari, Rebecca Jo. Cert. pratique de langue francaise ler Degre U. Rouen (France), 1967, diplome d'etudes françaises (2e Degre), 1967; BA, St. Lawrence U., 1968; J.D., Washington and Lee U., 1972. Bar: N.Y. 1972, U.S. Dist. Ct. (so. dist.) N.Y. 1977. Assoc. Johnson & Tannenbaum, N.Y.C., 1972-77; sole practice, N.Y.C., 1978—. Contbr. articles to profl. jours. Served with USAR, 1969-75. Mem. ABA (subcommittee chmn. 1977-82), N.Y. State Bar Assn., Copyright Soc. U.S.A., Phi Alpha Delta. Home: 8 High Point Ln Scarsdale NY 10583-3122 Office: Suite 306 1075 Central Park Ave Scarsdale NY 10583-3242

ANGEL, JAMES ROGER PRIOR, astronomer; b. St. Helens, Eng., Feb. 7, 1941; came to U.S., 1967; s. James Lee and Joan (Prior) A.; m. Ellinor M. Goonan, Aug. 21, 1965; children—Jennifer, James. B.A., Oxford (Eng.) U., 1963, D.Phil., 1967; M.S., Calif. Inst. Tech., 1966. From rsch. assoc. to assoc. prof. physics Columbia U., 1967-74; vis. assoc. prof. astronomy U. Tex., Austin, 1974; prof. astronomy U. Ariz., 1975—, prof. optical sci., 1984—, Regents prof., 1990—. Sloan fellow, 1970-74; hon. fellow St. Peter's Coll., Oxford U.; MacArthur fellow, 1996. Fellow Royal Soc., Royal Astron. Soc.; mem. Am. Astron. Soc. (v.p. 1987-90, Pierce prize 1976), Am. Acad. Arts and Scis. Research includes white dwarf stars, quasars, the search for extra-solar planetary systems, astronomical mirrors, telescopes and their instruments, and adaptive optics. Office: Univ Ariz Steward Obs Tucson AZ 85721

ANGEL, LARRY, business professional. With Koch Industries; pres. Reiss Remediation Inc. Office: Koch Industries PO Box 2256 Wichita KS 67201-2256*

ANGEL, STEVEN, musician; b. Bklyn., Aug. 2, 1953; s. Morris and Rosalyn (Sobiloff) A. Grad. H.S., L.I. Pres. Daystar Records, Santa Monica, Calif., 1991—; profl. drummer, 1960—; lectr. The Whole Life Expo, Pasadena, 1992-95, Inst. for the Advanced Studies of Human Sexuality, San Francisco; drum therapist, 1998—. Author (music and book) Angels Rejoice, 1976-80; wrote music for tv show Another World, 1987-91; wrote, recorded, produced three songs for Playboy album Music for Lovers, 1993; wrote, recorded, produced album The Erotic God, 1993; editor Unity and Difference Jour., 1994-97. Avocations: tennis, hiking, running. Home and Office: Daystar Records 2132 Montana Ave Apt B Santa Monica CA 90403-2017

ANGELAKIS, MANOS G(EORGE), filmmaker, communications executive; b. Athens, Mar. 27, 1941; came to U.S., 1967; s. George E. and Urania M. (Hadjioannou) A.; m. Barbara D. Pinkus, Sept. 7, 1969. Student, Athens (Greece) Coll., 1960, Ecole des Arts Decoratif, Paris, 1962-64. Sr. photographer R. Crandall Assocs., N.Y.C., 1970-72; owner Manos Angelakis Photography, N.Y.C., 1972-75; pres. EuroConference Mgmt., London, 1983-89; pres., creative dir. Trident Communications, N.Y.C., 1975-93; dir. Indsl. Strength Video, Ltd., N.Y.C., London, 1990—. Dir. (films) The Papermakers, 1983 (Gold award Internat. Film and TV Festival 1984), Impressions, 1986 (Silver award Visual Media Festival 1988, Telly award The Best of the Best, 1993); contbr. articles too profl. jours. Sgt. Royal Hellenic Airforce, 1960-62. Recipient Eagle award Visual Communications Congress, 1984, Best of Show award for video Visual Media Festival, 1988. Mem. Indsl. Photographers' Assn. of N.Y. (pres. 1977-79), Assn. for Multi-Image Internat. (treas. N.Y. chpt. 1984-88, pres. 1988-90, Best of Show award 1986). Home: 140 Prospect Ave Apt 11E Hackensack NJ 07601-2249 Office: Indsl Strength Video Interactive Ltd 140 Prospect Ave Hackensack NJ 07601-2255

ANGELAKOS, EVANGELOS THEODOROU, physician, physiologist, pharmacologist, educator; b. Tripolis, Greece, July 15, 1929; came to U.S., 1948, naturalized, 1966; s. Theodore A. and Aglaia (Tsiverioti) A.; m. Eleanor Pell, Aug. 28, 1954 (div. 1984); 1 son, Theodore; m. Elizabeth Hegnauer, Jan. 2, 1993. Student, Athens (Greece) U., 1947-48, Fordham U., 1948-50, Cornell U., 1950-51; MA, Boston U., 1953, PhD, 1956; MD, Harvard, 1959. Mem. faculty sch. medicine Boston U., 1955-68, prof. physiology, 1963-68; prof. dept. physiology and biophysics Hahnemann U., Phila., 1968-83, chmn. dept., 1968-85, prof. dept. pharmacology and medicine, 1982-95, interim dean sch. medicine, 1982-83, dean Grad. Sch., 1983-92, dep. dean sch. medicine, 1985-86, dir. Med. Sci. Track Program, 1982-95, prof. emeritus physiology, pharmacology and medicine, 1995—; chmn. adv. com. Biomed. Rsch. Inst. Ctr. Rsch. and Advanced Studies, U. Maine, Portland, 1971-80; dir., dept. chmn. physician assistance program Beaver Coll., 1995-96; provost, chief acad. officer Sch. Medicine Ross U., N.Y.C., 1996—; rsch. assoc. biomath. MIT, 1959-60; vis. scientist Karolinska Inst., Stockholm, 1962-63; cons. U.S. Army Labs. Environ. Medicine, Natick, Mass., 1964-72, NASA Electronics Rsch. Ctr., Cambridge, Mass., 1966-68; Trustee, sec. bd. Hahnemann Med. Coll. and Hosp., Phila., 1977-81. Contbr. articles to sci. jours. and textbooks. Med. Found. Research fellow, 1959-60; USPHS Research and Career Devel. grantee, 1960-68. Home: 109 Wayside Dr Cherry Hill NJ 08034-3350 Office: Ross U Adminstrn 460 W 34th St Fl 12 New York NY 10001-2369

ANGELIDES, DEMOSTHENES CONSTANTINOS, civil engineer; b. Thessaloniki, Greece, June 18, 1947; came to U.S., 1973; s. Constantinos D. and Chrysavgi (Papatsa) A.; m. Chryssanthi Koutsandrea, Dec. 25, 1991; 1 child, Constantine. Diplom. ingenieur, Aristotle U., Greece, 1970; MSCE, MIT, 1975, PhD, 1978. Registered profl. engr., Tex. Rsch. asst. MIT, Cambridge, 1973-78; supervising structural engr. Brian Watt Assocs., Inc., Houston, 1978-80; sr. cons. structural engr. McDermott, Inc., New Orleans, 1980-83, Hudson Engring./McDermott, Inc., Houston, 1983-85; sr. cons. engr. McDermott, Inc., New Orleans, 1985-90, mgr. total quality, 1990-93, dir. bus. process improvement, 1993-97; assoc. prof. civil engring. Aristotle U. Thessaloniki, Greece, 1997-99, prof. civil engring., 1999—; mem. tech. com. Am. Petroleum Inst., New Orleans, 1983-85; McDermott rep. Indsl. Liaison program MIT, New Orleans, 1981-89. Co-author: Offshore Structures, 1991; contbr. articles to Earthquake Engring. and Structural Dynamics, Jour. Engring. Mechanics, Jour. Structural Div., Jour. Offshore Mechanics and Arctic Engring. Mem. La. Fin. com. Dukakis for Pres., 1988; pres. Hellenic Arts Soc., New Orleans, 1986-88; bd. dirs. Trustees of Holy Trinity Greek Orthodox Ch., New Orleans, 1989-90; 2d lt. corps. engrs. Hellenic Army, Greece, 1971-73. Postdoctoral fellowship Coun. for Sci. and Indsl. Rsch., 1978; Govtl. scholar Aristotles U., Thessaloniki, 1965-70. Mem. ASCE, ASME (chmn. computer tech. comm. of offshore mechanics and arctic engring. div. 1985-88), Am. Assn. Artificial Intelligence, Am. Geophys. Union, Sigma Xi. Achievements include development and design of pioneering concepts of offshore oil platforms; applications of artificial intelligence in optimization of manufacturing and engineering design; planning and implementation of statistical methods for improving quality of products and processes in manufacturing, information technology, finance, administration and legal organizations; reengineering business processes in manufacturing, construction and finance organizations; knowledge management. Home: 31 Ethnikis Aminis, Thessaloniki 54621, Greece Office: Aristotle U Thessaloniki, Thessaloniki Greece

ANGELINE, MARY, poet; b. Youngstown, Ohio, Apr. 29, 1954; d. Dominic and Mary Louise Buzzacco. BA in Philosophy, Kent State U., 1983; MFA in Poetry, Brown U., 1989. Poetry editor Brown U. and R.I. Sch. of Design Jour. of Arts, 1989; instr. various coll. and univs., 1985-98. Author: Precise Intrigues, 1995; contbr. poetry and articles to profl. publs. Recipient Award Acad. of Am. Poets, 1989; McDowell Colony fellowship Sun and Moon Press, 1994. Mem. MLA, PEN Center West, Nat. Coun. of Tchrs. of English.

ANGELINI, EILEEN MARIE, foreign languages educator; b. Fitchburg, Mass., July 19, 1965; d. Joseph Anthony and Maureen Catherine (Kerrigan) A.; m. Robert Carl O'Malley, June 17, 1995. BA, Middlebury Coll., 1987; MA, Brown U., 1989, PhD, 1993. English lectr. U. Lyon (France) 2 and 3, 1992-93; assoc. prof. fgn. langs., dir. fgn. lang. program Phila. Coll. Textiles and Sci., 1993—; Advanced placement French reader Ednl. Testing Svc., Princeton, N.J., 1995—. Mem. methodology bd. Holt, Rinehart & Winston, Ft. Worth, 1997-98, accuracy editor, 1997—, textbook reviewer, 1993—, McGraw Hill textbook reviewer, 1999—; contbr. articles to profl. jours. Vol. interpreter Assn. Tennis Profls., Phila., 1994—, Women's Tennis Assn., Phila., 1994—; vol. tennis coach and cross-cultural communication facilitator, World Scholar-Athlete Games, U. R.I., Kingston, 1997, Ireland's Scholar-Athlete Games, U. Ulster, Jordanstown, No. Ireland, 1998, U.S. Scholar-Athlete Games, U. R.I., 1999. Grantee French Embassy, Grenoble, 1994-95, Am. Coun. on Edn., 1994-95, French Embassy, Strasbourg, 1994, 99, NEH, 1996, 98. Mem. MLA, Autobiography Soc., Am. Assn. French Tchrs. (nat. commn. on French for bus. and econ. purposes, task force on planning for the future), Am. Coun. Tchrs. Fgn. Langs., Assn. Bus. Lang. Educators (newsletter contbr.), French for Bus. and Internat. Trade (newsletter contbr.), Women in French. Avocations: tennis, poetry, watercolor painting, ballet, hiking. Office: Phila Coll Textiles and Sci School House Ln/ Henry Ave Philadelphia PA 19144-5497

ANGELIS, JANET IVES, executive; b. Meriden, Conn.; d. M. Edward and Clotilde Brazeau Ives; 1 child, Michael E. AB, Conn. Coll., 1968; MAT, Simmons Coll., 1970. Tchr. Brimmer & May Sch., Chestnut Hill, Mass., 1969-74, Lynnfield (Mass.) Jr. H.S., 1974-79; dir. pub. rels. Nutriwork, Andover, Mass., 1983-85; dir. comm. The Network, Andover, Mass., 1985-96; assoc. dir. Nat. Rsch. Ctr. on English Learning & Achievement, Albany, 1996—; cons. in field. Editor: Education by Charter, 1988, Copernican Plan, 1989. Bd. trustees U. Unitarian Ch., Haverhill, Mass., 1982-96; chair aquifer protection com. Town of Groveland (Mass.), 1982-92, water & sewer commr., 1985-91. Mem. Nat. Coun. Tchrs. English, Internat. Reading Assn., Burnt Hills Oratorio Soc., Phi Beta Kappa. Avocations: skiing, hiking, singing. Office: CELA U Albany ED-B9 1400 Washington Ave Albany NY 12222

ANGELL, JAMES BROWNE, electrical engineering educator; b. S.I., N.Y., Dec. 25, 1924; s. Robert Corson and Jessie (Browne) A.; m. Elizabeth Isabelle Rice, July 22, 1950; children: Charles Lawrence, Carolyn Corson. S.B., S.M., MIT, 1946, Sc.D. in Elec. Engring, 1952. Research asst. MIT, 1946-51; mgr. solid-state circuit research, research div. Philco Corp., Phila., 1951-60; mem. faculty Stanford U., 1960-95, prof. elec. engring., 1962-89, prof. emeritus, 1990—, dir. Solid-State Electronics Lab., 1964-71, assoc. dept. chmn., 1970-89; cons. to industry and govt., 1960—; Mem. electronics adv. group for comdg. gen. U.S. Army Electronics Command, 1964-74; mem. U.S. Army Sci. Adv. Panel, 1968-74; Carillonneur Stanford, 1960-91. Author sect. book. Area chmn. town incorporation com. Portola Valley, Calif., 1963-64; Bd. dirs. Portola Valley Assn., 1964-67. Fellow IEEE (life, chmn. internat. solid state circuits conf. 1964); mem. Am. Guild Organists, Guild Carillonneurs in N. Am. (dir. 1969-75, rec. sec. 1970-75). Home: 1400 Geary Blvd Apt 2309 San Francisco CA 94109-6574

ANGELL, KENNETH ANTHONY, bishop; b. Providence, Aug. 3, 1930; s. Henry L. and Mae T. (Cooney) A. AB in Philosophy, St. Mary's Sem., Balt., 1952, STB, 1954; STD (hon.), Our Lady of Providence Sem., 1975; JCD (hon.), Providence Coll., 1975. Ordained priest Roman Catholic Ch., 1956, consecrated bishop, 1974. Assoc. pastor St. Mark Ch., Jamestown, R.I., 1956; assoc. pastor Sacred Heart Ch., Pawtucket, R.I., 1956-60, St. Mary Ch., Newport, R.I., 1960-68; asst. chancellor and sec. to bishop Diocese of Providence, 1968-72, chancellor, 1972-74, aux. bishop, vicar gen., 1974-92; pastor St. John Ch., Providence, 1975-81; bishop Diocese of Burlington (Vt.), 92—. Bd. dirs. Sr. Thea Bowman Black Cath. Ednl. Fund, 1995—; trustee Wadhams Hall Seminary Coll., 1995—, Champlain Coll., 1995-98; v.p. Vt. Ecumenical Coun. & Bible Soc., 1997—. Mem. Nat. Conf. Cath. Bishops, U.S. Cath. Conf. Office: Diocese of Burlington 351 North Ave PO Box 526 Burlington VT 05402-0526

ANGELL, M(ARY) FAITH, federal magistrate judge; b. Buffalo, May 7, 1938; d. San S. and Marie B. (Caboni) A.; m. Kenneth F. Carobus, Oct. 27, 1973; children: Andrew M. Carobus, Alexander P. Carobus. AB, Mt. Holyoke Coll., 1959; MSS, Bryn Mawr Coll., 1965; JD, Temple U., 1971. Bar: Pa. 1971, U.S. Dist. Ct. (ea. dist) Pa. 1971, U.S. Ct. Appeals (3rd cir.) Pa. 1974, U.S. Supreme Ct. 1979; Acad. Cert. Social Workers. Dir. social work, vol. svcs. Wills Eye Hosp., Phila., 1961-64, 65-69; dir. soc. work dept. juvenile divsn. Defender Assoc., Phila., 1969-71; asst. dist. atty. City of Phila., 1971-72; asst. atty. gen. Commonwealth of Pa., Phila., 1972-74, deputy atty. gen., 1974-78; regional counsel ICC, Phila., 1978-80, regional dir., 1980-88; administrv. law judge Social Security Adminstrn., Phila., 1988-90; U.S. magistrate judge U.S. Dist. Ct. (ea. dist.) Pa., Phila., 1990—; adj. prof. Temple U. Law Sch., Phila., 1976-94, clin. instr., 1973-76; co-chmn. Commn. on Gender, 3d Cir. Task Force on Equal Treatment in Cts., 1994—. Federal trustee Defender Assn. Phila., 1985-90; bd. dirs. Child Welfare Adv. Bd., Phila., 1984-90, Federal Cts. 200 Adv. Bd., Phila., 1987-88, Phila. Woman's Network, 1986-88. Recipient Sr. Exec. Svc. award U.S. Govt., 1980. Mem. NASW, FBA (chair exec. com., pres. 1990-92, recognition 1992), Nat. Assn. Women Judges, Fed. Magistrate Judges Assn. (dist. dir. 1994-98), Phila. Bar Assn. (chmn. com. 1976-77), Temple Am. Inn of Cts. (master 1993-98), Third Circuit Task Force on Equal Treatment in the Courts (co-chair Commn. on Gender 1994-97), Temple Law Alumni Exec. Bd. (Women's Law Caucus Honoree 1996). Office: US District Court 601 Market St 3030 US Courthouse Philadelphia PA 19106

ANGELL, PHILIP ALVIN, JR., lawyer; b. Randolph, Vt., Dec. 22, 1936; s. Philip A. Sr. and Alice A. (Amee) A.; m. Rosalie Mogan, Aug. 3, 1963; children: Mark M., Matthew P., Rebecca. AB, The Citadel, 1959; LLB, Suffolk U., 1965. Bar: Vt. 1965. Ptnr. Angell & Angell, Randolph, Vt., 1965-96; ret., 1996. State rep. Vt. Legislator, Montpelier, 1993-94, 95-96, 97-98, 99—; chmn. Orange County Tax Appeal Bd., 1973-75, Orange County States Atty., 1967-72; mem. House Natural Resources and Energy Com., 1993—; bd. dirs. Green Mountain United Way, 1997—. Republican. Home and Office: PO Box 116 Randolph VT 05060-0116

ANGELL, RICHARD BRADSHAW, philosophy educator; b. Scarsdale, N.Y., Oct. 14, 1918; s. Stephen LeRoy and Alice (Angel) A.; m. Imogene Lucille Baker, June 4, 1949; children: John Baker, Paul McLean, James Bigelow, David Bradshaw, Kathryn Elizabeth. B.A., Swarthmore Coll., 1940; M. Govt. Adminstrn., U. Pa., 1948; M.A. in Philosophy, Harvard U., 1948, Ph.D. in Philosophy, 1954. Acting asst. prof. Fla. State U., 1949-51; asst. prof. Ohio Wesleyan U., 1954-58, asso. prof., 1958-63, prof., 1963-68; chmn. philosophy dept. Wayne State U., 1968-73, 76-78, prof., 1968-89, prof. emeritus, 1989—. Author: Reasoning and Logic. Chmn. bd. trustees Friends Sch., Detroit, 1978-80, 81-82; pres. Inner-City Sch. Endowment Fund, 1993—. Served to capt. Mem. AAUP, Am. Philos. Assn., ACLU, Mem. Soc. of Friends.

ANGELL, ROGER, writer, magazine editor; b. N.Y.C., Sept. 19, 1920; s. Ernest and Katharine Shepley (Sergeant) A.; m. Evelyn Ames Baker, Oct. 1942 (div. 1963); children—Caroline S., Alice; m. Carol Rogge, Oct. 1963; 1 child, John Henry. Grad., Pomfret Sch., 1938; A.B., Harvard, 1942. Editor, writer Mag. X, Curtis Pub. Co., 1946-47; sr. editor Holiday mag., 1947-56; fiction editor, gen. contbr. New Yorker mag., N.Y.C., 1956—. Author: The Stone Arbor, 1961, A Day in the Life of Roger Angell, 1971, The Summer Game, 1972, Five Seasons, 1977, Late Innings, 1982, Season Ticket, 1988, Once More Around the Park, 1991; editor: Nothing But You: Love Stories from the New Yorker, 1997. Served with USAAF, 1942-46, PTO. Recipient George Polk award for commentary, 1981. Mem. Authors Guild (nat. council, v.p.), Authors League (nat. council), P.E.N. Clubs: Century Assn., Coffee House. Office: New Yorker Mag 20 W 43rd St New York NY 10036-7400

ANGELL, WAYNE D., economist, banker; b. Liberal, Kans., June 28, 1930; s. Charlie Francis and Adele Thelma (Edwards) A.; children: Patrice, Wynne, Ryan, Wiley. BA, Ottawa U., 1952; MA, U. Kans., 1953, PhD, 1957. Instr. econs. U. Kans., Lawrence, 1954-56; prof. econs. Ottawa (Kans.) U., 1956-85, dean, 1969-72; pres., bd. dirs. Hume (Mo.) Bancshares, Inc., 1972-85; bd. dirs. Fed. Res. Bank, Kansas City, Mo., 1979-86, mem. bd. govs., 1986-94; chmn. com. on Fed. Res. Bank activities FRS, Washington, 1986-94; chmn. G-10 Com. on Payment and Settlement Systems, Basle, Switzerland, 1988-94; chief economist, sr. mng. dir. Bear, Stearns & Co., N.Y.C., 1994—; econ. cons. Franklin Savs. Assn., Ottawa, 1981-86; chmn. bd. dirs. 1st State Bank, Pleasanton, 1975-76. Rep. Kans. Ho. of Reps., Topeka, 1961-67; vice chmn. Rep. State Legis. Campaign Com., Topeka, 1964; chmn. Rep. Congl. Conv. 3d Dist., Overland Park, Kans., 1964. Mem. Am. Econ. Assn., Phi Beta Kappa. Republican. Baptist. Avocations: pvt. piloting, tennis, cycling. Home: 1600 N Oak St Arlington VA 22209-2751 Office: Bear Stearns & Co 245 Park Ave New York NY 10167-2500

ANGELO, ROBERT M., advertising executive; b. Balt.; married; 2 children. Grad., U. Tex. CPA, Tex. Acct. Grant Thornton, 1983-90; dir. fin. Earle Palmer Brown, Bethesda, Md., 1990-93, sr. v.p. fin. and adminstrn.,

1993-95, CFO, 1997—. Avocation: golf. Office: Earle Palmer Brown 6400 Goldsboro Rd Bethesda MD 20817

ANGELO, SANDRA MCFALL, television and video producer, writer; b. St. Louis, Apr. 24, 1950; d. Ernest Allison and Virginia Rose McFall. BA in Art, Seattle Pacific U., 1972; MBA in Mktg., Nat. U., San Diego, 1985. Cert. K-12 and cmty. coll. tchr., Calif. Tchr. art Downers Grove (Ill.) H.S., 1974-79, La Jolla (Ill.) Country Day Sch., 1981-86; prof. Palomar Coll., San Marcos, Calif., 1986—; video/TV prodr., exec. dir. Discover Art, San Diego, 1994—; nat. dir. Internat. Ann. Colored Pencil Symposium, San Diego, 1989—; columnist Arts and Crafts Mag., Decorative Painter, Dick Blick Catalog; contbr. The Artist's magazine American Artist. Author: So You Thought You Couldn't Draw, 1994, Colored Pencil Basics, 1994, Creating With Colored Pencils on Wood, 1996, Exploring Colored Pencil, 1999; author, developer Colored Pencil Art Kit, 1994, Madonna & Child needlepoint kit, 1995; contbg. editor Art Materials Today, 1994; writer, prodr., dir. (video series) The Easy Way to Draw Faces, 1994, The Easy Way to Draw Flowers, Landscapes and Water, 1994, The Easy Way to Draw Animals, 1994 (nominated for Emmy, winner 1st place Western Access Video Excellence (WAVE) award, Videographer award of excellence), Drawing Basics, 1994, (videos) Special Effects with Colored Pencils, 1994, Getting Started with Colored Pencils, 1994, Seven Common Drawing Mistakes and How to Correct Them, 1994, Color Theory Made Really Easy, 1995, Paint Like Monet in a Day with Oil Pastels, 1994, Easy Pen and Ink Techniques for Artists and Crafters, 1996, Realistic Colored Pencil Textures: A Mixed Media Approach, 1996, Time Saving Colored Pencil Techniques, 1996, Drawing Your Loved Ones: People, Building a Nature Sketchbook, 1997, Drawing Your Loved Ones: Pets, Creating with Colored Pencils on Wood, 1997, Creating Dynamic Compositions...with artist Steve Muller, 1997, Watercolor Pencils...the Portable Medium, 1999; contbr. articles to profl. jours. Recipient fellowship R.I. Sch. of Design, 1986, award Western Access Video Excellence, 1995; articles written about her in Creative Living Mag., 1995, Michael's Mag., 1996, Washington Post, 1998, Wall St. Jour., 1998. Republican. Avocations: water skiing, drawing, art shows, travel, sewing. Office: Discover Art PO Box 262424 San Diego CA 92196-2424

ANGELOFF, DANN VALENTINO, investment banking executive; b. Hollywood, Calif., Nov. 15, 1935; m. Jo Jeanne Ahlstrom, Sept. 26, 1964; children: Jennifer J., Dann V., Julie A. BS in Fin., U. So. Calif., 1958, MBA, 1963. Trainee Dean Witter & Co., Inc., L.A., 1957-60; v.p. Dempsey-Tegeler & Co., Inc., L.A., 1960-70; mng. dir. West Coast corp. fin. dept. Reynolds Securities, Inc., L.A., 1970-76; pres., bd. dirs. The Angeloff Co., L.A., 1976—; bd. dirs. Aremissoft Corp., London, Eng., SupraLife Internat., San Diego, Compensation Resource Group, Pasadena, Calif., Ready Pac Produce, Irwin Dale, Calif., Pub. Storage, Glendale, Calif., Nicholas-Applegate Growth Equity Fund, San Diego, Nicholas-Applegate Investment Trust, San Diego, Royce Med. Co., Westlake, Calif., World XChange Comm., San Diego, Balboa Capital Corp., Newport Beach, Calif., Consolidation Ptnrs., Pasadena, Calif., TopJob.Net, Manchester, Eng. Trustee U. So. Calif., 1979-86, univ. counselor; bd. dirs., chmn. Trojan Bd. Govs., 1990-92. Mem. Bond Club L.A., Commerce Assocs. U. So. Calif., Skull and Dagger, Cardinal and Gold, Calif. Club, Pacific Club, Valley Hunt Club, San Marino City Club, Kappa Beta Phi. Office: The Angeloff Co 727 W 7th St Los Angeles CA 90017-3707

ANGELOS, PETER G., professional sports team executive, lawyer; b. Pitts., July 4, 1929. LLB, U. Balt. Bar: Md. 1961, U.S. Dist. Ct. Md., 1962, U.S. Supreme Ct. 1974, U.S. Tax Ct., 1975, D.C. 1989, Tenn. 1990, U.S. Ct. Appeals (4th cir.) 1990. Pvt. practice atty. Balt., 1961—; mng. ptnr. Baltimore Orioles, 1993—; chmn., CEO Balt. Orioles, 1993—. Mem. Balt. City Coun. 1959-63; trustee Loyola Coll., Md. Mem. Am. Judicature Soc., Assn. Trial Lawyers Am., Criminal Def. Lawyers Assn., N Y State Trial Lawyers Assn., Md. Trial Lawyers Assn., Md. State Bar Assn., Tenn. Bar Assn., D.C. Bar, Bar Assn. Balt. City. Office: 100 N Charles St # 22D Baltimore MD 21202 Office: Baltimore Orioles 333 W Camden St Baltimore MD 21201-2435*

ANGELOU, MAYA, author; b. St. Louis, Apr. 4, 1928; d. Bailey and Vivian (Baxter) Johnson; 1 son, Guy Johnson. Studied dance with, Pearl Primus, N.Y.C.; hon. degrees, Smith Coll., 1975, Mills Coll., 1975, Lawrence U., 1976. Taught modern dance The Rome Opera House and Hambina Theatre, Tel Aviv; writer-in-residence U. Kans.-Lawrence, 1970; disting. vis. prof. Wake Forest U., 1974, Wichita State U., 1974, Calif. State U.-Sacramento, 1974; apptd. mem. Am. Revolution Bicentennial Council by Pres. Ford, 1975-76; 1st Reynolds prof. Am. Studies, Wake Forest U. since 1981, a lifetime appointment. Author: I Know Why the Caged Bird Sings, 1970, Just Give Me A Cool Drink of Water 'Fore I Diiie (nominated for Pulitzer Prize), 1971, Georgia, Georgia, 1972, Gather Together in My Name, 1974, Oh Pray My Wings are Gonna Fit Me Well, 1975, Singin' and Swingin' and Gettin' Merry Like Christmas, 1976, And Still I Rise, 1978, The Heart of a Woman, 1981, Shaker, Why Don't You Sing?, 1983, All God's Children Need Traveling Shoes, 1986, Now Sheba Sings the Song, 1987, I Shall Not Be Moved, 1990, On the Pulse of Morning: The Inaugural Poem, 1992, Lessons in Living, 1993, Wouldn't Take Nothing for My Journey Now, 1993, My Painted House, My Friendly Chicken, and Me, 1994, The Complete Collected Poems of Maya Angelou, 1994, Kofi and His Magic, 1996, Making Magic in the World, 1998; prodr.: Moon on a Rainbow Shawl, 1988 (by Errol John); appeared on TV in The Richard Pryor Special; author/prodr. Three Way Choice, Afro-American in the Arts (Golden Eagle award), in ltd. series Roots; appeared in revue Cabaret for Freedom and The Blacks (Obie award) with Godfrey Cambridge; adatped Ajax for Mark Taper Forum in L.A.; librettist, lyricist and composer: And Still I Rise, 1976; wrote and presented Trying to Make it Home, 1988; writer for Oprah Winfrey's Harpo Prodns.; poetry writer for film Poetic Justice, 1993; appeared in plays: Porgy and Bess, 1954-55 (Europe), 1957 (U.S.), Calypso, 1957, The Blacks, 1960, Mother Courage, 1964, Medea, Look Away, 1973; films: Roots (Emmy Nomination Best Supporting Actress), 1977, How to Make an American Quilt, 1995; contr. short stories and poems to mags.; also numerous appearances on network and local talk shows; articles, short stories, poems to Black Scholar, Chgo. Daily News, Cosmopolitan, Harper's Bazaar, Life Mag., Redbook, Sunday N.Y. Times, others. Mem. adv. bd. Women's Prison Assn.; apptd. by Dr. Martin Luther King Jr. No. Coord. Southern Christian Leadership Conf., 1959-60, apptd. by Pres. Ford to Bicentennal Commn., by Pres. Carter to Nat. Commn. on Observance of Internat. Women's Yr. Chubb fellowship award Yale U., 1970, named Woman of Yr. in Comm., 1976; Ladies Home Jour. Top 100 Most Influential Women, 1983, The Matric award, 1983, The North Carolina Award in Lit., 1987; named 1st Reynolds prof. Wake Forest U., 1981, a lifetime appointment, Woman of the Yr. Essence Mag., 1992, Disting. Woman of N.C., 1992, Horatio Alger award, 1992, Grammy award Best Spoken Word or Non-Traditional Album, 1994 (for recording of "On the Pulse of the Morning"). Mem. AFTRA, Dirs. Guild Am., Equity, Harlem Writers Guild, Am. Film Inst. (trustee), Women's Prison Assn., Horatio Alger Assn. Dist. Americans, Nat. Soc. Prevention of Cruelty to Children (Maya Angelou Ctr. opened 1992), ambassador, Unicef Internat., 1996. Office: care Dave La Camera Lordly and Dame Inc 51 Church St Boston MA 02116-5417

ANGELOV, GEORGE ANGEL, pediatrician, anatomist, teratologist; b. Bulgaria, May 12, 1925; came to U.S., 1978; s. Angel Christov and Maria Angelov; m. Olga Valerie Minkova, Dec. 21, 1952; 1 child, Angel. MD, Sch. of Medicine, Sofia, Bulgaria, 1952. Pediatrician Distric Hosp., Bulgaria, 1952-53; asst. prof. Sch. of Medicine, Sofia, Bulgaria, 1953-64; prof. anatomy and anthropology Sch. of Biology, Sofia, Bulgaria, 1964-77; mgr. reproductive toxicology Lederle Labs., Pearl River, N.Y., 1979-89; cons. reproductive toxicology pvt. practice, Laguna Niguel, Calif., 1989—; assoc. dean Sch. of Biology, Sofia, 1970-72; vis. scientist Sch. of Medicine, Geneva, 1971, 74. Author: (textbook) Anatomy, 1970; mem. glossary com. Teratology Glossary, 1987-89; reviewer several sci. jours.; contbr. numerous sci. publs. on anatomy, teratology, and growth and devel. of adolescents to profl. jours. Mem. Teratology Soc. USA, European Teratology Soc., Human Biology Coun. USA, Free Union of Univ. Profs. of Anatomy. East Orthodox. Avocations: bridge, chess, 20th century history.

ANGER, PAUL, newspaper editor. Broward editor Miami Herald, Hollywood, Fla. Office: The Miami Herald Pub Co 3325 Hollywood Blvd Ste 102 Hollywood FL 33021-6926*

ANGERMEIER, INGO, hospital administrator, educator; b. Berlin, Mar. 6, 1950; arrived in U.S., 1953; s. Karl Edward Angermeier and Margret (Schneider) Westphalen; m. L. Kaye Willis, July 12, 1992; children: Courtney, Katherine, Johnathan, T.J., Tiana, Tarryn. BA cum laude, Ripon Coll., 1972; MHA with honors, U. Minn., 1974. Assoc. adminstr. Marshfield (Wis.) Clinic, 1972-76; sr. v.p., acting COO Creighton-St. Joseph Hosp., Omaha, 1976-84; assoc. adminstr., COO Asbury Hosp., Salina, Kans., 1984-87; exec. v.p. St. Francis Hosp. and Med. Ctr., Topeka, 1987—; prof. med. ethics U. Kans., Lawrence, mem. adv. bd. program health svcs. adminstrn.; mem. clin. faculty U. Minn., Mpls. Tech. editor: Inquiry; contbr. articles to profl. jours. Recipient Ross Labs. award, 1974, Vernon E. Weckworth award U. Minn., 1983. Avocations: skiing, carpentry, boy scouts. Office: La State U Med Ctr 1501 Kings Hwy Shreveport LA 71103-4228

ANGIER, JOSEPH, television producer, writer; b. L.A., Sept. 10, 1953; s. Keith and Adele (Rosenthal) A. BA, SUNY, Binghamton, 1974. Prodr. HBO Am. Undercover, 1986-87, PBS-KCET, 1988-93, ABC News Turning Point, L.A., 1994-97, The Great War on PBS, 1996, Vital Signs, 1997, A&E Biography, 1998, Fox Files, 1998, Lifetime Intimate Portrait, ABC News 20/20, 1999. Author: Hollywood Remembers the Blacklist, 1997. Recipient Writers Guild Am. award, 1989, 91, Cine Golden Eagles, Emmy. Mem. Writers Guild Am. (Best Documentary Script 1989, 91), Acad. TV Arts and Scis. (Emmy for best documentary script 1984). Home: 2268 28th St Apt 6 Santa Monica CA 90405-1947 Office: PO Box 377 Santa Monica CA 90406-0377

ANGIER, NATALIE MARIE, science journalist; b. N.Y.C., Feb. 16, 1958; d. Keith and Adele Bernice (Rosenthal) A.; m. Richard Steven Weiss, July 27, 1991. Student, U. Mich., 1974-76; BA, Barnard Coll., 1978. Staff writer Discover Mag., N.Y.C., 1980-83, Time Mag., N.Y.C., 1984-86; editor Savvy Mag., N.Y.C., 1983-84; journalism educator NYU, N.Y.C., 1987-89; became reporter N.Y. Times, N.Y.C., 1990; now science correspondent N.Y. Times, Washington. Author: Natural Obsessions, 1988, The Beauty of the Beastly, 1995. Recipient Pulitzer Prize for beat reporting, 1991, Journalism award GM Ind. Bd., 1991, Lewis Thomas award Marine Biol. Labs., 1990, Journalism award AAAS, 1992, Disting. Alumna award Barnard Coll., 1993. Mem. Nat. Assn. Sci. Writers. Avocation: weightlifting. Office: NY Times Washington Bureau 1627 I St NW Fl 7 Washington DC 20006-4007*

ANGINO, ERNEST EDWARD, retired geology educator; b. Winsted, Conn., Feb. 16, 1932; s. Alfred and Filomena Mabel (Serluco) A.; m. Margaret Mary Lachat, June 26, 1954; children—Cheryl Ann, Kimberly Ann. B.S. in Mining Engring., Lehigh U., Bethlehem, Pa., 1954; M.S. in Geology, U. Kans., 1958, Ph.D. in Geology, 1961. Instr. geology U. Kans., Lawrence, 1961-62, prof. civil engring., 1971-99, prof. geology, 1972-99, chmn. dept. geology, 1972-86, dir. water resources ctr., 1990-99; asst. prof. Tex. A&M U., College Station, 1962-65; chief geochemist Kans. Geol. Survey, Lawrence, 1965-70, assoc. state geologist, 1970-72; cons. on water chemistry and pollution to various cos. and govt. agys. including Dow Chem. Co., Ocean Mining Inc., Envicon, Oak Ridge Lab., Fisheries Research Bd. Can., Midwest Research Inst., Coast and Geodetic Survey, U.S. Geol. Survey. Author: (with G.K. Billings) Atomic Absorption Spectrometry in Geology, 1967; author, editor: (with D.T. Long) Geochemistry of Bismuth, 1979; editor: (with R.K. Hardy) Proc. 3d Forum Geol. Industrial Minerals, 1967, (with G.K. Billings) Geochemistry Subsurface Brines, 1969; contbr. more than 125 articles to sci. and profl. jours. Mem. Lawrence City Police Rels. Commn., 1970-76, Lawrence City Commn., 1983-87, mayor, 1984-85; mem. Lawrence 2020 Planning Commn., 1992-94, Police Adv. Coun., 1994—, Crimestoppers Bd., 1994—. With U.S. Army, 1955-57. NSF fellow Oak Ridge Lab., 1963; recipient Antarctic Service medal Dept. Def., 1969; Angino Buttress named in his honor, 1967. Mem. Geochem. Soc. (sec. 1970-76), Soc. Environ. Geochemistry and Health (pres. 1978-79), Internat. Assn. Geochemistry and Cosmochemistry (treas. 1980-94), Forum Club (Factotum 1978-79), Rotary (pres. 1993-95). Republican. Roman Catholic. Avocations: philately, Western history, Indian lore. Home: 4605 Grove Dr Lawrence KS 66049-3777 Office: U Kans Dept Geology Lindley 120 Lawrence KS 66045-0294 *Knowledge is what really counts - the world does not owe anyone anything!.*

ANGIONE, HOWARD FRANCIS, lawyer, editor; b. N.Y.C., Aug. 3, 1940; s. Charles Francis Angione and Genevieve Rita (McCarthy) A.; m. Maryann Allgaier, June 24, 1971; children: Charles Francis, Mary Christine, Kathleen Elizabeth. B.A. in History, Holy Cross Coll., 1962; M.A. in Internat. Relations, Clark U., 1966; JD cum laude, St. John's U., Jamaica, N.Y., 1989. Bar: Conn. 1989, N.Y. 1990, D.C. 1991. Reporter, sci. writer Worcester Telegram, Mass., 1961-65; writer, day editor, sci. writer AP, Boston, 1965-69; editor, shift supr. Gen. Desk AP, N.Y.C., 1969-77; tech. editor N.Y. Times, 1977-87; assoc. Weil, Gotshal & Manges, N.Y.C., 1989-93; atty. pvt. practice, 1997—. Pub. N.Y. Region Lawyers Coop. Practice Guides, 1993-96; editor AP Stylebook, 1977; editor-in-chief N.Y. State Bar Jour., 1998—. Sec. Class of 1962 Holy Cross Coll., 1966-80. Mem. Harris Users Group (pres. 1980-84). Roman Catholic. Home: 80-47 192nd St Jamaica NY 11423-1042

ANGLAND, JOSEPH, lawyer; b. N.Y.C., Sept. 1, 1949; s. Patrick and Josephine (Woods) A.; m. Ida Wolff, Aug. 4, 1984. BS, MIT, 1972; JD, Harvard U., 1975. Bar: N.Y. 1977, D.C. 1988, U.S. Dist. Ct. (so. and ea. dists.) N.Y. 1978, U.S. Ct. Claims 1983, U.S. Tax Ct. 1985, U.S. Ct. Appeals (2d cir.) 1982, U.S. Ct. Appeals (D.C. cir.) 1988, U.S. Dist. Ct. D.C. 1988, U.S. Ct. Appeals (3d cir.) 1990, U.S. Ct. Appeals (D.C. cir.) 1992, U.S. Ct. Appeals (5th cir.) 1993, U.S. Ct. Appeals (7th cir.) 1993, U.S. Supreme Ct. 1990. Law clk. to presiding justice Calif. Supreme Ct., San Francisco, 1975-76; assoc. Dewey, Ballantine, Bushby, Palmer & Wood, N.Y.C., 1976-83; ptnr. Dewey Ballantine, N.Y.C., 1984—; dir. The Legal Aid Soc., 1993—. Chmn. editl. bd. Antitrust Law Devel. Mem. ABA (coun. antitrust sect.), N.Y. State Bar Assn., Assn. of Bar of City of N.Y. (com. on antitrust and trade regulation). Home: 292 Stanwich Rd Greenwich CT 06830-3528 Office: Dewey Ballantine 1301 Avenue Of The Americas New York NY 10019-6022

ANGLE, JOHN CHARLES, retired life insurance company executive; b. N.Y.C., Aug. 22, 1923; s. Everett Edward and Catharine Elizabeth (Dodge) A.; m. Catherine Anne Sellers, Oct. 4, 1945; children: Margaret Susan, James Sellers. SB, U. Chgo., 1944. With Union Nat. Life Ins. Co., Lincoln, Nebr., 1948-51; v.p., actuary Woodmen Accident and Life Co., Lincoln, 1953-73; dir. Woodmen Accident and Life Co., 1969-73; sr. v.p., chief actuary Guardian Life Ins. Co. Am., N.Y.C., 1973-77; exec. v.p. Guardian Life Ins. Co. Am., 1977-80, pres., 1980-84, chmn. bd., chief exec. officer, 1985-88, also bd. dirs.; pres. Probe, Inc. (ins. newsletter), 1990-97; adv. dir. Guardian Life Ins. Co., 1999—; dir. mutual funds Guardian Park Ave. Portfolio. Consulting editor: Life and Health Insurance Handbook, 2d edit., 1964. Pres. Lincoln Community Chest, 1965, Lincoln Community Coun., 1966-68, 14th St. - Union Sq. Bus. Improvement Dist., 1985-88, Nebr. Art Assn., 1992-94; trustee Am. Coll., 1987-92; bd. dirs. Lincoln Gen. Hosp., 1970-73; bd. visitors U. Nebr., Lincoln, 1994—. 1st lt. USAF, 1943-46, capt., 1951-52. Fellow Soc. Actuaries (dir. publs. 1975-79, bd. govs. 1980-83, 84-87); mem. Am. Acad. Actuaries (bd. dirs. 1977-79), Internat. Actuarial Assn. (v.p. U.S. sect.), Health Ins. Assn. Am. (bd. dirs. 1985-88), Life Office Mgmt. Assn. (bd. dirs. 1983-89, chmn. 1987), Am. Coun. Life Ins. (bd. dirs. 1986-88), Life Ins. Coun. N.Y. (bd. dirs. 1985-88), Lincoln Country Club, Lincoln Univ. Club. Home: 3800 S 42nd St Lincoln NE 68506-4209

ANGLE, MARGARET SUSAN, lawyer; b. Lincoln, Nebr., Feb. 20, 1948; d. John Charles and Catherine (Sellers) Angle. BA in Polit. Sci. with distinciton, U. Wis., 1970, MA in Scandinavian Studies, 1972, JD cum laude, 1976. Bar: Wis. 1977, Minn. 1978. Laaw clk. Madison, Mpls., Chgo., 1974-76; law clk. U.S. Dist. Ct., Mpls., 1977-78; mem. firm Faegre & Benson, Mpls., 1978-84; sr. atty., asst. gen. counsel, asst. sec. Nat. Car Rental System, Inc., Mpls., 1984-90; corp. sec. Car-Temps; CEO Angle & Assocs., Ltd., Eagan, Minn., 1980—. Note and comment editor U. Wis. Law Rev.; contbr. articles to profl. jours. NDEA fellow, 1972. Mem. ABA, Am. Car Rental Assn. (bd. dirs. 1987-90), Minn. Bar Assn., Wis. Bar Assn., Nennepin County Bar Assn., Alternative Dispute Resolution Com., Niños del Paraguay, Parents of Latin Am. Children, Order of Coif. Office: Angle & Assocs 8425 E Quarterhorse Trail Scottsdale AZ 85258-1365

ANGLEMAN-NOBLE, SHARON ANN, journalist; b. Houston, Apr. 14, 1961; d. Hildred Bruce Lockhart and Elizabeth Ann Davis; children: Justin Angleman, Thomas Angleman, Robert Angleman. BS in Journalism magna cum laude, Ark. State U., Jonesboro, 1998. Freelance journalist NobleInk Co., Jonesboro, 1997—; chair diversity SPJ, Jonesboro, 1997-98. Author numerous poems; photo editor Herald, 1997-98; contbr. articles to profl. jours. Recipient Udell Smith award Nat. Assn. Retired Employees, 1995, Foy Howard award Housing and Devel., 1996, 97, award Ark. Assn. Press, 1996, 97, 98. Mem. Ark. Press Photographer's Assn., Photographic Soc. (pres. 1998, Outstanding Sr. 1997), Bus. Profl. Women (Scholarship award 1997). E-mail: san@bscn.com. Home: 776 CR 912 Brookland AR 72417 Office: 776 CR 912 Brookland AR 72417

ANGLIN, FLORENCE See **AQUINO-KAUFMAN, FLORENCE**

ANGLIN, LINDA TANNERT, community health nurse, geriatrics nurse, educator; b. Chgo., Jan. 7, 1941; d. Fred Bruno and Mildred Violet (Schmude) Tannert; m. Edgar Allen Anglin, Nov. 21, 1961; children: George Walter, Paul Allen, Steven Eric, Melissa Renee. BSN, U. Ariz., 1962; MS in Nursing, U. Ill. at Chgo., Peoria, 1980; D of Arts, Ill. State U., 1990. RN; cert. gerontol. nurse specialist. Community health nurse Pima County Health Dept., Tucson; long term care relief nurse Washington (Ill.) Christian Village; assoc. prof. nursing Bradley U., Peoria; parish nurse cons. Regional Parish Nurse Network. Mem. Ill. State Task Force on Alzheimer's Disease. Mem. Ill. Nurses Assn., Epsilon Epsilon, Sigma Theta Tau, Phi Alpha Theta. Home: 629 E Grove Rd Metamora IL 61548-9804 Office: Dept of Nursing Coll Edn & Health Scis Bradley Univ Peoria IL 61625

ANGLIN, MICHAEL WILLIAMS, lawyer; b. Chelsea, Mass., Dec. 3, 1946; s. John M. and Lillian Rogene (Williams) A. BS, Tex. A&M Commerce, 1969; JD, U. Tex., 1976. Bar: Tex. 1976, U.S. Dist. Ct. (no. dist.) Tex. 1979, U.S. Dist. Ct. (we. and ea. dists.) Tex. 1987, U.S. Dist. Ct. Ariz. 1992, U.S. Ct. Appeals (5th and 11th cirs.) 1981, U.S. Supreme Ct. 1986. With Passman & Jones, Dallas, 1976-87; ptnr. Fulbright & Jaworski, LLP, Dallas, 1987—; trustee Official Panel Bankruptcy Trustees for No. Dist. Tex., 1980—. Corp. mem. Dallas Mus. Fine Arts, 1984; ct. apptd. spl. advocate, 1990—; bd. dirs. Dallas Opera, 1992-95; mem. Greater Dallas Planning Coun., 1994—; mem. Greater Dallas Crime Commn., 1994—; mem. Youth Crime Coun., 1994—. Mem. ABA, Tex. Bar Assn., Dallas Bar Assn., Am. Bankruptcy Inst. Office: Fulbright & Jaworski LLP 2200 Ross Ave Ste 2800 Dallas TX 75201-2784*

ANGLIN, WALTER MICHAEL, minister, law enforcement professional$D; b. Cheverly, Md., Jan. 10, 1958; s. Lawrence Tilmon and Margaret Lorraine (Thrash) A.; m. Meloene Alene Williams, Mar. 1, 1980; children: Walter Michael Jr., Mary Elizabeth. A in Practical Theology, Christ For The Nations Inst., 1979; BA in Pastoral Ministry, S.W. Assemblies of God Coll., 1991. Ordained to ministry Am. Bapt. Assn., 1978; ordained to ministry Faith christian Fellows. Internat., 1996; lic. to ministry Assemblies of God, 1980. Evangelist Assemblies of God, Duncanville, Tex., 1980-92; police officer Duncanville Police Dept., 1986-92, chaplain, 1990-92, high sch. liaison officer, 1990-92; pastor Immanuel Word Ctr., Homer, La., 1996—; chaplain Homer Police Dept., Homer, La., 1997—; youth sponsor Meml. Assembly of God, Duncanville, 1989-91; youth care leader Ch. on the Rock S., Duncanville, 1991-92; youth evangelist SWAT Youth Ministries, Duncanville, 1989-92; del. South Dallas sect. coun. Assemblies of God, Dallas, 1989, 90, Am. Bapt. Assn., Plain Dealing, La., 1974; youth pastor Word of Faith Joaquin, Tex., 1992-96. Exec. advisor local post Duncanville Law Enforcement Post, 1990-91; asst. coach Best S.W. Soccer Assn., Duncanville, 1989-91, YMCA Youth Baseball, Dallas, 1990;Southwest Baseball Umpire's Assn., 1993-96; La. High Sch. Athletic Assn. baseball umpire, 1996—; assoc. coord. Duncanville Citizen's Police Acad., 1990-91; head umpire Toledo Bend Dixie League, Joaquin, Tex., 1994-95. Fellow FOP (chaplain local chpt. 1989—); mem. Tex. Peace Officers Assn. (cert. advanced peace officer), Duncanville Youth Pastor's Assn., Tex. Sch. Resource Officer's Assn. (pres., founder 1992), Homer, LA Ministerial Alliance (pres. 1998—). Office: Immanuel Word Center 401 E 5th St Homer LA 71040-4005

ANGOFF, GERALD HARVEY, cardiologist; b. Cambridge, Mass., Feb. 6, 1944; s. Nathan Robert and Evelyn (Kanter) A.; m. Rosalind Norma Tarko, Nov. 23, 1975; children: Elizabeth, Rebekah. AB, Harvard Coll., 1966; MD, Harvard U., 1970. Diplomate Am. Bd. Internal Medicine, Am. Bd. Cardio Vascular Disease. Resident internal medicine Cleve. Met. Gen. Hosp., 1970-72; fellow in cardiology Harvard Med. Sch., Peter Bent Brigham Hosp., Boston, 1975-77, Harvard Sch. Pub. Health, Boston, 1977-78; cardiologist The Heart Ctr., Manchester, N.H., 1978—; chief cardiology Elliot Hosp., Manchester, 1979-82, 86-93; instr. Harvard Med. Sch., Boston, 1978-96 pres. The Heart Ctr., 1995—. Bd. dirs. Jewish Fedn. Greater Manchester, 1984-94; v.p. Temple Adath Yeshurun, Manchester, 1994-96, pres., 1996-98. Maj. U.S. Army, 1975-78. Fellow Am. Coll. Cardiology, Am. Heart Assn. (Coun. on clin. cardiology). Avocations: computers, skiing. Office: The Heart Ctr 57 Webster St Manchester NH 03104-2503

ANGST, GERALD L., lawyer; b. Chgo., Dec. 29, 1950; s. Gerald L. Sr. and Audrey M. (Hides) A.; m. Candace Simning, Jan. 29, 1983. BA magna cum laude, Loyola U., Chgo., 1972, JD cum laude, 1975. Assoc. Sidley & Austin, Chgo., 1975-82, ptnr., 1982—. Mem. ABA (constrn. litigation com. litigation sect.), Chgo. Bar Assn. (civil practice com.). Office: Sidley & Austin 1 First Natl Plz Chicago IL 60603-2003

ANGST, KAREN K., mental health nurse; b. Houston, Tex., May 16, 1948; d. Conrad Wilbur and Wanda Lee (Sullivan) A. Student, Sacred Heart Dominican Coll., Houston, 1966-68; cert., Houston C.C., 1972; student, U. Houston, 1977-78; ADN, Alvin (Tex.) C.C., 1979. RN, LVN, Tex.; cert. mental health nurse; RNC, ANCC. Staff nurse Gready Clinic, Houston, 1969-71; staff nurse St. Joseph Hosp., Houston, 1967-68, charge nurse cognitive impaired care unit and psychiat. acute care unit, 1971-98; staff nurse Vitas Hospice, Houston, 1998—; mem. planning com. Cognitive Impaired Care Unit, St. Joseph Hosp., Houston. Mem. Am. Assn. Ret. Persons, Alzheimer Assn., Houston Gerontol. Soc., Chi Sigma Nu. Lutheran.

ANGSTADT, F. V., language arts and theatre arts educator; b. Dover, Del., Oct. 11, 1953; d. T. Richard Sr. and Frances Virginia (Kohout) A. BA, Del. State U., 1976; MFA, Cath. U. Am., 1982. Lighting designer, assoc. dir. écarté dance Theatre, Dover, 1981-93; alternative tchr. Lake Forest H.S., Felton, Del., 1982-87; English tchr. Dover H.S., 1987-89; lang. arts and theater tchr. Ctrl. Mid. Sch., Dover, 1989—; lighting designer Harrisburg (Pa.) Ballet, 1991-93; lighting designer, artistic advisor Act I Players, Dover, 1983-93, lighting designer Kimberly Mackin Dance Co., Balt., Axis Theatre, 1996—, Women's Project at Theatre Project '97, 98, 99; adj. faculty Del. State U., Dover, 1985-89, Wilmington Coll., Dover, 1996—; tech. advisor, bd. dirs. 2nd St. Players, Milford, Del., 1993—; lighting designer Balt. Shakespeare Festival, 1994; mem. dance leadership Visual and Performing Arts Commn., Dover, 1994—; mem. English devel. com. state (testing) assessment team Dover Dept. of Edn., 1997—. Mem. Vietnam Vets. Meml. Com., Dover, 1985-87; sec., founding mem. Dover Arts Coun., 1988-93, tech. advisor, 1988-94; sec. Capital Educators Assn., Dover, 1993—; tecn. advisor City of Dover First Night, 1997—. Recipient scholarship All Am. Youth Honor Band, 1972, Del. State U., Dover, 1974-76; apptd. to adjudicator Del. Theatre Assn., 1986. Mem. ACLU, Nat. Coun. Tchrs. English, Theatre Communicators Group. Avocations: swimming, biking, voice, visual art, dance lighting. Home: 117 Wyoming Ave Dover DE 19904-6923 Office: Ctrl Mid Sch Delaware and Pennsylvania Dover DE 19901

ANGSTROM, WAYNE RAYMOND, communications executive; b. Chgo., Mar. 26, 1939; s. Raymond Harry and Dorothy Louise (Dixon) A.; m. Sandra Sue Weber, Oct. 5, 1963; children: Mark, Carl, David, Kristina. AA in Bus. Adminstrn., Chgo. City Coll., 1962; student, Northwestern U., 1963-68. Mfg. mgr. R.R. Donnelley & Sons Co., Chgo., 1962, div. dir., v.p., 1981-87; exec. v.p. Maxwell Communications Corp., St. Paul, 1987-90, Quebecor Printing Inc., Boston, 1990-91; pres., CEO, St. Ives Inc. U.S.A., 1992—; also bd. dirs. Home: 7082 Valencia Dr Boca Raton FL 33433-7404 Office: Saint Ives Inc 2025 Mckinley St Hollywood FL 33020-3139

ANGUIANO, LUPE, business executive; b. La Junta, Colo., Mar. 12, 1929; d. Jose and Rosario (Gonzalez) A. Student, Ventura (Calif.) Jr. Coll., 1948, Victory Noll Jr. Coll., Huntington, Ind., 1949-52, Marymount Coll., Palos Verdes, Calif., 1958-59, Calif. State U., L.A., 1965-67; M.A., Antioch-Putney-Yellow Springs, Ohio, 1978. S.W. regional dir. NAACP Legal Def. and Ednl. Fund, L.A., 1965-69; civil rights specialist HEW, Washington, 1969-73; S.W. regional dir. Nat. Coun. Cath. Bishops, Region X, San Antonio, 1973-77; pres. Nat. Women's Employment and Edn., Inc., L.A., 1979-91; pres., cons. Lupe Anguiano & Assocs., 1981—; cons. Tex. Dept. Human Resources, Dept. Labor, Women's Bur., U.S. Office Pers. Mgmt. and USCG, Washington, 1990-92; mem. part time faculty Ventura (Calif.) Coll.; proposal reader U.S. Office Edn.-Women's Equity Act; mem. Tex. Adv. Coun. on Tech.-Vocat. Edn. Calif. del. White House Conf. on Status Mexican-Ams. in U.S., 1967; founding mem. policy coun. Nat. Women's Polit. Caucus, from 1971; Tex. and nat. del. Internat. Women's Year, 1976-77; chmn. Nat. Women's Polit. Caucus Welfare Reform Task Force, from 1977; co-chmn. Nat. Peace Acad. Campaign, 1977-81; founder, bd. dirs. Nat. Chicana Found., Inc., 1971-78; bd. dirs. Calif. Coun. Children and Youth, 1967, Rio Grande Fedn. Chicano Health Ctrs., S.W. Rural States, 1974-76, Women's Lobby, Washington, 1974-77, Rural Am. Women, Washington, from 1978, Small Bus. Coun. Greater San Antonio; mem. Pres.'s Coun. on Pvt. Sector Initiatives, 1983. Recipient Community award Coalition Mexican-Am. Orgns., 1967, Outstanding Svc. award Washington, 1968, Thanksgiving award Boys' Club, 1976, Outstanding Svc. award Tex. Women's Polit. Caucus, 1977, Liberty Bell award San Antonio Young Lawyers, 1981, Vista award for exceptional svc. to end poverty, 1980, Headliner award San Antonio Women in Communications, 1978, Woman of Yr. award Tex. Women's Polit. Caucus, 1978, Pres.'s Vol. Action award 1983, Leadership award Nat. Network Hispanic Women, 1989; named Outstanding Woman of Yr., L.A. County, 1972, Woman of the 80s Ms. mag., 1980; Nat. Pres.'s award Nat. Image, Inc., 1981, Wonder Woman Found. award, 1982, Pres.' Vol. Action award 1983, Adv. of Yr. San Antonio SBA, 1984; selected Am. 100 Most Important Women, Ladies Home Jour., 1988, 89; featured in CBS TV series An Am. Portrait, 1985, Leadership award Nat. Network Hispanic Women, 1989. Mem. Assn. Female Execs., Pres.'s Assn., Am. Mgmt. Assn. Republican. Roman Catholic. Author: (with others) U.S. Bilingual Education Act, 1967, Texas A.F.D.C. Employment and Education Act, 1977; manuals Women's Employment and Education Model Program.

ANGUIZOLA, GUSTAV (ANTONIO), historian, educator, writer, consultant; b. Panama Canal Zone, Feb. 29, 1928; naturalized, U.S., 1961; s. Antonio Anguizola Palma and Melida Guerra Gómez; children: Phillip Anthony, Jerome James (dec.). B.A., Evansville Coll., 1948; M.A., Ind. U., 1951, Ph.D., 1954; Cert., Am. Sch. Classics, Athens, Greece, 1964, Stanford U., 1975. Sr. chem. tester Allby Corp., Gary, Ind., 1956-59; dept. chmn. Morris Coll., Sumter, S.C., 1959-62; spl. asst. Panam. Games Mayor of Chgo., 1959; vis. prof. SUNY, Geneseo, summers 1961, 62; chmn. dept. Elizabeth City State Coll., N.C., 1962-63; asst. prof. Purdue U., Lafayette, Hammond, Ind., 1963-66; asst. prof. history U. Tex., Arlington, 1966-82, research prof., 1982—; assoc. prof. Chgo. State U., 1967-69; chmn. midwest Collegiate Council UN, N.Y.C., 1962-76; cons. N.C. Bd. Edn., Raleigh, 1962-63, Hispanic Am. Hist. Rev., Austin, 1970-72, Gov. of Tex., Austin, 1980-82, Inter-Am. Security Council, Washington, 1977—; chmn. bd. The Freedom Fedn., Washington, 1982-86; mem. Minorities Commn. of Tex., 1980-82; mem. Gov. of Tex. Com., 1987—. Author: Isthmian Political Instability: 1821-76, 77, 78, Life of Philippe Bunau-Varilla, 1980, Violation of Human Rights in Panama, 1980, The Taft Convention, Research Sites Panama and Canal Zone, 1986; author: (with others) The Isthmus of Panama & Relations with U.S, Encyclopaedia Britannica, 1990 edit.; contbr. articles to profl. jours. Precinct chmn. Republican Party Tex., 1979—, election judge, 1985—; mem. Nat. Com. Rep. Party, Washington, 1982—; del. State Rep. Convention, Tex., 1978—, Nat. Rep. Conv., 1992; cons. Heritage Found., Washington, 1980—, Freedon Fedn. Recipient Hays-Mundt award U.S. Dept. State, 1953, Fulbright-Hays award, 1964, Andrew Mellon award, 1982; NEH grantee Stanford U., 1975, U. Chg., 1985—; named Alumnus of Yr., Evansville U., 1984. Mem. Am. Hist. Assn., AAUP (region sec. 1982—), Tex. State Tchrs. Assn., Conf. on Latin Am. History, Pacific Coast Council Latin Am. Studies, Nat. Soc. Sci. Assn., Dallas Men's Club, Arlington Rep. Club, Hispanic Assembly Tex., Pres.'s Club. Roman Catholic. Office: U Texas 920 Appleton Ste 17 Arlington TX 76019

ANGULA, HELMUT KANGULOHI, Namibian government official; b. Ontananga, Oshikoto, Namibia, Nov. 11, 1945; s. Onesmus and Adda (Thomas) A.; div. Nov. 1992; children: Adda Kaone, Vita, Priscilla, Magdalena, Monica. Cert., Nikumbi Internat. Coll., 1969; MSc in Biology, Voronezh State U., USSR, 1975. Cert. Tchr. Biology and Chemistry. Tchr. SWAPO Edn. Ctr., Nyango, Zambia, 1975-76; adminstr. SWAPO Edn. Ctr., Nyango, Zanbia, 1976-77; head of diplomatic mission SWAPO Mission, Havana, Cuba, 1977-86; head of mission SWAPO Observer Mission, UN, N.Y.C., 1986-89; deputy min. Ministry Mines and Energy, Republic of Namibia, 1990-91; min. Fisheries and Marine Resources, Republic of Namibia, 1991-95; min. of fin., 1995-96; min. Agr., Water and Rural Devel., 1997—. Author: Haimbodi Ya Haufiku 1000 Days, 1991. Activist South West Africa People's, Windhoek, 1964; youth activist Organization SWAPO, Zambia, 1966. Mem. Revival Volley Ball Club (patron), Parliamentary Football Team (capt. 1993—). Office: Embassy of Republic of Namibia 1605 New Hampshire Ave NW Washington DC 20009-2511

ANGULO, GERARD ANTONIO, publisher, investor; b. Havana, Cuba, Sept. 24, 1956; came to U.S., 1960; s. Ricardo A. and Rosario (Mestas) A. BA, Princeton U., 1978; MBA, Harvard U., 1980. With office of pres. Consol. Mining & Industries, N.Y.C., 1980-84; cons. in field; prof. grad. bus. sch. Columbia U., 1988-90, NYU, 1989-90; owner, pub. San Juan STAR, 1994—. Host TV show Capital Gains, 1990-91. Bd. dirs. YMCA of San Juan, P.R., Salvation Army; Ballet Concierto; pres., bd. dirs. Better Bus. Bur.; pres. Harvard Bus. Sch. Assn. P.R. Mem. New Eng. Soc. (bd. dirs. 1986-91, v.p., Achievement award 1979-80). Roman Catholic.

ANGUS, JOHN COTTON, chemical engineering educator; b. Grand Haven, Mich., Feb. 22, 1934; s. Francis Clark and Margaret (Cotton) A.; m. Caroline Helen Gezon, June 25, 1960; children—Lorraine Margaret, Charles Thomas. BSChemE, U. Mich., 1956, MS, 1958, PhD in Engring, 1960; DSc (hon.), Ohio U., 1998. Registered profl. engr., Ohio. Research engr. Minn. Mining & Mfg. Co., St. Paul, 1960-63; prof. Case Inst. Tech. (now Case Western Res. U.), Cleve., 1963-67; prof. chem. engring. Case Inst. Tech. (now Case Western Res. U.), 1967—, chmn. dept., 1974-80, interim dean engring., 1986-87; vis. lectr. U. Edinburgh, Scotland, 1972-73; vis. prof. Northwestern U., 1980-81; pres. Angus Engring, Inc. Trustee Ohio Scottish Games. NSF fellow, 1956-57; NATO sr. fellow, 1972-73. Fellow AIChE; mem. NAE, Am. Chem. Soc., Electrochem. Soc. (Pioneer award), Materials Rsch. Soc., Sigma Xi, Tau Beta Pi, Phi Lambda Upsilon. Research in fields of crystal growth, diamond synthesis, laser applications, electrochemical devices, thermodynamics. Office: Case Western Res U Dept Chem Engring Cleveland OH 44106-7217

ANGUS, ROBERT CARLYLE, JR., health facility administrator; b. Grand Rapids, Mich., July 23, 1946; s. Robert Carlyle Sr. and Vicki I. (Weidman) Deiters; m. Elizabeth T. Angus, May 1995; children: Tamra Ann, Robert M. BS, Donsbach U., Huntington Beach, Calif., 1985; PhD in Therapeutic Philosophy, World U., 1982. Registered cardiovascular technologist, pulmonary technologist, registered cardiology technologist, cert. respiratory therapist; lic. radiographer, respiratory care practitioner, hearing aid dispenser; cert. occupl. hearing conservationist; bd. cert. naturopathic physician; cert. colon hydrotherapist. Dir. cardiopulmonary St. Mary's Hosp., Grand Rapids, Mich., 1970-74; Lectr. Muskegon (Mich.) Community Coll., 1974-76; dir. respiratory therapy Hackley Hosp., 1974-76; dir. cardiovascular, cardiopulmonary Am. Internat. Hosp., Zion, Ill., 1976-78; physician's asst. Dr. William J. Mauer; dir. med. svcs., clinic adminstr. Kingsley Med. Ctr., Arlington Heights, Ill., 1978-90; dir. med. diagnostics, naturopathic physician Celebration of Health Ctr., Inc., Bluffton, Ohio, 1990—; edn. cons. Brookhaven Med. Care Facility; lectr., advisor Muskegon C.C., 1974-76; mem. Nat. Bd. Respiratory Care. Active Big Bros. Am., Muskegon, 1974-76. Mem. Nat. Bd. Cardiovascular Testing, Am. Cardiology Technologists Assn., Am. Assn. Respiratory Therapy, Am. Naturopathic Med. Assn., Nat. Soc. Cardiopulmonary Technologists, Am. Naturopathic Med. Assn., Coun. for Accreditation in Occupational Hearing Conservation, Internat. Assn. for Colon Hydrothrapy, Soc. for Noninvasive Vascular Tech., Cardiovascular Credentialing Internat. Avocations: canoeing, horses, antiques, old radios, reading.

ANIELLO, ANTHONY JOSEPH, information system executive; b. Hoboken, N.J., Aug. 24, 1941; s. Joseph Patrick and Louise (Gaetano) A.; m. Ann Elizabeth Brinkman, Aug. 10, 1963; children: Peter, Thomas, Catherine, Anthony. BS, St. Benedict's Coll., 1963; postgrad, Purdue U., 1963-64. Rsch. asst. Purdue U., West Lafayette, Ind., 1963-64; chemist Corn Products Co., Argo, Ill., 1964-65; programmer IBM Corp., Cocoa Beach, Fla., 1965-67; lead programmer Kennedy Space Ctr. Singer Corp., Link Div., 1967-69; section mgr. Control Data Corp., Arden Hills, Minn., 1969-75; asst. dir. U. Iowa Hosp. and Clinics, 1975-79; dir. U. Mo., 1979-85; assoc. v.p. U. Ill., Champaign, 1985—; mem. br. mgmt. adv. com. IBM, higher edn. adv. coun., IBM, 1994—. Mem. policy coun. Ill. Libr. Computing System Orgn. Grantee Ill. Bd. Higher Edn., 1987, Ill. State Libr., 1987—, NIH, 1963. Mem. Coll. and Univ. Systems Exch. Roman Catholic. Avocations: reading, weightlifting, golf. Home: 2115 Mayfair Rd Champaign IL 61821-6477

ANISKOVICH, PAUL PETER, JR., insurance company executive; b. New Haven, June 18, 1936; s. Paul Peter and Helen Adele (Postemsky) A.; m. Carol Lacey, Apr. 27, 1957; children: Michael, Nancy, Gary, Peter. Student, Fairfield U., 1956-57, Quinnipiac Coll., 1957-58. C.L.U. Sales mgr. Met. Life Ins. Co., New Haven, 1958-63; regional mgr. Puritan Life Ins. Co., Providence, 1963-67; 2d v.p. Life Ins. Mktg. & Research Assoc., Hartford, Conn., 1968-73; 2d v.p. mktg. Acacia Mut. Life Ins. Co., Washington, 1973-76; pres., dir. Patriot Gen. Life Ins. Co., Concord, Mass., 1976-78; dir. Middlesex Ins. Co., Concord, 1976-78; spl. asst. to pres. State Mut. Life Assurance Co., Worcester, Mass., 1978-80; exec. v.p. Union Central Life Ins. Co., Cin., 1980-87; pres., chief exec. officer Manhattan Life Ins. Co. and Manhattan Nat. Life Ins. Co., 1987-89, also bd. dirs.; vice chmn. Manhattan Nat. Corp., 1987-89, also bd. dirs.; chmn., pres., chief exec. officer U.S. Fin. Life Ins. Co., 1990—; pres., chief exec. officer Sagamore Fin. Corp., 1990—. Served with USMC, 1954-56. Mem. Am. Soc. C.L.U.s, Nat. Assn. Life Underwriters. Republican. Roman Catholic. Club: Hyde Park Country (Cin.). Home: 3435 Golden Ave Apt 1003 Cincinnati OH 45226-2026 Office: US Fin Life Ins Co PO Box 2347 201 E 4th St Cincinnati OH 45202-4122*

ANISMAN, MARTIN JAY, academic administrator; b. Bklyn., Nov. 4, 1942; s. Harry and Florence (Dobin) A.; children: Steve, Beth. BA, Syracuse U., 1963; MA, NYU, 1964, PhD, 1970. Asst. prof. English So. Conn. State U., New Haven, 1967-73, assoc. prof. English, 1973-77, prof. English, 1977-86, dean Sch. Arts and Scis., 1978-86; v.p. acad. affairs, dean of faculty Springfield (Mass.) Coll., 1986-89; pres. Sam Houston State U., Huntsville, Tex., 1989-95, Daemen Coll., Amherst, N.Y., 1996—; bd. dirs. Houston Advanced Rsch. Ctr., Tex. Internat. Ednl. Consortium; chmn. adv. com. Tex. Higher Edn. Coordinating Bd. Tchr. Edn. Editor: The Luck of Barry Lyndon: A Critical Edition, 1970. Divsn. chair United Way, 1996—; bd. dirs. Buffalo Conv. Ctr., 1997—, Erie County YMCA, 1997—. N.Y. State Regents fellow, 1963-67. Mem. MLA (bibiography com., sect. 6 1969-74), Edn. for Tomorrow Alliance (bd. dirs.). Avocations: photography, bicycling. Office: Daemen Coll 4380 Main St Amherst NY 14226-3544*

ANISTON, JENNIFER, actress; b. Sherman Oaks, Calif., Feb. 11, 1969; d. John Aniston. Actress Friends, 1994—. Stage appearances include For Dear Life, Dancing on Checkers' Grave; TV appearances include Molloy, The Edge, Ferris Bueller, Herman's Head, Quantum Leap, Burke's Law, She's the One, 1996, Dream for an Insomniac, 1996, Til There Was You, 1996, Picture Perfect, 1997, The Object of My Affection, 1998, Office Space, 1999. Office: care Hedrick Whitesell CAA 9830 Wilshire Blvd Beverly Hills CA 90212-1804*

ANJIER, JENNIFER J.M., librarian; b. Rockhampton, Australia, Dec. 24, 1937; came to U.S., 1953; d. John Mason Stringer and Decima Hogan Tipple; m. Joseph L. Anjier, Aug. 1, 1959; children: John Charles, Suzanne Christine. BA in Econs. cum laude, U. Colo., 1959; MLS, La. State U., 1980. Head circulation centroplex br. East Baton Rouge (La.) Parish Libr., 1980-85; head audio-visual resource ctr. State Libr. La., Baton Rouge, 1985-88, coord. spl. svcs. br., 1988—; sec. Jones Found. Blind & Physically Handicapped, Baton Rouge, 1988—. Mem. Baton Rouge Symphony Assn., 1985—, La. Hist. Found., Baton Rouge, 1997—, Hilltop Arboretum, Baton Rouge, 1998—. Mem. ALA, La. Libr. Assn., So. Conf. Librs. for Blind & Physically Handicapped, Beta Phi Mu. Office: State Libr La 701 N 4th St Baton Rouge LA 70802

ANKENBRAND, LARRY JOSEPH, physical education educator; b. Mt. Carmel, Ill., Jan. 5, 1935; s. William H. and Lorene (Wahler) A.; m. Maureen Kelly, Aug. 22, 1968; children: Laura, Eric, Jay, Ann. BS, Ea. Ill. U., 1959; MS, Ind. State U., 1966; PhD, U. Mo., 1972. Cert. in adminstrn. and spl. edn., Ill. Salesman Allyn & Bacon Inc., Chgo., 1962-64; tchr. Forrest Park Sch., Joliet, Ill., 1964-65, West View Sch., Romeoville, Ill., 1965-67; asst. prof. Chgo. State U., 1967-68; instr. U. Mo., Columbia, 1968-72; faculty assoc. Ill. State U., Normal, 1972-77; prof. phys. edn. Ea. Ill. U., Charleston, 1977—, chmn. dept., 1984-88, assoc. dean Coll. Health, Phys. Edn. and Recreation, 1989-91, dean, 1991-93, assoc. dean Coll. of Edn. and Profl. Studies, 1993—; cons. Ill. Bd. Edn., Springfield, 1982—; speaker in field. Meet dir. 9 Spl. Olympics, 1979—. With U.S. Army, 1958-62. Recipient Outstanding Tchr. award Ea. Ill. U., 1984. Mem. Am. Assn. Profl. Preparation in Health Phys. Edn. Recreation and Dance (pres. 1990-92, midwest chmn. 1984), Ill. Assn. Health Phys. Edn. Recreation and Dance (session chmn. 1968, 25th Anniversary award 1985, pres. 1989—), Panther Club, Trojan Boosters, P.E. Club, Univ. Club, KC, Moose, Elks. Republican. Roman Catholic. Avocations: sports, reading, collecting, community service. Home: 2418 Salem Rd Charleston IL 61920-4325 Office: Ea Ill U 115 Lantz Charleston IL 61920

ANKER, PEDER JOHAN, historian of sicence; b. Oslo, May 27, 1966; came to U.S., 1995; s. Erik and Bodil (Borchsenius) A. MA, U. Oslo, 1993, Harvard U., 1997. lectr., Oslo, 1993. Author: Critic of Deep Ecology, 1994; editor: Environmental Risk. Sgt. Norwegian Army, 1986. Rsch. fellow Ctr. Tech. and Culture, Oslo, 1993-94, Ctr. Environ. and Devel., Oslo, 1994-95. Mem. History of Sci. Soc. Office: Harvard U Sci Ctr 235 Cambridge MA 02138

ANKER, ROBERT ALVIN, retired insurance company executive; b. Austin, Minn., Dec. 24, 1941; s. Alvin J. and Ruth E. (McGuire) A.; m. Patricia M. Kennedy, Feb. 24, 1968; children—Sean, Kevin, Jennifer. B.A., Lawrence U., Appleton, Wis., 1964. CPCU, CLU. Actuary Employers of Wausau, Wausau, Wis., 1964-74; 2d v.p. Am. States Ins. Cos., Indpls., 1974-75, v.p., 1975-81, sr. v.p., 1981-84, exec. v.p., 1984-85, pres., 1985-91, chmn., chief exec. officer, 1991-92; pres., COO Lincoln Nat. Corp., Ft. Wayne, Ind., 1992-96, also bd. dirs.; chmn., CEO, bd. dirs. Lincoln Nat. Life Ins. Co.; chmn., CEO Am. States Fin. Corp., 1996-97; ret.; bd. dirs. Am. States Ins. Co., Ft. Wayne Nat. Corp. Contbr. articles to profl. jours. Mem. adv. bd. Repertory Theater, Christian Theol. Sem., Indpls., 1983-86; mem. sch. bd. Met. Sch. Dist., Washington Twp., Indpls., 1984-88, pres., 1987-88; bd. dirs. Ind. Repertory Theater, 1989-92, pres., 1990-92, Indpls. Symphony Orch., 1989—, Inroads/Indpls., 1992-96, Ft. Wayne Philharm., 1993—, St. Francis Coll., 1993-97. With Army N.G., 1964-70. Fellow Casualty Actuarial Soc. (bd. dirs. 1981-84, 90-93, v.p. 1983-85, pres. 1996-97, chmn. 1997—); mem. Am. Inst. CPCU (bd. dirs.), Am. Acad. Actuaries (bd. dirs. 1984-87, 94—), Midwestern Actuarial Forum (v.p. 1981-82, pres. 1982-83), Internat. Actuarial Assn., CPCU Soc., Indpls. C. of C. (bd. dirs. 1991-92), Ft. Wayne C. of C. (bd. dirs. 1994-96). *

ANKERSON, ROBERT WILLIAM, management consultant; b. Mt. Vernon, N.Y., Sept. 23, 1933; s. Paul Gustav and Virginia (Roberts) A.; children: Robert William Jr., Samuel B. AB, Dartmouth Coll., 1955. Indsl. rels. asst. Texaco Inc., N.Y.C., 1959-60; successively mktg. svcs. mgr., advt. sales rep., pub. affairs dir. Time Inc., N.Y.C., 1960-73; sr. v.p. Devine, Baldwin and Assocs., N.Y.C., 1973-75; v.p. and prin. Spencer Stuart and Assocs. Inc., N.Y.C., 1975-80; sr. v.p. and dir. Billington, Fox and Ellis, Inc., N.Y.C., 1980-82; sr. v.p. Haley Assocs. Inc., N.Y.C., 1982-86; ptnr. Ward Howell Internat. Inc., N.Y.C., 1986-93; pres. ConServ Inc., N.Y.C., 1993—. With USNR, 1956-59. Home: PO Box 1202 Seashore Ave East Quogue NY 11942 Office: 245 Fifth Ave Room 2304 New York NY 10016-8728

ANKROM, BARBARA BURKE, journalist; b. Upper Darby, Pa., May 30, 1943; d. Joseph Anthony and Teresa Gertrude (Smart) Burke; children: Joseph Burke Nied, Laura Ann Nied, Michele Marie Nied; m. Robert W. Ankrom, Sr. (dec.). AB, Wheeling Coll., 1965. Asst. editor Jones & Laughlin Steel Corp., Pitts., 1965-66; editor, reporter, pub. Dem. Messenger, Waynesburg, Pa., 1976, reporter/photographer, 1976-77; corr. McGraw-Hill & World News Pubs., N.Y.C., 1976—; writer Pitts. Bus. Times, 1981-82; tech. editor, writer JWK Internat. Corp., Pitts., 1982-84; writer-editor W.Va. U. Energy and Water Rsch. Ctr., 1985-88, Mining Ext. Svc. W.Va. U., 1988-89; staff writer News and Info. Svcs., 1989-98; freelance writer, 1976—'. Author: Individual Mine Rescue Team Training Module, 1989, Surface Oranization, 1989, Mine Gases, 1989, Mine Ventilation, 1989, Mine Exploration, 1989, Fires, Firefighting and Explosions, 1989, Rescue of Survivors and Recovery of Bodies, 1989, Mine Recovery, 1989, Mining Voice mag., 1997; asst. editor Men and Steel mag., 1965-66; editor Pa. chpts. Pan American's U.S.A. Guide Book, 1978, 80. Pub. rels. dir. Boy Scouts Am., Greene County, Pa., 1977-84. Mem. AAUW. Democrat. Roman Catholic. Home: RR 1 Box 234A Clarksville PA 15322-7720

ANKROM, CHARLES FRANKLIN, golf course architect, consultant; b. Parkersburg, W.Va., Nov. 7, 1936; s. Donsel and Elva Dale (Cale) A.; m. Evelyn Kay Smith, 1957 (div. Feb. 1966); children: Beverly Lyn, Jan Ellen; m. Alice Lynell Glass, Aug. 24, 1968; children: Steven Charles, Cheryl Lyn. Student, W.Va. U., 1955, Eli Frank Sch. Design Arts, Tampa, Fla., 1956, Indian River C.C., Stuart, Fla. Exec. dir. golf, corp. golf course architect Gen. Devel. Corp., Miami, Fla., 1964-70; exec. dir. golf, golf course architect Boise Cascade Recreation Communities Group, Palo Alto, Calif., 1970-73; pres. Charles F. Ankrom, Inc., Stuart, Fla., 1973—. Prin. works include Sabal Trace C.C., Port Charlotte, Fla., Sun 'N Lake Country Club, Sebring, Fla., Cocoa Beach Mcpl. Golf Course, Cocoa Beach City, Fla., Ft. Lauderdale (Fla.) Country Club, Boca Raton (Fla.) Mcpl. Golf Course, Woodmont Country Club, Tamarac, Fla., The Club at Emerald Hills, Hollywood, Fla., The Habitat Golf Course, Brevard County, Fla., Aquarina, Melbourne, Fla., Crane Creek C.C., Stuart, Fla., Meadowood C.C., Ft. Pierce, Fla., Indian River Planatation Resort, Jensen Beach, Fla., Metro Country Club, Dominican Republic, numerous others. Donated design & adminstrv. svcs. for Bulldog Sportsturf Complex, Martin County (Fla.) Schs. Recipient Outstanding Achievement by Ind. in Bus. or Industry award State of Fla. Coun. on Vocat. Edn., 1992, Bus. Ptnr. award Martin County Sch. Dist., 1991. Mem. Am. Soc. Golf Course Architects (bd. dirs., various nat. coms., Presdl. citation 1993), Nat. Golf Found. Home: 1831 SW Crane Creek Ave Palm City FL 34990-2215 Office: Charles F Ankrom Inc PO Box 898 Stuart FL 34995-0898

ANLYAN, WILLIAM GEORGE, surgeon, university administrator; b. Alexandria, Egypt, Oct. 14, 1925; s. Armand and Emmeraude (Nazar) A.; children: William George, John Peter, Louise. BS magna cum laude, Yale U., 1945, MD, 1949; DSc (hon.), Rush Med. Coll., 1973. Diplomate Am. Bd. Surgery, Am. Bd. Thoracic Surgery. Intern, resident, instr., assoc. in surgery Duke Hosp., Durham, N.C., 1949-53; asst. prof. surgery Duke Hosp., Durham, 1953-58; prof. surgery Duke Hosp., Durham, N.C., 1961-89; assoc. dean Sch. Medicine Duke, 1963, dean, 1964-69, v.p. health affairs, 1969-83, chancellor health affairs, 1983-88, exec. v.p., 1987-88; chancellor Duke U., 1988-90, chancellor emeritus, 1990—; chmn. Durham VA Chancellor's Com., 1963-89, Pearl Health Svcs., Inc., 1983-85; surg. cons. Durham VA Hosp.; Markle scholar med. sci., 1953-58; chmn. regents Nat. Libr. Medicine, 1971-72; bd. trustees N.C. Sch. Sci. and Math., 1978-85, chmn. phys. facilities com., 1979, vice-chmn. of bd. trustees, 1981-84; mem. bd. visitors The U. Tex. Health Sci. Ctr. at Houston, 1980-88, Stanford U., 1985-87; chmn. Yale U. Coun. Com. on Med. Affairs, 1985-93. Mem. editorial bd. Pharos, 1968-93. Trustee The Duke Endowment, 1990—, Commn. on Future Structure of Vet. Health Care, 1990-92; chmn. Gov.'s Task Force on Better Health for N.C. in 2000, 1991-97; mem. White House Sci. Coun., 1988-89. Recipient award for disting. achievement Modern Medicine, 1974; Gov.'s award for disting. meritorious service, 1978; Abraham Flexner award, 1980. Fellow ACS; mem. AMA (adv. com. med. sci. 1972—), Soc. Univ. Surgeons, Soc. Vascular Surgery, Internat. Cardiovascular Soc., Soc. Clin. Surgery, Am. Heart Assn., Soc. Med. Adminstrs. (pres. 1983-85), Inst. Medicine of Nat. Acad. Sci., Coun. Deans (chmn. 1968-69), AAMC Coun. Deans (chmn. 1968-69), So. Med. Assn., Coord. Coun. Med. Edn. (chmn. 1973-74), Surg. Biology Club II, Am. Surg. Assn., So. Surg. Assn., Halsted Soc., Allen O. Whipple Surg. Soc., Assn. Am. Med. Colls. (chmn. 1970-71), Ind. Rsch. Roundtable NAS, Assn. Acad. Health Ctrs. (pres. 1975), Rsch. Am. (bd. dirs. 1989—, chmn. 1992-96), Rotary, Phi Beta Kappa, Sigma Xi, Alpha Omega Alpha. Home: 1516 Pinecrest Rd Durham NC 27705-5817 Office: Duke Med Ctr PO Box 3626 Durham NC 27710-3626

ANMA, SO, engineering consultant; b. Hamamatsu, Shizuoka, Japan, Nov. 7, 1936; s. Yu and Chie (Matsumoto) A.; m. Fumie Kishikawa, Mar. 15, 1964; children: Ryo, Akitsu, Mizuho, Yashima. *Wife, Fumie received a BA, Ferris Women's College of Music, Yokohama, 1958. She taught piano for children privately for 35 years. Son Ryo received a BS and MS from Ryukyu University and a PHD from Uppsala University, Sweden, 1997. He's working for Tsukuba University, Ibaraki. Daughter Akitsu received a BA from the Toho-Gakuen School of Music, Tokyo, 1989. She was granted Diplome Superieur d'Execution, Ecole Normal de Musique de Paris 1993. She performs piano in France, Spain and Japan. Daughter Mizuho received a BS and MS from Hokkaido University, Sapporo, 1997. She studies volcanology of the Izu-Bonnin Islands. She married Hiroki Miyasaka. Daughter Yashima received a BJ from Hokkaido University, Sapporo 1997.* BS, Hokkaido U., Sapporo, Japan, 1959; DEng, Tokai U., Tokyo, 1987. Registered engrng. geologist; profl. civil engr. Rschr. Hukada Chisitsu Inst., Tokyo, 1959-67; pres. Kisokogaku Co., Tokyo, 1967-70; exec. Kensetsu Kiso Chosa Sekkei Co., Shimizu, Japan, 1970-91; pres. Kensetsu Kiso Chosa Sekkei Co., Shimizu, 1991—; lectr. Tokai U., Shimizu, 1988—; bd. dirs. Shizuoka (Japan) Environ. and Resources, 1989—; chapter vice chmn. Japanese Soc. of Snow and Ice, Tokyo, 1997—. Co-author: The First Ascent of Mt. Chamlang, 1965, Geology of Nepal Himalaya, 1967 (Chichibunomiya prize 1968), Patagonian Mountain Climb, 1968, Mt. Dhaulagiri-I Midwinter, 1985. Hazard reduction adviser Shizuoka Prefecture, 1984—. Recipient Chichibunomiya prize Chichibunomiya Meml. Found., Tokyo, 1968, Hokkaido prize Hokkaido Regional Govt., 1983, Asahi Sports prize Asahi Newspaper Inc., Tokyo, 1984. Mem. Internat. Geosynthetic Soc., Internat. Soc. Soil Mechanics and Found. Engring., Internat. Assn. Engring. Geology, Geol. Soc. Japan, Japanese Soc. Snow and Ice, Japanese Alpine Club (chpt. chmn. 1986-95). Avocations: mountaineering, forest watching. Office: Kensetsu Kiso Chosa Sekkei, 241-7 Kusunokishinden, Shimizu 424-0882, Japan

ANNABLE, JAMES EDWARD, economist; b. Grove City, Pa., May 26, 1943; s. James and Doris Jean (Burns) A.; m. Susan Virginia Bone, July 29, 1967. AB, Kenyon Coll., 1965; PhD, Princeton U., 1970. Asst. prof. MIT, Cambridge, Mass., 1969-74; sr. economist FRS, Washington, 1974-78; dep. asst. dir. Congl. Budget Office, Washington, 1978-81; chief domestic economist First Nat. Bank of Chgo., 1981-86, sr. v.p., chief economist, 1986—; bd. dirs. Unitrin, Inc.; sec. fed. adv. coun. Fed. Res. Bd., 1994—. Author: The Price of Industrial Labor, 1985; contbr. articles to profl. jours. Past chmn. bd. dirs. Goodman Theatre. Woodrow Wilson fellow, 1965. Mem. Am. Econ. Assn., Nat. Assn. Bus. Economists, Chgo. Assn. Commerce & Industry (v.p., bd. dirs.), Phi Beta Kappa. Home: 1214 N Astor St Chicago IL 60610-5211 Office: 1st Nat Bank Chgo 1 First Natl Plz Chicago IL 60603-2003*

ANNAKIN, KENNETH COOPER, film director, writer; b. Beverly, Yorkshire, England; came to U.S., 1979; s. Edward C. and Hannah J. (Gains) A.; m. Pauline Mary Carter, 1960; children: Jane, Deborah. Student, Hull U., 1934-35. Dir. The Swiss Family Robinson, 1960, A Very Important Person, 1961, The Hellions, 1961, Crooks Anonymous, 1962, The Fast Lady, 1962, The Longest Day, 1962, Those Magnificent Men in Their Flying Machines, 1965, The Battle of the Bulge, 1965, The Biggest Bundle of Them All, 1967, Those Daring Young Men in Their Jaunty Jalopies, 1969, Call of the Wild, 1972, Paper Tiger, 1974, The Fifth Musketeer, 1977, The Pirate Movie, 1982,

Pippi Longstocking, 1986; screenwriter Coco Chanel, 1999, Redwing, 1999. Office: 9233 Swallow Dr West Hollywood CA 90069-1145

ANNAN, KOFI A., diplomat; b. Ghana, 1938; married; 3 children. Grad., U. Sci. and Tech., Kumasi, Macalester Coll., St. Paul, Inst. des Hautes Etudes Internationales, Geneva, MIT. Held posts UN Econ. Commn. for Africa, Addis Ababa, Ethiopia, UN, N.Y.C., WHO, Geneva, 1962-71; adminstrv. mng. officer UN, Geneva, 1972-74; chief civilian pers. officer UN Emergency Force, Cairo, 1974; mng. dir. Ghana Tourist Devel. Co., 1974-76; dep. chief staff svcs. Office Pers. Svcs., Office of UN High Commn. for Refugees, Geneva, 1976-80, dep. dir. divsn. adminstrn., head pers. svc., 1980-83; chmn. bd. trustees UN Internat. Sch., 1987-95; dir. adminstrn. mgmt. svc., dir. budget Office Fin. Svcs. UN, N.Y.C., 1984-87, asst. sec-gen. Office Human Resources Mgmt., 1987-90, contr. Office of Programme Planning, Budget and Fin., 1990-92, asst. sec.-gen. dept. peace-keeping ops., 1992-93, under-sec.-gen. dept. peace-keeping ops., 1993-95, spl. rep. to sec.-gen. to former Yugoloavia, 1995-96, spl. envoy to NATO, 1995-96, sec. gen, 1997—. Alfred P. Sloan fellow MIT, 1971-72. Office: UN Pub Inquiries Unit Rm GA-57 UN Plz 46th St at First Ave New York NY 10017

ANNAU, RAYMONE JEANINE, cardiovascular nurse; b. Great Falls, Mont., May 27, 1942; d. Eugene F. and Lillian M. (Thompson) A. Diploma, Columbus Sch. Nursing, Great Falls, 1967; BSN, Mont. State U., 1991, MN, 1995. RN; CCRN; cert. United Care Reg. Nurse, 1996—; registered vascular technologist; cert. cardiopulmonary technologist; ACLS; BLS instr. Staff nurse Royal Berkshire Hosp., Reading, Eng., 1969-71, night sister, 1971-73; staff nurse Benefis Healthcare, Great Falls, 1967-69, 73-78; cardiovascular nurse Benefits Healthcare, Great Falls, 1978—; clin. instr. Mont. State U.-No., 1995-96, asst. prof. nursing, 1996-97. Gladys Ney Stevenson scholar, 1989. Mem. AACN (pres. Ctrl. Mont. chpt. 1995-96), Soc. Vascular Tech., Mont. Heart Assn. (bd. dirs. 1983-85). Home: 1812 Mountain View Dr Great Falls MT 59405-6522 Office: Benefits Healthcare PO Box 5013 Great Falls MT 59403-5013

ANNAUD, JEAN-JACQUES, film director, screenwriter; b. Juvisy, France, Oct. 1, 1943; s. Pierre and Madeleine (Tripoz) A.; m. Monique Rossignol, 1970 (div. 1980); 1 child, Mathilde; m. Laurence Duval; 1 child, Louise. Student, Ecole Louis Lumière, Institut Des Hautes Etudes Cinematographiques, Paris, 1966; Lic. Lettres, The Sorbonne, Paris, 1967. Freelance film dir., screenwriter Paris, 1967—. Sreenwriter, dir.: Black and White in Color, 1976 (Oscar award Best Fgn. Film 1977), Hot head, 1978, Quest for Fire, 1981, (César award 1982), Name of the Rose, 1986 (César award 1987, Donatello award), The Bear, 1988 (César award best dir. 1988), The Lover, 1991 (Best Dir. award Japan Critics Assn., 1992); screenwriter, dir., prodr.: Wings of Courage, 1994 (in IMAX 3D), Seven Years in Tibet, 1997 (Best Fgn. Film Gilde Filmpreis, Germany, 1998); prodr: Hoofbeat, 1999. Decorated commandeur Ordre des Arts et Lettres; recipient Grand Prix Nat. du Cinema, prix du Cinéma de L'Acadéemie Française, more than 100 awards for TV commercials, including Clios, Lions Cannes and Venice Festival, Art Dirs. Club. Mem. French Hollywood Cir. (pres.). Home: 9 rue Guénégaud, 75006 Paris France also: Repérage S A, Reperage SA, 10 rue Lincoln, 75008 Paris France also: ICM 8899 Beverly Blvd Los Angeles CA 90048-2412

ANNENBERG, LEONORE A., foundation administrator; m. Walter H. Annenberg; 2 children. BA, Stanford U.; PhD (hon.), Pine Manor Coll., LaSalle U., U. Pa., Brown U.; DHL (hon.), U. So. Calif., 1998. Former chief of protocol for U.S.A. Vice chmn., v.p. Annenberg Found.; founding mem. governing bd. Annenberg sch. comm. U. Pa., Annenberg sch. comm. U. So. Calif.; founder Am. Friends Covent Garden; past chmn., hon. chmn. Friends Art and Preservation Embassies; mem. trustee's coun. Nat. Gallery Art; mem. Com. Preservation White House; mng. dir. Met. Opera; mem. Acad. Music Com.; past pres., hon. trustee Palm Springs Desert Mus.; hon. trustee performing arts coun. L.A. Music Ctr.; trustee emeritus U. Pa.; former bd. dirs. Pa. Acad. Fine Arts, Phila. Orch. Assn.; bd. dirs. Met. Mus. Art, Phila. Mus. Art. Decorated Cavaliere Dell'Ordine Al Merito Della Republica Italiana, Grand Officio Order of Orange-Nassau (The Netherlands); recipient Wagner medal Robert F. Wagner grad. sch. pub. svc. NYU, Colonial Williamsburg Churchill Bell award, Nat. Medal of Arts, NEA, 1993. Mem. Disting. Daus. Pa. Office: The Annenberg Found St Davids Ctr 150 Radnor Chester Rd Ste A-200 Wayne PA 19087-5293*

ANNENBERG, WALTER H., philanthropist, diplomat, editor, publisher, broadcaster; b. Milw., Mar. 13, 1908; m. Veronica Dunkelman (div.); 1 child, Wallis; m. Leonore Cohn. Ed., The Peddie Sch., Wharton Sch., U. Pa.; hon. degree, Temple U., U. Pa., U. So. Calif., U. Notre Dame, Albert Einstein Coll. Medicine, Mt. Sinai Med. Coll., Hebrew U., Jerusalem, Northwestern U.; and others; hon. degree, Elizabethtown Coll., Howard U., Brown U., Brandeis U. Former pres., chmn., CEO Triangle Publs., Inc., including Phila. Inquirer, Phila. Daily News, Daily Racing Form, (founder) Seventeen Mag., (founder) TV Guide; also 6 AM, FM and TV Stas.; ret., 1988; U.S. ambassador to Great Britain and No. Ireland., 1968-74; chmn., pres. Annenberg Found.; founder Annenberg Sch. Comm., Grad. Sch. U. Pa., Annenberg Sch. Comm., Grad. Sch. U. So. Calif., Annenberg/Corp. Pub. Broadcasting Math/Sci. Project. Founder, trustee Eisenhower Exchange Fellowships, Eisenhower Med. Ctr., Rancho Mirage, Calif., hon. chmn. bd. trustees; trustee Winston Churchill Travelling Fellowships; emeritus trustee Met. Mus. Art, N.Y.C., Phila. Mus. Art, U. Pa., The Peddie Sch., Hightstown, N.J.; hon. mem. bd. overseers Albert Einstein Coll. Medicine, N.Y.C.; patron Churchill Archives Ctr. at Cambridge (Eng.) Coll. Former cmdr., USN. Decorated Knight Comdr., Order of Brit. Empire (hon.), Legion of Honor (France), Order of Merit (Italy), Order Crown (Italy), Order of the Lion (Finland), Bencher of Mid. Temple (hon.), Old Etonian (hon.); recipient Freedom medal for pioneering TV for ednl. purposes U.S. Pres. Reagan, Gold medal Pa. Soc., Linus Pauling medal for humanitarianism, George Foster Peabody award, Ralph Lowell award Corp. Pub. Broadcasting, Dwight D. Eisenhower medal for leadership and svc., Generous Am. award Town & Country Mag., Wagner medal for pub. svc. Robert F. Wagner Grad. Sch. Pub. Svc. NYU, Alumni Merit award U. Pa., William Penn award Greater Phila. C. of C., The Churchill Bell award, 1993, Nat. Arts medal NEA, 1993, Phila. award, 1994, Am. Legion award, 1994, Am. Assembly award, 1994, Arch of Peace award, 1995, George Peabody Edn. Philanthropy award, 1995, Thomas Jefferson award for outstanding pub. svc. by a pvt. citizen, 1995, Steven J. Ross/Time Warner award, 1996, World Class Philadelphians award, 1998 and others; named to Wharton Sch Hall of Fame, Mag. Pub. of Yr., 1984; apptd. by Pope John II as Knight Comdr. of Order of St. Gregory the Great, 1998. Fellow Am. Acad. Arts & Scis.; mem. AP, Am. Soc. Newspaper Pub., Am. Newspaper Pub. Assn., Am. Philos. Soc. (Benjamin Franklin award 1993), Internat. Press Inst., Nat. Press Club, Inter-Am. Press Assn., Overseas Press Club, Navy League U.S., Explorers Club, White's of London, Gulph Mills Golf Club, California Club, Green Valley Country Club, L.A. Country Club, The Racquet Club, Swinley Forest Club, The Club at Morningside, Century Country Club, Locust Club, U. Pa. Faculty Club, Eldorado Country Club (hon.).

ANNESE, DOMENICO, landscape architect; b. N.Y.C., June 9, 1919; s. Fedele and Antonia (Angelini) A.; m. Serafina Villanova, July 16, 1944; children: Donald F., Loretta S. Ed., SUNY Coll. Environ. Sci. and Forestry, 1942; B.S. in Landscape Architecture, Syracuse U., 1942. Registered landscape architect, N.Y., Pa., Conn., Mass., Ohio, Tenn. Landscape architect Clarence C. Combs, N.Y.C., 1946-50; assoc. Clarence C. Combs, 1955-56; asst. chief landscape architect Nat. Capital Parks, Washington, 1950-55; asso. Clarke and Rapuano, Inc., N.Y.C., 1956-72; v.p. Clarke and Rapuano, Inc., 1972-91; vice chmn. N.Y. State Bd. Landscape Architects, 1961-67, chmn., 1967-71; mem. Pleasantville (N.Y.) Parks and Recreation Bd., 1974-83; adj. prof. urban landscape architecture CCNY, 1975-76; vis. prof., lectr. in landscape architecture Sch. Planning and Architecture, New Delhi, India, 1977; pres. Landscape Architecture Found.; dir. N.Y. State Coun. Landscape Architects; dir. coll. environ. sci. and forestry ESF Found.; dir. N.Y. Parks and Conservation Assn. Served with Coast Arty., F.A. U.S. Army, 1942-46, ETO. Fellow Am. Soc. Landscape Architects, Sigma Lambda Alpha. Lutheran. Home: 315 Bedford Rd Pleasantville NY 10570-2212

ANN-MARGRET (ANN-MARGRET OLSSON), actress, performer; b. Stockholm, Sweden, Apr. 28, 1941; came to U.S., naturalized, 1949; d. Gustav and Anna Olsson; m. Roger Smith, 1967. Student, Northwestern U. Performer radio shows, band tours; appeared with: George Burns, Las Vegas, 1961; headliner numerous appearances, Las Vegas, 1961—; made NYC debut Radio City Music Hall, 1991; actress numerous films including Pocketful of Miracles, 1961, State Fair, 1961, Bye Bye Birdie, 1962, Viva Las Vegas, 1963, The Pleasure Seekers, 1964, Kitten With a Whip, 1964, Bus Riley's Back in Town, 1964, Once A Thief, 1965, Cincinnati Kid, 1965, Stagecoach, 1966, Made in Paris, 1966, The Swinger, 1966, Murderers' Row, 1967, The Tiger and the Pussycat, 1967, R.P.M., 1970, C.C. & Company, 1971, Carnal Knowledge, 1971, Train Robbers, 1972, Outside Man, 1972, Tommy, 1975, Joseph Andrews, 1976, The Last Remake of Beau Geste, 1977, Magic, 1978, The Cheap Detective, 1978, Lookin' To Get Out, 1978, The Villain, 1979, Middle-Age Crazy, 1980, The Return of the Soldier, 1982, I Ought To Be in Pictures, 1982, Twice in a Lifetime, 1985, 52-Pick-up, 1987, A Tiger's Tale, 1988, A New Life, 1988, Something More, Newsies, 1992, Grumpy Old Men, 1993, Grumpier Old Men, 1995, Seduced by Madness, 1996, The Limey, 1999, Any Given Sunday, 1999; several TV spls., 1975-76; TV films Who Will Love My Children, 1983, A Streetcar Named Desire, 1984, Our Sons, 1991, Nobody's Children, 1994, Seduced by Madness: The Diane Borchardt Story, 1996, Blue Rodeo, 1996, Life of the Party: The Pamela Harriman Story, 1998, Happy Face, 1999; mini-series The Two Mrs. Grenvilles, 1987, Alex Haley's Queen, 1993, Scarlett, 1994; TV series Four Corners, 1998; author: (with Todd Gold) Ann-Margret: My Story, 1994. Recipient 2 Acad. award nominations, 4 Emmy nominations, 5 Golden Globes. Office: William Morris Agy 151 S El Camino Dr Beverly Hills CA 90212-2775*

ANNS, ARLENE EISERMAN, publishing company executive; b. Pearl River, N.Y.; d. Frederick Joel and Anna (Behnke) E.; student Farleigh Dickenson U., 1946-48; BS, Utah State U., 1950; postgrad. Traphagen Sch. Design, 1957, NYU, 1958, Hunter Coll., 1959-60. Rsch. and promotion asst. Archtl. Record, N.Y.C., 1952-56; asst. rsch. dir. Esquire Mag., N.Y.C., 1956-62; rsch. mgr. Am. Machinist, publ. McGraw-Hill, Inc., N.Y.C., 1962-67, mktg. svc. mgr., 1967-69, 1969-71, sales mgr., 1976-77, dir. mktg., 1977-78; v.p. mktg. svcs. Morgan-Gramplan, Inc., N.Y.C., 1971-72; mktg. dir. Family Health & Diversion mag., 1972-74; dist. sales mgr. Postgrad. Medicine, 1974-76; advt. sales mgr. Contemporary Ob/Gyn, 1976-78; dir. profl. devel., 1978-80; pub. graduating engr. and dir. mktg. Aviation Week Group, 1980-90; pub. World Aviation Directory; dir. communications Aviation Week Group, 1990-92; v.p., Phase, Ltd., 1993—. Chair SCORE Resource for SBA. Mem. Am. Mktg. Assn., Pharm. Advt. Club, Advt. Women N.Y., Advt. Club N.Y., Sales Exec. Club, Employment Mgmt. Assn., Am. Soc. Pers. Adminstrs., Nat. Orgn. Disability (bd. dirs.), Internat. Platform Assn., Coll. Placement Coun., Svc. Corps Ret. Execs. (vice chair), Forestry Assn., Wings Club, Dir. Assn., Pi Sigma Alpha. Home: Barnhill Farm 6653 Celt Rd Stanardsville VA 22973-3638

ANNS, PHILIP HAROLD, international trading executive, former pharmaceutical company executive; b. London, Eng., June 24, 1925; came to U.S., 1950; s. Harold Falkner and Dorothy Louise (Torckler) A.; m. Jacqueline Estelle Wyrtzen, Dec. 27, 1952 (div. 1975); 1 child, Jean Anns; m. Arlene Claire Eiserman, Apr. 1, 1978. BA in Econs., Christ Coll., Cambridge, Eng., 1948, MA in Econs., 1950. Asst. to pres. BASF Inc., N.Y.C., 1954-58; gen. mgr. Squibb Australia E.R. Squibb and Sons, Princeton, N.J., 1958-68; dir. animal health E.R. Squibb and Sons, New Brunswick, N.J.; gen. mgr. animal health Am. Hoechst, Kansas City, Mo., 1968-72; exec. v.p. Lakeside Labs., Milw., 1972-75; sr. v.p., gen. mgr. internat. div. A.H. Robins Co., Inc., Richmond, Va., 1975-85; sr. v.p. corp. govt. relations A.H. Robins Co., Inc., Washington, 1986-90; pres. Phase Ltd., Arlington, Va., 1990—; with Va. Dist. Export Coun.; mem. Congl. staff U.S. Ho. of Reps., 1990—. Mem. Indsl. Devel. Authority, Greene County, Va. Served to lt. Brit. Royal Navy, 1943-46, ETO. Mem. Rotary. Republican. Episcopalian. Home and Office: 6653 Celt Rd Stanardsville VA 22973-3638

ANNUS, JOHN AUGUSTUS, artist; b. Riga, Latvia, Oct. 25, 1935; emigrated to U.S., 1949; s. Augustus and Irma (Gustavs) A.; m. Edite Zeile, Oct. 18, 1981; 1 dau., Aurelia 1 dau., by previous marriage, Fabiola. B.F.A., Pratt Inst., 1958; postgrad., Art Students League, 1958-59, Nat. Acad. Design, 1958-59, Academia de Belli Arti, Rome, 1962-64. One-man shows include Am. Acad. in Rome, 1960, Arte al Berge, Palermo, 1963, Archtl. League, N.Y., 1965, Vendo Nubes, Phila., 1965, 70, 76, Galleria del Vantaggio, Rome, 1962, 71, 73, 74, Galerie Clasing, Germany, 1982, T.L.C. Gallery, Toronto, 1985, Jacobi Gallery, Hamburg, 1987, 92, Raitern Gallery, Riga, Latvia, 1989, Gallery K. Munster, Germany, 1992, Internat. Mus., Riga, 1993, Jannus Image, Munster, 1993, 95, Design Technik GmbH Gallery-Verlag, Hamburg, 1995; group shows include Spectrum 5, N.Y.C., 1972, 73, Skidmore Coll., N.Y.C., 1975, U. Pa., 1976, NAD, 1958, 59, 64, 67, 68, 75, 80, 91, Nat. Acad. Design Mems. Show, 1993, Nat. Acad. Design Academician Show, 1995, Images Photokina, Cologne, Germany, 1996; 2nd internat. HRS Exhibition-Riga Latvia, 1998, represented in permanent collections NAD, Balt. Mus., Collection of the Italian Govt., Henry Ranger Fund, Am. Acad. in Rome. Recipient Gold medal for oil painting Labyrinth, 1962; recipient Wallace Truman prize for oil painting Agrigento, 1967, Ranger Purchase prize for By the Sea, 1965, Reflection, 1965, award of Excellence for By the Sea, 1982; Nat. Acad. Design grantee, 1958-59, Albert Hallgarten traveling grantee, 1958-59; Prix de Rome Am. Acad. in Rome, 1959-60; Italian Govt. grantee, 1962—. Mem. Nat. Acad. Design (academician), Soc. Fellows, Am. Acad. Rome (Centennial Directory listee), Nat. Soc. Mural Painters, others. Lutheran.

ANOATUBBY, BILL, governor; b. Nov. 8, 1945; m. Janice Marie Loman, Dec. 23, 1967; children: Chris, Brian. AS, Murray State Coll., 1970; BS, East Ctrl. State Coll., 1972. Acct., office mgr. Am. Plating Co., 1972-74; acct., systems & budgetary contr. Little Giant Corp., 1974-75; dir. health svcs. The Chickasaw Nation, Ada, Okla., 1975-76, dir. acctg., 1976-78, spl. asst. to gov., 1978-79, lt. gov., 1979-87; gov. The Chickasaw Nation, 1987—; Apptd. bd. trustees Morris K. Udall Scholarship and Excellence in Nat. Environ. Policy Found., 1994—. Mem. adv. com. Okla. Dept. Commerce, 1990; mem. Trail of Tears Nat. Historic Adv. Com., 1990-92; trustee Oklahoma City U., 1991-98; vol. Okla. Dukakis-Bentsen Campaign, 1988, Okla. Clinton-Gore Campaign, 1992. Named Okla. Minority Bus. Advocate of Yr., U.S. SBA, 1995. Mem. Inter-Tribal Coun. of Five Civilized Tribes (past v.p., pres.), United Indian Nations in Okla. (past pres.), Ada Area C. of C. (bd. dirs.), Okla. Indian Affairs Commn. Democrat. Office: Chickasaw Nation PO Box 1548 Ada OK 74821-1548

ANROMAN, GILDA MARIE, assistant director, lecturer, educator; b. New Haven, Conn., July 19, 1959; d. Owen Francis Anroman and Edera (Vagnini) Felice. BA, Trinity Coll., Washington, 1983; M in Applied Anthropology, U. Md., 1994, grad. cert. in historic preservation, 1997, postgrad., 1994—. Cert. yoga instr. Clin. technologist Nat. Health Lab., Vienna, Va., 1983-85; dept. mgr., clin. technologist Anmed/Biosafe Inc., Rockville, Md., 1985-92; rsch. asst. U. Md., College Pk., 1992-94, instr. dept. anthropology, 1994-97, acad. advisor, 1996—, asst. dir.; mem. search com. dept. anthropology U. Md., 1993-94. Rep. College Pk. Historic Dist. Commn., 1994-95. Scholar State of Conn., Hartford, 1977, Senatorial scholar, State of Md., Annpolis, 1995—, Del. scholar, Annapolis, 1998-99; recipient Margaret Cook award for historic preservation Prince George's County, Md., 1997. Mem. AAUW, Am. Anthropol. Assn., Am. Hist. Assn., Am. Soc. Environ. History, Am. Studies Assn., Inst. of Early Am. History/Culture, Orgn. Am. Historians, Soc. for Hist. Archaeology, Nat. Trust for Historic Preservation, Nat. Coun. on Pub. History. Home: 15526 Plaid Dr Laurel MD 20707-5317 Office: Dept Am Studies U Md 2125 Taliaferro Hall College Park MD 20742-7700

ANSAR, AHMAD, career counselor; b. Buffalo, Oct. 18, 1956; s. Robert Lee and Reva A. (Bowman) Parham; m. Jameelah Ali, Aug. 15, 1997. BA, Gannon U., 1978; D Clin. Hypnotherapy, Am. Inst. Hypnotherapy, 1991. Caseworker advocate Victim/Witness Asst. Program, Buffalo, 1986-87; field placement coord. St. Augustine Ctr., Buffalo, 1987-90; career planningand placement officer SUNY, Buffalo, 1990-97; assoc. prof. Erie C.C., Buffalo, 1992; lectr. SUNY, Buffalo, 1994-96; chmn. Mentor program, Buffalo, 1992-96. Mem. Internat. Assn. Counselors and Therapists (life),Assn. for Supervision and Curriculum Devel., Masons. Avocations: Aikido, Taoist Tai'chi. Home: 51 Burbank Ter Buffalo NY 14214-2640

ANSARI, MABOUD, education educator; b. Oct. 20, 1941. MA, Tehran U., 1968, New Sch. for Social Rsch., 1970; PhD, New Sch. for Social Rsch., 1974. Chancellor North Univ., Babolsar, Iran, 1978-79; rsch. advisor Welfare/Adult Literacy, Tehran, 1982-84; prof. William Paterson U., Wayne, 1985—. Office: William Paterson U 300 Pompton Rd Wayne NJ 07470-2103

ANSARY, CYRUS A., investment company executive, lawyer; b. Shoraz, Oram, Nov. 20, 1933; s. Adbul and Jamali (Mostmand) A.; m. Janet C. Hodges, Aug. 1, 1970; children: Douglas, Pary Ann, Jeffrey C., Bradley C. BS, Am. U., 1955; LLB, Columbia U., 1958. Bar: Md. 1959, D.C. 1960, Va. 1961. Pvt. practice Washington, 1959-72; sr. ptnr. firm Ansary, Kirkpatrick and Rosse, 1964-72; chmn. bd. Industry Reports, Inc., Washington, 1960-72; organizer, 1st chmn. bd., pres. Woodland Nat. Bank, Alexandria, Va., 1963-67; lectr. Sch. Bus. Adminstrn., Am. U., 1967-71; chmn. bd. Fin. Dynamics Corp., Washington, 1967-72, Campbell Music Co., Washington, 1968-72, John L. Lindstrom and Assocs., Inc., Washington, 1962-86; pres. IK Investment A.G., Zurich, Switzerland, 1974-79, Investment Svcs. Internat. Co., Washington, 1973—; chmn. MACO Bancorp Md., Washington, 1988-95; with Washington Mut. Investments Fund. Trustee Am. U., 1968—, chmn. bd., 1982—; trustee Internat. Law Inst., 1976-88, 82-90, Wolf Trap Found., Vienna, Va., 1977-82, Krupp Found., Essen, Germany, 1977-79, Washington Opera Soc., 1982-89; bd. trustees Am. U., 1968-96, chmn. bd.; dir. Metalurgica Campo Limpo Limitada, Sao Paulo, Brazil, 1976-80, Fried Krupp GmbH, Essen, 1975-79; pres. Ansary Found., Washington, 1983—; dir. Growth Fund Washington, 1985—, Am. Funds Tax-Exempt Series I, Washington, 1986—; chmn. bd. CorPay Solutions, Inc., Washington, 1999—. With USMCR, 1959-63. Mem. Washington Soc. Investment Analysts, Economic Club of Washington, Nat. Press Club, Metropolitan Club (Washington), Chevy Chase Country Club (Bethesda), Rotary. Office: 1725 K St NW Ste 410 Washington DC 20006-1401

ANSARY, HASSAN JABER, transportation executive; b. Tehran, Iran, May 3, 1949; arrived in Can., 1973; s. Aman-al-Allah J. and Robabeh (Naimi) A.; 1 child, Farrah R. BA in Bus., Tehran Bus. Coll., 1971; MA in Econ., Meml. U. Nfld., St. Johns, Can., 1975; MBA, Pitts. (Kans.) State U., 1976; PhD in Bus., Calif. Western U., 1982. Policy advisor Gov. Ont., Toronto, Can., 1977-78; mgr. strategic planning Domtar Inc., Montreal, Que., Can., 1978-81; mgr., planning coord. Polysar Ltd., Sarnia, Ont., 1981-83, mgr. planning and devel., 1983-84; dir. corp. devel. Ports Can., Ottawa, Ont., 1984-85, v.p. corp. svcs., 1985-88, exec. v.p., 1988-92, exec. v.p., COO, 1992-95; pres., CEO Canol Internat., Ottawa, Ont., Can., 1995-96, AmeriTest, Inc., Rock Springs, Wyo., 1996-97; COO Acosta Med. Testing Corp., Chgo., 1998—; sr. ptnr. The Maxxus Group, 1999—; bd. dirs., chmn. Electronic Data Interchange Coun. Can., Toronto, 1990; chmn. Total Electronic Commerce Svc. for Transp., 1993—. Founder, editor-in-chief quar. Portus, 1985-92. Bd. dirs. Carleton Condominium Corp., 1991-93, Can. Grain Coun., 1992—, Containerization and Intermodal Inst., 1993-94, The Van Horne Inst., 1993—. 2d lt. Armed Forces Iran, 1971-73. Fellow Chartered Inst. Transport; mem. Strategic Mgmt. Soc., Planning Forum, Am. Assn. Port Authorities (chmn. commerce com. 1993-94), Internat. Cargo Handling Coords. Assn. (internat. vice chmn. London 1992-94, chmn. 1994—, pres. Can. 1988—). Avocations: cinema, jogging. Home: 2822-186th St Ste 3N Lansing IL 60438

ANSBACHER, LEWIS, lawyer; b. Jacksonville, Fla., Nov. 23, 1928; s. Morris and Lillian (Pinkus) A.; m. Sybil Barnett, Oct. 27, 1957; children—Richard I., Lawrence V., Barry B. B.S. in Bus. Adminstrn., U. Fla., 1948, J.D., 1951; LL.M., George Washington U., 1955. Bar: Fla. 1951. Assoc. Philip Selber, Jacksonville, 1955-62; ptnr. Selber & Ansbacher, 1963-73; pvt. practice, Jacksonville, 1973-80; shareholder Ansbacher & Schneider, P.A., Jacksonville, 1981—; bd. dirs. CompassBank, Attys.' Title Ins. Fund Inc.; trustee 4th Cir. V.p. Jewish Family and Children's Service, Jacksonville, 1962-65, pres., 1965-68; v.p. Jacksonville Jewish Ctr., 1967-70; mem. planning bd. United Fund, 1965; mem. Duval County Legal Aid Assn., pres., 1964-65; mem. Gov.'s Ad Hoc Study Com. on Eminent Domain, 1984-85. Served to 1st lt. JAGC, U.S. Army, 1952-55. Named to Hall of Fame, U. Fla. Mem. ABA, Fla. Bar (exec. council real property and probate sect.). Jewish. Author in field. Home: 2008 Strand St Neptune Beach FL 32266-4863 Office: 100 Nat Fin Bldg 4215 Southpoint Blvd Jacksonville FL 32216-0976*

ANSBACHER, RUDI, physician; b. Sidney, N.Y., Oct. 11, 1934; s. Stefan and Beatrice (Michel) A.; m. Elisabeth Cornelia Vellenga, Nov. 19, 1965; children—R. Todd, Jeffrey N. Grad., Harvard Coll., 1951; B.A., Va. Mil. Inst., 1955; M.D., U. Va., 1959; M.S., U. Mich., 1970. Diplomate Am. Bd. Ob-Gyn. Staff ob-gyn, chief clin. investigation Brooke Med. Ctr., San Antonio, Tex., 1971-75, asst. chief ob-gyn, 1975-77; chief dept. ob-gyn Letterman Army Med. Ctr., San Francisco, 1977-80; prof. ob-gyn U. Mich., Ann Arbor, 1980—, asst. chmn. dept., 1980-88, acting chmn., 1984-85, interim chmn., 1991-93; cons. Biomed. Adv. Com. Population Resource Ctr., 1978-81, Assn. Voluntary Sterilization, Inc., 1982-95; bd. dirs. Health Policy Internat. Contbr. articles to profl. jours., chpts to books; mem. editorial bds., reviewer jours. Served to col. U.S. Army, 1960-80. Named Disting. Mil. Grad. Va. Mil. Inst., Lexington, Va., 1955; NIH grantee, 1973-78. Fellow ACOG (Chmn.'s award 1970), AAAS; mem. Am. Fertility Soc. (dir. 1979-82), Am. Soc. Andrology (sec. 1978-80, pres. 1984-85), Central Assn. Ob-Gyn, Assn. Mil. Surgeons U.S., Soc. for Study Reprodn., Mich. Med. Soc. (bd. dirs. 1995—). Republican. Presbyterian. Avocations: tennis; softball; gardening; skiing. Home: 3755 Tremont Ln Ann Arbor MI 48105-3022

ANSCHER, BERNARD, manufacturing executive, investor, management consultant; b. Bklyn., June 9, 1922; s. Abraham and Esther (Draznin) A.; children: William, Marlene, Joseph. *Son, William, former Executive Vice-President of National Molding, and a computer software and systems consultant. Son, Joseph, is president and CEO of National Molding Corporation, Farmingdale, L.I., N.Y., a leading plastic buckle and fastener manufacturer. Daughter Marlene Herring, is a lawyer and married to an art dealer in the Masters. Their Great Grandfather, Rabbi (and Teacher) Moshe Abraham Draznim, was killed in the Holocaust in 1942, together with his wife Rachel, their children and grandchildren that resided in Belarus.* Student, Sch. Tech., CCNY, 1939-42; BS in Mech. Engring., NYU, 1948, MBA, 1953, postgrad., 1953-65; postgrad., Fla. Internat. U., 1997—. Cert. mfg. engr. robotics, mfg. engr. Chief metall. and fabrication devel. reactor materials br. AED, N.Y.C., 1946-50; devel. mgr., gen. sales mgr. domestic sales, asst. v.p. Loewy-Hydropress, Inc., N.Y.C., 1950-55; cons., mfrs.' rep. Mervury Engring. Co., N.Y.C., 1955-65; founder, chmn. bd. dirs., pres. Nat. Molding Corp., Farmingdale, N.Y., 1965-87; pres. Anscher Mgmt. Corp. (formerly Custom Molds), Opa Locka, Fla., 1975—; founder, pres. Nat. Indsl. Robotic Controls, 1983-90; mfg. cons., 1991—; founder, instr. mktg. program in c.c., N.Y.C., 1962-65; mem. industry adv. group Underwriters Labs.; mem. robotics standards com. Robot Inst.; corp. mem. Automotive Industry Action Group, 1984-87. Reviewing editor Die Design Handbook, 1954-55; polit. columnist Miami Beach Sunpost, 1991-92; contbr. articles to profl. jours.; patentee in field. Queens County committeeman Rep. Party, 1960-68; mem. Dem. Exec. Com., Dade County, Fla., 1990-92; Dem. party nominee for Congress, 18th Dist., Fla., 1990; ind. candidate Congress, 22d Dist., Fla., 1992; mem. platform com. Dem. Party Presdl. Election, 1992; treas. Temple Emanu-el, 1994-95, Lehrman Day Sch., 1994-95. With AUS, 1943-46, PTO. Recipient Spl. award Manahttan Project, 1946; cert. mfg. engr. Mem. N.Y. State Mfg. Educators (chmn. curriculum rsch. com. 1964), Soc. Mfg. Engrs., Soc. Plastics Engrs., Robotics Internat., Am. Jewish Congress (commn. law and social action), Pres.' Club U. Miami, NYU Alumni Assn., Stuyvesant H.S. Alumni. Office: Anscher Mgmt Corp PO Box 610157 Miami FL 33261-0157

ANSCHUETZ, NORBERT LEE, retired diplomat, banker; b. Leavenworth, Kans., May 16, 1915; s. Otto William and Irma (Hilpert) A.; m. Roberta Cook, Mar. 13, 1943; children: Carol L., Ellen Anschuetz Lewis, Susan, Nancy Anschuetz Stahl. AB, U. Kans., 1936; LLB, Harvard U., 1939; grad., Nat. War Coll., 1957, State Dept. Sr. Seminar, 1967. Bar: Mo. 1939. Practice in Kansas City, Mo., 1939-41; with Bur. Near Ea., S. Asian and African Affairs Dept. State, 1946-51, fgn. service officer, 1951-68; assigned successively to Washington Athens, 1951-53; counselor Bangkok, 1954-56; minister-counselor Cairo, 1958-62, Paris, 1962-64, Athens, 1964-67; rep. for Middle East and Africa First Nat. City Bank N.Y., Beirut, 1968-70; fgn.

affairs rep. Citibank, N.Y.C., 1971-74; dir. Citicorp. Internat. Devel. Orgn., London, 1974-76; v.p. internat. relations Citibank, 1976-80; pres. Trans World Transactions, Inc., 1984—. Former mem. Coun. Fgn. Rels. Col. USAR., 1941-45, ETO. Hon. citizen Athens, 1967. Home: 4101 Cathedral Ave NW Washington DC 20016

ANSCHUTZ, PHILIP F., transportation executive, communications executive; b. Russell, Kansas, 1939. BS, Univ. Kansas, 1961. Dir. chair. QCC, 1993-, Anschutz Co., Denver, 1991-; ceo, dir. Anschutz Corp., Denver, 1992-; dir. So. Pacific Rail Corp., San Francisco, 1988-96; chair. So Pacific Rail Corp., 1988-96; vice chmn. (merger with So Pacific Rail Corp) Union Pacific, San Francisco, 1996-; dir. Forest Oil Corp., 1995-; dir., chair. Qwest Communications, 1997-; co-owner Los Angeles Kings, Los Angeles, 1995-; owner Los Angeles Galaxy, Los Angeles, 1996-; investor-operator Major League Soccer, 1995-; Board Mem: Am. Petroleum Inst., Nat. Petroleum Council, Nat. Hockey League, Kansas Univ. Endowment Assoc. Office: Southern Pacific Rail Corp 1 Market Plz San Francisco CA 94105 also: 555 17th St Ste 2400 Denver CO 80202-3941 Office: Los Angeles Kings 3900 W Manchester Blvd Inglewood CA 90305-2200

ANSELL, EDWARD ORIN, lawyer; b. Superior, Wis., Mar. 29, 1926; s. H. S. and Mollie (Rudnitzky) A.; m. Hanne B. Baer, Dec. 23, 1956; children: Deborah, William. BSEE, U. Wis., 1948; JD, George Washington U., 1955. Bar: D.C. 1955, Calif. 1960. Electronic engr. FCC, Buffalo and Washington, 1948-55; patent atty. RCA, Princeton, N.J., 1955-57; gen. mgr. AeroChem. Rsch. Labs., Princeton, 1957-58; patent atty. Aerojet-Gen. Corp., La Jolla, Calif., 1958-63, corp. patent counsel, 1963-82, asst. sec., 1970-79, sec., 1979-82, assoc. gen. counsel, 1981-82; dir. patents and licensing Calif. Inst. Tech., Pasadena, 1982-92; pvt. practice Claremont, Calif., 1992—; co-founder Gryphon Scis., South San Francisco, Calif., 93—, Ciphergen Biosystems, Palo Alto, Calif., 1993—; adj. prof. U. La Verne (Calif.) Coll. Law, 1972-78; spl. advisor, task force chmn. U.S. Commn. Govt. Procurement, 1971. Editor: Intellectual Property in Academe: A Legal Compendium, 1991; contbr. articles to profl. publs. Recipient Alumni Svc. award George Washington U., 1975. Mem. Am. Intellectual Property Law Assn., Assn. Corp. Patent Counsel, Ea. Bar Assn. Los Angeles County, L.A. Intellectual Property Law Assn., Licensing Execs. Soc., Assn. Univ. Tech. Mgrs., State Bar Calif. (exec. com. intellectual property sect. 1983-86), Internet Soc., Athenaeum Club Pasadena, Univ. Club Claremont, Internet Soc. Home and Office: 449 Willamette Ln Claremont CA 91711-2746

ANSELL, JULIAN S., physician, retired urology educator; b. Portland, Maine, June 30, 1922; s. Jacob M. and Anna Gertrude (Fieldman) A.; m. Eva Ruth Ballin, June 17, 1951; children: Steven, Jody, Carol, Ellen, Peter. BA, Bowdoin Coll., 1946; MD, Tufts U., 1951; PhD, U. Minn., 1959. Intern in surgery U. Minn. Hosps., Mpls., 1951-52, resident in urology, 1952-54; NIH fellow U. Minn., Mpls., 1954, instr., 1956-59; asst. prof., head urology U. Wash., Seattle, 1959-62, assoc. prof., head urology, 1962-64, prof., chair urology, 1965-87, prof. urology, 1987-92, prof. emeritus, 1992—. With U.S. Army, 1943-46. Mem. Am. Alpine Club. Office: 3827 49th Ave NE Seattle WA 98105-5233

ANSELME, JEAN-PIERRE LOUIS MARIE, chemist; b. Port-au-Prince, Haiti, Sept. 22, 1936; came to U.S., 1955, naturalized, 1960; s. Pierre F. and Jeanne (Kieffer) A.; m. Marie-Celine Carrie, Dec. 31, 1960; children: Fabienne, Veronika, Vanessa. B.A., St. Martial Coll., Haiti, 1955; B.S., Fordham U., 1959; Ph.D., Poly. Inst., Bklyn., 1963. Research asso. Poly. Inst. Bklyn., 1963, 65, sr. instr., 1965; NSF fellow Institut fur Organische Chemie, Munich, 1964; asst. prof. chemistry U. Mass. at Boston, 1965-68, asso. prof., 1968-70, prof., 1970—; pres. Organic Preparations and Procedures, Inc., Newton, Mass.; vis. prof. Research Inst. Indsl. Sci., Kyushu U., Fukuoka, Japan, 1972, U. Miami, Coral Gables, Fla., 1979. Author: (with others) Organic Compounds with Nitrogen-Nitrogen Bonds, 1966, N-Nitrosamines, 1979; founder, editor: Organic Preparations and Procedures, 1969-70, Organic Preparations and Procedures Internat, 1971—; contbr. (with others) articles to profl. jours. Recipient Seymour Shapiro award as outstanding grad. student organic chemistry Poly. Inst. Bklyn., 1963; Sloan fellow, 1969-71. Fellow Japan Soc. for Promotion Sci.; mem. Am. Chem. Soc., Chem. Soc. London, Sigma Xi, Phi Lambda Upsilon. Office: U Mass Dept Chemistry Harbor Campus Boston MA 02125-3393

ANSLEY, JULIA ETTE, educator, poet, writer, consultant; b. Malvern, Ark., Nov. 10, 1940; d. William Harold and Dorothy Mae (Hamm) Smith; m. Miles Ansley, Nov. 8, 1964 (div. June 1976); children: Felicia Dianne, Mark Damon. BA in Edn., Calif. State U., Long Beach, 1962; postgrad., UCLA Ext. Early childhood edn., life, gen. elem., kindergarten/primary, Miller-Unruh reading specialist credentials, Calif. Elem. tchr. L.A. Unified Sch. Dist., 1962—; coord. Proficiency in English Program, L.A., 1991-93, 98—; mem., advisor P.E.P. instrnl. tchrs. network, 1993—, workshop presenter, staff devel. leader, and classroom demonstration tchr. in field; also poetry presentations, L.A., 1989—; owner Poetry Expressions, L.A.; self-markets own poetry posters; creator, presenter KidChess integrated lang. arts program, 1987—. Author: (poetry vols.) Out of Heat Comes Light, From Dreams to Reality. Bd. dirs. New Frontier Dem. Club, L.A., 1990-93; mem. exec. bd. L.A. Panhellenic Coun., rec. sec., 1993-95; vol., cmty. orgns. Greater South L.A. Affirmative Action Project, 1995-96; elected tchr. rep. Ten Schs. Leadership Team, 1992-93. Honored by Teacher mag., 1990; recipient Spirit of Edn. award Sta. KNBC-TV, L.A., 1990, Shiny Apple award L.A. Tchr. Ctr., 1992, Dedicated Tchr. award Proficiency in English Program, 1994; grantee L.A. Edn1. Partnership, 1985, 87, 89, 93. Mem. L.A. Alliance African-Am. Educators (exec. bd. 1991-94, parliamentarian 1992-94), Black Women's Forum, Black Am. Polit. Assn. (edn. co-chair 1993-95), Sigma Gamma Rho. Mem. FAME Ch. Avocations: reading, listening to music, writing, playing chess (cert. chess instr. for grades K-3), political involvement. Home: 3828 Sutro Ave Los Angeles CA 90008-1925

ANSLEY, SHEPARD BRYAN, lawyer; b. July 31, 1939; s. William Bonneau and Florence Jackson (Bryan) A.; m. Boyce Lineberger, May 9, 1970; children-Anna Rankin, Florence Bryan. BA, U. Ga., 1961; LLB, U. Va., 1964. Bar: Ba. 1967. Assoc. Carter & Ansley and predecessor firm Carter, Ansley, Smith & McLendon, Atlanta, 1967-73, ptnr., 1973-84, of counsel, 1984-91; bd. dirs. Prime Bancshares, Inc., Prime Bank, FSB; chmn. bd. dirs., pres. Sodamaster Co. Am.; exec. v.p. Woodridge Realty, Inc.; sr. v.p., ACA Consulting, Inc.; fin. cons. Attkisson, Carter & Akers, Inc.; bd. dirs. Jour. Pub. Law Emory U., 1961-62; bd. dirs., sec. CRM Co., LLC, L.A. County, Calif. Mem. Vestry St. Luke's Episcopal Ch., Atlanta, 1971-74; treas., mem. exec. com., bd. dirs. Alliance Theatre Co., Atlanta, 1974-85; trustee Atlanta Music Festival Assn., Inc., 1975—; v.p., bd. dirs. Atlanta Preservation Ctr. Inc., pres., 1988-90; bd. visitors Lineberger Cancer Rsch. Ctr. U. N.C. at Chapel Hill, 1987-92; pres., bd. dirs. The Study Hall at Emmaus House, Inc.; bd. dirs., The Margaret Mitchell House, Inc. Served to capt. U.S. Army, 1965-67. Mem. ABA, Ga. Bar Assn., Atlanta Bar Assn., Atlanta Lawyers Club, Am. Coll. Mortgage Attys., Atlanta Jr. C. of C. (bd. dirs. 1968-72), Piedmont Driving Club.

ANSPACH, ERNST, economist, lawyer; b. Glogau, Germany, Feb. 4, 1913; came to U.S., 1936, naturalized, 1943; s. Hermann and Margarete (Gurassa) A.; m. Ruth Pietsch, Dec. 20, 1950; children: Paul David, Margaret Louise. Js.D., D Polit. Sci., U. Freiburg, Berlin, Munich, Breslau, 1935; M.Sc., New Sch. Social Research, N.Y.C., 1943. With German jud. service, 1934-36; fin. analyst Loeb, Rhoades & Co., N.Y.C., 1936-43; reorgn. of adminstrn. Justice in Bavaria and Hesse, 1946-49; gen. counsel and polit. adviser Dept. State, U.S. Land Commr. for Hesse, 1949-52; chief economist, gen. ptnr. Loeb, Rhoades & Co., Investment Bankers, N.Y.C., 1952-79; cons., 1980—; tchr. adult edn. program Henry St. Settlement, N.Y.C., 1939-43; lectr. Univs. Munich, Marburg, Frankfurt, 1948-52; lectr. fields econs., polit. sci., theology and primitive art, 1955—. Contbr. articles to sci. jours.; collection African Tribal Art; exhibited, Mus. Primitive Art, N.Y.C., 1967-68. Trustee Bleuler Psychotherapy Ctr., 1953-85, chmn. bd., 1956-65; trustee Nightingale-Bamford Sch., 1971-77; trustee Madison Ave. Presbyn. Ch., 1966—, chmn. bd. trustees, 1975-80; fellow in perpetuity and mem. vis. com. dept. primitive art Met. Mus. Art, N.Y.C.; bd. dirs. Mus. African Art, 1982-91, treas., 1982-87. Capt. AUS, 1943-46. Recipient Army commendation medal. Mem. Conf. Bus. Economists. Home: 118 W 79th St New York NY 10024-6445

ANSPACH, HERBERT KEPHART, retired appliance company executive, patent attorney; b. Ada, Ohio, Sept. 3, 1926; s. Eldred W. and Della (Kephart) A.; m. Elizabeth McKenzie, June 5, 1952; 1 dau., Heather. B.S. in Mech. Engring., U. Wis., 1947; J.D., U. Mich., 1952. Bar: Mich. 1953, Ohio 1953. Devel. engr. Goodyear Tire & Rubber Co., St. Mary's, Ohio, 1947-49; labor relations rep. Kaiser Motors, Willow Run, Mich., 1953; supr. indsl. relations Kaiser Motors, Shadyside, Ohio, 1953-54; patent examiner U.S. Dept. Commerce, Washington, 1954, patent atty., 1955-56, dir. patent sect., 1956-60, asst. sec., asst. gen. counsel, 1961-67; v.p. pers. Whirlpool Corp., 1967-74; chmn. bd., chief exec. officer Inglis Ltd., Toronto, Ont., Can., 1975-77; pres., chief operating officer Whirlpool Corp., Benton Harbor, Mich., 1977-83; mgmt. cons., 1983—; pres. Eagle Enterprises, 1985—. Served to 2d lt. USNR, 1944-46. Mem. Broken Sound Golf Club (Boca Raton), Toronto Club, Boca Raton Resort and Club. *

ANSPACHER, STEPHEN J., university official; b. Washington, Aug. 31, 1952; s. John M. and Ellinor J. (Feigl) A.; m. Joanna Gould, Dec. 13, 1997. BA, Columbia U., 1974, MA, 1992. Assoc. dir. intercultural rsch. Washington Internat. Ctr., 1974-76; cons. in internat. comm., Washington, 1976-83; dir. undergrad. rsch. U. N.C., Asheville, 1983-85; assoc. dir. Info. Tech. Inst., NYU, N.Y.C., 1985-89; mgr. acad. and career devel. AICPA, N.Y.C., 1989-93; dir. distance learning The New Sch., N.Y.C., 1993—. E-mail: sanspacher@dialsna.edu.

ANSPAUGH, DAVID, director, producer; b. Decatur, Ind., Sept. 24, 1946; s. Lawrence Earl and Marie Francis (DeMaio) A.; m. Tamara Kramer, Apr. 13, 1974; 1 child, Vanessa Christine. BS i Edn., Ind. U., 1970; MFA in Cinema, U. So. Calif., 1976. Tchr. Aspen (Colo.) Schs., 1970-74. Assoc. prodr. TV movies Paris, 1979, Vampire, 1979, Fighting Back, 1980; assoc. prodr. Hill St. Blues, 1980-81, prodr., 1981-84 (Emmy award for outstanding drama series 1982, 83, Golden Globe award for best TV series drama 1982, 83); dir. TV movies Deadly Care, 1987, In the Company of Darkness, 1993, TV spl. The Last Leaf, 1984; dir. films Hoosiers, 1987, Fresh Horses, 1988, Rudy, 1993, Moonlight and Valentino, 1995, Swing Vote, 1999. Mem. Dirs. Guild Am. (Outstanding Directorial Achievement award for TV 1982). Office: Creative Artists Agency 9830 Wilshire Blvd Beverly Hills CA 90212-1825*

ANSPAUGH, LYNN RICHARD, research biophysicist; b. Rawlins, Wyo., May 25, 1937; s. Solon Earl and Alice Henrietta (Day) A.; m. Barbara Anne Corrigan, Nov. 2, 1965 (div.); children: Gregory, Heidi; m. Larisa Fedorovna Kornushina, Sept. 27, 1993. BA, Nebr. Wesleyan U., 1959; M in Bioradiology, U. Calif., Berkeley, 1961, PhD, 1963. Biophysicist Lawrence Livermore (Calif.) Nat. Lab., 1963-74, group leader, 1974-75, sect. leader, 1976-82, div. leader, 1982-92, dir. Risk Scis. Ctr., 1992-95, dir. Dose Reconstruction program, 1995-96; rsch. prof. radiobiology divsn. Univ. Utah, Salt Lake City, 1997—; tchr. extension U. Calif., Berkeley, 1966-69; lectr. San Jose (Calif.) State U., 1975; guest lectr. UCLA, Stanford U., U. Calif., Davis, 1992—; faculty affiliate Colo. State U., Ft. Collins, 1979-83; cons. EPA, Washington, 1984-85, U. Utah, Salt Lake City, 1983-88, NAS/NRC, 1998; mem. U.S. del. UN Sci. Com. on Effects of Radiation, Vienna, 1987—; mem. Nat. Coun. on Radiation Protection and Measurements, 1989—. Contbr. articles to profl. jours. AEC fellow, 1959-61; fellow NSF, 1961-63. Fellow Health Physics Soc. (pres. environ. radiation sect. 1984-85, pres. No. Calif. chpt. 1986-87); mem. AAAS, Soc. for Risk Analysis, Internat. Union Radioecology, Radiation Rsch. Soc., Sigma Xi. Home: PO Box 171319 Salt Lake City UT 84117-1319 Office: U Utah Bldg 586 Salt Lake City UT 84112

ANSTAD, NEIL, director. Coord. humanities program Cleve. High Sch. Office: Humanitas Program Cleve High Sch 8140 Vanalden Ave Reseda CA 91335-1136*

ANSTATT, PETER JAN, marketing services executive; b. Haworth, N.J., Feb. 9, 1942; s. Herman E. and Margaret (Dunham) A.; m. Jean Ann Sorchiotti, Aug. 13, 1966; children: Christopher Ryan, Holley Elizabeth. B.S. in Printing Mgmt., Carnegie Mellon U., 1963; grad. program for mgmt. devel., Harvard U. Bus. Sch., 1977. Estimator Einson Freeman Inc., N.Y.C., 1963, project mgr., 1965-66; account exec. Einson Freeman Inc., Fairlawn, N.J., 1966-71; gen. mgr. Einson Freeman Inc., Fairlawn, 1971-76, pres., chief exec. officer, 1977-78; chmn., chief exec. officer Einson Freeman Inc., Paramus, N.J., 1978-93; pres. Enterprise Comms., Inc., Wyckoff, N.J., 1994—; exec. dir. Buehler Challenger & Sci. Ctr., Paramus, 1995—; v.p. ops. EAC Industires, Paramus, 1978. Mem. alumni bd. govs. Blair Acad., 1974-77; bd. dirs. Ridgewood YMCA, 1981-90, bd. trustees, 1991—. Served with C.E., U.S. Army, 1963-65, Korea. Recipient Jacob Van Dyke award for Outstanding Service, Ridgewood YMCA, 1985. Mem. Point of Purchase Advt. Inst. (chmn. trade ethics com. 1973-78, chmn. ann. exhibit com. 1979, dir. 1973-81, vice chmn. bd. 1979, chmn. 1980, speaker ann. industry seminar 1977-88, Producer/Supplier of Yr. 1984, inducted into Hall of Fame, 1994), Beta Theta Pi (pres. 1962-63). Republican. Methodist. Home: 63 Hunter Rd North Haledon NJ 07508-3303 *Undying belief in God, country and the free enterprise system. Adherence to the principles of respect, fairness, achievement through teamwork, and happiness.*

ANSTEAD, HARRY LEE, state supreme court justice. Former judge, chief judge U.S. Ct. Appeals. (4th dist.), Fla.; justice Fla. Supreme Ct., Tallahassee, 1994—. Office: Supreme Ct Bldg 500 S Duval St Tallahassee FL 32399-6556*

ANSTETT, PAT, newspaper editor. Med. writer Detroit Free Press. Office: Detroit Free Press 600 W Fort St Detroit MI 48226-3138*

ANTALFFY, LESLIE PETER, mechanical engineer; b. Budapest, Hungary, Oct. 31, 1942; came to U.S., 1973; s. Vilmos Leslie and Margo (Simay) A.; m. Barbara Ann Clark, Jan. 19, 1970; children: Julie, Michael, Nicole. B in Mech. Engring., U. Adelaide, Australia, 1970; MBA, Sam Houston State U., 1980. Registered profl. engr., Tex.; chartered profl. engr. Instn. Engrs. Australia. Mech. engr. T. O'Connor & Sons, Adelaide, 1968-69; vessel engr. Lummus Co. Can., Toronto, 1970-71, A.G. McKee Co. Can., Toronto, 1972; sr. vessel engr. Lummus Co. Can., Toronto, 1972-73; sr. vessel engr. Fluor Daniel, Houston, 1973-75, prin. engr., 1975-80, supervising mech. engr., 1980-89, mech. engring. dir., 1989-95, sr. mech. engring. dir., 1995—, sr. tech. fellow, 1996—. Contbr. articles to profl. jours.; presenter tech. papers at internat. confs. Fellow ASME (spl. working group on high pressure vessels, task group chmn. fabrication, examination testing of ASME VIII divsn. 3, 1992—, chmn. high pressure tech.-design 1993—). Republican. Roman Catholic. Achievements include patent for coke drum unheading device for coke drums on delayed coker units; patent for an automated chute system for delayed coker units; patent for a low headroom unheading device; patent for a coke drum system with movable floor pending. Home: 11946 Summerdale St Houston TX 77077-3022

ANTELL, DARRICK EUGENE, plastic surgeon; b. Cleve., Feb. 22, 1951; s. E. James and Wanda H. (Kociecki) A.; m. Elizabeth Ann Sobottka, July 14, 1984; children: Gillian Elizabeth, Darrick Eugene Jr., Leslie Jane, Helen Greer. BS in Biology, Hobart Coll., 1973; DDS, Case Western Res. U. Dental, 1978; MD, Med. Coll. of Ohio, 1982. Cert. Am. Bd. Plastic Surgery. Surgery intern Stanford (Calif.) U. Med. Ctr., 1982-83, surgery resident, 1983-85; plastic surgery resident N.Y. Hosp. Cornell, N.Y.C., 1985-87; plastic and reconstructive surgeon St. Luke's/Roosevelt, N.Y.C., 1987—; asst. clin. prof. plastic surgery Columbia U., N.Y.C., 1989—; med. dir., founder 850 Park Surg. Ctr., N.Y.C. *Dr. Antell has done more facelifts than anyone in the world on identical twins. His research on facial surgery and aging demonstrates that we can control the rate at which we age. Dr. Antell has made aesthetic (cosmetic) surgery a major focus of his practice. A Board Certified Plastic Surgeon and a member of the American Society for Aesthetic Plastic Surgery. In a survey of thousands of surgeons nationwide conducted by Town & Country magazine, Dr. Antell was picked as one of the "Top cosmetic Surgeons in the United States." Selected by NY Magazine as "One of the best Doctors in New York", and selected by his person for Town and Country's list of "The Best Cosmetic Surgeons in the Country", Dr. Antell has been featured in Town and Country, Vogue, Elle, The Wall Street Journal, as well as many national television and print media.* Author: Plastic Surgery, 1991; contbr. articles to profl. jours. Trustee East Side House Settlement, N.Y.C., 1991; trustee adv. Girl Scouts U.S.A., N.Y.C., 1991. Grantee Facial Proportions AM. Soc. for Aesthetic Plastic Surgery, 1987; recipient Pres. Citizenship award N.Y. State Med. Soc., 1992. Fellow ACS; mem. AMA, Am. Soc. Plastic and Reconstructive Surgeons, Am. Soc. Aesthetic Plastic Surgery, Am. Soc. Maxillofacial Surgeons Parliamentarian, N.Y. Regional Soc. Plastic and Reconstructive Surgeons, Internat. Soc. for Aesthetic Plastic Surgery, Internat. Acad. Dental Facial Aesthetics (founding), Am. Acad. Cosmetic Dentistry, Interplast, Lipoplasty Soc., Herbert Conway Soc., Univ. Sch. Alumni Adv. Coun., Union Club, Fishers Island Yacht Club, Cleve. Skating Club, Mill Reef Club (Antigua, W.I.). Avocations: squash, fly fishing. Office: 850 Park Ave New York NY 10021-1845

ANTEZZO, MATTHEW J., artist; b. Hartford, Conn., 1962. Degree, U. Utah, 1984, Parsond Sch. Design, N.Y.C., 1988. Office: Basilico Fine Arts 26 Wooster St New York NY 10013

ANTHOINE, ROBERT, lawyer, educator; b. Portland, Maine, June 5, 1921; s. Edward S. and Sarah B. (Pinkham) A.; children: Alison, Robert Neal, Nelson, Nina; m. Rebecca S. Rudnick, Dec. 2, 1990. AB, Duke U., 1942; JD, Columbia U., 1949. Bar: N.Y. 1949, U.S. Ct. Appeals (2d cir.) 1956, U.S. Supreme Ct. 1970. Research assoc. Am. Law Inst. fed income tax project Columbia U., N.Y.C., 1949-50; assoc. Cleary, Gottlieb, Friendly and Cox, N.Y.C., 1950-52; assoc. prof. law Columbia U., N.Y.C., 1952-56, prof. law, 1956-64, adj. prof., 1964-93; ptnr. Winthrop, Stimson, Putnam and Roberts, N.Y.C., 1963-86, sr. counsel, 1987—; in charge London office Winthrop, Stimson, Putnam and Roberts, 1972-76; vis. prof. U. Tex. Law Sch., Austin, 1988, U. N.C. Law Sch., Chapel Hill, 1991, U. Pa. Law Sch., Phila., 1996, Seattle U. Law Sch., 1997. Author, editor survey: Tax Incentives for Investment in Developing Countries, 1979; contbr. articles to profl. jours. Active Coun. Fgn. Rels.; bd. dirs. Feeling The Spirit Found.; pres. Line Circle Dot Found., S.K. Yee Found.; bd. govs. The Royal Shakespeare Theatre, Stratford-upon-Avon; vice-chmn., bd. dirs. Am. Friends Royal Shakespeare Theatre; chmn. bd. dirs. Aperture Found.; trustee, dir. Grosvenor Gallery (Fine Arts) Ltd., London; vice chair, trustee Internat. Photography Coun., Royal Shakespeare Theatre Trust, Seven Arts, Ltd., London; bd. dirs. emeritus Eric and Salome Estorick Found., Vol. Lawyers for the Arts. Lt. USN, 1942-46. Mem. ABA, Am. Law Inst. (life), Assn. Bar City N.Y. Internat. Fiscal Assn., Assn. Litéraire et Artistique Internat. (U.S.). Democrat. Clubs: The Century Assn., River (N.Y.C.); Queen's, Hurlingham (London). Office: Winthrop Stimson Et Al Battery Park Plz New York NY 10004-1490

ANTHONISEN, GEORGE RIOCH, sculptor, artist; b. Boston, July 31, 1936; s. Niels Landmark and Margaret (Rioch) A.; m. Ellen Friedman, Feb. 16, 1966; children: Rachel, Daniel. BA, U. Vt., 1961; postgrad., Nat. Acad. Design, N.Y.C., 1961-62, Art Students League, N.Y.C., 1962-64, Dartmouth U. Med. Sch., 1967. One-man shows include Hopkins Ctr. Dartmouth Coll., 1966, Ctr. Art Gallery, N.Y.C., 1969, Moody Gallery, Pasadena, Calif., 1979, Bjorn Lindgren Gallery, N.Y.C., 1981, 82, U. Scranton (Pa.) Art Gallery, 1986, Rotunda Cannon House Office Bldg., U.S. Capitol, Washington, 1989, The Woodmere Art Mus., Phila., 1992, Bianco Gallery, Buckingham, Pa., 1994, 98, Phila. Flower Show-Gale Nurseries, 1995, The Philip and Muriel Berman Mus. of Art, Ursinus Coll., Collegeville, Pa., 1996; exhibited in group shows NAD, N.Y., 1971, Port of History Mus., Phila., 1987, James A. Michener Art Mus., Doylestown, 1988, Millersville (Pa.) U., 1991, Nat. Sculpture Soc., 1993, Morani Gallery, Med. Coll. Pa., 1994, Monuments Conservancy, Samuel Dorsky Symposium on Pub. Monuments/Time and Life Bldg., N.Y.C., 1997; represented in permanent collections at WHO, Geneva, U.S. Capitol Bldg. Hall of Columns, Washington, Carnegie Hall, N.Y.C., Rittenhouse Hotel, Phila., Dartmouth-Hitchcock Med. Ctr., Lebanon, N.H., Washington Sch. Psychiatry, Germantown Hosp., Med. Ctr., Phila., Doylestown (Pa.) Hosp., Atlanta U. Trevor Arnett Libr., Trevor Arnett Libr., U. Alaska, Fairbanks, James Michener Art Mus., Doylestown, Phila. Coll. Osteo. Medicine, Wismer Ctr./Ursinus Coll., Collegeville, Pa. With U.S. Army, 1955-57. Sculptor-in-residence Augustus St. Gaudens Nat. Hist. Site, U.S. Dept. Interior, 1971; recipient James Augustus Suydam bronze medal, 1968, Sen. Ernest Gruening award Alaska State Coun. on Arts, 1976, Exemplary Achievement in Arts award Bucks County (Pa.) C. of C., 1985. Fellow Nat. Sculpture Soc. (bd. dirs. 1993-94). Avocations: fishing, baseball. Fax: 215-297-5162. E-mail: ellena@voicenet.com. Home and Office: PO Box 147 Solebury PA 18963-0147

ANTHONY, DONALD BARRETT, engineering executive; b. Kansas City, Kans., Jan. 28, 1948; s. Donald W. and Marjorie (Lifsey) A.; m. Darla S. Donovan, Dec. 16, 1972; children: Jennifer L., Danielle S. BSChemE, U. Toledo, 1970; MS, MIT, 1971, DSc, 1974. Asst. prof., practice sch. dir. dept. chem. engring. MIT, Cambridge, Mass., 1974-75; group supr. coal R&D Std. Oil Co. Ohio, Cleve., 1976-77, mgr. marine planning, 1978-79, mgr. synthetic fuels devel., 1980-83; v.p., gen. mgr. Pfaudler Divsn. Std. Oil Co. Ohio, Rochester, N.Y., 1983-85; v.p. R&D Std. Oil Co., Cleve., 1985-87, BP Am., Inc., Cleve., 1987-88, BP Exploration, Inc., Cleve., 1989-90; v.p. tech. Bechtel, Inc., Houston, 1990-94, v.p. ops., 1994-95, v.p. ref., 1995-96; pres. Bailey Controls Co., 1996-98, Process Ind. Group, ABB Automation, 1999—. Contbr. articles to profl. jours.; patentee in field. Capt. AUS, 1970-78. MIT Esso fellow, 1970-71, Little rsch.-devel. fellow, 1971-72, Procter & Gamble fellow, 1972-73, Bechtel fellow, 1992. Mem. AIChE, Am. Chem. Soc., Sigma Xi, Phi Kappa Phi, Tau Beta Pi, Pi Mu Epsilon, Phi Eta Sigma. Lutheran. Home: 6336 Canterbury Dr Hudson OH 44236-3488 Office: Bailey Controls Co 29801 Euclid Ave Wickliffe OH 44092-1898

ANTHONY, DONALD CHARLES, librarian, educator; b. N.Y.C., Mar. 29, 1926; s. Charles and Margaret Evelyn (Gleason) A.; m. Mary Miserez, Apr. 18, 1957; children—Stephen, Sheila, Irene. B.A., U. Wis., 1951, M.A., 1954; postgrad., U. Geneva, Switzerland, 1952-53. Library asst. Enoch Pratt Free Library, Balt., 1954-55; librarian Eleutherian Mills-Hagley Found., Wilmington, Del., 1955-59; dir. Fargo (N.D.) Pub. Library, 1959-61; asso. librarian N.Y. State Library, Albany, 1961-66; asst. dir. Columbia Libraries, 1966-69, acting dir., 1969, asso. dir., 1970-74; dir. Syracuse U. Libraries, 1974-85; cons. on preservation of library materials, 1986—; pres. Donmar Assocs., Clinton, N.Y., 1987—; adj. faculty Mohawk Valley Community Coll., Utica, N.Y., 1989-97; docent Munson-Williams-Proctor Arts Inst., Utica, 1999—; cons. N.Y. State Edn. Dept., 1967-97. Producer; host: TV Museum, KXGO-TV, Fargo, 1960; Contbr. articles to profl. jours. Trustee N.Y. Met. Reference and Research Library Agy., 1969-74, Cen. N.Y. Library Resources Council, 1983-86; chmn. bd. dirs. Five Asso. U. Libraries, Syracuse, 1975-76, 77-79; trustee Bd. Edn., Dobbs Ferry, N.Y., 1971-74, v.p., 1973-74. Served with USNR, 1944-46. Fellow Coun. on Libr. Resources. Home: 3654 State Route 12 Clinton NY 13323-4245

ANTHONY, EDWARD MASON, linguistics educator; b. Cleve., Sept. 1, 1922; s. Edward Mason and Elsie (Haas) A.; m. Ann Louise Terbrueggen, Sept. 18, 1946; children: Lynn Diane Anthony Higgins, Janice Louise, Edward Mason, 4th. AB, U. Mich., 1944, MA, 1946, PhD, 1954. From instr. English to prof. linguistics U. Mich., 1945-64; prof. U. Pitts., 1964-90, prof. emeritus, 1990—, chmn. dept. gen. linguistics, 1964-74; dir. Lang. Acquisition Inst., 1970, dir. lang. orientation programs, 1974-82, dir. Asian Studies program, 1977-82, dir. Lang. and Culture Inst, 1982-90; vis. lectr., Afghanistan, 1951, Thailand, 1955-57, Mexico, 1964, 65, Poland, 1977, Greece and Yugoslavia, 1981, Singapore and Thailand, 1984, Hong Kong, 1985, 86; dir. S.E. Asian English Project, Thailand, Laos, Vietnam, 1958-61, Rockefeller Found. Thai Project, 1967-72; vis. prof. Regional English Lang. Centre, Singapore, 1974-75, Peking Inst. Fgn. Lang., 1979-80; cons. in field; mem. Nat. Adv. Council Teaching English as a Fgn. Lang.; resource person Detroit Bd. Edn., 1964, Pitts. Bd. Edn., 1965; mem. adv. screening com. in linguistics Council for Internat. Exchange of Scholars, 1976; mem. adv. panel in English teaching to dir. USIA, 1987-93. Author: Reading Thai Syllables, 1962, (with others) Foundations of Thai, 2 vols, 1968, Towards a Theory of Lexical Meaning, 1975; book rev. editor: Lan. Learning, 1948; editor, 1949. Smith-Mundt grantee, 1951; recipient Fulbright award, 1955-57; NDEA lang. Rsch. grantee, 1965-67; State Dept. grantee, 1964, 65, 77, 81, 84, 90; plaque of Honor Ramkhamhaeng U., Bangkok, Thailand, 1986, USIA cert. appreciation, 1992. Mellon fellow Nat. Fgn. Language Ctr. Washington, 1990; mem. Linguistic Soc., Am. Assn. Applied Linguistics, Assn. Asian Studies, Siam Soc. (life), Assn. Tchrs. English to Speakers of Other Langs. (pres. 1967, Alatis award 1991), Nat. Council Tchrs. English. Democrat. Presbyterian. Home: 4118 Northampton Dr Allison Park PA 15101-1532 Office: Dept Linguistics U Pitts Pittsburgh PA 15260

ANTHONY, ELAINE MARGARET, real estate executive, interior designer; b. Mpls., Apr. 23, 1932; d. Jerome Pius and Adeline (Shea) Clarkin; m. Ronald Carl Anthony, Aug 28, 1954 (div. 1977); children: Richard, Lisa, Laura. Student, U. Minn., 1950-51; AA, Diablo Valley Coll., 1978; post-grad., San Jose (Calif.) State U., 1979, U. Calif., Berkeley, 1983-91. Agt., broker Sycamore Realty, Danville, Calif., 1972-75; broker, project sales mgr. Crocker Homes, Dublin, Calif., 1975-80; exec. v.p. BlackHawk Properties, Danville, 1980-82; broker, project sales mgr. Harold W. Smith Co., Walnut Creek, Calif., 1982-86; pres. Elaine Anthony & Assocs., Inc., Oakland, Calif., 1986—. Mem. vol. coun. San Francisco Symphony, 1986. Mem. Bldg. Industry Assn. (Outstanding Sales Person of Yr. No. Calif. chtp. 1983), Inst. Residential Mktg., Calif. Assn. Realtors, Contra Costa Assn. of Realtors, Nat. Assn. Realtors, Bellevue Club Oakland, Commonwealth Club (San Francisco). Republican. Roman Catholic. Avocations: traveling, food, theater. Home and Office: 1875 Grand View Dr Oakland CA 94618-2339

ANTHONY, ETHAN, architect; b. Iowa City, Oct. 14, 1950; s. Frank and Carol (Kessler) A.; m. Luz Eugenia, Feb. 18, 1984; children: Winston Eugene, Alexandra Luce, Edward Rey. Student, Boston Arch. Ctr., 1971-77; BArch, U. Oregon, 1980. Project architect Payette Assocs., Boston, 1980-83; prin. Anthony Assocs., Boston, 1983-90; pres. Hoyle, Doran Berry, Inc., Boston, 1991-98; cons. architect Phillips Exeter Acad., 1998—, St. George's Sch., 1999—; cons. N.E. MCI Worldcom, 1994—; instr. design Roger Williams Coll., Bristol, R.I., 1984-89; thesis advisor Boston Archtl. Ctr., 1985-87; speaker in field. Cons. architect Russell Sage First Presbyn. Ch., N.Y.C., 1994—, All Saint's Ch., Peterborough, N.H., 1998—. Recipient honor award Interfaith Forum on Religion, Art and Arch., 1993. Mem. AIA, Boston Soc. Archs. Avocations: painting, history. Office: Hoyle Doran and Berry Inc 38 Newbury St Boston MA 02116-3210

ANTHONY, HARRY ANTONIADES, city planner, architect, educator; b. Skyros, Greece, July 28, 1922; came to U.S., 1951, naturalized, 1954; s. Anthony G. and Maria G. (Ftoulis) Antoniades; m. Anne C. Skoufis, Sept. 23, 1950; children: Mary Anne Anthony Smith, Kathryn Harriet. B.Arch., Nat. Tech. U., Athens, Greece, 1945; student, Ecole Nat. Supérieure des Beaux Arts, Paris, 1945-46; M.City Planning, U. Paris, 1947; Docteur de l'Université, Sorbonne, Paris, 1949; Ph.D. in Arch. and Urban Planning, Columbia, 1955. Architect-planner with Constantinos A. Doxiadis, Athens, 1943-45, LeCorbusier, Paris, 1946-47, ECA, Paris, 1949-51; city planner with Maurice E.H. Rotival, N.Y.C., 1951-52; chief planner Brown & Blauvelt, N.Y.C., 1952-54; city planner, urban designer Skidmore, Owings & Merrill, N.Y.C., 1954-56; prin. planning cons. Brown Engrs. Internat., N.Y.C., 1956-60; prin. Brown & Anthony City Planners, Inc., N.Y.C., 1960-69; v.p. Doxiadis Assocs., Inc., Washington, 1971-72; mem. faculty Columbia U., 1953-72, from asst. to assoc. prof., 1956-63, prof. urban planning, 1963-72, dir. grad. div. urban planning Grad. Sch. Architecture and Planning, 1962-65; prof. urban planning Calif. State Poly. U., Pomona, 1972-83, prof. emeritus urban and regional planning, 1983—; chmn. dept. Calif. State Poly. U., 1972-76; vis. prof. urban design Tulane U., 1967-68; vis. lectr. U. Calif. at Berkeley, Stanford U., Dartmouth, San Diego State U., CUNY, U. Okla., Ohio U., Auburn U., Salk Inst. Biol. Studies, U.S. Internat. U.; lectr. urban studies and planning U. Calif., San Diego, 1980-82; scholar-in-residence U. B.C., Vancouver, 1978; planning, zoning, urban renewal and urban design cons. to several cities, U.S. and abroad; also cons. to UN, Am. Med. Bldg. Guild, corps. and pvt. firms, to govts. and univs.; planning commr., Leonia, N.J., 1958-64; master planner, cons. arch. for Ss. Constantine and Helen Greek Orthodox Ch. and Village for the Elderly, Cardiff-by-the-Sea, Calif., 1983-97 (AIA design awareness program orchid award 1997). Author, co-author, contbr.: Four Great Makers of Modern Architecture: Gropius, Le Corbusier, Mies Van Der Rohe, Wright, Dictionary of American History, The Challenge of Squatter Settlements-With Special Reference to the Cities of Latin America, La Défense à Paris et le Quartier d'Affaires de Vancouver: Une Comparaison Urbaine, New Orleans Air Rights Study, Woodstock Growth Plan and Land Use Controls, Mt. Vernon Planning Study, Corning Area, N.Y.: Conditions and Prospects, Metairie Shore, La.: Lakefront Recreation and Comty. Devel., U.S. Navy Multiple Activity Master Plan: Norfolk Complex, Aqaba, Jordan: Future Devel., Lands of Kapua, Hawaii: Feasibility Study for Urban, Agricultural and Recreational Devel.; several master plans, city and regional planning reports, urban design plans and programs, environ. impact reports, zoning ordinances, educational videocassettes on urban planning subjects; contbr. articles to profl. jours., mags., newspapers; acad. profl. writings, awards, plans, designs and reports included in Spl. Collections Libr., U. Calif. (San Diego), 1998. Recipient Premier Grand Prix Internat. Exhbn. Housing and City Planning, Paris, 1947; William Kinne Fellows travelling fellow in planning N.Am., 1956, French Govt. fellow, 1945-47; research award Urban Center of Columbia U., 1969; named Outstanding Prof. Calif. State Poly. U., 1975; founder Met. Opera House, Lincoln Ctr. for the Performing Arts, N.Y.C. Mem. AIA (Arnold W. Brunner scholar 1958), Am. Inst. Cert. Planners (bd. examiners), Am. Planning Assn. (Disting. Svc. award 1984, San Diego Cmty. Design Awareness Program Orchid award 1997), Order of Am. Hellenic Ednl. Progressive Assn., Hellenic Cultural Soc., Internat. Land Econs. Soc. of Lambda Alpha (Richard T. Ely Disting. Educator award 1988), Univ. Calif. San Diego Faculty Club. Home: 7665 Caminito Avola La Jolla CA 92037-3956

ANTHONY, JACQUELYN A., political scientist, educator; b. Flint, Mich., Apr. 5, 1963; d. Fred and Jacquelwyn (Willis) A. BA in English, Spelman Coll., 1985; MPA, Ga. State U., 1988, PhD, 1994. Pub. affairs specialist USDA Forest Svc., Atlanta, 1993—; program dir. Am. Project, Emory U. Carter Presdl. Ctr., Atlanta, 1994—, adj. prof., 1994—. Columnist Atlanta News Weekly, 1993; contbr. articles to profl. publs. Mem. Leadership DeKalb, Decatur, Ga., 1998; bd. dirs. Am. Cancer Soc., Atlanta, 1992-96, Ga. Environ. Orgn., Atlanta, 1997—. Named Outstanding Atlantan, 19967. Mem. ASPA, LWV, Am. Polit. Sci. Assn., Ga. State U. Alumni Assn. (bd. dirs. 1997—), Delta Sigma Theta (chpt. pres. 1997—). Avocations: swimming, reading, photography. Office: Emory U Carter Presdl Ctr PO Box 5317 Atlanta GA 31107-0317

ANTHONY, JOAN CATON, lawyer, writer; b. South Bend, Ind., July 28, 1939; d. Joseph Robert and Margaret Catherine (McMeel) Caton; m. Robert Armstrong Anthony, Jan. 3, 1980; 1 child, Peter. BA, Marquette U., 1961; MA, Northwestern U., Evanston, Ill., 1963; JD, Catholic U. Am., 1979. Bar: D.C. 1980, Va. 1982. Instr. English Marquette U., Milw., 1963-65; instr. English George Washington U., Washington, 1965-69, asst. prof., 1969-70; spl. asst. student affairs HEW, Washington, 1970-72; dir. Office Student and Youth Affairs U.S. Office Edn., Washington, 1972-74, legis. specialist, 1974-78; chief mgmt. ops. br. Fed. Wildlife Permit Office U.S. Fish and Wildlife Svc., Washington, 1978-81; assoc. Cate and Goodbread, Washington, 1981-86; atty., advisor office legis. counsel U.S. Dept. Interior, 1991-95; staff atty. Interior Bd. Land Appeals, 1995—; mem. U.S. del. to 2d meeting Conf. Parties to Conv. on Internat. Trade in Endangered Species of Wild Flora and Fauna, San Jose, Costa Rica, 1979. Contbr. lit. revs., essays and articles on univ.-cmty. rels., western settlement and internat. negotiations to various publs. Bd. dirs. McLean Citizens Assn., 1982-83, Fairfax County Humane Soc., 1983; pres. Franklin Forest Frolickers, 1985-86; treas. Greater McLean Rep. Women's Club, 1987-88; den leader cub scouts, com. mem. Boy Scouts Am., 1990—; parent vol. Fairfax County Pub. Schs., 1987—. Recipient Spl. Achievement award U.S. Fish and Wildlife Svc., 1981. Mem. D.C. Bar, Va. Bar, DAR (Freedom Hill chpt.). Roman Catholic. Home: 2011 Lorraine Ave Mc Lean VA 22101-5331

ANTHONY, JOHN H., college administrator. BS in Bus. Edn. and Acctg., Susquehanna U., 1958; MdD in Bus. Edn. and Psychology, Temple U., 1963, EdD in Bus. Edn. and Psychology, 1971. V.p. dean faculty, dean arts Coll. DuPage, 1967-73; pres. L.A. City Coll., 1973-77, Cayuga C.C., 1977-80, Portland C.C. Dist., 1980-85, Collin County C.C. Dist., 1985—. Past chair Med. Ctr. Plano; adv. bd. Plano Chamber Orch., Jr. League; mem. McKinney Econ. Devel. Coun., Plano Econ. Devel. Bd. Mem. Tex. Assn. C.C.s (pres.), So. Assn. Colls. and Schs. (mem. commn. of colls.), alliance for Hither Edn. (bd. dirs.), Assn. Tex. Colls. and Schs. (past pres.), Plano C. of C. (mem. adv. bd.). Address: 4800 Preston Park Blvd Plano TX 75093

ANTHONY, J(ULIAN) DANFORD, JR., lawyer; b. Boston, Oct. 23, 1935; s. Julian Danford and Eleanor Caroline (Hopkins) A.; m. Ellen Nora Brown, Apr. 8, 1961; children: Julian Danford III, Sarah Dodge, David Campbell. AB, Wesleyan U., 1957; LLB, Harvard U., 1960. Bar: Minn. 1961, Conn. 1965. Atty.-advisor U.S. Tax Ct., Washington, 1962-64; assoc. Day, Berry & Howard LLP, Hartford, Conn., 1965-70, ptnr., 1971—. Chmn. Conn. Red Cross Blood Svcs., Farmington, 1981-82; trustee J. Walton Bissell Found., Hartford, 1987—, pres., 1987—; bd. dirs. Hartford Symphony Orch., 1993—, Conn. Children's Med. Ctr., 1994—, pres., 1999—; bd. dirs. Coordinating Coun. for Founds., Hartford, 1994—; mem. adv. bd. dirs. Salvation Army, Hartford, 1990-96; elector Wadsworth Atheneum, Hartford, 1986-95; corporator Hartford Hosp., 1988—; bd. trustees Amistad Found., Hartford, 1997—. Mem. ABA, Nat. Assn. Bond Lawyers, Nat. Assn. Coll. and Univ. Attys., Fed. Tax Inst. New Eng. (exec. com. 1987—), Conn. Bar Assn. (chmn. tax sect. 1988-91), IRS Exempt Orgns. Liaison Group, Tax Club Hartford (pres. 1970-71). Office: Day Berry & Howard Cityplace Hartford CT 06103

ANTHONY, LANCE COLEMAN, marketing research executive; b. Columbus, Ga., Nov. 20, 1947; s. Noel Mercer and Mable Irene (Brookins) A.; B.A., Columbus State Univ., 1970; M.A., Stephen F. Austin State U., 1972. founder L.C.A. Enterprises, Inc., Phenix City, Ala., 1978—, pres., chief exec. officer, 1978—; social worker, State of Ala., 1991—. Recipient Blue Honor Key, R.D. award, Chevalier Degree, Internatl. Supreme Coun., 1967; Cross of Honor, ISC DeMolay, 1987. Mem. Mktg. Research Assn., Am. Mktg. Assn., mem. Ala. Coun. on Crime and Delinquency, 1991—, Democrat. Baptist. Lodge: Masons, (32 degree, master), K.T. (past comdr.), DeMolay (sr., Adv. Council Chmn., past high priest, past Illustrious Master). Home: PO Box 3050 Phenix City AL 36868-3050 Office: Bullock Correctional Facility Ala Dept Corrections US 82 E Union Springs AL 36089

ANTHONY, METROPOLITAN, OF SOUROZH (ANTHONY EMMANUEL GERGIANNAKIS), bishop; b. Heraklion, Crete, Mar. 2, 1935. Degree in theology, Theol. Sch., Halki, Constantinople, 1960; MDiv, Yale U., 1964; postgrad., U. Chgo., U. Wis. Ordained deacon Greek Orthodox Ch., 1958, ordained priest, 1960. Priest Holy Trinity Ch., Ansonia, Conn., 1961-64; priest Assumption Ch., Chicago Heights, Ill., 1964-69, Madison, Wis., 1969-73; dean St. George Cathedral, Montreal, 1974-78; titular bishop Ammissos, Denver, 1978-79; bishop San Francisco, 1979—; pres. Archdiocesan Council of Dept. of Edn.; founder St. Nicholas Ranch and Retreat Ctr., Dunlap Calif., northwest Orthodox Found. Retreat Facilities, Tacoma, Wash.; elected Met. of Dardanelles and Presiding Hierarch of San Francisco by Ecumenical Patriarchate, 1997. Office: Greek Orthodox Diocese 372 Santa Clara Ave San Francisco CA 94127-2090

ANTHONY, MICHAEL FRANCIS, lawyer; b. Chgo., Dec. 19, 1950; s. Rudolph A. and Margaret M. (Shea) A.; m. Megan P. O'Connell; children: Erin Christine, Ian O'Connell, Connor Cullerton, Madeline Shea, McKenzie Galligan. BS cum laude, Xavier U., Cin., 1972, MHA, 1974; JD, U. Balt., 1978. Bar: Md. 1978, Fla. 1979, Ill. 1980, D.C. 1989. Adminstrv. positions Johns Hopkins Hosp., Balt., 1973-78; assoc. Ober Kaler Grimes & Shriver, Balt., 1978-80; from assoc. to ptnr. McDermott, Will & Emery, Chgo., 1980-87, nat. head health law dept., 1989—; sr. v.p. for legal affairs Am. Hosp. Assn., Chgo., 1987-89. Contbr. articles to profl. jours. Mem. adv. bd. Loyola Inst. for Health Law. Fellow Am. Coll. Healthcare Execs. (various coms.), Am. Health Lawyers Assn. (pres.). Office: McDermott Will & Emery 227 W Monroe St Ste 3100 Chicago IL 60606-5096

ANTHONY, ROBERT ARMSTRONG, lawyer, educator; b. Washington, Dec. 28, 1931; s. Emile Peter and Martha Graham (Armstrong) A.; m. Ruth Grace Barrons, Feb. 7, 1959 (div.); 1 child, Graham Barrons; m. Joan Patricia Caton, Jan 3, 1980; 1 child, Peter Christopher Caton. BA, Yale U., 1953; BA in Jurisprudence, Oxford U., 1955; JD, Stanford U., 1957. Bar: Calif. 1957, N.Y. 1971, D.C. 1972. Assoc. Pillsbury, Madison & Sutro, San Francisco, 1957-62, Kelso, Cotton & Ernst, San Francisco, 1962-64; assoc. prof. law Cornell U. Law Sch., 1964-68, prof., 1968-75, dir. internat. legal studies, 1964-74; chief counsel, later dir. Office Fgn. Direct Investments, Dept. Commerce, 1972-73; cons. Adminstrv. Conf. U.S., Washington, 1968-71; chmn. Adminstrv. Conf. U.S., 1974-79; ptnr. McKenna, Conner & Cuneo, Washington, 1979-82; sole practice Washington, 1982-83; prof. law George Mason U., Arlington, Va., 1983—; Fulbright lectr., Slovenia, 1994; lectr. Acad. Am. and Internat. Law, Southwestern Legal Found., Dallas, summers 1967-72, instr. Golden Gate U., 1961. Mem. editorial adv. bd. Jour. Law and Tech., 1986-91; contbr. articles to profl. jours. Active Pres.'s Inflation Program Regulatory Coun., 1978-79, Fairfax County (Va.) Rep. Com., 1984-86; chmn. panel U.S. Dept. Edn. Appeal Bd., 1981-83; cons., chmn. pubs. adv. bd. Internat. Law Inst., 1984—; cons. Inst. Pub. Adminstrn., Slovenia, 1994—; bd. dirs. Marin Shakespeare Festival, San Rafael, Calif., 1961-64, Nat. Ctr. for Adminstrv. Justice, 1974-79, Va. Assn. Scholars, 1990-98; commr. Sausalito (Calif.) City Planning Commn., 1962-64. Mem. ABA (coun., sec. sect. adminstrv. law and regulatory practice 1988-94), Assn. Am. Rhodes Scholars, Am. Law Inst., Stanford U. Law Soc. Washington (pres. 1982), Cosmos Club. Home: 2011 Lorraine Ave Mc Lean VA 22101-5331 Office: George Mason U Law Sch 3401 N Fairfax Dr Arlington VA 22201-4411

ANTHONY, ROBERT NEWTON, management educator emeritus; b. Orange, Mass., Sept. 6, 1916; s. Charles H. and Grace (Newton) A.; m. Gretchen Lynch, Aug. 28, 1943; children: Robert N., Victoria Stewart; m. Katherine Worley, Aug. 4, 1973. AB, Colby Coll., 1938, MA (hon.), 1959, LHD (hon.), 1963; MBA, Harvard U., 1940, DCS, 1952. Mem. faculty Bus. Sch., Harvard U., 1940-42, 46-67, 68-83, Ross Graham Walker prof. mgmt. control, prof. emeritus, 1983—; pres. Mgmt. Analysis Ctr., Inc., 1955-63; asst. sec., contr. Dept. Def., 1965-68; prof. Mgmt. Devel. Inst., Switzerland, 1957-58; with Stanford Exec. Devel. Program, 1962; mem. adv. com. IMEDE, Switzerland, 1961-65, 68-77; spl. asst. to chmn. Price Commn., 1971-73; mem. educators cons. com. GAO, 1973-87; dir., chmn. audit com. Carborundum Co., 1971-77; dir. Warnaco, Inc., 1971-86; mem. adv. com. Kyoto Rsch. Inst., 1987-90, IPMI (Jakarta), 1983-90. Author: Management Controls in Industrial Research Organization, 1952, (with Dearborn and Kneznek) Shoe Machinery: Buy or Lease?, 1955, (with Reece) Accounting, Text and Cases, 1956, 10th edit., 1999, Office Equipment, Buy or Rent?, 1957, Essentials of Accounting, 1964, 6th edit., 1997, Accounting Principles, 1965, 7th edit., 1995, Planning and Control Systems: A Framework for Analysis, 1965, (with Govindarajan) Management Control Systems, 9th edit., 1998, (with Hekimian) Operations Cost Control, 1967, Plaid in Management Accounting, (with Welsch) Fundamentals of Financial Accounting, 1974, Fundamentals of Management Accounting, 1974, (with Young) Management Control in Nonprofit Organizations, 1975, 6th edit., 1999, Accounting for the Cost of Interest, 1976, Financial Accounting in Nonbusiness Organizations, 1978, Tell It Like It Was, 1983, Future Directions for Financial Accounting, 1984, Teach Yourself the Essentials of Accounting (computer software), 1999; (with Anderson) The New Corporate Director, 1986, The Management Control Function, 1988, Should Business and Nonbusiness Accounting Be Different?, 1989; editor Richard D. Irwin, Inc.; mem. bd. Harvard Bus. Rev., 1947-60; contbr. articles to profl. jours. Trustee Colby Coll., 1959-74, 75—, chmn., 1978-83; trustee Dartmouth Hitchcock Med. Ctr., 1983-93, treas., 1993; town auditor Town of Waterville Valley, N.H., 1976-92; mem. audit com. City of N.Y., 1977-85. Lt. comdr. USNR, 1941-46. Recipient Disting. Leadership award Fed. Govt. Accts. Assn., Disting. Pub. Svc. medal Dept. Def., Disting. Svc. award Harvard Bus. Sch., Marriner Disting. Svc. award Colby Coll., Meritorious Svc. award Exec. Office of Pres., CINPAC Letter of Commendation, Baker Scholar; named to Acctg. Hall of Fame. Fellow Acad. Mgmt.; mem. Am. Acctg. Assn. (v.p. 1959, pres. 1973-74, Outstanding Acctg. Educator of Yr. 1989), Fin. Exec. Inst., Inst. Mgmt. Accts. (chmn. cost concepts subcom., mgmt. acctg. practices com.), Assn. Govt. Accts., Am. Soc. Mil. Compts., Cosmos Club, Phi Beta Kappa, Pi Gamma Mu, Beta Alpha Psi. Home: 80 Lyme Rd Apt 332 Hanover NH 03755-1233

ANTHONY, SHEILA FOSTER, government official; b. Hope, Ark., Nov. 8, 1940; m. Beryl F. Anthony; children: Alison, Lauren. BA, U. Ark., 1962; JD, Am. U., 1984. Bar: Ark. 1985, D.C. 1985, U.S. Ct. Appeals (D.C. cir.) 1987, U.S. Supreme Ct. 1992. Tchr. Ark. Pub. Schs., 1962-63, 74-76; with Dow, Lohnes & Albertson, Washington, 1985-93; asst. atty. gen. Dept. of Justice, Washington, 1993-95; commr. FTC, Washington, 1997—. Del. Dem. Nat. Conv., 1980; justice of the peace Union County, Ark., 1969; trustee South Ark. U., 1971-75. Office: FTC 600 Pennsylvania Ave NW Washington DC 20580

ANTHONY, SUSAN, secondary education educator. Tchr. secondary geography Anchorage Sch. Dist. Recipient Disting. Tchr. K-12 award Nat. Coun. for Geog. Edn., 1992. Office: Anchorage Sch District PO Box 196614 Anchorage AK 99519-6614*

ANTHONY, SYLVIA, social welfare organization executive; b. Boston, Oct. 5, 1929; d. Charles and Josephine (Guastaferro) Caccamesi; children: Lyn Newbury, Edward Charles Souza Jr., Dean Souza. Student, Northeastern U., Boston, 1968-69, Lee Inst., 1966, 86-87. Lic. real estate broker, Mass. Founder, pres. Life for the Little Ones, Inc., Everett, Mass., 1987-94, Sylvia's Haven, Everett, 1994—. *Awarded 50 houses and Post Chapel through the McKinney Act by the U.S. Army for housing homeless women and children. To date, they have assisted over 200 families. This is a transitional shelter where the residents can stay up to 2 years. Its goal is to give them the support needed to become working citizens once more.Recognition awards received from the House of Representatives, 1999; Massachusetts Governor's Highway Safety Bureau; City of Leominster, Massachusetts, Mayor Dean J. Mazzarella.* Recipient Arthur L. Whitaker Recognition for Outstanding Cmty. Svc. award Am. Bapt. Chs. of Mass., 1992, Recognition awards Commonwealth of Mass. State Senate, Ho. of Reps., Gov. of Mass., 1997, 99, Mass. Gov.'s Hwy Safety Bur., 1998, Mayor Dean J. Mazzarella City of Leominster, 1999. Home: PO Box 1166 PO Box 1166 Groton MA 01450-1166 Office: Sylvia's Haven PO Box 2163 Devens MA 01432

ANTHONY, THOMAS DALE, lawyer; b. Cleve., July 23, 1952; m. Susan Shelly; children: Lara, Elizabeth. BS, Miami U., Oxford, Ohio, 1974; JD, Case Western Res. U., 1977. Bar: Ohio 1977. Tax specialist Ernst & Young, Cleve., 1977-79; ptnr. Benesch, Friedlander, Coplan and Aronoff, Cin., 1979-89, Frost and Jacobs, Cin., 1989-98; exec. v.p., chief legal officer, sec. Choice Care, 1996-98; pres., CEO PacifiCare of Ohio, 1998—; speaker various orgns. Mem. Cin. Coun. on World Affairs, 1980-82; vol. fundraising drive Sta. WVIZ, 1978-79, Sta. WCET, 1980-82; legal counsel Children's Internat. Summer Villages, 1979—; account capt. United Way of Hamilton County, 1986-88, cabinet mem., 1993; pres. State Libr. Bd., Ohio, 1987-89; mem. bus. adv. coun., subcom. ednl. legis. Mariemont City Schs. and Bd. of Edn.; bd. dirs. Greater Cin. Ctr. for Econ. Edn., Am. Heart Assn. (Cin. chpt.), Juvenile Diabetes Found. Mem. ABA (taxation sect., tax acctg. problems com., tax shelter subcom., small bus. com., mem. health law forum), Ohio State Bar Assn. (health law com., ins. sect.), Cin. Bar Assn. (chmn. tax. inst. com. 1990, adminstrn. and fin. com. 1991-93, chmn. tax sect. 1993, health law com.), Cin. C. of C., Miami U. Alumni Assn. (bd. dirs., treas. 1989-91, v.p. 1991-92), Nat. Health Lawyers Assn., Rotary (co-chair youth in city govt. program), Omicron Delta Kappa, Sigma Phi Epsilon. Home: 4337 Ashley Oaks Dr Cincinnati OH 45227-3947 Office: PacifiCare 11260 Chester Rd Ste 800 Cincinnati OH 45246-4056

ANTHONY, THOMAS RICHARD, research physicist; b. Pitts., June 27, 1941; s. Harry Louis III and Evelyn Gertrude (Fischer) A.; m. Angela Ute Klugert, Jan. 26, 1966; children: Wendy Christine, Jason Wayne. BS, U. Fla., 1962; MS, Harvard U., 1964, PhD, 1967. Rsch. physicist GE Corp. R&D Ctr., Schenectady, N.Y., 1967—. Assoc. editor Diamonds & Related Materials, 1991—; contbr. articles to profl. jours.; patentee in field. With USAF, 1959-63. Recipient IR. 100 award IRD Mag., 1977, U.S. Patent and Commerce Assn. medal, 1990, John A. Thornton Meml. award Am. Vacuum Soc., 1992, Best Product award Popular Sci., 1992, Best Product award Bus. Week, 1990, Inventor of Yr. award Ea. N.Y. Patent Lawyers Assn., 1994, Corp. Achievement award Inventors Assn. Conn., 1993; Coolidge fellow GE, 1978, NAE fellow, 1990, Woodrow Wilson fellow, 1963. Mem. Materials Rsch. Soc. (David Turnbull lectureship award 1992), Ea. N.Y. Patent Lawyers Assn. (inventor of yr. award 1994), Inventors Assn. Conn. (corp. achievement award 1993), Phi Beta Kappa, Phi Kappa Phi. Republican. Office: PO Box 8 Schenectady NY 12301-0008*

ANTHONY, VIRGINIA QUINN BAUSCH, medical association executive; b. Odessa, Tex., June 9, 1945; d. William Francis and Florence Elizabeth (Decker) Quinn; m. E. James Anthony; 1 child, Justin. B.A., Mt. Holyoke Coll., 1967. Exec. dir. Am. Acad. Child and Adolescent Psychiatry, Washington, 1973—. Mem. Am. Soc. Assn. Execs. Office: Am Acad Child & Adolescent Psychiatry 3615 Wisconsin Ave NW Washington DC 20016-3007

ANTHONY, WILLIAM GRAHAM, artist; b. Ft. Monmouth, N.J., Sept. 25, 1934; s. Emile Peter and Martha Graham (Armstrong) A.; m. Norma Neuman, Jan. 16, 1983. B.A. in European History, Yale U., 1958; student, San Francisco Art Inst., 1959. Author: A New Approach to Figure Drawing, 1965, Bible Stories, 1978, Bill Anthony's Greatest Hits, 1988; exhibited in one-man shows: Legion of Honor, San Francisco, 1962, Berland /Hall Gallery, N.Y.C., 1991, Stuart Katz Gallery, Laguna Beach, Calif., 1992, Cokkie Snoie Gallery, Rotterdam, 1995, others; exhibited in group shows: San Francisco Mus. Modern Art, Art Inst. Chgo., Whitney Mus. Am. Art, N.Y.C., Allan Stone Gallery, N.Y.C., St. Paul Art Center; works represented in collections: Art Inst. Chgo., Bklyn. Mus., Cleve. Mus. Art, Corcoran Gallery Art, Washington, Detroit Inst. Arts, Mus. Fine Arts, Houston, Met. Mus. Art, N.Y.C., Seattle Art Mus., Whitney Mus. Am. Art, N.Y.C., Guggenheim Mus., N.Y.C., others. Served with U.S. Army, 1953-55. Republican. Home and Studio: 463 West St Apt 903 New York NY 10014-2010

ANTHONY, YANCEY LAMAR, minister; b. Cordova, Ala., Feb. 13, 1922; s. Clifford Elmo and Tula (Barton) A.; m. Betty Pratt. B.A., Samford U., 1944; B.Th., So. Baptist Theol. Sem., 1947; Dr. è s scis., Paris; D.Th., Pioneer Theol. Sem., Rockford, Ill., Vanderbilt U., 1956, Galileo U., Italy; D.Ph., Accademia Universitaria Internazionale, Rome, 1957; D.D., Ministerial Tng. Coll., Sheffield, Eng., 1973; Ph.D. in History, Gt. China World U., Hong Kong. Ordained to ministry Baptist Ch., 1942; pastor Valley Grove Bapt. Ch., Tuscumbia, Ala., 1942-44, Walnut Grove Bapt. Ch., Lodiburg, Ky., 1945-47, First Bapt. Ch., Fort Walton Beach, Fla., 1947-53, Harsh Chapel Bapt. Ch., Nashville, 1953-56, Central Bapt. Ch., Fort Walton Beach, 1957-67; ambassador to all the Americas, Republik Danizig in Exile, N.Y.C., 1973-80; ambassador-at-large Principality of Sealand, 1980-98; moderator Okaloosa County Bapt. Assn., 1949-50; pres. Fort Walton Beach Ministerial Assn., 1952-55; mem. exec. bd. Fla. Bapt. Conv., 1948-56; pres. The Albert Schweitzer Internat. Open U., El Salvadore, 1989—. Pres. Okaloosa County Better Govt. League, 1950-52; mem. Fla. Bd. Social Welfare, 1959-68, chmn., 1960-64; dir. Ch. Missions Fund Bapt. Found., 1947—; dir. Ch. Devel. Found. Fla., 1962—; lt. col. and a.d.c. Gov. Ala.; a.d.c. Gov. Miss., 1976. Decorated Knights of Malta, 1973, knight Ordre dela Courtoisie Francais; Ordine Internazionale della Legion d'Onore de l'Immacolata (Italy); Gold medal of Labour (Netherlands), 1975; grand officier Ordre du Merite Africain; d'Honneur de l'Institut des Relations Diplomatiques, Brussels; Lit. award Belgian High Fidelity Inst., 1976; Legion of Honor, Chapel of Four Chaplains, Phila., 1981; numerous others; hon. academician W.A. Mozart (Germany), French Acad. Golden Letters. Fellow Brit. Inst. Adv. Cons.'s; mem. Accademia Delle Scienze di Roma (life), Inst. Diplomatic Relations Brussels (hon.), Royal Acad. Golden Letters (hon.), Accademia Gentium Populorum Progressie, Accademia Gentium Pro Pace, Nobility Acad. of Kaspis, Nat. Soc. Univ. Profs. (pres. 1981), Albert Schweitzer Soc. Internat. (pres. 1982-85, 90—), Internat. Assn. Educators for World Peace (v.p. fin. affairs 1989—), Sons of the Confederacy, Mt. Kenya Safari Club (exec. com.). Bd. editors Study Centre for Am. Indians, Antwerp, Belgium, 1989—. Home: 2328 River Rd Cordova AL 35550-3904

ANTIA, KERSEY H., industrial and clinical psychologist, consultant; b. Surat, Gujarat, India, Jan. 7, 1936; came to U.S. 1965; s. Hormasji and Dinsi R. (Mistry) A.; m. Dilshad K. Khambalta, Dec. 18, 1966; children: Anahita, Mazda, Jimmy. AB with honors, U. Bombay, 1958; MS, Tata Inst. Social Scis., Bombay, 1960, N.C. State U., 1969; PhD, Ind. No. U., 1976. Lic. psychologist, Ill.; cert. social worker, Ill. Personnel mgr., welfare officer Tata Steel and Tata Chem., 1960-65; research asst. psychology dept. N.C. State U., 1966-67, U. N.C., 1967-69; project dir. Behavior Systems, Inc., Raleigh, N.C., 1969-70; dir. Midwest Inst. Human Resources, Tinley Park, Ill., 1972—. Lang. scholar U. Bombay, 1954-56. Mem. Am. Psychol. Soc., Assn. for the Advancement of Psychology, Am. Acad. of Pain Mgmt., Am. Bd. of Profl. Disability Cons. Zoroastrian. Avocations: photography, yoga, jogging, hiking, traveling. Home: 8318 138th Pl Orland Park IL 60462-1746 Office: Tinley Ctr 17730 Oak Park Ave Ste B Tinley Park IL 60477-3918

ANTIN, DAVID, poet, critic; b. Bklyn., Feb. 1, 1932; s. Max and Mollie (Kitzes) A.; m. Eleanor Fineman, Dec. 16, 1961; 1 son, Blaise. BA, CCNY, 1955; MA (Herbert Lehman fellow), NYU, 1966. Prof. visual art U. Calif.-San Diego, 1968—; contbg. editor Alcheringa, 1972-80, New Wilderness 1979—; editorial com. U. Calif. Press, 1972-76; prof. emeritus visual arts U. Calif.-San Diego. Author: Definitions, 1967, Autobiography, 1967, Code of Flag Behavior, 1968, Meditations, 1971, Talking, 1972, Talking at the Boundaries, 1976 , Tuning, 1984, Selected Poems 1963-73, 1991, What It Means to be Avant Garde, 1993. Recipient Creative Arts award U. Calif., 1972; Guggenheim fellow, 1976-77; Nat. Endowment Humanities fellow, 1983-84. Home: PO Box 1147 Del Mar CA 92014-1147 Office: U Calif at San Diego Visual Arts Dept La Jolla CA 92037

ANTIN, MICHAEL, lawyer; b. Milw., Nov. 30, 1938; s. David Boris and Pauline (Mayer) A.; m. Evelyne Judith Hirsch, June 19, 1960; children: Stephanie, Bryan, Randall. BS, Univ. Calif., 1960; JD, U. Calif., 1963. Bar: Calif. 1963; cert. tax specialist. Tax atty. Cruikshank, Antin & Grebow, Beverly Hills, Calif., 1963-81, Antin, Litz & Grebow, Beverly Hills, 1981-91, Antin & Taylor, L.A., 1993—; bd. dirs. Small Bus. Counsel Am., Washington, The Group, Inc.; speaker in field; instr. Solomon S. Heubner Sch. CLU Studies, 1977-86. Author: How to Operate Your Trust or Probate, 1983; contbr. articles to profl. jours. With U.S. Air Force, 1959-67. Fellow Am. Coll. Tax Counsel, Am. Coll. of Trust & Estate Counsel, L.A. County Bowlers Assn. (bd. dirs. 1996). Avocations: jogging, tennis, cross country skiing, bowling. Office: Antin & Taylor Ste 1010 10880 Wilshire Blvd Los Angeles CA 90024

ANTIOCO, JOHN F., entertainment company executive. COO Pearle Vision, Dallas, 1990; pres., COO Circle K Corp, Phoenix, Ariz., 1991-96; pres., CEO Taco Bell Corp., 1996-97; chmn., CEO Blockbuster Entertainment, Dallas, 1997—. *

ANTIPAS, CONSTANTINE GEORGE, lawyer, civil engineer; b. N.Y.C., Mar. 8, 1962; s. George Spyro and Katina (Petropoulos) A.; m. Amy Lisa Scott, June 15, 1991. BSE, U. Conn., 1984; JD, Pace U., 1990. Bar: Conn. 1991, Mo. 1991, U.S. Dist. Ct. (we. dist.) Mo. 1991, N.Y. 1991, Kans. 1992, U.S. Dist. Ct. Kans. 1992, U.S. Dist. Ct. Conn. 1993; registered profl. engr. N.Y. Project engr./project mgr. Chas. H. Sells, Inc., Bedford Hills, N.Y., 1985-91, chmn. computer com., 1986-91; pvt. practice Overland Park, Kans., 1991-92; atty. Garcia & Assocs., P.C., New Haven, 1993-96, The Antipas Law Firm, Groton, Conn., 1996—; dir. Family Counseling Greater New Haven, Inc. Author: (legislation) Stamford Historic Preservation Ordinance, 1989. Active Vol.-Atty. Project, Kansas City, Mo., 1992. Named Stamford Found. Scholar, 1982. Mem. ABA, ASCE, Mo. Bar., Conn. Bar Assn. (legis. liaison, mem. exec. com. constrn. law sect.), Conn. Bldg. Congress (bd. dirs. 1998—), Conn. Design/Build Coalition, Order of Ahepa (sec. Rose of New Eng. chpt. 1997-99, lt. gov. Yankee Dist. 7, 1999—). Republican. Greek Orthodox. Avocations: sailing, history, linguistics, mountain hiking, scuba diving. Home: 164 Payer Ln Mystic CT 06355-1643

ANTLE, CHARLES EDWARD, statistics educator; b. East View, Ky., Nov. 11, 1930; s. Bayard Pierpoint and Mary Elizabeth (Blaydes) A.; m. Elna Thomas Hall, Nov. 25, 1953; children—James, Rebecca, Susan Hall, Mark Edward. A.A., Lindsey Wilson Coll., 1950; B.S., Eastern Ky. State U., 1954, M.A., 1955; postgrad., U. Ky., 1954-55; Ph.D. (NDEA fellow), Okla. State U., 1962. Sr. aerophysics engr. Gen. Dynamics Corp., Fort Worth, 1955-57; mem. faculty U. Mo., Rolla, 1957-60, 62-68; prof. math. U. Mo., 1966-68; asso. prof. statistics Pa. State U., University Park, 1968-70; prof. Pa. State U., 1970-92; prof. emeritus of stats. Pa. State U., University Park, 1992—. Contbr. articles to profl. jours. Served with AUS, 1951-53. Decorated Bronze Star medal. Mem. Am. Statis. Assn. Home: 2302 W Branch Rd State College PA 16801-8043 Office: Pa State U Dept Stats University Park PA 16802

ANTLEY, EUGENE BREVARD, sociology and religion educator; b. Brownwood, Tex., Aug. 2, 1929; s. George Brewton and Frances Nell (Brevard) A.; m. Dolores Stephan, July 12, 1953; children: Barbara, Corinne, Bruce. BA, Millsaps Coll., 1955; M Social Studies, U. Miss., 1956. Instr. Spartanburg (S.C.) Jr. Coll., 1957-58; asst. prof. Coll. of Ozarks, Clarksville, Ark., 1967-69; instr. history So. Oreg. Coll./Coll. of Siskiyous, Calif., 1958-67; assoc. prof. sociology Edinboro (Pa.) U. Pa., 1969—, also. instr. sociology of religion course. Author: Southern Families, 1988; co-editor Social Problems, 1990. Mem. Pa. Sociol. Soc., Assn. Pa. Schs., Colls. and Univ. Faculties, Fellowship of Reconciliation. Democrat. Home: 12241 Lakeview Dr Edinboro PA 16412-1429 Office: Edinboro U Pa 218 Hendricks Hall Edinboro PA 16412

ANTMAN, STUART SHELDON, mathematician, educator; b. Bklyn., June 2, 1939; s. Mitchell and Gertrude (Siegel) A.; m. Wilma Gail Richlin, Mar. 24, 1968; children: Rachel Alexandra, Melissa Dora. BS, Rensselaer Poly. Inst., 1961; MS, U. Minn., 1963, PhD, 1965. Lectr. U. Minn., 1965; vis. mem. Courant Inst. of NYU, 1965-67; asst. prof. math. and aeros. NYU, 1967-69, assoc. prof. math., 1969-72; sr. vis. fellow U. Oxford, 1969-70, Heriot-Watt U., Edinburgh, 1972, 77; prof. math. U. Md., College Park, 1972—; prin. investigator NSF grants, 1972—; mem. Applied Math. Summer Inst., Dartmouth Coll., 1973; prof. Ecole d'Eté d'Analyse Numérique, Bréau, France, 1974; vis. prof. U. Paris-Sud, Orsay, 1975, Brown U., Providence, 1978-79, Ecole Polytechnique, Palaiseau, France, 1979, U. Nacional Autónoma de México, 1981, Math. Scis. Rsch. Inst., Berkeley, Calif., 1983, Univ. P. and M. Curie, Paris, 1983, 92, Math. Rsch. Ctr., U. Wis., 1984, Inst. Math. and Applications, U. Minn., 1985, U. Bonn, 1987, U. Leipzig, 1995; mem. U.S. Nat. Com. on Theoretical and Applied Mechanics, 1980-88. Author: The Theory of Rods, 1972, Nonlinear Problems of Elasticity, 1995; co-editor: Bifurcation Theory and Nonlinear Eigenvalue Problems, 1969, Springer Tracts in Natural Philosophy, 1972-80, Metastability and Improperly Posed Problems, 1987, Analysis and Continuum Mechanics, 1989; mem. editorial bd. Archive for Rational Mechanics and Analysis, 1972-89, editor in chief, 1989—; mem. editl. bd. Acta Applicandae Mathematicae, 1982—, Jour. Elasticity, 1996—, Electronic Rsch. Announcements of Am. Math. Soc., 1997—, Quar. of Applied Math., 1999—; assoc. editor Notices of Am. Math. Soc., 1985-87; mem. editl. com. Proc. of Symposia on Applied Math, 1986-88; mem. editl. adv. bd. (Springer series) Applied Math. Scis.; mem. editl. bd. Interdisciplinary Applied Math., 1998—. Recipient D. Alcaraz medal U. Nacional Autónoma de México, 1997; John S. Guggenheim Meml. Found. fellow, 1978-79. Mem. Am. Math. Soc., Soc. Indsl. and Applied Math. (T. von Kármán prize 1999), Soc. for Natural Philosophy (sec. 1974-76), Soc. for Interaction of Mechanics and Math. (mem. exec. com. 1986-90), Math. Assn. Am. (L.R. Ford award 1987), Pi Mu Epsilon. Office: U Md Dept Math College Park MD 20742-4015

ANTOKOLETZ, ELLIOTT MAXIM, music educator; b. Jersey City, Aug. 3, 1942; s. Jack and Esther (Leiter) A.; m. Juana Canabal, May 28, 1972; 1 child, Eric. Student, Juilliard Sch. Music, 1960-65; BA in Musicology, Hunter Coll., 1968, MA in Musicology, 1970; PhD in Musicology, CUNY, 1975. Instr. violin Brearley Sch., N.Y.C., 1970-76; theory lectr., instr. chamber music Queens Coll., N.Y.C., 1973-76; prof. musicology U. Tex., Austin, 1976—. Author: The Music of Béla Bartók, 1984, Béla Bartók: A Guide to Research, 1988, Twentieth-Century Music, 1992; editor Internat. Jour. of Musicology; contbr. articles to prof. jours. and mags. Recipient Béla Bartók Memorial award Hungarian Govt., 1981, Tacquard Endowed Centennial Chair, U. Tex., 1983-84, Tching. Excellence award U. Tex., 1981, Achievement PhD Alumni award CUNY, 1987. Mem. Am. Musicol. Soc. (Subvention award 1982), Coll. Music Soc., Internat. Alban Berg Soc., Sonneck Soc., Internat. Musicol. Soc. Avocation: oil and water-color painting. Office: U Tex Music Dept Austin TX 78712

ANTON, BARBARA, writer; b. Pocono Pines, Pa., Apr. 3, 1926; d. Walter B. and Emma Agnes (Hess) Miller; m. Albert Anton, June 23, 1949. Grad. Gemologist, Gemol. Inst. of Am., 1964. Fashion and design editor Nat. Jeweler Mag., N.Y.C., 1956-58; freelance writer novels/plays, 1956—; staff writer Writer's Guidelines and News Mag. Contbr. articles to numerous nat. mags. including Cosmopolitan, Family Circle, Bride's Mag., Thema Lit. Mag., others; author plays (six winners Fla. Studio Theatre Shorts Competition 1995-98, Pa. Playwrighting award and prodn. 1994, 9 Off-Broadway Prodns., Theatre Row, N.Y.C., 1996-97, winner Lamia Ink Internat. Playwrighting Competition 1997); author: (novel) Egrets to the Flames (Top Ten/Fla. Writers Festival 1995, others); author short stories, anthologies (seven awards Writer's Digest, others). Nominated Best Of Off Broadway, Samuel French Play Festival, 1998-99. Mem. Internat. Women's Writing Guild, Nat. Writers Assn., Dramatists Guild.

ANTON, BRUCE NORMAN, textile company executive; b. N.Y.C., Dec. 27, 1951; s. Harvey and Betty L. (Weintraub) A.; m. Laurie Sue Weinberger, Mar. 7, 1981; children: Jamie Nicole, Ashley Blair, Emily Britt. BS in Textile Engring., Phila. Coll. Textile & Sci., 1973; MBA, Fairleigh Dickinson U., 1978. Salesman Robison-Anton Textile Co., Fairview, N.J., 1973-79, v.p., 1979-88, pres., 1988—; pres. Arrow Spinning Co., Inc., 1985-89; v.p. Bloomsburg Dye Co., Inc., 1984-94, pres., 1995—; pres. R.A. Mfg., 1990—. Mem. Am. Assn. Textile Tech. Office: Robison Anton Textile Co 175 Bergen Blvd Fairview NJ 07022-1619

ANTON, DANILO JOSE, geographer, writer; b. Montevideo, Uruguay, Dec. 2, 1940; s. Danilo Angel and Maria Sara (Guidile) A.; m. Elsa Lanza, May 4, 1968 (div. Oct. 1995); children: Carolina, Diego, Bruno; m. Maria Francia, Apr. 11, 1996. PhD, U. Louis Pasteur, Strasbourg, France, 1973. Prof., dir. U. de Guerrero, Acapulco, Mex., 1975-77; rsch. scientist McLaren Engrs., Toronto, Can., 1977-80; coord. divsn. U. Petroleum and Minerals, Dhah Rah, Saudi Arabia, 1980-84; sr. program officer Internat. Devel. Rsch. Ctr., Ottawa, Can., 1984-96; prof., dept. dir. U. de la Republica, Montevideo, Uruguay, 1993-98; invited prof. Macalester Coll., St. Paul, Minn., 1998-99; geomorphologist Ministry of Agr., Montevideo, 1973-75; rsch. prof. geology Inst. de Profesores, 1968-70; lectr. on water mgmt. U. de Costa Rica, 1997; lectr. devel. theory U. Pilar, Paraguay, 1997. Author: Thirsty Cities, 1993, Diversity, Globalization and the Ways of Nature, 1995; contbr. articles to profl. jours. Founder, pres. L.Am. Hidrologia Subterranea para Eldesarrouo, Montevideo, 1990-95. Recipient Huesped Ilustre award Mcpl. Merida, Venezuela, 1992. Fellow Consejo Interam. de la Espiritualidad Indigena (bd. dirs. 1996—), Authors Assn. Uruguay. Avocation: environmental activist. E-mail: danton@chasque.apc.org. Office: Macalester Coll 1600 Grand Ave Saint Paul MN 55105

ANTON, FRANK LELAND, insurance company executive; b. Mpls., Minn., Mar. 25, 1930; s. Arthur Fred and Gladys Mae (Miller) A.; m. Beverly Ann Johnson , June 11, 1955; children: Nancy Lynn, David Arthur. BA in journalism cum laude, U. of Minn., 1957. Editor Trane Co., LaCrosse, Wis., 1957-59; pub. rels. asst. Relia Star Fin. Corp., Mpls., 1959; editor Northwestern Nat. Life Ins., Mpls., 1960-64, supr. field svcs., 1964-66, advt. mgr., 1966-74, advt./sales promotion dir., 1974-88, dir. convs./meetings, 1988-96. Editor Kindley USAF Base Newspaper, Aquatennial Alumni Aqua Log, Rave Revs., Relia Star retiree publ.; author various articles to profl. jours. Mpls. Aquatennial Assc. (pres.) 1986, Mpls. Community Coll Bd. chmn., Mpls. Pub. Sch. Tchr. Recert. Comm. Chmn. Sl sgt. USAF, 1950-54. Recipient Good Neighbor award WCCO, Mpls., 1986, Rosarians Honoree award, 1986, Flying Col. award Delta, 1990, Conv. Liaison Coun. Hall of Leaders award, 1994, Aquatennial Lifetime Achievement award, 1995. Mem. Ins. Conf. Planners Assn. (pres. 1990-91), Life Ins. Communicators Assn. (pres. 1983-84, Lifetime Mem. award, Meritorious Svc. award 1992), Am. Coun. Life Ins. P.R., Mtg. Planners Internat., Soc. Incentive Travel Execs., Kiwanis, Aquatennial Admirals Club (grand admiral, past pres. and commodore). Lutheran. Avocations: writing, bridge, gardening, collecting poodle figurines. E-mail: faabaa@aol.com. Fax: 612-861-7113. Home and Office: 5712 Dupont Ave S Minneapolis MN 55419-1638

ANTON, JOHN PETER, philosopher, educator; b. Canton, Ohio, Nov. 2, 1920; s. Peter C. and Christine (Giannopoulos) A.; m. Helen Vezos, Nov. 26, 1955; children: James, Christopher, Peter. BS, Columbia U., 1949, MA, 1950, PhD, 1954; PhD, LHD (hon.), U. Athens, 1992. Instr. Pace Coll., 1953-54; vis. lectr. U. N.Mex., 1954-55; asst. prof. U. Nebr., 1955-58; assoc. prof. Ohio Wesleyan U., 1958-62; prof. SUNY, Buffalo, 1962-67, assoc. dean grad. sch., prof., 1967-69; Fuller E. Callaway prof. Emory U., 1969-81, chmn. dept. philosophy, 1969-76; prof., provost New Coll., U. South Fla., Tampa, 1982-83, disting. prof. Greek philosophy and culture, 1983—, dir. Ctr. Greek Studies; Woods vis. prof. Mills Coll., 1981; vis. prof. Columbia U., 1966. Author: Aristotle's Theory of Contrariety, 1957, Science, Philosophy and Educational Tasks, 1966, Naturalism and Historical Understanding, 1967, Philosophical Essays, 1969, Essays in Ancient Greek Philosophy (5 vols.), 1971-92, Science and the Sciences in Plato, 1980, Critical Humanism as a Philosophy of Culture, 1981, Upward Panic: The Autobiography of Eva Palmer-Sikelianos, 1993, The Poetry and Poetics of C.P. Cavafy, 1995, Categories and Experience, 1996; co-editor (jour.) Diotima: editl. cons. Jour. History of Philosophy, 1968—, The Humanist, 1967—; mem. editl. bd. So. Jour. Philos., 1974—, Eidos, 1974—, Ancient Philosophy, 1979, Idealistic Studies, 1981, Philos. Inquiry, 1981; founding editor (jours.) Jour. of Neoplatonic Studies, 1991, Revue de Philosophie Ancienne, 1984—, Skepsis, 1997. Bd. govs. St. Lawrence Coll., 1989. With U.S. Army, 1946-47. Named Disting.scholar U. South Fla., 1985; recipient Gold medal Hon. Citizen of Samos, Greece, 1988. Mem. Am. Philos. Assn., Soc. Advancement of Am. Philosophy (founding mem.), Am. Philol. Assn., Am. Soc. Aesthetics (trustee 1973-76, 81-84), Ga. Philos. Soc. (v.p. 1972, pres. 1973), Internat. Soc. Neoplatonic Studies (chmn. exec. com., pres. 1997—), Soc. Ancient Greek Philosophy (sec., treas. 1973-81, pres. 1981-83), Modern Greek Studies Assn. (v.p. 1969—), Soc. Macedonian Studies (hon.), Acad. Athens (corr.), Internat. Assn. Greek Philos. (hon. pres. 1993), Soc. Internat. pour l'Etude de la Philosophie Mediévale, Parnassos Lit. Soc. (hon.), Phi Beta Kappa, Eta Sigma Phi, Phi Sigma Tau. Home: 10012 Oxford Chapel Dr Tampa FL 33647-2870 Office: U South Fla Dept Philosophy Tampa FL 33620

ANTON, MACE DAMON, loan officer; b. N.Y.C., Mar. 18, 1961; s. Morris J. and Alice (Mayo) A.; m. Anna Kang, June 10, 1990; children: Joshua Benjamin, Juliet Alisha, Jennifer Carolyn. BA, Yeshiva U., 1982; MA, Columbia U., 1984. Cert. notary pub., N.Y. Credit investigator, analyst trainee James Talcott, Inc., N.Y.C., 1985-86; credit analyst commodity credit dept. Bear Stearns & Co. Inc., N.Y.C., 1986; comml. loan officer, asst. cashier Merchants Bank of N.Y., N.Y.C., 1986-93; comml. loan officer, treas. National Westminster Bank, USA, N.Y.C., 1993-94; bank contract analyst City of N.Y., 1994—. Mem. Nat. Rifle Assn., Nat. Geog. Soc., Smithsonian Inst., Kappa Delta Pi, Phi Delta Kappa. Republican. Jewish. Avocations: writing, politics, image consulting, travel, public relations. Home: Cathedral Sta PO Box 1642 New York NY 10025-1560 Office: Dept Fin 1 Centre St New York NY 10007-1602

ANTON, THOMAS JULIUS, political science and public policy educator, consultant; b. Worcester, Mass., Sept. 28, 1934; s. Julius and Irene (Dupsha) A.; m. Barbara Jane Lindblom, June 22, 1957; children: Lynn Allison, Leslie Carol, Thomas Rolf. AB, Clark U., 1956; MA, Princeton U., 1959; PhD, Prnceton U., 1961. Lectr. U. Pa., Phila, 1960-61; asst. prof. U. Ill., Urbana, 1961-63; assoc. prof. U. Ill., Urbana, Chgo., 1964-67; from assoc. prof. to prof. U. Mich., Ann Arbor, 1967-83, dir. PhD program in urban planning, 1977-80; prof. polit. sci., dir. A. Alfred Taubman Ctr. for Pub. Policy and Am. Instns. Brown U., Providence, 1983—, dean of faculty, 1990-91; vis. prof. U. Stockholm, 1968, 71; cons. State of Ill., Springfield, Chgo., 1963-70, State of Mich., Lansing, 1972-83, HEW, Washington, 1976-80, Brookings Instn., Washington, 1970—; cons. NAS, Washington, 1976-80, panel mem., 1981-82; mem. Swedish Fulbright Commn., Stockholm, 1971; vice chmn., bd. trustees Clark Univ., 1995—. Author: The Politics of State Expenditure in Illinois, 1966, Governing Greater Stockholm, 1975, Moving Money, 1980, Administered Politics, 1980, American Federalism and Public Policy: How the System Works, 1989; editor: Policy Scis., Amsterdam, 1977-80. Commr. Providence Housing Authority, 1986—, chmn., 1990—. J.F. Kennedy fellow Gov. of Sweden, 1977; NSF grantee, 1980; recipient Individual Recognition award HUD, 1992. Mem. Am. Polit. Sci. Assn. (Gladys M. Kammerer award 1989), Assn. Pub. Policy and Mgmt., Midwest Polit. Sci. Assn., Nat. Acad. Pub. Adminstrn. (panel on info. mgmt. 1993—), Princeton Club (N.Y.C.), Cosmos Club (Washington), Phi Beta Kappa. Democrat. Home: 13 Constitution Hl Providence RI 02904-5720 Office: Brown Univ Pub Policy Ctr PO Box 1977 Providence RI 02912-1977

ANTONACCI, ANTHONY EUGENE, controls engineer; b. Sept. 21, 1949; s. Salvatore Natali and Odile Estella (Stanton) A.; m. Sherry Lee Kessler, Mar. 6, 1971; children: Don Warren, Lance Anthony. Cadet, USAF Acad., 1968-69; AS, Forest Park Coll., 1971. Lic. power engr. Asst. supr. data processing ops. 1st Nat. Bank, St. Louis, 1969-71; engr. Installation & Svc. Engring. (Mech. & Nuclear) divsn. Gen. Electric Corp., St. Louis, 1971-76; engr. Anheuser-Busch Corp., St. Louis, 1976—; author software. Trustee, treas. Antonette Hills Trusteeship, Affton, Mo., 1976-80. Mem. Brewers and Maltsters Local 6 (del. 1982-83), Nat. Aerospace Edn. Coun., Apple Programmers and Developers Assn., Am. Legion. Republican. Roman Catholic. Avocations: classic auto restoration, trumpet music. Home: 8971 Antonette Hills Dr Saint Louis MO 63123-6503

ANTONACCIO, MARIO AMERICO, retired manufacturing executive; b. Harrison, N.J., Nov. 21, 1930; s. Antonio and Carmella (Comparelli) A.; m. Sonja Brunvatne, Apr. 24, 1954; 1 child, Carol. BSBA, Fairleigh Dickinson U., 1962. Billing clk. Worthington Pump Corp., Harrison, 1948-51, asst. supr., 1952-62, surp. payables, 1962-70; controller Worthington Div. Taneyton (Md.) Operation, 1970-74, mgr. fin., 1974-80, mgr. ops., 1980-81; gen. mgr. Worthington-Weir Joint Venture and Taneytown Operation, 1981-90; retired, 1991. Sgt. USAF, 1950-52. Mem. Am. Assn. Retired Persons, Am. Legion, U.S. Hist. Soc., Nat. Geographic Soc., DAV Commdrs. Club, The Statue of Liberty Ellis Island Found. Inc. (charter), Smithsonain Inst. Roman Catholic. Avocations: model trains, gardening, travel, reading, golf. Home: PO Box 544 RD # 6 Hanover PA 17331-0544

ANTONAKOS, STEPHEN, sculptor; b. So., Greece, Nov. 1, 1926; came to U.S., 1930; Ed., Bklyn. Community Coll. Lectr. Yale, New Haven, 1968; sculptor, working primarily in neon, vis. artist; artist-in-residence (U. Wis.), Madison, 1971, U. Calif.-Fresno, 1972. One-man shows U. Maine, 1958, Avant-Garde Gallery, N.Y., 1958, Miami Mus. Modern Art, 1964, Schramm Gallery, Ft. Lauderdale, 1964, Byron Gallery, N.Y.C., 1964, Fischbach Gallery, N.Y.C., 1967, 68, 69, 70, 72, John Weber Gallery, N.Y.C., 1974, 75, 76, 77, Ft. Worth Art Mus., 1970, 74-75, Contemporary Art Mus., Houston, 1971, SUNY, Albany, 1973, Bernier Gallery, 1977, Young Hoffman Gallery, Chgo., 1978, U. Mass., 1978, Bernier Gallery, 1977, Gillespie/de Laage Gallery, Paris, 1979, Albright-Knox Art Gallery, Buffalo, 1975, Wright State U., Dayton, Ohio, 1975, Galleria Marilena Bonomo, Bari, Italy, 1975, Galerie 26, Paris, 1975, Galleriaforma, Genoa, Italy, 1975, Galerie December, Dusseldorf, Germany, 1976, Art & Project, Amsterdam, 1976, Galerie Bonnier, Geneva, 1976, Nancy Lurie Gallery, Chgo., 1976, Galerie Aronowitsch, Stockholm, 1977, Galerie Tanit, Munich, 1978, 80, Lowe Art Mus., Miami, Fla., 1980, Nassau County Mus. Fine Art, Roslyn, N.Y., 1982, Maison de Culture de Nevers (France), 1983, Le Coin du Miroir, Dijon, France, 1983, Bonnier Gallery, N.Y.C., 1983, Jean Bernier Gallery, Athens, 1983, La Jolla (Calif.) Mus. Contemporary Art, 1984, Davenport (Iowa) Art Gallery, 1985, Ileana Tounta Contemporary Art Ctr., Athens, Greece, 1988, Rose Art Mus., Brandeis U., 1986, Elvehjem Mus. Art U. Wis., Madison, 1986, Burnett Miller Gallery, L.A., G.H. Dalsheimer Gallery, Balt., 1987, Kouros Gallery, N.Y.C., 1989, Galerie d'Art Contemporain, Geneva, 1990, Ileana Tounta Gallery, Athens, Greece, 1992, Carpenter Ctr., Harvard U., 1992-93, Rhodes (Greece) Contemp. Art Space, 1993, Mus. Contemporary Art, Salonika, 1993, Malibu (Calif.) Internat. Sculpt. Exhibition, 1993, Macedonian Mus. Modern Art, Salonika, Greece, 1993, The New Fort, Corfu, Greece, 1995, The Art Inst. Boston, 1996, Smith Coll. Mus. Art, Northampton, Mass., 1997, The Harn Mus., Gainesville, Fla., 1997, Stux Gallery, Athens Greece, 1997, Lucas Gallery Princeton U., 1998, Mitchell Algus Gallery, 1998, Gallery Camino Real, Boca Raton, Fla., 1999, St. Peter's Ch., 1999, Pub. Sch. 1, Long Island City, N.Y., 1999, others; exhibited in group shows Miami Mus. Modern Art, 1958, Martha Jackson Gallery, N.Y., 1960, Allan Stone Gallery, 1961, 62, 64, Byron Gallery, 1963, 64, PVI Gallery, N.Y., 1964, 65, Whitney Mus. Am. Art, 1966, 68, 69, 73, Newark Coll. Engring., 1968, U. N.C., 1968, R.I. Sch. Design, 1969, Worcester Art Mus., 1965, Nelson Gallery of Art, Kansas City, Mo., 1966, 68, Stedelijk von Abbemuseum, Eindhoven, 1966, Walker Art Ctr., Mpls., 1967, L.A. County Mus., 1987, N.J. State Mus. Cultural Ctr., 1967, Carnegie Internat. Mus., Pitts., 1967, Wadsworth Atheneum, Hartford, Conn., 1968, Fort Worth Art Mus., 1969, Smithsonian Instn., 1970, Portland Mus., Maine, 1971, Anne-Marie Verna Gallery, Zurich, 1972, San Francisco Mus. Art, 1973, Indpls. Mus. Art, 1974, Stadtischen Mus., Leverkusen, Federal Republic of Germany, 1975, MIT, Arts on the Line, 1980, Aldrich Mus., Ridgefield, Conn., 1979, 84, Corcoran Gallery of Art, Washington, 1987, Am. Craft Mus., N.Y.C., 1988, UCLA Art Gallery, 1969, U. Nebr., Lincoln, 1969, 70, Documenta 6, Kassel, W.Ger., 1977, Galerie Nancy Gillespie/Elisabeth de Laage, Paris, 1979, Wellesley (Mass.) Coll. Mus., 11th Internat. Sculpture Conf., Washington, 1980, Creative Time Inc., N.Y.C., Mus. Mod. Art, N.Y.C., 1981, Europalia, Brussels, 1982, Mus. Mod. Art of the City of Paris, 1983, 24th Annual Print Exbn. Bklyn. Mus., 1986, Sao Paulo Internat. Biennale, Brazil, 1987, Rose Art Mus. Brandeis U., 1987, archtl. show Montreal, 1988, Boston Atheneum, 1988, Ileana Tounta Contemporary Arts Ctr., Athens, Greece, 1988, Artec, Nagoya, Japan, 1989, Fawbush Gallery, N.Y.C., 1990, Nat. Gallery, Athens, 1992, Harn Mus. Art, Gainesville, Fla., 1998, Chrysler Mus. Art., Norfolk, 1999; represented in permanent collections Fed. Bldg., Dayton, Ohio, Hampshire Coll., Amherst, Mass., U. Mass., Amherst, Atlanta Internat. Airport, Whitney Mus. Am. Art, Mus. Modern Art, N.Y.C., Wadsworth Atheneum, Hartford, Conn., Phoenix Art Mus., Weatherspoon Art Gallery, U. N.C., Greensboro, Newark Mus., Milw. Art Center, Guggenheim Mus., La Jolla Mus. Contemporary Art; pub. commns. include Fed. Bldg., Dayton, Ohio, U. Mass., Amherst, Harstfield Internat. Airport, Atlanta, The Atheneum, U. Dijon, France, 14th Dist. Police Sta., Chgo., Hampshire Coll., U. Mass., 42d St, N.Y.C., Bagley Wright Theatre, Seattle, Tacoma (Wash.) Dome, La Jolla Mus. Contemporary Art, Rose Art Mus., Columbus (Ohio) Mus. Arts, Greektown Sta., Detroit, 59th St. Marine Transfer Sta., N.Y., 7475 Wis. Ave., Bethesda, Md., Back Bay/South Sta., Boston, Exch. Pl. Sta., Jersey City, 5th/Hill Sta. L.A., Lawrence St., Denver, Southwestern Bell, Dallas, Davenport (Iowa) Transit Ctr., Charles St. Sta., Balt., South Campus Sta., Buffalo, York Coll., Jamaica, N.Y., Embassy Stes., San Diego, Neon for the 59th St. Marine Transfer Station, N.Y., 1990, Neons for Buttonwood, Phila., 1990, Neons and Drawings Galerie d'Art Contemporain, Geneva, 1990, Neons for Momoci, Fukuoka, Japan, 1992, Neons for Messe Turm Frankfurt, Ger., 1993, Neons for the Stadtsparkasse, Cologne, 1993, Neons for Tachikawa, Tokyo, 1994, San Antonio Pub. Libr., 1995, Neons for Providence Convention Ctr., 1995, Neon for Granpark, Tokyo, 1996, Neon for William Paterson Coll., Wayne, N.J., 1995, Neuberger Gallery SUNY, Purchase, 1997, Neons Reading Power Plant, Tel Aviv, 1998—, Hot Glass, Flat Glass & Neon, Chrysler Mus., Norfolk, Va., 1999, Blue Cross: Meditation Chapel, Courthouse Gallery, Portsmouth, Va., 1999. Recipient award Nat. Endowment for Arts, 1973, N.Y. Creative Artists Pub. Service Program. Home and Studio: 435 W Broadway New York NY 10012-5902

ANTONE, NAHIL PETER, lawyer, civil engineer; b. Baghdad, Iraq, Jan. 17, 1952; came to U.S., 1978; s. Peter and Salima (Kammoo) A. BS in Civil Engring. with highest distinction, U. Baghdad, 1971; MS in Structural Engring., U. Surrey, 1974; JD summa cum laude, Detroit Coll. Law, 1985. Bar: Mich. 1985, U.S. Dist. Ct. (ea. dist.) Mich. 1985; registered profl. engr., Mich. Constrn. engr. Ministry Constrn., Baghdad, 1971-73; project mgr. Ministry Oil, Baghdad, 1974-78; design engr. Harley Ellington Pierce Yee, Southfield, Mich., 1978-79; v.p. Hennessey Engring. Co., Trenton, Mich., 1979-85; assoc. Bodman, Longley & Dahling, Detroit, 1985-88; owner N. Peter Antone Profl. Corp., Southfield, 1988—; ptnr. Antone & Kuhn Law Offices, Farmington Hills, Mich., 1989-93; pvt. practice Southfield, 1993—; lectr. Detroit Coll. Law, 1986-87. Govt. of Iraq scholar, 1974; scholar Det. Coll. Law, 1982. Mem. ABA, Detroit Bar Assn., ASCE (chmn. legis. com. Southeast Mich. chpt. 1981). Avocations: tennis, swimming, exercise, travel, music. Home: 28935 Murray Crescent Dr Southfield MI 48076-5563 Office: 16445 W 12 Mile Rd Southfield MI 48076-2949

ANTONECCHIA, DONALD A., principal. Prin. Pleasantville (N.Y.) High Sch., 1984-95; supt. Free Sch. Dist., Pleasantville, 1995—. Recipient Blue Ribbon Sch. award U.S. Dept. Edn., 1990-91. Office: Pleasantville High Sch Romer Ave Pleasantville NY 10570*

ANTONELLI, ANGELA MARIA, policy analyst; b. Aug. 4, 1963. BA, Cornell U., 1985; MPA, Princeton U., 1988. Asst. br. chief White House Office of Mgmt. and Budget, 1989-93; cons. Lewin-VHI, Inc., Vienna, Va., 1993-95; dir. Roe Inst. for Econ. Policy Studies Heritage Found., 1995—. E-mail: angela.antonelli@heritage.org. Office: 214 Massachusetts Ave NE Washington DC 20002

ANTONELLIS, PATRICIA ANNETTE, community health nurse; b. Jersey City, Feb. 3, 1939; d. Victor R. and Anne Marie (Davis) Fiore; children: Kevin, Christopher, Susan. Diploma, Jersey City Med. Ctr. Sch. Nursing, 1959; BSN, St. Peter's Coll., 1992. RN, N.J. Staff nurse, asst. head nurse surg. ICU Hackensach (N.J.) Med. Ctr., 1960-67; staff nurse Valley Nursing Home, Westwood, N.J., 1970-72; with surg. ICU Bergen Pines County Hosp., Paramus, N.J., 1975-79; discharge planner, home care intake coord. Community Health Care of No. Jersey, Orange, N.J., 1979-90; nursing supr. Patient Care Med. Svcs., Inc., West Orange, N.J., 1990-92; home care coord. Valley Home and Cmty. Health Care, Ridgewood, N.J., 1992—. Van Houten scholar, 1990, 91, Patricia Milewski Meml. scholar, 1990. Mem. ANA, N.J. Nurse's Assn., Sigma Theta Tau.

ANTONIC, JAMES PAUL, international marketing consultant; b. Milw., Mar. 29, 1943; s. George Paul and Betti Ware (Littler) A.; m. Irene Robson, Dec. 26, 1970; 1 child, Glenn. BS in Psychology, U. Wis., 1964; MBA, Boston U., 1976. Owner JPA Supply and Warehouse Co., Milw., 1966-68; product mgr., market mgr. Delta Oil Products, Milw., 1968-74; v.p. internat. ops. Delta Oil Products, Brussels, 1974-76; pres. Internat. Market Devel. Group, Barrington, Ill., 1976-98; CEO Internat. Market Devel. Group, LLC, Ft. Myers, Fla., 1998—; bd. dirs. ASG LLC, Schaumburg, Ill.; lectr. Cast Metals Inst., Am. Mgmt. Assn., U.S. Dept. Commerce, Ga. World Congress Inst., various colls. Contbr. articles to profl. jours. With U.S. Army Combat Engrs., 1964-66. Fellow Anglo-Am. Acad.; mem. Licensing Execs. Soc., Internat. Trade Club Chgo., MIT Enterprise Forum, World Trade Assn., Japan Mgmt. Cons. Assn., Am. Foundrymen's Assn. (chair legis. task force), Oak Brook Hounds (pres.). E-mail: jamesantonic@msn.com. Fax: 941-590-6061. Home: 9111 Southmont Cove # 406 Fort Myers FL 33908-6298 Office: 16481 Millstone Cir #201 Fort Myers FL 33908

ANTONIO, DOUGLAS JOHN, lawyer; b. N.Y.C., Sept. 14, 1955; s. John and Joan (Deitz) A.; m. Sarah Kathrine Nadelhoffer, Aug. 31, 1986; children: Zachary Douglas, Sophia Marie. BS, BA, U. Md., 1977, JD, 1980, MBA, 1981; LLM in Taxation, Georgetown U., 1983. Bar: Md. 1980, D.C. 1981, Mo. 1983, U.S. Ct. Claims 1983, Ill. 1984. Atty.-advisor U.S. Labor Dept., 1980-83; atty. Thompson & Mitchell, St. Louis, 1983-84; assoc. Blumenfeld, Sandweiss, Marx, Tureen, Ponfil & Kaskowitz, St. Louis, 1984-86; assoc. Sugar, Friedberg and Felsenthal, Chgo., 1986-87, ptnr., 1988-95; owner Antonio and Assocs., Chgo., 1995-98; ptnr. Holleb & Coff, Chgo., 1998—; adj. prof. law John Marshall Sch. Law, Chgo. Contbr. articles to profl. jours. Mem. Chgo. Bar Assn. (chair fed. taxation com. 1999—). Home: 1316 N Sutton Pl Chicago IL 60610-2008 Office: Holleb & Coff 55 E Monroe St Ste 4100 Chicago IL 60603

ANTONIOTTI, STEVE, broadcast executive; b. Davenport, Iowa; m. Alice Antoniotti; children: Justin, Christopher, Nicholas, Steven. B in Journalism, U. Mich., M in Journalism. News prodr. WDIV-TV (formerly WWJ-TV) Channel 4, Detroit, WUBK; exec. news prodr. WXYZ-TV, Channel 7, Detroit; news dir. KNBC-TV, L.A., KSDK-TV, St. Louis; sta. mgr. WJBK-TV2, Detroit, v.p. broadcasting ops., pres., gen., 1989-95; pres., gen. mgr. WTVS Channel 56/Detroit Pub. TV, 1995—. Avocation: tennis. Office: WTVS-Detroit Pub TV 7441 2nd Ave Detroit MI 48202-2701*

ANTONIOU, ANDREAS, electrical engineering educator; b. Yerolakkos, Nicosia, Cyprus, Mar. 3, 1938; immigrated to Can., 1969; s. Antonios and Eleni (Costi Coufou) Hadgisavva; m. Rosemary C. Kennedy, Mar. 7, 1964 (dec.); children: Anthony, David, Constantine, Helen. BSc with honors, U. London, 1963, PhD, 1966. Mem. sci staff GEC Ltd., London, 1966; sr. sci. officer P.O. Rsch. Dept., London, 1966-69; mem. sci. staff in R & D No. Electric Co., Ottawa, Ont., Can., 1969-70; successively asst. prof. elec. engring., assoc. prof., prof., dept. chmn. Concordia U., Montreal, Que., Can., 1970-83; prof. U. Victoria, B.C., Can., 1983—, founding chmn. elec. and computer engring. dept., 1983-90. Author: Digital Filters: Analysis, Design, and Applications, 1979, 2d edit., 1993; co-author: Two-Dimensional Digital Filters, 1992; contbr. articles to profl. jours. Fellow IEEE (assoc. editor Trans. on Cirs. and Sys. jour. 1983-85, editor 1985-87, mem. bd. govs. Cirs. and Sys. Soc.), Instn. Elec. Engrs. (Ambrose Fleming premium 1969); mem. Assn. Profl. Engrs. and Geoscientists B.C. (councilor 1988-90). Greek Orthodox. Fax: 250-721-6052. E-mail: andreas@ece.uciv.ca. Home: 4058 Jason Pl, Victoria, BC Canada V8N 4T6 Office: U Victoria Dep Elec Engring, PO Box 3055, Victoria, BC Canada V8W 3P6

ANTONOFF, STEVEN ROSS, educational consultant, author; b. Waukon, Iowa, Dec. 14, 1945; s. Ben H. and Florence R. A. BS, Colo. State U., 1967; MA, U. Denver, 1970, PhD, 1979. Spl. asst. to dean U. Denver, 1970-71, dean student life, 1971-74, dean Ctr. for Prospective Students, 1974-75, exec. dir. admissions and student affairs, 1975-78, dean admissions and fin. aid, 1978-81, adj. prof. speech communication, 1979-88; dir., now pres. Antonoff Assocs., Inc.; active Secondary Sch. Admission Testing Bd., Princeton, N.J. Author: College Match, The Coll. Finder; contbr. chpts. and articles to profl. jours. Chmn. Mayor's Commn. on Arts, Denver, 1979-81; trustee Congregation Emanuel, 1977-82; chmn. bd. dirs. Hospice of Met. Denver, 1970-84; mem. Denver Commn. on Cultural Affairs, 1984-86; mem. scholarship com. Mile High Cablevision, 1982-90; chmn. Cultural Affairs Task Force, City of Denver, 1988-89. Recipient Clara Barton award for meritorious vol. leadership ARC, 1992. Mem. ACA, Rocky Mountain Assn. Coll. Admissions Counselors, Am. Ednl. Rsch. Assn., New Eng. Assn. Coll. Admission Officers, Nat. Assn. Coll. Admissions Counselors, Ind. Ednl. Cons. Assn. (chmn. bd. 1992-94, chair nat. cert. commn. 1993—), Attention Deficit Disorder Advocacy Group, Rotary Internat., Zeta Beta Tau (found. bd. dirs. 1993-96). Office: 501 S Cherry St Ste 490 Denver CO 80246-1327

ANTONOVICH, MICHAEL D., city manager; b. L.A.. BA, Calif. State U., L.A., 1963, MA, 1967; grad., Pasadena Police Acad., 1967; postgrad., Harvard U., 1984, 87, Stanford U., 1968-70. Govt. and history instr. L.A. Unified Sch. Dist., 1966-72; Republican whip Calif. State Assembly, 1976-78, assemblyman, 1972-78; mem. bd. suprs. 5th Dist. L.A. County, 1983, 87, 91, 96—; instr. Calif. State U., 1979, 85, Pepperdine U., 1979. Trustee L.A. C.C., 1969-73; mem. Tournament of Roses Com., Glendale Symphony, L.A. Zoo. Assn., South Pasadena Police Dept. Res., Good Shepherd Luth. Home for Retarded Children; mem. Met. Transp. Authority, 1993—, chmn., 1994-95; mem. L.A. Conty Traps. Commn., 1980-93, chmn., 1984, 92; mem. L.A. Coliseum Commn., South Coast Air Quality Mgmt. Dist.; presdl. appointee U.S. Del. to UN Internat. Conf. on Indo-Chinese Refugees, Geneva, 1989, Com. on Privatization, 1987-88, U.S.-Japan Adv. Com., 1984, J. Fulbright Fgn. Scholarship Bd., 1991-93; mem. adv. bd. Atty. Gen.'s Missing Children, 1987-88. Recipient Pub. Ofcl. Yr., Nat. Fedn. Indian-Ams., 1989, Outstanding and Invaluable Svc. award Home Visitation Ctr., 1990, Brother's Keeper award Chaplain's Eagles, 1990, Responsible Citizen award Thomas Jefferson Rsch. Ctr., 1990, Outstanding Citizen award Internat. Footprint Assn., 1991, Recognition award Salvation Army, Leadership awards United Way, 1987, 91, 93, Hon. Svc. award PTA, 1991, San Fernando Valley Outstanding Leadership award Min.'s Fellowship and Focus 90s, 1991, Mental Health Assn. award of appreciation Antelope Valley Social Ctr., 1991, Recognition award MADD, 1992, Appreciation award Soc. Hispanic Profl. Engrs., L.A. chpt., 1992, awards Boy Scouts Am., 1992, 93, Recognition award Mex. Am. Correctional Assn., 1996. Mem. County Suprs. Assn. Calif. (bd. dirs.), Phila. Soc., Glendale C. of C., Elks, Sigma Nu. Lutheran. Office: 5th Dist LA County 869 Hall of Adminstrn 500 W Temple St Los Angeles CA 90012-2713*

ANTONS, PAULINE MARIE, mathematics educator; b. Monticello, Iowa, Jan. 15, 1926; d. Henry and Eliza (Zimmerman) Tobiason; m. Richard William Antons, Aug. 13, 1950; children: Sharon Kay, Karen Lyn. BS, U. Dubuque, 1948. Cert. secondary tchr., Iowa. Tchr. math. Elkader (Iowa) Community Sch., 1948-50, Onslow (Iowa) Ind. Schs., 1950-60, Midland Community, Wyoming, 1960-90, Kirkwood Coll., Cedar Rapids, Iowa, 1982-90; mem. scholarship adv. bd. Jones County Health Assn., Anamosa, Iowa, 1983—. Mem. adv. bd. Evang. Luth. Ch. Women; v.p. Limestone Bluffs Resource Conservation and devel.; co-treas. Jones County Soil & Water Commn., 1992-97 (Region 4 Commn. award 1997); del. Iowa League. Recipient Pres. award for excellence, 1988, Friends of Math. award Iowa Tchrs. of Math., 1992, Jones County Conservation Outstanding Tchr. award, 1988, 93; Pres.'s scholar U. Dubuque, 1945-48, NSF scholar Drake U., 1967, Clarke Coll., 1968, U. Iowa, 1969. Mem. Delta Kappa Gamma (treas. Beta Nu chpt.). Lutheran. Avocations: gardening, reading, travel. Home and Office: 13481 105th Ave Center Junction IA 52212-7502

ANTONSEN, ELMER HAROLD, Germanic languages and literature educator; b. Glens Falls, N.Y., Nov. 17, 1929; s. Haakon and Astrid Caroline Emilie (Sommer) A.; m. Hannelore Gertrude Adam, Mar. 24, 1956; children: Ingrid Carol, Christopher Walter. B.A., Union Coll., Schenectady, N.Y., 1951; postgrad., U. Vienna, 1951-52, U. Goettingen, 1956; M.A., U. Ill., 1957, Ph.D., 1961. Instr. German, Northwestern U., Evanston, Ill., 1959-61; asst. prof. U. Iowa, Iowa City, 1961-64, assoc. prof., 1964-67; assoc. prof. U. Ill., Urbana, 1967-70, prof. Germanic langs. and linguistics, 1970—, head dept. Germanic langs., 1973-82, head dept. linguistics, 1990-96, assoc. Ctr. for Advanced Studies, 1984; vis. prof. U. N.C., Chapel Hill, 1972-73, U. Goettingen, 1988. Author: A Concise Grammar of the Older Runic Inscriptions, 1975; editor: The Grimm Brothers and the Germanic Past, 1989, Studies in the Linguistic Sciences, 1995—; co-editor: Staefcraeft: Studies in Germanic Linguistics, 1991; contbr. articles to profl. jours. Served with AUS, 1953-56. Fulbright scholar, 1951-52. Mem. Linguistic Soc. Am., Royal Norwegian Soc. Scis. and Letters, Soc. Advancement of Scandinavian Study, Institut für Deutsche Sprache (corr. mem.), Selskab for nordisk filologi, Soc. for Germanic Philology, Archeol. Inst. Am., Phi Beta Kappa. Home: 2210 Plymouth Dr Champaign IL 61821-6542 Office: Univ Ill 4088 Flb Urbana IL 61801

ANTONUCCI, RON, librarian, editor; b. Akron, Ohio, Apr. 16, 1951; s. Dominic and Louisa (Conti) A.; m. Katherine Jean Lambert, Oct. 18, 1974 (div. Dec. 1991); four children. BS in Journalism, Ohio U., 1973; MLS, Kent State U., 1998. Owner, operator The Old Book Store, Akron, 1978-85; editor, reporter Maple Heights (Ohio) Press, 1985-89; mng. editor City Express Publs., Bklyn., 1989-90; cataloguer, bibliographer Strand Bookstore, N.Y.C., 1990-91; libr. Hudson (Ohio) Library & Hist. Soc., 1991—. Editor Ohio Writer Mag., 1996—. Mem. poetry coun. Cleve. State U., Writers Ctr. of Greater Cleve. Mem. Am. Libr. Assn., Poets League Greater Cleve. Home: PO Box 2115 Hudson OH 44236-0115

ANTONUCCIO, JOSEPH ALBERT, hospitality industry executive; b. San Pier Niceto, Sicily, Italy, Apr. 25, 1932; came to U.S., 1935, naturalized, 1941; s. Joseph and Nancy (Calogero) A.; m. Patricia B. Damon, June 1, 1957 (div. 1987); children—Joseph Russell, Louise Shaffer, Timothy Damon. A.B., Rutgers U., 1954. Vice pres. Deluxe Reading Corp., Elizabeth, N.J., 1962-67; ptnr. Peat, Marwick, Mitchell & Co., N.Y.C., 1967-88; exec. v.p. Lex Electronics Inc., Westbury, N.Y., 1988-90; v.p. Princess Hotels Internat., N.Y.C., 1990—. Contbr. aticles on computers to profl. jours. Vice pres., bd. dirs. Sutton-Area Community, Inc., N.Y.C., 1983—; mem. N.Y.C. Bd. Elections task force N.Y.C. Partnership, Inc., 1985. Served to sgt. U.S. Army, 1954-56. Mem. Data Processing Mgmt. Assn. (bd. dirs. 1962-67), Computer Security Inst. (lectr. 1979—), Assn. Systems Mgmt. (project chmn. 1972-79). Club: University (N.Y.C.). Avocations: hiking; skiing. Home: 405 E 56th St New York NY 10022-2412 Office: Princess Hotels Internat 805 3rd Ave New York NY 10022-7513

ANTONY, AJIT IVAN, urologist; b. May 1, 1945. B Medicine B Surgery, Seth Gordhandas Sunderas Med., Bombay, 1967; M Surgery, King Edward IV Meml. Hosp., Bombay, 1972. Resident in urology Beth Israel Med. Ctr., N.Y.C., 1973-77; physician Hudson Valley Urology Assoc., New Windsor, N.Y., 1977—. Mem. Am. Urol. Assn., Orange County Med. Soc., Med. Soc. State of N.Y. Office: Hudson Valley Urology Assoc PC 3074 Rte 9W Ste 100 New Windsor NY 12553

ANTOSZ, CANDACE ELIZABETH, health promotion educator; b. Billings, Mont., Nov. 11, 1946; d. Henry Joseph and Pamela Margaret (Sciacca) A. BS in Phys. Edn., Ithaca Coll., 1968; MA in Health Edn., NYU, 1970; MPH in Health Promotion, San Diego State U., 1984. Health edn. specialist Montgomery County Pub. Schs., Rockville, Md., 1970-71, White Plains (N.Y.) Pub. Schs., 1971-73; health promotion professional Milford (Conn.) Pub. Sch., 1973—; chair women and health care Women's Studies Conf. So. Conn. State U., 1991, 93. Author: (with others) School Intervention Report, 1991. Fund raiser Am. Cancer Soc., Milford, 1977-79; chmn. publicity Coalition Violence Against Women, New Haven, 1985. Recipient Merit cert. Am. Cancer Soc., 1979, Cardiovascular Fitness award Conn. Assn. Health Phys. Edn. Recreation and Dance, 1996, Outstanding Fitness Program award Am. Acad. Pediats. Sports Medicine Com., Conn. chpt., 1996-97; named Coach of Yr. CCIAC, 1980. Mem. AAHPERD, APHA. Avocations: masters swimming, tennis, golf, cross country skiing, hiking. Home: 19 School St Stony Creek Branford CT 06405 Office: Milford Pub Schs Parsons Complex Milford CT 06460

ANTREASIAN, GARO ZAREH, artist, lithographer, art educator; b. Indpls., Feb. 16, 1922; s. Zareh Minas and Takouhie (Daniell) A.; m. Jeanne Glascock, May 2, 1947; children: David Garo, Thomas Berj. BFA, Herron Sch. Art, 1948; DFA (hon.), Ind. U.-Purdue U. at Indpls., 1972. Instr. Herron Sch. Art, 1948-64; tech. dir. Tamarind Lithography Workshop, Los Angeles, 1960-61; prof. art U. N.Mex., 1964-87, chmn. dept. art, 1981-84; tech. dir. Tamarind Inst., U. N.Mex., 1970-72; vis. lectr., artist numerous univs.; Bd. dirs. Albuquerque Mus., 1980-90; printmaker emeritus Southern Graphics Coun., 1994. Prin. author: The Tamarind Book of Lithography: Art and Techniques, 1970; one-man shows include Malvina Miller Gallery, San Francisco, 1971, Marjorie Kauffman Gallery, Houston, 1975-79, 84, 86, U. Colo., Boulder, 1972, Calif. Coll. Arts & Crafts, Oakland, 1973, Miami U., Oxford, Ohio, 1973, Kans. State U., 1973, Atlanta Coll. Art, 1974, U. Ga., Athens, 1974, Alice Simsar Gallery, Ann Arbor, 1977-79, Elaine Horwich Gallery, Santa Fe, 1977-79, Mus. of N.Mex., Santa Fe, 1979, Robischon Gallery, Denver, 1984, 86, 90, Moss-Chumley Gallery, Dallas, 1987, Rettig-Martinez Gallery, Santa Fe, 1988, 91, 92, U. N.Mex. Art Mus., 1988, Albuquerque Mus., 1988, Louis Newman Gallery, L.A., 1989, Expositum Gallery, Mexico City, 1989, State U. Coll., Cortland, N.Y., 1991, Mus. Art, U. Ariz., Tucson, 1991, Indpls. Mus. Art, 1994, Ruschmon Gallery, Indpls., 1994, Mitchell Mus. Art, Vernon, Ill., 1995, Cline-Lewallen Gallery, Santa Fe, 1997, Anderson Gallery, Albuquerque, 1997, Feenix Gallery, Taos, NM State U., Las Crucis, 1998; exhibited group shows Phila. Print Club, 1960-63, Ind. Artists, 1947-63, White House, 1966, Nat. Lithographic Exhbn. Fla. State U., 1965, Library Congress, 1961-66, Bklyn. Mus., 1958-68, 76, U.S. Pavilion Venice Biennale, 1970, Internat. Biennial, Bradford, Eng., 1972-74, Internat. Biennial, Tokyo, 1972, City Mus. Hong Kong, 1972, Tamarind UCLA, 1985, Roswell Mus., 1989, Pace Gallery, 1990, Worcester (Mass.) Art Mus., 1990, Amon Carter Mus., Ft. Worth, 1990, Albuquerque Mus., 1991, 92, Art Mus. U. N.Mex., 1991, 92; represented in permanent collections: Bklyn. Mus., Guggenheim Mus., N.Y.C., Cin. Mus., Chgo. Art Inst., Ind. State Mus., Mus. Modern Art, N.Y.C., Library of Congress, Met. Mus., N.Y.C., N.Y. Pub. Libr., Mus. Fine Arts, Santa Fe, also, Albuquerque, Boston, Indpls., Seattle, Phila., San Diego, Dallas, N.Mex., Worcester Art Museums, Los Angeles County Mus., Roswell Mus. and Art Ctr., Tucson Mus., murals, Ind. U., Butler U., Ind. State Office Bldg. Fulbright vis. lectr. U. São Paulo and Found. Armando Alvares Penteado, Brazil, 1985. Combat artist with USCGR, World War II, PTO. Recipient Distinguished Alumni award Herron Sch. Art, 1972, N.Mex. Annual Gov.'s award, 1987; Grantee Nat. Endowment for Arts, 1983. Fellow NAD; mem. World Print Coun. (bd. dirs. 1980-87), Nat. Print Coun. Am. (co-pres. 1980-82), Coll. Art Assn. Am. (bd. dirs. 1977-80). Home: 11104 Academy Ridge NE Albuquerque NM 87111

ANTRIM, MINNIE FAYE, residential care facility administrator; b. Rochester, Tex., June 30, 1916; d. Charles C. Montandon and Myrtle Caldona (Brown) Montandon Taylor; m. Cecil C. Antrim, Jan. 1, 1938; children—Linda Faye Antrim Hathway, Cecil C. Student Central State Tchrs. Coll., Edmond, Okla., 1937. Asst. purchasing agt. Scenic Gen. Hosp., Modesto, Calif., 1955-68, Health Dept., Probation Dept., Stanislaus, Calif., 1955-68; owner, adminstr. Sierra Villa Retirement Home, Fresno, Calif., 1968-77, Mansion Home, Fresno, 1977—. Mem. Am. Coll. Health Care Adminstrs., Calif Bus. and Profl Club. Methodist. Club: Garden. Avocation: glee clubs. Home: 6070 E Townsend Ave Fresno CA 93727-5617

ANTRY, RONALD VIRGEL, county official; b. New Bern, Oct. 3, 1951; s. Virgel Earnest and Marie Margaret (Smith) A.; m. Judith Lynn Holzman, Oct. 8, 1990; 1 child, Christopher Holzman. AA, Craven C.C., 1976. Assessor Craven County, New Bern, N.C., 1981-87, tax adminstr., 1987—. Mem. N.C. Assn. Assessing Officers (cert., pres. 1993-94), N.C. Property Mappers Assn. (pres. 1991-92). Democrat. Baptist. Home: 5208 Trent Woods Dr New Bern NC 28562-7442 Office: Craven County Tax Admistr PO Box 1128 New Bern NC 28563-1128

ANTUNES, DANIEL L., sales consultant, camera operator; b. Portugal, June 24, 1971; came to U.S., 1986; s. Jose A. and Judite C. Antunes. AA, Union County Coll., 1991; BA, N.J. City U., 1994. Cameraman RTP-USA TV, Newark, 1988-90, tech. dir. news, 1990-93; actor, editor NBP Prodns., Lisbon, 1993; cameraman, robotics CN8, Union, N.J., 1997—; sales rep. Bell Atlantic Mobile, Paramus, N.J., 1994—. Avocations: snow boarding, tennis, soccer, online stock trading, video productions. E-mail: dantunes@aol.com. Home: 9 Radley St Kearny NJ 07032

ANTUPIT, SAMUEL NATHANIEL, art director; b. West Hartford, Conn., Feb. 14, 1932; s. Louis and Sylvia (Feinberg) A.; m. Rosalie Jane Littman, Dec. 30, 1956; children: Lisa Ruth, Jennifer Carol, Stephen Michael, Peter Louis. Grad., Loomis Sch., 1950; BA in English, Yale U., 1954, BFA in Graphic Design, 1956. Asst. art dir. Harper's Bazaar mag., 1958-61, Show mag., 1961-63; asst. corp. art dir. Conde Nast Publs., 1963, Pushpin Studios, 1963-64; art. dir. Art in Am., 1963-64, N.Y. Rev. Books, 1963-81, Esquire mag., 1964-68, 77; pres. Hess and/or Antupit, designer, publs., and cons., 1968-70; lectr. pub. procedures course Harvard-Radcliffe Coll., 1965-80, Stanford U., 1984-90; propr. Cycling Frog Press, Pound Ridge, N.Y., 1961—, Antupit & Others Inc., 1971—, Subsistence Press, 1971-81; exec. art dir. Book of the Month Club, 1977-81; v.p., dir. art and design, mem. pub. com. Harry N. Abrams, Inc., N.Y.C., 1981-97; pres. CommonPlace Books, New Canaan, Conn., 1995—; trustee Hiram Halle Meml. Libr.; bd. dirs. Summit Pubs. Author: (with Terry Clifford) Cures, 1980. Served with AUS, 1956-58. Recipient Design awards Art Dirs. Club N.Y.C., 1960—, Type Dirs. Club N.Y.C., 1961—, Soc. Illustrators, 1961—, Art Dirs. Club Boston, Emmy award NATAS, 1974; Am. fellow Nat. Endowment Arts, 1989. Mem. Nat. Acad. Rec. Arts and Scis., Am. Inst. Graphic Arts (bd. dirs. 1968-72, v.p. 1970-72, 90-93, Design awards 1965—), Yale U. Arts Assn. (exec. com. 1972-76), Alliance Graphique Internat., Documents of Am. Design (bd. dirs. 1983—), Century Assn., Univ. Glee Club, Small Press Ctr. (bd. advisors 1999—). Office: 2 Morse Ct New Canaan CT 06840-5505

ANTZELEVITCH, CHARLES, research center executive; b. Israel, Mar. 25, 1951; came to U.S., 1959; s. Chaim and Frida (Hassman) A.; m. Brenda Reisner, June 24, 1973; children: Daniel Avi, Lisa Rachel. BA, Queens Coll., 1973; PhD, SUNY, Syracuse, 1977. Postdoctoral fellow Masonic Med. Rsch. Lab., Utica, N.Y., 1977-80, rsch. scientist, 1980-83, sr. rsch. scientist, 1984, exec. dir., dir. rsch., 1984—; asst. prof. SUNY Health Scis. Ctr. Pharmacology, Syracuse, N.Y., 1980-83, assoc. prof., 1983-86; prof. of Pharmacology SUNY Health Scis. Ctr., Syracuse, N.Y., 1987—. Mem. editl. bd. Jour. Cardiovasc. Electrophysiology, 1990, NASPETAPES, Jour. of Cardiovascular Pharmacology and Therapeutics; contbr. articles to profl. jours. Com. mem. N.Y. State Heart Assn., Syracuse, 1982-87; bd. dirs. Clin. Med. Network, Utica, 1987-94, Jewish Cmty. Ctr., Utica, 1987-92, Royal Arch Masons Med. Rsch. Found., 1989, Ctrl. N.Y. Heart Assn., 1989; v.p. Temple Beth El, Utica, v.p., 1993-95, pres., 1995-97, mem. com., 1991—; mem. instnl. rev. bd. Faxton Hosp., Utica, 1990—. Recipient Van Horne award Ctrl. N.Y. Heart Assn., 1981-84, numerous grants; Gordon K. Moe scholar chair in exptl. cardiology, Masonic Med. Rsch. Lab., 1987—, Disting. Svc. award RAM Med. Rsch. Found., 1994, Charles Henry Johnson medal Grand Lodge Free and Accepted Masons N.Y., 1996. Fellow Am. Coll. Cardiology; mem. AAAS, Am. Heart Assn. (chmn. peer rev. com. 1997—), N.Y. Acad. Scis., Internat. Soc. for Heart Rsch., Cardiac Electrophysiol. Soc., Internat. Cardiac Electrophysiology Soc. (sec.-treas. 1994-96, pres. 1996-98, sec.-treas. 1998—), N.Am. Soc. Pacing and Electrophysiology (bd. dirs. 1997—, chmn. sci. com. 1995—, mem. long range planning com. 1997—, nominations com. 1997—), Masons. Avocation: swimming. Office: Masonic Med Rsch Lab 2150 Bleecker St Utica NY 13501-1738

ANUSZKIEWICZ, RICHARD JOSEPH, artist; b. Erie, Pa., May 23, 1930; s. Adam Jacob and Victoria (Jankowski) A.; m. Sarah Feeney, Nov. 26, 1960; children: Adam John, Stephanie, Christine. B.F.A., Cleve. Inst. Art, 1953; M.F.A., Yale U., 1955; B.S. in Edn., Kent State U., 1956. One-man shows at, Butler Art Inst., Youngstown, Ohio, 1955, The Contempories, N.Y.C., 1960, 61, 63, Sidney Janis Gallery, N.Y.C., 1965-67, Dartmouth Coll., 1967, Cleve. Mus. Art, 1967, Kent State U., 1968, Andrew Crispo Gallery, N.Y.C., 1975, 77, La Jolla (Calif.) Mus. Contemporary Art, 1976, Univ. Art Mus., Berkeley, Calif., 1977, Columbus (Ohio) Gallery of Fine Arts, 1977, Charles Foley Gallery, Columbus, 1982, Graham Modern, N.Y.C., 1984, Heckscher Mus., Huntington, N.Y., 1984, Schweyer-Galdo Galleries, Pontiac, Mich., 1985, Tampa (Fla.) Mus., 1986, Richard Green Gallery, N.Y.C., 1987, Galleria Sagittaria, Pordenone, Italy, 1988, Charles Foley Gallery, Columbus, 1988, Galleie Civiche D'Arte Moderna, Ferrara, Italy, 1989, Newark Mus., 1990, Maruzen Co., Ltd., Tokyo, 1990, 91, Abante Fine Art, Portland, Oreg., 1992, Ctr. fro Arts, Vero Beach, Fla., 1993, others; exhibited in group shows at, Mus. Modern Art, 1960-61, 63, 65, U. Ill., 1961, NYU, 1961, Pa. Acad. Design, 1962, Whitney Mus. Am. Art, 1962, 63-64, 70, 71, Inst. Contemporary Arts, Boston, 1962, Columbus (Ohio) Gallery Fine Arts, 1962, City Art Mus., St. Louis, 1962, Munson-Williams-Proctor Inst., Utica, N.Y., 1962, Tweed Gallery U. Minn., 1962, Silvermine (Conn.) Guild Artists, 1962, 63, Atheneum Sch., Helsinki, Finland, 1962, Mus. Modern Art, Sarasota, Fla., 1962, J.B. Speed Art Mus., Louisville, 1962, Meml. Art Gallery, Rochester, N.Y., 1962, Allentown (Pa.) Art Mus., 1963, Krannert (Ill.) Art Mus., 1963, De Cordova Mus., Lincoln, Mass., 1963, Washington Gallery Modern Art, 1963, U. Mich. Mus. Art, 1964, Sidney Janis Gallery, N.Y.C., 1964, 65, Art Inst., Chgo., 1964, 71, Tate Gallery, London, 1964, Far Gallery, 1964, Carnegie Inst., Pitts., 1964,, Corcoran Gallery Art, Washington, 1965, Art Fair Cologne, Germany, 1967, Larry Aldrich Mus., Ridgefield, Conn., 1968, 71, Hopkins Center Art Galleries Dartmouth Coll., Hanover, N.H., 1969, Denver Art Mus., 1969, Va. Mus. Fine Arts, Richmond, 1970, Ind. State U., Terre Haute, 1970, Masur Modern Art, Monroe, La., 1970, Birmingham (Ala.) Mus., 1971, Whitney Mus. Am. Art, N.Y.C., 1972, Hirshhorn Mus. and Sculpture Garden, N.Y.C., 1974, Bklyn. Mus., 1977, Albright-Knox Gallery, Buffalo, 1979, Met. Mus. Art, N.Y.C., 1982, Museo de Arts Moderno, Ciudad Bolivar, Venezuela, 1984, Tel Aviv Mus., 1986, Paris-New York-Kent Gallery, Kent, Conn., 1987, Guggenheim Mus., N.Y.C., 1987-88, Marilyn Pearl Gallery, N.Y.C., 1988, James A. Michener Arts Ctr. Bucks County, Doylestown, Pa., 1988, Centre d'Art Contempora, Geneva, 1989, Provincaal Mus., Hasselt, Belgium, Ctr. d'Art en Sante Monica, Barcelona, Spain, 1989, Galleri Civiche D'Arte Moderna, 1989, Samuel P. Harn Mus. Art, Gainesville, Fla., 1990, 92, DeCordova Mus., Lincoln, Mass., 1991, Nat. Gallery Art, Washington, 1991, Cummer Gallery Art, Jacksonville, Fla., 1992, Harmon Meek Gallery, Naples, Fla., 1993, Nat. Acad. Design, Washington, 1993, N.J. State Mus., Trenton, 1994, others; represented in permanent collections, Mus. Modern Art, Whitney Mus. Am. Art, Cleve. Mus. Art, Corcoran Gallery Art, Allentown Art Mus., Albright-Knox Art Gallery, Butler Art Inst., Akron (Ohio) Art Inst., Yale Art Gallery, Chgo. Art Inst., Larry Aldrich Mus., Ridgefield, Conn., Fogg Art Mus. of Harvard U., Hirshhorn Mus. and Sculpture Garden, artist-in-residence, Dartmouth Coll., 1967, U. Wis., 1968, Cornell U., 1968, Kent State U., 1968; Contbr. articles to profl. jours. Home and Office: 76 Chestnut St Englewood NJ 07631-3045*

ANVARIPOUR, M. A., lawyer; b. Tehran, Iran, Jan. 23, 1935; came to U.S., 1957; s. Ahmed and Monir (Georgi) A.; m. Patricia Matson Lynch (div. 1971); 1 dau., Sandra M.; m. Guilda Eshtehardi, Mar. 31, 1978 (div. 1984); 1 son, Cyrus Ramsey; m. Tess Temel, May 15, 1995. LLB, U. Tehran, 1956; BS, U. San Francisco, 1959; student, U. Calif. Hastings Coll. Law, San Francisco, JD, 1973. Bar: Ill. 1973, Fed. cts. Asst. field dir. Am. Friends of Middle East, Inc., Iran, 1962-64; field dir. Am. Friends of Middle East, Inc., 1964-66; asst. dean students, dean internat. students and faculty affairs Ill. Inst. Tech., Chgo., 1966-81; practiced in Chgo., 1973—, in San Francisco, 1985—; ednl. and legal advisor Consulate Gen. Iran, Chgo., 1973-79; aux. lawyer NAACP, Chgo., 1973-74; lectr. immigration and law seminar Ill. Inst. Tech.-Chgo.-Kent Coll. Law Sch., 1974. Mem. Am., Iran-Am. (sec.-gen. 1964-66), Chgo. Bar Assn. (chmn. immigration com. 1982-83), Iran Am. Alumni Assn. (sec. 1964-66), Nat. Assn. Fgn. Student Affairs (Ill. chmn. 1968-69), U. Tehran, U. San Francisco, Idaho State U. (hon.), Ill. Inst. Tech., Chgo.-Kent Coll. Law alumni assns., Am. Immigration Lawyers Assn. (sec.-treas. Chgo. chpt. 1976-78, v.p. 1978-80, pres. 1980-81), Phi Delta Phi. Club: Armour Faculty (pres. 1977-78). Home: 839 N Dearborn

St Chicago IL 60610-3373 Office: 180 N La Salle St Chicago IL 60601-2501 *My biases have made my life extremely rewarding. I have several. I have a strong bias against intolerance. I have a deep-seated bias against hate and bigotry, a bias against war, a bias for peace, and a bias which guides me to have faith in the basic goodness of my fellow human beings.*

ANWAR, GABRIELLE, actress; b. Laleham, Middlesex, Eng., Feb. 4, 1971; 1 child, Willow. Appeared in films Manifesto, 1988, If Looks Could Kill, 1991, Wild Hearts Can't Be Broken, 1991, Scent of a Woman, 1992, For Love or Money, 1993, The Three Musketeers, 1993, Body Snatchers, 1993, Things to Do in Denver when You're Dead, 1995, Halcyon Days, 1995, Whitechapel, 1997, Sub Down, 1997, Nevada, 1997, Kimberly, 1999, The Guilty, 1999, The Manor, 1999; song performer in For Love or Money, 1993; appeard on TV in First Born, 1989, In Pursuit of Honor, 1995, WonderWorks, 1990, Summer's Lease on Masterpiece Theatre, 1991, The Ripper, 1997. Office: United Talent Agy 9560 Wilshire Blvd Fl 5 Beverly Hills CA 90212-2400*

ANWYL-DAVIES, MARCUS JOHN, judge, arbitrator; b. London, July 11, 1923; came to U.S., 1993; s. Thomas Anwyl-Davies and Kathleen Beryl Oakshot; m. Eva Hilda Paulson, June 5, 1954 (div. Jan. 1974); children: Alexander Cornelia Eva, Nicholas Thomas Gustav; m. Myrna Ruth Berenbeim, Aug. 7, 1983. MA, Oxford U., 1956. Barrister Inner Temple, London, 1949, Queen's Counsel, 1967; cir. judge, 1972-93, arbitrator, 1993; pub. arbitrator Am. Arbitration Assn., 1993, Nat. Assn. Securities Dealers, 1994, Pacific Stock Exch., 1995; arbitrator Korean Comml. Arbitration Bd., 1996. Pres. Coun. of Her Majesty's Cir. Judges, Eng. and Wales, 1989; legal assessor Gen. Med. Coun., U.K., 1968-71, Gen. Dental Coun., U.K., 1968-71. Fellow Chartered Inst. Arbitrators; mem. Hertfordshire Magistrates Assn. (v.p.), Ctr. for Internat. Comml. Arbitration (bd. dirs.), London Ct. Internat. Arbitration. Avocations: photography, golf. E-mail: marcusanwyldavies@compuserve.com. Home: 16624 Calle Arbolada Pacific Palisades CA 90272-1923

ANYANWU, VICTOR O., criminologist, political scientist; b. Mbano, Imo, Nigeria, Jan. 5, 1967; came to the U.S., 1987; s. George A. Aguguesi and Catherine E. Anyanwu; m. Cathryn L. Mosley, June 2, 1990 (div. May 1996); m. Assumpta C. Ohanaja, June 27, 1996; children: Emmanuel Anyanwu, Janice Anyanwu. BS in Criminal Justice, Jackson State U., 1991, MA in Sociology, 1993, PhD in Pub. Adminstrn., 1998. Police officer Nigerian Police Force, Nigeria, 1982-87; rsch. analyst Jackson (Miss.) Pub. Sch. Dist., 1993-94; rsch. evaluator Jackson State U., 1994-95, rsch. cons., 1995-96; criminal justice instr. Durham (N.C.) Tech. C.C., 1998; adj. prof. N.C. Ctrl. U., Durham, 1998; computer ops. analyst Electronic Data Sys., Birmingham, Ala., 1999—; auditor, newsletter editor Nigerian Progressive Union, Jackson, 1993-98. Advisor Nigerian Peoples Party, 1994. Mem. ASPA, Conf. Minority Pub. Adminstrs., Toastmasters Club (chairperson 1994), Alpha Kappa Delta. Democrat. Avocations: soccer, swimming, reading, biking. E-mail: victor.anyanwu@bridge.bellsouth.com. Home: 3412 Hartwood Cir #4 Hoover AL 35216

ANYOMI, SAMUEL MAWUENA KWEKU, business educator; b. Adaklu, Ghana, Feb. 5, 1938; s. Noah Yao and Adzoa (Agamah) A. BS, Wilkes Coll., 1975, MBA, 1977; PhD, Calif. Coast U., 1982. Audit examiner Auditor-Gen.'s Dept., Accra, Ghana, 1966-69, examiner accounts, 1969-71; asst. mgr. United Bargain House, Columbia, S.C., 1977, Commissary Carolina Inn, Columbia, 1978, Sir George's Royal Buffet, Columbia, 1979; asst. prof. bus. adminstrn. and mgmt. Barber-Scotia Coll., Concord, NC, 1983-84; mem. adj. faculty dept. mgmt. and bus. adminstrn. Newport U., Newport Beach, Calif., 1983-95; prof. bus. adminstrn., chmn. dept. bus. and econs. Allen U., Columbia, 1994-95; prof. mgmt. and bus. adminstrn. Newport U. Grad. Sch. Bus. Adminstrn., Newport Beach, Calif., 1995—. Mem. Acad. Mgmt., Internat. Inst. Forcasters, Small Bus. Inst. Dirs. Assn. (pres. 1985—). Presbyn. Home: 4514 Clemson Ave Columbia SC 29206 Office: Newport Univ 20101 SW Birch St Newport Beach CA 92660

ANZALONE, FRANK MICHAEL, stage manager; b. Bklyn.. BA, St. Lawrence U., 1964; MA, Cath. U. Am., 1966. Dir. theater, tchr. High Point H.S., Bettsville, Md., 1966-71, 73-79; exec. asst. to CEO, Samuel French, Inc., N.Y.C., 1972; artistic dir. K & L Prodns., Burtonsville, Md., 1979-82; prodn. stage mgr. Walnut Street Theatre, Phila., 1983—; also stage dir. Vanities, 1995, Effect of Gamma Rays on Man-in-the-Moon Marigolds, 1996, 1776, 1997, Anything Goes, 1998. Mem. Soc. Stage Dirs. and Choreographers, Actors Equity Assn., Phi Beta Kappa. Democrat. Roman Catholic. Home: 233 S 6th St Apt 1304 Philadelphia PA 19106-3753 Office: Walnut Street Theatre 825 Walnut St Philadelphia PA 19107-5195

ANZEL, SANFORD HAROLD, orthopedic surgeon; b. Bayonne, N.J., Feb. 17, 1929; s. Jules and Faye (Morganstein) A.; m. Darlene J. Wilson, July 14, 1937; children: Linda, Jon. BA, Yale U., 1950; MD, N.Y. Med. Coll., 1954; MS in Orthopaedic Surgery, U. Minn., 1959; cer. Cert. Am. Bd. Orthopaedic Surgery; lic. Nat. Bd. Med. Examiners, Bd. Med. Examiners, Calif., Minn. State Bd. Med. Examiners. Intern U. Calif. Med. Ctr., San Francisco, 1954-55; fellow in orthopaedic surgery Mayo Clinic, Rochester, Minn., 1955-59; chief orthopaedic surgery Orange (Calif.) County Med. Ctr., 1965-71; assoc. clin. prof. orthopaedic surgery U. Calif., Irvine, 1971-79, clin. prof., 1979—; chief orthopaedic sect. Children's Hosp. Orange County, 1977-78; state co-chmn. Orthopaedic Research and Edn. Found., 1982-84; chief orthopaedics Long Beach (Calif.) Vet's. Hosp., 1986—; cons. Baden Powell Orthopaedic Unite, Anaheim, Calif., Foothill High Sch., Katella High Sch., Univ. High Sch., Mater Dei High Sch., Los Angeles Rams; 7th ann. former alumnus vis. prof. Mayo Clinic and Found., 1975. Contbr. numerous articles to profl. jours. Served to maj. USAF, 1959-64. S.H. Anzel Soc. named in his honor, 1985. Fellow ACS (select membership com. 1969-76), Am. Acad. Orthopaedic Surgeons (regional admission com. 11 1969-76, com. ann. meeting press relations 1975-77, 82, co-vice chmn. sci. com. 1981, chmn. sci. com. 1983, bd. councilors); mem. AMA, Western Orthopaedic Assn. (membership com. 1975-78, v.p. Orange County chpt. 1976 , pres.-elect 1988-89, pres. 1988-89, bd. dirs. 1985—), Calif. Med. Assn. Orange County Med. Assn., Am. Orthopaedic Soc. Sports Medicine, Arthritis Found. (Disting. Svc. award So. Calif. chpt. 1974, Humanitarian award Orange County chpt. 1968-79, Nat. Vol. Svc. Citation, 1981), Am. Soc. Shoulder and Elbow Surgeons, Am. Orthopaedic Assn., Wilson-Bost Interurban Club. Office: Orthopaedic Surgery Med Group Inc 1140 W La Veta Ave Ste 850 Orange CA 92868-4218

ANZIANO, GALE MARY, guidance counselor, social worker; b. N.Y.C., Dec. 8, 1943; d. Louis and Frances Regina Sileve Rear; m. Samuel Anziano, Oct. 8, 1978. MS in Edn., Hofstra U., 1969; MSW, Adelphi U., 1975, D of Social Work, 1985. Tchr. English Centrode Estudio, Valencia, Spain, 1965-66; tchr. U. Valencia, 1966; tchr. Spanish East Meadow (N.Y.) Schs., 1966-69; guodance counselor Freeport (N.Y.) Schs., 1969-73; cons. N.Y. State Dept. Social Svcs., N.Y.C., 1980; guidance counselor, social worker Glen Coves (N.Y.) Schs., 1973—. Chmn. Glen Cove Youth Bd., 1979-80, A.S. Pike, Nassau County, N.Y., 1993-97, Youth Commn., Garden City. Mem. NASW, ASPIRE, Kiwanis. Avocations: photography, writing, golf, screenwriting. Home: 147 Willow St Garden City NY 11530

AOYAMA, HIROYUKI, structural engineering educator; b. Shinjuku, Tokyo, Japan, July 14, 1932; s. Hidesaburo and Sadako (Nishimura) A.; m. Kikuko Sugiura, Apr. 16, 1960; children: Masako, Nobuyuki. B in Engring., U. Tokyo, 1955, M in Engring., 1957, DEng., 1960. Registered first class architect. Lectr. U. Tokyo, 1960-64, assoc. prof., 1964-78, prof., 1978-93, prof. emeritus, 1993—; prof. Nihon U., 1993-96, 98—; vis. rschr. U. Ill., Urbana, 1961-63, vis. prof., 1971-72; vis. prof. U. Canterbury, Christchurch, N.Z., 1980-81; fgn. assoc. Nat. Acad. Engring., 1996. Recipient Alfred E. Lindau award Am. Concrete Inst., 1995. Fellow Am. Concrete Inst. (award 1995), New Zealand Nat. Soc. Earthquake Engring.; mem. ASCE, Archtl. Inst. Japan (award 1976), Japan Concrete Inst. (award 1975), Japan Soc. Civil Engrs. Home: 4-2-13 Takadanobaba, Shinjuku-ku, Tokyo 169-0075, Japan Office: Aoyama Lab, 1-13-14 Sekiguchi, Bunkyo-ku Tokyo 112-0014, Japan

APANITES, JENNIFER MOORE, elementary educator; b. Cleve., July 29, 1965; d. John Wayne and Helen (Samardeya) Moore; m. John Michael Apanites, July 4, 1993; 1 child, Aaron. BS in Elem. Edn., Ohio State U., 1987; MA in Edn. with Reading Cert., John Carroll U., 1989. Cert. elem. tchr. K-8, reading cert. K-12. 3rd grade tchr. Solon (Ohio) City Schs., 1987-93; 4th grade tchr. Indian Hill Exempted Village Sch. Dist., Cin., 1993—. Mem. ASCD, Reading Assn., Nat. Bd. of Profl. Tchg. Stds. E-mail: apanitej@ih.k12.oh.us. Office: 6100 Drake Rd Cincinnati OH 45243

APARICIO, LUIS ERNESTO, retired baseball player; b. Maracaibo, Venezuela, Apr. 29, 1934. With Chgo. White Sox, 1958-62, 68-70, Balt. Orioles, 1963-67, Boston Red Sox, 1971-73. Named to Baseball Hall Fame, 1984; selected to Am. League All-Star Team 8 times, led league in stolen bases, 1956-64. Office: c/o Boston Red Sox Comm Dept Fenway Park Boston MA 02215*

APASSA, CYRIL OMO-OSAGIE, clergyman, educator; b. Aba, Abbia, Nigeria, Feb. 4, 1944; s. Emmanuel Agbonfiro and Agnes (Amobo) A. BD, Urban U., 1971; diploma in edn., U. Nigeria, 1977, MEd, 1986; EdD, U. San Francisco, 1996. Ordained to ministry, Roman Cath. Ch., 1971. Tchr. Govt. schs., Nigeria, 1964-77; pastor Roman Cath. chs., Nigeria, 1971-81; prin. Govt. H.S., Nigeria, 1981-90; assoc. pastor Our Lady of Lourdes Parish, Aba, Nigeria, 1990-91, Holy Angel's Parish, Arcadia, Calif., 1991, St. John Eudes Parish, Chatsworth, Calif., 1991-92, St. Theresa Little Flower Ch., Reno, 1996—; sch. counselor, chmn. disciplinary com. St. Ephrem's Secondary Sch., Owerrinta, Nigeria, 1975-79; mem. bd. govs., grad. coun. Mbutu Ngwa Secondary Sch., U. San Francisco, Owerrinta, 1984-89, San Francisco, 1995-96. Bd. dirs. Scholz Found. and Project Restart, 1998—. Mem. ASCD, K.C. (chaplain 1991—, Svc. award 1991, 96, 99). Avocations: photography, table tennis, traveling, soccer. Fax: 775-322-0176. Office: St Therese Ch of the Little Flower 875 E Plumb Ln Reno NV 89502

APATOFF, MICHAEL JOHN, finance executive; b. Harvey, Ill., June 12, 1955; s. William and Frances (Brown) A. BA, Reed Coll., 1980. Chief legis. asst. to U.S. Congressman Al Ullman, Chmn. Ways and Means Com., Washington, 1978-80; spl. asst. to U.S. Congressman Tom Foley, Majority Whip, Washington, 1981-85; exec. v.p., COO Chgo. Merc. Exch., 1986-90; pres., prin. Dresdner RCM Global Investors, San Francisco, 1991—. Democrat. Home: 2313 Broadway San Francisco CA 94115-1233 Office: Dresdner RCM Clobal Investors Four Embarcadero San Francisco CA 94111

APEL-BRUEGGEMAN, MYRNA L., entrepreneur; b. Cleve., July 19, 1942; d. Melvin Arthur and Merle Ruth (Hoffman) Rehlender; children: Timothy, Kristen, Michelle, Kim; m. Earl L. Brueggeman, May 7, 1994. BS in Edn., Kent State U., 1965, M. in Edn. Counseling, 1987. Cert. tchr., Ohio; lic. minister, Ohio. Owner, mgr. real estate investments Kent, Ohio; owner, founder IHS Counseling Ctr., Ravenna, Ohio; owner, mgr. Winning Edge, Kent, Ohio; founder, pres. IHS Sch. Personal Devel., Ravenna, Ohio; owner IHS Bookstore; co-owner Chapel on the Lakes. Mem. NAFE, Ohio Manufactured Housing Assn. (pres. We. Res. chpt.), Internat. Soc. Profl. Hypnotists, Sigma Epsilon, Chi Sigma Iota.

APFEL, GARY, lawyer; b. N.Y.C., June 2, 1952; s. Willy and Jenny (Last) A.; m. Serena Jakobovits, June 16, 1980; children: Alyssa J., I. Michael, Alanna J., Stephen J., Alexander. BA, NYU magna cum laude, 1973; JD, Columbia U., 1976. Bar: N.Y. 1977, Calif. 1988, U.S. Dist. Ct. (so. and ea. dists.) N.Y. 1977, U.S. Dist. Ct. (cen. dist.) Calif. 1988, U.S. Ct. Appeals (9th cir.) 1988. Assoc. Sullivan & Cromwell, N.Y.C., 1976-80; assoc. LeBoeuf, Lamb, Leiby & MacRae, N.Y.C., 1980-84, ptnr., 1985-88; ptnr. Kaye, Scholer, Fierman, Hays & Handler LLP, L.A., 1988-97, Akin, Gump, Strauss, Hauer & Feld, L.L.P., L.A., 1997—. Kent scholar Columbia U., 1976. Mem. ABA, Calif. State Bar Assn. (bus. law sect. corps. com.), Phi Beta Kappa. Office: Akin Gump Strauss Hauer & Feld LLP 2029 Century Park E Ste 2600 Los Angeles CA 90067-3012

APFEL, JOSEPH H., optical engineer, research scientist. AB in Physics, U. Calif., Berkeley, 1954, MA in Physics, 1956, PhD in Physics, 1959. With Optical Coating Lab., Inc., Santa Rosa, Calif., 1961—, former dir. corp. rsch., former v.p., chief tech. officer, now part-time staff mem. Contbr. articles to sci. jours. Recipient Joseph Fraunhofer award and Robert M. Burlez prize Optical Soc. Am., 1995. Office: Optical Coating Lab Inc 2789 Northpoint Pkwy Santa Rosa CA 95407-7397*

APFEL, KENNETH S., federal government official; b. Worcester, Mass., Oct. 10, 1948; s. Walter F. and Arlene (Fallstrom) A.; m. Caroline S. Hadley, Aug. 1, 1981; children: Derek, Dana. BA, U. Mass., 1970; MEd, Northeastern U., 1973; MPA, U. Tex., 1978. Dir. vets. svcs. Newbury Coll., Boston, 1973-76; presdl. mgmt. intern U.S. Dept. Labor, Washington, 1978-80; com. staff mem. U.S. Senate Com. on Budget, Washington, 1980-82; legis. asst. Senator Bill Bradley, Washington, 1982-89, legis. dir., 1989-93; asst. sec. for mgmt. and budget Dept. Health and Human Svcs., Washington, 1993-95; assoc. dir. Human Resources Off. Mgmt. & Budget, 1995-97; commr. of social security Balt., 1997—. Office: Social Security Adm Office of the Commr Ste 900 Altmeyer Bldg 6401 Security Blvd Baltimore MD 21235*

APFEL, ROBERT EDMUND, mechanical engineering educator, applied physicist, research scientist; b. N.Y.C., Mar. 16, 1943; s. Mark and Anita A.; m. Nancy Howe, July 13, 1968; children: Darren Alexander, Alison Anita. BA, Tufts U., 1964; MA, Harvard U., 1967, PhD, 1970. Postdoctoral research fellow Harvard U., 1970-71; asst. prof. mech. engring. Yale U., 1971-75, assoc. prof., 1975-81, prof., 1981—, chmn. dept., 1981-86, 92-94, chmn. Council of Engring., 1988-90, dir. external affairs engring., 1994—; Robert Higgin prof., chairperson mech. engring., 1991-95; prin., cons. Robert E. Apfel, Ph.D., New Haven, 1972—; pres. Apfel Enterprises, Inc., New Haven, 1987—; co-dir. Yale Ctr. for Ultrasonics and Sonics, 1994-96. Recipient A.B. Wood Medal and Prize, Inst. Physics, 1971, Ivy award Yale and New Haven Cmty. Award, 1996. Fellow Acoustical Soc. Am. (Biennial award 1976, v.p. 1991-92, pres. elect 1994-95, pres. 1995-96, Silver medal 1997); mem. ASME, Am. Phys. Soc., Am. Assn. Physics Tchrs., Health Physics Soc., Conn. Acad. Sci. and Engring., Sigma Xi (pres. Yale chpt. 1994—). Unitarian. Office: Yale U PO Box 208286 New Haven CT 06520-8286 also: Apfel Enterprises Inc 25 Science Park Ste 4 New Haven CT 06511-1984

APFELBAUM, MARC, lawyer; b. Phila., Apr. 30, 1955; s. Herbert and Beatrice Bernice (Bitman) A. BA cum laude, U. Pa., 1978; JD magna cum laude, Georgetown U., 1983. Bar: N.Y. 1984, U.S. Dist. Ct. (so. and ea. dists.) N.Y. 1984, Conn. 1991. Assoc. Cravath, Swaine & Moore, N.Y.C., 1983-89; v.p., assoc. gen. counsel, asst. sec. Time Warner Cable, Stamford, Conn., 1989-96, sr. v.p., gen. counsel, sec., 1996—. Editor Georgetown Law Jour., 1982-83. Mem. ABA. Home: 440 W End Ave Apt 14C New York NY 10024-5358 Office: Time Warner Cable 290 Harbor Dr Stamford CT 06902-7475

APGAR, JEAN E., artist, consultant; b. Rockford, Ill., May 19, 1949; d. Martin N. and Theodora F. (Rosander) Borsche; m. Richard R. Apgar, May 30, 1969; 1 child, Daniel. BFA, No. Ill. U., 1971, MA in Painting, 1978. Instr. continuing edn. Rock Valley Coll., Rockford, 1971-78; ptnr. Gallery Ten, Rockford, 1990-94; artist's cons. Jester Pubs., Rockford, 1995—; lectr. in field; condr. workshops in field. Co-author: Now what? This Art Business, 1994; one women shows include Third Floor Gallery, Union League Club of Chgo., 1981, Rockford Area Arts Coun., 1990, Gallery Ten, Rockford, 1991, Cannova's, Loves Park, Ill., 1992, LePetite Gallerie, Rockford, 1992, North End Gallery, Leonardtown, Md., 1992, Prairie Ctr. for the Arts, Schaumburg, Ill., 1992, Gallery 451, Rockford, 1994, 95; exhibited in group shows including Freeport Art Mus., 1980, The Parsonage, Rockford, 1981, Byron (Ill.) Gallery, 1981-82, Rockford Pub. Libr. Gallery Three, 1981-82, Images/4, 1980-82, North End Gallery, 1992, Charlotte Hackin Fine Arts Gallery, 1992, Gallery 451, 1991, Yvette's, Barrington, 1994, 317 Market St. Gallery, 1994, 95, Artisan Gallery, Paoli, Wis., 1996, Past Ptnrs. Plus, Gallery Ten, Rockford, 1996, Kebby Gallery, Rockford, 1996, Colonade Gallery, Chautauqua, N.Y., 1996, East Bank Gallery, Rockford, 1997; works in permanent collections at Gallery Ten, 1998, Gambino Gallery, 1998, Womanspace, Rockford, Ill., 1999, Beverly Bank, Chgo., Baarstad & Harris, Cherry Valley, Ill., Solar Flame, Genoa, Ill., Kishwaukee Coll., Malta, Ill., Winnebago County Title Ins., Swedish Am. Hosp., Rockford, Crusader Clinic, Rockford, many pvt. collections in U.S., Sweden, Gt. Britain. Advisor/cons. Arts against Violence, Rockford Area Arts Coun., 1994. Rockford Area Arts coun. City ArtsAction grantee, 1995, 96. Mem. Nat. Assn. Women Artists, Nat. Watercolor Soc. (assoc.), Am. Watercolor Soc. (assoc.), Tamaroa Watercolor Soc., Silk Painters Internat. Avocation: horseback riding. Home: 2513 Knight Ave Rockford IL 61101-4244

APICELLA, MICHAEL ALLEN, physician, educator; b. Bklyn., Apr. 4, 1938; s. Anthony D. and Fay (Kahn) A.; m. Agnes Dengler, Aug. 19, 1961; children: Michael P., Christopher A., Peter N. AB, Holy Cross Coll., 1959; MD, SUNY, Bklyn., 1963. Diplomate Am. Bd. Internal Medicine, Am. Bd. Infectious Disease. Postdoctoral fellow Johns Hopkins Hosp., Balt., 1966-68; asst. prof. microbiology SUNY, Buffalo, 1970-74, assoc. prof., 1974-78, prof., 1981-92; prof., chmn. dept. microbiology Coll. Medicine U. Iowa, Iowa City, 1993—. Contbr. over 100 articles to profl. jours. Maj. USAF, 1968-70. Office: U Iowa Coll Medicine Dept Microbiology Coll Medicine 3-403 Science Bldg Iowa City IA 52242*

APINIS, JOHN, chemist; b. Katvari, Latvia, Mar. 20, 1933; came to U.S., 1949, naturalized, 1954; s. Augusts and Marta (Gravelsins) A.; m. Johnnie Verena Burden, Feb. 6, 1960. B.S., Clemson U., 1960. Apprentice, Am. Thread Co., Willimantic, Conn., 1951-52, Leiss Velvet Mfg. Co., Willimantic, 1952-53; asst. plant chemist Burlington Industries, Wake Finishing Co., Raleigh, N.C., 1960-65, plant chemist, 1965-75, mgr. dept. dyeing, 1975-76, tech. coordinator, 1976-94; ret. Served with AUS, 1953-55. Mem. Am. Assn. Textile Chemists and Colorists. Clubs: Elks, Rotary (v.p. 1963-64, pres. 1964-65, dir. 1963-66), Raleigh Music, Questers (v.p. 1977-78, pres. 1978-79), Raleigh Clemson Alumni (pres. 1976-77). Research in textile color computer and chromosorter. Home: 225 Cherokee Dr Fair Play SC 29643-2308

APLAN, FRANK FULTON, metallurgical engineering educator; b. Boulder, Colo., Aug. 11, 1923; s. Frank Fulton Sr. and Helen Elizabeth (Fischer) A.; m. Clare Marie Donaghue, July 30, 1955; children: Susan M., Peter D., Lucy A. BS, S.D. Sch. Mines and Tech., 1948; MS, Mont. Sch. Mines, 1950; ScD, MIT, 1957; hon. degree in mineral engring., Mont. Tech. of U. of Mont., 1968. Mill engr. Climax Molybdenum Co., Climax, Colo., 1950-51, 53; asst. prof. U. Wash., Seattle, 1951-53; sr. scientist Kennecott Copper Corp., Salt Lake City, 1957; group mgr. mineral engring. R & D Mining and Metals div., Union Carbide Corp., Niagara Falls, Tuxedo, N.Y., 1957-67; prof. metallurgy and mineral processing Pa. State U., University Park, 1968—, Disting. prof., 1990, head dept. mineral preparation, 1968-71; chmn. mineral processing sect. Pa. State U., University Pk., 1971-77; chmn. metallurgy sect. Pa. State U., University Park, 1973-75; bd. dirs. Engring. Found., N.Y.C., 1977-90, chmn. 1985-87. Contbr. articles to profl. jours.; patentee in field. T/Sgt. U.S. Army, 1942-46, ETO. Decorated Bronze Star; recipient Engring. Found. award, 1989, Percy H. Nicholls award AIME/ASME Joint Soc., 1998; inductee S.D. Hall of Fame, 1998. Mem. Nat. Acad. Engring., AIME (hon. mem. 1991, Robert H. Richards award 1978, Mineral Industry Edn. award 1992), AIChE, ASM Internat., Archaeol. Inst. Am., Am. Filtration Soc., Am. Chem. Soc., Soc. Mining, Metallurgy & Exploration Engrs. (bd. dirs. 1973-76, chmn. mineral processing divsn. 1972-73, Arthur F. Taggart award 1985, Disting. Mem. award 1978, Antoine M. Gaudin award 1991), Minerals, Metals & Materials Soc., Mining History Assn. Home: 432 W Fairmount Ave State College PA 16801-4612 Office: Pa State U Dept Energy & Geo-Environ Engring 155 Hosler Bldg University Park PA 16802-5000

APLIN, JAMES GRANGER, artist; b. Chattanooga, Apr. 27, 1945; s. Charles Sewall and Carol Winnifred (Granger) A.; m. Jill Ann Sims, May 6, 1995; children: Benjamin, Matthew. BA, U. N.C., 1967; MFA, U. Ga., 1971; postgrad., Art Students League, N.Y.C., 1976. Art dir. Lavidge Assocs., Chattanooga, 1971-74; asst. prof. Coker Coll., Hartsville, S.C., 1974-76; freelance illustrator N.Y.C., 1976-82; faculty Parsons Sch. Design, N.Y.C., 1979-82, U. Tenn., Chattanooga, 1972-73, Am. Soc. for Emigres in Professions, N.Y.C., 1976-77. Exhbns. include Gotham Book Mart, N.Y.C., 1980, Hunter Mus., Chattanooga, 1996, The Legacy Lives, N.Y.C., 1996. Greenshields Found. grantee, 1976; Morehead Found. scholar, 1963-67. Mem. Soc. Illustrators, Phi Beta Kappa. Home: 124 N Forrest Ave Lookout Mountain TN 37350-1249

APOLINSKY, STEPHEN DOUGLAS, lawyer; b. Birmingham, Ala., Dec. 5, 1961; s. Harold Irwin and Sandra Jean (Rubenstein) A. BA, U. Mich., 1983; JD, Emory U., 1987. Bar: Ga. 1987, U.S. Dist. Ct. (no. dist.) Ga. 1987, D.C. 1989, Ala. 1994. Litigation assoc. Bentley, Karesh & Seacrest, Atlanta, 1987-94; mem. Eastman, Stapleton & Apolinsky, LLC, Atlanta, 1995-97, Eastman & Apolinsky, L.L.P., Atlanta, 1997—. Mem. ATLA, Ga. Trial Lawyers Assn., Atlanta Bar Assn., Atlanta Claims Assn., Am.-Israel C. of C. (bd. dirs. S.E. region). Avocations: travel and sports. Office: Eastman & Apolinsky Watkins Bldg 114 E Ponce De Leon Ave Decatur GA 30030-2526

APONE, CARL ANTHONY, journalist; b. Brownsville, Pa., July 9, 1923; s. Peter P. and Carmela (Puglia) A.; m. Kathleen King, Jan. 23, 1965; 1 dau., Elizabeth. B.A. cum laude, U. Notre Dame, 1949; M.A., Boston U., 1950. Dir. pub. rels., lectr. journalism and Am. lit. St. Mary's Coll., Notre Dame, Ind., 1950-53; staff writer UP, Detroit, 1953; city editor Brownsville Telegraph, 1953-57; staff writer Pitts. Sun- Telegraph, 1958-60; music editor Pitts. Press, 1960-89; mem. faculty journalism Duquesne U., 1967-72; freelance writer, 1950—; artistic dir. Music for Mt. Lebanon, Pitts., 1990—; Mem. penal com. St. Vincent DePaul Soc., 1963—. Served with inf. AUS, 1943-46. Recipient Golden Quill Journalism awards; Pa. Newspaper Pubs. Assn. awards. Mem. Third Order St. Francis. Home: 2016 Worcester Dr Pittsburgh PA 15243-1542 Office: Music for Mt Lebanon 2016 Worcester Dr Pittsburgh PA 15243-1542

APONTE, JOSE A., library director; b. Oct. 2, 1950; m. Cynthia Reyes; 2 children. BA, Bard Coll., 1973; MLS, U. Ariz., 1976. Br. libr. Tucson Pub. Libr., 1976-87; br. libr., coord. EOS Santa Barbara (Calif.) Pub. Libr., 1987-89; prin. adminstrv.libr. Orange County Pub. Libr., San Juan Capistrano, Calif., 1989-95; libr. dir. West Palm Beach (Fla.) Pub. Libr., 1995-96, Oceanside (Calif.) Pub. Libr., 1996—. Email: japonte@ci.oceanside.ca.us. Home: 3364 Ironwood Pl Oceanside CA 92056 Office: Oceanside Pub Libr 330 North Coast Hwy Oceanside CA 92054-2885

APONTE MARTINEZ, LUIS CARDINAL, archbishop; b. Lajas, P.R., Aug. 4, 1922; s. Santiago E. Aponte and Rosa Martinez. Student, San Ildefonso Sem., San Juan, P.R., 1944, St. John's Sem., Boston, 1950; LL.D. (hon.), Fordham U., 1965. Ordained priest Roman Cath. Ch., 1950; asst. in Patillas, P.R.; pastor in Maricao, P.R., Sta. Isabel, P.R., 1953-55; sec. to bishop of Ponce, P.R., 1955-57; pastor in Aibonito, P.R., 1957-60; aux. bishop of Ponce, 1960-63, bishop, 1963-64; archbishop of San Juan, 1964—; elevated to cardinal, 1973; Chancellor Cath. U. P.R., Ponce, 1963—; pres. Puerto Rican Episcopal Conf. Served as chaplain P.R. N.G., 1957-60. Mem. Lions. Address: Arzobispado Apdo S-1967 Calle del Cristo 50 San Juan PR 00902*

APOSTLE, CHRISTOS NICHOLAS, social psychologist; b. N.Y.C., Nov. 14, 1935; s. Nicholas Christos and Maria (Katsaros) A. BS, U. Colo., 1958; postgrad., New Sch. Social Rsch., CCNY, 1959, 69; MS in Social Psychology, U. Md., 1963. Interviewer Columbia U. Sch. Pub. Health, N.Y.C., 1962; rsch. supr. Nat. Opinion Rsch. Ctr., U. Chgo., N.Y.C., 1963; instr. Wagner Coll., S.I., N.Y., 1964, Hunter Coll., Bronx, N.Y., 1964, Hofstra U., Hempstead, N.Y., 1965; asst. prof. SUNY, Albany, 1965-68; founder, dir. rsch. Inst. Temporal and Durational Studies, Albany, 1970—; prin. scientist Booz-Allen Applied Rsch., Ft. Monmouth, N.J., 1968-70; instr. Rutgers U., Newark, 1968; bd. dirs. Effective Advt., Albany; arbitrator Better Bus. Bur., 1981-82. Author: Getting Through College Using Sociological Principles, 1966; editor Indian Sociol. Bull., 1966-69; contbr. articles to profl. jours. Bd. dirs. Albany Colonie C. of C., 1975-85, YMCA, Albany, 1979-82; committeeman Town of Colonie (N.Y.) Dem. Com., 1987-91. NYU fellow, 1963-65. Fellow Am. Sociol. Assn.; mem. N.Y. Acad. Scis., World Assn. Pub. Opinion Rsch. Democrat. Greek Orthodox. Achievements include development of concept of temporal sociology, establishment of influence of Karl Jaspers on Talcott Parsons suggesting possible plagarism; development of belted landing field for airplanes; creation of solution to remove plaster and adhesive from ceramic tile. Office: Inst Temporal Durational Studies PO Box 557 Newtonville NY 12128-0557

APOSTOLAKIS, JAMES JOHN, shipping company executive; b. N.Y.C., May 31, 1942; s. John George and Ann (Lampros) A. AB, U. Pa., 1962; LLB, Harvard U., 1965. Bar: N.Y. 1965. Atty. Dewey, Ballantine, Bushby, Palmer & Wood, N.Y.C., 1965-67; pres. Transoceanic Tank Ship Mgmt. Group, N.Y.C., 1968-72, Koplik Group Ltd., N.Y.C., 1983-84, A.G. Palmer & Co., Inc., N.Y.C., 1976—, Bradford Shipping, Inc., N.Y.C., 1973—, Bradmar Trading Corp., N.Y.C., 1975—; pres. Lexington Shipping and Trading Corp., N.Y.C., 1980—, Bedford Capital Corp., N.Y.C., 1989-93; vice chmn. Koplik Group Ltd., N.Y.C., 1988-93; bd. dirs. Macmillan, Inc., Grow Group, Inc., Columbia Labs., Inc.; vice chmn. Columbia Labs., Inc., Miami, 1999—. Mem. Phi Beta Kappa. Clubs: Union, Metropolitan. Home: 150 E 69th St New York NY 10021-5704

APOSTOLIDIS, PAUL C., political science educator; b. Phila., June 29, 1965; s. Panayotis Constantine and Daphne Padis Apostolidis; m. Jeanne Marie Morefield, June 1, 1996; 1 child, Anna Kathleen Apostlefield. BA, Princeton U., 1986; MA, Cornell U., 1993, PhD, 1996. Policy analyst Mass. Dept. Pub. Welfare, Boston, 1986-87; field coord., organizer Dukakis for pres., Dukakis-Bentsen '88, Des Moines, Tampa, Fla., Scranton, Pa., 1987-88; dep. fin. conv. mgr. Dem. Nat. Conv., Atlanta, 1988; legis. corr. U.S. Rep. Frank Guarini, Washington, 1989; issues dir. for Pa. Clinton-Gore '92, Phila., 1992; vis. asst. prof. govt. dept Cornell U., Washington, Ithaca, N.Y., 1996-97; asst. prof. politics dept. Whitman Coll., Walla Walla, Wash., 1997—; vis. asst. prof. Cornell U., Cornell-in-Washington, 1996-97. AD White fellow Cornell U. Grad. Sch., 1989-93. Mem. Am. Polit. Sci. Assn., Wash. Children's Alliance. Democrat. Avocations: piano, keyboard, guitar, singing, cooking. E-mail: apostopo@whitman.edu. Office: Whitman Coll Politics Dept Walla Walla WA 99362

APOSTOLOS-CAPPADONA, DIANE PAN, religion and art educator; b. Trenton, N.J., May 10, 1948; d. Vasilios Daniel and Stacia Elaine (Pappayliou) Apostolos. BA with spl. honors in religion, George Washington U., 1970, MA in Religion, 1973, PhD in Am. Civilization, 1988; MA in Religion and Culture, Cath. U. Am., 1979. Editl. asst. The George Washington U., 1970-73; asst. to dir. devel. Bellarmine Coll., 1974-75; professorial lectr. religion and art Georgetown U., 1978—, adj. prof. religion, art and gender studies, 1985—, rsch. prof. Ctr. for Muslim-Christian U., 1996—; lectr. religion and art Ctr. for Cmty. Edn., Bellarmine Coll., 1974, Humanities Inst., 1979-80; vis. lectr. in religion and art Inst. Religious Studies U. St. Thomas, 1979, Cath. U. Am., 1985, 86, 89; lectr. in religion Mount Vernon Coll., 1980-85, George Washington U., 1981-86; tchg. fellow Grad. Theol. Found., 1989-93; residential fellow Alden B. Dow Creativity Ctr., 1982, Edward F. Albee Found., 1983; core cons. PBS/BBC series Dancing, 1993; co-curator Noguchi at the Dance, N.Y. Pub. Libr. for the Performing Arts, 1994; sr. fellow Ctr. Study World Religions Harvard U., 1996-97; presenter and guest lectr. in field. Author: Dictionary of Christian Art, 1994, The Spirit and the Vision: The Influence of Christian Romanticism on the Development of 19th-century American Art, 1995, Encyclopedia of Women in Religious Art, 1996; editor: The Sacred Play of Children, 1983, Art, Creativity, and the Sacred, 1984, 95, Symbolism, the Sacred, and the Arts, 1985, Image and Spirit in Sacred and Secular Art, 1990; co-editor: Isamu Noguchi: Essays and Conversations with Bruce Altshuler, 1994; art editor: World Spirituality: An Encyclopedic History of the Religious Quest, 25 vols., 1985-94; co-translator A History of Religious Ideas, Vol. III, 1985; contbr. articles to profl. jours. Presenter adult edn. programs Blessed Sacrament Cath. Cmty., First Presbyn. Ch. Arlington, First Unitarian Ch. Washington, Smithsonian Resident Assoc. Program, Christ Episcopal Ch., others. Mem. AAUW, Am. Acad. Religion, Am. Assn. Mus., Am. Studies Assn., Assocs. for Religion and Intellectual Life, Coll. Art Assn., Coll. Theology Soc., Congress on Rsch. in Dance, Soc. for Art, Religion and Contemporary Culture. Office: Ctr Muslim-Christian Understanding Georgetown Univ ICC #260 Washington DC 20057

APP, JAMES LEONARD, assistant dean; b. Fairmont, Minn., Jan. 27, 1936; s. Leonard Walter and Lucia Irene (Hellbusch) A.; m. Diane Catherine Conoryea, July 5, 1957; children: Timothy, Lisa, Polly, Peter. BS, U. Minn., 1957; MS, U. Wis., 1960, PhD, 1961. Asst. prof. U. Minn., 1961-63, assoc. prof., 1963-72, prof., asst. dean, 1972-73; county extension dir. Manatee County Coop. Extension, Palmetto, Fla., 1973-75; dist. dir. U. Fla. Coop. Extension, Gainesville, 1975, asst. dean, 1975—; vice chmn. So. Region Extension Agrl. and Natural Resources, 1983-84, chmn., 1984-85, chmn. program planning, 1985-86; sec. So. Region Extension Cmty. Resource Devel. Com., 1986-87. Contbr. articles to profl. jours.; presenter in field. Mem. Community Leaders of Am. Recipient Spl. Accomplishments award Fla. Landscape Maintenance Assn., 1989, Innovative and Aggressive Program Support award U. Fla. Or. Hort. Extension Specialists, 1979, Davis Productivity award, 1998; named Hon. Fla. Master Gardener U. Fla. Cooperative Extension Specialists, 1984; Computerized Producers Guides grantee, 1978, 82. Mem. Am. Men of Sci., Gamma Sigma Delta. Office: Univ Fla Agr Programs PO Box 110210 Gainesville FL 32611-0210

APPEL, ALBERT M., lawyer; b. N.Y.C., May 26, 1945; s. Morris and Belle (Kaplan) A.; m. Irena Uhl, June 10, 1979; 1 child, Elliott. BS in Econs., U. Pa., 1966; JD, NYU, 1969. Bar: N.Y. 1969, U.S. Dist. Ct. (so. and ea. dists.) N.Y. 1971, U.S. Ct. Appeals (2d cir.) 1974, U.S. Ct. Appeals (4th cir.) 1979. Assoc. Spear and Hill, N.Y.C., 1969-75; assoc. Webster & Sheffield, N.Y.C., 1976-80, ptnr., 1981-91; spl. counsel Stroock & Stroock & Lavan LLP, N.Y.C., 1991-97, ptnr., 1998—. Mem. ABA, Am. Health Lawyers Assn., N.Y. State Bar Assn., Assn. of Bar of City of N.Y., Penn Club, Beta Alpha Psi. Home: 670 W End Ave New York NY 10025-7313 Office: Stroock & Stroock & Lavan LLP 180 Maiden Ln New York NY 10038-4925

APPEL, ANTOINETTE RUTH, neuropsychologist; b. N.Y.C., Mar. 31, 1943; d. Leon S. and Augusta (Marienberg) A. B.A., U. Vt., 1964; M.A., Mt. Holyoke Coll., 1965; postgrad., Yeshiva U., 1965-66, Hofstra U., 1966; Ph.D., CUNY, 1972. Diplomate Am. Bd. Profl. Neuropsychology, Am. Bd. Forensic Examiners, Am. Bd. Forensic Medicine, Am. Bd. Psychol. Spltys. (Forensic Neuropsychology). Instr. C.W. Post Coll., Greenvale, N.Y., 1968-69; lectr., instr. Queens Coll., Flushing, N.Y., 1970-71; fellow in neurology, instr. ophthalmology Mt. Sinai Sch. Medicine, N.Y.C., 1971-74; adj. asst. prof. St. Francis Coll., Bklyn., 1974; asst. prof. dept. psychology So. Ill. U. Sch. Medicine, Carbondale, 1974-76; USPHS intern Conn. Valley Hosp., Middletown, Conn., 1976-77; asst. prof., asst. project coordinator dept. psychiatry Nat. Alcohol Research Ctr., U. Conn. Health Ctr., Farmington, 1977-79; neuropsychologist, asst. prof. program in medicine Brown U., Providence, 1979-82; adj. asst. prof. psychology U. R.I., Kingston and Providence, 1979-83; pvt. practice psychology, 1981-83; dir. Neuropsychol. Assessment and Treatment Ctr., Ctr. for Neuropsychology Services, Ft. Lauderdale, 1983-90, So. Inst. Forensic Neuropsychology, 1990-97; adj. faculty Nova Southwestern U., 1997—; cons. Narco Bio-systems, 1974-75; cons. to commr. mental health State of Conn., 1978-79; invited spkr. NATO Neuropsychology Congress, 1980, Internat. Coun. Psychology, 1980, 22 Internat. Congress Psychology, 1980. Bd. dirs. Sojourner House, 1979-80, Combined Hosp. Alcoholism Program, 1978, Hartford Interval House, 1978. Served with WAC, 1963. CUNY fellow, 1972; recipient Hartford Salute award, 1979; USPHS tng. fellow, 1966-67, NIMH predoctoral fellow 1967-70. Fellow Am. Coll. Forensic Examiners; mem. APA (mem. exec. bd.), Assn. Women in Psychology (mem. steering com.), Eastern Psychol. Assn. (chmn. 1980 conv.), Conn. Psychol. Assn. (coun. 1978-79), R.I. Psychol. Assn., N.Y. Acad. Scis., Sigma Xi, Psi Chi. Home: 8714 NW 82nd St Tamarac FL 33321-1607 Office: 1200 N University Dr Plantation FL 33322-4734

APPEL, BERNARD SIDNEY, marketing consultant, former electronic company executive; b. Boston, Jan. 10, 1932; s. Max and Sophie (Altshuler) A.; m. Ellen Carey, July 1988; children: Ann, Sharon; children by previous marriage: Arlene R., Gerald I. AABA, Boston U., 1959; D Comml. Sci. (hon.), McKenzie Coll., 1991. Store mgr., buyer S & W Distbg. Co., Boston, 1949-59; buyer Radio Shack Co., Boston, 1959-66, mdse. mgr., Boston, 1966-70, v.p. merchandising, Ft. Worth, 1970-78, sr. v.p. merchandising and advt., 1978-80, exec. v.p. mktg., 1980-84, pres., 1984-92, chmn., 1992-93; sr. v.p. Tandy Corp., 1992-93, bd dirs., Curtis Mathes Holding Corp., 1995—, pres., Appel Assocs., mktg. cons., 1993—, vice chm., bd. dirs., Integrated Tech. Inc., 1994—. V.p. Holbrook (Mass.) Jewish Community Center, 1958-59; bd. dirs. Dan Danciger Jewish Community Ctr., Ft. Worth, 1989—; v.p., founder Temple Aliyah, Needham, Mass., 1969-70; pres. Congregation Ahavath Sholom, Ft. Worth, 1979-81, bd. dirs., 1972—; bd. dirs. Jewish Fedn. Ft. Worth, 1975—, v.p., 1981-85, pres., 1985-87; bd. dirs. Casa Mañana Mus., 1978-79; adv. bd. Arts Coun. Ft. Worth, 1985—; project renewal cluster chmn. Acco-East, Israel, 1981-94; mem. exec. com. United Jewish Appeal, So. Regional Campaign Cabinet, 1980-89; so. regional chmn. United Jewish Appeal's Passage to Freedom Campaign for Soviet Jewry, 1989; co-chmn. fin. rels. United Jewish Appeal Western Region, Jewish Agy. Com., 1992-93, United Jewish Appeal, Ctrl. Region, Jewish Agy. Com., 1993, Exec. Com., Network of Ind. UJA Coms., 1994—, bd. dirs. Family Svcs., Inc., 1990—; mem. Internat. Bd. Visitors M.J. Neeley Sch. Bus., Tex. Christian U., 1990—; hon. life mem. nat. commn. Anti-Defamation League, 1992. With USCG, 1951-54. Named B'nai Brith Ft. Worth Jewish Man of Yr., 1985, Man of Yr. Anti-Defamation League Ft. Worth, 1990; recipient Torch of Liberty award Anti-Defamation League of B'nai Brith Electronics and Appliances Div., 1988, Defender of Jerusalem award, 1990, Boston U. Sch. Mgmt. Alumni award, 1994. Mem. Electronic V.I.P. Club, Fort Worth C. of C. (bd. dirs. 1981-84). Clubs: Masons, Shriners, Frog (Tex. Christian U.), Colonial Country Club, City Country Club, Fort Worth. Home: 4917 Ranch View Rd Fort Worth TX 76109-3117 Office: Appel Assocs 301 Commerce St Ste 1415 Fort Worth TX 76102-4114

APPEL, GERALD, investment advisor; b. N.Y.C., June 2, 1933; s. Samuel and Vivian (Adlerstein) A.; m. Judith Kane, May 26, 1956; children: Marvin Laurence, Marion Fran. BA, Bklyn. Coll., 1954; MSW, NYU, 1956. Adminstr. social agy. Jewish Family Svc., Bklyn., 1958-73; pvt. practice as psychoanalyst Great Neck, N.Y., 1963-95; pres. Signalert Corp., Great Neck, 1973—, Appel Asset Mgmt. Corp., 1995—. Author: Winning Market Systems, 1972, Double Your Money Every Three Years, 1973, 99 Ways to Make Money in a Depression, 1974, Stock Option and No-Load Switch Fund Scalpers Manual, 1979, Winning Stock Selection Systems, 1979, The Big Move, 1981, Time-Trend III, 1988, Portraits of Nature, 1992, American Photographers at the Turn of the Century, Travel and Trekking, 1994, (with others) The Art of the Human Form, 1995, New Directions in Technical Analysis, 1976, Stock Market Trading Systems, 1980, Fast Away Faces—A Guide to Better Travel Portraits, 1998; (video) The MACD Trading System, 1990, Power Tools, 1992, Day Trading, 1990; contbr. articles to profl. jours. Bd. dirs. Keystone Ctr. of Music and Arts. Mem. Nat. Psychol. Assn. for Psychoanalysis (bd. dirs., v.p.), Am. Assn. Media Photographers. Avocations: photography, tennis, sailing, music. Home: 97 Myrtle Dr Great Neck NY 11021-1805 Office: Signalert Corp 150 Great Neck Rd Ste 301 Great Neck NY 11021-3339

APPEL, JOHN C., investment company executive. Pres., COO Dain Bosworth Inc., Mpls., 1992-98; vice chmn., CFO Dain Rauscher (formerly Dain Bosworth Inc.), Mpls., 1998—. Office: Dain Rouscher Inc Dain Rouscher Plaza 60 S 6th St Ste 1000 Minneapolis MN 55402-4422*

APPEL, JOHN C., communications company executive; m. Terry; two children. BSBA, U. Fla., 1971. From mgr. to divsn. mgr., dir. ops. GTE Comms. Corp., 1971-88; from south area dir. bus. svc. to regional v.p., mgr. Calif. GTE Tel. Ops., Irving, Tex., 1988-96, exec. v.p. network ops., 1996-97; pres. GTE Network Svcs., Irving, Tex., 1997—. Office: GTE Telephone Ops PO Box 152092 Irving TX 75015-2092*

APPEL, KENNETH I., mathematician, educator; b. Bklyn., Oct. 8, 1932; s. Irwin and Lillian (Sender) A.; m. Carole Stein, June 21, 1959; children—Andrew, Laurel, Peter. B.S., Queens Coll., 1953; M.A., U. Mich., 1956, Ph.D., 1959. Mem. tech. staff Inst. for Def. Analyses, Princeton, N.J., 1959-61; asst. prof. math U. Ill., Urbana, 1961-67; assoc. prof. U. Ill., 1967-77, prof., 1977-93; chair. dept. math. Univ. New Hampshire, 1993—. Alderman, City of Urbana, 1971-75, mem. zoning bd. of appeals, 1975—. Served as pfc. U.S. Army, 1953-55. Recipient Delbert Ray Fulkerson prize Am. Math. Soc. and Math. Programming Soc., 1979, Disting. Alumnus award Queens Coll., 1979. Mem. Am. Math. Soc., Math. Assn. Am., Assn. Symbolic Logic. Democrat. Jewish. Office: Univ New Hampshire Dept Math Kingsbury Hall Durham NH 03824

APPEL, MARSHA CEIL, association executive; b. N.Y.C., Dec. 3, 1953; d. Albert and Stella Joy (Glaser) A.; m. Mark D. Marcellus, Sept. 10, 1978; children: Sam, Jill. BA, SUNY, Albany, 1974; MSLS, Syracuse U., 1975. Info. specialist Am. Assn. Advt. Agys., N.Y.C., 1976-79, mgr. member info. svc., 1979-89, v.p., 1989-97, sr. v.p., 1997—. Author: Illustration Index IV, 1980, Illustration Index V, 1984, Illustration Index VI, 1988, Illustration Index VII, 1993, Illustration Index VIII, 1998; editor What's New in Advertising and Marketing, 1978-80; mem. adv. bd., contbr. Ency. Advt., 1999. Mem. Spl. Librs. Assn. (chmn. advt. and mktg. div. 1982-83). Office: Am Assn Advt Agys 405 Lexington Ave New York NY 10174-0002

APPEL, NINA SCHICK, law educator, dean; b. Feb. 17, 1936, Prague, Czech Republic; d. Leo and Nora Schick; m. Alfred Appel Jr.; children: Karen Oshman, Richard. Student, Cornell U.; JD, Columbia U., 1959. Instr. Columbia Law Sch., 1959-60; adminstr. Stanford U.; mem. faculty, prof. law, 1973—, assoc. dean 1976-83, dean Sch. Law, Loyola U., 1983—, dean Sch. Law, 1983—. Mem. Ill. Compensation Rev. Bd. Mem. Am. Bar Found., Chgo. Bar Found., Ill. Bar Found., Chgo. Legal Club, Chgo. Network. Jewish. Office: Loyola U Sch Law 1 E Pearson St Chicago IL 60611-2055

APPEL, ROBERT A., urologist; b. Feb. 22, 1955. BS, Villanova U., 1977; MD, U. Va., 1981. Staff urologist U.S. Naval Hosp., Charleston, S.C., 1986-90; pvt. practice urology Fayetteville, N.C., 1990—; chief surgery Highsmith-Rainey Meml. Hosp., Fayetteville, 1995-96. Mem. Cumberland County Med. Soc. (sec./treas. 1998-99). E-mail: Wahoos99@aol.com.

APPEL, ROBERT EUGENE, lawyer, educator; b. Cleve., Oct. 18, 1958; s. Robert Donald and Jean Ann (Crites) A.; m. Margaret Rose Curley, Aug. 24, 1985. BS, Cen. Conn. State U., 1980; JD, U. Bridgeport, Conn., 1982; MBA, U. Conn., 1984; LLM, Boston U., 1984. Bar: Conn. 1983. Asst. mgr. fin. services Lexington Ins. Co., Boston, 1984-85; tax. cons. Touche Ross and Co., Stamford, Conn., 1985-86; asst. dir. nat. design CIGNA Corp., Bloomfield, Conn., 1986-88; dir. nat. design CIGNA Corp., Bloomfield, 1988-98; asst. v.p. Lincoln Nat. Life Ins. Co., Hartford, 1999—; lectr. Real Estate Tng. and Ednl. Svcs., Bridgeport, 1985-88; lectr. real estate Dare Inst., Southbury, 1991—. Div. coord. United Way, 1988. Mem. ABA, Conn. Bar Assn. Republican. Roman Catholic. Avocations: investing, running, weightlifting, motorcycling. Home: 80 Kingston Dr East Hartford CT 06118-2450 Office: Lincoln Fin Group 350 Church St Hartford CT 06103-1106

APPEL, STANLEY HERSH, neurologist; b. Boston, May 8, 1933; widowed; 4 children. AB, Harvard U., 1954; MD, Columbia U., 1960. Diplomate Am. Bd. Psyciatry & Neurology. Intern medicine Mass. Gen. Hosp., 1960-61; resident neurology Mt. Sinai Hosp., 1961-62; rsch. assoc. Lab. Moleculat Biology NIH, 1962-64; chief rsch. assoc. Sch. Medicine U. Pa., 1965-66, asst. prof., 1966-67; assoc. of neurology Med. Ctr. Duke U., 1964-65, from assoc. prof. to prof. neurology, 1967-77, assoc. prof. biochemistry, 1968-77, chief divsn. neurology, 1969-77; prof. neurology, dept. chmn. Baylor Coll. Medicine, 1977—, chmn. program neurosci., 1977-89, dir. Jerry Lewis Neuromuscular Disorder Rsch. Ctr., 1977—. Recipient Rsch. Career Devel. award USPHS, 1965-70. Mem. Am. Acad. Neurology, Am. Soc. Biol. Chemistry, Am. Soc. Clin. Investigation, Am. Neurol. Assn. Achievements include research in etiology of amyotrophic lateral sclerosis, Parkinson's disease, and Alzheimer's disease. Office: Baylor Dept Neurology 6501 Fannin St NB302 Houston TX 77030-2703

APPEL, TRUMAN FRANK, surgeon; b. St. Louis, Apr. 4, 1936; s. Myron Henry and Ida Doris (Pearline) A.; children: Leslie Carol, Sarah Elizabeth. BS, Tulane U., 1956; MD, St. Louis U., 1960. Diplomate Am. Bd. Surgery, Am. Bd. Colon and Rectal Surgery. Pvt. practice Corpus Christi, Tex., 1969—; treas., bd. dirs. Coastal Bend Health Plan, Corpus Christi, 1984-92. Served to capt. USAF, 1961-64. Fellow AMA, ACS, Am. Soc. Colon and Rectal Surgeons Tex., Tex. Med. Assn., Masons, Shriners, Tex. Surg. Soc. Jewish. Avocations: hunting, fishing. Office: 307 Spohn Med Pl 1415 3rd St Corpus Christi TX 78404-2107

APPEL, WALLACE HENRY, retired industrial designer; b. Boston, Sept. 10, 1925; s. Wallace Henry and Isabella (Simpson) A.; m. Marjorie Jeanne Triebold, Nov. 22, 1948; children: Linda, Donna, Sandra. B.F.A., R.I. Sch. Design, 1950. Staff designer Westinghouse Electric, Mansfield, Ohio, 1950-55, mgr. indsl. design, 1955-75; mgr. indsl. design White-Westinghouse, Mansfield, 1975-80; v.p. design Advanced Food Systems, Columbus, Ohio, 1980-82; v.p. design and planning WCI Internat., Grand Rapids, Mich., 1982-87, Pitts., 1987-91. Contbg. author: World of Manufacturing, 1968; patentee in field. Served with USN, 1943-46. Fellow Indsl. Designers Soc. Am. (dir. 1975-80). Home: 1229 Schooner Ln Venice FL 34292-1437

APPEL, WILLIAM FRANK, pharmacist; b. Mpls., Oct. 8, 1924; s. William Ignatius and Elna Antonia (Mulzahn) A.; m. Louise D. Altman, Sept. 24, 1949; children—Nancy, Peggy, James, Elizabeth. B.S. in Pharmacy, U. Minn., 1949; D.Sc. (hon.), Phila. Coll. Pharmacy and Sci., 1978. Intern in pharmacy Northwestern Hosp., Mpls.; pres., pharmacist, mgr. Appel Com-Pharm, Inc., Mpls., 1949—; pres. Pharm. Cons. Services, P.A., St. Paul, 1960—; mem. Minn. Bd. Pharmacy, 1960-65, pres., 1965; preceptor internship requirement program; chmn. Minn. Gov's. Commn. on Drug Abuse, 1971-73; mem. Mpls. Health Dept. Task Force on Pub. Health Approaches to Chem. Dependency; clin. instr. U. Minn. Coll. Pharmacy, 1970—; cons. HEW; long term care facilities; rep. Nat. Pharmacy/Industry Com. on Nat. Health Ins.; mem. revision com. U.S. Pharmacopeial Conv., 1980—. Served with USN, 1942-46. Recipient Good Neighbor award Sta. WCCO, Mpls., 1973. Mem. Twin City Met. Drug Assn., Minn. Pharm. Assn. (v.p., Harold R. Popp award 1974, mem. continuing edn. faculty 1970—), Am. Pharm. Assn. (pres. N.W. br., nat. pres. 1976-77, Daniel B. Smith award 1970, treas. 1979—) pharm. assns), Minn. Gerontol. Soc., U. Minn. Coll. Pharmacy Alumni Assn. (v.p., Distinguished Pharmacist award 1971). Home: 7204 Trillium Ln Minneapolis MN 55435-4020 Office: PO Box 141024 Minneapolis MN 55414-6024

APPELBAUM, ANN HARRIET, lawyer; b. Decatur, Ill., Oct. 31, 1948; d. Irving and Cecelia (Hecht) A.; m. Neal Borovitz, July 4, 1982; children: Abby, Jeremy. BA, Barnard Coll., 1970; JD, Boston U., 1973. Bar: N.Y. 1974, U.S. Dist. Ct. (so. dist.) N.Y. 1975, U.S. Ct. Appeals (2nd cir.) 1975, U.S. Supreme Ct. 1978. Assoc. Hart & Hume, N.Y.C., 1974-76, Warshaw, Burstein, N.Y.C., 1976-80; counsel Jewish Theol. Sem. & Jewish Mus., N.Y.C., 1980—. V.p. Solomon Schechter Day Sch., N.J., 1992—. Mem. Nat. Assn. Coll. & Univ. Attys. Office: The Jewish Theological Seminary 3080 Broadway New York NY 10027-4650

APPELBAUM, DAVID MARC, magazine editor, philosophy educator; b. N.Y.C., Oct. 7, 1942; s. Henry and Anita (Volkert) A.; m. Amanda Ross, Sept. 14, 1965 (dec. Oct. 1975); 1 child, Susannah; m. Katy Bray, Oct. 25, 1984; 1 child, Joshua. BA, Williams Coll., Williamstown, Mass., 1964; MA, Exeter Coll., Oxford U., Eng., 1966; PhD, Harvard U., 1971. Prof. philosophy SUNY, New Paltz, 1971—; editor Parabola Mag., N.Y.C., 1994—. Author: Contact and Attention, 1986, Bringing the Body to Touch, 1988, Making the Body Heard, 1988, Voice, 1990, Everyday Spirits, 1993, The Stop, 1995, Disruption, 1996, Vision of Hume, 1996, Vision of Kant, 1997; co-author: (with Sarah Lawton) Ethics and the Professions, 1990, (with Jacob Needleman) Real Philosophy, 1991; contbr. numerous articles to profl. jours.; book rev. editor Parabola; series editor for SUNY Press: Visionary Worlds, Mysticism Examined, The Golden Fleece & Alchemy, Paranormal Experience & Survival of Death, Gnosis, Discovering the West, German Mysticism from Hildegard of Bingen to Ludwig Wittgenstein, Sacred Geography of the Ancient Greeks, The Masters Revealed, The Theosophical Enlightenment, Access to Western Esotericism, Mysticism, Death and Dying, The Brotherhood of the Common Life and Its Influence, What Number is God?, The Spiritual Wirings of Amir 'Abd-al-Kader, Initiates of Theosophical Masters, Yeats and Alchemy, Paranomral Experience & Survival of Death, Gnosis; series editor: Revisioning Philosophy, Peter Lang, various vols.; book reviewer. Moody fellow Williams Coll., 1964, Kent fellow Danforth Found., 1966. Avocations: biking, hiking. Home: 1 Arden Ln New Paltz NY 12561-3501 Office: Parabola Magazine 656 Broadway New York NY 10012-2317

APPELBAUM, JUDITH PILPEL, editor, consultant, educator; b. N.Y.C., Sept. 26, 1939; d. Robert Cecil and Harriet Florence (Fleischl) Pilpel; m. Alan Appelbaum, Apr. 16, 1961; children: Lynn Stephanie, Alexander Eric. BA with honors, Vassar Coll., 1960. Editor Harper's Mag., N.Y.C., 1960-74; mng. editor Harper's Weekly, 1974-76; sr. cons. Atlas World Press Rev., 1977; mng. editor Pubs. Weekly, 1978-81, contbg. editor, 1981-82; columnist N.Y. Times Book Rev., 1982-84; founder Sensible Solutions, Inc., 1979, mng. dir., 1984—; assoc. dir. Ctr. for Book Rsch., U. Scranton, 1985-88; book rev. editor Pub. Rsch. Quar., 1984-86, editor in chief, 1986-88, cons. editor, 1988—, chair book industry sys. adv. com. royalty subcom., 1996-98; chair Book and Serial Ind. Comm. Rights Com., 1998, mem. basic exec. com., 1998—; contbg. editor Small Press mag., 1991-96; mem. faculty Pub. Inst., U. Denver, 1981—, CUNY Edn. in Pub. Program, 1982—; chair Book Industry Study Group Publs., 1980—, Small Press Ctr., 1998—, adv. coun. mem.; mem. stats. com. Book Industry Study Group, 1984—, bd. dirs., 1997—, exec. com., 1998—; adv. bd. Coordinating Coun. Lit. Mags., 1980-84, PEN Ctr. USA West, 1988-90. Author: How to Get Happily Published, 1978, 5th edit., 1998, (with Fl. Janovic) The Writer's Workbook: A Full and Friendly Guide to Boosting Your Book's Soles, 1991; editor: (with T. Jones and G. Cravens) The Big Picture: A Wraparound Book, 1976, The Question of Size in the Book Industry Today, 1978, Getting a Line on Backlist, 1979, Paperback Primacy, 1981, Small Publisher Power, 1982. Mem. PEN, Authors Guild, Women's Media Group (bull. editor 1990-92), Pubs. Mktg. Assn. (bd. dirs. 1990-92, Benjamin Franklin Lifetime Achievement award 1995). Office: Sensible Solutions Inc 271 Madison Ave Ste 1007 New York NY 10016-1001

APPELBAUM, MICHAEL ARTHUR, finance company executive; b. N.Y.C., Nov. 7, 1945; s. Malvin and Dorothy (Gross) A.; m. Elizabeth Jane Urdang, June 1, 1969; children: Laura Beth, Mark David. BS, Fairleigh Dickinson U., 1967; JD, Suffolk U., 1970. Bar: N.J., 1974; CPA, N.J. Mgmt. trainee 1st Nat. Bank of Boston, 1970-71; sr. tax acct. Ernst & Whinney, Newark, 1971-75; from tax and ins. mgr. to dir. tax ins. and legal compliance Essex Chem. Corp., Clifton, N.J., 1975-82, v.p., treas., 1982-87, v.p., treas., chief fin. officer, 1987-88, chief oper. officer, 1988-89; chief fin. officer Ingersoll Publs. Co., Princeton, N.J., 1989-90; pres., chief exec. officer Alto Acquisition Cons., Inc., Morristown, N.J., 1990; v.p., chief fin. officer Hatco Corp., Fords, N.J., 1990-91; v.p., chief fin. officer Medarex, Inc., Annandale, N.J., 1991-93, sr. v.p. fin. and adminstrn., 1993—, also bd. dirs.; exec. v.p., CFO Medarex, Inc., Annandale, 1997—; pres., COO GenPharm Internat., Inc., 1997—, also bd. dirs.; bd. dirs. Ingersoll Newspapers, Inc., Community Newspapers, Inc.; pres. COO, bd. dirs. GenPharm Internat., Inc. Dir. Parsippany (N.J.) Soccer Club, 1981-84, treas. 1983-84. Mem. Nat. Assn. of Treas., Fin. Execs. Inst., Risk and Ins. Mgmt. Soc. Avocations: golf, skiing. Office: Medarex Inc Annandale NJ 08801

APPELBAUM, PAUL STUART, psychiatrist, educator; b. Bklyn., Nov. 30, 1951; s. Isidore W. and Celia (Bressler) A.; m. Diana Muir Karter, Nov. 9, 1953; children: Binyamin, Yonaton, Avigail. AB, Columbia U., 1972; MD, Harvard U., 1976. Diplomate Am. Bd. Psychiatry and Neurology. Intern Soroka Med. Ctr., Beersheva, Israel, 1976-77; resident Mass. Mental Health Ctr., Boston, 1977-80; Clin. fellow psychiatry Harvard Med. Sch., Boston, 1977-80; from asst. prof. to assoc. prof. psychiatry and law U. Pitts., 1980-84; assoc. prof. psychiatry Harvard Med. Sch., Boston, 1984-85; Zeleznik prof. psychiatry, dir. law and psychiatry program U. Mass. Med. Sch., Worcester, 1985—; chmn. dept. U. Mass. Med. Sch., Worcester, Mass., 1992—; vis. interdisciplinary prof. Law Ctr. Georgetown U., Washington, 1988-89; mem. commn. on mentally disabled ABA, Washington, 1982-87; task force on involuntary civil commitment Nat. Ctr. for State Cts., Williamsburg, Va., 1984-89, Rsch. Network on Mental Health and Law, John D. and Catherine T. Macarthur Found., Chgo., 1988-96; fellow Ctr. for Advanced Study in the Behavioral Scis., Stanford, Calif., 1996-97. Author: Clinical Handbook of Psychiatry and the Law, 1982 (M.F. Guttmacher award 1982), 2d edit., 1991, Informed Consent: Legal Theory and Clinical Practice, 1987, Paul Appelbaum on Law and Psychiatry, 1989, Almost A

Revolution: Mental Health Law and Limits of Change, 1994 (M.F. Guttmacher award 1996), Trauma and Memory: Clinical and Legal Controversies, 1997, Assessing Patients' Capacities to Consent to Treatment, 1998; contbr. articles to profl. jours. Nat. coord. Med. Mobilization for Soviet Jewry, Waltham, Mass., 1974-80; bd. dirs. Action for Soviet Jewry, Waltham, 1984-85, Torah Ctr., Sharon, Mass., 1987-88, Community Health Link, Worcester, Mass., 1992—. Recipient rsch. scientist devel. award NIMH, 1983; rsch. grantee President's Commn. on Ethical Problems in Medicine, Washington, 1982, John D. and Catherine T. MacArthur Found., 1988; fellow Ctr. for Advanced Study in Behavioral Scis., Palo Alto, Calif., 1996-97. Mem. Internat. Acad. Law and Mental Health, Am. Psychiat. Assn. (chair commn. on jud. action 1984-90, joint reference com. 1984-94, chair coun. on psychiatry and law 1990-94, sec. 1997-99, v.p. 1999—, Isaac Ray award 1990), Am. Acad. Psychiatry and the Law (councillor 1987-90, pres. 1995-96), Am. Soc. Law and Medicine, Mass. Psychiat. Soc. (pres. 1992-93). Jewish. Avocation: writing for popular mags. Office: U Mass Med Ctr Dept Psychiatry Worcester MA 01655

APPELL, KATHLEEN MARIE, management consultant, legal administrator; b. Phila., Apr. 20, 1943; d. Joseph F. and Catherine (Laing) Hudson; m. Vincent M. Mandes (div. Apr. 1968); children: Carren Lee, Vincent, Lori. Cert., Phila. Modeling Sch., 1960-61, Horsham Found., 1979-81, Behavioral Acad., 1981, Fashion Acad., 1984. Adminstr. Phila. Modeling and Career Sch., 1965-68; pres. KMA Enterprises Ltd., Rosemont, Pa., 1968—; exec. asst. Horsham Psychiat. Hosp., Ambler, Pa., 1976-84; cons. Horsham Psychiat. Hosp., Ambler, 1976-84; dir. admissions Career Inst., Phila., 1986-87; legal adminstr. Howson & Howson, Spring House, Pa., 1990-92; northeast regional dir. Gly Derm, Inc., Bloomfield Hills, Mich., 1992-94; pres. Preventif, Rosemont, Pa., 1994—; exec. dir. Ajune LLC, N.Y.C., 1999—; cons. Resource Spectrum, Ambler, 1979-82, Horsham Mgmt. Corp., Ambler, 1978-84. Contbr. articles to profl. jours. Mem. Rep. Task Force Com., Washington, 1981; mem. Ch. of Bethesda-By-the-Sea Episcopal Ch. Mem. Women's Econ. Devel., Assn. Fashion and Image Cons., Profl. and Exec. Women. Avocations: horseback riding, psychology, attitudinal tng.

APPELL, LOUISE SOPHIA, consulting company executive; b. Northampton, Mass., Sept. 22, 1930; d. Romeo Edward and Phyllis Teresa (Szynal) Fortier; m. Melville Joseph Appell, July 26, 1953 (div. 1975); children: Mellisande Foglio, David Maxcim; m. Clifford Harding Querolo, June 1, 1991 (dec. 1992). BA, Smith Coll., 1951; MA, U. Ky., 1966, PhD, 1972. Instr. U. Ky., 1966-68; dir. spl. edn. grad. program Catholic U. Am., Washington, 1969-76; assoc. dir. nat. com. Arts for the Handicapped, Washington, 1976-80; owner, pres. Louise Appell Cons. Svcs., Washington, 1980-82; assoc. Macro Systems, Inc., Silver Spring, Md., 1982-84, dir. edn. product devel., 1984-85, dir. ednl. product devel., 1985—, v.p., 1985—, ret., 1996, cons., 1996—.

APPELMAN, EVAN HUGH, retired chemist; b. Chgo., June 6, 1935; s. Harry Louis and Mollie Sarah (Hirsch) A.; m. Mary Frances Goold, Sept. 2, 1960; children: Harold Stewart, Hilary Louise. A.B., U. Chgo., 1953, M.S., 1955; Ph.D., U. Calif. at Berkeley, 1960. With Argonne (Ill.) Nat. Lab., 1960-95, chemist, 1963-76, sr. chemist, 1976-95, ret., 1995. Contbr. articles to profl. jours. Guggenheim fellow, 1973-74; Recipient award for service at Argonne Nat. Lab., U. Chgo., 1975, E.O. Lawrence award ERDA, 1976, Alexander von Humboldt Research award Fed. Republic Germany, 1988-89; vis. sr. rsch. fellow Brit. Sci. Rsch. Coun.-U. Oxford, 1983-84. Mem. AAAS, Am. Chem. Soc., Fedn. Am. Scientists, Phi Beta Kappa, Sigma Xi. Jewish. Home: 224 Lake Dr Kensington CA 94708-1132

APPELSON, MARILYN IRENE, director of college development; b. Bklyn., 1933; d. Abraham and Sophie (Porosoff) Backinoff; m. Wallace B. Appelson; children: Teri, Bruce, Andrew, CJ. BA, Bklyn. Coll., 1953; MA, Coll. of N.J., 1967; postgrad., Hunter Coll. Tchr. elem. Newport News (Va.) Pub. Sch., 1953-54; tchr. English, ESL White Plains (N.Y.) Pub. Sch., 1954-57; tchr. ESL Ewing Adult Schs., Ewing Twp., N.J., 1964-76; tchr. English, ESL Mercer County C.C., Trenton, N.J., 1974-76; coord. ESL Chgo. Urban Skills Inst., 1977-79; dir. vols. in tchg. adults Oakton C.C., Des Plaines, Ill., 1979-84, dir. coll. devel., 1984—; chair Fed. Funding Task Force, Washington, 1989-90. Author: (handbook) Handbook for Teachers of English & Citizenship, 1971; editor: (ann. report) NCRD: Federal Funding for Two Year Colleges, 1989-90, (news mag.) NCRD: Dispatch, 1993-94. Mem., v.p. LWV, Trenton, N.J., 1970, 72; mem. Nat. Libr. Literacy Coun., Cook County, Ill., 1997—. Mem. Nat. Coun. for Resource Devel. (pres. 1997—, v.p. programs 1991, Life Time Svc. award 1995), Ill. Resource Devel. Commn. (pres. 1986-87), Skokie Ill. Rotary (treas. 1997—). Avocations: tennis, skiing. Office: Oakton C C 1600 E Golf Rd Des Plaines IL 60016-1234

APPENZELLER, OTTO, neurologist, researcher; b. Czernowitz, Romania, Dec. 11, 1927; came to U.S., 1963; s. Emmanuel Adam and Josephine (Metsch) A.; m. Judith Bryce, Dec. 11, 1956; children: Timothy, Martin, Peter. MBBS, Sydney U., Australia, 1957, MD, 1966; PhD, U. London, Eng., 1963. Diplomate Am. Bd. Psychiatry and Neurology. Prof. U. N. Mex., Albuquerque, 1970-90; vis. prof. McGill U., Montreal, 1977; hon. rsch. fellow U. London, 1983; vis. scientist Oxygen Transport Program Lovelace Med. Found., Albuquerque, 1990-92; pres. N.Mex. Health Enhancement and Marathon Clinics Rsch. Found., Albuquerque, 1992—; prof. exptl. neurobiology Bogomoletz Inst. Ukrainian Acad. Sci., Kiev, 1995—; U.S.-India exch. scientist NSF, 1992; Fogarty internat. exch. scientist, Kiev, Ukraine, 1993; mem. rsch. com. UNESCO Internat. Coun. Sports and Phys. Edn., 1978—; ref. Med. Rsch. Coun. New Zealand, 1986—, reviewer, 1988—; mem. editl. bd. numerous peer reviewed med. jours. Author: The Autonomic Nervous System, 5th edit., 1997; co-author: Headache, 1984; editor: Pathogenesis and Management of Headache, 1976, Health Aspects of Endurance Training, 1978, Sports Medicine, 3d edit., 1988, Jour. Headache, 1975-77, Annals of Sports Medicine, 1984-88; translator: Neurologic Differential Diagnosis (M. Mumentaler), 2nd edit., 1992; vol. editor: Handbook of Clinical Neurology: The Autonomic Nervous System, Parts I and II, 1998. Grantee Diabetes Rsch. and Edn. Found., 1988, Instituto C. Mondino U. of Pavia, Italy, 1992, 95, 96; participant individual health scientist exch. program Fogarty Internat. Ctr., NIH to A.A. Bogomoletz Inst. Physiology, Kiev, 1993. Fellow ACP (sr.), Am. Acad. Neurology (sr.), Royal Australasian Coll. Physicians (sr.). Achievements include discovery of disease affecting peripheral nerves of Navajo children, of release of opioids and endothelin in human circulatory system after exercise, of chronic neurodegenerative disease in human T-lymphotropic viral II (HTLV II) infection, of peptidergic innervation of blood vessels supplying blood to peripheral nerves in present day and ancient mummified tissues; leader of Mt. Everest research expedition in 1987, Khachenjunga research expedition, 1989, Stock Kangri research expedition, 1992, Tso Moriri Lake (Ladakh) research expedition, 1994, Cerro de Pasco research expedition, 1997.

APPERSON, BERNARD JAMES, lawyer; b. Washington, June 28, 1956; s. Bernard James Jr. and Ann Wentworth (Anderson) A. BA in Polit. Sci., Am. U., 1978; JD, Cumberland Sch. Law, 1981; LLM in Internat. Law, Georgetown U., 1985. Bar: Fla. 1981, Ga. 1981, D.C. 1983, U.S. Supreme Ct. 1985. Atty., U.S. trustee for so. dist. N.Y. U.S. Dept. Justice, N.Y.C., 1981; atty. EPA, Washington, 1981-83; atty. civil rights div. U.S. Dept. Justice, Washington, 1983-84, atty. office legis. affairs, 1986-87; asst. U.S. atty. Ea. Dist. Va., Alexandria, 1987-97; counsel to dir. Legal Services Corp., Washington, 1985-86; commr. U.S. Dist. Ct., Ea. Dist. Va., Alexandria, 1996-97; sr. counsel com. on govt. reform and oversight, spl. counsel subcom. Nat. Econ. Growth, Resources etc. U.S. Ho. of Reps., Washington, 1997-98; assoc. ind. counsel Office of the Ind. Counsel, Washington, 1998-99, dep. ind. counsel, 1999—; instr. FBI Tng. Acad., Quantico, Va., 1990; lectr. law U. London and U. Ga., 1990. Assoc. editor Am. Jour. Trial Advocacy Cumberland Sch. Law, 1979-81. County chmn. Paula Hawkins for U.S Senate, Volusia County, Fla., 1974; nat. staff Citizens for Reagan, Fla., Kansas City, Mo., 1976; cons. Reagan for Pres., Detroit, 1980; dep. northeastern regional dir. Reagan-Bush 1984, Washington, 1984. Lewis F. Powell Medal for Excellence in Advocacy Am. Coll Trial Lawyers, 1980. Mem. Federalist Soc. for Law and Pub. Policy Studies, Order of Barristers, St. Andrew's Soc. Republican. Episcopalian. Home: 545 E Braddock Rd Apt 704 Alexandria VA 22314-2171 Office: Office Ind Counsel 4th Fl 1001 Pennsylvania Ave NW Ste 4 Washington DC 20004-2505

APPERSON, JACK ALFONSO, retired army officer, business executive; b. Fredericksburg, Va., Dec. 21, 1934; s. Claude Heywood and Mary Louise (Farmer) A.; m. Alexandra Maynard, Aug. 31, 1957 (dec. Aug. 1992); children: Melissa Heywood, Amy Alexandra, Robert Randall (dec.), Eric Edward; m. Marguerite M. Legin, Nov. 25, 1995. B.S. U.S. Mil. Acad., 1957; M.S. in Nuclear Physics, U. Ala., 1962; A.A. hon., Texarkana Community Coll., 1979. Commd. 2d lt. U.S. Army, 1957, advanced through grades to brig. gen.; platoon leader U.S. Army, Ft. Bragg, N.C., 1957-58, Ft. Knox, Ky., 1958-59; comdg. officer 546th Ordnance Co. U.S. Army-Europe, 1963-64, materiel officer 66th Maintenance Bn., 1964-65, exec. officer bn., 1965-66; asst. prof., instr. dept. ordnance U.S. Mil. Acad., 1967-69; bn. comdr. and materiel officer 801st Maintenance Bn., Vietnam, 1969-70; assignment officer ordnance br. Office of Personnel Ops., Dept. Army, Washington, 1970-71; chief co. grade assignments Office of Personnel Ops., Dept. Army, 1971-72; bn. comdr. 1st Inf. Div., Ft. Riley, Kans., 1973-74; office dep. chief of staff for logistics Dept. Army, Washington, 1974-75; chief war res. office Office Dep. Chief of Staff for Logistics, Dept. Army, Washington, 1975-76; exec. to asst. sec. Army Installations and Logistics, Washington, 1976-77; comdr. Red River Army Depot, Texarkana, Tex., 1977-79; dep. comdg. gen. U.S. Army Missile Materiel Readiness Command, Redstone Arsenal, Ala., 1979-81; comdg. gen. U.S. Army Depot System Command, Chambersburg, Pa., 1981-82; sr. v.p. ops. mgmt. div. Day & Zimmermann, Phila., 1982-83, also bd. dirs.; pres. Govt. Systems Group Day and Zimmerman, Phila., 1991-95, Systems Engring. Assocs. Corp., Mt. Laurel, NJ, 1983-91. Bd. dirs. Redstone Fed. Credit Union; vestryman Sharon Chapel Episcopal Ch., Alexandria, Va., 1975-77, St. Paul's Episcopal Ch., Phila., 1984-1988. Decorated DSM, Legion of Merit, Bronze Star (2), Meritorious Svc. medal, others; inducted into U.S. Army Ordnance Hall of Fame, 1994. Mem. Assn. Grads. U.S. Mil. Acad., West Point Soc. Phila. (bd. dirs.), Assn. U.S. Army (pres. chpt. 1983-85), Am. Def. Preparedness Assn., Alumni Assn. U.S. Army War Coll., Phila C. of C., Cherry Hill C. of C., Narragansett C. of C. (pres. 1996—), South County Hosp. Found., R.I. State Investment Commn., Rotary (pres. West Bay Rotary Coun. 1999), Sigma Pi Sigma. Republican. Home: 93 Old Boston Neck Rd Narragansett RI 02882-3007

APPERSON, JEAN, psychologist; b. Durham, N.C., June 8, 1934; d. James Harry and Dorothy Elizabeth (Johnson) Apperson; m. Calvin Adams Pope, Mar. 23, 1956 (div. 1967); 1 child, Richard Allan. BA, U. S. Fla., 1966; MA, Mich. State U., 1970, PhD, 1973. Cert. in psychoanalysis Mich. Psychoanalytic Coun., 1990. Teaching asst. Mich. State U., E. Lansing, 1968-69; psychiatric technician St. Lawrence Community Mental Health Ctr., Lansing, Mich., 1968-69; psychology intern St. Lawrence Community Mental Health Ctr., 1969-71, Mich. State U. Counseling Ctr., 1971-73; clin. psychologist U. Mich. Counseling Ctr., Ann Arbor, 1973-81; pvt. practice psychology and psychoanalysis Ann Arbor, 1974—; mem., chmn. Mich. Bd. Psychology, Lansing, 1984-91. Contbr. articles to profl. jours.; cons. editor Am. Psychol. Assn. Catalog of Selected Documents, 1975-80. USPHS grantee, 1969-70; NIMH grantee, 1970-71. Fellow Mich. Psychol. Assn. (chmn. women's issues com. 1981-83); mem. APA (com. on sci. and profl. ethics and conduct 1977-80), Mich. Soc. Psychoanalytic Psychology (treas. 1982-86), Mich. Psychoanalytic Coun. (tchg. and supervising analyst, mem. at large 1991-93, tng. com. 1992—, pres. 1995-97, v.p. for edn. and tng. 1998—), Asn. for Advancement of Psychology, Am. Women in Psychology, Mich. Women Psychologists. Democrat. Unitarian. Avocations: French language and culture, gardening, nature study, music. Home: 7224 Chelsea Manchester Rd Manchester MI 48158-9443 Office: 555 E William St Apt 23E Ann Arbor MI 48104-2428

APPERSON, JEFFREY A., lawyer; b. Zanesville, Ohio, July 1, 1954; s. Ronald L. and Rosemary (Carney) A.; m. Julie Brown; children: Tara Michelle, Jeffrey William, Justin Brown. BA, High Point Coll., 1979; JD, Samford U., 1982. Bar: Ala. 1982. Atty. Adminstr. Office of U.S. Cts., Washington, 1982-85; clk. U.S. Bankruptcy Ct. (we. dist.) Ky., Louisville, 1985-93, U.S. Dist. Ct. (we. dist.) Ky., Louisville, 1994—. Bd. dirs. Wayside Cristian Mission. Sgt. USAF, 1972-76. Mem. Louisville Bar Assn., Nat. Conf. Bankruptcy Clerks (sec. 1988-90, c.p. 1989-90, pres. 1990-91), Fed. Bar Assn. (Ky. chpt.), Kiwanis (pres. elect Metroban), Alpha Chi Omega (pres. 1979). Avocations: tennis, reading, hiking. Office: US Dist Ct 601 W Broadway Ste 106 Louisville KY 40202-2238

APPEZZATO, MARC ROBERT, graphic artist; b. Rahway, N.J., Jan. 22, 1973; s. Robert and Edith (Nardone) A. AA, Union County Coll., Cranford, N.J., 1995; BS, Kean Coll., Union, N.J., 1997. Graphic artist Vantage Custom Classics, Avenel, N.J., 1997—. Avocations: photography, writing, moviemaking/film. Home: 801 Garden St Rahway NJ 07065 Office: Vantage Custom Classics 100 Vantage Dr Avenel NJ 07001

APPIER, (ROBERT) KEVIN, professional baseball player; b. Lancaster, Calif., Dec. 6, 1967. Student, Fresno State U., Antelope Valley Coll. Pitcher Kansas City Royals, 1989—. Named Sporting News Rookie Pitcher of Yr., 1990; selected to Am. League All-Star Team, 1995. Office: Kansas City Royals PO Box 419969 Kansas City MO 64141-6969*

APPLBAUM, RONALD LEE, academic administrator; b. Charleroi, Pa., Dec. 14, 1943; s. Irwin and Marion (Caplan) A.; m. Susan Joy Stone, July 4, 1968; 1 child, Lee. BA, Calif. State U., Long Beach, 1965, MA, 1966; PhD, Pa. State U., 1969. Prof. Calif. State U., Long Beach, 1969-76, assoc. dean, 1976-77, dean, 1977-82; v.p. U. Tex.-Pan Am., Edinburg, 1982-90; pres. Westfield (Mass.) State Coll., 1990-96, Kean U., Union, N.J., 1996—; mem. bd. examiners Dept. Edn., 1997—; dir. N.J. Alliance, Inc., 1998—. Author: Fundamentals of Human Communication, 1973, Process of Group Communication, 1979, Organizational Communication, 1981, Business and Professional Speaking, 1982; co-author 7 textbooks; editor textbook series ModComm, MassCom, ProCom, 1973-80; contbr. articles to profl. jours. Bd. dirs.Temple Emanuel, McAllen, Tex., 1983-90, pres., 1987-89; v.p. McAllen chpt. B'nai Brith, 1984-89. Mem. Internat. Comm. Assn., World Comm. Assn. (sec.-gen. 1982-91, pres. 1991-95), Ea. Comm. Assn. (reviewer 1991-93, exec. coun. 1994-96), Speech Comm. Assn., Mass Comm. Assn., Assn. Comm. Adminstrs. (editor JACA 1992—), Westfield C. of C. (bd. dirs. 1991-96, vice-chair 1992-94, chair 1994-95), Westfield Comty. Devel. Corp. (pres. 1994, 95), Westfield Kiwanis (v.p. 1992-95, pres. 1995-96), Phi Kappa Phi (pres. Calif. State U. Long Beach chpt. 1976-77, Westfield State Coll. chpt. 1992-93), Union County Alliance (exec. bd. 1997—), Union County Twp. C.C. (bd. dirs. 1997—). Office: Kean U Office of Pres 1000 Morris Ave Union NJ 07083*

APPLE, B. NIXON, lawyer; b. Toronto, Ont., Can., 1924. Ed., U. Toronto, Osgoode Hall Law Sch. Ptnr. firm Torkin, Manes, Cohen & Arbus, Toronto; Queen's counsel. Home: Rural Route 3, Uxbridge, ON Canada L9P 1R3 Office: 151 Yonge St Ste 1500, Toronto, ON Canada M5C 2W7

APPLE, JACQUELINE B (JACQUELINE B. APPLE), artist, writer, educator; b. N.Y.C.. Student, Syracuse U.; BFA, Parsons Sch. Design. Curator exhbns. and performance Franklin Furnace, N.Y.C., 1977-80; prodr., host Sta. KPFK-FM, North Hollywood, Calif., 1982-95; mem. faculty Art Ctr. Coll. Design, Pasadena, Calif., 1983—; mem. faculty adv. com. Art Ctr. Coll. Design, Pasadena, 1993; vis. faculty UCSD, LaJolla. Contb. writer: L.A. Weekly, 1983-89; contbg. editor: Artweek, 1983-90, High Performance Mag., 1984-95; writer, performer, dir., prodr.: (record) The Mexican Tapes, 1979-80, (performance/radio work) Voices in the Dark, 1989-90, (radio art work) Swan Lake, 1989; artist, prodr.: (installations and audio work) The Culture of Disappearance, 1991-95; author, designer: (book, installation) Trunk Pieces, 1975-78, (cd) Thank You for Flying American, 1995; six part radio art series Redefining Democracy in America Parts, 1991-92; (site specific installation/projection) Zeitghosts: Angels in the Architecture, 1996; (photowork) ghost.dance series 1995—); pub. art project Aliso-Pico Cmty. Ctr., 1997—; author: Doing it Right in L.A., 1990. Recipient Vesta award Media Arts Women's Bldg., 1990; NEA visual artists fellow, 1979, 81; InterArts program grantee NEA, 1984-85, 91-92; Calif. Arts Coun. Visual Arts/New Genres fellowship, 1996. Mem. Internat. Art Critics Assn., Nat. Writers Union, Coll. Art Assn. Home: 3532 Jasmine Ave Los Angeles CA 90034-4947

APPLE, MARTIN ALLEN, scientific federation executive, educator; b. Duluth, Minn., Sept. 17, 1938; m. M. Daina; children: Deborah Dawn, Pamela Ruth, Nathan, Rebeccah Lynn. AB, ALA, U. Minn., 1959, MSc, 1962; PhD, U. Calif., 1968. Chmn. Multidisciplinary Drug Rsch. Group U. Calif., San Francisco, 1974-78; pres. Escagen-IPRI, San Carlos, Calif., 1978-81; with EAN-Tech., Inc., Daly City, Calif., 1982-84, chmn. bd., 1983-84; with Adytum Internat., Mountain View, Calif., 1982-90, CEO, 1983-90; CEO LEADERS, Washington, 1989—; exec. dir. Coun. Sci. Soc. Presidents, Washington, 1993—; CEO Sci. Watch, Inc., 1996—; with Hon. Doug Walgren co-chair Leadership Network, 1995-97; adj. prof. U. Calif., San Francisco, 1982-84; cons. SRI Internat. Dept. Edn., EPA, NIH, NSF, The Network, Hughes-GM, Nat. Cancer Inst., AAAS, Nat. Sci. Tchrs. Assn., others; adj. rsch. prof. George Mason U., Fairfax, Va., 1991-92; vis. scholar Nat. Humanities Ctr., 1990-91; nat. project mgr. NSTA Scope Sequence and Coordination Project, 1991-92; bd. dirs. Am. Med. Progress Ednl. Found.; bd. dirs. ACCTION, Inc., chmn. trustees, 1995-96; expert advisor Dept. of Edn., 1996—. Author: (with F. Myers) Review Medical Pharmacology, 1976; (with M. Fink) Immune RNA in Neoplasia, 1976; (with F. Becker et al) Cancer: A Comprehensive Treatise, 1977; (with M. Keenberg et al) Investing in Biotechnology, 1981; (with F. Ahmad et al) From Genes to Proteins: Horizons in Biotechnology, 1983; (with J. Kureczka) Status of Biotechnology, 1987; (with M. Baum) Business Advantage, 1987 (winner Excellence award Software Pubs. Assn. 1987); mem. editorial bd. Computers in Medicine. Mem. Calif. Coun. Indsl. Innovation, 1982. Recipient citation East West Ctr. Bd. of Govs., 1988, Leadership citation Coun. Sci. Soc. Pres., 1995. Fellow Am. Coll. Clin. Pharmacology, Am. Inst. Chemists; mem. Assn. Venture Founders (bd. govs. 1982-83), East-West Ctr. Assn. (trustee 1982-88, vice chmn. 1983-85), Profl. Software Programmers Assn., Leaders of Tomorrow (chmn. 1987-88), Commonwealth Club Calif., Phi Beta Kappa Assocs. (Disting. Svc. award 1984, 85), Phi Beta Kappa, Sigma Xi (bd. dirs., chmn. long-range strategic planning com. 1988-92). Office: Coun Sci Soc Presidents PO Box 33999 Washington DC 20033-0999

APPLE, RAYMOND WALTER, JR., journalist; b. Akron, Ohio, Nov. 20, 1934; s. Raymond Walter and Julia (Albrecht) A.; m. Betsey Pinckney Brown, July 14, 1982; stepchildren: Catherine St. George Brown, John Preston Brown. Student, Princeton U., 1952-56; AB, Columbia U., 1961; LHD (hon.), Denison U., 1989; LLD, Knox Coll., 1993, Gettysburg Coll., 1995. Reporter Wall St. Jour., 1956-57, 59-61; writer, corr. NBC News, 1961-63; mem. staff N.Y. Times, 1963—, Albany bur. chief, 1964-65, Vietnam corr., 1965-66, Vietnam bur. chief, 1966-68, Africa bur. chief, 1969, nat. polit. corr., 1970-76, London bur. chief, 1977-80, 81-85, Moscow bur. chief, 1980-81, Washington bur. chief, 1992-97, chief Washington corr., 1985-97, chief corr., 1998—; Theodore H. White Meml. lectr. Harvard U., 1989, Joe Alex Morris Jr. Meml. lectr., 1993; Herzberg lectr. Columbia U.; Kent Meml. lectr. Johns Hopkins U., 1990. Author: Apple's Europe, 1986; contbr. to nat. mags., books. Bd. visitors Western Res. Acad.; chmn. Rhodes Scholarship Com., Mid-Atlantic States. With AUS, 1957-59. Recipient Krout prize history Columbia U., 1961, award NATAS, 1963, George Polk Meml. award, 1967, Overseas Press Club award, 1967, Outstanding Alumnus award Columbia U., 1988, Western Res. Acad., 1976, Weintal award for diplomatic reporting, 1993, Lowell Thomas award for travel writing; Chubb fellow Yale U., 1998. Mem. AFTRA, Brit. Acad. Gastronomes (bd. dirs.), Am. Inst. Wine and Food (bd. dirs.), Gridiron Club, Princeton Club, Century Assn. N.Y., Army-Navy Club. Office: NY Times Washington Bur 1627 I St NW Washington DC 20006-4007

APPLEBAUM, CHARLES, lawyer; b. Newark, May 19, 1947; s. Harry I. and Francis (Gastwirth) A.; children: Matthew, David, Michael. BA, U. Pa., 1969; JD, Rutgers U., 1973; LLM, NYU, 1978. Bar: U.S. Dist. Ct. N.J. 1973. Law clk. to Hon. Samuel A. Larner Jersey City, 1973-74; assoc., then ptnr. Greenbaum, Rowe, Smith, Ravin & Davis, Woodbridge, N.J., 1974-89; gen. counsel Alfieri Orgn., Edison, N.J., 1989—; adj. prof. law Rutgers Law Sch., Newark, 1985-88. Co-author: New Jersey Real Estate Forms, 1988; contbr. articles to profl. jours. Mem. ABA (real property probate and trust, chmn. significant lit. and pubs. 1985-97, co-editor The Acrel Papers 1992, 93, 94), Am. Coll. Real Estate Lawyers (editor publs. 1991—). Office: M Alfieri Co Inc PO Box 2911 399 Thornall St Edison NJ 08837-2236

APPLEBAUM, EDWARD LEON, otolaryngologist, educator; b. Detroit, Jan. 14, 1940; s. M. Lawrence and Frieda (Millman) A.; m. Amelia J. Applebaum; children: Daniel Ira, Rachel Anne. A.B., Wayne State U., 1961, M.D., 1964. Diplomate: Am. Bd. Otolaryngology. Intern Univ. Hosp., Ann Arbor, Mich., 1964-65; resident Mass. Eye and Ear Infirmary Harvard Med. Sch., Boston, 1966-69; practice medicine specializing in otolaryngology Chgo., 1972—; assoc. prof. Northwestern U. Med. Sch., 1972-79; prof., head dept. otolaryngology, head and neck surgery Coll. Medicine, U. Ill., 1979—; mem. staffs U. Ill. Hosp., Westside VA Med. Ctr. Author: Tracheal Intubation, 1976; mem. editorial bd. Am. Jour. Otolaryngology, Laryngoscope. Served as maj. U.S. Army, 1969-71. Recipient Anna Albert Keller Rsch. award Wayne State U. Coll. Medicine, 1964, Disting. Alumni award, 1989, William Beaumont Soc. Original Rsch. award, 1964. Fellow ACS, Am. Soc. for Head and Neck Surgery, Am. Acad. Facial Plastic and Reconstructive Surgery, Am. Acad. Otolaryngology, Head and Neck Surgery, Am. Laryngol., Rhinol. and Otol. Soc. (v.p. 1993), Am. Laryngol. Assn., Am. Otol. Soc., Soc. Univ. Otolaryngologists, Head and Neck Surgeons (pres. 1988), Assn. Acad. Depts. Otolaryngology-Head and Neck Surgery (pres. 1995-96). Home: 161 E Chicago Ave Apt 42B Chicago IL 60611-6677

APPLEBAUM, GARY E., medical director, executive; b. Phila., Pa., Feb. 11, 1959; s. Louis and Arlene (Leonard) A.; m. Julie Ellen Levitt Applebaum, July 8, 1982; children: Michael Louis, Philip Ross. BA magna cum laude, U. Pa., 1981, MD, 1985. Diplomate Am. Bd. Internal Medicine, added qualifications in geriatric medicine. Intern, resident in gen. internal medicine Francis Scott Key Med. Ctr. (formerly Balt. City Hosp.), Balt., 1985-88; fellow in geriatric medicine Sch. of Med. Johns Hopkins U., Balt., 1988-89; attending physician St. Agnes Hosp., Catonsville, Md., 1989—; med. dir. Charlestown Care Ctr., Catonsville, Md., 1989-96; instr. in medicine Sch. of Medicine Johns Hopkins U., Balt., 1989-90, asst. prof. medicine Sch. of Medicine, 1991-99; sr. v.p., med. dir. Sr. Campus Living, Catonsville, Md., 1996-99, 1999—; cons. U.S. Ho. of Reps Select Com. on Aging, Subcommittee on Long Term Care, 1990-92; assoc. prof. medicine U. Md. contbr. numerous articles to profl. jours.; spkr. in field. Recipient Med. Resident award Francis Scott Key Med. Ctr., 1988. Mem. ACP, Am. Geriat. Soc. (Clinician of the Year award 1994), Am. Med. Dirs. Assn. (Ethics Com. 1992—). Jewish. Office: Senior Campus Living 701 Maiden Choice Ln Baltimore MD 21228-5968

APPLEBAUM, HARVEY MILTON, lawyer; b. Birmingham, Ala., Mar. 1, 1937; s. Oscar Arthur and Evelyn (Stein) A.; m. Elizabeth Bloom, June 23, 1962; children: Anne, Julie Flynn, Kathy. BA summa cum laude, Yale U., 1959; LLB magna cum laude, Harvard U., 1962. Bar: D.C. 1964, Ala. 1962, U.S. Ct. Appeals (D.C.) 1964, U.S. Ct. Internat. Trade 1976, U.S. Ct. Appeals (fed. cir.) 1984. Assoc. Covington & Burling, Washington, 1963-71, ptnr., 1971—; adj. prof. Georgetown U. Law Sch., Washington, 1968-72; lectr. U. Va. Law Sch., Charlottesville, 1975—. Chmn. editorial bd.: ABA Antitrust Law Developments, 1975; contbr. articles to profl. jours. Chmn. fair share dr. Sidwell Friends Sch., Washington, 1982-84; pres. Washington Area Tennis Patrons Found., 1986-90, bd. dirs., 1980—; trustee Levine Sch. of Music, 1983-96. Recipient Service award Sidwell Friends Sch., 1984, Yale medal, 1995; Sheldon traveling fellow Harvard U., 1962. Mem. ABA (chmn. antitrust law sect. 1980-81, mem. task force on global economy 1994—, mem. NAFTA task force 1993—, spl. com. on internat. antitrust 1990-91, D.C. Bar Assn., Ala. Bar Assn., Union Internationale des Avocats (del. 1991-93), Assn. Yale Alumni (bd. govs. 1985-94, chair 1990-92, chair Yale Alumni Mag. 1995—), Yale Club Washington (pres. 1981-82), City Club Washington, Edgemoor Club, Yale Club N.Y.C. Avocations: tennis, travel. Home: 2912 Albemarle St NW Washington DC 20008-2134 Office: Covington & Burling 1201 Pennsylvania Ave NW PO Box 7566 Washington DC 20044-7566*

APPLEBAUM, LOUIS, composer, conductor; b. Toronto, Ont., Can., Apr. 3, 1918; s. Morris Abraham and Fanny (Freiberg) A.; m. Janet Hershoff, July 19, 1940; 1 son, David Hersh. Student, U. Toronto, 1938-40; LLD (hon.), York U., 1979; Dr.Humanities (hon.), U. Windsor, Ont., 1994.

Music dir. Nat. Film Bd. Can., Ottawa, Ont., 1941-46; music cons. CBC, Toronto, 1960-61, Nat. Arts Centre, Ottawa, 1963-67; exec. dir. Ont. Arts Council, Toronto, 1971-80; chmn. Fed. Cultural Policy Rev. Com., 1980-82; lectr. York U., Toronto, 1974; artistic advisor Guelph Festival, 1988. Music dir. Stratford (Ont.) Festival, 1953-60; composer, condr. for films, TV, theatre; composed 400 scores for film, theatre, TV, ballets, symphonic, chamber, solo music; contbr. articles to jours. Pres. Socan Found., 1994; chmn. Laidlaw Found. Arts Panel, 1995-98. Decorated companion Order of Can.; recipient award Composers, Authors and Pubs. Assn. Can., 1938, Can. Film award, 1967, Can. Centennial medal, 1967, Wilderness award, 1973, Anik award, 1976, Jubilee medal, 1977, Gemini award, 1989, Arts Toronto Lifetime Achievement award, 1998, RoyThomson Hall award, 1999; nominee Acad. Award; named Arts Person of Yr., 1991. Fellow Ont. Inst. Studies in Edn. (hon.), Ont. Coll. Arts (hon., Juno Spl. Achievement award 1995, 97); mem. Can. Music Ctr., Can. League Composers, Soc. Composers, Authors and Music Pubs. Can. (past pres.), Guild Can. Film Composers, Can. Conf. Arts (Diplôme Honneur 1998), Assembly Arts Adminstrs., Arts and Letters Club Toronto. Home: 214-1210 Don Mills Rd, Don Mills, ON Canada M3B 3N9

APPLEBAUM, STUART S., public relations executive; b. N.Y.C., Sept. 19, 1949; s. Jack and Anne (Miller) A. BA, Queens Coll., 1971. Publicist Alfred A. Knopf Inc., N.Y.C., 1971-73, MGM Pictures, N.Y.C., 1973; publicist Bantam Books Inc., N.Y.C., 1974-77, mgr. publicity, 1977-79, dir. publicity, 1979-87, v.p., dir. pub. rels. and publicity, 1983-90, v.p., dir. pub. rels., 1990-91, v.p., dir. publicity and pub. rels., 1991—; sr. v.p., dir. pub. rels. Bantam Doubleday Dell Pub. Group, 1987-98, Random House, Inc., 1998—. Named as one of the People Who Shaped the Book Bus., Pubs. Weekly, 1997. Mem. Publishers Publicity Assn. (bd. dirs. N.Y.C. chpt. 1979-84). Office: Random House Inc 1540 Broadway New York NY 10036-4039

APPLEBERRY, JAMES BRUCE, higher education association executive; b. Waverly, Mo., Feb. 22, 1938; s. James Earnest and Bertha Viola (Lane) A.; m. Patricia Ann Trent, June 5, 1960; children: John Mark, Timothy David. BS, Central Mo. State Coll., 1960; MS, Cen. Mo. State Coll., 1963, EdS, 1967; postgrad., U. Kans., 1967; Ed.D., Okla. State U., 1969. Tchr. Knob Noster (Mo.) Pub. Sch., 1960-62; prin. Knob Noster Elem. Sch., 1962-63, Knob Noster Jr. High Sch., 1963-64; minister edn. Wornall Rd. Bapt. Ch., Kansas City, Mo., 1964-65; grad. fellow Cen. Mo. State Coll., Warrensburg, 1965-66, asst. dir. field service, 1966-67; grad. asst. Okla. State U., 1968-71, asst. prof. ednl. adminstrn., 1971-73, assoc. prof., 1971-73, prof., head dept. adminstrn. and higher edn., 1973-74; Am. Council on Edn. fellow acad. adminstrn. internship program U. Kans., Lawrence, 1973-74, dir. planning, prof. adminstrn., founds. and higher edn., 1975-76, asst. to chancellor, prof., 1976-77; pres. Pittsburg (Kans.) State U., 1977-83, No. Mich. U., Marquette, 1983-91, Am. Assn. of State Coll. and Univs., Washington, 1991-99; plenary rep. Univ. Council for Ednl. Adminstrn., 1968-72, mem. exec. com., 1973-76; ednl. adminstrn. rep. Council on Tchr. Edn., 1968-75; chmn. Am. Council Edn. Commn. Leadership Devel. and Acad. Adminstrn.; abstracter Univ. Council for Ednl. Adminstrn., Columbus, Ohio, 1969-75; asst. state liaison rep. to Am. Assn. Colls. for Tchr. Edn., 1971; coordinator Interested Profs. Ednl. Adminstrn.; cons. North Cen. Okla. Assn. Sch. Adminstrs.; vice chmn. adv. council Nat. Council Edn. Stats., 1980-83; Kans. rep. to Am. Assn. State Colls. and Univs., 1980-81; pres. Nat. Coll. Athletics Assn. Pres.'s Commn., 1988-89. Contbr. articles to ednl. jours. Trustee Marquette Gen. Hosp. Named Outstanding Alumnus Cen. Mo. State U., 1987, Disting. Alumnus Okla. State U., 1987. Mem. NEA, Am. Assn. for Higher Edn., Am. Assn. State Colls. and Univs. (chmn. policy and purposes com.), Am. Ednl. Rsch. Assn., Nat. Conf. Profs. Ednl. Adminstrn., Mace and Torch, Rotary, Masons (33 deg.), Phi Delta Kappa, Phi Kappa Phi, Kappa Delta, Phi Sigma Phi, Kappa Mu Epsilon, Alpha Kappa Psy. Home: 5610 Wisconsin Ave Apt 704 Bethesda MD 20815-4433 Office: 5th Fl 1307 New York Ave NW Fl 5 Washington DC 20005-4704

APPLEBROOG, IDA, artist; b. Bronx, N.Y., Nov. 11, 1929. Student, N.Y. State Inst. Applied Arts, 1948-50, Art Inst., Chgo., 1965-68. asst. instr. painting Art Inst., Chgo., 1962-66; instr. painting and sculpture U. Calif., San Diego, 1973-74. Prin. works Met. Mus. Art, Mus. Modern Art, New Mus. Contemporary Art, Guggenheim Mus., N.Y., Denver Mus. Art, Sol Lewitt Collection, Wadsworth Atheneum, Hartford, Conn.; one-person shows include Whitney Mus. Am. Art, N.Y., 1978, Chrysler Mus., Norfolk, Va., Ronald Feldman Gallery, N.Y., 1987, 89, 91, Contemporary Arts Mus., Houston, 1990, Kunsthallen Brandts Klaedefabrik, Odense, Denmark, 1992, Realistmus Studio, Berlin, 1992, Directions '83, Mus. Modern Art, N.Y., 1984, Documenta 8, Kassel, Germany, 1987, L.A. County Mus. Art, 1992, PS 1 Mus. L.I. City, N.Y., 1992, Corcoran Gallery of Art, Washington, 1998. Grantee Nat. Endowment Arts, 1980, 85; grantee N.Y. Found. Arts, 1986, 90; Guggenheim fellow, 1990, MacArthur fellow, 1998. Office: care Ronald Feldman Fine Arts 31 Mercer St New York NY 10013-2541

APPLEBY, JOYCE OLDHAM, historian; b. Omaha, Apr. 9, 1929; d. Junius G. and Edith (Cash) Oldham; children: Ann Lansburgh Caylor, Mark Lansburgh, Frank Bell Appleby. B.A., Stanford U., 1950; M.A., U. Calif., Santa Barbara, 1959; Ph.D., Claremont Grad. Sch., 1966. With Mademoiselle mag., 1950-52; asst. prof. history San Diego State U., 1967-70, asso. prof., 1970-73; prof. history, asso. dean Coll. Arts and Letters, 1973-75, prof., 1976-81; vis. asso. prof. U. Calif., Irvine, 1975-76; vis. prof. UCLA, 1978-79, prof. history, 1981—; vis. fellow St. Catherine's Coll., U. Oxford, 1983; Harmsworth prof. Am. History, U. Oxford, 1990-91; Bd. fellows Claremont Grad. Sch. and U. Center, 1970-73. Author: Economic Thought and Ideology in Seventeenth-Century England, 1978, Capitalism and a New Social Order, 1983, Liberalism and Republicanism in the Historical Imagination, 1992; co-author: Telling the Truth about History, 1994; co-editor: Knowledge and Postmodernism in Historical Perspective; mem. bd. editors Democracy, 1980-83, William and Mary Quar., 1980-83, 18th Century Studies, 1982-87, Ency. Am. Polit. History, Am. Hist. Rev., 1988—, Jour. Interdisciplinary History, 1989—, The Papers of Thomas Jefferson, 1988—, The Adams Papers, 1990—; contbr. articles to profl. jours.; mem. adv. bd. Am. Nat. Biography. Mem. Am. Acad. Arts and Scis., Am. Philos. Soc., Smithsonian Inst. (coun.), Am. Hist. Assn. (pres.), Orgn. Am. Historians (pres.), Inst. Early Am. History and Culture (coun. 1980-86, chmn. 1983-89). Home: 615 Westholme Ave Los Angeles CA 90024-3209 Office: UCLA Dept History Los Angeles CA 90024

APPLEGATE, CHRISTINA, actress; b. L.A., Calif., Nov. 25, 1971; d. Nancy Priddy. Film appearances include: Jaws of Satan, 1980, Streets, 1990, Don't Tell Mom the Babysitter's Dead, 1991, Across the Moon, 1994, Vibrations, 1995, Wild Bill, 1995, Mars Attacks!, 1996, Nowhere, 1997, Claudine's Return, 1998, The Big Hit, 1998, Mafia!, 1998; TV appearances include: (series) Days of Our Lives, 1974, Washingtoon, 1985, Heart of the City, 1986, Married...With Children, 1987-97, All My Life, 1998, (TV movies) Grace Kelly, 1983, Dance 'til Dawn, 1988, (spls.) Rate the '80's Awards, 1989, MTV's 1989 Ann. Emmy Awards, 1989, Time Warner Presents the Earth Day Special, 1990, The 4th Ann. Am. Comedy Awards, 1990, The 43d Ann. Primetime Emmy Awards Presentation, 1991, (episodes) Father Murphy, 1981, Quincy, 1983, Charles in Charge, 1984, 84, All Is Forgiven, 1986, Leave It to Beaver, 1986, Amazing Stories, 1986, Silver Spoons, 1986, Family Ties, 1987, 21 Jump St., 1988, Animal Crack-Ups, 1988, Hour Magazine, 1988, Win, Lose, or Draw, 1988, The Pat Sajak Show, 1989, Live with Regis and Kathy Lee, 1989, The Arsenio Hall Show, 1989, Jesse, 1998. *

APPLEGATE, JEFFREY SCOTT, social work educator; b. Carmel, Ind., Feb. 14, 1941; s. Frank and Alta Pearl (Hazelbaker) A.; m. Joan Louise Carter, Oct. 9, 1971; children: Lauren Elizabeth, Garth Andrew. BA, Ind. U., Bloomington, 1963; MA in Social Work, Ind. U., Indpla., 1965; DSW, Boston Coll., 1985. Lic. social worker, Pa. Psychiat. social worker Menninger Found., Topeka, 1965-69; psychotherapist Family Counseling and Guidance Ctrs., Inc., Boston, 1969-85; prof. Grad. Sch. Social Work and Social Rsch. Bryn Mawr (Pa.) Coll., 1985—. Author: Men as Caregivers to the Elderly, 1990, The Facilitating Partnership, 1995. Bd. dirs. Phila. Ctr. for Psychoanalytic Edn., 1994-97. Named Disting. Practitioner, Social Work divsn. Nat. Acads. Practice, 1994, Diane Davis Meml. Lectr., Smith Coll. Sch. for Social Work, 1996. Mem. NASW, Coun. on Social Work Edn., Pa. Soc. for Clin. Social Work. Avocations: 20th century art, jazz piano. Office: Bryn Mawr Coll 300 Airdale Rd Bryn Mawr PA 19010-1646

APPLEMAN, MARJORIE (M. H. APPLEMAN), playwright, educator, poet; b. Ft. Wayne, Ind.; d. Theodore E. and Martha C. Haberkorn; m. Philip Appleman. BA, Northwestern U.; MA, Ind. U.; degré supérieur, U. Paris, Sorbonne. Prof. in English and French Ind. U.; prof. English, playwriting NYU, Columbia U., N.Y.C.; mem. playwrights unit Circle Repertory Co., N.Y.C., 1978—. Author: (plays produced) Nice Place You Have Here, 1971, The Best Is Yet to Be, 1975, The Bedroom, 1978, Seduction Duet, 1982, Fox-Trot by the Bay, 1982, The Commuter, 1982, Thirty-Nine Seconds and Counting, 1983, Space, 1983, Intermission, 1985, Penelope's Odyssey, 1986, The Country House, 1988, Seduction Triangle, 1988, On the Edge, 1989, Happy New Year, 1990, Fox-Trot on Gardiner's Bay, 1991-92, Love Puzzles, 1992, Secrets, 1993, The Black Staircase, 1994, The Salt of Love, 1995, The Brunette, The Blonde, and the Mounties, 1996, Try, Try Again, 1996, The Shoot, 1997, The Salt of Love, 1997, Seduction Duet, 1997, Precipice, 1998, (plays published) Seduction Duet, 1982, The Commuter, 1985, (poetry) Against Time, 1994. Recipient Eugene O'Neill award Nat. Playwrights Conf., 1979, Double Image Short Play award Samuel French, Inc., 1981, 12th Ann. Playwriting award Jacksonville U., 1982, New Play Contest award John Drew Theatre, 1987; Hartford Found. fellow. Mem. PEN (membership com. Am. Ctr. 1980—), Dramatists Guild, Author's League Am., Acad. Am. Poets, Women's Project and Prodns., League Profl. Theatre Women (bd. dirs. 1989—), Poets and Writers, Inc. Home: PO Box 39 Sagaponack NY 11962-0039

APPLEMAN, PHILIP, poet, writer, educator; b. Feb. 8, 1926; m. Marjorie Haberkorn. BS in English, Northwestern U., 1950, PhD in English, 1955; AM in English, U. Mich., 1951; postgrad., U. Lyon, France, 1951-52. Teaching asst. Northwestern U., Evanston, Ill., 1953-55; instr. English Ind. U., Bloomington, 1955-58, asst. prof., 1958-62, assoc. prof., 1962-67, prof., 1967-82, disting. prof., 1982-86, disting. prof. emeritus, 1986—; dir., instr. in world lit. and philosophy Internat. Sch. Am., 1960-61, 62-63; vis. prof. lit. SUNY-Purchase, 1973; vis. prof. English Columbia U., 1974; panelist NEH, Washington, 1968, applications judge, 1978, 80; mem. adv. panel Ind. Arts Commn., 1971; cons. NEH-sponsored Project on Ethics and Values in Health Care Columbia U. Coll. Physicians and Surgeons, 1979-81; lectr. in field, poetry reader. Author: The Silent Explosion, 1965, (2d edit.), 1966, (Portuguese transl.), 1973; (poetry) Kites on a Windy Day, 1967 (Ind. Authors' Day citation 1968), Summer Love and Surf, 1968 (Friends of Lit. Soc. Robert F. Ferguson Meml. award 1969, Soc. Midland Authors Midland Poetry award 1969), Open Doorways, 1976, Darwin's Ark, 1984, Darwin's Bestiary, 1986, Let There Be Light, 1991, New and Selected Poems, 1956-96, 1996; (novels) In The Twelfth Year of the War, 1970, Shame the Devil, 1981, Apes and Angels, 1989; founding co-editor: Victorian Studies, 1957-63; co-editor: 1859: Entering An Age of Crisis, 1959; editor: The Origin of Species, 1975, An Essay on the Principle of Population, 1976, Darwin, 1970, 2d edit., 1979; contbr. numerous poems, articles, chpts. revs. to various publs.; pub. readings at Libr. of Congress, Poetry Ctr., N.Y.C., Guggenheim Mus. N.Y.C., Folger Shakespeare Libr., Washington, Huntington Libr., Calif., Internat. Poetry Forum, Pitts., Caxton Club, Chgo., Century Assn., N.Y.C., Nat. Pub. Radio, Am. Mus. Natural History, N.Y.C., Internat. Poetry Conf., Yugoslavia, Poets House, N.Y.C., Columbia U., Rutgers U., U. Calif., Berkeley, Irvine, UCLA, Wesleyan U., Tulane U., Temple U., CUNY, other colls. and univs. Co-founder Bloomington Civil Liberties Union; faculty adviser Ind. U. Civil Liberties Union, Bloomington. Served with AC U.S. Army, 1944-45; served with U.S. Mcht. Marine, 1946, 48-49. Recipient Citation for In the Twelfth Year of the War Ind. Authors's Day, 1971, Humanist Arts award, 1994; Fulbright scholar France, 1951-52; Huntington Hartford Found. fellow, 1964; Nat. Endowment for Arts fellow, 1975. Mem. AAUP (pres. Ind. U. chpt. 1968-69, mem. nat. council 1969-72), MLA (sec. English sect. II 1965, chmn. English sect. II 1966, chmn. exec. com. 1972), Nat. Council Tchrs. English, PEN, Poetry Soc. Am. (Christopher Morley Meml. award 1970, Alice Fay di Castagnola award 1975, awards judge 1970, 71, 74, 76, 79, mem. governing bd. 1981-83), Poets House (mem. poets adv. com. 1987—), Acad. Am. Poets, Authors Guild, Phi Beta Kappa. Home: PO Box 39 Sagaponack NY 11962-0039

APPLER, THOMAS L., lawyer; b. Washington, Oct. 12, 1943; m. Nancy J. Babb, Dec. 20, 1967; children: Alexandra, Whitney. AB in Politics, Princeton U., 1965; JD, George Washington U., 1968. Bar: Va. 1968. Atty. Office of Judge Adv., Surgeon Gen. of Army, 1969-70; ptnr. McGuire, Woods, Battle & Boothe (and predecessor firms), McLean, Va., 1970—. Co-author: Damages for Plaintiff and Defense Attorneys, 1987. USAR, 1970-76. Fellow Am. Coll. Trial Lawyers; mem. No. Va. Def. Attys. Assn. (pres. 1975), Va. Assn. Def. Attys. (v.p., bd. dirs. 1977-83), Va. Bar Assn. (bd. dirs. young lawyers sect. 1974-76, appellate judges com. 1989-91, Boyd-Graves Conf. com. 1988—), Va. State Bar (coun. 1985-92, malpractice ins. com. 1989—), Fairfax Bar Assn. (pres. 1984-85, bd. dirs. 1983-86), No. Va. Young Lawyers Assn. (pres. 1974). Home: 9717 Meadowlark Rd Vienna VA 22182-1951 Office: McGuire Woods Battle & Boothe LLP 8280 Greensboro Dr Ste 900 Mc Lean VA 22102-3892

APPLETON, DANIEL RANDOLPH, JR., optometrist; b. Boston, June 24, 1942; s. Daniel Randolph and Dorothy (Cheney) A.; m. Sandra Marshall Appleton; children: Carole Lee, Deborah Ann, Danielle Marie, Suzanne Estelle, Seth Marshall. BS, Tufts U., 1965; OD, Mass. Coll. Optometry, 1969. Pvt. practice optometry Newburyport, Mass., 1965—; dir. pediatric clinic Mass. Coll. Optometry, 1969-71, clin. cons., 1971-72; bd. dirs. 1st and Ocean Nat. Bank. Mem. bd. incorporators Anna Jacques Hosp., Newburyport, Sch. Com., 1975-79, Newburyport sewer commn., 1972-79; 2d v.p. ARC. Recipient Com. Svc. award United Fund, 1983, Disting. Svc. award Lions Club, 1989. Mem. Am. Optometric Found., Am. Optometric Assn., Mass. Soc. Optometrists (past dist. chmn., exec. bd. dirs.), Jaycees (past pres.). Lodges: Rotary (pres. 1988), Shriners. Home: 89 Scotland Rd Newburyport MA 01951-1002 Office: 39 Green St Newburyport MA 01950-2652

APPLETON, JAMES ROBERT, university president, educator; b. North Tonawanda, N.Y., Jan. 20, 1937; s. Robert Martin and Emma (Mollnow) A.; m. Carol Koelsch, Aug. 8, 1959; children: Steven, Jon, Jennifer. AB in Social Sci., Wheaton Coll., 1958; MA, PhD, Mich. State U., 1965. Lectr. Mich. State U., East Lansing, 1969-72; assoc. dean students Oakland U., Rochester, Mich., 1965-68, dean student life, 1968-72, assoc. prof. behavioral scis., 1969-72, v.p., 1969-72; v.p. student affairs U. So. Calif., L.A., 1972-82, v.p. devel., 1982-87; pres., Univ. prof. U. Redlands, Calif., 1987—. Author: Pieces of Eight: Rights, Roles & Styles of the Dean; guest editor Nat. Assn. Student Pers. Adminstrs. Jour., 1971; contbr. articles to profl. jours. Bd. dirs. So. Calif. Ind. Colls., Nat. Assn. Ind. Colls. and Univs.; mem. exec. com. Inland Empire Econ. Partnership; mem. nat. exec. com. Tuition Exch.; trustee San Francisco Presbyn. Sem. 1st lt. U.S. Army, 1958-60. Named One of 100 Emerging Young Leaders in Higher Edn., Am. Council Edn./Change, 1978; recipient Fred Turner award Nat. Assn. Student Personnel Adminstrs., 1980. Mem. NCAA (pres.'s commn.), Assn. Ind. Calif. Colls. & Univs. (govtl. rels. com.), Am. Assn. Higher Edn., Western Coll. Assn. (past pres.). Avocations: music performance and appreciation, athletics. Home: 1861 Rossmont Dr Redlands CA 92373-7219 Office: U of Redlands 1200 E Colton Ave PO Box 3080 Redlands CA 92373-0999

APPLETON, JOSEPH HAYNE, civil engineer, educator; b. Collinsville, Ala., Aug. 5, 1927; s. Shelton and Helen (Gower) A.; m. Patricia Ann Zimmerman, May 8, 1954; children—Joseph F., Sandra K., Jeffrey T., Tricia A., Kevin L., Kathryn L. B.C.E., Auburn U., 1947; M.S., U. Ill., 1949, Ph.D., 1959. Research asst. U. Ill., Urbana, 1947-49, research asso., 1951-54; structural engr. U.S. Bur. Pub. Rds., Washington, 1949-50; instr. N.C. State U., 1950-51; structural engr. Ala. Cement Tile Co., Birmingham, 1954-59; prof. engring. U. Ala., Birmingham, 1959-90, assoc. prof. dentistry, 1960-90, assoc. prof. physiology and biophysics, 1966-90, Disting. Service prof. civil engring., 1984-90, disting. svc. prof. emeritus civil engring., 1990—, dean Sch. Engring., 1971-78; cons. structural analysis and design, 1959—. Contbr. numerous articles to profl. jours. Mem. ASCE, NSPE, AAUP, Am. Soc. Engring. Edn., Am. Concrete Inst., Exchange Club of Birmingham (pres. 1981-82, Exchangite of Yr. 1992), Sigma Xi, Tau Beta Pi, Phi Kappa Phi, Chi Epsilon. Methodist. Home: 4237 Antietam Dr Birmingham AL 35213-3221

APPLETON, R. O., JR., lawyer; b. San Francisco, Aug. 17, 1945; s. Robert Oser and Leslie Jeanne (Roth) A.; m. Susan Frelich, June 3, 1971; children: Jesse David, Seth Daniel. AB, Stanford U., 1967; JD, U. Calif., San Francisco, 1970; postgrad., NYU, 1971. Bar: Calif. 1971, U.S. Dist. Calif. (no. dist.) Calif. 1971, Mo. 1973, U.S. Dist. Ct. (ea. dist.) Mo. 1974, U.S. Ct. Appeals (8th cir.) 1975, U.S. Ct. Internat. Trade, 1980. Assoc. Dinkelspiel & Dinkelspiel, San Francisco, 1971-73, Schramm & Morganstern, St. Louis, 1973-75; pvt. practice, 1975-77; ptnr. Braun, Newman, Stewart & Appleton, St. Louis, 1977-82, Appleton, Newman & Kretmar, St. Louis, 1982-84, Appleton, Newman & Gerson, St. Louis, 1984-89, Appleton & Kretmar, St. Louis, 1989—, Appleton, Kretmar & Beatty; adj. prof. pre-trial litigation Washington U. Sch. Law, St. Louis, 1985-88. Arbitrator, vol. Better Bus. Bur. of St. Louis, 1980—; St. Louis Gymnastic Centre, 1984—; bd. dirs. St. Louis Friends of Tibet, 1991-94. Mem. ABA, Calif. Bar Assn., Met. Bar Assn. of St. Louis, St. Louis County Bar Assn., Am. Arbitration Assn. (arbitrator comml. panel), Stanford Club (pres. 1991—). Democrat. Jewish. Avocations: jogging, swimming, cooking, model trains, reading. Home: 8317 Cornell Ave Saint Louis MO 63132-5025 Office: Appleton Kretmar Beatty & Stolze 8000 Maryland Ave Ste 900 Saint Louis MO 63105-3911

APPLETON, STEVEN R., electronics executive. BBA, Boise State U., 1982. Fab supr., prodn. mgr., dir. mfg., v.p. mfg. Micron Tech., Inc., Boise, Idaho, 1983-91, pres., COO, 1991, now chmn., CEO, pres.; chmn., CEO Micron Semiconductor, 1992. bd. dirs. Semiconductor Industry Asssn., St. Luke's Hosp.; trustee Boise State U.; mem. Coll. Bus. Adv. Coun., Semiconductor Tech. Coun. Office: Micron Tech PO Box 6 8000 Federal Way Boise ID 83707-0006

APPLEY, MORTIMER HERBERT, psychologist, university president emeritus; b. N.Y.C., Nov. 21, 1921; s. Benjamin and Minnie (Albert) A.; m. Dee Gordon, June 5, 1942 (div. Oct. 1969); children: Richard Gordon, John Benton; m. Mariann B. Hundahl, Jan. 10, 1971; stepchildren: Scott, Eric, Heidi Hundahl. BS, CCNY, 1942; MA, U. Denver, 1946; PhD, U. Mich., 1950; DSc (hon.), York U., 1975; DHL (hon.), Northeastern U., 1983; LittD (hon.), Am. Internat. Coll., 1984; LLD (hon.), Clark U., 1984. Instr. U. Denver, 1945-47; instr. U. Mich., 1947-49; asst. prof. Wesleyan U., Middletown, Conn., 1949-52; prof., chmn. psychology Conn. Coll., New London, 1952-60, So. Ill. U., Carbondale, 1960-62, York U., Toronto, Ont., Can., 1962-67; dean faculty grad. studies York U., 1965-68; prof., chmn. psychology U. Mass., Amherst, 1967-69; dean Grad. Sch., 1969-74, asso. provost, 1973-74; pres. Clark U., Worcester, Mass., 1974-84; vis. scholar psychology Harvard U., 1984-88, lectr., extension, 1985-95, vis. prof., 1985-86; exec. dir., Commn. on the Future of the Univ. U. Mass., Boston, 1988-89; cons. NSF, NIMH, NRC of Can., Can. Council, VA., AAAS, MacArthur Found. Author: (with C.N. Cofer) Motivation: Theory and Research, 1964, (with R. Trumbull) Psychological Stress, 1967, (with J. Rickwood) Psychology in Canada, 1967, (with R. Trumbull) Dynamics of Stress, 1986, (with L. Lasagna) Who are the Elderly, 1986, (with W.B. Maher) Social and Behavioral Sciences, 1989, Learning to Lead, 1989; editor: Adaption Level Theory: A Symposium, 1971, Motivation and Emotion, 1976-88; assoc. editor Psychol. Abstracts, 1961-62; editor, contbr. Internat. Ency. Neurology, Psychology, Psychoanalysis and Psychiatry; contbr. articles to profl. jours. Chmn. bd. mgrs. Unitarian Fellowship, Toronto; vestryman King's Chapel, Boston. With USAAF, 1942-45. NSF Sci. Faculty fellow, 1959-60, Fulbright fellow, Germany, 1973-74. Fellow AAAS, APA (past chmn. edn. and tng. bd.), Can. Psychol. Assn. (bd. dirs.); mem. Conn. Psychol. Assn. (past pres.), New Eng. Psychol. Assn. (past pres.), St. Botolph Club (Boston, pres. 1997—), Worcester Econ. Club (pres. 1980-81), Wharf Rats (Nantucket), Sigma Xi, Psi Chi, Phi Sigma. Democrat. Unitarian. Home: 221 Mt Auburn St Apt 606 Cambridge MA 02138-4851

APPLEYARD, DAVID FRANK, mathematics and computer science educator; b. South Haven, Mich., July 13, 1939; s. Edwin Ray and Hortense Ruth (Guilford) A.; m. Joey Hierlmeier, Aug. 5, 1967; children: David Wayne, Gregory Jay, Robert James. B.A., Carleton Coll., 1961; M.S., U. Wis., 1963, Ph.D., 1970. Teaching asst. in math. U. Wis., Madison, 1961-66; prof. math. and computer science Carleton Coll., Northfield, Minn., 1966—; Lloyd P. Johnson Norwest Found. prof. liberal arts Carleton Coll., 1993—; dean students Carleton Coll., Northfield, Minn., 1977-83, faculty pres., 1988-91; Carleton Coll. faculty athletic rep. to Midwest Collegiate Athletic Conf., 1975-83, pres., 1982-83. Trustee United Ch. Christ, Northfield, 1969-72. NSF fellow, 1964, grantee prin. investigator, 1993—; NASA traineeship, 1965-66; Sloan Found. grantee, 1969, 73, 84. Mem. Math. Assn. Am., Nat. Coun. Tchrs. Math., Sigma Xi. Avocations: long-distance running; canoeing. Home: 6450 134th St E Northfield MN 55057-4611 Office: Carleton Coll Northfield MN 55057

APRIL, MAX MICHAEL, otolaryngologist; b. 1959. MD, Boston U., 1985. Diplomate Am. Bd. Otolaryngology. Resident in otolaryngology Boston U., 1986-90, Tufts U., 1986-90; fellowship in pediat. otolaryngology Johns Hopkins, Balt., 1990-91; asst. prof. surgery and pediat. SUNY, Stony Brook, 1991-95; mem. staff Lenox Hill Hosp., N.Y.C., 1995—; asst. prof. surg. and pediat. SUNY, Stony Brook, 1991-95. Fellow ACS, Am. Acad. of Pediatrics; mem. AMA, Otolaryngology Head and Neck Surgery. Office: 186 E 76 St New York NY 10021

APRIL, RAND SCOTT, lawyer; b. Bklyn., Feb. 10, 1951; s. Arthur and Muriel (Marmorstein) A. BA, Northwestern U., 1972; JD, Columbia U., 1975. Bar: N.Y. 1976, U.S. Dist. Ct. (so. and ea. dists.) N.Y. 1976, Calif. 1989. Assoc. Marshall, Bratter, Greene, Allison & Tucker, N.Y.C., 1975-78, Gordon, Hurwitz, Butowsky, Baker, Weitzen & Shalov, N.Y.C., 1978-81; assoc. Skadden, Arps, Slate, Meagher & Flom, N.Y.C., 1981-83, ptnr., 1983—. Stone scholar Columbia U., 1974-75. Mem. Phi Beta Kappa. Avocation: skiing. Office: Skadden Arps Slate Meagher & Flom 300 S Grand Ave Los Angeles CA 90071-3109

APRISON, MORRIS HERMAN, biochemist, experimental and theoretical neurobiologist, emeritus educator; b. Milw., Oct. 6, 1923; s. Henry and Ethel (Mollin) A.; m. Shirley Reder, Aug. 21, 1949; children—Barry, Robert. BS in Chemistry, U. Wis., 1945, tchrs. cert., 1947, MS in Physics, 1949, PhD in Biochemistry, 1952. Grad. teaching asst. in physics U. Wis., Madison, 1947-49; grad. research asst. in pathology Sch. Medicine, 1950-51, grad. research asst. in biochemistry, 1951-52; tech. asst. in physics Inst. Paper Chemistry, Appleton, Wis., 1949-50; biochemist, prin. investigator, head biophysics sect. Galesburg (Ill.) State Research Hosp., 1952-56; prin. research investigator in biochemistry Inst. Psychiat. Research; asst. prof. depts. biochemistry and psychiatry Ind. U. Med. Sch., Indpls., 1956-60; asso. prof. Ind. U. Med. Sch., 1960-64, prof. biochemistry, 1964-78, distinguished prof. neurobiology and biochemistry, 1978-93, disting. prof. emeritus, 1993—, chief neurobiology sect., 1969-74; mem. exec. com. dept. psychiatry, exec. adminstr. Inst. Psychiat. Research, 1973-74, dir. inst., 1974-78, chief sect. applied and theoretical neurobiology, 1978-93; co-chmn. session on neurotransmitters 23d Internat. Physiol. Congress, 1965; chmn. session neurochemistry and neuropharmacology 25th Congress, 1971; ad hoc mem. study sect. psychopharmacology NIMH, 1967-71, mem. neuropsychology study sect., 1970-74; mem. molecular and cellular neurobiology program adv. panel NSF, 1984-86; mem. com. recommendations U.S. Army scientific research Nat. Research Council Bd. Physics and Astronomy, 1987-89; mem. gov. bd. Inst. for Advanced Study Ind. U., Bloomington, 1989-92; vis. prof. 4th ASPET Workshop, Vanderbilt U., 1972; guest scholar Grad. Sch., Kans. State U., 1973. Adv. editor Neurosci. Rsch., 1968-73, Jour. Biol. Psychiatry, 1968-83, Neuropharmacology, 1969-93, Jour. Neurochemistry, 1972-75, Pharmacology, Biochemistry and Behavior, 1973-89 , Jour. Comparative and General Pharmacology, 1974-75, Jour. Gen. Pharmacology, 1975-93, Jour. Developmental Psychobiology, 1974-77; regional editor Life Scis., 1970-73; co-editor Advances in Neurochemistry, 1973-92; mem. editorial bd. Jour. Neurochemistry, 1975-79, dep. chief editor, 1980-83; mem. editorial bd. Neurochem. Rsch., 1975-82, Jour. Neurosci. Rsch., 1984-92; co-editor 9 books; contbr. more than 365 rsch. articles to profl. jours., chpts. to books. Mem. Ind. regional adv. bd. Anti-Defamation League, 1973-76; bd. overseers St. Meinrad Sem., 1974-77. Served with USNR, 1944-46. Mem. Am. Physiol. Soc., Biophys. Soc., Soc. Biol. Psychiatry (program com. 1974-75, co-chmn. 1975-76, gold medal 1975), Internat. Brain Rsch. Orgn., Internat. Soc. Neurochemistry (co-chmn. session 1st internat. meeting Strasbourg, France 1967, 4th meeting Tokyo 1973, 7th meeting Jerusalem 1979, coun. 1973-75, sec. 1975-79, chmn. 1979-81, publicity com. 1975-83, nominating com. 1983-87, policy adv. com. 1985-97, ad hoc and founding rules com. 1998—), Am. Soc. Neurochemistry (co-chmn. sci. program com. 1972, mem. 1973), Soc. for Neurosci. (pres. Indpls. chpt. 1970-71), Sigma Xi. Home: 9268 Spring Forest Dr Indianapolis IN 46260-1266 Office: Ind U Sch Medicine Inst Psychiat Rsch 791 Union Dr Rm 113 Indianapolis IN 46202-2873

APT, CHARLES, artist; b. N.Y.C., Dec. 10, 1933; s. Gustav Lee and Tami (Vera Salzman) A.; m. Ursula Edith Betz, July 24, 1959; children—Gregory, Sam. B.F.A., Pratt Inst., 1956. Exhibited in group shows Mus. Fine Art, Springfield, Mass., 1966, Expn. Intercontinentale, Monaco, France, 1966, 68, NAD, 1965, 68, 77, 78, 79, 80, 81, 83, 85, 87, 99, Am. Watercolor Soc., 1965, 66, 68, 69, Allied Artists Am., 1964, 65, 67, 69, 70, 72, Nat. Mus. Racing, Saratoga, N.Y., 1967, Atlantic City Race Track, 1967, Nat. Arts Club, 1967; one-man shows Ground Floor Art Gallery, N.Y.C., 1967, 68, 69, Aqueduct Race Track Art Gallery, N.Y.C., 1967, Grand Central Art Galleries, 1969, Far Gallery, N.Y.C., 1972, 78, Palm Beach (Fla.) Galleries, 1973, Talisman Gallery, Bartlesville, Okla., 1976, Gallery 52, South Orange, N.J., 1976, 77, Lorings Gallery, Cedarhurst, N.Y., 1985, 87, Huntsman Gallery, Aspen Colo., Dassin Gallery, Los Angeles, Calif., Loring North Gallery, Sheffield, Mass., Off the Wall Gallery, Savannah, Ga. Served with AUS, 1956-58. Recipient Gold medal Am. Vets. Soc. Artists, 1965; Best in Show award Saratoga Mus. Racing Ann., 1967; 2d Benjamin Altman award for figure painting NAD, 1968; Le Prix Prince Souverain Monaco, 1968; hon. mention Allied Artists Am., 1970; Bronze medal Annual Open Watercolor Exhbn. Nat. Arts Club, 1971; Sutherland prize Annual Open Oil Exhbn., 1972; Ject-key prize Salmagundi Club, 1972, 1st prize Product Design award for Aquarelle fabric collection Resource Council, 1984. Mem. NAD (academician), Artists Equity Assn. N.Y. Home and Studio: 9 Saint Raphael Laguna Niguel CA 92677-2761

APT, LEONARD, physician; b. Phila., June 28, 1922; s. Morris and Rebecca A. AB with honors, U. Pa., 1942; MD with honors, Jefferson Med. Coll., 1945. Diplomate Am. Bd. Pediat., Am. Bd. Ophthalmology. Intern Jefferson Med. Coll. Hosp., Phila., 1945-46; rsch. fellow in pathology-hematology, resident in pediat. Children's Hosp., Detroit, 1946-49; resident in pediat. Children's Hosp., Cin., 1949-50; resident in pediat. Children's Med. Ctr., Boston, 1950-52, chief med. resident, 1952-53, asst. physician, 1953-55; resident in ophthalmology Wills Eye Hosp., Phila., 1955-57, fellow in pediat. ophthalmology rsch., 1959-61; fellow in pediat. ophthalmology NIH-Children's Hosp., Washington, 1957-59; practice medicine specializing in pediat. ophthalmology L.A., 1961—; assoc. prof. ophthalmology Sch. Medicine, UCLA, 1968-72, prof., 1972—; disting. prof. UCLA, 1993—; attending surgeon Jules Stein Eye Inst., UCLA, dir. pediat. ophthalmology, 1961-81, dir. emeritus, 1981—; tchg. fellow in pediat. Harvard U. Med. Sch., Boston, 1950-52, instr. pediat., 1953-55; sr. physician radioisotope unit Boston VA Hosp., 1953-55; cons. pediat. ophthalmology Cedars-Sinai Med. Ctr., L.A., St. John's Hosp., Santa Monica, Calif., Bur. Maternal and Child Health, Dept. Pub. Health, Calif., Dept. Health, L.A. Contbr. numerous articles on pediatric ophthalmology to med. books; editorial bd. numerous med. jours.; author: Diagnostic Procedures in Pediatric Ophthalmology, 1963. 1st lt. M.C. U.S. Army, 1943-46. Founder L.A. Philharmonic Assn.; presdl. circle mem. L.A. County Mus. of Art; v.p. fin. UCLA Grunwald Ctr. for Graphic Arts; steering com. UCLA Performing Arts Dept.; founder John Wooden UCLA Athletic Ctr.; judge ann. Wines of Am. competition. Recipient Disting. Alumnus Achievement award Jefferson Med. Coll., 1992, 1st Escalon Sci. award, 1992, Hall of Fame Distinction award Cin. Pediatric Hist. Soc., 1994, 1st Disting. Alumni award Sch. Arts and Scis. U. Pa., 1995, Alumni Univ. Svc. award UCLA 1996, William Feinbloom 1st Disting. Achievement award, 1999, Profl. Achievement award UCLA Med. Alumni and Aesculapians, 1999. Mem. AMA, Am. Acad. Ophthalmology (honor award 1968), Am. Acad. Pediats., Am. Ophthal. Soc., Assn. for Rsch. in Ophthalmology, Soc. Pediat. Rsch., Am. Assn. Pediat. Ophthalmology and Strabismus (1st Disting. Achievement award 1995, honor award 1995), Internat. Strabismol. Assn., Pacific Coast Oto-Ophthal. Soc., Am. Med. Writers Assn., Internat. Wine and Food Soc., Confrerie de la Chaine des Rotisseurs, Masons (32 degree), Shriner, Alpha Omega Alpha. Avocations: oenophile, gourmet food, theater, arts, sports. Fax: 310-206-3652. Office: UCLA Sch Medicine Jules Stein Eye Inst Los Angeles CA 90095-7000

APTED, MICHAEL DAVID, film director; b. London, Feb. 10, 1941. BA, Downing Coll., Cambridge, Eng., 1963. Dir.: (films) Triple Echo, 1972, Stardust, 1974, The Squeeze, 1976, Agatha, 1977, Coalminer's Daughter, 1980 (DGA nominee), Continental Divide, 1981, Gorky Park, 1983, Kipperbang, 1983 (Brit. Acad. TV and Film award nominee), Firstborn, 1984, Critical Condition, 1986, Gorillas in the Mist, 1988, Class Action, 1990, Thunderheart, 1991, Blink, 1993, Nell, 1994, Extreme Measures, 1996; (play) Strawberry Fields, 1978 (BAFTA, Emmy award); (documentaries) 14 UP, 21 UP (Internat. Emmy), 28 UP (Brit. Acad. award, Internat. Emmy), 1985, Bring On the Night, 1984 (Emmy, Grammy awards), The Long Way Home, 1989, Incident at Oglala, 1991, 35 UP, 1992 (BAFTA award), Moving the Mountain, 1993 (IDA award); (Brit. TV) Slattery's Mounted Foot, 1970 (Brit. Critics Best Play), The Mosedale Horshoe, 1971 (Brit. Critics Best Play), Another Sunday and Sweet F.A., 1972 (Brit. Critics Best Play), Follyfoot, 1972 (Best Children's Svcs.), Kisses at Fifty (Brit. Critics Best Play, SFTA Best Dir.), The Collection (Internat. Emmy), others. *

APTEKAR, KEN, painter; b. Detroit, May 13, 1950. BFA, U. Mich., 1973; MFA, Pratt Inst., 1975. Studio artist N.Y.C. Solo shows include Jack Shainman Gallery, N.Y.C., 1994, 96, Palmer Mus. Art Pa. State U., 1995, Corcoran Gallery of Art, 1997, Cummer Mus. of Art, Jacksonville, Fla., 1998, Steinbaum-Krauss Gallery, N.Y.C., 1999; exhibited in groups shows at Carnegie-Mellon U. Mus., Pitts., 1991, Corcoran Gallery, Washington, 1993-94, 95, Flint (Mich.) Inst. Art, 1993, Wight Gallery UCLA, 1994, Yerba Buena Ctr. Contemporary Art, San Francisco, 1994, Walters Art Gallery, Balt., 1995, Calif. Ctr. Contemporary Art, Escondido, 1996, Kohler Arts Ctr., Wis., 1996, Jewish Mus., N.Y.C., San Francisco, 1996, Armand Hammer Mus., L.A., 1996, Islip Art Mus., N.Y., 1998; represented in permanent collections Niagara U., Denver Mus. Art, Progressive Corp., Jewish Mus., Bell Atlantic Corp., Nat. Mus. Am. Art, Washington, Harvard U. Recipient Pollock-Krasner Found. award, 1989; NEA fellow, 1987, 95, Bellagio residency Rockefeller Found., 1992, artist residency Ucross Found., Wyo., 1992, painting residency Resident Artists Program Djerassi, 1991, 94, Mid Atlantic Arts Found. award, 1998. Home: 201 W 85th St Apt 7E New York NY 10024-3909

APTER, DAVID ERNEST, political science and sociology educator; b. N.Y.C., Dec. 18, 1924; s. Herman and Bella S. (Steinberg) A.; m. Eleanor Selwyn, Dec. 26, 1957; children: Emily Susan, Andrew Herman. B.A., Antioch Coll., 1950; M.A., Princeton U., 1952, Ph.D., 1954; M.A. (hon.), Yale U., 1969. Asst. prof. Northwestern U., 1954-57; assoc. prof. U. Chgo., 1957-61; prof. U. Calif., Berkeley, 1961-69, dir. Inst. Internat. Studies, 1963-69; H.J. Heinz prof. comparative polit. and social devel. Yale U., New Haven, 1969—, dir. social sci. div., 1978-81, chmn. Dept. Sociology, 1997-99; chmn. Coun. African Studies Yale U., 1995-99; dir. legitimization of violence project UN Rsch. Inst. for Social Devel., Geneva, 1989-94; exec. sec. com. comparative study of new nations U. Chgo., 1957-61; vis. fellow All Souls Coll., Oxford U., Eng., 1967-68, St. Anthony's Coll., 1972, Inst. for Advanced Studies, Princeton, N.J., 1973, 74, Kyoto Am. seminar, 1979; Halevy prof. Found. Nat. des Scis. Polit., Paris, 1981-82; vis. prof. U. Paris X, 1985; vis. fellow Magdalen Coll., Oxford U., spring 1988; fellow The Netherlands Inst. for Advanced Study, 1992; mem. Kennedy Task Force, Africa, 1957; Peace Corps dir. Ghana Tng. Program, 1961, 62; cons. Rand Corp., 1964-69, HUD, 1963, Coun. on Fgn. Relations, 1969—, State Dept. Adv. Com. for Africa, 1961-69; mem. U.S. Commn. for UNESCO, 1977-79. Author: Ghana in Transition, 1956; The Political Kingdom in Uganda, 1961; (with H. Eckstein) Comparative Politics, 1963; Ideology and Discontent, 1964; The Politics of Modernization, 1965; Some Conceptual Approaches to the Study of Modernization, 1968; (with C. Andrain) Contemporary Analytical Theory, 1972; Choice and the Politics of Allocation (Woodrow Wilson award Am. Polit. Sci. Assn), 1971; Political Change, 1973; Anarchism Today, 1973; Introduction to Political Analysis, 1977; (with L. Goodman) Multi-National Corporations and Social Change, 1977; (with Nagayo Sawa) Against the State, 1984, Rethinking Development, 1987; The New Realsim in Sub Saharas Africa, 1994; (with Carl Rosberg) Revolutionary Discourse in Mao's Republic, 1994; (with Tony Saich) Political Protest and Social Change, 1995, The Legitimization of Violence, 1997. Served with AUS, 1943-46. Fellow Social Sci. Rsch. Coun., Ghana, 1952-53, Ford Found., Uganda, 1955-56, Ctr. for Advanced Studies in Behavior Sci., 1957-59, Guggenheim Found., 1967-68, Fulbright Found., 1974, 79, Netherlands Inst. for Advanced Study, 1991-92; grantee Carnegie Found., 1955-60, Ford Found., 1967-71. Fellow Am. Acad. Arts and Scis., Coun. on Fgn. Rels.; mem. AAAS, Am. Polit. Sci. Assn., Internat. Polit. Sci. Assn. (pres. program com. 12th World Congress 1981), Century Assn. Club, Elizabethan Club. Democrat. Research in the politics of devel., comparative theory, and case studies in violent protest in different regions of the world. Office: Yale U Dept Polit Sci New Haven CT 06520 also: 7 rue Claude Bernard, Paris 75005, France

APTHEKER, HERBERT, historian, lecturer; b. Bklyn., July 31, 1915; s. Benjamin and Rebecca (Komar) A.; m. Fay Aptheker, Sept. 4, 1942; 1 dau., Bettina. B.S., Columbia U., 1936, A.M., 1937, Ph.D., 1943; Ph.D. (hon.), Martin Luther U., Halle, Germany, 1966; DHL (hon.), U. Mass., 1996. Editor Masses and Mainstream, 1948-52, Polit. Affairs, 1952-63; dir. Am. Inst. Marxist Studies, N.Y.C., 1964-85; prof. Hostos Community Coll., City U. N.Y., 1971-77; lectr. throughout, U.S. and Europe, 1946—; vis. lectr. dept. history Bryn Mawr Coll., 1969-71; vis. lectr. U. Mass., 1971-72, Yale U., 1976, U. Calif. at Berkeley Law Sch., 1978-91, U. Santa Clara, 1982-83; vis. prof. Afro-Am. studies U. Calif., Berkeley, 1984. Author: To Be Free: Studies in American Negro History, 1948, rev. edit., 1992, World of C. Wright Mills, 1960, Soul of the Republic, 1964, Negro Slave Revolts in the United States, 1939, Negro in the Civil War, 1938, Nat Turner's Slave Rebellion, 1966, Mission to Hanoi, 1966, Labor Movement in the South During Slavery, 1954, The Truth about Hungary, 1957, The Nature of Democracy, Freedom and Revolution, 1967, History of the American People, 3 vols, 1959, 60, Essays in the History of the American Negro, rev. edit, 1964, Era of McCarthyism, 1955, Dare We Be Free?, 1960, American Foreign Policy and the Cold War, 1962, American Negro Slave Revolts, 1943; rev. edit., 1963, 93, American Civil War, 1961, Urgency of Marxist-Christian Dialogue, 1970, Afro-American History: the Modern Era, 1971, Annotated Bibliography of the Published Writings of W.E.B. DuBois, 1973, Early Years of the Republic, 1783-1793, 1976, The Unfolding Drama: Studies in U.S. History, 1979, Racism, Imperialism and Peace, 1987, Abolitionism: A Revolutionary Movement, 1989, The Literary Legacy of W.E.B. DuBois, 1989, Marxism: Demise or Renewal, 1990, Anti-Racism in U.S. History, 1992; editor: Disarmament and American Economy, 1960, One Continual Cry, 1965, Marxism and Democracy, 1964, And Why Not Every Man, 1961, Marxism and Alienation, 1965, Documentary History of the Negro People in the United States, Vols. 1-7, 1951-94, Marxism and Christianity, 1967, Autobiography of W.E.B. DuBois, 1968, The Correspondence of W.E.B. DuBois, Vol. I, 1973, Vol. II, 1976, Vol. III, 1978, The Published Writings of W.E.B. DuBois, 40 vols, 1973-86, Education for Black People (DuBois), 1973, Prayers for Dark Folk (DuBois), 1980, Against Racism: 1887-1961 (DuBois), 1985. Ind. Peace candidate for U.S. Congress, 1966; candidate Communist party for U.S. Senate, 1976. Served to maj. F.A. AUS, 1942-46, ETO. Guggenheim fellow, 1946-47; grantee Social Sci. Research Council, 1961, Rabinowitz Found., 1965, Am. Council Learned Studies, 1974. Mem. Am. Hist. Assn., Assn. Study Negro Life (History award 1939, 69).

APUD, JOSE ANTONIO, psychiatrist, psychopharmacologist, educator; b. San Miguel de Tucuman, Argentina, May 25, 1948; came to U.S., 1987; s. Jose and Emelin (Chagra) A.; m. Graciela Varela, Jan. 25, 1979; children: Maria Macarena, Jose Sebastian. MD, U. Tucuman, 1975; degree in pharmacology, U. Milan, 1980, degree in exptl. endocrinology, 1983; PhD, U. Buenos Aires, 1985. Diplomate Am. Bd. Psychiatry and Neurology. Investigator CONICET, Buenos Aires, 1985—; prof. pharmacology U. Buenos Aires, 1985-93; psychiatrist in residence St. Elizabeth's Hosp., NIMH, Washington, 1991-95; clin. assoc. neuropsychiatry br. NIMH, Washington, 1995-98; faculty psychiatry residency tng. program CMHS, Washington, 1998—; dir. psychopharmacology divsn. SEH-CMHS, Washington, 1998—; cons. Farmitalia Carlo Erba Labs, Milan, 1979-83; vis. prof. pharmacology Georgetown U., Washington, 1987-91; mem. editorial bd. Endocrinologia Clinica y Metabolism, 1982—, Neuroendocrinologia Latinoamericana, 1982—; instr. dept. psychiatry George Washington U., 1995-98, clin. prof. psychiatry, 1998—. Contbr. numerous articles to profl. jours. Fellow Nat. Atomic Energy Commn., 1976, Dept. Endocrinology French Hosp., 1978, Inst. Pharmacology U. Milan, 1978-84, sr. staff fellow St. Elizabeth's Hosp. NIMH, 1994-98; recipient Cediquifa award in pharmacology, 1992, Upjohn award NIMH, 1993. Mem. AMA, Am. Psychiat. Assn. (sci. com. 1993-95, Burroughs Wellcome award 1993), Am. Soc. Clin. Psychopharmacology, Washington Psychiat. Soc., Italian Soc. Neurosci., Italian Soc. Pharmacology, Soc. for Neurosci., Sociedad Argentina de Farmacologia Exptl., Internat. Soc. Psychoneuroendocrinology, Internat. Soc. Neuroendocrinology, Argentina Soc. Biology and Nuclear Medicine, Serotonin Club. Roman Catholic. Achievements include identification of Gabaergic system in rats; study of the mechanism of action of psychotropic drugs; studies on schizophrenia and tardive dyskinesia; identification of an endogenous ligand for the serotonin-2 receptor in the rat brain. Avocations: reading, music, travel to foreign countries. Office: Neuropsychiatry Br NIMH St Elizabeth's Hosp 2700 ML King Jr Ave SE Washington DC 20032-2601

APURON, ANTHONY SABLAN, archbishop; b. Agana, Guam, Nov. 1, 1945; s. Manuel Taijito and Ana Santos (Sablan) P. BA, St. Anthony Coll., 1969; MDiv, Maryknoll Sem., 1972, M Theology, 1973; MA in Liturgy, Notre Dame U., 1974. Ordained priest Roman Catholic ch., 1972, ordained bishop, 1984, installed archbishop, 1986. Chmn. Diocesan Liturgical Commn., Agana, 1974-86; vice chmn. Chamorro Lang. Commn., Agana, 1984-86; aux. bishop Archdiocese of Agana, 1984-85, archbishop, 1986—; chmn. Interfaith Vols. Caregivers, Agana, 1984—; mem. Civilian Adv. com., Agana, 1986—; pres. Cath. Bishops' Conf. of Pacific, 1990—; v.p. Cath. Bishops' Conf. of Aceania, 1990—. Author: A Structural Analysis of the Content of Myth in the Thought of Mircea Eliade, 1973. Chmn. Cath. Ednl. Radio. Named Most Outstanding Young Man, Jaycees of Guam, 1984. Avocations: jogging, walking, swimming. Office: Archbishop's Office 196B Cuesta San Ramon Agana GU 96910*

APUZZIO, JOSEPH J., obstetrician-gynecologist; b. Elizabeth, N.J., 1947. MD, N.J. Med. Coll., 1973. Resident Martland Hosp., Newark, 1973-76; with U. Hosp., Newark, Clara Mass. Hosp., Belleville, N.J., Columbus Hosp., Newark, St. Elizabeth (N.J.) Hosp., Overlook Hosp., Summit, N.J. U. Hosp. fellow, Newark, 1980-82. Fellow ACS, ACOG, Maternal-Fetal Medicine; mem. Am. Coll. Ob-gyn. Office: Dept Ob-Gyn Med Sci Bldg E506 185 S Orange Ave Newark NJ 07103-2757

AQUADRO, JEANA LAUREN, graphic designer, educator; b. Key West, Fla., June 10, 1957; d. Charles Frasure and Geraldine Ferguson (Norton) A.; m. John A. Crawford. B Environ. Design magna cum laude, N.C. State U., 1979; MFA, Yale U., 1984. Graphic designer various projects for Cooper-Hewitt Nat. Mus. Design, Whitney Mus. Am. Art, Shearson Lehman Bros., Citicorp Investment Bank, Abbeville Press, UNICEF, others, N.Y.C., 1984-91; asst. dir. graphic design dept. Mus. Modern Art, 1988-89; design cons. Solomon R. Guggenheim Mus., 1989-91; prof. Savannah (Ga.) Coll., 1991—; mem. adv. bd. Wilderness S.E. Recipient The Am. Fedn. of Arts award of Excellence, 1988, Fed. design achievement award Nat. Endowment for Arts, 1992, Presidential award for design excellence Fed. Govt., 1994. Avocations: aquatic sports, dance, travel. Studio: 10033 Ferguson Ave Savannah GA 31406-8558

AQUILINA, ALAN T., physician; b. Buffalo, Apr. 1, 1948; s. Anthony M. and Jean D. (Schamber) A.; m. Suzanne Schlicht, July 22, 1972; children: Bethany A., Lindsay C. BA in Biology, Hobart Coll., 1970; MD with honors, U. Rochester, 1974. Diplomate in internal medicine and pulmonary/critical care medicine Am. Bd. Internal Medicine. Prof. clin. medicine SUNY, Buffalo, 1979—; attending physician Erie County Med. Ctr., Buffalo, 1979—, dir. pulmonary and critical care medicine and Tb, 1994—; cons. Buffalo Vets. Hosp., 1979—, Sisters Hosp., Buffalo, 1979—; cons. sleep medicine Assoc. Healthcare Co., Buffalo, 1994—. Fellow Am. Coll. Physicians, Am. Coll. Chest Physicians; mem. Am. Thoracic Soc., Am. Lung Assn. (bd. mem. 1995—), N.Y. State Thoracic Soc. (pres. 1994), We. N.Y. Critical Care Soc. (pres. 1992-95), Buffalo Yacht Club, Phi Beta Kappa. Avocations: sailing, running. Office: ECMC 462 Grider St Rm 162 Buffalo NY 14215-3098

AQUILINO, DANIEL, banker; b. Needham, Mass., Feb. 4, 1924; s. Michael Aquilino and Anna (Bruno) A.; m. Theresa H. Barberio, Nov. 9, 1946; children: Donna Lee, Daniel C., Michael D. B.S. magna cum laude, Northeastern U., 1949; grad., Stonier Grad. Sch. Banking, Rutgers U., 1962. With Fed. Res. Bank Boston, 1949-85, exec. v.p., 1970-85; exec. v.p. Bank of New Eng., Boston, 1985-89; cons. Boston, 1990—; dir. Secure Fin. Networks, Inc., Wakefield, R.I. Served with AUS, 1943-45. Recipient Sears B. Condit award Northeastern U., 1947, 49; recognition award Italian-Am. Soc., Inc., 1972. Home: 3 Bakers Hill Rd Weston MA 02493-1708

AQUILINO, THOMAS JOSEPH, JR., federal judge, law educator; b. Mt. Kisco, N.Y., Dec. 7, 1939; s. Thomas Joseph and Virginia Burr (Doughty) A.; m. Edith Luise Berndt, Oct. 27, 1965; children: Christopher T., Philip A., Alexander B. Student, Cornell U., 1957-59, U. Munich, 1960-61; BA, Drew U., 1962; postgrad., Free U., Berlin, 1965-66; JD, Rutgers U., 1969. Bar: N.Y. 1972, U.S. Dist. Ct. (so., ea. and no. dists.) N.Y. 1973, U.S. Ct. Appeals (2nd cir.) 1973, U.S. Supreme Ct. 1976, U.S. Ct. Appeals (3rd cir.) 1977, Interstate Commerce Commn. 1978, U.S. Ct. Claims 1979, U.S. Ct. Internat. Trade 1984. Law clk. to judge U.S. Dist. Ct. (so. dist.) N.Y., N.Y.C., 1969-71; atty. Davis Polk & Wardwell, N.Y.C., 1971-85; judge U.S. Ct. Internat. Trade, N.Y.C., 1985—; adj. prof. law Benjamin N. Cardozo Sch. of Law, 1984-95; mem. bd. visitors Drew U., 1997—. With U.S. Army, 1962-65. Mem. N.Y. State Bar Assn., Fed. Bar Coun. Roman Catholic. Avocations: sports, travel, linguistics, cinema. Office: US Ct Internat Trade 1 Federal Plz New York NY 10278-0001

AQUINO-KAUFMAN, FLORENCE (FLORENCE ANGLIN), actress, playwright; b. Bklyn., Sept. 21, 1918; d. Michael and Rebecca (Kaplan) Aquino; m. S. Jay Kaufman, June 3, 1945 (dec. June 1957). *The eighth of twelve children, her father, Michael Aquino left Avellino, Italy for New York in or about 1891. Her mother, Rebecca Kaplan Aquino, born in New York City of Russian/German parentage, was completely disowned by her family for marrying out of her Jewish religion. Her husband, S. Jay Kaufman was a New York columnist first for the New York Globe and then on the World-Telegram. He covered New York, London, Paris, Berlin and many other places and had a hand in establishing innumerable stars and people of the arts.* Studied acting, Lee Strasberg, Uta Hagan, Sandy Meisner; student, Empire State Coll., 1975. Legal sec., N.Y.C., 1936-43, freelance actress,, 1944—; founder, artistic and mng. dir. Knickerbocker Creative Theatre Found., Inc., N.Y.C., 1964-73; former co-prodr. Promenade Theatre, Bklyn.; crew chief Neighborhood Youth Corp., N.Y.C., 1964-73; dir. Urban Corps, N.Y.C., 1972-73. Author: (plays) It's Up to You!, 1964, The Winner!, 1971, Calling All Heroes/Shattered Idol, 1989, (with Ann Curry) I'd Rather Be Dead Than Alone, 1972; appeared as Florence Anglin on Broadway in Goodbye Fidel, Gideon, A Bell for Adano, Skipper Next to God, Winged Victory, Lower North; appeared in Romeo and Juliet, As You Like It, Much Ado About Nothing Shakespeare Theatre Workshop (now N.Y. Shakespeare Festival); TV appearances include Mrs. Pappas in Guiding Light, Felicia in One Life To Live, also Lucy Scheff in Love of Life, Freida in The Goldbergs, Naked City, Studio I, Philco TV Playhouse, Hallmark, U.S. Steel Hour, Late Night with Conan O'Brien, Staurday Night Live, also others; appeared in feature and TV films Law and Order, Falling in Love, Out of the Darkness, Trading Places, Author, Author, Lovers and Other Strangers, Mirage, Penelope, Cancel My Reservation, Giovanni and Ben; appeared on tour and summer stock in Prisoner of Second Avenue, Time of the Cuckoo, Middle of the Night, Man and Superman, Picnic, Gigi, Bad Seed, Harvey, Two Queens of Love and Beauty, also others; appearances in regional theatre and off-Broadway include Wrinkles, Steel Magnolias, You Can't Take It with You, Liliom, Bright and Golden Land, Coward in Two Keys, Medea, The Little Foxes, also others. Former mem. bd. dirs. Greenwich Mews Theatre; vol. 55th Street Block Assn. Grantee N.Y. State Coun. on Arts, 1970-72. Mem. AFTRA, SAG, Actors Equity Assn., Dramatists Guild, Inst. Noetic Scis. Avocations: ballet classes, yoga, ice skating, family.

ARABIA, PAUL, lawyer; b. Pittsburg, Kans., Mar. 28, 1938; s. John K. and Melva (Jones) A. B.A., Kans. State Coll.; J.D., Washburn U. Bar: Kans. 1966, U.S. Dist. Ct. Kans. 1966, U.S. Ct. Appeals (10th cir.) 1968. Ptnr., Fettis & Arabia, Wichita, 1968-74, Arabia & Wells, Wichita, 1974-78; pvt. practice, Wichita, 1978—. Program host Sta. KAKE-TV: Peoples Lawyer; TV host/producer: Legal Point. Mem. Kans. Bar Assn., Wichita Bar Assn. Office: PO Box 275 Wichita KS 67201-0275

ARABIAN, ARMAND, arbitrator, mediator, lawyer; b. N.Y.C., Dec. 12, 1934; s. John and Aghavnie (Yalian) A.; m. Nancy Arabian, Aug. 26, 1962; children: Allison Ann, Robert Armand. BSBA, Boston U., 1956, JD, 1961; LLM, U. So. Calif., L.A., 1970; LLD (hon.), Southwestern Sch. Law, 1990, Pepperdine U., 1990, U. West L.A., 1994, We. State U., 1997, Thomas Jefferson Sch. of Law, 1997. Bar: Calif. 1962, U.S. Supreme Ct. 1966. Dep. dist. atty. L.A. County, 1962-63; pvt. practice law Van Nuys, Calif., 1963-72; judge Mcpl. Ct., L.A., 1972-73, Superior Ct., L.A., 1973-83; assoc. justice U.S. Ct. Appeal, L.A., 1983-90, U.S. Supreme Ct. Calif., San Francisco, 1990-96; ret., 1996. 1st lt. U.S. Army, 1956-58. Recipient Stanley Litz Meml. award San Fernando Valley Bar Assn., 1986, Lifetime Achievement award San Fernando Valley Bar Assn., 1993/. Republican. Fax no.: (818) 781-6002; e-mail: honarabian@AOL.com. Office: 6259 Van Nuys Blvd Van Nuys CA 91401-2711

ARABIE, PHIPPS, marketing educator, researcher; b. Mar. 13, 1948; s. Wade Joseph and Betty Jo (Thomason) A. Diploma, Phillips Acad., Andover, 1966; A.B., Harvard U., 1970; Ph.D., Stanford U., 1974. Asst. prof. psychology U. Minn., Mpls., 1974-77, assoc. prof., 1977-80; prof. psychology and sociology U. Ill., Champaign-Urbana, 1980-90; prof. Rutgers U. Sch. Mgmt., Newark, 1990—, chair mktg., 1990-96; cons. AT&T Bell Labs, Murray Hill, N.J., 1975-82; Fulbright vis. prof. computer sci. U. Coll., Dublin, Ireland, 1986-87; vis. prof. psychology U. Santiago de Compostela, Spain, 1993. Co-author: Three-way Scaling and Clustering, 1987; co-editor: Clustering and Classification, 1996; editor Jour. Classification, 1983—; contbr. articles to profl. jours.; author computer programs for multidimensional analysis of data. Grantee NSF, Office Naval Research, Nat. Inst. Justice, AT&T; Beckman assoc. U. Ill., 1983-84. Fellow APA, AAAS, Am. Psychol. Soc., Am. Statis. Assn.; mem. Classification Soc. N.Am., Psychometric Soc. (trustee 1987-89, pres. 1990-91), Soc. Math. Psychology, Am. Mktg. Assn. Office: Rutgers U Sch Mgmt 180 University Ave Newark NJ 07102-1893

ARABNIA, HAMID REZA, computer scientist, educator; b. Tehran, Iran, June 24, 1958; came to U.S., 1987; s. Ahmad and Soghra (Homavandfar) A.; m. Rowshanak Mahin-Shirazi, Aug. 30, 1982; children: Samira, Omid, Amir Reza. BSc in Math., Computing, U. Glamorgan, Wales, 1983; PhD in Computer Sci., U. Kent, Eng., 1987. Cons. Caplin Cybernetics Corp., London, 1986-87; asst. prof. U. Ga., Athens, 1987-94, assoc. prof., 1994—; lectr. in field; keynote speaker in internat. rsch. confs. on parallel and distributed computing. Guest editor: Jour. Supercomputing, 1996, subject area editor, 1996—, editor-in-chief, 1997—; guest editor: Internat. Jour. Info. Scis., 1997; mem. editl. bd. Internat. Jour. Parallel Distbd. Sys. Networks, 1996—; reviewer Macmillan Pub. Co., W. Ednl. Pub., W. Pub. Co., Prentice Hall, Bus. Ednl. Tech. Pub., DC Heath Pub., Oxford U. Press, Kluwer Acad. Pub., Addison-Wesley Pub. Co., Addison Wesley, also numerous jours.; contbr. more than 60 rsch. articles to Internat. Jour. Eurographics Assn., Computer Jour., Jour. Parallel Distbd. Computing, Transputer Rsch. Applications, Internat. Jour. Pattern Recognition Artificial Intelligence, Jour. Supercomputing, Jour. Computer Comm. Recipient award Johns Hopkins U., 1991. Mem. N.Am. Transputer users Group Assn. (chmn. 1996—), Imaging Sci. Sys. Tech. Assn. (chmn., founder 1996—), Parallel Distributed Processing Techniques Applications Assn. (chmn., founder, 1995—), World Occam Transputer Users Group, Supercomputing Can. Office: U Ga Dept Computer Sci 415 GSRC Bldg Athens GA 30602

ARAI, TOSHIHIKO, retired microbiology and immunology educator; b. Niigata, Japan, Sept. 12, 1937; s. Hachiro Sisido and Kazue Arai; m. Hatsue Aoki, Dec. 1, 1963; children: Masako, Tomoko, Kazuhiko. MD, Keio U., Tokyo, 1962; PhD, Keio U., 1968. Instr. dept. microbiology Keio U. Sch. Medicine, 1967-73, asst. prof., 1973-85, assoc. prof., 1985; prof. microbiology and immunology Meiji Coll. Pharmacy, Tokyo, 1985-97; ret., 1997; rsch. assoc. U. Tex., Dallas, 1970-72; lectr. Ochanomizu U. Sch. Sci., Tokyo, 1978-79, Chiba (Japan) U. Sch. Medicine, 1978-82, Josai Dental U., Sakedo, Japan, 1978-87, Aoyama Gakuin U., Tokyo, 1988—; cons. Kitasato Inst., Tokyo, 1981-84. Author 15 books; contbr. over 200 articles to sci. and comml. jours. Mem. Japan Soc. Bacteriology (bd. dirs.), Japan Soc. Chemotherapy (bd. dirs.), Japan Antibiotic Rsch. Assn. (bd. dirs.), Am. Soc. Microbiology, N.Y. Acad. Scis. Zen Buddhist. E-mail: ya5-1-23@mxm.biglobe.ne.js. Home: 5-1-23 Yatsu, Narashino, Chiba 275-0026, Japan Office: Tsudanuma Ctrl Gen Hosp, 1-9-17 Yatsu, Narashino Chiba 275-0026, Japan

ARAIZA, FRANCISCO (JOSÉ FRANCISCO ARAIZA ANDRADE), opera singer; b. Mexico City, Oct. 4, 1950; s. José and Guadalupe (Andrade) A.; m. Vivian Jaffray, Sept. 30, 1977 (div. 1995); children: José Riccardo, Maria del Carmen Cecilia; children (from first marriage): Abessalom Rodrigo, Laura Imeda. Grad. in Bus. Adminstrn., U. Mexico City, 1972; grad., Nat. Sch. Music, Mexico City, 1974, Nat. Conservatory, Mexico City, 1974, Musikhochschule, Munich, 1975. Tenor roles (lyric repertory as well as dramatic parts till Wagner's Lohengrin in 1990) include performances in opera hos. Zurich, Munich, Vienna, Rome, Hamburg, Berlin, Milan, London, Parma, Florence, Venice, Barcelona, Madrid, Tokyo, Mexico City, Chgo., San Francisco, N.Y.C.; performed at Salzburg Festival, Bayreuth Festival; numerous recordings include works by Mozart, Rossini, Beethoven, Donizetti, Offenbach, Schubert, Verdi, Puccini, Gounod, Massenet, Weber and others; also six solo albums including opera arias, lieder, popular songs. Recipient Orphée d'Or, 1984, Deutscher Schallplattenpreis, 1984, Otello d'Oro performer prize, 1995, Golden Merkur award, 1996, Mozart medal of Mex., 1991; named Kammersänger of Vienna State Opera, 1988. Address: Wilford Divsn Columbia Artists 165 W 57th St New York NY 10019-2201

ARAKAWA, KASUMI, physician, educator; b. Toyohashi, Japan, Feb. 19, 1926; came to U.S., 1954, naturalized, 1963; s. Masumi and Fayuko (Hattori) A.; m. Juen Hope Takahara, Aug. 27, 1956; children: Jane Riet, Kenneth Luke, Amy Kathryn. MD, Tokyo Med. Coll., 1953; PhD, Showa U., Tokyo, 1984. Diplomate Am. Bd. Anesthesiology. Intern Iowa Meth. Hosp., Des Moines, 1954-56; resident in internal medicine U. Kans. Med. Ctr., Kansas City, 1956-58, instr. anesthesiology, 1961-64, from asst. prof. to prof., 1964-94; prof. emeritus, 1994—; Arakawa Disting. prof. anesthesiology U. Kans. Med. Ctr., Kansas City, 1990, Kasumi Arakawa professorship, 1994, prof. emeritus, 1994—; clin. assoc. prof. U. Mo.-Kans. City Sch. Dentistry, 1973—; dir. Kansas City Health Care, Inc. Fulbright scholar, 1954; civilian cons. USAF. Recipient Outstanding Faculty award Student AMA, 1970. Fellow Am. Coll. Anesthesiology; mem. Assn. Univ. Anesthetists, Acad. Anesthesiology (pres. 1986-87), Japan-Am. Soc. Midwest (v.p. 1965, 71). Home: 2913 W 112th St Leawood KS 66211-3088 Office: Univ Med Ctr 3901 Rainbow Blvd Kansas City KS 66160-0001

ARAKAWA, PETER STANHOPE, artist, educator; b. New Brunswick, N.J., Feb. 4, 1956; s. David Masaru Arakawa and Dorothy Hisako Umezawa. Student, Hampshire Coll., 1975-76; BFA, Rutgers U., 1982, MFA, 1984. Asst. in printmaking Oxbow Arts Inst., Saugatuck, Mich., 1981; asst. in ceramics Rutgrs U., New Brunswick, 1982-84, 88, Nantucket Island (Mass.) Sch. Design and Art, 1985-86; instr. ceramics, drawing and painting Raritan Valley C.C., Somerville, N.J., 1987-88, Middlesex C.C., Edison, N.J., 1995. One-man shows include Johnson & Johnson Internat. Hdqs., New Brunswick, N.J., 1990, Middlesex County Coll., Edison, N.J., 1997, Highland Park (N.J.) Pub. Libr., 1998; exhibited in group shows at The Morris Mus., Morristown, N.J., 1988, Newark Pub. Libr., 1991, Montclair (N.J.) State U., 1995, Hunterdon Mus. Art, Clinton, N.J., 1998; represented in pub. and pvt. collections. Recipient purchase award Jane Voorhees Zimmerli Art Mus., 1984, Johnson & Johnson Corp., 1990; painting fellow Rutgers U., 1981, Pollock-Krasner Found., 1994. Avocations: trout fishing, plastic model building, stamp collecting. Home: 210 Horizon Dr Edison NJ 08817 Studio: 1185 Stockton Pl North Brunswick NJ 08902

ARAKI, GREGG, film director, cinematographer; b. L.A.. Motion picture dir., writer, editor, prodr., ind. filmmaker. Films include Totally F***ed Up, 1993, The Doom Generation, 1995, Nowhere, 1997, Splendor, 1999; editor, dir., cinematographer The Living End, 1992; dir. 3 Bewildered People in the Night, 1987 (Ernest Artavia award Locarno Internat. Film Festival 1987), The Long Weekend (O'Despair), 1989 (L.A. Film Critics Assn. award 1989). Office: c/o DGA 7920 Sunset Blvd Los Angeles CA 90046

ARAKKAL, ANTONY LONA, engineering executive, researcher; b. Kattoor, Kerala, India, Dec. 15, 1937; came to U.S., 1969; s. Lona Joseph and Catherine N. A.; m. Bridget F. Fernandez, Feb. 4, 1967; 1 child, Antony, Jr. BS in Mech. Engring., U. Kerala, 1964; MS, Ill. Inst. Tech., Chgo., 1972. Mgr. mfg. engring. Black & Decker, Tarboro, N.C., 1977-86; pres. Arakkal Enterprises, Inc., Carlisle, Pa., 1986-93; v.p. advanced engring. Airtex Products, Inc., Fairfield, Ill., 1993—; cons. Fasco, Ozark, Mo., 1986-87, Ametek, Gram, N.C., 1990-91, Penn Ventilator, Phila., 1991, Fawn Industries, Middlesex, N.C., 1992. Mem. Soc. Auto. Engrs., Soc. Mfg. Engrs. (N.C. chmn. 1985-86), Internat. Rotary, Lions Club (v.p. 1985), Inst. Indsl. Engrs. (pres. Tri-state chpt.). Roman Catholic. Achievements include patent for Unipole Motor. Home: RR 3 Box 611E Fairfield IL 62837-9565 Office: Airtex Divsn UIS Fairfield IL 62837

ARAMIAN, MARC, composer, music producer; b. Chgo., Nov. 16, 1948; s. Samuel and Virginia A.; m. Debra Baker, July 19, 1976 (div. 1995); children: Gabriel, Lucas, Mason, Rose; m. Cly Wallace, May 24, 1997. BS in Indsl. Engring., Ga. Tech, 1970; studied with composer/condr., Robert G. Mann. Owner Sawdust Ltd., Atlanta, 1972-75; with Beck-Arabia, Ltd., Dharan, Saudi Arabia, 1975-76. Scored works for exercise video series The Firm, Discovery Channel's Invention series, Great Books series, themes for World Cup, Winter Olympics, PBS, TBS, AMC, among others, Walter Cronkite spls., Audubon Soc.; composed works for IBM, McDonald's, Coca-Cola, U.S. Marines, 3M, Pizza Hut, Nissan, CNN, for closing ceremonies Barcelona Olympics; scored Blacklist for AMC (Emmy, Presdl. award 1996), scored movie Heart of Christmas; prodr. records for Word Records, Star Records. Home: 1st Midland Office Condo, Gamboa St Rm 205, Legaspi Village Makati City The Philippines

ARAMS, FRANK ROBERT, electronics company executive; b. Danzig; came to U.S., 1939, naturalized, 1945; s. Richard and Alice (Frank) A.; m. Edith Knoll, July 24, 1952; children: Mark, Ronald. BEE, U. Mich., 1947; MS in Applied Physics, Harvard U., 1948; MS in Bus. Mgmt, Stevens Inst. Tech., 1953; PhD in Electrophysics, Poly. U. N.Y., 1961. Group leader RCA Microwave div., Harrison, N.J., 1948-56; cons. AIL div. Eaton Corp., Melville, N.Y., 1956-65; head electrooptics and infrared dept. Eaton Corp., 1965-71; v.p. LNR Communications, Inc., Hauppauge, N.Y., 1971—, also bd. dirs. Author: Infrared-to-Millimeter Wave Detectors, 1972; contbr. articles to profl. jours. Served with AUS, 1942-44. Fellow IEEE. Home: 37 School House Ln Great Neck NY 11020-1322 Office: 70 Suffolk Ct Hauppauge NY 11788-3714

ARANA, MARIE, editor, writer; b. Lima, Peru, Sept. 15, 1949; came to U.S., 1959; d. Jorge Enrique and Marie Elverine (Clapp) Arana; children: Hilary Brooks Ward, Adam Williamson Ward; m. Jonathan Yardley, Mar. 21, 1999. BA in Russian Lang. & Lit., Northwestern U., Evanston, Ill., 1971; cert. scholarship Mandarin lang., Yale U. in China, Hong Kong, 1976; MA in Linguistics, Brit. U. Hong Kong, 1977. Lectr. linguistics Brit. U. Hong Kong, 1978-79; sr. editor Harcourt Brace Jovanovich, Pubs., N.Y.C. and Washington, 1980-89; v.p., sr. editor Simon & Schuster Pubs., N.Y.C. and Washington, 1989-92; dep. editor, writer Washington Post, 1992—, editor Edn. Rev., 1992-97; bd. mem., dir. Ctr. Policy Rsch., Washington, 1994—, Nat. Book Critics Circle. Editor: Studies in Bilingualism, 1978. Recipient award for excellence in editing ABA, 1985, Christopher award for excellence in editing, 1986. Mem. Nat. Assn. Hispanic Journalists (bd. dirs. 1996—), Nat. Book Critics Cir. (bd. dirs. 1996—). Office: Washington Post 1150 15th St NW Washington DC 20071-0002

ARANDIA, CARMELITA S., school administrator; b. Lemery, Batangas, The Philippines, Sept. 29, 1944; came to U.S., 1970; d. Vivencio and Eugenia (Serrano) A. MEd, Loyola U., Chgo., 1975. Cert. tchr., adminstr., Ill. Head tchr. Head Start program Evanston (Ill.)-Skokie Sch. Dist., 1985-89, asst. coord. Head Start and Cmty. Child Care, 1989-94, interim coord. Head Start and child care programs, 1994-96, dir. Head Start Program, 1996—; mem. adv. bd. early childhood program Kendall Coll., Evanston, 1993—; mem. adv. bd. Early Start Local Interagy. Coun., Evanston, 1992—; mem. health adv. bd. Head Start Program, Evanston, 1989—. Democrat. Roman Catholic. Avocations: shopping, reading, health club. Office: Evanston/Skokie Sch Dist 3701 Davis St Skokie IL 60076-1744

ARANGO, JORGE SANIN, architect; b. Bogota, Colombia, Nov. 29, 1916; s. Fernando Arango and Maria Sanin A.; m. Elizabeth Leighton, 1944; 1 child, Pedro; m. Judith Brooks Wolpert, Dec. 14, 1951; children: Richard, Virginia; m. Penelope Corey, Aug. 18, 1976. Student, Universidad Catolica de Chile Sch. Architecture, 1935-42, Harvard Grad. Sch. Design, 1942-43. Head archtl. firm Arango & Murtra, Bogota, 1946-59; prof. architecture and urban design Nat. U., Bogota, 1945-47; vis. prof. Sch. Architecture U. Calif., Berkeley, 1956, 58; Pub. bldgs. dir. Colombia, 1948-49; pres. Colombian Soc. Architects, 1946-51, Colegio Engrs. and Architects of Colombia, 1955. Co-author basic plan for devel. Bogota, 1948; Author: (with C. Martinez) Architecture in Colombia, 1951, The Urbanization of the Earth, 1970, Segunda Edad Media, 1994; mem. Bd. Contbrs. Miami Herald. Recipient Excellence in Design awards Miami and Fla. chpts. AIA, 1967. Mem. AIA. Invited to U.S. by State Dept. and Mus. Modern Art, N.Y.C. Home: 5153 SW 71st Pl Miami FL 33155-5640

ARANGO, RICHARD STEVEN, architect, graphic and industrial designer; b. Bogota, Colombia, June 30, 1953; s. Jorge Arango Sanin and Judith (Wolpert) Arango; m. Maria Francesca Violich, Aug. 1977; children: Ruy Rafael, Antonia. AB in Architecture with honors, U. Calif., Berkeley, 1976, MArch, 1980. Registered architect. Prin. Arango Architects, Coconut Grove, Fla., 1993—; John K. Branner traveling fellow U. Calif.-Berkeley grad. div., 1980. Contbr. articles to profl. jours.

ARANI, ARDY A., professional sports marketing executive, lawyer; b. Bklyn., July 14, 1954; s. Aspee A. and Marie (Balandis) A. BBA, U. Miami, 1975; JD, Loyola U., New Orleans, 1978. Mktg. dir. Internat. Sports Mktg. Ltd., London, 1978-80; mng. dir. Championship Group Inc., Atlanta, 1980—. Mem. editl. bd. Sport Mktg. Quar.; contbr. articles to profl. jours. Bd. dirs. Atlanta Sports Coun., 1986—, Atlanta Olympic Organizing Com., 1988—; chmn. TEAM Ga. Mem. Am. Mktg. Assn., Sports Car Club of Am., Nat. Assn. Stock Car Auto Racing, Am. Motorcycle Assn., Internat. Motor Sports Assn. Home: PO Box 80489 Atlanta GA 30366-0489 Office: Championship Group Inc 3690 N Peachtree Rd Atlanta GA 30341-2340

ARANT, EUGENE WESLEY, lawyer; b. North Powder, Oreg., Dec. 21, 1920; s. Ernest Elbert and Wanda (Haller) A.; m. Juanita Clark Flowers, Mar. 15, 1953; children: Thomas W., Kenneth E., Richard W. B.S. in Elec. Engring, Oreg. State U., 1943; J.D., U. So. Calif., 1949. Bar: Calif. 1950. Mem. engring. faculty U. So. Calif., 1947-51; practiced in Los Angeles, 1950-51; patent atty. Hughes Aircraft Co., Culver City, Calif., 1953-56; pvt. practice, L.A., 1957-97, Ventura, Calif., 1997—. Author articles. Mem. La Mirada (Calif.) City Council, 1958-60; trustee Beverly Hills Presbyn. Ch., 1976-78. Served with AUS, 1943-46, 51-53. Mem. ABA, Am. Intellectual Property Law Assn., State Bar Calif., Ala. State Bar, Santa Barbara Rotary, Univ. Club Santa Barbara. Democrat. Home: 1248 Woodland Dr Santa Paula CA 93060-1263 Office: 674 County Square Dr Ste 205 Ventura CA 93003-9023

ARANT, PATRICIA, Slavic languages and literature educator; b. Mobile, Ala., Dec. 2, 1930. B.A., Ala. Coll., 1952; A.M., Radcliffe Coll., 1957; Ph.D., Harvard U., 1963. Researcher U.S. Govt., Washington, 1952-56; asst. prof. Russian Vanderbilt U., Nashville, 1963-65; asst. prof., assoc. prof., prof. Slavic langs. and lits. Brown U., Providence, 1965-97, chmn. dept., 1989—, assoc. dean Grad. Sch., 1981-88, prof. emerita Slavic langs. and lit., 1997—. Author: Russian for Reading, 1981, Compositional Techniques of the Russian Oral Epic, the Bylina, 1990. Grantee Am. Coun. Learned Socs.-Social Scis. Rsch. Coun., 1969, Internat. Rsch. and Exchs., 1973, 93, Kennan Inst., 1994. Mem. Am. Assn. Tchrs. Slavic and East European Langs., Am. Assn. Advancement Slavic Studies, Am. Folklore Soc. Home: 5 Squire Ln Apt D Riverside RI 02915-4012 Office: Brown U Box E Providence RI 02912

ARAPIAN, LINDA, pediatrics nurse; b. Portsmouth, N.H., July 7, 1949; d. William A. and Esther A. (Carlson) Niland; m. Stephen Graham Arapian, May 2, 1975; children: Stephanie, Michael, Jennifer. BSN, Boston Coll., 1971; MSN, Cath. U. Am., 1984. RN, D.C., Md.; cert. BLS, PALS instr., CPR instr. Staff nurse Portsmouth Regional Hosp., 1971-74; staff nurse II George Washington Univ. Hosp., Washington, 1974-75; sr. staff nurse emergency rm. Childrens Nat. Med. Ctr., Washington, 1975-80, with rheumatology clinic, 1980-83, clin. nurse III emergency rm., 1983-89, mem. float pool emergency rm., 1990-93, mem. pediatric transport team, 1993—; agy. nurse Md. Profl. Staffing, Bethesda, 1989-91; quality assurance specialist Dept. of Def. project Children's Nat. Med. Ctr., 1990-92, 93-94; health dir. Boy Scouts Goshen (Va.) Scout Camps, 1990, 91, 92; instr. emergency nursing pediatric course Emergency Nurses Assn. Author: (with others) Pediatric Emergencies: A Handbook for Nurses, 1990. Asst. scoutmaster Boys Scouts Am., Gaithersburg, Md., 1990—, active Order of Arrow. Recipient St. George medal Nat. Cath. Com. Boy Scouts, 1990, St. Eliz Seton medal Nat. Cath. Com. Girl Scouts, 1993. Mem. Emergency Nurses Assn. (instr. trauma nurse core curriculum, nat. pediatric com. 1997—), Soc. Pediat. Nurses, Am. Acad. Pediat. (affiliate mem. sect. on transport medicine). Democrat. Roman Catholic. Avocations: crafts, sewing, cross-stitch. Home: 12451 Quail Woods Dr Germantown MD 20874-1545 Office: Children's Nat Med Ctr 111 Michigan Ave NW Washington DC 20010-2916

ARAPOFF, JOHN RICHARD, artist; b. Beverly, Mass., June 1, 1935; s. Alexis Paul and Catherene (Green) A.; m. Rita Marie Crossman, Nov. 20, 1960; children: Anton A., Christopher J., Jason T., Alexis A.; 1 child from previous marriage, Steven P. Student, Vesper George, 1956-58. Artist Mass. Beverage Jour., Boston, 1958-60; fashion illustrator May D&F, Denver, 1961; artist A.B. Hirschfield, Denver, 1962; v.p., creative dir. South Shore Pub. Co., Scituate, Mass., 1965-88; pres. J. Arapoff Images, Marshfield, Mass., 1989—; artist, resident restorer South Shore Arts Ctr., Cohasset, Mass., 1964—; artist North River Arts Soc., Marshfield, 1975—; pub. dir. Mass. Cultural Coun., Marshfield, 1993-97. Exhibited in group shows at Denver Mus. Art, Central City (Colo.) Art Gallery, Colo. State Coll., South Shore Arts Festivals (prize 1986, 87), Scituate Arts Festival (1st prize 1966), North River Arts Soc. (Popular prize 1988), Boston Arts Festivals, Scituate Pub. Libr. (with cartoonist Paul Szep); one man shows include Thayer Gallery, Braintree, Mass., Habitat Belmont, Mass., Belmont Hill Sch., Artica Gallery, Duxbury, Mass., South Shore Conservatory of Music Staircase Gallery; represented in permanent collections Strohs Beer, Morris Alper & Sons, Am. Automobile Assn., Realtron Multi-List, Thayer Acad., Fitchburg State Coll., Tabloid Shippers, KTB Assocs., Taunton Regency Hotel, T.J. Clark Advt., Downtown Harvard Club, Mill Pond Tennis Club, 4 wall murals on Cuttyhunk Island, Mass.; numerous restorations including U.S. Postal Dept. and major librs. Mem. Am. Assn. Mus., Nat. Hist. Trust, Assn. Preservation Tech., Am. Inst. Conservation. Avocations: tennis, golf, biking. Office: PO Box 1080 Marshfield MA 02050-1080

ARASIMOWICZ, GEORGE ZBIGNIEW, composer, university dean; b. Ottawa, Ont., Can., Feb. 3, 1954; came to U.S., 1979; s. Stanley and Irene (Dubowik) A.; m. Lorraine Deborah Krawchuk, June 21, 1986; children: Andrew, Kimberly. BA with honors, Carleton U., Ottawa, 1976; BMus, U. Toronto, 1976; MA, McGill U., Montreal, 1979; postgrad., Chopin State Acad. Music, Warsaw, Poland, 1978-79; PhD, U. Calif., San Diego, 1982. Asst. prof. So. Calif. Coll., Costa Mesa, 1982-83, U. Alta., Edmonton, Can., 1984-89; assoc. prof. U. Colo., Denver, 1988-94, chair dept. music, 1994-97; dean Conservatory, Wheaton (Ill.) Coll., 1997—. Composer. Recipient 1st prize Internat. Excellence Chamber Music Composition, 1997, Kenneth Davenport Nat. Competition for Orchestral Works, 1996, commendation for excellence in composition Barlow Endowment, 1995, Covisions Recognition award in performing arts Colo. Coun. on the Arts, 1994, others; Guggenheim fellow, 1997. Mem. ASCAP, Coll. Music Soc., Am. Music Ctr., Computer Music Assn. Office: Conservatory Wheaton Coll Wheaton IL 60187

ARASKOG, RAND VINCENT, diversified telecommunications multinational company executive; b. Fergus Falls, Minn., Oct. 30, 1931; s. Randolph Victor and Hilfred Mathilda A.; m. Jessie Marie Gustafson, July 29, 1956; children: William Roy, Julie Kay, Kathleen Melinda. BSME, U.S. Mil. Acad., 1953; postgrad., Harvard U., 1953-54; LHD (hon.), Hofstra U., 1990. With Def. Dept., Washington, 1954-59, Spl. asst. to dir., 1958-59; dir. mktg. aero. div. Honeywell, Inc., Mpls., 1960-66; v.p. ITT Corp., 1971-76; exec. v.p. ITT Aerospace, Electronics, Components and Energy Group, Nutley, N.J., 1976-79; pres., CEO ITT Corp., N.Y.C., 1979—, chmn. bd., CEO, chmn. exec. and policy coms., 1980—; chmn., pres., CEO ITT Holdings Inc., N.Y.C.; bd. dirs. ITT Corp., Hartford Ins., Dayton-Hudson Corp., Shell Oil Corp., Dow Jones and Co., N.Y. Stock Exchange, Fed. Res. Bank of N.Y.; mem. Nat. Security Telecommunications Adv. Com., 1983—. Author: ITT Wars, 1989; contbr. articles to jours. including Reader's Digest, The New York Times. Mem. Bus. Coun., Trilateral Commn., Competitiveness Policy Coun.; bd. advisors N.Y. Zool. Soc.; mem. Rockefellow U. Coun. Served with U.S. Army, 1954-56. Decorated Officer of Nat. Order of Legion of Honor (France), Order of Merit of the Republic of Italy in the level of grand officer. Mem. The Bus. Coun., Aerospace Industries Assn. (bd. govs.), Air Force Assn. (mem. exec. coun.), Econ. Cub (chmn.), Bus. Roundtable, Coun. Fgn. Rels., Competitiveness Policy Coun., Trilateral Commn., Bus.-Higher Edn. Forum, West Point Soc. N.Y., N.Y.C. Partnership (bd. dirs.), Links Club, River Club, Meadow Club, Knickerbocker Club, Coun. U.S.-Italy (co-chmn.). Episcopalian. Office: ITT Corp 1330 6th Ave New York NY 10019-5400*

ARASTU, JAMEEL HUSAIN, neurologist; b. Mar. 22, 1956. MB, BChir, Osmania Med. Coll., Hyderabad, India, 1979. Diplomate Am. Bd. Psychiatry and Neurology. Pvt. practice Slocum-Dickson Med. Group P.C., New Hartford, N.Y., 1995—. Office: Slocum-Dickson Med Group PC 1729 Burrstone Rd New Hartford NY 13413-1093

ARAT, METIN, retired psychiatrist; b. Istanbul, Turkey; came to U.S., 1968; s. Esat and Saime A.; m. Sevinc Ulku, Feb. 29, 1952; children: Mustafa, Deger, Isil, Nese. MD, Med. Sch. Ankara, Turkey, 1951. Diplomate Turkish Bd. Psychiatry and Neurology. Commd. lt. Turkish Army, 1951, advanced through grades to col., 1968; intern Gulhane Mil. Med. Acad. and Sch. Medicine, Ankara, Turkey, 1952, resident, 1956-59; mil. physician Turkish Army, 1951-68, resigned, 1968; physician III, clin. dir. Farmington (Mo.) State Hosp., 1968-74; chief psychiatry VA Med. Ctr., Battle Creek, Mich., 1974-79; chief of staff VA Med. Ctr., Marion, Ind., 1979-97; ret., 197. Mem. Am. Psychiat. Assn. Moslem. Avocations: gardening, photography.

ARAU, ALFONSO, film producer and director, writer. Student, Seki Sano's Drama Sch., Mex., UCLA. Prodr., dir.: (films) Like Water For Chocolate, 1991 (Arieles awards for best film, best dir., Grand Prix for best fgn. film 1992, Unicorne d'Or for best fgn. film 1992, Best Film and Best Fgn. Film Ont. (Can.) Film Festival 1992); dir.: A Walk in the Clouds, 1995. Office: William Morris Agy 151 S El Camino Dr Beverly Hills CA 90212-2775*

ARBEIT, ROBERT DAVID, physician; b. Jersey City, Aug. 16, 1947; s. Sidney Robert and Marie (Gluck) A.; m. Susan Abelson, Dec. 20, 1970; children: Jeffrey, Miriam. BA, Williams Coll., 1968; MD, Yale U., 1972. Diplomate Am. Bd. Internat. Medicine, Am. Bd. Infectious Disease. Intern then resident Yale-New Haven Hosp., New Haven, 1972-74; clin. assoc. Nat. Cancer Inst., Bethesda, Md., 1974-76; fellow Sidney Farber Cancer Inst., Boston, 1976-79; staff physician VA Med. Ctr., Boston, 1979—, asst. chief med. svcs., 1989-91, dir. infectious diseases rsch., 1991—, assoc. chief of staff, rsch., 1991—; asst. prof. Sch. Med. Boston U., 1979-87, assoc. prof. Sch. Med., 1987-95, prof. Sch. Med., 1995—. Contbr. articles to profl. jours. and books. Fellow Infectious Diseases Soc. Am., Am. Coll. Physicians; mem. Am. Soc. for Microbiology, Soc. Rsch. Adminstrs., Phi Beta Kappa, Alpha Omega Alpha. Avocation: personal computers. Office: VA Med Ctr 150 S Huntington Ave Jamaica Plain MA 02130-4817

ARBEIT, WENDY SUE, researcher, writer; b. Jersey City, May 14, 1941; d. Carl and Ethel Arbeit. BA, Temple U., 1963; MA, Columbia U., 1968. Author: What Are Fronds For?, 1985, Baskets in Polynesia, 1990, Tapa in Tonga, 1994; assoc. editor Pacific Arts, 1992-98, co-editor, 1999—; prodr./dir. (video): From Mortal to Ancestor: The Funeral in Tonga, 1994, Pacific Passages, 1997. Mem. Pacific Arts Assn., Tongan History Assn., Cmty. TV Prodrs. Assn. (pres. 1997-98). Office: PO Box 23296 Honolulu HI 96823-3296

ARBELBIDE, C(INDY) L(EA), historian, author; b. Stockton, Calif., Aug. 4, 1949; d. Garrett Walter and Fern Mable (Lea) A. AA in History, Santa Barbara City Coll., Calif., 1969; BS in Health & Phys. Edn., Oreg. State U., 1972; M in Libr. Sci., Emporia State U., 1980; cert., Nat. Crisis Response Team Tng. Inst., 1991. Tchr. Petersburg (Ala.) Sch. System, 1972-73, Santa Barbara (Calif.) Sch. System, 1973-74, Linn Benton Community Coll., Oreg. State U., Albany, Corvallis, 1974-75, Can. Acad., Kobe, Japan, 1975-76; tchr., libr. Wichita (Kans.) Pub. Schs., 1976-81; mgr. Geol. Info. Libr., Dallas, 1982-84; coord., cons. North Tex. Libr. System, Ft. Worth, 1984-86; dir. libr., rsch. svcs. Nat. Victim Ctr., Ft. Worth, 1986-91; dir. tng., coord. tng. all insts. Nat. Orgn. for Victim Assistance, Washington, 1991-95; cons. Nat. Cmty. Response Team, N.J., Tex., 1992, FBI, Washington, 1994, NOVA, 1995. Author: Librarian's PLanning Handbook, 1986, National Library Resource Project on Crime Victimization, 1988, 89, Child Safety Curriculum Standards, 1989, The Story of Presidential Christmas Cards and Gift Prints, 1996, Diary of a White House Squirrel, 1996, The White House Easter Egg Roll, 1997. Named Woman of the Month Ladies Home Jour., 1973; recipient Yellow Rose of Tex. award Gov. Tex., 1992, Outstanding Contbn. letter U.S. Army, 1993, Recognition and Appreciation cert. Concerns of Police Survivors, 1994. Mem. ALA, Am. Assn. Law Librs., Spl. Librs. Assn. (chairperson catalog com. 1990-91, chairperson social sci. div. roundtable health and human svcs. 1990), Nat. Victim Ctr., Tex. Libr. Assn. (vice chairperson div. spl. librs. 1987-88, chairperson 1988-89), Critical Incident Stress Debriefing Soc. Internat. Assn. Trauma Counselors, Nat. Cmty. Crisi Response Team.

ARBER, WERNER, microbiologist; b. Gränichen, Switzerland, June 3, 1929; married; 2 children. Ed., Aargau (Switzerland) Gymnasium, Eidgenössische Technische Hochschule, Zurich. Asst. Lab. Biophysics, U. Geneva, 1953-58, docent, then extraordinary prof. molecular genetics, 1962-70; research assoc. dept. microbiology U. So. Calif., 1958-59; vis. investigator dept. molecular biology U. Calif., Berkeley, 1970-71; prof. microbiology U. Basel (Switzerland), 1971-96, rector, 1986-88. Co-recipient Nobel prize for physiology or medicine, 1978. Mem. Nat. Acad. Scis. (fgn. assoc.), Internat. Coun. Sci. (pres. 1996-99). Office: Biozentrum der Universität, 70 Klingelbergstrasse, CH-4056 Basel Switzerland

ARBETMAN, JEFFREY FARRELL, lawyer; b. Chgo., Jan. 23, 1941; s. Charles and Evelyn Mae (Honigberg) A.; m. Sara M. Amarilla, Apr., 1997. BA, U. Wis., 1963; JD, Loyola U., 1967. Bar: Ill. 1967, Calif. 1973, Ariz. 1978, U.S. Dist. Ct. (ea. dist.) Ill. 1968, U.S. Ct. Appeals (7th cir.) 1968, U.S. Ct. Appeals (9th cir.) 1972, U.S. Dist. Ct. (so. dist.) Calif. 1972, U.S. Dist. Ct. Ariz. 1982. Asst. house counsel Aldens Inc., Chgo., 1967-68; asst. U.S. atty. ea. dist. U.S. Dept. Justice, East St. Louis, Ill., 1968-72; asst. U.S. atty. so. dist. U.S. Dept. Justice, San Diego, 1972-78; asst. atty. gen. State of Ariz. Atty. Gen., Phoenix, 1978-86; atty. pvt. practice, Phoenix, 1986—. Co-author: Arizona Appellate Handbook, 1970-98. Mem. State Bar Ariz., State Bar Calif., Maricopa County Bar Assn. Independent. Avocations: classic and antique cars, collecting antiques. Home: 107 E Myrtle Ave Phoenix AZ 85020-4837 Office: 2702 N 3rd St Ste 3020 Phoenix AZ 85004-4607

ARBIB, MICHAEL ANTHONY, neuroscientist, educator, cybernetician; b. Eastbourne, U.K., May 28, 1940; came to U.S., 1961; s. John R. and Helen (Arbib) A.; m. Prue Hassell, Dec. 29, 1965; children: Phillipa Jane, Benjamin Giles. BSc with honors, U. Sydney, 1960; PhD in Math., MIT, 1963. Mem. faculty Stanford (Calif.) U., 1965-70, assoc. prof. elec. engring., 1969-70; adj. prof. psychology, prof. computer and info. sci. U. Mass., Amherst, 1970-86, chmn. dept. computer and info. sci., 1970-75; dir. Ctr. for Systems Neurosci., 1974-86, dir. Cognitive Sci. Program, 1980-82, dir. Lab. Perceptual Robotics, 1982-86; prof. biomed. engring., neurobiology, psychology U. So. Calif.,

L.A., 1986-94, prof. computer sci., elec. engring., dir. Ctr. for Neural Engring., 1987-94, dir. brain project Ctr. for Neural Engring., 1994—; vis. prof. U. Western Australia, Perth, 1974, 96, Technion, Israel, 1975, Washington U., St. Louis, 1976, U. Edinburgh, 1976-77, U. Calif., Irvine, 1980; vis. scientist Inst. Cybernetics, Barcelona, spring 1985, Cognitive Scis. Inst., U. Calif., San Diego, 1985-86; vis. lectr. U. New South Wales, Australia, 1962, 65, 68, Mont. State U., summers, 1963, 65, Imperial Coll. London, 1964; Gifford lectr. in natural theology U. Edinburgh, Scotland, 1983; John Douglas French lectr. Brain Rsch. Inst., UCLA, 1993; lectr. tours to U.S., USSR, Japan, Australia and China. Author: Brains, Machines and Mathematics, 1964, 2d. edit., 1987, Theories of Abstract Automata, 1969, The Metaphorical Brain, 1972, Computers and the Cybernetic Society, 1977, 2d edit., 1984, In Search of the Person, 1985, The Metaphorical Brain 2, 1989; (with others) Topics in Mathematical System Theory, 1969, System Theory, 1974, Discrete Mathematics, 1974, Conceptual Models of Neural Organization, 1974, Arrows, Structures and Functors, 1975, Design of Well-Structured and Correct Programs, 1978, A Basis for Theoretical Computer Science, 1981, A Programming Approach to Computability, 1982, Algebraic Approaches to Program Semantics, 1986, The Construction of Reality, 1986, From Schema Theory to Language, 1987, An Introduction to Formal Language Theory, 1988, Neural Organization: Structure, Function, Dynamics, 1997; editor: The Handbook of Brain Theory and Neural Networks, 1995, (with others) Algebraic Theory of Machines, Languages and Semigroups, 1968, Neural Models of Language Processes, 1982, Competition and Cooperation in Neural Nets, 1982, Adaptive Control of Ill-Defined Systems, 1983, Vision, Brain and Cooperative Computation, 1987, Dynamic Interactions in Neural Networks: Models and Data, 1988, Visuomotor Coordination: Amphibia, Comparisons, Models, and Robots, 1989, Natural and Artificial Parallel Computation, 1990, Visual Structures and Integrated Functions, 1991, Neuroscience: From Neural Networks to Artificial Intelligence; contbr. articles to profl. jours. Mem. IEEE, AAAS, Soc. Neurosci. Office: U So Calif Brain Project Los Angeles CA 90089-2520

ARBIT, BERYL ELLEN, legal assistant; b. L.A., Aug. 16, 1949; d. Harry A. and Norma K. (Michelson) A. BA, UCLA, 1970. From legal asst. to sr. legal asst. O'Melveny & Myers, L.A., 1977—; guest lectr. atty. asst. tng. program UCLA, 1991. Mem. UCLA Atty. Asst. Alumni Assn. (bd. dirs. 1980-82), Alpha Omicron Pi (treas. West L.A. alumnae chpt. 1993—), Nu Lambda (corp. bd. pres. 1978-80, chpt. adv. 1976-78). Avocations: travel, theater, needlework, bridge. Office: O'Melveny & Myers 400 S Hope St Los Angeles CA 90071-2899

ARBIT, BRUCE, direct marketing executive, consultant; b. Milw., Nov. 16, 1954; s. Saul B. and Naomi (Chase) A.; m. Tanya Arbit; children: Oren, Carmiel. Student, U. Haifa, Israel, U. Wis. Founder, co-mgr., dir. A B Data, Ltd., Milw., 1977—; chmn., bd. dirs. Integrated Mail Industries Ltd.; bd. dirs. State Fin. Bank, Asset Devel. Group, Inc., Integrated Mail Industries Israel, Ltd. Gen. campaign chmn., bd. dirs. Milw. Jewish Fedn., Milw. Jewish Day Sch., Habonim Dror Found.; mem. United Jewish Appeal Young Leadership Cabinet; mem. Wexner Heritage Found., Com. Econ. Growth Israel., United Israel Appeal., Non-profit Mailers Fedn., Campaign Cabinet Devel. Corp. for Israel. Recipient Benjamin E. Nickoll Young Leadership award Milw. Jewish Fedn., 1989. Mem. Direct Mktg. Assn., Israel Direct Mktg., Wis. Direct Mktg. Assn. (Direct Marketer of Yr. award 1997), Am. Assn. Polit. Cons. Office: AB Data Ltd 8050 N Port Washington Rd Milwaukee WI 53217-2600

ARBIT, TERRY STEVEN, lawyer; b. Chgo., May 11, 1958; s. Jack and Sandra (Dwork) A.; m. Rhona Sue Schwartz, July 21, 1985; children: Julie Lyn, Michael Colin. BA, U. Pa., 1980, MA, 1980; JD, U. Chgo., 1983. Bar: Ill. 1983, Mich. 1984, U.S. Dist. Ct. (no. dist.) Ill. 1985, U.S. Ct. Appeals (7th and 9th cirs.) 1988. Law clk. to justice Mich. Supreme Ct., Southfield, 1983-84; assoc. Karon, Savikas & Horn, Ltd., Chgo., 1984-88, Goldberg, Kohn, Bell, Black, Rosenbloom & Moritz Ltd., Chgo., 1989-90; counsel profl. liability sect. FDIC, Washington, 1991-95; trial atty. divsn. of enforcement Commodity Futures Trading Commn., Washington, 1996—. Mem. ABA, Phi Beta Kappa, Pi Gamma Mu, Pi Sigma Alpha. Avocations: polit. studies, swimming, cycling. Home: 8 Botany Ct North Potomac MD 20878-4208 Office: CFTC 1155 21st St NW Washington DC 20036-3308

ARBITELLE, RONALD ALAN, elementary school educator; b. Danbury, Conn., Aug. 1, 1949; s. Roxy Joseph and Janet Helen (Otto) A.; m. Ruth Ann Young, Aug. 6, 1977. BS, Western Conn. State U., 1971, MS, 1973; postgrad. in adminstrn., supervision, So. Conn. State U., 1983. Tchr. Shelter Rock Sch. Danbury (Conn.) Bd. Edn., 1977—; Mem. text selection coms., Shelter Rock Sch., Danbury. Active Shelter Rock PTO. Mem. NEA, Conn. Edn. Assn., Danbury Edn. Assn. Avocations: bowling, swimming, coin, baseball card and Jim Beam car collecting. Home: 7 Belmont Cir Danbury CT 06810-6426 Office: Shelter Rock Sch Shelter Rock Rd Danbury CT 06810

ARBITER, ANDREW RICHARD, accountant; b. Merrick, N.Y., May 12, 1958; s. Harold Irving and Marlene (Balfan) A.; m. Joan Sanalitro, Nov. 21, 1981; children: Heather, Aaron. BS in Acctg., U. Bridgeport, 1980; MBA in Taxation, Hofstra U., 1981. CPA, N.Y., N.C. Supr. Deloitte & Touche (formerly Deloitte Haskins & Sells), Woodbury, N.Y., 1981-85; prof. Dowling Coll., Oakdale, N.Y., 1985-86; dir. Andrew Richard Arbiter CPA, Massapequa, N.Y., 1985—; pres. Compucount Systems, Inc., Merrick, N.Y., 1988—; co-founder The Tax Shop, Massapequa, N.Y., 1995—. Author (computer software) lease analysis software for FASB-13 analysis, copyright, 1980; contbr. articles to mags. Councilman Day Care Coun. of Nassau County, Nassau, N.Y., 1979; treas. ChADD (Children and Adults with Attention Deficit Disorders) of Nassau County, N.Y.; trustee Beth Sholom Ctr. of Amityville and the Massapequas, N.Y., 1996—. Recipient Cert. of Qualification, Computer Assocs. Internat., San Jose, Calif., 1989. Mem. AICPA (tax divsn.), N.Y. State Soc. CPAs, Inst. Mgmt. Accts., Nat. Soc. Pub. Accts., N.C. Assn. CPAs, N.Y. Sport Fishing Fedn., NRA (affiliate). Republican. Jewish. Avocations: sport fishing, target shooting, photography. E-mail: andrew@arbitercpa.com. Office: 601 Broadway Massapequa NY 11758

ARBOGAST, GORDON WADE, systems engineer, executive, educator, consultant; b. Charleston, S.C., May 24, 1942; s. Valentine and Teresa Louise Arbogast; m. Dorothy Sheryl Blackwell, Mar. 5, 1966; children: Annette Marie, Christina Theresa, Valentine Scott. *Great, great grandfather Carl Bang was captian in 41st New York Volunteers Association, Union Army in Civil War. Lost arm during Battle of Gettysburg (1863). Father Valentine Arbogast was vice president of RCA Globecom (1963-75). He also served as officer in combat in Pacific Theater during World War II (1942-45). Son, Valentine Scott Arbogast is F16 fighter pilot for US Airforce. He flew missions over Iraq (Northern Watch 1998) and Kosovo, Yugoslavia (1999). Daughter Christina Teresa Arbogast is a Doctor of Naturpathy (ND). She has a practice in Bridgeport, Connecticut. Daughter Annette Marie Arbogast is a registered nurse.* BS, U.S. Mil. Acad., 1963; MSEE, MSIM, Ga. Inst. Tech., 1971; PhD, Clemson U., 1986. Commd. 2d lt. U.S. Army, 1963, advanced through grades to col., 1983, ret., 1990; head, assoc. prof. dept. engring. U.S. Mil. Acad., 1986-89; assoc. dir. engring. and tech. Def. Comm. Agy., 1989-90; v.p. sys. tech. Pacific Bell, San Ramon, Calif., 1990-93; prof. Jacksonville (Fla.) U., 1993—; prin. scientist Contel, Chantilly, Va., 1990; instr., cons. Learning Tree Internat., Reston, Va., 1994—. Contbr. articles to profl. jours. Lector, eucharistic min. Cursillo Cath. Ch., 1988—. Decorated Legion of Merit, Bronze Star, Air medal, Def. Superior Svc. meda. Mem. Inst. Indsl. Engrs. (sr.), Armed Forces Comm.-Electronics Assn. (pres. West Point chpt. 1987-89), West Point Soc. of North Fla. (pres. 1998—). Achievements include initiating systems engineering at U.S. Military Academy and major work in transforming Defense Communications Agency to Defense Information Systems Agency. Home: 4572 Oak Bay Dr W Jacksonville FL 32277-1016 Office: Jacksonville U Davis Coll Bus 2800 University Blvd N Jacksonville FL 32211-3321

ARBOUR, ALGER, professional hockey coach; b. Sudury, Ont., Can., Nov. 1, 1932; m. Claire Arbour; children: Julie, Janice, Jo-Anne, Jay. Defenseman Detroit Red Wings, Chgo. Black Hawks, Toronto Maple Leafs, St. Louis Blues of Nat. Hockey League, 1953-71; coach St. Louis Blues, 1970, 71-72, asst. gen. mgr., 1971; coach N.Y. Islanders, Uniondale, 1973-86, 1988-94, v.p. hockey opers., 1995—. Mem. 4 Stanley Cup championships teams, including Detroit Red Wings, 1954, Chgo. Black Hawks, 1961, Toronto Maple Leafs, 1964, 62; coach 4 Stanley Cup championship teams, 1980-83. Office: NY Islanders 1255 Hempstead Turnpike Nassau Vets Meml Colis Uniondale NY 11553*

ARBUCKLE, AVERIL DOROTHY (COOKIE ARBUCKLE), healthcare facility administrator; b. Bklyn., May 9, 1934; d. Arnold Drummond and Mildred (Engel) Lloyd; m. Robert V. Arbuckle (dec. Mar. 1990); children: Gregory, Jody, Leann, Kathleen, Mary. Student, Lamson Coll., Phoenix, 1968-71, Colo. State U., 1964-68, U. Ctrl. Okla., 1974, Okla. State U., Oklahoma City, 1976. Flight attendant Pacific Southwest Airlines, San Diego, 1952, Am. Airlines, Chgo., 1953; social worker Dept. Human Svcs., Oklahoma City, 1972-89; mem. task force Gov.'s Task Force on AIDS, Oklahoma City, 1987-88; exec. dir. Other Options, Inc., Oklahoma City, 1989—; adv. bd. Carter Hospice, Carter Home Health, Red Rock Mental Health Homeless Com., Okla. AIDS Coalition; cons. HIV-AIDS State of Okla., 1985-96. Author: Aids for HIV-AIDS, 4 edit. 1989 (award 1992), Accessing the System Directory, 1995, Physician Compassionate Use Directory, 1995. Bd. dirs. AIDS Support Program, 1986-88, Okla. Epilepsy Found., 1989-93; com. chmn. Cmty. Action Agy., Oklahoma City., 1994-95; bd. mem. Ven Cor Hosp. Ethics Com., 1998; HIV Care Consortium, Okla., 1998, 99, Okla. City Housing Com. HIV/AIDS, 1998, 99; Nat. Fin. Planning Bd. for Disabilities, 1998, 99. Recipient Jefferson award Presbyn. Health Found., Oklahome City, 1990, Jacqueline Kennedy award Am. Inst. Pub. Svc., Washington, 1990, Five Who Care award Gannett Found., Arlington, Va., 1992, merit award GLB Polit. Caucus, Oklahoma City, 1993, Book of Yr. award Woman's Front Page News, 1993, Friends of Libr. Book award City of Oklahoma City-Moore Libr., 1989, Cmty. Contbn. award, 1994. Mem. Case Mgmt. Soc. Am., Case Mgmt. Soc. Ctrl. Okla. Democrat. Avocations: writing, lecturing, consulting, horticulture, geology. Home: PO Box 36 Bethany OK 73008-0036 Office: Other Options Inc 5915 NW 23rd St Ste 219 Oklahoma City OK 73127-1254

ARBUCKLE, KURT, lawyer; b. Wichita, Kans., Nov. 18, 1949; s. Richard Thompson and Rheva Ruth (Casper) A.; m. Nancy Ann Blackmon, Apr. 8, 1978; children: Kelly Ruth, Ashley Ann. BA, U. Tex., 1972, JD, 1975. Bar: Tex. 1975, U.S. Dist. Ct. (so. dist.) Tex. 1975, U.S. Ct. Appeals (5th cir.) 1976, U.S. Ct. Appeals (11th cir.) 1981. Assoc. Morgan, Dudensing and Tullis, Houston, 1975-79; mng. atty. Emmott & Arbuckle, P.C., Houston, 1979—. Fellow Tex. Bar Found.; mem. Coll. of the State Bar of Tex., Tex. Ex-Students Assn. (life). Avocation: computer programming. Office: 2700 Post Oak Blvd # 950 Houston TX 77056

ARBURN, JERRY WILLIAM, farmer, vice president Indiana Farm Bureau; b. Princeton, Ind., Aug. 15, 1931; s. William Howard and Ruth T. (Kohlmeyer) A.; m. Mary Betty Pauley, Oct. 15, 1955; children: Gregory William, Mary Frances. Grad. h.s., Francisco, Ind.; student Agrl., Purdue U., 1952. Bd. dirs. Ind. Farm Bur. and Cos., Indpls., 1988-95; v.p. Ind. Farm Bur. Cos., Indpls., 1995—, Ind. Farm Bur. Ins., Indpls., 1995—; farmer Arburn Farms, Princeton, Ind., 1952—; pres. Gibson County Extension Bd., Princeton, Ind., 1980-86; mem. agrl. adv. com to U.S. Senator Dan Quayle, 1980-92. Contbr. articles to Hoosier Farmer, 1995—. Bd. dirs. Gibson Gen. Hosp. Health Found., Princeton, Ind., 1978-84. Mem. Princeton C. of C. (v.p. transportation), Kiwanis Internat. Methodist. Avocation: reading. Home: RR 2 Princeton IN 47670 Office: Ind Farm Bur Inc PO Box 1290 Indianapolis IN 46206-1290

ARBUTHNOT, ROBERT MURRAY, lawyer; b. Montreal, Quebec, Can., Oct. 23, 1936; s. Leland Claude and Winnifred Laura (Hodges) A.; m. Janet Marie O'Keefe, Oct. 6, 1968; children: Douglas, Michael, Mary Kathleen, Allison Anne. BA, Calif. State U., San Francisco, 1959; JD, U. Calif., San Francisco, 1966. Bar: Calif. 1967, U.S. Dist. Ct. (no. and cen. dists.) Calif. 1967, U.S. Ct. Appeals (9th cir.) 1967, U.S. Supreme Ct. 1975. Assoc. trial lawyer Rankin & Craddick, Oakland, Calif., 1967-69; assoc. atty. Ericksen, Arbuthnot, Brown, Kilduff & Day, Inc., San Francisco, 1970-73, ptnr., 1973-80, chmn. bd., mng. dir., 1980—; gen. counsel CFS Ins. Svcs., San Francisco, 1990—; pro tem judge, arbitrator San Francisco Superior Ct., 1990—; lectr. in field. Bd. regents St. Mary's Coll. High Sch., Berkeley, Calif., 1988-91. With U.S. Army, 1959-62. Recipient Honors plaque St. Mary's Coll. High Sch., 1989. Mem. Internat. Assn. of Ins. Counsel, No. Calif. Assn. of Def. Counsel, Def. Rsch. Inst., Assn. Trial Lawyers Am., San Francisco Lawyers Club. Avocations: boating, family activities. Office: Ericksen Arbuthnot Brown Kilduff & Day Inc 260 California St Ste 1100 San Francisco CA 94111-4300

ARBUTINA, PETRA, advertising executive. Sr. v.p., media dir. Ketchum Advt., Pitts., 1995—. Office: Ketchum Advt 6 Ppg Pl Fl 13 Pittsburgh PA 15222-5425*

ARCADI, JOHN ALBERT, urologist; b. Whittier, Calif., Oct. 23, 1924; s. Antonio and Josephine (Ramirez) A; m. Doris M. Bohanan, Apr. 11, 1951; children: Patrick, Michael, Judith, Timothy, Margaret, William, Catherine. BS cum laude, U. Notre Dame, 1947; MD, Johns Hopkins U., 1950; LHD (hon.), Whittier Coll., 1998. Diplomate Am. Bd. Urology. Intern Johns Hopkins Hosp., Balt., 1950-51, resident, 1951-52, 53-55; instr. urology Johns Hopkins U., Balt., 1953-55, U. So. Calif., L.A., 1955-60; research assoc. Whittier (Calif.) Coll., 1957-70, research prof., 1970—; coord. prostate cancer rsch. Huntington Med. Rsch. Inst., Pasadena, Calif., 1993—; emeritus staff mem. urology sect. Presbyn. Hosp., Whittier, 1960-97, dir. emeritus hosp. bd. Fellow AAAS, ACS; mem. Endocrine Soc., Am. Urology Assn., Am. Micros. Soc., Internat. Urol. Soc., Am. Assn. Clin. Anatomy, Am. Assn. Anatomists, Soc. for Basic Urologic Rsch., Soc. for Invertebrate Pathology. Republican. Roman Catholic. Avocations: photography, stamp and coin collecting, fishing. Address: 6202 Washington Ave Whittier CA 90601-3640

ARCAIN, JANETH, professional athlete. Forward Houston Comets, 1997—. Career highlights include winning Brazilian League Championships, 1990, 95, leading scorer Brazilian League, 1995, 96; played for Silver medalist team Brazil at 1996 Olympics, Atlanta, Brazilian Olympic team, 1992; mem. Brazilian World Championship team, 1990, 94; mem. Pan Am Games Team, 1987, 91, South Am. Championship team, 1986-88, 90, 95, Brazilian Championship team, 1987-89. Avocations: computers, movies. Office: Houston Comets Two Greenway Plaza Ste 400 Houston TX 77046-3865*

ARCARA, RICHARD JOSEPH, federal judge; b. Buffalo, June 6, 1940; s. Philip and Angela (Arcara); m. Gwendolyn White, July 1, 1976. B.A. in History, St. Bonaventure U., 1962; J.D., Villanova U., 1965. Bar: N.Y. bar 1966. Law clk. Legal Aid Bur., Buffalo, 1965; asso. firm Lipsitz, Green, Fahringer, Roll, Schuller & James, Buffalo, 1968-69; asst. U.S. atty. Western Dist. N.Y., 1969-73, 1st asst. U.S. atty., 1973-74, U.S. atty., after 1975; Erie County dist. atty., 1982-88; judge U.S. Dist. Ct. N.Y., Buffalo, 1988—. Capt. M.P., U.S. Army, 1966-68. Mem. Erie County Bar Assn., N.Y. State Bar Assn., Am. Bar Assn. Republican. Roman Catholic. Club: Buffalo Yacht. Office: US Dist Ct 609 US Courthouse 68 Court St Buffalo NY 14202-3405*

ARCE, A. ANTHONY, psychiatrist; b. San Juan, P.R., June 13, 1923; s. Angel and Juana (Baez) A.; m. Malvene Balkind, Oct. 7, 1971; children—Alan I. Scheer, Judith Ann Scheer, Michael Anthony Arce. B.S., Washington and Jefferson Coll., 1942; M.D., Temple U., 1946. Diplomate: Am. Bd. Psychiatry and Neurology; certified in adminstrv. psychiatry. Intern Mercy Hosp., Bay City, Mich. and; Frankford Hosp., Phila., 1946-47; dir. Aguadilla (P.R.) Dist. Hosp., 1947-48; chief health officer Utuado, P.R., 1950-51; physician U.S. Mil. Acad., West Point, N.Y., 1951-52; med. officer Pa. R.R., 1952-53; practice medicine Yonkers, N.Y., 1953-59; resident psychiatrist Payne Whitney Clinic, N.Y.C., 1959-62; assoc. dir. psychiatry Grasslands Hosp., Valhalla, N.Y., 1962-67; dir. psychiatry Lincoln Hall Sch., Lincolndale, N.Y., 1967-68; dir. Bur. Aftercare Services N.Y. State Dept. Mental Hygiene, 1968-71; dir. Manhattan Psychiat. Center, Ward's Island, N.Y., 1971-76, Hahnemann Community Mental Health and Mental Retardation Center, Phila., 1976-84; pvt. practice medicine specializing in psychiatry, 1962—; prof. psychiatry, dep. chmn. dept. mental health svcs. Hahnemann U., 1976-85, prof., chmn., 1985-87, prof., dir. amb. svcs., 1987-91; prof., dep. chmn. dept. psychiatry Med. Coll., U. Pa., Phila., 1991-96; chmn. dept. behavioral medicine Girard Med. Ctr., Phila., 1996—. Mem. president's council N.Y. U. Sch. Social Work, 1963-66; bd. dirs. P.R. Family Inst., N.Y.C., 1970-72. Served with AUS, 1943-46, 48-50. Mem. Am. Coll. Mental Health Adminstrs., Am. Coll. Psychiatrists, Am. Psychiat. Assn. (chmn. task force continuing care), Phila. Psychiat. Soc., Am. Assn. Psychiat. Adminstrs. (treas., pres.). Home: 7805 Chandler Rd Glenside PA 19038-7267 Office: Girard Med Ctr 2ADC 8th St & Girard Ave Philadelphia PA 19122-9999

ARCE, PEDRO EDGARDO, chemical engineering educator; b. Nogoya, Entre Rios, Argentina, Feb. 27, 1952; came to U.S., 1983; s. Pedro Ismael and Julia Celina (Traverso) A.; m. Maria Beatriz Trigatti, Feb. 9, 1978; children: Maria Paula, Andrea Lucia. Diploma in Chem. Engring., U. Nacional del Litoral, Santa Fe, Argentina, 1977; cert. of studies, Anglo-Continental Sch. of Eng., 1981; MSChemE, Purdue U., 1987, PhDChemE, 1990. Grad. fellow Coun. for Sci. Rsch. (CONICET), Argentina, 1978-84; lectr. Universidad Nacional de Litoral, Santa Fe, Argentina, 1980-87; instr. Purdue U., 1989; asst. prof. Fla. A&M U.-Fla. State U. Coll. Engring., Tallahassee, 1990-95, assoc. prof., 1995—, interim chair dept. chem. engring., 1995; elected mem. Sci. and Technol. Career Coun. of Rsch., Argentina, 1984-90; Fulbright lectr. for Latin Am., 1994; vis. scientist Smith Herchel Lab., U. Cambridge, Eng., 1995; assoc. faculty mem. Materials Rsch. Program, Fla. State U., 1991—, Geophys. Fluid Dynamics Inst., Fla. State U., 1997—; lectr. in field. Contbr. articles to profl. jours. including Chem. Engring. Sci., AIChE Jour., Comp. in Chem. Engring., I&E Chem. Rsch., Separations Tech., Hazardous Waste/Hazardous Materials, Internat. Comm. in Heat/Mass Transfer, Latin Am. Applied Rsch., Jour. Sci. Edn. and Tech., Jour. Chem. Engring. Edn. Argentina Coun. of Rsch. fellow, 1978, 80, 84, U. Queensland (Australia) fellow, 1982, Purdue U. fellow, 1988; recipient Excellence in Tchg. award Bd. Regents, U. Fla. Sys., 1994, Devel. Scholar award Fla. State U., 1996, Svc. award Fla. A&M U., 1996. Mem. ASME, AIChE (student chpt. Prof. of Yr. 1990-91, Invited lectr. 1994, vice chair divsn. applied math. and numerical methods 1996-98, chmn. exec. com., 1998—, program coord. 1998—, chair session honoring Prof. D. Ramkrishna 1999, Nat. Student Competition award 1998), TAPPI, Am. Filt. Soc., Am. Assn. Aerosol Rsch., Material Rsch. Soc., Am. Soc. Engring. Edn. (Thomas C. Evans award 1994), Am. Chem. Soc., Am. Phys. Soc., N.Am. Membrane Soc., Soc. Rheology, Fla. Acad. Scis., Sigma Xi, Phi Lambda Upsilon. Achievements include research in corona discharge in liquid phase for waste treatment; discovery of collaborative phenomena and pattern formation in catalytic reactors with implications for selectivity and yield improvement; of novel operator-theoretic structures in applied mathematics; development of the Integral-Spectral approach in computational methods, of the Colloquial Approach teaching technique. Fax: 850-410-6150. Office: Fla State U Chem Engring and GFDI 2525 Pottsdamer St Tallahassee FL 32310-6046

ARCE, PHILLIP WILLIAM, hotel and casino executive; b. N.Y.C., June 25, 1937; s. Joseph F. and Margaret (Degnan) A.; m. Dorothy Fiss, June 25, 1966; children: Joseph, William, Serena. Student, U. Notre Dame, 1955-56; AA, San Diego Jr. Coll., 1958; student, San Diego State U., 1958-60, San Diego U., 1960-62, LaSalle Law Sch., 1963-65. Various positions Del Webb Corp., Las Vegas and Reno, Nev., Oahu, Hawaii, 1963-75; exec. Caesars Palace, Las Vegas, 1975-78; pres. Frontier Hotel, Las Vegas, 1978-84; corp. v.p., v.p. mktg., sr. v.p. Dunes Hotel & Country Club, Las Vegas, 1985-88; hotel and gaming specialist Arce Cons., Las Vegas, 1988—; tchr. hotel div. U. Nev., Las Vegas, 1966-67, 1976-77. Mem. exec. com. Boulder Dam Area coun. Boy Scouts Am., 1976-88; vice chmn. United Way So. Nev., 1968-70; founder, chmn. Las Vegas Events, Inc., 1980-89; pres. Easter Seals Nev., 1974-76; bd. dirs. Air Force Acad. Found., 1982-89. Served with USMC, 1962. Recipient numerous awards including Appreciation awards Easter Seals, 1972, 73, United Way, 1975, Silver Beaver Boy Scouts Am., 1984. Mem. Am. Hotel and Motel Assn. (bd. dirs. 1979-82), Nev. Hotel and Motel Assn. (founder, pres. 1980, Hotelier of Yr. award 1981), Las Vegas C. of C. (dir. 1979-85, pres. 1984). Republican. Roman Catholic. Home: 4243 Ridgecrest Dr Las Vegas NV 89121-4949 Office: Arce Cons Hotel/Gaming Ind Specialists Ste 1 4460 W Hacienda Ave Las Vegas NV 89118-4909 also: Colo Belle Hotel & Casino PO Box 77000 Laughlin NV 89028-7000

ARCENEAUX, WILLIAM, historian, educator, association official; b. Scott, La., Aug. 19, 1941; s. Teddy and Regina (Begnaud) A.; m. Patricia Boozman; children—Ted, Angelle, Leah, Scott. BA, U. Southwestern La., 1962; MA, La. State U., 1965, PhD, 1969; LHD, Loyola U., 1982. Instr. La. State U., 1966-67; asst. prof. Northwestern State U., Natchitoches, La., 1967-69; assoc. prof., chmn. dept. history So. U., New Orleans, 1969-72; exec. dir. La. Coordinating Council for Higher Edn., Baton Rouge, 1972-75; commr. higher edn. La. Baton Rouge, 1975-87; pres. La. Assn. Ind. Colls. and Univs., 1987—; chmn. CSLA, Inc., Lajeunesse & Assocs., Inc. Author: Acadian General-Alfred Mouton and the Civil War, 1972, 2d edit., 1981, No Spark of Malice: The Murder of Martin Begnaud, 1999; editor: Postsecondary Education in Transition: Planning for Change in Louisiana, 1975. Bd. dirs., chmn. Student Loan Mktg. Assn., 1979-97; chmn. Devel. French in La. Found., 1993—; exec. com. La. Pub. Broadcasting. Decorated chevalier L'Ordre de la Pleiade, Association Internationale des Parlementaires de Langue Francaise, L'Ordre des Palmes Academique (France); named one of 100 Young Leaders of Academy Change mag., 1978; recipient Jefferson Davis medal UDC, E.T. Dunlap medal Southeastern Okla. State U. Mem. Nat. Assn. Ind. Coll. and Univ. State Execs., Am. Hist. Assn., Fgn. Relations Assn. New Orleans, La. Hist. Assn., City Club, Camelot Club, Omicron Delta Kappa, Phi Alpha Theta. Roman Catholic. Office: La Assn Ind Colls and Univs 700 N 10th St Ste 210 Baton Rouge LA 70802-4508

ARCHABAL, NINA M(ARCHETTI), historical society director; b. Long Branch, N.J., Apr. 11, 1940; d. John William and Santina Matilda (Giuffre) Marchetti; m. John William Archabal, Aug. 8, 1964; 1 child, John Fidel. BA in Music History cum laude, Radcliffe Coll., 1962; MAT in Music History, Harvard U., 1963; PhD in Music History, U. Minn., 1979. Asst. dir. humanities art mus. U. Minn., Mpls., 1975-77; asst. supr. edn. div. Minn. Hist. Soc., St. Paul, 1977-78, dep. dir. for program mgmt., 1978-86, acting dir., 1986-87, dir., 1987—. Trustee, bd. dirs. Am. Folklife Ctr., Libr. of Congress, 1989-98; bd. dirs. N.W. Area Found., 1989-98, St. Paul Acad. and Summit Sch., 1993—; v.p. Friends of St. Paul Pub. Libr., 1983-93; bd. regents St. John's U., Collegeville, Minn., 1997—; overseer Harvard Coll., Cambridge, Mass., 1997—. NDEA fellow U. Minn., 1969-72, U. Minn. grad. fellow, 1974-75. Mem. Am. Assn. State and Local History (sec. 1986-88), Am. Assn. Mus. (v.p. 1991-94, chair bd. dirs. 1994-96). Office: Minn Hist Soc 345 Kellogg Blvd W Saint Paul MN 55102-1906

ARCHAMBAULT, GEORGE FRANCIS, editor, pharmaceutical consultant; b. Springfield, Mass., Apr. 29, 1909; s. George Charles and Catherine V. (Mayette) A.; m. Lillian Herbert, Sept. 3, 1934; children: Joan Anne Archambault Rubis, Lillian Kathleen Archambault Matan, Patricia Gay Archambault Kachik, Frances Helen Archambault Parks, George Francis, William Herbert. Ph.G., Mass. Coll. Pharmacy, 1931, Ph.C., 1933, Pharm.D. (hon.), 1960; J.D., Northeastern U., 1941; D.Sc. (hon.), Phila. Coll. Pharmacy, 1951; LL.D. (hon.), Temple U., 1961. Bar: Mass. 1942, U.S. Supreme Ct. 1976, D.C. 1980; Registered pharmacist in Mass., 1932. Mem. faculty Mass. Coll. Pharmacy, 1933-45, lectr. pharmacy and bus. adminstrn., 1933-47; practiced in Belmont, Mass and Washington, 1945-47; dir. profl. relations in New Eng. states Liggett Drug Co., 1945-47; commd. pharmacist officer USPHS, 1947-67, pharmacist dir., 1952; chief pharmacy br., div. hosps. Bur. Med. Services, 1947-65; also pharmacy liasion officer Office Surgeon Gen. USPHS, 1960-67, medicare pharmacy planning cons. div. med. care adminstrn., 1965-67; dean, prof. pharmacy adminstrn. Coll. Pharmacy, U. Fla., Gainesville, 1967; editor Hosp. Formulary Jour., 1967-79; Washington editor Drug Intelligence and Clin. Pharmacy Jour., from 1979; cons. on pharmacy and instnl. and other drug distbn. systems, 1967—; cons. United Mine Workers Am. Health and Retirement Fund, 1971-76, Am. Soc. Cons. Pharmacists, 1972—, Hill-Burton program USPHS, 1969-79; mem. revision com. U.S. Pharmacopeia, 1950-60, trustee, 1960-75, USPHS del., mem.-at-large, 1975, cons. to exec. dir., 1976—, mem. subcoms. on external and internal preparations; hon. mem., 1980—; mem. faculty Inst. Hosp. Law of Am. Hosp. Assn., 1954-69; mem. joint com. Am. Soc. Hosp. Pharmacists and Am. Hosp. Assn., 1955-68; pharm. cons. Catholic Hosp. Assn., 1950—; pharmacy cons. profl. exam. service Am. Pub. Health Assn., 1949-59; adv. pub. health service pharmacy and prescription trend, div. prices and cost of living Bur. Labor Statistics, 1955-67; mem. nat. adv. com. Law-Medicine Research Inst., Boston U., 1960-65; lectr. law hosp. pharmacy and drugs including investigational drugs; Samuel Melendy Meml. lectr. U.

Minn. Coll. Pharmacy, 1962. Author numerous articles, chpts. in books. Recipient Harvey A. Whitney Hosp. Pharmacy award Am. Soc. Hosp. Pharmacists, 1956; Andrew Craigie award Assn. Mil. Surgeons, 1962; certificate of appreciation Cath. Hosp. Assn., 1956; certificate of appreciation Kappa Psi Pharm. Frat, 1962; certificate of appreciation U.S. Naval Sch. Hosp. Adminstrn., 1964; Disting. Service medal USPHS, 1965; Remington medal Am. Pharm. Assn., 1969; Disting. Alumni award Mass. Coll. Pharmacy, 1976; Disting. Alumni award Northeastern U. Sch. Law, 1980; named Man of Year Am. Druggist, 1966; George Archambault ann. award established in his honor by Am. Soc. Cons. Pharmacists, 1972; Pres.'s award Am. Soc. Pharmacy Law, 1982. Life mem. Am. Pharm. Assn. (chmn. council 1959-60, com. publs. 1958-59, pres. Washington chpt. 1950, nat. pres. 1962-63); fellow AAAS (v.p. 1958, mem. council from 1959), Am. Pub. Health Assn., Am. Soc. Hosp. Pharmacists (hon. charter, pres. 1954-55); mem. Commd. Officers Assn. USPHS (chmn. exec. com. 1961-62), Mass. Soc. Hosp. Pharmacists (founder, hon.), La. Socs. Hosp. Pharmacists (hon.), Nat. Health Lawyers Assn., Am. Soc. Law and Medicine, Am. Soc. Hosp. Attys., Am. Med. Writers Assn., Fed. Bar Assn., D.C. Bar Assn., Nat. Press Club, Am. Soc. Pharmacy Law, Nat. Assn. Uniformed Services, Ret. Officers Assn., Kappa Psi, Rho Chi.

ARCHAMBAULT, LOUIS, sculptor; b. Montreal, Que., Can., Apr. 4, 1915; s. Anthime Sergius and Annie (Michaud) A.; m. Mariette Provost, June 7, 1941; children: Aubert, Eloi, Eve, Patrice. Student, Coll. Jean-de-Brebeuf, Montreal; B.A., U. Montreal, 1936; Diploma, Ecole des Beaux Arts, Montreal, 1939. Former mem. faculty Musée des Beaux-Arts, Montreal, Ecole des Beaux-Arts, Montreal, U. B.C., Vancouver, Can., U. Que., Montreal, Concordia U., Montreal. Works exhibited Internat. Sculpture Exhbn., Festival of Gt. Britain, London, 1951, 10th Triennale, Milan, Italy, 1954, 28th Biennial, Venice, 1956, 11th Triennale, Milan, 1957, Brussels Universal and Internat. Exhbn., 1958, Pitts. Internat., 1958, Internat. Exhbn. Contemporary Sculpture, Expo '67, Montreal, 11th Biennial, Middelheim, 1971; several one-man shows in Can., France, Eng.; represented in permanent collections Nat. Gallery, Ottawa, Musée du Que., Quebec City, Musée d'art contemporain, Montreal, Musee des Beaux Arts, Montreal, Museo Internazionale della Ceramica, Faenza, Italy, Can. Imperial Bank of Commerce, Montreal, Art Gallery Ont., Toronto, Sun Life Bldg., Toronto, Upland Air Terminal, Ottawa, Place des Arts, Montreal, Malton Airport, Toronto, Scarborough Coll., Toronto, Macdonald Block, Queen's Park, Toronto, Centre D'Accueil, Longueuil, Que., Centre Hospitalier, Chateauguay, Que., Fed. Food and Drug Bldg., Longueuil, Can. Council Art Bank, Ottawa, Winnipeg Art Gallery, Justice Ct. Bldg., Quebec City, Faculté de Medicine Veterinaire U. de Montreal, also others. Decorated officer Order Can., 1968; recipient Allied Arts medal Royal Archtl. Inst. of Can., 1958; Recipient Diplome d'honneur Can. Conf. Arts, 1982; Canadian Govt. fellow for travel in France, 1953-54; Can. Council grantee, 1959, 62, 69. Academician Royal Canadian Acad. Arts. Address: 278 Sanford Ave, Saint Lambert, PQ Canada J4P 2X6

ARCHAMBAULT, PIERRE GUY, judge; b. Drummondville, Que., Can., May 22, 1949; s. René Guy and Paulette (Bergeron) A.; children: Patrick, Julie, Martin. BA, Sherbrooke U., 1969; B in Geography and Economy, U. Quebec, Montreal, Can., 1972; BCL, McGill U., 1975. With Vercheres & Gauthier, Montreal, Que., Can., 1976-78; assoc. to ptnr. Stikeman Elliott, Montreal, Que., Can., 1978-83, 83-93; judge Tax Ct. Can., Ottawa, Ont., Can., 1993—. Co-author: Canada Guide Fiscal, 1984, 90; contbr. articles to profl. jours. Recipient W.L. Jacob prize McGill U., Montreal, 1975. Mem. Can. Jud. Coun. (judges computer adv. com. 1994-98, chmn. 1996-98), Can. Inst. Adminstrn. Justice, Can. Judges Conf., Nat. Jud. Inst. Avocations: computers, golf, skiing, reading, travel. Office: Tax Ct Can, 200 Kent St, Ottawa, ON Canada K1A 0M1

ARCHARD, DOUGLAS BRUCE, foreign service officer; b. Queensbury, N.Y., Nov. 14, 1937; s. Wallace Henry and Pearl Ilene (Harris) A.; m. Mary A. Czechan, Jan., 1970 (div. 1985); adopted children: Wallace A. C., Malcolm A.H., Clea K.E.; m. E. Claire Curry, Dec. 15, 1990. BS, SUNY, Plattsburgh, 1963; MA, U. Wis., 1966; LittD (hon.), U. Ulster, Colerain, Northern Ireland, 1993. Vol. U.S. Peace Corps, The Philippines, 1963-64; instr. history Stout State U., Menomonie, Wis., 1966-69; advisor U.S. State Dept., Vietnam, 1970-72; polit. officer U.S. Embassy, Islamabad, Pakistan, 1973-76; desk officer U.S. State Dept., Washington, 1976-78; consul U.S. Consulate, Peshawar, Pakistan, 1978-82; polit. officer U.S. Embassy, Ankara, Turkey, 1983-87; polit. counselor U.S. Embassy, Khartoum, Sudan, 1987-89; consul gen. U.S. Consulate, Belfast, Northern Ireland, 1989-93; with Nat. Fgn. Affairs Tng. Ctr. U.S. State Dept., Washington, 1993-94; dep. chief mission U.S. Embassy, Ashgabat, Turkmenistan, 1994-96; consul gen. U.S. Consulate, Karachi, Pakistan, 96-99; diplomat in residence Carter Ctr., Atlanta, 1999—. With U.S. Army, 1956-58. Mem. Irish Assn., Kipling Soc. Avocations: trekking, birding, reading. Office: Carter Ctr Atlanta GA 30301

ARCHER, CHALMERS, JR., education educator; b. Tchula, Miss., Apr. 21, 1938; s. Chalmers Sr. and Eva Alcola (Rutherford) A. Asst. to the pres. Saints Coll., Lexington, Miss., 1968-72; asst. v.p. Tuskegee (Ala.) Inst., 1972-83; prof. No. Va. C.C., Manassas, 1983—. Author: Growing Up Black in Rural Mississippi (recipient Miss. Inst. of Arts and Letters award for Nonfiction); contbg. editor: The Jackson Advocate; contbr. articles to profl. jours. and newspapers. Mem. Dem. Spkr.'s Bur. for Clinton/Gore Re-election Campaign. Recipient Nat. Edn. Articulation Model, Conf. on Blacks in Higher Edn., Washington, 1986. Mem. Rotary. Democrat. Baptist. Avocations: acad. and cmty. program development; motivational speaking, writing. Home: 7885 Flager Cir Manassas VA 20109-7435 Office: No Va Comm Coll 6901 Sudley Rd Manassas VA 20109-2399

ARCHER, DAVID HORACE, process engineer, consultant; b. Pitts., Jan. 20, 1928; s. Horace G. and Inez E. (Eichholtz) A.; m. M. Justine Garnic, July 29, 1950 (dec. Sept. 1973); children: Catherine M.I., Miriam. A. J. Archer McCann, Amy C.A.; m. Alice Ann Parsons, July 2, 1976; 1 child, Martha J. Knezovich. BS, Carnegie Mellon U., 1948; PhD, U. Del., 1953. Instr. chem. enging. U. Del., Newark, 1951-53; asst. prof. to assoc. prof. Carnegie Mellon U., Pitts., 1953-60, prof., 1991—; successively sr. engr., fellow engr., supr. engr., sect. mgr. R & D, dept. mgr., cons. engr. Westinghouse Electric, Pitts., 1960-91; cons. Westinghouse Electric Corp., Pitts. Coke, Pa. Coke Tech., Pitts., 1954—, U.S. DOE, Caldon Inc., NAS-Nitrogen Oxides Panel, Washington. Co-contbr. numerous articles on process dynamics, optimization control, fuel cell power generation, fluidized bed combustion; holder 21 U.S. patents. Organist-choirmaster Mt. Zion Luth. Ch., Pitts., 1979—. Lt. U.S. Army, 1953-57. Mem. NAE, ASME, Am. Inst. Chem. Egrs., Am. Chem. Soc., Combustion Inst., Am. Soc. Engring. Edn. Republican. Lutheran. Home: 114 Kentzel Rd Pittsburgh PA 15237-2816 Office: Carnegie Mellon U Northern Pike & Mosside Blvd 216 Scaife Hall Pittsburgh PA 15213-3890

ARCHER, DENNIS WAYNE, mayor, lawyer; b. Detroit, Jan. 1, 1942; s. Ernest James and Frances (Carroll) A.; m. Trudy Ann DunCombe, June 17, 1967; children: Dennis Wayne, Vincent DunCombe. BS, Western Mich. U., 1965; JD, Detroit Coll. Law, 1970; LLD (hon.), Western Mich. U., 1987, Detroit Coll. Law, 1988, U. Detroit, 1988, John Marshall Law Sch., 1991, Gonzaga U., 1991, U. Mich., 1994; D in Pub. Svc. (hon.), Ea. Mich. U., 1994. Bar: Mich. 1970. Tchr. spl. edn. Detroit Bd. Edn., 1965-70; assoc. Gragg & Gardner, 1970-71; ptnr. Hall, Stone, Allen, Archer & Glenn, P.C., 1971-73, Charfoos, Christensen & Archer, P.C., 1973-85; assoc. justice Mich. Supreme Ct., 1986-90; ptnr. Dickinson, Wright, Moon, Van Dusen & Freeman, Detroit, 1991-93; mayor City of Detroit, 1994—; assoc. prof. Detroit Coll. Law, 1972-78; adj. prof. Wayne State U. Law Sch., Detroit, 1984-85; mem. Mich. Bd. Ethics, 1979-83; mem. adv. bd. U.S. Conf. Mayors, 1994—; bd. dirs. Nat. Conf. Black Mayors, 1994—; mem. intergovtl. policy adv. com. U.S. Trade Rep. Contbr. articles to legal jours. Bd. dirs. Legal Aid and Defenders Assn., Detroit, 1980-82, Nat. Conf. Black Mayors, 1994; co-chmn. Met. Detroit Cmty. Coalition for Dems., 1979-80; bd. trustees Olivet Coll., 1991-93; active numerous local Dem. campaigns, 1970-85; host local pub. svc. radio programs; co-chair platform com. Dem. Conv., 1996; pres. Nat. Conf. Dem. Mayors, 1996; mem. Nat. Com. on Crime Control and Prevention, 1995. Named Most Respected Judge in Mich. Mich. Lawyers Weekly Jour., 1990. Mem. ABA (ho. dels. 1979-93, chmn. drafting com. 1986-88, com. on scope and correlation of work sect. officers liaison 1987-90, chmn. gen. practice sect. 1987-88, chair commn. on opportunities for minorities in the profession 1987-91, sect. legal edn. and admissions to the bar, coun. mem. 1989-95, task force on profl. skills instrn. 1989-91, task force on law schs. and the profession, Narrowing The Gap, 1989-91, chmn. spl. com. prepaid legal svcs. 1981-83, chmn. sect. officers conf. 1988-90, resource devel. coun. 1988-91, bd. editors ABA Jour. 1988-94, bd. editors The Practical Litigator 1989-94, chmn. rules and calendar com. 1990-92, state del. 1990-96), ATLA, Nat. Bar Assn. (pres. 1983-84), Am. Judicature Soc. (bd. dirs 1977-81), State Bar Mich. (pres. 1984-85), Wolverine Bar Assn. (pres. 1979-80), Detroit Bar Assn. (bd. dirs. 1973-75), Mich. Trial Lawyers Assn. (exec. bd. 1973-74), Econ. Club, Alpha Phi Alpha. Roman Catholic. Office: City of Detroit 2 Woodward Ave Rm 1126 Detroit MI 48226-3413*

ARCHER, GLENN LEROY, JR., federal circuit judge; b. Densmore, Kans., Mar. 21, 1929; s. Glenn LeRoy and Ruth Agnes (Ford) A.; m. Carole J. Thomas, 1990; children: Susan, Sharon, Glenn, Thomas. B.A., Yale U., 1951; J.D. with honors, George Washington U., 1954. Bar: D.C. 1954. Asst. atty. gen. U.S. Dept. Justice, Washington, 1981-85; circuit judge U.S. Ct. Appeals (fed. cir.), Washington, 1985-94, chief judge, 1994-97, sr. cir. judge, 1997—. Republican. Methodist. Office: US Ct of Appeals Fed Circuit 717 Madison Pl NW Washington DC 20439-0002

ARCHER, HUGH MORRIS, consulting engineer, manufacturing professional; b. Dover, N.J., June 22, 1916; s. Harvey George and Helen Thomson (Morris) A.; m. Mary Jane Reed, May 11, 1940; children: June, Ruth, Lucy. BEE, Rensselaer Poly. Inst., 1937; D Engring., Milw. Sch. Engring., 1990. Registered profl. engr., Mich. Rsch. engr. Detroit Edison Co., 1937-51; founder, ptnr. Archer-Reed Co., Dearborn, 1951-63; ind. cons. engr. Dearborn, Mich., 1951—; founder, chmn. bd. dirs. Spiratex Co., Romulus, Mich., 1954—; chmn. Dearborn Bank and Trust Co., 1970-86, Alliance Fin. Corp., Dearborn, 1980-89; bd. dirs. Syncro Corp., Arab, Ala. Patentee in sci. instrumentation and mfg. processes. Active YMCA, Boy Scouts Am., others; bd. dirs. Greenfield Village Schs., 1948-52, Henry Ford Hosp., 1983-85; chmn. Fairlane Med. Ctr., 1980-85. Ensign USN, 1944-47, PTO, ETO. Recipient Gold award for engring. Affiliate Coun. Mich. Engrs., 1992. Mem. Dearborn Rotary Club (pres. 1957-58), Rotary Internat. (pres. 1989-90), Found. of Rotary Internat. (trustee 1990—). Republican. Presbyterian. Avocations: amateur radio, computer science, ancient technical books. Office: Spiratex Co 6333 Cogswell St Romulus MI 48174-4039

ARCHER, JAMES ELSON, engineering educator; b. Hedley, Tex., Dec. 1, 1922; s. James M. and Mary Minerva (Bolles) A.; m. Reta Faye Turner, Nov. 8, 1942; 1 son, James Elson. B.S., Tex. Tech. U., 1947; Ph.D., Mass. Inst. Tech., 1950. Instr. Mass. Inst. Tech., 1950-52, Sloan fellow in indsl. mgmt., 1963-64; researcher Pitts. Plate Glass Co., Pitts., 1952-53; asst. dir. Pitts. Plate Glass Co., 1953-54, asso. dir., 1954-56, dir. research, 1956-62; mng. partner Archer Assos., Dallas, 1962-64; corporate dir. mgmt. systems Tex. Instruments, Dallas, 1964-68; prof. Tex. Tech U., Lubbock, 1968-95, prof. emeritus, 1995—. Served with USAAF, 1943-46. Home: 6208 Lynnhaven Dr Lubbock TX 79413-5332 Office: PO Box 4200 Lubbock TX 79409-0006

ARCHER, J(OHN) BARRY, municipal official; b. Ft. Jackson, S.C., Mar. 21, 1946. BS in Civil Engring., Va. Mil. Inst., 1968; MA in Engring. Adminstrn., George Washington U., 1979; student, JFK Ctr. Spl. Warfare. Registered profl. engr.; cert. bldg. ofcl.; cert. profl. codes adminstr. Engr. trainee Va. Dept. of Transp.; project mgr. George Hyman Constrn. Co.; asst. city engr. Fairfax City, Va.; structural engr. Fairfax County, 1974-78; county bldg. ofcl., dep. dir. devel. adminstrn./pub. works Prince William County, Va., 1978-94; dir. dept. codes adminstrn. City of Kansas City, 1994—; chmn. Manufactured Homes Constrn. and Safety Stds. Code Change Com.; mem. manufactured home adv. com. U.S. Dept. HUD. Mem. rev. bd. Va. State Tech. Maj. U.S. Army Green Berets, 1969-70, Vietnam. Decorated Bronze Star with 1 oak leaf cluster, Combat Infantrymans Badge, Master Parachutist Wings, Vietnamese Spl. Forces Parachutist Wings; named Local Ofcl. of Yr. Northeastern Region Nat. Assn. Home Builders, 1992, Codes Adminstr. of Yr. Gtr. Kansas City Automatic Sprinkler Contractors Assn., 1997; recipient Meritorius Svc. award Va. Bldg. and Code Ofcls. Assn., 1994. Mem. NSPE, Am. Concrete Inst. Internat., Mo. Assn. Code Adminstrs., Internat. Conf. Bldg. Ofcls., Mo. Assn. Bldg. Ofcls. and Insps. Spl. Forces Assn. (life), Spl. Ops. Assn., Vietnam Vets. Assn. Am., VFW. Office: City of Kansas City Codes Adminstrn Dept City Hall 18th Fl 414 E 12th St Kansas City MO 64106-2702*

ARCHER, JOSEPH NEALE, industrial designer; b. Sistersville, W.Va., Apr. 14, 1933; s. Oliver William and Netta Lee (Davis) A.; m. Clara Mae Ash, Dec. 25, 1952 (dec. Oct. 1990); children: Kathy, Judith, Mary, William; m. Marie-Paule Cyrenne, Oct. 6, 1997. Grad. H.S., Middlebourne, W.Va. Draftsman Olin Aluminum, Hannibal, Ohio, 1956-67; estimator Ball Electric Co., Belpre, Ohio, 1967-78, Woodhurst Electric Co., Marietta, Ohio, 1978-80; cons. Indsl. Consultants, Sistersville, 1980—; designer GE Plastics, Parkersburg, W.Va., 1985-91, Parsons-SIP, Houston, 1991-93, Apex Engring., Parkersburg, W.Va., 1994—. Mem. Instrument Soc. Am. Achievements include systems design for petro-chem. industries and quality control rsch. using acoustic emission. Home: 2249 Next Rd Sistersville WV 26175-9063

ARCHER, MARY KATHRYN, elementary education educator; b. Traverse City, Mich., Feb. 3, 1956; d. Robert Allen and Arlene Vera Dean; m. William Allen Archer, Oct. 6, 1979; children: Alisha, Aimee. BS in Edn., Western Mich. U., 1978; MACT, Mich. State U., Traverse City, 1994. Cert. elem. edn. with early childhood endorsement. Tchr. Co-op Nursery, Interlochen, Mich., 1979-81; program dir. 4C, Traverse City, 1981-86; tchr. TCAPS, Traverse City, 1986—; mem. adv. bd. AEYC-Grand Traverse, Traverse City, 1981-83, 94-97, March of Dimes, Traverse City, 1985-87. Mem. ASCD, Grand Traverse Assn. for the Edn. Young Children (treas. 1981-83, newsletter chair 1994-97). Avocations: winter sports, gardening, traveling, reading. E-mail: archercnt1@aol.com.

ARCHER, RICHARD JOSEPH, lawyer; b. Virginia, Minn., Mar. 24, 1922; s. William John and Margaret Leanore (Duff) A.; m. Kristina Hanson, Jan. 29, 1977 (dec.); children: Alison P., Cynthia J. A.B., U. Mich., 1947, J.D., 1948. Bar: Calif. 1949, U.S. Supreme Ct. 1962, Hawaii 1982. Partner firm Morrison and Foerster, San Francisco, 1954-71, Sullivan, Jones and Archer, San Francisco, 1971-81, Archer Rosenak & Hanson, San Francisco, 1981-85, Archer & Hanson, San Francisco, 1985—. Served with USN, 1942-45. Decorated Bronze Star. Mem. ABA, Am. Bar Found. (life), Am. Law Inst. (life). Republican. Home: 3110 Bohemian Hwy Occidental CA 95465-9113 Office: Archer and Hanson 1426 Fillmore St Ste 213 San Francisco CA 94115-4164 also: Mauka Tower Ste 2920 737 Bishop St Honolulu HI 96813-3201

ARCHER, RONALD DEAN, chemist, educator; b. Rochelle, Ill., July 22, 1932; s. Don Adam and Irma Cecil (Olson) A.; m. Joyce Hilder Carlson, Jan. 31, 1954; children: Paul Dean, Lynn Sue, Sharon Jean, Julie Anne. B.S., Ill. State U., 1953, M.S., 1954; Ph.D., U. Ill., 1959. Tchr. Larson Jr. High Sch., Elgin, Ill., 1954; asst. prof. U. Calif., Riverside, 1959-63, Tulane U., New Orleans, 1963-65; assoc. prof. Tulane U., 1965-66, U. Mass., Amherst, 1966-70; prof. chemistry U. Mass., 1970—, head chemistry dept., 1977-83; vis. prof. Tech. U. Denmark, 1972, U. Vienna, 1987; research scientist Naval Research Lab., Washington, spring 1980; cons., 1960-63, 64-70, 72—; chief chemistry reader advanced placement program, Ednl. Testing Service, 1985-88. Contbr. chem. articles to research jours. Served with U.S. Army, 1954-56. Grantee USAF, Rsch. Corp., NSF, Am. Chem. Soc., NIH, Army Rsch. Office, Office Naval Rsch.; recipient Alumni Achievement award Ill. State U., 1989. Fellow AAAS; mem. Am. Chem. Soc. (chmn. Conn. Valley sect. 1979, councilor 1981—, chmn. com. on edn. 1987-89, nominating and election com. 1990-94, coun. policy com. 1996-98, exec. com. divsn. chem. edn. 1995-98, chair-elect, chair, past chair divsn. chem. edn. 1996-98, chair adv. bd. gen. chem. curriculum project 1997—), Royal Soc. Chemistry, Internat. Union Pure and Applied Chemistry, New Eng. Assn. Chemistry Tchrs., Sigma Xi, Phi Lambda Upsilon. Lutheran. Home: 19 Lantern Ln Amherst MA 01002-3222 Office: U Mass Grad Rsch Towers # A Amherst MA 01003 *Nothing surpasses the joy in the eyes of a student who has just synthesized a new chemical compound, especially if it has unique properties or may benefit the human endeavor.*

ARCHER, SARAH ELLEN, public health consultant; b. Chgo., Dec. 7, 1938; d. H. Ross and Helen Emily (Wason) A. BS, Ind. U., 1960; MPH, U. Mich., 1964; DPH, U. Calif., Berkeley, 1973. RN. Pub. health nurse Near East Christian Coun. Refugee Work, Jerusalem, Jordan, 1960-61, Marion County Health Dept., Indpls., 1962-63; instr. nursing W.Va. U., 1964-67; supervising public health nurse Santa Clara County Health Dept., San Jose, Calif., 1967-69; prof. U. Calif., San Francisco, 1972-84; maternal child health, nutrition and nursing cons. WHO, Dhaka, Bangladesh, 1985-90; tng. advisor German Govt. Tech. Assistance, Dhaka, 1990-94; emergency assessment coord. Internat. Med. Corps, Luanda, Angola, 1994; med. coord. and country dir. Internat. Med. Corps, Kigali, Rwanda, 1994-95; v.p. Shamitar, Inc., Indpls., 1993-98; vis. prof. cmty. health nursing U. Indpls., 1998; rsch. cons. Royal Australian Nursing Fedn., Melbourne, 1976, 82; curriculum cons. Coll. of Nursing Australia, Melbourne, 1976-82; mentor, external degree program Fielding Inst., Santa Barbara, Calif., 1975-81; founding trustee Nursing Dynamics Corp., Mill Valley, Calif., 1973-81; Humanitarian relief orgn. cons. Battle Command tng. program, U.S. Army, through Logicon Info. Tech Group, San Pedro, Calif., 1998—; health assessment cons. Internat. Med. Corps, Kosovo, Fed. Rep. Yugoslavia, 1998; cons. to dir. Divsn. of HIV/STD Ind. State Dept. of Health, Indpls., 1999—; cons. fetal and infant mortality program Marion County Health Dept., Indpls. Author: Implementing Change in Communities, 1984, Community, Health Nursing Patterns, 1976, 79, 85 (Book of Yr. 1976), Nurses: A Political Force, 1982; contbr. chpts. to books and articles to profl. jours. Parish rep. Episcopal Ch. St. Alban's Parish, Indpls., Bishop's Fund for World Relief. Fellow ANA (Pearl McIver pub. health nursing award 1982), APHA (chair exec. bd. 1980-81, Creative Achievement award 1978), Coll. of Nursing Australia, Royal Soc. for Health, Acad. of Nursing, Ind. Pub. health Assn. (legis. com. 1998—). Avocation: music, history. E-mail: drsearcher@aol.com.

ARCHER, STEPHEN MURPHY, retired theater educator; b. Winfield, Kans., N, May 14, 1934; s. William A. and Cecelia (Kumbera) A.; m. Paula Karalyn Agrelius, Aug. 3, 1959; 1 child, Steven Michael. BA, BS, Emporia State U., 1957, MS, 1958; PhD, U. Ill., 1964. Prof. theatre Kearney State U., Nebr., 1964-66, So. Ill. U.-Edwardsville, 1966-71, U. Mo., Columbia, 1971-98; ret., 1998. Author: How Theatre Happens, 1978, 83, American Actors and Actresses, 1983, Junius Brutus Booth: Theatrical Prometheus, 1992, Theatre: Its Art and Craft, 1993. Home: 715 Spring Valley Rd Columbia MO 65203-2248

ARCHER, VANESSA, education program director; b. Macon, Ga.; d. Curtis and Betty Power; m. Darnley Archer, Mar. 30, 1996. BFA, Valdosta State Coll., 1991; MEd, U. S.C., 1993; postgrad., Va. Poly. Inst. and State U. Area coord. Columbia (S.C.) Coll., 1991-93; dir. residence life Newberry (S.C.) Coll., 1993-94; asst. dir. leadership devel. and advisement St. Mary's Coll. Md., 1994-95; acad. coord. ednl. talent search Hampton (Va.) U., 1996, dir. ednl. talent search, 1996-98; project SAFE coord. Va. Poly. Inst. and State U., Blacksburg, 1998—; grad. asst. for minority student affairs U. S.C., Columbia, 1992; treas., student leadership conf. chair Mid-Eastern Assn. Ednl. Opportunity Program Pers., Washington, 1996-98; grant reader Dept. Edn. TRIO Programs, Washington. Vol. Food Bank, Norfolk, Va., 1996—; spokesperson Tidewater Literacy Coun., Portsmouth, Va., 1997—. Named Mrs. Chesapeake, Mrs. Va. Pageant, Roanoke, 1997-98; grad. scholar Sigma Gamma Rho Sorority, Inc., Columbia, 1992. Mem. Am. Coll. Pers. Assn. (exhibits co-chair nat. conv. planning team 1995-96), So. Assn. Coll. Student Affairs (chair small coll. com. chair 1996, 98), Nat. Assn. for Campus Activities (showcase selection com., ednl. svcs. coord. 1994-95). Avocations: singing, community activities. E-mail: varcher@vt.edu. Office: Dean Students Office Henderson Hall Blacksburg VA 24061

ARCHER, WILLIAM REYNOLDS, JR. (BILL REYNOLDS), congressman; b. Houston, Tex., Mar. 22, 1928; s. William Reynolds and Eleanor M. (Miller) A.; m. Sharon Sawyer; children: William Reynolds III, Richard M., Sharon, Elizabeth, Barbara. BBA, U. Tex., Austin, LLB with honors. Bar: Tex. Pvt. practice law; pres. Uncle Johnny Mills, Inc.; dir. Heights State Bank, Houston; councilman, mayor pro-tem Village of Hunters Creek, 1955-62; mem. Tex. Ho. of Reps., 1966-70, 92nd-104th Congresses from 7th Tex. dist., Washington, D.C., 1971—; chmn. House ways and means com., 1995—; mem. Joint Com. on Taxation, Rep. Policy Com., Rep. Leaders Task Force on Health. Bd. dirs. Houston Soc. Prevention Cruelty to Animals; past chmn. Rep. Study Com. Task Force on Regulatory Reform, Rep. Leadership's Econ. Task Force; mem. Rep. Leadership Task Force on Health, Nat. Commn. on Social Security Reform, 1982. Served with USAF, 1951-53. Recipient numerous svc. and honor awards, Taxpayer's Best Friend award Nat. Tax Payers Union, Taxpayer's Hero award Citizen Against Govt. Waste; named Most Respected Congressman from Tex., Tex. Bus. mag., Watchdog of the Treasury Nat. Associated Bus. Office: 1236 Longworth Bldg Washington DC 20515-4307*

ARCHERD, ARMY (ARMAND ARCHERD), columnist, television commentator; b. N.Y.C., Jan. 13; m. Selma Archerd. Grad., UCLA, 1941, U.S. Naval Acad. Postgrad. Sch., 1943. With Hollywood bur. AP, from 1945; columnist Herald-Express, Daily Variety, from 1953; master of ceremonies numerous Hollywood premieres, Acad. Awards shows; co-host People's Choice Awards shows. Served to lt. USN. Recipient awards Masquers, L.A. Press Club, Hollywood Fgn. Press Club, Newsman of Yr. award Publicists Guild, 1970. Mem. Hollywood Press Club (founder). Office: Daily Variety 5700 Wilshire Blvd Ste 120 Los Angeles CA 90036-5804

ARCHER-SORG, KAREN S., association coordinator; b. Ft. Wayne, Ind., Dec. 19, 1957; d. Paul Walter and Betty Irene (Harmon) Archer; m. Joseph Henry Sorg, Apr. 8, 1977; children: Joseph Henry II, Levi Paul. AA, Purdue U., 1987; BA, Ind. U., 1995. Cert. grantsmanship, Calif. Rsch. asst. Ind. U., Ft. Wayne, 1987-89; coord. Gov.'s Commn. for a Drug-Free Ind., Ft. Wayne, 1989—; staff Regional Adv. Bd., Ft. Wayne, 1989-97; mem. grants commn. Parks Bd., Ossian, Ind., 1990-97; mem. Stop Child Abuse and Neglect, Ft. Wayne, 1995-97. Past pres., co-founder No. Wells Soccer Club, Inc., Ossian, 1986-96; cons. Jr. Achievement, Ft. Wayne, 1994—; speaker Wells County Citizen's Against Drugs, Bluffton, 1993-96; vol. Smoke-Free Ind., Ft. Wayne, 1995—, schs. and town of Ossian, 1989-97. Recipient Appreciation award Ossian Fire Dept., 1993, Norwell Comm., Ossian, 1994, Dept. of Mental Health, Indpls., 1997. Mem. Wells County Citizens Against Drug Abuse. Office: Govs Comms for Drug-Free Ind 1 E Main St No Ste 710 Fort Wayne IN 46802-1815

ARCHIBALD, CHARLES ARNOLD, holding company executive; b. Louisville, Aug. 21, 1936; s. James Henry and Phyllis Maxine (Rice) A.; m. Rosa Jane Cusano, July 11, 1959; children: James Henry II (dec.), Diane Marie. BBA, U. Cin., 1959; postgrad., Xavier U., 1963-65. V.p., bd. dirs. J.H. Archibald Co., Cin., 1963-75; pres. J.H. Archibald Co., Springfield, Mo., 1975—; also chmn. bd. dirs. J.H. Archibald Co., Springfield; pres. C/D/R Assocs., Inc., Springfield, 1987—; ptnr. Bearcat Ltd., Springfield and La Habra, Calif., 1995—; v.p. The Oasis, Inc., Southgate, Ky., 1963-73, Crawford Sales of So. Ohio, Cin., 1965-73, Mid-Western Bldg. Sys., Norwood, Ohio, 1968-73; ptnr. TGA Publ. Palm Springs, Calif., 1985-96, The Graphic Arts Ctr., Cathedral City, Calif., 1985-96, (all affiliates of J.H. Archibald Co.), Bearcat Ltd., Springfield, Mo. and La Habra, Calif.; chmn. bd. dirs. Euro., S.A., Marbella, Spain, 1990—; pres. Euro. Svcs., Inc., Springfield, Mo. and Wilmington, Del.; bd. dirs. Archibald-Cowan-Ringer Comm., Inc., Springfield, Mo., Target Mktg., S.L., Madrid, SEDEF (Trading), Madrid; bd. dirs. Barna Catering, S.L., Barcelona; bd. dirs. SEDEF (Trading Co.), Mejorada del Campo, Madrid; ptnr. Bearcat, Ltd., Springfield, Mo., La Habra, Calif. Mem. Dem. Cen. Com., Hamilton County, Ohio, 1968-70. Served to lt. commdr. USN, 1959-62. Mem. Springfield C. of C., Tower Club, U. Cin. Alumni Assn., Pi Kappa Alpha (pres. local alumni chpt. 1980-90). Methodist. Home: 1224 W Highland St Springfield MO 65807-4626 Office: 3825 S Campbell Ave Ste 166 Springfield MO 65807-5339

ARCHIBALD, FRED JOHN, newspaper executive; b. Sept. 10, 1922; s. Fred Irwin and Edna Esther (Olson) A. BS, U.S. Mil. Acad., 1945. Commd. 2d lt. U.S. Army, 1945, advanced through grades to capt., 1951; served various assignments U.S. Army, U.S., Philippines, Japan; resigned U.S. Army, 1955; mng. editor Frederick (Md.) News-Post, 1956-78, assoc. pub., 1978-85; gen. mgr., editor News-Post News Svc., Frederick, 1985-87;

lectr. journalism and pub. relations, various instns., 1947—; cattle breeder Armadale Farms, Frederick, 1964—. Decorated Bronze Star. Mem. Airedale Terrier Club Am. (treas. 1959-61), Md. Hereford Assn. (pres. 1979-81), Mil. Order Carabao, Am. Legion, Nat. Press Club, Army and Navy Club, Georgetown Club, Overseas Press Club, Sigma Delta Chi, Sigma Alpha Epsilon. Democrat. Episcopalian. Avocations: theatrical productions, experimentl gardening, art collecting, press and garden photography. Home: Armadale Farms PO Box 74 Frederick MD 21705-0074 Office: Frederick News-Post PO Box 578 Frederick MD 21705-0578

ARCHIBALD, GEORGE, reporter; b. Newmarket, Eng., 1944. BA in Polit. Sci. and History, Old Dominion U., 1967. Editl. writer, columnist Arizona Republic, Phoenix, 1971-73; congrl. aide Washington, 1973-75, 78-81; assoc. staff Ho. Appropriations Com., 1979-81; Dep. Asst. Sec. Edn. Washington, 1981-82; nat. corr. Washington Times, 1982-93, 95—; editor, gen. mgr. The Warren Sentinel, Front Royal, Va., 1993-95; investigative reporter Washington Times, 1999—. Press sec., legis. asst. Rep. John B. Conlan, 1973-75, adminstrv. asst. Rep. Eldon Rudd, 1977-78; exec. dir. Am. Legis. Exch. Coun., Washington, 1976. With USAF, 1967-71. Office: Washington Times 3600 New York Ave NE Washington DC 20002-1996*

ARCHIBALD, JAMES DAVID, biology educator, paleontologist; b. Lawrence, Kans., Mar. 23, 1950; s. James R. and Donna L. (Accord) A. BS. in Geology, Kent State U., 1972; Ph.D. in Paleontology, U. Calif., Berkeley, 1977. Gibb's instr. dept. geology Yale U., New Haven, 1977-79, asst., then assoc. prof. dept. biology, 1979-83; curator of mammals Peabody Mus. Natural Hist., New Haven, 1979-83; assoc. prof., then prof. dept. biology San Diego State U., 1983—; extensive field expeditions in Mont., Colo., N.Mex., Pakistan, and former USSR, 1973—. Author: A Study of Mammalia and Geology Across the Cretaceous-Tertiary Boundary, 1982, Dinosaur Extinction and the End of an Era: What The Fossils Say, 1996; contbr. over 100 articles to profl. jours. Past trustee San Diego Natural History Mus. Scholar Yale U., San Diego State U.; fellow Alcoa Found., U. Calif.-Berkeley, fulbright fellow to Russia, 1996; Disting Lectr., grantee Sigma Xi, Nat. Geog. Soc., NSF, Petroleum Research Found., San Diego State U., Paleontology Soc. Mem. Soc. Vertebrate Paleontology, Geol. Soc. Am., Paleontol. Soc., Soc. Systematic Zoologists, Am. Soc. Mammalogists, Willi Hennig Soc., Soc. for Study of Evolution, Phi Beta Kappa Nu Chap lectr., Sigma Xi. Office: San Diego State U Dept Biology San Diego CA 92182

ARCHIBALD, JAMES KENWAY, lawyer; b. Mass., Mar. 29, 1949; s. John Lawrence and Jean (Kenway) A.; m. Joanne Mary Ricciuti, Aug. 16, 1975; children: Kathryn, John. BA, Johns Hopkins U., 1971; JD, U. Md., 1975. Bar: Md. 1975, D.C. 1985, U.S. Dist. Ct. Md. 1976, U.S. Ct. Appeals (4th cir.) 1978, U.S. Supreme Ct. 1979, U.S. Ct. Appeals (9th cir.) 1984, Maine 1998. Assoc. Venable, Baetjer and Howard, Balt., 1975-83, ptnr., 1983—. Co-author: Pleading Causes of Action in Maryland, 1990, Model Witness Examinations, 1997. Chmn. bd. trustees Md. State Colls. and Us., 1984-86; trustee Johns Hopkins U., 1997—; bd. dirs. Roland Park Country Sch., Inc., Balt., 1989-94; pres. Homeland Assn., Inc., Balt., 1990. Recipient Disting. Svc. award Litigation Sect. Md. State Bar, Md., 1981. Mem. ABA (litigation sect., co-chair com. 1987—), Internat. Assn. Def. Counsel, Def. Rsch. Inst. (Exceptional Performance award 1989, Md. state chair 1989-93), Md. Assn. Def. Trial Counsel (pres. 1988-89), Johns Hopkins Alumni Coun. (v.p. 1996-98, pres. 1998—), Johns Hopkins Second Decade Soc. (nat. chair 1989-91). Home: 115 Witherspoon Rd Baltimore MD 21212-3315 Office: Venable Baetjer & Howard 1800 Mercantile Bank Bldg 2 Hopkins Plz Ste 2100 Baltimore MD 21201-2982

ARCHIBALD, NATHANIEL, retired basketball player; b. N.Y.C., Sept. 2, 1948. Student, Ariz. Western Coll., U. Tex., El-Paso. With Cin. Royals, 1970-72, Kings, 1972-76, N.Y. Nets, 1976-77, Buffalo Braves, 1977-78, Boston Celtics, 1978-83, Milw. Bucks, 1983-84. NBA All-Star Game Most Valuable Player, 1981, Basketball Hall of Fame, 1991. Achievements include member All-NBA first team, 1973, 75, 76, All-NBA second team, 1972, 81, member NBA championship team, 1981. Office: care Basketball Hall of Fame PO Box 179 Springfield MA 01101-0179*

ARCHIBALD, NOLAN D., household and industrial products company executive; b. Ogden, Utah, June 22, 1943; m. Margaret Hafen, June 8, 1967. AA, Dixie Coll., 1966; BS, Weber State Univ., 1968; MBA, Harvard U., 1970. Exec. v.p., gen. mgr. Sno Jet, Inc. div. Conroy, Inc., Burlington, Vt., 1970-77; sr. v.p., and pres. non-foods cos. Beatrice Foods, Chgo., 1977-85; chmn., pres., chief exec. officer The Black & Decker Corp., Towson, Md., 1985—; former All Am. basketball player. Named One of 10 Most Wanted Execs in U.S., Fortune Mag., Six Best Mgrs. in U.S., Bus. Week Mag. Avocation: theater. *

ARCHIBALD, REGINALD MAC GREGOR, physician, chemist, educator; b. Syracuse, N.Y., Mar. 2, 1910; s. Eben Henry and Minnie (Archibald) A.; m. Evelyn Stroh, June 12, 1948; children: Ruth, Lawrence. BA, U. B.C., 1930, MA, 1932; PhD, U. Toronto, Ont., Can., 1934, MD, 1939. Tchr., rsch. asst. U. B.C., 1930-32; tchg. and rsch. asst. U. Toronto, 1932-33, fellow pathol. chemistry, 1933-35; intern pathology Hosp. for Sick Children, Toronto, 1937; surgery Hosp. for Sick Children, 1938, medicine, 1939; intern Toronto Gen. Hosp., 1939-40; fellow divsn. med. scis. NRC, 1940-42; asst. resident physician Rockefeller Inst. Hosp., 1941-46; assoc. Rockefeller Inst. Med. Rsch., 1946, mem., 1948—; prof. Rockefeller U., 1955-80, prof. emeritus, 1980—; sr. physician Rockefeller Hosp., 1955-80; prof. biochemistry Sch. Hygiene and Pub. Health Johns Hopkins U., 1946-48; mem. adv. bd. Hosp. of Rockefeller U., 1992-93. Mem. editorial bd.: Jour. Biol. Chemistry, 1948-58, Jour. Clin. Endocrinology and Metabolism, 1952-60, Child Development, 1954-56; adv. bd.: Analytical Chemistry, 1957-60. Mem. Am. Chem. Soc., Am. Soc. Biol. Chemists, Harvey Soc., Med. and Chirug. Faculty Md., Endocrine Soc., Soc. Rsch. in Child Devel., Brit. Biochem. Soc., Lawson Wilkins Soc. Pediatric Endocrinology, Soc. Adolescent Medicine, Nat. Acad. Clin. Biochemistry, N.Y. Met. Pediatric Endocrine Soc., Internat. Assn. for Adolescent Medicine, Explorers Club, Sigma Xi. Achievements include medical research in pediatric endocrinology and biochemistry; development of clinical laboratory methods; study of influence of hormones on enzymes, problems of physical growth and maturation of children. Home: 266 Ancon Ave Pelham NY 10803-2019 Office: Hosp of Rockefeller U 1230 York Ave New York NY 10021-6307

ARCHIBOLD, JOHN EWING, lawyer, consultant; b. Denver, Mar. 15, 1933; s. Robert French and Eleanor Eileen (Ewing) A.; m. Mary Ellen Ogelsby, Sept. 12, 1964; children: John Christopher, Stephen Ewing, Mary Elizabeth Eileen, Sarah Ellen Dean. AB, Princeton U., 1955; LLB, U. Denver, 1959; LLM, Georgetown U., 1965. Bar: Colo. 1960, D.C. 1964, U.S. Supreme Ct. 1965. Spl. liaison asst. U.S. Dept. State, Washington, 1960; trial atty. U.S. Dept. Justice, Washington, 1960-66; assoc. Grant, Shafroth, Toll & McHendrie, Denver, 1966-68; ptnr. Casey, Klene, Horan & Archibold, Denver, 1968-69; asst. atty. gen. Colo. Dept. Law, Denver, 1970-72; assoc. counsel Colo. Pub. Utilities Commn., Denver, 1972-74, chief counsel, 1974-90; of counsel Kelly, Stanfield & O'Donnell, Denver, 1991-1993; v.p. Info-Media, Inc., Denver, 1990—. Contbr. articles to legal pubs. Precinct committeeman Denver Rep. Party, 1958-59; chmn. Citizenship Day Com., Denver, 1967; dir. Rude Park Nursery, 1957-59; chancellor Anglican Cath. Ch. 1979-80, Diocese of Holy Trinity, 1977-90. Col. U.S. Army, 1955-86. Mem. Denver Bar Assn., Colo. Bar Assn. Avocations: reading, travel. Home: 1624 S Steele St Denver CO 80210-2940

ARCHIE, CAROL LOUISE, obstetrician and gynecologist, educator; b. Detroit, May 18, 1957; d. Frank and Mildred (Barmore) A.; m. Edward Louis Keenan III, Mar. 7, 1993. BA in History, U. Mich., 1979, postgrad. in Pub. Health Adminstrn., 1979-83; MD, Wayne State U., 1983. Diplomate Am. Bd. Ob-Gyn., Am. Bd. Maternal-Fetal Medicine. Resident ob-gyn. Wayne State U., Detroit, 1983-87; fellow in maternal fetal medicine UCLA, 1987-89, asst. prof. ob-gyn., 1989-97, asst. prof. dept of cmty. health scis., 1995-97, assoc. prof. ob-gyn. and cmty. health scis., 1997—; cons. Office Substance Abuse Prevention, Washington, 1989—, NIH, Bethesda, Md., 1990—, RAND, 1995—. Peer reviewer jours. Obstetrics and Gynecology, 1989—, Am. Jour. Pub. Health, 1994—, Am. Jour. Obstetrics and Gynecology, 1993—; contbr. chpts. to books. Mem. internal rev. bd. Friends Med. Rsch., 1991—; bd. dirs. Matrix Inst. on Addictions, L.A., 1993—; bd. dirs., vice chair Calif. Advocates for Pregnant Women, 1993—; bd. dirs., asst. v.p. med. svcs. Venice (Calif.) Free Clinic, 1994—, v.p. svcs., 1998—. Clin. Tng. grantee UCLA, 1993—; recipient Faculty Devel. award Berlex Found., 1992. Fellow ACOG; mem. AMA, APHA, Soc. Perinatal Obstetricians, Royal Soc. of Medicine (Eng.), Assn. Profs. of Gynecology and Obstetrics. Office: Dept Ob-gyn UCLA Sch Medicine Rm 22-132 10833 Le Conte Ave Los Angeles CA 90095-3075

ARCHULETA, LAURA LYNN, marketing executive; b. Fayette, Mo., Nov. 23, 1962; d. Warren W. and Nellie D. (Slocum) Hill. BA, William Woods U., 1985. Regional dir. admissions William Woods U., Fulton, Mo., 1985-87, adminstrv. asst. to v.p. admissions, retention and devel., 1985-87, dir. intramurals, recreation, 1987-92, dir. student fin. aid, 1987-98; mktg. mgr. USA Group, Inc., 1998—; fitness resource coord. William Woods U., 1992-93. Mem. strategic planning com. City of Fulton, also mem. mayor's adv. coun.; amb. Callaway County C. of C., bd. dirs., 1996-98; com. chair, program coord. Leadership Callaway, 1994-97. Mem. Nat. Assn. Student Fin. Aid Adminstrs., Midwest Assn. Student Fin. Aid Adminstrs. (state del. 1995, 96), Ill. Assn. Student Fin. Aid Adminstrn., Mo. Assn. Student Fin. Aid Pers. (chair budget and fin. com., sponsorship com., mem. program com., profl. devel. com., del. at large Com. of Yr. 1989, pres.-elect 1995, pres. 1996), Mo. Sch.-Coll. Rels. Com., chmn. North Cen. Accreditation Study, 1995-97). Avocation: reading. Office: USA Group 103 Collier Ln Fulton MO 65251

ARCHULETA, WALTER R., educational consultant, language educator; b. Embudo, N.Mex., Apr. 7, 1951; s. Luis M. and Josefina (Romero) A.; m. Carmel Bustos, Oct. 19, 1994. BS in Spanish and Social Sci., N.Mex. State U., 1974; MA in Spanish Linguistics, U. N.Mex., 1981, postgrad., 1991-93. Tchr. Spanish John F. Kennedy Jr. H.S., San Juan, N.Mex., 1974-76; oral history collector VISTA, Dixon, N.Mex., 1976-77; tchr. Spanish Santa Fe H.S., N.Mex., 1981-82, 85-88, Los Alamos (N.Mex.) H.S., 1982-85, Capital H.S., Santa Fe, 1988-91; edn. cons. N.Mex. State Dept. Edn., Santa Fe, 1995—; cons. Hispanic Culture Found., Albuquerque, 1991-93. U. N.Mex. Opportunity fellow, 1991-93, travel grantee, 1996. Mem. Am. Assn. Tchrs. Spanish and Portuguese, Am. Coun. on Tchg. of Fgn. Lang., Nat. Assn. Bilingual Edn. Democrat. Roman Catholic. Avocations: collecting oral history, writing poetry.

ARCINIEGA, TOMAS ABEL, university president; b. El Paso, Tex., Aug. 5, 1937; s. Tomas Hilario and Judith G. (Zozaya) A.; m. M. Concha Ochotorena, Aug. 10, 1957; children: Wendy M. Heredia, Lisa, Judy, Laura. BS in Tchr. Edn., N. Mex. State U., 1960; MA, U. N. Mex., 1966, PhD, 1970; postdoc., Inst. for Ednl. Mgmt., Harvard U., 1989. Asst. dean Grad. Sch. U. Tex.-El Paso, 1972-73; co-dir. Southwestern Schs. Study, U. Tex.-El Paso, 1970-73; dean Coll. Edn. San Diego State U., 1973-80; v.p. acad. affairs. Calif. State U., Fresno, 1980-83; pres. Calif. State U., Bakersfield, 1983—; prof. ednl. adminstrn. and supervision U. N.Mex., U. Tex.-El Paso, San Diego State U., Calif. State U., Fresno, Calif. State U., Bakersfield; cons. in edn. to state and fed. agys., instns.; USAID advisor to Dominican Republic U.S. Dept. State., 1967-68; dir. applied rsch. project U. N.Mex., 1968-69, dep. chief party AID Project, Colombia, 1969-70; cons. in field. Author: Public Education's Response to the Mexican-American, 1971, Preparing Teachers of Mexican Americans: A Sociocultural and Political Issue, 1977; co-author: Chicanos and Native Americans: The Territorial Minorities, 1973; guest editor: Calif. Jour. Tchr. Edn., 1981; editor Commn. on Hispanic Underrepresentation Reports, Hispanic Underrepresentation: A Call for Reinvestment and Innovation, 1985, 88; contbr. articles to profl. jours. Trustee emeritus Carnegie Corp. N.Y.; trustee Ednl. Testing Svc., Princeton, N.J., The Aspen Inst.; bd. dirs. Math., Engring., Sci. Achievement, Berkeley, Calif.; mem. bd. dirs. Air U., Nat. Hispanic Scholarship Fund; mem. Am. Coun. on Edn.; founding mem., trustee Tomas Rivera Policy Studies Ctr.; dir. Civic Kern Citizens Effective Local Govt.; mem. adv. bd. Beautiful Bakersfield; advisor Jr. League Bakersfield. Vis. scholar Leadership Enrichment Program, 1982; recipient Legis. commendation for higher edn. Calif. Legislature, 1975-78, Meritorious Svc. award Am. Assn. Colls. Tchr. Edn., 1977-78, Meritorious Svc award League United L.Am. Citizens, 1983, Pioneer award Nat. Assn. Bilingual Edn., 1994; named to Top 100 Acad. Leaders in Higher Edn. Change Mag., 1978. Mem. Am. Ednl. Rsch. Assn. (editl. com. 1979-82), Am. Assn. State Colls. and Univs. (bd. dirs.), Hispanic Assn. Colls. and Univs. (bd. dirs.), Assn. Mexican Am. Educators (various commendations), Am. Assn. Higher Edn. (instl. rep.), Western Coll. Assn. (past pres.), Rotary, Stockdale Country Club, Bakersfield Petroleum Club. Democrat. Roman Catholic. Home: 2213 Sully Ct Bakersfield CA 93311-1560 Office: Calif State U 9001 Stockdale Hwy Bakersfield CA 93311-1022 *Ensuring the right of every American youngster to a first-rate public education has been a driving interest in my life. I consider myself extremely fortunate in having had numerous opportunities to become involved in meaningful efforts to ensure that basic right in our country.*

ARCINO, MANUEL DAGAN, microbiologist, consultant; b. Manila, May 9, 1941; came to U.S., 1959; s. Francisco Villaneuva and Felicidad (Dagan) A.; m. Ofelia Caponpon Chavez, July 11, 1970; children: Jennifer Eillen, Michelle Monel, Catherine Anne, Mary Beth, Melissa Christy. BS in Bacteriology, Kans. State U., 1964; cert. in med. tech., St. Francis Hosp., 1966; MS in Microbiology, U. Bridgeport, Conn., 1974. Bench microbiologist Wesley Med. Ctr., Wichita, Kans., 1966-68; head microbiologist Mercy Hosp., Muskegon, Mich., 1968-70; specialist in microbiology Bridgeport Hosp., 1970-76; supervising microbiologist Lenoir Meml. Hosp., Kinston, N.C., 1976-81; cons. microbiologist Kinston Clinics, 1981—; teaching fellow, rsch. asst. Wichita State U., 1966-67; lectr. in microbiology Housatonic Coll., Bridgeport, 1973-74; med. lab. cons. Kinston Clinics/Tri-County Med. Health Ctr., 1981-91; presenter in field; coord. workshop/seminar. Member choir, cantor, eucharistic minister Holy Trinity Ch., Kinston, 1976-91, vice chmn. pastoral coun., 1989—; founder Evangelization program, Kinston, 1985; chmn. Evangelization Commn. & Spiritual Life Commn., renew coord. welcome com., bldg. com., liturgy commn., tchr. childrens' liturgy; facilitator Faith Sharing Group, Kinston, 1985-91. Wichita State U. fellow, 1967; recipient Greater Bridgeport Heart Assn., 1973, Teaching Recognition award Christ the King Sch., 1980. Mem. Am. Soc. Microbiology, Am. Soc. Clin. Pathologists, Assn. Practitioners in Infection Control, Southeastern Assn. Clin. Microbiologists, N.C. chpt. Am. Soc. Microbiology. Republican. Roman Catholic. Achievements include research on intestinal parasites among Puerto Ricans, differential diagnosis of Vibrio parahaemolyticus and its pathogenicity, yeast like fungi, family enterobacteriaceae, rapid diagnostic procedures in clinical microbiology, antimicrobial agents. Home: 2703 Fairfax Rd Kinston NC 28504-1154

ARCOS, CRESENCIO S., ambassador; b. San Antonio, Nov. 10, 1943; m. Patricia Cordova; 2 children. BA, U. Tex., 1966; MA, Johns Hopkins U., 1973. Various pub. and cultural affairs positions Leningrad, USSR, Sao Paulo, Brazil; consulate gen. Leningrad, Russia; various pub. and cultural affairs positions Am. Embassy, Lisbon, Portugal, from 1973; counselor pub. affairs Am. Embassy, Tegucigalpa, Honduras, 1980-85; dep. dir. Nicaraguan Humanitarian Assistance Office, U.S. Dept. State, Washington, 1985-86, dep. coord. Latin Am. and Caribbean pub. diplomacy, 1986-87, dep. asst. sec. state for Cen. Am., 1988-89; coord. pub. diplomacy White House Office Communications and Planning, Washington, 1987-88; amb. to Honduras, 1990-93; sr. dep. asst. Sec. State for Internat. Narcotics and Crime, 1993-95; v.p. AT&T Latin Am., Coral Gables, Fla., Latin Am., 1995—; mem. adv. group UN Drug Control Program Commn.; lectr. U. Calif. Irvine Regents, 1998—; mem. White House Pres.'s Fgn. Intelligence Adv. Bd., 1999—. Mem. Hispanic Coun. on Internat. Rels., Washington; bd. dirs. Caribbean-Latin Am. Action, Coun. of the Americas, N.Y.C.; adv. com. Fla. Internat. Univ. Latin Am. Carribean Ctr.; bd. visitors Zamorano Agr. Sch., Honduras; dir. United Negro Coll. Fund Inst. Internat. Pub. Policy. Recipient awards USIA, Superior Honor awards State Dept.; named to Orden de Morazan, Honduras; U. Calif. Regents' fellow, 1998-99. Mem. Coun. Fgn. Rels., Am. Fgn. Svc. Assn., Coun. of the Ams. (bd. dirs.). Office: 2333 Ponce De Leon Blvd Coral Gables FL 33134-5422

ARCURI, LEONARD PHILIP, elementary education educator; b. Bklyn., Apr. 28, 1947; s. Leonard James And Elizabeth Eleanor (Jaeger) A.; m. Lillian Campo, Aug. 11, 1979. BA, St. John's U., Jamaica, N.Y., 1969; MS, St. John's U., 1974; profl. diploma, C.W. Post, Greenvale, N.Y., 1980. Sci. educator St. Agnes Parish Sch., Bklyn., 1969-73; narcotics coord. Dist. 32 Drug Prevention Program, Bklyn., 1973-74; common branches tchr. P.S. 86 K, Bklyn., 1974-75; narcotics coord. Dist. 32 Drug Prevention Program, Bklyn., 1975-77; sci. educator P.S. 123 K, Bklyn., 1977—; tutor biology Empire State Coll., SUNY, N.Y.C., 1988-89; instr. sci. Coll. New Rochelle, N.Y., 1988-89; instr. camping St. John's U. Sch. Continuing Edn., Jamaica, 1989-91; del. to Assembly of United Fedn. Tchrs., 1996—. Pres. Greater Ridgewood (N.Y.) Hist. Soc., 1983-84; coun. commr. Boy Scouts Am., (Queens, N.Y.), N.Y.C. 1979-80; mem. nat. coun. Boy Scouts Am., Tex., 1979-80; scout master troop 154, Boy Scouts Am., Goldens Bridge, N.Y., 1994—. Recipient Energy Conservation Achievement award Dept. of Gen. Svcs. City of N.Y., 1983, Silver Beaver, 1980. Mem. Elem. Sch. Sci. Assn. N.Y., Planetary Soc., Astron. Soc. of the Pacific, Nat. Sci. Tchrs. Assn., Kiwanis. Democrat. Roman Catholic. Avocations: canoeing, hiking, camping, flyfishing. Office: PS 123 K 100 Irving Ave Brooklyn NY 11237-2952

ARD, HAROLD JACOB, library administrator; b. Herrick, Ill., Aug. 26, 1940; s. Jacob S. and Hazel E. (Taylor) A.; m. Erma Chapman, Jan. 30, 1960 (div. June 1974); children—Teri Ann, Mark Alan. B.S. in Edn, Ill. State U., 1962, M.S. in Psychology, 1964; M.L.S., Rosary Coll., River Forest, Ill., 1968. Tchr., materials cons. Decatur (Ill.) Pub. Schs., 1962-64; head librarian Barrington (Ill.) Pub. Library, 1964-68; exec. librarian Arlington Heights (Ill.) Meml. Library, 1968-72; library system dir. Jackson (Miss.) Met. Library System, 1972-77; assoc. dir. Rowland Med. Library, U. Miss. Med. Ctr., Jackson, 1978-84; mgr. bus., sci. and tech. units Fort Worth Pub. Libr., 1985-91; mgr. Wedgwood Libr., Ft. Worth, 1991-94; dir. S.W. Regional Libr., Ft. Worth, 1994-97; retired, 1997; cons., lectr. in field. Mem. ALA, Tex. Library Assn., Med. Library Assn., Beta Phi Mu. Methodist. Club: Rotary. Home: 1125 Clara St Fort Worth TX 76110-1026

ARD, PATRICIA, English language educator; b. Elizabeth, N.J., Aug. 1, 1955; d. John Lawrence and Millicent Nadine (McCrann) A.; m. Michael Aaron Rockland, July 16, 1978; children: Kate Sarah Rockland, Joshua Sean Ard Rockland. BA, Rutgers U., 1977; JD, Seton Hall U., 1980; PhD, Rutgers U., 1996. Asst. prof. LaGuardia C.C., CUNY, 1996—. Mem. Hist. Preservation Bd., Morristown, N.J., 1991-94. Mem. MLA, Nat. Coun. Tchrs. English, Phi Beta Kappa. Office: LaGuardia C C 31-10 Thomson Ave Long Island City NY 11101

ARDANS, ALEXANDER ANDREW, veterinarian, laboratory director, educator; b. Ely, Nev., June 6, 1941; s. Jean Baptiste and Eleanora (Campbell) A.; m. Janice Gae Sanford, Dec. 23, 1961; children: Tamara Marie, Stephanie Marie, Melanie Alexandra, Angela Rosanne, Jeanette Alison. Student, U. Nev., 1959-61; BS, U. Calif., Davis, 1963, DVM, 1965; MS, U. Minn., St. Paul, 1969. Instr. Colo. State U., Ft. Collins, 1965-66, U. Minn., St. Paul, 1966-69; asst. prof., Sch. Vet. Medicine U. Calif., Davis, 1969-74, assoc. prof., 1974-80, prof., 1980—, chmn. dept. medicine, 1983-87; dir. Calif. Vet. Diagnostic Lab., U. Calif., Davis, 1987—. Recipient Outstanding Tchr. award U. Calif.-Davis Sch. Vet. Medicine, 1970, 73. Mem. Nat. Acad. Practitioners, AVMA, Am. Assn. Vet. Lab. Diagnosticians, Calif. Vet. Med. Assn., Conf. Rsch. Workers in Animal Disease. Republican. Roman Catholic. Avocations: swimming, fishing, hunting. Office: Univ of Calif Davis Sch of Vet Medicine Vet Diag Lab Sys Davis CA 95616

ARDASH, GARIN, mechanical engineer; b. Detroit, July 14, 1963; s. Berge and Lucy Alice (Souldourian) A. BSME, U. Mich., 1986, MME, 1988. Grad. rsch. asst. U. Mich. Coll. Engring., Ann Arbor, 1986-87, Los Alamos (N.Mex.) Nat. Lab., 1987; analysis engr. Naval Reactors Facility, Idaho Falls, Idaho, 1989-92, rsch./analysis engr. materials tech. dept., 1992-94; sr. rsch./analysis engr. materials tech. dept. Bettis Atomic Power Lab. Bechtel Bettis Inc., West Mifflin, Pa., 1994—. U. Mich. Coll. Engring. fellow, 1986-87; State Mich. Coop. scholar, 1982-83. Mem. ASTM, AAAS, ASME (assoc.), Nat. Assn. Corrosion Engrs., Internat. Legion Intelligence, Mensa, Pitts. South Soccer Assn. Avocations: soccer, photography, skiing, chess. Home: 700 Penn Center Blvd #202 Pittsburgh PA 15235-5912 Office: Bettis Atomic Power Lab Materials Tech M/S O5N/MT PO Box 79 West Mifflin PA 15122-0079

ARDEN, BRUCE WESLEY, computer science and electrical engineering educator; b. Mpls., May 29, 1927; s. Wesley and Clare Montgomery (Newton) A.; m. Patricia Ann Joy, Aug. 25, 1951; children: Wayne Wesley, Michelle Joy. Student, U. Del., 1944; B.S. in Elec. Engring., Purdue U., 1949; postgrad., U. Chgo., 1949; M.A., U. Mich., 1955, Ph.D., 1965. Detail engr. Allison div. Gen. Motors Corp., Indpls., 1950-51; asst. prof. dept. computing and communication scis. U. Mich., Ann Arbor, 1965-67, assoc. prof., 1967-70, prof., 1970-73, chmn. dept., 1971-73, from research asst. to assoc. dir. Computing Facilities, 1951-73; prof., chmn. dept. elec. engring. and computer sci. Princeton U., 1973-85, Arthur Le Grand Doty prof. engring., 1981-86; prof. elec. engring., computer sci., dean engring. and applied sci. U. Rochester, 1986-94, vice provost computing, 1992-94, William F. May Prof. Engring., 1993-95, dean emeritus, 1994—; William F. May Prof. Engring. Emeritus, 1995—; vis. prof. U. Grenoble, France, 1971-72; guest prof. Siemens Research, Munich, Germany, 1983, also cons.; cons. to Gen. Motors Corp., Ford Corp., Westinghouse Co., RCA, Xerox Data Systems, IBM.; mem. sci. council USRA Inst. for Computer Applications in Sci. and Engring., 1973-79, 82-88; mem. sci coun. USRA Inst. Advanced Computer Sci., 1982-88; chmn. com. on anti-ballistic missile data processing Nat. Acad. Sci., 1966-71; mem. panel Inst. Computer Sci. and Tech., 1980-86; mem. acad. adv. council Wang Inst., 1978-87; mem. study sect. NIH, 1985-88; reviewer Guggenheim Found., 1985-91. Author: An Introduction to Digital Computing, 1963; (with K. Astil) Numerical Algorithms: Their Origins and Applications, 1970; editor: What Can Be Automated?, 1980. Served with USNR, 1944-46, 49-50. Fellow AAAS; mem. IEEE (sr.), Assn. for Computing Machinery, Univs. Space Research Assn. (bd. dirs. 1982-88), Sigma Xi, Tau Beta Pi, Eta Kappa Nu.

ARDEN, EUGENE, retired university provost; b. N.Y.C., June 25, 1923; s. Harry and Gussie (Shevach) A.; m. Sandra E. Rose, July 11, 1948; children: Stacey, Jonathan. BA, NYU, 1943; MA, Columbia U., 1947; PhD, Ohio State U., 1953. Mem. faculty Ohio State U., Columbus, Queen's Coll., Hofstra U., 1947-56; from asst. prof. to prof., chmn. dept. English and humanities div. C.W. Post Coll., Greenvale, N.Y., 1956-62, dean, 1962-64; dean grad. faculties L.I. U., 1964-70, dean Conolly Coll., 1970-71, exec. dean Bklyn. Ctr., 1971; vice chancellor, dean acad. affairs U. Mich., Dearborn, 1972-89, provost, 1989-91, ret., 1991. Editor: Boca Chase Newsletter, 1995—; contbr. articles to profl. jours., mags. Bd. dirs. Mid-Island YM and YWHA, 1962-64; mem. nat. exec. com. Hillel Founds.; asso. chmn. civil liberties com. Jewish Community Council, Met. Detroit. Served with AUS, 1943-46, ETO. Mem. AAUP (editor Academe jour. 1991-93), B'nai Brith (pres. Ctrl. Nassau lodge 1966-68). Home: 18102 Clearbrook Cir Boca Raton FL 33498-1943

ARDEN, SHERRY W., publishing company executive; b. N.Y.C., Oct. 18, 1930; d. Abraham and Rose (Bellak) Waretnick; m. Hal Marc Arden (div. 1974); children: Doren, Cathy; m. George Bellak, Oct. 20, 1979. Student, Columbia U. Publicity dir. Coward-McCann, N.Y.C., 1965-67; producer Allan Foshko Assoc., ABC-TV, N.Y.C., 1967-68; sr. v.p., pub. William Morrow & Co., N.Y.C., 1968-85; pres., pub. William Morrow & Co., 1985-89; owner Sherry W. Arden Lit. Agy., 1990—. Mem. Assn. Am. Pubs. (dir.). Club: Pubs. Lunch.

ARDERY, PHILIP PENDLETON, lawyer; b. Lexington, Ky., Mar. 6, 1914; s. William Breckenridge and Julia (Spencer) A.; m. Anne Stuyvesant Tweedy, Dec. 6, 1941; children: Peter Brooks (dec.), Philip Pendleton, Jr., Joseph Lord Tweedy, Julia Spencer. AB, U. Ky., 1935; JD, Harvard U., 1938; MBA, U. Louisville, 1957. Bar: Ky. 1938. Practice law Frankfort, 1938-40, 45-50, Louisville, 1952—; ptnr. Brown, Todd & Heyburn, 1972—; sec. Ky. Aero. Commn., 1946-48; commr. Jefferson County, 1958-61. Author: Bomber Pilot: A Memoir of World War II, 1978, Heroes and Horses, Tales of the Bluegrass, 1996; also articles. Bd. dirs. Frazier Rehab. Ctr., 1953-93, Schizophrenia Found., Ky., 1981—, Thomas D. Clark Found., 1994—, Nat. Alliance Rsch. in Schizophrenia and Depression, 1985-92, Norton Hosp. Found., 1985-94, Ky. Mental Health Assn., 1985—, Jewish Hosp. Healthcare Svcs., 1986—, Ky. Shakespeare Festival, 1989-90, Ky. Humanities Coun., 1989-94; pres. Ky. Heart Assn., 1955, chmn. bd., 1956;

incorporator, dir. Ballet Español, 1984—; chmn. bd. Am. Heart Assn., 1966-69; dep. Episcopal Gen. Convs., 1970, 73, 76, 79; mem. exec. com. Ky. Hist. Soc., 1983-95; trustee U. of South, 1977-80, Episcopal Theol. Sem. in Ky., 1985-90; sec. Ky. Horse Park Found., 1985—. Col. USAAF, 1940-45, col. USAF, 1950-52, maj. gen. USAFR, ret., 1974—. Decorated Silver Star, D.F.C. (2), Air medal (4); Croix de Guerre with palm (France). Mem. ABA, Ky. Bar Assn., Louisville Bar Assn., Soc. Cin., Order First Families of Va. (Burgess), Pendennis Club, Filson Club (bd. dirs. 1986-96), Phi Beta Kappa. Democrat. Episcopalian. Home: 448 Swing Ln Louisville KY 40207-1444 Office: 3200 Providian Ctr Louisville KY 40202-2873

ARDINGER, ROBERT HALL, JR., physician, educator; b. Corona, Calif., Dec. 4, 1956; s. Robert Hall Sr. and Alice Marie (Schaal) A.; m. Holly Hutchison, Nov. 6, 1982; children: Andrew, Patrick. BS, Calif. State Polytech. U., 1979; MD, U. Calif., San Diego, 1983. Diplomate Am. Bd. Pediats. Intern U. Iowa, Iowa City, 1983-84, resident, 1984-86, fellow, 1986-89; instr. U. Rochester, N.Y., 1989-90; asst. prof. U. Kans., Kansas City, 1990-96, assoc. prof., 1996—. Fellow Am. Acad. Pediats., Am. Coll. Cardiology. Office: Kans U Med Ctr Dept Pediats 3901 Rainbow Blvd Kansas City KS 66160-0001

ARDIRE, LINDA LEA, critical care nurse; b. Ocean City, N.J., July 12, 1953; d. William Henry and Antonia A. (Bruynincx) Bowers; m. Vincent J. Ardire, May 2, 1981. Diploma, Helene Fuld Sch. Nursing, 1974; ADS, Camden County Coll., 1985; BSN, Hahnemann U., 1987; MSN, U. Pa., 1989. Cert. acute care nurse practitioner. Nurse practitioner Alantic Gastroneterology Assocs., Egg Harbor Twp., N.J., 1997—. Mem. ANA, AACCN, N.J. State Nurses Assn., Sigma Theta Tau, Alpha Eta.

ARDITTI, FRED D., economist, former educator; b. N.Y.C., Jan. 30, 1939; s. David A. and Marie (Ben Nathan) A.; children: Elizabeth Marie, Anne Sarah, David Frederick. BS in Elec. Engring., MIT, 1960, MS in Indsl. Mgmt., 1962, PhD in Econs., 1966. Economist Rand Corp., Santa Monica, Calif., 1965-67; lectr., asst. prof. fin. U. Calif., Berkeley, 1967-71; from assoc. prof. to prof. fin. U. Fla., Gainesville, 1971-77; Walter J. Matherly chair fin. and econs. U. Fla., 1974-80, chmn. dept. econs., 1977-80; v.p. research, chief economist Chgo. Merc. Exchange, 1980-82; pres. GNP Fin. Inc., 1982-86, GNP Commodities Inc., 1984-86, Drexel, Burnham, Lambert Quantitative Asset Mgmt. Group, Chgo., 1986-89; fin. cons. Chgo., 1989—; prof. fin. DePaul U., Chgo., 1990-97; sr. exec. v.p. for planning and devel. Chgo. Merc. Exch., 1997—; vis. prof. Hebrew U., 1973, U. Toronto, 1976-77, U. Chgo., 1981-83, 90. Author: Derivatives: A Comprehensive Resource for Options, Futures, Interest rate Swaps and Mortgage Securities, 1996; contbr. articles to profl. jours., chpts. in books. NSF fellow; Ford Found. research grantee; NDEA fellow; other fellowships. Jewish. Office: Chgo Merc Exch 30 S Wacker Dr Fl 6N Chicago IL 60606-7473

ARDOIN, JOHN LOUIS, author; b. Alexandria, La., Jan. 8, 1935; s. Louis and Ruth (Herren) A. MusB, U. Tex., 1955; MusM, U. Okla., 1956; postgrad., Mich. State U., 1958-59; PhD (hon.), North Tex. State U., 1987. Asst. editor Mus. Am. mag., 1959-63, assoc. editor, 1963-64, editor, 1964; mng. editor Philharmonic Hall program; mem. music staff Saturday Rev., 1965-66; music critic Dallas Morning News, 1966-98; N.Y. music critic London Times, 1964-66, Opera mag., 1965-66; Guest lectr. Ind. U., 1971-72, Eastman Sch. Music, 1973, Am. Inst. Mus. Studies, 1973, 86; music cons. WNET-13, N.Y.C. Author: The Callas Legacy, 1977, The Stages of Menotti, 1985, Callas at Juilliard, 1987, The Furtwängler Record, 1994; co-author: Callas, 1974, The Tenors, 1974; author PBS film documentaries on Maria Callas, Bayreuth Festival, Spoleto U.S.A. Festival, Phila. Orch. Recipient Deems Taylor award Am. Soc. Composers, Authors and Pubs., 1979. Mem. N.Y. Music Critics Circle (1960-64). Home: 4305 Travis St Dallas TX 75205-4451

AREEN, GORDON E., finance company executive; b. Chgo., Feb. 10, 1918; s. Eric G. and Tillie S. (Nyberg) A.; m. Pauline J. Payberg, June 28, 1942; children: Judith Carol, Patricia Ann, Richard Gordon. Grad., Sch. Commerce, Northwestern U., 1940; LLD (hon.), Alma Coll., 1989. C.P.A., Ill. Acct. Arthur Andersen & Co. (C.P.A.s), 1945-46, Allstate Ins. Co., Chgo., 1946-47; asst. comptr. to exec. v.p. Assoc. Investment Co., South Bend, Ind., 1947-64; pres., dir., CEO Chrysler Fin. Corp., 1964-80, chmn. bd., CEO, dir., 1980-81; v.p. Chrysler Corp., 1974-81; pres., dir. Chrysler Ins. Co., 1964-81; pres., CEO, dir. Internat. Harvester Credit Corp., Chgo., 1981-84, chmn. bd., CEO, dir., 1984; v.p. Internat. Harvester Co., Chgo., 1981-84; dir. Onset BIDCO Inc., Farmington Hills, Mich., 1988-94, vice chmn. bd., 1989-94. Trustee Alma (Mich.) Coll., chmn. bd., 1981-85, vice chmn. bd., 1986-87, pres., 1987-88; past pres. Jr. Achievement S.E. Mich.; v.p., dir. Detroit Swedish Council, Inc., 1987-90; pres. bd. trustees Kirk in the Hills Presbyn. Ch., 1987-88. Served to maj. U.S. Army, 1940-45. Mem. Am. Inst. C.P.A.s, Alpha Kappa Psi,. Republican. Clubs: Masons. Home: 1729 Haggin Grove Way Carmichael CA 95608-5962

AREEN, JUDITH CAROL, dean; b. Chgo., Aug. 2, 1944; d. Gordon Eric and Pauline Jeanette (Payberg) A.; m. Richard M. Cooper, Feb. 17, 1979; children: Benjamin Eric (dec.), Jonathan Gordon. AB, Cornell U., 1966; JD, Yale U., 1969. Bar: Mass. 1970, D.C. 1972. Program planner for higher edn. Mayor's Office City of N.Y., 1969-70; dir. edn. voucher study Ctr. for Study Pub. Policy, Cambridge, Mass., 1970-72; mem. faculty Georgetown U., Washington, 1971—, assoc. prof. law, 1972-76, prof., 1976—, prof. cmty. and family medicine, 1980-89, assoc. dean Law Ctr., 1984-87; dean, exec. v.p. for law affairs Georgetown U, Washington, 1989—; gen. counsel, coord. domestic reorgn. pres.' reorgn. project Office of Mgmt. and Budget, Washington, 1977-80; spl. counsel White House Task Force on Regulatory Reform, Washington, 1978-80; cons. NIH, 1984; cons. NRC, 1985, mem. com. film badge dosimetry; bd. dirs. MCI World Comm., Safeguard Sci. Author: Youth Service Agencies, 1977, Cases and Materials on Family Law, 4th edit., 1999, Law, Science and Medicine, 1984, 2d edit., 1996. Mem. Def. Adv. Com. Women In Svcs., Washington, 1979-82; trustee Cornell Univ. Woodrow Wilson Internat. Ctr. for Scholars fellow, 1988-89, Kennedy Inst. Ethics Sr. Rsch. fellow, Washington, 1982—. Mem. ABA, D.C. Bar Assn., Am. Law Inst.

AREGOOD, RICHARD LLOYD, editor; b. Camden, N.J., Dec. 31, 1942; s. Lloyd Samuel and Ruby Odell (Trousdale) A.; m. Barbara Sue Wittenberger, Oct. 6, 1962 (div. June 1978); children: Laurie, Christopher; m. Doris Joan Sampieri, Apr. 21, 1979 (div. July 1992); children: Deborah, David, Jennifer, William Sampieri; m. Kathleen Shea, Feb. 20, 1993; 1 child, James. BA in English, Rutgers U., 1965. Reporter, editor Burlington County Herald, Mount Holly, N.J., 1964-65; reporter Burlington County Times, Willingboro, N.J., 1965-66; reporter Phila. Daily News, 1966-71, features editor, 1971-73, news editor, 1973-74, editor editorial page, 1975-95, dep. sports editor, 1976; editor the editl. page The Star Ledger of Newark (N.J.), 1995—. Pres. local 10 Newspaper Guild, Phila., 1978-79, v.p., 1973-77. Recipient Disting. Writing award Am. Soc. Newspaper Editors, 1984, 90, 92, Pulitzer prize for editorial writing, 1985, Walker Stone award Scripps-Howard Newspapers, 1993; inducted into Rutgers Hall of Disting. Alumni, 1993. Mem. Am. Soc. Newspaper Editors (dir. 1996—), Nat. Conf. Editl. Writers. Episcopalian. Office: The Star Ledger Star Ledger Pla Newark NJ 07102-1200

AREKAPUDI, KUMAR VIJAYA VASANTHA, compliance consultant, real estate agent; b. Angaluru, India, July 21, 1957; came to U.S., 1985, naturalized 1990; s. Rahgavendra Rao and Chandramma (Lingam) A.; m. Aruna Vallabhaneni, Sept. 4, 1988; 1 child, Raghava Chandra. BA, Osmania U., Hyderabad, India, 1984; MBA, Calif. Coast U., 1994. Patient transporter Ill. Masonic Med. Ctr., Chgo., 1985, psychiatric technician, 1985-88; communicable disease control investigator Chgo. Dept. Health, 1987-88, sanitarian, 1988-94; psychiatric technician Lincoln West Hosp., Chgo., 1988-91; real estate assoc. All Star Realty, Chgo., 1990; assoc. mgr. residential and comml. div. Century 21 Ben Garth Realty, Chgo., 1990-91; founder, pres., CEO Blue Planet Realty Inc., 1991-99; sanitarian/team leader Mayor's Health and Sanitation Task Force for City of Chgo., 1994-97; CEO Blue Planet Cons., St. Louis, 1997-98; mem. St. Charles (Mo.) Bd. Realtors, St. Louis Bd. Realtors. Chmn. Community Svcs. Indo Am. Dem. Orgn., Chgo., 1985-86, chmn. pub. relations, 1987-88; mem. 48th Ward Progressive Network, Chgo., 1985-90; voting mem. Multiple Listing Svc. No. Ill., 1992—; signatary fair housing and equal opportunity with U.S. Dept. Housing and Urban Devel, approved selling broker; active Ams. for Change, 1992—. Recipient Merit citation Indo-Am. Dem. Orgn., Chgo., 1985, Cert. of Recognition Mayor of City of Chgo. for Earth Day participation, Million Dollar Sales award Chgo. Assn. Realtors, 1991, Coop. Sales award N.W. Real Estate Bd., 1991, Man of Yr. medal honor ABI, 1994; named Man of Yr. 1986. Mem. Am. Fedn. State County Mcpl. Employees Union (pres. club), Congl. Network Team, Chgo. Assn. Realtors (voting mem. multiple listing svc. 1991—, leader comm. network team 1993, polit. affairs com., equal opportunity com. 1993), North Side Real Estate Bd. (Coop. Sales award 1991), N.W. Real Estate Bd. (Coop. Sales award 1991), N.W. Suburban Assn. Realtors (voting 1992-94), RNA, Euthanasia Club Ill., Real Estate Fin. Planners Inc., Lexington Blue Grass Assn. Realtors, Cumberland Valley Bd. Realtors. Hindu. Avocations: flying, boating, roller blading, golf. Home and Office: 1211 Crooked Creek Dr London KY 40744-8433

AREKAPUDI, VIJAYALAKSHMI, obstetrician-gynecologist; b. Davajigudem, Andhra Pradesh, India, Sept. 28, 1948; came to U.S., 1974; d. Subba Rao and Ramatulasamma (Ravi) Gondi; m. Bapu P. Arekapudi, May 5, 1974; children: Smitha, Swathi. MBBS, Guntur Med. Coll., Andhra Pradesh, India, 1970; diploma in ob/gyn., Coll. Physicians and Surgeons Bombay, 1973. Intern Ill. Masonic Med. Ctr., Chgo., 1975-76, resident in ob-gyn., 1976-79, jr. attending staff, 1979-82, assoc. attending staff, 1982-84, attending physician, 1985—; group practice Lake Shore Med. Assocs., Ltd., Chgo., 1979—, sec., treas., 1979-95; mem. med. staff exec. com. Ill. Masonic Med. Ctr., Chgo., 1994, 95. Fellow ACOG. Democrat. Hindu. E-mail: vijay@womendoc.md. Office: Lake Shore Med Assocs Ltd 2734 N Lincoln Ave Chicago IL 60614-1321

ARENA, ALBERT A., museum director; b. Waltham, Mass., Nov. 12, 1929; s. John Giovanni and Jennie (Inferrera) A.; m. Jean Marie MacDonald, Dec. 29, 1935; children: Albert A., Andrew A., Arthur A. BS, Mass. Maritime Acad., 1952. Licensed Chief Marine Engr. Marine engr. Gulf Oil Co., N.Y.C., 1952, Farrell Lines, Inc., Bklyn., 1952-54; naval engr. officer USS New Jersey, Norfolk, Va., 1954-56; engr. Commonwealth of Mass., various locations, 1957-59, Harvard U., Roxbury, Mass., 1960; marine engr. SS America, N.Y.C., 1960-62; boiler and machine inspector Factory Mutual Ins., Norwood, Mass., 1963-70; assoc. prof. Mass. Maritime Acad., Buzzards Bay, Mass., 1970-72; engr. instr. Raytheon Co., Lexington, Mass., 1973-74; chief stationary engr. Allied Maintenance Corp., Boston, 1974-80; museum dir. Waltham (Mass.) Museum, 1971—. Producer, narrator This Was Waltham for Waltham Cable Access TV, 1989-98. Recipient Ship Safety Achievement award Am. Merchant Marine Inst., 1962, Citation of Svc. for efforts associated with Waltham Mus. Mass. Ho. of Reps., 1994. Roman Catholic. Home: 17 Noonan St Waltham MA 02453-4212 Office: Waltham Mus 196 Charles St Waltham MA 02453-4206

ARENA, BLAISE JOSEPH, research chemist; b. Chgo., Nov. 17, 1948; s. Joseph R. and Margaret H. (Shogrin) A.; children: Evan, Eve, Carmen; m. Kathryn M. Zielnicki, Apr. 9, 1994. BS in Biology, Ill. State U., 1971; MSc in Chemistry, Northea. Ill. U., 1977. Rsch. specialist UOP Rsch. Ctr. UOP Inc., Des Plaines, Ill., 1978—. Contbr. articles Jour. Chem. Edn., Trans. Ill. State Acad. Sci. Mem. AAAS. Achievements include 42 patents in Catalysis and Carbohydrate Reactions. Office: UOP Inc 25 E Algonquin Rd Des Plaines IL 60016-6100 Address: 290 Ardmore Rd Des Plaines IL 60016-2119

ARENA, BRUCE, professional soccer coach; b. Brooklyn, N.Y., Sept. 21, 1951; m. Phyllis Arena; 1 child, Kenny. Student, Nassau (N.Y.) C.C., 1969-71; BS in Bus., Cornell U., 1971-73. Asst. lacrosse coach, asst. soccer coach Cornell U., Ithaca, N.Y., 1973-76; head soccer coach U. Puget Sound, Tacoma, Wash., 1976-78; head soccer coach, asst. men's lacrosse coach U. Va., Charlottesville, 1978-95; head coach DC United, Washington, 1995-98, U.S. Nat. Soccer Team, Chgo., 1998—; mem. U.S. nat. teams in both soccer and lacrosse and competed professionally in both sports; past chmn. ACC soccer coaches, ISAA Divsn. I nat. poll; "A" coaching lic. from U.S. Soccer Fedn.; mem. NCAA Divsn. I soccer com., 1989-95. Named ACC Coach of Yr., 1979, 84, 86, 88, 89, 91, South Atlantic Region Coach of Yr., 1982, 83, 87, nat. Coach of Yr. by Lanzera, 1993. Inducted into Cornell Athletic Field Hall of Fame, 1986, Long Island Lacrosse Hall of Fame, 1990. Head coach U.S. under-23 nat. team which will compete in 1996 Olympics. Achievements include career record of 295-58-32 (.808) in 18 yrs. at U. Va., leading U. Va. to NCAA titles in 1989, 91, 92, 93, 94, taking U. Va. to 6 or the last 7 NCAA semi-finals and 8 straight quarter finals, directing U. Va. to 15 straight NCAA tournament appearances (longest active streak in U.S.), Major League Soccer Cup Championships, 1996, 97, U.S. Open Cup Championship, 1996. Office: US Soccer 1801 S Prairie Ave Chicago IL 60616-1357*

ARENA, KELLI, news correspondent; b. Bklyn., N.Y., Dec. 17, 1963; d. Melvin Mullins and Mary Ann (Scafa) Tracy. BFA, NYU, 1985. Prodr. various shows CNN, N.Y.C., 1985-89, prodr. spl. reports, 1988-89, line prodr., 1989-90, supervising prodr., 1990-92; exec. prodr. CNN, London, 1992; news editor CNN, N.Y.C., 1992-93, reporter, anchor, 1993—. Youth dir. St. George's Ch., N.Y.C., 1989-93. Recipient Peabody award U. Ga., 1987, Cable Ace award, 1987, Gold award Houston Internat. Film Festival, 1987; named Topten Fin. Journalist Jour. Fin. Reporting, 1989-92. Mem. Soc. Am. Bus. Editors and Writers, Internat. Womens Media Found., N.Y. Fin. Writers Assn. Office: CNN Bus News 820 1st St NE Washington DC 20002-4243

ARENA, M. SCOTT, retired pharmaceutical company executive; b. Mt. Vernon, Ohio, Oct. 11, 1946; s. Ralph Michael and Nancy Jane (Frick) A.; m. Toni Gale Jackman, 1974; 1 child, M. Sean. BA, Ripon Coll., 1968; MA, Am. Grad. Sch. Internat. Mgmt., 1970; cert. program for mgmt. devel., Harvard Bus. Sch., 1986. Corp. banking mgr. Valley Nat. Bank, Phoenix, 1970-73; corp. treasury mgr. Bendix Corp., Southfield, Mich. and Paris, 1973-80; corp. mgr. internat. fin. G.D. Searle, Chgo., 1982; v.p., corp. treas. Alcon Labs., Ft. Worth, 1982-96; ret., 1996. Mem. Pharms. Mfrs. Assn. (treas. subcom.), Soc. Internat. Treas., Fin. Execs. Inst. Republican. Roman Catholic. Home: 5575 S Easy St Gold Canyon AZ 85219-4619 Office: Alcon Labs Inc 6201 South Fwy Fort Worth TX 76134-2099*

ARENAL, JULIE (MRS. BARRY PRIMUS), choreographer. Tchr. Herbert Berghof Studio; asst. on tng. program Lincoln Center Repertory Theatre. Dancer with cos. of Anna Sokolow, Sophie Maslow, John Butler, Jack Cole, Jose Limon; choreographer: Marat/Sade for, Theatre Co. of Boston, Harvard U. Loeb Theatre, Municipal Theatre, Atlanta, Hair, on Broadway (Most Original Choreographer of Year award Sat. Rev. 1968), also London; dir., choreographer Hair, Stockholm (Best Dir.-Choreographer of Year award 1969); choreographer, dir. Isabel's a Jezebel; choreographer: Indians on Broadway, Fiesta for Ballet Hispanico, 1972, 20008 1/2, Boccaccio, 1975, A Private Circus, 1975, Free to Be You and Me, 1976, The Referee, 1976, El Arbito, 1978; choreographer for San Francisco Ballet, Nat. Ballet de Cuba, (film) King of the Gypsies, Great Expectations, Fur. Friends, 1980, Mistress, 1991, Once Upon a Time in America, Houston Grand Opera Co., Porgy and Bess, 1995, Great Expectations, 1997; dir., choreographer (stage) Funny Girl, Tokyo, 1979-80; dir. N.Y. Express Hip Hop Dance Co., commd. by Spoleto Festival of the Two Worlds, N.C. and Italy; toured 7 cities in People's Republic of China. N.E.A. grantee for A Puerto Rican Soap Opera, Ballet Hispanico, 1973, Oreg. Shakespeare Festival, 1997, Porgy and Bess City Opera, N.Y.c. Opera, 2000.

ARENAS, JUSTO, federal judge. Bar: P.R. Magistrate judge for P.R., U.S. Magistrate Ct, San Juan, 1995—. Office: Ruiz-Nazario Courthouse 150 Ave Carlos Chardon # 198 San Juan PR 00918-1703

ARENBERG, IRVING KAUFMAN KARCHMER, ear surgeon, educator, entrepeneur; b. East Chicago, Ind., Jan. 10, 1941; s. Harry and Gertrude (Field) Kaufman; divorced; children: Daniel Kaufman, Michael Harrison, Julie Gayle. BA in Zoology, U. Mich., Ann Arbor, 1963; MD, U. Mich., 1967. Diplomate Am. Bd. Otolaryngology. Intern Chgo. Wesley Meml. Hosp., 1967-68; resident Barnes and Allied Hosps., St. Louis, 1969-74; asst. prof. surgery U. Wis., Madison, 1976-80, chief otolaryngology, 1976-80; clin. assoc. prof. otolaryngology U. Colo., Denver, 1980—; pres., CEO Ear Ctr. PC, Englewood, Colo., 1989-96; pres., chmn. bd., CEO IntraEar, Neurobiometrix Inc., IEMDS, Inc., 1994—; dir., founder Internat. Meniere's Disease Rsch. Inst., Denver, 1971—; guest of honor 39th Chinese Nat. ENT Congress, Taipei, 1985, U. Antwerp, 1995, West German ENT Soc., 1996; vis. scientist Swedish Med. Rsch. Coun., 1975-76, vis. surgeon, 1987; vis. prof. U. Mich., Ann Arbor, 1988, 94, St. Mary's Hosp. and Med. Sch., London, 1988, U. Verona (Italy) Med. Sch., 1989, U. N.C., Chapel Hill, 1989, U. Wurzburg (Germany) Med. Sch., 1989, 90, 92, U. Ark., Little Rock, 1990, 95, U. Innsbruck, Austria, 1991, U. Sydney, Australia, 1992, U. Tex., Dallas, 1993. Editor: Meniere's Disease, 1983, Inner Ear Surgery, 1991, Dizziness and Balance Disorders, 1993; assoc. editor AMA Archives of Otolaryngology, 1968-81; mem. editorial bd. Am. Jour. Otology, 1978-91, Head and Neck Surgery Jour., 1992—, Jour. Club Jour., 1993; guest editor Otolaryngologic Clinics N.Am., 1980, 83, Neurologic Clinics N.Am., 1990; editor Inner Ear Surgery, 1991; mem. rev. bd. Rev. de Laryngologie et Otology (France), 1984—; contbr. over 100 articles to profl. jours. Recipient Pietro Caliceti prize and Gold Medal Honor award U. Bologna, Italy, 1983, Spl. Tchr. Investigation Tng. award NIH; fellow Barnes and Allied Hosps., 1968-69, 75, NIH, 1971-76, U. Uppsala-Royal Acad. Hosp., Sweden, 1975-76; grantee NIH, 1971-77, Deafness Rsch. Found., 1971-73. Fellow ACS, Am. Acad. Otolaryngology, Am. Soc. Neurophysiologic Monitoring; mem. AMA, Am. Neurotology Soc., Am. Soc. Laser Medicine and Surgery, Am. Acad. Otolaryngic Allergy, N.Y. Acad. Scis., Colo. Orologic Rsch. Ctr. (pres., bd. dirs. 1980-88), Internat. Meniere's Disease Rsch. Inst. (founder, dir. 1971—), Internat. ECoG Monitoring Correspondence Group (founder), Internat. Electric Response Audiometry Study Group, Assn. Rsch. in Otolaryngology, Barany Soc., Triological Soc., Politzer Soc., Prosper Meniere Soc. (founder, exec. dir. 1981—), Children's Deafness Found. (pres., bd. dirs. 1983-88), Acoustical Soc. Am., Von Bekesy Soc., N.Am. Skull Base Soc. (founder), Ogura Soc., Sigma Xi. Avocations: skiing, golf, biking, tennis. Office: IntraEar Inc 7995 E Prentice Ave Ste 110 Greenwood Village CO 80111

ARENBERG, JULIUS THEODORE, JR., retired accounting company executive; b. Chgo., May 29, 1923; s. Julius Theodore and Ellen A. (Foran) A.; m. Jean E. Young, June 19, 1948; children—Robert, Thomas, Mary, James, Michael, Douglas. B.S. in Acctg, U. Ill., 1947. C.P.A., Ill. With Arthur Andersen & Co. (C.P.A.'s), Chgo., 1947—; partner Arthur Andersen & Co. (C.P.A.'s), 1962—, head fin. services div., 1975—; chmn. C.P.A. adv. com. Nat. Assn. Ins. Commrs., 1974-75; mem. faculty Bank Adminstrn. Inst. Sch., U. Wis., 1966-69, Nat. Installment Credit Sch., U. Chgo., 1965-70. Mem. Lombard (Ill.) Elementary Bd. Edn., 1960-66, pres., 1962-66. Served with USNR, 1943-46. Mem. Am. Inst. C.P.A.'s (chmn. com. ins. acctg. and auditing 1966-73), Ill. Soc. C.P.A.'s. Roman Catholic. Clubs: Attic (Chgo.); St. Charles Country, Bay Hill, Isleworth Golf.

AREND, ANTHONY CLARK, international relations educator; b. Balt., Oct. 24, 1958; s. Paul Joseph and Cora Allen (Clark) A. BSFS magna cum laude, Georgetown U., 1980; MA, U. Va., 1982, PhD, 1985. Rsch. asst. U. Va. Sch. Law, Charlottesville, Va., 1981-84, sr. fellow, 1985-86; professorial lectr. dept. govt. Georgetown U., Washington, 1986, asst. prof., 1988-93, assoc. prof., 1993—, chair main campus exec. faculty, 1997—; vis. asst. prof. Pa. State U., Harrisburg, 1987, Georgetown U., 1987-88. Author: Pursuing a Just and Durable Peace: John Foster Dulles and International Organization, 1988, Legal Rules and International Society, 1999; co-author: International Law and the Use of Force: Beyond the United Nations Charter Paridigm, 1993; editor: The United States and the Compulsory Jurisdiction of the International Court of Justice, 1986; co-editor: The Falklands War: Lessons for Strategy, Diplomacy and International Law, 1985, International Rules: Approaches from International Law and International Relations, 1996; mem. bd. advisors Va. Jour. Internat. Law, 1992—; contbr. chpts. to books, articles to profl. jours. Chmn. adminstrv. coun. Severn United Meth. Ch., 1984-89, lay leader, 1990—. Margaret Nils Butler Meml. DACOR fellow, 1980-81, Richard M. Weaver fellow, 1982-83, Lassen fellow, 1983-84, Philip Francis du Pont fellow, 1983-84. Mem. Am. Soc. Internat. Law, Phi Beta Kappa. Democrat. Avocations: golf, squash. Home: 1301 33rd St Apt 1 Washington DC 20007 Office: Georgetown U Dept Govt Washington DC 20057

ARENS, ALVIN ARMOND, accountant, educator; b. Marshall, Minn., Nov. 24, 1935; married, 3 children. BBA, U. Minn., 1960, M, 1967, PhD, 1970. CPA, Minn., 1963. Staff auditor Boulay, Anderson, Waldo & Co., Mpls., 1960-63, Ernst & Ernst, Mpls., 1963-64; lectr. U. Minn., Mpls., 1962-66; instr. Augsburg Coll., Mpls., 1966-67; asst. prof. Mich. State U., East Lansing, Mich., 1968-72; assoc. prof. Mich. State U., East Lansing, 1972-77, acting dept. chmn. acctg., 1976-77, prof., 1977—, dir. acad. initiatives for Ctr. for Internat. Bus. Edn., 1990-91, Price Waterhouse Auditing prof., 1978—, chmn. dept. acctg., 1994-97; tchr. auditing to local grain officials in China, June, 1986; lectr. at Univs. in Beijing, Shanghai, Wuhan, Chengdu, China; Jackarta, Jojakarta, Indonesia; Singapore; Bangkok, Thailand; Kuala Lumpur, Malaysia, 1988; guest spkr. Young Accts. Meeting, Kolding, Denmark, 1989, Copenhagen, Denmark, 1991, U. Denmark, Aarhus and Kolding, 1989, Oslo Sch. of Bus., 1989; tchr. Norwegian Sch. of Econs. and Bus. Adminstrn., Bergen, Norway, 1989; guest spkr. Conv. of Nat. Changchi U. and Fedn. of CPAs in Republic of China, Tapei, Taiwan, June, 1991, at Erasmus U., Rotterdam, the Netherlands, 1992; mem. evaluation team bus. sch. United Arab Emirates U., Al Ain, 1989, 90, 92; mem. vis. team to Bus. Sch. DeLaSalle U., Manila, 1993; co-chair Price Waterhouse Auditing Conf., 1988, Auditing Symposium, San Francisco, 1993; seminar leader Arthur Anderson's Symposium, St. Charles, Ill., 1992, 94; mem. Nat. Assn. State Bds. of Accountancy, 1988-89, Auditing Standards Bd. Attestation Compliance Guidance Task Force, 1991-94, Going Concern Task Force, 1992-94, Agreed Upon Procedures Task Force, 1994; mem. acad. adv. bd. Deloitte & Touche, 1991-97. Author: Auditing (CPA Rev. Manual), 1972, Statistical Sampling for Small Audit Clients, 1974, Statistical Sampling: Attributes for Small Audit Clients, 1976, CPA Review Manual, 1979, The Use of Attributes Sampling for Small Audit Clients, 1982; co-author: (with James K. Loebbecke) Auditing: An Integrated Approach, 1976, 6th rev. edit., 1994 (also Canadian, French-Canadian, Singaporean, Australian and Russian versions), Applications of Statistical Sampling to Auditing, 1981; (with D. Dewey Ward) Systems Understanding Aids for Auditing and Financial Accounting, 4th edit., 1995, Systems Understanding Aid-Microcomputer Version, 1985, 3d edit. 1989, (with David S. Kerr) Integrated Audit Practice Case, 1993; contbr. articles to profl. jours and chpts. to books. With U.S. Army, 1955-57. Named Price Waterhouse Auditing Prof., 1978—, Alumnus of Yr., 1993, Beta Alpha Psi, U. Minn., 1993; fellow Arthur Young & Co., 1965, Price Waterhouse & Co, 1966, Ernst & Whinney Dissertation 1967-68; grantee: Ford Found., 1967. Mem. AICPA (mem. statistical sampling in auditing com. 1974-76, sole acad. mem. auditing standards bd. 1992-94, founding ptnr., mng. ptnr. AHI Assocs., 1975—, joint venture with AICPA, 1990—, Educator of Yr. 1993), Am. Acctg Assn. (numerous coms. and offices including pres. auditing sect. 1977-78, mem. exec. com. and sec.-treas. 1983-85, pres. elect 1989-90, pres. 1990-91, Disting. Internat. Visiting Lectr. 1987-88), Mich. Assn. Cert. Pub. Accts. (mem. com. on profl. edn. 1971-74, mandatory continuing edn. com. 1974-75, accounting and auditing com., and industry govt. edn. com. 1975-76, Outstanding Acctg. Educator award 1992, 93), Mich. Soc. Cert. Pub. Accts., Beta Alpha Psi (acct. of yr. award 1995). Office: Mich State U Eli Broad Coll Bus Dept Acctg East Lansing MI 48824-1121*

ARENS, JAMES F., anesthesiologist, educator; b. Hamel, Minn., Apr. 20, 1934; s. Frederick and Aurelia (Boldwc) A.; m. Mary Helen, Feb. 9, 1960; children: Patricia, James F. M.D., Creighton U., Omaha, 1959. Cert. Am. Bd. Anesthesiology. Commd. officer USAF, advanced through grades to capt.; intern Tripler Army Med. Ctr., Honolulu, 1959-60; resident Charity Hosp., New Orleans, 1960-62; ret. USAF, 1966; dir. anesthesia Ochsner Clinic, New Orleans, 1967-72; prof., chmn. anesthesiology U. Miss. Med. Ctr., Jackson, 1972-77; prof., chmn. dept. anesthesiology U. Tex. Med. Br., Galveston, 1977—, dir. surg. operating and acute care support services, 1977—, med. dir. respiratory therapy dept., 1980-81, exec. dir. operating room, 1977—, v.p. of clinical affairs; chmn., sec. Joint Com. on Critical Care Medicine, 1982—. Mem. Am. Coll. Anesthesiology, Am. Bd. Med. Specialities (v.p.), Soc. Acad. Anesthesia Chmn. (pres. 1979), Am. Soc. Anesthesiologists. Roman Catholic. Home: 22 S Shore Dr Galveston TX 77551-4362 also: U Tex Med Br Hosps 5.118 Administrn Bldg 301 University Blvd Galveston TX 77555-5302*

ARENS, NICHOLAS HERMAN, bank executive; b. N.Y.C., Apr. 24, 1937; s. Nicholas and Sarah (Woods) A.; m. Eileen M. Casey, Jan. 27, 1960; children: Nicholas Jr., Steven, Cynthia, Linda. BBA, Pace U., 1969; postgrad., U. Wis., 1974. Audit officer Morgan Bank, N.Y.C., 1970-77, asst. auditor, 1978-80; chief auditor Algemene Bank Nederland, N.Y.C., 1981, sr.

v.p., 1982-84; auditor Nat. Bank Kuwait, N.Y.C., 1984, mgr. ops. div., 1985-88, mgr. human resources/adminstrn. div., 1988—. Served with U.S. Army, 1958-60. Mem. Council on Internat. Banking. Home: 95 Kime Ave North Babylon NY 11703-3316 Office: Nat Bank Kuwait 299 Park Ave New York NY 10171-0002

ARENS, WILLIAM EDWARD, social anthropology educator, writer; b. N.Y.C., Aug. 31, 1940; s. Nicholas and Sarah (Woods) A.; m. Diana Antos, Sept. 1, 1963; 1 child, Geoffrey W. Bachelors, Long Island U., 1963; Masters, U. N.Mex., 1966; PhD, U. Va., 1970; PhD (hon.), U. Gothenburg, Sweden, 1989. Asst. prof. anthropology SUNY, Stony Brook, 1970-76, assoc. prof., 1976-85, prof., 1985—; UN expert ILO, N.Y.C., 1990. Author: The Man-Eating Myth, 1979, On the Frontier of Change, 1979, The Original Sin, 1986. NIMH fellow NIH, 1968-70, rsch. fellow Social Sci. Rsch. Coun., 1978, Fulbright sr. rsch. fellow, 1989, fellow Rockefeller Found., 1999. Office: SUNY Anthropology Dept 100 Nicolls Rd Stony Brook NY 11794-4364

ARENSON, GREGORY K., lawyer; b. Chgo., Feb. 11, 1949; s. Donald L. and Marcia (Terman) A.; m. Karen H. Wattel, Sept. 4, 1970; 1 child, Morgan Elizabeth. BS in Econs., MIT, 1971; JD, U. Chgo., 1975. Bar: Ill. 1975, U.S. Dist. Ct. (no. dist.) Ill. 1975, N.Y. 1978, U.S. Dist. Ct. (so. and ea. dists.) N.Y. 1978, U.S. Supreme Ct. 1985, U.S. Ct. Appeals (2nd cir.) 1987, U.S. Dist. Ct. (ctrl. dist.) Ill. 1995, U.S. Ct. Appeals (7th cir.) 1997. Assoc. Rudnick & Wolfe, Chgo., 1975-77; assoc. Schwartz, Klink & Schreiber P.C., N.Y.C., 1977-81, ptnr., 1982-87; ptnr. Proskauer, Rose, Goetz & Mendelsohn, N.Y.C., 1987-93, Kaplan, Kilsheimer & Fox LLP, N.Y.C., 1993—; mediator U.S. Dist. Ct. (so. dist.) N.Y., 1993—; mem. MIT Corp., 1997—; mem. corp. devel. com. MIT, 1994—; mem. alumni/ae fund bd. MIT, 1989—, chair, 1994-96. Co-editor: Federal Rules of Civil Procedure, 1993 Amendments, A Practical Guide, 1994. Mem. ABA, N.Y. State Bar Assn. (comml. and fed. litigation sect., chair com. on discovery 1989-97, chair com. fed. procedure 1997—), Assn. of Bar of City of N.Y. Home: 125 W 76th St Apt 2A New York NY 10023-8334 Office: Kaplan Kilsheimer & Fox LLP 685 3rd Ave New York NY 10017-4024

ARENSTEIN, WALTER ALAN, environmental scientist; b. N.Y.C., Apr. 17, 1955; s. Fred and Evelyn (Eckhaus) A.; m. Gina Lilia Facca, June 6, 1993. BA in Human Ecology, Ramapo Coll. N.J., Mahwah, 1976; MA in Environ. and Urban Studies, CUNY, 1978; postgrad., U. Calif., Irvine. Cert. tchr. cmty. coll. ecology, Calif.; registered environ. assessor, Calif.; qualified environ. profl. Inst. Profl. Environ. Practice. Assoc. mem. profl. staff S.W. Regional Lab. for Ednl. Rsch. and devel., Orange County, Calif., 1979-80; mgr. L.A. Children's Mus., 1981-82; city coun. aide City of Irvine, 1983-86; pres. Writrac Cons., Iowa City, 1983—; instr. U. Calif., Irvine, 1985-87; cons. Rand Corp., Santa Monica, Calif., 1988; staff specialist South Coast Air Quality Mgmt. Dist., L.A., 1989-91; air pollution control officer Placer County Air Pollution Control Dist., Auburn, Calif., 1992-94; sr. scientist Midwest Rsch. Inst., Kansas City, Mo., 1994-95; instr. environ. sci. Scott C.C., Davenport, Iowa, 1997—, Kirkwood C.C.; program coord. environ. tng. ctr. and instr. environ. sci., Kirkwood C.C., 1997—. Contbr. articles to profl. jours. Organizer, spkr. Earth Day Activities, N.Y., Calif., 1970-90; mem. Calif. Uniform Air Quality Tng. Task Force, 1989—. Recipient Cert. of Appreciation, Placer County Econ. Devel. Bd., 1993. Mem. AAAS, Assn. Environ. Profls., Calif. Air Pollution Control Officers Assn. (bd. dirs. 1993-94), Air and Waste Mgmt. Assn. (chair cmty. rels. com. 1993—; chair land use and transp. policy com.). Avocations: tennis, computers, camping, music.

ARENT, ALBERT EZRA, lawyer; b. Rochester, N.Y., Aug. 25, 1911; s. Hyman J. and Sarah (Weller) A.; m. Frances Feldman, Nov. 23, 1939; children: Stephen Weller, Margery Arent Safir. A.B., Cornell U., 1932, LL.B., 1935. Bar: N.Y. 1935, D.C. 1945. Research asst. N.Y. State Law Revision Commn., 1934; atty. U.S. Bur. Internal Revenue, 1935-39; spl. asst. to Atty. Gen. U.S., 1939-44; chief trial atty. Alien Property Unit, U.S. Dept. Justice, 1942-44; pvt. law practice specializing in taxation; ptnr. firm Arent, Fox, Kintner, Plotkin and Kahn and (predecessor firms), Washington, 1944-86; counsel, 1986—; lectr. taxation Am. U., 1948-52; prof. taxation Georgetown Law Sch., 1951-73; also lectr. tax subjects before Practising Law Inst., NYU, U. Chgo. tax insts., Am., Fed., various local and state bar assns.; prosecuted leading fgn. agt. registration act cases, World War II.; chmn. adv. council Cornell Law Sch., 1979-82. Contbr. articles to legal publs. Vice pres. Jewish Community Council of Greater Washington, 1953-57, pres., 1957-61; chmn. Commn. on Social Action of Reform Judaism, 1973-77; chmn. Cornell Law Sch. Fund, 1975-77; mem. steering com. Nat. Urban Coalition, 1970-77, mem. exec. com., 1970-72; mem. governing bd. and exec. com. Common Cause, 1970-72; bd. dirs. Overseas Edn. Fund of LWV, 1961-79; vice chmn. Nat Jewish Community Relations Adv. Council, 1967-70, chmn., 1970-73; vice chmn. Conf. Pres.'s Major Jewish Orgns., 1970-73; trustee Cornell U., 1978-83, trustee emeritus, 1983—; 1st v.p. Washington Hebrew Congregation, 1978-80; v.p. United Jewish Appeal Fedn. Greater Washington, 1979-81. Recipient Stephen S. Wise medallion award Nat. Capital chpt. Am. Jewish Congress, 1965, Vicennial medal Georgetown U., 1971, Humanitarianism award B'nai Brith, 1975, Disting. Alumnus award Cornell U. Law Sch., 1982, award for outstanding service Overseas Edn. Fund, 1983, Disting. Service award Washington Lawyers Com. for Civil Rights Under Law, 1987, Judge Learned Hand award Am. Jewish Com., 1991. Mem. ABA, Am. Law Inst., Fed. Bar Assn., D.C. Bar Assn., Telluride Assn., Phi Beta Kappa, Phi Kappa Phi. Home: 6620 Boca Del Mar Dr Apt 608 Boca Raton FL 33433-5718 Office: 1050 Connecticut Ave NW Washington DC 20036-5303

ARESKOG, DONALD CLINTON, retired chiropractor; b. Bklyn., Aug. 6, 1926; s. Andrew Albert and Jennie Margaret (Dickson) A.; m. Julia Catherine Koskela, May 15, 1954. D Chiropractic, Logan Coll., St. Louis, 1950; Philosopher of Chiropractic, Atlantic States Chiropractic Coll. Ret., 1989; pvt. practice Bklyn., 1952-56, Wappingers Falls, N.Y., 1956-61, Poughkeepsie, N.Y., 1961-89; retired, 1989; bd. govs. Atlantic States Chiropractic Coll., Bklyn., 1954; research in field. Developer technique for removal of mental aberrations. Mem. Am. Chiropractic Assn. (speakers bur. 1964), Ednl. Rsch. Soc., Internat. Basic Rsch. Inst., Internat. Platform Assn., Wappingers Falls C. of C. (treas. 1959), Toastmasters. Achievements include developing a technique to create peak experiences known as "the flow", 1995. Home: 330 SE 20th Ave Apt 514 Deerfield Beach FL 33441-5181

ARESTY, JEFFREY M., lawyer; b. Framingham, Mass., Dec. 31, 1951; s. Victor Joseph and Pola (Granek) A.; m. Ellen Louise Gould, Aug. 15, 1976; children: Joshua, Abigail, Joanne. BA, Johns Hopkins U., 1973; JD, Boston U., 1976, LLM in Taxation, 1978, LLM in Internat. Banking, 1993. Bar: Mass. 1977, D.C. 1982. Tax specialist Coopers & Lybrand, Boston, 1976-78; assoc. Meyers, Goldstein & Crossland, Brookline, Mass., 1978-79; ptnr. Crossland, Aresty & Levin, Boston, 1979-87, Aresty & Levin, Boston, 1987-91; ptnr. Aresty Internat. Law Offices, Boston, 1992—. Cons. editor Tax Shelter Investment Rev., 1981-85. Recipient Disting. Achievement award Boston Safe Deposit and Trust, 1976, Grad. Banking Alumni Achievement award Boston U. Law Sch., 1993. Mem. ABA (membership chmn. 1981-84, coun. 1985-91, vice chmn. computer div. 1985-90, sect. law practice mgmt. 1985-91, chmn. internat. interest group 1992-96, chmn. internat. negotiations task force 1992-95, chmn. Mass. state membership com. 1985-91, internat. law sect., chair law practice com. 1995-98, co-editor ABA Guide Internat. Bus. Negotiations 1994, prodr. ABA/AT&T CD-Rom on Cross-Cultural Comm., 1997), Am. Bar Found., Mass. Bar Assn. (bd. dels., exec. com. 1981-83, chmn. law practice sect. 1983-85), Am. Bar Found. (standing com. tech. and info. svcs., 1998—, pub. bd. gen. practice, 1998—), Mass. Bar Found. Home: 35 Three Ponds Rd Wayland MA 01778-1732 Office: Aresty Internat Law Offices Bay 107 Union Wharf Boston MA 02109

ARETZ, BARBARA JANE, reading specialist, educator; b. Long Beach, Calif., Dec. 28, 1943; d. Raymond John and Violet Dorothy (Wurn) A. BA, U. San Diego, 1965; Cert. Elem. Tchr., Immaculate Heart Coll., 1968; MEd in Reading, Loyola U., 1975; postgrad. in Christian Spirituality, Creighton U., 1980-85. Cert. ESL tchr., reading specialist, alpha phonics tchr., lang. therapist. Tchr. 4th grade St. Laurence Sch., Amarillo, Tex., 1978-79; tchr. 6th grade, prin. St. Mary's Sch., Odessa, Tex., 1979-81; tchr. 6th grade Lamesa (Tex.) Mid. Sch., 1981-83; prin. St. Mary's Sch., 1983-85; tchr. reading Midland (Tex.) Ind. Sch. Dist., 1985—; team leader Midland Ind. Sch. Dist., 1997—, mem. Reading Club, San Jacinto Jr. H.S., 1997—. Recipient grant Diocese of Amarillo, 1981, Linda Laird Meml. award Acad. Lang. Therapy, 1993. Mem. Internat. Reading Assn., Tex. Classroom Tchr. Assn., Midland Reading Assn. (sec. 1986). Roman Catholic. Avocations: house remodeling, gardening, animal lover, miniature house building.

AREY, ROBERT JACKSON, JR., small business owner; b. Shelby, N.C., Apr. 7, 1952; s. Robert Jackson Sr. and Lorraine (Clay) A.; m. Nancy Candace Johnson, Dec. 8, 1973; children: Robert J. III, Mathew Johnson, Julian Clay. Student, Lenoir Rhyne Coll., Hickory, N.C., 1971-74. Driver, maintenance worker Arey Oil Co., Shelby, 1966-71, maintenance supr., 1972-74, v.p., 1975—; v.p. Arey Realty, Inc., Shelby, 1975—; gen. mgr. Robert Arey Oil Co., Shelby, 1975-77, pres., 1978—; founder, pres. One Stop Food Stores, Shelby, 1980—; pres. Arey Cos., Shelby, 1993—; brand chmn. N.C. Exxon Distbrs., 1982; nat. distbr. adv. coun. Exxon Co. U.S.A., Houston, 1984; founder, chmn. S.E. Petro-Food Exposition, Charlotte, N.C., 1983; bd. dirs. BB&T Bank. Lay leader Aldersgate United Meth. Ch., Shelby, 1985. Mem. Young Pres. Orgn., N.C. Petroleum Marketers Assn. (bd. dirs. 1983-85, treas. 1985, v.p. 1986, pres. 1987, Oil Industry Edn. award 1984), N.C. Assn. Convenience Stores (bd. dirs. 1989—, v.p. 1994, pres. 1995), Petroleum Marketers Assn. Am. (bd. dirs. 1988), Cleveland Country Club, Rotary (bd. dirs. Shelby 1984, 92). Democrat. Avocations: swimming, skiing, diving. Office: Arey Cos 1906 E Dixon Blvd Shelby NC 28152-6943

AREY, WILLIAM GRIFFIN, JR., former government official; b. Shelby, N.C., Feb. 18, 1918; s. William Griffin and Catherine (Roberts) A.; A.B., U. N.C. at Chapel Hill, 1939; m. Louise Turner Craft, Mar. 7, 1942 (dec. 1988); children—William Griffin III, John G. C.; m. Jean Getman, July 13, 1991. Publisher, editor Cleveland Times Pub. Co., Shelby, 1941-48; pub. affairs officer State Dept., Bogota, Colombia, 1948-51, Panama, Republic Panama, 1951-53; pub. relations officer Panama Canal Co., Balboa Heights, C.Z., 1954-62; with U.S. Travel Service, Commerce Dept., Washington, 1963-76, dir. travel promotion, 1963-67, dep. dir., 1967-70, exec. officer, 1970-73, exec. dir., 1973-76; asst. exec. v.p. Nat. Trust Hist. Preservation, 1976-81, corporate sec., 1981-83, ret., 1987. Served to 1st lt. USAAC, 1942-45. Recipient Silver medal Commerce Dept., 1973. Mem. Pub. Relations Soc. Am., Internat. Union Ofcl. Travel Orgns. (v.p.), Pacific Area Travel Assn. (dir.), Sigma Nu. Methodist. Clubs: Nat. Press, Cosmos, Rotary. Home: Wintergreen Resort RR 1 Box 563 Roseland VA 22967-9204 also: Four Seasons Resort Estates, Box 656, Charlestown Nevis Island, Leeward Islands

ARFSTEN, BETTY-JANE, nurse; b. N.Y.C., Sept. 28, 1946; d. William Paul and Jennie (Reyes) Brock; m. Oluf D. Arfsten, June 1, 1973 (dec.). BSN, Adelphi U., 1985; grad., Eastern Sch., 1966. Nurse clinician Meml. Sloan Kettering, N.Y.C., 1985-86; charge nurse Booth Meml. Med. Ctr., Flushing, N.Y., 1986-89; nurse coord. IVF Australia, Mineola, N.Y., 1990-93; occupl. health nurse Johnson Controls Inc., Tampa, Fla., 1994—. Mem. AACN, NAACOG, Am. Assn. Occupl. Health Nurses, ADA, Am. Hosp. Assn., Am. Assn. Diabetes Educators, Am. Fertility Soc., Oncology Nurses Soc. Home: 18821 Tournament Trl Tampa FL 33647-2459

ARGERIS, GEORGE JOHN, lawyer; b. Ten Sleep, Wyo., May 12, 1931; s. John Brown and Martha (Wilsonoff) A. BA, U. Colo., 1954; JD, U. Wyo., 1959. Bar: Wyo. 1959, U.S. Dist. Ct. Wyo. 1959, U.S. Supreme Ct. 1968. Asst. atty. gen. State of Wyo., Cheyenne, 1960-63; supervisory atty. Fgn. Claims Commn. U.S., Washington, 1963-68; dep. gen. counsel U.S. Info. Agy., Washington, 1972-74; ptnr. Guy, Williams, White & Argeris, Cheyenne, 1974-94; of counsel Orr, Buchhammer & Kehl (was Guy, Williams, White & Argeris), 1994-98. Assoc. editor U. Wyo. Law Rev., 1957-58. Mem. ABA, Assn. Def. Trial Lawyers, Wyo. Def. Lawyers Assn., Wyo. Trial Lawyers Assn., Omicron Delta Kappa, Chi Gamma Iota. Home: 3619 Carey Ave Cheyenne WY 82001-1227 Office: 1600 Van Lennen Ave Cheyenne WY 82001-4636

ARGEROS, ANTHONY GEORGE, lawyer; b. Moline, Ill., Dec. 1, 1964; s. George Anthony and Helen (Tsakanikas) A. BS, Ill. State U., 1987; JD, DePaul U., Chgo., 1990. Bar: Ill. 1990, U.S. Dist. Ct. (no. dist.) Ill. 1990, U.S. Dist. Ct. (cen. dist.) Ill. 1991, U.S. Dist. Ct. Ill. (trial bar) 1992, U.S. Ct. Appeals (7th cir.). Assoc. Elliott & McClure, P.C., Bourbonnais, Ill., 1990-93, Jack Samuel Ring & Assocs., Ltd., Chgo., 1993-97, Dennis T. Schoen, P.C., Chgo., 1997—. Mem. editl. bd. Jour. Health and Hosp. Law, 1988-89. V.p. membership devel. Kankakee (Ill.) Area Jaycees, 1991-92, v.p. community devel., 1992-93; bd. dirs. Kankakee Air Festival, 1991-92, Contemporary Coun. for Econ. Devel., Bourbonnais, Ill., 1992-93. Mem. ABA, ATLA (adv. Nat. Coll. of Advocacy 1991—), Ill. Trial Lawyers Assn., Chgo. Bar Assn., Ill. Bar Assn., Ill. State U. Alumni Assn. (bd. dirs. Chgo. Downtown and Northshore chpt. 1998-99), Order of Barristers, Phi Alpha Delta. Republican. Orthodox. Avocations: computers, hunting, fishing, golf, archery. Office: Dennis T Schoen PC 221 N Lasalle St Ste 663 Chicago IL 60601-1209

ARGIBAY, JORGE LUIS, information systems firm executive and founder; b. Montevideo, Uruguay, May 17, 1953; s. Candido Argibay and Blanca Martinez; m. Stella Gonzalez, Feb. 20, 1974 (div. Aug. 1981); children: Laura, Andres; m. M. Ines Sencion, Mar. 22, 1982; 1 child, Nicolas. Ingeniero de Sistemas, U. de la Republica, 1978. Cert. engring. Researcher laser optics Univ. Inst. of Physics, Montevideo, 1971-74; researcher operating systems Univ. Computing Div., Montevideo, 1975-77; prof. automata theory Faculty of Engring., Montevideo, 1977-81, prof. low level langs., 1977-81; pres. Swann S.A., Montevideo, 1980-91, Fla. Swan, Inc., Miami, 1991—; cons. Supreme Ct. of Justice, Montevideo, 1987—. Contbr. articles to profl. jours.; co-inventor DACOL programming lang. Avocation: boat sailing. Home and Office: 4726 NW 97th Ct Miami FL 33178-1977

ARGIRION, MICHAEL, editor; b. Chgo., May 2, 1940; s. Gus and Angela A.; m. Sherrie Berlant, Feb. 10; children: Carrie, Glen. Student, DePaul U., 1958-59, Northwestern U., 1959-60, U. Chgo., 1961-62. Copy editor Chgo.'s Am., 1959-68, wire editor, 1969; news editor Chgo. Today, 1970-71, Sunday and features editor, 1971-74; asst. Sunday editor Chgo. Tribune, 1974-75, features editor, 1975-79, asst. mng. editor features, 1979-81, asst. mng. editor news editing, 1981-82, exec. news editor, 1982-83, assoc. editor, 1983; editor Tribune Media Services, 1984, v.p., editor, 1985-93; co-creator internationally syndicated newspaper word puzzle Jumble, That Scrambled Word Game, 1994—. Editor: History of Your World, 1969. Served with U.S. Army, 1962. Mem. Trophy Club of Orlando. Office: Argco Inc Timber Ridge Dr Longwood FL 32779

ARGO, DOYLE W., federal magistrate; b. 1947. BA, U. Okla., 1969, JD, 1976. Atty. Lisle & Durbin, 1981-83, Welch & Argo, 1983-85, Bailey, Welch, Argo & Lillard, 1986-87; judge Norman (Okla.) Mcpl. Ct., 1984-87; magistrate judge U.S. Dist. Ct. (we. dist.) Okla., Oklahoma City, 1987—; gen. counsel Okla. Bar Assn., 1979-81; asst. dist. atty., 1976-79. Capt. USAF, 1969-73, col. USAFR, 1969-97. Recipient Golden Gavel award Okla. Bar. Mem. ABA, Fed. Bar Assn., Okla. Bar Assn., Oklahoma County Bar Assn., Cleveland County Bar Assn. Office: 1301 US Courthouse 200 NW 4th St Oklahoma City OK 73102-3026

ARGON, ALI SUPHI, mechanical engineering educator; b. Istanbul, Turkey, Dec. 19, 1930; came to U.S., 1948, naturalized, 1980; s. Mehmet Ali Suphi and Seniha Margaret (Grosche) A.; m. Xenia Mary Lacher, Sept. 6, 1953; children: Alice Leyla, Arif Kermit. B.S., Purdue U., 1952; S.M., MIT, 1953, Sc.D., 1956. Project engr. High Voltage Engring. Corp., Burlington, Mass., 1956-58; lectr. Middle East Tech. U., Ankara, Turkey, 1959; mem. faculty MIT, 1960—, prof. mech. engring., 1968—, Quentin Berg prof. mech. engring., 1982; vis. prof. polymer physics U. Leeds, 1972; cons. indsl. and govt. labs. Author: (with F.A. McClintock) Mechanical Behavior of Materials, 1966, (with U.F. Kocks and M.F. Ashby) Thermodynamics and Kinetics of Slip, 1975; editor: Physics of Strength and Plasticity, 1969, Constitutive Equations in Plasticity, 1975, Topics in Fracture and Fatigue, 1992; contbr. articles to profl. jours. Recipient Charles Russ Richards Meml. award ASME, 1976, Nadai medal, 1998, Humboldt award, 1992, Staudinger-Durren medal, 1999; hon. fellow Internat. Congress Fracture. Fellow Am. Phys. Soc.; mem. NAE, Soc. Engring. Sci. (bd. dirs.), Inst. Mech. Materials (bd. govs.). Home: 16 Plymouth Ave Belmont MA 02478-4220 Office: MIT Room 1-306 Dept of Mech Engring Cambridge MA 02139 *Always strive for perfection, but never take yourself seriously.*

ARGRAVES, HUGH OLIVER, poet, artist, playwright; b. Decatur, Ill., July 7, 1922; s. Wendell Oliver and Helen E. (Sax) A. Student, Beloit (Wis.) Coll., 1937. Retired. Author: Collected Poetry, 1960; contbr. poems to publs.; playwright: Osbert, 1978, The Great Depression, 1978, Greenwich Village, 1979, Hugh Oliver Argraves-Inferno, 1979, The Twenties, 1980, 2 One Act Plays, 1980, King Lear adaption, 1981, Skeleton Play, 1984, London Blitz-1941, 1984, Last Train to Berlin, 1985; various group shows include Lynn Kottler Galleries, 1961, 65, Ahda Artz Galleries, N.Y.C., 1962-66, Ligoa Duncan Gallery, 1968; represented in permanent collection Mus. Modern Art, N.Y. Served with U.S. Army, 1943-46. Republican. Presbyterian.

ARGYRIS, CHRIS, organizational behavior educator; b. Newark, July 16, 1923; s. Stephen and Sophia (Papasthathis) A.; m. Renee Brocoum, July 23, 1950; children: Dianne Ellen, James Phillip. AB, Clark U., 1947; MA, U. Kans., 1949; PhD, Cornell U., 1951; MA (hon.), Yale U., 1960, Harvard U., 1971; LLD, De Paul U., Buckingham U., Mc Gill U., 1977; D of Psychology, Pedagogy, U. Louvain, 1978, Stockholm Sch. Econ., 1979; LLD, Warwick U., Eng., 1996, HEC Sch. Mgmt., Paris, 1997; DBA, U. Piraeus, 1998; D in Econ. Sci., London Bus. Sch., 1998. From asst. prof. to prof. Yale U., 1951-60, Beach prof. adminstrv. sci., 1965-71; James Bryant Conant prof. edn., orgnl. behavior Harvard U. Grad. Schs. Bus., 1971—; cons. in field. Author: Intervention Theory and Method, 1970, Management and Organizational Development, 1971, The Applicability of Organizational Sociology, 1972, Organization and Innovation, 1965, Integrating the Individual and the Organization, 1965, Interpersonal Competence and Organizational Effectiveness, 1964, Behind the Front page, 1974, (with Donald Schon) Theory in Practice, 1974, Organizational Learning, 1978, Increasing Leadership Effectiveness, 1976, Inner Contradictions of Rigorous Research, 1980, Reasoning, Learning, Action, 1982, Strategy, Change, and Defense Routines, 1985, Action Science (with Robert Putnam, Diane Smith), 1985, Overcoming Organizational Defense, 1990, Organizational Learning, 1993, Knowledge for Action, 1993, Flawed Advice & the Managerial Trap, 1999; (with Donald Schon) Organizational Learning, 1996; also articles. Trustee Clark U., Mass., Nat. Tng. Labs. With Signal Corps, AUS, 1941-45. Recipient Irwin award for lifetime contbn. to discipline Acad. Mgmt., 1994, McKinsey prize Harvard Bus. Rev., 1994, gold medal for lifetime contbns. to applications of psychology APA, 1998, Life Time Achievement award ASTD, 1999; named Disting. Lifetime Contbr. to field of mgmt. Fin. Times Handbook of Mgmt., 1994, Disting. Contbr. to theory and practice of mgmt. Rev. Francaise de Gestron, 1994; Chris Argyris chair in social psychology of orgns. established at Yale U., 1994, Kurt Levin award, 1997. Fellow Nat. Acad. Human Resources; mem. Phi Beta Kappa, Sigma Xi, Phi Kappa Phi. Home: 58 Sylvan Ln Weston MA 02493-1028 Office: Harvard U Grad Sch Bus Baker Library Boston MA 02163 *Seeking valid information, enhancing human and organizational effectiveness, strengthening justice have been the foundations of my life.*

ARIAS, BRIDGET CARSER, elementary educator; b. Waterbury, Conn., May 11, 1967; d. Edmund William and Briday Elizabeth Carser; m. Luis Enrique, July 17, 1993. BA, Coll. of Mount Saint Vincent, 1989; MS, Ctrl. Conn. State U., 1996; postgrad., Trinity Coll. of Vt., 1997-99. Cert. tchr. pre K-6, Conn. Substitute tchr. Waterbury (Conn.) Pub. Schs., 1989-90, educator, 1990—. Mem. PTA, Waterbury, 1991—. Recipient Award of Appreciation U.S. Dept. Transp., 1984, Cert. of Appreciation Ptnrs. in Edn., 1995; scholarship Ctrl. Conn. State U., 1996, Pres. award Kingsbury Sch. PTA, 1996-97. Mem. NEA, ASCD, Conn. Edn. Assn. Roman Catholic. Avocations: walking, reading, swimming, music, peer relationships. E-mail: larias@snet.net. Office: Waterbury Pub Schs Dept Edn Kingsbury Sch 236 Grand St Waterbury CT 06702

ARIAS, DAVID, bishop; b. Mataluenga, Leon, Spain, July 22, 1929; came to U.S., 1958; s. Atanasio and Magdalena (Perez) A. Grad., St. Rita's Coll., San Sebastian, Spain, 1948, Good Counsel Theologate, Granada, Spain, 1952, Teresianum, Rome, 1964. Ordained priest Roman Catholic Ch., 1952, aux. bishop of Newark, 1983. Tchr. St. Rita Coll., San Sebastian, Spain, 1953; tchr., prefect St. Augustine Sem., Kansas City, 1964-66; assoc. pastor Lourdes Parish, Mexico City, 1952-58, 60-63; dir. Spanish Apostolate Archdiocese of N.Y., N.Y.C., 1978-83; vicar provincial Augustinian Recollects, West Orange, N.J., 1981-83; aux. bishop Archdiocese of Newark, 1983—; dir. Cursillo Movement, N.Y.C., 1966-78. Author: Luz y Vida, 1979, Presencia Nueva, 1988, Spanish Roots of America, 1992, Spanish Cross in Georgia, 1995. Mem. Nat. Conf. Cath. Bishops, U.S. Cath. Conf., N.J. Cath. Conf. Avocations: history, reading, music, golf. Home and Office: 6401 Palisade Ave West New York NJ 07093

ARIAS, INCENCIO F., diplomat; b. Albox, Spain, Apr. 20, 1940; married; 3 children. Degree in law, U. Complutense, Madrid. Mem. Spanish Diplomatic Svc., 1967—; dir. Diplomatic Info. Office Spain Fgn. Ministry, 1980-82, 85-88, 1996-97, undersec., 1988-91, state sec. internat. cooperation and Iberamerican affairs, 1991-93; permanent rep. of Spain UN, 1997—; mem. session European Coun., NATO summit, 1997; mem. conf. on environ. and devel. UN, 1992; participant 4 Iberoamerican summits, Mid. East summit, Madrid, 1991. Contbr. articles to profl. publs. Gen. dir. Real Madrid Soccer Club, 1993, 95.

ARIAS, OSCAR DAVID, computer programmer; b. Cleve., Feb. 24, 1970; s. Alan and Maria Delores Arias. AS in Info. Sys. and Analysis, Manatee C.C., Sarasota, Fla., 1994. Cert. Novell adminstr.; ordained min. Universal Life Ch. Stock clk. Winn-Dixie Stores, Inc., Sarasota, 1986-87; tchrs. aide Manatee C.C., Bradenton, Fla., 1992-94; applications developer Automation Scis. Inc., Sarasota, 1994-95; microcomputer hardware engr. Uptech Computers, Sarasota, 1995-96; computer sys. specialist Tropicana Products, Bradenton, 1997-98, Sarasota County Govt., 1998—; computer cons. in field. Programmer various applications software. With U.S. Army, 1988-91. Decorated Army Achievement medal U.S. Army, 1989. Mem. Karmann Ghia Club N.Am. Republican. Avocations: computer programming, antique automobiles. E-mail: oarias@co.sarasota.fl.us. Office: Sarasota County Govt 1660 Ringling Blvd Sarasota FL 34236

ARIENS, KARLA RAE, library director; b. Tremonton, Utah, July 3, 1966; d. Paul Elias and Lorna May Adams; m. Thaddeus William Ariens, Mar. 17, 1988; children: Talia Louise, Tori May, Terese Claire. BS in Elem. Edn., Utah State U., 1988. Tchr. asst. Children's Home, Logan, Utah, 1988-89; music specialist Hilltop Sch., Logan, Utah, 1988-89; chpt. I aide Adams Elem. Sch., Logan, Utah, 1989-90; gifted/talented specialist Cache County Sch. Dist., Logan, Utah, 1989-90; libr. dir. Brookville (Ind.) Town-Twp. Libr., 1991—. Sec. Franklin County Cmty. Network Com., Brookville, 1995. Mem. LDS Ch. Avocations: music, cooking, reading, piano, singing. E-mail: kariens@cnz.com. Office: Brookville Town-Twp Librr 919 Main St Brookville IN 47012

ARIS, RUTHERFORD, applied mathematician, educator; b. Bournemouth, Eng., Sept. 15, 1929; came to U.S., 1955, naturalized, 1962; s. Algernon Pollock and Janet (Elford) A.; m. Claire Mercedes Holman, Jan. 1, 1958. B.Sc. (spl.) with 1st class honours in Math, London (Eng.) U., 1948, Ph.D., 1960, D.Sc., 1964; student, Edinburgh (Scotland) U., 1948-50; D.Sc. (hon.), U. Exeter, 1984, Clarkson U., 1985; DEng honoris causa, U. Notre Dame, 1990; Ch.M., fellow, Inst. Math. Applications, 1992; D Engring. honoris causa, Tech. U., Athens, Greece. Tech. officer Billingham div. I.C.I. Ltd., 1950-55; research fellow U. Minn., 1955-56; lectr. tech. math. Edinburgh U., 1956-58; mem. faculty U. Minn., 1958—, prof. chem. engring., 1963—, Regents' prof., 1978-96, Regents prof. emeritus, 1996—; O.A. Hougen vis. prof. U. Wis., 1979; Sherman Fairchild Disting. scholar Calif. Inst. Tech., 1980-81; cons. to industry, lectr., 1961—; IXth Centennial lectr. in chem. engring. U. Bologna, 1988; mem. Inst. for Advanced Study, Princeton, 1994. Author: Optimal Design of Chemical Reactors, 1961, Vectors, Tensors and the Basic Equations of Fluid Mechanics, 1962, reprint edit., 1989, Discrete Dynamic Programming, 1964, Introduction to the Analysis of Chemical Reactors, 1965, Elementary Chemical Reactor Analysis, 1969, edn., 1990, (with N.R. Amundson) First-Order Partial Differential Equations with Applications, 1973, (with W. Strieder) Variational Methods Applied to Problems of Diffusion and Reaction, 1973, The

Mathematical Theory of Diffusion and Reaction in Permeable Catalysts, 1975, Mathematical Modelling Techniques, 1978, Chemical Engineering in the University Context, 1982; co-editor: Springs of Scientific Creativity, 1982, An Index of Scripts for E.A. Lowe's Codices Latini Antiquiores, 1982, (with Amundson and Rhee) First-order Partial Differential Equations, Vol. I Theory and Applications of Single Equations, 1986, Vol. II Theory and Applications of Systems of Quasilinear Hyperbolic Equations, Explicatio Formarum Litterarum—The Unfolding of Letterforms, 1990, (with K. Alhumaizi) Surveying A Dynamical System: The Gray/Scott Reaction In A Two-Phase Reactor, 1995, Mathematical Modeling--A Chemical Engineer's Perspective, 1999. Recipient E. Harris Harbison award for disting. teaching, 1969, Alpha Chi Sigma award Am. Inst. Chem. Engrs., 1969, Chem. Engring. lectr. award Am. Soc. Engring. Edn., 1973, Damköhler medal Deutsche Vereinigung fur Chemie and Verfahrenstechnik, 1991, Richard E. Bellman Control Heritage award Am. Automatic Control Coun., 1992, N.R. Amundson award Internat. Symposium on Chem. Reaction Engring., 1998; sr. rsch. fellow NSF, 1964-65, Guggenheim fellow, 1971-72. Fellow Am. Acad. Arts and Scis., Inst. Math. and Applications; mem. NAE, Soc. Nat. Philosophy, Soc. Indsl. and Applied Math., Am. Inst. Chem. Engrs. (R.H. Wilhelm award 1975, Inst. lectr. 1997), Mediaeval Acad. Am., Soc. Scribes and Illuminators, Internat. Soc. Math. Modeling. Lutheran. Office: Univ Minn Dept Chem Engring & Materials Sci Minneapolis MN 55455

ARISON, MICKY, cruise line company executive, sports team executive; b. Tel Aviv, June 29, 1949. Student, U. Miami. Reservations mgr. Carnival Corp., 1974-76, v.p. passenger traffic, 1976-79, pres., CEO, 1979-90, chmn., CEO, 1990—; managing gen. ptnr. Miami Heat, Miami; mng. gen. ptnr. Miami Heat. Office: Carnival Cruise Lines Inc 3655 NW 87th Ave Miami FL 33178-2428

ARISS, DAVID WILLIAM, SR., real estate developer, consultant; b. Toronto, Ont., Can., Nov. 29, 1939; s. William H. and Joyce Ethel (Oddy) A.; m. Lillie Ariss, Jan. 26, 1962 (div. 1989); m. Debra Ann Nocciolo, Nov. 17, 1990 (div. 1998); children: Katherine Joyce, David William Jr., Dylan William. BA, Claremont Men's Coll., 1961. Lic. real estate broker. Real estate broker Coldwell Banker, Torrance, Calif., 1971-75; v.p. The Lusk Co., Irvine, Calif., 1975-77; pres. DAL Devel. Co., Corona, Calif., 1977-84; mng. dir. Calif. Commerce Ctr. at Ontario, Ontario, Calif., 1984—. Chmn. Inland Empire Econ. Coun., Ontario, Calif., 1991-92; pres., adv. com. Chaffey Coll., Ontario, 1989; apptd. Calif. World Trade Commn., 1993, 95, 97. Maj. USMC, 1961-70, Vietnam. Decorated Silver Star, Disting. Flying Cross, two Purple Hearts, numerous Air medals. Mem. Urban Land Inst., Nat. Assn. Fgn. Trade Zone, Nat. Assn. Indsl. and Office Parks. Republican. Avocations: skiing, music, reading. Office: PIB Realty Advisors 3200 Inland Empire Blvd Ste 235 Ontario CA 91764-5513

ARITA, GEORGE SHIRO, biology educator; b. Honolulu, Oct. 9, 1940; s. Ichimatsu and Natsu (Kimoto) A.; m. Harriet Yooko Ide, Dec. 26, 1964; children: Laurie Reiko, Daren Shizuo. BA, U. Hawaii, 1962, MS, 1964; MS, U. B.C., Vancouver, 1967; postgrad., U. Calif., Santa Barbara, 1967-71. Cert. community coll. tchr., Calif. Prof. biology Ventura (Calif.) Coll., 1971—, curator fish collection, 1976-98. Author: (with others, lab. manual) Basic Concepts in Biology, 1981, Study Guide to Accompany Biology: Today and Tomorrow, 2d edit., 1984; contbr. articles on ichthyology to profl. jours. Fushiminomiya Meml. scholar U. Hawaii, 1961-62, Fisheries Assn. B.C. scholar U. B.C., 1964-65; NSF grad. trainee U. Calif. Santa Barbara, 1969-71. Mem. AAAS, Am. Soc. Ichthyologists and Herpetologists, Western Soc. Naturalists, Sigma Xi. Avocations: fishing, hiking, long distance running, photography. Home: 94 Howard Ave Oak View CA 93022-9524 Office: Ventura Coll Dept Biology Ventura CA 93003

ARIYAN, STEPHEN, surgeon; b. Egypt, July 30, 1941; m. Sandra Ariyan, June 25, 1967; children: Stephen, Christopher, Tiffany. BS, L.I. U., 1962; MD, N.Y. Med. Coll., 1966; MBA, U. New Haven, 1993; MA, Yale U., 1981. Diplomate Am. Bd. Surgery, Am. Bd. of Plastic Surgery. Intern in surgery UCLA, 1966-67; asst. resident in gen. surgery U. Calif., San Diego, 1967-68; asst. resident in gen. surgery Yale U., 1971-73, resident in plastic surgery, 1973-74, chief resident in gen. surgery, 1974-75, chief resident in plastic surgery, 1975-76, asst. prof. surgery, 1976-79, assoc. prof. surgery, 1979-81, prof. surgery, 1981-91, chmn. plastic surgery, 1979-91, clin. prof. surgery, plastic surgery, otolaryngology, 1994—; surg. dir. Yale Melanoma Unit, Yale Cancer Ctr., 1976—; cons. Am. Medico-Legal Found. Assoc. editor Plastic and Reconstructive Surgery, 1983-89; editl. bd. Annals of Surg. Oncology, 1993—. Vol. surgeon Hopital Albert Schweitzer, 1973, 82; mem. evaluation and treatment of injured victims Armenian Earthquake, U.S.S.R., 1989; med. dir. Tng. Soviet Med. Team in Plastic Surgery, 1990-91, Ministry of Health, 1989—. Named Best Breast Cancer Drs. Good Housekeeping mag., 1989, Outstanding Med. Specialists in U.S. Town and Country mag., 1989; recipient Disting. Svc. award Soc. of Head and Neck Surgeons, Presdl. award. Mem. ACS (Scholar award), Am. Coll. of Physician Execs., Am. Assn. of Plastic Surgeons, Am. Assn. of Hand Surgery, Am. Burn Assn., Am. Cleft-Palate-Craniofacial Assn., Soc. for Aesthetic Plastic Surgery, Am. Soc. of Maxillofacil Surgeons, Am. Soc. of Plastic and Reconstructive Surgeons, Am. Soc. for Reconstructive Microsurgery, Am. Soc. for Surgery of the Hand, Am. Surg. Assn., Assn. for Acad. Surgery, Assn. of Acad. Chmn. of Plastic Surgery, Assn. of Am. Med. Colls., Conn. Soc. of Am. Bd. Surgeons, Conn. Soc. of Plastic and Reconstructive Surgeons, Internat. Soc. of Reconstructive Microsurgery, New England Hand Soc., New England Soc. of Plastic and Reconstructive Surgeons (pres.), New England Surg. Soc., N.Y. Acad. Scis., N.Y. Regional Soc. of Plastic and Reconstructive Surgeons, Northeastern Soc. of Plastic Surgeons, Pan Pacific Surg. Assn., Plastic Surgery Rsch. Coun., Royal Soc. of Medicine (Eng.), Soc. of Head and Neck Surgeons, Soc. of Surg. Oncology, Soc. of Univ. Surgeons, Conn. Vis. Nurses Assn. (bd. dirs. 1996—), Alpha Epsilon Delta, Phi Sigma, Sigma Xi. Office: 60 Temple St #7C New Haven CT 06510

ARIZAGA, LAVORA SPRADLIN, retired lawyer; b. Garvin County, Okla., Apr. 29, 1927; d. Gervase Eugene and Donah Lavorah (Eddings) Spradlin; m. Francisco DePaula Arizaga, Aug. 10, 1946; children: F.D. III, Lavora Cristina Arizaga Ewan, Rebecca Maria Arizaga Armour, Nicolas Antonio. BA, U. Okla., 1952; JD, U. Houston, 1979. Bar: Tex. 1979. Sole practitioner Houston, 1979-92. Pres. United Meth. Women, St. Luke's United Meth. Ch., Midland, 1996-98; chmn. Affirmative Action Adv. Bd., City of Houston, 1984-86. Mem. AAUW, LWV (pres. Beaumont, Tex. 1960-61, v.p. Tex. 1983-85, pres. Houston 1985-87, Midland, Tex. 1997-99), UN Assn.-USA (bd. dirs.). Home: 1809 Kensington Ln Midland TX 79705-1706

ARIZMENDY, HELMER W., bank executive, lawyer; b. Pereira, Risaralda, Colombia, Apr. 20, 1962; came to U.S., 1980; s. Balmore and Gabriela (Cardona) A.; m. Adriana Celis, Aug. 3, 1985. BBA in Acctg., Pace U., 1989; JD, Touro Law Ctr., 1995. Bar: N.Y. 1997. V.p., tax cons. U.S. Trust Co. N.Y., N.Y.C., 1984-95, v.p., client svc. mgr., 1995-96; v.p., sr. fiduciary officer Bank Boston, White Plains, N.Y., 1996-97; v.p., internat. pvt. banker Citibank, N.A., N.Y.C., 1997—. Republican. Roman Catholic. Office: Citibank NA 153 E 53rd St New York NY 10022-4611

ARK, LAURINE, writer; b. Davenport, Iowa; d. Francis Leo Sr. and Burnetta Marie (Murray) A.; 1 child, Ben. BA, Humboldt State U., 1975. Creative cons. Fort Tryon Press Ltd., N.Y.C., 1994—. Author: Writing From the Exterior Dramatic Perspective: A New Vision for Literature, 1996, Book of Yr. 1997; contbg. author: Storming Heaven's Gate: Spiritual Writings by Women, 1997; contbr. short stories to profl. jours. Author: Writing From the Exterior Dramatic Perspective: A New Vision for Literature, 1996, Book of Yr. 1997; contbg. author Storming Heaven's Gate: Spiritual Writings by Women, 1997. Mem. Internat. Women's Writing Guild (workshop dir. 1993—).

ARKILIC, GALIP MEHMET, mechanical engineer, educator; b. Sivas, Turkey, Mar. 10, 1920; came to U.S., 1943, naturalized, 1960; s. Sabir Mehmet and Zahra Fatima (Hocazade) A.; m. Ann A. Bryan, Mar. 31, 1956. *Spouse, Ann Bryan, BSEd 1955, N.U., mother of four, porcelain artist with published works, and current president Virginia World Organization of China Painters. Son, Victor Mervin, BBA 1978, G.W. U., received certified purchasing manager certificate 1989, regional operations manager, Atlantic American Fire Equipment Co., performs as a drummer with his band around Washington. Son, Dennis Sabir, marine carpenter, Marine Concepts Inc., performs as guest harmonica player for bands around Fort Myers. Daughter Layla A. Hogan, BA Psychology 1982, G.W.U., BS Nursing 1985, JD 1991, G.M.U., trial attorney, solo-practice in Arlington, VA. Son, Errol Bernard, BS 1991, G.W.U., MS 1994, PhD 1997, MIT, principal engineer, Redwood Microsystems, Inc.* BME, Cornell U., 1946; MS, Ill. Inst. Tech., 1948; PhD, Northwestern U., 1954. Registered profl. engr., Va. Mech. engr. Miehle Printing Press and Mfg. Co., Chgo., 1948-49, analyst, 1954-56; research and devel. engr. Mech. and Chem. Industries, Turkey, 1949-52; asst. prof. Pa. State U., University Park, 1956-58; assoc. prof. dept. civil engring. George Washington U., Washington, 1958-63, prof. engring. and applied sci., 1963—, prof. emeritus, 1990—, chmn. dept. engring. mechanics, 1966-69, asst. dean, 1969-74. Contbr. articles to sci. jours. Vice pres. Courtland Civic Assn., Arlington, Va., 1965-66; pres. Am. Turkish Assn., Washington, 1967-71. Served to 2d lt. Turkish Army, 1939-41. Recipient Disting. Leadership award Am. Turkish Assn., 1972; Recognition of Service award Sch. Engring. and Applied Sci., George Washington U., 1976, Spl. Appreciation award Engring. Alumni Assn., George Washington U., 1990; Air Force Office of Sci. Research grantee, 1963-69. Mem. ASME, AAUP, Am. Acad. Mechanics, Math. Assn. of Am., Am. Math. Soc., Wash. Soc. Engrs., Sigma Xi. Club: George Washington U. (Washington). Home: 8403 Camden St Alexandria VA 22308-2111 Office: George Washington Univ Sch of Engring and Applied Sci Washington DC 20052

ARKIN, ADAM, actor; b. N.Y.C.; s. Alan Arkin; m. Linda Sublette; 1 child, Molly. Actor: (feature films) Under the Rainbow, Chu Chu and the Phillie Flash, Baby Blue Marine, Made for Each Other, Babies, 1990 (TV miniseries) Pearl; (TV series) Busting Loose, Teachers Only, A Year in the Life, Chicago Hope, 1994—; guest-star numerous TV shows including L.A. Law, Northern Exposure (recurring), Law & Order. Office: care CBS Entertainment 7800 Beverly Blvd Los Angeles CA 90036

ARKIN, MICHAEL BARRY, lawyer, arbitrator, writer; b. Washington, Jan. 11, 1941; s. William Howard and Zenda Lillian (Liebermann) A.; children and stepchildren from previous marriages: Tracy Renee, Jeffrey Harris, Marcy Susan, Chatom Callan, Michael Edwin, Samuel Hopkins, Brandon Maddox, Richards, Jessica Remaley, Brandi Remaley, Casey Remaley; m. Laura Dorene Haynes, Aug. 16, 1998. AA, George Washington U., 1961; BA in Psychology, U. Okla., 1962, JD, 1965. Bar: Okla. 1965, U.S. Ct. Claims 1968, U.S. Supreme Ct. 1968, Calif. 1970, U.S. Tax Ct. 1970, U.S. Ct. Appeals (3d, 5th, 6th, 9th, 10th cirs.) 1970, U.S. Dist. Ct. (cen. dist.) Calif. 1970, U.S. Dist. Ct. (so. dist.) Calif. 1970, U.S. Dist. Ct. (ea. dist.) Calif. 1987. Trial atty. tax divsn. U.S. Dept. Justice, 1965-68, appellate atty., 1968-69; ptnr. Surr & Hellyer, San Bernardino, Calif., 1969-79; mng. ptnr. Wied, Granby Alford & Arkin, San Diego, 1979-82, Lorenz Alhadeff Fellmeth Arkin & Multer, San Diego, 1982, Finley, Kumble, Heine, Underberg, Manley & Casey, San Diego, 1983; pvt. practice Sacramento and San Andreas (Calif.), 1984-86; ptnr. McDonough Holland & Allen, Sacramento, 1986-87; pvt. practice San Andreas, Calif., 1987—; chief counsel Calaveras County Child Protective Svcs., 1996—; judge pro-tem Calaveras County (Calif.) Consol. Cts., 1999—. Author: History of the Bench and Bar of Calaveras County California, 1997—. Bd. dirs. San Bernardino County Legal Aid Soc., 1971-73, sec., 1971-72, pres., 1973; mem. Calaveras County Adv. Com. on Alcohol and Drug Abuse, 1985-94, pres., 1991-92; treas. Calaveras County Legal Assistance Program, 1987—; trustee Calaveras County Law Libr., 1987-98; bd. dirs. Mark Twain Hosp. Dist., 1990—, treas., 1994—; mem. Calaveras County Rep. Ctrl. Com., 1990-92, 94-96; Calaveras County chmn. Wilson for Gov., 1994. Named to Hon. Order of Ky. Cols., 1967. Mem. ABA, Calif. Bar Assn. (Wiley F. Manuel pro bono pub. svc. award 1991), San Diego County Bar Assn., San Bernardino County Bar Assn. (bd. dirs., sec.-treas. 1973-75, pilot drug abuse program 1970), Calaveras County Bar Assn. (bd. dirs., v.p. 1988-90, pres. 1990-95), Am. Arbitration Assn. (arbitrator 1987—). Republican. Jewish. E-mail: markin2500@aol.com. Home: Fourth Mesa Murphys CA 95247 Office: PO Box 1210 7 Main St San Andreas CA 95249-9547

ARKIN, STANLEY HERBERT, retired construction executive, consultant; b. N.Y.C., Aug. 28, 1932; s. Joseph Lawrence and Mildred (Neidenberg) A.; m. Jill Theo Flitman, June 21, 1958; children: Bradley, Robert, Gregory. BBA cum laude, U. Miami, Coral Gables, Fla., 1954. Pres. Arkin Constrn. Co., Inc., Miami Beach, Fla., 1954-97. Life trustee, past mem. exec. com. U. Miami; cons. Greater Miami Jewish Fedn. Housing Corp.; chmn. bd. govs. Bascom Palmer Eye Inst./Ann Bates Leach Eye Hosp.; vice mayor, commr. City of Miami Beach, acting mayor, 1991; mem. Metro Dade County Performing Art Ctr. Trust. Mem. U. Miami Soc. Founders, Miami Beach Devel. Assn. (chmn.), Masons, Mahi Shrine, Iron Arrow, Phi Eta Sigma, Alpha Delta Sigma, Alpha Sigma Upsilon, Omicron Delta Kappa, Alpha Epsilon Pi. Republican. Avocations: skiing, golf, model railroads. Home and Office: Arkin Consulting Inc 5500 Collins Ave Apt 603 Miami Beach FL 33140-2537

ARKIN, STANLEY S., lawyer; b. L.A., Feb. 28, 1938; s. Jerome and Lillian (Rogo) A.; m. Suzanne Arkin, Mar. 3, 1963; children: Adam Arkin, Alexander Arkin, Anthony Arkin. AB, U. So. Calif., 1959; JD, Harvard U., 1962. Bar: N.Y. 1964, Calif. 1977, D.C. 1982. Sr. ptnr. Stanley S. Arkin, P.C., N.Y.C., 1969-90, Chadbourne & Parke, N.Y.C., 1990-93, Arkin Schaffer & Kaplan LLP, N.Y.C., 1994—; bd. dirs. Authentic Fitness Corp. Author: (with Matthew Bender) Business Crime, 1982, (with Matthew Bender) Hi Tech Crimes, 1989; contbr. articles to newspapers and profl. jour. Bd. dirs. Am. Craft Mus., Am. com. Weizman Inst. Sci. With JAGC Army, 1962-68. Fellow Am. Coll. Trial Lawyers; mem. Coun. on Fgn. Rels., Phi Beta Kappa. Office: Arkin Schaffer & Kaplan LLP 1370 6th Ave Fl 28 New York NY 10019-4602

ARKIN, WILLIAM MORRIS, military and political analyst, writer, consultant; b. N.Y.C., May 15, 1956; s. Donald and Lois (Halperin) A.; m. Susan Elizabeth Horn, Nov. 20, 1993; children: Rebecca, Hannah. BS in Govt. and Politics, U. Md., 1977; postgrad., Georgetown U., 1978-80. Sr. staff analyst Ctr. for Def. Info., Washington, 1980-81; dir. nat. security program and arms race and nuclear weapons research project, also fellow Inst. for Policy Studies, Washington, 1981-89; dir. nuclear info. unit, dir. military rsch. Greenpeace Internat./Greenpeace USA, 1989-94; polit. dir. Greenpeace USA, 1989-90; cons. Nat. Resources Def. Coun., Washington, 1980—, Bar Assn. P.R., San Juan, 1983—, Greenpeace Internat., Amsterdam, The Netherlands, 1987-89, Fedn. Am. Scientists, 1994-95, 98; Human Rights Watch Arms Divsn., 1994—, exec. office sec.-gen. UN, 1998-99, Legi-Slate, 1998—; vis. fellow Nat. Security Archive, 1994—; cons. Ctr. for Strategic Edn., Johns Hopkins U., 1997-98; mil. cons. Stern mag., Hamburg, Germany, 1981-88; on air mil. analyst MSNBC, 1998—, NBC Nightly News, 1998—, Washington Post, 1998—, Digital Ink (Washington Newsweek Interactive); lectr. and news analyst Air War Coll., Naval War Coll., Air Force Judge Advocate Gen. Sch., 1995-96; fellow Ctr. for Strategic Edn., Johns Hopkins U., Balt., 1999—. Author: Research Guide to Current Military and Strategic Affairs, 1981; co-author: SIOP: The Secret U.S. Plan for Nuclear War, 1983, Nuclear Battlefields: Global Links in the Arms Race, 1985, Encyclopedia of the U.S. Military, 1990, The Military Online: A Directory for Internet Access to the Department of Defense, 1997, 98; co-author, co-editor Nuclear Weapons Databook, Vols. 1-4, 1984-91; columnist Washington Post.com.; columnist, mem. editorial bd. Bull. Atomic Scientists, 1985—; editor Neptune Papers monographs; investigative reporter The Nation Institute, N.Y., 1995-96; contbg. editor Laser Report. Served with U.S. Army, 1974-78. John D. and Catherine T. MacArthur Found. rsch. and writing grantee, 1995-96, 97. Jewish. Home and Office: PO Box 149 South Pomfret VT 05067-0149

ARKING, LUCILLE MUSSER, nurse epidemiologist; b. Centre County, Pa., Jan. 26, 1936; d. Boyd Albert and Marion Anna (Merryman) Musser; m. Robert Arking, May 8, 1959; children: Henry David, Jonathan Jacob. RN, Episcopal Sch. Nursing, 1958; BSN, U. Pa., 1968; MSN, Wayne State U., 1986, postgrad., 1991—. Psychiat. rsch. nurse Boston City Hosp., 1958; hosp. supr. Phila. Psychiat. Ctr., 1959-61; pub. health nurse Cmty. Nursing Svc., Phila., 1961-64; DON Green Acres Nursing Ctr., Phila., 1966-67; head nurse U. Va., Charlottesville, 1967-68; asst. DON U. Ky., Lexington, 1968-70; asst. dir. nursing edn. Rio Hondo Hosp., Downey, Calif., 1973-75; DON Bellwood Hosp., Bellflower, Calif., 1974-75; nurse epidemiologist Henry Ford Hosp., Detroit, 1975-84, dir. hosp. epidemiology, 1984-89, sr. clin. epidemiologist, 1990-94; v.p. clin. svcs. Great Lakes Rehab. Hosp., Southfield, Mich., 1994-96; adminstr. Cadillac Nursing Ctr., Detroit, 1997-99; exec. dir. St. Anthony Nursing Care Ctr., Warren, Mich., 1999—; lectr. drug abuse Fountain Valley, Calif., 1970-75; instr. Santa Ana Coll., 1971-73; mem. HIV adv. com. Mich. Dept. Pub. Health, 1989-90. Contbr. articles to profl. jours. Co-founder Parents and Friends Learning Disabilities Orgn., 1968-70; dean leader Cub Scouts, Fountain Valley, 1968-75; bd. dirs. Wellness Networks, Detroit, 1982-86; mem. Mich. Gov. AIDS Task Force, 1985-86, Mich. Med. Soc. AIDS Task Force, 1986. Women's Club of Centre County scholar, 1954-58; grantee Cmty. Nursing Svc. Ednl., 1963-64; USPHS nursing trainee, 1965. Mem. APHA (mem. epidemiology sect. 1975—), ANA, Mich. Nurses's Assn. (AIDS task force 1987-89), Assn. Practitioners Infection Control, Sci. Rsch. Soc., Assn. Women in Sci., Sigma Xi. Home: 4705 Stoddard Dr Troy MI 48098-3504 Office: St Anthony Nursing Care Ctr 31830 Ryan Rd Warren MI 48092

ARKO, JOHN DAVID, transportation company driver; b. Cleve., June 17, 1949; s. John Frank and Rose Marie (Planisek) A. BA, John Carroll U., 1971; MPA, Cleve. State U., 1985. Instr. remedial reading Cuyahoga C.C., Cleve., 1976-77; benefits authorizer Social Security Adminstr., Chgo., 1977-80; home delivery staff N.Y. Times, Cleve., 1981-86; driver, warehouseman St. Vincent DePaul Soc., Cleve., 1986-93; driver Provide-A-Ride, Cleve., 1993—; Disaster relief vol. ARC, Cleve., 1980-85. With U.S. Army, 1967-70, Vietnam. Republican. Roman Catholic. Avocations: photography, history. Home: 20460 Lindbergh Ave Euclid OH 44119-2339

ARKOFF, SAMUEL Z., motion picture executive, producer; b. Ft. Dodge, Iowa, June 12, 1918; m. Hilda Rusoff. Student, U. Colo., U. Iowa; J.D., Loyola U., Los Angeles, 1948. Bar: Calif. Co-founder Am. Releasing, 1954, Am. Internat. Pictures, 1955; pres., chmn. bd. Am. Internat. Pictures, Inc., until 1979; pres., chmn. Samuel Z. Arkoff Co., Los Angeles, 1980—; pres., co-founder Am. Internat. Pictures, 1981—; lectr. Am. Film Inst., UCLA, Loyola Marymount U. Producer or co-producer: more than 500 films including The House of Usher, 1960, The Pit and the Pendulum, 1961, Beach Party, 1963, The Wild Angels, 1966, The Trip, 1967, Wild in the Streets, 1968, Wuthering Heights, 1971, Dillinger, 1973, Heavy Traffic, 1973, Cooley High, 1975, Futureworld, 1976, A Matter of Time, 1976, Empire of the Ants, 1977, The Island of Dr. Moreau, 1977, The People That Time Forgot, 1977, Our Winning Season, 1978, Love at First Bite, 1979, Something Short of Paradise, 1979, Meteor, 1979, Amityville Horror, 1979, How to Beat the High Cost of Living, 1980, Dressed to Kill, 1980, The Earthling, 1981, Underground Aces, 1981, The Final Terror, 1983, Up the Creek, 1984, Murders in the Rue Morgue, 1971, Cooley High, 1975; retrospectives: Mus. Modern Art, N.Y.C., 1979, Thalia Soho Theater, N.Y.C., 1986, U. S. Calif., 1986, Scottsdale (Ariz.) Film Festival, 1986. Trustee Loyola-Marymount U., Los Angeles, 1979—; exec. com. Permanent Charities of the Entertainment Industry. Served as cryptographer USAAF, World War II. Named with partner James H. Nicholson as Producers of Year Allied States Assn. Motion Picture Theatre Owners, 1963; Master Showman of Decade Theatre Owners Am., 1964; Producers of Year Show-A-Rama VIII; Motion Picture Pioneer of Yr. (with Nicholson) Found. Motion Picture Pioneers, Inc., 1971; decorated commendatore of Order of Merit Italy, 1970; named Internat. V.P. Variety Clubs Internat., 1973. Office: Arkoff Internat Pictures care Walt Disney Studios 500 S Buena Vista St Burbank CA 91521-7471*

ARKY, RONALD ALFRED, medical educator; b. New Brunswick, N.J., June 26, 1929; s. Eugene and Ida (Glick) A.; m. Marie Mahoney, Sept. 14, 1963. AB, Cornell U., Ithaca, N.Y., 1951; MD, Cornell U., N.Y.C., 1955. Intern Bellevue Hosp., N.Y.C., 1955-56; resident N.Y. VA Hosp., 1958-60; fellow Thorndike Meml. Lab., Boston City Hosp., 1961-63; dir. diabetes clinic Boston City Hosp., 1966-71; Charles S. Davidson prof. medicine Harvard U. Med. Sch., Cambridge, Mass., 1984—; chmn. dept. medicine Mt. Auburn Hosp., 1971-93; pres. Assocs. Program for Dirs. Internal Medicine, 1990-91; acting chief diabetes sect. Brigham Women's Hosp., Boston, 1996—. Fellow AAAS; Master ACP, Peabody Soc. Harvard Med. Sch.; mem. Am. Diabetes Assn. (pres. 1979-80), Am. Soc. Clin. Investigation, Endocrine Soc., Am. Clin. Climatol. Soc. Office: Francis W Peabody Soc Harvard Med Sch 260 Longwood Ave Boston MA 02115-5701*

ARL, ELLEN MARIE, English educator, television producer and host; b. Chgo., Jan. 12, 1943; d. John Francis and Helen Ruth (Lavicka) A.; m. Gary Wayne Chandler, May 21, 1977 (div. Sept. 1982). BA, St. Xavier Coll., Chgo., 1964; MFA, U. N.C., Greensboro, 1966; MA, Tulane U., 1971. Instr. U. Ga., Athens, 1966-67; rschr. Bacon's Rsch., Chgo., 1971-73; lectr. City Colls., Chgo., 1973-74; from instr. to prof. U. S.C., Sumter, 1974—. Prodr., host Ex Libris, WRJA-SCETV, Sumter, 1980—; sr. editor Continuum jour., 1991—. Named Gov.'s Prof., State Commn. on Higher Edn., S.C., 1993. Roman Catholic. Avocations: poetry, painting. Home: 236 N Purdy St Sumter SC 29150-4561 Office: U SC Sumter 200 Miller Rd Sumter SC 29150-2498

ARLEDGE, CHARLES STONE, former aerospace executive, entrepreneur; b. Bonham, Tex., Oct. 20, 1935; s. John F. and Mary Madeline (Jones) A.; m. Barbara Jeanne Ruff, June 18, 1966; children: John Harrison, Mary Katherine. B.S., Stanford U., 1957, M.S. (Standard Oil Co. Calif. scholar 1958), 1958, M.B.A., 1966. Engr. Shell Oil Co., Los Angeles, 1958-64; with Signal Cos., La Jolla, Calif., 1966-86; v.p. Signal Cos., 1970-79, group v.p., 1979-83, sr. v.p., 1983-86; v.p. Aerojet Gen. Corp., La Jolla, Calif., 1986-90; ptnr. Signal Ventures, 1990—. Republican. Presbyterian. Clubs: California; La Jolla Beach and Tennis. Home: PO Box 957 Rancho Santa Fe CA 92067-0957 Office: 777 S Pacific Coast Hwy Ste 107 Solana Beach CA 92075-2623

ARLEDGE, DAVID A., business executive; b. 1944. BBA, U. Tex., 1965, JD, 1968. With Touch Ross & Co., CPA's, 1968-72, ptnr., 1975-80; ptnr. Penfold & Arledge, 1972-75; pres., CEO, COO Coastal Corp., West Memphis, Ark., 1980—. Office: Coastal Corp Coastal Tower 9 E Greenway Plz Houston TX 77046-0905*

ARLEDGE, ROONE, television executive; b. Forest Hills, N.Y., July 8, 1931; m. Gig Shaw, May 21, 1994; children: Elizabeth Ann, Susan Lee, Patricia Lu, Roone Pinckney. BA, Columbia Coll., 1952; LHD (hon.), Boston U.; LLD (hon.), Wake Forest U. Prodr. network sports, Wide World of Sports ABC-TV, 1960-61, v.p. charge sports, 1964-68; pres. ABC Sports, Monday Night Football, 1968-85, ABC News, Nightline, 1977-98; group pres. ABC News and Sports, 1985-90; exec. prodr. all ABC sports programs, including 10 Olympic games, 1968; pres. ABC News, chmn., 1998—; bd. dirs. Coun. Fgn. Rels., ESPN, Arts & Entertainment Network, History Channel; dean's coun. Harvard U. JFK Sci. of Govt. Created ABC's Wide World of Sports, 1961, NFL Monday Night Football, 1970, ABC's World News Tonight, Nightline, 20/20, This Week with David Brinkley, PrimeTime Live, Viewpoint, Turning Point, Capital to Capital, World News This Morning, World News Now, Day One; responsible for most tech. and editorial innovations in sports coverage. Pres. Com. Meml. Sloan Kettering Hosp. com.; active Coun. Fgn. Rels.; bd. visitors Columbia Coll.; mem. Pres.' Coun. on Physical Fitness, also chmn. sports com.; trustee Columbia U. Served AUS, 1953-54. Recipient 36 Emmy awards, 4 George Foster Peabody awards, 2 Christopher awards, Broadcast Pioneers award, Gold medal Internat. Radio and TV Soc., 1983, Disting. Svc. to Journalism Honor medal U. Mo., John Jay Disting. Profl. Svc. award Columbia U., Lifetime Achievement award TV Critics Assn., Disting. Achievement award U. So. Calif. Journalism Assn., Founders award Acad. TV Arts and Scis. Inst., Grand Prix Montreux TV award, Olympic Order medal Internat. Olympic Com., Grand prize Cannes Film Festival; named Man of Yr. by Nat. Assn. TV Program Execs.; inducted into TV Acad. Arts and Scis. Hall of Fame, 1990, U.S. Olympic Hall of Fame, 1990, Nat. Assn. Broadcasters Hall of Fame, 1994. Mem. Royal and Ancient Golf Club (St. Andrews, Scotland), Shinnecock Hills Golf Club, Nat. Golf Links Am., Deepdale Golf Club, Winged Foot Golf Club, Castle Pines Golf Club, Portmarnock Golf Club (Dublin). Office: ABC News 47 W 66th St Fl 5 New York NY 10023-6201

ARLEDGE-BENKO, PATRICIA, retired minister; b. Pitts., Oct. 14, 1934; d. Raymond F. and Anna C. (Hoffman) O'Brien; m. James A. Arledge, Mar. 22, 1958 (dec. Nov. 1989); 1 child, Zeta Ann Turner; m. Frank Benko, Sept. 22, 1990. Diploma in Bible, Gt. Work Sch. Ministry, Monroeville, Pa., 1983; ThB, Internat. Sem., Plymouth, Fla., 1985, ThM, 1987, MA, 1987.

Ordained to ministry Full Gospel Ch., 1982, Bapt. Ch., 1987. Pastor, dir. Christian edn. Shiloh Bapt. Ch., Apollo, Pa.; ret. Leader Eastmont coun. Girl Scouts U.S.A., 1964, troup organizer, 1965-66; camping leader, 1967, neighborhood chmmn., 1968-74; vol. chaplain Presbyn. U., Eye and Ear and Children's hosps., Pitts., 1983-88; vol. nursing homes and hosps. Mem. Nat. Women's Ministerial Alliance, Pitts. Regional Assn. Women Ministers, Internat. Assn. Women Ministers (pres. 1996-97), Church Women United (pres. Apollo chpt. 1991-92, pres. Apollo ministerium 1994), Kiski Valley Union Chs., Allegheny Pekingese Kennel Club (pres. 1974-80), Order Ea. Star (matron 1967). Avocations: travel, sewing, golf, gardening, reading.

ARLEN, MICHAEL J., writer; b. London, Dec. 9, 1930; s. Michael and Atlanta (Mercati) A.; m. Ann Warner, 1957 (div. 1971); children—Jennifer, Caroline, Elizabeth, Sally; m. Alice Albright Hoge, 1972; stepchildren—Alicia, James Patrick, Robert Hoge. Grad., St. Paul's Sch., Concord, N.H., 1948, Harvard U., 1952; LLD (hon.), Colby Coll., 1984. Reporter Life mag., 1952-56; contbr., TV critic The New Yorker mag., 1957-82; juror Columbia U.-Dupont awards for broadcast journalism, 1969-72, 78-80; faculty Bread Loaf Writers Conf., 1980; bd. dirs. Nat. Arts Journalism Program. Author: Living-Room War, 1969, Exiles, 1970, An American Verdict, 1973, Passage to Ararat, 1975, The View from Highway 1, 1976, Thirty Seconds, 1980, The Camera Age, 1981, Say Goodbye to Sam, 1984. Recipient award for television criticism Screen Dirs. Guild, 1968; Nat. Book award for contemporary affairs, 1976; Le Prix Brémond, 1976. Mem. Authors Guild (exec. coun.), PEN Am. Ctr., Knickerbocker Club, Century Assn., Harvard Club of N.Y.

ARLIDGE, JOHN WALTER, utility company executive; b. Rochester, N.Y., Feb. 4, 1933; s. Harold Wesley and Grace Elizabeth (Kempshall) A.; m. Sandra Marie Koswar, Feb. 4, 1955; children: James William, Edward John. BS, L.A. State Coll., 1962. Registered profl. engr., Calif., Nev., Utah. With City of L.A., 1961-74, communications systems engring. design and purchase, 1961-62, power system resource planning research and devel., 1962-74; asst. to v.p. Nev. Power Co., Las Vegas, 1974-82, v.p. resource planning and power dispatch, 1982-89; sr. v.p. govt. affairs, 1989-93; v.p., dir. Nev. Electric Investment Co., 1982-89, adv. Elec./Lignite sector ministry Ind. and Trade, Warsaw, Poland, 1992-95; cons. Energy Resources and Regulation, 1995—; mem. State Engr.'s Adv. Com. on Geothermal Devel., 1974-76. State of Nev. Solar Energy Devel. Adv. Group, 1976-86; mem. energy task force WEST, 1972-84, mem. energy engring. planning com., 1978; mem. advanced energy systems divisional com. Electric Power Rsch. Inst., 1973-92; mem. Western Utility Group on Fed. Land, 1977; endangered species subcom., rail issues group Edison Elec. Inst., 1977; cons. on air, land and water Western Regional Coun., 1977; Nev. adv. bd. U.S. Bur. Land Mgmt., 1975-77, adv. coun. Las Vegas dist., 1980-92; rsch. adv. bd. U. Nev., bd. trustees Corp. Devel. Sci. Tech. State Nev. Contbr. articles on energy resources to pubis. Mem. Nature Conservancy Nev. adv. bd., Sec. of Energy's Nat. Coal Coun., 1988-93. Served with USMC, 1950-54. Mem. IEEE, Geothermal Resources Council (dir.), Utility Coal Gasification Assn. (chmn.), Internat. Solar Energy Assn., Nat. Coal Coun. (advisor to Sec. of Energy), Pacific Coast Elec. Assn., So. Nevada Off-Road Vehicle Assn., Slurry Transp. Assn. (dir. 1979). Clubs: Masons.

ARLING, BRYAN JEREMY, internist; b. Mpls., Dec. 10, 1944; s. Leonard Swenson and Marion (Schroeder) A.; m. Donna Dickson; children: Elissa, Jeremy, Timothy. BA summa cum laude, U. Minn., 1965; MD, Harvard U., 1969. Diplomate Am. Bd. Internal Medicine. Intern Stanford (Calif.) Affiliated Hosps., 1969-70, resident in internal medicine, 1970-71; spl. asst. to adminstr. health sci. mental health adminstrn. USPHS, Rockville, Md., 1971-73; instr., chief resident medicine George Washington U. Hosp., Washington, 1973-74; asst. prof. medicine George Washington U. Hosp., 1974-77; pvt. practice Washington, 1977—; clin. prof. medicine George Washington U., 1988—, Georgetown U., Washington, 1997—. Adminstrv. bd. Chevy Chase United Meth. Ch.; mem. devel. com. Maret Sch., 1985—, trustee, 1991—, v.p., 1994—; question relevance reviewer Am. Bd. Internal Medicine, 1991-92, com. on certifying and recertifying exam., 1992-93. Named One of Best Doctors in Town, Washington Mag, 1986, 95, 99, One of Best Pediatricians and Internists, 1987, Top Internist by other doctors, 1993, Best Doctors in Am., S.E. region, 1996. Fellow ACP; mem. AMA, Am. Soc. Internal Medicine, D.C. Med. Soc., Acad. Medicine, Smithsonian Assocs., Friends of Kennedy Ctr., Harvard Club Washington, Nat. Trust for Hist. Preservation, Friends of Nat. Zoo, Common Cause, ACLU, Physicians for Social Responsibility, Columbia Country Club, Bahamas Air-Sea Rescue Assn. Home: 3803 Taylor St Bethesda MD 20815-4117 Office: 2440 M St NW Ste 817 Washington DC 20037-1404 *1. Good medicine is more thoroughness than brilliance.2. The sickest body is smarter than the brightest doctor.3. Learn as though you'll never die - live as though you'll die tomorrow.*

ARLING, DONNA DICKSON, social worker; b. Jersey Shore, Pa., July 8, 1945; d. Eugene Robert and Helen (Bardo) Dickson; m. Bryan Jeremy Arling, Aug. 28, 1969; children: Elissa, Jeremy, Timothy. BS, Pa. State U., 1967; MSW, Smith Coll., 1969. Bd. cert. diplomate in clin. social work; cert. social worker, Md.; cert. ind. clin. social worker, D.C. Clin. social worker N. County Mental Health Ctr., Palo Alto, Calif., 1969-71, VA Hosp., Washington, 1971-77; pvt. practice clin. social work Washington, 1978—. Mem. Nat. Assn. Social Workers, Greater Washington Soc. Clin. Social Work, Smith Coll. Sch. Social Work Alumni Assn. (nat. exec. com. 1979-82, Washington exec. com. 1976-86). Home: 3803 Taylor St Chevy Chase MD 20815-4117 Office: 1015 33rd St NW Washington DC 20007-3523

ARLINGHAUS, SANDRA JUDITH LACH, mathematical geographer, educator; b. Elmira, N.Y., Apr. 18, 1943; d. Donald Frederick and Alma Elizabeth (Satorius) Lach; m. William Charles Arlinghaus, Sept. 3, 1966; 1 child, William Edward. AB in Math., Vassar Coll., 1964; postgrad., U. Chgo., 1964-66, U. Toronto, Ont., Can., 1966-67, Wayne State U., 1968-70; MA in Geography, Wayne State U., 1976; PhD in Geography, U. Mich., 1977. Vis. instr. math. U. Ill., Chgo., 1966; vis. asst. prof. geography Ohio State U., Columbus, 1977-78, lectr. math., 1978-79; lectr. math. Loyola U., Chgo., 1979-81, asst. prof. math., 1981-82; lectr. math. and geography U. Mich., Dearborn and Ann Arbor, 1982-83; founding dir. Inst. Math. Geography, Ann Arbor, 1985—; pres. Arlinghaus Enterprises, Ann Arbor, 1998—; guest lectr. U. Chgo., 1979, 87, U. Calif., 1979, Syracuse U., 1991, U. No. Iowa, 1991; guest lectr. U. Mich., Ann Arbor, 1983, 90-93, adj. prof. math. geography, population-environ. dynamics Sch. Natural Resources and Environ., 1994—, adj. prof. Coll. Architecture and Urban Planning, 1997; cons. Transp. Rsch. Inst., Coll. Architecture, 1985-86, Coll. Edn., 1992, Cmty. Sys. Found., 1993—; prodr. Ann Arbor Cmty. Access TV, 1988-90; dir. spatial analysis divsn. Cmty. Systems Found., 1996—, dir. fellowship tng. divsn., 1996—, dir. mapping, 1997—; co-founder Arlinghaus Enterprises, 1997. Author: Down the Mail Tubes: The Pressured Postal Era, 1853-1984, Essays on Mathematical Geography, 1986, Essays on Mathematical Geography-II, 1987, An Atlas of Steiner Networks, 1989, Essays on Mathematical Georgraphy-III, 1991; co-author: Population-Environment Dynamics, Sectors in Transition, 1992 and later editions through 1998, Mathematical Geography and Global Art, 1986, Environmental Effects on Bus Durability, 1990, Fractals in Geography, 1993; founder, editor, co-author Solstice, 1990—, Image Interactive Atlases, Image Game Series, Image Discussion Papers, Internat. Soc. Spatial Scis., 1995—; author, editor-in-chief Practical Handbook of Curve Fitting, 1994; co-author, editor-in-chief Practical Handbook of Digital Mapping: Terms and Concepts, 1994; editor-in-chief Practical Handbook of Spatial Stats., 1995; editor internat. monograph series; reviewer Mathematical Reviews, 1992—; contbr. articles, book reviews to profl. jours. in field of geography, psychology, math., biology, history, philately. Planning commr. City of Ann Arbor, 1995—, sec., 1997—; bd. dirs., mem. chmn. Bromley Homeowners Assn., Ann Arbor, 1989-93, pres., 1990-93, 95-96; co-vice chair citizens adv. com. North East Area Master Plan Revision, 1999—; bd. dirs. World Jr. Bridge Championships, Ann Arbor, 1990-91; bd. dirs. Dolfins Inc., 1993-96; artist Math. Awareness Week, Lawrence Tech. U., 1998; mem. bd. trustees Cmty. Sys. Found., 1995—; co-vice chair citizens adv. com. NE Ann Arbor master plan revision, 1999—. Fellow Am. Geog. Soc. (rep. search com. for curator of collection in Golda Meir Libr. U. Wis.-Milw. Libr. 1993-94); mem. AAAS, Am. Math. Soc., Math. Assn. Am., Assn. Am. Geographers, Internat. Soc. Spatial Scis. (founder), N.Y. Acad. Scis., Engring. Soc. Detroit, Regional Sci. Assn. Achievements include discovery of exact fractal characterization of the geometry of central place theory and its electronic interpretation; alignment of earth marking sculptures to solstices and equinoxes in Minnesota, Washington, Alaska, New Brunswick, Canada, and USSR; creator of one of world's first refereed electronic journals; creator of applications of chaos theory in geography and population environment dynamics, maps for major international projects for Syria and Pakistan. Office: U Mich Sch Natural Resources Ann Arbor MI 48109

ARLOOK, IRA ARTHUR, non-profit association executive; b. N.Y.C., Apr. 7, 1943; s. George G. and Shirley (Meyers) A.; m. Karen Beth Nussbaum, July 9, 1978; children: Gene, Jack, Eleanor. BA, Tufts U., 1964; MA in History, Stanford U., 1966; PhD in Pub. Policy, Union Inst., 1978. Asst. prof. Cleve. State U., 1975-80; exec. dir. Ohio Pub. Interest Campaign, Cleve., 1976-93, Citizen Action, Cleve., Chgo. and Washington, 1980-97; exec. dir. New Economy Comms., 1998. Woodrow Wilson Nat. fellow, 1965, NSF fellow, 1980. Mem. Citizens for Tax Justice (pres. 1980-97), Nat. Conf. Alternative State and Local Pub. Policies (bd. dirs. 1976-80), Citizen Labor Energy Coalition (bd. dirs. Washington 1978-90), Nat. Campaign Against Toxic Hazards (bd. dirs. 1983-87). Avocations: sports, music. Office: New Economy Comm 1320 18th St NW 5th fl Washington DC 20036-1811

ARLOW, ARNOLD JACK, advertising agency executive, artist; b. Bklyn., Sept. 29, 1933; s. Louis and Sylvia (Spitzberg) A.; m. Phyllis Banschick, Apr. 20, 1958 (div. 1990); children: Susan, Noah; m. Susan Gray, Nov. 22, 1992. B.F.A., Cooper Union, 1954. Art dir. N.Y. Times, 1958-61, Altman Stoller Advt., N.Y.C., 1961-65, Daniel & Charles Advt., N.Y.C., 1965, McCaffrey McCall Advt., N.Y.C., 1965-66; partner, creative dir. Martin Landey, Arlow Advt., N.Y.C., 1966-80; exec. v.p., creative dir. Geers Gross Advt., 1980-83; cons. communications industry, 1983-84.; exec. v.p., creative dir. TBWA Advt., 1984-94; ptnr., creative dir. Margeotes, Fertitta & Ptnrs., N.Y.C., 1994-98; creative cons., painter Amagansett, N.Y., 1998—; tchr. design Wagner Coll., Staten Island, 1964-69. Alumni trustee Cooper Union, 1982-85. Served with USAF Res., 1961-66. Recipient Augustus Saint-Gaudens award for profl. achievement in art Cooper Union, 1995; Fulbright-Hays grantee Paris, 1954-55; Kelly award MPA for Absolut Vodka Campaign, 1988, 90. Democrat. Jewish. Home: 31 W 12th St New York NY 10011-8500

ARLOW, JACOB A., psychiatrist, educator; b. N.Y.C., Sept. 3, 1912; s. Adolph A. and Ida (Feldman) A.; m. Alice Diamond, Oct. 31, 1936; children: Michael Saul, Allan Joseph, Seth Martin. B.S., N.Y. U., 1932, M.D., 1936; Grad., N.Y. Psychoanalytic Inst., 1947. Diplomate: Am. Bd. Neurology and Psychiatry. Rotating intern Harlem Hosp., N.Y.C., 1936-38; resident neuropsychiatrist USPHS Hosp., Ellis Island, N.Y., 1938-39; resident psychiatrist Kings County Hosp., Bklyn., 1939; asst. psychiatrist mental hygiene clinic Kings County Hosp., 1941; asst. resident neurologist Montefiore Hosp., Bronx, N.Y., 1940-41; asst. neurologist Montefiore Hosp., 1942-44; resident psychiatrist N.Y. State Psychiat. Inst. and Hosp., N.Y.C., 1940-41; cons. psychiatrist Pride of Judea Children's Home, Bklyn., 1940-45; pvt. practice N.Y.C., 1942-92; lectr. N.Y. Psychoanalytic Inst., 1948-50; instr. neurology Columbia Coll. Phys. and Surg., 1942-44, instr. psychiatry psychosomatic service of psychoanalytic clinic for tng. and research, 1947-51, John B. Turner vis. prof. psychiatry, 1967-68; research asso., instr. psychiatry Presbyn. Hosp.-Columbia Med. Center, 1944-51; clin. asst. prof. psychoanalytic medicine State U. N.Y. Coll. Medicine at N.Y.C., 1952-55, clin. assoc. prof., 1955-62, clin. prof., 1962-79; clin. prof. NYU, N.Y.C., 1979—; mem. faculty Ctr. Psychoanlytic Tng., N.Y.C.; prof. emeritus Albert Einstein Coll. Medicine, N.Y.C.; pvt. practice part-time N.Y.C., 1984—, Great Neck, N.Y., 1984—; faculty N.Y. Psychoanalytic Inst., 1956—; vis. prof. psychiatry La. State U. Sch. Medicine, 1969-70, Mt. Sinai Sch. Medicine, N.Y.C., 1972-73; vis. scholar Freud chair Hebrew U., Jerusalem, April, 1985; cons. Hillside Hosp., Glen Oaks, N.Y., 1989—. Author: Legacy of Sigmund Freud, 1956, (with Charles Brenner) Psychoanalytic Concepts and the Structural Theory, 1964, Psychoanalysis: Clinical Theory and Practice, 1991; editor: Selected Writings of Bertram D. Lewin; editor-in-chief Psychoanalytic Quar., 1970-79; mem. editl. bd. Psyche. Vice pres. Great Neck (L.I.) Coop. Sch.; trustee, sec. N.Y. Psychoanalytic Inst., 1956-59. Recipient Centennial award as Alumnus of Decade 1940-49, N.Y. State Psychiat. Inst., Heinz Hartmann award, 1980; Lenox Hill Disting. Clinicians award, 1980; Vexillarius Excellentae award Pride of Judea Mental Health Ctr., Mary Sigourney award Am. Coll. Psychoanalysts 1990, Henry Loughlin award 1991. Mem. AMA, Am. Psychoanalytic Assn. (pres. 1960-61, chmn. COPE 1962-66, bd. editors jours. 1958-60, chmn. bd. profl. standards 1967-70, Jour. award 1988); mem. Internat. Soc. Study of Time (coun.), Am. Psychiat. Assn., Psychosomatic Soc., N.Y. Psychoanalytic Inst. (pres. 1966-68), Internat. Psycho-Analytic Assn. (treas., v.p. 1961-69). Address: 94 Wildwood Rd Great Neck NY 11024-1223

ARMACOST, MARY-LINDA SORBER MERRIAM, former college president, educational consultant; b. Jeannette, Pa., May 31, 1943; d. Everett Sylvester Calvin and Madeleine (Case) Sorber; m. E. William Merriam, Dec. 13, 1969 (div. 1975); m. Peter H. Armacost, July 10, 1993. Student, Grove City Coll., 1961-63; BA, Pa. State U., 1963-65, MA, 1965-67, PhD, 1967-70; HHD (hon.), Carroll Coll., 1991; LLD (hon.), Wilson Coll., 1994. Rsch. assoc. Pa. State U., University Park, 1970-72; asst. prof. speech Emerson Coll., Boston, 1972-79, dir. continuing edn., 1974-77, spl. asst. to pres., 1977-78, v.p. adminstrn., 1978-79; asst. to pres. Boston U., 1979-81; pres. Wilson Coll., Chambersburg, Pa., 1981-91, Moore Coll. Art and Design, Phila., 1991-93; sr. fellow Office of Women in Higher Edn. Am. Coun. on Edn., 1994—; interim pres. Moore Coll. Art and Design, Phila., 1998-99; cons. Govt. Edn. and Secondary Edn. Act Title III, Alameda County, Calif., 1968. Bd. dirs. Sta. WITF, Inc., Harrisburg, Pa., 1982-91, chmn. bd., 1988-91; bd. dirs. Chambersburg Hosp., 1984-89, vice chmn. bd., 1987-89; bd. dirs. Elderhostel, 1997—, bd. of trustees, Monmouth U., NJ, 1994—, Sta. WHYY-FM-TV, Phila., 1992-93, Boston Zool. Soc., 1980-81, Arts Boston, 1979-81, Scotland Sch. Vets. Children, Pa., 1984-90; bd. dirs. Fla. Orch., 1993-97, co-chair edn. com., 1995-97, mem. exec. com., 1995-97; mem. exec. com. Found. for Ind. Colls., 1989-91, WEOU-TV, 1997—; pres. Chambersburg Area Coun. Arts, 1988-90; chmn. higher edn. com. Gen. Assembly Presbyn. Ch., 1987-90; elder Falling Spring Presbyn. Ch., 1988-90; fellow Am. Coun. Edn., 1977-78, commn. on govtl. rels., 1985-89, commn. on women, 1992-93; mem. exec. com. Pa. Assn. Colls. and Univs., 1984-90, mem. exec. com. Assn. Presbyn. Colls. and Univs., 1983-88, pres., 1986-87; mem. edn. adv. com. John S. & James L. Knight Found., 1998—. Recipient Disting. Alumna award Pa. State U., 1984, Disting. Dau. of Pa., 1986, Athena award Chambersburg C. of C., 1988, Outstanding Alumnae award Sch. Dist. Jeannette, 1991. Mem. NATAS (bd. govs. New Eng. chpt. 1980-81), AAUW, Cosmos Club (Washington), Soc. Arts and Letters, Phi Kappa Phi, Rho Tau Sigma, Phi Delta Kappa.

ARMACOST, MICHAEL HAYDEN, research institution executive, ambassador; b. Cleve., Apr. 15, 1937; s. George H. and Verda Gay (Hayden) A.; m. Roberta June Bray, Mar. 7, 1959; children: Scott, Timothy, Christopher. BA, Carleton Coll., 1958; postgrad., Friedrich Wilhelms U., 1959; MA, Columbia U., 1961, PhD, 1965. Assoc. prof. govt. Pomona Coll., Claremont, Calif., 1962-70, Wig Disting. prof., 1966; mem. policy planning staff State Dept., Washington, 1969-72; spl. asst. to ambassador Am. Embassy, Tokyo, 1972-74; mem. policy planning staff State Dept., Washington, 1974-77; sr. staff mem. NSC, Washington, 1977-78; dep. asst. sec. def. internat. security affairs Dept. Defense, 1978-80, prin. dep. asst. sec. East Asian and Pacific affairs, 1980-82; ambassador to Phillipines, 1982-84, under sec. for polit. affairs, 1984-89, ambassador to Japan, 1989-93; disting. sr. fellow, vis. prof. Stanford U., 1993-95; pres. The Brookings Instn., 1995—. Author: The Politics of Weapons Innovation, 1969, The Foreign Relations of United States, 1969, Friends or Rivals ? The Insider's Account of U.S.-Japan Relations, 1996. Recipient Superior Honor award State Dept., 1976, Disting. Civilian Svc. award Def. Dept., 1980, Presdl. Disting. Svc. award, 1987, 89; White House fellow, 1969-70; Sec.'s award State Dept., 1988. Mem. Coun. on Fgn. Rels., Am. Acad. Diplomacy. Office: Brookings Institution 1775 Massachusetts Ave NW Washington DC 20036-2188

ARMACOST, PETER HAYDEN, academic administrator; b. N.Y.C., July 12, 1935; s. George Henry and Verda Gay (Hayden) A.; m. Suzanne Lee Sadosky, June 22, 1957 (dec. Feb. 1991); children: Martha Hayden, David Keys, Sarah Jane, Rebecca Ann; m. Mary-Linda Merriam, July 10, 1993. BA, Denison U., 1957; PhD, U. Minn., 1963. Dean students, chmn. dept. psychology Augsburg Coll., Mpls., 1959-65; program dir. Assn. Am. Colls., Washington, 1965-67; pres., prof. psychology Ottawa U., (Kans.), 1967-77; pres. Eckerd Coll., St. Petersburg, Fla., 1977—. Author materials in field. Chmn. Kansas City (Mo.) Regional Coun. Higher Edn., 1972-74; pres. Am. Bapt. Chs. U.S., 1974-75, So. Univ. Conf., 1997; bd. dirs. United Way of Pinellas County, 1995—. Recipient Disting. Alumnus citation Denison U.; Woodrow Wilson fellow; Danforth fellow; named to Tampa Bay Bus. Hall of Fame, 1999. Mem. Assn. Am. Colls. (bd. dirs.), Am. Coun. Edn., Nat. Assn. Student Pers. Adminstrs. (bd. dirs. divsn. rsch., publs. and conf. chmn. Disting. Svc. award), Assn. Ind. Colls. Kans. (pres. 1970-72), Young Pres. Orgn. (chmn. Fla. chpt. 1983-84), So. Assn. of Colls. and Schs. (appeals com.), Am. Assn. Higher Edn., Soc. Values in Higher Edn., Nat. Assn. Ind. Coll. and U. Pres., Fla. Assn. Colls. and Univs. (pres. 1989-90), Ind. Colls. and Univs. Fla. (sec. 1984-86, treas. 1986-88, vice chmn. 1990-91, chmn. 1991-93), Coun. Ind. Colls. (bd. dirs. 1993—, sec. exec. com.), Nat. Assn. Ind. Colls. and Univs. (bd. dirs. 1995-98), Suncoast C. of C. (chmn. 1984-85), Pinellas Econ. Devel. Coun. (bd. dirs. 1989—), Fla. Coun. of 100, St. Petersburg C. of C. (bd. dirs. 1995—), St. Petersburg Yacht Club, Suncoasters Club, Rotary, SunTrust Bank of Tampa Bay (bd. dirs. 1983—), Blue Key, Phi Beta Kappa, Omicron Delta Kappa, Pi Gamma Mu, Psi Chi. Republican. Home: 6320 Bahama Shores Dr S Saint Petersburg FL 33705-5438 Office: Eckerd Coll 4200 54th Ave S Saint Petersburg FL 33711-4744

ARMACOST, ROBERT LEO, management educator, former coast guard officer; b. Balt., July 17, 1942; s. Leo Mathias and Margaret Virginia (Ruth) A.; m. Susan Marie Danesi, Jan. 16, 1965 (div.); children: Robert Leo, Andrew Paul, Kathleen Erin; m. Julia Johanna Agricola Pet, Apr. 17, 1999. BS with honors, USCG Acad., 1964; MS, USN Postgrad. Sch., 1970; DSc in Ops. Rsch., George Washington U., 1976. Engring. officer USCGC Cutter Mendota, Wilmington, N.C., 1964-66; ops. officer USCGC Cook Inlet, Portland, Maine, 1966-68; ops. rsch. analyst, ops. planning staff USCG Hdqrs., Washington, 1970-75, planning officer, aids to navigation divsn., 1976-78; comdr. Coast Guard Group USCG Hdqrs., Milw., 1978-81; comdg. officer USCG Marine Safety Office, Milw., 1981-84, capt. of port, 1981-84, officer in charge of marine inspection, 1981-84, ret., 1984; instr. computer sci. Milw. Area Tech. Coll., 1982-83; asst. prof. mgmt. sci. Marquette U., Milw., 1984-91, assoc. prof. mgmt. sci., 1991; asst. prof. ops. rsch. U. Ctrl. Fla., 1991-96, assoc. prof. ops. rsch., 1996—, IE Grad. Program Coord. Contbr. articles to profl. jours. First v.p. Md. Right to Life, 1976-78; active Milw. Pastoral Coun., 1984-89, vice chmn., 1986-87, chmn., 1987-88; bd. dirs. Nicholet H.S. Found., 1986-88. Recipient USCG commendation award, 1972, 74, 78, 81, 84; named Outstanding Civic Vol., Bowie, Md., 1976; nat. finalist White House fellow, 1977-78. Mem. Ops. rsch. Soc. Am. (com. 1983-94, chmn. 1990-94, fin. com. 1993-94), Math. Programming Soc., Inst. Mgmt. Sci., Decision Scis. Inst., Acad. of Mgmt., Inst. Ind. Engrs., Inst. Ops. Rsch. and Mgmt. Scis. (chair membership com. 1995-96, fin. com. 1995-97, dir. at large 1995-97, bd. dirs. 1995-97). Roman Catholic. Home: 602 Shorewood Dr Unit 402 Cape Canaveral FL 32920-5082 Office: U Ctrl Fla Dept IEMS Orlando FL 32816

ARMALY, MANSOUR F(ARID), ophthalmologist, educator; b. Shefa Amer, Palestine, Feb. 25, 1927; came to U.S., 1955, naturalized, 1965; s. Fareed M. and Fadwa M. (Bahouth) A.; m. Aida Makdisi, July 2, 1950; children: Raya, Fareed. B.A., Am. U., Beirut, 1947, M.D., 1952; M.Sc., U. Iowa, 1957. Diplomate: Am. Bd. Ophthalmology. Intern Am. U. Hosps., Beirut, Resident, 1952-55; research fellow U. Iowa, 1955-57, instr., 1957-58, asst. prof. ophthalmology, 1958-60, asso. prof., 1960-66, prof., 1966-70; prof., chmn. dept. ophthalmology George Washington U. Med. Center, 1970-97; prof. emeritus, 1997—; cons. in field; Univ. prof. U. Paraguay. Contbr. articles to profl. publs.; mem. editorial bd.: Investigative Ophthalmology, 1969-73, Ophthalmology Digest, 1971—; asso. editor: Archives Ophthalmology, 1970. Decorated knight Order of Cedars, Lebanon; recipient Alumni Gold Medal Am. U. Beirut; NIH grantee, 1957-69, 58-75, 58-63, 63-73, 68-73; Nat. Eye Inst. grantee, 1972, 73-76, 74-76. Fellow ACS, Internat. Coll. Surgeons; mem. AMA (Knapp award 1968, Hektoen Silver medal 1969, Merit award 1976), Am. Acad. Ophthalmology, Assn. for Research in Vision and Ophthalmology (Fight for Sight award 1966), Am. Ophthalmol. Soc., Internat. Glaucoma Com., Internat. Glaucoma Congress (Ann. Achievement award 1979), Pan Am. Glaucoma Soc. (pres. 1983-87), French Ophthalmologic Soc., Introcular Lens Implant Soc., Internat. Eye Found. Office: 2150 Pennsylvania Ave NW Washington DC 20037-3201

ARMAN, ARA, civil engineering educator; b. Istanbul, Turkey, Sept. 12, 1930; came to U.S., 1955; s. Hayg and Mary Ann (Papazian) A.; m. Claudia Catherine Carr, Nov. 30, 1963; children—Eric H., Michell M. B.S.C.E., U. Tex., 1955, M.S.C.E., 1956. Dist. lab. engr. La. Dept. Transp., Baton Rouge, 1956-60; sr. v.p. GEC, Inc., Baton Rouge, 1998—; soil design engr. La. Dept. Transp., Baton Rouge, 1960-63; asst. prof. civil engring. La. State U., Baton Rouge, 1963-67, assoc. prof., 1967-70, prof., 1970-76, asst. dir. engring. research, 1965-76, chmn. dept. civil engring., 1976-80, assoc. dean Coll. Engring., 1980-87; dir. La. Transp. Rsch. Ctr., Baton Rouge, 1987-90; v.p., prin. Woodward Clyde Cons., Baton Rouge, 1990-98; chair La. Bd. Registration for Profl. Engrs. and Land Surveyors, 1989-90, mem., 1987-93. Contbr. numerous articles on geotech. engring. to profl. jours. Active civic, county and parish assns. Mem. ASCE, ASTM, Nat. Acad. Scis., Transp. Research Bd., La. Engring. Soc., Am. Rd. and Transp. Builders Assn., Internat. Geotextiles Soc. (chmn. com. on rsch.), Internat. Soc. for Soil Mechanics and Found. Engring., Sigma Xi, Tau Beta Pi, Phi Kappa Phi. Mem. Armenian Apostolic Ch. Home: 1148 Verdun Dr Baton Rouge LA 70810-4683 Office: PO Box 84010 Baton Rouge LA 70884-4010*

ARMAN GELENBE, DENIZ, concert pianist; b. Ankara, Turkey, Oct. 8, 1944; came to U.S., 1962; d. Abdul Kerim and Ayse Mediha (Raif) A.; m. Erol Gelenbe, June 8, 1968; 1 child, Pamir Emre. Student, Eastman Sch. Music, 1962-64; MusB, Julliard, 1967, MusM, 1968; postgrad., U. Mich., 1970-71. Founder, artistic dir., prof. piano Paris U., 1979-90; founder, artistic dir. Arman Ensemble, N.C., 1994—, Paris, 1994—; vis. assoc. prof. piano U. Ctrl. Fla., Orlando, 1998—. Recitals in Salle Gaveau, Tonhalle, Zurich, Wigmore Hall, London, Concerts de Midi, Liege; soloist for Ensemble Orchestral Paris, Tokyo, Istanbul, Ankara Philharm., Spain, Philippines, N.C. Triangle Symphony; performance (CD's) with Hadyn Quartet, 1994, Arman Ensemble, 1996. Emerging Artist grantee, 1984. Mem. Nat. Music Tchrs. Assn., Chamber Music Am. Avocations: painting, reading, walking. Home: 100 Detmar Dr Winter Park FL 32789

ARMANIOS, ERIAN ABDELMESSIH, aerospace engineer, educator; b. Cairo, July 6, 1950; came to the U.S., 1980; s. Abdelmessih Armanios; m. Mahera S. Philobos, May 2, 1980; children: Daniel, Laura. BS in Aero. Engring., Cairo U., 1974, MS in Aero. Engring., 1979; PhD in Aerospace Engring., Ga. Inst. Tech., 1985. Teaching asst. U. Cairo, 1974-79, asst. lectr., 1979-80; grad. rsch. asst. Ga. Inst. Tech., Atlanta, 1980-84, rsch. engr. I, 1985-86, asst. prof., 1986-91, assoc. prof., 1991-97, prof., 1997—; cons. Bell Helicopter Textron Inc., Ft. Worth, 1984-85, Rolls-Royce Inc., Atlanta, 1989-95, Allison Engine Co., Indpls. 1995-96, Guided System Techs., 1991-92; judge Ga. Sci. and Engring. Fair, Atlanta, 1987; judge space sci. student program NASA, Atlanta, 1988-98, Internat. Sci. and Engring. Fair, 1998; dir. Ga. Space Grant Consortium, 1991—; adv. bd. mem. Ctr. of Excellence in Sci., Engring. and Math., Morehouse Coll., 1997—. Editor: Interlaminar Fracture of Composites, 1989, Fracture of Composites, 1996, Composite Materials: Fatigue and Fracture, 6th vol., 1997; mem. editl. bd. Jour. Composites Tech. and Rsch., 1992—, Jour. of Nat. Tech. Assn., 1995—; contbr. articles to profl. jours.; patentee in field. Recipient Tchg. Excellence award Ctr. for Enhancement of Tchg. and Learning, Amoco Found., 1990, Outstanding Paper award Jour. Aerospace Engring., 1990, Sigma Xi Outstanding PhD Thesis Advisor award, 1991, 98, Jr. Faculty award, 1991, Ga. Inst. Tech. Faculty Rsch. award 1996, Outstanding Tchr. award, 1999, Sci. Application Internat. Corp. cert. of award, 1990, 95, 97, Editor's Choice award Nat. Libr. of Poetry, 1996. Fellow AIAA (assoc.); mem. ASTM (com. on high modulus fibers and composites 1988); Am. Soc. for Composites, Am. Helicopter Soc. (com. on structures and materials). Office: Sch Aerospace Engring Ga Inst Tech Atlanta GA 30332

ARMBRECHT, WILLIAM HENRY, III, retired lawyer; b. Mobile, Ala., Jan. 13, 1929; s. William Henry and Katherine (Little) A.; m. Dorothy Jean Taylor, Sept. 1, 1951; children—Katherine Handley, William Taylor, Alexander Paterson. B.S., U. Ala., 1950, J.D., 1952. Bar: Ala. 1952, U.S.

Supreme Ct. 1972. Assoc. Inge, Twitty, Armbrecht & Jackson, Mobile, 1952-56; ptnr. Armbrecht, Jackson, McConnell & DeMouy, Mobile, 1956-65, Armbrecht, Jackson & DeMouy, Mobile, 1965-75, Armbrecht, Jackson, DeMouy, Crowe, Holmes & Reeves, Mobile, 1976-94, Armbrecht, Jackson, DeMouy, Crowe, Holmes & Reeves, LLC, 1994-96. Served to 1st lt. JAGC, AUS, 1952-54. Mem. ABA, Ala. Bar Assn. (chmn. grievance com. 1973-74, chmn. sect. corp. banking and bus. law 1976-78), Mobile Bar Assn., Mobile Area C. of C. Found. (bd. dirs. 1990-92), Southeastern Corp. Law Inst. (mem. planning com. 1967-96), Phi Delta Phi, Delta Kappa Epsilon. Episcopalian. Home: 600 Fairfax Rd E Mobile AL 36608-2931 Office: 1300 AmSouth Ctr PO Box 290 Mobile AL 36601-0290

ARMBRISTER, DOUGLAS KENLEY, surgeon; b. Emory, Va., Feb. 20, 1934; s. Victor Stradley and Naomi Lucile (Byrd) A.; m. Nancy Sheri Douglas, Apr. 30, 1960 (div. Sept. 1995); children: Valere Lynn, Victor Kenley, Christopher Douglas, Karen Leigh. BA in English/German, BS in Chemistry/Biology, Emory and Henry Coll., 1955; MD, U. Va., 1959, MS in Surg. Rsch., 1962. Diplomate Am. Bd. Surgery. Intern in surgery U. Va., 1959-60, resident in surgery, 1960-62, 64-67; pvt. practice Marion, Va., 1967—; regional adv. group Va. Regional Med. Program, 1971; subarea coun. chmn. Health Systems Agy.; bd. dirs. Va. Health Quality Ctr.; pres. Smyth County Cmty. Hosp. Med Staff, 1973, chair surg. svcs., 1978—. Bd. visitors Emory and Henry Coll., 1982—. Capt. USAF, 1962-64. Fellow Am. Col. Surgeons: mem. Va. Surg. Soc. (malpractice review panel mem. 1972—), Med. Soc. Va. (review bd. dirs. 1985-95), Southwest Va. Med. Soc., Muller Surg. Soc., Nat. Eagle Scout Assn., Blue Key Nat. Honor Soc. (pres. 1953). Methodist. Avocations: tennis, classical music, singing, piano. Office: 592 Radio Hill Rd Marion VA 24354-4224

ARMBRUST, DAVID B., lawyer; b. Silver City, N.Mex., July 21, 1947; s. Ervin F. and Mary G. (Kennedy) A.; m. Cheryl, Apr. 5, 1970; children: Allison, John. BA, N.Mex. State U., 1970; JD, St. Mary's U., 1974; LLM, U. Tex., 1975. Assoc. Brown, Maroney, Rose, Barbar et al, Austin, 1975-84, Armbrust & Brown, Austin, 1984-90, Strasburger & Price LLP, Austin, 1990-97; ptnr. Armbrust Brown & Davis L.L.P., Austin, 1997—; lectr. in field. Contbr. articles to profl. jours. Bd. dirs. Real Estate Coun. of Austin, 1991-99, Balcones Canyonlands Regional Conservation Plan, Austin, 1988-92; mem. Mayor's Task Force on Water Quality, Austin. Lt. U.S. Army, 1970-71. Recipient Disting. Svc. award City of Austin. Mem. Tex. Coll. Real Estate Attys. (dir. 1991-92), Metro. Club of Austin (dir. 1990-92). Office: Armbrust Brown & Davis LLP 100 Congress Ave Ste 1300 Austin TX 78701-4042

ARMELLINO, MICHAEL RALPH, retired asset management executive; b. Jersey City, Jan. 30, 1940; s. Ralph Michael and Florence (Arturo) A.; m. Patricia Ann Beckett, Mar. 3, 1963; children: Tracy, John, Joseph, Peter. BS in Econs., U. Pa., 1961; MBA, NYU, 1963. Chartered Fin. Analyst. Jr. analyst F.I. DuPont, N.Y.C., 1963-64; transp. analyst Standard & Poors, N.Y.C., 1964-67, Goodbody & Co., N.Y.C., 1967, Lord, Abbett & Co., N.Y.C., 1967-69; sr. transportation analyst Goldman, Sachs & Co., N.Y.C., 1970-90, dir. rsch., 1984-88, ptnr. in charge rsch., 1989-90; chmn., chief exec. officer Goldman, Sachs Asset Mgmt., 1991-94; ltd. ptnr. GS & Co., 1995—; mem. N.Y. Stock Exch. (allied); bd. dirs. Canadian Nat. Ry. Bd. Mem. bd. overseers Stern Sch. Bus. NYU, 1994—; trustee Peddie Sch., 1996—, chmn. investment com. Mem. Benjamin Franklin Soc., U. Pa. Alumni Assn., Soc. Airline Analysts (pres. 1983-84). Roman Catholic. Home: 9 Sigtim Dr Little Falls NJ 07424-2422

ARMENAKAS, ANTHONY EMMANUEL, aerospace educator; b. Mytilene, Greece, Aug. 23, 1924; came to U.S., 1946; s. Emmanuel Anthony and Efterpe (Sakis) A.; m. Stella Dimitri Petroutsa, Jan. 3, 1950 (dec. Jan. 1988); children: Alexandra Daphne, Noel Anthony, Melina Cybel. BSCE, Ga. Inst. Tech., 1950; MSCE, Ill. Inst. Tech., 1952; PhD in Applied Mechanics, Columbia U., 1959. Registered profl. engr., N.Y., N.J., Greece. Instr. Ill. Inst. Tech., Chgo., 1950-52; sr. structural engr. Edwards Kelcey and Beck Cons. Engrs., Newark, 1952-54; ptnr. Rynar Armenakas and McCann Cons. Engrs., Newark, 1954-59; lectr. civil engring. CUNY, N.Y.C., 1954-57; assoc. prof. civil engring. Cooper Union for the Advancement Sci. and Art, N.Y.C., 1958-65; prof. engring. sci. U. Fla., Gainesville, 1965-67; prof. aerospace Poly. U., Bklyn., 1967—; Fulbright lectr. to Greece, 1972-73, 73-74; prof., dir. Inst. Structural Analysis, Nat. Tech. U., Athens, Greece, 1977-84; vis. prof. divsn. engring. Brown U., Providence, 1964-65; cons. Vector Engring., Springfield, N.J., 1954-59; rsch. cons. Poly. Inst., Bklyn., 1962-67, Northwestern U., Evanston, Ill., 1962-65; pres. Stress-Optics, Inc., Queens, N.Y., 1970-72; bd. dirs. Greek r.r.s, 1978-80; vice-chmn. bd. dirs. Greek agy. for design and rsch. earthquake protection, 1989-92. Author: Free Vibrations of Circular Cylindrical Shells, 1969, Tensor Analysis for Engineers, 1974, Classical Structure Analysis-A Modern Approach, 1988, Modern Structural Analysis-The Matrix Method Approach, 1991; patentee in field; contbr. articles to profl. jours. Chmn. bd. dirs. Poulos Philanthropic Found., Athens, Greece. Fellow ASCE, ASME. Avocation: photography. Home: 52 Clark St Brooklyn NY 11201-2402 also: Kifissou, 3A Xalandri Attica, 15234 Athens Greece Office: Polytechnic Univ 333 Jay St Brooklyn NY 11201-2990

ARMENAKAS, NOEL ANTHONY, medical educator; b. Orange, N.J., Sept. 29, 1958; s. Anthony E. and Stella P. (Petroutsa) A.; m. Macrene R. Alexiades, Oct. 26, 1996. MD, U. Athens, Greece, 1985. Diplomate Am. Bd. Urology. Intern surgery Lenox Hill Hosp., N.Y.C., 1985-86; resident surgery Monmouth Med. Ctr., Long Branch, N.J., 1986-87; resident urology Lenox Hill Hosp., N.Y.C., 1987-91; fellow trauma and reconstructive surgery U. Calif., San Francisco, 1991-92, clin. instr. dept. urology, 1991-92; clin. instr. dept. surgery Cornell U. Med. Coll., N.Y.C., 1992-94; clin. asst. prof. dept. urology Cornell U. Med. Sch., N.Y.C., 1994—; mem. oper. rm. com. Lenox Hill Hosp., 1990, outpatient clinic com., 1993—; mem. ChubbHealth Physician Adv. Panel, 1994—; mem. scholarship com. Hellenic Med. Assn.; attending staff San Francisco (Calif.) Gen. Hosp., 1991-92; dir., physician-in-charge Outpatient Urologic Clinics; attending staff N.Y. Presbyn. Hosp., N.Y.C., 1992—, Lenox Hill Hosp., N.Y.C., 1992—; lectr. in field. Contbr. chpts. to books and articles to profl. jours. Fellow ACS; mem. AMA, Internat. Soc. Urology, Am. Assn. Clin. Urologists, Am. Urol. Assn., Hellenic Med. Assn., Soc. for Urology and Engring., Soc. Genitourinary and Reconstructive Surgeons. Avocations: skiing, tennis, traveling. Office: New York Urological Assocs 880 5th Ave New York NY 10021-4951

ARMENTROUT, DEBRA CATHERINE, neonatal nurse practitioner; b. Grand Forks, N.D., Mar. 26, 1953; d. Howard and Delores (Wilhelmi) Armentrout. BSN, U. N.D., 1975; MSN, U. Tex. Health Ctr., Houston, 1985. RN, Tex. Staff nurse Turner Newborn ICU, Hermann Hosp., Houston, 1975-79, 80-83; staff nurse, charge nurse newborn ICU/pediatrics Rogue Valley Meml. Hosp., Medford, Oreg., 1979-80; neonatal transport nurse Turner Newborn ICU, Hermann Hosp., Houston, 1984-86, 88-90, clin. nurse specialist, 1986-88; staff nurse nurseries and pediatrics Sierra Vista Regional Med. Ctr., San Luis Obispo, Calif., 1988; instr. clin. pediatrics, assoc. coord. neonatal nurse practioner U. Tex. Health Ctr., Houston, 1990-94, asst. prof. pediatrics, 1994—; clin. asst. prof. gen. instrn. Sch. Nursing U. Tex.; presenter in field. Contbr. articles to profl. publs. Mem. Nat. Assn. Neonatal Nurses (corr. mem. spl. interest group advanced practice role com., sec. practice com. 1990-94), Am. Acad. Nurse Practitioners, Houston Area Assn. Neonatal Nurses (sec. 1993-94, pres. 1995), Sigma Theta Tau. Office: 2 NT 9100 2C LBJ 5656 Kelley St Houston TX 77026-1967

ARMENTROUT, STEVEN ALEXANDER, oncologist; b. Morgantown, W.Va., Aug. 22, 1933; s. Walter W. and Dorothy (Gasch) A.; m. Johanna Ruszkay; children—Marc, Susan, Sandra, Nancy. A.B., U. Chgo., 1953, M.D., 1959. Intern U. Hosp., Cleve., 1959-60; resident in medicine, fellow Am. Cancer Soc. Western Res. U. Hosp., 1960-63; project dir. USPHS, 1963-65; asst. prof. Case Western Res. U. Med. Sch., 1965-71; mem. faculty U. Calif. Med. Sch., Irvine, 1971—; prof. medicine, chief divsn. hematology-oncology U. Calif. Med. Sch., 1978—, also dir. program in oncology.; pres. med. staff U. Calif.-Irvine Med. Ctr., 1983-85; researcher in multiple sclerosis. Mem. Am. Assn. Cancer Research, AAUP, ACP, Am. Cancer Soc. (chmn. bd. 1973, pres. Orange County chpt. 1985-86), AMA, Am. Soc. Clin. Oncology, Am. Soc. Hematology, Orange County Med. Assn., Am. Soc. Internal Medicine, Calif. Med. Assn., Cen. Soc. Clin. Research, Leukemia Soc. Am., Orange County Chief of Staff Council. Office: 101 The City Dr S Orange CA 92868-3201

ARMEY, RICHARD KEITH (DICK ARMEY), congressman; b. Cando, N.D., July 7, 1940; s. Glen Forest and Marion (Gutschlog) A.; m. Susan Byrd; children: Kathryn, David, Scott A., Chip, Scott Oxendine. B.A., Jamestown Coll., N.D., 1963; M.A., U. N.D., 1964; Ph.D., U. Okla., Norman, 1969. Mem. econs. faculty U. Mont., 1964-65; asst. prof. West Tex. State U., 1967-68, Austin Coll., 1968-72; assoc. prof. North Tex. State U., 1972-77, chmn. dept. econs., 1977-84; mem. 99th-104th Congresses from 26th Tex. dist., Washington, D.C., 1985—; former mem. edn. and labor com., chmn. ho. rep. conf. com., 1992-94, former mem. joint economic com., majority leader, 1995—. Author: Price Theory, 1977, The Freedom Revolution, 1995, The Flat Tax-A Citizen's Guide to the Facts on What it Will Do For You, Your Country, and Your Pocketbook, 1996. Office: Ste 3050 9901 Valley Ranch Pkwy E Irving TX 75063-6707 also: US Ho of Reps 301 Cannon Bldg Washington DC 20515-4326*

ARMFIELD, FRED MUNGER, minister; b. Woodruff, S.C., Sept. 23, 1949; s. Frank, Sr. and Minnie I. (Gist) A.; m. Deborah Ann Stackhouse, June 28, 1975; children: Phaedra, Xavier, Medea. BS, S.C. State Coll., 1975, MA, 1977; MDiv, Erskine Theol. Sem., Due West, S.C., 1990. Lic. minister African Methodist Episcopal Ch., 1987. Sch. tchr. McCormick (S.C.) Sch. System, 1977-79; program dir., coord. Multi-Mental Retardation Bd., Edgefield, S.C., 1979-81; masseur, counselor Greenwood, S.C., 1981-87; county councilman Greenwood County, 1995—; pastor Hist. Mt. Pisgah AME Ch., Greenwood, The Old Abbeville Cir./St. Paul - Mulberry AME, Calhoun Falls, S.C., The New Mt. Olive AME Ch., Donalds, S.C., St. Matthews AME Ch., Newberry, S.C. Bd. dirs. Upper Savannah Coun. of Govt., 1994—; bd. dirs. Greenwood City Zoning Bd. of Appeals, Greenwood, 1985-91, Greenwood City Adv. Bd., 1982-87; mem. Greenwood County Dem. Party, 1977—; officer Greenwood United Soc. of the Blind, 1987—; mgmt. v.p. Greenwood Jaycees; mem. Greenwood Black Ministerial Assn., Greenwood Grass Roots Com., others. Named Black male Citizen of the Yr., Greenwood County, 1982, Hero of Yr., Nat. Fedn. of Blind, Greenwood, 1981; recipient Jefferson award WYFF TV Greenville, 1987. Mem. Samaria Lodge #239 F & AM, Nat. Rehab. Orgn., Nat. Masseur's Orgn., Am. Psychol. Assn. Democrat. African Methodist Episcopal. Avocations: writing, croquet, organizing and planning programs. Home: 111 Wisewood Cir Greenwood SC 29646-8601

ARMIGER, GENE GIBBON, telecommunications executive, consultant; b. Balt., Oct. 17, 1931; s. Edward Gibbon and Irene Juliet (Peppler) A.; m. Cynthia Clare Carroll, Feb. 14, 1954 (div. 1971); children: Karen Lee, Scott Andrew; m. Dorothy Sue Looney, Feb. 17, 1979. Archtl. student, U. Md., 1951-52, Md. Inst., 1956-58. Cert. lic. capt. USCG. Project engr. Cook Electric Co., Chgo., 1958-62, U.S. Underseas Cable Corp., Washington, 1962; gen. mgr. sales/mktg. Superior Cable Corp., Hickory, N.C., 1963-74; dir. sales/mktg. No. Telecom Inc., Nashville, 1974-76, Porta Systems Inc., Syosset, N.Y., 1976-78; founder/chief exec. officer Armiger & Assocs. Inc., Ft. Worth, Tex., 1978-86; v.p. Richard Thomas & Assocs., Chgo., 1986-88, Suttle Armiger Telecom, Hector, Minn., 1988-90; cons. Telecom. Cons., Ft. Worth, 1990—; mem. FCC Telecom Industry Ad-hoc com. Washington, 1979-87. Contbr. articles to profl. jours. Bd. dirs. Telecommunications Industry Assocs., Washington, 1985-87. Sgt. U.S. Army, 1951-61, Korea. Mem. Am. Mgmt. Assn., U.S. Power Squadron, USCG Aux., Tel. Pioneer Assn., Ind. Tel. Pioneer Assn. (v.p. 1968-69), Va. Yacht Club, Petroleum Club, Ridglea Country Club, Masons. Republican. Episcopalian. Avocations: deep water sailing, golf, tennis, snow skiing, hunting. Home: 5330 Collinwood Ave Fort Worth TX 76107-3634

ARMINANA, RUBEN, academic administrator, educator; b. Santa Clara, Cuba, May 15, 1947; came to U.S., 1961; s. Aurelio Ruben and Olga Petrona (Nart) A.; m. Marne Olson, June 6, 1954; children: Cesar A. Martino, Maria G. Arminana. AA, Hill Jr. Coll., 1966; BA, U. Tex., 1968, MA, 1970; PhD, U. New Orleans, 1983; postgrad. Inst. of Applied Behavioral Scis., Nat. Tng. Labs., 1971. Nat. assoc. dir. Phi Theta Kappa, Canton, Miss., 1968-69; dir. ops. and tng. Inter-Am. Ctr., Loyola U., New Orleans, 1969-71; administrv. analyst City of New Orleans, 1972, adminstrv. analyst and organizational devel. and tng. cons., 1972-78; anchor and reporter part time STA. WWL-TV, New Orleans, 1973-81; v.p. Commerce Internat. Corp., New Orleans, 1978-83; exec. asst. to sr. v.p. Tulane U., New Orleans, 1983-85, assoc. exec. v.p., 1985-87, v.p., asst. to pres., 1987-88; v.p. fin. and devel. Calif. State Poly U., Pomona, 1988-92; pres. Sonoma State U., 1992—; TV news cons., New Orleans, 1981-88; lectr. Internat. Trade Mart, New Orleans, 1983-89, U.S. Dept. Commerce, New Orleans. Co-author: Hemisphere West-El Futuro, 1968; co-editor: Colloquium on Central America-A Time for Understanding, Background Readings, 1985. Bd. dirs. Com. on Alcoholism and Substance Abuse, 1978-79, SER, Jobs for Progress, Inc., 1974-82, Citizens United for Responsive Broadcasting, Latin Am. Festival Com; dir., bd. advisors Sta. WDSU-TV, 1974-77; mem. Bus. Govt. Rsch., 1987-88, Coun. Advancment of Support to Edn.; mem. League of United Latin Am. Citizens, Mayor's Latin Am. Adv. Com., Citizens to Preserve the Charter, Met. Area Com., Mayor's Com. on Crime. Kiwanis scholar, 1966, Books scholar, 1966. Mem. Assn. U. Related Rsch. Prks., L.A. Higher Edn. Roundtable, Soc. Coll. and U. Planning, Nat. Assn. Coll. and U. Bus. Officers Cou., Am. Econ. Assn., Assn. of Evolutionary Econs., Am. Polit. Sci. Assn., AAUP, Western Coll. Assn. (pres. 1994-95), Latin Am. C. of C. (founding dir. New Orleans and River Region 1976-83), Cuban Profl. Club, Phi Theta Kappa, Omicron Delta Epsilon, Sigma Delta Pi, Delta Sigma Pi. Democrat. Roman Catholic. Avocation: mask collecting. Office: Sonoma State U 1801 E Cotati Ave Rohnert Park CA 94928-3609

ARMISTEAD, JOHN GRAYSON, journalist; b. Mobile, Ala., June 4, 1941; s. William Linsey Armistead and Serena (Summersell) Tatum; m. Sandra Grant, July 12, 1968; children: William, David. BA, Miss. Coll., 1963; MDiv, Golden Gate Bapt. Theol. Sem., 1966; DMin, New Orleans Bapt. Theol. Sem., 1975; MA, U. Miss., 1987. Tchr. Meridian (Miss.) H.S., 1970-71; min. First Bapt. Ch., Meridian, 1971-75; pastor Waimea (Hawaii) Bapt. Ch., 1975-77, Kailua (Hawaii) Bapt. Ch., 1977-79, Calvary Bapt. Ch., Tupelo, Miss., 1979-94; religion editor N.E. Miss. Daily Jour., Tupelo, Miss., 1995—. Author: A Legacy of Vengeance, 1994, A Home Coming for Murder, 1995, Cruel as the Grave, 1996. Baptist. Office: NE Miss Daily Jour PO Box 909 Tupelo MS 38802-0909

ARMISTEAD, KATHERINE KELLY (MRS. THOMAS B. ARMISTEAD, III), interior designer, travel consultant, civic worker; b. Pitts., Apr. 14, 1926; d. Joseph Anthony and Katherine Arnold (Manning) Kelly; grad. Finch Jr. Coll., 1946; m. Thomas Boyd Armistead, III, Nov. 29, 1952; children: Katherine Kelly (Mrs. W. Michael Roark), Thomas Boyd IV. Editor news Sta. WOR, N.Y.C., 1946-51; with Dumont TV, 1951-52; editor Social Service Rev., L.A., 1956-57; interior designer, L.A., 1963—; travel cons. Gilner Internat. Travels, Beverly Hills, Calif., 1980—. Editorial bd. Previews Mag., 1984-87. Pres. Jrs. Social Svc., L.A., 1962-64; nat. chpt. chmn. Associated Alumnae of Sacred Heart, 1960-66; pres. Las Floristas, 1967-68; pres. L.A. Orphanage Guild, 1969-70; coord. Jr. Mannequin Assisteens, Assistance League So. Calif., 1971-72; pres. docent coun. L.A. County Mus. Art, 1976-77, pres. decorative arts coun., 1977-80, chmn. Am. Antiques Conf., 1979-81, mem. costume coun., mem. past pres.' coun., 1981—, mem. capital gifts campaign com.; bd. dirs. L.A. Orphanage Guild, 1970—; Cert. travel cons. Recipient Eve award Assistance League So. Calif. Mem. Am. Soc. Travel Agts., Inst. Cert. Travel Agts. (cert.), Lady Comdr. with star Equestrian Order of the Holy Sepulchre of Jerusalem. Republican. Roman Catholic. Clubs: Birnam Wood Golf (Santa Barbara, Calif.), Bel Air Garden.

ARMISTEAD, ROBERT ASHBY, JR., scientific research company executive; b. Roanoke, Va., Feb. 7, 1940; s. Robert Ashby and Lucille Denis (Owen) A.; m. Mona Thornhill, Dec. 26, 1965; children: Robert Ashby III, Wade Owen, Clay Thornhill. BS in Physics with highest honors, Va. Mil. Inst., 1962; MS in Physics, Carnegie Mellon U., 1963, PhD in Nuclear Sci. and Engring., 1966; MBA, U. Santa Clara, 1973. Physicist reactor divsn. Oak Ridge (Tenn.) Nat. Lab., 1964-67; nuclear weapons effects projecy officer Def. Atomic Support Agy., Washington, 1967-69; mgr. radiation physics Stanford Rsch. Inst., Menlo Park, Calif., 1969-77; pres., chmn. Advanced Rsch. and Applications Corp., Sunnyvale, Calif., 1977—; chmn. Calif. innovation com. 1986 White House Conf. Small Bus. Contbr. articles to profl. jours.; patentee x-ray imaging. Bd. dirs. Bay Area Regional Tech. Alliance, VMI Found., bd. trustees. Capt. U.S. Army, 1967-69. Named Innovator of Yr., U.S. Small Bus. Adminstrn., 1987, San Francisco Innovation Person of Yr. Small Bus. Adminstrn., 1987; Spl. fellow Atomic Energy Commn., 1963-64, Oak Ridge Grad. fellow, 1965-66. Mem. Am. Electronics Assn. (mem. procurement com. 1986-87, bd. dirs. 1987-90, mem. exec. com. 1989-90), Nat. Innovation Network (bd. dirs.). Avocations: tennis, golf. Office: Advanced Rsch Applications 425 Lakeside Dr Sunnyvale CA 94086-4704

ARMISTEAD, THOMAS BOYD, III, television and film producer; b. St. Louis, Feb. 18, 1918; s. Thomas Boyd and Alice Townsend (Jones) A; m. Katherine Kelly, Nov. 1952; children: Katherine Armistead Roark, Thomas Boyd IV. BA, Amherst Coll., 1939; B of Theater Arts, 1941; M of Theater Arts, State Theater of Calif., 1942. Producer, dir. Don Lee Mutual, Hollywood, Calif., 1945; dir., dept. head, instr. direction State Theater of Calif., Pasadena, 1946-50; TV dir. live Sta. KTTV, Hollywood, 1948-50; assoc. producer Bing Crosby Enterprises, Inc., Hollywood, 1951-52; owner, producer, dir. Pickwick Pictures, Hollywood, 1953; film producer, dir. J. Walter Thompson, New York City and Hollywood, 1954-58; producer, dir. TV and film for various studios including Screen Gems, Filmways, Paramount, Hollywood, 1959-62; v.p. executive producer Don Fedderson Prodns., Hollywood, 1962-64; producer, dir. various film cos., ABC TV film, Hollywood, 1964—. Producer, dir. TV film and commls.; dir. first full length live dramatic show produced on TV. With USAF, 1940-45. Recipient Christopher award Action for Children's TV Achievement award, 1979; 3 film works disply Mus. Moving Images, London. Mem. Dirs. Guild Am. (TV Council awards Com.), Nat. Acad. TV Arts and Scis. (edn. com.). Republican. Roman Catholic. Club: Les Ambassadeurs (London), Birnam Wood Golf. Avocations: photography, raising orchids, remodeling houses. Home and Office: Armistead Assocs 10373 Ashton Ave Los Angeles CA 90024-5372

ARMISTEAD, WILLIAM SPENCER, communications executive, political organization executive, political writer; b. Atlanta, Aug. 14, 1962; s. James Davenport and Rita Marie Armistead. BA in Philosophy, U. of South, 1984; MEd in Policy Analysis, Vanderbilt U., 1985. Rschr., speechwriter U.S. Dept. Edn., Washington, 1986-87; contbg. editor Conservative Digest mag., Washington, 1987-88; policy dir., speechwriter Office Rep. Beau Boulter, U.S. Ho. of Reps., Washington, 1988-89; speechwriter Rep. Nat. Com., Washington, 1989-90; mng. editor White House Bltn., Tysons Corner, Va., 1990-93; v.p. fed. and state campaigns Citizens for Sound Economy, Washington, 1993-99; v.p. sales and ops. Bull. News Network, Inc., McLean, Va., 1999—; sr. v.p. Bltn. News Network, Tysons Corner, 1990-93, corp. sec., 1993—. Mem. Univ. Club Washington. Republican. Episcopalian. E-mail: warmistead@bulletinnews.com. Home: 1003 Hillwood Ave Falls Church VA 22042 Office: Bulletin News Network Inc Ste 320 8260 Greensboro Dr Mc Lean VA 22102

ARMISTEAD, WILLIS WILLIAM, university administrator, veterinarian; b. Detroit, Oct. 28, 1916; s. Eber Merrill and Josephine Brunell (Kindred) A.; m. Martha Sidney Clark, Sept. 17, 1938 (dec. 1964); children: Willis William, Jack Murray, Sidney Merrill; m. Mary Wallace Nelson, 1967. D.V.M., Tex. A&M Coll., 1938; M.Sc., Ohio State U., 1950; Ph.D., U. Minn., 1955. Diplomate: hon. diplomate; Am. Coll. Veterinary Surgeons, Am. Coll. Veterinary Preventive Medicine. Pvt. practice veterinary medicine, 1938-40; instr. Sch. Veterinary Medicine Tex. A&M U., 1940-42, asst. prof. to prof. Sch. Veterinary Medicine, 1946-53, dean Sch. Veterinary Medicine, 1953-57; dean Coll. Veterinary Medicine Mich. State U., East Lansing, 1957-74; dean Coll. Veterinary Medicine, U. Tenn., Knoxville, 1974-79, chmn. strategic planning adv. com., 1988-89; v.p. agr. U. Tenn. System, 1979-87; collaborator animal diseases and parasite rsch. divsn. Dept. Agr., 1954-65; cons., adviser commn. veterinary edn. of South So. Regional Edn. Bd., 1953-56; mem. gov.'s sci. adv. bd., 1958-60; nat. cons. to Air Force Surgeon Gen., 1960-62; mem. adv. coun. Inst. Lab. Animal Resources, NRC, 1962-66; pres. Assn. Am. Veterinary Med. Colls., 1964-65, 73-74, Spl. award, 1983; veterinary med. resident investigators selection com. U.S. VA, 1967-70; veterinary medicine rev. com. Bur. Health Professions Edn. and Manpower Tng., HEW, 1967-71; mem. Nat. Bd. Veterinary Med. Examiners, 1970-74; mem. adv. panel for veterinary medicine Inst. Medicine, NAS, 1972-74; mem. bd. agr. and renewable resources NRC, 1976-77; 1st Allam lectr. Am. Coll. Veterinary Surgeons, 1972; Conti Meml. keynote lectr. Ariz.-Calif.-Nev. Veterinary Conf., 1994. Contbg. author: Canine Surgery, rev. edit, 1957, Canine Medicine, rev. edit, 1959; editor: The N.Am. Veterinarian, 1950-56, Jour. Veterinary Med. Edn, 1974-80; assoc. editor: Jour. Am. Animal Hosp. Assn., 1964-70; contbr. tech. articles to profl. jours. Bd. dirs. Tenn. Farm bur. Fedn., 1979-87, Tenn. Coun. Coops., 1982-87, Tenn. 4-H Club Found., 1979-87, Tenn. Agrl. Hall of Fame, 1979-87; mem. Tenn. State Soil Conservation Com., 1979-87; mem. Southwide adv. com. So. Agribus. Forum, 1979-87. Maj. Vet. Corps AUS, 1942-46. Recipient Meritorious Svc. award Selective Svc. System, 1972; hon. alumnus Mich. State U., 1972; recipient Disting. Alumnus award Coll. Vet. Medicine, Tex. A&M U., 1980, 75th Anniversary Achievement award Tex. A&M U. Coll. Vet. Medicine, 1991; named V.P Emeritus, U. Tenn., 1987—. Mem. AAAS, U.S. Animal Health Assn., Am. Vet. Med. Assn. (pres. 1957-58, award 1977), Tex. Vet. Med. Assn. (pres. 1947-48), Mich. Vet. Med. Assn. (trustee Edn. and Sci. Trust 1970-74), Fedn. Assns. Schs. of Health Professions (pres. 1975), Tenn. Vet. Med. Assn. (Lifetime Achievement award 1995), Inst. Medicine of NAS, N.Y. Acad. Scis., Rotary (pres. 1987-88), Sigma Xi, Phi Kappa Phi, Alpha Zeta, Phi Zeta, Omega Tau Sigma (nat. Gamma award Ohio State U. 1962), Phi Eta Sigma, Gamma Sigma Delta, Omicron Delta Kappa. Episcopalian. Lodge: Rotary. Home: 1101 Cherokee Blvd Knoxville TN 37919-7852

ARMITAGE, KENNETH BARCLAY, biology educator, ecologist; b. Steubenville, Ohio, Apr. 18, 1925; s. Albert Kenneth and Virginia Ethel (Barclay) A.; m. Katie Lou Hart, June 5, 1953; children: Carol, Keith, Kevin. BS summa cum laude, Bethany Coll., W.Va., 1949; MS, U. Wis.-Madison, 1951, PhD, 1954. Instr. U. Wis.-Green Bay, 1954-55; instr. U. Wis.-Wausau, 1955-56; asst. prof. biology U. Kans., Lawrence, 1956-62, assoc. prof., 1962-66, prof., 1966-96, William J. Baumgartner disting. prof., 1987-96, chmn. dept. systematics & ecology, 1982-88, dir. environ. studies program, 1976-82, dir. exptl. and applied ecology program, 1974-94, prof. emeritus, 1996—; vis. prof. U. Modena, Italy, 1989; mem. com. examiners Grad. Record Exam. Biology Test, 1986-92, chmn., 1988-92; sr. investigator Rocky Mountain Biol. Lab., Gothic, Colo., 1962—, trustee, 1969-86, pres. bd. trustees, 1985-86. Author: (lab. manual) Investigations in General Biology, (with others) Principles of Modern Biology; contbr. articles to profl. jours.; mem. editl. bd.: Ethology, Ecology and Evolution, 1989—, Ibex Jour. Mountain Ecology, 1994—, Oecologia Montana, 1996—. Pres. Douglas County chpt. Zero Population Growth, 1969-71; bd. dirs. Children's Hour, Inc., Lawrence, 1969-70. Served with U.S. Army, 1943-46, ETO. Recipient Antarctic medal NSF, 1968, Edn. Service award U. Kans., 1979, Alumni Achievement award Bethany Coll., 1989. Fellow AAAS, Animal Behavior Soc.; mem. Am. Soc. Naturalists (treas. 1984-86), Am. Inst. Biol. Scis. (mem. task force for 90s), Ecol. Soc. Am., Am. Soc. Zoologists, Am. Soc. Mammalogists (C. Hart Merriam award 1997), Orgn. Biol. Field Stations (v.p. 1986-87, pres. 1988-89), Sigma Xi, Phi Beta Kappa, Beta Beta Beta, Gamma Sigma Kappa. Avocations: stamp collecting, gardening, natural history, western history. Home: 505 Ohio St Lawrence KS 66044-2245 Office: Univ Kansas Dept Ecology & Evolutionary Biology Lawrence KS 66045-2106

ARMITAGE, SHANNON LYN, editor-in-chief newspaper; b. Hennepin County, Minn., June 10, 1971; d. Joseph and Marlene A. BA, Met. State U., St. Paul, Minn., 1994. Pub. affairs specialist Minn. ANG. Editor-in-chief The Metropolitan, St. Paul, 1992-94, The Alley, Mpls., 1994—. Editor: Minnesota Wing Tips (Minn. Civil Air Patrol, St. Paul), 1997—; contbr. articles to profl. jours. Vice-pres. Twin Cities Neighborhood and Comm. Press Assn., 1995—; bd. dirs. Cooperating Fund Drive. Sgt. USAFR, 1991-98. Mem. Soc. Profl. Journalists, AF Sgts. Assn., Minn. Nat. Guard Enlisted Assn. Office: The Alley 2600 E Franklin Ave Minneapolis MN 55406-1104

ARMITAGE, THOMAS EDWARD, library director; b. Torrington, Wyo., Dec. 11, 1946; s. Ross Eugene Armitage and Mary Kathleen (Donley) Wieland; m. Linda Lou Theisen, May 23, 1987; children: Anne, Nicholas,

Rachel. AA in History, Santa Barbara (Calif.) C.C., 1971; BA in History, Kans. State U., Pittsburg, 1973; MLS, U. Mo., 1974. Asst. dir. Ottumwa (Iowa) Pub. Libr., 1975-77; libr. dir. Ft. Dodge (Iowa) Pub. Libr., 1977-86, Cedar Rapids (Iowa) Pub. Libr., 1987—. With USN, 1967-69. Mem. ALA, Iowa Libr. Assn., Iowa Urban Pub. Libr. Assn. (pres. 1999—, sec. 1995-98), Linn County Libr. Assn. (v.p. 1993—), Linn County Libr. Consortium (sec. 1995—), Rotary, Greater Cedar Rapids C. of C. Office: Cedar Rapids Pub Libr 500 1st St SE Cedar Rapids IA 52401-2002

ARMOCIDA, PATRICIA ANNE, managed health care official; b. Portland, Maine, July 29, 1956; d. Gerald Arthur and Aileen Patricia (Malone) Faneuf; m. William Joseph Armocida, June 21, 1986. BS, Purdue U., 1980; MBA, Boston U., 1983. RN, Mass. Staff nurse New Eng. Med. Ctr., Boston, 1980-81, Mass. Gen. Hosp., Boston, 1981; cons. Health Data Inst., Boston, 1981-82; cons. Blue Cross/Blue Shield Assn., Chgo., 1983, asst. to the pres., 1983-85; mgr. health svcs. Blue Cross/Blue Shield Ill., 1985-86, dir. HMO, dir. utilization mgmt., 1987-90; v.p. mktg. Health Mgmt. Strategies, Alexandria, Va., 1990-91; dir. med. mgmt. Blue Cross and Blue Shield of the Nat. Capital Area, Washington, 1991-92; pres. Health Dimensions, Inc., Seattle, 1992—; lectr. George Washington U., 1991-94; surveyor Nat. Com. Quality Assurance, 1998—; compliance reviewer Medicare-Health Care Fin. Assn. Editor Health Plans, 1996-97. Vol. Harborview Hosp. Literacy Program; mem. rev. com. Nat. Inst. Drug Abuse Project; campaign vol. United Way, Chgo., 1988. Boston U. scholar, 1983; recipient Leadership award YWCA and Blue Cross/Blue Shield, 1988. Mem. Am. Assn. Health Plans (bd. dirs.), Case Mgmt. Soc. Am. Roman Catholic. Avocations: horse training, snow and water skiing, swimming.

ARMOR, DAVID J., sociologist; b. Long Beach, Calif., Nov. 11, 1938; s. John Edward Armor and Marie (Huffine) White; m. Marilyn Louise Sells, Sept. 7, 1958; children: Adrienne, Daniel. BA with highest honors, U. Calif., Berkeley, 1961; PhD, Harvard U., 1966. Asst. prof. sociology Harvard U., Cambridge, Mass., 1965-70, assoc. prof., 1970-73; sr. social scientist Rand Corp., Santa Monica, Calif., 1973-82; pres. Nat. Policy Analysts Inc., Santa Monica, 1981-86; acting asst. sec. Dept. Def., Washington, 1986-89; rsch. prof. George Mason U., 1992-95, 1995—; vis. prof. sociology UCLA, 1972-73, Rutgers U., 1991-92; cons. Nat. Inst. on Alcohol Abuse and Alcoholism, Washington, 1972-73, Dept. Def., Washington, 1982-83, U.S. Commn. on Civil Rights, Washington, 1984-86. Author: American School Counselor, 1968, The Data-Text Primer, 1972, Alcoholism and Treatment, 1976, Forced Justice: School Desegregation and the Law, 1995. Mem. L.A. Bd. Edn., 1985-86; assoc. Pepperdine U., Malibu, 1982-86; Rep. nominee for U.S. Congress 23d Calif. dist., 1982. Fellow Woodrow Wilson Found., 1961-62, Ph.D. fellow Russell Sage Found., 1963-65. Mem. Am. Sociol. Assn. Home: 5 Sharp Rock Rd Sperryville VA 22740-2333

ARMOR, JOHN N., chemical company scientist and research manager; b. Phila., Sept. 14, 1944; s. Lloyd N. and Cornelia Armor; m. Connie B. Korzuch, Dec. 17, 1966; children: Kimberly, Gregory, Jennifer. BS in Chemistry, Pa. State U., 1966; PhD, Stanford U., 1970. Asst. prof. chemistry Boston U., 1970-74; group leader Allied Signal Corp., Morristown, N.J., 1974-85; prin. rsch. assoc. Air Products and Chems. Inc., Allentown, Pa., 1985—; head corp. catalysis rsch. ctr. Air Products, 1999—; chmn. Inorganic Gordon Rsch. Conf., New London, N.H., 1988; gen. chmn. 2d World Congress on Environ. Catalysis. Editor Applied Catalysis, 1987-96; mem. editorial bd. Microporous Materials, Indsl. and Engring. Chemistry, Japanese Catalysis Surveys, others; contbr. more than 100 articles to profl. jours. Recipient Houdry award Excellence in Applied Catalysis N.Am. Catalysis Soc., 1997. Mem. AICE, Am. Chem. Soc. (organizer symposium on environ. catalysis 1993), Am. Ceramic Soc., Materials Rsch. Soc., N.Y. Acad. Scis. (chmn. catalysis sect. 1983-85), The N.Am. Catalysis Soc. (bd. dirs., treas. 1993—), Catalysis Club Phila. (award for Excellence in Catalysis 1995), Catalysis Club N.Y. (bd. dirs.). Achievements include more than 45 patents. Home: 1608 Barkwood Dr Orefield PA 18069-8923 Office: Air Products & Chem Inc 7201 Hamilton Blvd Allentown PA 18195-1526

ARMOUR, DAVID EDWARD PONTON, trade association administrator; b. Toronto, Ont., Can., Sept. 6, 1921; s. Ponton Edward Burton and Grace Marie (Magann) A.; m. Kathleen Marie Bridge-Williams, May 24, 1945 (div. Nov. 1974); children: Richard, Robin, Moira, Sheila, Anne; m. 2d Eve Denise Arnoldi, Oct. 8, 1974. Student, Trinity Coll., Port Hope, Ont.; BS Mil., Royal Mil. Coll., Kingston, Ont. Gen. mgr. woodland ops. Hammermill Paper, Erie, Pa.; gen. mgr. woodland ops. Howard Smith, Montreal, Que., Can., 1946-58; mgmt. cons. Currie, Cooper & Lybrands, Toronto, 1958-65; corp. dir. orgn. Salada Foods Ltd., Toronto, 1965-67; v.p., gen. mgr. Crush Internat., Toronto, 1967-75; pres. Elec. and Electronic Mfrs. Assn. Can., Toronto, 1976-86; chmn. exec. council Can. Soft Drink Assn., Toronto, 1969-74; bd. dirs. Fedn. Aggregate Studies, Toronto, 1981-83; dir. Yorkminster Realty, 1986-90; ret., 1992—; mem. sectoral adv. group on internat. trade Can./U.S. Free Trade Negotiations. Aide-de-camp Lt.-Gov. Ont., 1959-63; pres. Uxbridge Ratepayers Assn., Ont., 1970-74. Served to maj. Can. Army, 1942-46, ETO. Decorated Can. decoration Dept. Nat. Def., Ottawa. Progressive-Conservative. Clubs: Toronto North York Hunt (Aurora, Ont.); Royal Can. Mil. Inst. (Toronto).

ARMOUR, JAMES LOTT, lawyer; b. Jackson, Tenn., May 19, 1938; s. Quintin and Frances (Breeden) A.; m. Nancy Stokes Johnson, Mar. 17, 1962; 1 son, John Lawson. BA, Vanderbilt U., 1961, LLB, 1964; LLM, So. Meth. U., 1967. Bar: Tenn. 1964, Tex. 1965, U.S. Supreme Ct. 1967, N.Y. 1969, Okla. 1972. Assoc. firm Turner Rodgers Winn Scurlock & Terry, Dallas, 1965-67; internat. atty. Mobil Corp., N.Y.C. and London, 1967-71, Phillips Petroleum Co., Bartlesville, Okla., 1971-74; asst. gen. counsel Conoco, Inc., Stamford, Conn., 1974-83; ptnr. firm Locke Liddell & Sapp LLP, Dallas, 1984—. chair adv. bd. oil and gas SW Legal Fedn.; mem. Dallas Com. on Fgn. Rels.; former mem. alumni bd. Vanderbilt Law Sch. Mem. ABA, Assn. of Bar of City of N.Y., State Bar Tex., Dallas Bar Assn., Petroleum Club, Phi Delta Phi, Kappa Sigma. Episcopalian. Home: 4541 Belfort Pl Dallas TX 75205-3618 Office: Locke Liddell & Sapp LLP 2200 Ross Ave Ste 2200 Dallas TX 75201-2748

ARMSTRONG, ALEXANDRA, financial advisor; b. Washington, Sept. 26, 1939; d. Rhoda Elizabeth (Forbes) Armstrong; m. Robert B. Phillips III, Aug. 1966 (div. Mar. 1971). BA in History, Newton (Mass.) Coll. Sacred Heart, 1960. Cert. fin. planner. Exec. sec. Ferris & Co., Washington, 1961-66, registered rep., 1966-77; sr. v.p. Julia Walsh & Sons, Washington, 1977-83; pres. Alexandra Armstrong Advisors Inc., Washington, 1983-91; chmn. Armstrong, Welch & MacIntyre Inc., Washington, 1991—; bd. experts Boardroom Reports, 1987—, Bottom Line Personal, 1990—. Author: On Your Own: A Widow's Passage To Emotional and Financial Wellbeing, 1993. Mem. Washington Jr. League, 1961—; vice chmn. Nat. Coun. Friends of Kennedy Ctr., Washington, 1987-91; v.p. Deferred Giving Nat. Capital coun. Boy Scouts Am., 1988—; mem. bd. visitors Sch. Bus. Georgetown U., 1988-91; v.p. programs Internat. Women's Forum, 1991-93; bd. dirs. Reading is Fundamental, 1993—. Named Bus. Woman of Yr. Washington Bus. and Profl. Women's Club, 1978; recipient award of excellence for commerce Boston Coll. Alumni Assn., 1985, Woman Who Makes a Difference award Internat. Women's Forum, 1992, Silver Beaver award Boy Scouts Am., 1991, Beta Gamma Sigma chpt. honoree Georgetown U., 1992. Mem. Internat. Assn. for Fin. Planning (bd. dirs. 1980-87, chmn. emeritus, pres. 1986-87), Nat. Assn. Investment Clubs (columnist monthly mag. 1978—, Disting. Svc. award 1993), Nat. Assn. Securities Dealers (bus. conduct com. dist. 10 1986-89, vice chmn. 1988-89), Nat. Assn. Women Bus. Owners (pres. Capital Area chpt. 1980-81), Tax. Mgmt. and Fin. Planning Bd. (adv. bd. 1987—), Registry Fin. Planning Practitioners, D.C. Estate Planning Coun., Inst. Cert. Fin. Planners, Econ. Club (Washington), Cosmos Club (Washington). Republican. Roman Catholic. Home: 3560 Winfield Ln NW Washington DC 20007-2368 Office: 1155 Connecticut Ave NW Ste 250 Washington DC 20036-4314

ARMSTRONG, ANNE LEGENDRE (MRS. TOBIN ARMSTRONG), former ambassador, corporate director; b. New Orleans, Dec. 27, 1927; d. Armant and Olive (Martindale) Legendre; m. Tobin Armstrong, Apr. 12, 1950; children: John Barclay, Katharine A. Idsal, Sarita A. Hixon, Tobin and James L. (twins). BA in English, Vassar Coll., 1949. Co-chmn. Rep. Nat. Com., 1971-73; counsellor to U.S. Pres., 1973-74; U.S. amb. to Gt. Britain and No. Ireland, London, Gt. Britain, No. Ireland, 1976-77; chmn. adv. bd. Ctr. for Strategic and Internat. Studies (formerly affiliated with Georgetown U.), 1981-87, chmn. bd. trustees, 1987—; chmn. Pres.'s Fgn. Intelligence Adv. Bd., 1981-90; commn. on Integrated Long Term Strategy, 1987; bd. dirs. Halliburton Co., Boise Cascade Corp., Am. Express Co.; mem. adv. coun. GM Corp., 1998. Bd. regents Smithsonian Instn., 1978-94, emeritus, 1994; bd. overseers Hoover Instn., 1978-97; co-chmn. Reagan-Bush Campaign, 1980; bd. regents Tex. A&M U., 1997—. Recipient Gold Medal award for disting. svc. to humanity Nat. Inst. Social Scis., 1977, Rep. Woman of Yr. award, 1979, Texan of Yr. award, 1981, Presdl. Medal of Freedom award, 1987, Golden Plate award Am. Acad. Achievement, 1989; named to Tex. Women's Hall of Fame, 1986. Mem. English-Speaking Union (chmn. 1978-80), Coun. Fgn. Rels., Am. Assocs. of Royal Acad. Trust (trustee 1985—, vice chmn. 1996), Alfalfa Club, Washington Club, Phi Beta Kappa.

ARMSTRONG, BESS, actress; b. Balt., Dec. 11, 1953; m. John Fiedler. Student, Brown U. Appeared in films House of God, 1979, The Four Seasons, Jekyll and Hyde-Together Again, High Road to China, Jaws 3-D, Nothing In Common, Second Sight, Mother Mother, The Skateboard Kid, The Perfect Daughter, 1996, That Darn Cat, 1997, When it Clicks, 1998, Pecker, 1998; appeared in TV series On Our Own, All Is Forgiven, Married People, My So-Called Life; appeared in TV movies: Getting Married, How to Pick Up Girls, Walking Through the Fire, 11th Victim, This Girl For Hire, Lace, Take Me Home Again, She Stood Alone: The Tailhook Scandal, Stolen Innocence, Mixed Blessings, She Cried No, Christmas Every Day; spl. Barefoot in the Park. Office: c/o William Morris Agy 151 S El Camino Dr Beverly Hills CA 90212-2704*

ARMSTRONG, BILLIE BERT, retired highway contractor; b. Roswell, N.Mex., Apr. 18, 1920; s. Gayle G. and Murphy (Shannon) A.; m. Betty-Ellen Wilcox, Aug. 16, 1941; children: Billie B. Jr., Judith C., Robert G., Riley A. Student, N.Mex. Mil. Inst., 1935-39, Washington & Lee U., 1939-41. Mng. ptnr. Armstrong & Armstrong Ltd., Roswell, 1950—, G.G. Armstrong & Son, Ltd., Roswell, 1950—; chmn. bd. dirs. Sunwest Nat. Bank of Roswell, 1967-84; pres. Assoc. Gen. Contractors Am., Washington, 1966-67, Assoc. Contractors N.Mex., Santa Fe, 1952-53, 63; bd. dirs. Southwestern Pub. Svc. Co., Sunwest Fin. Svcs., Inc. Pres. Conquistador Coun. Boy Scouts Am., Roswell, 1981-82, bd. regents N.Mex. Mil. Inst., Roswell, 1960-62. Major U.S. Army, 1942-45. Named Citizen of Yr. Realtors N.Mex., 1969, Roswell, 1968, Jaycees, 1964; recognized for svc. to mankind Sertoma, 1966. Mem. Masons, Shriners, Jesters. Methodist. Avocation: golf. Home: 2619 Coronado Dr Roswell NM 88201-3404 Office: Armstrong & Armstrong Ltd PO Box 1873 Roswell NM 88202-1873

ARMSTRONG, BRUCE CHARLES, professional football player; b. Miami, Fla., Sept. 7, 1965. Student, Univ. Louisville. Offensive tackle New England Patriots, 1987—. Named offensive tackle The Sporting News NFL All-Pro team, 1988. Played in Pro Bowl, 1990, 91. Office: New Eng Patriots Foxboro Stadium 60 Washington St Foxboro MA 02035-1388*

ARMSTRONG, C. MICHAEL, communications company executive; b. Detroit, Oct. 18, 1938; s. Charles H. and Zora Jean (Brooks) A.; m. Anne Gossett, June 17, 1961; children: Linda, Julie, Kristy. B.S. in Bus. Econs, Miami U., Oxford, Ohio, 1961; grad., Dartmouth Inst., 1976; LLD (hon.), Pepperdine U., 1997, Loyola Marymount U., 1998. With IBM Corp., 1961-92, dir. systems mgmt. mktg. div., White Plains, N.Y., 1975-76, v.p. market ops. East, 1976-78, pres. data processing div., 1978-80, v.p., asst. group exec. plans and controls, data processing product group, 1980-83, v.p., group exec., 1983-84, sr. v.p., group exec., 1984-92; also pres. IBM Corp., Europe, Paris, until 1988; pres., dir. gen. World Trade Europe/Middle East/Africa IBM Corp., 1987-89, chmn. World Trade Corp., 1989-92; chmn., CEO Hughes Aircraft Co., L.A., 1992-93, GM Hughes Electronics (now Hughes Electronics Corp.), 1993—, AT&T, Basking Ridge, N.J., 1997—; Mem. GM Pres. Coun.; bd. dirs. Travelers Corp., Hartford, Conn., The Times-Mirror-Co., L.A., Citigroup; mem. supervisory bd. Thyssen-Bornemisza Group; chmn. Pres.'s Export Coun., The White House, 1994—. Trustee Johns Hopkins U., chmn. adv. bd. Johns Hopkins Med. Sch.; mem., CEO bd. of adv. U. So. Calif. Bus. Sch.; mem. bus. adv. coun. Miami U.; mem. Coun. on Fgn. Rels., Nat. Security Telecomm. Adv. Com., Def. Policy Adv. Com. on Trade (DPACT); mem. adv. bd. Yale Sch. Mgmt.; vice chmn. World Affairs Coun., L.A.; chmn. Sabriya's Castle of Fun Found.; bd. trustees Carnegie Hall. Mem. Calif. Bus. Roundtable. Office: AT&T Corp Corp Hdqs 295 N Maple Ave Basking Ridge NJ 07920-1025

ARMSTRONG, CHARLES G., professional baseball executive, lawyer; b. Louisville, Aug. 31, 1942; m. Susan; children—Dorrie, Katherine, Chuck. B.S., Purdue U., 1964; J.D., Stanford U., 1967. Bar: Calif. Practice law Hill Farrer & Burrill, Calif., 1971—; pres., chief operating officer Seattle Mariners Baseball Team, 1983—. Served with USN, 1967-70. Office: Seattle Mariners PO Box 4100 83 King St 3rd Floor Seattle WA 98104*

ARMSTRONG, C(HARLES) TORRENCE, lawyer; b. Charlotte, N.C., Aug. 7, 1945; s. George Rankin and Elizabeth (Torrence) A.; m. Mary Charles, Nov. 27, 1971; children: Charles Torrence Jr., Catherine McLean. BS in Commerce, Washington & Lee U., 1970; JD, U. N.C., 1972. Bar: N.C. 1973, Va. 1974, D.C. 1985. Ptnr. McGuire, Woods, Battle & Boothe, Alexandria, Va., 1973—. Pres. Ice Mountain Assn., Hampshire County, W.Va., 1990-93. Mem. Va. State Bar (bar coun., vice chmn. legal ethics com., chmn. grievance com.), Alexandria Bar Assn. (pres. 1983-84), No. Va. Young Lawyers Assn. (pres. 1977), Va. Bar Assn., Internat. Franchise Assn., Fed. Bar Assn. (v.p. North Va. chpt.), Alexandria C. of C. Home: 220 Virginia Ave Alexandria VA 22302-2906 Office: McGuire Woods Battle & Boothe 1750 Tysons Blvd Ste 1800 Mc Lean VA 22102-3915

ARMSTRONG, CLAY, physiology educator. Prof. physiology U. Pa., Phila. Recipient Louisa Horwitz prize Columbia U., 1996. Office: U Pa Dept Physiology B400 Richards Bldg Philadelphia PA 19104-6085*

ARMSTRONG, DANIEL WAYNE, chemist, educator; b. Ft. Wayne, Ind., Nov. 2, 1949; s. Robert Eugene and Nila Louise (Koeneman) A.; m. Linda Marilyn Todd, June 11, 1972; children: Lincoln Thomas, Ross Alexander, Colleen Victoria. BS, Washington and Lee U., 1972; MS in Chem. Oceanography, Tex. A&M U., 1974, PhD in Chemistry, 1977. Prof. Bowdoin Coll., Brunswick, Maine, 1978-79, Georgetown U., Washington, 1980-83, Tex. Tech. U., Lubbock, 1983-87; Curators' disting. prof., head ctr. environ. sci. and tech.; head dept. analytical chemistry U. Mo., Rolla, 1987—; bd dirs. Advanced Separations Techs., Whippany, N.J. Host Univ. Forum Radio Show, Washington, 1981-83; writer, host weekly radio show We're Sci. Nat. Pub. Radio, 1993—; author film, radio shows; contbr. articles to profl. publs.; patentee in field. Recipient Tchg. Excellence award U. Mo., 1985, 88, 89, 92, 94, Faculty Excellence award U. Mo., 1988, 89, Martin medal, 1991, EAS Chromatography award, 1990, Isco award, 1992, Presdl. award for rsch. and creativity, 1993, Perkin Elmer award for CE, 1994, R&D 100 award R&D Mag., 1995, Benedetti-Pichler award Am. Microchem. Soc. 1996; grantee Rsch. Corp., 1979, Petroleum Rsch. Fund, 1979, 91, NSF, 1981; Rsch. grantee Whatman Corp., 1981, Dept. Energy, 1984, 87, 91, 94, Dow Chem., 1985-90, NIH, 1986, 91, 95, EPA, 1995, Shell Co., 1989, 90-92. Fellow Am. Assn. Pharm. Scientists; mem. Am. Chem. Soc. (49th Midwest award for chemistry 1993, award in chromatography 1999), Sigma Xi, Phi Lambda Upsilon. Office: U Mo-Rolla Dept Chemistry 142 Schrenk Hall Rolla MO 65401-0249

ARMSTRONG, DAVID ANDREW, federal agency official, retired army officer; b. Washington, Sept. 6, 1940; S. William Hoye and Beatrice Pauline (Catey) A.; m. Helen Lynne Lanham, Dec. 28, 1968 (dec. Apr. 1990); 1 child, Anne Aileen; m. Cathy Jean Hammond, Mar. 28, 1997. BS, U.S. Mil. Acad., West Point, N.Y., 1962; MA, Duke U., 1970, PhD, 1975. Commd. 2d lt. U.S. Army, 1962, advanced through grades to brig. gen.; troop advisor 3d Armored Cavalry Squadron, II Corps Adv. Group, U.S. Mil. Assistance Command, Vietnam; sec. to gen. staff Adv. Team 21; instr., then asst. prof., rsch. officer dept. history U.S. Mil. Acad., West Point, N.Y.; exec. officer 5th Bn. 68th Armored Div.; comdg. officer 1st Bn. 37th Armored Div.; staff officer Army Planner, Office Dep. Chief of Staff for Ops. and Plans, Washington; comdr. 1st Brigade, 2d Inf. Div., Korea; asst. div. comdr. 5th Inf. Div., Ft. Polk, La.; comdg. gen. 1st Inf. Div. (Forward); ret., 1991; nat. intelligence officer Gen. Purpose Forces, Washington, 1989-93; dir. for joint history Office of Chmn. of Joint Chiefs of Staff, Washington, 1993—. Author: Bullets and Bureaucrats, 1982. Decorated D.S.M., Legion of Merit with 2 clusters, Bronze Star. Presbyterian. Avocations: military history, coin collecting. Office: The Pentagon Rm 1B707 Washington DC 20318

ARMSTRONG, DAVID ANTHONY, physical chemist, educator; b. Barbados, Aug. 27, 1930; came to Can., 1948, naturalized, 1962; m. Ruth Hallam; children: Graeme, Maureen, Andrew. BS with honors, McGill U., 1952, PhD in Phys. Chemistry, 1955. Brotherton research lectr. U. Leeds, Eng., 1955-57; NRC postdoctoral fellow U. Sask., Saskatoon, Can., 1957-58; from asst. prof. to assoc. prof. chemistry U. Calgary, Alta., Can., 1958-63, prof., 1968-91; prof. emeritus U. Calgary, 1991—; acting head dept. chemistry U. Calgary, Alta., Can., 1966-67, head dept., 1970-73, dean Faculty Sci., 1984-89; vis. scientist Atomic Energy of Can., Ltd., Chalk River, Ont., 1960, 1968-69, NRC of Can., Ottawa, Ont., 1966; participant numerous univ. coms. including mem. univ. space com., 1977-80, mem. Inst. for Humanities Council, 1979-82, pres.'s space mgmt. adv. com., 1980-82, mem. exec. com. dept. chemistry, 1983-84; mem. NRC Can. chem. grants selection com., 1971-73; grant referee for Nat. Scis. and Engring. Research Council, Materials Research Council; cons. Mountainview Provincial Health Unit, Union Carbide Can., P.R. Nuclear Ctr., Mayaguez, Alta. Govt., Edmonton, Algas Resources Ltd., Nova Co., NRC Can.; external examiner PhD theses U. Sask, 1959, 67, 84, McGill U., 1966, U. Alta., 1966, 87, Leeds U., 1967, U. Adelaide, 1970, U. Melbourne, 1987. Referee Can. Jour. Chemistry, Jour. Phys. Chemistry, Internat. Jour. Radiation Physics & Chemistry, Internat. Jour. Radiation Biology, Molecular Pharmacology, Jour. Am. Chem. Soc. Participant in ednl. activities for high sch. students Frontiers of Sci. lecture series and J.W. Young Meml. lectr., 1964; judge, screener sch. fairs; councilor Kiwanis Student Career Night meetings; active panel discussions for gen. pub. on environ. effects of radiation and current sci. issues; organizer joint Humanities-Sci. workshop, Kananaskis Ctr., 1981. Cominco fellow, 1954-55; Nuffield Found. grantee, 1969. Mem. Fellow Chem. Inst. Can. (sec. Calgary sect. 1959-60, treas. 1960-62, co-chmn. 1963-64, chmn. 1964-65, sci. council sub-com. on nuclear and radiation chemistry, exec. com. phys. chemistry div. 1981-84); mem. Am. Chem. Soc. (referee jour.), Sigma Xi. Office: U Calgary Dept Chem Fac Sci, 2500 University Dr NW, Calgary AB Canada T2N 1N4*

ARMSTRONG, DAVID LIGON, psychiatrist; b. Ontario, Calif., May 5, 1927; s. John Awdry and Ruth (Harrison) A.; m. Mary Meredith, Mar. 30, 1953 (dec. Feb. 1997); children: Meredith Richey, Paul, Adelaide Armstrong Butler. BS in Plant Sci., U. Calif., Berkeley, 1949; PhD in Genetics, U. Calif., Davis, 1956; MD, Creighton U., 1972. Diplomate Am. Bd. Psychiatry, Am. Bd. Neurology. Dir. rsch. Armstrong Nurseries, Inc., Ontario, Calif., 1953-68; resident in psychiatry U. Calif., Irvine, 1972-75; staff psychiatrist Met. State Hosp., Norwalk, Calif., 1975—; pres. med. staff Met. State Hosp., Norwalk, 1985-88, 97—. Patentee new varieties roses and peaches. Pres. West End United Fund, Ontario, 1958-60, Chaffey Young Reps., Ontario and Upland, Calif., 1958-60, West End Coun. Cmty. Svcs., Ontario, 1960-64; chmn. Rep. Ctrl. Com., San Bernardino County, Calif., 1960-62. With USNR, 1945-46. Mem. State Employed Physicians Assn. (pres. 1984-86), Sigma Xi, Alpha Zeta. Republican. Avocations: politics, travel, gardening. Fax: 562-651-5714. Home: 2809 E Hillside Ave Orange CA 92867-8413 Office: Met State Hosp 11400 Norwalk Blvd Norwalk CA 90650-2084

ARMSTRONG, DAVID LOVE, attorney general; b. Hope, Ark., Aug. 6, 1941; m. Carol Burress, 1963; 1 child, Bryce Shannon. B.S., Murray State U., 1966; J.D., U. Louisville, 1969; postgrad. Coll. Trial Advocacy, Harvard U., 1972; postgrad., U. Nev., 1973. Bar: Ky. 1969. Ptnr. firm Turner, McDonald & Armstrong Louisville, 1969-76; commonwealth atty. City of Louisville, 1976-83; atty. gen. State of Ky., 1983—; asst. prosecutor police ct., 1969-71; judge juvenile ct. Jefferson County, Ky., 1971-73; hearing officer Louisville-Jefferson County Bd. Health. Chmn. fund raising Brooklawn Home, Louisville; chair Ky. Child Sexual Abuse and Exploitation Prevention Bd., 1984—; appointed vice chair U.S. Atty. Gen. Adv. Bd. on Missing Children, 1985; bd. dirs. YMCA, Murray State U. Fleur de Lis award City of Louisville, 1973, Recipient/Outstanding Achievement award Nat. Assn. County Ofcls., 1977; recognized as one of Outstanding Pros. in Am. by Pres. Jimmy Carter, 1980. Mem. Am. Assn. Trial Lawyers (Human Rights award 1986), Ky. Bar Assn., Ky. Commonwealth Attys. Assn. (pres.), Nat. Dist. Attys. Assn. (sec.), ABA. Office: Office of Atty Gen 116 Capitol Ave Frankfort KY 40601-2831

ARMSTRONG, DAVID MICHAEL, biology educator; b. Louisville, July 31, 1944; s. John D. and Elizabeth Ann (Horine) A.; children: John D., Laura C. BS, Colo. State U., 1966; MA in Teaching, Harvard U., 1967; PhD, U. Kans., 1971. From asst. prof. to prof. natural sci. U. Colo., Boulder, 1971-85, prof. environ., population, and organismic biology, 1993—, assoc. chair, 1997—; sr. scientist Rocky Mountain Biol. Lab., Gothic, Colo., 1977, 79; resident naturalist Sylvan Dale Ranch, Loveland, Colo., 1984—; acting dir. Univ. Mus., 1987-88, dir., 1989-93; cons. ecologist. Author: Distribution of Mammals in Colorado, 1972, Rocky Mountain Mammals, 1975, 87, Mammals of the Canyon Country, 1982; co-author: Mammals of the Northern Great Plains, Mammals of the Plains States, Mammals of Colorado. Mem. non-game adv. council Colo. Div. Wildlife, 1972-76, Colo. Natural Areas Council, 1975-80. Mem. Am. Soc. Mammalogists (editor 1981-87), Southwestern Assn. Naturalists (editor 1976-80), Rocky Mountain Biol. Lab. (trustee 1979-83), The Nature Conservancy (Colo. chpt. trustee 1989—, chair 1996-98). Avocations: draft horses, conservation activities, writing. Office: U Colo EPO Biology PO Box 334 Boulder CO 80309-0334

ARMSTRONG, DENISE GRACE, medical association administrator. Mktg. diploma, Briarcliffe Coll., L.I., N.Y., 1974; student, Hofstra U., Nassau C.C. Staff asst. Klar, Klar & Tifford, law office, East Meadow, L.I., N.Y., 1974-76; exec. sec. Nassau Acad. Medicine and Nassau County Med. Soc., Garden City, L.I., N.Y., 1976-80; adminstr. Suffolk County Dental Soc., Hauppauge, L.I., N.Y., 1980-87; exec. dir. Suffolk County Dental Soc., Hauppauge, N.Y., 1988-89; dir. mktg. Med. Soc. of State of N.Y., 1989—. Mem. NAFE, Am. Soc. Assn. Execs., Am. Assn. Med. Soc. Execs., Mktg. Rsch. Assn. Office: 420 Lakeville Rd New Hyde Park NY 11042-1121

ARMSTRONG, DOUGLAS DEAN, journalist; b. Wichita, Kans., Mar. 12, 1945; s. H. Glenn and Emma F. (Starkey) A.; m. Paige Prillaman, Jan. 3, 1967 (div. Sept. 1982); children: David Douglas, Christine Elizabeth; m. Mary Alyce Dooley, Mar. 8, 1987; children: Patrick Glenn, Gillian Marie. BA, U. Minn., 1967. Entertainment writer Milw. Jour. Sentinel, 1967-72, editl. writer, 1972-74, consumer writer, 1974-81, movie critic, 1981-95, bus. writer, 1995—, personal fin. columnist, 1995—; guest lectr. U. Wis., Milw., 1982-89; movie reviewer WISN-TV, Milw., 1984-85; movie critic WKTI-FM, Milw., 1989-97; pres. Lexington Software Corp., 1996—. Contbr. short fiction to Ellery Queen's Mystery Mag., Alfred Hitchcock's Mystery Mag., Boys' Life. Recipient Pub. Interest award Ctr. for Pub. Representation, 1978. Mem. Mystery Writrs Am. Avocations: video, piano. Office: Milw Jour Sentinel 333 W State St Milwaukee WI 53203-1305

ARMSTRONG, EDWARD BRADFORD, JR., oral and maxillofacial surgeon, educator, naval officer; b. Teaneck, N.J., Sept. 24, 1928; s. Edward Bradford and Ruth Elizabeth (Fippinger) A.; AB, U. Pa., 1950; DDS, N.Y.U., 1954; m. Dusanka Vladimirovna Jakovljevic, Nov. 5, 1960; children: Edward Bradford, III, James B., Hugh B. Commd. lt. j.g. U.S. Navy, 1954, advanced through grades to capt. 1971; intern oral surgery Roosevelt Hosp., N.Y.C., 1958, assoc. attending oral surgery, 1959—, attending oral surgeon out-patient dept., 1959—, chmn., moderator Oral Surgery Staff Confs., 1963-70; resident Carle Hosp., Urbana, Ill., 1959; assoc. attending oral surgeon Flower and Fifth Ave. hosps., N.Y.C., 1960-78; asst. attending oral surgeon Hackensack (N.J.) Hosp., 1963-65; adminstrv. officer Naval Res. Dental Co. 3-2, 1965-68, exec. officer, 1968-71, comdg. officer, 1971-73; comdt.'s rep. 3d Naval Dist., Naval Acad., 1972-78, 3d Naval Dist for Dentistry, 1973-75, group staff officer for dentistry and medicine, 1973-75, Ready Res. Unit 502, 1975-77, VTU 0207, 1977-79, ret., 1979; assoc. clin. prof. oral surgery N.Y. Med. Coll., 1963-93; adj. assoc. clin. prof. oral surgery Columbia U. Sch. Dentistry, 1973-89; chmn. bd. E. & R. Armstrong, Inc., Albany, N.Y., 1966-77; pres. Edward B. Armstrong, P.C., N.Y.C., 1979-90; dir. Songtime, Inc.,

Boston; dir., mem. exec. com. PGP Internat. Corps, Inc. Bd. dirs., trustee Christian Mission Farms of Paraguay, Inc., 1974-84; pres., trustee Central Bible Chapel, Palisades Park, N.J.; area rep., ann. giving U. Pa., 1960-68; Blue and Gold officer Naval Acad. Admissions Com.; sec. bd. dirs., trustee Boys' Club of N.Y. Health Svcs., Inc. Diplomate Am. Bd. Oral Surgery. Fellow N.Y. Acad. Dentistry (sec., dir., pres. 1979-80), Am., Internat. Colls. Dentists (life), Am. Coll. Oral and Maxillofacial Surgeons (founding), Am. Dental Soc. Anesthesiology (hon. life); mem. ADA (life, 1st dist. life), Am. Assn. Oral and Maxillofacial Surgeons (life, N.J. rep. Ho. of Dels. 1963-65), N.Y. Soc. Oral Surgeons (life, chmn. audit and budget com. 1972-79), First Dist. Dental Soc. (life), N.Y. Dental Soc., Bklyn. Dental Soc., Yokosuka Dental Soc. (hon.), Assn. Mil. Surgeons U.S., Mil. Order World Wars, Naval Res. Assn. (life), Union League (chmn. art com. 1973-76, bd. govs. 1974-77, 82-84, v.p. 1977-80, 85-88), Met. Club (bd. gov. 1992-96, 98—), N.Y.C., U. Pa. Club, U. Pa. Club of Met. N.J. (dir. 1982—), Acacia, Xi Psi Phi, Psi Omega (hon.), Delta Sigma Delta. Mem. Plymouth Brethren Ch. Home: 110 Broad Ave Leonia NJ 07605-2003

ARMSTRONG, EDWIN ALAN, lawyer; b. Atlanta, June 20, 1950; s. Carl Edwin and Betty (Hawkins) A.; m. Marlene Bryant, Aug. 12, 1978. BA, Berry Coll., 1972; JD, Emory U., 1976. Bar: Ga. 1976, U.S. Dist. Ct. (no. dist.) Ga. 1977, U.S. Ct. Appeals (5th cir.) 1981, U.S. Ct. Appeals (11th cir.) 1982, U.S. Supreme Ct. 1989, U.S. Dist. Ct. (so. dist.) Ga., U.S. Ct. Appeals (4th cir.), U.S. Ct. Appeals (D.C. cir.) 1992, U.S. Ct. Appeals (6th cir.) 1992, U.S. Dist. Ct. (mid. dist.) Ga 1992. Atty. Flynt Jud. Cir. Pub. Defenders Office, McDonough, Ga., 1976-77; assoc. Neely, Neely & Player, Atlanta, 1977; pvt. practice, Atlanta, 1977-79, 81—; assoc. Stolz, Shulman & Loveless, Atlanta, 1979-81. Contbr. articles to profl. jours. Mem. ABA (forum com. on air and space law, tort and ins. practice sect.), ATLA, Atlanta Bar Assn., Decatur-DeKalb Bar Assn., State Bar Ga. (chmn. aviation law sect. 1998—), Ga. Trial Lawyers Assn., Nat. Transp. Safety Bd. Bar Assn. (founding, com. legis. and regulatory activity 1989—, editor newsletter 1991-92), Lawyer-Pilots Bar Assn. Episcopalian. Avocation: flying. Home: 4098 Northlake Creek Cv Tucker GA 30084-3416

ARMSTRONG, EDWIN RICHARD, lawyer, publisher, editor; b. Chgo., Sept. 25, 1921; s. Robert S. and Ella (Bremer) A.; m. Catherine Claire Graeber, June 29, 1957; children—Catherine Jane, Diane Claire, Douglas Edwin, Gregory Charles. B.A., Knox Coll., 1942; J.D., Northwestern U., 1948. Bar: Ill. 1949, U.S. Dist. Ct. (no. dist.) Ill. 1949, U.S. Ct. Appeals (7th cir.) 1949, U.S. Supreme Ct. 1961. Ptnr. Reimers & Armstrong, 1949-55; assoc. Friedman & Friedman, 1957-62; ptnr. Friedman, Armstrong & Donnelly, 1962-78, Armstrong & Donnelly, Chgo., 1978—. Mem. Oak Park (Ill.) Elem. Sch. Bd. 1963-69, pres. 1964-67; mem. exec. bd. Thatcher Woods Area council Boy Scouts Am. 1978-93, pres., 1983-84. Served to maj. USMCR 1942-46. Mem. Ill. Bar Assn., Chgo. Bar Assn. Club: Carlton. Home: 860 N Lake Shore Dr Apt 17M Chicago IL 60611-1788 Office: 77 W Washington St Ste 1009 Chicago IL 60602-2805

ARMSTRONG, ELIZABETH NEILSON, curator; b. Winchester, Mass., June 30, 1952; d. Douglas Byron and Ruth Mary (Publow) A.; m. Daniel Alexander Boone, Mar. 1, 1985; children: Olivia Armstrong Boone, Phoebe Elizabeth Boone. BA, Hampshire Coll., 1974; MA, U. Calif., Berkeley, 1982. Grants adminstr. NEH, Washington, 1976-79; rsch. asst. San Francisco Mus. Modern Art, 1979-81; cons. Lowie Mus. Anthropology, Berkeley, 1981-82; Nat. Endowment for Arts curatorial intern Walker Art Ctr., Mpls., 1982-83, asst. curator, 1983-86, assoc. curator, 1986-89, curator, 1989—; mem. adv. bd. Capp Street Project, San Francisco, 1987; guest curator Ctr. for Book Arts, N.Y.C., 1989; panelist NEA, Washington, 1988, 89, Pew Charitable Trust, 1994; cons., reviewer Nat. Gallery Art, Washington, 1990. Author: First Impressions, 1989; author, editor: Tyler Graphics: The Extended Image, 1987, Jasper Johns: Printed Symbols, 1990, In the Spirit of Fluxus, 1993. Mem. adv. com. Minn. Percent for Art Program, St. Paul, 1987; bd. dirs. Artpaper, Mpls., 1989-93. Recipient govt. merit award for outstanding performance NEH, 1979; humanities grad. rsch. grantee U. Calif., 1981; fellow for mus. profls. Nat. Endowment for Arts, 1989. Mem. Print Coun. Am., Minn. Ctr. for Book Arts. Avocations: snorkeling, tennis, skiing. Office: San Diego Museum of Contemporary Art 700 Prospect St La Jolla CA 92037-4228*

ARMSTRONG, F(REDRIC) MICHAEL, retired insurance company executive; b. Wichita, Kans., Dec. 20, 1942; s. Frederick Dale and Virginia Pauline A.; m. Patricia R. Latif, Dec. 13, 1976. BS in Elec. Engring., MIT, 1964; MBA, Stanford U., 1966. Mgr. capital appropriations Trans World Airlines, N.Y.C., 1966-69; corp. planner Transam. Corp., San Francisco, 1969-70; v.p. Transam. Film Service, Salt Lake City, 1970-73, also bd. dir.; v.p. fin. Europe Transam. Airlines, Madrid, Spain, 1973-75, v.p. planning and info. svcs., Oakland, Calif., 1975-77; exec. v.p. fin. Budget Rent a Car Corp., Chgo., 1977-83, also bd. dir.; exec. v.p., chief adminstrv. officer Transam. Ins. Group, L.A., 1983-93, also bd. dir.; pres. Century Indemnity Co., Century Reinsurance Co., 1995—, also bd. dirs.; bd. dirs. Melia Internat. Hotels, Panama, The Canadian Surety Co., Ins. Value Added Network Service, River Thames Ins. Co., London, Fairmont Fin. Inc., Mason-McDuffie Ins. Svc., Inc., The Completion Bond Co. Mem. adv. coun. Pierce Coll.

ARMSTRONG, GENE LEE, systems engineering consultant, retired aerospace company executive; b. Clinton, Ill., Mar. 9, 1922; s. George Dewey and Ruby Imald (Dickerson) A. m. Lael Jeanne Baker, Apr. 3, 1946; children: Susan Lael, Roberta Lynn, Gene Lee. BS with high honors, U. Ill., 1948, MS, 1951. Registered profl. engr., Calif. With Boeing Aircraft, 1948-50, 51-52; chief engr. astronautics divsn., corp. dir. Gen. Dynamics, 1954-65; chief engr. Def. Sys. Group TRW, Redondo Beach, Calif., 1956-86; pvt. cons. sys. engring. Def. Sys. Group TRW, 1986—; Mem. NASA Rsch. Adv. Com. on Control, Guidance & Navigation, 1959-62. Contbr. chpts. to books, articles to profl. pubs. 1st lt. USAAF, 1942-45. Decorated Air medal; recipient alumni awards U. Ill., 1965, 77;. Mem. Am. Math. Soc., AIAA, Nat. Mgmt. Assn., Am. Def. Preparedness Assn., Masons. Home: 5242 Bryant Cir Westminster CA 92683-1713 Office: Armstrong Sys Engring Co PO Box 86 Westminster CA 92684-0086*

ARMSTRONG, GIBSON E., state senator; b. Butler, Pa., Aug. 28, 1943; m. Martha Wilson, June 12, 1965; children: Gibson C., Erik, Kris, Erin. BBA in Econs., Wesminster Coll., 1965. Mem. Pa. Ho. of Reps., Harrisburg, 1976-84, Pa. Senate, Harrisburg, 1984—; mem. transp., fin. comm. and high tech. coms. Pa. Senate, chmn. labor and industry; mem. Rules & Exec. Nominations.; bd. dirs. Pa. State Employee's Retirement Bd. Bd. dirs. Water St. Rescue Mission, Ben Franklin Partnership, Lancaster Econ. Devel. Coun. Capt. USMC, 1966-69. Bd. dirs. Water St. Rescue Mission. Named Legislator of Yr., 1986, 87, Outstanding Young Men Am. Mem. Lions, VFW, Am. Legion. Office: Pa Senate PO Box 203013 Harrisburg PA 17120-3013*

ARMSTRONG, GILLIAN MAY, film director; b. Melbourne, Australia, Dec. 18, 1950. Student, Swinbourne Coll., Australian Film and TV Sch. Dir. (short films) One Hundred A Day, Gretel, the Singer and the Dancer, 1976 (documentaries) Satdee Night, Smokes and Lollies, 1975, Fourteen's Good, Eighteen's Better, 1980, Bingo, Bridesmaids, and Braces, 1988 (feature films) My Brillian Career, 1979, Starstruck, 1982, Mrs. Soffel, 1984, Hard to Handle, Hightide, 1987, Fires Within, 1991, The Last Days of Chez Nous, 1993, Little Women, 1994, Not Fourteen Again, 1996, Oscar and Lucinda, 1997. Office: c/o William Morris Agy 151 S El Camino Dr Beverly Hills CA 90212-2704*

ARMSTRONG, GREGORY DAVENPORT, arboretum administrator; b. LaCrosse, Wis., May 30, 1943; s. Miles Tymeson Armstrong and Beth (Davenport) Freiburger; m. Elizabeth Helen Marchant, July 1, 1972 (div. Apr. 1994); children: Miles S., Marjorie E. BS, U. Wis., 1967; Kew diploma, Royal Botanic Gardens, Surrey, Eng., 1970; MA, Smith Coll., Northampton, Mass., 1980. Dir. Botanical Garden Smith Coll., Northampton, Mass., 1971-83; dir. arboretum U. Wis., Madison, 1983—. Bd. dirs. Am. Assn. Botanical Garden and Arboreta, 1986-91, Child's Park, Northampton, 1979-83; advisor Historic Deerfield, Mass., 1976-83. Mem. Am. Assn. Mus. (program assessor 1988—, accreditation assessor 1991—), Rotary. Office: U Wis Madison Arboretum 1207 Seminole Hwy Madison WI 53711*

ARMSTRONG, GREGORY TIMON, religious studies educator, minister; b. Evanston, Ill., Dec. 23, 1933; s. John Robert and Clara Joanna A.; m. Edna Louise Stagg, May 11, 1957; children: Edna Montague, Elizabeth S. Roncace. BA with honors, Wesleyan U., 1955; BD with highest honors, McCormick Theol. Sem., 1958; ThD magna cum laude, U. Heidelberg, Germany, 1961. Ordained to ministry United Presbyn. Ch., 1961; instr. ch. history McCormick Theol. Sem., Chgo., 1961-62; asst. prof. ch. history Vanderbilt U. Div. Sch., Nashville, 1962-68; assoc. prof. religion Sweet Briar (Va.) Coll., 1968-75, prof., 1975-81, Charles A. Dana prof. religion, 1981-96; chmn. dept. religion Sweet Briar (Va.) Coll., 1972-74, 78-81, 83-88; chmn. dept. religion Sweet Briar (Va.) Coll., 1992-95, emeritus, 1997—; rsch. fellow U. Goettingen, Germany, 1974-75; vis. prof. hist. studies Union Theol. Sem., Richmond, 1983. Author: Die Genesis in der Alten Kirche, 1962; contbr. articles and book revs. on ch. history and art to scholary jours. and encys. Mem. Nashville United Givers Fund, 1966-68, Wesleyan U. Ann. Fund, 1971-74, 97—; pres. local PTA, Amherst, Va., 1971-72; mem. bd. suprs. Amherst County, Va., 1988-91, vice chmn., 1990, chmn., 1991; mem. Ctrl. Va. Cmty. Svcs. Bd., 1988-91, sec., 1990-91; fundraising chmn. Amherst County Habitat for Humanity, 1991-93; mem. Amherst County Social Svcs. Bd., 1989-91, 93-96, chmn., 1993-94, vice chmn., 1994-96; mem. Amherst County Sch. Bd., 1996—, vice chmn., 1998—. Rotary Internat. fellow, 1958-59; Rockefeller doctoral fellow, 1959-61; Nettie F. McCormick fellow, 1959-61; Presbyn. Grad. fellow, 1960-61; Am. Coun. Learned Socs. Study fellow, 1965-66, grantee, 1985; NEH grantee, 1971; Fulbright Hays sr. rsch. fellow, 1974-75; Sweet Briar faculty fellow, 1981-82; Vanderbilt U. Rsch. Coun. grantee, 1966-68; Am. Philos. Soc. grantee, 1981. Mem. AAUP (pres. chpt. 1976, mem. state exec. com. 1984-86, pres. Va. conf. 1986-87, chmn. state fin. com. 1993-94), Am. Hist. Assn., Am. Soc. Ch. History (membership chmn. 1972-74, mem. coun. 1985-87), Rotary (pres. Amherst club 1995-96), Phi Beta Kappa (chpt. pres. 1976-78). Address: PO Box 1253 Amherst VA 24521-1253

ARMSTRONG, HART REID, minister, editor, publisher; b. St. Louis, May 11, 1912; s. Hart Champlin and Zora Lillian (Reid) A.; m. Iona Rhoda Mehl, Feb. 21, 1932; 1 son, Hart Reed. Grad. Life Bible Coll., 1931; A.B., Christian Temples U., 1936; Litt.D., Geneva Theol. Coll., 1967; D.D. (hon.) Central Sch. Religion, Surrey, Eng., 1972; Th.M., Central Christian Coll., 1968, Th.D., 1970; Ph.D. in Religion, Berean Christian Coll., 1980. Ordained to ministry Assembly of God, 1932; pastor, 1932-34; dean Bible Standard Coll., Eugene, Oreg., 1935-40; missionary, Indonesia, 1941-42; editor Open Bible Pubs., Des Moines, 1944-46, Gospel Pub. House, Springfield, Mo., 1947-53, Gospel Light Pubs., Glendale, Calif., 1954; crusade adminstr. Oral Roberts Assn., Tulsa, 1955-62; exec. dir. Assembly Homes, Inc., Glenwood, Minn., 1963-66; pres. Defenders Christian Faith, Kansas City, Mo., 1967-80; founder, pres., editor Christian Communications, Inc., Wichita, Kans., 1981—; editor Devotional Letter Monthly. Fellow London Royal Soc. Arts; mem. Nat. Sunday Sch. Assn., Pope County Hist. Soc., Sigma Delta Chi. Lodge: Rotary (past charter pres. Glenwood, Minn.). Author: To Those Who Are Left, 1950; You Should Know, 1951; The Rebel, 1967; The Beast, 1967; How Do I Pray, 1968; All Things for Life, 1969; What Will Happen to the United States, 1969; Impossible Events of Bible Prophecy, 1979; All You Need to Know about Bible Prophecy, 1980; Thoughts at Three Score and Ten, 1981; The A-B-C of Last Day Events, 1982, The World that Then Was, How Great Thou Art!, The Gospel of John--A Commentary, 1983, The True Site of the Temple of Solomon, The Holy Jerusalem, UFOs--Are They for Real, Petra--the Mysterious City, 1984, The Seven Churches of Revelation, Verses from the Heart, Katherine Beard--A Life Poured Out, 1985, Let Them Speak to You, The Primary Movers (3 sects.), Where is the Ark of the Covenant?, The Sacred Festivals of the Lord, 1989, Commentary on the Book of Revelation (vols. I-IV), 1992, Why Not?-Biography of Dr. Frank Lindquest, Glory to Come!, 1993, The Olivet Discourse, The Last Seven on Earth, The Story of God, 1994, When Is the Rapture? I Found the Ark, The Last Great Day of God Almighty, 1995, The Miracle Voyage of the Ghost Ship, Visions Yet Future in the Book of Daniel, 1996, The Tribulation and the Martyrs, 1997, The Rebel and the Beast, 1998. Home: 6436 N Hillside St Wichita KS 67219-1805 Office: 6450 N Hillside St Wichita KS 67219-1805

ARMSTRONG, HENRY CONNER, former Canadian government official, consultant; b. Winnipeg, Man., Can., June 16, 1925; s. William Arthur Laird and Archena May (Conner) A.; m. Barbara Fay Jackson, May 20, 1950; children: Barbara E., Nancy M., Scott J. B.Sc. in Metall. Engring., Queen's U., Kingston, Ont., 1949; M.B.A. (Kresge fellow), U. Toronto, 1954; diploma in indsl. adminstrn. (Alcan fellow), Internat. Mgmt. Inst., Geneva, Switzerland, 1958. Various sales and marketing positions Aluminum Co. of Can., Ltd., 1954-64; commodity officer Dept. Trade and Commerce, Ottawa, Ont., 1964-66; comml. counsellor Canadian Embassy, Washington, 1966-74; chief research and planning div., resource industries and constrn. br. Dept. Industry, Trade and Commerce, Ottawa, Ont., Can., 1974-75; dir. minerals and metals div. Dept. Energy, Mines and Resources, Ottawa, Ont., 1975-81; exec. dir. internat. minerals Dept. Energy, Mines and Resources, 1981-82, mgr. spl. projects, 1982-83; counsellor (metals, minerals and energy) Can. High Commn., Canberra, Australia, 1983-86; counsellor (commercial) Can. Embassy, Washington, 1986-89; pvt. practice cons. Ottawa, 1989—. Served with RCAF and Royal Navy Fleet Air Arm, 1944-45. Mem. Assn. Profl. Engrs. Ont., Canadian Inst. Mining and Metallurgy, Am. Soc. Metals. Mem. United Ch. of Can. Home and Office: 2159 Delmar Dr, Ottawa, ON Canada K1H 5P6

ARMSTRONG, JACK GILLILAND, lawyer; b. Pitts., Aug. 10, 1929; s. Hugh Collins and Mary Elizabeth (Gilliland) A.; m. Ellen Lee Gliem, June 10, 1951 (dec.); children: Thomas G., Elizabeth Armstrong Pride; m. Elizabeth Lacewll White, March 27, 1993. AB, U. Mich., 1951, JD, 1956. Bar: Pa. 1956, Mich. 1956, U.S. Supreme Ct. 1968, Fla. 1981. Assoc. Buchanan, Ingersoll, Rodewald, Kyle & Buerger, Pitts., 1956-65; ptnr. Buchanan, Ingersoll, P.C., Pitts., 1965-90; counsel Buchanan, Ingersoll, P.C., 1990-94, of counsel, 1995; of counsel Rothman Gordon, P.C., 1996—; dir. Standard Steel Splty. Co., Greer, S.C. Trustee Union Dale Cemetery, 1972—, pres., 1992-95. Dir. Sigma Nu Ednl. Found., 1998—. Lt. U.S. Army, 1951-53. Mem. ABA (sects. taxation, real property, probate and trust law), Pa. Bar Assn. (real property, probate, and trust law sect., mem. coun. 1981-84, treas. 1985, vice chmn. probate divsn. 1986-88, chmn. 1988-89, tax law sect.), Fla. Bar (real property, probate and trust law sect., tax sect.), Allegheny County Bar Assn. (probate and trust law), Palm Beach County Bar Assn., Estate Planning Coun. Pitts., Am. Coll. Trust and Estate Counsel (Pa. state chmn. 1990-95), Am. Coll. Tax Counsel, U. Mich. Alumni Assn. (Disting. Alumni Svc. award 1981), Am. Arbitration Assn. (nat. panel 1965—), Order of Coif, Duquesne Club, Univ. Club (pres. 1988-89), St. Clair Country Club, Town Club Jamestown, Delray Beach Club, Chautauqua Golf Club, Pine Tree Golf Club, Masons, Shriners, Royal Order Jesters, Phi Alpha Delta, Signa Nu. Home: 4376 Pine Tree Dr Boynton Beach FL 33436-4818

ARMSTRONG, (ARTHUR) JAMES, educator, consultant, lecturer, writer; b. Marion, Ind., Sept. 17, 1924; s. Arthur J. and Frances (Green) A.; m. Sue Peterson, Dec. 10, 1988; children: Eve Stoughton, Allison; children from previous marriage: James, Teresa, John, Rebecca, Leslye Armstrong Hope. AB, Fla. So. Coll., 1948; BD, Candler Sch. Theology, Emory U., 1952; DD, Fla. So. U., 1960, DePauw U., 1965; LHD, Ill. Wesleyan U., 1970, Dakota Wesleyan U., 1970, Westmar Coll., 1971, Ind. Ctrl. U., 1982, Emory U., 1982. Ordained to ministry Meth. Ch., 1948; minister in Fla., 1945-58; sr. minister Broadway Meth. Ch., Indpls., 1958-68; bishop United Meth. Ch., Dakotas area, 1968-80, Ind. area, Indpls., 1980-83; exec. v.p. conflict resolution firm, Washington, 1984-87; vis. prof. preaching and social ministries Iliff Sch. Theology, Denver, 1985-91; sr. min. 1st Congl. Ch., Winter Park, Fla., 1991-99; exec. dir. Ctr. on Dialogue and Devel., Denver, 1984-96; adj. prof. Rollins Col., 1993—; instr. Christian Theol. Sem., Indpls., 1961-68; del. 4th Gen. Assembly, World Coun. Chs., 1968, 6th Gen. Assembly, 1983; pres. Nat. Coun. Chs., 1982-83; pres. bd. ch. and soc. United Meth. Ch., 1972-76, chmn. com. for peace and self devel. of peoples, 1972-76, pres. Commn. on Religion and Race, 1976-83; exec. v.p. Pagan Internat., 1982-87. Author: The Journey That Men Make, 1969, The Urgent Now, 1970, Mission: Middle America, 1971, The Pastor and the Public Servant, 1972, United Methodist Primer, 1973, 77, Wilderness Voices, 1974, The Nation Yet To Be, 1975, Telling Truth: The Foolishness of Preaching in a Real World, 1977, From the Underside, 1981; contbg. author: The Pulpit Speaks on Race, 1966, War Crimes and the American Conscience, 1970, Rethinking Evangelism, 1971, What's a Nice Church Like You Doing in a Place Like This?, 1972, The Miracle of Easter, 1980, Preaching on Peace, 1982, Ethics and the Multi-National Enterprise, 1986, The Best of the Circuit Rider, 1987. Vice-chmn. Hoosiers for Peace, 1968; mem. Ind. State Platform Com. Democratic Party, 1968, Nat. Coalition for a Responsible Congress, 1970. With USNR, 1942. Recipient distinguished service award Indpls. Jr. C. of C., 1959. Mem. Fla. Coun. Chs. (pres. 1996-97), Ctrl. Fla. Interfaith Alliance (co-chair 1994-96).

ARMSTRONG, JAMES LOUDEN, III, lawyer; b. Miami, Fla., Jan. 7, 1932; s. James Louden and Jean Macrea (Cawley) A.; m. Mary Elizabeth McCall, Aug. 25, 1955; children: Patricia Payan, James L. IV. BA, Yale U., 1955, LLB, 1958. Bar: Fla. 1958, U.S. Dist. Ct. (so. dist.) Fla. 1958, U.S. Dist. Ct. (middle dist.) Fla. 1960, U.S. Dist. Ct. (no. dist.) Fla. 1964, U.S. Ct. Appeals (5th and 11th cir.) 1962, U.S. Supreme Ct. 1962. Assoc. Smathers & Thompson, Miami, 1958-64, ptnr., 1964-87; ptnr. Kelley Drye & Warren LLP, Miami, 1987—. Pres. Orange Bowl Com., Miami, 1976; co-chmn. Cmty. Partnership for Homeless, Inc., 1994—. Fellow Am. Coll. Trial Lawyers, Internat. Acad. Trial Lawyers; mem. Dade County bar Assn.(pres. 1972), Yale Club (pres. 1966). Republican. Presbyterian. Avocation: golf. Home: 4911 Alhambra Cir Coral Gables FL 33146-1600 Office: Kelley Drye & Warren LLP 2400 Miami Ctr 201 S Biscayne Blvd Ste 400 Miami FL 33131-4324*

ARMSTRONG, JAMES SINCLAIR, foundation director, retired lawyer; b. N.Y.C., Oct. 15, 1915; s. Sinclair Howard and Katharine Martin (LeBoutillier) A.; m. Charlotte Peirce Horwood Faircloth, Nov. 22, 1978. Student, Milton (Mass.) Acad., 1934; AB cum laude, Harvard, 1938; JD, Harvard U., 1941; postgrad., Northwestern U., 1942-44, 46-48. Bar: Ill. 1941, N.Y. 1959. Assoc. Isham, Lincoln & Beale, Chgo., 1941-45, 46-49; ptnr. Isham, Lincoln & Beale, 1950-53; commr. SEC, Washington, 1953-57; chmn. SEC, 1955-57; asst. sec. navy for fin. mgmt., also compt. Dept. Navy, 1957-59; exec. v.p. U.S. Trust Co. of N.Y., 1959-80; ptnr. Whitman & Ransom, N.Y.C., 1980-84, of counsel, 1984-93; of counsel Whitman Breed Abbott & Morgan, N.Y.C., 1993-94, ret., 1995; bd. dirs., sec., treas. The Reed Found., Inc.; bd. dirs. The Bramwell Growth Fund, Inc. Chmn. emeritus English-Speaking Union U.S.; trustee emeritus, past pres. Gunnery Sch., Washington, Conn.; chmn. emeritus Nat. Inst. Social Scis.; sr. warden emeritus L'Eglise Francaise du St. Esprit; trustee Am. Friends Brit. Libr. Lt. (j.g.) USNR, 1945-46. Decorated officer Order Orange-Nassau (The Netherlands), comdr. Order of the Brit. Empire (U.K.). Mem. Am. Law Inst. (life), Practicing Law Inst. (mem. faculty The SEC Speaks program), Assn. of Bar of City of N.Y., Harvard Law Sch. Assn. (life), Navy League of U.S. (life), N.Y. Hist. Soc. (life), N.Y. Soc. Libr. (life), Am. Soc. Venerable Order St. John of Jerusalem, Pilgrims of U.S., St. Andrews Soc. State of N.Y. (life, past pres.), Huguenot Soc. Am. (life, past pres.), St. Nicholas Soc. City of N.Y. (life), Scottish Heritage USA (life), Soc. Colonial Wars of N.Y. (life), Squadron A Assn. (life), Victorian Soc. in Am. (life), Century Assn., Ch. Club of N.Y. (life, past pres.), Harvard Club, N.Y. Yacht Club, Thurs. Evening Club, Union Club, Chevy Chase (Md.) Club, Washington (Conn.) Club, Washington Garden Club, Edgartown (Mass.) Yacht Club, Edgartown Reading Rm. Home: 501 E 79th St Apt 3C New York NY 10021-0731 Office: The Reed Found Inc 444 Madison Ave Rm 2901 New York NY 10022-6903

ARMSTRONG, JEANETTE, education director; b. Montgomery County, Tenn., Oct. 4, 1939. BA, Tenn. State U., 1961, MA, 1979; MA, U. Mo., 1974; PhD, Vanderbilt U., 1986. Asst. prin. Met. Nashville Sch. Sys., 1985-88, cmty. edn. coord., 1988-91, dir. vocat., adult and cmty. edn., 1991—. Mem. Am. Vocat. Assn., United Tchg. Profls. Office: Met Nashville Edn Sys Cmty Edn Alliance 2601 Bransford Ave Nashville TN 37204-2811*

ARMSTRONG, JOANNA, education educator; b. Vienna, Austria, Feb. 3, 1915; came to U.S., 1946; m. David B. Armstrong, Mar. 12, 1946 (dec. Feb. 1992). Diploma, Kindergarten Tchr. State Coll., Vienna, 1933; diploma French Lit., Sorbonne, Paris, 1935; MA, U. Utah, 1951; EdD, U. Houston, 1959. Caseworker, interpreter Czech Refugee Trust Fund, London, 1939-41; tchr. French Gt. Missenden, Bucks, Eng., 1941-43; sec., translator-interpreter U.S. Army, England and France, 1943-46; instr. Coll. William and Mary, Williamsburg, Va., 1951-55, U. St. Thomas, Houston, 1957-59; chmn. langs. sect. South Tex. Coll., Houston, 1961-62; assoc. prof. fgn. langs. Tex. So. U., Houston, 1962-68; dir. NDEA Inst. U. Tex. at Houston, Houston, summer 1964, 65; assoc. prof. sch. eng. Headstart tchrs. U. Tex., El Paso, 1968-71; cons. office Child Devel. HEW, Kansas City, Mo., 1973-75; ret., 1975; cons. Tex. Edn. Agy., Austin, 1965; sec. U.S. Forest Svc., Ely, Nev., 1948; dir. summer programs U. Bordeaux at Pau, U. Zaragoza at Jaca. Author: (book) A European Excursion-From the Mediterranean to the Alps, 1967, Surprising Encounters, 1994; contbr. articles to profl. publs. Vol. Long Beach (Calif.) Symphony, 1978-81, Long Beach Opera, 1982-88, Long Beach Cambodian Scs., 1983-85; mem. Normandy Found. (participant 50th D-Day anniversary 1994). Decorated chevalier Ordre des Palmes Academiques, 1969; recipient award Heart Start, 1971, Pres. plaque Alliance Francaise El Paso, 1971, Commemorative Medal of Freedom, Coun. of Normandy, France, 1994. Mem. Long Beach Women's Music Club (program chmn. 1986-88, mem. choral sect. 1989-96, 1st v.p. 1990-92, rec. sec., chmn. opera sect. 1993-94), U.S.-China Peoples Friendship Assn. (rec. sec. 1987—), W.A.C. (Queen City chpt. 57). Avocations: walking, swimming, travel, photography, opera. Home: 215 Long Beach Blvd Ste 206 Long Beach CA 90802-3136

ARMSTRONG, JOANNE MARIE, clinical and consulting psychologist, business advisor, mediator; b. Cooperstown, N.Y., Nov. 26, 1956; d. William John and Joan Alice (Larsen) A.; m. Brian Joseph Yore, July 31, 1983; children: Mackensie A., Campbell A. BA, Trinity U., San Antonio, 1978; MA, U. Louisville, 1982, PhD, 1987. Lic. psychologist Wis., S.C. Mgmt. positions in ops., adminstrn. and purchasing Gentec Hosp. Supply Co., San Antonio and Dallas, 1978-79; rsch. asst. U. Louisville, 1980-81; therapist Seven Counties Svcs., Louisville, 1981-82; mental health profl. Head Start, Louisville, 1982-83; psychology intern Dallas VA Med. Ctr./Dallas Ghild Guidance Clinic, 1983-84; dir. Kaufman County Outreach Clinic, Tex. Dept. Mental Health-Mental Retardation, Terrell, 1984-85; clin. psychologist Nicolet Clinic/La Salle Clinic, S.C., Menasha, Wis., 1987-89; pvt. practice, Neenah, Wis., 1989-93; pvt. practice Spartanburg and Greenville, S.C., 1993—; founder Advisors to Bus. and Profls., 1995—; cons. Wellness Counseling Ctr., Appleton, Wis., 1989-93, Fox Valley Hosp., Green Bay, Wis., 1990-91, Greenville (S.C.) Hosp. Sys., 1993—. Mem. bd. Birthing Network, Neenah, 1988-93; mem. Citizens for Better Environ., Neenah, 1989-93. Rsch. fellow U. Louisville, 1985-86. Mem. APA, S.C. Psychol. Assn., S.C. Assn. Profl. Psychologists, Family Firm Inst., Upstate Mediation Network. Episcopalian. Avocations: renovating houses, bicycling, tennis, piano. Office: 2092A Woodruff Rd Greenville SC 29607-9457 also: 390 E Henry St Ste 206 Spartanburg SC 29302-2659

ARMSTRONG, JOHN ALLAN, business machine company research executive; b. Schenectady, N.Y., July 1, 1934; s. Orlo Lucius and Mary Kathryn (Moffitt) A.; m. Elizabeth Jean Saunders, Sept. 20, 1958; children: Sarah Richardson, Jennifer Mary. AB summa cum laude, Harvard U., 1956, MS, PhD, 1961. Rsch. fellow in applied physics Harvard U., Cambridge, Mass., 1961-63; mem. rsch. staff IBM, Yorktown Heights, N.Y., 1963-76; dir. phys. sci. Yorktown Heights, N.Y., 1976-80; mem. corp. tech. com. Armonk, N.Y., 1980-81; mgr. materials and tech. devel. East Fishkill, N.Y., 1981-83; v.p. rsch. div., logic and memory Yorktown Heights, 1983-86, dir. rsch., 1986-87, v.p., dir. rsch., 1987-89; v.p., sci. and tech. Armonk, 1989-93; ret., 1993; mem. Nat. Adv. Com. on Semicondrs.; mem. space studies bd. NRC; K.T. Compton lectr. MIT, 1993-94; mem. Nat. Sci. Bd, 1996—. Bd. overseers Harvard U., 1990-96; chair governing bd. Am. Inst. of Physics, 1998—. Fellow AAAS, IEEE, Am. Acad. Arts and Scis., Optical Soc. Am., Am. Phys. Soc. (Pake prize 1989); mem. NAE (elected councilor 1995—), Royal Swedish Acad. Engring. Scis. (Fgn. mem.).

ARMSTRONG, JOHN J., state agency administrator. AA, U. New Haven, 1976, BS cum laude, 1976, MS in Criminal Justice, 1982. With New Haven Correctional Ctr., 1977-82; various positions Conn. Dept. Correction, 1982—; dist. dir. Conn. Dept. Correction, Enfield, Conn., 1992-94; dep. commr. ctrl. office Conn. Dept. Correction, Hartford, 1994-95; commr. Conn. Dept. Correction, Wethersfield, 1995—; adj. instr. corrections Naugatuck Valley Cmty.-Tech. Coll., Waterbury, Conn., 1987—, U. New Haven, 1989—, Tunxis Cmty.-Tech Coll., 1995—; curriculum devel. advisor Ctrl. Conn. State U., New Britain, 1994—. Mem. Conn. Alcohol and Drug Policy

Coun.; mem. adv. bd. Criminal Justice Command Inst.; mem. Gov.'s Crime Coun.; mem. Sheriff's Adv. Bd.; mem. policy bd. Statewide Crime Task Force. Mem. Am. Correctional Assn., Am. Jail Assn., Am. Probation and Parole Assn., Assn. State Correctional Adminstrs. (exec. com.), Conn. Criminal Justice Assn., Internat. Cmty. Corrections Assn., Mid-Atlantic Correctional Assn., N.E. Assn. Correctional adminstrs. Office: State of Conn Corrections Dept 24 Wolcott Hill Rd Wethersfield CT 06109

ARMSTRONG, KENNETH, corporate lawyer. AB, Ind. U., 1969; JD, U. Chgo., 1972. Bar: Ohio 1973, Fla. 1987. Ptnr. Fuller & Henry, 1978-86; asst. gen. counsel Fla. Progress Corp., St. Petersburg, 1986-90, v.p., gen. counsel, 1990—. Office: Fla Progress Corp One Progress Plz Ste 2600 Saint Petersburg FL 33701

ARMSTRONG, KEVIN WILLIAM, marketing executive, researcher; b. Rockford, Ill., Apr. 29, 1958; s. William Robert and Dorothy Ellen (McCann) A.; children from previous marriage: Brian Kevin, Kathleen, Theodore Robert; m. Roxanne Lynn Grabow, Oct. 20, 1990; children: Kelly Erin, Megan Maureen. BA in History & Econ., Univ. Ill., 1980. Restaurant mgmt. Hardee's Food Systems, Inc., Rocky Mount, N.C., 1980-83, dir. fin., 1983-86, dir. devel., 1986, dir. sales analysis, 1986-87; dir. ops. Terratron, Inc., Salt Lake City, 1987-89; v.p. listening & responding Burger King Corp., Miami, 1989-91; pres. Armstrong Cons. Group, Delavan, Wis., 1991—; cons. Info. Resources, Inc., Chgo., 1989-96; pres. Pepsi-Cola Restaurant Cons. Group, Somers, N.Y., 1991-96; mem. bd. dirs. Lakeland Med. Ctr., Elkhorn, Wis., 1994—; bd. supr. Walworth County Bd. Supr., 1994—; mktg. dir. Subway Franchise Advt. Fund Trust, 1996—. Contbr. articles to profl. jours. Fin. chmn. Rock Island Sesquicentennial Soc., 1986; dir. Hardee's Golf Classic, Moline, Ill., 1985-86; mem. invesmtnet com., fin. com. Walworth County Bd. Suprs., 1994—; bd. dirs. Lakeland Med. Ctr., Inc. Mem. Wis. Hist. Soc., Delta Kappa Epsilon (pres. 1978-79), Phi Alpha Theta. Conservative. Avocations: football, politics, history, golf, gardening. Home: 216 N 4th St Delavan WI 53115-1204 Office: Armstrong Cons Group 216 N 4th St Delavan WI 53115-1204

ARMSTRONG, LANCE, professional cyclist; b. Plano, Tex., Sept. 8, 1972. Professional cyclist Motorola Team, 1990—. World Road-Racing Champion, 1993; US Professional Champion, 1993. Triathlete Rookie of the Year, 1988; winner Tour DuPont, 1995; winner 19 out of 21 stages Tourde France, 1999, overall winner, Tour de France, 1999. Former swimmer and triathlete. Office: care US Cycling Federation 1750 E Boulder St Colorado Springs CO 80909-5724 also: Lance Armstrong Found PO Box 27483 Austin TX 78755-2483*

ARMSTRONG, LINDA JEAN (GENE), writer, artist; b. L.A., Feb. 23, 1947; d. Charles Fred and Mary Eugenia (Gentry) Keck; m. Alden Arthur Armstrong, July 28, 1966; 1 child, Amy Alice. BA, Calif. State Coll., 1969. Tchr. elem. sch. L.A. Unified Sch. Dist., 1970-86; writer, artist, 1986—. Author: Early Tigers, 1995, Tanya's Desert Star, 1997. Fellow Woodstock (N.Y.) Sch. Art, 1993. Mem. Soc. Children's Book Writers and Illustrators. Home: PO Box 3151 Grand Junction CO 81502-3151

ARMSTRONG, LLOYD, JR., university official, physics educator; b. Austin, Tex., May 19, 1940; s. Lloyd and Beatrice (Jackson) A.; m. Judith Glantz, July 9, 1965; 1 son, Wade Matthew. BS in Physics, MIT, 1962; PhD in Physics, U. Calif., Berkeley, 1966. Postdoctoral physicist Lawrence Berkeley (Calif.) Lab., 1965-66, cons., 1976; sr. physicist Westinghouse Research Labs., Pitts., 1967-68, cons., 1968-70; research asso. Johns Hopkins U., 1968-69, asst. prof. physics, 1969-73, assoc. prof., 1973-77, prof., 1977-93, chmn. dept. physics and astronomy, 1985-87, dean Sch. Arts and Scis., 1987-93; provost, sr. v.p. for acad. affairs U. So. Calif., L.A., 1993—, prof. physics, 1993—; assoc. rsch. scientist Nat. Ctr. Sci. Rsch. (CNRS), Orsay, France, 1972-73; vis. fellow Joint Inst. Lab. Astrophysics, Boulder, Colo., 1978-79; program officer NSF, 1981-83, mem. adv. com. for physics, 1985-87, mem. visitors com. physics divsn., 1991; chmn. com. atomic and molecular scis. NAS/NRC, 1985-88, mem. bd. physics and astronomy, 1989-96; mem. adv. bd. Inst. for Theoretical Physics, Santa Barbara, 1992-96, chmn., 1994-95, Inst. Theoretical Atomic and Molecular Physics, Cambridge, Mass., 1994-97, Rochester Theory Ctr. for Optical Sci. and Enging., 1996—, chmn., 1997—; bd. dirs. So. Calif. Econ. Partnership, 1994—, Calif. Coun. on Sci. and Tech., 1994—, Pacific Coun. on Internat. Policy, 1996—. Author: Theory of Hyperfine Structure of Free Atoms, 1971; contbr. articles to profl. jours. NSF grantee, 1972-90; Dept. Energy grantee, 1975-82. Fellow Am. Phys. Soc. Office: U So Calif Office Provost University Park Los Angeles CA 90089-4019

ARMSTRONG, MARTHA SUSAN, accountant, educator; b. Harrisonburg, Va., Dec. 28, 1954; d. Harry Lee and Elizabeth (Roller) Anderson; m. Marvin Edward Armstrong, May 27, 1978; children: Nathaniel Roller, Andrew Michael. BBA cum laude, Bridgewater Coll., 1977; MS in Acctg., U. Va., 1985. CPA, Va. Asst. dir. of fin. aid Bridgewater (Va.) Coll., 1978-81, asst. prof. acctg. and bus. adminstrn., 1981-98; staff acct. Morris & Sprinkel CPA's, Harrisonburg, 1985—; cons. acctg. edn. WLR Foods, Hinton, 1990-95. Deacon Bridgewater Presbyn. Ch., 1982-85, v.p. Women of the Ch., 1983-85, asst. ch. treas., 1990-95; concert bell ringer Harrisonburg 1st Presbyn. Ch., 1987-91, treas. Dayton Nursery Sch., 1991-94; treas. PTA Pleasnat Valley Elem. Sch., 1998—. Named one of Outstanding Young Women Am., 1986; recipient Martha Thornton Tchg. award, 1998. Mem. AICPA, Va. Soc. CPAs. Home: 2644 Oscesta Springs Rd Harrisonburg VA 22801-8607 Office: Accounting Dept Bridgewater Coll Bridgewater VA 22812

ARMSTRONG, MICHAEL DAVID, investment banker; b. Bronxville, N.Y., May 7, 1955; s. Frank and Dorothy Armstrong; m. Deborah Jane Lauderdale, 1984. BA, Washington and Lee U., 1977; MBA, Coll. William and Mary, 1982. Prodn. mgr., account exec. Austin Kelley Adv., Atlanta, 1977-80; sr. assoc. 1st San Francisco Corp., Foster City, Calif., 1983-88, Bankers Trust Co., Atlanta, 1988-90; gen. mgr. Gimborn U.S., Atlanta, 1990-93; pres. New Market Beverage Co., Atlanta, 1994—. Mem. Atlanta Hist. Soc., Atlanta Bot. Gardens; trustee Washington and Lee U. Mem. Mu Beta Psi. Avocations: skiing, golf, swimming, reading, travel.

ARMSTRONG, MICHAEL J., federal agency administrator; b. Long Beach, Calif., June 24, 1955. BA in English, BS in Journalism, U. Colo.; JD, Pepperdine U. Asst. city atty. Aurora, Colo.; dep. dir. energy conservation Colo. Gov.'s Office; regional dir. Fed. Emergency Mgmt. Agy., Washington, 1994-97, assoc. dir. for mitigation, 1997—. Contbr. articles to newspapers. Office: Fed Emergency Mgmt Agy 500 C St SW Washington DC 20472

ARMSTRONG, NEAL EARL, civil engineering educator; b. Dallas, Jan. 29, 1941; m. Nancy L. Weinerth; 5 children. B.A., U. Tex., 1962, M.A., 1965, Ph.D., 1968. Research engr. Enging. Sci., Inc., 1967-68; asst. office mgr., cons. san. enging., 1968-70; mgr. Washington Research and Devel. Lab., 1970-71; assoc. prof. civil enging. U. Tex., Austin, 1971-79, prof., 1979—, assoc. chmn. dept., 1989-96, assoc. dean acad. affairs Coll. Enging., 1996—. Mem. ASCE, Water Environ. Fedn. (Svc. award 1976, 84, 96), Am. Acad. Environ. Engrs. (diplomate), Internat. Assn. on Water Quality, Am. Soc. Limnology and Oceanography, Estuarine Rsch. Fedn. (v.p. 1975-77), Am. Soc. Enging. Edn., Soc. Environ. Toxicology and Chemistry. Office: U Tex Dept Civil Enging Austin TX 78712

ARMSTRONG, NEIL A., former astronaut; b. Wapakoneta, Ohio, Aug. 5, 1930; s. Stephen A.; children: Eric, Mark. B.S. In Aero. Enging., Purdue U., 1955; M.S. in Aero. Enging., U. So. Calif. With Lewis Flight Propulsion Lab., NACA, 1955; then aero. research pilot for NACA (later NASA, High Speed Flight Sta.), Edwards, Calif.; astronaut Manned Spacecraft Center, NASA, Houston, 1962-70; command pilot Gemini 8; comdr. Apollo 11; dep. assoc. adminstr. for aeros. Office Advanced Research and Tech., Hdqrs. NASA, Washington, 1970-71; prof. aerospace engring. U. Cin., 1971-79; chmn. AIL Sys., Inc., 1989—. Mem. Pres.'s Commn. on Space Shuttle, 1986, Nat. Commn. on Space, 1985-86. Served as naval aviator USN, 1949-52, Korea. Recipient numerous awards, including Octave Chanute award Inst. Aero. Scis., 1962, Presdl. Medal for Freedom, 1969, Exceptional Service medal NASA, Hubbard Gold medal Nat. Geog. Soc., 1970, Kitty Hawk Meml. award, 1969, Pere Marquette medal, 1969, Arthur S. Fleming award, 1970, Congl. Space Medal of Honor, Explorers Club medal. Fellow AIAA (hon., Astronautics award 1966), Internat. Astronautical Fedn. (hon.), Soc. Exptl. Test Pilots; mem. Nat. Acad. Engring. *

ARMSTRONG, NELSON WILLIAM, JR., gaming company executive; b. Port Huron, Mich., Mar. 5, 1941; s. Nelson William and Kathryn J. (Clarke) A.; m. Judith A. Roth, Sept. 5, 1964; children: Nelson William III, Tad John. BA, Mich. State U., 1964. Acct., Gen. Motors Corp., Warren, Mich., 1964-66; in acctg. and fin. Consumers Power Co., Jackson, Mich., 1966-73; dir. acctg. Ramada Inns Inc., Phoenix, 1973-77, asst. contr., 1977-79, v.p. audit svcs., 1979-82, corp. contr., 1982-85, v.p. adminstrn., 1985—; v.p. audit and adminstrv. svcs., 1985—; v.p. corp. contr., 1987-90; v.p. adminstrn., sec. Aztar Corp., Phoenix, 1990.Mem. profl. adv. bd. Ariz. State U. Sch. Acctg. Mem. Fin. Execs. Inst. Republican. Office: Aztar Corp 2390 E Camelback Rd Phoenix AZ 85016-3448

ARMSTRONG, ORVILLE, judge; b. Austin, Tex., Jan. 21, 1929; s. Orville Alexander and Velma Lucille (Reed) A.; m. Mary Dean Macfarlane; children: Anna Louise Glenn, John M., Paul Jefferson. BBA, U. Tex., Austin, 1953; LLB, U. So. Calif., 1956. Bar: Calif., 1957, U.S. Ct. Appeals (9th cir.) 1958, U.S. Supreme Ct. 1980. Ptnr., Gray, Binkley & Pfaelzer, 1956-61, Pfaelzer, Robertson, Armstrong & Woodard, L.A., 1961-66, Armstrong & Lloyd, L.A., 1966-74, Macdonald, Halsted & Laybourne, L.A., 1975-88, Baker & McKenzie, 1988-90; judge Superior Ct. State of Calif., 1991-92, assoc. justice ct. appeal State of Calif., 1993—; lectr. Calif. Continuing Edn. of Bar. Served with USAF, 1946-49. Fellow ABA, Am. Coll. Trial Lawyers; mem. State Bar Calif. (gov. 1983-87, pres. 1986-87), L.A. County Bar Assn. (trustee 1971-72), Chancery Club (pres. 1988), Calif. Club. Baptist. Office: 300 S Spring St Los Angeles CA 90013-1230

ARMSTRONG, PHILLIP DALE, lawyer; b. Waukegan, Ill., Mar. 27, 1943; s. James Leonard and Bernice Frances (Nader) A.; m. Leila Robson; children: Leonard Hart, Theodore Nader, Leila VIII. BS in Chem. Enging., U. Mo., 1966; JD, Gonzaga U., 1978; LLM, U. Mo., Kansas City, 1979. Bar: N.D. 1979, U.S. Dist. Ct. N.D. 1979, U.S. Dist. Ct. Ariz. 1991, U.S. Tax Ct. 1980, U.S. Ct. Appeals 1983, U.S. Supreme Ct. 1984. Mktg. trainee Dow Chem. Co., Midland, Mich., 1966-68; chem. engr. Clark Oil and Refining, Hartford, Ill., 1968-70; life guard, pool attendant, pool mgr. various hotels and condominiums, Miami Beach, Fla., 1970-75; assoc. McCutcheon Law Firm, Minot, N.D., 1979-81; sole practice Minot, 1981—, Mandan, N.D., 1995—; founder, pres. Producers Oil & Gas Corp., 1992—; trustee in bankruptcy for chpts. 7, 12, and 13, N.W. and S.W. divs. Dist. of N.D., 1980-95; founder Armstrong Oilwell Ops., 1996. Mem. ABA, N.D. Bar Assn., Nat. Assn. Bankruptcy Trustees, Am. Bankruptcy Inst., Exch. Club (Minot). Republican. Episcopalian. Home: 1006 Valley View Dr Minot ND 58703-1642 Office: Armstrong Law Firm 12 Main St S Minot ND 58701-3871 also: 402 1st St NW Mandan ND 58554-3118

ARMSTRONG, RICHARD STOLL, minister, educator, writer, poet; b. Balt., Mar. 29, 1924; s. Herbert Eustace and Elsie Davis (Stoll) A.; m. Margaret Childs, Jan. 31, 1948; children: Ellen, Richard, Andrew, William, Elsie. BA, Princeton U., 1947; MDiv, Princeton Theol. Sem., 1958; DMin, Christian Theol. Sem.-Indpls., 1978; doctoral, Temple U., 1962-68. Ordained to ministry Presbyn. Ch., 1958. Pastor Oak Lane Presbyn. Ch., Phila., 1958-68; dir. devel. Princeton (N.J.) Theol. Sem., 1968-71, v.p. devel., 1971-74, prof. ministry and evangelism, 1980-90, prof. emeritus, 1990—; pastor 2d Presbyn. Ch., Indpls., 1974-80; life trustee Fellowship Christian Athletes, Inc., Kansas City, Mo., 1979—; mem. ch. mins. adv. bd. Christian Theol. Sem., 1975-80; bd. dirs. Nat. Conf. Christians and Jews, Ind., 1975-80, Ind. Inter-Religious Commn. on Human Equality, 1975-80. Author: The Oak Lane Story, 1971, Service Evangelism, 1979, The Pastor as Evangelist, 1984, The Pastor-Evangelist in Worship, 1986, Faithful Witnesses, 1987, The Pastor-Evangelist in the Parish, 1990, Enough, Already!, 1993, Now, That's A Miracle!, 1996, Faithful Witnesses MiniCourse, 1997, If I Do Say So Myself, 1997; contbg. author: Westminster Dictionary of Christian Theology, 1983. Bd. dirs. Indpls. Symphony Orch., 1978-80; trustee emeritus Am. Boychoir Sch., 1980—; trustee McDonogh Sch., Md., 1980-90; mem. adv. com., div. for contextual ministry Vista U., South Africa; mem. Nat. Coun. Presbyn. Men. 1995—; Lt. (j.g.) USN, 1942-46. Recipient Disting. Svc. award Fellowship of Christian Athletes, 1965, Branch Rickey Meml. award, 1974, Alumni Svc. award Princeton Theol. Sem., 1974, Outstanding Svc. award Nat. Conf. Christians and Jews, 1980, Robert L. Peters award Princeton U., 1990; named Man of Week, Princeton Town Topics, 1957, 68. Mem. Presbytery of New Brunswick (v.p.), Acad. for Evangelism Theol. Edn. (pres. 1989-91, Jour. editor 1991-97, Charles Grandison Finney award 1997), Presbyn. Writers' Guild, Poetry Soc. Am., Gallup Internat. Inst., Phila. A's Hist. Soc. Home: 3620 Lawrenceville Rd Princeton NJ 08540-4374 Office: Princeton Theol Sem PO Box 821 Princeton NJ 08542-0803

ARMSTRONG, RICHARD WILLIAM, bank executive, management consultant; b. Phila., June 18, 1932; s. Richard Mervyn and Elvina (Burns) A.; m. Barbara Robbins, Sept. 5, 1959; children: Richard W. Jr., James M. AB cum laude, Harvard U., 1954; MA, Johns Hopkins U., 1959. Fin. mgr. AEC, NASA and OEO, Washington, 1959-69; dep. mgr. Head Start, Washington, 1969-70; corp. budget dir. Chase Manhattan Bank, N.Y.C., 1970-78, chief fin. and adminstrv. officer real estate fin. bus., 1978-84, chief fin. and adminstrv. officer comml. sector, 1984-89, chief fin. and adminstrv. officer real estate fin. sector, 1989-91; mgmt. cons. N.Y.C., 1992—; prin. Coun. for Excellence in Govt., 1992—. Mem. audit com. Madison (N.J.) Presbyn. Ch., 1981; trustee, fin. officer Bethesda (Md.) Congl. Ch., 1965-67; mem. N.J. Harvard Schs. and Scholarship Com., 1983-88; bd. dirs. Family Svc. of Morris County, N.J., 1998. Lt. USN, 1954-57. Recipient Ford Found. award, 1967; Princeton U. fellow, 1968. Avocations: sailing, swimming, aquatic sports, hiking, travel. Home and Office: 10 Pomeroy Rd Madison NJ 07940-2619

ARMSTRONG, ROBERT, retired federal agency administrator. Asst. sec. land and minerals mgmt. Dept. of the Interior, 1993-98. Office: Dept of the Interior Land & Minerals Management 1849 C St NW Washington DC 20240-0002*

ARMSTRONG, ROBERT ARNOLD, petroleum company executive; b. Chgo., Feb. 17, 1928; s. Arnold Gustave and Lillian (Laver) A.; m. Jane Victoria Colestock, May 13, 1951 (dec. 1964); children: Michael, Richard, Patricia, Casey; m. Margaret Soden, Nov. 17, 1973; children: Gregory, Jennifer. Student, Mo. Sch. Mines, 1946-48; B.S., Stanford U., 1951; postgrad., Colo. Sch. Mines, 1956-58; M.S., U. So. Calif., 1961, postgrad., 1961-64. Petroleum engr. S.Am.; with Standard Oil Co. of Calif., 1951-58; research engr. Chevron Research Labs., La Habra, Calif., 1958-61; sr. evaluation engr. Union Oil Co., Los Angeles, 1961-63; v.p. Lee Keeling & Assocs., Los Angeles, 1963-65; pres. Armstrong Petroleum Corp., Newport Beach, Calif., 1965—; pres. West Newport Oil Co., 1983—, also bd. dirs.; pres. Los Amigos de Aviones, Tram Tower Comm. Assn.; bd. dirs. Armstrong Petroleum, Calif. Ind. Oil Producers; dir., pres. West Newport Oil Co., Newport Beach, Calif., Angel Flight; vis. prof. enging. U. So. Calif., Los Angeles, 1960-65. patentee in field of subsea prodn. systems. Mem. adv. bd. Stanford Bus. Sch.; chmn. U.S. Internat. U., Africa, chmn., San Diego. Mem. AAAS, Ind. Oilman's Assn., Calif. Conservation Comm., Am. Inst. Mining Engrs. (pres. jr. group, petroleum br. 1960-61), Am. Petroleum Inst., Orange County Petroleum Assn. (bd. dirs.). Office: 2244 W Coast Hwy Newport Beach CA 92663-4724

ARMSTRONG, ROBERT BEALL, physiologist; b. Hastings, Nebr., Nov. 13, 1940; s. Edwin Ollis and Elena (Beall) A.; m. Ingrid Elizabeth Vaiciulenas, Apr. 9, 1966; children: Edwin John, Andrew Niel, Sarah Elizabeth. BA, Hastings Coll., 1962; MS, Wash. State U., 1970, PhD, 1973. Asst. prof. biology Boston U., 1973-78; assoc. prof. physiology Oral Roberts U., Tulsa, Okla., 1978-81, prof. physiology, 1981-85; prof. U. Ga., Athens, 1985-90, rsch. prof., 1990-92; Omar Smith prof. health and kinesiology Tex. A&M U., College Station, 1992—, Omar Smith chair, 1995—; disting. prof., 1995—; assoc. zoology Harvard U., Cambridge, Mass., 1977-87; external examiner Nat. U. Singapore, 1984-85; rsch. com. Am. Heart Assn., Athens, 1987-89. Assoc. editor Med. Sci. Sports Exercise, Indpls., 1985-87; contbr. articles to Jour. Applied Physiology, Am. Jour. Physiology. NSF fellow, 1970-73; grantee NIH, 1975-97, Am. Heart Assn., 1981-89. Fellow Am. Coll. Sports Medicine (trustee 1986-88); mem. Am. Physiol. Soc. Office: Tex A & M U Dept Health & Kinesiology College Station TX 77843

ARMSTRONG, R(OBERT) DEAN, entertainer; b. Serena, Ill., July 2, 1923; s. Francis Robert and Viola D. (Thompson) A.; m. Ardith Roberta Taylor, Jan. 10, 1943; 1 child, Larry Dean. Grad. high sch., Serena, Ill.; student, Joliet (Ill.) Conservatory of Music, 1942. Host Dean Armstrong Show Sta. KOLD-TV, Tucson, 1953-75; leader, owner Ariz. Dance Hands, Tucson, 1946—. Served with U.S. Mil., 1943-45, ETO, PTO. Recipient Jefferson award Am. Inst. for Pub. Svc., 1992; inducted into Tucson Area Music Assn. Hall of Fame, 1994. Mem. Tucson Musicians Assn. (meritorious svc. award 1981), VFW, Western Music Assn. (charter mem.), Profl. Western Music Assn. Democrat. Methodist. Lodges: Elks, Eagles. Home and Office: 4265 N Avenida Del Cazador Tucson AZ 85718-7005

ARMSTRONG, ROBERT R., JR., federal judge; b. 1948. BA, U. Ala., 1970; JD, Cumberland U., 1974. Presiding judge Ala. Cir. Ct. 18th Jud. Dist., Shelby County, 1987-90; magistrate judge State of Ala., Birmingham, 1990—. Fax: 205-731-2326. Office: 274 US Courthouse 1729 Fifth Ave North Birmingham AL 35203

ARMSTRONG, ROBIN LOUIS, university official, physicist; b. Galt, Ont., Can., May 14, 1935; s. Robert Dockstader and Beatrice Jenny (Grill) S.; m. Karen Elisabeth Feilberg Hansen, July 8, 1960; children: Keir Grill, Christopher Drew. B.A., U. Toronto, 1958, M.A., 1959; Ph.D., 1961, FRSC, 1979. Rutherford Meml. fellow Oxford (Eng.) U., 1961-62; mem. faculty U. Toronto, 1962-90, prof. physics, 1971-90, chmn. dept., 1974-82, dean Faculty of Arts and Sci., 1982-90; prof. emeritus U. Toronto, Fredericton and Saint John, 1998—; pres. U. N.B., Fredericton, St. John, 1990-96, prof. physics, 1990—, Wilfrid Laurier U. spl. advisor to the pres., 1997—; pres. Can. Inst. Neutron Scattering, 1986-89; founding dir. Can. Inst. Advanced Rsch., 1981-82, mem. rsch. coun., 1982—; mem. coun. Nat. Sci. and Enging. Rsch. Coun., 1991-97 mem. exec., 1992-97, v.p., 1994-97. Co-author: Mechanics, Waves and Thermal Physics, 1970, Electromagnetic Interaction, 1973; contbr. articles to profl. jours. Recipient Commemorative medal for 125th Anniversary of Can. Confedn., 1992, Designated Visitante Distinguido U. Cordoba, Argentina, 1987. Mem. Can. Assn. Physicists (v.p. 1989-90, pres. 1990-91, Herzberg medal 1973, medal for achievement 1990), Can. Assn. Physics, Internat. Soc. Magnetic Resonance Medicine. Home: 540 Huron St, Toronto, ON Canada M5R 2R7 Office: U Toronto Dept Physics, 60 St George St, Toronto, ON Canada M5S 1A7

ARMSTRONG, RODNEY, librarian; b. Atlanta, Mar. 5, 1923; s. Harold Rodney and Mary Blair (Armstrong) A.; m. Katharine Price Cortesi, June 14, 1969; children: Louise Spencer, Robert Knowlton. BA, Williams Coll., 1948; MS, Columbia U., 1950. Libr. Phillips Exeter (N.H.) Acad., 1950-73; dir., libr. Boston Athenaeum, 1973-97, dir. and libr. emeritus, 1997—; N.E. assoc. Sotheby's. Pres., trustee Trustees For Edn. in Liberia, 1974—. Decorated Purple Heart; Benjamin Franklin fellow Royal Soc. Arts, 1974. Fellow Am. Acad. Arts and Scis., Soc. Antiquaries, Pilgrim Soc.; mem. ALA (life), N.H. Libr. Assn. (past officer, bd. dirs.), Am. Antiquarian Soc., Colonial Soc. Mass., Mass. Hist. Soc., Manuscript Soc. (bd. dirs., past pres.), New Eng. Hist. Geneal. Soc. (pres. 1977-82), Century Assn. (N.Y.C.), Grolier Club (N.Y.C.), Odd Volumes Club (pres. 1979-83). Episcopalian. Home: 101 Chestnut St Boston MA 02108-1032 Office: Sothebys 67 1/2 Chestnut St Boston MA 02108-1121

ARMSTRONG, SAUNDRA BROWN, federal judge; b. Oakland, Calif., Mar. 23, 1947; d. Coolidge Logan and Pauline Marquette Brown; m. George Walter Armstrong, Apr. 18, 1982. B.A., Calif. State U.-Fresno, 1969; J.D. magna cum laude, U. San Francisco, 1977. Bar: Calif. 1977, U.S. Supreme Ct. 1984. Policewoman Oakland Police Dept., 1970-77; prosecutor, dep. dist. atty. Alameda County Dist. Atty., Oakland, 1978-79, 80-82; staff atty. Calif. Legis. Assembly Com. on Criminal Justice, Sacramento, 1979-80; trial atty. Dept. Justice, Washington, 1982-83; vice chmn. U.S. Consumer Product Safety Commn., Washington, 1984-86; commr. U.S. Parole Commn., Washington, 1986-89; judge Alameda Superior Ct., 1989-91, U.S. Dist. Ct. (no. dist.) Calif., San Francisco, 1991—. Recipient commendation Calif. Assembly, 1980. Mem. Nat. Bar Assn., ABA, Calif. Bar Assn., Charles Houston Bar Assn., Black C. of C., Phi Alpha Delta. Republican. Baptist. Office: US Dist Ct Ste 400 S 1301 Clay St Oakland CA 94612-5217*

ARMSTRONG, SPENCE M., aerospace technology administrator; m. Beth Webb; 2 children. BS in Gen. Enging., U.S. Naval Acad., 1956; MS in Astron. Enging., MS in Instrumentation Enging., U. Mich., 1963; postgrad. in Bus. Adminstrn., Columbia U., 1976, Harvard U., 1978. Commd. 2d lt. USAF, advanced through grades to lt. gen.; ops. officer 34th Tactical Fighter Squadron, Korat Royal Thai Air Base, Thailand, 1967-68; various positions including comdr. Air Force Mil. Tng. Ctr., Randolph AFB, Tex.; chief U.S. Mil. Tng. Mission to Saudi Arabia, U.S. Ctrl. Command; vice comdr.-in-chief USAF Mil. Airlift Command; vice comdr. USAF Systems Command; ret. USAF, 1990; dir. program architecture Synthesis Group, 1990-91; assoc. adminstr. Human Resources and Edn., NASA, Washington, assoc. adminstr. Office of Aerospace Tech.,. Decorated D.F.C. with two oak clusters, Def. D.S.M. with one oak leaf cluster, D.S.M. with one oak leaf cluster, Legion of Merit with one oak cluster, Air medal with 14 oak leaf clusters, Meritorious Svc. medal, Saudi Arabian King Abdulaziz Badge 2d grade and 13 other ribbons. Office: Office of Aerospace Tech 300 E St SW Washington DC 20024-3210

ARMSTRONG, STEVEN HOLM, lawyer. AB in History and Lit., Harvard U.; JD, Columbia U., 1990. Bar: Conn. 1990, N.Y. 1991. Asst. city editor Miami (Fla.) Herald, 1982-87; atty. Townley & Updike, 1990-94; regulatory atty. in antitrust, contracts and govt. rels. Colgate Palmolive Co., N.Y.C., 1995—. Office: Colgate Palmolive Co 300 Park Ave Fl 8 New York NY 10022-7499*

ARMSTRONG, TERRY LEE, publishing executive, carpenter; b. Elgin, Nebr., Dec. 23, 1949; s. Lou Elvin and Donna Mae (Riggs) A.; m. Christine Angelina Alvarez, Nov. 15, 1991; 1 child, Rebecca Leigh. AA, San Antonio Coll., 1977. V.p. ArmWel, Inc., San Antonio, 1980-89; editor, pub. Lone Stars Mag., San Antonio, 1990—; carpenter San Antonio Indep. Sch. Dist., San Antonio, 1992—. Author: Wordweavers, 1992 (Hon. award), World of Poetry, 1992 (Golden Poet), Wordsmith, 1992 (Spl. Honor); editor, pub. Poet's Market, 1992. Recipient 1st pl. Nat. Libr. Poetry, 1990-91; named Poet of the Month Poetry of the People, 1990, Poet of the Yr. Poetry Break Jour., 1991.

ARMSTRONG, THEODORE MORELOCK, financial executive; b. St. Louis, July 22, 1939; s. Theodore Roosevelt and Vassar Fambrough (Morelock) A.; m. Carol Mercer Robert, Sept. 7, 1963; children: Evelyn Anne, Robert Theodore. BA, Yale U., 1961; LLB, Duke U., 1964. Bar: Mo. 1964. With Miss. River Transmission Corp. and affiliated cos., 1964-85; corp. sec. Mo. Pacific Corp., 1971-75, River Cement Co., 1968-75; asst. v.p. Miss. River Transmission Corp., 1974-75, v.p. gas supply, 1975-79, exec. v.p., 1979-83, pres., chief exec. officer, 1983-85; exec. v.p. Natural Gas Pipeline of Am., 1985; sr. v.p. fin. and adminstrn., chief fin. officer Angelica Corp., St. Louis, 1986—; bd. dirs. UMB Bank of St. Louis, Gen. Am. Capital Co., Walnut Street Funds, Inc. Bd. dirs. Ctrl. Inst. for Deaf; bd. dirs., chmn. Boys and Girls Town Mo.; mem., past pres. Tenn. Soc. St. Louis. Mem. ABA, Mo. Bar Assn., St. Louis Bar Assn., Bellerive Country Club, Saint Louis Club, Yale Club (St. Louis, N.Y.C.), Phi Alpha Delta. Republican. Presbyterian. Home: 43 Countryside Ln Saint Louis MO 63131-3310 Office: Angelica Corp 424 S Woods Mill Rd Chesterfield MO 63017-3431

ARMSTRONG, THOMAS ERROL, state legislator; b. Prescott, Ariz., Jan. 22, 1959; s. Paul David and Betty Jane (Muckey) A.; children: Thomas E. II, Christine Joy; m. Janice Christine, Sept. 13, 1980. A in Bus., Pa. State U., Reading, 1980. Owner, operator Remco Maintenance, Elizabethtown, Pa., 1981-84; asst. mgr. Roy Rogers, Lemoyne, Pa., 1984-85; comptroller Gordon Waste Co., Inc., Columbia, Pa., 1985-91; mem. Pa. Ho. of Reps., Harrisburg, 1991—; mem. labor rels. com., agrl. and rural affairs com., local govt. com., subcom. chmn. of boroughs, intergovtl. affairs and policy com. Pa. Ho. of Reps. Pres. Full Gospel Bus. Mens Fellowship Internat., Mt. Joy, Pa., 1994,

95. Mem. Kiwanis (pres. 1995). Avocations: music, home renovation. Home: 704 E Market St Marietta PA 17547-1810 Office: Ho of Reps PO Box 89 Bldg Harrisburg PA 17108-0089*

ARMSTRONG, THOMAS GLIEM, steel company executive; b. Ann Arbor, Mich., Nov. 28, 1953; s. Jack G. and Ellen Lee (Gliem) A.; m. Patricia Ann Markell, Oct. 22, 1977; children: Lauren, Susan. BS in Acctg., Washington & Lee U., 1975. CPA, Pa. Acct. Price Waterhouse & Co., Pitts., 1975-81; chief fin. officer HInkel-Hofmann Supply Co., Pitts., 1981-85; asst. to pres./plant mgr. Standard Steel Specialty Corp., Reidville, S.C., 1985-91, pres., CEO, 1991—. Mem. AICPAs, Young Pres. Orgn. Internat., Rotary, Scottish Rite. Presbyn. Avocations: golf, sailing. Office: PO Box 700 Reidville SC 29375-0700

ARMSTRONG, THOMAS NEWTON, III, American art and garden specialist, consultant; b. Portsmouth, Va., July 30, 1932; s. Thomas Newton, Jr. and Mary Saunders (Tabb) A.; m. Virginia Whitney Brewster, May 18, 1963; children: Thomas Newton IV, Whitney, Eliot, Amory. Student, Cornell U., 1950-54, Art Students League, summer 1953, Inst. Fine Arts, NYU, 1965-67. Personnel coordinator, asst. to chmn. bd. Stone & Webster, Inc., N.Y.C., 1957-65; curator, assoc. dir. Colonial Williamsburg-Abby Aldrich Rockefeller Folk Art Collection, Williamsburg, Va., 1967-71; dir. Pa. Acad. Fine Arts, Phila., 1971-73; dir. Whitney Mus. Am. Art, 1974-90, dir. emeritus, 1990—; dir. Andy Warhol Mus., Pitts., 1993-95; dir., pres. The Garden Conservancy; mem. selection com. Luce Scholars Program, Henry Luce Found., Inc.; dir. Nat. Bldg. Mus., 1999—. Trustee Nat. Bldg. Mus., Exhbns. Internat.

ARMSTRONG, VERNELIS K., federal magistrate judge; b. 1935. BA with distinction, Wayne State U., 1956, JD with distinction, 1960. Bar: Mich. 1961, Ohio 1973, U.S. Supreme Ct. 1980. Asst. atty. gen. Mich. Atty. Gen.'s Office, 1961-62; law clk. to Hon. Paul L. Adams Supreme Ct. of Mich., Lansing, 1962; asst. U.S. atty. civil divsn. U.S. Dist. Ct. (no. dist.) Ohio, 1979-94; magistrate judge U.S. Dist. Ct. (no. dist.) Ohio, Toledo, 1994—. Mem. ABA, State Bar Mich., Ohio State Bar, Ohio Women's Bar Assn., Toledo Bar Assn., Toledo Women's Bar Assn., Thurgood Marshall Bar Assn. Fax: (419) 259-3728. Office: US Dist Ct No Dist Ohio 318 US Courthouse 1716 Spielbush Ave Toledo OH 43624

ARMSTRONG, WILLIAM TUCKER, III, lawyer; b. Houston, Nov. 13, 1947; s. William Tucker Jr. and Jess (Nettles) A.; m. Nancy Bayliss Armstrong, Feb. 18, 1978; children: Will, Anne, Daniel. BA, Am. U., 1969; JD with honors, U. Tex., 1972. Bar: Tex. 1972, U.S. Ct. Appeals (5th cir.) 1972, U.S. Dist. Ct. (so. & we. dists.) Tex. 1978, U.S. Ct. Appeals (11th cir.) 1982, U.S. Ct. Appeals (D.C. cir.) 1983. Staff counsel for inmates Tex. Dept. Corrections, Huntsville, 1972-73; assoc. Foster, Lewis, Langley, Gardner & Banack, San Antonio, 1973-76, shareholder, 1976-96; shareholder Jeffers & Banack, 1996—. Active South Tex. Leukemia Soc., bd. dirs., 1989-92. Mem. Tex. State Bar Assn. (mem. coun. sch. law sect. 1985-87), San Antonio Longhorn Club (pres. 1993-94), San Antonio Tex. Exes (pres. 1995-96), Oak Hills Country Club (dir. 1998—). Methodist. Avocation: golf. E-mail: warmstrong@jeffersbanack.com. Office: Jeffers & Banack Inc 745 E Mulberry Ave Ste 900 San Antonio TX 78212-3154

ARMSTRONG-LAW, MARGARET, school administrator; b. Fargo, N.D., Jan. 21, 1931; d. Theron L. and Besse Ross Armstrong; m. Robert Harold Law, Sept. 6, 1952 (div. Oct. 1964); children: William Robert, Anne Elizabeth Law Buckingham, Amy Catherine Law Burman. BS in English, N.D. State U., 1952, MS Secondary Sch. Adminstrn., 1974; postgrad., UCLA, Moorhead State U., 1984, Mich. State U., 1985; Cert., Harvard Prin.'s Sch., London, 1986. Cert. tchr., ednl. adminstr.; speaker in field. Tchr. English Kamehameha Schs., Honolulu, 1967-68; tchr. English North High Sch., Fargo, N.D., 1968-74, asst. prin., 1974-78; secondary head Taipei Am. Sch., Taiwan, 1978-87, Vienna Internat. Sch., Austria, 1987-90; dir. Internat. Sch. Amsterdam, The Netherlands, 1990-97; internat. ednl. cons., 1998—; bd. dirs. European Coun. Internat. Schs., London, 1991-96, chair bd. dirs., 1994-96, prof. devel. com.; mem. No. European Coun. Internat. Schs., head coun., 1991-97. Author: (booklet, film) Future: The Quality of Life, 1975; contbr. articles to profl. jours. Mem. adv. bd. Coll. Arts, Humanities and Social Scis. N.D. State U., 1998—; chmn. Bd. Christian Edn. Plymouth Congl. Ch., Fargo, 1998—, mem. coun., 1998—, mem., vice chair women's fellowship bd., 1999—; active World Peace Com. in The Netherlands, 1997—, Fargo-Moorhead Opera Bd., 1999—. Recipient Bd. Dirs. award for Extraordinary Svcs. European Coun. Internat. Schs., Promotion of Internat. Edn. award, 1996; named hon. mem. for disting. svcs., European Coun. Internat. Schs., 1997; scholarship named in her honor by bd. govs. Internat. Sch. Amsterdam, 1997—. Mem. Assn. Advancement of Internat. Edn., Am. Assn. Sch. Adminstrs., Am. Women's Club/Amsterdam, Am. C. of C., Rotary (bd. dirs. 1993-94, program chair 1993-94, v.p. 1994-96, pres. 1995-96/Amsterdam), World Future Soc., World Peace Com. (The Hague, Netherlands), De Amsterdamschekring Club, Phi Kappa Phi. Republican. Congregational. Avocations: Chinese brush painting, music listening, reading, tennis, interior decorating.

ARNABOLDI, JOSEPH PAUL, retired veterinarian; b. W. Hoboken, N.J., Dec. 2, 1920; s. Joseph Paul and Gladys Evelyn (Wheeler) A.; m. Mary Louise Shoemaker, Aug. 24, 1944; children: Allan Charles, Sally-Jo Ann, Loren Joseph. DVM, Cornell U., 1943; postgrad., Liberty U., 1989—. Ordainded to ministry Africa Meth.-Episcopal Ch., 1966; cert. home health aide, N.Y. Veterinarian Port Jeff Animal Hosp., Port Jefferson, N.Y., 1946-81; min. Bethel AME Ch., Setauket, N.Y., 1966-84; first park commr. Inc. Village, Port Jefferson, N.Y.; bishop Eglise de Dieu Montagne de Sinai (parishes/orphanage), Haiti, 1982—; free-lance writer; mem. N.Y. State Vet. Cultural Exch. to Scandinavian and Iron Curtain countries, Eisenhower People-to-People program, 1964. Featured in L.I. sect. A Vet. Centennial in N.Y. State, 1890-1990; contbr. several articles to mags. Life mem., trustee Rep. Presdl. Task Force, 1981, Rep. Senatorial Inner Circle. Capt. AUS, 1943-46. Paul Harris fellow Rotary Internat., 1972; recipient Ronald Reagan medal of merit, Rep. Presdl. Legion of Merit medal, Rep. Senatorial medal of Freedom, Rep. Presdl. award, 1994. Mem. ASCAP (pub. songs), AVMA, L.I. Vet. Med. Assn. (pres. 1952), N.Y. State Vet. Med. Soc., Christian Vet. Mission World Concern (charter 1984—), Solar Cookers Internat. (founding mem. 1987—), Rotary Internat. (pres. Port Jefferson chpt. 1959-60, gov. L.I. dist. 725 1970-71, group study cultural exch. team leader to Japan 1993), Toastmasters Internat. (area gov. dist. 46 1962-63, Hall of Fame, recipient ATM award), No. Brookhaven Club (life, founder 1959-60, charter pres.). Republican. Avocations: tennis, piano, composing, public speaking, writing. Home and Office: 520 W Broadway PO Box 3 Port Jefferson NY 11777-1331

ARNALL, ROBERT ESRIC, physician, medical administrator; b. Griffin, Ga., Feb. 14, 1931; s. Paul Esric and Dolly (Henderson) A.; m. Sarah Maxwell, Jan. 18, 1933; children: Dana Kathryn, Robert Maxwell. BA, Emory U., 1953, MD, 1957. Diplomate Am. Bd. Pediatrics, Am. Bd. Med. Mgmt. Intern Atlanta VA Hosp., 1957-58; resident in pediat. Grady Meml. Hosp., Atlanta, 1958-60; chief resident Eggleston Hosp. for Children, Atlanta, 1960; med. dir., sys. v.p. Lee Meml. Health Sys., Ft. Myers, 1983—; pvt. practice pediatrics Atlanta, Fla., 1960-64; pvt. practice Ft. Myers, Fla., 1964-84; instr. pediat. Emory U., Atlanta, 1960-64; attending physician Eggleston Hosp. for Children, 1960-64, Grady Hosp., 1960-64; dir. continuing med. edn. Lee Meml. Hosp., Ft. Myers, 1987—, pres. med. staff, Ft. Myers, 1973-74, sys. v.p. physician integration, 1995—. Bd. dirs. Health Start, Ft. Myers, 1990-96, Goodwill Industries, Ft. Myers, 1989—, Edison-Ford Estates, 1991—, Healthy Start Dist. 8 Coalition; past bd. dirs. Edison Pageant of Light, pres.; past bd. dirs. Edison Festival of Light, Children's Home Soc., United Way of Lee County, Lee County Assn. Retarded Citizens, Easter Seal Soc., Nat. Found. March of Dimes, Cmty. Coord. Coun.; co-chmn. Healthy Start Regional Perinatal Network. With U.S. Army Res., 1960-68. Recipient Disting. Svc. awards Ft. Myers H.S., 1980, Lee County Sch. Bd., 1983, Fla. H.S. Athletic Assn., 1991. Fellow Am. Acad. Pediat. (subsect. adolescent medicine, past chmn. sch. health com. Fla. chpt.); mem. AMA (del. to hosp. med. staff sect. 1991-96, chmn. Southeastern Caucus 1994-96), Vol. Hosps. of Am. (task force on alternative delivery systems, task force on quality initiative, physician adv. bd., coun. med. dirs.), Fla. Med. Assn. (del. 1987-95, dist. rep. Coun. on Hosp. Med. Staffs 1989-93, vice chmn. 1991-93, chmn. 1993-95, chmn. governing coun. Organized Med. Staff sect. 1995-96, PRO com. 1991-95, long range planning com. 1995-96), Fla. Hosp. Assn. (quality assurance com.), Lee County Med. Soc. (chmn. sch. health adv. com. to Lee County sch. bd., chmn. sports medicine com. 1980-93), Rotary (past bd. dirs.), Alpha Omega Alpha. Democrat. Methodist. Avocation: golf. Home: 1324 Longwood Dr Fort Myers FL 33919-1821 Office: Lee Meml Health Sys Cleveland Ave Fort Myers FL 33902

ARNAUD, CLAUDE DONALD, JR., physician, educator; b. Hackensack, N.J., Dec. 4, 1929; s. Claude Donald and Alice Marie (Minnet) A.; m. Deborah Krupp; children: Claude Michael, Ellen Marie. B.A., Columbia Coll., 1951; M.D., N.Y. Med. Coll., 1955. Intern St. Luke's Hosp., N.Y.C.; also resident and endocrine fellow Milwaukee County Hosp.; fellow U. Wis.; instr. biochemistry U. Pa., 1959-66; cons. dept. endocrine research Mayo Clinic, Rochester, Minn., 1967-77; head mineral research unit Mayo Clinic, 1972-74, head endocrine research unit, mineral research lab., 1974-77, assoc. prof. medicine Grad. Sch. Medicine, 1970-74, prof., 1974-77; prof. medicine and physiology U. Calif., San Francisco, 1977—; chief endocrine unit San Francisco VA Med. Ctr., 1977-89, chief div. gerontology and geriatric medicine, 1989-91, dir. Ctr. for Biomed. Rsch. on Aging, 1989-91, dir. program osteoporosis and bone biology, 1991—. Contbr. numerous articles to profl. jours. Served with M.C. U.S. Navy, 1957-59. NIH grantee, 1968—. Fellow AAAS, Am. Coll. Endocrinologists, Am. Assn. Clin. Endocrinologists; mem. NAS (com. on diet, health and chronic disease 1985-88), NIH (musculoskeletal study sect. 1985-89), Am. Fedn. Clin. Rsch., Am. Soc. Biol. Chemists, Am. Soc. Clin. Investigation, Am. Physiol. Soc., Assn. Am. Physicians, Endocrine Soc., Western Assn. Physicians, Am. Soc. Bone Mineral Rsch. (past pres.), Nat. Rsch. Coun.

ARNBERGER, ROBERT, federal administrator. Supt. Grand Canyon Nat. Park, Ariz. Office: Grand Canyon Nat Park PO Box 129 Grand Canyon AZ 86023-0129*

ARNDT, JANET S., state legislator; b. Providence, May 23, 1947; m. Kenneth G. Arndt; 4 children. AB, Gordon Coll., 1968; MEd, Boston U., 1970; student, U. Mass., 1998—. N.H. state rep. Dist. 27, Rockingham, 1992—; mem. children, youth and juvenile justice com. N.H. Ho. of Reps., mem. const. and statutory rev. com.; specialist, counselor Early Childhood, 1987—; chmn. election law com., 1997—; adj. prof. Gordon Coll., 1995—, N.H. Tech. Coll., 1997—. Mem. Friends of the Libr. of Windham, chmn., 1991-92; active Girl Scouts Am., publicity chairperson; scholarship chmn. Nat. Order of Women Legislators; exec. bd. Rockingham County; events chairperson Nesmith Libr.; mem. edn. task force ALEC. Recipient M. Carter award for Outstanding Libr. Svc., 1995; named Leader of Yr. Windham Girl Scouts, 1995. Mem. N.H. Order Women Legislators, Gordon Coll. Alumni Coun. Address: NH House of Reps 8 Crestwood Rd Windham NH 03087-1429*

ARNDT, RICHARD TALLMADGE, writer, consultant; b. Phila., Oct. 28, 1928; s. Howard Wilcox Arndt and Eleanor (Shaw) Branigan; m. Edith Robichon (div. 1964); children: Skyler-Jennifer Arndt-Briggs, Matthew Wilcox; m. Dorothy Serlin (div. 1973); children: Daniel Serlin, Sarah L. Piazza; m. Lois W. Roth (dec. 1986). BA, Princeton U., 1949, postgrad., 1971-72; PhD, Columbia U., 1959. Instr., asst. prof. French Columbia U., N.Y.C., 1953-61; cultural attaché U.S. embassies, Beirut, 1961-63, Colombo, Sri Lanka, 1963-66, Tehran, Iran, 1966-71, Rome, 1974-78, Paris, 1978-80; dir. policy and plans Bur. Ednl. and Cultural Affairs, U.S. Info. Agy., 1980-83; cultural coord. Near East/So. Asia, USIA, Washington, 1983-85; dep. dir. L.Am., dir. youth and student programs Bur. Ednl. and Cultural Affairs Dept. State, Washington, 1972-74; diplomat-in-residence, dir. mid-career study dept. govt. U. Va., Charlottesville, 1986-89; bd. dirs. Fulbright Assn., Washington, 1986-92, v.p., 1986-89, pres., 1989-91; U.S. rep. Ctr. for Am. Studies, Rome; adj. prof. George Washington U., 1993-95; mem. faculty div. psychopolitics Ctr. Study Mind and Human Interaction, Charlottesville, 1988—; chmn. bd. Lois W. Roth Endowment, Washington, 1986—; mem. bd. Americans for UNESCO, 1992—. Prin. editor: The Fulbright Difference, 1948-92, Transaction, 1993; contbr. articles to profl. jours. Fulbright fellow U. Dijon, France, 1949-50, Coun. on Rsch. in Humanities fellow Columbia U., 1960, USIA mid-career fellow, 1971-72. Mem. Nat. Assn. Fgn. Student Affairs (bd. dirs. 1987-90), Internat. Soc. for Edn., Cultural and Sci. Interchange (pres. 1986-89), Coun. Internat. Programs, (1986-95, v.p. 1991-95), Nat. Peace Found. (bd. dirs. 1991, chmn. 1992-95, chmn. adv. coun. 1995—), Cosmos Club. Avocations: music, cultural diplomacy, political culture, theatre, history. Home: 1870 Wyoming Ave NW Washington DC 20009-1883

ARNDT, WALTER W., Slavic scholar, linguist, writer, translator; b. Constantinople, Turkey, May 4, 1916; came to U.S., 1949, naturalized, 1955; s. Fritz and Julia (Heimann) A.; m. Sophie Miriam Bach, Jan. 6, 1945; children: Robert Michael, Joachim David, Prudence Joy, Corinne Constance. Diploma in Econ. and Polit. Sci., Oriel Coll., Oxford (Eng.) U., 1936; postgrad. in ogmt., Sch. Bus. Adminstrn., Warsaw (Poland) U., 1939; BS Mech. Engring. summa cum laude, Robert Coll., Istanbul, Turkey, 1943; PhD in Linguistics and Classics, U. N.C., 1956; MA (hon.), Dartmouth Coll., 1967. Asst. dir. Turkey office Internat. Rescue and Relief Com., 1942-49, Intergovtl. Com. Refugees, 1945-47, UN Internat. Refugee Orgn., 1947-49; instr. Robert Coll., Istanbul, 1945-48; corr. The Economist, 1946-48; from instr. to asst. prof. classical and modern langs. Guilford Coll., 1950-56; from asst. prof. to assoc. prof. Slavic langs. and linguistics U. N.C., 1957-66, chmn. dept. linguistics, Slavic and Oriental langs., 1965-66; prof. Russian Dartmouth Coll., 1966-86, chmn. dept. Russian lang. and lit., 1967-70, now Sherman Fairchild prof. emeritus in the humanities, 1967-70; Fulbright prof. U. Münster, Germany, 1961-62; guest prof. Polish U. Colo., summer 1965. Author: Alexander Pushkin: Eugene Onegin, form-true English verse transl., 1963, 2d expanded edit., 1981; (with L. Levine) Grundzüge moderner Sprachbeschreibung, 1969, Pushkin Threefold, 1972, (verse transl.) Alexander Pushkin: Ruslan and Liudmila, 1974, (verse transl.) J.W. von Goethe, Faust: A Tragedy, 1976, (verse transl.) Anna Akhmatova, Selected Poems, 1976, (verse transl.) The Genius of Wilhelm Busch: Comedy of Frustration, 1982, (verse transl. with intro) Alexander Pushkin, Collected Narrative and Lyrical Poetry, 1984, (with Mark Harman) Robert Walser Rediscovered, 1985, (prose transl.) Uwe Johnson: Anniversaries IV, 1986, Bruno Schulz, Letters and Drawings, 1988, Pasternak, Tsvetaeva, Rilke, Letters, Summer, 1926, 1988, The Best of Rilke (72 form-true English verse transl., bilingual, intro. and comments), 1989; translator: (prose from Polish) Missing Pieces (Stanislaw Benski), 1989, New World Avenue and Vicinity (Tadeusz Konwicki), 1991, Ch. Morgenstern, Songs from the Gallows (bilingual, verse transl.), 1993, Heinrich Heine: Songs of Love and Grief (bilingual, verse transl.), 1995. With OSS, Office War Info., 1943-45. Co-recipient Bollingen prize for translation poetry, 1963; decorated Order of Merit, German Fed. Rep., 1995; rsch. grantee Am. Philos. Soc., 1967, 80, Rockefeller Found., 1975, Guggenheim Found., 1977-78, NEH, 1978-79; Ford Found. fellow U. Mich., 1952, Harvard U., 1956-57, Kennan fellow Wilson Ctr. Smithsonian Instn., 1981-82, Va. Ctr. for Creative Arts fellow, 1983, McDowell Colony fellow, 1985. Mem. Pen Club, Am. Assn. Advancement Slavic Studies, South Atlantic MLA (chmn. Slavic sect. 1959-60, sec. 1962-63, chmn. 1963-64), Am. Assn. Tchrs. Slavic and East European Langs. (v.p. 1964), So. Conf. Slavic Studies (v.p. 1964-65, pres. 1955-56, sr. scholar award 1993), Am. Lit. Transl. Assn., Polish Acad. Arts and Scis. in Am., Phi Beta Kappa (hon.). Home: 38 Maple St Hanover NH 03755-1922 Office: Dartmouth Coll Dept Russian Hanover NH 03755

ARNELL, RICHARD ANTHONY, radiologist; b. Chgo., Aug. 21, 1938; s. Tony Frank and Mary Martha (Oberman) Yaki; BA (Younker Achievement scholar), Grinnell Coll., 1960; MD, U. Iowa, 1964; m. Paula Ann Youngberg, June 28, 1964; children: Carla Ann, Paula Marie, Paul Anthony. With Innc., 1968—, v.p., 1970-78, sec., 1978-90, pres., 1990—, trustee pension and profit plan, 1979—; pres. Moline Radiology Assocs., S.C., 1990-93, Advanced Radiology, S.C., 1993—; mem. staff Luth. Hosp., Moline, 1968-88, dir. continuing med. edn. program for physicians, 1979-83, bd. dirs., 1977-83; mem. staff Moline Pub. Hosp., 1968-88, Hammond-Henry Dist. Ill., Geneseo, Ill., United Med. Ctr., 1989-92, chmn. radiology dept. United Med. Ctr., 1989-92; mem. staff Trinity Med. Ctr., 1992, chmn. radiology dept., 1992-94, med. dir. radiology dept., 1992—; pres. Moline Radiology Assocs., Inc., 1990-93; pres. Advanced Radiology, S.C., 1993—; mem. med. staff Mercer County Hosp., 1994—, Illini Hosp., 1995—, Trinity Med. Ctr., 1992; trustee Midstate Found. for Med. Care, 1975-79, exec. com., 1976-79; v.p. Quad City HMO Health Plan, 1979; clin. lectr. U. Iowa, 1980—; pres. med. staff, dir. Quad City MRI Inc., 1988-89; pres. Moline Mgmt. Assocs., Inc., 1990—; chmn. mng. com. Metro MRI Ctr., Ltd. Partnership. Supt. Sunday Ch. Sch. St. John's Luth. Ch., Rock Island, Ill., 1974-79, mem. ch. cabinet, 1975-76; del. Chs. United of Scott and Rock Island counties, Ill., 1977; mem. nat. exec. com. Augustana Coll., Rock Island, Ill., 1977-81; assoc. chmn. profl. div. United Way, 1985; bd. dirs. Luth. Hosp. Found., 1981-84, pres., 1982-84; bd. dirs. Quad Cities Health Care Resources, Inc., 1984-88 ; chmn. Luth. Health Care Found., 1984-88, chmn. United Health Care Found., 1989-91. Recipient David Theophillus trophy for outstanding athlete Grinnell Coll., 1960, Dr. Distinction award Rock Island Med. Soc. Alliance, 1998; diplomate Am. Bd. Radiology, Am. Bd. Nuclear Medicine. Mem. Am. Coll. Radiology, Ill. Radiol. Soc., Am. Coll. Nuclear Medicine, Soc. Nuclear Medicine, AMA, Ill. (ho. of dels. 1974-79), Rock Island County (exec. com. 1974-79, peer-rev. com. 1975-79), Iowa-Ill. Central (pres. 1978) med. socs., Central Ill. Med. Assn. (v.p. 1977, pres. 1978), Ind. Physicians Assn. Western Ill. (dir. 1984-86, v.p. 1985, pres. 1986), World Med. Assn., Am. Coll. Med. Imaging., Short Hills Country Club. Home: 3904 7th Ave Rock Island IL 61201-2246 Office: 3551 7th St Ste 101 Moline IL 61265-6156

ARNELL, WALTER JAMES WILLIAM, mechanical engineering educator, consultant; b. Farnborough, Eng., Jan. 9, 1924; came to U.S., 1953, naturalized, 1960; s. James Albert and Daisy (Payne) A.; m. Patricia Catherine Cannon, Nov. 12, 1955; children—Sean Paul, Victoria Clare, Sarah Michele Arnell. Aero. Engr., Royal Aircraft Establishment, 1946; BSc, U. London, 1953, PhD, 1967; MA, Occidental Coll., L.A., 1956; MS, U. So. Calif., 1958. Lectr. Poly. and Northampton Coll. Advance Tech., London, 1948-53; instr. U. So. Calif., L.A., 1954-59; asst. prof. mech. engring. Calif. State U., Long Beach, 1959-62, assoc. prof., 1962-66, prof., 1966-71, chmn. dept. mech. engring., 1964-65, acting chmn. divsn. engring., 1964-66, dean engring., 1967-69; rschr. Calif. State U. Ctr. Engring. Rsch., Long Beach; affiliate faculty dept. ocean engring. U. Hawaii, 1970-74; adj. prof. systems and insdl. engring. U. Ariz., 1981—; pres. Lenra Assocs. Ltd., 1973—; chmn., project mgr. Hawaii Environ. Simulation Lab., 1971-72. Contbr. articles to profl. jours. Trustee Rehab. Hosp. of the Pacific, 1975-78. Mem. Royal Aero. Soc., AIAA, IEEE Systems Man and Cybernetics Soc., AAUP, Am. Psychol. Assn., Soc. Engring., Psychology, Human Factors Soc., Ergonomics Soc., Psi Chi, Alpha Pi Mu, Tau Beta Pi, Phi Kappa Phi, Pi Tau Sigma. Home: 4491 E Fort Lowell Rd Tucson AZ 85712-1106

ARNESON, GEORGE STEPHEN, manufacturing company executive, management consultant; b. St. Paul, Apr. 3, 1925; s. Oscar and Louvia Irene (Clare) A.; children: George Stephen, Deborah Clare, Diane Elizabeth, Frederick Oscar. BS in Marine Transp., U.S. Mcht. Marine Acad., 1945; BEE, U. Minn., 1949. Certified mgmt. cons. Sales engr. Hubbard & Co., Chgo., 1949-54; cons. Booz, Allen & Hamilton, Chgo., 1954-57; mgr. mktg. cons. services, dir. mktg., plant mgr. Borg-Warner Corp., Chgo., 1957-60; asst. gen. mgr., then v.p., gen. mgr. Delta-Star Electric div. H.K. Porter Co., Inc., Pitts., 1960-63; v.p., gen. mgr. elec. divs. Delta-Star Electric div. H.K. Porter Co., Inc., 1963-65; v.p. mktg. Wheeling Steel Corp., 1965-66; pres., chief exec. officer Vendo Co., Kansas City, Mo., 1966-72, also dir., chmn. exec. com.; pres., chmn. Dun-Lap Mfg. Co., Newton, Iowa, 1973-77; pres. Arneson & Co., Overland Park, Kans., 1974—. Contbr. articles on mgmt. cons., bus. valuation and appraisal of mgmt. to profl. jours. Chmn. adv. bd. Kans. Dept. Corrections, Topeka, 1980-92. Lt. (j.g.) USNR, 1943-46. Recipient Outstanding Alumnus award U.S. Mcht. Marine Acad., 1968, Past Dir. award Automatic Merchandising Assn. Mem. Phi Gamma Delta (life), Alpha Phi Omega (life). Presbyterian. Clubs: Masons, KT, Shriners. Home: 5601 W 99th Ter Shawnee Mission KS 66207-2955

ARNETT, EDWARD MCCOLLIN, chemistry educator, researcher; b. Phila., Sept. 25, 1922; s. John Hancock and Katherine Williams (McCollin) A.; m. Sylvia Gettmann, Dec. 10, 1970; children: Eric, Brian; stepchildren: Elden, Byron, Colin Gatwood. B.S., U. Pa., 1943, M.S., 1946, Ph.D., 1949. Research dir. Max Levy and Co., Phila., 1949-53; asst. prof. Western Md. Coll., Westminister, 1953-54, assoc. prof., 1954-55; research fellow Harvard U., Cambridge, Mass., 1955-57; asst. prof. chemistry U. Pitts., 1957-61, assoc. prof., 1961-64, prof., 1964-80; R. J. Reynolds prof. Duke U., Durham, N.C., 1980-92, prof. emeritus, 1992—; vis. lectr. U. Ill., 1963; vis. prof. U. Kent, Canterbury, Eng., 1970; dir. Pitts Chem. Info. Ctr., 1967-70; mem. adv. bd. Petroleum Research Fund, 1968-71; mem. com. on chem. info. NRC, 1969-71. DuPont fellow, 1948-49; Guggenheim fellow, 1968-69; Mellon Inst. adj. sr. fellow, 1964-80; Inst. Hydrocarbon Chemistry sr. fellow, 1980. Fellow AAAS; mem. Am. Chem. Soc. (James Flack Norris award 1977, Pitts. award Pitts. chpt. 1976, Petroleum Chemistry award 1985), Nat. Acad. Scis., The Chem. Soc., Sigma Xi, Phi Lambda Upsilon. Author 210 papers in field.

ARNETT, FOSTER DEAVER, lawyer; b. Knoxville, Tenn., Nov. 28, 1920; s. Foster Greenwood and Edna (Deaver) A.; m. Jean Medlin, Mar. 3, 1951; children: Melissa Lee Arnett Campbell, Foster Jr. BA, U. Tenn., 1946; LLB, U. Va., 1948. Bar: Va. 1948, Tenn. 1948, U.S. Dist. Ct. (ea. dist.) Tenn. 1949, U.S. Ct. Appeals (6th cir.) 1954, U.S. Supreme Ct. 1958, U.S. Dist. Ct. (ea. dist.) Ky. 1978, U.S. Dist. Ct. (mid. dist.) Tenn. 1983, U.S. Dist. Ct. (ea. and we. dists.) Va. 1990. In practice Knoxville, 1948—; ptnr. Arnett, Draper & Hagood (and predecessors), 1954—; mem. Nat. Conf. Commrs. on Uniform State Laws, 1980-83; life mem. U.S. Ct. Appeals (6th cir.) Jud. Conf. Contbr. articles to profl. jours. Pres. Knox Children's Found., 1959-61, 75-76, East Tenn. Hearing and Speech Ctr., 1963-65, Knoxville Teen Ctr., 1969-71, Knoxville News-Sentinel Charities Inc., 1985—; v.p. Ft. Loudon Assn., 1972-75; del. Rep. Nat. Conv., 1964; bd. dirs., exec. com. Tenn. Mil. Inst., 1973-75; formerly active ARC, Am. Cancer Soc., United Fund. With AUS, 1942-46, PTO; to lt. col. USAR, ret. Decorated Silver Star, Bronze Star, Purple Heart. Fellow Am. Coll. Trial Lawyers (former chair legal ethics com., mem. atty.-client relationship com., mem. other coms.), Internat. Acad. Trial Lawyers (trustee Acad. Found. 1984-91, dean 1988-89, pres. 1992-93, mem. Found. Bd. 1983-92), Internat. Soc. Barristers, Am. Bar Found. (life), Tenn. Bar Found. (charter); mem. ATLA, ABA (mem. standing coms. on unauthorized practice of law and assn. comm., aviation and space law, state cert. legal specialist), Am. Bd. Trial Advs. (adv., charter, 1st pres. Tenn. chpt. 1985-86), Am. Inns of Ct. (charter, master of the bench emeritus Hamilton S. Burnett chpt.), Southea. Legal Found. (legal adv. bd.), Tenn. Bar Assn. (pres. 1968-69), Knoxville Bar Assn. (pres. 1959-60, Govs. award 1989), Internat. Assn. Def. Counsel (sec.-treas. 1981-84), S.E. Def. Counsel Assn. (v.p. 1966), Am. Acad. Hosp. Attys. of Am. Hosp. Assn. (charter), Tenn. Hosp. Assn., Am. Soc. Law, Medicine and Ethics, Fedn. Ins. and Corp. Counsel, Def. Rsch. Inst. (charter), U.S. Supreme Ct. Hist. Soc. (founder), Tenn. Supreme Ct. Hist. Soc. (founder), Federalist Soc., SAR, Scribes, U. Tenn. Nat. Alumni Assn. (pres. 1961-62, chmn. nat. ann. giving program 1961-63), Scabbard and Blade, Scarrabbean, Torchbearer, U. Va. Law Sch. Alumni Assn. (pres. 1991-93, nat. chmn. appeals Law Sch. Found. 1986-88), Raven Soc., 511th Parachute Infantry Regiment Assn., Civitan Club, Farmington Country Club, Charlottesville, Va.), Cherokee Country Club, LeConte Club, Univ. Club (hon.), Men's Cotillion (bd. dirs. 1960-61, 63-64, 66-68, trustee 1962—), Appalachian Club (pres. 1974-76), Phi Gamma Delta, Phi Delta Phi (hon.), Omicron Delta Kappa (hon.). Presbyterian. Home: 4636 Alta Vista Way Knoxville TN 37919-7605 Office: Arnett Draper & Hagood Ste 2300 First Tennessee Plaza Knoxville TN 37929-2300

ARNETT, LOUISE EVA, information records management executive; b. Cin., Sept. 8, 1945; d. Matthew Michael John Waldeck and Edith Louise (Reinholz) Driskell; m. Daniel L. Arnett, May 1, 1965; children: Matthew, Michael, John. Student, U. Cin., 1978-82, Thomas More, 1986—. Teller mgr. Tri State Savs., Cin., 1963-69; owner, operator Arnett's Hobby and Craft Shop, Inc., Erlanger, Ky., 1969-75; evening mgr. Wileswood Country Store, Greater Cin. Airport, Ky., 1975-78; records mgr. Federated Department Stores, Inc., Cin., 1978—. 1st commr. Tiger Cubs, Boy Scouts Am., Greater Cin., 1980-82; vol. Cin.'s 200th Birthday, 1988, Kenton County (Ky.) 150th Birthday, 1990; campaigner Kenton County Sch. Bd., 1987; booster alumna Dixie Band, Ft. Mitchell, Ky., 1986-92; vol. Tall Stacks, 1988, 92, 95, 99, United Way and Cmty. Chest Greater Cin., 1994—, mem. corp. vol. coun., 1994—, spl. projects liaison, 1994-97; vol. Cmty. Care Week, Nat. Vol. Week for the Elderly; founding mem. Keturah St. Kids' Cafe. Named for Meritorious Svc., Boy Scouts Am., 1979; recipient Order of the Heart, Boy Scouts Am., 1978, J.C. Penny Golden Rule award, 1998.

Mem. Assn. Records Mgrs. and Adminstrs. (dir. 1979-80, program chmn. 1980-81, pres. 1984-85, bd. dirs. Cin. chpt. 1986-92, chmn. bd. Cin. chpt. 1985, membership chmn. 1996—, Membership award 1982, Mem. of Yr. 1980), Federated Ptnrs. in Time (founding mem.), Keturah St. Kids Cafe (founding mem.). Republican. Avocations: walking, hobbies and crafts, tutoring, sewing. Office: Federated Dept Stores Inc 7 W 7th St Cincinnati OH 45202-2424

ARNETT, PETER, journalist; b. New Zealand, 1934; div.; 2 children. With Assoc. Press in various capacities AP, 1960—; war corr. Vietnam, 1962-75; White Horse corr. AP, 1970's; global corr. CNN (Cable News Network), Atlanta, Ga., 1981—; eyewitness corr. Persian Gulf War. CNN, 1991; chief fgn. corr. ForeignTV.com, N.Y.C., 1998—; Has covered 17 wars for various news orgn. Author: Live From the Battlefield: 35 Years Inside the World's War Zones, 1994. Collecting art, books, gourmet cooking. Office: ForeignTV.com Inc 162 5th Ave Ste 105A New York NY 10010*

ARNETT, RONALD CHARLES, communication educator; b. Ft. Wayne, Ind., Mar. 10, 1952; s. Arlo Guy and Dorothy Alice (Hennisa) A.; m. Mildred R. Bittinger, Jan. 30, 1972; children: Adam Geoffrey, Aimee Gabrielle. BS, Manchester Coll., 1974; MA, Ohio U., 1975, PhD, 1978; MDiv, Bethany Theol. Sem., 1983. Asst. prof., dir. basic comm. St. Cloud (Minn.) U., 1977-84; chair dept. comm. and rhetorical studies Marquette U., Milw., 1984-87; dean, v.p., prof. comm. Manchester Coll., North Manchester, Ind., 1987-93; chair dept. comm. and English Duquesne U., Pitts., 1993—, chair affiliate depts. comm. and English, 1999—; mem. various coms. Duquesne U., Pitts., 1993—. Author: Dialogic Education, 1992, Communication and Community, 1986, Dwell in Peace, 1980; editor: The Reach of Dialogue, 1994, Communication In An Age of Diversity, 1996, Dialogic Civility in a Cynical Age--Community, Hope and Interpersonal Relationships, 1999. Mem. adminstrv. bd. Ingomas Meth. Ch., Pitts., 1993; bd. dirs. On Earth Peace, Md., 1994; mem. North Manchester Aquatic, 1991-93, assoc. bd./ch. bd., 1985-88; vice chmn. Peace and Conflict Commn., 1993. Recipient Ohio U. Alumnus award, 1996. Mem. Ea. Comm. Assn., Nat. Comm. Assn. (chmn. ethics com. 1988). Avocation: camping. Office: Duquesne U Depts Comm and English Pittsburgh PA 15282

ARNETT, WARREN GRANT, interior designer; b. Charleston, W.Va., Aug. 16, 1923; s. Bernice Buell and Verla Dessie (Ash) A.; divorced; 1 dau., Linda Arnett McCulloch. Student, Carnegie Mellon Inst., 1941-42, Parsons Sch. Design, N.Y.C., 1959, N.Y. Sch. Interior Design, 1959-60. Studio mgr. NBC, N.Y.C., 1949-57; interior designer Myrick's Furniture, Inc., Orlando, Fla., 1957-59, W. and J. Sloane's, Manhasset, N.Y., 1959-60, Myrick's Interiors, Orlando, 1960-67; pres. Warren G. Arnett, Inc., Orlando, 1967—; sec., bd. dirs. Nat. Council Interior Design Qualifications, 1973-75, dir., 1979-81; mem. barrier free design com. President's Com. Employment Handicapped, 1971-72; rep. Fed. Design Assembly, 1972, 74; trustee Found. Interior Design Edn. Research, 1973-82, trustee emeritus, 1984—; lectr. in field, judge competitions. Free-lance actor radio, stage and TV, 1935—. Pres. Central Fla. Civic Theatre, Orlando, 1967-69, bd. dirs., 1963-87, chmn. bldg. com., 1968-73; founding mem., bd. dirs. Council Arts and Scis. Central Fla., 1967-71; bd. dirs. Participation Enriches Arts and Scis. Orgn. (PESO), 1968-88, sec., 1969-70, v.p., 1980-81, pres., 1981-82; bd. dirs. Orlando Loch Haven Park, 1977-87, chmn. bd., 1986-87. Served with U.S. Army, 1943-46. Decorated Bronze Star. Fellow Am. Soc. Interior Designers (founder, life mem., past pres., bd. dirs. 1976-81, Presdl. citation 1975, 80, Fla. North chpt. dir. emeritus 1996—); mem. Nat. Soc. Interior Designers (nat. pres. 1971-73, chmn. bd. 1973-75, bd. dirs. 1965-68, 69-75, Gold T Square award 1973); hon. mem. Interior Design Educators Coun. Home: 311 E Morse Blvd Apt 6-17 Winter Park FL 32789 Office: 745 N Thornton Ave Box 6967 Orlando FL 32803

ARNEZ, NANCY LEVI, educational leadership educator; b. Balt., July 6, 1928; d. Milton Emerson Levi and Ida Barbour (Rusk) Levi Washington. AB, Morgan State Coll., 1949; MA, Columbia U., 1954, EdD, 1958. Tchr. English Druid Jr. H.S., Balt., 1949-52, Houston Jr. H.S., Balt., 1952-57; asst. to admissions officer Tchrs. Coll., Columbia U., N.Y.C., 1957-58, grad. asst., 1957; head dept. English Cherry Hill Jr. H.S., Balt., 1958-62; assoc. prof., dir. student teaching Morgan State Coll., Balt., 1962-66; co-founder Cultural Linguistic Early Childhood Follow Through Approach; prof., asst. dir./dir. Ctr. for Inner City Studies, Northeastern Ill. U., Chgo., 1966-74; prof., assoc. dean, acting dean Sch. Edn. Howard U., Washington, 1974-80, chmn. dept. ednl. leadership, 1980-86, prof., 1980-93, prof. emeriti, 1993—. Author: Partners in Urban Education: Teaching the Inner City Child, 1973, The Struggle for Equality of Educational Opportunity, 1975, Administrative Issues in the Implementation of the Response to Educational Needs Project, 1979, The Besieged School Superintendent, 1981, School Based Administrator Training, 1982; mem. editorial bd.: Phi Delta Kappan, 1975-80, Jour. Negro Edn., 1975-80, Black Child Jour., 1980—; contbr. articles to profl. jours. State treas., mem. exec. com. Md. State council UN Children's Fund, 1965; founder Operation Champ, Balt, 1965; mem. adv. bd. Better Boys Found., Chgo., 1966-74, Mus. African-Am. History, 1969; state chmn. Right to Read, Washington, 1973-80; treas. Com. to Elect Douglass Moore to City Council, 1982. African Am. Inst. grantee, 1974; Spencer Found. grantee, 1976; AAUW grantee, 1977. Mem. Am. Assn. Sch. Adminstrs. (editorial bd. 1982), Assn. for Study of Afro-Am. Life and History, African Am. Heritage Assn., African Am. Writers Guild, Nat. Alliance Black Sch. Educators, D.C. Alliance Black Sch. Educators (pres. 1986-88), Phi Delta Kappa. Presbyterian. Home: 3122 Cherry Rd NE Washington DC 20018-1612

ARNHOFF, FRANKLYN NATHANIEL, psychologist, sociologist, educator; b. N.Y.C., Nov. 6, 1926; s. Abraham A. and Florence Wilner (Arnhoff); m. Lorraine Silver, Dec. 28, 1952; children: Stuart Brett, Gwen Alison. B.S., L.I. U., 1948; M.A., NYU, 1949; Ph.D., Northwestern U., 1953. Diplomate Am. Bd. Family Practice. Clin. psychology intern Elgin State Hosp., (Ill.), 1950, NRC fellow, 1950-51; USPHS fellow Northwestern U., Evanston, Ill., 1951-53, research assoc., instr. evening div., 1953-54; instr. med. psychology, chief psychologist adult out-patient services U. Nebr. Coll. Medicine, Omaha, 1954-56; research clin. psychologist VA Hosp., Salisbury, N.C., 1956-57; asst. prof. SUNY Upstate Med. Ctr., Syracuse, 1957-60; assoc. research scientst N.Y. Dept. Mental Hygiene, 1957-60; assoc. prof. psychology U. Miami, (Fla.), 1960-62, research assoc. prof. psychiatry Coll. Medicine, 1960-63; grants assoc. NIH, 1963-64; chief manpower and analytic studies br., div. manpower and tng. programs NIMH, 1964-70; John Edward Fowler prof. psychology U. Va., Charlottesville, 1970-92, Fowler prof. emeritus, 1992—, Univ. prof., 1975-92, Univ. prof. emeritus, 1992—, co-dir. pain studies clinic, head behavioral sci., 1970-75; cons., lectr. in field. Author: Manpower for Mental Health, 1969, Social Consequences of Policy Toward Mental Illness, 1975; The Sociology of Health, 1979, articles, reports. Served with USNR, 1944-46. Fellow Inst. Social Gerontology, U. Mich., 1958. Fellow AAAS, APA. Jewish. Home: 8400 Lee Jackson Cir Spotsylvania VA 22553-9426

ARNICK, JOHN STEPHEN, lawyer, legislator; b. Balt., Nov. 27, 1933; s. John and Josephine (Gaillardo) A. BS, U. Balt., 1956; LLD, U. Balt. Law Sch., 1961. Bar Assn. U.S. Marine Corps., 1956-59; magistrate Balt. County, 1966-67; del. Md. Gen. Assembly, Annapolis, 1967-79, 87-94, 1994—; atty. pvt. practice, Balt., Md., 1962—; del. Md. Gen. Assembly, Annapolis, 1983—. Mem. Twin Dist. Dem. Club, Battle Grove Dem. Club, Sons of Italy. Mem. Ea. Balt. C. of C., Moose Lodge, New 7th Dem. Club, South East Dem. Club. Democrat. Roman Catholic. Home: 7918 Diehlwood Rd Baltimore MD 21222-3316 Office: 7542 Holabird Ave Baltimore MD 21222-2104

ARNIS, EFSTATHIOS CONSTANTINOS, space naval designer; b. Thermon, Hellas, Greece, Apr. 14, 1931; s. Constantinos Efstathios and Joanna Andrew (Pachnis) A. Student, U. Athens, Hellas, 1950-51, 61-70; cert. in mech. engring. design, Technol. Sch. Benos-Palmer, Athens, 1972. Pvt. practice designer in mech. engring., 1952-94, ret., 1994; specialist in sci. field of energization of isolated phys. sys. Contbr. articles to profl. jours.; patentee in field of centrifugal space navigation. Mem. AIAA, AAAS, Hellenic Astron. Soc. (expert sec. 1992—), Planetary Soc., N.Y. Acad. Scis. (theoretician physicist). Avocations: astronomical obersvations, UFO investigator, Alpine climbing. Home: 10 Gortynos St, Hellas 112 54 Athens Greece Office: Hellenic Astron Soc, 14 Voulis St, Hellas 105 63 Athens Greece

ARNOLD, ALBERT JAMES, foreign language educator; b. Ballston Spa, N.Y., Nov. 8, 1939; s. Albert J. and Florence Emily (Cleveland) A.; m. Josephine Diane Valenza, June 8, 1963; 1 child, Elizabeth. AB, Hamilton Coll., 1961; MA, U Wis. Madison, 1964, PhD, 1968; cert French lang., lit., U. Paris, 1960. Instr. romance langs. Hamilton Coll., Clinton, N.Y., 1961-62; from asst. to prof. French U. Va., 1966—, chair com. comparative lit., 1974-79, 1986-89, co-chair comparative programs in literature and culture, 1989-95; dir. New World Studies, 1991-92; vis. exch. prof. U. de Paris III, 1981; external examiner Queensland U., Australia, 1986, U. West Indies, 1991—, N.Y. U., 1991, Yale U., 1994; spkr., cons. in field. Author: Paul Valéry, 1970, Sartre, 1973, Césaire, 1981, 90, Camus, 1983; gen. editor Caraf Books, 1987-93; editor New World Studies, 1992—; mem. internat. adv. bd. New West Indian Guide, 1992—; contbr. articles to profl. jours. ACLS fellow, 1975-76; NEH fellow Nat. Humanities Ctr., 1989-90; Fulbright fellow, 1995-96; trans. grantee NEH, 1991-92; grantee U. Va., 1969, 70, 72, 75-76, 78, 80, 81-82, 86, 95-96, Camargo Found., 1981-82, 86, Va. Found. Humanities, 1992, 94; Queensland U. fellow, Australia, 1995. Mem. Phi Beta Kappa. Democrat. Methodist. Avocations: gardening, photography, birding. Home: 310 E Beverley St Staunton VA 24401-4327 Office: New World Studies Dept of French University of Virginia 302 Cabell Hall Charlottesville VA 22903

ARNOLD, ALICE MARIE, real estate management executive; b. Beverly, Mass., Oct. 28, 1958; d. Donald Peyton and Barbara Marie (Maihos) Hayes; m. Mark McKay Arnold, July 12, 1986; children: Samuel Peyton, Amy Alice. Student, Salem State Coll., 1976-78, North Shore C.C., 1985-86. Art supr. Beverly (Mass.) Elem. Schs., 1976-78; clk. acctg. dept. Holyoke Mutual Insur. Co., Salem, Mass., 1978-80; asst. buyer Appleseeds, Inc., Beverly, Mass., 1980-82; property mgr. Battistelli Constr. Co., Beverly, 1982-87; prin. AMA Mgmt. Co., Beverly, 1986—. Mem. Beverly Hist. Soc., 1982—. Mem. Beverly Real Estate Bd., 1987—. Avocations: reading, handwork, boating, cooking, victorian period. Home and Office: AMA Mgmt Inc 38 Pemberton Rd Topsfield MA 01983-1808

ARNOLD, BARBARA EILEEN, state legislator; b. N. Adams, Mass., Aug. 3, 1924; d. Lester Flemming and Sarah (Van Hagen) Smith; m. William E. Arnold, Dec. 5, 1946; children: Wynn, Jeffrey, Gayle, Christopher. B.A. in Psychology, U. Mass.; postgrad. Keene State Coll. Spl. Edn. Clinic tchr. Keene State Coll., N.H., 1964-67; spl. edn. tchr. Easter Seal Rehab. Ctr., Manchester, N.H., 1967-74; state legislator N.H., 1982-95, Republican floor leader Ho. of Reps., 1989-95; mem. N.H. Coun. Vocat. Tech. Edn., 1986-95; mem. Ways and Means com., vice chmn., 1992-95; mem. State and Fed. Rels. commn.; chmn. Manchester Rep. Del.; Del. Bd. dirs. ARC, 1975-96, chmn. bd. dirs., 1977-80; Manchester chmn. Dole for Pres. Campaign, 1995—; Manchester campaign chmn. Warren Rudman for U.S. Senate, 1980, 86, Gov. Judd Gregg for U.S. Senate, 1992; chair Manchester Rep. Com., 1993-95; sec. N.E. State Coun. Vocational Edn.; mem. adv. bd. Greater Manchester Federated Women's Club; adv. bd. edn. N.H. Dept. Corrections; mem. adv. coun. adult rehab Easter Seal Soc., N.H., 1990—; mem. vestry, registered lay leader, mem. diocesan commns., del. gen. conv. Episcopal Ch.; mem. com. for children, families, social svcs. on the Nat. Conf. of State Legislatures; state adv. com. Vocat. Child Care Programs; chmn. Manchester Rep. Com., 1992-95. Address: 374 Pickering St Manchester NH 03104-2744

ARNOLD, BARRY RAYNOR, philosophy educator, minister, ethicist, counselor; b. Mooresville, N.C., Sept. 29, 1951; s. Adrian Leicester and Cleo Agnes (Fisher) A.; m. Margaret Elizabeth Morelock, Aug. 15, 1984. AB cum laude, Davidson Coll., 1973; MDiv magna cum laude, Emory U., 1976, PhD, 1986. Ordained to ministry Presbyn. Ch.; cert. Christian clin. counselor Am. Counseling Assn. Min. various parishes, Ga., Fla., 1976—; prof. Andrew Coll., Cuthbert, Ga., 1983-84; from asst. prof. to assoc. prof. U. West Fla., Pensacola, 1986-97, acting chmn. dept. philosophy/religion, 1997—; pvt. practice clin. counseling, Pace, Fla., 1996—; counselor Pace Counseling Ctr., 1996-97; spkr. in field. Author: The Pursuit of Virtue, 1989; editor: Essays in American Ethics, 1992; gen. editor (9 vols.) The Reshaping of Psychoanalysis, 1992-97; assoc. editor Explorations: Jour. Adventurous Thought, 1999—; contbr. articles to profl. jours. Pres., bd. dirs. Assn. for Retarded Citizens, Albany, Ga., 1978-79; bio-ethicist, bd. dirs. West Fla. Regional Med. Ctr., Pensacola, 1992-99. Recipient Disting. Tchg. award UWF and Fla. State Legislature, 1988, 90, 95; fellow Rice U., 1973-75, Emory U., 1975-76, 79-82, U. Glasgow, 1976. Mem. ACA, Am. Coll. Counselors (cert. Christian clin. counselor), Am. Acad. Religion, So. Soc. Philosophy/Psychology, Am. Bd. Child Mental Health Providers, Assn. for Cognitive Behavioral Therapists (cert. cognitive forensic therapist), Internat. Thomas Merton Soc., Phi Beta Kappa, Phi Kappa Phi (sec. 1988), Rotary (sgt.-at-arms 1982-83). Democrat. Avocations: antique cards, antique cars, birdwatching. Home: 5820 Kirkland Dr Milton FL 32570-8251 Office: Univ West Fla 11000 University Pkwy Pensacola FL 32514-5750

ARNOLD, BRIAN A., career officer. BS, California State U., 1971; student pilot tng., Webb AFB, Tex., 1972; student combat crew tng. sch., Castle AFB, Calif., 1973; MS in Adminstrv. Edn., Pepperdine U., 1976; student, Squadron Officer Sch., 1977, Air Command and Staff Coll., 1985, Nat. War Coll., 1992, Harvard U., 1995. Commd. 2d lt. USAF, 1971, advanced through grades to brig. gen., 1997; co-pilot 644th Bomb Squadron, K.I. Sawyer AFB, Mich., 1973-74; B-52D instr. pilot and flight examiner 60th Bombardment Squadron, Andersen AFB, Guam, 1974-78; stationed at Maxwell AFB, Ala., 1978-81, 95-97; FB-111 pilot, instr. 393rd Bomb Squadron, Pease AFB, N.H., 1981-84; various positions Pentagon, Washington, 1985-88, 89-91; comdr. 528th Bomb Squadron(FB-111), Plattsburgh AFB, N.Y., 1988-89; dep. dir. power projection requirements Hdqs. Air Force Air Combat Command, Langley AFB, Va., 1992-93; comdr. U.S. Forces Azores, Portugal, 1993-95, 65th Air Base Wing, Lajes Field, Azores, 1993-95; commdr. Squadron Ofcr. Sch., Maxwell AFB, AL, 1995-97; dir. requirements Hdqs. Air Force Space Command, Peterson AFB, Colo., 1997—. Office: HQ AFSPC/DR 150 Vandenberg St Ste 1105 Peterson AFB CO 80914-4580

ARNOLD, CECIL BENJAMIN, former small business owner; b. Bryantsville, Ky., Jan. 23, 1927; s. Walter Tribble and Ella Mae (Hagan) A.; m. Billie Jean Watkins, July 25, 1947; children: Mary Adrianne Davis, Cecil Benjamin Jr. Student, Heidelburg (Fed. Republic of Germany), 1945. Farmer Lancaster, Ky., 1947-50, grocery store owner, 1950-54; ins. agt. Commonwealth Life Ins., Lancaster, Ky., 1954-57; pres. Cecil Arnold Real Estate, Lancaster, Ky., 1957—; agt. Arnold & Boone Ins., Lancaster, Ky., 1957-81; owner Arnold's Furniture, Inc., Lancaster, Ky., 1971-90; ret., 1992; chmn. Lancaster-Garrard Indsl. Authority, 1993—. Pres. Lancaster-Garrard Indsl. Devel., 1984-90; mem. Exec. Com. Dem. Orgn., Lancaster, 1965-75; bd. dirs. Ky. Ins. Guaranty Bd., 1972-75; mem. Ky. legis. rsch. com. for revision of Commonwealth of Ky. Ins. Law, 1969-70; dir. Garrard County Habitat for Humanity, Lancaster, Ky., 1995—. Served with U.S. Army, 1945-47, ETO. Mem. Nat. Assn. Realtors, Ky. Assn. Realtors, Ky. Assn. Profl. Ins. Agts. (pres. 1968-69, bd. dirs. 1963-72, Mr. Chmn. award 1970, Mr. Profl. Agt. 1972, Profl. Agt. of Yr. 1975-76), Nat. Assn. Profl. Ins. Agts. (bd. dirs. 1972-80, v.p. 1979-80, Profl. Agt. of Yr. 1976-77), Dix River Bd. Realtors (pres. 1972), Nat. and Ky. Assn. Auctioneers, Lancaster-Garrard C. of C. (pres. 1966-68), Ky. Ins. Dept. (Ins. Svc. award 1969, 73; Special Recognition award 1975), Rotary (pres. 1966-68). Democrat. United Methodist. Avocations: basketball, golf, genealogy. Home: 641 Danville Rd Lancaster KY 40444-9327

ARNOLD, CHARLES BURLE, JR., psychiatrist, writer; b. Seattle, Aug. 13, 1934; s. Charles Burle and Ruth Helene (Hadley) A.; m. Sarah J. Slagle, Dec. 16, 1972; children: Geoffrey, Christopher, Jonathan. BS cum laude, U. Puget Sound, 1956; MD, CM, McGill U., 1960; MPH, U. N.C., 1965. Diplomate: Am. Bd. Preventive Medicine. Intern U. Wash. Hosp., Seattle, 1960-61; resident U. Wash. Hosp., 1961; physician Peace Corps, Bolivia, Washington, 1961-64; asst. prof. health adminstrn., asso. Carolina Population Center, U. N.C., Chapel Hill, 1965-69; asst. prof. Albert Einstein Coll. Medicine, Bronx, N.Y., 1969-72; prof. public adminstrn. and clin. assoc. prof. preventive medicine NYU, N.Y.C., 1972-83; adj. prof. pub. adminstrn. NYU, 1983—; med. dir., med. rels. Met. Life Ins. Co., 1983-91, v.p. med. rels., 1991-93; psychiat. resident North Shore Univ. Hosp., Manhasset, N.Y., 1993-96, chief resident, 1995-96; pvt. practice of psychiatry, 1996—; lectr. cmty. health Mt. Sinai Med. Sch., N.Y.C.; lectr. preventive medicine Downstate Med. Soc., SUNY, 1986-92; dir. Mahoney Inst. Health Maintenance, Am. Health Found., 1975-83, v.p. rsch., 1978-83, cons., 1983-86; chair Hitchcock Weekday Sch. Bd., 1986-92; chmn. Worksite Smoking subcom. N.Y. State Commn. on Smoking or Health, 1991-93; psychiatrist Drop-In Ctr., Ctr. Urban Cmty. Svcs., West Harlem, 1996-98; asst. attending psychiatrist N.Y. Presbyn. Hosp. Westchester Divsn.; dir. Open Arms Clinic; asst. clin. prof. psychiatry Cornell Med. Coll., 1998—. Editor, mem. exec. coun.: Transactions of Am. Acad. Ins. Medicine, 1988-93; assoc. editor Preventive Medicine Jour., 1975-83, sr. assoc. editor, 1983-85; editor Advances in Disease Prevention, 1981-83; editor-in-chief Statis. Bull., 1983-93; contbr. articles to profl. jours. Milbank Faculty fellow, 1967-74; OEO grantee, 1968-74; Population Council grantee, 1971-75; Health Research Council N.Y.C. grantee, 1972-75; Nat. Cancer Inst. grantee, 1975-83; Nat. Heart, Lung and Blood Inst. grantee, 1977-83; HEW Office Health Promotion grantee, 1978-80. Fellow Am. Coll. Preventive Medicine (pres. 1977-78); mem. N.Y. Acad. Medicine (com. on pub. health 1988—, vice chmn. 1992, chmn. 1993), Health Ins. Assn. Am. (chair com. on prevention and pub. health policy 1989-92). Office: 11 E 68th St # 1B New York NY 10021-4955

ARNOLD, CLAIRE GROEMLING, health care analyst; b. Chgo., Dec. 1, 1962; d. Robert Max and Dorothy Irene (Messerschmidt) Groemling; m. Daniel Lee Arnold, June 23, 1990; children: Christopher Alan, Andrew Lee. BS in Health Adminstrn., We. Ky. U., 1985; MBA, U. Louisville, 1989. Profl. rels. rep. Met Life Healthcare Network, Louisville, 1988-89; network devel. specialist Humana Inc., Louisville, 1989-90; program coord. U. Louisville Sch. Medicine, 1990-93, program mgr., 1993-95; dir. devel. Ky. Acad. Family Physicians Found., Louisville, 1995-97; health care analyst William M. Mercer, Inc., Louisville, 1998—. Contbr. articles to profl. jours. Bd. dirs. Goals for Greater Louisville, 1992, The Louisville Orch. Bd., 1993, Jr. League of Louisville, 1994, Tom Sawyer Park Found. Bd., 1996-97. Mem. Am. Coll. Healthcare Execs., Ky. Soc. Hosp. Planning and Mktg., Acad. for Health Svcs. Mktg. (pres. 1993-94), Discover the Louisville Orch. (sec. 1989-91, chmn. 1992-93), Western Ky. U. Alumni Assn. (pres.-elect 1998—, scholarship chmn. 1993-98), Phi Mu (pres. 1991-93). Democrat. Presbyterian. Office: William M Mercer Inc 462 S 4th Ave Ste 1500 Louisville KY 40202-3431

ARNOLD, DANIEL CALMES, finance company executive; b. Houston, Mar. 14, 1930; m. Beverly Bintliff; children:Mrs. Randy Helms, Mrs. Tom Martin, Steven Arnold. BBA, U. Tex.-Austin, 1951, LLB, 1953. Ptnr. Vinson & Elkins, Houston, 1953-83; pres., dir. First City Bancorp. Tex., Inc., Houston, 1983-85, chmn. pres., dir., 1985-88; chmn., CEO Farm & Home Fin. Corp., 1989-91, dir., 1991-94; bd. dirs. Belco Oil & Gas Corp., Parkway Properties, Inc., U.S. Physical Therapy; bd. dirs. Baylor Coll. Medicine, chmn. bd. trustees, 1996. Bd. dirs. Harris County Hosp. Dist., 1963-69, chmn. 1963-69; bd. dirs. Tex. Med. Ctr., Inc., 1963-89, Baylor Coll. Medicine, 1969—; bd. dirs. Houston-Harris County chpt. ARC, chmn. 1970-72; chmn. bd. dirs. Met. Transit Authority Harris County, Tex., 1980-84, bd. dirs. Tex. Medical Ctr., 1996—. Mem. ABA, Tex. Bar Assn., Houston Bar Assn. Methodist. Office: Ste 720 1001 Fannin St Houston TX 77002-6707*

ARNOLD, DAVID WALKER, chemical company executive, engineer; b. Dundee, Miss., Dec. 6, 1936; s. Jesse Braxton and Irene (Mitchell) A.; m. Barbara Ann Daves, Jan. 10, 1958; 1 child, Janet G. BS, U. Miss., 1958; MS, Iowa State U., 1963, PhD, 1966. Registered profl. engr., Miss. Jr. engr. Iowa State U., Ames, 1963-66; process study engr. Miss. Chem. Corp., Yazoo City, 1966-67, research project mgr., 1967-69, chief process engr., 1969-72, mgr. process engring., 1972-74, dir. engring., 1974-75, v.p. engring., 1975-81, sr. v.p. engring., 1981-87, sr. v.p. research and engring., 1987-91, sr. v.p. tech. group, 1991—; chmn. bd. dirs. Unifirst Bank, Yazoo City, 1982-89; mem. Miss. Bd. Registration for Profl. Engrs. and Land Surveyors, 1992-96. Contbr. articles in profl. jours. Commr. Pub. Svc. Commn., Yazoo City, 1980-95, chmn. commrs., 1987-95; chmn. Yazoo County Rep. Party, 1969-72; pres. Jr. Achievement Yazoo City, 1972; mem., chmn. Yazoo City Planning and Zoning Comm., 1972-78; pres. Yazoo County C. of C., 1981. Lt. USN, 1958-63. Mem. AIChE, NSPE, Am. Mgmt. Assn., Miss. Engring. Soc. (pres. 1986-87), U. Miss. Alumni Assn. (pres. 1989-90). Republican. Episcopalian. Club: Yazoo Country. Avocations: computers, reading. Office: Miss Chem Corp PO Box 388 Yazoo City MS 39194-0388

ARNOLD, DEBORRAH ANN, human services director; b. Elkins, W.Va., June 1, 1950; d. Lawrence Arnold and Sybil Dumire. ADN, Broome Community Coll., 1977; BSN, SUNY, Syracuse, 1987, MSN, 1987. Cert. clin. nurse specialist. Community health nurse Broome County Health Dept., Binghamton, N.Y., 1977-81, supr. home health aides, 1981-82, coord. employee health svcs., 1982-86; dir. profl. svcs. Kimberly Quality Care, Binghamton, N.Y., 1987-91; div. dir. clin. svcs. Kimberly Quality Care, Vestal, N.Y., 1991-93; quality assurance mgr. Olsten Kimberly Quality Care, Vestal, N.Y., 1993-96; clin. ops. edn. specialist Olsten Health Svcs., Endicott, N.Y., 1996-97, clin. ops. specialist, 1997-99, 3d pary liason coord., 1999—. Mem. N.Y. Nurses Assn. (dist. 5).

ARNOLD, DENNIS B., lawyer; b. Apr. 25, 1950. BA magna cum laude, SUNY Buffalo, 1972; JD, Yale U., 1975. Bar: Calif. 1976. Asst.-in-instrn. Yale Law Sch., New Haven, Conn., 1974-75; law clk. to Hon. Murray M. Schwartz U.S. Dist. Ct., Del., 1975-76; ptnr. Irell & Manella, 1980-88, Gibson, Dunn & Crutcher LP, L.A., 1988—; adj. assoc. prof. law Southwestern U. Sch. Law, 1980-82; advisor Restatement of Law, 2d edit., Suretyship and Guaranty, Am. Law Inst., 1989-95. Contbr. articles to profl. jours. Mem. ABA, Am. Law Inst., State Bar Calif. (standing joint com. anti-deficiency laws 1985-89, real property and bus. law sect. 1978—), L.A. County Bar Assn. (exec. com. commercial law and bankruptcy sect. 1987-90, 96—, exec. com. real property sect. 1987-92, steering com. real estate fin. subsect. 1987—), Fin. Lawyers Conf. (bd. govs. 1986-89, 92-95, 96—), Am. Coll. Real Estate Lawyers. Office: Gibson Dunn & Crutcher LP 333 South Grand Ave Los Angeles CA 90071-3197*

ARNOLD, DIETER KARL HEINRICH, Egyptologist; b. Heidelberg, Germany, Apr. 16, 1936; came to U.S., 1985; s. Franz and Franziska A.; m. Dorothea Emma Berta Schadewaldt, Apr. 9, 1963; children: Bernhard, Felix. DPhil, State U., Munich, Germany, 1962, D.habil., 1973. Resident archaeologist German Archaeol. Inst., Cairo, 1963-79; chmn. dept. Egyptology State U., Vienna, 1979-84; curator dept. Egyptian art Met. Mus. Art, N.Y.C., 1985—; prof. Egyptology State U., Vienna, 1979. Author 14 books. Mem. German Archaeol. Inst. (field dir. 1963-84). Avocations: mountaineering, opera, ballet. Office: Met Mus Art 1000 5th Ave New York NY 10028

ARNOLD, DON CARL, pastor, religious organization executive; b. Cassville, Mo., Jan. 25, 1936; s. Paul G. and Alva F. (Edens) A.; m. Jean G. Guest, Apr. 6, 1958; 1 child, Christina Lynne Arnold Mattox. DD, New Life Coll., 1985; D of Ministries, Logos U., 1992. Ordained to ministry Oak Park Grace Assembly Ch., Sand Springs, Okla., 1965. Mgr. Safeway Stores Inc., Tulsa, Okla., 1953-65; assoc. evangelist David Nunn Revivals, Dallas, 1965-66; assoc. pastor Souls Harbor Ch., Dallas, 1966-68; evangelist Full Gospel Fellowship, Dallas, 1968-69; sr. pastor The Tabernacle, Gadsden, Ala., 1969—; pres. full Gospel Fellowship of Chs. and Mins. Internat., 1988. Mem. All Am. City Com., Gadsden, 1994—, chmn. religious task force, 1994; bd. mem. Pentecostal/Charismatic Christian Edn. Alliance, 1994; founding mem. Life Springs Group, Religious Pub. Co., 1996. Recipient Cert. of Appreciation award for cmty. svc. All Am. City Com., 1993. Avocations: golf, travel, reading. Home: 108 Lakepoint Dr Gadsden AL 35901-5364 Office: The Tabernacle PO Box 324 1301 S 11th St Gadsden AL 35904-4901*

ARNOLD, DONALD RAYMOND, addiction consultant; b. Saskatoon, Sask., Can., Sept. 2, 1926; came to U.S., 1967; S. George Henry McKay and Christena (Hooff) A.; children from previous marriage: Richard, Maureen, Raymond; m. Virginia Ellen Love, July 14, 1974; stepchildren: Daniel, Sara, Matthew. Grad. high sch., Watrous, Sask. Sr. cert. alcoholism/drug addiction counselor. Machinist Can. Nat. Railway, Saskatoon, 1944-57; dist. mgr. Monarch Life Assurance Co., Saskatoon, 1957-61; alcohol counselor Bur. on Alcoholism, Regina, Sask., 1961-66; sr. alcoholism counselor Bur. on Alcoholism, Saskatoon, 1966-67; dir. of counseling Valley Hope Assn.,

Norton, Kans., 1967-71; program dir. Valley Hope Assn., Overland Park, Kans., 1971-74; adminstrv. cons. St. Joseph Med. Ctr., Wichita, 1975, program dir., 1975-90, sr. addictions counselor, 1990-91, parish health care liaison, 1991-94; ret., 1994; addiction consultant, Wichita, 1994—; lectr. in field. Mem. Sisters of St. Joseph Assocs., Wichita, 1989—; non-sexaholic trustee internat. bd. trustees Sexaholics Anonymous, 1997—. Ordinary seaman Royal Can. Navy, 1944-46. Mem. Kans. Alcoholism Counselor Assn. (pres. 1981, bd. mem. 1977-82), Kans. Alcoholism and Drug Addiction Counselors Assn. (chmn. ethics com. 1985-89, Counselor of Yr. award 1992). Avocations: antiques, furniture restoration. Home: 2535 Welgate Cir Wichita KS 67226-1044

ARNOLD, DONNA F., business educator; b. Charlotte, N.C., Aug. 16, 1947; d. Billy Lewis and Lily Frances (Wentz) Ferguson; m. Harvey Eugene Arnold, Feb. 3, 1979; 1 child, Sherry Lynne. BS in Fin., Fla. State U., 1982, MBA, 1983. Fin. cons. Ferguson Acctg., Ft. Pierce, Fla., 1982-83; account exec., broker Merrill Lynch, Ft. Pierce, Fla., 1983-85; prof. Indian River C.C., Ft. Pierce, Fla., 1985—. Treas., bd. dirs. Treasure Coast Deaf Svc. Ctr., Port St. Lucie, Fla., 1993-96; mem. Jud. Nominating Com., Port St. Lucie, 1992-95. Mem. Delta Epsilon Chi (Advisor of Yr. 1997). Home: 8007 Plantation Lakes Dr Port Saint Lucie FL 34986-3014 Office: Indian River CC 3209 Virginia Ave Fort Pierce FL 34981-5541

ARNOLD, DORIS FOLTZ, minister, former health care administrator; b. Hagerstown, Md., May 2, 1926; d. Xenia James and Elton Irene (Kline) Foltz; m. Raymond Merton Arnold, Apr. 1, 1953. AB, Lynchburg Coll., 1948; MRE, Lexington Theol. Sem., 1951; MA, Columbus U., 1964; postgrad., So. Ill. U., 1968—. Ordained to ministry Disciples of Christ (Christian Ch.), 1948; cert. spl. edn. tchr., N.Y. Asst. chaplain Lynchburg (Va.) Sch. for Retarded, 1944-48; chaplain Va. Indsl. Sch. for Delinquent Girls, Bon Air, 1948-51; assoc. min. Paris (Ky.) Christian Ch., 1951-55; psychologist Harlem Valley Psychiat. Hosp., Wingdale, N.Y., 1955-56, Cleve. Mental Hosp., 1956; edn. supr. Wassaic Developmental Ctr. for the Retarded, 1956-83; min. Dover Plains United Meth. Ch. and South Dover United Meth. Ch., 1978-90; min. part time Gallatin (N.Y.) Reformed Ch., 1989—; chaplain for mentally ill Veterans in a Gray Home, 1999—; dir. music Ky. Reform Sch., 1951; owner Past Times Gifts and Antiques Shop, Dover Plains, N.Y; speaker in field; organist Dover Plains United Meth. Ch., South Dover United Meth. Ch., Gallatin Reformed Ch. Author 4 books. Trustee Lynchburg Coll., 1979-80; mem. com. Dutchess County Battered Women, Boys Scouts Am., also Cub Scouts, Explorers; active various civic and community orgns. Mem. Mentally Retared Educators (sec. 1957-83), Am. Assn. for Mentally Defective, Order of Ea. Star (matron local lodge). Republican. Avocation: collecting antiques; restoring Greek Revival mansion. Home: RR 1 Box 246aa Dover Plains NY 12522-9726 *It is with a grateful living pattern that I feel I have been sent to this world by a Power of Creativity and ability to produce with my fellow travelers in this world. With the Lord Jesus Christ as my inspiration and director of my ways, my stewardship to my Creator will be a system filled with love, understanding and compassion. May each moment allow me to be accountable unto the Shepherd who allows me to work with His sheep.*

ARNOLD, DOROTHY HARRISON, assistant principal; b. Chgo., July 24, 1957; m. Earl Norman Arnold Sr., July 14, 1979; children: Erle Jr., Anthony, Daniel. BS, U. Dubuque, 1979; MEd, Emory U., 1994. Tchr. spl. edn. Des Moines (Iowa) Ind. Sch. Dist., 1979-84, DeKalb County Pub. Schs., Avondale Estate, GA., 1984-87; tchr. English, sci., TAG Fulton County Bd. Edn., Atlanta, Ga., 1987—; instrnl. specialist tchr., asst. prin. Fulton County Bd. Edn., Atlanta; mem. local sch. adv. bldg. planning/means com. Fulton County Bd. Edn. Mem. Hands on Atlanta, Gamma Sigma Sigma, 1994; campaigner Bd. Edn., Clayton County Schs., 1995. Avocations: traveling, reading, sewing. Home: 4981 Alexander Ave Union City GA 30291-1101

ARNOLD, ERIC DANIELL, budget analyst; b. Raleigh, N.C., Sept. 12, 1970; s. Earl Marvin Dunston and Mary Ann Arnold-Dunston; 1 child, Aarice Sharice. BA, N.C. Ctrl. U., Durham, 1993; MPA, N.C. Ctrl. U., 1998. Sr. materials/receiving clk. OMG Ams., Inc., Research Triangle Park, N.C., 1993—; budget analyst Office Mgmt. and Budget City Hall, Kansas City, Mo. Vol. David Price for Congress campaign, Cary, N.C., 1998; vol. intern Register of Deeds, Durham, 1991-92. Grad. Students Assn. scholar, 1998. Mem. Am. Soc. Pub. Adminstrn., Nat. Contract Mgmt. Assn. (scholar 1998), Internat. City/County Mgmt. Assn., Durham Alumni, Doric Lodge #28, Kappa Alpha Psi, Pi Alpha Alpha, Kappa Alpha Psi. Democrat. Baptist. Avocations: singing, basketball, running, bowling, mentoring. Home: 600 East 8th St Apt 1111 Kansas City MO 64106 Office: Mgmt and Budget Fl 13 Ste 1303 City Hall 414 East 12th St Kansas City MO 64106

ARNOLD, ERNEST WOODROW, minister; b. White Springs, Fla., Mar. 20, 1914; s. Turner Benjamin and Frances Essie (Wise) A.; m. Mildred Virginia Thomas, Jan. 26, 1945; children: Ernest Woodrow Jr., Cheryl Ruth Arnold Daves. BA magna cum laude, Furman U., 1943; BD, New Orleans Bapt. Theol. Sem., 1948; ThD, Luther Rice Sem., 1965. Ordained to ministry So. Bapt. Conv., 1942. Pastor East Pk. Bapt. Ch., Greenville, S.C., 1950-54, Brentwood Bapt. Ch., Charleston, S.C., 1955-58, Bethel Bapt. Ch., Shelby, N.C., 1958-72, Catawba Bapt. Ch., Rock Hill, S.C., 1972-75, 1st Bapt. Ch., Bostic, N.C., 1975-81, Lily Meml. Bapt. Ch., Shelby, 1987—; mem. faculty Luther Rice Sem., 1968-76. Author: Truth: Tried and Tested, 1996. With USMC, 1934-38. Recipient commendation USMC, 1935; New Orleans Bapt. Theol. Sem. fellow, 1948-50. Democrat. Home: 117 Ken Daves Rd PO Box 715 Boiling Springs NC 28017-0715 *Life can be a circle or it can be a line of movement to never ending joy and peace, accompanied by achievement, fulfillment and faith in God, the Eternal One.*

ARNOLD, G. DEWEY, JR., accountant; b. Montgomery, Ala., Jan. 30, 1925; s. G. Dewey and Janie Esther (Terry) A.; m. Dorothy Louise Wenger, Dec. 4, 1954; children: Susan O., G. Dewey III. B.A. in Econs, U. of South, 1949; postgrad. in acct., U. Tenn. C.P.A., Pa., D.C., Md. With Aladdin Industries, Inc., Nashville, 1949-50; with Price Waterhouse, 1950—, ptnr., 1961—; ptnr. in charge Washington office Price Waterhouse & Co., 1965-76, mem. policy com., 1975-80, regional mng. ptnr., 1976-85; exec. dir. Nat. Commn. on Fin. Fraud, 1985-87; dir. Audit-Intelsat., 1987—; instr. acctg. Robert Morris Sch. Acctg., 1952-53; lectr., course dir. mgmt. acctg. Inst. Mexicano de Administracion de Negocias, A.C., 1958-64; bd. dirs. Washington Bd. Trade, 1973-75; mem. audit adv. com. Sec. Navy, 1972-75. Bd. dirs. Jr. C. of C., 1954-55; trustee Fed. City Coun., 1966—; bd. dirs. Greater Washington Ednl. TV Assn., Inc., 1970-82, Minority Contractors Ctr., 1972-74, Redskins Found., 1973—; D. C. Mcpl. Rsch. Bur., 1974-76, Wolf Trap Found., 1975-90; chmn. bd. trustees Landon Sch., 1974-79; vice chmn. D.C. Bicentennial Commn., 1971-75. Served with USNR, 1943-45. Mem. AICPA, D.C. Inst. CPAs, Nat. Assn. Accts., Md. Inst. CPAs, Am. Arbitration Assn., Chevy Chase Club, Burning Tree Club, Pine Valley Golf Club, Rolling Rock Club, John's Island Club. Office: Intelsat 3400 PO Box 1B Washington DC 20044-0001

ARNOLD, GARY HOWARD, film critic; b. Princeton, Ind., Aug. 22, 1942; s. Charles Howard and Ferris (Smith) A.; m. Sue Datz, Dec. 29, 1967; children—Pauline, Jane, Esther. Student, NYU, 1959-60, U. Calif., Berkeley, 1960-63. Film critic Diplomat mag., 1966; film critic, reporter Ind. Film Jour., 1968-69; film critic Washington Post, 1969-84; co-host weekly TV commentary show The Moviegoing Family, 1985-90; arts critic The Connection, Reston, Va., 1987-89; movie critic The Washington Times, Washington, 1989—. Home: 5133 North 1st St Arlington VA 22203-1207 Office: The Washington Times 3600 New York Ave NE Washington DC 20002-1996

ARNOLD, GEORGE LAWRENCE, retired advertising company executive; b. Kansas City, Mo., Sept. 30, 1942; s. James Robert and Mary Virginia (Ellington) A.; m. Mary Antoinette Turrin, Dec. 31, 1964; children: Margery, Matthew, Molly, Sara. BJ magna cum laude, U. Tex., 1965, MA cum laude, 1966. Advt. and pub. relations trainee Gen. Electric Co., Phila., 1966; advt. asst. Dallas Power & Light Co., 1967-70; dir. communications Continuum Co. Inc., Austin, Tex., 1970-73; pres. Evans/Dallas Inc., Dallas, 1977-99; ret., 1999; bd. dirs. Evans Group, Inc., Salt Lake City, mem. operating com. Salt Lake City. Bd. dirs. United Way Met. Dallas, 1978, Lone Star council Camp Fire Girls, Dallas, 1978-84. Recipient Silver Anvil award Pub. Relations Soc. Am., 1980, Gold Effie award Am. Mktg. Assn., 1981. Mem. Tex. Pub. Relations Assn. (bd. dirs. 1978-80, 92-97, pres. 1998, Silver Spur award 1985), Dallas Advt. League (pres. 1981). Democrat. Roman Catholic. Home: 912 Kneese Rd Frederickburg TX 78624 Office: Evans Group Inc 3100 Monticello Ave Ste 600 Dallas TX 75205-3439

ARNOLD, GLORIA MALCOLM, artist, educator; b. Covington, Ga., July 16, 1945; d. George Clifford and Mildred Sarah (Johnson) Malcolm; m. John Edward Arnold, Feb. 12, 1966; 1 child, Troy Chandler. BS in Edn., U. Ga., 1966. Self-employed artist, tchr. Lee, Mass., 1984—. Executed mural Sweet Brook, 1990; contbr. Best Flower Painting 2, 1999; contbr. articles to profl. publs. Mem. Lee Cultural Coun., 1990-98; v.p. Pittsfield (Mass) Art League, 1987-89. Recipient Silver medal Nat. Parks Acad. Arts, 1996, 1st in Oils award Internat. Nature Fine Arts Competition, 1998. Fellow Am. Artists' Profl. League; mem. Oil Painters Am. (award of excellence 1997), Copley Soc. Boston, North Shore Arts Assn. (James G. Saunders Meml. award 1997), Acad. Artists Assn., Kent Art Assn. (v.p. 1994-96, bd. dirs. 1994—).

ARNOLD, HENRI, cartoonist; b. Bethlehem, Pa.; s. Samuel Max and Dora (Schnur) A.; m. Harriet Chefetz, Feb. 14, 1980; children by previous marriage—Nora Sally, Ned Michael. Student, Cooper Union, 1946. Editorial/sports cartoonist Bridgeport (Conn.) Sun. Herald; cartoonist weekly humor page Chgo. Tribune, 1955-65; art dir. Chgo. Tribune-N.Y. News Syndicate, Inc., N.Y.C., 1957-77; lectr. in field. Creator: This Man's Army, N.Y. Sun. News, 1954-64, Meet Mr. Luckey, N.Y. Daily News, 1991—; writer, cartoonist for Ching Chow, 1977—; producer Jumble, That Scrambled Word Game, 1960—; illustrator: The ABCs of Golf (by Tommy Armour), 63 vols. of Jumble, That Scrambled Word Game, 1962—, Super Jumble Puzzle Book, 1991, Jumble for Kids Book, 1992. Mem. Nat. Cartoonists Soc., Tamarack Country Club, Palm-Aire Country Club.

ARNOLD, HERBERT ANTON, German language educator; b. Buchau, June 23, 1935; came to U.S., 1963; s. Josef and Maria (Rothberger) A.; m. Annemarie Stuck, Feb. 11, 1961; children: Bettina, Corinna Maria, Christiane Vivien. Abitur, Oberrealschule Kaufbeuren, 1956; Staatsexamen, Julius-Maximilians U., Würzburg, Germany, 1962, Dr. Phil., 1966; M.A., Wesleyan U., 1980. Teaching asst. Liverpool (Eng.) Collegiate, 1959-60; referendar Siebold Realgymnasium, Würzburg, 1962-63; instr. Wesleyan U., Middletown, Conn., 1963-66, asst. prof., 1966-72, assoc. prof., 1972-80, prof. German and Letters, 1980—, dir. Wesleyan Program in Germany., 1967-69, 73, 81, 82, 85, 87, 91, 94, 99; chmn. dept. German Wesleyan U., 1982-85, co-dir. Coll. Letters, 1971-72, 79-82, dir. Coll. Letters, 1987-90, 93. Author: N. Chamberlain's Appeasement Policy, 1966; contbr. numerous articles, revs. on German lit. and history to profl. jours. Trustee Am. Field Svc., N.Y.C., 1970-73, 81-83, chmn. bd. dirs. Am. Field Svc.-USA, 1979-81, bd. dirs. 1981-87. Mem. Am. Assn. Tchrs. German (pres. Conn chpt. 1975-76), MLA, Northeast MLA, German Studies Assn. Home: 1 Edwards Rd Portland CT 06480-1521 Office: Wesleyan U Middletown CT 06459

ARNOLD, J. KELLEY, federal judge; b. 1937. JD, U. Idaho, 1961. Bar: Wash. Judge Wash. Superior Ct. Superior County, Tacoma, 1982-94; magistrate judge for western Wash., U.S. ct., Tacoma, 1994—. With U.S. Army, 1961-63. Office: US Ct 1717 Pacific Ave Rm 3409 Tacoma WA 98402-3234

ARNOLD, J(AMES) BARTO, III, marine archaeologist; b. San Antonio, Jan. 9, 1950; s. J. Barto Jr. and Wilnora (Barton) A.; m. Aurora Irene Foreman, Aug. 28, 1970; children: Kathryn, Julia, Jessica. BA cum laude, U. Tex., 1971, MA, 1973. Rsch. asst. Tex. Archeol. Rsch. Lab. U. Tex., Austin, 1970-72; asst. state marine archaeologist Tex. Antiquities Com., Austin, 1972-75; state marine archaeologist Tex. Hist. Com., Austin, 1975-97; dir. Tex. ops. Inst. of Nautical Archaeology, Tex. A&M U., College Station, 1997—; cons. NOAA, 1977-91, Nat. Trust Hist. Preservation, Washington, 1979-90, Congl. Office Tech. Assessment, Washington, 1986; mem. Md. Gov.'s Adv. Com. on Marine Archaeology, Annapolis, 1987-90; mem. history area com. nat. park sys. adv. bd. U.S. Dept. Interior, 1994-95; dir. La Salle Shipwreck Project, 1995-96, Confederate Blockade-Runner Denbigh Shipwreck Project, 1997—. Co-author: Nautical Archaeology of Padre Island, 1978, Documentary Sources for the Wreck of the New Spain Fleet of 1554, 1979 (Presidio La Bahaia 1979), others; Plenum series editor Underwater Archaeology, 1995—; contbr. articles to profl. jours. Recipient Achievement award for Hist. Preservation Dept. Interior, 1980. Mem. Soc. Profl. Archaeologists (cert.; sec.-treas. 1987-89, Spl. Achievement award 1990), Soc. Hist. Archaeology (pres. 1993), Tex. Archeol. Soc., Archaeol. Inst. Am., Explorers Club, Phi Beta Kappa. Methodist. Avocations: stamp collecting, science fiction. E-mail: barnold@tamu.edu. Office: Tex A&M U Inst Nautical Archaeology PO Drawer HG College Station TX 77841-5137

ARNOLD, JAMES PHILLIP, religious studies educator, history educator; b. Greenville, S.C.; s. David Lee and Vera Irene (Wilson) A. MA in Am. History, U. Houston, 1979; MA in Religious Studies, Rice U., 1984, PhD in Religious Studies, 1991. Instr. Am. History U. Houston, 1972-76; instr. religion Rice U., Houston, 1976-81; instr. ch. history, biblical studies, homiletics Houston Grad. Sch. Theology, 1984-86; instr. religion and history, exec. dir. The Reunion Inst., Houston, 1986—; pres. Living History Studies, Inc., Houston, 1993—; counselor families divided by religious cult issues; advisor to FBI on Branch Davidian crisis, Waco, Tex., 1993, Freeman crisis, 1996. Dir. Fine Arts Found., Houston, 1987—; founder Religion-Crisis Task Force, 1994. Rice U. fellow, 1980-91, U. Houston fellow, 1972-76; Tex. Com. for Humanities grantee, 1979. Mem. Am. Acad. Religion, Soc. Biblical Lit. Avocations: air-hockey, archaeology. Office: Reunion Inst 5508 Chaucer Dr Houston TX 77005-2632

ARNOLD, JAMES RICHARD, chemist, educator; b. New Brunswick, N.J., May 5, 1923; s. Abraham Samuel and Julia (Jacobs) A.; m. Louise Clark, Oct. 11, 1952; children: Robert C., Theodore J., Kenneth C. A.B., Princeton U., 1943, M.A., 1945, Ph.D., 1946. Postdoctoral fellow Inst. Nuclear Studies, U. Chgo., 1946-47, mem. faculty, 1948-55; NRC fellow Harvard U., 1947-48; mem. faculty chemistry Princeton U., 1955-58; assoc. prof. chemistry U. Calif., San Diego, 1958-60; prof. U. Calif., 1960-92, Harold C. Urey prof., 1983-92, chmn. dept. chemistry, 1960-63; assoc. Manhattan Project, 1943-46; dir. Calif. Space Inst., 1980-89, interim dir., 1996-97; prin. investigator Calif. Space Grant Consortium, 1989—; mem. various bds. NASA, 1959—; mem. space sci. bd. NAS, 1970-74, mem. com. on sci. and pub. policy, 1970-77. Mem. editorial bd.: Ann. Rev. Nuclear Chemistry, 1972; asso. editor: Revs. Geophysics and Space Physics, 1972-75, Moon, 1972—; contbr. articles to profl. jours. Pres. Torrey Pines Elem. Sch. PTA, 1964-65; pres. La Jolla Democratic Club, 1965-66; mem. nat. council World Federalists-U.S.A., 1970-72. Recipient E.O. Lawrence medal AEC, 1968, Leonard medal Meteoritical Soc., 1976, Kuiper award Am. Astron. Soc., 1993; asteroid 2143 named Jimarnold in his honor, 1980; Guggenheim fellow, India, 1972-73. Mem. Nat. Acad. Sci., Am. Acad. Arts and Scis., Internat. Acad. Astronautics, Am. Chem. Soc., AAAS, Fedn. Am. Scientists, World Federalist Assn. Office: U Calif San Diego Dept Chemistry Code 0524 La Jolla CA 92093

ARNOLD, JAMIE K., program management, safety and health, and training professional; b. Ann Arrundel County, Md.; d. J. David and Lynda Keplinger; m. Gregory D. Arnold, Oct. 31, 1993. BBA in Fin. and Mgmt., East Tenn. State U., 1989; MS in Safety, U. Tenn., 1995. Health physics technician Nuclear Fuel Svcs. Inc., Erwin, Tenn., 1990-93; sr. health physics technician Oak Ridge (Tenn.) Rsch. Inst., 1993-94; safety specialist PAI Corp., Oak Ridge, 1994-95, program mgr., 1995—. Office: 116 Milan Way Oak Ridge TN 37830-6913

ARNOLD, JAY, retired engineering executive, educator; b. Balt., Jan. 1, 1936; s. Otto Joseph and Margaret (Flannery) A.; m. Harriet Mary Metzbower, July 4, 1959; children: Kelly Marie Arnold Wood, Philip Driscoll Arnold, Michael Flannery Arnold. BS, Loyola Coll., Balt., 1965; MBA, Loyola Coll., Potomac, Md., 1977; postgrad., George Washington U., 1980-81, Berlitz Inst., Washington, 1987-90, U. So. Fla., 1994-95. With real times sys. IBM, Kingston, N.Y., 1962-65, Washington, 1962-65; software and systems engring. positions including mgt. NASA's Manned Space Program IBM, Houston, 1965-68; with FAA's Air Traffic Control, Atlantic City, 1968-73, FSD Advanced Tech., Bethesda, Md., 1973-78; vis. IBM prof. Morgan State U., Balt., 1978-79; planner of automation strategy Fed. Systems div. IBM, Gaithersburg, Md., 1979-81; sr. mgr. systems design depts. USAF Data Systems Modernization Fed. Systems div. IBM, Gaithersburg, 1981-83, sr. mgr. systems design depts. FAA Advanced Automation System, 1983-87; dir. network mgmt. and control Comsat Systems div. Communications Satellite Corp., Clarksburg, Md., 1987-88, sr. dir. Deutsche Fermelde Satellite program, 1988-90, sr. dir. MOSCOM program, 1990, sr. dir. engring. advanced systems, 1991-94; program dir. computer tech. St. Petersburg (Fla.) Jr. Coll., 1993-97; speaker, instr. and lectr. in field; tchr., entrepreneurial acad. Greater St. Petersburg C. of C., 1996—. Caregiver Frederick County Hospice, 1984-87; club leader Frederick County 4-H, 1975-80; pres./v.p. Frederick County Sheep Breeders Assn., 1983-84; chmn. bd. govs. Am. Bouviers Des Flandres Club, 1981-82; mem. St. Peter's Ch. Parish Coun., 1991-92; active Suncoast Tiger Bay, 1994-98, Leadership St. Pete Alumni, 1995—, Leadership Tampa Bay Alumni, 1997—. With USAF, 1958-62, Korea, 1960-61. Recipient Parenting awards Future Farmers of Am., 1978-80, Award for Advancement of Human Rights UN Assn., 1984; named Alumni of Yr. Mt. St. Joseph Coll. H.S., 1989. Mem. Am. Assn. for Retired Persons, St. Petersburg Yacht Club, St. Petersburg Sail and Power Squadron, Kiwanis Club St. Petersburg (Outstanding Chmn. 1997-98), St. Petersburg Cmty. Alliance. Roman Catholic. Avocations: farming, golf, personal computing, boating. Home: 1120 N Shore Dr NE Apt 903 Saint Petersburg FL 33701-1425

ARNOLD, JEANNE ELOISE, anthropologist, archaeologist, educator; b. Cleve., July 9, 1955; d. Lawrence Fred and Marybelle Eloise (Culp) A. BA, U. Mich., 1976; MA, U. Calif., Santa Barbara, 1979, PhD, 1983. Prof. anthropology U. No. Iowa, Cedar Falls, 1984-88; assoc. dir. Inst. Archaeology UCLA, 1988—, prof. anthropology, 1988—; vis. instr. anthropology Rice U., Houston, 1981; vis. prof. anthropology Oreg. State U., Corvallis, 1983-84; sr. archaeologist Infotec Rsch., Inc., Sonora, Calif., 1986-87; cons. in field. Author 3 books; contbr. over 40 articles and revs. to profl. jours. and over 15 chpts. to books. Rsch. grantee NSF, 1988-91, 95—; Rsch. and Ednl. grantee U. Calif. at L.A. and Santa Barbara, 1977—. Mem. Am. Anthropol. Assn., Soc. Am. Archaeology, Soc. Calif. Archaeology, Inst. Archaeology (mem. editorial bd. 1988—), Sigma Xi, Phi Beta Kappa. Avocations: photography, cinema. Office: UCLA Dept Anthropology PO Box 951553 Los Angeles CA 90095-1553

ARNOLD, JEROME GILBERT, lawyer; s. Edward F. and Annastacia (Thielen) A.; m. Judith Lindor, Dec. 18, 1971; children: Thomas, Mark, John, Jason, Maria. BS, U. Minn., 1964; LLB, U. N.D., 1967. Bar: Minn. 1967, S.D. 1967, U.S. Dist. Ct. S.D. 1967, U.S. Dist. Ct. Minn. 1973, U.S. Ct. Appeals (8th cir.) 1986. Law clk. U.S. Dist. Ct., Aberdeen, S.D., 1967-68; asst. city atty. City of Duluth, Minn., 1968-69; asst. county atty. St. Louis County, Duluth, 1969-70, chief criminal prosecutor, 1970-71; spl. asst. to county atty. County of Carlton, Minn., 1971; ptnr. Hunt & Arnold, Duluth, 1971-86; U.S. atty. U.S. Dist. Ct. Minn., Mpls., 1986-91; ptnr. Larson, Husby. Brodin & Arnold, Duluth, Md., 1992-93; compensation judge State of Minn., 1993—; mem. adv. com. Supreme Ct. Appointments, St. Paul, 1980; chmn. selection com. 6th Jud. Dist., Duluth, 1978-83. Chmn. St. Louis City (Minn.) Bd. Adjustment, 1978-82; Rep. nominee 8th Congl. Dist, Minn., 1974; mem. state steering com. Reagan for Pres., 1976, 80, 84. Mem. Fed. Bar Assn. (bd. dirs. 1986-91), Minn. Bar Assn. Roman Catholic. Avocations: fishing, hunting.

ARNOLD, JOHN DAVID, management counselor, catalyst; b. Boston, May 14, 1933; s. Israel and Edith (Gordon) A.; BA cum laude in Social Relations, Harvard U., 1955; children from previous marriage: Derek, Keith, Craig; m. Diane Summers, Sept. 1994. Prodn. supr., dealer service mgr. Arnold Stretch Mates Corp., Boston, 1957-59; asst. dir. manpower and orgn. devel. Polaroid Corp., Waltham, Mass., 1959-63; dir. internat. ops. Kepner-Tregoe & Assocs., Princeton, N.J., 1963-68; pres. John Arnold ExecuTrak Systems Inc., Boston, 1968—; merger integration catalyst, conflict resolution/prevention counselor, conf. leader numerous firms; speaker in field. 1st lt. U.S. Army, 1955-57. Author: Make Up Your Mind, 1978, The Art of Decision Making, 1978, Shooting the Executive Rapids, 1981, How to Make the Right Decisions, 1982, Trading Up-A Career Guide: How to Get Ahead Without Getting Out, 1984, How to Protect Yourself Against a Takeover, 1986, The Complete Problem Solver! A Total System of Competitive Decision Making, 1992, When The Sparks Fly: Resolving Organizational Conflict, 1993; contbr. articles to bus. mags. Bd. Dirs. World Music. E-mail: jarnold917@aol.com. Fax: 617-536-2228. Office: John Arnold ExecuTrak Systems Inc 256 Beacon St Boston MA 02116-1214

ARNOLD, JOHN FOX, lawyer; b. St. Louis, Sept. 17, 1937; s. John Anderson and Mildred Chapin (Fox) A.; m. Martha Ann Freeman, June 29, 1963 (div. Oct. 1993); children: Lisa A. Galena, Laura Wray, Lynne A. Binder, Lesli Freeman. A.B., U Mo, 1959, LLB, 1961. Bar: Mo. 1961, U.S. Dist. Ct. (ea. dist.) Mo. 1961, U.S. Ct. Appeals (8th cir.) 1961, U.S. Supreme Ct. 1971. Ptnr. Green, Hennings, Henry & Arnold, St. Louis, 1963-70; mem. Lashly & Baer, P.C., St. Louis, 1970—, chmn., 1987—. Mem. St. Louis County Charter Revision Com., Mo., 1968; chmn. bd. overseers, Lindenwood Coll., 1992-93, mem. bd. dirs. 1993-95; chmn. St. Louis County Bd. Election Commrs., 1981-86, Downtown St. Louis Inc., bd. dirs., 1992-98, chmn. bd. dirs., 1996-98; chmn. bd. dirs. Downtown St. Louis Partnership, Inc., 1997—. Lt. USAR, 1961-63. Recipient citation of merit U. Mo. Law Sch., Columbia, 1984. Fellow Am. Bar Found.; mem. ABA (mem. house of dels. 1986-90), Bar Assn. Met. St. Louis (pres. 1975-76), Mo. Bar (pres. 1984-85), Nat. Conf. Commrs. on Uniform State Laws (chmn. Securities Act 1978-90, chmn. rev. com. Partnership Act 1991-92, drafting com. article 2 sales, 2A leases and 8 investment securities of uniform comml. code), Am. Law Inst. Republican. Presbyterian. Office: Lashly & Baer 714 Locust St Saint Louis MO 63101-1699

ARNOLD, KAREN L., writer, consultant; b. East Chicago, Ind., July 2, 1945; d. Glenn T. and Lillian (Helding) Bovard; m. Gary G. Arnold, Dec. 16, 1967; children: Sara, Jenny, Emily. BA, No. Ill. U., 1967; MA, U. Md., 1983, PhD, 1994. Poet-in-residence Montpelier Cultural Arts Ctr., Laurel, Md., 1985—; scholar, lectr. NEH and Howard County Libr. Sys., Columbia, Md., 1988—; lectr., discussion moderation Balt. City Libr. Sys., 1994—, Montgomery County Libr. Sys., Rockville, 1993—, Prince George's County Libr. Sys., Adelphi, 1988—, Frederick (Md.) County Libr. Sys., 1998; vis. prof. U. Lund, Sweden, 1997; writing workshop leader, cons., Md., 1982—; adj. faculty, vis. prof. U.S. Naval Acad., Annapolis, 1988-90, 97-98; pres., mem. adv. bd. Montpelier Cultural Arts Ctr., Laurel, Md., 1983-94. Author: Border Crossings, 1997; editor: Impetus III, 1988, Montpelier Plus 4, 1988. Vol. workshop leader Prince George's County Schs., Laurel, 1974-83, Howard County Schs., Columbia, Md., 1983—. Fellow Am. Scandinavian Found., 1998, Am. Women's Club in Sweden, 1997-98, Soc. for Advancement Scandinavian Studies, 1988; recipient Outstanding Arts Conf. award Mid-Atlantic Recreation Assn., 1984. Avocations: beach time, visits to Maine coast, embroidery. E-mail: grshtct@aol.com. Home and Office: 12213 Green Shoot Ct Columbia MD 21044

ARNOLD, KATHRYN, artist, educator; b. Kansas City, Mo.. Student, Kansas City Art Inst.; BFA in Painting and Drawing, U. Kans., 1991, MFA in Art, 1993. Represented by Duane Reed Gallery St. Louis; Leedy-Voulkos Gallery, Kansas City, Ellen Paustcher Fine Arts Cons., (Chgo.); tchg. asst. U. Kans., Lawrence, 1993; adj. instr. Johnson County C.C., Overland Park, Kans., 1997; adj. asst. prof. Washburn U., Topeka, 1994-97; mem. faculty Kansas City Art Inst., 1995-97; resident Contemporary Artists Ctr., North Adams, Mass., 1995; lectr., panel participation David Levik Gallery, 1995, U. Minn., 1996, St. Cloud State (Minn.) U., 1996, U. Wis., Madison, 1997. One-woman shows include U. Kans., 1993, 94, Nat. Computer Tng. Ctr., Kansas City, 1994, Park Coll., Parkville, Mo., 1994, David Levik Gallery, Wesport, Kans., 1994, 95, B.Z. Wagman Art Inc., St. Louis, 1994, Rockhurst Coll., 1996, U. Minn., 1996, Las Vegas Cultural Ctr., 1996, 97, Duane Reed Gallery, 1997, 90; group shows include Wichita Kans. Art Ctr., 1993, State of the Art Gallery, Ithaca, N.Y., 1993, David Levik Gallery, 1993-94, 95, Kansas City Artist's Coalition, 1994, 95, George Walter Vincent Smith Art Mus., Springfield, Mass., 1994, An Art Place, Inc., Chgo., 1994, 95, The Gallery Ctr., Indpls., 1994, New Harmony Gallery of Contemporary Art, 1994, Washburn U., Topeka, 1994, Contemporary Artists Ctr., North Adams, Mass., 1995, Tustin Renaissance, Calif., 1995, Roger Guffey Gallery, Kansas City, 1995, Art Inst. Chgo., 1996, Riverside Arts Ctr., Chgo., 1996,

Korean Cultural Ctr., L.A., 1996, Johnson County C.C. Gallery of Art, 1996, Mulvane Art Mus., Topeka, 1996, 97, Ohio State U., 1996, Morgan Gallery, Kansas City, 1997, Leedy-Voulkos Gallery, Kansas City, 1997, Pelham (N.Y.) Art Ctr., 1997, U. Hawaii, Hilo, 1997, Lakelake Coll., Sheboygan, Wis., 1999; permanent collections include Thompson & Mitchell Attys. at Law, Corp. Skills Internat., Sch. Fine Arts U. Kans., Bryan Cave Law Firm, Am. Kenpo Karate Acad. Kans., Topeka Pub. Libr., Ramada, McDonald-Douglas Corp., United Mo. Bank, U. Minn., Am. Legacy. Vol. Accessible Arts, Kansas City, 1997. NEA fellow, 1996; Kans. Arts Commn. Profl. Devel. grantee, 1993-94; recipient Recognition of Merit award Contemporary Artists Ctr., 1995, award Mass. Art League, 1994. Mem. Chgo. Artists Coaltion, Kansas City Artists Coalition, Coll. Art Assn., Phi Kappa Phi. Office: # 404 1427 W 9th St Kansas City MO 64102

ARNOLD, KEVIN DAVID, psychologist, educational researcher; b. Massilon, Ohio, Jan. 7, 1957; s. Jack Olen and Arlene Adele (Harrold) A.; m. Cindi Englefield. BS, Grace Coll., 1979; MA, Ohio State U., 1981; PhD, Ohio State U., N.Y., 1983; advanced cert., Ctr. for Cognitive Therapy, N.Y., 1994, Atlanta Ctr. Cognitive Therapy, 1994. Fellow and diplomate Am. Bd. Med. Psychotherapists; diplomate in behavioral psychology Am. Bd. Profl. Psychology (bd. dirs.); cert. treatment of alcohol and other psycho-active substance use disorders, APA Coll. Profl. Psychology; lic. psychologist, Ohio; listed divorce mediator Franklin County (Ohio) Ct. Common Pleas. Grad. rsch. assoc. Ohio State U., Columbus, 1980-83, rsch. assoc., 1983-84, prin. investigator deaf and blind project, 1984-92, asst. dir. Ctr. Spl. Needs Populations, 1988-93, asst. prof., 1988-92; psychologist Columbus, 1991—; dir. Ctr. for Cognitive and Behavioral Therapy Greater Columbus, 1995—; founder, CEO Ohio Proficiency Test Rev., Inc., 1990-95; v.p. Englefield & Arnold Pub., 1995—; bd. dirs. Am. Bd. Behavioral Psychology, also work sample coord. Co-author: Passing the Ohio Proficiency Test, 1993, Passing the Ohio Ninth Grade Proficiency Test, 1996, (test) Social Behavior Assessment Inventory, 1992; contbr. chpts. to books and articles to profl. jours. Fundraiser, cons. Dem. gubernatorial campaign, 1989-90, 1989-90. Deaf and Blind Ctr. grantee U.S. Dept. Edn., 1984-94, Sch. Psychology grantee, 1987-93, Evaluation Intervention Teams Ohio Dept. Edn. grantee, 1988-93, Drop-out Cost Study Ctr. Labor Rsch. grantee, 1990-91, Parent Satisfaction Study Ohio Devel. Disabilities Planning Coun. grantee, 1989-90, Tchr. Compentency Survey Study grantee, 1992-93. Fellow Am. Acad. Behavioral Psychology; mem. APA, Am. Psychol. Soc. (del. state leadership conf.), Assn. for Advancement of Behavior Therapy, Acad. Family Mediators, Ohio Psychol. Assn. (former mem. continuing edn. com., trustee, former chmn. publs. coun., former co-editor Ohio Psychologist, former co-editor Ohio Psychol. Rev., pres.-elect 2000-2001), Am. Assn. Mental Retardation, Ctrl. Oho Psychol. Assn., Am. Psychology-Law Soc., Soc. Rsch. in Child Devel., Soc. Personality Assessment, Zinfandel Advocates and Producers. Roman Catholic. Avocation: wine collecting. Office: CCBT 2121 Bethel Rd Ste C Columbus OH 43220-1804

ARNOLD, LARRY K., major general United States Air Force; m. Linda Smith; 2 children. BA in Polit. Sci., Wake Forest U., 1964; grad., Squadron Officer Sch. USAF, 1972; MBA, Auburn U., 1977; student, Air War Coll., 1984; studnt Nat., Internat. Security Mgmt., Kennedy Sch Govt Harvard U., 1994. Commd 2d lt. USAF, 1965, advanced through grades to maj. gen., 1998; fighter pilot 390th Fighter Squadron USAF, Da Nang Air Base, Republic Viet Nam, 1966-67; student combat crew tng., F-106 tng. USAF, Perrin and Tyndall AFBs, Tex., Fla., 1967-68; pilot instr. USAF, Langley AFB, Va., 1968-72, Tyndall AFB, Fla., 1972-73; instr., pilot tng. officer Air Nat. Guard, Atlantic City Airport, N.J., 1973-76, cmmdr., 1977-83; dep. comdr. ops. Fighter Interceptor Group Air Nat. Guard, Atlantic City Airport, 1984-86; air nat. guard advisor to comdr. Air Univ and faculty mem. Air War Coll., Maxwell AFB, Ala., 1986-88; comdr. 147th fighter interceptor group Air Nat. Guard, Ellington AFB, Tex., 1988-89; asst. dir. readiness support Air Nat. Guard Readiness Ctr., Andrews AFB, Md., 1989-92; asst. dir. Air Nat. Guard Bur. Pentagon, Washington, 1994-97; vice comdr. First Air Force, Tyndall AFB, 1997; comdr. 1st Air Force Air Combat Command, Tyndall AFB, Fla., 1997—. Decorated Legion of Merit, Disting. Flying Cross with oak leaf cluster, Meritorious Svc. medal with oak leaf cluster, Air medal with 14 oak leaf clusters, Air Force Commendation medal, Air Force Achievement medal, Combat Readiness medal with 3 oak leaf clusters, Republic of Vietnam Gallantry Cross with one device, Vietnam Armed Forces Honor medal, Republic of Vietnam Campaign medal, Vietnam Svc. medal with two bronze stars, others. Office: 1st Air Force Office Pub Affairs Tyndall AFB FL 32403-5428

ARNOLD, LEE, library scientist; b. Waukegan, Ill., Oct. 18, 1959; s. Louis Douglas and Verona Christina (Lemke) A. BA cum laude, Edgewood Coll., Madison, Wis., 1982; M of Libr. and Info. Sci., U. Wis., Milw., 1987. Sales support mgr. Marshall Field and Co., Milw., Wis., 1982-88; asst. univ. libr. for adminstrv. svcs. Princeton (N.J.) U., 1988-92; English tchr. Berlitz Schs. of Lang., Princeton, N.J., 1990-92; dir. coll. mgmt. and spl. projects Hist. Soc. of Pa., Phila., 1992—. Contbr. articles to profl. jours.; numerous book reviews and presentations in field. Mem. Delta Epsilon Sigma. Democrat. Roman Catholic. Avocations: reading, travel, outdoors. Office: Hist Soc PA 1300 Locust St Philadelphia PA 19107-5661

ARNOLD, LEONARD J., construction executive; b. San Diego, Mar. 17, 1947; s. William W. and Thelma C. (Cook) A.; m. Judy Lynn Keeton, Aug. 30, 1969; children: Alyssa Noelle, Lorienne Eve. BS in Constrn. Mgmt., Colo. State U., 1970. V.p. G. E. Johnson Constrn., Colorado Springs, Colo., 1970-76; pres. Wyoming Johnson Inc., Casper, 1976-79; v.p. Hensel Phelps Constrn. Co., Greeley, Colo., 1979-88, Phelps, Inc., 1988-89, Hensel Phelps Constrn. Co., Greeley, Colo., 1990-94; pres. Lighthouse Group, Greeley, Colo., 1994—, Rainbow Lake Investments, 1994—. Chmn. Weld County Econ. Devel., Greeley, 1986-88. Mem. Urban Land Inst., Associated Gen. Contractors Am., Soc. Am. Mil. Engrs., U.S. Space Found., Colo. Assn. Sch. Bds., Sigma Lambda Chi. Republican. Club: Greeley Country. Avocations: fishing, classic car collection, auto racing, outdoors activities. Home: 527 Hickory Dr Lyons CO 80540-8031 Office: Rainbow Lake Investments LLC 308 E Elkorn Estes Park CO 80517

ARNOLD, LESLIE ANN, special education educator; b. St. Louis, Oct. 20, 1953; d. Eugene L. and Louisa French (Gale) A. BS, Central State U., 1975, MEd, 1981. Cert. spl. edn.; learning disabilities, mental retardation tchr., Kans. Tchr. level III educable mentally handicapped Unified Sch. Dist. 345, Topeka, Kans., 1976-82; tchr., specialist mentally retarded and occupationally handicapped Sch. Dist. 619, Wellington, Kans., 1982-87; coord. vocat. options level IV educable mentally handicapped Wellington Unified Sch. Dist. 353, 1987—; coord. spl. edn. Wellington Unified Sch. Dist., 1995-98, dir. spl. edn., 1998; cons. in field. Grantee Vocat. Rehab., 1992-95, Kansas Transition Network, 1994-98, Charter Sch., 1997.

ARNOLD, MARSHA DIANE, writer; b. Kingman, Kans., July 7, 1948; d. Eugene Willard Krehbiel and Elsie Irene (Lippincott) Raymond; m. Frederick Oak Arnold, Jan. 25, 1970; children: Amy Marie, Calvin Diedrich Oak. BA in English cum laude, Kans. State U., 1970. Cert. secondary English tchr., Kans., standard elem. tchr., Calif. Eligibility worker Dept. Social Svcs., San Mateo, Calif., 1970-71, San Rafael, Calif., 1971-79; eligibility worker Calif. Children Svcs., Dept. of Health, San Rafael, 1979-81; kindergym tchr. Calif. Parenting Inst., Petaluma, 1981; writer children's books, columnist Sebastopol, Calif., 1985—; tchr.'s aide Twin Hills Sch. Dist., Sebastopol, 1991-94; spkr. in field. Author: Heart of a Tiger, 1995 (Jr. Lib. Guild selection 1995, 1997-98 Show Me Readers Award Master List, Internat. Reading Assn. Children's Disting. Book award 1996, Young Hoosier Book Award selection, Houston Chronicle Best Book of '95 Christmas Roundup), Quick, Quack, Quick, 1996; contbr. columns, stories and articles to mags. Animal care vol. Boyd Mus. Sci., San Rafael, 1974-75, Calif. Marin Mammal Rehab. Ctr., Marin County, Calif., 1976; v.p. PTA, Sebastopol, 1985. Recipient Best Local Columnist award Calif. Newspaper Pubs. Assn., 1986, 87, 93, Marion Vannett Ridgway award for outstanding first published picture book for children by an author or illustrator, 1996. Mem. Soc. Childrens' Book Writers and Illustrators, Phi Kappa Phi, Kappa Delta Pi. Avocations: scuba diving, travel, nutrition. Home: 350 Mcgregor Ln Sebastopol CA 95472-5375*

ARNOLD, MICHAEL NEAL, real property appraiser, consultant; b. Madera, Calif., June 6, 1947; s. John Patrick and Patricia (Neal) A.; m. Suzanne Elizabeth Badal, Aug. 31, 1968; children: C. Matthew Neal Arnold, Nathaniel T. Badal Arnold, Andrew T. White Arnold, Thomas A. Badal Arnold. BA in Geography, U. Calif., Santa Barbara, 1974. Cert. appraiser. Assoc. R.W. Raymond & Co., Santa Barbara, 1974; appraiser Madera County Assessor Office, 1975; assoc. Pickthorne & Assocs., San Bruno, Calif., 1975-76; ptnr. Hammock, Arnold, Smith, Santa Barbara, 1976—; instr. Santa Barbara City Coll., 1980-85, 99. Contbr. articles to profl. jours. Coach AYSO, Santa Barbara, 1978—; cub master Boy Scouts Am., Santa Barbara, 1985. Mem. Appraisal Inst., Vieja Valley Site Coun., Santa Barbara Coun. Real Estate Appraisers (founder, sec., speaker bur.), Appraisal Inst. (instr. 1990—, grader, com. chair, officer, chpt. pres.), Amateurs Club, Santa Barbara City Coll. (adv. coun. mem.). Anglican-Episcopalian. Avocations: reading, walking, skiing, talking, genealogy. Home: 521 N Ontare Rd Santa Barbara CA 93105 Office: Hammock Arnold Smith & Co 215 W Figueroa St Fl 2 Santa Barbara CA 93101-3602

ARNOLD, MORRIS SHEPPARD, judge; b. Texarkana, Tex., Oct. 8, 1941. BSEE, U. Ark., 1965, LLB, 1968; LLM, Harvard U., 1969, SJD, 1971; MA (hon.), U. Pa., 1977, JD (hon.), 1986; LLD (hon.), U. Ark., Little Rock. Bar: Ark. 1968, Pa. 1985. Tchg. fellow law Harvard U., 1969-70; from asst. prof. to prof. Ind. U. Law Sch., 1971-76, prof., 1976-77, dean, 1985; prof. law, history U. Pa., 1977-81; Ben J. Altheimer disting. prof. law U. Ark., Little Rock, 1981-84; judge U.S. dist. Ct. (we. dist.) Ark., Ft. Smith, 1985-92, U.S. Cir. Ct. (8th cir.), 1992—; vis. fellow commoner Trinity Coll., Cambridge U., 1978; v.p., dir. office of pres., U. Pa., 1980-81; vis. prof. Stanford (Calif.) U. Law Sch., 1985. Author: Old Tenures and Natura Brevium, 1974, Yearbook 2 Richard II, 1378-79, 1975, On the Laws and Customs of England, 1980, Unequal Laws Unto a Savage Race, 1985, Select Cases of Treespass from the King's Courts, 1307-1399, 2 vols., 1985, 87, Arkansas Colonials, 1986, Colonial Arkansas 1686-1804: A Social and Cultural History, 1991. Rep. gen. counsel, Ark., 1982, chmn., 1983; bd. dirs. Nature Conservancy of Ark., 1982-87, Ark. Arts Ctr., 1981-84. Decorated Chevalier Ordre Palmes Acad. (France); Frank Knox fellow Harvard U., U. London, 1970-71, Mus. Sci. Natural History, 1986. Fellow Am. Soc. Legal History (hon.), Athenaeum Club London, Union League Club Phila., Country Club Little Rock. Office: US Cir Judge PO Box 2060 Little Rock AR 72203*

ARNOLD, P. A., special education educator; b. Toledo; d. Mattie Spear; m. Earl E. Arnold. BA, BS, David Lipscomb Coll., 1960; MA, Wayne State U., 1962; MS, Nova U., 1986. Cert. spl. edn., psychology, speech, mental retardation, emotional disturbance, Bible, Fla. Tchr. dactyology, interpreter for deaf, 1960—; tchr. Hobbs (N.Mex.) Mcpl. Schs., 1981-82; tchr. spl. edn. City Systems, Rockford and Warren, Mich., 1960-67; dir. Four-County Ctr. Handicapped, Ark., 1977-81; dir. model project ACTION; Project TREE Tech. Resources in Exceptional Edn.; conf. presenter in fields. Author: Instructor, Light for Deaf, 1992, Ol' Time Preacher Man, 1995, Little Red Schoolhouse, 1998, Trapezoid of Children, 1999. Bd. dirs., deaf advisor Hearing Soc. Volusia County; mem. project TREE-Tech. Resources in Exceptional Edn.-Tech. Exceptional Edn.-SY 2000, Dept. Edn., Fla. State U. Ctr. Ednl. Tech. Grantee Pub. Welfare, Nat. Gardening Assn., FUTURES, Newspapers in Edn. Mem. NEA, ARC, ASCD, Volusia Ednl. Assn., Fla. Edn. Assn., Coun. for Exceptional Children, Am. Assn. on Mental Deficiency, Nat. Assn. Deaf.

ARNOLD, PERI ETHAN, political scientist; b. Chgo., Sept. 21, 1942; s. Joseph Evon and Eve (Jacobs) A.; m. Beverly Ann Kessler, Aug. 22, 1965; children: Emma, Rachel. BA, Roosevelt U., Chgo., 1964; MA, U. Chgo., 1967, PhD, 1972. Lectr. Roosevelt U., Chgo., 1966-68; instr. polit. sci. Western Mich. U., Kalamazoo, 1970-71; asst. prof. polit. sci. U. Notre Dame, Ind., 1971-76, assoc. prof. govt., 1976-86, prof. of govt. and internat. studies, 1986; chair dept. govt., 1986-92; Compton vis. prof. of world politics Miller Ctr., U. Va., 1993-94; dir. Hesburgh Program in Pub. Svc., 1995—; dir. Notre Dame Semester in Washington, 1997—. Author: Making the Managerial Presidency, 1986 (Louis Brownlow Book award 1987), 2nd rev. ed., 1998; mem. editl. bd. Am. Jour. Polit. Sci., 1991-94, Polity, 1995—, Presdl. Studies Quar., 1997—; co-editor Jour. of Policy History, 1987-88; contbr. articles to profl. jours. Bd. dirs. South Bend Hebrew Day Sch., Mishawaka, Ind., 1985-88; chair Comty. Rels. Coun. of Jewish Fedn. of St. Joseph Valley, South Bend, Ind., 1990-94; bd. trustees Congregation Beth El, South Bend, 1994—; mem. acquisitions com. Snite Mus. Art, Notre Dame, Ind; bd. dirs. Jewish Fedn. of St. Joseph Valley, 1999—. Recipient Spl. Presdl. award U. Notre Dame, 1993, Marshall Dimock award Am. Soc. Pub. Adminstrn., 1996; grantee Am. Coun. Learned Socs., 1974; rsch. grantee Herbert Hoover Libr. Assn., 1993-94; Ford Found. fellow, 1978-81. Mem. Am. Polit. Sci. Assn. (program chmn., exec. com. presidency sect.), Midwest Polit. Sci. Assn., Univ. Club. Democrat. Jewish. Avocations: literature, music, drama. Home: 1419 E Colfax Ave South Bend IN 46617-3307 Office: U Notre Dame Dept Govt Internat Studies Notre Dame IN 46556

ARNOLD, PETER GORDON, communications consultant; b. Newton, Mass., Jan. 25, 1943; s. Israel Isaac and Edith (Gordon) A.; m. Kirsten Ellen Arnold, July 25, 1966 (div. 1979); 1 child, Jeremy Gordon; m. Margery Loewenberg, July 27, 1980; 1 child, Jessica Beth. BA, U. Mich., 1966; MA, U. So. Calif., 1969. Writer, producer Universal Studios, Hollywood, Calif., 1969-70; exec. v.p. Cameo Pictures, Hollywood, 1971-72; devel. writer Calif. Inst. Tech., Pasadena, 1973; dir. spl. projects Occidental Coll., Los Angeles, 1974-75; exec. dir. Hugh O'Brian Youth Found., Los Angeles, 1976; pres. Peter Arnold Assocs., Boston, 1977—. Author: Lady Beware, 1973, Emergency Handbook, 1980 (Literary Guild selection 1980), Job and Career Building, 1980, Packaging Your House for Profit, 1986 and seven other books. Mem. Writers Guild Am., Authors League, Advt. Club Greater Boston. Office: 1 Hollis St Ste 350 Wellesley MA 02482-4673

ARNOLD, RICHARD SHEPPARD, federal judge; b. Texarkana, Tex., Mar. 26, 1936; s. Richard Lewis and Janet (Sheppard) A.; m. Gale Hussman, June 14, 1958 (divorced); children: Janet Sheppard, Arnold Hart, Lydia Palmer, Arnold Turnipseed; m. Kay Kelley, Oct. 27, 1979. BA summa cum laude, Yale U., 1957; LLB magna cum laude, Harvard U., 1960; LLD, U. Ark., 1992, U. Richmond, 1998. Bar: D.C. 1961, Ark. 1960. Pvt. practice Washington, 1961-64, Texarkana, Ark., 1964-74; law clk. to justice Brennan U.S. Supreme Ct., 1960-61; assoc. Covington & Burling, 1961-64; ptnr. Arnold & Arnold, 1964-74; legis. sec. Gov. of Ark., 1973-74, staff coord., 1974; legis. asst. Senator Bumpers of Ark., Washington, 1975-78; judge U.S. Dist. Ct. (ea. and we. dists.) Ark., 1978-80, U.S. Ct. Appeals (8th cir.), Little Rock, 1980—; chief judge U.S. Ct. Appeals (8th cir.), 1992-98; part-time instr. U. Va. Law Sch., 1962-64; mem. Ark. Constl. Revision Study Commn., 1967-68. Case editor: Harvard Law Rev., 1959-60; contbr. articles to profl. jours. Gen. chmn. Texarkana United Way Crusade, 1969-70; pres. Texarkana Community Chest, 1970-71; mem. vis. com. Harvard Law Sch., 1973-79, U. Chgo. Law Sch., 1983-86, 94-97; candidate for Congress 4th Dist. Ark., 1966, 72; del. Democratic Nat. Conv., 1968, Ark. Constl. Conv., 1969-70; chmn. rules com. Ark. Dem. Com., 1968-74, mem. exec. com., 1972-74; mem. Com. on Legis. Orgn., 1971-72; trustee U. Ark., 1973-74; chmn. budget com. Jud. Conf. of U.S., 1987-96. Fellow Am. Bar Found.; mem. Am. Law Inst. (coun.), Jud. Conf. U.S. (exec. com. 1992-98), Cum Laude Soc., Phi Beta Kappa. Episcopalian. Office: 600 W Capitol Ave Ste 208 Little Rock AR 72201-3321

ARNOLD, ROBERT JEFFREY, musician; b. San Marcos, Tex., Apr. 28, 1959. Student, U. North Tex., 1977-80, Baylor U., 1982-83. Concert pianist, organist radio and TV, N.Am. and Europe, 1967—; exec. dir. Dallas Inst. Vocal Arts, 1988-89; exec. artistic dir. Lee County Opera, Giddings, Tex., 1989-92; accompanist, coach Opera Ensemble of San Antonio, 1994; voice tchr. and coach, 1977—; artistic dir. Lake Shore Art Song Ensemble, Chgo., 1996-98; duo pianist Arnold-Harman Piano Duo, 1993—. Recital debuts Carnegie Hall, N.Y.C., 1989, 95, St. Mary Magdalene Ch., Picton, Ont., 1993, Countess of Huntingdon Hall, Worcester, Eng., 1995. Mem. Opera Am., Organ Hist. Soc.

ARNOLD, ROBERT LLOYD, investment broker, financial advisor; b. Seattle, June 18, 1952; s. Vern Lloyd and Ruth Francis (Bruty) A. Student, Bellevue Coll., Wash., 1971-72; BS magna cum laude, U. Wash., 1975; MS, Yale U., 1977. Lic. fed. securities agt. Group leader U.S. Govt., Miramonte, Calif., 1977-78; economist U.S. Govt., Walla Walla, Wash., 1978-79; gen. mgr. Full Value Roofing, Bellevue, 1979-81; transp. mgr. N.W. Hydra-Line, Inc., Seattle, 1981-83; owner Fairfields, Seattle, 1982—; sr. fin. advisor Waddell & Reed, Inc., Bellevue, 1983—; coord. Charles Givens Found., Seattle, 1984-85, 88-90; lectr. Comty. Sch., Seattle, 1984-91; guest spkr. Kiwanis, Puyallup, Wash., 1985; seminar leader Chgo. Title Ins. Co., Seattle, 1985-90. Fund raiser ARC, Seattle, 1984-85; chmn. fin. com. Unity Ch. of Seattle, 1988-90. Grantee Bloedel Found., 1973-74, Bishop Soc. grantee, 1974-75; fellow Yale U., 1975-77. Mem. Rainier Club (reciprocity com. 1994—, young Rainiers com. 1994-95, arts and libr. com. 1996-98), Seattle Delta Group (life, chmn. 1985-87), Letip Internat. Eastside (v.p. 1996, pres. 1996), Inglewood Beach Club (trustee 1996—, v.p. 1996, pres. 1997—), Bellevue Master Mind (pres. 1996-97), Rolls Royce Owners Club, Xi Sigma Pi (treas. 1974-75). Republican. Avocations: fishing, exploring ghost towns. Office: 12340 NE 8th St Ste 100 Bellevue WA 98005-3189

ARNOLD, ROBERT MORRIS, banker; b. Seattle, June 6, 1928; s. Lawrence Moss and Grace Elizabeth (Heffernan) A.; children: Grace Arnold Loes, Lauren McLellan Gorter. BA in Fin. and Bus. Adminstrn., Yale U., 1951; grad., Pacific Coast Sch. Banking, 1963. With Seattle-1st Nat. Bank, 1951, 1955—, v.p., 1965-73, mgr. nat. accounts dept., 1969-73, sr. v.p., mgr. corp. bus. devel., 1973-81, bd. dirs.; bd. dirs. Seafirst Corp. Bd. dirs. Centrum Found., Fred C. Hutchinson Cancer Rsch.; trustee Poncho; bd. dirs., exec. com., fin. com. Seattle Art Mus., also mem., joint founder its Contemporary Art Coun. Officer USNR, 1951-55. Mem. Am. Inst. Banking, Mcpl. League Seattle, Yale Assn. Western Wash., Newcomen Soc. (treas. Pacific N.W. com.), Seattle Golf Club, Seattle Tennis Club, Seattle Yacht Club, University Club (Seattle), Bohemian Club (San Francisco), Thunderbird Golf Club (Palm Springs, Calif.), O'Donnell Golf Club (Palm Springs), Mission Hills Country Club (Palm Springs). Home: 1535 Parkside Dr E Seattle WA 98112-3719 Office: 1001 4th Ave Ste 4710 Seattle WA 98154-1198 also: 50 Hilton Head Dr Rancho Mirage CA 92270-1607*

ARNOLD, ROLAND R., dental educator and researcher; b. Denver, Dec. 18, 1946. BS, La. State U., 1972, PhD in Microbiology, 1975. Assoc. dean dental rsch. Emory U., 1988-91; mem. study sect. NIH, 1983-91; prof. periodontics and diagnostic scis. U. N.C., Chapel Hill, 1991—, dir. Dental Rsch. Ctr., 1991-96. Mem. Am. Assn. Immunologists, Am. Assn. Dental Rsch., Am. Soc. for Microbiologists, Omicron Kappa Upsilon. Office: Dental Rsch Ctr Univ NC Campus Box 7455 Chapel Hill NC 27599-7455*

ARNOLD, RONALD HENRI, nonprofit organization executive, consultant; b. Houston, Aug. 8, 1937; s. John Andrew and Carrie Virginia (Henri) A.; m. Phoebe Anne Trogdon, Oct. 12, 1963 (dec. Feb. 1974); 1 child, Andrea; m. Janet Ann Parkhurst, Aug. 8, 1974; stepchildren: Andrea Wright, Rosalyn Wright. Tech. publ. Boeing Co., Seattle, 1961-71; cons. Northwoods Studio, Bellevue, Wash., 1971—; exec. v.p. Ctr. for Def. of Free Enterprise, Bellevue, 1984—; advisor Nat. Fed. Lands Conf., 1988-92. Author: James Watt and the Environment, 1981, Ecology Wars, 1987, The Grand Prairie Years, 1987, (with Alan Gottlieb) Trashing the Economy, 1993, Politically Correct Environment, 1996, Ecoterror, 1997, Battered Communities, 1998; editor: Stealing the National Parks, 1987; contbg. editor Logging Mgmt. mag., 1978-81, Western Conservation Jour., 1974-81. Recipient Editorial Achievement award Am. Bus. Press, 1981. Mem. AFTRA, Forest History Soc. Republican. Avocation: music. Home: 12605 NE 2nd St Bellevue WA 98005-3206

ARNOLD, ROY, provost, university administrator; m. Jane Kay Price, 1963; children: Jana Lynn Hoffman, Julie Kay Salvi. BS with distinction, U. Nebr., 1962; MS, Oreg. State U., 1965, PhD, 1967. Asst. prof. food sci. and tech. U. Nebr., Lincoln, 1967-71, assoc. prof., 1971-74, prof., 1974-87; provost, exec. v.p. Oreg. State U., 1991—; head dept. food sci. and tech. U. Nebr., 1973-79, dean, dir. agrl. experiment sta., 1980-82, vice chancellor for agrl. and natural resources, 1982-87; dean Coll. Agrl. Sci., Oreg. State U., 1987-91. Recipient Carl R. Fellers award Inst. of Food Technologists, 1998. Fellow AAAS, Inst. of Food Technologists (pres. 1994-95). Fax: roy.arnold@orst.edu. Office: Oreg State U Office Acad Affairs 624 Kerr Adminstrn Bldg Corvallis OR 97331-2153

ARNOLD, RUTH ANN, elementary education educator; b. Lebanon, Pa., June 3, 1955; d. Earl Edwin and Joan Marie (Meyer) Rittle; m. Elijah Joseph Arnold III, July 17, 1976; 1 child, Nathan Joseph. BS, Lebanon Valley Coll., 1977; MEd, Millersville U., 1982. Cert. reading recovery tchr. Elem. reading specialist, reading recovery tchr. Palmyra (Pa.) Area Sch. Dist., 1980—. Vol. Local 4-H Club, Lebanon, Pa., 1973-98; organist, choir dir. Tulpehocken United Ch. of Christ, Richland, Pa., 1982-95. Mem. Internat. Reading Assn., Keystone State Reading Assn., Lebanon-Lancaster Reading Coun., Reading Recovery Coun. North Am. Avocation: music.

ARNOLD, SCOTT GREGORY, computer information systems specialist; b. Wabash, Ind., June 23, 1961; s. Don H. and Martha S. (Gregor) A.; m. Jerri Sue Malan, May 20, 1995. BS in Computer Sci., Ball State U., 1983; postgrad., St. Francis Coll., 1985, Ind. U./Purdue U., 1985, Ind. Vocat. Tech. Coll., 1985, Moraine Park Tech. Coll., 1987-89. Programmer Slater Steel Corp., Ft. Wayne, Ind., 1983-85; programmer II, N.Am. Van Lines, Ft. Wayne, 1985-86; programmer, analyst Speed Queen Co., Ripon, Wis., 1986-90, Direct Transit, Inc., Sioux City, Iowa, 1990; programming cons. Turille and Assocs., Omaha, 1991; programmer, analyst Warren Distbn., Inc., Omaha, 1991; programmer CMS-Tempro, South Bend, Ind., 1992; programmer, analyst Heaters Engring., Inc., North Webster, Ind., 1992; software support analyst NACCO Materials Handling Group, Inc., Danville, Ill., 1992-98; cons. Computer Application Solutions, Inc., Springfield, Ill., 1998—; cert. mgr. Bus. and Econ. Inst., 1994-95; cert. 21st Century Computer Assocs. Resource Mgmt. Sys., Sys. Start-up Ltd., 1997; cert. in Electronic Data Interchange, Whittman-Hart, 1997. Chmn. Circus Vegas, 1993-97; bd. dirs. Jr. C. of C., 1985-97, Riponfest, 1987-89, Springfest, 1992-95, Internat. Mgmt. Coun., 1993-97. Mem. Toastmasters. Republican. Mem. Ch. of Christ. Avocation: bowling. Home: 1024 Sunset Rdg Danville IL 61832-2083

ARNOLD, SKIP, performance artist; b. Binghamton, N.Y.. BFA, State U. Coll., Buffalo, 1980; MFA, UCLA, 1984. One artist performances include (video installation) Dizzy, Newport Harbor Art Mus., 1992, (performance/activity) Spin, Jack Tilton Gallery, N.Y., 1994, Burnett Miller Gallery, Santa Monica, Calif., 1995, Roger Merians Gallery, N.Y., 1995, others; selected group exhbns. include Long Beach (Calif.) Mus. Art, 1990, Infermental 10, Osnabruck/Skopje, Germany, 1991, American Gallery, L.A., 1991, San Francisco Cameraworks, 1991, Kim Light Gallery, L.A., 1992, Gallery 400, U. Ill., 1992, others; also videos, ad campaigns, campaign billboards. Video grantee Found. for Art Resources, 1990, Visual Arts fellowship grantee NEA, 1993, Guggenheim Fellowship grantee, 1995; Performance fellow Brody Arts Found., 1992, Art Matters, Inc., 1992. Address: Miller Burnett Gallery Apt 803 2934 1/2 N Beverly Glen Cir # 395 Los Angeles CA 90077-1724*

ARNOLD, STANLEY NORMAN, manufacturing consultant; b. Cleve., May 26, 1915; s. Morris L. and Mildred (Stearn) A.; m. Barbara Anne Laing, Aug. 31, 1946; 1 child, Jennifer Laing. B.S. in Econs., U. Pa., 1937. Co-founder, exec. v.p. Pick-N-Pay Supermarkets, Cleve., 1937-51; exec. v.p., dir. Cottage Creamery Co., Cleve., 1937-51; dir. sales promotion div. Young & Rubicam, N.Y.C., 1952-58; founder, pres. Stanley Arnold & Assocs., Inc., N.Y.C., 1958—; cons. Ford Motor Co., United Airlines, Gen. Electric, Nat. Cash Register, IBM, Philip Morris, Am. Express, Bank of America, DuPont, Goodyear, Quaker Oats, Readers Digest, Continental Can, Hunt Foods, Moet-Hennessy, Seagram, Pan Am, Chrysler Corp., Pillsbury, Coca Cola, Gen. Mills, Lever Bros., Exxon, Arco, Hallmark, others; mem. adv. bd. Bank of Palm Springs div. Bank of Calif. subs. Mitsubishi Corp., 1989—; vis. exec. prof. Freeman Sch. Bus., Tulane U., 1998—. Author: Tale of the Blue Horse, 1968; Magic Power of Putting Yourself Over with People, 1961; I Ran Against Jimmy Carter, 1977. Syndicated daily columnist, 1943-48. Architect of plan to install new office of v.p. in White House. Contbr. articles to profl. jours. Pres. Ind. Sch. Fund of N.Y.C., 1960-66; mem. fund raising com. U.S. Olympic Team, 1984. Founding mem. Nat. Businessmen for Humphrey, 1968, Nat. Citizens for Humphrey, 1968; candidate for Dem. nomination for v.p. U.S., 1972; chmn. White House Libr. Fund Raising Com., 1961-63; corp. sponsor for The Rose as Nat. Flower, 1983-86; nat. chmn. Golf's Tribute to Ike, 1980; mem. Clinton adv. com., 1991-92. Recipient Sales Exec. award Sales Exec. Club N.Y., 1965; Wisdom award of

Honor Wisdom Soc., 1979. Clubs: Les Amis D'Escoffier, Doubles, Dutch Treat (N.Y.C.); 7 Lakes Country, La Quinta Country, Racquet, Tennis, Indian Wells Racquet, Desert Riders, La Quinta Fishing, Oasis Water Park (Palm Springs, Calif.); Balboa Bay (Newport Beach, Calif.), Outrigger Canoe Club of Honolulu. Home: 162 Desert Lakes Dr Palm Springs CA 92264-5521 also: 2895 Kalakaua Ave Honolulu HI 96815-4003 Office: Stanley Arnold & Assocs Inc PO Box 2865 Palm Springs CA 92263-2865 also: 375 Park Ave New York NY 10152-0002

ARNOLD, STEPHEN PAUL, investment professional; b. San Antonio, Mar. 26, 1957; s. Francis Andrew and Charlene (Tyler) A.; m. Kenzie Lou Box, Dec. 16, 1978; children: Stephen Kameron, Kalen Lou. BS in Agrl. Econs., Tex. A&M U., 1979. Rsch. specialist Employee's Retirement System of Tex., Austin, 1982-84, adminstr. of spl. programs, 1984-85, dir. of spl. programs, 1985-87, asst. investment officer, 1987-91, investment portfolio mgr., 1991-94; strategist and portfolio mgr. Bluestone Investments, 1994-96; v.p., trust investment officer San Antonio, Tex.-Norwest Bank Tex., N.A., San Antonio, 1997—; mem. Tex. Econ. Forum, Austin, 1989-92; adv. bd. Internat. Bus. Forum, N.Y.C. Del. Tex. Rep. Party, Austin, 1980-86. Named to Outstanding Young Men of Am., 1983. Mem. Austin Investment Assn., Fin. Analyst Assn., Capitol City A&M Club, Former Student Assn./Tex. A&M. Baptist. Avocations: reading, parenting. Home: 25110 Summit Cove San Antonio TX 78258-1930 Office: Norwest Bank Tex 40 NE Loop 410 Ste 301 San Antonio TX 78216-5826

ARNOLD, THOMAS IVAN, JR., legislator; b. Paterson, N.J.; s. Thomas Ivan and Marjorie Lewis (Eccles) A.; m. Barbara Jane Phinney, July 25, 1953 (dec. June 1985); children: Thomas I., Barbara J., Edward H., Patricia J., Peter S., Dennis L., Nancy L., Richard B., Susan D., Charles P. ME, Stevens Inst. Tech., Hoboken, N.J., 1950, MS, 1954. Registered profl engr., N.H. Asst. to quality mgr. Curtiss-Wright Corp., Wood Ridge, N.J., 1950-58; mgr. corp. quality control ops. Sanders Assocs., Inc., Nashua, N.H., 1958-67; mgr. quality assurance RCA Corp., Burlington, Mass., 1967-72; mgr. product assurance and quality control Compugraphic Corp., Wilmington, Mass., 1972-81; mgr. quality assurance GE, Burlington, 1981-91; state rep. dist. Hillsborough 20 N.H. Gen. Ct., 1992—, vice chair com. on election laws, 1997-98, mem. sci. tech. and energy com., 1999—, mem. com. on children and family law, 1999—. Moderator Sch. Dist., Brookline, 1960—, Town of Brookline, 1976—, selectman, 1968-69; chmn. Zoning Bd. Adjustment, Brookline, 1970-82; chmn. Rep. town com.; mem. N.H. State Rep. Com., 1999—; mem. EMT Brookline Vol. Ambulance, 1976-86; mem. N.H. Indsl. Heritage Commn., 1995-96. With USAAF, 1946-47. Mem. NRA, Soc. for Quality Control (sect. chmn. 1964), Mensa, GO N.H., Order of Daedalians. Republican. Episcopalian. Avocations: fixing things, wood working. Home: 10 Milford St Brookline NH 03033-2446 Office: NH House State House Concord NH 03301

ARNOLD, TOM, actor, comedian, producer; b. Ottumwa, Iowa; s. Jack and Ruth (stepmother) A.; m. Roseanne Arnold, Jan. 1990; 3 stepchildren. Actor, co-exec. producer, writing supr. Roseanne, 1990-94; actor, co-exec. producer The Jackie Thomas Show, 1992-93, Tom, 1994, (movie) McHale's Navy, 1997; actor, co-exec. producer HBO Tom Arnold the Naked Truth I, II, III; dir. HBO's Roseanne Live from Minn.; TV movies include Backfield in Motion, 1991, Graced Land, 1992; film appearances in Hero, 1992, Undercover Blues, 1993, True Lies, 1994, Nine Months, 1995, Big Bully, 1995, The Stupids, 1996, Carpool, 1996, Touch, 1997, Austin Powers: International Man of Mystery, 1997, Buster and Chauncey's Silent Night (voice), 1998, Golf Punks, 1998, The Day October Died, 1999, Bar Hopping, 1999. Office: William Morris Agency care Michael Gruber 151 S El Camino Dr Beverly Hills CA 90212-2775*

ARNOLD, VLADIMIR IGOREVICH, mathematics researcher; b. Odessa, USSR, June 12, 1937; s. Igor Vladimirovich and Nina Alexandrovna (Isakovich) A.; m. Nadejda Nikolaevna Brouchlinskaia (div.); 1 child, Igor; m. Elionora Alexandrovna Voronina, Dec. 25, 1976; 1 child, Dimitri. PhD, Moscow State U., 1959; candidate phys. math. sci., Keldysh Applied Math. Inst., Moscow, 1962, D. in Phys. Math. Sci., 1963; doctorate honoris causa, U. P. et M. Curie Paris,, Warwick, Utrecht, Bologna, Madrid, Toronto. Dozent math. faculty Moscow State U., 1963-65, prof., 1965-86; prof. Steklov Math. Inst., Moscow, 1986—, U. Paris-Dauphine, 1993—. Author: (with A. Avez) Ergodic Problems in Classical Mechanics, 1967, Mathematical Methods of Classical Mechanics, 1974, Catastrophe Theory, 1981, Singularity Theory and its Applications, Vol.1, 1982, Vol. 2, 1984, Hygens and Barrow, Newton and Hooke, 1990, others. Recipient Lenin prize, 1965, Crafoord prize Swedish Acad. Sci., 1982, Harvey Prize, Israel Institute of Technology, 1994, Lobachevski prize Russian Acad. Sci., 1992. Fellow Russian Acad. Scis., Russian Natural Scis. Acad., Moscow Math. Soc. (v.p. 1966, pres. 1996), Am. Phil. Soc. (fgn.), London Math. Soc. (hon.), NAS (fgn.), Am. Acad. Arts and Scis. (fgn.), Royal Soc. London (fgn.), Acad. des Scis. Paris (fgn. assoc.), Acad. Lincei Rome (fgn.), Acad. Europaea. Avocations: skiing, canoeing, hiking. Office: Steklov Math Inst, 8 Gubkina St, GSP-1 Moscow 117966, Russia also: Ceremade, U de Paris-Dauphine, Pl du Mal de Lattre de Tassigny, Paris 75775, France

ARNOLD, WILLIAM EDWIN, foundation administrator, consultant; b. Charleston, S.C., Aug. 13, 1938; s. Edwin Gustaf and Sara Louise (Hitchcock) A. BA, Yale U., 1960. Pres., Dixon & Rippel, Inc., Saugerties, N.Y., 1965-70; v.p. Taj Enterprises Ltd., 1965-67, Bellern Rsch. Corp., pres. Dixon & Rippel div., Saugerties, 1970-75; v.p. H & G Industries, Inc., pres. Indsl. Brush Div., Belleville, N.J., 1975-82; pres. World Brushworks, Inc., 1982-84; v.p., CFO Optimax III, Inc., N.Y.C., 1983-84; mng. dir. Brush Trading, Ltd., 1983-87; pres. Chestnut Holdings Ltd., 1985-91; part time mng. dir. Cassi Properties, 1984—; pres. Swan Holding Ltd., 1985-88; bd. dirs. ARCS, 1991-92; chair Dutchess County AIDS Consortium, 1989-95, Dutchess County HIV Health Svcs. Planning Coun., 1995-96; bd. dirs. Multi County Cmty. Devel. Corp., 1990-96, ARCS Cmty. Educator, 1989-91; pres. Hudson AIDS Cmty. Progress, Inc., 1992—; dir. Cmty. AIDS Nat. Alert Network, 1995—; AIDS cons.; exec. dir. Title II Nat. AIDS Coalition, 1994-95; CEO Title II Cmty. AIDS Nat. Network, Washington, 1995—; co-chair working group AIDS Drug Assistance Program, Washington, 1995—. 1st lt. U.S. Army, 1961-63. Mem. Res. Officers Assn. Home: 1755 Seaton Pl NW Washington DC 20009-2625 Office: 1775 T St NW Washington DC 20009-7124

ARNOLD, WILLIAM HOWARD, retired nuclear fuel executive; b. Jefferson Barracks, Mo., May 13, 1931; s. William Howard and Elizabeth Welsh (Mullen) A.; m. Josephine Routheau, June 13, 1952; children: William, Frances, Edward, David, Thomas. AB, Cornell U., 1951; AM, Princeton U., 1953, PhD, 1955. Registered profl. engr., Pa. Sr. engr. comml. and atomic power Westinghouse Elec. Corp., Pitts., 1955-61, program mgr. Nerva project, 1962-68, engring. mgr. pressurized water reactor div., 1971-72, gen. mgr. pressurized water reactor div., 1972-78, gen. mgr. nuclear internat. div., 1979-80; gen. mgr. AESD div. Westinghouse Elec. Corp., Madison, Pa., 1981-86; mgr. Westinghouse Def. Ctr., Balt., 1968-70; v.p. engring. and devel. Westinghouse Hanford Co. (subs. Westinghouse Elec. Corp.), Richland, Wash., 1987-89; pres. La. Energy Svcs., 1989-96, ret., 1996. Contbr. articles to profl. jours.; patentee in field. Fellow AAAS, Am. Nuclear Soc.; mem. Nat. Acad. Engring. (elected), Am. Phys. Soc., Sigma Xi.

ARNOLD, WILLIAM MCCAULEY, lawyer; b. Waco, Tex., May 3, 1947; s. Watson Caulfield and Mary Rebecca (Maxwell) A.; m. Karen Axtell, May 17, 1980; children: Margaret McCauley, William Axtell. BA, Duke U., 1969; JD, U. Tex., 1972. Bar: Tex. 1973, Va. 1975, D.C. 1977, Md. 1983, U.S. Dist. Ct. (ea. dist.) Va. 1975, U.S. Ct. Appeals (4th cir.) 1977, U.S. Ct. Claims 1977, U.S. Supreme Ct. 1978. Spl. atty. U.S. Dept. Justice, Newark, 1973-75; asst. county atty. County of Fairfax, Va., 1975-78; ptnr. Cowles, Rinaldi & Arnold, Ltd., Fairfax, 1978-95; ptnr. McCandlish & Lillard, Fairfax, 1995—; instr. No. Va. Community Coll., Alexandria. Pres. Clifton Betterment Assn., Va., 1979-81; chmn. Clifton Planning Commn., 1980-85; mem. Clifton Town Council, 1985—; bd. dirs. Clifton Gentlemen's Social Club, 1981-84. Mem. ABA, Va. State Bar Assn., Fairfax County Bar Assn., Va. Trial Lawyers Assn., Am. Arbitration Assn. (arbitrator), Associated Builders and Contractors (counsel to bd. dirs.). Office: McCandlish & Lillard PC 11350 Random Hills Rd Ste 500 Fairfax VA 22030-6044

ARNOLD, WILLIAM PARSONS, JR., retired internist; b. Waterbury, Conn., May 10, 1922; s. William Parsons and Dorothy Amanda (Granniss) A.; m. Mildred Opal Beleu, Oct. 27, 1948; children: Susan Emerson Arnold Brainerd, Jane Elizabeth Arnold Pittari. BS, Yale U., 1943; MD, Columbia U., 1946. Diplomate Am. Bd. Med. Examiners. Intern St. Luke's Hosp., N.Y.C., 1946-47, resident in medicine, 1949-51, chief resident in medicine, 1951-52; pvt. practice Middlebury, Conn., 1952-89; attending physician medicine Waterbury (Conn.) Hosp., 1952-89; assoc. attending physician St. Mary's Hosp., Waterbury, 1952-89; dir. health Middlebury (Conn.) Dept. Health, 1954—; sch. physician Region 15 Elem. Schs., Middlebury, 1955-92; asst. med. examiner Conn. State M-E Office, Middlebury, 1956-84; surgeon Middlebury Vol. Fire Dept. and Middlebury Police Dept., 1964—. Capt. U.S. Army Med. Corps, 1947-49, ETO. Recipient John N. Lewis Founders award Waterbury Vis. Nurse Assn., 1988. Mem. AMA, ACP, Conn. State Med. Soc., New Haven County Med. Assn., Waterbury Med. Assn. Republican. Congregational. Avocations: western riding, rodeos. Home: 142 White Deer Rock Rd Middlebury CT 06762-1314

ARNOLD, WINNIE JO, retired mental health nurse, nursing administrator; b. Cromwell, Okla., May 21, 1939; d. Robb Henry and Luella (Odom) Boatman; widowed; children: Linda, Cherie. BSEd, Okla. U., 1962; ADN, Amarillo Coll., 1974; BSN, St. Joseph's Coll., 1977. RN, Tex. Charge nurse Northwest Tex. Hosp., Amarillo; staff nurse, team leader High Plains Bapt. Hosp., Amarillo; adminstr. Healthcare Svcs., Amarillo; dir. nurses Tex. Dept. Corrections, Amarillo, 1989-97. Vol. ARC. Recipient Vol. award ARC, 1989, Pilot Club, 1989. Mem. Am. Kidney Found., Women's Bus. Assn. (Bus. Woman of Yr. 1989). Home: 216 Ramada Trl Amarillo TX 79108-1128

ARNOLD HUBERT, NANCY KAY, writer; b. Kalamazoo, Mich., May 9, 1951; d. Byron Lyle and Ada (Doorlag) Arnold; m. Louis Scott Hubert, May 5, 1989. BFA in Painting, Western Mich. U., 1983, postgrad., 1985-86. Writer Advanced Systems & Designs, Inc., Farmington Hills, Mich., 1987-89; pres., owner TechWrite, Kalamazoo, 1989—. Author: (poetry) Tetragonal Pyramids, 1982; exhibited in group shows, Kalamazoo, 1983, Western Mich. U., 1982, 85. Mem. AAUW, NAFE, Kalamazoo County C. of C., Humane Farming Assn. Am. People for Ethical Treatment of Animals. Libertarian. Avocations: bike riding, reading, piano, singing, cross-country skiing. Office: 3857 Wolf Dr Kalamazoo MI 49009-8527

ARNOLDSON, EARL RANDON, educator; b. Mt. Pleasant, Utah, Oct. 13, 1962; s. Elliot J. and R. LaRane (Bjerregaard) A. AS, Snow Coll., Ephraim, Utah, 1984; BS, Utah State Univ., 1986; MEd, Univ. So. Miss., 1992. Cert. elem. sch. tchr., adminstr. Tchr. Millard Sch. Dist., Delta, Utah, 1987-98, contract negotiator, 1990-93, head tchr., 1996-98; prin. Anna Smith Elem. Tooele Sch. Dist., 1998—. Dist. chmn. Delta Dem. Com., 1992-94; coord. drug prevention Delta North Elem. Sch., 1994-96; referee Delta Youth Football, 1995-96. mem. ASCD, NEA, Utah Edn. Assn., Tooele Edn. Assn., Phi Delta Kappa. Avocations: fly fishing, hunting, mountain biking. Office: PO Box 879 731 N Aria Blvd Wendover UT 84083-0879

ARNONE, MICHAEL J., state legislator, dentist; b. Red Bank, N.J., Sept. 10, 1932; m. Barbara Covert, 1956; children: John Stephen, Suzanne, Mark Raymond, Paul Xavier, Michael David. Student, Seton Hall U.; DDS, Temple U., 1958. Pvt. practice dentistry; mem. from dist. 12 N.J. State Assembly, 1989—, chmn. local govt. and housing com., 1992—. Chmn. Red Bank Zoning Bd., 1969; councilman City of Red Bank, 1970-73, mayor, 1979-90; mem. Monmouth County Rep. Exec. Com. Mem. KC, Elks. Address: 258 Broad St Red Bank NJ 07701-2003*

ARNONE, WILLIAM J., executive; b. Bronx, Nov. 9, 1948; s. John A. and Lucia D'Errico; m. Caren Ray, Sept. 7, 1985; 1 child, Allyson Lee. BA, Fordham Coll., 1970; JD, NYU, 1973. Exec. dir. Project Hand, Bronx, 1974-76; program dir. N.Y.C. Dept. Aging, 1976-79; cons. Florence Burden Found., N.Y.C., 1980-81; benefit cons. Buck Cons., N.Y.C., 1981-94; ptnr. Ernst & Young, N.Y.C., 1994—; bd. trustees Employees Benefits Rsch. Inst., Washington, 1997—; founding mem. Nat. Acad. Social Ins., 1986—. Author: Ernest & Young Retirement Planning Guide, 1996; editor: Columbia University Retirement Guide, 1984. Democrat. Roman Catholic. Office: Ernst & Young 787 7th Ave New York NY 10019

ARNOT, ANDREW H., art gallery director; b. Detroit, Nov. 28, 1960. BA in History of Art, Mich. State U., 1984; postgrad., Ball State U., 1985-86. Grad. asst. Ball State U. Art Gallery, Muncie, Ind., 1985-86; slide libr. Fogg Art Mus., Harvard U., Cambridge, Mass., 1987-89; adminstrv. asst. PSG Framing, Boston, 1987-89; asst. dir. Tibor de Nagy Gallery, N.Y.C., 1989-90, dir., 1990—. Avocations: foreign languages, ultimate frisbee, clarinet. Office: Tibor de Nagy Gallery 724 5th Ave New York NY 10019-4106*

ARNOTT, HOWARD JOSEPH, biology educator, university dean; b. Los Angeles, Mar. 9, 1928; s. Andrew Hugh and Evelyn Leonore (Donnelly) A.; m. Wanda Jean Cross, Jan. 28, 1950; children: John Joseph, Catherine Jean Arnott-Thornton, Susan Leonore Arnott Garrett, Virginia Anne Arnott Scott. AB, U. So. Calif., 1952, MS, 1953; PhD, U. Calif., Berkeley, 1958. Asst. prof. biology Northwestern U., Evanston, Ill., 1958-64; assoc. prof. dept. botany U. Tex., Austin, 1965-68, prof., 1968-72, acting chmn. dept., 1970-71; prof., chmn. dept. biology U. So. Fla., Tampa, 1972-74; dean Coll. Sci. U. Tex., Arlington, 1974-90, prof. biology, 1974-91, Ashbel Smith prof. biology, 1991-96, dir. Ctr. for Electron Microscopy Coll. Sci., 1984—, Jenkins Garrett prof., 1996—; vis. mem. dept. biology Tex. A&M U., 1971-75; cons. Ency. Brit. Films, NASA, Alcon Labs., Frito-Lay; bd. dirs. Ft. Worth Nature Ctr., 1985-91; chmn. 2nd Gordon Conf. Calcium Oxalate, 1989, main spkr. 4th Conf., 1993; vis. prof. Purdue U., 1990-91; Bessey lectr. Iowa State U., 1993. Advisory editor: Protoplasma; Contbr. articles, abstracts to sci. jours., chpts. to books. With USN, 1946-48. Recipient award for disting. and continued research U. Tex. at Arlington, 1984; postdoctoral fellow U. Tex., NIH, 1964-65; NSF grantee, 1963-65, NIH grantee, 1989. Mem. Am. Soc. Plant Physiology, Bot. Soc. Am., Mycol. Soc. Am., Microscopy Soc. Am., Tex. Soc. Microscopy (hon., pres. 1988-89), Sigma Xi (bd. dirs. S.W. region 1984-91), Phi Sigma.

ARNOTT, ROBERT DOUGLAS, investment company executive; b. Chgo., June 29, 1954; s. Robert James Arnott and Catherine (Bonnell) Cameron; children: Robert Lindsay, Sydney Allison. BA, U. Calif., Santa Barbara, 1977. V.p. Boston Co., 1977-84; pres., chief exec. officer TSA Capital Mgmt., L.A., 1984-87; v.p., strategist Salomon Bros. Inc., N.Y.C., 1987-88; mng. ptnr. First Quadrant L.P., Morristown, N.J., Pasadena, Calif., and London, 1988-96, First Quadrant, L.P., Pasadena, London, Boston, 1996—; mem. chmn.'s adv. coun. Chgo. Bd. Options Exch., 1989—; bd. dirs. Internat. Faculty in Fin.; mem. product adv. bd. Chgo. Mercantile Exch., 1990. Editor: Asset Allocation, 1988, Active Asset Allocation, 1992, Handbook of Equity Style Management, 1997; mem. editorial bd. Jour. of Investing, 1990—, Jour. Portfolio Mgmt., 1984—; contbr. articles to profl. jours. and chpts. to books. Mem. Inst. Internat. Rsch. (adv. bd. 1990—), Assn. for Investment Mgmt. and Rsch., Inst. Quantitative Rsch. in Fin., Toronto Stock and Futures Exch. (adv. coun. 1992—). Avocations: motorcycling, billiards, sommelier, travel. Office: 1st Quadrant LP 800 E Colorado Blvd Ste 900 Pasadena CA 91109-7183

ARNOULD, RICHARD JULIUS, economist, educator, consultant; b. Rochelle, Ill., Nov. 18, 1941; s. Elliott and Blanch (Colwell) A.; m. Carol Foster, Aug. 27, 1960; children: Debra, Laura. BS, Iowa State U., 1963, MS, 1965, PhD, 1968. Instr. Iowa State U., Ames, 1963-65; asst. prof. econs. and bus. adminstrn. U. Ill., Champaign, 1967-72, assoc. prof., 1973-82, prof., 1982—, dir. Coll. Rsch. Office, 1995-96, assoc. dean for acad. affairs, Coll. Commerce and Bus. Adminstrn., 1979-87, prof. econs., Coll. Medicine, 1984—, adj. prof. Inst. of Govt. and Pub. Affairs, 1987—, head dept. econs., 1996—, dir. Program in Health Econs., Mgmt. & Policy, 1989—; acting dir. Exec. Devel. Ctr., part-time 1982, 84, mem. Med. Scholars Steering Com., active numerous other univ., coll. and dept. coms.; rsch. economist pricing and competition grp., USDA, 1965-67; vice chmn. Dept. Econs., U. Ill., 1970-73; vis. economist Econ. Policy Office, U.S. Justice Dept., 1973-74; regional economist U.S. Comptroller of Currency, 1976-79; vis. rsch. prof. Duke U., 1977-78; vis. rsch. scholar York (Eng.) U.; cons. Carle Found., chmn. bd., 1989-91; mem. Gov's. Task Force on Health Care Reform, 1992—; cons. Auditor Gen. State of Ill., GAO, Health Care Financing Adminstrn., Anti-trust div. U.S. Justice Dept., ABA, AMA, Prepaid Legal Svcs. Inst., others; bd. dirs. First Busey Trust & Investment Co.; expert witness numerous law firms; speaker profl. meetings. Author: Extra Territorial Application and Effects of Certain U.S. and Canadian Laws, 1978, (monograph) Blue Shield Fee Setting in the Physicians' Service Market: A Theoretical and Empirical Analysis, (pamphlets) Diversification and Profitability Among Large Food Processing Firms, USDA, 1970, (with R. Resek) A Comparative Cost Study of Staff Panel and Participating Attorney Panel Prepaid Legal Servcie Plans, ABA, 1982; editor spl. issue Quar. Rev. of Econs. and Bus., 1990, also book chpts. and revs.; co-editor: (with R. Rich and W. White) Competitive Approaches to Health Care Reform, 1993; contbr. numerous articles to profl. jours. Bd. dirs. City Bank Champaign, First Basey Trust and Investment Co.; trustee Carle Found., 1981-93, chmn. fin. com., 1982-86, chmn. bd., 1989-91; elder 1st Presbyn. Ch., Champaign; mem. Gov.'s Task Force on Health Care Reform; mem. U.S. Govt. Study of Econ. Underpinning of Vaccine Markets. Brookings Inst. Econ. Policy fellow, 1973; recipient Outstanding Service award, U.S. Justice Dept., 1974; grantee Internat. Bur. Edn., 1979, Carle Found., 1982-83, Grad. Research Bd., 1983-86; named Outstanding Tchr. U. Ill. various yrs. Mem. Am. Econ. Assn., So. Econ. Assn., Internat. Health Econs. Assn., Midwest Econ. Assn. Avocation: golf. Office: U Ill 1206 S 6th St Champaign IL 61820-6915

ARNOVE, ROBERT FREDERICK, education educator; b. Chgo.; s. Isadore and Julie (Zeplowitz) A.; m. Toby Strout; 1 child, Anthony Keats. BA, U. Mich., 1969; MA, Tufts U., 1961; PhD, Stanford U., 1969. Vol. tchr. Peace Corps, Venezuela, 1962-64; Ford Found. edn. advisor Bogota, Colombia, 1969-71; prof. comparative edn. Ind. U., Bloomington, 1969—, Ind. U.-Hangzhou, People's Rep. China, 1983; vis. prof. Stanford U., McGill U.; edn. cons. to Latin Am. ministries and agys.; dir. Overseas Study Program of Ind., Purdue, and Wis. univs. in Madrid, 1989—; USIA Exch. scholar, Ryazan, Russia, 1996, Yaounde, Cameroon, 1997; UNESCO-chair vis. scholar U. Palermo, Buenos Aires, 1997. Author, editor, co-editor: Student Alienation, Educational Television, Education and American Culture Comparative Education, Philanthropy and Cultural Imperialism, Education and Revolution in Nicaragua, National Literacy Campaign: Historical and Comparative Perspectives, Emergent Issues in Education: Comparative Perspectives, Education as Contested Terrain: Nicaragua 1979-93, 1994, Comparative education: The Dialectic of the Global and the Local, 1999; prodr. documentary film Alternative Public Schools, 1978, Asi Fue: Election Time Nicaragua, 1984; also articles. Citizens Party candidate for U.S. Congress, 8th dist. Ind., 1982. Fulbright grantee, India, 1982; Fulbright lectr. Fed. U. Bahai, Brazil, 1995. Mem. Comparative and Internat. Edn. Soc. (v.p., pres.-elect), Latin Am. Studies Assn., Phi Delta Kappa. Office: Ind U Sch Edn Bloomington IN 47405

ARNOVITZ, BENTON MAYER, editor; b. Butler, Pa., July 21, 1942; s. Paul and Miriam (Shapiro) A. A.B., Cornell U., 1964; M.A., NYU, 1969; grad., U.S. Army Command and Gen. Staff Coll., 1982; grad. Nat.Security Mgmt. Program, Nat. Def. U., 1986. Editor Macmillan Pub. Co., N.Y.C., 1966-73; sr. trade editor Chilton Book Co., Radnor, Pa., 1973-76; exec. editor Stein and Day Pubs., Briarcliff Manor, N.Y., 1976-85, v.p., 1984-85; ind. editorial svcs., 1985-89, 91-93; editorial dir. Scarborough House Pubs. div. BookCrafters, Peekskill, N.Y., 1989-91; dir. acad. pubs. U.S. Holocaust Meml. Mus., Washington, 1994—. Contbr. articles to scholarly jour. and newspapers. Trustee Field Libr. Inc., 1985-94, Westchester Libr. Sys., 1992-94. Capt. U.S. Army, 1964-66, 70; lt. col. USAR. Mem. Alpha Phi Delta. Home: 13439 Overbrook Ln Bowie MD 20715-1159 Office: 100 Raoul Wallenberg Pl SW Washington DC 20024-2126

ARNOWITT, RICHARD LEWIS, physics educator, researcher; b. N.Y.C., May 3, 1928; s. Leon and Belle (Feinberg) A.; m. Young In Rhee, Apr. 21, 1961; children: Michael Paul, Myron Philip. BS, MS, Rensselaer Poly. Inst., 1948; PhD, Harvard U., 1953. Rsch. assoc. Radiation Lab. U. Calif., Berkeley, 1952-54; mem. Inst. Advanced Study, Princeton, N.J., 1954-56; asst. prof. Syracuse (N.Y.) U., 1956-59, assoc. prof., 1959-62; prof. Northeastern U., Boston, 1962-86; prof. Tex. A&M U., College Station, 1986-88, disting. prof. physics, 1988—, dir. Ctr. Theoretical Physics, 1986-95, head dept. physics, 1987-93. Contbr. over 200 articles to profl. jours. Fellow Guggenheim Found., 1975-76. Fellow Am. Phys. Soc.(Dannie N. Heineman prize 1994, Burgess chair high energy physics 1997—). Office: Texas A & M U Dept Physics College Station TX 77843-4242

ARNSTEIN, WALTER LEONARD, historian, educator; b. Stuttgart, Germany, May 14, 1930; came to U.S., 1939, naturalized, 1944; s. Richard and Charlotte (Heymann) A.; m. Charlotte Culver Sutphen, June 8, 1952; children: Sylvia, Peter. B.S.S., CCNY, 1951; M.A., Columbia U., 1954; Ph.D., Northwestern U., 1961; postgrad., U. London, Eng., 1956-57. Asst. prof. history Roosevelt U., Chgo., 1957-62, assoc. prof., 1962-66, prof., acting dean grad. div., 1966-67; prof. history U. Ill., Urbana, 1968-98, LAS Jubilee prof. history, 1989-98, prof. history and LAS Jubilee prof. history emeritus, 1998—, chmn. dept., 1974-78, assoc. Ctr. for Advanced Study, 1972-73; vis. assoc. prof. history Northwestern U., 1963-64; vis. fellow Clare Hall, Cambridge U., 1982; hon. fellow U. Edinburgh, 1989. Author: The Bradlaugh Case: A Study in Late Victorian Opinion and Politics, 1965, 2d edit., 1984, Britain Yesterday and Today, 1966, 7th edit., 1996, Protestant Versus Catholic in Mid-Victorian England, 1982, (with the late William B. Willcox) The Age of Aristocracy, 3d edit., 1976, 7th edit., 1996; editor: The Past Speaks: Sources and Problems in British History Since 1688, 1981, 2d edit. 1993; editor: Recent Historians of Great Britain, 1990; bd. editors The Historian, 1976—, Am. Hist. Rev., 1982-85, Albion, 1988-93; mem. bd. advisers: Victorian Studies, 1966-75; contbr. articles profl. jours. Vice chmn. Ill. Humanities Council, 1983-84. Served with AUS, 1951-53, Korea. Fulbright scholar, 1956-57; Fellow Am. Council Learned Socs., 1967-68. Fellow Royal Hist. Soc.; mem. Am. Hist. Assn., Brit. Hist. Assn., N.Am. Conf. Brit. Studies (exec. com. 1971-76, v.p. 1993-95, pres. 1995-97), Midwest Conf. on Brit. Studies (pres. 1980-82), Midwest Victorian Studies Assn. (pres. 1977-80), Phi Beta Kappa, Phi Alpha Theta. Home: 804 W Green St Champaign IL 61820-5017 Office: U Ill Dept History 309 N Gregory Hall 810 S Wright St Urbana IL 61801-3611

ARNTSEN, ARNT PETER, engineer, consultant; b. Hvaler, Norway, Oct. 23, 1921; s. Arnt Peter and Helene Oleane (Helgesen) A.; m. Margot Petra Nilsen, Oct. 24, 1953; children: Tom David, Carol Ann, John Frederick. Registered profl. engr., Mass. Engr., Westinghouse Research Center, Pitts., 1962-64; sr. engring. scientist RCA Corp., Burlington, Mass., 1964-89; cons., 1989-96, ret., 1996. Patentee in field. Home and Office: 9 Lincoln Ave Manchester MA 01944-1119

ARNTSON, PETER ANDREW, lawyer; b. Washington, May 23, 1938; s. Paul Lee and Mary Ellen (Garrigan) A.; m. Colette Rousseau, July 11, 1962; 1 child, Eric Paul. BA, U. Va., 1960, JD, 1965; LLM in Taxation, Georgetown U., 1971; postgrad., U.S. Army War Coll., 1981. Bar: Va. 1965, U.S. Supreme Ct. 1973. Assoc., then ptnr. Phillips, Kendrick, Gearheart & Aylor, Arlington, Va., 1965-75; ptnr. McCandlish, Lilliard, Church & Best, Fairfax, Va., 1975-84, Miles & Stockbridge, Fairfax, 1984-95, McCandlish & Lillard, Fairfax, 1995—; chmn. com. on taxation Va. State Bar, 1978; dep. commr. accts. County of Fairfax, 1994—. Chmn. bd. dirs. No. Va. Am. Heart Assn., 1978; bd. dirs. Benedictine Sch. Exceptional Children, Ridgely, Md., 1985—, Arlington Cmty. Found., 1992-96, No. Va. Cmty. Found., 1991—; mem. exec. coun. Nat. Capital Area coun. Boy Scouts Am., 1993—; founder, pres. Wakefield Ednl. Found., 1986—; trustee Claude Moore Charitable Found. 1st lt. U.S. Army, 1960-62, col. AUS, ret. Mem. ABA, Va. Bar Assn., Fairfax Bar Assn., Assn. U.S. Army , Rotary. Methodist. Home: 4047 27th Rd N Arlington VA 22207-5237 Office: McCandlish & Lillard 11350 Random Hills Rd Ste 500 Fairfax VA 22030-6044

ARNTZEN, CHARLES JOEL, bioscience educator; b. Granite Falls, Minn., July 20, 1941; s. George Otto and Irene G. (Skrukrud) A.; m. Kathleen Rae Lang, Dec. 28, 1962; 1 child, Christopher James. BS, U. Minn.-St. Paul, 1965, MS, 1967; PhD in Cell Biology, Purdue U., 1970, DSc (hon.), 1997. Postdoctoral fellow C. F. Kettering Research Ctr., Yellow Springs, Ohio, 1969-70; educator U. Ill., Urbana, 1970-80; prof. U. Ill.; plant physiologist USDA Agrl. Rsch. Svc., 1975-80; prof., dir. Dept Energy Plant Research Lab., Mich. State U., East Lansing, 1980-84; research dir. E. I. Du Pont de Nemours & Co., Wilmington, Del., 1984-88; dep. chancellor, dean of agr. The Tex. A&M Univ. System, College Station, 1988-92; prof., dir. plant biotech. program Tex. A&M Inst. Biosci. and Tech., Houston, 1992-95; pres., CEO Boyce Thompson Inst. for Plant Rsch., Ithaca, N.Y., 1995—; bd. govs. Argonne Nat. Lab., U. Chgo., 1990-97; bd. dirs. DeKalb Genetics Inc. Author books and jour. articles. Recipient Superior Service award USDA, 1980. Fellow AAAS; mem. NAS (U.S. and India chpts.), Am. Soc. Plant Physiologists (pres.-elect 1984-85, pres. 1985-86, Charles A. Shull award 1979, Dennis R. Hoaglund award 1994), Am. Biophys. Soc., Am. Soc. Cell Biology, Internat. Plant Molecular Biology Soc. (bd. dirs. 1985-88), Nat. Wildflower Res. Ctr. (trustee 1989-92). Office: Boyce Thompson Inst Tower Rd Ithaca NY 14853-1801*

AROMIN, MERCEDES FUNG, portfolio manager, investment advisor, consultant; b. Kowloon, Hong Kong, Dec. 1, 1956; came to U.S., 1974; d. Remigio N. and Josephine (Fung) A. BS in Bus. Adminstrn., U. Tenn., Knoxville, 1978; MBA, Ga. State U., 1989. Mgr. Ramada Inn, Scottsburg, Ind., 1978; asst. mgr. York Steak House, Nashville, 1978-80; asst. terminal mgr. Greyhound Lines Inc., Atlanta, 1980-84; staff asst. The Coca-Cola Co., Atlanta, 1985-87; staff asst. Coca-Cola Enterprises Inc., Atlanta, 1987-89, shareholder rels. mgr., 1989-92; pres., CEO MFA Fin. Asset Mgmt., Atlanta, 1992—; sec.-treas. Coca-Cola Enterprises Inc. Employee Nonpartisan Com. for Good Govt., Atlanta, 1989-91; founder, pres. Woodstock Investment Group, 1997—. William Way scholar, 1976, Alcoa Found. scholar, 1977. Mem. Ga. State U. MBA Alumni Group (charter). Roman Catholic. Avocation: international travel. Office: 2040 Bascomb Carmel Rd Woodstock GA 30189-3545

ARON, EVE GLICKA SERENSON, personal care industry executive; b. N.Y.C., Sept. 5, 1937; d. Max and Edith (Gitelson) Serenson; m. Joel Edward Aron, Dec. 13, 1964; children: Jennifer, Joshua, Eric. BS, CCNY, 1958; MS, Yeshiva U., 1960; MBA with honors, Iona Coll., 1985. Med. technician Albert Einstein Coll. Medicine, Bronx, N.Y., 1959-60; chemist Strasenburgh labs., Belleville, N.J., 1961-63, Roche Labs., Nutley, N.J., 1963-67; sr. chemist Pantene Labs. div. Roche, Nutley, 1967-69; mgr. R&D Combe Inc., White Plains, N.Y., 1978-85, assoc. dir. R&D, 1985-95, dir. tech., 1995—. Contbr. articles and book revs. to profl. jours. Tutor Literacy Vols. of Am. mem. NOW, Am. Chem. Soc., Soc. Cosmetic Chemists (sec. Conn. chpt. 1989-90, chair 1992, chpt. advisor 1993, hospitality/membership chair 1994-96, program com. co-chair 1997, employment chair 1999). Avocations: golf, walking, swimming. Home: 470 Park Ave Rye NY 10580-1213 Office: Combe Inc 1101 Westchester Ave White Plains NY 10604-3597

ARON, JERRY E., lawyer; b. Lancaster, Pa., Oct. 1, 1951. BS, Drexel U., 1974; JD, Stetson U., 1977. Bar: Fla. 1977. Lawyer Gunster, Yoakley, Valdes-Fauli & Stewart, West Palm Beach, Fla.; teaching asst. legal rsch. and writing Stetson Coll. Law, 1975-76; chmn. Palm Beach County Realtor/Atty. Joint Com., 1983-84. Editor-in-chief Stetson Law Rev., 1976-77. Mem. ABA (real property, probate and trust law sect., econs. of law practice sect., chmn. standing com. lawyers' title guaranty funds), Am. Coll. Real Estate Attys., Fla. Bar (exec. coun. real property probate and trust law sect. 1980—, exec. com. 1985—, sec. 1985-88, dir. real property divsn. 1988-90, chmn.-elect. 1990-91, chmn. 1991-92, chmn. publs. 1980-85, co-chair action line com. 1984-85, liason with title insurers 1984-85, energy law com., environ. land use sect., pub. utilities law com., Annual Svc. award), Palm Beach County Bar Assn., Blue Key, Phi Delta Phi. Office: Phillips Pt 777 S Flagler Dr Ste 500 West Palm Beach FL 33401-6161*

ARON, MARK G., lawyer, transportation executive; b. Hartford, Conn., Jan. 27, 1943; s. Samuel H. and Florence A.; m. Cindy Sondik, June 1, 1966; 1 child, Samantha. B.A. summa cum laude, Trinity Coll., 1965; LL.B., Harvard U., 1968. Bar: Va., Mass., D.C. Asst. prof. law Osgood Hall Law Sch., York U., Toronto, 1968-70; assoc. Goulston & Storrs, Boston, 1970-71; atty., asst. gen. counsel then dep. gen. counsel U.S. Dept. Transp., Washington, 1971-81; asst. gen. counsel CSX, Richmond, Va., 1981-83, gen. counsel spl. projects, 1983-85; sr. v.p. corp. svcs. Chessie System R.R., Balt., 1985-86; sr. v.p. law and pub. affairs CSX Corp., Richmond, 1986-95, exec. v.p. law and pub. affairs, 1995—. Trustee Va. Union U.; bd. dirs. Va. Literacy Found., Theatre IV, Ctrl. Va. Pub. Broadcasting; mem. Or Ami Cong. Mem. Va. Bar Assn., Mass. Bar Assn., D.C. Bar Assn., Country Club Va. Office: CSX Corp One James Ctr PO Box 85629 901 E Cary St Richmond VA 23285-5629*

ARON, PETER ARTHUR, charitable foundation executive, private investor; b. Memphis, May 26, 1946; s. Jack R. and Jane (Baerwald) A.; m. Erika Maria Kostron, Mar. 11, 1972; children: Heather Jane, Holly Frances. BA, Tulane U., 1969. Asst. v.p. J. Aron & Co., Inc., N.Y.C., 1965-83; v.p., treas. Lafayette Enterprises, Inc., N.Y.C., 1983—; pres., exec. dir. J. Aron Charitable Found., N.Y.C., 1974—; dir. William B. Reily Co., New Orleans, 1993—; dir., sec. J. Aron & Co., Inc., New Orleans, 1988—; trustee FTI Funds, Pitts., 1995—. Editor: Aspiration and Perseverance, 1984. Chmn. bd. trustees South St. Seaport Mus., N.Y.C., 1987—; chmn. bd. dirs. Avon (Conn.) Old Farms Sch., 1992—; trustee Lenox Hill Hosp., N.Y.C., 1975—; vice chmn. Tulane U., New Orleans, 1981-96; hon. life trustee The Asia Soc., N.Y., 1997—; chmn. bd. appeals Village of Kings Point, N.Y., 1997—. 1st lt., U.S. Army, 1970-71, Vietnam. Decorated Bronze Star; recipient Pub. Svc. award Nat. Neurofibromatosis Found., N.Y.C., 1994, Disting. Trustee award United Hosp. Found., N.Y.C., 1995. Mem. Asia Soc. Galleries Friends (past chmn.), N.Y. Yacht Club, Univ. Club (N.Y.C.). Avocations: yachting, Asian art, scuba diving.

AROND, MIRIAM, magazine editor, writer; b. Bklyn., Oct. 31, 1955; d. Lionel and Irma (Krasna) Arond; m. Samuel L. Pauker, June 11, 1981; children: Sarah, Elizabeth. BA, U. Pa., 1977; MA, NYU, 1981. Editl. asst. Doubleday Book Pub., N.Y.C., 1977-78; sr. assoc. editor Bride's Mag., N.Y.C., 1981-83; staff feature writer New York Daily News, 1983-84; sr. editor Child Mag., N.Y.C., 1990-93, articles editor, 1993-95, exec. editor, 1995-96; exec. editor Am. Health for Women mag., N.Y.C., 1996-98; editor-in-chief Am. Health Mag., N.Y.C., 1998—. Co-author: The First Year of Marriage: What to Expect, What to Accept and What You Can Change for a Lasting Relationship, 1987. Recipient Sigma Delta Chi Deadline club award, 1980, 81. Mem. Authors Guild, Phi Beta Kappa. Home: 116 Tewkesbury Rd Scarsdale NY 10583-6024

ARONIAN, SUNA, Russian and women's studies educator; b. Lynn, Mass.; d. Arshag and Arousiag Opsoyan Aharonian; m. Geoffrey D. Gibbs, Sept. 3, 1972; stepchild, Allegra. BA, Boston U., 1960; PhD, Yale U., 1971. Instr. U. Pitts., 1965-66, U. Pa., Phila., 1966-69; from asst. to assoc. prof. U. R.I., Kingston, 1970-87, prof., 1987—. Mem. MLA, ACLU (bd. dirs. 1998—), Am. Assn. Advancement Slavic Studies (bd. dirs. 1988-90), Am. Assn. Tchrs. Russian and E. European Studies, Nat. Assn. Am. Studies and Rsch., R.I. Fgn. Lang. Assn. (K-12 adv. com. 1998—). Avocation: amateur pianist. Office: U RI 60 Upper College Rd Ste 3 Kingston RI 02881

ARONIN, LEWIS RICHARD, metallurgical engineer; b. Norwood, Mass., Aug. 4, 1919; s. Samuel and Celia (Acoff) A.; B.S., M.I.T., 1940; m. Natalie Eleanor Wolfson, June 19, 1947; children—Marlene Aronin Sigel, Terry Aronin Dubow. Asst. to research dir. Waltham Watch Co. (Mass.), 1940-48; staff mem. M.I.T. Metall. Project, Cambridge, 1949-54; mgr. research and devel. dept. Nuclear Metals, Inc., Concord, Mass., 1954-65; cons. Kennecott Copper Corp., Lexington, Mass., 1966-67; materials engr. Army Materials Tech. Lab., Watertown, Mass., 1967-90; pvt. cons. advanced materials devel., 1990—. Registered profl. engr., Mass. Mem. AIME, Am. Soc. Metals, AIAA, Soc. Advancement Materials and Process Engring. (treas. Boston chpt. 1976-89), Engring. Socs. New Eng. (dir. 1984-87), Sigma Xi. Lodges: Lions, Masons. Research and publs. on nuclear materials, radiation effects, beryllium, refractory materials, and advanced structural composites; patentee in field. Home and Office: 20 Ingleside Rd Lexington MA 02420-2522

ARONIN, MARC JACOB, playwright, artistic director, director; b. Queens, N.Y., July 24, 1964; s. Carl and Phyllis (Montesano) A. BFA in Theatre, MA in Ednl. Theatre magna cum laude, Adelphi U., 1987. Prof. Adelphi U., Garden City, N.Y., 1986-91; gen. mgr. Larkspur Dance Theatre, N.Y.C., 1986-92; lit. agt. Profl. Artists Unltd., N.Y.C., 1987-1988; mng. dir. Olmsted Theatre, Garden City, 1990-92; asst. dir. Joyce Trisler Danscompany, N.Y.C., 1991-92; artistic dir. E.M. Arrow Prodns., N.Y.C., 1991—; freelance prodn. mgr. Amblin/Putnam, Talking Books, N.Y.C.; adminstrv. dir. Sch. for Film and TV Three of Us Studios, 1992—; theatre cons. Vanishing Glory, Vicksburg, Miss., 1991-96; talent cons. Internat. Modeling and Talent Assn., 1993—; guest lectr. Internat. Thespian Soc., 1996—; curriculum and accredidation evaluator Nat. Assn. Schs. of Theatre, 1996—; instr. Colo. Thespian Soc., Fla. State Thespians, Caryn Internat. Mpls., Barbizon Apollo Denver, Fam-J Talent and Modeling, Anchorage. Author: (drama) State of Mind, 1990, Best Laid Plans, 1991, Minstrel Melodies, 1991, Party Time, 1992, 93, (fiction) Preconception, 1993, Marking Time, 1991, Bohemia Bound, 1991, The Face of Pain, 1994, Dearly Departed, 1995, Princess and the Pee Pot, 1996, Traveling Man, 1997, (film) Best Laid Plans, 1994, (TV) Coed Call Girls, 1996, South Beach Story, 1996, Kips Bay Commons, 1998. Fundraiser Fortune Soc. for High Risk Youths, 1992—, Family Health Ctr., Garden City, 1990-91. Named Alexander Barnes Scholar, Adelphi. U., 1982-86. Mem. NATAS. Avocation: cultural outreach to rural children. Home: 240 E 30th St New York NY 10016-8222

ARONOFF, CRAIG ELLIS, management educator, consultant; b. Atlanta, May 18, 1951; s. Marvin Charles and Patricia (Sabin) A.; children: Lara Lorena, Emily Rose. BS in Journalism, Northwestern U., 1971; MA, U. Pa., 1974; PhD, U. Tex., 1975. Asst. prof. mgmt. Ga. State U., Atlanta, 1975-79, assoc. prof., 1979-83; prof. mgmt. Kennesaw State U., Marietta, Ga., 1983—, Dinos disting. prof. pvt. enterprise, 1983—, chmn. dept. mgmt., 1984-86; dir. Family Enterprise Ctr., 1987—, eminent scholar, 1999—; chmn. Cobb Transit Adv. Bd., Marietta, 1988-90; exec. dir. Bus. Owner Resources, Marietta, 1989—; CEO Family Bus. Comm., Inc., 1989—, Family Bus. Cons. Group, Inc. 1994—. Co-author: Public Relations: The Profession and the Practice, 4th edit., 1996, Family Business Leadership Series, 11 vols., 1992—; co-editor: The Future of Private Enterprise, 3 vols., 1982-84; also author, co-author, editor other books, 1979—; contbg. editor, columnist Family Bus. Planning, Nation's Bus. mag., 1990-99; mem. editl. bd. Jour. Pvt. Enterprise Edn., 1986—, Family Bus. Rev., 1992—; exec. editor Family Bus. Advisor, 1991—. Commr. Marietta Bd. Zoning and Planning, 1987-90; bd. dirs. Temple Kol Emeth, Marietta, 1989-92; mem. Leadership Cobb, 1986-87; co-pres. West Side Elem. Sch. PTA, 1992-93. Recipient Leavey award Freedoms Found., 1987, Outstanding Educator award Nat. Fedn. Ind. Bus. Found., 1989, Disting. Leadership award Leadership Cobb, 1988. Mem. Assn. Pvt. Enterprise Educators (pres. 1978-79, bd. dirs. 1977-91, Kent-Aronoff award 1988), Family Bus. Forum (founder, bd. dirs. 1987—), Family Firm Inst. (bd. dirs. 1989-94, sec., treas. 1990-92, pres. 1992-94, Richard Beckhard award 1997), Southeastern Legal Found. (bd. dirs. 1990-97), Ga. Coun. Econ. Edn. (trustee 1983—), Cobb C. of C. (vice chmn. 1986, 91-93), Progressive Club (pres. 1976-77), Kiwanis (pres. Marietta chpt. 1990, Outstanding Kiwanian award 1989). Home: 1852 Bishops Green Dr Marietta GA 30062-6079 Office: Kennesaw State U 1000 Chastain Rd Kennesaw GA 30144-5588

ARONOFF, DONALD MATTHEW, mental health facility administrator; b. Red Bank, N.J., Jan. 19, 1949; s. Milton and Frances (Webber) A.; m. Carol Sena, June 1, 1979 (div. Jan. 1982); m. Sandra Rockwell, July 3, 1983. BA, New Coll., 1970; MA, West Ga. Coll., 1973. Cert. clin. social worker, nursing home adminstr., Ga. Coord. stds. and licensure Ga. Divsn. of Mental Health, Atlanta, 1974-76; dir. Columbus (Ga.) Area Mental Health/Mental Retardation Program, 1976-82; exec. dir. So. Hills Counseling Ctr., Jasper, Ind., 1982—; adj. prof. U. So. Ind., Evansville, 1995. Book rev. editor Human Services in the Rural Environment, 1989-90, Spencer County Leader, 1996—. Bd. dirs. Metro Columbus Urban league, 1980-81, Linconland Econ. Devel. Corp., 1996; pres. Santa Claus Town Bd., Ind., 1996-98, Leadership Spencer County, 1996-99. Mem. Jasper C. of C. (bd. dirs. 1986-88), Kiwanis (bd. dirs. Jasper chpt. 1982-94), Santa Claus Optimist Club. Office: So Hills Counseling Ctr PO Box 769 Jasper IN 47547-0769

ARONOFF, MARK H., linguistics educator, author, consultant; b. Montreal, Que., Can., Jan. 9, 1949; came to U.S., 1970; s. Moses and Grace (Rosenberg) A.; m. Frances A. Kelley, Jan. 16, 1976; children: Catherine, Peter, Ruth. BA, McGill U., 1969; PhD, MIT, 1974. Asst. prof. linguistics SUNY, Stony Brook, 1974-80, assoc. prof., 1980-85, prof., 1985—, assoc. provost, 1998—. Author: Word Formation, 1976, Morphology by Itself, 1993; editor: Juncture, 1980, Language Sound Structure, 1984; editor Language, The Jour. of the Linguistic Soc. Am., 1995—. NEH fellow, 1980, 93, Am. Inst. Indian Studies fellow, India, 1987. Mem. Linguistic Soc. Am., Sigma Xi. Office: SUNY Dept Linguistics SBS S-211 Stony Brook NY 11794-4376

ARONOFF, MICHAEL STEPHEN, psychiatrist; b. Phila., Aug. 5, 1940; s. William Richard and Reva (Miller) A.; m. Carol R. Aronoff, Nov. 27, 1966; m. Dara Welles Aronoff, June 17, 1984; children: Amanda Susan, Jessica Ann. BA, Haverford Coll., 1962; MD, U. Pa., 1966; radiation biophysics cert., NIH, 1967; psychoanalysis cert., Columbia U., 1976. Diplomate Am. Bd. Forensic Examiners; cert. Am. Bd. Psychiatry and Neurology, Am. Bd. Forensic Psychiatry, Qual's Forensic Psychiatry. Intern medicine U. Chgo., 1966-67; staff assoc. NIMH, Bethesda, Md., 1967-69; resident psychiatry Columbia U., NYSPI, N.Y.C., 1969-72, chief resident, 1971-72; rsch. adminstr. unit for volitional disorders NYSPI, 1972-74; chief psychiat. outpatient svcs. Lenox Hill Hosp., N.Y.C., 1976-79, dir. rsch. dept. psychiatry, 1988, attending physician, sr. med. staff, 1976—; clin. prof. psychiatry NYU Med. Ctr., N.Y.C., 1995—; adj. assoc. prof. psychiatry N.Y. Med. Coll., Valhalla; radio talkshow host WFAS, White Plains, N.Y. Author: Sleep and Its Secrets: The River of Crystal Light, 1991; host, assoc. editor The Elderly; contbr. 2 book chpts, 50 articles to profl. jours.; host, assoc. editor 2 PBS TV series on elderly; commentator Courtroom TV Network, 1997-99; co-host PBS TV Calling for Health. Pres. Black Lake Assn., White Lake, N.Y., 1989-99, bd. dirs., 1999—. Lt. comdr., surgeon USN/USPHS, 1967-69. Fellow APA (Falk fellow 1970, chmn. pub. affairs NYCDB, cons., sec. NYCDB 1999-2000), Am. Coll. Psychoanalysts, Am. Acad. Psychoanalysts (bd. trustees 1996-99), The Pacific Rim Coll. of Psychiatrists; mem. Am. Pain Soc. (charter), N.Y. Soc. for Ericksonian Psychotherapy and Hypnosis (past exec. v.p.). Jewish. Avocations: photography (fantascenes), martial arts. Office: 60 Riverside Dr Apt 16E New York NY 10024-6171

ARONOW, EDWARD, psychologist, educator; b. Dec. 22, 1945; s. Hyman and Gertrude (Bakst) A.; m. Anna Aronow; children: David, Rebecca. BA in Psychology, CUNY, 1967; MA in Psychology, Fordham U., 1969, PhD in Clin. Psychology, 1973. Psychology trainee VA, N.Y.C., 1968-72; prof. psychology Montclair (N.J.) State U., 1972—; sr. clin. psychologist St. Vincent's Hosp., N.Y.C., 1972-79; clin. psychologist Verona, N.J., 1974—. Author: Rorschach Content Interpretation, 1976, A Rorschach Introduction: Content and perceptual Approaches, 1982, The Rorschach Technique, 1994. Fellow Am. Bd. of Assessment Psychology; mem. APA, Ea. Psychol. Assn., N.J. Psychol. Assn., Soc. Personality Assessment. Office: 69 Forest Ave Verona NJ 07044-1217

ARONOW, SAUL, radiological physicist, consultant; b. N.Y.C., Oct. 4, 1917; s. Abraham and Minnie (Mirel) A.; m. Alice Pearlman, Feb. 12, 1942; children: Victor A., Frederick D., David B., Nathan J., Louise G., Jessie P. Kravette. BEE, Cooper Union, 1939; PhD, Harvard U., 1953. Registered profl. engr., Mass.; cert. radiol. physicist. Engr. Harvey Radio Labs., Cambridge, Mass., 1946-49; med. physicist Mass. Gen. Hosp., Boston, 1953-81; clin. engr. Project Hope, Jamaica, W.I., 1981-83; treas., chmn. bd. Tech. in Medicine, Inc., Milford, Mass., 1972—, FDA, 1976—; adj. prof. Northeastern U., Boston, 1975—; instr. MIT, Cambridge, 1969-83. Editor: The Fallen Sky, 1963. Served to 1st lt. Signal Corps, U.S. Army, 1942-46. NSF fellow Harvard U., 1950, Fulbright fellow Danmarks Tekniske Hojskole, Lynbgy, Denmark, 1969; recipient Gano Dunn medal Cooper Union Inst. Tech., N.Y.C., 1981. Mem. Newton Dem. City Com. Fellow IEEE; mem. Am. Assn. Physicists in Medicine (dir. 1979-82), Assn. Advancement Med. Instrumentation (dir. 1966-71), Nat. Fire Protection Assn. (mem. standards coun. 1983-89), Newton Recycling Com., Soc. Nuclear Medicine. Democrat. Jewish. Club: Folk Song Soc. Greater Boston, Harvard Musical Assn. Avocations: hiking, folk music. Home: 86 Crofton Rd Newton MA 02468-2115 Office: Mass Gen Hosp Dept Radiology Boston MA 02114

ARONOW, WILBERT SOLOMON, physician, educator; b. N.Y.C., Oct. 30, 1931; s. Simon and Bella (Safrin) A.; m. Ina Gloria Brody, Sept. 20, 1958; children—Michael Steven, Janice Susan. BS, Queens Coll., 1953; MD, Harvard U., 1957. Diplomate Am. Bd. Internal Medicine. Intern Michael Reese Hosp. and Med. Ctr., Chgo., 1957-58, resident, 1958-61; practice medicine specializing in internal medicine and cardiology; cardiologist, chief Noninvasive Cardiovascular Lab., Long Beach (Calif.) VA Hosp., 1964-72, chief cardiovascular diseases, 1973-82, asst. chief medicine for rsch., 1975-80; asso. prof. medicine U. Calif., Irvine, 1972-75, prof. medicine, 1975-82, prof. cmty. and environ. medicine, 1975-82, prof. pharmacology and therapeutics, 1976-82, vice chief cardiovascular div., chief cardiovascular research, 1974-82; prof. medicine, chief cardiovascular rsch. Creighton U., Omaha, 1982-84; vis. prof. U. Tex. Southwestern Med. Sch., Dallas, 1976, U. Man., 1979, U. Toronto, 1979, Tex. Tech U. Sch. Medicine, Lubbock, 1983, U. Medicine and Dentistry of N.J.-Rutgers Med. Sch., 1983; vis. prof. geriatrics Rochester Sch. Medicine, 1999; cons. cardiology Orange County Med. Center, 1968-82; staff cardiology service St. Joseph Hosp., Omaha, 1982-84; cons. FDA, 1970-77, mem. ad hoc sci. ad. coms., 1970-72, mem. cardiovascular and renal advisory com., 1973-76; cons. U. Calif. Project Clear Air, 1970, Calif. Air Resources Bd., 1973, 78, 80, EPA, 1973, 78, 79, 80, 81, 82, 83, dept. drugs AMA, 1974, 78, 81, 93, NIH, 1976, 80, W. Ger. Dept. Health, 1978, U.S. Dept. Justice Law Enforcement Assistance Adminstrn., 1978, NHLBI, 1979, FTC, 1980, 81, Dept. Health and Environ. Scis., State of Mont., 1980, Nat. Ctr. Health Stats., 1981; cons. and chmn. spl. rev. com. Nat. Cancer Inst., 1980; cons. and mem. subcom. on smoking Am. Heart Assn., 1980-83; med. dir. Hebrew Hosp. Home, 1984—; cons. in medicine Albert Einstein Coll. Medicine, 1990—, State of N.Y. Dept. of Health Office of Pub. Health, 1986, 93, 94; adj. prof. geriatrics and adult devel. Mt. Sinai Sch. Medicine, 1992—. Mem. editorial bd. Jour. Pharmacology and Exptl. Therapeutics, guest field editor, 1981; editorial bd.: Am. Jour. Cardiology, 1980-82, Jour. Circulation, 1980-83, E R Reports, 1981-84, Physician's Drug Alert, 1982—, Jour. Cardiovascular and Pulmonary Technique, 1983-86, Clin. Pharmacology and Therapeutics, 1977-83, Jour. ACC, 1982-83, Drugs and Aging, 1990—, Am. Jour. Noninvasive Cardiology, 1996-95, Jour. Cardiovascular Diagnosis and Procedures, 1992—, Jour. Nonvasive Cardiology, 1996—, Preventive Cardiology, 1998—; contbr. to research publs. Served to capt., M.C. AUS, 1961-63. Fellow A.C.P., Am. Geriatrics Soc., Am. Coll. Cardiology, Am. Coll. Chest Physicians (vice-chmn. coronary disease sect. 1978-79, gov. So. Calif. 1977-83, chmn. coronary disease sect. 1979-81, vice chmn. gov.'s council, mem. exec. council 1979-81, chmn. forum on cardiovascular disease 1980-81, sec. council on govs. 1981-82), Council Clin. Cardiology of Am. Heart Assn., Coun. on Geriatric Cardiology (chmn. program com. 1993—, bd. dirs. 1994—); mem. Am. Soc. Clin. Pharmacology and Therapeutics (chmn. cardiovascular and pulmonary diseases sect. 1973-74, 1975-77), Am. Fedn. Clin. Research, Assn. VA Cardiologists (pres. 1975-77), Long Beach Heart Assn. (dir. 1972-75), Orange County Heart Assn. (dir. 1979-81), Phi Beta Kappa. Jewish. Home: 23 Pebbleway Rd New Rochelle NY 10804-3914 Office: Hebrew Hosp Home 801 Co Op City Blvd Bronx NY 10475-1603 *Concern for the public health as well as for individual patient care has been the motivating force behind my medical research, teaching, and patient care. Performing work in a very careful, scientific fashion, being honest, being helpful and supportive to others, working very hard and efficiently, and being true to my principles of conduct has contributed to my success.*

ARONOWITZ, ALFRED GILBERT, writer; b. May 20, 1920; s. Morris and Lena Aronowitz; children: Myles, Brett, Joel. BL, Rutgers U., 1950. Reporter Newark Evening News, 1952-57, N.Y. Post, N.Y.C., 1957-60; contbg. editor Saturday Evening Post, N.Y.C., 1960-64; columnist N.Y. Post, N.Y.C., 1969-72; freelance writer, 1972-95; blacklisted journalist On Internet, 1995—. Home: PO Box 964 Elizabeth NJ 07208-0964

ARONOWITZ, JULIAN, management consultant; b. N.Y.C., June 27, 1949; s. George and Sophie (Bailin) A. Cert. in Computer Programming, NYU, 1980; BBA, CUNY, 1989. Data analyst Bunker Ramo, N.Y.C., 1974-76; mktg. rep. Cen. Hosiery Sales Co., Inc., N.Y.C., 1977-87; project asst. dept. mgmt. Baruch Coll./CUNY, 1988, 1990; computer instr. adult edn. program Norwood Triangle, Bronx, N.Y., 1989-92; computer profl. Bob Malmet Enterprises, Bronx, 1985-96; bus. advisor N.Y.C., 1991-97; Beta tester Expansion Systems, Fremont, Calif., 1992—; project leader Jay Miner Soc., Inc., N.Y.C., 1998-99; resource for Software Mag., N.Y.C., 1991—; instr. Amiga Users' Group of N.Y., 1995—; demonstrator Users' groups and other orgns., N.Y.C.; adj. lectr. Lehman Coll. CUNY, Bronx, 1998—. Columnist: BUG News; author: (tutorials) File for BBS's, Files for Disk Libraries. Exec. trustee U.S. Assn. Evening Students, N.Y.C., 1983-86; exec. v.p. Com. for Equality in Edn., N.Y.C., 1988. Regents scholar N.Y. State Dept. Edn., 1967, others. Mem. IEEE Computer Soc., Assn. Computing Machinery, Amiga Users' Group of N.Y., Bronx Users' Group (v.p. 1991—), Westchester Amiga Users' Group, Knights of Pythias (past dep. grand chancellor), Royal-Hartman Lodge (knight, Man of Yr. 1993, 97). Jewish. Avocations: swimming, drawing, billiards, walking. Home: 3390 Wayne Ave Apt G52 Bronx NY 10467-2454

ARONS, ARNOLD BORIS, physicist, educator; b. Lincoln, Nebr., Nov. 23, 1916; s. Solomon and Esther (Rosen) A.; m. Jean M. Rendall, Aug. 17, 1942; children: Marion, Janet, Kenneth, Paul. ME, Stevens Inst. Tech., 1937, MS, 1940; PhD, Harvard U., 1943; MA (hon.), Amherst (Mass.) Coll., 1953; DE (hon.), Stevens Inst. Tech., 1982. Rsch. scientist Woods Hole (Mass.) Oceanographic Inst., 1942-68; from asst. to assoc. prof. Stevens Inst. Tech., Hoboken, N.J., 1946-52; prof. physics Amherst Coll., 1952-68; prof. physics U. Wash., Seattle, 1968-82, prof. emeritus, 1982—; cons. in field, 1946-65; mem. Commn. on Coll. Physics, 1962-68. Author: A Guide to Introductory Physics Teaching, 1990, Teaching Introductory Physics, 1997; contbr. articles to profl. jours. Guggenheim Found. fellow, 1957-58, NSF fellow, 1962-63. Fellow AAAS, Am. Phys. Soc.; mem. Am. Assn. Physics Tchrs. (pres. 1966-67, Oersted medal 1972), Am. Geophys. Union, Nat. Sci. Tchrs. Assn. Achievements include patent for piezoelectric guage for explosion pressure measurement, experimental and theoretical work on phase distortion of acoustic pulses reflected from the sea bed; research on model of abyssal oceanic circulation, cognitive development, teaching and learning of physics. E-mail: arons@phys.washington.edu. Home: 10313 Lake Shore Blvd NE Seattle WA 98125-8160 Office: Dept Physics U Wash PO Box 351560 Seattle WA 98195-1560

ARONS, BERNARD S., psychiatrist, educator, health services director. Grad., Oberlin Coll.; MD, Case Western Res. U. Psychiatrist, adminstr., instr. psychiat. residents St. Elizabeths Hosp. NIMH, Washington, dir. Dixon implementation office, 1980, chief clin. advisor, dir. med. nursing, psych. social work; assoc. dir. mental health fin. NIMH; legis. asst. to chair Health Subcom. Ways and Means Com., Washington; dir. Ctr. Mental Health Svcs. U.S. Dept. Health and Human Svcs., Washington, 1993—; advisor to Mrs. Tipper Gore Office of V.P. U.S.; instr. Ctr. Mental Health Inc., Washington; clin. prof. psychiatry Georgetown U. Office: Ctr Mental Health Svcs Rm 17-99 5600 Fishers Ln Rockville MD 20857-1750*

ARONS, MARVIN SHIELD, plastic and hand surgeon; b. Derby, Conn., Feb. 13, 1931; m. Moira Fitzsimmons, 1952 (dec. 1988); children: Kathryn Barry, Mark David, Jeffrey Alan, Megan Fitzsimmons; m. Gloria Whison McLennan, 1992. BS, Yale U., 1952; DMD, Harvard U., 1955; MD, U. Md., 1957. Diplomate Am. Bd. Plastic Surgery. Intern in straigh surgery Duke U. Hosp., Durham, N.C., 1957-58; jr. resident in surgery Duke U. Hosp., Durham, 1958-59; clin. assoc. head and neck surgery Nat. Cancer Inst. NIH, Bethesda, Md., 1959-61; sr. resident in surgery Georgetown U. Hosp., Washington, 1961-62; resident, chief resident in plastic surgery U. Tex. Medical Br., Galveston, 1962-65, instr. plastic and maxillofacial surgery, 1964-65; clin. instr. plastic surgery Med. Sch. Yale U., New Haven, Conn., 1965-68; clin assoc. plastic surgery Yale U., 1968-70, asst. clin. prof. plastic surgery, 1970-78, assoc. clin. prof. plastic surgery, 1978-89; clin. prof. plastic surgery $D, $D, 1989—; attending staff plastic surgery Hosp. St. Raphael, New Haven, 1965—; chief sect. plastic surgery Hosp. of St. Raphael, New Haven, 1974—; attending staff plastic surgery Yale-New Haven Hosp., 1965—; attending plastic surgeon VA Hosp., West Haven, Conn., 1965—; cons. plastic surgery Laurel Heights Hosp., Shelton, 1965-85, Bur. Vocat. Rehab. State of Conn., 1967—, cons. in hand surgery Worker's Comp. Commn., 1965—; cons. in hand surgery Worker's Comp. Bd. Fed. Dist. New Eng., 1989—; vis. prof. plastic surgery U. Tex. Med. Br., Galveston, 1977, Sch. Medicine Washington U., 1978, Health Sci. Ctr. Coll. Medicine SUNY, 1995; presenter in field. Contbr. numerous articles to profl. jours. Bd. trustees Hosp. St. Raphael Found., 1975-90, Hopkins-Day Prospect Hill Sch., 1978-80; chmn. physician gifts United Way New Haven, 1984-85, co-chmn., 1997-98; bd. permanent officer Yale Med. Sch., 1989—; bd. dirs. Ind. Practice Assn. Hosp. St. Raphael, 1986-90, New Haven Jewish Cmty. Coun.,

1968-75, Congregation B'nai Jacob, Woodbridge, 1972-74. Fellow Am. Cancer Soc., 1963-64, 64-65; recipient award Am. Acad. Dental Medicine, 1957. Fellow Saybrook Coll. (assoc.); mem. Am. Assn. Hand Surgery, Am. Assn. Plastic Surgeons, Am. Cleft Palate Assn., ACS, Am. Soc. Maxillofacial Surgeons, Am. Soc. Plastic and Reconstructive Surgeons, Am. Soc.Peripheral Nerve, Conn. Soc. Plastic and Reconstructive Surgeons, Conn. State Med. Soc., Lipoplasty Soc. North Am., New Eng. Soc. Plastic and Reconstructive Surgeons, New Haven Med. Assn., New Haven County Med. Assn., Singleton Surg. Soc., U. Md. Med. Alumni Assn. (regional v.p. 1991-92), Yale Cancer Ctr. (assoc.), Blocker-Lewis Plastic Surgery Soc. (pres. 1990-91), New Haven Colony Hist. Soc. (bd. dirs. 1992-97, v.p. 1997—), Woodbridge Country Club (bd. dirs. 1971-74), Friends of Am. Art at Yale, Yale Golf Club, New Haven Lawn Club, Qunnipiack Club, Sigma Xi. Home: 66 Hunting Hill Rd Woodbridge CT 06525 Office: 205 Orchard Med Ctr 330 Orchard St New Haven CT 06511

ARONS, MYRON MILFORD, psychology educator; b. Detroit, Oct. 17, 1929; s. William Arons and Edna (Auslander) Arons Perskey; m. Christiane Hugette Feve; 1 child, Sandrine. BA in Psychology, Wayne State U., 1961; PhD, Sorbonne U., 1965; MA, Brandeis U., 1967. Prof. Coll. Moderne, Oyem, Gabon, Africa, 1962-63; assoc. prof., chmn. dept. psychgology Prince of Wales Coll., Charlottetown, Can., 1967-68; assoc. prof., head dept. psychgology West Ga. Coll., Carrolltown, 1968-73, prof., chmn. dept. psychology, 1974-93, prof. psychology, 1994—; vis. prof. U. Aarhus, Denmark, 1985. Mem. editorial bd. Jour. Humanistic Psychology, 1992—; contbr. articles to sci. and profl. jours. With USN, 1948-49. Mem. APA (pres. APA divsn. #32, 1974-75, exec. bd. 1994—), Nat. Assn. Humanistic Psychology (exec. bd. dirs. 1973-74, pres. 1992-93). Home: 2077 Clem Lowell Rd Carrollton GA 30116-9220 Office: State U of West Ga Maple St Carrollton GA 30118

ARONSON, ARTHUR LAWRENCE, veterinary pharmacology and toxicology educator; b. Mpls., Aug. 24, 1933; s. Arthur Theodore and Thorene (Elfstrand) A.; m. Marilyn Ann Lundeen, Sept. 15, 1956; children: Brenda Louise, Mark Theodore, Luann Marie. BS, U. Minn., 1955, DVM, 1957, PhD, 1963; MS, Cornell U., 1959. Asst. prof. pharmacology Cornell U., 1964-67, assoc. prof., 1967-71, prof., 1971-80; prof., head dept. anatomy, physiol. sci., and radiology Coll. Vet. Medicine, N.C. State U., Raleigh, 1980-99; prof. emeritus, 1999—; mem. com. biologic effects atmospheric pollutants NRC; mem. vet. medicine adv. com. FDA.; mem. U.S. Pharmacopeia Adv. Panel Vet. Medicine; chmn. com. recognition of pain and distress in lab. animals, Inst. Lab. Animal Resources, NAS, 1988. Co-editor Jour. Vet. Pharmacology and Therapeutics, 1992-99. Mem. Friends of Scandinavia, Carl Larsson Vasa Lodge; pres. Wake County Literacy Coun., 1997-99. Mem. AVMA (chmn. coun. on biologic and therapeutic agts. 1986-87), Am. Soc. Pharmacology and Exptl. Therapeutics, Soc. Toxicology (animals in rsch. com.), N.C. Soc. Toxicology (pres. 1985-86), am. Acad. Vet. Pharmacology and Therapeutics (pres. 1987-89), Am. Coll. Vet. Clin. Pharmacology (pres. 1993-95), Wake County Literacy Coun. (bd. dirs. 1991—, pres. 1997-99), Sigma Xi, Phi Zeta. Lutheran. Home: 1213 Glendale Dr Raleigh NC 27612-4772 Office: Coll Vet Medicine N C State U Raleigh NC 27606

ARONSON, BENJAMIN, artist; b. Boston, Oct. 4, 1958; s. David and Georgianna (Nyman) A.; m. Margaret Ray Combs, Nov. 5, 1983; children: Jesse Benjamin, Alexander Raymond. BFA in Painting, Boston U., 1980, MFA in Painting, 1982. tchg. asst. Boston U. Sch. Fine Art, 1980-82; tchr. Beaver Country Day Sch., Chestnut Hill, Mass., 1983-90; mem. U.S. Supreme Ct. Portrait Painting Team, 1989-97; guest lectr. Boston U. Summer Art Inst., 1985, Deerfield Acad., Old Deerfield, Mass., 1986, Salve Regina Coll., Newport, R.I., 1987, Mass. Coll. Art, Boston, 1987, Worcester Craft Ctr., Boston Globe Scholastic Art Awards, 1988, Boston U. Sch. Art Edn., 1988, art dept. Southeastern Middlesex U., 1988, Gordon Coll., Wenham, Mass., 1989, painting dept. Boston U. Sch. Visual Art, 1989, R.I. Sch. Design, 1990, Charrette Corp., 1991, Harvard Grad. Sch. Design, 1995, 96, 97, 98, 99; artist in residence Beaver Country Day Sch., Chestnut Hill, Mass., 1985-88. One-man shows include Nancy Lincoln Gallery, Chestnut Hill, Mass., 1983, 89, Lane Gallery, Gordon Coll., Wenham, Mass., 1986, Julia-Saul Gallery, Sudbury, Mass., 1987, Louis Newman Galleries, Beverly Hills, Calif., 1994, Jerry Solomon Gallery, Hollywood, Calif., 1996, Horwitch Newman Gallery, Scottsdale, Ariz., 1996, M B Modern, N.Y.C., 1997, 99, Sydne Bernard Fine Arts, Hollywood, 1998; exhibited in group shows at Boston U. Art Gallery, 1980, 82, Dana Hall Gallery, Wellesley, Mass., 1984, Quadrum Gallery, Chestnut Hill, 1984, DeCordova Mus., Lincoln, Mass., 1988, Copley Soc., Boston, 1990, Nat. Acad. Design, N.Y.C., 1990, 92, Urban Ctr. Mcpl. Art Soc., N.Y.C., 1991, Mickelson Gallery, Washington, 1992, Security Pacific Gallery, Seattle, 1992, Gwenda Jay Gallery, Chgo., 1992, Louis Newman Galleries, Beverly Hills, 1993, 94, Koplin Gallery, Santa Monica, Calif., 1995, Horwitch Newman Gallery, Scottsdale, 1995, 96, Jerry Solomon Gallery, Hollywood, 1996, 97, Sydne Bernard Fine Arts, Hollywood, 1997, 98, Pepper Gallery, Boston, 1997, M B Modern, N.Y.C., 1997, 98, Mangel Gallery, Phila., 1998, Soma Gallery, la Jolla, Calif., 1998, Alpha Gallery, Boston, 1999; represented in permanent collections at Reading (Pa.) Pub. Fine Art Mus., MIT, Woodshole Oceanographic Inst., Mass.; also corp. and pvt. collections; contbr. articles to profl. jours. Recipient Blanche E. Colman award for painting, 1986, 88, 1st prize in drawing Sudbury Art Assn., 1987, Mass. Lottery grant for painting, 1987, St. Botolph Club Found. grant for painting, 1988, R.I. State Coun. for Arts grant, 1989, William P. and Gertrude Schweitzer painting prize, Nat. Acad. of Design, 1990, Thomas Fisher award Am. Soc. Archtl. Perspectivists, N.Y.C., 1991, Ogden M. Pleissner painting award Nat. Acad. Design, N.Y.C., 1992. Home: 33 Wayside Inn Rd Framingham MA 01701-3021

ARONSON, CARL EDWARD, pharmacology and toxicology educator; b. Providence, Mar. 14, 1936; s. Carl Ivar and Ruth (Workman) A.; m. Marjorie Peck Boutelle, Dec. 17, 1960; children—Linda J., Kristen L. A.B., Brown U., Providence, 1958; Ph.D., U. Vt., Burlington, 1966; M.A., U. Pa., Phila., 1973. Asst. prof. pharmacology U. Pa. Sch. Medicine, Phila., 1971-75, assoc. prof. pharmacology, 1975-92; asst. prof. pharmacology and toxicology dept. animal biology U. Pa. Sch. Vet. Medicine, Phila., 1971-73, head labs. of pharmacology and toxicology, 1972-86, assoc. prof. pharmacology and toxicology, 1973-96; retired to emeritus status, 1996; instrument specialist, dept. chemistry Haverford (Pa.) Coll., 1996—. Editor Veterinary Pharmaceuticals and Biologicals, 1978-79, 80-81, 82-83, 85-86; contbr. chpts. to books, articles to profl. jours. Active local sch. dist. coms. and other civic assns. Served to 1st lt. USAFR, 1958-65. Recipient Norden award for disting. tchg. U. Pa. Sch. Vet. Medicine, 1972, Legion of Honor, Chapel of the Four Chaplains, 1984. Fellow Am. Acad. Vet. Pharmacology and Therapeutics (pres. 1983-85, Svc. award 1994), Am. Acad. Vet. and Comparative Toxicology; mem. Am. Soc. Pharmacology and Exptl. Therapeutics, Am. Vet. Med. Assn., AAUP, Sigma Xi. Lutheran. Club: Bay Region Mariners Sailing Assn. (treas. 1981-83, vice comdr. 1986, commodore 1987). Lodge: Masons (Greenville, R.I.). Avocations: sailing; photography. Office: Haverford Coll Dept Chemistry 370 Lancaster Ave Haverford PA 19041-1392 also: Haverford Coll Dept Chemistry 370 Lancaster Ave Haverford PA 19041-1392

ARONSON, DAVID, artist, retired art educator; b. Shilova, Lithuania, Oct. 28, 1923; came to U.S., 1929, naturalized, 1931; s. Peisach Leib and Gertrude (Shapiro) A.; m. Georgianna B. Nyman, June 10, 1956; children: Judith, Benjamin, Abigail. Certificate, Boston Mus. Sch., 1946; LHD (hon.), Hebrew Coll., 1993. Instr. painting Boston Mus. Sch., 1943-54; prof. art Boston U., 1962-89, chmn. div., 1952-62, chmn. painting dept., 1962-89, prof. emeritus, 1989—. Contbr. articles to profl. jours.; one man shows include Niveau Gallery, N.Y.C., 1945, 56, Mus. Modern Art, N.Y.C., 1946, Boris Mirski Gallery, Boston, 1951, 59, 64, 69, Downtown Gallery, N.Y.C., 1953, Nordness Gallery, N.Y.C., 1960, 63, 69, Rex Evans Gallery, Los Angeles, 1961, Long Beach (Calif.) Mus., 1961, Westhampton (N.Y.) Gallery, 1961, J. Thomas Gallery, Provincetown, Mass., 1964, Zora Gallery, Los Angeles, 1965, Hunter Gallery, Chattanooga, 1965, Kovler Gallery, Chgo., 1966, Bernard Danenberg Galleries, N.Y.C., 1969, 72, Pucker Gallery, Boston, 1976, 78, 86, 90, 94, Phila. Mus. Judaica, 1990, Louis Newman Gallery, L.A., 1977, 81, 84, 86, 89, 92, Sadye Bronfman Art Ctr., Montreal, Que., Can., 1982, Horwitch Newman Gallery, Scottsdale, Ariz., 1995, 96, MB Modern Gallery, N.Y., 1997; group shows include N.Y. World's Fair, 1964-65, Bridgestone Gallery, Tokyo, Royal Acad. London, Mus. Modern Art, Paris, Palazzo Venezia, Rome, Congresse Halle, Berlin, Charlottenborg, Copenhagen, Palais Des Beaux Arts, Brussels, Smithsonian Instn., 1965, retrospective exhbns. include Rose Mus., Brandeis U., Waltham, Mass., 1978, Jewish Mus., N.Y.C., 1979, Nat. Mus. Am. Jewish History, Phila., 1979, So. Middlesex U., South Dartmouth, Mass., 1983, Mickelson Gallery, Washington, 1985; represented in permanent collections Art Inst. Chgo., Va. Mus. Fine Arts, Richmond, Bryn Mawr Coll., Brandeis U., Tupperware Mus., Orlando, Fla., Decordova Mus., Lincoln, Mass., Mus. Modern Art, Atlanta U., Atlanta Art Assn., U. Nebr., Krannert Art Mus. of U. Ill., Whitney Mus. Am. Art, Colby Coll., U. N.H., Portland Mus. Art, Corcoran Gallery Art, Washington, Munson Williams Proctor Art Inst., Ithaca, N.Y., Boston Mus. Fine Arts, Smithsonian Instn., Washington, Milw. Art Inst., Pa. Acad. Fine Arts, Johnson Found., Racine, Wis., Worcester (Mass.) Art Mus., Brockton (Mass.) Mus. Art, Longy Sch. Music, Cambridge, Mass., Boston U., Jewish Community Ctr., Boston, Joseph Hirschhorn Collection, Hebrew Coll., Brookline, Mass., David and Alfred Smart Mus., U. Chgo., Two-Ten Found., Boston, Pa. State U. Mus. Art, Syracuse (N.Y.) U., Beth Israel Hosp., Boston, U. Judaism, Los Angeles, Guilford Coll., N.C., Fine Arts Ctr., Cheekville, Tenn.; numerous others; sculpture commns. Container Corp. Am., 1963, 65, Reform Jewish Appeal, 1980, Combined Jewish Philanthropies, 1981, Temple Beth Elohim, Wellesley, Mass., 1982, Brandeis U. Library, Waltham, Mass., 1983, Brandeis U. Berlin Chapel, 1996. Recipient 1st Judges prize Inst. Modern Art, Boston, 1944, 1st Popular prize, 1944; Choice Friends of Art Art Inst. Chgo., 1946; Purchase prize Va. Mus. Fine Arts, 1946; Travelling fellow Boston Mus. Sch., 1946; Grand prize Boston Arts Festival, 1952, 54; 2d prize, 1953; 1st prize Tupperware Art Fund, 1954, cert. of merit for sculpture NAD, 1990; grantee in Art Nat. Inst. Arts and Letters, 1958; Purchase prize, 1961, 62, 63; purchase prize Pa. Acad. Fine Arts, also other purchase prizes; Samuel F.B. Morse Gold medal NAD, 1973; Isaac N. Maynard prize NAD, 1975; Joseph S. Isidor gold medal NAD, 1976; Guggenheim fellow, 1960; Adolph and Clara Obrig prize NAD, 1968, Academician NAD, 1970. Home: 137 Brimstone Ln Sudbury MA 01776-3200

ARONSON, DONALD ERIC, professional services firms consultant, value added tax consultant; b. Boston, Feb. 24, 1934; s. Harry and Nathalie (Snyder) A.; m. Margery Roth, Sept. 27, 1955 (dec. 1981); children: Nancy, Helaine; m. Joan Gelman, Jan. 12, 1986. AB, Dartmouth Coll., 1955; MBA, Columbia U., 1959. CPA, N.Y., N.J. Mem. audit and tax staff Arthur Young & Co., N.Y.C., 1959-63, tax mgr., 1963-68, tax ptnr., 1968-72; office mng. ptnr. Arthur Young & Co., Saddle Brook, N.J., 1972-80; dir. mktg. Arthur Young, N.Y.C., 1980-89; dir. tax mktg. Ernst & Young, N.Y.C., 1989-92; prin., profl. svcs. firms cons. Aronson/Heintz Assocs., N.Y.C., 1995—; value added tax recovery advisor, cons. and prin. VATAm., L.P., N.Y.C. and Princeton, N.J., 1993—; Asst. prof. acctg. Upsala Coll., East Orange, N.J., 1963-65; asst. prof. Columbia U. Grad. Sch. Bus., N.Y.C., 1966-67; acctg. adv. bd. Columbia U. Grad. Sch. of Bus., N.Y.C., 1981-89; assoc. prof. bus. NYU, 1992-97; cons. and lectr. in field. Contbr. articles to bus. and profl. jours. Served to 1st lt. USAF, 1955-57. Recipient Montgomery prize Columbia U. Grad. Sch. Bus., 1959; award N.Y. Soc. C.P.A.s, 1959. Mem. AICPA, N.Y. State Soc. CPAs, N.J. Soc. CPAs (trustee 1975-78). Democrat. Jewish. Avocations: tennis, skiing, boating. Office: 530 Park Ave Ste 4D New York NY 10021-8015

ARONSON, EDGAR DAVID, venture capitalist; b. N.Y.C., June 17, 1934; s. Aaron Solomon and Ida Claire (Minevitch) A.; m. Nancy Carol Pforzheimer, Dec. 23, 1956; children: Edgar David, Alison C., Edith S., Peter Borrah. A.B., Harvard U., 1956, M.B.A., 1962. Successively trainee, asst. cashier, v.p. 1st Nat. Bank of Chgo., 1962-67; v.p. Republic Nat. Bank of N.Y., 1968; trainee Salomon Bros., N.Y.C., 1968-69; ltd. partner Salomon Bros., 1970, v.p., 1971-72, gen. partner, 1972-79; mng. dir. Salomon Bros. Internat. Ltd., London, 1971-76; chmn. bd. Dillon, Read Internat., 1979-81; pres. EDACO, Inc., 1981—; bd. dirs. APL N.V., Curacao, Petrogas Ltd., Hong Kong, MidAmEnergy Holdings, Inc., Omaha, H.L. Oakes & Co., Inc., Panama, Hertford Internat., N.V., Curacao. Author: (with others) New Old World, 1962, Response to Change, 1963. Trustee Lesley Coll., Cambridge, Mass., 1981-84,South St. Seaport Mus., N.Y.; bd. dirs. Carl and Lily Pforzheimer Found., N.Y.C. 1st lt. USMCR, 1956-60, maj. FMF ret. res. Mem. Marine Corps Res. Officers Assn., 1st Marine Divsn. Assn., The Cruising Assn. (U.K.), Mensa, N.Y. Yacht Club, Bass Harbor Yacht Club, Harvard Club N.Y.C., Royal Cork Yacht Club, The Brook (N.Y.C.), Eire, Annabel's (London). Office: EDACO Inc 551 Fifth Ave Rm 512 New York NY 10176-0599

ARONSON, HOWARD ISAAC, linguist, educator; b. Chgo., Mar. 5, 1936; s. Abe and Jean A. B.A., U. Ill., 1956; M.A., Ind. U., 1958, Ph.D., 1961. Asst. prof. Slavic langs. and lit. U. Wis., Madison, 1961-62; asst. prof. Slavic linguistics U. Chgo., 1962-65, asso. prof. depts. slavic langs. and lit. and linguistics, 1965-73, prof., 1973—, chmn. dept. linguistics, 1972-80, chmn. dept. Slavic langs. and lits., 1983-91. Editor: Annual of the Society for the Study of Caucasia, 1989—. Mem. Am. Assn. Advancement Slavic Studies, Am. Assn. Tchrs. Slavic and East European Langs. Jewish. Home: 415 W Aldine Ave Apt 7B Chicago IL 60657-3601 Office: U Chgo Dept Slavic Langs and Lit Chicago IL 60637

ARONSON, JASON, publisher; b. Minn., Jan. 25, 1928; s. Louis and Mollie (Weiner) A.; div.; 1 child, Jane; m. Joyce Kraus. BA, U. Minn., 1949, MD, 1953. Resident in psychiatry U. Minn. Hosps., 1954-57; asst. psychiatrist Harvard Med. Sch. and Mass. Gen. Hosp., 1959-64; editor-in-chief Internat. Jour. Psychiatry, 1962-70; pres. Jason Aronson Pubs. Inc., Northvale, N.J., 1964—. Capt. U.S. Army, 1957-59. Fellow Am. Psychiat. Assn. Office: Jason Aronson Inc 230 Livingston St Northvale NJ 07647-1731

ARONSON, JAY RICHARD, economics educator, researcher, academic administrator; b. N.Y.C., Aug. 26, 1937; s. Lester and Rose (Hacken) A.; m. Judith Libby Klein, Sept. 13, 1959; children: Sarah, Miriam, Anne. A.B., Clark U., 1959, Ph.D., 1964; M.A., Stanford U., 1961. Asst. prof. econs. Worcester Poly. Inst. (Mass.), 1961-65; asst. prof. econs. Lehigh U., Bethlehem, Pa., 1965-68, assoc. prof., 1968-72, prof., 1972—; dir. Martindale Ctr. for Study Pvt. Enterprise Lehigh U., Bethlehem, 1980—; William L. Clayton prof. bus. and econs. Lehigh U., 1984—; vis. scholar U. York (Eng.), 1973; cons. Internat. City Mgmt. Assn.; commr. Pa. Pension Fund Study Commn. Author: books including (with J. Hilley) Financing State and Local Governments, Public Finance; editor: books including (with E. Schwartz) Management Policies in Local Government Finance, 1975, 3d edit., 1987; contbr. articles to profl. publs. Recipient Lindback award Lehigh U., 1968; recipient Stabler award Lindback award, 1974; Rockefeller fellow, 1959-61; named hon. fellow Clark U., 1962; grantee Ford Found., 1971-72, 76-77, HEW, 1978-79, Scaife Found., 1982; Fulbright research scholar, 1978, 96. Mem. Am. Econ. Assn., Nat. Tax Assn., Am. Fin. Assn., Roya Econ. Soc. Democrat. Jewish. Home: 1804 Jennings St Bethlehem PA 18017-5235 Office: Lehigh U Dept Economy Bethlehem PA 18015

ARONSON, LOUIS VINCENT, II, manufacturing executive; b. Newark, Jan. 18, 1923; s. Alexander H. and Leona L. (Lazarus) A.; m. Joan Barbara Fisch, Nov. 2, 1945; children: James Richard, Robert A., Kathryn Ann, Diane Barbara. BS, U.S. Naval Acad., 1945. Methods engr. Ronson Corp., Newark, 1947-48, supr. prodn. control, 1948-50, v.p. charge material procurement, 1950-52, v.p. charge ops., 1952-53, pres., 1952—, also bd. dirs. Bd. dirs. NCCJ. Served as ensign USN, 1945-47. Mem. U.S. Naval Acad. Athletic Assn. Home: PO Box 9 Oldwick NJ 08858-0009 Office: Ronson Corp PO Box 6707 Somerset NJ 08875-6707

ARONSON, LUANN MARIE, actress; b. Ithaca, N.Y., Nov. 18, 1964; d. Arthur Lawrence and Marilyn Ann (Lundeen) A. MusB, Ithaca Coll., 1986; MusM, Southern Meth. U., Dallas, 1988. Appeared as Guenevere in the Nat. Tour of Camelot, 1991; originated the role of Betty Schaefer in the workshop prodn. of Sunset Boulevard at Andrew Lloyd Webber's Sydmonton Festival, London, 1992; features soloist in the Music of Andrew Lloyd Webber, Radio City Music Hall, N.Y.C., 1992; as Maria in the Far East Tour of the Sound of Music, 1992; as Christine Daaé on Broadway in Phantom of the Opera, N.Y.C., 1992-94; as Christine Daaé in the Internat. Tour of The Phantom of the Opera, 1995; as Marian Paroo in The Music Man, 1997; as Laurie in Oklahoma!, 1997; as Sharon in Master Class, 1999; participant Encores Series City Ctr., 1998. Recipient Outstanding Young Alumni award Ithaca Coll. Alumni Assn., 1994; Blossom Music Festival scholar, 1988, Tanglewood Summer Music Festival scholar, 1986. Mem. Actor's Equity Assn.

ARONSON, MARC, artist; b. Seattle, June 26, 1948; s. Leonard and Marian (August) A.; m. Sue Elizabeth Steiner, June 28, 1971; 1 child, Elliot. BA, Western Wash. U., Bellingham, 1971; MA, NYU, 1989, postgrad., 1989—. Exhibited in group shows Seattle Art Mus. Pavilion, 1971, Warren Benedek Gallery, N.Y.C., 1974, U. Denver Sch. Art, 1975, Orgn. Ind. Artists Fed. Courthouse, Bklyn., 1977, Aldrich Mus. Contemporary Art, Ridgefield, Conn., 1978, Foster White Gallery, Seattle, 1980, Renssellaer Poly. Inst., Troy, N.Y., 1980, Sci. Mus. Tokyo, 1985, Embellishment of Statue of Liberty Barneys N.Y., 1986, Island Introductions Galveston (Tex.) Arts Ctr., 1990, Art of N.E. USA Silvermine Guild Arts Ctr., New Canaan, Conn., 1991, Nat. Midyear Exhbn. Butler Inst. Am. Art, Youngstown, Ohio, 1991, Am. 500 Centro Cultural Recoleta, Buenos Aires, 1992, The Emerging Collector, N.Y.C., 1992, Art of Northeast USA Silvermine Guild Arts Ctr., New Canaan, Conn., 1993, Butler Inst. Am. Art, Youngstown, Ohio, 1994, Washington Sq. East Galleries, N.Y.C., 1995, Art of Northeast USA Silvermine Guild Arts Ctr., New Canaan, Conn., 1996., Nat. Competition Finalists' Exhibition Provincetown Art Assn. and Museum, 1998, S.I. (N.Y.) Biennial Juried Art Exhibition, 1998, Art of N.E. Silermine Guild Arts Ctr., New Canaan, Conn., 1999; represented in permanent collection Time Warner Inc. Nat. Endowment for Arts fellow, 1976, N.Y. Found. Arts fellow, 1980. Mem. Kappa Delta Pi. Jewish. Avocation: racquetball.

ARONSON, MARGARET R., school psychologist; b. Lewistown, Pa., Dec. 12, 1921; d. Frederick Augustine and Claire S. (Schellenberg) Rupp; m. Morton Jerome Aronson, Oct. 31, 1948; children: Eric L. Aronson Simmonds, Frederick Rupp, Scott Charles. BA, Pa. State U., 1942, MS, 1943. Nat. cert. sch. psychologist. Clin. psychologist Inst. Pa. Hosp., Phila., 1943-48, Georgetown Hosp., Washington, 1948-50; ind. cons. Patchogue (N.Y.) Pub. Schs., 1986-96, Luth. Ministries, Queens and Nassau County, N.Y., 1996—. Editor Winter Olympics Pindar Press, 1980-82. Mem. MGA, Phi Beta Kappa, Phi Kappa Phi, Psi Chi. Avocation: golf. Home: Windsor Gate Great Neck NY 11020

ARONSON, MARK BERNE, consumer advocate; b. Pitts., Aug. 24, 1941; s. Richard J. and Jean (DeRoy) A.; m. Ellen Jane Askin, July 20, 1970 (div. Oct. 1993); children: Robert M., Andrew A., Michael D. BS in Econs., U. Pa., 1962; JD, U. Pitts., 1965. Pvt. practice Pitts., 1965-90; sr. ptnr. Behrend & Aronson, Pitts., 1967-80, Behrend, Aronson & Morrow, Pitts., 1980-83; pres. Current Concepts Corp., Pitts., 1992—; real estate broker, 1972-94; cons. to attys., 1991—; pvt. consumer advocate, 1991—. Past pres. Community Day Sch., Pitts., Rodef Shalom Jr. Congregation; trustee Rodef Shalom Congregation, Pitts, 1979-87, Pitts. Child Guidance Found., 1987-90; mem. Pitts. Coun. on Edn., 1986-89. Mem. Am. Arbitration Assn. (mem. nat. panel arbitrators), Masons (master). Republican. Jewish. Address: Ste 506-507 Churchill Mansions 2525 Greensburg Pike Churchill Borough PA 15221-3686

ARONSON, MICHAEL ANDREW, editor; b. Bklyn., Apr. 27, 1939; s. Jesse Besthoff and Marcia (Sacks) A. B.A., Johns Hopkins, 1960. Asst. dir. Ind. U. Press, Bloomington, 1966-69; London editor U. Chgo. Press, 1970, sci. editor, 1971-73; editor-in-chief Johns Hopkins U. Press, Balt., 1973-78; sr. editor social scis. Harvard U. Press, Cambridge, Mass., 1978—. Office: Harvard U Press 79 Garden St Cambridge MA 02138-1423

ARONSON, NORMAN LEONARD, publishing executive, consultant; b. Washington, June 7, 1924; s. Herman and Bertha Martha (Miller) A.; m. Marcia Ross Rosey, Mar. 29, 1952 (dec. Nov., 1989); children: Susan Elizabeth Aronson Baratta, John Michael. BS in Bus. and Pub. Adminstrn., Georgetown U., 1947, JD, 1949. V.p. Esquire Mag., N.Y.C., 1951-75; publisher Univ. Comms., Rahway, N.J., 1975-76; advt. dir. Signature Mag., N.Y.C., 1976-82; pres. Best Publs. Inc., N.Y.C., 1982-86; CEO Musculoskeletal Transplant Found., Little Silver, N.J., 1986-88; editor, publisher "Q" Physicians Guide to Quality, Princeton, N.J., 1988—; entrepreneur, investor founder, pres. The Kings Ct. Restaurants, Princeton, N.J., Charlottesville, Va., Bostons Restaurant, Trenton, N.J., 1977-80; pres. The Svc. News Stands, Pentagon Bldg., Washington, 1965-75; cons. Universal Press Syndicate, Kansas City, Mo., 1988-89, Target Mktg., Kansas City, 1988—. Publisher The Book of Bests, 1983-84. Lt. j.g. US Navy, 1942-46 PTO. Recipient Lone Sailor award, U.S. Navy, Washington, 1990. Mem. The Nassau Club. Avocations: wine, cooking.

ARONSON, PETER SAMUEL, medical scientist, physiology educator; b. Bklyn., Feb. 3, 1947; s. Harry and Sydelle (Pincus) A.; m. Marie Louise Landry, Sept. 25, 1977; children: Paul L., William L. AB, U. Rochester, 1967; MD, NYU, 1970; MA (hon.), Yale U., 1987. Diplomate Nat. Bd. Med. Examiners, Am. Bd. Internal Medicine (subspeciality Nephrology). Intern and resident in internal medicine U. N.C. Sch. Medicine, Chapel Hill, 1970-72; clin. assoc. Gerontology Rsch. Ctr., NIH, Balt., 1972-74; fellow in nephrology Yale U. Sch. Medicine, New Haven, 1974-77, asst. prof. medicine and physiology, 1977-81, assoc. prof. medicine and physiology, 1981-87, prof. medicine and cellular and molecular physiology, 1987—, C.N.H. Long prof. internal medicine, 1995—; chief sect. nephrology Yale U. Sch. Medicine, New Haven; established investigator Am. Heart Assn., 1981-86. Mem. editl. bd. Am. Jour. Physiology, 1982-86, 87-90, 96—, Kidney Internat., 1990-94, Jour. Biol. Chemistry, 1995—; cons. editor Jour. Clin. Investigation, 1993-98; contbr. rsch. articles to profl. jours. With USPHS, 1972-74. Recipient Solomon Berson Med. Alumni Achievement award NYU, 1996. Fellow AAAS; mem. Assn. Am. Physicians (editl. bd. Proc. 1997-99), Am. Fedn. for Med. Rsch., Am. Physiol. Soc., Am. Soc. for Clin. Investigation (councillor 1986-88, editl. com. 1993-98), Am. Soc. Nephrology (Young Investigator award 1985, Homer Smith award 1994), Am. Heart Assn. (exec. com. coun. on the kidney 1986-90), Internat. Soc. Nephrology, Soc. Gen. Physiologists, Salt and Water Club (sec. 1985-87), Phi Beta Kappa. Office: Yale School of Medicine Dept of Medicine/Nephrology PO Box 208029 New Haven CT 06520-8029

ARONSON, STANLEY MAYNARD, physician, educator; b. N.Y.C., May 28, 1922; s. Eliuh and Lena (Hassner) A.; m. Betty Ellis, June 3, 1947; children: Susan, Lisa, Sarah. BS, CCNY, 1943; MD, NYU, 1947; MA, Brown U., 1971; MPH, Harvard U. Sch. Pub. Health, 1981. Diplomate: Am. Bd. Pathology., Am. Bd. Neuropathology. Resident Bellevue Hosp., Sydenham Hosp., Meml. Sloan-Kettering Ctr. for Cancer., N.Y.C., 1946-51; fellow Mt. Sinai Hosp., N.Y.C., 1951-54; faculty Columbia Coll. Physicians and Surgeons, 1951-54; prof. pathology, asst. dean SUNY, Bklyn., 1954-70; prof. med. sci., dean medicine Brown U., 1970-81, Univ. prof. med. sci., 1981-87, dean medicine emeritus, 1987—; dir. labs. Kings County Hosp. Center, Bklyn., 1965-70; pathologist-in-chief Miriam Hosp., Providence, 1970-75; vis. prof. community medicine Dartmouth Coll. Med. Sch., 1982—; lectr. Yale Sch. Medicine, 1964-65; lectr. pathology Tufts U. Sch. Medicine, 1978—; professorial lectr. Bklyn. Health Ctr., SUNY, 1970—; cons. physician neuropathology Jewish Chronic Disease Hosp., Bklyn., 1951—, NIH, 1962—, R.I. Hosp., Roger Williams Hosp., Meml. Hosp., Miriam Hosp., Providence VA Hosp., Butler Hosp., Providence, R.I. Med. Ctr., Luth. Med. Center, N.Y.C. Author: (with B.W. Volk) Cerebral Sphingolipidoses, 1962, Inborn Disorders of Sphingolipid Metabolism, 1966, Sphingolipids, Sphingolipidoses and Allied Disorders, 1972, (with A. Sahs and E Hartman) Guidelines for Stroke Care, 1976; (with Adachi and Hirano) The Pathology of the Myelinated Axon, 1985, Tapestry of Medicine, 1999, also numerous articles; mem. editorial bd. Jour. Submicroscopic Cytology, Jour. Neuropathology and Exptl. Neurology; editorial bd., editor-in-chief R.I. Med. Jour.; weekly columnist Providence Jour.-Bull. Commr. U.S. Commn. Control of Huntington's Disease, 1976-79; chmn. Legis. Commn. Dementia Related to Aging; vice chmn. R.I. Bd. of Med. Licensure and Discipline, 1993—; pres. Hospice R.I., 1989—, Interfaith Health Care Ministries, 1989-91; mem. Nat. Adv. Commn. on Multiple Sclerosis, 1973-74, NIH Perinatal Rsch. Commn., Joint Commn. on Stroke Facilities, med. adv. bd. Nat. Multiple Sclerosis Soc., Dysautonomia Found., Nat. Tay-Sachs Assn., Nat. Fund for Med. Edn.; trustee Univ. Health Scis., Chgo.; cons. for internat. epidemiology programs The Rockefeller Found., 1990—; chmn. bd. trustees Jewish Home for Aged, R.I., 1993-94; pres. Shalom Housing for Elderly, 1993-94. With U.S. Army, 1942-46. Inductee R.I. Hall of Fame, 1997. Mem. AMA, Am. Neurol. Assn., Am. Assn. Neuropathology (pres. 1971-72), N.Y. Acad. Medicine, Am. Acad. Neurology, Am. Assn. Pathologists and Bacteriologists, Internat. Soc. Neuropathology, Assn. Am. Med. Colls., N.Y. Neurol. Soc., Am. Pub. Health Assn., Am. Osler Soc., Am. Coll. Epidemiology, Nat. Acad. Sci. (com. on nutrition in med. edn. 1983-85, com. on dietary guidelines implementation 1988-90). Research on genetics, epidemiology, pathology and diagnostic features of cerebral degenerative diseases, population dynamics, pathology and epidemiology of cerebral vascular disease and organic dementia. Home: 26 Elm St Rehoboth MA 02769-2304 Office: Brown U Office Med Affairs Providence RI 02912

ARONSON, VIRGINIA L., lawyer; b. Bremerton, Wash., June 4, 1947. BA, U. Chgo., 1969, MA, 1973, JD, 1975. Bar: Ill. 1975. Ptnr. Sidley & Austin, Chgo.; staff mem. Univ. of Chgo. Law Review, 1974-75. Contbr. articles to profl. jours. Mem. Am. Coll. Real Estate Lawyers, Chgo. Mortgage Atty.'s Assn., Chgo. Fin. Exchange, Legal Club Chgo (dir. Chgo. ctrl. area com.). Office: Sidley & Austin 1 First Natl Plz Chicago IL 60603-2003*

ARONSTAM, NEIL LEE, media marketing firm executive; b. N.Y.C., Jan. 25, 1945; s. H.J. and Annette (Moldow) A.; m. Vicki F. Elgisser, June 9, 1974; children: Eve Rachel, Pamela Joy. AB in Journalism, U. Ga., 1965. Media staff asst. Benton & Bowles, N.Y.C., 1965; sr. media buyer Ted Bates, N.Y.C., 1966; dir. mktg. Allied Foods, Atlanta, 1967-68; pres. Ind. Media Services, N.Y.C., 1969—; mem. journalism adv. bd. Henry W. Grady Coll. of Journalism and Mass Communication, U. Ga., 1988-94; mem. George Foster Peabody Awards Nat. Adv. Bd., 1994—, chmn. 1998—. Recipient AIDE to Advt. award, 1997. Mem. Nat. Acad. TV Arts & Scis., Internat. Radio & TV Soc., Sigma Delta Chi. Office: Ind Media Svcs Inc 880 3rd Ave New York NY 10022-4730

ARONSTEIN, JACQUELINE BLUESTONE, psychoanalyst, counselor, educator; b. Bklyn., Aug. 29, 1939; d. Michael J. and Reneé (Schillinger) Bluestone; m. Richard L. Aronstein; children: Steven, Jonathan. BA, Adelphi U., 1959; MS, Yeshiva U., 1960; PsyD, Heed U., 1980. Cert. psychoanalyst, hypnotherapist, N.Y.; cert. validator and custody expert, N.Y. Counselor, psychologist N.Y.C. Bd. Edn., 1959-90; dir. Northshore Midtown Consultation Ctr., N.Y.C., 1971—; psychology instr. SUNY Empire State Coll., 1996—; guest cons. NBC News, Good Day N.Y., Channel 12 News, News Talk TV, 1993-96; workshop presenter. Mem. Nat. Assn. for the Advancement of Psychoanalysis (v.p.), Nat. Guild Hypnotists, Am. Counseling Assn., L.I. Ctr. for Bus. and Profl. Women (bd. dirs.). Democrat. Jewish. Home and Office: 159 Soundview Dr Port Washington NY 11050-1748 Office: Midtown Consultation 488 7th Ave New York NY 10018-6806

ARONSTEIN, MARTIN JOSEPH, lawyer, educator; b. N.Y.C., Jan. 25, 1925; s. William and Mollie (Mintz) A.; m. Sally K. Rosenau, Sept. 18, 1948; children: Katherine Aronstein Porter, David M., James K. BE, Yale U., 1944; MBA, Harvard U., 1948; LLB, U. Pa., 1965. Bar: Pa. 1965. Bus. exec. Phila., 1948-65; assoc. firm Obermayer, Rebmann, Maxwell & Hippel, Phila., 1965-67; partner Obermayer, Rebmann, Maxwell & Hippel, 1968-69; assoc. prof. law U. Pa., 1969-72, prof., 1972-78; counsel firm Ballard, Spahr, Andrews & Ingersoll, Phila., 1978-80; partner Ballard, Spahr, Andrews & Ingersoll, 1980-81; prof. law U. Pa., 1981-86, prof. emeritus, 1986—; of counsel firm Morgan, Lewis & Bockius, Phila., 1986-95. Contbr. articles to law revs.; mem. Permanent Editorial Bd. Uniform Comml. Code, 1978-80, counsel, 1980-87, counsel emeritus, 1987—. Served with USN, 1943-46. Mem. Am. Law Inst., ABA (reporter com. on stock certs. 1973-77, chmn. subcom. on investment securities 1982-84), Phila. Bar Assn., Order of Coif, Sigma Xi, Tau Beta Pi. Home: 1820 Rittenhouse Sq Philadelphia PA 19103-5832 Office: 1701 Market St Philadelphia PA 19103

ARORA, JASBIR SINGH, engineering educator; b. Tarn-Taran, India, Apr. 13, 1943; came to U.S., 1965; naturalized 1977; m. Rita Paul, June 21, 1972. BS in Engring. with honors, Punjab U., India, 1964; MS, Kans. State U., 1967; PhD, U. Iowa, 1971. Asst. prof. G.N. Engring Coll., Ludhiana, India, 1964-65; asst. prof. U. Iowa, Iowa City, 1972-76, assoc. prof., 1976-81, prof. engring., 1981—, dir. optimal design lab., 1984—. Author: Introduction to Optimum Design, 1989; co-author: Applied Optimal Design, 1979; contbr. articles to profl. jours. Mem. AIAA, ASME, ASCE. Home: 1262 Oakes Dr Iowa City IA 52245-5730 Office: U Iowa # 2130 SC Iowa City IA 52242

AROUH, JEFFREY ALAN, lawyer; b. N.Y.C., May 2, 1945; s. Isaac E. and Jean J. (Halfon) A.; m. Karen Ann Wieder, Feb. 1, 1969; children: Russell Andrew, Ilonne A. BA, U. Mich., 1966; JD cum laude, NYU, 1969. Bar: N.Y. 1970; sr. cert. relocation profl. Assoc., Gilbert, Segall and Young, N.Y.C., 1969-74, ptnr., 1975—; speaker in field. Editor: NYU Law Rev., 1969; contbr. articles to legal publs. Recipient Founders Day award NYU. Mem. ABA, N.Y. State Bar Assn., Assn. of Bar of City of N.Y., Employee Relocation Coun. (law and govt. rels. com.), Order of Coif, Hampshire Country Club, Tennis Club of Palm Beach. Home: 3 Ridgeway Rd Larchmont NY 10538-1123 Office: 430 Park Ave New York NY 10022-3505

ARP, DANIEL JAMES, biochemistry educator; b. Henderson, Nebr., Mar. 14, 1954; s. Jack Jr. and Delores Lucille (Brown) A.; m. Wanda Hofmann, Aug. 10, 1974; children: Sarah, James. BS in Chemistry with distinction, U. Nebr., 1976; PhD in Biochemistry and Bacteriology, U. Wis., Madison, 1980. NATO postdoctoral fellow U. Erlangen, West Germany, 1980-82; from asst. prof. to assoc. prof. dept. biochemistry U. Calif., Riverside, 1982-89; assoc. prof., dir. Lab. for Nitrogen Fixation Rsch., Dept. Botany and Plant Pathology Oreg. State U., Corvallis, 1990-92, prof., dir. Lab. for Nitrogen Fixation Rsch., Dept. Botany and Plant Pathology, 1992—, dir. molecular biology program, 1993—; adminstr. dept. botany and plant pathology Oreg. State U., affiliate mem. dept. biochemistry and biophysics, mem. molecular and cellular biology grad. program, grant panel mem. various agys. and programs including Dept. of Energy, 1988, USDA, 1989, 91, EPA, 1994, NIH, 1996, 97; numerous presentations and seminars. Contbr. numerous chpts. to books, articles to profl. jours. including Applied Environ., Microbiology, Jour. Bacteriology, Biochemistry, Jour. Biol. Chemistry. Vol. demonstrator of sci. concepts to elem. schs., youth groups; co-founder Partnership for Sci. Edn. Com. Grantee NSF, 1983-85, 85-88, 86-87, Dept. Energy, 1984-86, 86-88, 88-91, 91-94, 94-97, 97—, USDA, 1984-86, 88-90, 90-94, 91-94, 94-96, EPA, 1990-93, 94-97, NIH, 1997—; Regent's scholar U. Nebr., 1972; Evelyn Steenbock fellow, 1977, Wharton fellow, 1979. Mem. AAAS, Am. Soc. for Microbiology, Am. Chem. Soc., Am. Soc. for Biochemistry and Molecular Biology, Phi Beta Kappa, Am. Acad. Microbiologists. Achievements include research in biochemistry and physiology of the microbial N cycle, biological N2 fixation, H2-utilizing microorganisms, biochemistry, physiology and molecular biology of nitrification, enzymology of gas-utilizing metalloenzymes; enzyme inhibitors as probes of enzyme mechanism and physiological function; bioremediation. Home: 1999 NW Lantana Dr Corvallis OR 97330-1016 Office: Oreg State U Dept Botany and Plant Path 2082 Cordley Hall Corvallis OR 97331-8530

ARP, ELIZABETH KENCH, psychotherapist, social worker; b. Morrisville, Pa., Jan. 17, 1913; d. John Edward and Anna Elizabeth (Goodnoe) Kench; m. William F. Arp, Aug. 10, 1945; children: Mary E. Hardy, Edward, Gerald K. BA in Psychology, Temple U., 1936; MSW, U. Denver, 1965. Lic. clin. social worker; cert. psychotherapist. Liason City and County Denver, Colo. State Hosp.; psychiatric and med. social worker Dept. Social Svcs., Denver; clin. social worker Denver Gen. Hosp.; pvt. practice Golden, Colo.; clin. psychotherapist Colo. Trauma Ctr., P.C., Denver. Mem. NASW. Home: 90 Corona St Denver CO 80218-3817 Office: Colo Trauma Ctr PC Ste 875 3773 Cherry Creek North Dr Denver CO 80209-3826

ARPINO, GERALD PETER, performing company executive; b. Staten Island, N.Y., Jan. 14, 1928; s. Luigi and Anna (Santanastasio) A. Student, Wagner Coll., PhD (hon.), 1980; student ballet under Mary Ann Wells, student modern dance under May O'Donnell and Gertrude Shurr. Dancer Ballet Russe, 1951-52; co-founder Joffrey Ballet, 1956, dancer, to 1962; former assoc. artistic dir., now artistic dir. Joffrey Ballet, Chgo., resident choreographer, until 1990; with faculty Joffrey Ballet Sch. N.Y.C., from 1953, now artistic dir., assoc. dir., to 1988, prin. choreographer, to 1988; bd. dirs. Dance Notation Bur., Dancers in Transition; mem. adv. coun. to dept. dance Calif. State U., Long Beach, also mem. Disting. Artists Forum. Choreographer ballets including Incubus, 1962, Viva Vivaldi!, 1965, Olympics, Nightwings, both 1966, Cello Concerto, Arcs and Angels, Elegy, all 1967, Secret Places, The Clowns, Fanfarita, A Light Fantastic, 1968, Animus, The Poppet, 1969, Confetti, Solarwind, Trinity, all 1970, Reflections, Valentine, Kettentanz, all 1971, Chabriesque, Sacred Grove on Mount Talmalpais, both 1972, Jackpot, 1973, The Relativity of Icarus, 1974, Drums, Dreams on Banjos, 1975, Orpheus Times Light 2, 1976, Touch Me, 1977, Choura, L'Air d 'Esprit, Suite Saint-Saens, all 1978, Epode, 1979, Celebration, 1980, Ropes, Partita for Four, Sea Shadow, Diverdissement, 1980, Light Rain, 1981, Round of Angels, 1982, Italian Suite, Quarter-Tones, 1983, Jamboree (commd. by City of San Antonio). Adv. Sportsmedicine Edn. & Rsch. Found., L.A.; mem. adv. com. N.Y. Internat. Festival of the Arts; mem. nat. adv. coun. ITI/USA Internat. Ballet Competition; mem. hon. com. The Yard Benefit-Vineyard Celebration, 1989; mng. dir., bd. dirs. Found. for Joffrey Ballet, Inc. Served with USCG, 1945-48. Recipient Dancemagazine award, 1974, Bravo award San Antonio Performing Arts Assn., 1984, Disting. Achievement award Nat. Orgn. Italian-Am. Women, 1987, Tiffany award Internat. Soc. Performing Arts Adminstrs., 1989, Outstanding Artistic Achievement award Staten Island Coun. on Arts, 1990, Ammy award Am. Express Corp. Office: Joffrey Ballet Chgo 70 E Lake St Fl 1300 Chicago IL 60601-5913*

ARP LOTTER, DONNA, investor, venture capitalist; b. Henrietta, Tex., Dec. 17, 1950; d. T.S. Jr. and Coy Lee (Howard) Grimsley; m. Bruce D. Lotter, Feb. 18, 1984; children: Brandon, Collin. BS, Midwestern State U., 1975, M in Counseling, 1979. Sales rep. Burroughs-Wellcome Co., Fort Worth, Tex., 1978-79; sales mgr. Procter & Gamble Co., Dallas, 1979-84; pres. Arp-Lotter Investments, Colleyville, Tex., 1984—; mayor City of Colleyville, Tex., 1999—; prin. DBL Investments, Inc.; sec., officer KCB Corp., Inc.; bd. dirs. Landmark Bank. Chmn., trustee Baylor Hosp., Grapevine, Tex., 1998; bd. dirs. Am. Cancer Soc., North Tex. Commn., Am. Heart Assn.; bd. govs. N.E. Arts Coun.; city councilperson, City of Colleyville, 1996-98, mayor (pro tem.). 1997-98. Named Alumnus of Yr., Midwestern State U., 1995, Hardin scholar, 1975; recipient Legacy of Women award Am. Heart Assn., 1995, Vol. of Yr. award, Colleyville, 1996; voted Most Influential Female of Tarrant County, Tex., 1997, 98, 99. Mem. Bus. Profl. Womens Club, Nat. Assn. Women Bus. Owners, Colleyville C. of C. (pres. 1995). Republican. Methodist.

ARPS, DAVID FOSTER, electronics engineer; b. Napoleon, Ohio, July 28, 1948; s. Fred B. and Melba Lavern (Harrison) A.; m. Vickie Lee Westrick, Mar. 19, 1982; children: Derek, Elizabeth. BS in Astronomy, Case Inst. Tech., 1970; MAT in Physics, Bowling Green State U., 1975; MS in Atmospheric Physics, U. Nev., Reno, 1977. Cert. secondary edn. and community coll. tchr. Astronomy instr. U. Toledo, Ohio, 1970; physics tchr. Napoleon (Ohio) High Sch., 1970-74; teaching asst. Bowling Green (Ohio) State U., 1974-75; rsch. fellow Desert Rsch. Inst., Reno, 1975-78; mech. engr., physicist Naval Air Warfare Ctr., Aircraft Div., Indpls., 1978-84, elec. engr., failure analyst, 1984-96; elec. engr. component specification Def. Supply Ctr., Columbus, Ohio, 1996—; astronomical rschr. Ritter Obs., U. Toledo, Ohio, 1970; solar radiation rschr. Desert Rsch. Inst., Reno, 1975-78. Mem. PTA, Mt. Comfort (Ind.) Elem., 1989-95; asst. coach Mt. Comfort (Ind.) Elem. Sports, 1992-95; coach Youth Softball, Pickerington, Ohio, 1998—. Recipient Rsch. fellowships Desert Rsch. Inst., Reno, 1975-78. Mem. Sigma Pi Sigma. Methodist. Achievements include numerous technical reports on component failure analysis and x-ray microanalysis; defense specification preparing activity for fiber optic, electron tube, and microwave components. Home: 13314 Princeton Ln Pickerington OH 43147-8324 Office: Defense Supply Ctr 3990 E Broad St Columbus OH 43216-5000

ARPS, JOYCE ANN, librarian; b. Gilmer, Tex., May 28, 1950; d. Leon and Christene (Walker) Jones; m. Carl Wayne Arps, Nov. 11, 1975; children: Shana, Shantee', Ke'Amber, Ke'Andria. BS, Tex. Coll., 1972; MS, East Tex. State U., 1984. Cert. tchr., Tex. Clk. Tex. Coll., Tyler, 1972-74, tech. svc. asst., 1974-79, reference libr., circulation libr., 1979—. Mem. Zeta Pi Beta. Democrat. Baptist. Avocations: gardening, reading, crossword puzzles. Office: Tex Coll 2404 N Grand Ave Tyler TX 75702-1962

ARQUETTE, PATRICIA, actress; b. Apr. 8, 1968; d. Lewis and Mardi A.; m. Nicolas Cage, 1995. Actress: (films) A Nightmare on Elm Street 3: Dream Warriors, 1987, Far North, 1988, The Indian Runner, 1991, Prayer of the Rollerboys, 1991, Ethan Frome, 1993, Trouble Bound, 1993, Inside Monkey Zetterland, 1993, True Romance, 1993, Holy Matrimony, 1994, Ed Wood, 1994, Infinity, 1995, Flirting with Disaster, 1996, Los Highway, 1996, Nightwatch, 1998, In the Boom Boom Room, 1999, Goodbye Lover, 1999, Stigmata, 1999, Bringing Out the Dead, 1999, (TV movies) Daddy, 1987, Dillinger, 1991, Wildflower, 1991, Betrayed by Love, 1994, Lost Highway, 1996, Nightwatch, 1996, Goodbye Lover, 1996, Beyond Rangoon, 1995, The Secret Agent, 1996, Flirting with Disaster, 1996, Toby's Story, 1998, The Hi-Lo Country, 1998. Office: UTA 9560 Wilshire Blvd Fl 5 Beverly Hills CA 90212-2401*

ARQUETTE, ROSANNA, actress; b. N.Y.C., Aug. 10, 1959; d. Lewis and Mardi A.; m. John Sidel, Dec. 1993. Actress: (films) S.O.B., 1981, Baby it's You, 1983, Desperately Seeking Susan, 1985, After Hours, 1985, Silverado, 1985, The Aviator, 1985, 8 Million Ways To Die, 1986, Nobody's Fool, 1986, The Big Blue, 1988, New York Stories, 1989, The Linguini Incident, 1992, Fathers and Sons, 1992, Nowhere to Run, 1993, Pulp Fiction, 1994, Search and Destroy, 1995, Crash, 1996, Liar, 1997, Gone Fishin', 1997, Buffalo '66, 1997, Cite de la peur: une comedie familiale, 1994, White Lies, 1996, Hell's Kitchen, 1997, Do Me a Favor, 1997, Palmer's Pick Up, 1998, I'm Losing You, 1998, Homeslice, 1998, Floating Away, 1998, Hope Floats, 1998, Fait Accompli, 1998, Sugar Town, 1999, Palmer's Pick Up, 1999; actress (TV mini-series) The 60's; TV guest appearances include Eight Is Enough, 1977, Homicide: Life on the Street, 1993; TV appearances include Having Babies II, 1977, Zuma Beach, 1978, Dark Secret of Harvest Home, 1978, The Ordeal of Patty Hearst, 1979, A Long Way Home, 1981, The Wall, 1982, Johnny Belinda, 1982, Executioner's Song, 1982, The Parade, 1984, Survival Guide, 1985, Promised a Miracle, 1988, Separation, 1990, Sweet Revenge, 1990, Son of the Morning Star, 1991, In the Deep Woods, 1992, The Wrong Man, 1993, Nowhere to Hide, 1994, I Know What You Did, 1998. Office: 8033 W Sunset Blvd # 16 Los Angeles CA 90046-2427*

ARQUIT, KEVIN JAMES, lawyer; b. Ithaca, N.Y., Sept. 11, 1954; s. Gordon James and Nora (Harris) A. BA cum laude, St. Lawrence U., 1975; JD cum laude, Cornell U., 1978. Bar: Ohio 1978, N.Y. 1980, U.S. Dist. Ct. (so. and ea. dists.) N.Y. 1980, U.S. Dist. Ct. (we. dist.) N.Y. 1983, U.S. Dist. Ct. (no. dist.) Calif. 1983, U.S. Ct. Appeals (3d cir.) 1983,, U.S. Dist. Ct. (no. dist.) N.Y. 1985, U.S. Ct. Appeals(2d cir.) 1985, U.S. Supreme Ct. 1989. Assoc. Arter & Hadden, Cleve., 1978, Fish & Neave, N.Y.C., 1978-83, Harris, Beach & Wilcox, Rochester, N.Y., 1983-86; atty. advisor to chmn. FTC, Washington, 1986-87, chief staff, 1987-88, gen. counsel, 1988-89; dir. Bur. Competition, Washington, 1989-92; ptnr., head Rogers & Wells Antitrust Practice Group, N.Y.C., 1992—. Republican. Roman Catholic. Office: Rogers & Wells 200 Park Ave Fl 8E New York NY 10166-0800

ARRAF, SHREEN, school system administrator; b. Acre, Israel, Nov. 19, 1950; came to U.S., 1985; d. Eli and Laura Tabrizi; m. Rakad Arraf, Aug. 18, 1974. BA, U. Haifa, Israel, U. Haifa; MEd, Wayne State U., PhD. Cert. sch. adminstr., Mich. Tchr., 1970-85; field experience supr. U. Haifa, 1983-85; asst. prin. Min. Edn., Israel, 1974-85; rsch./tchg. asst. Wayne State U., Detroit, 1987-90; edn. analyst Access, Dearborn, Mich., 1990-93; adminstr. bilingual and comp. edn. Dearborn Pub. Schs., 1993-97, adminstr. planning and rsch., 1997—; ednl. cons. Mich. Dept. Edn., Lansing; mem. adv. bd. Grolier's Pub., Danbury, Conn. V.p. adv. bd. YWCA, Inkster, Mich., vol., Detroit, 1995—, v.p. 1995-97; vol. Access, Dearborn, 1993—. Recipient Women of Achievement award YWCA, 1995, Cmty. Appreciation award Cmty. Coalition, 1997. Mem. ASCD, AAUW, Mich. Assn. Bilingual Edn. (pres. 1997). Avocations: reading, writing, singing, violin, guitar. E-mail: arrafs@db.k12.mi.us. Home: 785 Laguna Dr Wolverine Lake MI 48390

ARRASTIA, JAVIER ARMANDO, administrative law judge; b. Havana, Cuba, Sept. 1, 1948; s. Cecilio and Palmira (Marrero) A.; m. Ruth Ennes Littrell, May 26, 1979. BA, Swarthmore (Pa.) Coll., 1970; postgrad., Princeton U., 1970-72; JD, Temple U., Phila., 1979. Law clk. U.S. Ct. Appeals (3d cir.), Phila., 1979-80; asst. regional counsel U.S. HHS, Phila., 1980-95; U.S. adminstrv. law judge Office Hearings and Appeals Social Security Adminstrn., Newark, 1995-98, Phila., 1998—. Office: Office Hearings and Appeals Social Security Adminstrn 1601 Market St Fl 9 Philadelphia PA 19103-2311

ARRATHOON, LEIGH ADELAIDE, medievalist, editor, writer; b. N.Y.C., Nov. 30, 1942; d. Henry and Peggy Adelaide (Weed) A.; m. Raymond Arrathoon, June 10, 1967. Cours de vacances, U. de Genève, L'Université de Lilla à Boulogne sur Mer, Lausanne, 1961-63; AB in French and Spanish, Hunter Coll., 1963; MA in French, Stanford U., 1966, MA in Spanish, 1968; MA in Medieval French Lit., Princeton U., 1975, PhD in Medieval French Lit., 1975. Mem. UN Secretariat, N.Y.C., 1963-64; tchg. asst. Stanford U., 1964-66; tchr. Spanish and French Convent of Sacred Heart, Menlo Park, Calif., 1966-67; asst. prof. Spanish Rider Coll., Trenton, N.J., 1970-71; pub. editor-in-chief Solaris Press, Troy, Idaho, 1975-80, Rochester, Mich., 1980-86; pres. Solaris Press II, 1986—; pres., advt./mktg. A.D. Images, Inc., 1986-96; pres. Paint Creek Press, 1996—; v.p. John J. Davio, Rochester, Mich., 1996—; enrichment tchr. French and creative writing Rochester Pub. Schs., 1996—; facilitator French and ESL PALS Internat., 1997—; adj. prof. French and Spanish Oakland C.C., Auburn Hills, Mich., 1998—. Author: Who Changed the World: The Henry Ford Story, 1997, The First Birdmen: The Wright Brothers, 1997, Great Places: Jody's Michigan Adventures, Vol. I Frankenmuth, Vol. II Holland, Mich., Vol. III Mackinac Island, 1997, reprinted 1999, Michigan's Upper Penninsula, Vol. IV, Detroit, Vol. V, Northwest Michigan, Vol. VI, Greenfield Village, Vol. VII, 1999, Great People: Men & Women Who Changed the World, 1999; contbg. editor: The Craft of Fiction: Essays in Medieval Poetics, 1984; editor, translator The Lady of Vergi, 1984; contbg. editor: Chauncer and the Craft of Fiction, 1986, numerous fictional short stories, articles to South Hill Gazette (weekly periodical), 1985-90; contbr. articles to profl. jours. Scholar Centre d'Art Dramatique, 1957. Mem. MLA, Medieval Acad. Am., Courtly Lit. Soc., Sigma Delta Pi, Alpha Gamma Delta. Office: PO Box 80547 Rochester MI 48308-0547

ARREOLA, JOHN BRADLEY, diversified financial service company executive, financial planner; b. San Fernando, La Union, Philippines, Mar. 20, 1935; came to U.S., 1950; naturalized, 1960; s. Juanito Antonio and Catalina (Bacalzo) A.; m. Judith Anne Hughes, June 26, 1965; children: Bradley, Christopher. Student, Hartnell Coll., Salinas, Calif., 1950-52; BA, San Jose State Coll., 1955. Cert. real estate appraiser; cert. internat. financier; CFP. Statistician O'Connor Hosp., San Jose, Calif., 1955-60; tax cons. Arreola-Comita & Assocs., San Jose, 1960-63; cost acct. Granger & Assocs., Palo Alto, Calif., 1963-64; mgr. cost acctg. Gen. Micro-Electronics, Santa Clara, Calif., 1964-65; chief acct. Kaiser Engrs., Calif. and Venezuela, 1965-67; comptr. Aluminio del Caroni, S.A. (Reynolds Alumnium subs.), Caracas, Venezuela, 1967-78; bus. cons. Venezuela and U.S., 1978-83; pres. Arreola, Hughes & Co. Inc., Sarasota, Fla., 1983—; CEO, pres. MAP Fin. Group of Cos., Inc., Sarasota, 1985-92; pres. J&J Enterprises, Sarasota, 1992—. Mem. Internat. Assn. for Fin. Planning (pres. Sarasota chpt. 1988-89), Inst. Cert. Fin. Planners, Tournament Players Club of PGA at Prestancia, Sarasota Ski Club. Republican. Roman Catholic. Avocations: golf, snow skiing, photography, football, baseball, gardening. Home: 3900 Torrey Pines Blvd Sarasota FL 34238-2833

ARRIETA, MARCIA, poet, editor, publishing executive, educator; b. Santa Monica, Calif., Aug. 24, 1952; d. Cecil and Dora Teresa (Ramos) A.; m. Kevin Timothy Joy, June 10, 1978; children: Matthew Kevin, Brendan Yeats, Dylan James. BA, UCLA, 1975; MFA, Vt. Coll., 1999. Lic. profl. clear tchg. credential, Calif. Tchr. English L.A. Unified Sch. Dist., 1985—; editor, publ. Indefinite Space, Pasadena, Calif., 1992—; participant The Frost Place, Franconia, N.H., 1993; leader poetry workship, tchr. Pasadena (Calif.) Citywide Arts Program, 1991-92. Contbr. poems to The Midwest Quarterly, Wind, Bitterroot, Minotaur, Small Pond, Abbey, Perceptions, Pacific Rev., The? WHY? Project, Blue Unicorn, Sierra Nevada Coll. Rev., Psychopoetica, Riverrun, Abraxas, Atticus Rev., Tight, Camellia, West/Word, Bogg, Elf, Big Scream, Generator, So To Speak, Yefief, Juxta, Lost and Found Times, Atelier, Plainsongs, Hyphen, Tin Wreath, Pacific Coast Journal, NRG, Gestalten, others. Grantee Literary Arts Pasadena City Arts Commn., 1991; recipient Literary Arts award Pasadena Arts Coun., 1993. Mem. Am. Fedn. Tchrs., Assoc. Writing Program. Avocations: travel, gardening, hiking, art. Office: Indefinite Space PO Box 40101 Pasadena CA 91114-7101

ARRILLAGA, MARIA, foreign language educator; b. Mayagüez, P.R.; m. Joseph M. Gutiérrez; 1 child, Maria Ana McDonough. BS, St. Louis U., 1961; MA, NYU, 1966; postgrad., U. Dijon, France, 1976; PhD magna cum laude, U. P.R., 1987. Typist, translator, interpreter St. Luke's Hosp., 1962-63; Spanish tchr. Yeshiva Rabbi Samson Raphael Hirsch, N.Y.C., 1965-66, O. Henry Sch., N.Y.C., 1966-67; recreational dir. I Spy Health Program Beth Israel Hosp., N.Y.C., 1967-68; Spanish instr. SEEK program CUNY, N.Y.C., 1968-69; substitute tchr. Onteora H.S., Woodstock, N.Y., 1969-70; instr. art and music of P.R. N.Y.C. Tech. Coll., Bklyn., 1970-71; writer Dept. Edn. Press, Hato Rey, P.R., 1971-73; Spanish prof. Coll. Gen. Studies U. P.R., Río Piedras, 1973—; vis. prof. York Coll., CUNY, Queens, 1993-94. Author: (poetry) Life in Time, 1974, New York in the Sixties, 1976, Cascade of Sun, 1977, Poems 747, 1977, Freshness, 1981, (novel) Mañana Valentina, 1995; works included in anthologies; author of poetry, short stories, essays and articles. Recipient First prize Inst. Puerto Rican Lit., 1981, first prize Inst. Bus. Adminstrn., P.R. Jr. Coll., Mayagüez, 1982, 84, Luis Lloréns Torres award Puerto Rican Acad. of the Spanish Lang., 19887, medal of honor Josefina Romo Arregui Meml. Found. for Contbn. to Lit., N.Y., 1990, others. Home: Apt 8E 140 Charles St New York NY 10014 Office: U PR Sta PO Box 21910 Rio Piedras PR 00931

ARRINGTON, BARBARA, public health educator; b. Honolulu, Feb. 7, 1948; d. Wade Hampton Arrington III and Marie E. (Kaleda) Arrington Bailey. BS, Columbia U., 1970; MS in Pub. Health, U. Mo., 1976; PhD, St. Louis U., 1985. Planning asst./extern State Office Comprehensive Health Planning, Jefferson City, Mo.; asst. DON Mid-Mo. Mental Health Ctr., Columbia; instr. nursing Luth. Med. Ctr., St. Louis; home care coord. N.Y. Hosp.-Cornell Med. Ctr., N.Y.C.; staff pub. health nurse Vis. Nurse Svc. N.Y., N.Y.C.; sr. planner, planning assoc. Greater St. Louis Health Systems Agy., 1976-79; with sch. pub. health, health scis. ctr. St. Louis U., 1979—, asst. prof. community health, 1981—, assoc. prof. health adminstrn., 1994—, chair health adminstrn., 1993-94, assoc. dean, 1997—; chair planning and mktg. com. People's Clinic; cons. Region VII Ctr. Health Planning, Columbia, 1977-78, Nat. Assn. Community Health Ctrs., Washington, 1978-79; mem. planning and devel. com. St. Mary's Hosp. East St. Louis, 1983-90, chair, 1987-90, mem. exec. com., 1984—, bd. dirs.; cons. strategic planning and mktg. Mercy Health Svcs., Farmington Hills, Mich., 1986-88; chair ad hoc com. sabbatical leave Sisters Mercy Health System, St. Louis, 1986; mem. exec. strategic planning com. of corp. bd. Ancilla Systems, Inc., 1988, 91-93; mem. exec. com. St. Joseph's Hosp., Alton, Ill., 1988-89; strategic design and visioning cons. and facilitator Soc. Bioethics Consultation, 1989; mem. strategic learning orgn. design and facilitation regional cmty. Detroit Sisters Mercy Ams., 1990-92; cons. leadership devel. task force Franciscan Health System, Aston, Pa., 1991-92, mem. leadership adv. coun., 1993—, retained cons. and facilitator area common interests operational mgmt. group, 1993-94; mem. univ. support health care task force Mo. Ho. Reps., 1992; course dir. Inst. Healthcare Improvement, Boston, 1992-94, mem. governance curriculum devel., 1992-94, mem. strategy planning group, 1993; cons., facilitator master affiliation agreement SSM Health Care System/health scis. ctr. St. Louis U., 1994—; strategy cons. grad. med. edn. com., sch. medicine St. Louis U., 1994—; mem. needs assessment/focus group facilitation St. Jane's Cmty. Ctr., St. Louis, 1994; cons. governance facilitation and leadership devel. Ea. Mercy Health System, Radnor, Pa., 1994—; presenter in field. Author and editor: (with others) The Evolution of Strategy: Case Studies in Health Administration, Vol. VIII, 1991; author: (with others) Strategic Management of Human Resources in Health Services Organizations, 1993; reviewer Health Progress, 1980—, Hosp. and Health Svcs. Adminstrn., 1984—, Health Svcs. Rsch., 1997—; contbr. articles to profl. jours. Named Leader Honoree, St. Louis YWCA, 1994; grantee Agy. Health Care Policy and Rsch., 1984, Nat. Inst. Alcohol Abuse and Alcoholism/Nat. Inst. Drug Abuse, 1990-93, Beaumont Faculty Devel. Fund, 1992, Sisters Mercy Ams., 1993; fellow Agy. Health Care Policy and Rsch., 1984. Fellow Am. Coll. Healthcare Execs.; mem. Cath. Health Assn. U.S. (cons. and facilitator divsn. theology, mission and ethics 1988-90, mem. task force tax exemption, 1991-93, mem. leadership devel. focus group 1991, 93, mem. leadership devel. steering com. 1993-94), Assn. Univ. Programs Health Adminstrn. (mem. ad hoc com. curriculum health planning 1980-83, mem. com. minority group affairs 1980-82, mem. strategic planning and mktg. faculty forum 1984—, chair 1988-89, mem. governance task force 1987-91, mem. program dirs. group 1993-94, mem. continuous improvement interest group 1994—, mem. govtl. affairs com. 1994—), Greater St. Louis Assn. Women Health Adminstrn. (co-founder Am. Coll. Healthcare Execs.-Affiliated Women's Network 1981-85, various offices), Sigma Theta Tau. Office: St Louis U Health Scis Ctr Sch Pub Health 3663 Lindell Blvd Saint Louis MO 63108-3342

ARRINGTON, CAROLYN RUTH, education consultant; b. May 20, 1942; d. Robert Ray and Grace Dotson; m. Wayne Vernon Arrington; children: Kevin Ray, Kemp Gray, Korey shay, Wayne, Kimberly. AA, Ohio Valley Coll., 1962; BA, Fairmont State Coll., 1964; MA, W.Va. U., 1966, EdD, 1994. Cert. pub. sch. adminstr., 1993. Tchr. Greenbrier Bd. Edn., Lewisburg, W.Va., 1964-68; supr. Mason County Bd. Edn., Point Pleasant, W.Va., 1968-70; media specialist Kanawha County Bd. Edn., Charleston, W.Va., 1970-71; asst. dir., dir., asst. divsn. chief W.Va. Dept. Edn., Charleston, 1971-89, asst. state supt. schs., 1989-98; v.p. Arrington Assocs., Inc., 1998—; edn. and bus. cons. in field. Author numerous poems and children's books; developer workshop materials. Bd. dirs. YWCA, Charleston, 1988-91. Recipient medal of merit Edn. Ohio Valley Coll.; SEA fellow U.S. Dept. Edn., 1984. Mem. Assn. Ednl. Comm. and Tech. (pres. 1979-80, Edgar Dale award 1975, Spl. Svc. award 1982), Wva. Ednl. Media Assn. (pres. 1975-76). E-mail: Warrington@earthlink.net. Office: Arrington Assocs Inc PO Box 3912 Charleston WV 25339-3912

ARRINGTON, CHARLES HAMMOND, JR., retired chemical company executive; b. Rocky Mount, N.C., Dec. 23, 1920; s. Charles Hammond and Annie (Barrett) A.; m. Elsie Jane Woodlief, Aug. 20, 1941; children: Charles Hammond III, Roger W. B.S., Duke U., 1941; Ph.D., Calif. Inst. Tech., 1949. Research chemist E.I. DuPont De Nemours & Co. Inc., Wilmington, Del., 1949-52, research supr., 1952-57, assoc. research dir., 1957-67, dir. research, 1967-74, asst. gen. dir. research and devel., 1974-78, gen. dir. research and devel., 1978-84; ret. E.I. DuPont De Nemours & Co. Inc. Served to lt. USNR, 1943-46. Mem. AAAS, Am. Chem. Soc., Am. Phys. Soc., Wilmington Country Club, DuPont Country Club, Sigma Xi. Episcopalian. Home: 711 Greenwood Rd Wilmington DE 19807-2935

ARRINGTON, JOHN LESLIE, JR., lawyer; b. Pawhuska, Okla., Oct. 15, 1931; s. John Leslie and Grace Louise (Moore) A.; m. Elizabeth Anne Waddington, 1956 (div.); children: Elizabeth Anne, John Leslie III, Winifred L., Katherine M.; m. Linda Vance, 1972. Grad., Lawrenceville Sch., 1949; AB, Princeton U., 1953; JD, Harvard U., 1956, LLM, 1957. Bar: Okla. 1956, U.S. Supreme Ct. 1960. Assoc. Arrington, Kihle, Gaberino & Dunn and predecessor firms, Tulsa, 1957-61, ptnr., 1961-93, chmn., CEO, 1994-96; gen. counsel ONEOK, Inc., 1997-98; of counsel Gable & Gotwals, Tulsa, 1998—; chmn. bd. dirs. Woodland Bank of Tulsa, 1979-94. Prin. draftsman Okla. Supreme Ct. rules governing disciplinary proceedings, 1980-81; bd. dirs. Tulsa County Legal Aid Soc., 1965-70, pres. 1967-70; bd. dirs. Tulsa Family Mental Health Ctr., 1982-89. Named Outstanding Young Man, Tulsa Jaycees, 1963. Mem. ABA, Tulsa County Bar Assn. (Young Lawyer award 1962, pres. 1970, Pres.'s award 1984, Professionalism award 1993), Okla. Bar Assn. (mem. profl. responsiblity commn. 1977-84, vice chmn. 1983-84, Disting. svc. award 1984, Golden Gavel award 1985, Pres.'s award 1991, Masonic award for ethics 1995), So. Hills Country Club (Tulsa), Princeton Club (N.Y.C.). Republican. Episcopalian. Home: 2300 Riverside Dr Unit 3E Tulsa OK 74114-2402 Office: 100 W 5th St Ste 1000 Tulsa OK 74103-4293

ARRINGTON, RICHARD, JR., mayor; b. Livingston, Ala., Oct. 19, 1934. A.B., Miles Coll., 1955; M.S., U. Detroit, 1957; Ph.D. in Zoology, U. Okla., 1966. Asst. prof. Miles Coll., 1957-63, prof., 1966-70; exec. dir. Ala. Ctr. for Higher Edn., 1970-79; mayor City of Birmingham, Ala., 1979—; counselor Miles Coll., 1962-63, dir. summer sch., acting dean, 1966-67, dean, 1967-70. Mem. Birmingham City Council, 1971-79. Office: Office of Mayor 710 20th St N Birmingham AL 35203-2216

ARROTT, PATRICIA GRAHAM, artist, art instructor; b. Pitts., July 27, 1931; d. George Patterson and Helen (Gilleland) Graham; m. Anthony Schuyler Arrott, June 6, 1953; children: Anthony Patterson, Helen Graham, Matthew Ramsey, Elizabeth. BFA in Painting and Design, Carnegie-Mellon Univ., 1954; postgrad., Nat. Acad. Design, N.Y.C., 1985-87, Art Students League, N.Y.C., 1980-91. Cert. tchr. art, Pa. Instr. children's ceramics Handcraft House, Vancouver, B.C., Can., 1970-72; courtroom artist Vancouver, B.C., Can., 1972-73; pvt. portrait artist Vancouver, N.Y.C., 1975—; instr. Art Students League, N.Y.C., 1993-99. Group shows include Nat. Acad. Design Ann. Exhbn., 1990, 92, 94, Cork Gallery, Lincoln Ctr., N.Y.C., 1991, Pen & Brush Club, N.Y.C., 1988-98, Silver Point Etc. traveling exhbn., 1992-93; represented by Eleanor Ettinger Gallery, N.Y.C., 1997-98, 99. Recipient Helen M. Loggie Prize, 1990, and cert. of merit, 1994, Nat. Acad. Design; recipient Emily Nicholas Hatch award Pen & Brush Club, 1989-91, Elizabeth Morse Genius award, 1988, 90, 93, 95, others. Mem. Art Student's League (life; mem. bd. 1989-92, women's v.p. 1991-92), Am. Fine Arts Soc. (mem. bd. 1991-92), Mayflower Soc. (life), Kappa Kappa Gamma (life). United Presbyterian.

ARROW, KENNETH JOSEPH, economist, educator; b. N.Y.C., Aug. 23, 1921; s. Harry I. and Lillian (Greenberg) A.; m. Selma Schweitzer, Aug. 31, 1947; children: David Michael, Andrew. BS in Social Sci., CCNY, 1940; MA, Columbia U., 1941, PhD, 1951, DSc (hon.), 1973; LLD (hon.), U. Chgo., 1967, CUNY, 1972, Hebrew U. Jerusalem, 1975, U. Pa., 1976, Washington U., St. Louis, 1989; D. Social and Econ. Scis. (hon.), U. Vienna, Austria, 1971; LLD (hon.), Ben-Gurion U. of the Negev, 1992; D. Social Scis. (hon.), Yale, 1974; D (hon.), Université René Descartes, Paris, 1974, U. Aix-Marseille III, 1985, U. Cattolica del Sacro Cuore, Milan, Italy, 1994, U. Uppsala, 1995; Dr.Pol., U. Helsinki, 1976; MA (hon.), Harvard U., 1968; DLitt, Cambridge U., Eng., 1985. Rsch. assoc. Cowles Commn. for Research in Econs., 1947-49; asst. prof. econs. U. Chgo., 1948-49; acting asst. prof. econs. and stats. Stanford, 1949-50, assoc. prof., 1950-53, prof. econs., stats. and ops. rsch., 1953-68; prof. econs. Harvard, 1968-74, James Bryant Conant univ. prof., 1974-79; exec. head dept. econs. Stanford U., 1954-56, acting exec. head dept., 1962-63, Joan Kenney prof. econs. and prof. ops. rsch., 1979-91, prof. emeritus, 1991—; economist Coun. Econ. Advisers, U.S. Govt., 1962; cons. RAND Corp.; Fulbright prof. U. Siena, 1995; vis. fellow All Souls Coll., Oxford, 1996. Author: Social Choice and Individual Values, 1951, Essays in the Theory of Risk Bearing, 1971, The Limits of Organization, 1974, Collected Papers, Vols. I-VI, 1983-85; co-author: Mathematical Studies in Inventory and Production, 1958, Studies in Linear and Nonlinear Programming, 1958, Time Series Analysis of Inter-industry Demands, 1959, Public Investment, The Rate of Return and Optimal Fiscal Policy, 1971, General Competitive Analysis, 1971, Studies in Resource Allocation Processes, 1977, Social Choice and Multicriterion Decision Making, 1985. Served as capt. AUS, 1942-46. Recipient Alfred Nobel Meml. prize in econ. scis. Swedish Acad. Scis., 1972, Kempé de Feriet medal, 1998, medal U. Paris, 1998; Social Sci. Rsch. fellow, 1952; fellow Ctr. for Advanced Study in the Behavioral Scis., 1956-57, Churchill Coll., Cambridge, Eng., 1963-64, 70, 73, 86; Guggenheim fellow, 1972-73. Fellow AAAS (chmn. sect. K. 1983), Am. Acad. Arts and Scis. (v.p. 1979-81, 91-93), Econometric Soc. (v.p. 1955, pres. 1956), Am. Statis. Assn., Inst. Math. Stats., Am. Econ. Assn. (exec. com. 1967-69, pres. 1973, John Bates Clark medal 1957), Internat. Soc. Inventory Rsch. (pres. 1983-90); mem. NAS (mem. coun. 1990-93), Internat. Econs. Assn. (pres. 1983-86), Am. Philos. Soc., Inst. Mgmt. Scis. (pres. 1963, chmn. coun. 1964, Von Neumann prize 1986), Finnish Acad. Scis. (fgn. hon.), Brit. Acad. (corr.), Western Econ. Assn. (pres. 1980-81), Soc. Social Choice and Welfare (pres. 1991-93), Pontifical Acad. Social Scis. Fax: (650) 725-5700. E-mail: arrow@leland.stanford.edu.que. Office: Stanford U Dept Econs Stanford CA 94305-6072

ARROYO, RODNEY LEE, city planning and transportation executive; b. Miami, Fla., Dec. 31, 1958; s. Julian Avelino and Marilyn (Marsh) A.; m. Leslie Ponessa; children: Nicholas Julian, Anthony Eugene. BA cum laude, U. South Fla., 1980; M in city planning, Ga. Inst. Tech., 1982. Asst. dir. South Fla. Regional Planning Coun., Hollywood, Fla., 1982-86; sr. assoc. Barton Aschman Assocs., Inc., Southfield, Mich., 1986-89; v.p. Birchler Arroyo Assoc., Inc., Southfield, 1989—; founder and editor, Planning Mich. Magazine, 1988-91. Contbr. articles to profl. jours. Recipient Outstanding Planning Project award Mich. Soc. Planning Ofcls. and Mich. chpt. Am. Planning Assn., 1997, 98. Mem. Inst. Transp. Engrs. (sub. com. mem. 1986—), Am. Planning Assn. (Mich. exec. com. 1989-91, award for excellence in small town and rural planning Small Town & Rural Planning Divsn. 1998), Am. Inst. Cert. Planners. Avocations: golfing, running, geneaology, photography. Office: Birchler Arroyo Assocs Inc 20245 W 12 Mile Rd Ste 200 Southfield MI 48076-6407

ARSHAD, M. KALEEM, psychiatrist; b. Islam Garh Gujrat Dist, Punjab, Pakistan, Nov. 8, 1955; came to U.S., 1981; s. Amir and Rasool (Bibi) Bakhsh; m. Jameela Yasmeen, Nov. 26, 1982; 1 child, Nadeem Sohail. FSc, Govt. Nat. Coll., Karachi, Pakistan, 1973; MBBS, Dow Med. Coll., Karachi, 1981. Diplomate Am. Bd. Psychiatry and Neurology, Am. Bd. Forensic Medicine, Am. Bd. Geriatric, Forensic and Addiction Psychiatry. House officer psychiatry Dow Med. Coll. and Civil Hosp., 1981, Provident Hosp., Inc., Balt., 1983-85; resident in psychiatry Tex. Tech U. Health Scis. Ctr., El Paso, 1985-88; resident in internal medicine Tulane U. Med. Ctr., New Orleans, 1988-89; program dir. admission svcs. East La. State Hosp., Jackson, 1989; med. dir. Metairie (La.) Ctr. Psychotherapy, 1990-91, Meth. Psychiat. Pavillion, New Orleans, 1991—, Meth. Behavior Resources, New Orleans, 1992—; pvt. practice cons. First pres., founder Anjamane Nawjawanane Ahle Sunnat, Karachi. 1980, pres. Pakistan Muslim Student Fedn., Dow Med. Coll., 1979-80. Mem. Am. Psychiat. Assn. (resident rep. 1987), Dow Med. Coll. Alumni Assn. (regional councilor 1989-90, sec.-treas. 1997-98, pres.), Assn. Pakistani Physicians N.Am. (pres. So. chpt. 1993—), Dow Alumni Assn. N.Am. (pres.-elect 1998—). Islam. Avocations: fishing, swimming, golf. Home: 133 Chateau St Michel Dr Kenner LA 70065-2037 Office: Meth Psychiat Pavillion 5610 Read Blvd New Orleans LA 70127-3106

ARSHAM, HOSSEIN, operations research analyst; b. Mashhad, Iran, Mar. 28, 1947; came to U.S., 1978; s. Gholam Reza and Habebeh (Babai) A.; m. Elaheh-Naaze Khoshghadam, Dec. 20, 1984; 1 child, Aryana. BSc in Physics, Arya-Mehr U. Tech., Tehran, Iran, 1971; MSc, Cranfield Inst., Eng., 1978; DSc, George Washington U., 1982. Cert. info. scientist, specialized in telecom. Postdoctoral rschr. Internat. Water Resources Inst., Washington, 1982-83; prof. U. Balt., 1983—, Harry Wright disting. rsch. prof. mgmt. sci. and stats.; rsch. prof. Info. Systems Rsch. Ctr., Balt., 1996—; faculty advanced studies Calif. Nat. U., 1991—; faculty cons. Kennedy-Western U., 1995—; tech. lectr. Bethlehem Steel Co., Balt., 1983-84; sci. cons. in field. Editor: InterStat: Stats. on the Internet, Jour. of Interdisciplinary Math., assoc. editor Computational Stats. and Data Analysis and Jour. of Applied Statistical Reasoning; editorial bd. mem. Jour. of End User Computing, Internat. Jour. Ops. and Quantitative Mgmt.; mem. internat. sci. com. Advances in Intelligent Data Analysis, 1997—; contbr. articles to profl. jours. Commn. on Office Lab. Accreditation grantee, 1993, NSF grantee, 1995; recipient Black & Decker Corp. Rsch. award, 1987, 88, 98. Fellow Royal Statis. Soc., Operational Rsch. Soc., Inst. Combinatorics and Applications; mem. AAAS, IEEE, Am. Math. Soc., Internat. Assn. Math. and Computer Modeling, Internat. Forecasting Soc., Am. Statis. Assn., Assn. for Computing Machinery, Digital Equipment Computer Users Soc., Info. Resources Mgmt. Assn., Math. Assn. Am., London Math. Soc., Inst. for Ops. Rsch. and Mgmt Scis., Soc. Indsl. and Applied Math., Soc. for Info. Mgmt., N.Y. Acad. Scis., Beta Gamma Sigma, Omega Rho. Achievements include research in statistics, applied probability, discrete-event systems simulation, and mathematical programming and modeling. Office: U Balt 1420 N Charles St Baltimore MD 21201-5720

ARSTARK, LESTER D., advertising agency executive; b. Hoboken, N.J., Sept. 7, 1924; s. Maurice T. and Sophia L. (Solomon) A.; m. Janice M. Corn, June 29, 1952; children: Kim A. (dec.), Dru A. AB, Brown U., 1948; postgrad., Columbia U., 1951-52. News editor Bristol (R.I.) Phoenix, 1948-49, New Bedford (Mass.) Standard-Times radio stas., 1949-51; account exec. Kenyon & Eckhardt, N.Y.C., 1951-53, supr. promotion food products, 1954-57; mgr. advt. and sales promotion Hudson Pulp and Paper Corp., 1957-59, dir. comm., 1959-60; pres. L.D. Arstark & Co., N.Y.C., 1961—; lectr. pub. rels. C.W. Post Coll., 1960-61; lectr. mktg. Bernard Baruch Sch., CCNY, 1959-61; adj. assoc. prof. N.Y. Inst. Tech., Old Westbury, 1985-91; dir., exec. com. Programming & Systems, Inc., 1961-70. Bd. dirs. Nat. Parkinson Found., exec. com., 1962-64; trustee Roslyn Landmark Soc., 1981—, pres. 1996—; trustee Roslyn Preservtion Corp., 1981—, pres., 1997—; pres. Roslyn Village Civic Assn., 1985-87; cmty. rep./police liaison Village of Roslyn, N.Y., Inc., 1995—, hist. dist. bd., 1999. With USAAF, 1943-46. Mem. Brown Club of L.I. (pres. 1979-81), bd. dirs. 1979-86), Hempstead Harbour Club, Two Rivers Country Club. Home: 190 Main St Roslyn NY 11576-2131 Office: PO Box 72 Roslyn NY 11576-0072

ARTERS, LINDA BROMLEY, public relations consultant, writer, lecturer; b. Phila., Dec. 18, 1951; d. Edward Pollard and Rosalyn Irene (Bromley) A. BA, Thiel Coll., 1973. Cert. emergency med. tech., Ariz. Dir. customer rels. Artmann Devel. Corp. Inc., Media, Pa., 1973-74; with S.E. Nat. Bank, Malvern, Pa., 1974-78, coord. pub. rels., 1976-78; pvt. practice pub. rels. consultant Media, 1978-84, Phoenix, 1984-88; mgr. community rels. City of Tempe, Ariz., 1988-96; pub. rels. cons. Tempe, 1996—; lectr. in field; past mem. pvt. industry coun. County Del (Pa.) Comprehensive Emplyment Tng. Act Program. free lance writer for local, regional and nat. mags. and newspapers. Past chmn. Emergency Dept. Vols. Chandler Regional Hosp.; past bd. dirs. South Chester County Advanced Life Support, Inc., United Cerebral Palsy of Del County; former mem. Phila. Indoor Tennis Corp., 1977-82; past mem. com., Az Hum. Soc., East Valley steering com. Ariz. Humane Soc.; past mem. Critical Incident Stress Debriefing Team Phoenix Fire Dept.; past coord. CISD program City of Tempe; com. mem. Fiesta Bowl, 1996—, Publicity and Media Hotel Subcoms., 1990-96; Parade and Media Ops. Subcom., 1997—; parade dir., sales/mktg., 1999, former v.p. pub. awareness Ariz. affiliate Found. Fighting Blindness, media rels. chair, rescue a Golden of Arizona, vice pres. Comm. Rels., East Valley Ptnrshp. Mem. Pub. Rels. Soc. Ariz. (past mem. eligibility com. Phoenix chpt., mem. counselors group), Stress Mgmt. Nat. Network (past chmn. S.W. region critical incident). Republican. Presbyterian. Home: 1303 W Lisa Ln Tempe AZ 85284-5121

ARTERTON, JANET BOND, judge; b. 1944. BA, Mt. Holyoke Coll., 1966; JD, Northeastern U., 1977. Law clk. to Hon. Herbert J. Stern U.S. Dist. Ct. N.J., 1977-78; ptnr. Garrison & Arterton, 1978-95; judge U.S. Dist. Ct. Conn., New Haven, 1995—. Fellow Am. Bar Found., Conn. Bar Found.; mem. ATLA, Nat. Employment Lawyers Assn., Conn. Employment Lawyers Assn., Conn. State Trial Lawyers Assn. (bd. govs. 1990-95), Conn. Bar Assn. (mem. adv. com. state ct. rules 1992, mem. fed. jud. selection com. 1991-93, mem. exec. com. women and the law sect. 1990-93, chairperson fed. practice sect. 1993-95. Office: US Dist Ct Conn 141 Church St New Haven CT 06510-2030

ARTH, LAWRENCE JOSEPH, insurance executive; b. Lincoln, Nebr., July 8, 1943; s. William John and Josephine Marie (Willie) A.; children: Laura, Susan, William. BBA, U. Nebr., 1965, MA in Bus. Adminstrn., 1969. Asst. v.p. securities Bankers Life Ins. Co. Nebr., Lincoln, 1973-78, 2nd v.p. fin., 1978-83, v.p. fin., 1983, v.p. fin. treas., 1983-85, sr. v.p. investents, treas., 1985-88; chmn. Ameritas Investment Advisors, Inc., Lincoln, 1986—; pres., COO Ameritas Life Ins. Corp., Lincoln, 1988-94, chmn., CEO, 1995—; chmn., CEO Ameritas Acacia Mutual Holding Co., Lincoln, 1999—. Fellow Fin. Analysts Fedn.; mem. Omaha/Lincoln Soc. Fin. Analysts (bd. dirs. 1978-84, pres. 1983-84), Lincoln C. of C. (chmn. 1997), Lincoln Country Club (bd. dirs. 1984-87). Republican. Roman Catholic. Avocations: hunting, fishing, golf, tennis. Office: Ameritas Life Ins Corp PO Box 81889 Lincoln NE 68501-1889

ARTHER, RICHARD OBERLIN, polygraphist, educator; b. Pitts., May 20, 1928; s. William Churchill Sr. and Florence Lind (Oberlin) A.; m. Mary-Esther Wuensch, Sept. 12, 1951; children: Catherine, Linda, William III. BS, Mich. State U., 1951; MA, Columbia U., 1960. Chief assoc. John E. Reid and Assocs., Chgo., 1951-53; dir. N.Y.C. office John E. Reid and Assocs., 1953-58; pres. Sci. Lie Detection, Inc., N.Y.C., 1958—, Nat. Tng. Ctr. Polygraph Sci., N.Y.C., 1958—. Author: Interrogation for Investigators, 1958, The Scientific Investigator, 1964, 5th edit., Arther Polygraph Reference Guide, 1964—; editor: Jour. Polygraph Sci., 1966—. Fellow Acad. Cert. Polygraphists (exec. dir. 1962—), Am. Polygraph Assn. (founding mem.), Am. Assn. Police Polygraphists (founding mem., Polygraphist of Yr. 1980), N.Y. State Polygraphists (founder), N.J. Polygraphists (founder). Office: Sci Lie Detection Inc 200 W 57th St Ste 1400 New York NY 10019-3211

ARTHUR, BEATRICE, actress; b. N.Y.C., May 13, 1926; d. Philip and Rebecca Frankel; m. Gene Saks, May 28, 1950 (div.); 2 sons. Student, Blackstone Coll., also Franklin Inst. Sci. and Arts; student acting with, Erwin Piscator, Dramatic Workshop, New Sch. Social Research. Theatrical appearances include: Lysistrata, 1947, Dog Beneath the Skin, 1947, Gas, 1947, Yerma, 1947, No Exit, 1948, The Taming of the Shrew, 1948, Six Characters in Search of An Author, 1948, The Owl and the Pussycat, 1948, Le Bourgeois Gentilhomme, 1949, Yes Is for a Very Young Man, 1949, Creditors, 1949, Heartbreak House, 1949, Three Penny Opera, 1954, 55, Shoestring Revue, 1955, Seventh Heaven, 1955, The Ziegfield Follies, 1956, What's The Rush?, summer 1956, Mistress of the Inn, 1957, Nature's Way, 1957, Ulysses in Nightown, 1958, Chic, 1959, Gay Divorcee, 1960, A Matter of Position, 1962, Mame, 1966 (Tony award best supporting mus. actress), Fiddler on the Roof, 1964, Bermuda Avenue Triangle, 1996, For Better or Worse, 1996; stock appearances with Fiddler on the Roof, Circle Theatre, Atlantic City, summer 1951, State Fair Music Hall, Dallas, 1953, Music Circus, Lambertville, N.J., 1953, resident commedienne, Tamiment (Pa.) Theatre, 1953; numerous TV and nightclub appearances, 1948—; motion picture appearances That Kind of Woman, 1959; Lovers and Other Strangers, 1970, Mame, 1974, History of the World Part I, 1981, Stranger Things, 1995; TV movie: My First Love, 1988; TV appearances include All in the Family, 1971, leading role in TV series Maude, 1972-78 (Emmy award for Best Actress in a Comedy Series 1977), The Golden Girls, 1985-92 (Emmy award for Best Actress in a Comedy Series 1988), The Beatrice Arthur Spl., TV series 30 Years of TV Comedy's Greatest Hits. Mem. Artists Equity Assn., SAG, AFTRA.

ARTHUR, CHARLES GEMMELL, IV, accountant; b. St. Louis, Jan. 28, 1965; s. Charles Gemmell III and Mary Elizabeth (Senes) A.; m. Denise Renee Dougherty, June 13, 1987. BSBA in Acctg. and BS in Econs., S.E. Mo. State U., 1987; MBA in Internat. Studies, Lindenwood Coll., 1990. CPA. Fiscal analyst McDonnell Douglas Corp., St. Louis, 1987-90, sr. acct., 1990-93, sr. spl. acct., 1993-97; sr. spl. bus. analyst Boeing Co., St. Louis, 1997—. Recipient U.S. Congl. Gold medal for svc., achievement and initiative, 1987. Mem. Mensa. Methodist. Home: 13192 Weatherfield Dr Saint Louis MO 63146-3656

ARTHUR, GREER MARTIN, maritime container leasing firm executive; b. Champaign, Ill., Feb. 15, 1935; s. Greer Martin and Olive Loretta (Simard) A.; m. Veronica Lattman, Nov. 30, 1968; children: Alexandra, Vincent, Tanya, Greer III. BA, Lafayette Coll., 1956; JD, Columbia U., 1961. Bar: N.Y. 1961. Account exec. tng. program Young & Rubicam, 1957-58; firm assoc. Havens, Wandless, Stitt & Tighe, N.Y.C., 1961-62; mgmt. cons. McKinsey & Co., 1962-67; asst. to v.p. internat. Scovil Mfg. Co., Waterbury, Conn.; internat. market mgr. Scovil France, Paris, market mgr. Hamilton Beach div. Scovil, Waterbury, 1967-69; pres., CEO SSI Container Corp., subs. Itel Corp., San Francisco, 1969-73; founder, chmn., pres., CEO, dir. Trans Ocean Ltd, San Bruno, Calif., 1973—; founder, dir., bd. dirs. Inst. Internat. Container Lessors, 1970-73, dir., 1977—, pres. 1982-84, 89-90, 94—. Treas., trustee Phillips Brooks Sch., Menlo Park, Calif., 1980-83; bd. dirs. Alzheimer's Assn., 1994—; dir. San Francisco Opera; active Lafayette Coll. Nat. Coun., 1981-83. Mem. Assn. Corp. Growth, Chief Exec. Orgn. (bd. dirs. 1988-91), World Pres. Orgn. (No. Calif. chpt. chmn. 1991-92, bd. dirs. 1994—). Clubs: Bankers, World Trade (San Francisco); Club at World Trade Center (N.Y.C.); Family, Commonwealth. Office: Trans Ocean Distribution 2500 Sand Hill Rd Ste 215 Menlo Park CA 94025

ARTHUR, JAMES ALLEN, telecommunications systems engineer; b. Memphis, Oct. 29, 1950; s. Allen Ward and Erma Faye (Walls) A.; m. Donna Georgene Schaefer, July 2, 1970; children: Kristina Lynn Arthur Porterfield, Jennifer Lea Soles. AA in Liberal Arts, St. Leo Coll., 1985, BA in Bus. Adminstrn./Computer Info. Sys, 1988. Constrn. worker Messick & Gray Constrn., Bridgeville, Del., 1968; fork lift operator Penco, Seaford, Del., 1972-73; svc. ctr. mgr. Exide Power Sys., Tampa, Fla., 1977-78; sr. test tech. Paradyne Corp., Largo, Fla., 1980-85, sr. engring. tech., 1985-88; prin. engr. products, svcs. AT&T Paradyne, Largo, 1988-94; cons. sys. engr. Paradyne Corp., Largo, 1994-97, mgr. Tech. Support Ctr., 1997—. With USAF, 1968-72, 73-77. Avocations: playing 12 string guitar, singing, songwriting. Home: 6707 S Gabrielle St Tampa FL 33611-5213 Office: Paradyne Corp 8545 126th Ave Largo FL 33773-1502

ARTHUR, JAMES GREIG, mathematics educator; b. Hamilton, Ont., Can., May 18, 1944; s. John Greig and Katherine Mary Patricia (Scott) A.; m. Dorothy Pendleton Helm, June 10, 1972; children: James Pendleton, David Greig. B.Sc., U. Toronto, 1966, M.Sc., 1967; Ph.D., Yale U., 1970. Instr. Princeton U., 1970-72; asst. prof. Yale U., 1972-76; prof. Duke U., 1976-79, U. Toronto, 1979—. Contbr. articles to profl. jours. Sloan fellow, 1975-77. Fellow Royal Soc. Can. (Synge award in Math. 1987, Henry Marshall Tory medal 1997, Can. Gold medal for sci. and engring. 1999), Royal Soc. London; mem. Can. Math. Soc., Am. Math. Soc. Address: 23 Woodlawn Ave W, Toronto, ON Canada M4V 1G6

ARTHUR, JEWELL KATHLEEN, dental hygienist; b. Bloomington, Ind., Apr. 12, 1947; d. Gerald E. and Wilma Kathleen (McDonald) Beyers; m. Leland Stanley Arthur, Sept. 21, 1968; children: Sherri Kay, Brian Lee. AS in Dental Hygiene, Ind. U., 1968. Lic./registered dental hygienist. Infection control mgr., dental hygienist Office Dr. Thomas Watkins, DDS, Bloomington, Ind., 1990—; spkr., presenter in field. Vice-chmn. precinct Rep. Com., Batholomew, 1987—; chmn. Batholomew Consolidated Sch. Aids Com., Columbus, 1988—; vice chair City of Columbus Bd. Zoning Appeals, 1989-93, Bartholomew County Pers. Adminstrn. Com., 1993—; councilwoman Batholomew County Coun., Columbus, Ind., 1993—; chmn. AIDS Com., Columbus, 1988-98. Mem. Am. Assn. Ret. Persons, Am. Dental Hygienists Assn. (liaison 1989—, Disting. Svc. award 1994), Ind. Dental Hygienists Assn. (pres. 1986-87, del. 1991—, Comty. Svc. award 1991, Outstanding Dental Hygienists of Yr. award 1991), Ind. Pub. Health Assn. (chair legislation 1986-89), Driftwood Valley Dental Hygienists Assn. (trustee 1989-91, 98—), Assn. Ind. Counties, DAR-Joseph Hart, Order Eastern Star. Republican. Methodist. Avocations: antiques, pottery, old toys, music. Home: 1800 Clover Ct Columbus IN 47203-3615

ARTHUR, JOHN MORRISON, retired utility executive; b. Pitts., Aug. 17, 1922; s. Hugh Morrison and Anna Matilda (Crowe) A.; m. Sylvia Ann Martin, June 19, 1948; children: William Robert, John Martin, Andrew Scott. BEE, U. Pitts., 1944, MEE, 1947. With Duquesne Light Co., Pitts., 1944-87, asst. to chmn. bd. and pres., 1966-67, pres., 1967-68, chmn. bd., chief exec. officer, 1968-83, chmn. bd., pres., 1983-85, chmn. bd., 1986-87; ret. Duquesne Light Co., 1987. Trustee emeritus U. Pitts. With AUS, 1942-43. Mem. Duquesne Club, Montour Heights Country Club, Rolling Rock Club.

ARTHUR, LINDSAY GRIER, retired judge, author, editor; b. Mpls., July 30, 1917; s. Hugh and Alice (Grier) A.; m. Jean Johansen, Sept. 19, 1940; children: Lindsay G., Mollie K., Julie A. AB, Princeton U., 1939; postgrad., Harvard U., 1939-40; LLB, JD, U. Minn., 1946. Bar: Minn. 1946, U.S. Dist. Ct. Minn. 1948, U.S. Supreme Ct. 1964. Lawyer Nieman, Bosard & Arthur, Mpls., 1946-54; alderman Mpls. City Coun., 1951-54; judge Mcpl. Ct., Mpls., 1954-61; chief judge juvenile div. Dist. Ct., Mpls., 1961-79, 87-93, judge felony, civil div., 1979-83; chief judge mental health div. Dist. Ct., 1983-87; mediator, 1987—; arbitrator civil and family cts., 1991—. Author: Twin Cities Uncovered, 1996, A Manual for Mediators, 1995; editor: Digest of Juvenile and Family Law, 1983-93; contbr. articles to profl. jours. Bd. dirs. Nat. Ctr. State Cts., Williamsburg, 1974-77, Metro YMCA, Mpls. area, 1981-85; chmn. trustees Bethlehem Luth. Ch., 1979-80. Lt. USNR, 1942-45, PTO. Mem. Nat. Coun. Juvenile Ct. Judges (pres. 1972-73, Jud. scholar 1985—), ABA (disabilities com. 1984-89), Am. Law Inst. (advisor divorce law 1989-93). Avocations: writing, walking. Home: 1201 Yale Pl Apt 205 Minneapolis MN 55403-1955

ARTHUR, MICHAEL ELBERT, lawyer; b. Seattle, Oct. 9, 1952; s. Theodore E. and Gladys L. (Jones) A.; m. Claire C. Meeker, Dec. 23, 1974; children: Christine, Conor. BA, U. Calif., Santa Barbara, 1974; JD, Stanford U., 1977. Bar: Oreg. 1977, U.S. Dist. Ct. Oreg. 1977, U.S. Ct. Appeals (9th cir.) 1984. Assoc. Miller, Nash, Wiener, Hager & Carlsen LLP, Portland, Oreg., 1977-84, ptnr., 1984—. Trustee Chiles Found. Mem. ABA, Oreg. Bar Assn., Order of Coif, Phi Beta Kappa. Home: 13535 NW Lariat Ct Portland OR 97229-7001 Office: Miller Nash Wiener Hager & Carlsen LLP 111 SW 5th Ave Ste 3500 Portland OR 97204-3699

ARTHUR, PAUL KEITH, electronic engineer; b. Kansas City, Mo., Jan. 14, 1931; s. Walter B. and Frieda J. (Burckhardt) A.; m. Joy N. Lim, Apr. 26, 1958; children: Gregory V., Lia F. Student, Ohio No. U., 1947, Taylor U., Upland, Ind., 1948-49; BSEE, Purdue U., 1956; postgrad., N.Mex. State U., 1957-78. Registered profl. engr., N.Mex.; cert. army acquisition profl.; cert. Naval engring. duty officer, Navy material profl. With White Sands Missile Range, N.Mex., 1956—; electronic engr. field engring., group missile flight surveillance office, 1956-60; chief field engring grouop, 1960-62; project engr. Pershing Weapon Sys. Army Missile Test and Evaluation Directorate, 1962-74; chief high altitude air def. projects br., 1974-82, chief air def. materiel test divsn., 1982-91, dep dir. Materiel Test Directorate, 1991-95, dir., 1995-98, exec. dir. Nat. Range, 1998—; spl. asst. to WSMR comdr. for Space Programs, 1994—; mem. N.Mex. Spaceport Commn., Southwest Regional Space Task Force, Metro Planning Orgn.; past pres. missile range pioneer group; bd. dirs. Daugupan Electric Corp. of the Philippines. Author numerous plans and reports on weapon systems test and evaluation and topics in naval engring. Chmn. adminstrv. bd. Meth. Ch., 1992-95. Served with USN, 1949-53, USNR, 1954-87, rear adm. and sr. engring. duty officer, 1984-87. Decorated Legion of Merit, Meritorious Svc. medal, Navy Achievement medal, Mil. Order St. Barbara, others. Mem. AIAA (past vice chmn.), Internat. Test and Evaluation Assn., Am. Def. Preparedness Assn. (past pres.), Assn. Old Crows, Naval Res. Assn., Res. Officers Assn. (pres. 1983-85), United Vets. Coun. (chmn. 1984-85), Am. Soc. Naval Engrs., Naval Inst., Navy League, Surface Navy Assn., Assn. U.S. Army, U.S. Field Arty. Assn., Purdue U. Alumni Assn. (past pres.), N.Mex. State U. Alumni Assn., Mesilla Valley Track Club, Bujutsukan Acad. Martial Arts. Home: 2050 San Acacio St Las Cruces NM 88001-1570 Office: Nat Range White Sands Missile Range NM 88002

ARTHUR, ROCHELLE LINDA, creative director; b. N.Y.C., Mar. 24, 1937; d. Arthur Greenberg and Dorothy (Wool) Greenberg Lucas; 1 child, Adam Israel Aryeh Lapidus. BFA, Pratt Inst., 1958. Art dir. Harcourt, Brace, Jovanovich, N.Y.C., 1977-79, The Seabury Press, N.Y.C., 1979-83, office comm. nat. exec. hdqs. Episc. Ch., N.Y.C., 1983-94; creative dir. Food for the Poor, Deerfield Beach, Fla., 1994-95; advt. advisor South Fla. Newspaper Network, Deerfield Beach, Fla., 1996-98; cons. in field.

ARTHUR, WILLIAM LYNN, environmental foundation administrator; b. Spokane, Wash., May 22, 1954; s. Robert Cyril and Mabel Mildred (Collison) A.; m. Debora Lee Donovan, Feb. 2, 1975; children: Kathleen, Jonathan. BA in Econs., Wash. State U., 1976, postgrad., 1982-83. Rsch. asst. Wash. State U., 1976-77; project mgr. Ctr. Environ. Understanding, Cheney, Wash., 1977-78; program dir. Wash. Energy Extension Svc., Spokane, 1978-79; econs. instr. Spokane Falls Community Coll., 1977-81; economist, cons. Biosystems Analysis Inc., Spokane, 1983; assoc. N.W. rep. Sierra Club, Seattle, 1983-87, N.W. rep., 1987-91, N.W. regional dir., 1992—; also mem. nat. wildlands campaign com. Sierra Club, —; chmn. bd. N.W. Conservation Act Coalition, Seattle, 1982-83; adv. com. N.W. Renewable Resources Ctr., Seattle, 1987-91; cons. energy workshops N.W. Regional Found., Spokane, 1982; mem. exec. com. Save Our Wild Salmon Coalition, 1991-95 (bd. dirs. 1999—); mem. adv. com. Inland Empire Pub. Lands Coun., 1990—; mem. steering com. Campaign for the Northwest, 1998—. hmn., mem. city commn. Environ. Quality Commn., Pullman, Wash., 1976-77; bd. di rs. Ryegrass Sch., Spokane, 1978-81; conservation rep. Internat. Mountain Caribou Tech. Com., 1978-81; bd. dirs. Wash. Citizens for Recycling, Seattle, 1980-82; chair Wash. State Environmentalists for Clinton/Gore Com., 1992, 96; environ. rep. N.W. Forest Conf. convened and chaired by Pres. Clinton, Apr. 2, 1993; mem. steering com. on No Initiative 164 Coalition, 1995; mem. Wash. State Steering Com. to Re-elect Clinton/Gore, 1996. Avocations: hiking, rafting, fishing, playing guitar. Office: Sierra Club NW Office 180 Nickerson St Ste 103 Seattle WA 98109-1631

ARTHURS, HARRY WILLIAM, legal educator, former university president; b. Toronto, Ont., Can., May 9, 1935; s. Leon and Ellen (Dworkin) A.; m. Penny Milnes, June 22, 1974. BA, U. Toronto, 1955, LLB, 1958; LLM, Harvard U., 1959; LLD (hon.), Sherbrooke, Brock Law Soc. Upper Can., McGill U.; D.Litt. (hon.), Lethbridge U. Prof. Osgoode Hall Law Sch., York U., Toronto, Ont., 1961-95; dean Osgoode Hall Law Sch., York U., 1972-77, pres. univ., 1985-92; univ. prof. York U., 1995—; chief adjudicator Pub. Svc. of Can., 1967-68; assoc. Can. Inst. Advanced Rsch., 1995-98; arbitrator, mediator. Author various books and articles on labor law, legal history, adminstrv. law and legal edn. to profl. jours. Vice pres. Can. Civil Liberties Assn., 1964-76, pres., 1976-77; mem. U.A.W. Pub. Rev. Bd., 1967-77; vice chmn. Ont. Ednl. Relations Commn., 1976-77; chmn. S.S.H.R.C. Study on Legal Research and Edn. in Can., 1980-83; bencher Law Soc. Upper Can., 1979-83; mem. Econ. Council Can., 1978-81. Officer Order of Can., 1989; mem. Order of Ont., 1995. Fellow Royal Soc. Can. Home: 11 Hillcrest Pk, Toronto, ON Canada M4X 1E8 Office: York U, 4700 Keele St, Toronto, ON Canada M3J 1P3

ARTIGLIERE, RALPH, lawyer, educator; b. Morristown, N.J., Mar. 1, 1947; s. Fiore Joseph and Mary (Bolcar) A.; m. Gale Anderson, June 14, 1969; children: William Michael, Adam Robert. BS in Engring., U.S. Mil. Acad., 1969; JD, U. Fla., 1977. Bar: Fla. 1977, U.S. Dist. Ct. (mid. dist.) Fla. 1978, U.S. Ct. Appeals (11th cir.) 1981, U.S. Dist. Ct. (no. dist.) Fla. 1984. Project mgr. Ryder System, Inc., Miami, Fla., 1974-75; cons. Ryder System, Inc., Gainesville, Fla., 1975-77; atty. Holland & Knight, Lakeland, Fla., 1977-81, Lane, Trohn, Clarke, Bertrand & Williams, Lakeland, Fla., 1981-91, Anderson & Artigliere, P.A., Lakeland, Fla., 1991—; mem. jury instrn. com. Fla. Supreme Ct., Tallahassee, 1990—; aj. prof. U. South Fla., Tampa, 1991-92; instr. legal writing U. Fla. Law Sch., Gainesville, 1976-77. Author: (chpt.) Florida Forms of Jury Instruction, 1990, Drafting and Using Jury Instructions in Civil Cases, 1998. Pres. Santa Fe High Sch. Bd., Lakeland, 1985; chmn. 10th Cir. Jud. Nominating Commn., Polk County, Fla., 1985-86; bd. dirs. Polk Pub. Mus., Lakeland, 1987-89, United Cerebral Palsy of Polk County, Lakeland, 1980-82. Capt. U.S. Army, 1969-74, Vietnam. Decorated Bronze Star, Air medal with "V"; recipient Fla. Bar Pro Bono award Fla. Supreme Ct., 1982. Fellow Am. Coll. Trial Lawyers; mem. ABA, FBA, Fla. Bar (cert. civil trial lawyer 1993—, chmn. CLE com. 1996-97), Polk County Trial Lawyers Assn. (pres. 1995-96), Phi Kappa Phi, Order of Coif. Republican. Avocations: fly fishing. Home: 138 Sands Point Dr Tierra Verde FL 33715-2211 Office: Anderson & Artigliere PA 4927 Southfork Dr Lakeland FL 33813-2043

ARTILES, NEMUEL OTHNIEL, hospital executive; b. Mayaguez, P.R., Nov. 20, 1954; s. Gertrudis and Celinda (Montalvo) A.; m. Mayra Fonseca, Dec. 22, 1985; children: Sharlenne, Cristina, Mayrel. AS in Bus. Adminstrn., U. P.R., Aguadilla, 1974; BS in Bus. Adminstrn., U. P.R., Mayaguez, 1977; MS in Pub. Health Adminstrn., Loma Linda U., 1979. Adminstrv. resident Fla. Hosp. Med. Ctr., Orlando, 1979; adminstr. Bella Vista Hosp. & Polyclinic, Mayaguez, 1980-84; assoc. adminstr. Bella Vista Hosp., Mayaguez, 1984-85, CEO, 1985—; pres. Yauco (P.R.) Area Hosp.; former prof. Antillian Adventist U.; cons. in field., Mex., Jamaica, Guyana, Dominican Republic; mem. com. Interam. divsn. SDA Health and Hosp.; mem. enterprise coun. adv. com. Interam. U., San Germán, P.R., 1992; chmn. bd. Bella Vista Health Svcs. HMO. Bd. dirs. Antillian Adventist U., Mayaguez, 1987; treas. Neighborhood Watch Coun., Cerro Las Mesas, Mayaguez, 1994; co-founder I Can Cope program Mayaguez chpt. Am. Cancer Soc., 1988; chmn. bd. Bella Vista Adventist Acad.; bd. dirs. P.R. Union 7th-day Adventist; elder, bd. dirs., Bible tchr., song dir. Bella Vista 7th-day Adventist Ch.; past instr., dir. Pathfinder Club; former 1st aid instr., lifeguard ARC; former 1st aid instr., shelter adminstr. Civil Def. Fellow Am. Coll. Healthcare Execs. (mem. regent adv. coun. 1993-94); mem. P.R. Indsl. Assn., P.R. Hosp. Assn. (v.p. 1992-94, pres. elect 1995, pres. 1997—), Am. Hosp. Assn. (mem. ho. of reps., mem. regional policy bd. 1994-97), P.R. Coll. Health Svcs. Adminstrs., Assn. Adventist Healthcare Execs., Loma Linda (Calif.) U. Sch. Pub. Health Alumni Assn. Achievements include transforming Bella Vista Hospital from general acute hospital to terciary specialized institution. Avocations: music, civic activities, outdoor activities. Office: Bella Vista Southwestern Hosp PO Box 68 Yauco PR 00698-0068

ARTIN, MICHAEL, mathematics educator; b. June 28, 1934. PhD in Mathematics, Harvard U., 1960. Prof. Mathematics MIT, Cambridge, Mass., 1963—. Mem. Nat. Acad. Scis. Office: MIT Dept Math Rm 2-236 77 Massachusetts Ave Cambridge MA 02139 Home: Cambridge MA 02139*

ARTINIAN, NANCY TRYGAR, critical care nurse, researcher; b. Detroit, Aug. 13, 1951; d. Michael Henry and Honor (Burke) Trygar; m. James Haig Artinian, Apr. 19, 1980. BSN cum laude, Mercy Coll. of Detroit, 1973; MS in Nursing, Wayne State U., 1975, PhD, 1988; postdoctoral rsch. fellow, U. Mich., 1995-96. Staff nurse surg. care unit and ICU Grace N.W. Hosp., Detroit, 1973-75; staff nurse, asst. clin. coord. ICU William Beaumont Hosp., Royal Oak, Mich., 1975-78, staff nurse, 1979-85, staff nurse, contingent surg. stepdown unit, 1989-91; postdoctoral rsch. fellow U. Mich., Ann Arbor, 1995-96; asst. prof. nursing Mercy Coll. of Detroit, 1982-83; assoc. prof. Wayne State U., Detroit, 1988—, coord. acute care nurse practitioner program, critical care. Contbr. articles to profl. jours. Grantee Am. Heart Assn. of Mich., 1987-88, 89-92; Advanced Nurse Edn. Program grantee, Wayne State U., 1992-95. Mem. ANA, AACN (bd. dirs. S.E. Mich. 1992-94), Am. Acad. Nurse Practitioners, Am. Health Coun. Cardiovasc. Nursing, Midwest Nursing Rsch. Soc., Nat. Coun. on Family Rels., Sigma Theta Tau (rsch. grantee 1985-86).

ARTL, KAREN ANN, business owner, author; b. Bainbridge, N.Y., July 4, 1950; d. Douglas Robert and Beverly Florence (Schofell) Moore; m. Robert Edward Gurney, June 15, 1969 (div. June 1981); children: Douglas Albert Gurney, Rebecca Susan Gurney; m. Jeffrey Joseph Artl, Nov. 8, 1986; 1 child, Grace Beverly. BA in Edn., SUNY Coll. at Oneonta, 1972; MA in Reading and Edn., Cleve. State U., 1981. Tchr. reading Independence (Ohio) Mid. Sch., 1979-81; sr. editor Am. Greetings Corp., Cleve., 1981-87; mem. adj. faculty Lorain Community Coll., Cleve., 1987-89; creative dir. Gibson Greetings, Inc., Cin., 1994-97; owner Cresta Creative, 1999—; owner, pres. WordsWorth Studio, Inc.; conf. speaker, trainer, cons. Social Expression Industry. Author: You can Write Greeting Cards, 1999, M. Washington, etc., 1991, (children's book) I'm Me and You're Not, 1991, Now Noah Knew What to Do!, 1998, The Baby King, 1999, Babies of the Bible, 1999; inspirational plaque line for Christian market; editor CR Gibson/Gift Books, 1993, Gibson Greetings, 1993. Vol. Am. Cancer Soc., Cleve., 1991. Mem. AAUW, NAFE, Greeting Card Assn., Greeting Card Creative Network, Soc. Children's Book Writers. Lutheran. Avocations: writing inspirational materials, activities to combat illiteracy. Home and Office: Cresta Creative 1980 Diplomat Vw Apt 1826 Colorado Springs CO 80906-8346

ARTNER, ALAN GUSTAV, art critic, journalist; b. Chgo., May 14, 1947; s. Gustav and Katherine Rose (Lucas) A. B.A., Northwestern U., 1968, M.A., 1969. Apprentice music critic Chgo. Tribune, 1972-73, art critic, 1973—; contbg. editor The Art Gallery Mag., 1975-76; corr. Artnews Mag., 1977-80. Contbr. to Playbill, 1994—. Decorated Chevalier de l'ordre des Arts et des Lettres; Rockefeller Found. grantee, 1971-72. Office: Chgo Tribune Co 435 N Michigan Ave Chicago IL 60611-4066*

ARTSCHWAGER, RICHARD ERNST, artist; b. Washington, Dec. 26, 1923; s. Ernst and Eugenia (Brodsky) A.; m. Elfriede Wejmelka, 1947 (div. 1970); 1 child, Eva; m. Catherine Kord, 1972 (div. 1989); m. Molly O'Gorman (div. 1993); children: Clara, Augustus; m. Ann Sebring, 1995. A.B., Cornell U., 1948; pupil of Amedee Ozenfant, N.Y.C., 1949-50. One-man shows include Leo Castelli Gallery, N.Y.C., 1965, 67, 72, 73, 75, 76, 78, 79, 89, 91, Kunstverein, Hamburg, Germany, 1979, Albright-Knox Art Gallery, Buffalo, 1979, Inst. Contemporary Art, U. Pa., Phila., 1979, La Jolla (Calif.) Mus. Contemporary Art, 1980, Mus. Contemporary Art, Houston, 1980, Mary Boone Gallery, N.Y.C., 1983, 86, 90, 93, 94, 97, Kunsthalle, Basel, Switzerland, 1985, Van Abbe Mus., Eindhoven, Netherlands, 1985, Whitney Mus. Retrospective, 1988 (travelled to San Francisco Mus. Modern Art, Mus. Contemporary Art, L.A., Palacio de Velasquez, Madrid, Spain, Mus. Nat. d'Art Moderne, Ctr. Georges Pompidou, Paris, Stadtische Kunsthalle, Dusseldorf, Fed. Republic Germany), Mus. Fine Arts, Boston, 1992, Kunstnernes Hus, Oslo, 1992, Portikus, Frankfurt, 1993, Fondation Cartier, Paris, 1994; mus. and gallery shows include Documenta IV, 1967, V, 1972, VII, 1982, VIII, 1987, IX, 1992, Kassel, Germany; outdoor sculpture commns. include Battery Park City, N.Y.C., 1984-88, Gen. Mills Corp. Hdqrs., Mpls., 1988, Elvehjem Mus. Art, Madison, Wis., 1990-91; represented in permanent collections Mus. Modern Art, N.Y., Whitney Mus., Centre Georges Pompidou, Paris, Emily Fisher Landau Found., N.Y., San Diego Mus. Contemporary Art, Mus. Ludwig, Cologne, Germany, Detroit Art Center, Met. Mus., N.Y.C., Walker Art Ctr., Mpls., Wadsworth Athenaeum, Conn., Rotterdam (Netherlands) Mus., Basel Mus., also pvt. collections; contbr. articles to profl. jours. With U.S. Army, 1944-46. Address: PO Box 12 Hudson NY 12534-0012

ARTURI, ANTHONY JOSEPH, engineering executive, consultant; b. Paterson, N.J., Sept. 6, 1937; s. Emanuel and Mary (Territo) A.; m. Betty Jane Hanner, July 14, 1962; children: Anthony David, Dawn Elizabeth. Degree in mech. engring., Stevens Inst. Tech., 1959, MS in Math., 1966. Registered profl. engr., N.J. Project engr. Gen. Precision-Kearfott, Wayne, N.J., 1962-64, Bendix Corp., Teterboro, N.J., 1964-66; engr. supr. Singer Kearfott Divsn., Wayne, 1966-74; project mgr. Lummus Co., Bloomfield, N.J., 1974-77, GE Info. Svcs., N.Y.C., 1977-82; pres. ARTECH Assocs., Wayne, 1982—; trustee Stevens Inst. Tech., Hoboken, N.J., 1986-88; adj. faculty Fairleigh Dickinson U., Teaneck, N.J., 1968-75. Presenter in field. Organizer, panelist Stevens Enterprise Forum, 1985-90. Recipient Alumni Achievement award Stevens Alumni Assn., 1979. Mem. IEEE, Drug Info. Assn., Stevens Entrepreneurs Club (organizer small bus. network 1986), Lions. Home: 13 Miller Rd Wayne NJ 07470-3620 Office: ARTECH Assocs 1341 Hamburg Tpke Wayne NJ 07470-4042

ARTZ, FREDERICK JAMES, diversified manufacturing company executive; b. Pitts., Dec. 28, 1949; s. Ray Edison and Jean Elizabeth (McClurg) A.; m. Donna Marie Moschella, Dec. 16, 1977; children: James Randall, BrieAnn Elizabeth. BS in Adminstrn. and Mgmt. Sci., Carnegie Mellon U., 1972; MBA, U. Pitts., 1973. Indsl. engr. Spang and Co., Butler, Pa., 1973-74; retail buyer Sun Drug div. Spang Stores, Butler, 1974-79, internal auditor, 1979-82, acctg. mgr., 1982-88, treas., adminstr. pension plan, 1988—; v.p. Spang & Co. Mem. Beta Gamma Sigma. Office: Spang & Co PO Box 751 Butler PA 16003-0751

ARTZ, JOHN CURTIS, lawyer; b. Columbus, Ohio, Mar. 4, 1946; s. Curtis Price and Kathryn Lucille (Risley) A.; m. Nancy Eileen Jones, Apr. 5, 1969; children: John Curtis Jr., Alexander Hardie, Kathryn Cullen. BA with distinction, Allegheny Coll., 1968; JD magna cum laude, U. S.C., 1976. Bar: Pa. 1976, U.S. Dist. Ct. (we. dist.) Pa. 1976, U.S. Ct. Appeals (3d and 6th cirs.) 1996, U.S. Supreme Ct. 1980. From assoc. to ptnr. Eckert Seamans Cherin & Mellott, Pitts., 1976-94; shareholder, dir. Polito & Smock, P.C., Pitts., 1994—; adj. asst. prof. Grad. Sch. Pub. Health U. Pitts., 1988-92; part-time instr. Robert Morris Coll., Pitts., 1998—; seminar and workshop presenter Nat. Safety Coun., Western Pa. Safety Coun., Pa. Bar Inst., Allegheny County Bar Assn., Pitts. Human Resources Assn., Butler county Pers. Assn., Pa. Inst. CPAs, Western Pa. Cmty. Accts. Notes editor U. S.C. Law Rev., 1975-76; contbr. articles to profl. jours. Dir. Jr. Achievement S.W. Pa., Pitts., 1994—, vice-chair adminstrn., 1998—. Capt. USAF, 1968-73. Recipient Bronze Leadership award Jr. Achievement S.W. Pa., 1993. Fellow Allegheny County Bar Found.; mem. Soc. for Human Resource Mgmt., Pa. Self-Insurer's Assn., Pa. Bar Assn. (com. on legal ethics and profl. responsibility 1987-94, com. on occupl. safety and health law 1981—), Pitts. Human Resources Assn. (treas. 1997, sr. profl. human resources 1998—), Omicron Delta Kappa. Avocation: USSF soccer referee. Office: Polito & Smock PC 444 Liberty Ave Pittsburgh PA 15222-1220

ARTZT, EDWIN LEWIS, consumer products company executive; b. N.Y.C., Apr. 15, 1930; s. William and Ida A.; m. Ruth Nadine Martin, May 12, 1950; children—Wendy Anne, Karen Susan, William M., Laura Grace, Elizabeth Louise. B.J., U. Oreg., 1951. Account exec. Glasser Gailey Advt. Agy., L.A., 1952-53; with Procter & Gamble Co., Cin., 1953-95, brand mgr. advt. dept., 1956-58, asso. brand promotion mgr., 1958-60, brand promotion mgr., 1960, 62-65, copy mgr., 1960-62, advt. mgr. paper products div., 1965-68, mgr. products food div., 1968-69, v.p., 1969, v.p., acting mgr. coffee div., 1970, v.p., group exec., 1970-75, dir., 1972-75, 80-95, exec. v.p. then vice chmn., 1980-89; group v.p. Procter & Gamble Co., Europe, Belgium, 1975-80; pres. Procter & Gamble Internat., 1984-89, chmn., chief exec. officer, 1995—; bd. dir. GTE Corp. Past chmn. residential div. United Appeal; past chmn. Public Library Capital Funds campaign; past dist. chmn. Capital Fund Raising dr. Boy Scouts Am., past leadership tng. chmn.; past chmn. advt. com. Sch. Tax Levy, County Govt. Issue; past trustee Kansas City Philharmonic, Nutrition Found., Boys' Clubs Greater Cin.; past bd. dirs. Kansas City Lyric Theater; past bd. govs. Kansas City Art Inst. Mem. Am. C. of C. Belgium (v.p.), Conf. Bd. Europe (adv. council), Internat. C. of C. (exec. com. U.S. council), Nat. Fgn. Trade Council. Clubs: Queen City (Cin.), Cin. Country (Cin.), Comml. (Cin.). Home: 9495 Whitegate Ln Cincinnati OH 45243-1647 Office: Procter & Gamble Co 1 Procter And Gamble Plz Cincinnati OH 45202-3393*

ARTZT, RUSSELL M., computer software company executive; b. 1947. B.S., Queens Coll., 1968; M.S., NY U., 1975. With Riverside Rsch. Corp. N.Y.C., 1968-72, with Standard Data Corp., 1972-76; with Computer Assocs. Internat. Inc., 1976—; v.p. Computer Assocs. Internat. Inc., 1978-83, sr. v.p. devel., from 1983; now exec. v.p. Office: Computer Assocs Internat Inc 1 Computer Associates Plz Hauppauge NY 11788-7000*

ARUM, ROBERT, lawyer, sports events promoter; b. N.Y.C., Dec. 8, 1931; s. Samuel and Celia (Baumgarten) A.; m. Barbara Mandelbaum, July 2, 1960 (div. 1977); children: John, Richard, Elizabeth; m. Sybil Ann Hamada, Dec. 18, 1977 (div. 1991); m. Lovee Du Boef Hazan, Sept. 14, 1991. BA, NYU, 1953; JD cum laude, Harvard U., 1956. Bar: N.Y. 1956. Atty. firm Root, Barrett, Cohen, Knapp & Smith, N.Y.C., 1956-61; asst. U.S. atty., chief tax sect. U.S. Atty.'s Office, So. Dist. N.Y., 1961-64; partner firm Phillips, Nizer, Benjamin, Krim & Ballon, N.Y.C., 1964-72, Arum & Katz, N.Y.C., 1972-79; chmn. Top Rank, Inc.; Promoter Ali-Frazier Super Fight II, 1974, Evel Knievel Snake River Canyon Jump, 1974, Ali-Norton World Heavyweight Championship, 1976, Monzon-Valdez World Middleweight Championships, 1976, 77, Ali-Spinks Championships, 1978, Leonard-Duran Championships, 1980, 89, Top Rank/ESPN Boxing Series, 1980—, Arguello-Pryor Championship, 1983, Moore-Duran Championship, 1983, Hagler-Duran Championship, 1983, Hagler-Hearns Championship, 1985, Hagler-Leonard Superfight Championship, 1987, Leonard-Hearns "The War" Championship, 1989-91, Holyfield-Foreman World Heavyweight Championship, 1991, Holyfield-Holmes World Heavyweight Championship, 1992, Foreman/Morrison Heavyweight Championship, 1993, De la Hoya/Whitaker, 1997, De la Hoya/Chevez, 1996, 98, De la Hoya/Quartey, 1999. Elected to Boxing Hall of Fame, 1999. Mem. ABA, Assn. Bar City N.Y., Friars Club. Home: 36 Gulf Stream Ct Las Vegas NV 89113-1354 Office: 3980 Howard Hughes Pkwy Las Vegas NV 89109-0992

ARUMUGHAM, GAYATHRI SHAKTHI, healthcare activist, educator; b. Batavia, N.Y., Sept. 30, 1973; d. Rangaswamy and Visa Arumugham. BA in Sociology and Criminology, U. Mich., 1996; postgrad., NYU, 1997-99. GED tchr. Washtenaw County Jail and Juvenile Ctr., Dept. Corrections, Ann Arbor, Mich., 1992-95; counselor Concord-Assabet, Boston, N.Y., 1995-97; sexual health educator Asian Pacific Islander Coalition on HIV-AIDS, N.Y.C., 1997—; dir. Diva Creations, Bklyn., 1995—; tour mgr., dancer Kanya/Nrityanjali, North Potomac, Md., 1996-97; cons. Yagna Rama Gaitonde AIDS Care, Madras, India, 1997—. Mem. South Asian Students Soc. (founder, head), South Asian Progressive Task Force, Nat. Asian Women's Health Orgn. Hindu. Avocations: cooking, languages. E-mail: gaiaka@mailcity.com.

ARUNDEL, JOHN HOWARD, financial consultant; b. Washington, June 4, 1965; s. Arthur W. and Margaret C. (McElroy) A. BA in Polit. Sci., Duke U., 1988; MA in Internat. Econs., Johns Hopkins U., 1995. Registered fin. cons. Reporter, trainee The New York Times, N.Y.C., 1988-90; bur. chief States News Svc., Washington, 1991-92; corr. The Washington Post, Kuwait City, Kuwait, 1991; fin. cons. Smith Barney, Inc., Washington, 1996—; bd. mem. Va. Film Found.; mem. Gore 2000, Washington, 1995-96; bd. dirs. The Kennedy Ctr. Camelot Circle, Washington, 1995—. Author: The Student Guide to Duke, 1988; co-author: U.S.-Japan Relations, 1994; contbr. articles to profl. jours. Mem. Nat. Press Club. Democrat. Episcopalian. Avocation: collector of presidential documents. Home: 4 Muirs Ct Alexandria VA 22314-2415 Office: Smith Barney Inc 1776 Eye St NW Ste 900 Washington DC 20006-3713

ARVAI, ERNEST STEPHEN, consulting executive; b. Detroit, Sept. 9, 1950; s. Ernest and Maria Magdolna (Horvath) A.; m. Mary Ann Hughes, Oct. 11, 1980; 1 child, Marc Alexander. BS in Indsl. Engring. with high distinction, U. Mich., Dearborn, 1971; MS in Indsl. Adminstrn., Carnegie Mellon U., 1974. CPA, N.H. Rsch. asst. Hwy. Safety Rsch. Inst., Ann Arbor, Mich., 1970-73; sr. cons. Arthur Andersen & Co., Detroit, 1974-77; dir. N.Am. mgmt. cons. Arthur D. Little Inc., Cambridge, Mass., 1978-90; v.p., mng. dir. tech. mgmt. Battelle Meml. Inst., Columbus, Ohio, 1990-91; pres., CEO Arvai Group, Inc., Windham, N.H., 1991—; bd. advisors Cislunar Corp., Madison, Conn., 1992—. Author newsletter The Expert Network, 1994; contbr. articles to profl. jours. Bd. dirs., coord. Windham Baseball League, 1993. Mem. AICPA, N.H. Inst. CPAs, Internat. Order Characters, Wings Club. Republican. Avocations: aviation, skiing, golf. Home: 16 Telo Rd Windham NH 03087-1151 Office: Arvai Group Inc PO Box 468 Windham NH 03087-0468

ARVESON, RAYMOND GERHARD, retired state official; b. Jamestown, N.D., May 11, 1921; m. Adelaide Arveson; children: Raymond, Susan Aden, John. BA, Mayville State U., 1942; MA, U. Minn., 1948; EdD, U. Calif., Berkeley, 1962. High sch. prin. Pub. Schs., Alamo and Langdon, N.D., 1942-44; supt. Langdon (N.D.) Pub. Schs., 1944-45, Leeds (N.D.) Pub. Schs., 1945-57; counselor, social sci. tchr. Hayward (Calif.) Union High Sch., 1957-58; dean of boys Tennyson High Sch. and Hayward Union High Sch., 1958-59, vice prin., 1958-59, prin., 1960-63; asst. supt. Hayward (Calif.) Union Sch. Dist., 1963-68; supt. Hayward (Calif.) Unified Sch. Dist., 1968-76, Mpls. Pub. Schs., 1976-80, East Baton Rouge (La.) Parish Pub. Schs., 1980-87, East Feliciana Parish Pub. Schs., 1989-90; asst. supt. acad. programs La. Dept. Edn., Baton Rouge, 1991, state supt. edn., 1991-96; ret., 1996; bd. dirs. Operation Upgrade, S.W. Ednl. Devel. Lab., La. Edn. TV Authority, La. Sch. for Math., Sci. and Arts, La. Drug Policy, La. Children's Cabinet; co-chmn. bd. dirs. Satellite Ednl. Rsch. Consortium; co-project dir. La. Systemic Initiatives Program; bd. trustees La. Tchrs. Retirement System; mem. supts. adv. coun. State Bd. Elem. and Secondary Edn.; active Coun. Chief State Sch. Officers, Govs. Cabinet. Mem. joint adv. bd. Baton Rouge Gen. Hosp.; bd. dirs. Baton Rouge Symphony, La. Youth Orch., Playmakers, Crime Stoppers, Fairview Hosp., Tau Ctr.; trustee La. Arts and Scis. Coun., Our Lady of Lake Coll.; mem. visitation com. and bd. dirs. United Way, also ednl.hmn.; mem. standing com. for rsch. and analysis Am. Luth. Ch.; mem. tchr. edn. coun. La. State U.; and numerous others; mem. La. LEARN Commn. Recipient State Farmer award La. Assn. Future Farmers Am., Boss of Yr. award Am. Bus. Women's Assn. Mem. NEA (life), Am. Assn. Sch. Adminstrs. (emeritus), Nat. Sch. Bds. Assn. (mem. liaison com.), Nat. Speech Assn. (pres. debate and discussion divsn.), Nat. Soc. Study of Edn., Nat. PTA, La. Assn. Sch. Execs. (Outstanding Educator award), La. Assn. Sch. Supts. (bd. dirs.), Far West Lab. Ednl. Rsch. and Devel. (bd. dirs.), Assn. Supervision and Curriculum Devel. (bd. dirs.), Large City Schs. Supts. Assn. (pres.), PTA (hon. life), Baton Rouge C. of C. (mem. edn. com.) Horace Mann League, Phi Delta Kappa, Lambda Delta Lambda. Avocations: golf, tennis, camping, fishing, gardening. *

ARVESON, WILLIAM BARNES, mathematics educator; b. Oakland, Calif., Nov. 22, 1934; s. Ronald Magnus and Audrey Mary (Hichens) A.; m. Lee A. Kaskutas. B.S. in Math, Calif. Inst. Tech., 1960; M.A., UCLA, 1963, Ph.D., 1964. Benjamin Peirce instr. Harvard U., 1965-68; lectr. dept. math. U. Calif., Berkeley, 1968-69; assoc. prof. U. Calif., 1969-74, prof.,

1974—, Miller rsch. prof., 1985-86, 99—. Author: An Invitation to C*-algebras, 1976; assoc. editor: Duke Math. Jour, 1975-86, Jour. of Operator Theory, 1977-87, editor, 1987—; contbr. articles to math. jours. Served with U.S. Navy, 1952-55. John Simon Guggenheim fellow, 1976-77. Mem. Am. Math. Soc. (assoc. editor bulletin 1988-91), Edinburgh Math. Soc. (assoc. editor proceedings 1989—). Office: U Calif Dept Math Berkeley CA 94720

ARVIDSON, ROBERT BENJAMIN, JR., geneticist, consultant; b. Lafayette, Ind., June 10, 1920; s. Robert Benjamin Sr. and Ollie Blanche (Ice) A.; m. Rose Janet Gaylord, Sept. 2, 1943; children: Cheryl R., James R., Kay E. BSA, Purdue U., 1942, MS, 1950. Poultry geneticist Hy-Line Internat. Div. Pioneer Hi Bred Internat., Des Moines, 1947-50; dir. rsch. Hy-Line Internat., Des Moines, 1951-79, ret., 1979; cons. World Bank, Washington, 1979-80. Precinct committeeman Rep. Party, Des Moines, 1970. Capt. Q.M.C., U.S. Army, 1942-46. Mem. World Poultry Sci. Assn., Poultry Sci. Assn., Kiwanis (pres. 1979). Methodist. Avocations: golf, fishing, gardening, Dahlia growing. Home: 4010 Adams Ave Des Moines IA 50310-4036

ARVISAIS, KARI LYNN, marriage and family therapist; b. Hayward, Calif., July 25, 1967; d. Edward A. and Carolyn J. (Edgar) A. BA in Psychology, U. Mass., 1989; postgrad., UNLV, 1991, 93-94; MS in Counseling Psychology, St. John's U., 1993. Lic. marriage and family therapist. Marriage and family therapist Charter Behaviorial Health, Las Vegas, 1994-95; marriage and family therapist, drug and alcohol counselor Cmty. Counseling, Las Vegas, 1995-97; marriage and family therapist HBI, Las Vegas, 1997; pvt. practice Las Vegas, 1995—. Hot-line counselor Suicide Prevention, Las Vegas, 1992; vol. homeless shelter Market Ministries, New Bedford, Mass., 1989-90. Mem. Am. Assn. of Marriage and Family Therapists, Nev. Assn. of Marriage and Family Therapy (clin. mem.), Am. Orthopsychiat. Assn. (clin. mem.). Avocations: animal lover, reading, movies, music, computers.

ARVIZU, CHARLENE SUTTER, elementary education educator; b. San Jose, Calif., Mar. 1, 1947; d. Joseph Carl and Marjorie Loreen (Nylin) Sutter; m. Ambrose Emanuel Arvizu, Apr. 7, 1980; children: Joseph Todd Nottingham, Matthew Sutter. BA in Art, San Jose State U., 1964, lifetime tchg. credential grades K-9, 1969, lifetime spl. edn. grades K-14, 1969, specialist/learning handicapped, 1969. Tchr. edn. mentally retarded class grades K-12 Berryessa Union Sch. Dist., 1969-71, resource ctr. dir. grades K-5, 1971-73, kindergarten tchr. Ruskin Sch., 1974—; instr. Ohlone Coll., Fremont, Calif., 1980-89, Chapman Coll., 1985-88, San Jose County Office Edn., 1985-94; cons., lectr. Bur. Edn. & Rsch., 1991—; nat. lectr., cons. and presenter in field. Author: Whole Language Strategies in the Classroom, 1991, Strengthening Your Kindergarten Using Thrmatic, Integrate Literature Based Strategies, 1993, Kindergarten 5 Day Institute Book, 1994, Read It Again, 1998, Current Best Strategies to Help All Your Kindergartens to be Successful, 1998, Management for Kindergarten Success, 1999. Recipient Disting. Sch. award Office of Mayor of San Jose, Calif., 1987, Award Bur. of Edn. and Rsch., 1998. Mem. Internat. Reading Assn., Calif. Reading Assn., Internat. Book Assn. for Young Readers, Children's Book Coun. Inc., Calif. Sch. Age Consortium, Planetary Citizens-One World-One People, Soc. Children's Book Writers, Delta Kappa Gamma. Avocations: animals, horseback riding. Home: 3010 Daurine Ct Gilroy CA 95020-9552 Office: Ruskin Sch 1401 Turlock Ln San Jose CA 95132-2399

ARVYSTAS, MICHAEL GECIAUSKAS, orthodontist, educator, sculptor; b. Vilnius, Lithuania, Dec. 18, 1942; came to U.S., 1949; naturalized, 1961; s. Mykolas and Antanina (Kleiza) A.; m. Jane Grannis, 1969 (div. 1978); m. Mary Ruth Buchness, Nov. 2, 1992. B.A., Colgate U., 1965, D.M.D., Tufts U., 1969; cert. Columbia U., 1973. Diplomate Am. Bd. Orthodontics. Chief orthodontic sect. Morrisania City Hosp., Bronx, N.Y., 1973-76; dir. orthodontics ctr. for cranio facial disorders and cleft palate ctr. Montefiore Hosp. and Med. Ctr., Bronx, 1973—; chief orthodontic sect. N. Central Bronx Hosp., 1976-83; clin. prof. N.J. Dental Sch., Newark, 1974—, dir., lectr. undergrad. and postgrad. dental students, 1974—; lectr. in field; vis. prof. Albert Einstein Coll. Medicine, Bronx. Contbr. numerous articles to profl. jours., also chpts. to books. Served to capt. Dental Corps, USAF, 1969-71. Mem. ADA, First Dist. Dental Soc. N.Y.C., Am. Assn. Orthodontists, Northeastern Soc. Orthodontists, N.Y. Acad. Dentistry, Am. Acad. Esthetic Dentistry, Tufts U. Dental Alumni Assn., Orthodontic Alumni Soc. Columbia U., Colgate U. Alumni Assn., Sigma Xi. Office: 24 Washington Sq N New York NY 10011-9168

ARWINE, ALAN TROY, political educator; b. Albuqueque, Mar. 15, 1963; s. James Ronnie and Doris Marie (Oliver) A. BS, Kansas State U., 1986; MS, Fort Hays State U., 1989; PhD, So. Ill. U., 1996. Head coach, rifle team Kans. State U., Manhattan, 1984-86; instr. Kansas City (Kans.) C.C., 1990, McKendree Coll., Lebanon, Ill., 1995, So. Ill. U., Carbondale, 1994-96; asst. prof. MacMurray Coll., Jacksonville, Ill., 1996-97; rsch. scientist U. Ill., Urbana, 1997—; instr. Parkland Coll., Champaign, Ill., 1998—. Author: The Use of U.S. Aid as a Tool to Improve Human Rights Performance, 1996; (with others) The Political Behavior of Older Americans, 1994, Birth Order and Political Behavior, 1996, Recent Explorations in Biology and Politics, 1997. Mem. Am. Polit. Sci. Assn., Midwest Polit. Sci. Assn., NRA (coach rifle team, 11 time nat. rifle champion 1983-86, All-Am. rifle team 1985). E-mail: arwine@uiuc.edu. Home: 2606 Heritage Dr Champaign IL 61822

ARYA, SATYA PAL, meteorology educator; b. Mavi Kalan, Dist Meerut, India, Aug. 24, 1939; came to U.S., 1965.; BE (Civil), U. Roorkee (India), 1961, ME (Civil), 1964; PhD, Colo. State U., 1968. Asst. engr. Irrigation Dept., Lucknow, India, 1961-62; lectr. U. Roorkee, 1963-65; rsch. asst. Colo. State U., Ft. Collins, 1965-68, rsch. assoc., 1968-69; rsch. asst., assoc. prof. U. Wash., Seattle, 1969-76; assoc. prof. N.C. State U., Raleigh, 1976-81, prof. meteorology, 1981—, acting head MEAS dept., 1982-83; vis. prof. Indian Inst. Tech., Delhi, 1983-84. Author: Introduction to Micrometeorology, 1988, Air Pollution Meteorology and dispersion, 1999; contbr. sci. articles to jours. of atmospheric scis., applied meteorology, fluid mechanics, others. Fellow AAAS, Am. Meteorol. Soc.; mem. Am. Geophys. Union. Achievements include research in atmospheric sciences, applied meteorology, fluid mechanics, atmospheric environment, geophysical research, environmental pollution. Office: NC State U Dept Marine Earth & Atmospheric Sci Raleigh NC 27695-8208

ARZOUMANIDIS, GREGORY G., chemist; b. Thessaloniki, Greece, Aug. 16, 1936; came to U.S., 1964, naturalized, 1976; s. Gerasimos and Sophia A.; m. Anastasia Anastasopoulos, Jan. 2, 1966; children: Sophia, Alexis. B.S. in Chemistry, U. Thessaloniki, 1959, M.S. in Chemistry, 1959; Ph.D. in Inorganic Chemistry, U. Stuttgart, (Germany), 1964; M.B.A., U. Conn., 1979. Research assoc. MIT, 1964-66; research chemist Monsanto, Everett, Mass., 1966-69; sr. research chemist Am. Cyanamid Co., Stamford, Conn., 1969-72, Stauffer Chem. Co., Dobbs Ferry, N.Y., 1972-79; research assoc. Amoco Chem. Co., Naperville, Ill., 1979-94, Argonne (Ill.) Nat. Lab., 1995-96; with Oakwood Cons., 1996—. Inventor comml. catalysts for polypropylene plastics, new processes; patentee (U.S. and fgn.); prin. co-inventor Amoco supported polypropylene catalyst; contbr. articles to profl. jours. Served to 2d lt. Greek Army, 1959-61. Recipient acad. award Govt. of W.Ger., 1963, Presdl. award Amoco Chem. Co., 1990. Mem. AAAS, Am. Chem. Soc., Sigma Xi. Greek Orthodox. Home: 7 S 610 Carriage Way Naperville IL 60540

ARZT, NOAM H., academic administrator, consultant; b. Portsmouth, Va., Oct. 31, 1961; s. A. David and Edya S. Arzt; m. Heidi Lynn Steinberg, June 12, 1983; children: Jeremy, Jesse. BS, U. Pa., 1983, MSEd, 1987, PhD, 1993. Assoc. dir. Wharton Sch. Dean's Office U. Pa., Phila., 1983-90, exec. dir. info. sys. and computing, 1990-97, sr. fellow, 1997—; pres. HLN Consulting, LLC, Marlton, N.J., 1997—. Author: The Business of Higher Education, 1995. Recipient Commr.'s award N.J. Dept. Health and Sr. Svsc., 1996. E-mail: arzt@hln.com. Home and Office: HLN Consulting LLC 105 Peabody Ln Marlton NJ 08053

ASA, CHERYL SUZANNE, biologist; b. Herrin, Ill., Feb. 21, 1945; d. Robert Adron Asa and Dorotha Elnora (Cravens) Asa Armentrout; children: Brett Clavenna, Scott Clavenna. BA, U. Wis., 1976, MS, 1979, PhD, 1981. Rsch. biologist U. Minn., St. Paul, 1981-84; rsch. fellow Rockefeller U./N.Y. Zool. Soc., N.Y.C., 1985-87; field rsch. in ecology U. Minn., Mpls., 1986-88; dir. rsch. St. Louis Zool. Park, 1988—; cons. Sci. Mus. Minn., St. Paul, 1982-84, Equus mag., 1985—. Contbr. articles to profl. jours. Vol. Planned Parenthood, St. Louis, 1989—; chair Meso-Am. Fauna Interest Group, 1994—. NSF fellow, 1977-80; Noyes Found. fellow, 1985-88; grantee Nixon Griffis Fund, 1989-92, Inst. for Museum Svcs., 1989—. Mem. Internat. Union for Conservation Nature (Survival Svc. commn. Equids, 1992—), Am. Assn. Zool. Parks and Aquariums (chmn. contraception com. 1989—, chmn. cryopreservation com. 1989-90), Am. Soc. Mammalogists, Animal Behavior Soc., Soc. for Conservation Biology, Captive Breeding Specialist Group, Soc. Study of Fertility, Soc. Study Reprodn., Equid Taxon Adv. Group (chmn. 1991—), St. Louis (Mo.) Rsch. Coun. (pres. 1992-93), Sigma Xi. Avocations: photography, piano, dance. Office: St Louis Zool Pk Forest Pk Saint Louis MO 63110

ASADI, ANITA MURLENE, business educator; b. Kirksville, Mo., Feb. 2, 1948; d. James Murl and Norma Waneva (Schillie) Wallace; m. Asad Asadi, Feb. 25, 1972; children: Soraya, Ali. BS in Bus. Edn., N.E. Mo. State U., 1970, MA, 1971. Grad. asst. N.E. Mo. State U., Kirksville, 1970-71; instr. bus. edn. Muscatine (Iowa) C.C., 1971-76; mem. faculty St. Ambrose U., Davenport, Iowa, 1977-83; instr. mgmt. support sys., chmn. dept. Scott C.C., Davenport, 1977—; adminstrv. asst. Stanley, Lande, Coulter & Pearce, Muscatine, 1971-74; cons. Rock Island (Ill.) Arsenal, 1983-85; writer Sci. Rsch. Assocs. a.k.a. SRA/Pergamon, Chgo., 1987-88, Paradigm Pub. Internat., Eden Prairie, Minn., 1989—. Author: (textbook) Stenoscript ABC Shorthand, 1989; mem. editorial bd. Answer Book, Illinois Legal Handbook; contbr. articles to profl. jours. Mem Pres. Club Rep. Nat. Com., 1990, Talent Identification Program Parent/Alumni Network, Duke U., Durham, N.C., 1989-90, Scott County Family YMCA, Davenport, 1984-90. Recipient Bus. Edn. award, 1990, Disting. Svc. and Scholarship award IBEA, 1990, Chancellor's award, 1991, Phebe Sudlow award Quad Cities Encouragement Bd., 1991; named Outstanding Postsecondary Bus. instr., IBEA, 1991. Mem. NAACP, NEA, Am. Vocat. Assn., Iowa Vocat. Assn., Bus. Profl. Educators Iowa, Iowa Bus. Edn. Assn., Office Automation Network, Assn. Info. System Profl., Bus. Profl. Am., Iowa Women Ednl. Leadership, Internat. Soc. Bus. Educators, Delta Pi Epsilon. Avocations: Mideast artifacts, Am. antiques, music boxes, reading autobiographies. Home: 5075 Crestview Heights Dr Bettendorf IA 52722-5626 Office: Scott CC 306 W River Dr Davenport IA 52801-1201

ASADI, ROBERT SAMIR, high school principal; b. Salt Lake City, Dec. 21, 1953; s. Abdul-Aziz and Wilma (Craig) A.; m. Karen Lee Schenk, June 16, 1990; children: Scott, Ryan. BS, U. Wyo., 1986; MEd, No. Ariz. U., 1994. Cert. tchr. and adminstr. Tchr., coach Cactus H.S., Glendale, Ariz., 1986-89, Holbrook (Ariz.) H.S., 1989-91; tchr., adminstrv. asst., coach Agua Fria Union H.S. South, Avondale, Ariz., 1991-94; prin. Agua Fria Union H.S.-North, Goodyear, Ariz., 1994-98, Millennium H.S., 1998—. mem. West Valley Fine Arts Coun., Avondale, 1995-96, Leadership West II, Avondale, 1995-96. Mem. ASCD, Tri City West C. of C., Ariz. Sch. Adminstrs., Nat. Assn. of Secondary Sch. Prins. Avocations: computers, golf, backpacking, spectator sports. Home: 9139 W Evans Dr Peoria AZ 85381-3784 Office: Millennium High Sch 14802 W Wigwam Blvd Goodyear AZ 85338

ASAHINA, ROBERT JAMES, editor, publishing company executive; b. Toledo, 1950; s. Shoichi and Katherine A. AM, NYU, 1974; B in Gen. Studies, U. Mich., Ann Arbor, 1972. Mng. editor The Pub. Interest, N.Y.C., 1975-78; adminstrv. editor GEO, N.Y.C., 1978-79; editor N.Y. Times, N.Y.C., 1979-82; arts editor Harper's Mag., N.Y.C., 1982-83; v.p., sr. editor Simon & Schuster, N.Y.C., 1983-96, editorial dir. Summit Books, 1990-92; pres. adult pub. group Golden Books Family Entertainment, N.Y.C., 1996-98; editor in chief Broadway Books, N.Y.C., 1999—; chmn. Tokunaga Dance Co., N.Y.C., 1985—. Contbr. numerous articles to jours. and mags., including Wall Street Jour. Office: Broadway Books 1540 Broadway New York NY 10036

ASAI-SATO, CAROL YUKI, lawyer; b. Osaka, Japan, Oct. 22, 1951; came to U.S., 1953; d. Sumiko (Kamei) Asai; 1 child, Ryan Makoto Sato. BA cum laude, U. Hawaii, 1972; JD, Willamette Coll. Law, 1975. Bar: Hawaii 1975. Assoc. firm Ashford & Wriston, Honolulu, 1975-79; counsel Bank of New Eng., Boston, 1979-81; assoc. counsel Alexander & Baldwin, Honolulu, 1981-83, sr. counsel, 1984-88; of counsel, Rush, Moore, Craven, Sutton, Morry, Beh, 1988-89, ptnr., 1989-97; ptnr. Alston Hunt Floyd & Ing, 1997—. Willamette Coll. Law Bd. Trustees scholar, 1972-73. Mem. ABA, Hawaii Bar Assn., Hawaii Women Lawyers, Phi Beta Kappa, Phi Kappa Phi. Democrat. Office: Alston Hunt Floyd & Ing Pacific Tower 18th Fl 1001 Bishop St Ste 1800 Honolulu HI 96813-3689

ASAKAWA, TAKAKO, dancer, dance teacher, director, choreographer; b. Toyko, Feb. 23, 1939; came to U.S., 1962; d. Kamenosuke and Chiaki Asakawa. Student, Tokyo schs., 1962-91. Prin. dancer Martha Graham Dance Co., N.Y.C., 1962-76, 81—; dancer Alvin Ailey, 1968-69, Pearl Lang, 1967, Lar Lubovitch, 1974-80; guest tchr. at numerous schs. and univs. throughout world, including Moscow Culture Exch. Program, Martha Graham Sch., Juilliard Sch.; co.-founder Asakawalker Dance Co.; dir. Paris Opera Ballet Co. and various univs. throughout world. Performed all major roles in GRaham reperatory throughout world, including Paris Opera House, Covent Garden; Broadway and TV performances include Eliza in The King and I, Bell Tel. Hour. Named Legendary Woman of Am., St. Vincent's Hosp. Mem. Am. Guild Musical Artists. Home and Office: 20 West 64 St Apt E/F New York NY 10023

ASANUMA, HIROSHI, physician, educator; b. Kobe, Japan, Aug. 17, 1926; s. Kisaburo and Yukiko (Takahashi) A.; m. Reiko Shimazu, Dec. 15, 1953; children—Chisato, Mari. M.D., Keio U., Tokyo, 1952; D.M.S., Kobe Med. Coll., 1959. Instr., Kobe Med. Coll., 1953-59; asst. prof. Osaka City U., Japan, 1959-65; guest investigator Rockefeller Inst., N.Y.C., 1961-63; assoc. prof. N.Y. Med. Coll., N.Y.C., 1965-71, prof., 1971-72; prof. Rockefeller U., N.Y.C., 1972-96, emeritus prof., 1996. Contbr. articles to profl. jours. and books. Mem. Am. Physiol. Soc., Soc. for Neurosci., Harvey Soc., Japanese Physiol. Soc. Home: 505 E 79th St New York NY 10021-0709 Office: Rockefeller U Dept of Motorphysiology 1230 York Ave Dept Of New York NY 10021-6399

ASARE, KAREN MICHELLE GILLIAM, reading, math and English language educator; b. Bklyn., Jan. 21; d. James Henry and Frances (Walker) Gilliam; m. William Kofi, May 4, 1977; 1 child, Anton William Kwaku Asare Jr. BA, Hunter Coll., 1976, MS in Edn., 1979. Cert. tchr., N.Y. state. Tchr. Women's Prison Assn., N.Y., 1977-78, St. Augustine's Sch., Bronx, N.Y., 1978—. Ednl. Opportunity Ctr. of SUNY, 1989—. Mem. NAACP, Nat. Coun. Tchrs. English, Reading Reform Found., Nat. Cath. Edn. Assn., Profl. Staff Congress, Sigma Gamma Rho-Delta Nu Sigma. Avocations: reading, art, creative writing. Office: Saint Augustine's Sch 1176 Franklin Ave Bronx NY 10456-4306

ASARO, V. FRANK, lawyer; b. San Diego, July 28, 1935; s. Frank B. and Josephine (Quinci) A.; m. Barbara A. Mansfield, Aug. 16, 1958 (div. Mar., 1988); children: Dean, Valerie, Stephanie, Audrey. BA, San Diego State U., 1957; postgrad., Loyola U., L.A., 1957-60; JD, LLB, Southwestern U., L.A., 1961. Bar: Calif. 1962; U.S. Dist. Ct. (so. dist.) Calif. 1962, U.S. Dist. Ct. Ala. 1990; U.S. Ct. Appeals (9th cir.) 1965, U.S. Ct. Appeals (6th cir.) 1983. Clk. to the Hon. Justice Coughlin Calif. Dist. Ct. Appeal (4th dist.), San Diego, 1961-62; assoc. atty. Jenkins & Perry, San Diego, 1962-65, partner, 1965-70; partner Gant & Asaro, San Diego, 1970-80; sr. partner Asaro, Gattis & Sullivan, San Diego, 1980-82, Asaro & Long, San Diego, 1982-85, V Frank Asaro and Assocs., San Diego, 1985—; judge pro-tem San Diego Superior Ct., 1975—; arbitrator, San Diego Superior Ct., 1975, 1997; lectr. Practicing Law Inst. Author: Balance Between Order and Chaos, 1988, A Primal Wisdom, 1997; contbr. columnist Dicta County Bar Journal, 1965-70. Chairman Harborview Redevelopment Com., San Diego, 1975-85; mem. County Airport relocation SANPAT Com., San Diego County, 1970-75, City Center Planning Com., San Diego, 1986-90. Recipient citation for pub. svc., Mayor San Diego, 1989. Mem. Calif. State Bar Assn. (del.), San Diego County Bar Assn., Rotary Club (program chair 1996—, pres. 1998—), Barristers Club San Diego (dir.). Achievements include patent for avalanche rescue markers. Avocations: writing, music, philosophy. Office: Ste 400 4370 La Jolla Village Dr San Diego CA 92122-1249

ASATO, SUSAN PEARCE, business executive, educator; b. Dallas, Dec. 29, 1949; d. Joe Camp and Sue (Dickey) Pearce; m. Morris T. Asato, Apr. 1, 1973. Student, U. Internat., Saltillo, Mex., 1968; BE, U. Tex., 1973; MBA, Calif. State U., San Bernardino, 1981. Tchr. Austin (Tex.) Ind. Sch. Dist., 1972-73; rsch. assoc. U. Tex., Austin, 1973-77; dir. Tairyu (Japan) English Ctr., 1977-78; purchasing agt. U. Calif., Riverside, 1978-83; gen. mgr. corp. purchasing ABC-TV, Hollywood, Calif., 1983-90; dir. purchasing and material mgmt. Mira Costa Coll., Oceanside, Calif., 1990—; instr., lectr. U. Calif., Riverside, 1981-83. Bd. dirs. Santa Margarita YCMA, 1996—, Oceanside Mus. of Art, 1998—. Mem. Nat. Assn. Purchasing Mgrs., Nat. Assn. Ednl. Buyers, Nat. Contract Mgmt. Assn., Calif. Assn. Sch. Bus. Ofcls., Calif. Assn. Pub. Purchasing Ofcls., Oceanside Rotary Internat. (bd. dirs., Paul Harris fellow 1998). Episcopalian. Home: Mira Costa Coll 1 Barnard Dr Oceanside CA 92056-3820

ASBELL, BERNARD, author, English language educator; b. Bklyn., May 8, 1923; s. Samuel and Minnie (Zevin) A.; m. Mildred Sacarny, Jan. 2, 1944; children: Paul, Lawrence, Jonathan, Jody; m. 2d, Marjorie Baldwin Farrell, June 11, 1971 (div. Aug. 1977); m. 3d, Jean Brenchley, July 21, 1990. Student, U. Conn., 1943-44; L.H.D., U. New Haven, 1978. Reporter Richmond (Va.) Times-Dispatch, 1945-47; engaged in pub. relations Chgo., 1947-55; mng. editor Chgo. mag., 1955-56; tchr. non-fiction writing U. Chgo., 1956-60, Bread Loaf Writers Conf., Middlebury (Vt.) Coll., 1960, 61, U. Bridgeport, 1961-63; vis. lectr. Yale U., 1979-80; vis. lectr. Pa. State U., 1984-85, assoc. prof. English, 1985-92; dir. New Eng. Writers Ctr., 1979-84; writer in residence Clark U., 1982; freelance author, 1956—; cons. Ednl. Facilities Labs., 1963, U. Ill., 1964, Ford Found., 1965, 1968-69; cons. to sec. HEW, 1965-68, IBM Corp., Carnegie Corp. N.Y.; assoc. fellow Trumbull Coll., Yale U., 1981—; vis. lectr. Duke U., 1998-99. Author: When F.D.R. Died, 1961, The New Improved American, 1965, What Lawyers Really Do, 1970, Careers in Urban Affairs, 1970, The F.D.R. Memoirs, 1973, (under pseudonym Nicholas Max) President McGovern's First Term, 1973, (with Clair F. Vough) Productivity, 1975, The Senate Nobody Knows, 1978, (with David Hartman) White Coat, White Cane, 1978; editor: Mother and Daughter: The Letters of Eleanor and Anna Roosevelt, 1982, Transit Point Moscow, 1985, (with Joe Paterno) Paterno by the Book, 1989, What They Know About You, 1991, The Book of You, 1992, The Pill: A Biography of the Drug That Changed the World, 1995; contbr. to nat. mags. Justice of peace, Wilton, Conn., 1966-67; chmn. Wilton Democratic party, 1964-66. Served with AUS, 1943-45. Recipient Sch. Bell award NEA, 1965; Edn. Writers Assn. 1st prize mag. coverage, 1965; spl. citation, 1966. Mem. Am. Soc. Journalists and Authors (pres. 1963, exec. coun. 1964-66, Author of Yr. award 1996), Authors Guild, Nat. Press Club. Address: 237 Wooded Way State College PA 16803-1239

ASBELL, FRED THOMAS, government executive; b. Birmingham, Ala., May 23, 1948; s. George Thomas and Dorothy Elizabeth (Wood) A. B.S. in Bus. Adminstrn., Jacksonville State U., 1973. Dir. sales Gulf Hills Inn, Ocean Springs, Miss., 1974-76; dir. sales The Read House, Chattanooga, 1976-77; adminstrv. asst. U.S. Rep. Clay Shaw, Washington, 1981-83; dep. polit. dir. Republican Nat. Com., Washington, 1983-84; dir. com. service Nat. Republican Congressional Com., Washington, 1984-85; exec. asst. to sec. U.S. Dept. Labor, Washington, 1985-87; exec. asst. to chmn. Dole for Pres. Com., Washington, 1987-88; cons. The Brock Group (formerly William Brock Assocs.), Washington, 1988-89; v.p. Am. Viewpoint Inc., Alexandria, Va., 1989-90; cons. The Brock Group, Washington, 1993; pres. Friends of Bill Brock for U.S. Senate, Inc., Annapolis, 1993-94, Internat. Mobile Comm., Inc., Bethesda, Md., 1994-97; exec. dir. U.S. Census Monitoring Bd., Suitland, Md., 1998—. Baptist. Home: 141 12th St NE # 15 Washington DC 20002 Office: Ste 1230 4700 Silver Hill Rd Suitland MD 20746

ASBURY, ARTHUR KNIGHT, neurologist, educator; b. Cin., Nov. 22, 1928; s. Eslie and Mary (Knight) A.; m. Carolyn Holstein, May 17, 1980; children by previous marriage: Dana, Patricia Knight, William Francis. Grad., Phillips Acad., Andover, Mass., 1946; student, Stanford, 1947-48; BS, U. Ky., 1951; MD, U. Cin., 1958; MA (hon.), U. Pa., 1974. Intern in medicine Mass. Gen. Hosp., Boston, 1958-59; resident Mass. Gen. Hosp., 1959-63, fellow, 1963-65, staff neurologist, 1965-69; chief neurology San Francisco VA Hosp., 1969-74; prof. dept. neurology U. Pa., Phila., 1974—, chmn. dept. neurology, 1974-82; Van Meter prof. neurology U. Pa., 1983-97; acting dean, exec. v.p. U. Pa. Sch. Medicine, 1988-89, vice dean for rsch., 1990-93, vice dean for faculty affairs, 1993-97; teaching fellow Harvard Med. Sch., 1958-65, instr., 1965-68, assoc., 1968-69; assoc. prof. neurology U. Calif. at San Francisco, 1969-73, vice-chmn., 1969-74, prof., 1973-74; mem. nat. adv. neurol. disease & stroke coun. NIH, 1990-93; hon. prof. med. scis. Hebei Med. Coll., China, 1995. Sr. editor Blue Books of Practical Neurology, 1980—; assoc. editor Archives of Neurology, 1975-76; assoc. editor Annals of Neurology, 1976-81, chief editor, 1985-93; mem. editorial bd. Muscle and Nerve, 1977-89, Neurology, 1981-85, Jour. Neuropathology and Exptl. Neurology, 1981-83, Jour. Neurol. Scis., 1989—; contbr. chpts. to med. textbooks, articles to med. jours. V.p., bd. dirs. Forest Retreat Farms Inc., Carlisle, Ky., 1970-92. With AUS, 1951-53. Recipient Daniel Drake medal U. Cin., 1988; grantee UPHS, 1967-93, Muscular Dystrophy Assn., 1974-82. Fellow AAAS, Am. Acad. Neurology (v.p. 1977-79); mem. Inst. Medicine, Am. Neurol. Assn. (councillor 1976-81, pres. 1982-83, hon. 1995), Am. Assn. Neuropathologists (v.p. 1983-84), Soc. Neurosci., Assn. Univ. Profs. Neurology (pres. 1980-82), World Fedn. Neurology (v.p. 1989-93), European Neurol. Soc. (hon.). Home: 408 S Van Pelt St Philadelphia PA 19146-1233 Office: U Pa Hosp Dept Neurology 3400 Spruce St Philadelphia PA 19104-4204

ASCH, ARTHUR LOUIS, environmental company executive; b. N.Y.C., July 4, 1941; s. Alexander and Esther W. A.; m. Anita S.; children: Michael, Lisa. BS in Econ., U. Pa., 1963. Fin. analyst Schlumberger Ltd., N.Y.C., 1966-68, Colt Industries Inc., N.Y.C., 1968-69; chmn. bd. Rexx Environ Corp (previously Oak Hill Sportswear Corp.), N.Y.C., 1969—. Bd. dirs. Nassau County chpt. Assn. for Help Retarded Children, Brookville, N.Y., 1987—. Office: REXX Environmental Corp 350 Park Ave Fl 14 New York NY 10022-6022

ASCH, FRANK, writer children's books, illustrator; b. Somerville, N.J., Aug. 6, 1946; s. John Louis and Margaret (Giasullo) A.; m. Jan Pizzutello, Mar. 27, 1975; 1 child, Devin. BFA, Cooper Union, 1969. Author: George's Store, 1968, Yellow Yellow, 1971, Good Lemonade, 1976, The Last Puppy, 1980, Mooncake, 1983, Pearl's Promise, 1984, Journey to Terezor, 1989, Dear Brother, 1992, The Earth and I, 1994, One Man Show, 1997, and numerous others. Mem. John Burroughs Assn. (Outstanding Nature Writing for Children award Am. Mus. Natural History 1996). Home: 277 Spruce Knob Rd Middletown Springs VT 05757

ASCHAFFENBURG, WALTER EUGENE, composer, music educator; b. Essen, Germany, May 20, 1927; came to U.S., 1938, naturalized, 1944; s. William Arthur and Margarete (Herz) A.; m. Nancy Dandridge Cooper, Aug. 14, 1951 (div.); children: Ruth Margareta, Katherine Elizabeth; m. Rayna Klatzkin Barroll, Aug. 5, 1987. Diploma, Hartford Sch. Music, 1945; BA, Oberlin Coll., 1951; MA, Eastman Sch. Music, 1952. Prof. composition and music theory, former chmn. composition dept. Oberlin (Ohio) Coll. Conservatory of Music, prof. emeritus, 1987—, also former chmn. dept. music theory, 1952-87. Composer: TRIO for piano, violin, cello, 1951, Divertimento for Trumpet, Horn Trombone 1952, Chaconne for Brass Ensemble, 1952, Ozymandias-Symphonic Reflections for Orch., 1952, cello Sonata, 1953, Sonata for Solo Violin, 1954, Piano Sonatina, 1954, String Quartet, 1955, Bartleby-opera, 1962, Elegy for Strings, 1961, The 23d Psalm for chorus, tenor solo, and oboe, 1963, Three Dances for Orch., 1966, Three Shakespeare Sonnets for tenor and piano, 1967, Quintet for Winds, 1967, Proem for Brass and Percussion, 1969, Blossom Music Ctr. Fanfare, 1970, Duo for Violin and Cello, 1971, Conversations-Six Pieces for Piano, 1973, Summit Records, 1994, Libertatem Appellant for Tenor, Baritone and Orch., 1976, Carrousel—24 Pieces for Piano, 1980, Concertino for Violin, Ten Winds and Contrabass, 1982, Laughing Time for Mixed Chorus, 1983, Festive Fanfare and Hymn for Brass and Percussion, 1983, Concerto for Oboe and Orch., 1985, New World Records, 1997. From South Mountain for Brass Quintet, 1988, Coalescence for Oboe and Cello, 1989, Sonata for the

Fortepiano or Pianoforte, 1990, Parings for Clarinet and Piano, 1993. Served with AUS, 1945-47. Recipient award Fromm Music Found., 1953; Nat. Inst. Arts and Letters award, 1966; Cleve. arts prize, 1980; Guggenheim fellow, 1955-56, 73-74. Mem. ASCAP, Soc. Composers, Am. Music Ctr., Soc. Music Theory. Home: 4639 E Monte Way Phoenix AZ 85044-7517

ASCHAUER, CHARLES JOSEPH, JR., corporate director, former company executive; b. Decatur, Ill., July 23, 1928; s. Charles Joseph and Beulah Diehl (Kniple) A.; m. Elizabeth Claire Meagher, Apr. 28, 1962; children: Karen A. Vorwald, Thomas Arthur, Susan A. Baisley, Karl Andrew. B.B.A., Northwestern U., 1950; certificate internat. bus. adminstr., Centre d'Etudes Industrielles, Geneva, Switzerland, 1951. Prin. McKinsey & Co., Chgo., 1955-62; v.p. mktg. Mead Johnson Labs. div. Mead Johnson & Co., Evansville, Ind., 1962-67; v.p., pres. automotive group Maremont Corp., Chgo., 1967-70; v.p., group exec. Whittaker Corp., Los Angeles, 1970-71; v.p., pres. hosp. products div. Abbott Labs., North Chicago, Ill., 1971-76; v.p., group exec. Abbott Labs., 1976-79, exec. v.p., dir., 1979-89, ret., 1989; bd. dirs. Trustmark Ins. Co., Lake Forest, Ill., The Linc Group, Chgo., Boston Sci. Corp., Natick, Mass. Lt. Supply Corps, USNR, 1951-55. Mem. Univ. Club Chgo., Econs. Club Chgo., Sunset Ridge Country Club, Fairbanks Ranch Country Club.

ASCHEN, SHARON RUTH, genetic counselor, psychotherapist, nurse; b. Chgo., May 10, 1948. MA, Loyola U., 1979; MS, U. Ill., 1978, BS, 1972; postgrad., Ind. U. Med. Sch., Indpls., 1993—. RN, Ind. Mental health clinician Northwestern Inst. of Psychiatry, Chgo., 1974-79; lectr. Loyola U., Chgo., 1979-81; staff therapist Edgewater-Uptown Community Mental Health Clinic, Chgo., 1980-81, dir. emergency svcs., 1981-84; pvt. practice counselor and psychotherapist Chgo., 1984-87; psychiat. nurse Charter Hosp. of Indpls., Indpls., 1988-92; nurse LaRue Carter Meml. Hosp., Indpls., 1992-93, CPC Valle Vista Hosp., Greenwood, Ind., 1993-94, Koala Hosp., Indpls., 1995—; pvt. practice psychotherapy Indpls., 1995—; clin. therapist Schizophrenic Treatment Ctr, Indpls., 1996—. Author (handbook) Mental Status Examination, 1981, rev. 1991. Grantee Gt. Lakes Regional Genetics Group Edn. Initiative in Psychiat. Genetics, 1995—, NIMH Svcs.-Rsch. Br. Psychiat. Genetic Svcs. and Related Rsch. Mem. APA (assoc.), Am. Soc. for Genetic Counselors, Internat. Soc. for Nurses in Genetics, Ill. Psychol. Assn. (sec. 1983-84). Avocations: outdoor sports, old movies, Trivial Pursuit, cooking. Home and Office: 6218 Eastridge Dr Indianapolis IN 46219-4628

ASCHER, DAVID MARK, lawyer; b. Bklyn., Nov. 6, 1952; s. Bert A. and Adeline (Rose) A.; m. Joani S. Wolf, June 17, 1973; children: Ari, Shonna. BA, SUNY, Buffalo, 1973, JD, 1978; M of Community Planning, U. Cin., 1975. Bar: Ohio 1978, U.S. Dist. Ct. (no. dist.) Ohio 1978, U.S. Ct. Appeals (6th cir.) 1979, U.S. Ct. Appeals (3d cir.) 1994. Assoc. Squire, Sanders & Dempsey, Cleve., 1978-82; litigation counsel White Motor Corp., Cleve., 1982-83; gen. atty. Sea-Land Corp., Menlo Park, N.J., 1983-86; sr. atty./group counsel C.R. Bard, Inc., Murray Hill, N.J., 1986-91; v.p., gen. counsel, corp. sec. Vickers Am. Holdings, Inc., Paramus, N.J., 1991-98; v.p., gen. counsel The Newark Group, Inc., Cranford, N.J., 1999—. Editor: Coastal Zone Legal References, 1976. Pres. South Orange-Maplewood (N.J.) Spl. Edn. PTA, 1987-89; mem. South Orange-Maplewood Bd. Edn., 1989-98; bike ride com. Union County affiliate Am. Diabetes Assn., Clark, N.J., 1988-91, Essex County affiliate Am. Diabetes Assn., Roseland, N.J., 1994-96. Mem. ABA, Am. Corp. Counsel Assn. Avocations: bicycling, N.Y. Times crossword puzzles, tennis, cooking. Office: The Newark Group 20 Jackson Dr Cranford NJ 07016-3609

ASCHER, JAMES JOHN, pharmaceutical executive; b. Kansas City, Mo., Oct. 2, 1928; s. Bordner Fredrick and Helen (Barron) A.; m. Mary Ellen Robitsch, Feb. 27, 1954; children: Jill Denise, James John, Christopher Bordner. Student, Bergen Jr. Coll., 1947-48, U. Kans., 1946-47, 49-51. Rep. B.F. Ascher & Co., Inc., Memphis, 1954-55; asst. to pres. B.F. Ascher & Co., Inc., Kansas City, Mo., 1956-57, v.p., 1958-64, pres., 1965—. Bd. dirs. Childrens Cardiac Ctr., 1964-70, pres., 1968-70; mem. cen. governing bd. Children's Mercy Hosp., 1968-80; bd. dirs. Jr. Achievement of Middle Am., 1970-90, pres., 1973-76, chmn., 1979-81; edn. chmn. Young Pres.'s Orgn. 6th Internat. Univ. for Pres., Athens, 1975. 1st. lt. inf., U.S. Army, 1951-53, Korea. Decorated Bronze Star, Combat Infantryman's Badge. Mem. VFW, Am. Mgmt. Assn. (pres.'s assn.), Lenexa City C. of C., Drug, Chem. and Allied Trades Assn., World Pres.'s Orgn., Consumer Health Care Products Assn., Chief Execs. Orgn., Midwest Healthcare Mktg. Assn., Lotos Club, N.Y. Athletic Club, Kansas City Club, Mercury Club, Indian Hills Country Club, Delta Chi. Home: 6706 Glenwood St Shawnee Mission KS 66204-1451 Office: 15501 W 109th St Lenexa KS 66219-1307

ASCHER, MARIA LOUISE, translator, editor; b. N.Y.C.. AB, Cornell U., 1973; AM, U. Mass., 1978, Harvard U., 1989; PhD, Harvard U., 1997. Tchg. fellow dept. comparative lit. Harvard U., Cambridge, Mass., 1990-93; editor Harvard U. Press, 1979-89, sr. editor, 1994—. Translator: Souvenirs Pieux (Marguerite Yourcenar) (pub. in English as Dear Departed), 1992, Archives du Nord (Yourcenar) (pub. in English as How Many Years), 1995. I.H. Levin fellow Harvard U., 1987-88. Mem. MLA, Am. Comparative Lit. Assn., New Eng. Translators Assn. Office: Harvard U Press 79 Garden St Cambridge MA 02138

ASCHER, MICHAEL CHARLES, transportation executive; b. 1944. B in mech. engring., City Coll. of N.Y., 1966; MS, Long Island Univ., 1971. Plant engr. Long Island Lighting Co., Long Island, N.Y., 1966-72; dir. nuclear projects, deputy dir., project mgr. Burns & Roe, Inc., Oradell, N.J., 1972-84; deputy v.p. N.Y.C. Transit Authority, 1984-85, v.p., chief engr., 1985-87; exec. v.p., chief engr. Triborough Bridge and Tunnel Authority, N.Y.C., 1988-90, pres., COO, 1990—. Office: Triborough Bridge Tunnel Authority Randalls Is New York NY 10035*

ASCHER, ROBERT, anthropologist, archaeologist, educator, filmmaker; b. N.Y.C., Apr. 28, 1931; s. Alfred and Claire (Eliscue) A.; m. Marcia Alper, Mar. 10, 1956. Ph.D., UCLA, 1960. Prof. dept. anthropology Cornell U., Ithaca, N.Y., 1960—; fieldwork in Turkey, Mex., Eng., Peru, U.S., Israel, 1960—. Co-author: Mathematics of the Incas, 1997; contbr. articles to Anthropology and Humanism Quar., Sci., History of Sci., Visual Anthropology, other profl. jours.; filmmaker: Cycle: An Australian Myth, 1984-86, Bar Yohai: In Celebration of a Visionary, 1987-88, Blue: A Tlingit Odyssey, 1989-91, The Golem, 1992-95. Office: Cornell Univ Dept Of Anthropology Ithaca NY 14853

ASCHERMAN, JEFFREY ALAN, plastic and reconstructive surgeon; b. Erie, Pa., Mar. 19, 1962; s. Herbert Stanley and Dorothy Rose A.; m. Corinne Fortunee Rouah, June 9, 1988; children: Jeremy, Benjamin, Jonathan, Sarah. Student, Am. U. Paris, 1983; BA, Harvard U., 1984; MD, Columbia U., 1988. Diplomate Am. Bd. Plastic Surgery. Resident in gen. surgery Columbia-Presbyn. Med. Ctr., N.Y.C., 1988-91, rsch. fellow, 1991-92, resident in plastic surgery, 1992-94; fellow in craniofacial and pediat. plastic surgery Hôpital Necker-Enfants Malades, Paris, 1994-95; instr. clin. surgery Columbia U., N.Y.C., 1995-97, asst. prof. surgery, 1998—; assoc. adj. N.Y. Eye and Ear Infirmary, N.Y.C., 1995—; asst. attending physician N.Y. Presbyn. Hosp., N.Y.C., 1988—. Patent pending palatal distractor; contbr. articles to profl. jours. Active mem. local synagogues Kehilath Jeshurun, Ohab Zedek, N.Y.C., 1996—. Palatal Distraction Rsch. grantee Columbia U., 1996; Palatal Distraction Rsch. grantee Plastic Surgery Edn. Found., 1997; Cranial Ossification Rsch. grantee Columbia U., 1997; Retention Suture Rsch. grantee Columbia U., 1998. Mem. AMA, Am. Soc. Plastic and Reconstructive Surgeons, Am. Cleft Palate-Craniofacial Assn., Am. Soc. Peripheral Nerve, Med. Soc. State N.Y., N.Y. Regional Soc. Plastic and Reconstructive Surgery. Republican. Avocations: downhill skiing, tennis, travelling. E-mail: jaa7@columbia.edu. Office: Columbia-Presbyn Med Ctr 161 Fort Washington Ave New York NY 10032

ASCHHEIM, EVE MICHELE, artist, educator; b. N.Y.C., Aug. 30, 1958; d. Emil and Lydie Aschheim. BA, U. Calif., Berkeley, 1983; MFA, U. Calif., Davis, 1987. Asst. prof. Occidental Coll., L.A., 1990, Sarah Lawrence Coll., Bronxville, N.Y., 1994-97; vis. critic Md. Inst. Coll. Art, Balt., 1998; lectr. Princeton (N.J.) U., 1991, 93, 98. Solo shows include Stefan Stux Gallery, 1997, Galerie Rainer Borgemeister, Berlin, 1999, Galleri Magnus Åklundh, Lund, Sweden, 1999, Galerie Benden and Klimczak, Cologne, Germany, 1999; group exhbns. include Sackler Mus., Cambridge, Mass., 1997, Kunstmuseum Winterthur, Switzerland, 1998, Akademie der Künste, Berlin, 1998, Fonds régional d'art contemporain de Picardie and Museé de Picardie Amiens, 1997, Stark Gallery, N.Y.C., 1999, U. Calif., San Diego, 1999; represented in permanent collections at The Nat. Gallery, Washington; artist (catalog) Eve Aschheim, Paintings and Drawings, 1999. Recipient Rosenthal award AAAL, 1997; fellow NEA, 1989, Pollock-Krasner Found., 1990, N.Y. Found. for Arts, 1991; grantee Elizabeth Found., 1997. Mem. Am. Abstract Artists. Home: 67 Hudson St Apt 3C New York NY 10013-2852

ASCHHEIM, JOSEPH, economist, educator; b. Hanover, Germany, May 28, 1930; s. Max and Sarah (Pfeffer) A.; married; 1 child. A.B. with highest honors, U. Calif. at Berkeley, 1951; A.M. (Charles H. Smith scholar), Harvard U., 1953, Ph.D. (Thayer scholar, Willard scholar), 1954. Mem. faculty Johns Hopkins U., 1956-63; mem. faculty George Washington U., Washington, 1963—; prof. econs. George Washington U., 1964—; cons. to U.S. govt. and internat. orgns.; dir. rsch., econ. advisor to gov. Ctrl. Bank Kenya, 1971-72; vis. scholar, vis. fellow, lectr. Brit. univs.; vis. lectr. European and Asian univs.; faculty advisor D.C. univs. consortium U.S. Naval Res. Officers Tng. Corps Unit, 1984—; affiliated scholar Ctr. for Study of Ctrl. Banks, NYU Sch. of Law, 1995—. Author books and numerous articles in profl. jours.; editorial bd. So. Econ. Jour, 1960-63, Atlantic Econ. Jour, 1973—. Served with AUS, 1954-56. Ford Found. Faculty Research fellow. Mem. Am. Econ. Assn., Atlantic Econ. Soc. (v.p. 1973-76), Royal Econ. Soc., Arts Club Chgo., Phi Beta Kappa. Jewish. Office: George Washington U Dept Econs Washington DC 20052

ASCHLEMAN, JAMES ALLAN, lawyer; b. Auburn, Ind., June 1, 1944. BA, Manchester Coll., 1966; JD, Harvard U., 1969. Bar: Ind. 1969, U.S. Dist. Ct. (so. dist.) Ind. 1969, U.S. Ct. Appeals (7th cir.) 1969. Ptnr. Baker & Daniels, Indpls., 1969—. Fellow Ind. Bar Found.; mem. ABA, Ind. Bar Assn., Indpls. Bar Assn., Highland Golf and Country Club. Office: Baker & Daniels 300 N Meridian St Ste 2700 Indianapolis IN 46204-1782

ASCHOFF, LAWRENCE MICHAEL, computer information scientist; b. N.Y.C., Feb. 14, 1950; s. Edward William and Marie Louise (Marshall) A. BA in Art History, U. Fla., 1971; MBA in Fin., NYU, 1984, advanced profl. cert. in computer applications and info. systems, 1988. Sales rep. VIP Fabrics, N.Y.C., 1978-81; asst. to v.p. mktg. RAM Data, N.Y.C., 1981-82; sales agt. Equitable Life Assurance Soc., N.Y.C., 1982; programmer/analyst Drexel Burnham Lambert, N.Y.C., 1984-86, sr. programmer/analyst, 1986-88, project leader, 1988-89, project mgr., asst. v.p., 1989-90; mgr. project mgmt. competency ctr., nat. consumer svcs. strategic tech. Chase Manhattan Bank (formerly Chem. Bank), N.Y.C., 1990-91, officer, 1991—; treas. Saunders Owners of Queens, Ltd., 1989-91, pres., 1991—. Clin. assoc. Suicide and Crisis Prevention Ctr., Gainesville, Fla., 1972; mem. pres.'s coun. U. Fla., 1992—; vol. fundraiser Walk Am. program March of Dimes. Mem. Mensa, Phi Beta Kappa (sec. L.I. Alumni Assn. 1985-87, pres. 1987-93), Alpha Lambda Delta. Democrat. Avocations: photography, travel, fitness, music, science fiction. Office: Chase Manhattan Bank 4 New York Plz New York NY 10004-2413

ASCOLESE, MICHAEL J., corporate communications executive. AB in English, St. Peter's Coll., Jersey City, N.J., 1968. Reporter Bayonne (N.J.) Times, 1968; gen. assignment and beat reporter Star Ledger, Newark, 1972-79, asst. city editor, 1979-81, bus. and fin. editor, 1981-83; press rep. Allied-Signal, Inc., Morris Twp., N.J., 1983-86, media rels. mgr., 1986-88, pub. rels. dir., 1988-92, corp. comm. dir., 1992-94; dir. pub. rels. Price Waterhouse, 1994-98; dir. comms. PricewaterhouseCoopers, N.Y.C., 1998—. Bd. dirs. Voluntary Action Ctr., 1987-91, Am. Diabetes Assn., N.J., 1988-90, Morris Ctr. YMCA, 1992-98. Vol. U.S. Peace Corps, 1968-72; mem. Internat. Assn. Bus. Communicators, N.Y. Fin. Writers Assn., Pub. Rels. Soc. Am.,. Office: PricewaterhouseCoopers 1301 Avenue Of The Americas New York NY 10019-6022

ASENSI, GUSTAVO, advertising executive, filmmaker; b. Vitoria, Spain; came to the U.S., 1992; s. Gustavo Asensi. Student, Sch. Dramatic Arts, Madrid, 1983, Sch. Cinematography, Madrid, 1983. Copywriter Delvico Bates, Madrid, 1985-86, J. Walter Thompson, Madrid, 1986-87; creative dir. HDM, Madrid, 1987-89; exec. creative dir., v.p. Publinsa, Madrid, 1989-92; sr. v.p., exec. creative dir. Font & Vaamonde Advt., N.Y.C., 1993-94, mng. ptnr., CCO, 1994—. *As early as age 12, Mr. Asensi explored the world of filmmaking in the quiet town of Vitoria, Spain. At age 15, he broadcasted his own local radio show. The following years were dedicated to theatrical studies. It was during these years that he joined the movement of experimental filmmakers led by Movida Madilena. He entered the world of advertising in 1986, as one of Madrid's finest Executive Directors. Since his move to New York in 1992, he has won more than 16 internationally acclaimed awards for his television commercials, among them, the Gold Clio Award.* Recipient Bronze medal Festival San Sebastian, 1990, Silver medal, 1991, Gold medal Houston Internat. Film Festival, 1995, 96, Bronze medal, 1995, Gold medal Charleston Internat. Film Festival, 1995, Grand award, 1995, Gold Clio award, 1995. Office: FSA Comm 235 Park Ave South New York NY 10003

ASGAR, KAMAL, dentistry educator, consultant; b. Tabriz, Iran, Aug. 28, 1922; s. Salmon and Rogheye Asgarzadeh; m. Safieh Seyedi, Sept. 4, 1948; children: Alexander (dec.), Andrew. BA in Chemistry, Tech. Coll., Tehran, 1945; MS, U. Mich., 1948, BSChemE, 1950, PhD, 1959. Paint chemist Tehran, 1945-46; rsch. asst. U. Mich., Ann Arbor, 1949-56, rsch. assoc., asst. prof., 1956-62, assoc. prof., 1962-66, prof. dentistry, 1966-88, prof. emeritus dentistry, 1988—; cons. U.S. Army, U.S. Navy. Contbr. articles to sci. jours.; patentee in field. Recipient Gibbon award U. Mich., 1963, 70, 80, Hollenback meml. prize Acad. Operative Dentistry, 1984, Mitch Nakayama award Piere Forchad Acad. Japan. Fellow Internat. Coll. Dentistry; mem. Internat. Assn. Dental Rsch. (Souder award 1970), Am. Electon Probe Assn., Am. Soc. Metals, Fedn. Dentaire Internationale. Fax: 201-391-5645. Office: Sch Dentistry Univ Mich Ann Arbor MI 48109 Home: 209 Bearwoods Rd Park Ridge NJ 07656-2614

ASH, DOROTHY MATTHEWS, civic worker; b. Dresden, Germany, Nov. 10, 1918; came to U.S., 1924; d. Kurt Horst and Ana (Sekes) Matthesius; m. Harry A. Ash, Apr. 13, 1941 (dec. June 1981); children: Fredrick Curtis, Dorothea Ash Linklater. *Mrs. Ash's late husband Harry Ash was born in Chicago, 1894. He received a LLB from Chicago Kent College of Law, 1915. He specialized in legal work with investment houses 1918-1925; first assistant Attorney General of Illinois and inheritance tax attorney for Cook County, 1925-1933. He served the U.S. Army 1917-1918 and was Chairman of the Chicago Draft Board 1940-1942. He was the director of Illinois crime prevention 1945-47. He was also on the board of commissioners of the Cook County Board of Forest Preserve Commissioners of Cook County, 1949. He was a member of the American Bar Association, American Legion, Masons, Elks, Binai B'rith.* Dancer, 1933-40; treas. Inheritance Abstractors Inc., Chgo., 1949-70; reporter Miami (Fla.) Sun Post, 1983; reporter, columnist Social Mag., Miami, 1984—; chmn. Miss Universe Pageant, 1983-85; cruise chmn. Miami U., 1984, mem. Pres.'s Club, 1983. Pres. Big Bros. and Big Sisters, 1982-83; founding mem. World Sch. of Arts, 1985—; founding Notable Douglas Gardens 1988: Pres.'s Club U. of Miami, 1989; founding and bd. mem. Cancer Link Rsch., 1990; mem. Bd. Animal Welfare; active Project: Newborn, Am. Cancer Soc., March of Dimes, chmn. quest for the best, 1988-92, winner gourmet gala, 1988, leading lady 1998; active Children's Resource, Erase Diabetes, founding and bd. mem. 1990, Cerebral Palsy Found., Theatre Arts League, Linda Ray Infant Ctr., Miami City Ballet, Am. Ballet; bd. dirs. Greater Miami Opera, 1975—, Leading Ladies, Inc. 1997; pub. rels. vol. Miami Heart Inst., 1988—; com. mem. Miami Beach (Fla.) Beautification Program, 1984; mem. bd. Miami Mayor's Ad Hoc Com., 1984; mem. com. Challenger Seven Meml., 1988; active Cousteau Soc.; numerous others. Named Woman of Yr., Big Bros. and Big Sisters, Miami, 1981, Best Dressed, Am. Cancer Soc., 1981, Outstanding Humanitarian and Civic Leader, Mayor City of Miami, 1985, Woman of the Yr., Project: New Born, 1985, Miss Charity, Biscayne Bay Hosp., 1986, Queen of Hearts, Miami Children's Hosp., 1988, Leading Lady, March of Dimes, 1998; recipient Shining Star award Bon Secours Hosp., 1993, Patron Recognition award Mia Heart Rsch. Inst., 1993, Goddess of Love award Villa Maria Hosp., 1995. Mem. Miami Internat. Press Club. Avocations: reading, writing, painting. Home: 10245 Collins Ave Bal Harbour FL 33154-1407 also (summer): 330 W Diversey Pkwy Chicago IL 60657-6231

ASH, FREDERICK MELVIN, manufacturing company executive; b. Columbus, Ohio, June 15, 1941; s. Melvin Edward and Ida Belle (Berry) A.; student U. Cin., 1959-61; B.S. in B.A., Ohio State U., 1963; M.B.A. in Mgmt., Rutgers U., 1982; m. Karen Persichetti, Apr. 7, 1979; children—Jason, Carrie. Staff acct. chem. plastics div. Gen. Tire & Rubber Co., Akron, Ohio, 1963-65, office mgr., 1965-67, acctg. mgr., Lawrence, Mass., 1968, controller, Newcomerstown, Ohio, 1968-70, Lawrence, 1971-73, plant mgr., 1974-76, v.p. film, Jeannette, Pa., 1977; pres. Gen. Tire & Rubber Plastic Film Co., Jeannette, 1977-78; bus. dir. plastics Tenneco Chems., Inc., Piscataway, N.J., 1978-80, gen. mgr. plastics, 1980-82; v.p., gen. mgr. plastics Nuodex, Inc., Edison, N.J., 1982-84; v.p. mktg. and sales Am. Maize Products, 1985-89, v.p. ops., 1990-92, pres. ingredients divsn., 1993-95, pres., comml. dir. Cerestar USA, Inc., 1995-99, ret., 1999. Adv. Jr. Achievement, Akron, 1965; mem. budget com. Merrimack Valley United Fund, Lawrence, 1973-74, budget com. chmn., 1975, campaign chmn., 1976, dir., 1975-76; bd. dirs. Tradewinds Rehab. Ctr., Lakeshore Devel. Coun., United Way of Westmoreland County, 1977-78, Lake Area United Way, NW Ind. Forum, Olympia Fields/Flossmoor United Way, 1985, pres. 1986-87; v.p. Village 2 Homeowners Assn. U.S. Rubber scholar, 1961-63; recipient Pace Setter award Ohio State U., 1963. Mem. Soc. Plastics Industry (vice chmn. film group), Ind. Mfrs. Assn. (mem. bd. dirs.), Corn Refiners Assn. (bd. dirs.), Westmoreland County C. of C., Nat. Assn. Accts., Ohio State U. Alumni Assn., Rutgers U. Alumni Assn., Sigma Chi, Beta Gamma Sigma. Republican. Presbyterian. Lodges: Masons, Scottish Rite. Home: 928 Elm St Flossmoor IL 60422-2231 Office: Cerestar USA Inc 1100 Indianapolis Blvd Hammond IN 46320-1019

ASH, GORDON IAN, professional sports team executive; b. Toronto, Ont., Can., Dec. 20, 1951; m. Susan Cutajar; children: Christie, Carrie, Aaron. BA in History and Sociology, York U., 1974. With Can. Imperial Bank of Commerce, 1974-78; ticket office clk. Toronto Blue Jays, 1978-79, ops. supr., 1979-80, asst. dir. ops., 1980-84, adminstr. player personnel, 1984-89, asst. gen. mgr., 1989-94, v.p. baseball, gen. mgr., 1994-97, exec. v.p., 1997—. Office: Toronto Blue Jays, One Blue Jays Way Ste 3200, Toronto, ON Canada M5V 1J1*

ASH, HERBERT LEONARD, lawyer; b. N.Y.C., Sept. 9, 1941; m. Sandra Joyce Engel, Dec. 25, 1963; children: Scott, Michael. BA, Queens Coll., 1962; LLB, Columbia U. Sch. Law, 1965. Ptnr. Hahn & Hessen, L.L.P., N.Y.C., 1965—; bd. dirs. Donnkenny, Inc., Hampton Industries, Inc. Trustee Nat. Jewish Med. and Rsch. Ctr., Denver, 1988—; mem. bd. zoning appeals Village of Flower Hill, N.Y., 1976-83; assoc. trustee North Shore Univ. Hosp., Manhasset, 1982-89. Fellow Am. Coll. Comml. Fin. Attys.; mem. North Shore Country Club, Knickerbocker Yacht Club. Office: Hahn & Hessen LLP 350 5th Ave New York NY 10118-0075

ASH, HIRAM NEWTON, graphic designer; b. Paterson, N.J., Dec. 9, 1934; s. Newton Briton Todd and Ellen Sproule (Bowman) A.; m. Marilyn Ruth Robinson, 1957 (div. 1972); children: Erica Robinson, Jennifer Hamilton; m. Susan Main Humes. Student, Hobart Coll., 1952-56, Columbia U., 1956-58; BFA Sch. Art & Architecture, Yale U., 1960. Graphic designer Styling div. GM Tech. Ctr., Warren, Mich., 1959; art dir. N.W. Ayer & Sons, Phila., 1960-61; graphic designer George Nelson & Co., N.Y.C., 1961-62; ptnr. Ash/Reller Assocs., N.Y.C., 1962-63; pres. Hiram Ash, Inc., N.Y.C., 1963-70; prin. Hiram Ash, Colebrook, Conn., 1970—; founder, proprietor private press Orchard Press, Winsted, Conn., 1993—; asst. in instrn. Sch. Art and Arch., Yale U., New Haven, Conn., 1959-60; adj. instr. graphic design Cooper Union, N.Y.C., 1965-67; designer TriVers Exhbn. Systems, 1964; designer numerous album covers Caedmon Records, N.Y.C., 1960s; designer theatre posters Rugoff Theatres, N.Y.C., 1960s; designer set and program graphics Pub. Broadcast Lab. of NET, Ford Found., 1966-67; designer signature trademark and graphics implementation Am. Shakespeare Theatre, Stratford, Conn., 1980; mktg. and product devel. cons. Indian jewelry Zuni Community Action Program, Zuni Pueblo, N.Mex., 1967-68. Designer numerous books; work presented in Graphis Anns., Indsl. Design, Trademarks & Symbols of the World, Trade Marks U.S.A. Chmn. Colebrook Town Hall/Fire House Bldg. com., 1988-91. Recipient Design and Printing for Commerce and 50 Books of Yr. awards Am. Inst. Graphic Arts, N.J. Art Dirs. Club awards. Mem. Am. Inst. Graphic Arts, Fine Press Book Assn., Am. Printing History Assn., Printing Hist. Soc., Letterpress Guild of New England, Typophiles, Colebrook Hist. Soc. (pres. 1987-90, bd. dirs. 1993-96), Colebrook Land Conservancy, Inc. (trustee 1991—), Conn. Trust for Hist. Preservation, Millbrook Mount Assembly, Sandanona Harehounds, Yale Club (N.Y.C.), Book Club Calif. Republican. Episcopalian. Avocations: antiquarian and private press book dealer, photography, beagling. Address: PO Box 309 61 Church Hill Rd Colebrook CT 06021-0309

ASH, J. MARSHALL, mathematician, educator; b. N.Y.C., Feb. 18, 1940; s. Barney and Rosalyn (Hain) A.; m. Alison Igo, Nov. 24, 1977; children: Michael A., Garrett A., Andrew A. SB, U. Chgo., 1961, SM, 1963, PhD, 1966. Joseph Fels Ritt instr. Columbia U., N.Y.C., 1966-69; asst. prof. math. DePaul U., Chgo., 1970-72, assoc. prof., 1972-74, prof., 1975—; vis. prof. Stanford U., 1977; cons. PWS Pub., Saunders Coll. Pub., Dover Pub., Marcel Dekker, Gordon and Breach Pub. Author: Studies in Harmonic Analysis, 1976; contbr. articles to profl. jours. George Westinghouse fellow, 1961, NSF fellow, 1962-66. Mem. AAUP, Am. Math. Soc., Math. Assn. Am., Sigma Xi. E-mail: mash@math.depaul.edu. Home: 662 Maple St Winnetka IL 60093-2312 Office: De Paul U Math Dept Chicago IL 60614-3504

ASH, JAMES LEE, JR., academic administrator; b. Palestine, Tex., Mar. 29, 1945; s. James Lee and Ruth Agnes (Walling) A.; m. Patricia Bryan, Aug. 24, 1969; children: Erin Patricia, Eleanor Ruth. BA, Abilene Christian Coll., 1968; ThM, So. Meth. U., 1972; MA, U. Chgo., 1974, PhD, 1976. Ordained to ministry Presbyn. Ch., 1978. Asst. prof. religious studies Oreg. State U., Corvallis, 1975-77; asst. prof. religious studies U. Miami, Fla., 1977-81, assoc. prof., 1981-89, chmn. dept., 1979-81, assoc. dean, Coll. Arts and Scis., 1981-83, dir. Honors and Privileged Studies, 1981-83, assoc. provost, Honors and Undergrad. Studies, 1983-87, vice provost, 1987-89; pres. Whittier (Calif.) Coll., Calif., 1989—. Author: Protestantism and the American University, 1982; contbr. articles to profl. jours. Named Outstanding Tchr. Humanities, Premed. Student Soc., U. Miami, 1980, Prof. of Yr. Undergrad. Student Body, U. Miami, 1981, Prof. of Yr. Honors Student Assn., U. Miami, 1985. Mem. Am. Acad. Religion, Am. Soc. Ch. History. Democrat. Avocations: racquetball, gardening. Office: Whittier Coll Office of President 13406 Philadelphia St Whittier CA 90601-4446

ASH, MAJOR MCKINLEY, JR., dentist, educator; b. Bellaire, Mich., Apr. 7, 1921; s. Major McKinley Sr. and Helen Marguerite (Early) A.; m. Fayola Foltz, Sept. 2, 1947; children: George McKinley, Carolyn Marguerite, Jeffrey LeRoy, Thomas Edward. BS, Mich. State U., 1947; DDS, Emory U., 1951; MS, U. Mich., 1954; Doctoris Medicine Honoris Causa, U. Bern, 1975. Instr. sch. dentistry Emory U., Atlanta, 1952-53; instr. U. Mich., Ann Arbor, 1953-56, asst. prof., 1956-59, assoc. prof., 1959-62, prof., 1962—, chmn. dept. occlusion, sch. dentistry, 1962-89, dir. stomatognathic physiology lab., sch. dentistry, 1969-89, dir. TMJ/oral facial pain clinic, sch. dentistry, 1983-89, Marcus L. Ward prof. dentistry, 1984-89, prof. emeritus, rsch. scientist emeritus, 1989—; cons. N.E. Regional Dental Bd., 1988-92; vis. prof. U. Bern, 1989, U. Tex., San Antonio, 1990-98; pres. Basic Sci. Bd., State of Mich., 1962-74; cons. over the counter drugs FDA, Washington, 1985-89. Author, co-author 66 textbooks, 1958—; editor 4 books; contbr. over 181 articles to profl. jours. Served to tech. sgt. Signal Corps, U.S. Army, 1942-45, ETO. Nat. Inst. Dental Research grantee, 1962-85. Fellow Am. Coll. Dentists, Internat. Coll. Dentists, European Soc. Craniomandibular Disorders, European Soc. Oral Physiology; mem. AAAS, Am. Dental Assn. (cons. coun. on dental therapeutics 1982—, cons. coun. sci. affairs 1995—), N.Y. Acad. Scis., Washtenaw Dist. Dental Soc. (pres. 1963-64), Phi Kappa Phi. Presbyterian. Avocations: photography, bird watching. Office: U of Mich Sch of Dentistry Ann Arbor MI 48109

ASH, MARY KAY, cosmetics company executive; b. Hot Wells, Tex., May 12; d. Edward Alexander and Lula Vember (Hastings) Wagner; m. Melville

Jerome Ash, Jan. 6, 1966 (dec.); children: Marylyn Theard (dec.), Ben Rogers, Richard Rogers. Student, U. Houston, 1942-43. Mgr. Stanley Home Products, Houston, 1939-52; nat. tng. dir. World Gift Co., Dallas, 1952-63; founder, chmn. emeritus Mary Kay Cosmetics, Inc., Dallas, 1963—; speaker to various orgns. Bd. dirs. Horatio Alger Assn.; hon. chmn. Tex. Breast Screening Project. Office: Mary Kay Inc 16251 Dallas Pkwy Dallas TX 75248-2603 *After 25 years in direct sales, I retired for a month. During that time I decided to start a company that would give women an "open end opportunity", a privilege not enjoyed by women at that time. It would be based on the golden rule and a philosophy of God 1st, family 2d, career 3d. Women have embraced this philosophy and we are now a Fortune 500 Co.**

ASH, PHILIP, psychologist; b. N.Y.C., Feb. 2, 1917; s. Samuel Kieval and Estella (Feldstein) A.; m. Ruth Clyde, Sept. 16, 1945 (div. Dec. 1972); children—Peter, Sharon; m. Judith Nelson Cates, June 6, 1973; 1 son, Nelson E. B.S. in Psychology, City U. N.Y., 1938; M.A. in Personnel Adminstrn, Am. U., 1949; Ph.D. in Psychology, Pa. State U., 1949. Diplomate: Indsl. Psychlogy Am. Bd. Profl. Psychology. Analyst to unit chief occupational research Dept. Labor, 1940-47; research fellow Pa. State U., 1947-49, asso. prof., 1949-52; asst. to v.p. indsl. relatons Inland Steel, 1952-68; prof. psychology U. Ill., Chgo., 1968-80; prof. emeritus U. Ill., 1980—; dir. rsch. John E. Reid Assocs., Chgo., 1969-87; v.p. rsch. Reid Psychol. Sys., 1985-87; cons. London House, Inc., Park Ridge, Ill., 1987-94; dir. Ash, Blackstone & Cates, Blacksburg, Va., 1975—. Author: Guide for Selection and Placement of Employees, 2d edit., 1977, Volunteers for Mental Health, 1973, The Legality of Preemployment Inquiries, 1989, The Construct of Employee Theft Proneness, 1991, Preparing for Retirement: Guidelines and Information Sources, 1993, also other books, monographs and articles; editor: Forensic Psychology and Disability Evaluation, 1972; editor-in-chief The Va. Psychologist, 1996—. Mem. public adv. com. Chgo. Commn. Human Relations, 1957-80; retirement com. Chgo. Commn. Sr. Citizens, 1960-80; chmn. Ill. Psychologist Examining Com., 1963-72. Fellow AAAS, Am. Psychol. Assn. (pres. div. indsl. psychology 1968-69); mem. Ill. Psychol. Assn. (pres. 1963-64), Chgo. Psychol. Assn., Va. Psychol. Assn. (editor-in-chief Va. Psychologist 1996—), Va. Applied Psychology Acad. (pres. 1992-93), Midwest Psychol. Assn., Am. Pers. and Guidance Assn., Acad. for Criminal Justice Scis., Am. Criminology Assn., Internat. Assn. Applied Psychology, Sigma Xi, Phi Beta Kappa, Psi Chi. Home: 817 Hutcheson Dr Blacksburg VA 24060-3211 *Try to formulate clear objectives for your life. If possible, those objectives should provide purpose for yourself, and contributions to the welfare of your contempories, and additions, however small to human knowledge.*

ASH, ROY LAWRENCE, business executive; b. Los Angeles, Oct. 20, 1918; s. Charles K. and Fay E. (Dickinson) A.; m. Lila M. Hornbek., Nov. 13, 1943; children—Loretta Ash Danko, James, Marilyn Ash Hanna, Robert, Charles. M.B.A., Harvard, 1947. Chief fin. officer Hughes Aircraft Co., 1949-53; co-founder Litton Industries, Inc., Beverly Hills, Calif., 1953-72; dir. Litton Industries, Inc., 1953-72, pres., 1961-72; chmn. Pres.'s Adv. Coun. on Exec. Orgn., 1969-71; asst. to Pres. U.S.; dir. Office Mgmt. and Budget, Washington, 1973-75; chmn. bd., chief exec. officer AM Internat., 1976-81; co-chmn. Japan-Calif. Assn., 1965-72, 80-81; mem. vis. com. Harvard U. Kennedy Sch. Govt., 1992-98; mem. Bus. Roundtable, 1977-81. vice chmn. Los Angeles Olympic Organizing Com., 1980-85, chmn. fin. com.; trustee Calif. Inst. Tech., 1967-72, Com. for Econ. Devel., 1970-72, 75—; dir. Los Angeles World Affairs Council, 1968-72, 78—, pres., 1970-72; chmn. adv. council on gen. govt. Rep. Nat. Com., 1977-80; chmn. L.A. Music Ctr. Opera Assn., 1988-93. From pvt. to capt. Army Air Corps, 1942-46. Mem. C. of C. U.S. (bd. dirs. 1979-85, chmn. internat. policy com. 1979-85). Clubs: Bel Air Country, Harvard, California (Los Angeles). Office: Ste 1600 1900 Avenue Of The Stars Los Angeles CA 90067-4407

ASH, SHARON KAYE, real estate company executive; b. Altus, Ark., July 21, 1943; d. William Clyd and Odus Marie (Drew) Cline; m. J.W. Ash, June 1, 1966 (div. Oct. 1978); 1 child, Brian Edward. BS, S.W. Mo. State U., 1985; grad., Realtor Inst. cert. residential splst.; accredited buyer rep.; lic. real estate broker, Mo. Personal lines asst. Squibb Ins., Springfield, Mo., 1967-69; bookkeeper Hood-Rich, Architects and Engrs., Springfield, 1969-89; owner Ash Computer Svc., Springfield, 1985—; pres. Ash Real Estate Inc., Ash Real Estate Assocs., Inc. Featured in Home Gym and Fitness mag. Avocations: golf, sailing, reading, collecting clowns. Home: 630 N Washington St Strafford MO 65757-8486 Office: Ash Real Estate 1340 W Battlefield St Ste 114 Springfield MO 65807-4102

ASH, THOMAS PHILLIP, superintendent of schools; b. East Liverpool, Ohio, June 4, 1949; s. Bobby and Elizabeth Ann (Ludwig) A.; m. Nancy Elizabeth Gauron, June 8, 1951; children: Megan Elizabeth, John Gauron. BS in Edn., Bowling Green (Ohio) State U., 1971; MS in Edn., Youngstown (Ohio) State U., 1974. Tchr. East Liverpool City Schs., 1971-73, project coord., 1973-78, asst. supt., 1978-84, supt., 1984—; bd. dirs. Ctrl. Fed. Savs. & Loan, Columbiana County Mental Health Assn.; chmn. Lincoln Way Spl. Edn. Resource Ctr., 1988-89, 93-94. Mem. exec. coun. Columbiana County coun. Boy Scouts Am., 1989-91; pres. East Liverpool Area United Way, 1990-92; mem. State Supt. Adv. Commn. for Spl. Edn., 1993-95. Recipient Disting. Alumni aaward East Liverpool High Sch. Alumni Assn., 1987, Ohio Adminstr. of Yr. award Ohio Ednl. Libr. and Media Assn., 1990. Mem. Am. Assn. Sch. Adminstrs., Buckeye Assn. Sch. Adminstrs. (pres. 1999—), East Liverpool Area C. of C. (bd. dirs. 1985—, Outstanding Educator award 1982, Disting. Svc. award 1982). Office: E Liverpool City Sch Dist 202 Maplewood Ave East Liverpool OH 43920-1461

ASH, WILLIAM JAMES, geneticist, scientific consultant, educator; b. N.Y.C., Nov. 3, 1931; s. William and Anna Marie (Ruegg) A.; m. Gertrude Louise Kehm, June 15, 1953; children: Annalee M., Barbara A. (dec.), William J., Jr., James J., Lydia A. BS, Cornell U., 1953, MS, 1958, PhD, 1960. Grad. research asst. Cornell U., 1955-59; dir. research Crescent Corp., Aquebogue, N.Y., 1964-65; research geneticist Cornell U., Ithaca, N.Y., 1959-64; asst. prof. W.Va. U., Morgantown, 1965-66; prof. St. Lawrence U., Canton, N.Y., 1966-81, Kuwait U., Arabian Gulf, 1976-78; program officer NSF, Washington, 1979-81; mem. sr. staff U.S.-Saudi Joint Commn., Riyadh, Saudi Arabia, 1982-83; pres. Adv. Assocs. Internat., Westhampton, N.Y., 1981-94; prof. SUNY-Stony Brook, 1985-91; prof. Emeritus SUNY-Stony Brook, 1991—. Contbr. articles to profl. jours.; comdr.Peconic Bay Power Squadron, Riverhead, N.Y., 1986-88; scoutmaster Boy Scouts Am., Canton, 1967-69; coach U.S. Amateur Ice Hockey Assn., Canton, 1970-75. Served to capt. U.S. Army, 1953-65. Recipient Travel award Cornell U., 1963, Travel award NSF, 1983; NSF grantee, 1970-72, 79-81. Fellow Am. Dermatoglyphics Assn.; mem. Sigma Xi, Beta Beta Beta. Roman Catholic. Republican. Clubs: Cape Lookout Sail and Power Squadron, Alpenverein. Avocations: sailing; gardening; photography; travel; amateur radio, genealogy, celestial navigation. Home: 3507 Canterbury Rd New Bern NC 28562-7703

ASHBERY, JOHN LAWRENCE, language educator, poet, playwright; b. Rochester, N.Y., July 28, 1927; s. Chester Frederick and Helen (Lawrence) A. Grad., Deerfield Acad., 1945; B.A., Harvard U., 1949; M.A., Columbia U., 1951; postgrad., NYU, 1957-58; D.Litt. (hon.), Southampton Coll. of L.I.U., 1979. Copywriter Oxford U. Press, N.Y.C., 1951-54; copywriter McGraw Hill Book Co., N.Y.C., 1954-55; art critic European edit. N.Y. Herald Tribune, Paris, 1960-65; Paris corr. Art News, 1964-65; exec. editor Art News, N.Y.C., 1966-72; prof. English Bklyn. Coll., 1974-90, Disting. prof., 1980-90, Disting. emeritus prof., 1990; Charles P. Stevenson prof. langs. and lit. Bard Coll., 1990—; editor quar. rev. Art and Lit., Paris, 1963-66; art critic Art Internat., Lugano, Switzerland, 1961-64; editor Locus Solus, Lans-en-Vercors, France, 1960-62; poetry editor Partisan Rev., 1976-80; art critic New York Mag., 1978-80, Newsweek, 1980-85; Charles Eliot Norton prof. poetry Harvard U., 1989-90; conducted spl. rsch. on life and work of Raymond Roussel. Author: (poems) Turandot and Other Poems, 1953, Some Trees, 1956, 70, 78, The Poems, 1960, The Tennis Court Oath, 1962, Rivers and Mountains, 1966, 77, Selected Poems, 1967, Three Madrigals, 1968, Sunrise in Suburbia, 1968, Fragment, 1969, The Double Dream of Spring, 1970, 76, The New Spirit, 1970, Three Poems, 1972, 77, The Vermont Notebook, 1975, Self-Portrait in a Convex Mirror, 1975, 76, 77, Houseboat Days, 1977, As We Know, 1979, Shadow Train, 1981, 82, A Wave, 1984, Selected Poems, 1985, 86, 87, April Galleons, 1987, 88, Flow Chart, 1991, 92, Hotel Lautréamont, 1992, And the Stars Were Shining, 1994, Can You Hear, Bird, 1995, Wakefulness, 1998; (plays) The Heroes, 1952, The Compromise, 1956, The Philosopher, 1963; author: (novel) (with James Schuyler) A Nest of Ninnies, 1969, 76, 87; works represented in numerous anthologies, including Reported Sightings: Art Chronicles, 1957-87, 89, 90; also author numerous articles art criticism, chronicles, translations; contbr. verse to lit. periodicals; verse set to music. Recipient Yale Series of Younger Poets prize, 1956, Harriet Monroe Poetry award Poetry Mag., 1963, 75, Union League Civic and Arts Found. prize, 1966, Nat. Inst. Arts and Letters award, 1969, Shelley award Poetry Soc. Am., 1973; guest of honor Poetry Day Modern Poetry Assn., 1974; Pulitzer prize, 1976; Nat. Book award, 1976; Nat. Book Critics Circle award Harvard U., 1976; poetry award English-Speaking Union, 1979; Mayor's award N.Y.C., 1983; Charles Flint Kellogg award Bard Coll., 1983; Jerome J. Shestack poetry award Am. Poetry Rev., 1984, Bollingen prize in poetry Yale U. Library, 1985, Lenore Marshall poetry prize the Nation, 1985, Common Wealth award in lit. MLA, 1986, Creative Arts award Brandeis U., 1989, Ruth Lilly Poetry prize Poetry Mag. and Modern Poetry Assn. and Am. Coun. for Arts, 1992, Robert Frost medal Poetry Soc. of Am., 1995, Grand Prize Biennales Intnernat. Poetry, Belgium, 1996; named Phi Beta Kappa Poet Harvard U., 1979, Literary Lion, N.Y. Pub. Libr., 1984, Poet of Yr. Pasadena City Coll., 1984; Fulbright scholar U. Montpellier, France, 1955-56; Fulbright scholar Paris, France, 1956-57; Poets' Found. grantee, 1960, 64; Ingram Merrill Found. grantee, 1962, 72; Guggenheim fellow, 1967, 73; Rockefeller Found. grantee, 1979-80, Wallace Stevens Fellow Yale U., 1985; McArthur Found. Fellow, 1985-90. Fellow Acad. Am. Poets; mem. Am. Acad. and Inst. Arts and Letters (Gold Medal 1997), Acad. Am. Poets (chancellor 1988—), Am. Acad. Arts and Scis. Office: c/o George Borchardt Inc 136 E 57th St New York NY 10022-2707 Address: Dept Langs and Lit Bard Coll PO Box 5000 Annandale-on-Hudson NY 12504-5000*

ASHBURN, ANDERSON, magazine editor; b. Winston-Salem, N.C., Aug. 24, 1919; s. Arthur Lee and Nonnie Mae (Boyles) A.; m. Sue Shermer, Aug. 4, 1941; children: Kit (Mrs. Robert Champlin), Terri (Mrs. Robert Higgins), Edward Lee. BSE, U. Mich., 1940. Editor Mich. Technic, Ann Arbor, 1939-40; assoc. editor Tool Engr., Detroit, 1940-41; asst. editor Am. Machinist (McGraw-Hill Publs. Co., now Penton Pub.), N.Y.C., 1942, assoc. editor, 1946-54, mng. editor, 1955-64, chief editor, 1965-87, editor emeritus, 1987—; chief editor Product Engrng., N.Y.C., 1970-71; mem. mfg. studies bd. NRC. Dir., past pres. Asbury Terr. Housing Devel. Fund; trustee Am. Precision Mus.; treas. Meth. Ch. of Tarrytown. Recipient Jesse H. Neal Editorial Achievement awards, 1966, 68, 71, 76, 78, Nat. Mag. award Columbia Grad. Sch. Journalism, 1969, Crain award Am. Bus. Press, 1st McGraw-Hill Disting. Editorial Career award, 1987. Fellow Soc. Mfg. Engrs. (bd. dirs. 1993-94, Disting. Contbns. award 1985); mem. ASME, Soc. Automotive Engrs. (past v.p., chmn. mfg. activity), Am. Soc. Mag. Editors (chmn. 1973-75), Computer and Automated Sys. Assn., Dutch Treat Club (N.Y.C.), Kappa Sigma, Tau Beta Pi. Home and Office: 45 Highland Ave Tarrytown NY 10591-4204

ASHBY, DENISE STEWART, speech educator, communication consultant; b. Charleston, W.Va., Aug. 15, 1941; d. Dennison Elmer and Marie Juanita (Queripel) Ellis; m. Rudolph Krutzner III, Dec. 6, 1958 (div. 1961); m. Garth Rodney Ashby, Feb. 15, 1976; children: Kevin Krutzner, Kevin Ashby, Lisa Ashby, Scott Ashby. AA with highest honors, Diablo Valley Coll., Pleasant Hill, Calif., 1981; BA in Speech summa cum laude, Calif. State U., Hayward, 1982; MA in Speech and Communication summa cum laude, Calif. State U., 1983. Lic. beautician N.J. Bd. Cosmetology. Owner Salon 105, Somerville, N.J., 1964-66; pres. Second Hand Rose, New Providence, N.J., 1966-76, The Place to be Beauty Salon, New Providence, 1966-76, The Place to be Boutique, New Providence, 1966-76; mgr. LaTortuga Boutique, 1977-81; instr. Los Positas Coll., Livermore, Calif., 1985-90; tenured instr. Diablo Valley Coll., Pleasant Hill, 1982—; pres. Ashby & Assocs., Danville, Calif.; AAUW liaison Ctr. for Higher Edn., San Ramon, 1988-90. Vice pres. Danville United Presbyn. Women, 1978-79. Recipient Pres.'s award, Calif. State U., 1983. Mem. AAUW (bd. dirs. 1988-90), NAFE, Speech Comm. Assn., Pi Lambda Theta, Pi Kappa Delta (pres. 1982). Home: 82 Cumberland Ct Danville CA 94526-1819 Office: Diablo Valley Coll Golf Club Rd Pleasant Hill CA 94523

ASHBY, EUGENE CHRISTOPHER, chemistry educator; b. New Orleans, Oct. 25, 1930; s. Anthony and Ida (Bruno) A.; m. Carolyn Turner, Sept. 13, 1952; children: Chris, Steven, Terry, Marie, Angela, Julie, Rachel. BS in Chemistry, Loyola U., New Orleans, 1951; MS in Chemistry, Auburn U., 1953; PhD in Chemistry, U. Notre Dame, 1956. Rsch. chemist Ethyl Corp., Baton Rouge, 1956-59, rsch. assoc., 1959-63; asst. prof. Ga. Inst. Tech., Atlanta, 1963-65, assoc. prof., 1965-69, prof., 1969-73, Regents prof., 1973-93, Regents prof. emeritus, 1993—; cons. Ethyl Corp., 1980-91, Conoco, Ponca City, Okla., 1972-76, U.S. Dept. Energy, 1990-98, Ga. Dept. Edn., 1994-97, Pfizer Pharm., 1996. Contbr. over 270 articles to profl. jours. Recipient Lavoisier medal French Chem. Soc., 1971, Sigma Xi rsch. award, 1968, 75, Herty medal Am. Chem. Soc., 1983, Disting. Prof. award Ga. Inst. Tech., 1988. Avocations: tennis, cattle farming. Home: 2516 Flair Knoll Dr NE Atlanta GA 30345-1316 Office: Sch Chemistry Ga Inst Tech Atlanta GA 30332

ASHBY, RICHARD JAMES, JR., bank executive, lawyer; b. Lancaster, Pa., Aug. 18, 1944; s. Richard James and Gloria Marie (Mayer) A.; m. Claire Lundberg, July 1, 1967; children: Douglas R., Elizabeth, Brian J. AB, Wittenberg U., 1966; JD, Ohio State U., 1969. Bar: Pa. 1969, Ohio 1969. Assoc. Arnold Bricker Beyer & Barnes, Lancaster, 1969-71; trust officer First Nat. Bank Strasburg (Pa.), 1971-73, v.p., 1973-78; v.p. Fulton Bank, Lancaster, 1978-80, sr. v.p., 1980-86, exec. v.p., 1986-91; pres. Lafayette Bank, Easton, Pa., 1991-98; pres., COO Fulton Bank, Lancaster, Pa., 1999—; vice chmn. Lehigh Valley Econ. Devel. Corp., 1995-98. Author: Profitability in Community Bank Trust Department, 1977. Mem. adv. bd. pa. Joint State Govt. Commn., Harrisburg, 1984—; commr. Manheim Twp., Lancaster County, 1988-92; mus. dir. Lancaster Red Rose Chorus, 1976-91; pres. Parish Resource Ctr., Lancaster, 1984—, Northampton C.C. Found., 1991-98, pres., 1994-96, State Theatre, Easton, 1991-98, pres., 1993-94, Easton Hosp., 1991-98, dir. Valley Health Found., 1992—; dir. Northampton County Devel. Corp., 1994—; dir. LeHigh Valley Partnership, 1993-98. Staff sgt. U.S. Army, 1970-76. Recipient George Beneman Meml. award Ohio State U. Coll. Law, Columbus, 1969, Am. Spirit Honor medal Army & Navy Vets Aux., Ft. Ord, Calif., 1970. Mem. Pa. Bar Assn., Lancaster Bar Assn., Am. Bankers Assn., Pa. Bankers Assn., Two Rivers Area C. of C. (dir., vice chmn. 1993—), Lancaster C. of C. (bd. dirs. 1999), Hamilton Club, Lancaster Country Club, Northampton Country Club. Republican. Lutheran. Avocations: barbershop quartet singing, golf, fishing, squash. Office: 1 Penn Sq Lancaster PA 17602

ASHCRAFT, KIMBERLY M., nursing administrator; b. Welch, W.Va., June 19, 1957; d. John M. and Nellie (Pais) Moore; m. Gregory Alan Ashcraft, Dec. 4, 1982 (div. Jan. 1999); children: Heather Lynne, Nathan Gregory. BSN, W.Va. U., 1978, MS in Exercise Physiology, 1986. RN, W.Va. Rehab. nurse Monongalia Gen. Hosp., Morgantown, W.Va., staff nurse; staff nurse surg. ICU Charleston (W.Va.) Area Med. Ctr., rehab. nurse, dir. cardiac rehab.; charge nurse VA Med. Ctr., Beckley, W.Va., program dir. med. cardiology cardiac svcs. adminstrn. Mem. AACN, Am. Heart Assn. (program cir. Kanawha County chpt.), Am. Coll. Sport Medicine (cert. exercise specialist), W.Va. Nurses Assn. (faculty annual meeting 1989), W.Va. Assn. Cardiovascular and Pulmonary Rehab. (pres.).

ASHCROFT, JOHN DAVID, senator; b. Chgo., May 9, 1942; m. Janet Elise; children: Martha, Jay, Andrew. B cum laude, Yale U., 1964; JD, U. Chgo., 1967. Bar: Mo., U.S. Supreme Ct. Assoc. prof. S.W. Mo. State U., Springfield, 1967-72; pvt. practice Springfield, 1967-73; state auditor State of Mo., 1973-75, asst. atty. gen., 1975-77, atty. gen., 1977-84, gov., 1985-92; atty. Suelthaus and Kaplan P.C., 1993-94; U.S. senator from Mo., 1995—; mem. commerce, sci. and transp. coms., aviation subcom., comm. subcom., consumer affairs subcom., chmn. fgn. commerce & tourism subcom., mem. fgn. rels. com., European affairs subcom., Near Ea. & South Asian affairs subcom., chmn. African affairs subcom., mem. jud. com., chmn. constitution subcom., fedn. and property rights; mem. Presdl. Adv. Coun. Intergovtl. Affairs; nat. chmn. Edn. Commn. States, 1987-88, Jud. Com., Subcom., chmn. constn.; chmn. Nat. Govs. Assn. Task Force on Coll. Quality, 1985, Nat. Govs. Assn. Task Force on Adult Literacy; co-chair Renewal Alliance. Gospel singer: records include In the Spirit of Life and Liberty, The Gospel According to John; author: Lessons from a Father to a Son, 1998, (with wife) College Law for Business, 7th, 8th, 9th, 10, 11th edits., It's the Law, 1979-91; contbr. articles to profl. jours. Chmn. Task Force on Adult Literacy, Task Force on College Quality Nat. Gov.'s Assn., 1991; chmn. Rep. Gov.'s Assn., 1990; co-chmn. Rep. Platform Com., 1992. Recipient Nat. Sheriffs Assn. award, 1996; named Christian Statesman of Yr., 1996. Mem. ABA (ho. of dels.), Mo. Bar Assn., Cole County Bar Assn., Nat. Assn. Attys. Gen. (pres. 1980-81, chmn. budget com., exec. com., Wyman award 1983), Nat. Govs. Assn. (vice chmn. 1990, chmn. 1991-92, chmn. Pres.'s Commn. on Urban Families 1992). Republican. Mem. Assembly of God Ch. Office: 316 Hart Senate Office Bldg Washington DC 20510-2504

ASHCROFT, NEIL WILLIAM, physics educator, researcher; b. London, Nov. 27, 1938; m., 1961; 2 children. BSc, U. New Zealand, 1958, MSc with honors, 1960; PhD, U. Cambridge, 1964; DSc (hon.), Victoria U., Wellington, New Zealand. Sci. rsch. coun. sr. fellow Cavendish Lab. U. Cambridge, Eng., 1973-74, vis. fellow Clare Hall, 1973-74; assoc. theoretical physics Cornell U., Ithaca, N.Y., 1965-66, from asst. prof. to assoc. prof., 1966-75, prof. physics, 1975—, Horace White Chair of Physics, 1990, various adminstrv. and acad. coms., dir. Lab. of Atomic and Solid State Physics, 1979-84; dep. dir. Cornell High Energy Synchrotron Source, Ithaca, N.Y., 1978-97; dir. Cornell Ctr. for Materials Rsch., Ithaca, 1997—; chaire municipale Joseph Fourier U., Grenoble, France, 1989-93; sci. cons. Los Alamos Nat. Lab., 1977-93; adv. com. High Flux Beam Reactor, Brookhaven, 1984—; sci. cons. Lawrence Livermore Nat. Lab., 1985—; chmn. Gordon Rsch. Conf. on Rsch. at High Pressure, 1986—, trustee 1988—, chmn. bd. trustees, 1991—; liasion rep. Nat. Rsch. Coun. Rev. Panel on Materials, Am. Phys. Soc. div. of Condensed Matter Physics Physics; vis. com. Brookhaven Nat. Lab., 1986—; Gordon Godfrey vis. prof. U. New South Wales, Australia, 1988—; mem. rsch. briefing panel on high temperature superconductivity NAS, adv. panel solid state div. Oak Ridge Nat. Lab.; Erskine fellow Canterbury U., New Zealand, 1990, Ehrenfest lectr. U. Leiden, The Netherlands, 1991; Faraday bicentennial lectr. Electrochem. Soc., 1991; mem. solid state scis. com. NRC, 1993—. Co-author: Solid State Physics, 1975; mem. editl. bd. Jour. of Physics, 1988—, The Phys. Rev., 1996-98, Australian Jour. of Physics, 1997—; contbr. numerous articles to profl. jours. Guggenheim fellow, 1984-85, Royal Soc. guest fellow, 1984-85, overseas fellow, Churchill Coll., Cambridge U., 1984—, Erskine fellow Canterbury U., 1990. Fellow AAAS, Am. Phys. Soc., Royal Soc. New Zealand (hon.); mem. Assn. Internat. pour L'Avancement de la Recherche et de la Technologie Aux Hautes Pressions (exec. com. 1995—), Nat. Acad. of Sci. Office: Cornell U Clark Hall Ithaca NY 14853-2501

ASHCROFT, RICHARD CARTER, controller; b. East Orange, N.J., Sept. 6, 1942; s. Herbert and Grace Alberta (Schwalb) A.; m. Gail P. Cook, Sept. 12, 1964 (div. May 1, 1981); children: Janet Lynn, Scott Carter; m. Marlene Ann Krueger, Jan. 23, 1982. BA in Econs., Grove City Coll., 1964; postgrad., U. Rochester, 1964-66. Asst. controller Schlegel Corp., Rochester, N.Y., 1972-73; adminstrv. mgr. Schlegel Tenn., Inc., Maryville, Tenn., 1973-74, controller, 1975-76, controller, asst. treas., 1977-79; group fin. dir. Schlegel U.K. Ltd., Leeds, Eng., 1979-80; corporate mgr. acctg. Schlegel Corp., Rochester, N.Y., 1980-83; controller, chief fin. officer Sugardale Foods, Inc., Canton, Ohio, 1983-86; pres., dir. Rotek, Inc., Aurora, Ohio, 1986-88; corporate controller Nesco, Inc., Cleve., 1988—; pres. Ashcroft Assocs. Inc., 1989—; also chmn., 1993-98; pres. Interim Settlement Funding Corp. Fin. chmn. St. Luke's Episc. Ch., Fairport, N.Y., 1983; chmn. Girls Clubs Am., Maryville, Tenn., 1978, treas., 1977. Mem. Prestwick Country Club (Uniontown, Ohio). Democrat. Methodist. Avocations: golf, travel, reading, swimming, history. Home: 98 Jefferson Dr Hudson OH 44236-2110

ASHDOWN, CHARLES COSTER, lawyer; b. N.Y.C., 1961; s. Cecil Spanton Jr. and Marie Antoinette Ashdown; m. Philomena Saldanha, Sept. 16, 1989; children: Marygrace, Helen. BA magna cum laude, Fordham U., 1983; JD, U. Notre Dame, 1986. Bar: Ohio 1986, U.S. Dist. Ct. (so. dist.) Ohio 1987, U.S. Ct. Appeals (6th cir.) 1994. Student law clk. to Hon. John E. Sprizzo U.S. Dist. Ct. (so. dist.) N.Y., N.Y.C., 1984; ptnr. Strauss & Troy, Cin., 1986—. Trustee Cin. Opera Assn., 1987-93, mem. adv. bd., 1998—; judge Midwest Concours d'Elegance, Cin., 1992-95, chief judge, 1997—; planned giving adv. com. Episcopal Retirement Homes, Inc., 1998—. Mem. ABA, Cin. Bar Assn., Black Lawyers Cin. Roundtable, Univ. Club Cin., Alpha Sigma Nu, Phi Kappa Phi. Home: 1739 Churchwood Dr Cincinnati OH 45238-1901 Office: Strauss & Troy The Fed Reserve Bldg 150 E Fourth St 4th Fl Cincinnati OH 45202-4018

ASHDOWN, FRANKLIN DONALD, physician, composer; b. Logan, Utah, May 2, 1942; s. Donald and Theresa Marie (Hill) A. BA, Tex. Tech. U., 1963; MD, U. Tex., 1967. Chief of med. Holloman Air Force Base, New Mexico, 1971-73; chief of staff Gerald Champion Mem. Hosp., Alamogordo, N.M., 1976, 91, 92; pvt. practice Alamogordo, 1973—; pres. Otero County Concerts Assn., Alamogordo, 1985-94, Otero County Med. Soc., Alamogordo, 1986; cons. New Mexico Sch. for Visually Handicapped, Alamogordo, 1973-76. Composer of more than 60 published and recorded works. Bd. dirs. Otero County Mental Health Assn., Alamogordo, 1973-77, Flickinger Found. for Performing Arts, 1995; bd. trustees Gerald Champion Meml. Hosp., 1992. Mem. Gerald Champion Mem. Hosp., N.M. Med. Soc., Am. Soc. Internal Med., ASCAP. Republican. Office: 1301 Cuba Ave Alamogordo NM 88310-5727

ASHDOWN, MARIE MATRANGA (MRS. CECIL SPANTON ASHDOWN, JR.), writer, lecturer; b. Mobile, Ala.; d. Dominic and Ave (Mallon) Matranga; m. Cecil Spanton Ashdown Jr., Feb. 8, 1958; children: Cecil Spanton III, Charles Coster; children by previous marriage: John Stephen Gartman, Vivian Marie Gartman. Student, Maryville Coll. Sacred Heart; student, Springhill Coll. Feature artist, women's program dir. daily program Sta. WALA, WALA-TV, Mobile; v.p., dir. Met. Opera Guild, N.Y.C., opera instr. in-svc. program, 1970-80; opera instr. in-svc. program Marymont Coll., N.Y.C., 1979-85; exec. dir. Musicians Emergency Fund, Inc., N.Y.C., 1985—; mem. internat. adv. coun. Van Cliburn Found., 1998—; cons. No. Ill. U. Coll. of Visual and Performing Arts, 1985—; lectr. in field. Author: Opera Collectables, 1979, contbr. articles to profl. jours. Internat. cons. Van Cliburn Found. Recipient Extraordinary Service award March of Dimes, 1958, Medal of Appreciation award Harvard Bus. Sch. Club N.Y.C., Cert. Appreciation, Kiwanis Internat., Arts Excellence award N.J. State Opera, Ciparío award. Mem. AAUW, Nat. Inst. Social Scis., Com. for U.S.-China Rels. Avocations: collecting art, antique ceramics and porcelains, bookbinding. Home: 25 Sutton Pl S Apt 16K New York NY 10022-2456 Office: Musicians Emergency Fund Inc PO Box 1256 New York NY 10150-1256

ASHE, ARTHUR JAMES, III, chemistry educator; b. N.Y.C., Aug. 5, 1940; s. Arthur James and Helen Louise (Hawelka) A.; m. Penelope Guerard Vaughan, Aug. 25, 1962; children: Arthur J., Christopher V. B.A., Yale U., 1962, M.S., 1965, Ph.D., 1966; postgrad., Cambridge U., 1962-63. Asst. prof. chemistry U. Mich., Ann Arbor, 1966-71; assoc. prof. U. Mich., 1971-76, prof., 1976—, chmn. dept., 1983-86; vis. scientist Phys. Chemistry Inst., U. Basle, Switzerland, 1974. Mem. editorial avd. bds. profl. jours, 1984—. Alfred P. Sloan fellow, 1972-76. Mem. Am. Chem. Soc. Office: U Mich Dept Chemistry Ann Arbor MI 48109

ASHE, BERNARD FLEMMING, arbitrator, educator, lawyer; b. Balt., Mar. 8, 1936; s. Victor Joseph Ashe and Frances Cecelia (Johnson) Flemming; m. Grace Nannette Pegram, Mar. 23, 1963; children: Walter Joseph, David Bernard. BA, Howard U., 1956, JD, 1961. Bar: Va. 1961, D.C. 1963, Mich. 1964, N.Y. 1971. Tchr. Balt. Pub. Schs., 1956-58; atty. NLRB, Washington, 1961-63; asst. gen. counsel Internat. Union United Auto Workers, Detroit, 1963-71; gen. counsel N.Y. State United Tchrs., Albany, 1971-96, arbitrator, 1996—; mem. adj. faculty Cornell Sch. Indsl. and Labor Rels., Albany div., 1981, 87, Fordham U. Law Sch., 1996—, Roger Williams U. Law Sch., 1996-98. Contbr. articles on labor and constnl. law to profl. jours. Bd. dirs. Urban League Albany, 1979-85, 1st v.p., 1981-85; trustee N.Y. Lawyers Fund for Client Protection, 1981—, Adelphi Univ., Garden City, N.Y., 1997—. Fellow Am. Bar Found. (life), Coll. Labor and Employment Lawyers (emeritus); mem. ABA (chmn. sect. labor and employment law sect. 1982-83, consortium on legal svcs. and the pub. 1979-84, commn. on pub. understanding about the law 1987-91, mem. standing com.

on group and prepaid legal svcs. 1996-97, ho. of dels. 1985-96, 97—, nominating com. 1988-91, bd. govs. 1991-94, exec. com. 1993-94, accreditation com. sect. legal edn. and admission to the bar 1994-98, chmn. standing com. on group and prepaid legal svcs. 1996-97, sr. lawyers divsn. coun. 1996—, chair drafting com. 1998—), Am. Law Inst., Nat. Bar Assn., Am. Arbitration Assn. (bd. dirs. 1982-98, Whitney North Seymour Sr. medal 1989), N.Y. State Bar Assn., Albany County Bar Assn.

ASHE, KATHY RAE, special education educator; b. Bismarck, N.D., Oct. 24, 1950; d. Raymond Charles and Virginia Ann (Mason) Lynch; m. Barth Eugene Olson, Aug. 11, 1973; 1 child, William Raymond; m. Fredrick A. Ashe, Aug. 5, 1994. BS, U. N.D., 1972; MS in Spl. Edn., U. N.D., 1987. Cert. elem. tchr. with spl. edn. credential, N.D. Instr., Grafton State Sch., N.D., 1972-74; tchr. spl. edn. Grand Forks Sch. Dist., N.D., 1974—; bd. dirs. Agassiz Enterprises; mem. RAD com. Valley Jr. High; mem. transition governing bd., Region IV. Bd. dirs. Assn. Retarded Citizens, Devel. Homes, Inc., N.D. Sch. Blind Found., pres. 1997—; spl. needs recreation program Grand Forks Park Bd., 1973-76; mem. Spl. Olympics Area Mgmt. Team, 1984—. Named N.D. Tchr. of Yr., Coun. of Chief State Sch. Officers, 1981. Mem. AAUW (pres. 1998—), Delta Kappa Gamma (sec. 1984-86, pres. 1990-94), Alpha Phi (alumni pres. 1984-86, 90-91, alumni treas. 1995—), Pi Lambda Theta., Phi Delta Kappa. Republican. Roman Catholic. Avocations: sporting events, civic work, cross stitch, bowling. Home: 3208 Walnut St Grand Forks ND 58201-7665

ASHE, LINCOLN EMIL, police officer; b. Balt., Mar. 13, 1962; s. Thomas Jacobe and Mattie Mae (Thompson) A.; m. Bernadette Gray, Sept. 3, 1983. Mil. police diploma, VA diploma, Fort McCallan, 1981. Missionary Child Evangelism Fellowship, Balt., summer 1980; mil. police officer N.G., Towson, Md., 1980-81; mil. police officer U.S. Army, Ft. Myer, Va., 1981-82, Ft. McNair, Washington, 1982-84; police officer VA, Washington, 1985-86; spl. police officer security co. Washington, 1986-87; treasury police Bur. of Engraving, Washington, 1987—. Author: (book) Melodies of the Heart, 1996. With U.S. Army, 1981-84. Recipient Good Citizenship award SAR, 1981. Baptist. Avocations: writing poetry and short stories, movies, video games, fixing things. Home: 13803 Palmer House Way Silver Spring MD 20904-4861 Office: Dept of Treasury 301 14 & C St SW Washington DC 20228

ASHE, REID, publishing executive; b. 1948. Student, MIT. With Tech. Rev., Boston, 1971-72; asst. editor Washington (N.C.) Daily News, 1972-73; reporter, editl. writer, editl. page editor Jackson (Tenn.) Sun, 1973-84, exec. editor, 1974-78, editor, pub., pres., 1978-84; gen. exec. Knight-Ridder Inc., 1984; CEO Viewdata Corp. (a subsidiary of Knight-Ridder Inc.), 1984-87; pres., pub. The Wichita (Kans.) Eagle, 1987-96, Tampa Tribune, 1996—. Office: The Tampa Tribune 202 S Parker St Tampa FL 33606-2395*

ASHEN, PHILIP, chemist; b. Bklyn., Nov. 5, 1915; s. Joel and Fannie (Hirt) A. BA in Chemistry, Bklyn. Coll., 1936; MBA, NYU, 1957, PHD, 1968. Cert. profl. chemist. Chief chemist Alco Mfg. Corp., Bklyn., 1936-48; mgr. chem. div. M.W. Hardy & Co., Inc., N.Y.C., 1948-63, v.p., 1963-77, pres., chief exec. officer, 1977—; lectr. grad. sch. NYU, N.Y.C., 1954-56; lectr. chem. warfare U.S. Citizens Def. Corps., 1940-45, gas reconnaissance officer, 1940-45; cons. in field, 1957—. Author: Foreign Chemical Companies Engaged in International Trade, 1957, The American Selling Price Method of Valuation in U.S. Chemical Imports, 1969. Bd. dirs. Bklyn. Coll. Alumni Assn., Bklyn., 1969-86. Recipient citation, U.S. Treasury Dept., 1944, Nat. War Fund Commn., 1945, Civilian Def. Vol. Office, 1945, War Finance Com. U.S. Treasury Dept., 1945, award ARC, 1945, Founders Day award NYU, 1969, Roosevelt medal Theodore Roosevelt Assn., Bklyn. Coll. Svc. Merit award, 1987, Merit award chemistry dept. Bklyn. Coll., 1982. Fellow Am. Inst. Chemists (chmn. profl. accreditation com. N.Y. chpt. 1964-68, treas. N.Y. chpt. 1970-76, councillor N.Y. chpt. 1964-70), AAAS; mem. SACI, Am. Chem. Soc., N.Y. Acad. Sci., Chemistry Alumni Soc.-Bklyn. Coll. (pres. 1966—), Chemists Club (resident). Home: 2315 Avenue I Brooklyn NY 11210-2825 Office: M W Hardy & Co Inc 111 Broadway Rm 806 New York NY 10006-1985

ASHENFELTER, DAVID LOUIS, reporter, former newspaper editor; b. Toledo, Oct. 20, 1948; s. Duaine Louis and Betty Jean A.; m. Barbara Ann Dinwiddie, Feb. 22, 1974. B.S. in Edn., Ind. U., 1971. Reporter Kokomo Morning Times, Ind., 1966-67, Bloomington Daily Herald-Telephone, Ind., 1968-69, Bloomington Courier-Tribune, 1970-71, Detroit News, 1971-82, Detroit Free Press, 1982—. Recipient Pulitzer prize for meritorious pub. service Columbia U., 1982, Silver Gavel award ABA, 1986, Worth Bingham Prize, 1986, and more than 24 local, state and nat. newswriting awards. Mem. Soc. Profl. Journalists (Disting. Svc. award 1981, 83, 85), Sigma Chi. Office: Detroit Free Press 600 W Fort St Detroit MI 48226

ASHENFELTER, ORLEY CLARK, economics educator; b. San Francisco, 1942. BA in Econs., Claremont Coll., 1964; PhD in Econs., Princeton U., 1968. Dir. office evaluation U.S. Dept. Labor, 1972-73; now prof. econs., dir. indsl. rels. sect. Princeton (N.J.) U., N.J., 1971-95; vis. prof. U. Bristol, 1981; Meyer vis. rsch. prof. law NYU, 1990. Author: Discrimination in Labor Markets, 1974, Evaluating the Labor Market Effects of Social Programs, 1976; assoc. editor Jour. Urban Econs., 1975-76; mng. editor Am. Econ. Rev.; contbr. articles to profl. jours. Bd. trustees Ctr. for Advanced Study in Behavioral Scis., 1994—. Guggenheim Meml. Found. fellow, 1976, Ctr. for Advanced Study in Behavioral Scis. fellow, 1989. Fellow Econometric Soc., Am. Acad. Arts & Scis. Research on determinants of labour supply and unemployment, arbitration and dispute resolution systems. Office: Princeton U Indsl Rels Sect Firestone Libr Princeton NJ 08540

ASHER, AARON, editor, publisher; s. Samuel and Henny (Meyer) A.; m. Linda Wolfsey, Oct. 11, 1956; children—Rachel, Abigail. BA with honors, U. Chgo., 1949, MA, 1952. Mem. editorial staff Alfred A. Knopf, Inc., N.Y.C., 1956-58; exec. editor Meridian Books, Inc., N.Y.C., 1958-64; sr. editor Viking Press, Inc., N.Y.C., 1964-69; dir. gen. book dept. Holt, Rinehart and Winston, Inc., N.Y.C., 1969-74; editor in chief Macmillan Pub. Co., Inc., N.Y.C., 1974; editor in chief, v.p. Farrar, Straus and Giroux, Inc., N.Y.C., 1975-81; exec. editor Harper & Row, N.Y.C., 1981-86; pub. Grove Press, N.Y.C., 1986-89, Grove Weidenfeld, N.Y.C., 1989-90, Aaron Asher Books, Harper Collins, N.Y.C., 1990-93; pub. cons., editor, translator, 1993—. Served with AUS, 1953-55. Home and Office: 201 W 86th St New York NY 10024-3328

ASHER, BETTY TURNER, academic administrator; b. Booneville, Ky., Oct. 19, 1944. BA, Ea. Ky. U.; MA, Western Ky. U.; EdD, U. Cin. Sr. assoc. vice provost U. Cin., 1978-80; assoc. vice chancellor acad. affairs Minn. State U. System, 1981-82; v.p. student affairs Ariz. State U., Tempe, 1982-89; pres. U. S.D., Vermillion, 1989-1996, Bus., Industry Tng., Destin, Fla., 1997—. Office: Bus and Industry Tng 898 Highway 98 E Destin FL 32541-2700*

ASHER, DANA, publishing executive. BS, Syracuse U. Editor-in-chief Meadow Publs. Inc., Mamaroneck, N.Y. Office: Meadow Publs Inc 126 Libr Ln Mamaroneck NY 10543

ASHER, GARLAND PARKER, investment holding company executive; b. Richmond, Va., Sept. 6, 1944; s. Harry Garland and Margie Gregory (Duke) A.; m. Elizabeth Tinkham Deszyck, June 29, 1968; children: Elaine Tinkham, Timothy Duke. BA in Polit. Sci., Randolph-Macon Coll., 1967; MBA in Internat. Fin., U. Pa., 1970. Fin. analyst Ford Motor Co., Dearborn, Mich., 1970-71; asst. v.p. research Kidder Peabody & Co., Inc., N.Y.C., 1971-77; dir. fin. planning Tandy Corp., Ft. Worth, 1977-86; v.p., CFO InterTAN, Inc., Ft. Worth, and Brussels, Belgium, 1986-91; v.p. adminstrn. and CFO Intelligent Electronics, Exton, Pa., 1991-92; pres. G. Parker Holdings Inc., Ft. Worth, Tex., 1992—; bd. dirs. Craddock Allied Corp., Ft. Worth. Bd. dirs. Tarrant County Soc. Crippled Children and Adults, 1978-87; mem. bd. assoc. Randolph-Macon Coll., 1986-92. Mem. Inst. Chartered Fin. Analysts, Fin. Execs. Inst., Newcomen Soc., Commanderie de Bordeaux. Republican. Presbyterian. Avocations: wine, oriental carpets. Office: G Parker Holdings Inc 4001 Monticello Dr Fort Worth TX 76107

ASHER, SANDRA FENICHEL, author, playwright; b. Phila., Oct. 16, 1942; d. Benjamin and Fanny (Weiner) Fenichel; m. Harvey Asher, Jan. 31, 1965; children: Ben, Emily. BA, Ind. U., 1964. cert. in elem. edn., Mo. Writer-in-residence Drury Coll., Springfield, Mo., 1986—; Bd. dirs. Mo. Ctr. for the Book, Jefferson City, 1990-98; literary mgr. Good Co. Theater, Springfield, 1997—. Author: (plays) Little Old Ladies in Tennis Shoes, 1989, A Woman Called Truth, 1993, Dancing With Strangers, 1994, Across the Plains, 1997. Grantee NEA; recipient Nat. Playwriting Symposium award Ind. U./Purdue U. Indpls./ Bonderman, 1987, 89, 95, New Visions/New Voices award Kennedy Ctr., Washington, 1995, Joseph Campbell meml. award The Open Eye Theater, N.Y.C., 1992. Mem. Soc. Children's Book Writers & Illustrators (bd. dirs. 1988-97), Am. Alliance Theater & Edn., Dramatists Guild. Office: Drury Coll 900 N Benton Ave Springfield MO 65802-3712

ASHFORD, CLINTON RUTLEDGE, judge; b. Honolulu, Mar. 23, 1925; s. Huron Kanoelani and Lillian Radcliffe (Cooke) A.; m. Joan Beverly Schumm, Aug. 24, 1951; children: Marguerite, Frank, Bruce, James. B.A., U. Calif.-Berkeley, 1945; J.D., U. Mich., 1950. Bar: Hawaii 1950, U.S. Supreme Ct. 1967, Republic of Marshall Islands 1985. Ptnr. Lee & Ashford, Honolulu, 1951-53; dep. atty. gen. Hawaii, 1953-55; ptnr. Ashford & Wriston, Honolulu, 1955-89, of counsel, 1990—; chief justice Supreme Ct., Republic of Marshall Islands, 1989-96. Bd. dirs. Child and Family Svc., Honolulu, 1967-73, pres., 1971; bd. dirs. Health and Cmty. Svcs. Coun., 1973-75, Neighborhood Justice Ctr., Aloha United Way, 1975-81, exec. com., 1977-79; bd. dirs. Hawaii Justice Found., 1994-99, pres., 1996. With USNR, 1943-46, res., 1950-64, ret. lt. comdr. Fellow Am. Bar Found., Am. Coll. Trust and Estate Counsel, Am. Coll. Real Estate Lawyers, Am. Coll. Trial Lawyers, Am. Acad. Appellate Lawyers, Coll. Law Office Mgmt.; mem. ABA (bd. govs. 1979-82, exec. com. 1981-82), Hawaii Bar Assn. (pres. 1972), Am. Law Inst., Am. Judicature Soc. (bd. dirs. 1981-86, chpt. bd. dirs. 1998—), Internat. Acad. Estate and Trust Law, Order of Coif, Lambda Alpha (Aloha chpt.). Avocations: amateur radio operator, blue water sailor. Email: cashford@awlaw.com. Home: 45-628 Halekou Pl Kaneohe HI 96744-5203 Office: Ashford & Wriston PO Box 131 1099 Alakea St Fl 14 Honolulu HI 96813-4500

ASHFORD, EVELYN, former track and field athlete; b. Shreveport, LA, Apr. 15, 1957; m. Ray Washington; 1 child, Rana. Student, UCLA. Track and field athlete, 1976-92. Competed in 1976 Olympics; winner 2 Gold medals, 1984 Olympics (Women's 100 Meters, Women's 4x100-Meter); winner Gold medal, 1988 Olympics (Women's 4x100-Meter); recipient Flo Hyman award Women's Sport Found., 1989; winner Gold medal, 1992 Olympics, Barcelona, Spain (4x100-Meter), inducted Track & Field Hall of Fame, 1997. Address: USA Track & Field 1 Rca Dome Ste 140 Indianapolis IN 46225-1023*

ASHFORTH, ALDEN, musician, educator; b. N.Y.C., May 13, 1933; m. Nancy Ann Regnier, June 12, 1956 (div. 1980); children—Robyn Richardson, Melissa Adams, Lauren Elizabeth. A.B., Oberlin Coll, 1958, B.Mus., 1958; M.F.A., Princeton U., 1960, Ph.D., 1971. Instr. Princeton U., N.J., 1961; instr. Oberlin Coll., Ohio, 1961-65, N.Y.U., N.Y.C., 1965-66, Manhattan Sch. Music, N.Y.C., 1965; lectr. CUNY, N.Y.C., 1966-67; asst. prof. music UCLA, 1967-72, assoc. prof. music, 1972-80, prof., 1980—; coordinator electronic music studio, 1969-86. Composer numerous instrumental, vocal and electronic works including: Episodes (chamber concerto for 8 instruments), 1962, The Unquiet Heart (cycle for soprano and chamber orch.), 1968, Big Bang (piano-four hands) 1970, Byzantium (organ and electronic tape), 1971, Sailing to Byzantium (organ and electronic tape), 1973, Aspects of Love (song cycle), 1978, Christmas Motets (a cappella chorus), 1980, The Miraculous Bugle (flugelhorn and percussion), 1989, Palimpsests (organ), 1997; producer, recorder New Orleans Jazz including, New Orleans Parade: The Eureka Brass Band Plays Dirges and Stomps, 1952, Doc Paulins Marching Band, 1982, Last of the Line: The Eagle Brass Band, 1984; contbr. articles to profl. jours. and to New Grove Dictionary of Jazz. Office: UCLA Music Dept Los Angeles CA 90095-1616

ASHHURST, ANNA WAYNE, foreign language educator; b. Phila., Jan. 5, 1933; d. Astley Paston Cooper and Anne Pauline (Campbell) Ashhurst; m. Ronald G. Gerber, July 22, 1978. AB, Vassar Coll., 1954; MA, Middlebury Coll., 1956; PhD, U. Pitts., 1967. English tchr. Internat. Inst. Spain, Madrid, 1954-56; asst. prof. Juniata Coll., Huntingdon, Pa., 1961-63; asst. prof. Spanish dept. Franklin and Marshall Coll., Lancaster, Pa., 1968-74, acting chmn. Spanish dept., 1972, convenor, fgn. lang. council, 1972-74; assoc. prof. dept. modern fgn. langs. U. Mo., St. Louis, 1974-78. Author: La literatura hispano-americana en la critica española, 1980. Mem. Welcome Wagon of Lancaster, Pa., 1968-70, 71-74. Fulbright-Hays grantee, Colombia, S.Am., summer 1963; Ford Humanities fellow, summer 1970; Mellon fellow, 1970-71. Mem. AAUW (pres. Ferguson-Florissant br. 1989-91, 95-98, chmn. St. Louis area interbranch coun. 1992-94, chair environ. task force Mo. 1992-95, local arrangements chair for Mo. state conv. 1997, Woman of Distiction award 1998), Internat. Inst. in Spain, Instituto Internacional de Literatura Iberoamericana, Am. Assn. Tchrs. Spanish and Portuguese. Home: 2105 Barcelona Dr Florissant MO 63033-2805

ASHINGTON-PICKETT, MICHAEL DEREK, construction company executive, journalist; b. London, Oct. 11, 1931; s. Edward Robert and Mary Dorothy (Trewhella) Ashington-Pickett; came to U.S., 1965, naturalized, 1971; Civil and Structural Engrng. degrees London U., 1956; m. Sandra Helen Smart, Nov. 20, 1976; children: Michael Derek II, Claire Amanda. Constrn. mgr. various firms in Eng., 1956-63; pres. So. Precast Holdings, London, Eng., 1963-65, The Ashington-Pickett Group of Cos., 1965—; chmn. Ashington-Pickett Found., Inc., 1986—, Orlando Constrn. and Licensing Bd., 1974-78, 82-88, bd. dirs., 1978-80; lectr. for Brit. Council, 1963-65; chmn. Mid-Pac, 1982-88. Editor, pub. The Ashington-Pickett Airlines & Travel Report, 1982—, The Ashington-Pickett Wine Rev., 1992—. Chmn. Ashington-Pickett Found. Inc., 1985—. Served as officer Brit. Army, 1950-52; Korea. Recipient Disting. Svc. award Orange County Bicentennial Commn., 1976; cert. of merit ComitéNational des Vins de France; decorated Chaine De Rotisseurs, Order de Mondial, Campanion Order of Beaujolais, Chevalier Ordre des Chevaliers Bretvins. Mem. Home Builders Assns. Am. (pres., dir. Mid-Fla. chpt.; Disting. Svc. award 1973, life dir. Fla. chpt., Builder of Yr. award 1981), Econs. Club (dir. 1986-96, pres. 1992-93), Orlando C. of C. (dir., v.p. 1981-83), Orlando Jaycees, Kiwanis, Citrus Club. Presbyterian. Home: 1307 Montcalm St Orlando FL 32806-7055 Office: PO Box 149044 Orlando FL 32814-9044

ASHKENAZY, VLADIMIR DAVIDOVICH, concert pianist, conductor; b. Gorky, USSR, July 6, 1937; s. David and Evstolia (Plotnova) A.; m. Thorunn Johannsdottir, Feb. 25, 1961; children—Vladimir Stefan, Nadia Liza, Dimitri Thor, Sonia Edda, Alexandra Inga. Student, Cen. Music Sch., Moscow, Moscow Conservatory; studies with, Sumbatyan, Lev Oborin. Condr., music dir. Royal Philharm. Orch., London, 1987-95; prin. guest conductor Cleve. Orch., 1987-94; music dir. Deutsches Symphonie Orchester (formerly Radio Symphony Orch.), Berlin, 1989-99; music. dir. Czech Philharm. Orch., 1998—. London debut, London Symphony Orch. under George Hurst, later solo recital, Festival Hall, 1963, recs., concerts throughout world. Music dir. Czech Philharm. Orch., Prague, 1998. Recipient 2d prize Internat. Chopin Competition, Warsaw, 1955, Gold medal Queen Elizabeth Internat. Piano Competition, Brussels, 1956, Grammy awards 1973, 78, 81, 85, 87; co-recipient Tchaikovsky Piano Competition award, Moscow, 1962. Office: care Harrison/Parrott Ltd, 12 Penzance Pl, London W11 4PA, England

ASHKIN, MICHAEL, artist; b. Morristown, N.J., 1955. BA, U. Pa., 1977; MA in Mid. East Langs. and Cultures, Columbia U., 1980; MFA in Painting and Drawing, Sch. Art Inst. Chgo., 1993. One-man shows include Peter Miller Gallery, Chgo., 1992, 94, Bronwyn Keenan Gallery, N.Y., 1996, Feigen Inc., Chgo., 1996, Galerie Jousse Seguin, Paris, 1997, Andrea Rosen Gallery, N.Y.C., 1998; exhibited in group shows at Peter Miller Gallery, Chgo., 1992, Sch. Art Inst. Chgo., 1993, Gallery 2, Sch. Art Inst. Chgo., 1994, 450 Gallery, N.Y., 1995, Andrea Rosen Gallery, N.Y.C., 1996, Rosenberg Gallery, Hofstra U., Hempstead, N.Y., 1997, Kerlin Gallery, Dublin, Ireland, 1997, Mus. Contemporary Art, Miami, Fla., 1997, New Mus. Contemporary Art, N.Y.C., 1997, Turner & Runyon, Dallas, 1998, Saatchi Gallery, London, 1998, Four Walls Gallery, Bklyn., 1998, S.E. Ctr. Contemporary Art, Winston-Salem, N.C., 1999, numerous others. Recipient award The Pollock-Krasner Found., Inc., 1997; Hon. Pres. fellow Columbia U., 1978; Full Merit scholar Sch. Art Inst. Chgo., 1991-93. Office: care Andrea Rosen Gallery 525 West 24th St New York NY 10011

ASHKIN, RAJASPERI MALIAPEN, marketing executive; b. Penang, Malaysia, Mar. 1, 1956; came to U.S., 1984; d. Maliapen A.M.N. (Annasamy) and Jayaletchemi (Chelliah) M.; m. Ronald Evan Ashkin, Nov. 25, 1984; 1 child, Jacqueline Ariel. BS in Forestry, U. Canterbury, 1978, DBA, 1979. Mktg. asst. Forest Rsch. Inst., Rotorua, Nw Zealand, 1978-79; mktg. officer Consulate Gen. India, Sydney, Australia, 1980-81; nat. mktg. coord. Estee Lauder Ltd., Sydney, 1981-84; assoc. buyer Brown Store Group, Terre Haute, Ind., 1984-85; mktg. mgr. A.T.C. Time Inc., Terre Haute, 1985-87; v.p. New Concepts Inc., Terre Haute, 1987-90; chief exec. officer, mng. dir. Excelsior Corp., Terre Haute, 1990—, also bd. dirs.; mktg. & advt. cons. in field; organizer Christmas Food Drive Salvation Army, Terre Haute, 1985-86; vol. reader Vigo County Pub. Libr. Literacy Program, 1989—. Mktg. com. Leadership Terre Haute, 1986-87; TV moderator Valley Point of View, Terre Haute, 1986—; bd. dirs. YWCA, Terre Haute, 1986—; internat. rels. chairperson Altrusa Club, Terre Haute, 1985-87; cake bake chairperson, on site rep. Century Club, YWCA, 1986. Recipient Letter of Commendation Ralph Davidson Time Inc., 1986, Nat. System Mktg. award A.T.C. Time Inc., 1986, Grand Prize HBO Summer Sales Campaign, 1986, Letter of Commendation Disney Channel, 1986, Outstanding Creative Contbrn. award, 1987, Tempo TV award, 1987; named to Scholastic Honor Soc. Pamarista Ind. State U., 1989, Literacy Grante Internat. Network for Women, 2000 Notable Am. Women Hall of Fame, A.B.I., 1990, Woman of Yr., A.B.I., 1990, Internat. Leaders in Achievement, IBC, 1990. Mem. NAFE, India Assn. Terre Haute, United Hebrew Congregation Terre Haute, Country Club of Terre Haute, M.V.P. Club Larry Bird, Altrusa Club of Terre Haute, YWCA, Leadership Terre Haute. Avocations: travel, gardening, music, fine arts, skiing.

ASHKIN, RONALD EVAN, international executive; b. New Rochelle, N.Y., Apr. 5, 1957; s. Abraham and Arleen (Wollins) A.; m. Rajasperi Maliapen, Nov. 25, 1984; 1 child, Jacqueline Ariel. AB magna cum laude, Harvard U., 1977; MBA, Wharton Sch., U. Pa., 1982; postgrad., Harvard U., 1993, 96. Cert. fin. planner. V.p. Continental Chem. Corp., Terre Haute, Ind., 1978-83, pres., 1983-86; pres. New Concepts Inc., Terre Haute, 1987-90, Excelsior Corp., Terre Haute, 1990-92; dir. internat. sales Gold Eagle Co., Chgo., 1992-95, v.p. internat., 1995-97; dir. cons. The Recovery Group, Boston, 1998—, USAID Bus. Cons., Sarajevo, Bosnia, 1998—; adj. faculty Sch. Bus., Ind. State U., 1991-92. Moderator TV show, Terre Haute, 1985-86. Mem. Terre Haute sch. adv. com., 1984-86; bd. dirs. Glenn Civic Ctr., Terre Haute, 1985-88; mem. mktg. edn. curriculum study com. Ind. Dept. Edn. Group study exch. grantee Rotary Found., Sri Lanka and India, 1985-86; Harvard U. scholar, 1973-76; recipient Ill. Gov.'s Export award, 1995, 96. Mem. Leadership Terre Haute Alumni Assn. (chmn. 1986), Am. Prodn. and Inventory Control Soc. (local v.p. 1982-84, 86, local pres. 1985), Overseas Automotive coun., Automotive Exporters Coun. (v.p. 1994—, pres. 1995—), Jr. Achievement (vol. cons.), Toastmasters (local v.p. 1981-82), Phi Beta Kappa. Avocations: music, outdoor recreation, travel. Home: 270 Congress St Boston MA 02210-1037

ASHKINAZY, LARRY ROBERT, dentist; b. N.Y.C., Feb. 12, 1952; s. Philip and Kate (Scherer) A. BS, Bklyn. Coll., 1973; DDS, NYU, 1976. Cert. Nat. Bd. Dental Examiners. Gen. dental practice residency Cabrini Health Care Ctr., 1977; pvt. practice dentistry N.Y.C., 1977—; assoc. attending dentist Cabrini Healthcare Ctr., 1984—, assoc. attending in implantology, 1983-86, postgrad. instr. Inst. for Grad. Dentists, 1981-82; guest lectr. various pub. and profl. edn. instns.; health and sci. corr. Sta. WWOR-TV. Author: Dentistry, 1982; contbr. articles to profl. jours.; mem. editorial bd. Internat. Congress Oral Implantologists newsletter, 1982; various radio and TV appearances; patentee in field; trademarks Bionic Tooth, Tooth Plant. Health care providor Drs. with a Heart, N.Y.C., 1987; health care spokesman Jr. League, N.Y.C., 1978, Community Fair, N.Y.C., 1983. Recipient Cert. of Appreciation Greater N.Y. Dental Meeting, 1981, 87, Cert. of Appreciation NYU Dental Ctr., 1981. Fellow Acad. Gen. Dentistry, Acad. Dentistry Internat., Acad. Implants and Transplants, Am. Endodontic Soc., Internat. Congress Oral Implantologists; mem. Am. Dental Assn. (cert. appreciation 1980), Am. Acad. Oral Medicine, Internat. Analgesia Soc., 1st Dist. Dental Soc. (oral health clinician 1978, speakers bur. subcom.chmn. 1984pub. and profl. relations com. 1982), Am. Prosthodontic Soc., Sociedad Venezolana de Implantodontologos, Am. Acad. Implant Dentistry (chmn. sci. exhibit com., 1984, edn. com. 1984, library com. 1984, membership com. 1983, N.Y. chmn. 1983 ann. meeting and world assembly. Dentistry Alumni, Alpha Omega. Club: Greater N.Y. Implant Study (pres. 1981—). Home and Office: 200 Central Park S New York NY 10019-1415

ASHLEIGH, CAROLINE, art and antiques appraiser. BA, Worcester (Mass.) Coll., 1973; cert. in appraisal studies, NYU, 1994. Profl. lectr. on connoisseurship; appraiser Home and Garden TV Sta. WJBK-TV2, Bloomfield Hills, Mich., 1995; appraiser Media-One TV, 1997—, PBS, Sta. WTVS, Southfield, Mich., 1997—; edn. dept. staff Cranbrook Acad. of Art, Bloomfield Hills, 1997—; columnist Detroit Monthly Mag., 1988—, Detroit Met. Woman, 1997—; edn. dept. staff Detroit Inst. Art, 1988—; regional rep. William Doyle Auctioneers, N.Y.C., 1997—; columnist Detroit Legal News, 1998—; appraiser Chubbs Antique Roadshow, WGBH-TV, Boston, 1996—; lectr. in field; columnist Hour Detroit Mag., Detroit Legal News, 1999. Columnist Detroit Monthly, 1995-96. Mem. Appraisers Assn. of Am., Nat. Mus. of Women in the Arts, Cranbrook Art Mus. Home: 800 E Lincoln St Birmingham MI 48009-1784

ASHLER, PHILIP FREDERIC, international trade and development advisor; b. N.Y.C., Oct. 15, 1914; s. Philip and Charlotte (Barth) A.; m. Jane Porter, Mar. 4, 1942 (dec. 1968); children: Philip Frederic, Robert Porter, Richard Harrison; m. Elise Barrett Duvall, June 21, 1969; stepchildren: Richard Edward Duvall, Jeffries Harding Duvall. BBA cum laude, St. Johns Coll., 1935; MBA, Harvard U., 1937; grad., Indsl. Coll. Armed Forces, 1956; ScD, Fla. Inst. Tech., 1969; LLD (hon.), U. West Fla., 1969; postgrad., U. Oxford, Eng., 1988, 89, 91. Enlisted USMCR, 1932; commd. ensign USN, 1938, advanced through grades to rear adm., 1959; served in Normandy, So. France, Iwo Jima, Korea; dir. Office Small Bus., Dept. Def., Washington, 1948-49; mem. joint staff Joint Chiefs Staff, 1957-59; ret., 1959; dir. devel. Pensacola Jr. Coll., 1960-68; vice chancellor adminstrn. State Univ. System Fla., 1968-70, exec. vice chancellor, 1970-75; treas., ins. commr., fire marshal State of Fla., 1975-76, sec. of commerce, 1977-79; pres. Philip F. Ashler & Assos., Tallahassee, 1979—; chmn. bd. Cambridge Community Care, Inc., Tallahassee, 1981-86, Circle Seven Internat., Tampa, 1988-91; past dir. Fidelity Guaranty Life Ins. Co., Balt., U.S. Fidelity & Guaranty Co., 1st Fla. Bank N.A., Tallahassee; sec., dir. Fringe Benefits Mgmt. Co., Tallahassee, 1987—; mem. Fla. Edn. Council, 1967-68; commr. from Fla. Edn. Commn. States, 1967-68; mem. U.S. Dept. Commerce Dist. Export Council, 1978-92; chmn. bd., dir. Fla. Internat. Vol. Corps., 1988-90; mem. legis. adv. council So. Regional Edn. Bd., 1966-68; mem. Fla. Bd. Ind. Colls. and Univs., 1971-75, mem. adv. council for mil. edn., 1980-85; bd. advisors Ctr. Profl. Devel., Fla. State U., 1988-96; chmn. Fla. Civil Def. Adv. Council, 1966-69; mem. Fla. Council Internat. Devel., 1973-92, vice chmn., 1979-80, chmn., 1980-82, chmn. emeritus, 1990—; mem. Select Council on Post High Sch. Edn., 1967-68; chmn. Fla. Med. Liability Ins. Commn., 1975-76, Fla. Task Force on Auto and Workers Compensation, 1975-76; mem. Yugoslavia Adv. Council, 1976-87, InterAm. Congress on Psychology, Bogota, Colombia, 1974, NATO Advanced Sci. Inst., W.Ger., 1973; guest lectr. U. Belgrade, Yugoslavia, 1973; adviser econ. devel. to gov. Fla., 1977-78; mission leader Japan/S.E. U.S. Assn., Tokyo, 1977; trustee Fla. Council on Econ. Edn., 1979-81; mem. services policy adv. com. Office of U.S. Trade Rep., Exec. Office of Pres., Washington, 1980-85; mem. Republic of China/U.S.A. Econ. Council, 1979-92. Mem. Fla. Ho. of Reps., 1963-68; chmn. bd. dirs. Fla. Heart Assn., 1969-71; bd. dirs., treas. Internat. Cardiology Found.; bd. dirs. Tallahassee Meml. Hosp., Easter Seal Soc., 1963-68; bd. dirs., mem. exec. com. Am. Heart Assn., 1971-77, Internat. Cardiology Fedn., Geneva, 1975-77; founding chmn. Tallahassee Symphony Orch., 1981-82; trustee So. Ctr. Internat. Studies, Atlanta, 1988-91; mem. adv. bd. Fla./China Inst., Miami, Fla./Japan Inst., Tampa, Fla./Brazil Inst. Decorated Bronze Star with Combat V, Korean Presdl. citation; recipient Internat. Distinguished Service award Kiwanis Internat., 1965; Distinguished

Service award Am. Heart Assn., 1965, 71; Distinguished Achievement award, 1975; Legislative award St. Petersburg Times, 1967. Mem. Fla. Med. Malpractice Joint Underwriting Assn. (chmn. bd. govs. 1975-76), Nat. Assn. Ins. Commrs. (vice chmn. exec. com. 1976), Internat. C. of C. (U.S. coun. 1979-87), U.S. S.E./Japan Assn. (chmn. 1981-83), S.E. U.S./Korea Econ. Coop. Coun. (bd. dirs.), Capital Tiger Bay Club (chmn. bd. dirs.), Govs. Club (bd. govs. 1989-93, v.p. for fin. 1992-93, bd. govs. 1994-96, treas. 1996), Econ. Club Fla. (chmn. 1987-90, chmn. emeritus 1991—), Masons (32 degree), Shriners, Rotary, Kappa Delta. Episcopalian (lic. lay eucharistic minister). Home: 2115 E Randolph Cir Tallahassee FL 32312-3325 also: 11 Riad Sultan Kasbah, Tangier Morocco Office: Fringe Benefits Mgmt Co PO Box 1878 Tallahassee FL 32302-1878

ASHLEY, DARLENE JOY, psychologist; b. N.Y.C., Oct. 29, 1945; d. George Geiger and Ann Debra (Bernstein) Munzer; m. Joseph Michael O'Brien, Sept. 23, 1974 (div. June 1981); 1 child, Sundara Amber; m. Roy William Fagan, Aug. 16, 1991. BA with honors, Antioch Coll., 1966; MA, NYU, 1973; PhD, Calif. Grad. Sch., San Rafael, 1987. Lic. clin. psychologist, Hawaii, Calif.; diplomate Am. Bd. Med. Psychotherapists; lic. marriage, family and child counselor, Calif.; Biofeedback Cert. Inst. of Am. Psychology instr. Coll. of the Redwoods, 1977-82; instr. psychology North Am. Coll., San Rafael, 1980; cons., psychol. examiner Hawaii Bd. Edn., Hilo, 1982; lectr. U. Hawaii, Hilo, Manoa, 1982—; predoctoral clin. psychology intern Redwood Ctr., Berkeley, Calif., 1983-85; pvt. practice San Rafael, Berkeley, 1985-87, Darlene Ashley, PhD and Assocs., Kailua Kona, Hawaii, 1988—; presenter in field; instr. psychology Coll. of Redwoods, Ft. Bragg, Calif., 1978-82; presenter AM-FM Sta. KMPO, Caspar, Calif., AM-FM Sta. KKON, Kealakekua, Hawaii. Author: Voluntary Controls Training Handbook, 1982; author: (cassette) Deep Relaxation, 1983. Bd. dirs. Friends of Child Advocacy Ctr., 1995—, Island Crisis Help, 1996—; mem. Task Force on Worker's Compensation Reform for Hawaii, 1994-95; proponent Hawaii bill pertaining to psychologists, 1988; mem. com. Rep. Virginia Isbell's Fundraiser, Kailua-Kona, 1988—. Rsch. grantee NSF, Mus. Natural History, N.Y.C., 1965, NIMH, NYU, 1968-70, fellowship NIMH, 1969, Outstanding Rsch. award Biofeedback Soc. Calif., 1987. Mem. APA, Hawaii Psychol. Assn., Hawaii Island Psychologists Assn. (pres.-elect 1997). Avocations: tennis, running, travel. Office: 75-5744 Alii Dr Ste 237 Kailua Kona HI 96740-1740

ASHLEY, ELEANOR TIDABACK, retired elementary educator; b. Yonkers, N.Y., May 29, 1910; d. Frederick Victor and Bessie (Van Tassel) Tidaback; m. Kenneth Miller Ashley, June 25, 1938; 1 child, Robert Bruce. Grad., New Paltz Tchrs. Coll., 1931; BS in Edn., NYU, 1936. Tchr. 3d grade Spring Valley, N.Y., 1931-36, tchr. jr. high sch. English, 1936-38; tchr. 5th and 6th grades Elementary Sch., New City, N.Y., 1938-44; tchr. 2d grade Elementary Sch., Ossining, N.Y., 1941-67; introduced moral values program Ossining (N.Y.) Pub. Schs. Mem. AAUW, Sr. Citizens Club of Niantic (Conn.), Am. Assn. Ret. Persons. Home: 81 Quarry Dock Rd Niantic CT 06357-1908

ASHLEY, ELIZABETH, actress; b. Ocala, Fla., Aug. 30, 1941; d. Arthur Kingman and Lucille (Ayer) Cole; m. George Peppard (div.); 1 son, Christian Moore; m. James Michael McCarthy. Student ballet with, Tatiana Semenova; student, La. State U., 1957-58; grad., Neighborhood Playhouse, N.Y.C., 1961. Apptd. Pres.'s council 1st Nat. Council on the Arts, 1965-69; dir. Am. Film Inst., 1968-72. Appeared on Broadway in The Highest Tree, 1961, Take Her, She's Mine, 1962, Barefoot in the Park, 1963; motion pictures include The Carpet Baggers, 1963, Ship of Fools, 1964, The Third Day, 1965, Marriage of a Young Stockbroker, 1971, Paperback Hero, 1974, Golden Needles, 1974, Rancho Deluxe, 1975, 92 in the Shade, 1976, The Great Scout and Cathouse Thursday, 1976, Coma, 1978, Windows, 1980, Paternity, 1981, Lookin' to Get Out, 1982, Split Image, 1982, Dragnet, 1987, Dangerous Curves, 1987, A Man of Passion, 1988, Vampire's Kiss, 1989, Mallrats, 1995, Sleeping Together, 1997, Happiness, 1998, Just the Ticket, 1999; TV work includes (series) Evening Shade, CBS, 1990-94; TV movies include When Michael Calls, 1972, Second Chance, 1972, The Heist, 1972, Your Money or Your Wife, 1972, One of My Wives is Missing, 1976, The War Between the Tates, 1977, A Fire in the Sky, 1978, Svengali, 1983, Stage Coach, 1986, He's Fired, She's Hired, 1984, Warm Hearts, Cold Feet, 1987, The Two Mrs. Grenvilles, 1987, Orleans (series), The Rope, Blue Bayou, 1990, Reason for Living: The Jill Ireland Story, 1991, In the Best Interest of the Children, 1992, (mini series) The Buccaneers, 1995; stage appearances include The Enchanted, Washington, 1973, The Skin of Our Teeth, Washington, Broadway, 1975, Cat on a Hot Tin Roof, Stratford, Conn. and Broadway, 1974, Agnes of God; author: Postcards from the Road, 1978; TV guest appearances include Murder, She Wrote, Law & Order, The Larry Sanders Show, B.L. Stryker, Women ot the House, Burke's Law, others. Recipient Antoinette Perry award, 1962. Mem. Actors Equity, Screen Actors Guild, AFTRA. Office: Writers and Artists Agy 19 W 44th St Ste 1000 New York NY 10036-6095*

ASHLEY, HOLT, aerospace scientist, educator; b. San Francisco, Jan. 10, 1923; s. Harold Harrison and Anne (Oates) A.; m. Frances M. Day, Feb. 1, 1947 (wid.). Student, Calif. Inst. Tech., 1940-43; BS, U. Chgo., 1944; MS, MIT, 1948, ScD, 1951. Mem. faculty MIT, 1946-67, prof. aero., 1960-67; prof. aeros. and astronautics Stanford U., Palo Alto, Calif., 1967-89, prof. emeritus, 1989—; spl. rsch. aeroelasticity, aerodynamics; cons. govt. agys., rsch. orgns., indsl. corps.; dir. office of exploratory rsch. and problem assessment and div. advanced tech. applications NSF, 1972-74; mem. sci. adv. bd. USAF, 1958-80, rsch. adv. com. structural dynamics NASA, 1952-60, rsch. adv. com. on aircraft structures, 1962-70, chmn. rsch. adv. com. on materials and structures, 1974-77; mem. Kanpur Indo-American program Indian Inst. Tech., 1964-65, governing bd. Nat. Rsch. Coun., 1988-91; AIAA Wright Bros. lectr., 1981; dir. Rann Inc. Co-author: Aeroelasticity, 1955, Principles of Aeroelasticity, 1962, Aerodynamics of Wings and Bodies, 1969, Engineering Analysis of Flight Vehicles, 1974. Recipient Goodwin medal M.I.T., 1952; Exceptional Civilian Service award U.S. Air Force, 1972, 80; Public Service award NASA, 1981; named one of 10 outstanding young men of year Boston Jr. C. of C., 1956; recipient Ludwig-Prandtl Ring, West German DGLR, 1987, Spirit of St. Louis Medal, ASME, 1992. Fellow AIAA (hon., assoc. editor jour., v.p. tech. 1971, pres. 1973, Structures, Structural Dynamics and Materials award 1969), Am. Acad. Arts and Scis., Royal Aero. Soc. (hon.); mem. AAAS, NAE (aeros. and space engrng. bd. 1977-79, mem. coun. 1985-91), Am. Meterol. Soc. (profl., 50th Ann. medal 1971), Phi Beta Kappa, Sigma Xi, Tau Beta Pi. Home: 475 Woodside Dr Woodside CA 94062-2375

ASHLEY, JAMES MACGREGOR, management consultant; b. Little Falls, N.Y., July 29, 1941; s. Robert Cudworth and Vivien Arlene (McCaughan) A.; m. Jane Staszewski, Apr. 20, 1995; children: Christopher Robert, Kimberly Dawn. BA, U. Miami, 1964. Program dir. Sta. VUNC Radio, Okinawa, Japan, 1965-67; photographer Sta. WOKR-TV, Rochester, N.Y., 1968-70; film dir. Sta. WVNY-TV, Burlington, Vt., 1969-71; mng. dir. Champlain Coun. Holiday Magic Dist., Burlington, 1971-72; sales mgr. MAICO Hearing Aid Ctr., Burlington, 1972-77; buyer IBM, Burlington, 1978-83; internat. contract cons. IBM, Boca Raton, Fla., 1983-87, mgr., 1987—; pres. Procurement Arts Internat., Boca Raton, 1988—. Co-author: Handbook of Buying and Purchasing Management, 1992; author: International Purchasing Handbook, 1998, numerous quick study guides for colls. and univs. Capt. U.S. Army, 1964-67. Mem. ASTD (past pres.), Am. Mgmt. Assn. (faculty), Am. Purchasing Soc. (exec. bd.), Inst. Mgmt. Cons. (past v.p.). Episcopalian. Avocation: USCG aux. Home and Office: 744 NE 12th Ter Boynton Beach FL 33435-3272

ASHLEY, JOHN BRYAN, software executive, management consultant; b. Lake Charles, La., Dec. 1, 1955; s. John Nathaniel and Anne Lee (Baker) A.; m. Peggy Anne Daly, Mar. 21, 1988; children: John B. Jr., Robert Lee, Elizabeth Anne. BS, La. Tech. U., 1977, MS in Econs., 1977. Mktg. rep. IBM, Shreveport, La., 1978-81, acct. mgr., 1981-84; product mgr. IBM, Rochester, Minn., 1984-88; product cons. IBM, Atlanta, 1988-93; v.p. mktg., sr. ptnr. Distbr. Solutions Internat., Alpharetta, Ga., 1993-95; dir. strategic alliances Infinium Software, Inc., Hyannis, Mass., 1995-97, also London, Paris, Singapore; mng. dir. Europe, Mid. East, Africa Infinium Software, Inc., 1996-97, v.p. bus. devel., 1997—; cons. to IBM Corp., USA, 1993, IBM Europe, Paris, 1994, 95, Russian Fedn., 1995; market cons. to European Software Vendors, 1994, 95. Del. Ga. State Rep. Party, 1992-93, Cobb Rep. Party, 1992-93. Mem. Sons of Confederate Vets., Colonial Williamsburg Found., Ravinia Club Atlanta, Ams. for Hope, Growth and Opportunity, Kappa Sigma (pres.). Presbyn. Avocations: wine, African safaries, oriental arts, horticulture, realist art and Am./English antiques, equestrian activities. Home: 4750 Talleybrook Dr NW Kennesaw GA 30152-5484 Office: Infinium Software 2500 Northwinds Pkwy Alpharetta GA 30004-2243 also: Crosby House Meadow Bank, Bourne End, Bucks United Kingdom

ASHLEY, LINDA ANN, nurse; b. Milford, Del., Feb. 8, 1950; d. Alton O. and Annie E. (Barrett) King; m. Walton Ashley, Apr., 1988; children: Robin, Robert, Rachel, Caleb. ADN, De Tech Community Coll., Georgetown, Del., 1979; BSN, Wilmington Coll., 1989, MSN, 1995. Cert. family nurse practitioner. Staff nurse Milford (Del.) Manor Nursing Home; staff nurse surg. dept. Beebe Hosp., Lewes, Del.; staff nurse Vis. Nurses' Assn., Milford; instr. in nursing De Tech Community Coll., Georgetown; pub. health nurse Div. Pub. Health State of Del., Dover; nurse practitioner Nanticoke Meml. Hosp.; pvt. family practice. Home: RR 3 Box 204 Lincoln DE 19960-9715

ASHLEY, PERRY JONATHAN, journalism educator; b. West Lebanon, Ind., May 1, 1928; s. Terrell Garner and Viola Ethel (Whitmer) A.; m. Lita Grey Cochran, Nov. 29, 1952; children: Jonathan Edward, Richard Douglas. AB in Journalism, U. Ky., 1956, MA in Polit. Sci., 1966; PhD in Journalism, So. Ill. U., 1968. Instr. Sch. Journalism U. Ky., Lexington, 1956-65; teaching assoc. Sch. Journalism So. Ill. U., Carbondale, 1965-67; prof. Coll. Journalism and Mass Comm. U. S.C., Columbia, 1967-93, interim dean Coll. Journalism, 1985-86, assoc. dean, 1986-92, disting. prof. emeritus, 1993—; dir. Ky. Scholastic Press Assn., U. Ky., 1956-65; dir. media rsch. Coll. Journalism, U. S.C., 1970-90; dir. S.C. Scholastic Press Assn., U. S.C., 1971-74; cons.on audience analysis S.C. Ednl. TV System, 1969-72. Editor: Newspaper Publishing in South Carolina, 1980, American Newspaper Journalists, 1873-1900, 1983, American Newspaper Journalists, 1901-1925, 1984, American Newspaper Journalists, 1926-1950, 1984, American Newspaper Journalists, 1690-1872, 1985, American Newspaper Publishers, 1951-1990, 1993. Mem. Gov.'s Safety Coun., Commonwealth of Ky.; mem. East Richland Pub. Svc. Commn., Columbia, 1972-79, chmn., 1973-77; trustee Richland County Sch. Dist. 2, Columbia, 1981-87, chmn., 1985. Cpl. U.S. Army, 1950-52, Germany. Named Nation's Outstanding Yearbook Adviser Nat. Coun. Coll. Publs. Advisers, 1964. Mem. Am. Journalism Historians Assn. (program chmn., bd. dirs. 1988-91), Assn. Edn. in Journalism and Mass Comm., Soc. Profl. Journalists (Disting. Campus Chpt. Adviser 1982), Alpha Delta Sigma, Kappa Tau Alpha, Alpha Epsilon Rho, Phi Alpha Theta, Psi Sigma Alpha, Omicron Delta Kappa. Independent. Presbyterian. Avocations: miniaturist, travel, reading, amateur photography, gardening, backyard birdwatching. Home: 3747 Greenleaf Rd Columbia SC 29206-3362

ASHLEY, RAYMOND WELDON, writer; b. Muenster, Tex., Aug. 27, 1942; s. Noble Preston and Velma Modene (Reed) A.; m. Cecilia Mackie Boyd, Dec. 19, 1964; children: Gregory Wayne, Audrey Rae, Laura Nell. BA, U. North Tex., 1963; MA, Mich. State U., 1970; postgrad., U. Nebr., Omaha, 1973-75, Midwestern State U., 1996—. Commd. 2d lt. USAF, 1963, advanced through grades to lt. col., 1980, various positions in comm., resource mgmt., logistics, 1987; tchr. social studies St. Jo (Tex.) H.S., 1992; adult edn. instr. Region IX Edn. Svcs. Ctr., Wichita Falls, Tex., 1994-95; spkr. in field. Author (videotape) Victor Guriev, Profile of a Soviet Officer, 1977, Tsar and Commissar, A History of Russia 862-1945, 1978; author: Old School Scholastics, A History of Education in Saint Jo, Texas, 1872-1922, 1995; writer Saint Jo Tribune, Nocona and Bowie News, Wichita Falls Times-Record News, 1991-96. Reporter Illinois Bend (Tex.) Civic Assn., 1991-93; trustee Illinois Bend Cemetery Assn., 1996—, Illnois Bend Civic Assn., 1998—. Decorated Bronze Star, Meritorious Svc. Medal with 2 oak leaf clusters, Air medal, Air Force Commendation medal with 2 oak leaf clusters, Air Force Achievement medal; honor medal 1st class (Vietnam); Ten Films scholar U. North Tex. Philosophy Club, 1962-63, merit scholar Midwestern State U., 1996-98. Mem. Retired Officer Assn., Montague County Hist. Commn., Masons, Phi Alpha Theta, Sigma Tau Delta. Avocations: landscaping, researching local history, gardening, reading. Home and Office: PO Box 430 Saint Jo TX 76265-0430

ASHLEY, SHARON ANITA, pediatric anesthesiologist; b. Goulds, Fla., Dec. 28, 1948; d. John H. Ashley and Johnnie Mae (Everett) Ashley-Mitchell; m. Clifford K. Sessions, Sept. 1977 (div. 1985); children: Cecili, Nicole, Erika. BA, Lincoln U., 1970; postgrad., Pomona Coll., 1971; MD, Hahnemann Med. Sch., Phila., 1976. Diplomate Am. Bd. Pain Mgmt., Am. Bd. Anesthesiologists. Intern pediatrics Martin Luther King Hosp., L.A., 1976-77, resident pediatrics, 1977-78, resident anesthesiology, 1978-81, mem. staff, 1981—. Named Outstanding Tchr. of Yr., King Drew Med. Ctr., Dept. Anesthesia, 1989, Outstanding Faculty of Yr., 1991. Mem. Am. Soc. Anesthesiologists, Calif. Med. Assn., L.A. County Med. Soc., Soc. Regional Anesthesia, Soc. Pediatric Anesthesia. Democrat. Baptist. Avocations: reading, crocheting, sailing. Office: Martin Luther King Hosp 12021 Wilmington Ave Los Angeles CA 90059-3099

ASHLEY, WILLARD WALDEN C., SR., minister; b. N.Y.C., Nov. 16, 1953; s. Will and Clara (Peterkin) A.; m. Veronica Lamb, June, 1975 (div. Sept., 1976); 1 child, Willard W. C. Ashley, Jr.; m. Diane Theresa Manning, Sept. 29, 1979. AAS, Fashion Inst. Tech., N.Y.C., 1974; BA, Montclair (N.J.) State Coll., 1981; MDiv, Andover Newton Sch. Theol., 1984, D Ministry, 1992. Ordained to ministry Am. Bapt. Ch., 1982. Seminarian First Bapt. Ch., Tewksbury, Mass., 1981-82; pastor New Hope Bapt. Ch., Portsmouth, N.H., 1982-84; asst. dean students, dir. recruitment Andover Newton Theol. Sch., Newton, Mass., 1984-86; pastor Monumental Bapt. Ch., Jersey City, N.J., 1986-96; founder Abundant Joy Bapt. Ch., Jersey City, 1996—; pastoral psychotherapy resident Blanton-Peale Counseling Ctr., N.Y.C., 1996—; mem. Am. Bapt. Statement of Concerns Com., 1988-90, North N.J. Missionary Bapt. Assn., 1988—; co-chmn. Interfaith Cmty. Orgn., Jersey City, strategy team, 1988-95, Indsl. Areas Found., Nat. Leaders Team, 1991-92; assoc. prof. N.Y. Theol. Sem., 1992—, Drew Theol. Sem., 1996-98, Auburn Sem., 1998—; coord. pastoral care Barnert Hosp., Patterson, N.J., 1994-97; psychotherapist Montclair Counseling Ctr., Upper Montclair, 1998—. Preacher weekly radio program WNJR, Hillside, N.J., 1987-92. Bd. dirs. Visiting Homemakers of Hudson, Jersey City, 1988-93, YMCA of Jersey City, 1989-93; bd. regents St. Peter's Coll., 1995—. Recipient Montclair State Coll. award, 1981, H. Otherman Smith Preaching award, 1984, Citation, Phi Delta Kapppa, 1989, Appreciation award, Alpha Kappa Alpha, 1990, Humanitarian award, Nat. Conf. Christians and Jews. Mem. Am. Assn. Pastoral Counselors, Am. Assn. Marriage and Family Therapists (student mem.), Clin. Pastoral Edn., Ministers Coun. Am. Bapt. Ch. Home: Society Hill at U Heights 16 Krueger Ct Newark NJ 07103-3466 Office: Abundant Joy Bapt Ch 137 Bowers St Jersey City NJ 07307-2905

ASHLEY-FARRAND, MARGALO, lawyer, mediator, private judge; b. N.Y.C., July 26, 1944; d. Joel Thomas and Margalo (Wilson) Ashley; m. Marvin H. Bennett, Mar. 5, 1964 (div. June 1974),; children: Marc, Aliza; m. Thomas Ashley-Farrand, Dec. 11, 1981. Student, UCLA, 1962-63, U. Pitts., 1972-74; BA cum laude, NYU, 1978; JD, Southwestern U., 1980. Bar: D.C. 1981, Md. 1981, Calif. 1983, U.S. Dist. Ct. (ctrl. and no. dists.) Calif. 1984; cert. family law specialist Calif. State Bar. Pvt. practice law Washington, 1981-82; ptnr. Ashley-Farrand & Smith, Glendale, Calif., 1983-87; pvt. practice law, 1987-95; pvt. practice Pasadena, Calif., 1995—; v.p. Legal Inst. Fair Elections, 1995—; settlement officer L.A. Mcpl. Ct., 1990—; judge pro tem L.A. Mcpl. Ct., 1989—, L.A. Superior Ct., 1993—. Convenor, pres. East Hills chpt. NOW, 1972-74, mem. Pa. state bd., 1972-74, pres. Hollywood chpt. 1974-75, mem. bd. N.Y.C. chpt. 1975-78; convenor, coord. L.A. Women's Coalition for Better Broadcasting, 1974-75; Dem. nominee Calif. State Assembly, 1994. Themis soc. scholar, 1980; named one of Outstanding Young Women of Am., 1980. Mem. ABA, ACLU, NOW, NWPC, League of Conservation Voters, Calif. Women Lawyers, Women Lawyers Assn. L.A., Pasadena Interracial Women's Club (pres. 1993-94). Office: 215 N Marengo Ave Fl 3 Pasadena CA 91101-1504

ASHMAN, ALICIA KONINSKA, civic activist; b. Syracuse, N.Y., July 18, 1923; d. Edward and Stanislawa (Tomaszewska) Koninski; m. Hubert C. Ashman, Apr. 28, 1945; children: Wanda Lorain, Alice Barbara, Philip Richard, Martha Jane. RN, Kings County Sch. Nursing, Bklyn., 1945. Nurse eye dept. Mayo Clinic, Rochester, Minn., 1945-47; alderwoman City of Madison, Wis., 1968-77, coun. pres., 1974; served on more than 30 civic coms., including parks, welfare, libr., re-devel., equal opportunities, housing, others. Co-founder 10th Dist. Assn., Regent Neighborhood Assn. Capital Cmty. Citizens, 1960s, Dane County Aux. Med. Soc.; mem. State of Wis. Environ. Coun., 1978-80; activist LWV, Dane County, 1948—; pres. bd. trustees Madison Pub. Libr., 1989-96, 1969-75. Recipient Capital Community Citizen Orchid award 1970, cert. of appreciation Wis. Legis. Coun., 1976, LWV, Dane County, Inc., 1995, cert. of recognition Women's Issues and Affirmative Action Office, 1977, The Madison Equal Opportunities Commn., 1983; Alicia Ashman Pedestrian Overpass dedicated in her name, City of Madison, 1979; Trustee of Yr. South Ctrl. Libr. System, 1994. Avocations: travel, reading, gardening, sewing.

ASHMAN, CHARLES H., retired minister; b. Johnstown, Pa., June 1, 1924; s. Charles H. Sr. and Flora A.; m. Frances Marie Bradley, July 12, 1946; children: Kenneth W., Judy Ashman Fairman, Karl W. BA cum laude, Westmont Coll., 1947; MDiv magna cum laude, Grace Theol. Seminary, Winona Lake, Ind., 1950. Ordained to ministry Grace Brethren Ch., 1950. Sr. pastor Grace Brethren Ch., Rittman, Ohio, 1950-55, Phoenix, 1955-62; sr. pastor Grace Brethren Ch., Winona Lake, Ind., 1962-89, pastor emeritus, 1989—; asst. coord. Fellowship of Grace Brethren Chs., Winona Lake, Ind., 1979—; prof. Grace Theol. Sem., 1969-89. Mem. Nat. Fellowship Grace Brethren Ministers (pres. 1984, Pastor of Yr. 1989, moderator nat. conf. 1973-74), Kiwanis (pres. 1991-92). Home: 1531 S Cherry Creek Ln Warsaw IN 46580-7691 Office: Fellowship Grace Brethren PO Box 386 Winona Lake IN 46590-0386

ASHMAN, MARTIN C., federal judge; b. 1931. JD, DePaul U., 1953. Bar: Ill. 1953, U.S. Surpeme Ct. 1959. Atty. Ashman & Jaffe, 1954-70, Martin C. Ashman, Ltd., 1970-87; commr. Ill. Ct. Claims, 1974-87; corp. counsel Village of Morton Grove, Ill., 1977-87; cir. judge domestic rels. divsn., law divsn. State of Ill., 1987-95; magistrate judge U.S. Dist. Ct. (no. dist.) Ill., 1995—; vol. Legal Svcs. Found., Chgo. Recipient Spl. Tribute award Ill. Coun. Against Handgun Violence. Mem. ABA, Fed. Bar Assn., Fed. Magistrate Judges Assn., Ill. State Bar Assn., Decalogue Soc. Lawyers, Ill. Judges Assn., Chgo. Bar Assn. (Cert. of Appreciation). Office: US Dist Ct 2206 Dirksen Bldg 219 S Dearborn St Chicago IL 60604-1702

ASHMAN, STUART, museum director; b. N.Y.C., Apr. 10, 1948. BA, CUNY, 1972. Mus. intern in mus. studies and cinematography Staten Island (N.Y.) Inst. Arts and Scis., 1970-72; with Apeiron Workshops in Photography, Rochester Inst. Tech., 1972-78; gallery dir., visual arts coord. Armory for the Arts, Santa Fe, 1978-80; art instr. Santa Fe Preparatory Sch., 1980-82; artist in residence N.Mex. rural pub. schs., 1982-84; art instr. Penitentiary of N.Mex., 1984-86; studio artist Santa Fe, 1986-90; founder, coord. Mus. on Wheels program Santa Fe Children's Mus., 1990-92; Art with Elders coord. Open Hands Inc., 1990-92; artist in residence N.Mex. Arts Divsn., Santa Fe, 1990-92; curator/dir. The Gov.'s Gallery Mus. Fine Arts, Mus. N.Mex., Santa Fe, 1992-95, dir., 1995—; chmn. acquisitions com. Mus. N.Mex.; adv. bd. Georgia O'Keeffe Mus., SITE Santa Fe; bd. dirs. N.Mex. Counseling and Therapy Bd., Art Therapy Standards Com., Capitol Arts Found., Santa Fe Children's Mus. Mem. Am. Assn. Muss., Am. Fedn. Arts, Mus. N.Mex. Found., Friends of Contemporary Art, Folk Art Soc. Am. Home: RR 4 Box 16K Santa Fe NM 87501-7021 Office: Mus Fine Arts PO Box 2087 Santa Fe NM 87504-2087*

ASHMANSKAS, DONALD C., federal judge; b. 1935. AB, Rutgers U., 1960; JD, NYU, 1966. Revenue officer Dept. of Treasury, N.Y.C., 1959-61; asst. prof. Bur. Govtl. Rsch. and Svc. U. Oreg., 1966-68; legal counsel, field cons. League of Oreg. Cities, 1968-79; city atty. Beaverton, Oreg., 1970-75; judge U.S. Dist. Ct. Oreg., 1975-77, Oreg. Cir. Ct., 1977-92; apptd. magistrate judge U.S. Dist. Ct. Oreg., 1992. With USMC, 1954-57. Mem. Oreg. State Bar. Fax: (503) 326-8289. Office: 1127 US Courthouse 1000 SW 3d Ave Portland OR 97204-2902

ASHMEAD, ALLEZ MORRILL, speech, hearing, and language pathologist, orofacial myologist, consultant; b. Provo, Utah, Dec. 18, 1916; d. Laban Rupert and Zella May (Miller) M.; m. Harvey H. Ashmead, 1940; children: Harve DeWayne, Sheryl Mae Harames, Zeltha Janeel Henderson, Emma Allez Broadfoot. BS, Utah State U., 1938; MS summa cum laude, U. Utah, 1952, PhD summa cum laude, 1970; postgrad., Idaho State U., Oreg. State Coll., U. Denver, U. Utah, Brigham Young U., Utah State U., U. Washington, U. No. Colo. Cert. secondary edn., remedial reading, spl. edn., learning disabilities; cert. ASHA clin. competence speech pathology and audiology; profl. cert. in orofacial myology. Tchr. pub. schs. Utah, Idaho, 1938-43; speech and hearing pathologist Bushnell Hosp., Brigham City, Utah, 1943-45; sr. speech correctionist Utah State Dept. Health, Salt Lake City, 1945-52; dir. speech and hearing dept. Davis County Sch. Dist., Farmington, Utah, 1952-65; clin., field supr. U. Utah, Salt Lake City, 1965-70, 75-78; speech pathologist Box Elder Sch. Dist., Brigham City, 1970-75, 78-84; teaching specialist Brigham Young U., Provo, 1970-73; speech pathologist Primary Children's Med. Ctr., Salt Lake City, 1975-77; pvt. practice speech pathology and orofacial myology, 1970-88; del. USSR Profl. Speech Pathology seminar, 1984, 86; participant numerous internat. seminars. Author: Physical Facilities for Handicapped Children, 1957, A Guide for Training Public School Speech and Hearing Clinicians, 1965, A Guide for Public School Speech Hearing Programs, 1959, Impact of Orofacial Myofunctional Treatment on Orthodontic Correction, 1982, Meeting Needs of Handicapped Children, 1975, Relationship of Trace Minerals to Disease, 1972, Macro and Trace Minerals in Human Metabolism, 1971, Electromotive Potential Differences Between Stutterers and Non-stutterers, 1970, Learning Disability, An Educational Adventure, 1969, New Horizons in Special Education, 1969, Developing Speech and Language in the Exceptional Child, 1961, Parent Teacher Guidance in Primary Stuttering, 1951, numerous others; contbr. research articles to profl. jours. Student Placement chair Am. Field Service, Kaysville, Utah, 1962-66; ednl. del. Women's State Legis. Council, Salt Lake City, 1958-70; chairwoman fund raising Utah Symphony Orch., Salt Lake City, 1970-71; sec., treas. Utah chpt. U.S. Council for Exceptional Children, 1958-62, membership com. chair, 1962-66, program com. chair, 1966-68. Recipient Scholarship award for Higher Edn. U. Utah, Salt Lake City, 1969; Phi Kappa Phi scholar, Delta Kappa Gamma scholar, 1968; rsch. grantee Utah Dept. Edn., 1962. Mem. NEA, Utah Ednl. Assn., Am. Speech, Lang. Hearing Assn. (life, continuing edn. com. 1985, Ace award for Continuing Edn. 1984), Western Speech Assn., Internat. Assn. Orofacial Myology (life, bd. examiners, Sci. Contribution award 1982), Utah Speech, Hearing and Lang. Assn. (life, sec., treas. 1956-60), AAUW (Utah state bd. chair status of women 1959-62, Kaysville br. 1957-60, bd. dirs. Kaysville-Davis br. 1987-92, chair internat. rels. 1987-91, chair cultural interests Kaysville-Davis br. 1991-92), Delta Kappa Gamma (state scholarship award 1968, del. Woman's State Legis. Coun. 1958-70, profl. affairs chair 1963-67, tchr. of yr. award 1978), AAUW (bd. dirs. internat. rels. Kaysvile-Davis br., 1988-91), Daus. Utah Pioneers (parliamentarian Kaysville 1980-92, historian 1974-80, lesson leader 1992-95, capt. 1996-98), Soroptimists (charter, bd. dirs. 1954-56, pres. Davis County chpt. 1965-69, Rocky Mountain regional bd. dirs. 1965-70, cmty. svc. award 1968, pub. svc. award 1970), Sigma Alpha Eta, Theta Alpha Phi, Psi Chi, Zeta Phi Eta, Phi Kappa Phi. Republican. Mem. LDS Ch. Avocations: international travel, reading, boating, sports, fine and performing arts. Home: 719 E Center St Kaysville UT 84037-2138

ASHMUS, KEITH ALLEN, lawyer; b. Cleve., Aug. 19, 1949; s. Richard A. and Rita (Petti) A.; m. Marie Sachiko Matsuoka, Dec. 15, 1973; children: Emmy Marie, Christopher Todd. BA in Policy Sci., Mich. State U., 1971, MA in Econs., 1972; JD, Yale U., 1974. Bar: Ohio 1974, Calif. 1991, U.S. Dist. Ct. (no. dist.) Ohio 1975, U.S. Dist. Ct. (no., so. and cen. dists.) Calif. 1991, U.S. Ct. Appeals (6th cir.) 1975, U.S. Supreme Ct. 1980. Assoc. Thompson Hine & Flory LLP, Cleve., 1974-82, ptnr., 1982—; ptnr.-in-chg. Cleve. office Thompson Hine & Flory LLP, 1996—; mediator/arbitrator Am. Arbitration Assn. Securities and Comml. Employment Panels, 1995—. Co-author: Public Sector Collective Bargaining: The Ohio System, 1984. Trustee community arts Baycrafters, Bay Village, Ohio, 1981-84, Hospice Council No. Ohio, 1982-84, Inst. for Personal Health Skills, Cleve. 1985-90, Coun. Smaller Enterprises, 1990-96, 98—, Village Found., 1997—; sec. George W. Codrington Charitable Found., 1994—; chmn. job placement for older persons Skills Available, Cleve., 1980-87; gov.'s appointee to Health Care Quality Adv. Coun., 1996; mem. adv. bd. Greater Cleve. Salvation

Army, 1997—. Named one of Outstanding Vols. award Nat. Hospice Orgn., 1982, Vol. of Yr. Vocat. Guidance and Rehab. Services, 1985, 86. Mem. ABA, State Bar Calif., Ohio Bar Assn. (coun. dels. 1995—, bd. govs. 1998—), Cleve. Bar Assn. (trustee 1985-88, 98—, chmn. labor law sect. 1983-84), Def. Rsch. Inst., Pub. Sector Labor Rels. Assn. (exec. com. 1989-93). Avocation: fishing. Office: Thompson Hine & Flory LLP 3900 Key Center 127 Public Sq Cleveland OH 44114-1216

ASHTON, BETSY FINLEY, broadcast journalist, author, lecturer; b. Wilkes-Barre, Pa., May 13, 1944; d. Charles Leonard Hancock Jones and Margaretta Betty (Hart) Jones Layton; m. Arthur Benner Ashton, Nov. 5, 1966 (div. 1972); m. Robert Clarke Freed, May 18, 1974 (div. 1981); m. Jacob B. Underhill III, Oct. 17, 1987. BA, Am. U., 1966; postgrad., Corcoran Sch. Art, 1968; postgrad. in fine arts, Am. U., 1969-71; student in painting, Corcoran Sch. Art, 1968. Tchr. art Fairfax County (Va.) Pub. Schs., 1967-70; reporter, anchor Sta. WWDC, Washington, 1972-73, Sta. WMAL-AM-FM, Washington, 1973-75; corr. Sta. WTTG-TV, Washington, 1975-76, Sta. WJLA-TV, Washington, 1976-82; consumer corr. CBS News and Sta. WCBS-TV, N.Y.C., 1982-86; sr. corr. Today's Bus., 1986-87; personal fin. contbr. CBS Morning Program, 1987, Lifetime Cable TV, 1988—; anchor FNN Money Talk, 1989; bd. dirs. Lowell E. Mellett Fund for a Free and Responsible Press, Washington, 1979-82; courtroom artist numerous trials, Washington, 1978-81. Reporter TV news report Caffeine, 1981 (AAUW award 1982); reporter spot news 6 P.M. News, 1979 (Emmy award); author: Betsy Ashton's Guide to Living on Your Own, 1988. Concert master of ceremonies Beethoven Soc., Washington, 1979-82. Recipient Laurel award Columbia Journalism Rev., 1984, Outstanding Alumna award Am. U., 1985, Outstanding Media award Am. U., 1986, Best Consumer Journalism citation Nat. Press Club, 1983. Mem. AFTRA, NATAS, Author's Guild, Newswomen's Club N.Y., Soc. Profl. Journalists (pres. N.Y. chpt. 1994, Washington chpt. 1980-81, bd. dirs. N.Y. chpt. 1989—), Friends of Thirteen (bd. dirs. 1995—), Sigma Delta Chi Found. (bd. dirs. 1996—), Alpha Chi Omega (v.p. chpt. 1964-66). Episcopalian. Avocations: painting, drawing, golf.

ASHTON, DORE, author, educator; b. Newark; d. Ralph N. and Sylvia (Ashton) Shapiro; m. Adja Yunkers, July 8, 1952 (dec. 1983); children—Alexandra Louise, Marina Svietlana; m. Matti Megged, 1985. BA, U. Wis., 1949; MA, Harvard U., 1950; PhD honoris causa, Moore Coll., 1975, Hamline U., 1982. Asso. editor Art Digest, 1951-54; asso. critic N.Y. Times, 1955-60; lectr. Pratt Inst., 1962-63; head humanities dept. (Sch. Visual Arts), 1965-68; prof. Cooper Union, 1968—; art critic, lectr., dir. exhbns. in arts; mem. adv. bd. John Simon Guggenheim Found. Author: Abstract Art Before Columbus, 1957, Poets and the Past, 1959, Philip Guston, 1960, The Unknown Shore, 1962, Rauschenberg's Dante, 1964, Modern American Sculpture, 1968, Richard Lindner, 1969, A Reading of Modern Art, 1970, Pol Bury, 1971; Cultural Guide for New York, 1972; Picasso on Art, 1972, The New York School: A Cultural Reckoning, 1973, A Joseph Cornell Album, 1974, Yes, But, A Critical Biography of Philip Guston, 1976, A Fable of Modern Art, 1980, American Art Since 1945, 1982, About Rothko, 1983, Jacobo Borges, 1984, 20th Century Artists on Art, 1985, Out of the Whirlwind, 1987, Fragonard in the Universe of Painting, 1988, Terence La Noue, 1992, Noguchi East and West, 1992, Ursula van Rydingsvard, 1995, The Delicate Thread: Teshigahara's Life in Art, 1997, A Rebours: La Rebelión Informalista, 1999; also monographs; co-author: (with Denise Browne Hare) Rosa Bonheur, A Life and Legend, 1981; co-editor: Redon, Moreau, Bresdin, 1961; N.Y. contbg. editor Studio Internat, 1961-74, Opus Internat, 1968-74, XXième Siècle, 1955-70; assoc. editor Arts, 1974-92; contbr. to: Vision and Value series (Gyorgy Kepes), 1966, The New Art Anthology (Gregory Battcock), 1966. Adv. bd. Guggenheim Found. Recipient Mather award for art criticism Coll. Art Assn., 1963, Art Criticism prize St. Louis Art Mus., 1988; Guggenheim fellow, 1964; Graham fellow, 1963; Ford Found. fellow, 1960; Nat. Endowment for Humanities grantee, 1980. Mem. Internat. Assn. Art Critics, Phi Beta Kappa. Home: 217 E 11th St New York NY 10003-7302 Office: Cooper Union Advancement Sci and Art 41 Cooper Sq New York NY 10003-7136

ASHTON, GEOFFREY CYRIL, geneticist, educator; b. Croydon, Eng., July 5, 1925; s. Cyril Hanniss and Ethel (Pate) A.; m. Kathleen J. Stanley, Feb. 25, 1951; children—Carolyn Joy, Kathryn Alison, Melinda Jane, Jonathan Geoffrey. B.Sc., Liverpool U., 1943, Ph.D., 1958, D.Sc. 1967. Research asst. U. Toronto, Ont., Can., 1948-50; sect. leader Glaxo Labs., Eng., 1951-56; sr. sci. officer Farm Livestock Research Centre, Eng., 1956-58; prin. research officer Commonwealth Sci. and Indsl. Research Orgn., Australia, 1958-64; prof. genetics U. Hawaii, 1964-95; prof. emeritus, 1995—; chmn. dept. U. Hawaii, 1979-88, asst. vice chancellor, 1972-74, vice chancellor, 1974-78, dir. health, instr. research unit, 1986-93; pres. MedMedia Inc., 1994—; mem. blood group scientists panel FAO, 1963—, chmn. subcom. on protein polymorphism nomenclature, 1963—. Mem.Brit. Commonwealth Club of Hawaii (pres. 1993), Phi Delta Kappa. Home: 5414 Kirkwood Pl Honolulu HI 96821-1938

ASHTON, HARRIS JOHN, business executive; b. Elizabeth, N.J., June 21, 1932; s. Earle S. and Dorothy (Black) A.; m. Angela Murphy, Oct. 20, 1962; children: Kelly Elizabeth, Victoria Catherine. BA, Yale U., 1954; LLB, Columbia U., 1959. Bar: N.Y. 1960. Assoc. Breed, Abbott & Morgan, 1959-62, Lovejoy, Wasson, Lundgren & Huppuch, 1962-64; partner Lovejoy, Wasson, Lundgren & Ashton, 1964-75, of counsel, 1975-81; pres., chief adminstrv. officer Gen. Host Corp., 1967-69, chmn., pres., chief exec. officer, 1970-97; bd. dirs. Bar-S Foods Co., of 50 Franklin Templeton Group of Funds, RBC Holdings (U.S.A.), Inc. Bd. dirs. Madison Square Boys and Girls Club; trustee Greenwich Acad., 1977-81, Miss Porter's Sch., 1981-85, United Cerebral Palsy Rsch. and Ednl. Found., Inc.; mem. bd. visitors Columbia U. Sch. Law, 1982—, Yale New Haven Hosp., 1990-95. Mem. Yale Club (N.Y.C.), Sky Club (N.Y.C.), Blind Brook Club, Stanwich Club, Lyford Cay Club, Bohemian Club.

ASHTON, JEAN WILLOUGHBY, library director; b. Detroit, Mar. 1, 1938; d. Gerald Woodrow and Dorothy (McEwen) Willoughby; m. Robert William Ashton, Mar. 30, 1960; children: Katherine, Susanna, Emily, Isabel. BA, U. Mich., 1959; MA, Radcliffe Coll., 1961; PhD, Columbia U., 1970; MLS, Rutgers U., 1985. Lectr. Fisk U., Nashville, 1962-64; asst. prof. English L.I. U., Bklyn., 1969-73; reference libr. N.Y. Hist. Soc., N.Y.C., 1984-87, assoc. libr. pub. svcs., 1987-89, acting libr., 1989-90, dir. libr., 1990-93; dir. rare books and manuscripts libr. Columbia U., N.Y.C., 1993—; vis. lectr. N.Y. area Colls., 1976-80; lectr. N.Y. Coun. for the Humanities, 1988-92; coord. Comm. for Resources in N.Y. History, 1987-90. Author: (book) Harriet Beecher Stowe: A Reference Guide, 1976; contbr. articles to N.Y. Times, Am. Lit. Realism, Prospects, Magill's Lit. Ann., New Bklyn., Imprint, Biblion, RQ. Vol. BAM Theater Co., Bklyn., 1980-81; mem. bd. govs. Rsch. Librs. Group, 1989-91.; mem. Metro Adminstrv. Svcs. Com., 1990-92. Recipient Avery Hopwood Writing award U. Mich., 1959; Woodrow Wilson fellow Woodrow Wilson Found., 1959; faculty scholar Columbia U., 1966-67. Mem. ALA, Am. Printing History Assn., Bibliog. Soc. Am., Soc. History Authorship, Readership and Pub. Librs., The Grolier Club. Home: 300 W 108th St Apt 14B New York NY 10025-2705 Office: Rare Book and Manuscript Libr Columbia U 535 W 114th St New York NY 10027-7035

ASHTON, MARK RANDOLPH, lawyer; b. Abington, Pa., Sept. 10, 1955; s. Frank E. and Charlotte (Wagenbaur) A. BA in Internat. Affairs, George Washington U., 1977; JD, John Marshall U., 1980. Bar: Pa. 1980. Law clk. to Hon. Mason Avrigian Ct. of Common Pleas of Montgomery County, Norristown, Pa., 1980-81; assoc. Abrahams & Loewenstein, Norristown, 1982-87; dept. chmn. Riley, Riper, Hollin & Colagreco, 1987-90; ptnr. Fox, Rothschild, O'Brien & Frankel, Exton, Pa., 1990—. Mem. Montgomery Bar Assn. (bd. dirs. 1985-87), Chester County Bar Assn. (chmn. family law sect. 1988-90), Wissahickon Valley Hist. Soc. (pres.), D.J. Freed Am. Inn of Ct. (sec.-treas.). Republican. Episcopalian. Home: 413 Stratford Ave Collegeville PA 19426-2553 Office: Fox Rothschild O'Brien & Frankel 760 Constitution Dr Ste 104 Exton PA 19341-1149

ASHTON, SISTER MARY MADONNA, healthcare administrator; b. St. Paul; d. Avon B. and Ruth (Fehring) A. BA, Coll. St. Catherine, St. Paul, 1944; LHD (hon.), Coll. St. Catherine, 1996; MSW, St. Louis U., 1946; MHA, U. Minn., 1958; LHD (honorary), Hamline U., 1997. Joined Congregation Sisters of St. Joseph of Carondelet, Roman Cath. Ch., 1946. Dir. med. social service dept. St. Joseph's Hosp., St. Paul, 1949-56; dir. outpatient dept. St. Mary's Hosp., Mpls., 1958-59; asst. adminstr. St. Mary's Hosp., 1959-62, adminstr., 1962-68, exec. v.p., 1968-72, pres., 1972-82; commr. health State of Minn., 1983-91; pres. Carondelet LifeCare Ministries, St. Paul, 1991—; dir. Client Security Bd. of Minn. Supreme Ct., 1993-98, St. Catherine's Coll., St. Paul; mem. bd. sci. counselors Nat. Cancer Inst. Recipient Sabra Hamilton award Program in Hosp. Adminstrn. U. Minn., 1958; Minn. Health Citizen of Yr. award, 1977, Gaylord Anderson Leadership award, 1988; Bush summer fellow Harvard Sch. Bus., 1976. Fellow Am. Coll. Healthcare Execs.; mem. Nat. Cath. Health Assn. (sec.). Home: 5101 W 70th St Apt 120 Minneapolis MN 55439-2105 Office: Carondelet LifeCare 1884 Randolph Ave Saint Paul MN 55105-1747

ASHTON, RICHARD M., federal lawyer. BA, Catholic U., JD. Lawyer honors program FDIC, 1974-76; staff atty. Fed. Res. Bd., 1976-82, asst. gen. counsel, 1982-85, assoc. gen. counsel, 1985—. Office: Federal Reserve System Board Members Office 20th & C Sts NW Washington DC 20551*

ASHTON, RICK JAMES, librarian; b. Middletown, Ohio, Sept. 18, 1945; s. Ralph James and Lydia Marie (Thornbery) A.; m. Marcia K. Zuroweste, Dec. 23, 1966; children: Jonathan Paul, David Andrew. AB, Harvard U., 1967; MA, Northwestern U., 1969, PhD, 1973; MA, U. Chgo., 1976. Instr., asst. prof. history Northwestern U., Evanston, Ill., 1972-74; curator local and family history Newberry Libr., Chgo., 1974-77; asst. dir. Allen County Pub. Libr., Ft. Wayne, Ind., 1977-80, dir., 1980-85; city libr. Denver Pub. Libr., 1985—; mem. Ind. Coop Libr. Svcs. Authority, 1980-85, pres., 1984-85; cons. NEH, Nat. Ctr. Edn. Stats., Northwestern U. Office Estate Planning, Snowbird Leadership Inst. Author: The Life of Henry Ruiter, 1742-1819, 1974, The Genealogy Beginner's Manual: A New Edition, 1977, Stuntz, Fuller, Kennard and Cheadle Ancestors, 1987 (with others) Trends in Urban Library Management, 1989. Bd. dirs. Cmty. Coordinated Child Care, Evanston, 1972-74, Three Rivers Montessori Sch., Ft. Wayne, 1977-80; bd. dirs., sec. Allen County-Ft. Wayne Hist. Soc., 1977-83; conscientious objector. Recipient Old City Hall Hist. Svc. award, 1985, Phil Milstein award Denver AIA, 1998; NDEA fellow, 1967-69, Downtown Denver award, 1996, 97; Woodrow Wilson fellow, 1971-72. Mem. ALA, Colo. Libr. Assn., Colo. Alliance Rsch. Librs. (pres. 1987-88, sec. 1993-95, chmn. 1995—), Cactus Club. Home: 217 S Jackson St Unit A Denver CO 80209 Office: Denver Pub Libr 10 W 14th Avenue Pkwy Denver CO 80204-2731

ASHTON, TAMARAH M., special education educator; b. Toledo, Dec. 5, 1961; d. Harold Leroy and Patricia Marie (Casto) Ashton; m. John G. Coombs, Feb. 11, 1989; 1 child, Rebecca Marie. MusB, Western Mich. U., 1984; MS, San Diego State U., 1988, MA, 1990, PhD, 1997. Cert. tchr., Calif. Asst. project dir. San Diego State U., 1994-98; asst. prof. dept. of spl. edn. Calif. State U., Northridge, 1998—; pvt. practice ednl. cons., San Diego, 1990-98; rsch. asst. doctoral program edn. San Diego State U., 1990-93. Mem. Coun. for Learning Disabilities. Mem. Coun. for Exceptional Children, Phi Kappa Phi, Pi Lambda Theta. Avocation: needlework. Home: 4689 49th St San Diego CA 92115-3240

ASHTON, THOMAS WALSH, investment banker; b. Rochester, N.Y., May 11, 1929; s. Charles Edward and Marie Margaret (Walsh) A.; m. Frances E. Hickey, May 16, 1953 (div. 1977); children: Lucy M. Van Atta, Mary B. Ashton Anders, Monica H., William T; m. Mary K Joy, Dec. 20, 1978. B.S., U.S. Mil. Acad., 1952; M.B.A., Harvard U., 1957. Assoc. corp. fin. Eastman Dillon Union Securities, N.Y.C., 1957-61, gen. ptnr., 1967-69; asst. v.p. Harris Upham & Co., N.Y.C., 1961-67; v.p. duPont Glore Forgan, Inc., N.Y.C., 1971-73; sr. v.p. ABD Securities Corp., N.Y.C., 1973-75; fin. cons. Am. Cancer Soc. of N.Y.C., East View Group Inc.; chmn. Peninsular Investments, Treasure Island, Fla., 1977-87; cons. Dept. Commerce, 1971; chmn. Ashton Investments, Inc., 1987—. Chmn. parent's coun. Smith Coll., 1974-76. With AUS, 1946-48, 52-55. Mem. Soc. Harvard Engrs. & Scientists (gov. 1974-75), West Point Soc. N.Y. (dir. 1971-75), Army and Navy Club (Washington), Treasure Island Yacht Club. Republican. Office: 153d Ave Madeira Beach FL 33708

ASHWELL, G. GILBERT, biochemist; b. Jersey City, July 16, 1916; married, 1942; children: Jonathan D., Ariel J. BA, U. Ill., 1938, MS, 1941; MD, Columbia U., 1948; Dr, U. Paris-Sud, 1988. Rsch. fellow Columbis U., 1948-50; med. dir. NIH, 1950-78, chmn., 1978-84, inst. scholar, lab biochemistry and metabolism, 1984—, emeritus scientist, 1995—. Recipient Outstanding Achievement in Field of Med. Sci. Gairdner Found., 1982, Sr. Scientist award Alexander von Humboldt Found., 1989. Mem. NAE, Am. Soc. Biology Chemists (Merck prize 1984). Office: NIH Lab Cell Biochemical & Biol Rm 415 Bldg 8 Bethesda MD 20892

ASHWORTH, BRENT FERRIN, lawyer; b. Albany, Calif., Jan. 8, 1949; s. Dell Shepherd and Bette Jean (Brailsford) A.; m. Charlene Mills, Dec. 16, 1970; children: Amy, John, Matthew, Samuel (dec.), Adam, David, Emily, Luke, Benjamin. BA, Brigham Young U., 1972; JD, U. Utah, 1975. Bar: Utah 1977. Asst. county atty. Carbon County, Price, Utah, 1975-76; assoc. atty. Frandsen & Keller, Price, Utah, 1976-77; v.p. legal affairs, sec., gen. counsel Nature's Sunshine Products, Provo, Utah, 1977—. Bd. dirs., gen. counsel Carbon County Nursing Home, Prize, 1976-77; mem. Provo Landmarks Commn., 1997—, co-chair sesquicentennial com., 1998—; chmn. Utah County Cancer Crusade Com., 1981-83; chmn. Provo LCOC Arts subcom.; city councilman Payson City, Utah, 1980-82, mem. planning commn., 1980-82, mayor pro tem, 1982; bd. dirs. ARC, Utah County chpt., 1988-94, Springville Mus. Art, 1998—; pres. Deseret Village Spani Fork, Utah, 1988-90; gen. counsel Brigham Young Acad. Found., 1995—; co-chair Provo Utah Sesquecentennial com., 1998—. Mem. ABA, SAR (pres. Utah County chpt. 1989-90, state chpts. 1st v.p. 1990-91, state soc. pres. 1991-92, chancellor 1992-94), ATLA, Southeastern Utah Bar Assn. (sec. 1977), Utah State Bar, Am. Corp. Counsel Assn. (sec. Intermountain chpt. 1990-91), Emily Dickinson Soc. Utah (pres. 1995-97), Sons Utah Pioneers, Kiwanis Club (v.p. 1995-96, pres. 1997-98), Phi Kappa Phi, Phi Eta Sigma. Home: 1965 N 1400 E Provo UT 84604-2106 Office: Natures Sunshine Products 1655 N Main St Spanish Fork UT 84660-1007

ASHWORTH, JULIE, elementary education educator. Tchr. Hawthorne Elem. Sch., Sioux Falls, S.D., 1990—; participant Internat. Space Camp, Huntsville, Ala., 1993; S.D. tchr. participant Goals 2000 Forum, U.S. Dept. Edn., Washington, 1993; mem. S.D. Gov.'s Adv. Coun. on Cert. for Tchrs., 1994—; mem. exceptional needs standards com. Nat. Bd. for Profl. Tchg. Stds., Washington, 1994—; initiator, organizer S.D. Tchrs. Forum, 1994. Named S.D. Tchr. of Yr., Sioux Falls Sch. Dist., 1992, S.D. Elem. Tchr. of Yr., 1993. Home: 2015 Pendar Ln Sioux Falls SD 57105-3022 Office: Hawthorne Elem Sch 601 N Spring Ave Sioux Falls SD 57104-2721*

ASHWORTH, KENNETH HAYDEN, public affairs specialist, educator; b. Abilene, Tex., Feb. 24, 1932; s. Harold Laverne and Mae Beatrice (Grote) A.; m. Emily Yaung; children: Rodney Brian, Karen Grace Saulsberry. B.A., U. Tex., 1958, Ph.D., 1969; M. Pub. Adminstrn., Syracuse U., 1959. Asst. commr. Tex. Higher Edn. Coordinating Bd., Austin, 1965-69; commr. higher edn. Tex. Higher Edn. Coordinating Bd., 1976-97; vice chancellor for acad. affairs U. Tex. System, Austin, 1969-73; exec. v.p. U. Tex. at San Antonio, 1973-76; vis. prof. govt. and pub. affairs U. Tex., Austin, 1997—, Tex. A &M U., College Sta., 1997—. Author: Scholars and Statesmen, 1972, American Higher Education in Decline, 1979, (with Norman Hackerman) Conversations on the Uses of Science and Technology, 1996. Served with USN, 1951-55. Mem. Philos. Soc. Tex., Phi Beta Kappa, Phi Delta Kappa, Phi Kappa Phi, Pi Sigma Alpha. Democrat. Unitarian. Club: Town and Gown. Home: 7616 Rustling Rd Austin TX 78731-1365 Office: LBJ Sch Pub Affairs PO Box Y U Tex Austin TX 78713-8925 also: Tex A&M U Bush Sch Govt and Pub Svc College Station TX 77843-4220

ASHWORTH, ROBERT VINCENT, data processing executive; b. Kingsport, Tenn., Sept. 3, 1952; s. Ivan Henry and Mary Ann (Greene) A.; m. Nancy Marie Fricke, Oct. 15, 1983; children: Rachael, Sarah. BS in Tourism, Food and Lodging, U. Tenn., 1978; AS in Computer Sci., State Tech. Inst., Knoxville, Tenn., 1981. Cert. info. systems auditor, 1995. Computer programmer City of Knoxville, 1981-87; systems analyst Knoxville Utilities Bd., 1987-88; data processing auditor Piedmont Bank-Group, Inc., Martinsville, Va., 1988-95; quality assurance analyst Shaw Industries, Inc., Dalton, Ga., 1995-98; sr. info. systems auditor Lowe's Cos., Inc., North Wilkesboro, N.C., 1998—. Mem. Big Bros./Big Sisters, Knoxville, 1987, 88. Mem. Electronic Data Processing Auditors Assn., KC. Avocations: bicycling, camping, reading, cooking. Home: 124 Hunter Cir Wilkesboro NC 28679-7413 Office: Lowe's Cos Inc PO Box 1111 North Wilkesboro NC 28656

ASIJA, S(ATYA) PAL, lawyer; b. Leiah, India, Apr. 26, 1942; came to U.S., 1967, naturalized, 1972; s. Chander Bhanu and Radha Bai (Chugh) P.; m. Madeline Rich Magill, June 1, 1974 (dec. June 1982); m. Terry Aguilar, July 15, 1989. Grad. IERE (Lond), Southampton, Eng., 1964; postgrad. diploma U. Wales, Cardiff, 1967; MBA, U. Dayton, 1970; JD, No. Ky. U., 1974. Bar: U.S. Patent Office 1974, U.S. Supreme Ct. 1978, Conn. 1983, U.S. Ct. Appeals (fed. cir.) 1984. Supr. electronics AEC Radiation Lab. U. Notre Dame, Ind., 1967-68; rsch. & devel. systems engr. NCR, Dayton, Ohio, 1968-71; systems analyst Police Dept., Dayton, 1971-73; exec. dir. MINCIS, State of Minn., St. Paul, 1974-76; systems engr. Sperry Univac, Eagan, Minn., 1977-80; sr. mem. tech. staff ITT, Shelton, Conn., 1980-84; cons., avionics engr. Sikorsky Aircraft, Div. United Technologies Corp., Stratford, Conn., 1985-88; pvt. practice law, Shelton, Conn., 1988—; advisor Computer Users Legal Reporter, Westport, Conn., 1984—, Yale Sci. Park Legal Clinic, New Haven, 1984—; mem. on-line faculty U. Phoenix, 1996—. Author: 4 books; editor newsletter Chasette, 1972; contbr. articles to profl. jours.; 6 patents, 4 trademarks. Inventor Swiftanswer, 1977 (3d pl. award 1977), Magicfold, 1976 (2d pl. award 1976). Candidate for Minn. Ho. of Reps., 1976; capt. CAP, 1979-80. Named to Hall of Fame Engring., Sci, and Tech., 1990. Mem. ABA, IEEE (sr.), Am. Arbitration Assn. (panelist 1972—), Internat. Bar Assn., Minn. Computer Soc. (pres. 1977), Toastmasters (able toastmaster 1972, pres. 1972). Republican. Mormon. Home and Office: 7 Woonsocket Ave Shelton CT 06484-5536

ASKANAS-ENGEL, VALERIE, neurologist, educator, researcher; b. Poland, May 28, 1937; came to U.S., 1969, naturalized, 1975; d. Marian and Leontyne Hornik; m. W. King Engel; 1 dau., Eve Monique Kerr. MD, Warsaw Med. Sch., Poland, 1960, PhD, 1967; Doctor honoris causa, U. d'Aix-Marseille, France, 1987. Rotating intern Univ. Hosp. Warsaw Med. Sch., 1960-61, resident in neurology, 1961-64, fellow in neuromuscular diseases, 1964-65; asst. prof. neurology Warsaw Med. Sch., 1965-69; assoc. mem. Inst. Muscle Diseases, N.Y.C., 1969-73; asst. prof. NYU Med. Sch., 1973-77; sr. investigator NIH, Bethesda, Md., 1977-81; prof. neurology and pathology U. So. Calif., L.A., 1981—; co-dir. Neuromuscular Ctr. at Hosp. Good Samaritan, 1981—, Muscular Dystrophy Assn. Clinic, 1981—, The Jerry Lewis ALS Clin. and Rsch. Ctr., 1988—; v.p. 6th Internat. Congress on Neuromuscular Diseases, 1986, 7th, 1990, 8th, 1994; vis. prof. internat. congresses, Europe, S.Am., Can., Far East. Contbr. numerous articles, chpts., abstracts to med. publs.; sr. editor: (book) Inclusion-Body Myositis and Myopathies, 1998. Recipient Dean's prize for outstanding research, 1967; Premio Associazione Stampa Medica Italiana Di Giurnal Italianalsmo Medico, 1980; grantee NIH, 1974-77, 83—, Muscular Dystrophy Assn., 1969-77, 81—. Fellow Am. Acad. Neurology, L.A. Acad. Medicine; mem. Soc. for Neurosci., Am. Neurol. Assn., d'Honneur de la Soc. Francaise de Neurologie, Am. Soc. Cell Biology, Am. Assn. Neuropathology, Histochem. Soc., Uruguayan Neurological Assn. (hon. mem.), L.A. County Med. Assn., Polish Neurol. Assn. (hon.). Home: 527 S Arden Blvd Los Angeles CA 90020-4737 Office: U So Calif Neuromuscular Ctr Good Samaritan Hosp 637 Lucas Ave Los Angeles CA 90017-1912

ASKENASE, PHILIP WILLIAM, medicine and pathology educator; b. Bklyn., June 7, 1939; s. Irving and Hilda Askenase; m. Marjorie Dopkin, June 21, 1967; children: Hilary, Isabel. BA in Physics magna cum laude, Brown U., 1961; MD cum laude, Yale U., 1965. Diplomate Am. Bd. Internal Medicine, Am. Bd. Allergy and Immunology. Intern, asst. resident in medicine Boston City Hosp., 1965-67; clin. assoc. arthritis and rheumatism sect. Nat. Inst. Arthritis and Metabolic Disease, NIH, 1957-59; Brit. Am. Heart fellow of Am. Heart Assn., London Hosp. Med. Coll., 1969-70; postdoctoral trainee in inflammatory diseases Yale U. Sch. Medicine, New Haven, 1970-71, asst. prof. medicine, 1971-75, assoc. prof., 1975-82, assoc. prof. pathology, 1981-82, prof. medicine and pathology, 1982—, chief sect. clin. immunology dept. medicine, 1985—; attending physician Yale-New Haven Hosp., 1971—, West Haven (Conn.) VA Hosp., 1971—; vis. scientist immunoparasitology div. Nat. Inst. Med. Rsch., London, 1977-78; lectr. biology Yale U., 1981—, vis. prof. molecular immunology unit, 1991; hon. rsch. fellow tumor immunology unit dept. zoology Univ. Coll., London, 1984-85; mem. Yale Comprehensive Cancer Ctr., 1987—; ad hoc reviewer numerous med. jours; vis. prof., Woods Hole, Mass., 1980-84; mem. U.S.-Israel Binat. Sci. Found., 1982—, Med. Rsch. Coun. Can., NSF, Netherlands Cancer Found., Wellcome Truste, London, Med. Rsch. Coun., London, Can. Med. Rsch. Coun.; mem. adv. bd. spl. program in tropical diseases WHO; mem. pathology-A/study sect. NIH, 1976, mem. immunol. scis. study sect., 1983-87, ad hoc mem. allergy and immunology study sect. NIH, 1987-89. Mem. editl. bd. Jour. Clin. Immunology, 1983-88, Jour. Allergy and Clin. Immunology, 1980-85, Clin. and Diagnostic Lab. Immunology, 1983—; assoc. editor Jour. Immunology, 1976082; mem. editl. adv. bd. Jour. Molecular and Cellular Immunology, 1983—; contbr. over 200 articles, abstracts and revs. to med. jours., chpts. to books. Laurens Hammond grantee for cancer rsch., 1975-77, grantee NIH, 1987—. Fellow Am. Acad. Allergy; mem. AAAS, Am. Assn. Immunologists (membership com. 1978-82), Am. Assn. Physicians, Am. Fedn. Clin. Rsch., Am. Rheumatism Assn., Am. Soc. Clin. Investigation, Am. Soc. Tropical Medicine and Hygiene, Am. Thoracic Soc., Brit. Soc. Immunology, Clin. Immunology Soc., Collegium Internat. Allergogium, Conn. Allergy Soc., Histamine Rsch. Soc. N.Am., Reticuloendothelial Soc., Serotonin Soc., Skin. Pharmacology Soc., Soc. Investigative Dermatology, Interurban Clin. Club, Polish Acad. Arts and Scis. (fgn. corr.), Phi Beta Kappa, Alpha Omega Alpha. Office: Yale U Sch of Medicine PO Box 208013 333 Cedar St New Haven CT 06510-3289*

ASKER, JAMES ROBERT, magazine editor; b. Louisville, 1952. BA, Rice U., 1974. Reporter, columnist Houston Post, 1974-88; freelance reporter, 1988-89; mng. editor Electronic Bus., 1989-95; space tech. editor Aviation Week & Space Tech., Washington, 1989-95; Washington bur. chief Aviation Week & Space Tech., 1995—. Knight Sci. Journalism fellow MIT, Cambridge, 1987-88. Office: Aviation Week & Space Tech 1200 G St NW Ste 900 Washington DC 20005-3814

ASKEW, DENNIS LEE, poet; b. Las Vegas, Apr. 19, 1953. Grad. high sch., Las Vegas. Columnist Las Vegas Sun Newspaper, 1980-85; customer svc. Charles Schwab, Inc., Newport Beach, Calif.; credit specialist Dean Witter, Inc., Santa Ana, Calif.; trade adminstrn. mgr. Bankers Pension Svcs., Tustin, Calif.; writer Quest Capital Mgmt., Laguna Hills, Calif. Author: (novel) A Handful of Dreams, 1990, (stageplay) The Paint Box, 1992, (poetry) Big World of Love Vol. I, 1993, Vol. II, 1995, Vol. III, 1996. Vol. Street Svcs., Santa Ana, 1992—. Democrat. Avocations: jazz, painting.

ASKEW, LAURIN BARKER, JR., architect, executive; b. Richmond, Va., May 29, 1942; s. Laurin Barker and Ellen (White) A.; m. Theda Bundy; children: Laurin Barker, Portia Elizabeth. N.C. State U., Sch. Design, 1965. Registered architect, Md. Designer Architecture Coop., Stockholm, Sweden, 1964; designer and job capt. RTKL Assocs. Inc., Balt., 1965-68; designer Gehry, Walsh, O'Mally, Balt., 1968-69; designer and job capt. Ballard McKim & Sawyer, Wilmington, N.C., 1969; dir. design, v.p. The Rouse Co., Columbia, Md., 1969—; adv. bd. Md. Inst. Coll. of Art; selection com. The Vernon F. Shogren Endowment N.C. State U. Fellow AIA. Office: Rouse Co 10275 Little Patuxent Pkwy Columbia MD 21044-3455*

ASKEW, PENNY SUE, choreographer, artistic director, ballet instructor; b. Fairview, Okla., Oct. 8, 1967; d. Donald Lee and Susan Lea (Johnson) A. BS in Psychology, Southwestern Okla. U., 1989, MS in Applied Psychology, 1996. Ballet tchr. Western Okla. Ballet Acad., Clinton, 1986-88, owner, dir., 1988—; artistic dir. Western Okla. Ballet Theatre, Clinton, 1988—. Choreographer: (musical theater) Oklahoma!, 1990, Kiss Me Kate, 1992, Quilters, 1993, Nunsense, 1993, Annie Get Your Gun, 1993, Guys and Dolls, 1994, Nunsense II, 1995, over 40 dance works. Named Outstanding Choreographer of 1996 RDA Nat. Performance/Choreography Conf., 1996. Mem. Regional Dance Am./S.W. (sec. 1991—), Clinton C. of C. (Art in the Park com. 1990—), Kiwanis (bd. dirs. Clinton club 1996-97). Democrat. Avocations: reading, attending arts events. Office: Western Okla Ballet Theatre PO Box 1602 512 Frisco Ave Clinton OK 73601-3442*

ASKEY, RICHARD ALLEN, mathematician; b. St. Louis, June 4, 1933; s. Philip Edwin and Bessie May (Yates) A.; m. Elizabeth Ann Hill, June 14, 1958; children: James, Suzanne. B.A., Washington U., St. Louis, 1955; M.A., Harvard U., 1956; Ph.D., Princeton U., 1961. Instr. in math. Washington U., 1958-61, U. Chgo., 1961-63; asst. prof. math. U. Wis., Madison, 1963-65, asso. prof., 1965-68, prof., 1968-86, Gabor Szego prof., 1986-95, John Bascom prof., 1995—. Author: Orthogonal Polynomials and Special Functions, 1975; Author: (with G.E. Andres and R. Roy) Special funcitons, 1999; editor: Theory and Application of Special Functions, 1975, Collected Papers of Gabor Szego, 1982, (with George E. Andrews and Ranjan Roy) Special Functions, 1999;. Guggenheim fellow, 1969-70. Fellow AAAS, Indian Acad. Sci. (hon.), Am. Acad. Arts and Scis.; mem. Am. Math. Soc., Nat. Acad. Sci., Math. Assn. Am., Soc. Indsl. and Applied Math. Home: 2105 Regent St Madison WI 53705-3941 Office: Van Vleck Hall U Wis Madison WI 53706

ASKEY, WILLIAM HARTMAN, magistrate, lawyer; b. Williamsport, Pa., June 21, 1919; s. Charles Fisher and Marguerite Kirlin (Hartman) A.; m. Betty Arlene Moore, July 3, 1942; 1 dau., Elizabeth Powell. BA, Bucknell U., 1941; JD, U. Pitts., 1951. Bar: Lycoming County Cts., 1951, Pa. 1952, U.S. Dist. Ct. (mid. dist.) Pa. 1952, U.S. Supreme Ct. 1960. Sole practice Williamsport, Pa., 1951—; U.S. commr. U.S. Dist. Ct. (mid. dist.) Pa., 1964-71; part-time U.S. magistrate, judge, 1971—; with AAA, North Penn. Bd. dirs. Appalachia Ednl. Lab., Charleston, W.Va., 1967-85; mem. Vestry Episcopal Ch., Williamsport, Pa., jr. warden, 1989. Served to maj. USAAF, 1941-46. Mem. Lycoming Law Assn. (pres. 1968-69), Pa. Bar Assn., ABA (Nat. Conf. Spl. Ct. Judges), Fed. Bar Assn. (hon.), Fed. Magistrate Judges Assn., Masons, Ross Club (Williamsport).

ASKIN, FRANK, law educator; b. Balt., Jan. 8, 1932; s. Abraham and Rose (Mervis) A.; m. Marilyn Klein, Aug. 6, 1960; children: Andrea Marcy, Jonathan Michael, Daniel Simon; 1 son from previous marriage, Steven. B.A., CCNY, 1966; J.D., Rutgers U., 1966. Bar: N.J. 1966, N.Y. 1983, U.S. Dist. Ct. (ea. dist.) N.Y., U.S. Ct. Appeals (2d, 3d cirs.), U.S. Supreme Ct. 1971. Former journalist N.Y. Post, Bergen Record, Newark Star-Ledger; Disting. prof. law Rutgers Law Sch., Newark, 1975—; vis. prof. U. Hawaii Law Sch., 1975; spl. counsel edn. and labor com. U.S. Ho. of Reps., 1976-77, cons. govt. ops. com., 1989-92; gen. counsel ACLU, 1976—. Author: Defending Rights: A Life in Law and Politics, 1997; co-editor Enforcing Fair Housing Laws, 1970; dem. candidate 11th dist. U.S. Ho. of Reps., N.J., 1986—. Contbr. articles to profl. jours. Del., Democratic Nat. Conv., 1980, 88; nat. bd. dirs. ACLU, 1968—, sec., 1971-75, gen. counsel, 1976—. Robert Knowlton scholar Rutgers Law Sch. Mem. Soc. Am. Law Tchrs. (treas. 1974-75). Office: Rutgers Law Sch 15 Washington St Newark NJ 07102-3192

ASKIN, MARILYN, lawyer, educator; b. N.Y.C.; d. Simon and Lena (Merker) Klein; m. Frank Askin, Aug. 6, 1960; children: Andrea, Jonathan, Daniel. B.S. in Edn., CCNY, 1954; postgrad. Russian Inst., Columbia U., 1958-60; J.D., Rutgers U., 1970. Bar: N.J. 1970. U.S. Dist. Ct. N.J. 1970, U.S. Supreme Ct. 1977, N.Y. 1983; cert. in elder law, 1995. Journalist The Record, Hackensck, N.J., 1956-62; tchr. high sch. English, Newark, 1964-67; regional dir. Am. Jewish Congress, Newark, 1971-76; counsel Pub. Documents Com., Washington, 1976-77; sr. atty. Essex Newark Legal Services, Orange, N.J., 1978-93; of counsel, Fein, Such, Kahn & Shepard, Parsippany, N.J., 1993-95; lectr. Inst. Continuing Legal Edn., 1983, 87—; adj. faculty Rutgers Law Sch., 1984—; mem. ethics com. Supreme Ct. Dist., 1985—, adj. faculty Seton Hall U. Law Sch., 1992—; mem. Supreme Ct. Com. on Rels. with Media, 1990—, Supreme Ct. Com. on Women in the Cts., 1994—; Editl. bd. N.J. Lawyer Mag., 1987—. Rev. bd. Children in Placement, Essex County, 1980—; bd. trustees Chr-Ill. (home health non-profit), 1983—. Author: ABC's of Elder Law, 1990, Elder Law, 1993, Elder Law Made Easy!, 1995, Elder Law for Neophytes, 1997, Long-Term Care Insurance, 1995, Reverse Mortgages, 1993, Nursing Home Residents As Clients, 1994, Elder Law for Neophytes. Mem. Nat. Acad. Elder Law Attys. Essex County Bar Assn. (chair com. on rights of elderly 1981—), N.J. State Bar Assn. (chair aging and the law com. 1985-89), N.J. Women Lawyers (pres. 1997—), Essex County Women Lawyers (pres. 1989-91), Nat. Legal Aid and Defender Assn. (chair sr. citizen sect. 1986-89), Rutgers Law Sch. Alumni Assn. (pres. 1993-94). Office: 193 Zeppi Ln West Orange NJ 07052-4129

ASKIN, WALTER MILLER, artist, educator; b. Pasadena, Calif., Sept. 12, 1929; s. Paul Henry and Dorothy Margaret (Miller) A.; child from previous marriage, Nancy Carol Oudegeest; m. Elise Anne Doyle, Apr. 17, 1993. B.A., U. Calif.-Berkeley, 1951, M.A., 1952; postgrad., Ruskin Sch. Drawing and Fine Art, Oxford. Asst. curator edn. Legion of Honor Mus., San Francisco, 1953-54; prof. art Calif. State U., Los Angeles, 1956-92; pub. Nose Press, Pasadena, Calif., 1984—; vis. artist Pasadena Art Mus., 1962-63, U. N.Mex., 1972, Calif. State U.-Long Beach, 1974-75, Cranbrook Acad. Art, Mich., 1978, Ariz. State U., Tempe, 1979, Art Ctr. Athens Sch. Fine Arts, Mykonos, Greece, 1973, Kelpra Studio, London, 1969, 73; chief reader Advanced Placement Program Ednl. Testing Service, 1982-85; chmn. visual arts panel Art Recognition and Talent Search Nat. Found. Advancement in Arts-Commn. on Presdl. Scholars; mem. advanced placement studio art examinaton com. Coll. Bd., 1985—, chmn., 1992—; mem. Commn. of Future of Advanced Placement Program, The Coll. Bd., 1999—; mem. acad. coun. Coll. Bd., 1989-94, chair arts adv. com., 1987-93; adj. prof. Ariz. State U., 1986-90; artist-in-residence Ragdale Found., Lake Forest, Ill., 1986, John Michael Kohler Art Ctr., Sheboygan, Wis., 1987, Hambidge Ctr. for Arts & Sci., Georgia , 1991, Vt. Studio Colony, 1988; co-dir. 1st Internat. Conf. on Humor in Art, Chateau de la Bretsche, Brittany, France, 1989, 92; spkr., juror nat. travel show So. Graphics Coun. Conf., Ohio U., Athens, 1998. Numerous exhbns. including one-man shows, Kunstlerhaus, Vienna, Austria, 1981, Santa Barbara Mus. Art, 1966, Hellenic-Am. Union, Athens, Greece, 1973, Hank Baum Gallery, San Francisco, 1970, 74, 76, Ericson Gallery, N.Y.C., 1978, Abraxas Gallery, Calif., 1979, 80, 81, Fla. State U., Tallahassee, 1988, Lizardi/Harp Gallery, Pasadena, 1988, 91, 95, L.A. Valley Coll., 1989; one-man traveling show U.S. Info. Agy., Yugoslavia, 1985-86, 15th Internat. Biennale of Prints and Drawings, Taipei Mus. Art, 1998; Pasadena's choice exhbn., Armory Ctr. for Arts, 1991, Contemporary Art in Pasadena, 1960-74, Norton Simon Museum, 1999 ; author: A Briefer History of the Greeks, 1983, Another Art Book to Cross Off Your List, 1984, Modern Manifesto Match Game, 1998, Hidedus Headlings, 1998, Womsters and Foozlers, 1998, On Becoming an Artist, 1999; contbr. articles to profl. jours. and mags. Trustee Pasadena Art Mus., 1963-68; bd. dirs. Los Angeles Inst. Contemporary Art., 1978-81, Pasadena Gallery Contemporary Arts; bd. govs. Baxter Art Gallery, Calif. Inst. Tech., 1980-86; bd. dirs. The Calif. Artist, Book Program, 1985—; dir. The Visual Humor Project, 1989—. Recipient Outstanding Prof. award Calif. State U., 1973, Artists award Pasadena Arts Council, 1970; grantee Pasadena Arts Commn., 1990; also over 50 awards in competitive exhbns. art. Mem. Coll. Art Assn. Am. Home and Office: PO Box D South Pasadena CA 91031-0120 *What can we do today that has any kind of meaning and value? We can search for a means to escape from conventions, from ordinariness, and from the limitations of everyday existence. We can help create the emergent fiction that is the world we live in. We can regenerate the key myths and archetypes so that life doesn't seem worth living unless one is on the side of the liberating and transformative. We can learn to play again - to not know what we are looking for, to break through the ice of habit, to know what it means to be truly alive and to experience the specialness of even the most ordinary things. We can find the god within, inspiration, magic, once again be visionaries, bring peace. The real joy is in making a better, more calm, more serene, more alive, more playful, more energized, more focused, more directed, more life filled existence for the time we're here.*

ASKINS, ARTHUR JAMES, accountant, finance management and auditing executive; b. Phila., Dec. 12, 1944; s. William J. and Rita M. (O'Brian) A.; m. Nancy E. Paulsen, Apr. 28, 1979. BS, LaSalle U., 1967; MA, Rider Coll., 1971; cert. of specialization Hospitality Acctg. and Mgmt., Am. Hotel and Motel Assn., 1989. CPA, Pa., N.J.; cert. fraud examiner, hotel adminstr. Tchr. Cardinal Dougherty H.S., Phila., 1967-70; pvt. practice acctg., 1967—; staff acct. Gross Master & Co., Jenkintown, Pa., 1970-74; asst. contr. Hankin Trustee, Willow Grove, Pa., 1974-79; mgr. internal audit Resorts Internat. Hotel Casino, Atlantic City, N.J., 1979-87, dir. revenue acctg., 1987-89, hotel contr., 1989; dir. internal audit Divi Resorts, 1989-91, Steamboat Devel., Corp., Bettendorf, Iowa, 1991-92; dir. internal audit, Casino Am., Inc, 1992-93; v.p. fin. Sea Escape Cruises, Inc., 1993-94; dir. fin., CFO Castle Beach Casino Hotel, Biloxi, Miss., 1994-95; dir. internal audit Lady Luck Gaming Corp., Las Vegas, Nev., 1995-96, fin. cons., 1996—, dir. internal audit Hollywood Casino-Hotel, 1997—. Recipient cert. of Commendation Twp. of Abington (Pa.), 1967, Disting. Service award Cmty. Accts., Phila., 1982, Superstar award Resorts Ir award Resorts Internat. Casino-Hotel, 1982, Brotherhood award NCCJ, Atlantic City, 1983, Mgmt. award Resorts Internat. Casino Hotel, 1986, 1st Mgrs. award Resort Internat. Casino-Hotel, 1986, Outstanding Vol. Service award Big Bros./Big Sisters, 1987. Mem. Nat. Assn. Accts. (nat. bd. dirs. 1983-85), pres. South Jersey Shore chpt. 1979-81, Community Affairs award Suburban Northeast Phila. 1978), Inst. Internal Auditors (bd. dirs. 1984-89), AICPA, N.J. Soc. CPAs, Pa. Inst. CPAs, Greater Mainland C. of C., Nat. Assoc. Cert. Internat. Fraud Examiners (audit com. 1979-83), Internat. Assn. Hosp. Accts. Republican. Roman Catholic. Home: 5155 Lake Ridge Dr Apt 1D Southaven MS 38671-8542 Office: Hollywood Casino-Tunica PO Box 218 Robinsonville MS 38664-0218

ASKINS, BILLY EARL, education educator, consultant; b. Burkburnett, Tex., Dec. 28, 1930; s. Sidney Earl and Nellie Alice (Johnson) A.; m. Sydney Loraine Gamblin, Feb. 21, 1954; 1 child, Dewayne Earl. BS, East Tex. State U., 1953; MEd, Midwestern U., 1959; EdD, U. North Tex., 1967. Instr., edn. specialist Sheppard Tech. Tng. Ctr., Wichita Falls, Tex., 1955-65; asst. dir. tchr. adminstrn. U. North Tex., Denton, 1965-66; tchr. Ft. Worth Pub. Schs., 1966-67; from asst prof. to prof. Tex. Tech. U., Lubbock, 1967-77, assoc. dean Coll. Edn., 1978-90, prof. edn., 1991—; cons. to univs., fedn. edn. labs., state edn. svc. ctrs., pub. schs., state prisons schs., schs. of nursing, community colls., state bar assns., and pvt. agys., 1980—; presenter at profl. confs. Contbr. to profl. publs. 1st lt. USAF, 1953-55, lt. col. Res. to 1981. Mem. Am. Ednl. Rsch. Assn., Assn. Tchr. Educators (Disting. Maj. Prof. award 1982), Nat. Staff Devel. Coun., Tex. Staff Devel. Coun. (bd. dirs. 1989-92), Tex. Assn. Tchr. Educators (exec. bd. 1987-89), Internat. Rotary Club, Order Ky. Cols. Avocations: photography, fly fishing, travel. Home: 5214 28th St Lubbock TX 79407-3508 Office: Tex Tech U PO Box 41071 Lubbock TX 79409-1071

ASKINS, WALLACE BOYD, manufacturing company executive; b. Chgo., June 2, 1930; s. Wallace Fay and Evelyn Mae (Baker) A.; m. Trieste M. Olivieri, May 20, 1954 (div. Sept. 23, 1994); 1 child, Justin Wallace. B.A., Lake Forest (Ill.) Coll., 1952; J.D. with honors, John Marshall Law Sch., Chgo., 1961. Bar: Ill. 1961; CPA, Ill. Sr. accountant Ernst & Young (CPAs), Chgo., 1952-55; controller, house counsel Nat. Lock Co., Rockford, Ill., 1955-65; asst. corp. controller Xerox Corp., Stamford, Conn., 1965-77; exec. v.p., chief fin. officer White Motor Corp., Cleve., 1977-81, chmn. bd., chief exec. officer, 1981-84; exec. v.p., chief fin. officer Armco Inc., Parsippany, N.J., 1984-92, also bd. dirs.; bd. dirs. Enviro-Source, Trump Hotel and Casino Resorts, Inc. Mem. ABA, AICPA, Ill. Soc. CPA's, N.Y. Soc. CPA's, Ill. Bar Assn.

ASKOV, EUNICE MAY, adult education educator; b. St. Louis, Nov. 20, 1940; d. David Hull and Marjorie Jane (Gutgsell) Nicholson; m. Warren Hopkins Askov, Jan. 22, 1967; children: David, Karen. BA in English, Denison U., 1962; MA in English, U. Wis., 1966, PhD in Curriculum and Instrn., 1969. English and reading tchr. Rich Twp. High Sch., Park Forest, Ill., 1962-64; reading svc. reading specialist U. Wis., Madison, 1965-66, project asst. Wis. R & D Ctr. for Cognitive Learning, 1966-67, rsch. assoc., 1969-72, lectr. dept. curriculum and instrn., 1968-69; coord. adult basic edn. programs U. Wis. Extension, 1966-67; remedial reading specialist Lincoln Jr. High Sch., Madison, 1966; adult basic edn. tchr. Madison Vocat., Tech. and Adult Schs., 1967-68; asst. prof. elem. edn. Minn. State U., Bemidji, 1972-74; assoc. prof. Pa. State U., University Park, 1974-79, prof., 1980—; presenter seminars on adult edn., Germany, 1986, 93; cons., speaker in field; mem. editorial bd. Jour. Ednl. Rsch., Adult Edn. Quarterly, Adult Basic Edn., Am. Reading Forum Yearbook; mem. steering com. Adult Literacy and Tech.; mem. panel nat. work group on cancer and literacy Nat. Cancer Inst.; organizer, coord. Pa. State Coalition for Adult Literacy; mem. adv. coun. Nat. Coalition for Literacy. Contbr. articles to profl. publs. Mem. celebration com. Pa., Yes!, 1990; mem. Pa. task force Project Literacy U.S.; adv. mem. goal 5 task force Pa. 2000. Fulbright sr. scholar, 1983; Literacy Leader fellow Nat. Inst. for Literacy, 1994-95; recipient Alumni Achievement award U. Wis.-Madison Sch. of Edn., 1994; Disting. fellow Flinders U. Inst. Internat. Edn., Australia. Mem. Am. Assn. Adult and Continuing Edn. (chair, mem. various coms., bd. dirs.),Commn. Profs. of Adult Edn., Am. Edn. Rsch. Assn., Am. Reading Forum, Internat. Reading Assn. (chair, mem. various coms.), Keystone State Reading Assn., Mid-State Literacy Coun. (bd. dirs., pers. com., long range planning com.), Mid-State Reading Coun. (pres.), Pa. Assn. Adult and Continuing Edn., Phi Beta Kappa, Phi Delta Kappa. Democrat. Methodist. Avocations: travel, aerobics, hiking, reading. Office: Pa State U Inst for Study Adult Lit 102 Rackley Bldg University Park PA 16802-3202

ASLAM, MUHAMMED JAVED, physician; b. Shillong, India, June 27, 1938; came to U.S., 1963; m. Tasnim Qadir, Feb. 5, 1967; children: Anissa, Shaazia, Sohail. MBBS, King Edward Med. Coll., Lahore, Pakistan, 1962. Diplomate Am. Bd. Internal Medicine, Am. Bd. Hematology; Fellow Royal Coll. Physicians/Can. Hematologist Winnipeg (Can.) Clinic, 1971-77; pvt. practice, hematologist Houston, 1977—; pres. Tess Data Systems, Houston, 1985—. Author: (computer software) Dietician, 1980, Tess System One, 1985, Tess System Two, 1987, Tess System Three, 1990; co-author: (computer software) Dietician Dietwae, 1984. Mem. Tex. Med. Assn., Harris County Med. Soc., N.Y. Acad. Scis. Office: Tess Data Systems Inc 13910 Champion Forest Dr Houston TX 77069-1882

ASLAM, SYED, chemist, research; b. Patna, Bihar, India, Dec. 25, 1938; came to the U.S., 1970; s. Syed Abdul Aziz and Bibi Rakeya Khatoon; m. Shahnaz Ahmad Aslam, Mar. 13, 1967; children: Faiz, Amir, Shazia. BS with honors, Patna U., 1959, MS in Chemistry, 1961; MS in Chemistry, Ea. Mich. U., 1973; cert. in Infra Red Spectroscopy, Bowdoin Coll., 1980. Cert. lab. analyst Mich. Water Pollution Control Assn. Lectr. chemistry Magadh U., Patna, 1961-69; rsch. asst. Ea. Mich. U., Ypsilanty, 1971-73; rsch. assoc. Detroit Med. Ctr., 1973-76; chemist County of Wayne Dept. Pub. Works, Wyandotte, MIch., 1976-92; asst. lab. dir. County of Wayne Dept. Pub. Works, Wyandotte, 1992—; cons. Alfa Tech. Svcs., Trenton, Mich., 1989-91. Author: Elements of Organic Chemistry, 1965; inventor in field. Pres. Assn. Indian Muslim, Canton, Mich., 1993—. Mem. Water Environment Fedn. Avocations: gardening, hunting, woodworking, glass blowing. Home: 1180 Mill Brook Rd Canton MI 48188-5088 Office: County of Wayne Dept Environment 797 Central St Wyandotte MI 48192-7307

ÅSLUND, ANDERS, economist; b. Karlskoga, Sweden, Feb. 17, 1952; s. Ivan and Ingrid (Åblad) A. BA, U. Stockholm, Sweden, 1976; MSc, Stockholm Sch. Econs., 1976; PhD, U. Oxford, England, 1982. Second sec. Swedish Embassy, Kuwait, 1977-78; first sec. Swedish Permanent Delegation, Geneva, 1982-84, Swedish Embassy, Moscow, 1984-87; rsch. scholar Kennan Inst. Advanced Russian Studies, Washington, 1987-88; prof., dir. Stockholm Inst. E. European Econs., Stockholm Sch. Econs., 1989-94; sr. assoc. Carnegie Endowment for Internat. Peace, Washington, 1994—; fellow World Econ. Forum, Geneva, 1991—. Author: Private Enterprise in Eastern Europe, 1985, Gorbachev's Struggle for Economic Reform, 1989, 91, Post-Communist Economic Revolutions: How Big a Bang?, 1992, How Russia Became a Market Economy, 1995; editor 7 books on Soviet and Russian econ. affairs. Sr. econ. advisor to Russian Govt., 1991-94, Ukrainian Govt., 1994-97. Mem. Cosmos Club (Washington). Office: Carnegie Endowment Internat Peace 1779 Massachussetts Ave Washington DC 20036

ASMA, LAWRENCE FRANCIS, priest; b. Waukegan, Ill., Oct. 21, 1947; s. Francis Victor and Isabelle Amelia (Recktenwald) A. BA in English, U. Wis., Whitewater, 1969; MA in English, Ill. State U., 1974; MA in Scripture magna cum laude, De Andreis Sem., 1982, MDiv, 1983. Ordained priest Roman Cath. Chr., 1983. Dir. spritual formation Cardinal Glennon Coll., St. Louis, 1983-85, instr. theology dept., 1983-85; chaplain St. Vincent's Div. DePaul Health Ctr., St. Louis, 1985—; Bd. dirs. Rosati Stabilization Ctr., St. Louis, 1988-94; vice chmn. Rosati Stabilization Ctr., 1990-94; advisor Explorers, 1991-92. Local religious superior Congregation of the Mission, 1994—; chaplain Knights Columbus, 1996—. With USNR, 1970-72, Vietnam. Mem. Assn. Mental Health Clergy (bd. cert.), Assn. Profl. Chaplains (bd. cert.), Cath. Biblical Assn., Congregation of Mission, Sigma Tau Delta. Avocations: ornithology, photography, drawing. Office: DePaul Health Center 12303 De Paul Dr Bridgeton MO 63044-2588

ASMAN, ROBERT JOSEPH, lawyer; b. St. Louis, Feb. 7, 1924; s. Robert J. and Anna M. (Spaeth) A.; student Holy Cross Coll., 1941-43; A.B., Cath. U. Am., 1948; LL.B., Georgetown U., 1951; m. Mary Elizabeth Kane, Sept. 8, 1948; children—Kathryn Anne, Robert Joseph III, Peter Kane, Teresa Elizabeth, Suzanne Marie, Elizabeth Jane. Admitted to D.C. bar, 1952, Ohio bar, 1961; asso. firm Cummings, Truitt & Reeves, Washington, 1956; trial atty. anti-trust div. Dept. Justice, 1952-53; asst. U.S. atty. D.C., 1953-60; counsel flight propulsion lab. dept. Gen. Electric Co., 1960-63; v.p., sec., gen. counsel Pneumo Dynamics Corp., Cleve., 1963-70; pres., chief exec. officer Ohio State Bar Assn. Automated Research, Cleve.; mem. firm Van Aken, Bond, Withers, Asman & Smith, Cleve. Mem. Bd. Zoning Appeals, Cleveland Heights, Ohio; mem. Ohio Mental Health and Mental Retardation Adv. Council, 1972—, mem. com. Met. Health Planning Corp.; mem. Cuyahoga County Community Mental Health and Retardation Bd., 1972—. Pres. Hill House, Cleve., 1964; trustee Cleve. Mental Health Assn., 1966-68, St. John's Coll., Hill House. Served with AUS, 1943-45; ETO. Decorated Bronze Star. Mem. Am., Fed., D.C., Ohio bar assns., Greater Cleve. Growth Assn., Phi Delta Phi. Clubs: Clevelander, Union, Rowfant Skating (Cleve.). Home: 2676 Berkshire Rd Cleveland OH 44106-3364 Office: 1519 Nat City Bank Bldg Cleveland OH 44114

ASMODEO GIGLIO, ELLEN THERESA, advertising executive; b. N.Y.C., Dec. 25, 1961; d. Elizer and Michelina (Barilla) A.; m. Stephen A. Giglio, May 8, 1993. AD, Fashion Inst. Tech., 1981; BA, Baruch Coll., 1983. With Conn. Mut. Life Inst. Co., 1978-83; acct. rep. MJM Advt., N.Y.C., 1983-87, The Travel Channel, N.Y.C., 1987-89; account mgr. Travel & Leisure mag., N.Y.C., 1989-93, advt. dir., 1995-98, v.p. sales and mktg., 1998—; travel mgr. Departures mag., 1993-95; bd.dirs. Caribbean Tourism ORgn., N.Y.C. Treas. Audrey Palmer Hawks Scholar Fund, N.Y.C., 1990-97. Office: Travel & Leisure 1120 Avenue Of The Americas New York NY 10036-6700

ASMUS, JOHN FREDRICH, physicist; b. Pasadena, Calif., Jan. 20, 1937; s. William F. and Eleanor E. (Kocher) A.; m. Barbara Ann Flaherty, Feb. 23, 1963; children—Joanne M., Rosemary H. BSEE, Calif. Inst. Tech., 1958, MSEE, 1959, PhDEE and Physics, 1965. Head optical systems dept. Aero Geo Astro Corp., Alexandria, Va., 1960-64; head laser dept. Gulf Gen. Atomic, San Diego, Calif., 1964-69; research staff Inst. Def. Analyses, Arlington, Va., 1969-71; v.p., bd. mem. Sci. Applications, Inc., Albuquerque, 1971-73; lectr. U. Calif., Davis, 1974; research physicist, co-founder art and sci. center U. Calif., San Diego, 1973—; co-dir. JASON nat. laser program study Office of Pres. of U.S., 1971; cons. in field; mem. adv. group on electron devices Smithsonian Assocs.; featured cable, PBS TV documentaries, 1975—. Contbr. sci. articles to profl. jours. Recipient Rolex Laureate for Enterprise award for restoration Xian terra cotta warriors Montres Rolex SA, Geneva, 1990, Best Scholarly Article award Soc. for Tech. Com., 1988; named George Eastman lectr. Optical Soc. Am., 1994; winner IBM Supercomputing Competition for Image Enhancement of Mona Lisa, 1989; Schlumberger fellow, 1959-60, Tektronix fellow, 1960-61, Getty fellow, 1989, Oberlin Coll. fellow, 1990, Explorers Club fellow, 1997; decorated knight of Holy Sepulchre of Jerusalem, 1993. Mem. Internat. Inst. Conservation of Historic and Artistic Works, IEEE, Am. Inst. Conservation, Nat. Trust Historic Preservation, Venice Soc., Bay Area Art Conservation Guild, Soc. Photo-Optical Instrumentation Engrs., Lasers for the Conservation of Artworks (sci. bd. mem.), Sigma Xi, Tau Beta Pi. Patentee metallic vapor laser, embedded pinch laser, plasma pinch annealing system, chemical decontamination with ultraviolet; introduced laser, ultrasonic and computer image enhancement techniques to art conservation, introduced laser cleaning to the field of paleontology, and revealed new features of da Vinci's Mona Lisa; restored Cremona Cathedral, Calif. State Capital, White House mural, Washington, Arches Nat. Pk. Pictograph, Venice Ducal Palace Sculpture, office of Galileo in U. Padova using laser radiation; development of laser-robotic technique for the decontamination of the Hanford nuclear weapons facility of the U.S. Dept. of Energy; laser system for branding bowhead whales at a distance. Home: 8239 Sugarman Dr La Jolla CA 92037-2222 Office: IPAPS 0360 U Calif San Diego 9500 Gilman Dr La Jolla CA 92093-5003 *The lessons and adventures that pervade our stories are manifestations of God's grace.*

ASMUSSEN, J. DONNA, educational administrator, consultant; b. Woonsocket, R.I., Aug. 22, 1951; d. John E. and Marion Annette (Fanning) A. BS in Edn., R.I. Coll., 1974, MEd, 1984. Cert. elem. and spl. edn. tchr., R.I., Maine, spl. edn. dir., spl. edn. cons., Maine. Spl. edn. tchr. Lincoln (R.I.) Sch. Dept., 1974-78, diagnostician, 1978-85; tchr. spl. edn. Maine Sch. Adminstrv. Dist. 36, Livermore Falls, 1985-89, composite rm. tchr., cons., 1989-90; dir. spl. svcs. Maine Sch. Adminstrv. Dist. 34, Belfast, 1990-95; cons. State Dept. Edn., Augusta, 1995—; presenter in field. Internat. Paper Co. fellow; State of Maine grantee, Univ. Affiliated Programs grantee, U. Maine, Orono. Mem. ASCD (presenter conf. 1995), Coun. Exceptional Children (intern, presenter conf. 1991), Coun. Adminstrs. Spl. Edn., Maine Assn. Dirs. Svcs. Children with Exceptionalities. Home: PO Box 381 East Winthrop ME 04343-0381 Office: Maine Dept Edn 23 State House Sta Augusta ME 04333-0023

ASNER, EDWARD, actor; b. Kansas City, Mo., Nov. 15, 1929; s. Morris David and Lizzie (Seliger) A.; m. Nancy Lou Sykes, Mar. 23, 1959; children: Matthew and Liza (twins), Kathryn, Charles. Student, U. Chgo., 1947-49. Debut at Playwrights Theatre, Chgo., 1953; appeared on TV, in Off-Broadway and Broadway shows, N.Y.C., 1955-61; appeared in numerous motion pictures and TV shows, Los Angeles, 1961—; appeared in TV miniseries Rich Man, Poor Man, 1976, Roots, 1977; appeared on Slattery's People, CBS-TV, 1964-65, Mary Tyler Moore Show, CBS-TV, 1970-77, Lou Grant Show, CBS-TV, 1977-82, Off The Rack, ABC-TV, 1985, This Side of Eden, The Bronx Zoo, 1987-88, The Trials of Rosie O'Neil, 1991, Fish Police (voice) 1991, Hearts Afire, 1992-93, Thunder Alley 1994-95; narrator TV film Narco; appeared in cable and TV films The Doomsday Flight, 1966, Doug Selby, D.A., 1969, House on Greenapple Road, 1969, Daughter of the Mind, 1970, The Old Man Who Cried Wolf, 1970, The Last Child, 1971, The Haunts of The Very Rich, 1971, Hey, I'm Alive, 1975, Life and Assassination of the Kingfish, 1977, The Gathering, 1977, The Family Man, 1979, A Small Killing, 1981, A Case of Libel, 1983, Anatomy of an Illness, 1984, Tender Is The Night, 1985, Vital Signs, 1986, The Christmas Star, 1986, Cracked up, 1987, Friendship in Vienna, 1988, Not a Penny More, Not a Penny Less, 1990, Switched at Birth, 1991, Yes, Virginia, There Is a Santa Claus, 1991, Silent Motive, 1991, Cruel Doubt, 1992, Gypsy, 1993; appeared in motion pictures Kid Gallahad, 1962, The Slender Thread, 1965, The Satan Bug, 1965, The Venetian Affair, 1967, Peter Gunn, 1967, Change of Habit, 1969, Halls of Anger, 1970, They Call Me Mister Tibbs, 1970, Skin Game, 1971, Gus, 1976, Fort Apache, The Bronx, 1980, O'Hara's Wife, 1982, Daniel, 1983, Moon Over Parador, 1988, JFK, 1991, (voice) Happily Ever After, 1993. Down on the Watefront, 1993; Higher Education (tv); Gargoyles: The Heroes Awaken (voice), 1994; Gargoyles (tv series, voice), 1994; Spider-Man (tv series), 1995; Freakazoid (tv series, voice), 1995; The Story of Santa Claus (tv), 1996; Gargoyles: The Goliath Chronicles (tv series, voice), 1996; Bruno the Kid (tv series, voice), 1996; Prep, 1997;Dog's Best Friend (tv), 1997; 187 Documented, 1997; Batman: Gotham Knights (tv series, voice), 1997; Payback (tv), 1997; The Long Way Home (voice), 1997; Ask Harriet (tv series), 1998; Hard Rain (aka The Flood), 1998; The Closer (tv series), 1998; More Tales of the City (aka Armistead Maupin's More Tales of the City, tv series), 1998. Served with Signal Corps U.S. Army, 1951-53. Recipient 5 Golden Globe Awards, 7 Emmy Awards, Flame of Truth Award, Fund for Higher Education, 1981; inducted into TV Acad. Hall of Fame, 1996. Mem. Screen Actors Guild (pres. 1981-85). Office: William Morris Agency care Brian Dubin 1325 Avenue Of The Americas New York NY 10019-6026*

ASOKAN, UNISA, information professional; b. Augusta, Ga., May 8, 1969; d. S.K. and Kathleen (McGuirk) A. BA, NYU, 1991; MLS, San Jose State U., 1993. Libr. Printed Circuit Builders, Inc., Santa Clara, Calif., 1991-93; tech. writer Atre Assocs., Port Chester, N.Y., 1992-94; dir. info. svcs. Fin. World Mag., N.Y.C., 1994-96; rsch. libr. The Atlanta Jour. Constn., 1997—; editor Fifth Planet Press, Atlanta, 1992—; bd. dirs. AtreNet, Inc., Santa

Cruz, Calif. Author: Non-Prophet, 1994. Recipient Youth Leadership award Congl. Youth Leadership Coun., 1987. Mem. Spl. Libs. Assn.

ASP, WILLIAM GEORGE, librarian; b. Hutchinson, Minn., July 4, 1943; s. George William and Blanche Irene (Mattson) A. BA, U. Minn., 1966, MA, 1970; postgrad., U. Iowa, 1972-75. Dir. East Cen. Regional Libr., Cambridge, Minn., 1967-70; asst. prof. Sch. Libr. Sci. U. Iowa, 1970-75; dir. Minn. Office Libr. Devel. and Svcs., St. Paul, 1975-96, Dakota County Libr., Eagan, Minn., 1996—; mem. Nat. Coun. Quality Continuing Edn. for Info., Libr. and Media Pers., 1979-85; bd. dirs. Bakken Libr. Electricity and Life, Mpls.; vice chmn. White House Conf. on Libr. and Info. Svcs. Task Force, 1980-81, chmn., 1982, mem. adv. com., 1989-91; pres. Continuing Libr. Edn. Network and Exch., 1986-87. Mem. Minn. Regional Network Bd., 1992-96. Mem. ALA (mem. coun. 1985-88), Minn. Libr. Assn., Chief Officers State Libr. Agys. (chmn. 1979-80), Minn. Ednl. Media Orgn., Minn. Assn. Continuing and Adult Edn., Assn. Specialized and Coop. Libr. Agys. (pres. 1989-90), Am. Field Svc. Home: 4137 42nd Ave S Minneapolis MN 55406-3530

ASPEN, ALFRED WILLIAM, international trading company executive; b. Phila., Aug. 22, 1927; s. Alfred W. and Theresa D. A.; B.A., Gettysburg Coll., 1951; m. Katherine LeVan, July 14, 1962 (div.); children—Carolyn S., Cynthia L., Alfred L. Asst. v.p. Far East, Woodward & Dickerson, 1956-63, Korea, 1956-61; mgr. S.E. Asia, Hong Kong, Singapore Internat. Minerals & Chem. Corp., 1966-73, v.p. trading, 1973-75, exec. v.p. Continental Fertilizers subs., N.Y.C., 1973-75; pres., gen. mgr. Transcontinental Fertilizer Co., Phila., 1975—, also dir.; dir. Coromandel Fertilizers, India. Served with USAF, 1945-47, 51-55. Decorated Air medal, D.F.C. Mem. Internat. Fertilizer Assn., Fertilizer Inst. Republican. Clubs: Phila. Country, Hong Kong, Am. of Hong Kong, Royal Hong Kong Golf, Tanglin.

ASPEN, MARVIN EDWARD, federal judge; b. Chgo., July 11, 1934; s. George Abraham and Helen (Adelson) A.; m. Susan Alona Tubbs, Dec. 18, 1966; children: Jennifer Marion, Jessica Maile, Andrew Joseph. BS in Sociology, Loyola Univ., 1956; JD, Northwestern U., 1958. Bar: Ill., 1958. Individual practice Chgo., 1958-59; draftsman joint com. to draft new Ill. criminal code Chgo. Bar Assn.-Ill. Bar Assn., 1959-60; asst. state's atty. Cook County, Ill., 1960-63; asst. corp. counsel City of Chgo., 1963-71; pvt. practice law, 1971; judge Cir. Ct. Cook County, Ill., 1971-79; judge U.S. Dist. Ct. (ea. dist.) Ill., Chgo., 1979-95, chief judge, 1995—; Edward Avery Harriman adj. prof. law Northwestern U. Law Sch.; past chmn. new judges, recent devels. in criminal law, and evidence coms. Ill. Judicial Conf., adv. bd. Inst. Criminal Justice, John Marshall Sch. Law; past mem. Ill. Law Enforcement Commn., Gov. Ill. Adv. Commn. Criminal Justice, Cook County Bd. Corrections; past chmn. assoc. rules com. Ill. Supreme Ct., com. on ordinance violation problems; past vice chmn. com. on pattern jury instrns. in criminal cases; lectr. at judicial confs. and trial advocacy programs nationally and internationally; planner, participant in legal seminars at numerous schools including Harvard U., Emory U., U. Fla., Oxford U. (Eng.), U. Bologna, Nuremberg (Germany) U., U. Cairo, Egypt, U. Zimbabwe, U. Malta, U. The Philippines, U. Madrid; past mem. Georgetown U. Law Ctr. Project on Plea Bargaining in U.S., spl. faculty NITA advanced Trial Advocacy Program introducing Brit. trial techniques to experienced Am. litigators, spl. faculty of ABA designed to acquaint Scottish lawyers with modern litigation and tech.; frequent faculty mem. Nat. Judiciary Coll., Fed. Judicial Ctr., U. Nev. (Reno), Nat. Inst. for Trial Advocacy, Colo.; bd. dir. Fed. Judicial Ctr.; past mem. Judicial Conf. Com. on Adminstrn. of the Bankruptcy System, Trial Bar Implementation Com. on Civility of the 7th Fed. Cir.; exec. bd. Fed. Jud. Ctr. Co-author Criminal Law for the Layman-A Citizen's Guide, 2d edit., 1977, Criminal Evidence for the Police, 1972, Protective Security Law, 1983; contbr. over two dozen articles to legal publs. Past mem. vis. com. Northwestern U. Sch. Law, chmn. adv. com. for short courses (post law sch. ednl. program); mem. vis. com. U. Chgo. Law Sch.; organizer, past pres. Northwestern Univ. Sch. of Law chpt. Amincourt Program U.S. Judicial Conf; past mem. Cook County Bd. Corrections, John Howard Assn. With USAF, 1958-59; trustee Am. Inns Ct. Recipient Nat. Ctr. Freedom of Info. Studies award, Ctr. for Pub. Resources award, Nat. Ctr. for Freedom of Info. Studies award, Merit award Northwestern U. Alumni Assn.; named Person of Yr. Chgo. Lawyer, 1995. Mem. Am. Bar Found. (bd. dirs.), Judicature Soc. Ill. (past chmn. coms.), Chgo. Bar Assn. (bd. mgrs. 1978-79, past chmn. criminal law com., past bd. editors Chgo. Bar Record, mem. commn. on criminal justice. coms. on cont. legal edn., devel. of law, civil disorder and others), Ill. State Bar Assn. (past chmn. pub. rels., corrections, fair trial/free press, criminal law coms., mem. others), Northwestern U. Law Alumni Assn. (past pres., Merit award), past mem. ABA bd. govs., mem. house dels., past chmn. exec com., Nat. Conf. Fed. Trial Judges, past mem. coun. sect. litigation, past chmn., coun. sect. criminal justice, past co-chmn. liason jud. com. sect. litigation, mem. jury comprehension study com., pres. ABA Mus. Office: US Dist Ct 2548 US Courthouse 219 S Dearborn St Chicago IL 60604-1702

ASPENBERG, GARY ALAN, personnel and labor relations professional; b. Darby, Pa., Jan. 13, 1945; s. Albert Alexander and Edith Ellen (Ware) A.; m. Vicki Ann Carlson, Oct. 15, 1979; children: Carla Fay Lynn, Derek Alan. BA, Drew U., 1967, MA, 1972. Asst. pers. dir. Woodhull Med. Group, Bklyn., 1986, dir. pers. and labor rels., 1987-98, exec. dir. pers., labor. rels. and adminstrn., 1998—. Author: Bus Poems, 1993. Avocation: poet. Home: 323A E 89th St New York NY 10128-5007 Office: Woodhull Med Group 760 Broadway Brooklyn NY 11206-5317

ASPER, SAMUEL PHILIPS, medical administrator, educator; b. Oak Park, Ill., July 14, 1916; m.Ann Carver, 1942; children: Ann, Lucy. AB, Baylor U., 1936; MD, Johns Hopkins U., 1940. House officer in medicine Johns Hopkins Hosp., Balt., 1940-41; rsch. fellow Thorndike Meml. Lab., Harvard U., 1941-42, 46-47; from instr. to prof. Sch. Medicine Johns Hopkins U., 1947-85, assoc. dean, 1957-68; v.p. med. affairs Johns Hopkins Hosp., 1970-73; emeritus prof. medicine Johns Hopkins U., 1985—; prof. internal medicine, dean faculty med. sci. Am. U., Beirut, 1973-78; chief staff Univ. Hosp., 1973-78; dep. exec. v.p. ACP, 1979-81; pres. Edn. Com. Fgn. Med. Grads., 1982-85, emeritus pres., 1985—. Major U.S. Army Med. Corps, 1942-45. Master ACP (pres. 1969-70, emeritus pres. 1985—); mem. Inst. Medicine/Nat. Acad. Sci., Endocrine Soc. (v.p. 1966-67), Assn. Am. Physicians, Am. Soc. Clin. Investigation. Address: 830 W 40th St Apt 603 Baltimore MD 21211-2116

ASPERO, BENEDICT VINCENT, lawyer; b. Newton, N.J., Sept. 3, 1940; s. Umberto S. and Rose (Cerreta) A.; m. Sally Hennen, June 26, 1971; children: Benedict Vincent Jr., Alexander Morgan. AB, U. Notre Dame, 1962, J.D., 1966. Bar: N.J. 1970, N.Y. 1982, D.C. 1983, U.S. Dist. Ct. N.J. 1970, U.S. Supreme Ct. 1981. Assoc., then ptnr. Meyers, Lesser & Aspero, Sparta, N.J., 1971-76, Benedict V. Aspero, Sparta and Morristown, N.J., 1976-82; ptnr. Broderick, Newmark, Grather & Aspero, Morristown, N.J., 1982-89, Courter, Kobert, Laufer, Purcell & Cohen, 1989-91; prin. Benedict V. Aspero, Morristown, 1992-96; ptnr. Aspero & Aspero, P.C., Morristown, 1996-97, Benedict V. Aspero, Esq., P.C., 1997—; mem. adv. bd. Summit Bank. Trustee, pres. Harding Twp. Civic Assn., 1982-85; trustee, pres. Craig Sch., Loyola Retreat House. Mem. ABA, N.J. Bar Assn., Morris County Bar Assn., Sussex County Bar Assn., Sorin Soc. Republican. Roman Catholic. Clubs: Morristown, Essex Hunt. Office: 222 Ridgedale Ave PO Box 1573 Morristown NJ 07962-1573

ASPINALL, MARA GLICKMAN, marketing and general management professional; b. N.Y.C., Aug. 14; d. Alvin and Betty Glickman. BA, Tufts U., 1983; MBA, Harvard U., 1987. Assoc. First Boston Corp., N.Y.C., 1986; cons. Bain & Co., Inc., Boston, 1987-90; dir. mktg., client svcs. Hale and Dorr LLP, Boston, 1990-97; v.p. corp. devel. Genzyme Corp., Cambridge, Mass., 1997—; pres. Genzyme Pharms., Genzyme Corp., Cambridge, 1997—; mem. biotech project adv. group Radcliffe Pub. Policy Inst. Mem. editorial bd. Rainmaker's Quar. Chmn. Am. Cancer Soc., Mass., 1996—; bd. dirs. Arts Boston, 1996—, Dana-Farber Cancer Inst., Boston, 1998—; dir. Success by 6 Leadership Coun., United Way, 1998—; dir. Mus. Fine Arts Corp. Coun., 1999—. Recipient Woman of Vision award Mass. Prevent Blindness Assn., 1995, Pinnacle award for Emerging Exec. of Yr. Greater Boston C. of C., 1997; named among Forty under Forty Top Bus. Execs., Boston Bus. Jour. Mem. Nat. Assn. Law Firm Mktg. (pres. New Eng. 1992-94), Assn. Tufts Alumnae (pres. 1988-90, 92-94, alumni trustee rep. bd. trustees), Harvard Bus. Sch. Assn. (chairperson reunion com.), Harvard Bus. Sch. Network for Women (dir. 1995-98), WGBH Corp. Exec. Coun. (dir. 1997—), The Children's Mus. Boston (trustee 1996—). Office: Genzyme Corp 1 Kendall Sq Cambridge MA 02139-1562

ASPLIN, EDWARD WILLIAM, retired packaging company executive; b. Mpls., June 25, 1922; s. John E. and Alma (Carlbom) A.; m. Eleanor Young Rodgers, Oct. 20, 1951; children—Sarah L., William R., Lynn E. B.B.A., U. Minn., 1943; postgrad., U. Mich., 1947-48, Wayne State, 1949-50, Rutgers U. Sch. Banking, 1957-59. Cost accountant Nat. Bank Detroit, 1947-50; asst. v.p. adminstrn. Northwest Bancorp., Mpls., 1950-59; v.p. mktg. Northwestern Nat. Bank, Mpls., 1959-67; chmn. Bemis Co., Inc., Mpls., 1967-88. Advisor Opportunity Ptnrs., Inc.; hon. bd. dirs. Mpls. YMCA, Minn. Hist. Soc.; adv. bd. dirs. U. Minn. Cancer Adv. Bd. Mem. Woodhill County Club, Mpls. Club. Office: 730 2nd Ave S Ste 825 Minneapolis MN 55402-2450

ASPLUNDH, CHRISTOPHER B., tree service company executive; b. 1939. With Asplundh, Willow Grove, Pa., 1963—, v.p., 1966, pres., 1992—, also bd. dirs. Office: Asplundh Tree Expert Co 708 Blair Mill Rd Willow Grove PA 19090-1784*

ASPNES, DAVID ERIK, physicist, educator; b. Madison, Wis., May 1, 1939; s. Erik A. and Anita L. (Knabe) A.; m. Edna Joyce Hall, Jan. 27, 1964 (dec. 1996); children: James D., Gary E., Ann K.; m. Cynthia Jean Ball, July 26, 1997. BSEE, U. Wis., 1960, MSEE, 1961; PhD, U. Ill., 1965. Postdoctoral rsch. assoc. U. Ill., Urbana, 1965-66, Brown U., Providence, 1966-67; mem. tech. staff Bell Labs., Murray Hill, N.J., 1967-83; sr. scientist Max-Planck-Inst., Stuttgart, Fed. Republic Germany, 1976-77; dist. mgr. Bellcore, Red Bank, N.J., 1983-92; prof. physics dept. N.C. State U., 1992-99, Disting. Univ. prof. physics, 1999—. Contbr. more than 350 articles to Phys. Rev., Applied Optics, Thin Solid Films and other jours.; U.S. editor Applied Surface Sci., 1996—. Recipient Sr. Scientist award Alexander von Humboldt Found., 1976-77, John Yarwood medal Brit. Vacuum Coun., 1993, Max Planck Rsch. Award for Internat. Coop., 1997, Outstanding Rsch. award N.C. State U. Alumni Assn., 1997. Fellow Am. Phys. Soc. (councillor divsn. condensed matter physics 1996—, exec. coun. 1998-99, Frank Isakson prize 1996), Optical Soc. Am. (Wood prize 1987), Am. Vacuum Soc. (chmn. electronic materials and processing divsn. 1982-83, chmn. electronics materials and processing divsn. internat. Union Vacuum Sci., Techniques and Applications 1986-89, bd. dirs. 1991-92, Medard W. Welch award 1998), Soc. Photo-Optical Instrumentation Engrs.; mem. AAAS, IEEE, Nat. Acad. of Scis., Materials Rsch. Soc., Alexander von Humboldt Assn. Am., Sigma Xi. Mem. LDS Ch. Achievements include discovery and development of reflectance-difference spectroscopy and low-field electroreflectance; development of spectroscopic ellipsometry with applications to process control; contributions to solid-state physics including 3rd derivative interpretation of low-field electroreflectance, ordering of the lower conduction bands of GaAs, elucidation of the kinetics of crystal growth by organometallic chemical vapor deposition, virtual-interface theory. Office: Physics Dept NC State U Raleigh NC 27695-8202

ASSADOURIAN, SARKIS, member of parliament; b. Aleppo, Syria, Jan. 25, 1948; arrived in Can., 1970; m. Zaza Assadourian; children: Raffi, Tamar, Vatche, Gacia. Student, Chgo. Acad. Fine Arts. Exec. dir. Armenian Cmty. Ctr., North York, Ont., 1985-93; mem. Can. Parliament for Don Valley North, 1993-97, mem. Can. Parliament for Brampton Ctr., 1997—; mem. standing com. on fgn. affairs and internat. trade, standing com. on ofcl. langs., 1997—; mem. standing comm. on human rights and status of persons with disabilities, sub-com. on dispute settlements, 1993-97; mem. ho. of commons standing com. on citizenship and immigration, sub-com. to investigate immigration consultants, 1994-95. Mem. Liberal Task Force on De-industrialization of Can., Ont. Adv. Coun. on Multiculturalism, Can. Consultative Coun. on Multiculturalism; past treas., bd. dirs. Willowdale Cmty. Legal Svcs.; bd. dirs. Armenian Cmty. Ctr., founder Outstanding Can. award; fundraiser Heart and Stroke Found., Arthritis Soc., others; hon. mem. Armenian Relief Soc., Can. Armenian Bus. Coun., Syro-Can. Union of Montreal. Recipient Vol. Svc. award Ont. Govt., 1988, Outstanding Father award St. Mary's Armenian Ch., 1992. Office: Ho of Commons, 120 Confederation Bldg, Ottawa, ON Canada K1A 0A6*

ASSAEL, HENRY, marketing educator; b. Sofia, Bulgaria, Sept. 12, 1935; s. Stanley Isaac and Anna (Behar) A.; m. Alyce Friedman, Aug. 19, 1961; children: Shaun Eric, Brenda Erica. B.A. cum laude, Harvard U., 1957; M.B.A., U. Pa., 1959; Ph.D., Columbia, 1965. Asst. prof. mktg. Sch. Bus. St. John's U., Jamaica, N.Y., 1962-65; asst. prof. mktg. Hofstra U., Hempstead, N.Y., 1965-66; prof. mktg. Stern Sch. Bus. NYU, 1966—, chmn. dept., 1979-91; cons. AT&T, N.Y. Stock Exchange, Nestle Co., Inc., GTE, CBS, Am. Can Co. Author: Educational Preparations for Positions in Advertising Management, 1966, The Politics of Distributive Trade Associations: A Study in Conflict Resolution, 1967, Consumer Behavior and Marketing Action, 1981, 6th edit. 1997, Marketing Management: Strategy and Action, 1985, Marketing: Principles and Strategy, 1990, 2d edit., 1993, Marketing: Core Concepts, 1997; editor: A Century of Marketing, 33 vols., 1978, Early Development and Conceptualization of the Field of Marketing, 1978, History of Advertising, 40 vols., 1985; contbr. numerous articles to profl. jours. Mem. Am. Mktg. Assn., Assn. Consumer Research. Office: 44 W 4th St New York NY 10012-1106

ASSAEL, MICHAEL, lawyer, accountant; b. N.Y.C., July 20, 1949; s. Albert and Helen (Hope) A.; m. Eiko Sato. BA, George Washington U., 1971; MBA., Columbia U. Grad. Sch. Bus., 1973; JD, St. John's Law Sch., 1977. Bar: N.Y. 1978, U.S. Dist. Ct. (so. and ea. dists.) N.Y. 1980, U.S. Supreme Ct. 1982; CPA, N.Y. Tax sr. Price Waterhouse & Co., N.Y.C. and Tokyo, 1977-78; pvt. practice law, N.Y.C., 1978—; pvt. practice acctg., N.Y.C., 1978—. Author: Money Smarts, 1982. Pres. bd. dirs. 200 Block East 74th Street Assn., 1982; bd. dirs. 200 E 74 Owners Corp., 1981—, treas., 1983-84, pres., 1984-85; mem. Yorkville Civic Council, tenant adv. com. Lenox Hill Neighborhood Assn., 1981-82. Recipient N.Y. Habitat/Citibank mgmt. achievement award, 1985. Mem. ABA, N.Y. State Bar Assn., N.Y. County Lawyers Assn., Am. Inst. CPA's, Am. Assn. Atty. CPA's, Inc., Nat. Assn. Accts., N.Y. State Soc. CPA's, Aircraft Owners and Pilots Assn. Clubs: N.Y. Road Runners, Columbia Bus. Sch. (N.Y.).

ASSANIS, DENNIS N. (DIONISSIOS ASSANIS), mechanical engineering educator; b. Athens, Greece, Feb. 9, 1959; came to U.S., 1980; s. Nicholas and Kyriaki Assanis; m. Helen Stavrianos, Aug. 25, 1984; children: Nicholas, Dimitris. BSc in Marine Engring. with distinction, Newcastle U., U.K., 1980; SMME, SM in Naval Arch. Marine Engring., MIT, 1982, PhD in Power and Propulsion, 1985, SM in Mgmt., 1986. Asst. prof. mech. engring. U. Ill., Urbana-Champaign, 1985-90, assoc. prof. mech. engring., 1990-94; assoc. prof. Nat. Ctr. for Supercomputing Applications, 1992-94, head thermal scis./systems divsn., 1992-94; prof. mech. engring. U. Mich., Ann Arbor, 1994—, dir. program automotive engring., 1995—, elected senator, 1995-98, Arthur F. Thurnau prof., 1999—; part-time rsch. staff energy and environ. systems divsn. Argonne Nat. Lab., 1978—; cons. in field. Assoc. editor ASME Transactions, Jour. Engring. for Gas Turbines and Power, 1996—; contbr. over 100 articles to profl. jours.; presenter in field. Univ. scholar, 1991-94, Athens Coll. Acad. scholar, 1967-77; recipient IBM Rsch. award, 1991, NSF Presdl. Young Investigator award, 1988-93, NSF Engring. Initiation award, 1987, NASA Cert. of Recognition for Creative Devel. of a Tech. Innovation, 1987; Lilly Endowment Teaching fellow, 1988. Mem. ASME (faculty advisor U. Ill. student sect. 1989-91, ASME/Pi Tau Sigma Gold Medal award 1990, Internal Combustion Engine Divsn. Speaker award 1993, 94, Meritorious Svc. award 1997), Soc. Automotive Engrs. (faculty advisor U. Mich. student sect. 1997—, Ralph Teetor award 1987, Russell Springer Best Paper award 1991), Am. Soc. for Engring. Edn., Combustion Inst., Sigma Xi. Achievements include development of comprehensive models of internal combustion engine processes. Office: U Mich Dept Mech Engring & Applied Mechanics 2045 WE Lay Automotive Lab Ann Arbor MI 48109-2121

ASSANTE, ARMAND, actor; b. N.Y.C., Oct. 4, 1949. Student, Am. Acad. Dramatic Art, N.Y.C. Actor on stage in The Lake of the Woods, 1971, Comedians, 1976, Romeo and Juliet, 1977, Kingdoms, 1982, Yankees 3, Detroit 0, Rubbers, Boccaccio, in feature films Paradise Alley, 1978, Prophecy, 1979, Love and Money, 1979, Little Darlings, 1980, Private Benjamin, 1980, I, The Jury, 1982, Unfaithfully Yours, 1984, Belizaire the Cajun, 1985, The Penitent, 1986, Animal Behavior, 1989, Q&A, 1990, Eternity, 1990, The Marrying Man, 1991, The Mambo Kings, 1992, 1492, 1992, Hoffa, 1992, Fatal Instinct, 1993, Trial by Jury, 1994, Judge Dredd, 1995, Striptease, 1996, Looking for an Echo, 1999, Hunt for the Devil, 1999, in TV movies Human Feelings, 1978, The Lady of the House, 1978, The Pirate, 1978, Sophia Loren: Her Own Story, 1980, Rage of Angels, 1983, Why Me?, 1984, A Deadly Business, 1986, A Stranger in My Bed, 1986, Hands of a Stranger, 1987, Jack the Ripper, 1988, Passion and Paradise, 1989, Fever, 1991, Blind Justice, 1994, Kidnapped 1995, Gotti, 1996, C.S.S. Hunley, 1999, in TV mini-series Napoleon and Josephine, 1987, The Odyssey, 1997. *

ASSIBEY-MENSAH, GEORGE OSSEI, political science educator; b. Kumasi, Ashanti, Ghana, Jan. 23, 1950; s. Ossei and Rosina (Howard) A.-M.; m. Naana O. Assibey-Mensah; children: Godfred, Priscilla, Vanessa, Rosina, Laretta. BSBA, Ky. State U., 1977; M Public and Internat. Affairs, U. Pitts., 1979; PhD in Pub. Adminstrn. and Pub. Policy, Va. Poly. Inst. and State U., 1993. Asst. prof. Shaw U., Wilmington, N.C., 1993; asst. prof. polit. sci. Ind. U. Sch. Pub. and Environ. Affairs, Gary, 1994—, mem. adv. panal N.W. Ind. Ctr. for Data and Analysis, 1996—, mem. cmty. outreach group, 1995—; cons., mem. evaluation geam Gary Weed and Seed Program Com., 1994-95; cons. Kent Goldmining Co., Kumasi, 1994—, Gary Mayor's Office, 1995-96. Contbr. articles to profl. jours., including Jour. Black Studies, Western Jour. Black Studies, Pub. Budgeting and Fin., Jour. Ind. Acad. Social Scis. Mem. Willowpong Apts. Self-Sufficiency Program, Wilmington, 1994-95; mentor Values Partnership Program for African-Am. Male Youth, Hammond, 1995-96, 21st Century Scholars Program, Gary, 1995-96. With U.S. Army, 1983-85. Overseas rsch. dissertation grantee Va. Poly. Inst. and State U. Grad. Sch., 1991; grantee Ind. U. N.W. Sch. Pub. and Environ. affairs and Internat. Programs, 1995, 96, overseas rsch. grantee, 1998. Mem. ASAP (ethics co-coord. N.W. Ind. chpt. 1995—), Midwest Polit. Sci. Assn., Ind. Acad. Social Scis. Avocations: walking and jogging, photography, sight-seeing, travel, jazz music. E-mail:gassibey@iunhaw1.iun.indiana.edu. Office: Ind U Sch Pub-Env Affairs Lindenwood Hall 108 3400 Broadway Gary IN 46408

ASSUNTO, RICHARD ANTHONY, payroll executive; b. New Haven, Conn., Nov. 15, 1942; s. Joseph and Anne Maude (Tull) Martin. BA, Biola U., 1970; MBA, U. Hartford, 1987. Mgr. life issue Aetna Life Ins., Hartford, Conn., 1973-81, mgr. payroll, 1981-89, mgr. purchasing, 1989-92; mgr. payroll Allied Signal, Tempe, Ariz., 1992-94; dir. payroll Norrell Corp., Atlanta, 1994-97; exp. mgr. Andersen Consulting, Atlanta, 1997—. Chmn. United Way Aetna Life Ins., 1983; treas. Hill Ctr., Hartford, 1983-85. With USAF, 1961-65. Mem. Am. Payroll Assn. (pres. 1983-85, v.p. 1993-94, Communications award 1989, Speakers award 1989), Am. Soc. Payroll Mgrs. Avocations: bicycling, swimming, basketry, golf.

AST, STEVEN TODD, executive search firm executive; b. Washington, June 11, 1943; s. Harold Gerken and Mary Ann (Lynn) A.; m. Maria Kelly Stevens, Dec. 1995. BA, Georgetown U., 1965. Cert. fund raising exec. Dir. devel. U. Chgo., 1970-73; prin. Steven T. Ast Assocs., Chgo., 1973-75; dir. devel. U. Calif., San Francisco, 1975-76, The Salk Inst., La Jolla, Calif., 1976; exec. dir. That Man May See, San Francisco, 1976-79; dir. devel. Arlington (Va.) Hosp., 1979-82; v.p. Brakeley, John Price Jones, Stamford, Conn., 1982-83; pres. Brakeley Recruiting, Stamford, 1983-89; chmn. AST/BRYANT, Stamford, Conn., 1989—. Office: AST/BRYANT One Atlantic St Stamford CT 06901

ASTAIRE, CAROL ANNE TAYLOR, artist, educator; b. Long Beach, Calif., Aug. 26, 1947; d. John Clinton and Carolyn Sophie (Wright) Taylor; m. Frederic Astaire, Jr., Feb. 14, 1971; children: John Carroll, Johanna Carolyn. BFA, UCLA, 1969; grad. summer studies, Salzburg Summer Sch., Klessheim, Austria, 1969; cert. secondary sch. tchr., Calif. State U., Long Beach, 1971; postgrad., Calif. Polytechnic State U., San Luis Obispo, 1986-87. Cert. secondary sch. tchr. life, Calif. Tchr., tutor, cons. art edn. San Luis Coastal Unified Sch. Dist., San Luis Obispo, 1980-89. Author: (book) Left Handed Poetry from the Heart, 1993; artist: work in permanent collections. Yergeau Musée Internat. Art, Montreal, Can., 1991, Travis (Calif.) AFB Mus., 1990. Founder, trustee, San Luis Coastal Unified Sch. Dist./Found. Arts Art Core, 1988-92; mem. adv. coun. Coastal Cmty. Edn. and Svcs., San Luis Obsipo, 1989-92, screening com. UCLA Alumni scholarship, 1993-95. Nat. finalist Kodak Internat. Newspaper Snapshot award, 1993. Mem. Nat. Mus. of Women in Arts (charter), Fine Arts Coun., San Luis Obispo Art Ctr., San Luis Obispo Art Coun., Oil Pastel Acrylic Group Brushstrokes (hon. mention 1994), Ctrl. Coast Watercolor Soc., Ctrl. Coast Photo. Soc. Republican. Episcopalian. Avocations: classical ballet, architectural design, swimming, gardening, reading.

ASTE, MARIO ANDREA, foreign language educator; b. Carloforte, Italy, Jan. 11, 1943; came to U.S., 1966; s. Stefano and Francesca A.; m. Dorothy Elaine Balbirer, June 6, 1970; children: Stephen Robert, Marie Francesca, Kristina Elizabeth. BA in Philosophy, Philos. Inst., Torino, Italy, 1966; MA in Italian, Cath. U. Am., 1969, PhD, 1971, MA in Spanish, 1978. Prof., chmn. langs. U. Mass., Lowell, 1971—; bd. dirs. Internat. Inst., Lowell, pres., 1980-99. Author: La Narrativa Di Luigi Pirandello, 1979, Two Novels of Pirandello: An Essay, 1979, Grazia Deledda: Ethnic Novelist, 1989, They Came in Hope, 1995; editor: Technology Industry Labor and the Italian American Communities, 1997. Housing rev. bd. City of Lowell, 1981-84; pastoral fin. coun. St. Michael Parish, Lowell, 1987—. Teaching fellow Cath. U. Am., Washington, 1967; NEH grantee Stanford U., 1979, Princeton U., 1983, Cath. U., 1988. Mem. MLA (chair exec. com. 20th century Italian lit. divsn. 1996-97), Am. Assn. Tchrs. Italian, Am. Assn. Italian Studies (jour. editor 1989-98, mng. editor 1998—), Am. Italian Hist. Assn. (exec. bd. 1992—, treas. 1997—), N.E. MLA (exec. bd. 1998—), Mass. Soc. Prof. (pres. 1988—), K.C. Democrat. Roman Catholic. Avocations: Lowell folk life festivals, soccer, scouting. Home: 115 Reservoir St Lowell MA 01850-2244 Office: U Mass 1 University Ave Lowell MA 01854-2827

ASTHANA, RAJIV, engineering educator, researcher; b. Lucknow, India, June 18, 1957; s. Hari S. and Kamala Asthana; m. Neerja Prakash, Apr. 22, 1987; children: Ankur, Akansha. BS, Indian Inst. Tech., Kharagpur, 1980, MS, 1983; PhD, U. Wis., Milw., 1991. Staff scientist Coun. Sci. and Indsl. Rsch., Bhopal, India, 1983-87; tchg. and rsch. asst. U. Wis., Milw., 1987-91; resident rsch. assoc. NASA Lewis Rsch. Ctr., Cleve., 1991-95, project scientist, 1993; asst. prof. mfg. engring. U. Wis. Stout, Menomonie, 1995—; vis. asst. prof. U. Wis., Milw., summers 1996, 97; faculty adviser Am. Foundrymen's Soc., Menononie, 1996—. Author: Solidification Processing for Reinforced Metals, 1998; contbr. articles to profl. jours. NRC postdoctoral rsch. assoc., 1994, 95; Barker Meml. fellow, 1988, 89. Mem. Am. Soc. for Materials, The Minerals, Metals and Materials Soc., Am. Foundrymen's Soc., Am. Soc. for Engring. Edn. Home: 412 21st St N # 1 Menomonie WI 54751-2230 Office: U Wis Stout 326 Fryklund Dr Menomonie WI 54751-3841

ASTIGARRAGA, JOSE I(GNACIO), lawyer; b. Havana, Cuba, July 20, 1953; came to U.S., 1960, naturalized 1974; AA with honors, Miami Dade Community Coll., 1973; BBA summa cum laude, U. Miami, 1975; JD magna cum laude, 1978. Bar: Fla. 1978, U.S. Dist. Ct. (so. dist.) Fla. 1979, U.S. Dist. Ct. (mid. dist.) 1988, U.S. Ct. Appeals (5th and 11th cir.) 1981, U.S. Supreme Ct. 1990. Chief bailiff Dade County Juvenile and Family Ct., Miami, Fla., 1972-74; law clk.-bailiff 11th Jud. Cir., Miami, 1974-77; with firm Steel, Hector & Davis, Miami, 1978-84, ptnr., 1984—; adj. faculty U. Miami Sch. Law, Coral Gables, Fla., 1980-81; cons. World Bank; mem. U.S. del. Org. Am. States 6th Conf. on pvt. internat. law; Little Havana Activities and Nutrition Ctrs. of Dade County, Inc., 1987-94, NAFTA adv. comm. on the resolution of private commercial disputes, 1994-96; mem. panel arbitrators Comml. Arbitration and Mediation Ctr. for Ams., 1996; founder Latin Am. users coun. London Ct. Internat. Arbitration. Co-author: Secured Lenders Beware: Particular Issues Affecting Secured Lenders, 1993; adminstrv. hearing officer Dade County Sch. Bd., Miami, 1982-90; bd. dirs. Miami Children's Hosp., 1985-88, also chmn. quality assurance com., mem. fin. com.; bd. dirs. Miami Children's Hosp. Rsch. Inst., Inc., 1986-87, chmn. nominating com.; bd. dirs. Dade County Beacon Coun. Inc., 1985-95, Miami Coalition, Inc., 1988-94; mem. exec. com., chmn. schs. task force, 1988-90; trustee Fla. Internat. U. Found., 1988—. Named Harvey T. Reid scholar U.

Miami Sch. Law, 1975-78, Leonard T. Abess scholar, U. Miami, 1974-75; recipient Up and Comers Law award Price Waterhouse and South Fla. Bus. Jour., 1988. Mem. ABA (com. on comml. fin. svcs., Uniform Comml. Code com., com. bus. bankruptcy 1990—, Internat. Bar Assn. (com. arbitration, insolvency), Am. Arbitration Assn. (panel on commercial fin. disputes 1994—), Am. Law Inst. (adv. transnat. insolvency project 1997), Fla. Bar Assn. (bus. law sect., sec. civil procedure rules com. 1979-84, bankruptcy UCC com. 1992—, lectr. bankruptcy seminar 1993, 94), Dade County Bar Assn. (commr. jud. campaign practices commn. 1986-87), Cuban-Am. Bar Assn., Bankruptcy Bar Assn. (v.p. 1992-94), U. Miami Sch. Law Alumni Assn. (bd. dirs. 1981-88), Greater Miami C. of C. (bd. govs. 1985-86, group chmn. econ. devel. sect. 1986-87). Office: 200 S Biscayne Blvd Fl 41 Miami FL 33131-2310

ASTILL, KENNETH NORMAN, mechanical engineering educator; b. Westerly, R.I., July 16, 1923; s. John Henry and Mabel Nellie (Robotham) A.; m. Hazel Patricia Lamb, Apr. 10, 1948; children: Kenneth John, Robert Michael. BS, U. R.I., 1944; MA in Engring., Chrysler Inst. Engring., 1946; MS, Harvard U., 1953; PhD, MIT, 1961. Lab engr. Chrysler Corp., Detroit, 1944-47; prof. mech. engring. Tufts U., Medford, Mass., 1947-91, assoc. dean engring., 1980-88, prof. emeritus, 1991—; mem. energy facilities siting coun. Commn. of Mass., 1989-92; mng. dir. U. Rsch. Engring. Assn., 1989—; cons. Sylvania Electric Co., Natick Labs., Kaye Instruments, C.S. Draper Labs.; vis. fellow U. Leeds, 1976, U. Sussex, 1983. Author: (with B. Arden) Numerical Algorithms, 1970, Elementary Experiments in Mechanical Engineering, 1971, (with others) Laboratory Demonstrations in Heat Transfer and Fluid Mechanics, 1968. Trustee Charles River Mus., 1992—. Recipient Ralph R. Teeter award Soc. Automotive Engrs., 1981; NSF fellow, 1968. Fellow ASME (life, chmn. Boston sect. 1981-82); mem. AAUP, Am. Soc. Engring. Edn., Engring. Soc. New Eng. (bd. dirs. 1982-87), Sigma Xi, Tau Beta Pi. Home: 72 Yale St Winchester MA 01890-2331 Office: Tufts U Anderson Hall Medford MA 02155

ASTILL, ROBERT MICHAEL, credit manager; b. Winchester, Mass., Apr. 11, 1960; s. Kenneth Norman and Hazel Patricia (Lamb) A. BA in Psychology and Polit. Sci., Merrimack Coll., 1982. Credit mgr. Kazmaier Internat., Concord, Mass., 1983-90; cons. Astill Group, Winchester, Mass., 1990-92; credit mgr. Internat. Ice Cream, Boston, 1992-93; corp. credit mgr. New Eng. Frozen Foods, Southborough, Mass., 1993-97; mgr. spl. credit and collection activities West Lynn Creamery, Lynn, Mass., 1997—. Bd. dirs. Friends of Winchester (Mass.) Libr., 1990-94; mem. New Eng. Steamship Found., 1997—. Mem. NACM (chmn. bd. dirs. New Eng. wholesale provision 1992-97), New Eng. Steamship Found., Psi Chi. Roman Catholic. Avocations: photography, music, travel. Home: 5 Glen Rd Apt 208 Stoneham MA 02180-3128

ASTLE, JOHN CHANDLEE, state legislator; b. Charleston, W.Va., Mar. 31, 1943; m. Jayne Asher; children: Jay, David. BA, Marshall U., 1966; postgrad., Cath. U., 1972-74. Md. state del. Dist. 30, 1983-94; chmn. Ann Arundel County Delegation, 1986-91; Md. state senate Dist. 30, 1995—. Col. USMCR, 1975-96, ret. Decorated 31 air medals, Purple Heart, Legion of Merit, Meritorious Svc. medal, Presdl. Svc. badge. Mem. Marine Corps. Res. Officers Assn., Am. Legion, VFW, DAV. Address: Presidential Wing James Senate Office Bldg Annapolis MD 21401

ASTMAN, BARBARA ANN, artist, educator; b. Rochester, N.Y., July 12, 1950; d. George William and Bertha Dinah (Meisel) A.; m. Noel Robert Harding, Feb. 23, 1977 (div. 1983); m. Joseph Anthony Baker, Aug. 29, 1984; children: Amy Astman Baker, Laura Astman Baker. A degree, RIT, 1970; grad., Ont. Coll. Art, Toronto, 1973. Mem. faculty Ont. Coll. Art and Design (formerly Ont. Coll. Art), Toronto, 1975—, York U., Toronto, 1978-80, 86; lectr. in field. Solo exhbns. include Baldwin St. Gallery Photography, Toronto, 1973, Ryerson Photo Gallery, Toronto, 1974, Nat. Film Bd. Can., Ottawa, 1975, S.A.W. Gallery Inc., 1976, The Sable-Castelli Gallery Ltd., Toronto, 1977, 79-84, 86, 88, 90, The Jean Marie Antone Gallery, Annapolis, Md., 1979, Whitewater Gallery, North Bay, Ont., Bruce Art Gallery, Canton, N.Y., 1980, The Mendel Art Gallery, Saskatoon, Sask., 1981, The So. Alberta Art Gallery, Edmonton, Alta., 1981, The Art Gallery Peterborough, Ont., 1982, Galerie du Musee, Musee du Quebec, 1986, Ctr. d'Animation et de Diffusion de la Photographie, Quebec, 1986, Thunder Bay Art Gallery, Ont., 1992, The Robert McLaughlin Gallery, Oshawa, Ont., 1993, McIntosh Gallery, London, Ont., 1994, Gallery Stratford, Stratford, Ont., 1994, Art Gallery of Hamilton, 1995; The Edmonton Art Gallery, Edmonton, Alberta, The Kamloops Art Gallery, Kamloops, B.C., 1996—, June Corkin Gallery, 1997; group exhbns. include Lamkin Camerawork Gallery, San Francisco, 1975, Art Gallery Ont., Toronto, 1975, 80, 84, 93, Rochester (N.Y.) Meml. Art Gallery, Montreal Mus. Fine Arts, 1975, Harbourfront Art Gallery, Toronto, 1977, 80, The Sable-Castelli Gallery Ltd., 77, 81, Anna Leonowens Gallery, Halifax, N.S., 1977, London (Ont.) Regional Art Gallery, 1978, 83, Edmonton (Ont.) Art Gallery, 1978, The Winnipeg Art Gallery, 1979, Everson Mus., Syracuse, N.Y., 1979, Galerie Luca Polazzoli, Milan, 1979, H.F. Johnson Mus. Art, Ithaca, N.Y., 1979, George Eastman House, Rochester, N.Y., 1979, The Hamilton (Ont.) Art Gallery, La Galerie Powerhouse, Montreal, 1981, YYZ Gallery Toronto, 1982, Forum des Halles, Paris, 1985, Graves Art Gallery, Sheffield, U.K., 1985, San Diego Art Ctr., 1986, Hallwalls Gallery, Buffalo, 1986, La Galerie des Arts Lavalin, Montreal, 1988, Pro Mus. Contemporary Art, Finland, 1988, The Kamloops (B.C.) Art Gallery, 1989, The Koffler Gallery, Toronto, 1990, Art Gallery of Peterborough, Ont., 1992, Art Gallery of Hamilton, Ont., 1993, Southern Alberta Art Gallery, Lethbridge, 1994; Art Gallery Hamilton, Gallerie Arts Tech., Montreal, P.Q., Basel Art Fair, Basel, Switzerland, 1998, Chgo. Art Fair, 1999; public collections include Agnes Etherington Art Ctr., Kingston, Ont., Art Gallery Hamilton, Art Gallery Ont., Toronto, Bibliotheque Nationale, Paris, The Gallery/Stratford, The Nickle Arts Mus., Calgary, Alta., The Robert McLaughlin Gallery, Oshawa, The Winnipeg Art Gallery, Victoria and Albert Mus., London; also involved with other pub. art projects. Coord. Colour Xerox Artists' Program, Visual Arts Ont., Toronto, 1977-83; bd. dirs. Art Gallery at Harbourfront, Toronto, 1983-85; apptd. mem. City of Toronto Pub. Art Commn., 1986-89; mem. curatorial team WaterWorks Exhbn., Toronto, 1988; chmn. Toronto Arts Awards, Visual Arts Jury, 1988; bd. dirs. Arts Found. of Greater Toronto, 1989-92. Office: Ont Coll Art and Design, 100 McCaul St, Toronto, ON Canada M5T 1W1 Dealer address: Jane Corkin Gallery, 179 John St, Toronto, ON Canada

ASTON, EDWARD ERNEST, IV, dermatologist; b. Jersey City, Jan. 14, 1944; m. Kirsten Anita. B.A., U. Md.-College Park, 1968; M.D., U. Md.-Balt., 1969. Diplomate Am. Bd. Dermatology. Intern, Orange County Med. Ctr., Orange, Calif., 1969-70; resident U. Calif.-Irvine-Orange County Med. Ctr., 1971-74; practice medicine specializing in dermatology Fullerton Med. Clinic of Dermatology, Calif., 1974—. Office: 301 W Bastanchury Rd Ste 220 Fullerton CA 92835-3424

ASTON, STEVEN WESLEY, production manager; b. Burbank, Calif., June 30, 1953; s. Beverly Baugh Aston and Theresa Joan (Rivelli) James. Student, UCLA, 1971-75. Cert. tchr., Calif. Stage mgr. Knott's Berry Farm, Buena Park, Calif., 1971-75, prodn. mgr., 1975-82; prodn. mgr. Long Beach (Calif.) City Coll., 1983—, Internat. City Theatre, Long Beach, 1985—; instr. theatre arts Long Beach City Coll., 1986—; cons. Walt Disney Entertainment Arts Program, Long Beach, 1989-91; stage mgr. numerous orgns. Mem. USO, 1975. Mem. So. Calif. Arts Adminstrs., Nat. Mgmt. Assn. (pres. 1981-82). Office: Long Beach City Coll 4901 E Carson St Long Beach CA 90808-1706

ASTOR, DAVID WARREN, journalist; b. Bronx, Mar. 29, 1954; s. Harold Milton and Thelma (Oppenberg) A.; m. Kathy Barbara Kattenburg, Jan. 12, 1985; 1 child, Maggie Elizabeth. BA in English, Rutgers U., 1976; MS in Journalism, Northwestern U., 1978. Rutgers corres. New York Times, N.Y.C., 1974-76; reporter Red Bank Register, Shrewsbury, N.J., 1976-77, Passaic (N.J.) Herald-News, 1978; assoc. editor and sr. editor Mktg. Communications Mag., N.Y.C., 1978-83; assoc. editor and syndication reporter Editor & Pub. Mag., N.Y.C., 1983—. Avocations: reading, guitar-playing, bicycling, baseball, cartooning. Office: Editor and Publisher 11 W 19th St New York NY 10011-4209

ASTRACHAN, BORIS MORTON, psychiatry educator, consultant; b. N.Y.C., Dec. 1, 1931; s. Isaac and Ethel (Kahn) A.; m. Batja Sanders, June 17, 1956; children: David Isaac, Joseph Henry, Michael Sanders, Ellen Beth Astrachan-Fletcher. *Son David is in otolaryngology practice in New Haven, Hamden, and Madison, Connecticut. He and Karen are parents of Ariel, Daniel, and Brian. Son Joseph holds the Wachovia Chair of Family Business at Kennesaw University, Georgia and has extensive national and international consulting practice. Children are Winston and Quinn. Son Michael is an award-winning computer artist. He and Bethany are parents of Benjamin. Ellen is assistant professor of psychology in Psychiatry at University of Illinois, Chicago, and her husband Tony Fletcher is at the Isaac Ray Forensic Center in Chicago and in private practice. Their children are Noah and Sara.* BA cum laude, Alfred (N.Y.) U., 1952; MD, Albany Med. Coll., 1956. Lic. Ill.; bd. cert. in psychiatry. Intern, resident USN Hosp., St. Albans and Phila., N.Y., 1956-57, 57-58; asst. depot psychiatrist recruitment tng. depot USMC, Parris Island, S.C., 1958-61; resident in psychiatry dept. psychiatry Yale U., New Haven, 1961-63, from asst. prof. to assoc. prof. dept. psychiatry, 1963-71; dir. Conn. Mental Health Ctr., New Haven, 1971-87; prof. dept. psychiatry Yale U., New Haven, 1971-90; prof., head dept. psychiatry U. Ill., Chgo., 1990-98, disting. prof. psychiatry, 1998—; mem. NIMH Initial Rev. Group, Rockville, Md., 1987-90, chmn., 1989-91; mem. IBM Mental Health Adv. Bd., White Plains, N.Y., 1990—; mem. adv. bd. Alcohol, Drug Addiction, Mental Health Adminstrn., Washington, 1985-86; mem. rsch. task force Pres. Commn. on Mental Health and Illness, Washington, 1977-78; vis. prof. U. Rotterdam, Amsterdam, 1986, Boston U., 1996. Co-author: (with Tischler) Quality Assurance in Mental Health, 1983; contbr. articles to profl. jours. (Citation classic 1986). Mem. State Health Clin. Coordinating Com., Hartford, Conn., 1980s; mem. clin. adv. com. Ill. Dept. Mental Health and Devel. Disabilities, Chgo., 1995-97; chair mental health task force Ill. Dept. Children and Family Svcs., Chgo., 1993-97; chair Mental Health Svc. Sys. Adv. Coun., Springfield and Chgo., Ill., 1992-95. Lt. comdr. USN, 1955-61. Recipient Disting. Faculty award U. Ill., Chgo., 1997; named Alumnus of Yr., Albany Med. Coll., 1999. Fellow Am. Coll. Psychiatrists, Am. Psychiat. Assn. (life, trustee-at-large, Adminstrv. Psychiatry award 1995), Am. Assn. Psychiat. Adminstrs. (Past. Pres. award 1992); mem. AMA. Jewish. Avocations: time with family, listening to music, reading. Home: 333 E Ontario St Apt 2902B Chicago IL 60611-4882 Office: Dept Psychiatry M/C 913 912 S Wood St Chicago IL 60612-7325

ASTRIAB, STEVEN MICHAEL, army officer; b. Pitts., Mar. 10, 1952; s. Steven Leonard and Anna (Popivchak) A.; m. BettyLou Elaine Gimmi, Dec. 27, 1975. BA in Psychology, Washington and Jefferson Coll., 1974; MS in Manpower Planning, W.Va. U., 1976. Commd. 2d lt. U.S. Army, 1974, advanced through grades to lt. col., 1992; div. social work officer 1st Cav. Div., Ft. Hood, Tex., 1976-77, med. platoon leader, then med. co. comdr. 15th med. bn., 1977-79; med. ops. officer 1st Cav. Div. Hdqs., Ft. Hood, Tex., 1979-81; chief M.C. procurement Office Army Surgeon Gen., Washington, 1982-85; chief combat medicine Office Project Mgr., Saudi Arabian Nat. Guard, Riyadh, 1985-88; pers. officer 62 Med. Group, Ft. Lewis, Wash., 1988-90; asst. chief staff for med. civil and mil. ops. 3d U.S. Army (Army Cen. Command), Riyadh, 1990-91; med. ops. officer Hdqrs. I Corps, Ft. Lewis, 1991-93; chief med. plans for S.W. Asia Hdqs. 3d U.S. Army, Atlanta, 1993-95; chief coalition integration for S.W. Asia Hdqs. 3d U.S. Army, 1995-96; chief med. plans and intelligence S.W. Asia Hdqrs. 3d U.S. Army, 1996; sr. med. and fgn. mil. sales advisor U.S. Mil. Tng. Mission for Saudi Arabia, Riyadh, 1996-98; chief of ops. Divsn., exec. officer Pacific Regional Med. Command, 1998—; assoc. faculty Ctr. Excellence for Disaster Mgmt. and Humanitarian Assistance, 1999—. Decorated Bronze Star medal, Def. Meritorious Svc. medal, Meritorious Svc. medal (6), Joint Svc. Commendation medal, Army Commendation medal (2), Nat. Def. Svc. medal (2), S.W. Asia Campaign medal (3), Armed Forces Expeditionary Medal, liberation of Kuwait medal (Saudi Arabia), Liberation of Kuwait medal (Kuwait). Republican. Baptist. Avocations: running, weight training, computer applications. also: 1328 Parks Pl Honolulu HI 96819-2127

ASTUCCIO, SHEILA MARGARET, educational administrator; b. Biddeford, Maine, Apr. 24, 1943; d. James T. III and Margaret H. (Cameron) Rollinson; m. Joseph Kevin Astuccio, Aug. 22, 1976 (dec. Apr. 1992); children: James M., Sheila E. BS in Edn., Salem (Mass.) State Coll., 1968, MEd, 1975; cert. advanced grad. studies, Lesley Coll., Cambridge, Mass., 1983. Cert. elem. tchr. and prin., supr., dir., Mass. Elem. educator Hood Elem. Sch., Lynn, Mass., 1968-79; tchr. grades 3 and 4 Lynn (Mass.) Pub. Schs., comp. coord., facilitator, 1981-84, tchr. academically talented, 1979-81, 84-85, computer program specialist, 1986-87, computer implementation team leader, MIS dir., 1987-98; adminstr. IS/MIS, 1998—; owner operator Pilot Imaging Computer Imaging, Lynn, Mass., 1991-92; tchr. adult edn. North Shore C.C., 1982-87; part-time real estate broker, 1979—; part-time mktg. cons. IDN, 1993-95. Mem. Chpt. II adv. coun., 1979-83; nat. grad. alumni rep. Lesley Coll., 1984-85; chair Mayor's Computer Adv. Com., 1985-86; participant Educators in Industry GE/Salem State Coll., 1983. Recipient Educators in Industry cert., 1983, Novell Netware Adminstr. and Sys. Installation/Configuration certs., 1994-95; Chpt. II grantee, 1984. Mem. ASCD, AAUW, NAFE, NSBA, DECUS, PEI Nat. Users Group, New Eng. Pentamation Users Group, Boston Computer Soc. Office: Data Center LVTI 80 Neptune Blvd Lynn MA 01902-4570 also: PO Box 2613 South Hamilton MA 01982-0613

ASTUTO, PHILIP LOUIS, retired Spanish educator; b. N.Y.C., Jan. 5, 1923; s. Salvatore and Anna (Insalaco) A.; m. Natella M. Digia, July 4, 1953; children: Philip, Anne Marie. BA, St. John's U., 1943; MA, Columbia, 1947; PhD, Columbia U., 1956. Mem. faculty St. John's U., 1947-89, prof. Spanish, 1958-89, prof. emeritus, 1991—, dir. Latin Am. studies, 1957-60, chmn. dept. modern fgn. langs., 1961-65; Participant Prof.-Student Summer Seminar, sponsored State Dept., 1950; OAS research fellow, Quito, Bogota, 1973-74. Contbr. articles to profl. jours. Mem. coll. coun. SUNY, Farmingdale, 1988—. 1st lt., inf. AUS, 1943-46, ETO. Recipient Pietas medal St. John's U., 1977, Faculty Outstanding Achievement medal, 1986. Mem. Am. Assn. Tchrs. Spanish and Portuguese, Am. Hist. Assn., Assn. Latin Am. Studies, MLA, Nat. Acad. History of Ecuador (fgn. corr.). Home: 11 Steuben Dr Jericho NY 11753-1414

ASTWOOD, WILLIAM PETER, psychotherapist; b. N.Y.C., May 18, 1940; s. Henry Kenneth and Rose Margit (Eastby) A.; m. Sharon Lisa Sprung, June 10, 1979; 1 child, Jesse Jack. BA, CUNY, 1962; MA, NYU, 1967, PhD, 1975. Case worker, supr. dept. social services City N.Y., 1964-67; community orgn. trainer Block Communities, Inc., N.Y.C., 1967-68; field rep. Office Econ. Opportunity, N.Y.C., 1968-70, U.S. Dept. Health, Edn., Welfare, N.Y.C., 1970-71; pvt. practice Bklyn., 1971—; dir. family therapy div. DiMele Ctr. for Psychotherapy, N.Y.C., 1990—; bd. dirs. South Beach Psychiat. Ctr., Bklyn., 1976-78, N.Y. Group for Comprehensive Family Therapy, Mineola, 1988—; exec. bd. Met. Ctr. for Psychotherapy, N.Y.C., 1969-72. Co-author: Practicing Psychotherapy, 1980. Exec. bd. Social Service Employees Union, N.Y.C., 1965-67. Staff sgt. USANG, 1963-69. Mem. N.Y. Acad. Scis., Assn. for Humanistic Psychology, Am. Assn. Marriage and Family Therapy (clin.). Home: 394 Atlantic Ave Brooklyn NY 11217-1703 Office: 163 Clinton St Brooklyn NY 11201-4601

ATAIE, ATA JENNATI, oil products marketing executive; b. Mashad, Iran, Mar. 15, 1934; s. Hamid Jennati and Mohtaram (Momeni) A.; came to U.S., 1957, naturalized, 1969; B.S. in Agr., Fresno (Calif.) State U., 1964; B.A. in Econs., San Francisco State U., 1966; m. Judith Garrett Bush, Oct. 7, 1961; children—Ata Jennati, Andrew J. Mktg. exec. Shell Oil Co., Oakland, Calif., 1966-75; pres. A.J. Ataie & Cos., Danville, Calif., 1975—; Am. Value Inc., 1976—. Served as 2d lt. Iranian Army, 1953. Mem. Nat. Petroleum Retailers Assn. Democrat.

ATAIE, JUDITH GARRETT, middle school educator; b. San Francisco, July 24, 1941; m. A.J. Ataie Sr., Oct. 7, 1961; children: A.J. Jr., Andrew Jennati. BA, U. Calif., Berkeley, 1980; postgrad., U. Hawaii, Manoa, 1982—. Art instr., dean faculty The Athenian Sch., Danville, Calif., 1980—.

ATAL, BISHNU SAROOP, speech research executive; b. Kanpur, Uttar Pradesh, India, May 10, 1933; came to U.S., 1961; s. Jagannath Prasad and Lakshmi Devi (Lakshmi) A.; m. Kamla Atal, July 3, 1959; children: Alka, Namita. BS with honors, U. Lucknow, India, 1952; elec. engring. degree, Indian Inst. Sci., Bangalore, 1955; PhD in Elec. Engring., Poly. Inst. Bklyn., 1968. Sr. rsch. asst. Indian Inst. Sci., Bangalore, 1955-56, lectr., 1957-60; sr. rsch. fellow Cen. Elec. Engring. Rsch. Inst., Pilani, Rajasthan, India, 1960-61; mem. tech. staff AT&T Bell Labs., Murray Hill, N.J., 1961-85, head acoustics rsch., 1985-90, head speech rsch., 1990-97; tech. dir. AT&T Labs., Florham Park, N.J., 1997—. Contbr. articles to various publs. Fellow Acoustical Soc. Am., IEEE (Acoustics, Speech and Signal Processing Sr. Tech. Achievement award 1975, ASSP Sr. award 1980, Centennial medal 1984, Morris N. Liebman Meml. Field award 1986); mem. NAE, NAS. Office: AT&T Labs Rsch 180 Park Ave Florham Park NJ 07932-1004

ATALLAH, MIKHAIL JIBRAYIL, computer science educator; b. Aleppo, Syria; came to U.S., 1979; s. Gabriel M. and Nadia C. Atallah; m. Karen A. Atallah, Dec. 27, 1980; children: Nadia M., Christina M. BSEE, Am. U., Beirut, Lebanon, 1975; MSEE, Johns Hopkins U., 1980, PhD in computer sci., 1982. Asst. prof. computer sci. Purdue U., West Lafayette, Ind., 1982-86; assoc. prof. computer sci. Purdue U., West Lafayette, 1986-89, prof. computer sci., 1989—, assoc. head computer sci. dept., 1994-96; vis. scientist NASA Ames Rsch. Ctr., 1988. Contbr. chpts. to books, numerous articles to profl. jours.; editor: SIAM Jour. on Computing, 1988-98, Jour. of Parallel and Distributed Computing, 1993—, Info. Processing Letters, 1991-97, Computational Geometry: Theory & Applications, 1990—, Internat. Jour. on Computational Geometry & Applications, 1990—, Methods of Logic in Computer Sci., 1990-96, Algorithmica (guest editor for spl. issue on computational geometry), 1990-91; mem. editl. bds.: Handbook of Algorithms and Theory of Computation, 1995—, Handbook of Parallel and Distributed Computing, 1993—, Handbook of Computer Sci. and Engring., 1994-97; spkr., presenter in field. Recipient NSF Presdl. Young Investigator award, 1985. Fellow IEEE; mem. Assn. for Computing Machinery (spl. interest group on automata and computability theory), IEEE Computer Soc., Soc. for Indsl. and Applied Math., Upsilon Pi Epsilon. Office: Computer Sci Dept Purdue U West Lafayette IN 47907

ATCHER, RANDY, musician, narrator, entertainer, retired realtor; b. Tip Top, Ky., Dec. 7, 1918; s. George Christopher and Mary Agnes (Ray) A.; m. Daphne Lilian Fuller, Dec. 24, 1943 (dec. Dec. 1977); children: Randall Mark, Christopher Clay; m. Elizabeth Thorne, July 14, 1979; stepchildren: Laura, Judy, Kathy, John. Student, Western Ky. U., 1936-37. Musician, singer Sta. WHAS, Louisville, 1932-38, musician, singer, bandleader, 1947-49; musician, singer Sta. WIND, Sta. WJJD, Gary, Ind. and Chgo., 1938-41, Sta. WBBM, Chgo., 1941; musician, singer, disc jockey Sta. WKLO, Louisville, 1949; bandleader, singer, announcer, master of ceremonies Sta. WHAS Radio-TV, Louisville, 1950-70; narrator Am. Printing House, Louisville, 1970—; realtor Coldwell Banker (formerly Gibson/Pfannenschmidt Inc.), Louisville, 1970-80, Atcher-Goff Realtors, 1979-84; ret., 1984; realtor Atcher-Goff Realtors, 1980-92; recorded with Columbia Records and MGM Records. Songwriter numerous works. Chmn. Muscular Dystrophy Assn., Louisville, 1951-92; master of ceremonies, musician, singer Sta. WHAS Crusade for Children Telethon, 1953-70, 92—; active Country Music Found. and Hall of Fame, Nashville; mem. adv. bd. The Dream Factory; active Western Singing Trio High, Wide and Handsome, 1993—. Served to maj. Air Corps U.S. Army, 1942-46. Recipient numerous awards and certificates Ky. Derby Festival, Muscular Dystrophy Assn., Multiple Sclerosis, Am. Heart Assn., Cystic Fibrosis, Key to the City of Louisville, 1991. Alexander Scourby award Found. for the Blind; named Man of Yr., Firemans Assn., Louisville, 1956, Man of Yr., Police Assn., Louisville, 1957, Musician of Yr., Louisville Fedn. of Musician, 1989. Mem. Am. Fedn. Musicians. Democrat. Roman Catholic. Club: Wildwood (Louisville). Avocations: golf, tennis. Home: 1900 Manor House Dr Louisville KY 40220-1405

ATCHESON, RICHARD, editor. Exec. editor Modern Maturity Am. Assn. Retired Persons, Washington. Office: Am Assn Retired Persons 601 E St NW Washington DC 20049-0001

ATCHESON, SUE HART, business educator; b. Dubuque, Iowa, Apr. 12; d. Oscar Raymond and Anna (Cook) Hart; m. Walter Clark Atcheson (div.); children: Christine A. Hischar, Moffet Zoe Onofrei, Claye Williams. BBA, Mich. State U.; MBA, Calif. State Poly. U., Pomona, 1973. Cert. tchr. and adminstr. Instr. Mt. San Antonio Coll., Walnut, Calif., 1968-90; bd. dirs. faculty assn. Mt. San Antonio Coll.; mem. acad. senate Mt. San Antonio Coll.; originator vol. income tax assistance Mt. San Antonio Coll.; speaker in field; adj. lectr. in bus. mgmt. Calif. State Polytech U., Pomona, 1973-75; adj. lectr. macroecons. Colo. Mountain Coll., Salida, 1999. Author: Fractions and Equations on Your Own, 1975. Charter mem. Internat. Commn. on Monetary and Econ. Reform; panelist infrastructure funding reform, Freeport, Ill., 1989. Mem. Cmty. Concert Assn. Inland Empire (bd. dirs.), Scripps Coll. Fine Arts Found., Recyclers Club (pres. 1996).

ATCHISON, CHRISTOPHER GEORGE, public health director. AB in Pol. Sci., Loyola U., Chgo., 1971; MPA, U. Ill., Springfield, 1990; student, Harvard U., 1996. Chief staff Office Lt. Gov., Springfield, Ill., 1978-81; exec. dir. Ill. Rep. State Com., Springfield, 1981-85; spl. asst. to dir. Ill. Dept. Pub. Health, Springfield, 1985-87; acting chief epidemiological studies Ill. Dept. Pub. Health, 1987, asst. dir., 1987-91; dir. Iowa Dept. Pub. Health, Des Moines, 1991-99, Ctr. Pub. Health Practice, U. Iowa, Iowa City, 1999—. Chair One Gift Campaign, Iowa, 1993, Health Data Commn., Iowa, 1993-96, Health Regulation Task Force, Iowa, 1996—; sec. Prospective Minor Parent Program Adv. Commn., Iowa, 1996—; vice chair Long Term Care Coord. Unit, Iowa, 1993—; mem. Iowa Leadership Consortium, 1991-92, Govs. Health Care Reform Council, Iowa, 1993-94. Pub. Health scholar Pub. Health Leadership Inst., 1992-93. Mem. AMA, Am. Pub. Health Assn. (pres. Iowa chpt. 1994-95, Ill. chpt., pub. health medicine steering com. 1995—), Assn. State Territorial Health Ofcls. (pres. 1994-95, chair nominations com. 1995—, exec. com. 1992—, chair primary care com. 1992-93, chair joint council official pub. health agys. 1994-95), N.Y. Acad. Med. (medicine pub. health panel 1996—), Milbank Found. (reforming states group 1995—), Pub. Health Leadership Inst., Am. Soc. Pub. Adminstrn. (Iowa chpt., pres. ctrl. Ill. chpt. 1990-91, exec. council Ill. 1987-91). Office: Iowa Dept Public Health Planning & Admin Division Lucas State Off Bldg 4th Fl 321 E 12th St Des Moines IA 50309-5636*

ATCHISON, RICHARD CALVIN, trade association director; b. Altadena, Calif., Aug. 4, 1932; s. Floyd and Clara (Warwick) A.; m. Mildred Platt, Jan. 24, 1957; children: Tracey, Hayley. B.S., UCLA, 1958. Salesman, product mgr. Lever Bros., N.Y.C., 1958-61; group product mgr., then regional sales mgr. Purex Corp.; pres. Van Camp Seafood Co. div. Ralston Purina Co., 1965-81; pres. Mitsubishi Foods (USA) Inc., 1981-91; exec. dir. Am. Tuna Boat Assn., San Diego, 1991-93; pres. Internat. Bus. Cons., 1993—. With USAF, 1952-56.

ATCHLEY, ANTHONY ARMSTRONG, physicist, educator; b. Lebanon, June 23, 1957. BS, U. South, 1979; MS, NMex. Tech., 1982; PhD in Physics, U. Miss., 1984. Asst. prof. physics Naval Post Grad. Sch., 1985-90, assoc. prof., 1990-96, prof., 1996—, chmn. dept., 1996-97; chmn. grad. program in acoustics Pa. State U., State College, Pa., 1997—. Recipient R. Bruce Lindsay award Acoustical Soc., 1992. Fellow Acoustical Soc. Am.; mem. Am. Physics Soc., Am. Assn. Physics Tchrs. Achievements include research in Thermoacoustic heat transport. Office: Pa State Univ Grad Program Acoustics PO Box 30 State College PA 16804-0030

ATCHLEY, CURTIS LEON, mechanical engineer; b. Lexington, Okla., June 3, 1940; s. Curtis Marvin and Hazel (Franks) A.; m. Barbara Ann Bryant, Feb. 14, 1976; children: Jeffrey Allen, Eric Andrew. BSME, U. Okla., 1970. Engr. Halliburton Oil Svc. Co., Enid, Okla., 1970-71, Tinker AFB, Midwest City, Okla., 1971-79; supervisory gen. engr. Lajes AFB, Azores, Portugal, 1979-80; gen. engr. Hdqrs. USAFE, Ramstein AFB, Fed. Republic Germany, 1980-82, Hdqrs. Air-Edn. and Tng. Command, Randolph AFB, 1985—; mem. staff Air Force Civilian Pers. Ctr., Randolph AFB, Universal City, Tex., 1983-85. U.S. and fgn. patentee in solar tech., U.S. patentee for light intensifying device for cameras and telescopes. Mem. Dem. Nat. Com., 1996. Sgt. USAF, 1964-68. Mem. Amnesty Internat. (freedom writer), Internat. Soc. Poets (life, charter), Nashville Song Writers Assn., Broadcast Music Inc. Avocations: golf, skiing, camping, backpacking, swimming. Home: 7531 Oriental Trl San Antonio TX 78244-2400 Office: Hdqrs AETC Randolph AFB Universal City TX 78150

ATCHLEY, WILLIAM REID, geneticist, evolutionary biologist, educator; b. Stilwell, Okla., Sept. 6, 1942; s. Reid Kenneth and Velma Alice (Mays) A.; m. Wilinda Landon, Sept. 4, 1964; children: Erika Leigh, Kevin Landon. BS, Ea. N.Mex. U., 1964; MA, U. Kans., 1966, PhD, 1969. Postdoctoral fellow U. Melbourne, 1969-70; postdoctoral fellow U. Wis., 1976-77; NSF trainee U. Kans., 1966-69, asst. prof. entomology, 1970-71; asst. prof. biology and stats. Tex. Tech U., Lubbock, 1971-74, assoc. prof., 1974-77; assoc. prof. entomology and genetics U. Wis., Madison, 1977-80, prof. entomology and genetics, 1980-84, prof. genetics, 1984-86; James prof. pure and applied sci. St. Francis Xavier U., Can., 1991; prof. genetics, prof. stats. N.C. State U., Raleigh, 1986-93, William Neal Reynolds prof. genetics and stats., 1993—; head dept. genetics N.C. State U., 1986-90, dir. Ctr. for Quantitative Genetics, 1993—; vis. rsch. fellow U. Melbourne, Australia, 1974; vis. fellow Australian Nat. U., 1980-81. Author: Multivariate Statistical Methods, 1975, Evolution and Speciation, 1981; contbr. numerous articles to profl. jours. NIH postdoctoral fellow, 1977, NSF mid-career fellow, 1989-90, Alfred Sloan Found. fellow, 1993-94; Fulbright scholar, 1969-70; Alexander von Humboldt grantee, 1999—. Fellow AAAS; mem. Soc. Study Evolution (councillor 1980-82, assoc. editor 1984-86), Soc. Systematic Zoology (councillor 1981-83), Am. Soc. Naturalists (v.p. 1986-87). Office: NC State U Dept Genetics Raleigh NC 27695-7614

ATHANASSOULAS, SOTIRIOS (SOTIRIOS OF TORONTO), bishop; b. Epirus, Greece, Feb. 19, 1936; s. George and Anastasia A. B.D., U. Athens, 1961; M.A., U. Montreal Scis. Religieuses, 1971. Ordained priest Greek Orthodox Ch., 1962; priest St. George Ch., Edmonton, Alta., Can., 1962-65, St. George Cathedral, Montreal, Que., Can., 1965-73; consecrated bishop, 1973; bishop of Toronto, Ont., Can., 1979-96; met. archbishop Toronto, 1996—; head Greek Orthodox Ch. of Can., 1979—; mem. archdiocese council Greek Orthodox Archdiocese, 1968-96 , pres. diocesan council, 1974, mem. holy synod, 1977-96 , mem. archdiocese council, 1968, pres. diocesan council, 1974—; mem. exec. com. Can. Council Chs., 1974—; hon. pres. Thalassemia Found., 1975—; mem. Presbyters Council, 1970-73. Vice pres. Christian Pavilion, Expo 67; mem. governing council U. Toronto, 1975-78. Recipient Centennial medal of Can., 1967. Office: Greek Orthodox Metropolis, 86 Overlea Blvd, Toronto, ON Canada M4H 1C6

ATHANS, SISTER MARY CHRISTINE, church history educator; b. Joliet, Ill., Apr. 7, 1932; d. Christophil Nicholas and Mary Elizabeth (Anderson) A. BS in Humanities, Loyola U., Chgo., 1954; MA in History, Cath. U. Am., 1966; MA in Theology, U. San Francisco, 1975; Licentiate in Sacred Theology, Jesuit Sch. Theology, Berkeley, Calif., 1982; PhD in Hist. Theology, Grad. Theol. Union, Berkeley, Calif., 1982. Joined Sisters of Charity of Blessed Virgin Mary Religious Order, 1955. Exec. dir. N. Phoenix Corp. Ministry, 1970-76; asst. acad. dean/dean students Sch. Theology, Claremont, Calif., 1979-80; adj. faculty U. San Francisco and U. Santa Clara, 1980-82; asst. prof. religious studies U. Ill., Urbana-Champaign, 1982-84; prof. ch. history The St. Paul Sem. Sch. of Div., U. St. Thomas, St. Paul, 1984—, full prof. ch. history, 1995—; mem. numerous religious and civic bds. and commns. Author: The Coughlin-Fahey Connection: Father Charles E. Coughlin, Father Denis Fahey C.S.Sp., and Religious Anti-Semitism in the United States, 1938-54, 1991, To Work for the Whole People: The History of St. Paul Seminary, 2000; co-editor: In Service of the Church, 1993; editor: Proceedings of the Ctr. for Jewish-Christian Learning, 1993-96; contbr. articles to profl. jours. and chpts. to books. bd. dirs. Minn. Interreligious Com., Mpls.; trustee Mundelein Coll., Chgo., 1984-87, Grad. Theol. Union, Berkeley, 1978-79. Recipient Humanitarian of Yr. award B'nai B'rith, Phoenix, 1974, Sisterhood award, Nat. Conf. Christians and Jews, 1994; named fellow Inst. for Ecumenical and Cultural Rsch., 1990. Mem. Am. Acad. Religion, Am. Cath. Hist. Assn., Cath. Theol. Soc. Am., U.S. Cath. Hist. Soc., Phi Alpha Theta. Democrat. Office: U St Thomas Sch Div 2260 Summit Ave Saint Paul MN 55105-1010

ATHANSON, MARY CATHERYNE, school system administrator. Area III supt. Pinnellas County Sch. Dist., Gulfport, Fla., 1998—. Office: Pinellas County Sch Dist Office Area III 1001 51st St S Gulfport FL 33707-3638

ATHAS, GUS JAMES, lawyer; b. Chgo., Aug. 6, 1936; s. James G. and Pauline (Parhas) A.; m. Marilyn Carres, July 12, 1964; children: Paula C., James G., Christopher G. BS, U. Ill., 1958; JD cum laude, Loyola U., Chgo., 1965. Bar: Ill. 1965, U.S. Dist. Ct. (no. dist.) Ill. 1965, U.S. Ct. Appeals (7th cir.) 1970. Assoc., Isham, Lincoln & Beale, Chgo., 1965-69; group gen. counsel, asst. sec. ITT, Skokie, Ill., 1969-87; assoc. gen. counsel Itel Corp., Chgo., 1987; sr. v.p., gen. counsel, sec. Eagle Industries Inc., Chgo., 1987-97; exec. v.p. adminstrn., gen. counsel, sec. Falcon Bldg. Products, Inc., Chgo., 1994—; sr. v.p., gen. counsel Great Am. Mgmt. and Investment Inc., Chgo., 1995—; dir. Signet Armorlite, Inc. Contbr. articles to profl. jours. 1st lt. U.S. Army, 1958-62. Mem. ABA, Am. Corp. Counsel Assn., Ill. Bar Assn., Chgo. Bar Assn. Greek Orthodox. Home: 1240 Hawthorne Ln Downers Grove IL 60515-4503 Office: Falcon Bldg Products Inc Sears Tower 233 S Wacker Dr Ste 3500 Chicago IL 60606-6383

ATHERTON, ALFRED LEROY, JR., former foreign service officer; b. Pitts., Nov. 22, 1921; s. Alfred Leroy and Joan (Reed) A.; m. Betty Wylie Kittredge, May 26, 1946; children: Lynne Kittredge, Michael Anton, Reed Wylie. BS, Harvard U., 1943, MA, 1947; PhD (hon.), Muskingum Coll., 1984; spl. student econs., U. Calif. at Berkeley, 1961-62. Joined U.S. Fgn. Service, 1947, accorded rank of career amb., 1981; vice consul Stuttgart, Germany, 1947-50, Bonn, Germany, 1950-52; 2d sec. Damascus, Syria, 1953-56; consul Aleppo, Syria, 1957-58; internat. relations officer Bur. Near Eastern and South Asian Affairs, State Dept., 1959-61; consul Calcutta, India, 1962-65; dep. dir. Office Near Eastern Affairs, State Dept., 1965-66; country dir. Arab States North, State Dept., 1966-67, country dir. Israel and Arab Israel affairs, 1967-69; dep. asst. sec. Bur. Near East and South Asian Affairs, State Dept., 1970-74; asst. sec. Bur. Near East and South Asian Affairs, 1974-78, ambassador-at-large, 1978-79; amb. to Egypt Cairo, 1979-83; dir. gen. Fgn. Service, dir. personnel State Dept., 1983-85; dir. The Harkness Fellowships, 1985-91; vis. Sol M. Linowitz prof. Hamilton Coll., 1988, 92, 94; vis. Cyrus Vance prof. Mt. Holyoke Coll., 1991; vis. prof. Birmingham So. Coll., 1992, 93, 95, 98. Trustee, The Una Chapman Cox Found., 1985-87, chmn. policy coun., 1987-88, exec. dir., 1989-98; pres. Egyptian-Am. C. of C., 1985-87; chmn. N.Y.-Cairo Sister City Com., 1986-98; mem. adv. bd. Hariri Found., 1986—; mem. nat. coun. Near East Found., 1986—; bd. dirs. U.S. New Zealand Coun., 1987—, adv. commn. on Fgn Svc. Pers. System, 1988-89; mem. adv. com. Initiative for Peace and Coop. in Middle East of Search for Common Ground, 1991—, chmn., 1992—. 1st lt. F.A., AUS, 1943-45, ETO. Decorated Air medal, Silver Star; recipient Career Svc. award Nat. Civil Svc. League, 1975, Pres.'s award for disting. fed. civilian svc., 1980, State Dept. Disting. Svc. award, 1985, Wilbur Carr award, 1985, Fgn. Svc. Dir. Gen.'s cup, 1988, commendation for svc. to nation in sense of Senate resolution, 1979. Mem. Am. Fgn. Svc. Assn., Coun. on Fgn. Rels., Am. Acad. Diplomacy, Middle East Inst., Washington Inst. Fgn. Affairs, Harvard Club (N.Y.C. and Washington). Unitarian. Home: Apt 5003 4301 Massachusetts Ave NW Washington DC 20016-5569

ATHERTON, CHARLES HENRY, federal commission administrator; b. Kingston, Pa., June 24, 1932; s. Thomas Henry and Mary A.; m. Mary Bringhurst Davis, Dec. 15, 1967; children: Sarah Scott, Thomas Henry, Charles Henry. BA summa cum laude, Princeton U., 1954, MFA, 1957. Registered architect, D.C. Asst. sec. Fine Arts Commn., Washington, 1960-64, sec., adminstrv. officer, 1964—. Trustee Nat. Child Rsch. Ctr., 1975-79; v.p. Washington Hist. Soc.; bd. dirs. Hist. Am. Bldgs. Survey Found., Navy Art Found., Parks and History Assn.; mem. Citizens Commemorative Coin Adv. Com., 1994—. Lt. (j.g.) USNR, 1957-60. Recipient Martin Luther King Leadership award D.C. Pub. Libr. Sys., 1992, Centennial medal Washington chpt. AIA, 1993. Mem. Potomac Boat Club, Cosmos Club. Home: 3127 Newark St NW Washington DC 20008-3344 Office: Fine Arts Commn 441 F St NW Washington DC 20001-2728

ATHERTON, WILLIAM, actor; b. New Haven, July 30, 1947; s. Robert Atherton Knight and Myrtle (Robison) Raymond; m. Bobbi Goldin, Dec. 8, 1980. BFA, Carnegie-Mellon U., 1969. Film appearances include The Sugarland Express, The Day of the Locust, The Hindenburg, Looking for Mr. Goodbar, Real Genius, Ghostbusters, No Mercy, Die Hard, Die Hard 2: Die Harder, Grim Prairie Tales, Oscar, The Pelican Brief, Frank and Jesse, Biodome; stage appearances include title roles in The Basic Training of Pavlo Hummel and Suggs (Drama Desk award, Outer Circle Critics award, two Obie nominations, Theatre World award), role of Ronnie in original prodn. of House of Blue Leaves, Kennedy Ctr. prodn. The Scarecrow, Misalliance. Broadway prodn. The American Clock, The Caine Mutiny Court Martial; TV appearances include mini-series Centennial, The House of Mirth, Tomorrow's Child; series The Equalizer; numerous other made-for-TV movies; also actor, singer in musical comedies; sang theme song What'll I Do? in movie The Great Gatsby.

ATHREYA, BALU H., pediatrics educator; b. Tamil Nadu, India, July 7, 1933; came to U.S., 1958; s. Hariharan and Meenakshi Athreya; m. Ramaa Devi, July 1, 1965; children: Bama, Hari, Sheela. Degree in sci., Loyola Coll, Madras, India, 1951; MD, Madras Med. Coll., 1956. Diplomate Am. Bd. Pediat., Am. Bd. Pediat. Rheumatology. Intern Binghamton (N.Y.) Gen. Hosp., 1958-59; resident in internal medicine Childrens Hosp., Phila., 1959-60; clin. dir. Children's Seashore House, Atlantic City, N.J., 1970-86; from asst. prof. to prof. pediat. U. Pa., Phila., 1970-96; prof. pediat. Thomas Jefferson U., Phila., 1996—. Author: Differential Diagnosis of Pediatrics, 1970, Pediatric Physical Diagnosis, 1983. Recipient Earl Brewer award Am. Juvenile Arthritis Orgn., 1991, Joseph Lee Hollander award Ea. Pa. chpt. The Arthritis Found., 1997. Avocations: music, literature, travel, photography. Office: Dupont Hosp for Children PO Box 269 1600 Rockland Rd Wilmington DE 19899-3607

ATIBA, JOSHUA OLAJIDE O., internist, pharmacologist, oncologist, educator; b. Enugu, Nigeria, July 6, 1956; s. Joseph Ojo and Abigail Olayo A.; m. Stella N. Mordi, June 26, 1981; children: April, Annamarie, Joseph. MD, U. Lagos, Nigeria, 1979; MHA, St. Mary's Coll., 1999. Diplomate Am. Bd. Internal Medicine, Am. Bd. Oncology. Rotating intern Ahmadu Bello U. Tchg. Hosp., Kaduna, Nigeria, 1979-80; resident in internal medicine Lagos U. Tchg. Hosp., 1981-83; fellow in med. oncology Cancer Control Agy., Vancouver, B.C., Can., 1988-90; fellow in clin. pharmacology Stanford U. Med. Ctr., Palo Alto, Calif., 1983-86; pvt. practice Irvine, Calif.; dir. clin. investigation U. Calif., Irvine, 1991-95; mem. U. Calif. Irvine Med. Ctr., Orange, North Bay Med. Ctr., Fairfield, Calif., Vaca Valley Hosp., Vacaville, Calif.; asst. prof. medicine, pharmacology U. Calif., Irvine. Med. dir. North Bay Hospice, Fairfield, Calif.; pres. Newport Oncology and Healthcare. Fellow Royal Coll. Physicians Can.; mem. ACP, AMA, Am. Fedn. for Clin. Rsch., Am. Soc. of Clin. Pharmacology and Therapeutics, Am. Soc. Clin. Oncology, Calif. Med. Assn., Solano County Med. Soc. (sec./treas.), KC (knight 1997). Republican. Roman Catholic. Office: North Bay Cancer Ctr 1860 Pennsylvania Ave Ste 230 Fairfield CA 94533-3550

ATIEH, MICHAEL GERARD, accountant; b. Paterson, N.J., Aug. 8, 1953; s. Michael and Evelyn (Makoujy) A.; m Mary P. Higgins, May 9, 1976; children: Allison, Michael, Steven, Kevin. BA in Acctg. and Econs., Upsala Coll., 1975. CPA, N.J. Audit mgr. Arthur Young & Co., Newark, 1975-81; dir. acctg. stds. Merck & Co., Whitehouse Station, N.J., 1981-82; dir. acctg., 1983-86, dir. investor rels., 1986-88; v.p. govt. rels. Merck & Co., Rahway, N.J., 1988-90, treas., 1990-93; v.p. pub. affairs, 1994; sr. v.p. Merck-Medco, 1994—; bd. dirs. Ace Ltd. Mem. AICPA, N.J. State Soc. CPAs. Republican. Roman Catholic. Avocation: golf. Office: Merck & Co One Merck Dr Whitehouse Station NJ 08889

ATIGBI, KOFITUNDE JOLOMI, telecommunications professional; b. Bklyn., July 10, 1961; s. Ignatius Amaduwa and Joan Akwasiba (Derby) A.; m. Jueth McIntosh. Student, Thomas Edison State Coll., Trenton, N.J. Mktg. rep. Radio Shack Computers, N.Y.C., 1984-86; dir. recruitment Robert Fiance Co., N.Y.C., 1986-88; ptnr. Ednl. Vocat. Alliance, Bklyn., 1987-89; rep. Nynex, N.Y.C., 1988-94; field technician Bell Atlantic, 1994—; sales adminstr. Wireless Cable of N.Y., L.I., 1989-90; mem. network mktg. staff KT Svcs., East Orange, N.J., 1991-94; owner Top Class Cleaning Svc., Selden, N.Y., 1994—; cons. Higher Ednl. Devel. Fund, Bronx, N.Y., 1988-90. Recipient Community Svc. award Holy Spirit Ch., Bronx, 1979, St. Augustine Ch., Bronx, 1981. Mem. Internat. Assn. Approved Basketball Ofcls., Sports United Boro-Wide Alliance Inc. (Most Improved Ofcl. 1989), Inst. of Inspection Cleaning and Restoration Certification, Assn. Specialists in Cleaning and Restoration. Avocations: sports, officiating. Office: Bell Atlantic 84 King St New York NY 10014-4807

ATIYAH, SIR MICHAEL FRANCIS, mathematician; b. London, Apr. 22, 1929; s. Edward Selim and Jean (Levens) A.; m. Lily J. Brown, July 30, 1955; children: John, David, Robin. BA, Trinity Coll., Cambridge, 1952, PhD, 1955; DSc (hon.), Warwick and Bonn, 1968, U. Durham, 1977, U. Dublin, U. Chgo., Cambridge (Eng.) U.; others. Fellow Trinity Coll., Cambridge, 1954-58, 97—, hon. fellow, 1976-97, master, 1990-97; hon. prof. dept. math. U. Scotland, Edinburgh, 1997—; lectr., fellow Pembroke Coll., Cambridge, 1958-61, hon. fellow, 1983; Commonwealth Fund fellow Princeton, 1955-56, prof. Inst. Advanced Study, 1969-72; reader Oxford U., 1961-63, Saviliam prof. geometry, 1963-69, Royal Soc. rsch. prof., fellow St. Catherine's Coll., 1973-90, hon. fellow, 1991; dir. Isaac Newton Inst. for Math. Scis., Cambridge, Eng., 1990-96; chancellor Leicester U., 1995—; pres. Pugwash Confs. Sci. and World Affairs, 1997—. Author: K-Theory, 1966, Commutative Algebra, 1969; contbr. articles to math. jours., also collected works, 1987. Decorated Knight; recipient Fields medal Internat. Congress Mathematicians, Moscow, 1996, DeMorgan medal London Math. Soc., 1980, Feltrinelli prize Accademia Nazionale dei Lincei, 1982, King Faisal Found. Internat. prize for sci., Saudi Arabia, 1987, Order of Merit, 1993. Fellow Royal Soc. (pres. 1990-95, Royal medal 1969, Copley medal 1988), Royal Soc. Edinburgh (hon.), Royal Instn. (hon.), Royal Acad. Engring. (hon.); mem. Internat. Math. Union (exec. com. 1966-74), Math. Assn. (pres. 1981), London Math. Soc. (pres. 1975-77), Nat. Acad. Scis. U.S.A. (fgn.), Leopoldina Acad. (fgn.), Am. Acad. Arts and Scis. (fgn.), Swedish Royal Acad. (fgn.), Academie des Scis. (fgn.), Royal Irish Acad. (fgn.), Am. Philos. Soc. (fgn., Benjamin Franklin medal 1993), Third World Acad. Scis., Indian Nat. Sci. Acad. (fgn.), Chinese Acad. Sci. (hon. prof.), Ukrainian Acad. Scis. (fgn.), Venezuelan Acad. Sci., Australian Acad. Sci., Russian Acad. Sci., Georgian Acad. Sci., Order Andres Bello. Office: James Clerk Maxwell Bldg, Dept Math/Stats Mayfield Rd, Edinburgh EH9 3JZ, Scotland Home: 3/8 West Grange Gardens, Edinburgh EH9 2RA, Scotland

ATKIN, ANDREW SCOTT, artist; b. San Antonio, Mar. 16, 1955; s. Robert Byron and Jean Elizabeth (Bell) A.; m. Margaret Ethel Peyronel, Aug. 10, 1997; 1 child, Ian Scott. BFA with honors, Ea. Ky. U., 1981; MA in Fine Arts, Western Carolina U., 1988pol. Represented by Gallery 9 Boone and Blowing Rock, N.C. Exhibit in solo shows at Thomas Wolfe Auditorium and Gallery, Asheville, N.C., Broadway Arts Complex, Asheville, Caldwell Arts Coun., Lenoir, N.C., Rococo Fish Art Gallery, Charlotte, N.C., numerous others; exhibited in group shows including Am. Soc. Interior Designers Gallery, Washington, Earth Art, Sawtooth Bldg. Art Galleries, Winston-Salem, RJR Art Galleries, Winston-Salem, Ctr. for Creative Leadership, Greensboro, N.C., Dickson Found. Gallery, Charlotte, McDonald's Corp., Valdese, N.C.; works in permanent collections at Western N.C. Diocese of the Episc. Ch., Ch. of the Ascension, Hickory, N.C., Suzuki Sch. Arts, Hickory, Caldwell C.C., Hudson, N.C., Caldwell County Sch. Sys., Burke County Coun. of the Arts, Jailhouse Art Gallery, Morganton, N.C., Mercy Children's Home, Chgo., Sipes Orchard Children's Home, Convover, N.C., Lincolnton (N.C.) Arts Coun., numerous pvt./corp. collections. Recipient 34 awards for various categories in art including 10 first place awards, 4 purchase awards, 4 best-in-show awards, 2 awards in excellence, Bernard Industries Award in Excellence in the Visual Arts, 1995, Satie Broyhill award, 1993; Nancy T. Alexander Emerging Artist grantee, Caldwell Arts Coun., 1992, 93. Mem. Caldwell Arts Coun., Assoc. Artists of Winston-Salem, the Other Group, N.C. Coun. of the Arts. Republican. Methodist. Avocations: hunting, fishing, gardening. Home and Office: PO Box 957 4564 Carswell Rd Valdese NC 28690-9647

ATKIN, GARY EUGENE, lawyer; b. Salt Lake City, Oct. 7, 1946; s. Henry Eugene and Dolores Heckman (Dykes) A.; m. Marsha Selin, June 12, 1967; children: Kathryn Dawn, Kenneth Eugene. BS in Acctg., U. Utah, 1967, JD, 1970. Bar: Utah 1970, U.S. Dist. Ct. Utah 1970, U.S. Ct. Appeals (10th cir.) 1978, U.S. Supreme Ct. 1978. Assoc. Rawlings, Roberts & Black, Salt Lake City, 1970-74; assoc. counsel Utah State Legislature, Salt Lake City, 1974-79; ptnr. Gustin, Adams, Kesting & Liapis, Salt Lake City, 1979-81, of counsel, 1981-82; ptnr. Atkin & Anderson, Salt Lake City, 1982-91, Atkin & Assocs., Salt Lake City, 1992—. Mem. Assn. Trial Lawyers Am., Fed. Bar Assn., Utah Trial Lawyers Assn. (bd. dirs. 1980-90, pres. 1984-85). Avocation: announcer. Home: 4498 Adonis Dr Salt Lake City UT 84124-3923 Office: Atkin & Assocs 311 S State St Ste 380 Salt Lake City UT 84111-5215

ATKIN, J. MYRON, science educator; b. Bklyn., Apr. 6, 1927; s. Charles Z. and Esther (Jaffe) A.; m. Ann Spiegel, Dec. 25, 1947; children—David, Ruth, Jonathan. B.S., CCNY, 1947; M.A., NYU, 1948, Ph.D., 1956. Tchr. sci. Ramaz High Sch., N.Y.C., 1948-50; tchr. elem. sch. sci. Great Neck (N.Y.) pub. schs., 1950-55; prof. sci. edn. Coll. Edn., U. Ill., Urbana, 1955-79, assoc. dean, 1966-70, dean, 1970-79; prof. Sch. Edn., Stanford (Calif.) U., 1979—, dean, 1979-86; cons. OECD, Paris, Nat. Inst. Edn.; mem. edn. adv. bd. NSF, 1973-76, 84-86, vice-chmn., 1984-85, sr. advisor, 1986-87; mem. Ill. Tchr. Certification Bd., 1973-76; Sir John Adams lectr. U. London Inst. Edn., 1980, vis. scholar com. scholarly commn. Nat. Acad. Scis., People's Republic China, 1987; math. sci. edn. bd. NRC, 1985-89, nat. com. sci. edn. standards and assessment, 1992-96, com. on sci. edn. K-12, 1996—, vice chair, 1998—; invited lectr. Nat. Sci. Coun., Taiwan, 1989—. Author children's sci. textbooks. Served with USNR, 1945-46. Fellow AAAS (v.p. sect. Q 1973-74); mem. Coun. Elem. Sci. Internat. (pres. 1969-70), Am. Ednl. Rsch. Assn. (exec. bd. 1972-75, chmn. govt. and profl. liaison com.), Sigma Xi (chair com. on sci., math. and engring. edn.). Office: Sch Edn Stanford U Stanford CA 94305

ATKINS, AARON ARDENE, lawyer; b. Du Quoin, Ill., July 17, 1960; s. Thornton A. and Venita Lee (Thornton) A. BA, So. Ill. U., 1982, JD, 1985. Bar: Ill. 1985, U.S. Dist. Ct. (so. dist.) Ill. 1986. Ptnr. Miller & Atkins, Du Quoin, 1985-87; pvt. practice Du Quoin, 1987—; city atty. City of Du Quoin, Ill.; village atty. Village Dowell, Ill.; atty. Consol. Pub. Water Dist., Perry County Housing Authority, 1995—. Bd. dirs. Boys Club, Du Quoin, 1986-87, United Way, Du Quoin, 1987-94; cons. Sacred Heart Endowment Fund, Du Quoin, 1987-94; active in Sacred Heart Parish Coun., 1987-94, organist, 1974—. Mem. Ill. State Bar Assn., Perry County Bar Assn. (sec.-treas. 1995—), Du Quoin Bus. Assn., K.C. (4th degree), Elks (organist Du Quoin club 1992-94). Roman Catholic. Avocation: antiques. Home: 2372 Magnolia Rd Du Quoin IL 62832-9755 Office: 18 N Oak St Du Quoin IL 62832-1615

ATKINS, C(ARL) CLYDE, federal judge; b. Washington, Nov. 23, 1914; s. C. C. and Marguerite (Criste) A.; m. Esther Castillo, Jan 18, 1937; children: Julie A. Landrigan, Carla A. Schulte (dec.), Carl Clyde (dec.). Student, U. Miami, Fla., 1931-32; LLB, U. Fla., 1936; LLD, Barry Coll. (now Barry U.), Miami Shores, 1966; JD, U. Fla., 1967; LLD (hon.), U. Miami, Miami Shores, 1970; LLD, St. Thomas of Villanova U. (formerly Biscayne Coll.), Miami, 1970. Bar: Fla. 1936. Pvt. practice Stuart, Fla., 1936-41, Miami, Fla., 1941-66; ptnr. firm Walton, Lantaff, Schroeder, Atkins, Carson & Wahl (and predecessors), 1941-66; judge U.S. Dist. Ct. (so. dist.) Fla., 1966—, chief judge, 1977-82, sr. judge, 1983—; founder-trustee Lawyers Title Guaranty Fund (now Atty.'s Title Ins. Fund, Inc.), 1948-66, treas., 1963-66. Contbr. articles to profl. jours. Pres. St. Augustine Diocesan Union of Holy Name Societies, 1950-51, Miami Archdiocesan Coun. Cath. Men, 1959-70. Recipient Outstanding Cath. award NCCJ, 1959, Lifetime Achievement award Attys. divsn. Greater Miami Jewish Fed., 1997; establishment of C. Clyde Atkins Moot Ct. Series by U. Miami Sch. Law, 1997. Fellow Am. Coll. Trial Lawyers; mem. ABA, (jud. adminstrv. divsn. Ho. of Dels., 1960-66, 79-80), Dade County Bar Assn. (pres. 1953-54), The Fla. Bar (bd. govs. 1954-59, pres. 1960-61), Nat. Conf. Fed. Trial Judges (chmn. exec. com. 1975-77, del. Jud. Adminstrn. Coun. 1979-82), Nat. Conf. Christians and Jews (chmn. Miami region 1989-95), Miami Kiwanis Club (past dir.), Coral Gables Country Club, Century Club of Coral Gables (past dir.), Serra Club (pres. 1965-66, 91-92), Tau Kappa Alpha, Phi Kappa Tau, Phi Alpa Delta. Office: US Dist Ct Rm 417 301 N Miami Ave Miami FL 33128-7705

ATKINS, CLAYTON H., family physician, epidemiologist, educator; b. Beech Grove, Ind., Nov. 12, 1944; s. Amos H. Atkins and Edythe E. (Dale) Heneghan; m. Carole A. Kirlin, Aug. 2, 1974; children: Brenda M. Spencer, Craig N., Angela C. AB in Chemistry, Ind. U., Bloomington, 1965, MAT in Chemistry, 1967; MD, Ind. U., Indpls., 1969; BS in Math. summa cum laude with highest honors, Butler U., 1980. Diplomate Am. Bd. Family Practice. Rotating intern Meth. Hosp. Ind. Inc., Indpls., 1969-70; pvt. practice Greenwood, Ind., 1970-94; mem. active staff family practice dept., 1970—, hosp. epidemiologist, 1989—; with med. exec. commn. St. Francis Hosp. and Health Ctrs., Beech Grove, 1993-96; pres. med. staff St. Francis Hosp. and Health Ctrs., Beech Grove, Ind., 1995; mem. exec. mgmt. com. St. Francis Hosp. and Health Ctrs., Beech Grove, 1995-96; pvt. practice associated with St. Francis Med. Group, Beech Grove, Ind., 1995—; mem. courtesy med. staff family practice dept. Cmty. Hosp. South, Indpls., 1970—; instr. NSF math. for high sch. tchrs. Ind. U., Bloomington, 1966-67; instr. microgiology Ind. Ctrl. Coll. (now U. Indpls.), 1968; adj. asst. prof. Butler U. Cll. Pharmacy, Indpls., 1991-95; mem. Ops. Coun. St. Francis Med. Group, 1998-99, Mgmt. Coun. 1999—. With USAFR, 1971-77; maj. med. corps, 1991—. Fellow Am. Acad. Family Physicians; mem. AMA, Ind. State Med. Assn., Inpls. Med. Soc., Assn. for Practitioners in Infection Control and Epidemiology, Epidemiology Inc., Soc. for Hosp. Epidemiology in Am., Math. Assn. Am., Sigma Xi, Phi Kappa Phi, Phi Delta Kappa, Alpha Epsilon Delta, Phi Lambda Upsilon, Phi Eta Sigma, Mu Alpha Theta. Avocations: astronomy, cosmology, mathematics, gardening, mountain hiking. Home: 7610 W Banta Woods Dr Bargersville IN 46106 Office: 8778 Madison Ave Ste 200 Indianapolis IN 46227-7202

ATKINS, DALE MORRELL, retired physician; b. Somerset, Colo., Jan. 20, 1922; s. James Perry and Lura May (Morrell) A.; m. Loretta Ilene Davidson, June 20, 1943 (dec.); children—Loretta, Linda, Peter, John. B.A., U. Colo., 1943, M.D., 1945, M.S., 1953. Intern Mass. Meml. Hosp., 1945-46; resident medicine Colo. U. Sch. Medicine, 1948-50, resident urology, 1950-53; pvt. practice genitourinary surgery Denver, 1953-96; Mem. bd. regents U. Colo., 1963-74. Served to capt., M.C. AUS, 1946-48. Mem. Phi Beta Kappa. Home: 3860 S Dahlia St Denver CO 80237-1004

ATKINS, DIXIE LEE, critical care nurse; b. Elkin, N.C., Oct. 8, 1953; d. Charles Lee and Betty Lou (Southard) Cook; m. Ronnie Steven Atkins, Aug. 30, 1984; children: Sarah Kathryn, Carl Steven, William Shane. AD in Applied Sci., Surry C.C., Dobson, 1973; student, St. Joseph's Coll., North Windham, Maine, 1990—. Cert. provider ACLS, NRP, Am. Heart Assn. Indsl. nurse Brown-Wooten Mills Inc., Mount Airy, N.C.; relief charge nurse pediatrics Forsyth Meml. Hosp., Winston-Salem, N.C., 1973-78; charge nurse emergency rm. No. Hosp. Surry County, Mount Airy, 1979—; nursing supr. No. Hosp. of Surry County, Mount Airy, 1995—; instr., CEN, basic trauma life support, CPR; mobile intensive care nurse; provider advanced cardiac life support, PALS; provider NRP; neonatal recussitation provider; part-time instr. Surry C.C.; profl. photographer Images Studio, Dobson, N.C. Mem. Surry County chpt. MADD; bd. dirs. Dobson Rescue Squad; chairperson Surry Nursing Domiciliary Home Cmty. Adv. Com.; vol. ARC. Named Vol. of Yr. Surry County, 1999. Mem. Emergency Nurses Assn. Home: PO Box 992 407 Marion St Dobson NC 27017-8473

ATKINS, HONEY JEAN, retired business executive; b. Chgo., Mar. 6, 1932; d. Anthony Theophane and Mary Jean (Barrett) Shelvis; m. Robert Claremore Atkins, Aug. 30, 1975; stepchildren: Brett, Cary, Dean, Dana, Christopher, Mary Clare, Patrick. Grad., Rome City H.S., Rome City, Ind., 1948. Mgr. Pacific Telesis, Santa Ana, Calif., 1956-82. Commr. cultural commn. City of La Quinta (Calif.), 1994-98; mem. adv. com. Riverside County Free Libr., La Quinta, 1995-97; mem. adv. bd. CVC Concert Assn., 1995—; bd. dirs. Friends of Libr., v.p., 1993—. Named Citizen of Yr., La Quinta C. of C., 1996, Woman of Distinction, Soroptimists, 1995. Mem. La Quinta Arts League (pres., 1995-97), La Quinta Arts Found. (bd. dirs. 1995—), La Quinta Hist. Soc. (fundraising chair 1994-95), Round Table West (founder Desert chpt., chair), La Quinta On Stage (pres.). Home: 52470 Avenida Madero La Quinta CA 92253-3315

ATKINS, PETER ALLAN, lawyer; b. N.Y.C., June 29, 1943; m. Lorraine Marilyn Feuerstadt, Apr. 3, 1966; children: Aileen Debra, Karen Jennifer. BA magna cum laude, CUNY, 1965; LLB cum laude, Harvard U., 1968. Bar: N.Y. 1969. Assoc. Skadden, Arps, Slate, Meagher & Flom LLP, N.Y.C., 1968-74, ptnr., 1975—; mem. dean's adv. com. Harvard Law Sch.; bd. dirs. A Better Chance, Inc. Contbr. articles to profl. jours. Mem. ABA,

N.Y. State Bar Assn., Assn. of Bar of City of N.Y. Office: Skadden Arps Slate Meagher & Flom LLP 919 3rd Ave New York NY 10022-3902

ATKINS, PHYLLIS HALSEY, federal judge. Apptd. magistrate judge U.S. Dist. Ct. Nev., 1982. Fax: (702) 784-5326. Office: Fed Bldg and Courthouse 400 S Virginia St Reno NV 89501-2193

ATKINS, RICHARD BART, film, television producer; b. Paterson, N.J., May 11, 1951; s. S. Stephen and Alice B. (Stein) A.; m. Joanna Pang; 1 child, David. AB in Polit. Sci., Princeton U., 1973. With Cadence Industries, N.Y.C., 1973-74; mgr. TV program devel. Benton & Bowles, N.Y.C., 1977-79, mgr. daytime programming, 1980; v.p. prodn. Telecom Entertainment, N.Y.C., 1981-83; pres. Atkins Pictures Inc./A-Films, Florham Park, N.J., 1984—; programming and prodn. cons. Hearst Entertainment, Whittle Communications, D'Arcy Masius Benton & Bowles, King World Prodns., 1989-91, Quartier Latin, Paris, 1992, TeleVest, 1997-98. Prodr. (TV films) Murder in Coweta County, 1983, The Gift of Love: A Christmas Story, 1983, Trapped in Silence, 1986; exec. in charge prodn. About Sarah, 1998; prodr., writer (videocassette) Knowing Childbirth, 1985; prodr., writer (feature film) Forced March, 1989; producer: (feature film) Asunder, 1998; dir. (documentary) Mongolia, 1995; author: Method to the Madness: Hollywood Explained, 1975, (musical plays) Getting to Know You, 1994, 97, In the Mirror, 1995, Independence, 1996. Mem. Friar's Club, Princeton Club. Jewish. Avocations: golf, computers. Home and Office: A-Films 149 Ridgedale Ave Florham Park NJ 07932-1708

ATKINS, RONALD RAYMOND, lawyer; b. Kingston, N.Y., Mar. 8, 1933; s. A. Raymond and Charlotte S. A.; m. Mary-Elizabeth Empringham, June 23, 1956; children: Peter Herrick, Timothy Barnard, Suzanne Elizabeth. BS in Econs., U. Pa., 1954; JD, Columbia U., 1959. Bar: N.Y. 1959. Assoc. Pell, Butler, Curtis & LeViness, N.Y.C., 1959-61, ptnr., 1962-67; ptnr. Bisset & Atkins, N.Y.C., 1967—, also Greenwich, Conn., 1982—; also of counsel Davidson, Dawson & Clark, LLP, N.Y.C.; trustee Mianus Gorge Preserve, Inc., chmn., 1984-94. 1st lt. U.S. Army, 1954-56. Fellow Frick Collection, Piermont Morgan Libr.; mem. ABA, N.Y. State Bar Assn., Assn. Bar City N.Y. Republican. Episcopalian. Club: University (N.Y.C.), Grolier Club (N.Y.C.), Field Club (Greenwich, Conn.), U. Pa. Club (N.Y.C.). Home: Hobby Hill Farm Mianus River Rd Bedford NY 10506 also: 777 North St Greenwich CT 06831-3105

ATKINS, VICTOR KENNICOTT, JR., investment banker; b. Seattle, Feb. 8, 1945; s. Victor Kennicott and Elizabeth (Tanner) A. AB, Harvard U., 1967, MBA, 1972. Assoc. Blyth Eastman Dillon & Co., N.Y.C., 1972-75, v.p., 1976-78, 1st v.p., 1978-79; 1st v.p. E.F. Hutton & Co., N.Y.C., 1979-81, sr. v.p., 1981-84; pres. Covington Ptnrs., 1984-85; pres. Equity Income Ptnrs. Capital Corp., Southampton, 1987-94, also bd. dirs.; chmn. Polaris Industries Capital Corp., Southampton, 1987-94, also dir.; pres., dir. Am. Nat. Security Inc., Omaha, 1992-95; internat. adv. bd. Laidlaw Holdings, Inc., N.Y.C., 1995-96. Lt. USNR, 1967-70, Vietnam. Decorated Bronze Star, Cross of Gallantry Republic of Vietnam. Mem. The Brook Club (N.Y.C.), Southampton Club, Nat. Golf Links, Pacific Union Club (San Francisco), Bohemian Club (San Francisco), Meadow Club of Southampton, The Valley Club (Montecito). Home: PO Box 310 Boyeson Rd Southampton NY 11969-0310 Office: 33 Flying Point Rd Ste 219 Southampton NY 11968-5276

ATKINS, WILLIAM ALLEN, academic administrator; b. St. Louis, Sept. 19, 1934; s. William Allen and Nancy Lou (Hunter) A.; m. Joan Markmann, Feb. 6, 1954 (div. Feb. 25, 1977); children: Andrew Bennett, Stephen Hunter; m. Maxine Stegman, Apr. 6, 1977. BA, U. Denver, 1955; MA in Edn., Washington U., 1958; CAS, Harvard U., 1962, EdD, 1965. Cert. Supt., N.Y., Mass., Vt. Elem. tchr. Univ. (Mo.) City Pub. Schs., 1956-61; asst. supt. Williamstown (Mass.) Pub. Schs., 1963-65; supt. Rutland (Vt.) Pub. Schs., 1965-68; mgr. Gen. Learning Corp., Washington, 1968-71; assoc. dean Hofstra U. Sch. Edn., Hempstead, N.Y., 1971-77; exec. dir. Sexton Ednl. Ctr., Massapequa, N.Y., 1977-82; dir. Queensborough Community Coll., Bayside, N.Y., 1982-85; exec. dir. S.I. Continuum of Edn., Inc., 1985-90; asst. dean Nassau Community Coll., Garden City, N.Y., 1990-92; v.p. Nassau Community Coll., Garden City, 1992-93, exec. asst. to pres., 1993-95, assoc. dean for acad. affairs, 1995—; adj. prof. in field; edn. dir. Episcopal Diocese L.I., Garden City, 1973-77; pres. N.Y. State Coun. for Resource Devel., 1994-96; dir. region II Nat. Coun. Resource Devel., 1996-98. Co-author: Developing An Educationally Accountable Program, 1973. Chair United Way, Garden City, 1972-77; bd. dirs. St. Mary's and St. Paul Episcopal Schs., Garden City, 1973-77, Rutland (Vt.) Hosp., 1965-68, Urban League L.I., 1994—; v.p. fin. Northgate Homeowners Assn., 1993—; treas. Wantagh Jewish Ctr., v.p., 1995-97. Recipient Faculty Disting. Svc. award Hofstra U., 1977, Internat. Reading Assn., 1987, Presdl. award L.I. Univ., 1989, Disting. Kappan award, 1989. Mem. NEA, Am. Assn. Sch. Adminstrs., Coun. for Resource Devel., Kappa Delta Pi (faculty sponsor 1971-77), Phi Delta Kappa (pres. 1989-90). Democrat. Jewish. Avocations: reading, photography, travel, golf. Home: 8 Northgate Ct Melville NY 11747-3046 Office: Nassau Community Coll Garden City NY 11530-6793

ATKINS, WILLIAM AUSTIN, SR. (BILL ATKINS), former state legislator; b. Tate, Ga., Aug. 16, 1933; s. Austin and Gladys Atkins; m. Mary Jo Ellerbee; children: Chip, Paige. BS in Pharmacy, Mercer U., 1954. Former owner Atkins Pharmacy, Smyrna, Ga.; mem. Ga. Ho. of Reps., 1982-94, mem. appropriations, regulated beverages and industry coms.; dir. Drugs and Narcotics Agy. State of Ga., 1994—; past chair Cobb County Joint House and Senate Legis. Delegation; past chmn. Ga. State Bd. Pharmacy. Leader, vocalist Bill Atkins Band. Past mem. adminstrv. bd. 1st United Meth. Ch.; bd. dirs. Mercer U. Sch. Pharmacy; mem. governing bd. Brawner Hosp., 1993-96; mem. long-range planning bd. Smyrna Hosp., 1993-96. Recipient Appreciation plaque Ga. div. Am. Cancer Soc., 1991, Legislator of Yr. Friendship award Personal Care Homes of Ga., 1991, Liberty Bell award Cobb County Bar Assn., 1991, Pharmacist of Yr. in Ga. award, Phi Delta Chi, 1978, One of a Kind award Cobb Clean Commn., 1992, Meritorious Svc. award Mercer U., So. Sch. Pharmacy, 1992, others. Mem. Ga. Pharm. Assn. (award for dedication and svc. to profession of pharmacy 1986, Cmty. Svc. award 1997), Ga. Pharmacists Assn. (past bd. dirs.), Ga. Assn. Chiefs of Police, 7th Dist. Pharmacists Assn. (past pres.), Atlanta Metropol, Cobb C. of C., Moose (named Mr. Cobb County 1993). Home: 4719 Windsor Dr SW Smyrna GA 30082-4465

ATKINSON, A. KELLEY, insurance company executive; b. Tulsa, Okla., July 7, 1947; s. Milton A. Atkinson and Helen G. Brower; m. Patricia L. Morton, June 28, 1969 (dec. 1991); children: Gregory, Brent; m. Pamela A. Bender, Feb. 14, 1993. BS, Tex. Christian U., 1969; MBA, Ariz. State U., 1972. Sales rep. Mallinckrodt, Inc., Saint Louis, 1972-73, assoc. product mgr., 1973-74, regional sales mgr., 1974-76, mgr. market rsch. & data systems, 1976-77; mgr. product mktg. Intermedics, Inc., Freeport, Tex., 1977-79, dir. mktg., 1979-82, v.p. mktg., 1982-83; pres., COO Neuro Systems, Inc., Garland, Tex., 1983; pres. BoMed Mfg., Irvine, Calif., 1984; pres., CEO Physicians Health Plan Utah, Salt Lake City, 1984-87, United Health Care Ga., Atlanta, 1987—; Pres. Ga. Assn. HMOs, Atlanta, 1989, 94-96; adj. prof. Mercer U., Atlanta, 1990-92. Treas. Windward Cmty. Svcs. Assn., Alpharetta, Ga., 1995-96. Avocations: computer science, fly fishing. Office: United Healthcare Ga 2970 Clairmont Rd NE Ste 300 Atlanta GA 30329-4415*

ATKINSON, ARTHUR JOHN, JR., clinical pharmacologist, educator; b. Chgo., Mar. 22, 1938; s. Arthur John and Inez (Hill) A.; m. Mary Jo Yunker, May 12, 1984; AB in Chemistry, Harvard U., 1959; MD, Cornell U., 1963. Intern and asst. resident in medicine Mass. Gen. Hosp., Boston, 1963-65, chief resident and Howard Carroll fellow in medicine Passavant Meml. Hosp., Chgo., instr. in medicine Northwestern U., Chgo., 1967-68; fellow in clin. pharmacology U. Cin., 1968-69, asst. prof. pharmacology, 1969; vis. scientist dept. toxicology Karolinska Inst., Stockholm, Sweden, 1970; asst. prof. medicine and pharmacology Northwestern U., Chgo., 1970-73, assoc. prof., 1973-76, prof., 1976-94; corp. v.p. clin. devel. and med. affairs Upjohn Co., 1994-95; v.p. clin. R & D and worldwide clin. pharmacology Pharmacia & Upjohn, Inc., 1995-96; adj. prof. pharmacology Ctr. for Drug Devel. Sci., Georgetown U., 1996—; sr. advisor clin. pharmacology to dir. clin. ctr. NIH, 1998—; with NIH, USPHS, 1965-67. Recipient Faculty Devel. award in clin. pharmacology Pharm. Mfrs. Assn., 1970-72; Burroughs Wellcome scholar in clin. pharmacology, 1972-77. Fellow ACP; mem. Ctrl. Soc. Clin. Rsch., Am. Soc. for Clin. Investigation, Am. Soc. Pharmacology and Exptl. Therapeutics (Harry Gold award 1989), Am. Soc. Clin. Pharmacology and Therapeutics (pres. 1995-96, Rawls Palmer award 1983), Am. Bd. Clin. Pharmacology (pres. 1996-98), Assn. Am. Physicians, Chgo. Soc. Internal Medicine (pres. 1984-85), Alpha Omega Alpha. Clubs: Chgo. Yacht. Mem. editl. bd. jours. Rational Drug Therapy, 1972-83, Clin. Pharmacology and Therapeutics, 1973—, Pharm. Revs., 1977—, Therapeutic Drug Monitoring, 1979-94. Home: 5000 Battery Ln PH - 204 Bethesda MD 20814-2655

ATKINSON, BARBARA FRAJOLA, pathologist; b. Mpls., Oct. 19, 1942. BA, Coll. of Wooster, Ohio, 1964; MD, Thomas Jefferson U., 1974. Diplomate Am. Bd. Pathology in clin. and anatomic pathology and cytopathology; lic. physician, Pa. Intern in clin. and anatomic pathology U. Pa., Phila., 1974-75, resident, 1975-78, NIH pulmonary tng. fellow in pulmonary pathology, 1976-77, NIH rsch. fellow in pulmonary pathology, 1977-78; asst. instr. pathology dept. pathology U. Pa. Sch. Medicine, Phila., 1974-78, asst. prof. dept. pathology and lab. medicine, 1978-84, assoc. prof., 1985-87; mem. pathology grad. group U. Pa. Sch. Medicine, 1985-87; prof., chair dept. pathology and lab. medicine Med. Coll. of Pa. and Hahnemann U., Phila., 1987-94; sr. mem. Ctr. for Gerontol. Rsch. Med. Coll. Pa., Phila., 1994-96; Annenberg dean Med Coll Pa and Hahnemann Sch. Medicine MCP Hahnemann Sch. Med. Allegheny U. Health Scis., 1996-99; assoc. scientist Wistar Inst. Anatomy and Biology, 1983-87; mem. staff dept. pathology Hosp. of U. Pa., 1978-87, dir. cytopathology, 1978-87, med. program dir. Sch. Cytotech., 1978-86; chair dept. pathology and lab. medicine Med. Coll. Pa., 1987-94; dir. Delaware Valley Regional Lab. Svcs., Med. Coll. Hosps. and St. Christopher's Hosp. for Children, 1991-96; chair dept. pathology and lab. medicine Med. Coll. Pa. and Hahnemann U., 1994-96; trustee Am. Bd. Pathology, 1992-95, pres., 1998—. Mem. editl. bd. Lab. Investigation, 1988-94, Modern Pathology, 1990-94, Human Pathology, 1992-94; manuscript reviewer Cancer, Diagnostic Cytopathology, Modern Pathology, 1988-94; abstract rev. bd. U.S. and Can. Acad. Pathology, 1989-92; rev. panel Am. Soc. Clin. Pathology Abstract, 1991-96; contbr. articles to profl. jours., chpts. to books. Bd. dirs., treas. Laennec Soc. Phila., 1979-81; bd. dirs. Thyroid Soc. Phila., 1982-84; exec. com., bd. dirs. Med. Coll. Pa., 1994-96; bd. trustees Hahnemann U., 1994-96. Recipient Golden Apple Teaching award for excellent sci. teaching, 1994; grantee NIH, 1985-88, Takeda-Abbott R&D, 1989-94, NIA, 1991-94. Mem. AMA, Am. Soc. Cytology, Coll. Am. Assn. Exptl. Biologists, Am. Med. Women's Assn. (Janet M. Glasgow Meml. Scholarship 1974), Am. Soc. Clin. Pathologists (coun. on cytopathology 1989-94), Assn. Pathology Chmn. (v.p. 1992-94), Am. Assn. Cancer Rsch., Internat. Acad. Cytopathology, Phila. Pathology Soc., Pa. Assn. Pathologists, Coll. Physicians Phila., Phila. Cancer Rsch. Assn., Phila. County Med. Soc., Papanicolaou Soc. Cytopathology, Coun. of Deans of AAMC, Am. Bd. Pathology (Treasurer, 1998—). Home: 3111 Spring Mill Rd Plymouth Meeting PA 19462 Office: MCP Hahnemann Sch Med 245 N 15th St M5441 Philadelphia PA 19102-1192

ATKINSON, BILL, artistic director. Studied with various tchrs., N.Y.C. Artistic dir. Dallas Met. Ballet; founder Etgen-Atkinson Ballet Sch., 1960—. Performances include Royal Winnipeg (Can.) Ballet, Ballet AAA, South Am., Dallas State Fair Musicals, Jacobs Pillow Dance Festival, Mass.; appeared in Broadway in My Fair Lady, Oh Captain, Happiest Girl in the World. Mem. S.W. Regional Ballet Assn. (membership chmn.). Office: Dallas Met Ballet 6815 Hillcrest Ave Dallas TX 75205-1308*

ATKINSON, DONNA DURANT, research and evaluation consultant; b. Jan. 23, 1954. AB, Wellesley Coll., 1976; MS, U. Pitts., 1980, PhD, 1984. Asst. dir. rsch. Greater Detroit Area Health Coun., 1985-87; cons. Applied Mgmt. Sci., Silver Spring, Md., 1987-91; prin. cons. Birch & Davis Assoc., Inc., Silver Spring, 1991—. E-mail: datkinson@birchdavis.com.

ATKINSON, G. DOUGLAS, SR., marketing executive, consultant; b. Missoula, Mont., Feb. 8, 1943; s. George Stanford and Armene J. (Stinger) A.; m. Judythe Ann Reed, Aug. 11, 1967; children: G. Douglas Jr., Robert S., Emily A., Anne Marie. BS in Pharmacy, Drake U., 1966; MBA in Hosp. Adminstrn., Xavier U., 1970. Lic. pharmacist, Iowa. Adminstrv. resident St. Joseph's Hosp. and Med. Ctr., Phoenix, 1969-70, asst. adminstr., 1970-74; chief exec. officer Holy Rosary Hosp., Miles City, Mont., 1974-78; dir. mgmt. service Brim & Assoc. Inc., Portland, Oreg., 1978-79, v.p. cons. div., 1979-80, v.p. corp. devel., 1980-88; regional v.p. Brim Healthcare, Inc., 1988-93, v.p. of mktg. and devel., 1994—; assoc. dean, v.p. networks Bowman Gray/Bapt. Hosps. Med. Ctr., Winston-Salem, N.C., 1983; instr. health care mktg. Oreg. State U., Corvallis, 1984—; pres. Med. Mktg. Services Inc., Portland, 1987—. Deck ofcl. U.S. Swimming Assn., 1986—; chmn. bd. dirs. Community Decision Making in Rural Hosp. Project, Boise, Idaho, 1988—; Rep. precinct capt., Multomah County, Oreg., 1987; alternate del. Rep. State Conv., Oreg., 1988. Named one of Outstanding Young Men in Am., Oreg. C. of C., 1978. Fellow Am. Coll. Health Care Execs., Am. Mktg. Assn. (Oreg. chpt. pres. 1987); mem. Mt. Hood Swim Team (Gresham, Oreg.) (pres. 1986-88). Congregationalist. Home: 1008 Glousman Rd Winston Salem NC 27104-1274 Office: Wake Forest U Bapt Med Ctr Med Ctr Blvd Winston Salem NC 27157

ATKINSON, GORDON, chemistry educator; b. Bklyn., Aug. 29, 1930; s. John and Margaret (Barrie) A.; m. Betty Lou Dilmore, Apr. 1, 1976; children: Alan Gordon, Gwyneth, Valerie. B.S. in Chemistry, Lehigh U., 1952; Ph.D. in Phys. Chemistry, Iowa State U., 1956. Instr chemistry U. Mich., Ann Arbor, 1957-61; asst. prof. U. Md., College Park, 1961-64, assoc. prof., 1964-67, prof., 1967-71; prof. chemistry U. Okla., Norman, 1971—; chmn. dept. chemistry U. Okla., 1971-74; dean Grad. Coll., 1974-79, vice provost for research adminstrn., 1974-79; cons. in field.; Fulbright prof. Copenhagen U., 1967-68. Author: Reactions and Reason, 1973; Contbr. articles to profl. jours. Recipient Excellence in Teaching award U. Md., 1963, Regent's award for research U. Okla., 1983. Fellow N.Y. Acad. Sci., Am. Inst. Chemists; mem. Am. Chem. Soc., AAAS, AAUP, Sigma Xi, Phi Beta Kappa, Tau Beta Pi, Phi Kappa Phi, Phi Lambda Upsilon, Kappa Sigma. Democrat. Unitarian-Universalist. Home: 1419 Greenbriar Dr Norman OK 73072-6858 Office: Okla U Dept Chemistry 620 Parrington Oval Norman OK 73019-3050

ATKINSON, HOLLY GAIL, physician, journalist, business executive, author, lecturer, human rights activist; b. Detroit, Oct. 20, 1952. BA in Biology magna cum laude, Colgate U., 1974; MD, U. Rochester, 1978; MS in Journalism, Columbia U., 1981. Diplomate Nat. Med. Bds. Intern in internal medicine Strong Meml. Hosp., Rochester, N.Y., 1978-79; rschr. Walter Cronkite's Universe show CBS News, N.Y.C., 1981-82; med. reporter CBS Morning News, N.Y.C., 1982-83; on-air co-host Bodywatch health show PBS, 1983-88; contbg. editor and health columnist New Woman mag., 1983-88; on-air corr., med. editor, sr. v.p. programming/med. affairs Lifetime Med. TV, 1985-93; assoc. editor Journal Watch, 1986-90; med. corr. Today Show NBC News, N.Y.C., 1991-94; exec. v.p. Reuters Health, N.Y.C., 1994-98; editor HealthNews, 1994—; pres., CEO Reuters Health, 1998—; lectr. Dept. Pub. Health Cornell U. Med. Coll., 1997—. Author: Women and Fatigue, 1986. Vol. nat. and local level Am. Heart Assn., 1984-91, bd. dirs., chmn. nat. comms. com. Am. Heart Assn., 1987-91; bd. dirs. Phys. Human Rights, 1994—, NOW Legal Def. and Edn. Fund, 1996—, Soc. Advancement Women's Health Rsch., 1997-99, Am. Lyme Disease Found, 1997-98. Recipient Young Achievers award Nat. Coun. Women, 1986, Achievement award Soc. Advancement Women's Health Rsch., 1995. Mem. Phi Beta Kappa. Office: Reuters Health Info Svc 1700 Broadway Fl 20 New York NY 10019-5905

ATKINSON, JOHN T., treasurer City of Virginia Beach; b. Norfolk, Va., Feb. 9, 1941. Student, Fredrick Coll., 1959. Owner, mgr. Frank Atkinson Real Estate, Virginia Beach, Va., 1963-78; city treas. City of Va. Beach, 1978—. With U.S. Navy, 1959-63. Office: Office City Treas 2401 Court House Dr # 2401 Virginia Beach VA 23456-9121*

ATKINSON, PATRICIA, minister of health; b. Biggar, Sask., Can., Sept. 27, 1952; d. Robert Roy and Edna (Aylward) A. BA with honors, U. Sask., Can., 1976, B of Edn., 1976. Min. social svcs. Govt. of Sask., Can., 1992-93, min. edn., tng. & employment, 1993-95, min. edn., 1995-98; min. health Govt. of Sask., 1998—. Active Big Sisters; mem. Nutana Neighbor to Neighbor Program; past v.p. Saskatoon Cmty. Clinic; founding dir. Coop Housing Assn.; former Sask. rep. to Can. Daycare Advocacy Assn. Mem. Pub. Rels. Com. Avocations: hiking, Irish music, resoration of antique furniture and early 1900's home. Home and Office: Legis Bldg, Regina, SK Canada S4S 0B3

ATKINSON, PERRY, political organization administrator. Chair Oreg. Rep. Party, Beaverton. Fax: (503) 587-9244. Office: Oreg Rep Party PO Box 789 Salem OR 97308

ATKINSON, REGINA ELIZABETH, medical social worker; b. New Haven, May 13, 1952; d. Samuel and Virginia Louise Griffin. BA, U. Conn., Storrs, 1974; MSW, Atlanta U., 1978. Social work intern Atlanta Residential Manpower Center, 1976-77, Grady Meml. Hosp., Atlanta, 1977-78; med. social worker, hosp. coordinator USPHS, Atlanta, Palm Beach County (Fla.) Health Dept., West Palm Beach, 1978-81; dir. social services Glades Gen. Hosp., Belle Glade, Fla., 1981-95; case mgr. divsn. sr. svcs. Palm Beach County Cmty. Svcs., West Palm Beach, Fla., 1996—; instr. Palm Beach Jr. Coll.; participant various work shops, task forces. Vice pres. Community Action Council South Bay, 1978-79. Whitney Young fellow, 1977; USPHS scholar, 1977. Mem. NAFE, NAACP, Am. Hosp. Assn. (soc. for social work adminstrn. in health care), Soc. Hosp. Social Work Dirs., Assn. State and Territorial Pub. Health Social Workers, Nat. Assn. Black Social Workers, Nat. Assn. Social Workers, Fla. Soc. for Hosp. Social Work Dirs. (adminstrn. in health care), Glades Area Assn. for Retarded Citizens. Home: 525 1/2 SW 10th St Belle Glade FL 33430-3712 Office: 810 Datura St Ste 100 West Palm Beach FL 33401-5204

ATKINSON, RICHARD CHATHAM, university president; b. Oak Park, Ill., Mar. 19, 1929; s. Herbert and Margaret (Feuerbach) A.; m. Rita Loyd, Aug. 20, 1952; 1 dau., Lynn Loyd. Ph.B., U. Chgo., 1948; Ph.D., Ind. U., 1955. Lectr. applied math. and stats. Stanford (Calif.) U., 1956-57, assoc. prof. psychology, 1961-64, prof. psychology, 1964-80; asst. prof. psychology UCLA, 1957-61; dep. dir. NSF, 1975-76, acting dir., 1976, dir., 1976-80; chancellor, prof. cognitive sci. U. Calif., San Diego, 1980-95; pres. U. Calif. Sys., 1995—. Author: (with Atkinson, Smith and Bem) Introduction to Psychology, 12th edit., 1996, Computer Assisted Instruction, 1969, An Introduction to Mathematical Learning Theory, 1965, Contemporary Developments in Mathematical Psychology, 1974, Mind and Behavior, 1980, Stevens' Handbook of Experimental Psychology, 1988. Served with AUS, 1954-56. Guggenheim fellow, 1967; fellow Ctr. for Advanced Study in Behavioral Scis., 1963; recipient Distinguished Research award Social Sci. Research Council, 1962. Fellow APA (Disting. Sci. Contbn. award 1977, Thorndike award 1980), AAAS (pres. 1989-90), Am. Psychol. Soc. (William James fellow 1985), Am. Acad. Arts and Scis.; mem. NAS, Soc. Exptl. Psychologists, Am. Philos. Soc., Nat. Acad. Edn., Inst. of Medicine, Cosmos Club (Washington), Explorer's Club (N.Y.C.). Home: 70 Rincon Rd Kensington CA 94707-1047 Office: U Calif Office of Pres 1111 Franklin St Oakland CA 94607-5200

ATKINSON, RICHARD LEE, JR., internal medicine educator; b. Petersburg, Va., May 15, 1942; s. Richard Lee and Ruth (Scarborough) A.; m. Susan Stayner Hume, Aug. 13, 1966; children: Catherine Crane, Barbara Hill, Deborah Gildea. BA, VA Mil. Inst., 1964; MD, Med. Coll. Va., 1968. Liaison endocrinologist Vanderbilt U., Nashville, 1973-74; adj. asst. prof. UCLA, 1975-77; asst. prof. internal medicine U. Va. Sch. Medicine, Charlottesville, 1977-83; assoc. prof. internal medicine U. Calif., Davis, 1983-87; prof. internal medicine Ea. Va. Med. Sch., Norfolk, 1987-93; assoc. chief staff for rsch. VA Med. Ctr., Hampton, Va., 1987-93; prof. medicine and nutritional scis., dir. Beers-Murphy Clin. Nutrition Ctr. U. Wis., Madison, 1993—; mem. nutrition study sect. NIH, 1991-95, chair, 1993-95. Contbr. articles to profl. jours. Maj. U.S. Army, 1970-74. Mem. N.Am. Assn. Study Obesity (pres. 1990-91), Am. Soc. Clin. Nutrition (pub. info. com. 1988-91, membership com. 1986-90, pres. 1994-95), Am. Obesity Assn. (pres.). Home: 2132 Vintage Dr Fitchburg WI 53575-1928 Office: U Wis Nutritional Scis Bldg 1415 Linden Dr Madison WI 53706-1527

ATKINSON, SANDRA MILLER, marketing educator; b. Jamestown, N.C., Oct. 2, 1958; d. Thomas Raymond and Sandra (James) Miller; m. Richard Dillon Atkinson, May 15, 1982; children: Richard Miller, Elizabeth James. BS, Va. Commonwealth U., 1981; MEd, Old Dominion U., 1993. Mktg. tchr. Windsor (Va.) H.S., 1981-85; mktg. tchr. Franklin (Va.) H.S., 1985—, HSTW site coord., 1995-97; presenter Southern Region Edn., Atlanta, 1995-96, presider, 1997; facilitator H.S. That Works, Richmond, 1997; presider Ken. SREB, 1996, 97. HSTW grant Va. Dept. Edn., 1993—. Mem. Va. Assn. Mktg. Edn., Mktg. Edn. Assn. Democrat. Methodist. Avocations: reading, computers, crafts, traveling, beaches. Office: Franklin High Sch 310 Crescent Dr Franklin VA 23851-2341

ATKINSON, SUSAN D., producing artistic director, theatrical consultant; b. Phila., May 23, 1944; d. Joseph A. and Josephine (Mierley) Davis; m. Robert Atkinson, 1971 (div. 1986). BA, Juniata Coll., 1966; postgrad., San Francisco State Coll., 1968-69, U. Calif., Berkeley, 1968-69. Dir. Am. Conservatory Theatre, San Francisco, 1967-72; guest dir. Berkeley Repertory Theatre Co., 1968-69; dir. Marin Shakespeare Festival, Marin County, Calif., 1968-69; producing artistic dir. Repertory Theatre Co. Bucks County, Doyleston, Pa., 1980-86, Bristol (Pa.) Riverside Theatre, 1986—; guest dir. Grove Shakespeare Festival, 1992. Bd. dirs. Pa. Coun. on the Arts, Harrisburg, Pa., 1989—. Mem. Soc. Stage Dirs. and Choreographers (sec.). Office: Bristol Riverside Theatre PO Box 1250 Bristol PA 19007-1250

ATKINSON, TOMMY RAY, sportscaster, sportswriter; b. Charleston, W.Va., Jan. 29, 1973; s. Tommy David and Sandra Kay (Powers) A.; m. Tracie Lynn McNiel, June 7, 1997. BS, W.Va. State Coll., 1996. Sports editor The Yellow Jacket, Institute, W.Va., 1995-96; sports asst. The Charleston Gazette, 1995—; sportscaster W.Va. Radio Corp., Charleston, 1996—. Republican. Baptist. Avocations: sports, reading, writing. Home: 3309 33rd St Nitro WV 25143-1630

ATKINSON, WILLIAM JAMES, JR., retired cardiologist; b. Mobile, Ala., July 4, 1917; s. William J. and Gertrude (Smith) A.; m. Glenda E. Street, Oct. 29, 1949; children: Glenda Street, Regina Creswell, William James III. BA, Amherst Coll., 1939; MD, U. Pa., 1943; MS in Internal Medicine, St. Louis U., 1949. Intern, Phila. Gen. Hosp., 1943-44; resident in medicine St. Louis City Hosp., 1946-48; resident in cardiology St. Louis U., 1948-49; practice medicine specializing in internal medicine and cardiology, Mobile, Ala., 1949—; chief cardiac clinic Mobile City Hosp., 1950-60; electrocardiographer Mobile Infirmary, 1949-92, Providence Hosp., 1949-75; cardiologist Diagnostic and Med. Clinic, 1949-92; mem. staff U. South Ala. Med. Ctr. Hosp., Mobile Infirmary, Providence Hosp.; chmn. bd. Diagnostic and Med. Clinic P.A., 1973-92; clin. assoc. prof. medicine U. Ala., 1964-89; clin. assoc. prof. medicine U. South Ala., 1973-92; ret. Served as capt. M.C., AUS, 1944-46. Decorated Bronze Star. Diplomate Am. Bd. Internat. Medicine, Am. Bd. Cardiovascular Disease. Fellow ACP, Am. Coll. Cardiology, Am. Coll. Chest Physicians; mem. Am. Heart Assn., Ala. Heart Assn. (chmn. bd. 1956), AMA, Am. Soc. Clin. Pharmacology and Therapeutics, Mobile C. of C. Republican. Episcopalian. Clubs: Rotary, Mobile Country, Mobile Yacht. Home: 3965 Byronell Ct Mobile AL 36693-5502

ATKYNS, ROBERT LEE, communications research professional; b. Boston, Jan. 20, 1948; s. Glenn C. and Syme M. (Vataja) A. BA, Rutgers U., 1971; MA, U. Conn., 1974; PhD, Temple U., 1986. Grad. asst. communication div. U. Conn., Storrs, 1971-73; communications researcher drug abuse info. rsch. project, 1971-74; instr. U. Conn., Hartford, 1973-74; health care analyst The Phila. Health Plan, 1974-76, asst. dir. rsch. and evaluation, 1976-78, dir. rsch. and evaluation, 1978-80; mktg. scientist mktg. rsch. and forecasting div. AT&T Long Lines, Bedminster, N.J., 1980-82, mktg. rsch. staff mgr. AT&T Gen. Depts., Basking Ridge, N.J., 1982-83, mktg. staff mgr. AT&T Communications, Basking Ridge, N.J., 1984-85, advt. staff mgr., 1985-93, multimedia svcs. rsch. staff mgr., 1994-95; reg. mktg. scis. mgr. AT&T, 1996, new product devel., 1997, dist. mgr. pub. policy and comms. rsch., 1997; cons. Chmn., Cheltenham Twp. Drug, Alcohol and Mental Health Com. Mem. Flemington Presbyn. Ch. Recipient Community Svc. award Cheltenham Twp., AT&T Eagle award, 1986, AT&T Spirit Communication awards 1990, 91. Mem. AAAS, Internat. Communication Assn., Am. Assn. Pub. Opinion Rsch., Am. Mktg. Assn., Am. Pub. Health Assn., Am. Acad. Polit. and Social Sci. Contbr. to profl. jours. and confs. Home: 263

Kingwood Station Rd Frenchtown NJ 08825-3615 Office: AT&T Hdqrs 295 N Maple Ave Basking Ridge NJ 07920-1025

ATLAS, DAVID, meteorologist, research scientist; b. Bklyn., May 25, 1924; s. Isadore and Rose (Jaffee) A.; m. Lucille Rosen, Sept. 26, 1948; children: Joan Linda, Robert Fred. BSc, NYU, 1946; MSc, MIT, 1951, DSc in Meteorology, 1955. Chief weather radar br. Air Force Cambridge Research Labs., Bedford, Mass., 1948-66; prof. meteorology U. Chgo., 1966-72; dir. atmospheric tech. div. Nat. Center for Atmospheric Research, Boulder, Colo., 1972-73; dir. nat. hail research expt. Nat. Center for Atmospheric Research, 1974-75; dir. lab. for atmospheric sci. Nasa Goddard Space Flight Ctr., Greenbelt, Md., 1977-84, disting. vis. scientist, 1988—; sr. research assoc. dept. meteorology U. Md., 1985-87; disting. vis. scientist Jet Propulsion Lab. Calif. Inst. Tech., 1984-92; chmn. panel on remote atmospheric probing, also mem. com. on atmospheric scis., NAS, 1975-82, mem. on modernization of the Nat. Weather Svc., 1996—; vis. scientist Coop. Inst. for Marine and Atmospheric Scis., U. Miami, 1988—. 1st lt. USAAF, 1943-46. Recipient Loeser award Air Force Cambridge Research Labs., 1957, O'Day award, 1964; Robert M. Losey award AIAA, 1966; NASA Outstanding Leadership medal, 1982; Presdl. Meritorious Sr. Exec. award, 1983; NSF sr. postdoctoral fellow Imperial Coll., London, Eng., 1959-60. Fellow Am. Meteorol. Soc. (councilor 1961-64, 72-74, Meisinger award 1957, assoc. editor publs. 1957-74, pres. 1975, Cleveland Abbe award 1983, Remote Sensing award 1991, Carl Gustav Rossby medal 1996), Am. Geophys. Union, Am. Astron. Soc., Royal Meteorol. Soc. (Symons Meml. medal 1989), AAAS (chmn. atmospheric and hydrospheric scis. sect. 1986); mem. NAE, Internat. Radio Sci. Union (pres. inter-union commn. on radio meteorology 1969-72). Inventor weather radar devices. Home: Apt 302 1610 Golf Club Rd Weston FL 33326

ATLAS, JAMES ROBERT, magazine editor, writer; b. Chgo., Mar. 22, 1949; s. Donald and Nora (Glassenberg) A.; m. Anna O'Conor Sloane Fels, Aug. 2, 1975; children: Amelia Eyre, William Easton. BA, Harvard U., 1971; postgrad. (Rhodes scholar), Oxford (Eng.) U., 1971-73. Staff writer Time, N.Y.C., 1977-78; asst. editor N.Y. Times Book Rev., N.Y. Times, 1978-81; assoc. editor Atlantic Monthly, 1981-85; contbg. editor Vanity Fair, N.Y.C., 1985-87; asst. editor N.Y. Times Mag., 1987-97; gen. editor Lives series Lipper Viking Penguin. Author: Delmore Schwartz: The Life of an American Poet, 1977, The Great Pretender, 1986; (novel) Battle of the Books, 1992; contbr. articles to various nat. mags. Home: 40 W 77th St New York NY 10024-5128 Office: Lipper & Co 101 Park Ave Fl 6 New York NY 10178-0002

ATLAS, JAY DAVID, philosopher, consultant, linguist; b. Houston, Tex., Feb. 1, 1945; s. Jacob Henry and Babette Fancile (Friedman) A. AB summa cum laude, Amherst (Mass.) Coll., 1966; PhD, Princeton (N.J.) U., 1976. Mem. common rm. Wolfson Coll., Oxford, Eng., 1978, 80; vis. fellow Princeton U., 1979; rsch. assoc. Inst. for Advanced Study, Princeton, 1982-84; vis. lectr. U. Hong Kong, 1986; prof. Pomona Coll., Claremont, Calif., 1989—; sr. assoc. Jurecon, Inc., L.A.; lectr. 2d European Summer Sch. in Logic, Lang. and Info., 1990; examiner U. Edinburgh, Scotland, 1993, U. Groningen, The Netherlands, 1991, 93-97, vis. rsch. prof., 1995; vis. prof. UCLA, 1988-95, Max. Planck Inst. for Psycholinguistics, Nijmegen, The Netherlands, 1997. Author: Philosophy Without Ambiguity, 1989; contbr. to PC Laptop Computer Mag., 1994, articles to profl. jours. Mem. Am. Philos. Assn., Linguistic Soc. Am. Office: Pomona Coll 551 N College Ave Claremont CA 91711-4410

ATLAS, LIANE WIENER, writer; b. N.Y.C.; d. Louis and Frances (Ferne) Wiener; m. Martin Atlas, Mar. 5, 1944 (dec. Mar. 1997); children: Stephen Terry, Jeffrey L. AB, Vassar Coll., 1943; postgrad., Johns Hopkins U., 1953-55. Cert. fin. planner. Fgn. affairs officer Dept. State, Washington, 1962-68; sr. economist U.S. Commerce Dept., Washington, 1968-75, U.S. Treasury Dept., Washington, 1975-79, Riggs Nat. Bank, Washington, 1980-82; v.p. Fintapes Inc., Washington, 1984-87, pres., 1987-95; freelance writer Washington, 1995—; mem. U.S. delegation UN Econ. Orgns., N.Y.C., Geneva, 1963, 64, 68, 79. Author: Middle East Financial Institutions, 1977, (audio cassettes) What Every Wife Should Know, 1986, rev., 1992, Financial Planning for Divorce, rev. edit. 1992; freelance writer Changing Times and other mags., 1982-87. Treas. Entertaining People/Washington Home, 1986-90, Smithsonian Craft Show, 1993-95, Smithsonian Women's Com., 1996-98. Fellow in econs. Johns Hopkins U., Balt., 1954-55; recipient Cert. of Appreciation U.S. Treasury Dept., Washington, 1977. Mem. Inst. CFPs, Am. Econ. Assn., Washington Ind. Writers, Vassar Club. Avocations: print collecting, skiing, tennis. Home: 2254 48th St NW Washington DC 20007-1035

ATLAS, NANCY FRIEDMAN, judge; b. N.Y.C., May 20, 1949. BS, Tufts U., 1971; JD, NYU, 1974. Bar: N.Y. 1975, U.S. Dist. Ct. (so. and ea. dists.) N.Y. 1975, U.S. Ct. Appeals (2nd cir.) 1975, U.S. Dist. Ct. (so. dist.) Tex. 1982, U.S. Ct. Appeals (5th cir.) 1982, U.S. Dist. Ct. (no. dist.) Tex. 1989. Law clk. to Hon. Dudley B. Bonsal U.S. Dist Ct. (so. dist.) N.Y., 1974-76; assoc. Webster & Sheffield, 1977-78; asst. U.S. atty. So. Dist. N.Y., 1979-82; shareholder Sheinfeld, Maley & Kay, P.C., Houston, 1982-95, also bd. dirs.; judge U.S. Dist. Ct. Tex., Houston, 1995—; lectr. numerous programs CLE. Mng. editor NYU Ann. Survey Am. Law, 1973-74; contbr. numerous articles to profl. jours. Chair Tex. Higher Edn. coord. Bd., 1992-95; mem. Tex. Coun. Workforce and Econ. Competitiveness, 1993-95. Fellow ABA Found., State Bar Tex., Houston Bar Assn.; mem. ABA (co-divsn. dir. litigation sect. 1996-98, co-chair ADR com. litigation sect. 1994-95, bus. and litigation joint task force on bankruptcy practice 1994-98), FBA (trustee), Houston Bar Found., Phi Beta Kappa. Office: US Courthouse 515 Rusk St Ste 9015 Houston TX 77002-2605*

ATLAS, RANDALL IVAN, architect, criminologist; b. Miami Beach, Fla., Mar. 6, 1953; s. Fred and Janet (Radoff) A.; m. Gaile Esko, Oct. 31, 1989. BArch, U. Fla., 1974; B in Criminal Justice, U. South Fla., 1976; MArch, U. Ill., 1976; PhD in Criminology, Fla. State U., 1982. Registered profl. architect, Fla. Archtl. intern Fla. Dept. Corrections, Tallahassee, 1976-78; architect Harper & Buzinec, Coral Gables, Fla., 1983; pres. Atlas & Assocs., Miami, Fla., 1984-88; tech. assistance cons. Nat. Inst. Corrections, Boulder, Colo., 1983—; v.p. Atlas Safety & Security Design, Inc., Miami, 1989—; adj. prof. criminal justice Fla. Internat. U., Miami, 1984-89, adj. prof. U. Miami Sch. Architecture, 1994—; co-chmn. Greater Miami C. of C. Crime Prevention Commn., 1991-95. Author: Preventing Slip & Fall Accidents, 1987, Preventing Inmate Suicide, 1987. Mem. AIA (architecture for justice com.), Am. Correctional Assn. (design and tech. com.), Am. Soc. Indsl. Security (security architecture/engring. com.), Nat. Safety Coun. (falls prevention com.), Am. Soc. Safety Engrs. Avocations: windsurfing, tennis, scuba diving, target shooting.

ATLAS, TERRY, journalist; b. Washington, 1952. BA in Econs. and Polit. Sci., U. Rochester, 1974. Energy reporter Chgo. Tribune, 1978-83; Washington corr. Chgo. Tribune, Washington, 1983-86, chief diplomatic corr., Washington bur., 1986-97, Washington news editor, 1997—. Office: Chicago Tribune DC Bureau 1325 G St NW Ste 200 Washington DC 20005-3112

ATLEE, JOHN LIGHT, physician; b. Lancaster, Pa., Feb. 22, 1941; s. John Light Jr. and Ann (Stevens) A.; m. Barbara Sheaffer, June 20, 1964 (dec. Apr. 14, 1967); m. Barbara Sanford, Feb. 3, 1968; children: Sarah Sanford, John Light. BA, Franklin & Marshall Coll., 1963; MD, Temple U., 1967, MS in Pharmacology, 1971. Diplomate Am. Bd. Anesthesiology. Intern Germantown Hosp., Phila., 1967-68; resident in anesthesiology Temple U. Hosp., Phila., 1968-70; postdoctoral rsch. fellow pharmacology Temple U. Grad. Sch. Medicine, 1970-71; staff anesthesiologist U.S. Naval Hosp, Bethesda, Md., 1971-73; asst. prof. anesthesiology U. Wis., Madison, 1973-78, assoc. prof. anesthesiology, 1978-85, prof. anesthesiology, 1985-88; prof. anesthesiology Med. Coll. Wis., Milw., 1988—; mem. editl. bd., referee, cons. peer rev. jours. Anesthesia & Analgesia, Am. Jour. of Physiology, Anesthesiology, Med. and Biol. Engring. and Computing, Jour. of Cardiothoracic and Vascular Anesthesia; chmn., CEO Cardiac Control Techs.; cons. Medtronic Inc., Wyeth-Ayerst, Ebewe Pharms., Sensor Devices, Aristo-MED. Author: Perioperative Cardiac Arrhythmias, 1985, 2d edit., 1990, Arrhythmias and Pacemakers, 1996; editor: Perioperative Management of Pacemaker Patients, 1992, Complications in Anesthesia, 1999; Cardiovascular & Thoracic Anesthesia Jour. Club Jour.; contbr. articles to profl. jours.; patentee in field. Lt. comdr. USN, 1971-73. NIH grantee, 1978—. Fellow Am. Coll. Cardiology and Anesthesiology; mem. Am. Soc. Anesthesiologists, Assn. Univ. Anesthesiologists, N.Am. Soc. Pacing and Electrophysiology, Am. Soc. Exptl. Pharmacology and Therapeutics, Soc. Register Assn., Sigma Xi. Republican. Episcopalian. Achievements include development of a new transeosphageal stimulation and recording technology for use in anesthesiology, cardiology, emergency medicine and intensive care. Home: N71w29436 Tamron Ln Hartland WI 53029-9249 Office: Froedert Meml Luth Hosp E Med Coll Wis 9200 W Wisconsin Ave Milwaukee WI 53226-3522

ATLURI, SATYA N(ADHAM), aerospace engineering educator; b. Gudivada, Andhra, India, Oct. 7, 1945; came to U.S., 1966, naturalized, 1976; s. Tirupati Rao and Tulasi (Devi) A.; m. Revati Adusumilli, May 17, 1972; children: Neelima, Niroupa. B.E., Andhra U., Vizag, 1964; M.E., Indian Inst. Sci., Bangalore, India, 1966; DSc, MIT, 1969; DSc honoris causa, Nat. U. Ireland, Dublin, 1989. Researcher MIT, Cambridge, 1966-71; Jerome Clarke Hunsaker vis. prof. aeronautics and astronautics MIT, 1990-91; asst. prof. U. Wash., Seattle, 1971-74; assoc. prof. engring. sci. and mech. Ga. Inst. Tech., Atlanta, 1974-77, prof., 1977-79, Regents' prof. mechanics, 1979—, dir. Ctr. for Advancement Computational Mechanics, 1980—, inst. prof., 1991—, Regents' prof. aerospace engring., 1991—; White House nominee Com. for Evaluation Nat. Medal of Tech. Dept. Commerce, 1992—; mem. rsch. engring. & devel. adv. com. FAA, Washington, 1994—; co-chmn. Internat. Conf. on Computational Engring. Sci., Tokyo, 1986, Atlanta, 1988, Melbourne, Australia, 1991, Patras, Greece, 1991, Hong Kong, 1992, Hawaii, 1995; gen. lectr., invited keynote speaker over 250 internat. tech. confs.; adv. prof. Southwestern Jiaotong U., Emei, Sichuan, China, 1988; bd. dirs. FAA Ctr. for Excellence in Computational Modeling of Aerospace Structures, Ga. Inst. Tech., 1992; White House nominee Evaluation Com. for Nat. Medal of Tech., U.S. Dept. Commerce, 1992; mem. adv. com. rsch., engring. and devel. FAA, 1995—. Contbr. over 500 articles to profl. jours.; gen. editor: Springer Verlag Series on Computational Mechanics, 1988-91, 91, Structural Intgegrity of Aging Airplanes, 1991, Frontiers in Computational Mechanics, 1989—; author 25 books, including Computational Methods in the Mechanics of Solids and Structures, 1984; editor: books including Hybrid and Mixed Finite Element Methods, 1983, Computational Methods in the Mechanics of Fracture, 1985 (Russian transl. 1989), Handbook of Finite Elements, 1986, Dynamic Fracture Mechanics, 1986, Computational Mechanics 86, 1986, Large-Space-Structures: Dynamics and Control, 1987, Computational Mechanics '88, 1988, Computational Mechanics '91, 1991, Frontiers in Computational Mechanics, 1989, Computational Mechanics '91, 1991, Structural Integrity of Aging Airplanes, 1991, Durability of Metal Aircraft Structures., 1992, Nonlinear Computational Mechanics in Aerospace Engineering, 1992; editor-in-chief Internat. Jour. Computational Mechanics, Computer Modeling and Simulation in Engineering; mem. editorial bd. Computers and Structures, Engring. Fracture Mechanics, Internat. Jour. Plasticity, Internat. Jour. for Numerical Methods in Engring., Acta Mecanica Solida Sinica, also others. Grantee NSF, 1975—, USAF Office Sci. Research, 1973—, Office Naval Research, 1978—, Air Force Rocket Propulsion Lab., 1976-79, NASA, 1980—, NRC, 1978-80, Dept. Transp., 1987—, ARO, 1988—, FAA, 1991—, Dept. Energy, 1994—; recipient V.K. Murti Gold medal Andhra U., India, 1964, Roll of Honors award Indian Inst. Sci., 1966, Disting. Alumnus award, 1991, Class of 1934 Disting. Prof. award for 1986 Ga. Inst. Tech., Outstanding Faculty Research award Ga. Inst. Tech., 1986, 91, Survey Paper Citation AIAA Jour., 1988, Monie Ferst Meml. award for Sustained Research, Sigma Xi, 1988, Outstanding Rsch. award, 1991, Tech. Achievement award Nat. Acad. Engring., 1995; fellow Japan Soc. for Promotion Sci., 1987—, Computational Mechanics Div. medal Japan Soc. Mech. Engrs., 1991, ICES Gold medal, 1992, A.C. Eringen medal of the Soc. of Engring. Sci., 1995; named Southwest Mechanics lectr., 1987, Midwestern Mechanics lectr., 1988. Fellow Internat. Congress on Fracture (hon.), ASME (chmn. com. computing in applied mechanics 1983-85, assoc. editor Applied Mech. Revs.), AIAA (assoc. editor AIAA Jour. 1983—, Structures Dynamics and Materials award 1988), Am. Acad. Mechanics, Aero. Soc. India, U.S. Assn. Computational Mechanics (founder, mem. exec. com.); mem. ASCE (assoc. editor Jour. Engring. Mechanics 1982-84, mem. exec. com., Aerospace Structures and Materials award 1986), U.S. Nat. Acad. Engring., Internat. Assn. for Computational Mechanics (founding mem., exec. coun.), Internat. Assn. Boundary Element Methods (mem. exec. com.). Home: 424 Hilgard Ave Los Angeles CA 90024-2593 Office: Ga Inst Tech Ctr Computational Modeling and Infrastructure Rehab Atlanta GA 30332-0356

ATNIP, BETTY LOUISE, accountant; b. Llano, Tex., Dec. 1, 1946; d. Travis Alger and Edith Lucile (Tate) N.; m. Vernon George Mangold (div. July 1981); 1 child, Ian Keith; m. Jimmy Ray Atnip, Nov. 1998. Student, San Antonio Jr. Coll., 1965-66; BBA, U. Tex., San Antonio, 1985. Data claims analyst Blue Cross/Blue Shield, San Antonio, 1980-82; regional sec., acct. BioMed. Applications, San Antonio, 1982-83; with acctg. dept. Comprehensive Bus. Svcs., Boerne, Tex., 1983-84; acct. Cadwallader Ins. Agy., San Antonio, 1986, Data Processing Support, Inc., San Antonio, 1986-87, Archive Retrieval Sys., Inc., San Antonio, 1986-87; pvt. practice acctg. San Antonio, 1987—; acct. Aircraft Techs., San Antonio, 1997—; acct. atty., 1989-92; acct. Night in Old San Antonio, 1996; personal fin. analyst Primerica Fin. Svcs., 1994—. Vol. Boy Scouts Am., San Antonio, 1978-89, unit commr., 1989; bd. dirs. San Antonio Met. Ministries, 1987-90. Scholar Women in Bus., 1983. Mem. Nat. Assn. Accts. (assoc. bd. dirs. 1988-90), Inst. Mgmt. Accts., Leon Springs Bus. Assn., Am. Luth. Women. Avocations: music, grandchildren, crafts, sewing. Home and Office: 25403 Brewer Dr San Antonio TX 78257-1139

ATREYA, SUSHIL KUMAR, space science educator, astrophysicist, researcher; b. Apr. 15, 1946; came to U.S., 1966, naturalized, 1975; s. Harvansh Lal and Kailash Vati (Sharma) A.; m. Evelyn M. Bruckner, Dec. 31, 1970; 1 child, Chloë E. ScB, U. Rajasthan, India, 1963, MSc, 1965; MS, Yale U., 1968; PhD, U. Mich., 1973. Rsch. assoc. physics U. Pitts., 1973-74; asst., then assoc. rsch. scientist U. Mich., Ann Arbor, 1974-78, ast. prof., 1978-81, assoc. prof. atmospheric sci., 1981-87, prof. atmospheric and space sci., 1987—, dir. planetary sci. lab.; assoc. prof. U. Paris, 1984-85; vis. sr. rsch. scientist Imperial Coll., London, 1984; mem. sci. and exptl. team Cassini-Huygens Probe to Saturn-Titan, Galileo Jupiter Probe, Planet-B Japanese Mars Mission, Mars Express Mission, Russian Mars '96 and Soviet Phobos projects, Voyager spacecraft missions to the giant planets, Comet Rendezvous/Asteroid Flyby, 1986-92, and SpaceLab I; guest observer/investigator on Hubble Space Telescope, Internat. Ultraviolet Spectrometer and Copernicus Orbiting Astron. Obs.; mem. sci. working groups NASA, Jet Propulsion Lab., European Space Agy. Author: Atmospheres and Ionospheres of the Outer Planets and their Satellites, 1986; co-editor: Planetary Aeronomy and Astronomy, 1981, Outer Planets, 1989, Cometary Environments, 1989, Origin and Evolution of Planetary and Satellite Atmospheres, 1989; contbr. numerous articles to books and profl. jours. Recipient NASA award for exceptional sci. contbns. Voyager Project, 1981, NASA Group Achievement award for Voyager Ultraviolet Spectrometer Investigations, 1981, 86, 90, NASA Group Achievement awards for Galileo Probe Mass Spectrometer experiment, and for Significant Outstanding Contbns. to the Galileo Probe and Orbiter to Jupiter, Excellence in Rsch. award U. Mich. Coll. Engring., 1995. Mem. AAAS, Internat. Assn. Meteorology and Atmospheric Scis. (pres. commn. planetary atmospheres and their evolution 1987-95, sec. 1983-87), Am. Geophys. Union (assoc. editor Geophys. Rsch. Letters jour. 1986-89), Internat. Astron. Union, Am. Astron. Soc., Internat. Acad. Astronautics. Office: U Mich Dept Atmospheric Oceanic and Space Sci 2455 Hayward St Ann Arbor MI 48109-2143

ATRISTAIN-CARRION, RAMIRO JAVIER, investment company executive; b. La Paz, Bolivia, May 19, 1962; s. Javier and Miriam (Carrion) Atristain. AA, Elgin C.C., Ill., 1991; BA, Dominican U., 1989, The-otokeoion (hon.), 1989; MBA, Ill. Inst. Technology, Chgo., 1993. Analyst The Dai-Ichi Kangyo Bank, Chgo., 1989-93; v.p. CAPRI Capital L.P., Chgo., 1994-98, sr. v.p., 1998—; vis. faculty De Paul U., Chgo., 1996—, Grant Hosp., Chgo., 1997—; investment advisor Alivio Med. Ctr., Chgo., 1995—. Founder Info. Technology Devel. Assn., Cache Assn., 1991. Mem. fundraising com. R. Durbin's Campaign, Chgo., 1996; treas. fundraising com. Miriam Santos Campaign, Chgo., 1995; vol. Summer Enrichment Program, Chgo., 1993—, Support Ctr. of Chgo., 1992. Mem. Nat. Soc. Hispanic MBAs (nat. pres. 1997-98, chpt. pres. 1995-97), Acad. of Mgmt. (hon.), Sigma Iota Epsilon. Roman Catholic. Avocations: photography, equestrian sports, langs. (fluent in Spanish, Italian; knowledge of Japanese and German). Home: 850 W Margate Ter Apt 3A Chicago IL 60640-3945 Office: CAPRI Capital LP 10 S La Salle St Ste 3712 Chicago IL 60603-1002

ATSADA, CHAIYANAM, diplomat. Rep. to UN Govt. of Thailand, N.Y.C., 1997—. Office: Permanent Mission Thailand to UN 351 E 52nd St New York NY 10022-6302*

ATSBERGER, DEBORAH BROWN, clinical nurse specialist; b. Detroit, Apr. 6, 1954; d. Robert Gerald and Virginia (Van Kleek) Brown; m. William Robert Atsberger, Jan. 26, 1980; children: Rebecca May, Stefanie Lyn. BSN, Ohio State U., 1976; MSN, Kent State U., 1994. RN, Ohio; cert. post anesthesia nurse, Ohio. Staff nurse Med. Coll. Va. Hosps., Richmond, 1976-78; staff nurse Cleve. Clinic Found., 1978-80, critical care clin. instr., 1980-94, clin. nurse specialist, 1994—; critical care and post anesthesia cons. Resource Applications, Inc., 1987-90; case mgr. Cleve. Clinic Found., 1994—; asst. clin. instr. Case Western Res. U. Sch. Nursing, 1990-97. Mem. AACN, Am. Soc Post Anesthesia Nurses, Assn. Oper. Rm. Nurses.

ATTAL, GENE (FRED EUGENE ATTAL), hospital executive; b. Austin, Tex., Oct. 6, 1947; s. Sam Arthur and Olga (Johns) A.; B.J. with spl. honors (NDEA fellow in langs. 1968-69), U. Tex., 1970; M.S. (Internat. fellow 1972), Columbia U., 1972; m. Marsha Ablah, July 26, 1970; children—Christopher, Allison, Anne. Public relations exec. Westinghouse Electric Corp., 1972-75; v.p. pub. affairs Seton Med. Center, Austin, 1975—; pres. The Seton Fund; mem. faculty U. Tex. Recipient Telstar Excellence in Communication award, annually 1978-81, Arthur W. Page award U. Tex., 1986. Mem. Am. Soc. Hosp. Public Relations (regional dir.), Assn. Healthcare Philanthropy (internat. bd. dirs.), Tex. Soc. Hosp. Public Relations (pres. 1981), Barton Creek Country Club. Greek Orthodox. Home: 1201 Constant Springs Dr Austin TX 78746-6615 Office: 1201 W 38th St Austin TX 78705-1006

ATTANASIO, JOHN BAPTIST, law educator; b. Jersey City, N.J., Oct. 19, 1954; s. Gaetano and Madeline (Germinario) A.; m. Kathleen Mary Spartana, Aug. 20, 1977; children: Thomas, Michael. BA, U. Va., 1976; JD, NYU, 1979; diploma in law, Oxford U., 1982; LLM, Yale U., 1985. Bar: Md. 1979, U.S. Dist. Ct. Md. 1980, U.S. Ct. Appeals (4th cir.) 1980, U.S. Supreme Ct. 1983. Pvt. practice Balt., 1979-81; vis. asst. prof. law U. Pitts., 1982-84; assoc. prof. law U. Notre Dame, Ind., 1985-88, prof. law, 1988-92; Regan dir. Kroc Inst. for Internat. Peace Studies, 1991-92; dean Sch. of Law St. Louis U., 1992-98; dean, William Hawley Atwell chair constnl. law So. Meth. U. Sch. Law, Dallas, 1998—. Co-author: Constitutional Law 1989. Chair adv. bd. Ctr. for Civil and Human Rights, 1990-92; mem. Fulbright awards area com., 1994-96; bd. dirs. Legal Svcs. Ea. Mo., 1996-98; bd. dirs. Ctr. for Internat. Understanding, 1993—. Recipient Legal Teaching award Sch. of Law, NYU, 1994. Mem. Ctrl. States Law Sch. Assn. (v.p. 1992-94), Phi Beta Kappa, Alpha Sigma Nu. Democrat. Roman Catholic. Office: So Meth U Sch Law PO Box 750116 3315 Daniel Ave Dallas TX 75275-0116

ATTAWAY, DAVID HENRY, retired federal research administrator, oceanographer; b. Sterling, Okla., June 9, 1938; s. Fred John and Minnie Ora (Yandell) A. BS in Chemistry, U. Okla., 1960, PhD in Biochemistry, 1968. Phys. oceanographer U.S. Naval Oceanog. Office, Suitland, Md., 1962-65; postdoctoral scholar, Marine Sci. Inst. U. Tex., Port Aransas, 1968-69; chief, geochemistry U. Kans., State Geol. Survey, Lawrence, 1969-71; chem. oceanographer USCG, Washington, 1971-72; rsch. and grants adminstr. Nat. Sea Grant Coll. Program, Washington, 1972-97, ret., 1997; cons., 1997—. Contbr. articles to profl. jours. Mem. AAAS, Am Chem. Soc., Inst. Food Tech., Marine Tech. Soc., Am. Geophys. Union, Sigma Xi, Phi Lambda Upsilon, Phi Sigma. Office: 609 7th St NE Washington DC 20002-5209

ATTEBERY, LOUIE WAYNE, English language educator, folklorist; b. Weiser, Idaho, Aug. 14, 1927; s. John Thomas Attebery and Tressie Mae (Blevins) Attebery Miller; m. Barbara Phyllis Olson, Dec. 31, 1947; children: Bobby Lou, Brian Leonard. BA, Albertson Coll. of Idaho, 1950; MA, U. Mont., 1951; PhD, U. Denver, 1961. Tchr. Middleton H.S., Idaho, 1949-50, Payette H.S., Idaho, 1951-52, Nyssa H.S., Oreg, 1952-55, East H.S., Denver, 1955-61; prof. English Albertson Coll. Idaho, Caldwell, 1961—, Eyck-Berringer chmn. English, 1987—, acting acad. v.p., 1983-84; vis. fellow Harvard U., Cambridge, Mass., 1993-94. Author: The College of Idaho, 1981-91, A Centennial History, 1991, Sheep May Safely Graze: A Personal Essay on Tradition and A Contemporary Sheep Ranch, 1993, The Most of What We Spend, 1998, Albertson College of Idaho: The Second Hundred Years, 1999; editor: Idaho Folklife: Homesteads to Headstones, 1985; editor Northwest Folklore, 1985-91; gen. editor U. Idaho Northwest Folklife series, 1991—. Trustee Idaho Hist. Soc., 1984-91. With USN, 1945-46. Bruern fellow U. Leeds, Eng., 1971-72. Mem. Western Lit. Assn. (exec. com. 1964-65), Assn. Lit. Scholars and Critics, 1995—. Methodist. Office: Albertson Coll Idaho 2112 Cleveland Blvd Caldwell ID 83605-4432

ATTEBURY, JANICE MARIE, accountant; b. Sterling, Ill., Sept. 8, 1954; d. Carl Edwin and Eileen Marie (Gilley) McDonald; m. Rudy Joe Attebury, July 8, 1972 (div. 1977); 1 child, Nicole Marie. Student, Okaloosa Walton Jr. Coll., Fort Walton Beach, Fla., Sauk Valley Coll., Dixon, Ill., Houston Community Coll.; BSBA in Acctg., Calif. U. for Advanced Studies, 1990; grad., Rhema Bible Tng. Ctr., 1992. Office mgr. Diamond Jim Enterprises, 1973-74; mgr. data processing dept. Sterling High Sch., 1974-75; bookkeeper 3-G Care Mgmt., Inc., 1977-78, office mgr., 1978-81; staff acct. Jerry T. Paul, CPA, 1982-84; staff acct. Lindgren, Callihan, Van Osdol and Co., Ltd., 1984-85, jr. acct., 1985-89; mgr. Riverside Cemetery, Sterling, 1989-90; pvt. practice J.M. Attebury Acctg. & Bookkeeping Svc., 1989-90; mgr. tng. dept., mgr. cons. dept. Omega C.G. Ltd., Lombard, Ill., 1993-95; CEO, pres., owner Attebury Acctg. & Cons. Svc., Sterling, Ill., 1990—. Mem. corp. bd. dirs., CFO Abiding Word Christian Ctr., Sterling, 1985-94, fin. adminstr., 1985-94; mem. corp. bd. Twin City Crists Pregnancy Ctr., Sterling, 1988-90. Mem. NAFE, Nat. Soc. Pub. Accts., Nat. Soc. of Tax Profls. Republican. Mem. Charismatic Ch. Avocations: travel, reading, swimming. Office: 409 4th Ave Sterling IL 61081-3750

ATTENBOROUGH, BARON RICHARD SAMUEL, actor, producer, director, goodwill ambassador; b. Cambridge, England, Aug. 29, 1923; s. Frederick Attenborough; m. Sheila Beryl Grant Sim; 3 children. Leverhulme scholar to Royal Acad. Dramatic Art, 1941 (Bancroft Medal); DLitt (hon.), U. Leicester, 1970, U. Kent, 1981, U. Sussex, 1987; DCL (hon.), U. Newcastle, 1974; LLD (hon.), Dickinson Coll., 1983; DLit (hon.), Am. Internat. U., 1994. Fleming Meml. lectr. R.T.S., 1989; Cameron Mackintosh vis. prof. of theatre Oxford U., 1996; pro-chancellor U. Sussex, 1970-98, chancellor 1998—. First stage appearance as Richard Miller in Ah, Wilderness, Intimate Theatre, Palmers Green, 1941; Ralph Berger in Awake and Sing, Arts (West End debut), 1942; The Little Foxes, Piccadilly, 1942; Brighton Rock, Garrick, 1943. Joined RAF 1943; seconded to RAF Film Unit for Journey Together, 1944; demobilised, 1946. Returned to stage in The Way Back (Home of the Brave), Westminster, 1949; To Dorothy a Son, Savoy, 1950, Garrick, 1951; Sweet Madness, Vaudeville, 1952; The Mousetrap, Ambassadors, 1952-54; Double Image, Savoy, 1956-57, St. James's, 1957; The Rape of the Belt, Piccadilly, 1957-58; film appearances: In Which We Serve (screen debut), 1942; School for Secrets, The Man Within, Dancing With Crime, Brighton Rock, London Belongs to Me, The Guinea Pig, The Lost People, Boys in Brown, Morning Departure, Hell is Sold Out, The Magic Box, Gift Horse, Father's Doing Fine, Eight O'Clock Walk, The Ship That Died of Shame, Private's Progress, The Baby and the Battleship, Brothers in Law, The Scamp, Dunkirk, The Man Upstairs, Sea of Sand, Danger Within, I'm All Right Jack, Jet Storm, SOS Pacific; The Angry Silence (also co-prod.), 1959; The League of Gentlemen, 1960; Only Two Can Play, All Night Long, 1961; The Dock Brief, The Great Escape, 1962; Seance On a Wet Afternoon (also prod.) Best Actor, San Sebastian Film Festival and Brit. Film Acad.), The Third Secret, 1963; Guns at Batasi (Best Actor, Brit. Film Acad.), 1964; The Flight of the Phoenix, 1965; The Sand Pebbles (Hollywood Golden Globe), 1966; Dr. Dolittle (Hollywood Golden Globe), The Bliss of Mrs. Blossom, 1967; Only When I Larf, 1968; The Last Grenade, A Severed Head, David Copperfield, Loot, 1969; 10 Rillington Place, 1970; And Then There Were None, Rosebud, Brannigan, Conduct Unbecoming, 1974; The Chess Players, 1977; The Human Factor, 1979, Jurassic Park, 1992, Miracle on 34th St., 1994, The Lost World, 1996,

Elizabeth, 1997; producer: Whistle Down the Wind, 1961; The L-Shaped Room, 1962; producer, dir.: Oh! What a Lovely War (16 Internat. Awards including Hollywood Golden Globe and BAFTA UN Award), 1968; dir.: Young Winston (Hollywood Golden Globe), 1972; A Bridge Too Far (Evening News Best Drama Award), 1976; Magic, 1978; producer, dir.: Gandhi (8 Oscars, 5 Brit. Acad. TV and Film Artists Awards, 5 Hollywood Golden Globes, Dirs.' Guild of Am. Award for Outstanding Directorial Achievement), 1980-81, Cry Freedom (Berlinale Kamera, BFI award tech. achievement), 1987, Chaplin, 1992, Shadowlands, 1992 (Alexander Korda award for outstanding Brit. film of yr., BAFTA), In Love and War, 1997, Grey Owl, 1998; publications: In Search of Gandhi, 1982, Richard Attenborough's A Chorus Line (with Diana Carter), 1986, Cry Freedom, A Pictorial Record, 1987. Goodwill amb. UNICEF, 1987—; mem. Brit. Actors' Equity Assoc. Council, 1949-73, Cinematograph Films Council, 1967-73, Arts Council of Great Britain, 1970-73; formed Beaver Films with Bryan Forbes, 1959, Allied Film Makers, 1960; dir. Chelsea Football Club, 1969-82 (life v.p. 1993—); dir. Young Vic, 1974-84; chmn. The Actor's Charitable Trust, 1956-88, pres., 1988—; chmn. European Script Fund, 1988-96, (hon. pres. 1996—), Combined Theatrical Charities Appeals Council, 1964-88, pres., 1988—; chmn. Brit. Acad. TV and Film Artists (v.p. from 1971-94, chmn. trustees, 1970—), 1969-70, Royal Acad. Dramatic Art, mem. council 1963—, chmn., 1972—, Capital Radio, 1972-92, life pres., 1992—, Help a London Child, 1975—; chmn. U.K. Trustees Waterford-Kamhlaba Sch., Swaziland (gov. 1987—), 1976—, Duke of York's Theatre, 1979-92, Brit. Film Inst., 1981-92, Goldcrest Films & TV, 1982-87, Com. of Inquiry into the Arts and Disabled People, 1983-85, Channel Four TV (dep. chmn. 1980-86), 1987-92, Brit. Screen Adv. Council, 1987—; Gov. Nat. Film Sch., 1970-81, pres. 1997; pres. Muscular Dystrophy Group of Great Britain (v.p. 1962-71), 1971-96, hon. pres. 1996—; pres. The Gandhi Found., 1983—, Brighton Festival, 1984-85, Brit. Film Yr., 1984-86; trustee Tate Gallery, 1976-82, 94-96, Tate Found., 1986—, Found. Sport and Arts, 1991—; pres. Arts for Health, 1989—, Gardner Centre Arts, Sussex U., 1990—; gov. Motability, 1977—; patron Kingsley Hall Community Ctr., 1982—; R.A. Centre Disability & Arts, Leicester, 1990—. Decorated Commander Brit. Empire, 1967, Knighted 1976; recipient Evening Std. Film award, 40 yrs. svc. to Brit. Cinema, 1983, Praemium Imperiale award, 1998, Martin Luther King Jr. Peace Prize, 1983, Padma Bhushan, India, 1983, award of merit for humanitarianism in film making, European Film awards, 1988, Shakespeare prize Outstanding Contbn. European culture, 1992; named Commandeur, Ordre des Arts et des Lettres, France, 1985; Chevalier, Order de la Legion d'Honneur, France, 1988; named Freeman of City of Leicester, 1990; named fellow Kings Coll. London, 1993; named Baron, Life Peer of Long Borough of Richmond upon Thames, 1993; recipient hon. fellowship U. Wales, 1997. Fellow BAFTA, Brit. Film Inst.; mem. Garrick Club, Beefsteak Club. Avocations: collecting paintings and sculpture, listening to music, watching football. Home: Old Friars, Richmond Green Surrey, England Office: Richard Attenborough Prodns, Beaver Lodge, Richmond Surrey TW9 1NQ, England

ATTERBURY, ROBERT RENNIE, III, lawyer; b. Englewood, N.J., July 11, 1937; s. Robert Rennie Jr. and Beatrice May (Tether) A.; m. Lynda Duer Smith, Sept. 14, 1963; children: Stockton Ward, Kendall C. B. BA, U. Pa., 1960, LLB, 1963. Bar: N.Y. 1963, Ill. 1966. Assoc. Donovan, Leisure, Newton & Irvine, N.Y.C., 1963-66; atty. Caterpillar Tractor Co., Peoria, Ill., 1966-73; sr. atty. Caterpillar Overseas S.A., Geneva, Switzland, 1973-78; gen. atty. Caterpillar Tractor Co., Peoria, 1978-83; assoc. gen. counsel Caterpillar Inc., Peoria, 1983-91, v.p., sec., gen. counsel, 1991—; mem. planning com. Ray Garrett Jr. Corp. and Securities Law Inst., Chgo., 1991—; mem. adv. coun. Asia/Pacific Ctr. for Resolution of Internat. Bus. Disputes, San Francisco, 1991—; mem. Mfrs. Alliance Law Coun. I., Arlington, Va., 1992-98, vice chair, 1998—; mem. The Forum for U.S.-European Union Legal-Econ. Affairs, Boston, 1995—, large law dept. coun., 1996—; mem. corp. counsel com. Nat. Ctr. for State Cts., 1998—. Pres. AMC Found., 1991—; bd. dirs. Peoria Symphony Found., 1991—; bd. dirs. Lakeview Mus. Arts and Scis., 1995-98, vice chmn., 1998—; bd. dirs., sec. Lakeview Mus. Found., 1998—. Mem. ABA, SAR, Am. Corp. Counsel Assn., Am. Soc. Corp. Secs., Assn. Gen. Counsel, Country Club Peoria (dir.), Rotary. Home: 315 W Crestwood Dr Peoria IL 61614-7328 Office: Caterpillar Inc 100 NE Adams St Peoria IL 61629-0002*

ATTIYEH, RICHARD EUGENE, economics educator; b. Bklyn., Oct. 8, 1937; s. Semeer Mathew and Dorothy (Krentz) A.; m. Jessica Falikman, July 20, 1958; children: Michael Richard, Amy Lauren, Gregory Moss. BA, Williams Coll., 1958; PhD, Yale U., 1966. Staff economist Pres.'s Council of Econ. Advisers, Washington, 1961-62; asst. prof. Econs. Stanford U., Palo Alto, Calif., 1962-64, Yale U., New Haven, 1964-67; assoc. prof. then prof. U. Calif.-San Diego, La Jolla, 1967—, dean grad. studies and research, 1982-94, vice chancellor for rsch., dean grad. studies, 1994—, interium sr. vice chancellor acad. affairs, 1996-97. Mem. Grad. Record Examinations Bd., 1987-92, chair, 1990; bd. dirs. Coun. Grad. Schs., 1990-93, chair, 1992. Mem. Am. Econ. Assn., Assn. Grad. Schs. (pres. 1996), Calif. Biomed. Rsch. Assn. (bd. chair 1997-99), Calif. Soc. for Biomed. Rsch. (treas. 1998—). Office: U Calif San Diego Office Grad Studies La Jolla CA 92093

ATTKISSON, SHARYL T., newscaster, correspondent, writer; b. St. Petersburg, Fla.; d. Robert F. Thompson and Judith Jon (Starr) Crist; m. James H. Attkisson, Feb. 18, 1984; 1 child, Sarah Judith Starr Attkisson. BS in Broadcast Journalism, U. Fla., 1982. Reporter, prodr. Sta. WTVX-TV, Ft. Pierce, Fla., 1982-85; reporter Sta. WBNS-TV, Columbus, Ohio, 1985-86, Sta. WTVT-TV, Tampa, Fla., 1986-90; anchor, corr. Cable News Network, Atlanta, 1990-93, CBS News, N.Y.C., 1993-94, CBS News Washington, 1995—; mem. adv. bd. Coll. Journalism, U. Fla., Gainesville, 1994-97, chmn. telecom. adv. bd., 1996-97; host Healthweek series PBS, 1997—. Author: Unreliable Sources, 1993, (booklet) So...You Want an Agent?, 1997. Recipient 1st place TV Reporting Communicator's award Fla. Agribus. Inst., 1983, 1st place award Mature Media Nat. Awards, 1993, bronze medal Mature Media Nat. awards, 1994, 1st place sports reporting award Sigma Delta Chi, 1990, U. Fla. Alumnae Outstanding Achievement honor, 1997, 1st place pub. affairs award Nat. Assn. Black Journalists, 1994, Silver Medal award Mature Media, 1998, Alumni of Distinction Honor award U. Fla. Journalism Coll., 1999; named 1st female journalist to fly on a B-52 combat mission from Fairford Royal AFB to Yugoslavia, 1999. Avocations: writing, gardening. Office: CBS News Washington 2020 M St NW Washington DC 20036-3368

ATTRIDGE, PATRICK J., federal judge; b. 1929. BA, St. Johns U., 1951; LLB, Georgetown U., 1956. Bar: D.C. Atty. Doherty, Attridge & Doherty, 1957-69, Attridge & Harig, 1969-80, MacLeay, Lynch, Bernard, Gregg & Attridge, 1980-83; magistrate judge U.S. Dist. Ct. D.C., Washington, 1983—; mem. security, space and facilities com. Jud. Conf. U.S., 1990-96. Mem. D.C. Bar Assn., Bar Assn. D.C. Office: US Dist Ct 333 Constitution Ave NW Washington DC 20001-2802

ATTRIDGE, RICHARD BYRON, lawyer; b. Atlanta, Oct. 14, 1933; s. Archibald Angus and Katherine Elizabeth (Babb) A.; m. Florence Law, Dec. 14, 1963; children: Anne Habersham, Elizabeth Barnes, R. Byron Jr. BA, Princeton U., 1955; LLB, Emory U., 1961. Bar: Ga. 1960. Ptnr. King & Spalding, Atlanta, 1960—; chmn. State Bd. of Bar Examiners, Ga., 1978-83. Vice chmn. Cmty. Rels. Com., Atlanta, 1968-73; various local charities; vestry Episc. Ch. 1st lt. U.S. Army, 1956-57. Fellow Am. Coll. Trial Lawyers; mem. ABA, State Bar Ga. (bd. govs. 1974-83), Atlanta Bar Assn. (pres. 1971-72), Lawyers Club Atlanta, Capital City Club (bd. dirs. 1989—), Piedmont Driving Club. Avocations: hunting, fishing, tennis. Home: 2820 Habersham Rd NW Atlanta GA 30305-2959 Office: King & Spalding 191 Peachtree St NE Atlanta GA 30303-1740

ATTWOOD, JAMES ALBERT, JR., telecommunications industry executive; b. Lake Forest, Ill., Apr. 20, 1958; s. James Albert and Pauline Veryl (Ellwood) A.; m. Leslie Kim Williams. BA, MA, Yale U., 1980; MBA, JD, Harvard U., 1985. Bar: Mass., N.Y., D.C. Assoc. Hewitt Assocs., Rowayton, Conn., 1980-81; v.p. Goldman, Sachs & Co., N.Y.C., 1985-96; exec. v.p. strategic devel. and planning GTE Corp., Irving, Tex., 1996—. Mem. Am. Soc. Actuaries. Democrat. Presbyterian. Office: GTE Corp 1225 Corporate Dr Irving TX 75015-2257

ATWA, SALEM ALDASOUKI, entrepreneur; b. Benha, Kalubia, Egypt, Dec. 4, 1968; s. Salem Aldasouki and Eatemad Kandel (Elsayed) Atwa; m. Kathryn Janette Gettles, July 12, 1996. Student in elec. engring., Ain Shamps, Cairo, 1990-92. Mgr. Thompson Gourmet, N.Y.C., 1995-98; buyer and seller of small businesses, 1998—. With Egyptian Army, 1989-90. Muslim. Home: 1276 Lexington Ave Apt 3C New York NY 10028-2069

ATWAN, HELENE, publishing executive; b. Paris, July 2, 1953; naturalized Am. citizen, 1980; m. Robert Atwan; children: Gregory, Emily. BA, U. S.C., 1975; MA in English Lit., U. Va., 1976. Asst. editor Random House Coll. Divsn., N.Y.C., 1976; publicity assoc. Alfred A. Knopf, N.Y.C., 1977-79; assoc. dir. publicity The Viking Press, N.Y.C., 1979-81; dir. publicity Farrar, Straus and Giroux, N.Y.C., 1981-83, v.p., 1987-93, assoc. publisher, 1991-93; v.p., dir. mktg. Pocket Books, N.Y.C., 1993-95; publisher Beacon Press, Boston, 1995—; lectr. U. Va., Radcliffe Publishing Procedures, N.Y.U. Publishing Inst., U. Pa. Seton Hall U., Emerson Coll., Boston Coll. Founder, NYU Pub. Inst./ Publishers' Publicity Assn. Scholarship Fund; chair Am. Found. AIDS Rsch. Benefit, 1989; co-chair Goddard Riverside Project for Homeless, 1990, Union Settlement Assn., 1991 (Publishers' Publicity Assn. Benefits). Mem. Publishers' Publicity Assn. (bd. dirs. 1983-93). Home: 1134 Canton Ave Milton MA 02186-2411 Office: Beacon Press 25 Beacon St Boston MA 02108-2824*

ATWATER, JULIE DEMERS, critical care nurse; b. Santa Maria, Calif., Aug. 29, 1945; d. Julian G. and Luella M. (Drown) Demers; m. Roy Michael Atwater, Jan. 29, 1977; children: Michael J. Kawecki, Joel M. LPN, Fanny Allen Sch. for Practical Nursing, Winooski, Vt., 1967; ADN, Weber State Coll., Ogden, Utah, 1982, BS in Allied Health, 1987, BSN, 1989. Lic. practical nurse, Vt., Mass., N.H.; RN, Utah. Practical nurse Brattleboro (Vt.) Meml. Hosp.; practical nurse ICU, Cooley Dickerson Hosp., Northampton, Mass., Cheshire Meml. Hosp., Keene, N.H.; clin. nurse ICU/CCU Evanston (Wyo.) Regional Hosp., 1978-87; clin. nurse VA Hosp., Salt Lake City, 1985-87; critical care nurse McKay Dee Hosp., Ogden, Utah, 1978-92, level IV nurse, 1989-92, clin. head nurse ICU, 1992-95, critical care svc. line shift coord., 1995-97, emergency rm. nurse, 1997—; com. mem. ICU and Heart Right Group, mem. ICU adv. com. and critical care re-eingring. com., 1992-95, organ donor liason, 1982—, trauma com., 1982-97. Recipient Utah Critical Care Nurse of Yr. award, 1991. Mem. AACN, No. Utah AACN, Emergency Nurses Assn. E-mail: Juliedka@aol.com. Home: 3191 S 3500 W Hooper UT 84315-9624

ATWATER, STEPHEN DENNIS, professional football player; b. Chicago, Oct. 28, 1966. BS in Bus. Adminstrn., U. Ark., 1989. Safety Denver Broncos, 1989-98, N.Y. Jets, 1999—. Named to Sporting News NFL All-Pro team, 1992, Pro-Bowl, 1990-96. Office: New York Jets 1000 Fulton Ave Hempstead NY 11550*

ATWATER, TANYA MARIA, marine geophysicist, educator; b. Los Angeles, Aug. 27, 1942; d. Eugene and Elizabeth Ruth (Ransom) A.; 1 child, Alyosha Molnar. Student, MIT, 1960-63; BA, U. Calif., Berkeley, 1965; PhD, Scripps Inst. Oceanography, 1972. Vis. earthquake researcher U. Chile, 1966; research assoc. Stanford U., 1970-71; asst. prof. Scripps Inst. Oceanography, 1972-73; U.S.-USSR Acad. Scis. exchange scientist, 1973; asst. prof. MIT, 1974-79, assoc. prof., 1979-80, research assoc., 1980-81; prof. dept. geoscis. U. Calif., Santa Barbara, 1980—; chairperson ocean margin drilling Ocean Crust Planning Adv. Com.; mem. pub. adv. com. on law of sea U.S. Dept. State, 1979-83; mem. tectonics panel Ocean Drilling Project, 1990-93; Sigma Xi lectr., 1975-76. Sci. cons.: Planet Earth: Continents in Collision (R. Miller), 1983; contbr. articles to profl. jours. Sloan fellow, 1975-77; recipient Newcomb Cleveland prize AAAS, 1980; named Scientist of Yr. World Book Ency., 1980. Fellow Am. Geophys. Union (fellows com. 1980-81, 94-95, Ewing award subcom. 1980., McElwane award subcom. 1994), Geol. Soc. Am. (Penrose Conf. com. 1978-80); mem. AAAS, Assn. Women in Sci, Am. Geol. Inst., Nat. Acad. Scis., Phi Beta Kappa, Eta Kappa Nu. Office: U Calif Dept Geoscis Santa Barbara CA 93106

ATWATER, VERNE STAFFORD, finance educator; b. Pitts., Aug. 22, 1920; s. Verne L. and Priscilla (Brodeur) A.; m. Evelyn Lowe, May 29, 1943; children: Lynda Mary Atwater Pyfrin, Louise Christine Atwater Cross. *Verne Atwater has three grandchildren: Evelyn Pyfrin Stapelton, Steven John Atwater Pyfrin, and Christopher Stafford Reinhart.* BA, Heidelberg Coll., 1943; MBA, Harvard U., 1943; PhD, NYU, 1961; LHD, Heidelberg Coll., 1989. Asst. prof. bus. adminstrn. Syracuse U., 1946-50; asst. to chmn. bd. N.J. Bank, Paterson, 1950-56; dir. adminstrn. Ford Found., 1956-61; rep. Argentina/Chile, 1961-63; dir. Latin Am. and Caribbean Program, 1963-64, v.p., 1964-68; pres. Westinghouse Learning Corp., N.Y.C., 1968-71; chmn., chief exec. officer Central Savs. Bank, N.Y., 1971-81; prof. fin. Lubin Grad. Sch. Bus., Pace U., N.Y.C., 1981-90, vice dean, 1984-86; pres. Sing n Do Co., Inc.; prof. emeritus in residence Pace U., N.Y.C., 1990—; bd. dirs. Hudson City Savs. Bank N.J., Marcel Dekker Inc.; mem. Nat. Commn. on Electric Fund Transfers, 1975-77; mem. Pres.'s Task Force on Career Devel., 1967-68, N.J. Housing Fin. Agy., 1966-70. Chmn. bd. trustees Heidelberg Coll., 1982-89; chmn. Woodlawn Cemetery, 1994-98, James T. Lee Found; founder Tribute to Women in Industry Program of YMCA (TWIN), 1974—; church soloist. Lt. USNR, 1943-46. Recipient Disting. Svc. award Outstanding Cmty. Leadership, YMCA Bergen County, The American Red Cross, Crossroads Chpt., the United Way, Vol. Ctr. Bergen County, Ramapo Coll., Heidelberg College and the Heritage. Mem. Arcola Country Club (dir., Paramus, N.J.), Univ. Club (N.Y.C.). Home: 500 Clinton Ave Wyckoff NJ 07481-1432 Office: Pace U Lubin Grad Sch Bus Pac Plz New York NY 10038

ATWELL, CONSTANCE WOODRUFF, health services executive, researcher; b. Jan. 27, 1942. AB with high honors in psychology, Mount Holyoke Coll., 1963; MA, UCLA, 1965, PhD, 1968. Asst. prof. psychology Pitzer Coll., Claremont (Calif.) Grad. Sch., 1967-72, assoc. prof. psychology, 1972-77, prof. psychology, 1977-78; grants assoc. div. of rsch. grants NIH, Bethesda, Md., 1978-79; chief, Office of Clin. Applications of Vision Rsch. Nat. Eye Inst., NIH, Bethesda, 1979-88, asst. chief, Strabismus, Amblyopia and Visual Processing Br., 1980-81, chief, Strabismus, Amblyopia and Visual Processing Br., 1981-92, dep. assoc. dir. Extramural and Collaborative Programs, 1988-92; assoc. dir. for extramural activities Nat. Inst. Neurol. Disorders and Stroke, Bethesda, 1992—, acting dep. dir., 1997-98; rsch. proposal reviewer for the Nat. Found. March of Dimes, Nat. Inst. of Disability and Rehab. Rsch., Nat. Soc. to Prevent Blindness, U.S. Dept. Edn., NIH office of Program Planning and Evaluation, co-chair adv. com. women's health issues; various adv. bds., exec. coms. and rsch. projects, co-chair improving peer rev. reinvention com. Contbr. articles to profl. publs. Reader for Recording for the Blind, 1973-78; trustee Claremont Collegiate Sch., 1975-77; chmn. guidance adv. com. Cabin John Jr. High Sch., 1980-81, exec. com., 1980—, pres. parent tchrs. assn., 1981-82; mem. exec. com. Winston Churchill High Sch. PTA, 1982-85. Recipient Nat. Merit scholarship, 1959-63; named Sara Williston scholar, Mary Lyon scholar. Mem. AAAS, Soc. for Neurosci., Assn for Women in Sci., Phi Beta Kappa, Sigma Xi. Office: Ninds 7550 Wisconsin Ave Bethesda MD 20814-3559

ATWELL, ROBERT HERRON, higher education executive; b. Washington, Pa., Jan. 26, 1931; s. R. Boice and Elsie (Herron) A.; m. Suzanne Fogg, Apr. 22, 1989; children by previous marriages: Mary, Robert, John, Nancy, Carl, Catherine, Cynthia. BA, Coll. Wooster, 1953; MA in Pub. Adminstrn, U. Minn., 1957. Budget examiner U.S. Bur. Budget, Washington, 1957-60; fiscal economist, loan officer U.S. Devel. Loan Fund, Dept. State, 1960; budget examiner, program analyst for higher edn. and med. research programs U.S. Bur. Budget, 1961-62; program planning officer, asst. chief Cmty. Mental Health Ctrs. br. NIMH, HEW, 1962-65; vice chancellor for adminstrn. U. Wis., Madison, 1965-70; pres. Pitzer Coll., Claremont, Calif., 1970-78; v.p. Am. Coun. Edn., 1978-84; pres. Am. Coun. Edn., 1984-96, pres. emeritus, 1996—; chmn. coun. Claremont Coll., 1971-72; pres. Ind. Colls. So. Calif., 1974-75; trustee Tchrs. Ins. Annuity Assn./Coll. Retirement Equities, Eckerd Coll., Collegis Corp., Edn. Mgmt. Corp.; sr. cons. A.T. Kearny Inc. With AUS, 1953-55. Home: 447 Bird Key Dr Sarasota FL 34236

ATWOOD, EDWARD CHARLES, economist, educator; b. N.Y.C., Dec. 2, 1922; s. Edward Charles and Bertha Margaret (Moloney) A.; m. June Matilda Ruschmeyer, Mar. 30, 1946; children—Edward Terrell, Jeffrey Terrell. A.B., Princeton U., 1946, M.A., 1950, Ph.D. in Econs, 1959. Teaching fellow U. Buffalo, 1946-47; part-time instr. Princeton U., 1948-50; instr. Denison U., 1950-52; from asst. to assoc. prof. Washington and Lee U., 1952-60, dean students, 1961-69, dean Sch. Commerce, 1969-86, Lewis W. Adams Prof. of Econs., 1986-93, prof. econs. emeritus, 1993—; econ. cons. Bankers Trust Co., N.Y.C., 1956; economist Gen. Electric Co., 1960-61; tchr. courses Am. Inst. Banking, Va. Sch. Banking, 1957-59; co-chmn. Va. Council Higher Edn. Bus. Adminstrn. Task Force, 1985-86; dir. United Va. Bankshares/Rockbridge, Lexington; vis. prof. Tamkang U., Taiwan, Fall, 1986; vis. fellow U. Coll., Oxford U., Spring, 1987. Pres. Rockbridge Area Housing Corp., 1974-75; trustee Lawrenceville Fathers Assn. Served with USNR, 1942-46. Mem. Am. Assembly Collegiate Schs. Bus. (initial accreditation com., continuing accreditation com. 1969-86), Am., So. econ. assns., Am. Bankers Assn (selection com. 1973-74), Beta Gamma Sigma, Omicron Delta Kappa, Omicron Delta Epsilon. Presbyterian. Home: 389B Heritage Vlg Southbury CT 06488-1717

ATWOOD, HAROLD ASHLEY, retired historian; b. Antioch, Ill., Dec. 18, 1921; s. Charles and Elaine (Pritchard) A.; m. Georgia Elnora Christlieb, Aug. 21, 1954. BA, U. Ill., 1948; MA, U. Wis., 1950; MLS, Western Mich. U., 1976. Tchr. Benton Harbor (Mich.) H.S., 1952-72; adminstrv. asst. hist. preservation City of Benton Harbor, 1979-80; history cons. Benton Harbor Area Schs., 1989-91. Home: 234 Searles Ave Benton Harbor MI 49022-5431

ATWOOD, HAROLD LESLIE, physiology and zoology educator; b. Montreal, Que., Can., Feb. 15, 1937; s. Carl Edmond and Margaret (Killam) A.; m. Lenore Gertrude Mendelson, Dec. 23, 1959; children: David, Robert, Evan. BA, U. Toronto, 1959; MA, U. Calif.-Berkeley, 1960; PhD, Glasgow U., 1963, DSc, 1978. Research assoc. U. Oreg., Eugene, 1962-64; research fellow Calif. Inst. Tech., Pasadena, 1964-65; asst. prof. U. Toronto, 1965-68, assoc. prof., 1968-72, prof. zoology, 1972—, chmn. dept. physiology, 1981-91; vis. Forchheimer prof. Hebrew U., Jerusalem, 1987-88; dir. Med. Rsch. Coun. of Can. Group in Nerve Cells and Synapses, 1991—. Guggenheim fellow U. Calif.-San Diego, 1972; Med. Rsch. Coun. Can. Disting. Scientist, 1997—. Fellow Royal Soc. Can.; mem. AAAS,Soc. Neurosci., Can. Soc. Zoologists, Am. Physiol. Soc., Can. Physiol. Soc. (editor jour. 1987-91), Can. Assn. Neurosci. (pres. 1993-95). Office: U Toronto, Dept Physiology, Toronto, ON Canada M5S 1A8

ATWOOD, HOLLYE STOLZ, lawyer; b. St. Louis, Dec. 25, 1945; d. Robert George and Elise (Sauselle) Stolz; m. Frederick Howard Atwood III, Aug. 12, 1978; children: Katherine Stolz, Jonathan Robert. BA, Washington U., St. Louis, 1968; JD, Washington U., 1973. Bar: Mo. 1973. Jr. ptnr. Bryan Cave, St. Louis, 1973-82, ptnr., 1983—, exec. com., 1995—. Bd. dirs. St. Louis council Girl Scouts U.S., 1976-86; trustee John Burroughs Sch., St. Louis, 1983-86. Mem. ABA, Met. St. Louis Bar Assn., Washington U. Law Sch. Alumni Assn. (pres. 1983-84). Club: Noonday (St. Louis) (bd. govs. 1983-86). Office: Bryan Cave 1 Metropolitan Sq 211 N Broadway Saint Louis MO 63102-2733

ATWOOD, JAMES R., lawyer; b. White Plains, N.Y., Feb. 21, 1944; s. Bernard D. and Joyce Rose A.; m. Wendy Fisler, Aug. 22, 1981 (div. July 1993); children: Christopher Charles, Carl Fisler. BA, Yale U., 1966; JD, Stanford U., 1969. Bar: Calif. 1969, D.C. 1970. Law clk. to judge U.S. Ct. Appeals, L.A., 1969-70; law clk. to Chief Justice Warren Burger U.S. Supreme Ct., 1970-71; mem. Covington & Burling, Washington, 1971-78, ptnr., 1977-78, 81—; dep. asst. sec. for transp. affairs U.S. Dept. State, Washington, 1978-79, dep. legal adviser, 1979-80; acting prof. Law Sch. Stanford U., 1980. Author: (with Kingman Brewster) Antitrust and American Business Abroad, 2nd edit, 1981. Mem. bd. visitors Law Sch. Stanford U., 1995-97. Mem. ABA, Am. Soc. Internat. Law, Washington Inst. Fgn. Affairs, D.C. Bar Assn. Home: 8020 Greentree Rd Bethesda MD 20817-1304 Office: Covington & Burling PO Box 7566 1201 Pennsylvania Ave NW Washington DC 20044-7566

ATWOOD, JOHN BRIAN, federal agency administrator; b. Wareham, Mass., July 25, 1942; s. Ellsworth Savary and Bernice Anita (Perkins) A.; m. Susan Johnson, Aug. 3, 1991; children: John, Deborah. BA, Boston U., 1964; postgrad., Am. U., 1970. Mgmt. intern Nat. Security Agy., Washington, 1964-66; fgn. service officer U.S. Dept. State, Washington, 1966-71; legis. asst. to Senator Thomas F. Eagleton, 1971-77; dep. asst. sec. for congl. relations U.S. Dept. State, Washington, 1977-79, asst. sec., 1979-81; dean, profl. studies and acad. affairs Fgn. Service Inst., Washington, 1981-82; v.p. Internat. Reporting and Info. Systems, Washington, 1982—; exec. dir. Dem. Senatorial Campaign Com., Washington, 1982-84; pres. Nat. Dem. Inst. for Internat. Affairs, Washington, 1985-93; adminstr. U.S. AID, Washington, 1993—. Recipient Harvard Prize Book award, 1959. Mem. Boston U. Alumni Assn. Home: 3009 Mckinley St NW Washington DC 20015-1265 Office: US Agency for International Development 1300 Pennsylvania Ave NW Washington DC 20523*

ATWOOD, MARGARET ELEANOR, author; b. Ottawa, Ont., Can., Nov. 18, 1939; d. Carl Edmund and Margaret Dorothy (Killam) A. BA, U. Toronto, 1961; AM, Radcliffe Coll., 1962; postgrad., Harvard U., 1962-63, 65-67; LittD (hon.), Trent U., 1973, Concordia U., 1980, Smith Coll., Northampton, Mass., 1982, U. Toronto, 1983, U. Waterloo, 1985, U. Guelph, 1985, Mt. Holyoke Coll., 1985, Victoria Coll., 1987, Univ. de Montréal, 1991, McMaster U., 1996; LLD (hon.), Queen's U., 1974. Lectr. in English U. B.C., 1964-65, Sir George Williams U., 1967-68, U. Alta., 1969-70; asst. prof. English York U., Toronto, 1971-72; writer-in-residence U. Toronto, 1972-73, U. Ala., Tuscaloosa, 1985; Berg Chair NYU, 1986; writer-in-residence Macquarie U., Australia, 1987, Trinity U., San Antonio, 1989. Author: (poetry) Double Persephone, 1961, The Circle Game, 1967, The Animals in That Country, 1968, The Journals of Susanna Moodie, 1970, Procedures for Underground, 1970, Power Politics, 1973, Poems for Voices, 1970, You Are Happy, 1975, Selected Poems, 1976 (Am. edit. 1978), Selected Poems, 1966-84, 1990, Margaret Atwood Poems, 1965-75, 1991, Two Headed Poems, 1978, True Stories, 1981, Interlunar, 1984, Selected Poems II: Poems Selected and New, 1976-1986, 1986, Morning in the Burned House, 1995; (novels) The Edible Woman, 1969 (Am. edit. 1970), Surfacing, 1972, (Am. edit. 1973), Lady Oracle, 1976, Life Before Man, 1979, Bodily Harm, 1981, The Handmaid's Tale, 1985, Cat's Eye, 1988 (City Toronto Book award 1989, Coles Book of the Yr. 1989, Can. Booksellers Assn. Author of the Yr., 1989, Book of the Yr. award Found. for Advancement of Can. Letters, Periodical Marketers Can., 1989, Torgi Talking Book award 1989), The Robber Bride, 1993 (award for Fiction Can. Authors Assn., 1993, Trillium award for Excellence in Ont. Writing 1993, Regional Commonwealth Lit. award), Alias Grace, 1996 (Giller Prize 1996, Medal of Honor for Literature, Nat. Arts Club 1997); (short stories) Dancing Girls, 1977, Bluebeard's Egg, 1983, Murder in the Dark, 1983, Wilderness Tips, 1991 (Trillium award 1992, Book of the Yr. award Periodical Marketers of Can., 1992), Good Bones, 1992; (juvenile) Up in the Tree, 1978, Anna'a Pet, 1980, For the Birds, 1990, Princess Prunella & the Purple Peanut, 1995; (non-fiction) Survival; A Thematic Guide to Canadian Literature, 1972, Second Words: Selected Critical Prose, 1982, Strange Things: The Malevolent North in Canadian Literature, 1995;. Recipient E.J. Pratt medal, 1961, Pres.'s medal U. Western Ont., 1965, YWCA Women of Distinction award, Gov. Gen.'s award, 1966, 1st pl. Centennial Commn. Poetry Competition, 1967, Union Poetry prize Chicago, 1969, Bess Hoskins prize of Poetry Chicago, 1974, City of Toronto Book award, 1977, Can. Booksellers Assn. award, 1977, award for short fiction Periodical Distbr. Can., 1977, St. Lawrence award for Fiction, 1978, Radcliffe Grad. medal, 1980, Molson award, 1981, Internat. Writer's prize Welsh Arts Council, 1982, Book of Yr. award Periodical Distbrs. of Can. and Found. for Advancement Can. Letters, 1983, Los Angeles Times Fiction award, 1986, Gov. Gen.'s Lit. award, 1986, Ida Nudel Humanitarian award, 1986, Toronto Arts award, 1986, Arthur C. Clarke award for Best Sci. Fiction, 1987, shortlisted for Ritz Hemingway prize, Paris, 1987, Commonwealth Lit. Prize regional award, 1987, 94, Silver medal for Best Article of Yr. Council for Advancement and Support of Edn., 1987, Nat. Mag. award 1st prize, 1988, Sunday Times award for literary excellence, YWCA Women of Distinction award 1988, Centennial medal Harvard U., 1990, John Hughes prize Welsh Devel. Bd., 1992, Commemorative medal 125th Anniversary of Can. Confedn., 1992, Trillium award for excellence in Ont. writing, 1995; Guggenheim fellow, 1981; decorated companion Order of Can., 1981, Order of Ont., 1990; named Woman of Yr. Ms. Mag., 1986, Humanist of Yr., 1987, Chevalier de l'Ordre des Arts et des Lettres, 1994. Fellow Royal Soc. of Can., Am. Acad. Arts and Scis. (fgn. hon. lit. mem. 1988). Address: care Oxford U Press, 70 Wynford Dr, Don Mills, ON Canada M3C 1J9

AUBAIN, JOSEPH F., municipal official. Exec. dir. St. Thomas-St. John C. of C. Office: St Thomas-St John C of C PO Box 324 6-7 Dronningens Gade Charlotte Amalie VI 00804-0324*

AUBERJONOIS, RENÉ MURAT, actor; b. N.Y.C., June 1, 1940; s. Fernand and Laura (Murat) A.; m. Judith Helen Mihalyi, Oct. 19, 1963; children: Tessa Louise, Rémy-Luc. BFA, Carnegie-Mellon U., 1962. Tchr. acting U. Calif. at Berkeley, San Francisco State U., Julliard Sch.; bd. dirs. Calif. Theatre Council, Calif. State U. Summer Sch. of the Arts; mem. artistic advancement panel NEA; bd. dirs. Calif. State Summer Sch. Arts. Appeared in films M*A*S*H, 1969, Brewster McCloud, 1970, McCabe and Mrs. Miller, 1970, Pete N' Tillie, 1972, Images, 1972, The Hindenberg, 1973, King Kong, 1976, Eyes of Laura Mars, 1978, Where the Buffalo Roam, 1980, 3:15, 1985, Walker, 1987, My Best Friend is a Vampire, 1987, Police Academy V, 1988, The Feud, 1989, The Little Mermaid, 1989, Star Trek: The Undiscovered Country, The Ballad of Little Jo, 1993, Batman Forever, 1995, Los Locos, 1997, Burning Down the House, 1997, Snide and Prejudice, 1997, Cats Don't Dance, 1997, Inspector Gadget, 1999; appeared in repertory theatre Arena Stage, Washington, 1962-65, A.C.T., San Francisco, 1965-68, B.A.M. Rep., 1976-77, Mark Taper Forum, Los Angeles, 1980-83; Broadway plays Fire!, 1968, Coco, 1970 (Tony award), The Good Doctor, 1974 (Tony nomination), Tricks, 1972, Break a Leg, 1979, Big River, 1985 (Tony nomination), Every Good Boy Deserves Favor, 1986, Metamorphosis, 1989, City of Angels, 1990 (Tony nomination); star TV series Benson, 1980-86 (Emmy nomination); created role of Odo, shape shifter on Star Trek, Deep Space Nine, other TV appearances include (mini-series) Ashenden, Lost Language of Cranes (BBC and PBS), 1993, Outer Limits, 1998, Poltergeist, 1998; dir. TV: Marblehead Manor; actor, dir. TV Star Trek: Deep Space Nine.

AUBERT, KENNETH STEPHEN, guidance and counseling administrator, educator; b. Lowell, Mass., Aug. 19, 1952; s. Harvey A. and Irene A. (Genest) A. BS, U. Mass., 1974; MEd, Tufts U., 1976. Cert. sch. psychologist, guidance counselor, guidance dir., Mass. Psychotherapist Reading, Mass., 1976-78; guidance counselor Parker Jr. H.S., Chelmsford, Mass., 1976-78; clin. psychologist Angel Guardian Home, Bklyn., 1978-83; guidance counselor Foxborough (Mass.) H.S., 1983—, dir. guidance, 1986—; ednl. cons. Carol Gill Assocs., Brookline, Mass., 1987-92. Pres., bd. dirs. Chambers Ballet Co., Randolph, Mass., 1987—. Mem. NEA, ACA, Nat. Assn. for Coll. Admission Counseling, Mass. Sch. Counselor's Assn., New England Assn. for Coll. Admission Counseling, Mass. Tchrs. Assn., Greater Boston Guidance Assn. Avocations: gardening, landscaping, skiing, sailing. Home: 279 Poplar St Boston MA 02131-3651 Office: Foxborough High Sch 120 South St Foxboro MA 02035-1723

AUBIN, BARBARA JEAN, artist; b. Chgo., Jan. 12, 1928; d. Philip Theodore and Dorothy May (Chapman) A. BA, Carleton Coll., 1949; B Art Edn., Sch. Art Inst. Chgo., 1954, M Art Edn., 1955. Lectr. Centre D'Art & Haitian Am. Inst., Port-Au-Prince, Haiti, 1958-60; asst. prof. Sch. Art Inst. Chgo., 1960-67, Loyola U., Chgo., 1968-71; lectr. Calumet Coll., Hammond, Ind., 1971-75; prof. art Chgo. State U., 1971-91; ret., 1991; vis. prof., artist Wayne State U., Detroit, Mich., 1965; vis. artist St. Louis C.C., Forest Park, Mo., 1980, 81, U. Wis., Green Bay, 1981; co-curator Art for the Next Millennium Kimo Theatre Gallery, Albuquerque, 1997. One-woman shows include Countryside Arts Ctr., Arlington Heights, Ill., 1954, Avant Arts Gallery, Chgo., 1954, Riccardo's Restaurant and Gallery, Chgo., 1956, Evanston (Ill.) Twp. H.S., 1958, Centre d'Art, Port-au-Prince, Haiti, 1960, Chgo. Pub. Libr., 1960, Chgo. Acad. Fine Arts, 1965, Oxbow Summer Sch. Fine Arts, 1965, Lewis Towers Gallery, Loyola U., Chgo., 1970, Chgo. State U., 1971, 74, 85, North River Cmty. Gallery, Northeastern Ill. U., Chgo., 1974, Ill. Arts Coun., Chgo., Crossroads-Jr. Mus., Art Inst. Chgo., 1976, Fairweather Hardin Gallery, Chgo., 1978, 80, 85, 90, U. Wis., 1981, Illini Union Gallery, U. Ill., Urbana, 1986, Countryside Art Ctr., Arlington Heights, 1987, Artemisia Gallery, Chgo.; exhibited in group shows at Art Inst. Chgo., 1960, 78, 80, 85, 89, Vanderpoel Art Assn., Beverly Art Ctr., Chgo., 1992, Ancient Echoes, Chgo., 1992, Renaissance Ct., Chgo. Cultural Ctr., 1993, Artemisia Gallery, Chgo., 1994, Art Place Gallery, Chgo, 1994, Chgo. State U., 1994, Chgo. Women's Caucus for Art, 1994, 98 Eastern Ill. U., Charleston, 1994, ARC Gallery, Chgo., 1995, 97, N.Mex. Art League, Albuquerque, 1996, Mirage Gallery, Albuquerque, Barrington Arts Coun., 1997, Meridian Ctr., Washington, 1997, Chgo. Women's Caucus for Art No. Ill. U., 1998, Springfield Art Mus. (Patron Purchase award for Watercolor U.S.A. '99), Mo., 1999 ; represented in permanent collections at Art Inst. Chgo., Ill. State Mus., Ball State Mus., Calumet Coll., Hammond, Ind., Shimer Coll., Waukegon, Ill., Kemper Group Collection, Long Grove, Ill., State of Ill. Bldg., Chgo., Seyfarth, Shaw, Fairweather & Geraldson, Washington, Ernst & Ernst, Chgo., Foote, Cone & Belding, Chgo., U.S. League of Savs. and Loans, Chgo., Northside Industries, Chgo., Keck, Cushman, Mahin & Cate, Chgo., Gould, Inc., Rolling Meadows, Ill., First Nat. Bank Chgo., Ill. Tool Works, Chgo., Internat. Mineral and Chem., Skokie, Ill.; reporter Women Artists News, 1977, 80, 83-86; pvt. collections. V.p. Midwest region Womens Caucus for Art, Chgo., 1982-88; founding mem. local chpt. Chgo. Women's Caucus for Art, 1973; bd. dirs. Chgo. Artists Coalition, 1992-94. Recipient George D. Brown Fgn. Travel fellowship Sch. Art Inst. Chgo., 1955-56, Art grant Fulbright Found., 1958-60, grant Huntington Hartford Fedn., 1963, Project Completion grant Ill. Arts Coun., 1978, 79. Mem. Arts Club Chgo., Chgo. Artists' Coalition, Chgo. Womens Caucus for Art, Albuquerque United Artists. Home: 5101 Glenwood Pointe Ln NE Albuquerque NM 87111-2976

AUBREY, BRYAN, educator, writer, editor; b. Beckenham, Kent, Eng., Sept. 6, 1949; came to U.S., 1981; s. Ronald Edmund and Mignon Estelle (Clifford) A. BA in Religious Studies, U. Lancaster, Eng., 1977; PhD in English Lit., U. Durham, Eng., 1982. Asst. prof. lit. Maharishi Internat. U., Fairfield, Iowa, 1981-84, assoc. prof. lit., 1985-86, adj. assoc. prof. lit., 1987—; editor, writer Fast Times Mag., San Marcos, Calif., 1988—. Author: Watchmen of Eternity, 1986, English Romantic Poetry, 1991; contbr. articles to Studies in Mystical Lit., Studia Mystica, Aligarh Critical Miscellany. Avocations: opera, current affairs, meditation and spirituality. Home: 1100 E Madison Ave Fairfield IA 52556-3737

AUBREY, JAMES REYNOLDS, English educator; b. Kittanning, Pa., Dec. 3, 1945; s. Samuel Moss and Alice (Reynolds) A.; m. Marilyn Sue Awbrey, June 8, 1968; children: Sarah Elizabeth, Meredith Anne. BS, USAF Acad., 1968; MA, Northwestern U., 1973; PhD, U. Wash., 1979. Commd. 2d lt. USAF, 1968, advanced through grades to lt. col., 1984; ret., 1989; intlligence briefer hq. mac Met. State Coll., Scott AFB, 1970-72; chief of intelligence 42ECS, 8TFW, RAF Upper Meyford, 1983-86; prof. English USAF Acad., 1973-76, 79-83, 86-89; prof. English Met. State Coll., Denver, 1989—. Author: John Fowles, 1991.

AUBREY, SHERILYN SUE, elementary school educator; b. Louisville, Nov. 7, 1951; d. Sheridan and Alice (Rivera) A. BA in Edn., U. Ky., 1974; MA in Edn., Murray State U., 1979. Cert. elem. tchr., Ky. Primary tchr. Hopkins County Bd. Edn., Madisonville, Ky., 1975—; early childhood edn. rank I Murray State U., 1999—; mem. coun. site-base com. Grapevine Sch., Madisonville, 1991—. Mem. NEA, Ky. Edn. Assn., Hopkins County Edn. Assn. (rep. 1986-90), Alpha Delta Kappa (chair altruistic com. Omicron chpt. 1988-91). Baptist. Avocations: travel, reading, theater. Home: 501 E Morehead St Central City KY 42330-1238 Office: Grapevine Sch Hayes Ave Madisonville KY 42431-3296

AUBURN, MARK STUART, educator, administrator; b. Cin., Dec. 9, 1945; s. Norman Paul and Kathleen (Montgomery) A.; m. Sandra Korman, Jan. 25, 1969; children: David Andrew, Benjamin Max Joseph. BS in Math., BA in English, U. Akron, 1967; A.M. in English, U. Chgo., 1968, PhD, 1971. Mem. faculty Ohio State U., 1971-83, assoc. prof. English, 1977-83, asst. vice provost, sec. Coll. Arts and Scis., 1980-82, assoc. vice provost, 1982-83; dean Coll. Arts and Scis., prof. English, Ark. State U., 1983-85; v.p. for planning and mgmt. support U. Ark. System, 1985-88; vice chancellor acad. affairs Ind. U.-Purdue U., Ft. Wayne, Ind., 1988—; prof. English Ind. U., 1988—; cons. various univs., founds.; bd. dirs. Ark. Endowment for Humanities, pres., 1987-88, Ind. Humanities Coun., 1990—. Trustee First Unitarian Ch. Columbus, 1976-79, pres., 1977-78, moderator, 1979-80. Grantee Am. Philos. Soc., 1972, Ohio State U., 1972, 73, 75, 76, 78, 80, NEH, 1984. Mem. Am. Soc. 18th Century Studies, MLA, AAUP, Coll. English Assn. Ohio (exec. com. 1979), Am. Soc. Theater Rsch., Midwest MLA, S.W. MLA, Lambda Chi Alpha, Phi Kappa Phi, Phi Delta Kappa, Omicron Delta Kappa. Author: Sheridan's Comedies, 1977; (with others) Drama Through Performance, 1977. Editor: Marriage a la Mode, 1981; editorial bd. Theatre Ann., Restoration and 18th Century Theatre Rsch. Home: 2101 E Coliseum Blvd Fort Wayne IN 46805-1445 Office: Indiana U-Purdue U E Coliseum Blvd Fort Wayne IN 46805

AUBURN, NORMAN PAUL, university president; b. Cin., May 22, 1905; s. Joseph and Huldah A.; m. Kathleen Montgomery, June 28, 1930 (dec. 1974); children: Ames Auburn Latta, Richard, Mark, David Bruce; m. Virginia Kirk, Jan. 4, 1977. AB, U. Cin., 1927, postgrad., 1927-28, 34-35, LLD, 1952; LLD, Parsons Coll., 1945, U. Liberia, 1959, U. Akron, 1971; DSc, U. Tulsa, 1957; LittD, Washburn U., 1961; LHD, Coll. of Wooster, 1963; DCL, Union Coll., 1979. Editor Cin. Constructor, 1928-33; asst. mgr. Asso. Gen. Contractors of Am., 1928-33; publicity mgr. Allied Constrn. Industries, 1930-33; exec. sec. U. Cin. Alumni Assn., 1933-36; editor Cin. Alumnus, 1929-36; asst. dir., asst. prof. Evening Coll., U. Cin., 1936-38; assoc. prof. U. Cin., 1938-40, acting dean, 1940-41, dean and prof., 1941-43, dean of univ. adminstrn., clk. bd. dirs., 1943-51, v.p., 1943-51, acting pres., 1949; exec. dir. U. Cin. Research Found., 1943-51; pres. U. Akron, 1951-71, pres. emeritus, cons., 1971—; acting pres. Council Fin. Aid to Edn., N.Y.C., 1957-58, bd. dirs., 1957-71; spl. asst. univ. relations AID, U.S. State Dept., 1965-66, cons., 1966—; cons. Acad. Ednl. Devel., Inc., N.Y.C., 1965-70, sr. v.p., dir. institutional ops., 1971-89, sr. v.p., emeritus, 1989—; acting pres. Poly. Inst., Bklyn., 1973, Stephens Coll., Columbia, Mo., 1974-75, Cedar Crest Coll., Allentown, Pa., 1977-78, Union Coll., Schenectady, N.Y., 1978-79; acting chancellor Union U., Albany, N.Y., 1978-79; sr. v.p., provost Widener U., Chester, Pa., 1979-82; acting pres. Salem Coll., W.Va., 1982-83, Lincoln U., Jefferson City, Mo., 1987-88; spl. asst. to pres. for planning W.Va. U., Morgantown, 1983-86; chmn. Univ. Council on Edn. for Pub. Responsibility, 1965-66; dir. Great Lakes Megalopolis Research Project, 1968-74; vice chmn. Am. Council Edn., 1963-64, dir., 1969-72; bd. dirs. First Fed. Savs. and Loan Assn., Akron, 1963, chmn., 1973—; bd. dirs. Charter One Fin., Cleve., 1988—, Charter One Bank, 1988—, 1st Nat. Bank Akron, emeritus; hon. pres. Lane Theol. Sem., Cin., 1990—. Contbr. articles to ednl. jours. Bd. dirs. Akron Gen. Hosp., U. Akron Devel. Found., 1967—; trustee Greater Akron Musical Assn., 1967—; trustee, sec. Lane Theol. Sem., Cin., 1945—, hon. pres., 1990—; trustee Ohio Coll. Assn., pres., 1960-61; mem. Air Force ROTC Adv. Panel to Dept. USAF, 1960-64; mem. exec. com. Ohio Research and Devel. Bd., 1962-65; pres. Herman Muehlstein Found., 1965—; mem. U. Cin. Endowment Fund Assn. Fellow AAAS; mem. Assn. Am. Colls. (vice chmn. commn. coll. adminstrn. 1965-68), Am. Soc. Engring. Edn., Am. Assn. State Colls. and Univs. (chmn. com. on internat. programs 1970-71), Assn. Univ. Evening Colls. (pres. 1944), Assn. Urban Univs. (pres. 1955-56, sec.-treas. 1956-65), Newcomen Soc., Cincinnatus Soc., Summit County Hist. Soc. (trustee 1975-80), Queen City Assn., Alpha Kappa Psi, Phi Alpha Delta, Lambda Chi Alpha, Omicron Delta Kappa, Scabbard and Blade. Presbyterian. Clubs: Rotary (pres. Cin. 1950-51, Akron 1958-59), Commonwealth (Cin.), Univ. (N.Y.C., Columbus, Ohio), City, Portage Country (Akron), Lago Mar Beach (Ft. Lauderdale, Fla.). Home: 2385 Covington Rd Akron OH 44313-4335 Office: U Akron Office Of Pres Emeritus Akron OH 44325

AUCH, FRED H., JR., company executive. BSCE, U. Mich., 1951. CEO George W. Auch Co., 1982—. Office: 735 S Paddock St Pontiac MI 48341

AUCH, WALTER EDWARD, securities company executive; b. Detroit, Apr. 12, 1921; s. Fred J. and Beatrice H. (Higgins) A.; m. Patricia H.; children: Walter Edward, Timothy R., Terrance H. Student, Albion Coll., also U. Detroit, 1939-42, Cornell U., 1959. Stockbroker William C. Roney & Co., Detroit, 1946-55; sr. partner Bache & Co., N.Y.C., 1955-64, Paine, Webber, Jackson & Curtis, N.Y.C., 1964-70; pres. Nat. Securities & Research Corp., N.Y.C., 1970-72; exec. v.p. duPont, Glore, Forgan, Inc., N.Y.C., 1972-73; pres. duPont Walston, Inc., 1973-74; exec. v.p. Paine, Webber, Jackson & Curtis, N.Y.C., 1974-79; chmn., chief exec. officer Chgo. Bd. Options Exchange, 1979-86, cons., 1987—; bd. dirs. Ft. Dearborn Fund, Pimco Advisors, L.P., Smith Barney Concert Series Fund, Smith Barney Trak Fund, Advisors Series Trust, Nicholas/Applegate Funds, Banyan Land Trust, Semele Group, Inc., Legend Properties, Inc., Brinson Ptnrs. Funds, Pilgrim Funds. Trustee Hillsdale Coll., Ariz. Heart Inst. With USAAF, 1942-45. Mem. Bond Club N.Y., Bond Club Chgo., N.Y. Stock Exch. Club, Chgo. Club, Greenwich Country Club, Troon Golf and Country Club, Paradise Valley Country Club (Scottsdale), Crystal Downs Country Club (Crystal Lake, Mich.), Sigma Chi. Summer Home: 2700 Crystal Dr Crystal Lake Beulah MI 49617 *When I was a boy, my grandfather advised me to "live every day in such a way that the line behind the hearse gets longer." I've tried hard to follow that advice.*

AUCHINCLOSS, KENNETH, magazine editor; b. N.Y.C., July 3, 1937; s. Douglas and Eleanor (Grant) A.; m. Eleanor Muir Johnson, June 5, 1971; children: Malcolm Grant, Emily Johnson. A.B., Harvard U., 1959; B.A., M.A. (Henry fellow), Balliol Coll., Oxford (Eng.) U., 1961. Asst. to dep. asst. sec. commerce Washington, 1962-63, exec. asst. Pres.'s spl. rep. for trade negotiations, 1963-65; asst. to trustees Inst. for Advanced Study, Princeton, N.J., 1965-66; assoc. editor Newsweek, N.Y.C., 1966-69, gen. editor, 1969-72, sr. editor, 1972, exec. editor, 1973-75, mng. editor, 1975-95, editor internat. edits., 1986-95, editor-at-large, 1996—. Home: 40 E 62nd St New York NY 10021-8017 Office: 251 W 57th St New York NY 10019-1802

AUCHINCLOSS, LOUIS STANTON, writer; b. Lawrence, N.Y., Sept. 27, 1917; s. Joseph Howland and Priscilla (Stanton) A.; m. Adele Lawrence, Sept. 1957; children: John, Blake, Andrew. Student, Yale U., 1939; LLB, U. Va., 1941; LittD, N.Y. U., 1974, Pace U., 1979, U. of the South, 1986. Bar: N.Y. bar 1941. Assoc. Sullivan & Cromwell, 1941-51; assoc. Hawkins, Delafield & Wood, N.Y.C., 1954-58, ptnr., 1958-86. Author: The Indifferent Children, 1947, The Injustice Collectors, 1950, Sybil, 1952, A Law for the Lion, 1953, The Romantic Egoists, 1954, The Great World and Timothy Colt, 1956, Venus in Sparta, 1958, Pursuit of the Prodigal, 1959, The House of Five Talents, 1960, Reflections of a Jacobite, 1961, Portrait in Brownstone, 1962, Powers of Attorney, 1963, The Rector of Justin, 1964, Pioneers and Caretakers, 1965, The Embezzler, 1966, Tales of Manhattan, 1967, A World of Profit, 1968, Motiveless Malignity, 1969, Second Chance, 1970, Edith Wharton, 1971, I Came As a Thief, Richelieu, 1972, The Partners, A Writer's Capital, 1974, Reading Henry James, 1975, The Winthrop Covenant, 1976, The Dark Lady, 1977, The Country Cousin, 1978, Persons of Consequence, 1979, Life, Law and Letters, 1979, The House of the Prophet, 1980, The Cat and the King, 1981, Watchfires, 1982, Exit Lady Masham, 1983, The Book Class, 1984, Honorable Men, 1985, Diary of a Yuppie, 1986, Skinny Island, 1987, The Golden Calves, 1988, Fellow Passengers, 1989, The Vanderbilt Era, 1989, The Lady of Situations, 1991, False Gods, 1992, Three Lives, 1993, Tales of Yesteryear, 1994, The Style's The Man, 1994, Collected Stories, 1994, The Education of Oscar Fairfax, 1995, The Man Behind the Book, 1996, LA Gloire, 1996, The Atonement, 1997. Trustee emeritus Josiah Macy, Jr., Found.; chmn. Mus. City of N.Y. Lt. USNR, 1941-45. Mem. AAAL (pres.), Assn. Bar City N.Y., Century Assn. Episcopalian. Home: 1111 Park Ave New York NY 10128-1234

AUCHTERLONIE, DAVID THOMAS, quality assurance professional; b. Newcastle Upon Tyne, Eng., June 15, 1946; s. Joseph and Anne (Burn) A.; m. Carla Reed; children: Jane, Sarah. B of Metallurgy, Sir John Cass Coll., London, 1970, Teeside Poly., 1972; MBA, Newcastle U., 1983. Chartered engr. Brit. Inst. Engrs. Tech. trainee, mem. ironmaking devel. staff Brit. Steel Corp., Consett Works, Eng., 1964-69, tech. asst. to ironmaking mgr., 1969-72; sr. process engr. Lynemouth (Eng.) Smelter, Brit. Alcan, 1972-78, tech. mgr. casting, 1978-84; sr. devel. metallurgist, cons. metallurgist Ingot Products div. Alcan Smelters & Chems., Jonquiere, Que., Can., 1984-89; mgr. improvement process Alcan Smelters & Chems., Jonquiere, 1989-92; dir. quality improvement Alcan Rolled Products Co., Oswego, N.Y., 1992-96; tech. and quality assurance mgr. Alcan Rolled Products Co., Warren, Ohio, 1996-98, bus. unit mgr. automotive Sheet Divsn, 1998-99; plant mgr. Wabash Alloy LLC, Dickson, Tenn., 1999—. Mem. Am. Soc. for Quality Control, AMinerals, Metals and Materials Soc. Office: 600 Printwood Dr Dickson TN 37055

AUCLAIR, LOUISE A., education educator; b. Somersworth, N.H., Feb. 25, 1941; d. Alphonse J. and Alice M. (Chretien) A. BA in English and Elem. Edn., Notre Dame Coll., 1968; MEd in Reading, Salem State Coll., 1973; PhD in Higher Edn., Boston Coll., 1990. Mem. Sisters of Holy Cross, 1958—. Elem. sch. tchr. New Bedford (Mass.) Schs., 1960-61, Nashua and Rochester (N.H.) Schs., 1963-70; elem. sch. prin. Suncook and Nashua, N.H., 1970-74; reading specialist Rochester Cath. Sch., 1974-75, Nashua Cath. Sch., 1975-80; grad. divsn. chair Notre Dame Coll., Manchester, N.H., 1981-87, 90-91, dean edn., 1991-95, prof. edn., 1995—; dean faculty edn. Regina Assumpta Coll., Cap Haitien, Haiti, 1995—. Author: Ideas for Teachers from Teachers, 1983, Historical Development of Departmental Leadership in American Higher Education, 1990. Mentor College Bound program Boston Coll., Chestnut Hill, Mass., 1988-90; usher Palace Theater, Manchester, 1995—. Named Moreau Disting. Svc. Prof., Notre Dame Coll., 1995. Mem. Internat. Reading Assn., New Eng. Reading Assn., Phi Delta Kappa (v.p. 1982-84, pres. 1984-85, coll. rep. 1985-87, 90—, historian 1995—), Alpha Sigma Nu. Roman Catholic. Avocations: reading, travel, sewing. Home: 68 Mammoth Rd Londonderry NH 03053-4024 Office: Notre Dame Coll 2321 Elm St Manchester NH 03104-2213

AUCUTT, RONALD DAVID, lawyer; b. St. Paul, Dec. 28, 1945; s. Howard Lewis and Eleanor May (Malcolm) A.; m. Grace Diane Kok, Apr. 3, 1976; children: David Gerard, James Andrew. BA, U. Minn., 1967, JD, 1975. Bar: Minn. 1975, D.C. 1976, Va. 1978, U.S. Supreme Ct. 1978, U.S. Tax Ct. 1980, U.S. Dist. Ct. D.C. 1980, U.S. Ct. Appeals (D.C. cir.) 1980, U.S. Ct. of Claims 1980, U.S. Claims Ct. 1982, U.S. Ct. Appeals (fed. cir.) 1982, U.S. Dist. Ct. (ea. dist.) Va. 1986, U.S. Ct. Appeals (4th cir.) 1986. Assoc. Miller & Chevalier, Chartered, Washington, 1975-81, ptnr., 1982-98; ptnr. McGuire, Woods, Battle & Boothe, L.L.P., McLean, Va., 1998—; mem. bd. advisors IRS Practice Alert, N.Y.C., 1987-93; adj. prof. Sch. Law U. Va., 1998—. Mem. bd. advisors Jour. Taxation Exempt Orgns., 1989—, Bus. Entities, N.Y.C.; mem. editl. bd. Estate Planning, N.Y.C., 1993—, mem. adv. bd. Tax Mgmt. Estates, Gifts, and Trusts Jour., 1999—; editl. adv. bd. Judges and Lawyers Bus. Valuation Update, Portland, Oreg., 1999—; contbr. articles to profl. publs. Sec.-treas. Miller and Chevalier Charitable Found., Washington, 1980-82, pres., 1993-97; bd. dirs. Evang. Free Ch. Am., Mpls., 1986-92, vice moderator, chmn. bd. dirs., 1993-95, moderator, 1995-97; bd. dirs. Coun. for Ct. Excellence, Washington, 1993—, Advocates Internat., Fairfax, Va., 1997—, vice chmn. 1999—; Orgn. Security and Coop. in Europe internat. observer Bulgarian Parliamentary election, 1997; mem. adv. bd. Trinity Law Sch., Santa Ana, Calif., 1998—; bd. visitors U. Minn. Law Sch., 1998—. Lt. USN, 1970-73. Fellow Am. Bar Found., Am. Coll. Tax Counsel, Am. Coll. Trust and Estate Counsel (bd. regents 1996—, chmn. bus. planning com. 1997—, sec. 1999—); mem. ABA (chair taxation sect., com. on estate and gift taxes 1986-88, vice chmn. com. on govt. submissions 1989-91, chmn. 1991-93, coun. 1993-97, liaison to sect. real property, probate and trust law 1990—, vice chair com. ops. 1998—), Internat. Acad. Estate and Trust Law (academician), Christian Legal Soc., Met. Club Washington, Univ. Minn. Law Alumni Assn. (bd. dirs. 1998—). E-mail: rdaucutt@mwbb.com. Home: 3417 Silver Maple Pl Falls Church VA 22042-3545 Office: McGuire Woods Battle & Boothe LLP 1750 Tysons Blvd Ste 1800 Mc Lean VA 22102-3915

AUDET, HENRI, retired communications executive; b. Montreal, Que., Can., Aug. 7, 1918; s. Victor F. and Alice (Turgeon) A.; m. Marie Labelle, June 24, 1950; children: Louis, François, Denise, Bernard, Geneviève. BA, U. Montreal, BA in Sci.; MSEE, MIT; DSc (hon.), U. Que., 1979. Staff CBC, 1945-47, engr.-in-charge Montreal dist., 1948-52, regional engr. Que., spl. TV com., 1953-57; pres. TV St. Maurice Inc., 1957-72, La Belle Vision, Inc., 1973, TV St. François, Inc., 1974-76; chmn., CEO Cogeco Inc., 1976-93, chmn. bd. dirs., 1993-96; chmn. bd. dirs. Cogeco Cable, Inc., 1993-96; chmn. emeritus, ret., 1996; chmn. bd. Publ. Dumont Inc., 1988, TV de l'Est du Can., 1982; pres. Cogeco Devel. Fund, 1992-96. Past chmn. Que. U., Trois Rivières, Com. Trifluvien des Concerts Symphonique de Que., Cultural Ctr.; past dir. Symphonic Concerts Que., Ctr. Hospitalier Ste.-Marie; active Festivals de Musique Que., Counseil des gouverneurs associés des U. Montreal; bd. govs. Fondation U. Ctr. Que., 1989; mem. hon. coun. Montreal Symphonic Orch.; pres. Fondation du Theatre du Rideau Vert, Fonds du Patrimoine de laa paroisse St-Viateur d'Outremont. Decorated Order of Can.; recipient Prix de comm. Govt. of Que., 1989, Prix Mérite, Assn. Anciens de Poly., 1991; named to honors list Can. Cable TV Assn., 1994. Mem. l'ACRTF (Can. French lang. broadcasters, pres. 1962-64, Grand Prix 1987), IEEE, Can. Assn. Broadcasters (pres. 1971, Golden Ribbon award 1989), Engring. Inst. Can. (past dir.), Hall of Fame of the Canadian Assn. Broadcasters, Broadcast Execs. Soc., Found. Des Ingenieurs du Quebec (bd. dirs.), Hydro-Quebec (bd. dirs.), Can. Acad. Engring, Order of Egrs., Can. C. of C., Que. C. of C., Montreal C. of C., Montreal Bd. Trade, Thelma Finlayson Soc., Mount-Royal Club, St. Denis Club, St. Maurice Yacht Club, Laviolette Club, Radisson Club, Ki-8-Eb Golf Club, Club des Ambassadeurs de la CEDIC, Pres. Club. Roman Catholic. Avocation: travel, sailing, arts, photography. Home: 169 Maplewood Ave, Outremont, Que, PQ Canada H2V 2M6 Office: Cogeco Inc, 1 Pl Ville Marie Ste 3636, Montreal, PQ Canada H3B 3P2

AUDET, LEONARD, theologian; b. Maria, Que., Can., Nov. 26, 1932; s. Ernest and Emilie (Loubert) A. DTh, U. Montreal, 1964; Licence en Ecriture Sainte, Pontificium Institutum Biblicum, Rome, 1964. Prof. Scolasticat de Theologie de Joliette, Que., Can., 1965-67; prof. Bible, Faculty of Theology U. Montreal, 1967-77, 85-94, dean Faculty of Theology, 1977-85; superior gen. Clerics of St. Viator, 1988—. Author: Résurrection: Espérance humaine et don de Dieu, 1971, Jésus? de l'histoire à la foi, 1974, Neuve est ta Parole, 1974, Apres Jesus, Autorite et Liberte dans le peuple de Dieu, 1977, A Companion to Paul, 1975, Vivante est ta parole, 1975, Je crois en Dieu, 1989; contbr. numerous articles to Can. periodicals. Mem. Can. Cath. Soc. of the Bible, Can. Soc. Theology, Cath. Assn. Bibl. Study of Can. (treas. 1968-77). Home: Chierici di San Viatore, Casella Postale 10793, 00144 Rome Italy

AUDET, PAUL ANDRE, retired newspaper executive; b. Quebec, Can., Mar. 14, 1923; s. Sylvio and Rose Aimee (Cloutier) A.; m. Michele Richard, Sept. 13, 1947; children: Francine, Andre, Marc. D. Honoris Causa (hon.), U. Québec, 1985. Newspaper reporter L'Evenement Jour., 1942-44; staff writer The Canadian Press, 1944, asst. mng. editor, 1945-48, sales and sales mgr. printing dept., 1948-54; advt. dir. Le Soleil Quebec, 1955-74; pres., gen. mgr., 1974-88; past pres. Edimedia, Inc.; v.p. Que. Mil. Inst., Que. Opera Co.; bd. dirs. Que. Mil. Inst. Named hon. col. Les Voltigeurs de Que. Regt. Mem. Ordre des Chevaliers de Meduse, Garrison Club, Officers Mess Citadelle de Québec, Order of Can. Roman Catholic. *Whatever you do or you are, try to be the best. Somehow, some day, someone is bound to find out and you will be rewarded accordingly.*

AUDREY-TAYLOR, DAVIDA, secondary education educator; b. Washington, Sept. 16, 1963; d. Jacob and Doris (Davis) Audrey; m. Anthony Robinson, Sept. 16, 1984 (dec.); 1 child, Deneira Laaontrey Audrey; m. Brian Anthony Taylor, Feb. 19, 1993; children: Brian Leroy Taylor, Denina Levern Taylor. BA, U. D.C., 1992; MEd, Nat.-Louis U., 1992; cert. advanced studies, Johns Hoopkins U., 1999; postgrad. in instrnl. tech., Nova Southeastern U. TV editor D.C. Pub. Schs., 1992-94, secondary sch. tchr., 1994—; video cons., W.B. Video Svc., Washington, 1992—. mem. Kappa Delta Pi. Home: 4956 Astor Pl SE Washington DC 20019-6251

AUDY, LYNN, editor; b. Jan. 23, 1973. B in Journalism, U. Mo., 1996. Mng. editor Weekend mag., Columbia, Mo., 1996; asst. editor Asay Publ. Co., Joplin, Mo., 1996-98; editor First Mktg. Co., Pompano Beach, Fla., 1998-99. E-mail: laudy@hotmail.com. Home: 11509 Oak St # 201 Kansas City MO 64114

AUEL, JEAN MARIE, author; b. Chgo., Feb. 18, 1936; d. Neil Solomon and Martha Amelia (Wirtanen) Untinen; m. Ray Bernard Auel, Mar. 19, 1954; children: RaeAnn Marie, Karen Jean, Lenore Jerica, Kendall Poul, Marshall Philip. MBA, U. Portland, 1976, LittD (hon.), 1984; HHD (hon.), U. Maine, 1986; LHD (hon.), Mt. Vernon Coll., 1986; HHD (hon.), Pacific U., 1995. Office and tech. positions, then tech. writer, credit mgr. Tektronix,

Inc., Beaverton, Oreg., 1964-76. Author: The Clan of the Cave Bear, 1980 (Friends of Lit. award 1980, finalist Best First Novel Nat. Book Awards 1980), The Valley of Horses, 1982, The Mammoth Hunters, 1985, The Plains of Passage, 1990 (Waldo award Waldenbooks 1990, Persie award WIN/WIN 1990). Bd. dirs. Oreg. Mus. Sci. and Industry, 1993-96; hon. campaign chair Oreg. Coun. for Humanities, 1991; speaker, fund raiser various charitable and ednl. orgns. Recipient Excellence in Writing award Pacific N.W. Booksellers Assn., 1980, award Scandinavian Kaleidoscope of Art and Life, 1982, Bronze Sculpture award Publieksprijs voor het Nederlandse Boek, 1990, Silver Trowel award Sacramento Archeol. Soc., 1990, contbn. award Dept. Interior/Soc. for Am. Archaeology, 1990, Nat. Zoo award, Centennial medal Smithsonian Instn., 1990, Golden Plate award Am. Acad. Achievement, 1986. Mem. PEN, Authors Guild, Willamette Writers (life), Oreg. Writers Colony (charter mem.), Internat. Women's Forum (bd. dirs. 1985-93), Mensa (hon. v.p. 1990—). Avocation: travel. Office: Jean V Naggar Lit Agy Ste 1 E 217 E 75th St New York NY 10021-2902*

AUER, JAMES MATTHEW, art critic, journalist; b. Neenah, Wis., Dec. 2, 1928; s. Matthew George and Charlotte Agnes (Friedland) A.; m. Marilyn Mills, Feb. 1, 1964; 1 son, Charles William. B.A., Lawrence Coll., Appleton, Wis., 1950. With accounting dept. George Banta Co., 1950-51; reporter Twin City News-Record, 1953-56, asst. to editor, 1957-60, news editor, 1960-61; asst. Sunday editor Appleton Post-Crescent, 1960-65, Sunday editor, 1965-72; art critic Milw. Jour., 1972—. Author: The Spirit is Willing, 1960; plays: The City of Light, 1961, Tell It to Angela, 1971; motion pictures: The Magic World of Patrick Farrell, 1978, The Bohrod Touch, 1984, An Artist's Vision: Born on the Stone, 1986, Olgivanna Lloyd Wright: A Partner to Genius, 1993, In Your Face: The Distorted World of John Kascht, 1994, Etched in Acid: Warrington Colescott, 1998. Presiding officer Attic Theatre, Inc., 1959-62; pres. Friends of Bergstrom Art Center, 1967-68; mem. Neenah Municipal Mus. Found., Inc. Recipient Pres.'s award Wis. Heart Assn., 1969. Mem. Am. Assn. Sunday and Feature Editors (pres. 1972-73), State Hist. Soc. Wis. (award of merit 1962), Soc. Profl. Journalists, Milw. Press Club, Phi Kappa Tau. Congregationalist. Home: 1849 N 72nd St Wauwatosa WI 53213-2353 Office: Milw Jour Sentinel 333 W State St Milwaukee WI 53203-1305 *Art is not a luxury or a frill. It is a quality-of-life issue. That is why I have spent so much of my life enjoying, collecting and writing about it.*

AUERBACH, ALAN JEFFREY, economist; b. N.Y.C., Sept. 27, 1951; s. William and Tess (Kasper) A.; m. Gay Cameron Quimby, June 25, 1978; children: Ethan, Andrew. BA, Yale U., 1974; PhD, Harvard U., 1978. Asst. prof. dept. econs. Harvard U., Cambridge, Mass., 1978-82, assoc. prof., 1982-83; assoc. prof. dept. econs. U. Pa., Phila., 1983-85, prof., 1985-94, chmn. dept., 1988-90, prof. Sch. Law, 1990-94; Robert D. Burch prof. of tax policy and pub. fin. U. Calif., Berkeley, 1994—. Author: The Taxation of Capital Income, 1983 (David A. Wells prize); co-author: Dynamic Fiscal Policy, 1987, Macroeconomics: An Integrated Approach, 1995; editor: Corporate Takeovers, 1988, Mergers and Acquisitions, 1988, Fiscal Policy: Lessons from Economic Research, 1997; co-editor: Handbook of Public Economics, Vol. I, 1985, Vol. II, 1987; editor jour. Econ. Perspectives, 1995-96. Fellow Econometric Soc.; mem. Am. Econ. Assn. (exec. com. 1992-94, v.p. 1999), Phi Beta Kappa. Home: 110 El Camino Real Berkeley CA 94705-2823 Office: U Calif Berkeley Dept Econs 549 Evans Hall Berkeley CA 94720-1775

AUERBACH, ARNOLD (RED AUERBACH), professional basketball team executive; b. N.Y.C., Sept. 20, 1917; s. Hyman and Marie (Thompson) A.; m. Dorothy Lewis, June 6, 1941; children: Nancy, Randy. BS in Phys. Edn., George Washington U., 1940, MA in Edn., 1941; LHD (hon.), Franklin Pierce Coll., 1981, U. Mass., 1982, Boston U., 1984; D in Bus. Adminstrn. (hon.), Cen. New Eng. Coll., 1986; ArtsD (hon.), Stonehill Coll., 1988; HHD (hon.), Am. Internat. Coll., 1988; D. Pub. Svc., George Washington U., 1993. Coach Washington Capitols, 1946-49, Tri-Cities Blackhawks, 1949-50, Boston Celtics, 1950-66; gen. mgr. Boston Celtics Basketball Team, 1964-84, pres., 1970—; Rep. State Dept. for clinics, demonstrations, exhbns.; dir. basketball sch. Camp Milbrook, Marshfield, Mass.; sports commentator, lectr.; dir. Seacrest Hotel, North Falmouth, Mass. Author: Fan and Coach, 1953, (with Paul Sann) Red Auerbach: Winning the Hard Way; (with Joe Fitzgerald) Red Auerbach: An Autobiography, Red Auerbach On and Off the Court; (with Ken Dooley) MBA (Management By Auerbach); producer: (instructional video) Winning Basketball, 1987. Chmn. Mass. chpt. Easter Seal Soc. Served to lt. USN, 1943-46. Recipient Arch McDonald Achievement award, 1962, Boston's Disting. Achievement medal, 1965, Sports Achievement award B'nai B'rith; named Nat. Basketball Assn. Coach of Year, 1965; named to Nat. Basketball Hall of Fame, 1968, Naismith Meml. Basketball Hall of Fame, 1968; chosen All-Time NBA Coach; coach 11 consecutive all star games; winner 12 Ea. div. titles, 9 world titles, 16 World Titles as pres., gen. mgr., coach. Mem. Nat. Coaches Assn., Omicron Delta Kappa, Colonials (George Washington U.). Club: Touchdown (award) (Washington). Office: Boston Celtics 151 Merrimac St Ste 5 Boston MA 02114-4717*

AUERBACH, BOB SHIPLEY, librarian; b. N.Y.C., Dec. 14, 1919; s. Leo and Gertrude Anne (Shipley) A.; m. Mary Carson, July 13, 1954 (div. Mar. 1976); children: Hopi, Jennine. BA, NYU, 1948; MA in Libr. Sci., Vanderbilt U., 1956. Asst. libr. Shepherd Coll., Shepherdstown, W.Va., 1956-57, Coll. Steubenville (Ohio), 1957-58; libr. Tecumseh High Sch, New Carlisle, Ohio, 1958-59, Urbana (Ohio) Coll., 1959-61; dir. Capital Libr. Svc., Greenbelt, Md., 1961-72; reference libr. U. D.C., Washington, 1972-87; libr. World Hunger Edn. Svc., Washington, 1988-91; retired, 1991—. Chair Peoples Party Md., 1972-73; mem. Green coun. Green Nat. Com., Lawrence, Mass., 1995-97; chair Greenbelt Greens, 1990—, Socialist Discussion Group, Washington, 1975—; mem. Nat. Com. Socialist Party, 1991-95, alt. mem. nat. com., 1995-997, nat. com. mem., 1997—. Mem. ALA, AAUP, Am. Polit. Sci. Assn., Washington Independent Writers Assn. Avocations: stamp collecting, button collecting. Home: 22 Ridge Rd Apt 234 Greenbelt MD 20770-0746

AUERBACH, ERNEST SIGMUND, lawyer, company executive, writer; b. Berlin, Dec. 22, 1936; s. Frank L. and Gertrude A.; m. Jeanette Taylor, 1990; 1 child, Hans Kevin. AB, George Washington U., 1958, JD, 1961; postgrad., U.S. Army Gen. Staff Coll., 1975. Bar: D.C. 1962, Pa. 1978. Atty. So. Ry. Co., Washington, 1961-62; commd 1st lt. U.S. Army, 1962, advanced through grades to col.; served in Germany, Vietnam, Pentagon; div. counsel Xerox Corp., Stamford, Conn., 1970-75; mng. atty. NL Industries, Inc., N.Y.C., 1975-77; from asst. to assoc. gen. counsel, staff v.p. INA Corp., Phila., 1977-79; sr. v.p. INA Svc. Co., 1979-82; sr. v.p., chief of staff INA Internat., 1982-83; pres. internat. life and group ops. CIGNA Worldwide Corp. div. CIGNA Corp., 1984-89; mng. dir. Crusader Life Ins. PLC, Reigate, Eng., 1984-86, chmn., 1986-89; pres., COO N.Y. Life Worldwide Holding, Inc., N.Y.C., 1989-90; pres., CEO Paperless Claims, Inc., N.Y.C., 1991-92; dir. gen. Seguros Azteca Ins. Co., Mexico City, 1992-93; sr. cons. Anderson Consulting, Mexico City, 1993-95; sr. v.p. United Ins. Cos., Inc., Irving, Tex., 1995-97, also pres., CEO student ins. divsn., 1996-97, pres., CEO ins. group, 1997; pres., COO Software Testing Assurance Corp., N.Y.C., 1998; pres., CEO Paperless Adjudication, LLC, N.Y.C., 1998—. Author: Joining the Inner Circle: How To Make It As A Senior Executive, 1990; contbg. author: The Wall St. Jour. on Mng., 1990; contbr. articles to legal, fin., news, and def. jours. Mem. Am. Coun. on Germany; computer sys. tech. adv. com. Dept. Commerce, 1974-76; mem. bd. adv. dirs. Salvation Army, Mexico City, 1993-94; commr. bd. adjustment City of Coppell, Tex., 1996-97. Ret. col. USAR, 1985. Decorated Legion of Merit with oak leaf cluster, Bronze Star. Mem. ABA, Westchester-Fairfield Corp. Counsel Assn. (founding officer), Audubon Soc. (bd. dirs. Greenwich chpt. 1999—), Univ. Club, Nat. Arts Club (N.Y.C.), Army and Navy Club (Washington chpt.). Home: 36 E Lyon Farm Dr Greenwich CT 06831-4349

AUERBACH, JEROLD S., university educator; b. Phila., May 7, 1936; s. Morry M. and Sophie (Soloff) A.; m. Susan H. Levin, May 16, 1982; children: Shira, Rebecca; children from previous marriage Jeffrey, Pamela. BA, Oberlin Coll., 1957; MA, Columbia U., 1959, PhD, 1965. Lectr. Queens Coll. CUNY, 1964-65; asst. prof. Brandeis U., Waltham, Mass., 1965-71; asst. prof. Wellesley (Mass.) Coll., 1971-72, assoc. prof., 1972-77, prof., 1977—; vis. scholar Harvard Law Sch.; Fulbright lectr. Tel Aviv U., 1974-75. Author: Labor and Liberty, 1966, Unequal Justice, 1976, Justice Without Law?, 1983, Rabbis and Lawyers, 1990, Jacob's Voices, 1996. Guggenheim Meml. Found. fellow, 1974-75; fellow NSF, 1979-80, NEH, 1986-87, 91-92. Office: Wellesley Coll 106 Central St Wellesley MA 02481-8203

AUERBACH, JONATHAN LOUIS, securities trader; b. Phila., Nov. 25, 1942; s. Joseph and Judith (Evans) A.; m. Ann Gardner Luce, Nov. 10, 1989; children: Gabrielle, Jake, Nicholas, Patrick (dec.), Alexander. BA, Yale Coll., 1964. Asst. v.p. Bache & Co., N.Y.C., 1966-71; v.p. F.S. Smithers & Co., N.Y.C., 1971-73; sr. v.p. Atlantic Capital Corp., N.Y.C., 1973-80, Dillon Read & Co. Inc., N.Y.C., 1980-84; mng. dir. Dillon Read Ltd., London, 1984-86, J.L. Auerbach & Co., London, 1986-88; chmn. Cresvale, Internat. Inc., N.Y.C., 1988-92, Auerbach Grayson & Co. Inc., 1992—. Producer: (film) Vortex, 1983. Bd. dirs. Shakespeare Globe, N.Y.C., 1989—, Russia Privitization Fund. Mem. Downtown Assn., Nat. Assn. Securities Dealers (dist. 12 com. 1989-92, dist. 10 vice chmn. 1992).

AUERBACH, JOSEPH, lawyer, educator; b. Franklin, N.H., Dec. 3, 1916; s. Jacob and Besse Mae (Reamer) A.; m. Judith Evans, Nov. 10, 1941; children: Jonathan L., Hope B. Pym. AB, Harvard U., 1938, LLB, 1941. Bar: N.H. 1941, Mass. 1952, U.S. Ct. Appeals (1st, 2d, 3d, 5th, 7th and D.C. cirs.), U.S. Supreme Ct. 1948. Atty. SEC, Washington and Phila., 1941-43, prin. atty., 1946-49; fgn. service staff officer U.S. Dept. State, Dusseldorf, W. Ger., 1950-52; ptnr. Sullivan & Worcester, Boston, 1952-82, counsel, 1982—; lectr. Boston U. Law Sch., 1975-76; lectr. Harvard Bus. Sch., Boston, 1980-82, prof., 1982-83, Class of 1957 prof., 1983-87, prof. emeritus, 1987—; prof. Harvard Extension Sch., 1988, 91-95; bd. dirs. Nat. Benefit Life Ins. Co., N.Y.C., Inacom Corp., Omaha, Auerbach, Christenson, Tagiuri, Inc., Boston; past dir. The Williams Cos., Old Colony Trust Co., Manhattan Fund, Liberty Fund, Hemisphere Fund, Harvard Bus. Sch. Pub. Co. Author: (with S.L. Hayes, III), Investment Banking and Diligence, 1986, Underwriting Regulation and Shelf Registration Phenomenon in Wall Street and Regulation, 1987, also chpt. to book, papers and articles in field. Trustee Mass. Eye and Ear Infirmary, Boston, 1981—, chmn. devel. com., 1985-88, chmn. nominating com., 1993-94; mem. adv. bd., former chmn. devel. com. Am. Repertory Theatre, Cambridge, Mass., 1985—; bd. dirs., past pres. Friends of Boston U. Librs., 1972—; past v.p., bd. dirs. Shakespeare Globe Ctr., N.A., 1983-90; overseer New Eng. Conservatory of Music, 1992-98, mem. fin. com.; bd. dirs. English Speaking Union, Boston, 1995-98; chair 1938 Harvard Pres. Assn.; active Harvard Coll. Fund, Harvard Law Sch. Fund. Decorated Army Commendation medal; recipient Disting. Svc. award Harvard Bus. Sch., 1996, Disting. Teaching award 1993, Exemplary Svc. award Harvard Extension Sch., 1995. Mem. ABA, Mass. Bar Assn., Boston Bar Assn., Harvard Mus. Assn., St. Botolph Club, Harvard Club N.Y.C., Shop Club, Downtown Club. Home: 300 Boylston St Apt 512 Boston MA 02116-3923 Office: Sullivan & Worcester 1 Post Office Sq Ste 2300 Boston MA 02109-2129 also: Harvard Bus Sch Cumnock Hall Rm 300 Boston MA 02163

AUERBACH, MARSHALL JAY, lawyer; b. Chgo., Sept. 5, 1932; s. Samuel M. and Sadie (Miller) A.; m. Carole Landsberg, July 3, 1960; children—Keith Alan, Michael Ward. Student, U. Ill.; J.D., John Marshall Law Sch., 1955. Bar: Ill. 1955. Sole practice Evanston, Ill., 1955-72; ptnr. in charge matrimonial law sect. Jenner & Block, Chgo., 1972-80; mem. firm Marshall J. Auerbach & Assocs., Ltd., Chgo., 1980—; mem. faculty Ill. Inst. Continuing Legal Edn. Author: Illinois Marriage and Dissolution of Marriage Act, enacted into law, 1977; Historical and Practice Notes to Illinois Marriage and Dissolution of Marriage Act, 1980-88; contbr. chpts. to Family Law, Vol. 2. Fellow Am. Acad. Matrimonial Lawyers; mem. Ill. State Bar Assn. (chmn. family law sect. 1971-72), ABA (vice-chmn. family law sect. com. for liaison with tax sect. 1974-76). Home and Office: 180 N La Salle St Ste 2307 Chicago IL 60601-2703*

AUERBACH, PHILIP GARY, lawyer; b. Irvington, N.J., Sept. 26, 1932; s. Sam and Nettie (Walsh) A.; m. Cynthia Auerbach, June 30, 1962; children: Lisa, Jon, Lauren. BS, Ohio State U., 1954; JD, U. Pa., 1959. Atty. Plone & Tomar, Camden, N.J., 1959-60; ptnr. Drazin, Warshaw, Auerbach & Rudnick, Red Bank, N.J., 1960-71; sr. ptnr. Auerbach, Rudnick, Waldman, Ford, Addonizio & Pappa, Red Bank, 1971-86; pvt. practice Red Bank, 1986-88; ptnr. Auerbach, Melody & Cox, Red Bank, 1988-92, Auerbach & Cox, Red Bank, 1992-94; pvt. practice, 1994—; adj. prof. Rutgers Law Sch., Newark, 1971—; vis. prof. Ct. Practice Inst., Chgo., Willamette Sch. Law, Salem, Oreg.; speaker nationally; keynote speaker Willamette U., Salem, Oreg., 1991. Author: Try It, 1976, Try It Again, 1992; contbr. articles to profl. jours., chpts. to books. Atty. Bd. Adjustment, Red Bank, 1968-69, Millstone, N.J., 1973-74; mem. Supreme Ct. Com. Civil Procedure. Mem. ABA, N.J. State Bar Assn., N.J. Trial Attys. (pres. 1970-71, chmn. 1971-72, Trial Bar award 1992), Inns of Ct. (pres. Monmouth County Haydn proctor 1994-95). Avocations: skiing, jogging, tennis. Office: 231 Maple Ave Red Bank NJ 07701-1727

AUERBACH, RITA ARGEN, artist, educator; b. Buffalo, Mar. 28, 1933; d. Ralph Joseph and Helen Margarite (Catalano) Argen; m. Richard Carlton Auerbach, Dec. 30, 1952; children: Bradford, Carolyn, Glenn. AA, Albright Art Sch., Buffalo, 1954; BS in Art Edn., SUNY, Buffalo, 1954, MS in Art Edn., 1974. Tchr. art Clarence (N.Y.) Ctrl. Schs., 1974-94; mem. spl. studies program faculty Chautauqua (N.Y.) Instn., 1994—; travel, workshop instr. tours to Costa Rica and France Splty. Tours, 1996—; chairperson dist. art dept. Clarence Ctrl. Schs., 1991-93. Author: Sketches and Reflections of a Journey to Soviet Union, 1987; contbr. monthly column to Living Prime Time, 1997; one-woman shows include Nat. Acad. Art, Riga, Latvia, Patterson Art Gallery, Westfield, N.Y., SUNY, Buffalo, Garret Club, Buffalo, Kenan Ctr., Lockport, N.Y., Art Dialogue, Buffalo, Spencer Hotel, Chautauqua, Chautauqua Art Assn., 1990-96, Burchfield-Penney Art Ctr., Buffalo, 1997; exhibited in group shows at Pa. Watercolor Soc., Pitts. Watercolor Soc., Batavia (N.Y.) Nat. Exhbn., Niagara Frontier Watercolor Soc., Lockport, N.Y., Albright-Knox Art Gallery, Buffalo Soc. Artists, Mpls. City of Lakes Exhbn. (1st pl. 1988), Adirondacks Nat. Exhbn. Am. Watercolors, 1984-86, others; represented in permanent collections, orgns. including City Hall, Buffalo, Law Offices Peter J. Sullivan, Marina del Ray, Calif., U. Buffalo Sch. Dentistry, Key Bank, Buffalo, J.M. Smucker Corp., Orrville, Ohio, Std. Oil, Miami, Fla., Rich Products, Buffalo, Burchfield-Penney Art Ctr., also pvt. collections. Bd. dirs. Big Orbit Gallery, Buffalo, 1991-94; mem. coun. Burchfield-Penney Art Ctr., 1994—; mem. coxswain coun. East Hill Found., Akron, N.Y., 1992-95. Named Art Educator of Yr., Western N.Y. br. N.Y. State Art Tchrs. Assn., 1993; arts grantee Nat. League Am. PEN Women, Washington, 1988. Mem. Pa. Watercolor Soc. (signature, Pres.'s award nat. exhibit 1987), Niagara Frontier Watercolor Soc. (charter, v.p. 1985-86, 1st pl. award 1985, 86), Buffalo Soc. Artists (exhibiting, pres. 1988, 91). Avocations: travel, golf, snokeling, volunteering at art galleries. Studio: 33 Delaware Rd Kenmore NY 14217-2742

AUERBACH, SEYMOUR, architect; b. N.Y.C., May 28, 1929; s. Nathan and Jennie (Norman) A.; m. Alyce Kelly, Oct. 21, 1963 (div. 1977); children: Kalin Marie Hyman, Alison Kelly; m. Patricia Sullivan, July 31, 1985 (div. 1991). B.Arch., Yale U., 1951. Asso. firm Satterlee & Smith (Architects), Washington, 1955-59; partner Cooper & Auerbach (Architects), Washington, 1960-69, Walton, Madden, Cooper & Auerbach (Architects), Washington, 1970-71; prin. Offices Seymour Auerbach (Architect), Washington, 1971—; pres. Kamak Enterprises, Inc., sole propr. for patent commercialization; developer, architect Battery Subdiv., Washington, Buck's Knoll Farm, Yellow Spring, W.Va.; prof. architecture Cath. U. Am., 1960-99. Prin. works include Nat. Visitor Ctr., Washington, campus plan and dormitories, Georgetown U., Olam Tikvah Synagogue, Fairfax, Va., Brith Sholom Synagogue, Bethlehem, Pa., resort cmtys., Rehoboth Beach, Del., campus for Bowling Brook prep; patentee in unrelated fields. Bd. mgrs. Chevy Chase Village, Md., 1973-77, vice chmn. bd., 1976-77; mem. archtl. adv. panel Union of Am. Hebrew Congregations. Served with C.E. U.S. Army, 1951-54. Decorated knight honor and merit Imperial Russian Order St. John of Jerusalem; recipient award excellence in architecture Met. Washington Bd. Trade, 1964, Papal Benemerenti medal, 1994; winner award competition for design of Copley Plaza, Boston, 1967; William Wirt Winchester fellow, 1951. Fellow AIA (1st award for excellence in design Potomac Valley chpt. 1964); mem. AAUP, Soc. Archtl. Historians, Guild Religious Architecture, Cosmos Club Washington, Yale Club Washington. Republican. Jewish. Home and Office: 115 Hesketh St Chevy Chase MD 20815-4222 *I consider it to be of the highest calling to be involved in the improvement of man's physical environment: not only his shelter, but also his public environment and the implements he uses. In this context I have held architecture to be an Applied, rather than a Fine, Art. I consider it to be a higher calling to be a designer than to be an architect and I find the greatest of personal pleasure in solving individual problems of design for man, by myself, without regard to "style", and without regard to political or other irrelevant considerations.*

AUERBACH, STANLEY IRVING, ecologist, environmental scientist, educator; b. Chgo., May 21, 1921; s. Abraham and Carrie (Friedman) A.; m. Dawn Patricia Davey, June 12, 1954; children: Andrew J., Anne E., Jonathan B., Alison M. BS, U. Ill., 1946, MS, 1947; PhD, Northwestern U., 1949. Instr., then asst. prof. Roosevelt U., Chgo., 1950-54; assoc. scientist, then scientist health physics divsn. Oak Ridge (Tenn.) Nat. Lab., 1954-59, sr. scientist, sect. leader, 1959-70, dir. ecol. sci. divsn., 1970-72, dir. environ. scis. divsn., 1972-86, sr. rsch. advisor, 1986-90; adj. prof. ecology U. Tenn., 1965-90; adj. rsch. prof. radiation ecology U. Ga., 1964-90; mem. U.S. exec. com. Internat. Biol. Program, co-chmn. program coord. com., dir. deciduous forest biome project, 1969-74; mem. exec. com. Sci. Adv. Bd. U.S. EPA, 1986-92; adv. com. Sci. and Tech. NSF, 1989-91; environ. adv. bd. U.S.C.E., 1989-93; mem. NAS Adv. Com. on Rsch. to Sec. Agr., 1969-70, NAE Power Plant Siting Program Commn., 1970-71, mem. bd. energy studies, 1974-77, chmn. com. on energy and environ., 1974-77, chmn. environ. studies bd., 1983-86, mem. com. on phys. scis., math. and resources, 1982-83, mem. com on natural resources, 1979-82; chmn. archtl. rev. com. Oak Ridge Nat. Lab., 1971-84; mem. ecol. adv. bd. Bur. Reclamation; mem. NAS-NAE Bd. on Energy Studies, 1974-77; mem. C.E. bd. environ. cons. Tenn.-Tombigbee Waterway, 1975-86; mem. ad hoc com. on transuranic burial ERDA (Dept. Energy, 1976-78; mem. Pres.' Spl. Com. on Health and Environ. Effects of Increasing Coal Utilization, 1977-78, Resources for the Future Rsch. Adv. Com., 1978-81; mem. commn. natural resources NRC, 1979-81; mem. adv. coun. Water Resources Rsch. Ctr. U. Tenn., 1980-91; mem. NAS-NRC Com. on Bldg. an Environ. Mgmt. Sci. Program for DOE, 1996-97. Ecology editor Environ. Internat., 1979-94; mem. adv. bd. Environ. and Exptl. Botany, 1967-92; mem. bd. editors Radiation Rsch., 1975-77. 2nd lt. AUS, 1942-44. Recipient Dist. Achievement award U.S. Dept. Energy, 1987, Comdr.'s award U.S. Dept. Army, 1990. Fellow AAAS; mem. Am. Inst. Biol. Scis. (bd. govs.), Soc. Zoology (chmn. ecology div.), Am. Soc. Agronomy, Brit. Ecol. Soc., Health Physics Soc., Entomol. Soc. Am., Soc. Systematic Biology, Ecol. Soc. Am. (chmn. com. radioecology 1963-65, sec. 1964-69, chmn. fin. com. 1969, pres. 1971-72, Disting. Service award 1985), Internat. Union Radioecology (pres. 1984-87, mem. of honour 1991), Sigma Xi (pres. Oak Ridge br. 1972-73, chmn. admissions 1980-82), Alpha Epsilon Pi. Achievements include research on ecology centipedes, radioecology and radioactive waste disposal; on environmental behavior of radionuclides and ecosystem analysis. Home: 103 Wildwood Dr Oak Ridge TN 37830-8624

AUERBACH, STUART CHARLES, development loan fund administrator, journalist; b. N.Y.C., Oct. 28, 1935; s. Jack and Betty (Segnes) A.; m. Lena F. Lee, Sept. 29, 1995. B.A., Williams Coll., 1957. Reporter Berkshire Eagle, Pittsfield, Mass., 1957-60, Miami (Fla.) Herald, 1960-66; reporter, then sci.-med. corr. Washington Post, 1966-76, Middle East corr., 1976-77, legal corr., columnist, 1977-79, South Asia corr., 1979-83, econ. corr., 1983-93, health corr., 1995-97; chmn. bd. Media Devel. Loan Fund, Washington, 1996-97, dir. devel., trustee, 1997—. Recipient Pub. Service award Nat. Kidney Found., 1973; certificate commendation Am. Acad. Family Physicians, 1976. Mem. Nat. Assn. Sci. Writers (Sci.-in-Society award 1976). Clubs: Nat. Press, Fed. City (Washington); Overseas Press (N.Y.C.); Delhi Gymkhana. Home: 2812 28th St NW Washington DC 20008-4110 Office: Media Devel Loan Fund 2812 28th St NW Washington DC 20008-4110

AUERBACH, WILLIAM, lawyer; b. N.Y.C., Aug. 14, 1914; s. Max and Jennie (Geller) A.; m. Tess Kasper, Mar. 15, 1946; children: Sue Ellen, Alan Jeffrey, Melissa Jo. B.S.S., CCNY, 1936; J.D., Harvard U., 1939. Bar: N.Y. 1940; Certificate Far Eastern Specialization, AUS Specialized Tng. Program, 1944. Practiced in N.Y.C., 1939-43, 46—; assoc. firms Hirson & Bertini, 1939-41, Morris A. Edelman, 1941-43; partner firm Cohen & Auerbach, 1949-51, Auerbach & Labes,, 1967—; sr. atty. Office Price Adminstrn., Washington, 1946. Served as cryptanalyst and intelligence analyst OSS AUS, 1943-46. Mem. Assn. Bar City N.Y. Jewish. Home: 61 Paine Ave New Rochelle NY 10804-4146 Office: 605 3rd Ave New York NY 10158-0180

AUERBACK, SANDRA JEAN, social worker; b. San Francisco, Feb. 21, 1946; d. Alfred and Molly Loy (Friedman) A. BA, U. Calif., Berkeley, 1967; MSW, Hunter Sch. Social Work, 1972. Diplomate clin. social work. Clin. social worker Jewish Family Services, Bklyn., 1972-73; clin. social worker Jewish Family Services, Hackensack, N.J., 1973-78; pvt. practice psychotherapy San Francisco, 1978—; dir. intake adult day care Jewish Home for the Aged, San Francisco, 1979-91. Mem. NASW (cert., bd. dirs. Bay Area Referral Svc. 1983-87, chmn. referral svc. 1984-87, state practice com. 1987-91, regional treas. 1989-91, rep. to Calif. Coun. Psychiatry, Psychology, Social Work and Nursing, 1987-95, chmn. 1989, 93, v.p. cmty. svcs. 1991-93, chair Calif. polit. action com. 1993-95), Am. Group Psychotherapy Assn., Mental Health Assn. San Francisco (trustee 1987—). Home: 1100 Gough St Apt 8C San Francisco CA 94109-6638 Office: 450 Sutter St San Francisco CA 94108-4206

AUFDERHEIDE, ARTHUR CARL, pathologist; b. New Ulm, Minn., Sept. 9, 1922; s. Herman John and Esther (Sannwald) A.; m. Mary Lillian Buryk, Jan. 26, 1946; children: Patricia Ann, Tom Paul, Walter Herman. MD, U. Minn., 1946; DSc (hon.), Coll. of St. Scholastica, 1983. Chief dept. pathology Mpls. VA Hosp., 1952-53, St. Mary's Hosp., Duluth, Minn., 1953-57; chief dept. pathology Sch. Medicine U. Minn., Duluth, 1970-87, dean Sch. Medicine, 1974-75, dir. paleobiology lab. Sch. Medicine, 1977—; mem. Plaisted Polar Expdn., 1968; rsch. cons. anthropology lab. U. Colombia, Bogota, 1989—, Pigorini Mus., Rome, 1988, Archeol. Mus. of Tenerife, Canary Islands, 1989-90; chmn. sci. com. Cronos Rsch Project, Santa Cruz, Tenerife, 1991—. Author: Cambridge Ency. Human Paleopathology, 1998; co-editor: Paleopathology, 1991; author: (documentary film) Copper Eskimo, 1970; contbr. numerous articles to profl. publs. Chmn. civil com. to devel. a degree-granting med. sch., Duluth, 1988. Capt. U.S. Army, 1947-49. Mem. Paleopathology Assn., N.Y. Acad. Scis. Democrat. Lutheran. Achievements include research in soft tissue paleopathology. Home: 4711 Colorado St Duluth MN 55804-1512 Office: U Minn 10 University Dr Duluth MN 55812-2403

AUFSES, ARTHUR H(AROLD), JR., surgeon, medical educator; b. N.Y.C., Feb. 8, 1926; s. Arthur Harold and Beatrice (Hauser) A.; m. Harriet Whitman, Dec. 28, 1947; children: Arthur Harold III, Carolyn Aufses Blashek. Student, Columbia U., 1942-43; BS, Union Coll., 1944; MD, Columbia U. Coll. Physicians and Surgeons, 1948. Diplomate Am. Bd. Surgery. Intern Presbyn. Hosp., N.Y.C., 1948-49; resident in surgery Presbyn. Hosp., 1950-51, 53-54, Mt. Sinai Hosp., N.Y.C., 1954-56; practice medicine specializing in surgery N.Y.C., 1956-97; prof. Mt. Sinai Med. Ctr., N.Y.C., 1974—, chmn. dept. surgery, 1974-96; chmn. dept. surgery L.I. Jewish Med. Ctr., 1971-74; prof. surgery SUNY-Stony Brook, 1971-74; surgeon-in-chief Mt. Sinai Hosp., N.Y.C., 1974-96. Contbr. articles to med. jours. Bd. dirs. 92d St. YMHA, 1974—. 1st lt. U.S. Army, 1951-53. Recipient Jacobi medallion Mt. Sinai Med. Ctr., 1979; recipient Gold Headed Cane award Mt. Sinai Med. Ctr., 1982. Fellow ACS (2nd v.p. 1996-97), Am. Surg. Assn. (2nd v.p. 1995-96), Am. Coll. Gastroenterology (pres. 1986-87), Assn. of Program Dirs. (pres. 1989-91), N.Y. Acad. Medicine; mem. Soc. Surg. Oncology, Am. Gastroent. Assn., N.Y. Surg. Soc. (pres. 1979-80), Soc. Surgery Alimentary Tract, Brazilian Coll. Surgeons, Chilean Congress Surgeons, Portuguese Soc. Gastroenterology. Jewish. Home: 1185 Park Ave New York NY 10128-1308 Office: Mt Sinai Med Ctr 1 Gustave L Levy Pl New York NY 10029-6500

AUFZIEN, ALAN L., professional sports team executive. Owner N.J. Nets (NBA), sec., treas.; former chmn. The RAL Corp., Fairfield, N.J. Office: NJ Nets 405 Murray Hill Pkwy East Rutherford NJ 07073-2136*

AUG, JONATHAN VINCENT, federal bankruptcy judge; b. Indpls., Feb. 16, 1946; m. Mary Joseph Aug; children: Katherine, Lauren. Student, U. Fribourg, Switzerland, 1966-67; BA, Georgetown U., 1968; JD, U. Cin.,

1973. Bar: Ohio 1973, D.C. 1974. With Peace Corps, Kenya, 1968-69; reporter Cin. Post, 1970; staff atty. Jud. Panel on Multidist. Litigation, Washington, 1973-74; pvt. practice Neiman, Aug, Elder & Jacobs, Cin., 1974-76; spl. counsel Ohio Atty. Gen., 1974-76; columnist Cin. Enquirer, 1978-83; U.S. magistrate judge So. Dist. Ohio, Cin, 1976-88, bankruptcy judge, 1988—; adj. faculty Midwest Regional Bankruptcy Law Inst. Contbr. articles to profl. jours. Bd. visitors U. Cin. Coll. Law; former mem. Hamilton County Dem. Steering Com. Recipient Nicholas Longworth III Alumni Achievement award U. Cin. Coll. Law, 1992, Outstanding Journalism award Ohio Trial Lawyers Assn. Mem. Am. Inns of Ct. (master of bench emeritus), Fed. Bar Assn. (pres. Cin. chpt. 1984). Democrat. Roman Catholic. Avocations: motorcycling, sailing, muzzleloading rifle shooting. Office: US Courthouse 221 E 4th St Cincinnati OH 45202-4124*

AUGELLI, JOHN PAT, geography educator, author, consultant, rancher; b. Celenza, Italy, Jan. 30, 1921; s. Pat John and M. Antoinette (Iacaruso) A.; divorced; children: John, Robert. BA, Clark U., 1943; MA, Harvard U., 1949, PhD, 1951. Teaching fellow Harvard U., Cambridge, Mass., 1948-49; from asst. to assoc. prof. geography U. P.R., Rio Piedras, 1949-51; assoc. prof. U. Md., College Park, 1952-61; prof. U. Kans., LAwrence rk, 1961-70, 71-91; lectr., travel cons. Mediterranean and Latin Am. cruises, 1991-95; mem. Bd. Fgn. Scholarships, Washington, 1967-70; cons. Nat. Geographic Soc., Washington, 1984-87; del. U.S. Acad. Scis., New Delhi, 1968; sec. Coun. of Inter-Am. Affairs, Washington, 1959-60. Author: Carribean Lands, 1965, Puerto Rico, 1973, Middle America, 3d edit., 1989; cons.: (atlas) World & North America, 1984; contbr. 76 articles to profl. jours. Served to 1st lt. U.S. Army, 1943-46, PTO, Res., 1949-51. Recipient Fulbright research grant, 1982. Fellow Am. Geog. Soc.; mem. Assn. Am. Geographers (sec. 1966-69), Latin Am. Studies Assn. (pres. 1969), Nat. Council Geographic Edn. (master tchr. 1979), Conf. of Latin Americanist Geographers (outstanding contbn. to research and teaching award 1982). Democrat. Roman Catholic. Avocations: travel, fishing. Mailing: 35 Mediterranean E Port St Lucie FL 34952

AUGELLO, WILLIAM JOSEPH, lawyer; b. Bklyn., Apr. 5, 1926; s. William J. and Catherine (Ehalt) A.; m. Elizabeth Deasy, July 1, 1950; children: Thomas, Charles, Patricia, William, Peggy Ann, James. LLB, Fordham U., 1950; BA, Dartmouth Coll., 1946. Bar: N.Y. 1951. Individual practice law N.Y.C., 1953-71; mem. firm Augello, Deegan & Pezold, Huntington, N.Y., 1971-78; sr. mem. firm Augello, Pezold & Hirschmann, Huntington, 1978—; treas., dir. Transp. Arbitration Bd., Inc., 1978—; chmn. accreditation com. Certified Claims Profl. Accreditation Council, Inc., Washington, 1981—; exec. dir., gen. counsel Transp. Consumer Protection Coun. Inc., Huntington, 1974—; adv. com. pvt. internat. law study group maritime matters Dept. State; co-chmn. uniform liability regime working group Ctr. Inter-Am. Trade; bd. dirs. U. Denver Intermodal Transportation Inst.; bd. dirs. Inst. Logistical Mgmt. Author: Freight Claims in Plain English, 1979, 82, 95, Transportation Insurance in Plain English, 1985, Defending and Avoiding Undercharge Claims and Suits, 1991, Doing Business Under the New Transportational Law: The Negotiated Rates Act of 1993, 94, How to Read Tariffs to Avoid Surprises, 1994, A Guide to Transportation After the I.C.C., 1996, Protecting Shippers Interests, 1997, Corporate Procedures for Shipping and Receiving, 1998; co-author: Freight Claim Prevention in Plain English, 1985, Transportation Contracts in Plain English, 1991; author, lectr. Beginning of Freight Claims-Bill of Lading Contract, 1979, Documenting Claims, 1980, Liability Rules and Shipping/Receiving Practices Affecting Loss, Damage and Delay, 1981, Changes in Carrier Liability: Court Decisions, Statutes and Regulations, 1983, Legal Principles of Freight Claims From Claimant's Standpoint, 101 Declinations-And What To Do About Them, Differences Between Can. and U.S. Carrier Liability, Negotiating Liability in Today's Transp. Environment. Served with USN, 1944-46. Recipient Harry E. Salzberg Medallion award Syracuse U., 1994, Transp. Educator of Yr. award Operation Stimulus, 1996; named Nat. Transp. Man of Yr., Delta Nu Alpha, 1979-80. Mem. Maritime Law Assn., Transp. Lawyers Assn. (Disting. Svc. award 1988), Suffolk County Bar Assn., Assn. Transp. Law, Logistics and Policy, Indian Hills Country Club (ft. Salonga, N.Y.), El Con Conquistador Country Club (Tucson), Delta Nu Alpha. Republican. Roman Catholic. Office: Augello Pezold & Hirschmann 120 Main St Huntington NY 11743-6906 also: 11520 N Palmetto Dunes Ave Tucson AZ 85737-7205 *Few things in life are more gratifying than helping others reach their full potential or just providing them with a means to advance up the corporate ladder with their heads higher than before.*

AUGENBRAUM, HAROLD, library director, editor; b. N.Y.C., Mar. 31, 1953; s. Samuel and Ada (Baker) A.; m. Carla S. Scheele, Sept. 23, 1989; 1 child, Audrey Baker Scheele. BA, Boston U., 1976. Dir. external affairs Brookdale Ctr. on Aging, N.Y.C., 1984-87; assoc. dir. for external affairs Mus. City N.Y., 1987-89; dir. Merc. Libr. N.Y., N.Y.C., 1990—. Editor: Latinos in English, 1992, Bendíceme, America, 1993, Growing Up Latino, 1993, The Latino Reader, 1997. Mem. bd. N.Y. Coun. for Humanities, N.Y.C., 1993-98, vice chmn., 1996. Grantee NEH, 1992, 95, 96, Florence Gould Found., 1999. Mem. Proust Soc. Am. (pres. 1997—). E-mail: mercantilelibrary@msn.com. Office: Merc Libr NY 17 E 47th St New York NY 10017

AUGENSTEIN, BRUNO W., research scientist; b. Germany, Mar. 16, 1923; came to U.S., 1927, naturalized, 1935; s. Wilhelm C. and Emma (Mina) A.; m. Kathleen Greenlaw, May 27, 1950; children: Karen, Eric, Christopher. Sc.B. in Physics and Math, Brown U., 1943; M.S. in Aero, Calif. Inst. Tech., 1945. Supr. N.Am. Aviation Co., 1946-48; asst. prof. Purdue U., 1948-49; Navaho project leader, 1948; sr. scientist Rand Corp., 1949-58; ICBM project leader, 1952-56; chief scientist satellite programs; dir. planning Lockheed Missiles & Space Co., 1958-61; spl. asst. for reconnaisance and intelligence, dep. dir. Office Sec. Def., 1961-65; now cons.; rsch. adviser Inst. Def. Analyses, 1965-67; v.p. research Rand Corp., Santa Monica, Calif., 1967-71; chief scientist Rand Corp., 1971-72, resident cons., 1972—, sr. scientist, 1976—, emeritus scientist, 1995—; cons., NAS, Bur. Budget, 1965—, Nat. Bur. Standards, 1971—, Xerad, Inc., 1972—, Dept. Navy, NSF, NASA, 1973—, Dept. Def., 1978—, Hi Tech Investment Mgmt., Inc., 1983; chmn. naval health systems rev. com. Office Sci. Tech. Policy, 1975—, cons., 1978—; v.p. rsch., bd. dirs. Spectravision, Inc.; bd. regents, asst. chmn. Nat. Libr. Medicine, HEW, 1967-73; mem. NAS computer sci. com. Nat. Bur. Standards, 1971-79, chmn., 1973-76. Guest contbr., editor Chaos, Solitons and Fractals Jour., 1995, 99. Recipient Distinguished Pub. Service award Dept. Def., 1965. Mem. Am. Inst. Physics, AIAA, AAAS, IEEE, Am. Nuclear Soc., Philosophy of Sci. Assn., N.Y. Acad. Scis., Beta Theta Pi. Home: 1144 Tellem Dr Pacific Palisades CA 90272-2244 Office: Rand Corp 1700 Main St Santa Monica CA 90401-3297

AUGHENBAUGH, DEBORAH ANN, mayor, retired educator; b. Bklyn., Oct. 15, 1922; d. James R. and Alice Lillian (Walsh) Donecho; m. William Irving Hopwood, Mar. 31, 1946 (dec. July 1966); 1 child, William James; m. Kenneth Merle Aughenbaugh, Oct. 20, 1973 (dec. Sept. 1997). BS, Towson (Md.) State Coll., 1952; MS, Shippensburg (Pa.) U., 1967. Cert. elem. tchr., guidance counselor, Md. Tchr. Balt. City Pub. Schs., 1952-54, St. John's Cath. Ch., Frederick, Md., 1960-63, Frederick County Bd. Edn., Frederick, 1963-84; mem. city coun. City of Burkittsville, Md., 1971-74, 80-83, mayor, 1986-95; ret., 1995; mem. Gov.'s Policy Com. on Edn., 1994-95, Frederick County Bd. Edn., 1995—, Md. Assn. Bds. of Edn. legis. com., 1995-97, 98-99. Chmn. Burkittsville Planning and Zoning Commn., 1969-79; mem. Frederick Recycling Com., 1989-91, Frederick Solid Waste Adv. Bd., 1991-93; mem. Frederick County Bd. of Edn. Mem. Frederick County Ret. Tchrs. Assn., Md. Mcpl. League (pres. Frederick County chpt. 1992, state legis. com. 1985-95, chair 1992-93, bd. dirs. 1985-95, pres. 1992, 94), Nat. League Cities (human devel. com. 1991-95), Frederick County Future Growth and Sch. Schedule Advisory Com. Democrat. Avocations: reading, travel, crocheting. Home: 8 W Main St Box 408 Burkittsville MD 21718-9200

AUGSBURGER, AARON DONALD, clergyman; b. Elida, Ohio, Dec. 21, 1925; s. C.A. and Estella R. (Shenk) A.; m. Martha L. Kling, June 5, 1948; children: Phyllis Augsburger Ressler, Patricia Augsburger, Don Richard. BA, Mennonite Coll., 1949; MRE, Ea. Bapt. Sem., Phila., 1956; DEd, Temple U., 1963. Ordained to ministry Mennonite Ch., 1951. Mem. pers. and student svcs. coms. Mennonite Bd. Missions and Charities, 1954-70; pastor students, tchr. Christian edn. Ea. Mennonite Coll., Harrisonburg, Va., 1958-64; asst. dean Goshen (Ind.) Sem., 1964-65; pastor, bishop North Goshen (Ind.) Mennonite Ch., 1965-70; tchr. psychology Goshen (Ind.) Coll., 1965-66; pastor Park View Mennonite Ch., Harrisonburg, 1974-80; prof. Ea. Mennonite Sem., 1980-89; pastor Bahia Vista Mennonite Ch., Sarasota, Fla., 1989-96; dir. pastoral care Mennonite Home, Lancaster, Pa., 1996—. Author: Creating Christian Personality, 1966, A Pattern for Living, 1993; editor: Marriages That Work, 1984, Reshaping Your Marriage, 1996. Guidance counselor Bethany Christian High Sch., Goshen, 1966-68, supr., 1968-70; moderator Gen. Assembly of Mennonite Chs., 1971-73. Home: 535-D Abbeyville Rd Lancaster PA 17603-6347

AUGUR, MARILYN HUSSMAN, distribution executive; b. Texarkana, Ark., Aug. 23, 1938; d. Walter E. and Betty (Palmer) H.; m. James M. Augur, Dec. 29, 1962; children: Margaret M. Hancock, Elizabeth H. Taylor, Ann Louise. BA, U. N.C., 1960; MBA, So. Meth. U., 1989. Pres. North Tex. Mountain Valley Water, Dallas, 1989—; bd. dirs. Camden News Pub. Co., Little Rock. Trustee Hussman Found., Little Rock, 1991—, U. Tex. Southwestern Med. Found., 1993—, Nat. Jewish Hosp., 1993—, Marilyn Augur Found., Dallas, 1991—; bd. dirs. Baylor Health Sys. Found., 1992—, chmn., 1995; bd. dirs. Dallas Summer Musicals, 1992-95, mem. exec. com., 1992-94; bd. dirs. Tate Lectr. Series, 1994—, Salvation Army, 1996—, adv. bd.; mem. Tex. Bus. Hall of Fame, 1992—, exec. com., 1994-95; mem. Dallas Citizens Coun., 1994—, Dallas County C.C., Dist. Found., 1995—, Dallas Helps, 1995—, Charter 100. Mem. Dallas Country Club, Crescent Club, Dallas Women's Club, Beta Gamma Sigma. Episcopalian. Avocations: travel, skiing, treking. Office: North Tex Mountain Valley Water 3131 Turtle Creek Blvd Ste 1000 Dallas TX 75219-5439

AUGUST, ALBERT T., III, publishing executive; b. Richmond, Va., Dec. 19, 1939. BA, Randolph-Macon Coll., 1964. Classified advt. acct. exec. Richmond (Va.) Newspapers, Inc., 1964-71, classified advt. sales supr., 1971-73, advt. sales devel. mgr., 1973-74, dept. circulation subscriber rels. mgr., 1974-75, circulation sales, svc., promotion mgr., 1975-78, times dispatch circulation mgr., 1978-81, asst. circulation dir., 1981-82, asst. advt. dir., 1982-89, v.p., bus. mgr., 1989-93, sr. v.p., gen. mgr., 1993, pres., gen. mgr., 1994—. Office: Richmond Times-Dispatch 333 E Franklin St Richmond VA 23219 also: Richmond Times-Dispatch PO Box 85333 Richmond VA 23293

AUGUST, BILLE, film director; b. Denmark, 1948. Grad., Danish Film Sch., 1971. Cinematographer: Miesta ei voi raiskata, Kaleken, The Grass is Singing; dir., screenwriter: Honnig Mane, 1978, Zappa, 1983, Twist and Shout, 1984, Buster's World, 1985, Pelle the Conqueror (Oscar award 1988, Golden Palm Cannes Film Festival 1988); dir.: The Best Intentions, 1992 (Golden Palm Cannes Film Festival 1992), The House of the Spirits, 1993, Jerusalem, 1996, Smilla's Sense of Snow, 1997, Les Miserables, 1997. Office: CAA 9830 Wilshire Blvd Beverly Hills CA 90212-1804*

AUGUST, DIANE L., independent education consultant, policy researchr; b. N.Y.C., May 28, 1948; d. Burton and Flora A.; m. Michael Anthony Fainberg, Sept. 7, 1986; children: Nina Anne, Elisabeth Renee. BA, Wheaton Coll., 1970; MA, Stanford U., 1971, PhD, 1981, postgrad., 1982. Cert. tchr. administr., Calif. Tchr. Whisman Sch. Dist., Mountain View, Calif., 1972-79, program mgr., 1979-82; congl. sci. fellow AAAS, Washington, 1982-83; grants officer Carnegie Corp., N.Y.C., 1984-87; dir. edn. divsn. Children's Defense Fund, Washington, 1986-88; edn. cons. August & Assocs., Washington, 1988-95, 97—; sr. program officer Nat. Acad. Sci., Washington, 1995-97; mem. social policy com. Soc. Rsch. in Child Devel., Washington, 1988-91. Author: Language Minority Education in the United States, 1988; editor: Improving Schooling for Language Minority Children: A Research Agenda. Mem. Am. Ednl. Rsch. Assn. Office: 4500 Wetherill Rd Bethesda MD 20816-1813

AUGUST, LOUISE, artist, illustrator, educator; b. N.Y.C.; 3 children. Artist N.Y.C., 1960—; painter, printmaker, instr. New Sch. Social Rsch., N.Y.C., 1991—; children's book illustrator N.Y.C., 1992—; gbuest lectr. pub. and pvt. orgns. and founds.; color cons. A.I.D. One-man shows include HIgh Gate Gallery, N.J., Gillary Gallery, N.Y., Downtown Gallery, N.C., Swain's Art Gallery, N.J., Fromuth's Gallery, Pa., Lucinda Gallery, N.J., Art Shop Gallery, N.Y., The Little Gallery, Pa., West Side Synagogue, Tenn., Middletown Art Gallery, N.Y., Jan Mitchell Gallery, N.Y., Sprai Home Art Gallery, N.Y.; group exhbns. include Saltsman Gallery, Fla., White House Gallery, N.Y., Scotti Sheldon Gallery, Mass., Pandemonium, Inc., Pa., Galleries III, Va., Miller Gallery, Ohio, others; represented in permanent collections Phila. Mus. Art, Butler Inst. Am. Art, Youngstown, Ohio, Newark (N.J.) Pub. Libr. Collection, Yale U. Mus. Fine Art, New Haven, U. N.C., Durham, Princeton (N.J.) U., N.C. Coll., Greensboro, Cheekwood Fine Art Ctr., Nashville, other pub. and pvt. collections in U.S. and abroad; commd. murals include S.C. State Bank, Columbia, Gilbert Hotel, Fallsburgh, N.Y., Grand Ctrl. Sta., N.Y.C., Summit Hotel, N.Y., The Essex, N.Y., Schraft's, N.Y., Harry's Restaurant, N.Y., others; children's book illustrations include In the Month of Kislev, Sunday Potatoes, Monday Potatoes, Night Lights, Milk and Honey, The Way Meat Loves Salt; book jackets include The Woman Who Lived in a Prologue, After Goliath, Black Robes, Among the Volcanoes, Under the Domim Tree. Mem. Nat. Guild Mural Artists (v.p.).

AUGUST, ROBERT OLIN, journalist; b. Ashtabula, Ohio, Oct. 6, 1921; s. Frank and Lillian (Olin) A.; m. Marilynn Eccles, Sept. 23, 1943; 1 dau., Alison. B.A., Coll. Wooster, 1943. With Cleve. Press, 1946-82, staff sports dept., 1950—, covered profl. football, 1953-58, exec. sports editor, 1957-58, sports editor, 1958-64, sports columnist, 1964-67, sports columnist, sports editor, 1967-79, gen. columnist, asst. to editor, 1979-81, assoc. editor, 1981-82; sports editor Lake County News-Herald, 1982-89; sports columnist 4 Ingersoll newspapers, 1982—; nationally syndicated columnist Wiser Side of 60 Universal Press Syndicate, 1982-86. Served from ensign to lt. (j.g.) USNR, 1943-46. Recipient Cleve. Newspaper Guild awards, 1958, 61, 81, 82, 83; inducted into Cleve. Journalism Hall of Fame, 1988. Mem. Sigma Delta Chi (Disting. Svc. award 1981). Home: 1140 Hedgecliff Dr Wooster OH 44691-3088

AUGUST, ROBERT WILLIAM, designer, educator; b. Chgo., Mar. 31, 1944; s. Benjamin R. and Lillian (A.) A.; m. Lois J. Yoder, Feb. 19, 1977; children: Kristen J., Michael M. BA, L.I. U., 1970; MA, Nat.-Louis U., 1995. USNR, 1965-70; pres. Design Agy. Inc., Chgo., 1976-77; pres., chief exec. officer Expocom Inc., Elgin, Ill., 1977—. Elected to bd. edn. Sch. Dist. U-46, Elgin, 1989-93. Mem. North Suburban Assn. Commerce and Industry, Elgin Area C. of C. Avocations: gardening, historical restoration work, arts, personal computers, amateur astronomy.

AUGUST, RUDOLF See SCHLOEMANN, ERNST FRITZ

AUGUSTA, JUDITH WOOD, librarian; b. Apr. 29, 1940. BA, Wellesley Coll., 1962; MLS, So. Conn. State U., 1994. Adminstrv. asst. Joint Ctr. for Urban Studies of Harvard and MIT, Cambridge, Mass., 1966-72; indexer Rsch. Publs. Inc., Woodbridge, Conn., 1980-90; head libr. Derby (Conn.) Neck Libr., 1994—. E-mail: laughter@ix.netcom.com. Office: 307 Hawthorne Ave Derby CT 06418

AUGUST-DEWILDE, KATHERINE, banker; b. Bridgeport, Conn., Feb. 13, 1948; d. Edward G. and Benita Ruth (Miller) Burstein; m. David deWilde, Dec. 30, 1984; children: Nicholas Alexander, Lucas Barrymere. AB, Goucher Coll., 1969; MBA, Stanford U., 1975. Cons. McKinsey & Co., San Francisco, 1975-78; dir. fin. Itel Corp., San Francisco, 1978-79; sr. v.p., chief fin. officer PMI Group, San Francisco, 1979-85, pres., CFO, 1988-91; CEO, pres. First Republic Thrift & Loan of San Diego, 1988-96; exec. v.p. First Republic Bank, San Francisco, 1987—, sr. v.p. , chief fin. officer, 1985-87, COO, 1996—; mem. policy adv. bd. Ctr. for Real Estate and Urban Econs., U. Calif., Berkeley, 1987—; bd. dirs. First Republic Bank, Trainer, Wortham & Co., Inc. Bd. dirs. San Francisco Zool. Soc., 1993—, vice-chair, 1995—; trustee Carnegie Found., 1999—, Town Sch. for Boys, San Francisco, 1999—. Mem. Women's Forum (bd. dirs.), Bankers Club, Belvedere Tennis Club, Univ. Club. Home: 2650 Green St San Francisco CA 94123-4607 Office: First Republic Bank 111 Pine St San Francisco CA 94111-5311

AUGUSTINE, HILTON H., JR., computer company executive. Degree in elec. engring., U. Wis. Salesman IBM; founder Global Mgmt. Sys. Inc., 1988—; chmn., CEO Global Mgmt. Sys. Inc., Bethesda, Md., 1996—. Office: Global Mgmt Sys Inc 6707 Democracy Blvd Bethesda MD 20817

AUGUSTINE, JEAN, member of parliament. BA, U. Toronto, Ont.; MEd, U. Toronto, LLD (hon.). Elem. sch. prin. Met. Toronto Separate Sch. Bd.; chair bd. dirs. Met. Toronto Housing Authority; mem. Can. Parliament for Etobicoke-Lakeshore, 1993—; past Parliamentary sec. to Prime Minister, vice chair ministerial task force on social security reform; mem. standing com. on fgn. affairs and internat. trade, standing com. on citizenship and immigration; vice chair standing com. on human resources devel, mem. standing com. on human rights and status of persons with disabilities Ho. of Commons. Bd. dirs. Harbourfront, Cath. Children's Aid Soc., Can. Adv. Coun. on Status of Women, Ont. Jud. Coun., Urban Alliance on Race Rels., Grenada Assn., Metro Action Com. on Pub. Violence Against Women and Children, Etobicoke Social Devel. Coun.; mem. Toronto Mayor's Task Force on Drugs, Metro Toronto Drug Abuse Prevention Task Force, Toronto Crime Inquiry, 1991; chair women's caucus Nat. Liberal Caucus, Ont. Caucus Comm. Com., Social Policy Sub-Com. on Housing. Recipient Vol. award and pin Govt. Ont., Caribana Achievement award, Bob Marley award, Kay Livingstone award, Women of Distinction award YWCA, Women on the Move award Toronto Sun, Can. Black Achievement award 1994. Mem. Can. Assn. for Parliamentarians on Population and Devel. (chair), Nat. Sugar Caucus (chair). Office: Ho of Commons, 433 W Block, Ottawa, ON Canada K1A 0A6*

AUGUSTINE, JEROME SAMUEL, merchant banker; b. Racine, Wis., May 7, 1928; s. Lester Samuel and Pearl (Hilker) A.; m. Camilla Sewell, Feb. 7, 1953; children: Theodore Samuel Purnell, Julia Sewell Augustine Marshall, Elizabeth Stroebel Augustine Burgoyne. AB cum laude, Harvard U., MBA, 1952. Cons. Scudder, Stevens & Clark, Boston, 1952-56; founder, treas., dir. Vencap, Inc., Boston, 1956-58; treas., dir. Consumer Products, Inc., Boston, 1956-58; founder, treas., dir. Microsonics, Inc., Hingham, Mass., 1956-58; treas., dir. Capitol Mgmt. Corp., Boston, 1956-58; cons. Kidder, Peabody & Co., Boston, 1958-64; pres. Cosmos Am. Corp., N.Y.C., 1964-66; founder, pres., dir. Cosmos Securities Corp., 1965-70, Cosmos (Bahamian) Ltd., Nassau, 1964-70; mng. dir. J. Samuel Augustine & Co., Ltd., Toronto, Ont., Can., 1966—; 1st v.p. Van Alstyne, Noel & Co., N.Y.C., 1973-74; v.p. Wright Investors' Svc., Bridgeport, 1974-87, sr. v.p., 1987-92; pres. Kredietbank (Belgium) Global Asset Mgmt., Stamford, 1992-94; bd. dirs. Chicken Soup, Plus, Inc. Trustee Low-Heywood Sch.; trustee The Augustine Family Charitable Trust. Named to Washington Hall of Fame, 1986. Mem. Boston Fin. Rsch. Assocs. (gov. 1960-64, v.p. 1963-64), New Eng. Amateur Rowing Assn. (past pres.), Union Boat Club, Harvard Club, Noroton Yacht Club, Royal Canadian Yacht Club, Ox Ridge Hunt Club, Calif. Polo Club, Royal Ascot Polo Club, East India Club (London). Anglican. Fax: (206) 374-6442. E-mail: augustco@concord.net. Office: Ste F24, 122 St Patrick St, Toronto, ON Canada M5T 2X8

AUGUSTINE, KATHY, state official. BA, Occidental Coll., L.A.; MPA, Calif. State U., Long Beach. Assemblywoman Nev. State Legislature, Carson City, 1992-94; senator State of Nev., Carson City, 1994-98, controller, 1999—. Bd. dirs. Alzheimer's Assn., hon. chmn. Memory Walk; trustee Cath. Charities So. Nev. Housing Corp.; mem. Family and Child Treatment Adv. Com.; bd. dirs. NCSL Women's Network, 1996-98. Recipient Am. Legion Achievement medallion, Legislator of Yr. awrd Nat. Rep. Legislators ASsn., 1998; Henry Toll fellow Coun. State Govts.; Flemming fellow, 1996; Lyndon B. Johnson Internship grantee, 1975; Congl. intern, Washington. Office: Controller's Office 101 N Carson St Ste 5 Carson City NV 89701

AUGUSTINE, NORMAN RALPH, industrial executive, educator; b. Denver, July 27, 1935; s. Ralph Harvey and Freda Irene (Immenga) A.; m. Margareta Engman, Jan. 20, 1962; children: Gregory Eugen, René Irene. BSE magna cum laude, Princeton U., 1957, MSE, 1959; DEng (hon.), Rensselaer Poly. Inst., 1988; DSc (hon.), U. Colo., 1989; ED (hon.), Western Md. Coll., 1990; DEng (hon.), U. Md., 1992; D Aerospace Mgmt. (hon.), Embry Riddle U., 1992; DEng (hon.), Stevens Inst., 1993; HHD (hon.), Wheeling Jesuit Coll., 1994; DSc (hon.), SUNY, 1994; DEng (hon.), U. Ctrl. Fla., 1995, Worcester Polytech., 1996; LHD (hon.), U. Denver, 1996, Georgetown U., 1997, Trinity Coll., 1997; DEng (hon.), U. Ariz., 1997; LLD (hon.), Duke U., 1997; DEng (hon.), Milw. Sch. Engring., 1998. Rsch. asst. Princeton U., 1957-58; program mgr., chief engr. Douglas Aircraft Co., Inc., Santa Monica, Calif., 1958-65; asst. dir. def. rsch. and engring. U.S. Govt., Office of Sec. Def., Washington, 1965-70; v.p. advanced systems Missiles and Space Co., LTV Aerospace Corp., Dallas, 1970-73; asst. sec. army The Pentagon, Washington, 1973-75; undersec. army The Pentagon, 1975-77; v.p. ops. Martin Marietta Aerospace Corp., Bethesda, Md., 1977-82; pres. Martin Marietta Denver Aerospace Co., 1982-85, sr. v.p. info. systems, 1985, from pres., COO to chmn., CEO, 1986-95, also bd. dirs.; pres. Lockheed Martin Corp., Bethesda, 1995-96, pres., CEO, 1996-97; lectr. (rank of prof.) Princeton Univ.Faculty, 1997—; bd. dirs. Phillips Petroleum Co., Procter & Gamble Co., New Am. Schs. Devel. Corp.; cons. office Sec. of Def., 1971—, Exec. Office Pres., 1971-73, Dept. Army, Dept. Air Force, Dept. Navy, FAA, Dept. Energy, Dept. Transp.; mem. USAF Sci. Adv. Bd.; chmn. Def. Sci. Bd., Exel Comm., 1997—; mem. NATO Group Experts on Air Def., 1966-70, NASA Rsch. and Tech. Adv. Coun., 1973-75, chmn. Space Sys. and Tech. Adv. Bd., 1985-89; mem. Chief of Naval Ops. Exec. Bd., 1989-92; chmn. def. policy adv. com. on trade, 1988-91, 93—; lectr. Princeton U., 1997—. Author: Augustine's Laws; co-author: The Defense Revolution, 1990, Augustine's Travels, 1997; mem. adv. bd. Jour. Def. Rsch., 1970—; assoc. editor Def. Systems Mgmt. Rev., 1977-82; mem. editorial bd. Astronautics and Aerospace. Trustee Johns Hopkins U., Princeton U., MIT; mem. bd. govs. Colonial Williamsburg, 1996—; chmn. White House/NASA Adv. Com. on Future of U.S. Space Program, 1991, Nat. Security Telecomm. Adv. Com., U.S. Antarctic Program Rev. Com., 1996-97; nat. program evaluation com., coun. v.p. Boy Scouts Am., pres., 1993—; chmn. ARC; mem. Pres.'s Com. of Advisors on Sci. and Tech. Recipient Meritorious Svc. medal Dept. Def., 1979, 5 Disting. Civilian Svc. medals Dept. Def., Nat. Engring. award Am. Assn. Engring. Socs., 1991, Am. Acad. Achievement Golden Plate award, 1995, James Madison medal Princeton U., 1995, Blumenthal award Johns Hopkins U. Sch. Engring., 1996, Gold Eagle award Soc. Am. Mil. Engrs. Acad. of Fellows, 1996, Ralph Coates Roe medal ASME, 1996, M. Eugene Merchant Mfg. medal, 1997, Nat. Medal of Technology, 1997; named Personality of Yr., Flight Internat. Aerospace, 1996. Fellow IEEE (Founders' award 1996), AIAA (hon., bd. dirs. 1978-85, pres. 1983-84, Goddard medal 1988), Am. Astron. Soc., Am. Helicopter Soc. (dir. 1974-75), Royal Aero. Soc.; mem. NAE (chmn. 1994—, Arthur M. Bueche award 1991), Am. Acad. Arts and Scis., Internat. Acad. Astronautics, Assn. U.S. Army (pres. 1980-84, chmn. 1990—, George C. Marshall medal), Nat. Security Indsl. Assn. (Forrestal medal 1988), Indsl. Coll. Armed Forces (Eisenhower award 1990), Armed Forces Comm. and Electronics Assn. (Sarnoff medal 1990), Nat. Space Club (Goddard Trophy 1991), Rotary (Nat. Space Trophy 1992), Planetary Soc. (bd. dirs.), Phi Beta Kappa, Sigma Xi, Tau Beta Pi. Presbyterian. Office: Lockheed Martin Corp 6801 Rockledge Dr Bethesda MD 20817-1877

AUGUSTUS, SUSAN J., nurse anesthetist; b. Providence, Aug. 10, 1947; d. Kenneth Francis and Jean Eleanor (Hennessey) Pettee; m. Peter Augustus III, Apr. 29, 1984. Diploma, R.I. Hosp., 1968, St. Joseph Hosp., 1980; BS, St. Joseph Coll., 1993. RN, Mass., R.I.; cert. RN anesthetist. Staff nurse MICU-SICU R.I. Hosp., Providence, asst. head nurse recovery rm.; staff nurse anesthetist, clin. instr. St. Joseph Hosp., Providence; staff nurse anesthetist Charlton Meml. Hosp., Fall River, Mass. Col. R.I. Air NG, Oper. Desert Shield/Storm (1st woman comdr. and col.), ret. Mem. AANA, Assn. Air Nat. Guard Nurses.

AUGUSTYN, FREDERICK JOHN, JR., librarian; b. Stamford, Conn., Aug. 4, 1951; s. Fred John and Helen Josephine (Bienkowski) A. BA, Boston U., 1973; student, U. Wis., 1973-77; MA, MLS, U. Md., 1983, PhD, 1996. Tchg./rsch. asst. dept. history U. Md., College Park, 1979-83; libr. Libr. of Congress, Washington, 1984—; Congl. Constituent tour guide, 1992—. Book reviewer Libr. of Congress. Mem. ALA, Am. Hist. Assn., Orgn. Am. Historians, Popular Culture Assn., Phi Alpha Theta, Beta Phi Mu. Avocations: political campaign collectibles, sport history, popular culture, linguistics. Home: 7800 Hanover Pky # 301 Greenbelt MD 20770-2620 Office: Libr of Congress Washington DC 20540

AUGUSTYNSKI, ADAM J., lawyer; b. Chgo., June 16, 1965; s. Marian Marcin and Genowefa (Jedrzejek) A.; m. Michele Honora Thorne, Sept. 28, 1991; 1 child, Alexander Thorne. AB with honors, Harvard U., 1986; JD, Northwestern U., 1990. Bar: Ill. 1990. Asst. legis. office U.S. Senator Alan Dixon, Washington, 1984; asst. office of chief of staff U.S. Senator Paul Simon, Washington, 1985; spl. asst. to pres. Polish Nat. Alliance, Chgo., 1989-94; pvt. practice Chgo., 1991—. Democrat. Roman Catholic. Avocations: sports, international politics. Office: 5850 W Bryn Mawr Chicago IL 60646

AUH, YANG JOHN, librarian, educational administrator; b. Chulla Namdo, Korea, Mar. 18, 1934; s. Sam Hyuck and So Yae (Suh) A.; came to U.S., 1962, naturalized, 1971; B.A., Chung-ang U., 1957; M.A. in Library Sci., Western Mich. U., 1964; cert. in library adminstrn. devel. (HEW fellow) U. Md., 1973; cert. in advanced librarianship Columbia U., 1975; cert. in mgmt., librarian's program (HEW fellow), Clarkson U., 1978; M.B.A., St. John's U., 1979; postgrad. NYU, 1996, Oxford (Eng.) U., 1997; m. Karen Kyung-ja Kim, Mar. 11, 1969; 1 dau., Alice Kim. Asst. librarian Korean Nat. Library, Seoul, 1957; tech. services librarian Korean Mil. Acad. Library, Seoul, 1958-61; asst. librarian Branch County Library, Coldwater, Mich., 1964; head union catalog L.I. U. Libraries, Greenvale, N.Y., 1965-68; head catalog dept., tech. services coordinator Wagner Coll. Library, S.I., N.Y., 1968-71, library dir., 1972-84, dir. Library and Learning Resources Ctr., 1984; pres. Highland Realty Mgmt., 1984—. Evaluator, Commn. Higher Edn., Middle States Assn. Colls. and Schs., 1984; trustee Am. Friends of Chung-ang U., 1979—. Mem. ALA, N.Y. State Library Assn., Korean Library Assn. Club: N.Y. Librarians, Omicron Delta Kappa (nat. mem., administrv. mem. Circle Wagner Coll. chpt. 1995). Office: Wagner Coll Horrmann Libr 631 Howard Ave Staten Island NY 10301-4428

AUKLAND, DUNCAN DAYTON, lawyer; b. Delaware, Ohio, July 6, 1954; s. Merrill Forrest and Elva Sampson (Dayton) A.; m. Diane Sue Clevenger, Aug. 7, 1982. BA, Va. Polytech. Inst., 1978; JD, Capital U., 1982. Bar: Ohio 1982, U.S. Dist. Ct. (so. dist.) Ohio 1982. Legal intern Ohio EPA, Columbus, 1982, staff atty., 1982-83, legal cons., 1983; sole practice Columbus, 1983-90; judge adv. USNG, Columbus, 1990—. Atty. Clean Up and Recycling Backers of Clintonville, Columbus, 1983-89; deacon Overbrook Presbyn. Ch., Columbus, 1986-89. With JAGC, USAR, 1984-90. Mem. Ohio Bar Assn., Va. Poly. Alumni Assn. Cen. Ohio (pres. 1984-85), Ohio Gamma Alumni Corp. (trustee 1983-88, 91-95). Republican. Avocations: golf, home repairs. Home: 5789 Crescent Ct Worthington OH 43085-3804 Office: Ohio Adj Gen's Dept Attn: AGOH-JA 2825 W Dublin Granville Rd Columbus OH 43235-2789

AUKOFER, FRANK ALEXANDER, journalist; b. Milw., Apr. 6, 1935; s. Herbert Anselm and Wanda Mary (Kaminski) A.; m. D. Sharlene Talatzko, Aug. 6, 1960; children: Juliann Navarrete, Matthew P., Becky Hawryluk, Joseph J. BA in Journalism, Marquette U., 1960; Fellowship Cert., Northwestern U., 1967. With The Milw. Jour. Sentinel (merger The Milw. Jour., Sentinel), 1960—; with Washington Bur. The Milw. Jour. Sentinel, 1970—, bur. chief; writer syndicated column on automobiles DriveWays, 1985—. With USAF Res., 1952-60. Recipient Byline award for lifetime achievement in journalism Marquette U., 1992, Profl. Merit award Marquette U., awards from Wis. Press. Assn., Milw. Press Club, Soc. Profl. Journalists; Vis. Profl. Freedom Forum First Amendment scholar Vanderbilt U., 1994-95. Mem. Nat. Press Club (pres. 1978, bd. dirs. bldg. corp., Corr. award), Nat. Press Found. (pres., chmn. bd. 1980-85, bd. dirs.), Soc. Profl. Journalists, Standing Com. Corr. U.S. Congress (sec. 1976), Washington Automotive Press Assn. (pres. 1987-88), Gridiron Club Washington. Roman Catholic. Home: 6136 Beachway Dr Falls Church VA 22041-1428 Office: Milw Jour 940 National Press Building Washington DC 20045-1901

AULBACH, GEORGE LOUIS, property investment company executive; b. York, Pa., July 9, 1925; s. George A. and Mary N. (Goulden) A.; m. Gertrude Frisby, June 24, 1949; children; Jeanne, Cynthia, Patricia, Kathleen, Barbara. BSCE, Villanova U., 1945. Registered prof. engr., Pa., Ga. Dield engr., estimator, chief engr., project mgr., exec. v.p R.S. Noonan, Inc., York, Pa., 1946-63; pres., CEO R.S. Noonan, Inc. & Noonan Engring. Corp., York, Pa., 1963-72; pres. systems bldg. divsn. McCrory-Sumwalt, Columbia, Columbia, S.C., 1972-76; pres., CEO Laing Properties, Inc., Atlanta, 1976-90; retired; adv. bd. dirs. Bank South, Atlanta, Ga. Tech. Rsch. Inst. bd. dirs. Northside Hosp. Found., Cath. Housong Initiative; trustee So. tech. Found.; cons. non-profit corp. developing affordable housing; chmn. sch. implementation com. Cath. Archdiocese of Atlanta. Lt. (j.g.) USN, 1943-46. Recipient Highest Papal Honor for a Layman Knight Comdr. St. Gregory, 1998. Mem. NSPE, Ga. Soc. Profl. Engrs., Soc. Internat. Bus. Fellows, York Are C. of C. (pres. 1965), Pa. Jeystone Chpt. AGC Bldg Contractors Assn. (pres. 1969-70), Urban Land Inst., Cherokee Town and Country Club. Roman Catholic.

AULD, ALBERT MICHAEL, sculptor; b. Kingston, Jamaica, Aug. 15, 1943; s. Ian Sturdee and Phylis Mae (Campbell) A.; m. Rose Amelia Powhatan, June 11, 1966; children: Ian, Alexei, Kiros. BFA, Howard U., 1966, MFA, 1980. Graphic designer Lindo, Norman, Craig, Kumel, Kingston, Jamaica, 1966; designer, illustrator NEA, Washington, 1967-72; art tchr. Sidwell Friends Sch., Washington, 1972-76; founder, dir. A&B Assocs. Adv., Washington, 1973-82; founder, co-dir. Opus 2 Gallery, Washington, 1973-80; lectr. design dept. Howard U., Washington, 1976-82; tchr., sculpture Duke Ellington Sch. of Arts, Washington, 1982—; cultural chmn. Caribbean/Am. Intercultural Orgn., Washington, 1976-84; chmn. artist's bd. Fondo del Sol Mus., Washington, 1982-86; co-founder, designer Pure Jamaican, Inc., L.A., 1995. Creator: (comic strip) Anansesem, 1968; sculptor: Powhatan Totems, 1987 (grantee 1986), Jamestown Totem Poles, 1994-95; vicео artist: Taino/Carib Esthetics, 1992 (grantee); one-man show: (sculpture) Honoring the Memory of Itiba Cahubaba, 1996-97. Active Native Am. Issues, Am. Indian Soc., Va., 1991—; co-founder Powhatan Cultural Arts, Columbia, Md., Washington, 1990—. Cmty. Svc. award Fondo del Sol Mus., Washington. Democrat. Lutheran. Avocations: writing, researching indigenous aesthetics, participating in Indian Pow Wows. Home: 1519 Monroe St NW Washington DC 20010-3140

AULD, FRANK, psychologist, educator; b. Denver, Aug. 9, 1923; s. Benjamin Franklin and Marion Leland (Evans) A.; m. Elinor James, June 29, 1946 (dec. June 1990); children—Mary, Robert, Margaret; m. Elinor Leah Levine, Dec. 8, 1996. A.B., Drew U., 1946; M.A., Yale U., 1948, Ph.D., 1950. Cert. psychologist, Mich., Ont. Instr. psychology Yale U., New Haven, 1950-52, asst. prof., 1952-59; asso. prof. Wayne State U., Detroit, 1959-61; prof. Wayne State U., 1961-67, dir. clin. psychology tng. program, 1960-66; prof. U. Detroit, 1967-70, dir. psychol. clinic, 1967-69; prof. U. Windsor, Ont., Can., 1970-91, prof. emeritus, 1992—; cons. in field. Author: Steps in Psychotherapy, 1953, Scoring Human Motives, 1959, Resolution of Inner Conflict, 1991; contbr. articles to profl. jours. Chmn. Dearborn (Mich.) Community Council, 1962; mem. adv. com. on coll. work Episcopal Diocese Mich., 1962-71. Recipient Alumni Achievement award Drew U., 1965. Fellow Am. Psychol. Assn. (evaluation com. 1961-66); mem. Can. Assn. U. Tchrs., Can., Mich. psychol. assns., Ont. Psychol. Assn. (edn. and tng. bd. 1976-91, Lifetime Achievement award 1998), Conn. State Psychol. Soc. (pres. 1958), Soc. Psychotherapy Research, Phi Beta Kappa, Sigma Xi. Home: 5436 Fairway Ct West Bloomfield MI 48323-3463 Office: U Windsor, Dept Psychology, Windsor, ON Canada N9B 3P4

AULD, JAMES S., educational psychologist. Grad., U. Nebr. Cert. sch. counselor, profl. counselor. Dir. testing, asst. prof., K-12 dir. guidance, kindergarten-12 dir. psychol. svcs. Author: Real Personality. Mem. APA, AACD, ASCD, Can. Psychol. Assn., Nebr. Profl. Counselors, Gold Key, nat. Disting. Svc. Registry for Counselors, Phi Delta Kappa. Office: PO Box 6228 Lincoln NE 68506-0228

AULD, LARRY ELWOOD, foundation executive; b. Miami Beach, Fla., Sept. 14, 1945; s. Andrew Joseph and Margarette Delane (Bush) A. AA, Miami Dade Community Coll., 1964; BA, Fla. State U., 1966; MA, U. Ky., 1968. Instr. theatre and eng. U. Ky., Hopkinsville, 1968-69; resident actor and coord. children's theatre Players State Theatre, Miami, 1969-73; actor Regional Theatres, 1973-79; supr. Met. Opera, N.Y.C., 1979-81; assoc. dir. devel. Am. Coun. for the Arts, N.Y.C., 1981-85; adminstrv. mgr. mktg. svcs. Hill & Knowlton, Inc., N.Y.C., 1985-90; dir. devel. The Pearl Theatre Co., N.Y.C., 1991-93; program dir. The Lifebridge Found., N.Y.C., 1993—; cons., fundraising, 1982—; acting coach, 1984—. Editor The Bridging Tree. Bd. adv. N.Y. Children's Theatre, 1988—; bd. dirs., 1985-88, Theatre Sports N.Y., 1988-90; co-artistic dir. The Tuesday Group, Inc., 1981-84. Mem. AEA, SAG, The Lifebridge Found. (sec. bd. dirs. 1994—). Democrat. Office: The Lifebridge Found PO Box 793 New York NY 10108-0793

AULETTA, JOAN MIGLORISI, construction company executive, mortgage and insurance broker; b. N.Y.C., July 23, 1940; d. Angelo George and Ann (Passa) Miglorisi; ABS, Bklyn. C.C., 1957; m. E.V. Auletta, Oct. 5, 1958; children—Ann, Vincent, George, Jeanne. Owner-mgr. Auletta Realty, also owner-mgr. E&J Pancake House, L.I., N.Y., 1947-76; office and fin. mgr. Larchwood Constrn. Co., Farmingville, N.Y., 1976-77; prodn. mgr. Lawlor Industries, Holtsville, N.Y., 1977-79; real estate and fin. adv. Family Home Improvement Corp., Queens Village, N.Y., 1979-81; co-owner Total Home Constrn. Co., N.Y.C., 1981-86; owner-mgr. Century 21, Echo Hills Realtors Inc., Miller Place, N.Y., 1987-92 , Auletta Realty, 1989—, Tone-O-Matic, 1988-89; owner-mgr. comml. property, 1970—; bd. dirs. Multiple Listing Svc. of L.I., 1986-91, L.I. Bd. Realtors, 1986-92, Fin. Dept. Waste Industry, 1992—. Mem. Miller Pl.-Mt. Sinai C. of C. (pres. 1988-90). Roman Catholic. Home: 6715 NW 71st Ct Tamarac FL 33321-5447

AULETTA, KEN, writer, columnist; b. Bklyn., 1942. BA in History, SUNY, Oswego, 1963; MA in Polit. Sci., Syracuse U., 1965. Polit. columnist Daily News, N.Y.C., 1977-93; media columnist New Yorker mag., N.Y.C. Author 7 books, including: Three Blind Mice: How the TV Networks Lost Their Way. Office: The New Yorker 20 W 43d St New York NY 10036-7441

AULL, JAMES STROUD, retired bishop; b. Winnsboro, S.C., Mar. 3, 1931; s. Luther Bachman and Ruth (Bull) A.; m. Virginia Kloeppel, Aug. 9, 1958; children: Diane, James Jr. (dec.), Virginia Ruth. AB magna cum laude, Newberry Coll., 1953; MDiv cum laude, Luth. Theol. So. Sem., Columbia, S.C., 1960; M in Systematic Theology, Luth. Sch. Theology, Chgo., 1970; PhD, Duke U., 1971; DD (hon.), Newberry Coll., 1988. Ordained to ministry United Luth. Ch. in Am., 1961. Pastor St. Timothy Luth. Ch., Camden, S.C., 1961-62; instr., staff mem. Luth. Theol. So. Sem., Columbia, S.C., 1962-79; sec. S.C. Synod, Luth. Ch. in Am., Columbia, 1979-87, bishop, 1988-96; ret., 1996. Author: Obey My Voice: a Form Critical Study of Selected Prose in the Book of Jeremiah", 1971. Trustee Newberry Coll., 1972-96, sec., 1977-82; trustee Luth. Home, White Rock, S.C., 1988-96, Lutheridge/Lutherock Ministries, Inc., 1988-96; bd. dirs. divsn. for edn. Evang. Luth. Ch. Am., Chgo., 1988-91, mem. ch. coun., 1991-96, bd. trustees, bd. pensions, 1997—. Mem. Soc. Bibl. Lit., Rotary (bd. dirs. 1987-90, pres. 1996-97). Home: 413 Challedon Dr Columbia SC 29212-3210

AULL, SUSAN, physician; b. N.Y.C.; d. Eugene and Ines Aull. BA, Vassar Coll., 1981; MD, N.Y. Med. Coll., 1986. Diplomate Am. Acad. Phys. Medicine and Rehab., Am. Acad. Pain Mgmt. Intern internal medicine L.I. Coll. Hosp., Bklyn., 1986-87; phys. medicine and rehab. PGY II, III Westchester County Med. Ctr., Valhalla, N.Y., 1987-89; phys. medicine and rehab. PGY IV Lincoln Hosp., Bronx, N.Y., 1989-90; med. dir. dept. phys. medicine and rehab. Halifax Med. Ctr., Daytona Beach, Fla., 1992—; med. dir. 21st Century Rehab. and Wound Mgmt. Ctr., Maitland, Fla., 1992; mem. staff dept. internal medicine Winter Park (Fla.) Meml. Hosp., 1991-96; pvt. practice Winter Park, 1991—; multi-specialty group practice, dir. phys. medicine and rehab. Ctrl. Fla. Physicians Rehab., Orlando, 1990-91; electrodiagnostic cons. SEA Med. Svcs., P.A., Goldenrod, Fla., 1990-96; adj. clin. prof. U. Ctrl. Fla., Orlando, 1991-96. Author: (with others) Strength Conditioning for Preventive Medicine, 1992, ISC Control Points - New Generation of Pressure Points, 1993. Recipient Leadership award Defensive Tactics Newsletter, 1993; grantee PPCT Mgmt. Systems, Inc., 1992. Fellow Am. Acad. Phys. Medicine and Rehab.; mem. AMA, Am. Congress Rehab., Am. Coll. Sports Medicine, Fla. Med. Soc., Orange County Med. Soc. Office: Winter Woods Physical Medicine PO Box 32 Sarasota FL 34230-0032

AULT, ETHYL LORITA, special education educator, consultant; b. Bklyn., May 30, 1939; d. Albert Nichols Fadden and Marion Cecil (Corrigan) Snow; (div.); children: Debra Marie Ault Butenko, Milinda Lei Jones, Timothy Scott. BS, Ga. State U., MEd, 1976, cert. in spl. edn. 6th yr., 1984. Tchr. spl. edn. Butts County Sch. System, Jackson, Ga., 1972-73; tchr. spl. edn. Rockdale County Sch. System, Conyers, Ga., 1973-75, lead tchr., 1975-77; cons. spl. edn. Newton County Sch. System, Covington, Ga., 1977-79; curriculum specialist spl. edn. La Grange (Ga.) Sch. System, 1979-83, dir. spl. edn., 1983-94, dir. accredited studies curriculum, 1994—, dir. student svcs., 1995—; collaboration process trainer State of Ga., 1990—, dir. student svcs./spl. program, 1996—; instr. La Grange Coll., 1984—; mem. Tchr. Competency Testing Commn., Atlanta, 1988—, Task Force Documentation and Decision Making, Atlanta, 1988—. Contbg. editor: (manual) Mainstream Modification Handbook, 1989. Chairperson Jud. Adv. Panel, LaGrange, 1988; bd. dirs. Crawford Tng. Ctr. Adv. Panel, La Grange, 1985—; pres. West Ga. Youth Coun. Bd., La Grange, 1980—; mem. State Adv. Panel for Spl. Edn.; bd. dirs. Troup County Hist. Soc., 1999—; mem. State of Ga. Task Force on Alt. Edn., 1998—. Mem. Coun. Exceptional Children, Ga. Assn. Edn. Leaders, Ga. Assn. Curriculum and Instrn. Supervision, Ga. Coun. Adminstrs. Spl. Edn. (v.p. 1988—, pres.-elect 1989, pres. 1992—, Gifted State Task Force 1994—), La Grange Women's Club (v.p. 1989—), Profl. Assn. Ga. Spl. Educators (Adminstr. of Yr. 1993), Ga. Supporters of the Gifted, Nat. Assn. for Gifted Edn. Democrat. Episcopalian. Avocations: swimming, fishing, walking, gardening. Home: 441 Gordon Cir Lagrange GA 30240 Office: 2828 Westpoint Rd Lagrange GA 30240-6423

AULT, JAMES MASE, bishop; b. Sayre, Pa., Aug. 24, 1918; s. Tracey Everett and Bessie (Mase) A.; m. Dorothy Mae Barnhart, Dec. 22, 1943; children: James Mase, Kathryn Louise, Elizabeth Ann, Christopher John (dec.). AB magna cum laude, Colgate U., 1949; BD magna cum laude, Union Theol. Sem., N.Y.C., 1952, STM, 1964; postgrad., St. Andrews U., Scotland, 1966; DD, Am. U., Washington, 1968; LLD (hon.), Albright Coll., 1973, Ohio Wesleyan U., 1973; DHL (hon.), Drew U., 1986; LHD (hon.), Allegheny Coll., 1987. Ordained to ministry Meth. Ch. as deacon, 1951, as elder, 1952. Tool engr. Ingersoll-Rand Co., 1936-42; pastor Meth. Ch., Preston, N.Y., 1946-49, Carlton Hill Meth. Ch., East Rutherford, N.J., 1951-53, Meth. Ch., Leonia, N.J., 1953-58, First Meth. Ch., Pittsfield, Mass., 1958-61; dean students, asso. prof. practical theology Union Theol. Sem., N.Y.C., 1961-64; prof. practical theology, dir. field edn. Union Theol. Sem., 1964-68; dean, prof. pastoral theology Theol. Sch., Drew U., Madison, N.J., 1968-72; bishop Phila. area United Meth. Ch., 1972-80, bishop Pitts. area, 1980-88, bishop Wyo. conf., 1990; prof. contemporary ministries Theol. Sch. Drew U., Madison, N.J., 1988-91, interim dean Theol. Sch., 1990-91; sec. council of bishops United Meth. Ch., 1980-84, pres. council bishops, 1986-87; mem. governing bd. Nat. Coun. Chs. of Christ in U.S.A., 1981-84; mem. central com. World Coun. Chs., 1981-91; mem. exec. com. World Meth. Coun., 1981-88. Author: Responsible Adults for Tomorrow's World, 1962. Mem. sr. exec. ecumenical seminar Hartford Theol. Sem. and the Lilly Endowment, 1989-92; chair U.S. Bossey com. World Coun. Chs., 1994—. Lt. U.S. Army, 1942-46. Faculty fellow Am. Assn. Theol. Schs., 1965-66. Mem. AAUP, Acad. Polit. and Social Sci., Phi Beta Kappa. Home: 1 Amoskegan Dr Brunswick ME 04011-9524

AULT, JEFFREY MICHAEL, investment banker; b. Norfolk, Va., Jan. 20, 1947; s. Frank Willis and Helen Blake (Hamner) A.; 1 child, Jeffrey Franklin. BS, U. Calif., San Diego, 1974; postgrad., U. San Diego, 1975-84, Word of Faith Bible Inst., Dallas. Ordained to ministry Fedn. Gen. Assemblies Internat., 1988. Dir. nat. bus. devel. Mayflower, San Diego, 1970-75; dir. new accounts Aero-Mayflower Transit Co., Alexandria, Va., 1976-78; v.p. Mchts. Mgmt. Co., Washington, 1976-78; v.p. mktg. Stevens Van Lines, various states, 1978-80; exec. v.p. Fla. Am. Van Lines Inc., Tampa, 1980-84; pres. Victory World Trade Corp., Washington, 1984-85; chmn., CEO Maranatha Van Lines, Inc., Tampa, 1984-90; exec. dir. Maranatha Vision Ministries Inc., Tampa, Swords Into Plowshares, France, Russia, Vietnam, U.S.; pres. Ea. Star Trading Co., Minsk, Belarus; pres. JRW Corp., S.A., Santiago, Tampa, Seattle, Moscow, Bangkok, Mpls., Buenos Aires, Miami, Zurich; v.p., sr. ptnr. Noord Prince Mchts. Bank, Curacao; sr. ptnr. Geneses Group, Mpls.; trustee Gold-Lyon Trust, The Bear Trust, Vaduz, Leichtenstein. Mem. U.S. Senate Trust, Hillsborough County Republican Party; sustaining mem. Rep. Nat. Com. Sgt. USMC, 1966-72, Vietnam. Mem. DAV, Aircraft Owners and Pilots Assn., U. Calif. at San Diego Alumni Assn., First U.S. Marine Div. Assn., USMC Combat Corrs. Assn., Mensa. Home: PO Box 811 18026 Lindawoods St Odessa FL 33556-4713 Office: JRW Corp SA PO Box 391 Tampa FL 33601-0391 also: Samarkandsky Bulvar 15/1, Flat 142, Moscow Russia

AULTMAN, WILLIAM ROBERT, career officer; b. Ft. Benning, Ga., July 15, 1953; s. William Wilmer and Kazuko Suzie (Sano) A.; m. Barbara Ellen Tison, Dec. 22, 1979; children: Sara Alexandra, Nicholas Christian. BS in Engring, U.S. Military Acad., 1975; MSSM, USC, 1987; MS in Strategic Intelligence, Joint Mil. Intelligence Coll., 1994; diploma, U.S. Army War Coll., 1996. Commd. 2d lt. U.S. Army, 1975, advanced through grades to col., 1998; platoon leader, bn. S-2 intelligence officer 3rd infantry div. U.S. Army, Aschaffenburg, Fed. Republic Germany, 1975-78; tactical reconnaissance officer 82nd Airborne Div., Ft. Bragg, N.C., 1980-81; co. commdr. 1st Mil. Intelligence Battalion, Ft. Bragg, 1981-82; ops. officer Ft. Shafter, HI, 1982-85; plans officer Defense Intelligence Agy., Washington, 1985-88; chief intelligence collection mgmt. Combined Field Army, Camp Red Cloud, Korea, 1988-89; chief ADP applications Intelligence Ctr. Pacific, Camp Smith, Hawaii, 1989-91; VII Corps G2 staff Operation Desert Storm, Persian Gulf, 1991; chief logistics mgmt. Joint Intelligence Ctr., Pacific, Pearl Harbor, Hawaii, 1992-93; chief project mgmt. U.S. Army Info. Systems Command Pentagon, Arlington, Va., 1993-95; project officer TAADS-R U.S. Army, Ft. Belvoir, Va., 1995-97; dep. for Army electronic warfare programs OUSD (A&T)/S&TS/EW Pentagon, Washington, 1997—. Mem. NRA, Ret. Officers Assn., Assn. Grads. U.S. Mil. Acad., Va. Shooting Sports Assn., Army War Coll. Alumni Assn., Assn. Old Crows, Def. Sys. Mgmt. Alumni Assn. Baptist. Avocations: travel, reading, Japanese swords, beaches. Home: 8811 Telegraph Crossing Ct Lorton VA 22079-4411 Office: OUSD (A&T)/S&TS/EW Pentagon Washington DC 20301-3100

AUMACK, SHIRLEY JEAN, financial planner, tax preparer; b. Newark, May 17, 1949; d. Herbert O. and Edythe V. (England) Marlatt; m. Kenneth J. Aumack, Oct. 25, 1969; children: Douglas, Steven. BA in Econs., Wilson Coll., 1971. Cert. fin. planner, enrolled agt.; registered investment advisor; registered rep., investment exec. Fin. Network Investment Corp. Account exec. N.J. Bell Telephone, Scotch Plains, N.J., 1972-76; ptnr., ind. contr. Personal Mgmt. and Planning Inc., Matawan, N.J., 1982-90; pvt. practice fin. planner tax and fin. aspects of divorce Fair Haven, 1990—; mng. supr. Employee Fin. Edn. Divsn. Fin. Network Investment Corp., 1998—; instr. fin. planning Momouth County Park System, Lincroft, N.J., 1991, Rutgers U., 1993, 94, Rumson Cmty. Edn., 1995—. Pres. Performing Arts Soc., Rumson Fair-Haven Regional High Sch., 1992-94. Mem. Internat. Assn. for Fin. Planning (seminar speaker 1990), Inst. Cert. Fin. Planners, Nat. Assn. Enrolled Agts., Accreditation Coun. for Accountancy and Taxation (tax advisor). Office: 21 Cedar Ave # E Fair Haven NJ 07704-3264 also: 2 Ethel Rd Bldg 201A Edison NJ 08817-2839

AUMICK, AMALIA, legislative staff member; b. Port Jervis, N.Y., Oct. 30, 1935. Dist. dir. Office of Rep. Benjamin Gilman, Middletown, N.Y., 1989—. Office: Dist Dir Office Rep Benjamin Gilman PO Box 358 419 E Main St Middletown NY 10940*

AUNGST, BRUCE JEFFREY, pharmaceutical company scientist; b. Pottsville, Pa., Nov. 22, 1952; s. Roy Stewart and Grace M. (Rupp) A.; m. Judith M. Smith, Aug. 23, 1980; children: Matthew, Colleen, Christopher, Keenan, Mariette, Nelson. BS, Pa. State U., 1974, MS, 1977; PhD, SUNY, Buffalo, 1982. Rsch. pharmacist DuPont, Wilmington, Del., 1981-85, sr. rsch. pharmacist, 1985-91; prin. rsch. scientist DuPont Merck, Wilmington, 1991-98, DuPont Pharm. Co., Wilmington, 1998—. Contbr. articles to profl. jours.; patentee in field. Mem. Am. Assn. Pharm. Scientists, Controlled Release Soc. Office: DuPont Pharm Co PO Box 80400 Wilmington DE 19880-0400

AUNG-THWIN, MICHAEL ARTHUR, history educator; b. Rangoon, Burma, 1946. BA, Doane Coll., 1969; MA, U. Ill., Urbana, 1971; PhD, U. Mich., 1976. Asst. prof. Asian history Elmira (N.Y.) Coll., 1980-87; assoc. prof. history No. Ill. U., DeKalb, 1987-95; dir. Ctr. S.E. Asian Studies No. Ill. U., DeKalb, Ill., 1987-95; prof. Asian Studies U. Hawaii, Honolulu, 1995—; vis. prof. Cornell U., 1981; vis. scholar Ctr. for S.E. Asian Studies, Kyoto, Japan. Contbr. articles to profl. jours. NEH fellow, 1977-80. Mem. Assn. for Asian Studies (bd. dirs. 1980-83, mem. S.E. Asia Coun.), Burma Studies Found. (sec.-treas.). Office: U Hawaii Sch Hawaiian Asian Studies 413 Moore Hall Honolulu HI 96822*

AUPING, MICHAEL G., curator; b. Portland, Oreg., Oct. 17, 1949; s. Jack Louis and Jane (Hammel) A.; m. Patricia Contreras, Aug. 22, 1974; children: Alicia Contreras, Jonathan Contreras. AA, Santa Ana Coll., 1969; BA, Calif. State U., Fullerton, 1971; MA, Calif. State U., Long Beach, 1975. Editor #1 Powell Libr. UCLA, 1975-77; assoc. curator Univ. Art Mus., Berkeley, Calif., 1977-80; head of curatorial, curator 20th century art Ringling Mus. Art, Sarasota, Fla., 1980-84; chief curator Albright-Knox Art Gallery, Buffalo, 1984-93, Modern Art Mus. of Ft. Worth, 1993—; instr. art history Citrus Coll., Azusa Calif., summer 1977, San Francisco Art Inst., spring 1978; adj. lectr. U. Calif., Santa Barbara, fall 1977, U. Buffalo, 1988-89; guest curator Artist's Space, N.Y., 1988; panelist mus. aid program N.Y. State Coun. on Arts, 1988-89, Fed. Adv. Com. for Internat. Exhibitions, NEA and Rockefeller Found., 1992—; cons., commr. Am. Pavilion 1990 Venice Biennale, Italy; mem. adv. com. Intermus. Conservation Lab., CARE Publication., Art in Pub. Places, Met.-Dade area, 1984—, The Bush Found., St. Paul, 1985; cons. L.A. county Dept. Parks Cultural Arts sect., 1973; grant panelist mus. programs spl. exhbns. NEA, Washington, 1985, panelist, on-site evaluator Artists' Orgn. N.Y.C., 1983; visual arts panelist Div. Cultural Affairs State of Fla., Tallahassee, 1980, 81. Author: Francesco Clemente, 1985, Jenny Holzer, 1992, Drawing Rooms: Jonathan Borofsky, Sol LeWitt, Richard Serra, 1994, Arshile Gorky: The Breakthrough Years, 1995, Tatsuo Miyajima: Big Time, 1996, Susan Rothenberg Paintings, 1996, Georg Baselitz: Portraits of Elke, 1997, Agnes Martin/Richard Tuttle, 1998; TV appearances including CBS Sunday Morning, 1988; mng. editor L.A. Inst. Contemporary Art Jour., 1976-77; contbr. articles to profl. jours.; organizer exhbns. Office: Modern Art Mus 1309 Montgomery St Fort Worth TX 76107-3015

AURAND, CHARLES HENRY, JR., music educator; b. Battle Creek, Mich., Sept. 6, 1932; s. Charles Henry and Elisabeth Dirk (Hoekstra) A.; m. Donna Mae Erb, June 19, 1954; children: Janice, Cheryl, Sandra, Charles III, William. MusB, Mich. State U., 1954, MusM, 1958; PhD, U. Mich., 1971. Cert. tchr., Mich., Ohio. Asst. prof. music Hiram Coll., Ohio, 1958-60; dean, prof. music Youngstown State U., 1960-73; dean No. Ariz. U., Flagstaff, 1973-88, prof. music, 1988-94, prof. emeritus, 1994—; chmn. Ariz. Alliance for Arts Edn., 1974-77; solo clarinetist Flagstaff Symphony; solo, chamber music and orch. musician, 1973-86; fine arts cons. Miami U. of Ohio, 1982. Author: Selected Solos, Methods, 1963. Elder Presbyterian Ch., 1965; chmn. Boy Scouts Am., Coconino dist., 1974-78; bd. dirs. Ariz. Com. Arts for the Handicapped, 1982-88, Flagstaff Symphony Orch., 1973-85, Flagstaff Festival of Arts, 1973-89; bd. dirs. Sedona Chamber Mus. Soc., 1989—, Sedona Med. Ctr., 1998—; conf. dir. Internat. Clarinet Soc., 1991; pres. Citizens for an Alt. Rt., 1995—. Served to 1st lt. USAF, 1955-57. Recipient award of merit Boy Scouts Am., 1977; cert. appreciation John F. Kennedy Ctr. Performing Arts, 1985. Mem. Am. Assn. Higher Edn., Ariz. Humanities Assn., Music Educators Nat. Conf., State Adminstrs. of Music Schs. (chmn. 1971-73), Internat. Clarinet Soc./ClariNetwork Internat. (conf. dir. 1991), No. Ariz. U. Retirees Assn. (pres. 1997-98). Republican. Presbyterian. Lodge: Kiwanis (pres. 1984-85). Avocations: golf, tennis, bridge. Home: 140 Fairway Oaks Ln Sedona AZ 86351-8835 Office: No Ariz U Box 6040 Flagstaff AZ 86011

AURBACH, HERBERT ALEXANDER, sociology educator; b. Cleve., Aug. 6, 1924; s. Nate and Sara (Munitz) A.; m. Rebecca Rachel Blumenfeld, Nov. 2, 1952; children—Jacquelyn Aurbach Scheidlinger, Seth Jacob. B.S., Western Res. U., 1948; Ph.D., U. Ky., 1960. Asst. rural sociologist Miss. State Coll., 1954-55; asst. prof. sociology and research asso. N.C. State Coll.,

Raleigh, 1955-57; research dir. Pitts. Commn. Human Relations, 1957-61; rsch. assoc., asst. prof. sociology U. Pitts., 1961-66; assoc. prof. edn. and sociology Pa. State U., 1966-70; prof. sociology Buffalo State Coll., 1970-93, chmn. dept. sociology, 1970-74, prof. emeritus, 1993—; assoc. dir. Nat. Study Am. Indian Edn., 1968-69. Author: (with Estelle Fuchs) The Status of American Indian Education, 1970; Assoc. editor: Social Problems, 1966-74; Contbr. profl. jours. Bd. dirs. Citizens Commn. Criminal Justice, Buffalo and Erie County, 1972-74, Anti-Defamation League of B'nai B'rith, Buffalo, 1971-75, 97—, Coun. of Sr. Citizens Clubs of Buffalo and Erie County, 1996—; pres. Amherst chpt. Nat. Coun. Sr. Citizens, 1996-99; co-chmn. Self-Study Task Force Bur. Jewish Edn., Greater Buffalo, 1979-80, bd. trustees, 1998—; co-chair adult edn. com. Temple Shaarey Zedek, Buffalo, 1995—; mem. sr. svcs. adv. bd. Town of Amherst, 1997—. Decorated Air medal with 4 clusters; recipient N.Y. State/United Univ. Professions Excellence award, 1991; fellow So. Fellowship Fund, 1956-57. Mem. Soc. Study Social Problems (sec. 1965-69, treas. 1966-74, exec. officer 1975-86, v.p. 1987-88, chair bylaws com. 1988—, chair youth, aging and life course divsn. 1993-94), Am. Assn. Retired Persons/VOTE (27th congl. dist. coord. 1993-95). Home: 23 Millbrook Ct Buffalo NY 14221-4312

AURBACH, ROBERT MICHAEL, lawyer, consultant, photographer; b. Chgo., Mar. 12, 1952; s. Arthur B. and Helen T. Aurbach; m. Elizabeth Cervantes, Aug. 7, 1994; children: Elyse Louise, Rebecca Michelle. BA summa cum laude, Boston U., 1974; JD, Cornell U., 1979; postgrad., U. N.Mex., 1992, 98. Bar: N.Mex. 1979, U.S. Dist. Ct. N.Mex. 1979, U.S. Ct. Appeals (10th cir.) 1979, U.S. Supreme Ct. 1984. Assoc. Montgomery & Andrews, P.A., Santa Fe, 1979-80; asst. dist. atty. 1st Jud. Dist. Atty.'s Office, Santa Fe, 1980-84; exec. dir. N.Mex. Adminstrv. Office of Dist. Attys., Santa Fe, 1984-89; sr. assoc. U. N.Mex. Inst. Criminal Justice, Albuquerque, 1989-90; pvt. practice law Santa Fe, 1989-90; gen. counsel N.Mex. Workers' Compensation Adminstrn., Albuquerque, 1990—; cons. Navajo Nation Workers' Compensation Task Force, Windowrock, Ariz., 1993-97, U.S. V.I. Workers Compensation Adminstrn., Charlotte Amalie, 1992-93; chmn. Children's Justice Act Adv. Group, Albuquerque, 1989; instr. N.Mex. Law Enforcement Acad., Santa Fe, 1985-90; del. to working group on cross border workers' compensation issues Secretariat, Commn. on Labor Coop., N.Am. Agreement of Labor Coop., 1997—. Author: (handbook) Peace Officer Prosecutions, 1985. Mem. bar coun. Disciplinary Bd. of N.Mex. Supreme Ct., 1979—; em. com. Unauthorized Practice of Law Com., 1991-97; bd. dirs. Albuquerque Met. Crimestoppers, 1994-95; docent Albuquerque Aquarium. Mem. Internat. Assn. Indsl. Accident Bds. (legal editor jour. 1997—, co-chair coverage and compliance com. 1998—), So. Assn. WCA, Western Assn. Workers Compensation Bds., Phi Beta Kappa. Avocations: golf, scuba diving, fishing. Home: 819 Suzanne Ln SE Albuquerque NM 87123-4502 Office: NMex Workers Compensation 2410 Centre Ave SE Albuquerque NM 87106-4190

AURELL, JOHN KARL, lawyer; b. Tulsa, Sept. 26, 1935; s. George E. and Maxine (Reagor) A.; m. Jane Brevard Collins, Oct. 1, 1960; 1 child, Jane B. BA, Washington and Lee U., 1956; LLB, Yale U., 1964. Bar: Fla. 1964, D.C 1971, U.S. Dist. Ct. (no., mid. and so. dists.) Fla., U.S. Ct. Appeals (5th and 11th cirs.), U.S. Supreme Ct. Gen. counsel to Gov. State of Fla., Tallahassee, 1979-80; ptnr. Ausley & McMullen, Tallahassee, 1994—; mem. Fed. Jud. Nominating Commn. Fla.; chmn. No. Dist. Fla., 1993-97. Mem. exec. com., v.p. Yale Law Sch. Assn., 1975-80; mem. Orange Bowl Com. 1st lt. U.S. Army, 1956-57. Fellow Am. Bar Found., Internat. Soc. Barristers, Am. Coll. Trial Lawyers; mem. ABA, Fla. Bar Assn. (bd. govs. young lawyers sect. 1966-71), Am. Law Inst., Gov.'s Club, Exch. Club, Yale Club (N.Y.C.), Econ. Club Fla. (chmn. 1997-98), Capital City Country Club. Democrat. Home: 920 Live Oak Plantation Rd Tallahassee FL 32312-2415 Office: Ausley & McMullen PO Box 391 Tallahassee FL 32302-0391

AURIEMMA, GENO, university athletic coach; m. Kathy; children: Jenna, Alysa, Michael. BA, West Chester U., 1981. Coach boys' basketball Bishop Kenrick High Sch., 1979-81; asst. women's basketball coach U. Va., 1981-85, St. Joseph's U., Phila., 1984; head coach U. Conn., 1985—; mem. Kodak All-Am. Selection Com., chair, 1992; voting mem. USA Today/WBCA Topo 25 Poll-In; co-head coach Nat. Sr. All-Stars; coach USA Basketball Select Team, Colorado Springs, Colo.; asst. coach USA World U. Games Women's Basketball Team, 1995; head coach West Team U.S. Olympic Festival, San Antonio, 1993; spkr. Nat. High Sch. Coaches Assn. Convention, Conn. Chair Why-Me of New Eng.; chair (hon.) AHA. Named Women's Basketball Nat. Coach of Yr. (4), Naismith Nat. Coach of the Yr., Coach of Yr. AP, Nat. Coach of Yr. Women's Basketball Coaches Assn., Coach of Yr. Big East, 1988-89, 94-95, 96-97; recipient Victor award Women's Basketball Coaches Assn. Office: U Conn 2095 Hillside Rd Storrs Mansfield CT 06269-9017*

AURIEMMO, FRANK JOSEPH, JR., financial holding company executive; b. N.Y.C., Mar. 16, 1942; s. Frank Joseph and Jean (Celano) A.; m. Annette Marie Rounds, Oct. 14, 1967; children: Frank Bertram, Adam Rounds, Lucas James. BBA in Corp. Fin., Iona Coll., 1964; postgrad., NYU, 1967-69. Trust adminstr. Chase Manhattan Bank, NA, N.Y.C., 1965-67; investment analyst Paine, Webber, Jackson & Curtis, N.Y.C., 1967-69; sr. investment analyst Hayden, Stone, Inc., N.Y.C., 1970, Bache & co., N.Y.C., 1970-72, Hornblower & Weeks, Hemphill, Noyes, N.Y.C., 1972-74; with USLIFE Corp., N.Y.C., 1974-97, 2d v.p., analyst, 1979-83, 2d v.p. corp. fin., 1983-84, v.p. fin. ops., 1984, v.p., treas., 1984—, sr. v.p., treas., 1995-97; founder, pres., CEO, Kittiwake Assocs., LLC, Bronxville, N.Y., 1997—; v.p. subs. U.S. Life Ins. Co., All Am. Life Ins. Co., Old Line Life, USLIFE Credit Life, 1984-97; bd. dirs., v.p., treas. New D Corp., Iowa, 1983—; dir. Midwest Property Mgmt. Co. With U.S. Army and N.Y. Army N.G., 1964-70. Mem. Nat. Assn. Bus. Economists, The Planning Forum, N.Y. Soc. Security Analysts, Assn. Ins. and Fin. Analysts, Fin. Analysts Fedn. Mem. Conservative Party. Avocations: hunting, fishing, target shooting, reading military history. Home: 35 Tanglewylde Ave Bronxville NY 10708-3131 Office: Kittiwake Assocs LLC PO Box 233 Bronxville NY 10708-0233

AURILIA, ANTONIO, physicist, educator; b. Napoli, Italy, May 14, 1942; came to U.S., 1986, naturalized, 1993; s. Clemente and Assunta (Ligesto) A.; m. Elizabeth Christine Adams, Dec. 1, 1972; children: Darius Matthew, Alexandra Rebecca. Laurea in Physics, U. Naples, Italy, 1966; PhD in Physics, U. Wis., Milw., 1970. Postdoctoral fellow dept. physics U. Alta., Edmonton, 1970-72; rsch. assoc. dept. physics Syracuse (N.Y.) U., 1972-74; rsch. scientist Internat. Ctr. Theoretical Physics, Trieste, Italy, 1974-75, Nat. Inst. Nuclear Physics, Trieste, 1975-86; prof. dept. physics Calif. State Poly. U., Pomona, 1986—. Mem. Am. Phys. Soc., Am. Assn. Physics Tchrs., N.Y. Acad. Sci., Sigma Xi. Democrat. Roman Catholic. Achievements include research in theoretical physics. Office: Calif State U Dept Physics 3801 W Temple Ave Pomona CA 91768-2557

AURILIA, CHRISTINE MARIE, administrative assistant; b. Bklyn., Mar. 23, 1962; d. Anthony Neil and Christina Mary (Chernega) A. BA in Journalism, Rutgers U., 1984. Editorial asst. Marvel Entertainment Group, N.Y.C., 1985-87, adminstrv. asst., 1987-96. Sponsor Futures for Children, Albuquerque, 1988, Childreach, 1996-97; active Am. Friends of the Royal Shakespeare Co., London, 1985, Amnesty Internat., 1990, Oxfam Am., 1991, Greenpeace, 1991; supporter Colonial Williamsburg Found., 1994. Mem. Am. Mus. Natural History. Avocations: reading, writing. Office: Marvel Entertainment Group 387 Park Ave S New York NY 10016-8810

AURIN, ROBERT JAMES, entrepreneur; b. St. Louis, Feb. 13, 1943; s. George Henry and Elizabeth Anastasia (Krauska) A.; m. Kathryn L. Engel., 1998. B in Journalism, U. Mo., 1965. Copywriter Leo Burnett Co., Chgo., 1971-72, Young & Rubicam, Inc., Chgo., 1972-73; from copywriter to v.p., creative dir. Foote, Cone & Belding, Inc., Chgo., 1973-79; exec. v.p., dir. creative services Grey-North Inc., Chgo., 1979-82; pres. Robert Aurin Assocs., Chgo., 1982—; owner ROMAR Investments Co., Chgo., 1984—; exec. dir. DraftWorldwide, Inc., 1996—. Served to lt. USN, 1965-70, Vietnam. Mem. Art Inst. Chgo.

AURIOL, YVES, university women's head fencing coach; b. Aug. 12, 1937; m. Georgette Auriol; 1 child, Stephane. Grad., Lycee de Toulouse, France, 1955; MS, Inst. Nat. du Sport, Paris. Founder Salle Auriol Fencing Club; fencing coach Portland State U., 1975-85; phys. edn. instr. Cmty. Coll.; head coach Notre Dame U.; Coach U.S. Olympic fencing squad, 1980, 84, 88, 92, Jr. World Championship, 1976-79. Office: U of Notre Dame Womens Athletic Dept Joyce Ctr Notre Dame IN 46556

AURNER, ROBERT RAY, author, corporate executive; b. Adel, Iowa, Aug. 20, 1898; s. Clarence Ray and Nellie (Slayton) A.; m. Kathryn Dayton, June 16, 1921; 1 son, Robert Ray II. B.A. summa cum laude, U. Iowa, 1919, M.A., 1920, Ph.D., 1922. Dir. customer relations, new bus. The State Bank, Madison, Wis., 1925-28; research dir. Walker Co., 1925-30; established Aurner and Assocs., Cons. to Mgmt., bus. adminstrn., market distbn. and human relations, pres., chmn., chief exec. officer, 1938—, pres., 1988—; v.p., dir. Pacific Futures, Inc., 1962—; dir., chmn. bus adv. com. VNA Corp., 1959-62; fin. cons., dir. Carmel Savs. & Loan Assn., Calif., 1960-71; lectr. NBC Station WTMJ, 1929-30; state commr. Wis. Library Certification Bd., 1931-38; pres. Am. Bus. Communication Assn., 1939-40; mem. faculty, adminstrv. staff U. Wis., 1925-48, ranking research prof. bus. adminstrn., chmn. adminstrn. and mgmt. div., mem. univ. lectr. bur., 1930-48; vis. prof. bus. mgmt. U. Pitts., 1934, 36, 39; vis. research prof. Rare Book Rm., Huntington Library, San Marino, Calif., 1941; adminstrv. cons. Internat. Cellucotton Products Co., Chgo., 1947-52; cons., dir. Communications Div., Fox River Paper Corp., Appleton, Wis., 1947-60; v.p., gen. cons., dir. Scott, Inc., Milw. and Carmel, 1949—; cons. U.S. Naval Postgrad. Sch., Mgmt. Sch. Div., Dept. Navy, Dept. Def., 1957—, Jahn & Ollier Corp., Morris, Schenker, Roth, Inc., First Nat. Bank, Chgo., Library Research Service, New Haven, Nat. Assn. Real Estate Bds., N.Y.C., Allis-Chalmers Corp., Milw.; ltd. partner Salinas-Peninsula Investment Co., 1963-72; cons. Wis. Div. Vital Statistics, 1930-48; Dean Coll. of Commerce, Biarritz Am. U., France, U.S. Army Univ. Center No. 2, ETO, 1945-46; attached U.S. Army, USFET, I. and E. Div., Field Grade, rank of col., 1945-46; spl. lectr. Netherlands Sch. Econs., Rotterdam, 1945; U.S. State Dept. rep. Dutch-Am. Conf., The Hague, Holland, 1945; mem. nat. adv. com. Conf. Am. Small Business Orgns., 1947—; Dir. SAE Corp. Evanston, Ill., 1943-53, pres., chmn. bd., chief exec. officer, 1951-53, Eminent Supreme Archon; mem. nat. adv. counsel Atlantic Union, Inc., 1949—. Author: Specialized Field Approach, 1963, Language Control for Business, 1965, Success Factors in Executive Development, 1967, Effective English for Colleges, 6th edit., 1980, Effective English for Business Communication, 8th edit., 1982, Effective Communication in Business with Management Emphasis, 8th edit., 1988; contbg. editor: Am. Ency. Social Scis.; co-author, contbg. editor, American Business Practice (4 vols.). Trustee Levere Meml. Found., Chgo., 1943-53, pres., chmn. bd., chief exec. officer, 1951-53; chmn. bd., pres., chief exec. officer Carmel Found., Calif., 1981-85, v.p., 1977-81, dir., past chmn. fin. com., past chmn. meml. policy com. mem. internal trusteeship com., exec. com., 1954-83; mem. bd. investment mgmt. Hazeltine Fund Calif., 1963-83; adv. gov., bd. dirs. Monterey Fund Edn., 1965—; dir., chmn. com. endowments York Sch., 1966-69; bd. dirs. Wis. div. AAA, 1936-47. Recipient Disting. Service award with gold medal Sigma Alpha Epsilon, 1967; Championship Gold Medal award N.O.L. Big Ten Univ. Debate Competition, 1919. Fellow Assn. Bus. Communication (hon.); mem. Am. Mktg. Assn., Nat. Assn. Mktg. (v.p. 1931), Smithsonian Instn. Nat. Assos., Wis. Acad. Scis., Arts and Letters, State Hist. Soc. Iowa, Phi Beta Kappa, Delta Sigma Rho, Alpha Kappa Psi (vice chmn. com. profl. programs, exec. group 1955—), Sigma Alpha Epsilon (supreme council 1943-53, nat. pres. 1951-53). Clubs: Continental (Chgo.); Highlands (Monterey Peninsula), Decemvir (Monterey Peninsula), Convivium (Monterey Peninsula); Statesman's (Los Angeles); The Group (Pebble Beach, Calif.). also: Bristlecone Trading and Devel Corp Executive Campus Ste D3 703 Mill Creek Rd Manahawkin NJ 08050-3828 *Hold forever in trust the advantages you have enjoyed; and to the peak of your powers, let it be your mandated obligation to pass these advantages on to all who come within your sphere of influence.Died Dec. 1997.*

AURNER, ROBERT RAY, II, oil company, auto diagnostic, restaurant franchise and company development executive; b. Madison, Wis., Mar. 24, 1927; s. Robert Ray and Kathryn (Dayton) A.; m. Phyllis Barrett, 1951 (div. 1966); children: Sheryl, Roxanne, Kathryn, Suzanne, Robert III; m. Deborah Marion Lucas, Jan. 31, 1976 (div. 1999); children: William Lucas, Christopher Ray. Grad., Shattuck Mil. Sch., 1945; BA, Calif. State U., Fresno, 1950; postgrad., U. Calif. Berkeley, Monterey, Peninsula Coll., Duquesne U. Lic. real estate broker, Calif., Pa., N.Y.; registered investment advisor. Announcer Radio Sta. WSUI, Iowa City, 1946-48; featured celebrity Cowboy Bob, William Randolph Hearst Radio Sta. WISN-CBS, Milw., 1951-52; sr. sales supr. Shell Oil Co., San Francisco, 1952-60; dir. west coast real estate devel. Gulf Oil Corp., no. Calif. region, 1960-67; dir. Midwest ops. Sunray DX Oil Co. (merger Sunoco), Tulsa, 1967-72; mgr. site devel. franchising Milex Auto Diagnostic Franchise, Inc., Plymouth Meeting, Pa., 1972-74; dir. real estate store devel. Pitts. divsn. Atlantic & Pacific Tea Co. Supermarkets, 1974-77; real estate adminstr. store devel. N.E. U.S. region Steak and Ale Restaurant divsn. Pillsbury Cos., Dallas, 1977-80; real estate mgr. N.Y. and Phila. regions Burger King Corp. divsn. Pillsbury Cos., 1980-87; real estate mgr. Ky. Fried Chicken divsn. Pepsi Co. (formerly owned by Heublein) and Pizza Hut divsn. Pepsi-Cola Inc., N.Y.C. Metro and SMSA, 1987-89; nat. dir. real estate and franchising, resturant devel. Nathan's Famous Restaurants, Inc., N.Y.C., 1989-90; bd. dirs. Bristlecone Trading and Devel., Inc., Carmel, Calif., Manahawkin, N.J.; pres., CEO Aurner and Assocs. Mktg. Cons., Carmel, 1987—, chmn. bd. dirs., 1990—; tower devel. mgr. So. N.J. Nextel Wireless Telecom. Corp., N.J., 1994-95; founder Trader Bob, Inc., Western Fashion Wear for Ladies and Gentlemen, Carson City, Nev., 1997. With USNR, 1944-46, PTO. Named to Hon. Order Ky. Col., Gov. of Ky., Commodore in Okla. Navy Gov. of Okla. Mem. USS Yellowstone Assn. (USNR), U. Iowa and Calif. State U. Fraternity, Sigma Alpha Epsilon, Buccaneer Club (pres. N.Y. and Conn.), Elks, Rotary. Republican. Episcopalian. Avocations: golf, precious metals conniseuer, Civil War buff. Office: Aurner & Assocs PO Box 222135 Carmel CA 93922 also: Bristlecone Trading & Devel Ste 300 26544 Carmel Rancho Blvd Carmel CA 93922-2135 also: Trader Bob Inc 251 Jeanell Dr Ste 3 Carson City NV 89703-2129

AUSBURN, LYNNA JOYCE, vocational and technical curriculum developer, consultant; b. Austin, Tex., July 18, 1944; d. Richard F. and Mary Joyce (Aab) Burt; m. Floyd B. Ausburn, July 30, 1966. BS, U. Tulsa, 1966, MA, 1970; PhD, U. Okla., 1976. English and drama tchr. John Marshall High Sch., Oklahoma City, 1966-67; English and speech tchr. West Jr. High Sch., Muskogee, Okla., 1967-70; lang. arts tchr. Muskogee High Sch., 1970-73; grad. teaching asst. clin. instrnl. media and devel. Coll. Edn., U. Okla., 1974-76; edn. svcs. coord. Swinburne Coll. of Tech. and Further Edn., Melbourne, Australia, 1976-84; head planning and rsch. Frankston Coll. Tech. and Further Edn., Melbourne, 1984-89; curriculum devel. coord. Okla. Dept. Vocat. and Tech. Edn., Stillwater, 1990-99; adj. faculty Okla. State U., 1999; sessional lectr. Monash U., Melbourne, 1976-83, external PhD thesis examiner, 1980-84; sessional lectr. State Coll. Victoria, Melbourne, 1980-81; rsch. cons. Vocat. Orientation Ctr., Royal Melbourne Inst. Tech., 1979; vis. rschr. Papua New Guinea U. Tech., Lae, 1980; cons., instr. Colombo Plan Staff Coll., Singapore, 1983, Australian Devel. Assistance Bur., Dept. Fgn. Affairs, Bangladesh, 1985, Regional Edn. Ctr. Sci. and Math., Penang, Malaysia, 1986, 88; resource speaker UNESCO Workshop on Tech. Edn. and Nat. Productivity, Colombo, Sri Lanka, 1995; sr. rschr. USAF, 1977-79, Nat. Ctr. R & D, Adelaide, 1983-84; project instr. Indonesian Roads Project, Okla. State U., 1995-98, Jamaican Tech. Edn. Project, 1996, China Ministry of Labor Project, 1996, 97; spkr. in field. Co-author Evaluation Basics for Instructional Methods and Materials, 1981, Instructional Development Skills for Teaching, 1985; contbr. articles to profl. publs., chpt. to book. Recipient Hon. Mention article award Writer's Digest Nat. Competition, 1991, 92; award-winning photographer, 1990-99; named Bus. Assoc. of Yr., Am. Bus. Women's Assn., 1995. Mem. Australian Coll. Edn., Okla. Vocat. Assn., Assn. Career and Tech. Edn., Okla. Vocat. Instrnl. Materials (state advisor 1992-98), Phi Delta Kappa. Republican. Avocations: writing, travel, fishing, diving, photography.

AUSENBAUM, HELEN EVELYN, social worker, psychologist; b. Chgo., May 16, 1911; d. Herbert Noel and Mayme Eva A. AB, U. Calif., Berkeley, 1938, MSW, 1956. Social worker Alameda Welfare Commn., Oakland, Calif., 1939-42; exec. dir. ARC, Richmond, Calif., 1943-51; tchr. fifth grade Castro Elem. Sch., El Cerrito, Calif., 1951-53; guidance cons. Oakland Pub. Schs., 1953-76; founder, dir. Orinda Counseling Ctr., 1959-95; program dir. Support Svcs., Walnut Creek, Calif., 1978-84; chair Rossmoor Com. for Common Concern, 1994-96, Mental Health Task Force Contra Costa County, 1978-84; mem. Contra Costa County Adv. Coun. on Aging, 1984-97. Mem. chair nominating com. Rossmoor Dem. Club, 1996; mem. and cochair Mental Health Profls. of Rossmoor. Mem. NASW, Rotary. Democrat. Presbyterian. Avocations: stamps, freighter travel, reading. Home: 1637 Skycrest Dr # 7 Walnut Creek CA 94595-1872

AUSLANDER, MARC ALAN, computer scientist; b. Bklyn., May 12, 1942; s. David and Mildred (Burke) A.; m. Rochelle Judith Griffithskig, July 5, 1963; children: Kyra Joan, Joel Edward. AB, Princeton U., 1963. Programmer IBM, Cambridge, Mass., 1963-68; mem. rsch. staff IBM T.J. Watson Rsch. Ctr., Yorktown Heights, N.Y., 1968-91; fellow IBM, Yorktown Heights, 1991—. Inventor in field. Fellow IEEE, Assn. Computing Machinery; mem. NAE, Shattemnc Yacht Club. Jewish. Avocations: sailing, bridge, reading.

AUSMAN, ROBERT K., surgeon, research executive; b. Milw., Jan. 31, 1933; s. Donald Charles and Mildred (Shafrin) A.; m. Christine McCann, 1992. Ed., Kenyon Coll., 1953; M.D., Marquette U., 1957. Damon Runyon cancer fellow U. Minn., 1958-61; dir. Health Research Inc. Roswell Park Meml. Inst., 1961-69; dep. dir. Fla. Regional Med. Assn., 1969-70; v.p. clin. research Baxter Travenol Labs., 1970-82, pres. advanced devel. group, 1982-90; pres. Mildon Corp., 1985—, Citation Pub. Co., 1991—; clin. prof. surgery Med. Coll. Wis., 1972—. Named Outstanding Young Man in N.Y. Buffalo Evening News, 1966, Citizen of Year, 1967. Mem. Am. Soc. Clin. Oncology, Am. Assn. Cancer Rsch., Masons. Home: PO Box 3538 Long Grove IL 60047 Office: Willow Valley Rd Long Grove IL 60047

AUSNEHMER, JOHN EDWARD, lawyer; b. Youngstown, Ohio, June 26, 1954; s. John Louis and Patricia Jean (Liguore) A.; m. Carole Marie Ausnehmer; children: Jill Ellen, Amber Layne. BS, Ohio State U., 1976; JD, U. Dayton, 1980. Bar: Ohio 1980, U.S. Dist. Ct. (no. dist.) Ohio 1981, U.S. Supreme Ct. 1984, U.S. Ct. Appeals (6th cir.) 1984. Law clk. Ohio Atty. Gen., Columbus, 1978, Green, Schiavoni, Murphy, Haines & Sgambati Co., L.P.A., 1978; assoc. Dickson Law Office, Petersburg, Ohio, 1979-85 ; sole practice, Youngstown, Ohio, 1984—; asst. prosecuting atty. Mahoning County, Ohio, 1986-89, 92—. Mem. Ohio Acad. Trial Lawyers, ABA, Ohio State Bar Assn., Mahoning County Bar Assn., Columbiana County Bar Assn., Phi Alpha Delta. Democrat. Roman Catholic. Club: Mahoning Valley Soccer (rep. 1982-84). Home: 51 S Shore Dr Boardman OH 44512-5926 Office: PO Box 3965 721 Boardman Poland Rd Ste 201 Youngstown OH 44512-5105

AUSPITZ, JOSIAH LEE, writer, foundation administrator; b. Phila., Feb. 5, 1941; s. Herman Jacob Auspitz and Gabriella (Hartstein) Auspitz-Labson; m. Katherine Holahan, Oct. 10, 1965; children: Rachel Berthe, Benjamin Adam. BA, Harvard U., 1963; postgrad., Oxford (Eng.) U., 1963-64. Rsch. dir. Pres.'s Adv. Coun. on Exec. Orgn., 1969-70; tutor in govt. Harvard U., Cambridge, Mass., 1969-73; dir. philosophy program Sabre Found., Cambridge, 1978—, founder, cons. sci. assistance project, 1986-98; cons. computer firms dealing in data analysis and natural lang. processing, 1995—; mem. metadata and ontology stds. com. Am. Nat. Stds. Inst., 1996—. Contbr. articles to profl. jours. Mem. organizing com. Davis Sq. Task Force, Somerville, Mass., 1974—; sec. bd. dirs. Sabre Found., 1985—. Marshall scholar, 1963-64; fellow NEH, 1975-76, Internat. Rsch. Exch. Bd., 1986-87, 88, Earhart Found., 1996—. Mem. Coun. on Fgn. Rels., Com. for Study of Am. Electorate, Learned Soc. Praxiology (hon. charter mem.). Republican. Jewish. Home: 17 Chapel St Somerville MA 02144-1901

AUST, JOE BRADLEY, surgeon, educator; b. Buffalo, Sept. 8, 1926; s. Joe Bradley and Edith (Derby) A.; m. Constance Ann MacMullin, June 18, 1949; children—Jay Bradley, Bonnie Jean, Barbara Ann, Linda Lee, Mary Louise, Tracey Roberta. M.D., U. Buffalo, 1949; M.S. in Physiology, U. Minn., 1957, Ph.D. in Surgery, 1958. Diplomate: Am. Bd. Surgery, Am. Bd. Thoracic Surgery. Intern U. Minn. Hosps., 1949-50, resident, 1950-58; scholar Am. Cancer Soc. U. Minn., 1957-62, mem. faculty, 1957-66, prof. surgery, 1964-66; prof. surgery, chmn. dept. U. Tex. Med. Sch., San Antonio, 1966-96, prof. dept. surgery, 1996—; cons. Minn. State Prison, 1958-62, Anoka State Hosp., 1962-65, Brooke Army Med. Hosp., 1967—, Wilford Hall USAF Hosp., 1967—, Audie Murphy Meml. VA Hosp., 1973—; nat. cons. to surgeon gen. USAF, Washington, 1975-78. Served with M.C. USNR, 1950-52. Fellow ACS; mem. Am. Surg. Assn., Western Surg. Assn., So. Surg. Assn., Cen. Surg. Assn., Soc. U. Surgeons, Soc. Head and Neck Surgeons, Am. Assn. Cancer Rsch., Soc. Surg. Oncology, San Antonio Surgical Soc., Am. Assn. Cancer Edn., Halsted Soc., Soc. Clin. Oncology, Transplantation Soc., Sigma Xi, Alpha Omega Alpha, Phi Ch. Spl. research cancer immunity, regional cancer chemotherapy, shock, homotransplantation. Office: U Tex Med Sch 7703 Floyd Curl Dr San Antonio TX 78284-6200

AUST, STEVEN DOUGLAS, biochemistry, biotechnology and toxicology educator; b. South Bend, Wash., Mar. 11, 1938; s. Emil and Helen Mae (Crawford) A.; m. Nancy Lee Haworth, June 5, 1960 (dec.); children: Teresa, Brian. BS in Agr., Wash. State U., 1960, MS in Nutrition, 1962; PhD in Dairy Sci., U. Ill., 1965. Postdoctoral fellow dept. toxicology Karolinska Inst., Stockholm, 1966; N.Z. facial exzema sr. postdoctoral fellow Ruakura Agrl. Research Ctr., Hamilton, 1975-76; mem. faculty dept. biochemistry Mich. State U., East Lansing, 1967-87, prof., 1977-87, assoc. dir. Ctr. for Environ. Toxicology, 1980-85, dir. Ctr. for the Study of Active Oxygen, 1985-87; dir. biotech. ctr. Utah State U., Logan, 1987-91, prof. chem. biochemistry, 1987—; dir. basic rsch. and tng. program Super Fund Nat. Inst. Environ. Health Scis., 1988-96; mem. toxicology study sect. NIH, 1979-83; mem. environ. measurements com., mem. sci. adv. bd. EPA, 1980-83; mem. toxicology data bank, mem. peer rev. com. Nat. Libr. Medicine, 1983-85; mem. Mich. Toxic Substance Control Commn., 1979-82, chmn., 1981-82; exec. v.p. rsch. Intech One-Eighty Corp., North Logan Utah, 1993—; mem. adv. panel for metabolic biochemistry program NSF, 1998—; mem. EPA/DOE/NSF/ONR Joint Program on Bioremediation, 1998. Contbr. articles to profl. jours. Recipient Nat. Rsch. Svc. award NIH, USPHS, Dupont Sci. and Engring. award, 1988, Alumni Achievement award Wash. State U., 1998; NRC facial eczema fellow Ruakura Agrl. Rsch. Ctr., Hamilton, New Zealand, 1975. Fellow Acad. Toxicology Scis., Oxygen Soc.; mem. Am. Soc. Biol. Chemists, Am. Soc. Pharmacology and Exptl. Therapeutics, Soc. Toxicology, Am. Soc. Photobiology, Am. Soc. Microbiology. Office: Utah State U Biotech Ctr Logan UT 84322-4705 also: Intech One-Eighty Corp 1770 Research Park Way North Logan UT 84341-1978

AUSTELL, EDWARD CALLAWAY, banker; b. Spartanburg, S.C., Aug. 9, 1937; s. Edward and Frances Roberta (Glenn) A.; m. Louise Arnold Zimmerman, May 14, 1966; children: Frances Barrett, Elizabeth Callaway. A.B., Davidson Coll., 1959; M.B.A., U.N.C., 1960; postgrad., Nat. Trust Sch. Northwestern U., 1968. Vice pres. trust dept. First Nat. Bank S.C., 1964-71; sr. v.p. trust dept. Ga. R.R. Bank & Trust Co., Augusta, 1971-83; sr. v.p. Wachovia Bank, N.A., Winston-Salem, NC, 1983—. Served with AUS, 1960-62. Mem. N.C. Soc. Fin. Analysts, Ga. Bankers Assn. (past pres. trust div.), Beta Theta Pi. Presbyterian (elder). Home: 1241 Kent Place Ln Winston Salem NC 27104-1140 Office: Wachovia Bank NA PO Box 3099 Winston Salem NC 27150-3099

AUSTEN, K(ARL) FRANK, physician, educator; b. Akron, Ohio, Mar. 14, 1928; s. Karl and Bertle (Jehle) A.; m. Joycelyn Chapman, Apr. 11, 1959; children: Leslie Marie, Karla Ann, Timothy Frank, Jonathan Arthur. AB, Amherst Coll., 1950; MD, Harvard U., 1954. Intern in medicine Mass. Gen. Hosp., 1954-55, asst. resident, 1955-56, sr. resident, 1958-59, chief resident, 1961, asst. in medicine, 1962-63, asst. physician, 1963-66, chief pulmonary unit, 1964-66; also cons. in medicine; practice medicine, specializing in internal medicine, allergy and immunology Mass. Gen. Hosp., Boston, 1962-66; USPHS postdoctoral research fellow Nat. Inst. Med. Research, Mill Hill, London, 1959-61; asst. in medicine Harvard Med. Sch., 1961, instr., 1961-62, asso. in medicine, 1962-64, asst. prof., 1965-66, assoc. prof., 1966-68, prof., 1969-72, Theodore B. Bayles prof., 1972—; physician-in-chief Robert B. Brigham Hosp., Boston, 1966-80; chmn. dept. rheumatology and immunology Brigham and Women's Hosp., Boston, 1980-95, dir. lab. inflammation and allergic disease rsch. sect., 1995—; mem. fellowship subcom. Arthritis Found., 1968-71, chmn., 1971; mem. coun. Infectious Disease Soc. Am., 1969-71; mem. arthritis tng. grants com. Nat. Inst. Arthritis and Metabolic Diseases, NIH, 1970-73, NHLB adv. coun., 1994—; mem. directing group, task force on immunology and disease Nat. Inst. Allergy and Infectious Diseases, 1972-73; bd. dirs. Arthritis Found., 1972-75, chmn. manpower study com., 1972-73, chmn. rsch. com. Multipurpose Arth. Ctr.,

1972-76; chmn. rsch. com. Med. Found., Inc., 1972-76; mem. Am. Bd. Allergy and Immunology, 1973-78, Nat. Commn. on Arthritis and Related Musculoskeletal Diseases, 1975-76, Allergy and Immunology Rsch. com., NIAID, 1975-79, chmn., 1976-79; chmn. nomenclature com. Internat. Union Immunological Socs., 1983—; mem. adv. com. to the dir. NIH, 1986-90, mem. nat heart, lung and blood adv. coun., 1966-80. Mem. editorial bd. Arthritis and Rheumatism, 1968-81, Proc. of Transplantation Soc., 1968-82, Jour. Infectious Diseases, 1969-79, Jour. Exptl. Medicine, 1971—, Immunol. Communications, 1972-85, Clin. Immunology and Immunopathology, 1972-89, Proc. of Nat. Acad. Scis., 1978-83, Clin. and Exptl. Immunology, 1978-88, Internat. Jour. Immunopharmacology, 1984, Advances in Immunology, 1985—, Advances in Pharmacology, 1989—; contbr. articles to profl. jours. Trustee Amherst Coll., 1981—. Served to capt., M.C. U.S. Army, 1956-58. Mem. NAS (chmn. sect. on med. microbiology and immunology 1983-86), Inst. Medicine, Am. Soc. Pharm. and Exptl. Therapeutics, Am. Soc. Exptl. Pathology, Am. Assn. Immunologists (pres. 1977-78), Brit. Soc. Immunology, Am. Soc. Clin. Investigation, Am. Rheumatism Assn., ACP, Transplantation Soc., Am. Acad. Arts and Scis., Assn. Am. Physicians (recorder 1978-84, pres. 1989-90), Am. Acad. Allergy and Immunology (exec. com. 1970-72, sec. 1977-80, pres. 1981), Interurban Clin. Club, Fedn. Am. Soc. Exptl. Biology, Internat. Assn. Allergology and Clin. Immunology, Internat. Soc. Immunopharmacology (pres. 1994). Office: Smith Bldg One Jimmy Fund Way Rm 638 Boston MA 02115*

AUSTEN, SHELLI OETTER, radio news anchor, consultant; b. Tulsa, Sept. 8, 1954; m. Fred Chris Sorenson, Dec. 31, 1984 (div. Oct. 1988); 1 child, Kristen Amara; m. John R. Oetter, May 16, 1998. BA, U. Calif., Santa Barbara, 1974. Actress Starlight Theatre, Pasadena Playhouse, 1974; with various improvisational acting troupes, 1974-80; news dir. Sta. KMVI, Maui, Hawaii, 1980-83; v.p. Bill Baker Advt., Honolulu, 1983-85; advt. dir. Ground Swell Mag., Haleiwa, 1985-87; prodr., reporter, anchor Sta. KHVH, Honolulu, 1987-92; dir. adv. Beachcomber Mag., 1992-93; disc jockey Sta. KGY, Olympia, Wash., 1994—; reporter Alameda (Calif.) Times Star, 1994-96; morning news anchor KSRO AM Radio, Santa Rosa, Calif., 1996—; pres. In House Prodns. Media Consulting Firm, 1997-98; pres., news anchor KSSK-AM Radio, Honolulu, 1998—; media cons. Rep. Party of Hawaii, Honolulu, 1987—; actress Altarina Playhouse, 1994-95, News Anchor KSSK, Honolulu. Contbr. articles to profl. jours. Media coord. Merimed found., Honolulu, 1988; del. Rep. Party, Honolulu, 1989, mem. presdl. task force, Honolulu, 1989-90. Christian. Home: 58-032 Kapuai Pl Haleiwa HI 96712-9730

AUSTEN, W(ILLIAM) GERALD, surgeon, educator; b. Akron, Ohio, Jan. 20, 1930; s. Karl A. and Bertl (Jehle) A.; m. Patricia Ramsdell, Jan. 28, 1961; children: Karl Ramsdell, William Gerald, Jr., Christopher Marshall, Elizabeth Patricia. BS, MIT, 1951; MD, Harvard U., 1955; HHD (hon.), U. Akron, 1980; DSc (hon.), U. Athens, Greece, 1981, U. Mass., 1985, Northeastern Ohio U. Coll. Medicine, 1996. Diplomate Am. Bd. Surgery, Am. Bd. Thoracic Surgery. Intern, then resident surgery Mass. Gen. Hosp., Boston, 1955-61, chief surg. cardiovascular rsch. unit, 1963-69, chief surgery, 1969-97, surgeon-in-chief, 1989-97, surgeon-in-chief emeritus, 1997—; surgeon clinic surgery Nat. Heart Inst., 1961-62; pres. Mass. Gen. Physicians Orgn., 1994-98, CEO, chmn., 1998—; assoc. in surgery Harvard Med. Sch., 1963-65, assoc. prof. surgery, 1965-66, prof. surgery, 1966-74, Edward D. Churchill prof. surgery, 1974—; mem. residency review com. surgery Accreditation Coun. Grad. Med. Edn., 1988-93. Author, editor med. textbooks; contbr. articles to profl. jours. Mem. corp. MIT, 1972—, life mem. corp., 1982—, mem. exec. com. corp., 1986-98; trustee John S. and James L. Knight Found., 1986—, vice chmn., 1991-96, chmn., 1996—; bd. dirs. Found. Biomed. Rsch., 1988—; trustee Mass. Eye and Ear Infirmary, 1991—, Ptnrs. HealthCare System Inc., 1994-97, Gen. Hosp. Mass. Gen. Hosp., 1997—. Markle scholar, 1963-68. Fellow AAAS, Royal Coll. Surgeons Eng. (hon.), Am. Acad. Arts & Scis.; mem. NAS Inst. Medicine, Am. Heart Assn. (pres. 1977-78), Am. Surg. Assn. (sec. 1979-84, pres. 1985-86), Am. Assn. Thoracic Surgery (v.p. 1987-88, pres. 1988-89), Am. Bd. Surgery (mem. bd. 1969-74, sr. 1974—), Am. Bd. Thoracic Surgery (bd. dirs. 1984-90), ACS (regent 1982-91, chmn. bd. regents 1989-91, pres. 1992-93), Assn. Acad. Surgery (pres. 1970), Soc. Univ. Surgeons (sec. 1967-70, pres. 1972-73), New Eng. Cardiovascular Soc. (pres. 1972-73), Mass. Heart Assn. (pres. 1972). Home: 330 Beacon St Apt C66 Boston MA 02116 Office: Mass Gen Hosp BUL 208C Boston MA 02114-2696

AUSTER, CAROL JEAN, sociology educator; b. Bloomington, Ind., Mar. 2, 1954; d. Donald and Nancy Eileen (Ross) A.; children: Lauren Jean, Lisa Amy. AB in Social Rels., Colgate U., 1976; MA in Sociology, Princeton U., 1979, PhD in Sociology, 1984. Instr. sociology Franklin and Marshall Coll., Lancaster, Pa., 1981-84, asst. prof., 1984-88, assoc. prof., 1988-96, prof., 1996—, acting chair dept., 1982-83, chair dept., 1988-91; NSF rsch. assoc. N.H. Coll., Manchester, 1974, Hampshire Coll., Amherst, Mass., 1975; cons. dept. planning Lancaster (Pa.) Gen. Hosp., 1984—. Author: The Sociology of Work: Concepts and Cases, 1996; contbr. articles, revs. to profl. jours. N.Y. State Regents scholar Colgate U., 1976; Princeton U. fellow, 1977-80; Rockefeller Found. grantee U. Ill., 1979-80, Alfred P. Sloan Found. grantee, 1993-96. Mem. AAUP (dist. VII rep. to nat. coun. 1986-89, com. F. on cons. 1986-92, memberships grants com. 1987-89, 2d v.p. 1990-92, chair com. B. on ethics 1994—), Am. Sociol. Assn. (com. on employment 1994—), Soc. for Study Social Problems, Sociologists for Women in Society, Ea. Sociol. Soc., So. Sociol. Soc. Office: Franklin and Marshall Coll Dept Sociology Lancaster PA 17604

AUSTER, PAUL, writer; b. Newark, Feb. 3, 1947; s. Samuel and Queenie (Bogat) A.; m. Lydia Davis, Oct. 6, 1974 (div. 1979); 1 child, Daniel; m. Siri Hustvedt, June 16, 1981; 1 child, Sophie. BA, Columbia U., 1969, MA, 1970. Lectr. Princeton (N.J.) U., 1986-90. Author: (poetry) Unearth, 1974, Wall Writing, 1976, Fragments From Cold, 1977, Facing the Music, 1980, Disappearances: Selected Poems, 1988, (non-fiction) White Spaces, 1980, The Invention of Solitude, 1982, The Art of Hunger, 1982, expanded edit., 1992, Why Write?, 1996, Translations, 1997, Hand to Mouth, 1997, (novel) City of Glass, 1985, Ghosts, 1986, The Locked Room, 1986, In the Country of Last Things, 1987, Moon Palace, 1989, The Music of Chance, 1990, Leviathan, 1992, Mr. Vertigo, 1994, Timbuktu, 1999, (film) Smoke, 1995, Blue in the Face, 1995, Lulu on the Bridge, 1998; editor: The Random House Book of Twentieth-Century French Poetry, 1982. Decorated chevalier de l'Orde des Arts et des Lettres (France), Prix Médicis Etranger, 1993; fellow Nat. Endowment for the Arts, 1979, 85; recipient Ind. Spirit award, 1996. Mem. PEN. Office: care Carol Mann Agy 55 5th Ave New York NY 10003-4301

AUSTILL, ALLEN, dean emeritus; b. Newton, Mass., June 22, 1927; s. William E. and Anna (Pifer) A.; m. Joan Mildred Sellery, June 4, 1950; children: Randolph Allen, Christopher Scott, Lara Anne. B.A., U. Chgo., 1948, M.A., 1951; LHD (hon.), New Sch. Social Rsch., 1987. Research asso. Council State Govts., Chgo., 1951-52; mem. faculty, dir. admissions and placement St. Johns Coll., 1953-55; dir. student housing U. Chgo., 1955-57; tchr., dean students SUNY-Stony Brook, 1957-61; cons. Ford Found., Middle East, Amman, Jordan, 1962; mem. faculty, asso. dean New Sch. Social Research, 1962-64, dean, 1964-79, v.p. acad. affairs and exec. dean, 1979-82, dean, 1982-87, chancellor, 1987-89; cons. title I Higher Edn. Act, State N.Y.; mem. council academic fellows Shimer Coll., 1971-80; mem. N.Y. Regents Adv. Task Force for Adult Edn., 1972-77, chmn., 1976-77; chmn. bd. dirs. Harpers Mag. Found., 1988—; bd. dirs. Ednl. Mgmt. Network, 1985—; chmn. vis. com. Am. Mus. Natural History, 1990. Author: (with others) Higher Education in the Forty-Eight States, 1952; Summary of State Legislation and Elections (with others), 1953. Pres. Friends of Cresskill Libr., 1969-71; mem. vis. com. continuing edn. Harvard U., 1977-83; mem. Boston Ctr. for Adult Edn., 1990—, chair bd. trustees, 1991-95. With AUS, 1945-46. Home: 6 Hammersmith Dr Saugus MA 01906-4168

AUSTIN, ARTHUR DONALD, II, lawyer, educator; b. Staunton, Va., Dec. 2, 1932; s. George Milnes and Mae (Eichner) A.; m. Irene Clara Wittenberg, June 12, 1960; 1 son, Brian Carl. B.S. in Commerce, U. Va., 1958; J.D., Tulane U., 1963. Bar: Va. 1964, D.C. 1970. Asst. prof. Coll. of William and Mary, Williamsburg, Va., 1963-64, Bowling Green State U., Ohio, 1964-66; asst. prof. law Cleve. State U., 1966-68; prof. law Case Western Res. U., Cleve., 1968-70, 72-78; Edgar A. Hahn prof. jurisprudence Case Western Res. U., 1978—; atty. Dept. Justice, Washington, 1970-71. Author: Antitrust: Law, Economics, Policy, 1976, Complex Litigation Confronts the Jury System, 1984, The Empire Strikes Back: Outsiders and the Struggle Over Legal Education, 1998; contbr. articles to law revs. Served with U.S. Army, 1952-54. Decorated Bronze Star medal with V, Purple Heart. Home: 1174 Stony Hill Rd Hinckley OH 44233-9538 Office: 11075 East Blvd Cleveland OH 44106-5409

AUSTIN, CHARLES, Olympic athlete; b. Bay City, Tex., Dec. 19, 1967; married; children: Camron, Allex. Grad., S.W. Tex. State U., 1990. Recipient Gold medal high jump Atlanta Olympics, 1996; winner NCAA, 1990, World Championships, 1991, USA Championships, 1995, USA Indoor Championships; 8th place Barcelona Olympics, 1992; winner 2d USA Indoor, 1994, 4th, 1996, 1st Pl., 1997, 98, among others. Office: USA Track & Field 1 RCA Dome Ste 140 Indianapolis IN 46225*

AUSTIN, CHARLES JOHN, health services educator; b. Cin., Nov. 28, 1934; s. Charles D. and Catherine (Shields) A.; m. Mary Carroll Nurre, June 4, 1955; children—Mary Lynn, Charles, Christopher, Andrew, Carroll Jane. B.S. summa cum laude, Xavier U., 1956; M.S., U. Colo., 1969; Ph.D., U. Cin., 1972. Systems analyst, programmer Procter & Gamble Co., Cin., 1957-60; data processing mgr., mgmt. analyst HEW, Washington, 1960-66; computer ctr. dir., prof. dept. preventive medicine U. Colo. Med. Ctr., 1967-69; prof. dept. hosp. adminstrn. Xavier U., Cin., 1970-72; study dir. Commn. on Edn. for Health Adminstrn., Washington, 1972-74; dean grad. studies Trinity U., San Antonio, 1974-78; v.p. Ga. So. Coll., Statesboro, 1978-82; pres. East Tex. State U., Commerce, 1982-86; prof., chmn. health svcs. adminstrn. Sch Health Related Professions, U. Ala., Birmingham, 1987-94; prof. dept. health adminstrn. and policy Med. U. S.C., Charleston, 1995—. Author: The Politics of National Health Insurance, 1975, Information Systems for Health Services Administration, 1979, 5th edit., 1998; contbr. articles to profl. jours. Served with U.S. Army, 1957-58. Fellow Am. Pub. Health Assn., Am. Acad. Med. Adminstrs. (hon.); mem. Tex. Assn. Grad. Schs. (pres.), Conf. So. Grad. Schs. (bd. dirs.), Assn. Univ. Programs in Health Adminstrn., Torch Club, Rotary. Home: 34 Edgewood Dr Hilton Head Island SC 29926-6703 Office: Med U SC Dept Health Admin/Policy 171 Ashley Ave Charleston SC 29425-0001

AUSTIN, DAN, retired dean; b. DeKalb County, Ala., Aug. 24, 1929; s. William J. and Edwina (Murphy) A.; m. Myra Sue Emmett, Jan. 14, 1951; 1 child, Deborah Elaine Austin Land. B.S. in Edn., Jacksonville U., 1964, M.S. in Edn., 1971. Tchr., Etowah County Bd. Edn., Gadsden, Ala., 1964-65, Anniston City Bd. Edn., Ala., 1965-66; faculty Ayers State Tech. Coll., Anniston, 1966-67, dean of instrn., 1967-88; ret 1988. Bd. dirs. Jacksonville Hosp.; mem. Jacksonville City Bd. Edn.; adv. bd. Ayers State Tech. Coll. Served as sgt. U.S. Army, 1951-53. Mem. Dean's Assn. Ala. (pres. 1969-70, treas. 1972-74). Democrat. Baptist. Avocations: photography, camping, gardening. Home: 600 11th St NE Jacksonville AL 36265-1129

AUSTIN, DANFORTH WHITLEY, newspaper executive; b. Hutchinson, Kans., Sept. 21, 1946; s. Whitley and Mary Frances (Danforth) A.; m. Gail Ellen Davenport, Sept. 2, 1967; children: Stephen D., Richard D. BS, U. Kans., 1968. Staff reporter The Wall St. Jour., Dallas, Detroit, 1970-76; spl. writer The Wall St. Jour., N.Y.C., 1976-78, news editor, 1978; bur. chief The Wall St. Jour., Pitts., 1978-83; from asst. to deputy nat. editor The Wall St. Jour., N.Y.C., 1984-86, spl. reports editor, 1986-87; dir. corp. rels. Dow Jones and Co. Inc., N.Y.C., 1987-89; dir. circulation Wall St. Jour., Barron's, Princeton, N.J., 1989-95; v.p. circulation Wall St. Jour., 1992-95, v.p., gen. mgr., 1995—. Sr. warden St. Peter's Episcopal Ch., Brentwood, Pa., 1981; lay reader Episcopal Diocese of Pitts., 1981-83; vestryman St. George's Episcopal Ch., Maplewood, N.J., 1985-88; trustee William Allen White Found., U. Kans., Lawrence, Kans., 1996—. Sgt. U.S. Army, 1968-70, Vietnam. Decorated Bronze Star, Air medal. Mem. Soc. Profl. Journalists, Kappa Sigma. Home: 51 Joanna Way Short Hills NJ 07078-3206 Office: Dow Jones and Co 200 Liberty St Fl 11 New York NY 10281-1099

AUSTIN, DANIEL WILLIAM, lawyer; b. Springfield, Ill., Feb. 24, 1949; s. Daniel D. and Ruth A. (Ahrenkiel) A.; m. Lois Ann Austin, June 12, 1971; 1 child, Elizabeth Ann. BA, Millikin U., 1971; JD, Washington U., 1974. Bar: Ill. 1974, U.S. Dist. Ct. (cen. dist.) Ill. 1979, U.S. Ct. Appeals (7th cir.) 1980, U.S. Supreme Ct. 1980, U.S. Tax Ct. 1986. Assoc. Miley & Meyer, Taylorville, Ill., 1974-78; ptnr. Miley, Meyer & Austin, Taylorville, 1978-81; prin. Meyer, Austin & Romano P.C., Taylorville, 1981—. Pres. United Fund, Taylorville, 1980, Christian County YMCA, Taylorville, 1983-85, St. Vincent Meml. Hosp. Found., 1998—. Named one of Outstanding Young Men Am., 1985, Outstanding Citizen of City of Taylorville, 1993. Mem. ABA, Ill. Bar Assn., Christian County Bar Assn., Order of Barristers. Democrat. Presbyterian. Club: Taylorville Country (pres. 1985). Lodge: Sertoma (Taylorville pres. 1976). Avocations: golf, photography. Home: 14 Westhaven Ct Taylorville IL 62568-9064 Office: Meyer Austin & Romano PC 210 S Washington St Taylorville IL 62568-2245

AUSTIN, DAVID GEORGE, dentist; b. Dayton, Ohio, Sept. 11, 1951; s. Donald Edward and Mary Josephine (Thompson) A.; m. Mary Allene Allen, Dec. 23, 1977; children: Jonathon David, Jennifer Mary. BA, Ohio Wesleyan U., 1973; DDS, Ohio State U., 1977; MS, U. Med. Dentistry N.J., 1992. Diplomate Am. Bd. Orofacial Pain, Am. Acad. Pain Mgmt. Sr. assoc. dentist Dr. Deeds and Assocs., Inc., Columbus, Ohio, 1980-82, clinic dir., 1982-85; gen. practice dentistry Columbus, 1981-88; fellow TMJ/Orofacial Pain Ctr. Univ. Med. Dentistry N.J., 1988-90; clin. asst. prof. neurology Coll. Medicine Ohio State U., Columbus, 1992-98, asst. dir. dept. neurology headache clinic, 1994-98; dental cons. Franklin County Dept. Human Svcs., Columbus, 1982-88; bd. dirs. Found. Pedodontique d'Haiti, Port-au-Prince; pres. Brineserve, Inc., Columbus, 1985-88; adj. assoc. prof. Coll. Dentistry Ohio State U., 1986-88; chmn. Coll. Dentistry Almni Assn. Class Reunion Ohio State U., 1997. Patents in apparatus/method for processing oil well brine, 1988; in apparatus and method for measuring human mandibular movement, 1990; in apparatus and method for craniovertebral imbalance and headache during sleep, 1992. Pres., founder Vol. Health Svcs. Found., Columbus, 1982—. Served to capt. U.S. Army, 1977-80. Mem. ADA (Fgn. Vol. Svc. award 1988), Am. Pain Soc., Am. Acad. Orofacial Pain (mem. specialty status com.), Am. Assn. for Study of Headache, Am. Acad. Pain Mgmt., Ohio Headache Assn., Ohio Dental Assn. (Humanitarian of Yr. 1986, alt. del. 1994-96, 98), Ohio Oil and Gas Assn., Columbus Dental Assn. mem. speaker's bur. 1982-88, Pub. Rels. Coun. 1984-88, vice chmn. radio com. 1985-88), U. Med. Dentistry N.J.-TMJ Alumni Soc., Xi Psi Phi (pres. Kappa chpt. 1976-77), Sigma Xi. Home: 1218 Millcreek Ln Columbus OH 43220-4961 Office: Ste 5C 3600 Olentangy River Rd Columbus OH 43214-3437

AUSTIN, DAVID JOHN, curriculum developer, writer; b. Northamptonshire, Eng., Sept. 15, 1947; s. Derrick William and Doris Kathleen (Vendy) A.; 1 child, Alton Montcrieff. BA, U. Colo., Denver, 1979, MS, 1987. Mgr. Nat. Jewish Ctr. for Immunology and Respiratory Medicine, Denver, 1980-83, Arthur Young and Co., Denver, 1983-84; sr. tech. cons. DTSS Inc., Denver, 1984-88; sys. mgr., DBA, Hughes Aircraft Co., Fullerton, Calif., 1988-92; sr. prin. curriculum developer Oracle Corp., Costa Mesa, Calif., 1992—. Author: Using Oracle 8, 1998, co-author spl. edit., 1998. Mem. L.A. Oracle User Group (hon.), Phi Beta Kappa. Avocations: home sound reproduction, life music, performing arts. Fax: 949-458-7557. E-mail: daustin@us.oracle.com. Office: Oracle Corp 600 Anton Blvd Costa Mesa CA 92626

AUSTIN, DAVID MAYO, social work educator; b. New Haven, June 9, 1923; s. Ralph Vernon and Helen Howe (Mayo) A.; m. Zuria Farmer; Clayton Mayo, Judith Ann, Paul Farmer. BA, Lawrence Coll., 1943; MS Social Adminstrn., Western Res. U., 1948; PhD, Brandeis U., 1969. Cert. social worker, Tex. Group worker U. Settlement, Cleve., 1948-51; assoc. neighborhood svcs. United Community Svcs. Met. Boston, 1951-54; planner, exec. dir. Spl. Youth Program, Roxbury, Mass., 1953-56; exec. sec. group work coun. Welfare Fedn. Cleve., 1957-61; planning dir. Greater Cleve. Youth Svcs. Planning Commn., 1961-63; assoc. dir. planning and rsch. Community Action Youth Cleve., 1963-64; lectr. Sch. Applied Social Scis. Case Western Res. U., Cleve., 1964-65; lectr. Florence Heller Grad. Sch. for Advanced Studies in Social Welfare Brandeis U., Waltham, Mass., 1968-71, assoc. prof., 1971-73; prof. Sch. Social Work U. Tex., Austin, 1973—, Bert Kruger Smith Centennial prof., 1987-98, acting dean, 1991-92; vis. prof. Coll. Social Work U. Tenn., Knoxville, 1985-86, cons., 1979; vis. scholar Nelson Rockefeller Coll. Pub. Affairs and Policy, SUNY, Albany, 1986; chmn. state adv. bd. Mass. Dept. Pub. Welfare, Boston, 1970-73; chmn. task force on social work rsch. NIMH, 1988-91; cons. Hogg Found. for Mental Health, Austin, 1989; external reviewer Sch. Social Work Rutgers U., New Brunswick, N.J., 1985; vis. com. Mandel Sch. Applied Social Scis., Case Western Res. U., Cleve., 1993—. Author: (with others) Organization and the Human Services: Cross-Disciplinary Reflections, 1981, (monograph) A History of Social Work Education, 1986, The Political Economy of Human Service Programs, 1988; mem. editorial bd. Social Work , 1983-89; interim co-editor Jour. Applied Behavioral Sci., 1988-89; contbr. articles to profl. jours., publs. including Ency. of Social Work. Bd. dirs. Unitarian Universalist Svc. Com., Boston, 1983-88. Sgt. U.S. Army, 1943-46. Named Alumnus of Yr. Sch. Applied Social Scis. Case Western U., 1980; fellow NIMH, 1965-68; named Outstanding Grad. Tchr. U. Tex. at Austin, 1989. Mem. Acad. Cert. Social Workers (cert.), Nat. Assn. Social Workers (bd. dirs. 1963-66, chmn. human rights commn. 1964-67, pres. award Excellence Social Work Rsch. 1992), Coun. on Social Work Edn. (ho. dels. 1975-78, 79-82, ednl. planning commn. 1979-82, significant lifetime achievement award 1997), Am. Pub. Welfare Assn. (bd. dirs. 1980-82), Am. Soc. Pub. Adminstrn., Nat. Conf. Social Welfare (bd. dirs. 1980-83), Phi Beta Kappa, Phi Kappa Phi. Office: U Texas Sch of Social Work Austin TX 78712

AUSTIN, EDWARD MARVIN, retired mechanical engineer, researcher; b. Rome, Ga., Nov. 15, 1933; s. Marvin Hart and Sarah Katherine (Youngblood) A.; m. Elizabeth Maria Geisz, Dec. 17, 1955; children: Jean, Diane, Judy. BS in Mech. Engring., Ga. Inst. Tech., 1955, MS in Mech. Engring., 1957. Registered profl. engr., N.C., cert. quality engr., nuclear weapon devel. With Sandia Nat. Labs., Albuquerque, 1957-94; cons., project engring. and quality mgmt., 1994—. Vol. examiner, Quality N. Mex., 1993-98. Mem. ASME (life, chmn. N.Mex. sect. 1991, bd. dirs. 1992-94, region XII industry rels. com. 1992-98), Am. Soc. Quality (sr.), Sigma Xi, Tau Beta Pi. Avocations: reading, camping. Home: 3017 Matador Dr NE Albuquerque NM 87111-5620

AUSTIN, GABRIEL CHRISTOPHER, publisher; b. N.Y.C., Sept. 3, 1935; s. Robert and Gabrielle (Connolly) A.; m. Florence Heilbrun, Oct. 16, 1967; 1 dau., Louise. B.A., St. John's U., Jamaica, N.Y., 1956; M.S. in L.S, Pratt Inst., 1957. Reference librarian N.Y. Pub. Library, 1952-62; librarian Grolier Club, N.Y.C., 1963-69; asst. v.p. Sotheby Parke Bernet, N.Y.C., 1969-75; pres. Wittenborn Art Books, Inc., N.Y.C., 1975-91. Author: Iter Italicum, 1962, Library of Jean Grolier, 1970. Fellow Pierpont Morgan Library, since 1963. Mem. Grolier Club, Bibliog. Soc. Am., Internat. Assn. Bibliophiles. Democrat. Roman Cath. Club: Century Assn. (N.Y.C.). Home: 528 E 79th St Apt 2E New York NY 10021-1574

AUSTIN, GRANT WILLIAM, real estate appraiser; b. Toronto, Ont., Canada, July 15, 1954; m. Joanne; 1 child, Kelly Rae. BA summa cum laude, York U., 1983. Cert. genl. appraiser, Fla., mem. Appraisal Inst. Pres. Am. Valuation, Inc., Ft. Lauderdale, Fla., 1998—. Author: Calculator Skills for the HP 19B, 1995, The Property Owner's Guide to Condemnation, 1998, The Valuation of Retail Gasoline Outlets, 1999. Mem. Appraisal Inst. (chair pub. rels. com. 1995-97), Assn. Eminent Domain Profls. (v.p., dir. 1994-95, bd. dirs. 1993-94), Lambda Alpha Internat. (pres. 1997—). Avocations: golf, tennis. Office: Am Valuation Inc Weston FL 33326

AUSTIN, H(ARRY) GREGORY, lawyer; b. N.Y.C., Mar. 18, 1936; s. Harry Gregory and Pauline (Moore) A.; m. Deanna Ruth Anderson, Nov. 28, 1970; children: Sabrina Elizabeth, Harry Gregory III, Anne Catherine. BE, Yale U., 1957, postgrad., 1958; JD, U. Mich., 1961; LLD (hon.), Lincoln U., 1976. Bar: Colo. 1961, U.S. Supreme Ct. 1974. Assoc., then ptnr. Holland & Hart, Denver, 1962-73, ptnr., 1977—; gen. counsel U.S. SBA, Washington, 1973-75; solicitor, gen. counsel U.S. Dept. Interior, Washington, 1975-77. Trustee Colo. Legal Aid Found., Denver, 1984-91, chmn., 1988-91; bd. dirs. Children's Hosp., Denver, 1985-97. 1st lt. USAR, 1957-64. Mem. Am. Law Inst., Colo. Bar Assn. (chmn. bus. entities subsect. bus. law sect. 1987-89, vice chmn. bus. law sect. 1989-91, chmn. 1991-93, chmn. partnership laws com. 1993—), Denver Bar Assn., Metro Denver C. of C. (bd. dirs., sec. 1995-97). Republican. Office: Holland & Hart 555 17th St Ste 2900 Denver CO 80202-3979

AUSTIN, HARRY GUIDEN, engineering and construction company executive; b. Belton, Tex., Dec. 10, 1917; s. Harry Guiden and Emma Lena (Brown) A.; m. Elizabeth Ann Heard, Aug. 31, 1940; children—Lucy Ann, Elizabeth Austin Page, Catherine Austin Wyatt. B.S. in Elec. Engring, Tex. A&M Coll., 1938; M.B.A., Harvard U., 1940; H.H.D., Wiley Coll. Registered profl. engr., Tex. With Pan Am. Airways, Miami, Fla., 1940-41; elec. engr. Brown Shipbldg. Co., Houston, 1941-45; with Brown & Root, Inc., Houston, 1945—; v.p. Brown & Root, Inc., 1960-65, sr. v.p., 1965-68, sr. group v.p., 1968-70, exec. v.p. engring. and constrn., 1970-78; also dir.; pres. Hael, Inc., Houston, 1978—; mem. Tex. A&M Geosci. Coun. Bd. dirs. Retina Rsch. Found. Mem. NSPE, IEEE, Mus. Fine Arts, Petroleum Club, Houston Country Club, Ramada Club (Houston), Riverhill Country Club (Kerrville, Tex.). Methodist. Home: 267 Pine Hollow Ln Houston TX 77056-1501 Office: Hael Inc 267 Pine Hollow Houston TX 77056-1501

AUSTIN, HUGH S., JR., city official; b. Houston, Dec. 27, 1953. AA, U. Md., Munich, Germany, 1974; BS in BA, Auburn U., 1980. Dir. Montgomery (Ala.) Civic Ctr., 1993—. Office: Montgomery civic Ctr PO Box 4037 Montgomery AL 36103-4037*

AUSTIN, HUGH SAM, municipal department administrator; b. Mooringsport, La., Apr. 10, 1931. BA, La. Tech. U., 1953; MA, George Washington U., 1967. Commd. 2nd lt. USAF, 1955, ret., 1976; dir. fin. dept. City and County of Montgomery, Ala., 1976—. Mem. Govt. Fin. Officers Assn., Cert. Govt. Fin. Officers (cert.). Office: City and County of Montgomery Finance Dept PO Box 1111 Montgomery AL 36101-1111*

AUSTIN, JACOB (JACK AUSTIN), Canadian senator; b. Calgary, Alta., Can., Mar. 2, 1932; s. Morris and Clara Edith (Chetner) A.; m. Natalie Veiner Freeman, Apr. 2, 1978; children: Edith Clare, Sharon Jill, Barbara Joan. BA, LLB, U. B.C.; LLM, Harvard U.; postgrad., U. Calif., Berkeley; ScD in Social Sci., U. East Asia. Bar: B.C. 1958, Yukon 1966. Prin. sec. to prime minister, 1974-75, dep. minister energy, mines and resources, 1970-74; mem. Senate, 1975—; minister of state, 1981-82, minister of state for social devel., 1982-84. Mem. Vancouver Club, Rideau Club, Le Cercle Universitaire d'Ottawa Club, Met. Club (N.Y.C.). Liberal. Jewish. Home: 3439 Point Grey Rd, Vancouver, BC Canada V6R 1A6 Office: The Senate, Victoria Bldg Rm 304, Ottawa, ON Canada K1A 0A4

AUSTIN, JAMES GROVER, JR., theologian, pastor, telecommunications manager; b. Phila., May 12, 1951; s. James G., Sr. and Florence (Hendon) A.; m. Valerie Gills, June 9, 1989; children: Asanti, Tyshan; 1 step-child, Angela. AA, L.A. City Coll., 1976; BA in Theology, Christian Bible Coll. Seminary, 1992, MA in Exegetical Theology, 1993, PhD, 1994; grad. summer program in theology, Oxford U., 1997, 98; D in Ministry, Grad. Theol. Found., 1998. Cryptologist U.S. Navy, 1971-89; chief secure comm. svcs. br. U.S. Coast Guard, Alexandria, Va., 1993—; educator D.C. Bible Inst., 1997—. Mem. Chief of Police Adv. Coun., Fairfax, Va., 1995—. Mem. ASCD, Am. Assn. Christian Counselors, Assn., Am. Soc. Christian Therapist (cert. Christian marriage family therapist, cert. pastoral addictions counselor, cert. domestic abuse counselor), Evang. Tng. Assn., Christian Soc. for the Healing of Dissociative Disorders, World Pastoral Care Ctr. Baptist. Home: 4384 Stepney Dr Gainesville VA 20155-1246

AUSTIN, JANET HAYS, artist; b. Phila., Nov. 20, 1926; d. Francis Baumer and Marjorie (Edwards) Hays; m. H. Philips Austin Jr., June 23, 1951 (dec. Dec. 30, 1982); children: Jeremiah Hays Austin, Clare Edwards Austin Roberts. Student, U. Pa., Fleischer Meml. Sch. of Art, Cornell U. adult program. artist-in-residence Holy Cross Monastery, West Park, N.Y.; art coord. Lower Makefield Soc. for the Performing Arts; juror Arts Alliance of Bucks County, Yardley (Pa.) Art Assn.; chair centennial Art Exhibit, Friends' Sch., Haverford, Pa., Haverford Coll.; co-founder Friends of Lake Afton. Co-author: Alleluia: The Parish Family Celebrates; co-author, rschr.: The History and Ecology of Lake Afton, 1970; exhbns. in group shows include Nat. Mid-Summer Exhibit, Cape May, N.J., Allied Artists of Am.,

N.Y.C., 1976, 77, Audubon Artists, Inc., N.Y.C., 1978, Internat. Soc. Artists, N.Y.C., 1978, Salmagundi Club, N.Y.C., 1976, Knickerbocker Artists, N.Y.C., 1978, Am. Watercolor Soc., N.Y.C., 1977, Multiple Sclerosis Invitational Show, Trenton, N.J., 1966, 68, 70, 71, Garden State Watercolor Soc., Princeton, N.J., Levittown (Pa.) Artists Assn., Yardley (Pa.) Art Assn., Phillips Mill, New Hope, Pa., Morrisville-Trenton (N.J.), Art Group, Princeton (N.J.) Art Assn., 1967, 68, 69, 72, Woodmere Art Gallery, Phila., 1976, 78, Phila. Sketch Club, Arts Alliance Bucks County, Lahaska, Pa., Wayne (Pa.) Art Ctr., 1989-91, 92, 93, Main Line Ctr. Arts, 1992, 93, Haverford, Pa., Villanova U./Am. Coll., 1989, 91, Valley Forge Hist. Soc., 1994. Machine inspector Rep. Orgn. Ward 3-2, Wayne, Pa., 1990, 91, 92, 93, 94, 95; worker Clinton Victory '92 Campaign, Phila., 1992; mem. Wayne Art Ctr., Main Line Ctr. of the Arts; one of the founders Bucks County Arts Alliance; sec., pres. PTA Yardley Elem. Sch.; co-founder, co-chair Friends of Lake Afton, Artemis; trustee, co-founder Yardley-Makefield Free Libr., sec., pres., del. to county libr. workshops, del. state libr. conv.; vestry St. Andrew's Ch., Yardley, del. diocesan conv.; horticulture therapy vol. Magee Rehab. Hosp.; publicity writer Yarley-Makefield Free Libr.; writer parish newsletter St. Andrew's Ch.; census taker Yardley Borough. Mem. NOW, Nat. Audubon Soc. (illus. Valley Forge chpt. newsletter), Nat. Mus. Am. Indian (charter), Am. Hort. Therapy Assn. (Delaware Valley chpt.), Yardley Ecol. Soc. (co-founder, co-chair), Internat. Soc. Artists (Bucks county corr., columnist Communicator), Cornell Lab. of Ornithology, Pa. Hort. Soc., Embroiderers' Guild of Am. (Phila. area chpt.), Cape May Bird Observatory, Birding Club Del. Co. (charter mem., illus. newsletter), Order of the Holy Cross, Friends' Sch. Haverford Alumni/Alumnae Coun. Episcopalian. Avocations: gardening, ecology, writing, embroidery, Internet.

AUSTIN, JEAN PHILIPPE, medical educator, radiologist. BA, NYU, 1980; MD, SUNY, N.Y.C., 1985. Diplomate Am. Bd. Radiology. Intern in internal medicine Orlando (Fla.) Regional Med. Ctr., 1985-86; chief resident, resident in radiation oncology SUNY Health Sci. Ctr., 1986-89; clin. fellow in radiation oncology Harvard U. Med. Sch., Boston, 1989-90; mem. jr. staff in radiation oncology Mass. Gen. Hosp., Boston, 1989-90; asst. prof. radiation oncology La. State U. Med. Ctr.-Tulane U. Med. Ctr., New Orleans, 1990-96; dir. radiation oncology Convenant Med. Ctr., Champaign, Ill., 1996—; med. dir. radiation oncology Christie Clinic, Champaign, Ill.; papers presented at New Eng. Cancer Soc., 1989, Am. Radium Soc. Proceedings, 1990, A.S.T.R.O. Ann. Meeting, 1990, La. Soc. Radiologic Technologists Acadian Soc., 1991, Internat. Conf. of Hematology and Oncology, Cali, Colombia, 1992, 74th Ann. Meeting of the Am. Radium Soc., Orlando, 1992, La. Med. Assn. and Pelican State Dental Assn., Lafayette, 1992, New Orleans Med. Assns., 1992, Physician Assn. La., 1993, Am. Coll. Chest Physicians, New Orleans, 1993; with cancer com. Children's Hosp, La. State U. Med. Ctr.; affiliated physician VA Hosp., Mercy Hosp., Med. Ctr. La. New Orleans, United Med. Ctr., Univ. Hosp., Children's Hosp., Tulane U. Med. Ctr.; med. dir. Radiation/Oncology, Covenant Med. Ctr. Contbr. articles to profl. jours. Bd. dirs. Christie Clinic Assn., 1998—. Mem. Am. Soc. for Therapeutic Radiology and Oncology, Am. Radium Soc., Nat. Med. Assn., Orleans Parish Med. Soc., Physicians Assn. La., New Orleans Med. Assn., Radiation Therapy Oncology Group, S.W. Oncology Group, Christie Clinic Assn. (bd. dirs. 1998—). Office: Covenant Med Ctr 1400 W Park St Urbana IL 61801-2396

AUSTIN, JOAN D., personal care industry executive. Grad. h.s. Sr. v.p., treas. A-dec, 1963; pres. Austin Industries, Newberg, Oreg. Chmn. bd. Drug and Alcohol Treatment Ctr. at Springbrook N.W., Newberg. Mem. Internat. Women's Forum, Found. for Women's Resources. Office: 2601 Crestview Dr Newberg OR 97132

AUSTIN, JOHN DAVID, retired financial executive; b. Memphis, Jan. 16, 1936; s. Thomas L. and Vela M. (Davis) A.; m. Dorothy Clemens, Dec. 31, 1959 (div.); children— Laura Jan, David John; m. Marilyn C. Brewster, Nov. 2, 1985; 1 son, Christopher Brewster. BBA, Ga. State U., 1961. Acct., Price Waterhouse & Co. Atlanta, 1961-64; sr. tax acct. Price Waterhouse & Co., Miami, 1964-67; audit mgr. N.C. Nat. Bank Corp., Greensboro, 1968; v.p., gen. auditor N.C. Nat. Bank Corp., Charlotte, 1969-73; sr. v.p., dir. corp. planning 1st Nat. Bank Mobile, Ala., 1973-74; sr. v.p. Southeast Nat. Bank. Pa., Malvern, 1974-75, exec. v.p., 1975-83, acting pres., chief exec. officer, 1978-80; sr. v.p. Va. Fed. Savs. and Loan, Richmond, 1984, exec. v.p., 1985, pres., 1986-88, also bd. dirs.; exec. v.p. and chief oper. officer, Citizens Fed. Savs. & Loan, Salisbury, N.C., 1988-90, also bd. dirs.; self employed, Marietta, Ga., 1990-91; v.p., chief fin. officer Atlanta Cutlery Corp., Conyers, Ga., 1991-96, chief oper. officer, 1993-96; ret.; former pres. United Arts Coun. of Rowan; former bd. dirs. Chester County Mental Health/Mental Retardation Bd., The Chester Group, Del. County Econ. Devel. Com., Del. County Community Coll. Found., St. John's Hosp. With U.S. Army, 1957-59. Home: 1303 Spring Gate Cir Woodstock GA 30189-5489

AUSTIN, JOHN DELONG, judge; b. Cambridge, N.Y., May 31, 1935; s. John DeLong and Mabel Cowles (Bascom) A.; m. Marcia Kay Behan, Aug. 15, 1969 (dec.); children: John DeLong, Susan Behan. AB, Dartmouth Coll., 1957; postgrad., u. Minn., 1959; JD, Albany Law Sch., 1969. Bar: N.Y. 1970. Editl. dir. Glens Falls (N.Y.) Times, 1960-66; sole practice Glens Falls, 1970-79; law asst. Warren County Judge and Surrogate, 1975-79, N.Y. State Supreme Ct., 1980-84; judge Warren County Family Ct., N.Y., 1984-98, Warren County Ct. and Surrogate's Ct., 1998—; judge; b. Cambridge, N.Y., May 31, 1935; s. John DeLong and Mabel Cowles (Bascom) A.; m. Marcia Kay Behan, Aug. 15, 1969 (dec.); children: John DeLong, Susan Behan. AB, Dartmouth Coll., 1957; postgrad. U. Minn., 1959; JD, Albany Law Sch., 1969. Bar: N.Y. 1970. Editorial dir. Glens Falls (N.Y.) Times, 1960-66; sole practice, Glens Falls, 1970-79; law asst. Warren County Judge and Surrogate, 1975-79; law asst. N.Y. State Supreme Ct., 1980-84; judge Warren County Family Ct. (N.Y.), 1984-98; judge Warren County Court and Surrogates Court, 1998— ; instr. Adirondack Community Coll., Glens Falls. Councilman, Town of Queensbury (N.Y.), 1969-71, supr., 1972-74; budget officer Warren County, N.Y., 1974; mem. N.Y. State Local Govt. Records Adv. Coun. Editor New Eng. Hist. and Geneal. Register, 1970-73; contbr. hist. and geneal. articles to various periodicals. Served with U.S. Army, 1958-60. Recipient Adminstrv. Law prize Albany Law Sch., 1969. Fellow Am. Soc. Genealogists; mem. N.Y. State Bar Assn., Warren County Bar Assn., Mohican Grange, Elks. Republican. Editor New Eng. Hist. and Geneal. Register, 1970-73; contbr. hist. and geneal. articles to various periodicals. Councilman Town of Queensbury, N.Y., 1969-71, supr., 1972-74; budget officer Waren County, N.Y., 1974; mem. N.Y. State Local Govt. Records Adv. Coun. With U.S. Army, 1958-60. Recipient Adminstrv. Law prize Albany Law Sch., 1969. Fellow Am. Soc. Genealogists; mem. N.Y. State Bar Assn., Warren County Bar Assn., Mohican Grange, Elks. Republican. Office: Warren County Mcpl Ctr Lake George NY 12845

AUSTIN, JOHN NORMAN, classics educator; b. Anshun, Kweichow, China, May 20, 1937; s. John Alfred and Lillian Maud (Reeks) A. B.A., U. Toronto, Ont. Can., 1958; M.A., U. Calif.-Berkeley, 1959, Ph.D., 1965. Vis. lectr. Yale U., New Haven, 1971; asst. prof., then assoc. prof. UCLA, 1966-76; Aurelio prof. Greek Boston U., 1976-78; prof., chmn. dept. classics U. Mass., Amherst, 1978-80; prof. classics U. Ariz., Tucson, 1980—, acting dean humanities, 1987-88, head, dept. classics, 1995—. Author: Archery at the Dark of the Moon, 1975, Meaning and Being in Myth, 1990, Helen of Troy and Her Shameless Phantom, 1994; editor: (with others) The Works of John Dryden, vol. III; sr. editor Calif. Studies Classical Antiquity, vols. VI and VII. Jr. fellow Ctr. for Hellenic Studies, 1968-69, J.S. Guggenheim Found. fellow, 1974-75. Mem. Am. Philol. Assn. (bd. dirs. 1983-86). Episcopalian. Home: 2939 E 3rd St Tucson AZ 85716-4122 Office: U Ariz Dept Classics PO Box 210067 Tucson AZ 85721-0067

AUSTIN, JUDY ESSARY, scriptwriter; b. Jackson, Tenn., Apr. 7, 1948; d. Hershel Dee and Elizabeth Sue (Rhodes) Essary; m. James Michael Austin, July 4, 1965; children: James Allan Austin, Julia Ann Austin Patterson. AS, DeKalb Coll., 1988; BA in Communications and Journalism, Mercer U., 1989. Retail mgr. Bankers Note, Atlanta, 1980-84, Le Chocolat Elegant, Atlanta, 1984-85; student asst. student affairs DeKalb Coll., Dunwoody, Ga., 1987-88; asst. art dir. Sportime, Atlanta, 1990-92; writer, prodr. CAMA, Atlanta, 1993-94; freelance scriptwriter Atlanta, 1994—; bd. dirs. Second Wind Orgn., Dekalb Coll., Dunwoody, 1987-88. Scholar Am. Bus. Womens Assn., 1987. Mem. Women in Communications, NAFE, Phi Kappa Phi. Avocations: photography, reading, flying, fishing, writing. Home: 3133 Raymond Dr Atlanta GA 30340-1826

AUSTIN, MAX EUGENE, horticulture educator; b. Pine Grove, Pa., July 17, 1933; s. Russell Lyle (dec.) and Hilda Havena (Hilkes) (dec.) A.; m. Eleanor Mae Fessenden, Aug. 29, 1953; children: Susan, Becky, Max Jr., Robin. BS in Landscape Design, U. R.I., 1955, MS in Pomology/Botany, 1960; PhD in Olericulture/Mech. Harvesting, Mich. State U., 1964. Jr. rsch. asst. U. R.I., Kingston, 1957-60; assoc. researcher Mich. State U., East Lansing, 1960-64, dist. hort. extension agt., 1964-65; asst. prof. horticulture Va. Poly. Inst. and State U., 1965-70, assoc. prof., 1970-72; assoc. prof. U. Ga. Coastal Plain Experiment Sta., Tifton, 1972-79, prof., 1979-93; prof. emeritus U. Ga. Coastal Plain Experiment Sta., 1993—; head dept. horticulture U. Ga. Coastal Plain Experiment Sta., Tifton, 1972-85; acting head dept. horticulture Va. Poly. Inst. and State U., 1970-71; 1st Kagoshima (Japan) U. exch. prof. U. Ga., 1981; Blue Max cons. Contbr. numerous articles to profl. jours. 1st lt. inf. U.S. Army, 1955-57, Korea. Kagoshima U. fellow, 1990; grantee Va. Sweet Potato Commn., Va. Agrl. Found. Fellow Am. Soc. Hort. Sci. (pres. so. region 1985-86, v.p. internat. affairs div. 1991-92); mem. Ga. Hort. Soc. (bd. dirs. 1991-92), Internat. Soc. Hort. Sci., Internat. Soc. Tropical Root Crops, So. Assn. Agrl. Scientists, N.Am. Blueberry Coun. (rsch. com. 1989-95), Alpha Zeta, Gamma Sigma Delta, Phi Sigma, Sigma Xi, Phi Beta Delta. Episcopal. Achievements include production of Rabbiteye blueberries from breeding to post-harvest handling; release of 3 blueberry cultivars, Brightwell, Baldwin, and Georgiagem.; 1 rabbiteye blueberry cultivar named Austin. Home: 2202 N Ridge Ave Tifton GA 31794-2835

AUSTIN, MICHAEL CHARLES, insurance company executive; b. Syracuse, N.Y., Dec. 7, 1955; s. Harold Ernest and Helen (Sanderson) A.; m. Patricia Farrell, Aug. 12, 1978; 1 child, Bryan Michael. AA in Liberal Arts, Mohawk Valley Community Coll., 1974; BA in English, SUNY, Oswego, 1976. Dir. pub. rels. United Way of Greater Utica, N.Y., 1976-79; asst. mgr. advt. and pub. relations Utica Nat. Ins. Group, 1979-81, asst. dir. corp. communications, 1981-89, dir. corp. communications, 1989—; v.p. Utica (N.Y.) Mut. Ins. Co., 1994; adj. faculty Mohawk Valley Community Coll., Utica, 1982. Contbr. articles to profl. jours. Bd. dirs. United Cerebral Palsy Found., Utica, 1987—, pres., 1992-95, 98-99; pres. bd. trustees Mohawk Valley C.C. Found., 1990-95; chmn. Mohawk Valley Stop-DWI, Utica, 1994—; Mohawk Valley Coun. on Alcoholism, Utica, 1987-93, United Way, Utica, 1982. Recipient Alumni Merit award Mohawk Valley C.C., 1989, Honor Roll award SUNY Alumni, 1996, STOP-DWI Cmty. Svc. award 1997; named Outstanding New Yorker Jaycees, 1994. Mem. Ins. Consumer Affairs Exch., Ins. Mktg. Comm. Assn., Utica C. of C. (bd. dirs. 1998—), Mohawk Valley Advt. Club (pres. 1989-90, dir. 1982-93, awards excellence, Ad Person of Yr. 1992, 95), Syracuse Ad Club, MV Ad Club, Profl. Ins. Comm. Am. Roman Catholic. Avocations: photography, comic book collecting, autograph collecting. Office: Utica Nat Ins Group 180 Genesee St Utica NY 13502-4324

AUSTIN, PHILIP EDWARD, university president; b. Fargo, N.D., 1942; s. William and Angelyn A.; m. Susan Gates; children: Patrick William, Philip James. B.S., N.D. State U., 1964, M.S., 1966; M.A., Mich. State U., 1968, Ph.D., 1969; hon. doctorate, Autonomous U. Guadalajara, Mexico, N.D. State U., U. Ala. Economist U.S. Office of Mgmt. and Budget, Washington, 1971-74; dep. asst. sec. HEW, Washington, 1974-77; acting asst. sec. HEW, 1977; dir. doctoral program in pub. policy George Washington U., Washington, 1977-78; v.p. for acad. affairs, prof. econs. and fin. Bernard Baruch Coll., N.Y.C., 1978-84; pres., prof. econs. Colo. State U., Fort Collins, 1984-89; chancellor U. Ala. System, Tuscaloosa, 1989-96; pres. U. Conn., Storrs, 1996—; bd. dirs. Fleet Bank. Served with U.S. Army, 1969-71. Decorated Bronze Star. Office: U Conn Gulley Hall 352 Mansfield Rd Storrs Mansfield CT 06269-9000

AUSTIN, ROBERT BRENDON, civil engineer; b. West Point, N.Y., Aug. 10, 1956; s. Thomas and Margaret Ann (Hart) A. BS, U. Conn., 1979; M Civil Engring., U. Tex., Arlington, 1992. Registered profl. engr., Tex., La., Colo., Ga., Fla., S.C. Resident engr. Stone & Webster Engring. Corp., Dallas, 1979-94; rsch. assoc., instr. U. Tex., Arlington, 1990-95; city engr. City of Arlington, 1994-95; tech. dir. Nat. Precast Concrete Assn., Indpls., 1995-98; mgr. engring. Quikset Orgn., 1998—. Contbr. articles to profl. jours. Recipient Constrn. Innovation award Stone & Webster Engring., Boston, 1987. Mem. ASCE, NSPE, ASTM, Am. Concrete Inst., Constrn. Specifications Inst. Address: 130 Willowdale St Toccoa GA 30577-1830

AUSTIN, ROBERT CLARKE, naval officer; b. Cleve., Sept. 5, 1931; s. Clarke Albert and Margaret Jane (Richardson) A.; m. Joyce Ann Bisese, Apr. 22, 1957; children—Susan Lynn, James Holden, Robert Clarke, Cecelia Ann. BS, U.S. Naval Acad., 1954; MS in Physics, Naval Postgrad. Sch., 1963. Enlisted U.S. Navy, 1948, commd. ensign, 1954, advanced through grades to rear adm., 1980; commdg. officer USS Finback, 1968-72; comdr. Submarine Devel. Group Two, 1974-76; commdg. officer Naval Submarine Sch., 1976-78; chief of staff submarine force U.S. Atlantic Fleet, 1979-80; dep. dir. for internat. negotiations for Plans and Policy Directorate, Joint Chiefs of Staff, Pentagon, Washington, 1981-82; chief naval tech. ing., 1982-86; supt. Naval Postgrad. Sch., 1986-89; ret. USN, 1989; pres. Austin Assocs., Inc., Alexandria, Va., 1989-97. Decorated Def. Superior Service Medal, Legion of Merit with 4 gold stars, Meritorious Service medal, others. Mem. Sigma Xi. Episcopalian.

AUSTIN, ROBERT EUGENE, JR., lawyer; b. Jacksonville, Fla., Oct. 10, 1937; s. Robert Eugene and Leta Fitch A.; children: Robert Eugene, George Harry Talley; m. Carolyn Rhea Songer. BA, Davidson Coll., 1959; JD, U. Fla., 1964. Bar: Fla. 1965, D.C. 1983, U.S. Supreme Ct. 1970; cert. in civil trial law Nat. Bd. Trial Advocacy, Fla. Bar. Legal asst. Fla. Ho. Reps., 1965; assoc. firm Jones & Sims, Pensacola, Fla., 1965-66; ptnr. firm Warren, Warren & Austin, Leesburg, Fla., 1966-68, McLin, Burnsed, Austin & Cyrus, Leesburg, 1968-77, Austin & Burleigh, Leesburg, 1977-81; sole practice Leesburg, 1981-83, Leesburg and Orlando, Fla., 1984-86; ptnr. firm Austin & Lockett P.A., 1983-84; ptnr. Austin, Lawrence & Landis, Leesburg and Orlando, 1986-92, Austin & Pepperman, Leesburg, 1992—; asst. state atty., 1972; mem. Jud. Nominating Commn. and Grievance Com. 5th Dist. Fla.; gov. Fla. Bar, 1983; trustee U. Fla. Law Ctr. Chmn. Lake Dist. Boy Scouts Am.; asst. dean Leesburg Deanery Diocese Cen. Fla.; trustee Fla. House, Washington, U. Fla. Law Ctr., 1983—, chmn., 1988-90. Mem. Acad. Fla. Trial Lawyers, Am. Arbitration Assn., Am. Law Inst., Nat. Inst. Trial Advocacy, Lake County Bar Assn., Roscoe Pound Am. Trial Found., Timuquana Country Club (Jacksonville), Kappa Alpha, Phi Delta Phi. Democrat. Episcopalian. Home: PO Box 490200 Leesburg FL 34749-0200 Office: Austin & Pepperman 1321 Citizens Blvd Ste C Leesburg FL 34748-3946

AUSTIN, SAM M., physics educator; b. Columbus, Wis., June 6, 1933; s. A. Wright and Mildred G. (Reinhard) A.; m. Mary E. Herb, Aug. 15, 1959; children: Laura Gail, Sara Kay. BS in Physics, U. Wis., 1955, MS, 1957, PhD, 1960. Rsch. assoc. U. Wis., Madison, 1960; NSF postdoctoral fellow Oxford U., Eng., 1960-61; asst. prof. Stanford U., Calif., 1961-65; assoc. prof. physics Mich. State U., East Lansing, 1965-69, prof., 1969-90, univ. disting. prof., 1990—, chmn. dept., 1980-83; acting dean Coll. Natural Sci., 1994; assoc. dir. Cyclotron Lab. Mich. State U., 1976-79, rsch. dir., 1983-85, co-dir., 1985-89, dir., 1989-92; guest Niels Bohr Inst., 1970; guest prof. U. Munich, 1972-73; sci. collaborator Saclay and Lab. Rene Bernas, 1979-80; vis. scientist Triumf-U. B.C., 1993-94; invited prof. U. Paris, Orsay, 1996; mem. grant selection com. for sub-atomic physics, NSERC (Can.), 1996-99; mem. com. on nuc. physics Nat. Rsch. Coun., 1996-99; mem. steering com. Nuc. Physics Summer Sch. Author, editor: The Two Body Force in Nuclei, 1972, The (p,n) Reaction and Nucleon-Nucleon Force, 1980; editor Phys. Rev. C, 1988—; assoc. editor Atomic Data and Nuc. Data Tables, 1990—. Fellow NSF, 1960-61, Alfred P. Sloan Found., 1963-66; recipient Mich. Assn. of Governing Bds. Disting. Prof., 1992. Fellow AAAS (mem. nominating com.), Am. Phys. Soc. (vice chmn. nuc. physics divsn. 1981-82, chmn. 1982-83, exec. com. 1983-84, 86-89, coun. 1986-89, coun. exec. com. 1987-88, panel on pub. affairs 1996-98); mem. APS, Sigma Xi (Sr. rsch. award 1977). Achievements include research in nuclear physics, nuclear astrophysics and nitrogen fixation. Home: 1201 Woodwind Trl Haslett MI 48840-8994 Office: Mich State U Nat Supercondr Cyclotron Lab East Lansing MI 48824

AUSTIN, SANDRA IKENBERRY, nurse educator, consultant; b. Lexington, Va., Dec. 22, 1941; d. William Peters and June Virginia (Blackwell) Ikenberry; m. Joseph M. Austin, Apr. 10, 1965; children: Joseph M. Jr., Susan C., Christopher M. BSN, U. Va., 1963; MSN, U. Calif., L.A., 1967; EdD, U. Mass., 1997. RN, Mass. Pub. health nurse Dept. Health, Waynesboro, Va., 1963-64; instr. U. Va., Charlottesville, 1964-65; staff nurse Santa Monica (Calif.) Hosp., 1965-66; faculty nursing Boston U., 1968-69, Quinsigamond C.C., Worcester, Mass., 1969-70, Fitchburg (Mass.) State Coll., 1973-96; asst. prof. nursing Framingham (Mass.) State Coll., 1997—; project dir., sr. health edn. cons. HealthCo Consulting Inc., Shrewsbury, Mass., 1996—. Mem. Shrewsbury Town Meeting, 1992-95; chair steering com. Framingham State Coll. Nursing Honor Soc., 1998, faculty counselor/advisor, 1999. HBO and Co. Nurse scholar, 1995. Mem. Am. Ednl. Rsch. Assn., Assn. Woman's Health, Obstetric and Neonatal Nurses, Nat. League Nursing, Assn. Critical Care Nurses, Framingham State Coll. Nursing Honor Soc. (chair steeing com. 1998, faculty counselor, advisor 1999), Sigma Theta Tau (Epsilon Beta edn. chair 1993-95, rsch. grant 1996), Pi Lambda Theta. Republican. Congregational. Avocations: computer multimedia production, reading, walking. Home: 100 Harrington Farms Way Shrewsbury MA 01545-4081 Office: Framingham State Coll Nursing Dept Framingham MA 01701

AUSTIN, SCOTT RAYMOND, lawyer; b. Newark, Ohio, Jan. 14, 1956; s. Frank W. and Donna J. (Essig) A.; m. Jilise B. Bushling, May 27, 1989; children: Alec Steven, Luke William. BS summa cum laude, Ohio U., 1979, MBA, 1981; JD, Georgetown U., Washington, 1984. Bar: Fla. 1984, U.S. Dist. Ct. (so. dist.) Fla. 1986, U.S. Dist. Ct. (mid. dist.) Fla. 1991, U.S. Ct. Appeals (11th cir.) 1995. Law clk. Nat. Assn. Broadcasters, Washington, 1982-83; assoc. Ruden, Barnett et al., Ft. Lauderdale, Fla., 1984-92; ptnr. Houston & Shahady, P.A., Ft. Lauderdale, 1992-97, English, McCaughan & O'Bryan, P.A., Ft. Lauderdale, 1997—. Sr. editor, mem. exec. editl. bd. Law and Policy in Internat. Bus., 1983-84; contbr. articles to profl. jours. Mem. ABA (mem. corp., banking and bus. law sect., chmn. ltd. liability co. legis. revisions com.), Fed. Bar Assn., Broward County Bar Assn., The Fla. Bar, Georgetown Club (pres. 1994—), Beta Gamma Sigma. Avocations: computer music development, programming, international travel. Office: English McCaughan & O'Bryan 100 NE 3rd Ave Ste 1100 Fort Lauderdale FL 33301-1144

AUSTON, DAVID HENRY, university administrator, educator; b. Toronto, Ont., Can., Nov. 14, 1940; came to U.S., 1963; BS, U. Toronto, 1962, MS, 1963; PhD, U. Calif. at Berkeley, 1969. Rsch. physicist GM, Santa Barbara, Calif., 1963-66; tech. staff AT&T Bell Labs., Murray Hill, N.J., 1969-82, head dept., 1982-87; prof. Columbia U., N.Y.C., 1987—, chmn. elec. engring. dept., 1990, dean sch. engring. and applied sci., 1991-94; provost Rice U., Houston, 1994-99; pres. Case Western Res. U., Cleve., 1999—. Author: 1 book; also numerous sci. papers; holder 7 patents. Fellow IEEE (Quantum Electronics award 1990, Morris E. Leeds award 1991), Optical Soc. Am. (R.W. Wood prize 1985), Am. Acad. Arts and Scis., Am. Phys. Soc.; mem. Nat. Acad. Scis., NAE. Office: Case Western Res U Office of the Pres Cleveland OH 44106-7021

AUSTRIAN, NEIL R., football league executive; b. N.Y.C., Feb. 21, 1940; s. Joseph H. and Jessie Davis A.; m. Nancy Hewitt, Sept. 8, 1962; children: Neil, John, Jennifer, Jessie Davis, Patrick. B.C.E., Swarthmore Coll., 1961; M.B.A. (Baker scholar), Harvard U., 1968. Vice-pres. Laird Inc., N.Y.C., 1968-70; founder, pres. Dryden & Co., N.Y.C.; investment banker Dryden & Co., 1970-74; exec. v.p. fin., adminstrn. Doyle Dane Bernbach Internat. Inc., N.Y.C., 1974-76, pres., COO, 1976-82, pres., CEO, 1982-84; chmn., CEO Showtime/The Movie Channel Inc., N.Y.C., 1984-86; mng. dir. Dillon Read & Co., 1987—; pres., COO NFL, N.Y.C., 1991—; bd. dirs. Bankers Trust Co., Refac Techs., Viking Office Products. Chmn. bd. Swarthmore Coll. Lt. USNR, 1963-66. Office: NFL 280 Park Ave New York NY 10017-1216*

AUSTRIAN, ROBERT, physician, educator; b. Balt., Apr. 12, 1916; s. Charles Robert and Florence (Hochschild) A.; m. Babette Friedmann Bernstein, Dec. 29, 1963; stepchildren: Jill Bernstein, Toni Bernstein. AB, Johns Hopkins U., 1937, MD, 1941; DSc honoris causa, Hahnemann Med. Coll., 1980, Phila. Coll. Pharmacy and Sci., 1981, U. Pa., 1987, SUNY, 1996. Diplomate: Am. Bd. Internal Medicine. House officer Johns Hopkins Hosp., 1941-50, asst. dir. med. out-patient dept., 1951-52; assoc. prof. medicine, then prof. medicine SUNY Coll. Medicine, 1952-62; John Herr Musser prof., chmn. rsch. medicine U. Pa. Sch. Medicine, 1962-86, prof. emeritus, chmn. emeritus, 1986—; attending physician Hosp. U. Pa.; Tyndale vis. lectr. and prof. Coll. Medicine U. Utah, 1964; spl. research on infectious diseases, bacterial genetics; mem. Meningococcal Infections Commn., 1964-72, Commn. on Acute Respiratory Disease, 1965-72, Commn. Streptococcal and Staphylococcal Diseases, 1970-72, Armed Forces Epidemiol. Bd.; cons. surg. gen. U.S. Army Research and Devel. Command, 1966-69; mem. subcom. streptococcus and pneumococcus Internat. Com. Bacteriol. Nomenclature; mem. allergy and immunology study sect. Nat. Inst. Allergy and Infectious Diseases, 1965-69, mem. bd. sci. counselors, 1967-70, chmn., 1969-70; mem. WHO Expert adv. panel Acute Bacterial diseases, 1979—. Mem. editorial bd.: Jour. Bacteriology 1964-69, Am. Rev. Respiratory Diseases, 1963-66, Bacteriol. Rev., 1967-71, Jour. Infectious Diseases, 1969-74, Antimicrobial Agents and Chemotherapy, 1972-86, Infection and Immunity, 1973-81, Revs. of Infectious Diseases, 1979-89, Vaccine, 1983—. Trustee Johns Hopkins U., 1963-69. Served to capt. M.C. AUS, 1943-45. Recipient U.S. Typhus Commn. medal, 1947; Albert Lasker Clin. Med. Research award, 1978; Phila. award, 1979; Willard O. Thompson award Am. Geriatric Soc., 1981, others; lifetime sci. award Inst. Advanced Studies in Immunology & Aging, 1997; disting. svc. medal Coll. Physicians Phila., 1997, Pasteur Merieux MSD award 1st Internat. Symposium on Pneumococci and Pneumococcal Diseases, 1998. Fellow ACP (master, James D. Bruce Meml. award 1979), N.Y. Acad. Scis., Am. Acad. Microbiology, AAAS (chmn. sect. on med. scis. 1975); mem. Assn. Am. Physicians, Am. Soc. Clin. Investigation, Am. Clin. and Climatol. Assn. (pres. 1984), Am. Soc. Microbiology (v.p. N.Y. br. 1961-62), Am. Philos. Soc., Nat. Acad. Scis., Soc. Exptl. Biology and Medicine, Harvey Soc., Am. Fedn. Clin. Rsch., Inst. Medicine (sr.), Balt. Med. Soc., Am. Assn. Immunologists, N.Y. Acad. Medicine (sec. sect. microbiology 1961-62), Phila. County Med. Soc. (Strittmatter award 1979), Coll. Physicians Phila. (Meritorious Svc. award 1980, pres.-elect 1986, pres. 1988-89, Disting. Svc. medal 1997), Interurban Clin. Club (pres. 1970), Infectious Disease Soc. Am. (pres. 1971, Maxwell Finland lecture award 1974, Bristol award 1986), Johns Hopkins Soc. Scholars, Phi Beta Kappa, Sigma Xi, Alpha Omega Alpha, Omicron Delta Kappa. Club: 14 W. Hamilton Street (Balt.). Achievements include demonstration of the continuing importance of lobar pneumonia as a cause of death despite treatment with antibiotics and of the efficacy of polyvalent pneumococcal vaccine in preventing such illness, leading to its relincensure. Office: U Pa Sch Medicine Dept Rsch Medicine 552 Johnson Pavilion Philadelphia PA 19104-6088

AUSTRIN, MICHAEL STEVEN, health care consultant, strategic planner; b. Columbus, Ohio, Jan. 24, 1957; s. Harvey Robert and Miriam Charlotte (Gottschalk) A.; m. Linda Sheryl Goldstein, Apr. 12, 1986; children: Brian, Bradley, Brandon. BA, St. Louis U., 1980, MA, 1986. Strategic planner Emerson Electric, St. Louis, 1986-91; head planning and rsch. Metaphase Corp., St. Louis, 1991-94; dir. strategic planning Right CHOICE Managed Care, St. Louis, 1994-96, BJC Health Sys., 1999—; cons. DataHounds, St. Louis, 1996-99. Contbr. editor: Learning Med. Terminology, 1997; contbr. articles to profl. jours. Recipient Silver Rsch. award Bus. Week./IDSA, 1992, 94. Mem. Am. Mktg. Assn. (contbr. editor), Strategic Leadership Forum. Home: 1641 Redbluff Ct Saint Louis MO 63146-3915 Office: BJC Health Sys 600 S Taylor Ave Saint Louis MO 63110

AUSUBEL, DAVID PAUL, retired psychiatrist, author; b. Bklyn., Oct. 25, 1918; s. Herman and Lillian (Leff) A.; m. Pearl Leibowitz, Nov. 23, 1943 (div. 1979); m. Gloria Grace George, Sept. 24, 1983; children: Frederick Michael, Laura Ruth. BA, U. Pa., Phila., 1939; MA, Columbia U., 1940, PhD, 1950; MD, Middlesex U., Waltham, Mass., 1943. Intern Gov. Hosp., N.Y.C., 1943-44; resident USPHS Hosp., Lexington, Ky., 1946-47, Buffalo (N.Y.) Psychiat. Ctr., 1947-48; profl. ednl. psychology U. Ill., Urbana, 1950-

66; prof. med. edn. rsch. U. Toronto Grad. Sch., 1966-68; prof. ednl. psychology, program head CUNY, N.Y.C., 1968-73; resident Albert Einstein Coll. Medicine/Bronx Psychiat. Ctr., 1976-77; psychiatrist N.Y. State Divsn. Youth, Highland, 1986-94; vis. prof. psychology Salesian U., Rome, 1964-65, Hochschule der Bundeswehr, Munich, Germany, 1980; cons. U.S. Office Edn., Washington, 1968-70; mem. internat. adv. bd. Psychologie in Erziehung und Unterwicht, 1981-85. Author: Ego Development and the Personality Disorders, 1952, Theory and Problems of Adolescent Development, 1954, Theory and Problems of Child Development, 1957, Ego Development and Psychopathology, 1996; mem. editl. bd. Child Devel. Monograph Social Rsch. Child Devel., 1963-65, Internat. Jour. Addictions, 1963—. Capt. USPHS, 1945-47. Recipient Fulbright award to New Zealand, 1957. Fellow APA (Thorndike award 1976); mem. Am. Psychiat. Assn., Am. Psychol. Soc., Am. Ednl. Rsch. Assn. Democrat. Roman Catholic. Avocations: gardening, music (CD's), hiking, boating. Home: 2 The Hls Port Ewen NY 12466-5015

AUSUBEL, HILLEL, librarian; b. N.Y.C., Nov. 25, 1924; s. Herman and Lillian Leah (Leff) A.; m. Lucille Whintrop, June 19, 1949; children: Joan Ellen, Carol Ruth, Lawrence Marc. BA, Yale U., 1947; MA, Columbia U., 1948, MS in Libr. Svc., 1949, PhD in Music, 1953. Cert. pub. and sch. librarian, N.Y. Librarian Bklyn. Pub. Libr., 1949-50, Queens Pub. Libr., Jamaica, N.Y., 1954-63, Mt. Vernon (N.Y.) Schs., 1963-66, New Rochelle (N.Y.) Pub. Libr., 1968-89; head librarian N.Y. Coll. Music, N.Y.C., 1966-68; adj. librarian Queens (N.Y.) Coll., 1996—; music book reviewer Libr. Jour., 1980-89; pvt. music tchr., 1945—. Composer various works for piano, voice and chamber music. Bd. dirs. Dems. for New Politics, Flushing, N.Y., 1990—. Mem. Ret. Educators & Profls., Queens Oratorio Soc. (trustee 1982-90). Democrat. Jewish. Avocations: music, gardening. Home: 46-10 216th St Bayside NY 11361 Office: Queens Coll Music Libr Kissena Blvd Flushing NY 11365

AUTEN, DAVID CHARLES, lawyer; b. Phila., Apr. 4, 1938; s. Charles Raymond and Emily Lillian (Dickel) A.; m. Suzanne Crozier Plowman, Feb. 1, 1969; children: Anne Crozier, Meredith Smedley. BA, U. Pa., 1960, JD, 1963. Bar: Pa. 1963. Ptnr. Reed Smith Shaw & McClay (and predecessor), Phila., 1963—. Author articles in field. V.p. N.E. Cmty. Mental Health Ctr., 1971-72; vice chmn. alumni ann. giving U. Pa., 1975-77, 81-82, chmn., 1982-84, trustee, 1977-80, 83-88; pres. Gen. Alumni Soc., 1977-80; chmn. Benjamin Franklin Assocs., 1975-77, 81-82, bd. overseers Sch. Arts and Scis., 1983-96; trustee U. Pa. Health Sys., 1995—, Springside Sch., 1985-88, v.p., 1987-88; pres. Soc. of Coll., 1975-77; v.p. Assn. Reps. for Educated Action, 1971-79; bd. mgrs. Presbyn.-U. Pa. Med. Ctr., 1980—, vice chmn., 1983-85, 88-95; trustee Presbyn. Found. for Phila., 1986—, vice chm., 1996-98, chmn., 1998—; bd. mgrs. Phila. City Inst., 1981—, treas., 1990-99; bd. dirs. Kearsley Home, 1974—, treas., 1990-96, chmn., 1996—; bd. mgrs. St. Peter's Sch., 1975-88, pres., 1978-79; bd. dirs. Greater Phila. Internat. Network, 1989-94, Com. of Seventy, 1990—, Courtland Found., Del Pres Health Care Inc., Courtland Health Care, chmn., 1998—; mem. econ. devel. com. Greater Phila. First Corp.; rector's warden Christ Ch., Phila., 1996—. Mem. ABA, Pa. Bar Assn. (vice chmn. real property sect. 1985-87, chmn. 1987-88), Am. Land Title Assn., Phila. Bar Assn. (vice chmn. young lawyers sect. 1971-72), Juristic Soc. (pres.), Am. Coll. Real Estate Lawyers, Interfrat. Alumni Coun. U. Pa. (pres. 1970-74), French Am. C. of C. (bd. dirs. 1989—), Phi Beta Kappa, Theta Xi (pres. 1974-76, chmn. found. 1977-86), Rittenhouse Club (pres. 1979-82), Union League (bd. dirs., v.p., pres. 1993-94, chmn. Lincoln Found. 1996—), Fourth St. Club (bd. dirs. 1998—), Phila. Club. Episcopalian (vestryman). Home: 120 Delancey St Philadelphia PA 19106-4303 Office: Reed Smith Shaw & McClay 2500 One Liberty Pl Philadelphia PA 19103

AUTEN, JOHN HAROLD, government official; b. Ames, Iowa, June 29, 1922; s. John T. and Dorothy (Davis) A.; m. Ethel Anne Pye, Jan. 20, 1951; children—Susan Irene, John Aaron, Joanne Marie. B.Sc., Ohio State U., 1947; Ph.D., Mass. Inst. Tech., 1954. Instr. Ohio State U., 1952; from instr. to prof. econs. Rice U., 1952-64; with Office Fin. Analysis, Treasury Dept., 1963—, dir., 1966—. Contbr. articles to profl. jours. Served with USAAF, 1943-46. Home: 2816 8th St S Arlington VA 22204-2230 Office: Treasury Dept 15th and Pennsylvania Ave NW Washington DC 20220

AUTERI, ROSE MARY PATTI, school system administrator; b. N.Y.C., June 6, 1928; d. Francesco and Stefana (Patti) A. BS, Hunter Coll., 1950; MA, Columbia U., 1962; EdD, Nova-Southeastern U., 1975; postdoctoral, Columbia U., 1976-77. Tchr. Howell Rd Sch., Valley Stream, N.Y., 1951-58, asst. prin., 1958-64; prin. Centennial Ave Sch., Roosevelt, N.Y., 1964-69, Northside Sch., Levittown, N.Y., 1969-83, Abbey Ln. Sch., Levittown, 1983-89; adminstr. in charge elem. schs. Levittown Pub. Schs., 1989-90; prin. Abbey Ln. Sch., Levittown, 1990—. Mem. Nassau County Youth Bd.; coord. Nassau County Mentoring Program; trustee Sacred Heart Roman Cath. Ch., Merrick. Recipient Disting. Prin. award State of N.Y., 1988, 89, Disting. Svc. award Nat. PTA; named Italian Am. Woman of Yr. Consortium L.I. Italian Am. Orgns., 1990, Woman of Yr. Societa Scarese D Am., 1998. Mem. Am. Assn. Sch. Adminstrs., Nat. Assn. Elem. Sch. Prins., Nat. Assn. Supervision and Curriculum Devel., Nassau County Elem. Prins. Assn. (pres.), L.I. Assn. Supervision and Curriculum Devel. (bd. dirs.), N.Y. State Assn. Devel., Am. Assn. Electroencephalographic Technologists, Am.-Italian Hist. Assn. (sec. 1988—, pres., editor L.I. regional chpt.). Home: 1816 Thomas St Merrick NY 11566-2652 Office: Levittown Pub Schs Abbey Ln Levittown NY 11756

AUTH, JUDITH, library director. BA in English Lit., U. Calif., Riverside, 1968, grad. advanced mgmt. program, 1990; MLS, UCLA, 1971. Children's libr. Marcy br. Riverside City & County Pub. Libr., 1971-73, ctrl. libr. children's rm., 1973-75, coord. children's svcs., 1975-80, area br. supr., 1980-85, head ctrl. libr., 1985-87, acting head tech. svcs., 1987-88, asst. libr. dir., 1988-91, libr. dir., 1991—; asst. to city mgr. in charge of entrepreneurial mgmt. program City of Riverside, 1988-91. Mem. ALA, Am. Soc. Pub. Adminstrn., Calif. Libr. Assn. (leadership inst. task force 1992-93, mem. assembly 1994), Calif. County Librs. Assn. (sec. 1992-94), So. Calif. Coun. Lit. for Children and Young People (bd. dirs. 1975-90). Office: Riverside City & County Libr 3581 Mission Inn Ave Riverside CA 92501-3306*

AUTIO, RUDY, artist educator; b. Butte, Mont., Oct. 8, 1926. BS, Mont. State U., 1950; MFA, Wash. State U., 1952; DFA, Md. Inst. Coll. Art, Balt., 1986. resident artist dir. Archie Bray Found., 1952-56; asst. curator Mont. Mus. Hist. Soc., 1955; prof. ceramics and sculpture U. Mont., 1957-84. Author: About Drawing, 1985; one-man shows include Henry Gallery, U. Wash., Seattle, 1963, Toledo Art Mus., 1965, Retrospectives, Am. Crafts Mus., N.Y., 1983, John Michael Kohler Art Mus., Sheboygan, Wis., 1983, Bellevue Art Mus., Wash., 1983, Mont. Horses, Ryijy Tapestry, Taideteollisuusmuseo, Helsinki, 1985, Everson Mus., Syracuse, 1964; group shows include Chgo. Art Mus., 1968, Am. Studio Potters & Victoria & Albert Mus., London, 1972, San Francisco Mus. Modern Art, 1972, Mus. Contemporary Crafts, N.Y., 1974, Seattle Art Mus., 1979; retrospectives includes Am. Crafts Mus., N.Y. and Bellevue Mus. Seattle, 1984, Western States Arts Found. 3d Ann. Exhbn. Bklyn. Mus., 1986, Contemporary Am. Ceramics, Nat. Mus. Modern Art, Seoul, 1987; prin. works exhibited Renwick Gallery, Smithsonian Mus., Everson Mus., Syracuse, N.Y., Victoria & Albert Mus., London, Nat. Mus. Stockholm, Taideteollisusmuseo, Helsinki. Recipient Tiffany Found. award, 1963, Purchase award Everson Mus., 1964, Ceramic Art award, Am. Ceramic Soc., 1978, NEA, 1980, 1st Gov.'s award in Visual Arts' Most Outstanding Artist, 1980, Disting. scholar award U. Mont., 1984. Fellow Am. Craftsmen Coun., Archie Bray Found. (trustee 1974), Internat. Ceramic Soc. Geneva; mem. Nat. Coun. Edn. Ceramic Arts. Office: Dorothy Weiss Gallery 256 Sutter St San Francisco CA 94108-4409*

AUTOLITANO, ASTRID, consumer products executive; b. Havana, Cuba, Aug. 25, 1938; came to U.S., 1966; d. Manuel and Efigenia (Giquel) Rodriguez; m. Dominick Autolitano, July 23, 1977; children: Astrid Martinez, Manuel Martinez. Student, U. Havana, 1962-64, El Camino Coll., Torrance, Calif., 1968-71, UCLA, Westwood, 1973-75, Columbia U., 1983. Multi-lingual sec. Mattel Toys, Hawthorne, Calif., 1966-69, coord. internat. sales, 1969-73, mgr. Pan Am. sales, 1973-78, dir. export sales and licensees, 1978-83, v.p. Latin Am., 1983-89; sr. v.p. Latin Am. Mattel Toys, El Segundo, Calif., 1989-95, exec. v.p. Latin Am., 1995-96, exec. v.p. Ams., 1996; pres. internat. Mattel Toys, 1996—. Office: Mattel Toys 333 Continental Blvd El Segundo CA 90245-5012

AUTRY, CAROLYN, artist, art history educator; b. Dubuque, Iowa, Dec. 12, 1940; d. William Tilden and Vela (Laseman) A.; m. Peter Elloian, May 27, 1966; 1 dau., Cybele Justine. BA, U. Iowa, 1963, MFA, 1965. Instr. art, art history Baldwin-Wallace Coll., Berea, Ohio, 1965-66; adj. assoc. prof. art history dept. art Ctr. for Visual Arts U. Toledo, 1966—; artist-in-residence Sch. Arts in France, Lacoste, 1984, 87, adj. instr. in printmaking, 1987. Exhbns. include San Francisco Mus. Art, 1973, Oakland Mus., 1975, Santa Barbara Mus., 1975, U. Mo., 1975, Ljubljana Internat. Biennial, 1975, 81, 87, Internationale Grafik Biennale, Frechen, W. Ger., 1976, Biella, Italy, 1976, Genoa, Italy, 1976, Leverkusen, Fed. Republic Germany, 1977, Phila. Mus. Art, 1980, 97, Visual Arts Ctr., Anchorage, Alaska, 1980, U. Louisville, 1981, U. Dallas, 1981, Grunwald Ctr. Graphic Arts, UCLA, 1981, Ohio State U., 1982, Belle Arts & Graphic Inc., Nyack, N.Y., 1982, Mus. Arts and Scis., Macon, Ga., 1983, U. Tenn., Knoxville, 1983, Pratt Graphics Ctr., N.Y.C., 1983, Calif. State Coll., San Bernardino, 1983, Taipei Fine Arts Mus., 1983, 85, 87, 89, 91, 95, Museo Arte Contemporaneo, Ibiza, Spain, 1984, Drake U., 1985, Fla. State U., 1985, Am. Embassy Cultural Ctr., Belgrade, Yugoslavia, 1983, Irvine (Calif.) Fine Arts Ctr., 1986, Inter-graphic Internat., East Berlin, 1984, 87, Met. Mus. Art Ctr., Coral Gables, Fla., 1987, Fifth Internat. Graphic Exhbn., Catania, Italy, 1988, Korean Cultural Svc. Gallery, L.A., Walker Hill Gallery, Seoul, Korea, and Korean Embassy Cultural Ctr., Paris, 1989, Barbican Art Centre, London, Salford (Gt. Britain), Mus., Mead Gallery, U. Warwick, Coventry, Gt. Britain, Brighton and Poly. Gallery, Brighton, Gt. Britain, 1989, Internat. Exhbn. Prints, Kanagawa, Japan, 1989, 90, 95, 97, Gallery Fine Arts Ctr. Seoul, 1989, Nat. Exhbn. Prints, Ringling Sch. Art and Design, Sarasota, Fla., 1990, Internat. Impact Art Festival, Kyoto City Mus., Japan, 1990, 91, 92, 93, 94, Ohio Drawing and Printmaking Invitational, Upper Arlington, 1991, Fondation Mona Bismarck, Paris, 1991, Fine Arts Assn. Gallery, Hanoi, Republic of Vietnam, 1991, Prints Internat., 1992, Silvermine Guild Arts Ctr., New Caanan, Conn., 1993, Taejon (Korea) Expo Graphic Art, 1993, Soc. Am. Graphic Artists 65th Nat., N.Y.C., 1993, Architecture in Contemporary Print Making, Boston Archtl. Ctr., 1994, Am. Inst. Architecture, Washington, 1994, U. N.H., 1995, Midwest Select, South Bend Regional Mus. of Art, Ind., 1994, Triton Mus., Santa Clara, Calif., 1995, Mansfield (Ohio) Art Ctr., 1995, 20th Harper Nat. Exhbn., Macomb, Ill., 1996, Hunterdon Art Ctr., Clinton, N.J., 1996, Soc. Am. Graphic Artists 66th Nat. Print Exhbn., Hanover, N.J., 1997, Internat. Print Triennial, Cracow, Poland, 1997, Fla. Print Makers 9th Ann. Nat. Print Exhbn., Jacksonville, Fla., 1997, Institut Franco-Américain, Rennes, France, 1997, Prized Impressions, Internatl. Exhbn. of Prints, Philadelphia Mus. of Art, 1997, Natl. Print Exhbn., Calif. State Univ. at Chico, 1997, 22nd natl. Print Biennal Silvermine Guild Arts Ctr., Conn., 1998, Counterpoint 30th Natl. Exhbn. Hill Country Arts Found., Tex., 1998, Printmakers 98, Pittsburgh Ctr. for the Arts, Penn., 1998, numerous others; represented in permanent collections Libr. of Congress, Phila. Mus. Art, Worcester Art Mus., Mount Holyoke Coll., U. Colo., Bradley U., Calif. State U., San Diego, Ga. State U., U. S.D., U. N.D., U. Louisville, St. Lawrence U., U. Dallas, Hunterdon Art Ctr., Clinton, N.J., Fitchburg (Mass.) Mus., Duxbury (Mass.) Art Complex, Elvehjem Mus. Art U. Wis.-Madison, Inst. per la Cultura E L'Arte, Catania, Italy, Lakeview Mus. Arts and Scis., Peoria, Ill., Nat. Mus. Fine Arts, Hanoi. Recipient Ture Bengtz Meml. prize, 1981, Pennell award Libr. Congress, 1971, 75, Phila. Print Club awards, 1972, 75, 79, Wesleyan Coll. Internat. award of merit, 1980, Anne Steele Marsh award Hunterdon Art Ctr., Clinton, N.J., 1991, Bradley U. Nat. award, 1991, Friends of the Janet Turner Gallery Nat. Exhbn. award Chico State U., Calif., 1995, Exhbn. award 16th Nat. Print Exhbn., Artlink, 1996, Exhbn. award 17th Nat. Print Exhbn., 1997; Ford Found. grantee, 1961-63, Ohio Arts Coun. grantee, 1979, 90, Yale-Norfolk Summer Sch. Art and Music scholar, 1962. Mem. Boston Printmakers (Louis Black award 1971), L.A. Printmakers Soc., Soc. Am. Graphic Artists (Jo Miller award 1985, Phillip Monteith award 1986), Calif. Soc. Printmakers, Coll. Art Assn. Am., The Print Club of Albany, N.Y. (Ledyard Logswell, Jr. Meml. prize 1995), Phi Beta Kappa. Address: 26114 W River Rd Perrysburg OH 43551-9128

AUVENSHINE, ANNA LEE BANKS, school system administrator; b. Waco, Tex., Nov. 27, 1938; d. D.C. and Lois Elmore Banks; B.A., Baylor U., 1959, M.A., 1968, Ed.D., 1978, postgrad., 1989—, Colo. State U., 1970-71, U. No. Colo., 1972; m. William Robert Auvenshine, Dec. 21, 1963; children—Karen Lynn, William Lee. Tchr. math. and English, Lake Air Jr. High Sch., Waco Ind. Sch. Dist., 1959-63, Ranger (Tex.) Ind. Sch. Dist., Ranger High Sch., 1964, Canyon (Tex.) Ind. Sch. Dist., Canyon Jr. High Sch., 1964-66; instr. English, Baylor U., 1963; tchr. math. Canyon Ind. Sch. Dist., Canyon High Sch., 1968-70; tchr. math. and English, St. Vrain Sch. Dist., Erie (Colo.) High Sch., 1970-71; tchr. English and reading Thompson Sch. Dist., Loveland (Colo.) High Sch., 1971-72; instr., reading program dir. Ranger Jr. Coll., 1972-84, chmn. humanities div., 1978-82; tchr. math. Hillsboro High Sch., 1984-85, adminstr. Hillsboro Ind. Sch. Dist., 1985-92. Trustee, Ranger (Tex.) Ind. Sch. Dist., 1979-84, v.p. bd. trustees, 1980-82, pres., 1982-84; community chmn., publicity chmn., troop leader Ranger Girl Scout Assn., 1974-77; sec. Eastland County Heart Assn., 1975-77; ch. sch. supt. First United Meth. Ch., Ranger, 1979-81, organist, 1974-77, mem. adminstrv. bd., 1979-84; assoc. program dir. community and tech. colls. and fed. projects, equity dir. Tex. Higher Edn. Coordinating Bd., Austin, 1992—. Mem. Internat. Reading Assn., Assn. Supervision and Curriculum Devel., Western Coll. Reading Assn., Tex. Assn. Sch. Adminstrs., Tex. Assn. Gifted and Talented, Tex. Jr. Coll. Tchrs. Assn. (cert. of appreciation 1979, mem. profl. devel. com. 1974-79, vice chmn. 1976-77, mem. resolutions com. 1979-80), Ranger PTA (parliamentarian 1978-79), Ranger Jr. Coll. Faculty Orgn. (pres. 1980-81), Baylor Alumni Assn. (life, bd. dirs. 1988-94), director, Baylor Alum. Assn., 1988-92, Delta Kappa Gamma (pres. Beta Upsilon chpt. 1978-80, pres. Gamma Delta chpt. 1986—, achievement award 1980). Methodist. Clubs: 1947 (pres. 1977-78) (Ranger); Baylor Bear (Waco). Home: 1107 E Walnut St Hillsboro TX 76645-2637 Office: Texas Higher Edn Coordinating Bd PO Box 12788 7745 Chevy Chase Dr Bldg 5 Austin TX 78752-1508

AUVENSHINE, WILLIAM ROBERT, academic administrator; b. Waco, Tex., June 21, 1937; s. E.H. and Corinne (Clark) A.; m. Anna Banks, Dec. 21, 1963; children: Karen, Lee. AA, Arlington State Jr. Coll., 1957; BS, Tex. Christian U., 1959; MS, West Tex. State U., 1967; EdD, U. No. Colo., 1973. Tchr. music Chico (Tex.) Pub. Schs., 1957-60, Ranger (Tex.) Pub. Schs., 1960-64; mgr., part-owner Megert Music Co., Amarillo, Tex., 1964-70; counselor Loveland (Colo.) Pub. Schs., 1970-72; dean Ranger Jr. Coll., 1972-84; pres. Hill Coll., Hillsboro, Tex., 1984—. Mem. Heritage League, Hillsboro, 1984—; chmn. State Task Force on C.C. Annexation, 1993; chmn. bd. dirs. Eastland County Tax Appraisal Dist., 1979-84; mem. Indsl. Com., Cleburne, 1984—, Hillsboro, 1984—; mem. First United Meth. Ch., Hillsboro; mem. gen. bd. discipleship com. that rewrote Book of Worship for Meth. Ch.; past lay leader Ctrl. Tex. Conf., leader del. to gen. conf.; bd. dirs. Nat. Jr. Coll. Atletic Assn., 1993—, Harris Meth. Hosp. Sys., 1997—. Recipient Disting. Alumni award West Tex. State U., Canyon, 1983, Jefferson Davis award United Daus. of Confederacy, 1991; named Man of Yr., Ranger C. of C., 1963. Mem. Tex. Jr. Coll. Assn. (pres. 1991-92), Tex. Pub. Community Jr. Coll. Assn. (sec., treas. 1985-90), Tex. Assn. for C.C. Chief Student Affairs Adminstrs. (pres. 1982-83), Tex. C.C. Ins. Consortium (pres. 1992—), Hillsboro C. of C., Lions (dist. gov. 1977-78, Internat. Press award 1983, Lion of Yr. award Ranger chpt. 1975, Citizen of Yr. award Hillsboro chpt. 1986), Sons of Confederate Vets. (past comdr. 1988-90), Sons of Union Vets. of Civil War (chaplain), Masons (32d degree), Shriners, Hillsboro Country Club (pres. 1993-95), Phi Delta Kappa. Avocations: golf, restoring antique cars, reading. Home: 1107 E Walnut St Hillsboro TX 76645-2637 Office: Hill Coll 111 Lamar Dr Hillsboro TX 76645-2712

AUVILLE, FRANCES CARTER, educational administrator; b. Fayetteville, N.C., Dec. 26, 1935; d. C. Alexander and Ida Mae (Melvin) Carter; m. John Joe Auville, Aug. 17, 1958 (div. Apr. 1981); children: Nicole, Michèle, John. BA in English, Concord Coll., Athens, W.Va., 1965; MA in English, Marshall U., 1970, postgrad., 1994—. Payroll clk. Concord Coll., 1959-64; ins. auditor Treadwell & Harry Brokers, Memphis, 1964-66; tchr. St. John Sch., Memphis, 1966-67, Mercer County Schs., Princeton, W.Va., 1967-69, 83-89; supr. Mercer County Schs., Princeton, 1989-92, asst. prin., 1992—; instr. Bluefield (W.Va.) State Coll., 1969-74; participant seminars NEH, Washington, 1988, 92. Contbr. poetry to Am. Poetry, World of Poetry (Golden Poet award 1988, 91), Am. Poetry Anthology, 1985, 88, 91, Art of Poetry, 1985, Treasures of the Precious Moment, 1985 (Oustanding Poets 1994); mem. adv. bd. Children's Album mag., Concord, Calif., 1987-90. Vol. hosp., Bluefield, 1974-86; Rep. poll worker, Bluefield. Mem. Nat. Coun. Tchrs. of English, W.Va. English Lang. Arts Coun. (Lang. Arts Tchr. of Yr. 1986), W.Va. Writing Project (cons.), Phi Delta Kappa. Presbyterian. Avocations: tennis, golf, reading. Home: 510 Mountain View Ave Bluefield WV 24701-4121

AUWERS, STANLEY JOHN, motor carrier executive; b. Grand Rapids, Mich., Mar. 22, 1923; s. Joseph T. and Cornelia (Moelhoek) A.; m. Elizabeth Kruis, Apr. 6, 1946; children—Ellen (Mrs. William Northway), Stanley John, Thomas. Student, Calvin Coll., 1940-41; B.B.A., U. Mich., 1943. C.P.A., Mich. With Ernst & Ernst, Detroit, 1943-51; controller Interstate Motor Freight System, Grand Rapids, Mich., 1951-61; v.p., controller Interstate Motor Freight System, 1961-65, v.p. finance, 1965-69, exec. v.p., 1969-72; also dir.; pres. Transam. Freight Lines, Detroit, 1973—; Chmn. cost com. Mich. Trucking Adv. Bd. to Mich. Pub. Service Commn., 1958-63; mem. citizens com. to study Mich. tax structure advisory Mich. Ho. Reps., 1958. Mem. Am. Motor Carriers Central Freight Assn. (gov. regular common carrier conf.), Mich. Motor Carriers Central Freight Assn. (v.p., gov.), Tax Execs. Inst., Am. Inst. C.P.A.s, Trucking Employers. Presbyn. Home: 3099 Lakeshore Dr Douglas MI 49406 Office: 3684 28th St SE Grand Rapids MI 49512-1606

AUXENTIOS (BISHOP AUXENTIOS), clergyman; b. June 28, 1953. BA in Religion, Princeton U., 1976; Lic. Theol., Ctr. for Traditionalist Orthodox Studies, 1986; ThD, Grad. Theol. Union, Berkeley, Calif., 1992. Ordained as rasophore monk, then hierodeacon Old Calendar Greek Orthodox Ch., 1976, hieromonk, 1977, great schema, 1986, oikonomos, 1989, archimandrite, 1989, titular bishop of Photiki, 1991. Co-dir. Ctr. for Traditionalist Orthodox Studies, 1987—. Author: (with Chrysostomos and Akakios) Contemporary Eastern Orthodox Thought: The Traditionalist Voice, 1982, (with Chrysostomos and Ambrosios) Scripture and Tradition, 1982, (with Chrysostomos) The Roman West and the Byzantine East, 1988, The Holy Fire, 1991; translator: (with Chrysostomos) The Future Life According to Orthodox Teaching (Constantine Cavarnos), 1988, The Monastic Life (Met. Cyprian of Oropos and Fili), 1988; (with others) The Evergetinos: A Complete Text, Vol. I of the First Book, 1988, Vol. II, 1990; editor Orthodox Tradition, 1989—; contbr. articles to profl. jours. Address: St Gregory Palamas Monastery Etna CA 96027

AVAKIAN, LAURA ANN, hospital administrator; b. DeSoto, Mo., July 6, 1945; d. Edward Ernest and Elizabeth (Gamel) McClary; m. Stephen Avakian, Dec. 30, 1969. BA, U. Mo., 1967; MA, Northwestern U., 1968. Instr. Sacramento (Calif.) State Coll., 1968-69; tchr. English Hathaway Brown Sch., Cleve., 1969-73; pers. profl. Huron Rd. Hosp., Cleve., 1974-76, dir. human resources, 1978-80; dir. employment Cleve. Clinic Found., 1976-78; sr. v.p. human resources Beth Israel Deaconess Med. Ctr., Boston, 1980-96, Beth Israel Deaconess Med. Ctr. and Care Group, Boston, 1996—. Assoc. editor Yearbook of Healthcare Management, 1990, 91, 92, 93. Mem. Mayor's Commn. on Comparable Worth, Boston, 1989-90; trustee Pine Manor Coll., 1997—. Mem. Am. Soc. Healthcare Human Resources Adminstrn. (bd. dirs. 1989-93, Pres. Leadership award 1989, Lit. award 1992, pres. 1994-95, Disting. Svc. award 1997), Soc. Human Resource Mgmt. (Profl. Excellence award 1996), Mass. Health Care Human Resources Assn. (pres. 1987-88). Avocation: crossword puzzle construction. Office: Beth Israel Deacones Med Ctr 330 Brookline Ave Boston MA 02215-5400

AVAKOFF, JOSEPH CARNEGIE, medical and legal consultant; b. Fairbanks, Alaska, July 15, 1936; s. Harry B. and Margaret (Adams) A.; m. Teddy I. Law, May 7, 1966; children: Caroline, Joey, John. AA, U. Calif., Berkeley, 1956, AB, 1957; MD, U. Calif., San Francisco, 1961; JD, Santa Clara U., 1985. Bar: Calif. 1987; diplomate Am. Bd. Surgery, Am. Bd. Plastic Surgery. Physicist U.S. Naval Radiol. Def. Lab., San Francisco, 1957, 59; intern So. Pacific Gen. Hosp., San Francisco, 1961-62; resident in surgery Kaiser Found. Hosp., San Francisco, 1962-66; resident in plastic surgery U. Tex. Sch. Medicine, San Antonio, 1970-72; pvt. practice specializing in surgery Sacramento, 1966-70; pvt. practice specializing in plastic surgery Los Gatos and San Jose, Calif., 1972-94; cons. to med. and legal professions, 1994—; clin. instr. surgery U. Calif. Sch. Medicine, Davis, 1967-70; chief dept. surgery Mission Oaks Hosp., Los Gatos, 1988-90; chief divsn. plastic surgery Good Samaritan Hosp., San Jose, 1989-91; expert med. reviewer Med. Bd. Calif., 1995—; spl. cons. Calif. Dept. Corps., 1997—; presenter numerous med. orgns. Contbr. numerous articles to med. jours. Mem. San Jose Adv. Commn. on Health, 1975-82; bd. govs. San Jose YMCA, 1977-80. Mem. AMA, Calif. Med. Assn., Santa Clara County Bar Assn., Santa Clara County Med. Assn., Union Am. Physicians and Dentists, Phi Beta Kappa, Phi Eta Sigma. Republican. Presbyterian. Avocations: music, photography, computer programming. Home: 6832 Rockview Ct San Jose CA 95120-5607

AVANT, GRADY, JR., lawyer; b. New Orleans, Mar. 1, 1932; s. Grady and Sarah (Rutherford) A.; m. Katherine Willis Yancey, Feb. 23, 1963; children: Grady M., Mary Willis Yancey. B.A. magna cum laude, Princeton U., 1954; J.D., Harvard U., 1960. Bar: N.Y. 1961, Ala. 1962, Mich. 1972. Assoc. Bradley, Arant, Rose & White, Birmingham, Ala., 1961-63; assoc., ptnr. Long, Preston, Kinnaird & Avant, Detroit, 1972-87; ptnr. Dickinson, Wright, Moon, Van Dusen & Freeman, Detroit, 1988-94; sr. v.p. investment banking North Am. Capital Advisors, Inc., Bloomfield Hills, Mich., 1995-96; pvt. practice Grosse Pointe, Mich., 1996—. Contbr. articles to legal jours. Served to lt. USMC, 1954-57. Mem. ABA (bus. law sect., fed. regulation of securities com.), Am. Law Inst., Assn. of Bar of City of N.Y., State Bar of Mich. (coun. sect. antitrust law 1978-85, chmn. sect. 1983-84, bus. law sect.), Detroit Com. on Fgn. Rels. (exec. com. 1979—, chmn. 1986-88), Grosse Pointe Club, Mountain Brook Club, Knickerbocker Club, Met. Club, Princeton Club of Mich. (pres. 1976-77, 94-95). Episcopalian. Fax: 313-886-6556. Home and Office: 406 Lincoln Rd Grosse Pointe MI 48230-1607

AVANT, PATRICIA, nursing educator; b. Dallas, Aug. 15, 1941; d. Lem Barrett and Georgia Evelyn (Mullennix) Coalson; m. Gayle R. Avant, Sept. 6, 1963; children: Samantha Gay Foss, Celia Kay Drews. RN, Methodist Hosp., Dallas, 1962; BSN, Tex. Christian U., 1963; MSN, U. N.C., Chapel Hill, 1965; PhD, Tex. Woman's U., Denton, 1978. cons. in field. Fellow: Am. Acad. Nursing; mem. Royal Coll. Nursing (Australia), ANA (pres. Dist. 10 1983-84), Nat. League Nursing, (1st v.p. Tex. 1985-89), N.Am. Nursing Diagnosis Assn. (taxonomy chair 1994-98, pres.-elect 1998—). Democrat. Baptist. Fax: (254) 741-9850. E-mail: KAvant@mail.utexas.edu. Home: 7601 Tallahassee Rd Waco TX 76712-3814 Office: U Tex 1700 Red River St Austin TX 78701-1412

AVANT, ROBERT FRANK, physician, educator; b. Chisholm, Minn., 1937; m. Betty Jensen, Dec. 28, 1962; children: Paul, Gregory, Todd. MD, U. Minn., 1963. Intern San Bernardino, Calif. County Hosp., 1963-64; chief of family practice Glenwood Hills Hosp., 1970-71, chief of staff, 1972; dir. family practice residency North Meml. Hosp., Mpls., 1973-77; asst. prof. dept. family practice and cmty. health U. Minn., 1973-77; chmn. dept. family medicine Mayo Clinic, Rochester, Minn., 1977-91, assoc. prof. family medicine, 1977-84; prof. family medicine Mayo Med. Sch., Rochester, 1984-93; Sanders prof. primary care Mayo Clinic, Rochester, 1986-93; chmn. dept. family medicine Mayo Clinic Jacksonville, 1991-93; dep. exec. dir. Am. Bd. Family Practice, Lexington, Ky., 1991-97, exec. dir., 1998—. Capt. MC, USAF, 1964-66. Office: Am Bd Family Practice 2228 Young Dr Lexington KY 40505-4219

AVARD, STEPHEN LEWIS, finance educator; b. Chgo., Feb. 16, 1940; s. William Richard and Helen M. (Gundy) A.; m. Bonnie J. Fulford, Sept. 1, 1962; children: Margaret, Stephen Jr., Jean. BA, Northwestern U., 1961; MBA, Tex. A&M U., Commerce, 1976; PhD, U. North Tex., 1983. CFA. Asst. city m gr. City of Highland Park, Ill., 1961-64; treas., asst. hosp. adminstr. Sherman (Tex.) Cmty. Hosp., 1964-69; hosp. cons. and zone supr. Tex. State Dept. Health, Austin, 1969-71; real estate broker John King Realtors, Sherman, 1971-73; pres. Miracle Gardens of Tex., Sherman, 1973-79; sec., gen. mgr. Med. Mart, Inc., Sherman, 1979-83; prof. fin. Tex. A&M U., Commerce, 1984—, head dept. econs. and fin., 1995—. Co-author (monographs): Feasibility Study for a Graduate Program in Health Care

Administration, 1984, Accounting for the Non-Accounting Manager, 1984, Overview of the Petroleum Industry, 1983, 89, 98; contbr. articles to refereed profl. jours. and conf. procs. (Top Six Best Articles, bd. editors Rsch. Mgmt. jour., 1983). Grad. fellow Gulf Oil, Inc., 1982. Mem. Assn. Investment Mgmt. and Rsch. (cons. higher order knowledge testing project 1999, active in testing process 1987—), Fin. Execs. Inst. (mem. acad. rels. com. Dallas chpt. 1988—), Dallas Assn. Investment Analysts, Rotary Internat. Avocation: sailing. Home: 1619 Crescent Dr Sherman TX 75092-5523 Office: Tex A&M U Econs-Finance Dept Commerce TX 75429

AVARY, ROGER ROBERTS, film director, writer; b. Flin Flon, Manitoba, Canada, Aug. 23, 1965; s. Edwin Roberts and Brigitte (Bruninghaus) A. Student, Art Ctr., Pasadena, Calif., 1985-88. Writer D'Arcy, Masius, Benton & Bowles, L.A., 1989-90, J. Walter Thompson, L.A., 1990—. Writer: (film) 99 Days, 1991, (with Mario Puzo) The Lorch Team, 1992; writer, dir. (film): Killing Zoe, 1993 (Yubari Internat. Film Festival Best Film award, 1994, Mystfest Best Film award, 1994, Mystfest Critics prize, 1994, Cannes Prix Tres Spl. Best Film award, 1994), True Romance, 1993; exec. prodr. (film): The Last Man, 1999; co-exec. prodr. (film): Boogie Boy, 1997; co-writer (film): Pulp Fiction, 1994 (L.A. Film Critics Assn. Best Screenplay award, 1995, N.Y. Film Critics Cir. Best Screenplay award, 1995, Boston Soc. Film Critics Best Screenplay award, 1995, Nat. Soc. Film Critics Best Screenplay award, 1995, Chgo. Soc. Film Critics Best Screenplay award, 1995, BAFTA Best Screenplay award, 1995, Acad. award best screenplay 1995), Hatchetman, 1995, (children's book) Marshall's Dreams, 1991, (music video) for the group The Go Go's song The Whole World Lost Its Head, 1994; writer, dir., prodr. (TV movie) Mr. Stitch, 1995. Office: DGA 7920 Sunset Blvd Los Angeles CA 90046*

AVED, BARRY, retail executive, consultant; b. Mpls., Mar. 27, 1943; s. Alick Leonard and Marna Claire (Sandon) A.; m. Marlys Sandra Drentlaw, Sept. 3, 1961; children: Andrea, Nicole Aved Badeau, Danielle, Rachelle. Grad. high sch., Mpls., 1961. Buyer Dayton Hudson Co., Mpls., 1963-72; v.p. Ltd. Stores, Columbus, Ohio, 1972-82; pres. Id, Inc., Green Bay, Wis., 1982-86; pres., CEO Brooks Fashion Stores, N.Y.C., 1986-89; pres. Ormond Stores, Inc., North Bergen, N.J., 1989-90; pres., CEO Lerner N.Y., N.Y.C., 1991-95; prin. Aved Cons., Lakeville, Minn., 1995—; bd. dirs. Tarrant Apparel Group. Avocations: swimming, fishing, reading.

AVEDISIAN, ARCHIE HARRY, community organization executive; b. Binghamton, N.Y., June 22, 1928; s. Harry and Charlotte (Charkjian) A.; m. Gloria Ann Rogers; children: Debra Ann, Anthony Joseph. BS in Edn., SUNY, Cortland, 1951; MA in Orgn. and Adminstrn., NYU, 1954, postgrad. Phys. dir. Jamestown Boys Club, N.Y.C., 1951-53; program dir. Flatbush Boys Club, Bklyn., 1953-56; exec. dir. Boys Clubs of East St. Louis, Ill., 1956-59, Columbia Park Boys Club, San Francisco, 1959-60, Santa Rosa Boys Clubs, Calif., 1960-67, Boys Clubs of Seattle and King County, 1967-72; pres. Boys and Girls Clubs of Greater Washington, D.C., 1972-95; pres. emeritus Boys & Firls Group Homes & Shelters, Balt. and Annapolis, Md., 1996-98; pres., CEO Archie Avedisian & Co., Montgomery Village, Md., 1998—; cons. Boys Clubs of Am. tng. program, 1974-75; tchr. Montgomery Coll., 1998—. Chmn. Seattle-King County Youth Commn., 1967-72, Congress for Community Programs, Santa Rosa, 1964, Calif. Youth Authority Sch. for Girls, 1961-66; United Way of Am., Washington, San Francisco, East St. Louis, Seattle, 1957—; bd. govs. Congress for Community Progress, East St. Louis, 1958; active President's Commn. on White House Fellowships, 1993, D.C. Bar Assn. Anti-Drug Coalition, 1993, Inst. of Internat. Edn. Met. Washington Consortium on Alcohol and Drug Abuse, 1992, Nat. Partnership Alcohol and Drug Abuse, 1986—, Greater Washington Billy Graham Crusade Adv. Com., 1986, Met. Washington Bd. Trade, 1973—, Montgomery County Employment Devel. Commn., 1978-82, Sonoma County Community Action Council, 1969, Govs. Conf. on Youth, Sonoma County, 1965, Gen. Plan Program, Santa Rosa, 1964. Recipient Disting. Svc. award Jr. C. of C., 1958, various gov. commd. awards, 1970-73, various United Way Am. awards, 1974-79, H. Roe Bartle Am. Humanities Recruiting award, 1979, Cmty. Svc. award Sales and Mktg. Execs. of Met. Washington, 1985, Chmns. award Greater Washington Soc. Assn. Execs., 1986, Cmty. Leadership award FBI Dirs., 1990, Alumni award SUNY, Golden Links award Bd. of Trade, Disting. Alumni award SUNY, Cortland; named one of Outstanding Young Men Am., 1965; named Outstanding Young Man of Yr., East St. Louis, 1958, Businessman of Day, Santa Rosa, 1967; presented key to San Francisco, 1959; Archie and Gloria Avedisian Ednl. Scholarship Fund established in his name, Boys and Girls Clubs. Mem. NAACP, Boys Clubs Profl. Assn. (numerous local and nat. offices 1953—), Boys Clubs Am. (numerous local and nat. offices 1951—), Nat. Soc. Fund Raisers (mem. membership com.), Greater Washington Soc. Assn. Execs. (chmn. various coms.), Am. Soc. Assn. Execs., Internat. Platform Assn., Ctr. for Devel. and Population Activities, Inst. Internat. Edn., D.C. C. of C. (various com. memberships, mem. bd. dirs. 1985—), Upper Montgomery County C. of C., 1986—, Jr. League of Washington Community (mem. adv. bd. 1991—). Republican. Roman Catholic. Clubs: Washington, D.C. Touchdown, Montgomery Village Golf (Gaithersburg, Md.), Tam O'Shanter Country (Bellevue, Wash.). Lodges: Rotary, Elks, Lions. Home and Office: 9832 Meadowcroft Ln Montgomery Village MD 20886-1337

AVEDISIAN, EDWARD, artist; b. Lowell, Mass., 1936. Student, Boston Museum Sch. Art. artist-in-residence U. Kans., 1969; instr. Sch. Visual Arts, N.Y.C., 1969-70, U. Calif. Irvine, 1972, U. La., 1973. One-man shows include Boyston Print Ctr. Gallery, Cambridge, Mass., 1957, Hansa Gallery, 1958, Tibor de Nagy Gallery, 1959, 60, Robert Elkon Gallery, N.Y.C., 1962-75, Galerie Zigler, Zürich, 1964, Nicholas Wilder Gallery, L.A., 1966, 68, 69, Kasmin Gallery, London, 1966, 67, Bucknell U. Art Gallery, 1970, Walter Moos Gallery, 1971, Jack Glenn Gallery, Corona del Mar, Calif., 1971, Janie C. Lee Gallery, Houston, 1974, Carriage House, Buffalo, 1975, 78, Fishback Gallery, 1979, Jason McCoy, Inc., N.Y.C., 1984, Mitchel Algus Gallery, 1995; exhibited in group shows at Tibor de Nagy Gallery, Tony Shafrazi, 1987, Boston Mus. Art, Mus. Modern Art, Washington, Whitney Mus. Art, Dayton (Ohio) Art Internat., Kasmin Gallery, Mus. Modern Art, N.Y.C., Jewish Mus., N.Y.C., Larry Aldrich Mus., San Francisco Mus. Art, Paintings From Expo '67, Boston Inst. Contemporary Art, Berkshire Mus., 1980; represented in permanent collections at Guggenheim Mus., Whitney Mus. Art, Mus. Modern Art, L.A. Mus. Art, Pasadena (Calif.) Mus. Art, Larry Aldrich Mus., Wadsworth Atheneum, Met. Mus., N.Y.C., others. Address: 26 Warren St Hudson NY 12534-3119

AVEDON, RICHARD, photographer; b. N.Y.C., May 15, 1923; s. Jack and Anna (Polonsky) A.; m. Dorcas Nowell, 1944; m. Evelyn Franklin, Jan. 29, 1951; 1 child, John. Student, Columbia U., 1941-42; studied with Alexey Brodovitch, Design Lab. New Sch. for Social Rsch., N.Y.C., 1944-50; DSc (hon.), Royal Coll. Art, London, 1989, Parsons Sch. Design, N.Y.C., 1994, Kenyon Coll. Staff photographer Jr. Bazaar, 1945-47, Harper's Bazaar, 1945-65; photographer French collections, 1947-84; staff photographer, editor Theatre Arts, 1952-53; staff photographer Vogue mag., 1966-90; first staff photographer The New Yorker, 1992—; Visual cons. for film: Funny Face, Paramount Studios, 1957; conducted master class in photog. (with Marvin Irael), Avedon studio, 1967. Author: (comments by Truman Capote) Observations, 1959, (text by James Baldwin) Nothing Personal, 1964, (intro. by Harold Rosenberg) Portraits, 1976, (essay by Harold Brodkey) Avedon Photographs, 1947-1977, 1978, In the American West, 1985; author spl. bicentennial edit. Rolling Stone mag. The Family, 1976; editor: Diary of a Century (photographs by Jacques Henri Lartigue), 1970, (with Doon Arbus) Alice in Wonderland: The Forming of a Company, The Making of a Play, 1973, An Autobiography, 1993, (essays by Jane Livingston, Adam Gophik) Evidence: 1944-94, 1994; photographs in permanent collections: Smithsonian Instn., Met. Mus. Art, N.Y.C., Mus. Modern Art, N.Y.C., Amon Carter Mus., Fort Worth, San Francisco Mus. Modern Art, Mus. Fine Arts, Houston, Victoria and Albert Mus., London, Nat. Portrait Gallery, Washington, Nat. Portrait Gallery, London, Ctr. for Creative Photography U. Ariz., Tucson, Kunstaus Zurich, Switzerland, Kunstaus, Basel, Switzerland, Andreas Reinhart Found., Winterthur, Switzerland; one-man retrospective exhbn. Smithsonian Instn., Washington, 1962, Mpls. Inst. Arts, 1970, Univ. Art Mus., Berkeley, Calif., 1980, Whitney Mus. Am. Art, 1994; one-man shows: Mus. Modern Art, 1974, Marlborough Gallery, 1975, Met. Mus. Art, N.Y.C., 1978, Amon Carter Mus., 1985, Corcoran Gallery of Art, Washington, DC, San Francisco Mus. Modern Art, Art Inst. Chgo., Phoenix Art Mus., Inst. Contemporary Art, Boston, The High Museum, Atlanta, 1985, Installation Brandenburg Gate, Carnegie Mus. of Art, Pitts., 1991; group shows include: Mus. Modern Art, 1955, Met. Mus. Art, 1959, 60, 63, 67, Musée Réattu, Arles, France, 1965, N.Y. World's Fair, 1965-66, Fogg Art Mus., Cambridge, Mass., 1967, Mus. Modern Art, N.Y.C., 1964, 65, 69, Expo '70, Osaka, Japan, 1970, Whitney Mus. Am. Art, 1974, Corcoran Gallery Art, Washington, 1985, Nat. Gallery Art, Washington, 1989; photographed civil rights movement in the South, 1963, anti-war movement across U.S., 1969, Vietnam, 1971, Am. Working Class, 1978-84. With USMC, 1942-44. Recipient highest achievement medal awards Art Dirs. Show, 1950—; voted one of world's ten greatest photographers Popular Photography, 1958; citation of dedication to fashion photography Pratt Inst., 1976; Nat. Mag. award Visual Excellence, 1976; Pres.'s fellow RISD, 1978; Chancellor's citation U. Calif., Berkeley, 1980; named to Hall of Fame Art Dirs. Club, 1982; Photographer of Yr., Am. Soc. Mag. Photographers, 1985; Best Photog. Book of Yr. award Maine Photog. Workshop, 1985; Dir. of Yr., Adweek mag., 1985; Comml. Dir. of Yr. award of excellence Eastman Kodak, 1985; Lifetime Achievement award Coun. Fashion Designers Am., 1989.; Internat. Photography prize Erna and Victor Hasselblad Found., 1991; Master of Photography award Internat. Ctr. Photography, 1993, Prix Nadar Bibliotheque Nationale, 1994, Humanitarian award Mental Health Assn., N.Y.C., 1996. Office: The New Yorker 20 W 43rd St New York NY 10021-3102

AVELLA, JOHN THOMAS, principal, school administrator; b. Passaic, N.J., June 23, 1957; s. John T. and Margaret Louise (Watson) Avella; m. Jane Marie Myers; children: Katelyn Mary, Shaylyn Clare. BS in Spl. Edn., Trenton State Coll., 1981; MA in Ednl. Adminstrn., Georgian Ct. Coll., 1986; postgrad., Nova Southeastern U., 1997—. Tchr. Lacey Twp. (N.J.) Bd. Edn., 1982-88; supr. Union City Edn. Svcs. Commn., Westfield, N.J., 1988-89; prin., sch. supt. Monmouth Ocean Edn. Svcs. Commn., Freehold, N.J., 1989—. Mem. Nat. Assn. Secondary Sch. Prins. Avocations: sports, music. Address: 3435 Hwy 9 PO Box 1264 Freehold NJ 07728

AVELLA, JOSEPH RALPH, university executive; b. N.Y.C., Nov. 13, 1942; s. Salvatore Ralph and Bianca (Artoni) A.; m. Elizabeth Theresa Eberhardt, Aug. 12, 1967 (div. May 1991); children: Edward Jay, James Joseph. BS in Chemistry, Rensselaer Poly. Inst., 1964; MA, Cath. U. Am., 1992, PhD, 1995. Mgr. Md. ops. The Great Atlantic and Pacific Tea Co., Inc., 1978-83; program mgr. Honeywell Fed. Sys., Inc., McLean, Va., 1984-86, mgr. integration svcs., 1987-89; dep. dir. mobilization Office of Sec. Def., Washington, 1990-92, dir. internat. programs, 1992-93; sr. fellow global strategy program Potomac Found., McLean, 1995-98; prof. and acad. dean Am. Mil. U., Manassas, Va., 1995-98; cons. Masi Rsch. Cons., Inc., Washington, 1995-97; exec. sec. NATO Forces Com., Brussels, Belgium, 1992-94; seminar moderator U.S. Naval War Coll., Newport, R.I., 1989-91; pres. Delphic Consulting Inc., 1998; exec. v.p. Capella U., 1998—. Contbr. articles to profl. jours. With USNR, 1970-95. Recipient Achievement award No. Va. Navy League, 1989, Cert. of Apprecation Sec. of Navy, 1986, 88, Award of Appreciation U.S. Naval Sea Cadet Corps, 1986. Mem. Am. Polit. Sci. Assn., Ctr. for Study of Presidency (contbg. author), U.S. Strategic Inst., Assn. Naval Aviation (past cpt. sec.), Navy League of U.S. (former mem. bd. dirs.), U.S. Naval Inst. (contbg. author), Pi Sigma Alpha. Home: 20 2nd St NE Apt 2105 Minneapolis MN 55413-4207 Office: Capella Univ 330 2nd Ave S Ste 550 Minneapolis MN 55401-2213

AVENT, CHARLES KIRK, medical educator; b. Memphis, Oct. 27, 1939; s. C. Harold and Emily Schoolfield (Wallace) A.; m. Rosalie Phillips Adams, Aug. 16, 1962 (div. Mar. 1981); children: Emily Wallace, Mary Adams Avent Mezera; m. Nancee Ruth Neel, Dec. 17, 1983; 1 child, Clayton B. Neel. BA, Vanderbilt U., 1961; MD, Harvard Med. Sch., 1965. Diplomate Am. Bd. Internal Medicine. Resident in medicine Univ. Hosp., Birmingham, 1965-68; fellow in infectious disease U. Washington, Seattle, 1968-70; from instr. medicine to prof. U. Ala. Sch. Medicine, Birmingham, 1970—; dir. med. clerkships U. Ala. Sch. Medicine, Birmingham, 1981—, title IX coord., 1976-78. Author: Medicine for Mountaineering, 1992. Mem. Am. Coll. Physicians, Infectious Disease Soc. Am., Phi Beta Kappa, Alpha Omega Alpha. Office: U Ala Sch Medicine 609 MEB UAB Sta Birmingham AL 35294

AVENT, SHARON H., consumer products company executive. Sr. v.p. Smead Mfg. Co., Hastings, Minn. Office: Smead Mfg Co 600 Smead Blvd Hastings MN 55033-2219*

AVERCH, HARVEY ALLAN, economist, educator, academic administrator; b. Denver, Dec. 18, 1935; s. Louis and Gussie (Weiner) A.; m. Barbara Ann Duvall, July 5, 1962; children: Elizabeth, Caroline. AB. summa cum laude (Univ. scholar), U.Colo., 1957; Ph.D. (Univ. fellow, Ford Found. fellow), U. N.C., 1962. Sr. staff economist Rand Corp., Santa Monica, Calif., 1961-71; dir. Div. Social Systems and Human Resources, Research Applications Directorate, NSF, Washington, 1971-74; dep. asst. dir. for analysis and planning Div. Social Systems and Human Resources, Research Applications Directorate, NSF, 1974-75, acting asst. dir. for sci. edn., 1975-76, asst. dir. for sci. edn., 1976-77, asst. dir. sci., technol. and internat. affairs, 1977-82, sr. staff assoc. Office of Dir., 1985-89; prof. pub. adminstrn., acting dir. Fla. Internat. U., 1989-90, prof., dir., 1990-94, prof., 1994—; mem. faculty UCLA, 1963-64, Calif. Inst. Tech., 1967, Rand Grad. Inst., 1970-71; vis. prof. policy scis. and econs. U. Md.-Baltimore County, 1982-85, adj. prof. policy scis. and econs., 1985—. Author: Behavior of the Firm Subject to Regulatory Constraint, 1962, Asymmetry and Arms Control: Some Basic Considerations, 1963, (with M. Lavin) Simulation of Decision-Making in Crisis: Three Manual Gaming Experiments, 1964, (with F. Denton and J. Koehler) A. Crisis of Ambiguity: Political and Economic Development in the Philippines, 1970, The Matrix of Policy in the Philippines, 1971, (with others) How Effective is Schooling: A Critical Review and Synthesis of Research Findings, 1972, How Effective is Schooling: A Critical Review of Research, 1974, A Strategic Analysis of Science and Technology Policy, 1985, Applied Social Science, Policy Science, and The Federal Government, 1987, Measuring The Cost-Efficiency of Basic Research Investments, 1987, Exploring the Cost-Efficiency of Basic Research Funding in Chemistry, 1989, Policy Research for the University Research System, 1989, Private Markets and Public Interventions, 1990, The Political Economy of R&D Taxonomies, 1991, Practice of Research Evaluation in the United States, 1991, Evaluation of Projects and Portfolios, 1992, Systematic Use of Expert Judgment, 1994, Evaluation of Urban Model, 1997; chief coeditor Policy Studies Rev., 1990—; contbr. articles to profl. jours. Chmn. U.S./Israel Binat. Sci. Found., 1979. Recipient Meritorious Service award NSF, 1973, Disting. Service award, 1977. Mem. Phi Beta Kappa. Office: Fla Internat U Sch Policy & Mgmt Aca #1 North Miami FL 33181

AVERILL, BRUCE ALAN, chemistry educator; b. Bucyrus, Ohio, May 19, 1948; s. Kenneth L. Averill and Mildred (Reid) Krug; m. Patricia Ann Eldredge, Aug. 23, 1986; children: Lindsay Patricia, Alan Eldredge, Ryan Eldredge. BS, Mich. State U., 1969; PhD, MIT, 1973. Asst. prof. chemistry Mich. State U., East Lansing, 1976-81, assoc. prof. chemistry, 1981-82; assoc. prof. chemistry U. Va., Charlottesville, 1982-88, prof. chemistry, 1988-94; prof. biochemistry U. of Amsterdam, 1994—; mem. biophysics adv. panel NSF, Washington, 1985-88; mem. faculty forum for sci. rsch. U. Va., Charlottesville, 1984-88; group leader protein rsch. and coord. chemistry working parties Dutch Found. Chem. Rsch., 1995—, mem. exec. com. protein rsch. working party, 1996-99. Contbr. over 125 articles to sci. jours. A.P. Sloan fellow, 1981-83; recipient creativity award NSF, 1991. Mem. AAAS, Am. Soc. Biochemistry and Molecular Biology, Am. Chem. soc., Royal Soc. Chemistry, Soc. Biol. Inorganic Chemistry, Dutch Soc. for Biochemistry and Molecular Biology, Sigma Xi. E-mail: baa@chem.uva.nl. Office: EC Slater Inst U Amsterdam, Plantage Muidergracht 12, 1018 TV Amsterdam The Netherlands

AVERILL, ELLEN CORBETT, secondary education science educator, administrator; b. Milledgeville, Ga.; d. Felton Conrad and Vivian Iris (Brookins) Corbett; m. George Edmund Averill, July 31, 1971; 1 child, John Conrad. BS, U. Ga., 1966, MS, 1971; teaching cert., Columbus Coll., 1979, EdS, 1994. Grad. teaching asst. U. Ga., Athens, 1966-68; tchr. sci. Decatur (Ga.) City Schs., 1971-72; tchr. sci., chair dept. Kendrick High Sch., Columbus, Ga., 1980—; rsch. asst. Caretta Rsch. Project, Savannah (Ga.) Sci. Mus., 1985, NEWMAST, Kennedy Space Ctr., 1986; rsch. assoc. Inhalation Toxicology Rsch. Inst., Albuquerque, summer, 1990; instr. sci. Gov.'s Honor Program Valdosta State Coll., summer, 1991, Woodrow Wilson Biotechnology Inst., Princeton, N.J., 1993. Contbr. articles to newspapers, jours.; inventor The Wrap-All, 1992. Mem. Nat. Sci. Tchrs. Assn. (program com., regional conf. 1993), Nat. Assn. Biology Tchrs. (Outstanding Biology Tchr. 1990-91), Ga. Sci. Tchrs. Assn. (dist. VI rep. 1988-90, secondary rep. 1990-91, pres.-elect 1991-92, pres. 1992-93, conf. coord. ann. conf. 1992, Dist. VI Sci. Tchr. of Yr. 1995), Coalition for Excellence in Sci. Edn. (orgnl. com. 1992-93), Ga. Sci. Tchrs. Edn. Found. (chair 1994-98), Valley Area Sch. Tchrs. (charter, pres.-elect 1996-97, pres. 1997-98), Muscogee Area Literacy Assn. (treas. 1992-93), Phi Delta Kappa (PDK Tchr. of Yr. 1992), Delta Kappa Gamma Edn. Soc. Unitarian-Universalist. Avocations: procelain art, gardening, amateur radio operator. Home: 126 Waterway Dr Cataula GA 31804-4077 Office: Kendrick High Sch 6015 Georgetown Dr Columbus GA 31907-4698

AVERILL, JAMES REED, psychology educator; b. San Francisco, Nov. 29, 1935; s. Dupree Reed and Rosalie (Diamond) Averill. B.A., San Jose U., 1959; Ph.D., UCLA, 1966. Psychologist U. Calif.-Berkeley, 1966-71; mem. faculty U. Mass., Amherst, 1971—, prof. psychology, 1976—. Served with U.S. Army, 1954-57. Fulbright fellow W. Germany, 1959-60. Mem. APA, Am. Psychol. Soc., Internat. Soc. for Rsch. on Emotion. Office: U Mass Dept Psychology Amherst MA 01003

AVERILL, RONALD HENRY, political science educator, retired military officer; b. L.A., Jan. 9, 1938; s. Alexander Anthony Averill and Anita Marie (Moser) Mitchell; m. Janice Louise Vaughan, Apr. 4, 1961; 1 child, Ella Louise Averill Morales. BA in Fgn. Svc., U. So. Calif., 1959; MA, Am. U., 1974. Lt. U.S. Army, Darmstadt, Germany, 1959-62; asst. prof. Mil. Sci. Okla. St. U., Stillwater, 1963-66; staff officer U.S. Army, 1968-73, comdr., 1974-89; instr. Hawaii Pacific U., Honolulu, 1989-91, South Puget Sound C.C., Olympia, Wash., 1992—. Chmn. St. Mary's Parish Coun., Centralia, 1993-96, Lewis County Nat. Resources Com., Chehalis, 1994—, Lewis County Solid Waste Adv. Com., Chehalis, 1994—, Lewis County Rep. Cen. Com., 1997—. Mem. Am. Legion (post 17), Nat. Intersch. Coaches Assn. (soccer coach 1969-97), Assn. U.S. Army, The Retired Officers Assn., Lewis County Farm Bur. (legis. liaison 1994), Knights of Columbus (past grand knight, recorder, 1995—), VFW. Republican. Roman Catholic. Avocation: soccer coach. Home: 2523 Graf Rd Centralia WA 98531-9087 Office: S Puget Sound C C 2011 Mottman Rd SW Olympia WA 98512-6218

AVERITT, RICHARD GARLAND, III, financial services company executive; b. Kearney, Nebr., Jan. 27, 1945; m. Sandra Louise Smith, June 7, 1967; children: Dawn, Rick, Scott. BA, Duke U., 1967. Cert. fin. planner. Account exec. Merrill Lynch, Pierce, Fenner & Smith, Atlanta, 1976-78; v.p. Consol. Planning Co., 1978-84; v.p. mktg. Investment Mgmt. & Rsch. Inc. (now Raymond James Fin. Scvs.), Atlanta, 1984-87, lst v.p., dir. mktg., 1987-91, sr. v.p., nat. sales mgr., 1991-97, exec. v.p., 1997—, also bd. dirs. Founding chmn. Atlanta Area Marine Corps Coord. Coun. Col. USMCR ret. Mem. Internat. Assn. Fin. Planning (bd. dirs. Ga. chpt. 1978-79), Inst. Cert. Fin. Planners, Mensa. Republican. Office: Raymond James Fin Svcs 3 Ravinia Dr Ste 1950 Atlanta GA 30346-2145

AVERITTE, CLINTON E., federal judge; b. 1948. BS, U. Tex., 1971; JD, So. Meth. U., 1974. Asst. atty. gen. Atty. Gen.'s Office, Tex., 1974-77; ptnr. Hiersche, Martens & Averitte, Dallas, 1977-78; asst. dist. atty., chief bus. crimes divsn. Lubbock County Dist. Atty.'s Office, 1979-80; asst. U.S. atty. U.S. Dist. Ct. (no. dist.) Tex., Lubbock, 1980-85, magistrate judge, 1987—; asst. U.S. atty., chief Amarillo divsn. U.S. Dist. Atty.'s Office, 1985-87. Mem. Amarillo Bar Assn., Order of Coif. Office: US Dist Ct No Dist Tex 205 E 5th St Amarillo TX 79101

AVERY, A. NELSON, physician, medical educator; b. Austin, Tex., June 1, 1947; s. Charles N. Jr. and Lucille S. Avery; 1 child, Mary. BA, U. Tex., 1969; MD, U. Tex., Galveston, 1973. Diplomate Am. Bd. Internal Medicine, Am. Bd. Preventive Medicine. Resident in internal medicine U. Tex. Med. Br., Galveston, 1973-76; ptnr. Capital Med. Clinic, Austin, Tex., 1976-93; dir. Ctr. for Occupl. and Corp. Health, Austin, Tex., 1993-96; assoc. prof., dir. environ. health U. Tex. Med. Br., Galveston, 1996—, dir. occupl. med. residency, 1998—; sr. occupl. med. cons. Motorola Semiconductor Products Sector, 1992—; sr. med. cons. Tex. Workers Compensation Ins. Fund, Austin, 1994—. Pres. Old Enfield Homeowners Assn., Austin, 1984-88. Mem. AMA, APHA, Am. Coll. Occupl. and Environ. Medicine, Soc. for Occupl. and Environ. Health, Semiconductor Safety Assn., Tex. Med. Assn., U. Tex. Med. Br. Alumni Assn. (pres. 1993-94, chmn. devel. bd. dirs. 1995-97), Alpha Omega Alpha. Avocation: scuba diving. E-mail: navery@utmd.edu. Office: U Tex Med Br 301 University Blvd Galveston TX 77555-0826

AVERY, BRUCE EDWARD, lawyer; b. Boonville, N.Y., Aug. 16, 1949; s. Edward Cecil and Marian Alma (Pierce) A.; m. Margaret Calvert, June 21, 1969; children: Sarah, Prudence. BA in Sociology, Polit. Sci., Hobart Coll., 1971; JD, U. Louisville, 1976. Bar: Ky. 1976, U.S. Ct. Mil. Appeals 1977, U.S. Army Ct. Mil. Rev. 1984, U.S. Supreme Ct. 1984, Md. 1992, D.C., 1993, U.S. Ct. Vet. Appeals 1992, U.S. Dist. Ct. Md. 1993. Commd. capt. U.S. Army, 1976, advanced through grades to maj., 1983; rschr. U.S. Army Rsch. Inst., Ft. Knox, Ky., 1972-76, atty., 1976-77; atty. U.S. Army, Camp Zama, Japan, 1977-80, U.S. Army Recruiting, Ft. Meade, Md., 1980-83, U.S. Army Claims Svc., Ft. Meade, 1984-87, U.S. Armed Forces Claims Svc., Seoul, Korea, 1987-89; chief claims V Corps, Frankfort, Germany, 1989-91; pvt. practice Rockville, Md., 1991—. Mem. Ft. Knox Bd. Edn., Ky., 1975-76. Mem. ABA, ATLA, FBA, D.C. Bar, Md. State Bar., Ky. Bar Assn. Office: 51 Monroe St Ste 1509 Rockville MD 20850-2408

AVERY, BYLLYE YVONNE, health association administrator. BA in Psychology, Talladega Coll., 1959; MEd in Spl. Edn., U. Fla., 1969; LHD (hon.), Thomas Jefferson U., 1990, SUNY, Binghamton, 1990, Bowdoin Coll., 1993; LLD (hon.), Bates Coll., 1995. Occupl. and recreational therapy aide N.E. Fla. State Hosp., 1959-65; resource tchr. for emotionally disturbed Richard L. Brown Elem. Sch., Jacksonville, Fla., 1966-68; learning disabilities resource tchr. Waldo (Fla.) Cmty. Sch., 1969-70; head tchr. children's mental health unit U. Fla., Gainesville, 1970-76, instr. dept. psychiatry, 1970-76; co-founder, dir. edn. Gainesville, 1976-78; co-founder, dir. pub. rels. Birthplace: An Alternative Birth Environment, Gainesville, 1978-80; dir. CETA Santa Fe C.C., Gainesville, 1980-82; exec. dir., founder Nat. Black Women's Health Project, Atlanta, 1982-90, founding pres., 1990-97; founding pres. Nat. Black Women's Health Project, Washington, 1997—; vis. fellow dept. health and social behavior Sch. Pub. Health Harvard U., 1991-93; cons. in field. Contbr. articles to profl. publs.; prodr. films: It's Up To Us (PBS documentary), 1985, On Becoming A Woman: Mothers and Daughters Talking Together, 1987. Bd. dirs. Nat Women's Health Network, 1976-81, New World Found., 1986-91, W.K. Kellogg Internat. Friendship Program, 1989-94, Boston Women's Health Book Collective, 1990-92, Global Fund for Women, 1989—, Internat. Women's Health Coalition, 1989—; bd. visitors Tucker Found. Dartmouth Coll., 1990—; mem. women's cancer adv. bd. Dana Farber Cancer Ctr., Boston; mem. adv. com. on rsch. on women's health Office Rsch. on Women's Health, NIH, Bethesda, Md. Recipient Outstanding Woman of Color award Nat. Inst. Women of Color, 1987, NOW, 1987, Svc. award Religious Coalition for Abortion Rights, 1988, Outstanding Svc. to Women and Children award Children's Def. Fund, 1988, award for cmty. svc. in sci., health and tech. award Essence mag., 1989, John D. and Catherine T. MacArthur Found. Fellowship award, 1989, Women of Achievement award YWCA, Atlanta, 1990, Orthro Woman of 21st Century award Orthro Pharm., 1991, Cmty. Svc. award Spelman Coll., 1991, Trends Setters award Nat. Health Coun., 1993, Woman of Achievement award Ms. Found., 1993, Grassroots Realist award Ga. Legis. Black Caucus, 1994, Gustav O. Lienhard award Inst. of Medicine, 1994, Dorothy I. Height Lifetime Achievement award, 1995, Pres.' citation Am. Pub. Health Assn., 1995. Office: Nat Black Women's Health Project 1211 Connecticut Ave NW Ste 310 Washington DC 20036-2709

AVERY, DONALD HILLS, metallurgist, educator, ethnographer; b. Hartford, Conn., May 7, 1937; s. Charles Raymond and Loma Ellinor (Mulholland) A.; children: Jon Weymouth, Nathaniel Caleb, Jessica van Voast; m. Mariana Pinchot, Dec. 3, 1994. Student, Loomis Inst., 1951-55; BS, MIT, 1959, ScD, 1962; MA, Brown U., 1969. Lic. profl. engr.; lic. pvt. detective. Pres. Strathmore Research Co., Cambridge, Mass., 1961-69; dir.

research Armor Flite Group, Rangely, Maine, 1973-83; pres. A.T.S. Cons. Engrs., 1980—; dir. A.P.C. Engrs., East Providence, R.I., 1977-82; asst. prof. M.I.T., 1962-66; asst. prof. Brown U., 1966-69, asso. prof., 1969-74, prof. engring., 1974-97, prof. emeritus, 1997—; vis. scholar, prof. U. Capetown, 1974, 76, 79, 82, 83; vis. fellow Yale U. Sch. Forestry, New Haven. Contbr. articles to profl. jours.; patentee in field. NSF fellow, 1959-62; Ford fellow, 1965; research scholar Tanzania, 1976, 79; research scholar Malawi, 1982, 83. Mem. AIME (Metall. Soc.), AAAS, AAU, Am. Soc. Metals (past chmn. R.I., Howe medal 1965), Soc. Plastics Engrs., Soc. Automotive Engrs., Hist. Metall. Soc., History Sci. Soc., Soc. History Tech., Hope Club, Explorers Club, Athenaeum, Barrington Yacht Club, Kasungu Farmers. Home: 142 Toandos Rd Quilcene WA 98376-9687 Office: Brown U Div Engring Providence RI 02912

AVERY, EVELYN MADELINE, English language educator; b. Bklyn., Jan. 18, 1940; d. Jack Gross and Faye Pittelman; m. Sheldon B. Avery, Dec. 5, 1936; children: Peter, Daniel. BA, Bklyn. Coll., 1961; MA in English, U. Oreg., 1968, PhD in English, 1976. Instr. English Aga Khan Secondary Sch., Kampala, Uganda, 1961-63, Lane C.C., Eugene, Oreg., 1969-72; instr. English Towson (Md.) U., 1974, prof. English, 1976—. Author: (book) Rebels and Victims: Fiction of Richard Wright and Bernard Malamud, 1980. Recipient summer stipend NEH, 1980. Mem. Nat. Assn. Scholars (steering com., bd. trustees 1987—), Assn. for Jewish Studies, N.E. MLA (exec. bd. 1992-95). Independent. Home: 3317 Marnat Rd Baltimore MD 21208-4508 Office: Towson U English Dept 8000 York Rd Towson MD 21252

AVERY, JAMES STEPHEN, oil company executive; b. Cranford, N.J., Mar. 24, 1923; s. John Henry and Martha Ann (Jones) A.; m. Joan Avery; children: Sheryl Ann, James Stephen. B.A., Columbia U., 1948, M.A., 1949. Pub. relations rep. Esso Standard Oil Co. (named changed to Exxon Co. U.S.A.), N.Y.C., 1956-63; coordinator community relations Humble Oil and Refining Co. (named changed to Exxon Co. U.S.A.), N.Y.C., 1963-68; mgr. pub. relations Exxon Co., Pelham, N.Y., 1968-71; mgr. pub. affairs Exxon Co. U.S.A., 1971-83, pub. affairs cons., 1983-86, ret. Vice-chmn., chmn. adv. com. to Vice Pres.'s Task Force on Youth Motivation, 1966-69; chmn. Union County (N.J.) Coordinating Agy. for Higher Edn., 1968-81; nat. vice-chmn. ann. campaigns United Negro Coll. Fund, 1962, 63, 64; trustee N.Y. and N.J. State Councils Econ. Edn., 1974-86, N.Y. State Traffic Coun., 1974-81, Coun. Mcpl. Performance, 1983-86; vice chmn. Phila. Regional Intro. to Minorities to Engring. and Other Sci-Math. Based Professions, 1986-95; bd. dirs. N.J. State Bd. Higher Edn.'s Opportunity Fund, 1988—, assistance bd., 1993—; trustee Lincoln U., Pa., 1994—. With AUS, 1942-46. Named one of 100 most influential blacks in Am. Ebony Mag., 1973. Mem. Nat. Assn. Market Devel. (pres. 1964-66, chmn. bd. 1967), Omega Psi Phi (Grand Basileus 1970-73). Baptist. Home: 201 Hidden Hollow Ct Edison NJ 08820-1054

AVERY, JAMES THOMAS, III, lawyer, management consultant; b. Richmond, Va., July 21, 1945; s. James Thomas Jr. and Hester Vail (Kraemer) A.; m. Nancy Carolyn Hoag, June 22, 1968; children: James Thomas IV, Carolyn Sears, John Dolph II. AB magna cum laude, Princeton U., 1967; MBA, JD, Harvard U., 1975. Bar: Mass. 1975, U.S. Dist. Ct. Mass. 1975, U.S. Ct. Appeals (1st cir.) 1975. Assoc. Choate, Hall & Stewart, Boston, 1975-79; dir. Cambridge (Mass.) Research Inst., 1979-85; pres. The Avery Co., Boston, 1985—; prin. Symmetrix, Inc., Lexington, Mass., 1992-94; pres., CEO PHH Fantus Cons., Inc., Hunt Valley, Md., 1995-97; bd. dirs. Boston Pub. Co. Treas. All Saints Ch., Brookline, Mass., 1976-78; vestryman Ch. of Redeemer, Chestnut Hill, Mass., 1985-89. Capt. U.S. Army, 1967-71, Vietnam. Decorated Bronze Star, Air medal. Mem. ABA, Phi Beta Kappa. Republican. Episcopalian. Clubs: Somerset, Harvard, The Second (trustee, sec. 1980-85) (Boston); Brookline Thursday. Avocations: tennis, golf, skiing.

AVERY, JULIA MAY, speech pathologist, organizational volunteer; b. Holly, Colo., May 2, 1917; d. Willard Smith and Bertha Eudora (Knuckey) A. AA, Colo. Women's Coll., 1936; BA, U. Colo., 1939; postgrad., UCLA, 1942, U. Calif., 1944, SUNY, Buffalo, 1946; MA in Speech Pathology, U. Colo., 1960. Cert. life tchr. and speech pathologist, Colo. Tchr. 4th-8th grades Mt. Harris (Colo.) Pub. Schs., 1939-41; tchr. 2d grade, spl. edn., speech pathology Pueblo (Colo.) Pub. Schs., 1941-77, spl. edn. tchr. physically handicapped, 1946-54; speech pathologist Pueblo, 1954—. Co-author: DiBur Speech Therapy Card Games (32 sets), 1959. Mem. adv. bd. Area Agy. on Aging; active United Way, Retarded Citizens Assn., bdd. dirs. YWCA, also past pres.; past pres., sec. Greehorn Valley Arts Coun., 1994-96; bd. dirs. Pueblo Arts Coun., also past pres. Named Tchr. of Yr., Star Jour., 1971, Chieftain, 1949-50; recipient Community Svc. award Optimists, 1985, 86, 87, numerous others. Mem. AARP (Colo. state legis. com. 1984-88, program dir. Community Housing Info. Sr. Svcs. 1991-93, health advocacy svc. local coord. 1993-96, state dental com., info. ctr. vol., local coord., treas. chpt. 2808 health advocacy svc.)), NEA (life), DAR (past pres. local chpt.), Am. Bus. Women's Assn. (scholarship chmn.), Colo. Gerontol. Soc. (bd. dirs. 1989-99), United Srs. of Colo. (pres. 1989, Colo. sr. lobby, area rep., lobbyist), Am. Speech and Hearing Assn. (past local pres.), Colo. Speech and Hearing Assn., Southeastern Colo. Hist. Soc. (pres. 1990-96), Colo. Archeol. Soc. (past state pres, C.T. Hurst award for extraordinary svc. 1992), League Club Bus. and Profl. Women (pres. 1991-95), Terr. Daus. Colo., Pueblo Beautiful Assn. (pres. 1994-96). Republican. Episcopalian. Avocations: history, archaeology, philately, music, drama, art. Home: 725 W Grant Ave Pueblo CO 81004-1414

AVERY, KAY BETH, secondary school educator; b. Pueblo, Colo., Apr. 11, 1950; d. John S. and Juanita M. (Burrus) Faris; m. Charles W. Avery, May 21, 1971; children: Cassie Louise, Carrie Leigh. BA in Speech and English, Ft. Hays (Kans.) State U., 1982; MS in Edn. Media tech., U. Miami, 1984, EdD in Instrnl. Leadership, 1986. Cert. tchr. speech, English, media, supervision and adminstrn. Tchr. English Unified Sch. Dist. 211, Norton, Kans., 1973-74; tchr. English, speech Dededo (Guam) Mid. Sch., 1974-78; tchr. English Bur. Indian Affairs, Ft. Wingate, N.Mex., 1979-80, Gallup (N.Mex.) H.S., 1980-83; media specialist Oak Ridge H.S., Orlando, Fla., 1986-90; tchr. English Gallup (N.Mex.) H.S., 1991-93; curriculum resource tchr. Osceola H.S., Kissimmee, Fla., 1990-93; tchr. English Poinciana H.S., Kissimmee, 1993—; facilitator of new methods, such as CRISS reading strategies and coop. learning. Contbr. articles to profl. jours. Co-chairperson sch. renewal com. Poinciana in Osceola Sch. Dist. Grantee Osceola County, 1991, 94, 95, 96, Found. for Osceola Edn., 1994, 96, Fla. Dept. Edn., 1990, Orange County, 1989, 90. Mem. NEA, ASCD, Internat. Reading Assn., Fla. Reading Assn., Nat. Coun. Tchrs. English, Fla. Coun. Tchrs. English, Phi Delta Kappa. Home: 219 Iowa Woods Cir W Orlando FL 32824-8638 Office: Poinciana High Sch 2300 S Poinciana Blvd Kissimmee FL 34758-2404

AVERY, MARY ELLEN, pediatrician, educator; b. Camden, N.J., May 6, 1927; d. William Clarence and Mary (Miller) A. AB, Wheaton Coll., Norton, Mass., 1948, DSc (hon.), 1974; MD, Johns Hopkins U., 1952; DSc (hon.), Trinity Coll., 1976, U. Mich., 1975, Med. Coll. Pa., 1976, Albany Med. Coll., 1977, Med. Coll. Wis., 1978, Radcliffe Coll., 1978; MA (hon.), Harvard U., 1974; LHD (hon.), Emmanuel Coll., 1979, Northeastern U., 1981, Russell Sage Coll., 1983, Meml. U., Newfoundland, 1993; DHL, Johns Hopkins U., 1999. Intern Johns Hopkins Hosp., 1953-54, resident, 1954-57; research fellow in pediatrics Boston, 1957-59, Balt., 1959-69; assoc. prof. pediatrics Johns Hopkins U., 1964-69; prof., chmn. dept. pediatrics McGill U. Med. Sch., 1969-74; prof. pediatrics Harvard U., 1974-97; physician-in-chief Montreal Children's Hosp., 1969-74, Children's Hosp. Med. Center, Boston, 1974-85; mem. Med. Rsch. Coun. Can.; mem. study sect. NIH, 1968-71, 84-88. Author: The Lung and Its Disorders in the Newborn Infant, 4th edit., 1981, (with A. Schaffer) Avery's Diseases of the Newborn, 7th edit., 1998, (with H.W. Taeusch and R. Ballard), 1998; (with G. Litwack) Born Early, 1984; author, editor: (with L. First) Pediatric Medicine, 1988, 2d edit., 1994; also articles; mem. editorial bd. Pediatrics, 1965-71, Am. Rev. Respiratory Diseases, 1969-73, Am. Jour. Physiology, 1967-73, Jour. Pediatrics, 1974-84, Medicine, 1985, Johns Hopkins Med. Jour., 1978-82, Clin. and Investigative Critical Care Medicine, 1990-96, New Eng. Jour. Medicine, 1990-95. Trustee Wheaton Coll. (1965-85), Radcliffe Coll., Johns Hopkins U., 1982-88. Recipient Mead Johnson award in pediatric rsch., 1968, Trudeau medal Am. Thoracic Soc., 1984, Nat. Medal of Sci. NSF, 1991, Marta Philipson award Karolinska Inst., Stockholm, 1998; Markle scholar in med. scis., 1961-66. Fellow AAAS (dir. 1989), NAS (mem. coun. 1997—), Internat. Pediatric Assn. (standing com. 1986-89), Am. Acad. Pediat., Am. Acad. Arts and Scis.; mem. Can. Pediatric Soc., Am. Physiol. Soc., Soc. Pediatric Rsch. (pres. 1972-73), Royal Coll. Paediatrics and Child Health (hon.), Inst. Medicine (coun. 1987), Am. Pediatric Soc. (pres. 1990), Phi Beta Kappa, Alpha Omega Alpha. Address: 65 Grove St Wellesley MA 02482-7810

AVERY, ROBERT DEAN, lawyer; b. Youngstown, Ohio, Apr. 23, 1944; s. Donald Carson and Alta Belle (Simon) A.; m. Ann Mitchell Lashen, May 16, 1993; 1 child from previous marriage: Benjamin Robert. BA, Northwestern U., 1966; JD, Columbia U., 1969. Bar: Ohio 1971, Calif. 1973. Law clk. to Hon. Robert P. Anderson U.S. Ct. Appeals 2d Cir., N.Y.C., 1969-70; assoc. lawyer Jones, Day, Reavis & Pogue, Cleve., 1970-74; assoc. lawyer Jones, Day, Reavis & Pogue, L.A., 1974-76, ptnr., 1977-98, adminstrv. ptnr., 1990-92; ptnr. Jones, Day, Reavis & Pogue, Chgo., 1999—. Editor: Columbia Law Rev., 1968-69. Dir. Wilshire YMCA, L.A., 1981-88. Harlan Fiske Stone Scholar. Home: 45 E Divsion St Chicago IL 60601 Office: Jones Day Reavis & Pogue 77 W Wacker Dr 35th Fl Chicago IL 60601

AVERY, ROBERT NEWELL, sculptor; b. May 22, 1940; s. Robert Newell and Margaret (Andrews) A.; m. Karen Lissol, Aug. 27, 1963 (div. 1978); 1 child, Robert Walter; m. Amanda Fair Jones, May 5, 1979; 1 child, Melinda Hopkins. BFA, Calif. Coll. Arts and Crafts, Oakland, 1962; postgrad., Coll. of San Mateo, Calif., 1969-70, Coll. of Redwoods, 1975-76. Freelance comml. artist Mendocino, Calif., 1971-75; exec. dir. Mendocino Art Ctr., Inc., 1975-79; proprietor Missing Link Prodns., Mendocino, 1979-93; mng. dir. Mezzanine Gallery at Daly's, Ft. Bragg, Calif., 1986-87, 91-93; exec. dir. Staunton/Augusta Art Ctr., Staunton, Va., 1995-96; proprietor Avery Studio Gallery, Staunton, 1996—; art dir. The Mendocino Rev., 1983-91; judge Sonoma County Fair, Santa Rosa, Calif., 1977; auctioneer many arts/ednl./polit. events; art dir. The Mendocino Rev. #3, 1975; disc jockey Radio Sta. KMFB-FM, Mendocino, 1971-73, KJAZ-FM, Berkeley, Calif., 1960-61; lead player (play) The Great American Desert, 1975, Candida, 1977, Mousetrap, 1978, Rain, 1979, The Real Inspector Hound, 1984; prodr.: Twin Peaks (stage play), 1985; host interviewer: Art View, 1987-89, The Now and Then Show, 1985-91; prodr., programmer radio show: Odd Bob Comedy Show, KZYX-FM, 1989-90. Contbr. articles, photographs, illustrations to profl. jours.; columnist The Mendocino Daily Planet, 1972-73, The Mendocino Beacon, 1975-79, The New Settler Interview, 1986, Mendocino Grapevine, 1977-82; illustrator: The House that Jack Built; one man shows include Winona Gallery, Mendocino, 1990, Stock Exch. Deli, Waynesboro, Va., 1995, Augusta County Libr., Fishersville, Va., 1996; group shows include Mendocino Art Ctr., 1986, 1990, 91-93, Mayhew Wildlife Gallery, Mendocino, 1986-93, Mezzanine Gallery, Ft. Bragg, 1986-88, Caspar Studios Gallery, 1990, Shenandoah Valley Art Ctr., Waynesboro, Va., 1994-95, Beverley St. Studio Sch., Staunton, Va., 1995, Jordan Gallery, Charlottesville, Va., 1995, Lynchburg Fine Arts Ctr., 1995, Augusta Art Ctr., 1997, others;. Master of ceremonies 4th of July Parade, Mendocino, 1976-93; judge Bodega Bay Fisherman's Festival Ann. Arts Show, 1976; chmn. art acquisition com. Augusta Hosp. Corp., 1997; mem. founding bd. Mendocino Performing Arts Co., Inc.; past pres. Mendocino Cmty. Land Trust, Inc.; trustee Mendocino Unified Sch. Dist., 1973-77, pres., 1977; past dir. Mendocino Bus. and Profl. Coun.; mem. citizen's adv. coun. Coll. of the Redwoods, 1979-80; mem. exec. com. Calif. Arts Coun., Rural Arts Svcs., 1978-79; trustee Mendocino Art Ctr., Inc., 1980-85, chmn. citizen's adv. com., 1991, hon. life mem. Recipient numerous sculpture awards various art assns. Mem. Assn. of Sci. Fiction Artists, Internat. Sculpture Commn. Home and Office: Route 1 Box 91 Swoope VA 24479-9714

AVERY, STEPHEN GOODRICH, marketing professional, consultant; b. Bklyn., Apr. 22, 1938; s. Charles Leslie and Virginia (Cox) A.; m. Frona Sinexon (div. 1980); children: Heather Brodie, Wyckham Christie; m. Ellen Lowe, 1993. Student, Cornell U., 1962-64. Dir. food svc. Rutgers U., Camden, N.J., 1962-66, Franklin Pierce Coll., Rindge, N.H., 1967; advt. mgr. Keen (N.H.) Sentinel, 1967-68; advt. sales mgr. Yankee Pub. Co., Dublin, N.H., 1968-91; exec. commr. N.H. Highland Games, 1992-98; bd. dirs., New Eng. Travel and Tourism Rsch. Assn. Producer, dir. N.H. Internat. Mil. Tattoo, 1997—. Mem. N.H. Ho. of Reps., Concord, 1988—; del. White House Conf. Tourism, 1995; mem. Gov.'s tack Force Travel & Tourism; vice chmn. N.H. Commn. Smithsonian Festival, 1997. Fellow Soc. Antiquaries (Scotland); mem. Internat. Festival and Event Assn., N.H. Lodging and Restaurant Assn. (bd. dirs. 1983-87), Vt. Lodging and Restaurant Assn. (bd. dirs. 1982-88), Yankee Festival and Event Assn. (chmn. 1997), N.H. Gathering of Scottish Clans (bd. dirs. 1985-91), St. Andrews Soc. (bd. convenors 1999—). Republican. Episcopalian.

AVERY, STEVEN THOMAS, professional baseball player; b. Trenton, Mich., Apr. 14, 1970; s. Ken Avery. Pitcher Atlanta Braves, 1990-96, Boston Red Sox, 1996-98, Cin. Reds, 1999—. Named to Sporting News Nat. League All-Star Team, 1993. Office: Cin Reds Cinergy Field 100 Cinergy Field Cincinnati OH 45202*

AVERY, WILLIAM HINCKLEY, physicist, chemist; b. Ft. Collins, Colo., July 25, 1912; s. Edgar Delano and Mabel Abbey (Gordon) A.; m. Helen Wallace Palmer, July 18, 1938; children—Christopher, Patricia (Mrs. W. Randolph Bartlett, Jr.). AB, Pomona Coll., 1933; AM, Harvard, 1935, PhD in Phys. Chemistry, 1937. Postdoctoral research asst. infrared spectroscopy Harvard, 1937-39; research chemist Shell Oil Co., St. Louis, Houston, 1939-43; head propulsion div. Allegany Ballistics Lab., Cumberland, Md., 1943-46; cons. in physics and chemistry Arthur D. Little Co., Cambridge, Mass., 1946-47; profl. staff mem. Applied Physics Lab., Johns Hopkins Univ., Laurel, Md., 1947-73; asst. dir. exploratory devel. Applied Physics Lab., Johns Hopkins Univ., 1973-78, dir. ocean energy programs, 1978-89, ret., 1989; mem. various coms. DOD, NASA, NRC, Nat. Acad. Scis.; Nat. Acad. Engring., 1955—; mem. tech. adv. bd. panel on SST environ. research Dept. Commerce, 1971; mem. subcom. AEC, Pres.'s Energy Report, 1973. Author: Renewable Energy from the Ocean: A Guide to OTEC, 1994; contbr. articles to profl. jours. Recipient C.N. Hickman award, 1951, Presdl. certificate of merit, 1948, Naval Ordnance Devel. award, 1945, IR 100 award, 1979, Sir Alfred Egerton award, 1972, William H. Avery Propulsion Rsch. Lab. established in his honor Johns Hopkins U., 1989, renamed William H. Avery Advanced Tech. Devel. Lab., 1996. Fellow AIAA (tech. dir. 1968-71); mem. Am. Chem. Soc., Combustion Inst. (dir. 1960-80, Sir Alfred C. Egerton Gold medal 1971), Marine Tech. Soc., Cosmos Club (Washington), Phi Beta Kappa. Home: 237 N Main St # 353 South Yarmouth MA 02664 Office: Johns Hopkins U Applied Physics Lab Johns Hopkins Rd Laurel MD 20723

AVERY, WILLIAM JOSEPH, packaging manufacturing company executive; b. Chgo., June 20, 1940; s. Floyd Joseph and Margaret Mildred (Musard) A.; m. Sharon Bajorek, Sept. 5, 1959; children: Michelle, Martin, Sheryl. Grad. in indsl. mgmt., U. Chgo., 1968. With Crown Cork & Seal Co. Inc., Phila., 1959—, v.p. sales, 1974-79, sr. v.p. mfg. and sales, 1979-80, exec. v.p., 1980-81, pres., 1981-96, chmn., CEO, 1990—. Roman Catholic. Office: Crown Cork & Seal Co Inc 1 Crown Way Philadelphia PA 19154-4599*

AVERYT, GAYLE OWEN, insurance executive; b. Montgomery, Ala., Oct. 13, 1933; s. Edwin Franklin and Asenath Pratt (Murfee) A.; m. Margaret Rosborough Finlay, June 15, 1963; children: Caroline Elliott, Margaret McQueen, Elinor Finlay. BS cum laude, Davidson Coll., 1955; MBA, Harvard U., 1958; D Pub. Svc. (hon.), U. S.C., 1989. Chmn. bd. Colonial Cos., Inc., Columbia, S.C., 1970-93; bd. dirs. UNUM Cor., 1993—; bd. dirs., treas. Palmetto Bus. Forum, 1977-94; mem. S.C. Ins. Commn., 1976-84, S.C. State Ports Authority, 1994—, S.C. State Ports Authority, 1994—. Trustee Davidson Coll., N.C., 1980-84; pres. S.C. Orch. Assn., 1986-88. Recipient Order of Palmetto State of S.C., 1994, Disting. Alumnus award Davidson Coll., 1997—; named Business Man of Yr. S.C. C. of C., 1989; inducted into S.C. Bus. Hall of Fame, 1998. Mem. Phi Beta Kappa. Home: 1717 Greene St Columbia SC 29201-4014 Office: Colonial Cos Inc 1200 W Colonial Life Blvd Columbia SC 29210-7646

AVGERAKIS, GEORGE HARRIS, video producer; b. Trenton, N.J., July 4, 1948; s. Anastasios and Katherine (Harris) A.; m. Rarie R. Pastorelli, June 13, 1976; children: Stephanie, Alex. BA, U. Md., 1972; diploma, London Film Sch., 1974. Asst. prodr. Grey Advt., N.Y.C., 1975-78; prodr. Girl Scouts USA, N.Y.C., 1978-79; art dir. BASF-FD&O Divsn., N.Y.C., 1979-80; video prodr. Nabisco Brands, N.Y.C., 1980-82; v.p. exec. dir. Avekta Prodns. Inc., N.Y.C., 1982—. Contbg. editor Videography Mag., N.Y.C., 1991—; writer, dir. Russian situation comedy: Living Room, 1995; writer TV and home video: Celebrity Cooking with Jerry Lewis, 1994; animation designer TV program Horatio Alger Awards Ceremony, 1997; writer, prodr. JVC Booth at Nat. Assn Broadcasters Convention, 1998-99. Avocations: scuba diving, flying, sailing. Office: Avekta Prodns Inc 145 E 48th St New York NY 10017-1254

AVIAN, BOB, choreographer, producer; b. N.Y.C., Dec. 26, 1937; s. John Hampar and Esther (Keleshian) Avedisian. B.F.A., Boston U., 1959. Dancer, 1959-68; danced in: West Side Story, Broadway, 1960, Funny Girl, Broadway, 1964-65, assoc. choreographer, dir., Michael Bennett Prodns., N.Y.C., 1967-89, choreographer-producer, 1975—; Broadway prodns. include: Henry, Sweet Henry, 1967, Promises, Promises, 1968, Coco, 1969, Company, 1970, Follies, 1971, Twigs, 1971, Seesaw, 1973, God's Favorite, 1974, A Chorus Line, 1975 (Tony award for best choreography 1976, Los Angeles Drama Critics award for best choreography 1977), Ballroom (Tony award for best choreography 1979, Drama Desk award for choreography 1979); choreographer (London premieres): Follies, 1987, Miss Saigon, 1989, Sunset Boulevard, 1993 (Tony nomination, 1995), Martin Guerre, London, 1996 (Laurence Olivier award for best choreography 1996); prodr.: Dreamgirls, 1981.

AVIL, RICHARD D., JR., lawyer; b. Phila., Nov. 28, 1948; s. Richard Daniel and Elizabeth (McGinley) A.; m. Karen Mudry, May 27, 1972; children: Sierra Soo, Brier Sung, Winston Richard. BEE, Villanova U., 1970; JD, Cornell U., 1974. Law clk. U.S. Dist. Ct. Northern Dist. N.Y., 1974-75, 75-76, U.S. Ct. Appeals Second Cir., N.Y.C., 1976-77; assoc. Jones, Day, Reavis and Pogue, Cleve., 1977-83, ptnr., 1984-91; ptnr. Jones, Day, Reavis and Pogue, Washington, 1991—. Speaker in field. Mem. Fed. Energy Bar Assn. Home: 51 Louisiana Ave NW Washington DC 20001 Office: Jones Day Reavis & Pogue Met Sq 1450 G St NW Washington DC 20005-2088

AVILA, ARTHUR JULIAN, metallurgical engineer; b. Hoboken, N.J., July 9, 1917; s. Michael Angel and Caroline Elizabeth (Bauman) A.; m. Mary Noreen DeMartino, Oct. 23, 1948; children: Susan Ekkebus, Philip, Stephen, John. BSCE, NYU, 1946; MS in Metallurgy, Stevens Inst. Tech., 1952. cert. profl. chem. and metall. cons., N.J. Prodn. engr. Western Electric Co., Kearny, N.J., 1943-57; sr. staff engr. Western Electric Co., Chgo., 1967-72; rsch. supr. W.E. Engring. Rsch. Ctr., Princeton, N.J., 1957-67; tech. dir. TRW Cinch, Chgo., Elk Grove, Ill., 1973-74; cons. Avila Engring. Svcs., Des Plaines, Ill., 1974—. Author: Production Pulse Plating, 1984; co-author: Theory and Practice of Pulse Plating, 1986; patented in field. Commr. Cub Scouts, Middlesex, N.J. 1970; chmn. Boy Scouts Am., Middlesex, 1971-72; chmn. Cath. Youth Orgn. St. Mary's Parish, Flemington, N.J., 1960-65. Mem. Am. Soc. Metals, Am. Electroplaters Soc. Home and Office: 502 W Huntington Commons Rd Mount Prospect IL 60056-5278

AVILA, FERNANDO, automotive company executive; b. Mexico City, Mex., Nov. 12, 1951; came to U.S., 1996; s. Fernando and Maria Elena A.; m. Maria Guadalupe Salgado, Apr. 30, 1982; children: Fernando, Adriana. Diploma in engring., Univ. Nat. Autonoma Mex., Mexico City, 1975. Design engr. product engring. Ford, Mexico City, 1977-80, fin. analyst product planning, 1980-81, sr. analyst, 1981-85, chief product planning, 1987-90, chief imports, 1990-94, fgn. svc. specialist bus. planning, product devel., 1986-87, mktg. plan mgr. mktg. & sales, 1994-95, advtg. & sales promotions mgr., 1995-96; cross-vehicle mktg. plans mgr. mktg. sales & svc. Ford, Dearborn, Mich., 1996—, large vehicle ctr. mktg. plans and brand devel., 1997-98; trucks group brand mgr. Ford, Mex., 1999—; prof. calculus Univ. Nat. Autonoma Mex., 1975-82, indsl. designs Univ. Anahuac, Mexico City, 1988-89. Mem. Soc. Automotive Engrs. (v.p. 1991-92). Roman Catholic. Avocations: oil painting, tennis, travel. Office: PO Box 2053 MD1140 2000 Rotunda Dr Dearborn MI 48121-2053

AVILDSEN, JOHN GUILBERT, film director; b. Ill., Dec. 21, 1935; s. Clarence John and Ivy (Guilbert) A.; m. Tracy Brooks Swope, Feb., 1987; children: Anthony Guilbert, Jonathan, Bridget Emily Margaret. Student, NYU, 1955. Advt. mgr. Vespa Motor Scooters, 1959. Asst. dir. Greenwich Village Story, 1961; prodn. mgr.: Mickey One, 1964; 2d unit dir.: Hurry Sundown, 1964; with Muller, Jordan & Herrick Indsl. Films, 1965-67; dir. photography Out of It, 1967; dir. films Turn on to Love, 1967, Sweet Dreams, 1968, Guess What We Learned in School Today, 1969, Joe, 1970, Cry Uncle, 1971, Save the Tiger, 1972, Inaugural Ball, 1973, W.W. and the Dixie Dancekings, 1974, Rocky, 1976 (Acad. award for best direction), Slow Dancing in the Big City, 1978, The Formula, 1980, Neighbors, 1981, A Night in Heaven, 1983, The Karate Kid, 1984, Happy New Year, 1985, The Karate Kid II, 1986, For Keeps, 1987, The Karate Kid III, 1989, Lean on Me, 1989 (Image award NAACP), Rocky V, 1990, The Power of One, 1992, 8 Seconds, 1994, Coyote Moon, 1998; prodr., dir. documentary film Traveling Hopefully, 1982 (Acad. nomination for best documentary). Served with U.S. Army, 1959-61. Mem. Dirs. Guild Am., Motion Picture Photographers Union, Motion Picture Editors Union, Writers Guild Am. Office: care United Talent Agy Dan Aloni 9560 Wilshire Blvd Fl 5 Beverly Hills CA 90212-2401

AVILES, ALICE ALERS, psychologist; b. N.Y.C; d. Jose Oscar and Pauline (Irizarry) Alers; m. Jose A. Aviles, Aug. 13, 1954 (div. Oct. 1981); children: Jeffrey (dec.), Brian, Gregory; m. Clifford M. Goldman, June 29, 1997. BS magna cum laude, SUNY, Oswego, 1955; MA, Queens Coll., 1978; PhD, Yeshiva U., 1984; postdoctoral diploma in psychoanalysis, Adelphi U., 1991. Lic. psychologist, N.Y. Tchr. elem. schs. Spring Valley, N.Y., 1955, Erlangen (Fed. Republic Germany) Am. Sch., 1955-56; tchr. elem. schs. Uniondale, N.Y., 1956, Freeport, N.Y., 1957-58, Island Park, N.Y., 1973-75; psychology clk. Fifth Ave. Ctr. for Counseling and Psychotherapy, N.Y.C., 1978-80; psychology intern St. Vincent's Hosp. and Med. Ctr., N.Y.C., 1980-81; psychologist Kingsboro Psychiat. Ctr., Bklyn., 1981-84; psychologist to assoc. psychologist South Beach Psychiat. Ctr., Bklyn., 1984-86; pvt. practice Valley Stream, N.Y., 1985—; from staff psychologist to sr. psychologist Luth. Med. Ctr., Bklyn., 1986-95; cons. Beach Terrace Care Ctr., Long Beach, N.Y., 1995-97; mem. adv. com. Hispanic Counseling Ctr. of Family Svc. Assn. of Nassau County, Hempstead, N.Y., 1978-80; cons. Nassau County Extended Care Ctr., Hempstead, 1997-99, Resort Nursing Home, Far Rockaway, N.Y., 1998—. Ford found. grad. fellow, 1978-81. Mem. APA, N.Y. State Psychol. Assn., Nassau County Psychol. Assn. (mem. pvt. practice com. 1992-93), Adelphi Soc. Psychoanalysis and Psychotherapy. Office: 10 Valley Ln E North Woodmere NY 11581

AVISE, JOHN CHARLES, geneticist, educator; b. Grand Rapids, Mich., Sept. 19, 1948; s. Reginald Dean and Edith Dorothy (Johnson) A.; m. Joan Marie Yanov, Dec. 24, 1979; 1 child, Jennifer Ann. BS, U. Mich., 1970; MA, U. Tex., 1971; PhD, U. Calif., Davis, 1975. Asst. prof. U. Ga., Athens, 1975-79, assoc prof., 1980-84, prof., 1985—. Author: Molecular Markers, Natural History and Evolution, The Genetic Gods: Evolution and Belief in Human Affairs; contbr. articles to profl. jours. Recipient William Brewster Meml. award Am. Ornithologists' Union, 1997. Mem. AAAS, NAS. Avocations: nature study, sports. Office: Univ of Ga Dept of Genetics Athens GA 30602

AVISHAI, SUSAN E., artist, illustrator; b. Montreal, Que., Can., Mar. 18, 1949; came to U.S., 1980; d. Maurice Lawrence and Alice June (Weigensberg) Cheifetz; m. Bernard Israel Avisha, June 8, 1969 (div.); children: Benjamin, Ellie, Tamar. Student, Ont. Coll. Art, 1968-70; BFA, Sir George Williams U., Montreal, 1971. Freelance illustrator Boston, 1985—; guest lectr. Art Inst. Boston, 1995-96, Babson Coll., Wellesley, Mass., 1997-98. Illustrator: The House on Walenska Street (Charlotte Herman), 1990, Talking About Death: A Dialogue Between Parent and Child (Earl Grollman), 1990, By Brother's Bar Mitzvah (Janet Gallant), 1991, Bat Time (Ruth Horowitz), 1991, Sophie and the Sidewalk Man (Stephanie Tolan), 1992, A Visit to the Big House (Oliver Butterworth), 1993, A Friend for Life (Susan Nessim), 1994, When the Big Dog Barks (Munzee Curtis), 1996, Israel: The Founding of a Modern Nation (Maida Silverman), 1997.

Recipient drawing prize Cornerstone Gallery 1st Nat. Open, Falls Village, Conn., 1991, merit award Springfield (Mass.) Art League, 1992, 2nd pl. award Lake Worth (Fla.) Art League, 1993, Gallery Alliance award Colored Pencil Soc. Exhbn., Birmingham, Mich., 1993, 2nd pl. award Parkersburg (W.Va.) Art Ctr., 1994, 1st pl. award All New Eng. Color Show, Cohasset, Mass., 1997; one-woman shows include The Artists' House, Jerusalem, 1979, Rutgers U., MIT Faculty Club, Cambridge, Mass., 1981, Newton (Mass.) Pub. Libr., 1993, Lighthouse Gallery, Tequesta, Fla., 1995; exhibited in group shows at Bridgewater (Mass.) State Coll., Columbia (Mo.) Coll., 1982, Berkshire Artisan's Gallery, Pittsfield, Mass., 1985, Milton (Mass.) Art Mus., 1990, Radcliffe Coll., Cambridge, 1991, Rye (N.Y.) Arts Ctr., 1991, Cornerstone Gallery, Falls Village, Conn., 1991, Slater Meml. Mus., Conn., 1992, Springfield (Mass.) Mus., 1992, Francesca Anderson Fine Arts, Lexington, Mass., 1992, 93, 94, 95, 96, Boston Ctr. Arts, 1993, 95, Parkersburg (W.Va.) Art Ctr., 1993, 94, Lake Worth (Fla.) Art League, 1993, Andrea Marquit Gallery, Boston, 1994, Starr Gallery, Newton, Mass., 1994, 96, Chase/Freedman Gallery, Hartford, Conn., 1994, South Shore Arts Ctr., Cohasset, Mass., 1995, U. Mass. Med. Ctr., Worcester, 1995, Creative Arts Workshop, New Haven, 1995, Erector Square Gallery, New Haven, 1996, Perkins Gallery, Stoughton, Mass., 1997, All New Eng. Color Show, Cohasset, Mass., 1997, Horn Gallery Babson Coll., Wellesley, Mass., 1998. Democrat. Avocations: canoeing, hiking, camping. Home: 28 Marlboro St Newton MA 02458-2121

AVISON, DAVID, photographer; b. Harrisonburg, Va., July 13, 1937; s. Charles and Kathryn (Driver) A.; July 10, 1973. Sc.B., MIT, 1959; Ph.D., Brown U., 1966; M.S., Ill. Inst. Tech., 1974. Tchr. photography Columbia Coll., 1970-86; owner, operator Avison Photo Products. Exhibitions include Mus. Contemporary Photography, Chgo., 1973-76, 80, 81, 84-89, 95, 97, 98, Art Inst. Chgo., 1977, 78, 79, 80, 81, 82, 83, 84, 89, Grey Art Gallery, NYU, 1977, Dittmar Meml. Gallery, Northwestern U., 1974-76, 78, Crocker ARt Gallery, Sacramento, 1978, Block Gallery, Northwestern U., 1984, Burden Gallery, N.Y.C., 1985, Macintosh Mus., Scotland, 1985, Photography Archives U. Louisville, Ky., 1988, Chgo. Hist. Soc., 1989, Mesa (Ariz.) SW Mus., 1989, Davenport Mus. Art, 1992, Contemporary Arts Ctr., Cin., 1993, Musée des Beaux Arts, Reims, France, 1994, Addison Gallery Am. Art, Andover, Mass., 1998; represented in permanent collection, Mus. Modern Art, Art Inst. Chgo., Mus. Fine Art, Boston, Internat. Mus. Photography at George Eastman House, Rochester, N.Y., Dallas Mus. Fine Arts, Hallmark Collection, Kansas City, Mo., Exchange Bank, Chgo., Mus. Contemporary Photography, Chgo., Ball State U. Gallery, Muncie, Ind., No. Ill. U. Sven Parson Gallery, DeKalb. Photographers fellow NEA, 1977; Focus Infinity Fund grantee, 1987-88; recipient Time-Life Search for Photog. Talent award 1974. Studio: 300 Summer St Ste 58 Boston MA 02210-1115

AVIV, JONATHAN ENOCH, otolaryngologist, educator; b. N.Y.C., Aug. 24, 1960; s. David Gordon and Rena (Rod) A.; m. Robin Kiam, Nov., 1998. BA, Columbia U., 1981, MD, 1985. Diplomate Am. Bd. Otolaryngology, Nat. Bd. Med. Examiners. Resident dept. surgery Mount Sinai Med. Ctr., N.Y.C., 1985-87, resident dept. otolaryngology, 1987-90, fellow microvascular surgery, 1990-91; assoc. prof., dir. divsn. head and neck surgery Coll. Physicians and Surgeons, Columbia U., N.Y.C., 1991—; Co-founder AP Healthcare, L.L.C. Contbr. articles to profl. jours., numerous book chpts. Fellow Am. Soc. Head and Neck Surgery; mem. AMA, ACS (faculty), Am. Acad. Otolaryngology, Am. Acad. Facial, Plastic and Reconstructive Surgery, Am. Broncho-Esophagological Assn., N.Am. Skull Base Soc., N.Y. Head and Neck Soc., N.Y. Laryngological Soc. Achievements include development of and a patent for method and device to endoscopically measure sensory discrimination in throat and voice box. Office: Columbia-Presbyn Med Ctr Dept Otolaryngology 630 W 168th St New York NY 10032-3702

AVLON, HELEN DAPHNIS, artist; b. Manhattan, N.Y., June 18, 1932. BFA, Hunter Coll., 1975; MA in Art, Bklyn. Coll., 1976. Home: 463 West St Westbeth 632B New York NY 10014

AVNET, JONATHAN MICHAEL, motion picture company executive, film director; b. Bklyn., Nov. 17, 1949; m. Barbara Brody; children: Alexandra, Jacob, Lily. BA, Sarah Lawrence Coll., 1971; postgrad., U. Pa., 1967-69; student, Conservatory for Advanced Film Studies, 1972-73. Reader United Artists, L.A., 1974; dir. creative affairs Sequoia Pictures, L.A., 1975-77; pres. Tisch/Avnet Prodns., L.A., 1977-85; chmn. Avnet/Kerner Co., L.A., 1985—; pres. Allied Communications, Inc. Dir., producer: (motion pictures) Fried Green Tomatoes (3 Acad. award nominations, 3 Golden Globes, Writers Guild Gladd best feature film award), The War; producer, writer, dir. (TV series) Call To Glory, 1984-85 (Golden Reel award), Between Two Women (1 Emmy award); producer, exec. producer: (motion pictures) Risky Business, Men Don't Leave, Less Than Zero, When a Man Loves a Woman, Mighty Ducks(all three), Deal of the Century, Miami Rhapsody, Three Musketeers, and others; exec. producer: (movies of the week) The Burning Bed (8 Emmy nominations), Silence of the Heart, Heatwave (4 Cable Ace awards, including Best Picture), Do You Know the Muffin Man, No Other Loved, others. Trustee L.A. County Opera. Am. Film Inst. fellow. Mem. Am. Film Inst., Dir.s Guild of Am., Writers Guild of Am., Acad. Motion Pictures Arts and Scis., Producers Caucus. Avocations: basketball, skiing, biking.

AVRAM, HENRIETTE DAVIDSON, librarian, government official; b. N.Y.C., Oct. 7, 1919; d. Joseph and Rhea (Olsho) Davidson; m. Herbert Mois Avram, Aug. 23, 1941; children: Lloyd, Marcie, Jay. Student, Hunter Coll., N.Y.C., George Washington U.; ScD (hon.), So. Ill. U., 1977; DLitt (hon.), Rochester Inst. Tech., 1991; DSc (hon.), U. Ill., 1993. Systems analyst, methods analyst, programmer Nat. Security Agy., 1952-59; systems analyst Am. Rsch. Bur., 1959-61, Datatrol Corp., 1961-65; supervisory info. systems specialist Libr. of Congress, Washington, 1965-67, asst. coord. info. systems, 1967-70, chief MARC Devel. Office, 1970-76, dir. Network Devel. Office, 1976-80, dir. processing systems, network and automation planning, 1980-83, asst. libr. for processing svcs., 1983-89, assoc. libr. Collection Svcs., 1989-92; ret. Libr. Congress, 1992; chmn. network adv. com. Libr. of Congress, Washington, 1981-92, chmn. emerita network adv. com., 1992—; chair subcom. 2 sectional com. Z39 Am. Nat. Standards Inst., 1966-80, RECON Working Task F, 1968-73, Internat. Rels. Round Table, 1986=87, subcom. 4 working group 1 on character sets Internat. Orgn. for Standardization, 1971-80; lectr. sch. of info. and libr. sci. Cath. U. Am., Washington, 1973—, com. mem. strategies for 80's, 1980-81; bd. visitors libr. and learning resources com., 1980; mem. internat. standards coord. com. Info. Sys. Standards Bd., 1983-86; del. to U.S. nat. com. UNESCO/Gen. Info. Program, 1983; chair internat. rels. com. Nat. Info. Standards Orgn., 1983-92. Bd. editors: Jour. Library Automation, 1970-72; contbr. articles to profl. jours. Recipient Superior Svc. award Libr. of Congress, 1968, Margaret Mann citation, 1971, Fed. Woman's award, 1974, Achievement award ALA/Libr. Info. Tech. Assn., 1980, Meritorious Svc. award ANSI, 1992, Disting. Exec. Svc. award Fed. Govt., 1990; co-recipient Rsch. Libr. of Yr. award Assn. Coll. and Rsch. Libr. Acad., 1979. Fellow Internat. Fedn. Libr. Assns. and Instns. (chair working group on content designators 1972-77, chair profl. bd. 1979-81, mem. program mgmt. com. 1983-90, mem. exec. bd. 1983-87, 1st v.p. 1985-87); mem. ALA (bd. dirs., past pres. info sci. and automation div., John Ames Humphrey Forest Press award 1990, Melvil Dewey award 1981, Lippincott award 1988, Hon. Membership award 1997), Am. Soc. Info. Sci. (spl. interest group on libr. automation and networks 1965), Spl. Librs. Assn. (Recognition award 1990), Assn. Libr. and Info. Sci. Edn. (Libr. of Congress disting. svc. award 1992), Assn. Bibliog. Agys. Gt. Britain, Australia, Can. and U.S. (del. 1977—). Home: 44041 Fieldstone Way California MD 20619-2097

AVRIT, RICHARD CALVIN, defense consultant; b. Tilamook, Oreg., Feb. 18, 1932; s. Roy Calvin and Mary Louise (Morgan) A.; m. Alice Jane Tamminga, July 10, 1959; 1 dau., Tamra Jane. B.S. in Engring., U.S. Naval Acad., 1953; M.S. in Engring. Electronics, U.S. Naval Postgrad. Sch., 1960; postgrad., U.S. Naval War Coll., 1971-72. Commd. ensign U.S. Navy, 1953, advanced through grades to rear adm., 1979; served weapons dept. U.S.S. George K. Mackenzie, 1953-54; ops. dept. U.S.S. Willis A. Lee, 1954-57; comdg. officer U.S.S. Sumner County, 1960-63; project officer, staff of comdr. Operational Test and Evaluation Force, Key West, Fla., 1963-66; exec. officer U.S.S. Berkeley, 1966-68; ops. officer, AAW project officer Comdr. Cruiser Destroyer Florilla Nine, 1968-70; comdg. officer U.S.S. Sellers, 1970-71; mil. asst. for surface guns and missiles to asst. dir. Ocean Control Directorate, Def. Research and Engring., Office Sec. of Def., 1972-76; comdg. officer U.S.S. Harry E. Yarnell, 1976-78; chief of staff, comdr. Naval Surface Force U.S. Atlantic Fleet, 1978-79; project mgr. for Saudi Naval Expansion Program, Naval Material Command, Washington, 1979-82; dir. navy logistics plans Office Chief of Naval Ops., Washington, 1982-84; cons. Info. Spectrum, Inc., 1984-88; pres. Mil. Data Corp., Arlington, Va., 1989-91; small bus. cons., 1992—. Decorated D.S.M., Legion of Merit (3), Bronze Star with Combat V, Meritorious Service Medal (2). Mem. Naval Inst., IEEE. Methodist. Home: 4839 Keswick Ct Dumfries VA 22026-1084 Office: 1254 W Cedar Ave Denver CO 80223-1728

AWACHIE, PETER IFEACHO ANAZOBA, chemistry educator, research chemist; b. Umunnachi, Anambra, Nigeria, Aug. 31, 1952; came to U.S., 1994; s. Ifejika Okonkwo and Juliana Uluji (Malobi) A.; m. Miriam Nwaka Akudu, Dec. 23, 1988; children: Ifeanyichukwu Onefolu, Chisom Ogonna, Tochukwu Onyedikachi, Ifeacho Ifejika. BSc, U. Nigeria, Nsukka, 1978; PhD, U. Nigeria, 1986. Tutor chemistry State Edn. Commn., Enugu, Nigeria, 1979-89; rsch. assoc. U. Nigeria, Nsukka, 1982-89, asst. prof., 1989-94; rsch. fellow Shaman Pharms., Inc., South San Francisco, Calif., 1994-95; resource person Raw Materials R & D coun., Lagos, Nigeria, 1992—; rsch. assoc. Internat. Orgn. Chemistry in Devel., 1992—; faculty rep. Senate of U. Nigeria, 1993-94. Discovered organic reaction mechanism, 1990. Tchr., mentor Nat. Youth Svc. Corps, Lagos, 1978-79; co-founder Grad. Students' Union U. Nigeria, Nsukka, 1982, chmn. Kwame Nkrumah Hall, 1982-83. Rsch. grantee Stiftung Volkswagenwerk, Hannover, Germany, 1991; grad. scholar Fed. Ministry of Edn., Nigeria, 1982-84. Mem. AAAS, Am. Chem. Soc., Soc. Free Radical Rsch. (assoc. editor 1992—), Nigerian Soc. Pharmacognosy. Roman Catholic. Avocations: jogging, reading, hiking, classical music. Home: 417 Valley Hill Rd SW Apt K8 Riverdale GA 30274-2773

AWAIS, GEORGE MUSA, obstetrician, gynecologist; b. Ajloun, Jordan, Dec. 15, 1929; came to U.S., 1951; s. Musa and Meha (Koury) A.; m. Nabila Rizk, June 24, 1970. AB, Hope Coll., 1955; MD, U. Toronto, 1960. Diplomate Am. Bd. Obstetrics and Gynecology. Intern U. Toronto Hosps., Ont., Can., 1960-61, resident in obstetrics and gynecology, 1961-64, chief resident, 1965; chief resident Harlem Hosp., Columbia U., N.Y.C., 1966; asst. obstetrician and gynecologist Cleve. Met. Gen. Hosp., 1967, assoc. obstetrician and gynecologist, 1969; instr. obstetrics and gynecology Case Western Res. U., Cleve., 1967-70, asst. obstetrician and gynecologist MacDonald House, 1970, asst. prof., 1970, asst. clin. prof. dept. reproductive biology, 1971, asst. obstetrician and gynecologist Univ. Hosps., 1971; mem. staff, dept. gynecology Cleve. Clinic Found., 1971-91; chmn. dept. ob-gyn. King Faisal Specialist Hosp. and Rsch. Ctr., Riyadh, 1975-76; cons. panel mem. Internat. Corr. Soc. Obstetricians and Gynecologists, 1971; emeritus staff Cleve. Clinic Found., 1991; pres. Task Force on Humanitarian Aid and Relief Inc., 1997. Contbr. articles to publs. in field, papers, reports to confs., TV appearances, Saudi Arabia. Named Grand Officer of Order of Independence His Majesty King Hussein of Jordan, 1992. Fellow ACS, Am. Coll. Obstetricians and Gynecologists, Royal Coll. Surgeons Can.; mem. AMA, AAAS, Am. Infertility Soc., Arab Am. Med. Assn. (pres. 1991—, chmn. humanities relief 1996), Acad. Medicine of Cleve. Office: Cleve Clinic Found Emeritus Office EE/40 9500 Euclid Ave Cleveland OH 44195-0001

AWALT, MARILENE KAY, principal; b. Mineral Wells, Tex., Mar. 20, 1942; d. Pat O. T. and Mary Lee (Curry) Morse; children: Stacy (dec.), Bradley. BS, Tex. Wesleyan Coll., 1966; MS in Edn., Baylor U., 1972; PhD, George Peabody Coll., Vanderbilt U., 1988. Cert. tchr., prin., supr. Elem. tchr. San Antonio Pub. Schs., 1966, LaVega Pub. Schs., Waco, Tex., 1966-68; with reading clinic Baylor U., Waco, 1969-70; tchr. reading Franklin Spl. Schs. (Tenn.), 1970-71, first grade tchr., 1971-80, asst. prin., 1980-84, prin., 1984-90; prin. Moore Elem. Sch., Franklin, 1990-97, assoc. supt., 1997—. Mem. adv. council for tchr. cert. and edn. Tenn. State Sch. Bd., 1977-86; adminstr. career level III State of Tenn., 1987—. Tenn. spl. scholar, 1983-84. Named Tenn. Elem. Prin. of Yr., 1994, Nat. Disting. Prin. Tenn., 1996. Mem. ASCD (bd. dirs. 1992-95, exec. coun. 1995-98), Mid. Tenn. Coun. Internat. Reading Assn., Internat. Reading Assn., Tenn. Assn. Supervision and Curriculum Devel. (pres. 1986-87, 92-93, exec. sec. 1993—), Tenn. Bd. of Examiners for State for Approval of Tchr. Edn., Delta Kappa Gamma (pres. Rho chpt.). Baptist. Co-author Religious Christian Day Sch. Curriculum, 1978; author: Study Book for 6-8 Year Olds, 1980; chmn. for revision elem. cert. State of Tenn. Office: Franklin Schs 507 New Highway 96 W Franklin TN 37064-2470

AWAN, AHMAD NOOR, civil engineer; b. Chakwal, Punjab, Pakistan, June 2, 1942; came to U.S., 1969; s. Ghulam Hussain and Sayada Awan; m. Nargis Parveen Janjua, Dec. 24, 1972; children: Monazza, Shujah, Noureen, Farah. BSc in Civil Engring., U. Engring., Lahore, Pakistan, 1965; MS in Civil Engring., U. Pa., Phila., 1971; grad. project mgmt. program, Poly. Inst. N.Y., 1976. Registered profl. engr., N.Y., N.J., Pa. Civil engr. Water & Power Devel. Authority of Govt. Pakistan, Lahore, 1965-66; project resident engr., cons. Govt. Libya, El Beida, 1966-68; sr. structural engr. Stone & Webster Engring. Corp., N.Y.C., 1971-79; sr. project mgr., mgmt. cons. U.S. Army C.E. Middle East, Saudi Arabia, 1979-83; sr. staff engr. project Port Authority of N.Y. and N.J., N.Y.C., 1985—; Mem. internat. roster of experts in fields of engring., constrn. bldg., fin. and contracts and tenders Habitat, UN Centre for Human Settlements, 1980. Recipient Exceptional Svc. award Port Authority N.Y. and N.J. Mem. ASCE, Am. Concrete Inst. Achievements include development of computerized project management system for U.S. Army Corps of Engineers for 10 billion dollar super construction project; managed major restoration team after New York World Trade Center bombing, 1993. Home: 6 Silver Holw New Brunswick NJ 08902-2600

AWTREY, JIM L., sports association executive; b. Oakland, Calif., Nov. 18, 1943; s. Hal G. and Betty D. (Kieff) A.; m. Jeannie M. Scott, Feb. 8, 1968; children: Jena, Julie, Justin. BABA, U. Okla., 1966. Asst. profl. Okla. City Country Club, 1966-69, Siwanoy Country Club, Bronxville, N.Y., 1968-69; profl. golfer PGA Tour, 1970-71; coach, gen. mgr. Univ. Golf Club, Norman, Okla., 1972-77; head Heritage Hills Golf Club, Claremore, Okla., 1977-80, Dornick Hills Golf Club, Ardmore, Okla., 1980-82; gen. mgr. The Trails Golf Club, Norman, 1982-86; mgr. tournament ops. PGA, Palm Beach Gardens, Fla., 1986-87; exec. dir., CEO PGA, Palm Beach Gardens, 1987—; chief exec. officer PGA, 1988—; sec.-treas., pres. South Cen. sect. PGA, 1975-76, co-vice chmn. rules com, 1984-86, co-vice chmn. jr. golf, 1985-86, vice chmn. info. svcs., 1987, vice chmn. tournament 1987; head coach golf team U. Okla., Norman, 1972-77. Mem. Econ. Coun., Palm Beach, Fla., 1989-92; bd. dirs. Fellowship Christian Athletes, Palm Beach Gardens, 1989-92. Recipient Golf Profl. of Yr. award South Ctrl. PGA, 1977, Horton Smith award, 1979. Republican. Methodist. Avocation: fishing. Office: PGA 100 Avenue of Champions PO Box 109601 Palm Beach Gardens FL 33410-9601*

AX, EMANUEL, pianist; b. Lvov, Poland, June 8, 1949; s. Joachim and Hellen (Kurtz) A.; m. Yoko Nozaki, Nov. 23, 1974; 2 children. Student of Mieczyslaw Munz, Juilliard Sch. Music; BA, Columbia U. Appeared as soloist Chgo., Los Angeles, Phila., Rochester, Seattle, St. Louis and London, Philharm. orchs., N.Y. Philharm., Israel Philharm., Pitts. Symphony; recitalist (with Yo-Yo Ma) Avery Fisher Hall, Carnegie Hall, N.Y.C., festival at Tanglewood, Hollywood Bowl and Ravinia; toured extensively in C.Am. and S.Am., performed in joint recital (with violinist Nathan Milstein), extensive tours, Europe, Japan; with major orchs.; also recs. Winner Arthur Rubinstein Internat. Competition 1974, Avery Fisher prize 1979; recipient Young Concert Artist's Michaels award 1975; 4 Grammy awards. Office: care ICM Artists 40 W 57th St New York NY 10019-4001 or: care Harold Holt Ltd, 31 Sinclair Rd, London W14 ONS, England*

AXE, JOHN RANDOLPH, lawyer, financial executive; b. Grand Rapids, Mich., Apr. 30, 1938; s. John Jacob and Elizabeth Katherine (Lynott) A.; m. Linda Sadlier Stroh, June 1, 1989; children from previous marriage: Catherine, Peter, Meredith, Sara, Jay, stepchildren: Suzanne Stroh, Greg Stroh. AB, U. Mich., 1960; LLB, Harvard U., 1963. Bar: Mich. 1964. Ptnr. Dickinson, Wright, McKean, Cudlip, Detroit, 1972-80, Martin, Axe, Buhl & Schwartz, Bloomfield Hills, Mich., 1981-82, Axe & Schwartz, Bloomfield Hills, 1983-85, Dykema, Gossett, Spencer, Goodnow, Detroit, 1985-89; prin. John R. Axe and Assocs., Detroit, 1989—; pres. Mcpl. Fin. Cons., Inc., Detroit, 1982—; adj. prof. Wayne State U. Law Sch., 1992—. Mem. Mich. Higher Edn. Assistance Authority, Lansing, Mich., 1977-83. Served to lt. USNR, 1965-69. Mem. Nat. Assn. Bond Lawyers (steering com. 1981-83, 86, bd. dirs. 1987-90), Mich. Assn. County Treas. (gen. counsel 1977-88), Downtown Assn. Club (N.Y.C.), Doubles Club (N.Y.C.), Mill Reef Club (Antigua). Office: John R Axe and Assocs 21 Kercheval Ave Ste 360 Grosse Pointe MI 48236-3633

AXEL, RICHARD, pathology and biochemistry educator; b. N.Y.C., July 2, 1946. A.B. magna cum laude, Columbia U., 1967; M.D., Johns Hopkins U., 1970. Intern dept. pathology Columbia U. Coll. Physicians and Surgeons, N.Y.C., 1970-71; fellow Inst. Cancer Research, 1971-72; vis. fellow dept. pathology Columbia U., 1971-72; research assoc. USPHS, NIH, 1972-74; asst. prof. dept. pathology Inst. Cancer Research, Columbia U., 1974-78, prof. depts. pathology and biochemistry, 1978—; mem. molecular biology study sect. NIH, 1981—; Univ. lectr. Columbia U., 1983. Assoc. editor: Cell, 1976—; contbr. articles to profl. jours. Recipient Irma T. Hirschl Career Scientist award, 1976; recipient Young Scientistaward Passano Found., 1979, Alan T. Waterman award, 1982, Eli Lilly award, 1983, Scientific Award, Moet Hennessy, Louis Vuitton, 1992. Mem. NAS (Richard Lounsbery award 1989), Am. Acad. Arts and Scis., Phi Beta Kappa. Office: Howard Hughes Med Inst 701 W 168th St New York NY 10032*

AXELROD, GLEN SCOTT, publishing company executive; b. Newark, Nov. 4, 1953; s. Alan Robert and Janet Lee Axelrod; m. Jennifer Anderson, June 24, 1979; children: Jason Aaron, Daniel Jay. BA in Biology, Rutgers U., 1975; MSc in Zoology/Ichthyology, Rhodes U., Grahamstown, South Africa, 1978. Asst. to pres., sr. editor TFH Pubs., Inc., Neptune City, N.J., 1979-81; asst. to prin. Six Star Cablevision Group, Englewood, N.J., 1981-82; exec. v.p. Breckenridge Devel. Corp., Wayne, N.J., 1985-92; pres., CEO Design Svcs., Riverdale, N.J., 1992-95; pres. GJA Prodn. Corp., Mahwah, N.J., 1982—; exec. v.p. TFH Pubs., Inc., Neptune City, 1996-97, pres., CEO, 1997—; bd. dirs. TFH Pubs., Inc. Exec. editor zool. mags.; patentee in field; contbr. articles to profl. jours. Trustee, treas. Deerhaven Assn., Mahwah, 1990-97. Fellow The Zool. Soc. London (sci.), Masons. Achievements include taxonomic description of new Pisces species. Avocations: skiing, diving, hiking, aquarium hobbyist, writing. Office: TFH Publications Inc One TFH Plz 3d & Union Neptune City NJ 07753

AXELROD, JONATHAN GANS, lawyer; b. N.Y.C., Oct. 23, 1946; s. Arthur and Rosalind (Gans) A.; m. Carol Jean Zachary, Jan. 16, 1983; children: Zachary Arthur, Tristan Gans. AB Dartmouth Coll. 1968; JD Columbia U. 1971; LLM in Labor Law George Washington U. 1975. Bar: N.Y. 1971, D.C. 1975. Trial atty. App. ct. br. NLRB 1971-74; asst. gen. csl. Ea. Conf. Teamsters 1974-80; ptnr. Beins, Axelrod, Osborne, Mooney & Green, P.C., Washington, 1980-96; ptnr. Beins, Axelrod & Kraft, P.C., Washington, 1996—. Mem. ABA, D.C. Bar Assn. (co-chmn. sect. on labor law 1985-89, steering com. 1990-91). Contbr. articles to profl. jours. Office: Beins Axelrod & Kraft PC 1717 Massachusetts Ave NW Washington DC 20036-2001

AXELROD, JULIUS, pharmacologist, biochemist; b. N.Y.C., May 30, 1912; s. Isadore and Molly (Leichtling) A.; m. Sally Taub, Aug. 30, 1938; children: Paul Mark, Alfred Nathan. BS, CCNY, 1933; MA, NYU, 1941, DSc (hon.), 1971; PhD, George Washington U., 1955, LLD (hon.), 1971; DSc (hon.), U. Chgo., 1965, Med. Coll. Wis., 1971, Med. Coll. Pa., 1974, U. Pa., 1986, Hahnemann U., 1987; LLD (hon.), CCNY, 1972; D honoris causa, U. Panama, 1972, U. Paris (Sud), 1982, Ripon Coll, 1984, Tel Aviv U., 1984; DSC (hon., McGill U., Montreal, 1989. Chemist Lab. Indsl. Hygiene, 1935-46; research assoc. 3d N.Y. U. research divsn. Goldwater Meml. Hosp., 1946-49; assoc. chemist sect. chem. pharmacology Nat. Heart Inst., NIH, 1949-50, chemist, 1950-53, sr. chemist, 1953-55; acting chief sect. pharmacology Lab. Clin. Sci. NIMH, 1955, chief sect. pharmacology, 1955-84; guest worker Lab. Cell Biology NIMH, 1984—; scientist emeritus NIH, 1996; Otto Loewi meml. lectr. N.Y. U., 1963; Karl E. Paschkis meml. lectr. Phila. Endocine Soc., 1966; NIH lectr., 1967; Nathanson meml. lectr. U. So. Calif., 1968; James Parkinson lectr. Columbia U., 1971; Wartenberg lectr. Am. Acad. Neurology, 1971; Arnold D. Welch lectr. Yale U., 1971; Harold Carpenter Hodge distinguished lectr. toxicology U. Rochester, 1971; Bennett lectr. Am. Neurol. Assn., 1971; Harvey lectr., 1971; Mayer lectr. Mass. Inst. Tech., 1971; distinguished prof. sci. George Washington U., 1972; Salmon lectr. N.Y. Acad. Medicine, 1972; Eli Lilly lectr., 1972; Mike Hogg lectr. U. Tex., 1972; Fred Schueler lectr. Tulane U., 1972; numerous other hon. lectures; vis. scholar Herbert Lehman Coll. City U. N.Y., 1973; professorial lectr. George Washington U., 1959—; panelist U.S. Bd. Civil Service Examiners, 1958-67; mem. research adv. com. United Cerebral Palsy Assn., 1966-69; mem. psychopharmacology study sect. NIMH, 1970-74; mem. Internat. Brain Research Orgn.; mem. research adv. com. Nat. Found.; vis. com. Brookhaven Nat. Lab., 1972-76; bd. overseers Jackson Lab., 1974-88. Mem. editorial bd. Jour. Pharmacology and Exptl. Therapeutics, 1956-72, Jour. Medicinal Chemistry, 1962-67, Circulation Research, 1963-71, Currents in Modern Biology, 1966-72; mem. editorial adv. bd. Communication in Behavioral Biology, 1967-73, Jour. Neurobiology, 1968-77, Jour. Neurochemistry, 1969-77, Jour. Neurovisceral Relation, 1969, Rassegna di Neurologia Vegetativa, 1969—, Internat. Jour. Psychobiology, 1970-75; hon. cons. editor Life Scis, 1961-69; co-author: The Pineal, 1968; contbr. papers in biochem. actions and metabolism of drugs, hormones, action of pineal gland, enzymes, neurochem. transmission to profl. jours. Recipient Meritorious Rsch. award Assn. Rsch. Nervous and Mental Diseases, 1965; Gairdner award disting. rsch., 1967; Nobel prize in med. physiology, 1970; Alumni Disting. Achievement award George Washington U., 1968; Superior Service award HEW, 1968; Disting. Svc. award, 1970; Claude Bernard professorship and medal U. Montreal, 1969; Disting. Svc. award Modern Medicine mag., 1970; Albert Einstein award Yeshiva U., 1971; medal Rudolf Virchow Med. Soc., 1971; Myrtle Wreath award Hadassah, 1972; Leibniz medal Acad. Sci. East Germany, 1984; Salmon medal N.Y. Acad. Medicine, Bristol-Myers award for disting. rsch. in neurosci., 1989, Thudicum medal Brit. Biochem. Soc. (lectr.), 1989, Gerard medal Soc. Neuroscience, 1991. Felow AAAS, Am. Acad. Arts and Scis., Am. Soc. Neuropsychopharmacology; mem. German Pharmacol. Soc. (corr.), Am. Chem. Soc., Am. Soc. Pharmacology and Exptl. Therapeutics (Torald Sollmann award 1973), Nat. Acad. Scis., Am. Neurol. Assn. (hon.), Royal Soc. London (fgn.), Inst. Medicine (sr.), Am. Philos. Soc., Deutsche Academie Naturfoucher (East Germany), Am. Psychopathol. Assn. (hon.), Sigma Xi. Home: 10401 Grosvenor Pl Rockville MD 20852-4646 Office: NIH Dept Health Edn & Welfare 9000 Rockville Pike Rm 3a-15 Bethesda MD 20892-0003

AXELROD, NORMAN N(ATHAN), technical planning and technology application consultant; b. N.Y.C., Aug. 26, 1934; s. Louis E. and Sadie (Katz) A.; m. Victoria Ann Grant, Mar. 21, 1975; children: Lauren Grant, Brian George. AB, Cornell U., 1954; postgrad., U. Paris, France, 1958; PhD in Optics and Physics, U. Rochester, 1959. Aerospace scientist NASA, Goddard Space Flight Ctr., Washington, 1959-60; rsch. fellow U. London, 1960-61; asst. prof. U. Del., 1961-65; mem. tech. staff Bell Labs., Murray Hill, N.J., 1965-72; prin. Axelrod Assocs., N.Y.C., 1972—; bd. dirs. World Resources Devel. Corp., Input-Output Tech., Inc.; mem. adv. bd. Del. Dept. Edn., 1963-64; participant vis. scientist program Am. inst. Physics, 1963-64; cons. Met. Mus. Art, N.Y.C., 1969-72; advisor to White House, 1969-70, French Ministry Nat. Def. and War, 1971, Alliance Found., Am. Consumer Products, Inc., Bausch & Lomb, Calor plc, Compuscan, Corning, CPC, Delco, GE, IBM, ITT, Konishiroku, Johnson & Johnson, Labatt, Lear Siegler, Medtronic, Recognition Equipment Inc., Perkin-Elmer, Sharp, Proctor & Gamble, RCA, Sensar, Teradyne, Timken Co., Wall St. Jour., Wheatland Tube, Woodgram Millwork; guest cons. Marine Biol. Lab., Woods Hole, Mass., 1993—. Editor: Optical Properties of Dielectric Films, 1968; book reviewer, cons. John Wiley & Sons, 1965-68, Rheinhold-Van Nostrand, 1968-70, Pergamon Press, 1969-70; contbr. articles to profl. jours. Patentee in field. Boldt scholar; recipient Fortune 500 Corp. award for tech. contbn., 1990; grantee NATO, NSF, Office of Naval Rsch. Fellow AAAS; mem. IEEE, Am. Phys. Soc., Am. Optical Soc., Soc. Mfg. Engrs. (cert. by stature as CMfgE in machine vision), Del. Acad. Sci., N.Y. Acad. Sci., Electrochem. Soc., Sigma Xi, Sigma Pi Sigma, Pi Mu Epsilon. E-mail: naxelrod@axelrodassociates.com. Home: 445 E 86th St New York NY 10028-6433 Office: Norman Axelrod Assocs 28 W 44th St New York NY 10036-6600*

AXELROD, SUSAN L., fundraiser; b. Orange, N.J., June 8, 1962; d. Asher Arthur and Therese Deborah (Albach) Lowenthal; m. Howard Michael Axelrod, Sept. 13, 1987; children: Rebecca Fay, Sarah Michelle. BA, Mount Holyoke Coll., 1984. Cert. fund raising exec. Campaign coord. George Washington U., Washington, 1985-86; dir. devel. Hillel Harvard U., Cambridge, Mass., 1986-88; asst. dir. devel. Rensselaer Poly. Inst., Troy, N.Y., 1988-92; dir. devel. Unity House, Troy, N.Y., 1992-95; found. officer Ellis Hosp. Found., Schenectady, N.Y., 1995-98; campaign dir. Albany (N.Y.) Jewish Cmty. Ctr., 1998—; tchr. fundraising class Knowledge Network, Albany, N.Y., 1996-97; instr., fundraising cert. program Siena Coll., Londonville, N.Y., 1996-98. Contbr. articles to profl. jours. Bd. dirs. Congregation Aqudat Achim, Hebrew Acad. Mem. Nat. Soc. Fund Raising Execs. (presenter internat. confs.), Gift Planning Gorup Northeastern N.Y. Democrat. Jewish. Avocations: piano, public speaking, jewish involvement. Office: Albany Jewish Cmty Ctr 340 Whitehall Rd Albany NY 12208

AXELSON, CHARLES FREDERIC, retired accounting educator; b. Chgo., Apr. 24, 1917; m. Dorothy L. Jepson, July 23, 1940 (dec. Oct. 1994); children: Linda Axelson Masters, Fred, Lorraine Axelson Gresty; m. Marion I. Murray, Mar. 11, 1995. AB, MBA, U. Chgo., 1937. Staff acct. Lybrand, Ross Bros. & Montgomery, Chgo., 1938-41; with U.S. Gypsum Co., Chgo., 1941-70; asst. controller U.S. Gypsum Co., 1946-52, controller, 1952-60, controller, asst. treas., 1960-70; v.p. controller Libby, McNeill & Libby, Chgo., 1970-78; v.p., chief fin. officer Lawry's Foods, Inc., Los Angeles, 1978-82; prof. acctg. U. So. Calif., Los Angeles, 1982-85; vis. lectr. Darling Downs Inst. Advanced Edn., Toowoomba, Queensland, Australia, 1985; lectr. acctg. Calif. State Poly. U., Pomona, 1985-92; lectr. emeritus, 1992; lectr. acctg. Northwestern U., 1946-53; bd. dirs. Air Conditioning Co., 1982-96; bd. dirs. Goodwill Industries So. Calif., 1982—. Trustee emeritus Nat. Louis U.; former chmn. Crippled Children's Soc. So. Calif., vice chmn., 1990—, also bd. dirs. Named to Calif. Poly. Acctg. Hall of Fame, 1996; named Lipton Vol. of Yr., 1997. Mem. AICPA, Fin. Execs. Inst. (past dir. L.A. chpt., past pres. Chgo. chpt., past nat. dir., past v.p. Midwestern area), Phi Delta Theta. Presbyterian. Club: Town Hall (Los Angeles). Home: 888 S Orange Grove Blvd # 2-w Pasadena CA 91105-1790 *Whatever successes I've had - business and personal - can be traced to self-discipline, a good education, a reputation for integrity, much reading, good health, outside interests to offset business pressures and lots of advance planning.*

AXELSON, JOSEPH ALLEN, professional athletics executive, publisher; b. Peoria, Dec. 25, 1927; s. Joseph Victor Axelson and Florence (Ealen) Massey; m. Malcolm Rae Smith, Oct. 7, 1950 (dec.); children: David Allen, Mark Stephen, Linda Rae. B.S., Northwestern U., 1949. Sports info. dir. Ga. So. U., Statesboro, 1957-60, Nat. Assn. Intercollegiate Athletics, Kansas City, Mo., 1961-62; tournament dir. Bowling Proprs. Assn. Am., Park Ridge, Ill., 1963-64; asst. exec. sec. Nat. Assn. Intercollegiate Athletics, Kansas City, Mo., 1964-68; exec. v.p., gen. mgr. Cin. Royals Profl. Basketball Team, Cin., 1969-72; mgr. Cin. Gardens, 1970-72; pres., gen. mgr. Kansas City Kings Profl. Basketball Team, Kansas City, Mo., 1972-79, 82-85; pres., gen. mgr. Sacramento Kings Profl. Basketball Team, 1985-88, exec. v.p., 1988-90; pres. Arco Arena, Sacramento, 1985-88; exec. v.p. Sacramento Sports Assn., Arco Sports Complex, 1988-90, Profl. Team Publs., Inc., Stamford, Conn., 1991-92; pub. Between The Vines Newsletter, 1993—; exec. v.p. ops. NBA, N.Y.C., 1979-82, chmn. competition and rules com., 1975-79; trustee Naismith Basketball Hall of Fame; co-host The Sports Page, Sta. KFMB-AM, San Diego, 1994-97. Author: Basketball Basics, 1987. Mem. Emil Verban Meml. Soc., Washington. Capt. Signal Corps. AUS, 1949-54. Named Nat. Basketball Exec. of Yr. The Sporting News, St. Louis, 1973, Sportsman of Yr., Rockne Club, Kansas City, 1975; recipient Annual Dirs. award Downtown, Inc., Kansas City, Mo., 1979, Nat. Assn. Intercollegiate Athletics Frank Cramer Nat. Svc. award, 1983, Man of Yr. award Sacramento (Calif.) C. of C., 1986; named to Ga. So. U. Sports Hall of Fame, 1990. Mem. Am. Philatelic Soc., Phi Kappa Psi. Republican. Presbyterian. Office: 1112 1st St Ste 410 Coronado CA 92118-1407

AXFORD, ROY ARTHUR, nuclear engineering educator; b. Detroit, Aug. 26, 1928; s. Morgan and Charlotte (Donaldson) A.; m. Anne-Sofie Langfeldt Rasmussen, Apr. 1, 1954; children: Roy Arthur, Elizabeth Carole, Trevor Craig Charles. B.A., Williams Coll., 1952; B.S., Mass. Inst. Tech., 1952, M.S., 1955, Sc.D., 1958. Supr. theoretical physics group Atomics Internat., Canoga Park, Calif., 1958-60; assoc. prof. nuclear engring. Tex. A&M, 1960-62, prof., 1962-63; assoc. prof. nuclear engring. Northwestern U., 1963-66; assoc. prof. U. Ill., Urbana, 1966-68, prof., 1968—; cons. Los Alamos Nat. Lab., 1963—. Vice-chmn. Mass. Inst. Tech. Alumni Fund Drive, 1970-72, chmn., 1973-75; sustaining fellow MIT, 1984. Recipient cert. of recognition for excellence in undergrad. teaching U. Ill., 1979, 81; Everitt award for teaching excellence, 1985. Mem. ASME, Am. Nuclear Soc. (Excellence in Undergrad. Teaching award 1990, 95, 97, 99, Disting. faculty Alpha Nu Sigma 1991), SAR (sec.-treas. Piankeshaw chpt. 1975-81, v.p. chpt. 1982-3, pres. chpt. 1984-86), Kiwanis (charter life patron fellow 1992), Sigma Xi, Tau Beta Pi, Phi Kappa Phi. Home: 2017 S Cottage Grove Ave Urbana IL 61801-6353

AXILROD, STEPHEN HARVEY, global economic consultant, economist; b. N.Y.C., June 21, 1926; s. Jacob James and Pearl (Feltenstein) A.; m. Katherine Podolsky, July 1, 1950; children: Peter, Emily Axilrod Hildner, Richard. Student, So. Meth. U., 1943-44; AB magna cum laude, Harvard U., 1948; MA, U. Chgo., 1950, postgrad., 1951-52. Assoc. dir. div. research and statistics Fed. Res. Bd., Washington, 1970-73, advisor to bd. govs., 1973-76, staff dir. for monetary and fin. policy, 1976-86; economist domestic fin. Fed. Open Market Com., Washington, 1974-78, economist, 1978-81; staff dir., sec. Fed. Open Market Commn., Washington, 1981-86; vice chmn. Nikko Securities Internat., N.Y.C., 1986-94; cons. internat. orgns. and ctrl. banks on policy ops., 1994—; cons. global econs. and markets pvt. practice, 1994—; advisor Brookings Panel on Econ. Activity, Washington, 1986-89; mem. investment com. Japan Soc.; mem. adv. coun. Ctrl. Bank of Oman. Contbr. articles on monetary policy, credit and securities markets, transformation of policy ops. and markets in emerging countries and related matters to books, newspapers, mags. and profl. jours. Bd. overseers Lemberg program on internat. fin., Brandeis U. With USN, 1944-46. Mem. Phi Beta Kappa. Avocations: flute, tennis, reading, hiking.

AXINN, DONALD EVERETT, real estate investor, developer; b. N.Y.C., July 13, 1929; s. Michael and Ann (Schneider) A. AB, Middlebury Coll., 1951, LittD (hon.), 1989; MA, Hofstra U., 1975, LLD (hon.), 1991; LittD (hon.), So. Vt. Coll., 1989; LHD (hon.), SUNY, Farmingdale, 1996. Founder, owner Donald E. Axinn Co., Jericho, L.I., N.Y., 1958—; dir. Farrar, Straus & Giroux, Inc., N.Y.C., 1971-94; assoc. dean Hofstra Coll. Liberal Arts and Scis., Hempstead, N.Y., 1971-72; also dir. Inst. Arts. Chmn., commr.; Nassau County Fine Arts Commn., 1970-73; mem. Gov.'s Task Force on Cultural Life and Arts, 1975—; trustee N.Y. Ocean Scis. Labs., Montauk, N.Y., 1969-71, Waldemar Cancer Rsch. Inst., Woodbury, N.Y., 1966-68, North Shore U. Hosp., 1980-91, N.Y. State Nature and Hist. Preserve Trust, 1978-83, Nassau County Mus., 1980-83; trustee Hofstra U., 1970, 72—, sec., 1973-74, vice chmn., 1974—; trustee emeritus The Nature Conservancy, 1990—, chmn. Long Island chpt., 1997—; bd. dirs. Pro Arte Symphony Orch., 1967-70, N.Y. Quar. Poetry Rev. Found., Inc., 1969—, Eglevsky Ballet Co., Outward Bound, Inc.; v.p. bd. dirs. Leukemia Soc.; treas. Interfaith Nutrition Network, 1984-85. Author: Sliding Down the Wind, 1978, The Hawk's Dream and Other Poems, 1982, Against Gravity, 1986, The Colors of Infinity, 1990, Spin, 1992, Dawn Patrol, 1992, The Latest Illusion, 1995, The Ego Makers, 1998. Recipient archtl. design and community enhancement awards L.I. Assn. and Plainview C. of C., 1962-70, Brotherhood award NCCJ, 1977, Humanitarian award Am. Jewish Com., 1978, Interfaith Nutrition Network, 1989, hon. award Beta Gamma Sigma, 1978, L.I. Disting. Leadership award, 1979, Estabrook award Hofstra U., 1987, also others; Tennessee Wiliams fellow in poetry Bread Loaf, 1979. Mem. PEN, Nat. Pilots Assn., Poets and Writers, Aircraft Owners and Pilots Assn., L.I. Early Fliers Club, Poetry Soc. Am. (bd. govs. 1987-95), Acad. of Am. Poets (bd. dirs. 1996—), L.I. Regional Econ. Devel. Coun., Poets House, Middlebury Coll. Alumni Assn. (v.p., adv. bd. 1978), Players Club (N.Y.C.), Sands Point Country Club (L.I.), Old Westbury Racquet Club (N.Y.), Delta Upsilon. Designer, developer Long Island Office Park, Engineers Hill Indsl. Parks, Montvale Office Park, The Ellipse at Garden City, Montvale III, Montvale IV, Meadow Hill Office Plz. Office: 131 Jericho Tpke Jericho NY 11753-1060 *A wonderful characteristic of this great democracy of ours is the right to fail—which is, of course, the opportunity to succeed. As we pursue some goal, especially a noble one, we learn about the aspects and degrees of success or failure. The aspiration, therefore, becomes a worthwhile endeavor in itself.*

AXINN, GEORGE HAROLD, rural sociology educator; b. Jamaica, N.Y., Feb. 1, 1926; s. Hyman and Celia (Schneider) A.; m. Nancy Kathryn Wigsten, Feb. 17, 1945; children: Catherine, Paul, Martha, William. B.S., Cornell U., 1947; M.S., U. Wis., 1952, Ph.D., 1958. Editorial asst. Cornell U. Geneva, N.Y., 1947; bull. editor U. Md., College Park, 1949; chmn. dept. rural communication U. Del., Newark, 1950; mem. faculty Mich. State U., East Lansing, 1953—; assoc. dir. coop. extension service Mich. State U., 1955-60; coordinator U. Nigeria program, 1961-65, prof. agrl. econs., 1970-85, prof. emeritus resource devel., 1985-95, prof. emeritus, 1996—, asst. dean internat. studies and programs, 1964-85; pres., exec. dir. Midwest Univs. Consortium for Internat. Activities, Inc., 1969-76, 1969-76; FAO rep. to Nepal, 1983-85, India and Bhutan, 1989-91; cons. World Bank, 1973-74, Ford Found., 1968, UNICEF, 1978, FAO, 1974, 87, 89, Govt. of India, 1988; vis. prof. Cornell U., Ithaca, N.Y., 1958-60, U. Ill., Urbana, 1969-70. Author: Modernizing World Agriculture: A Comparative Study of Agricultural Extension Education Systems, 1972, New Strategies for Rural Development, Rural Life Associates, 1978, FAO Guide Alternative Approaches to Agricultural Extension, 1988, Collaboration in International Rural Development - A Practitioner's Handbook (with Nancy W. Axinn), 1997; contbr. articles to various publs. Served with USNR, 1944-46. Recipient Outstanding Alumni award Cornell U. Coll. Agrl. and Life Sci., 1993; W.K. Kellogg Found. fellow, 1956-57. Mem. AAAS, Rural Sociol. Soc., Soc. Internat. Devel., Soc. Applied Anthropology, Indian Soc. Extension Edn., Assn. Farming Systems Rsch. and Extension, Phi Kappa Phi. Clubs: Lansing Tennis, Michigan State U. Home: 2513 Bentley Ct East Lansing MI 48823-2972 Office: Mich State U 313 Natural Resources East Lansing MI 48824-1222

AXINN, STEPHEN MARK, lawyer; b. N.Y.C., Oct. 21, 1938; s. Mack N. and Lili H. (Tannenbaum) A.; m. Stephanie Chertok, May 12, 1963; children: Audrey, David, Jill. BS, Syracuse U., 1959; LLB, Columbia U., 1962. Bar: N.Y. 1962, U.S. Supreme Ct. 1962. Assoc. Cahill & Gordon, N.Y.C., 1963-64, Malcolm A. Hoffman, N.Y.C., 1964-66; assoc. Skadden, Arps, Slate, Meagher & Flom, N.Y.C., 1966-69, ptnr., 1970-97; ptnr. Axinn, Veltrop & Harkrider LLP, N.Y.C., 1997—; adj. prof. Law Sch. NYU, 1981-83, Law Sch. Columbia U., 1983-85. Author: Acquisitions Under H-S-R, 1980; contbr. articles to profl. jours. Chmn. lawyers div. United Jewish Appeal, N.Y.C., 1985-87; mem. exec. com., treas. Jewish Theol. Sem. Am., 1984-96; mem. bd. visitors Columbia Law Sch., 1993—; mem. adv. panel on environ. crimes by orngs. U.S. Sentencing Commn., 1992-94. Capt. U.S. Army, 1965-68. Mem. ABA (council antitrust sect. 1983-85), N.Y. State Bar Assn. (chmn. antitrust sect. 1982-83). Office: Axinn Veltrop & Harkrider LLP 1633 Broadway New York NY 10019-6708

AXLEY, DIXIE L., insurance company executive. B in Social Welfare, Ill. Wesleyan U. Chartered property casualty underwriter. Pers. devel. specialist State Farm Mutual Automobile Ins. Co., Bloomington, Ill., 1987-88, supt., 1988-91, dir. mgmt. planning and info., 1991-93, mgr. pub. affairs, 1993-94, asst. divsn. mgr., 1994-95, asst. dir.- pub. affairs, then dir.- pub. affairs, 1995-96, asst. v.p.- pub. affairs, 1996—, v.p. pub. affairs, 1997. Office: State Farm Ins Cos Pub Affairs Dept 1 State Farm Plz Bloomington IL 61710-0001*

AXLEY, FREDERICK WILLIAM, lawyer; b. Chgo., June 23, 1941; s. Frederick R. and Elena (Hoffman-Pinther) A.; m. Cinda Jane Russell, Mar. 29, 1969; children: Sarah Elizabeth, Elizabeth Jane. BA, Holy Cross Coll., 1963; MA, U. Wis., 1966; JD, U. Chgo., 1969. Bar: Ill. 1969, U.S. Dist. Ct. (no. dist.) Ill. 1969, U.S. Ct. Appeals (7th cir.) 1970. Assoc. McDermott, Will & Emery, Chgo., 1969-74, jr. ptnr., 1974-80, sr. ptnr., 1980—. Trustee Wilmette Elem. Sch. Dist. #39, Ill., 1976-81, Ill. chpt. Nature Conservnacy, 1983-91; bd. dirs. Bus. and Profl. People for the Pub. Interest, Chgo., 1984—; bd. dirs. Friends of the Chgo. River, 1994—, pres., 1998—; bd. dirs. Shore Line Place, 1994—. Served to lt. USN, 1963-65. Mem. Mich. Shores Club (Wilmette). Democrat. Roman Catholic. Home: 112 Lawndale St Wilmette IL 60091-3211 Office: McDermott Will & Emery 227 W Monroe St Ste 3100 Chicago IL 60606-5096*

AXLEY, HARTMAN, underwriter; b. Madison, Wis., Apr. 17, 1931; s. Ralph Emerson and Katharine Nella (Hartman) A.; m. Marguerite Ann Thessin, Sept. 4, 1954; children: Colleen Lynn Axley Patrick, Timothy Hartman Axley. BA, U. Wis., 1952, JD, 1956; MSFS, Am. Coll., Bryn Mawr, Pa., 1983. CLU, cert. fin. planner, accedited estate planner; chartered fin. cons.; registered health underwriter. Assoc. atty. Holland & Hart, Denver, 1956-58; life underwriter Colo. Assocs. of Allmerica Fin. (formerly State Mut. Cos.), Denver, 1958—; mem. bd. editl. advisors Fin. Svc. Advisors (formerly Life and Health Insurance Sales), Lexington, Ky.; mem. Colo. Ethics in Bus. Award Bd., 1995—; mem. Denver Estate Planning Coun., pres., 1968-69. Author: National Ski Patrol Ski Lift Evacuation Manual, 1975, National Ski Patrol Awards Manual, 1980. Bd. dir. Met. Denver YMCA, 1978-81; bd. dirs. S.W. Denver Family YMCA, 1973—, chmn. bd. dir., 1978-81; mem. First Aider Mile High chpt. ARC, Denver, 1956-86; bd. dir., officer Community Concert Assn. Denver, 1962-65; bd. dir. Colo. Ski Mus., 1994—; chair Colo. Ski Hall of Fame, 1996-99; mem. Nat. Ski Patrol System, 1948—, asst. nat. dir., 1969-76, Rocky Mountain div. dir., 1963-69 (Minnie Dole award 1988, Schobinger Outstanding Adminstr. award 1973); mem. Olympic Ski Patrol, Squaw Valley, Calif., 1960; mem., patroller Arapahoe Basin Ski Patrol, 1956-85, front range dir., 1961-63; coord. badminton Rocky Mountain Sr. Games, 1987—. Capt. USAF (JAG), 1952-60. Named to Roll of Honor, Mile High ARC, 1974, to Denver YMCA Hall of Fame, Met. Denver YMCA, 1987, to Colo. Ski Hall of Fame, 1993; recipient Award of Merit (Lifesaving) ARC, 1959, J. Stanley Edwards award Colo. and Denver Assn. Life Underwriters, 1980, Badminton medal Rocky Mountain Sr. Games, 1987—, U.S. Badminton Assn. Sr. Championship, 1988, 92, U.S. Nat. Sr. Games, 1991, 93, 95, 97. Mem. ABA (real property, probate and trust sect.), Nat. Assn. Estate Planning Cons. (bd. dirs. 1970-76, pres. 1974-75, dir. emeritus 1989—, patron chair 1975—, accreditation com. 1991—), Nat. Assn. Estate Planners (founding mem. bd. dirs. 1987), Am. Soc. CLU and ChFC (bd. dirs. 1992-95, western region v.p. 1994-95, nat. pub. rels. com. 1990-94, vice chair 1992, chair baby boomer rsch. project 1990, Colo.-Wyo. liaison 1992-97), Estate Law Specialists Bd. Inc. (founding mem., bd. dirs. 1996—), Am. Soc. CLU and ChFC (Rocky Mountain chpt. bd. dirs. 1985-91, pres. 1989-90), Assn. for Advanced Life Underwriters (Colo. liaison, 1996—), Denver Assn. Life Underwriters (Wesley Whitney award 1995, qualifying and life mem., Million Dollar Round Table 1970-85), Colo. Ins. Commr.'s Adv. Coun. (chmn. 1990—), Colo. Assn. Commerce and Industry (Health Care Task Force 1990-94), Colo. Assn. Life Underwriters, Nat. Assn. Life Underwriters (Nat. Quality award, Nat. Sales Achievement award), Life Underwriter Charities, Inc. (founding mem. bd. dirs. 1989-92), Wis. Bar Assn., Metro Denver Assn. Health Underwriters (founding mem. bd. dirs. 1990-92, legis. chair 1990-92), Colo. State Assn. Health Underwriters (charter 1986—, founding mem. bd. dirs. 1986-92, legis. chair 1986-92), Nat. Assn. Health Underwriters (leading producers roundtable 1981-89), U.S. Badminton Assn. (staff vol. Olympic Games 1996), U. Wis. Alumni Assn. (bd. dirs. 1970-89, Spark Plug award 1977), Wis. Bar Assn., Denver Athletic Club (bd. dirs. 1984-87, Sr. Athlete of Yr. 1997). Congregationalist. Avocations: skiing, badminton, deltiophile, singing, travel. Office: State Mutual Cos 720 South Colorado Blvd Denver CO 80246-1905

AXON, DONALD CARLTON, architect; b. Haddonfield, N.J., Feb. 27, 1931; s. William Russell Sr. and Gertrude L. (Ellis) A.; m. Rosemary Smith, Sept. 1952 (div. Oct. 1967); children: Donald R., James K., Marianne Axon Flannery, Darren H., William R. II; m. Janice Jacobs, Mar. 16, 1968; stepchildren: Jonathan Lee, Elise Marie. BArch, Pratt Inst., 1954; MS in Arch., Columbia U., 1966. Registered architect, N.Y., Pa., Calif. Designer, drafter Keith Hibner, Assoc., Hicksville, N.Y., 1954-56; designer Charles Wood, Riverhead, N.Y., 1956-59; architect, prin Donald C. Axon, Assoc., Wantaugh, N.Y., 1959; ptnr. Bailey-Axon & Assoc., Long Beach, N.Y., 1960-66; project mgr. Caudill Rowlett Scott, Houston, 1966-69; in-house architect Kaiser Permanente Hosp., L.A., 1969-75; dir. med. facilities Daniel Mann Johnson Mendenhall, L.A., 1975-78, Lyon Assocs., L.A., 1979-80; pres. Donald C. Axon, FAIA, Inc., L.A., 1980—; tchr. bldg. sci. program U. So. Calif., 1978-82; lectr. in field; profl. advisor dept. architecture U. Tex., 1968-69; advisor to chmn. Sch. Architecture Rice U., Houston, 1968-69; profl. dir. Future Architect Am., 1965-66. Mem. Crestwood Hills Assn., bd. dirs. 1971-75, pres., 1973-75, archtl. rev. com., 1987—; bd. dirs. Brentwood Community Fedn., 1973-75, v.p., 1974-75. Recipient L.A. Beautiful award KPH Norwalk Hosp. Fellow AIA (Calif. regional bd. dirs. 1987-89, mem. various subcoms., chair steering com. 1980, liaison 1991—, bd. dirs. L.A. chpt. 1983-84, pres. 1986, chair com. on architecture for health 1974, chair health facilities com. Calif. coun. 1975, Disting. Svc. citation 1992), Royal Soc. Health, Health Facilities Inst., Hosp. Facilities Inst.; mem. Archtl. Found. L.A. (founding, v.p. 1985-89, pres. 1989-90), Internat. Conf. Bldg. Ofcls., Am. Hosp. Assn., Forum for Health Care Planning (bd. dirs. 1982—, pres. 1993-94). Fax: 949 360 8112. E-mail: donaxon@aol.com. Office: 24302 Carlton Ct Laguna Niguel CA 92677-3718

AXON, MICHAEL, education association field representative; b. Bradenton, Fla., Aug. 15, 1957; s. Gladys C. (Thomas) A. Student, Campbell U., 1975-77; BA in Social Sci. Edn., U. South Fla., 1979; MEd in Adminstrn. and Supervision, West Ga. Coll., 1995. Asst. mgr. Nat. Shirt Shop, Bradenton, 1979; account rep. Avco Fin. Svcs., Bradenton, 1979-80; tchr. Palm Beach County Sch. Bd., Palm Beach, Fla., 1980-86; customer svc. rep. Best Products Co., Inc., West Palm Beach, Fla., 1981-83; field rep. Atlanta Fedn. Tchrs., 1986—; v.p. Am. Fedn. Tchrs. of Palm Beach County, 1982-86; rep. Palm Beach County Cen. Labor Coun., West Palm Beach, 1982-86; commn. mem. Pres.'s Commn. on Excellence in Edn., Fla. Edn. Assn./United, Tallahassee, 1985; v.p. exec. coun. Fla. Edn. Assn./United, Tallahassee, 1985-86; staff coord. union newspaper Atlanta Fedn. Tchrs., 1988—. Membership chairperson Metro-Atlanta A. Philip Randolph Inst., 1987-89; editor vision newsletter Cathedral of Faith Ch. of God in Christ, Atlanta, 1989-95; counselor Juvenile Alt. Svc. Program, West Palm Beach, 1982-85; faculty sponsor key club Palm Beach Garden (Fla.) H.S., 1980-84. Avocations: poetry, cooking, walking, gardening. Office: Atlanta Fedn Tchrs Ste 439 2001 Martin Luther King Dr Atlanta GA 30310-5806

AXTELL, CLAYTON MORGAN, JR., lawyer; b. Deposit, N.Y., Aug. 4, 1916; s. Clayton Morgan and Olive Aurora (Vosburgh) A.; m. Margaret Williamson RitchieApr. 24, 1943; children: Margaret R. Axtell Stevenson, Clayton Morgan III, Karen R. Axtell Arnold, Susan R. Axtell. AB, Cornell U., 1937, JD, 1940. Bar: N.Y. 1940, U.S. Dist. Ct. (no. dist.) N.Y. 1941, U.S. Supreme Ct. 1964. Assoc. Hinman, Howard & Kattell, Binghamton, N.Y., 1940-48; ptnr. Hinman, Howard & Kattell, Binghamton, 1948—; former mem. adv. bd. First-City Nat. Bank, Binghamton; bd. dirs. Farmers Nat. Bank, Deposit, N.Y., First City Nat. Bank, Binghamton. Pres. N.Y. State Sch. Bd. Attys., Albany, 1962-63, Broome County Bar Assn., Binghamton, 1967-68, Conrad and Virginia Klee Found.; mem. N.Y. State Rep. Com., Binghamton, 1988-93. 1st lt. US Army, 1942-46 ETO. Decorated Bronze Star U.S. Army, 1945, Croix de Guerre, Govt. of France, 1945; recipient Disting Svc. award U.S. Jr. C. of C., 1942; named Young Man of Yr. Binghamton Jr. C. of C., 1949. Mem. ABA, N.Y. State Bar Assn., Hillcrest -Port Dick Kiwanis (pres.), Binghamton Club. Republican. Lutheran. Home: 1338 Chenango St Binghamton NY 13901-1539 Office: Hinman Howard & Kattell 80 Exchange St Ste 700 Binghamton NY 13901-3490

AXTELL, JAMES LEWIS, history educator; b. Endicott, N.Y., Dec. 20, 1941; s. Arthur James Axtell and Laura (England) Levinsky; m. Susan Carol Hallas, Aug. 31, 1963; children: Nathaniel Harsen, Jeremy England. BA, Yale U., 1963; PhD, U. Cambridge, Eng., 1967. Asst. prof. Yale U., New Haven, Conn., 1966-72; assoc. prof. Sarah Lawrence Coll., Bronxville, N.Y., 1972-75; vis. prof. Northwestern U., Evanston, Ill., 1977-78; prof. Coll. of William and Mary, Williamsburg, Va., 1978—, William R. Kenan Jr. prof. of humanities, 1986—. Author: The Educational Writings of John Locke, 1968, The School Upon a Hill, 1974, The European and the Indian, 1981, The Invasion Within, 1985 (prize 1985, 2 prizes 1986), After Columbus, 1988, Beyond 1492, 1992; The Indians' New South, 1997, The Pleasures of Academe, 1998, editor: The Indian Peoples of Eastern America, 1981; contbr. articles to jours. in field. Recipient Outstanding Faculty award Va. State Coun. Higher Edn., 1988; NEH fellow, 1975-77, 86, 92, J.S. Guggenheim Meml. Found. fellow, 1981-82, Am. Coun. Learned Socs. fellow, 1987. Mem. Soc. Am. Historians, Am. Soc. for Ethnohistory (pres. 1988-89), The Champlain Soc., Am. Hist. Assn., Orgn. Am. Historians, Colonial Soc. Mass., Pilgrim Soc., Mass. Hist. Soc. Democrat. Avocations: book collecting, track. E-mail: jlaxte@wm.edu. Home: 109 Walnut Hills Dr Williamsburg VA 23185-3426 Office: Coll of William & Mary Dept History Williamsburg VA 23187-8795

AXTELL, JOHN DAVID, genetics educator, researcher; b. Mpls., Feb. 5, 1934; s. Maynard J. and Caroline (Kolstad) A.; m. Susan Dee Kent, Aug. 17, 1957; children—Catherine Dee, John D. Jr., Laura Jean. B.S., U. Minn., St. Paul, 1957, M.S., 1965; Ph.D., U. Wis., Madison, 1967. Research asst. U. Minn., St. Paul, 1957-59; research assoc. U. Wis., Madison, 1959-67; prof. agronomy Purdue U., West Lafayette, Ind., 1967-84; Lynn Disting. prof. Purdue U., West Lafayette, 1984—; Mem. Research Adv. com. AID, Washington, 1983—, sci. liaison officer, 1984—. Contbr. chpts. to books, articles to profl. jours. Nat. Inst. Gen. Med. Scis. fellow; recipient Cert. of Appreciation award U.S. AID, 1975; Alexander Von Humboldt award, 1976; Research award Crop Sci. Soc. Am., 1977; Internat. award Disting. Service to Agr., 1984. Fellow AAAS, Am. Soc. Agronomy; mem. NAS, Am. Soc. Agronomy, Crop Sci. Soc. Agronomy, Sigma Xi, Gamma Sigma Delta, Alpha Zeta. Home: 1824 Sheridan Rd West Lafayette IN 47906-2226 Office: Purdue U Agronomy Dept Life Sci Bldg West Lafayette IN 47907

AXTELL, KEITH ELTON, federal agency administrator; b. San Bernardino, Calif., Mar. 10, 1942; s. John Dewey and Nelta (George) A.; m. Patricia Boster, Dec. 1964 (div. Oct. 1980); children: Andrea Miriam, Jonathan Patrick; m. Holly Berna Handler, Nov. 30, 1980. BA, U. Calif., Berkeley, 1965, MA in Pub. Adminstrn., 1966. Dir. housing programs br. U.S. Dept. Housing and Urban Devel., San Francisco, 1971-74, asst. regional adminstr. for adminstrn. Regional Office, 1974-78, dir. Office of Indian Programs, 1978-79, exec. asst. to regional adminstr., 1979-83, dir. Regional Office of Housing, 1983-94, dir. Office of Housing FHA, 1995-97, cmty. resources rep., 1998—; mem. adv. bd. pub. adminstrn. dept. Calif. State U., Hayward, 1988—; cons. Calif. State Legis., Sacramento. Commr. Met. Transp. Commn., San Francisco Bay Area, 1996—. Recipient Pres.'s Spl. award Pres. Richard Nixon, Washington, 1970. Mem. ASPA (exec. com. Bay area 1981-93, pres. Bay area 1990-91, nat. coun. mem., regional rep. 1994-95, Achievement award 1993, Chpt. Contbr. award 1993), Rotary Internat. Avocations: hiking, gardening. Office: US Dept HUD Box 36003 450 Golden Gate Ave San Francisco CA 94102-3661

AXTON, HOYT WAYNE, singer, composer; b. Duncan, Okla., Mar. 25, 1938; s. John Thomas and N. Mae (Boren) A.; children: Michael Stephen, April Laura, Matthew Christopher. Student, Okla. State U., 1957-58. Singer, rec. artist, performer, 1961—, albums recorded on Horizon, VeeJay, Columbia, Capitol, MCA and A&M labels, latest being Hoyt Axton Live; TV performances include Bonanza, 1964, I Dream of Jeannie, 1964, Chryslers Theatre, 1965, Johnny Carson Shows (10), 1976-77, Dinah Shore Show (4), 1975-77, Smothers Bros. Show, 1975, The Hoyt Axton Country Western, Boogie Woogie, Gospel, Rock and Roll Show, 1975, Bionic Woman, 1976, McCloud, 1976, Hee Haw, 1977, 79, 82, 84, Music Hall America, 1977, Midnight Special, 1975-77, Nashville On The Road, 1980-81, Barbara Mandrell Show, 1981, Dukes of Hazard, 1981, Diff'rent Strokes, 1984, Glitter, 1984, Star Search, 1984, Cover-Up, 1984, Nashville Now, 1984, Flo, 1982, Faerie Tale Theatre, 1983-84, numerous others; movie appearances include The Story of a Folk Singer, 1963, Smoky, 1966, Black Stallion, 1980, Junk Man, 1981, Liar's Moon, 1982, Endangered Species, 1983, Gremlins, 1984. Composer numerous recorded songs, including Greenback Dollar, 1962, The Pusher, 1964, Snowblind Friend, 1967, Joy to the World (Jeremiah), 1971, Never Been to Spain, 1972, When the Morning Comes, 1974, Boney Fingers, 1974, Ease Your Pain, 1973, Less Than The Song, 1973, Lion in the Winter, 1974, The No, No, No Song, 1975, Fearless Free Sailin', Life Machine, My Griffin Is Gone, Southbound; a musical The Happy Song, 1972, Outlaw Blues; movie sound track, 1977. Record producer, song pub., pres. bd., Jeremiah Records, from 1979, now chmn. bd.; performer Grand Ole Opry, Nashville, 1974, 75, 76, 80, 82, 83, Ernest Tubb Record Shop, Nashville, 1974-75, 79, Ralph Emery Show, Nashville, 1974-76; performed at Jimmy Carter Inaugural Ball. Author, illustrator: Line Drawings, Vols. I-V, 1974-

78; author song books Life Machine, 1973, Southbound, 1975, Less Than the Song, 1977. Spokesman Am. Heart Assn., 1975, UNICEF, 1975-76; organizer fund raising INTERPLAST, for Stanford U. dept. reconstructive surgery, 1975-76; fund raiser Free Clinics, Calif., 1971-74, Redwing Found., 1976, 77; subsidizing founder Bread and Roses Found., Mill Valley, Calif., 1974—; performer at numerous state and fed. prisons, including San Quentin, 1965-75; Active Democratic presdl. campaigns Eugene McCarthy, Sen. McGovern, Dem. gubernatorial campaigns Gov. Edmond Brown, Calif., Gov. David Boren, Okla.; served as Grand Marshall Special Games, Los Angeles, 1984, Will Rogers Day, Claremore, Okla., 1984. Served with USN, 1958-62. Recipient award Bread and Roses Found., 1984. Mem. Country Music Assn., Am. Fedn. Musicians, AFTRA, Screen Actors Guild, Broadcast Music Inc., Okla. Cattlemen's Assn. Mem. Christian Ch. Office: 1601 Jacksons Valley Pl Hermitage TN 37076-4319

AXWORTHY, LLOYD, Canadian government official; b. North Battleford, Sask., Can., Dec. 21, 1939; s. Norman Joseph and Gwen Jane A.; m. Denise Ommanney, Aug. 3, 1984; 1 child, Stephen. BA, U. Winnipeg; MA, Princeton U., PhD. Min. employment and immigration Canada, 1980-83, min. responsible for status of women, 1980-81, min. transp., 1983-84; critic on internat. trade Official Opposition, 1984-88; critic Liberal Caucus Com. on External Affairs and Nat. Defense, 1988—; vice chmn. Standing com. on External Affairs and Internat. Trade, 1991—; dir. U. Rsch. Inst, assoc. prof.; min. human resources devel., western econ. diversification Canada, 1993-96; min. fgn. affairs Canadian Govt., Ottawa, 1996—; elected to various positions. Office: House of Commons, Rm 418-N Centre Block, Ottawa, ON Canada K1A 0A6*

AYAD, JOSEPH MAGDY, psychologist; b. Cairo, Egypt, May 21, 1926; s. Fahim Gayed and Victoria Gabour (El-Masri) A.; came to U.S., 1949, naturalized, 1961; B.A. in Social Scis., Am. U., Cairo, 1946; M.A. in Clin. Psychology (Univ. scholar), Stanford U., 1952; Ph.D. in Clin. Psychology (Univ. scholar), U. Denver, 1956; m. Widad Fareed Bishai, May 29, 1954; children—Fareed Merritt, Victor Maher, Michael Joseph, Mona Elaine. Translator Hoover Inst. War and Peace, Stanford U., 1950-51; asst. to chief psychologist Colo. Psychopathic Hosp., 1952-54; cons. Child Guidance Clinic, State Dept. Pub. Welfare, Denver, 1953-56; cons. psychologist Dept. Pub. Welfare, State of Tex., 1957-72; cons. psychologist Dept. Insts., Social and Rehab. Svc., State of Okla., 1960-72, N.Mex. Dept. Pub. Welfare, 1960-72; lectr. Fitzsimmons Army Hosp., Denver, 1953-54; vis. psychologist State Dept. Pub. Welfare, Child Guidance Clinic, Pueblo, Colo., 1953-54; staff psychologist Cons. Psychol. Svc., Denver, 1956-57, High Plains Neurol. Ctr., Amarillo, Tex., 1957—; pres. JMA Cattle Co., Amarillo, 1973—; v.p., treas. Filigon Inc., Amarillo, 1962-75, pres., 1976—. Mem. profl. adv. bd. Amarillo Mental Health Assn., 1968-69. Mem. Amarillo Child Welfare Bd., 1961-63; area chmn. U. Denver Fund Raising Campaign, 1963; mem. profl. adv. bd. St. Paul's Meth. Ch. Sch. for Children with Learning Disabilities, Amarillo, 1969-70. Recipient Grad. Sr. award in Philosophy Am. U. at Cairo, 1946. Mem. Am. Psychol. Soc., Am. Psychol. Assn., Internat. Assn. Applied Psychology, Am. Assn. Marriage and Family Therapists, Potter-Randall County (Tex.) Psychol. Soc. (pres. 1974), Tex. Psychol. Assn., Calif. Psychol. Assn. Presbyn. Club: Amarillo Country. Contbr. articles to profl. jours. Home: 4239 Erik Ave Amarillo TX 79106-6008 Office: High Plains Neurological Ctr 2301 W 7th Ave Amarillo TX 79106-6601

AYADI, OLUSEGUN FELIX, finance educator; b. Erinje, Ondo, Nigeria, Mar. 7, 1956; came to the U.S., 1987; s. Thompson Morayo and Dorcas Metele Ayadi; m. Morenike Elizabeth Oyinsulu, Dec. 26, 1986; children: Olufemi, Olukemi, Olusegun Jr. BS in Banking and Fin., U. Lagos, Nigeria, 1980; MS in Fin., U. Lagos, 1983; PhD in Fin., U. Miss., 1991. Lectr. U. Lagos, 1980-87; asst. prof. Lemoyne-Owen Coll., Memphis, 1991-92; asst. prof. Savannah (Ga.) State U., 1992-94, acting dean, 1993; assoc. prof. Fayetteville (N.C.) State U., 1994-97, prof. fin., 1997—; assoc. grad. faculty Ga. So. U., Statesboro, 1992-94. Author: Modern Commerce in West Africa, 1995; guest editor Managerial Fin., 1996-98; contbr. numerous articles to profl. jours. Cons. Jr. Achievement, Savannah, 1992-94, Cumberland County Planning Com., Fayetteville, 1996-97; adv. bd. mem. Savannah Youth Entrepreneur, 1993-94; spkr. C. of C., Savannah, 1992, Cumberland County Schs., Fayetteville, 1995, 98. Recipient Positive Image award Pee Dee Newspaper Group, Greenville, S.C., 1996; named Tchr. of Yr., Sch. Bus. and Econs., Fayetteville State U., 1998-99; Nissan fellow in fin. Nissan Corp./Ednl. Testing Svc./Historically Black Colls. and Univs., Chgo., 1994. Mem. Am. Fin. Assn., Am. Acad. Econs. and Fin., Assn. for Global Bus., Fin. Mgmt. Assn., Ea. Fin. Assn., Nat. Assn. African Am. Studies (N.C. state chair 1995-99). Avocations: reading, tennis, fishing, traveling, watching television. E-mail: fayadi@sbe1.uncfsu.edu. Office: Fayetteville State Univ 1200 Murchison Rd Fayetteville NC 28301

AYALA, FRANCISCO JOSÉ, geneticist, educator; b. Madrid, Mar. 12, 1934; came to U.S., 1961, naturalized, 1971; s. Francisco and Soledad (Pereda) A.; m. Hana Lostakova, Mar. 8, 1985; children by previous marriage: Francisco José, Carlos Alberto. BS, Universidad de Madrid, 1954, D. honoris causa, 1986; MA, Columbia U., 1963, Ph.D., 1964; D. honoris causa, Universidad de León (Spain), 1982, Universidad de Barcelona, Spain, 1986, U. Athens, Greece, 1991, U. Vigo, Spain, 1996, U. Islas, Baleares, Spain, 1998. Research assoc. Rockefeller U., 1964-65; asst. prof. Providence Coll., 1965-67, Rockefeller U., 1967-71; assoc. prof. to prof. genetics U. Calif., Davis, 1971-87; disting. prof. biology U. Calif., Irvine, 1987-89; Donald Bren prof. of Biol. scis., 1989—; bd. dirs. basic biology NRC, 1982-91, chmn., 1984-91, mem. commn. on life scis., 1982-91; mem. nat. adv. coun. Nat. Inst. Gen. Med. Scis.; mem. exec. com. EPA, 1979-80; mem. adv. com. directorate sci. and engring. edn. NSF, 1989-91; mem. nat. adv. coun. for human genome rsch. NIH, 1990-93; mem. Pres. com. advisors sci. and tech., 1994—. Author: Population and Evolutionary Genetics, 1982, Modern Genetics, 1980, 2d edit., 1984, Evolving: the Theory and Processes of Organic Evolution, 1979, Evolution, 1977, Molecular Evolution, 1976, Studies in the Philosophy of Biology, 1974. Recipient medal Coll. de France, 1979, Mendel medal Czech Republic Acad. Scis., 1994; Guggenheim fellow, Fulbright fellow. Fellow AAAS (Sci. Freedom and Responsibility award 1987, bd. dirs. 1989-93, pres.-elect 1993-94, pres. 1994-95, chmn. of bd. 1995-96, chmn. com. on health of sci. enterprise 1991—, mem. nat. coun. for sci. and edn. for phase II, project 2061 1990—); mem. NAS (sect. population biology evolution and ecology chmn. 1983-86, councillor 1986-89, bd. dirs. Nat. Acad. Corp. 1990—), Am. Acad. Arts and Scis., Am. Soc. Naturalists (sec. 1973-76), Genetics Soc. Am., Am. Genetic Assn. (hon. life, Wilhelmine E. Key award), Ecology Soc. Am., Am. Philos. Soc., Soc. Study Evolution (pres. 1979-80), Royal Acad. Scis. Spain (fgn. mem.), Russian Acad. Natural Scis. (fgn. mem.), Mex. Acad. Scis. (fgn. mem.). Home: 2 Locke Ct Irvine CA 92612-4034 Office: U Calif Dept Ecology and Evolutionary Biology Irvine CA 92697-2525

AYALA, JOHN, librarian, dean; b. Long Beach, Calif., Aug. 28, 1943; s. Francisco and Angelina (Rodriguez) A.; m. Patricia Marie Dozier, July 11, 1987; children: Juan, Sara. BA in History, Calif. State U., Long Beach, 1970, MPA, 1981; MLS, Immaculate Heart Coll., L.A., 1971. Library paraprofl. Long Beach Pub. Library, 1963-70; librarian L.A. County Pub. Libr., 1971-72; librarian Long Beach City Coll., 1972-90, assoc. prof., 1972-90, pres. acad. senate, 1985-87; dean, Learning Resources Fullerton (Calif.) Coll., 1990—, evening/weekend supr., 1997—; chmn. Los Angeles County Com. to Recruit Mexican-Am. Librs., 1971-74; mem. acad. senate Calif. Cmty. Colls., 1985-90; pres. Latino Faculty/Staff Assn., NOCCD, 1993—. Editor Calif. Librarian, 1971. Served with USAF, 1966-68, Vietnam. U.S. Office Edn. fellow for library sci., 1970-71. Mem. ALA (com. mem. 1971—, Melvil Dewey award com. 1998—), Calif. Libr. Assn., REFORMA Nat. Assn. to Promote Spanish Speaking Libr. Svc. (founding mem., v.p., pres. 1973-76). Democrat. Roman Catholic. Office: Fullerton College Library 321 E Chapman Ave Fullerton CA 92832-2011

AYASO, MANUEL, artist; b. Coruna, Galicia, Spain, Jan. 1, 1934; came to U.S., 1947, naturalized, 1955; s. Jose and Dolores (Dios) A.; m. Lucia Rivas, May 2, 1959; children: Monica, Jose Luciano. Student, Newark Sch. Fine and Indsl. Art, N.J., 1953-56. Exhibited one-man shows, Cober Gallery, N.Y.C., 1961-63, 65, 66, 68, Forum Gallery, 1970, 72, 74, Ft. Worth Art Ctr., 1964, SUNY-Oswego, 1965, Witt Meml. Mus., San Antonio, 1967, Casa de Galicia, Madrid, Spain, 1994, N.Y. Armory, 1995, Casa da Parra, Santiago de Compostela, Spain, 1997; group shows include 22d Biennial Internat. Watercolor Exhbn., Bklyn. Mus., 1963, U. Mex., Mexico City, 1963, Exhibit Contemporary Am. Artists, Nat. Inst. Arts and Letters, 1962, 63, 64, 71, Whitney Mus. Am., 1963, Vatican Exhibit Contemporary Am. Spiritual Art, Rome, 1976, traveling exhbn., The Fine Line: Drawing with Silver in Am., 1985-86, Objects and Drawings from the Sanford M. and Diane Besser Collection, 1992-93, Casa da Cultura, Riveira La Coruna. Served with U.S. Army, 1956-58. Recipient St. Paul Gallery and Sch. Art Purchase award, 1961; Tiffany Found. Award, 1962; Ford Found. grantee, 1964; recipient Nat. Inst. Arts and Letters Childe Hassam Purchase award, 1971, hon. mention 2d Ann. Int. Exhibit of Miniature Art, Del Bello Gal, Toronto, Can., 1987. Mem. Nat. Geog. Soc., Smithsonian Instn., Whitney Mus. Am. Art, N.J. State Mus. Roman Catholic. Address: 12 Vincent Pl Verona NJ 07044-3022

AYBAR, CHARLES ANTON, aviation executive; b. N.Y.C., Sept. 27, 1956; s. Louis Adolf and Elisabeth A. (Schwarz) A.; m. Deborah Ann Benson, May 1, 1988; children: Heidi Brita, Aric Anton. AS in Aeronautics, Embry-Riddle Aero. U., 1987; BS in Aviation Mgmt., Pacific-Western U., 1988, MBA in Mktg., 1988, PhD in Mgmt., 1993. Lic. airline transport pilot; cert. FAA flight instr. and aircraft dispatcher. V.p. mktg. Commuter Air Tech., Inc., Scottsdale, Ariz., 1996—; written test examiner FAA, Orlando, Fla., 1989-91, accident prevention counselor, 1991—; cons. CBS TV Network, 1979-80; prodr., host TV show series Flightline, Aviation Today in Ariz., 1994-98. Recipient Silver medal award FAA, 1995, A.C.E. award FAA, Flight Instr. of Yr. award FAA, 1994. Avocations: roller skating, ice skating, swimming, electronics. Home: 3922 E Kimberly Way Phoenix AZ 85050-6334

AYBAR, ROMEO, architect; b. Buenos Aires, Argentina, Feb. 8, 1930; came to U.S., 1960, naturalized, 1965; s. Aristobulo Romeo and Maria Sara (Figoli) A.; m. Rose Delia Caceres, Oct. 18, 1954; children: Patricia Monica Aybar Smith, Viviana Sylvia Aybar Pugaczewski, Cynthia Jenny Aybar Giordano. B.Arch., U. Buenos Aires, 1954. Lic. architect, N.J., Pa., Del., Md., Vt., Va.; registered planner, N.J.; cert. Dept. Def. fall-out shelter analyst. Pvt. practice architecture Buenos Aires, 1955-60; sr. draftsman Widersum Assocs., N.Y.C., 1960-61; job capt. Mahony Troast, Clifton, N.J., 1961-63; project mgr. R. Cadien Architect, Cliffside Park, N.J., 1963-67; ptnr. Cadien & Aybar, Cliffside Park, N.J., 1968-69; sr. ptnr. The Aybar Partnership-Architects and Planners, Ridgefield, N.J., 1969—; organizer, dir. First Fed. Bank, Clifton, N.J.; mem. adv. bd. archtl. drafting course The Plaza Sch., Paramus, N.J., 1971—; lectr. Ft. Lee High Sch., Ridgefield High Sch., N.J. Sch. Architecture, N.J. Inst. Tech., others; mem. adj. faculty Montclair State Coll., 1971-74. Mem. Indsl. Safety Council N.J., 1973-78; mem. Ridgefield Zoning Bd. Adjustments, 1969-71, chmn., 1972-73; mem. Hudson Riverfront Planning Commn. State of N.J., 1979-81; acting bldg. insp. City of Ridgefield, 1968; mem. planning commn. Ellis Island & Statue of Liberty Restoration Master Plan, 1979-80. 1st lt., pilot N.J. wing CAP, 1978. Recipient Dir.'s award Architects League N.J., 1971, 84, 86, Vegliante Meml. award Architects League N.J., 1973, Outstanding Excellence in Design award N.J. Soc. Architects, 1971, 73, citation for Outstanding Svcs. Am. Concrete Assn., 1979; named Jerseyan of Week Star Ledger Publs., 1979. Fellow AIA (N.J. regional dir. 1981-83, 125th Anniversary Presdl. citation 1982, Presdl. citation 1982, citation Dedicated Svcs. 1983); mem. Archtl. League N.J. (pres. 1975), N.J. Soc. Architects (dir. 1971, established Romeo Aybar Scholarship 1973, treas. 1974-75, pres. 1979, award of Honor 20 Yrs. Meritorious Accomplishments 1988, regional dir. 1983), Aircraft Owners and Pilots Assn., Nat. Pilots Assn. Republican. Club: Ridgefield Exchange (pres.) (1972-73); Ridgefield Exchange (dir. N.J. dist.) (1973-74). Home: 2150 Center Ave Fort Lee NJ 07024-5806 Office: Aybar Partnership 605 Broad Ave Ridgefield NJ 07657-1697*

AYDELOTTE, MYRTLE KITCHELL, nursing administrator, educator, consultant; b. Van Meter, Iowa, May 31, 1917; d. John J. and Larava Josephine (Gutshall) Kitchell; m. William O. Aydelotte, June 22, 1956; children—Marie Elizabeth, Jeannette Farley. B.S., U. Minn., 1939, M.A., 1947, Ph.D., 1955; postgrad., Columbia U. Tchrs. Coll., summer 1948. Head nurse Charles T. Miller Hosp., St. Paul, 1939-41; surg. teaching St. Mary's Hosp. Sch. Nursing, Mpls., 1941-42; instr. U. Minn., 1945-49; dir., dean State U. Iowa Coll. Nursing, 1949-57, prof., 1957-62; assoc. chief nurse VA Hosp. Rsch. for Nursing, Iowa City, 1963-64, chief nursing rsch., 1964-65; prof. U. Iowa Coll. Nursing, 1964-76, 82-88; exec. dir. Am. Nurses Assn., 1977-81; dir. nursing U. Iowa Hosps. and Clinics, 1968-76; mem. sci. adv. bd. Ctr. for Health Rsch. Wayne State U., 1972-76, Inst. Medicine, 1973—; cons. U. Minn., 1970, 82, 90, U. Rochester, 1971, U. Mich., 1970, 73, U. Colo., 1970-71, U. Hawaii, 1972-73, Ariz. State U., 1972, U. Nebr., 1972-73. Contbr. articles to profl. jours.; editorial bd.: Nursing Forum, 1969-72, Jour. Nursing Adminstrn, 1971. Mem., v.p. Iowa City Library Bd., 1961-67; mem. Johnson County Bd. Health, 1967-70; mem. adv. com. on family living courses Iowa City Bd. Edn., 1970-72. Served with Army Nurse Corps, 1942-46. Mem. Am. Nurses Assn., Inst. Medicine, Am. Acad. Nursing, Sigma Theta Tau (research com. 1968-72). Home: 41 Menlo Pl Rochester NY 14620-2717

AYER, DONALD BELTON, lawyer; b. San Mateo, Calif., Apr. 30, 1949; m. Anne Norton; children: Christopher, Alison. BA in History with great distinction and honors, Stanford U., 1971; MA in History, Harvard U., 1973, JD cum laude, 1975. Bar: Calif. 1975, D.C. 1978. Law clk. to judge U.S. Ct. Appeals D.C. Cir., 1975-76; law clk. to Justice William H. Rehnquist, U.S. Supreme Ct., Washington, 1976-77; asst. U.S. atty. criminal div. No. Dist. Calif., San Francisco, 1977-79, in charge San Jose office, 1978-79; assoc. Gibson Dunn & Crutcher, San Jose, Calif., 1979-81; U.S. atty. Eastern Dist. Calif., Sacramento, 1982-86; prin. dep. solicitor gen. Dept. Justice, 1986-88; ptnr. Jones, Day, Reavis & Pogue, Washington, 1988-89, adminstrv. ptnr., 1991-93, chair gov. disputes sect., 1993-96; dep. atty. gen. U.S. Dept. Justice, Washington, 1989-90. mem. Atty. Gen.'s Adv. Com. of U.S. Attys., 1986; mem. exec. com. 9th Cir. Jud. Conf., 1983-85; mem. Calif. State Bar Fed. Cts. Commn., 1983-86; pubs. com. U.S. Supreme Ct. Hist. Soc., 1991—; mem. adv. com. state and local legal ctr.; 1992—. Articles editor Harvard U. Law Rev., 1974-75; contbr. articles to legal jours. Bd. dirs. Langley Non-Profit Housing Corp., 1990-98; mem. vestry St. Mary's Episc. Ch., 1987-90; trustee Potomac Sch., McLean, Va., 1994—; bd. dirs. Am. Rivers, Inc., 1997—, treas., 1998—; pres. Stanford Young Reps., 1970-71; mem. adv. com. State and Local Legal Ctr., 1992—; mem. Fed. City Coun., 1991-93. Fellow Am. Bar Found. (life); mem. ABA (litigation sect., task force on internat. criminal ct. 1991-94, adv. bd. state and local legal ctr.), Am. Bar Found., Am. Acad. Appellate Lawyers (mem. com. 1997—), Am. Law Inst., D.C. Bar Found. (adv. bd. 1992—), Calif. State Bar, D.C. Bar Assn. Episcopalian. Office: Jones Day Reavis & Pogue 1450 G St NW Washington DC 20005-2001

AYER, RAMANI, insurance company executive. BS, Indian Inst. Tech., Bombay; MS in Chem. Engring., D in Chem. Engring., Drexel U. With The Hartford, Hartford, Conn., 1973—, asst. sec., staff asst. to chmn. and chief exec., 1979-83; v.p. HartRe, 1983-86; pres. Hartford Specialty Co., 1986-89; sr. v.p. The Hartford, 1989-90, exec. v.p., 1990-91; pres., COO property-casualty ops. Hartford Fire Ins. Co., 1991-97; chmn., CEO, pres. The Hartford, 1997—; mem. listed co. adv. com. N.Y. Stock Exch. Bd. Dirs.; past chmn. Ins. Svcs. Office. Trustee Mark Twain House, Hartford, Conn. Mem. Am. Ins. Assn. (bd. dirs., past chmn. task force catastrophic issues, past vice chmn. spl. bd. com. workers compensation), Am. Inst. Property and Liability Underwriters (trustee), Ins. Inst. Am. (trustee). Office: The Hartford Hartford Plz 690 Asylum Ave Hartford CT 06115*

AYERS, CHARLES ALLEN, insurance risk management executive; b. Jamestown, N.Y., Nov. 5, 1941; s. Allen Franklin and Margaret Clarice (Graham) A.; divorced; children: Mark, Suzanne. BA in Psychology, U. Buffalo, 1963, LLB, 1966. Multi line adjuster Nationwide Ins. Co., Buffalo, 1966; field rep. Gates, McDonald & Co., Buffalo and Atlanta, 1966-70; br. mgr. Gates, McDonald & Co., Atlanta, 1970-74, dist. mgr., 1974-78; regional/gen. mgr. Gates, McDonald & Co., Columbus and Tampa, 1978-87; v.p. Sedgwick James, Orlando, Fla., 1988-90; workers compensation and benefits ins. mgr. Walter Industries, Inc., Tampa, Fla., 1991—; self ins. cons. Bradham & Bennett, P.A., 1990-91; Fla. industry rep. Fla.Dept. Labor Self Ins. Rules Adv. Com., Tallahassee, 1983-91. Mem. Fla. Assn. Self Ins. (bd. dirs. 1983—, chair self ins. rules com., Pres.'s award for Contbns. to Self Ins. Industry 1990, pres. 1995-97), So. Assn. Workers Compensation Adminstrs. (select com. on self ins. 1979-91). Avocations: tennis, golf, table tennis. Office: Walter Industries Inc 1500 N Dale Mabry Hwy Tampa FL 33607-2551

AYERS, HARRY BRANDT, editor, publisher, columnist; b. Anniston, Ala., Apr. 8, 1935; s. Harry Mell and Edel Olga (Ytterboe) A.; m. Josephine Ehringhaus, Dec. 9; 1 child, Margaret. BA in History, U. Ala., Tuscaloosa, 1959; LHD (hon.), U. Ala., Birmingham, 1994, U. Ala., 1994. Polit. writer The Raleigh (N.C.) Times, 1959-61; corr. Bascom Timmons Bur., Washington, 1961-63; mng. editor The Anniston Star, 1963-69, editor, pub., 1969—; chair Consolidated Publ. Co., 1998—; commentator Pub. Radio, NPR "Morning Edition." Mem. adv. bd. Inside Story, Pub. Broadcasting System, N.Y.C., 1981-85; co-editor: You Can't Eat Magnolias, 1972; co-author: A Bicentennial Portrait of the American People, U.S. News Books, 1976, Inaugural Book President Carter, 1977, Dixie Dateline, 1983; frequent contbr. to internat. and nat. newspapers. Trustee Talladega (Ala.) Coll., 1972-89, Wooster Sch., Danbury, Conn., 1989-90, 20th Century Fund, 1985—, Ctr. for Excellence in Govt., 1985-88, Am. Com., Internat. Press Inst., Vienna, 1985—; bd. dirs. So. Ctr. for Internat. Studies, Atlanta, 1979—, Bd. Fgn. Scholarships, Washington, 1981-84; mem. adv. bd. Am. Ditchley Found., London; mem. Coun. Fgn. Rels., N.Y.C., 1983—; bd. dirs. Inter-Am. Press Assn., Miami, 1992-93. Named Disting. Journalism Grad., U. Ala., 1967; recipient Human Rels. award Am. Jewish Com., 1977, Green Eyeshade award Soc. Profl. Journalists, 1985; named to Ala. Acad. Honor, 1991; fellow Nieman Found., Harvard U., 1968, sr. fellow Gannett Ctr., Columbia U., 1989. Mem. Ala. Press Journalism Found. (founding pres. 1969), Am. Soc. Newspaper Editors, So. Newspaper Pubs. Assn. (dir. 1981-84), Century Assn. N.Y.C., Met. Club Washington, The Summit Club Birmingham. Democrat. Episcopalian. Home: 1 Booger Holw Anniston AL 36207-6805 Office: Anniston Star PO Box 189 Anniston AL 36202-0189

AYERS, JEFFREY DAVID, lawyer; b. Grant, Nebr., Nov. 30, 1960; s. William D. and Lela R. (Gilmore) A.; m. Shelly Jo Dodds, June 11, 1988; children: Sydney Elizabeth, Bailey Anne. BS, Graceland Coll., 1982; MBA, JD, U. Iowa, 1985. Bar: Mo. 1985. Assoc. Stinson, Mag & Fizzell, Kansas City, Mo., 1985-88, Bryan, Cave, McPheeters & McRoberts, Kansas City, 1989-92; ptnr. Blackwell Sanders Peper Martin LLP, Kansas City, Mo., 1992—; mayor City of Lake Tapawingo, Mo., 1993-96. Trustee Little Blue Valley Sewer Dist., 1994-95. Democrat. Reorganized Ch. Latter-Day-Saints. Office: Blackwell Sanders et al 2300 Main St Ste 1100 Kansas City MO 64108-2416

AYERS, RICHARD WAYNE, electrical company official; b. Atlanta, Aug. 23, 1945; s. Harold Richard and Martha Elizabeth (Baughan) A.; m. Nancy Katherine Martin, Aug. 9, 1969. BBA, Ga. State Coll., 1967; MBA, Ind. U., 1969. Specialist mktg. comm. rsch. GE Co., Schenectady, N.Y., 1969-70; copywriter lamp divsn. GE Co., Cleve., 1970-73, supr. distbr. advt. & sales promotion, 1973-75; supr. comml. & indsl. promotional programs GE Lighting Bus. Group, 1975-79, mgr. comml. & indsl. market distbr. and promotional programs, 1979-87, mgr. comml. & indsl. comm., 1987-91, mgr. mktg. comms., 1992—; lectr. in field. Author: Winning Through Promotion, 1987, 93, 96. Dir.-at-large Ga. Young Reps., 1966-67. Recipient Best Indsl. Promotion award Advt. Age, 1974, Incentive Showcase award Nat. Premium Sales Exec. Assn., 1975, 76, 87, 91, Gold Key award Nat. Assn. Incentive Mktg., 1976, 77, 87, Golden Communicators award Factory mag., 1976, Leader award Direct Mktg. Assn., 1983, Top prize Am. Lighting Assn., 1990, 91, 92, 95, 96, 97, 98, Addy award Am. Advt. Assn., 1992. Mem. Elfun Soc., Blue Key, Delta Sigma Pi, Beta Gamma Sigma. Home: 12550 Lake Ave Apt 1309 Lakewood OH 44107-1570 Office: Nela Park Bldg 307 Cleveland OH 44112

AYKAL, GÜRER, conductor; b. Eskisehir, Turkey, May 22, 1942; s. Tevfik and Sadiye (Kaftan) A.; m. Duygu Aykal, Jan. 4, 1964 (dec. Jan. 1988); children: Kerem Tim, Emre T., John M. Student, Santa Cecilia Acad., Rome, 1971-73; Diploma di Merito in Advanced Conducting, Academia Musicale Chigiana; grad. degrees, Academia Chigiana, Siena, Italy, Academia Santa Cecilia, Rome, Royal Acad. Music, London, Guildhall Sch. Music, London, Ankara State Conservatory, Turkey; studied with Franco Ferrara, Andre Previn, George Hurst. Asst. condr. to Franco Ferrara Academia Santa Cecilia, Rome; violinist Presdl. Symphony Orch., Ankara, condr., music dir., 1975—; condr., music dir. Lubbock (Tex.) Symphony Orch.; founder, music dir. Ankara Chamber Orch.; prin. guest condr. Oulu State Orch., Finland; guest condr. various prominent orchs. in Eng., Ireland, Italy, France, Spain, Belgium, The Netherlands, Yugoslavia, Finland, Norway, Fed. Republic Germany, German Dem. Republic, Czechoslovakia, Bulgaria, Romania, Poland, Hungary, USSR, Singapore; condr. English Chamber Orch. for tour of South Am. and Caribbean, Moscow State Symphony Orch. for tour of USSR, Istanbul Symphony Orch. on tour or Greece, 1989, Amsterdam Concertgebow Chamber Orch. on tour of Germany, 1989; past condr. Ankara State Conservatory Orch., Turkish State Opera and Ballet Co.; tchr. conducting Ind. U., Tex. Tech. U. Recordings include work with London Philharm. Orch. Named Turkish State Artist, 1981. Avocation: soccer. Home: 108 Westminister Rd Scarsdale NY 10583-2425 Office: Lubbock Symphony Orch 1721 Broadway St Lubbock TX 79401-3013

AYKROYD, DANIEL EDWARD, actor, writer; b. Ottawa, Ont., Can., July 1, 1952; came to U.S., 1975; s. Peter Hugh and Lorraine G. (Gougeon) A.; m. Maureen Lewis, May 10, 1974 (div.); children: Mark, Lloyd, Oscar; m. Donna Dixon, 1984; children: Danielle, Belle Kingston. Mem. Toronto Co. of Second City Theater; star in CBS TV series Coming Up Rosie; writer, actor: NBC's Saturday Night Live, 1975-79; other TV appearances include All You Need is Cash, Steve Martin's Best Show Ever, Tales From the Crypt, HBO, 1992, Soul Man, 1997; motion picture appearances include (actor) Love at First Sight, 1974, 1941, 1979, Mr. Mike's Mondo Video, 1979, Neighbors, 1981, Doctor Detroit, 1983, Trading Places, 1983, Twilight Zone, 1983, Nothing Lasts Forever, 1984, Into the Night, 1985, Caddyshack II, 1988, The Great Outdoors, 1988, My Stepmother is an Alien, 1988, Driving Miss Daisy, 1989, My Girl, 1991, Sneakers, 1992, Chaplin, 1992, My Girl 2, 1994, Exit to Eden, 1994, (actor, co-screenwriter) The Blues Brothers, 1980, Ghostbusters, 1984, Spies Like Us, 1985, Dragnet, 1987, Ghostbusters II, 1989, Coneheads, 1993, Canadian Bacon, 1994, Tommy Boy, 1995, Rainbow, 1995, Casper, 1995, Sgt. Bilko, 1996, My Fellow Americans, 1996, getting Away With Murder, 1996, Feeling Minnesota, 1996, Celtic Pride, 1996, Grosse Pointe Blank, 1997, Blues Brothers 2000, 1997, The Arrow, 1997, Susan's Plan, 1998, Antz (voice), 1999, Diamonds, 1999, (actor, dir., screenwriter) Nothing But Trouble, 1991, (exec. prodr.) One More Saturday Night, 1986; performed (with John Belushi) as the Blues Brothers; albums include: Briefcase Full of Blues, Made in America, The Blues Brothers (motion-picture soundtrack), Best of the Blues Brothers, The Essential Blues Brothers; guest-columnist for Premiere magazine, 1992; tv guest appearances The Nanny, 1993, Home Improvement, 1991. Recipient Emmy award 1976-77. Mem. Writers Guild Am. West, AFTRA. Office: CAA care Fred Specktor 9830 Wilshire Blvd Beverly Hills CA 90212-1804*

AYLIN, ELIZABETH TWIST PABST, real estate broker, developer; b. Pueblo, Colo., Aug. 22, 1917; d. Earl Joshua and Mabel Prudence (Benning) Twist; m. Julius Frohne Pabst, Apr. 16, 1944 (dec. Mar. 1984); children: Rachel Pabst Mrvichin, Jane Selkirk Pabst; m. Robert Norman Aylin, May 5, 1990 (dec. Nov. 1997). AB, U. No. Colo., 1939. English lang. teacher high sch., Holyoke, Colo., 1939-40; sec. to chancellor U. Denver, 1940-41; sec. to regional dir. Civil Svc., Denver, 1941-42; pers. dir. Denver Med. Depot, U.S. Quartermaster Corps, 1942; bus. adminstr. Pabst Home Builders and Lumber Co., Houston, 1945-84; owner, pres. Selkirk Island Corp., Houston, 1984-99, Selkirk Island Utilities Corp., Houston, 1984-99, Pabst Corp., Houston, 1984-99. Wave ensign USN, 1942-44. Recipient Alumni Contbn. to Bus. award U. No. Colo., 1991. Mem. Houston Area Ret. Officers Assn. (v.p. 1986-90, 92-93). Home: 3835 Olympia Dr Houston TX 77019-3031 Office: 1 Selkirk Rd Bay City TX 77414-9341

AYLING, HENRY FAITHFUL, writer, editor, consultant; b. Bklyn., Dec. 30, 1931; s. Albert Edward John and Mina Campbell McCurdy (Lindsay) A.; m. Julia Corinne Gornto, 1954; children: Campbell, Eben, Corey, Harry, Faith. BA, Grinnell Coll., 1953; MA, Columbia U., Calif. State U., Carson, 1984; 2 grad. teaching certs., Calif. State U., Carson, 1985. Asst. to registrar Columbia U., N.Y.C., 1958-59; supr. crew scheduling Pan Am World

Airways, Jamaica, N.Y., 1959-62, supr. payload control, 1963-65; mgr. crew scheduling Seabd. World Airlines, Jamaica, 1962-63, 65-68, mgr. system control, 1968-80; mgr. ops. control Flying Tiger Line, 1980-84; instr. English, ESL Long Beach (Calif.) City Coll., 1984-85; mng. editor IEEE Expert, IEEE Computing Futures IEEE Computer Soc., Los Alamitos, Calif., 1985-90, editorial dir. Computer Soc. Press, 1990-93; writer, editor, cons., 1993—. Mem. editorial bd. Expert Mag., 1986-90, CamAm Programming Inc., 1987-88; columnist Mag. Design and Prodn. mag., 1988-89; contbr. articles to profl. mags. and tech. books; contbr. poetry to various mags. and anthologies. Bd. dirs. Playa Serena Home Owners Assn., Playa Del Rey, Calif., 1983-85. Recipient Maggie awards Western Publs. Assn., 1988-89. Avocations: music, fine arts. Home and Office: 78291 Allegro Dr Palm Desert CA 92211-1894

AYLOR, DONALD EARL, biophysicist, research meteorologist, plant pathology educator and reseacher; b. Hunt, N.Y., Dec. 22, 1940; married Ruthann Brody, 1964; children: Adam, Rachel. BES, SUNY, Stony Brook, 1964; MS, SUNY, 1966, PhD in Mechnical Engring., 1970. Asst. scientist, 1969-75; chief scientist biophysicist Dept. Ecology & Climatology, 1976-83; chief scientist dept. plant pathology and ecology Conn. Agrl. Expt. Sta., 1984—; mem. com. aerobiol. Nat. Rsch. Coun., 1976-80. Guggenheim fellow, 1980. Fellow Am. Meteorological Soc., Am. Phytopath Soc., AAAS. Research in turbulent dispersion of particles and gases in the atmosphere and of solutes in rivers; plant disease epidemiology; noise propagation outdoors; mechanics of plant cells. Office: Conn Agrl Expt Sta Dept Plant Pathology & Ecology PO Box 1106 New Haven CT 06504-1106

AYLOUSH, CYNTHIA MARIE, financial executive; b. Jackson, Mich., July 2, 1950; d. Leonard Edward and Violet Caroline (Kroeger) Ullrich; m. Abbott Selim Ayloush, June 21, 1980; children: Sasha Christine, Nadia Marie, Ramsey Abbott. AA, Fullerton Coll., 1970; diploma in fashion mdse., Brooks Coll., 1975; BS, Pepperdine U., 1980. Receptionist, Hydraflow, Commerce, Calif., 1968-74, pers. mgr., Cerritos, Calif., 1979—, treas., 1979—, corp. sec., 1985—, exec. v.p., CFO, 1995—; with sales dept. Robinson's, Cerritos, Calif., 1974-75, dept. mgr., 1975-79. Mem. Am. Soc. Pers. Adminstrs., Pers. Indsl. Rels. Assn., Mchts. and Mfrs. Assn., Cerritos C. of C. (bd. dir. 1983-89). Republican. Roman Catholic. Clubs: Soroptimist (sec. 1979—, pres. 1993-94), Damas de Caridad (sec. 1992-93), Century, Pepperdine U. Office: Hydraflow 13259 166th St Cerritos CA 90703-2269

AYLWARD, PAUL LEON, lawyer, banker, rancher; b. Stonington, Ill., Mar. 1, 1908; s. Dennis E. and Via (Holben) A.; m. Karma Golden, Oct. 30, 1929; children: Paul, Patricia Thompson, Peter. BS, U. Ill., 1928; LLB, Chgo. Kent Coll. Law, 1930. Bar: Ill. 1930, Kans. 1931, U.S. Dist Ct. Kans. 1931, U.S. Ct. Appeals (10th cir.) 1941. Sole practice, Elsworth, Kans., 1931-40; county atty. Ellsworth, 1933-39; atty. city of Ellsworth, 1938-63, 66-72; spl. atty. U.S. Dept. Justice, 1940-53; ptnr. Aylward, Svaty & Sherman, Ellsworth, 1940-88; dir. First Nat. Bank Holcomb (Kans.), Citizen's State Bank, Ellsworth. Trustee, past pres. Ellsworth County Vet. Meml. Hosp., 1946-91; bd. dirs. Ellsworth Devel. Assn.; past chmn. Kans. Park Resources Authority; chmn. Kans. Joint Council on Recreation, 1967-74; active Rural Area Devel. Nat. Adv. Com., 1963-63; trustee, past pres. Smoky Hills Art Found., 1968—; mem. exec. com. Coronado council Boy Scouts Am., 1970—, pres., 1977-78; county chmn. Democratic party, 1946-74, chmn. 1st Dist., 1964-68, 70-74; del. Dem. Nat. Conv., 1960, 68, 72, 76; chmn. Kansans for Carlin for Gov., 1977; mem. Kans. for Carter Com., 1976, Kans. Vets. Commn., 1986-90. Served to lt. USN, 1943-45. Mem. ABA, Kans. Bar Assn., Kans. Assn. Def. Counsel (dir. 1967-72), Am. Legion (comdr. Kans. 1953; nat. legis. com. 1954-57; others). Roman Catholic. Home and Office: 306 Forest Dr Ellsworth KS 67439-3520

AYLWARD, RONALD LEE, lawyer; b. St. Louis, May 30, 1930; s. John Thomas and Edna (Ketcherside) A.; m. Margaret Cecilia Hellweg, Aug. 10, 1963; children: Susan Marie, Stephen Ronald, Carolyn Ann. AB, Washington U., St. Louis, 1952, JD, 1954; student, U. Va., 1955. Bar: Mo. 1954, Ill. 1961, U.S. Supreme Ct. 1968. Assoc. Heneghan, Roberts & Cole, St. Louis, 1958-59; asst. counsel Olin Corp., East Alton, Ill., 1960-64; asst. gen. counsel INTERCO, Inc., St. Louis, 1964-66; asso. gen. counsel, mgr. law dept. INTERCO, Inc., 1966-69, asst. sec., 1966-74, gen. counsel, 1969-81, mem. operating bd., 1970-92, v.p., 1971-81, mem. exec. com., dir., 1975-92, exec. v.p., 1981-85, vice chmn. bd. dirs., 1985-92; chmn., pres. Aylward & Assocs., Inc., St. Louis, 1992—; mem. dist. export coun. U.S. Dept. Commerce, 1974-77; dir., mem. exec. com. Boatmen's Nat. Bank St. Louis, 1982-91, trust estates com., 1982-85, chmn. audit com., 1986-91; bd. dirs. Boatmen's Bancshares, Inc., mem. audit com., 1984-91, mem. compensation com., 1986-91; trustee Maryville U., 1989-92, chmn. bd., 1991-92. Bd. dirs. St. Louis chpt. Nat. Found. March of Dimes, 1974-84, sec., 1976-78, chmn., 1979-82; bd. dirs. Cardinal Ritter Inst., 1975-90, chmn. pers. com., 1986-90; bd. dirs. St. Louis chpt. ARC, 1977-82, Linda Vista Montessori Sch., 1975-77, BBB Greater St. Louis, 1978-81, YMCA Greater St. Louis, 1981—, NCCJ, 1992-93; bd. dirs. Cardinal Glennon Children's Hosp., 1991-96, mem. exec. com., 1992-96, bd. dirs. Found., 1996—; bd. dirs. Cath. Charities of St. Louis, 1994—, vice chmn., 1995-97, chmn. 1997—; mem. coun. Archdiocesan Devel. Appeal, 1994-97, chmn. 1996-97, vice chmn ., 1995-97, mem. exec. com., 1995-97, chmn. rev./planning com., 1995-96, chmn., 1996-97, hon. life mem.; mem. fin. coun. Archdiocese of St. Louis, 1995-98, mem. investment com., 1995-97; bd. dirs., fin. United Way Greater St. Louis, 1986—; mem. in vestment com. St. Louis Cmty. Found., 1993-95; trustee St. Louis Coun. World Affairs, sec., 1977-84; chmn. lay bd. DePaul Health Ctr., 1979-81; mem. exec. com. lay bd., 1981-89; mem. lay adv. bd. Chaminade Coll. Prep Sch., 1980-84, chmn. bd. trustees, 1981-84; mem. lay bd. Acad. of the Visitation, 1981-85. With AUS, 1955-58. Recipient of Order of St. Louis's King, Archdiocese of St. Louis. Mem. Mo. Bar Assn., St. Louis Bar Assn., Am. Footwear Industries Assn. (nat. affairs vice chmn. 1970, chmn. 1971-75), Am. Apparel Mfrs. Assn. (dir. 1983-85), NAM (taxation com. 1970-76, pub. affairs com. 1973-76, govt. ops./expenditures com. 1973-78), St. Louis C. of C. (legis. and tax com. 1966-74, vice chmn. 1970-71), Assoc. Industries Mo. (dir. 1973-80, exec. com. 1974-80, 2d v.p. 1974-76, pres. 1976-78), Am. Soc. Corp. Secs. (pres. St. Louis regional group 1972-73), Creve Coeur C. of C., Rotary (bd. dirs. St. Louis Club 1976-79), Knights of Malta, Knights of Holy Sepulcher, Order of St. Louis King, Legatus, Mo. Athletic Club, Bellerive Country Club (dir. 1981-84), Delta Theta Phi (dist. chancellor Mo. 1970-79, pres. St. Louis Alumni 1963). Clubs: Mo. Athletic, Bellerive Country (dir. 1981-84). Home: 55 Muirfield Saint Louis MO 63141-7372 Office: Aylward and Assoc Inc One City Plaza Dr Saint Louis MO 63141 *Having something to achieve is the essence of my career. Continuing to set higher goals throughout life has made it both interesting and rewarding.*

AYMAN, IRAJ, international education consultant; b. Tehran, Feb. 9, 1928; came to the U.S., 1978; s. Abbas and Lagha (Hamidi) A.; m. Lily Ahy; children: Roya, Saba, Rama. BA, Tehran U., 1949; EdD, Edinburgh U., 1952; PhD, U. So. Calif., 1957; postgrad., Harvard U., 1963. Cert. tchr. Assoc. prof. applied psychology, dir. Pers. Mgmt./Rsch. Ctr. U. Tehran, Iran, 1957-70; prof., chair psychology dept. Nat. U. Tchr. Edn., Tehran, 1963-70; dir. Inst. Ednl. Studies, Tehran, 1963-70; pres. Nat. Inst. Psychology, Tehran, 1970-80; rsch. assoc. U. Chgo., 1979-83; regional edn. advisor Asia and Pacific UNESCO, Bangkok, 1983-87; chief tng. ednl. pers. UNESCO, Paris, 1987-88; dir. internat. programs Human Resource Inst., Westport, Conn., 1979-83; founder, dir. Landegg Acad., Wienacht, Switzerland, 1988-94; dir. Inst. Internat. Edn., St. Gallen, Switzerland, 1988-94; internat. cons. Internat. Edn. Systems, L.A., 1994-96; dean Wilmette (Ill.) Inst., 1995—; faculty Capella U., 1996—; program evaluation cons. IIT, 1975—; vis. prof. grad. colls. edn. & mgmt. scis. UCLA, 1974-75; vis. prof., Ford Found. cons. grad. colls. edn. & pub. adminstrn. U. Philippines, Mania, 1965-67; dir. inst. edn. Nat. Tchr. Edn. U., Tehran, 1960-63; tng. advisor Pakistan Internat. Airline, Karachi, 1969-70; faculty Grad. Sch. Am., 1996—. Author, co-editor: Personnel Administration, 1955; author: Merit Rating, 1958; gen. editor: Educational Psychology, 1960; author, editor: A New Framework for Moral Education, 1993; co-editor: Transition to Global Society, 1993. Cons. UN Devel. Program, N.Y.C., Sri Lanka, 1993; exec. sec., coord. Internat. Dialogue on Transition to Global Soc., Switzerland, 1989-94; cons. Activity Ctr. for Edn., Beijing, 1988—; commr. of audit Eastern Regional Orgn. for Pub. Adminstrn., Manila, 1962-82. Specialist grantee Govt. of U.S., 1963, U.K. Tech. Cooperation Dept., 1962, USAID, 1955-57. Fellow Chinese Assn. Local Edn. Annals (sr., advisor Coun. Edn.-Bus. Partnership 1995—); mem. Am. Ednl. Rsch. Assn., Religious Edn. Assn. U.S.A. and Canada (exec. bd. 1994—), Am. Psychol. Assn., Internat. Assn. Ednl. Assessment (v.p. 1975-82), Internat. Test Commn. (pres. 1978-82), Internat. Assn. Applied Psychology (pres. divsn. 1978-82), Internat. Union Sci. Psychology (adminstrv. coun. 1960—). Avocations: mountaineering, swimming, stamp collecting, hiking, chess playing. Home: 5715 S Kenwood Ave Apt 3N Chicago IL 60637-1742

AYMOND, GREGORY M., academic administrator. Pres. Grad. Sch. Theology, Notre Dame Sem., New Orleans, bishop, rector, pres., most reverant, 1997—. Office: Bishop of New Orleans 2901 S Carrollton Ave New Orleans LA 70118-4301*

AYOTTE, RICHARD L., architect; b. Webster, Mass., Oct. 23, 1954; s. Lionel Armand and Yvonne Therese (Pelletier) A. BArch, Cornell U., 1977. Lic. architect, N.Y. Intern architect Kopple, Sheward & Day, Phila., 1978-79; assoc. Peix & Ptnr., N.Y.C., 1979; project architect Hardy Holzman Pfeiffer Assocs., N.Y.C., 1980-84; prin. Richard Ayotte Architecture, PC, N.Y.C., 1984—. Exhbn. N.Y. Design Ctr., 1990. Recipient Design awards N.Y. Soc. Architects, 1995. Mem. N.Y.C. Soc. of Am. Registered Architects. Office: Richard Ayotte Architecture PC 200 Park Ave S New York NY 10003-1503

AYOUB, RAYMOND GEORGE, mathematics educator; b. Sherbrooke, Que., Can., Jan. 2, 1923; came to U.S., 1949; s. George Ferris and Nazeera Rizk Ayoub; m. Christine Williams, July 11, 1950; children: Cynthia, Daphne. BSc, McGill U., Montreal, Can., 1943, MSc, 1946; PhD, U. Ill., 1950. Forecaster Can. Meteorol. Svc., Ottawa, Ont., 1943-45; instr. McGill U., Montreal, 1945-47; Peirce instr. Harvard U., Cambridge, Mass., 1950-52; asst. prof. Pa. State U., University Park, 1952-54, 1954-58, prof., 1958-84, prof. emeritus, 1984—, head math. dept., 1968-72; vis. prof. King Saud U., Riyadh, Saudi Arabia, 1984-85; Fulbright prof. Bethlehem U., 1986-87. Author: Introduction to Analytical Theory of Numbers, 1963. Recipient Ford award Math. Assn. Am., 1982. Mem. English Speaking Union. Democrat. Mem. Soc. of Friends. Avocations: Quaker history, linguistics. E-mail: ayoub@math.psu.edu. Home: 500 E Marylyn Apt 142 State College PA 16801 Office: Pa State U McAllister Bldg University Park PA 16802

AYRES, DAVID T., senatorial administrator; b. Feb. 12, 1964. Chief of staff to Senator John Ashcroft U.S. Senate, Washington, 1995—. Office: 316 Senate Hart Office Bldg Washington DC 20510-2504

AYRES, EDWARD HUTCHINSON, editor; b. Summit, N.J., Oct. 11, 1941; s. John Underwood and Alice (Hutchinson) A.; m. Sharon Lee Talbott, May 5, 1980; 1 child, Elizabeth. BA, Swarthmore Coll., 1963. Tchr. George Sch., Newtown, Pa., 1963-68; sci. writer Internat. Rsch. & Tech. Corp., Washington, 1969-76; founding editor, pub. Running Times mag., Washington, 1977-91, Running Time Mag., Beverly Hills, Calif., 1977-91; editor World Watch Mag., Washington, 1991—; editl. dir. Worldwatch Inst., Washington, 1994—. Author: What's Good for GM, 1970, God's Last Offer, 1999. Named Top 25 Censored or Under-reported Stories award Project Censored, 1997. Mem. Soc. of Friends. Avocations: long distance running, sculpture. Office: Worldwatch Inst Ste 800 1776 Massachusetts Ave NW Washington DC 20036-1995

AYRES, ELIZABETH, educator; b. Elsmere, Nebr., Mar. 23, 1937; d. Paul L. and Irene F. (Paine) Weber; m. Harold D. Gibbons, May 24, 1959 (dec. May 1992); children: Jerry, Wayne, Kristi; m. Dee Ayres, Oct. 20, 1996. AA in Arts Edn., Chadron State Coll., 1958, BE, 1988. Tchr. Cherry County (Nebr.) Rural Schs., 1955-59, Crawford (Nebr.) City Schs., 1959-60; substitute tchr. Sioux and Dawes County (Nebr.) Schs., 1960—; freelance writer and photographer Nebr., 1971—; program asst. Dawes County Ext. Office, 1992—; examiner U.S. Office Personnel Mgmt. Nebr., 1993-96; treas. Sch. Dist. # 25, Crawford, 1965-75; pres. Dawes County Ext. Bd., Chadron, 1992-94; dir. State Panhandle Family & Cmty. Edn., 1995-97. Co-author: Leaning Into The Wind, 1997; editor: (periodical) Dawes County 4-H Special, 1979—. Gt. Am. Smokeout facilitator Am. Cancer Soc., Dawes County, 1996-97; organizer Panhandle Citizens Against Tobacco, 1997. Recipient various 4-H Alumni medals Univ. Nebr. Ext. Svc., 1993-94; Family & Cmty. Leadership scholar, Kearney, Nebr., 1993, 95. Home: 660 Squaw Creek Rd Crawford NE 69339-2113 Office: Dawes County Extension Off PO Box 670 337 Main St Chadron NE 69337-2357

AYRES, JANICE RUTH, social service executive; b. Idaho Falls, Idaho, Jan. 23, 1930; d. Low Ray and Frances Mae (Salem) Mason; m. Thomas Woodrow Ayres, Nov. 27, 1953 (dec. 1966); 1 child, Thomas Woodrow Jr. (dec.). MBA, U. So. Calif., 1952, M in Mass Comms., 1953. Asst. mktg. dir. Disneyland, Inc., Anaheim, Calif., 1954-59; gen. mgr. Tamasha Town & Country Club, Anaheim, Calif., 1959-65; dir. mktg. Am. Heart Assn., Santa Ana, Calif., 1966-69; state exec. dir. Nev. Assn. Mental Health, Las Vegas, 1969-71; exec. dir. Clark Co. Easter Seal Treatment Ctr., Las Vegas, 1971-73; mktg. dir., fin devel. officer So. Nev. Drug Abuse Coun., Las Vegas, 1973-74; exec. dir. Nev. Assn. Retarded Citizens, Las Vegas, 1974-75; assoc., cons. Don Luke & Assocs., Phoenix, 1976-77; program dir. Inter-Tribal Coun. Nev., Reno, 1977-79; exec. dir. Ret. Sr. Vol. Program, Carson City, Nev., 1979—; chair sr. citizen summit State of Nev., 1996; presenter in field. Bd. suprs. Carson City, Nev., 1992—; commr. Carson City Parks and Recreation, 1993—; obligation bond com., legis. chair Carson City; bd. dirs. Nev. Dept. Transp., 1993; active No. Corp. for Nat. and Cmty. Svc. by Gov., 1994, V&TRR Commn., 1993, chair, 1995, vice-chair, chair pub. rels. com., bd. dirs. Hist. V&TRR Bd., chair PR Cmty./V&RR Commn., vice-chair Carson City Gen. Obligation Bond Commn., Nev. Home Health Assn.; appointed liaison Carson City Sr. Citizens Bd., 1995; chair summit Rural Nev. Sr. Citizens, Carson City; pres. No. Nev. R.R. Found., 1996—; chair Tri-Co-R.R. Commn., 1995; chair Gov.'s Nev. Commn. for Corp. in Nat. and Cmty. Svc., 1997—, pres. 1998., Carson City Pub. Transp. Commn., 1998—, Carson City Commn. for Clean Groundwater Act, 1998—. Named Woman of Distinction, Soroptimist Club, 1988, Outstanding Dir. of Excellence, Gov. State of Nev., 1989, Outstanding Dir., Vol. Action Ctr., J.C. Penney Co., Outstanding Nev. Women's Role Model Nev. A.G., 1996. Mem. AAUW, Am. Mgmt. Assn. (bd. dirs.), Am. Mktg. Assn. (bd. dirs. 1999—), Internat. Platform Assn., Pub. Rels. Soc. Am. (chpt. pres., Silver Spike award 1996), Women Radio and TV, Nat. Soc. Fund Raising Execs., Nev. Fair and Rodeo Assn. (pres.), Nev. Assn. Transit Svcs. (bd. dirs., legis. chmn.), Nev. Women's Polit. Caucus, Nat. Women's Polit. Caucus, Am. Soc. Assn. Execs., No. Nev. Railroad found. (pres. 1996). Home: 1762 Montelena Ct Carson City NV 89703-7383 Office: Ret Sr Vol Program 501 E Caroline St Carson City NV 89701-4054

AYRES, JAYNE LYNN ANKRUM, community health nurse; b. Reed City, Mich., Oct. 12, 1944; d. Quinten Wayne and Marshia Agetha (Crum) Ankrum; m. Ronald Francis Ayres, Apr. 16, 1977; children: Linda, Michele, Julie. ADN, Manatee C.C., Bradenton, Fla., 1975. RN, Fla., Ga. Staff nurse med.-surg., cardiac, oncology and float team Sarasota (Fla.) Meml. Hosp., 1975-77; nursing supr. Upjohn Healthcare Svcs., Sarasota, 1981-85; staff nurse Devereux Found., Kennesaw, Ga., 1986-89; staff nurse, supr. Vis. Nurse Health Sys., Metro, Atlanta, 1989-97; entertainer JPM Prodn. Co., 1996—; adv. bd. Waldrop Personal Care, Inc., 1998—; mem. adv. subcom. Waldrop Personal Care, Inc., 1998—. Vol. ARC, M.U.S.T. Ministries Health Clinic for Homeless, Summer Olympics Games, 1996. Mem. Am. Legion (hon.), Fla. Nurses Assn. (hon.), Beta Sigma Phi. Achievements include invention of the syringe filling monitor. Address: 6520 Dodgen Rd SW Mableton GA 30126-4406

AYRES, JEFFREY PEABODY, lawyer; b. Waltham, Mass., Sept. 23, 1952; s. John Cecil and Dora Hoxie A.; m. Janet Diehl, May 31, 1980; children: Brendan Peabody, Caroline Bradfield, Gordon Pettit. BA, Harvard U., 1974; JD, George Washington U., 1977. Bar: D.C. 1977, Md. 1978, U.S. Ct. Appeals (3d, 4th and D.C. cirs.), U.S. Dist. Ct. Md., U.S. Dist. Ct. D.C., U.S. Supreme Ct. 1985. Assoc. Arent, Fox, Kintner, Plotkin & Kahn, Washington, 1977-78; assoc. Venable, Baetjer & Howard, Balt., 1978-85, ptnr., 1986—. Contbr. articles to profl. jours. Del. Episcopal Diocesan Conv. Mem. ABA, Md. Bar Assn., Balt. Bar Assn. (chair labor and employment sect. 1998—), Harvard Club Md. (pres. 1989-94, v.p. 1994—), Harvard Alumni Assn. (regional dir. 1995-98). Democrat. Episcopalian. Avocations: running, bicycling. Home: 7120 Sheffield Rd Baltimore MD 21212-1629 Office: Venable Baetjer & Howard 1800 Mercantile Bank & Trust Blg 2 Hopkins Plz Ste 2100 Baltimore MD 21201-2982

AYRES, MARY ELLEN, government official; b. Spokane, Wash., June 23, 1924; d. Frank H. and Marion (Kellogg) A. Student, U. Wash., 1942-43; B.A., Stanford U., 1946; postgrad., Am. U., 1960. With Henry von Morpurgo, Advt., 1946-47; reporter Wenatchee Daily World, Wash., 1947-50, Washington Post, 1951-52; with U.S. Fgn. Service, Dept. State, 1950-51; mem. editorial staff Changing Times, 1952-61; editor Family Guide, Kiplinger Washington Editors, 1958-61, Bur. Labor Stats., Manpower Adminstrn., U.S. Dept. Labor, 1962-67; pub. info. specialist Bur. Indian Affairs, U.S. Dept. Interior, 1967-75; writer-editor Bur. Labor Stats., 1975—; tchr. newsletter class Dept. Agriculture Grad. Sch., 1975-89, editing style and technique class, 1987-89; past treas. Govt. Info. Orgn. Mem. publicity com. Nat. Capitol YWCA, 1982-83; dir. Wenatchee High Sch. Scholarship Found., 1988—. Mem. Nat. Assn. Govt. Communicators (founding treas., dir. 1975-80, 89-91, chmn. Blue Pencil Contest 1987, nat. capital chpt. treas. 1989), Am. News Women's Club, Am. Econ. Assn., Stanford U. Alumnae Assn., Kappa Kappa Gamma. Episcopalian. Club: Nat. Press (Washington). Home: 2400 Virginia Ave NW Apt C802 Washington DC 20037-2612 Office: Bur Labor Stats 2 Massachusetts Ave NE Washington DC 20212-0022

AYRES, PAUL ERDMAN, artist; b. Detroit, Apr. 13, 1921; s. Harry Erdman and Bessie Marie (Friedman) A.; m. Marianne Elizabeth Kuhn, May 29, 1944 (dec. Sept. 1995); children: Martha, Jeffrey, Christopher. DVM, Mich. State U., 1943; student, Oakland C.C., Rochester, Mich., 1981-83, Coll. of Charleston, S.C., 1983-91. Lic. DVM, Mich. Tech. asst. Parke Davis & Co., Detroit, 1944-53; mgr. vet. dept. Parke Davis & Co., Rochester, Mich., 1953-74; mgr. lab. Parke Davis & Co., Rochester, 1974-76; mgr. indsl. hygiene dept. Parke Davis & Co., divsn. Warner Lambert Co., Rochester, 1976-83. One-man shows include Lowcountry Artists, Ltd., Charleston, 1984—; represented in numerous pvt. collections. Pres. Cmty. Chest, Oakland Twp., Mich., 1962-65; bd. dirs. Print Studio South, Charleston, 1994-96; treas., bd. dirs. Charleston Artists Guild, 1987-90. Roman Catholic. Avocation: sailing. Home and Office: 1161 Shadow Lake Cir Apt A Mount Pleasant SC 29464-9060

AYRES, RICHARD EDWARD, lawyer; b. Salem, N.J., Feb. 2, 1942; s. John Lecroy and Mary Sayre (Fogg) A.; m. Margaret Alice Miles, Aug. 29, 1964; (div. 1985); children: Alice Elizabeth Hutchinson, Richard Alden; m. Merribel Symington, May 17, 1986. AB, Princeton U., 1964; MA in Politics, LLB, Yale U., 1969. Bar: N.Y. 1971, U.S. Ct. Appeals (D.C. cir.) 1971, U.S. Ct. Appeals (1st, 2nd, 5th, 9th, and 10th cirs.) 1972, U.S. Ct. Appeals (8th cir.) 1973, D.C. 1975, U.S. Supreme Ct. 1976. Atty. Vera Inst. Justice, N.Y.C., 1969-70; co-founder, sr. atty. Natural Resources Def. Coun., N.Y.C., 1970-73; sr. atty. Natural Resources Def. Coun., Washington, 1973-91; ptnr. O'Melveny & Myers, Washington, 1991-96; chmn. Nat. Clean Air Coalition, 1975-91; commr. Nat. Commn. Air Quality, 1978-81; mem. Clean Air Act adv. com. U.S. EPA, 1995—; mem. adv. coun. Gas Rsch. Inst., 1991-93; mem. Carnegie Commn. Sci., Tech. and Govt. Task Force Sci. and Tech. in Jud. and Regulatory Decision Making, 1991-93; mem. mayor's environ. adv. coun., Washington, D.C., 1999—. Contbr. articles to profl. jours. Bd. dirs. League Conservation Voters, 1975-94; mem. bd. trustees Natural Resources Def. Coun., 1992—; mem. bd. Clean Air Action Corp., 1993—, New Century Fund, 1993—, Breakthrough Technologies Inst., 1993—. Recipient citation Outstanding Svc. to Pub. Interest, Yale Law Sch., for role in creating pub. interest law movement, 1989; trustee Keystone Ctr., 1998—. Mem. ABA (chmn. environ. values com. sect. adminstrv. law and regulatory practice 1991—, sect. natural resources, energy and environ. law 1995—). Democrat. Office: Howrey & Simon 1299 Pennsylvania Ave NW Washington DC 20004-2420

AYRES, ROBERT MOSS, JR., retired university president; b. San Antonio, Sept. 1, 1926; s. Robert Moss and Florence (Collett) A.; m. Patricia Ann Shield, Sept. 10, 1955; children: Robert Atlee, Vera Patricia. Student, Tex. Mil. Inst., 1944; BA, U. of the South, 1949, DCL, 1974; postgrad., Oxford (Eng.) U., 1949; MBA, U. Pa., 1952. With Kidder, Peabody & Co., Phila., N.Y.C., 1950-52; with Dittmar & Co., San Antonio, 1952-53; pres., dir. Russ & Co., Inc., San Antonio, 1953-73; sr. v.p., dir. Rotan Mosle Inc., San Antonio, 1973-77; pres. U. South, Sewanee, Tenn., 1977-88, pres. emeritus, 1988—; past pres. So. Univ. Conf.; chmn. So. Coll. and Univ. Union; former allied mem. N.Y. Stock Exch., Am. Stock Exch.; bd. dirs. Rail Tex. Corp., Howell Corp., James Avery Craftsman. Past pres. Assn. Alumni U. of South; past pres. bd. dirs. Bexar County chpt. ARC; past pres. bd. trustees Tex. Mil. Inst.; trustee, past chmn. bd. regents U. of South; trustee Brother's Bro. Found.; mem. exec. coun. Episcopal Ch., 1976-82, also mem. nat. and world mission com., dir., past pres. St. Mary's Episcopal Ctr.; mem. Commn. on Ministry Com. Diocese of Tex.; past bd. dirs. Inst. European Studies, Presiding Bishop's Fund World Relief, Alfalit, Internat.; vol. exec. dir. Vol. in Mission, 1976; bd. dirs. Inst. of Servant Leadership, Soc. Promotion of Christian Knowledge/U.S.A., Salvation Army, Episcopal Hist. Soc. With USN, 1944-46; lt. Res. 1949-60. Mem. San Antonio Soc. Fin. Analysts (past pres.), Securities Industries Assn. (past mem. governing coun.), Investment Bankers Assn. Am. (past chmn. Tex. group), Nat. Assn. Securities Dealers (past mem. dist. com.) Young Pres. Orgn., Order of Alamo, Tex. Cavaliers, Argyle, Am. Soc. Order of St. John, Sigma Alpha Epsilon. Episcopalian (mem. exec. bd. diocese W. Tex.; vestryman). Clubs: San Antonio German, San Antonio Country. Home: 5705 Scout Island Cv Austin TX 78731-3386

AYRES, ROBERT UNDERWOOD, environmental economics and technology educator; b. Plainfield, N.J., June 29, 1932; s. John Underwood and Alice Conrow (Hutchinson) A.; m. Leslie Wentz, June 26, 1954; 1 dau., Jennifer Leigh. BS in Math., U. Chgo., 1954; MS in Physics, U. Md., 1956; PhD, U. London, 1958. Research assoc. Hudson Inst., Croton-on-Hudson, N.Y., 1962-67; vis. scholar Resources for Future, 1967-68; v.p., dir. Internat. Research & Tech. Corp., Washington, 1968-76, Delta Research Corp., Arlington, Va., 1976—; prof. engring. and pub. policy Carnegie-Mellon U., 1979-92; chmn. bd. Variflex Corp., Pitts., 1969-87; cons. in field; mem. tech. and water com. Nat. Acad. Scis., 1971, new transp. systems and tech. com., 1971—, strategic and critical materials com., 1971-72, com. steel rsch., 1978, com. alts. for reduction chlorofluorocarbon emissions, 1979; mem. com. on engring. edn. Nat. Acad. Engring., 1984; dep. program leader, project leader Internat. Inst. Applied Systems Analysis, 1986-90; prof. environ. econs., Sandoz prof. environ. mgmt., dir. Ctr. for Mgmt. of Environ. Resources, INSEAD, Fontainebleau, France, 1992—. Author: Technological Forecasting and Long Range Planning, (with others) Economics and the Environment, 1971, Alternatives to the Internal Combustion Engine, 1972, Resources, Environment and Economics, 1978, Uncertain Futures, 1979, Robotics: Applications and Social Implications, 1983, The Next Industrial Revolution: Reviving Industry Through Innovation, 1984, CIM: Revolution in Progress, 1991, Information, Entropy and Progress: A New Evolutionary Paradigm, 1994, Industrial Metabolism, 1994, Industrial Ecology: Closing the Materials Cycle, 1996, Turning Point: An End to the Growth Paradigm, 1998, Accounting for Resources Materials and Waste, 1998; contbr. articles to profl. jours.; assoc. editor: Jour. Transp. Tech. and Planning, 1970-74. Fellow AAAS (coun., com.-at-large sect. indsl. sci. 1972-74, World Econ. Forum 1994); mem. Internat. Soc. Ecol. Econs., Am. Econ. Assn., Assn. Environ. and Resource Economists, Schumpeter Soc., Sigma Xi. Office: INSEAD, Fontainebleu 77305, France

AYRES, STEPHEN MCCLINTOCK, physician, educator; b. Elizabeth, N.J., Oct. 29, 1929; s. Malcolm B. and Florence M. A.; m. Dolores Kobrick, June 11, 1955; children—Stephen (dec. May 1998), Elizabeth, Margaret. B.A., Gettysburg Coll., 1951; M.D., Cornell U., 1955. Intern N.Y. Hosp., N.Y.C., 1955; resident N.Y. Hosp., 1958-61; dir. cardio-pulmonary lab. St. Michael's Hosp., Newark, 1961-63, St. Vincent's Hosp. and Med. Center, N.Y.C., 1963-73; physician-in-chief St. Vincent Hosp., Worcester, Mass., 1973-75; prof., chmn. dept. internal medicine St. Louis U. Med. Center, 1975-85; dean Med. Coll. Va., Richmond, 1985-93; dean emeritus, dir. office internat. health program Med. Coll. Va./Va. Commonwealth U., Richmond, 1993—. Author: Care of the Critically Ill, 3d edit., 1988; coauthor: Textbook of Critical Care, 1988, Nutritional Support of the Critically Ill, 1988; editor: Major Issues in Critical Care Medicine, 1984; contbr. articles to profl. jours. Chmn. bd. Found. for Critical Care, 1985—. Served with M.C., U.S. Army, 1956-58. Fellow A.C.P., Am. Coll. Cardiology, Am. Coll. Chest Physicians; mem. Soc. Critical Care Medicine (pres. 1979-80), Am. Lung Assn., Assn. Am. Physicians, Am. Soc. Clin. Investigation. Home: 5103 Cary Street Rd Richmond VA 23226-1644 Office: Med Coll Va PO Box 565 Richmond VA 23218-0565

AYRES, TED DEAN, lawyer, academic counsel; b. Hamilton, Mo., July 14, 1947; m. Marcia Sue Busselle; children: John Corbett, Jackson Frazer, Joseph Dean. BSBA, Ctrl. Mo. State Coll., 1969; JD, U. Mo., 1972. Bar: Mo. 1972, U.S. Dist. Ct. (we. dist.) Mo. 1972, U.S. Ct. Appeals (8th cir.) 1977, U.S. Supreme Ct. 1977, Colo. 1984, U.S. Dist. Ct. Colo. 1984, U.S. Ct. Appeals (10th cir.) 1984, Kans. 1987. Law clk. to presiding justice Mo. Supreme Ct., Jefferson City, 1972-73; ptnr. Stubbs & Ayres, Chillicothe, Mo., 1973-74; atty. Southwestern Bell Tel. Co., St. Louis, 1974-76; counsel U. Mo., Columbia, 1976-84; univ. counsel U. Colo., Boulder, 1984-86; gen. counsel Kans. Bd. Regents, Topeka, 1986-92, gen. counsel, dir. govtl. rels., 1992-96; acting pres. Pitts. State U., 1995; gen. counsel, assoc. to pres. Wichita (Kans.) State U., 1996—; adj. asst. prof. coll. bus. adminstrn. U. Colo., Denver, 1984-85, adj. assoc. prof., 1985-86; spl. asst. atty. gen. State of Colo., 1984-86, State of Kans., 1987—; presenter region II conf. Assn. Coll. Unions Internat., U. Mo., Rollas, 1983; spkr. Soc. Colo. Archivists, U. Colo., Boulder, 1985; adj. prof. Washburn U., Topeka, 1989; adj. prof. kinesiology and sport studies Wichita State U., 1999—. Contbr. articles to profl. jours. Active adv. com. Boone County (Mo.) Cmty. Svcs.; mem. com. social concerns Mo. United Meth. Ch., 1979-81, supervisory com. Mothers' Morning Out program, 1980-84; adminstv. bd., com. on fin. and stewardship 1st United Meth. Ch., Topeka, 1989-91, family life coun., 1994-95; trustee Mid-Mo. chpt. Nat. Multiple Sclerosis Soc., 1981-84; mem. bd. mgrs. Topeka YMCA-Downtown Br., 1991-96, fedn. coun. Indian Guides program, 1988-91; treas. pack 175 Cub Scouts, 1990-95; bd. dirs. Innovative Tech. Enterprise Corp., 1991-94, S.W. Youth Athletic Assn., Inc., 1994-96, Friends of Topeka Zoo, 1995—, Wichita Tech. Corp., 1997—, Wichita State U. Hist. Preservation Commn., 1998—, parents coun. Truman State U., 1997-99. Curator scholar, 1969-70, Omar E. Robinson scholar, 1970-71, John M. Dalton Ednl. Trust scholar 1971-72. Mem. Mo. Bar Assn., Nat. Assn. Coll. and Univ. Attys. (chairperson Southwestern region 1979-81, bd. dirs. 1985-88, various coms. 1979—, del. and presenter numerous CLE workshops), Friends of Topeka Zoo, U. Mo. Alumni Assn. (life). Home: 2214 SW Brookfield St Topeka KS 66614-4236 Office: Wichita State Univ 201 Morrison Hall Wichita KS 67260-0001

AYSCUE, EDWIN OSBORNE, JR., lawyer; b. Monroe, N.C., May 21, 1933; s. Edwin Osborne and Grace Elizabeth (Fields) A.; m. Emily Mizell Urquhart, Aug. 17, 1957; children: Grace Thompson, E. Osborne, Emily Hassell, Margaret Certain. Grad. cum laude, Phillips Acad., Andover, Mass., 1951; AB in Polit. Sci., U. N.C., Chapel Hill, 1954, LLB with honors, 1960. Bar: N.C. 1960, U.S. Supreme Ct. 1979. Ptnr. Smith Helms Mulliss & Moore, L.L.P. (and predecessor firms), Charlotte, 1960—; mem. Civil Justice Reform Act Com., Western Dist. N.C., 1991-95. Editor-in-chief N.C. Law Rev., 1959-60. Contbr. articles to profl. jours. Alumni rep. Phillips Acad., 1964-90; bd. dirs. Legal Services of So. Piedmont, 1983-85, Legal Services of N.C., 1984-85, 88-94; sr. warden Christ Episcopal Ch., 1990-91; bd. dirs. Friends of U. N.C. Libr., 1989-92. Lt. USNR, 1955-57. Fellow Am. Coll. Trial Lawyers (regent 1991—, sec. 1995-97, pres.-elect 1997-98, pres. 1998-99), Am. Bar Found. (life); mem. ABA (ho. of dels. 1991-95), N.C. Bar Assn. (pres. 1984-85, Gen. Practice Hall of Fame), N.C. State Bar (mandatory continuing edn. com, 1987-92, vice chair 1990-93), Mecklenburg County Bar Assn. (pres. 1980-81), U. N.C. Hapel Hill Law Alumni Assn. (pres.-elect 1998-99), Mecklenburg Bar Found. (trustee 1987-93), Am. Judicature Soc. (bd. dirs. 1985-89), Order Golden Fleece, Nat. Conf. Bar Pres., 4th Cir. Jud. Conf., Charlotte Country Club, Order of Coif, Phi Beta Kappa. Democrat. Episcopalian. Office: Smith Helms Mulliss & Moore PO Box 31247 Charlotte NC 28231-1247

AYUB, YACUB, financial consultant; b. Bombay, India, May 14, 1944; s. Ayub and Aziza Abbas; children: Murtaza, Marzia. *Son Murtaza Ayub, M.I.M. 1997, American Graduate School of International Management (Thunderbird) Arizona, is currently employed as manager, Emerging Markets, Citibank, N.A., 111 Wall Street, New York. Daughter Marzia Ayub, BA 1998, Rutgers University, is currently pursuing a Masters in Human Relations. Yacub Ayub celebrated his 30th wedding anniversary with his wife Rashida, who is the backbone of their happy family.* MBA, U. Karachi, Pakistan, 1966. CPC, CFP. Rep. officer United Bank of Pakistan, Tehran, 1966-73; calling officer Bank Credit and Commerce Internat. (Iran Arab Bank), Tehran, 1974-78; audit officer Bank Credit and Commerce Internat., London, 1978-79; mgr. br. ops. Bank Credit and Commerce Internat., Panama City, Panama, 1979-83; mgr. mktg. and bus. devel. Bank Credit and Commerce Internat., N.Y.C., 1983-88; fin. cons. Investment & Mgmt. Cons. Inc., Holmdel, N.J., 1988—. Fellow Life Underwriters Tng. Coun. Republican. Home: 38 Bayberry Dr Holmdel NJ 07733-1040 *Perseverance, hard work, faith and hope are the true ingredients to success. Add to it honesty and trust which leads to great achievements in business and life.*

AYYILDIZ, JUDY LIGHT, writer, poet, educator; b. Teays, W.Va., Feb. 9, 1941; d. Jewel Garnet and Laura Gladys (Perry) Light; m. Vedii Ayyildiz, Nov. 20, 1962; children: Kent, Kevin, Karen. BA in Music Edn., Marshall U., 1963; MA in Liberal Arts, Hollins U., Roanoke, Va., 1980, MA in English and Creative Writing, 1981. Music tchr. Buffalo Pub Schs., 1964-65, Roanoke City Schs., 1965-66; writing cons. Roanoke City and County, 1983—; writing cons. Hollins Summer Program, Richmond City, Salem, Roanoke Coll.; writing instr. and cons. Hollins Women's Ctr.; founding bd. mem. Blue Ridge Writers Conf., Roanoke, 1984-93; bd. dirs. Appalfolks of Am., Clifton Forge, Va., 1987-94. Author: (poetry) Smuggled Seeds, 1979 (Gusto Poet Discovery award), Mud River, 1989, Sky Hooks and Grasshopper traps, 1987, Creative Writing Across the Curriculum, 1995, Critical Thinking Quick and Easy, 1996, The Writer's Express, 1999; editor Artemis mag., 1980-93, Collage mag., 1978. Pres. Roanoke Acad. Medicine Aux., 1973; bd. dirs. S.W. Va. Opera Co., Roanoke, 1971; dir. Med. Aux. Chorus, Roanoke, 1968-78. Recipient Emma Trigg Meml. prize Poetry Soc. Va., 1980, 1st place award, 1979, Jim Wayne Miller 1st place poetry award, 1994, others. Mem. Poets and Writers, Assoc. Writing Programs, Am. Acad. Poets (Hollins Coll. Gertrude Claytor prize 1981), Artemis/Artists and Writers. Avocations: singing, acting, boating, walking. Home: 4930 Hunting Hills Cir Roanoke VA 24014-4961

AYYUB, BILAL M., civil engineering educator, researcher, executive; b. Shweikeh, Tulkaram, Palestine, Jan. 5, 1958; came to U.S., 1980; s. Mohammed S. and Thuraya Ayyub; m. Deena L. Ziadeh, June 27, 1987; children: Omar, Rami, Samar, Ziad. BSCE, U. Kuwait, 1980; MSCE, Ga. Inst. Tech., 1981, PhD, 1983. Registered profl. engr., Md. Asst. prof. dept. civil engring. U. Md., College Park, 1983-88, assoc. prof., 1988-93; prof. U. Md., 1993—, dir. Ctr. for Tech. and Sys. Mgmt.; pres. BMA Engring. Inc., Md., 1988—; cons. prof. Carderock divsn. of Naval Surface Warfare Ctr., USN; cons. USCG, Groton, Conn., 1987-90, USN, Crystal City, Va., 1990—, ASME, Washington, 1990—, Internat. Monetary Fund, Washington, 1993, Chevron Rsch. and Tech. Corp., Richmond, Calif., 1992-94, U.S. Army Corps. of Engrs., Washington, 1994—; mem. adv. bd. to internat. jours. and Naval Engrs. Jour., 1989—; gen. chmn. Internat. Symposium on Uncertainty Modeling and Analysis, 1990, 93, 95; dir. Ctr. for Tech. and Sys. Mgmt. Editor: Analysis and Management of Uncertainty, 1992, Uncertainty Modeling and Analysis, 1995, Uncertainty Modeling in Finite Element, Fatique, and Stability of Systems, 1997, Uncertainty Modeling in Vibration, Control, and Fuzzy Analysis in Structural Systems, 1997, Uncertainty Modeling and Analysis in Civil Engineering, 1998, Uncertainty Modeling and Analysis in Engineering and the Sciences, 1997; (textbooks) Numerical Methods for Engineers, 1995, Probability, Statistics and Reliability for Engineers, 1997; contbr. over 250 articles to profl. jours. Grantee NSF, 1985-92, Md. State Hwy. Adminstrn., 1986-90, USN, 1990-95, U.S. Army Corps. Engrs., 1994-95; recipient Cert. of Appreciation U.S. Army Corps. Engrs., 1995. Fellow ASCE (Outstanding Rsch. Oriented Paper award 1988, Edmund Friedman award 1989, Walter L. Huber Civil Engring. Rsch. award 1997, chmn. reliability of offshore structures com. 1993-96, assoc. editor Jour. Structural Engring., mem. com. on fatugue and fracture reliability, mem. tech. adminstrv. com. on structural safety and reliability 1993-96); mem. ASME (polit. action com. 1990—, risk-based tech. rsch. com.), IEEE, NRC (working groups of marine bd.), Am. Soc. Naval Engrs. (life, Jimmie Hamilton award 1986, 93), Soc. Naval Archs. and Marine Engrs. (chmn. panel on design procedure and philosopy of the hull structures com., Jour. Ship Rsch. com.), Am. Concrete Inst., Am. Acad. Mechanics, N.Am. Fuzzy Info. Processing Soc. (K.S. Fu award 1995, gen. chmn. ann. conf. 1995), Computer Soc. Achievements include risk and uncertainty analysis in engineering, design guidelines for posttensioned composite bridges, general guidelines for risk-based inspection, structural reliability assessment using variance reduction techniques, uncertainty modeling and analysis in engineering, fuzzy logic in civil engineering, reliability-based design of marine structures, reliability assessment and reliability-based design of navigation structures. Office: U Md Dept Civil Engring College Park MD 20742

AZANK, ROBERTO, artist; b. Buenos Aires, Nov. 3, 1955; came to U.S., 1979; s. Neazi and Dora Margarita (Estevez) A.; m. Monika Schifler, Oct. 20, 1990; 1 child, Rudi Vinicius. Student, U. Arch., Buenos Aires, 1975-78. One-man shows include Marcos J. Alegria Sch. Fine Arts, P.R., 1991, Consulate Gen. of Argentina, N.Y.C., 1997, Lizan Tops Gallery, East Hampton, N.Y., 1998, Albers Fine Arts, Memphis, 1998, Albert White Gallery, Toronto, Can., 1998, Hooks-Epstein Galleries, Houston, Tex., 1998, Brewster Arts Limited, N.Y.C., 1999, Addison-Ripley Gallery, Washington .C., 1999, Byron Cohen Gallery, Kansas City, Mo., 1999, Albert Einstein U., N.Y.C., 1999; group exhbns. include Olympia and York Gallery, N.Y., 1991, Galaxy Gallery, Miami Beach, Fla., 1990, SUNY, Albany, 1993, Ramis Barquet Gallery, Miami, 1997, N.Y. Arts Mag. 2d City-wide Biennial, 1997, Mulligan Shanoski Gallery, San Francisco, 1998, Elite Fine Art, Miami, 1998, Art Miami, '98, 1998, Lyons. Wier Gallery, Chgo., 1998, Artspace/Va. Miller Gallery, Miami, 1998, Meredith Kelly Fine Arts, Santa Fe, 1998, Kougeas Gallery, Boston, 1999, William Havu Gallery, Denver, 1999, Navy Pier Art Show, Chgo., 1999; represented by Robert Miller Gallery, N.Y., Brewster Arts Ltd., N.Y.C., Addison-Ripley Gallery, Washington, Artspace/Virginia Miller Gallery, Miami, Albers Gallery, Memphis; works featured in publs. including N.Y. Arts Mag., New Am. Painting, Waterfront Week, Kansas City Star, The Washington Post; pvt. collections;. Avocations: classical music, astronomy. Office: Roberto Azank Studio 1073 Lorimer St Brooklyn NY 11222-2644

AZAR, HENRY AMIN, medical historian, educator; b. Egypt, Dec. 21, 1927; s. Amin Antonios and Agnes Garabed (Nazaretian) A.; m. Rose Theresa Connell, Apr. 19, 1960; children: Henry Amin Jr., Philip John. BA, Am. U., Beirut, 1948, MD, 1952; PhD in History, U. N.C., 1998. Diplomate Am. Bd. Pathology. Intern N.Y.C. Hosp., 1952-53; resident Columbia-Presbyn. Hosp. Med. Ctr., N.Y.C., 1955-56, N.Y.-Cornell, Med. Ctr., N.Y.C., 1956-57, Mass. Meml. Hosp., Boston, 1957-58; asst. prof. pathology Am. U., Beirut, 1958-60; asst. prof. and assoc. prof. pathology Coll. Physicians and Surgeons, Columbia U., 1960-70; dir. surg. pathology, prof. U. Kans., 1970-72; chief lab. service James A. Haley Vets. Hosp., Tampa, Fla., 1972-83, chief anatomic pathology, 1983-92; prof. U. South Fla., 1973-92, prof. emeritus, 1992; rsch. prof. pathology U. N.C., 1998—. Author: Multiple Myeloma and Related Disorders, 1973, Diagnostic Electron Microscopy: The Hemopoietic System, 1979, Pathology of Human Neoplasms, 1988, Ibn Zuhr (Avenzoar): The Translation of His Work into Latin and His Image in Medieval Europe, 1998; contbr. articles to profl. jours. Fellow Coll. Am. Pathologists; mem. Assn. Vet. Chiefs Lab. Svc. (pres. 1981-83), Arthur Purdy Stout Soc. (sec. 1983-87, pres. 1990-91), Pathology Alumni Found. (emeritus trustee) Harvey Soc., Internat. Acad. Pathology (emeritus), Hematopathology Soc., Am. Assn. for History of Medicine, Soc. Internat. History of Sci. and Philosopy Arab Islam, Am. U. Beirut Alumni Assn. (pres. Tampa Bay chpt. 1985-87), History of Pathology Soc. (pres. 1996-97, trustee 1996—, editor history sect. Annals of Diagnostic Pathology 1997—). Syrian Orthodox. Home: 1700 Old Oxford Rd Chapel Hill NC 27514-2132

AZARIA, HANK, actor; b. N.Y.C., Apr. 25, 1964; m. Helen Hunt, 1995. Motion picture and T.V. actor. Films include Cool Blue, 1998, Pretty Woman, 1990, Quiz Show, 1994, Now and Then, 1995, Heat, 1995, The Birdcage, 1996, Grosse Pointe Blank, 1997, Godzilla, 1998, Homegrown, 1998, The Cradle Will Rock, 1999, Alligatropolis, 1999, Mystery Men, 1999, others; voice characterizations The Simpsons, 1989—, Spider-Man, 1995, Anastasia, 1997, Stressed Eric, 1998; T.V. guest appearances include Tales from the Crypt, 1989, Growing Pains, 1985, Spider-Man, 1995, Friends, 1994, others. Office: c/o CAA 9830 Wilshire Blvd Beverly Hills CA 90212*

AZARIAN, MARTIN VARTAN, publishing company executive; b. N.Y.C., May 5, 1927; s. Marderos and Altoon (Toutoian) A.; m. Margaret Emery, Aug. 9, 1980; 1 dau., Carol Lydia. BA, CUNY-Hunter Coll., 1950; MS, NYU, 1954; student, Bklyn. Poly. Inst., 1957. Mgr. Claremont Polychem. Corp., Roslyn, N.Y., 1953-54; tech. dir. Borden Chem. Co., Fairlawn, N.J., 1957-63; pres. Internat. Univs. Press Inc., N.Y.C., 1963—. Trustee Austin Riggs Found., 1985-89; dir. Found. for Armenian Recovery, 1988—. With AUS, 1945-46. Mem. Am. Chem. Soc., Chemists Club N.Y. (trustee 1972-87, chmn. libr. com. 1972-74), Nat. Headache Found. (bd. dirs. 1989—), Turf and Field Club, N.Y. Athletic Club, Acad. Medicinae and Psychiatriae Found. Home: 85 Long Hill Rd Guilford CT 06437-1827 Office: Internat U Press Inc 59 Boston Post Rd Madison CT 06443-2130

AZARNOFF, DANIEL LESTER, pharmaceutical company consultant; b. Bklyn., Aug. 4, 1926; s. Samuel J. and Kate (Asarnow) A.; m. Joanne Stokes, Dec. 26, 1951; children: Rachel, Richard, Martin. BS, Rutgers U., 1947, MS, 1948; MD, U. Kans., 1955. Asst. instr. anatomy U. Kans. Med. Sch., 1949-50, research fellow, 1950-52, intern, 1955-56, resident, Nat. Heart Inst. research fellow, 1956-58, asst. prof. medicine, 1962-64, assoc. prof., 1964-68, dir. clin. pharmacology study unit, 1964-68, assoc. prof. pharmacology, 1965-68, prof. medicine and pharmacology, 1968, dir. Clin. Pharmacology-Toxicology Ctr., 1967-78, Disting. prof., 1973-78, also prof. medicine, 1965-67, pres. Sigma Xi Club, 1968-69, clin. prof. medicine, 1982-96; Nat. Inst. Neurol. Diseases and Blindness spl. trainee Washington U. Sch. Medicine, St. Louis, 1958-60; asst. prof. medicine St. Louis U. Sch. Medicine, 1960-62; vis. scientist, Fulbright scholar Karolinska Inst., Stockholm, Sweden, 1968; sr. v.p. worldwide research and devel. G.D. Searle & Co., Skokie, 1978; pres. Searle Research and Devel., Skokie, 1979-85, Azarnoff Assocs., Inc., Evanston, Ill., 1986-87, D.L. Azarnoff Assocs., So. San Francisco, Calif., 1987—; prof. pathology, clin. prof. pharmacology Northwestern U. Med. Sch., 1978-85; commr. Nat. Commn. on Orphan Diseases, 1985-87; chmn. bd. dirs. Alpha RX Corp., South San Francisco, Calif., 1992-94; clin. prof. med. Stanford U. Sch. Med., 1998—; professorial lectr. U. Chgo., 1978-86; dir. Second Workshop on Prins. Drug Evaluation in Man, 1970; chmn. com. on problems of drug safety NRC-NAS, 1972-76; bd. dirs. Oread, Inc., Lawrence, Kans., 1994—, chmn., 1998—; CEO Cibus Pharms., Burlingame, Calif., 1996-97; cons. numerous govt. agys.; chmn. bd. dirs. Cibus Pharm., Inc., 1996-97; bd. dirs. Entropin, Inc., 1997—. Editor: Devel. of Drug Interactions, 1974-77, Yearbook of Drug Therapy, 1977-79; series editor: Monographs in Clin. Pharmacology, 1977-84; mem. editorial bd. Drug Investigation, 1989—, others. Served with U.S. Army, 1945-46. Recipient Ginsburg award in phys. diagnosis U. Kanas. Med. Ctr., 1953, Outstanding Intern award, 1956, Ciba award for gerontol. rsch., 1958, Rectors medal U. Helsinki, 1968; named Disting. Med. Alumnus, U. Kans. Coll. Health Sci., 1995; John and Mary R. Markle scholar, 1964, William N. Creasy vis. prof. clin. pharmacology Med. Coll. Va., 1975; Bruce Hall Meml. lectr. St. Vincents Hosp., Sydney, 1976, 7th Sir Henry Hallett Dale lectr. Johns Hopkins U. Med. Sch., 1978. Fellow ACP, N.Y. Acad. Scis., Am. Assn. Pharm. Scientists (Rsch. Achievement award in clin. scis. 1995); mem. Am. Soc. Clin. Nutrition, Am. Nutrition Instn., Am. Soc. Pharmacology and Exptl. Therapeutics (chmn. clin. pharmacology divsn. 1969-71, mem. exec. com. 1966-73, 78-81, del. 1975-78, bd. publ. trustees), Am. Soc. Clin. Pharmacology and Therapeutics (Oscar B. Hunter Meml. award 1995), Am. Fedn. Clin. Rsch., Brit. Pharmacol. Soc., AMA (vice chmn. coun. on drugs 1971-72, editl. bd. jour.), Ctrl. Soc. Clin. Rsch., Royal Soc. for Promotion Health, Inst. Medicine of Nat. Acad. Scis., Soc. Exptl. Biology and Medicine (councillor 1976-80), Internat. Union Pharmacologists (sec. clin. pharmacology sect. 1975-81, internat. adv. com. Paris Congress 1978), GPIA (blue ribbon com. on generic medicine 1990), Sigma Xi.

AZAROFF, LEONID VLADIMIROVITCH, physics educator; b. Moscow, June 19, 1926; came to U.S., 1939, naturalized, 1945; s. Vladimir Ivanovitch and Maria Yulievna (Odlen) A.; m. Carmen Wade, Mar. 9, 1946 (div. July 1968); m. Beth Sulzer, Mar. 4, 1972; children: David, Richard, Lenore. BS cum laude, Tufts Coll., 1948; PhD, MIT, 1954. Research physicist Armour Research Found., Chgo., 1953-54, sr. scientist, 1954-57; asso. prof. metall. engring. Ill. Inst. Tech., Chgo., 1957-61, prof., 1961-66; prof. physics, dir. Inst. Material Sci., U. Conn., Storrs, 1966-92; guest physicist Brookhaven Nat. Lab., 1961, 62, 64; vis. prof. U. Mass., 1978-79, 85-86; cons. Owens-Ill., Philips Electronics, Hilger-Watts, Inc.; U.S. del. Internat. Union Crystallography, teaching commn., 1963-69; dir. Conn. Product Devel. Corp., Rogers Corp., Conn. Devel. Corp., 1977-92, Conn. Innovations Inc., 1990-92; pres. Conn. Acad. Sci. and Engring., Hartford, Conn., 1976-82; translation editor Am. Inst. Physics, N.Y.C., 1958; bd. dirs. Conn. Product Devel. Corp., Hartford. Author 8 books, including X-Ray Diffraction and X-Ray Spectroscopy, 1973, Physics Over Easy, 1996; also articles. With AUS, 1944-46. Recipient ofcl. citation Conn. Gen Assembly, 1982, 91. Fellow Am. Phys. Soc. (cons. editor), Mineral. Soc. Am.; mem. AAAS (dir.), IEEE (sr.), Am. Soc. Engring. Edn., Conn. Acad. Sci. and Engring. (pres. 1976-82), Am. Crystallographic Assn., Am. Inst. Mining Engrs., Am. Inst. Electronic Engrs., Internat. Union Physics, Internat. Union Crystal Growth, Sigma Xi (pres. Medford, Mass. chpt. 1947-48), Phi Kappa Phi, Sigma Pi Sigma. Republican. Russian Orthodox. Home: 5555 Heron Point Dr Naples FL 34108-2708 Office: U Conn Inst Materials Sci PO Box 136 Storrs Mansfield CT 06268-0136 *I have always adhered to the principle that anything worth doing at all is worth doing as well as possible. Therefore, I select very carefully the tasks to undertake.*

AZARYAN, ANAHIT VAZGENOVNA, biochemist, researcher; b. Yerevan, Armenia, Jan. 9, 1950; came to U.S., 1991; d. Vazgen Kh. and Dazy T. (Mirzoyan) A.; m. David B. Akopian, Jan. 30, 1981; 1 Child, Tigran. MD, Med. Sch., Yerevan, 1972; PhD, Inst. Molecular Biology, Moscow, 1979; Dr. Sc., Inst. Biochemistry, Yerevan, 1988. Prin. investigator Inst. Biochemistry, Yerevan, 1980-84, head proteolysis group, 1984-90; Fogarty rsch. program vis. scientist Nat. Inst. Child Health and Human Devel./NIH, Bethesda, Md., 1991; rsch. assoc. dept. biochemistry Uniformed Svcs. U. Health Scis., Bethesda, 1992-94, sr. rsch. scientist dept. pharmacology, 1994—. Author: Brain Peptide Hydrolases and Their Biological Functions, 1989; contbr. articles to Jour. Biol. Chem., Neurochem. Rsch., Jour. Neurosci. Rsch., others. Recipient fellowship Martin Luther U., Halle, Germany, 1983, fellowship N. Kline Inst. Psychiat. Rsch., N.Y.C., 1988, Travel award Internat. Soc. Neurochem.-FIDIA, Washington, 1991; Fogarty Internat. Ctr. Rsch. fellow, 1991. Mem. Internat. Soc. for Neurochemistry, European Soc. for Neurochemistry, Am. Soc. for Neuroscience, N.Y. Acad. Scis. Achievements include characterization of ATP-Ubiquitin-dependent protease in brain proves the existence of cytosolic ATP-Ub-dependent proteolysis pathway in that tissue; characterization of YAP3, a novel yeast aspartic protease and chromaffin granule convertases PC1/PC2 involved in the activitation of prohormones and proneuropeptides. Office: USUHS Dept Pharmacology 4301 Jones Bridge Rd Dept Bethesda MD 20814-4799

AZCARRAGA, GASTON, hotel executive; b. Nov. 19, 1955. Indsl. engring., U. Anahuac, Mexico City, Mex.; MBA, Harvard U. Chmn. bd., CEO Grupo Posadas, S.A. de C.V.; bd. dirs. Bancomer, Seguros Comercial América, Grupo Embotellador Mexicano, Walworth de México, Corp. Mexicana de Restaurantes. Mem. Asociacion de Inversionistas en Hoteles y Empresas Turisticas, A.C. (pres.), Consejo Mexicano de Promocion Turistica (v.p.), Consejo Nacional de Certification y Normalizacion de las Competencias Laborales (rep.). Office: Posadas USA Inc 5950 Berkshire #990 Dallas TX 75225

AZCUENAGA, MARY LAURIE, government official; b. Council, Idaho, July 25, 1945. AB, Stanford U., 1967; JD, U. Chgo., 1973. Atty. FTC, Washington, 1973-75, asst. to gen. counsel, 1975-76, staff atty. San Francisco regional office, 1977-80, asst. regional dir., 1980-81, asst. to exec. dir., 1981-82, litigation atty. Office of Gen. Counsel, 1982, asst. gen. counsel for legal counsel, 1983-84, commr., Washington, 1984-98; mem. Adminstrv. Conf. of the U.S., 1990-95. Trustee Food and Drug Law Inst., 1990-97, Advisory Bd. FDLI, 1997-98, Natl. Advertising Review Bd., 1998—, ERA Review Bd., 1998—. Office: 815 Connecticut Ave NW Ste 200 Washington DC 20006-4004*

AZHAR, RUBAINA SHAMEEM, journalist; b. May 21, 1971. BA, Claremont McKenna Coll., 1993; MS, Columbia U., 1996. Copy editor Newsday/N.Y. Newsday, Melville, N.Y., 1993-94; reporter, copy editor The Hartford (Conn.) Courant, 1994-98; copy editor L.A. Times, 1998—. E-mail: rubaina.azhar@latimes.com.

AZINGER, PAUL, professional golfer; b. Holyoke, Mass., Jan. 6, 1960; m. Toni Azinger; 2 children. Student, Broward Jr. Coll., Fla., Fla. State U. Profl. golfer, 1982—; mem. Ryder Cup Team, 1993. Winner Phoenix Open, 1987, Las Vegas Invitational, 1987, Canon Greater Hartford Open, 1987, 89, Bay Hill Classic, 1988, Tournament of Champions, 1990, AT&T Nat. Pro-Am, 1991, Tour Championship, 1992, Meml. Tournament, 1993, PGA Championship, 1993, New England Classic, 1993; named PGA Tour Player of Yr., 1987. Office: PGA Tour 112 Tpc Blvd Ponte Vedra Beach FL 32082-3077*

AZIZ, KHALID, petroleum engineering educator; b. Bahawalpur, Pakistan, Sept. 29, 1936; came to U.S., 1952; s. Aziz Ul and Rshida (Atamohammed) Hassan; m. Mussarrat Rizwani, Nov. 12, 1962; children: Natasha, Imraan. BS in Mech. Engring., U. Mich., 1955; BSc in Petroleum Engring., U. Alta., 1958, MSc in Petroleum Engring., 1961; PhD in Chem. Engring., Rice U., 1966. Jr. design engr. Massey-Ferguson, 1955-56; various position to asst. prof. petroleum engring. U. Alta., 1960-62; various positions, chmn. bd. Neotech. Cons. Ltd., 1972-85; mgr., dir. Computer Modelling Group, Calgary, Alta., 1977-82; various positions to chief engr. Karachi (Pakistan) Gas Co., 1958-59, 62-63; various positions to prof. chem. and petroleum engring. U. Calgary, 1965-82; hon. prof., 1994—; prof. petroleum engring. dept. Stanford (Calif.) U., 1982—, assoc. dean rsch. Sch. Earth Scis., 1983-86, chmn. petroleum engring. dept., 1986-91, 94-95, Otto N. Miller prof. in earth scis., 1989—; hon. prof. chem. and petroleum engring. U. Calgary, 1994—. Co-author: Flow of Complex Mixtures in Pipes, 1972, Petroleum Reservoir Simulation, 1979; contbr. articles to profl. jours. Recipient Diploma of Honor, Pi Epsilon Tau, 1991; Chem. Inst. Can. fellow, 1974, Killam Resident fellow U. Calgary, 1977. Mem. Soc. Petroleum Engrs. (disting. mem., Ferguson award 1979, Reservoir Engring. award 1987, Lester C. Uren award 1988, Disting. Achievement award for Petroleum Engring. Faculty 1990, hon. mem. 1996), Am. Inst. Mining, Metall. and Petroleum Engrs. (hon. mem.), Soc. Indsl. and Applied Maths., Assn. Profl. Engrs. Geologists, Geophysicists (Alta., Can.), Nat. Acad. Engring., Russian Acad. Natural Scis. (fgn.), Sigma Xi. Muslim. Achievements include rsch. in multiphase flow of oil/gas mixtures & steam in pipes & wells, multiphase flow in porous media, reservoir simulation (black-oil, compositional, thermal, geothermal), natural gas engring., hydrocarbon fluid phase behavior. Home: 112 Peter Coutts Cir Stanford CA 94305-2517 Office: Stanford U Dept Petroleum Engring Stanford CA 94305-2220

AZIZKHAN, RICHARD GEORGE, pediatric surgeon, educator; b. London, Aug. 10, 1953; came to U.S., 1964; s. Reza George and Helga Marianne (Behnke) A.; m. Geralyn Brindisi; children: Richard Anthony, Kathryn Marie, Christine Elizabeth Ann, Aaron Brindisi. BS with honors, Dickinson Coll., Carlisle, Pa., 1972; MD, Pa. State U., 1975. Diplomate in gen. surgery, pediat. surgery and surg. critical care Am. Bd. Surgery. Resident in surgery U. Va., Charlottesville, 1976-78, 80-83; rsch. fellow in pediat. surgery Harvard Med. Sch. Boston Children's Hosp., 1978-80; fellow in pediat. surgery Johns Hopkins Univ., Balt., 1983-85; chief pediat. surgery U. N.C., Chapel Hill, 1985-93; surgeon-in-chief Child Hosp., Buffalo, 1993-98; prof. surgery and pediats. SUNY, Buffalo, 1993-98; surgeon-in-chief Children's Hosp. Med. Ctr., Cin., 1998—; prof. surgery and pediats., vice chair dept. surgery U. Cin., 1998—; surg. adv. bd. Smith, Kline, Beecham, Phila., 1990-95; dir. Pediatric Surgery Tng. Program, U. Cin., 1998—. Author: Congenital Malformations: Prenatal Diagnosis and Management, 1990, A Geneology of Pediatric Surgery of North America, 1997; contbr. over 100 articles to profl. jours. Recipient Upjohn Achievement award U. Va. Sch. Medicine, 1981, Hugh J. Warren Tchg. award, 1983, Battle Disting. Excellence in Tchg. award U. N.C. Sch. Medicine, 1988, Disting. Alumnus award Pa. State U., 1995; Schering scholar ACS, 1982; SmithKline & French fellow ACS, 1986, Pa. State U. Alumnae fellow, 1995. Fellow ACS, Am. Acad. Pediats. (chair program com. 1995, surg. sect. exec. com. 1997—), Am. Pediat. Surgery Assn. (program com. 1990-93, bd. govs. 1998—), Pa.

State U. Alumnae Assn. (life); mem. Assn. of Acad. Surgery (exec. coun. 1986-89), Alpha Omega Alpha. Roman Catholic. Achievements include research that helped illucidate the importance of heparin in the growth of new blood vessels (angiogenesis); development of novel technique utilizing fiberoptic laser to treat bronchial stenosis in infants. Office: Childrens Hosp Med Ctr 3333 Burnet Ave Cincinnati OH 45229

AZOLA, MARTIN PETER, civil engineer, construction manager; b. Elmhurst, Ill., Jan. 12, 1947; s. Joseph Ramon and Lillian Alice (Zeeman) A.; m. Lone Tidemand, June 29, 1968; children: Anthony, Matthew, Kirsten. BSCE, Va. Polytechnic Inst., 1968, MSCE, 1969. Registered profl. engr., Md. V.p. J.R. Azola and Assocs., Balt., 1973-80; pres. M.P. Azola, Inc., Balt., 1980-90, Azola and Assocs., Inc., Balt., 1990—; commr. Balt. County Landmarks Com., Towson, Md., 1983-93; chmn. Nat. Remodelers Coun., Washington, 1988-89; instr. Goucher Coll., Towson, 1992-93. Contbr. articles to profl. jours. Pres. Charles St. Assoc., Balt., 1978; dir. Soc. For Preservation of Md. Antiques, Balt., 1988; trustee Children's Hosp., Balt., 1992, Md. Hist. Trust, 1996—. Recipient Preservation Svc. award State of Md., 1988, Profl. Achievement award Profl. Builder, Washington, 1987, Renaissance Grand award Nat. Assn. Home Builders, Washington, 1991; named Builder of Yr. Home Builders Assn. Md., 1988, Remodeler of Yr., 1991. Mem. ASCE, Nat. Soc. Profl. Engrs., Soc. Am. Mil. Engrs., Home Builders Assn. Md. (v.p. 1997—), Engring. Soc. Balt. (dir. 1980), Md. Jockey Club (v.p. 1996—), Omicron Delta Kappa (pres. 1967), Chi Epsilon. Office: Azola and Assocs PO Box 140 Brooklandville MD 21022-0140

AZOPARDI, KORITA MARIE, secondary school educator; b. Galveston, Tex., Jan. 30, 1941; d. John and Cecil Marie (Kierbow) Hamilton; m. Benny Lee Azopardi, May 27, 1960; children: Connie, B. Lee Jr. BS in Edn. and Math., S.W. Tex. State U., 1961; MA in Math., St. Louis U., 1970. Tchr. Navarro Pub. Schs., Geronimo, Tex., 1961-62, Victoria (Tex.) Ind. Sch. Dist., 1962-65, St. Louis Ind. Sch. Dist., 1965-67, Normandy Ind. Sch. Dist., St. Louis, 1967-69, Mary Inst., St. Louis, 1969-71, Corpus Christi (Tex.) Ind. Sch. Dist., 1979-84, Calallen Ind. Sch. Dist., Corpus Christi, 1984—. Mem. NEA, Nat. Coun. Tchrs. of Math., Math. Assn. Am., Tex. Coun. Tchrs. of Math., Tex. Tchrs. Assn., Tex. Computer Edn. Assn. Republican. Presbyterian. Avocation: ranching. Home: 4705 Gayle Dr Corpus Christi TX 78413-3322 Office: Calallen Ind Sch Dist 4001 Wildcat Dr Corpus Christi TX 78410-5105

AZOULAY, BERNARD, chemicals company executive; b. 1940. Grad., Ecole Polytechnique, Paris. With Societe Nat. Elf Aquitaine, Paris, 1966-77, M&T Chem., Inc., Phila., 1977-79, Elf Atochem, Paris, 1979-89; COO Elf Atochem N.A., Inc., Phila., 1990-93; pres., CEO Elf Atochem N.Am., Inc., Phila., 1993—. Office: Elf Atochem North America Inc 2000 Market St Ste 2200 Philadelphia PA 19103-3399

AZRACK, JOAN M., judge; b. 1951. BS, Rutgers Univ., N.J., 1974; JD, N.Y. Law Sch., 1979. With U.S. Dept. of Justice, 1979-81, U.S. Attorney's Office (N.Y. ea. dist.), 1982-90; magistrate judge U.S. Dist. Ct. (N.Y. ea. dist.), 2nd circuit, Brooklyn, 1991—. Office: US District Court 225 Cadman Plz E Rm 333 Brooklyn NY 11201-1818

AZRAEL, JUDITH ANNE, educator; b. Balt., July 28, 1938; d. Maurice and Altie A.; m. Herbert Greenberg, Dec. 20, 1960; children: Denise, Jeffrey. BA, U. Wis., 1939; MFA, U. Oreg., 1974. Tchr. U. Oreg., Eugene, 1973; vis. writer Western Wash. U., Bellingham, 1978-80. Author 4 vols. of poetry; contbr. short stories and essays to mags. Recipient Helene Werlitzer Found. award, Taos, N.Mex., 1973. Avocations: travel, hiking, reading.

AZRIELANT, AYA, jewelry manufacturing executive; Came to U.S. 1981.; m. Ofer; 3 children. Haifa U. Designer, owner Aya Azrielant, N.Y.C. Avocation: collector of modern art. Fax: 212-886-6006. Office: Andin International Inc 609 Greenwich St New York NY 10014-3683

AZRIN, NATHAN HAROLD, psychologist; b. Boston, Nov. 26, 1930; s. Harry and Esther (Alper) A.; m. Victoria Behar Besalel, Jan. 25, 1953; children—Rachel, Michael, David, Richard. B.A. cum laude, Boston U., 1951, M.A., 1952; Ph.D., Harvard U., 1956. Mem. faculty So. Ill. U., Carbondale, 1958-80; prof. rehab. So. Ill. U., 1959-80; rsch. dir. Anna (Ill.) Mental Health Ctr., 1958-80; prof. Nova Psychol. Clinic, Nova U., Ft. Lauderdale, Fla., 1980-87, Nova Southeastern U., Ft. Lauderdale, 1980—. Author: Token Economy, 1968, Toilet Training in Less than a Day, 1974, Toilet Training the Retarded, 1973, Habit Control, 1977, Job Club, 1980, Finding a Job, 1982. Editor psychol. jours. Served with AUS, 1956-58. Mem. Am. Psychol. Assn. (pres. div. 25 1963, ann. award applications in psychology 1975), Fla. Assn. Behavior Analysis (pres.), Midwestern Psychol. Assn. (pres.), Assn. Advancement Behavior Therapy (pres., Lifetime Achievement award 1997), Midwestern Analysis of Behavior Assn. (pres.). Home: 5151 Bayview Dr Fort Lauderdale FL 33308-3433 Office: Nova Southeastern U 3301 College Ave Fort Lauderdale FL 33314-7796

AZUAJE, RAFAEL, computer scientist, educator; b. Trujillo, Venezuela, Aug. 19, 1957; came to U.S., 1981; s. Marcial Azuaje and Aurelia Linares; m. Stella Azuage, Aug. 19, 1979; children: Aurelia, Rafael, Consuelo. BS in Computer Sci., Poly. U. Madrid, 1979; MS in Computer Info. Sys., St. Mary's U., 1998. Engr. Datapoint, San Antonio, 1981-89; sys. analyst U. Tex., San Antonio, 1989-94; sys. adminstr., prof. Our Lady of the Lake U., San Antonio, 1994—; pres. MicroSystems Internat., San Antonio, 1995-98. Baptist. Home: 1715 W Craig Pl San Antonio TX 78201-5402 Office: Our Lady of the Lake U 411 SW 24th St San Antonio TX 78207-4666

AZUMA, TAKAMITSU, architect, educator; b. Osaka, Japan, Sept. 20, 1933; s. Yoshimatsu and Yoshiko (Ikeda) A.; m. Setsuko Nakaoka, Mar. 17, 1957; 1 child, Rie. BArch, Osaka U., 1957, DArch, D. of Engring, 1985. Designer, Ministry of Postal Svcs., Osaka, 1957-60; chief designer Junzo Sakakura Architect and Assocs., Osaka, 1960-63; chief designer Junzo Sakakura Architect and Assocs., Tokyo, 1963-67; prin. Takamitsu Azuma Architect & Assocs., Tokyo, 1967-85; instr. Tokyo U. Art and Design, 1976-78, Tokyo Denki U., 1980-82, Tokyo U., 1983-85; instr. Osaka U., 1981-85, prof., 1985-97, emeritus prof., Osaka U., 1997—; instr. Osaka Art U., 1985-87; architect Azuma Architects & Assocs., 1985—; vis. prof. Sch. Architecture Washington U., St. Louis, 1989; prof. Chiba Inst. Tech., 1997—. Recipient Diplomatic Design prize Kinki Br. of Archtl. Inst. Japan Competition, 1957. Author: Reevaluation of the Residence, 1971, On the Japanese Architectural Space, 1981, Takamitsu Azuma-Contemporary Japanese Architects Series (4), 1982, Philosophy of Living in the City, 1983, Device from Architecture, 1986, Space Analysis of Urban Residence, 1986, 100 Chpt. for Children's Place, 1987, White Book about Tower House, 1987, Cities and Urban Residences, 1998. Mem. Archtl. Inst. Japan (Archtl. Design prize 1995), Japan Inst. Archs. Home: 3-39-4 Jingumae, Shibuya-ku, Tokyo 150-0001, Japan Office: 3-6-1 Minami-Aoyama Minato-ku, Tokyo 107-0062, Japan

AZZARONE, CAROL ANN, marketing executive; b. Jersey City, Aug. 1, 1946; d. Paul Buglione and Catherine (DellaFave) LiCalsi; m. Dominick L. Azzarone, May 13, 1967 (div. 1989); children: Anthony Paul, Kathryn Ann. AA, Bergen C.C., 1982; BA, Ramapo Coll., 1984. Editl. asst. McGraw-Hill, Inc., N.Y.C., 1964-69; real estate agt. Auburn Realty, Inc., Bergenfield, N.J., 1975-80, Weichert Realty, Morris Plains, N.J., 1975—; pub. rels. coord. Ridgefield (N.J.) Bd. Edn., 1982-84; mktg. dir. Spa Lady Corp., Fairfax, Va., 1984-86, Newson Fitness, Morristown, N.J., 1986-88; creative dir. Publ. Corp., Morristown, 1988-90; advt. dir. Ronton Advt., Union, N.J., 1990-98; mktg. v.p. Dynamic Tech. Group, Inc., Parsippany, N.J., 1998—; advt. cons. Editor (newsletters) Ridgefield Sch. News, 1982-84, Cliffside Park Sch. News, 1984-85, The Grapevine, 1985-86. Mem. NOW, 1989—. N.J. Bell scholar N.J. Bell Corp., 1980, Bergen Community Coll. Alumni scholar, 1981. Mem. NOW, NAFE (First Place Award of Excellence 1996, Jersey award for web-site adv.), Advt./Pub. Rels. Assn., N.J. Advt. Club, Phi Theta Kappa. Democrat. Roman Catholic. Avocations: cross country skiing, horseback riding, biking, reading. Office: Dynamic Tech Group Inc 1055 Parsippany Blvd Parsippany NJ 07054-1230

AZZOLI, VAL, music company executive. Co-chmn., co-CEO Atlantic Recording Corp., N.Y.C. Office: Atlantic Group 1290 Avenue Of The Americas New York NY 10104-0101*

AZZOLINA, DAVID SEAN, librarian; b. East Orange, N.J., May 22, 1957; s. Alexander and Helen (Fitzpatrick) A. BA, U. Pa., 1978, MA, 1991, PhD, 1996; MS, Columbia U., 1979. Social sci. libr. Rice U., Houston, 1980-82; ref. libr. Johns Hopkins U., Balt., 1982-86; ref. libr. U. Pa., Phila., 1986—, adj. prof. folklore/folklife, 1997—; Author: Tale Type and Motif Indexes, 1987; contbr.: (book) Guide to Reference Books, 11th edit., 1997; reviewer various jours. Democrat. Episcopalian. Home: 256 S 44th St Philadelphia PA 19104-2944 Office: University of Pennsylvania Library 3420 Walnut St Philadelphia PA 19104-3411

AZZOPARDI, MARC ANTOINE, astrophysicist, scientist; b. Philippeville, Algeria, Oct. 28, 1940; s. Antoine Philippe and Marie Madeleine (Grech) A.; divorced; children: Pauline, Mathilde, Marceau; m. Alexandra L. Giorla, June 30, 1994; children: Anne-Sophie, Mary. Lic. es sci., Algeria and Marseilles U., France, 1963; DSc, Toulouse U., France, 1981. Astronomy aide U. Toulouse, 1964-81, adj. astronomer, 1981-83; adj. astronomer U. Marseilles, France, 1983-87, astronomer 2d class, 1987-92, astronomer 1st class, 1992—; astronomer in charge European South Obs. Sta., Zeekoegat, South Africa, 1964; vis. scholar U. Tex., Austin, 1982-83; mem. sci. adv. coun. Can.-France-Hawaii Telescope Co., Hawaii, 1984-87, vis. scientist, 1994-96; sci. assoc. European So. Obs., Garching, Germany, 1983-87, mem. users com., 1988-91, chmn., 1990-91, guest prof., 1992-93, panel mem. observing program com., 1996-97. Contbr. articles to profl. jours. Recipient NSF-Ctr. Nat. Sci. Rsch. award, 1982-83. Mem. Soc. French Specialists in Astronomy, Am. Astron. Soc., European Astron. Soc. Roman Catholic. Office: Observatoire de Marseilles, 2 place le Verrier, F-13248 Marseilles Cedex 4, France

BAAB, CARLTON, advertising executive. COO, CFO CKS Ptnr., Cupertino, Calif. Office: CKS Partners 10443 Bandley Dr Cupertino CA 95014-1912

BAADE, HANS WOLFGANG, legal educator, law expert; b. Berlin, Dec. 16, 1929; s. Fritz and Edith (Wolff) B.; m. Anne Adams Johnston; children—Friedrich James, Hans Alastair. A.B., Syracuse U., 1949; J.D., Kiel U. (Germany), 1951; LL.B., LL.M., Duke U., 1955, diploma Hague Acad. Internat. Law, 1956. Assoc. Inst. Internat. Law, Kiel, 1955-60; assoc. prof. law Duke U., 1960-64, prof. law, 1964-70; prof. law U. Toronto, 1970-71; Hugh Lamar Stone prof. civil law U. Tex., Austin, 1971—; arbitrator internat. comml. matters; dir. Am. Soc. Comparative Law. Mem. Am. Arbitration Assn. (nat. panel arbitrators); assoc. mem. Internat. Acad. Comparative Law. Editor: Law and Comparative Problems, 1961-66; bd. editors Am. Jour. Comparative Law, 1960—; editorial sec. German Yr. Book Internat. Law, 1956-60; contbr. numerous articles to profl. jours. Hon. fellow faculty of law U. Edinburgh (Scotland), 1997—. Home: 6002 Mountainclimb Dr Austin TX 78731-3822 Office: U Tex Sch Law Austin TX 78705

BAAKLINI, ABDO ISKANDAR, educator; b. Dhourshweir, Lebanon, Mar. 7, 1938; s. Iskandar A. Baaklini and Sa'ada Ya'coub; children: Farid, Iskandar. BA, Am. U., Beirut, 1960, MA, 1963; PhD, SUNY, Albany, 1972. Tchr. Govt. of Iraq, Amara, 1960-61; acad. councillor U.S. Embassy, Beirut, 1962-68; prof. SUNY, Albany, 1972—; dir. Ctr. for Legis. Devel., SUNY, 1976—; advisor USAID, 1971—, various govts., 1971—. Author: Legislatures in the Middle East: Their Role During Transition to Democracy, 1999, Viable Constitutionalism and Democratic Political Stability, 1997, The Brazilian Legislature and Political System, 1992, Legislative and Political Development: Lebanon, 1842-1972, Legislative Institution Building in Brazil, Costa Rica and Lebanon, 1976; contbr. articles to profl. jours. Mem. Am. Soc. Pub. Adminstrn., Am. Polit. Sci. Assn. E-mail: aib71@cnsvax.albany.edu. Home: 96 Alpine Dr Latham NY 12203 Office: Ctr for Legis Devel SUNY 423 State St Albany NY 12222

BAAR, DIANE, advertising executive. Sr. v.p., media svcs. dir. The Martin Agy., Richmond, Va. Office: The Martin Agy 1 Shockoe Plz Richmond VA 23219-4132*

BAAR, JAMES A., public relations and corporate communications executive, author, consultant, internet publisher, software developer; b. N.Y.C., Feb. 9, 1929; s. A.W. and Marguerite R. B.; m. Beverly Hodge, Sept. 2, 1948; 1 son, Theodore Hall. AB, Union Coll., Schenectady, 1949. Washington corr. UPI, also other wire service burs. and newspapers, 1949-59; sr. editor Missiles and Rockets mag., 1959-62; mgr. various news bur. ops. Gen. Electric Co., 1962-66; mgr. European Mktg. Communications Ops., 1966-70; pres. Gen. Electric subs. Internat. Mktg. Communications Cons., 1970-72; sr. v.p., dir. public relations Lewis & Gilman, Inc., Phila., 1972-74; exec. v.p. Creamer Dickson Basford, Inc., 1974-78; pres. Creamer Dickson Basford-New Eng., 1978-83; sr. v.p./mgr. Northeast region Hill & Knowlton, Inc., Boston, 1983-84; v.p. communications Computervision Corp., 1984-86; sr. v.p. Gray & Co. Pub. Communications and gen. mgr. Gray & Co., N.Y., 1986-87; exec. v.p., worldwide dep. dir. advanced tech. practice Hill & Knowlton, Inc., 1987-90; pres., mng. cons. Omegacom, Inc., Boston, 1990—; cons. Internet Pub.; corp. comms. and internet software developer and strategic comms. cons., 1990—. Author: Polaris, 1960, Combat Missileman, 1961, Spacecraft and Missiles of the World, 1962; (novel) The Great Free Enterprise Gambit, 1980, The Careful Voters Dictionary of Language Pollution, 1999; also numerous articles. Bd. overseers New Eng. Conservatory Music. Mem. Nat. Investor Relations Inst., Pub. Relations Soc. Am., Counselors Acad., Internat. Pub. Relations Assn., Chi Psi, Nat. Press Club, Overseas Press Club, English Speaking Union (bd. dirs. Boston), Univ. Club (Providence). Republican. Roman Catholic. E-mail: jimber@omewgacom.com. Office: 24 Thayer St Providence RI 02906-1021

BAAS, JACQUELYNN, art historian, museum administrator; b. Grand Rapids, Mich., Feb. 14, 1948. BA in History of Art, Mich. State U.; Ph.D. in History of Art, U. Mich. Registrar U. Mich. Mus. Art, Ann Arbor, 1974-78, asst. dir., 1978-82; editor Bull. Museums of Art and Archaeology, U. Mich., 1976-82; chief curator Hood Mus. Art, Dartmouth Coll., Hanover, N.H., 1982-84, dir., 1985-89; dir. U. Calif. Berkeley Art Mus. and Pacific Film Archive, Calif., 1989-99; cons. in field; organizer exhbns. Contbr. articles to jours. and catalogues. NEH fellow, 1972-73; Nat. Endowment Arts fellow, 1973-74, 87-88. Mem. Coll. Art Assn. Am., Am. Assn. Mus. Address: 225 Alvarado Rd Berkeley CA 94705

BABA, ISAMU, construction company executive; b. Oita, Japan, June 13, 1923; s. Gunroku and Kimiko Baba; m. Fumiko Takita, Nov. 3, 1948; children: Shiro, Kyoko Kojima. B in Engring., Osaka (Japan) U., 1945; PhD, Waseda U., Japan, 1990. Cert. architect, cons. engr., value specialist. Mgr. R & D Fujita Corp., Tokyo, 1965-75, dir., 1975-85, exec. v.p., 1985-90, sr. exec. v.p., 1990-94, exec. adviser, 1994—. Author: The Method of Value Engineering in the Construction Industry, 1975, Basics of Construction Value Engineering, 1983, Application of Construction Value Engineering, 1983, Illustration of the Method of Keeping Costs Down in the Construction Industry, 1984, The Study of Development and Application of Value Engineering For Construction Site Management, 1990, Terminos Practicos de Ingenieria Civil y Arquitectura, 1993. Chmn. bd. trustees Tottori Women's Coll., Japan, 1991—. Recipient Presdl. Citation Soc. Am. Value Engrs., 1981, Soc. award Associated Gen. Contractors of Japan, 1985, Presdl. Citation Archtl. Inst. Japan, 1992, 4th Order of Merit with the Rising Sun, 1998. Mem. Internat. Coun. Bldg. Rsch., Studies and Documentation, Soc. Japanese Value Engrs. (trustee, Best Paper prize 1973, Promotional Achievment award 1984, Presdl. Citation 1990), Soc. Korean Value Engrs. (adviser), Archtl. Inst. Japan, Japanese Value Engring. (Soc. award 1990), Soc. Japanese Value Specialis (pres.). Avocation: noh (Japanese classic art). Home: 2-29-21 Irima-cho, Chofu Tokyo 182, Japan Office: Fujita Corp, 4-6-15 Sendagaya, Shibuya-ku, Tokyo 151, Japan

BABA, MARIETTA LYNN, business anthropologist, b. Flint, Mich., Nov. 9, 1949; d. David and Lillian (Joseph) Baba; m. David Smokler, Feb. 14, 1977 (div. 1982); 1 child, Alexia Nicole Baba Smokler. BA with highest distinction, Wayne State U., 1971, MA in Anthropology, 1973, PhD in Phys. Anthropology, 1975; MBA Mich. State U., 1994. Asst. prof. sci. and tech. Wayne State U., Detroit, Mich., 1975-80, assoc. prof. anthropology, 1980-88, prof., 1988—, spl. asst. to pres., 1980-82, econ. devel. officer, 1982-83, asst. provost, 1983-85; assoc. provost, 1985-89, dir. Internat. Programs and Interim Assoc. Dean of Grad. Sch., 1988-89, assoc. dean grad. sch., 1989-90, acting chair Dept. Anthropology, 1990-92; program dir. transformations to quality orgns., dir. social, behav. and econ. scis. NSF, 1994-96, chair, dept. anthropology Wayne State U., 1996—; founder, corp. officer Applied Rsch. Teams Mich., Inc., Detroit, Intelligent Techs., Inc., Detroit; evolution researcher Wayne State U., 1975-82; cons. GM Rsch. Labs., 1988-92, Electronic Data Systems, 1990-93, McKinsey Global Inst., 1991; rsch. contractor GM/EDS, 1990-94. With USAF, SBIR, 1992-94; lectr. nat. and internat. symposia, profl. confs. Contbr. numerous papers and abstracts to tech. jours; patentee in field. Bd. dirs. City-Univ. Consortium, Detroit, 1980-83; v.p. Neighborhood Svc. Orgn., Detroit, 1980-85; mem. State Rsch. Fund Feasibility Rev. Panel, 1982-94; mem. adv. panel on tech., innovation and U.S. trade U.S. Congl. Office Tech. Assessment, 1990-91, mem. panel on electronic enterprise, 1993-94; active Leadership Detroit Class IV, 1982-83; dir. Mich. Tech. Coun. (SE div.), 1984-85. Job Partnership Tng. Act grantee, 1981-90; NSF grantee, 1982, 84-85. Adv. editor for orgnl. anthropology American Anthropologist, 1990-93; Issued letters patent for method to map joint ventures and maps produced thereby. Fellow Am. Anthrop. Assn. (bd. dirs. 1986-88, exec. com. 1986-88, del. to the Internat. Union Anthrop. and Ethnol. Sci. 1990-94, chair global commn. anthropology, 1993—), Nat. Assn. Practice Anthropology (pres. 1986-88), Soc. Applied Anthropology, Phi Beta Kappa, Sigma Xi (Morton Fried award, 1991), Beta Gamma Sigma. Office: Wayne State U 137 Manoogian Hall Detroit MI 48202

BABA, THOMAS FRANK, corporate economist, economics educator; b. Yonkers, N.Y., Mar. 10, 1957; s. Frank Thomas and Teresa Helen (Kratjeski) B.; 1 child, Frank Thomas. BA, Manhattan Coll., 1979; MA, Fordham U., 1982, postgrad., 1984—. Prof. Rose Hill campus Fordham U., N.Y.C., 1985-89; prof. Iona Coll., New Rochelle, N.Y., 1986-90; sr. U.S. economist, mgr. rsch. and planning group Toyota Motor Corp., N.Y.C., 1989-97; corp. economist, mkt. rsch, mgr. Mercedes Benz North Am., Montvale, NJ, 1998—. Mem. Nat. Assn. Bus. Economists, Am. Econ. Assn., N.Y. Assn. Bus. Economists, Am. Acad. Polit. Sci., World Assn. Former U.N. Interns and Fellows, Soc. Automotive Analysts. Home: 46 Linn Ave Yonkers NY 10705-2503 Office: Mercedez Benz North Am Inc 1 Mercedes Dr Montvale NJ 07645-1815

BABAO, DONNA MARIE, community health, psychiatric nurse, educator; b. St. Louis, May 6, 1945; d. Wilbert C. and Cecelia (Hogan) Bremer; widowed; 1 child, Tonya J. Diploma, Henry Ford Hosp. Sch. Nursing, Detroit, 1966; BSN, Calif. State U., Sacramento, 1978, MS in Nursing, 1989; MA in Edn., Calif. State U., Chico, 1985. Cert. pub. health nurse; master tchr. cert.; cert. clin. use of interactive guided imagery. Staff nurse U. Calif. Med. Ctr., San Francisco, 1968-72; staff and charge CCU nurse Children's Hosp. of San Francisco, 1972-78; pub. health nurse Sutter-Yuba Health Dept., Yuba City, Calif., 1979-81; instr. nursing Yuba Coll., Marysville, Calif., 1981—; psychiat. charge nurse Sunridge Hosp., Yuba City, 1994-96; mem. exam. item writing panel NCLEX-RN, 1998. Writer health column, 1986-90; chpt. to textbooks; reviewer nursing textbooks; contbr. articles to profl. jours. 1st lt. Nurse Corps, U.S. Army, 1966-68. Mem. Nat. League Nursing, Calif. Tchrs. Assn., Vietnam Vets. Am., Am. Holistic Nurses Assn. Office: Yuba Coll Dept Nursing 2088 N Beale Rd Marysville CA 95901-7605

BABAR, RAZA ALI, industrial engineer, utility consultant, futurist, management educator, marketing strategist, author, publisher; b. Shujabad, Punjab, Pakistan, May 29, 1947; came to U.S., 1972; s. Syed Mohammad Ali Shah and Syeda Hafeeza (Gilani) Bukhari; m. Sufia K. Durrett, July 23, 1974 (div. 1983); children: Azra Yasmeen, Imran Ali, Amenah Andaleep; m. Syeda Afshan Gilani, Aug. 23, 1983; children: Abdullah Ali, Hammad Ali, Omaima Ali, Mustafa Ali. Pre Engring. student, Govt. Coll., Lahore, Pakistan, 1965; BS in Mining Engring., U. Engring. and Tech., Lahore, 1969; MS in Indsl. Engring., Wayne State U., 1978; postgrad., Detroit Coll. Law, 1982; postgrad. U.S. Econ. Outlook Conf., U. Mich., 1977-84. Engr., planner Bukhari Elec. Concern, Multan, Pakistan, 1969-70; mgr. mining ops. Felezzate Yazd Co., Iran, 1970-72; salesman Great Books, Inc., Chgo., 1972-73; field underwriter N.Y. Life Ins. Co., 1972-73; indsl. engr. Ellis/Naeyaert Assocs., Inc., Warren, Mich., 1973-74; grad. asst. dept. indsl. engring. and ops. rsch. Wayne State U., Detroit, 1974-75; prin. engr., work leader project svcs. divsn. Generation Constrn. Dept., Detroit Edison Co., 1975-79; tech. advisor Ministry of Prodn., Govt. Pakistan, Islamabad, 1979-80; chmn. dept. bus. adminstrn. Zakariya U., Multan, Pakistan, 1980-83; prin. engr. project controls Enrico Fermi 2 Detroit Edison Co., 1981-82, supr. Fermi 2 rate case task force, 1982-84, spl. projects engr. planning, 1984-88; mgr. econ. support svc. Syndeco, Inc., 1985-88; market planner Detroit Edison Co., 1988-89, sr. mktg. strategist, 1989-90; dir. global rsch. and intelligence, 1990-92, project dir. bus. customer satisfaction, new products and svcs. rsch., 1992-93, dir. demand side mgmt., 1993-95, dir. customer energy solutions, 1995-96, dir. ethnic mktg., 1996-98, dir. svc. ctr. oper., 1998—; nat. tech. adv. bd. E-Source; vis. prof. Grad. Sch. Bus. Adminstrn., Wayne State U., 1987—. Author rsch. papers and articles, presentations in field. Founder Fedn. Engring. Assns. Pakistan, 1969; pres. acad. staff assn., mem. chancellor's com. Zakariya U., Pakistan, 1980-81; pres. Pakistan Cultural Group, Detroit, 1975-76, Pakistan Students Assn., 1975-76; bd. dirs. Detroit Islamic Libr., 1976-77; mem. Econ. Outlook Conf., U. Mich., Ann Arbor, 1977-84, Rep. Presdl. Task Force Honor Roll, Rep. Nat. Com.; charter mem. Rep. Congl Task Force, Rep. Presdl. Legion Merit; vol. planning advisor Cmty. Tng. and Devel. Orgn., Beginning Experience and Mich. Tng. and Resource Ctr.; tchg. cons. applied econs. Jr. Achievement; vol. cons. Detroit Area Agy. on Aging; industry rep. U. Mich. Global Citizenship Program; mem. adv. com. bus. and internat. edn. program Mott C.C.; bd. dirs. Wayne County Foster Care Rev. Bd.; mem. adv. panel Office Tech. Assessment U.S. Congress; mem. bd. dirs. Asian Am. Ctr. for Justice, 1998—; founder Asian and Mid. Eastern Am. Forum, 1996; bd. dirs. IAATRADE U.S.A., 1998—. Recipient Pride of Performance medal Engring. U. Pakistan, 1967; Acad. Merit scholar Detroit Coll. Law, 1982. Mem. IEEE, Am. Mgmt. Assn., Am. Mgmt. Assn. Internat., Econ. Club Detroit, Am. Inst. Indsl. Engrs., Am. Assn. Cost Engrs., Engring. Soc. Detroit, ESD Profl. Activities Coun. (co-chmn. civic affairs com., emerging techs. com.), Pakistan Engring. Congress, Pakistan Inst. Mining Engrs., Am. Assn. MBA Execs., Assn. Muslim Scientists and Engrs., Assn. Muslim Social Scientists, Internat. Platform Assn., Islamic Soc. N.Am., Am. Moslem Soc., Islamic Cultural Inst., Islamic Assn. Mich. (chmn. Islamic edn. com., mem. editl. bd. Muslim News), Tanzeem-e-Islami Pakistan and N.Am., Pakistan Assn. of Am., Internat. Assn. Bus. Communicators (bd. dirs., chmn. multicultural communicators com.), Soc. Competitor Intelligence Profls. (steering com.), Assn. Energy Svcs. Profls., Assn. Demand Side Mgmt. Profls., World Future Soc. Avocations: reading, writing, public speaking, sports, travel. E-mail: babarr@dteenergy.com. Home: 627 Weybridge Dr Bloomfield Hills MI 48304-1083 Office: 6301 23 Mile Rd Shelby Township MI 48316

BABAYANS, EMIL, financial planner; b. Tehran, Iran, Nov. 9, 1951; came to U.S., 1969; s. Hacob and Jenik (Khatchatourian) B.; m. Annie Ashjian. B.S., U. So. Calif., 1974, M.S., 1976; Cert. fin. planner; chartered life underwriter, fin. cons. Pres. Babtech Internat., Inc., Sherman Oaks, Calif., 1975-85; sr. ptnr. Emil Babayans & Assocs., Woodland Hills, Calif., 1985—. Mem. Am. Mgmt. Assn., Nat. Assn. Life Underwriters, Inst. Cert. Fin. Planners, Internat. Assn. Fin. Planners, Am. Soc. CLU and Chartered Fin. Cons., Million Dollar Round Table. Armenian Orthodox. Office: 21700 Oxnard St Ste 1100 Woodland Hills CA 91367-7574

BABB, ALBERT LESLIE, biomedical engineer, educator; b. Vancouver, B.C., Can., Nov. 7, 1925; came to U.S., 1948, naturalized, 1954; s. Clarence Stanley and Mildred (Gutteridge) B.; m. Marion A. McDougall; children—Eugene Matthew, Philip Leslie, Christine Louise. B.A.Sc., U. B.C., 1948; M.S., U. Ill., 1949, Ph.D., 1951; student Internat. Sch. Nuclear Sci. and Engring., Argonne Nat. Lab., 1956, 57. Chem. engr. Nat. Research Council Can., 1948; research engr. Rayonier, Inc., 1951-52; faculty U. Wash., Seattle, 1952—; chmn. nuclear engring. group U. Wash., 1957-65, prof. chem. engring., 1960—, acting chmn. dept. chem. engring., 1985, dir. nuclear reactor labs., 1962-72, prof. nuclear engring., 1965-91, prof. emeritus nuclear engring. and chem. engring., 1991—, chmn. dept. nuclear engring., 1965-81, acting chmn. dept. nuclear engring., 1984-86, adj. prof. bioengring., 1985-91; v.p. rsch. Meridian Med. Corp., Seattle, 1991—; del. Japan-U.S. Seminar on

Nuclear Engring. Edn., 1974; lectr. hemodialysis engring. USSR Ministry of Health, Moscow, 1976; lectr. biomed. engring. Norwegian Nephrological Soc., Oslo, 1980; lectr. hemodialysis engring. Kuratorium für Hemodialyse, Münster, Germany, 1980, Clinique Iser, Munich, Germany, 1980, Mcpl. Hosp., Hvidovre, Denmark, 1980, State Hosp., Copenhagen, 1980; mem. Assembly Engring., NRC, Com. Transp. Plutonium by Air; cons. med. engring., 1952—. Contbr. chpts. to books, profl. jours. Trustee Pacific Sci. Center Found., mem. exec. com., 1973-80. Recipient citation Wash. Joint Legis. Com. Nuclear Energy, 1968, Disting. Teaching award Coll. Engring. U. Wash., 1987, Clyde Shields Disting. Svc. award N.W. Kidney Found., 1992, U. Ill. Alumni Achievement award, 1993, tchg. excellence award Aspen Tech. Inc., 1999, Am. Engr. Specifying award for excellence in design artificial kidney systems, 1970, Nat. Kidney Found. Pioneer award, 1982, Sigma Xi award, 1982; named Engr. of Yr. Wash. State Profl. Engrs. Assn., 1969. Fellow Am. Inst. Chemists, Am. Inst. Chem. Engrs. (Engr. Distinction award), Am. Nuclear Soc. (v.p. 1982-83, chmn. 1983-84), Am. Inst. Med. and Biol. Engring.; mem. NAS (chmn. com. on future devel. nuclear power 190, mem. Inst. Medicine), NAE (memberships com.), Engrs. Joint Coun., Am. Soc. Engring. Edn. (chmn. nuclear engring. divsn. 1965-66), Internat. Soc. Artificial Organs, Am. Soc. Artificial Internal Organs, European Dialysis and Transplantation Assn., Inst. Medicine, Biomed. Engring. Soc., Sigma Xi, Tau Beta Pi, Pi Mu Epsilon, Alpha Chi Sigma. Presbyterian. Clubs: U. Wash. Pres.', Wash. Athletic. Co-inventor continous central artificial kidney system for low cost treatment in centers, also co-inventor automatic artificial kidney system for overnight unattended hemodialysis of patients in homes, and techniques for early diagnosis of cystic fibrosis in children using a nuclear reactor; formulated dialysis index for prescribing minimum adequate treatment for patients undergoing hemodialysis; co-inventor, dir. design and devel. extracorporeal system for treatment of sickle cell anemia; co-developer computerized wearable insulin pump for diabetics; patentee systems for stblzn. of structures in permafrost, also field of artificial kidney, artificial pancreas, and respiratory diagnostics. Home: 3237 Lakewood Ave S Seattle WA 98144-7229

BABB, ELIZABETH, artist, graphic artist; b. Salem, Ohio, July 27, 1966; d. Roger Hal and Florence (March) B. BFA, Kent (Ohio) State U., 1988; MFA, Tyler Sch. Art Temple U., Pa., 1993. Graphic artist MacMillan Office Supply, Salem, Ohio, 1993—; $D. Exhbns. include Salem Pub. Libr., 1999, Ohio River Arts Festival, 1997, Trumball Art Gallery, 1996, Butler Inst. Am. Art, 1995, CASA Gallery Group Shows, 1994 Last Show of the Eighties, 1989, KSU Filmakers Show, 1988, Butler Area Artists Exhbn., 1984, City of N.Y., North Winds Gallery, Chappell's House of Pictures, Ohio River Arts Gallery, Tomorrow's Treasures, Ctr. Frame Warehouse, Inc.; One woman shows include Butler Inst. Am. Art, 1998. E-mail address: rhb@rayex.com. Home: 1449 Manor Dr Salem OH 44460

BABB, FRANK EDWARD, lawyer, executive; b. Maryville, Mo., Dec. 22, 1932; s. Dale Victor and Esther (Hull) B. B.S., Northwest Mo. State U., Maryville, 1954; LL.B., Harvard U., 1959. Bar: Ill. 1959, D.C. 1980. Ptnr. McDermott, Will & Emery, Chgo., 1959-90, of counsel, 1991—; chmn. AF Ptnrs., Morgantown, W.Va., 1991—; ptnr. Critical Capital Growth Fund, N.Y.C., 1997—. With CIC U.S. Army, 1954-56. Mem. D.C. Bar, Ill. Bar, Univ. Club Chgo., Am. Alpine Club.

BABB, HAROLD, psychology educator; b. Mosheim, Tenn., Sept. 4, 1926; s. Ray Edward and Mary Louise (Brown) B.; m. Marjorie Craig Leask (Sept. 27, 1947); children: Patricia Craig, Barbara Lou, David Edward. BA, Wayne State U., 1950; MA, Ohio State U., 1951, PhD, 1953. Asst. prof., assoc. prof., chmn. dept. psychology Coe Coll., 1953-58; prof., chmn. dept. psychology Hobart and William Smith Colls., 1958-63; NIH, NIMH exec. sec., grants specialist, 1963-64; prof., chmn. dept. psychology U. Mont., Missoula, 1964-71; prof. psychology SUNY-Binghamton, 1971-95, prof. emeritus, 1995—, chmn. dept., 1971-74. Contbr. articles on psychology to profl. jours. Served with USNR, 1944-46. NIMH research grantee, 1960-62; NSF research grantee, 1968-69. Fellow Am. Psychol. Assn., Am. Psychol. Soc.; mem. AAAS, AAUP, Ea. Psychol. Assn., Midwestern Psychol. Assn., Psychonomic Soc., Sigma Xi. Home: RR 1 Box 1957 Stanley Lake Rd Friendsville PA 18818 Office: Binghamton U Dept Psychology PO Box 6000 Binghamton NY 13902-6000

BABB, MICHAEL PAUL, engineering magazine editor; b. Logansport, Ind., May 17, 1944; s. Paul G. and Eleanor Ruth (Berg) B.; m. Sharon Jean Spence, Dec. 8, 1973; children—Sara, Melissa. B.S. in Physics, Ind. U., 1967. Teaching asst. U. Nebr., Lincoln, 1967-68; programmer Atomic Energy of Can., Pinawa, Man., 1968-70; tchr. high sch., jr. coll., Shawinigan, Que., Can., 1971-78; mgr. engring. services Nuclear Data, Schaumburg, Ill., 1979-85; assoc. editor Control Engring. Mag., Barrington, Ill., 1985-86, mng. editor, 1986, editor-in-chief, 1987—, sr. editor internat. edit., 1994; European editor Cahners Bus. Info., London. NSF research fellow, 1966; U. Nebr. Grad. Sch. teaching asst., 1968. Mem. IEEE, Am. Phys. Soc., Instrument Soc. Am., Soc. Mfg. Engrs., Soc. Tech. Communications, Ind. U. Alumni Assn. Home: 4A Cavendish Rd, Redhill Surrey RH1 4AE, England Office: Control Engring Mag, Cahners Pub Co/Quadrant Ho, Surrey SM2 5AS, England

BABB, RALPH W., JR., banker; b. Sherman, Tex., Feb. 4, 1949; s. Ralph Wheeler and Billie Margaret (Odneal) B.; m. Barbara Louise Alexander, Aug. 30, 1970; children: Dana P., Derek R. BS in Acctg., U. Mo., Columbia, 1971. CPA, Mo. Audit mgr. Peat, Marwick, Mitchell & Co., CPA's, St. Louis, 1971-78; sr. v.p., treas. Mercantile Bancorp. Inc., St. Louis, 1978-82, sr. v.p. fin., comptr., 1982-83, exec. v.p., CFO, 1983-87; exec. v.p., CFO Mercantile Bank N. A., St. Louis, 1983-87; vice-chmn., CFO Mercantile Bancorporation Inc., St. Louis, 1987-95; vice chmn., CFO Comerica, Inc., Detroit, 1995—. Mem. Fin. Execs. Inst. (pres. St. Louis chpt. 1986-87). Methodist. Office: Comerica Inc PO Box 75000 Detroit MI 48275-3388

BABB, ROBERTA JOAN, educational administrator; b. East Chicago, Ill., Jan. 5, 1944; d. Joseph A. and Katherine Phillips; m. Donald L. Babb, July 30, 1966; children: Sasha M., Holly S. BS in Edn., Ind. U., 1966; postgrad., De Paul U. Tchr. East Chicago Pub. Schs., 1969-70, Hammond (Ind.) Pub. Schs., 1966-68, 70-71; head tchr. The Lab Sch., Washington, 1968-69, 74-79; co-founder, dir. Creme de le Creme, Houston. Scholar Ind. U., PTA. Mem. Nat. Child Care Assn., Tex. Lic. Child Care Assn; bd. dirs. Crem dela Creme Inc., Denver.

BABB, VALERIE M., English educator, writer. BA, CUNY, 1973; MA, SUNY, Buffalo, 1977, PhD, 1977. Prof. Georgetown U., Washington; mem. faculty Bread Loaf Sch. English, Middlebury (Vt.) Coll., summers 1993, 94, 98, 99; lectr. Phillips Collection Mus., Washington, 1994, 97, Libr. of Congress, 1989. Author: Black Georgetown Remembered, 1991, Ernest Gaines, 1991, Whiteness Visible, 1998; creator video Black Georgetown Remembered, 1989. Keck fellow Am. Studies Program, 1992. Office: Georgetown U Dept English Box 571131 Washington DC 20057-1131

BABB, WYLIE SHERRILL, college president; b. Greenville, S.C., Aug. 20, 1940; s. J. Wylie and Sally P. B.; m. Linda Witmer, June 30, 1963; children: Corinne, Michelle, David. B.A. in History, Post Coll., 1963; Th.M., Dallas Theol. Sem., 1967; Ph.D. in Ednl. Adminstrn, U. Pitts., 1979. Ordained to ministry Scottsdale, Ariz., 1967; pastor Bible Ch., 1967-71; dean acad. affairs Lancaster (Pa.) Bible Coll., 1971-76; dean faculty Moody Bible Inst., Chgo., 1976-79; pres. Phila. Coll. Bible, 1979—; speaker, cons. in field. Mem. Am. Assn. Higher Edn., Doctoral Assn. Educators, Am. Assn. Bible Colls. (pres.), Lower Bucks County C. of C., Middle States Assn. Commn. for Higher Edn., Phi Delta Kappa. Home: 805 S Pine St Langhorne PA 19047-2924 Office: Phila Coll Bible Langhorne Manor 200 Manor Ave Langhorne PA 19047-2943

BABBEL, DAVID FREDERICK, finance and insurance educator; b. Salt Lake City, Apr. 12, 1949; s. Frederick William and June (Andrew) B.; m. Mary Jane Benson, Aug. 27, 1975; children: Tara Nicole, Elise Kiera, Karisa Rose, Tyson Frederick. *David has four sisters: Bonnie Lewis, Julene Updike, Judy Cloward, and Joanne Smith. Parents Frederick W. and June A. Babbel authored several books and articles on religion. Wife Mary Jane serves as Stake Young Women President and Stake Organist for the LDS Church in Philadelphia. Daughter Tara Nicole, BA 1999 Wellesley College, is an economist and organist. Daughter Elise Kiera is a student at Stanford University. She has won many piano competitions. Daughter Karisa Rose is president of her junior class at Harrington High. Son Tyson Frederick is a student at Welsh Valley MS and is a Boy Scout.* BA, Brigham Young U., 1973; MBA, U. Fla., 1975, PhD, 1978; MA (hon.), U. Pa., 1986. Prof. of fin. U. Calif., Berkeley, 1978-85; prof. fin. and ins. U. Pa. Wharton Sch., Phila., 1985—; v.p. Goldman, Sachs & Co., N.Y.C., 1987; pres. A/L Tech. Bryn Mawr, Pa.; prin. LECG, Inc.; cons. IBM Morgan Guaranty, World Bank, Bell Atlantic, Morrison-Knudson, Goldman Sachs, Aetna, G.E. Capital, Met Life, 1978—. Author 6 books on fin. and ins.; contbr. 80 articles to profl. jours. Fulbright fellow, 1976-77. Republican. Mormon. Office: Wharton Sch U Pa 303 Colonial Penn Ctr Philadelphia PA 19104 *Any idea, without at least some element of absurdity, is probably not worth further consideration.*

BABBITT, BRUCE EDWARD, federal official; b. June 27, 1938; m. Hattie Coons; children—Christopher, T.J. BS magna cum laude, U. Notre Dame; MS, U. Newcastle, Eng., 1962; LL.B., Harvard U., 1965. Bar: Ariz. 1965. Assoc. Brown and Bain, Phoenix, 1965-74; atty. gen. State of Ariz., Phoenix, 1975-78; gov. State of Ariz., 1978-87; ptnr. Steptoe & Johnson, Phoenix; sec. U.S. Dept. Interior, Washington, 1993—; mem. President's Commn. on Accident at Three Mile Island, 1979-80; chmn. Nuclear Safety Oversight Com., 1980-81, Western Govs.' Policy Office, 1982; mem. Adv. Commn. on Intergovtl. Relations, 1980-84; chmn. task force on fed. budget deficit Roosevelt Ctr. for Am. Policy Studies, 1984; chmn. Nat. Groundwater Policy Forum, 1984—. Author: Color and Light: The Southwest Canvases of Louis Akin, 1973, Grand Canyon: An Anthology, 1978. Trustee Dougherty Found.; candidate for Dem. Party nomination for Pres. of U.S. Recipient Thomas Jefferson award Nat. Wildlife Fedn., 1981, spl. conservation award Nat. Wildlife Fedn., 1983. Mem. Nat. Govs. Assn. (chmn. subcom. on water resources), Democratic Govs. Assn. (chmn. 1985). Democrat. Office: US Dept Interior Office of Secretary 1849 C St NW Washington DC 20240-0001*

BABBITT, DONALD PATRICK, radiologist; b. Oshkosh, Wis., Aug. 24, 1922; s. James Sylvester and Loretta Gertrude (Sensenbrenner) B.; m. Elizabeth May Gerhard, Apr. 28, 1945 (dec. Nov. 1971); children—Patrick, Ann, James; m. Jill Ann Sieg, Jan. 29, 1975 (div. Apr. 1984); m. Katherine J. Zehren, Dec. 12, 1987. Student, U. Wis., River Falls, 1939-42; M.D., Med. Coll. Wis., 1946. Diplomate Am. Bd. Radiology. Intern Meth. Hosp., Indpls., 1946-47; resident Milw. Hosp. and Milw. Ch. Hosp., 1949-52; practice medicine specializing in radiology Milw.; mem. staff Milw. Children's Hosp., 1952—, chief radiology, 1964-82; mem. staff Milw. County Gen. Hosp., 1964—; cons. St. Mary's Hosp., Milw., 1968-76, attending staff, 1982-95; instr. radiology Med. Coll., Wis., 1958; assoc. prof. radiology Med. Coll., 1964-70, clin. prof. pediatrics, 1979—; assoc. clin. prof. radiology U. Wis. Center Health Scis., Madison, 1968-70, clin. prof., 1970—. Active Boy Scouts Am. (century mem.). Served to capt. M.C., AUS, 1947-49. Named Tchr. of Yr. Milw. Children's Hosp. Dept. Pediatrics, 1980. Fellow Am. Coll. Radiology (medallion in nuclear medicine 1959), Am. Acad. Pediatrics; mem. Am. Roentgen Ray Soc., European Soc. Pediatric Radiology, Soc. Pediatric Radiology, Radiol. Soc. N.Am., Wis. Radiol. Soc. (pres. 1976), Wis. State Med. Soc., Milw. Surg. Soc. (pres. 1978), Milw. Roentgen Ray Soc. (pres. 1975-77), Milwaukee County Med. Soc. (pres. 1974), Milw. Acad. Medicine, Milw. Pediatric Soc., AMA Med. Coll. Wis. Alumni Assn., Alpha Omega Alpha, Phi Chi. Roman Catholic. Club: Flying Physicians. Lodge: Rotary (Milw.). Home: 5904 Eagle Point Rd Hartford WI 53027-9211

BABBITT, GEORGE T., career officer; m. Louise Babbitt; children: Ian, Megan. BSME, U. Wash., 1965; MS in Logistics Mgmt., Air Force Inst. Tech., 1970. Commd. 2d lt. USAF, 1965, advanced through grades to lt. gen., 1995; maintenance officer Royal Air Force Sta. Alconbury, Eng., 1966-69; squadron maintenance officer 12th Tactical Reconnaissance Squadron, Tan Son Nhut Air Base, South Vietnam, 1970-71; maintenance planner B-1A Sys Program Office Rockwell Internat., L.A., 1971-73; support equipment and spares mgr. B-1A Sys. Program Office, Wright-Patterson AFB, Ohio, 1973-76; dep. program mgr. logistics Precision Location Strike Sys. Program Office, Wright-Patterson AFB, Ohio, 1976-78; from maintenance officer to comdr. 1st Aircraft Generation Squadron, Langley AFB, Va., 1978-80; comdr. 36th Aircraft Generation Squadron, Bitburg Air Base, West Germany, 1980-81; from asst. dep. comdr. maintenance to dep. comdr. maintenance 36th Tactical Fighter Wing, Bitburg Air Base, West Germany, 1981-85; from divsn. chief to dep. dir. logistics plans and programs Hdqs. USAF, Washington, 1986-90, dir. supply, 1993-94, dep. chief staff logistics, 1995-96; dir. logistics Hdqs Air Tng. Command, Randolph AFB, Tex., 1990-92, Hdqs. USAF Europe, Ramstein Air Base, Germany, 1992-93; dep. dir. material mgmt. Def. Logistics Agy., Alexandria, Va., 1994-95; dir. Def. Logistics Agy., Ft. Belvoir, Va., 1996-97; comdr. Air Force Material Command, Wright Patterson AFB, Ohio, 1997—. Decorated Legion of Merit, Bronze Star medal. Office: Wright Patterson AFB 4375 Childliw Ave Ste 1 Wright Patterson AFB OH 45433-5001*

BABBITT, ROBERT T., municipal official; b. Tulsa, July 11, 1955. Bachelors, U. Tex., Arlington, 1976, PhD, 1984. CPA, Tex. V.p. McDonnell Transit Assn., Ft. Worth, 1984-87; v.p./dir. fin. and adminstrn. City Ft. Worth, 1987-90; exec. dir. Nashville Met. Transit Authority, 1990—. Mem. Rotary. Office: Nashville Met. Transit Authority 130 Nestor St Nashville TN 37210-2124*

BABBITT, SAMUEL FISHER, retired university official; b. New Haven, Feb. 22, 1929; s. Theodore and Margaret (Fisher) B.; m. Natalie Zane Moore, June 28, 1954; children: Christopher Converse, Thomas Collier, Lucy Cullyford. BA, Yale U., 1953, MA, 1957, PhD, 1965; LLD (hon.), Hamilton Coll., Clinton, N.Y., 1968. Asst. dean Yale Coll. Grad. Sch., New Haven, 1953-57, 63-66; dean of men Vanderbilt U., Nashville, 1957-62; chief coll. and univ. liaison Office Pub. Affairs, U.S. Peace Corps, Washington, 1962-63; pres. Kirkland Coll., Clinton, N.Y., 1966-78; v.p. program planning and resources Meml. Sloan-Kettering Cancer Ctr., N.Y.C., 1979-83; v.p. devel. Brown U., Providence, 1982-90, sr. v.p. The Campaign, 1990-93, sr. advisor to pres. for Far Eastern Affairs, 1993-96; mem. N.Y. State Commn. on Civil Rights, 1968-76. Author: The 49th Magician, 1966; producer: (film) The Eyes of the Amaryllis, 1981. Pres., bd. dirs. Sandra Feinstein-Gamm Theatre, 1993—. With inf. U.S. Army, 1948-51, Korea. Decorated Silver Star. Mem. Century Assn. (N.Y.C.). Democrat.

BABBY, ELLEN REISMAN, education administrator; b. Montreal, Que., Can., Oct. 21, 1950; came to U.S., 1973; d. Mark Reisman and Rose Gutwillig (Reisman); m. Lon Scott Babby, June 17, 1973; children—Kenneth Robert, Heather Lynn. Student, McGill U., 1968-70; B.A., Beaver Coll., 1972; M.A., Lehigh U., 1973, Yale U., 1976; M.Phil., Yale U., 1977, Ph.D., 1980. Tchr. elem. schs. to coll. levels; instr. resident assoc. program Smithsonian Instn., Washington, 1980-82; exec. dir. Assn. for Can. Studies in U.S., Washington, 1982-92; with Nat. Fgn. Lang. Ctr. Johns Hopkins U., Washington, 1992-94; sr. dir. planning and devel. Nat. Assn. Fgn. Student Affairs Assn. Internat. Educators, Washington, 1995-99; sr. devel. officer Am. Counsel On Edn., Washington, 1999—. Author: Play of Language and Spectacle: A Structural Reading of Selected Texts by Gabrielle Roy, 1986. Contbr. articles on Quebec lit. to profl. jours. Mem. Assn. for Can. Studies in U.S., Am. Soc. Assn. Execs., Nat. Soc. Fund Raising Execs., Yale Alumni (del. 1989-92). Email: ellenbab@aol.com. Office: Am Counsel On Edn One Dupont Cir #800 Washington DC 20036

BABBY, LON S., lawyer; b. Bklyn., Feb. 21, 1951. BA, Lehigh U., 1973; JD, Yale U., 1976. Bar: Conn. 1976, D.C. 1977, U.S. Supreme Ct. 1981, U.S. Claims Ct., 1986; cert. agt. Nat. Basketball Players Assn., Nat. Football League Players Assn. Law clk. to Hon. M. Joseph Blumenfeld Dist. Conn., 1976-77; mem. Williams & Connolly, Washington, 1977—; adj. faculty George Washington U. Law Sch., 1991-92. Editor Yale Law Jour., 1974-76; contbr. articles to profl. jours. Mem. ABA, D.C. Bar, Conn. Bar Assn., Phi Beta Kappa, Omicron Delta Kappa. Office: Williams & Connolly 725 12th St NW Washington DC 20005-5901

BABCOCK, BARBARA ALLEN, lawyer, educator; b. Washington, July 6, 1938; d. Henry Allen and Doris Lenore (Moses) B.; m. Thomas C. Grey, Aug. 19, 1979. AB, U. Pa., 1960; LLB, Yale U., 1963. Bar: Md. 1963, D.C. 1964, JD (hon.), U. San Diego 1983, U. Puget Sound, 1988. Law clk. U.S. Ct. Appeals D.C., 1963; assoc. Edward Bennett Williams, 1964-66; staff atty. Legal Aid Agy., Washington, 1966-68; dir. Pub. Defender Svc. (formerly Legal Aid Agy.), 1968-72; assoc. prof. Stanford U., 1972-77, prof., 1977—; asst. atty. gen. U.S. Dept. Justice, 1977-79. Ernest W. McFarland Prof. Law, 1986-97; Judge John Crown Prof. of Law, 1997—. Democrat. Author: (with others) Sex Discrimination and The Law, 1975, Sex Discrimination and The Law: History, Theory and Practice, 1996; (with Carrington) Civil Procedure, 1977, (with Massaro) Babcock, Civil Procedure: Problems and Cases, 1997; contbr. articles to profl. jours. Home: 835 Mayfield Ave Palo Alto CA 94305-1052 Office: Stanford U Sch Law Stanford CA 94305*

BABCOCK, CATHERINE MARLY, public relations executive; b. Mpls., Mar. 23, 1954; d. Edmund Page and Madolyn Evelyn (Yousse) B.; m. Jeffrey C. Beyer, Jan. 20, 1979; children: Marly Elizabeth, James Conrad. BA in Polit. Sci., Macalester Coll., St. Paul, 1976; MA in Pub. Adminstrn., Univ. Wash., 1981. Welfare specialist Minn. Dept. Pub. Welfare, St. Paul, 1976-79; cmty. affairs officer First Interstate Bank, Seattle, 1981-85; asst. v.p. cmty. rels. Seattle First Nat. Bank, 1985; comm. coord. Huntington Libr., San Marino, Calif., 1988-92; comm. dir. Huntington Libr., San Marino, 1992—. Editor Huntington Calendar. Mem. Am. Assn. Mus., Pub. Rels. Soc. Am., Women in Comm. Avocations: riding, reading, skiing, gardening, cooking. Office: Huntington Libr Art Collection Botanical Gardens 1151 Oxford Rd San Marino CA 91108-1218

BABCOCK, CHARLES LUTHER, classics educator; b. Whittier, Calif., May 26, 1924; s. Robert Louis and Margarette Estelle (Fuller) B.; m. Mary Ayer Taylor, Aug. 6, 1955; children: Robert Sherburne, Jennie Rownd Chapman, Jonathan Taylor. AB in Latin, U. Calif., Berkeley, 1948, MA in Latin, 1949, PhD in Classics, 1953. Asst. in classics U. Utah, Salt Lake City, 1949-50; instr. classics Cornell U., Ithaca, N.Y., 1955-57; acting. instr. Stanford U., Calif., summer 1956; asst. prof. classical studies U. Pa., Phila., 1957-62, assoc. prof., 1962-66, asst. dean, vice dean of coll., 1960-62, 62-64, acting dean, spring 1964; prof. classics Ohio State U., Columbus, 1966-92, prof. emeritus, 1992—, chmn. dept., 1966-68, 80-88, dean Coll. of Humanities, 1968-70; prof.-in-charge summer sch. Am. Acad. in Rome, 1966, resident in classical studies, 1986, acting Mellon prof.-in-charge sch. classical studies, 1988-89, chmn. adv. coun. sch. classical studies, 1992-94; mem. Latin exam. com. Advanced Placement Program, 1967-74, chmn., 1972-74; prof.-in-charge Intercollegiate Ctr. Classical Studies, Rome, 1974, chair mng. com., 1975-82; scholar in residence Hope Coll., 1993. Co-author: Aspects of Roman Civilization, 1980; contbr. articles on Latin lit. (especially Horace), Latin epigraphy, Roman civilization. Served to capt. inf. U.S. Army, 1943-47, ETO. Recipient Alumni Disting. Teaching award Ohio State U., 1982, Exemplary Faculty award Coll. Humanities, Ohio State U., 1989, Disting. Svc. award, 1996; Univ. fellow in classics U. Calif., Berkeley, 1951-53; fellow Am. Acad. in Rome, Fulbright scholar in classics, Rome, 1953-55. Fellow Am. Acad. in Rome (trustee 1981-83, trustee emeritus 1994); mem. Am. Philol. Assn. (bd. dirs. 1968-72), Classical Assn. of Mid. West and South (Ovatio award 1982, pres. 1977-78), Vergilian Soc. Am. (pres. 1975-76), Assn. Depts. Fgn. Langs. (pres. 1986), Phi Beta Kappa (pres. Epsilon of Ohio 1969-70), Phi Kappa Phi, Phi Sigma Kappa (former pres. U. Calif., regional dep. 1949-51). Clubs: Scabbard and Blade (U. Pa.) (hon.), Philomathean Soc. (hon.). Home: 973 Lynbrook Rd Columbus OH 43235-3307 Office: Ohio State U Dept Greek & Latin 230 N Oval Mall Columbus OH 43210-1319

BABCOCK, CHARLES R., columnist; b. Pitts., 1944. Diploma in History and Journalism, Ohio Wesleyan, 1966; Diploma, Fletcher Sch. of Law and Diplomacy, 1967. Reporter Louisville Courier-Jour., 1970-75; columnist The Washington Post, 1976—. Office: The Washington Post 1150 15th St NW Washington DC 20071-0001*

BABCOCK, CHARLES WITTEN, JR., lawyer; b. Kansas City, Mo., Dec. 6, 1941; s. Charles W. and Esther L. (Marcy) B.; m. Sharon K. Chamberlain, June 26, 1976; children: David, William, Susan, Stephen. BA with honors, U. Mo., 1963; JD, Harvard U., 1966. Bar: Mo. 1966, Mich. 1971. Judge advocate USMC, various locations, 1966-69; assoc. Blackwell, Sanders, Kansas City, 1969-71; staff atty. Gen. Motors Corp., Detroit, 1971—. Contbr. articles to profl. jours. Dir. Mothers Against Drunk Driving, 1992—. Avocation: amateur radio. Home: 917 Grand Marais St Grosse Pointe MI 48230-1867 Office: Gen Motors Corp PO Box 33122 Detroit MI 48232-5122

BABCOCK, JO, artist, educator; b. St. Louis, Feb. 24, 1954; s. Boyd Leon and Shirley Lynn (Hamm) B.; m. Diane DeVoto, Aug. 20, 1973 (div. June 1975); domestic ptnr. Kitty Costello, Oct. 1991—. Student, UCLA, 1975; BFA, San Francisco Art Inst., 1976, MFA, 1979. Color printer Rolling Stone mag., San Francisco, 1976, Outside mag., San Francisco, 1977; cameraman 1st Calif. Press, San Francisco, 1977-80; electrician Bros. Electric, San Francisco, 1984-89; assoc. prof. San Francisco Art Inst., 1989-93; exhibit designer Levi Strauss & Co., 1989—. One-man shows include Zwinger Gallery, Berlin, 1987, Marcuse Pfeiffer Gallery, N.Y.C., 1988, Artspace, San Francisco, 1989, Visual Studies Workshop, Rochester, N.Y., 1990, Ctr. for the Arts, San Francisco, 1995, Oakland (Calif.) Mus., 1997, Kyle Roberts Gallery, San Francisco, 1992, Addison Gallery Am. Art, Andover, Mass., 1997, Chgo. Art Inst., 1982, CEPA, Buffalo, 1988, others; exhibited in group shows at Friends of Photography Gallery, Carmel, 1976, Sao Paulo (Brazil) Bienal, San Francisco Mus. of Modern Art, 1989, Rena Bransten Gallery, San Francisco, 1991, Oliver Art Ctr., CCAC, 1991, Lieberman & Saul, N.Y., 1991, Tampa Mus. Art, 1992, San Jose Mus. Art, 1992, Palm Springs Desert Mus., 1993, 100 Years of Landscape Art in the Bay Area, M.H. de Young Mus., San Francisco, 1995, Bay Area Landscapes, 1995, Addison Gallery of Am. Art, Andover, Mass., 1997, The Alternative Mus., N.Y., 1981, Wooster St. Gallery, N.Y., 1981, Living Mus., Rejkjavik, Iceland, 1983, 10 on 8, N.Y., 1983, Windows on White, N.Y., 1984, Public Image, N.Y., 1984, Otis Parsons Gallery, L.A., 1985, Hotel Project, Oakland, Calif., 1986, Roanoke Mus. Fine Art, Va., 1988, Ctr. for Contemp. Arts, Santa Fe, 1988, Artists at the Rock, Alcatraz, Calif., 1988, others; represented in permanent collections at San Francisco Mus. Modern Art, Bklyn. Mus., Newport Harbor Art Mus., Lightwork, Syracuse, N.Y., La Biblioteque, Avignon, France, San Francisco Pub. Libr., San Francisco Arts Commn., George Eastman House, Rochester, N.Y., Nat. Collection, Smithsonian Instn., others. Grantee City of Oakland, 1985, N.Y. State Coun. on Arts, 1988, Nat. Endowment for Arts, 1990. Mem. Primitive Hunting Soc. Avocations: building pinhole cameras. Studio: 378 San Jose Ave Apt B San Francisco CA 94110-3700

BABCOCK, JUDY ANN, auditor; b. New Hampton, Iowa, June 30, 1949; d. George and Lois Rose (Drewelow) Eichenberger; m. Douglas W. Babcock, Apr. 12, 1969; children: Jeffrey, Mark (dec.), Laura. Tax dep., co-treas. Chickasaw County, New Hampton, 1968-73, 78-96, auditor, 1997—. Democrat. Roman Catholic. Avocations: sewing, quilting, gardening. Home: 1997 235th St New Hampton IA 50659-9160 Office: Chickasaw County 8 E Prospect St New Hampton IA 50659-1345

BABCOCK, KEITH MOSS, lawyer; b. Camden, N.J., Aug. 5, 1951; s. William Strong Jr. and Dinah Leslie (Moss) B.; m. Jacquelyn Sue Dickman, Aug. 16, 1975; children: Michael Arthur, Max William. AB, Princeton U., 1973; JD, George Washington U., 1976. Bar: S.C. 1977, U.S. Dist. Ct. S.C. 1977, U.S. Ct. Appeals (4th cir.) 1977, U.S. Supreme Ct. 1980. Staff atty. S.C. Atty. Gen.'s Office, Columbia, 1977-78, state atty., 1978-79, asst. atty. gen., 1979-81; ptnr. Barnes & Austin, Columbia, 1981-82, Austin & Lewis, Columbia, 1982-84, Lewis, Babcock & Hawkins, Columbia, 1984—; mem. civil justice adv. com. for dist. S.C., 1991-94. Bd. dirs. Columbia Jewish Community Pre-Sch., 1984, chmn., 1985-86; bd. dirs. Columbia Jewish Community Ctr., 1986-88. Mem. ABA, S.C. Bar Assn. (chmn. prof. resp. com. 1985-86), Richland County Bar Assn., Princeton Alumni Assn. of S.C. (v.p. 1980-86, 88-89, pres. 1990-93, 96-98), George Washington U. Law Sch. Alumni Assn. (bd. dirs. 1983-87), Summit Club, Spring Valley Country Club (Columbia). Democrat. Episcopalian. Home: 233 W Springs Rd Columbia SC 29223-6912 Office: Lewis Babcock & Hawkins 1513 Hampton St Columbia SC 29201-2928

BABCOCK, LEO ALOYSIUS, architect, scenic designer; b. Detroit, Oct. 4, 1961; s. James Ludwig and Mareda (Witte) B.; m. Barbara Goldstein, Sept. 15, 1990; children: Charlotte, Ella. BS, U. Mich., 1983, MArch, 1986. Registered architect, Mass. Draftsman Diehl & Diehl Architects, Detroit, 1984,

Engring Svcs., U. Mich., Ann Arbor, 1985; job capt. Steffian Bradley Assocs., Boston, 1986-88, project mgr., 1989-91; prin. Babcock Design Studio, Saline, Mich., 1991—; guest lectr. Saline Drama Club, 1994, Saline Hist. Soc., 1996. Chmn. Saline Hist. Dist. Commn., 1999. Office: Babcock Design Studio 309 N Ann Arbor St Saline MI 48176-1140

BABCOCK, LEWIS THORNTON, federal judge; b. 1943. BA cum laude, U. Denver, 1965, JD, 1968; LLM, U. Va., 1968. Ptnr. Mitchell and Babcock, Rocky Ford, Colo., 1968-76; atty. City Las Animas, Colo., 1969-74, City Rocky Ford, 1970-76; asst. dist. atty. 11th Jud. Cir., La Junta, Colo., 1973-76, dist. judge, 1978-83; judge Colo. Ct. Appeals, 1983-88, U.S. Dist. Ct. Colo., Denver, 1988—; escrow and loan closing agt. FHA, Rocky Ford, 1973-76. Bd. dirs. Colo. Rural Legal Svcs. Inc., 1974-76. With Colo. N.G., 1968-74. Named to Order St. Ives. Mem. ABA, Colo. Bar Assn., Denver Bar Assn., Colo. Bar Found., North Ind. Dist. Bar Assn. Office: US Dist Ct C-502 US Courthouse 1929 Stout St Rm C550 Denver CO 80294-0001*

BABCOCK, LYNDON ROSS, JR., environmental engineer, educator; b. Detroit, Apr. 8, 1934; s. Lyndon Ross and Lucille Kathryn (Miller) B.; m. Betty Irene Immonen, June 21, 1957; children—Lyndon Ross III, Sheron Lucille Babcock Fruehauf, Susan Elizabeth Babcock Williams, Andrew Dag. BSChemE, Mich. Tech. U., 1956; MSChemE, U. Washington, 1958, PhD in Environ. Engring., 1970. Registered profl. engr., Ill. Chem. engr. polymers Shell Chem. Co., Calif., N.J., N.Y., 1958-67; assoc. prof. environ. engring., geography, pub. health U. Ill., Chgo., 1970-75, prof. environ. engring., geography, pub. health, 1975-90, prof. emeritus, 1990—, dir. environ. health scis. program Sch. Pub. Health, 1978-79, dir. environ. and occupational health scis. program Sch. Pub. Health, 1979-84, assoc. dean Sch. Pub. Health, 1984-85; cons. WHO, 1985, Interam. Devel. Bank, 1990-91, Environ. Secretariat Fed. Dist., Mexico City, 1995-97; USA coord. air quality project for Gestión de la Calidad del Aire, Mexico City, 1986-92; environ. cons./lectr. Tech. Instns., Mexican Secretariat of Pub. Edn., 1993-95; vis. prof. El Colegio de Mexico, Mexico City, 1996—. Mem. editorial bd. The Environ. Profl., 1979-90; contbr. environ. articles to profl jours.; patentee plastics composition and processing. Bd. dirs. Chgo. Lung Assn., 1981-92. Fulbright lectr., Turkey and India, 1975-76, Mexico, 1986-87, 1992-93; fed. and state environ. research and edn. grantee. Mem. Air and Waste Mgmt. Assn. (chmn. Lake Michigan sect. 1977-78), League Am. Bicyclists, Chicagoland Bicycle Fedn. (v.p. 1985-86). Home: 4934 Wildwood Dr Bridgman MI 49106-9553 Office: U Ill Sch Pub Health EOHS MC922 2121 W Taylor St Chicago IL 60612-7260

BABCOCK, MARGUERITE LOCKWOOD, addictions treatment therapist, educator, writer; b. Jacksonville, Fla., Jan. 1, 1944; d. Allen Seaman and Emilie (Lockwood) B. BA in Art History, Am. U., 1965; M Counselor Edn., U. Pitts., 1982. Cert. addictions counselor, Pa.; nat. cert. counselor. Addictions therapist South Hills Health Sys., Pitts., 1978-81; addiction therapist, clin. supr., clin. dir. Alternatives- Turtle Creek Mental Health/Mental Retardation/D&A Ctr., Pitts., 1981-86; addictions therapist, coord. Ligonier Valley Treatment Ctr., Stahlstown, Pa., 1987-88; addictions clin. supr., unit dir. Ctr. for Substance Abuse Mon-Yough, McKeesport, Pa., 1988-96; utilization mgmt. and coordination Mon-Yough, McKeesport, 1996-97; clin. supr. Sojourner House, Pitts., 1997—; adj. instr. in addictions courses Seton Hill Coll., Greensburg, Pa., 1989-91, C.C. Allegheny County, West Mifflin, Pa., 1989-91, Pa. State U., McKeesport, 1993—; pvt. trainer, writer, Acme, Pa., 1985—; founder addictions home-study bus.; cons. in field. Co-author, co-editor: Challenging Codependency: Feminist Critiques, 1995; contbr. articles to profl. jours. Fellow Andrew Mellon Found., 1966-68, NSF, 1967. Mem. Pa. Assn. Alcoholism and Drug Abuse Counselors (bd. dirs. 1994-97), Ligonier Valley Writers, Phi Kappa Phi, Alpha Lambda Delta. Avocation: herpetology. Home and Office: RR 1 Box 138 Acme PA 15610-9712

BABCOCK, PETER HEARTZ, professional sports executive; b. Bangor, Maine, May 12, 1949; s. Bernard Roland and Jeanne Sargent (Heartz) B.; m. Yolanda Marie Cava; children: Amy, Katherine. BA, Ariz. State U., 1971, MA, 1976. Tchr., coach Glendale Union High Sch. Dist., Phoenix, 1972-80; asst. coach San Diego Clippers, 1980-82, dir. player pers., 1982-83, v.p. basketball ops., 1983-84; dir. player pers. Denver Nuggets, 1984-85, dir. basketball ops., 1985-86, v.p. basketball ops., 1986-87, pres., gen. mgr., 1987-90; exec. v.p., gen. mgr. Atlanta Hawks, 1990—; mem. competition and rules com., dir. Chgo. pre-draft camp NBA, 1985—, mem. steering com., 1995—; mem. USA Basketball Sr. National Team Com., 1995—. Mem. bd. addiction rsch. and treatment svcs. U. Colo. Med. Sch., 1986—, vis. mem. dept. psychiatry, 1989—; mem. bd. Adopt-A-Sch., Denver Pub. Schs., 1985-89; adv. bd. Big Bros., Denver, 1985—, Kops N Kids, 1987—; exec. com. Cmtys. for Drug Free Colo., Denver, 1987—; pres. NET Found./Charitable Fundraising, 1987-90; mem. Mayor's Coun. on Phys. Fitness, 1987-90; bd. dirs. Ga. Alliance for Children, 1996—, Yes! Atlanta, 1990—, Atlanta Urban League. Recipient Golden Apple award Atlanta Pub. Schs., 1996; named Outstanding Sports Personality of Ga., Spl. Olympics, 1992. Mem. Atlanta Tip Off Club (mem. nat. adv. bd. 1990—). Episcopalian. Avocations: jogging, weight-lifting, swimming, reading. Office: Atlanta Hawks S Tower 1 Cnn Ctr NW Ste 405 Atlanta GA 30303-2762 *Learn to respect others for their differences rather than to discriminate due to those differences. Tolerance, acceptance, and understanding are necessary for us to grow as human beings.*

BABEL, DEBORAH JEAN, social worker, paralegal; b. Fulton, N.Y., Oct. 12, 1959; d. Sheldon Rowell and Mary Jane (Dimon) Ford; m. Charles Jacob Babel III, Sept. 7, 1984 (seperated); children: Casandra Jane, Stefan Michael (dec.). BA in Acctg., Aurora (Colo.) C.C., 1981; BS in Social Wk., U. Boulder, 1982, MS in Social Work, 1984; cert., Denver Paralegal Inst., 1995. Cert. respite care for abused children; paralegal cert. Denver Paralegal Inst., 1986. Acct. Dale Conklin and Assocs. CPA Firm, Englewood, Colo., 1981-84, Beechcraft Aviation Inc., Denver, 1985-92; pres., founder The Parents Help Network, Aurora, 1993—; adv. Adoptive Families of Am., Mpls., 1989—, Colo. Coalition for Children, Denver, 1989—, Fedn. of Families for Childrens Mental Health, Alexandria, Va., 1989—; parent rep. N.Am. Coun. on Adoptable Children. Contbr. articles to profl. jours. Mem. NAFE, NASW, Nat. Com. on the Prevention of Child Abuse, Attachment Disorder Parents Network (v.p. 1988—, Parent Advocacy award 1989), N.Am. Coun. on Adoptable Children (Warmline and Parent Advocate). Democrat. Roman Catholic. Avocations: adoption and foster care legislation, abuse and neglect issues in children, swimming, crafts, spending time with children. Home and Office: Parents Help Network 10555 W Jewell Ave #4-208 Lakewood CO 80232

BABER, RALPH KING, writer, publisher; b. Huntington, W.Va., Nov. 7, 1930; s. Elwin Harold and Juanita (King) B.; m. Lorentz Schultz Baber, Mar. 20, 1999. AAS in Real Estate, Tidewater Cmty. Coll., Virginia Beach, 1977-78; AA, San Antonio Coll., 1951; BS in Indsl. Engring., Ga. Inst. Tech., Atlanta, 1954. Lt. col. USAF, Washington, 1955-77; v.p. real estate sales C21 Truitt Realty, Norfolk, Va., 1977-84; publisher, editor Ogden Press, Tow, Tex., 1990—; writer Tow, 1984—; Dir. NetSmart, San Antonio, 1997—. Author: (book) From the A. Front, 1993, Goddess of Mystery, 1991, (weekly column) it happened this way..., The Picayune, Marble Falls, Tex., 1997, On This Day in U.S. History, 1997. Rep. Llano Co. Republican Com., 1992. Mem. Toastmasters Club, Masons. Avocations: music, public speaking, theatre. Home: 6162 Birkewood Rd Huntington WV 25705-2202 Office: Ogden Press 6162 Birkewood Rd Huntington WV 25705-2202

BABER, WILBUR H., JR., lawyer; b. Shelby, N.C., Dec. 18, 1926; s. Wilbur H. and Martha Corinne (Allen) B.; BA, Emory U., 1949; postgrad. U. N.C., 1949-50, U. Houston, 1951-52; JD, Loyola U., New Orleans, 1965. Bar: La. 1965, Tex. 1966. Sole practice, Hallettsville, Tex., 1966—. Trustee Raymond Dickson Found. Served with U.S. Army. Mem. ABA, ASCE, La. Bar Assn., Tex. Bar Assn., La. Engring. Soc., Tex. Surveyors Assn. Methodist. Lodge: Rotary. Office: PO Box 294 Hallettsville TX 77964-0294

BABIN, CLAUDE HUNTER, history educator; b. Baton Rouge, Feb. 6, 1924; s. Ventress Victor and Essie (Bond) B.; m. Barbara Ann Murphy, Dec. 29, 1947; 1 son, Claude Hunter. B.A., La. State U., 1945; M.A., U. Wis., 1946; Ph.D., Tulane U., 1954; LL.D., Hendrix Coll., 1965. Instr. history U. Miami, Fla., 1946-49; grad. fellow Tulane U., 1949-54; asst. prof., asso. prof., then prof. history Ark. A. and M. Coll., Monticello, 1954-60; acad. dean Ark. A. and M. Coll., 1960-62, pres., 1962-71; chancellor U. Ark. at Monticello, 1971-77, prof. history, 1977-92, chancellor, prof. emeritus, 1992—. Ford fellow, 1951-52. Mem. Am. Hist. Assn., Ark. Hist. Assn., Ark. Farm Bur. Fedn., Drew County Hist. Soc., Kappa Sigma, Phi Alpha Theta, Pi Sigma Alpha. Democrat. Methodist. Home: 135 Ross Ave Monticello AR 71655-4249

BABIN, CLAUDE HUNTER, JR., marketing executive; b. Pensacola, Fla., Aug. 23, 1952; s. Claude Hunter and Barbara Ann Murphy; m. L. Joyce Bradley, Sept. 28, 1988; 1 child, Catherine Joyce. BA, U. Ark., 1975, M of Pub. Adminstrn., 1979. Acctg. supr. Ark. La. Gas Co., Little Rock, 1975-78, budget analyst, 1978-80; sr. sales rep. Sperry Corp., Little Rock, 1980-84; mktg. rep. Systematics, Inc., Little Rock, 1984; acct. rep. Wang Labs., Little Rock, 1985-96, team leader southern region; acct. mgt. Cisco Systems, 1996—. Moderator local issues TV program, 1983. Bd. dirs. Little Rock Multiple Sclerosis Soc., 1979, Cen. Ark. chpt. March of Dimes, 1980; charter mem. com. for the future Ark. Children's Hosp., 1987—; mem. exec. bd. Quapaw coun. Boy Scouts Am., 1990—. Mem. Ark. Leadership Seminar (founder, bd. dirs. 1980-86), Alpha Kappa Lamdba. Methodist. Avocations: tennis, golf. Home: 29 Ledgelawn Dr Little Rock AR 72212-2650

BABIN, STEVEN MICHAEL, atmospheric scientist, researcher; b. Lawton, Okla., Sept. 6, 1954; s. Cleveland Victor Jr. and Delys Lilian (Lowry) B.; m. Pamela Gail Nee, June 23, 1990. BS in Engring. Physics spl. distinction, U. Okla., 1976; MD, U. Okla., Oklahoma City, 1980; MSEE, U. Pa., 1983; MS in Meteorology, U. Md., 1994, PhD in Meteorology, 1996. Diplomate Am. Bd. Med. Examiners. Assoc. instr. pathology and lab. medicine U. Pa. Hosp., Phila., 1980-82; sr. engr. Applied Physics Lab. Johns Hopkins U., Laurel, Md., 1983—; Presenter in field. Contbr. articles to profl. jours. Engring. scholar Frontiers Sci. Found., 1972, Spl. scholar Nat. Merit Found., 1972. Mem. IEEE (sr.), Am. Meteorol. Soc., Am. Geophysics Union (life), Am. Mensa (life), Sigma Xi, Tau Beta Pi, Alpha Epsilon Delta, Phi Eta Sigma. Achievements include investigation of meteorological effects on microwave propagation in the marine boundary layer; design and development of data acquisition and analysis software in use on helicopters, rocketsondes, buoys, etc.; development of optical waveguide pH sensor; design and creation of working proportional counter for exo-electron research. Office: John Hopkins U Applied Physics Lab Johns Hopkins Rd Laurel MD 20723-6099

BABÍNEAU, MARGARET LOUISE, music educator; b. Norway, Maine, July 16, 1947; d. Raymond Francis and Elizabeth Frances (Collins) B. BS in Music Edn., Gorham (Maine) State Coll., 1969; MusM in Music Edn., U. Mich., 1970. Cert. music tchr., Mich. Vocal/gen. music educator Livonia (Mich.) Pub. Schs., 1970—, facilitator of music, 1997—; choir mem., accompanist Grace Bible Ch., Ann Arbor, Mich., 1970-72; soprano Ann Arbor Choral Union, 1970-73; asst. accompanist Livonia Youth Choir, 1971-72; mem. choir, pianist Covenant Community Ch., Redford, Mich., 1972-74. Apptd. del. U.S.-Asian Joint Conf. on Edn., People to People Internat. divsn. Eisenhower Found., Beijing, China, 1992; organist, choir dir. 1st Bapt. Ch. of Ferndale, deacon, 1986-89, chair activities com., 1989; organist Milford Presbyn., 1993—. Mem. ASCD, Am. Guild Organists, Paris (Maine) Cape Hist. Soc., Music Educators Nat. Conf. Republican. Avocations: golf, reading, travel, hiking, sailing. Home: 1800 W Dawson Rd Milford MI 48380-4154 Office: Livonia Pub Schs 15125 Farmington Rd Livonia MI 48154-5413

BABINGTON, CHARLES MARTIN, III, lawyer; b. St. Louis, Mar. 15, 1944; s. Charles Martin Jr. and Sarah Elizabeth (Karraker) B.; m. Ann Baker, July 6, 1974; children: Martin, Anthony, Liza. AB, Dartmouth Coll., 1965; JD, U. Mich., 1968; LLM in Tax, Washington U., St. Louis, 1975. Bar: Mo. 1968, U.S. Dist. Ct. (ea. dist.) Mo. 1968, U.S. Ct. Appeals (8th cir.) 1973, U.S. Ct. Claims 1974, U.S. Tax Ct. 1975. Judge adv. USAF, Beale AFB, Calif., 1968-72; assoc. Thompson & Mitchell, St. Louis, 1972-77, ptnr., 1978-95; of counsel Thompson Coburn, 1996-98; ret., 1999. Dir., sec. St. Louis Steam Tain Assn., 1986—; dir. Ecumenical Housing Prodn. Corp., 1992-97, U. Club. St. Louis, 1994-98. Capt. USAF, 1968-72. Mem. ABA, Mo. Bar Assn. (mem. staff benefits com. 1979-96), Bar Assn Met. St. Louis (chmn. tax sect. 1982-83). Republican. Episcopalian. Avocations: steam locomotive restoration, photography. Home: 25 Warson Ter Saint Louis MO 63124-1680 Office: Thompson Coburn 1 Mercantile Ctr Ste 3300 Saint Louis MO 63101-1643

BABITZKE, THERESA ANGELINE, health facility administrator; b. Madison, Ill., Dec. 19, 1925; d. Victor Joseph and Angela (Ziolkowski) Sobolewski; m. Douglas Christ Babitzke, May 2, 1953; children: Charlotte, Mary Ann, Rose Marie, Helen. Student, Quincy Coll., 1943; diploma, St. John's Sch. Nursing Edn., Springfield, Ill., 1949; student, U. Ill., Chgo., 1970; BA, St. Francis Coll., 1973; MA in Geronology summa cum laude, Sangamon State U., 1982. Co-founder, admin. dir. Mayslake Village, Oakbrook, Ill., 1962, St. Paschal's Infirmary, Oakbrook, 1962; night supr. Godair Home, Hinsdale, Ill., 1958-72; DON King Bruwaert House, Hinsdale, 1973-76; head nurse Mt. Sinai Hosp., Chgo., 1976-82; DON Rosary Hill Home, Justice, Ill., 1989—. Election judge Rep. Com. DuPage County, 1953-98; mem. adv. bd. Gower Grade Sch., 1973-76; mem. adv. com. Burr Ridge Marriot Brighton Gardens Assisted Living, 1996—. Named Ill. Nurse of Yr. of the Midwest, 1981, Catholic Woman of Yr. 1962, St. Mary's Ch., Joliet, Ill. Mem. Downers Grove and Suburban Nurses Club (pres. Downers Grove chpt.), U. of Ill. Gerontology, Sigma Phi Omega (Eta chpt. U. Ill.). Roman Catholic. Avocations: travel, bicycling, doll collecting, reading.

BABIUK, LORNE ALAN, virologist, immunologist, research administrator; b. Canora, Sask., Can., Jan. 25, 1946; s. Paul and Mary (Mayden) B.; m. Betty Lou Carol Wagar, Sept. 29, 1973; children: Shawn, Kimberley. BSA, U. Sask., Saskatoon, 1967, MSc, 1969, DSc, 1987; PhD, U. B.C., Vancouver, 1972. Postdoctoral fellow U. Toronto, Ont., Can., 1972-73; asst. prof. We. Coll. Vet. Medicine, Saskatoon, Sask., 1973-75, assoc. prof., 1975-79, prof., 1979—; assoc. dir. rsch. Vet. Infectious Disease Orgn., Saskatoon, 1984-93, dir., 1993—; cons. Molecular Genetics, Mpls., 1980-84, Genetech., San Francisco, 1981-84, Ciba Geigy, Basel, Switzerland, 1984-91. Contbr. some 300 articles to refereed publs., 60 chpts. to books. Recipient award Can. Soc. Microbiology, 1990, Am. Vet. Immunology, 1992, Xerox-Can. Forum., 1993, Emerging Sci. and Tech. award for innovation, 1995, Pfizer award in animal health 1998, Nat. Merit award 1998. Fellow Infectious Disease Soc. Am., Royal Soc. Can.; mem. Internat. Soc. Interferon Rsch., Am. Soc. Microbiology, Am. Soc. Virology, Can. Soc. Microbiology, Soc. Gen. Microbiology, Internat. Soc. Antiviral Rsch. Achievements include six patents in field. Home: 245 East Pl, Saskatoon, SK Canada S7J 2Y1 Office: Vet Infectious Disease Orgn, 120 Veterinary Rd, Saskatoon, SK Canada S7N 5E3

BABLER, WAYNE E., retired telephone company executive, lawyer; b. Orangeville, Ill., Dec. 8, 1915; s. Oscar E. and Mary (Bender) B.; m. Mary Blome, Dec. 27, 1940; children: Wayne Elroy Jr., Marilyn Anne Monson, Sally Jane Sperry. BA, Ind. Cen. Coll., 1935; JD, U. Mich., 1938; LLD, Ind. Cen. U., 1966. Bar: Mich. 1938, N.Y. 1949, Mo. 1955, Wis. 1963, U.S. Supreme Ct. 1963. Assoc. Bishop & Bishop, Detroit, 1938-42; ptnr. Bishop & Bishop, 1945-48; atty. AT&T, 1948-55; gen. solicitor Southwestern Bell Tel. Co., St. Louis, 1955-63; v.p., gen. counsel, sec. Southwestern Bell Tel. Co., 1965-80, ret., 1980; v.p., gen. counsel Wis. Tel. Co., Milw., 1963-65. Bd. dirs., chmn. St. Louis Soc. Crippled Children; bd. dirs. St. Louis Symphony Soc. Mem. ABA (chmn. pub. utility sect. 1978-79), Fed. Communications Bar Assn., Wis. Bar Assn., Mo. Bar. Assn., Delray Dunes Country Club, Ocean Club. Home: 11943 Date Palm Dr Boynton Beach FL 33436-5534

BABLER, WAYNE E., JR., lawyer; b. Detroit, Apr. 29, 1942; s. Wayne E. and Mary E. (Blome) B.; m. Patricia A. Ward, Feb. 5, 1972; children: Dean W., Anne E. BA, Wittenberg U., 1964; JD, U. Wis., 1967. Bar: Wis. 1967, U.S. Ct. Appeals (7th cir.) 1971, U.S. Supreme Ct. 1980, U.S. Dist. Ct. (ea. and we. dists.) Wis., 1967, U.S. Dist. Ct. (cen. dist.) Ill. 1987, U.S. Dist. Ct. (ea. and we. dists.) Mich. 1990; U.S. Ct. Appeals (9th and 10th cirs.) 1981, U.S. Ct. Appeals (D.C. cir.), 1983. Assoc. Quarles, Herriott, Clemons, Teschner & Noelke, Milw., 1971-74; assoc. Quarles & Brady, Milw., 1974-76, ptnr., 1976—; rep. of chief justice Wis. Supreme Ct. to Wis. Jud. Compensation Com., 1983-84. Author: (with others) Business and Commercial Litigation in Federal Court, 1998; Rsch. editor Wis. Law Rev., 1966-67, Antitrust, Federal Civil Litigation, State Civil Litigation. Mem. U. Wis. Benchers Soc.; campaign cabinet United Performing Arts Fund, Inc., Milw., 1977-78; bd. dirs. Milw. Bar Found., 1976-79, treas., 1977-78; bd. dirs. Wis. Bar Found., 1983—, pres., 1985-87; bd. dirs. Legal Aid Soc. Milw., 1997—. With JAGC, USN, 1967-71. Fellow Am. Bar Found., Am. Coll. Trial Lawyers; mem. ABA (ho. of dels. 1984-96), Milw. Bar Assn. (bd. dirs. 1976-83, pres. 1981-82), Wis. Acad. Trial Lawyers, State Bar Wis. (bd. govs. 1983-87), Nat. Conf. Bar Pres., Nat Inst. Trial Advocacy Advocates Assn., Bar Assn. 7th Fed. Cir., Milw. Yacht Club, Univ. Club, Order of Coif. E-mail: web@quarles.com. Home: 1475 E Fairy Chasm Rd Milwaukee WI 53217-1433 Office: Quarles & Brady 411 E Wisconsin Ave Milwaukee WI 53202-4497

BABLITCH, WILLIAM A., state supreme court justice; b. Stevens Point, Wis., Mar. 1, 1941. B.S., U. Wis., Madison, 1963, J.D., 1968. Bar: Wis. 1968. Pvt. practice law Stevens Point, Wis.; mem. Wis. Senate, 1972-85, senate majority leader, 1976-82; justice Wis. Supreme Ct., Madison, 1985—; dist. atty. Portage County, Wis., 1969-72. Mem. Nat. Conf. State Legislators (exec. com. 1979). Office: Wis Supreme Ct PO Box 1688 Madison WI 53701*

BABSON, IRVING K., publishing company executive; b. Tel Aviv, Apr. 15, 1936; came to U.S., 1940; s. Matthew and Miriam B.; m. Laurie Sher; children: Stacey B., Mia L., Christopher. BBA, CCNY, 1957; postgrad. NATO seminars, Harvard U., 1965. Dir. Tribune/Fox Cos., 1987-90; chmn. BMT Publs., Inc., Tulsa, 1989-91, Convenience Store News, U.S. Distbn. Jour., Gaming Bus. Mag., Smokeshop Mag., N.Y.C., Jour. Petroleum Mktg., N.Y.C.; mng. ptnr. Babson Capital Ventures, J.V., 1995—, Holdsworth Investments Inc., Belize, 1995—; ptnr. Mag. Devel. Fund, Babson Family Investment, J.V., N.Y.C., Babson Capital, 1988. With AUS, 1956-57. Mem. Nat. Assn. Corp. Dirs. Club: Friars. Home: 19707 Turnberry Way Aventura FL 33180-2566

BABULA, WILLIAM, university dean; b. Stamford, Conn., May 19, 1943; s. Benny F. and Lottie (Zajkowski) B.; m. Karen L. Gemi, June 19, 1965; children: Jared, Joelle. BA, Rutgers U., 1965; MA, U. Calif., Berkeley, 1967, PhD, 1969. Asst. prof. English U. Miami, Coral Gables, Fla., 1969-75; assoc. prof. U. Miami, Coral Gables, 1975-77, prof., 1977-81, chmn. dept. Eng., 1976-81; dean of arts and humanities Sonoma State U., Rohnert Park, Calif., 1981—. Author: Shakespeare and the Tragicomic Archetype, 1975, Shakespeare in Production, 1935-79, 1981; (short stories) Motorcycle, 1982, Quarterback Sneak, 1983, The First Edsel, 1983, Ransom, 1983, The Last Jogger in Virginia, 1983, The Orthodontist and the Rock Star, 1984, Greenearth, 1984, Football and Other Seasons, The Great American Basketball Shoot, 1984, Ms. Skywriter, Inc., 1987; (plays) The Fragging of Lt. Jones (1st prize Gualala Arts Competition, 1983), Creatures (1st prize Jacksonville U. competition 1987), The Winter of Mrs. Levy (Odyssey Stage Co., New Play Series 1988), Nat. Playwright's Showcase, 1988, Theatre Americana, 1990 (James Ellis award), Basketball Jones, Black Rep of Berkeley, 1988, West Coast Ensemble, Festival of One Acts, 1992, Mark Twain Masquers, 9th Ann. Festival One Act Plays, 1994 (2d Place award), The Last Roundup, 1991 (Odyssey Stage Co.); (novels) The Bombing of Berkeley and Other Pranks (1st prize 24th Ann. Deep South Writers' Conf. 1984), St. John's Baptism, 1988, According to St. John, 1989, St. John and the Seven Veils, 1991, St. John's Bestiary, 1994; contbr. articles to profl. pubs. and short stories to lit. mags. Mem. Dramatists Guild, Assoc. Writing Programs, Mystery Writers Am., Phi Beta Kappa. Office: Sonoma State U Sch Arts and Humanities Rohnert Park CA 94928

BABYAR, MARGARET, school counselor; b. Elmhurst, Ill., Jan. 18, 1950; d. Frank and Janet (Leuser) Gross; m. Tom Babyar, Sept. 30, 1972; children: Megan, Molly, Marc. BS, So. Ill. U., 1972; MS, No. Ill. U., 1981. Tchr. Dist. 205, Elmhurst, 1972-83, counselor, 1983—. Pres. PTA, Elmhurst, 1993; ECAF pres. Children's Found., Elmhurst; rel. edn. tchr. Immaculate Conception Ch., Elmhurst, 1983—; soccer coach Ayso, Elmhurst, 1983, 85, 89. Mem. AAUW. Roman Catholic. Home: 600 Chatham Ave Elmhurst IL 60126-4047

BABYFACE (KENNY EDMONDS), popular musician; b. Inpls., Apr. 10, 1959. Co-songwriter Lucky Charm, 1988, The Lover In Me, 1988, Love Saw It, 1988, Every Little Step, 1988, Dial My Heart, 1988, It's No Crime, 1989, Whip Appeal, 1989, Tender Lover, 1989, Ready or Not, 1989, My Kinda Girl, 1989, Can't Stop, 1989, Lovers, 1989, Giving You the Benefit, 1990, I'm Your Baby Tonight, 1990, My, My, My, 1990, On Our Own, A Closer Look, 1991, For the Cool in You, 1993, The Day, 1996, others; soundtrack Ghostbusters II, 1989, Waiting to Exhale, 1995; CDs include Babyface Unplugged NYC, 1997, Christmas with Babyface, 1998; singles include This is For the Lover in You, 1996. Grammy nomination (Best Rhythym & Blues Male Vocal, 1994) for "For All the Cool in You"; recipient Grammy award, 1997. Office: Solar Epic Recordings Sony Music Distbr 550 Madison Ave New York NY 10022-3211*

BACA, EDWARD DIONICIO, national guard officer; b. Santa Fe, July 27, 1938; s. Ernest J. and Delphine (Garcia) B.; m. Rita Ann Hennigan, Apr. 12, 1957; children—Brian Edward, Brenda Anne, Karen Lynne, Mark Andrew, Michelle Marie, David William, Daniel Patrick. Student, Coll. of Santa Fe, N.Mex. Nat. Guard's Officer Candidate Sch., 1962, Chem., Biol. and Radiol. Sch., 1965, U.S. Command and Gen. Staff Coll., 1976; BS, SUNY, 1986. Administrv. asst. N.Mex. Army N.G., Santa Fe, 1957-58; procurement-contracting staff N.Mex. Army N.G., 1958-59, clk., traffic mgr., supply clk., 1959-62, field account clk., 1962, field auditor, 1962-64, air nat. guard insp., 1964, supply officer, 1966-69, supervisory auditor Army-air, 1969-71, logistics officer, 1971-75, comptroller, 1975-77, mil. personnel mgmt. officer, 1977-81, command adminstrv. officer, 1981-83, adjutant gen. of N.Mex., 1983—; chief Natl Guard Bureau DOD, Washington, 1994—; dir. CEPD, Santa Fe. Bd. dirs. Vietnam Vets. Chapel, Angel Fire, N.Mex.; past pres. St. Francis Sch. Bd., Santa Fe; mem. parish council St. John the Bapt. Cath. Ch., Santa Fe. Served with ARNG, 1984—. Decorated Army Commendation ribbon, Meritorious Service medal; recipient Meritorious Service award Nat. Guard Assn., 1981. Mem. Mil. Order of World Wars, Vietnam Vets., DAV, U.S. Nat. Guard, N.Mex. Nat. Guard, Assn. U.S. Army. Democrat. Roman Catholic. Office: Natl Guard Bureau 2500 Army Pentagon Washington DC 20310-2500

BACA, JIM, mayor. BSBA, U. N.Mex. Mayor City of Albuquerque, 1997—; former dir. alcohol and beverage control State of N.Mex., press sec. to gov., commr. pub. lands; past asst. to mayor, gen. mgr. Rio Grande Conservancy Dist.; former dir. Fed. Bur. Land Mgmt.; nat. cons. pub. land and conservation issues. Served with USAF. Office: Mayors Office PO Box 1293 Albuquerque NM 87103*

BACA, JOSEPH FRANCIS, state supreme court justice; b. Albuquerque, Oct. 1, 1936; s. Amado and Inez (Pino) B.; m. Dorothy Lee Burrow, June 28, 1969; children: Jolynn, Andrea, Anna Marie. BA in Edn., U. N.Mex., 1960; JD, George Washington U., 1964; LLM, U. Va., 1992. Asst. dist. atty. 1st Jud. Dist., Santa Fe, 1965-66; pvt. practice Albuquerque, 1966-72; dist. judge 2d Jud. Dist., Albuquerque, 1972-88; justice N.Mex. Supreme Ct., Santa Fe, 1989—; spl. asst. to atty. gen. Office of N.Mex. Atty. Gen., Albuquerque, 1966-71. Dem. precinct chmn., albuquerque, 1968; del. N.Mex. Constl. Conv., Santa Fe, 1969; bd. dirs. State Justice Inst., 1994—. Recipient Judge of Yr. award Peoples Commn. for Criminal Justice, 1989, Quincentennial Commemoration Achievement award La Hispanidad Com., 1992, Luchando por la Justicia award Mex. Am. Law Students Assn. U. N.Mex. Law Sch., 1993; J. William Fulbright Disting. Pub. Svc. award George Washington U. Alumni Assn., 1994, Recognition and Achievement award Commn. on Opportunities for Minorities in the Profession, 1992, others; named one of 100 most influential Hispanics Hispanic Bus. Mag., 1997, 98. Mem. ABA, Hispanic Nat. Bar Assn., N.Mex. Bar Assn. (outstanding jud. svc. award 1998), Am. Law Inst., Scribes, Am. Jud. Soc., Albuquerque Bar Assn., Santa Fe Bar Assn., N.Mex. Hispanic Bar Assn., Alumni Assn. (pres. 1980-81), Kiwanis (pres. Albuquerque chpt. 1984-85), KC (dep. grand knight 1968). Roman Catholic. Avocation: reading history. Office: Supreme Ct NMex Supreme Court Bldg PO Box 848 Santa Fe NM 87504-0848

BACA, KELLY MAE, marketing communications director; b. Denver, Mar. 15, 1960; d. Errol H. and Virginia A. Klein; m. Paul A. Baca, May 26, 1979; children: Amber Nicole, Natalie Faye. Student, U. Md., San Vito Air Station, Italy, 1983-85. Pub. rels. mgr. Morale, Welfare and Recreation, San Vito Air Station, 1983-85; prodn. mgr. Morrison & Morrison Advt., Biloxi, Miss., 1986-87; ops. mgr. DeOlivera Creative, Denver, 1988-90; newspaper mgr. May D&F, Denver, 1990-92; mktg./location specialist Colo. Film Commn., Denver, 1993-95; dir. mktg. Colo. Studios, Denver, 1995-97; mktg. comms. dir. Gart Sports/Sportsmart, Denver, 1997—; mem. adv. bd. Colo. Motion Picture and TV Commn., Denver, 1993-95. Editor, author: (quar. newsletter) Wrap Sheet, 1993-95; contbr. poetry to anthologies. Mem. Denver Advt. Fedn. Avocations: writing screenplays, poetry and children's books, snow skiing, shooting pool, biking. Office: Gart Sports 1000 Broadway Denver CO 80203

BACA ARCHULATA, MARGIE, city clerk; b. Albuquerque, May 18, 1948. City clk. Office of Mayor, Albuquerque, 1997—. Office: Office of City Clk/Govt Bld 1 Civic Plz NW Rm 11110 Albuquerque NM 87102-2167*

BACALL, LAUREN, actress; b. N.Y.C., Sept. 16, 1924; m. Humphrey Bogart, May 21, 1945 (dec. 1957); children: Stephen, Leslie; m. Jason Robards, July, 1961 (div.); 1 son, Sam. Student pub. schs., Am. Acad. Dramatic Art. Actress in Broadway plays Franklin Street, 1942, Goodbye Charlie, 1959; motion picture actress, 1944—, film appearances include To Have and Have Not, 1945, Confidential Agent, 1945, The Big Sleep, 1946, Dark Passage, 1947, Key Largo, 1948, Young Man With a Horn, 1949, Bright Leaf, 1950, How To Marry a Millionaire, 1953, Woman's World, 1954, The Cobweb, 1955, Blood Alley, 1955, Written on the Wind, 1956, Designing Woman, 1957, The Gift of Love, 1958, Flame Over India, 1959, Shock Treatment, 1964, Sex and the Single Girl, 1965, Harper, 1966, Murder on the Orient Express, 1974, The Shootist, 1976, Health, 1980, The Fan, 1981, Tree of Hands, 1987, Appointment With Death, 1987, Mr. North, 1988, Misery, 1990, A Star for Two, 1991, All I Want for Christmas, 1991, Ready to Wear (Prêt-à-Porter), 1994, My Fellow Americans, 1996, The Mirror Has Two Faces, 1996, The Line King: Al Hirschfield, 1996, Le Jour et la Nuit, 1997; appeared in Broadway play Cactus Flower, 1966-68, Applause, 1969-71 (Sarah Siddons award 1975); also road co., 1971-72, London co., 1972-73 (Tony award for best actress in a musical 1970); Broadway play Woman of the Year, 1981 (Tony award for best actress in a musical 1981, Sarah Siddons award 1983), Sweet Bird of Youth, 1983 (London, 1985, Australia, 1986, L.A., 1987; TV spl. The Paris Collections, 1968, Applause, 1973, A Commercial Break (Happy Endings), 1975; TV movies: Perfect Gentlemen, 1978, Dinner at Eight, 1989, The Portrait, 1992, A Foreign Field, 1993, From the Mixed Up Files of Mrs. Basil E. Frankweiler, 1995; author: Lauren Bacall By Myself, 1978, Lauren Bacall Now, 1994. Recipient Am. Acad. Dramatic Arts award for achievement, 1963, Standard award London Evening, 1973, Nat. Book award, 1979; decorated comdr. Order of Arts and Letters (France), 1995. Office: care Johnnie Planco William Morris Agy 1325 Avenue Of The Americas New York NY 10019-6026*

BACALOGLU, RADU, chemical engineer; b. Bucharest, Romania, July 21, 1937; came to the U.S., 1985; s. Dan and Elena (Lazarescu) B.; m. Ilze Irina Schiff, Aug. 29, 1963; 1 child, Radu Dan. MSChE, Poly. Inst., Romania, 1959, PhD in Organic Chemistry, 1968. Asst. prof. Poly. Inst., Timisoara, Romania, 1959-79, prof. chemistry, 1979-85; rsch. assoc. U. Calif., Santa Barbara, 1985-89; asst. prof. Rutgers U., New Brunswick, N.J., 1989-91; group leader R&D vinyl Witco Corp., Oakland, N.J., 1991-97; mgr. R&D vinyl Witco Corp., Tarrytown, N.Y., 1997—; dir. rsch. group of homogeneous and enzymatic catalysis Inst. Chem. Energetics, Bucharest, 1981-85. Author 2 books, more than 180 papers; contbr. articles to Rev. Roumaine Chemie, Tetrahedron, Spectrochimica Acta, Jour. Am. Chem. Soc. Phys. Chem. Polymer Degree Stabilization, others. Recipient 1st prize for scientific rsch. Ministry of Edn., Romania, 1965, G. Spacu award for rsch. in chemistry Romanian Acad., 1981. Mem. Am. Chem. Soc., N.Y. Acad. Scis., Soc. Plastic Engrs., AAAS. Achievements include 13 patents in organic chemistry; research in physical and synthetic organic chemistry, kinetic study of degradation and stabilization of polymers, especially polyvinyl chloride. Home: 27 Burlington Ct Hamburg NJ 07419-1320 Office: Witco 771 Old Saw Mill River Rd Tarrytown NY 10591

BACCARELLA, THERESA ANN, primary school educator; b. Bayonne, N.J., June 8, 1960; d. George Thomas and Antoinette (Barresi) Nolan; m. John Richard Baccarella, Oct. 27, 1984; children: Jaclyn Marie, Ryan Thomas. BA in Early Childhood Edn. summa cum laude, Jersey City State Coll., 1982, MBA, Reading Specialist, 1994. Cert. tchr. nursery, kindergarten, elem. Head tchr., asst. coord. Jersey City State Coll. Child Care Ctr., 1982-84; basic skills tchr. kindergarten, 1st grade Bayonne (N.J.) Pub. Sch. System, 1984-88; tchr. 1st grade, kindergarten, 2nd grade Hazlet (N.J.) Twp. Sch. System, 1988—; mem. curriculum coms. Hazlet Bd. Edn., 1988-90. Confraternity of Christian Doctrine tchr. Ch. of the Ascension, Bradley Beach, N.J., 1991—. Recipient Tchr. Recognition award, 1990-91. Mem. Monmouth Art Alliance, Hudson Reading Coun. (rec. sec. 1994-95, corr. sec. 1995-96), Hudson Reading Coun. (v.p. 1996-97), Alpha Upsilon Alpha (co-pres. 1993-94, v.p. 1994-96), Kappa Delta Pi. Roman Catholic. Avocations: drawing, painting, collage. Home: 53 Wyncrest Ln Neptune NJ 07753-7421

BACCIGALUPPI, ROGER JOHN, agricultural company executive; b. N.Y.C., Mar. 17, 1934; s. Harry and Ethel (Hutcheon) B.; m. Patricia Marie Wier, Feb. 6, 1960 (div. 1978); children: John, Elisabeth, Andrea; m. Iris Christine Walfridson, Feb. 3, 1979; 1 child, Jason. B.S., U. Calif., Berkeley, 1956; M.S., Columbia U., 1957. Asst. sales promotion mgr. Maco Mag. Corp., N.Y.C., 1956-57; merchandising asst. Honig, Cooper & Harrington, San Francisco and L.A., 1957-58, 1958-60; asst. dir. merchandising Honig, Cooper & Harrington, 1960-61; sales rep. Blue Diamond Growers (formerly Calif. Almond Growers Exch.), Sacramento, 1961-64, mgr. advt. and sales promotion, 1964-70; v.p. mktg. Blue Diamond Growers (formerly Calif. Almond Growers Exch.), 1970-73, sr. v.p. mktg., 1973-74, exec. v.p., 1974-75, pres., 1975-91; founder RB Internat., Sacramento, 1992—; bd. dirs. Mad Rover Records, Inc.; vice chmn., bd. dirs. Agrl. Coun. Calif., 1975-91; mem. consumer-prodr. com., adminstrn. com.; mem. U.S. adv. com. Trade Policy and Negotiations, 1983—; mem. U.S. adv. bd. Rabobank Nederlands, 1988-91; mem. Calif. World Trade Commn., 1993—; mem. adv. coun. Nat. Ctr. for Food and Agr. Policy Resources for Future, 1990—. Vice chmn. Calif. State R.R. Mus. Found.; chmn. Cmty. Colls. Found.; vice chmn. Grad. Inst. Cooperative Leadership, 1986-87, chair, 1987-89. With AUS, 1957. Mem. Calif. C. of C. (chmn. internat. trade com. 1988-94, bd. dirs. 1988—, vice chmn. bd. 1992-94, chmn. bd. 1995, Sacramento Host Com. (chmn. 1997, 98), Calif. for Higher Edn., Grad. Inst. Coop. Leadership (chmn., trustee), Grocery Mfrs. Am., Inc. (bd. dirs. 1988-91), Sutter Club. Office: RB Internat 777 Campus Commons Rd Ste 200 Sacramento CA 95825-8343

BACCINI, LAURANCE ELLIS, lawyer; b. Darby, Pa., Nov. 16, 1945; m. Tracey Judith Lane, Dec. 20, 1969; 1 child, Allyson Alexandra Lane. BS, Drexel U., 1968; JD, Villanova U., 1971. Bar: Pa. 1971, U.S. Dist. Ct. (ea. dist.) Pa. 1973, U.S. Ct. Appeals (3d cir.) 1979. Law clk. to chief judge U.S. Dist. Ct. (ea. dist.) Pa., 1971-73; assoc. Schnader, Harrison, Segal & Lewis, Phila., 1973-78, ptnr., 1979—, mem. exec. com., 1990-91; ptnr. Wolf, Block, Schorr and Solis-Cohen, 1991—; speaker, faculty mem. on labor law Practising Law Inst., N.Y.C.; trustee Phila. Bar Found., 1986—; bd. dirs. Interest on Lawyers Inst. Account Bd. Author: NLRA Supervisor's Handbook; assoc. editor Villanova Law Rev. Recipient Drexel One Hundred honor award, 1992. Mem. Phila. Bar Assn. (bd. govs. 1978—, chmn. 1982, vice chancellor 1986, chancellor-elect 1987, chancellor 1988, commn. on jud. selection, retention and evaluation 1978-79), chmn. exec. com. young lawyers sect., chmn. long range planning com.), Pa. Bar Assn. (ho. of dels. 1983—), ABA (former chair, and dir. young lawyers div. 1981-82, chair long-range planning com., young lawyers div.'s Fed. practice com., fed. judicial standards com., judicial conf. for 3d cir., house of dels. 1988—, mem. editorial bd. The Labor Lawyer), Greater Phila. C. of C.(bd. dirs. 1988). Office: Wolf Block Schorr and Solis-Cohen Packard Bldg 12th Flr SE Corner 15 St & Chestnut St Philadelphia PA 19102

BACH, BETTY JEAN, health services educator; b. Jackson, Ky., Dec. 25, 1952; d. Eugene Parker and Celeste White B. AA, Ea. Ky. U., 1975, BS, 1995; student, Ohio U., 1984, Morehead U., 1986. RN, Ky.; cert. ob-gyn. nurse practitioner, advanced RN practitioner. Staff nurse, nurse practitioner Breathitt County Health Dept., Jackson, Ky., 1975-80; sch. health nurse, health svcs. coord. Breathitt County Bd. Edn., Jackson, 1983-88; health svcs. instr. Breathitt Area Vocat. Edn. Ctr., Jackson, 1988—. Mem. NEA, Ky. Edn. Assn. Am. Vocat. Assn., Vocat. Assn. Kappa Delta Pi. Home: Highway 30 E Rousseau KY 41366

BACH, CYNTHIA, educational program director, writer; b. Oct. 28. BA in Art Edn., UCLA, 1955; MPA, U. So. Calif., 1978; LDS, Calif. Luth., 1993. Cert. gen. elem., spl. secondary art, and gen. jr. h.s. tchr. Staff asst. L.A. Unified Sch. Dist., 1976; rainbow tchr., gifted coord. Trinity Elem. Sch., L.A., 1978-81; field worker/in-svc. for parents and staff educator Hubbard Elem. Sch., Sylmar, Calif., 1981-90; student observer Liggett Elem. Sch., Panorama City, Calif., 1990-92; tng. tchr. Calif. State U. (Northridge)-Vena Sch., Arleta, Calif., 1992-93; pres. Comprehensive Learning Systems; rsch. bd. advisors Am. Biograph. Inst., Inc. Author: Alternatives to Retail Marketing for Seniors (Bur. of Consumer Affairs). Lectr. Sr. Citizens Bur of Consumer Affairs, City Hall; past pres. local PTA; lay eucharistic min., 1998; del. Children's Def. Fund Conf., 1998; sch. bd. mem. St. Martin-in-the-Fields Parish Sch. Nat. Art scholar, Chouinard Art Inst. scholar., Special Recognition, 79 State Evaluation Mar Team-outstanding educator, Phi Alpha Alpha, Nat. Acad. Hon. Soc. Pub. Affairs Admin., Order of Internat. Fell.(-500 persons worldwide)-Edn., Nat. Div. Research Brd. Advisors Amer. Biographical Inst., elected assoc. mem., Nat. Mus. Women in Arts, elected Internat. Platform Assn., 21st Century Award for Achievement. Mem. NAFE, AAUW, 1st Century Soc. UCLA, Nat. Mus. Women in Arts (assoc.), Phi Alpha Alpha. Avocations: reading, theology, old movies, writing, gardening. Home: 5140 White Oak Ave Apt 214 Encino CA 91316-2435

BACH, JAN MORRIS, composer, educator; b. Forrest, Ill., Dec. 11, 1937; s. John Nicholas and Anne (Morris) B.; m. Dalia Zakaras; children: Dawn, Eva. MusB, U. Ill., 1959, MusM, 1961, MusD, 1971; postgrad., U. Va., Arlington, 1963-65, Yale U., summer 1960, Berkshire Music Ctr., summer 1961. Instr. music U. Tampa, Fla., 1965-66; prof. music No. Ill. U., DeKalb, 1966—; Presdl. Rsch. prof. No. Ill. U., Dekalb, 1982-86, Disting. Rsch. prof., 1986—; composer-in-residence Institut de Hautes Etudes Musicales, Montreux, Switzerland, 1976; editor for brass compositions M.M. Cole, Chgo., 1969-72; mem. Ill. Arts Coun., 1986-89, Ind. Arts Coun., 1992. Composer: Skizzen, 1967, Woodwork, 1970, Eisteddfod, 1972, Turkish Music, 1968, Four Two-Bit Contraptions, 1971, The System, 1973, Dirge for a Minstrel, 1974, Three Choral Dances, 1975, Laudes, 1975, Piano Concerto, 1975, Three Bagatelles, 1978, Hair Today, 1978, The Happy Prince, 1978, My Wilderness, 1979, Student from Salamanca, 1979, Rounds and Dances, 1980, Horn Concerto, 1982, Helix, 1984, Escapade, 1984, Dompes & Jompes, 1986, Harp Concerto, 1986, Trumpet Concerto, 1987, A Solemn Music, 1987, Triptych, 1989, Euphonium Concerto, 1990, With Trumpet and Drum, 1991, Anachronisms String Quartet, 1991, People of Note, 1993, Concerto for Steelpan and Orchestra, 1994, The Last Flower, 1995, Foliations, 1995, Bassoon Concertino, 1996, Pilgrimage, 1997, Variations on a Theme of Brahms, 1997, Kimberly's Song, 1998, Dear God, 1998. Served with AUS, 1962-65. Recipient BMI student composers 1st prize, 1957, Koussevitsky composition award, 1961, Harvey Gaul composition award, 1973, Mannes Opera award, 1973, Pulitzer prize nomination, 1973, 81, 82, 84, 92, SAI composition award, 1974, Excellence in Tchg. award No. Ill. U., 1978, choral composition award Brown U., 1978, Nebr. Sinfonia Chamber Orch. contest, 1979, N.Y.C. Opera contest, 1980; commns. include Tuba Brotherhood, 1977, Internat. Trumpet Guild, 1978, 86, Internat. Brass Congress, 1980, Greenwich Philharmonia, 1981, Orch. of Ill., 1982, NACWPI, 1982, Minot Symphony, 1984, Am. Brass Quintet-Chamber Music Am., 1988, Sacramento Symphony-N.C. Symphony, 1989, Camarata Singers, 1991, WFMT-Vermeer Quartet, 1991, Woodstock Chimes Fund, 1994, Ronen Chamber Ensemble, 1994, Stockholm Chamber Brass, 1994, Eileen Gress-N.C. Symphony, 1995, Elmhurst Symphony, 1996, Ramon Parcells, 1996. Mem. Coll. Mus. Soc., Broadcast Music, Phi Eta Sigma, Phi Mu Alpha, Phi Kappa Phi, Pi Kappa Lambda., Omicron Delta Kappa. Office: No Ill U PO Box 403 Wasco IL 60183-0403

BACH, JEAN ENZINGER, filmmaker; b. Chgo., Sept. 27, 1918; d. George Enzinger and Gertrude Cole Passmore; m. Clarence Francis Sherock, Feb. 3, 1941 (div. Sept. 1947). Student, Vassar Coll., 1936-37. Journalist Chgo. Times, 1937-38, Jour. Am., Chgo., 1938-40; writer WNEW Radio, N.Y.C., 1947-48; pub. rels. specialist Edward L. Bernays, N.Y.C., 1948-50, Virginia Wicks, N.Y.C., 1950-52, Harry Sobol, N.Y.C., 1952-53; writer, prodr. Dumont-TV, N.Y.C., 1953, ABC-TV, N.Y.C., 1953-55; writer, rschr., prodr. WOR Radio, N.Y.C., 1960-84; freelance filmmaker N.Y.C., 1989—. Prodr., dir., writer documentaries: A Great Day in Harlem, 1995 (Acad. award nomination), The Spitball Story, others. Bd. dirs. Ellington Meml. Com., 1984-98. Grantee J. & L. Pettit Found., 1994, Dallas Film Found., 1998. Mem. Fortue Soc. (bd. dirs.), Silurians, Vassar Club.

BACH, MÁRIA-CATHÉRINE, writer, researcher, translator; b. Kleinbettange, Luxembourg, Feb. 6, 1910; came to U.S., 1946; naturalized, 1950.; d. Dominique and Marie (Müller) Bach; m. James Dunn, Dec. 23, 1946. Student, Institut Ste Anne Soeurs du Sacré Coeur, Hougaerde, Belgium, 1926-28, Lycée Esch-Alzette, Luxembourg, 1922-26. interpreter, translator, negotiator hist. documents, 1967-71; translator ednl. program Voice Am., N.Y. State Hist. Assn., Cooperstown, 1953; initiator, sponsor Bibliotheque Luxemburgiana, St. Thomas U., St. Paul, 1993; active Mária Bach scholarship Miami U. European Ctr., Luxembourg Program, Oxford, Ohio, 1992. Contbg. editor: Luxembourg News Am., 1959-96. Vol. Mary Imogene Bassett Hosp., Cooperstown, 1950-55; contbg. mem. Luxembourg Heritage Soc. Inc.; charter mem. U.S. Holocaust Mus.; sponsor Maria Bach scholarship Miami U. Dolibois European Ctr., Luxembourg, 1993—. Recipient award of merit regional chpt. Nat. Red Cross Am., 1950, 52, Nat. Medal of Merit, Luxembourg Govt., 1993, Achievement and Contbn. recognition Rollingstone (Minn.) Luxembourg Mus., 1997. Mem. NOW, ACLU. Democrat. Roman Catholic. Avocations: traveling, book collecting, reading, music, theater.

BACH, MARTIN WAYNE, stockbroker, owner antique clock stores; b. Milw., Mar. 30, 1940; s. Jack Baer and Rose (Weiss) B.; m. Roberta Sklar, Aug. 19, 1962; children: David Louis, Emily Elizabeth. BA, U. Wis., 1963. Stockbroker J. Barth & Co., Oakland, Calif., 1966-72, v.p., 1970-72; sr. v.p., stockbroker Dean Witter & Co., Oakland, 1972—; founder The TimePeace, Carmel, Calif., 1972-83, San Francisco, 1975-83, La Jolla, 1977-83; instr. fin. San Leandro, Lafayette and Hayward (Calif.) Adult Sch., 1970—. Chmn. bd. dirs. Diablo Light Opera Co., 1985-87; bd. dirs. East Bay Hosp., 1985-90. 1st lt. U.S. Army, 1963-65. Mem. Calif. Thoroughbred Breeders Assn., Calif. Thoroughbred Assn., Nat. Assn. Clock and Watch Collectors, Am. Horse Coun., East Bay Brokers Club, Blackhawk Country Club, Dean Witter Chairmen's Club, B'nai B'rith. Avocations: breeder, owner thoroughbred race horses. Home: 4431 Deer Ridge Rd Danville CA 94506-6019 Office: 2 Theatre Sq Ste 322 Orinda CA 94563-3346

BACH, STEVE CRAWFORD, lawyer; b. Jackson, Ky., Jan. 31, 1921; s. Bruce Grannis and Evelyn (Crawford) B.; m. Rosemary Husted, Sept. 6, 1947; children—John Crittenden, Greta Christine. AB, Ind. U., 1943, JD, 1948; postgrad. Eastern studies, U. Mich., 1944, Nat. Trial Judges Coll., 1966; U. Minn. Juvenile Inst., 1967. Bar: Ky. 1948, Ind. 1948. Atty. Bach & Bach, Jackson, Ky., 1948-51; investigator U.S. CSC, Indpls., 1951-54; sole practice Mt. Vernon, Ind., 1954-65, 83—; judge 11th Jud. Circuit, Mt. Vernon, Ind., 1965-82; pres. Internat. Inst. for Youth, Inc., Mt. Vernon, 1985-90; sr. judge Posey County Superior Ct. State of Ind., 1997—; spl. overseas rep. Nat. Council Juvenile and Family Ct. Judges, 1983-86, bd. trustees, 1979-83; moderator Ind. Conf. Crime and Delinquency, Indpls., 1968; tchr. seminar on juvenile delinquency, Ind. Trial Judges Assn., 1969, del. Internat. Youth Magistrates Conf., Geneva, 1970, Oxford, Eng., 1974, Can., 1977; faculty adviser Criminal Law Inst., Nat. Trial Judges Coll., 1973; treas. Ind. Council Juvenile Ct. Judges, 1975, v.p., 1976, pres., 1978-79; bd. dirs. Jud. Conf., Ind. Jud. Ctr., 1978-79; faculty adviser Nat. Jud. Coll., 1978; mem. faculty Seminar for Inst. for New Judges, State of Ind., 1979. Pres. Greater Mt. Vernon Assn., 1958-59; past mem. Juvenile Justice divsn. Ind. Jud. Study Commn.; mem. Ind. Gov.'s Juvenile Justice Delinquency Prevention Adv. Bd., 1976-78, community adv. coun. Ind. U. Sch. Medicine, 1986-96. With intelligence Signal Corps, AUS, 1943-46. Mem. Nat. Coun. Juvenile Ct. Judges, Am. Legion, Ind. Bar Assn. (del.), Ind. Judges Assn. (mem. bd. mgrs. 1966-71), Masons, Elks, Kiwanis, Sigma Delta Kappa, Delta Tau Delta. Democrat. Methodist. Home and Office: 512 Walnut St Mount Vernon IN 47620-1862

BACH, THOMAS HANDFORD, lawyer, investor; b. Vineland, N.J., Dec. 25, 1928; s. Albert Ludwig and Edith May (Handford) B. A.B., Rutgers U., 1950; LL.B., Harvard U., 1956. Bar: N.Y. State bar 1957. Asso. firm Hawkins, Delafield & Wood, N.Y.C., 1956-61, Reed, Hoyt, Washburn & McCarthy, N.Y.C., 1961-62; ptnr. Bach & Condren, N.Y.C., 1963-71, Bach & McAuliffe, N.Y.C., 1971-79, Stroock & Stroock & Lavan, N.Y.C., 1979-88, Sullivan & Donovan, N.Y.C., 1989—; co-counsel N.Y. State Senate Housing and Urban Devel. Com., 1971; fiscal cons. N.Y.C. Fin. Adminstrn., 1967-70; asst. counsel State Fin. Com., N.Y. State Constl. Conv. of, 1967; del. U.S./Japan Bilateral Session, 1988, Moscow Conf. on Law and Bilateral Econ. Rels., 1990; spkr. Practicing Law Inst., Mcpl. Bond Workshop, N.Y., 1995-97. Contbr. articles to profl. jours.; co-author: A Guide to Certificates of Participation, 1991, the Handbook of Municipal Bonds, 1994. Mem. N.Y. State Commn. to Study Constl. Tax Limitations, 1974-75; chmn. subcom. Pub. Securities Assn.; dir. Citizens Union of N.Y. Served with U.S. Army, 1951-53, 1st lt. U.S. Army, 1952-53, Japan. Mem. Am. Bar Assn., N.Y. State Bar Assn. (internat. law. sect.), Assn. of Bar of City of N.Y., N.J. Bar Assn., N.Y. Mcpl. Analysts Group (chmn. 1973-74), Mcpl. Forum of N.Y., Tax Collectors and Treas. Assn. of N.J., Market Technicians Assn., Internat. Fin. Svcs. Vol. Corps. Episcopalian. Home: 4 E 89th St New York NY 10128-0636 Also: 615 W Oak Rd Vineland NJ 08360-2262 Office: Sullivan & Donovan 415 Madison Ave New York NY 10017-1111

BACHAND, STEPHEN E., retail company executive; b. 1938; married. BA, Williams Coll., 1960; MBA, U. Va., 1962. With Gen. Motors Corp., Washington, 1962-63; sr. v.p. fin. Hechinger Co. Inc., Landover, Md., 1963, exec. v.p., 1986-87, also bd. dirs.; COO Home Quarters divsn. Hechinger Co., 1987-93; pres., CEO Can. Tire Corp. Ltd., Toronto, 1993—. Office: Canadian Tire Corp Ltd, Box 770 Station K, Toronto, ON Canada M4P 2VB

BACHARACH, BURT, composer, conductor; b. Kansas City, Mo., May 29, 1929; s. Bert and Irma (Freeman) B.; m. Paula Stewart; m. Angie Dickinson (div.); 1 child, Lea Nikki; m. Carole Bayer Sager, Mar. 30, 1982 (div.); 1 child, Cristopher Elton. Student, McGill U., Montreal, 3 years; pupil, Darius Milhaud at New Sch. for Social Research, Henry Cowell at Music Acad. West, Santa Barbara, Calif. Accompanist, Vic Damone,, 1952; accompanist, Polly Bergen, Georgia Gibbs, Joel Gray, Ames Bros., Marlene Dietrich; now composer songs, film scores, stage musicals; frequent collaborator Carole Bayer Sager. Composer: Raindrops Keep Fallin' on My Head, Magic Moments, The Story of My Life, Don't Make Me Over, Walk on By, Trains and Boats and Planes, Close to You, Anyone Who Had a Heart, What the World Needs Now, I'll Never Fall in Love Again, Do You Know the Way to San Jose?, The Look of Love, One Less Bell to Answer, Alfie (Grammy award 1967), Heartlight, Power, On My Own, Arthur's Theme, That's What Friends Are For (Grammy award 1986); film scores The Man Who Shot Liberty Valence, 1962, Wives and Lovers, 1963, Send Me No Flowers, 1964, A House is Not a Home, 1964, Who's Been Sleeping in My Bed, 1964, What's New Pussycat?, 1965, Alfie, 1966, Promise Her Anything, 1966, After the Fox, 1966, Casino Royale, 1967, The April Fools, 1969, Butch Cassidy and the Sundance Kid, 1969 (Acad. awards 1969), Lost Horizon, 1972, Together?, 1979, Arthur, 1981 (Acad. award), Night Shift, 1982, Best Defense, 1984, Baby Boom, 1987, Arthur 2: On the Rocks, 1988; composer music for play Promises, Promises, 1969 (Drama Desk award 1968, Grammy award 1969); recs. for A&M Records, Kapp Records; author: The Bacharach-David Song Book, 1970. Served with AUS, 1950-52. Named (with David) Entertainers of Yr., Cue mag., 1969; recipient 3 Acad. awards, 5 Grammy awards, 2 Emmy awards, Tony award. *

BACHARACH, MELVIN LEWIS, retired venture capitalist; b. Oakland, Calif., May 14, 1924; s. Max and Ellen Mildred (LeValley) B.; m. Vera Patricia Mortimer, Aug. 20, 1950; children: Kimberly Bacharach Arnone, Craig Ronald. BSBA, U. Calif., Berkeley, 1948. With Levi Strauss & Co., 1948-79, v.p., then exec. v.p., 1973-79, pres. U.S. group, 1975-79, also bd. dirs., mem. exec. com.; pres., chief exec., officer Internat. Bus. Sponsors, Inc., 1979-86, also bd. dirs.; pres., chief exec., officer VMB, Inc., San Rafael, Calif., 1986-98; ret., 1998; bd. dirs. Internat. Bus. Sponsors, Inc., Above the Belt, Inc. Served as pilot USNR, 1942-46, 51-53. Decorated Air medal. Mem. U. Calif. Bus. Adminstrn. Alumni Assn., Beta Gamma Sigma, Pi Lambda Phi. Clubs: Marine Meml., Mira Vista Country, Concordia Argonaut, Palm Valley Country, Avondale Golf Club. Patentee in apparel field.

BACHELDER, JOSEPH ELMER, III, lawyer; b. Fulton, Mo., Nov. 13, 1932; s. Joseph Elmer and Frances Evelyn (Gray) B.; m. Louise Este Mason, June 12, 1955; children: Louise Stewart Bachelder Alcock, Christina Cathryn Bachelder Dufresne, Hilary Houston. BA magna cum laude, Yale U., 1955; LLB, Harvard U., 1958. Bar: N.Y. 1959. Assoc. Mudge, Rose, Guthrie & Alexander, N.Y.C., 1958-67, McKinsey and Co., Inc., N.Y.C., 1967-69; ptnr. Satterlee and Stephens, N.Y.C., 1969-72, Leboeuf, Lamb, Lieby & MacRae, N.Y.C., 1972-80; founder, sr. ptnr. Law Offices Joseph E. Bachelder, N.Y.C., 1980—; chmn. The Bachelder Group, Inc., 1989—; pub. The Bachelder CEO Bull., 1990—; lectr. NYU Ann. Inst. on Fed. Taxation, 1972-74, Practicing Law Inst., 1977-80, Am. Law Inst., 1980, The Conf. Bd., 1986. Co-author, editor: Employee Stock Ownership Plans, 1979; columnist N.Y. Law Jour. Mem. Princeton Twp. (N.J.) Zoning Bd., 1981-82; trustee Concord (Mass.) Acad., 1986-92. Fellow Am. Coll. Tax Counsel; mem. ABA, N.Y. State Bar Assn., Assn. of Bar of N.Y.C., The DownTown Assn. Republican. Congregationalist. Clubs: Yale Club N.Y.; Bedens Brook (Princeton), Nassau (Princeton); Siasconset Casino (Nantucket, Mass.). Home: 226 Constitution Dr Princeton NJ 08540-6712 Office: 780 3rd Ave New York NY 10017-2024

BACHELDER, ROBERT STEPHEN, minister; b. Middletown, N.Y., Nov. 2, 1951; s. Stephen and Dorothy Esther (Gunderson) B.; m. Beverly June Brandt, Sept. 17, 1977; children: Stephen, Elizabeth. AB, Dartmouth Coll., 1973; MDiv, Yale U., 1978. Ordained to ministry United Ch. of Christ, 1978. Money markets trader R.I. Hosp. Trust Nat. Bank, Providence, 1973-75; pastor United Ref. Ch., Pangbourne, Eng., 1978-79; min. 1st Congl. Ch., Shrewsbury, Mass., 1980-84; min. for mission and svc. Worcester (Mass.) Area Mission Soc., 1984—; advisor to religious congregations for charitable giving. Author: Mystery and Miracle, 1983, Between Dying and Birth, 1983; contbr. chpts. to books, articles to profl. jours. Bd. dirs. Mass. Coun. of Chs., 1991-93, Worcester Interfaith, 1992-94, Worcester County Ecumenical Coun., 1992-96, Mass. Conv. Congl. Mins., 1983-85, Ctrl. Assn. Mass. Conf., United Ch. of Christ, 1983—, Worcester Coop. Coun., 1985-89, Accord: The Ctr. for Human Rels., 1991-93, Corx, Inc., 1993—, Martin Luther King Jr. Bus. Empowerment Ctr., 1993—, WCHR Securities, Inc., 1993—, Mass. Congl. Fund, 1999—, New Am. Cmty. Forum, 1995-97, Pakachoag Cmty. Music Sch., 1996-98, Congl. Christian Hist. Soc., 1997—, Worcester Pastoral Counseling Ctr., 1998—, Geater Worcester Cmty. Found. Exec. Com., 1998—, Colony Retirement Homes, 1998, Worcester Area Campus Ministry, 1998—; pres. Habitat Worcester, 1984-86, Worr Cmty. Loan Fund, 1986-90, Worcest er Com. on Homelessness and Housing, 1988-91, Worcester Cmty. Housing Resources, 1993-95; mem. City Mgr.'s Housing Task Force, 1990-92; v.p. Worcester Housing Partnership, 1991-93; distbn. com. mem. Fed. Emergency Mgmt. Agy., Ctrl. Mass., 1984-86, Housing Ind. Fund, 1989-92, Greater Worcester Cmty. Found., 1994—, chair, 1998—; v.p. Higgins Armory Mus., 1994-97, pres., 1997-99; v.p. New Horizons Ret. Homes, 1992-97; chair Worcester Housing Summit,1990-91; mem. adv. com. Clara Barton Birthplace Mus., 1996—; cmty. trustee United Way of Ctrl. Mass., 1995-98; incorporator Protestant Youth Ctr., 1995-98; co-founder Greater Worcester Interreligious Legis. Network, 1985, Worcester AIDS Housing Task Force, 1993; co-founder, chair The Neighborhood Forum, 1996—; mem. steerng com. Main South Credit Union, 1997—; founder Neighborhood Leaders Fund, 1996. Recipient award Pernet Family Svc., 1993, Outstanding Charitable Svc. award United Ch. of Christ, 1995. Mem. St. Wulstan Soc., United Ch. of Christ Ministers' Fellowship (pres. 1982-83), Worcester Econ. Club, Dartmouth Club of Ctrl. Mass. (pres. 1991-93). Home: PO Box 67 North Oxford MA 01537-0067 Office: Worcester Area Mission Soc 128 Central St Auburn MA 01501-2820

BACHENHEIMER, RALPH JAMES, merchant banker; b. Frankfurt, Fed. Republic Germany, Jan. 24, 1928; came to U.S., 1946; s. Ferdinand and Louise (Felber) B.; m. Clare Conway (dec. Feb. 1991); children: Lisa Clare, Cara Conway; m. Brith Bore. Student, Coll. Marianum, Vaduz, Liechtenstein, Switzerland, U. Zürich, Switzerland, Columbia U. V.p. Iselin-Jefferson Co., Inc., N.Y.C., 1946-66; pres., chief exec. officer Indian Head Yarn Co., N.Y.C., 1966-69; v.p. Europe Internat. Standard Brands Inc., N.Y.C., 1970-71; corp. v.p. Genesco, Inc., Nashville, 1971-76; exec. v.p., dir. Corland Corp., N.Y.C., 1976-84; mng. dir. E. S. Jacobs & Co., N.Y.C., 1985-93, S.N. Phelps & Co., Greenwich, Conn., 1993-95; self-employed Greenwich, 1995—; bd. dirs., past v.p. N.Y. Bd. Trade; bd. dirs. numerous corps. Founding mem. Rep. Nat. Senatorial Inner Cir., Washington; mem. Nat. Panel Arbitrators, N.Y.C. Named to Jaycees Hall of Fame, 1983. Mem. Vets. the 7th Regiment, Met. Club (N.Y.C., gov.), Fripp Island Club, Greenwich Country Club, Dataw Island Club. Republican. Avocation: golf. Home and Office: 5 Hill Rd Greenwich CT 06830-4024

BACHER, LUTZ, film, video and photography educator; b. Karlsruhe, Fed. Republic Germany, May 2, 1941; came to U.S., 1965; s. Ludwig and Liselotte (Hauth) B.; m. Patricia Delores Stamp, Dec. 18, 1964; children: Brent, Burton, Dara. B of Commerce, U. Windsor, Can., 1964; MA, Wayne State U., 1976, PhD, 1984. Owner, mgr. LBJP Concert Agy., Detroit, 1964-74; freelance prodn. asst. Detroit, 1975-76; asst. dir. Roger Jackson Prodns., Detroit, 1976-78; instr. Wayne State U., Detroit, 1978-80; asst. prof. film, video, photography Robert Morris Coll., Coraopolis, Pa., 1981-97; assoc. prof. Robert Morris Coll., Coraopolis, 1998—. Author: The Mobile Mise-en-Scene, 1978, Max Ophuls in the Hollywood Studios, 1996; writer, dir. Interstate Incident, 1972, Changes, 1973. Mem. Univ. Film-Video Assn., Soc. for Cinema Studies. Avocations: jazz, travel, swimming. Home: 17616 Wisconsin St Detroit MI 48221-2504 Office: Robert Morris Coll Narrows Run Rd Coraopolis PA 15108-1189

BACHER, ROBERT NEWELL, church official; b. Houston; m. Shirley Ann Good; children: Carol Lynn March, Laurie Ann Andrews, Joy Marie. BA in English, BS in Indsl. Engring., Tex. A&M U., 1957; MDiv, Luth. Sch. Theology, Chgo., 1961; MEd in Edn. Psychology, Temple U., 1970; MPA, DPA, U. So. Calif., 1981. ordained, 1961. Pastor St. Mark Luth. Ch., Lakewood, Colo., 1961-66; assoc. youth dir. Commn. Youth Ministry Luth. Ch. in Am., Phila., 1966-72; project mgr. action rsch., dept. rsch. and planning Divsn. for Parish Svcs., Luth. Ch. in Am., Phila., 1972-75, asst. dir. dept. rsch. and planning, 1975-77, asst. exec. dir. planning and budgeting, 1977-85, exec. dir., 1985-87; exec. for adminstrn., asst. to bishop Evang. Luth. Ch. in Am., 1987—. Contbr. articles to profl. jours. Office: Evang Luthern Church in Am 8765 W Higgins Rd Chicago IL 60631-4101*

BACHMAN, ARTHUR, lawyer; b. Phila., Nov. 18, 1947; s. Stanley Bachman and Ann (Rosen) Flashner; m. Linda Kay Moss, June 8, 1969; children: Helene, Allison. BBA, Temple U., 1969, JD, 1972, postgrad., 1980. Bar: Pa. 1972. Atty., advisor legis./regulations divsn. Office Chief Coun. IRS, Washington, 1972-76; assoc. Fox, Rothschild, O'Brien & Frankel, 1976-79; ptnr. Blank, Rome, Comisky & McCauley, Phila., 1979—; instr. Am. Coll., 1986, 88, Temple U., 1988; lectr. Estate Planning Coun. Lehigh Valley, 1983, C. of C. of Cherry Hill, N.J., 1985, Nat. Conf. CPA Practitioners, 1988, Am. Soc. Pension Actuaries, 1988, Internat. Soc. Employee Benefit Specialists, 1991; guest speaker Harry S. Gross radio program Sta. WCAU, 1987, 88, 89. Co-author: (booklets) The REA's Joint and Survivor Annuity Rules--Coping with the Regulations, 1986, How to Defer Income with IRA's and Sec. 401(k) Plans, 1987, Evaluation of Probable Impact of Proposed Nondiscrimination Regs: An Interview with 8 Pension Experts, 1990, An Evaluation of the Proposed Regulations on Separate Lines of Business, 1991, ERISA: A Comprehensive Guide, 1991-96; contbr. articles to jours., chpts. to books. Mem. Pa. Bar Assn., Phila. Bar Assn., Phi Alpha Delta, Alpha Epsilon Pi, Beta Gamma Sigma. Office: Blank Rome Comisky et al Fls 10-13 One Logan Square Philadelphia PA 19103-2521

BACHMAN, CAROL CHRISTINE, trust company executive; b. Buffalo, Jan. 20, 1959; d. Christian George and Joan Marie (French) B. Student, Grad. Inst. Internat. Study, 1979-80; AB, Smith Coll., 1981; grad., New Eng. Sch. Banking, 1987. Trust asst. BayBank Middlesex, Burlington, Mass., 1984-85, sr. trust asst., 1985-87, trust adminstr., 1987, trust officer, 1987-88; estate settlement specialist Bank of Boston, 1988-90, system cons., 1990, mgr. adminstrv. support svcs., asst. v.p., 1990-96; sr. sys. analyst Bank Boston, Westwood, Mass., 1996—. Office: BankBoston 858 Washington St Dedham MA 02026

BACHMAN, DAVID, neurologist, pediatric neurologist; b. Savannah, Ga., Apr. 22, 1944; s. Henry and Ilse Bachman; m. Bunnie Blanken; children: Eric, Kevin. BA, Harvard U., 1965; MD, Johns Hopkins U., 1969. Diplomate Am. Bd. Psychiatry and Neurology, Am. Bd. Pediat. Intern Pitts. Children's Hosp., 1969-70; resident in pediat. Johns Hopkins U., Balt., 1972-73, resident in neurology, 1973-76; pvt. practice Wilmington, N.C.; pres., med. dir. Wilmington Health. Officer USPHS, 1970-72. Office: Wilmington Health 1202 Medical Center Dr Wilmington NC 28401-7307

BACHMAN, DAVID CHRISTIAN, orthopedic surgeon; b. Peoria, Ill., Apr. 11, 1934; s. Leland Alvin and Elsie May (Springer) B.; m. Betty June Foster, Sept. 9, 1956; children: Lynne Allison, Laura Ailene. BA, Goshen Coll., 1958; MD, Northwestern U., 1962. Intern Cook County Hosp., Chgo., 1962-63; resident in orthopaedic surgery Northwestern U. Med. Sch., 1963-67; practice medicine specializing in orthopaedic surgery Chgo., 1967-80; practice specializing in ski injuries, 1980-93; with Mountain Med. Services, Telluride, Colo., 1982-87, Ouray Mountain Rescue Team, Inc., Ouray Med. Ctr., Ouray, Colo.; coroner Ouray County, Colo., 1982-93; mem. staffs Northwestern Meml. Hosp., Children's Meml. Hosp., Grant hosp., (all Chgo.), 1967-80, Montrose Meml. Hosp., Colo., 1984-93; med. cons. Western Area U.S. Postal Svc.; dir. Ctr. for Sports Medicine, Northwestern U. Med. Sch., 1978-80; team physician Chgo. Bulls, Nat. Basketball Assn., 1967-80; asst. prof. dept. orthop. surgery Northwestern U. Med. Sch., 1967-80; syndicated columnist on sports medicine Dr. Jock, 1976-90; cons. Western area U.S. Postal Svc., 1996-97; sr. area med. dir. Western Area U.S. Postal Svc., 1997. Author: (with Marilyn Preston) Dear Doctor Jock . . .The Peoples Guide to Sports and Fitness, 1980, (with others) The Diet That Lets You Cheat, 1983, (with Tod Bacigalupi) The Way it Was, 1990, (with Robert Pickering) The Use of Forensic Anthropology, 1996. Elder Presbyn. Ch., 1965—; rsch. assoc. anthropology dept. Denver Mus. Natural History, 1994—. Mem. ACS, Am. Acad. Orthop. Surgery, Am. Orthop. Soc. for Sports Medicine, Phi Rho Sigma. Presbyterian. Home: 23 Tamarade Dr Littleton CO 80127-3518

BACHMAN, DAVID M., ophthalmologist; b. Scranton, Pa., Aug. 10, 1951; s. Seymour W. and Natalie (Goodman) B. BA, Johns Hopkins U., 1973, MD, 1976. Resident in ophthalmology Stanford (Calif.) U. Hosp., 1977-80; fellow Nat. Eye Inst.-NIH, Bethesda, Md., 1980-82; pvt. practice ophthalmology Washington, 1982—; sr. ophthalmic surgeon Washington Hosp. Ctr., Washington, 1982—; clin. instr. ophthalmology George Washington Hosp., Washington, 1990-98. Manuscript reviewer Archives of Ophthalmology; contbr. articles to profl. jours. Bd. dirs. Myasthenia Gravis Found., Washington, 1986—, Young Concert Artists, Washington, 1983—. Recipient Physician's Recognition award AMA, 1980, 83, 86, 93. Fellow Am. Acad. Ophthalmology; mem. Washington Ophthalmol. Soc., Med. Soc. D.C. Jewish. Avocation: classical pianist. Office: 1133 20th St NW Ste B-150 Washington DC 20036-3424

BACHMAN, GEORGE, mathematics educator; b. N.Y.C., Jan. 17, 1933; s. Frederick Joseph and Ruth (Benson) B.; m. Joan Caggiano. B.E.E., N.Y. U., 1950, M.S., 1952, Ph.D. in Math, 1956. Asst. prof. math. Rutgers U., New Brunswick, N.J., 1957-60; mem. faculty Bklyn. Poly. Inst., 1960—, assoc. prof., 1962-66, prof., 1966—. Author: (with L. Narici and E. Beckenstein) Functional Analysis and Valuation Theory, 1971, (with L. Narici) Functional Analysis, 1966, Elements of Abstract Harmonic Analysis, 1964, Introduction to p-adic Numbers and Valuation Theory, 1964; Contbr. articles to profl. jours. Recipient Disting. Teaching award Bklyn. Poly. Inst., 1974, Disting. Research award Sigma Xi, 1982; NSF grantee, 1968—. Mem. Am. Math. Soc., Math. Assn. Am. Home: 27 Summit Rd Riverside CT 06878-2104 Office: 333 Jay St Brooklyn NY 11201-2907

BACHMAN, HENRY LEE, electrical engineer, engineering executive; b. Bklyn., Apr. 29, 1930; s. Solomon and Frances (Cortese) B.; m. Doris Engelhardt, Dec. 8, 1951; children: Steven, Diane, Lorraine. BEE, Poly. U., N.Y., 1951, MSEE, 1954; postgrad. Advanced Mgmt. Program, Harvard U., 1972. Engr., mgr. Wheeler Labs., Great Neck, N.Y., 1951-55, exec. v.p., dir., 1967-68, pres., dir., 1968-70; product line dir. advanced systems divsn. Marconi Aerospace Systems, Green Lawn, N.Y., 1970-72, v.p. quality assurance and logistics, 1973-75, v.p. quality assurance and customer svc., 1975-78, v.p. ops., 1978-84, v.p. engring., 1985-90, v.p. market planning, 1991, v.p. spl. projects, 1992-95, ret. v.p., 1996, dir. tech. mktg., 1996—; chmn. L.I. Forum for Tech., 1985-86; mem. corp. bd. Poly. U., 1988—. Contbr. articles to profl. jours. Pres., bd. dirs. Friends of L.I. Mus. Sci. and Tech., 1994-96; bd dirs. Huntington Arts Coun., 1994-96; mem. Pres.'s Adv. Com. on Indsl. Innovation, 1979. Named Fellow and Disting. Alumnus Poly. Inst., N.Y., 1986; recipient Engring. Mgr. of Yr. award IEEE/Engring. Mgmt. Soc., 1985. Fellow AAAS, IEEE (Centennial medal 1984, Haradem Pratt award 1995, exec. v.p. 1984, treas. 1985, pres. 1987, pres. IEEE Found. 1994—); mem. Sigma Xi, Eta Kappa Nu, Tau Beta Pi. Avocations: sailing, opera, piano. Home: 5 Brandy Rd Cold Spring Harbor NY 11724-2401 Office: Marconi Aerospace Systems Inc Advanced Systems Divsn Mail Sta 1-73 Greenlawn NY 11740

BACHMAN, SISTER JANICE, health care executive; b. Coshocton, Ohio, Oct. 25, 1945; d. Edward Michael and Kathryn Elizabeth (Norris) B. Student, Ohio Dominican Coll., 1963-67; BS in Pharmacy, Ohio State U., 1971; MBA in Mgmt., Xavier U., 1976; M in Christian Spirituality, Creighton U., 1989. Joined Dominican Sisters, 1963. Staff pharmacist St. George Hosp., Cin., 1971-73, dir. pharmacy svcs., 1973-76; instr. pharmacology and related courses Coll. Mt. St. Joseph, Cin., 1973-74; instr. pharmacology Sch. Nursing Bethesda Hosp., Cin., 1975; adminstrv. resident St. Joseph Hosp., Mt. Clemens, Mich., 1976-77, adminstrv. asst., 1977-78, asst. adminstr., 1978-79; corp. dir. religious programs St. Francis-St. George Hosp., Inc., Cin., 1979-80, asst. v.p. hosp. support svcs., 1980-82, v.p. therapeutic and diagnostic svcs., 1983-89; dir. exec. affairs Benedictine Health Sys., Inc., Duluth, Minn., 1989-90; vicaress Dominican Sisters St. Mary of the Springs, Columbus, Ohio, 1990-96. Editor: Guidelines for Developing an IV Admixture, 1976. Trustee Ohio Dominican Coll., 1980-96, mem. devel. com., 1984-94, physical facilities com., 1994-96; mem. radiologic tech. adv. bd. Xavier U., Cin., 1983-89; mem. MLT adv. bd. Coll. Mt. St. Joseph, 1983-85; trustee Program for Medically Underserved dba Health Moms and Babes, 1986-91, co-founder, chair, 1986-89; bd. dirs. Franciscan Health Sys. Cin., 1990-92; chmn. bd. dirs. Nazareth Towers, Columbus, 1990-94; bd. dirs. Dominican Acad., N.Y.C., 1990-95; trustee St. Mary of the Springs Montessori Sch., Columbus, 1990-95; trustee Milford (Ohio) Spiritual Ctr., 1993—, Ohio, vice chair, 1993-94, chair, 1994—; mem. fin. com. Dominican Leadership Conf., 1994-96; bd. dirs. Westwood Civic Assn., Cin., 1979-86, past sec., past 1st v.p., past pres.; mem. steering com. Cong. Neighborhood Groups, Cin., treas., 1981-84; mem. planning divsn. bd. Cmty. Chest and Coun., Cin., 1981-88, chair single parent task force study, 1983-85; mem. rev. bd. City of Cin. Commercial/Indsl. Revolving Loan Fund, 1982-84; bd. dirs. Cin. Area Chpt. ARC, 1982-89, chair nursing and health com., 1983-87, bd. exec. com., 1987-89; bd. dirs. SW Ohio Residences, Cin., 1983-89, vice chair, 1984-87, chair, 1987-89; trustee Providence Fund, Franciscan Sisters of Stella, Niagara, N.Y., 1996—, C.G. Jung Assn. Ctrl. Ohio, co-chair program com., 1996—; trustee Las Casas (Ministry to Cheyenne and Arapaho Native Ams.), Canton, Okla., 1996, treas., 1997—. Recipient Cmty. Leadership award United Appeal and Cmty. Chest, 1985. Fellow Am. Coll. Healthcare Execs.; mem. Nat. Assn. Treas. of Religious Insts. Avocations: swimming, cross-country skiing, biking. Office: St Mary of the Springs 2320 Airport Dr Columbus OH 43219-2098

BACHMAN, KENNETH LEROY, JR., lawyer; b. Washington, Aug. 24, 1943; s. Kenneth Leroy and Audrey Teresa (Torrence) B.; m. Sharon Abel, June 18, 1966; children—Laura Ann, Eric Kenneth. A.B. summa cum laude, Ohio U., 1965; J.D. cum laude, Harvard U., 1968. Bar: D.C. 1968, U.S. Ct. Appeals (D.C. cir.) 1971, U.S. Supreme Ct. 1981. Law clk. to judge U.S. Dist. Ct. So. Dist. N.Y., 1968-70; assoc. Cleary, Gottlieb, Steen & Hamilton, Washington, 1970-76, ptnr., 1976—. Mem. ABA. Contbg. editor Oil and Gas Price Regulation Analyst, 1978-83, Natural Gas Journal, 1983-85; contbr. articles to profl. jours. Home: 5332 Falmouth Rd Bethesda MD 20816-2915 Office: 1752 N St NW Washington DC 20036-2907

BACHMAN, LEONARD, physician, retired federal official; b. Balt., May 20, 1925; m. Sarah Jaffe; children: Emily, L. Joseph, Daniel, Jacob. BS, Franklin and Marshall Coll., 1946; MD, U. Md., 1949; MS (hon.), U. Pa., 1969; LHD (hon.), Pa. Coll. Podiatric Medicine, 1975, Hahnemann Med. Coll., 1977. Diplomate Am. Bd. Anesthesiology (assoc. examiner 1965). Asst. resident in anesthesiology U.S. Naval Hosps., Bethesda, Md. and Chelsea, Mass., 1950-52; resident Children's Med. Ctr., Boston, 1952-53; fellow in anesthesiology N.E. Deaconess Hosp., Boston, 1952-53; anesthesiologist, instr. anesthesiology, pharmacology and exptl. therapeutics Johns Hopkins U. Med. Sch., 1953-55; dir. div. anesthesiology Children's Hosp., Phila., 1955-72; dir. health svcs. Commonwealth of Pa., 1972-75, chmn. Gov.'s health care task force, 1971, sec. of health, 1975-79; dir. div. hosps. and clinics HEW, Washington, 1979-83; med. dir. NOAA, Washington, 1983-88; dir. med. affairs, Office Surgeon Gen. USPHS, Washington, 1988-90; dir. med. svcs. USPHS, 1990-94; ret. USPHS, Washington, 1994; asst. prof. anesthesiology U. Pa., 1955-61, assoc. prof., 1961-66, prof., 1966-72; vis. anesthesiologist VA Hosp., Loch Raven, Balt., 1953-55; cons. VA Hosp., Phila., 1961—; hon. vis. prof. U. Iowa, 1964, Einstein Coll. Medicine, N.Y.C., 1970; clin. prof. anesthesiology George Washington U. Sch. Medicine, 1982—. Campaign chmn. Delaware County Dem. Com., 1965; bd. dirs. Cen. Phila. Reform Dems., 1967, pres. 1968; chmn. Health Profls. for Humphrey/Muskie, 1968; mem. Urban Coalition Phila.; bd. dirs. Society Hill Civic Assn., 1968; active Boy Scouts Am. With USNR, 1943-46, lt. M.C., 1950-52. Fellow Am. Acad. Pediatrics, Am. Coll. Chest Physicians, Am. Coll. Anesthesiology; mem. Am. Soc. Anesthesiologists, Pa. Soc. Anesthesiologists (pres. 1968-69), Phila. Soc. Anesthesiologists (pres. 1965-67), AMA, Pa. Med. Soc., Balt. City Med. Soc., Phila. County Med. Soc., N.Y. Acad. Scis., Physiol. Soc. Phila., Sigma Xi. Home: 3830 Harrison St NW Washington DC 20015-1926

BACHMANN, BILL, photographer; b. Pa., Mar. 4, 1946; s. Ernest Edward and Helen May (Himler) B. BS, Roberts Wesleyan Coll., Rochester, N.Y., 1967; MBA, SUNY, Brockport, 1971; postgrad., U. London, U. Calif., Berkeley, Rochester Inst. Tech., U. Pitts., Ft. Lauderdale Art Inst. Freelance comml. and advt. photographer Miami, N.Y.C., Orlando, 1972—; worked in over 100 countries worldwide; instr. photography Triangle Inst., 1992, S.E. Ctr. for Creative Arts, Daytona, 1990—; dir. TV commls. and co. videos; vis. instr. photography at several colls. and univs.; guest numerous TV programs, 1978—; lectr. in field, 1980—. *One of the top five stock photographers in the world, Bachmann has reps marketing his photography in 25 countries. His work appears regularly in many international consumer magazines. Bachmann's commercial photography and television directing has won numerous Gold and Addy awards. He is the author of 3 books, 1 screenplay and many magazine articles. He has lectured to advertising and motivational seminars in many countries. Bachmann has traveled on assignment to over 100 countries on all the continents. His newest book, Introspective World, is a large coffee-table fine arts masterpiece.* Prin. works include Miami Herald, 1978-80, Fla. Tourism, 1982-, Sheraton Hotels, 1982-, Gen. Mills Restaurants, 1983-, Olive Garden, 1986-, Marriott Hotels, 1992-, Bahamas Tourism, Radisson Hotels, 1986-, Grosvenor Hotels, 1988-, Revlon, 1991—, Harris Corp., 1993—, Sea Escape Cruises, 1988—, Burger King, 1988—, Caribbean Travel & Life, 1990—, Fuji, 1990—, Nickelodeon, 1989—, Merv Griffin's Paradise Island, Bahamas, 1990—, Kodak Films, 1976—, McDonalds, 1987—, Stern Mag., 1987—, Regal Boats, 1990—, Renaissance Cruises, 1996—, Universal Studios, 1990—, Citibank VISA, 1990—, Delta Airlines, 1991—, Am. Showcase, 1991—, Creative Black Book, 1994—, Hilton Hotels Internat., 1992—, NuSkin, 1995—, Pizza Hut, 1996—, Grey Poupon, 1995—, Home Depot, 1996—, Whale Cay, 1997—, People Mag., 1998—, Pitcom, 1999; dir. TV commls. and videos, 1987—; author: Clicking the Shutter is the Easy Part, 1988, Introspective World, 1996, Welcome Back Berlin, 1990, Bali-Paradise in Indonesia, 1994, Shooting Figure Studies, 1990, Kathmandu, A Jewel Discovered, 1996, One Dream Too Many, 1989, Images of Women, 1997, Treasures of the Caribbean, 1992, China's Greatest Resource, It's Diverse People, 1997, Orlando-The City Beautiful, 1998; photographer 295-Day Kodak World Photo Tour, 1992-95, Photo Pro Mag., 1991—; photgraphed over 700 mag. covers. Bd. dirs. Big Bros.; active Vols. in Action, 1989—. Named Photographer of Yr. Fla. Peoples Choice Awards, 1987, Photographer of Yr. Asia, 1993; recipient Addy awards, 1976—. Mem. One Club (bd. dirs. 1988—), Sales and Mktg. Execs. (bd. dirs., officer), Am. Soc. Media Photographers N.Y., Orlando C. of C. (pres.' club 1983—), Cen. Fla. Photographers Assn. (v.p., bd. dirs. 1983—), Fla. Motion Pictures and TV Guild, Heathrow Club (social dir. 1986—), Rotary. Republican. Methodist. Avocations: snow skiing, tennis, golf, writing. Home and Office: PO Box 950833 Lake Mary FL 32795-0833

BACHMANN, JOHN WILLIAM, securities firm executive; b. Centralia, Ill., Nov. 16, 1938; s. George Adam and Helen (Johnston) B.; m. Katharine I. Butler; children: John C., Kristene Ellen Bachmann Dorcey. AB, Wabash Coll., 1960; MBA, Northwestern U., 1962; LLD (hon.), Wabash Coll., 1990. Researcher Edward Jones, St. Louis, 1962-63, investment rep., 1963-70, gen. ptnr., 1970-80, mng. ptnr., 1980—; bd. dirs. TWA. Trustee Wabash Coll., Crawfordsville, Ind., 1980—; chmn. bd. visitors Drucker Ctr. Claremont (Calif.) Grad. Sch., 1987—; past chmn., bd. dirs. Arts and Edn. Coun. Greater St. Louis; commr. St. Louis Art Mus.; chmn. St. Louis Symphony Soc. Mem. Nat. Assn. Securities Dealers (past dist. chmn.), Securities Industry Assn. (bd. dirs., chmn. 1976-79), Securities Industry Found. for Econ. Edn. (chmn. trustees 1988-92), Civic Progress, U.S. C. of C. (dir.), St. Louis Club, Bogey Club. Office: Edward Jones 12555 Manchester Rd Saint Louis MO 63131-3729

BACHMANN, RICHARD ARTHUR, oil company executive; b. Green Bay, Wis., Dec. 6, 1944; s. Richard Arthur and Anita Sidonia (Dohmeyer) B.; children: Richard A., Joseph E., Christina J.; m. Susan Dawn Minney, July 31, 1993. BBA, Wis. State U., 1967; MBA, U. Wis., 1968. Mgr. fgn. fin. Exxon Corp., N.Y.C., 1968-78; v.p., treas. Itel Corp., San Francisco, 1978-81; sr. v.p. fin. and adminstrn., chief fin. officer La. Land and Exploration Co., New Orleans, 1981-85, exec. v.p. fin. and adminstrn., chief fin. officer, 1985-97; pres., COO, 1995-97; pres., CEO, chmn. bd. Energy Ptnrs., Ltd., New Orleans, 1997—; also bd. dirs. La. Land and Exploration Co., New Orleans; bd. dirs. Univ. Health Care Sys. Gov. Com., Penn Va. Corp. Bd. dirs., mem. exec. com., sustaining membership com. chmn. New Orleans coun. Boy Scouts Am., 1984—, pres., mem. exec. bd., 1988-92, nat. bd. coun. fin. cabinet mem., chmn. supply com., 1990-92; bd. dirs. Audubon Park and Zool. Garden, Audubon Inst.-Aquarium of Ams., Covenant House, 1990—; bd. dirs., chmn. fin. oversight com. met. Arts Fund; bd. govs. Isadore Newman Sch., bd. dirs., 1990—; adv. bd. Summerbridge, 1989—. Office: Energy Partners Ltd 201 Saint Charles Ave Ste 3400 New Orleans LA 70170-1026

BACHMANN, WILLIAM THOMPSON, dermatologist; b. Orange, N.J., Mar. 21, 1940; s. George Kirsten and Agnes Mary (Cunningham) B.; m. Carolyn Emily Loeber, Dec. 28, 1961 (div. June 1971); children: John Kirsten, William Thompson; m. Judith Richmond, June 20, 1981; 1 stepchild, Julia Garriga. AB, Williams Coll., 1962; MD, Boston U., 1966. Diplomat Am. Bd. Internal Medicine, Am. Bd. Dermatology. Intern St. Francis Hosp., Hartford, Conn., 1966-67, resident, 1967-68; resident Yale New Haven (Conn.) Hosp., 1971-72, 72-74; dermatologist Westerly (R.I.) Hosp. Lt. comdr. USN, 1969-71. Fellow Am. Coll. Physicians, Am. Acad. Dermatology; mem. New England Dermatological Soc., R.I. Med. Soc., Yale Soc. Attendings in Dermatology (st. attending mem.), Alpha Omega Alpha. Avocations: boating, photography. Office: 39 East Ave Westerly RI 02891-3113

BACHMEYER, STEVEN ALLAN, secondary education educator; b. Queens, N.Y., Feb. 8, 1945; s. Harold Frederick and Dorothy (Blackstone) B.; m. Mary Louise Bachmeyer, June 18, 1968; children: Steven Adam, Melanie Hope. AA, Miami Dade C.C., 1966; BEd in Indsl. Arts Edn., U. Miami, 1969; MS in Computer Edn. Tech., Barry U., 1995. Cert. tech. edn. Tchr. indsl. arts Miami Springs (Fla.) Jr. High Sch., 1969-73, dept. chmn., 1972-73; tchr. indsl. arts Hialeah-Miami Lakes Sr. High Sch., Hialeah, Fla., 1973-86, chmn. graphic arts, architecture and engring. drafting dept., 1986; instr. architecture and engring. drafting, tech. studies and aerospace tech. South Dade Sr. High Sch., Homestead, Fla., 1988—; part-time dir. Camp Adventure, Black Mountain, N.C., 1984-86, dir., 1986-88; chmn. tech. edn. dept. South Dade Sr. High Sch., Homestead, Fla., 1991—; founder/exec. dir. Aerospace Edn. Alliance, 1997; dir. Tech. Concepts, Homestead, Fla., 1991—; instr. part-time dept. indsl. arts edn. U. Miami, Coral Gables, Fla., 1971-72; instr. part-time bldg. constrn. drawing and archtl. history dept. arch./bldg. constrn. Miami Dade C.C., 1980-84; writer curriculum framework aerospace tech. program Fla. State Dept. Edn., 1991; mem. equity com. South Dade Sr. H.S., 1989-90, mem. tchrs. as advisors steering com., 1989-91, mem. sch. based mgmt. team, 1990-91, mem. tech. com. for tech. edn. Fla. Dept. Edn., 1991, 92, 93, Fla. Tchr. Cert. Devel. Com., 1992-93; mem. state tech. com. Tech. Ed.; chmn. bd. Fla. Tech. Student Assn. and Found., Inc., 1993; demonstration tchr. Fla. Acad. Excellence in Teaching, Fla. Dept. Edn., 1993; part-time instr. Fla. Internat. Univ., 1996—; presenter blueprint workshop Fla. Dept. Edn., 1991, aerospace tech. curriculum project, Lakeland, Fla., 1993, aerospace tech. curriculum project Nat. Congress Aviation and Aerospace Edn., Orlando, Fla., 1993, Norfolk, Va., 1994, NASA Internat. Space Camp, Huntsville, Ala., 1993; workshop instr. Dade County Pub. Schs., 1993; adj. prof. dept. vocat./adult edn. U. South Fla., 1994, dept. vocat. edn., 1995; cons. in field. Author: Aerospace Technology Curriculum Project--Principles of Aeronautics, 1991-93, Technology in Action Project Series, 1994, Parachutes Yesterday, Today, Tomorrow, 1993, Up From Clay A Beginners Guide to R/C, Space-Science and Technology Series, 1996; author The World of Comms. visual media, 1972, The World of Comms. audio visual media, 1973, An Introduction to Comms. Careers, 1974. Asst. supt. Dade County Youth Fair, 1990-95; supt. aerospace tech. divsn. Dade County Youth Fair, 1997; waterfront dir. McGregor-Smith Scout Reservation, Inverness, Fla., 1981, program dir., 1982-83; cert. camp dir. Boy Scouts Am., cubmaster, scoutmaster, explorer advisor troop 124, Hollywood, Fla., 1980-86, scoutmaster troop 811, Old Fort, N.C., 1987-88; mem. sch. bd. Prince of Peace Luth. Ch./Sch. 2d lt. U.S. Army. Recipient Graphic Arts Tchr. Excellence award Kiwanis Club Miami, 1981, Tchr. Excellence award Dade County DAVACCE, 1990, Newsmast Honor award NASA, 1990, scholarship Fla. Assn. Ednl. Data Systems, 1991, Tchr. Excellence award Internat. Tech. Edn. Assn., Fla., 1993, Excellence in Aviation Edn. award Gen. Aviation Mfrs. Assn., 1993, Best Practice award Fla. Vocat. Assn., 1993, 94, Ednl. Profl. Excellence award Kelvin Found. Tech., 1994, Tandy Tech. scholar, 1993-94/nat. hon. mention, 2 nat. awards, 1997, 1 regional award, Regional Tchr. of the Yr., DCPS, Dade County, Fla., 1997, Janice M. Dwyer Aviation Edn. award ADMA, 1998, Christa McAuliffe award AFA/Nat. Aerospace Tchr. of the Yr., 1998, A. Scott Crossfield award Civil Air Patrol-Crown Cir., 1998. Mem. Am. Vocat. Assn., Fla. Aerospace Edn. Assn. (mem. exec. bd. 1993), Fla. Vocat. Assn. (presenter conf. 1991-94), Fla. Tech. Edn. Assn. (conf. presenter 1989-94, pres. region V 1989-91, bd. dirs. 1989-91, pres.-elect 1992, pres. 1993, Tchr. of Yr. finalist 1990, 1, 92, Tchr. of Yr. award 1993), Fla. Assn. Computers Edn., Dade County Tech. Edn. Assn., Internat. Tech. Edn. Assn. (presenter nat. conf. 1992, 93, 94, 95, scholarship 1992, Program Excellence award Fla. chpt. 1992, Tchr. Excellence award 1993), Internat. Soc. Tech. Edn., Tech. Student Assn. (event chmn. aerospace tech. nat. conf. 1991-95, Outstanding Advisor award Fla. chpt. 1990, chmn. adv. coun. 1990-92, dir. adv. tng. conf. 1990, presenter nat. conf. 1990-92, instr. profl. workshop 1992, state advisor Vocat. Student Orgn., 1993, region tchr. year, 1997), Aerospace Edn. Found., Assn. Ednl. Comm. and Tech. (divsn. interactive systems and computers), Am. Camping Assn. (advanced campcraft, tripmaster and campcraft instr. certs.), Am. Canoe Assn. (whitewater canoe instr.), Epsilon Pi Tau (pres. Alpha Omega chpt.). Democrat. Avocations: sailing, photography. Home: 1721 NW 11th Ave Homestead FL 33030-2943 Office: South Dade Sr High Sch 28401 SW 167th Ave Homestead FL 33030-2005

BACHOVE, JASON FROST, musician; b. L.A., Nov. 11, 1972; s. L. and J. (Free) B. B, Evergreen Coll., 1996. Promoter, distributer Planet Sun, 1993-97; with Blue Moon & Co., L.A., 1997—. author, performer numerous recordings. Office: Blue Moon & Co 10619 W Atlantic Blvd Ste 235 Coral Springs FL 33071-5610

BACHRACH, CHARLES LEWIS, advertising agency executive; b. N.Y.C., Feb. 22, 1946; s. Herbert and Lilla Clare (Blumberg) B.; m. Lois Susan

Davis, Sept. 12, 1968; 1 dau., Jennifer Leigh. B.S., Ithaca (N.Y.) Coll., 1968. Assoc. producer MPO Sports Co., N.Y.C., 1968-69; unit mgr. NBC, N.Y.C., 1969; with Ogilvy & Mather, Inc., N.Y.C., 1969—; sr. v.p. broadcast Ogilvy & Mather, Inc., 1978-83, dir. Network and Programming Dept; sr. v.p. network and programming Western Internat. Media, 1983-89, exec. v.p., 1989—; pres. Western Internat. Syndication, 1983—; sr. v.p., dir. network and program purchasing Rubin Postaer & Assocs., L.A., 1990-92, exec. v.p., dir. media and resources and programming, 1992—; vis. prof. Ithaca Coll. Sch. Communications; vis. lectr. New Sch.; guest lectr. UCLA, Calif. State, L.A., Marymount Coll.; guest commentator NPR, CNN, NBC. Contbr. articles to profl. publs. Judge Internat. Emmy Awards.; Lobbyist N.Y. State pvt. colls.; bd. dirs. Caption Ctr., 1992. Recipient Disting. Alumni award Ithaca Coll., 1980, Aid to Advt. Edn. award Am. Advt. Fedn., 1986, Media Maven award Advt. Age, 1996; named One of Top 100 Young People in Advt., 1985. Mem. AAAA (com. broadcast network and programming), TV Acad. Arts and Scis., L.A. Advt. Club (bd. dirs. 1989). Home: 3121 Dona Marta Dr Studio City CA 91604-4327 Office: Rubin Postaer and Assocs 1333 2d St Santa Monica CA 90401-1100

BACHRACH, EVE ELIZABETH, lawyer; b. Oakland, Calif., July 4, 1951; d. Howard Lloyd and Shirley B. AB cum laude, Boston U., 1972; JD with honors, George Washington U., 1976. Bar: D.C. 1976, U.S. Dist. Ct. D.C. 1976, U.S. Ct. Appeals (D.C. cir.) 1976. Assoc. Stein, Mitchell & Mezines, Washington, 1976-79; assoc. gen. counsel Cosmetic, Toiletry, and Fragrance Assn., Washington, 1979-85; v.p., assoc. gen. counsel, corp. sec., 1985-95; v.p., deputy gen. counsel, corp. sec. Nonprescription Drug Mfrs. Assn., Washington, 1995-98, sr. v.p., gen. counsel, sec., 1998—; guest lectr. Am. U., Washington, 1986—, George Washington Nat. Law Ctr., Washington, 1986—, Cath. U. Law Sch., 1988—. Contbr. numerous articles on food and drug law and advt. law. Vol. lawyer Legal Counsel for the Elderly, Washington, 1978—. Mem. ABA (food and drug com., antitrust sect., adminstrv. law sect.), D.C. Bar Assn., Fed. Bar Assn. (chmn. food and drug com. 1986-90), Food Drug Law Inst. (chmn. writing awards com. 1982-88, vice chmn. 1987-89, chmn. 1990, editl. adv. bd. Food Drug Law Jour., mem. adv. bd. 1998—). Avocations: classical pianist. Office: Nonprescription Drug Mfrs Assn 1150 Connecticut Ave NW Washington DC 20036-4104

BACHRACH, HOWARD L., biochemist; b. Faribault, Minn., May 21, 1920; s. Harry and Elizabeth (Panovitz) B.; m. Shirley F. Lichterman, June 13, 1943; children: Eve E., Harrison J. BA in Chemistry, U. Minn., 1942, PhD in Biochemistry, 1949. Research chemist synthetic rubber Jos. E. Seagram & Co., 1942; Research asst. explosives research lab. Nat. Def. Research Com. project Carnegie Inst. Tech., Pitts., 1942-45; research asst. U. Minn., Mpls., 1945-49; biochemist, foot-and-mouth disease mission USDA, Denmark, 1949-50; research biochemist virus lab. U. Calif-Berkeley, 1950-53; chief scientist, head biochem. and phys. investigation Plum Island Animal Disease Ctr., Greenport, N.Y., 1953-80, research chemist, advisor to dir., 1981-89, sci. collaborator, 1989—; charter mem. Sr. Exec. Svc. U.S. Govt., 1979; mem. viral and rickettsial grants subcom. Walter Reed Army Inst. Tsch., 1982-85; cons. Pan Am. Health Orgn., Brazil, 1981, Coop. State Res. Svcs. USDA, 1982-83, Report Rev. Com. NAS, 1984; contbr. reports to Office Tech. Assessment U.S. Congress, 1984-85, 88-89, cons. Nat. Cancer Inst., 1984-87, Tex. A&M U. Inst. Bioscis. and Techs., 1987-89; Theobald Smith lectr. Am. Soc. Microbiology, 1981. Contbr. 20 chpts. to books, more than 150 original articles to sci. publs. Recipient Naval Ordnance Devel. award, 1945, Cert. of Merit USDA, 1960, Disting. Svc. award USDA, 1982, U.S. Presdl. citation, 1965, U.S. Sr. Exec. Svc. award, 1980, Newcomb Cleveland prize AAAS, 1982, Nat. Award for Agrl. Excellence, 1983, Alexander von Humboldt award, 1983, Nat. Medal Sci., 1983, ISI Citation Classics Publ., 1986; named to USDA Agr. Sci. Hall of Fame, 1987. Fellow N.Y. Acad. Sci.; mem. Nat. Acad. Scis. U.S., Am. Coll. Veterinary Microbiologists (hon.), Am. Chem. Soc. (Kenneth A. Spencer medal 1983, 50 yr. mem. 1997), Am. Soc. Virology, Sigma Xi., Gamma Alpha, Phi Lambda Upsilon. Achievements include first purification and electron microscopic visualization of polio and foot-and-mouth disease viruses; subunit vaccines--protection of swine with a protein isolated from foot-and-mouth disease virus; reported first effective recombinant DNA cloned viral protein vaccine for use in animals or humans; described comparative molecular pathways of replication for all classes of animal and human viruses. Home: 355 Dayton Rd. P.O. Box 1054 Southold NY 11971-0932 also: 10220 Andover Coach Cir Apt G2 Lake Worth FL 33467-8137

BACHTEL, ANN ELIZABETH, educational consultant, researcher, educator; b. Winnipeg, Man., Can., Dec. 12, 1928; d. John Wills. and Margaret Agnes (Gray) Macleod; m. Richard Earl Bachtel, Dec. 19, 1947 (dec.); children: Margaret Ann, John Macleod, Bradley Wills; m. Louis Philip Nash, June 30, 1978 (div. 1987). AB, Occidental Coll., 1947; MA, Calif. State U., L.A., 1976; PhD, U. So. Calif., 1988. Cert. life tchr., adminstr., Calif. Elem. tchr. various pub. and pvt. schs., Calif., 1947-50, 64-77; dir. emergency sch. aid act program, spl. projects, spl. art State of Calif., 1977-80; leader, mem. program rev. team Calif. State Dept. Edn., 1981-85; cons. Pasadena Unified Sch. Dist., 1981-85; cons. Pasadena Unified Sch. Dist., 1981-86; tchg. asst., adj. prof. U. So. Calif.; cons., presenter in field. Editor: Arts for the Gifted and Talented, 1981; author Nat. Directory Programs for Artistically Gifted and Talented Students K-12; contbr. articles to profl. jours. Active legis. task forces; chair resource allocation com. City of Pasadena, 1982-90, Pasadena-Mishima (Japan) Sister Cities Internat. Com., 1983—; asst. chair Pasadena-Jarvenpaa, Finland, 1990-92, chair, 1992-95; asst. chair Pasadena-Mishima, 1996-97; active L.A. World Affairs Coun., Bonita Unified Sch. Dist. Curriculum Coun., 1990-93, Dist. Task Force Fine Arts, 1990-93, Dist. Task Force Tech., 1990-93, Dist. Handwriting Task Force, 1993, Pasadena Hist. Soc., Pasadena Philharm. Com., Womens Com. Pasadena Symphony Assn.; deacon Pasadena Presbyn. Ch., 1989-92, elder, 1997—. Emergency Sch. Aid Act grant, 1977-81; named to Bonita Unified Sch. Dist. Hall of Fame, 1990-91. Mem. World Coun. Gifted and Talented Children, Internat. Soc. Edn. Through Art, Nat. Art Educators Assn. (dels. assembly 1988-92), Clan MacLeod Soc. (bd. dirs. So. Calif. chpt.), Phi Delta Kappa, Kappa Delta Pi, Pi Lambda Theta (pres. L.A. chpt. 1991-95, nat. rsch. awards com. 1989-91, chair 1991-95, co-pres. region V 1993-97, Ella Victoria Dobbs Nat. Rsch. award 1989, Outstanding Pi Lambda Thetan in region V 1993-95), Assistance League Pasadena.

BACHULA, GARY R., federal official; b. Saginaw, Mich., Jan. 1, 1947; s. Joseph F. and Frieda P. Rexius; m. Jane D. Woodfin, Mar. 29, 1984; 1 child. AB cum laude, Harvard Coll., 1968; JD cum laude, Harvard U., 1973. Chief of staff Rep. Bob Traxler, 1975-86; chmn. Gov.'s Cabinet Coun. Human Investment State of Mich., 1987-90; v.p. Consortium Internat. Earth Sci. Info. Network, 1991-93; dep. under sec. tech. Tech. Adminstrn., Dept. Commerce, Washington, 1993-97, acting under sec. tech. Tech. Adminstrn., 1997—. With U.S. Army, 1968-70. Lutheran. Office: Tech Adminstrn 14th & Constitution Ave NW Washington DC 20230-0002

BACHUR, NICHOLAS ROBERT, SR., research physician; b. Balt., July 21, 1933. BA, Johns Hopkins U., 1954; MD, PhD, U. Md., 1961. Research asst. McCollum-Pratt Inst., Balt., 1951-55; research fellow dept. pediatrics U. Md. Sch. Medicine, Balt., 1955-60, intern dept. medicine, 1961-62; head sect. biochemistry Nat. Cancer Inst., Balt. Cancer Ctr., NIH, Balt., 1966-76, chief lab. clin. biochemistry, 1976-83; dir. rsch. U. Md. Cancer Ctr., Balt., 1983-89, acting dir., 1985-87; chmn. anthracycline coordination Nat. Cancer Inst., NIH, Bethesda, Md., 1976-85. Contbr. over 400 articles to profl. jours. and 15 chpts. to books. Mem. merit rev. bd. VA, Washington, 1986-90; bd. dirs. Md. div. Am. Cancer Soc., Balt., 1966—, Right to Vote, Balt., 1985—. Md. dir. surgeon USPHS, 1962-85. Tobacco Research fellow, 1955-56, Lederle Med. Research fellow, 1956-57, NIH Med. Research fellow, 1957-60. Mem. Am. Soc. Biochem. and Molecular Biology, Am. Soc. Pharmacol. and Exptl. Therapy, Am. Assn. Cancer Research (program com. 1980-81), Am. Soc. Clin. Oncology, Am. Soc. Clin. Pharmacol. and Therapy. Office: U Md Cancer Ctr 655 W Baltimore St Baltimore MD 21201-1509*

BACHUS, BENSON FLOYD, mechanical engineer, consultant; b. LeRoy, Kans., Aug. 10, 1917; s. Perry Claude and Eva Pearl (Benson) B.; m. Ruth Elizabeth Beck, May 31, 1942; children: Carol Jean Schueler, Bruce Floyd, Linda Ruth Gadway. Degree, Hemphill Diesel Sch., Chgo., 1937; student, Sterling Coll., 1937-39; BSME, Kans. State U., 1942; postgrad., Ohio State U., 1961, Stevens Inst., 1964; MBA, Creighton U., 1967. Registered profl. engr., Ariz., Ill., Nebr. Researcher, mech. engr. Naval Ordnance Rsch. Lab., Washington, 1942-43; jr. product engr. Western Electric Co., Inc., Chgo. and Eau Claire, Wis., 1944-46; sr. devel. engr. Western Electric Co., Inc., Chgo., 1946-56; devel. engr. Western Electric Co., Inc., Omaha, 1960-66; product engr. mgr. Century Electronics and Instruments, Inc., Tulsa, Okla., 1956-60; sr. staff engr. Western Electric Co. div. AT&T Techs., Phoenix, 1966-85; cons. in field, Phoenix, 1985—; chmn. energy conservation AT&T Techs., Inc., 1973-85; advisor to student engrs. Ariz. State U., 1967-87. Patentee in field (9). Trustee Village of Westchester (Ill.), 1949-53; sec.-treas. Westchester Broadview Water Commn., 1949-53; Sunday Sch. supr. Westchester Cmty. Ch., 1949-56; vol. campaign worker, precinct committeeman, capt. Phoenix Rep. Party, 1986—. Named Westchester Family of Yr., Westchester Cmty. Ch., 1952; recipient Centennial medal Am. Soc. Engrs., 1979, Recognition and Appreciation award Sterling Coll., 1996; inducted Kans. State U. Coll. Engring. Hall of Fame, 1995. Fellow ASME (state legis. coord. 1985-86, 88-93, treas. Ariz. sect. 1971-72, sec. 1972-73, vice chmn. 1973-74, chmn. 1974-75, 50-Yr. Membership award, President's Dedicated Svc., Devotion, Leadership, Performance award 1992, Dedicated Svc. award 1993); mem. TAPPI, NSPE (Engr. of Yr. award 1979), Soc. Profl. Engrs. (editor mag. 1972-86), Ariz. Coun. Engring. and Sci. Assn., Am. Security Coun., Soc. Plastics Engrs., Weoma Sci. Club (pres. 1963-66), Tel. Pioneers Am., Order of Engrs., Elks, Airstream Wally Byam Caravan Club Internat. Trailer Club. Avocations: woodworking, hiking, fishing, tennis, writing. Home and Office: 5229 N 43d St Phoenix AZ 85018-1671

BACHUS, SPENCER T., III, congressman, lawyer; b. Rocky Ridge, Ala., 1948; m. Linda; children: Warren, Stuart, Elliott, Candance, Lisa. BA, Auburn U., 1969; JD, U. Ala., 1972. Atty., 1972—, U.S. senator from Ala. 17th dist., 1982-83, U.S. rep. from Ala. 46th dist., 1983-86; sr. ptnr. Bachus, Dempsey, Carson, & Steed, 1992—; mem. 103rd-105th Congress from 6th Ala. dist., 1993—; mem. com. banking and fin. svcs., com. trans. and infrastructure, com. vets. affairs; vice chmn. Jefferson County Legis. Del. Mgr. Guy Hunt's Gubernatorial campaign, 1986; del. Rep. Nat. Conv., 1988; mem. Ala. Bd. Edn.; chmn. Ala. State Rep. Exec. Com., 1991. Recipient Commr's. merit award as Outstanding Rep. Ala. Dept. Human Resources, 1986, Henry M. Somerville award U. Ala. Office: US Ho of Reps 442 Cannon Bldg Washington DC 20515-0106*

BACHUS, WALTER OTIS, retired army general, former association executive; b. Grand Saline, Tex., Oct. 27, 1926; s. Walter Harry and Gladys Marie Bachus; m. Helen Singer, Dec. 12, 1946; children: Bruce, Leslie. BSCE, Tex. A&M U., 1950; M in Indsl. Engring., NYU, 1957; grad., Army War Coll., 1968; grad. Advanced Mgmt. Program, Harvard U., 1973. Registered profl. engr., Tex., D.C., Wash. Officer Corps Engrs. U.S. Army, 1950, advanced through grades to brig. gen.; ret., 1978; exec. dir. Soc. Am. Mil. Engrs., Alexandria, Va., 1978-93; ret. Soc. Am. Mil. Engrs., 1993. Decorated D.S.M., Legion of Merit, Bronze Star, Army Commendation medal; recipient Sec. of Def. Pub. Svc. medal. Christian Scientist. Home: 3808 Great Neck Ct Alexandria VA 22309-2634*

BACHYNSKI, MORREL PAUL, physicist; b. Bienfait, Sask., Can., July 19, 1930; s. Nick and Karolina (Bachynski) B.; m. Slava Krkovic, May 1959; children—Caroline Dawn, Jane Diane. B.Eng., U. Sask., 1952, M.Sc., 1953; Ph.D., McGill U., 1955; LLD (hon.), U. Waterloo, 1993; DSc (hon.), McGill U., 1994; LLD (hon.), Concordia U., 1997. Mem. sci. staff RCA Ltd., Montreal, Que., 1955-58; dir. microwave physics lab. RCA Ltd., 1958-65, dir. research, 1965-72, dir. research and devel. labs., 1972-75, v.p. research and devel., 1975-76; pres. MPB Technologies Inc., Pointe Claire, Que., 1976—; Scitec, 1974-75. Author: (with Johnston and Shkarofsky) The Particle Kinetics of Plasmas, 1968; contbr. Recipient David Sarnoff Gold medal, 1963, Prix Scientifique du Quebec, 1973, Can. Enterprise Devel. award, 1977, Prix PME Que., 1984, Medal of Achievement Can. Rsch. Mgmt. Assn., 1988, Can. awards for Business Excellence-Entrepreneurship, 1989, 90, Prix award Assn. Que. Dirs. Indsl. Rsch., 1991. Fellow IEEE, Am. Phys. Soc., Royal Soc. Can., Can. Aero. and Space Inst., Can. Acad. Engring.; mem. Can. Assn. Physicists (pres. 1968, medal of achievement 1984, Applied Physics medal 1995), Sci. Coun. Can., Engring. Inst. Can. (hon.). Home: 78 Thurlow Rd, Montreal, PQ Canada H3X 3G9 Office: MPB Techs Inc, 151 Hymus Blvd, Pointe Claire, PQ Canada H9R 1E9

BACIGALUPO, ANA MARIELLA, anthropology educator; b. Lima, Peru, Dec. 4, 1964; d. Antonio Andres and Ivonne Meriel (Gittins) B. MA, U. Catolica de Santiago, Chile, 1988; MA in Anthropology, UCLA, 1991, PhD in Anthropology, 1994. Rsch. assoc. Carleton U., Ottawa, Can., 1993-94; asst. prof. U. Bollivariana, Santiago, Chile, 1994-95, U. Catolica, Santiago, Chile, 1992-95, Whittier (Calif.) Coll., 1996-98; vis. asst. prof. Harvard U., Cambridge, Mass., 1998—; cons. in field. Contbr. articles to profl. jours. Rsch. grantee Internat. Fedn. U. Women, 1994, Fundacion Andes, Chile, 1995; rsch. fellow Centro Estudios Realidad Contemporaneo, Santiago, 1994-95, U. Catolica, Temuco, Chile, 1994-95, Women Studies Religion Program, Harvard U., 1998-99. Mem. Am. Anthropol. Assn., Am. Acad. Religion, Soc. Anthrop. Consciousness, Anthropology Religion, Assn. L.Am. Anthrop., Soc. Femnist Anthropology. Hme: 260 Beacon St Apt 2R Somerville MA 02143 Office: Harvard Div Sch 45 Fiarcos Ave Cambridge MA 02138

BACIGALUPO, CHARLES ANTHONY, brokerage company executive; b. Hempstead, N.Y., June 4, 1934; s. Charles R. and Eleanor (Ferrara) B.; m. Eileen B. Summers, Apr. 4, 1959; children: Tracy Ann, Thomas M., Scott S. BA, St. Lawrence U., 1956. Broker, analyst Hayden Stone & Co., N.Y.C., 1959-63; sr. v.p., dir. Legg Mason, Inc., Balt., 1981—, Legg Mason Wood Walker Inc., Balt., 1983; bd. dirs. Legg Mason Fund Adviser, Inc., Legg Mason Capital Mgmt., Inc. Balt., Legg Mason Wood Walker Realty Inc., Legg Mason Fin. Services. With AUS, 1957-59. Mem. Bond Club Balt., Washington Soc. Security Analysts. Republican. Roman Catholic. Office: Legg Mason Inc 100 Light St Ste B2 Baltimore MD 21202-1099

BACK, ROBERT WYATT, investment executive, pharmaceutical company executive, consultant; b. Omaha, Dec. 22, 1936; s. Albert Edward Jr. and Edith (Elliott) B.; m. Linaya Gail Hahn, Aug. 30, 1964; children: Christopher Frederick, Gregory Franklin. BA, Trinity Coll., 1958; postgrad. London Sch. Econs. and Polit. Sci., 1959-60, Harvard U., 1960-61; MA, Yale U., 1960. CLU, chartered fin. analyst, fin. cons. Head trader, reinsurance rep., security analyst Lincoln Nat. Life Ins. Co., Fort Wayne, Ind., 1964-69; sr. investment analyst Allstate Ins. Co., Northbrook, Ill., 1969-72; investment adv. acct. mgr. Brown Bros. Harriman & Co., Chgo., 1972-74; asst. v.p., investment analyst Harris Trust & Savs. Bank, 1974-82; v.p. instl. research Prescott Ball & Turben, 1982-83, Blunt, Ellis & Loewi, Inc., 1983-84; v.p. instl. equity sales Rodman & Renshaw, Inc., 1984-87; v.p. instnl. rsch. ins. Legg, Mason, Wood & Walker, Inc., 1987-89; mng. dir. instl. dept. J.E. Liss & Co., 1989-92; mng. dir. SNC Capital Mgmt., 1991—; mng. dir. Backfocus Cons. & Referrals, Wheaton, Ill., 1954—; mng. dir. investor pub. rels. CCR Assocs. Contbr. numerous articles to profl. jours. Mem. long-range planning com. Adlai Stevenson H.S., Prairie View, Ill., 1980-82; chmn. investments Ill. Police Pension Fund Assn., Chgo., 1985-87; pres. Buffalo Grove Police Pension Fund, 1973-90; deacon Presbyn. Ch; active Founding Coun. Nat. Edn. Access Fund, 1992; chmn. emeritus Biolipids Pharm. Corp., 1992; fund mgr. AIDS/HIV Select Fund, 1992—. Capt. USAFR, 1961-64. Woodrow Wilson fellow Yale U., 1958, English-Speaking Union fellow London Sch. Econs., 1959, Russian Research fellow Harvard U., 1960-61; subject of Superanalyst profile Crains Chgo. Bus., 1987. Fellow Fin. Analysts Fedn. (internat. del. 1974—), Assn. for Investment Mgmt. and Rsch.; mem. Inst. Chartered Fin. Analysts (sec., bd. dirs. Chgo. chpt. 1980-84), Am. Coll. CLUs and Chartered Fin. Cons. (bd. dirs. 1986-87), Yale Club Chgo. (bd. dirs. alumni assn. del. 1972—, coord. grad. and profl. alumni), Yale Club Fort Wayne (pres. 1964-69), Trinity Club (mem. exec. com. Chgo. chpt. 1987-90), Wheaton AM Rotary Club (charter, Paul Harris fellow 1995), Phi Beta Kappa, Pi Gamma Mu. Republican. Avocations: skiing, international travel. Home: 225 N Dorchester Ave Wheaton IL 60187-4707

BACKAS, JAMES JACOB, foundation administrator; b. Chgo., May 3, 1926; s. John and Ernestine (Harms) B.; m. Margot Wells Schutt, Dec. 1973; 1 dau., Amy Elizabeth. B.A., Mich. State U., 1950; postgrad., U. Mich., 1953-54; M.A., U. Iowa, 1960. Teaching fellow U. Iowa, Iowa City, 1958-59; research fellow U. Iowa, 1959-60; mgr. Coll. div. Doubleday & Co., N.Y.C., 1962-66; mktg. dir. publs. Brookings Instn., Washington, 1966-69; mng. editor Am. Mus. Digest, N.Y.C., 1969; exec. dir. Md. State Arts Council, 1972-76; spl. cons. to chmn. Nat. Endowment for Arts, 1976-78; exec. dir. Am. Arts Alliance, 1978-80; mgmt. cons. Washington, 1980-82; exec. dir. So. Arts Fedn., Atlanta, 1982-84, D.C. Commn. on Arts and Humanities, Washington, 1984-86, Md. State Arts Council, 1986—; music critic Washington Star, 1966-76; lectr. music history Peabody Conservatory, Balt., 1970-73; mem., co-chmn. music adv. panel Nat. Endowment Arts, 1982-87. Contbr. numerous articles on arts administration to profl. and govt. publs. Mem. adv. bd. ESEA Title III, Md., 1972-76; mem. policy com. for cultural affairs Johns Hopkins U., 1974-76; mem. exec. bd. Nat. Assembly State Arts Agy.; bd. dirs. Nat. Pub. Radio, Kennedy Ctr., Community Fedn. Greater Balt., Mid-Atlantic Arts Fedn., 1987—. Mem. Assn. Univ. Presses, AAUP, Music Critics Assn., Phi Mu Alpha. Club: National Press. Home: 3315 Q St NW Washington DC 20007-2717 Office: 601 N Howard St Baltimore MD 21201-4589

BACKER, MATTHIAS, JR., obstetrician-gynecologist; b. St. Louis, Dec. 19, 1926; s. Matthias Henry Sr. and Louise (Jokisch) B.; m. Laverne Elizabeth Knapp, June 4, 1949 (dec. Oct. 15, 1992); children: Mary Kathryn, Matt III, Marilyn Ann, Mary Lou, Donald, Robert, Edward, Mary Susan, Mary Carol, Mary Patrice, Joseph, Brian, Denis; m. Georgia Lynn Garrison, Apr. 28, 1997. MD, St. Louis U., 1950. Diplomate Am. Bd. Ob-Gyn. (examiner 1986-93), Nat. Bd. Med. Examiners. Intern Nat. Naval Med. Ctr., Bethesda, Md., 1950-51; resident in ob-gyn St. Louis U. Hosps., 1951-54; practice medicine specializing in ob-gyn St. Louis, 1954-85; instr. ob-gyn St. Louis U. Sch. Medicine, 1954-60, sr. instr., 1960-63, asst. clin. prof., 1963-66, assoc. clin. prof., 1966-72, clin. prof., 1972-85, prof. ob-gyn., chmn. dept., 1985-92, prof. and chmn. emeritus, 1992—, dir. ob-gyn outpatient clinic, 1967-69, mem. com. faculty appointments and promotions, 1972-81, mem. exec. com. faculty, 1972-76, mem. faculty affairs com., 1975-78, dir. residency program, 1985-92; staff cons. tchg., rsch, patient care Naval Med. Ctr., San Diego; adj. prof. ob-gyn. Uniformed Svc. Univ. of the Health Scis., 1994—; chief ob-gyn St. Joseph's Hosp., Kirkwood,, 1959-62, St. Anthony's, St. Louis, Hosp., 1966-69; pres. St. Louis U. Hosps. Med. Staff, 1968-69; mem. governing bd. St. Louis U. Hosps., 1969-70; pres. med. and dental staff St. Anthony's Med. Ctr., 1984-85; lectr. Archdiocesan PreCana Council, 1955-58, Archdiocesan Sch. Commn., 1969-72; pres. Backer & Probst Inc., St. Louis, 1967-85. Contbr. numerous articles to profl. jours. Bd. dirs. St. Louis chpt. Am. Cancer Soc., 1970-76, Blue Shield Mo. Med. Svc., 1970-80; lector Our Lady of Providence Ch., St. Louis, 1969-92; guardian ad litem for unborn Mo. Supreme Ct., 1971. Served to rear adm. M.C., USNR, 1944-84. Decorated Legion of Merit, Dept. Def. Superior Service medal; recipient Backer award St. Louis U. High Sch., 1983. Fellow ACS, ACOG (Adm. Robert A. Ross award Armed Forces dist. 1993); mem. AMA, Mo. Med. Assn., St. Louis Med. Soc., Soc. Mil. Surgeons U.S., Ctrl. Assn. Obstetricians and Gynecologists, St. Louis Gynecol. Soc. (pres. 1969-70), Naval Res. Assn. (past pres. Spirit of St. Louis chpt.). Roman Catholic. Home and Office: 3903 California St Unit 5 San Diego CA 92110-2157 also: 101 Flamingo Dr Saint Louis MO 63123-1007

BACKES, BETTY LOU, city clerk; b. Little Falls, Minn., Aug. 2, 1941; d. Sigfred Arthur and Ruth Wilhelmina (Gebert) Nelson; m. Melvin Robert Bell, Mar. 12, 1960 (div. Aug. 31, 1983); m. Ronald James Backes, June 1, 1985. Grad., Minn. Sch. of Bus., 1960; Grad. Mcpl. Clks. Inst., Iowa State U., 1977; student in records mgmt., U. N.D. Cert. mcpl. clk., Minn. Sec. No. Ordnance, Fridley, Minn., 1960-62; part-time sales assoc. Sears, Anoka, Minn., 1964-71; dep. city clk. City of Coon Rapids, Minn., 1971-74, city clk., 1974—. Staff liaison Coon Rapids Charter Commn., 1973—; bd. dirs. Coon Rapids Firefighters Relief Assn., 1980-85, Munici-Pals, 1976-82, chairperson, 1976, v.p., 1975, Intergovernmental Info. Sys. Adv. Coun., 1984-86; mem. Clerks's Election Adv. Bd. to Sec. of State, 1980-81. Recipient Woman of Achievement award for outstanding career achievements and contbns. to cmty. and church North Metro Bus. & Profl. Women's Club, 1981, 85, William Olsten award for Excellence in Records Mgmt.-Hon. Mention, Assn. Records Mgrs. & Adminstrs., 1981, 82. Mem. Internat. Inst. Mcpl. Clks. (conf. resource panelist 1977, membership co-chair 1977-79, nominating com. 1979, 81, 83, goals com. 1980, 84, 85, fed. legislation com. 1982, word processing com. 1983, Mpls. cons. spl. event com. co-chair 1983, pub. info. com. 1986, internat. com. 1991-92, 50th anniversary com. 1992-96, bd. dirs. 1984-89, Quill award 1989), Mcpl. Clks. & Fin. Officers Assn. of Minn. (certification com. 1976-81, region 4 v.p. 1976, treas. 1977, sec. 1978, dir. at large 1981, pres. 1980, publicity chair 1982, 90, 91), Assn. Records Mgrs. & Adminstrs., Nat. Alliance for Cmty. Media. Lutheran. Avocations: sewing, crafts, flower gardening. Home: 12191 Grouse St NW Apt 402 Coon Rapids MN 55448-1996 Office: City of Coon Rapids 11155 Robinson Dr NW Coon Rapids MN 55433-7453

BACKES, JOAN, artist; b. Milw., Jan. 31, 1950; d. Gilbert Frances and Jeanne (Vogt) B.; m. Thomas Deeg Sills, June 14, 1975; children: Joseph Backes Sills, Elizabeth Backes Sills. BA, U. Iowa, 1972; MA, U. Mo., 1983; MFA, Northwestern U., Evanston, Ill., 1985. Adj. asst. prof. U. Mo., Kansas City, 1985-88; instr. Kansas City Art Inst., 1988-94; vis. prof. U. Chile, Santiago, 1994-95; adj. asst. prof. Brown U., Providence, 1997—; resident artist Nova Scotia Coll. Art and Design, Halifax, Can., 1999; resident artist Aberdeen Art Mus., Scotland, 1986-87, Nat. Gallery, Reykjavik, Iceland, 1989, Edward Munch Studio Ekely, Olso, Norway, 1991, Yellowstone (Wyo.) Nat. Park, 1992; artist-in-residence Ragdale Found., 1998, 99, Hafnarborg Inst. Culture and Fine Art, 1998, 99. One-man shows include Aberdeen Art Mus., Scotland, 1987, Hafnarborg Art Mus., Iceland, 1991, 98, Dorry Gates Gallery, Kansas City, 1988, 90, 94, Virginia Lynch Gallery, Tiverton, R.I., 1995, Museo de Arte Contemporaneo, Santiago, Chile, Mus. Contemporary Art, Santiago, 1996, Virginia Lynch Gallery, Tiverton, R.I., 1995, 97, Centro Cultural Recoleta, Buenos Aires, 1997, James Baird Gallery, St. Johns, Newfoundland, 1998, Nova Scotia (Can.) Coll. Art and Design, 1999; exhibited in group shows at Chgo. Art Inst., 1990, Joslyn Art Mus., 1990, New Bedford (Mass.) Art Mus., 1997, Museo de Arte Contemporaneo, Santiago, Chile, 1998; represented in permanent collections at Milw. Art Mus., Nelson-Atkins Mus., Kansas City, Aberdeen Art Mus., Scotland, Hafnarborg Art Mus., Wustum Mus. Fine Arts, Racine, Wis., Joslyn Art Mus., Omaha, Nova Scotia Coll. Art and Design, Halifax, Can. Grantee Kans. Arts Commn./NEA, 1986, 92, Am.-Scandinavian Found., N.Y., 1991; Fulbright scholar 1994-95; recipient award Ragdale Found., 1998, 99. Mem. Coll. Art Assn., Kansas City Artists Coalition, Phi Kappa Phi. Avocations: swimming, hiking, travel. Office: PO Box 100 Seekonk MA 02771-0100

BACKHERMS, KATHRYN ANNE, parochial school educator; b. Cin., Aug. 19, 1955; d. Francis Walter and Mary Elizabeth (Healy) B. BA, Coll. Mount St. Joseph (Ohio), 1977; MusM, U. Cin., 1981. Cert. tchr., Ohio. Music specialist 1-8 St. Ursula Villa, Cin., 1977-79; choral music dir. McAuley High Sch., Cin., 1980-86; chairperson music dept. Coll. Mt. St. Joseph, 1986-89; music dir. St. Ursula Acad., Cin., 1989—; mem. rev. teams area high schs. North Cent. Assn., Cin., 1987-89; presenter Archdiocesan In-Svc. Day, Cin., 1988; adjudicator Ohio Fedn. Music Clubs, Cin., Ohio Fedn. Music Clubs Collegiate Solo Auditions, Columbus, 1989. Composer: (musicals) Musical, 1973, Just Like Me, 1975, Take A Chance, 1976, Nothing Can Stop Us Now, 1979, Heaven Help Us, 1983, Some Things Never Change, 1984, The Real Me, 1985, Something Special, 1997. Recipient Tchr. award Greater Cin. Found., 1984; profl. devel. grantee St. Ursula Acad., 1997. Mem. Music Educators Nat. Conf., Mu Phi Epsilon (v.p. Cin. alumnae chpt. 1992-94), Kappa Gamma Pi (treas. Cin. alumnae chpt. 1988-89). Avocations: composing, playing instruments, Volksmarching, pets, astronomy. Office: Saint Ursula Acad 1339 E Mcmillan St Cincinnati OH 45206-2180

BACKLIN, JIM, legislative staff member; b. Mpls., July 4, 1942. Grad., West Point, 1966. With mfg. dept. Procter & Gamble; plant mgr. Potlatch Corp., Scranton, Pa.; with Nat. Life Vt.; v.p. Anderson Products Inc.; chmn. Minn. Ronald Reagan Presdl. Campaign; with office intergovtl. affairs Sec. VA; chief of staff U.S. Rep. Roscoe G. Bartlett. Founder, organizer Cheboygan Mich. Hockey Assn.; active Harvest Christian Fellowship, Frederick, Md. Office: US Rep Roscoe G Bartlett 2412 Rayburn Ho Office Bldg Washington DC 20515

BACKMAN, ALAN GREGORY, health sciences technologist; b. Bklyn., Sept. 11, 1950; s. Gustav Adolf and Maude Therese (Darcy) B.; m. Mary Rose Vincent, Aug. 18, 1978; children: Gregory Alan, Lynsey Ann. Student, L.I. U., 1971, Thomas Edison Coll. Cert. respiratory therapy technician; cert. and registered cardiopulmonary technician; registered polysomnographic technologist. Respiratory technician St. Peter's Hosp., New Brunswick, N.J., 1969-71; biomed. engr. and dir. pulmonary Raritan Valley Hosp., Greenbrook, N.J., 1971-80; respiratory therapist NYU Hosp., N.Y.C., 1980-81; supr. pulmonary lab. Middlesex Gen. Hosp., New Brunswick, 1981-85; tech. dir., pulmonary diagnostics Deborah Heart and Lung Ctr., Browns Mills, N.J., 1985—; cons. Rutgers Occupational Health Div., New Brunswick, N.J., 1980—, Environ. Health Insp., Lakewood, N.J., 1988—, N.J. State Dept. Health, Trenton, 1987—, Health Adv. Bd., Washington, Amb. Med. Svcs., Marlton, N.J.; educator Rutgers U., Piscataway, N.J., 1981—, Environ. Orgnl. Safety Health Inst., Univ. Medicine and Dentistry N.J.; adj. prof. Sch. Allied Health Professions; rschr. air pollution and effects Deborah Heart and Lung Rsch. Ctr. Contbr. articles to profl. jours. Lector Mt. Virgin Ch., Middlesex, 1988-89; speaker's bur. Deborah Heart and Lung Ctr., 1985-88. With USAF, 1968-69. Recipient Contbr. award, Nat. Bd. Respiratory Care, Kans., 1987. Mem. Nat. Bd. Respiratory Care, Assn. Polysomnographic Tech., Am. Sleep Disorders Assn., Am. Inventors Soc., Am. Assn. Respiratory Care, Acad. Med. Arts and Scis. Democrat. Roman Catholic. Avocations: electronics, chemistry, woodworking, reading, physical fitness. Office: Deborah Heart and Lung Ctr 200 Trenton Rd Browns Mills NJ 08015-1799

BACKMAN, GERALD STEPHEN, lawyer; b. N.Y.C., Apr. 16, 1938; s. Morris and Marion (London) B.; m. Susan Pergament, Sept. 3, 1961 (dec. May 1978); children: Jonathan A., Kenneth S.; m. Barbara Fried Kaynes, Nov. 3, 1979; children: Jonathan J. Kaynes, Adam R. Kaynes. BA, U. Pa., 1959; LLBcum laude, Harvard U., 1962. Assoc. Weil, Gotshal & Manges LLP, N.Y.C., 1962-70, ptnr., 1970—; house counsel The Associated Merchandising Corp., N.Y.C., 1965-68; lectr. N.Y.U., 1973, Irving Trust Co., N.Y.C., 1981-88; mem. Blue Ribbon Commission on Audit Coms. of Nat. Assn. Corp. Dirs. Bd. dirs. Hewlett-East Rockaway (N.Y.) Jewish Ctr., 1976-97, chmn. legal com., 1974-85, sec., 1980-82; bd. dirs. 25 E. 86th St. Corp., N.Y.C., 1996-99. Mem. ABA, Am. Arbitration Assn. (arbitrator), N.Y. State Bar Assn. (trustee bus. law sect.), Assn. Bar N.Y.C. (commr. Blue Ribbon commn. on audit com.), Masons. Republican. Jewish. Avocations: golf, skiing, tennis, fishing. Home: 25 E 86th St Apt 9G New York NY 10028-0553 Office: Weil Gotshal & Manges LLP 767 5th Ave New York NY 10153

BACKMAN, ROBERT MARC, television and radio station executive; b. Phila., Jan. 13, 1949; s. Irving William and Beatrice (Belovsky) B.; m. Sara Lea Reed, Sept. 1, 1972; children: Marta, Lauren, Elizabeth. On-air personality WHAT/WWDB-FM, Phila., 1966-70; on-air personality, asst. program dir. WRCP-AM-FM, Phila., 1970-72; music dir. KTTS-AM-FM, Springfield, Mo., 1972; prodn. dir. WSGA-AM, Savannah, Ga., 1973; morning drive air personality KELI-AM, Tulsa, Okla., 1973-74; sales mgr. KBUL-AM, Wichita, Kans., 1974-77; gen. mgr. KTFX, Tulsa, 1977-81; group v.p. Katz Broadcasting Co., Atlanta, 1981-85; gen. mgr. WDJO-AM, WUBE-FM, Cin., 1986-89, WPPX-TV, Phila., 1995—. Co-author: Think Big! Event Marketing for Radio, 1995. Recipient Best of the Best award Nat. Assn. Broadcasters, 1984, Winner of Gavin award for Major Mktg. Sta., 1988, Winner of the Radio Billboard Air Personality award, County Radio, 1972, Winner of The Master Class Strategic award, The Rsch. Group. Office: WPPX 520 N Columbus Blvd Philadelphia PA 19123-4226

BACKSTEDT, ROSEANNE JOAN, artist; b. San Francisco, Dec. 15, 1941; d. Anthony and Tillie LaRocca; m. Lawrence Henry Backstedt, Aug. 9, 1964; 1 child, Simone Rose. Student, San Francisco Art Inst., 1960-64, U. Oreg., 1966-68, Aesthetic Realism Found., 1976—. One-woman shows include Sullivan County Mus., Hurleyville, N.Y., 1972, Hansen Gallery, N.Y.C., 1973-77, The Viewing Rm., N.Y.C., 1978, Noho Gallery, N.Y.C., 1987, Ceres Gallery, N.Y.C., 1991—; group shows include Elysian Art Gallery, San Francisco, 1962-64, Portland Art Mus., 1969, Terrain Gallery, N.Y.C., 1979-85, Ligoa Duncan Gallery, N.Y.C., 1980, Krasdale Food Corp., Bronx, 1989, 91, 94, Z Gallery, N.Y.C., 1991, 92, World Trade Ctr., N.Y.C., 1991, Triplex Gallery, N.Y.C., 1992, Snug Harbor Cultural Ctr., S.I., N.Y., 1992, Lincoln Ctr., N.Y.C., 1994, Cedco Calendars, 1994-97, JCB Internat. Co., N.Y.C., 1996, Univ. Luth Ch., Harvard Square, Mass., 1996, Mills Pond Ho., St. James, N.Y., 1997, Künstlerforum, Bonn, 1998, Orange County C.C., Middletown, N.Y., 1998, Soho 20 Gallery, N.Y.C., 1999, Kingsbourgh C.C., Bklyn., 1999; presenter ART TAlk, Aesthetic Realism Found., N.Y.C., 1998. Mem. Women's Caucus for Art Ct. Democrat. Roman Catholic. Office: Ceres Gallery 584 Broadway Rm 306 New York NY 10012-3271

BACKSTROM, WILLIAM M., JR., lawyer; b. Clarksdale, Miss., Nov. 26, 1954. BS, Miss. State U., 1976; JD, U. Miss., 1979; LLM in Taxation, NYU, 1980. Ptnr. Jones, Walker, Waechter, Poitevent, Carrere & Denegre, L.L.P., New Orleans; La. correspondent for "State Tax Notes", "State and Local Taxes Weekly". Contbr. articles to law jours. Mem. ABA (mem. taxation sect. 1980—, state and local tax com., co-author La. property tax chpt. Property Tax Handbook), La. State Bar Assn. (mem. tax. sect. chmn. 1993-94), Miss. State Bar (mem. tax sect.). Office: Jones Walker Waechter Poitevent Carrere & Denegre LLP 1st NBC Bldg 201 St Charles Ave New Orleans LA 70170-1000*

BACKUS, GEORGE EDWARD, theoretical geophysicist; b. Chgo., May 24, 1930; s. Milo Morlan and Dora Etta (Dare) B.; m. Elizabeth Evelyn Allen, Nov. 15, 1961 (div. 1971); children: Benjamin, Brian, Emily; m. Varda Esther Peller, Jan. 8, 1977. PhB, U. Chgo., 1947, BS in Math., 1948, MS in Math. and Physics, 1950, 53, PhD in Physics, 1956; D honoris causa, Inst. de Physique de Globe, Paris, 1995. Jr. mathematician Inst. for Air Weapons, Chgo., 1951-53; physicist Project Matterhorn, Princeton, N.J., 1957-58; asst. prof. math. MIT, Cambridge, 1958-60; assoc. prof. geophysics U. Calif. San Diego, La Jolla, 1960-62, prof. geophysics, 1962-94, rsch. prof. geophysics, 1994—; mem. vist. com. Institut de Physique du Globe de Paris, 1987; co-chmn. Internat. Working Group on Magnetic Field Satellites, 1983-90; chair acad. senate U. Calif., San Diego, 1992-93. Contbr. articles to profl. jours. Guggenheim Found. fellow, 1963, 71; Royal Soc. Arts fellow, London, 1970—. Fellow Royal Astron. Soc. (Gold medal 1986), Am. Geophys. Union (John Adam Fleming medal 1986); mem. NAS (com. on grants and fellowships Day Fund 1974-79, com. on sci. and pub. policy 1971-74), Académie des Sciences (France), Am. Acad. Arts and Scis., Am. Phys. Soc., Am. Math. Soc., Math. Assn. Am., Soc. for Indsl. and Applied Math., Seismol. Soc. Am. Avocations: skiing; swimming; bicycling; hiking; history. Office: U Calif Inst Geophysics and Planetary Physics La Jolla CA 92093

BACKUS, JOHN, computer scientist; b. Phila., Dec. 3, 1924; m. Una Stannard, 1968; children: Karen, Paula. BS, Columbia U., 1949, AM, 1950; D.Univ. (hon.), U. York, Eng., 1985; ScD (hon.), U. Ariz., 1988; Docteur honoris causa, Université de Nancy 1, France, 1989; ScD (hon.), Ind. U., 1992. Programmer IBM, N.Y.C., 1950-53, mgr. programming rsch., 1954-59; staff mem. IBM T.J. Watson Rsch. Ctr., Yorktown Heights, N.Y., 1959-63; IBM fellow IBM Rsch., Yorktown Heights and San Jose, Calif., 1963-91; mgr. functional programming IBM Almaden Rsch. Ctr., San Jose, 1980-91; cons., 1991—. Mgr. Incest Info. Bay Area, 1992—. With AUS, 1943-46. Recipient W. Wallace McDowell award IEEE, 1967; Nat. medal of Sci., 1975; Harold Pender award Moore Sch. Elec. Engring., U. Pa., 1983; Achievement award Indsl. Research Inst., Inc., 1983. Fellow Am. Acad. Arts and Scis.; mem. NAS, NAE (Charles Stark Draper prize 1993), Assn. Computing Machinery (Turing award 1977). Achievements include system design of IBM 704, Fortran programming lang., Backus-Naur Form Lang., function-level programming; mem. design group ALGOL 60 lang. E-mail: jbackus@jps.net. Home: 91 Saint Germain Ave San Francisco CA 94114-2129

BACKUS, JOHN CARLTON, JR., venture capitalist; b. Bloomington, Ind., Oct. 24, 1958; s. John Carlton and Nancy A. Backus; m. Margaret Ann Weiland, Sept. 8, 1990; children: John III, Ben. BA in Econs., Stanford U., 1981, MBA, 1984. Mgmt. cons. Bain & Co., Palo Alto, Calif., 1981-85; CFO Key Airlines, Las Vegas, Nev., 1985-86; v.p. corp. devel. WorldCorp, Herndon, Va., 1987-90; pres., CEO InteliData Techs., Herndon, 1990-98; mng. ptnr. Draper Atlantic Venture Fund, Reston, Va., 1999—; bd. dirs. InteliData Techs., World Airways, Herndon. Bd. dirs. No. Va. Tech. Coun., Herndon, 1998—; mem. Bus. Roundtable, McLean, Va., 1998—;mem. Greater Washington Area Bd. Trade, 1998—. Recipient # 1 Fastest Growing Tech. Co. Va., D&T Fast 50, 1997, Top 50 Fastest Growing Cos. in Va., 1998, top 500 Fastest Growing Cos. Nationally, 1997, 98. Avocations: golf, running, mechanical watches. Fax: (703) 757-9296. E-mail: backus@draperatlantic.com. Office: Draper Atlantic 11600 Sunrise ValleyDr Reston VA 20191

BACKUS, JOHN KING, former chemical company research administrator; b. Buffalo, May 22, 1925; s. Arthur Osgood and Lois V. (King) B.; m. Marjorie North, June 18, 1950; children: David King, Lois Victoria, Laura North Scott, Ruth Ellen Grillo. B.A. in Chemistry and Math., Hamilton Coll., 1947; M.S. in Phys. Chemistry, Cornell U., 1950, Ph.D., 1952. Research chemist Procter & Gamble Co., Cin., 1952-53; rsch. chemist, supr. Gen. Mills, Inc., Tonawanda, N.Y., 1953-61; rsch. specialist Mobay Corp., Pitts. (now Bayer Corp.), 1962-64, group leader, 1964-67, mgr. applications rsch., 1967-68, mgr. rsch. svcs., 1968-1990, ret.; participant profl. confs. Patentee in field (3); contbr. articles to tech. jours. Chmn. bd. dirs. Bach Choir Pitts., 1969-70; bd. dirs. Western Pa. Safety Council, 1975-90, mem. exec. com., 1983-90, chair safety and health conf., 1980; mem. Pitts. Concert Chorale, 1989—; mem. council First Lutheran Ch., Pitts., 1978-80, 84-87, 92-93, pres., 1979; mem. coun. southwestern Pa. synod Evang. Luth. Ch. in Am., 1992-97; co-pres. chpt. AFS Internat. Scholarships, 1972-75, host parent, 1969-70, 79; pres. High Sch. Parent-Faculty Assn., 1970-71; advisor Explorer Post, 1967-68; chair corp. sect. United Way Western Pa., 1981-82; organizer, dir. Bayer Choir, 1978-90. With U.S. Army, 1944-46. Mem. Am. Chem. Soc. (environ. improvement com. 1990-95, chairman elect Pitts. sect. 1992, chmn. 1993, dir. 1995—), N.Y. Acad. Scis., AAAS, Soc. Plastics Industry (chair tech. conf. of urethane div. 1977), Sigma Xi. Republican. Avocations: music; gardening; swimming. Home: 9441 Katherine Dr Allison Park PA 15101-2020

BACKUS, KEVIN MICHAEL, minister; b. Holyoke, Mass., Oct. 27, 1956; m. Sharon Diane Marshall, Aug. 16, 1980. BA in Bibl. Lit., Shelton Coll., Cape Canaveral, Fla., 1978; MDiv, Faith Theol. Sem., Elkins Park, Pa., 1982; STM, Whitefield Theol. Sem., 1995, PhD in Bibl. Counseling, 1997. Cert. tchr. Bible, history, and langs., cert. sch. adminstr.; ordained to ministry Bible Presbyn. Ch., 1982. Asst. pastor Armor Bible Presbyn. Ch., Orchard Park, N.Y., 1977; asst. pastor Bible Presbyn. Ch., Grand Island, N.Y., 1978-80, assoc. pastor, 1982-99; pastor, 1999—; stated supply pastor Calvary Bible Presbyn. Ch., Trenton, N.J., 1980-82; dir. devel. Faith Christian Sch., Collingswood, N.J., 1981-82; adminstr. Grand Island Christian Sch., 1986-92; adj. prof. Biblical counseling Western Ref. Sem., 1995—; dir. grad. Sch. biblican counseling Whitefield Theol. Sem., 1996—; pres. Internat. Christian Youth, Collingswood, 1982-86; stated clk. Bible Presbyn. Ch.-Gen. Synod, Grand Island, 1989-95, chmn. interchurch rels.,1 989—; bd. dirs. United Reformed News Svc. Staff editor Christian Observer, 1994—; contbr. articles to profl. jours. Fellow Nat. Assn. Nouthetic Counselors; mem. Presbyn. Missionary Union (coun. mem. 1989—, exec. mem. 1989—, v.p. 1991-95, pres. 1996-98, v.p. 1998—), N.Y. State Sunday Sch. Assn. (bd. dirs. 1994, cons. 1995). Office: Bible Presbyn Ch 1650 Love Rd Grand Island NY 14072-2311 *Two things I constantly underestimate in life: the depravity of man, and the grace of God. Thankfully sovereign grace is greater.*

BACKUS, ROBERT COBURN, biophysical chemist; b. Carroll, Iowa, Aug. 25, 1913; s. Roy Eugene and Ethel (Coburn) B.; m. Beverly Helen Torwelle, July 5, 1940; children: Byron Torwelle, Robley Dean. BS, Dakota Wesleyan U., 1937; MS in Biochemistry, U. Mich., 1944, PhD in Bacteriology/Immunology, 1951. Instr. field army sanitation, rsch. viral hepatitis Sch. Pub. Health (U.S. Army contracts), 1942-45; rschr. physics dept. U. Mich., Ann Arbor, 1946-50; rschr. Virus Lab. U. Calif., Berkeley, 1950-56; cons. rsch. grants, contracts Am. Cancer Soc., N.Y.C., 1957; rsch. grants adminstr. Nat. Cancer Inst.-NIH, Bethesda, Md., 1958-61, Nat. Inst. Allergy, Infectious Disease, NIH, Bethesda, Md., 1962-65; office of dir. NIH, Bethesda, Md., 1965-87; ret.; biophysicist U.S. Dept. Agrl. European Commn. Foot and Mouth Disease, Pirbright, Eng., 1951; staff Surgeon Gen.'s Ad Hoc Adv. Com. on Quarantine, Washington, 1967; staff HEW Tuskegee Syphilis Study Ad Hoc Adv. Panel, Washington, 1972-73; acting exec. sec. HEW Ethics Adv. Bd., 1978; bd. trustees Am. Type Culture Collection, 1962-68; mem. Civil Svc. Exam. Bd. for Health Scientist Adminstrn. Applicants, 1962-68. Contbr. articles to profl. jours. Mem. Electron Microscope Soc. Am. (bd. dirs. 1954-57), Sigma Xi (life). Achievements include electron microscopic counts of virus particles and determination of macromolecular weights; correlation of bacteriophage counts with infectivity; invention of field aligning capsule centrifugation; others. Home: 5305 Roosevelt St Bethesda MD 20814-1431

BACON, A(DELAIDE) SMOKI, public relations consultant, television host; b. Brookline, Mass., Jan. 29, 1928; d. Alfred Leon and Ruth Dorothy (Burns) Ginepra; m. Edwin Conant Bacon, May 11, 1957 (dec. July 1974); children: Brooks Conant, Hilary Conant; m. Richard Francis Concannon, Oct. 13, 1979. Student, Art Inst. Boston, 1947; grad., Jackson Von Ladau Sch. Design, Boston, 1951. Pub. rels. cons. Boston, 1968—; pres. Bacon-Concannon Assocs., Boston, 1979-95; dir. craftsmobiles Summerthing Program, Boston, 1968-73; dir. exhibits Citifair, Boston, 1974; dir. Victorian exhibits Bicentennial Boston 200, 1975, dir. spl. events, 1976; cons. spl. events. Inst. Contemporary Art, 1977-78, Boston Tea Party Ship, 1978-79; fundraiser Mass. Assn. Mental Health, 1979; dir. promotions Met. Ctr., 1979; coord. grand finale celebration Boston Jubilee 350, 1979-80; coord. Elliot Norton Awards, 1983; pub. rels. Dyansen Gallery, Boston, 1987-88, French Speaking League, 1987; cons. spl. events Jordan Marsh, 1987; fundraiser, pub. rels. Boston Philharmonic, 1988; coord. 30th anniversary celebration Charles Playhouse, 1988; fundraiser Elliot Norton Awards, 1989; coord. benefit New Eng. Premiere of film Glory Afro-Am. Mus., 1990; pub. rels. cons. Boston Chamber Music Soc., 1990; pub. rels. Paul Sorota Gallery of Fine Arts, 1990-91; fundraising cons. Internat. Inst., 1991; pub. rels., fundraiser Brookline H.S. Sesquicentennial Celebration, 1992-93; co-host radio show Celebrity Time, 1980—; co-host TV show On the Town; guest lectr. Boston U. Sch. Pub. Rels., 1979, ARC, 1987, Radcliffe Coll. 4'O'Clock Forums, 1989; contbg. editor Design Times Mag. Social calendar editor Boston Tab Newspaper, 1987-90; contbg. editor Design Times Mag.; columnist BeaconHill News. Candidate Dem. State Rep., Mass., 1980; Bastille Day chmn. French Libr. Boston, 1994—; local adv. com. Nat. Trust for Historic Preservation; bd. dirs. Boston Lit. Hour; host parents com. Harvard Coll.; bd. dirs. Mugar Libr., Spl. Collections, 1994—; vis. com. Mus. Fine Arts, Eqyptian Dept., 1994—; bd. trustees Boston Arts Festival, 1960-63; bd. dirs., treas. Samaritans, Boston, 1974-84; art auction chairperson WGBH-Pub. Radio-TV, Boston, 1969-70; bd. dirs. Urban League Ea. Mass., Boston, 1975-85; former mem. numerous civic coms. Recipient Woman of Great Achievement award Cambridge Young Women's Assn., 1991; named One of Boston's 100 Female Leaders, Boston Mag., 1980; Guest of Honor, Womens' City Club Ann. Dinner Dance, 1979. Democrat. Avocation: artistics graphics. Home: 9 Fairfield St Boston MA 02116-1601 Office: Bacon Concannon Assocs 94 Beacon St Boston MA 02108-3329

BACON, BENJAMIN B., title designer; b. Savannah, Ga., June 12, 1957; s. Leroy Nathaniel and Gracie Mae B. BA in Music magna cum laude, Fisk U., 1979; BS in Computer Sci., Elec. Engring. summa cum laude, Savannah State U., 1992. Rsch. asst. dept. chemistry Savannah State U., 1990-92; rschr./designer AT&T Bell Labs, Holmdel, N.J., 1990, Murray Hill, N.J., 1991; owner, artistic/ tech. designer Plane Space, Savannah, 1993—; math. tutor Ga. U. Sys., Savannah, 1994-97. author: Theoretical Foundations of Inertial Mass Acceleration, 1994; pioneer in field. Thomas J. Watson fellow The Watson Found., 1979, GTE Minority fellowship MIT, 1992. Mem. Phi Mu Alpha. Avocations: mathematics, rocketry, creative arts, astrophysics, cybernetics.

BACON, BRETT KERMIT, lawyer; b. Perry, Iowa, Aug. 8, 1947; s. Royden S. and Aldeen A. (Zuker) B.; m. Bonnie Jeanne Hall; children: Jeffrey Brett, Scott Michael. BA, U. Dubuque, 1969; JD, Northwestern U., 1972. Bar: Ohio 1972, U.S. Ct. Appeals (6th cir.) 1972, U.S. Supreme Ct. 1980. Assoc., Thompson, Hine & Flory, Cleve., 1972-80, ptnr., 1980—; speaker in field. Author: Computer Law, 1982, 1984. V.p. profl. sect. United Way, Cleve., 1982-86; pres. Shaker Heights Youth Ctr., Inc., Ohio, 1984-86; elder Ch. of Western Res., 1996—. Mem. Fedn. Ins. and Corp. Counsel, Bar Assn. Greater Cleve., Cleve. Play House Club (officer 1986-94, pres. 1991-93, pres. men's com. 1993-96), Pepper Pike Civic League (trustee and treas. 1994-97). Home: 33076 Woodleigh Rd Cleveland OH 44124-5257 Office: Thompson Hine & Flory 3900 Key Ctr 127 Public Sq Cleveland OH 44114-1216

BACON, BRUCE RAYMOND, physician; b. Amherst, Ohio, Nov. 7, 1949; s. Raymond Clifford and Cathryn E. (Fowell) B.; m. Joan Laurie Benson, June 26, 1971; children: Jeffrey Dale, Laurie Katherine. BA in chem., Coll. Wooster, 1971; MD, Case Western Reserve U., 1975. Diplomate Am. Bd. Internal Medicine and Gastroenterology. Asst. prof. medicine Case Western Reserve U., Cleve., 1982-87, assoc. prof. medicine, 1987-88; assoc. prof. medicine, chief gastroenterology sect. La. State U., Shreveport, 1988-90; prof. internal medicine, dir. gastroenterology divsn. St. Louis U. Sch. Medicine, St.Louis, 1990—; chair subspecialty bd. gasteroenterology Am. Bd. Internal Medicine, 1999—. Co-author: Essentials of Clinical Hepatology, 1993; co-editor: Liver Disease: Diagnosis and Management, 1999; contbr. numerous articles to profl. jours. Fellow Am. Coll. Physicians, Am. Coll. Gastroenterology, Am. Soc. Clin. Investigation. Presbyterian. Avocation: photography. Office: St Louis U Health Sci Ctr 3635 Vista Ave PO Box 15250 Saint Louis MO 63110-0250

BACON, DAVID WALTER, chemical engineering educator; b. Peterborough, Ont., Can., Sept. 12, 1935; s. Arthur and Eleanor (Bothwell) B.; m. Lucille Ann Parks, July 6, 1963 (wid. Aug. 1998); children: Ann Marie, David Eric. B.A.Sc., U. Toronto, Can., 1957; M.S., U. Wis., 1962, Ph.D., 1965. Registered profl. engr., Ont., Can. Computations analyst Canadian Gen. Elect. Co., Peterborough, 1957-60; research group leader Du Pont Can. Inc., Kingston, Ont., 1965-67; assoc. prof. chem. engring. Queen's U., Kingston, Ont., 1968-73, prof., 1973—; dean applied sci. Queen's U., Kingston, 1980-90, acting head chem. engring., 1996-97; cons. N.Am. Mfg., 1997—. Contbr. book chpts., articles to profl. jours. Bd. dirs. Kingston Gen. Hosp., 1983-85. Recipient Excellence in Teaching award Ont. Confdn. U. Faculty Assns., 1978. Fellow Am. Statis. Assn., Can. Soc. Chem. Engring., Chem. Inst. Can.; mem. Statis Soc. Can., Am. Soc. Quality Control. Home: RR 1, Picton, ON Canada K0K 2T0 Office: Queen's Univ, Dept Chem Engring, Kingston, ON Canada K7L 3N6

BACON, DIANA HOLFORD, hydrologist, researcher; b. Fairfax, Va., Aug. 4, 1961; d. Donald Lloyd and Eunice Stunkard (Smith) Holford; m. John Anthony Bacon, May 22, 1993; 1 child, Evan Jeffrey. BS in Geology, George Mason U., 1983; MS in Hydrology, N.Mex. Inst. of Mining/Tech., 1986; PhD in Geology, Wash. State U., 1997. Sr. rsch. scientist Pacific N.W. Nat. Lab., Richland, Wash., 1986—. Contbr. articles to profl. jours. Mem. Am. Geophys. Union, Geol. Soc. of Am. E-mail: diana.bacon@pnl.gov. Office: Pacific NW Nat Lab 3200 Q Ave Richland WA 99352

BACON, DONALD CONRAD, author, editor; b. Jacksonville, Fla., Jan. 15, 1935; s. Francis Herbert and Myrtis Ann (Gunter) B.; m. Barbara Lee Barnwell, June 22, 1957; children—Elizabeth, Jennifer (dec.). B.S. in Journalism, U. Fla., 1957. Staff writer Wall St. Jour., 1957-61; Congl. fellow, 1961-62; staff writer Washington Star, 1962-63; successively Congl. corr., White House corr., sr. corr. and columnist Newhouse News Service, 1963-75; asso. editor U.S. News & World Report mag., Washington, 1975-79, sr. editor, 1979-81, asst. mng. editor, 1981-88; sr. editor Nation's Business, 1988-89; project dir. Ency. of U.S. Congress, Washington, 1989-95; pres. Fund for the Study of Congress, 1989—. Author: Congress and You, 1969; co-author: The New Millionaires, 1961, Rayburn-A Biography, 1987 (Best Biography award Tex. Hist. Commn. 1987, Best Book award Washingtonian mag. 1987); co-editor: Encyclopedia of the United States Congress, 1995 (Best Reference Source Libr. Jour., 1995). Recipient (with others) Loeb award U. Conn., 1961; award for excellence in journalism Lincoln U., Jefferson City, Mo., 1977. Mem. Cosmos Club (Washington). Home: 3809 East-West Hwy Chevy Chase MD 20815-5918

BACON, EDMUND NORWOOD, city planner; b. Phila., May 2, 1910; s. Ellis W. and Helen (Comly) B.; m. Ruth Holmes, Sept. 16, 1938 (dec. May 1991); children: Karin Ellis, Elinor Ruth, Hilda Holmes, Michael Comly, Kira, Kevin Norwood. B.Arch., Cornell U., 1932. Archtl. designer Shanghai, China, 1934; with W. Pope Barney, architect, Phila., 1935; supr. city planning Inst. Research and Planning, Flint, Mich., 1937-39; mng. dir. Phila. Housing Assn., 1940-43; co-designer Better Phila. Exbn.; also sr. land planner Phila. City Planning Commn., 1946-49, exec. dir., 1949-70, also devel. coordinator, 1968-70; v.p. design devel. Mondev Internat. Ltd., 1972-87; prof. adviser in Franklin D. Roosevelt Meml. Competition, 1959; adj. prof. U. Pa., 1950-87. Author: Design of Cities, 1967, rev. edit., 1974; prod.: Understanding Cities film series Rome: Impact of an Idea, Paris: Living Space, John Nash and London, The American Urban Experience, The City of the Future, 1983. Mem. Pres.'s Citizen's Adv. Com. Recreation and Natural Beauty, 1966-69; Trustee Am. Acad. in Rome, 1965-76. Recipient Art Alliance Phila. medal achievement, 1961, Man of Yr. award City Bus. Club Phila., 1962, Brown medal award Franklin Inst., 1962, R.S. Reynolds award for community architecture, 1976, Fairmount Park Art Assn. medal of honor, 1976, Gold medal Royal Instn. Chartered Surveyors, 1974, Chgo. Archtl. award, 1989, Sir Patrick Abercrombie prize Internat. Union Architects, 1990, Planning Pioneer award Am. Inst. Cert. Planners, 1993; Ford Found. travel fellow, 1959; Rockefeller fellow, 1963; Nat. Endowment for the Arts Disting. Designer fellow, 1987, emeritus fellow Urban Land Inst., 1989, Plym disting. professorship in architecture U. Ill. Fellow AIA (medal 1976), Am. Inst. Planners (Distinguished Service award 1971, Phila. award 1983, Penn Club award 1984). Address: 2117 Locust St Philadelphia PA 19103-4802

BACON, ELINOR R., goverment agency administrator; b. Phila., July 30, 1941. BA, New Sch. for Social Rsch., 1964; MA in Chinese Studies, U. Calif., Berkeley, 1967. Insp., adminstr. of rehab. City of Balt. Dept. Housing and Comml. Devel., 1974-80; with office of urban revitalization Dept. HUD, Washington, 1980-82; dir. commn. devel. Johns Hopkins Hosp., Balt., 1982-85; pres. Bacon & Co., Balt., 1985-97; dep. asst. sec. for pub. housing investments Dept. HUD, Washington, 1997—. Office: Dept HUD 451 7th St SW Rm 4138 Washington DC 20410-0001

BACON, ELIZABETH MORROW, librarian, writer, editor, educator; b. L.A., Sept. 15, 1914; d. James Edwin and Elizabeth Margaret (Hodenpyl) Morrow; m. George Richards Bacon, Sept. 7, 1939 (div. June 1963); children: David Nathaniel, Daniel Carl. BA, Bryn Mawr Coll., 1935; MLS, U. Calif., Berkeley, 1958. Children's book editor various publishing firms, N.Y.C., 1935-52; ctrl. children's svcs. librarian Contra Costa County Libr., Pleasant Hill, Calif., 1959-70; dir. children's svcs. Solano County Libr., Vallejo, Calif., 1970-78; lectr., Sch. of Libr. and Info. Studies U. Calif., Berkeley, 1978-84; lectr. extension classes Calif. State U. Sonoma, Solano Cmty. Coll., U. Calif. Berkeley, 1970-82. Author: See Through the Sea, 1955, See Up the Mountain, 1958, Jewish Holidays, 1967, A Great Miracle, 1968, People at the Edge of the World, 1991; editor: How Much Truth Do We Tell the Children?, 1988; contbr. articles and book revs. to profl. jours. Mem. exec. com. Friends Com. on Legis., Sacramento, Calif., 1974—; mem. adv. com. Criminal Justice Project, Am. Friends Svc. Com., Oakland, Calif., 1994—; vol. organizer Am. Fedn. Tchrs. AFL-CIO, Berkeley, 1979-86. Recipient spl. recognition Bay Area Storytelling Festival, Berkeley, 1994, Tribute of a Lifetime Com. of Correspondence, San Francisco, 1994. Mem. Assn. Children's Librarians (book rev. chair 1971), Soc. Children's Book Writers (spkr. 1977), Calif. Libr. Assn. (various coms. 1968-78). Mem. Soc. of Friends. Avocations: travel, bird watching, needlepoint, archeology. Home: 1320 Addison St Apt C-232 Berkeley CA 94702-1738

BACON, GEORGE EDGAR, pediatrician, educator; b. N.Y.C., Apr. 13, 1932; s. Edgar and Margaret Priscilla (Anderson) B.; m. Grace Elizabeth Graham, June 30, 1956; children: Nancy, George, John. BA, Wesleyan U., 1953; MD, Duke U., 1957; MS in Pharmacology, U. Mich., 1967. Diplomate Am. Bd. Pediatrics, subsplty. Bd. Pediatric Endocrinology. Intern in pediatrics Duke Hosp., Durham, N.C., 1957-58; resident in pediatrics Columbia-Presbyn. Med. Ctr., N.Y.C., 1961-63; instr. U. Mich., Ann Arbor, 1963, asst. prof., 1968, assoc. prof., 1971, prof. pediatrics, 1974-86, prof. emeritus, 1986—, chief pediatric endocrinology svc., dept. pediatrics, 1970-83, dir. house officer programs, dept. pediatrics, 1981-86, assoc. chmn. dept. pediatrics, 1983-86, mem. senate assembly, 1978-80; vice chmn. dir.'s adv. coun. Univ. Hosp., Ann Arbor, 1981-82; prof. pediatrics Tex. Tech U., Lubbock, 1986-89, chmn. dept., 1986-89, chmn. med. practice income plan,

1989; chief staff pediatrics Lubbock Gen. Hosp., 1986-89; dir. med. edn. and rsch. Butterworth Hosp., Grand Rapids, Mich., 1990-91, med. dir. dept. pediatrics, 1991-94; prof. pediatrics Mich. State U., East Lansing, 1990-94; pediatric endocrinologist Univ. Mich. Hosp., Ann Arbor, 1995—, Detroit Medical Ctr., Southfield, Mich., 1996—; coord. profl. svc. C.S. Mott Children's Hosp., 1973-83, mem. exec. com. for clin. affairs, 1975-76, 77-79, assoc. vice chmn. med. staff, 1978-79; chmn. exec. com. Women's Hosp., Holden Hosp., Ann Arbor, 1973-82. Author: A Practical Approach to Pediatric Endocrinology, 1975, 3d edit., 1990; contbr. articles to profl. jours. Capt. U.S. Army, 1958-61. Fellow Am. Acad. Pediatrics (treas. Mich. chpt. 1983-86, alt.-at-large 1995—, coun. Tex. chpt. 1986-89); mem. Am. Pediatric Soc., Pediatric Endocrine Soc. Home: 3911 Waldenwood Dr Ann Arbor MI 48105-3008 Office: U Mich Med Ctr PO Box 718 Ann Arbor MI 48109-0718

BACON, GEORGE HUGHES, JR., systems analyst, consultant; b. Phila., Mar. 4, 1935; s. George Hughes Sr. and Alice Olive (Campbell); divorced; children: Christopher Scott, Melissa Anne Hinkle. *Geneological studies have traced Mr. Bacon's parental line to Samuel Bacon, married in 1797, and the maternal line to Archibald Campbell, born in 1795. Great Grandfather Joseph Cornet taught in Flandreau, Territory of Dakota, was a civil war veteran, and served for a short time as principal of the Jenkintown (PA) schools.* BA in English Lit. and Music, Temple U., 1957; MS in Ednl. Adminstrn., U. Pa., 1968. Cert. info. scis., tchr. Computer programmer 1st Pa. Bank, Phila., 1960-62; tchr. Bucks County, Pa., 1962-72; assoc. dir. Kranzley and Co., Cherry Hill, N.J., 1973-74; computer programmer Phila. Nat. Bank, 1975-77; cons. Sci. and Computer Tech. Inc., Malvern, Pa., 1978-79; lead systems analyst Ednl. Testing Svc., Princeton, N.J., 1979-86; cons. in field, 1986—; cons., lectr. computer literacy and software Abington (Pa.) Pub. Libr., 1983-84, Jenkintown (Pa.) Music Sch., 1984, Fudan U., Shanghai, China, 1985; invited lectr., sr. tech. advisor UN Devel. Program Jao Tong U., Shanghai, 1988. Vol. aide Mercer County Geriatric Unit, Lawrenceville, N.J., 1986, Holy Redeemer Hosp., Meadowbrook, Pa., 1988-98, Rydal Park Retirement Home, 1988-98; cons. Abington Sch. Bd., 1989—; tutor Abington Pub. Libr. Literacy Project, 1988; mem. headmaster's coun. Am. Boychoir, Princeton, 1987, Abington Presbyn. Ch.; Friend, Princeton U. Mem. Temple U. Coll. Arts and Scis. Alumni Assn., U. Pa. Grad. Sch. Edn. Alumni Assn., Phila. Orch. Assn. Avocations: theater, concerts, piano, reading, walking. Home: 1515 The Fairway #425 Rydal PA 19046

BACON, JENNIFER GILLE, lawyer; b. Kansas City, Kansas, Dec. 26, 1949. BA with honors, U. Kansas, 1971, JD, 1976; MA, Ohio State U., 1973. Bar: Mo. Ptnr. Shughart, Thompson & Kilroy, Kansas City, Mo. Contbr. articles to profl. jours. Mem. ABA, Kansas City Metro. Bar Assn., Lawyers Assn. Kansas City. Office: Shughart Thompson & Kilroy 12 Wyandotte Plz 120 W 12th St Ste 1500 Kansas City MO 64105-1929*

BACON, KENNETH H., federal agency administrator, editor, journalist; b. Bronxville, N.Y., Nov. 21, 1944; s. Theodore S. and Sarah (Hogate) B.; m. Darcy; children: Katharine, Sarah. BA in English, Amherst Coll., 1966; MS in Journalism, MBA, Columbia U., 1968. Enlisted civil affairs unit U.S. Army Reserve, 1968-74; legis. asst. Sen. Thomas J. McIntyre, New Hampshire, 1968-69; various editl. pos. Wall Street Jour., 1969-94; apptd. asst. to Sec. of Defense for pub. affairs, 1994—; asst. Sec. Defl, 1996—. Office: Dept of Defense Public Affairs 1400 Defense Pentagon Washington DC 20301-1400*

BACON, KEVIN, actor; b. Phila., July 8, 1958; m. Kyra Sedgwick; 2 children: Travis and Sosie Ruth. Actor: (off-Broadway debut) Getting Out, Marymount Manhattan Theatre, 1978, (Broadway debut) Slab Boys, Playhouse Theatre, 1983, other stage prodns. include Glad Tidyings, 1979-80, Mary Barnes, 1980, Album, 1980, Forty-Deuce, 1981, Flux, 1982, Poor Little Lambs, 1982, Men Without Dates, 1985, Loot, 1986, (feature films) National Lampoon's Animal House, 1978, Starting Over, 1979, Hero at Large, 1980, Friday the 13th, 1980, Only When I Laugh, 1981, Diner, 1982, Footloose, 1984, Quicksilver, 1985, White Water Summer, 1987, Planes, Trains and Automobiles, End of the Line, 1988, She's Having a Baby, 1988, Criminal Law, 1989, The Big Picture, 1989, Tremors, 1990, Flatliners, 1990, Queens Logic, 1991, He Said/She Said, 1991, Pyrates, 1991, JFK, 1992, A Few Good Men, 1992, The Air Up There, 1994, The River Wild, 1994, Murder in the First, 1995, Apollo 13, 1995, Sleepers, 1996, Telling Lies in America, 1997, Picture Perfect, 1997, Digging to China, 1997, , My Dog Skip, 1999, The Hollow Man, 1999, Stir of Echoes, 1999; (TV episodes) The Guiding Light, Search for Tomorrow, (TV movies) The Gift, 1979, Enormous Changes at the Last Minute, 1982, The Demon Murder Case, 1983, Frasier (voice), Mad About You, 1992, Happy Birthday Elizabeth: A Celebration of Life, 1997, (TV spl.) Mister Roberts, 1984, (video) Destination Anywhere, 1997; actor, prodr. The Wild Things, 1998; actor, dir; Losing Chase, 1996. Office: William Morris Agy Frank Frattaroli 9830 Wilshire Blvd Beverly Hills CA 90212*

BACON, LEONARD ANTHONY, accounting educator; b. Santa Fe, June 10, 1931; s. Manuel R. and Maria (Chavez) Baca; m. Patricia Balzaretti; children—Bernadine M., Jerry A., Tiffany A. B.E., U. Nebr.-Omaha, 1965; M.B.A., U. of the Americas, Mexico City, 1969; Ph.D., U. Miss., 1971. CPA; cert. mgmt. acct., internal auditor. Commd. 2d lt. U.S. Army, 1951, advanced through grades to maj., 1964, served fin. and acctg. officer mainly Korea, Vietnam; ret., 1966; asst. prof. Delta State U., Cleveland, Miss., 1971-76; assoc. prof. West Tex. State U., Canyon, 1976-79; prof. acctg. Calif. State U., Bakersfield, 1979—; cons. Kershen Co. (now Atlantic Richfield Oil Co.), Canyon, 1979-80. Contbr. articles to profl. jours. U.S., Mex., Can., papers to profl. confs. Leader Delta area Boy Scouts Am., Cleveland, 1971-76; dir. United Campus Ministry, Canyon, 1976-79; min. Kern Youth Facility, Bakersfield, 1983—, Christians in Commerce, 1990—. Paratrooper Brazilian Army, 1955. Mem. Am. Acctg. Assn., Am. Inst. CPA's, Am. Assn. Spanish Speaking CPA's, Inst. Mgmt. Accts. (pres. Bakersfield chpt. 1981-82, Most Valuable Mem. award 1981), Am. Mgmt. Assn., Inst. Mgmt. Acctg., Calif. Faculty Assn., Acad. Internat. Bus., Inst. Internal Auditors, Inst. Cost Estimators and Analysts, Alpha Kappa Psi (Dedicated Service award 1979), Omicron Delta Epsilon, Beta Gamma Sigma. Clubs: Jockey (Rio de Janeiro). Lodges: Lions (v.p. Cleveland 1971-73), Kiwanis (v.p. 1974-79, A Whale of a Guy award, Cleveland 1975, Plaque of Appreciation, 1992-93). Office: Calif State U 9001 Stockdale Hwy Bakersfield CA 93311-1022

BACON, LOUIS ALBERT, retired consulting civil engineer; b. Champaign, Ill., Apr. 10, 1921; s. Harrison Waxler and Mabel Mae (Watson) B.; m. Clara Elizabeth Manny, Aug. 28, 1943; children: Robert Louis, David Kenneth, William Harrison. BSCE, U. Ill., 1943. Registered profl. engr., Ga., Ill.; registered structural engr., Ill. Wing designer Douglas Aircraft Co., El Segundo, Calif., 1943-44; structural designer C.A. Metz Engring. Co., Chgo., 1946-47; chief structural engr. Shaw, Metz & Dolio, architects-engrs., Chgo., 1947-53; chief structural engr., assoc. ptnr. Shaw, Metz & Assocs., Chgo., 1953-66; pres. P&W Engrs., Inc., cons., Chgo., 1966-74; v.p., head Atlanta div. Stanley Cons., Inc., 1974-76; v.p., dir. engring. div. Heery Internat., Inc., Atlanta, 1976-84, dir. mktg. to fed. govt., 1984-89; ret.; founder, co-chmn. Ga. Prostate Cancer Coalition, 1997—. Mem. planning com. City of Brookfield, Ill., 1951-54, mem. bd. local improvements, village trustee, 1954-59; mem. Glen Ellyn (Ill.) Environ. Protection Commn., 1971-74; pres. Ridgeview Neighborhood Civic Assn., Atlanta, 1980-82, sec.-treas. 1995—; chmn. Fulton County Developers Adv. Com., 1981; bd. dirs. Literacy Vols. Am.-Met. Atlanta, 1992-95, 96—, pres., 1993-94; commr. Housing Authority Fulton County, 1995—, vice chmn., 1998-99, chmn., 1999—; vol. Habitat for Humanity, Atlanta, 1994-96; bd. dirs. Cancer Network St. Joseph's Hosp. Atlanta, 1995—. With USNR, 1944-46. Recipient Outstanding Achievement award Engrs. of Met. Atlanta, 1980; named Engr. of Yr., Engrs. of Met. Atlanta, 1984. Fellow ASCE, Soc. Am. Mil. Engrs. (v.p. 1988-89); mem. NSPE (life, dir. 1966-69, v.p. 1969-71, pres.-elect 1982-83, pres. 1983-84, div. chmn. profl. engrs. in pvt. practice 1971-72, Chmn.'s award profl. engrs. in pvt. practice 1972, PEPP award 1976, Disting. Svc. award 1993), Ill. Soc. Profl. Engrs. (hon. mem., pres. 1964-65, Ill. award 1968), Ga. Soc. Profl. Engrs. (Pres.'s award Sandy Springs chpt. 1980, Engr. of Yr. award 1982), Engrs. Greater Atlanta (Engr. of Yr. 1984), U. Ill. Civil Engring. Alumni Assn. (pres. 1980-82, Disting. Alumnus award 1985), U. Ill. Alumni Assn. (Loyalty award 1985, Constituent award 1988), Chi Epsilon (hon.). Methodist. Club: Dunwoody (Ga.) Country. Home: 5240 W Kingston Ct NE Atlanta GA 30342-2129

BACON, MARTHA BRANTLEY, small business owner; b. Wrightsville, Ga., Apr. 20, 1938; d. William Riley and Susie Mae (Colston) B.; m. Albert Sidney Bacon, Jr., Aug. 3, 1958; children: Albert Sidney, III, Gregory Riley. BS, Ga. So., Statesboro, 1959; grad., Realtors Inst., 1959; Post Grad., U. Va., Charlottesville, 1978-80, Adrian Hall Interior Design, Savannah, Ga., 1984. Lic. real estate broker, Ga., Va. Tchr. Chatham Bd. Edn., Savannah, Ga., 1961; co-owner mgr. Two Kentucky Fried Chicken Restaurants, Charlottesville, Va., 1967-80; real estate broker Real Estate III, Charlottesville, Va., 1978-83, Landmark Realty, Statesboro, Ga.; tree farmer Johnson Co., Ga., 1980—; mgr., co-owner Restaurant, 1987-92; co-owner Plunderosa Antiques and Collectibles, Statesboro, Ga., 1993—; v.p. Bd. Realtors Statesboro Ga. 1985; regional franchise agt., owner Ice Cream Churn of South Ga. Chmn. Jaycettes Gov. Columbus, Ga., 1962; vol. First Bapt. Ch. Pers. Com., Charlottesville, 1978, U. Va. Hosp., 1980-83; com. mem. Athletic Hall of Fame Ga. So. U.; mem. Ga. Forestry Stewardship, 1991—. Recipient Outstanding Sales award Real Estate III Co. Charlottesville 1980; named Outstanding Jaycette 1961, Jaycettes Gov. Columbus, 1962. Mem. AAUW, Charlottesville Restaurant Assn., Westchester Garden Club, Ga. Restaurant Assn., Ga. So. Univ. Alumni Bd., Ga. So. Symphony Guild, Ga. So. Univ. Athletic Boosters Club, Pilot Club, Evergeen Garden Club, Ga. (v.p.), Optimist (Stateboro essay chmn.),. Baptist. Avocations: bridge, auctions, theatre. Home: 30 Golf Club Cir Statesboro GA 30458-9160

BACON, PHILLIP, geographer, author, consultant; b. Cleve., July 10, 1922; s. Hollis Phillip and Emma (Schneider) B.; m. Jane Lowrie, 1980 (dec. 1991); children by previous marriage: Laura Bacon Fraser, Phillip Everett; m. Sandra Sullivan, 1995. Cadet, The Citadel, 1940-42; AB, U. Miami, 1946; MA, George Peabody Coll. for Tchrs. (now Vanderbilt U.), 1951, EdD, 1955. Tchr. social studies, tactical officer Castle Heights Mil. Acad., Lebanon, Tenn., 1946-47; Tchr. social studies Army and Navy Acad., Carlsbad, Calif., 1948-53; grad. asst. geography George Peabody Coll. for Tchrs. (now Vanderbilt U.), 1953-55; dean Grad. Sch., 1963-64; acting dir. Library Sch., 1964; asst. prof. geography U. Pitts., 1955-57; vis. asst. prof. geography Columbia U. Tchrs. Coll., 1956-57, assoc. prof., 1957-60, prof., 1960-63, 64-66; prof. geography and social studies edn. U. Wash., Seattle, 1966-71; co-dir. tri-univ. project in elementary edn. U. Wash., 1967-71; prof. geography U. Houston, 1971-85, chmn. dept., 1973-78, prof. geography and anthropology emeritus, 1985—; instr. history George Peabody Coll. for Tchrs., summer 1951; vis. prof. geography U. Colo., 1961, U. Wash., 1965, 79; Jennings lectr., 1963; vis. scholar N.C. Central U., 1966; vis. lectr. geography U. Tex., 1966, NSF vis. scientist, 1970-72; Disting. vis. prof. social studies edn. and geography Seattle Pacific U., 1977, 78, 79, vis. prof., geographer-in-residence, Coll. of Edn., U. N.Mex., 1993-95; co-coord. N.Mex. Geog. Alliance, 1993-97; mem. editl. adv. bd. World Book Ency., 1965-84; bd. cons. World Book Atlas, 1965-70; cons. editor Golden Press, 1958-61; ednl. dir. Golden Book Inst. Knowledge, 1960-61; cons. book div. Time, Inc., 1960-69; cons. social sci. project Ednl. Research Council Am., 1962-70; mem. steering com. High Sch. Geography Project, 1965-70; cons. U.S. Office Edn., 1964-71; mem. Wash. Social Studies Adv. Commn., 1968-71; dir. Follett Social Studies Program, 1980-83, Allyn and Bacon elem. social studies program, 1983-85, dir. Summer Geography Inst., N.Mex. Geographic Alliance, 1993-97; social scis. cons. Harcourt Brace, 1985-98, Holt, Rinehart and Winston, 1989-97; prof. geography grad. faculty U. Colo., Boulder, 1999—; geography cons. SWAP Project, Colo. Dept. Edn., 1998; curriculum cons. Author: Australia, Oceania, and the Polar Lands, 1961, North America, 1961, Children's Picture Atlas of the World, 1966, (with Norman Carls and Frank E. Sorenson) Knowing Our Neighbors in the United States and Canada, 1966, Regions Around the World, 1970, (with R.R. Boyce) Towns and Cities, 1970, (with others) The United States and Canada, 1970, (with P.V. Greco) The Story of Latin America, 1970, (with others) America: In Space and Time, 1976, Exploring Our World, 1982, (with Donald C. Fairweather) World Regions, 1983, (with James B. Kracht) Our World Today, 1983, (with M. Evelyn Swartz) Our State: California, 1983, World Geography, The Earth and Its People, 1989; editor: Focus on Geography, Key Concepts and Teaching Strategies, 1970; co-editor (with Lorrin G. Kennamer) Foundations of World Regional Geography Series, 1970; cons. editor: (with others) Life Pictorial Atlas of the World, 1961; mem. adv. bd.: (with others) Jour. of Geography, 1967-70, Social Edn., 1975-78; editl. dir.: (with others) Field Social Studies Program, 1972-73; co-dir.: (with others) Addison-Wesley Elementary Social Studies Program, 1973-80; ednl. cons. The American Nation, Reconstruction to the Present, 1986, The American Nation, Beginnings Through Reconstruction, 1986, Triumph of the American Nation, 1986, World History: People and Nations, 1990, The Story of America, 1994; sr. editl. advisor HBJ Social Studies, K-7, Landmark edits., 1988; geography cons. Harcourt Brace Elem. Social Studies Program Stories in Time, 1997; contbr. articles to profl. jours., chpts. to books, yearbooks. Mem. adv. bd. Grad. Sch., U. Colo., 1987-93. With USNR, 1942-45. Recipient Teaching Excellence award U. Houston, 1975, 79, 80. Mem. NEA (life), Assn. Am. Geographers (coun. 1976-79, chmn. publs. com. 1976-78), Nat. Coun. for Geog. Edn. (life, pres. 1966, disting. svc. award 1974), Alaska Geog. Soc., Nat., Tex., N.Mex. (exec. bd. 1992-95), Social Studies Couns. (exec. bd. 1992-95), Vanderbilt U. Alumni Assn. (dir. 1979-83), Peabody Coll. Alumni Assn. (pres. 1981-83, Disting. Alumnus award 1986, alumni bd. 1994-95), Peabody Coll. Roundtable, Sigma Xi, Sigma Alpha Epsilon, Phi Delta Kappa, Kappa Delta Pi, Kappa Phi Kappa (life), Omicron Delta Kappa, Gamma Theta Upsilon, Pi Gamma Mu. Lutheran. Home: 2718 Caribbean Dr Grand Junction CO 81506-1712

BACON, VICKY LEE, lighting services executive; b. Oregon City, Oreg., Mar. 25, 1950; d. Herbert Kenneth and Lorean Betty (Boltz) Rushford; m. Dennis M. Bacon, Aug. 7, 1971; 1 child, Randene Tess. Student, Portland Community Coll., 1974-75, Mt. Hood Community Coll., 1976, Portland State Coll., 1979. With All Electric Constrn., Milwaukie, Oreg., 1968-70, Lighting Maintenance Co., Portland, Oreg., 1970-78; svc. mgr. GTE Sylvania Lighting Svcs., Portland, 1978-80, br. mgr., 1980-83; div. mgr. Christenson Electric Co. Inc., Portland, 1983-90, v.p. mktg. and lighting svcs., 1990-91, v.p. svc. ops. and mktg., 1991—; chmn. Oreg. Ltd. Energy Com., 1993—; vice chmn. to labor commr. Oreg. State Apprenticeship Coun., 1996—. Mem. Energy Contractors Assn., Illuminating Engring. Soc., Nat. Elec. Contractors Assn. (bd. dirs. Oreg. Columbia chpt. 1997—), Nat. Assn. Lighting Maintenance Contractors, Elec. Contractors Assn.,. Office: Christenson Electric Co Inc 111 SW Columbia St Ste 480 Portland OR 97201-5886

BACON, VINTON WALKER, civil engineer; b. Estelline, S.D., Dec. 21, 1916. BS, Univ. Calif., 1940; diploma, Am. Acad. Environ. Engrs., 1956. Engr. East Bay City Sewage Disposal Svc., Berkeley, 1940-41; designer L.A. County Sanitary Dist., 1941-43; office engr. Orange County Sewerage Svc., 1946-49; exec. officer Calif. State Water Pollution Control Bd., 1950-56; exec. sec. NW Paper & Pulp Assn., Tacoma, Wash., 1956-62; gen. supr. Metro Sanitary Dist. Greater Chgo., 1962-70; prof., 1970-82; prof. civil engr. Univ. Wis., Milw., 1982; cons. civil engr., chmn. Wis. Gov. Solid Waste Recycling Task Force, 1971-76. Active Wis. Solid Waste Recycling Authority, 1974-76; city councilman Mill Creek, Wash., 1992-96. Mem. Am. Soc. Civil Engrs., Nat. Acad. Engring., Am. Pub. Health Assn., Water Pollution Control Fedn., Am. Water Works Assn. Home: 2616 143rd Pl SE Mill Creek WA 98012-5733*

BACON, WALLACE ALGER, speech communications educator, author; b. Bad Axe, Mich., Jan. 27, 1914; s. Russell Alger and Mana (Wallace) B. A.B., Albion Coll., 1935, Litt. D., 1967; A.M., U. Mich., 1936, Ph.D., 1940; LL.D., Emerson Coll., 1975. Instr. English U. Mich., 1941-47; chmn. dept. interpretation Northwestern U., Evanston, Ill., 1947-79; asst. prof. English and speech Northwestern U., 1947-50, assoc. prof. English and speech, 1950-55, prof. speech, 1955-80, prof. emeritus, 1980—; Fulbright lectr., Philippines, 1961-62, Fulbright-Hays lectr., 1964-65; vis. prof. U. Calif.-Berkeley, U. Wash., Nihon U., Tokyo, U. N.C., Chapel Hill, N.Mex. State U., U. Philippines, Santo Tomas U., Philippines; mem. adv. bd. Inst. for Readers Theatre, 1974-85; mem. adv. bd. Harwood Found. of U. N.Mex., 1982-91, pres., 1984-87, 90-91, v.p. 1988-89. Author: verse play Savonarola, 1950 (Bishop Sheil award 1946), William Warner's Syrinx, 1950, (with Robert S. Breen) Literature as Experience, 1959, Literature for Interpretation, 1961, (with N. Crame-Rogers and C. V. Fonacier) Spoken English, 1962, (with C.V. Fonacier) The Art of Oral Interpretation, 1965; The Art of Interpretation, 1966, 3d edit., 1979, Oral Interpretation and the Teaching of Literature in Secondary Schools, 1974, also articles, poetry, monographs.; editor: Festschrift for Isabel Crouch: Essays on the Theory, Practice and Criticism of Performance, 1988; assoc. editor: Performance of Literature in Historical Perspectives, 1983; editor Text and Performance Quar., 1989-91, assoc. editor, 1992—; assoc. editor Quar. Jour. Speech, 1957-59, 63-65, 75-77, Speech Monographs, 1966-71; adv. editor Lit. in Performance, 1980-82, assoc. editor, 1983-88. Served with AUS, 1942-46. Decorated Legion of Merit; Alfred Lloyd postdoctoral fellow U. Mich., 1940-41; Rockefeller fellow, 1948-49; Ford Found. fellow, 1954-55; recipient Hopwood Major Writing Drama award U. Mich., 1936; spl. citation U. Philippines, 1965, 70; spl. commendation Ednl. Found. Philippines, 1965; Disting. Alumnus award Albion Coll., 1986. Mem. Nat. Communication Assn. (Golden Anniversary Prize Fund award 1965, 74, disting. svc. award 1983, disting. scholar award 1995, awards com. 1967, 85, 2d v.p. 1975, 1st v.p. 1976, pres. 1977), Western States Communication Assn., Malone Soc., AAUP, Phi Beta Kappa, Delta Sigma Rho, Theta Alpha Phi, Zeta Phi Eta. Home: PO Box 2257 Taos NM 87571-2257 *I believe in the significance of man as a social creature, and in the importance of service. No person has ever found himself or herself except through becoming aware of others. A sense of the otherness of others—in a word, a knowledge of love—is for me the greatest of human virtues.*

BACON-SMITH, CAMILLE, educator, writer; b. Phila., July 13, 1949; d. John P. and Elizabeth (Revis) Bacon; children: Erik, David. MA, U. Penn., 1985, PhD, 1989. Author: Enterprising Women, 1992, Eye of the Daemon, 1996, Face of Time, 1996, Eyes of the Empress, 1998, Science Fition Culture, 1999; dir. Philadelphia Fantastic Reading Series; moderator: New Directions in Folklore. Avocations: theatre, action movies.

BACOT, JOHN CARTER, retired banking executive; b. Utica, N.Y., Feb. 7, 1933; s. John Vacher and Edna (Gunn) B.; m. Shirley Schou, Nov. 26, 1960; children: Elizabeth, Susan. AB, Hamilton Coll., Clinton, N.Y., 1955; LLB, Cornell U., 1958. Bar: N.Y. 1959. With firm Utica, 1959-60; with Bank of N.Y., N.Y.C., 1960—, pres., 1974-84, chief exec. officer, chmn., 1982-98; also bd. dir. Bank of N.Y.; ret., 1998; bd. dirs. Home Life Ins. Co., Atlantic Reins. Co., Centennial Ins. Co., Bank of N.Y. Internat. Corp., Bank of N.Y. Co., Inc.; trustee Atlantic Mut. Ins. Co.; chmn. bd. trustees Hamilton Coll. Mem. Econ. Club N.Y., Pilgrims of U.S., Assn. Res. City Bankers, N.Y. State Bar Assn., Coun. on Fgn. Rels., Montclair Golf Club, Links Club, Union Club. Episcopalian. Home: 48 Porter Pl Montclair NJ 07042-2036 Office: Bank of NY 1 Wall St New York NY 10286*

BACOT, MARIE, management consultant, researcher; b. Jackson, Miss., Oct. 2, 1942; d. James Peter and Marie (Moore) B. BA, Millsaps Coll., 1964; MEd, U. New Orleans, 1974, PhD, 1992. Tchr. Houston Ind. Sch. Dist., 1964-68, Jefferson Parish Sch. Bd., Gretna, La., 1968-86; dir. Ednl. Testing Assocs., New Orleans, 1982-86, Marie Bacot Innovation & Creativity Cons., New Orleans, 1987—; presenter Acad. Mgmt., 1989, So. Mgmt. Assn., 1989, Decision Scis. Inst., 1990. Co-author chpt.: Understanding Students with High Incidence Exceptionalities: Categorical and Non-categorical Perspectives, 1991; contbr. articles to profl. jours. Recording sec. The New Orleans City Ballet, 1986-87; publicity chmn. book fair New Orleans Symphony Orch., 1986-87; spl. donor chmn. opera ball New Orleans Opera Assn. 1986-87; soloist, quartet/trio choir mem. Trinity Episcopal Ch., 1981-88. Mem. Ctr. for Rsch. in Applied Creativity, Creative Edn. Found., Acad. Mgmt., Am. Soc. for Quality Control. Republican. Episcopalian. Developer Bacot Organizational Learning and Innovation Scale (BOLIS), instrument used to assess organizations. Avocations: music, physical fitness, snow skiing, tennis, hiking. Office: PO Box 15695 New Orleans LA 70175-5695

BACUS, TERRENCE LEE, labor relations consultant; b. Vinton County, Ohio, Sept. 30, 1944; s. John E. and Margery A. (Jeffers) B.; m. Mary K. Kerr, July 11, 1964; children: Terrence L. Jr., Sherri D. BS in Indsl. Mgmt., Franklin U., 1975. Staff rep. AFSCME-AFL/CIO, Columbus, Ohio. Subchmn. Columbus Vets. Day Com., 1987-96, Armed Forces Day, Columbus, 1989; pres. Music Boosters, Canal Winchester, Ohio, 1983-84, Cmty. Labor Day Festival, Canal Winchester, 1985-86. Mem. Am. Soc. Pers. Adminstrs., Ohio Head Injury Assn. (past exec. dir.), AMVETS, Am. Legion, Vietnam Vets. Am., (vets. svc. rep.), F&A Masons, Shriners, Order Ea. Star, Sigma Kappa Phi (nat. pres. 1974). Avocations: photography, sports. Home: 240 Cherokee Ct N Canal Winchester OH 43110-1027

BADAL, DANIEL WALTER, psychiatrist, educator; b. Lowellville, Ohio, Aug. 22, 1912; s. Samuel S. and Angelina (Jessen) B.; m. Julia Lovina Cover, June 1939 (dec. May 1968); children: Petrina Badal Gardner, Julia Badal Graf, Peter C.; m. Eleanor Bosworth Spitler, Sept. 5, 1969 (dec. Feb. 1994). A.B., Case Western Res. U., 1934, M.D., 1937. Resident in medicine, neurology and psychiatry Peter Bent Brigham Hosp., Mass. Gen. Hosp., Boston City Hosp., 1937-41; fellow in psychiatry and neurology Harvard U., Boston, 1941-45; asst. prof. psychiatry Washington U., St. Louis, 1945; mem. faculty Sch. Medicine Case Western Res. U., Cleve., 1946—, assoc. clin. prof. emeritus psychiatry, 1983—; practice medicine specializing in psychiatry and psychoanalysis Cleve., 1955—; mem. faculty Cleve. Psychoanalytic Inst., Cleve., 1975—. Author: Treatment of Depression and Related Moods, 1988; contbr. articles to profl. jours. NRC Office Sci. Research and Devel. fellow, 1941-45. Fellow Internat. Psychoanlytic Assn. (life), Am. Psychiat. Assn.; mem. AMA, Ohio Med. Assn., Cleve. Psychiat. Soc., Acad. Medicine Cleve., Am. Psychoanalytic Assn., Phila. Assn. Psychoanalysis, Cleve. Psychoanalytic Soc. (pres. 1963). Home: 2432 Kenilworth Rd Cleveland Hts OH 44106-2730 Office: 11328 Euclid Ave Ste 201 Cleveland OH 44106-3959

BADALAMENT, ROBERT ANTHONY, urologic oncologist; b. Detroit, Mar. 20, 1954; s. Louis F. and Grace D. (Costello) B.; m. Providence F. Vitale, Nov. 9, 1980; children: Louis F., Peter P., Grace F. BS in Biology, So. Meth. U., 1976; MD, Emory U., 1980. Diplomate Am. Bd. Urology. Surg. intern Henry Ford Hosp., Detroit, 1980-81, surg. resident, 1981-82, urologic resident, 1982-85; fellow in urologic oncology Meml. Sloan Kettering Cancer Ctr., N.Y.C., 1985-87; asst. prof. Ohio State U., Columbus, 1987-92, assoc. prof., 1992-95, prof. Sch. Pub. Health, 1995—; mem. attending staff Arthur James Cancer Ctr., Columbus, 1990-95, Crittenton Hosp., Rochester Hills, Mich., 1995—. Contbr. chpt. to book, articles to profl. jours. Fellow ACS; mem. AMA, Am. Soc. Clin. Oncology, Soc. Univ. Urologists, Soc. Urologic Oncology, Soc. for Basic Urologic Rsch., Am. Cancer Soc. (bd. trustees Mich. divsn.). Office: Rochester Urology PC 1135 W University Dr Ste 420 Rochester Hills MI 48307

BADALAMENTI, ANGELO, composer, conductor. Music dir., orchestrator, composer: (TV series) Twin Peaks, 1990-91 (Emmy award nominations outstanding achievement in music and lyrics and outstanding achievement in music composition 1990, BPI award for best soundtrack album 1992), (films) Tough Guys Don't Dance, 1987, Cousins, 1989; music dir., condr., composer: Blue Velvet, 1986; composer: (film scores) Gordon's War, 1973, Law and Disorder, 1974, A Nightmare on Elm Street Part III: Dream Warriors, 1987, Weeds, 1987, Parents, 1989, National Lampoon's Christmas Vacation, 1989, Wait Until Spring, Bandini, 1989, Wild at Heart, 1990, The Comfort of Strangers, 1990 (Anthony Asquith award 1992), Twin Peaks: Fire Walk with Me, 1992 (Spirit awards 1993), Naked in New York, 1993, The Witch Hunt, 1994, Invasion of Privacy, 1995, The City of Lost Children (Cesars mus. score nominee), 1995, Lost Highway, 1996, (TV movie scores) Hotel Room, 1993, (film songs) (from Across the Great Divide) Across the Great Divide, 1976, (from Blue Velvet) Blue Star, 1986, (from Blue Velvet) Mysteries of Love, 1987, (from Tough Guys Don't Dance) You'll Come Back, 1987, Real Man, 1987, (from Cousins) I Love You for Today, 1989, (from Wild at Heart) Up in Flames, 1990, Sycamore Trees, 1990-91, (TV songs) (from Twin Peaks) Twin Peaks Theme, 1990-91 (Emmy award nomination in main title theme music 1990, Grammy award best pop instrumental performance 1990), The Nightingale, 1990-91, Falling, 1990-91; composer, conductor (torch theme 1992 Summer Olympics) The Flaming Arrow; composer, prodr. (album) Marianne Faithfull-A Secret Life, 1995, (album, with Tim Booth) Booth and the Bad Angel, 1996.

BADALAMENTI, ANTHONY, financial planner; b. St. Louis, Apr. 1, 1940; s. Sebastino and Grace (Orlando) B.; 1 child, Annette Marie. BS in Acctg., Washington U., 1970. CPA, Mo.; registered investment advisor. Staff acct. Fischer & Fischer, CPAs, St. Louis, 1959-63; acct. McDonnell Aircraft Corp., St. Louis, 1963-65; asst. chief acct. Dempsey Tegler, Inc., St.

Louis, 1965-66; contr. Cummins Mo. Diesel, Inc., St. Louis, 1966-67; sr. acct. Elmer Fox & Co., CPAs, St. Louis, 1967-71; pvt. practice St. Louis, 1972-94; fin. planner Asset Builders Fin. Planners, St. Louis, 1995—; tchr. Meramec C.C., St. Louis, 1973-75. Mem. Mo. Soc. CPAs, Crestwood-Sunset Hills C. of C. (pres. 1980-81, Bus. Profl. Month award 1986, 91), Rotary (pres. Crestwood-Sunset Hills chpt. 1982-83). Republican. Roman Catholic. Avocations: basketball, softball, dancing. Home: 1865 Locks Mill Dr Fenton MO 63026-2662 Office: 4400 S Lindbergh Blvd Ste 3 Saint Louis MO 63127-1603

BADALAMENTI, FRED LEOPOLDO, artist, educator; b. Long Island City, N.Y., June 25, 1935; s. Leopoldo and Concetta (Vitali) B.; m. Barbara J. Frankenfield, June 14, 1959; children: Katherine, Alexander, Frederick. Student, Pratt Inst., 1953-55, U. Alaska, 1957-58; BS, SUNY, New Paltz, 1961; MFA, Bklyn. Coll., 1967. Art tchr. Newburgh (N.Y.) Pub. Schs., 1960-63, Deer Park (N.Y.) High Sch., 1963-65; prof. emeritus Bklyn. Coll., 1967-92; vis. prof. art, lectr. SUNY, Stony Brook, 1977-78, 80, 81, 83; dep. chmn. for studio art Bklyn. Coll., 1990-92, dep. chmn. for grad. art, 1972-89; dir. First St. Gallery, N.Y.C., 1978; adj. faculty art dept. Bklyn. Coll., 1992-93, Stony Brook U., 1993-99. One man shows include Suffolk Community Coll., 1971, First Street Gallery, 1973, 76, 80, 89, Nassau County Mus. of Fine Arts, 1987, St. Joseph's Coll., 1987, The Alfred Van Loen Gallery, South Huntington, N.Y., 1998; exhibited paintings and drawings of representational art in N.Y.C. and L.I., 1967—. With USAF, 1955-59. Bklyn. Coll. grad. fellow, 1965-67. Mem. Coll. Art Assn., AAUP. Avocations: travel, tennis, gardening. Home: 182 Lower Sheep Pasture Rd East Setauket NY 11733-1826

BADASH, LAWRENCE, science history educator; b. Bklyn., May 8, 1934; s. Joseph and Dorothy (Langa) B.; children: Lisa, Bruce. BS in Physics, Rensselaer Poly. Inst., 1956; PhD in History of Sci., Yale U., 1964. Instr. Yale. U., New Haven, Conn., 1964-65, research assoc., 1965-66; from asst. to assoc. prof. U. Calif., Santa Barbara, 1966-79, prof. history of sci., 1979—; dir. summer seminar on global security and arms control U. Calif., 1983, 86, energy rsch. group, 1992, pacific rim program mem., 1993-95; cons. Nuclear Age Peace Found., Santa Barbara, 1984-90. Author: Radioactivity in Am., 1979, Kapitza, Rutherford, and the Kremlin, 1985, Scientists and the Development of Nuclear Weapons, 1995; editor: Rutherford and Boltwood, Letters on Radioactivity, 1969; Reminiscences of Los Alamos, 1943-45, 1980. Bd. dirs. Santa Barbara chpt. ACLU, 1971-86, 96-99, pres., 1982-84, 96—; nat. bd. dirs. Com. for a Sane Nuclear Policy, Washington, 1972-81; mem. Los Padres Search and Rescue Team, Santa Barbara, 1981-94. Lt. (j.g.) USN, 1956-59. Grantee, NSF, Cambridge, Eng., 1965-66, 69-72, 90-92, Am. Philos. Soc., New Zealand, 1979-80, Inst. on Global Conflict and Cooperation, Univ. Calif., 1983-87; J.S. Guggenheim fellow, 1984-85. Fellow AAAS (sect. mem. at large 1988-92), Am. Phys. Soc. (chmn. divsn. of history of physics 1988-89, exec. com. forum on physics and society 1991-93); mem. History of Sci. Soc. (founder West Coast chpt., chpt. bd. dirs. 1971-73, nat. coun. 1975-78). Democrat. Jewish. Avocation: backpacking. Office: Univ Calif Dept History Santa Barbara CA 93106

BADDERS, REBECCA SUSANNE, military officer, educator, writer; b. Knoxville, Tenn., Jan. 6, 1962; d. John Albert and Tamara Elizabeth (Day) B. BA in Edn., U. Fla., 1984; MA in Edn., U. South Fla., Tampa and St. Petersburg, 1997. Cert. profl. tchr., Fla. Commd. ensign USN, 1984, advanced through grades to lt. commdr., 1995; oceanographic watch officer Naval Facility Brawdy, Wales, 1984-86; oceanographic officer anti-submarine warfare Comdr. Undersea Surveillance, Norfolk, Va., 1986-90; dept. head Readiness Tng. Facility, Dam Neck, Va., 1990-93; tchr. Pinellas County Schs., Largo, Fla., 1994-97; commanding officer Naval Weapon Sta., Charleston, S.C., 1995-97; exec. officer Naval Res. Ctr., Kearny, N.J., 1997—; faculty rep. Pinellas County Tchrs. Assn., Largo, 1994-97. Author: Maddy and the Peek-A-Boo Moon, 1995. V.p., bd. dirs. Pilot Club Internat., Mid-Pinellas, Fla., 1993—. Recipient Navy Achievement medal, 1990, 93, 96. Mem. Naval Res. Officer Assn., Navy League of U.S., Coun. for Exceptional Children, Internat. Order of Rainbow (worthy advisor, pres. 1975-82), Scabbard and Blade, Kappa Delta Pi. Republican. Episcopalian. Avocations: travel, computers, reading, gourmet cooking, arts. Office: Naval Res Ctr Kearny 53 Hackensack Ave Kearny NJ 07032

BADDING, JOHN VICTOR, chemistry educator; b. Buffalo, May 6, 1962; s. Victor George and Nancy (Clark) B.; m. Mizue Abe, Dec. 28, 1993. BS, Manhattan Coll., N.Y.C., 1984; PhD, U. Calif., Berkeley, 1989. Asst. prof. chemistry Pa. State U., University Park, 1991-97, assoc. prof. chemistry, 1997—. Contbr. articles to profl. jours. Packard fellow, 1993; NSF Young Investigator awardee, 1993. Office: Pa State U Dept Chemistry University Park PA 16802

BADDOUR, ANNE BRIDGE, pilot; b. Royal Oak, Mich.; d. William George and Esther Rose (Pfiester) Bridge; m. Raymond F. Baddour, Sept. 25, 1954; children: Cynthia Anne, Frederick Raymond, Jean Bridge. Student, Detroit Bus. Sch., 1948-50; BA, Pine Manor Coll. Stewardess Eastern Airlines, Boston, 1952-54; instr. aero. Powers Sch., Boston, 1958; co-pilot, flight attendant Raytheon Co., Bedford, Mass., 1958-63; flight dispatcher, ferry Pilot Comerford Flight Sch., Bedford, 1974-76; adminstrv. asst., ferry pilot Jenney Beachcraft, Bedford, 1976; mgr., pilot Balt. Airways, Inc., Bedford, 1976-77; rsch. pilot Lincoln Lab. Flight Test Facility MIT, Lexington, 1977-97; aviation cons., corp. pilot Energy Resources, Inc., Cambridge, Mass., 1974-84; holder World Class speed records for single-engine aircraft; Boston to Goose Bay, Labrador, 1985, Boston to Reykjavik, Iceland, 1985, Portland, Maine to Goose Bay, 1985, Portland to Reykjavik, 1985, Goose Bay to Reykjavik, 1985; records for twin-engine aircraft: Sept Isles to Goose Bay, 1988, Mont Joll to Goose Bay, 1988, Presque Isle to Goose Bay, 1988, Millinocket to Goose Bay, 1988, Bedford to Goose Bay, 1988, Goose Bay to Narssassrag, Greenland, 1988, Narssassrag to Klevelevic, Iceland, 1988, Narssassrag to Reykjavik, 1988, Bedford to Narssassrag, 1988, Millinochet to Narssassrag, 1988, Presque Isle to Narssassrag, 1988, Bedford to St. John, 1991, Bedford to Charlottetown, 1991, Charlottetown to Kennebunk, 1991, Charlottetown to Portsmouth, 1991, Muncton to Bedford, 1991, St. John, to Kennebunk, 1991, St. John to Bedford, 1991. Bd. dirs. Cambridge Opera, 1977-79; mem. campaign coun. Mus. Transp., Boston; mem. coun. assocs. French Libr. in Boston; commr. Commonwealth of Mass., Mass. Aero. Commn., 1979-83; chmn. regional adv. coun. FAA, 1984-88; trustee bd. adminstrn. Amelia Earhart Birthplace Mus., 1992-93; trustee Daniel Webster Coll., Nashua, N.H., 1995—; trustee Friends of the Libr. Spl. Collections Boston U., 1997—; bd. dirs. Smithsonian Nat. Air & Space Mus., 1998—. Winner trophy Phila. Transcontinental Air Race, 1954, New Eng. Air Race, 1957, Clifford B. Harmon trophy Internat. Aviatrix, 1988; recipient Spl. Recognition award FAA, 1990; honoree Internat. Aviation Forest of Friendship, Atchison, Kans., 1991; named Pilot of the Year, New Eng. sect. Internat. Women Pilots Orgn./The Ninety-Nines, Inc., 1992. Mem. DAR, Fedn. Aeronautique Internat., Nat. Aero. Assn., Ninety-Nines (New Eng. Safety trophy 1986), Aero Club New Eng. (v.p. 1978-80, dir. 1978—), Aircraft Owners Pilots Assn., Nat. Pilots Assn., U.S. Sea Plane Pilots Assn., Assn. Women Transcontinental Air Race, Bostonian Soc., English Speaking Union, Soc. Exptl. Test Pilots, Friends of Switzerland, French Ctr. Libr., Belmont Hill Club, St. Botolph Club, Chilton Club, Boston Women's Travel Club, Harvard Travellers Club, Fairchild Tropical Garden Club. Republican. Episcopalian.

BADDOUR, RAYMOND FREDERICK, chemical engineer, educator, entrepreneur; b. Laurinburg, N.C., Jan. 11, 1925; s. Frederick Joseph and Fannie (Rizk) B.; m. Anne M. Bridge, Sept. 25, 1954; children: Cynthia Anne, Frederick Raymond, Jean Bridge. B.S., U. Notre Dame, 1945; M.S., Mass. Inst. Tech., 1949; Sc.D., 1951; D (hon.), St. Andrew's Coll., 1999. Asst. dir. Engring Practice Sch., Oak Ridge, 1948-49; asst. prof. Mass. Inst. Tech., 1951-57, asso. prof., 1957-63, prof. chem. engring, 1963-89, Lammot du Pont prof. chem. engring., 1973-89, prof. emeritus, 1989—, also head dept., 1969-76; dir. Environ. Lab., 1970-76; mem. project separation AEC, 1954; Am. Inst. Chem. Engrs. del. Mendeleev Conf. on Pure and Applied Chemistry, Moscow, 1959; lectr. Max Planck Insts., Germany, 1962; Shell lectr. Cambridge (Eng.) U., 1962; P.C. Reily lectr. Notre Dame U., 1964; Dr. Warren K. Lewis lectr., chmn. engring. MIT, 1998; mem. sci. adv. com. Gen. Motors Corp., 1971-82; co-founder, chmn. Abcor, Inc., Cambridge, Mass., 1963-72; dir. Raychem Corp., 1972-80; founder, chmn. Energy Resources Co., Inc. (ERCO), 1974-83; chmn. ERCO AG, 1980-83; co-founder dir. Amgen, Inc., 1980-97, Lam Research, 1980-82; co-founder BREH, Inc., 1983; co-founder, dir. SKB, Inc., 1984, MatTek Corp., 1985, BLW Corp., 1985, Enterprise Mgmt. Corp., 1985, Ascent Pediat., Inc., 1989—; cons. Mobil Chem. Co., N.Y.C., 1963-84, U.S. Dept. Commerce, 1960-62, Freeport Minerals Co., N.Y.C., 1976-83, Allied Chem. Co., 1980-81; dir. HYSEQ, Inc., 1993—, Scully Signal, 1996—. Mem. corp. Boston Museum Sci.; mem. sci. and tech. adv. bd. Field Enterprises, Chgo. (World Book Ency.), 1966-68. United Engrs. and Constructors preceptorship, 1956; NSF sr. post-doctoral fellow, 1967-68; recipient honor award U. Notre Dame Coll. of Engring., 1976. Fellow Am. Inst. Chem. Engrs., Am. Inst. Chemists, Am. Acad. Arts and Scis., N.Y. Acad. Scis.; mem. AAAs, Am. Chem. Soc., St. Batalph Club. Research publs. and patents in field.

BADDOURA, RASHID JOSEPH, emergency medicine physician; b. Beirut, Aug. 4, 1947; came to U.S., 1974; s. Joseph and Renée Baddoura; m. Rola Tohme, July 15, 1989; children: Joseph, Philip, Karen. BS, Am. U. Beirut, 1970, MD, 1974. Diplomate Am. Bd. Emergency Medicine (examiner 1984-89), Am. Bd. Internal Medicine, Am. Bd. Pulmonary Diseases. Intern Am. U. Med. Ctr., Beirut; resident in internal medicine St. Joseph's Hosp. & Med. Ctr., Paterson, N.J., 1974-76; fellow in pulmonary and critical care Duke U., 1976-79; dir. emergency dept. Meml. Hosp., Danville, Va., 1981-84; corp. med. officer, mem. med. adv. bd. Coastal Healthcare Group, Durham, N.C., 1981-86; assoc. dir. emergency dept. Valley Hosp., Ridgewood, N.J., 1986-90, dir. emergency dept., 1990—; mem. bd. Coastal Found. for Med. Edn., Durham, 1984-89; clin. asst. prof. emergency medicine Georgetown U., Washington, 1986-89. Fellow Am. Coll. Emergency Physicians; mem. Am. Coll. Physician Execs. Avocations: hunting, fishing, philosophy, classical music. Office: Valley Hosp Dept Emergency Medicine Ridgewood NJ 07451

BADE, CARL AUGUST, retired secondary education educator; b. St. Louis, Dec. 6, 1924; s. Carl William and Lena Wilhelmina Christina (Gruendler) B.; m. Marie Hoefer, Sept. 11, 1954; children: Steven Carl, Paul Martin, David Edward. BS in Edn., Washington U., St. Louis, 1949, MA in Edn., 1951. Cert. secondary edn. tchr., Mo. Jr. H.S. tchr. Normandy (Mo.) Sch. Dist., 1949-51; youth assoc. Evangelical and Reformed Ch., Phila., 1951-52; cmty. outreach worker Zion Evangelical and Reformed Ch., St. Louis, 1952-54; assoc. dir. voluntary svc. Evangelical and Reformed Ch., Pottstown, Pa., 1954-61; co-dir. voluntary svc. United Ch. of Christ, Pottstown, Pa., 1961-74; dir. voluntary svc. United Ch. of Christ, N.Y.C., 1975-91; ret., 1991; pres. Commn. on Voluntary Svc., N.Y.C., 1960-66; mem. exec. com. Christian Ministry in Nat. Pks., N.Y.C., 1991—; sec. Prisoner Visitation and Support, Phila., 1991—; bd. dirs. Waldensian Aid Soc., N.Y.C., 1985—. With U.S. Army, 1943-45. Democrat. Mem. United Ch. of Christ. Avocations: reading, world travel.

BADEAUX, DIANE MARIE, mental health nurse; b. Thibodaux, La., Oct. 19, 1943; d. Jessie Joseph Sr. and Agnes Marie (Zeringue) Pertuit; m. Freddie Badeaux Jr., June 24, 1961; children: Tyrome, Troy, Agnes. Tab. AD, Nicholls State U., 1975, BSN, 1992; M Nursing, La. State U. Med. Ctr., 1995. Staff nurse St. Anne Gen. Hosp., Raceland, La., 1975-76, 88-89; critical care nurse Terrebonne Gen. Hosp., Houma, La., 1976-78, 89-90; dept. head supply, processing, and distbn. S. La. Med. Ctr., Houma, 1978-88; nurse, adminstrv. supr. Bayou Oaks Hosp., Houma, 1988-94; nurse Behavioral Health St. Anne Gen. Hosp., Raceland, 1994-96; asst. prof. nursing Nicholls State U., 1996—; nurse Lafourche Mental Health Clinic, Raceland, 1995, mem. adv. bd., 1995, pres. adv. bd., 1996—. Mem. Am. Psychiat. Nurses, Sigma Theta Tau (bd. dirs. Xi Zeta chpt. 1997-98), Alpha Lambda Delta. Roman Catholic. Avocations: travel, reading, arts and crafts.

BADEER, HENRY SARKIS, physiology educator; b. Mersine, Turkey, Jan. 31, 1915; came to U.S., 1965, naturalized, 1971; s. Sarkis and Persape Hagop (Koundakjian) B.; m. Mariam Mihran Kassarjian, July 12, 1948; children: Gilbert H., Daniel H. M.D., Am. U., Beirut, Lebanon, 1938. Gen. practice medicine Beirut, 1940-51; asst. instr. Am. U. Sch. Medicine, Beirut, 1938-45; adj. prof. Am. U. Sch. Medicine, 1945-51, asso. prof., 1951-62, prof. physiology, 1962-65, acting chmn. dept., 1951-56, chmn., 1956-65; research fellow Harvard U. Med. Sch., Boston, 1948-49; prof. physiology Creighton U. Med. Sch., Omaha, 1967-91, emeritus prof., 1991—; acting chmn. dept. Creighton U. Med. Sch., 1971-72; vis. prof. U. Iowa, Iowa City, 1957-58, Downstate Med. Center, Bklyn., 1965-67; mem. med. com. Azounieh Sanatorium, Beirut, 1961-65; mem. research com. Nebr. Heart Assn., 1967-70, 85-88. Author textbook Spanish translation; contbr. chpts. to books, articles to profl. jours. Recipient Golden Apple award Students of AMA, 1975, Disting. Prof. award, 1992; Rockefeller fellow., 1948-49; grantee med. research com. Am. U. Beirut, 1956-65. Mem. Internat. Soc. Heart Rsch., Am. Physiol. Soc., Internat. Soc. for Adaptive Medicine (founding mem.). Home: 2808 S 99th Ave Omaha NE 68124-2603 Office: Creighton U Med Sch 2500 California Plz Omaha NE 68178-0001 *My success seems to be related to having set a goal and persevering in achieving it; satisfaction in or enjoyment of the performance of my daily task no matter how mundane; and eagerness to learn from personal experience or the experience of others.*

BADEL, JULIE, lawyer; b. Chgo., Sept. 14, 1946; d. Charles and Saima (Hyrkas) B.D. 1986). Student, Knox Coll., 1963-65; BA, Columbia Coll., Chgo., 1967; JD, DePaul U., 1977. Bar: Ill. 1977, U.S. Dist. Ct. (no. dist.) Ill. 1977, U.S. Ct. Appeals (7th and D.C. cirs.) 1981, U.S. Supreme Ct. 1985, U.S. Dist. Ct. (ea. dist.) Mich. 1989. Hearings referee State of Ill., Chgo., 1974-78; assoc. Cohn, Lambert, Ryan & Schneider, Chgo., 1978-80; assoc. McDermott, Will & Emery, Chgo., 1980-84, ptnr., 1985—; legal counsel, mem. adv. bd. Health Evaluation Referral Svc. Chgo., 1980-89; bd. dirs. Alternatives, Inc., Chgo. chpt. Asthma and Allergy Found., 1993-94, Glenwood Sch. for Boys. Author: Hospital Restructuring: Employment Law Pitfalls, 1985; editor DePaul U. Law Rev., 1976-77. Mem. ABA, Chgo. Bar Assn., Labor & Employment Alliance for Women, Columbia Coll. Alumni Assn. (1st v.p., bd. dirs. 1981-86), Pi Gamma Mu. Office: McDermott Will & Emery 227 W Monroe St Ste 3100 Chicago IL 60606-5096

BADENHAUSEN, JOHN PHILLIPS, II, mental health facility administrator; b. Bryn Mawr, Pa., Jan. 2, 1954; s. Bayard and Cintra (Morgan) B.; m. Cidney Lynn Pardue, Mar. 17, 1990 (dec. July 10, 1990); 1 child, Zohar Roy. BSEE, U. Pa., 1976; MA, Lesley Coll., 1992. VISTA vol. Wilson (N.C.) Cmty. Improvement Assn., 1976-77; design engr. Teledyne TAC, Woburn, Mass., 1978-80; sr. design engr. U.S. Windpower, Burlington, Mass., 1980-88; field application engr. Inmos/SGS Thompson, Lincoln, Mass., 1988-90; counselor Ctr. Cmty. Counseling, Walpole, Mass., 1992-95; dir. Westborough (Mass.) Youth & Family Svcs., 1995—. Mem. Mass. Mental Health Counselors Assn. (treas. 1994-96). Office: Westborough Youth & Family Svcs 34 W Main St Westborough MA 01581-1902

BADENHOP, SHARON LYNN, psychologist, educator, entrepreneur; b. Roswell, N.Mex., Feb. 21, 1946; d. Charles Theodore and Anna (Burke) B.; BA in Ednl. Psychology, SUNY-Oneonta, 1967, MS, 1969, MS in Counselor Edn., 1971. Cert. mental health adminstr. Tchr. Gilbertsville (N.Y.) Central Sch., 1968-70; guidance counselor Delaware Acad., Delhi, N.Y., 1970-71; instr. SUNY-Oneonta, 1971-75; prof. SUNY-Delhi, 1974-75; psychol. case worker United Cerebral Palsy Assn., 1977-78; psychologist in psychogeratrics Rochester (N.Y.) Psychiat. Center, 1979, dir. edn. and tng. dept., 1979-81, psychologist, 1981-90; instr. U. Rochester, 1978-91, Rochester Inst. Tech., 1981-83, 92—; psychologist Securecare, 1985-91; founder, pres. USA East Assocs., Inc., 1991—; founder, sec. Internat. Resource Group; adj. faculty summer Shenandoah U., Winchester, Va., 1998. Bd. dirs. East House. Lic. guidance counselor, N.Y. State; cert. mental health adminstr.; cert. tchr. grades 1-6, N.Y. State, GEMS cons. Mem. NAFE, APA, SIETAR, Clin. Sociology Assn., Soc. Internat. Devel., Assn. Mental Health Adminstrs., Rochester Profl. Cons. Network, Coun. on Fgn. Rels., Internat. Soc. for Intercultural Edn., Tng. and Rsch. Home and Office: 18 Hollingham Rise Fairport NY 14450-1609

BADER, ALFRED ROBERT, chemist; b. Vienna, Austria, Apr. 28, 1924; came to U.S., 1947, naturalized, 1964; s. Alfred and Elizabeth Maria (Serenyi) B.; m. Isabel Overton, Jan. 26, 1982; children from previous marriage: David, Daniel. BS in Engring. Chemistry, Queens U., Can., 1945, BA in History, 1946, MS in Organic Chemistry, 1947, LLD, 1986; MA, Harvard U., 1948, PhD, 1949; DS (hon.), U. Wis.-Milw., 1980, Purdue U., 1984, U. Wis.-Madison, 1984, Northwestern U., 1990; D.Univ. (hon.), U. Sussex, Eng., 1989. Rsch. chemist PPG Co., Milw., 1950-54, group leader, 1953-54; chief chemist Aldrich Chem. Co., Milw., 1954-55, pres., 1955-81, chmn., 1981-91; pres. Sigma-Aldrich Corp., 1975-80, chmn., 1980-91, chmn. emeritus, 1991-92; pres. Alfred Bader Fine Arts, Milw., 1991—. Author: Adventures of a Chemist Collector, 1995. Guest curator Milw. Art Mus., 1976, 89—. Recipient Winthrop-Sears medal Chem. Industry Assn., 1980, J.E. Purkyne medal Acad. Scis., Czech Republic, 1994, Gold medal Am. Inst. Chemists, 1997, Boron USA award, 1997; named Entrepreneur of Year Research Dirs. Assn., 1980, Hon. Citizen, U. Vienna, 1995, Comdr. of the Brit. Empire, 1998. Fellow Royal Soc. Arts, Royal Soc. Chemistry (hon.); mem. Am. Chem. Soc. (award Milw. sect. 1971, Parsons' award, 1995, named one of the top 75 disting. contbrs. to the chem. enterprise in the last 75 years 1998), Chem. Soc. London, Coll. Art Assn. Jewish. Club: University (Milw.). Patentee in field. Office: Alfred Bader Fine Arts 924 E Juneau Ave Milwaukee WI 53202-2748

BADER, DIEDRICH, actor; b. Alexandria, Va., Dec. 24, 1968. Actor in feature film debut in dual role as twins Jethro and Jethrine in remake of tv series: The Beverly Hillbillies; actor (film): Teresa's Tattoo, 1994, Office Space, 1999, The Assassination File, (tv movies) Preppie Murder, 1989, (tv series): Danger Theatre, 1993, The Drew Carey Show, 1995—, Hercules, 1998; tv guest appearances include: 21 Jump Street, 1987, Fresh Prince of Bel-Air, 1990, Star Trek: The Next Generation, 1987, Cheers, 1982, Quantum Leap, 1989, Broken Badges, 1990, Flying Blind, 1992, Diagnosis Murder, 1993, Frasier, 1993, Gargoyles, 1994, Murphy Brown, 1988, Happy Hour, 1999. Office: Warner Bros Domestic TV Dist 4001 N Olive Ave Burbank CA 91522*

BADER, JOHN BURKHARDT, political scientist, educator; b. Washington, Jan. 8, 1963; s. William Banks and Gretta (Lange) B.; m. Amy Christine DeLouise, June 15, 1996; 1 child, Calvin James DeLouise Bader. BA in History, Yale U., 1985; MA in Polit. Sci., U. Wis., 1990, PhD in Polit. Sci., 1994. History tchr. Fairfax (Va.) County Schs., 1986-87; polit. rschr. ABC News, N.Y.C., 1987-88, asst. editor '88 election, 1988-89; project. asst. U. Wis., Madison, 1989-92; asst. prof. polit. sci., assoc. dir. Washington programs UCLA Ctr. Am. Politics & Pub. Policy, Washington, 1994—. Author: Taking the Initiative, 1996. Trustee Western Presbyn. Ch., Washington, 1997—; singer The Tone Rangers, Washington, 1995—. Fulbright scholar to India, 1985-86, Dirksen Congrl. scholar, 1997-98; fellow Brookings Inst., Washington, 1992-93, U. Wis., 1993-94. Avocation: singing. Office: UCLA Ctr Am Politics 2301 M St NW Washington DC 20037-1427

BADER, JOHN MERWIN, lawyer; b. Wilmington, Del., June 29, 1919; s. Merwin Oldrin and Escelyn (Connell) B.; m. Constance Wulffaert, Dec. 27, 1944 (div. Oct. 1965); children: Andrew M., Mary Drakely Donley, Eileen Williams, Matthew J.; m. Anne S. Shane, Jan. 15, 1973. BA, Villanova U., 1941; LLB, U. Pa., 1948. Bar: Del. 1948, U.S. Supreme Ct. 1956. Pvt. practice law Wilmington, 1948-56, 66-70; ptnr. Balick and Bader, Wilmington, 1956-59, Bader and Biggs, Wilmington, 1959-66, Bader, Dorsey & Kreshtool, Wilmington, 1970-81; pvt. practice Wilmington, 1981-85; ptnr. Bader & Williams, Wilmington, 1985-87; of counsel Tomar, Simonoff, Adourian & O'Brien, Wilmington, 1988—. Counsel Rep. State Com., Wilmington, 1975-85. Served to 1st lt. U.S. Army, 1941-45. Mem. Del. Bar Assn. (v.p. 1969-71), Assn. Trial Lawyers Am. (bd. govs. 1969-73, 75-80), Del. Trial Lawyers Assn. (pres. 1977-80). Club: Univ. & Whist (Wilmington). Lodge: Elks, Kiwanis. Home: 402 Rockwood Rd Wilmington DE 19802-1238 Office: Tomar Simonoff Adourian & O'Brien 919 N Market St Wilmington DE 19801-3023

BADER, LORRAINE GREENBERG, textile stylist, designer, consultant; b. Bklyn., Sept. 5, 1930; d. Isidore and Sadie (Schreier) Greenberg; m. Martin Bader, June 24, 1950; children: Evan Ashley, Reid Scott, Wade. Student, Parsons Sch. Design, 1948-49. Textile stylist, dir. design, fashion and spl. creative projects, color coord. Cortley Fabrics Corp., N.Y.C., 1950-64, Avon Fabrics, N.Y.C., 1964-67, R.S.L. Fabrics Corp., N.Y.C., 1967-71; textile stylist, fashion dir. Shirley Fabrics Corp., N.Y.C., 1971-76; interior designer, decorator Lorraine Bader Interiors, Lawrence, N.Y., 1976-79; textile stylist, dir. design, fashion, and spl. projects, color coord. Lida Inc., N.Y.C., 1979-81; textile designer Fresh Paint, N.Y.C., 1981-87; textile designer for women's wear, children's wear, fabrics, sweaters, scarves, dinnerware, tablecloths, placemats and bedding for home furnishings Lorraine Bader Designs, Hackensack, N.J., 1987—. Scholar Parsons Sch. Design, 1948. Mem. The Fashion Group. Avocations: painting all mediums, antiquing, interior decorating, faux decorative art.

BADER, ROBERT SMITH, biology, zoology educator and researcher; b. Falls City, Nebr., June 18, 1925; s. Ray Jay and Grace (Smith) B.; m. Joan Larson; children: Douglas, Jonathan, Eric, Joel. BS, Kans. State U., 1949; PhD, U. Chgo., 1954. From instr. to asst. prof. biology U. Fla., 1952-56; from asst. prof. to prof. zoology U. Ill., Urbana, 1956-68; prof. biology, dean Coll. Arts and Scis., U. Mo., St. Louis, 1968-83, rsch. prof., 1983-85; rsch. assoc. U. Kans., 1985-91; adj. prof. Kans. State U., 1986-91. With USNR, 1943-45. Achievements include research on Kansas history, prohibition history, Biblical theology. Home: 2165 Squirrel Rd Neosho Falls KS 66758-7122

BADER, ROCHELLE LINDA (SHELLEY BADER), educational administrator. BA in Speech Arts, BA in Edn., Hofstra U., 1970; MLS, U. Md., 1973; EdD, George Washington U., 1993. Mgmt. intern Office Civil Pers., Dept. of the Army, Pentagon, Washington, 1971; circulation libr. George Washington U. Med. Libr., Washington, 1971-73; head reference libr. Himmelfarb Health Scis. Libr./George Washington U. Med. Ctr., Washington, 1973-75, head Audio Visual Study Ctr., 1975-78, chief Access and Facilities Svcs. Divsn., 1978-79, chief Reader Svcs. Divsn., 1979-80, assoc. dir., 1980, dir., 1980-90; dir. ednl. resources George Washington U. Med. Ctr., Washington, 1990—, assoc. v.p. ednl. resources, 1998—; audio visual cons. Regional Med. Libr. Program, D.C. Metro area, 1977-79; mem. nat. adv. com. U. Iowa, 1984-85; mem. Med. Ctr. Faculty Senate Com. on Health Scis. Programs, George Washington U., Washington, 1989, chmn. Health Scis. Programs Ednl. Evaluation Com., 1993—, many other coms.; adv. com. Found. for Health Svcs. Rsch., 1992-93; presenter in field. Consulting editor: Biomedical Comms., 1983-84; mem. editorial rev. bd.: The Jour. of Biocommunication, 1988-92, Annual Statistics of Medical School Libraries in the United States and Canada, 12th, 13th and 14th edits., 1989-93; contbr. articles to profl. jours. Grantee Coun. on Libr. Resource, 1989-90, Nat. Libr. Medicine, 1991, NSF, 1993-94; recipient Disting. Svc. award Health Scis. Comms. Assn., 1986. Mem. Am. Med. Informatics Assn. (exec. com. edn. workshop group 1991—, MLA rep. to adv. coun. 1992—), Assn. Am. Med. Colls. (group on med. edn., coun. on acad. scos. 1991—), Assn. Acad. Health Scis. Libr. Dirs. (pres. 1986-87, chmn. fin. com. 1987-88), Assn. Biomedical Comms. Dirs. (membership com. 1989-91, program com. 1991), Health Scis. Comms. Assn. (coord. interactive media festival 1990-91, chmn. awards com. 1992, pres. 1984-85), Med. Libr. Assn. (bd. dirs. 1995—), Beta Phi Mu. Home: 12225 Seline Way Potomac MD 20854-2872 Office: George Washington U Med Ctr 2300 I St NW Washington DC 20037-2336

BADER, RONALD L., advertising executive; b. 1931. With Amana (Iowa) Refrigeration, 1949-55, Gittens Co., Milw., 1955-60, Brady Co., Milw., 1961-70, Hoffman, York, Baker & Johnson, Milw., 1971-74; with Bader Rutter & Assocs., Inc., Brookfield, Wis., 1975—, now pres, sec., treas., CEO. Office: Bader Rutter & Assoc Inc Bishop's Wood Ctr 13555 Bishops Ct Ste 300 Brookfield WI 53005-6231*

BADER, WILLIAM BANKS, historian, foundation executive, former corporate executive; b. Atlantic City, Sept. 8, 1931; s. Edward L. and Celeste Bader (Burkard) B.; m. Gretta Lange, Dec. 19, 1953; children: Christopher, Katharine, John, Karl Diedrich. B.A., Pomona Coll., Claremont, Calif., 1953; M.A., Princeton U., 1960, Ph.D., 1964. With Library of Congress, 1954-55; with Office Nat. Estimates, 1962-64; lectr. history Princeton U., 1964-65; with Dept. State, 1965-66, U.S. Senate Fgn. Relations Com., 1966-69; program officer, then European rep. Ford Found., 1969-73; program officer Office European and Internat. Affairs, Washington and; N.Y.C., 1973-74; fellow Woodrow Wilson Internat. Ctr. Scholars, 1974-75; dir. fgn. intelligence task force U.S. Senate, 1975-76; asst. dep. under sec. for policy Dept. Def., 1976-78; staff dir. U.S. Senate Fgn. Relations Com., 1978-81; v.p.

SRI Internat.-Washington, Arlington, Va., 1981-87; sr. v.p. SRI Internat., Menlo Park, Calif., 1988-92; pres. Eurasia Found., Washington, 1992-96; with World Bank Group, Washington, 1996-97, Ctr. Strategic and Internat. Studies, 1997—; assoc. dir. Ednl. and Cultural Affair US Information Agency, 1998—; adj. prof. Georgetown U. Author: Austria Between East and West: 1945-1955, 1966, The U.S. and the Spread of Nuclear Weapons, 1968, The Taiwan Relations Act: A Decade of Implementation, 1989; also articles. Bd. dirs. Samuel H. Kress Found., Am. Inst. for Contemporary German Studies, New Ind. States. Served as officer USNR, 1955-58, capt. Res. ret. Recipient Meritorious Service medal Dept. State, 1966, Sec. Def. medal for outstanding pub. service, 1979, Osterreichische Ehrenkreuz fur Wissenschaft und Kunst 1. Klasse (officer's cross), Republic of Austria, 1991. Mem. Council Fgn. Relations, Internat. Inst. Strategic Studies. Roman Catholic. Club: Cosmos (Washington). Office: Ctr Strategic and Internat Studies 301 4th St SW Rm 849 Washington DC 20547

BADER, W(ILLIAM) REECE, lawyer; b. Portland, Oreg., Oct. 31, 1941; s. William Lange and Phyllis Harriet (Cole) B.; m. Jean McCarty, Aug. 3, 1963 (div. 1993); children: Lawson R., Cole R.; m. Alicia Spatafore, June 14, 1998. BA, Williams Coll., 1963; JD, Duke U., 1966. Bar: D.C. 1967, Calif. 1969, U.S. Dist. Ct. D.C., U.S. Dist. Ct. (no., ctrl., ea. and so. dists.) Calif., U.S. Ct. Appeals (D.C., 2d, 3d, 7th, 9th and fed. cirs.), U.S. Tax Ct., U.S. Claims Ct., U.S. Supreme Ct. Law clk. to judge U.S. Ct. Appeals (D.C. cir.), Washington, 1966-68; assoc. Orrick, Herrington & Sutcliffe LLP, San Francisco, 1968-74, ptnr., 1974—; mem. legal adv. bd. Hastings Law Ctr. Found., 1981-87; mem. securities disputes resolution com. Ctr. for Pub. Resources, 1990—; mem. nat. arbitration and med. com. NASDR, 1994-98; mem. ad hoc com. on ct. facilities and design U.S. Jud. Conf., 1969-72, mem. adv. com. on civil rules, 1982-87, mem. standing com. on rules of practice and procedure, 1987-90; lectr., panelist Practicing Law Inst., ABA Am. Law Inst., Internat. Franchise Assn., Calif. Electronic Assn., many others; arbitrator, mediator Nat. Assn. Securities Dealers Regulation Inc., 1979—, Am. Arbitration Assn., 1979—, N.Y. Stock Exch., 1984—, Nat. Futures Assn., 1985—, Pvt. Adjudication Found., 1987-96. Mem. editl. bd. Alternatives, 1991—; editor: Securities News, 1993-94, Securities Arbitration, 1999, Private Securities Litigation Reform Act Reporter, 1996—; contbr. article to profl. jours. Trustee North Park Coll. and Theol. Sem., Chgo., 1984-89, sec., 1985-86, chmn., 1986-89. Fellow Am. Bar Found., Pvt. Adjudication Found., Environ. Law Inst.; mem. ABA (litig., bus., natural resources sects.), State Bar Calif. (litig., pub. law sects.), Securities Industry Assn. (compliance and legal divsn.), Futures Industry Assn. (compliance and legal divsn.), Bar Assn. San Francisco, D.C. Bar Assn. Avocations: collecting toy trains, squash, reading, travel. Home: 62 Lloyden Dr Atherton CA 94027-3834 Office: Orrick Herrington Sutcliffe LLP 1020 Marsh Rd Menlo Park CA 94025-1021

BADERTSCHER, DAVID GLEN, law librarian, consultant; b. Morrow, Ohio, Jan. 31, 1935; s. Glen C. and Blanche (Cluff) B.; m. Betty Jo Shafer, June 25, 1965. BS, Ind. State U., 1957, MS, 1962; MS, Rosary Coll., 1967. Tchr. Rockville High Sch., Ind., 1957-59, Medinah Elem. Sch., Ill., 1961-63; libr. Elgin Acad., Ill., 1963-64; tchr. Beachwood High Sch., Ohio, 1964-65; libr. Chgo. Pub. Libr., 1965-66; circulation, asst. reference libr. U. Chgo. Law Sch., 1966-70; libr. Schiff Hardin Waite Dorschel & Britton, Chgo., 1970-73; exec. libr. Georgetown U. Law Ctr., Washington, 1973-78; dir. libr. Milbank, Tweed, Hadley & McCloy, N.Y.C, 1978-80; prin. law libr. N.Y. Supreme Ct., N.Y.C., 1980—; cons. Urban Research Corp., Chgo., 1970-73, Herner & Co., 1977—, R.R. Bowker & Co., 1981-91, Nat. Ctr. for State Courts, 1992-96; advisor Computer Law Svc., 1972-82, EIS, 1978—; adj. prof. Baruch Coll., 1982—, bd. dirs. N.Y. Met. Reference and Rsch. Libr. Agy., chmn. bd. pers. com., 1989-93; mem. judges com. on automation and tech. State of N.Y. Unified Ct. Sys., 1994-96. Contbr. articles to profl. jours. Mem. corp. adv. bd. Tech. Forum Internat., 1997—. Served with AUS, 1959-61. Mem. ABA (assoc.), Medinah Tchrs. Assn. (pres. 1962-63), Am. Assn. Law Librs. (chmn. com. on automation, sci. devel. 1970-72, chmn. state, city and county law librs. sect. 1989-90, mem. adv. com. law libr. jour. 1989-91, conv. grantee 1970), Chgo. Assn. Law Librs. (pres., conf. chmn. 1970-72, mem. com. on automation and tech. for judges in N.Y. 1994-96), Am. Soc. Info. Sci. (editor SIG/Law Newsletter 1975-79), Assn. Info. Mgrs. Home: 257 Orchard St Apt 8 Westfield NJ 07090-3130 Office: NY Supreme Ct 100 Centre St New York NY 10013-4308

BADERTSCHER, DORIS RAE, elementary education educator; b. Akron, Ohio, May 10, 1935; d. Ray and Doris Ada (Lee) Shanaberger; m. James Lee Badertscher, Feb. 2, 1958; children: Leslie, Lynn. BS, Kent State U., 1957; MS, Calif. State U., Dominguez Hills, 1987. Tchr. Marion (Ohio) City Schs., 1968—; supr. Saturday sch., 1989-90; coach Odyssey Mind, 1984-85; chmn. Marion City Schs. divsn. Marion Art Fair, 1970; drama coach for 54 programs, 1968—, dir. make up, 1975-79. Author: (children's books) The Prying Princess, 1990, The Dragon Dilemma, 1990. Vol. Marion Gen. Hosp., 1970; mem. Marion Little Theatre, 1975-79, com. Teach-In Day, 1980, com. ednl. fair, 1990, Marion Women's Roundtable, 1987; coord. Black History Month, 1990; participant sexual assault and abuse prevention workshop, 1990, Jennings Scholar Alumni workshop, 1986; mem. Christian edn. com., deacon 1st Presbyn. Ch., Marion, 1986-88; founding mem. Guild One Grady Meml. Hosp., past pres., sec., 1986—; founder Kids for Grady Christmas News Paper; chair Right-to-Read Week, 1989-90; wedding coord., stewardship com. Emanuel Luth. Ch., 1996, bd. edn., chmn. of day care bd., 1997. Martha Holden Jennings scholar, 1980-81, Ohio Theatre Alliance scholar, 1984, 86; Career Exploration grantee, 1987; recipient Disting. Alumni award Cuyahoga Falls (Ohio) High Sch., 1991, Golden Apple Achiever award Ashland Oil Co., 1990. Mem. AAUW (pres. 1986-87, pres. 1993-94), Phi Delta Kappa, Alpha Gamma Delta, Alpha Psi Omega. Avocation: theatre, travel, knitting, reading, interior decoratin. Home: 1660 Westminster Rd Marion OH 43302-5854

BADGER, DAVID HARRY, lawyer; b. Indpls., June 16, 1931; s. David Henry and Mayme Pearl (Wright) B.; m. Donna Lee Bailey, June 24, 1954; children: David Mark, Lee Ann, Steven Michael. BEE, Rose Poly. Inst., 1953; JD, Ind. U., 1964. Bar: Ind. 1964, U.S. Dist. Ct. (so and no. dists.) Ind. 1964, U.S. Patent Office 1964, U.S. Ct. Customs and Patent Appeals 1971, U.S. Ct. Appeals (fed. cir.) 1982. Engr. GE, 1953-56, Ransburg Corp., Indpls., 1956-62; chief elec. engr. Rex Metal Craft, Inc., Indpls., 1963-64; patent counsel Ransburg Corp., Indpls., 1964-74, sec., 1974-76; legal counsel Ball Corp., Muncie, Ind., 1976-77; ptnr. Jenkins, Coffey, Hyland, Badger & Conard, Indpls., 1977-82; mng. ptnr. Brinks, Hofer, Gilson & Lione, Indpls., 1982-98. Contbr. articles to profl. jours.; patentee in U.S. and fgn. countries. With USN, 1953-55, lt. comdr. USNR. Named Hon. Alumnus Rose Hulman Inst. Tech., 1987. Mem. ABA (various coms.), IEEE, Ind. Bar Assn. (various coms.), Am. Intellectual Property Law Assn. (various coms.), Licensing Execs. Soc. (various coms.), Indpls. Bar Assn., Internat. Assn. Intellectual Property Law, Indpls. Jazz Club (bd. dirs. 1983-85, 95-97), Junto of Indpls. (bd. dirs. 1997—). Home: 938 E 58th St Indianapolis IN 46220-2606 Office: 1 Indiana Sq Ste 2425 Indianapolis IN 46204-2045

BADGER, SANDRA RAE, health and physical education educator; b. Pueblo, Colo., Nov. 2, 1946; d. William Harvey and Iva Alberta (Belveal) Allenbach; m. Graeme B. Badger, Oct. 9, 1972; 1 child, Jack Edward. BA in Phys. Edn., U. So. Colo., Pueblo, 1969; MA in Arts and Humanities, Colo. Coll., 1979; postgrad., Adams State U., Alamosa, Colo., 1980-91. Cert. tchr., secondary endorsement in health and phys. edn., Colo. Head women's swimming coach Mitchell High Sch., Doherty High Sch., Colorado Springs, Colo., 1969-90; head dept. Health Edn. Doherty High Sch., 1979—; asst. coach cross country men & women U. Colo., 1996—; trainer student asst. program CARE, Colorado Springs, 1983—; trainer drug edn. U.S. Swim Olympic Tng. Ctr., Colorado Springs, 1988-89; coach in track and field, Colorado Springs, 1989, 91; cons. Assocs. in Recovery Therapy, 1989—; speaker in field. Author, editor: Student Assistant Training Manual, 1983-95. Bd. dirs. ARC, Colo. Springs, 1990-96, sec., 1991-92, mem. health and safety com., 1990-95; reviewer ARC/Olympic Com. Sports Safety Tng. Manual Handbook Textbooks; mem. comprehensive health adv. com. Dept. Edn., State of Colo., Denver, 1991. Recipient Svc. award ARC, 1985, Coach of Yr. award Gazette Telegraph, 1979, 84, CARE award State of Colo., 1988, others; Gamesfield grantee, 1985; Nat. Coun. on Alcoholism grantee, 1990; named Readers' Digest Tchr. of Yr., 1998-99. Mem. NEA, Colorado Springs Edn. Assn. Avocations: scuba diving, running, travel. Office: Doherty High Sch 4515 Barnes Rd Colorado Springs CO 80917-1599

BADGEROW, JOHN NICHOLAS, lawyer; b. Macon, Mo., Apr. 7, 1951; s. Harry Leroy Badgerow and Barbara Raines (Buell) Novaria; m. Teresa Ann Zvolanek, Aug. 7, 1976; children: Anthony Thornton, Andrew Cameron, James Terrill. BA in Bus. and English with honors, Principia Coll., 1972; JD, U. Mo., Kansas City, 1975. Bar: Kans. 1976, U.S. Dist. Ct. Kans. 1976, U.S. Ct. Appeals (10th cir.) 1977, U.S. Ct. Appeals (4th cir.) 1979, U.S. Supreme Ct. 1982, U.S. Ct. Appeals (fed. cir.) 1985, U.S. Ct. Appeals (8th cir.) 1986, Mo. 1986, U.S. Dist. Ct. (we. dist.) Mo. 1986. Ptnr. McAnany, VanCleave & Phillips, P.A., Kansas City, Kans., 1975-85; ptnr.-in-charge Spencer, Fane, Britt & Browne, Kansas City, Mo. and Overland Park, Kans., 1986—; Co-author, co-editor: Kansas Lawyer Ethics, 1996. Co-author: Kansas Employment Law, 1992. Co-chmn. Civil Justice Reform Act Commn., Dist. of Kans., 1995-96. Mem. ABA, Kans. Jud. Coun., Kans. Bar Assn. (employment seminars, bd. editors 1982-88, CLE com. 1989-95, Outstanding Svc. award 1995, mem. ethics adv. opinion com. 1997—), Kans. Met. Bar Assn. (chmn. civil rights com.), Lawyers' Assn. Kansas City, Kans. Assn. Def. Counsel (age discrimination seminar), Mission Valley Hunt Club (Stilwell, Kans.). Republican. Christian Scientist. Avocations: horseback riding, carpentry, reading. Office: Spencer Fane Britt & Browne Ste 700 9401 Indian Creek Pky Shawnee Mission KS 66210-2005

BADGLEY, JOHN ROY, architect; b. Huntington, W. Va., July 10, 1922; s. Roy Joseph and Fannie Myrtle (Limbaugh) B.; m. Janice Atwell, July 10, 1975; 1 son, Adam; children by previous marriage: Dan, Lisa, Holly, Marcus, Michael. AB, Occidental Coll., 1943; MArch, Harvard, 1949; postgrad., Centro Internazionale, Vincenza, Italy, 1959. Pvt. practice, San Luis Obispo, Calif., 1952-65; chief architect, planner Crocker Land Co., San Francisco, 1965-80; v.p. Cushman & Wakefield Inc., San Francisco, 1980-84; pvt. practice, San Rafael, Calif., 1984—; tchr. Calif. State U. at San Luis Obispo, 1952-65; bd. dirs. Ft. Mason Ctr., Angel Island Assn. Served with USCGR, 1942-54. Mem. AIA, Am. Arbitration Assn., Golden Gate Wine Soc. Home and Office: 1356 Idylberry Rd San Rafael CA 94903-1074

BADGLEY, THEODORE MCBRIDE, psychiatrist, neurologist; b. Salem, Ala., June 27, 1925; s. Roy Joseph and Fannie (Limbaugh) B.; m. Mary Bennett Wells, Dec. 30, 1945; children: Justice Badgley O'Neil, Jan Badgley, Mona Jean Badgley Covey, Jason Wells, James John, Mary Rose Badgley Bleier. Student, Occidental Coll., 1942-44; M.D., U. So. Calif., 1949. Diplomate: Am. Bd. Psychiatry and Neurology. Intern Letterman Gen. Hosp., San Francisco, 1949-50; resident in psychiatry Letterman Gen. Hosp., 1950-53; commd. capt. M.C. U.S. Army, 1950, advanced through grades to lt. col., 1967; chief mental hygiene cons. service Ft. Gordon, Ga.; and asso. clin. prof. psychiatry and neurology Med. Coll. Ga., 1954-55; resident in neurology Walter Reed Gen. Hosp., Washington, 1955-57; asst. chief psychiatry service Walter Reed Gen. Hosp., 1957-59, chief psychiatry service, 1959-62, asst. chief dept. psychiatry and neurology, 1962-63, dir. edn. and tng. psychiatry, 1957-63; chief dept. psychiatry and neurology U.S. Army Gen. Hosp., Landstuhl, Germany, 1963-66; chief psychiatry outpatient dept. Letterman Gen. Hosp., 1966-67; ret., 1967; dir. Kern View Mental Health Center, Bakersfield, Calif., 1967-69; pvt. practice medicine specializing in med. and forensic neuropsychiatry Bakersfield, 1967-93; pres. Sans Doloroso Inst., Bakersfield, 1969-93; lectr. community health service orgns., profl. confs., seminars. Contbr. articles to profl. jours. Fellow Am. Psychiat. Assn. (life); mem. Kern County Psychiat. Soc. (pres. 1972-93), Kern County Med. Soc. (pres. 1981). Home: 21508 Indian Wells Dr Tehachapi CA 93561-8029 *My father is—will always be—30 years older than I.*

BADHAM, JOHN MACDONALD, motion picture director; b. Luton, Eng., Aug. 25, 1939; came to U.S., 1945; s. Henry Lee and Mary Iola (Hewitt) B.; 1 child, Kelly MacDonald; m. Julia Laughlin, 1992. BA, Yale U., 1961, MFA, 1963. Assoc. producer Universal Studios, 1969-70; pres. Gt. Am. Picture Show; chmn. bd. JMB Films, Inc.; pres. Badham Co.; guest lectr. UCLA, Yale U., U. So. Calif., Amherst Coll. Assoc. producer TV movies Night Gallery, 1969, Neon Ceiling, 1970; assoc. producer, dir. TV movies The Senator, 1970 (Emmy award nomination 1971); dir. numerous episodes of The Bold Ones, others; motion pictures for TV include The Law (Emmy nomination 1974), 1974 (ARD reihe 'das film festival award 1975), Isn't It Shocking, 1973, Reflections of Murder, 1973, The Impatient Heart (Christopher award 1971), The Gun, (So. Calif. Motion Picture Council award 1974), The Godchild, 1974, Sorrow Floats, 1998; theatrical motion pictures include The Bingo Long Travelling All Stars and Motor Kings (NAACP image award nomination 1976), Saturday Night Fever, 1977, Dracula, 1979 (Grand prize 9th Internat. Sci. Fiction Festival of Paris, Best Horror Film award and, 1st George Pal Meml. award, both Acad. of Sci. Fiction Fantasy and Horror Films), Whose Life Is It Anyway, 1981, Blue Thunder, 1983, War Games (Best Dir., Acad. of Sci. Fiction Fantasy and Horror Films), 1983, American Flyers, 1985, Short Circuit, 1986, Stakeout, 1987, Bird on a Wire, 1989, The Hard Way, 1990, Point of No Return, 1993, Another Stakeout, 1993, Drop Zone, 1994, Nick of Time, 1995, Incognito, 1998, Floating Away, 1998, The Jack Bull, 1999; exec. prodr. motion picture Rebound, 1996. Bd. dirs. Indian Spring Sch. Served with U.S. Army, 1963-64. Mem. Dirs. Guild Am., Am. Film Inst., Acad. Motion Picture Arts and Scis., Yale Drama Alumni Fund (chmn.).

BADHAM, JULIA AILEEN, artist; b. San Francisco, July 23, 1945; d. Thomas Floyd and Aileen Mary (Koeber) Laughlin; m. Dean Tussey Hallo, Nov. 22, 1985 (div. Apr. 1992); m. John MacDonald Badham, July 11, 1992. Student, Calif. State U., Northridge, L.A. Pierce Coll., Woodland Hills, Otis Art Inst., L.A., UCLA. Art dir., set decorator Pytka, Venice, Calif., 1984-90, Angel City Prodns., Hollywood, Calif., 1990-94; set decorator Warner Bros., Burbank, Calif., 1992, Disney, Glendale, Calif., 1993, Paramount Pictures, Hollywood, Calif., 1995. Art dir., set decorator over 200 TV commls., 1984-94; set decorator Point of No Return movie, 1992, Another Stakeout, 1993, Nick of Time, 1995. Mem. Set Decorators Soc. Am., Internat. Alliance of Theatrical and Stage Employees. Avocations: painting, sculpting. Office: c/o Elkins and Elkins 16830 Ventura Blvd Ste 300 Encino CA 91436-1715

BADIAN, ERNST, history educator; b. Vienna, Austria, Aug. 8, 1925; came to U.S., 1968; m. Nathlie A. Wimsett, 1950; children: Hugh I., Rosemary J. BA, U. N.Z., 1945, MA, 1946; BA, Oxford (Eng.) U., 1950, MA, 1954, DPhil, 1956; LittD, Victoria U., Wellington, N.Z., 1962; DLitt (Hon.), Macquarie Univ., 1993; LittD (Hon.), U. Canterbury, 1999. Jr. lectr. classics Victoria U., 1947-48; asst. lectr. classics and ancient history U. Sheffield, Eng., 1952-54; lectr. classics U. Durham, Eng., 1954-65; prof. ancient history U. Leeds, Eng., 1965-69; prof. classics and history SUNY, Buffalo, 1969-71; prof. history Harvard U., 1971-82, John Moors Cabot prof. history, 1982-98, John Moors Cabot prof. history emeritus, 1998—; vis. prof. univs. Colo., Oreg., Wash., South Africa, Heidelberg, Tel-Aviv, Western Australia, UCLA; Sather prof. U. Calif., Berkeley, 1976; vis. mem. Inst. Advanced Study, Princeton, fall 1980, fall 1992, Nat. Humanities Ctr., fall 1988, Kommission für Alte Geschichte, Munich, May 1989. Author: Foreign Clientelae, 264-70 B.C., 1958 (Conington prize Oxford U.), Studies in Greek and Roman History, 1964, Roman Imperialism in the Late Republic, 1967, Publicans and Sinners, 1972, From Plataea to Potidaea: Studies in the History and Historiography of the Pentecontaetia, 1993, Zöllner und Sünder, 1997; editor: Polybius, 1966, Ancient Society and Institutions, 1966, Sir Ronald Syme, Roman Papers vols. 1-2, 1979, Am. Jour. Ancient History, 1976—. Fellow Am. Coun. Learned Socs., 1972-73, 82-83, Leverhulme fellow, Eng., 1973, Guggenheim fellow, 1984, hon. fellow Univ. Coll., Oxford, Eng. Fellow Brit. Acad., Am. Acad. Arts and Scis., Am. Numismatic Soc.; hon. mem. Soc. Promotion Roman Studies; corr. mem. Austrian Acad. Scis., German Archeol. Inst.; fgn. mem. Finnish Acad. Scis.; mem. Am. Philol. Assn., Assn. Ancient Historians, Classical Assn. Can., U.K. Classical Assn., Soc. Promotion Hellenic Studies, Virgil Soc. Office: Harvard U Robinson Hall Cambridge MA 02138

BADICS, ZSOLT, electrical engineer, researcher; b. Budapest, Hungary, Nov. 29, 1959; s. Tibor and Margit (Nagy) B.; m. Magdolna Szorcsok, Apr. 9, 1982; children: Andras, Aron. DiplEng, Tech. U. Budapest, 1984, DrTech, 1992. Asst. prof. Tech. U. Budapest, 1987-92; chief engr. Nuclear Fuel Industries, Ltd., Osaka, Japan, 1992-97; rsch. and dev. engr. Ansoft Corp., Pittsburgh, Pa., 1997—. Contbr. articles to tech. jours. Mem. (sr.) IEEE, Internat. Compumag Soc., Soc. for Indsl. and Applied Math. Avocations: jazz, jogging, skiing, tennis. Office: Ansoft Corp 4 Station Sq Ste 660 Pittsburgh PA 15219-1119

BADIE, RONALD PETER, banker; b. Elizabeth, N.J., Dec. 13, 1942; s. R. Peter and Madeline E. (Knoop) B.; m. Fabiana Duclos; children: Tracey, Tamara, Tara, Gabrielle, Alexandra. B.S., Bucknell U., 1964; M.B.A., NYU, 1971. Sr. v.p. Bankers Trust Co., N.Y.C., 1979-86; mng. dir. Bankers Trust Co., L.A., 1986-96; sr. mng. dir. Bankers Trust Co. Calif., L.A., 1996—, also bd. dirs.; mem. adv. bd. Merrill Lynch Capital Appreciation Fund II, Green Equity Investors II. Mem. adv. bd. entrepreneurial studies program UCLA Sch. Mgmt., Stonington Capital Appreciation Fund. Republican. Home: 3747 Chevy Chase Dr La Canada Flintridge CA 91011-4163 Office: Bankers Trust Co 300 S Grand Ave Los Angeles CA 90071-3109

BADLER, NORMAN IRA, computer and information science educator; b. L.A., May 3, 1948; s. Bernard and Lillian Lorraine Badler; m. Virginia Renke, June 14, 1968; children: Jeremy, David. BA in Creative Studies, U. Calif., Santa Barbara, 1970; MS in Computer Sci., U. Toronto, Toronto, 1971, PhD in Computer Sci., 1975. Lectr. U. Toronto, 1973-74; asst. prof. computer and info. sci. U. Pa., Phila., 1974-79, assoc. prof., 1979-86, prof., 1986—, Cecilia Fitler Moore prof., 1990-94, dir. Ctr. for Human Modeling and Simulation, 1994—; mem., chmn. program coms. numerous confs. and workshops. Co-author: Simulating Humans, 1993; co-editor: Making Them Move, 1990; contbr. numerous articles to profl. jours. Grantee Advanced Rsch. Projects Agy., NSF, Nat. Libr. of Medicine, U.S. Army, USAF. Mem. IEEE Computer Soc., Assn. for Computing Machinery (vice chmn. spl. interest group on graphics 1979-81, mem. spl. interest group on artificial intelligence), Cognitive Sci. Soc., Am. Assn. for Artificial Intelligence, Phi Beta Kappa. Democrat. Jewish. Avocations: home renovation, cooking. Office: U Pa Computer & Info Sci Dept Philadelphia PA 19104-6389

BADO, KENNETH STEVE, automotive company administrator; b. Amherst, Ohio, Mar. 13, 1941; s. Steve and Hildegarde Paulene (Gutosky) B.; m. Linda Bonita Crabtree, May 30, 1962 (div. Oct. 1989); children: Bradley Steve, Cheryl Lynn Smith, John Robert; m. Polly Ann Steele, Nov. 28, 1989. Student, Ohio U., 1958-60, Lorain County Community Coll., 1960-62. Mfg. planning specialist Ford Motor Co., Lorain, Ohio, 1961-97; farmer Henrietta, Ohio, 1972—; owner, mgr. The Galleon, Lorain, 1986—; leader Sub-System Group (Group Tng.), Lorain, 1987-92. Advisor Lorain County Steer Club (4-H), Lorain County, 1977-93, Henrietta Hazers Club (4-H), Lorain County, 1976-88. Mem. Am. Quarter Horse Assn., Ohio Quarter Horse Assn., Moose, Masons (32 degree), Scottish Rite Soc. Republican. Lutheran. Avocations: boating, fishing, horseback riding, computer work. Home: 12359 Baird Rd # 2 Oberlin OH 44074-9632 Office: The Galleon 4875 W Erie Ave Lorain OH 44053-1331

BADR, GAMAL MOURSI, legal consultant; b. Helwan, Egypt, Feb. 8, 1924; came to U.S., 1970; s. Ahmad Moursi and Aisha Morshida (Al-Alaily) B.; m. Fatima al-Zahraa Barakat, June 18, 1950; children: Hefni, Hussein. LLB, U. Alexandria, Arab Republic of Egypt, 1944, LLD summa cum laude, 1954; diploma in econs., U. Cairo, 1945, diploma in pvt. law, 1946. Asst. dist. atty. Mixed Cts. Egypt, Alexandria, 1945-49; from assoc. to ptnr. Vatimbella, Catzeflis, Garrana & Badr, Alexandria, 1949-63; legal advisor UN Congo Operation, Kinshasa, Congo, 1963-64; justice Supreme Ct. Algeria, Algiers, 1965-69; from mem. to dep. dir. legal dept. UN Secretariat, N.Y.C., 1970-84; legal advisor Mission of Qatar to UN, N.Y.C., 1984-94; advisor Mission of Saudi Arabia to UN, N.Y.C., 1998—; permanent bur. mem. Pan-Arab Lawyers' Fedn., Cairo, 1959-61; adj. prof. law NYU, 1982—; lectr. The Hague Acad. Internat. Law, 1984. Author: Agency, 1980, State Immunity, 1984; gen. editor Commercial Law of the Middle East; contbr. articles to profl. jours. Mem. Internat. Law Assn. (London), Am. Soc. Internat. Law, Am. Arbitration Assn. (panel of arbitrators), Am. Fgn. Law Assn. (v.p. 1985-87, 89-92), Egyptian-Am. Assn. (pres. 1987-90), Rotary (pres. Alexandria Club 1962-63). Muslim. Home: 18 Peter Lynas Ct Tenafly NJ 07670-1115

BADRA, ROBERT GEORGE, philosophy, religion and humanities educator; b. Lansing, Mich., Dec. 8, 1933; s. Razouk Anthony and Anna (Paul) B.; m. Maria Teresa Beer, Oct. 25, 1968 (div. 1973); m. Kristen Lillie Stuckey, Dec. 30, 1977; children: Rachal Jennifer, Danielle Elizabeth Jane. BA, Sacred Heart Sem., 1957; MA, Western Mich. U., 1968; MDiv, St. John's Provincial Sem., 1985. Ordained priest Roman Cath. Ch., 1961. Mem. faculty Kalamazoo Valley C.C., 1968—, prof. philosophy, religion and humanities, 1968—; adj. prof. Nazareth Coll., 1985-91, Siena Heights Univ., 1993—; mem. faculty ministry formation, Cath. Diocese of Kalamazoo, 1999—. Author: Meditations for Spiritual Misfits, 1983; columnist Western Mich. Cath., Grand Rapids, 1983-88. Bd. dirs. Kalamazoo Coun. for Humanities, 1983-86, Van Buren Youth Camp, 1993-95. Recipient Edn. award Exxon, 1996; NEH grantee 1991—. Mem. Assn. Religion and Intellectual Life. Office: Kalamazoo Valley CC PO Box 4070 Kalamazoo MI 49003-4070

BADUR, DIANA ISABEL, English language educator; b. Mayaquez, P.R., Sept. 26, 1957; d. Fred V. and Nilda C. (Flores) Soltero; m. Gultekin Badur, May 21, 1985; children: Ahmet, Mehmet. BA magna cum laude, U. P.R., 1978; MA, U. Wis., 1979, PhD, 1982. Asst. prof. Sacred Heart U., San Juan, P.R., 1982-84; lectr. U. Houston, Houston C. C., 1985-87; vis. asst. prof. Tex. A&M U., Coll. Sta., 1987-88; lectr. U. Md. extension, Izmir, Turkey, 1989; vis. asst. prof. Inter-Am. U., San German, P.R., 1991; prof. Black Hawk Coll., Moline, Ill., 1991—; translator Ctr. for Environ. Rsch., San Juan, 1983, 84, P.R. Water Resources Authority, San Juan, 1983, 84. Mem. Logan Elem. PTA Bd., Moline, 1996-97; bd. dirs. Moline Coun. for Gifted. Mem. NCTE, Ill. Assn. Tchrs. English, Butterworth PTA, Washington PTA. Office: Black Hawk Coll 6600 34th Ave Moline IL 61265-5870

BAE, FRANK S. H., law educator, law librarian; b. Chung King, Szechuan, China, Dec. 19, 1941; came to U.S., 1967; s. Tse H. and Yu F. (Wang) B.; m. Anne Rita Donavan, March 15, 1975; children: Stephen, David, Marie, Elizabeth. LLB, Nat. Chung Shing U., Taipei, Taiwan, 1965; MCL, U. Miami, Fla., 1968; MS, U. Wis., 1970; JurD (hon.), New England Sch. Law, Boston, 1977. Dir. law libr. New England Sch. Law, 1970—, asst. prof. law, 1970-73, assoc. prof. law, 1973-74, prof. law, 1974—. Co-author: Searching the Law, 2nd edit., 1999. Mem. New England Law Libr. Consortium (bd. dirs.). Office: New Eng Sch Law Libr 154 Stuart St Boston MA 02116-5616

BAECHLER, DONALD, painter; b. Hartford, Conn., 1956. Student, Md. Inst. Art, 1974-76, Cooper Union, N.Y.C., 1977-78, Staatliche Hochschule Kunste, Frankfurt, Germany, 1978-79. Exhibited in group shows at Wadsworth Atheneum, Hartford, Conn., 1975, Whitney Mus. Am. Art, N.Y.C., 1989, Parallel Visions, Modern Artists and Outsider Art, L.A. County Mus. Art, 1992; one-man shows include Sperone Westwater, N.Y.C., 1993, 95, Paul Kasmin Gallery, N.Y.C., 1993, Erika and Otto Friedrich, Bern, Switzerland, 1994, Pace Prints, N.Y.C., 1994, Stephen Wirtz Gallery, San Francisco, 1994, Laura Carpenter Fine Art, Santa Fe, 1994, Galerie Thaddaeus Ropac, Paris, 1994-95; rep. in permanent collection Barbara Krakow Gallery, Boston, 1994, Matthew Marks Gallery, N.Y.C., 1994, Eva Menzio, Turin, Italy, 1994, Tony Shafrazi Gallery, N.Y.C., 1995. Office: Paul Kasmin Galleryl 74 Grand St New York NY 10013-2235*

BAECKSTROM, MARIANNE, actuary; b. Stockholm, Mar. 16, 1925; came to U.S., 1959; d. Carl Emil Leonard and Anna Brita Marianne (Eastman) Liedstrand; m. Gosta Michael Baeckstrom, July 8, 1947; children: Christer Gustav, Monica Ann. BS, Stockholm U., 1948. Actuarial asst. Towers Perrin, Phila., 1950-65, actuarial supr., 1965-74, asst. mgr., 1974-79, mgr. actuarial ops., 1979-85, prin., 1976-85, outside cons., 1985-93; retired. Mem. Am. Swedish Hist. Mus. (bd. dirs. women's aux. 1995—), Swedish Colonial Soc., Swedish Women's Ednl. Assn., Vasa Order Am. Home: 1321 Carol Rd Meadowbrook PA 19046-2505

BAEHR, STEPHEN LESSING, Russian langauge educator, researcher; b. Hartford, Conn., Aug. 23, 1945; s. Lawrence Lessing and Sophie Sylvia Baehr; m. Irina Leonidovna Mess, July 30, 1977. BA in Econs. magna cum laude, Clark U., 1967; MA in Slavic Langs., Columbia U., 1970, PhD with distinction, 1972. Asst. prof. Russian U. Va. Dept. Slavic Langs., Charlottesville, 1972-78; Andrew Mellon Faculty Fellow in Humanities Harvard U., Cambridge, Mass., 1978-79; assoc. prof. Russian & humanities Va. Poly. Inst. & State U., 1979-88, assoc. prof. Russian, 1988-94, prof., 1994—. Author: The Paradise Myth in Eighteenth-Century Russia, 1991; editor

Slavic and East European Jour., 1999—; contbr. articles to profl. jours. Fulbright-Hays rsch. fellow U.S. Dept. Edn. U. Helsinki, Finland, 1991, Coun. Internat. Exch. Scholars/Finland-U.S. Ednl. Exch. Commn., 1990-91, Nat. Endowment Humanities rsch. fellow, 1984-85, rsch. fellow Harvard U., 1975-76, U. Va. Summer Faculty rsch. fellow, 1973, 74, jr. fellow Columbia U. Russian Inst., 1971-72, Edward John Noble Leadership fellow Columbia U., 1967-71. Mem. Am. Assn. Advancement Slavic Studies, Am. Assn. Tchrs. Slavic & Eastern European Langs. & Lit., Phi Beta Kappa. Avocations: travel, walking, music. Office: Va Poly Inst & State U Dept Fgn Langs Blacksburg VA 24061-0225

BAEHR, THEODORE, religious organization administrator, communications executive; b. May 31, 1946; m. Liliana Milani, 1975; children: Thedore Peirce, James Stuart Castiglioni, Robert Gallatin, Evelyn Noelle. *His father Theodore Baehr starred in stage and screen under the name Robert (Bob Tex) Allen. As a cowboy star, he rated next to Tim McCoy. As a Hollywood star, he received a box office award in the 1930s. On Broadway, he starred in Showboat, Auntie Mame and Whoopie. His mother Evelyn Pierce starred in many movies in the 1930s* Student in French lit. U. Bordeaux and Toulouse, France, 1967; student English lit. Cambridge (Eng.) U., 1967; student German lit. U. Munich, 1968; BA in Comparative Lit. with high distinction, Dartmouth Coll., 1969; JD, NYU, 1972; postgrad. Inst. Theology, Cathedral St. John the Divine, N.Y.C., 1978-80. Rsch. engr. Precision Sci. Co., Chgo., 1964-65; legal cons. firm Dandeub, Fleissig & Assocs., N.Y.C., 1970-71; law student asst. U.S. Atty.'s Office, So. Dist. N.Y., 1971-72; pres. Agape Prodns., N.Y.C., 1972-79, chmn. bd., 1979-82; exec. dir. Good News Comms., Inc., N.Y.C., 1978-80, chmn. bd., 1980—; pres. Episc. Radio-TV Found., Inc., Atlanta, 1981-82, Trinity Concepts, 1982; cons. media; dir. TV Center, CUNY at Bklyn. Coll., 1979-80, 82—; Episc. Communicators, 1981-84; exec. prodr. Ch.'s Presence at World's Fair, Knoxville, Tenn., 1982; dir. Am. Theater Actors, Episc. Comms. Editor, Commentator, NYU Law Sch. newspaper, 1969-72, Contemporary Drug Problems, 1971-72, Atlanta Area Christian News; creator, coord. Communicate Workshops, 1979; creator, writer, editor Episc. Ch. Video Resource Guide and Episcopal Video/TV Newsletter, 1979; prodr., dir., writer various TV and radio programs including Movieguide, Joy of Music, Perspectives, PBS, 1981-82, Religionwise on WGST, CBS, 1981— (Religion in Media award), Searching, 1978-80, others; editor, writer various books, including TV and Reality, Asking the Right Questions, Tangled Christian Communications, Getting the Word Out (Wilbur award), Movie and Video Guide for Christian Families (Religion in Media award), Hollywood's Reel of Fortune, 1991, The Media-Wise Family, 1998; dir. Runaways (Chgo. Intercom Gold Plaque and Religion in Media award 1989); prodr. In Their Own Words, Was It Love (Religion in Media award). V.p. Ctr. for TV in Humanities, 1982; chmn. bd. Christian Film & TV Commn., 1990—; bd. dirs. Celebrate Life, Christian Conciliation Svc., Dorsey Theatre, SUP, Inc., Coalition on Revival, Habitat for Humanity; mem steering com. Theol. Summit Conf. Mem. Nat. Assn. TV Arts and Scis., Nat. Religious Broadcasters (dir., chmn. TV com.), Bishop in Ind. Christian Chs. Internat., Seawanhaka Corinthian Yacht Club, Nat. Press Club.*After putting together financing for five feature films, Dr. Baehr went to seminary and headed up the TV Center at City University of New York. In the late 1970s, he instituted comprehensive research on the influence of the mass media. Next, Dr. Baehr went on to head the denominational organizations that produced C.S. Lewis' The Lion, The Witch, and the Wardrobe on CBS. This C.S. Lewis TV program won an Emmy Award. Dr. Baehr now dedicates his career to redeeming the values of the media. He accomplishes this by informing media executives about the concerns of Christian families and by helping Christian families become media-wise*

BAEHRE, EDNA VICTORIA, college president; b. Dreisen, Germany, Mar. 15, 1949. BA, Paedagogische Hochschule, Heidelberg, Germany, 1971; MA, SUNY, Buffalo, 1973, PhD, 1977. Pres. Harrisburg (Pa.) Area C.C., 1998—. Office: 1 Harrisburg Area CC Dr Harrisburg PA 17110-2999

BAEK, PAUL, neurological surgeon; b. Mar. 5, 1961; m. Sandy Abler. MD, Med. Coll. Wis., Milw., 1988. Diplomate Am. Bd. Neurol. Surgeons. Resident in neurosurgery Med. Coll. Wis., Milw., 1988-95; neurol. surgeon U.S. Navy, San Diego, 1995-98, Bay Care, Green Bay, Wis., 1998—. Lt. comdr. USNR, 1995-98. Office: Neurol Surgeons 720 S Van Buren St # 302 Green Bay WI 54301

BAER, ADAM SCOTT, artist; b. Portchester, N.Y., Mar. 16, 1969; s. Stephen Samuel Baer and Linda Elaine (Kassed) Nieberg. BFA in Photography, SUNY, Purchase, 1992. Mem. People for the Ethical Treatment of Animals, Greenwich, Conn., 1994—. Fellowship in photography J.S. Guggenheim Meml. Found., 1998, The Aaron Siskind Found., 1995, N.Y. Found. for the Arts, 1994. Mem. Sierra Club. Avocations: hiking, theater, arts and dance, music. Home: 7 Riverview Ct Greenwich CT 06831-4127

BAER, ERIC, engineering and science educator; b. Nieder-Weisel, Germany, July 18, 1932; came to U.S., 1947, naturalized, 1952; s. Arthur and Erna (Kraemer) B.; m. Ana Golender, Aug. 5, 1956; children: Lisa, Michelle. M.A., Johns Hopkins, 1953, D. of Engring., 1957. Research engr., polychems. dept. E.I. du Pont de Nemours & Co., Inc., 1957-60; asst. prof. chemistry and chem. engring. U. Ill., 1960-62; assoc. prof. engring. Case Inst. Tech., 1962- 66; prof., head dept. polymer sci. Case Western Res. U., 1966-78; dean Case Inst. Tech., 1978-83, Leonard Case prof. macromolecular sci., 1984-89, Herbert Henry Dow prof. sci. and engring., 1989—; cons. to industry, 1961—, Edison Polymer Innovations Corp. Author articles in field.; Editor: Engineering Design for Plastics, 1963, Polymer Engineering and Science, 1967-90, Journal of Applied Polymer Science, 1988—. Recipient Curtis W. McGraw award ASEE, 1968. Mem. Am. Chem. Soc. (Borden award 1981), Am. Phys. Soc., Am. Inst. Chem. Engring., Soc. Plastics Engring. (internat. award 1980), Plastics Inst. Am. (trustee). Home: 2 Mornington Ln Cleveland Heights OH 44106 Office: Case Western Reserve Univ Engring Dept Cleveland OH 44106*

BAER, GEORGE MARTIN, veterinarian, researcher; b. London, Jan. 12, 1936; came to U.S., 1940; s. Curtis Otto and Kathi (Meyer) B.; m. Maria Olga Lara, June 13, 1960; children: Katherine, Yvette, Isabella. DVM, Cornell U., 1959; MPH, U. Mich., 1961. Pvt. equine practice Calif., 1959-60; epidemiologist Ctrs. Disease Control, Albany, N.Y., 1961-63; acting chief rabies div. Ctrs. Disease Control, Atlanta, Ga., 1963-64, S.W. Rabies Investigations Ctr., Las Cruces, N.Mex., 1964-66; rabies cons. Pan Am. Health Orgn., Mex. City, 1966-69; chief rabies lab. Ctrs. Disease Control, Atlanta, 1969-91; dir. Collab Lab. for Reference and Rsch. in Rabies, WHO, 1970-91, Laboratorios Baer, Mex., 1991—. Editor: The Natural History of Rabies, 1975, 2d edit., 1991. Mem. Am. Vet. Med. Assn., Am. Pub. Health Assn., N.Y. Acad. Scis. Democrat. Mem. Soc. of Friends. Office: Labs Baer, Calle Cuautla # 150, Mexico City 06140, Mexico

BAER, HAROLD, JR., judge; b. N.Y.C., Feb. 16, 1933; s. Harold and Edna (Jacobus) B.; grad. magna cum laude, Hobart Coll., 1954; LLB, Yale U., 1957; m. Suzanne Harris, Aug. 18, 1957; children: Elizabeth Jane, Linda Gail. Bar: N.Y. 1959, U.S. Supreme Ct. 1964, U.S. Ct. Appeals (2d cir.) 1961, U.S. Dist. Ct. (so. dist.) N.Y. 1961. Asst. U.S. atty. So. Dist. N.Y., chief organized crime unit, 1961-66; exec. dir. civilian complaint rev. bd. N.Y.C. Police Dept., 1966-67; 1st dep. asst. U.S. atty., chief criminal div. U.S. Atty.'s Office So. Dist. N.Y., 1970-71; partner Guggenheimer & Untermyer, N.Y.C., 1968-70, 72-82; justice N.Y. State Supreme Ct., 1982-92; exec. jud. officer Jud. Arbitration and Mediation Svcs. (JAMS)/Endispute, 1992-94; apptd. U.S. Dist. judge So. Dist. N.Y., 1994—; mem. N.Y.C. mayoral com. alleged police corruption, 1993, 94. Mem. N.Y. County Lawyers Assn. (pres. 1979-81, dir., mem. exec. com.), N.Y. State Bar Assn. (ho. dels. 1977-89, 93-96), Assn. Bar City N.Y. (criminal justice coun. 1980-82, mem. judiciary com. 1993-94), Network Bar Leaders (founder, chmn. 1981-83), Assn. Justices of N.Y.C. and N.Y. State(officer). Contbr. articles to profl. jours. Office: US Courthouse 500 Pearl St New York NY 10007-1316

BAER, JO, painter; b. Seattle, Aug. 7, 1929; d. Lester M. and Hortense Z. (Kalisher) Kleinberg; 1 child, Joshua. Student, U. Wash., New Sch. Social Rsch., N.Y. One-woman shows include Fischbach Gallery, N.Y., 1966, Gaelrie Ricke, Köln, 1968, 73, 78, Noah Goldowsky Gallery, N.Y., 1970, Locksley-Shea Gallery, Mpls., 1970, Toselli Gallery, Milan, Italy, 1974, Whitney Mus. Am. Art, 1975, Lisson Gallery, London, 1977, Mus. Modern Art, Oxford, 1977, Scottish Arts Coun. Gallery, Edinburgh, 1978, Douglas Hyde Gallery, Trinity Coll., Dublin, 1978, Stedelijk Van Abbemuseum, Eindhoven, 1978, 86, Oliver Dowling Gallery, Dublin, 1978, Lisson Gallery, London, 1980, Paul Andriesse Gallery, Amsterdam, 1988, 90, 99, Rhona Hoffman Gallery, 1989, Paley/Levy Gallery, Moore Coll., Phila., 1993, Rijksmuseum Kröller Müller, Otterloo, 1993, Paula Cooper Gallery, N.Y.C., 1995, Stedelijk Mus., Amsterdam, 1999, (with Bruce Robbins) Oliver Dowling Gallery, Dublin, 1980, 84, 112 Workshop, N.Y.C., 1980, Mary Boone Gallery, N.Y., 1982, Lisson Gallery, London, 1982, Riverside Studios, London, 1982; exhibited in group shows at Kaymar Gallery, N.Y., 1964, Guggenheim Mus., 1966, 70, Dwan Gallery, N.Y., 1966, 67, Whitney Mus. Am. Art, N.Y.C., 1967, 69, Museum Friedericianum, Kassel, 1968, Ulmer Mus., Ulm, West Germany, 1968, Museum Athenaum, Helsinki, Finland, 1969, Corcoran Mus., Washington, 1969, Seattle Art Mus., 1969, Kolnischer Kunstverein, Koln, 1969, Mus. Modern Art, 1969, Art Inst. Chgo., 1971, Centro Communitario di Brero, Milan, 1973, Mus. Contemporary Art, Chgo., 1974, Lisson Gallery, London, 1975, 78, 81, 82, Fort Worth (Tex.) Art Mus., 1976, Tacoma Art Mus., 1977, Art Net, London, 1977, Worcester (Mass.) Art Mus., 1978, Cincinnati Art Mus., 1979, Galerie Ricke, Cologne, 1981, Stadtische Kunsthalle, Dusseldorf, 1982, Neuberger Mus. CUNY, 1986, Musée St. Pierre, Lyon, France, 1988, Mus. Modern Art, 1990, 96, Mus. Wiesbaden, 1990, Galerie Metropole, Wien, Austria, 1991, Museum Haus Lange, Krefeld, 1992, 93, Aargauer Kunsthaus, Aarau, Switzerland, 1995, Mus. Winterthei, Switzerland, 1995, Nat. Gallery Australia, Canberra, 1995, Galerie Ricke, Köln, 1996, Kunstverein, Winterthur, Switzerland, 1996, Snug Harbor Cultural Ctr., N.Y.C., 1997, Irish Mus. Modern Art, Dublin, 1997; represented in permanent collections Albright-Knox Art Gallery, Buffalo, N.Y., Arts Coun. G.B., London, Australian Nat. Gallery, Canberra, Australia, Chase Manhattan Bank, N.Y.C., Ft. Worth Mus., Balt. Mus. of Art, Gemeentemuseum Arnhem, NL, Haags Gemeentemuseum, Den Haag, NL, Kaiser Wilhelm Mus., Krefeld, Germany, Kunstmusem Winterthur, Switzerland, Ludwig Coll., Kolnischer Kunstverein, Koln, Germany, Suermondt Mus., Aachen, West Germany, Levi-Strauss Coll., San Francisco, U. Tex. Austin, Mus. Contemporary Art, Chgo., Mus. Modern Art, N.Y.C., Mus. Modern Art, San Francisco, Nat. Gallery Art, Washington, SUNY, Norton Simon Mus., Rijksdienst Beeldende Kunst, The Hague, Rijksmuseum Kröller-Müller, Otterlo, The Netherlands, Guggenheim Mus., N.Y.C., Stedelijk Mus., Amsterdam, Stedelijk Van Abbemuseum, Eindhoven, NL, Tate Gallery, London, U. N.C., Whitney Mus. Am. Art, N.Y.C. Office: Rozengracht 207, Amsterdam 1016 LZ, The Netherlands

BAER, JOHN METZ, entrepreneur; b. Md., June 30, 1908; s. Adam Daniel and Leah Bertie (Metz) B.; BS, Goshen Coll., 1932; m. Joan Cushwa, Oct. 16, 1976; children: John Metz, Deborah Ann. Food distribution cons.; pres. Profl. Arts Assocs. Inc., Greencastle (Pa.) Ice and Cold Storage Inc., Baer Packing Corp., Greencastle; Nat. Frozen Foods Assn. ofcl. rep. to 1st Internat. Foods Conf., Paris, 1950; participant numerous internat. food confs. Pres. Washington County Hosp., Hagerstown, 1958-60, Washington County Bd. Edn., 1962-68; bd. dirs. Am. Heart Assn. of Md. Trustee Hagerstown Jr. Coll.; Chmn. United Way of Washington County, hon. mem. Greater Hagerstown Club, chmn. Hagerstown Parking Authority. Mem. Produce Mktg. Assn. (past pres.); bd. dirs. Md. Symphony Orch. Republican. Methodist. Clubs: Fountainhead Country, Assembly of Hagerstown. Lodge: Rotary. Home: 13217 Hillandale Rd Hagerstown MD 21742-2647 Office: 5 Public Sq Hagerstown MD 21740-5528

BAER, JOHN METZ, JR., psychology educator; b. Hagerstown, Md., Dec. 22, 1948; s. John Metz and Janice Margaret (Magaha) B.; m. Sylvia Judith Kuhner, Nov. 25, 1985; 1 child, Heather Ann. BA, Yale U., 1972; MS, Rutgers U., 1989, PhD, 1991. Guide, interpretor U.S. Pavilion World's Fair, Osaka, Japan, 1970; reporter, columnist The Japan Times, Tokyo, 1972-73; program coord. Brook Lane Psychiatric Ctr., Lettersburg, Md., 1973-78; tchr., supr. Washington County Bd. Edn., Hagerstown, Md., 1978-88; examiner Edn. Testing Svc., Princeton, N.J., 1990-92; prof. Rider U., Lawrenceville, N.J., 1992—; cons. in field. Author: Creativity and Divergent Thinking, 1993, Creative Teachers, Creative Students, 1997; mem. editl. bd. Transformations, 1991-94; contbr. chpts. to books; contbr. articles to profl. jours.; contbr. items for profl. testing svcs. Cons. Goals 2000 Lawrence Twp., 1995-97. Recipient Berlyne prize Am. Psychol. Assn., Washington, 1993, Innovative Excellence award 8th Nat. Conf. Coll. Tchg. Learning, 1997; Nat. Merit scholar Yale U., 1966-72; Nat. Science Found. fellow Rutgers U., 1988-91. Office: Rider Univ 2083 Lawrenceville Rd Lawrenceville NJ 08648-3099

BAER, JOHN RICHARD FREDERICK, lawyer; b. Melrose Park, Ill., Jan. 9, 1941; s. John Richard and Zena Edith (Ostreyko) B.; m. Linda Gail Chapman, Aug. 31, 1963; children: Brett Scott, Deborah Jill. BA, U. Ill., Champaign, 1963, JD, 1966. Bar: Ill. 1966, U.S. Dist. Ct. (no. dist.) Ill. 1967, U.S. Ct. Appeals (7th cir.) 1969, U.S. Ct. Appeals (D.C. cir.) 1975, U.S. Ct. Appeals (9th cir.) 1979, U.S. Supreme Ct. 1975. Assoc. Keck, Mahin & Cate, Chgo., 1966-73, ptnr., 1974-97; of counsel Sonnenschein Nath & Rosenthal, Chgo., 1997—; mem. Ill. Atty. Gen.'s Franchise adv. bd., 1992-94, 96—, chair 1996—. Mem editl. bd. U. Ill. Law Forum, 1964-65, asst. editor, 1965-66; contbg. editor: Commercial Liability Risk Management and Insurance, 1978. Mem. Plan Commn., Village of Deerfield (Ill.), 1976-79, chmn., 1978-79, mem. Home Rule Study Commn., 1974-75, mem. home rule implementation com., 1975-76. Mem. ABA (topics and articles editor Franchise Law jour. 1995-96, assoc. editor 1996—), Internat. Franchise Assn. (legal/legis. com. 1990—), Inter-Pacfic Bar Assn., Ill. Bar Assn. (competition dir. region 8 nat. moot ct. 1974, profl. ethics com. 1977-84, chmn. 1982-83, spl. com. on individual lawyers advt. 1981-83, profl. responsibility com. 1983-84, standing com. on liaison with atty. registration and disciplinary commn. 1989-93), Internat. Bar Assn. E-mail: jrb@sonnenschein.com. Office: 8000 Sears Tower 233 S Wacker Dr Chicago IL 60606-6404

BAER, JON ALAN, political scientist; b. Southampton, N.Y., June 25, 1945; s. Kosty Joseph and Mary Olive (Klingler) B. BA, LIU, 1970; MA, SUNY, Albany, 1977, MA, 1978, PhD, 1993. Entertainer, Sta. WLNG, Sag Harbor, N.Y., 1969-70, 74-75; rsch. fellow, rsch. assoc. U.S. Adv. Commn. on Intergovtl. Rels., 1978-80; rschr. N.Y. State Legis. Commn. on Expenditure Rev., 1979-81 lectr. polit. sci. Siena Coll., 1980; instr. polit. sci. Russell Sage Coll., 1981-82; rsch. assoc. SUNY, Albany, 1977-93; polit. analyst, news anchor Main Street Broadcasting, Sag Harbor, 1993—; cons. Office of Intergovtl. Rels., Suffolk County, N.Y., 1978-79. With U.S. Army, 1970-73. Decorated Army Commendation medal, N.Y. State Conspicuous Svc. Cross. Mem. Acad. Polit. Sci., Am. Polit. Sci. Assn., Am. Soc. Public Adminstrn., Ctr. for Study of Presidency, Conf. Fedn. Studies, Nat. Civic League. Episcopalian. Contbr. articles to profl. jours. Home: PO Box 743 Sag Harbor NY 11963-0019 Office: Main Street Broadcasting PO Box 2000 Sag Harbor NY 11963-0075

BAER, JOSEPH WINSLOW, retired lawyer, mediator, arbitrator; b. Chgo., Sept. 15, 1917; s. Joseph Louis and Gretchen Winslow (Shattuck) B.; m. Nanette Talbot, June 14, 1952; children—Richard, Elizabeth, Jennifer. A.B., U. Chgo., 1938, J.D., 1940. Bar: Ill. 1940, U.S. Dist. Ct. 1946. Ptnr. Davis, Boyden, Jones & Baer, Chgo., 1947-85; sr. ptnr. Baer, Davis, Zavett, Kane & Mac Rae, Chgo., 1985-86; chmn. divorcee div. Endispute of Chgo., 1986-89; lectr. in matrimonial law; instr. John Marshall Law Sch., 1956-61. Author: The Last "Good" One; co-author: Merit in No Fault Divorce; contbr. articles on matrimonial law to profl. jours. Active amateur theater; Rep. candidate for mcpl. ct. judge, Chgo., 1956; mem. Gov. Athletic Supporters Inst., 1946-75; pres. Captiva Island (Fla.) Civic Assn., 1991-93. Lt. comdr. USNR, 1940-45, PTO. Fellow Am. Acad. Matrimonial Lawyers (founding); mem. ABA, Ill. Bar Assn., Chgo. Bar Assn. (chmn. com. entertainment 1976-77), Adventurers Club Chgo., Law Club Chgo., Tavern Club Chgo., Psi Upsilon, Phi Delta Phi. Home: 1109 Old Elm Ln Glencoe IL 60022-1234 also (winter): PO Box 123 Captiva FL 33924-0123

BAER, KENNETH PETER, farmer cooperative executive; b. Deer Creek, Okla., May 20, 1930; s. Samuel Benjamin and Viola Emelia (Peter) B.; m. Annette Robertson, Jan. 9, 1999; children: Jeff Wayne, James Lee. Grad. exec. program, Stanford U. Salesman Summerfield Farmers Coop Grain Co., Ill., 1948-52; mgr. grain and farm supplies Bond County Service Co., Greenville, Ill., 1952-53; with Growmark, Inc., 1955-87; dir. market devel., then v.p. field services Growmark, Inc., Bloomington, Ill., 1966-76; group v.p. supply ops. Growmark, Inc., 1976-82, exec. v.p., chief exec. officer, 1982-87; chmn. bd. CF Industries, Inc., Long Grove, Ill., 1979-87; internat. mgmt. cons., agri-bus.; dir. Nat. Coop. Refinery Assn., McPherson, Kans., Archer-Daniels-Midland Co. Vice pres. bd. Mennonite Hosp., Bloomington. Served with AUS, 1953-55. Home: 29 Diamante Blvd Hot Springs National Park AR 71909

BAER, LEDOLPH, oceanographer, meteorologist; b. Monroe, La., Nov. 21, 1929; s. Leo M. and Leonora (Lieber); m. Inge Rosenbaum, Dec. 22, 1957; children: Teresa, Margaret, Leonard. Student, Tulane U., 1946-48; BS, La. Poly., 1950; MS, Tex. A&M U., 1955; PhD, NYU, 1962. Meteorologist Gulf Cons., Houston, 1955-57; from oceanographer to mgr. divsn. ocean scis. Lockheed Corp., Sunnyvale, Burbank, Calif., 1959-74; dir. ocean svcs. to chief policy staff NOAA, Rockville, Md., 1974-93; oceanographer to chief phys. oceanography-ocean observations divsns. NOAA/Nat. Ocean Svc., Rockville, Silver Spring, Md., 1993-95; pvt. cons., Potomac, Md., 1995—. Contbr. articles to profl. jours. Staff sgt. USAF, 1950-54. Fellow AAAS; mem. Am. Meteorol. Soc. (profl.), Am. Geophys. Union. E-mail: Peinge@iname.com. Home and Office: 9920 Bedfordshire Ct Potomac MD 20854-2015

BAER, MICHAEL ALAN, political scientist, educator; b. Atlanta, Feb. 4, 1943; s. Kurt Arthur and Beulah (Mendelson) B.; m. Charlotte Glazer, Aug. 16, 1964; children: Daniel Noach, Naomi Aviva. BA, Emory U., 1964; MA, U. Oreg., 1966, PhD, 1968. Rsch. asst. Center Advanced Study Ednl. Adminstrn., U. Oreg., 1964-68; faculty U. Ky., Lexington, 1968-90, prof. polit. sci. and pub. adminstrn., 1980-90, chmn. dept. polit. sci., 1977-81, dean Coll. Arts and Scis., 1981-90; polit. analyst WAVE-TV, Louisville; prof. polit. sci. Northeastern U., Boston, 1990—, provost, sr. v.p. acad. affairs, 1990-98; sr. v.p. for programs and analysis, dir. Ctr. for Policy Analysis, Am. Coun. on Edn., Washington, 1998—. Co-author: Lobbying: Influence and Interaction in American State Legislatures, 1969; co-editor: Political Science in America, 1991; mem. editorial bd.: State and Local Govt. Rev, 1977-81; contbr. articles to profl. jours. Bd. dirs. Ctrl. Ky. Civil Liberties Union, 1973-77, Congragation Ohavay Zion, Lexington, 1976-78, Ctrl. Ky. Jewish Assn., 1970-74, 79-84, pres. 1973-74, Bluegrass chpt. NCCJ, 1980-81, Coun. Colls. Arts and Scis., 1983-89, pres. 1988, Jamaica Pond Assn., 1992-97; rec. sec. Bluegrass chpt. Ky. Assn. Gifted Edn., 1983-85; mem. Mayor's com. to establish Lexington Children's Mus., 1988-90, bd. dirs., 1990; mem. coun. Inter Univ. Consortium for Polit. and Social Rsch., U. Mich, 1988-94, chmn. 1990-92. Leverhulme fellow, 1974-75. Mem. Am. Polit. Sci. Assn. (endowed programs com. 1993-94, 95-98), Midwest Polit. Sci. Assn. (exec. coun. 1980-83), Brit. Politics Group (exec. coun. 1978-80), So. Polit. Sci. Assn. (chmn. nominating com. 1993-94, 96), Ky. Conf. Polit. Sci., Nat. Assn. Univ. and Land Grant Colls. (commn. on arts and scis. 1986-90, chmn. 1990). Home: 4103 38th St NW Washington DC 20016-2217 Office: Am Coun on Edn 1 Dupont Cir NW Washington DC 20036-1110

BAER, MICHAEL SHELLMAN, III, lawyer, Louisiana Senate secretary; b. New Orleans, Apr. 10, 1947; s. Michael Shellman Jr. and Gwendolyn Marie (Willis) B.; m. Alice Marie Lejuay, Nov. 23, 1964 (div. July 1979); children: Deborah Ann, Michael Shellman IV, Katherine Gwen; m. Mary Deborah Harkins, Sept. 5, 1980; children: Christian Price, Andrew Chase. BS in fin., La. State U., 1969, JD, 1974. Bar: La. 1974, U.S. Dist. Ct. (mid. and ea. dists.) La. 1974, U.S. Ct. Appeals (5th cir.) 1975. Sawmill mgr. Pearl River Lumber Co., 1969-71; law clerk La. Legis. Budget Com., Baton Rouge, 1971-72; rschr. La. Constl. Conv., Baton Rouge, 1973; rsch. dir. La. Dome Stadium Investigating Com., Baton Rouge, 1974; counsel to gov. La. Gov.'s Office, Baton Rouge, 1975-78; atty. Camille Gravel Law Firm, Baton Rouge, 1974—; sec. of senate La. Senate, Baton Rouge, 1979—; lectr. So. U. Law Sch., Baton Rouge, 1985-94, La. State U., Baton Rouge, 1985—, Tulane U., New Orleans, 1995—; mem. Gov.'s Mansion Commn., 1995—; mem. adv. bd. Acad. Politics La. State U., 1995—; adj. prof. law So. U., 1997—. Clerk La. State Dem. Ctrl. Com., Baton Rouge, 1989-96; chmn. Old State Capitol Found., Baton Rouge, 1990—; mem. Old State Capitol Adv. Com., Baton Rouge, 1992—. Recipient Youth Legis. award YMCA, Baton Rouge, 1992. Mem. ABA, Nat. Assn. Legislators, So. Legis. Conf., Am. Soc. Clks. and Secs., L.A. Bar Assn. Presbyterian. Avocations: deep sea fishing, aviculture. Home: 300 Highland Crossing St Baton Rouge LA 70810-5813 Office: PO Box 44183 Baton Rouge LA 70804-4183

BAER, RICHARD MYRON, retired college administrator; b. Chgo., May 26, 1928; s. Ernest Conroy and Elma Harriet Baer; m. Carol Louise Moyer, Aug. 31, 1956; children: Dana, David, Caron, John. BS in Edn., No. Ill. State Tchrs. Coll., 1954; MS in Bus. Adminstrn., No. Ill. U., 1962, Cert. of Advanced Standing in Bus. Mgmt., 1967. Dist. field engr. Barber-Colman Co., Rockford, Ill., 1957-62; coord., ctrl. stores No. Ill. U., DeKalb, 1962-67; dean, bus. svcs. Rock Valley Coll., Rockford, 1967-73; bus. mgr. Rockford Coll., 1973-81; v.p. fin., adminstrv. svcs. Met. Com. Coll., Omaha, 1981-94. Sgt. U.S. Army, 1952-53, Korea. Mem. Nat. Assn. Coll. and Univ. Bus. Officers, Assn. Sch. Bus. Ofcls. (registered sch. bus. adminstr.), Nebr. Cmty. Coll. Bus. Officers (chmn. 1993-94), Rotary, Sigma Iota Epsilon. Avocations: camping, fishing. Home: 15927 Nottingham Dr Omaha NE 68118-2033

BAER, ROBERT J., transportation company executive; b. Oct. 25, 1937, St. Louis; s. Charles A. and Angeline Baer; m. Jo Baer, Aug. 27, 1960; children: Bob Jr., Angie, Tim, Cathy, Kristen. BA, So. Ill. U., 1962, MS, 1964. Regional supr. div. recreation City of St. Louis, 1957-64; dep. dir. Human Devel. Corp., St. Louis, 1964-70; chief of staff to co. exec. St. Louis County Govt, 1970-74; exec. dir. Bi-State Devel. Agy., St. Louis, 1974-77; v.p., gen. mgr. United Van Lines Inc. and subs., Fenton, Mo., 1977-80, exec. v.p., 1980-82, pres., COO, 1982-95; CEO United Van Lines Inc., Fenton, 1995—; CEO Vanliner Ins. Co., Fenton, Total Transp. Svcs. Inc., Mayflower Transit Inc., Fenton, 1995—, UniGroup Worldwide Inc., Fenton, 1996—, Pinnacle Group Assocs., Inc., Omaha, 1998—; pres., COO UniGroup, Inc. Fenton. Mo., 1987—; bd. dirs. Mercantile Bank of St. Louis. Pres. St. Louis Bd. Police Commn., 1984-89; chmn. St. Louis Regional Conv. and Sports Complex Authority, 1990-96; bd. trustees St. Louis U.; mem. chancellor's coun. U. Mo.; mem. Civic Progress, Inc., 1996—; mem. bd. govs. Cardinal Glennon Children's Hosp., St. Louis, 1998—. Office: UniGroup 1 Premier Dr Fenton MO 63026-2535

BAER, ROBERT JACOB, retired army officer; b. Jamestown, Mo., Aug. 12, 1924; s. John William and Esther Elizabeth (Knipker) B.; m. Ann O'Hara, Dec. 31, 1948; children: John, Thomas, Stephen, Teresa. B.S., U.S. Mil. Acad., 1947; grad., Army War Coll., 1967. Commd. 2d lt. U.S. Army, 1947, advanced through grades to lt. gen., 1977; service in ETO, Japan, Korea, Vietnam; staff div. chief Dept. Army, 1969-71; dir. devel. office Chief R & D, 1971-72; project mgr. XM-1 Tank Systems Tank Automotive Command, Warren, Mich., 1972-77; dep. comdr. Army Devel./Readiness Command, Alexandria, Va., 1977-80; ret., 1980; sr. v.p. XMCO, Inc., 1980-90; pvt. cons., 1990; mem. U.S. Army Sci. Bd., 1982-88; dir. Western Design Howden Corp. Contbr. to mil. jours. Decorated D.S.M., Silver Star, Legion of Merit with oak leaf cluster, Def. Superior Svc. medal, Meritorious Svc. medal, Air medal with 11 oak leaf clusters, Army Commendation medal with oak leaf cluster, Combat Inf. badge. Mem. U.S. Armor Assn. (past pres.), Assn. U.S. Army, German-Am. Bus. Assn. (mem. adv. bd.), Kappa Alpha, Country Club of Fairfax. Roman Catholic. Home: 6213 Militia Ct Fairfax VA 22039-1325

BAER, RUDOLF LEWIS, dermatologist, educator; b. Strasbourg, France, July 22, 1910; came to U.S., 1934, naturalized, 1940; s. Ludwig and Clara (Mainzer) B.; m. Louise Jeanne Grumbach, Nov. 6, 1941; children: John Reckford, Andrew Rudolph. MD, U. Basel, Switzerland, 1934; postgrad. dermatology, N.Y. Postgrad. Med. Sch., 1937-39; MD (hon.), U. Munich, 1981. Diplomate Am. Bd. Dermatology (mem. 1964-72, pres. 1969-70). Intern Beth Israel Hosp., N.Y.C., 1934-35; resident dermatology Montefiore Hosp., N.Y.C., 1936-37; faculty Columbia U. Sch. Medicine, 1939-48; dir. dept. dermatology Univ. Hosp., 1961-81; faculty NYU Sch. Medicine, 1948—, prof. dermatology, 1961—, chmn. dept. dermatology, 1961-81, George Miller MacKee prof., 1961-81; dir. dept. dermatology Bellevue Hosp. Center, 1961-81; surgeon gen. U.S. Army, FDA; mem. Internat. Com. Dermatology, 1967-82, pres., 1972-77; mem. com. on revision U.S.

Pharmacopeia, 197--75; mem. commn. cutaneous diseases Armed Forces Epidemiologic Bd., 1967-72. Editor: Office Immunology, 1947, Atopic Dermatitis, 1955, Year Book Dermatology, 1955-65; also past mem. numerous editorial bds.; Author over 300 articles. Chmn. bd. Dermatology Found., 1974-77; bd. dirs. Rudolf L. Baer Found. for Skin Diseases, 1975—. Decorated Order of the Rising Sun (Japan), 1991; Dohi lectr. and recipient Dohi medal Japanese Dermatol. Soc., 1965; Von Zumbusch lectr. Munich, 1967, Hellerstrom lectr. Stockholm, 1970, O'Leary lectr. Mayo Clinic, Rochester, Minn., 1971, Robinson lectr. U. Md., 1972, Barrett Kennedy lectr., 1973, Louis A. Duhring lectr., 1974, Samuel M. Bluefarb lectr., 1975, Frederick J. Novy Jr. vis. scholar, 1978, Morris Samitz lectr., 1979, Ruben Nomland-Robert Carney lectr., 1979, Barrett Kennedy meml. lectr., 1980, A. Harvey Neidorff lectr., 1985, Ferdinand von Hebra meml. lectr., 1988, Alexander A. Fisher lectr., 1989, Stuart B. Fisher lectr., 1991, Tamotsu Imaeda lectr., 1991, Hermann Pinkus lectr., 1992; Walter C. Lobitz Jr. lectr., 1994; recipient von Hebra medal U. Vienna, 1988, Discovery award Dermatology Found., 1993. Fellow N.Y. Acad. Medicine (chmn. sect. dermatology 1963-64), Am. Acad. Dermatology (pres. 1974-75, Dome lectr. 1976, gold medal 1978, hon. mem. 1980), Am. Acad. Allergy, Am. Coll. Allergists; mem. AMA (chmn. sect. dermatology 1965-66), Am. Dermatol. Assn. (pres. 1977, hon. mem. 1992), Soc. Investigative Dermatology (pres. 1963-64, Stephen Rothman medal 1973, hon. mem. 1980), Am. Contact Dermatitis Soc. (hon.), Bronx Dermatol. Soc. (pres. 1952), N.Y. Dermatol. Soc. (pres. 1982-83, hon. mem. 1991), N.Y. Allergy Soc., N.Y. Acad. Scis., N.Y. County and State Med. Soc., World Congress Dermatology (hon. pres. 1992), Internat. League Dermatol. Socs. (pres. 1972-77, Alfred Marchionini gold medal 1977), Argentinian Dermatol. Soc. (hon. mem.), Austrian Dermatol. Soc. (hon. mem.), Brit. Dermatol. Soc. (hon. mem.), Brazilian Dermatol. Soc. (hon. mem.), Danish Dermatol. Soc. (hon. mem.), Finnish Dermatol. Soc. (hon. mem.), German Dermatol. Soc. (hon. mem., Karl Herxheimer medal 1995), Iranian Dermatol. Soc. (hon. mem.), Israeli Dermatol. Soc. (hon. mem.), Italian Dermatol. Soc. (hon. mem.), Japanese Dermatol. Soc. (hon. mem.), Mex. Dermatol. Soc. (hon. mem.), Polish Dermatol. Soc. (hon. mem.), Swedish Dermatol. Soc. (hon. mem.), Yugoslav Dermatol. Soc. (hon. mem.), Venezuelan Dermatol. Soc. (hon. mem.), Brazilian Nat. Acad. Medicine, Pacific Dermatol. Soc. (corr. mem.), Cuban Dermatol. Soc. (corr. mem.), French Dermatol. Soc. (corr. mem.), French Allergy Soc. Office: 566 1st Ave New York NY 10016-6402

BAER, SUSAN M., airport executive. Gen. mgr. LaGuardia Airport, Flushing, N.Y., 1994-98, N.J. Airports, Newark, 1998—. Office: Port Authority of NY/NJ Newark Internat Airport Tower Rd Bldg 10 Newark NJ 07114*

BAER, WALTER S., research executive; b. Chgo., July 27, 1937; s. Walter S., Jr. and Margaret S. (Mayer) B.; m. Miriam R. Schenker, June 18, 1959 (div. 1987); children: David W., Alan B.; m. Jeri Weiss, Oct. 23, 1988. B.S., Calif. Inst. Tech., 1959; Ph.D. (NSF fellow), U. Wis., 1964. Research physicist Bell Telephone Labs., Murray Hill, N.J., 1964-66; White House fellow Washington, 1966-67; White House sci. adv. staff, 1967-69; cons. and sr. scientist RAND Corp., Santa Monica, Calif., 1970-81; dir. energy policy program RAND Corp., 1978-81; dir. advanced tech. Times Mirror Co., Los Angeles, 1981-89; deputy v.p. domestic rsch. RAND Corp., Santa Monica, Calif., 1990—; cons. UN, maj. U.S. corps, 1970—; dir. Aspen (Colo.) Cable TV Workshop, 1972-73, L.A. Ednl. Partnership; pres. KCRW Found., Santa Monica, Calif.; adv. bd. Columbia U. Inst. Tele-Info., U.S. Com. for Internat. Inst. Applied Systems Analysis; dir. Am. Tng. Internat.; mem. gov. coun. on info. tech. State of Calif. Author: Interactive Television, 1971, Cable Television: A Handbook for Decisionmaking, 1973, also articles; editor: The Electronic Box Office, 1974, wc/ RAND Cable Television Series, 1974; editorial bd.: Telecommunications Policy, 1976—, Internat. Ency. Communications. Mem. European Community Visitor, 1978. Recipient U. Wis. award for excellence in teaching, 1960; Preceptor award Broadcast Industry Conf., 1974—. Fellow AAAS (chmn. Indsl. Sci. Sec. 1992-93); mem. IEEE (mem. com. on comm. and info. policy 1994—), Am. Phys. Soc., Internat. Inst. Communications, Sigma Xi. Office: RAND 1700 Main St Santa Monica CA 90401-3297

BAER, WERNER, economist, educator; b. Offenbach, Ger., Dec. 14, 1931; came to U.S., 1945, naturalized, 1952; s. Richard and Grete (Herz) B. BA, Queens Coll., N.Y.C., 1953; MA, Harvard U., 1955, PhD, 1958; Doctor honoris causa, Fed. U. of Pernambuco, Brazil, 1988. Instr. Harvard U., 1958-61; asst. prof. Yale U., New Haven, 1961-65; asso. prof. Vanderbilt U., Nashville, 1965-69; prof. Vanderbilt U., 1969-74; prof. econs. U. Ill., Urbana, 1974—; vis. prof. U. São Paulo, Brazil, 1966-68, Vargas Found., Brazil, 1966-68; Rhodes fellow St. Antony's Coll., Oxford (Eng.) U., 1975. Author: The Brazilian Economy: Growth and Development, 4th edit., 1995, Privatization in Latin America, vol. 17, 1994, The Changing Role of International Capital in Latin America, 1998; co-editor: Paying the Costs of Austerity in Latin America, 1989, U.S. Policies and the Latin American Economies, 1990, Latin America: The Crisis of the Eighties and the Opportunities of the Nineties, 1992, Latin America-Privatization, Property Rights and Deregulation, 1993, Neo-Liberalism and Income Dristribution in Latin America, 1997. Decorated Order So. Cross (Brazil). Mem. Am. Econ. Assn., Latin Am. Studies Assn. Home: 1703 Devonshire Dr Champaign IL 61821-5901 Office: U Ill 1407 W Gregory Dr Urbana IL 61801-3606

BAER, WILLIAM J., lawyer; b. May 31, 1950; s. Joseph and Roses B.; m. Nancy Hendry; children: Michael Hendry, Andrew Hendry. BA, Lawrence U., 1972; JD, Stanford U., 1975. Bar: Wis., 1975, D.C., 1981, U.S. Ct. Appeals D.C., 1989, U.S. Supreme Ct. 1999. Trial atty. divsn. nat. advertising FTC, Washington, 1975-76, asst. to dir. bureau consumer protection, 1976-77, atty. advisor to chmn., 1977-78, asst. gen. counsel for legis., 1978-80; assoc. Arnold & Porter, Washington, 1980-83, ptnr., 1984-95; dir. Bur. of Competition FTC, Washington, 1995—. Contbr. articles to numerous publs. Chmn. Lobbyists and Lawyers for Campaign Fin. Reform, 1987-92. Mem. ABA. Democrat. Avocations: tennis, jogging. Office: FTC Bur of Competition # H-374 6 Pennsylvania Ave NW Washington DC 20580-4316

BAERENKLAU, ALAN H., hotel executive; b. N.Y.C.. Grad., Cornell U. V.p. ops. Howard Johnson Co.; pres., COO MOA Hospitality; also bd. dirs.; founder, pres. Fla. Hospitality Group; lectr. Cornell U., Hillsborough Cmty. Coll; mem. Howard Johnson Internat. Operators Coun. Mem. Walt Disney Hotel Assn. Office: MOA Hospitality Inc 701 Lee St Ste 1000 Des Plaines IL 60016-4547

BAERG, RICHARD HENRY, podiatrist, surgeon; b. L.A., Jan. 19, 1937; s. Henry Francis and Ruth Elizabeth (Loven) B.; children from previous marriage: Carol Elizabeth, William Richard, Michael David, Yvette Marie, Brie Ann, Nicolo, Monica, Devon, Arianna. AA, Kings River Coll., 1956; BS, Calif. Coll. Podiatric Medicine, 1965, DPM, 1968, MSc in Foot Surgery, 1970; MPH in Med. Adminstrn., U. Calif., Berkeley, 1971; ScD (hon.), N.Y. Coll. Podiatric Medicine, 1980; LittD (hon.), Ohio Coll. Podiatric Medicine, 1984; postgrad. Sch. Edn. and Pub. Health, U. Mich., 1973-1974; postgrad. Sch. of Bus. and Sch. of Edn., Harvard U., 1975. Diplomate Am. Bd. Podiatric Surgery (foot and ankle surgery), Am. Bd. Podiatric Orthopedics and Primary Podiatric Medicine (exec. dir. 1980-90), Am. Bd. podiatric Pub. Health (bd. dirs. 1980-89). Intern Highland Alameda County Gen. Hosp., Oakland, Calif., 1969; resident in surgery Calif. Podiatry Hosp. (Pacific Coast Hosp.), San Francisco, 1970; acad. dean N.Y. Coll. Podiatric Medicine, N.Y.C., 1971-74; v.p., dean Calif. Coll. Podiatric Medicine, San Francisco, 1974-76; chief podiatric medicine Los Angeles County-U. So. Calif. Med. Ctr., 1976-78; dir. So. Calif. Podiatric Med. Ctr., 1976-78; pvt. practice Beverly Hills, Calif., 1976-78; pres. Ill. Coll. Podiatric Medicine, Chgo., 1978-79; mem. spl. med. adv. group to sec. Dept. Vets. Affairs, Washington, 1976-79, dir. podiatric service, dept. medicine and surgery, 1979-84, acting dir., 1984-86; health resources adminstrn. cons. Dept. Health and Human Svcs., Washington, 1974-88; chief podiatry VA Med. Ctr., Loma Linda, Calif., 1984-89; dir. residency tng. Loma Linda Foot Clinic, 1990; exec. v.p., med. dir. Dr. Footcare Corp., Montclair, Calif., 1988-90; faculty podiatry U. N.C. Hosps., Chapel Hill, 1992—; clin. prof. Sch. of Podiatric Medicine Barry U., Miami, Fla., 1993—; clin. prof. Med. Sch., U. N.C., 1992—; staff podiatrist LTCA, Inc., 1997—; mem. podiatric staff Chapel Hill Surg. Ctr., 1993—; chief of podiatry Umstead Hosp., Butner, N.C., 1997—; assoc. clin. prof. Stanford U. Med. Sch., 1974-76; clin. prof. Pa. Coll. Podiatric Medicine, 1979-86, U. Osteo. Medicine and Health Sci., 1984-92; pres. Baerg & Assocs.; mem. podiatry adv. panel NAS Inst. Medicine, 1974; mem. bd. podiatric medicine Calif. dept. Consumer Affairs, 1989-90, chmn. residency, edn. and hosp. inspection com. Contbg. author: (text) Podiatric Medicine and Public Health, 1987; mem. editl. bd. Jour. Podiatric Edn., Yearbook of Podiatric Medicine and Surgery, Mil. Medicine Jour.; contbr. over 30 articles to profl. jours., 3 chpts. to textbooks. With M.C. U.S. Army and USN, 1958-64. Mead-Johnson fellow, 1968-69. Fellow USPHS, Am. Podiatric Med. Assn. (com. on pub. health 1971-84, coun. podiatric edn. 1975-84, chmn. profl. edn. com. 1977-78, com. on hosp. 1980-85, Kenison award 1984, cert. appreciation 1990, com. on pub. health and preventive medicine), Am. Coll. Foot and Ankle Surgeons, Am. Coll. Foot & Ankle Orthopedics and Medicine (exec. dir. 1980-90), Acad. Ambulatory Foot Surgery; mem. APHA (governing coun. 1977-80, chmn. podiatric health sect. 1991-94, chmn. nominating com. 1994-96), Am. Acad. Podiatric Adminstrs. (exec. dir. 1990-91), Nat. Bd. Podiatric Med. Examiners (bd. dirs.), Assn. Podiatrists in Fed. Svc., Am. Assn. Colls. Podiatric Medicine (exec. com. 1973, pres. 1980-81), Assn. Mil. Surgeons U.S., Nat. Acads. of Practice (podiatric medicine 1985), N.C. Foot and Ankle Soc. (bd. dirs. ins. com. 1994-97, cons. 1997—, chmn. zone III 1994-97, rep. N.C. Health Care Reform Com. 1994-97), Coun. Med. Sch. Affiliated Podiatrists (bd. dirs., dir. region 10), N.C. Symphony Assn., Mason (Scottish Rite, 32 degree), Sigma Pi Epsilon, Pi Delta. Republican. Office: PO Box 4741 Chapel Hill NC 27515-4741

BAERMANN, DONNA LEE ROTH, property executive, retired insurance analyst; b. Carroll, Iowa, Apr. 28, 1939; d. Omer H. and Mae Lavina (Larson) Real; m. Edwin Ralph Baermann, Jr., July 8, 1961 (dec. Aug. 1997); children: Beth, Bryan, Cynthia. BS, Mt. Mercy Coll., 1973; student Iowa State U.-Ames, 1957-61. Cert. profl. ins. woman; fellow Life Mgmt. Inst. Ins. agt. Lutheran Mut. Ins. Co., Cedar Rapids, Iowa, 1973; home economist Iowa-Ill. Gas & Electric Co., Cedar Rapids, Iowa, 1973-77; supr. premium collection Life Investors Ins. Co. (now Aegon USA), Cedar Rapids, 1978-83, methods and procedures analyst, 1987-94, sr. supr. policy svc., 1987-84; v.p. bd. dirs. Roth & Assocs., Roth Farms, Roth Inc. & Readymix, Roth Apts. Inc., 1988-90; pres. bd. dirs. Roth & Assocs., Roth Farms, Roth, Inc., Roth Readymix, Roth Apts. Inc., 1990-96; pres., CEO Roth Apt. Corp., 1990—, Baermann Apts Inc., 1992-94; pres. Baermann Apts. Inc., 1992—; mem. telecom. study group com. 1982-83, mem. productivity task force, 1984-94. Mem. Internat. Platform Assn., Citizens Com. for Persons with Disabilities, Nat. Assn. Ins. Women, Nat. Mgmt. Assn. (bd. dirs. Cedar Rapids chpt.), DAR, Knights of Malta (named Damsel of Ancient Order of St. John, N.Y.C.), Chi Omega. Republican. Presbyterian. Home: 361 Willshire Ct NE Cedar Rapids IA 52402-6922

BAERNSTEIN, ALBERT, II, mathematician; b. Birmingham, Ala., Apr. 25, 1941; s. Albert and Kathryn (Wiesel) B.; m. Judith Haynes, June 14, 1962; children—P. Renée, Amy. Student, U. Ala., 1958-59; A.B., Cornell U., 1962; M.A., U. Wis., 1964, Ph.D., 1968. Instr. math. U. Wis., Whitewater, 1966-68; asst. prof. math. Syracuse U., N.Y., 1968-72; assoc. prof. math. Washington U., St. Louis, 1972-74, prof. math., 1974—. Fulbright sr. research scholar Imperial Coll., London, 1976-77. Mem. Am. Math. Soc., Math. Assn. Am. Office: Washington U Dept Math Saint Louis MO 63130

BAERWALD, JOHN EDWARD, traffic and transportation engineer, educator; b. Milw., Nov. 2, 1925; s. Albert J. and Margaret M. (Brandt) B.; m. Elaine S. Eichstaedt, Apr. 3, 1948 (dec.); children: Thomas J., James K., Barbara Baerwald Bowman; m. Donna D. Granger, May 24, 1975. Student, Valparaiso U., 1943, 46-48; BSCE, Purdue U., 1949, MSCE, 1950, PhDCE, 1956. Registered profl. engr., Calif., Ill., Ind. Rsch. asst. Purdue U., 1949-50, rsch. assoc., instr. hwy. engring., 1950-52, rsch. engr., instr. hwy. engring., 1952-55; asst. prof. traffic engring. U. Ill., Champaign-Urbana, 1955-57, assoc. prof. traffic engring., 1957-60, prof. traffic engring., 1960-69, prof. transp. and traffic engring., 1969-83, univ. traffic engr., 1957-63, dir. Hwy. Traffic Safety Ctr., 1961-83, prof. emeritus, 1983—; staff assoc. Police Tng. Inst., 1969-91; cons. traffic engr., 1952—; pres. John E. Baerwald P.C., Santa Fe, 1982—; chmn. Champaign Parking and Traffic Commn., Ill., 1960-69; liaison mem. staff subcom. Ill. Gov.'s Ofcl. Traffic Safety Coordination Com., 1962-69, mem. subcom. hwy. safety program deficiencies, 1970-72; mem. Champaign-Urbana Urbanized Area Transp. Study, 1963-83, tech. adviser to policy com., 1963-75, chmn. policy com., 1977-83; mem. Ill. Sec. State Adv. Com. Vehicle Registration and Titling Matters, 1973-74; trustee Champaign-Urbana Mass Transit Dist., 1973-83, chmn., 1975-83; mem. tech. adv. com. Ill. Transp. Study Commn., 1977-81. Editor: Traffic Engineering Handbook 3rd edit., 1965; sr. editor: Transportation and Traffic Engineering Handbook 1st edit., 1976; contbr. over 100 articles and papers to profl. jours. With AUS, 1943-46. Recipient Pub. Svc. award Ill. Sec. State, 1976, past. pres. award Ill. Sec. Inst. of Transp. Engrs., 1983. Fellow ASCE, Inst. Transp. Engrs. (internat. pres. 1970, dir. 1964-65, 67-71, internat. coun. 1977-83, dir. Ill. sect. 1963-64, exec. com. expert witness coun. 1986-90, vice-chmn. 1988, chmn. 1989, exec. com. transp. safety coun. 1992-95, vice chmn. 1993, chmn. 1994, other offices and coms., Past Pres.' award 1953, Theodore M. Matson Meml. award for outstanding contbns. to the traffic engring. profession 1988, Burton W. Marsh Disting. Svc. award 1996); mem. Transp. Rsch. Bd. (divsn. B coun. 1974-83, other offices and coms.), Pan Am. Hwy. Congress (best tech. paper award 1963, 67), Santa Fe Host Lions Club (pres. 1994-95, Melvin Jones Internat. fellow 1997), Am. Legion, Masons, Sigma Xi, Chi Epsilon. Lutheran. Home: 35 Shilo Rd Santa Fe NM 87505-7004 Office: 1221 C S St Francis Dr Santa Fe NM 87505-4033

BAESEL, STUART OLIVER, architect; b. Charlotte, N.C., Feb. 5, 1925; s. Edward Franklin and Rose (Engel) B.; m. Betsey London Cordon, Nov. 23, 1949; children—Stuart Oliver, Betsey London, Cordon Telfair. Student, U. N.C., 1940-42, Ecole des Beaux Arts, Fountainbleau, France, 1948; B.Arch., N.C. State U., 1950; M.Arch., Cranbrook Acad. Art, 1951. Architect A.G. Odell, Jr. & Assocs., Charlotte, 1951-55; architect-designer Skidmore, Owings, Merrill, N.Y.C., 1955-59, LBC & W Assocs., Columbia, S.C., 1959-65; dir. design J.N. Pease Assocs., Charlotte, 1965-72; mem. faculty Architecture Sch. Calif. State U., Pomona, 1972-74; prin. Stuart Baesel, Architect, Design Group, La Jolla, Calif., 1972—; dir., sec. treas. Design World, Inc., Charlotte, 1968-72; dir., pres. Space Planning Assocs., Charlotte, 1966-72. Editor: Rev. Architecture, Columbia, S.C., 1962-65. Cons. Charlotte Planning Bd., 1954. Served with USAAF, 1943-46, PTO. Recipient various profl. awards, including Honor award S.C. chpt. AIA, 1964, 65, 66, N.C. chpt. AIA, 1956, 66, 68, 69, 70, 72. Fellow AIA (bd. dirs. N.C.); mem. N.Y. Archtl. League, Phi Delta Theta. Episcopalian. Club: La Jolla Beach and Tennis. Home: 303 Coast Blvd Apt 1 La Jolla CA 92037-4635 Office: PO Box 1237 La Jolla CA 92038-1237 also: Les Flots Bleus, 06230 Villefranche Sur Mer France

BAESLER, SCOTTY, lawyer, former congressman. Mayor City of Lexington, Ky., until 1993; mem. 103rd-105th Congresses from 6th Ky. dist., 1993-99; lawyer Wyatt, Tarrant & Combs, Lexington, Ky., 1999—; mem. forestry, resource conservation & rsch., risk mgmt. & specialty crops and agr. budget coms. Office: 1700 Lexington Fin Ctr 250 W Main St Lexington KY 40507*

BAESSLER, CHRISTINA A., medical/surgical nurse; b. Phila., Feb. 10, 1948; d. Harry and Mary (Moreken) B. Diploma, St. Agnes Sch. Nursing, 1968; student, Neumann Coll., 1977-81; BSN, LaSalle U., 1987, MSN, 1993. RN, Pa.; cert. CPR, BCLS. Project coord., asst. adminstr. Nat. Cardiovascular Rsch. Ctr., Haddonfield, N.J.; cardiac arrhythmia suppression trial project coord. Hahnemann U. Hosp., Phila.; grad. hosp. nurse researcher in cardiology Hahneman U. Hosp., Phila.; gallstone lithotripsy nurse clin. coord. Hahnemann U. Hosp., Phila., coord. electrophysiology rsch. and quality assurance, 1990—, antiarrhythmics verses implantable defibrillators rsch. coord., 1993—, allhat coord., 1994, affirm coord., 1995—, invest htn coord., 1998—, ramp coord., 1996—, defibrillator implant coord., 1996—. Contbr. articles to profl. publs. Recipient Vol. Recognition award S.E. Pa. chpt. Am. Heart Assn., 1982. Mem. AACN (life, pres. S.E. Pa. chpt. 1975-76), Am. Heart Assn. (nursing com. 1994—), Sigma Theta Tau (v.p. Kappa Delta chpt. 1989-94, rsch. award, 1995). Home: 848 Windermere Ave Drexel Hill PA 19026-1534 Office: MCP Hahnemann EPS/Cardiology MS-470 Broad & Vine Sts Philadelphia PA 19102

BAETZ, W. TIMOTHY, lawyer; b. Cin., Aug. 5, 1944; s. William G. and Virginia (Fauntleroy) Baetz. BA, Harvard U., 1966; JD, U. Mich., 1969. Bar: Ill. 1969, D.C. 1980. Assoc. McDermott, Will & Emery, Chgo., 1969-74, income ptnr., 1975-78, capital ptnr., 1979—; mem. mgmt. com. McDermott, Will & Emery, 1987-92, 95—. With U.S. Army, 1969-75. Fellow Am. Coll. Trust and Estate Counsel; mem. ABA, Ill. Bar Assn., Chgo. Bar Assn., Chgo. Coun. Lawyers, D.C. Bar Assn. Republican. Episcopalian. Home: 940 Golfview Rd Glenview IL 60025-3116 Office: McDermott Will & Emery 227 W Monroe St Ste 3100 Chicago IL 60606-5096

BAETZHOLD, HOWARD GEORGE, English language educator; b. Buffalo, Jan. 1, 1923; s. Howard Kuster and Harriet Laura (Hofheins) B.; m. Nancy Millard Cheesman, Aug. 5, 1950; children: Howard King, Barbara Millard. Student, Brown U., 1940-43, MIT, 1943-44; A.B. magna cum laude, Brown U., 1944, A.M., 1948; Ph.D., U. Wis., 1953. Asst. dir. Vets. Coll., Brown U., Providence, 1947-48, dir., 1948-49, admissions officer, 1948-50; teaching asst. U. Wis.-Madison, 1950-51; asst. to assoc. dean Coll. Letters and Sci., 1951-53; asst. prof. English Butler U., Indpls., 1953-57, assoc. prof., 1957-67, prof. English, 1967-88, Rebecca Clifton Reade prof., 1981-88, Rebecca Clifton Reade prof. emeritus, 1988—, head dept., 1981-85; vis. prof. U. Del., summer 1963. Author: Mark Twain and John Bull: The British Connection, 1970; co-editor: The Bible According to Mark Twain: Writings on Heaven, Eden and the Flood, 1995, paperback edit., 1996, Three Decades of Odes, 1997; contbr. articles to profl. jours., Dictionary Lit. Biography, Mark Twain Ency. Mem. OASIS (Older Adult Svcs. and Info. Agy.) adv. coun., 1996—, Indpls. Art Ctr., Indpls. Mus. Art, Indpls. Opera Guild. Named Sagamore of the Wabash, 1988; Faculty fellow Butler U., 1957-58, 69-70, Butler U. fellow, 1986, 87, Butler U. Soc. of Fellows, 1988—, John S. Tuckey Meml. Rsch. fellow Elmira Coll. Ctr. for Mark Twain Studies at Quarry Farm, 1990—; grantee Am. Philos. Soc., 1967, Am. Coun. Learned Socs., 1958. Mem. AAUP (v.p. state conf. 1955), MLA, Ind. Coll. English Assn. (exec. bd. 1983-85), Am. Lit. Assn., Mark Twain Cir. Am. (exec. com. 1987-88, hon. life mem. 1995), Am. Philatelic Soc., Greater Ind. Masters Swimming Assn., Indpls. Lit. Club (2d v.p. 1985-86, 1st v.p. 1987-88, 92-93, pres. 1993-94), Butler U. Odd Topics Soc., Ovid Butler Soc. (exec. com. 1998—), Delta Upsilon. Home: 6723 Riverview Dr Indianapolis IN 46220-1628

BAEZ, JOAN CHANDOS, folk singer; b. S.I., N.Y., Jan. 9, 1941; d. Albert V. and Joan (Bridge) B.; m. David Victor Harris, Mar. 1968 (div. 1973); 1 son, Gabriel Earl. Appeared in coffeehouses, Gate of Horn, Chgo., 1958, Ballad Room, Club 47, 1958-68, Newport (R.I.) Folk Festival, 1959-69, 85, 87, 90, 92, 93, 95, extended tours to colls. and concert halls, 1960s, appeared Town Hall and Carnegie Hall, 1962, 67, 68, U.S. tours, 1970—, concert tours in Japan, 1966, 82, Europe, 1970-73, 80, 83-84, 87-90, 93—, Australia, 1985; rec. artist for Vanguard Records, 1960-72, A&M, 1973-76, Portrait Records, 1977-80, Gold Castle Records, 1986-89, Virgin Records, 1990-93, Grapevine Label Records (UK), 1995—, Guardian Records, 1995—, European record albums, 1981, 83, award 8 gold albums, 1 gold single; albums include Gone From Danger, 1997, Rare, Live & Classic (box set), 1993; author: Joan Baez Songbook, 1964, (biography) Daybreak, 1968, (with David Harris) Coming Out, 1971, And a Voice to Sing With, 1987, (songbook) An Then I Wrote, 1979. Extensive TV appearances and speaking tours U.S. and Can. for anti-militarism, 1967-68; visit to Dem. Republic of Vietnam, 1972, visit to war torn Bosnia-Herzegovina, 1993; founder, v.p. Inst. for Study Nonviolence (now Resource Ctr. for Nonviolence, Santa Cruz, Calif.), Palo Alto, Calif., 1965; mem. nat. adv. coun. Amnesty Internat., 1974-92; founder, pres. Humanitas/Internat. Human Rights Com., 1979-92; condr. fact-finding mission to refugee camps, S.E. Asia, Oct. 1979; began refusing payment of war taxes, 1964; arrested for civil disobedience opposing draft, Oct., Dec., 1967. Office: Diamonds & Rust Prodns PO Box 1026 Menlo Park CA 94026-1026

BAEZ, MANUEL, health care executive; b. Havana, Cuba, Oct. 25, 1941; came to U.S., 1962; s. Manuel and Esther (Cano) B.; m. Rebecca Sue Miller, June 4, 1967; children: Daniel, Michael, Jennifer. BA, Ind. U., 1969. Gen. mgr. export Baxter/Travenol, Miami, Fla., 1977-80; gen. mgr. Mexico Baxter/Travenol, Mexico City, 1981-84; v.p. Latin Am. Baxter/Travenol, Chgo., 1984-85, pres. L.A. and Spain, 1985-87; pres. internat. div. Baxter/Travenol, Miami, 1987-89; corp. v.p. Baxter Internat., Inc., Miami, 1989-90, group v.p., 1990-95, exec. v.p., 1995-96; exec. v.p., pres. Analytical Instruments Perkin-Elmer Corp., Norwalk, Conn., 1996—; bd. dirs. Celotex Corp. Mem. Nephrology Soc. Mexico (hon.). Avocations: chess, fishing, boating. Office: Perkin-Elmer Corp 761 Main Ave Norwalk CT 06859-0003

BAFFONI, FRANK ANTHONY, biomedical engineer, consultant; b. Cranston, R.I., Aug. 3, 1954; s. Anthony Frank and Margaret Rose (Mastrati) B. BChem, U. R.I., 1977; MD, Ross U., 1986. Diplomate Am. Bd. Internal Medicine. Biomed. engr. artificial internal organs Brown U., Providence, 1977-79; intern, resident R.I. Hosp., Providence, 1986-90; doctor internal medicine State of Conn., Southbury, 1990-93; pvt. practice Warwick R.I., 1993-95; biomed. cons. Davol, Inc., Cranston, 1989-91; cons. Intellitech, 1990-95, Medicore, Hungary, 1988-90, COMED, U.S.S.R., 1988-90, EDL, Can., 1988-91; spl. adv. com. mem. Blue Cross/Blue Shield, Providence, 1994-95. Author: Situational Soloing-A Systematic Approach to Guitar Phrasing, 2d edit., 1985; patentee multiple phase stethoscope. Mem. breast cancer com. Am. Cancer Soc., Providence, 1994-95; mem. state bd. HIV/AIDS Significant Exposure, Hartford, Conn., 1992-93. Mem. Am. Soc. Internal Medicine, Kent County Med. Soc. Avocations: music, computer art, computer animation, billiards. Office: 300 Toll Gate Rd Ste 304 Warwick RI 02886-4447

BAGA, MARGARET FITZPATRICK, nurse, medical office manager; b. Mount Vernon, N.Y., Mar. 20, 1951; d. John James and Margaret Mary (Wade) F.; m. Victor Bonoan Baga, June 22, 1974; children: Jessica Margaret, Victoria Lynn, Kathryn Naomi. RN, Misericordia Hosp. Sch. Nursing, Bronx, N.Y., 1971; student, Eckerd Coll., 1997—. RN, N.Y., Fla. RN Fordham Hosp., Bronx, 1971-74, Coney Island Hosp., Bklyn., 1974-75; RN, office mgr. Victor B. Baga M.D., P.A., Venice, Fla., 1975-98. Mem. women's bd. Venice (Fla.) Hosp. Found., nominating chair, project chair, patrons party chair, ann. gala chair, v.p., 1988-94, edn. grant screening com., 1995-96, chair, 1996-97, grant steering com., 1996; bd. dirs. The Venice Cotillion, 1991-94; mem. Congrl. Club-Dan Miller, 1995—; mem. sch. bd. Cardinal Mooney H.S.; mem. parent network for admissions, mem. parents com. Phillips Exeter Acad.; cmty. adv. bd. PALS Sarasota County, 1996—; mem. sch. bd. Cardinal Mooney H.S., 1994—; mem. Parents Network for Admissions, parents com., Phillips Exeter Acad., 1995-97; cmty. adv. bd. PALS Sarasota County, 1996-98; ballet amb. Sarasota Ballet of Fla., 1989-91; bd. dirs. Ballet Eddy Toussaint, Sarasota, 1992-94, Edn. Found. Sarasota County, 1998—; apptd. parliamentarian Sarasota County Med. Soc. Alliance, 1996-97; mem. Rollins Coll. Parents Com., 1998—. Mem. Fla. Med. Assn. Alliance (fall conf. co-chair 1993-94, south west dist. v.p. 1994-95, state chair 1995-96, mem. com. physicians resource network 1995-96, apptd. state chmn. 1996—, mem. fin. com., nominating com., long range planning com., awards chair 1996-97, co-chair ann. meeting Miami Beach 1997, interim treas. 1997, treas. 1997-98), AMA Alliance (del. ann. conv.), Sarasota County Med. Soc. Aux. (pres. county coun. 1992-93, corr. sec. south br. 1985-86, v.p. south br. 1989-90, recording sec. 1994-95), Venice Area Toastmasters. Republican. Roman Catholic. Avocations: reading, skiing, fitness, computers. Home: 708 Laguna Dr Venice FL 34285-1300

BAGAN, MERWYN, neurological surgeon; b. Phila., Jan. 25, 1936; s. Frank and Shirley (Lindenbaum) B.; m. Carol Augusta Joseph, Nov. 14, 1964; children: Eric, Seth, Karin. AB, Dartmouth Coll., 1957; MD, Boston U., 1962, MPH, 1995. Diplomate Am. Bd. Neurol. Surgery. Neurol. surgeon Surg. Neurology Profl. Assn., Concord, N.H., 1970-93; chmn. Healthsource, Inc., Hooksett, 1985-97; chmn., pres. Healthsource N.H., Concord, 1985-93; adj. asst. prof. clin. surgery (neurosurgery) Dartmouth Med. Sch., 1981-88; vis. prof. dept. surgery Tribhuvan U. Inst. Medicine, Kathmandu, Nepal, 1997—. Lt. comdr. USPHS, 1963-65. Recipient Disting. Alumnus award Boston U. Sch. Medicine, 1993. Fellow ACS; mem. AMA, Am. Assn. Neurol. Surgeons (pres. 1992-93), N.H. Med. Soc. (pres. 1983), Congress of Neurol. Surgeons (Disting. Svc. award 1990), Alpha Omega Alpha. Home: 173 School St Concord NH 03301-2568

BAGBY, GEORGE FRANKLIN, JR., English language educator; b. Washington, Dec. 10, 1943; s. George F. and J. Mildred (Ilgenfritz) B.; m. Susan

M. Hrom, Nov. 20, 1971; children: Elizabeth S., Joseph L. BA in English with high honors, Haverford Coll., 1965; MA, Yale U., 1968, PhD, 1975. Asst. prof. English, Woodrow Wilson teaching intern LeMoyne-Owen Coll., Memphis, 1968-70; instr. U. Va., 1970-72; from asst. to assoc. prof. Hampden-Sydney (Va.) Coll., 1972-88, prof., 1988—, chair dept. English, 1981-82, 84-87; vis. Lilly scholar program continuing edn. Coll. Faculty, Duke U., 1977-78; mem. NEH summer seminar U. Ariz., 1988; Fulbright lectr. U. Zulia, Maracaibo, U. Andes, Mérida, Venezuela, 1992-93; presenter in field. Author: (with others) American Literature, 1986, Twentieth Century Literature, 1992, Frost and the Book of Nature, 1993. Organizer, bd. dirs., chair, vol. Farmville (Va.) Area Community Emergency Svcs., 1988—; vol. Robert R. Moton Mus. project, 1997—. Woodrow Wilson fellow Yale U., 1965-66. Mem. AAUP, MLA (Am. lit. sect.), James Fenimore Cooper Soc., Robert Frost Soc., Assn. Study Afro-Am. Life and History, Phi Beta Kappa. Home: 304 1st Ave Farmville VA 23901-1902 Office: Hampden-Sydney Coll English Dept PO Box 26 Hampden Sydney VA 23943*

BAGBY, JOSEPH RIGSBY, financial investor; b. Banner Elk, N.C., Aug. 23, 1935; s. Wesley Marion and Ila Paunee (Rigsby) B.; m. Martha Green, Jan. 1, 1965; 1 child, Meredith Elaine. Student, Fla. State U., 1955; BBA, U. Miami, 1959; MCR, Inst. Corp. Real Estate, West Palm Beach, Fla., 1977. Employee and supr. Miami Herald Pub. Co., 1953-63; rsch. and sales asst. Oscar Dolly Assocs., Miami, 1961-63; sales, appraising and property mgr. Jack Thomas Realty, Miami, 1963-65; dir. corp. real estate Burger King Corp., Miami, 1965-70; founder, pres. Internat. Assn. Corp. Real Estate Execs., Coral Gables, Fla., 1969-88; chmn. bd. trustees Nat. Assn. Corp. Real Estate Execs., Coral Gables, Fla., 1973-88, bd. dirs., 1971—; pres., founder Property Resources Corp. and 14 other investment cos., Miami and Palm Beach, 1970—; founder merger and acquisition investment co., 1997; mem. businessman's adv. com. U.S. Postal Svc., Washington, 1984-88. Author: Real Estate Financing Desk Book, 1975, rev. edits. 1977, 81, Real Estate Directory, 1975. Pres. interfraternity coun. U. Miami (co-editor campus newspaper); mem., chmn. fin. com. St. Edward's Cath. Ch., Palm Beach, Fla., 1985-93. With U.S. Army, 1959-61. Named to Hall of Fame, Nat. Assn. Corp. Real Estate Execs., 1991. Mem. Nat. Assn. Location Analysts and Negotiators (founder), Progress Club of Miami (co-founder), Optimist (founding mem. Miami Downtown club), Rotary (Harris fellow), Interfaith Cotillian (co-founder), Sigma Chi (past pres.), Alpha Kappa Psi. Democrat. Avocations: swimming, tennis. Home: 125 Brazilian Ave Palm Beach FL 33480-4221 Office: Property Resources Corp PO Box 3120 Palm Beach FL 33480-1320

BAGBY, MARTHA L. GREEN, real estate holding company executive, novelist, publisher; b. West Palm Beach, Fla., June 17, 1937; d. Hampton and Louise (Lambert) Green; m. Joseph R. Bagby, 1966; 1 child, Meredith E. AA, Palm Beach Jr. Coll., 1957; AB, U. Miami, 1959; MA, Pa. State U., 1964. Tchr. journalism, English, Palm Beach County, 1959-62; instr. journalism Pa. State U., 1962-63; city editor, writer Palm Beach News & Life, 1963-64; editor Alfred Hitchcock Mag., Riviera Beach, Fla., 1964; editor, supr. editorial services, pub. relations employee newspaper Nat. Airlines, Inc., Miami, Fla., 1965-73; corp. sec., chmn. bd. Property Resources Co., Palm Beach, Fla., 1971—; Ill. franchisee Burger King Corp.; founder Internat. Health Awareness Assn.; lectr. journalism, Dade, Palm Beach counties; instr. Barry Coll., Miami; pub. The Bagby's Health Digest, 1985—. Author: Stranglehold, 1977, The Complete Real Estate Dictionary, 1992, The Real Estate Financing Deskbook, 1979-90; (with others) The Complete Real Estate Book. Mem. exec. bd. Childbirth and Parent Edn. Assn., Miami. Mem. Fla. Pub. Relations Assn., S. Fla. Indsl. Chmn. Internat. Council Indsl. Editors, Airline Editors Conf. (chmn.), Air Transport Assn. Am., Women in Communications (pres.), Internat. Assn. Corp. Real Estate Execs. (founder, trustee, exec. editor, dir. life); founder Internat. Health Awareness Assn. Office: 125 Brazilian Ave Palm Beach FL 33480-4221

BAGBY, ROSE MARY, pollution control administrator, chemist; b. Jackson, Miss., Feb. 18, 1947; d. Woodrow Lewis and Mary Alice (Wolverton) Holley; m. Barry Alan Bagby Sr., June 1, 1974 (div. Mar. 1978); 1 child, Barry Alan II. AA, Hinds Cmty. Coll., 1967; BS in Chemistry, Miss. Coll., 1970; Cert. in Med. Tech., St. Sch. Med. Tech., Vicksburg, Miss., 1970. Cert. class IV pollution control operator, Miss. Med. technologist Jeff Davis Meml. Hosp. Clin. Lab., Natchez, Miss., 1970-73, Vicksburg (Miss.) Hosp. Clin. Lab., 1973-74; lab. mgr. Vicksburg Water Pollution Control Ctr., 1973-92, plant mgr./lab. mgr., 1992—; mem. adv. bd. for certification Miss. Dept. Environ. Quality, Jackson, Miss., 1989-91, adv. bd. revolving fund, 1988-94. Mem. Miss. Rep. Party, Jackson, 1990—. Mem. Water Environ. Fedn. (dir. 1976—), Miss. Water Environ. Assn. (charter, pres. 1976—, com. chmn., Past Pres. award 1989, Dir. award 1994, Arthur Sidney Bedell award 1995), Miss. Water and Pollution Control Ops. Assn. (dir. 1989-92, pres. 1992-93, Howard K. Williford Svc. award 1992, 94, Past Pres. award 1994, Pollution Control Operator of Yr. 1985), Vicksburg Warren C. of C. (Edn. 2000 com. 1993—), United Way Warren County (Vol. award 1986). Republican. Baptist. Avocations: photography, floral arranging, water sports. Home: 211 Kendra Dr Vicksburg MS 39180-8986

BAGBY, WILLIAM RARDIN, lawyer; b. Grayson, Ky., Feb. 19, 1910; s. John Albert and Nano A. (Rardin) B.; m. Mary Carpenter, Sept. 3, 1939; 1 child, John Robert; m. Elizabeth Hinkel, Nov. 22, 1975. AB, Cornell U., 1933; JD, U. Mich., 1936; postgrad., Northwestern U., 1946-47. Bar: Ky. 1937, Ohio 1952, U.S. Tax Ct. 1948, U.S. Supreme Ct. 1950, U.S. Ct. Appeals (6th cir.) 1952. Pvt. practice Grayson, 1937-43; atty., judge City of Grayson, 1939-43; counsel Treasury Dept., Chgo., Cleve. and Cin., 1946-54; pvt. practice Lexington, Ky., 1954—; prof. U. Ky., 1956-57; gen. counsel Headley-Whitney Mus., 1974-84; mem. Bd. of Adjustment, Lexington-Urban County City Govt., 1965-97, chmn., 1980-97. Trustee Bagby Found. Musical Arts, N.Y.C., 1963-74; trustee, gen. counsel McDowell Cancer Found., 1979-91, pres., 1988-91. Lt. USN, 1943-46. Mem. ABA (hon. life), Am. Judicature Soc., Ky. Bar Assn. (hon. life), Fayette County Bar Assn., Lexington Club, U. Ky. Faculty Club, Rotary. Democrat. Home: 228 Market St Lexington KY 40507-1030 Office: 1107 1st National Bldg Lexington KY 40507

BAGDIKIAN, BEN HAIG, journalist, emeritus university educator; b. Marash, Turkey, Jan. 30, 1920; came to U.S., 1920, naturalized, 1926; s. Aram Theodore and Daisy (Uvezian) B.; m. Elizabeth Ogasapian, Oct. 2, 1942 (div. 1972); children: Christopher Ben, Frederick Haig; m. Betty L. Medsger, 1973 (div.); m. Marlene Griffith, 1983. A.B., Clark U., 1941, LittD, 1963; LHD, Brown U., 1961, U. R.I., 1992. Reporter Springfield (Mass.) Morning Union, 1941-42; assoc. editor Periodical House, Inc., N.Y.C., 1946; successively reporter, fgn. corr., chief Washington corr. Providence Jour., 1947-62; contbg. editor Saturday Evening Post, 1963-67; project dir. study of future U.S. news media Rand Corp., 1967-69; asst. mng. editor for nat. news Washington Post, 1970-71, asst. mng. editor, ombudsman, 1971-72; nat. corr. Columbia Journalism Review, 1972-74; prof. Grad. Sch. Journalism U. Calif., Berkeley, 1976-90, dean, Grad. Sch. Journalism, 1985-88, prof. emeritus, Grad. Sch. Journalism, 1990—. Author: In the Midst of Plenty: The poor in America, 1964, The Information Machines: Their Impact on Men and the Media, 1971, The Shame of the Prisons, 1972, The Effete Conspiracy, 1972, Caged: Eight Prisoners and Their Keepers, 1976, The Media Monopoly, 1983, 5th edit., 1997, Double Vision: Reflections on My Heritage, Life and Profession, 1995; also pamphlets; contbr.: The Kennedy Circle, 1961; editor: Man's Contracting World in an Expanding Universe, 1959; bd. editors Jour. Investigative Reporters and Editors, 1980-88. Mem. steering com. Nat. Prison Project, 1974-82; trustee Clark U., 1964-76; bd. dirs. Nat. Capital Area Civil Liberties Union, 1964-66, Com. to Protect Journalists, 1981-88, Data Ctr., Oakland, Calif., 1990-97; pres. Lowell Mellett Fund for Free an Responsible Press, 1965-76; acad. adv. bd. Nat. Citizens Com. for Broadcasting, 1978—; judge Ten Most Censored Stories, 1976-98. Recipient George Foster Peabody award, 1951, Sidney Hillman Found. award, 1956, Most Perceptive Critic citation Am. Soc. Journalism Adminstrs., 1978, Career Achievement award Soc. Profl. Journalists, John and Catherine Zenger award, 1996, James Madison award ALA, 1998; named to R.I. Journalism Hall of Fame, 1992; fellow Ogden Reid Found., 1956, Guggenheim fellow, 1961-62. Mem. ACLU. Home: 25 Stonewall Rd Berkeley CA 94705-1414 *Personal philosophy: The most compelling principles in my life have been, in private life the pervasive need of love and trust in human relations, in public life dignity of the individual combined with devotion to the common good, in intellectual life a distrust of detachment from the human condition, and in journalism honesty and clarity.*

BAGG, ROBERT ELY, poet; b. Orange, N.J., Sept. 21, 1935; s. Theodore Ely and Elma Hague (White) B.; m. Sarah Frances Robinson, Aug. 24, 1957 (div. 1996); children: Theodore, Christopher, Jonathan, Melissa, Hazzard; m. Mary L. Bauman, July 27, 1996. AB, Amherst Coll., 1957; MA, U. Conn., 1961, PhD, 1965. Instr. English, U. Wash., Seattle, 1963-65; asst. prof., then prof. U. Mass., Amherst, 1965-96, chmn. dept. English, 1986-92; stage prodm. selection, U Utah,; lectr. Smith Coll., Northampton, Mass., 1967; assoc. prof. classics U. Tex., Austin, 1971; vis. artist Rome Am. Acad. Arts and Letters, 1980, 96; cons. in field. Author: (poems) Madonna of the Cello, 1961, The Scrawny Sonnets, 1973, Body Blows, 1988; translator: (Greek dramas) Hippolytos, 1973, The Bakkhai, 1977, Oedipus the King, 1982, Women of Trachis, 1993. Recipient Prix de Rome Am. Acad. Arts and Letters, 1959; fellow Am. Acad. in Rome, 1958-59; vis. artist Ingram Merrill Found., 1961, 62, 63, 74, NEA, 1975, Guggenheim Found., 1980; Bellagio residency Rockefeller Found., 1999. Mem. MLA. Democrat. Avocations: golf, horseback riding, sailing, flyfishing. Home: 582 Pfersick Rd Shelburne Falls MA 01370-9590 Office: U Mass Dept English Bartlett Hall Amherst MA 01003

BAGGE, CARL ELMER, association executive, lawyer, consultant; b. Chgo., Jan. 12, 1927; s. Hjalmar and Adele (Elmquist) B.; m. Margaret Evelyn Carlson, June 27, 1953; children: Carol Eileen, Charles Edward, Barbara Ann, Beverly Jean. B.A. summa cum laude, Augustana Coll., 1949; postgrad., Uppsala (Sweden) U., 1949, U. So. Calif., 1956; J.D., Northwestern U., 1952; LL.D. (hon.), Alderson Broaddus Coll., 1980. Bar: Ill. 1951, U.S. Supreme Ct. 1962, D.C. 1982. Pvt. practice Chgo., 1951-52; atty. A., T. & S.F. Ry., Chgo., 1952-62; asst. gen. atty. A., T. & S.F. Ry., 1962-63, spl. asst. exec. dept., 1963-64, gen. atty., 1964-65; commr. FPC, Washington, 1965-70; vice chmn. FPC, 1966-67; pres., chief exec. officer, dir. Nat. Coal Assn., Washington, 1971-87; mem. gen. tech. adv. com. to Energy R & D Adminstrn.; mem. nat. adv. com. Project Independence; mem. nat. coal adv. com. FEA; mem. coal adv. com. to sec. U.S. Dept. Interior; co-founder, dir., vice chmn. Internat. Coal Rsch. Commn., 1974-87; bd. dirs. U.S. Nat. Com. World Energy Conf. Contbr. articles to legal and bus. publs.; contbr. to: The Supreme Court, 1961. Bd. dirs. Nat. Energy Found.; mem. commn. ch. and econ. life Nat. Coun. Chs. of Christ; mem. Deerfield Zoning Bd. Appeals, 1955-58, Deerfield Planning Commn., 1958-62; bd. dirs. Augustana Coll., Bituminous Coal Rsch.; trustee Luth. Student Found. Met. Chgo., Internat. Energy Rev. Ensign USNR, 1945-46. Mem. Nat. Assn. R.R. and Pub. Utility Commrs. (exec. com.), ABA, Ill. Bar Assn.,Chgo. Bar Assn., ICC Practitioners Assn., Legal P.C. Club Chgo., Econ. Club Chgo., Assn. Western Ry. Counsel, Lexington Group Ry. Historians, Ill. Jr. C. of C., Am. Scandinavian Found., Ill. Hit. Soc., Ry. Systems and Mgmt. Assn., Phi Beta Kappa, Phi Alpha Delta, Pi Kappa delta. Republican. Lutheran. Clubs: Capitol Hill (Washington), Nat. Press (Washington), University (Washington), Congressional Country (Washington), Peridia Golf and Country, Bradenton Yacht. Home: 4229 Augusta Ter E Bradenton FL 34203-4016 Office: 808 17th St NW Washington DC 20006-3910

BAGGER, RICHARD HARTVIG, lawyer; b. Plainfield, N.J., Mar. 27, 1960; s. Donald Hartvig and Elizabeth Claire (Broback) B.; m. Barbara Jane Laird, May 14, 1988; Katherine Bianca, Jennifer Anne, Meredith Skye. AB, Princeton U., 1982; JD, Rutgers U., 1986. Bar: N.J. 1986, U.S. Dist. Ct. N.J. 1986. Legis. aide N.J. Gen. Assembly, Trenton, 1979-82; mem. profl. staff Select Com. on Aging U.S. Ho. Reps., Washington, 1982-83; assoc. McCarter & English, Newark, 1986-91; asst. gen. counsel Blue Cross and Blue Shield of N.J., Inc., Newark, 1991-93; mgr. civic affairs Pfizer, Inc., N.Y.C., 1993-96, dir., state corp. affairs, 1996—; trustee N.J. Hist. Trust, Trenton, 1986-89, Westfield Found., 1995—; bd. govs. N.J. Hist. Soc., 1989-98. Editor, author Rutgers Law Rev., 1985-86. Councilman Town of Westfield (N.J.), 1984-90, mayor, 1991-92; mem. N.J. Gen. Assembly, 1992—, chair appropriations com.; mem. Westfield Planning Bd., 1987-92; dist. committeeman Union County Rep. Com., Elizabeth, N.J., 1980-83, 87. Episcopalian. Avocations: Tennis, swimming, reading. Office: Pfizer Inc 235 E 42nd St New York NY 10017-5755

BAGGEROER, ARTHUR BERNARD, electrical engineering educator; b. Weymouth, Mass., June 9, 1942. BSEE, Purdue U., 1963; DSc, MIT, 1968. Asst. prof., assoc. prof. elec. and ocean engrng. MIT, Cambridge, 1963-80, prof. elec. and ocean engrng., 1980—, Ford prof. engrng., 1991—, sec. of navy, chief of naval ops., chair ocean sci., 1999—. Contbr. articles to profl. jours. Fellow NSF, 1963-67; Cecil and Ida Green scholar Scripps Instn. Oceanography, 1990. Fellow Acoustical Soc. Am. (exec. com. 1994—), IEEE (Disting. Tech. Achievement award 1992); mem. NAE. Office: MIT Dept Elec Engrng & Ocean Engineering 77 Mass Ave Cambridge MA 02139-4307

BAGGETT, ALICE DIANE, critical care nurse; b. Louisville, Dec. 27, 1964; d. Stanley Wayne and Pauline (Stearman) B. BSN cum laude, Spalding U., Louisville, 1988. Nurses aide Wesley Manor-Meth. Retirement Homes, Louisville, 1983-88, medication technician; staff nurse, charge nurse TCU, ICU nurse, relief house supr. Columbia Hosp.-Suburban, Louisville, 1988—. Home: PO Box 85 DePauw IN 47115

BAGGETT, DONNIS GENE, journalist, editor; b. Livingston, Tex., July 16, 1952; s. Sam Jr. and Mavis (Baxley) B.; m. Jean Shaddix, May 18, 1974; children: Valerie Shaddix, David Shaddix. BA, Stephen F. Austin State U., 1973. Reporter, photographer East Tex. Eye, Livingston, Tex., 1973-74, coeditor, 1974; reporter Longview (Tex.) Morning Jour., 1974-75, East Tex. editor, 1975-76; reporter The Dallas Morning News, 1976, asst. night city editor, 1977, asst. state editor, 1977-82, state editor, 1982-94, asst. mng. editor, 1994-95; pub., editor The Eagle, Bryan-College Station, Tex., 1996—. Chmn. Tex. Agrl. Summit Exec. Com., 1997—. Mem. Press Club of Dallas (pres. 1992-94, treas. 1991-92, sec. 1990-91). Methodist. Avocation: ranching.

BAGGETT, JANET ROSALIND, secondary education educator; b. Greeneville, Tenn., Oct. 28, 1933; d. Samuel Ranklin and Reba Kathleen (Broyles) Bacon; m. Victor Lee Baggett, Sept. 18, 1953 (div. Nov. 1970); children: Victor Lee Jr., Ben Bailey. BS in English and Music, Tenn. Technol. U., 1952; MA in Curriculum and Instrn., Austin Peay State U., 1958; postgrad., Northwestern U., Trevecca Nazarene Coll., Fisk U., Seattle Pacific U.; MA, Tenn. State U., 1982. Cert. permanent profl. secondary and elem. tchr., Tenn. Tchr. English and Latin, band and choral dir. Jo Byrns H.S., 1952-57; elem. tchr., supervising tchr. Austin Peay State U., New Providence Sch., 1957-59; elem. tchr. Glengary Elem. Sch., 1966-67; ESEA tchr. reading Rosa Park Jr. H.S., 1967-71, J.T. Moore Jr. H.S., 1971-76; tchr. English and class piano, band and choral dir. Pearl H.S., Nashville, 1976-83; tchr. English and class piano, choral dir. Pearl-Cohn Comprehensive H.S., Nashville, 1983—; instr. Ningxia (China) Edn. Coll., 1990. Participant Internat. Conf. for Women, Moscow, 1994; music dir. Crievewood United Meth. Ch., 1967-69, also former Sunday Sch. tchr., mission worker; bd. stewards Forest Hills United Meth. Ch., disciple 1 tchr.; organist All Faiths Chapel, Mid. Tenn. Mental Health Inst., 1986; active Nashville Symphony Guild, Nashville Inst. for Arts, Leonard Bernstein Ctr. Named Terrific Tchr. Sta. WSM-TV, 1990. Mem. EA, Music Educators Nat. Conf., Nat. Coun. Tchrs. English, Tenn. Edn. Assn., Tenn. Coun. Tchrs. English, Met. Nashville Edn. Assn., Metro-Nashville Coun. Tchrs. English (pres. 1991-92), Delta Kappa Gamma, Phi Delta Kappa. Democrat. Avocations: music, reading, gardening, travel. Office: Pearl-Cohn Comprehensive HS 904 26th Ave N Nashville TN 37208-3202

BAGGETT, STEVEN RAY, lawyer; b. Fayetteville, Ark., July 3, 1963; s. Harold Ray and Norma June (King) B.; m. Amy Lynn Griggs, Jan. 2, 1999. BA, U. Ark., 1985; JD, So. Meth. U., 1988. Bar: Tex. 1988, U.S. Dist. Ct. (no. dist.) Tex. 1988, U.S. Ct. Appeals (5th cir.) 1992. Assoc. Thompson & Knight, Dallas, 1988-95, shareholder, 1996—. Recipient Am. Jurisprudence awards Bancroft-Whitney Co., 1985-86. Mem. Tex. Bar Assn., Dallas Bar Assn. (spkrs. com. 1997, state fair trial by jury com. 1998—, jud. com. 1999, cmty. involvement com. 1999, law in the schs. and cmtys. com. 1999), Ark. U. Alumni Assn., So. Meth. U. Alumni Assn., Phi Beta Kappa. Avocations: weight training, running, ice skating, music. Office: Thompson & Knight 1700 Pacific Ave Ste 3300 Dallas TX 75201-4693

BAGGETT, W. MIKE, lawyer; b. Waco, Tex., Nov. 8, 1946; s. Bill R. and Jenna (Robertson) B.; m. Jo Kilpatrick, May 28, 1968; children: Carl, Cary. BBA, Tex. A&M U., 1968; JD cum laude, Baylor U., 1973. Bar: Tex. 1973. Briefing atty. Tex. Supreme Ct., Austin, 1973-74; assoc. Winstead, Sechrest & Minick, Dallas, 1974-79, shareholder, 1979—, chmn. and chief exec. officer, 1992—. Author: Texas Foreclosure: Law & Practice, 1983; co-author: Lender Liability Law and Litigation, 1989. Trustee Tex. A&M Found., 1989—, chmn., 1992-93; mem. Joint Select Com. on Judiciary, 1988; bd. dirs. Tex. Higher Edn. Coordinating Bd., 1989-95, North Tex. Commn., Dallas Citizens Coun., State Fair of Tex., GTE-SMU Athletic Forum; chmn. Dallas/Ft. Worth Sports Commn.; mem. devel. coun. Tex. A&M U. Coll. Bus. Adminstrn.; chmn., CEO, Cotton Bowl Athletic Assn. 1st lt. U.S. Army, 1968-71, Vietnam. Decorated Bronze Star. Fellow Tex. Bar Found., Dallas Bar Found. (trustee), Southwestern Legal Found., Am. Bd. Trial Advocates; mem. Tex. Bar Assn. (adminstrn. justice com., bd. cert. civil trial com. 1983), Dallas Bar Assn. (pres.-elect chmn., bd. dirs., chmn. Tex. Supreme Ct. Home Equity Loan Foreclosure Rules Com.), Ctrl. Dallas Assn. (chmn.), Transp. Mgmt. Assn., Assn. Former Students Tex. A&M U. (pres. 1988, Outstanding Alumni Coll. Bus. 1996, Disting. Alumni 1998), Baylor Law Sch. Alumni Assn. (pres., bd. dirs.), Royal Oaks Club, City Club. Methodist. Office: Winstead Sechrest & Minick 5400 Renaissance Tower 1201 Elm St Ste 5400 Dallas TX 75270-2199

BAGGOTT, BRENDA JANE LAMB, elementary educator; b. Augusta, Ga., Nov. 10, 1948; d. Morgan Barrett Jr. and Ollie Virginia (Toole) Lamb; m. John Carl Baggott, July 8, 1967 (div. Jan. 1998); children: Carla Baggott Walczak, John Carl Jr. Student, Truett McConnel Jr. Coll., 1966-67; BS in spl. Edn., Augusta Coll., 1974; postgrad., Southeastern La. U., 1976-77, U. New Orleans, 1977-78, U. Ctrl. Fla., 1987, 97—; MEd, Nova Southeastern U., 1997. Cert. spl. edn. tchr., elem. tchr., coach, Fla. Spl. Olympics tchr. Copeland Elem. Sch., Augusta, Ga., 1973-74; spl. edn. tchr. Percy Julian Spl. Sch., Marrero, La., 1974-78; Spl. edn. resource tchr. Rosemary Mid. Sch., Andrews, S.C., 1978; spl. edn. tchr. Bynum Elem. Sch., Gerogetown, S.C., 1979, Ridgewood Park Elem. Sch., Orlando, Fla., 1979-97; reading recovery tchr. Rock Lake Elem. Sch., Orlando, 1997—; curriculum coord. Percy Julian Spl. Sch., 1975-77; mem. state tchr. mentally handicapped exam validation team Inst. for Instnl. Rsch. and Practice, Fla. Dept. Edn., Tampa, 1990—. Coord. Orange County Spl. Olympics, Orlando, 1984-85, coach, 1974—. Mem. Coun. for Exceptional Children, Internat. Reading Recovery Coun., Orange County Reading Coun. Democrat. Baptist. Avocations: directing children's choirs, coaching Special Olympics. Home: 5528-C Cinderlane Pkwy Orlando FL 32808 Office: Rock Lake Elem Sch 408 N Tampa Ave Orlando FL 32805-1296

BAGLEY, CHARLES FRANK, III, lawyer; b. Dec. 3, 1944; m. Kirsten L., Aug. 19, 1967; children: Charles F. IV, Gordon T. BA, Southwestern U., 1966; JD, Washington & Lee U., 1969. Judge advocates gen. ct. lt. U.S. Navy, 1969-74; ptnr. Campbell, Woods, Bagley, Emerson, McNeer & Herndon, 1974—. pres. bd. dirs. tri state coun. Boy Scouts of Am., 1982-85; mem. bd. dirs. Contact Huntington, Hospice Huntington, chmn. 1987-89; active Huntington Area C. of C., Enslow Park Presbyn. Ch. Mem. ABA, Va. Bar Assn., W.Va. State Bar Assn. (mem. bd. govs. 1986-93, pres. 1991-92), W.Va. Bar Assn. (mem. exec. coun. 1986-95, pres. 1993-94), Def. Trial Coun. W.Va. (mem. bd. govs. 1985-90), Cabell County Bar Assn. (pres. 1985-86), Internat. Assn. Ins. Coun., Def. Rsch. Inst., Inc. (state chmn. 1985-90). Address: 1123 12th Ave Huntington WV 25701-3423

BAGLEY, EDYTHE SCOTT, theater educator; b. Marion, Ala.; d. Obie and Bernice (McMurry) Scott; m. Arthur Moten Bagley, June 5, 1954; 1 child, Arturo Scott. BEd, Ohio State U., 1949; MA in English, Columbia U., 1954; MFA in Theater Arts, Boston U., 1965. Instr. Elizabeth City (N.C.) State Coll., 1953-56; asst. prof. Albany (Ga.) State Coll., 1956-57, A&T U., Greensboro, N.C., 1957-58, Norfolk (Va.) State Coll., 1963-65; assoc. prof. theater Cheyney (Pa.) U., 1971—, chair dept. theater arts; cons. in black theater Mich. State U., East Lansing, 1969-71. Dir. coll. prodns., 1968-71. Spl. asst. to Coretta Scott King. Mem. NAACP, AAUW, NAFE, Nat. Coun. Negro Women, Theater Assn. Pa., The Links Inc. (chair com. on arts 1972-80), Womens Internat. League for Peace and Freedom, Nat. Assn. Dramatic and Speech Arts, Nat. Assn. Schs. of Theater, The Pa. Martin Luther King Jr. Assn. for Nonviolence (bd. dirs.), The Martin Luther King Jr. Ctr. for Nonviolent Social Change (bd. dirs.). Featured in book Sisters. Home: 2 Derry Dr Cheyney PA 19319 Office: Cheyney U Cheyney PA 19319

BAGLEY, MARK JOSEPH, investment analyst; b. Altoona, Pa., Aug. 17, 1972; s. Walter William Jr. and (Jean Piotrowski) B.; m. Christine Noel Wawraszko, June 14, 1997. B of Acctg., Pa. State U., 1994. CPA Pa. Staff acct. Deloitte & Touche, Pitts. & Phila., 1994-97; investment analyst CMS Cos., Phila., 1997-99, Hirtle, Callaghan & Co., 1999—. Mem. AICPA. Republican. Roman Catholic. Home: 3117 William Rd Boothwyn PA 19061-2045

BAGLEY, STEVEN ROBERT, food bank organization executive, consultant; b. Rocky Mount, N.C., Mar. 9, 1958; s. Frank Arthur and Frances May (Milton) B. BS in Criminal Justice, Appalachian State U., 1985, MA in Polit. Sci., 1987. Personal cons. in security mgmt. Commonwealth Suma Corp., Toronto, Ont., Can., 1979-85, Pan Egypt Internat., Cairo, 1980-84; exec. v.p., CFO Fed. Trust Corp., Blowing Rock, N.C., 1985-91; exec. cons. Hill Pub., Inc., Hilton Head, S.C., 1991-93; exec. dir. Food Bank of Coastal Carolina, Wilmington, N.C., 1994—. With USMC, 1976-80. Recipient Vol. of Yr. award Brigade Boy's and Girl's Club, Wilmington, 1997. Republican. Avocation: philatelist.

BAGLEY, THOMAS STEVEN, private equity investor; b. Chgo., Oct. 25, 1952; s. James A. and Corinne M. (Catania) B.; m. Christine A. Elliott; 1 child, Derek Elliott Bagley. BA in Econs. cum laude, North Park Coll., Chgo., 1974; MBA in Fin., DePaul U., 1977. Mgr. contr. divsn. Continental Ill. Nat. Bank, Chgo., 1975-78, officer Cleve. Office, 1978-81, asst v.p. Corr. Banking, 1981, v.p. mgr. Ill. & Wisc., 1981-84; v.p. area mgr. of Midwest Area of Leveraged Capital Group Citicorp North Am., Inc., Chgo., 1984-88; founder, gen. ptnr. Pfingsten Ptnrs., Deerfield, Ill., 1989—; founder, gen. ptnr. Chgo. Assocs. Internat., 1988-89; bd. dirs. Woodall Pub. Group, Inc., Hallcrest, Inc., Huebcore Comm., Inc., Am. Acad. Suppliers, Inc., Park Foods, L.P., Barjan Products, L.P., Norcraft Cos. LLC, Pfingsten Pub. LLC. Blum Glover scholar, 1973-74. Mem. Union League Club of Chgo., Conway Farms Golf Club, Execs. Club Chgo., Econs. Club Chgo., Delta Mu Delta. Republican. Lutheran. Home: 1155 Ashlawn Dr Lake Forest IL 60045-1504 Office: Pfingsten Ptnrs Corporate 500 Centre 520 Lake Cook Rd Ste 375 Deerfield IL 60015-5632

BAGLEY, WILLIAM THOMPSON, lawyer; b. San Francisco, June 29, 1928; s. Nino J. and Rita V. (Thompson) Baglietto; m. Diane Lenore Oldham, June 20, 1965; children: Lynn Lorene, William Thompson, Walter William, Shana Angela, Tracy Elizabeth. AB, U. Calif.-Berkeley, 1949, JD, 1952. Bar: Calif. 1953, U.S. Supreme Ct. 1967. Atty., Pacific, Gas & Electric Co., 1952-56; assoc. Gardiner, Riede & Elliott, San Rafael, Calif., 1956-60; ptnr. Bagley & Bianchi, San Rafael, 1961-74; mem. Calif. Legis., 1961-74; chmn. Commodity Futures Trading Commn., Washington, 1975-79; ptnr. Nossaman, Guthner, Knox and Elliott, San Francisco, 1980—; mem. Calif. Pub. Utilities Commn., 1983-86; mem. Calif. Transp. Commn., 1983-89, chmn., 1987-88. Bd. Regents U. Calif., 1989—; bd. dirs. Nat. Futures Assn., Calif. Council Environ. and Econ. Balance, Edmund G. Brown Inst. Govtl. Affairs, Los Angeles; chmn. bd. Calif. Republican League, 1980-82. Recipient Freedom of Info. award Sigma Delta Chi, 1970; Golden Bear award Calif. Park Commn., 1973; named Most Effective Assemblyman, Capitol Press Corps, 1969, Legislator of Yr., Calif. Trial Lawyers Assn., 1970. Mem. ABA, Calif. State Bar Assn., San Francisco Bar, Marin County Bar Assn., Phi Beta Kappa, Alpha Tau Omega. Presbyterian. Clubs: World Trade, Elks (life). Bd. editors Calif. Law Rev., 1951-52.

BAGLIO, VINCENT PAUL, aeronautical engineer; b. Patchogue, N.Y., Feb. 18, 1960; s. Lorenzo and Nancy (Morello) B.; m. Donna Marie Cappo, Sept. 8, 1985. BS, Princeton U., 1982; MS, Poly. U., Bklyn., 1986; MBA, Hofstra U., 1993. Product mgr. integrated sys. and aerostructures sector Northrop Grumman Corp., Bethpage, N.Y., 1982-99; mgmt. cons. Beacon Cons. Svcs. Inc., 1999—. Contbr. articles to profl. jours. Alumni schs. com.

Princeton (N.J.) U.; chmn. Princeton Alumni Assn. of L.I. Mem. AIAA (tech. com. 1995-97), Soc. Automotive Engrs. (indsl. lectr. 1990-91), Internat. Coun. Aero. Scis. (program com. 1989-93), Friends Princeton Football. Avocations: golf, running.

BAGLIVO, MARY L., client services administrator. Bachelors, Rutgers U.; M in Advt., Northwestern U. Account exec. Euro RSCG Tatham, Chgo., 1981-91, sr. ptnr., 1991-94, mng. ptnr., 1994-96, CEO, 1996—; Bd. dirs. Evanston Northwestern Healthcare. Office: Euro RSCG Tatham 980 N Michigan Ave Chicago IL 60611-4501

BAGSHAW, BRADLEY HOLMES, lawyer; b. Salem, Mass., Mar. 26, 1953; s. James Holmes and Hope (Bradley) B.; m. Suzanne LuBien, Aug. 23, 1975. AB summa cum laude, Bowdoin Coll., 1975; JD cum laude, Harvard U., 1981. Bar: Wash. 1981, U.S. Dist. Ct. (we. dist.) Wash. 1981, U.S. Dist. Ct. (ea. dist.) Wash. 1989, U.S. Ct. Appeals (9th cir.) 1989. Assoc. Helsell Fetterman, Seattle, 1981-88, ptnr., 1988—, mng. ptnr., 1991-97, ptnr., 1997—. Home: 6240 27th Ave NE Seattle WA 98115-7114 Office: Helsell Fetterman 1325 4th Ave Ste 1500 Seattle WA 98101-2569

BAGSHAW, JOSEPH CHARLES, molecular biologist, educator; b. Niagara Falls, N.Y., Sept. 2, 1943; s. Joseph Stanley Pash and Nancy Jo (Panabaker) Pash; m. Elizabeth Brevoort Potts, Nov. 27, 1971; children: Joseph Scott, Alan David. BA, Johns Hopkins U., 1965; PhD, U. Tenn., Oak Ridge, 1969. Research fellow Mass. Gen. Hosp., Boston, 1970-71; asst. prof. molecular biology Wayne State U., Detroit, 1971-77, assoc. prof., 1977-84; prof. biology and biotech. Worcester (Mass.) Poly. Inst., 1984—; dir. Worcester Consortium Ph.D. Program in Biomed. Sci., 1985—. Editor: (with others) Cell and Molecular Biology of Artemia Development, 1989. Predoctoral fellow NSF; research grantee NSF, NIH, USDA. Mem. Am. Soc. Biochemistry and Molecular Biology, Am. Soc. Cell Biology, AAAS. Office: Worcester Poly Inst Dept Biology/Biotech Worcester MA 01609

BAGSHAW, MALCOLM A., radiation oncologist, educator; b. Adrian, Mich., 1925. BA, Wesleyan U., 1946; MD, Yale U., 1950. Diplomate Am. Bd. Radiology. Surg. intern Grace-New Haven Hosp., 1950-51, resident in surg. pathology, 1951-52; resident in radiology U. Mich., 1953-56, clin. instr. radiology, 1955-56; instr. Stanford U., Palo Alto, Calif., 1956-59, asst. prof., 1959-62, assoc. prof., 1962-69, prof., 1969-92, Henry S. Kaplan-Harry Lebeson prof. emeritus, 1992—, dir. div. radiation therapy, 1960-92, chmn. radiology dept., 1972-86, chmn. radiation oncology dept., 1986-92; resident etranger Inst. Gustave-Roussy, France, 1962-63; cons. radiation therapy VA Hosp., Palo Alto, Calif., 1960-92. Recipient Disting. Alumnus award Wesleyan U., 1996, Charles P. Kettering Gold medal Gen. Motors Co., 1996. Mem. AMA, Radiological Soc. of N.Am. (Gold Medal 1999). Office: Stanford U Med Ctr 300 Pasteur Dr Palo Alto CA 94304-2203

BAGWELL, JAMES EMMETT, history educator; b. Plains, Ga., Mar. 16, 1941; s. Henry Lafayette and Floy Howell Bagwell; m. Cynthia Baker, June 8, 1980; childrne: James Bradford, Victoria Floy. BSEd in History, U. Ga., 1963; MA in History, Ga. So. U., 1967; PhD in History, U. So. Miss., 1978. Prof. history Ga. S.W. State U., Americus, 1967—. Author: James Hamilton Cooper and Plantation Life in the Georgia Coast, 1999. Home: 517 Thomas St Plains GA 31780

BAGWELL, JEFF (JEFFREY ROBERT BAGWELL), professional baseball player; b. Boston, May 27, 1968. Grad., Hartford Coll. With Boston Red Sox, 1989-90; first baseman Houston Astros, 1990—; mem. Nat. League All-Star Team, 1994, 96. Recipient Nat. League Gold glove, 1994; named Ea. League MVP, 1990, Nat. League Rookie Player of Yr., Sporting News, 1991, Nat. League Rookie of Yr., Baseball Writers' Assn. Am., 1991, Nat. League MVP, 1994, Major League Player of Yr., Sporting News, 1994, First Baseman, Sporting News Nat. League All-Star Team, 1994, First Baseman, Sporting News Nat. League Silver Slugger Team, 1994. Office: Houston Astros PO Box 288 Houston TX 77001-0288*

BAHAR, EZEKIEL, electrical engineering educator; U.S. citizen; s. Silas and Hannah (Gubbay) B.; m. Ophira Rodoff; children: Zillah, Ruth Iris, Ron Jonathan. BS, Technion IIT, Haifa, Israel, 1958, MS, 1960; PhD, U. Colo., 1964. Instr. Technion, Haifa, Israel, 1960-62; research assoc. U. Colo., Boulder, 1962-64, asst. prof., 1964-67; assoc. prof. U. Nebr., Lincoln, 1967-71, prof., 1971-80, Durham prof., 1981-89, George Holmes Disting. prof., 1989—, dir. program revs., 1981-83; vis. prof. NOAA, Boulder, 1979. Prin. investigator radio wave propagation research, 1964—. Pres. faculty senate U. Nebr., Lincoln, 1980. Recipient Outstanding Research and Creative Activities award U. Nebr., Lincoln, 1980, Scholarship citation U. Colo., Boulder, 1964. Fellow IEEE (life); mem. Internat. Union Radio Sci. (rep. 1978, 81, 84, 87, 90, 93, 96). Avocation: swimming. Home: 2431 Bretigne Dr Lincoln NE 68512-1913 Office: U Nebr WSEC 218 N Lincoln NE 68588-0511

BAHBAH, BISHARA ASSAD, editor; b. Jerusalem, Apr. 10, 1958; came to U.S., 1976; s. Assad R. and Filomene H. Bahbah; m. Heather Del Parsons, Sept. 24, 1983; children: Leila Jean, As'ad Victor, Jubran Ronald, Remzi Robert. BA, Brigham Young U., 1979; MA, Harvard U., 1981, PhD, 1983. Editor-in-chief Al-Fajr Newspaper, Jerusalem, 1983-84; dir. United Palestinian Appeal, Washington, 1985-87; pres. Internat. Mktg. and Fund Raising Assocs., Inc., Woodbridge, Va., 1987—; editor-in-chief The Return Mag., Washington, 1988-90; exec. com. mem. Ctr. Policy Analysis on Palestine, Washington, 1990-96; assoc. dir. Middle East Inst., Kennedy Sch., Harvard U., 1992-96; pres., CEO TV Devel. Ptnrs., Inc., N.Y.C., 1997; regional rep. Middle East and Africa RSL COM and RSL Studios, N.Y.C., 1997-98; pres., CEO BHB Enterprises, Woodbridge, Va., 1998—; vis. prof. Brigham Young U., Provo, Utah, 1985, adj. prof. polit. sci., 1985-90; sr. fellow Kennedy Sch. Govt. Harvard U., 1996-98. Author: Israel and Latin America--The Military Connection, 1986; mem. adv. bd. Internat. Ency. Communications, 1984—. Bd. dirs. Palestine Children's Relief Fund, USA; mem. Nat. Policy Coun., Arab Am. Inst., Washington; mem. Palestinian Del. to the Multi-Lateral Peace Talks on Arms Control and Regional Security, 1991—. Mem. Am. Polit. Sci. Assn., Nat. Soc. Fund Raising Execs., Direct Mktg. Assn. Washington.

BAHCALL, NETA ASSAF, astrophysicist; b. Israel, Dec. 16, 1942; d. Yehezkel Oscar and Gita (Zilberstein) Assaf; m. John Norris Bahcall, Mar. 21, 1966; children: Ron Assaf, Dan Ophir, Orli Gilat. BS, Hebrew U., Jerusalem, 1963; MS, Weizmann Inst. Sci., Israel, 1965; PhD, Tel Aviv U., 1970. Rsch. asst. astrophysics Calif. Inst. Tech., 1965-67; rsch. fellow Calif. Inst. Tech., 1970-71; rsch. assoc. at observatory Princeton U., 1971-74, rsch. staff mem. 1974-75, rsch. astronomer, 1975-79, sr. rsch. astronomer, 1979-83, chief gen. observer br., from 1983; with Space Telescope Sci. Inst., Balt.; prof. dept. astronomy Princeton (N.J.) U., 1990—. Contbr. articles to profl. jours. Mem. Am. Astron. Soc., Nat. Acad. Sci. Office: Princeton U Dept Astro-Physics Peyton Hall Princeton NJ 08544

BAHL, ROY WINFORD, economist, educator, consultant; b. Miami, Fla., June 28, 1939; s. Roy Winford and Vista Lee (Becks) B.; m. Marilyn Seifried, Dec. 22, 1963; children: Renee, Alexandra, Martin, Ashley. BA, Greenville (Ill.) Coll., 1961; MA, U. Ky., 1963, PhD in Econs., 1965. Asst. prof. econs. W.Va. U., Morgantown, 1965-67; economist IMF, Washington, 1967-71; prof. econs. Syracuse (N.Y.) U., 1971-88, Maxwell prof. polit. economy, 1985-88; prof. econs. Ga. State U., Atlanta, 1988-96, dir. Policy Rsch. Ctr., 1988-96, dean Sch. Policy Studies, 1996—; bd. dirs. N.Y. State Energy Authority, Albany, 1979-87, Lincoln Found., Phoenix, 1986-93; cons. World Bank, Washington, 1971—. Author: Urban Public Finance in LDCs, 1992, Economic Growth and Fiscal Plan, 1992, Fiscal Policy in China, 1999; editor: The Jamaican Tax Reform, 1991. Recipient Fiscal medal Govt. of Philippines, 1986, Disting. Economist award State of Ky., 1989. Mem. Nat. Tax Assn. (pres. 1986), Am. Econs. Assn., So. Econs. Assn. (v.p. 1993). Democrat. Office: Ga State U Sch Policy Studies 35 Broad St Ste 602 Atlanta GA 30329

BAHL, SAROJ MEHTA, nutritionist, educator; b. New Delhi, India, Apr. 4, 1946; came to U.S., 1972; d. L.D. and G.D. Mehta; m. Vishwa Mittar Bahl; children: Rahul, Ragini. BS in Home Sci., Delhi U., 1965, MS in Nutrition, 1967, PhD in Nutrition, 1973. Lectr. Lady Irwin Coll., New Delhi, 1970-71; instr. U. N.D., Grand Forks, 1972-74; rsch. assoc. U. Tex. Med. Sch., Houston, 1976-78; asst. prof. U. Tex. Sch. Allied Health, Houston, 1979-87, assoc. prof., 1987—; program dir. Peace Corps, Houston, 1984. Author: Nutritional Management of the AIDS Patient; contbr. articles to profl. jours. Den leader Boy Scouts Am., Hosuton, 1983; mem. ednl. com. March of Dimes, Houston, 1986—; mem. exec. bd. Indo-Am. Charity Found. of Houston, 1995-98. Recipient several awards for tchg. excellence including John P. McGovern award, 1992, 95; named Outstanding Dietetic Educator Tex. Tex. Dietetic Assn., 1995; nominated for U.S. Prof. of Yr., 1993, 94. Mem. Am. Inst. Life Threatening Illness (assoc.), Soc. Nutrition Edn. (editor newsletter), Minority Faculty Assn. (pres. 1996-97), Vivekananda Vedanta Soc. (pres. 1993—). Avocations: painting, music, reading. Office: U Tex Dental Sch 3 112J 6516 John Freeman St Houston TX 77030-3402

BAHLER, GARY M., lawyer. BA, Houghton Coll., 1973; JD, Cornell U., 1976. Bar: N.Y. 1977. Sec., dep. gen. counsel Woolworth Corp., N.Y.C., 1991-93; sr. v.p. Venator Group Inc., N.Y.C., 1993—. Office: Venator Group Inc 233 Broadway Fl 3N New York NY 10279-0003

BAHLMAN, WILLIAM THORNE, JR., retired lawyer; b. Cin., Jan. 9, 1920; s. William Thorne and Janet (Rhodes) B.; m. Nancy W. DeCamp, Mar. 21, 1953; children: Charles R., William Ward, Baker D. B.A., Yale U., 1941, LL.B., 1947. Bar: Ohio 1947. Prin. Paxton & Seasongood, L.P.A., Cin., 1947-67, 73-88; ptnr. Paxton & Seasongood, Cin., 1954-67, Thompson, Hine & Flory, Cin., 1989-94; prof. law U. Cin. Coll. Law, 1967-73, lectr., 1965-67, 73-77; ret., 1994. Served with USAAF, 1942-46. Mem. Am. Law Inst., ABA, Ohio State Bar Assn., Cin. Bar Assn. Office: Thompson Hine & Flory 312 Walnut St Fl 14 Cincinnati OH 45202-4024

BAHLS, GENE CHARLES, agricultural products company executive; b. Danville, Ill., June 9, 1929; s. Martin Joseph and Renetta Johanna (Rook) B.; m. Marilyn Bernice Lane, June 9, 1951; children: Steven Charles (dec.), Sara Lynn Bahls Durre, David Lane. BMechE, Purdue U., 1951; postgrad., Miami (Ohio) U., 1958-59, Western Mich. U., 1965-66. Indsl. engr. Gardner Board & Carton Co., Middletown, Ohio, 1951-60; mgr. insdl. engring. Brown Paper Co., Kalamazoo, 1960-70; dir. engring. Armour Pharm. Co., Kankakee, Ill., 1970-76; dir. engring. Corn Processing div. Am. Maize Products Co., Hammond, Ind., 1976-80, v.p. ops., 1980-86, sr. v.p. mfg., 1986-89, sr. v.p. venture tech., 1989-96; sr. v.p. venture tech. Cerestar (merger), Hammond, 1996-97; cons. Wet Corn Milling Industry, 1997—; bd. dirs. Renewable Fuel Assn. Bd. dirs. Kankakee Symphony Assn., 1986—. Served with U.S. Army, 1954-56. Mem. Corn Refiners Assn. (bd. dirs. 1979-89), Renewable Fuel Assn. (bd. dirs. 1993-96). Republican. Lutheran. Avocations: sailing, skiing, golf. Home: 2 Bristol Grn Bourbonnais IL 60914-1603

BAHN, GILBERT SCHUYLER, retired mechanical engineer, researcher; b. Syracuse, N.Y., Apr. 25, 1922; s. Chester Bert and Irene Eliza (Schuyler) B.; m. Iris Cummings Birch, Sept. 14, 1957 (dec.); 1 child, Gilbert Kennedy. BS, Columbia U., 1943; MS in Mech. Engring., Rensselaer Poly. Inst., 1965; PhD in Engring., Columbia Pacific U., 1979. Chem. engr. GE Co., Pittsfield, Mass., 1946-48, devel. engr., Schenectady, 1948-53; sr. thermodynamics engr. Marquardt Co., Van Nuys, Calif., 1953-54, rsch. scientist, 1954-64, rsch. cons., 1964-70; engring. specialist LTV Aerospace Corp., Hampton, Va., 1970-88; ret.; freelance rsch. FDR at Nadir, 1988—. Mem. JANNAF performance standardization working group, 1966-83, Thermochemistry Working Group, 1967-72; propr. Schuyler Tech. Libr., 1952—. Air raid warden, 1941-43; active Boy Scouts Am., 1958-78. Served to capt. USAAF, 1943-46. Recipient Silver Beaver award Boy Scouts Am., 1970. Registered profl. engr., N.Y., Calif. Mem. ASME, Combustion Inst. (sec. western states sect. 1957-71), Soc. for Preservation Book of Common Prayer. Episcopalian (vestryman 1968-70). Author: Reaction Rate Compilation for the H-O-N System, 1968, Blue and White and Evergreen: William Byron Mowery and His Novels, 1981, Oliver Norton Worden's Family, 1982, Studies in American Historical Demography to 1850, Vol. 1, 1987, Overall Population Trends, Age Profiles, and Settlement, Vol. 2, 1987, The Wordens, Representative of the Native Northern Population, Vol. 3, 1994, Computerized Treatment and Statistical Evaluation of the 1790 Federal Census for the Northern Half of the State of New York, The Ancient Worden Family in America: A Story of Growth and Migration, 1988, FDR at Nadir: 1937 & 1938, 1993, Senator Alva B. Adams of Colorado, 1993, Senator Bennett Champ Clark of Missouri, 1993, Senator Walter F. George of Georgia, 1993, Senator Guy Mark Gillette of Iowa, 1993, Senator Augustine Lonergan of Connecticut, 1993, Senator Frederick Van Nuys of Indiana, 1993, Senator Patrick Anthony Mc Carran of Nevada, 1994, Senator Ellison D. Smith of South Carolina, 1995, Senator Millard E. Tydings of Maryland, 1996, Franklin D. Roosevelt's Appointments and Itineraries for the New Deal Years in Alphabetical Fashion, 1996, Infestation of Yankees: Reference Guide to Union Troops In Confederate Territory, 1998, American Place Names of Long Ago, 1998; founding editor Pyrodynamics, 1963-69; proceedings editor Kinetics, Equilibria and Performance of High Temperature Systems, 1960, 63, 67; contbr. articles to profl. jours.; discoverer free radical chem. species diboron monoxide, 1966. Home: 4519 N Ashtree St Moorpark CA 93021-2156

BAHNER, SUE (FLORENCE SUZANNA BAHNER), radio broadcasting executive; b. Phila.; d. William and Florence (Quinlivan) McElwee; m. David S. Bahner; children—Suzanna Elizabeth, Caryl Aileen. Grad. Columbia Bus. Coll., 1950. Various exec. sec. positions, 1954-74; office mgr. Sta. WYRD, Syracuse, N.Y., 1974, gen. mgr., 1974-80; gen. mgr. Sta. WWWG-AM, Rochester, N.Y., 1980-93; gen. mgr. WDCW, Syracuse, N.Y., 1993—; pres. The Cornerstone Group, 1986—, Crossway Cons., 1997—. Bd. dirs. Rescue Mission, Syracuse; active Eastern Hills Bible Ch. Mem. Greater Syracuse Assn. Evangelicals (treas. 1993—), N.Y. State Assn. Evangelicals (sec. 1998—), Nat. Religious Broadcasters (pres. ea. chpt. 1984-98, bd. dirs. 1983—, 2d v.p., 1992—). Office: Nat'l Religious Broadcasters 7839 Ashton Ave Manassas VA 20109-2883

BAHNIUK, EUGENE, mechanical engineering educator; b. Weirton, W.Va., Mar. 10, 1926; s. Michael and Mary (Sikora) B.; m. Margaret J. Hilton, June 11, 1977; children—Douglas Eugene, Joy Ruth, Barbara Jane, Becky Lynn, David Robert. BS, Case Inst. Tech., 1950, MS, 1961; PhD, Case Western Res. U., 1970. Registered profl. engr., Ohio. Devel. engr. Air Brake, Watertown, N.Y., 1950-54; project engr. Lear Corp., Elyria, Ohio, 1954-56; supr. Borg Warner Corp., Bedford Heights, Ohio, 1956-61; mgr. research and devel. Weatherhead Corp., Cleve., 1961-68; faculty Case Western Res. U., Cleve., 1970—, prof. mech. engring., 1972—. Contbr. articles to profl. jours.; patentee in field. Served to 1st lt., inf. U.S. Army, 1944-46. NIH fellow, 1969-70, NSF fellow, 1968-69, NASA fellow, 1982. Fellow ASTM (award of merit 1988); mem. Am. Soc. Biomechanics, Internat. Soc. Ski Safety, Sigma Xi. Home: 7629 Cairn Ln Gates Mills OH 44040-9738 Office: Case Western Reserve Univ Engring Dept Cleveland OH 44106

BAHR, CARMAN BLOEDOW, internist; b. Middletown, Ohio, Mar. 24, 1931; d. Edwin Louis and Berneice Mae (Bacon) Bloedow; m. Walter Julien Bahr, Aug. 28, 1968 (dec. Sept. 1971). BA cum laude, Miami U., Oxford, Ohio, 1952; MD, Ohio State U., 1956; MS, U. Okla., 1996. Cert. diabetes educator, 1986, 92. Intern St. Luke's Hosp., Chgo., 1956-57; resident U. Okla. Health Sci. Ctr., 1957-60; assoc. prof. medicine Okla. Health Sci. Ctr., 1971-93, prof. emeritus, 1993. Fellow ACP, 1986; mem. AMA (Physician's Recognition award 1976, 79, 82, 85, 88, 91, 93, 97), Am. Diabetes Assn. (chpt. pres. 1989, Robert Endress award 1985), Am. Assn. Diabetes Educators, Western Okla. Diabetes Educators, Am. Med. Women's Assn. Home: 5609 N Everest Ave Oklahoma City OK 73111-6729 Office: VA Med Ctr 921 NE 13th St Oklahoma City OK 73104-5007

BAHR, DONALD WALTER, chemical engineer; b. Chgo., Dec. 13, 1927; s. Walter James and Justine Antonia (Schwegler) B.; m. Mary Estelle Zieverink, Oct. 15, 1960; children: Donald Walter Jr., Susan Mary. BSChemE U. Ill., 1949; MSChemE, Ill. Inst. Tech., 1951, MS in Gas Tech., 1951. Registered profl. engr., Ohio. Aero. research scientist Lewis Flight Propulsion Lab., NASA, Cleve. 1951-54; chem. engr. Gen. Electric Co., Cin., 1956-62, engring. mgr., Phila., 1962-68, engring. mgr. GE Aircraft Engines, Cin., 1968-94; vice chmn. jet engine fuels panel NASA Lewis Research Ctr., Cleve., 1973-76. Contbr. articles to profl. jours. Patentee in field. Served to 1st lt. USAF, 1954-56. Recipient Outstanding Engring. Achievements award Gen. Electric Co., 1982; named to The Propulsion Hall of Fame for GE, 1995. Fellow ASME (combustion and fuels com. 1975—, vice chmn. 1985-87, chmn. 1987-89, R. Tom Sawyer award 1998), AIAA (Outstanding Achievement award air breathing propulsion, 1983); mem. NAE, Combustion Inst. (bd. advisors ctrl. states sect. 1986—, chmn. bd. advisors 1993-95, chmn. ctrl. states sect. 1995-97), Aerospace Industries Assn. (chmn. aircraft engine emissions com. 1971-95), Gen. Aviation Mfrs. Assn. (environ. com.), Coordinating Rsch. Coun. (aviation fuel, lubricant and other equipment com.). Republican. Roman Catholic. Avocations: golf, duplicate bridge. Home: 6576 Branford Ct Cincinnati OH 45236-2212

BAHR, EHRHARD, Germanic languages and literature educator; b. Kiel, Germany, Aug. 21, 1932; came to U.S., 1956; s. Klaus and Gisela (Badenhausen) B.; m. Diana Meyers, Nov. 21, 1973; stepchildren: Gary, Timothy, Christopher. Student, U. Heidelberg, Germany, 1952-53, U. Freiburg, Germany, 1953-56; M.S. Ed. (Fulbright scholar), U. Kans., 1956-58; postgrad., U. Cologne, 1959-61; Ph.D., U. Calif., Berkeley, 1968. Asst. prof. German UCLA, 1968-70, assoc. prof., 1970-72, prof., 1972—, chmn. dept. Germanic langs., 1981-84, 93-98, chair grad. council, 1988-89; Author: Irony in the Late Works of Goethe, 1972, Georg Lukacs, 1970, Ernst Bloch, 1974, Nelly Sachs, 1980; editor: Kant, What is Enlightenment?, 1974, Goethe, Wilhelm Meister's Journeyman Years, 1982, History of German Literature, 3 vols., 1987-88; co-editor: The Internalized Revolution: German Reactions to the French Revolution, 1789-1989, 1992; commentary: Thomas Mann: Death in Venice, 1991; contbr. articles to profl. jours. Author: Irony in the Late Works of Goethe, 1972, Georg Lukacs, 1970, Ernst Bloch, 1974, Nelly Sachs, 1980; editor: Kant, What is Enlightenment, 1974, Goethe, Wilhelm Meister's Journeyman Years, 1982, History of German Literature, 3 vols., 1987-88, 2nd edit., 1998-99, The Novel as Archive: The Genesis, Reception and Criticism of Goethe's Wilhelm, 1998; co-editor: The Internalized Revolution: German Reactions to the French Revolution, 1789-1989, 1992; commentary: Thomas Mann: Death in Venice, 1991; contbr. articles to profl. jours. Recipient Disting. Teaching award UCLA, 1970, Humanities Inst. award, 1972, summer stipend NEH, 1978. Mem. MLA, Am. Soc. 18th Century Studies, Am. Assn. Tchrs. German, Western Soc. 18th Century Studies, German Studies Assn. (pres. 1987-88), Philol. Assn. Pacific Coast, Lessing Soc., Goethe Soc. N.Am. (exec. sec. 1979-89, pres. 1995-97). Office: UCLA Dept Germanic Langs Los Angeles CA 90095-1539

BAHR, HOWARD MINER, sociologist, educator; b. Provo, Utah, Feb. 21, 1938; s. A. Francis and Louie Jean (Miner) B.; m. Rosemary Frances Smith, Aug. 28, 1961 (div. 1985); children: Bonnie Louise, Howard McKay, Rowena Ruth, Tanya Lavonne, Christopher J., Laura L., Stephen S., Rachel M.; m. Kathleen Slaugh, May 1, 1986; children: Alden Keith, Jonathan Andrew. B.A. with honors, Brigham Young U., 1962; M.A. in Sociology, U. Tex., 1964, Ph.D., 1965. Research assoc. Columbia U., N.Y.C., 1965-68; vis. lectr., summer 1968; lectr. in sociology N.Y. U., 1967-68, Bklyn. Coll., City U. N.Y., 1967; asso. prof. sociology Wash. State U., Pullman, 1968-73; prof. Wash. State U., 1972-73, chmn. dept. rural sociology, 1971-73; prof. sociology Brigham Young U., Provo, Utah, 1973—; dir. Family Research Inst., 1977-83; fellow David M. Kennedy, 1992; Virginia F. Culter lectr., 1997; vis. prof. sociology U. Va., 1976-77, 84-85. Author: Skid Row: An Introduction to Disaffiliation, 1973, Old Men Drunk and Sober, 1974, Women Alone: The Disaffiliation of Urban Females, 1976, American Ethnicity, 1979, Sunshine Widows: Adapting to Sudden Bereavement, 1980, Middletown Families, 1982, All Faithful People: Change and Continuity in Middletown's Religion, 1983, Life in Large Families, 1983, Divorce and Remarriage: Problems, Adaptations and Adjustments, 1983, Social Science Research Methods, 1984, Recent Social Trends in the United States 1960-90, 1991, Dine' Bibliography to the 1990's, 1999; contbr. articles to profl. jours.; asso. editor: Rural Sociology, 1978-83, Jour. Marriage and the Family, 1978-83. NIMH grantee, 1968-70, 71-73; NSF grantee, 1971-72, 76-80. Mem. Soc. Applied Anthropology, Rural Sociol. Assn., Nat. Coun. Family Rels. Mem. LDS Ch. Office: Brigham Young U Dept Sociology 842 SWKT Provo UT 84602

BAHR, JANE MARIE, writer, retired English educator. BA in English, U. Wis., River Falls, 1971; MA in English, U. Wis., Whitewater, 1978. English tchr. Whitewater (Wis.) H.S., 1973-82, Eau Claire (Wis.) Meml. H.S., 1985, Glenwood City H.S., summers 1990-91; freelance writer Wis. Regional Writers' Assn., 1985—, Wis. Fellowship of Poets, 1981—, Wis. Arts Bd. Grant, 1998. WRWA Soar scholar Sch. of Arts, U. Wis., Madison, 1999.

BAHR, LAUREN S., publishing company executive; b. New Brunswick, N.J., July 3, 1944; d. Simon A. and Rosalind J. (Cabot) B. Student, U. Grenoble, France, 1964; BA (Branstrom scholar), MA, U. Mich., 1966. Asst. editor New Horizons Pubs., Inc., Chgo., 1967, Scholastic Mags., Inc., N.Y.C., 1968-71; supervising editor Houghton Mifflin Co., Boston, 1971; product devel. editor Appleton-Century-Crofts, N.Y.C., 1972-74; sponsoring editor McGraw-Hill, Inc., N.Y.C., 1974-75; editor Today's Sec. mag., 1975-77; sr. editor Media Systems Corp., N.Y.C., 1978; sr. editor coll. dept. CBS Coll. Pub., N.Y.C., 1978-82, mktg. mgr. fgn. langs., dir. mktg. adminstrn., 1982-83; from dir. devel. Coll. divsn. to pub. cons. Harper & Row, N.Y.C., 1983-91; v.p., editl. dir. Atlas Edits., Inc., N.Y.C., 1991-98. Democrat. Jewish. Home: 444 E 82nd St New York NY 10028-5903

BAHR, MORTON, trade union executive; b. Bklyn., July 18, 1926; s. Martin and Elizabeth B.; m. Florence Bahr, 1945; 2 children. Student, Bklyn. Coll., 1942-43. Pres. Local 1172 Communications Workers Am., 1954-58, Organizer Dist. 1, 1958-61, dir. N.Y. State, 1961-63, asst. to v.p. Dist. 1, 1963-69; now pres. Communications Workers Am., Washington. Dir. Myasthenia Gravis Found, 1962—; trustee Maritime Port Coun. AFL-CIO, 1973—; mem. exec. coun. N.Y. State AFL-CIO, 1974. Office: Comm Workers Am 501 3rd St NW Washington DC 20001-2760*

BAHR, SHEILA KAY, physician; b. Highland Park, Mich., June 2, 1956; d. Thomas Joseph and Kathryn Mary (McCrohan) Bernhardt; m. Wayne Edward Bahr, June 19, 1981. BS, U. Mich., Dearborn, 1978; DO, Mich. State U., 1982. Diplomate Am. Osteo. Bd. of Internal Medicine. Intern Botsford Gen. Hosp., 1982-83, resident in internal medicine, 1983-86; staff physician Health Alliance Plan, Livonia, Mich., 1986-87; pvt. practice, 1987-95; staff physician Henry Ford Health Sys., 1996; asst. clin. prof. Coll. Osteo. Medicine Mich. State U., 1991—; resident in psychiatry Wayne State U., Detroit, 1998—. Regent's scholar U. Mich., 1974; named Physician Trainer of Yr., Garden City (Mich.) Osteo. Hosp., 1990. Fellow Am. Coll. Osteo. Internists; mem. Am. Osteo. Assn., Mich. Osteo. Assn., Oakland County Osteo. Assn.

BAHRANI, AL SATTAR, mechanical engineer; b. Baghdad, Iraq, Jan. 21, 1932; came to U.S., 1949; s. Abdul Hussain and Fahima Ali B.; m. Krystine Whiting, June 5, 1955 (div. 1974); children: Neda, Linda, Steve; m. Inga-Maj Kristina Frieberg, Sept. 24, 1982. BA, Dartmouth Coll., 1953; MSME, U. Mich., 1955. Cert. TPM mgmt, instr. Engr. Am. Std., Detroit, 1955-60, dept. mgr., 1960-62; product engr. Procter & Gamble Co., Cin., 1962-72, group leader, 1972-75, sect. head, 1976-82, mgr. tech., 1982-90, assoc. dir. mfg., 1990-94; pres., prin. TPM Mgmt. Inc., 1994—; cons. HP, Toyota Motors, Exxon, Motorola, Devro. 9 patents in field. Recipient First Tech. award Procter & Gamble Co., 1992. Avocations: windsurf, dance, swimming. Home: 3855 Poole Rd Cincinnati OH 45251-2828

BAHRE, JEANNETTE, English language educator, education educator, librarian; b. Darby, Pa., Dec. 28, 1948; d. Paul Florent and Jeanne (Shangraw) Gibson; m. Stephen Alan Bahre, May 14, 1974; children: Kimberly, Christian, Rachael. BA, Merrimack Coll., 1970; MEd, U. Ariz., 1979. Cert. experienced tchr., N.H.; cert. English tchr., Mass. Tchr., 1970—; libr. St. Augustine Sch., Andover, Mass., 1980-83; Beverly (Mass.) Sch. for Deaf,

1988-89; instr. No. Essex C.C., Haverhill, Mass., 1982-84, libr. evening svc., 1986-88; tchr., advisor Linton Hall Sch., Bristow, Va., 1985-86; lectr. George Mason U., Fairfax, Va., 1985-86; tchr., tutor Even Start: Family Lit. Project, Amesbury, Mass., 1990-93; Chpt. I tutor Seabrook (N.H.) Elem. Sch., 1994-95; libr. South Hampton (N.H.) Pub. Libr., 1994—; summer seminar for tchrs. Univ. N.H., N.H. Humanities Found., 1997; tchr. Family Scrapbooks program New England Found. Humanities, Lawrence, Mass., 1997. Editor Four Winds Lit. Jours., 1992, 93, 94, 95, 96. Completed CCD master tchr.'s program Archdiocese of Boston, Aquinas Coll., 1991-92. Grantee NEH, 1988. Avocation: reading literature.

BAHRET, MARY ELLEN, press secretary. BA in Polit. Sci. and Urban Studies, U. Pitts., 1994. Adminstrv. asst., recruiting asst. McKinsey and Co., Inc., 1993-95; exec. asst. J. Michael Eakin for Superior Ct. Judge Campaign, 1995; adminstrv. & policy asst. strategic planning/congl. affairs Rep. Nat. Com., 1995-96, coord. congl. comm. Office Congl. Affairs, 1996; asst. to the chief of staff Office of Senator Larry E. Craig, Washington, 1997, dep. press sec., 1997-98, legis. asst., 1997—. Office: 520 Hart Senate Office Bldg Washington DC 20510-1203

BAI, NINA BEATE, senior software engineer, consultant; b. Orange, N.J., Dec. 7, 1963; d. Karl Dieter and Sylvia Ellinor (Von Hodenberg) Moeller; m. Mark Aristide Bai, Sept. 21, 1985; 1 child, Natalie Ann. BS in Computer Sci., Fairleigh Dickinson U., 1985, MS in Computer Sci., 1992. Software engr. Singer Kearfott, Wayne, N.J., 1985-87, Applied Biosystems, Ramsey, N.J., 1988-90; sr. software engr. Philips Electronics, Mahwah, N.J., 1991-96, Beckman Coulter, Allendale, N.J., 1996—; cons. C++ for Windows, 1996—. Asst. editor: Optics, 1985. Mem. Phi Zeta Kappa, Phi Omega Epsilon. Republican. Achievements include development of first Windows application for analysis and display of energy dispersive spectra using C++. Home: 64 Van Buren St Little Ferry NJ 07643-1335 Office: Beckman Coulter 90 Boroline Rd Allendale NJ 07401-1613

BAIER, EDWARD JOHN, former public health official, industrial hygiene engineer, consultant; b. Pitts., Apr. 1, 1925; s. Edward O. and Lucy M. Baier; m. Grace Cecelia McDonald, Jan. 15, 1947; children: Edward Michael, Grace Cecelia. BS, U. Pitts., 1946, MPH (fellow), 1955. Lic. indsl. hygienist, Ill.; cert. in comprehensive practice of indsl. hygiene Am. Bd. Indsl. Hygiene, internat. hazard control mgmt. Hazard Control Mgr. Cert. Bd., hazardous materials mgmt. Inst. Hazardous Materials Mgmt.; cert. safety profl. Bd. Cert. Safety Profls. Chief indsl. hygiene sect. Dept. Health State of Pa., 1956-68, dir. divsn. occupl. health, 1968-71; dir. divsn. occupl. health Dept. Environ. Resources, 1971; dir. Bur. Mines and Occupl. Health and Safety, 1971-72; dep. dir. Nat. Inst. for Occupl. Safety and Health, HEW, Rockville, Md., 1972-78; corp. dir. indsl. hygiene and toxicology Diamond Shamrock Corp., Cleve., Dallas, 1978-82; dir. tech. support OSHA, Dept. Labor, 1982-89; cons. in occupl. and environ. health and safety, 1989—; lectr. in field. Contbr. articles to profl. jours. Chmn. West Shore coun. Boy Scouts Am., 1970-71; sec. Upper Allen Twp. (Pa.) Sewer Authority, 1970-72. Fellow Am. Indsl. Hygiene Assn. (pres. 1975-76, Cummings Meml. award 1982, Edward J. Baier Tech. Achievement award 1984); mem. Am. Conf. Govt. Indsl. Hygienists (chmn. 1968-69), Am. Acad. Indsl. Hygiene (founder, pres. 1987-88), Indsl. Hygiene Roundtable (steward 1975-76), Inst. Hazardous Materials Mgmt. (cert. hazardous materials mgrs. bd. examiners 1991—, bd. dirs. 1992—, vice chmn. 1993—), Nat. Am. Indian Safety Coun., N.Y. Acad. Scis., Pa. Soc. Profl. Engrs., Am. Bd. Indsl. Hygiene (bd. dirs. 1970-76). Roman Catholic.

BAIG, MUKARRAM, internist; b. Rawalpindi, Pakistan, July 10, 1963. MBBS, Aga Khan U. Med. Coll., Pakistan, 1988. Diplomate in internal medicine and cardiology Am. Bd. Internal Medicine. Internist Johns Hopkins Hosp., Balt., 1990-91; internist East Tenn. State U., Johnson City, 1991-92, resident, 1993-94, chief resident in internal medicine, 1993-94; fellow in surgery Johns Hopkins Hosp., Balt., 1989-90; fellow in cardiology Barnes-Jewish Hosp., Washington U., St. Louis, 1994-97; fellow in interventional cardiology U. Louisville, 1997-98, lectr. in cardiology, 1997-98. Mem. Am. Coll. Cardiology. Address: Profl Office Bldg Ste 206 11301 Fallbrook Dr Houston TX 77065-4237

BAIGIS, WENDY SUE, probation and parole officer; b. Bellefonte, Pa., Sept. 25, 1967; d. Andrew J. and Judith A. (Miga) B.; m. John R. Freas, Nov. 25, 1994. BS, West Chester U., 1989, MS, 1995. Rsch. asst. U. Pa., Phila., 1985-86; pub. safety officer West Chester (Pa.) U., 1987-90; probation and parole officer Chester County Adult Parole and Probation Dept., West Chester, 1989-92, probation and parole officer specialist, 1992—; adj. faculty Chestnut Hill Coll., Phila., 1999—. Mem. Acad. Criminal Justice Scis., Lambda Alpha Epsilon (nat. conf. coord. 1995).

BAIK-KROMALIC, SUE S., metallurgical engineer; b. June 21, 1965. BS in Metallurgical Engring., Ohio State U., Columbus, 1990. Project engr. Cummins Engine Co., Columbus, Ind, 1988-89; engring. staff, materials testing and devel. engr. Honda Am. Mfg., Inc., East Liberty, Ohio, 1990-92; trainer problem solving Honda Am., Inc., East Liberty, Ohio, 1992-93, new model project engr., 1993-94, leader tech. devel., 1994; prodn. planning ops. and control, 1994-95; engring. coord. mfg. ops., cost & manpower resources control Honda of Am. Mfg., Inc., 1995-97, with ops. office gen. planning and control, 1997-99, asst. mgr. bus. mgmt. sys. reporting, 1999—; guest speaker Ohio State U., Columbus, 1991. Mem. ASM Internat. (Columbus chpt. awards chmn. 1992-94, mem. chpt. devel. task force 1993-94, Columbus chpt. sec. 1994-95, Columbus chpt. task force 1993-94, membership devel. com. 1994-97, Columbus chpt. treas. 1994-96, chpt. coun. 1994-97, Columbus chpt. chairperson 1996-97, vice chair membership devel. com. 1996-97, chair membership devel. com. 1997-98). Roman Catholic. Avocation: golf. Office: Honda of Am Mfg Inc Honda Ops Office 24000 Honda Pkwy Marysville OH 43040-9251

BAIL, JOE PAUL, agricultural educator emeritus; b. Herold, W.Va., May 12, 1925; s. Alva Edward and Prudence (Wood) B.; m. Nelma Louise Rapp, Oct. 20, 1945; 1 son, David Joe. B.S., W.Va. U., 1947, M.S., 1947; Ph.D., Mich State U., 1958. Tchr. agr. Spencer (W. Va.) High Sch., 1947; head dept. agr. Glenville (W. Va.) State Coll., 1948-51; asst. prof., assoc. prof. agrl. edn. W.Va. U., 1951-57; asst. prof., then assoc. prof. Cornell U., Ithaca, N.Y., 1957-67; prof. agrl. edn. div. Cornell U., 1967-90, prof. edn. emeritus, 1990—, chmn. agrl. edn. div., 1963-71, chmn. dept. edn., 1978-87; vis. prof. U. Ariz., U. Fla.; Cons. pub. schs., N.Y., Mass., W.Va., Ariz, Fla.; mem. com. Nat. Acad. Scis.; field review officer U.S. Office Edn. Contbg. author: Teacher Education in Agriculture, 1967, 79; contbr. articles to profl. jours. Dist. chmn. Boy Scouts Am., 1972-73; mem. Ch.-Community Action, Inc., 1968—; past pres. N.Y. Council on Rural Edn. Served to 1st lt. USAAF, 1943-45, ETO. Decorated Soldier's medal, Air medal with four oak leaf clusters; recipient 30-yr. award in agrl. edn. N.Y. Assn. Tchrs. Agr., 1977, Outstanding Educator award N.Y. State Rural Schs., 1987, Outstanding Alumni award W.Va. U., 1990; named Hon. Am. Farmer Future Farmers Am., 1978, Paul Harris fellow. Mem. Am. Vocat. Assn. (past nat. com. chmn.), Assn. Higher Edn., N.Y. Assn. Deans of Edn. (coun.), Rotary (past pres.), Alpha Zeta, Kappa Delta Pi, Delta Tau Delta, Alpha Tau Alpha. Democrat. Baptist. Home: 111 Winston Dr Ithaca NY 14850-1935

BAILAR, BARBARA ANN, statistician, researcher; b. Monroe, Mich., Nov. 24, 1935; d. Malcolm Laurie and Clara Florence (Parent) Dezendorf; m. John Francis Powell (div. 1966); 1 child, Pamela; m. John Christian Bailar; 1 child, Melissa. BA, SUNY, 1956; MS, Va. Poly. Inst., 1965; PhD, Am. U., 1972. With Bur. of Census, Washington, 1958-88, chief Ctr. Rsch. Measurement Methods, 1973-79, assoc. dir. for statis. standards and methodology, 1979-88; exec. dir. Am. Statis. Assn., Alexandria, Va., 1988-95; v.p. for survey rsch. Nat. Opinion Rsch. Ctr., Chgo., 1995—; instr. George Washington U., 1984-85; head dept. math. and stats. USDA Grad. Sch., Washington, 1972-87. Contbr. articles, book chpts. to profl. publs. Pres. bd. dirs. Harbour Sq. Coop., Washington, 1988-89. Recipient Silver medal U.S. Dept. Commerce, 1980. Fellow Am. Statis. Assn. (pres. 1987); mem. AAAS (chair sect. stats. 1984-85), Internat. Assn. Survey Statisticians (pres. 1989-91), Internat. Statis. Inst. (Pres.'s invited speaker 1983, v.p. 1993-95), Cosmos Club. Office: NORC 1155 E 60th St Chicago IL 60637-2745

BAILAR, BENJAMIN FRANKLIN, academic administrator, administration educator; b. Champaign, Ill., Apr. 21, 1934; s. John C. and Florence (Catherwood) B.; m. Anne Tveit, Aug. 22, 1958; children: Christina, Benjamin Franklin Jr. BA, U. Colo., 1955, DHL (hon.), 1989; MBA, Harvard, 1959; DPA (hon.), Monmouth Coll., 1976. With Continental Oil Co., Houston, 1959-62; with Am. Can Co., N.Y.C., 1962-72; v.p. Am. Can Co., 1967-72; sr. asst. postmaster gen. U.S. Postal Service, Washington, 1972-74; dep. postmaster gen. U.S. Postal Service, 1974-75, postmaster gen., 1975-78; exec. v.p., dir. U.S. Gypsum Co., Chgo., 1978-82; pres., chief exec. officer Scott Pub. Co., N.Y.C., 1983-85; pres. Franklin Fin. Corp., 1985-87; dean, prof. adminstrn. Jones Grad. Sch. of Adminstrn. Rice U., Houston, 1987-97; bd. dirs. Dana Corp., Toledo, Smith Internat., Inc., Houston, U.S. Can Corp., Oak Brook, Ill., Trico Marine Svcs., Inc., Houston. Mem. Chgo. Club, Tau Kappa Epsilon.

BAILAR, JOHN CHRISTIAN, III, public health educator, physician, statistician; b. Urbana, Ill., Oct. 9, 1932; married; 4 children. BA, U. Colo., 1953; MD, Yale U., 1955; PhD in Stats., Am. U., 1973. Intern U. Colo. Med. Ctr., Denver, 1955-56; field investigator, biometry br. Nat Cancer Inst., NIH, Bethesda, Md., 1956-62, head demography sect., 1962-70, dir. 3d nat. cancer survey, 1967-70, dep. assoc. dir. for cancer control, 1972-74; editor-in-chief JNCI, 1974-80; dir. research service VA, Washington, 1970-72; lectr. in biostats. Harvard U., Cambridge, Mass., 1980-87; prof. McGill U., Montreal, 1987-95; chair dept. epidemiology and biostats. McGill U., Can., 1993-95; sr. scientist Office Disease Prevention and Health Promotion, Dept. HHS, Washington, 1983-92; chair dept. health studies U. Chgo., 1995-98; sr. scientist health and environ. rev. divsn. EPA, 1980-83; lectr. epidemiology and pub. health Yale U., New Haven, Conn., 1958-83; mem. faculty math. and stats. USDA Grad. Sch., Washington, 1966-76; vis. prof. stats. SUNY, Buffalo, 1974-80; professorial lectr. George Washington U., Washington, 1975-80; cons. in biostats. and epidemiology Dana-Farber Cancer Inst., Boston, 1977-83; vis. prof. Harvard U., 1977-79; spl. appointment grad. faculty U. Colo. Med. Ctr., Denver, 1979-81; scholar in residence NAS, 1992-96. Mem. editorial adv. bd. Cancer Rsch., 1968-72; statis. cons. New Eng. Jour. Medicine, 1980-91; mem. bd. editors New England Jour. Medicine, 1992—; contbr. numerous articles to profl. jours.; editor JNCI, 1974-80. John D. and Catherine T. MacArthur Found. fellow, 1990-95. Fellow AAAS, Am. Coll. Epidemiology, Am. Statis. Assn. (chair-elect and chair biometric sect. 1979-81, founding chair sect. stats. and environment 1990); mem. AMA (hon.), Inst. of Medicine, Internat. Statis. Inst., Coun. Biology Editors (chair publishing policy com. 1983-89, pres.-elect, pres., past pres. 1986-89), Soc. Risk Analysis (founding chair Boston chpt. 1985-86). Office: U Chgo Divsn Biol Scis MC-2007 5841 S Maryland Ave Chicago IL 60637-1463

BAILE, CLIFTON A., biologist, researcher; b. Warrensburg, Mo., Feb. 8, 1940; s. Harold F. and Salome (Mohler) B.; m. Beth Lucile Hoover, Aug. 21, 1960; children: Christopher A., Marisa B. BS in Agr., Bus., Cen. Mo. State U., 1962; PhD in Nutrition, U. Mo., 1965; MA (hon.), U. Pa., 1979. NIH rsch. fellow Sch. Pub. Health Harvard U., Boston, 1964-66, from. instr. to asst. prof. Sch. Pub. Health, 1966-71; mgr. neurobiol. rsch. SmithKline Animal Health, Phila., 1971-75; from assoc. prof. to prof. Sch. Vet. Medicine U. Pa., Phila., 1975-82; disting. fellow, dir. R & D Monsanto Agrl. Co., St. Louis, 1982-95; adj. prof. nutrition Sch. Medicine Washington U., St. Louis, 1982-95; adj. prof. dept. animal sci. U. Mo., 1982-95; dist. prof. animal sci. and food and nutrition U. Ga., Athens, 1995—; Ga. Rsch. Alliance Eminent scholar Agrl. Biotech., Athens, 1996—; presenter numerous seminars and symposiums. Contbr. over 250 articles and 230 abstracts to sci. jours. Ralston Purina rsch. fellow, 1962-64, NIH spl. postdoctoral fellow, 1969. Mem. Am. Soc. Animal Sci. (bd. dirs. 1990-93, animal growth and devel. award 1989), Am. Physiol. Soc., Am. Inst. Nutrition, Am. Dairy Sci. Assn. (Am. Feed Mgmt. award 1979), Soc. Neurosci. Achievements include 16 patents in field; research in control and feed intake and regulation of energy balance. Office: U Ga 444 ADS Complex Athens GA 30602-2771

BAILEY, AMOS PURNELL, clergyman, syndicated columnist; b. Grotons, Va., May 2, 1918; s. Louis Willian and Evelyn (Charnock) B.; m. Ruth Martin Hill, Aug. 22, 1942 (dec. 1992); children: Eleanor Carol Bailey Harriman, Anne Ruth Bailey Page, Joyce Elizabeth Bailey Richardson, Jeanne Bailey Dodge-Allen; m. Betty Lou Sheffield, Mar. 5, 1994. BA, Randolph-Macon Coll., 1942, DD, 1956; BD, Duke U., 1948; ThM, Union Theol. Sem., 1957; postgrad., Ecumenical Inst., Jerusalem, 1977. Ordained to ministry United Meth. Ch., 1942; pastor Emporia, Va., 1938, Beulah UMC Ch., Richmond, Va., 1938-43, New Kent circuit, 1943-44, Oak Grove United Meth. Ch., Norfolk, Va., 1948-50, Grace United Meth. Ch., Newport News, 1950-54, Centenary Ch., Richmond, 1954-61; supt. Richmond dist. United Meth. Ch., 1961-67; sr. minister Reveille Ch., Richmond, 1967-70; assoc. gen. sec., div. chaplains Bd. Higher Edn. and Ministry United Meth. Ch., Washington, 1970-79; v.p. Nat. Meth. Found., 1979-82; interim minister Herndon Ch., 1985-86; pres., CEO Nat. Temple Ministries, Inc., Arlington, Va., 1982—; pres. S.E.J. and S.C.U. Comms., 1968-76; dir. Reeves-Parvin Co., 1978-85; v.p. Va. Conf. Bd. Missions, 1955-61, Meth. Commn. Town and Country Work, 1956-67; mem. Meth. Commn. on Higher Edn., 1960-70, Meth. Interbd. Coun., 1960-70; del. Southeastern Jurisdictional Conf., 1964, 68, Gen. Conf., 1964, 66, 68, 70, World Meth. Conf., London, 1966, Denver, 1970, Dublin, 1976, Rio de Janeiro, 1996; exec. com. Congress, 1987-88; fin. com. Nat. Ch. Growth Rsch. Ctr., 1986-89; frequent chaplain U.S. Senate, U.S. Ho. of Reps., Va. Gen. Assembly; mem. coun., exec. com., pres. comms. com. Southeastern Jurisdiction, 1968-76; pres. Joint Comms. Com., 1968-76; vice chmn. Ministry to Svc. Pers. in East Asia, 1972-79; mem. Commn. on Interpretation, Va. Conf. Bd. Ordained Ministry, 1974-82; participant Ednl. Study Mission to Eng., 1988. Writer syndicated column Daily Bread, 1945— (50th Anniversary award 1995), syndicated radio devotional, 1945-69; condr. weekly radio counseling program The Night Pastor, 1955-69, Sunshine and Shadows, 1967-70; contbr. articles to profl. jours. Mem. exec. com. Va. Conf. Bd. Edn., 1968-72; mem. World Meth. Coun., Va. Commn. Aging; pres. adv. bd. Richmond Welfare Dept., 1956-68, Va. Conf. Bd. Ministry, Richmond Pub. Assistance Com., Richmond Coun. Alcoholism, Citizen Adv. Bd. Duke U. Comprehensive Cancer Ctr., 1995—; group chmn. industry divsn. Richmond United Givers Fund, 1961; chmn. chaplains adv. coun. VA, Washington; bd. mgrs. Richmond YMCA, 1961-69; bd. dirs. Va. Meth. Advisers; trustee Randolph-Macon Coll., 1960-82, trustee emeritus, 1986; bd. visitors Duke Div. Sch., 1964-70; trustee So. Sem., 1961-76. With Chaplains Corps AUS, 1945-47. Mem. DAV (life), Meth. Hist. Soc., Duke Div. Alumni Assn. (pres.). Club: Kiwanis. Home: Apt 1312 12100 Chancellors Village Ln Fredericksburg VA 22407-6595 Office: PO Box 41296 Fredericksburg VA 22404-1296 *Life for me is rich and meaningful in a Christian commitment which allows a free and unfettered search for truth. Discipline of time and resources, the love of persons in my sphere of activity, a devoted family —all are part of the life I cherish daily.*

BAILEY, ANDREW DEWEY, JR., accounting educator; b. St. Paul, Feb. 18, 1942; s. Andrew D. and Lorraine L. (LaBelle) B.; m. Irene S. Femrite, Mar. 22, 1964; children: Andrew D. III, Rachelle I. BSB, U. Minn., 1964, MS, 1966; PhD, Ohio State U., 1971. CPA, Ind.; cert. mgmt. acct.; cert. internal auditor; cert. fraud examiner. Teaching assoc. Ohio State U., Columbus, 1967-70; asst. prof. acctg. U. Maine, Orono, 1970-72; from asst. prof. to assoc. prof. acctg. U. Iowa, Iowa City, 1972-74; from assoc. prof. to prof. acctg. Purdue U., West Lafayette, Ind., 1974-80; prof., chair dept. acctg. U. Minn., Mpls., 1980-85; Arthur Young prof. Ohio State U., 1985-89; Deloitte and Touche prof., head dept. acctg. U. Ariz., Tucson, 1990-94; Ernst & Young prof., head acctg. dept. U. Ill., Champaign, 1994-97; dir. Ctr. for Internat. Edn. and Rsch. in Acctg., Champaign, 1997-99; vis. prof. U. Queensland (Australia), 1978-79, U. Otago, Dunedin, N.Z., 1986, Norwegian Grad. Sch. Mgmt., 1994, 95, 96, ESCP, Paris, 1994. Author: (with J. Gerlach and A.B. Whinston) Office Systems Technology and Organizations, 1985; Statistical Auditing: Review, Concepts and Problems, 1981; contbr. chpts. to books, articles to profl. jours.; editor Internat. Jour. Acctg., 1997—. Mem. AICPA (Elijah Watts Sells awrd 1976), Am. Acctg. Assn. (pres. 1993-94, chmn. auditing sec. 1989-90, Innovation in Acctg. Edn. award 1991), Inst. Internal Auditiors (Cert. of Excellence 1981), Fin. Execs. Inst., Inst. Mgmt. Accts. (Beyer Gold medal 1977), Inst. Cert. Fraud Examiners, Beta Alpha Psi (Acct. of Yr. Educator 1996). Republican. Office: U Ill Dept Acctg 1206 6th St Dept Acctg Champaign IL 61820

BAILEY, BARRY STONE, sculptor, educator; b. High Point, N.C., Oct. 21, 1952; s. Richard Junior and Dorothy (Harris) B. MFA, East Carolina U., 1978. Sculptor New Orleans, 1980—; curator, visual arts coord. Contemporary Arts Ctr., New Orleans, 1980-82; curator La. World Expo., New Orleans, 1984; instr. La. State U., Baton Rouge, 1985; prof. U. Ga., Cortona, Italy, 1992, 96; asst. prof. Tulane U., New Orleans, 1989-93, assoc. prof., 1993—. Grantee: Sculpture grant for Italy, Ford Found., Cortona, Italy, 1977, NEA/So. Arts Found., 1987. Office: Tulane U Art Dept New Orleans LA 70118

BAILEY, BETTY L., federal agency administrator; m. Charles Bailey; 3 children. BA, Golden Gate U., MBA; PhD, Calif. Coast U. Civil servant Edwards Air Force Base, 1977; chief rsch. devel. Air Force Astronautics Lab.; dir. policy mgmt., dir. contracting, space divsn. L.A. Air Force Base, 1987-90; dir. contracting Air Force Comm. Command Hdqs., Scott Air Force Base, Ill., 1990—; dir. office acquisition mgmt. U.S. EPA, Washington, 1993—. Office: EPA Office Acquisition Mgmt 401 M St SW Washington DC 20024-2610*

BAILEY, BRENDA MARIE, accountant; b. Chgo., June 21, 1940; d. Walter E. and Dorothy Virginia (Seyl) B.; m. Norman R. Hill, Nov. 30, 1985 (dec. Nov. 1993); 1 stepchild, Andrea M. Hill. BS, So. Ill. U., 1966. CPA, Calif. U.S. govt. gen. svcs. adminstrn. auditor U.S. Navy, Barstow, Calif., 1966-69; staff acct. Stanford Bruns & Co., San Diego, 1969-74; pvt. practice La Mesa, Calif., 1974-91; ptnr. Bailey & Dana CPAs, La Mesa, 1991—; cons. to dirs. Santa Fe Rlwy. Hist. Soc., L.A., 1988-95; treas. Pacific S.W. Rlwy. Mus., San Diego, 1979-86, San Diego Rlwy. Mus. of Balboa Park, 1981—. Co-host, treas. 1998 ann. conv. Lionel Operating Train Soc. Mem. AICPAs, Calif. Soc. CPAs (vol. Tax Hotline 1996—), Am. Soc. Women Accts. (bd. dirs. 1975-77, pub. editor 1976-77), Nat. Model R.R. assn. (mem. planning and asminstrv. com. Pacific S.W. divsn. conv. 1994), Santa Fe Rlwy. Hist. Soc. (mem. planning com., treas. ann. conv. 1986, 94, 97, 98, treas. 1995—), La Mesa C. of C. Republican. Presbyterian. Avocations: photography, hiking. Home: 1931 Aspen Ln El Cajon CA 92019-4178 Office: 4817 Palm Ave # 3 La Mesa CA 91941-3861

BAILEY, BYRON JAMES, otolaryngologist, medical association executive; b. Okla. City, Apr. 5, 1934; s. Jay Gordon and Christine F. (Koehn) B.; m. Margaret Ann Whale, June 6, 1957; children: Michael Jon, Debra Lynn, James Grant, Jennifer Leigh, John Albert. BA, U. Okla., 1955, MD, 1959. Intern UCLA Med. Ctr., Los Angeles, 1959-60; resident in gen. surgery UCLA Med. Ctr., 1960-61, resident, head and neck specialist, 1961-64, asst. prof., 1964-68; Wiess prof., chair dept. otolaryngology U. Tex., Galveston, 1968—; treas. Am. Bd. Med. Specialties. Editor The Laryngoscope, 1994—. Chmn. Emergency Med. Svcs. Commn., Galveston, 1975-80. Recipient Mosher award Triological Soc., 1971, Harvey W. Wiley medal U.S. FDA, 1988. Mem. Am. Acad. Otolaryngology (pres. 1988-89), Am. Bd. Otolaryngology (pres. 1992-94), Am. Soc. Head and Neck Surgery (pres. 1992-93), Soc. Univ. Otolaryngologists (pres. 1976), Assn. Acad. Dept. Otolaryngology (pres. 1984), Am. Laryngol. Assn. (pres. 1993-94), Am. Bd. Med. Specialities (treas. 1993-97), Galveston C. of C. (v.p. 1978), Cosmos Club, Triological Soc. (v.p. 1997-98), Nat. Assn. fo Physicians for the Environ. (pres. 1998—). Office: U Tex Med Br Dept Otolaryn 7104 JSA 301 University Blvd Galveston TX 77555-5302*

BAILEY, CECIL DEWITT, aerospace engineer, educator; b. Zama, Miss., Oct. 25, 1921; s. James Dewitt and Matha Eugenia (Roberts) B.; m. Myrtis Irene Taylor, Sept. 8, 1942; children: Marilyn, Beverly. B.S., Miss. State U., 1951; M.S., Purdue U., 1954, Ph.D., 1962. Commd. 2d lt. USAF, 1944, advanced through grades to lt. col., 1965, pilot, 1944-56, sr. pilot, 1956-60, command pilot, 1960-67, asst. prof. Air Force Inst. Tech., 1954-58, assoc. prof., 1965-67, ret., 1967; assoc. prof. aero. and astronautical engring. Ohio State U., Columbus, 1967-69; prof. Ohio State U., 1970-85, prof. emeritus, 1985—; dir. USAF-Am. Soc. Engring. Edn. summer faculty research program Wright-Patterson AFB, Ohio, 1976-78. *The demonstration of the meaning of the Law of Varying Action caused much controversy and criticism. Professor D.H. Hodges was more perceptive and observed that something worthwile had been accomplished. In 1978, he wrote, "(1) People have always stopped short of Hamiltons' Law...thus they haven't been able to do what you have done. (2) You have shown a beautiful parallel between obtaining solutions for the time and space domains....(3) With the use of power series, you have laid the foundation for a new generation of finite elements...". In 1989, he wrote "The technical community owes you some gratitude...".* Contbr. numerous articles to profl. jours. Mem. Soc. Exptl. Stress Analysis, Am. Soc. Engring. Edn., Am. Acad. Mechanics, Res. Officers (life), Ret. Officers Assn. (life), Am. Legion (life), Sigma Xi, Sigma Gamma Tau. Club: USAF Officers. Research into a unified theory of mechanics, dynamics and the calculus of variations, the general energy equation. Demonstrated in 1975, for the first time in the history of applied mathematics, direct analytical solutions (i.e., solutions obtained without the mathematical theory of differential equations) to the time dependent problems of the motion of matter in time and space. A significant application, recently demonstrated in papers by Oz and Adiguzal, results in the elimination of the coupled nonlinear "Riccati" differential equations from the mathematics of control calculations. Home and Office: 4176 Ashmore Rd Columbus OH 43220-4683

BAILEY, CHARLES RICHARD, political consultant; b. Logan, Utah, Nov. 16, 1929; s. Charles Bradshaw and Laura (Merrill) B.; m. Janice Johnson, Jan. 12, 1949; children: Steven, Kenneth, Rodger. Student, Utah State Coll., 1947-50. Salesman Am. Greetings Co., Cleve., 1955-60; wage and salary analyst The Boeing Co., Seattle, 1960-69; dep. chmn. Rep. Nat. Com., Washington, 1969-80, dir. U.S. senate campaigns, 1980-81, dep. chmn., 1981-82; chmn. Bailey Polit. Consultants, Washington and Ogden, Utah, 1982—; mem. Nat. Policy Forum Rep. Nat. Com., Washington, 1994-96; cons. Vietnam Meml. Fund, Washington, 1982; creator coll. degree program Am. Inst. Applied Politics, 1980, Utah State U., lecture series Politics=Power, 1996. Developer Sunset (Utah) city recreation programs, 1954-64; v.p. Jaycees, Sunset, 1955; mem. City Coun. Sunset, 1959, mayor, 1965. Recipient Leadership award Sunset Recreation Programs, 1961. Mem. LDS Ch. Avocation: collecting Santa Clauses. Office: Bailey Consulting 1104 Country Hills Dr Ste 304 Ogden UT 84403-2493

BAILEY, CHARLES WALDO, II, journalist, author; b. Boston, Apr. 28, 1929; s. David Washburn and Catherine Ruth (Smith) B.; m. Ann Card Bushnell, Sept. 9, 1950; children: Victoria Britton, Sarah Tilden. Grad., Phillips Exeter Acad., 1946; AB magna cum laude, Harvard U., 1950. Reporter, Mpls. Tribune, 1950-54; reporter, corr. Washington bur. Mpls. Tribune, Des Moines Register, Look mag., 1954-67; chief Washington bur. Mpls. Tribune, 1968-72, editor, 1972-82; editor Mpls. Star and Tribune, 1982; Washington editor Nat. Pub. Radio, 1984-87; mem. Standing Com. Corr., Washington, 1962-63; pres. White Ho. Corr. Assn., 1969-70. Author: Conflicts of Interest: A Matter of Journalistic Ethics, 1984, The Land Was Ours, 1991; co-author: (with Fletcher Knebel) No High Ground, 1960, Seven Days in May, 1962, Convention, 1964; contbr. to Candidates 1960, 1959, Exeter Remembered, 1965, The President's Trip to China, 1972, The Media and Foreign Policy, 1990. Trustee Carnegie Endowment for Internat. Peace, Henry L. Stimson Ctr. Mem. Overseas Writers, Coun. on Fgn. Rels., Gridiron Club, Cosmos Club. Home: 3001 Albemarle St NW Washington DC 20008-2102

BAILEY, CHARLES WILLIAM, management consultant, researcher; b. Mpls., May 26, 1932; s. Charles Nelson and Ruth Elthleen (Brower) B.; m. Anne G. Stultz (div. 1979); children: Charles R., George L., Dana R., William W., Jonathan D., Margaret R. BBA in Indsl. Rels. and Psychology, U. Minn., 1955. Orgn. analyst Duluth Missabe & Iron Range Railway, 1958-60, supr. orgn. planning, 1960-67; dir. safety Duluth (Minn.) Missabe and Iron Range Ry., 1967-86; pres. Bailey and Assocs., Duluth, 1986—; cons. rail safety com. NRC, Washington, 1979-80; chmn. adv. com. masters program-indsl. safety U. Minn., 1976—. Author: Using Behavioral Techniques to Improve Safety Program Effectiveness, 1989; Inventor system for digital computer rec. of petroglyphs, 1991. Advisor Minn. Safety Coun., Mpls., 1982-86; bd. dirs., treas. Duluth Pub. Schs. Bd. of Edn., 1967-71. With U.S. Army, 1955-58, Korea. Mem. Nat. Safety Coun. (gen. chmn. r.r. sect. 1973-74), Assn. Am. R.R.s Washington (chmn. safety rsch. com. 1976-86), No. Lakes Archaeol. Soc. (sec., treas. 1988-91), Inst. for Study of Am. Cultures (researcher), Epigraphic Soc. (contbr.), Am. Rock Art Rsch. Assn., Kiwanis. Republican. Presbyterian. Office: Bailey and Assocs 530 N 40th Ave E Duluth MN 55804-2158

BAILEY, CHARLES-JAMES NICE, linguistics educator; b. Middlesborough, Ky., May 2, 1926; s. Charles Wise and Mary Elizabeth (Nice) B. AB in Classical Philology with highest honors, Harvard U., 1950, MTh, 1955; DMin, Vanderbilt U., 1963; AM, U. Chgo., 1966, PhD, 1969. Mem. faculty dept. linguistics U. Hawaii, Manoa, 1968-71, Georgetown U., 1971-73; prof. Technische U. Berlin, 1974-91, univ.-prof. emeritus, 1991—; vis. prof. U. Mich., Ann Arbor, 1973, U. Witwatersrand, Johannesburg, 1976, U. Brunei, Darussalam, 1990; Forcheimer prof. U. Jerusalem, 1986; proprietor Orchid Land Publs.; hon. col. Staff Gov. of Ky. Fellow Netherlands Inst. Advanced Study (life), Internat. Soc. Phonetic Scis.; mem. AAAS, Linguistic Soc. Am. (life), European Acad. Scis., Arts and Letters (corr.), N.Y. Acad. Scis., Soc. Linguistica Europaea, Am. Dialect Soc., Internat. Palm Soc.

BAILEY, CLARK TRAMMELL, II, public relations/public affairs professional; b. Chickasha, Okla., Jan. 28, 1961; s. Clark Trammell and Virginia (Anderson) B. BS with honors, Okla. State U., 1983; MBA with high honors, Okla. City U., 1990. Pub. rels. coord. Sta. KOSU-FM, 1981-83; advt. coord. Dallas Downtown News, 1983-84; voter registration coord. Reagan-Bush '84, Austin, Tex., 1984; campaign mgr. Buechner for Congress, St. Louis, 1986; asst. to gov. Office of the Gov., Oklahoma City, 1986-89; dir. pub. affairs Southwestern Bell, Oklahoma City, 1989—. Founding editor newsletter Telecomms.: Advantage Okla., 1993-95. Mem. exec. edn. program Class I Okla. Partnership, 1995; co-chair pub. rels. Oklahoma City Nat. Meml. Found., 1995—; chmn. Excellent Educator Awards Okla. City Pub. Schs. Found., 1996, 97, 98; chmn. Friends of Oklahoma City Pub. Schs., 1998-99, bd. trustees, 1998-99; mem. Class XIII Leadership Oklahoma City, 1994-95; v.p., bd. dirs. Downtown Now, 1995-97; bd. dirs. Okla. Alliance on Aging, 1997—; mem. exec. com. Stage Ctr. Recipient B.L. Semtner Meml. award of excellence United Way Ctrl. Okla., 1991, award of merit Internat. Assn. Bus. Communicators, 1992, 93, 94, Group Gold Vail award for noteworthy pub. svc. SBC Comms., 1995; named 40 Under 40, Metro Jour. Mem. Pub. Rels. Soc. Am. (accredited; bd. dirs. Oklahoma City chpt. 1995, 99, Upper Case award Oklahoma City chpt. 1990, 94, 95, nat. assembly del. 1999), Okla. Acad. for State Goals, Oklahoma City U. Alumni Assn. (bd. dirs. 1995—). Republican. Episcopalian. Avocations: travel, physical fitness, reading, writing, personal finance. Office: Southwestern Bell Telephone 800 N Harvey Ave Rm 378 Oklahoma City OK 73102-2813

BAILEY, DANA KAVANAGH, radiophysicist, botanist; b. Clarendon Hills, Ill., Nov. 22, 1916; s. Dana Clark and Dorothy (Kavanagh) B. B.S. with highest distinction, U. Ariz., 1937; postgrad., Harvard U., 1940; B.A. (Rhodes scholar) Queen's Coll., Oxford U., 1940, M.A., 1943, D.Sc., 1967. Astronomer expdn. to Peru for Hayden Planetarium, N.Y.C., 1937; physicist Antarctic expdn. U.S. Antarctic Service, 1940-41; project engr. Project RAND Douglas Aircraft Co., Santa Monica, Calif., 1946-48; physicist Nat. Bur. Standards, Washington, 1948-55; physicist, cons. Nat. Bur. Standards, Boulder, Colo., 1959-66; radiophysicist, research botanist Space Environment Lab., Environ. Research Labs., Nat. Oceanic and Atmospheric Adminstrn., Boulder, 1966-76; sci. dir. Page Communications Engrs., Inc., Washington, 1955-59; U.S. Exchange rep. Brit. Antarctic Survey, Falkland Islands and Antarctica, 1967-68; research assoc. in physics Rhodes U., Grahamstown, Republic South Africa, 1970-71; assoc. in gymnosperms U. Colo. Mus., 1972—; internat. chmn. study group internat. radio consultative com. Internat. Telecommunication Union, Geneva, 1956-78. Contbr. articles to profl. jours. Served to maj., Signal Corps AUS, 1941-46. Decorated Legion of Merit; recipient Arthur S. Flemming govt. award Washington Jr. C. of C., 1951; Silver medal Dept. Commerce, 1952; Gold medal, 1956. Fellow AAAS, Am. Phys. Soc., Am. Geog. Soc., Royal Astron. Soc., Royal Geog. Soc.; mem. Sci. Research Soc. Am. (pres. Boulder br. 1967-68), Am. Geophys. Union, Am. Astron. Soc., Geog. Soc. Lima (hon.), Phi Beta Kappa, Sigma Xi. Clubs: Cosmos (Washington); Explorers (N.Y.C.). Home: 624 Pearl St Apt 403 Boulder CO 80302-5073 Office: Univ Col Mus Botany Dept Boulder CO 80309

BAILEY, DANIEL ALLEN, lawyer; b. Pitts., Aug. 31, 1953; s. Richard A. and Virginia (Henry) B.; m. Janice Abraham, Oct. 10, 1981; children: Jeffrey, Megan. BBA, Bowling Green State U., 1975; JD, Ohio State U., 1978. Bar: Ohio 1978, U.S. Dist. Ct. (so. dist.) Ohio 1978, U.S. Tax Ct. 1979. Ptnr. Arter & Hadden, Columbus, Ohio, 1978—. Co-author: Handbook for Corporate Directors, 1985, Liability of Corporate Officers and Directors, 6th edit., 1998. Bd. dirs. Columbus Met. Community Action Orgn., 1979-80, Franklin County Head Start, Columbus, 1979-80, Faith Luth. Ch., Whitehall, Ohio, 1985-90, Luth. Social Svcs. Cen. Ohio, 1991—. Mem. ABA, Ohio Bar Assn., Columbus Bar Assn., Phi Kappa Phi, Beta Gamma Sigma, Omicron Delta Kappa. Office: Arter & Hadden 10 W Broad St Ste 2100 Columbus OH 43215-3422

BAILEY, DARLYNE, social worker, educator; b. N.Y.C., July 21, 1952; d. Arthur and Iris B. AB in Pyschology and Secondary Edn., Lafayette Coll., 1974; MSc in Pychiatric Social Work, Columbia U., N.Y.C., 1976; PhD Orgn. Behavior, Case Western Reserve U., 1988. Lic. ind. social worker, Ohio. Coord. specialized treatment Essex County Guidance Ctr., East Orange, N.J., 1976-82; dir. emergency access svcs. Cmty. Mental Health Orgn., Englewood, N.J., 1980-83; field instr. NYU Sch. of Social Work, 1981-82; instr. Case Western Reserve U. Weathered, Cleve., 1986-87; program faculty Case Western Reserve U. Mandel Ctr., Cleve., 1988-94; asst. prof. Case Western Reserve U. Mandel Sch., Cleve., 1988-94; rsch. faculty assoc. prof. Case Western Reserve U. Mandel Sch. Ctr. for Urban Poverty, Cleve., 1991—, dean and assoc. prof., 1994-99, dean, prof., 1999—; cons. to numerous profl. groups; orgnl. devel. specialist Mid-Atlantic Regional Med. Edn. Ctr. VA, Brecksville, Ohio, 1985-88, Shaker Heights (Ohio) Sch. Dist., 1988-90, Cuyahoga Plan, Cleve., 1989-90; trainer 9-to-5 Nat. Assn. Working Women, Cleve., Family Children and Adult Svcs., Columbus, 1988, Exec. Tng. Inst., 1988-90, The Free Med. Clinic of Greater Cleve., Cuyhoga County Dept. Human Svcs., Sr. and Adult Svcs., Luth. Chaplaincy Svc., Cleve., 1993, KPMG Peat Marwick project, Chgo., 1990-91, Ghana Assn. Pvt. Vol. Orgns. in Devel., Accra, 1992-94, Old Stone Ch. Project, Cleve., 1994, Cleve. Rape Crisis Ctr. Project, 1995; chair secretariat Mandel Ctr., 1994—. Contbr. articles to profl. jours., also book reviews and chpts. to books. Mem. exec. com. bd. trustees Heights Youth Ctr., Inc., Cleveland Heights, Ohio, 1983-95; mem. Human Resources Devel. Com., Neighborhood Ctrs. Assn., Cleve., chair mgmt. and governance task force, 1988-90; bd. trustees Neighborhood Ctrs., Cleve., 1991-94, Tiffin U., 1992-95, Fedn. for Cmty. Planning, Cleve., 1995—, Nat. Coun., Cleve., 1995—; mem. book rev. com. NASW Press, Washington, 1992-95; cons. editor Social Work, 1996—; mem. philantropy and volunteerism adv. com. Kellogg Found., Battle Creek, Mich., 1992—, and many others. Named Nat. Fellow W.K. Kellogg Found., Battle Creek, Mich., 1993-94; recipient George Washington Kidd award Lafayette Coll., Easton, Pa., 1994. Fellow Am. Othopsyciatric Assn., Nat. Assn. Social Workers; mem. Nat. Bd. Organizational Behavior Tchg. Soc. (co-chair). Home: 915 Keystone Dr Cleveland Hts OH 44121-2035 Office: Case Western Res U Ctr Urban Poverty and Social Change 10900 Euclid Ave Cleveland OH 44106-7164*

BAILEY, DAVID NELSON, pathologist, educator; b. Anderson, Ind., June 21, 1945; s. Omer Nelson and Louise Genevieve (Hurst) B. BS with high distinction, Ind. U., 1967; MD, Yale U., 1973. Diplomate Nat. Bd. Med. Examiners, Am. Bd. Pathology (Clin. and Chem. Pathology). Clin. fellow dept. lab. medicine Yale U., 1973-75; asst. resident specializing in clin. pathology Yale-New Haven (Conn.) Hosp., 1975-76, chief resident specializing in clin. pathology, 1976-77; asst. prof. pathology U. Calif. San Diego, 1977-81, assoc. prof. pathology, 1981-86, prof. pathology, 1986—, head div. lab. medicine, 1983-89, 94-98; acting chmn., 1986-88; chmn. dept. pathology U. Calif. San Diego, 1988—; dir. toxicology lab. U. Calif. Med. Ctr., San Diego, 1977—, dir. clin. labs., 1982—. Mem. editorial bd. Jour. Analytical Toxicology, 1979—, Clin. Chemistry Jour., 1983-93, Am. Jour. Clin. Pathology, 1991—; contbr. articles to profl. jours. Recipient Gerald T. Evans award Acad. Clin. Lab. Physicians and Scientists, 1993; Merit scholar Ind. U., 1963-65, Arthur R. Metz scholar, 1965-67. Mem. Calif. Assn. Toxicologists (pres. 1981-82), Acad. Clin. Lab. Physicians and Scientists (pres. 1988-89), Am. Assn. Clin. Chemistry, Am. Chem. Soc., Assn. Pathology Chmn. (sec.-treas. 1996—), Phi Lambda Upsilon, Alpha Omega Alpha. Office: U Calif Med Ctr San Diego Dept Pathology 200 W Arbor Dr Dept San Diego CA 92103-1911

BAILEY, DAVID ROY SHACKLETON, classics educator; b. Lancaster, Eng., Dec. 10, 1917; came to U.S., 1968; s. John Henry Shackleton and Rosamund Maud (Giles) B.; m. Kristine Zvirbulis, 1994. B.A., Gonville and Caius Coll., Cambridge, 1939, M.A., 1943, Litt.D., 1958; Litt.D. (hon.), U. Dublin, 1984. Fellow Gonville and Caius Coll., 1944-55, praelector, 1954-55, dep. bursar, 1964, sr. bursar, 1965-68, Univ. lectr. Tibetan, 1948-68; fellow, dir. studies in classics Jesus Coll., Cambridge, 1955-64; vis. lectr. classics Harvard U., 1963, prof. Greek and Latin, 1975-82, Pope prof. Latin lang. and lit., 1982-88, prof. emeritus, 1988—; prof. Latin U. Mich., Ann Arbor, 1968-75, adj. prof., 1989—; vis. Andrew V.V. Raymond prof. classics SUNY, Buffalo, 1973-74; vis. fellow Peterhouse, Cambridge, 1980-81, Inst. For Advanced Study, Princeton U., 1986. Author: The Satapancasatka of Matrceta, 1951, Propertiana, 1956, Cicero's Letters, 10 vols., 1965-81, Cicero, 1971, Profile of Horace, 1982, Anthologia Latina I, 1982, Horatius, 1985, Cicero's Philippines, 1986, An Onomasticon to Cicero's Speeches, 1988, Ciceronis Epistulae, 4 vols., 1987-88, Lucanus, 1988, Quintilianus, Declamationes Minores, 1990, Martialis, 1990, Martial, 3 vols., 1993, Back From Exile, 1994, Homoeoteleuton in Latin dactylic poetry, 1994, Onomasticon to Cicero's Letters, 1995, Onomasticon to Cicero's Treatises, 1996, Selected Classical Papers, 1997, Cicero Letters To Atticus, 4 vols., 1999, others; contbr. articles on Oriental and classical subjects to profl. jours.; editor Harvard Studies in Classical Philology, 1978-84. Recipient Charles J. Goodwin award of merit, 1978; Nat. Endowment for Humanities fellow, 1980-81; Kenyon medal, Brit. Acad., 1985. Fellow Brit. Acad., Am. Acad. Arts and Scis.; mem. Am. Philos. Soc., Soc. for Promotion of Roman Studies (hon.).

BAILEY, DENNIS, state official; b. Livermore Falls, Maine; 1 child, Heather. BJ, U. Maine, 1975. Reporter Lewiston Daily Sun, Biddeford Jour. Tribune, Maine Times, Portland Press Herald/Maine Sunday Telegram; press sec. U.S. Rep. Tom Andrews, Maine, 1990-93; dir. comm. State of Maine Gov. Angus King, 1994—. Contbr. articles to Time, Wall St. Jour., and other newspapers and mags.; singer, guitarist Van Gogh Go's. Office: Office of Gov 1 State House Station Augusta ME 04333-0001

BAILEY, DONNIS AARON DAVID, county official; b. Tacoma, Wash., Mar. 9, 1970; s. Jack Lee and Victoria Renel (Theopolis) B.; m. Charla Marie Salyers, July 18, 1992; 1 stepson, Barry Duane. Cert. Acctg., Clark State C.C., Springfield, Ohio, 1992. Registered svc. worker, Ohio; CPR instr.; notary public; ordained minister Progressive Univerasal Life Ch. Night auditor Imperial House Motel, Springfield, Ohio, 1990; workshop specialist I Clark County Bd. of MR/DD, Springfield, 1990-96, registered svc. worker, 1996—, fiscal clk., 1996—; tax preparer, Springfield, 1992—. Mem. Masons. Roman Catholic. Avocations: woodworking, weight lifting, bowling, fishing, camping.

BAILEY, DONOVAN, Olympic athlete; b. Manchester, Jamaica, Dec. 16, 1967; 1 child, Adrienna. Diploma in bus. adminstrn., Sheridan Coll. Recipient Silver medal in 100 and 200 meters, Pan Am Trials, 1991, in 400 meter relay, Pan Am Games, 1991, in 100 meters, Harry Jerome Classic, 1991, Gold medal in 100 meters, 1996, Bronze medal in 200 meters, Can. Nat. Indoor Championship, 1992, Meeting der Spitzenklasse, Lindau, Germany, 1993, Silver medal in 100 meters, Rendez-Vous MontrCal, 1993, in 200 meters, Can. Nat. Championships, 1993, Bronze medal in 100 meters, 1993, Silver medal in 100 meters, Jeux de la Francophonie, Paris, 1994, Gold medal in 4x100 meter relay, Commonwealth Games, 1994, Silver medal, Comunidad de Madrid, 1995, Lausanne Grand Prix Meeting, 1995, Bronze medal, Gateshead Games, 1995, Gold medal, Mutual Games, 1995, Internat. Quelle Fest in Narnberg, 1995, Ill. State Championships, 1995, in 4x100 meter relay, World Outdoor Championships, Giteborg, Sweden, 1995, Bronze medal in 100 meters, Atlanta Grand Prix, 1996, Gold medal in 100 meters, Brazil Grand Prix, 1996, Can. Olympic Trials, 1996, in 4x100 meter relay, 1996, Olympic Games, Atlanta, 1996; winner World's Fastest Man Race, 1997. Office: c/o Flynn Sports MGmt 625-A Hales Chapel Rd Gray TN 37615*

BAILEY, ELIZABETH ANNE, middle school education educator; b. Stillwater, Okla., Sept. 5, 1950; d. John Henry and Ione Elizabeth (Schroeder) Steichen; children: Brian, Kevin. BA in English, Okla. State U., 1972, MA in English, 1974. Cert. tchr., Okla.; cert. tchr. in early adolescence/English lang. arts. Instr. composition Okla. State U., Stillwater, 1972-74; tchr. jr. and sr. English, Stillwater Pub. Schs., 1974-77; asst. editor Quarter Racing Record, Ft. Worth, 1977-78; mid. sch. tchr. Edmond (Okla.) Pub. Schs., 1978-82; tchr. English, Cimarron Mid. Sch., Edmond, 1982—; mentor tchr. Edmond Pub. Schs., 1994-99; presenter in field; tech./internet trainer Okla. State Dept. Edn., 1996. Contbr. articles to profl. publs. Neighborhood welcomer St. John the Bapt. Cath. Ch., Edmond, 1994-98. Mem. Nat. Coun. Tchrs. English, Okla. Coun. Tchrs. English, Edmond Reading Assn. (sec. 1995-96), Delta Kappa Gamma (scholar 1997-98). Avocations: reading, travel. Office: Cimarron Mid Sch 3701 S Bryant Ave Edmond OK 73013-6300

BAILEY, EXINE MARGARET ANDERSON, soprano, educator; b. Cottonwood, Minn., Jan. 4, 1922; d. Joseph Leonard and Exine Pearl (Robertson) Anderson; m. Arthur Albert Bailey, May 5, 1956. B.S., U. Minn., 1944; M.A., Columbia U., 1945; profl. diploma, 1951. Instr. Columbia U., 1947-51; faculty U. Oreg., Eugene, 1951—, prof. voice, 1966-87, coordinator voice instrn., 1969-87, prof. emeritus, 1987—; faculty dir. Salzburg, Austria, summer 1968, Europe, summer 1976; vis. prof., head vocal instrn. Columbia U., summers 1952, 59; condr. master classes for singers, developer summer program study for h.s. solo singers, U. Oreg. Sch. Music, 1988—, mem. planning com. 1998-99 MTNA Nat. Convention. Profl. singer, N.Y.C.; appearances with NBC, ABC symphonies; solo artist appearing with Portland and Eugene (Oreg.) Symphonies, other groups in Wash., Calif., Mont., Idaho, also in concert; contbr. articles, book revs. to various mags. Del. fine arts program to Ea. Europe, People to People Internat. Mission to Russia for 1990. Recipient Young Artist award N.Y.C. Singing Tchrs., 1945, Music Fedn. Club (N.Y.C.) hon. award, 1951; Kathryn Long scholar Met. Opera, 1945. Mem. Nat. Assn. Tchrs. Singing (lt. gov. 1968-72), Oreg. Music Tchrs. Assn (pres. 1974-76), Music Tchrs. Nat. Assn. (nat. voice chmn. high sch. activities 1970-74, nat. chmn. voice 1973-75, 81-85, NW chmn. collegiate activities and artists competition 1978-80, editorial com. Am. Music Tchr. jour. 1987-89), AAUP, Internat. Platform Assn., Kappa Delta Pi, Sigma Alpha Iota, Pi Kappa Lambda. Home: 17 Westbrook Way Eugene OR 97405-2074 Office: U Oreg Sch Music Eugene OR 97403 *My chief goal in life is to realize my potentials through perfecting my innate talents and capabilities.*

BAILEY, FRANCIS LEE, lawyer; b. Waltham, Mass., June 10, 1933; m. Florence Gott (div. 1961); m. Froma Portney (div. 1972); m. Lynda Hart, Aug. 26, 1972 (div. 1980); m. Patricia Shiers, June 10, 1985. Student, Harvard U., 1950-52, 57; LL.B., Boston U., 1960. Bar: Mass. 1960, U.S. Dist. Ct. Mass., 1961, U.S. Ct. Appeals (1st cir.) 1963, U.S. Tax Ct. 1964, U.S. Ct. Appeals (6th cir.) 1964, U.S. Supreme Ct. 1964, U.S. Ct. Appeals (2d cir.) 1967, U.S. Ct. Appeals (10th cir.) 1968, U.S. Ct. Appeals (3d cir.) 1969, U.S. Ct. Appeals (9th cir.) 1970, U.S. Ct. Appeals (4th and 7th cirs.) 1971, U.S. Dist. Ct. (we. and no. dists.) Tex. 1980, U.S. Ct. Mil. Appeals 1981, U.S. Ct. Appeals (8th and 11th cirs.) 1984, U.S. Ct. Appeals (5th cir.) 1985, Fla. 1989, U.S. Dist. Ct. (ea. dist.) Wis. 1991. Prin. Law Offices of F. Lee Bailey, West Palm Beach, Fla. Author: (with Harvey Aronson) The Defense Never Rests, 1971, Cleared for the Approach, 1977, (with John Greenya) For the Defense, 1976; novel Secrets, 1979; How to Protect Yourself Against Cops In California and Other Strange Places, 1982, To Be a Trial Lawyer, 1983; numerous works in field of criminal law (with Henry Rothblatt). Lt. USMC, 1952-56. Mem. ABA, ATLA. *

BAILEY, FRED COOLIDGE, retired engineering consulting company executive; b. Claremont, N.H., Oct. 5, 1925; s. Howard Perry and Helen Gare (Coolidge) B.; m. Mary Beecroft Cunningham, June 26, 1948; children: Susan Bailey Hunter (dec.), Stephen Coolidge, Elizabeth Bailey George. BS, MIT, 1948, MS, 1949. Registered profl. engr., Mass. Research engr. Caterpillar Tractor Co., Peoria, Ill., 1949-51; asst. tech. dir. com. ship structural design Nat. Acad. Scis., Washington, 1952-55; pres. Teledyne Engring. Services, Waltham, Mass., 1955-86, chmn., 1986-87; group exec. Teledyne Inc., Waltham, Mass., 1983-87, cons., 1987-90, ret., 1990; chmn. exec. com. Lexington Savs. Bank, 1989-94, chmn. bd. dirs., 1994-97; dir. Affiliated Cmty. Bancorp, 1995-98. Chmn. bd. Fire Commrs., Lexington, Mass., 1964-69; mem. Bd. Selectmen, 1969-78p; trustee Cary Meml. Libr., Lexington, 1971-78, pres., 1972-77; trustee Symmes Hosp., Arlington, Mass., 1969—, mem. exec. com., 1977-89, v.p., 1978-80, pres., 1980-81; trustee, chmn., pres. Brookhaven at Lexington, 1994-96; chmn. Choates-Symmes Health Svcs., 1981-83; v.p. Charles River Mus. Industry, 1983-86, trustee, 1984—, pres., 1986-89. With USNR, 1944-46. Fellow Soc. for Exptl. Mechanics (pres. 1968-69, recipient Tatnall award 1974, hon. mem. 1992); mem. Soc. Naval Architects and Marine Engrs. (recipient Linnard prize 1972), ASME, Am. Welding Soc. Home: 48 Coolidge Ave Lexington MA 02420-1838

BAILEY, GEORGE SCREVEN, lawyer; b. Columbia, S.C., Feb. 7, 1951; s. Edward E. and Mary S. (Simpson) B. BA in Econs., Wofford Coll., 1972; JD, U.S.C., 1975; LLM in Taxation, NYU, 1976. Bar: S.C. 1976, U.S. Tax Ct. 1979, U.S. Ct. Appeals (4th cir.) 1982. Cert. tax specialist. Assoc. Johnson, Smith et al, Sparantanburg, S.C., 1976-77, Law Offices R. Young, Columbia, S.C., 1976, O'Connor & Young, Columbia, 1976-79; sec.-treas. O'Connor & Bailey, P.A., Columbia, 1979-84; ptnr. Nelson, Mullins, Riley & Scarborough, L.L.P., Columbia, 1984—; state rep. to spl. liaison tax com. of southeastern region, Atlanta, 1980-83. Mem. Am. Coll. Tax Counsel, S.C. Bar Assn. (chmn. tax sect. 1986-87, sect. estate planning, probate and trust law, chmn. taxation law specialization adv. bd. 1990-91), So. Fed. Tax Inst. (trustee 1994—), Richland County Bar Assn., Forest Lake County Club, Columbia Cotillion Club, Pine Tree Hunt Club, Palmetto Club, Columbia Taxation Study Group. Office: Nelson Mullins Riley & Scarborough LLP 1330 Lady St Columbia SC 29201-3300*

BAILEY, GRACE DANIEL, retired secondary school educator; b. Wilson, N.C., Dec. 7, 1927; d. James Clenon and Ella Mae (West) Daniel; m. Hubert Jesse Bailey, Apr. 27, 1951; 1 child, Vicky Lynette Bailey Freeman. BS in Bus. Edn. and English, East Carolina U., 1950, MAE in Guidance and Counseling, 1966. Tchr. bus. edn., English Apex (N.C.) H.S., 1950-51; tchr. bus. edn. Atlantic Christian Coll., Wilson, N.C., summer 1951; tchr. bus. edn., English Lucama (N.C.) H.S., 1951-53, 1956-75, tchr. bus. edn., counselor, 1975-77, counselor, 1977-78; counselor Hunt H.S., Wilson, 1978-79, counselor, dept. chair, 1979-86, ret., 1986. Sec. adv. com. Cmty. Manpower and Tng., Wilson, 1973-74; organizer Wilson Cmty. Coun., 1973-74; sec. Wilson County Humane Soc., 1978; mem. edn. com. Am. Cancer Soc., Wilson, 1987-88. Recipient award Am. Legion, Wilson, 1986; grantee Wilson County Mental Health Assn., 1964. Mem. AAUW, N.C. Assn. Educators (treas. Wilson County chpt. 1974-75), Wilson County Guidance Pers. Assn. (organizer, 1st pres. 1966-67), Wilson Women's Club (co-chairperson comm. com. 1993-94), Delta Kappa Gamma (v.p. Gamma Mu chpt. 1986-88, pres. 1988-90). Methodist. Avocations: gardening, growing roses, reading. Home: 4904 Pebble Beach Cir Wilson NC 27896-0916

BAILEY, HAROLD RANDOLPH, surgeon; b. Palestine, Tex., Jan. 20, 1943; m. Kelly Curry Bailey. BA in Biology summa cum laude, Rice U., 1964; MD, U. Tex., 1968. Diplomate Am. Bd. Surgery, Am. Bd. Colon and Rectal Surgery. Intern straight surg. Parkland Hosp., Dallas, 1968-69; resident gen. surgery U. Tex. Med. Sch./Hermann Hosp., Houston, 1969-73; fellow colon and rectal surgery Ferguson-Droste-Ferguson Hosp., Grand Rapids, Mich., 1973-74; clin. faculty U. Tex. Med. Sch., Houston, 1974—, dir. residency tng. program colon and rectal surgery, 1984—, clin. prof. surgery, 1986—; clin. asst. prof. surgery Baylor Coll. Medicine, 1980-86, clin. faculty, 1986—; assoc. examiner Am. Bd. Colon and Rectal Surgery, 1985-89, bd. dirs., chmn. exam. com., 1994—, exam. com., 1992—, residency rev. com. colon and rectal surgery 1993—, pres. 1996-97; chief staff Park Plaza Hosp., Houston, 1988-90. Bd. dirs. Am. Cancer Soc., Greater Houston unit, 1989—, v.p., 1991-93, pres., 1993-95; mem. vestry Palmer Meml. Episcopal Ch., Houston, 1979-83, 84-86, chmn. fin. com., 1984-86; mem. fund coun. Rice U., Houston, 1993-94, class fund drive chmn. 1993-95). Recipient George Waldron award Hermann Hosp., 1970, Violet Keller award, 1973; named to Good Housekeeping mag. 400 Best Doctors in U.S., 1991, Good Housekeepingmag. Best Cancer Doctors in U.S., 1993. Fellow ACS (chmn. adv. coun. colon & rectal surgery 1996—), Internat. Soc. Univ. Colon and Rectal Surgeons (program com. 1986), Am. Soc. Colon and Rectal Surgeons (treas., exec. coun. 1993—), Tex. Surg. Soc.; mem. AMA, Tex. Soc. Colon and Rectal Surgeons (pres. 1981, exec. sec. 1982-88), Soc. Am. Gastrointestinal Endoscopic Surgeons, Tex. Med. Assn., Tex. Soc. Gastrointestinal Endoscopy, Harris County Med. Soc., Houston Surg. Soc., Phi Beta Kappa, Alpha Omega Alpha. Office: Colon & Rectal Clinic 6550 Fannin St Ste 2307 Houston TX 77030-2723*

BAILEY, HELEN MCSHANE, historian; b. Gardner, Kans., Oct. 17, 1916; d. Harry Cramer and Maude Ethel (Kramer) McShane; m. James Edwin Bailey, Feb. 23, 1946; children: James Edwin, Barbara Ann Bailey Crawford. B.A., Bethany Nazarene Coll., 1938. Adminstrv. asst. Office Chief of Staff, U.S. Army, Washington, 1941-48; historian U.S. Army ofcl. history of World War II, U.S. Army, Washington, 1948-58; research asst. George C. Marshall Research Found., Washington, 1958-59; historian Orgn. Joint Chiefs of Staff, Dept. Def., Pentagon, Washington, 1968-87; cons., 1987—. Mem. Am. Hist. Assn., Soc. Historians of Am. Fgn. Relations, World War Two Studies Assn., Soc. History in the Fed. Govt. Republican. Lutheran. Home: 9451 Lee Hwy Apt 415 Fairfax VA 22031-1812

BAILEY, HENRY JOHN, III, retired lawyer, educator; b. Pitts., Apr. 4, 1916; s. Henry J. and Lenore Powell Bailey Cahoon; m. Marjorie Jane Ebner, May 30, 1949 (dec. July 1998); children: George W., Christopher G., Barbara W., Timothy P. Student, U.S. Naval Acad., 1934-36; B.A., Pa. State U., 1939; J.D., Yale U., 1947. Bar: N.Y. 1948, Mass. 1963, Oreg. 1974. Ins. investigator Liberty Mut. Ins. Co., N.Y.C., 1941-42; atty. Fed. Res. Bank of N.Y., N.Y.C., 1947-55; asst. v.p. Empire Trust Co., N.Y.C., 1955-56; atty., legal dept. Am. Bankers Assn., N.Y.C., 1956-62; editor Banking Law Jour., Boston, 1962-65; asso. prof. law Willamette U., Salem, Oreg., 1965-69; prof. Willamette U., 1969-81, prof. emeritus, 1981—, adj. prof., 1981-83, scholar in residence, 1987; counsel firm Churchill, Leonard, Brown & Donaldson, Salem, 1981-85; vis. prof. sch. law U. Akron, 1983-84; vis. prof. coll. of law Fla. State U., 1984-85; vis. prof. sch. law Rutgers U., Camden, N.J., 1985-87; cons., lectr. to bar and banking groups; lectr. Banking Sch. of South, Baton Rouge, 1972, 73, 75. Author: Brady on Bank Checks (The Law of Bank Checks), 1960, 3d edit., 1962, 4th edit., 1969, 5th edit., 1979, 6th edit., 1987 and periodic supplements, 7th edit. (with Richard B. Hagedorn), 1992, (with Richard B. Hagedorn) rev. edit. 2 vols., 1997, periodic supplements, Uniform Commercial Code Forms, 1963, (with Clarke and Young) Bank Deposits and Collections, 1972, UCC Deskbook: A Short Course in Commercial Paper, 1973, (with Robert D. Hursh) The American Law of Products Liability, 2d edit., 1984, (with William D. Hawkland) The Sum and Substance of Commercial Paper, 1976, 80, 88, Secured Transactions in a Nutshell, 1976, 2d edit., 1981, 3d edit. (with Richard B. Hagedorn), 1988, Oregon Uniform Commercial Code, 3 vols., 1983, 84, 86, 88, 2d edit. 3 vols., 1990, New 1990 Uniform Commercial Code: Article 3, and 4, periodic supplements; contbr. articles on sales, products liability, comml. paper and secured transactions to legal jours. 1st lt. USAAF, 1942-45; lt. col. Res.; ret. Mem. Am. Bar Assn. (chmn. subcom. on comml. paper 1965-66, 79-81), Am. Law Inst. (mem. editorial bd. The Practical Lawyer 1981-93, emeritus mem. editorial bd. 1993—), Oreg. State Bar, Lambda Chi Alpha. Republican. Roman Catholic. Office: Coll Law Willamette U Salem OR 97301

BAILEY, HERBERT SMITH, JR., retired publisher; b. N.Y.C., July 12, 1921; s. Herbert Smith and Viola (Howe) B.; m. Elizabeth M. Brown, June 26, 1943; children: John R., James C., Robin E., George W. AB, Princeton U., 1942, LLD (hon.), 1986; LHD (hon.), Yale U., 1976. Sci. editor Princeton U. Press, 1946-52, editor, 1952-54, dir., 1954-86; ret., 1986; past bd. dirs. Nat. Enquiry into Scholarly Publ., Franklin Book Programs, Princeton Bank; past mem. adv. com. on tech. publs. AEC; bd. govs. Wesleyan U. Press; past mem. bd. visitors Duke U. Press; past chmn. sci. info. coun. NSF; vis. fellow Nat. Humanities Ctr., 1984; R.R. Bowker lectr., 1977; mem. publs. com. Am. Scientist. Author: The Art and Science to Book Publishing, 1970; contbr. articles to profl. jours. Past mem. Princeton Regional Bd. Edn.; past mem. and chmn. long range planning Princetown Twp. Bd. of Edn.; past commr. Comm. on Preservation and Access; bd. dirs. Triangle Opera. Lt. USNR, 1942-45. Mem. Am. Book Pubs. Coun. (past bd. dirs.), Assn. Am. Pubs. (past bd. dirs., Curtis Benajmin award for creative pub. 1987), Assn. Am. Univ. Presses (past bd. dirs. and pres.), Am.

Philos. Soc. (mem. publs. and program coms.), Sigma Xi. Home: 248 Fearrington Post Pittsboro NC 27312-5501

BAILEY, HUGH COLEMAN, university president; b. Berry, Ala., July 2, 1929; s. Coleman Costello and Susie (Jenkins) B.; m. Ahleida Joan Seever, Nov. 17, 1962; children: Debra Jane, Laura Joan. A.B. with honors, Samford U., 1950; M.A., U. Ala., 1951, Ph.D., 1954. Instr. history and polit. sci. Samford U., 1953-54, asst. prof., 1954-56, assoc. prof., 1956-59, prof., 1959-75, chmn. dept., head div. social scis., 1967-70; dean Howard Coll. Arts and Scis., 1970-75; v.p. for acad. affairs Francis Marion U., Florence, S.C., 1975-78; pres. Valdosta (Ga.) State Univ., 1978—; Mem. commn. colls. So. Assn. Colls. and Schs., 1974-75; v.p. Ala. Acad. Sci., 1968-69; pres. Ala. Writers Conclave, 1971-73. Author: John Williams Walker, 1964, Hinton Rowan Helper: Abolitionist-Racist, 1965, Edgar Gardner Murphy: Gentle Progressive, 1968, Liberalism in the New South, Southern Social Reformers and the Progressive Movement, 1969, America: The Framing of a Nation, 2 vols, 1975; Editorial bd.: Social Sci. Vice pres. Homewood City Bd. Edn., 1972-75; bd. dirs. Valdesta chpt. ARC, Salvation Army. Guggenheim fellow, 1963-64; Am. Council Learned Socs. fellow, 1965-66; recipient award merit Am. Assn. State and Local History, 1967. Fellow Royal Soc. Arts; mem. South Ga. C. of C. (bd. dirs.), Pi Gamma Mu (trustee, nat. trustee-at-large 1969-71, nat. 1st v.p. 1978-84, pres. 1984-90), Kiwanis. Episcopalian. Home: 222 Georgia Ave Valdosta GA 31602-3843 Office: Valdosta State Univ 1500 N Patterson St Valdosta GA 31602-3847

BAILEY, JAMES (JIM BAILEY), lawyer, professional football team executive; b. Wilmington, Oreg., Aug. 21, 1946; m. Ann Bailey; children: Sarah, Jenny. Grad., Fla. State U.; J.D., U. Mich. Assoc. Guren, Merritt, Sogg & Cohen, Cleve., 1971-76, ptnr., 1976; v.p., gen. counsel Cleve. Browns, NFL, 1978-84; exec. v.p. legal and adminstrn. Balt. Ravens, NFL, 1984—. Office: Baltimore Ravens 200 Saint Paul Pl Ste 2400 Baltimore MD 21202-2003*

BAILEY, JAMES ANDREW, middle school educator; b. Jackson, Tenn., Mar. 15, 1957; s. John Truman and Hazel (Cox) B.; m. Lisa McDaniel, June 13, 1992; 1 child, Abby E. AS, Jackson (Tenn.) State C.C., 1977; BS, Memphis State U., 1980; MA, Bethel Coll., 1989. Cert. tech. edn. instr., Tenn. Indsl. arts instr. Kirby High Sch., Memphis, 1980-83; tech. edn. instr. Parkway Mid. Sch., Jackson, 1983—; writing team mem. State Tenn. Tech. Edn. Curriculum Project, 1984-90; tech. edn. participant People to People/Citizen Amb. Program, People's Republic China, summer 1991. Co-author: Instructor's Guide to Metric 500, 1980; contbg. author: Production Technology, 1991. Chmn. Madison-Chester Assn. Bapt. Singles Coun., Jackson, 1990-91; mem. West Jackson (Tenn.) Bapt. Ch., dir., tchr. singles Sunday sch. Named Outstanding Young Man of Am., 1985, Indsl. Arts Advisor of Yr., Tenn. Indsl. Arts Students Assn., 1987, 2000 Notable Am. Men, 1994. Mem. NEA, Tenn. Edn. Assn. (Disting. Classroom Tchr. 1997), Am. Vocat. Assn., Jackson-Madison County Edn. Assn. (pres. 1998—, exec. bd. 1995-97, chmn. instruction and profl. devel. com. 1995-97, mem. legis. com. 1995-98), Tenn. Vocat. Assn. (Tech. Tchr. of Yr. 1989), Internat. Tech. Edn. Assn. (area rep. 1991-92), Tenn. Tech. Edn. Assn., West Tenn. Tech. Edn. Assn. (bd. mem. 1990-92). Avocations: tennis, spelunking, hunting, fishing. Home: 20 London Park Pl Jackson TN 38305-3547 Office: Parkway Middle Sch 1341 N Parkway Jackson TN 38305-4699

BAILEY, JAMES EDWIN, chemical engineer; b. Great Falls, Mont., Feb. 28, 1944. BA, Rice U., 1966, PhD, 1969; PhD (hon.), U. Brussels, 1988. Engr. Shell Devel. Co., Calif., 1969-71; from asst. prof. to prof. U. Houston, 1971-80, assoc. dean, 1976-78; prof. chem. engring. Calif. Inst. Tech., Pasadena, Calif., 1980-92; Chevron prof. Calif. Inst. Tech., Pasadena, 1989-92; chem. engr. Inst. Biotechnology, Zurich, Switzerland, 1992—; disting. biotechnology lectr. U. Fla., 1988; disting. vis. lectr. U. Alta., Can., 1988. Recipient Amgen Biochem. Engring. award, 1993. Fellow AAAS; mem. NAE, AIChE (Allan T. Colburn award, 1979, Profl. Progress award 1987, Food, Pharm. and Bioengring. divsn. award 1991), Am. Chem. Soc. (Marvin J. Johnson award 1990) Sigma Xi. Office: Inst Biotechnology, ETH HPT, CH-8093 Zurich Switzerland

BAILEY, JANET DEE, publishing company executive; b. Newark, Aug. 23, 1946; d. Richard and Mary Louise (Dee) Shapiro; m. John Frederick Bailey, May 9, 1971; children: Jason David, Juliana Dee. BA, U. Del., 1968; MBA, Pace U., 1981. Prodn. editor Prentice-Hall, Inc., Englewood Cliffs, N.J., 1968-70; dir. publs. Spl. Libraries Assn., N.Y.C., 1970-76; dir. mktg. services Knowledge Industry Publs., White Plains, N.Y., 1978-81, v.p., 1984-85; dir. inventory and contracts Macmillan Book Clubs, N.Y.C., 1981-84; group pub. Elsevier Sci. Pub. Co., N.Y.C., 1985-95, v.p. global mktg., 1996-99; exec. pub. John Wiley & Sons, 1999—. Mem. Assn. Am. Publishers (chmn. jours. com., PSP exec. coun.), Soc. for Scholarly Publishing. Office: Elsevier Sci Pub Co 655 Avenue Of The Americas New York NY 10010-5107

BAILEY, JOHN, cinematographer; b. Mo., Aug. 10, 1942; m. Carol Littleton, Mar. 11, 1972. Student, U. Santa Clara, Loyola U., U. So. Calif., U. Vienna. Lectr. Am. Film Inst., 1982, 84, 94. Cinematographer: (feature films) Premonition, 1972, End of August, 1974, Legacy, 1976, The Mafu Cage, 1978, Boulevard Nights, 1979, American Gigolo, 1980, Ordinary People, 1980, Honky Tonk Freeway, 1981, Continental Divide, 1981, Cat People, 1982, That Championship Season, 1982, Without a Trace, 1983, The Big Chill, 1983, Racing with the Moon, 1984, The Pope of Greenwich Village, 1984, Mishima: A Life in Four Chapters, 1985 (Cannes Film Festival award for Artistic Achievement 1985), Silverado, 1985, Crossroads, 1986, Brighton Beach Memoirs, 1986, Light of Day, 1987, Swimming to Cambodia, 1987, Tough Guys Don't Dance, 1987, The Accidental Tourist, 1988, My Blue Heaven, 1989, A Brief History of Time, 1990, (TV movies) Battered, 1978, City in Fear, 1980; photographer, dir.: The Search for Signs of Intelligent Life in the Universe, 1990 (Cable Ace nomination); dir. China Moon, 1991, Mariette In Ecstasy, 1995; photographer: Groundhog Day, 1992, In the Line of Fire, 1993, Nobody's Fool, 1994, Passion, 1995, Extreme Measures, 1996, As Good as it Gets, 1997, Always Outnumbered, 1998. Mem. Am. Soc. Cinematographers (sec.), Acad. Motion Picture Arts and Scis. (bd. govs.). Office: United Talent Agy 9560 Wilshire Blvd Fl 5 Beverly Hills CA 90212-2400 also: Am Soc Cinematographers 1782 N Orange Dr Los Angeles CA 90028-4307*

BAILEY, JOHN MARTIN, retired transportation planner, educator; b. Lakewood, Ohio, Feb. 23, 1928; s. Frank Moherman and Elma (Keener) B.; m. Dorothy Jane Stubbs, Apr. 9, 1960; children: Leslie Jane, Brian John. B.A., Hiram Coll., 1949; M.S., MIT, 1951; Ph.D., U. Va., 1959, postgrad., 1977-78. Aero. research scientist NASA, Cleve., 1951-55; mem. faculty dept. physics Beloit (Wis.) Coll., 1959-76; transp. planner Balt. Regional Coun. Govs., 1976-89, Md.-Nat. Capital Pk. and Planning Commn., 1989-95; ret., 1995; sabbatical research Cambridge U., 1965-66; dir. Overseas Seminar in Quantum Physics, Copenhagen, Denmark, 1970. Author: Liberal Arts Physics, 1974. Mem. Am. Planning Assn., Transp. Research Bd. Presbyterian. Home: 9502 Good Lion Rd Columbia MD 21045-3948

BAILEY, JOHN TURNER, public relations executive; b. Cleve., Dec. 2, 1926; s. Theodore Litchfield and Helen (Moyle) B.; m. Katherine Gerwig, June 21, 1952; children: Theodore Gerwig, Mary Katherine. AB, Harvard U., 1950; student, Columbia Grad. Sch., 1950-51. Circulation mgr. internat. edits. N.Y. Times, N.Y.C., 1952-58; mgr. profl. relations Lederle Labs., Am. Cyanamid Co., Pearl River, N.Y., 1958-61; partner firm Edward Howard & Co., Cleve., 1961-67; exec. v.p. Edward Howard & Co., 1967-72, pres., 1972-77, chmn. bd., 1977-86, dir., 1967-98; urban scholar Cleve. State U., 1988. With USCG, 1944-46. Clubs: Rowfant, Hatvard (Cleve.); Chautauqua (N.Y.) Yacht (commodore 1970-71). Home: 1433 Sanderling Cir Sanibel FL 33957-3640 also: 29 N Lake Dr Chautauqua NY 14722

BAILEY, JONATHAN E., photographer; b. Rutland, Vt., Dec. 19, 1954; s. Arthur Edward and Mary Ellen (Howell) B. BS, U. Vt., 1976. guest curator Maine Art Commn., Augusta. One-man shows include Musee Francaise de la Photographie, Bievres, France, 1998, Mus. of Art, U. Maine, Orono, 1998, Farnsworth Mus., Rockland, Maine, 1998; groups shows include Farnsworth Mus., Rockland, Maine, 1997, Old Dominion U., Norfolk Va., 1997, Unity Coll. Art Gallery, Maine, 1996, AfterImage Gallery, Dallas, 1996, Southeast Mus. Photography, Daytona Beach, Fla., 1996, The Creative Photograhic Art Ctr. of Maine, Lewiston, 1996, Main Coast Artists Gallery, Rockport, 1995, others; work collected in The Bibliotheque Nat., Paris, Ctr. for Creative Photography, Tucson, Ariz., Southeast Mus. of Photography, Daytona Beach, Fla., Robert Hull Fleming Mus., U. Vt., Burlington, Colección Imagen Alterna Merida, Yucatan, Mexico, Brindl Fine Arts, Thomaston, Maine, Regency Hotel, Portland, Maine; handmade books include: Alchemy, 1993, Prickles and Goo, 1992, Deer Camp, 1979, The Bar Book, 1979; contbr. photographs, art to various projects and publs. Recipient artist fellowship Vt. Coun. on Arts, Montpellier, 1982. Avocation: wine making. Home and Office: HC 61 Box 346 Saint George ME 04857-9704

BAILEY, JOY HAFNER, counselor, educator; b. Weehawkin, N.J., Aug. 15, 1928; d. Elmar William and Fern (Williams) Hafner; children: Kerry, Jan, Leslie, Liza, Annie Laurie, Kristin. BA, Austin Coll., 1974; MS, Tex. A&M U., 1975, EdD, 1977. Lic. marriage and family therapist, profl. counselor; nat. cert. counselor. Counselor, instr. Tex. A&M U., Commerce, 1976-80; dir. student support svcs. acad. and counseling program Ga. State U., Atlanta, 1980—, asst. prof. counseling and psychol. svcs., 1988—; pvt. practice marriage and family therapy. Mem. APA, ACA, Am. Assn. Marriage and Family Therapists (approved supr.), Ga. Assn. Marriage and Family Therapists, Atlanta Mallet Club (v.p. 1989-92, pres. 1999-00), Psi Chi. Office: Ga State U 152 Sparks Atlanta GA 30303-2948

BAILEY, JUDITH IRENE, university official, consultant; b. Winston-Salem, N.C., Aug. 24, 1946; d. William Edward, Jr. and Julia (Hedrick) Hege; m. Brendon Stinson Bailey, Jr., June 8, 1968. BA, Coker Coll., 1968; MEd, Va. Tech., 1973, EdD, 1976; Ednl. Mgmt. Program, Harvard U., 1994; Leadership Maine Course, 1994-95. Tchr. Chariho Regional high sch., Wood River Junction, R.I., 1969-70, Prince William County Pub. Schs., Woodbridge, Va., 1968-72; asst. prin. Osbourn high sch., Manassas, Va., 1973; secondary sch. coord. Stafford (Va.) County Schs., 1973-74; middle sch. coord. Stafford County Schs., 1975-76; human rels. coord. Coop. Extension Svc. U. Md., College Park, 1976-79; dep. dir. Coop. Extension Svc. U. D.C., Washington, 1980-88; asst. v.p., dir. Coop. Extension U. Maine, Orono, 1988-92, interim v.p. for rsch. and pub. svc., 1992-93, v.p. rsch. and pub. svc., 1993-95; v.p. acad. affairs, provost U. Maine, Orono, MI, 1995-97; pres. No. Mich. U., Marquette, 1997—; adj. prof. George Mason U., Fairfax, Va., 1978; Grad. Student advisor, U. Md., 1979-80; speaker in field; cons. in field. Co-author: Contingency Planning for a Unitary School System; contbr. to profl. jours. Bd. dirs. Maine Toxicology Inst., 1992-95, Bangor (Maine) Symphony Orch., 1991-97, Pine Tree State 4-H Found., 1988-97; bd. trustees Marquette (Mich.) Gen. Hosp., 1998—. Recipient Disting. Alumni Achievement award Coker Coll., 1998; Susan Coker Watson fellow, 1967. Mem. AAUW, Rotary Internat. (Marquette chpt. 1997—), Lake Superior Cmty. Partnership (co-chair 1997—), Phi Delta Kappa, Phi Kappa Phi, Epsilon Sigma Phi (sec. Mu. chpt. 1987, v.p. Mu chpt. 1988, State Disting. Svc. award). Republican. Avocations: gourmet cooking, antique jewelry, hiking. Home: 1440 Center St Marquette MI 49855-1625 Office: Northern Mich U Office of the President 1401 Presque Isle Ave Marquette MI 49855-5305

BAILEY, JULIA NANCY, geneticist; b. Van Nuys, Calif., Aug. 13, 1965; d. David Bertram and Elizabeth Mary (Kiss) B. BSc with honors, Concordia U., Montreal, Que., 1988; PhD, Yale U., 1996. Rsch. asst. Yale U., New Haven, 1989-96; rsch. assoc. U. Miami, Fla., 1990-94; postdoctoral fellow UCLA, 1996—. Contbr. articles to profl. jours. Yale U. fellow, 1989-96, NIMH fellow, 1996, CAN fellow 1998. Mem. Am. Soc. Human Genetics, Internat. Soc. Genetic Epidemiology, Soc. for Creative Anacronism. Office: UCLA 760 Westwood Plz # 47421 Los Angeles CA 90095-8353

BAILEY, K. RONALD, lawyer; b. Sandusky, Ohio, July 30, 1947; s. Kenneth White and Virginia McClung (Sheddan) B.; m. Sara Ann Geary Bressler, Mar. 14, 1969 (div. June 1973); 1 child, Matthew Scott; m. Lynn Darlene Kammer, Aug. 31, 1973; children: Thomas Keith, Kenneth Richard. B in Liberal Studies summa cum laude, Bowling Green State U., 1979; JD, Cleveland-Marshall Law Sch., 1982; grad., Gerry Spence's Trial Lawyers Coll., 1994. Bar: Ohio 1983, U.S. Dist. Ct. (no. dist.) Ohio 1983, U.S. Ct. Appeals (6th cir.) 1985, U.S. Supreme Ct. 1992. Tool, diemaker Gen. Motors, Sandusky, 1968-84; sole practice Huron, Ohio, 1983-87; sr. trial atty. K. Ronald Bailey & Assocs. Co., Legal Profl. Assn., Sandusky, 1987—; chmn. Charter Rev. Com. of Huron, 1984. Mem. ATLA, Nat. Assn. Criminal Def. Lawyers, Ohio Bar Assn. (coun. dels. 1998—), Erie County Bar Assn., Ohio Assn. Criminal Def. Lawyers (bd. dirs. 1988—, v.p. publs. 1991-93, 97-98, treas. 1994, pres. 1995-96, chmn. capital litigation 1997—, Pres.'s award 1989-95, 97-98, v.p. CLE 1997-98). Democrat. Pentecostal. Avocations: reading, photography, painting, swimming, drag racing. Home: 513 Williams St Huron OH 44839-2535 Office: 220 W Market St Sandusky OH 44870-2515

BAILEY, KATHERINE CHRISTINE, artist, writer; b. Glendale, Calif., Dec. 1, 1952; d. Carl Leonard and Anna Alice (Dzamka) Abrahamson; m. David Francis Bailey, Sept. 27, 1975. BA, Calif. State U., L.A., 1974, MA, 1975; PhD, U. N.Mex., 1982. Exhbns. include Miniature Painters Sculptors & Gravers Soc., Washington, Oil Pastel Assn., N.Y.C., Mont. Miniature Art Soc. Internat., many others; author: (novel) Brush With Death; also numerous short stories; participant in Cyberspace Exhbn. on internet. Recipient hon. mention in mixed media category Nat. Western Small Painting Show, Bosque Art Gallery, N.Mex., 1985, 2d pl. award in pastels, 1986, Cert. of Merit award 4th Ann. Holiday Exhbn. of Oil Pastel Assn., 1994; tuition fellow U. N.Mex., 1977; Alpha Gamma Sigma scholar, 1972. Mem. Oil Pastel Assn., Nat. Mus. Women in Arts, Mont. Miniature Art Soc., Laramie Art Guild, N.W. Pastel Soc., Phi Kappa Phi, Alpha Gamma Sigma. Avocations: playing piano, photography, hiking. Home and Studio: PO Box 301 Daggett CA 92327-0301

BAILEY, KEITH E., petroleum pipeline company executive; b. 1942; married. B.S., Mo. Sch. Mines, 1964. With Continental Pipe Line, 1964-66; with Yellowstone Pipeline, 1966, Continental Pipeline, 1966-73, William Pipe Line Co. Inc., Tulsa, 1973-83; past pres. William Pipe Line Co. Inc.; pres., chief oper. officer N.W. Central Pipeline Corp., Tulsa; past exec. v.p. fin. and adminstrn. The Williams Cos., Tulsa, pres., 1992; now chmn., pres., CEO, dir. The Williams Cos., Inc., Tulsa. Office: Williams Cos Inc 1 Williams Ctr Tulsa OK 74172-0150*

BAILEY, KENNETH KYLE, history educator; b. nr. Coldwater, Miss., Dec. 3, 1923; s. John Parham and Ruby Ross (Allen) B.; m. Mary Lou Crain, Aug. 5, 1961. Student, Northwest Miss. Jr. Coll., 1941-42, 45-46; B.A., Vanderbilt U., 1947, M.A., 1948, Ph.D., 1953. Instr. social sci. Cumberland (Ky.) Coll., 1949-50; instr. social sci. N.M. Mil. Inst., 1952-53, asst. prof., 1953-55; instr. history Ind. U., 1955-56, Tex. Western Coll., 1956-57; asst. prof. North Tex. State Coll., 1957-58, La. State U., 1958-60; assoc. prof. history U. Tex., El Paso, 1960-63, prof., 1963-91, prof. emeritus, 1991—; chmn. dept. U. Tex. at El Paso, 1968-71, 74. Author: Southern White Protestantism in the Twentieth Century, 2d edit, 1968; bd. editors: Jour. So. History, 1975-79. Mem. City of El Paso Historic Landmark Commn., 1983-90, chmn., 1986-90; pres. El Paso Landmarks, Inc., 1992-96. With AUS, 1942-45. Social Sci. Research Council grantee, 1955; Guggenheim Meml. fellow, 1966-67. Mem. Am., So. hist. assns., Orgn. Am. Historians (mem. Pelzer meml. award com. 1965-69). Presbyterian. Home: 3033 Federal Ave El Paso TX 79930-4307

BAILEY, LINDA A., educator; b. Jan. 26, 1953. BS, Cheyney U., 1975, MEd, 1999. Special needs tchr., 1979-85, tchr., 1985-94, tchr., mentor, 1994—. Home: 102 Lucas Ln Voorhees NJ 08103

BAILEY, MARIANNE THERESE, social service administrator; b. Evanston, Ill., Dec. 26, 1949; d. Eugene Thomas and Marguerite O'Brien B. Student, Sorbonne, Paris, 1970, San Francisco Coll. Women, 1967-69; BA, Barat Coll. of Sacred Heart, 1971; cert., U. Paris, Sorbonne, 1972; ancien élève, Ecole du Louvre, Paris, 1973-74. Cert. cmty. transp. mgr. Tchr. 2d and 3d grade Marymount Internat. Sch., Neuilly, France, 1971-72; dir. Ctr. Audio Visuel des Langues, Enghien, France, 1973-76; pre-sch. dir. P.L. Child Care Ctrs., Glenview, Ill., 1976-81; with dept. def. civilian Child Support Svcs., Ft. Sheridan, Ill., 1981-82; dir. tng. and spl. events N.W. Mcpl. Conf., Mt. Prospect, Ill., 1982-84; exec. dir. PRC Paratransit Svcs., Park Ridge, Ill., 1984—; mem. Nat. Transp. Cert. Coun., 1996—. V.p. N.W. Suburban chpt. Citizens with Disabilities; lobbyist disabled and sr. citizens State of Ill.; bd. dirs. 10th Congl. Dist. Women's Rep. Club, sec. 1997-98; treas., exec. bd. Wheeling Twp. Rep. Org., 1988—; del. Rep. State Conv., Ill., 1994, 96, 98; pres. N.W. Suburban Coun. for Cmty. Svcs., 1989-91; v.p. Twp. Ofcls. Ill. Disabled Advocacy, 1985-90, pres., 1990—; active Chgo. Area Transp. Study, 1984—, Gov.'s Task Force on Aging and Disability, 1987-97, PACE-ADA Adv. Com., 1990—, Sage Sr. Advocacy Group, 1990—; mem. Twp. Ofcls. of Cook County, N.W. Suburban Regional Transp. Consortium, 1992—, Project Action Ill. steering com., 1995—; treas. Friends of Wheeling Twp., 1997—; mem. access com. Ill. Capital Devel. Bd. Mem. AAUW, ALTRUSA, Am. Pub. Transit Assn., Am. Pub. Works Assn., Cmty. Transp. Assn. Am. (state del. 1992—), Ill. Paratransit Assn. (bd. dirs., sec. 1987-91), Ill. Assn. for Cmty. Transp. (bd. dirs.), Ill. Alliance Info. and Referral, Cmty. Transp. Assn. Am. (state del. 1992—), Lions Club (v.p. 1990-92, pres. 1992-93, Lion of the Yr. 1991-92, mem. bd. dirs. 1988-94, dist. diabetes awareness chmn. 1991-93), Pi Delta Phi. Roman Catholic. Office: PRC Paratransit Svcs 1700 Ballard Rd Park Ridge IL 60068-1006

BAILEY, NANCY JOYCE, educator; b. Detroit, May 9, 1942; d. Thomas Hill and Margaret (McGrath) Rainey; m. Carl John Bailey, June 12, 1963; 1 child, John. BA, Vanderbilt U., 1960; internat. exchange student, Stuttgart, Germany, 1960; postgrad., U. Mex., 1957, U. Santa Clara, 1975, George Washington U., 1979-80. Cert. early childhood edn. tchr., early childhood specialist. Hostess Brentwood (Tenn.) Country Club, 1960; adminstrv. aide U.S. Senate, Washington, 1966; sec. U.S. Ho. of Reps., Washington, 1971-74; tchr. D.C. Pub. Schs., 1961—; bd. dirs Cabvin Internat. Corp., 1985—; rep. Washington Tchrs. union, 1982-94; founder David Lipscomb U., Nashville, 1988; participant Internat. Tchr. Exch. Program, Korea, 1994; mem. Ednl. Delegation to China, 1996; mem. postgrad. program NIH, Bethesda, Md., 1996. Keyperson United Way Campaign, Washington, 1974-93; docent The White House, Exec. Office of the Pres., Washington, 1987—; vol. First Lady's Corr., The White House, Washington, 1990—, Social Sec.'s Office, East Wing, 1993, 98—, Office of First Lady, 1993; coord. Presdl. Youth Vol. Day, 1993; mem. Nat. Trust for Historic Preservation, 1990—, Friendship Force of Nat. Capital Area, 1993—, People to People Internat. of Nat. Capital Area, 1993—; mem. adv. bd. New Visions for Child Care, Inc., 1993; chair Local Schs. Restructuring Team, 1992-93; participant Internat. Tchr. Exch. Program, Korea, 1994; mem. exec. com. YWCA Internat. Fair, Washington, 1994; del. Internat. Women's Friendship Conf. World Peace, Washington, 1995; mem. World Affairs Coun., Washington, 1995—; mem. Internat. Policy Inst., Washington, 1997—, v.p. edn., 1998—; mem. ARK Found. Mission to Africa, RUVU Project, Tanzania, 1997; supr. mcpl. elections Orgn. for Security and Coop. in Europe Mission in Bosnia/Herzegovina, 1997, supr. presdl. elections out of country voters, Croatia, 1998. Recipient Internat. Cooperation award Am. Fgn. Study Program, Am. Study Program, 1984-86, Am. Student Ednl. Travel. Mem. Delta Group (mem. coun. 1989-92), Am. Fedn. Tchrs., Internat. Reading Assn., World Affairs Coun., Delta Kappa Gamma. Avocations: antiques, numismatics, flying, boating. Home: 10729 Deborah Dr Potomac MD 20854-2714 Office: La Salle Sch Riggs Rd and Madison St NE Washington DC 20011

BAILEY, PHILIP SIGMON, JR., university official, chemistry educator; b. Charlottesville, Va., Mar. 17, 1943; s. Philip Sigmon Bailey and Marie Jeanette (Schultz) Hatch; m. Christina Anne Wahl; children: Karl, Jennifer, Kristen, Michael. Student, Am. U., Cairo, 1961; BS in Chemistry, U. Tex., 1964; PhD, Purdue U., 1969. Asst. prof. chemistry Calif. Poly. State U., San Luis Obispo, 1969-73, prof., assoc. dean, 1973-83, prof. chemistry, dean Coll. Sci. and Math., 1983-89, v.p. acad. affairs, sr. v.p., 1989-90, dean, 1990—. Author: (lab texts) Experimental Chemistry for Contemporary Times, 1975, Organic Chemistry, 1978, (textbook) Organic Chemistry, 1978, 5th edit., 1995. Mem. Am. Chem. Soc., Alpha Chi Sigma. Home: 1628 Royal Way San Luis Obispo CA 93405-6334 Office: Calif Poly State U Coll Sci And Math San Luis Obispo CA 93407

BAILEY, REBECCA L., writer; b. Dayton, Ohio, Dec. 16, 1958; d. Randolph and Marjorie Rose Bailey. BS, Morehead State U., 1982, MA, 1986. Mapping technician Ky. Revenue Cabinet, Frankfort, 1983-85; instr. English Morehead (Ky.) State U., 1987-94, publ. asst., 1995-96, publs. editor, 1996-98. Author: Reign of the Girl-King, 1998, A Wild Kentucky Garden, 1998; co-author: Three Women Alone in the Woods, 1992; contbg. author, editor: The Kinks: Reflections on Thirty Years of Music, 1994. Bd. dirs. Ky. Writers Coalition, Louisville, 1998—. Recipient Al Smith Profl. Devel. award in Poetry, Ky. Arts Coun., 1995. Mem. Wolfe County Arts Assn., Phoenix Writers, Poets & Writers, Ky. State Poetry Soc. Home: 2465 Rock Fork Rd Morehead KY 40351-8134

BAILEY, REEVE MACLAREN, museum curator; b. Fairmont, W.Va., May 2, 1911; s. Joseph Randall and Elizabeth Weston (Maclaren) B.; m. Marian Alvinette Kregel, Aug. 13, 1939; children—Douglas M., David R., Thomas G., Susan Helen. Student, Toledo U., 1929-30; A.B., U. Mich., 1933, Ph.D., 1938. Instr. zoology Iowa State Coll. (now univ.), 1938-42, asst. prof., 1942-44; asst. prof. zoology U. Mich., 1944-50, asso. prof., 1950-59, prof., 1959-81, prof. emeritus, 1981—; assoc. curator Mus. Zoology, 1944-48, curator, 1948—; rsch. assoc. Am. Mus. Nat. History, 1964—. Contbr. over 150 articles, bulls., revs. to profl. jours. on ichthyology and herpetology. Fellow Iowa Acad. Sci.; mem. Am. Soc. Ichthyologists and Herpetologists (editl. bd., v.p. 1954, pres. 1959, Robert H. Gibbs Jr. Meml. award 1995), Am. Fisheries Soc. (pres. 1974, hon. mem. 1979—, recipient Award of Excellence 1980, Meritorious Svc. award 1989, Justin W. Leonard award of excellence Mich. chpt. 1985), Am. Inst. Fisheries Rsch. Biologists (Outstanding Achievement award 1996), AAAS (coun. 1968-72), Ecol. Soc. Am., Soc. Study Evolution, Soc. Systematic Biologists, Soc. Limnology and Oceanography, Mich. Acad. Sci., Arts and Letters. Ichthyol. expdns. in U.S., Bermuda, Bolivia, Guatemala, Paraguay, Zambia. Home: 2730 Whitmore Lake Rd Ann Arbor MI 48105-9226 Office: Univ Mich Museum Zoology Ann Arbor MI 48109

BAILEY, REGENIA DEE, non-profit executive; b. Knoxville, Iowa, Dec. 24, 1959; d. Marvin Lee and Lorraine Janice (Clark) B.; m. Jay Robert Berry Jr., Nov. 25, 1989. MusB, U. Iowa, 1982, MusM, 1988, MBA, 1995. Grades K-12 vocal/gen. music tchr. Remsen (Iowa) Union Schs., 1982-83, NESCO Schs., Zearing, Iowa, 1984-87, Regina Schs., Iowa City, 1988-89; capital campaign dir. Domestic Violence Intervention Program, Iowa City, 1996-97; exec. dir. Iowa Women's Found., Iowa City, 1997—; bd. dirs., v.p. Emma Goldman Clinic for Women, Iowa City, 1995-98. Mem. Nat. Soc. for Fundraising Execs., Iowa City C. of C. (participant leadership program 1996-97). Office: Iowa Womens Found 220 Lafayette St Iowa City IA 52240-1746

BAILEY, RICHARD BRIGGS, investment company executive; b. Weston, Mass., Sept. 14, 1926; s. George William and Alice Gertrude (Cooper) B.; m. Rebecca C. Bradford, June 20, 1950 (div. Dec. 1974); children: Ann, Elizabeth, Richard, Rebecca; m. Anne D. Prescott, Dec. 14, 1974 (div. 1980); m. Anita S. Lawrence, Sept. 12, 1980 (div. 1990); 1 child, Alexandra; m. Nanette Sexton, Sept. 27, 1993. B.A., Harvard, 1948, M.A., 1951; postgrad., Grad. Sch. Bus. Adminstrn., 1966. Prodn. engr. C. Brewer & Co., Honolulu, 1951-53; prodn. engr. Raytheon Co., Waltham, Mass., 1953-54; security analyst Keystone Custodian Funds, Boston, 1955-59; industry specialist Mass. Investors Trust, 1959-69; v.p. Mass. Fin. Svcs., Co., Boston, 1969-77, pres., 1978-82, chmn., dir., 1982-91, ret., 1991; bd. dirs. Cambridge Trust Co., Sun Life Assurance Co. Can. (U.S.); trustee MFS Family Funds, Lifetime Family Funds, Meridian Family Funds; chmn. Lincoln (Mass.) Fin. Com., 1966-68; ind. fund trustee Mass. Fin. Svcs., Inc. Trustee Plimoth Plantation, Inc., Plymouth, Mass., Phillips Exeter Acad., Exeter, N.H., 1978-82, Handel and Haydn Soc.; mem. adv. bd. Coll. Mental Health Ctr. of Boston. 2d lt. Signal Corps, AUS, 1944-46. Decorated Letter of Commendation. Mem. Boston Security Analysts Soc., Harvard Club (N.Y.C.), Somerset Club (Boston). Republican. Episcopalian. Home: 3321 Hanover Cir Loxahatchee FL 33470-2417 Office: Mass Fin Svcs Co Ste 19 500 Boylston St Boston MA 02116-3740*

BAILEY, RICHARD WELD, English language educator; b. Pontiac, Mich., Oct. 26, 1939; s. Karl Deanor and Elisabeth Phelps (Weld) B.; m. Margaret Louise Bowman, 1960 (div. 1976); children—Eleanor Bowman (dec.), Charles Andrew Stuart; m. Julia Ruth Huttar, 1990. Student, U. Edinburgh, Scotland, 1959-60; AB, Dartmouth Coll., 1961; MA, U. Conn.,

1963, PhD, 1965. From asst. prof. English to assoc. prof. U. Mich., Ann Arbor, 1965-76, prof., 1976—; del. ACLS, 1996—. Author: Images of English, 1991, Nineteenth-Century English, 1996; editor: (with others) English Stylistics, 1968; Computing in the Humanities, 1982; Michigan Early Modern English Materials, 1975; English as a World Language, 1982, Literacy for Life, 1983, Dictionaries of English, 1987. Trustee Washtenaw C.C., Ann Arbor, 1974—, chair, 1985-95, 1999—; del. platform com. Nat. Dem. Conv., 1976; sr. warden St. Clare of Assisi Episcopal Ch., Ann Arbor, 1981-82, guild of scholars, 1997—. Grantee NEH, 1971-75, 78, 85, 91-92, Ford Found., 1978-82; Inst. for Advanced Studies in the Humanities fellow, 1971. Mich. Linguistic Soc. (pres. 1975-76), Commn. on English Lang., Nat. Council Tchrs. of English, Am. Dialect Soc. (exec. council 1980-84, v.p. 1985-87, pres. 1987-88), Dictionary Soc. N.Am. (exec. com. 1992-95, pres. 1999—), Assn. Computing in the Humanities (v.p. 1980-83), Am. Coun. Learned Socs. (del. 1996—). Clubs: Flounders (Ann Arbor); The Athenaeum (London). Home: 1609 Cambridge Rd Ann Arbor MI 48104-3520 Office: U Mich Dept English Ann Arbor MI 48109-1003

BAILEY, RITA MARIA, investment advisor, psychologist; b. Frankfurt, Germany, June 10, 1949; came to U.S., 1957; d. Ludwig and Gertrude (Cierniak) Fleischmann; m. William W. Bailey, Feb. 17, 1974; children: Anne Christine, Cynthia Patricia. BS in Psychology, Austin Peay U., 1975, MA in Psychology, 1977, postgrad., 1977-79. Cert. counselor, Tenn. Editor U.S. Army Spl. Warfare Inst., Ft. Bragg, N.C., 1967-74, edn. officer, 1979-82; edn. officer Augsburg (Germany) Cmty. Ctr., 1982-85; pvt. practice counseling Leavenworth, Kans., 1985-90; pvt. practice investments, 1990—; sr. investment advisor pvt. orgns., Washington, 1991—. Author: Extroversion and Introversion, 1978, Special Warfare Training Plan, 1981; author, editor tng. manual Foreign Small Arms, 1982. Dir. Energy Conservation Campaign, Clarksville, 1976; founder, dir. Women's Support Ctr., Leavenworth, 1986. Mem. Nat. Assn. Investors, Alpha Mu Gamma. Roman Catholic. Avocations: long distance swimming, gardening, German poetry.

BAILEY, ROBERT, JR., advertising executive; b. Kans. City, Apr. 27, 1945; s. Robert and Sarah (Morgan) B.; m. Rita Carol Burdine, June 26, 1971; children: Rebecca, Sarah. AB, U. Kans., 1967; MA, Northwestern U., Ill., 1968; PhD, Northwestern U., 1972, MM, 1979. Research supr. BBDO Chgo., 1973-78, v.p. research dir., 1978-82, sr. v.p., mktg. services dir., 1982-85, exec. v.p., rsch. and planning dir. Author: Radicals In Urban Politics, 1974; contbr. articles to profl. jours. Am. Mktg. Assn.. Office: BBDO Chgo 410 N Michigan Ave Ste 8 Chicago IL 60611-4226

BAILEY, ROBERT C., opera company executive; b. Metropolis, Ill., Dec. 28, 1936; m. Sally McDermott, July 13, 1958. BA in Speech, U. Ill., 1958, MA in English, 1960; BM in Applied Voice, Eastman Sch. Music, 1965; MM in Applied Voice, New Eng. Conservatory Music, 1969. Music prodr. Nat. Pub. Radio, Washington, 1971-73, dir. cultural programming, 1973-75; mgr. Western Opera Theatre, San Francisco, 1975-79; instr. arts mgmt. Golden Gate U., San Francisco, 1977-82; cons. arts mgmt. San Francisco, 1980-82; gen. dir. Portland Opera Assn., Oreg., 1982—; dir. Opera Am., 1995—; cons. On-Site Program Nat. Endowment Arts, Washington, 1982—; judge Met. Opera Auditions, 1977—. Recipient Chevalier in the Order of Arts and Letters French Govt., 1999. Mem. Bohemian Club (San Francisco), City Club (Portland), Arlington Club, Rotary Club. Office: Portland Opera Assn Inc 1515 SW Morrison St Portland OR 97205-1814

BAILEY, ROBERT ELLIOTT, financial executive; b. Logansport, Ind., Mar. 29, 1932; s. Edwin William and Elizabeth Carolyn (Elliott) B.; m. Geraldine E. Hershberger, Jan. 31, 1954; children: Susan Elaine, Kathryn Jane. BS in Acctg., Ind. U., 1954; LLB, Tex. A&M U., Houston, 1962. CPA, Tex. Ptnr. Arthur Andersen & Co., Chgo., 1958-72; exec. v.p., dir., CFO Damson Oil Corp., N.Y.C., 1972-82; exec. v.p., CFO ENI Cos., Seattle and Houston, 1982-85; exec. v.p., CFO, dir. Gearhart Industries, Inc., Ft. Worth, Tex., 1985-88; corp. fin. cons., 1988-91; chmn. fin. The Turner Corp., N.Y.C., 1991-93; sr. v.p., CFO Rotondo Cos., Avon, Conn., 1993-94; dir. fin. UCAR, Danbury, Conn., 1995-96, Tauck Tours, Inc., Westport, Conn., 1996-98. Capt. USAFR, 1958. Mem. AICPA, Tex. Bar Assn., N.Y. CPA Soc., Fla. CPA Soc. Home: 58 S Washington Dr Sarasota FL 34236-1434

BAILEY, ROBERT SHORT, lawyer; b. Bklyn., Oct. 17, 1931; s. Cecil Graham and Mildred (Short) B.; m. Doris Furlow, Aug. 29, 1953; children: Elizabeth Jane Goldentyer, Robert F., Barbara A. Jongbloed. A.B., Wesleyan U., Middletown, Conn., 1953; J.D., U. Chgo., 1956. Bar: Ill. 1965, U.S. Dist. Ct. D.C. 1956, U.S. Supreme Ct. 1960. Atty. U.S. Dept. Justice, criminal div., 1956-61; asst. U.S. atty. No. Dist. Ill., 1961-65; ptnr. LeFevour & Bailey, Oak Park, Ill., 1965-68; pvt. practice, Chgo., 1968—; panel atty. Fed. Defender Program, 1965—. Mem. NACDL (mem. faculty 1976-78, legis. chmn. 1976-78). Home: 17 Timber Trl Streamwood IL 60107-1353 Office: 53 W Jackson Blvd Ste 918 Chicago IL 60604-3813

BAILEY, ROBIN KEITH, physician assistant, perfusionist; b. St. Petersburg, Fla., Jan. 8, 1951; s. Albert Hugh and Kathleen Elizabeth (Badgley) B. AA, St. Petersburg Jr. Coll., 1973; BS in Pub. Rels. in Criminal Justice, U. Fla., 1976, B Health Sci., 1984; cert., Newark Beth Israel Med. Ctr., 1990; Masters in Physician Assts. Studies, U. Nebr., 1998. Cert. physician Nat. Cert. Commn. of Physician Assts., ATLS, PHTLS. Paramedic Alachua County Emergency Med. Svc., Gainesville, Fla., 1972-78; perfusionist U. Fla./VA Med. Ctr., Gainesville, 1980-96; physician asst. U. Fla., 1984-96; with U. South Fla.-VA Med. Ctr., Tampa, 1996—; air ambulance medic/perfusionist Shands Hosp., Gainesville, 1995-97; cons. in field. Contbr. articles to profl. publs. Lt. col. U.S. Army, 1978-81, USAFR, 1981—. Mem. Am. Acad. Physician Assts., Fla. Acad. Physician Assts., Assn. Mil. Surgeons, Am. Heart Assn. (exec. com., ACLS instr., BCLS instr./trainer). Avocations: golf, fishing. Home: 200 SW Lincoln Cir N Saint Petersburg FL 33703-1311

BAILEY, STEPHEN, history educator; b. Chgo., Apr. 4, 1939; s. Roland James Bailey and Zena Karras Sutherland; m. Susan Wood, Aug. 9, 1966; children: James, Andrew, Elisabeth. BA, U. Chgo., 1960, PhD, 1966. Prof. history Knox Coll., Galesburg, Ill., 1965—; mem. acad. coun. Coll. Bd., N.Y.C., 1997—; cons. Javits Fellowship, U.S. Dept. Edn., Washington, 1987—; reader, table leader Ednl. Testing Svc., Princeton, N.J., 1980-93; grant cons. Joyce Found., Chgo., 1991-94. Contbr. more than 100 book revs. to Choice, 1977—. Vol. Galesburg Humane Soc., 1996—. Recipient Phillip Green Wright Tchg. prize Knox Coll., 1984. Democrat. Avocations: reading, gardening. Home: 1215 N Cherry St Galesburg IL 61401-1814 Office: Knox Coll Galesburg IL 61401

BAILEY, STEPHEN FAIRCHILD, museum director and curator, ornithologist; b. Stamford, Conn., Feb. 7, 1948; s. Edwin Montgomery and Frances (Sherman) B.; m. Karen Lynn Burtness Bailey, Aug. 18, 1971 (div. July 1987); divorced. BA in Biology magna cum laude, Beloit Coll., 1971; PhD in Zoology, U. Calif., Berkeley, 1978. Museum dir. and curator Pacific Grove Mus. of Natural Hist., Calif., 1992—; collections mgr. for ornithology and mammalogy Calif. Acad. Scis., San Francisco, 1984-92; biological cons., 1979-92; adj. prof. biology San Francisco State U., 1986—; teaching Albany Adult Sch., Calif., 1979-85. Co-author Atlas of the Breeding Birds of Monterey County, 1993; co-author, photographer Audubon Society Master Guide to Birding 3 vols., 1983; regional editor Field Notes, 1985-98; contrb. articles to profl. jours. Rsch. fellowship Christensen Rsch. Inst., Papua New Guinea, 1989. Mem. Am. Birding Assn. (elected), Ecological Soc. Am. (life), Am. Ornithologists Union, Cooper Ornithological Soc. (life), Pacific Seabird Group, Soc. Preservation of Natural Hist. Collections, Phi Eta Sigma, Phi Beta Kappa. Avocations: birding, travel, nature study, military history. Home: 830 Sunset Dr Apt J Pacific Grove CA 93950-4729 Office: Pacific Grove Museum Natural History 165 Forest Ave Pacific Grove CA 93950-2612

BAILEY, STEVEN FREDERICK, publishing executive; b. Bremmerton, Wash., Dec. 13, 1943; s. Robert Frederick and Cora Lois (Wieher) B.; m. Raydell Joan Walton, Sept. 4, 1965 (div. Jan. 1986); children: Scott F., Tara E.; m. Jill Elizabeth Manee, Aug. 15, 1988. BS, No. Ill. U., 1966. Unit sales mgr. Procter and Gamble, Chgo., 1966-71; area sales mgr. Cheseborough Ponds, St. Louis, 1971-74; regional v.p. Time Distbn. Svcs., N.Y.C., 1974-77; zone sales mgr. Pillsbury Co., N.Y.C., 1977-82; pub. Lebhar Friedman Inc., N.Y.C., 1982-91; pub. Travel Weekly Reed Elsevier, Secaucus, N.J., 1991—, 1991-98; v.p. of custom publ. and product devel. Reed Elsevier, Secaucus, 1998—. Mem. Am. Soc. Travel Agts., Assn. Corp. Travel Execs., Nat. Bus. Travelers Assn., Pacific Area Travel Assn, Inst. Cert. Travel Counselors. Office: Cahners Travel 500 Plaza Dr Secaucus NJ 07094-3619*

BAILEY, STEVEN SCOTT, operations research analyst; b. Ft. Benning, Ga., Dec. 9, 1948; s. Claude Esmond and Marietta (Tanzola) B.; m. Wendy Cropf, Dec. 10, 1988; 1 child, Michael. BS, U.S. Mil. Acad., 1970; MPA, U. Colo., Denver, 1977, MS, 1981; PhD, Colo. Sch. of Mines, 1989. Cert. prodn. and inventory mgmt. Commd. 2nd lt. U.S. Army, 1970, advanced through grades to lt. col., 1987; asst. prof. U.S. Mil. Acad., West Point, N.Y., 1981-84; ops. rsch. analyst Concepts Analysis Agy. U.S. Army, Bethesda, Md., 1984-86; asst. prof. Park Coll., Denver, 1986-89; ops. rsch. analyst RAND Corp., Santa Monica, Calif., 1989-92; rsch. analyst Ctr. for Naval Analyses, Alexandria, Va., 1992—; dir. analysis COMUSNAVCENT, Bahrain, 1994—; instr. C.W. Post Coll., L.I. (N.Y.) U., 1982-84, Colo. Sch. Mines, Golden, 1988-89, UCLA Extension, 1990-91, CSUN, 1991-92, Amideast, 1996—, U. Md., 1997—. Mem. Am. Prodn. and Inventory Control Soc., Inst. Mgmt. Sci., RAND Scuba Club (pres. 1989-92), Phi Kappa Phi. Avocation: scuba. Office: Psc 451 Box 643 FPO AE 09834-2800

BAILEY, SUSAN CAROL, commercial banking executive; b. Muskogee, Okla., Apr. 10, 1954; d. William E. and Lula M. (Holloway) Green; m. Wayne M. Bailey, Aug. 6, 1976; 1 child, Nathan W. BS in Fin., So. Ill. U., 1982, MBA, 1983. Tech. asst. ops. Marsh Stencil Machine Co., Belleville, Ill., 1973-85; loan officer Delmar Fin. Co., Belleville, 1985-86; asst. v.p., asst. br. mgr. Fidelity Fed. Savs. and Loan Assn., Fairview Heights, Ill., 1986; asst. v.p., br. mgr. Fidelity Fed. Savs. and Loan Assn., Belleville, 1986-87, v.p., br. mgr., 1987-89, v.p., br. mgr., Metro E. Deposit Acquisition & Fin. Svcs. officer, 1989-90; v.p., comml. loan officer, dir. mktg. Union Bank Ill., Swansea, 1991-96; v.p., comml. loan officer Bank of Alton, Ill., 1996-97; comml. relationship mgr., v.p. Nations Bank, Belleville, Ill., 1997—; fin. cons., Caseyville, Ill., 1985-86. Mem., treas. Belleville Welcome Wagon; mem. allocations bd. United Way Greater St. Louis; active leadership program Leadership Ctr. St. Louis, 1993-94, Civic Leader Tour, Scott AFB, 1994; chairperson teleparty St. Clair County Am. Heart Assn., 1995; indsl. divsn. chairperson River Bend United Way. Mem. St. Louis Fedn. Socs. for Coating Tech. (exec. com. 1980-85, chmn. edn. com. 1983-84), Belleville Bd. Realtors, Edwardsville-Collinsville Bd. Realtors, Women's Coun. Realtors, Homebuilders Assn., Belleville Econ. Progress (amb.), Belleville Postal Coun. (bd. dirs.), Ill. Bankers Assn., So. Ill. Network of Women (alliance rep., pres. 1991—), Fin. Women Internat., Noon Networking of Women, Fairview Hts. C. of C. (amb.), Metro East Profl. Women, Swansea C. of C. (bd. dirs.), Rotary. Home: 710 Belleville Rd Caseyville IL 62232-1142 Office: Nations Bank 23 Public Sq Belleville IL 62220-1627

BAILEY, SUZANNE K., health care consultant; b. Pigeon, Mich., Jan. 19, 1955; d. Willard G. Horton and Peggy A. Hoffman; m. Robert M. Bailey III, July 1977 (div. Aug. 1998); children: Christopher D., Mathew R. AA, Tallahassee C.C., 1985; BS, Fla. State U., 1996, MS, 1997, grad. cert. in pub. adminstrn.; grad. cert. in gerontology, Fla. State Pepper Inst. Cert. assisted living facility adminstr. Med. and charter coord. Tallahassee (Fla.) Flight Line, 1983-85; materials mgr. Gadsden Meml., Quincy, Fla., 1985-86; med. edn. and outreach coord. Tallahassee Meml. Hosp., 1986-95; med. edn. cons. Dept. Corrections Office of Health Svcs., State of Fla., Tallahassee, 1998. Vol. Fla. State Ctr. for Civic Edn. and Svc., Tallahassee, 1995-96. Mem. Am. Soc. Pub. Adminstrs. Avocations: fishing, reading, traveling. E-mail: suzyûbailey@tallahassee.net. Home: PO Box 37304 Tallahassee FL 32315-7304

BAILEY, THOMAS C., conservancy executive; b. Jackson, Mich.; s. Ralph E. and E. Jean Bailey; m. Jane M. Bailey; 1 child, John T. BS, Mich. State U., 1976. Seasonal park ranger U.S. Nat. Park Svc., Isle Royale, Mich., 1974-76; resource specialist Mich. Dept. Natural Resources, Lansing, 1978-84; exec. dir. Little Traverse Conservancy, Harbor Springs, Mich., 1984—; chair tech. adv. bd. Mich. Gt. Lakes Protection Fund, Lansing, 1994—. Mem. Mich. Water Resources Commn., Lansing, 1993. Recipient Charles Poell award for professionalism Mich. State U., 1976, Olals Murie-Harvey Broome award Wilderness Soc., 1972. Mem. Nat. Land Trust Coun. Avocations: hunting, sailing, navigation, outdoor activities. Office: Little Traverse Conservancy 3264 Powell Rd Harbor Springs MI 49740-9469

BAILEY, THOMAS CHARLES, lawyer; b. Rochester, N.Y., Nov. 26, 1948; s. Charles George and Teckla Barbara (Driscoll) B.; m. Rosalie Stoll, Sept. 24, 1974; children: Leah Isabelle, Molly Driscoll, Elizabeth Rose. BA, Princeton U., 1970; JD, SUNY, Buffalo, 1974. Bar: N.Y. 1975, Fla. 1977. Assoc. Little & Burt, Buffalo, 1974-78, ptnr., 1978-80; ptnr. Saperston & Day, PC, Buffalo, 1980-92; pvt. practice Buffalo, 1992-97; mem. Albrecht Maguire Heffern and Gregg PC, Buffalo, 1997—; bd. dirs., sec. Buffalo Therapeutic Riding Ctr. Inc., 1999—. Pres. St. Thomas Moore Guild, 1981; trustee Shea's O'Connell Preservation Guild, 1986-96, chmn., 1994. Mem. ABA, N.Y. State Bar Assn. (exec. com. of real property law sect.), Fla. Bar Assn., Am. Assn. Franchisees and Dealers (fair franchising standards com.), Saturn Club, Mathais Soc., Princeton U. Alumni Assn. Western N.Y. (pres. 1990-91), Brookhaven Trout Club. Avocations: fly fishing, boating, horses. Office: 2100 Main Place Tower Buffalo NY 14202-3721

BAILEY, THOMAS EVERETT, engineering company executive; b. Atlantic, Iowa, Mar. 30, 1936; s. Merritt E. and Clara May (Richardson) B.; m. Elizabeth Jane Taylor, Sept. 9, 1956; children: Thomas E., Douglas L., Steven W. BS, U. Iowa, 1959. Registered profl. engr., environ. assessor, expert witness. Engr. Calif. Dept. Water Resources, Sacramento, 1960-67; sr. engr. Calif. Water Quality Control Bd., San Luis Obispo, 1967-72; asst. div. chief, dir. water quality planning State Water Resources Control Bd., Sacramento, 1972-75, chief div. planning rsch., 1975-77, chief tech. support br., 1977-79; sr. tech. advisor Yemen Arab Republic, Sana'a, 1979-81; chief Calif. superfund program Calif. Dept. Health Svcs., Sacramento, 1982-86; prin., v.p. Kleinfelder Inc., Walnut Creek, Calif., 1986-92; also bd. dirs. Kleinfelder Inc., Walnut Creek; pres. Bailey Environ., Goodyear, Ariz., 1992—; cons. engr. Contbr. articles to profl. jours. Mem. San Luis County Obispo Rep. Ctrl. Com., 1969-72, vice-chmn., 1970-71, chmn., 1971-72; vice-chmn. bd. trustees Meth. Ch., San Luis Obispo, 1970-72; mem. Contra Costa County Hazardous Materials Com., 1988-89; chmn. bus. practices com. Hazardous Waste Action Coalition, 1991-93, bd. dirs., 1992-93; mem. Calif. Remedial Action Group, co-chmn., 1991-92. With U.S. Army, 1959-60. Office: 15434 W Piccadilly Rd Goodyear AZ 85338-8805

BAILEY, WILFORD SHERRILL, retired parasitology educator, science administrator, university president; b. nr. Hartselle, Ala., Mar. 2, 1921; s. Ollis Wilford and Bessie (Widener) B.; m. Cratus Hester, May 30, 1942; children: Wilford Edward, Joe Sherrill, Margaret Ann, Sarah Jane. D.V.M., Auburn U., 1942, M.S., 1946, H.H.D., 1984; Sc.D., Johns Hopkins U., 1950. Instr. to head prof. dept. pathology and parasitology Sch. Vet Medicine, Auburn U., 1942-62; asso. dean Grad. Sch. and coordinator research, 1962-66, v.p. for academic affairs, 1966-72; health scientist adminstr. Inst. Allergy and Infectious Diseases, NIH, 1972-74; prof. dept. pathology and parasitology Auburn (Ala.) U., 1974-92, assoc. dean vet. medicine, 1979-80, pres., 1983-84, Univ. prof., 1984-92; research leader Regional Parasite Research Lab., U.S. Dept. Agr., Auburn, 1980-82; custodian Am. Soc. Parasitologists, 1952-79. Mem. NRC Coun., 1962-68; mem. tng. grant com. Nat. Inst. Allergy and Infectious Diseases, 1964-69, Nat. Adv. Allergy and Infectious Disease Coun., 1971-72, 75-78; mem. com. on animal health NRC, Nat. Acad. Sci., 1980-84; trustee Internat. Christian U., Vienna, Austria, 1990-95. Research fellow Am. Vet. Med. Assn.; Johns Hopkins Univ. scholar; NSF Sci. Faculty fellow; Rockefeller Found. scholar; named Ala. Disting. Sportsman of Yr., Ala. Sports Hall of Fame, 1995. Mem. Am. Vet. Med. Assn., Am. Soc. Parasitologists (pres. 1971), Am. Soc. Tropical Medicine and Hygiene (pres. 1977), Mortar Bd., Nat. Collegiate Athletic Assn. (sec.-treas. 1985-86, pres. 1987-88), Sigma Xi, Phi Kappa Phi, Alpha Phi Omega, Phi Zeta, Omicron Delta Kappa, Phi Beta Delta. Mem. Ch. of Christ. Home: 778 Moores Mill Rd Auburn AL 36830-6032

BAILEY, WILLIAM HAROLD, medical educator; b. Ft. McKinley, Philippines, Mar. 27, 1947; s. Jamie Morris and Nancy (Weinstein) B.; m. Kathy P. Bailey, July 23, 1983; children: Nancy M., William L. BA, Tulane U., New Orleans, 1969, MD, 1976. Diplomate Am. Coll. Cardiology, Am. Bd. Internal Medicine, Am. Acad. Family Medicine. Resident family medicine Baylor Coll. Medicine, Houston, 1976-79; resident internal medicine U. Tex. Med. Sch., Houston, 1979-81, fellow cardiology, 1981-83; cardiologist South Tex. Cardiology Assn., San Antonio, 1983-93; fellow cardiac electrophysiology Tex. Heart Inst., Baylor Coll. Medicine, Houston, 1993-94; prof. medicine Tex. A&M Med. Sch., Temple, 1996—; chmn. dept. cardiology and electrophysiology Olin Teague VA Med. Ctr., Temple, 1996—; pvt. practice South Tex. Cardiology Assocs., San Antonio, 1984-93, Houston Heart Ctr., 1994, Ctrl. Tex. VA Med. Ctrs., 1995—. Lt. col. USAF, 1982—. Rsch. grantee cardiology NIH, Temple, 1997, rsch. grantee CIBA-Geigy, Bristol Meyer, Fujisaws, Merck & CPI, Temple. Fellow Am. Coll. Cardiology, Am. Heart Assn.; mem. N.Am. Soc. Pacing and Electrophysiology, ACP, Am. Heart Failure Soc., Res. Officers Assn., Soc. Aerospace Medicine. Republican. Roman Catholic. Avocations: bagpipes, jogging, sailing, writing novels. Office: Temple VA Med Ctr Chmn Cardiology 111-C 1901 S 1st St Temple TX 76504-7451*

BAILEY, WILLIAM HARRISON, artist, educator; b. Council Bluffs, Iowa, Nov. 17, 1930; s. Willard Kendall and Marjorie Esther (Cheyney) B.; m. Sandra Stone, May 28, 1958; children: Ford Hamilton, Alix Brook. Student, U. Kans., 1948-51; BFA, Yale U., 1955, MFA, 1957; HHD (hon.), U. Utah, 1987; DFA (hon.), Adelphi U. Instr. art Yale U., New Haven, 1957-61, asst. prof., 1961-62, adj. prof., 1969-73, prof. art, 1973-79, dean Sch. Art, 1974-75, Kingman Brewster prof., 1979-95, Kingman Brewster prof. emeritus, 1995—; asst. prof. art Ind. U., 1962-65, assoc. prof., 1965-68, prof., 1968-69; mem. Nat. Coun. on the Arts, 1992-97. Exhbns. include Robert Schoelkopf Gallery, N.Y.C., 1968, 71, 74, 79, 82, 86, 90, 91, Galerie Claude Bernard, Paris, 1978, Galleria il Gabbiano, Rome, 1989, 85, 93, 97, John Berggruen Gallery, San Francisco, 1988, Andre Emmerich Gallery, N.Y.C., 1992, 94, 95, Alpha Gallery, Boston, 1998, Robert Miller Gallery, N.Y.C., 1999; represented in permanent collection Mus. Modern Art, Whitney Mus., Hirshorn Mus., St. Louis Art Mus., Neu Galerie Der Stadt Aachen, West Germany Pa. Acad., Yale Art Gallery. Served with U.S. Army, 1951-53. Alice Kimball English traveling fellow, 1955; Guggenheim fellow, 1965; Ingram Merrill fellow, 1979. Mem. Nat. Acad. Design, Nat. Coun. Arts, Am. Acad. Arts and Letters, Acad. San Luca, Rome, Conn. Commn. on the Arts, Academia di Belli Arti, Perugia, Tiffany Found. (bd. dirs.), Yaddo (mem. corp.). Office: Yale U Sch Art Dept Painting Printmaking New Haven CT 06520

BAILEY, WILLIAM NATHAN, systems engineer; b. Thomasville, N.C., Nov. 30, 1955; s. Charlie Franklin and Bonnie Mae (West) B.; m. Joy Linda Wagner, June 10, 1978 (dec. Feb. 1987); m. Belinda Carol Church, Aug. 8, 1988; 1 child, Benjamin Franklin. BFA, U. N.C., Greensboro, 1978; MA, Life Christian U., 1996, PhD, 1997. Sr. programmer CIBA-GEIGY Corp., Greensboro, N.C., 1986-88, sr. system analyst, 1990-95; system mgr. N.C. A&T State U., Greensboro, 1988-90; cons. CIBA-GEIGY Corp., Greensboro, N.C., 1995-96; sr. systems engr. BizNetz, Inc., Greensboro, 1996-97; engr. Ctr. for Creative Leadership, Greensboro, 1998—; chmn. DECUS PT-LUG, Greensboro, 1987-88, 90-96, asst. chmn., 1988-89; cons. Ciba-Geigy Corp., 1995-96; prof. LCU, Greensboro campus, 1996—. Contbr. articles to profl. jours. Tchr. Faith & Victory Ch., Greensboro, 1988—. Mem. Window NT System Profls. Assn., Internet Developers Assn., Digital Equipment Computer Users Soc., Piedmont Triad Nt Users Group (chmn. 1997—). Republican. Office: Ctr for Creative Leadership One Leadership Pl PO Box 26300 Greensboro NC 27438-6300

BAILEY, WILLIAM RAY, transportation planner; b. L.A., Feb. 11, 1961; s. Merlyn Ray and Patsy Darlene (Goble) B.; m. Judy Edwards, May 27, 1989. BA in Pub. Adminstrn., U. Ctrl. Fla., 1995, MPA, 1998. Planning intern Ctrl. Fla. Regional Planning Coun., Winter Park, Fla., 1995, City of Altamonte Springs, Fla., 1995-96; coord. Fla. Work Experience program U. Ctrl. Fla., Orlando, 1995; transp. planning intern City of Orlando, Fla., 1996-98; transp. planner City of Orlando, 1998—. Chair marriage retreat com. First Presbyn. Ch., Orlando, 1995-98. Mem. ASPA, Am. Planning Assn., U. Ctrl. Fla. Alumni Assn. (chair pub. adminstrn. chpt. 1998—). Republican. Avocation: volleyball. E-mail: wbailey@integrityonline15.com. Home: 403 Bonifay Ave Orlando FL 32825-8001 Office: City of Orlando Transp Planning Bur 400 S Orange Ave Orlando FL 32801-3302

BAILEY, WILLIAM WADDELL, writer, communications executive; b. Gordonsville, Va., May 25, 1951; s. George W. and Phyllis K. (Kennon) B.; m. Rita Maria Fleischmann, Feb. 17, 1974. BA in Psychology, U. Miss., 1973; MA in Internat. Rels., U. So. Calif., 1985; disting. grad., Command and Gen. Staff Coll., 1987. Cert. software engr. Commd. 2d lt. U.S. Army, 1973, advanced through grades to lt. col.; officer U.S. Army, Ft. Bragg, N.C., 1973-82; software mgr. U.S. Govt., Augsburg, Germany, 1982-85; modernization mgr. U.S. Govt., Leavenworth, Kans., 1985-90; divsn. chief U.S. Govt., Arlington, Va., 1990-92, spl. exec., 1992-93; sr. advisor to pvt. orgns. Washington, 1993-97; pres. Writer's Ink, Fayetteville, N.C., 1997—; resident artist Urban Arts Prgm., 1998; cons. Sierra Cybernetics, Yorba Linda, Calif., 1993—. Author, editor: 2004 Future Architecture, 1987, Modernization Plan, 1989; author: Desert Storm Lessons Learned, 1991; contbr. articles, stories and poems to mags. and jours. Mem. fundraising com. Hist. Mus., Fayetteville, 1981; mem. Arts Coun., 1996—. Decorated Legion of Merit. Avocations: astronomy, fencing. Fax: (910) 423-6667.

BAILLIE, ALEXANDER CHARLES, JR., banker; b. Orillia, Ont., Can., Dec. 20, 1939; s. A. Charles and Jean G. Baillie; m. Marilyn J. Michener, June 25, 1965; children: A. Charles M., Matthew D.G., Jonathan E.M., Alexandra C.M. BA in Polit. Sci. and Econs. with honors, U. Toronto, 1962; MBA, Harvard U., 1964. With Toronto Dominion Bank, Toronto, Can., 1964—, v.p., gen. mgr. USA divsn., 1979-81, sr. v.p. USA divsn., 1981-84, exec. v.p. corp. and investment banking group, 1984-92, vice chmn. corp. and investment banking group, 1992-95, pres., 1995—; pres. and CEO Toronto Dominion Bank, Toronto, 1997—, chmn., 1998—; bd. dirs. Toronto-Dominion Bank; mem. Ont. Bus. Adv. Coun., Brit.-N.Am. Com. Mem. Corp. of Trinity Coll.; bd. govs. Shaw Festival, treas., chmn. fin. and audit com.; active capital campaign U. Toronto; areawide chairperson United Way Campaign. Fellow Inst. Can. Bankers. Office: Toronto Dominion Bank TD Tower, PO Box 1 T D Center, Toronto, ON Canada M5K 1A2

BAILLIE, CHARLES DOUGLAS, banker; b. Bklyn., Sept. 12, 1918; s. Charles Tupper and Nina (Vincent) B.; m. Helene Elizabeth Kuehn, Feb. 15, 1941 (dec. Apr. 1979); children—Barbara Ann (Mrs. John Roland Obenchain), Charles Douglas, Nancy Helene (Mrs. Michael Malke); m. Nancy Lee Anderson, Oct. 22, 1982. B.S. in Bus. Adminstrn. with distinction, Ind. U., 1940; certificate exec. program, UCLA, 1956. Pers. and credit supervision Continental Ill. Nat. Bank, Chgo., 1940-52; v.p. treas., dir. Nat. Discount Corp., South Bend, Ind., 1952-54; with United Calif. Bank, Los Angeles, 1954-75, asst. v.p., 1955-56, v.p., 1956-68, sr. v.p., 1968-70, exec. v.p., 1970-75; v.p. Mfrs. Bank, Los Angeles, 1975-78, sr. v.p., dir., 1978-81; sr. v.p., dir. Mitsui Mfrs. Bank, Los Angeles, 1981-86, cons., 1986-89. Bd. dirs. Mitsui Mfrs. Bank Found., 1981-86, San Marino Community Council, 1968-76, AID-United Givers, 1977-80, United Way Los Angeles County, 1980-86; councilman City of San Marino, 1972-76; trustee San Marino Community Ch. Served from ensign to lt. Supply Corps USNR, 1942-46. Mem. Am. Inst. Banking, UCLA Exec. Program Alumni Assn., 1 Men's Assn., Robert Morris Assos., Town Hall, Delta Sigma Pi, Phi Gamma Delta, Beta Gamma Sigma (dirs. table). Clubs: Rotarian, San Marino City (gov. 1979-80), San Gabriel (Calif.) Country. Home: 118 W Las Flores Ave Arcadia CA 91007-8223

BAILLIE, STUART GORDON, research technician; b. Plainfield, N.J., Jan. 23, 1962; s. Gordon Richard and Pauline (Balicki) B.; m. Tammy Marie Chelel, Apr. 28, 1990. Grad. high sch., North Plainfield, N.J. Asst. mgr. Carousel Enterprises, Inc., Piscataway, N.J., 1979-82; bus. mgr. C.R.D. Enterprises, Inc., Greenbrook, N.J., 1982-92; lab. rschr. Sandoz Pharms., Est Hanover, N.J., 1992-96; rsch. tech. Novartis Pharms., East Hanover, N.J., 1995—. Vol. Children's Specialized Hosp., Mountainside, 1997. Mem. Am. Assn. Lab. Animal Scis., N.J. Assn. Lab. Animal Sci., NRA. Republican. Avocations: travel, stock market, sports, family. Office: Novartis Pharms 59 Rt 10 Bldg 406 East Hanover NJ 07936

BAILLIE-DAVID, SONJA KIRSTEEN, controller; b. Lac Megantic, Quebec, Canada, Mar. 26, 1961; came to the U.S., 1964; d. Patrick Eugene and Erika (Bagdonowich) Baillie-David; m. Glenn Frank Skoff, Nov. 12, 1988; 1 child, Elaine Elise Skoff. AA, Joliet Jr. Coll., 1983; BBA, Coll. St. Francis, 1985; MBA in Entrepreneurship, DePaul U., 1992. CPA, Ill. Auditor Peat, Marwick Main, Chgo., 1985-87; auditor Ill. Tool Works, Chgo., 1987-88, fin. analyst, 1988-89; fin. systems project mgr. Ill. Tool Works, Glenview, Ill., 1989-94; controller U.S. Wire-Tie Systems, Woodridge, Ill., 1994-96, Pennysaver Publs., Inc., Tinley Pk., Ill., 1996-97, Littell Internat., Inc., Addison, Ill., 1997—. Mem. Ill. CPA Soc., NAFE, Am. Mgmt. Assn. Roman Catholic. Avocations: scuba diving, underwater photography, travel, refinishing antiques, reading. Office: Littell Internat Inc 145 N Swift Rd Addison IL 60101-1407

BAILON, GILBERT, newspaper editor. V.p. and exec. editor Dallas Morning News. Office: The Dallas Morning News PO Box 655237 508 Young St Dallas TX 75202-4828

BAILYN, BERNARD, historian, educator; b. Hartford, Conn., Sept. 10, 1922; s. Charles Manuel and Esther (Schloss) B.; m. Lotte Lazarsfeld, June 18, 1952; children: Charles David, John Frederick. AB, Williams Coll., 1945, LittD (hon.), 1969; MA, Harvard U., 1947, PhD, 1953; LHD (hon.), Lawrence U., Bard Coll., Clark U., Yale U., Grinnell Coll., Trinity Coll., Manhattanvill Coll., Dartmouth Coll., U. Chgo., Coll. of William and Mary; LittD, Rutgers U., Fordham U., La Trobe U., Australia, Washington U., St. Louis. Faculty Harvard U., Cambridge, Mass., 1953—, prof. history, 1961-66, Winthrop prof. history, 1966-81, Adams Univ. prof., 1981-93, prof. emeritus, 1993—, James Duncan Phillips prof. early Am. history, 1991, prof. emeritus, 1993—, editor in chief John Harvard Library, 1962-70, dir. Charles Warren Ctr. for Studies in Am. History, 1983-94; dir. Internat. Seminar on the History of Atlantic World, 1995—, sr. fellow Soc. Fellows, Harvard U.; Colver lectr. Brown U., 1965; Phelps lectr. NYU, 1969; Trevelyan lectr. Cambridge U., 1971; Becker lectr. Cornell U., 1975; Walker-Ames lectr. U. Wash., 1983; Curti lectr. U. Wis., 1984; Lewin vis. prof. Washington U., St. Louis, 1985; Pitt prof. Am. history Cambridge U., 1986-87; Thompson lectr. Pomona Coll., 1991; Montgomery fellow Dartmouth Coll., 1991; mem. Inst. Advanced Study, Princeton U., 1980-81, Trustee, 1989-94. Author: New England Merchants in the 17th Century, 1955, (with Lotte Bailyn) Massachusetts Shipping, 1697-1714, A Statistical Study, 1959, Education in the Forming of American Society, 1960, The Ideological Origins of the American Revolution, 1967 (Pulitzer and Bancroft prizes 1968), The Origins of American Politics, 1968, The Ordeal of Thomas Hutchinson, 1974 (Nat. Book award 1975), The Peopling of British North America: An Introduction, 1986, Voyagers to the West, 1986 (Pulitzer Prize, Saloutos award Immigration History Soc., Triennial Book award Soc. of the Cin.), Faces of Revolution, 1990, On The Teaching and Writing of History, 1994; co-author: The Great Republic, 1977; editor: Pamphlets of the American Revolution, 1750-1776, Vol. 1, 1965, The Apologia of Robert Keayne, 1965, The Debate on the Constitution, 2 vols., 1993; co-editor: The Intellectual Migration, Europe and America, 1930-1960, 1969, Law in American History, 1972, Perspectives in American History, 1967-77, 81-86, The Press and The American Revolution, 1980, Strangers Within the Realm, 1990. Served with AUS, 1943-46. Recipient Robert H. Lord award Emmanuel Coll., 1967, Jefferson Lectr. Nat. Endowment of Humanities, 1998, first millenium lectr. White House, 1998, medal Fgn. Policy Assn., 1998; hon. fellow Christ Coll., Cambridge U. Fellow Royal Hist. Soc. (corr.); mem. Am. Hist. Assn. (pres. 1981), Am. Acad. Arts and Scis., Nat. Acad. Edn., Am. Philos. Soc. (Thomas Jefferson medal 1993, Henry Allen Moe prize, 1994), Mass. Hist. Soc., Brit. Acad. (fgn.), Mex. Acad. History and Geography (fgn.),Russian Acad. Scis. (fgn.), Academia Europaea (fgn.). Home: 170 Clifton St Belmont MA 02478-2604 Office: Harvard U History Dept Cambridge MA 02138

BAIMAN, GAIL, real estate broker; b. Bklyn., June 4, 1938; d. Joseph and Anita (Devon) Yalow; children: Steven, Susan, Barbara. Student Bklyn. Coll., 1955-57. Lic. real estate broker, N.Y., Pa., Fla.; hynotherapist, stress mgmt. cons.; firewalk instr. Pers.-pub. rels. dir. I.M.C., Inc., N.Y.C., 1970-72; pres., broker Gayle Baiman Assocs., Inc., N.Y.C., 1972-74; v.p., broker Tuit Mktg. Corp., Mt. Pocono, Pa., 1974-83; pres., broker Ind. Timeshare Sales, Inc., St. Petersburg, Orlando, 1983—. Author: Vacation Timesharing, A Real Estate, 1992. Mem. Am. Resort Developers Assn., Better Bus. Arbitrator Assn., Internat. Resale Brokers Assn. (co-founder), Chmn. League, Better Bus. Bur. Arbitrators. Office: Ind Timeshare Sales Inc 5680 66th St N Saint Petersburg FL 33709-1515

BAIN, C. RANDALL, lawyer; b. Greeley, Colo., Feb. 1, 1934; s. Walter Lockwood and Harriet Lucille (Stewart) B.; m. Joanne Berg, Aug. 4, 1956 (div.); children: Jennifer Harriet, Charles Alvin; m. Lois Jean Frazier, Feb. 1, 1973; 1 child, Frazier. BA, Yale U., 1955, LLB, 1960. Bar: Ariz. 1961, U.S. Dist. Ct. Ariz. 1961, U.S. Ct. Appeals (9th cir.) 1963, U.S. Supreme Ct. 1968, U.S. Ct. Appeals (fed. cir.) 1992. Ptnr. Brown & Bain, Phoenix, 1961—, pres., 1972-87, exec. v.p., 1987—; bd. dirs. UDC Homes, Inc., Tempe, Ariz., 1974-95. Trustee Phoenix Country Day Sch., 1983-94. Mem. ABA, Ariz. Bar Assn. (chmn. fee arbitration com. 1982-86), Am. Law Inst., Yale U. Law Sch. Alumni Assn. (exec. com. 1982-85, 93-97). Office: Brown & Bain PA 2901 N Central Ave Ste 2000 Phoenix AZ 85012-2788

BAIN, CONRAD STAFFORD, actor; b. Lethbridge, Alta., Can., Feb. 4, 1923; came to U.S., 1946, naturalized, 1946; s. Stafford Harrison and Jean Agnes (Young) B.; m. Monica Marjorie Sloan, Sept. 4, 1945; children: Kent Stafford, Mark Alexander, Jennifer Jean. Grad., Am. Acad. Dramatic Art, 1948. Founder Actors Fed. Credit Union, 1962. Broadway appearances include Candide, 1957, Lost in the Stars, 1958, Hot Spot, 1963, Advise and Consent, 1961, Twigs, 1971, Uncle Vanya, 1973, On Borrowed Time, 1991; off-Broadway appearances include The Iceman Cometh, 1957, Hogan's Goat, 1966, Scuba Duba, 1967, The Kitchen, 1968, Steambath, 1969, The Dining Room, Pasadena Playhouse, 1991, On Borrowed Time, 1992; film appearances A Lovely Way to Die, 1967, Who Killed Mary Whats er Name, 1968, Up the Sand Box, 1970, C.H.O.M.P.S, 1979, Child Bride of Short Creek, 1982, Postcards from the Edge, 1990; Pasadena Playhouse The Dining Room, 1991; co-star: (TV) Maude, 1971-78; star: (TV) Diff'rent Strokes, 1978-86, Mr. President, 1987—. Served with Canadian Army, World War II. Mem. Actors Equity Assn. (councilor 1962-76), ANTA West (dir. since 1977). Club: Players (N.Y.C.). Office: 1230 Chicory Ln Los Angeles CA 90049-1403 *I have come to realize that each job no matter how small must be an end in itself, and that each day of whatever character must be lived for that day, in all its fullness. Yesterday is gone, regret is a waste, and tomorrow is unknown.*

BAIN, DIANE MARTHA D'ANDREA, clinical nurse specialist in critical care; b. Westfield, Mass., June 29, 1949; d. John Anthony and Eva Margaret (Gerulis) D'Andrea; m. John Kenneth, Sept. 24, 1972. AS with hons., Quinsigamond Community Coll., 1971; BS with high hons., Worcester State Coll., 1977; MS with highest honors, U. Mass., Worcester, 1987. Staff and asst. head nurse MICU and crit. care St. Vincent Hosp., Worcester, 1971-77; instr. St. Vincent Hosp. Sch. Nursing, 1977-79; nurse educator critical care U. Mass. Hosp., Worcester, 1979-87, clin. nurse specialist critical care, 1987-93; assoc. faculty U. Mass. Grad. Sch. Nursing, Worcester, 1987-93, Worcester State Coll., 1987-93; presenter, lectr., cons. for regional orgns., agencies, and hosps. Reviewer for Applied Rsch. nursing jour., 1988-89; contbr. articles to profl. jours. Mem. AACN, Sigma Theta Tau, Iota Phi.

BAIN, DONALD KNIGHT, lawyer; b. Denver, Jan. 28, 1935; s. Francis Marion and Jean (Knight) B.; divorced; children: Stephen A., Andrew K., William B. AB, Yale U., 1957; LLB, Harvard U., 1961. Bar: Colo. 1961. From assoc. to ptnr. Holme Roberts & Owen, Denver, 1961-93, chmn. exec. com., 1988-90; ptnr. Holme Roberts & Owen LLP, Denver, 1993—; chmn. Colo. Rep. Com., 1993-97; bd. dirs. Fairmount Cemetery Co.; mem. grievance com. Colo. Supreme Ct., 1975-80, chmn., 1980. Active Rep. Nat. Com., Washington, 1993-97; bd. dirs. Rocky Mountain Corp. Pub. Broadcasting, 1975-83, Downtown Denver, Inc., 1977—, Greater Denver Corp., 1987-91, Denver Metro C. of C., 1998—; trustee Denver Pub. Libr. Friends Found., 1978-96, Denver Found., 1989-95, chmn., 1993-95; trustee Berger Found., 1994-96; trustee, chmn. Colo. Coun. on Arts, 1999—; trustee Human Svcs., Inc., 1970-81, chmn., 1979-80; trustee Colo. Humanities Program, 1975-78; bd. dirs. Auraria Higher Edn. Ctr., 1978-89, chmn., 1986-89; bd. dirs. Auraria Found., 1986—, Legal Aid Found., Colo., 1999—; mem. Denver Pub. Libr. Commn., 1983-91; candidate for mayor of Denver, 1987, 91. Fellow Royal Geog. Soc., Am. Coll. Trial Lawyers, Explorers Club; mem. ABA, Colo. Bar Assn., Denver Bar Assn., Colo. Yale Assn. (pres. 1974-76), Assn. Yale Alumni (bd. govs. 1982-85), Selden Soc., Am. Antiquarian Soc., Internat. Wine and Food Soc., Confrerie des Chevaliers du Tastevin, Cactus Club, Denver Country Club, Mile High Club, Denver Law Club, Grolier Club, Yale Club, Colo. Mountain Club, Capitol Hill CLub. Republican. Avocations: antiquarian book collecting; mountaineering. Home: 1177 Race St Apt 805 Denver CO 80206-2840 Office: Holme Roberts & Owen LLP 1700 Lincoln St Ste 4100 Denver CO 80203-4541

BAIN, GERI, magazine editor; b. N.Y.C., Aug. 7, 1951; d. Sanford K. and Ruth (Lseman) B.; m. Robert D. Kesoock, Apr. 4, 1994; 1 child, Jenny Keroack. BA in Philosophy, U. Colo., 1973. Freelance writer N.Y.C., 1978-85; Caribbean/features editor Travel Agt. Mag., N.Y.C., 1985-88; travel editor Modern Bride, N.Y.C., 1988—. Author: Bruce Springsteen, 1984, New Jersey, 1985, Modern Bride: Honeymoons and Weddings Away, 1997. Mem. N.Y. Travel Writers (sec.-treas. 1997-98). Office: Modern Bride 249 W 17th St New York NY 10011-5300

BAIN, JAMES ARTHUR, pharmacologist, educator; b. Langdon, N.D., May 22, 1918; s. James Hamilton and Mabel (Aldritt) B.; m. Eleanor Theo Hohaus, Dec. 5, 1947; children: Andrew J., Peter T. A.A., Wayland Jr. Coll., 1938; B.S., U. Wis., 1940, Ph.D., 1944. Research asst. McArdle Meml. Lab., U. Wis., 1940-44, Rockefeller fellow, 1946-47; research asso. U. Ill., 1947-50, asst. prof., then asso. prof., 1952-54; mem. faculty dept. pharmacology Emory U., 1954—, prof., 1954-89, chmn. dept., 1957-62, dir. div. basic health scis., 1960-76; exec. asso. dean Emory U. (Sch. Medicine), 1976-88, prof. emeritus, 1988—, cons. to dean, v.p., 1989-93; cons. to govt., nat. agys., industry, 1954—. Contbr. articles profl. jours. Mem. Am. Chem. Soc., Am. Soc. Pharmacology and Exptl. Therapeutics, AAAS. Home: 2275 Tanglewood Rd Decatur GA 30033-1915

BAIN, JAMES WILLIAM, lawyer; b. Suffern, N.Y., Dec. 19, 1949; s. William James and Agnes (Hoey) B.; m. Colleen K., Mar. 23, 1974; children: Rebecca, Meghan. BA, U. Conn., 1972; JD, U. Fla., 1976. Bar: Fla. 1977, U.S. Dist. Ct. (ea. dist.) Tenn. 1980, Tenn. 1984, U.S. Ct. Appeals (11th cir.) 1984, U.S. Ct. Appeals (D.C. cir.) 1984, Colo. 1986, U.S. Dist. Ct. Colo 1986, U.S. Ct. Appeals (10th cir.) 1988, U.S. Supreme Ct. 1998. Atty. trial Tenn. Valley Authority, Knoxville, 1977-85; atty. dir. Roath & Brega, P.C., Denver, 1985-89, Brega & Winters, P.C., Denver, 1989—; instr. U. Fla., Gainesville, 1976, U. Colo., Boulder, 1987-90; seminar chmn. Inst. for Advanced Legal Study, Denver, 1987. Contbr. articles to profl. jours.; editor constrn. law column Colo. Lawyer. Recipient Civil Litigation Writing award for 1986-87, Denver Colo. Bar Assn., 1987. Mem. ATLA, Colo. Bar Assn., Fla. Bar Assn., Am. Judicature Soc., Am. Arbitration Assn. (arbitrator 1986), Internat. Platform Assn. Avocations: soccer, skiing, biking, basketball. Office: Brega & Winters PC 1700 Lincoln St Ste 2222 Denver CO 80203-4522

BAIN, LINDA L., academic administrator. BS in Phys. Edn. summa cum laude, Ill. State U., 1962, MS in Phys. Edn., 1968; PhD in Phys. Edn. and Learning Theory, U. Wis., 1974. Instr. Lowell Elem. Sch., Wheaton, Ill., 1962-64, East Peoria (Ill.) H.S., 1964-68, U. Mich., Ann Arbor, 1968-69; asst. prof. U. Ill., Chgo., 1969-75; asst. prof. U. Houston, 1975-78, assoc. prof., 1978-83, prof., 1983-88, chmn. dept. health, phys. edn. and recreation, 1980-82, assoc. dean rsch. Coll. Edn., 1982-88; prof. Calif. State U., Northridge, 1988-95, dean Sch. Commn., Health and Human Svcs., 1988-95; prof. San Jose (Calif.) State U., 1995—, provost, v.p. acad. affairs, 1995—; Alderson lectr. U. Tex., 1982; Amy Morris Homans lectr. Nat. Assn. Phys. Edn. in Higher Edn., 1989; Ethel Martus Lawther lectr. U. N.C., Greensboro, 1992; Scholar lectr. Ill. State U., 1993; presenter in field. Co-author: Transition to Teaching: A Guide for the Beginning Teacher, 1983, The Curriculum Process in Physical Education, 1985, 2d edit., 1995; reviewer Rsch. Quar. for Exercise and Sport, 1977-95, Jour. Phys. Edn., Recreation and Dance, 1976-88; mem. editl. adv. bd. Youth and Soc., 1984-95, Jour. Phys. Edn., Recreation and Dance, 1984-87; editl. bd. Jour. Tchg. in Phys. Edn., 1985-95, Quest, 1991-94; book rev. editor Rsch. Quar. for Exercise and Sport, 1991-94; contbr. articles to profl. jours., chpts. to books. Bd. dirs. Am. Cancer Soc., San Fernando Valley, Calif., 1993-95; mem. health project policy bd. Calif. Phys. Edn., 1994-95; mem. met. bd. YMCA of Santa Clara Valley, 1998—; bd. dirs. Met. San Jose Collaborative for Acad. Excellence, 1998—; mem. hon. com. No. Exposure: New Art from Japan, San Jose Inst. Contemporary Art, 1999. Marie L. Carns fellow, 1972-73, Fellow AAH-PERD, 1980, Am. Leadership Forum Silicon Valley, 1999; recipient Rsch. award So. Assn. Phys. Edn. of Coll. Women, 1983, Honor award AAH-PERD, 1990, Jose Maria Cagigal Scholar lectr. Assn. Internat. Ecoles Superieures d'Edn. Physique, 1990, Disting. Adminstrn. award Nat. Assn. Phys. Edn. in Higher Edn., 1993, Alumni Achievement award Ill. State U., 1995, U. Wis. Sch. Edn., 1997, Tribute to Women in Industry award YWCA, Santa Clara Valley, 1999. Fellow Am. Acad. Kinesiology and Phys. Edn. Office: San Jose State U 1 Washington Sq San Jose CA 95192-0001

BAIN, TRAVIS WHITSETT, II, manufacturing and retail executive; b. San Antonio, Mar. 4, 1934; s. Travis Whitsett and Zelma Gladys (Middleton) B.; m. Karlen Jo Bruner, May 30, 1957; children: Travis W. III, James Henry III. B in Chem. Engring., U. Tex., 1956; MBA, Harvard U., 1958. Mfg. supt. Tex. Instruments, Dallas, 1958-61; sr. assoc. McKinsey and Co., L.A. and Chgo., 1961-65; exec. v.p., COO Trend Line Corp., Jackson, Miss., 1965-81; pres., CEO W.E. Walker Stores, Inc., Jackson, 1981-86, Sunbelt Nursery Group, Inc., Ft. Worth, 1986-87; investor, cons. Bain Assocs., Ft. Worth, 1987-88; pres. Jarman Shoe Co. div. Genesco Inc., Nashville, 1988-92, Bain Enterprises, Inc. dba Sandler Pools, Plano, Tex., 1993—; bd. dirs. Atmos Energy Corp., Dallas, 1988—, Tex. Commerce Bank, Ft. Worth, 1986-88, Delta Industries, Inc., Jackson, 1984—; chmn. bd. dirs. Master Pools Guild, 1997—; pres. Dallas Exec. Assn., 1998—. Bd. dirs. New Stage Theatre, Jackson, 1980-86, Boy Scouts Am., Ft. Worth, 1986-88, Miss. Ballet Internat., Jackson, 1984-86; bd. dirs., exec. com. Nashville Ballet, 1989-92; mem. placement coun. Owen Sch. Mgmt. Vanderbilt U., Nashville, 1984-92; mem. adv. bd. CBA Found. U. Tex., Austin, 1987—. Republican. Presbyterian. Avocations: gardening, tennis, jogging, travel, scuba diving. Office: Bain Enterprises Inc 2001 Coit Rd Ste 130 Plano TX 75075-3728

BAIN, WILLIAM DONALD, JR., lawyer, chemical company executive; b. Rochelle, Ill., July 1, 1925; s. William Donald and Gretchen (Kittler) B.; m. Pauline Thomas, Jan. 14, 1950 (dec. Nov. 1991); children: Elizabeth Kittler Zibart, Anne Alexander, Nancy Hemenway Coté; m. Barrie Feighner, Mar. 30, 1996. BS in Econs, U. Pa., 1947; JD, Washington and Lee U., 1949. Bar: S.C. 1952. Mortgage loan field rep. Travelers Ins. Co., Hartford, Conn., Cleve.; Orlando, Fla., 1949-51; with Moreland-McKesson Chem. Co., Spartanburg, S.C., 1951-83, pres., 1965-83, also dir.; v.p., gen. mgr. McKesson Chem. Corp., San Francisco, 1982-84; bd. dirs. Cote Color & Chem. Co., Inc., Spartan Comms. Corp., Tietex Corp.; co-founder, bd. dirs. Affiliated Chem. Group, Bermuda; ptnr. Triple B Ptnrs. Mem. Spartanburg Sch. Bd., 1958-72, chmn., 1963-72; trustee Converse Coll., 1968-92, chmn. bd., 1985-92; chmn. alumni bd. Washington and Lee U., 1979-82; trustee Hollins (Va.) Coll., 1992—; bd. dirs. Mary Black Meml. Hosp., 1975—, chmn., 1980-82; trustee Mary Black Found., 1996—; trustee, former chmn. Spartanburg County Found.; mng. dir. Bain Found. With USAAC, 1943-45. Mem. S.C. Bar Assn., Rotary. Republican. Presbyterian.

BAIN, WILLIAM JAMES, JR., architect; b. Seattle, June 26, 1930; s. William James and Mildred Worline (Clark) B.; m. Nancy Sanford Hill, Sept. 21, 1957; children: David Hunter, Stephen Fraser (dec.), Mark Sanford, John Worthington. BArch, Cornell U., 1953. Lic. 1st class architect, Japan. Ptnr. NBBJ (formerly Naramore, Bain, Brady & Johanson), Seattle; lectr. U. Wash., Seattle, mem. affiliate program steering com. Coll. Architecture and Urban Planning, 1969-71; lectr. Wash. State U.; organizer founding bd. dirs. Pacific N.W. Bank. Prin. works include U. Wash. South Campus, U.S. Pavilion at Expo '74 Worlds Fair, Honolulu Mcpl. Bldg., Two Union Square High-Rise Office Bldg., Four Seasons Olympic Hotel and Sun Mountain Lodge, Bagley Wright Theater and Paramount Theater renovation, Saitama Prefecture Demonstration Housing, Japan, Pacific Place Retail Complex, others. Bd. dirs. Corp. Coun. for Arts, 1989—, Arboretum Found., 1971-74; bd. dirs. Downtown Seattle Assn., 1980—, 1st vice-chmn., 1990-91, chmn., 1991-92; bd. dirs. Seattle Symphony Orch., 1974-87, pres., 1977-79; mem. coun. Cornell U., 1987-91, 94—; mem. Seattle Pub. Libr. Citizen's Adv. Bd., 1997. With C.E., U.S. Army, 1953-55. Recipient Cert. of Achievement Port of Whittier, Alaska, 1955, Disting. Alumnus award Lakeside Sch., 1985. Fellow AIA (pres. Seattle chpt. 1969, chmn. N.W. regional student profl. fund 1971, pres. Wash. coun. 1974, co-commn. Seattle centennial yr., Seattle medal 1997), N.W. Regional Archtl. Found. (pres. 1975); mem. Royal Inst. Brit. Architects, Royal Archtl. Inst. Can., Seattle C. of C. (bd. dirs. 1980-83), Urban Land Inst., N.W. Real Estate Inst., N.W. Forum, Am. Arbitration Assn. (comml. panel 1975—), L'Ogive Soc., Seattle Athletic Club, Seattle Tennis Club, Rotary (bd. dirs. 1970-72, svc. found. bd. 1976-80), Lambda Alpha, Phi Delta Theta. Episcopalian. Clubs: Rainier, Wash. Athletic, Tennis (Seattle); University, Columbia Tower (founding bd. dirs.). Home: 2033 1st Ave Seattle WA 98121-2132 Office: NBBJ 111 S Jackson St Seattle WA 98104-2881

BAINBRIDGE, FREDERICK FREEMAN, III, architect; b. Charlottesville, Va., Sept. 15, 1927; s. Frederick Freeman and Cornelia Winston (Burnley) B.; m. Binki Baker, Jan. 6, 1948 (div. Nov. 1972); children—Burnley, Susan Winifred, Meriwether, Robin; m. Anna Bacon, Jan. 1976; 1 son, Nicholas Gordon. B.Arch., U. Va., 1950; M. Indsl. Design, Kansas City Art Inst., 1952. Asst. prof. Sch. Architecture Clemson (S.C.) U., 1952-55; asso. firm Toombs, Amisano & Wells (Architects), Atlanta, 1955-62; prin. firm Martin & Bainbridge, Atlanta, 1962-70, Bainbridge & Assos., 1970—; Southeastern project architect U. Ky. civil defense research project, 1964; vis. critic Ga. Inst. Tech., 1964-67. Chmn. archtl. rev. com. Atlanta Civic Design Commn., 1967—. Served with USNR, 1944-46. Recipient honor awards S. Atlantic Region AIA, 1964, 66, 68, 70; honor award prestressed Concrete Inst., 1967. Mem. AIA. Clubs: Fairington Golf and Tennis, Amelia Island Plantation; Farmington Country (Charlottesville, Va.). Home: Oldham Farm PO Box 317 Ivy VA 22945-0317 Office: 6795 Brandon Mill Rd NW Atlanta GA 30328-2028

BAINE, RICHARD JOSEPH, vocational rehabilitation counselor; b. Louisville, Mar. 19, 1944; s. Robert Parnell and Catherine Veronica (Maloney) B.; m. Elizabeth Amber Phair, Aug. 9, 1968; children: Kristin Elisabeth, Richard J. Jr., Catherine Anne, Patrick Harold. BA in History, Bellarmine Coll., 1966; MA in Am. History, St. Louis U., 1968; postgrad., U. Mo., Kansas City, 1975-77, Columbia Pacific U., 1994. Diplomate Am. Bd. Vocat. Experts (credentials com. 1990—); cert. Nat. Commn. Rehab. Counselors, Mo.; cert. Nat. Commn. Ins. Rehab. Specialists; cert. vocat. expert Social Security Adminstrn., R.R. Retirement and Disability Bd.; cert. vocat. cons. VA. Rehab. cons. Mo. Div. Vocat. Rehab., Kansas City, 1971-74, sr. counselor, 1974-77; rehab. cons. Vocat. Cons., Inc., Kansas City, 1974-77; dir. Phila. Office, Crawford Rehab. Svcs., Inc., 1977-81; dir. rehab. svcs. Hoover Rehab. Svc., Inc., King of Prussia, Pa., 1981-83; propr., dir. rehab. svcs. Mid Atlantic Rehab. Mgmt. Inc., Blue Bell, Pa., 1983—; instr. vocat. rehab. Upjohn Healthcare, Bala Cynwid, Pa., 1980-83; instr. rehab. Employers Ins. Wausau, 1979; mem. faculty Ins. Soc. Phila., 1985-93, instr. rehab., 1986—, mem. curriculum adv. coun., 1985—; faculty rehab. vocat. experts at seminar Pa. Bar Inst., 1995, social security disability practice lectr., 1996. Mo. del. White House Commn. on Disabled, 1975; mem. cmty. svc. coun. UpJohn Health Care Svcs., 1979-83; mem. vets. adv. com. Montgomery County Commrs., 1991-95; mem. Ctrl. Montgomery County All Vets. Coun., 1994—. With U.S. Army, 1968-70; mem. USAR, 1971-79. Mem. Nat. Rehab. Assn. (del. Gt. Plains regional conv. 1975), Nat. Rehab. Counselors Assn., Nat. Assn. Svc. Providers in Pvt. Rehab., Pa. Rehab. Assn. (past bd. dirs.), Pa. Rehab. Counselors Assn., Cath. War Vets., Vietnam Vets. Am. (del. Pa. coun. 1992-96, v.p., bd. dirs. chpt. 349 1991-94, chpt. pres. 1994-99, chmn. state econ. affairs com. 1995-96, chmn. state veteran's benefits com. 1998—, bd. dirs. region III 1995—, Pa. del. nat. conv. 1993, mem. nat. leadership conf. 1996, mem. vets. adv. com. for Congressman Jon Fox 1995-99, vets. adv. com. Congressman Joseph Hoeffle 1999—, Chpt. Vet. of Yr. award 1994), elected, mem. Natl. Bd. Dirs., ABVE, 1999—. Republican. Avocations: golf, hiking, swimming, travel. Office: Mid Atlantic Rehab Mgmt Inc 650 Sentry Pkwy Ste 1 Blue Bell PA 19422-2318

BAINER, PHILIP LA VERN, retired college president; b. Pomona, Kans., Aug. 10, 1931; s. Raymond and Ina Leona (Ward) B.; m. Jane Kristine Huhtala, July 1, 1967 (div.); children: Angela Dawn, Jeffrey Philip. A.B. in Biology, Ottawa U., 1953; M.S. in Biology, Kans. State Tchrs. Coll., 1957. Tchr. Turner High Sch., Kansas City, Kans., 1957-63; instr. Clatsop Community Coll., 1963-64, chmn. div. liberal arts, 1964-66, dean instrn., 1966-70, pres., 1970-90, ret., 1990. Pres. Columbia River Maritime Mus., Astoria, Oreg., 1977. Served with Signal Corps, U.S. Army, 1954-56. Mem. Astoria C. of C. Mem. Astoria C. of C. (bc. dirs. 1998-99). Republican. Mem. Brethren Ch. Home: 186 Kensington Ave Astoria OR 97103-6443

BAINES, ANDREW DEWITT, medical biochemist; b. July 17, 1934; m. Cornelia Johanna Van Erk, 1956; children: Nicole DeWitt, Nigel Eric. MD, U. Toronto, Can., 1959, PhD, 1965. Intern Toronto Western Hosp., 1959-60; fellowship Med. Rsch. Coun., 1960-63; rsch. fellow dept. medicine U. N.C., Chapel Hill, 1965-68; McLaughlin fellow dept. physiology Commissariat à l'Energie Atomique, Saclay, France, 1967-68; lectr. dept. path. chemistry U. Toronto, 1963-65, assoc. prof. dept. clin. biochemistry, 1968-73, grad. faculty, 1968—, prof. dept. clin. biochemistry, 1973—, chmn. dept. clin. biochemistry, 1988-95, vice dean edn. Faculty of Medicine, 1994—; out-patient staff Renal Clinic Toronto Western Hosp., 1970-72, Toronto Gen. Hosp., 1972-77; assoc. physician dept. medicine Toronto, 1972—; out-patient staff Hypertension Clinic Mt. Sinai Hosp., 1977-84, assoc. staff clin. biochemistry, 1978-84; sr. fellow Massey Coll., U. Toronto, 1982—; chmn. sci. coun. Kidney Found. Can., 1990-93, co-chair rsch. steering com., 1993-95; lectr. in field. Mem. editl. bd. Am. Jour. Physiology, 1993—, Clin. Biochemistry, 1994—; contbr. chpts. to books and over 72 articles to profl. jours. Recipient Bronze T award Toronto Athletics, 1957, Cybermedics award Can. Soc. Clin. Chemists, 1982, Med. award Kidney Found. Can., 1994, and numerous rsch. grants, 1978—. Fellow Royal Coll. Physicians and Surgeons Can.; mem. Am. Physiol. Soc., Am. Fedn. for Clin. Rsch., Am. Soc. Nephrology, Can. Soc. Nephrology, Can. Physiol. Soc., Can. Soc. for Clin. Investigation, Can. Hypertension Soc., Can. Soc. Clin. Chemists, Can. Acad. Clin. Chemists, Internat. Soc. Nephrology, Ont. Med. Assn., Can. Assn. Med. Biochemistry. Office: Cir Med Scis Bldg, 1 Kings Coll Rm 2113, Toronto, ON Canada M5S 1A1

BAINES, GWENDOLYN L., university office manager; b. Nashville, Aug. 7, 1943; d. Geneva Baines; 1 child, Rosita Delaine Baines Lee. Student, Tenn. State U., Nashville, 1961-63, 68-69. Sec. State Govt., Nashville, 1965-68, Kelly Svcs., N.Y.C., 1969-70; sec. Meharry Med. Coll., Nashville, 1970-73, office mgr., 1973-88; office asst. Manpower Svcs., Long Beach, Calif., 1988-91; office specialist Vanderbilt U., Nashville, 1992-96, adminstrv. asst., office mgr., 1996—; workshop presenter African-Am. Women on tour (AAWOT), Atlanta, Ga., 1998, Washington, 1999. Author: People in the Web of Life, 1978, 92, Sassy, Secure and Over Sixty, 1997; nat. one-woman show Sassy, Secure, and Over Sixty, debut Literary Cafe, Nat. Assoc. Black journalists meeting, Chgo., 1997; columnist Ask Gwendolyn Baines, 1989—. Recipient Certificate, African Am. Cultural Complex, Raleigh, N.C., 1997, NAACP, Nashville, 1979. Mem. Assn. Black Women Entrepreneurs. Baptist. Avocation: going to movies. Office: Nevada Pub Co PO Box 78246 Nashville TN 37207-8246

BAINES, HAROLD DOUGLASS, professional baseball player; b. St. Michaels, Md., Mar. 15, 1959; m. Marla Henry, Oct. 29, 1983; 4 children: Antoinette, Britni, Harold, Jr., and Courtney. With Chgo. White Sox, 1980-89, 96-97, Texas Rangers, 1989-90, Oakland Athletics, 1990-92, Balt. Orioles, 1993-95, 97—. Named to Am. League All-Star Teams, 1985, 86, 87, 89, 91; named Outfielder Am. League Sporting News All-Star Team, 1985, designated hitter, 1988-89, Sporting News Am. League Silver Slugger Team, 1989. Office: Balt Orioles Oriole Park at Camden Yards 333 W Camden St Baltimore MD 21201-2435*

BAINES, KEVIN HAYS, planetary scientist, astronomer; b. Norwalk, Conn., Feb. 11, 1954; s. Elliot A. and Martha Ellen (Ashcroft) B.; m. Jenine Bsharah, June 4, 1982; children: Emily Ansara, Christopher Lewis. BA, Amherst Coll., 1976; MA, Washington U., St. Louis, 1978, PhD, 1982. Resident rsch. assoc. NRC-JPL, Pasadena, Calif., 1982-84; rsch. scientist Jet Propulsion Lab. Calif. Tech. Inst., Pasadena, 1984—; co-investigator Galileo

Near-Infrared Mapping Spectrometer and Cassini Visual-Infrared Mapping Spectrometer expts. Contbr. articles to profl. jours. Flight dir. Aero Assn. Calif. Tech. Inst., 1986, treas., 1987—. Virgil I. Grissom Astronaut fellow Washington U., 1976-79. Mem. AAAS (planetary scis. divsn.). Republican. Achievements include research in determination of vertical cloud/haze structures of Uranus and Neptune; determination of methane and ortho/para hydrogen above averages in Uranus and Neptune; near-infrared imagery and analysis of Jupiter's cloud structure from the Galileo spacecraft; near-infrared imagery of Venus surface; role of asteroid-impact generated sulfuric gases on dinosaur extinctions. Avocations: flight instructor (FAA cert.), multi-engine and single-engine aircraft, airline transport and rotorcraft pilot, scuba diver (cert.). Home: 778 Forest Green Dr La Canada CA 91011

BAINES, RHUNELL (NELL BAINES), nurse; b. Eden, N.C., Feb. 1, 1929; d. Robert Moses and Ruby (Boone) Freeman; m. Lloyd B. Baines (dec.), Apr. 17, 1954; 1 child, Kenneth Orrin. Nursing asst. cert., Danville Meml. Hosp., 1947; cert. nurse asst., Rowan Tech. Coll., Salisbury, N.C., 1981; cert. in emergency care and pharmacology, Rowan Cabarrus Community Coll., Salisbury, 1982. CRNA, N.C., 1989. Nursing asst. Jolenes Nursing Home, Salisbury, N.C., Tricounty Vis. Nurses, Charlotte, N.C.; pvt. duty nurse N.C. Lutheran Home, Salisbury, N.C.; pvt. duty practical nurse Autumn Care Nursing Home, Salisbury, N.C.; pvt. duty nurse Rowan Meml. Hosp.; pres. Nursing Assistance Svcs., Salisbury, N.C., 1990—. Mem. Patient Helpers Club (chmn. hiring com., pres.). Home: 221 Dunham Ave Salisbury NC 28146-5817

BAINS, HARRISON MACKELLAR, JR., financial executive; b. Pasadena, Calif., July 8, 1943; s. Harrison MacKellar and Celeste Adele (Callahan) B.; m. Leslie E. Tawney, Mar. 7, 1970; children: Harrison MacKellar, III, Tawney Elizabeth. B.A., U. Redlands, 1964; M.B.A., U. Calif., Berkeley, 1966. Asst. v.p. Citibank N.A., 1968-72; asst. treas. Richardson-Merrell Inc., 1972-76; v.p. treas. Nabisco Inc., East Hanover, N.J., 1976-81; sr. v.p., treas. Nabisco Brands, Inc., East Hanover, N.J., 1981-85; v.p., treas. RJR Nabisco, Inc., Winston-Salem, N.C., 1985-87; sr. v.p. Chase Manhattan Bank, N.Y.C., 1987-88; v.p., treas. Bristol-Myers Squibb Co., N.Y.C., 1988—. Mem. Fin. Execs. Inst., Food Safety Council (treas. 1980—). Office: Bristol-Myers Squibb Co 345 Park Ave New York NY 10022-6000

BAINS, LEE EDMUNDSON, state official; b. Birmingham, Ala., June 18, 1912; s. Herman Lipsey and Myrtle (Edmundson) B.; m. Ruel Eneida Burton, Jan. 1, 1938; children: Sandra Anita (Mrs. Henry Barnard Hardegree), Myrtle Lee, Lee Edmundson. Student, Birmingham So. Coll., 1930-31; B.S., U. Ala., 1934, J.D., 1936. Bar: Ala. 1936, U.S. Supreme Ct 1936; diplomate: Nat. Coll. Advocacy. Practiced in Bessemer, 1936-94, city atty., 1950-58; instr. Birmingham Sch. Law, 1937-41; faculty Nat. War Coll., 1960; atty. for Ala. Power Co., South Central Bell Telephone Co., Phillips Petroleum Co., AmSouth Bank; apptd. by gov. as spl. asst. atty. gen. State Ala., 1980—. Contbr. article to profl. jour.; Author: Basic Legal Skills, 1976. Pres. Bessemer Bd. EDn., 1955-58, Bessemer YMCA, 1961; advisor Bd. Family Ct., Jefferson County, 1966-74; chmn. fin. com. Nat. Vets. Day for Birmingham, 1973; alt. del. Dem. Nat. Conv., 1941; tchr. men's Bible class First United Meth. Ch., 1966-93; tchr. Bible classes Canterbury Meth. Ch., Mountain Brook, 1994—. Rear adm. USNR, 1930-72, WWII. Fellow Am. Coll. Trial Lawyers; mem. ABA (vice chmn. environ. law sect. 1979), ATLA, Ala. Assn. Trial Lawyers, Ala. Bar Assn. (chmn. unauthorized practice com. 1977-79, mem. mil. law com.), Bessemer Bar Assn. (pres. 1983-84), Birmingham Bar Assn., Res. Officers Assn., Naval Res. Assn., Soc. Colonial Wars (state gov. 1972-73, corr. sec. 1976-80), SAR (pres. Ala.), Kiwanis, Birmingham Ski Club, Downtown Club, The Club, Phi Gamma Delta, Beta Gamma Sigma. Winner numerous swimming, jogging, skiing and figure skating awards, Presdl. sports award. Home: Fair Haven 1624 Montclair Rd Birmingham AL 35210 Office: 1813 3rd Ave N Bessemer AL 35020-4963 *If your goal is happiness, you most likely will accomplish little, and not be happy in your pursuit. If your objective is the pursuit of excellence - doing the very best you can with the task upon which you are working now - then there is a probability of producing good and, perhaps, an excellent work product, and finding happiness as an unsought reward. The pursuit of happiness is a political phrase that represents tolerance and the freedom to pursue individual goals. As a personal objective it will not lead to worthwhile achievement. To the contrary, the pursuit of excellence will lead to the highest and best accomplishments, and happiness will come as an unsought-for reward.*

BAINS, LESLIE ELIZABETH, banker; b. Glen Ridge, N.J., July 28, 1943; d. Pliny Otto and Dorothy Ethel (Keeley) Tawney; m. Harrison Mackellar Bains Jr.; Harrison III, Tawney Elizabeth. BA, Am. U., 1965. Asst. treas. Citicorp, N.Y.C., 1965-73; v.p. Mfrs. Hanover, N.Y.C., 1973-80; v.p., divsn. exec. Chase Manhattan Bank, N.Y.C., 1980-86, v.p., group exec., 1986-87, sr. v.p. group exec., 1987-91; mng. dir. Citibank, N.Y.C., 1991-93; exec. v.p. Republic Nat. Bank, N.Y.C., 1993—; chair fin. com. Interplast, 1991, also bd. dirs. Chmn. Ednl. Cable Consortium, Summit, N.J., 1987-91; exec. com., bd. visitors Kogod Sch. Bus., Am. U., 1992—; trustee Am. U., 1994—; chair exec. com., bd. dirs. Jr. Achievement, N.Y.C., 1996—, Duke U. Inst. for Pub. Policy; mem. Coun. Fgn. Rels., 1991—; mem. exec. com. bd. visitors Sch. Pub. Policy, Duke U. Named Achiever of Yr. YWCA, 1985, One of Top 100 Women in Corp. Am., Bus. Month., 1989. Mem. Am. Bankers Assn. (bd. dirs. pvt. banking coun.), Fin. Women Internat. (treas. 1981-83, v.p. 1983-84, pres. 1984-85, vice chmn. Edn. Found. 1980-81), Fin. Women's Assn., Women and Founds. Office: Republic Nat Bank 452 5th Ave New York NY 10018-2706*

BAINTON, DONALD J., diversified manufacturing company executive; b. N.Y.C., May 3, 1931; s. William Lewis and Mildred J. (Dunne) B.; m. Aileen M. Demoulins, July 10, 1954; children—Kathryn C., Stephen L., Elizabeth A., William D. BA, Columbia U., 1952, postgrad., 1960. With The Continental Group, Inc., 1954-83, gen. mgr. prodn. planning, 1967-68, gen. mgr. mfg. Eastern divsn., 1968-73, gen. mgr. Pacific divsn., 1973-74, gen. mgr. Eastern divsn., 1974-75; v.p., gen. mgr. ops. U.S. Metal, 1975-76; exec. v.p., gen. mgr. CCC-USA, 1976-78, corp. exec. v.p., pres. diversified ops., 1978-79; pres. Continental Can Co., 1979-81; pres. Continental Packaging, 1981-83, exec. v.p., operating officer parent co., bd. dirs., 1979-83; chmn., CEO, dir. Viatech Inc., Syosset, N.Y., 1983-92; chmn., CEO Continental Can Co., Inc., Boca Raton, Fla., 1992—; bd. dirs. Dixie Union, Ferembal S.A., Continental Plastic Containers, Complete Cable, Inc. Bd. dirs. Columbia Coll. With USN, 1952-54, Korea. Mem. Inst. Applied Econs. (dir.), Milbrook Country Club (Greenwich, Conn.), Winged Foot Club (Mamaroneck, N.Y.), Union League Club (N.Y.C.), Royal Palm Yacht and Country Club (Boca Raton, Fla.). Republican. Roman Catholic. Office: Sanctuary Tower 4400 N Federal Hwy Ste 125 Boca Raton FL 33431-5180

BAINTON, DOROTHY FORD, pathology educator, researcher; b. Magnolia, Miss., June 18, 1933; d. Aubrey Ratcliff and Leta (Brumfield) Ford; m. Cedric R. Bainton, Nov. 28, 1959; children: Roland J., Bruce G., James H. BS, Millsaps Coll., 1955; MD, Tulane U. Sch. of Medicine, 1958; MS, U. Calif., San Francisco, 1966. Postdoctoral rsch. fellow U. Calif., San Francisco, 1963-66, postdoctoral rsch. pathologist, 1966-69, asst. prof. pathology, 1969-75, assoc. prof., 1975-81, prof. pathology, 1981—, chair pathology, 1987-94, vice chancellor acad. affairs, 1994—; mem. Inst. of Medicine, NAS, 1990—. NIH grantee, 1978—. Fellow AAAS, Am. Acad. Arts & Scis.; mem. FASEB (bd. dirs.), Am. Soc. for Cell Biology, Am. Soc. Hematology, Am. Soc. Histochemists and Cytochemists, Am. Assn. of Pathologists. Democrat. Mem. Soc. of Friends. Office: Office of Acad Affairs U Calif San Francisco Med Scis Bldg Rm 115 San Francisco CA 94143-0400

BAINTON, J(OHN) JOSEPH, lawyer; b. Long Branch, N.J., May 21, 1947; s. Robert L. and Elizabeth (Dowling) B.; 1 child, John Joseph Jr. BA, Kenyon Coll., 1969; JD, Rutgers U., Newark, 1973. Bar: N.Y. 1973. Assoc. Burke & Burke, N.Y.C., 1972-76; ptnr. Reboul, MacMurray, Hewitt, Maynard & Kristol, N.Y.C., 1976-89, Shea & Gould, N.Y.C., 1989-90, Whitman & Ransom, N.Y.C., 1991-92, Ross & Hardies, N.Y.C., 1993-98, Bainton McCarthy & Siegel, LLC, N.Y.C., 1998—. Contbr. articles to legal jours. Mediator Mandatory Mediation Program So. Dist. N.Y. Mem. U.S. Trademark Assn. (editor 1976), Internat. Anticounterfeiting Coalition (bd. dirs. 1986-92), Products Liability Adv. Coun., Nat. Inst. Trial Advocacy (faculty). Avocation: yacht racing. Office: Bainton McCarthy & Siegel LLC 130 E 35th St New York NY 10016-3815

BAINUM, PETER MONTGOMERY, aerospace engineer, consultant; b. St. Petersburg, Fla., Feb. 4, 1938; s. Charles J. Bainum and Mildred (Trincher) Salyer; m. Carmen Cecilia Perez, Sept. 7, 1968; 1 child, David P. BS, Tex. A&M U., 1959; SM, MIT, 1960; PhD, Cath. U., 1967. Asst. engr. MIT Naval Supersonic Lab., Cambridge, Mass., 1959-60; sr. engr. Martin Co., Orlando, Fla., 1960-62; staff engr. IBM Fed. Systems Div., Bethesda, Md., 1962-65; sr. staff, aerospace engr., cons. Johns Hopkins U. Applied Physics Lab., Laurel, Md., 1965-69, 69-72; assoc. prof. Howard U., Washington, 1969-73, prof., 1973-90, disting. prof., 1990—; v.p. rsch., cons. WHF & Assocs., Bethesda, 1977-86; mem. NASA/PSN Tether Applications Simulation Working Group, 1987; lectr. various internat. univs., rsch. ctrs. and confs.; hon. vis. prof. Universidad Francisco Marroquin, Guatemala, 1991. Editor, co-editor 16 books, 1981-98; author tech. reports and conf. procs.; contbr. numerous articles to profl. jours. Judge, D.C. Sci. Fair, Washington, 1973. Recipient Ralph R. Teetor award Soc. Automotive Engrs., 1971. Fellow AIAA (capital sect. cmty. action com. 1975-76, astrodynamics com. 3 terms, space transp. com. 1989-93), AAAS, Am. Astronautical Soc. (v.p. internat. 1986-96, bd. dirs. 1996—, Brouwer award 1990), Brit. Interplanetary Soc.; mem. Internat. Acad. Astronautics, Internat. Astronautical Fedn. (materials and structures com. 1992—), Sigma Xi. Office: Howard Univ Dept of Mechanical Engr Washington DC 20059 *With a doctoral degree comes significant responsibilities: to search out truth scientifically, to safeguard it, and to apply it to the shaping of both private and public life.*

BAINUM, STEWART WILLIAM, JR., health care and lodging company executive; b. Takoma Park, Md., Mar. 25, 1946; s. Stewart William Sr. and Jane Loretta (Goyne) B.; m. Sandra Ann Yarish, Sept. 26, 1987. BA, Pacific Union Coll., 1968; MBA, UCLA, 1970; postgrad. theology, Andrews U., 1971-72. V.p. Manor Care Inc., Silver Spring, Md., 1973-79, vice chmn., 1982-87; chmn., chief exec. officer HCR Manor Care Inc., Silver Spring, Md., 1987—, also bd. dirs.; mem. Md. Ho. of Dels., Annapolis, 1979-83, Md. State Senate, Annapolis, 1983-87. Bd. dirs. Invest in Am., Washington, 1987; co-chmn. Dem. Forum, Montgomery County, Md., 1987; alt. del. Dem. Nat. Conv., San Francisco, 1984. Named Outstanding State Ofcl. of Yr., Young Democrats of Md., 1981; recipient Cert. of Merit, Common Cause of Md., Annapolis, 1982, 85, Torch of Liberty award Anti-Defamation League, Washington region, 1984. Avocations: tennis, physical fitness, reading. Office: NCR Manor Care Inc 7361 Calhoun Pl Ste 300 Rockville MD 20855 Also: 4 Seasons Nursing Ctrs 10750 Columbia Pike Silver Spring MD 20901-4427*

BAIOCCO, SHARON A., college administrator; b. Buffalo, N.Y., Dec. 31, 1943; d. Kenneth C. and Beatrice R. (Lanich) Quackenbush; m. John D. Baiocco, June 4, 1966; children: Lara L., Deanna M. BA, St. Lawrence U., 1965; EdM, SUNY, Buffalo, 1971, PhD, 1985. Cert. tchr. secondary English, N.Y. Reporter UPI, Buffalo, 1965, 66; tchr. Orchard Park (N.Y.) H.S., 1966-67; instr. Erie C.C., Williamsville, N.Y., 1976-78; asst. prof. to assoc. prof. D'Youville Coll., Buffalo, 1980-95, prof. English, chair dept. liberal arts, 1996-97; asst. dean arts and scis. Jacksonville (Fla.) U., 1997—.

BAIR, BRUCE B., lawyer; b. St. Paul, May 26, 1928; s. Bruce B. and Emma N. (Stone) B.; m. Jane Lawler, July 19, 1952; children: Mary Jane, Thomas, Susan, Barbara, Patricia, James, Joan, Bruce, Jeffrey. BS, U. N.D., 1950, JD, 1952. Bar: N.D. 1952, U.S. Dist. Ct. N.D. 1955, U.S. Ct. Appeals (8th cir.) 1971, U.S. Supreme Ct. 1974. Assoc. Lord and Ulmer, Mandan, N.D., 1955-57; ptnr. Bair, Bair & Garrity and predecessors, Mandan, 1957—; spl. asst. atty. gen. State of N.D., 1967—; chmn. bd. Bank of Tioga, 1984—, also dir. Rep. precinct committeeman, 1956-70, chmn. Morton County Rep. Com., 1958-62, mem. N.D. Rep. State Cen. Com., 1962-67; pres. sch. bd. St. Joseph's Cath. Ch., 1967-68; mem. bd. Mandan Pub. Sch. Dist. #1, 1971-77; mem. exec. com. Internat. Assn. Milk Control Agys., 1970—; mem. bd. regents U. Mary, Bismarck, N.D., 1984—. Served to 1st lt. JAG Corps USAF, 1952-55. Fellow Am. Coll. of Trust and Estate Counsel; mem. ABA, N.D. Bar Assn., Big Muddy Bar Assn., Am. Legion, Rotary, Elks. Roman Catholic. Home: 901 3rd St NW Mandan ND 58554-2537 Office: 210 1st St NW Mandan ND 58554-3115

BAIR, MYRNA LYNN, state senator; b. Huntington, W.Va., Oct. 26, 1940; d. Charles Thomas and Velma Elvera (Schoenlein) North; B.S. in Chemistry, U. Cin., 1962; Ph.D., U. Wis., 1968, DHL (hon.) WilsonColl.; m. Thomas Irvin Bair, Mar. 12, 1966; children—Thomas Irvin, Catherine Lynn. Asst. prof. chemistry Beaver Coll., Glenside, Pa., 1966-70; instr. chemistry U. Del., 1974-76, asst. prof. edn., 1977-79; asst. dir. pub. info. Del. Energy Office, Wilmington, 1978-79; mem. Del. Senate, 1981—; past pres. women's network Nat. Conf. of State Legislatures; sr. mgmt. advisor Coll. Urban Affairs and Pub. Policy, dir. women's leadership tng. program, 1989—. Contbr. articles to sci. jour. Pres. Women's Leadership Ctr. Del.; mem. Nat. Republican Com. Recipient Freshman award Chem. Rubber Co., 1959; DuPont Co. Teaching award, 1963, Pres.'s award Jr. League, 1988; NSF fellow, 1964-66. Mem. AAUW, Internat. Women's Forum (pres. Del. chpt.), Wilmington Rep. Women's Club, Phi Beta Kappa, Iota Sigma Pi, Alpha Lambda Delta. Methodist. Office: Legislative Hall State Capital Bldg Dover DE 19903*

BAIR, ROBERT RIPPEL, lawyer; b. New London, Conn., Nov. 24, 1925; s. Bruce Thomas and Alga (Smith) B.; m. Dorothy Burke Dorsey, June 1, 1957; c. Student, Johns Hopkins U., 1943; AB summa cum laude, Brown U., 1947; JD, Harvard U., 1950. Law clk. to cir. judge U.S. Ct. Appeals (4th cir.), 1950-51; atty. Bur. Legis. Reference, Md. Gen. Assembly, Annapolis, 1951-52; assoc. Venable, Baetjer and Howard, Balt., 1951-59, ptnr., 1960-89, sr. of counsel, 1990—; asst. U.S. atty. U.S. Atty.'s Office, Balt., 1954-56; lectr. estate and tax planning Renaissance Inst., Coll. Notre Dame, 1991—. Contbr. articles to profl. jours. Chmn. Balt. City Zoning Com., 1958-61; gen. counsel Mayor's Balt. City Housing Code Com., 1962-64. Lt. SC USNR, 1946-66. Fellow Am. Coll. Trust and Estate Counsel, Md. Bar Found.; mem. ABA, Am. Judicature Soc., Md. State Bar Assn. (sec. 1965-71), Balt. City Bar Assn., Supreme Ct. Hist. Soc., Wednesday Law Club. Avocations: piano, oil and water color painting, tennis, golf, skiing. E-mail: rbair@venable.com. Office: Venable Baetjer & Howard 1800 Merc Bank & Trust Bldg 2 Hopkins Plz Ste 2100 Baltimore MD 21201-2982

BAIR, ROYDEN STANLEY, architect; b. New Rochelle, N.Y., Jan. 21, 1924; s. Roy S. and Ruth Irene (Farmer) B.; m. Margaret Davis Powell, Sept. 7, 1946 (dec. July 1972); children: Katherine, David, Laurence (dec.), Andrew, Matthew; m. Martha Ann Cooper, July 7, 1973. BS in Civil Engring., Purdue U., 1947; BArch, MIT, 1950. Registered architect, Tex, Fla.; registered profl. engr., Tex. Construction adminstrn. Skidmore, Owings & Merrill, Chgo., 1950-53; draftsman J.N. MacCammon, Dallas, 1953-56; sr. assoc. Harrell & Hamilton, Dallas, 1956-67; sr. architect Lloyd Morgan Jones, Houston, 1967-68; architect R.S. Bair, Architects, Houston, 1969-95; ptnr. Turner & Bair Architects, Houston, 1996—. Capt. U.S. Army, 1942-46, 51-53. Mem. AIA (fellowship 1988, pres. Houston chpt. 1982), Construction Specifications Inst. (nat. pres. 1979, fellowship 1972), Construction Scis. Rsch. Found. (v.p. 1980-87), Tex. Soc. Architects. Home: 9573 Doliver Dr Houston TX 77063-1010 Office: Turner & Bair Architects 303 Stafford St Ste 100 Houston TX 77079-2345

BAIR, WILLIAM ALOIS, engineer; b. Bklyn., Aug. 13, 1931; s. Henry Auchu and Anna Margaret (Zidar) B.; m. Patricia Anne Doyle, July 23, 1955; children: William A. Jr., Joseph M. Student, Pa. State U., 1949-51; BS in Engring., U.S. Naval Acad., 1955; BS in Civil Engring., Rensselaer Poly. Inst., 1958; MS in Nuclear Engring., U. Calif., 1966; grad. advanced mgmt. program, Wharton Sch., 1987. Registered profl. engr., N.Y., N.J., Pa., Conn., Md., Del., Va., S.C., Ga., D.C. Commd. ensign USN, 1955, advanced through grades to comdr., 1969; with USN Civil Engr. Corps, 1955-77; ret. USN, 1977; project mgr. Raytheon Engrs. and Constructors Inc., Princeton, N.Y., 1977-85, 88-96; dir. program planning and devel. Ebasco Svcs. Inc., N.Y.C., 1985-88; pres. Bair Engring. Cons., 1996—; appointed mem. spl. 3 man NATO tech. com. to evaluate effectiveness of European Airfield Phys. Protection Program to counter damage from attack by Warsaw Pact Nations, 1972. Author: Helium 3 Neutron Spectrometer, 1966; contbr. articles to profl. jours. Scoutmaster Boy Scouts Am., Rockville, Md., 1969-70; coun. mem. European br., CAsteau, Belgium, 1971-75. Decorated Legion of Merit, Bronze Star with V; Vietnamese Cross of Gallantry, Medal of Honor 1st class, Joint Svc. Commendation medal. Mem. ASCE, VFW, Am. Nuclear Soc., Soc. Am. Mil. Engrs., Nat. Contract. Mgmt. Assn., Am. Legion. Republican. Roman Catholic. Achievements include research and innovative process/procedures for decontamination and demolition of radioactive structures. Home and Office: Bair Engring Cons 21 Lorrie Ln Princeton Junction NJ 08550-5112

BAIR, WILLIAM J., radiation biologist; b. Jackson, Mich., July 14, 1924; s. William J. and Mona J. (Gamble) B.; m. Barbara Joan Sites, Feb. 16, 1952; children: William J., Michael Braden, Andrew Emil. B.A. in chemistry, Ohio Wesleyan U., 1949; Ph.D. in Radiation Biology, U. Rochester, 1954. NRC-AEC fellow U. Rochester, 1949-50, research asso. radiation biology, 1950-54; biol. scientist Hanford Labs. of Gen. Electric Co., Richland, Wash., 1954-56, mgr. inhalation toxicology sect., biology dept., 1956-65; mgr. inhalation toxicology sect., biology dept. Battelle Meml. Inst., 1965-68; mgr. biology dept. Pacific Northwest Labs., Richland, Wash., 1968-74, dir. life scis. program, 1973-75, mgr. biomed. and environ. research program, 1975-76, mgr. environ. health and safety research program, 1976-86, mgr. life scis. ctr., 1986-93, sr. advisor health protection rsch., 1993—; demonstrated toxicology of plutonium and carcinogenisis of radioactive particles in lung; lectr. radiation biology Joint Ctr. Grad. Study, Richland, 1955-75; cons. to adv. com. on reactor safeguards Nuclear Regulatory Commn., 1971-87; mem. several coms. on plutonium toxicology; mem. subcom. inhalation hazards, com. pathologic effects atomic radiation NAS, 1957-64, mem. ad hoc com. on hot particles of subcom. biol. effects ionizing radiation NAS-NRC, 1974-76, vice chmn. com. on biol. effects of ionizing radiation, BEIR IV Alpha radiation, 1985-88, mem. battlefield radiation exposure com., 1997-99; chmn. task force on biol. effects of inhaled particles Internat. Commn. on Radiol. Protection, 1970-79, mem. com. 2 on permissible dose for internal radiation, 1973-93, chmn. task group on respiratory tract models, 1984-93; mem. Nat. Coun. on Radiation Protection and Measurements, 1974-92, hon. mem., 1992, bd. dirs., mem. com. of radionuclides on maximum permissible concentration of occupl. and nonoccupl. exposure, 1970-74, mem. com. basic radiation protection criteria, 1975-92, chmn. ad hoc com. on hot particles, 1974, chmn. ad hoc com. internal emitter activities, 1976-77, mem. com. on internal emitter stds., 1977-92; mem. radiation adv. com. and sci. adv. bd. EPA, 1993-99. Author 200 books, articles, reports, chpts. in books. With AUS, 1943-46. Decorated Bronze Star; recipient E.O. Lawrence Meml. award AEC, 1970, cert. of appreciation AEC, 1975, Alumni Disting. Achievement citation Ohio Wesleyan U., 1986. Fellow AAAS, Health Physics Soc. (bd. dirs. 1970-73, 83-86, pres. elect 1983-84, pres. 1984-85, Disting. Sci. Achievement award 1991, Herbert H. Parker award Columbia chpt. 1998); mem. Radiation Rsch. Soc., Nat. Coun. Radiation Protection measurement (hon., Lauriston S. Taylor lectr. 1997), Soc. Exptl. Biology and Medicine (vice chmn. N.W. chpt. 1967-70, 74-75), Sigma Xi, Kiwanis (dir.). Home: 102 Somerset St Richland WA 99352-1966 Office: Battelle Pacific NW Labs PO Box 999 Richland WA 99352-0999

BAIRD, ALAN C., screenwriter; b. Waterville, Maine, Jan. 5, 1951; s. Chester A. and Beverly E. B. BA, Mich. State U., 1973. Pres. Souterrain Teeshirts, Nice, France, 1977-78; page NBC, N.Y.C., 1979-80; producer, dir. Random Prodns., Hollywood, Calif., 1981; writer, producer Preview STV, N.Y.C., 1982-83, Sta. KCOP-TV, Hollywood, 1983-84; writer Vidiom Prodns., Hollywood, 1985-95; screenwriter, 1995—. Author: ATS Operations, 1976, Writes of Passage, 1992, 9TimeZones.com, 1999; prodr. TV script Live at the Palomino, 1981; designer Screenwright Screenplay Formatting Software, 1985; writer TV scripts Night Court, 1986, 20/60, 1986, Golden Girls, 1986, Family Ties, 1986, Max Headroom, 1987, Dave's World, 1993, movie scripts Trading Up, 1988, Merlinsky, 1989, Eleven Thousand Virgins, 1994, The Fall in Budapest, 1997; play script Twisted Pair, 1998. Crisis counselor San Francisco Suicide Prevention, 1975; prodn. asst. March of Dimes Telethon, Hollywood, 1985; escort, host, vol. Verdugo Hills Hosp., 1994-96. Recipient Harvard Book prize Harvard U., Cambridge, Mass., 1969. Avocations: flying, running, scuba diving, parachuting, competitive driving.

BAIRD, BRIAN N., congressman; b. Chama, N.Mex., Mar. 7, 1956; m. Mary Baird; 2 stepchildren. BS, U. Utah, 1977; MS, U. Wyo., 1980, PhD, 1984. Mem. faculty dept. psychology Pacific Luth. U., 1986—; mem. 106th Congress from 3d Wash. dist., 1999—; mem. transp. and infrastructure and small bus. coms.; cons. clin. psychologist St. Charles Med. Ctr., 1994-96. Mem. NOW, APA, Wash. State Psychol. Assn., Amnesty Internat. Address: 1721 Longworth Washington DC 20515-4703*

BAIRD, BRUCE ALLEN, lawyer; b. Cin., Mar. 26, 1948; s. William Wendell and Audrey (Geignetter) B.; m. Erica Borden, July 27, 1975 (div. 1993); 1 child, Jessica; m. Nicolette Adair Heidepriem, Sept. 17, 1993; 1 child, William. BA, Cornell U., 1970; JD, NYU, 1975. Spl. asst. to dep. atty. gen. U.S. Dept. Justice, Washington, 1975-76; law clk. to presiding judge U.S. Ct. Appeals (2d cir.), Brattleboro, Vt. and N.Y.C., 1976-77; assoc. Davis, Polk & Wardwell, N.Y.C., 1977-80; asst. U.S. atty. U.S. Attys. Office (so. dist.) N.Y., N.Y.C., 1980-86, dep. chief criminal div., 1986-87, chief narcotics unit, 1987, chief securities and commodities frauds unit, 1987-89; of counsel Covington & Burling, Washington, 1989-91, ptnr., 1991—. Editor in chief NYU Law Rev., 1974-75. Mem. ABA (co-chair securities and commodities fraud subcom. of white collar crime com. of criminal justice sect. 1994—), N.Y. State Bar Assn. (profl. jud. ethics com. 1982-89), Assn. of Bar of City of N.Y. (profl. jud. ethics com. 1979-82, 86-89), Fed. Bar Council, D.C. Bar Assn. Republican. Presbyterian. Home: 5404 Edgemoor Ln Bethesda MD 20814-1326

BAIRD, CHARLES BRUCE, lawyer, consultant; b. DeLand, Fla., Apr. 18, 1935; s. James Turner and Ethelyn Isabelle (Williams) B.; m. Barbara Ann Fabian, June 6, 1959 (div. Dec. 1979); children: C. Bruce Jr., Robert Arthur, Bryan James; m. Byung-Ran Cho, May 23, 1982; children: Merah-Iris, Haerah Violet. BSME, U. Miami, 1958; postgrad UCLA, 1962-64; MBA, Calif. State U., 1966; JD, Am. U., 1971. Bar: Va. 1971, U.S. Dist. Ct. (ea. dist.) Va. 1971, D.C. 1973, U.S. Dist. Ct. D.C. 1973, U.S. Ct. Appeals (4th cir.) 1974, U.S. Supreme Ct. 1975. Rsch. engr. Naval Ordnance Lab., Corona, Calif., 1961-67; aerospace engr. Naval Air Systems Command, Washington, 1967-69; cons. engr. Bird Engring. Rsch. Assts., Vienna, Va., 1969-71; prof. Def. Systems Mgmt. Coll., Ft. Belvoir, Va., 1982; spl. asst. for policy compliance USIA Voice of Am., Washington, 1983-84; cons. Booz, Allen & Hamilton, Inc., Bethesda, 1975-82, IBM, Bethesda, Md., 1984, Logistics Mgmt. Inst., McLean, Va., 1986-98; adj. prof. Fla. Inst. Tech., 1988. Contbr. articles to profl. jours. Inventor computer-based communications systems for the gravely handicapped. Bd. govs. Sch. Engring. U. Miami, 1957; trustee Galilee United Meth. Ch., Arlington, Va., 1983-87. Mem. ATLA, Internet Soc., Fed. Comm. Bar Assn., United We Stand Am. (founding mem.), Sigma Alpha Epsilon. Republican. Home and Office: 5396 Gainsborough Dr Fairfax VA 22032-2744

BAIRD, CHARLES F., state supreme court justice; b. Texas, Mar. 3, 1955; m. Elizabeth Margaret Garcia Baird. Student, Kilgore Jr. Coll., 1973-74; BBA, U. Tex., 1976; student, Georgetown U., 1976-77; graduated, So. Tex. Coll. of Law, 1980; M of Laws in the Judicial Process, U. Va. Law Sch., 1995. Pvt. practice Houston, 1980-90; judge Tex. Ct. Criminal Appeals, Austin, 1990—. Contbr. articles to profl. jours. Regional adv. com. Am. Acad. Jud. Edn.; mem. Austin Rape Crisis Ctr. Adv. Bd., St. Luke United Meth. Ch. (v.p., trustee); co-chair implementation com. Tex. Supreme Ct.'s Gender Bias Task Force. Recipient So. Tex. Coll. Law Disting. Alumnus award, 1993, Harris County Dems. State Jud. award, 1992. Mem. State Bar of Tex. (past mem. ct. cost, efficiency and delay com., past mem. continuing legal edn. com.), Tex. Bar Found., State Bar Coll., Travis County Bar Assn. Methodist. Office: Tex Ct Criminal Appeals PO Box 12248 Capitol Sta Austin TX 78711-2308 Office: Tex Ct Criminal Appeals Supreme Court Bldg 201 W 14th St Austin TX 78701-1614*

BAIRD, CHARLES FITZ, retired mining and metals company executive; b. Southampton, N.Y., Sept. 4, 1922; s. George White and Julia (Fitz) B.; m. Norma Adele White, Sept. 13, 1947; children: Susan Baird Creyke, Stephen White, Charles Fitz, Nancy Baird Harwood. AB, Middlebury (Vt.) Coll., 1944; grad., Advanced Mgmt. Program, Harvard, 1960; LLD (hon.), Bucknell U., 1976. With Standard Oil Co., N.J., 1948-65; dep. European fin. rep. Standard Oil Co., London, 1955-58; asst. treas. Standard Oil Co., 1958-62; dir. Esso Standard SA Française, 1962-65; asst. sec. of navy (fin. mgmt.),

1966-67, undersec. of navy, 1967-69; v.p. fin. Inco Ltd., 1969-72, sr. v.p., 1972-76, vice-chmn., 1976-77, pres., 1977-80, chmn., CEO, 1980-87; chmn. CNA Corp., 1992-97; past trustee Mgmt. Logistics Inst.; mem. Pres.'s Commn. on Marine Sci., Engring. and Resources, 1967-69, Nat. Adv. Commn. on Ocean and Atmosphere, 1972-74. Trustee Bucknell U., 1969-95, chmn. bd. trustees, 1976-82; bd. advisers Naval War Coll., 1970-74. Capt. USMC, 1943-46, 51-52. Mem. Coun. Fgn. Rels., Chevy Chase Club (Md.), Maidstone Club (East Hampton, N.Y.), Bridgehampton Club (N.Y.). Home: 4423 Boxwood Rd Bethesda MD 20816-1817 also (summer): PO Box 421 Bridgehampton NY 11932-0421

BAIRD, DAVID BRYAN, architect; b. Omaha, Sept. 12, 1964; s. Robert Dallen and Patty Jo (Lutz) B.; m. Sarah Beth Baird, July 6, 1991. BS in Arch., U. Ill., 1987; BArch, U. Ariz., 1990, MArch, 1991. Registered architect, Ariz. Architect AS Tegnestven, Copenhagen, 1988; intern architect O.P.N. Architects, Cedar Rapids, Iowa, 1988-89; prin. Vineyard Christian Sch., Tucson, 1992-94; archtl. designer Architecture One, Tucson, 1994-95; asst. prof. arch. La. State U., Baton Rouge, 1995—. Artist sculpture Faith and Form, 1993, Yeiser Art Ctr., 1996, Alexandria Mus. Art, 1996, Folio Weekly, 1995. Recipient Sax Art award San Bernardino Mus. Art, 1993, Honor award Inter-Faith Forum on Religious Art and Arch., 1992, Best of Show award Gallery Latreuro, Jacksonville, Fla., 1995, 1st place/Best of Show Ink People Ctr. for Arts, Eureka, Calif., 1996. Mem. Christians in Visual Arts. Home: PO Box 16805 Baton Rouge LA 70893-6805 Office: Louisiana State Univ 136 Atkinson Hall Baton Rouge LA 70803

BAIRD, DAVIS W., philosophy educator; b. Boston, Apr. 12, 1954; s. Walter Scott and Mary Warren (Davis) B.; m. Linda Weingarten, June 10, 1982 (dec. June 1992); 1 child, Ian; m. Deanna Leamon, Apr. 11, 1994. BA, Brandeis U., 1976; MA, Stanford U., 1981, PhD, 1981. Vis. asst. prof. U. Ariz., Tucson, 1981-82; asst. prof. U. S.C., Columbia, 1983-88, chmn. dept. philosophy, 1992—, assoc. prof., 1988—. Author: Inductive Logic, 1992; editor: Heinrich Hertz, 1997; contbr. articles to profl. jours. Office: U SC Dept Philosophy Columbia SC 29208

BAIRD, DONALD ROBERT, secondary school educator; b. Boise, Idaho, June 26, 1941; s. Donald Whitney and Pauline June (Cox) B.; m. Donna Colleen Karnes, Sept. 18, 1970; children: Patricia Colleen Baird Duffey, Diane Marie Baird Henry. BS, Coll. Idaho, 1963; MS, Boise State U., 1980. Advanced secondary teaching cert. Instr. NESEP USN, San Diego, summers 1969-75; tchr. South Jr. H.S., Boise, 1969-80, Capital H.S., Boise, 1980—; instr. BOOST USN, San Diego, summers 1984-89; tchr. Boise State U., 1981-82; computer cons. Capital H.S., Boise, 1990—; dept. chmn. South Jr. H.S., Boise, student body advisor, 1975-76. Info. officer U.S. Naval Acad., Annapolis, Md., 1991—. Comdr. USN, 1963-66, res., 1967-89. Recipient Outstanding Educator award Acad. of Am. Educators, 1973. Mem. Nat. Coun. Tchrs. Math., Idaho Coun. Tchrs. of Math. (sec.-treas. 1983-85), Naval Res. Assn. (chpt. pres. 1985-89), Boise Edn. Assn. (rep.), Order of Demolay (chevalier 1959), Masons (Master # 39). Republican. Presbyterian. Avocations: tennis, golf, computers, chess, model ship building. Office: Capital H S 8055 Goddard Rd Boise ID 83704-3100

BAIRD, DOUGLAS GORDON, law educator; b. Phila., July 10, 1953; s. Henry Welles and Eleanora (Gordon) B. BA, Yale U., 1975; JD, Stanford U., 1979; LLD, U. Rochester, 1994. Law clk. U.S. Ct. Appeals (9th cir.), 1979, 80; asst. prof. law U. Chgo., 1980-83, prof. law, 1984—, assoc. dean, 19984-87, Bigelow prof. law, 1988—, dean, 1994-99. Author: (with others) Security Interests in Personal Property, 1984, 2d edit., 1987, Bankruptcy, 1985, 2d edit., 1990, Elements of Bankruptcy, 1992, (D. Baird, R. Gertner, R. Picker) Game Theory and the Law, 1994. Mem. AAAS, Order of Coif. Office: U Chgo Sch Law 1111 E 60th St Chicago IL 60637-2702

BAIRD, DUGALD EUAN, oil field service company executive; b. Aberdeen, Scotland, Sept. 16, 1937; came to U.S., 1979; s. Dugald and Matilda Deans (Tennant) B.; m. Angelica Hartz, May 24, 1961; children—Camilla N., Maiken E. Student, Aberdeen U., Scotland, Trinity Coll., Cambridge, 1957-60; MA in Geophysics, Cambridge U., 1960; LLD, Aberdeen U., 1995, Dundee U., 1998; DSc, Heriot-Watt U., 1999. Joined Schlumberger, 1960, various field assignments in Europe, Asia, Mid. East, Africa, 1960-74; pers. mgr., v.p. ops. Schlumberger Tech. Svcs., Paris, 1974-79; exec. v.p. in charge of worldwide wireline ops. Schlumberger Ltd., N.Y.C., 1979-86, chmn. bd., pres., CEO, 1986—. Office: Schlumberger Ltd 277 Park Ave Fl 41 New York NY 10172-0266

BAIRD, EDWARD ROUZIE, JR., lawyer; b. Norfolk, Va., Aug. 29, 1936; s. Edward Rouzie and Eleanor Gray (Perry) B.; m. Nell McGlaughon, Oct. 8, 1967 (dec. Oct. 1973); 1 child, Eleanor Gray; m. Abby St. John Starke, Feb. 5, 1977; children—Abby St. John, Edward Rouzie V. B.A., U. Va., 1960, LL.B., 1967. Bar: Va. 1967. Assoc. Baird, Creshaw & Ware, Norfolk, 1967-68; asst. dist. counsel U.S. Army C.E., Norfolk, 1968-73; asst. U.S. atty. U.S. Atty.'s Office, Norfolk, 1973-77; sole practice, Norfolk, 1977-82; ptnr. Willcox & Baird, Norfolk, 1982—. Served to lt. (j.g.) USN, 1960-63. Mem. Va. Bar Assn., Norfolk-Portsmouth Bar Assn., Soc. of Cincinnati. Club: Virginia (Norfolk). Home: 1711 Cloncurry Rd Norfolk VA 23505-1717 Office: Willcox & Baird 210 Monticello Ave Norfolk VA 23510-2301

BAIRD, ELLEN TAYLOR, art historian, educator; b. Baton Rouge, La., Aug. 28, 1943; d. Cecil and Ellen Taylor; m. Charles M. Baird (div.); 1 child, Ellen; m. Thomas H. Bestul (div.). BA, Emory U., 1968; MA, Tulane U., 1970; PhD, U. N.Mex., 1979. Asst., assoc. prof. art history, chair modern langs. and lit U. Nebr., Lincoln, 1975-92; prof. art history, dean Coll. Architecture and Art U. Ill., Chgo., 1992—. Author: The Drawings of Sahagun's Primeros Memoriales: Structure and Style, 1993; contbr. numerous articles to profl. jours. Mem. Coll. Art Assn. (bd. dirs. 1996—). Office: U Ill Chgo Dept Art History 935 W Harrison St Chicago IL 60607-7039

BAIRD, GORDON PRENTISS, publisher; b. York, Pa., July 12, 1950; s. Gordon P. Baird and Ann Raymond Luce; m. Jo Ann Hart, Aug. 25, 1979; children: Abigail Hart, Morgan Raymond, Wilder Pollard. BA, Marlboro Coll., Vt., 1972. Dir. Marlboro Theater Co., Vt., 1972-74; assoc. publisher Musician's Guide, Boston, 1974-76; pub., founder Musician Mag., Gloucester, Mass., 1976—; pub. Billboard Pub., N.Y.C., 1981—; dir., pres. Amordian Press, Boulder, Colo., 1976—; founder, dir. Gloucester Kids Theater Club, 1995—. Host (TV) Gloucester Chicken Shack. Asst. chmn. mayor's housing com. Gloucester, Mass., 1985; pres. Internat. 210 Racing Assn., Ea. Point Residents Assn., 1993—; founder, dir. Gloucester Kids' Theater Club, 1995—. Mem. Mag. Pubs. Assn., Nat. Assn. Music Mchts., Internat. 210 Class Racing Assn. (pres. 1992—), Mass. Bay Sailing (v.p. design sailing 1995—). Club: Eastern Point Yacht (bd. dirs. Gloucester chpt.). Office: Musician Mag 27 Fort Hill Ave Gloucester MA 01930-4434 also: Musician Mag Billboard Pub 1515 Broadway New York NY 10036-8901

BAIRD, GREG ROSS, university program director, theater educator; b. Lapeer, Mich., Feb. 13, 1961; s. Ronald Edwin Baird and Marjorie Ruth Weston. Student, North Ctrl. Mich. Coll., Petoskey; degree in speech/theater edn., Ctrl. Mich. U., Mt. Pleasant, 1992. Cert. secondary edn. speech/theater tchr., Mich. Performing arts dir. Camp Sloane, Lakeville, Conn., 1989-91, 93-96; hall dir. Interlochen (Mich.) Ctr. for the Arts, 1994-96; residence life/student activities dir., theater educator North Ctrl. Mich. Coll., Petoskey, 1996—; dir. lecture series North Ctrl. Mich. Coll., 1996—, mem. hall coun., 1996—, guest lectr., 1996—, advisor student senate, 1996—. Author: (plays) Mime, Music & Mayhem, 1989, Mime, Music & an Evening of Imagination, 1994, Mime, Music & an Encore for the Audience, 1996. Bd. dirs. Friends North, Traverse City, Mich., 1993-95. Excellence scholar Ryan White Youth Conf., 1997-99. Avocations: swimming, travel, directing theater, public speaking, hiking. Home: 1525 Howard St Petoskey MI 49770 Office: North Ctrl Mich Coll 1515 Howard St Petoskey MI 49770

BAIRD, HAYNES WALLACE, pathologist; b. St. Louis, Jan. 28, 1943; s. Harry Haynes and Mary Cornelia (Wallace) B.; m. Phyllis Jean Tipton, June 26, 1965; children: Teresa Lee, Christopher Wallace, Kelly Wallace. BA, U. N.C., 1965, MD, 1969. Diplomate Am. Bd. Pathology. Radio announcer, disc jockey, 1961-63; intern N.C. Meml. Hosp., Chapel Hill, 1969-70, resident in pathology, 1970-72, chief resident in pathology, 1972-73; practice medicine specializing in pathology, Greensboro, 1973—; assoc. pathologist Moses H. Cone Meml. Hosp., Greensboro, N.C., 1973-98; chief pathology Moses Cone Health Sys., Greensboro, 1998—; adj. asst. prof. U. N.C., Chapel Hill, 1978-96, adj. assoc. prof., 1996—; clin. lectr. chemistry U. N.C., Greensboro, 1973—. Mem. adminstrv. bd. West Market St. United Meth. Ch., 1985-88, usher, 1988—; bd. dirs. Greensboro unit Am. Cancer Soc., 1980-81; mem. com. protection of rights of human subjects (Instl. Rev. Bd.) Moses H. Cone Meml. Hosp., 1989-98. Fellow Coll. Am. Pathologists (ho. of dels. 1983-85, insp. commn. on lab. accreditation); mem. AMA, So. Med. Assn., Am. Soc. for Clin. Chemistry, Am. Soc. Cytology, Papanicolaou Soc. of Cytopathology, Am. Soc. Clin. Pathologists, U.S. & Can. Acad. Pathology, N.C. Med. Soc., Greater Greensboro Soc. Medicine, N.C. Soc. Pathologists (sec.-treas. 1977-79). Methodist. Home: 2805 New Hanover Dr Greensboro NC 27408-6705 Office: 1200 N Elm St Greensboro NC 27401-1004

BAIRD, IRENE CEBULA, educational administrator; b. Ware, Mass.; d. Frank M. and Ann Elizabeth (Bigda) Cebula; m. Irwin Lewis Baird, Aug. 30, 1949 (dec. Apr. 1981); children: Lisa M., Nina J., Mara L. AB, Smith Coll., 1945; MA, U. Kans., 1947; DEd, Pa. State U., 1994. Rsch. assoc. PROBE, Pa. State Harrisburg, Middletown, 1982-88, coord./facilitator Job Link Program, 1988-91, supr./facilitator Adult Basic Edn./Gen. Edn. Devel. program, 1991-92; project dir. Pa. Commn. for Women, Harrisburg, 1992; dir. Women's Enrichment Ctr. Pa. State Harrisburg, 1994—, affiliate asst. prof., 1995—; Spanish instr. U. Kans., U. Mass. Author: Unlocking the Cell: A Humanities Model for Incarcerated Women, 1996; contbr. chpts. to Pa. Vocat. Edn. Mktg. Manual; mem. editl. bd. Alumnae Quar., Smith Coll., 1987-91; contbr. articles to profl. jours.; presenter in field. Mem. task force Adult Literacy and Lifelong Learning, Capital Region 2000, 1991—; mem. exhibits/cmty. edn. coms. Susquehanna Art Mus., 1991—, bd. dirs., 1991—; bd. dirs. Children's Play Room Inc., 1994—, Concertante Chamber Ensemble, 1996-98, Harrisburg Arts Factory, 1996; mem. career edn. adv. bd. Harrisburg Sch. Dist., 1986-92, mem. cmty. adv. com., 1991-93. Named one of Initial 75 Pa. Honor Roll Disting. Women; recipient Alumni Achievement award Pa. State U., Mae Carvell award for contbg. to advancement of women, 1998, Harrisburg/Hershey Cmty. Woman of Yr. AAUW, 1999, Women Helping Women award, Soroptomost Internat., 1999. Mem. Am. Assn. Adult and Continuing Edn. (presenter nat. and internat. adult edn. confs. 1991—, Non-formal Edn. award 1997), Am. Assn. Tchrs. Spanish and Portuguese, Ctrl. Pa. Assn. Women Execs., Nat. Assn. Women in Edn., Pa. Assn. Adult and Continuing Edn. (one of Outstanding Adult Students in Higher Edn. 1995), Women's Legis. Exch. Avocations: reading, theater, chamber music, gardening, travel. Home: 115 Rodney Ln Camp Hill PA 17011-1323 Office: Pa State Harrisburg-Eastgate 1010 N 7th St Harrisburg PA 17102-1400

BAIRD, JOHN ABSALOM, JR., college official; b. Honolulu, Sept. 13, 1918; s. John Absalom and Helen (Bates) B. m. Virginia Walton, Mar 8, 1941 (dec. 1983); children: Suzanne W. Baird Perot, Linda Baird Woodruff, Barbara Baird Rogers; m. Clare A. Emmons, May 12, 1984 (dec. 1998). AB, Princeton U., 1940; postgrad., Johns Hopkins U., 1941. Asst. supt. Charles S. Walton Co., 1942-47, asst. sec. and dir., 1947-52, v.p., 1952-72; asst. pres. Ea. Bapt. Theol. Sem., Phila.; asst. pres. Ea. Coll., St. Davids, Pa., 1952-61, v.p., 1961-88, advisor to pres., 1988—. Author: A Leap of Faith, 1972, The Whole Gospel for the Whole World, 1975, All Things Are Thine, 1976, Profile of a Hero, 1977, The Shining Fire, 1979, Horn of Plenty, 1982, Great House, 1984, Promises to Keep, 1989, More Than Knowledge, 1992, The Power of One, 1997; contbr. articles to profl. jours. Bd. corporators, bd. dirs. Covenant Life Ins. Co., 1971-94; Phila. Main Line dist. chmn. Valley Force Coun. Boy Scouts Am., 1952-54, dist. commr., 1954-56; vice chmn. Main Line br. YMCA Greater Phila., 1947-63; trustee, v.p. Pa. Lupus Found.; v.p. Pa. chpt. Lupus Found. Am., 1973-95; trustee Vol. Svcs. for the Blind, Phila., 1971-85; mem. adv. bd. Phila. Inglis House, Union League; chmn. bd. trustees Shipley Sch., Bryn Mawr, Pa., 1972-78; trustee 4th Bapt. Mission Found., 1976-80, Ludington Libr., Bryn Mawr, Ralston House, Phila., Seaman's Ch. Inst., Phila.; v.p., bd. dirs. Am. Sunday Sch. Union (Phila.) 1957-69; bd. dirs. Watchman Examiner Corp. (N.Y.C.), 1958-70, Pa. United Theol. Sem. Found. (Pitts.), Am. Ednl. Film & Video Ctr., Std. Davids, Athenaeum, Phila. Recipient Freedom Founds. Honor medal, 1973. Mem. Am. Bapt. Pub. Rels. Assn., Am. Alumni Coun., Am. Coll. Pub. Rels. Assn., U.S. Naval Inst., U.S. Naval Found., Loyal Legion, Soc. of Cin. (pres. Del. 1972-75, sec. gen. 1977-83), Colonial Soc. Pa. (gov. 1994-97), Soc. Colonial Wars (gov. 1991-94), Order Fgn. Wars, S.R., Am. Assn. Sem. Staff Officers (pres. 1966-68), Pa. Acad. Fine Arts, Am. Rose Soc., Am. Philatelic Soc., English-Speaking Union, Hist. Soc. Pa. (dir. 1992—), Penn Club, Right Angle Club, Merion Cricket Club (Haverford, Pa.), Geneal. Soc. Pa. (dir. 1988—),. Republican. Presbyterian. Home: 74 Pasture Ln # 116 Bryn Mawr PA 19010-1797 Office: Ea Coll Off of Advisor to Pres Saint Davids PA 19087

BAIRD, JOHN MICHAEL, lawyer, non-profit organization executive; b. Champaign, Ill., May 5, 1966; s. Rodman Bradley and Beryla Joy (Boyer) B.; m. Martha Marie Kondalski, May 16, 1992; children: Cassidy Marie, Dustin Joseph. BA, Walsh U., 1988; JD, U. Toledo, 1991. Bar: Ind. 1991. Law clk. Robert M. Anspach Assocs., Toledo, 1989-91; assoc. David A. Retherford & Assoc., Indpls., 1991-93; pvt. practice John M. Baird & Assocs., Indpls., 1993-94; compliance coord. Anthem Life Ins. Co., Indpls., 1994-95; dir. The Daniel Wolf Meml. Found. for Children, Inc., Indpls., 1995—; tax-deferred annuity/deferred compensation plan compliance supr., atty. Gardner & White, Indpls., 1996-98; staff atty. The Nyhart Co., Inc., Indpls., 1998—. Mem. Indpls. Jr. C. of C., 1992-95, dir. cmty. devel., 1993-94; vol. Habitat for Humanity, Indpls. Named Jaycee of the Month, Indpls. Jr. C. of C., 1993. Roman Catholic. Avocations: history, politics, sports. Home: 7341 Donegal Dr Indianapolis IN 46217-5476 Office: The Nyhart Co Inc 9320 Priority Way West Dr Indianapolis IN 46240-1468

BAIRD, LARRY DON, minister, nurse; b. Abilene, Tex., Sept. 23, 1949; s. Delmar Lee baird and Frances Elizabeth Weathers; m. Mary Margaret Ledbetter, Dec. 22, 1970; 1 child, Shannon Kirk; 1 adopted child, Walter Dale. Student, San Diego State U., 1971-72, Cisco Jr. Coll., Clyde, Tex., 1977-78; diploma in nursing, Hendrick Meml. Hosp., Abilene, 1972-73. Ordained to ministry United Pentecostal Ch. Internat., 1973-84, Assemblies of Lord Jesus Christ, 1984. Evangelist United Pentecostal Ch., 1973-78; pastor United Pentecostal Ch., Hamlin, Tex., 1979-82; residential dir. Tupelo (Miss.) Children's Mansion, 1982-84, campus dean, 1983-84; co-pastor 1st Pentecostal Ch., Abilene, 1984; DON Valley View Care Ctr., Anson, Tex., 1990-91; unit dir. Hill Resources Inc., Abilene, Tex., 1992—; asst. choir dir., musician, dir. and interpreter for deaf United Penecostal Ch., Abilene, 1984—; dir. Spirit of Freedom Alcoholic Ministries, 1984—; pvt. nurse coord. Health Care Svcs., Abilene, 1984-85; sr. pastor Abundant Life Apostolic Ministries, Abilene, 1984—; dir. home missions Tex.-N.Mex. Distr. for Assemblies of Lord Christ Jesus Christ, 1986-91; bd. dirs. Blue Mountain (Miss.) Childrens Home. Active various health support groups, Abilene, 1984—; chmn., mem. exec. bd. Abilene Coord. Coun., 1984—; chmn. adv. com. Home Cmty. Svc. Mental Health-Mental Retardation Program, Abilene, 1994—. With USNR, 1970-76. Fellow Ministerial Alliance (pres. 1980-82). Republican. Home: PO Box 5677 Abilene TX 79608-5677 Office: Abundant Life Apostolic Ministries 741 S 11th St Abilene TX 79602-3852 *Life is like jig saw puzzle. Many pieces seem unnecessary, however, the true beauty is only seen at the time of completion, when all pieces fit perfectly together. It is finished—so also is a finished life in Christ.*

BAIRD, LOURDES G., federal judge; b. 1935. BA with highest honors, UCLA, 1973, JD with honors, 1976. Asst. U.S. atty. U.S. Dist. Ct. (ctrl. dist.) Calif., L.A., 1977-83, U.S. atty., 1990-92; ptnr. Baird & Quadros, 1983-84, Baird, Munger & Myers, 1984-86; judge East L.A. Mcpl. Ct., 1986-87; adj. prof. law Loyola U., L.A., 1986-90; judge L.A. Mcpl. Ct., 1987-88, L.A. Superior Ct., 1988-90; U.S. atty. ctrl. dist. Calif., 1990-92; judge U.S. Dist. Ct. (ctrl. dist.) Calif., L.A., 1992—; faculty civil RICO program Practicing Law Inst., San Francisco, 1984-85, western regional program Nat. Inst. Trial Advocacy, Berkeley, Calif., 1987-88; adj. prof. trial advocacy Loyola U., L.A., 1987-90. Recipient Silver Achievement award for the professions YWCA, 1994; named Woman of Promise, Hispanic Womens' Coun., 1991, Alumnus of Yr., UCLA Sch. Law, 1991. Mem. Mexican-Am. Bar Assn., Calif. Women Lawyers, Hispanic Nat. Bar Assn., UCLA Sch. Law alumni Assn. (pres. 1984). Office: US Dist Ct Ctrl Dist Calif Edward R Roybal Bldg 255 E Temple St Ste 770 Los Angeles CA 90012-3334*

BAIRD, MARIANNE SAUNORUS, critical care clinical specialist; b. Chgo., Dec. 15, 1953; d. John and Irene (Lameka) Saunorus; m. Thomas W. Baird, Sept. 10, 1983; 1 child, Rachel. BSN, Loyola U., Chgo., 1975; MSN, Emory U., 1982. Critical care RN, cert. advanced cardiac life support affiliate faculty mem., Ga. Supr. surg. nursing Rush-Presbyn. St. Lukes Med. Ctr., Chgo.; staff nurse, clin. mgr. intensive care unit St. Joseph's Hosp., Atlanta, dir. meg.-surg. unit, clin. specialist, case mgr.; mem. clin. assoc. faculty Emory U., Ga. State U., Atlanta; mem. RN preceptor, ednl. staff Genentech, Inc., 1995—. Author several nursing textbooks; contbr. articles to profl. jours. Mem. med. supply com. Atlanta Com. for Olympic Games, 1994-96. Recipient Fed. traineeship Emory U., 1980-81; named one of Outstanding Young Women of Am., 1991. Mem. AACN (bd. dirs. Atlanta chpt. 1984-86), Soc. Critical Care Medicine, Am. Holistic Nurses Assn., Blue Key, Kappa Gamma Pi, Sigma Theta Tau. Home: 3788 Glengarry Way Roswell GA 30075-2615

BAIRD, MELLON CAMPBELL, JR., electronics industry executive; b. Corsicana, Tex., Feb. 24, 1931; s. Mellon Campbell and Katherine (Wasson) B.; m. Mary Beth Norman, Dec. 27, 1956. BBA, North Tex. State U., 1957, MBA, 1961. Adminstrv. asst. VARO Inc., Garland, Tex., 1957-59; western region mgr. VARO Inc., Los Angeles, 1959-61; dir. mktg. VARO Inc., Santa Barbara, Calif., 1961-63; exec. v.p., pres. F&M Systems Co., Dallas, 1963-74; pres., bd. dirs. fed. systems group Sanders Assocs. Inc., Nashua, N.H., 1974-81; pres. def. and electronics group Eaton Corp., Cleve., 1981-86; pres., chief oper. officer, bd. dirs. Tracor Inc., Austin, 1986-87, pres., CEO, 1988-89; pres., CEO, chmn. bd. dirs. Delfin Systems, Sunnyvale, Calif., 1990—; pres., CEO TITAN Techs. and Info. Sys. Corp., San Diego, 1998—; bd. dirs. Software Spectrum Inc., Dallas, EDO Corp., College Point, N.Y., Hawker Pacific Aerospace, Sun Valley, Calif. Served with USN, 1951-55. Mem. Nat. Security Indsl. Assn. (trustee 1974—), Navy League U.S. (life), Armed Forces Communications & Electronics Assn., Assn. Old Crows (life, tech. symposium chmn. 1987), Security Affairs Support Assn. (bd. dirs. 1988-91), Tex. Assn. Taxpayers (bd. dirs. 1988-91). Home: 4204 Green Cliffs Rd Austin TX 78746-1241 Office: TITAN Corp 3033 Science Park Rd San Diego CA 92121-1199

BAIRD, PATRICIA ANN, physician, educator; b. Rochdale, Eng.; came to Can., 1955; d. Harold and Winifred (Cainen) Holt; m. Robert Merrifield Baird, Feb. 22, 1964; children—Jennifer Ellen, Brian Merrifield, Bruce Andrew. BSc with honors, McGill U., 1959, MD, CM, 1963; DSc (hon.), McMaster U., 1991; D Univ. (hon.), U. Ottawa, 1991. Intern Royal Victoria Hosp., Montreal, Que., Can., 1963-64; resident, fellow in pediat. Vancouver Gen. Hosp., B.C., Can., 1964-67; instr. pediat. U. B.C., Vancouver, 1968-72, from asst. prof. to prof., 1972-94, Univ. Killam Disting. prof., 1994—; head dept. med. genetics Grace Hosp., Vancouver, 1981-89, Children's Hosp., Vancouver, 1981-89, Health Scis. Centre Hosp., 1986-89; med. cons. B.C. Health Surveillance Registry, 1977-90; chmn. genetics grants com. Med. Rsch. Coun., Ottawa, Ont., Can., 1982-87, mem. coun., 1987-90; mem. Nat. Adv. Bd. on Sci. and Tech. to Fed. Govt., 1987-91; mem. genetic predisposition study steering com. Sci. Coun. Can., 1987-90; chair Royal Commn. on New Reproductive Technologies, 1989-93; co-chair Nat. Forum Sci. and Tech. Couns., 1991; v.p. Can. Inst. for Advanced Rsch., 1991—; bd. dirs. Biomed. Rsch. Centre, 1986-89. Contbr. articles to med. jours. Bd. govs. U. B.C., 1984-90. Decorated Order B.C., 1992, Commemorative medal for Confedn. of Can., 1992. Fellow RCP Can., Can. Coll. Med. Geneticists (v.p. 1984-86); mem. Am. Soc. Human Genetics (chair nominating com. 1987-89), B.C. Med. Assn., Can. Med. Assn., Genetics Soc. Can., Genetic Epidemiology (adv. bd. 1991-94). Avocations: skiing, cycling, music. Office: U BC, Dept Med Genetics, Vancouver, BC Canada V6T 1Z3

BAIRD, ROBERT DAHLEN, religious educator; b. Phila., June 29, 1933; s. Jesse Dahlen and Clara (Sonntag) B.; m. Patty Jo Lutz, Dec. 18, 1954; children: Linda Sue, Stephen Robert, David Bryan, Janna Ann. BA, Houghton Coll., 1954; BD, Fuller Theol. Sem., 1957; STM, So. Meth. U., 1959; PhD, U. Iowa, 1964. Instr. philosophy and religion U. Omaha, 1962-65; fellow Asian religions Soc. for Religion in Higher Edn., 1965-66; asst. prof. religion U. Iowa, Iowa City, 1966-69, assoc. prof., 1969-74, prof., 1974-88, 89, acting dir. Sch. Religion, 1985; Leonard S. Florsheim Sr. Eminent Scholar's chair New Coll., U. South Fla., Sarasota, 1988-89; dir., Sch. of Religion U. Iowa, Iowa City, 1995—; faculty fellow Am. Inst. Indian Studies, India, 1972, sr. fellow, 1992; vis. prof. Grinnell Coll., 1983. Author: Category Formation and the History of Religions, 1971, 2d paperback edit., 1991, (with W.R. Comstock et al) Religion and Man: An Introduction, 1971, Indian and Far Eastern Religious Traditions, 1972; editor, contbr.: Methodological Issues in Religious Studies, 1975, Religion in Modern India, 1981, 2d edit., 1988, 3rd rev. edit., 1995, Essays in the History of Religion, 1991; editor, contbr. Religion and Law in Independent India, 1993; book rev. editor: Jour. Am. Acad. Religion, 1979-84; contbr. articles to profl. jours. Ford Found. fellow, 1965-66; U. Iowa Faculty Devel. grantee, 1979, 86, 92; Am. Inst. Indian studies sr. fellow, 1972, 92. Mem. Am. Acad. Religion, Assn. Asian Studies, N.Am. Assn. for the Study Religion. Democrat. Presbyterian. Office: U Iowa Sch of Religion Iowa City IA 52242

BAIRD, ROBERT DEAN, mission director; b. Hereford, Tex., Aug. 12, 1933; s. Kay and Maybelle (Witherspoon) B.; m. Margaret Ann Roberts, Aug. 27, 1953; children: Sandy, Deana Young. AA, Amarillo Jr. Coll., 1953; BTh., Bapt. Bible Coll., 1970, DD (hon.), 1986; DD (hon.), Atlantic Bapt. Bible Coll., 1986. Ordained to ministry Bapt. Ch., 1969. Asst. pastor High St. Bapt. Ch., Springfield, Mo., 1969-72; missionary Bapt. Bible Fellowship Internat., Springfield, 1972-77, asst. mission dir., 1977-81; pastor Hallmark Bapt. Ch., Fort Worth, 1981-86; mission dir. Bapt. Bible Fellowship Internat., Springfield, 1986—. Mem. Internat. Conf. on World Evangelism (steering com. 1990—). Office: Bapt Bible Fellowship Inter PO Box 191 Springfield MO 65801-0191*

BAIRD, ROBERT MALCOLM, philosophy educator, researcher; b. Memphis, May 30, 1937; s. Robert Locke and Lelia Christine (Bobbitt) B.; m. Alice Elizabeth Cheavens, Aug. 29, 1959; children: Katherine, Robert David, Susan Christine. BA, Baylor U., 1959, MA, 1961; BD, So. Bapt. Sem., 1964; PhD, Emory U., 1967. Lectr. philosophy Baylor U., Waco, Tex., 1960-61, asst. prof., 1968-70, assoc. prof., 1970-79, prof., 1979-87, prof., chair dept. philosophy, 1987—; designated master tchr. Baylor U., Waco, 1993; asst. prof. philosophy Oglethorpe Coll., Atlanta, 1966-67, Nebr. Wesleyan U., Lincoln, 1967-68; Piper prof. Tex. Piper Found., 1995. Editor: The Philosophical Life, 1983, Philosophy of Punishment, 1988, Morality and the Law, 1988, The Ethics of Abortion, 1989, Euthanasia, 1989, Animal Experimentation, 1991, Pornography: Private Right or Public Menace?, 1991, Bigotry, Prejudice and Hatred, 1992, Punishment and the Death Penalty, 1995, Homosexuality, 1995, Same Sex Marriage, 1997, Media and Morality, 1999. Bd. dirs. The Freeman Ctr., Waco, 1974-82, pres. bd., 1977; mem. bd. Vanguard Preparatory Sch., Waco, 1985-88. Mem. Am. Philos. Soc., Southwestern Philos. Soc., AAUP (pres. Baylor U. chpt. 1973-74, 95-96). Democrat. Baptist. Home: 212 Guittard Ave Waco TX 76706-1516 Office: Baylor U Dept Philosophy PO Box 97273 Waco TX 76798-7273

BAIRD, STUART, film editor, director. Editor: (films) Lisztomania, 1975, Tommy, 1975, The Omen, 1976, Welcome to My Nightmare, 1976, Valentino, 1977, Superman, 1978 (Academy award nomination best film editing 1978), Altered States, 1980, Superman II, 1980, Outland, 1981, Five Days One Summer, 1982, Beyond the Limit, 1983, Revolution, 1985, Ladyhawke, 1985, Lethal Weapon, 1987, Gorillas in the Mist, 1988 (Academy award nomination best film editing 1988), (with Hubert de la Boullerie and Robert Ferretti) Tango & Cash, 1989, Leathal Weapon 2, 1989, (with Ferretti) Die Hard 2, 1990, Radio Flyer, 1992, Demolition Man, 1993, Marverick, 1994; Director: Executive Decision, 1996, U.S. Marshals, 1998. Office: United Talent 9560 Wilshire Blvd Ste 500 Beverly Hills CA 90212-2427*

BAIRD, WILLIAM DAVID, retired anesthesiologist; b. Dallas, Feb. 17, 1922; s. John B. and Sue S. B.; m. Virginia Claye Sanders, June 27, 1948; children: Linda B. Moore, Cynthia B. Matthews, C. Sanders Baird, Ginger B. Stark, J. Davies Baird. BA, Rice Inst., Houston, 1949; MD, U. Tex., 1953. Diplomate Am. Bd. Anesthesiologists. Intern U. Tex. Med. Br. Hosps., Galveston, 1953-54; resident in anesthesiology U. Tex. Med. Br.

Hosps., 1954-56, fellow, instr. anesthesiology, 1956-57; pvt. practice anesthesiology Garland, Tex., 1957-80; med. cons. Garland Cmty. Hosp., 1980-81, Branson & Misko, 1981-93; clin. instr. U. Tex. SW Br., 1963-80; chief anesthesiology Garland Clinic and Hosp., 1957-75, Garland Meml. Hosp., 1975-78; exec. staff com. Meml. Hosp. Garland, 1975-78; adv. bd. Presbyn. Hosp. Dallas, 1969. Author: Some Descendants of John Baird, A Genealogy, 1997; editor, pub.: The 17th Sortie Newsletter of the 17th Bomb Group/Wing Reunion Assn. Precinct chmn. Rep. party, Garland, 1969-74; bd. dirs. Garland YMCA, 1972-74. Fellow Am. Coll. Anesthesiologists; mem. AMA, Am. Soc. Anesthesiologists, Tex. Med. Assn., Dallas County Med. Soc., Tex. Soc. Anesthesiologists, Dallas County Anesthesiology Soc., Dallas County Hist. Soc., Dallas County Pioneer Assn., Marauder Men of Metroplex, B-26 Marauder Hist. Soc. Republican. Avocations: genealogy, 17th bomb group history, farming, hunting, fishing.

BAIRD, WILLIAM MCKENZIE, chemical carcinogenesis researcher, biochemistry educator; b. Phila., Mar. 23, 1944; s. William Henry Jr. and Edna (McKenzie) B.; m. Elizabeth A. Myers, June 21, 1969; children: Heather Jean, Elizabeth Joanne, Scott William. BS in Chemistry, Lehigh U., 1966; PhD in Oncology, U. Wis., 1971. Postdoctoral fellow Inst. Cancer Research, London, 1971-73; from asst. to assoc. prof. biochemistry Wistar Inst., Phila., 1973-80; assoc. prof. medicinal chemistry Purdue U., West Lafayette, Ind., 1980-82, prof., 1982-97, Glenn L. Jenkins prof. medicinal chemistry, 1989-97, dir. Cancer Ctr., 1986-97; faculty participant cancer ctr., biochemistry program Purdue U., 1980-97; dir. Environ. Health Scis. Ctr., Oreg. State U., Corvallis, 1997—, prof. dept. environ. and molecular toxicology, 1997—, prof. dept. biochemistry and biophysics, 1997—, dir. environ. Heatlh Sci. Ctr. ; adv. com. on biochemistry and chem. carcinogenesis Am. Cancer Soc., 1983-86; mem. chem. pathology study sect. NIH, 1986-90. Contbr. articles to profl. jours.; assoc. editor Cancer Rsch. Grantee NCI. Mem. ISSX, AAAS, Am. Assn. Cancer Rsch., Am. Chem. Soc., Am. Soc. Biochemistry and Molecular Biology, Environ. Mutagen Soc., Soc. Toxicology. Office: Oreg State U Environ Health Scis Ctr 1011 ALS Bldg Corvallis OR 97331-7302*

BAIRD, ZOË, lawyer, insurance company executive; b. Bklyn., June 20, 1952; d. Ralph Louis and Naomi (Allen) B.; m. Paul Gewirtz, June 8, 1986; 1 child, Julian Baird Gewirtz. AB, U. Calif., Berkeley, 1974, JD, 1977. Bar: Washington, 1979, Calif. 1977, Conn. 1989. Law clk. Hon. Albert Wollenberg, San Francisco, 1977-78; atty., advisor Office Legal Counsel U.S. Dept. Justice, Washington, 1979-80; assoc. counsel to the Pres. The White House, Washington, 1980-81; assoc., then ptnr. O'Melveny & Myers, Washington, 1981-86; counsellor, staff exec. GE, Fairfield, Conn., 1986-90; v.p., gen. counsel Aetna Life & Casualty, Hartford, 1990-93, sr. v.p. gen. coun., 1993-96; pres. John & Mary R. Markle Found., N.Y.C., 1998—; bd. dirs. Sci. Pk. Devel. Corp., New Haven, So. New Eng. Telecom. Corp., mem. bd. contbrs. Mem. Am. Lawyer Media, N.Y.C. (bd. contbrs.). Office: John & Mary Markle Found 75 Rockefeller Plz Rm 1800 New York NY 10019-6908

BAIREY, MARIE, principal. Prin. Sonoma Elem. Sch., Modesto, Calif., 1988-98; resource tchr. Beard Elem. Sch., Modesto, Calif., 1998—. Recipient DOE Elem. Sch. Recognition Program award, 1989-90. Office: Beard Elem Sch 915 Bowen Ave Modesto CA 95350*

BAIRSTOW, FRANCES KANEVSKY, labor arbitrator, mediator, educator; b. Racine, Wis., Feb. 19, 1920; d. William and Minnie (DuBow) Kanevsky; m. Irving P. Kaufman, Nov. 14, 1942 (div. 1949); m. David Steele Bairstow, Dec. 17, 1954; children: Dale Owen, David Anthony. Student U. Wis., 1937-42; BS, U. Louisville, 1949; student Oxford U. (Eng.), 1953-54; postgrad. McGill U., Montreal, Que., 1958-59. Rsch. economist U.S. Senate Labor-Mgmt. Subcom., Washington, 1950-51; labor edn. specialist U. P.R., San Juan, 1951-52; chief wage data unit WSB, Washington, 1952-53; labor rsch. economist Canadian Pacific Ry. Co., Montreal, 1956-58; asst. dir. indsl. rels. ctr. McGill U., 1960-66, assoc. dir., 1966-71, dir., 1971-85, lectr., indsl. rels. dept. econs., 1960-72, asst. prof. faculty mgmt., 1972-74, assoc. prof. faculty mgmt., 1974-83, prof., 1983-85; lectr. Stetson Law Sch., Fla. spl. master Fla. Pub. Employees Rels. Commn., 1985-97; dep. commr. essential svcs. Province of Que., 1976-81; mediator So. Bell Telephone, 1985—, AT&T and Comm. Workers Am., 1986—; cons. on collective bargaining arbitrator to OECD, Paris, 1979; cons. Nat. Film Bd. of Can., 1965-69; arbitrator Que. Consultative Coun. Panel of Arbitrators, 1968-83, Ministry Labour and Manpower, 1971-83, United Airlines and Assn. Flight Attendants, 1990-95, Am. Airlines and Transport Workers Union, 1997-98, State U. System of Fla., 1990-97; FDA, 1996-98, Social Security Adminstrn., 1996-97, Am. Airlines, 1997—; arbitrator Tampa Gen. Hosp., 1996—, mediator Canadian Public Svc. Staff Rels. Bd., 1973-85; contbg. columnist Montreal Star, 1971-85. Chmn. Nat. Inquiry Commn. Wider-Based Collective Bargaining, 1978. Fulbright fellow, 1953-54. Mem. Canadian Indsl. Rels. Rsch. Inst. (exec. bd. 1965-68), Indsl. Rels. Rsch. Assn. Am. (mem. exec. bd. 1965-68, chmn. nominating com. 1977), Nat. Acad. Arbitrators (bd. govs. 1977-80, program chmn. 1982-83, v.p. 1986-88, nat. coord. 1987-90), Ctrl. Fla. Indsl. Rels. Rsch. Assn. (pres. 1999). Home and Office: 1430 Gulf Blvd Apt 507 Clearwater FL 33767-2856

BAIRSTOW, RICHARD RAYMOND, retired lawyer; b. Waukegan, Ill., Sept. 26, 1917; s. Fred Raymond and Mildred (Wright) B.; m. Mary Kelley, Aug. 8, 1942 (dec. June 19, 1979); children: Kathleen Bairstow Young, Suzanne Bairstow Hicks, Mary Bairstow Neely; m. Agnes Macaitis Caldwell, July 22, 1980 (dec. July 22, 1995). AB, U. Ill., 1939, JD, 1947; postgrad., George Washington U., 1939-41. Bar: Ill. 1947, U.S. Dist. Ct. (no. dist.) Ill. 1964, U.S. Ct. Mil. Appeals 1963, U.S. SUpreme Ct. 1963. Assoc. Hall, Meyer & Carey, Waukegan, 1947-49; asst. state's atty. Lake County, Waukegan, 1949-53; ptnr. McClory & Bairstow, Waukegan, 1953-60, McClory, Bairstow, Lonchar & Nordigan, Waukegan, 1960-66; prin. Richard R. Bairstow & Assocs., Waukegan, 1966-98; ret., 1998; dist. atty. Fox Lake Fire Protection Dist., Ingleside, Ill., 1948-98; adminstrv. law judge Ill. Dept. Revenue, Chgo., 1953-87. Bd. dirs. ARC, Lake County, 1947-73; mem., pres. Salvation Army, Waukegan, 1954-66; bd. dirs. Lake County Family YMCA, 1990-91. Col. AUS, 1941-46, ETO, USAR, 1946-71, ret. U.S. Army Command and Gen. Staff Coll., 1965. Mem. ABA, Ill. Lake County Bar Assn., Assn. U.S. Army, The Ret. Officers Assn., Am. Legion, Glen Flora Country Club, Waukegan City Club, Delta Tau Delta, Phi Alpha Delta. Republican. Episcopalian. Home: 2122 Ash St Waukegan IL 60087-5033

BAISDEN, ELEANOR MARGUERITE, airline compensation executive, consultant; b. Bklyn., Nov. 7, 1935; d. Vernon McKee and Ethel Mildred (Cockle) Baisden. BA, Hofstra U., 1970. Clk., Trans World Airlines, N.Y.C., 1953-55, sec., 1955-64, compensation analyst, 1964-75, compensation mgr., 1975-85, dir. compensation and orgn. planning, 1985-88, dir. compensation and adminstrn., 1988-97. Bd. dirs./treas. Weatherby Lake Improvement Co., 1997—. Mem. Airline Pers. Dirs. Conf. (pers. com. 1984-85), Airline Tariff Pub. Co. (pers. com. 1978-96), Nat. Fgn. Trade Coun. (compensation com. 1980-84), Internat. Pers. Assn. (co. rep. 1980-84), Mensa, Weatherby Lake Yacht Club (Mo.), BIG Investment Club (treas. 1998—), Alpha Sigma Lambda (scholar 1965-66). Republican. Methodist. Avocations: boating, swimming, piano, travel. Home: 7818 NW Scenic Dr Kansas City MO 64152-1643

BAISHANSKI, JACQUELINE MARIE, foreign language educator; b. Plouguernevel, France, Feb. 20, 1944; came to U.S., 1970; d. Jerome Marie and Marcelle Nicolas; m. Bogdan M. Baishanski, Sept. 23, 1972; childre: Yelena, Ana, Vanya, Tatyana. MS in Math., Sorbonne, Paris, 1964, DEA, 1966; PhD in French Lit., Ohio State U., 1998. Math., statis. Inst. Nat. Statis., Paris, 1966-67, French Coop., Libreville, 1967-68; asst. prof. U. Reims, France, 1969-70; teaching asst. Ohio State U., Columbus, 1970-73, lectr. math., 1978-80, 81-82, teaching asst. French, 1991-98, lectr. French, 1998—. Judge Ann. Lang. Olympics, Columbus, 1990; bd. dirs. early childhood edn. Ohio State U., 1985-86. Recipiuent Fawcett award Ohio State U., 1987. Mem. Modern Lang. Assn. Am., Midwest Modern Lang. Assn. Avocations: reading, writing, classical music, travel. Home: 367 Blenheim Rd Columbus OH 43214

BAISIER, MARIA DAVIS, English language educator, theater director; b. Louisville, Aug. 15, 1947; d. Alvin Joseph and Alice Josephine Davis; children: Bernard Paul Leon, Aimée Louise Davis. BA, St. Mary's Dominican Coll., 1969; secondary cert. in English, Tulane U., 1992. Asst. mng. editor So. Ins. Mag., New Orleans, 1979-85; tchr. St. Catherine of Siena Sch., Metairie, La., 1969-75, 85—, chair English dept., 1985—, dir. theatre, 1991—. Creator, dir. Camp Big Foot Summer Camp, Metairie, 1974, 75; v.p. Sacred Heart Sch. PTA, Anniston, Ala., 1977; vol. worker Sta. WYES-TV Auction, New Orleans, 1978-83; mem. women's com. New Orleans Opera Assn., 1979—, chair Opera Ball, 1984; various com. positions Women's Guild, 1980-84; chair ann. fundraiser fair St. Francis Xavier Ch., 1982-84; mem. hospitality com. Rep. Nat. Conv., 1988; mem. Les Amies Ensembles, 1996—, St. Patrick's Ch. Performing Choir, 1998—. Mem. Nat. Coun. Tchrs. English, Kappa Delta Pi, Phi Beta. Avocations: theatre, opera, museum, travel, reading. Home: 226 Phosphor Ave Metairie LA 70005-3733

BAISLEY, ROBERT WILLIAM, music educator; b. New Haven, Apr. 5, 1923; s. Joseph V. and Mary (Bergin) B.; m. Jean Shanley, July 30, 1955; children: Joan Ann, Susan Jean, Elizabeth Veronica. Mus.B., Yale U., 1949; M.A., Columbia U., 1950. Tchr. Cherry Lawn Sch., Darien, Conn., 1950-51; dir. Neighborhood Music Sch., New Haven, 1951-56; asst. prof. piano, exec. officer Sch. Music Yale U., New Haven, 1956-65; prof. music Pa. State U., University Park, 1965-87, chmn. dept. music, 1965-79. Concert pianist in various concerts, recitals, radio and TV. Vol. United Fund, New Haven, 1951-65; rep. to Coun. of Social Agys., 1951-60; mem. adv. coun. Salvation Army, 1963-65; bd. dirs. Ctrl. Pa. Festival of Arts (pres. 1969-71). Served with AUS, 1942-45. Recipient cert. of merit Yale U., 1979. Mem. Coll. Music Soc., Yale U. Sch. Music Alumni Assn. (pres. 1979-82, 89-94, exec. com. 1977—). Home: 454 Park Ln State College PA 16803-3207 Office: Pa State U Music Dept University Park PA 16802

BAITSELL, WILMA WILLIAMSON, artist, educator, lecturer; b. Palmyra, N.Y., July 5, 1918; d. Glen Hiram and Luetta (Newell) Williamson; m. Victor Harry Baitsell, Oct. 29, 1941; children: Corin Victor, Coby Allan, Corrine Luetta. BSE, SUNY, Oswego, 1957, MSE, 1964; postgrad. Iowa State Tchrs. Coll., Syracuse U., Ind. State U., Cooper Union, McGill U. Montreal, Western State U.; HHD, World U., 1982; PhD, U. Cambridge, Eng., 1981. Tchr. rural sch., 1939-41, Phoenix Central Sch., 1957-71, SUNY, Oswego, 1971-77; ret., 1977; cons. area schs., 1965-68; art cons. N.Y. State Dept. Edn., summers 1968-70. Author: Creativity and Intelligence, 1965, Art for Campers, 1972, Crafts for Children, 1976, Christianity, Creativity and Democracy, 1978, Create or Destroy, Love or Hate, Peace or War, 1983; editor Summer Art mag., 1957-71. Chmn. Republican Twp. Com.; pres. Oswego County Women's Rep. Club; chmn. Sch. Bldg. and Orgn. Com., 1954; mem. ch. adminstrv. bd., 1948—, Ford Found. sci. and math. grantee, 1958-59; recipient 1st prize Mid-States Art Show, 1981, hon. mention for painting, Yamiguchi, Japan, 1981, 1st prize Am. Craftsman's Show, 1973. Mem. N.Y. State Ret. Tchrs. Assn. (life), Internat. Soc. Edn. Through Art, Oswego Art Guild (life), Nat. Ret. Tchrs. Assn., Oswego County and Scriba Hist. Soc. (life), SUNY Oswego Alumni Assn. (life), N.Y. State Grange, AAUW, DAR, Order Eastern Star. (life, mem. adminstrv. bd.). Methodist. Home and Office: 104 Whittemore Rd Oswego NY 13126-6613

BAITY, JOHN COOLEY, lawyer; b. South Bend, Ind., June 22, 1933; s. Roscoe Flake and Gladys Paula (Kline) B.; m. Patricia Ann Bowen, Nov. 9, 1985; children: Keith F., John C. Jr., Cheryl R., Michael P., Philip J., Mark A. AB, U. Mich., 1955, JD, 1958. Bar: Ill. 1958, N.Y. 1961, Calif. 1977, D.C. 1979. Assoc. Cravath, Swaine & Moore, N.Y.C., 1960-62; assoc. Donovan Leisure Newton & Irvine, N.Y.C., 1962-65, ptnr., 1966-83; ptnr. Hunton & Williams, N.Y.C., 1983-84, Baity & Joseph, Los Angeles, 1984-86, Milbank, Tweed, Hadley & McCloy, N.Y.C., 1986—; gen. counsel U.S. Golf Assn., Far Hills, N.J., 1980-85. Trustee Nat. Hypertension Assn., N.Y.C., 1981-91; bd. dirs. Am. Cancer Soc., Atlanta, 1983-87, 90—, treas., 1994-98, vice chmn., 1999—; chmn. fin. com., mem. coun. and exec. com. Union Internationale Contre le Cancer, 1995—; dir. The Walt and Lilly Disney Found. and Walt Disney Family Ednl. Found. Mem. N.Y. State Bar. Assn., Calif. Bar Assn., Order of Coif, Phi Beta Kappa, Phi Kappa Phi. Office: Milbank Tweed Hadley & McCloy 1 Chase Manhattan Plz Fl 47 New York NY 10005-1413

BAITY, WILLIAM F., federal agency administrator; married; two children. BS in Math., N.C. Coll., 1969; MS in Indsl. Adminstrn., Carnegie-Mellon U., 1971; JD, Vanderbilt U., 1976. Bar: Tenn., La. Econ. and bus. analyst Exxon Co., 1971-73; asst. dir. legal officer USCG, 1976-80; asst. U.S. atty. Ea. Dist. La., New Orleans, 1980-88, chief civil divsn., 1984-88; adminstr. region 15 Jud. Dist. So. Calif., Hawaii and Guam, 1990; U.S. trustee region 5 Jud. Dist. La. and Miss.; dep. dir. U.S. Bankruptcy Trustee Program Dept. of Justice, 1991-94, acting dir., 1994; dep. dir. Fin. Crimes Enforcement Network, U.S. Dept. Treasury, 1995—, acting dir., 1998—. Office: Dept of the Treasury Ste 200 2070 Chain Bridge Rd Vienna VA 22182

BAITZEL, GREGORY WILSON, accounting executive; b. Lansdale, Pa., Dec. 18, 1955; s. Wilson Gregory and Anne Marie (Lubisco) B.; m. Karen Anne Cocchi, Aug. 6, 1977; children: Jonathon, Nickolas. BS, St. Joseph's U., 1981. CPA, Pa. Staff acct. W.G. Baitzel Acctg. and Tax Svc., Haverford, Pa., 1976-81, Rainer and Co., Newtown Square, Pa., 1981-82; sr. acct. McQuay, Garrett & Sullivan, Tampa, Fla., 1982-83; sr. acct., mgr. H.R. Margolis Co., Bala Cynwyd, Pa., 1983-91; ptnr. Leibowitz & Gold, Phila., 1991-95; with Baitzel & Co., CPAs, 1995—; bd. dirs. The Bala House, Bala Cynwyd; cons. Innovation Printing, Phila., 1992. Mem. AICPA, Pa. Inst. CPAs, Young Printers Exec. Club. Avocations: golf, reading, basketball. Home: 122 Sloan Rd Springfield PA 19064-1625 Office: Baitzel & Co 12 S Monroe St Media PA 19063-2915

BAIUL, OKSANA, figure skater; b. Dnepropetrovsk, Ukraine, Nov. 16, 1977; d. Marina Baiul. Skating tours include Champions on Ice, 1993, 94, 95, 96, 97, 98, The Great Skate II: Charity Event, 1995, Great Skate III, 1997, Nutcracker on Ice, 1995, CBS Spl.: Too Hot to Skate, 1995, 96, Sergei Grinkov: Celebration of a Life, 1996, CBS Spl.: Wizard of Oz on Ice, 1996, An Evening with Champions: Charity Benefit, 1997, 98, Fire on Ice: Charity Event, 1998, 75 Yrs. of Disney Magic, 1998, FTD Champions on Ice, 1999. Recipient 2d Pl. award women's figure skating European Championships, 1993, 1st Pl. award women's figure skating World Figure Skating Championships, 1993, Gold medal women's figure skating Olympic Games, 1994, 2d Pl. Nikon Championship, 1994, 4th Pl. Am. Skating Invitational, 1994, 2d Pl. Ice Wars Overall Team Results, 1995, 98, 2d Pl. Gold Championships, 1995, 2d Pl. Rock'n' Roll Championships, 1996, 1st Pl. Ice Wars Overall Team Results, 1997, 3d Pl. Skate TV Championships, 1998, among others. Address: c/o Fred Rust Ice Arena U Del Newark DE 19716*

BAJAJ, CELINE COSME, medical/surgical and pediatric nurse; b. Manila, Nov. 21, 1948; d. Jose R. and Gloria LL. (Umale) Cosme; m. Narain Bajaj; children: Alejandro, Nicolai. Diploma, De Ocampo Meml. Sch. Nursing, Manila, 1970; BSN, Philippine Women's U., Manila, 1971. Pvt. nurse Sloan-Kettering Hosp., N.Y.C.; nurse Indian River Meml. Hosp., Vero Beach, Fla.; head nurse Coler Meml. Hosp., N.Y.C.; owner, treas. BASM Systems Inc., Rockville Center, N.Y. Home: 12 Stratford Rd Rockville Centre NY 11570-2141

BAJARIA, BHARAT JAMNADAS, accountant; b. Bombay, India, Mar. 22, 1949; s. Jamnadas Naranji and Shavitri Jamnadaj (Neghathi) B.; m. Kokila Narandas Sampat, July 6, 1976; children: Radhika, Shyam. BS in Acctg., A.P. Coll. Commerce, Surat, India, 1971. Came to U.S., 1976;. Acctg. clk. W.G.P.R. Inc. CH 62, Detroit, 1977-79; acct. Plymouth Gen. Hosp., Detroit, 1979-84, Blue Cross Blueshield of Mich., Detroit, 1984—. Mem. Nat. Mgmt. Assn. Home: 154 Amboy St Dearborn Heights MI 48127-3604

BAJCSY, RUZENA KUCEROVA, computer science educator; b. Bratislava, Czechoslovakia, May 28, 1933; came to U.S., 1968; d. Felix and Marguita (Weisz) Kucerova; m. Sherman Frankel. PhD in Elec. Engrin., Slovak Tech. U., Bratislava, 1967; PhD in Computer Sci., Stanford U., 1972. Asst. prof. elect. engrin. Slovak Tech. U., 1967-68; rsch. scientist artificial intelligence lab. Stanford (Calif.) U., 1968-72; prof. computer science U. Pa., Phila., 1972—, chair computer and info. sci. dept., 1985-90, dir. Grasp Lab., 1985—; dir. Nat. Sci. Found. Washington, 1998—; vis. scientist INRIA, France, 1979; vis. prof. U. Copenhagen, Denmark, 1984, 1988, U. Pisa, Italy, 1988; Forsythe lectr. Stanford U., 1989; cons. in field. Editor periodicals including Computer Vision. Fellow IEEE, Assn. Computing Machinery; mem. Inst. Medicine NAS. *

BAJEK, FRANK MICHAEL, career officer, retired, financial consultant; b. Chgo., July 4, 1950; s. Edward Joseph and Anna J. (Banik) B.; m. Renee Ann Kaspar, Aug. 1, 1981; children: David, Amanda, Erica. BBA, Loyola U., Chgo., 1972; MBA, Keller Grad. Sch. Mgmt., 1981. CPA, Ill.; cert. govt. fin. mgr., Assn. Govt. Accts. Asst. mgr. svc. auditing Aldens, Inc., Chgo., 1976-78, indsl. engr., 1978-79, internal auditor, 1979-80; field auditor Stewart-Warner Corp., Chgo., 1980-81; commd. 2d lt. USAR, 1972; active duty, 1981; advanced through grades to lt. col. USAR, 1992; retired, 1996; tax, fin. cons. Ill., 1989—; adj. instr. acctg. Nat.-Louis U., 1994, Northwestern Bus. Coll., 1997-99, Robert Morris Coll., 1998—; asst. prof. Nasson U., The Univ. of the U.S. Mem. AICPA, Am. Soc. Mil. Comptrollers, Ill. CPA Soc., Assn. Govt. Accts. Roman Catholic. Home and Office: 26 W 58th St Westmont IL 60559-2315

BAJOR, JAMES HENRY, musician, jazz pianist; b. Detroit, May 7, 1953; s. Henry Stanley and Irene (Hetmanski) B. Student, Wayne State U., 1976. Rec. artist Sugo Music, Half Moon Bay, Calif. Produced albums of own piano compositions: Awakening, 1987 (nominated for New Age solo acoustic Grammy award 1987), Gentle Images, 1988; appears regularly on radio and TV programs. Mem. ASCAP, NARAS. Office: Ste 304 340 1st St Apt 304 Rochester MI 48307-2673

BAJURA, RICHARD ALBERT, university administrator, engineering educator; b. Duquesne, Pa., Feb. 2, 1941. BSME, Notre Dame, 1962, MSME, 1964, PhD, 1967. Energy rsch. dir. W.Va. U., Morgantown, 1984-90; rsch. engr. Babcok & Wolcox R&D Ctr., Alliance, Ohio, 1967-68; postdoctoral researcher Johns Hopkins U., Balt., 1968-69; prof. mech. engring. W.Va. U., Morgantown, 1969—, assoc. provost, 1990-94; dir. Nat. Rsch. Ctr. for Coal and Energy, 1994—. Editor: Polyphase Flow Transport Technology, 1980. Mem. ASME (v.p. basic engring. 1998—). Office: WVa U Nat Rsch Ctr for Coal & Energy PO Box 6064 Morgantown WV 26506-6064

BAKAKOS, DIANA, middle school educator; b. N.Y.C., Apr. 2, 1952; d. Michael and Catherine (Itsines) Constant; m. Constantine Bakakos, Nov. 24, 1974; children: Chris Fotis, Vikki. BA with honors, Coll. of S.I., 1973, MS in Edn., 1976; PhD in Psychology, Neotarian Coll. of Philosophy, 1979; MS in Computer Edn., L.I. U., 1987. Tchr. I.S. 391 Bd. of Edn., Bklyn., 1978—; instr. adult edn. Bklyn. Coll., 1988; adj. prof. Fordham U., Bronx, 1990; tchr. asst. Peer Intervention Program, N.Y.C., 1995; instr. grad. credits QUIPP N.Y.C. Pub. Schs., Bklyn., 1990. Civilian vol. N.Y.C. Police Dept., Bklyn., 1978; mem. Petrina Brotherhood Assn., Bklyn., 1978—, Laconian Assn. of Can. and N.Am., Bklyn., 1978—, Hellenic Am. Edn. Assn., N.Y.C., 1982. Recipient Tchr. of Yr. Arista, 1988, N.Y. Alliance award, 1990. Mem. Doctorate Assn. of N.Y. Educators, United Fedn. of Tchrs. (chpt. mem.-at-large), Epsilon Delta Chi. Democrat. Greek Orthodox. Avocations: travel, swimming, dancing, art, word games. Home: 8620 21st Ave Brooklyn NY 11214-4004

BAKAL, CARL, writer, public affairs consultant, photojournalist; b. N.Y.C., Jan. 11, 1918; s. William and Esther (Tutelman) B.; m. Shirley Sesser, 1956; children: Stephanie, Emilie, Amy, Wendy. B.S., CCNY, 1939; postgrad., Columbia, 1949. Advt. mgr. Fotoshop, N.Y.C., 1939-41; editor Fotoshop Almanac, 1939-41; assoc. editor, contbg. editor U.S. Camera, 1939-43; sales promotion mgr. Universal Camera Corp., 1941-43; editorial chief information control div. Mil. Govt., Germany, 1947-48; writer N.Y. Mirror, 1948-50; assoc. editor Coronet mag., N.Y.C., 1950-55; free-lance writer, photojournalist, 1955—; editor Real, See mags., 1957-58; pub. affairs cons. U.S. Dept. Commerce, 1961-62; sr. assoc. Howard Chase Assocs., N.Y.C., 1962-65; dir. mag. dept. Carl Byoir & Assocs., 1966-68; account supr. Anna M. Rosenberg Assocs., 1968-84; sr. v.p. Jack Raymond & Co., Inc., N.Y.C., 1984-86; pres. Carl Bakal Assocs., N.Y.C., 1986—; guest lectr. photojournalism U. Wis., 1953. Author: Filter Manual, 1953, How to Shoot for Glamour, 1955, The Right to Bear Arms, 1966, No Right to Bear Arms, 1968, Charity U.S.A, 1979; contbr. articles and photographs to publs. including McCall's, Redbook, Life, Reader's Digest, Harper's, Town & Country, Esquire, Good Housekeeping; contbr. to Ency. Photography, 1942, Treasury of Tips for Writers, 1965, Tools of the Writer's Trade, 1990; photojournalism columnist Writers Digest.; travel editor Sylvia Porter's Personal Fin. mag., 1984-86. Served to 1st lt. AUS, 1942-46, 51-52. Recipient 1st prize Popular Photography $25,000 picture contest, 1956. Mem. Author's Guild, Violoncello Soc., P.E.N., Am. Soc. Journalists and Authors (v.p. 1968), Dutch Treat Club, Nat. Coun. for Responsible Firearms Policy (founder, v.p.). Home and Office: 225 W 86th St New York NY 10024-3330

BAKALAR, JOHN STEPHEN, printing and publishing company executive; b. Lynn, Mass., Feb. 10, 1948; s. Leo and Ann Beatrice (Lepie) B.; m. Christine Lake Heilman, Sept. 24, 1972; children—Brooke Heilman, Jessica Heilman, Luke Heilman. B.A., U. Pa., 1970; M.B.A., Stanford U., 1973. Investment mgr. First Chgo. Corp., Chgo., 1973-76; treas. Rand McNally & Co., Skokie, Ill., 1976-78; v.p. fin., treas. Rand McNally & Co., 1978-86, exec. v.p., 1986-93, pres., chief oper. officer, 1993-98; dir. Racing Champions. Adv. bd., dir. Broader Urban Involvement and Leadership Devel., Chgo., 1976—; fellow Leadership Greater Chgo., 1987-88; trustee, treas. North Shore Country Day Sch., Winnetka, Ill., 1989-98. Mem. Econ. Club Chgo., Northmoor Country Club (Highland Park, Ill.), Country Club of the Rockies (Edwards, Colo.). Home: 1760 Dale Ave Highland Park IL 60035-3303

BAKALY, CHARLES GEORGE, JR., lawyer, mediator; b. Long Beach, Calif., Nov. 15, 1927; s. Charles G. Sr. and Doris (Carpenter) B.; m. Patricia Murphey, Oct. 25, 1952; children: Charles G. III, John W., Thomas B. A.B., Stanford U., 1949; J.D., U. S.C., 1952. Assoc. O'Melveny & Myers, L.A., 1956-63, ptnr., 1963-94; spokesman Office Ind. Counsel, Washington, 1998-99; mem. Commn. on Calif. State Govt. Orgn. and Economy, President's Nat. Commn. on Employment Policy, 1992-94; mem. 9th Cir. Jud. Conf. Lawyer Del. Ch., 1984-87, mem. indigent def. panel, 1992-94; chmn. Calif. Dispute Resolution Adv. Coun., 1987-88; pres. Dispute Resolution Svcs. Bd. Dirs., Calif. Dispute Resolution Coun. Author: (with Joel M. Grossman) Modern Law of Employment Relationships, 1983, 2d edit. 1989; contbr. chpts. to books. Capt. JAG, U.S. Army, 1952-56. Fellow Am. Coll. Trial Lawyers, Assn. Atty.-Mediators (pres. So. Calif. chpt. 1995—); mem. ABA (chmn. sect. labor and employment law 1981-82, sect. dispute resolution), L.A. County Bar Assn. (trustee, chmn. labor law sect. 1976-77, dispute resolution sect.), Lincoln Club (pres. 1989-91), Chancery Club, Valley Hunt Club (Pasadena, Calif.), Calif. Club (L.A.), Bohemian Club (San Francisco). Office: 521 Michigan Blvd Ste 2 Pasadena CA 91107-4928 also: 445 S Figueroa St Ste 2600 Los Angeles CA 90071-1630*

BAKANOWSKY, LOUIS JOSEPH, visual arts educator, architect, artist; b. Conn., Oct. 8, 1930; s. Louis Joseph Bakanowsky and Alice (Sullivan) Debra; m. Marie A. Golas, Jan. 27, 1951; 1 child, Louis J., III. BFA, Syracuse U., 1957; MArch, Harvard U., 1961. Registered architect, Mass., N.Y., N.J., Conn., N.H. Asst. prof. architecture Cornell U., Ithaca, N.Y., 1961; assoc. prof. Harvard U., Cambridge, Mass., 1963-71, prof. architecture, 1972—, prof. visual arts., 1975-97, Osgood Hooker prof. visual studies emeritus, 1997—, chmn. dept. visual and environ. studies, 1976-86; dir. Carpenter Ctr. for Visual Arts, 1984-90; prin. Cambridge Seven. Assocs., 1962—. Prin. works include U.S. Pavillion for Expo '67, Montreal, Can., Henry DuPont Libr., Pomfret Sch., Conn., Columbia Sch., Rochester, N.Y., Rostropovich residence; (sculpture) Carl Siembab Gallery, Boston, 1958; represented in various pub. an pvt. collection. With USAF, 1951-53. Grantee Nat. Endowment Arts, 1979, 83, Graham Found. for Advanced Studies in Fine Arts, 1983. Fellow AIA (design awards 1967, 70). Office: Harvard U Carpenter Ctr for Visual Arts 24 Quincy St Cambridge MA 02138-3804

BAKAY, ROY ARPAD EARLE, neurosurgeon, educator; b. Chgo., Mar. 5, 1949; s. Archie Joseph and Marjorie (Jordal) B.; m. Joann P. Feiertag; children: Mark, Scott, Candace, Jacqueline. BS, Beloit Coll., 1971; MD, Northwestern U., 1975. Diplomate Am. Bd. Med. Examiners, Am. Bd. Neurol. Surgeons. Intern U. Mich., Ann Arbor, 1975-76; resident in neurosurgery U. Wash., Seattle, 1976-82; acting instr., asst. in neurosurgery U. Wash. Med. Sch., Seattle, 1980-82, NIH fellow, 1981-82; asst. prof. sect. neurol. surgery Emory U. Med. Sch., Atlanta, 1982-88, dir. neurol. surgery resident rsch., 1984—, assoc. prof., 1988-93, prof., 1993—; mem. R & D Com. VA Med. Ctr., Decatur, Ga., 1982-86, sect. chief neurol. surgery, 1982-95; affiliate scientist neurobiology Yerkes Regional Primate Rsch. Ctr., Atlanta, 1982—; vice chmn. dept. neurol. surgery, 1995—. Author: (with others) Yearbook of Science and Technology, 1989; abstractor Jour. Surg. Gynecology and Obstetrics, 1978-86; mem. editorial bd. Jour. Contemporary Neurosurgery, 1987-93; mem. editorial rev. bd. Neurosurgery, 1994—; contbr. articles to profl. jours., chpts. to books. Chmn. profl. adv. bd. Ga. chpt. Epilepsy Found. Am., 1987-88; mem. adv. panel U.S. Congl. Office Tech. Assessment, Washington, 1988-90; profl. rep. Am. Cancer Soc., Atlanta, 1987-90. Recipient Resident Rsch. award Western Neurosurgery Soc., 1979, No. Pacific Soc.Neurology and Psychiatry, 1979, Soc. Neurology Anesthesists and Neurology Supportive Care, 1981; named one of Outstanding Athletes of Am., 1971, Am. Best Doctor, 1994—. Mem. AAAS, Soc. Neurosci., Am. Stereotactic and Functional Neurosurgeons (v.p. 1988-91, pres. 1991-93), Am. Assn. Neurol. Surgeons (chmn. GRAFT Registry Com. 1987-95), Congress Neurol. Surgeons (v.p. joint com. 1988-91, pres. 1991-93), Am. Soc. Neural Tranplantation and Repair (founding 1992, counsilor, 1992-99, pres.-elect 1999). Presbyterian. Avocations: hiking, camping, skiing, fishing, team sports. Office: The Emory Clinic 1327 Clifton Rd NE Atlanta GA 30322-1013

BAKEMAN, CAROL ANN, travel and administrative services manager, singer; b. San Francisco, Oct. 27; d. Lars Hartvig and Gwendolyne Beatrice (Zimmer) Bergh; student UCLA, 1954-62; m. Delbert Clifton Bakeman, May 16, 1959; children: Laurie Ann, Deborah Ann. Singer, Roger Wagner Chorale, 1954-92, L.A. Master Chorale, 1964-86, The Wagner Ensemble, 1991—; libr. Hughes Aircraft Co., Culver City, Calif., 1954-61; head econs. libr. Planning Rsch. Corp., L.A., 1961-63; corp. libr. Econ. Cons., Inc., L.A., 1963-68; head econs. libr. Daniel, Mann, Johnson & Mendenhall, archs. and engrs., L.A., 1969-71, corporate libr., 1971-77, mgr. info. svcs., 1978-81, mgr. info. and office svcs., 1981-83, mgr. adminstrv. svcs., 1983-96, sr. assoc., 1996-98, assoc. v.p., 1998—; travel mgr. AECOM Tech. Corp., 1996—; pres., Creative Libr. Sys., L.A., 1974-83; libr. cons. ArchiSystems, divsn. SUMMA Corp., L.A., 1972-81, Property Rehab. Corp., Bell Gardens, Calif., 1974-75, VTN Corp., Irvine, Calif., 1974, William Pereira & Assos., 1975; mem. office sys. and bus. edn. adv. bd. Calif. State U. Northridge, 1992. Mem. Assistance League, So. Calif., 1956-86, nat. auxilaries com. 1968-72, 75-78, nat. by laws com. 1970-75, assoc. bd. dirs., 1966-76. Mem. AFTRA, SAG, Am. Guild Musical Artists, Adminstrv. Mgmt. Soc. (v.p. L.A. chpt. 1984-86, pres. 1986-88, internat. conf. chmn. 1988-89, internat. bd. dirs. 1988-90, internat. v.p. mgmt. edn. 1990-92), L.A. Master Chorale Assn. (bd. dirs. 1978-83), L.A. Bus. Travel Assn. (bd. dirs. 1995, sec. 1997, v.p. 1998, pres. 1999), Nat. Bus. Travel Assn. (nat. conv. seminar com. 1994-95). Office: DMJM 3250 Wilshire Blvd Los Angeles CA 90010-1577

BAKER, ALTON FLETCHER, III, newspaper editor, publishing executive; b. Eugene, Oreg., May 2, 1950; s. Alton Fletcher Jr. and Genevieve (Mertzke) B.; m. Wendy Walker, Jan. 27, 1979; children: Benjamin A., Lindsay A. BA in Comms., Washington State U., 1972. Reporter Associated Press, 1972-79; asst. city editor The Register-Guard, Eugene, 1979-80, city editor, 1980-82, mng. editor, 1982-86, editor, 1986-87, editor, publisher, 1987—; pres. Guard Publishing Co., Eugene, 1987—; pres. Cmty. Newspapers, Inc., Portland. Pres. YMCA, Eugene, 1989, United Way of Lane County, Eugene, 1985-99, Eugene Festival Musical Theatre, 1990-94. Avocation: golf. Office: Guard Publishing Co 3500 Chad Dr Eugene OR 97408-7348

BAKER, ANDREW HARTILL, clinical laboratory executive; b. London, Dec. 7, 1948; came to U.S., 1976; s. Charles David and Isobel Joyce (Taylor) B.; m. Susan Nancy Spector, Oct. 24, 1986; children: Laura, Sally, Thomas; 1 stepchild, Jason Fredson. Student, Framlingham Coll., Suffolk, Eng.,, 1961-66; diploma accountancy, City of London Polytechnique, 1968. Auditor Touche Ross, London, 1968-73; contr. Corning Ltd., Essex, Eng., 1974-76; div. contr. Corning Med., N.Y., 1977-79; asst. contr. Corning Glass Works, N.Y., 1980-82; sr. v.p. Metpath, Teterboro, N.J., 1982-85, pres., 1985-92; chmn., CEO Unilabs Corp., Hackensack, N.J., 1989-97, chmn. emeritus, 1998; pres. Corning Lab Svcs., Inc., Teterboro, 1990-92; founder, dir. Med. Diagnostic Mgmt., Inc.; proprietor, chmn. Hartill Ltd. Investment Co.; chmn. Unilabs (UK) Ltd.; sr. ptnr. Focused Healthcare Ptnrs. Treas. United Way of Steuben County, Corning, N.Y., 1978-82; trustee Wayne Gen. Hosp., N.J., 1982-87. Fellow Inst. Chartered Accts. in Eng. and Wales, Honourable Arty. Co. Club (London). Mem. Ch. of Eng. Avocation: duck hunting, motor racing. Home: Apt 49C One Central Park West New York NY 10023 Office: Unilabs Corp 401 Hackensack Ave Hackensack NJ 07601-6411

BAKER, ANITA DIANE, lawyer; b. Atlanta, Sept. 4, 1955; d. Byron Garnett and Anita (Swanson) B.; m. Thomas Johnstone Robison III, Sept. 26, 1995. BA summa cum laude, Oglethorpe U., 1977; JD with distinction, Emory U., 1980. Bar: Ga. 1980. Assoc. Hansell & Post, Atlanta, 1980-88, Kitchens, Kelley, Gaynes, Huprich & Shmerling, 1989-90; asst. gen. counsel NationsBank Corp., 1991-97; v.p., gen. counsel Adaris Corp., 1997—. Mem. Ga. Bar Assn., Atlanta Bar Assn., Southeastern Software Assn., Atlanta Hist. Soc., pace Acad. Alumni Assn. (bd. dirs.), Oglethorpe U. Alumni Assn. (bd. dirs.), Order of Coif, Phi Alpha Delta, Phi Alpha Theta, Alpha Chi, Omicron Delta Kappa. Office: Adaris Corp Glenridge 400 Bldg 3 5825 Glenridge Dr NE Ste 101 Atlanta GA 30328-5387

BAKER, BERNARD ROBERT, II, lawyer; b. Toledo, Nov. 19, 1915; s. Joseph Lee and Grace (Baker) O'Neil; m. Elinor Shutts, Oct. 16, 1943; children: Bernard Robert III, Lynn Agnes. *Maternal grandfather, Bernard R. Baker, was a prominent merchant in the Toledo and Cleveland areas. He established specialty stores in their respective areas in 1893 and 1915. He treated his grandson, Bernard R. Baker II, as his son and provided him with guidance and educational opportunities for which he is eternally grateful.* AB, Kenyon Coll., 1936; JD, Harvard U., 1941. Bar: Ohio 1946. Practice in Toledo, 1947—; ptnr. Brown, Baker, Schlageter & Craig and predecessor firm, 1950-91, now of counsel; pres. B.R. Baker Co., 1946-60; dir. emeritus First Nat. Bank Toledo, First Ohio Bankshares; ret. sec., dir. Toledo Blade Co., Blade Comm., Inc. Regional vice chmn. U.S. Com. for UN, 1955-62; past pres. St. Vincent Hosp., Toledo United Appeal, Toledo C. of C.; past trustee Med. Coll. Ohio at Toledo, Salvation Army, Toledo, Goodwill Industries, Toledo, St. Vincent Hosp. Found.; trustee emeritus Rutherford B. Hayes Presdl. Ctr., Fremont, Ohio; past trustee Boys Clubs Toledo; past pres., trustee Med. Coll. Ohio Found., Toledo. Lt. comdr. USNR, 1940-45. Recipient Boys Club Bronze Keystone award, 1965, Disting. Citizen award Med. Coll. Ohio, 1986; named Toledo Outstanding Man of Year, 1948. Mem. ABA, English Speaking Union, Harvard Club (N.Y.C.), Belmont Country Club, Carranor Hunt and Polo Club (Toledo), Bath and Tennis Club, Beach Club, Chevaliers du Tastevin (Palm Beach), Psi Upsilon. Roman Catholic. Home: 1801 S Flagler Dr Ph 9 West Palm Beach FL 33401-7348

BAKER, BETTY LOUISE, retired mathematician, educator; b. Chgo., Oct. 17, 1937; d. Russell James and Lucille Juanita (Timmons) B. BE, Chgo. State U., 1961, MA, 1964; PhD, Northwestern U., 1971. Cert. tchr. secondary and elem. grades 3-8 math., Ill. Tchr. math. Harper H.S., Chgo., 1961-70, Hubbard H.S., Chgo., 1970-85; also chmn. dept. Hubbard H.S.; tchr. Bogan H.S., 1985-94; ret., 1994; part-time instr. Moraine Valley C.C., 1982-83, 84-86, 94—; reader AP calculus exams. Ednl. Testing Svc. Contbr. articles to profl. jours. Cultural arts chmn. Hubbard Parents-Tchrs.-Students Assn., 1974-76, 1st v.p., program chmn., 1977-79, 82-84, pres. 1979-81; organist Hope Luth Ch., 1964-95, accompanist S.W. Luth. Chorus, 1987—; organist and choir dir. Faith Luth. Ch., Oak Lawn, 1995—. Chorus Univ. fellow, 1969-70. Mem. ASCD, Nat. Coun. Tchrs. Math., Ill. Coun. Tchrs. Math., Chgo. Tchrs. Union, Nat. Coun. Parents and Tchrs. (life), Sch. Sci. and Math. Assn., Am. Guild of Organists, Luth. Collegiate Assn., Walther League Hiking Club, Met. Math. Club Chgo., Kappa Mu Epsilon, Rho Sigma Tau, Mu Alpha Theta (sponsors), Kappa Delta Pi, Pi Lambda Theta, Phi Delta Kappa. Home: 6330 Pine Ridge Dr Apt 1D Tinley Park IL 60477-4927

BAKER, BONNIE BARBARA, mental health and school counselor, educator; b. Bklyn., Aug. 22, 1949; d. Irving Charles and Martha (Besner) B.; m. Thomas Andrew Ridgik, Aug. 4, 1990. BAE, U. Fla., 1971, PhD, 1985; MEd, U. N.C., 1972. Lic. mental health counselor, Fla. Sch. counselor Alachua County Schs., Gainesville, Fla., 1972—; mental health counselor Gainesville Counseling and Devel. Ctr., 1985—. Contbr. book chpt. to Managing Your School Counseling Program; editor (booklet) How to Choose a College: A Guide to Students with a Disability. Vol. counselor U. Fla. Student Svcs., 1991—. Recipient Joe Wittmer Leadership award Chi Sigma Iota, 1994. Mem. ACA (mem. ethics com. 1987-88), Am. Sch. Counselor Assn., Am. Mental Health Counselors Assn., Fla. Counseling Assn. (treas. 1979-82, chair govt. rels. 1988-89, Leadership award 1989), Fla. Sch. Counselor Assn. (treas. 1978-80, pres. 1983-84). Avocations: travel, theater, reading. Home: PO Box 14155 Gainesville FL 32604-2155 Office: Gainesville Counseling & Devel Ctr 2831 NW 41st St Ste F Gainesville FL 32606-6690

BAKER, BRENT, dean. Dean Coll. comm. Boston U., 1992—. Office: Boston U Coll Communications 640 Commonwealth Ave Boston MA 02215-2422*

BAKER, BRIDGET DOWNEY, newspaper executive; b. Eugene, Oreg., Sept. 14, 1955; d. Edwin Moody and Patricia B.; m. Guy Dominique Wood, June 30, 1977 (div. Oct. 1981); m. Rayburn Keith Kincaid, June 27, 1987; stepchildren: Benjamin, Jacob. BA in English, French and Theatre, Lewis and Clark Coll., 1977; MA in Journalism, U. Oreg., 1985. Circulation dist. supr. The Register-Guard, Eugene, 1978-80, pub. relations coordinator, 1980-83, promotion dir., 1983-86, mktg. dir., 1986-88; corp. pub. rels. dir., 1989—; bd. dirs. Guard Pub. Co., Eugene. Bd. dirs. Wilani Coun. Camp Fire, 1982-88, pres. bd. dirs., 1986-88; bd. dirs. Lane County United Way, 1982-88, community info. com. chairperson, 1982-84; chair planning com., 1987-88; bd. dirs. Eugene Opera, 1988-91, pres. bd. dirs., 1990-91. Recipient 1st pl. advt. award Editor and Pub. Mag., N.Y.C., 1984, also 1st pl. TV promotion, 1st pl. newspaper rsch. award, 1988, Best Mktg. Idea/Campaign award Oreg. Newspaper Pub. Assn., 1984, 85; named Woman of Yr., Lane County Coun. of Orgns., 1994. Mem. Internat. Mktg. Assn. (bd. dirs. Western region 1986-88, internat. bd. dirs. 1995—, 8 1st pl. Best in the West awards 1983-91), Pub. Rels. Soc. Am. (pres. Greater Oreg. chpt. 1995-96, Spotlight award 1986), Eugene C. of C. (bd. dirs. 1989-92), U. Oreg. Alumni Assn. (bd. dirs. 1990-93), Lane C.C. Found. (bd. dirs. 1995-97), Town Club (bd. dirs. 1995-97), Downtown Athletic Club, Eugene Yacht Club, Zonta Internat. (pres. Eugene Club 1994-96, area dir. 1997-98, lt. gov. Dist. 8, 1998—). Republican. Avocations: sailing, folk dance, outdoor activities, piano. Office: Guard Pub Co PO Box 10188 Eugene OR 97440-2188

BAKER, BRUCE EDWARD, orthopedic surgeon, consultant; b. Oswego, N.Y., Mar. 22, 1937; s. Elbert J. and Reatha (Hartranft) B.; m. Patricia Therese Gormel, Aug. 19, 1961; children: Brett, Clayton, Sean, Reatha. BSME, Syracuse U., 1959; MD, SUNY-Syracuse, 1965. Intern State U. Iowa, Iowa City, 1965-66, asst. resident, 1966-67; resident orthopaedics SUNY-Upstate Med. Ctr., Syracuse, 1969-72, NIH orthopaedic rsch. fellow, 1972-73, asst. prof. orthopaedic surgery, 1973-79, assoc. prof., 1979-86, prof., 1986-89; dir. univ. sports medicine svc. divsn. dept. orthopaedic surgery 1980-89; team physician, dir. sports medicine athletic dept., Syracuse U., 1973-93, orthopaedic cons. Student Health Ctr., 1973-93, staff SUNY Hosp., Syracuse, 1973-89, Syracuse VA Hosp., 1973-89, A.C. Silverman Pub. Health Hosp., 1973-77, Crouse-Irving Meml. Hosp., 1973—; cons. in field. Contbr. numerous articles to profl. jours. Capt. USAF, 1967-69. Recipient AMA Physicians Recognition award, 1978, Bronze medal award Am. Roentgen Ray Soc., 1980, Gold medal award Sound Slide Prodn. Conditioning, 1977; Syracuse U. scholar, 1955; N.Y. State Regents scholar, 1955-59; USPHS grantee, 1973-74; Hendricks Research fund grantee, 1973-75; NIH grantee, 1974-76, 76-77. Fellow ACS, Am. Acad. Orthop. Surgeons; mem. AMA, Med. Soc. State N.Y., Onondaga County Med. Soc., Orthop. Rsch. Soc., Am. Coll. Sports Medicine, N.Y. Soc. Orthop. Surgeons, Royal Soc. Medicine, Internat. Soc. Arthroscopy, Knee Surgery and Orthop. Sports Medicine, Am. Orthop. Soc. Sports Medicine, European Soc. Sports Trauma, Knee Surgery and Arthroscopy, Arthroscopy Assn. N. Am. Office: 600 E Genesee St Ste 117 Syracuse NY 13202-3108

BAKER, BRUCE J., lawyer; b. Balt., Apr. 2, 1954; s. John J. and Kathryn (Fusetti) B.; m. Pamela Ross Fennell, Nov. 17, 1984; children: Elizabeth Jordan, Julia Hayes, Katharine Ross. BA, U. Pa., 1976; JD, Harvard U., 1979. Bar: N.Y. 1980, U.S. Dist. Ct. (so. and ea. dists.) N.Y. 1980, U.S. Dist. Ct. (we. dist.) N.Y. 1986. Assoc. Milbank, Tweed, Hadley & McCloy, N.Y.C., 1979-83; sr. atty. office of gen. counsel U.S. Synthetic Fuels Corp., Washington, 1983-85; assoc. Nixon, Hargrave, Devans & Doyle, LLP, Rochester, N.Y., 1985-94; of counsel Nixon, Hargrave, Devans & Doyle, LLP, Rochester, 1994-98, ptnr., 1999—. Dist. committeeman, dep. leader 21st legis. dist. Monroe County Reps., Rochester, 1986-90; dist. committeeman Pittsford Rep. Com., 1991—. Mem. ABA, N.Y. State Bar Assn., Monroe County Bar Assn. (chair bus. law sect. 1998—), Rep. Nat. Lawyers Assn. Roman Catholic. Home: 500 Allens Creek Rd Rochester NY 14618-3406 Office: Nixon Hargrave Devans & Doyle PO Box 1051 Rochester NY 14603-1051

BAKER, BRUCE JAY, lawyer; b. Chgo., June 18, 1954; s. Kenneth and Beverly (Gould) B. Student, U. Leeds, Eng., 1974-75; BS, U. Ill., 1976; JD, Washington U., 1979. Bar: Ill. 1979, U.S. Dist. Ct. (no. dist.) Ill. 1984. Asst. atty. gen. antitrust divsn. State of Ill., Chgo., 1979-83; assoc. Mass, Miller & Josephson Ltd., Chgo., 1983-86; sr. counsel Discover Card Services Inc., Riverwoods, Ill., 1986-89; sr. legis. counsel Dean Witter Fin. Svcs. Group, Riverwoods, 1989-91; gen. counsel Ill. Commr. Banks and Trust Cos., Chgo., 1991-94; ptnr. Schiff Hardin & Waite, Chgo., 1994-99, of counsel, 1999—; gen. counsel Bankers Assn., 1999—. Contbr. articles to profl. jours. Registered lobbyist Ill. Legislature, Springfield, 1985-91, 94—. Named Ill. State scholar, 1972. Mem. ABA (antitrust com., banking com.), Ill. State Bar Assn. (comml. banking and bankruptcy sect.), Chgo. Bar Assn. (fin. insts. com.), Ill. Bankers Assn. (legis. counsel 1985-86, gen. counsel 1994—, Disting. Bank Counsel award 1991, 97). Office: Schiff Hardin & Waite 7200 Sears Tower Chicago IL 60606

BAKER, BRUCE ROY, retired art educator, artist; b. Syracuse, N.Y., July 18, 1937; s. Morse Roy and Gladys Irene (Hilton) B.; m. Helen Louise Butler, Apr. 16, 1965; children: Paul, Suzanne, Diana, Amy. BS in Art Edn., New Paltz Coll., 1959; MS in Art Edn., Syracuse U., 1966. Cert. tchr. N.Y. Tchr. art Catskill (N.Y.) Pub. Schs., 1959-62, Cortland (N.Y.) City Schs., 1964-66, Marcellus (N.Y.) Ctrl. Schs., 1966-92; pvt. practice artist, illustrator Marcellus, 1992—; tchr. art Mex. (N.Y.) Acad., 1975-76. Works exhibited in group shows Artists of Ctrl. N.Y.-Munson-Williams-Procter Inst., Utica, 1969, N.Y. State Fair, Syracuse, 1973, 74, 75, Cooperstown (N.Y.) Ann., 1974; contbg. painter Leopold F. Landsberger, N.Y.C., 1979-86; contbg. illustrator Firestone Pub. Corp., Miami Lakes, Fla., 1982—, Spartacus/Centurian, Garden Grove, Calif., 1983—, Quadriga Art, Inc., N.Y.C., 1993—; illustrator (book) Erotic Art of Bruce Baker, 1995; contbr. articles to profl. jours. With U.S. Army, 1962-64. Recipient Hon. Mention (sculpture) N.Y. State Fair, 1975. Avocation: reading. Home: 11 1st St Marcellus NY 13108-1114

BAKER, C. B., retired day care director, organizer, communicator; b. Ft. Wayne, Ind.; d. James Edwin Doelling Sr. and Susie Mae Nutter; m. Gerald R. Baker, June, 1962 (div. 1966); 1 child, Erin Lee; m. Jeffrey E. Baker, June, 1967 (div. 1972); 1 child, Shannon Rae. Student, Internat. Bus. Coll., Ft. Wayne, 1961. Expeditor Wayne Fabricating, Ft. Wayne, 1971; county adminstr. Champaign (Ill.) County Bd., 1974-76; sec. WICD-TV, Champaign, 1976-77; ops. chmn. 40 Plus of Colo., Inc., Denver, 1983, v.p., 1984-85, pres., 1985-86; co-dir. St. Anne's Extended Day Program, Denver, 1986-88; self-employed organizer Denver, 1988—. Editor The Village Voice newsletter, Savoy, Ill., 1974. Chmn. Winfield Village Swimming Pool Com., Savoy, 1975; dir. Mich. Sugar Festival, Sebewaing, 1991. Mem. Am. Bus. Women's Assn., Colo. Women's C. of C. Avocations: reading, horseback riding, weights, walking.

BAKER, CAMERON, lawyer; b. Chgo., Dec. 24, 1937; s. David Cameron and Marion (Fitzpatrick) B.; m. Katharine Julia Solari, Sept. 2, 1961; children: Cameron III, Ann, John. Student, U. Notre Dame, 1954-57; AB, Stanford U., 1958; LLB, U. Calif., Berkeley, 1961. Bar: Calif. 1962, U.S. Dist. Ct. (so. dist.) Calif. 1962, U.S. Dist. Ct. (no. dist.) Calif. 1963, U.S. Ct. Appeals (9th) 1963. With Adams, Duque & Hazeltine, Los Angeles, 1961-62; with Pettit & Martin, San Francisco, 1962-95, mng. ptnr., 1972-81, 84-87, mem. exec. com, 1971-82, 84-88; with Farella, Braun & Martel, San Francisco, 1995—; mayor City of Belvedere, Calif., 1978-79; arbitrator Am. Arbitration Assn.; owner Larkmead Vineyands, Napa Valley, Calif. Dir. Lassen Nat. Park Found., 1992—; trustee Belvedere Cmty. Found. Mem. ABA (sects. on bus. law and internat. law and practice), Calif. Bar Assn. (sect. bus., real property and internat. law), Bar Assn. San Francisco (bd. dirs. 1966, 72-73), Boalt Hall Alumni Assn. (dir. 1982-84), Bohemian Club, Tiburon Peninsula Club. Home: 38 Alcatraz Ave Belvedere CA 94920-2504 Office: Farella Braun & Martel 235 Montgomery St Fl 31 San Francisco CA 94104-3159

BAKER, CARL LEROY, lawyer; b. Woodland, Calif., Nov. 9, 1943; s. Elmer L. and Lucea G. (Tickner) B.; m. Suzon L. Lockhart, June 13, 1966; children: Michele S., Eric L. BA, Sacramento State Coll., 1965; JD, Ind. U., 1968. Bar: Ind. 1968, U.S. Dist. Ct. (no. and so. dists.) Ind. 1968, U.S. Supreme Ct. 1978. Atty. Lincoln Nat. Corp., Ft. Wayne, Ind., 1968-74, asst. gen. counsel, 1974-77, assoc. gen. counsel, 1977-81, 2d v.p., 1979-85, v.p., 1985—, v.p., deputy gen. counsel, 1992—; mem. assoc. faculty Ind.-Purdue U. at Ft. Wayne, 1976—. Mem. staff Law Jour. Ind. U. Sch. Law, 1966-67. Bd. dirs., v.p. Garrett (Ind.) Pub. Libr., Ch. Builders, Inc., Ft. Wayne, 1986—, pres., 1994; pro bono atty. indigent clients, Ft. Wayne, 1968—; mem. adv. bd. Lincoln Mus. Mem. Ind. Bar Assn. (conf. speaker 1988), Am. Coun. Life Ins. (legal sect. 1972—), Assn. Life Ins. Counsel, Am. Judicature Soc., Ind. Trial Lawyers Assn., Am. Corp. Counsel Assn., Nat. Lawyers Club (Washington), Delta Theta Phi, Sigma Phi Epsilon. Avocations: trout fishing, splitting firewood, hiking, Indiana U. basketball. Office: Lincoln Nat Corp 1300 S Clinton St Fort Wayne IN 46802-3506

BAKER, CARLETON HAROLD, physiology educator; b. Utica, N.Y., Aug. 2, 1930; s. Harold George and Loretta (Darling) B.; m. Sara Frances Johnson, July 20, 1963; children: Elizabeth Ann, Janet Lee. BA, Utica Coll. of Syracuse U., 1952; MA, Princeton U., 1954, PhD, 1955. Asst. instr. Princeton (N.J.) U., 1952-54, asst. in research, 1954-55; asst. prof. Med. Coll. Ga., Augusta, 1955-61, assoc prof., 1961-67, prof., 1967; prof. physiology and biophysics U. Louisville Health Scis. Ctr., 1967-71; prof., chmn. dept. physiology and biophysics U. South Fla. Coll. of Medicine, Tampa, 1971-92, dep. dean for research and grad. studies, 1980-82, prof surgery, physiology and biophysics, dir. surg. rsch., 1992-95; prof. emeritus U. South Fla., 1995—; rsch. prof. physiology U. S.C. Coll. Medicine, Columbia, 1994—; rsch. com. mem. Am. Heart Assn., Louisville, 1969-71; rsch. com., bd. dirs. Am. Heart Assn. of Fla., Tampa, 1971-85; NIH program project site visit team, 1982-84, mem. LCME Accreditation Survey Team, 1980-81; vis. prof. U. S.C., 1994-95; cons. U. Louisville Grad. Sch., East Carolina U. Grad. Program. Editor: Microcirculatory Technology, 1986; mem. numerous editorial bds.; contbr. numerous articles in field. Pres. Augusta Choral Soc., 1963; v.p. Blount Rd. Homeowners Assn., Lutz, Fla., 1986-93. Grantee NIH, 1960-92, Am. Heart Assn., 1968-97; recipient Svc. awards Am. Heart Assn. Fla., 1974, 77, Disting. Scientist award U. South Fla. Coll. Medicine, 1981, Outstanding Artist/Scholar award Phi Kappa Phi, 1991, Dean's Citation U. So. Fla. Coll. Medicine, 1991, Founder award, 1992. Fellow: Am. Physiol. Soc. (fellow cardiovascular sect. mem. com. 1982-85); mem. Microcirculatory Soc., European Microcirculatory Soc., Shock Soc. (mem. program coms.). Republican. Avocations: golfing, fishing. Home: 4039 Old Waynesboro Rd Augusta GA 30906-9254 Office: U SC Coll Medicine Dept Physiology VAH Bldg 1 Columbia SC 29208-9999

BAKER, CAROL ANN, elementary school educator; b. Milw., Dec. 6, 1958; d. Alfred Walter and Gertrude Marian (Grabler) Krause; m. Donald Albert Baker, Aug. 11, 1984; 1 child, Caitlin Ann. BA in Psychology, Cardinal Strich Coll., 1982. Cert. tchr. grades kindergarten through 3rd, cert. tchr. spl. edn. grades kindergarten through 8th, Wis. Elem. tchr. St. Josaphat Sch., Milw., 1982-90; substitute tchr. Mukwonago Sch. Dist., 1997—. Mem. Psi Chi, Kappa Delta Pi (charter). Democrat. Roman Catholic. Avocations: needle crafts, fishing, gardening.

BAKER, CAROLYN, musician; b. Corona, Calif., Sept. 4, 1953; d. Earl Ross and Mary Louise (Stanley) Baker; children: Jaime Ann, Samuel Earl. BS in Phys. Edn., Ariz. State U., 1981, MA in Human Rels., 1988. Lic. realtor, Ariz. Mem. faculty Rio Salado C.C., Phoenix, 1981-92; pvt. practice Wickenburg, Ariz., 1995—; mem. faculty Glendale C.C. and Rio Hondo C.C., 1998—. Composer lyrics and music (song) Home Remedy, 1995; musician (mandolin and vocals) Daughters of the Purple Sage, Wickenburg, 1998 (Rising Star of Yr. Acad. Western Artists 1998). Cons. Wickenburg Bd. Edn., 1995; commr. Wickenburg Revitalization Adv. Commn., 1996. Mem. Ariz. Assn. Healthcare Philanthropy, Wickenburg Bus. and Profl. Women. Avocations: hiking, water sports, gardening, travel, dancing. E-mail: carolyn@primenet.com. Home: PO Box 408 Wickenburg AZ 85358-0408

BAKER, CHARLES DEWITT, research and development company executive; b. Dayton, Ohio, Jan. 5, 1932; s. Donald James and Lillian Mae (Pund) B.; m. June Thordis Tandberg, June 25, 1954; children: Charles, Robert, Thomas, Michael. AA in Elec. Engring., Long Beach City Coll., 1953; ed., Boston U., 1954, Pacific Coast U., 1963, U. Utah, 1980. Registered profl. mfg. engr., Calif. Chemist Shell Oil, Torrance, Calif., 1957-60; materials and process engr. Northrop Corp., Hawthorne, Calif., 1960-63; packaging engr. Jet Propulsion Lab., Pasadena, Calif., 1963-71; med. design engr. Utah Biomed. Test Lab., Salt Lake City, 1971-78, sect. mgr., 1978-83; v.p. Tech. Rsch. Assocs., Salt Lake City, 1983-88, pres., 1988—; pres. Thordis Corp., 1980—. Contbr. articles to profl jours.; 20 patents in field. Chmn. bd. dirs. Care Holder Group, 1996—; mem. cmty. adv. com. Heart and Lung Inst., spl. study sect rev. NIH, Tech. Transfer Forum, U. Utah, 1984. Recipient Cost Reduction award NASA, 1969, New Tech. award, 1969, 71, 75. Mem. ASME, Soc. Mfg. Engrs., Utah Mfg. Assn., Acad. of Tech., Entrepreneurs and Innovators. Republican. Avocations: teaching, reading, car rebuilding. *

BAKER, CHARLES DUANE, business administration educator, former management executive; b. Newburyport, Mass., June 21, 1928; s. Charles Duane and Eleanor (Little) B.; m. Alice Elizabeth Ghormley, 1955; children: Charles D., Jonathan G., Alexander K. A.B., Harvard, 1951, M.B.A., 1955. With Westinghouse Electric Corp., Elmira, N.Y., 1955-57, Jersey City, 1957-61; v.p., treas. United Research, Inc., Cambridge, Mass., 1961-65; various positions through chmn., chief exec. Harbridge House, Inc., Boston, 1965-69, 72-83; prof. bus. adminstrn. Northeastern U., Boston, 1985—; dep. under sec. U.S. Dept. Transp., Washington, 1969-70, asst. sec. policy and internat. affairs, 1970-71; under sec. U.S. Dept. HHS, Washington, 1984-85; presiding dir. Millipore Corp., 1986-87. Author various studies dealing with mgmt. transp., health care, pub. policy. Mem. vis. com. Harvard U.; bd. dirs. Caring for Children Found., Pioneer Inst. for Pub. Policy, Millipore Corp., Am. Med. Response, Inc.; trustee, chmn. McLean Hosp.; pres. Hall-Mercer Hosps.; trustee Harvard Med. Ctr., 1996—; mem. Group Ins. Commn. Lt. (j.g.) USNR, 1946-48, 51-53. Recipient Award for Outstanding Achievement U.S. Govt., 1971. Mem. Pi Eta. Republican. Congregationalist. Clubs: Essex County; Harvard, Comml., Clover (Boston); E. India (London); Metropolitan (Washington). Home: 81 Marmion Way Rockport MA 01966-1928 Office: Northeastern U 319 Hayden Hall 360 Huntington Ave Boston MA 02115-5000

BAKER, CHARLES LYNN, management consultant; b. Dallas, Mar. 17, 1934; s. Leonard Allan and Nellie (Boals) B.; m. Joan Heverly, June 1, 1968; 1 child, Annette Lynn. BS in Internat. Rels. summa cum laude, Syracuse U., 1967; MA in Polit. Sci. cum laude, Auburn U., 1975. Commd. USAF, advanced through grades to col.; dep. inspector gen. USAF, Washington, 1975-80; retired USAF, 1980; mng. ptnr. T.Z. Assocs., Balt., 1980-83; pres. McDermott Internat. Trading A.G., Zurich, 1983-88; mng. dir. McDermott Internat. Gen. Svcs., Hong Kong, 1983-88; pres. Baker Assocs., Redlands, Calif., 1988—; bd. dirs. T.Z. Assocs., Balt., Environ. Scis., San Diego, Broadleaf Industries, San Diego; adj. prof. U. Redlands Grad. Bus. Sch. Author: Strategic Planning, 1987. Pres. Redlands Ballet Co., 1987-89; chmn. Redlands Cultural Art Commn., 1988—. Mem. Am. C. of C. (v.p. Hong Kong br. 1984-86), Rotary (pres. Redlands chpt. 1989-90, bd. dirs. internat. chpt. in Hong Kong 1983-85), Pres.'s Assn. (chmn. 1988—), Calif. Cultural Arts Commn. Republican. Episcopalian. Avocations: golf, tennis, reading. Office: Baker Assocs 16047 Via Galan Rancho Santa Fe CA 92091-4014

BAKER, CHARLES STEPHEN, music educator; b. Cleve., July 25, 1942; s. LeRoy Williams and Nellie Angela (Burskey) B. MusB, Oberlin Coll. Conservatory, 1964; MA, Case Western Reserve U., 1967. Cert. music educator, Ohio. Tchr. music Madison Local Schs., Mansfield, Ohio, 1964-65, Wickliffe (Ohio) City Schs., 1967-96; pvt. clarinet instr., freelance clarinet performer Sch. of Fine Arts, Willoughby, Ohio, 1969—; prin. clarinet, assoc. condr. Lakeland Civic Orch., Mentor, Ohio, 1972—. Recipient Disting. Svc. award Sch. of Fine Arts, 1992. Mem. NEA, Ohio Music Edn. Assn. (gen. music com. mem. 1972—, 25 Yr. Svc. award 1991), Music Educators Nat. Conf. (N.E. region chair 1986-92, 94—, all-state orch. chair 1990-92), Lake County Music Educators (sec. v.p., pres.), Ohio Edn. Assn., Am. Fedn. Musicians, U.S. Figure Skating Assn. Roman Catholic. Avocations: figure skating, photography, gardening, travel. Home: 5476A Wildwood Ct Willoughby OH 44094-3256

BAKER, CLAUDE DOUGLAS, biology educator, researcher, environmental activist; b. El Dorado, Ark., Aug. 10, 1944; s. Claude Austin and Margaret Ester (Norman) B.; m. Karen Lee Sutterfield, Feb. 19, 1987; 1 child, Jessica Elizabeth. BS, U. Ark., 1966, MS, 1968; PhD, U. Louisville, 1972; postgrad., Fla. Atlantic U., 1985. Rsch. assoc. U. Ill., Champaign-Urbana, 1971-73; prof. biology Ind. U. S.E., New Albany, 1976—, preprofl. coord., 1994-98, coord. biology, 1996-97; mem. adj. faculty Fla. Atlantic U., 1997-99; vis. scientist Ind. U., 1976—; selected spkr. Ind. Sci. Edn. Fund, Indpls., 1978-90; reviewer NSF, Washington, 1980-90; tchr. Ind. U./Aramco, Ras Tanura, Saudi Arabia, 1983. Contbr. chpts. to books, articles to profl. jours.; developer award winning field biology program, Fla., Hawaii, Belize. Tchr. extracurricular program Ind. U., 1976-90; co-dir. S.E. Regional Sci. Fair, New Albany, 1976-83; bd. dirs. Protect Our Woods, Protect Our River Environment; bd. dirs., environ. adviser Save Our Rivers. Mem. Fla. Audubon Soc., Nat. Soc. SAR, Pi Kappa Alpha. Democrat. Avocations: scuba diving, photography, computers, travel, genealogy. Office: Ind U SE Dept of Biology 4201 Grantine Rd New Albany IN 47150

BAKER, CORNELIA DRAVES, artist; b. Woodbury, N.J., Mar. 2, 1929; d. Carl Zeno and Cornelia (Powell) Draves.; m. Philip Douglas Baker, July 16, 1955; children: Brinton, Todd, Claudia, Samuel. Student, Ohio Wesleyan U., 1947-50, Goethe U., Frankfurt, Germany, 1950-52. Travel dir. Am. Youth Hostels, Inc., N.Y.C., 1953-57; artist Cornelia Gallery, Kumamoto, Japan, 1994—; gallery dir. Presbyn. Ch., Franklin Lakes, N.J., 1988-97, Marcella Geltman Gallery, New Milford, N.J., 1993-96; bd. dirs. Bergen Mus. Art and Sci., N.J., 1996—, corr. sec., mem. exec. com., 1999—. One-woman shows include Ramapo Coll., 1986, Shimada Mus., Kumamoto, 1990, Sekaikan Gallery, Tokyo, 1990, Am. Ctr., Fukuoka, 1990, Bergen Mus. Art and Sci., 1993, L'Atelier Inc. Gallery, 1994, N.Y. Theol. Sem., N.Y.C., 1996, The Gallery, Franklin Lakes, 1997, Office Congressman S.R. Rothman, Hackensack, N.J., 1997, Lee Hecht Harrison, Paramus, N.J., 1998; represented in permanent collections Bergen Mus. Art and Sci., Paramus, Beekley Internat. Skiing Fine Art and Graphics. Chair social problems com. Borough of Franklin Lakes Coun., 1973-76. Recipient Best of Show award Ringwood Manor Assn. of the Arts, 1987, Bergen Mus. Art and Sci., 1989, Emeriti award for excellence N.J. Ctr. for Visual Arts, 1989, Excellence cert. Internat. Art Competition, 1988, Women Making History in Arts award Bergen County, N.J., 1993, Crabbie award Art Calendar, 1994, Gold prize RISO Edn. Found., Japan, 1997. Mem. Nat. Assn. Women Artists (printmaking jury chmn. 1992-94), Salute to Women in the Arts (pres. 1988-90), Mastodon Artists Soc. (life), Altrusa Club of Bergen County, N.J. Republican. Presbyterian. Avocations: skiing, traveling, tennis. Home: 293 Green Ridge Rd Franklin Lakes NJ 07417-2011

BAKER, COSETTE MARLYN, religion writer, editor; b. Miami, Fla., Sept. 22, 1933; d. Juel Marlyn and Corene Frances (Emery) Baker; BBA, U. Miami, Fla., 1955; MRE, So. Bapt. Theol. Sem., 1959. Dir. childhood edn. First Bapt. Ch., Knoxville, Tenn., 1959-63; minister to children South Main Bapt. Ch., Houston, 1964-73; asst. to minister of edn. Central Bapt. Ch., Miami, Fla., 1973-74; cons. in Sunday Sch. Dept., Bapt. Sunday Sch. Bd., Nashville, 1974-92, children's program editor, 1974-92, children's program design editor, 1985-92, cons. Recipient YWCA award outstanding woman in religious work U. Miami, 1955, cert. achievement award for Bible Study Resource Kit for Children's Worship, 1991.. Mem. Tenn. Assn. for Edn. Young Children, Gamma Alpha Chi. Baptist. Author: God's Outdoors, 1967; writer children's teaching tapes for Broadman Press, 1979-81; writer, on-camera person Bapt. Telecomm. Network, 1984—; editor Children's Leadership, 1985-91, design editor, 1991—; design team chairperson The Sunday Sch. Leader Smaller Ch. Edit.; writer Sunday Sch. Bd. Younger Children's Leadership Tng. Video, 1993, life and work curriculum writer, 1994-95; ret. Home: 100 Longwood Pl Nashville TN 37215-1927

BAKER, D. JAMES, oceanographic and atmospheric administrator; b. Long Beach, Calif., Mar. 23, 1937; m. Emily Lind Baker. BS in Physics, Stanford U., 1958; PhD in Exptl. Physics, Cornell U., 1962; LHD (hon.), Nova U., 1993. Rsch. assoc. in phys. oceanography U. R.I., Kingston, 1962-63; NIH postdoctoral fellow in chem. biodynamics U. Calif., Berkeley, 1963-64; NIH postdoctoral fellow in chem. biodynamics Harvard U., Cambridge, Mass., 1964-66, asst. prof. oceanography, 1966-70, assoc. prof., 1970-73; group leader deep-sea physics Pacific Marine Environ. Lab. Nat. Oceanog. and Atmospheric Adminstrn., Seattle, 1977-79; rsch. assoc. prof. dept. oceanography U. Wash., Seattle, 1973-75, rsch. prof. dept. oceanography, 1975-79, sr. oceanographer Applied Physics Lab.,, 1973-86, adj. prof. dept. atmospheric scis., prof. Sch. Oceanography, 1979-86, chmn. dept. oceanography, 1979-81, dean Coll. Ocean and Fishery Scis.,, 1981-83; disting. vis. scientist Jet Propulsion Lab., Calif. Inst. Tech., Pasadena, 1982-93; pres., bd. govs. Joint Oceanog. Instns. Inc., Washington, 1983-93; under sec. of commerce for oceans and atmosphere, adminstr. Nat. Oceanic and Atmospheric Adminstrn., Washington, 1993—; guest investigator Woods Hole Oceanographic Instn., 1968-69, vis. scholar, 1970; mem. adv. com. NAS, Nat. Oceanic and Atmospheric Adminstrn. and other internat. bodies; co-chair environ. and natural resources com. Nat. Sci. and Tech. Coun., 1993—; ex-officio mem. Pres.'s Coun. on Sustainable Devel., 1993—; chair Fed. Com. for Meteorol. Svcs. and Supporting Rsch., 1993—; mem. Govt.-Univ.-Industry Rsch. Roundtable Coun., NAS/NRC, 1993—. Author: Planet Earth-The View from Space, 1990; co-editor-in-chief Geophys. Fluid Dynamics 1975-79; mem. editl. bd. Dynamics of Atmospheres and Oceans, 1979-88, Marine Tech. Soc. Journ., 1986-89, Oceanus Mag., 1992-93; contbr. articles to profl. jours.; patentee in field. Recipient COSPAR Vikram Sarabhai award, 1998. Recipient COSPAR Vikram Sarabhai award, 1998. Fellow AAAS, Am. Meteorol. Soc. (coun. 1982-88, pub. awareness com. 1991-93); mem. Am. Geophys. Union, The Oceanography Soc. (climate change com. 1977-80, cinterim pres. 1988-89, pres. 1989-92, past pres. 1992-93), Marine Tech. Soc., Challenger Soc. for Marine Sci., Can. Meteorol. and Oceanog. Soc., Am. Soc. Limnology and Oceanography, Sigma Xi. Office: US Dept Commerce Hoover Bldg Rm 5128 14th St & Constitution Ave Washington DC 20230

BAKER, DANIEL NEIL, physicist; b. Postville, Iowa, Nov. 10, 1948; s. Joseph N. and Alvira H. (Amundson) B.; m. A. Victoria Vaughan, Aug. 14, 1971. BA, U. Iowa, 1969, MS, 1973, PhD, 1974. Research aide dept. physics U. Iowa, Iowa City, 1967-69, grad. research asst., 1970-74, postdoctoral research assoc., 1974-75; research fellow Calif. Inst. Tech., Pasadena, 1975-78; mem. staff Los Alamos (N.Mex.) Nat. Lab., 1978-81, group leader, 1981-87; chief Lab. for Extraterrestrial Physics NASA, Goddard Space Flight Ctr., Greenbelt, Md., 1987-94; dir. Lab. for Atmospheric and Space Physics U. Colo., Boulder, 1994—; chmn. data sys. users group NASA, Washington, 1982-90, tech. cons., 1985—, mem. space physics mgmt. and ops. com., adv. coun. Space Sci. and Applications, 1988-92, grand tour cluster mission study scientist, 1991-95; mem. com. solar and space physics NAS, Washington, 1983-86, com. data mgmt. and computation, 1986-88, space studies bd., 1995—; mem. panel on long-term observations NRC, Washington, 1985-88, commn. D Sci. Com. on Solar-Terrestrial Physics, 1986-90, U.S. coordinating com. Solar Terrestrial Energy Program, 1988—, U.S. STEP project scientist, 1990-97, chair results, analysis, modeling phase (S-Ramp), 1997—, Geospace Environ. Modeling com. NSF, 1988-91; project sci. NASA small explorer program, prin. investigator NASA rocket program, numerous NASA ESA satellite missions in field; project sci. Internat. Solar-Terrestrial Physics POLAR Spacecraft Mission, 1992-94; U.S. rep. Internat. Assn. Geomagnetism and Aeronomy, 1996—. Assoc. editor Geophys. Research Letters, Washington, 1986-88, Jour. of Atmospheric and Solar-Terrestrial Physics, 1998—; mem. space tech. rev. bd. Los Alamos Nat. Lab.; contbr. numerous articles to profl. jours. Mem. external adv. com. Boston U. Ctr. for Space Rsch., 1989-94; mem. sci. vis. com. U. Md. Inst. Phys. Sci. and Tech., 1990-94; mem. external adv. com. Solar-Terrestrial Environ. Lab., Nagoya (Japan) U., 1995-97. NSF research fellow U. Iowa, 1970-74; grantee Inst. Geophys. and Planetary Physics U. Calif., 1980-89. Fellow Am. Geophys. Union (mem. natural hazards panel 1996—); mem. AAAS, Am. Geophys. Union (geomagnetism assessment panel 1987-88, sec. magnetospheric sect. 1988-90), Internat. Acad. Astronautics, Univs. Space Rsch. Assn. (chair coun. of instns. 1996-97), Sigma Xi. Avocations: jogging, creative writing, basketball, cinema. Office: U Colo Lab Atmospheric & Space Physics PO Box 590 Boulder CO 80309-0590

BAKER, DANIEL RICHARD, computer company executive, consultant; b. Copenhagen, Mar. 19, 1932; came to U.S., 1936; s. Arthur and Molly (Needman) B.; m. June Ellin Nebenzahl, Oct. 2, 1960; children: David Charles, Jill Alison. Student, Tufts Coll., 1949-51; BA, Bklyn. Coll., 1957; postgrad, Fairleigh Dickinson U., 1961-64, Am. U., 1968-69; graduate, Realtors Inst., 1973. Math tchr. N.Y.C. Pub. Schs., 1958-59; computer programmer Sys. Devel. Corp., Paramus, N.J., 1959-61; programmer analyst ITT, Paramus, N.J., 1961-64; sr. mathematician Melpar Corp., Falls Church, Va., 1964-65; sys. analyst Wolf R & D Corp., Bladensburg, Md., 1965-66, Aries Corp., McLean, Va., 1966-68; sr. sys. analyst N. Am. Rockwell Corp., Roslyn, Va., 1968-70; pres. Data Assocs., Fairfax Station, Va., 1970—; Real estate broker. Group leader Dale Carnegie Sales Courses; vol. Ann. Fund Campaign Tufts Coll., 1976—. With AUS, 1954-55. Mem. Nat. Assn. Realtors (No. Va. chpt. multilist com., edn. com., pub. rels. com., 5-yr. Million Dollar Sales Club award, Va. chpt. Assn. Realtors dir. 1977-80, 83-97, Lifetime award 1992, 94-98), Am. Soc. Cybernetics, Silvanus Packard Soc., Wash. Tufts Club (v.p. 1975). E-mail: dan baker@email.com. Office: Data Assocs 5622-G Ox Rd Fairfax VA 22039-1018

BAKER, DAVID A., federal judge; b. Arlington, Va., Aug. 13, 1951; married; 3 children. AB, U. N.C., 1973; JD, U. Va., 1976. Bar: U.S. Supreme Ct., U.S. Ct. Appeals (7th & 11th cirs.), U.S. Dist. Ct. (mid. & so. dists.) Fla., U.S. Dist. Ct. (ea. & we. dists.) Wis. Law clk. to Hon. J. Calvitt Clarke, Jr. U.S. Dist. Ct., Norfolk, Va., 1976-77; assoc., ptnr. Foley & Lardner, Milw., 1977-85; ptnr. Foley & Lardner, Orlando, Fla., 1985-91; fed. magistrate U.S. Dist. Ct. (mid. dist.) Fla., Orlando, 1991—; adj. instr. legal studies dept. U. Cen. Fla., Orlando, 1993-95; mem. com. automation and tech. Jud. Conf. U.S., 1996—. Chmn. parks & recreation adv. bd. City of Maitland, Fla., 1990-91, mem. comprehensive devel. plan update com.; coach Little League, Youth Soccer, 1985-94. Mem. State Bar Fla., State Bar Wis., Orange County Bar Assn., Order of Coif, Phi Beta Kappa. Office: US Magistrate Judge 80 N Hughey Ave Orlando FL 32801-2231*

BAKER, DAVID ARTHUR, small business owner, manufacturer; b. Cranston, R.I., Jan. 5, 1941; s. Andrew Harris and Phyllis Evelyn (Partridge) B.; m. Anne Marie Perron, July 14, 1959; children: Susan Marie, Pamela Phyllis. Diploma, Brit. Inst. Homeopathy, Middlesex, Eng., 1995, DHM, 1996. Garment cutter Supreme Coat Co., Worcester, Mass., 1960-74; owner D.A. Baker Mfg. Co., Auburn, Mass., 1975—, Eagle's Nest Video Prodns., Auburn, 1985—; bd. dirs. Royal Arts Found. of Belcourt Castle, Newport, R.I. Producer (ednl. video) Popular Amazons, 1986, Macaws, 1987, Cockatoos, 1988, Parrot Keeping, 1989, and others. Treas. Boston Soc. Aviculture, 1983-85; co-founder, bd. dirs. Exotic Cage Bird Soc., 1986-88; mem. Plaza Club, Worcester, 1985-91; res. dep. sheriff Worcester County. Recipient Outstanding Svc. award Boston Soc. Aviculture, 1984, Exotic Cage Bird Soc. New Eng., 1985, Cert. of Merit, Les Comité des Vins de France, 1982. Fellow Brit. Inst. Homeopathy; mem. Homeopathic Acad. Naturopathic Physicians, Internat. Platform Soc., Internat. Soc. Food and Wine, Nat. Trust Hist. Preservation, Boston Soc. Aviculture (treas. 1983-85), Prservation Soc. Newport County, Exotic Cage Bird Soc. (co-founder, bd. dirs. 1986-88), Friends Ballroom Dancing, Friends of the Royal Arts Found. (v.p.), Rolls Royce Owners Club, Daimler and Lanchester Club, Club Maxine's, Health Scis. Inst., Leicester Bus. Assn. (v.p.), Knight Cottage Assn. (pres.). Republican. Avocations: art and antiques collector, shooting, boating, aviculturist. Home: Knight Cottage Bellevue Ave Newport RI 02840 Office: Eagles Nest Villa 196 Leicester St Auburn MA 01501-0637

BAKER, DAVID HIRAM, nutritionist, nutrition educator; b. DeKalb, Ill., Feb. 26, 1939; s. Vernon T. and Lucille M. (Severson) B.; m. Norraine A. Baker; children: Barbara G., Michael D., Susan G., Debora A., Luann C., Beth A. BS, U. Ill., 1961, MS, 1963, PhD, 1965. Sr. scientist Eli Lilly & Co., Greenfield, Ind., 1965-67; mem. faculty U. Ill., Champaign-Urbana, 1967—, prof. nutrition, dept. animal sci., nutritional biochemist, 1974—, dept. head, 1988-90. Author: Sulfur in Nonruminant Nutrition, 1977, Bioavailability of Nutrients for Animals, 1995; mem. editorial bd. Jour. Animal Sci., 1969-73, Jour. Nutrition, 1975-79, 89-99, Poultry Sci., 1978-84, Nutrition Revs., 1983-92; contbr. numerous articles to sci. jours. Chmn. bd. Champaign-Urbana Teen Challenge Drug Rehab. Program, 1977-80. Recipient Disting. Svc. award USDA, 1987; Univ. Scholar award, 1986; Nutrition Rsch. award, 1986; Am. Feed Mfrs., 1973; Merck award, 1977; Paul A. Funk award, 1977; H. H. Mitchell teaching award, 1979, 85; Broiler Rsch. award, 1983. Mem. Am. Soc. Animal Sci. (Young Scientist award 1971, Gustaf Bohstedt award 1985, Hoffman LaRoche award 1985, Morrison award 1994), Poultry Sci. Assn., Am. Inst. Nutrition (Borden award 1986), Fedn. Am. Socs. Exptl. Biology, Sigma Xi, Phi Kappa Phi, Alpha Zeta, Gamma Sigma Delta. Home: 2609 Wadsworth Ln Urbana IL 61802 Office: U Ill Nutrition Dept Urbana IL 61801

BAKER, DAVID REMEMBER, lawyer; b. Durham, N.C., Jan. 17, 1932; s. Roger Denio and Eleanor Elizabeth (Ussher) B.; m. Myra Augusta Mullins, Nov. 2, 1955. PhB, U. Chgo., 1949; BA, Birmingham-So. Coll., 1951; JD, Harvard U., 1954. Bar: Ala. 1954, N.Y. 1963, U.S. Supreme Ct. 1972. Assoc. Cabaniss & Johnston, Birmingham, Ala., 1957-62; assoc. Chadbourne, Parke, Whiteside & Wolff, N.Y.C., 1962-66, ptnr., 1967-86; ptnr. Jones, Day, Reavis & Pogue, N.Y.C., 1986-93, ret. ptnr., 1993—; ptnr. Afridi, Angell & Baker, N.Y.C., 1993-96, Gersen, Baker & Wood LLP, N.Y.C., 1997-98; gen. counsel Econ. Club of N.Y., N.Y.C., 1977—, Baker, Johnston & Wilson LLP, Birmingham, Ala., 1998—; counsel Afridi & Angell, 1997—; gen. counsel Econ. Club of N.Y., N.Y.C., 1977—; pres. Remember Baker Corp. Co-editor Due Diligence, Disclosures and Warranties in the Corporate Acquisition Practice, 1988, 2d edit., 1992; author articles and book chpts. Pres. N.Y. Legis. Svc., N.Y.C., 1975-98, chmn., 1998—; mem. adv. com. to Sec. of State of N.Y. on Access to Corps. Database, 1988-92; sec., dir. Jr. Achievement of N.Y., 1973-99; dir. Jr. Achievement of Greater Birmingham, 1999—; trustee Birmingham-So. Coll., 1985—. With U.S. Army, 1954-57. Mem. ABA (liaison com. fin. acctg. stds. bd.), Am. Arbitration Assn. (nat. panel), Am. Law Inst., Am. Fgn. Law Assn., Am. Soc. Internat. Law, Am. Judicature Soc., Assn. Bar City N.Y. (chmn. com. on state legis. 1968-70), Ala. Bar Assn., Birmingham Bar Assn., Internat. Bar Assn. (vice chmn. bus. orgn. com. 1986-90, chmn. com. on trusts for bus. 1990-94, rep. to U.S. members N.Y. area 1988—, prin. rep. to UN in N.Y. 1993—), Internat. Law Assn., Assn. Lloyd's Mems. (N.Am. adv. bd.), N.Y. State Bar Assn. (exec. com. bus. law sect. 1987-89, exec. com. internat. law and practice sect. 1991-92, chmn. internat. investment and devel. com. 1991-92), Internat. Ins. Soc., Musica Viva N.Y. (pres. 1994-96), Harvard Club, Met. Club. Democrat. Unitarian. Avocation: bridge (life master Am. Contract Bridge League). Home: 1200 Beacon Pkwy E Apt 500 Birmingham AL 35209-1041 also: 315 E 72d St Apt 2-J New York NY 10021 Office: Baker Johnston & Wilson LLP 1 Independence Plz Ste 322 Birmingham AL 35209-2634 also: 126 E 56th St 17th Fl New York NY 10022

BAKER, DAVID S., architect; b. Warsaw, N.Y., June 5, 1940; s. G. Stanley and Isabelle Mae (Payn) B.; m. Vera Elaine Shaffner, July 5, 1963; children: Nicole Jean, Lynette Ann, Lorrin Paul. Student, Columbia U., 1957-59; BA in Sociology, Syracuse U., 1963, BArch, 1965. Registered architect, Mass. Architect Christopher Kantianis, 1965-67, McClintock & Craig, Springfield, Mass., 1967-76, Cannon Design, Springfield, 1976-83, Timothy Murphy Architects, Holyoke, Mass., 1983—. Office: Timothy Murphy Architects 380 High St Holyoke MA 01040-4937

BAKER, DEBORAH, editor, writer; b. Charlottesville, Va., Mar. 28, 1959; d. Jeffrey John Wheeler and Barbara Ann Baker; m. Amitav Ghosh, Feb. 15, 1990; children: Lila, Nayan. Affiliated degree, Cambridge (Eng.) U., 1980; BA, U. Va., 1981. Editl. dir. Overlook, N.Y.C., 1986-88; assoc. pub. Sheep Meadow, The Bronx, 1993-95; exec. editor Kodansha, N.Y.C., 1995—. Author: In Extremis: The Life of Laura Riding, 1993 (finalist for Pulitzer prize), Making a Farm: The Life of Robert Bly, 1982. Office: care Georges Borchardt Inc 136 E 57th St New York NY 10022-2707

BAKER, DEBORAH KAY, secondary education educator; b. McAllen, Tex., Sept. 28, 1950; d. Dwight Menherion and Doris Marie (Poellot) Tresidder; m. Marvin Lee Baker, Dec. 28, 1971; children: Andrew Dwight, Jerrod Shane. BA, Sam Houston State U., 1971; MA in Edn., U. North Tex., 1982. Cert. secondary sch. tchr. English and history, all levels, Tex.; cert. master tchr., region 7, Tex. Edn. Assn., 1986, cert. gifted/talented tchr. 1983, advanced placement 1995. 6th grade reading tchr. Copperas Cove (Tex.) Jr. H.S., 1972-73; tchr. Ft. Collins (Colo.) Jr. and Sr. H.S., 1973-74; history and lang. arts tchr. grades 5-8 Keller (Tex.) Ind. Sch. Dist., 1976-87; devel. reading instr. Tyler (Tex.) Jr. Coll., 1988-89; English and reading tchr. Chapel Hill H.S., Tyler, 1987—; mem. Dist. Ednl. Improvement Com., Chapel Hill, 1995—; coord. advanced placement Chapel Hill Ind. Sch. Dist., 1998. Vol. Meals on Wheels, Tyler and Whitehouse, Tex., 1988—, Literacy Coun., 1988—, Mothers Against Drunk Driving, 1988—, Am. Cancer Soc., 1988—; bd. mem., chair various coms. Whitehouse Meth. Ch., 1988—. Mem. AAUW (v.p. 1980—, scholarship award 1981), Internat. Reading Assn. (program chair 1982—), Tex. Gifted & Talented Assn., Tex. Classroom Tchrs. Assn., Phi Kappa Phi. Avocations: reading, swimming, hiking. Home: 18280 FM Rd 3341 Troup TX 75789 Office: Chapel Hill High Sch 13172 State Highway 64 E Tyler TX 75707-5340

BAKER, DEXTER FARRINGTON, manufacturing company executive; b. Worcester, Mass., Apr. 16, 1927; s. Leland Dyer and Edith (Quimby) B.; m. Dorothy Ellen Hess, June 23, 1951; children: Ellen L., Susan A., Leslie A., Carolyn J. B.S., Lehigh U., 1950, M.B.A., 1957. Sales engr. Air Products & Chems., Inc., Allentown, Pa., 1952-56, gen. sales mgr., 1956-57, mng. dir., 1957-64, chief exec. ops. in Europe, bd. dirs., 1964-67, exec. v.p., 1967-78, pres., 1978-86, 90-91, chmn., pres., 1990-91, chmn., chief exec. officer, 1986-92, chmn. exec. com.bd. dirs., 1992-98; former chmn. investment policy U.S. Trade Rep. Bd. assocs. Muhlenberg Coll.; trustee Harry C. and Mary M. Trexler Found. Served with USNR, 1945-46; with U.S. Army, 1950-52. Mem. AIChE, Am. Mgmt. Assn., Nat. Assn. Mfrs. (former chmn.), Theta Chi. Presbyterian (elder). Office: Air Products and Chems Inc 7201 Hamilton Blvd Allentown PA 18195-1526

BAKER, DIANE R.H., dermatologist; b. Toledo, Nov. 17, 1945. BS, Ohio State U., 1967, MD cum laude, 1971. Diplomate Am. Bd. Dermatology. Intern U. Wis. Hosp., Madison, 1971-72, resident in dermatology, 1972-74; resident in dermatology Oreg. Health Sci. Ctr., Portland, 1974-76; pvt. practce, Portland, 1976—; clin. prof. dermatology Oreg. Health Sci. U., 1986—; mem. med. staff Meridian Park Hosp., Tualatin, Oreg., 1981—; dir. Am. Bd. Dermatology, 1995—. Mem. AMA (del. 1995—), Am. Acad. Dermatology (v.p. 1990), Am. Dermatol. Assn., Oreg. Derm. Soc., Alpha Omega Alpha. Office: Dermatol Assocs 9495 SW Locust St Portland OR 97223-6683*

BAKER, DON ROBERT, chemist, inventor; b. Salt Lake City, Apr. 6, 1933; s. Ralph H. and Ruth Eve (Thalmann) B.; m. Shirley May Nelson, Nov. 20, 1954 (dec. 1993); children: Robert, David, George, Barbara; m. Shirlee Ann Call, Sept. 17, 1994. AA, Sacramento City Coll., 1953; AB, Calif. State U., Sacramento, 1955; PhD, U. Calif., Berkeley, 1959. Sr. rsch. chemist Stauffer Chem. Co., Richmond, Calif., 1958-72, rsch. assoc., 1970-74, supr., 1974-85; sr. rsch. assoc. ICI Ams. Inc. Zeneca Ag Products, Richmond, 1985-97; cons. in chemistry and chem. safety, 1998—; lectr. family history topics. Editor Calif. Chemists Alert, 1986—, Synthesis and Chemistry of Agrochems., 1987, 90, 92, 95, 98; contbr. articles to profl. jours.; holder more than 200 U.S. patents. Recipient Zeneca Patent award, 1996. Fellow Am. Chem. Soc. (chmn. Calif. sect. 1973, councilor 1971—, chmn. nat. divsn. profl. rels. 1980, coordinating com. Calif. sects. 1970—, vice-chmn. agrochem. divsn. 1993, chmn. agrochems. divsn. 1995, Walter Petersen award 1991, fellow award 1991, ACS Internat. award for agrl. rsch. 1999); mem. Orchid Soc. Calif. (pres. 1979-80), Oakland Family History Ctr. (libr. 1967—). Republican. Mormon. Avocations: orchid growing, mineralogy, genealogy. Home: 15 Muth Dr Orinda CA 94563-2805 Office: Zeneca Ag Products 15 Muth Dr Orinda CA 94563-2805

BAKER, DONALD, lawyer; b. Chgo., May 28, 1929; s. Russell and Elizabeth (Wallace) B.; m. Gisela S. Carli, Oct. 6, 1960; children: Caryna, Andrew, Russell. Student, Deep Springs Coll., Calif., 1947-49; J.D.S., U. Chgo., 1954. Bar: Ill. 1955, N.Y. 1964. Ptnr. Baker & McKenzie, Chgo., 1955-94, ret., 1994; sec., gen. counsel, bd. dirs. Air South, Inc., Columbia, S.C., 1994-95; bd. dirs. Trimedyne, Inc. Bd. dirs. exec. com. Mid-Am. Com., Chgo., 1980—. Mem. ABA. Club: Michigan Shores (Wilmette, Ill.).

BAKER, DONALD G., social sciences educator; b. Elgin, Ill., Feb. 16, 1932; s. Glenn O. and Helen K. Baker; m. Barbara L. Sands; 1 child, Catherine K. BA in Polit. Sci., Denver U., 1953; MA in Polit. Sci., Syracuse U., 1957, PhD in Social Scis., 1961. Asst. prof., dir. dept. Am. studies Skidmore Coll., Saratoga Springs, N.Y., 1959-64; assoc. prof., then prof. Southampton (N.Y.) Coll. of L.I. U., 1964—, dir. social scis. divsn., 1964-70; cons. Peace Corps, Washington, 1964-67, N.Y. State Dept. Edn., Albany, 1964-66, AID, Washington, 1977-79; dir. Grad. Legis. Intern Program, Albany, 1962-67. Author: Politics of Race, 1975, Race, Ethnicity and Power, 1983. Cpl. U.S. Army, 1954-56. Rsch. fellow U. Rhodesia, 1976-78, U. Zimbabwe, 1981, Victoria U., New Zealand, 1993; assoc. rsch. fellow Yale U., 1992-93; rsch. grantee St. Antony's Coll., Oxford U., Eng., 1980-81, 86. Democrat. Avocations: travel, writing. Home: PO Box 701 Hampton Bays NY 11946-0607

BAKER, DONALD GARDNER, retired soil science educator; b. St. Paul, July 20, 1923; s. William E. and Florence A. (Kirkendall) B.; m. Jacqueline M. Mouzel, Feb. 14, 1953; 1 child, William G. Student, U. Wis., 1943, U. Chgo., 1943-44; BS, U. Minn., 1949, MS, 1950, PhD, 1958. With U. Minn., St. Paul, 1958-94, instr., 1958-61, asst. prof., 1961-65, assoc. prof., 1965-69, prof., 1969-94, prof. emeritus, 1994—. Lt. USAAF, 1943-46, ETO, 51-52, Korea. Decorated Bronze Star. Fellow AAAS, Am. Soc. Agronomy; mem. Am. Meteorol. Soc., Am. Geophys. Union, Royal Meteorol. Soc. (London), Soil Sci. Soc. Am. Office: U Minn Soil Water and Climate Dept 439 Borlang Hall Saint Paul MN 55108*

BAKER, DONALD PARKS, journalist, educator; b. Wheeling, W. Va., Nov. 20, 1932; s. Clarence Parks and Katherine Ruth (Rapp) B.; m. Nancy Cottrell, Aug. 30, 1959; children—Lisa Dawn, Amanda Jean. AB in Journalism, W. Va. Inst. Tech., 1954. Reporter Daily Record, Wooster, Ohio, 1954-57; reporter Courier Press, Evansville, Ind., 1957-60; reporter, editor Indpls. Times, 1960-66, Cleve. Press., 1966-70, Washington Post, Washington, 1970—; adj. prof. Am. U., Washington, 1971-76; part-time faculty Marymount Coll., Arlington, Va., 1984-85, U. Md., College Park, 1980-83, Va. Commonwealth U., 1986-89, 92-97; journalist-in-residence Coll. of William and Mary, 1998. Author: Wilder: Hold Fast to Dreams, 1989. Alicia Patterson fellow, 1995. E-mail: Bakerdp@aol.com. Office: Washington Post 1001 E Broad St Ste 410 Richmond VA 23219-1928

BAKER, DOUGLAS FINLEY, library director; b. Highland, Ill., July 21, 1950; s. Elmer Eugene and Winifred Ilona (Timmons) B.; m. Susan Diane Siewert, June 6, 1989; children: Gretchen, Richard, Charles. BA with distinction, U. Iowa, 1972, MA in Libr. Sci., 1973. Libr. West Side Br., Des Moines Libr., 1974; I-LITE coord. State Libr. of Iowa, 1974-77, dir. office in interlibr. cooperation, 1977-78; dir. N.W. Wis. Libr. System (now No. Waters Libr. Svc.), Ashland, 1978-86, Kenosha (Wis.) Pub. Libr., 1986—. Mem. ALA, System and Resource Libr. Adminstrs. Assn. of Wis., Wis. Libr. Assn., Wis. Assn. of Pub. Librs. Office: Kenosha Pub Libr PO Box 1414 812 56th St Kenosha WI 53141-1414

BAKER, DUSTY (JOHNNIE B. BAKER, JR.), professional baseball team manager; b. Riverside, Calif., June 15, 1949. Student, Am. River Coll. Player Atlanta Braves, 1968-75, L.A. Dodgers, 1976-83, San Francisco Giants, 1984, Oakland A's, 1985-86; coach San Francisco Giants, 1988-92, mgr., 1993—; mem. Nat. League All-Star Team, 1981-82. Recipient Silver

Slugger award, 1980-81, Gold Glove, 1981; named to Sporting News All-Star Team, 1980. Office: San Francisco Giants 3 com park at Candlestick Point San Francisco CA 94124*

BAKER, EDITH MADEAN, counselor; b. Greeley, Colo., Oct. 7, 1942; d. Richard Luther and Catherine Jane (John) Tatman; m. Richard Dennis Baker, Oct. 25, 1964; children: Kimberly Baker Parker, Gregory. Student, U. No. Colo., 1961; BA, U. Colo., 1964; postgrad., San Jose (Calif.) State U., 1969-70; EdM, Oreg. State U., 1978. Cert. counselor, Oreg. Tchr. Spaulding Sch. Dist., Waukegan, Ill., 1965-67, Alhambra Pvt. Sch., Phoenix, 1968-69; pvt. practice Corvallis, Oreg., 1977-80; counselor Salem (Oreg.) Sch. Dist., 1978-79; testing specialist Corvallis Sch. Dist., 1980, counselor, 1980-88; counselor Springfield (Oreg.) Sch. Dist., 1988—; chair activity curriculum com. Corvallis Sch. Dist., 1984, chair prin. selection com., 1985. Member Symphony Guild, Eugene, Oreg., 1988—, PTA; bd. dirs. Boys and Girls Club, Corvallis, 1984-88, Assn. for Retarded Citizens, Eugene, 1989-90; chair Parent Graduation Celebration, Corvallis, 1985, 88. Mem. NEA, Oreg. Counseling Assn., Oreg. Edn. Assn., Mental Health Assn. of Oreg., Springfield Edn. Assn., Univ. Women's League, Delta Kappa Gamma, Kappa Delta Pi, Delta Delta Delta. Democrat. Avocations: traveling, reading, camping, music. Home: 2011 Dogwood Dr Eugene OR 97405-5848 Office: Thurston High Sch 333 N 58th St Springfield OR 97478-6999

BAKER, EDWARD KEVIN, retail executive; b. Chester, Ill., Nov. 25, 1948; s. Edward Louis and Betty Lou (Huch) B.; m. Janet Lynn Verbal, Oct. 26, 1967 (div. 1973); 1 child, Shawn Allen; m. Doris Mary Kubala, June 12, 1975; stepchildren: Jimmy Lee, Jennifer Lou Godard. Mgr. F.W. Woolworth Co., St. Louis, then Dallas, 1968-74; pres. Baker Mktg. Co., Dallas, 1974-76; mgr. E.B. Mott Co., Dallas, 1976-83; mkt. mgr. Michaels Stores Inc., San Antonio, 1983-86; dir. merchandising Michaels Stores Inc., Irving, Tex., 1986-88, dir. mgmt. devel., 1988-89, v.p. ops., 1989-91; sr. v.p. ops., distbn. mktg. Silk Greenhouse Inc., Tampa, 1990-91; dir. ops. mdse. Crafts & More div. Ames Dept. Stores, Rocky Hill, Conn., 1991-92; pres. E.K. Baker Group, Inc., Treasure House Stores, Inc., Seattle, 1993—; chief oper. officer, bd. dirs. Treasure House Stores, Inc.; bd. dirs. H. Mangelsen & Sons Inc., Omaha, Nebr., 1997—. Author The Edge 1988; producer (video) Framing Technique 1989; editor (video) Art Materials 1989. Mem. Southwest Craft & Hobby Assn. (bd. dirs. 1987-93), Am. Soc. Tng. Dirs., Art Materials Trade Assn., Am. Soc. Decorative Painters, Profl. Picture Framers Assn. Lutheran. Avocation: restoring antique furniture.

BAKER, EDWARD L., JR., physician, science facility executive; b. Chattanooga, Nov. 18, 1946; s. Edward Lamar and Sue B. Baker; m. Pamela Taylor, June 21, 1969; children: Justin, Ryan, Lindsay. BA, Vanderbilt U., 1968; MD, Baylor U., 1972; MPH, Harvard U., 1979, MS, 1980. Diplomate Am. Bd. Internal Medicine, Am. Bd. Occupational Medicine. Commd. USPHS, 1974—, advanced through grades to rear adm., 1995, asst. surgeon gen.; asst. prof. Harvard U. Sch. Pub. Health, Boston, 1980-82, assoc. prof., 1982-85; asst. dir. Nat. Inst Occupl. Safety and Health Ctr. Disease Control, Atlanta, 1985-88, dep. dir. Nat. Inst. Occupl. Safety and Health, 1988-90, asst. surgeon gen., dir. Pub. Health Practice Program Office, 1990—; bd. dirs. Internat. Commn. on Occupl. Health, 1986-92. Author, editor 100 sci. articles and book chpts. Fellow Am. Coll. Epidemiology; mem. APHA, Am. Coll. Occupl. and Environ. Medicine (authorship award 1988), Soc. Occupl. and Environ. Health, Royal Soc. Medicine (London, vis. fellow). Home: 755 Kirk Rd Decatur GA 30030-4529 Office: Ctr Disease Control Pub Health Practice Program Office (K36) 2877 Brandywine Rd Atlanta GA 30341-3724

BAKER, EDWARD MARTIN, engineering and industrial psychologist; b. Bklyn., Mar. 13, 1941; s. Harold H. and Paula B.; m. Shige Jajiki; 1 son, Evan Keith. B.A., CCNY, 1962, M.B.A., 1964; Ph.D. (Research fellow), Bowling Green State U., 1972. Human factors research engr. environ. and safety engrng. staff Ford Motor Co., Dearborn, Mich., 1972-77; tech. tng. assoc. mgmt. and tech. tng. dept. Ford Motor Co., Detroit, 1977-79; orgn. devel. cons., personnel and orgn. staff Ford Motor Co., 1979-81, statis. assoc., ops. support product quality office,, 1981-83, statis methods mgr. Asia-Pacific and Latin-Am. automotive ops., 1983-87, dir. total quality planning, cons. and statis. methods corp. quality office, 1987—, dir. quality strategy and ops. support, 1990-92; sr. fellow Aspen Inst., Wye, Md., 1992-95; mgmt. cons., 1993—. Author: Scoring a Whole in One, 1999; contbr. articles to profl. jours.; editorial referee: Jour. Quality Tech, 1974-75, 77-81. Trustee The W. Edwards Deming Inst., Washington, 1993—. Fellow Am. Soc. Quality (Brumbaugh award 1975, Craig award 1976, 79, 86, 88, Ishikawa medal 1995, Deming medal 1997). Office: PO Box 279 Farmington MI 48332-0279

BAKER, EDWIN MOODY, retired newspaper publisher; b. Cleve., Dec. 20, 1923; s. Alton Fletcher and Mildred Elizabeth (Moody) B.; m. Patricia Petersen, 1954 (dec. 1983); children: Bridget Baker Kincaid, Amanda Baker Barber, Jonathan; m. Marie Kottkamp Randall, 1984; step children: Steven, Mark, Bruce Randall. B.S. in Bus. Adminstrn., U. Oreg., 1948. With Eugene (Oreg.) Register-Guard, 1948-88, successively advt. mgr., bus. mgr., gen. mgr., pub., pres., chmn. bd. Guard Pub. Co. Mem. exec. bd. Oreg. Trail Council, Boy Scouts Am., 1953—, pres. 1960-61, chmn. Region XI Area I (Northwest) 1971, pres., 1972, mem. nat. exec. bd., 1971-72, nat. adv. council, 1972-82; trustee U. Oreg. Found., 1975-90, Lane C.C. Found. Bd.; bd. dirs. Oreg. Community Found., 1982-90; Oreg. Hist. Soc., 1988-92; trustee Eugene Arts Found., 1980-85; pres. Oreg. Pacific Econ. Devel. Corp., 1984-85; 2d v.p. Eugene Springfield Met. Ptnrship.; mem., chmn. Kakegawa Sister City com., 1986-88; co-chmn. Birth to Three Capital Campaign, 1997; chmn. United Way Leadersip, 1997-98. Served with AUS, World War II. Decorated Bronze Star, Purple Heart; recipient Silve r Beaver award, Boy Scouts Am., 1962, Silver Antelope, 1965, Pioneer award U. Oreg., 1982, Distng. Eagle Scout, 1982, Awbrey Watzig award Lewis and Clark Coll., 1988; named Eugene First Citizen, 1983. Mem. Am. Newspaper Pubs. Assn. (research inst. lab. com. 1978-79), Oreg. Newspaper Pubs. Assn. (dir. 1982-90, pres. 1988-89), U. Oreg. Pres. Assocs., Nat. Assn. Fund Raising Execs. (vol. 1994 Oreg. chpt., Fund Raiser of Yr. 1993), Rotary, Eugene Country Club. Home: 2121 Kimberly Cir Eugene OR 97405-5821 Office: PO Box 10188-2188 Eugene OR 97401-3204

BAKER, EDWIN STUART, retired computer consultant; b. Ottumwa, Iowa, Feb. 14, 1944; s. Edwin Moore and Geraldine Vivian (Irby) B; m. Wilma Jeanne Parker, 1968 (div. 1970). Student, Whitman Coll., 1962-64; BS, Oreg. State U., 1978. Programmer agrl. engrng. dept. Oreg. State U., Corvallis, 1977-78, rsch. asst., 1979-83, sr. rsch. asst., 1984-89; measurement standards specialist Oreg. Dept. Agr., Salem, 1990-93; cons. in field. Mem. IEEE, Assn for Computing Machinery, Am. Legion, DAV, NRA, Nat. Intercollegiate Ro-deo Assn., 59ers Svc. Club. Avocations: photography, horses. Home: PO Box 370 Lebanon OR 97355 Office: Oreg Dept Agr Measurements Standards Divsn Salem OR 97310

BAKER, ELAINE R., radio station executive. V.p., gen. mgr. WOMC-FM, Detroit, Mich. Office: WOMC-FM 2201 Woodward Hts Ferndale MI 48220-1511*

BAKER, ELIZABETH CALHOUN, magazine editor; b. Boston; d. John Calhoun and Elizabeth Marshall Evans B. B.A. cum laude, Bryn Mawr Coll.; M.A., Radcliffe Coll. Fulbright scholar Inst. d'Art et d'Archeologie and Ecole du Louvre, Paris; Instr. art history Boston U., Wheaton Coll., Norton, Mass.; assoc. editor Art News, N.Y.C., 1963-65; mng. editor Art News, 1965-73; editor Art in Am. mag., N.Y.C., 1973—; instr. art history Sch. Visual Arts, N.Y.C., 1968-74; freelance art criticism. Recipient Lifetime Achievement award Coll. Art Assn., 1992; Nat. Endowment for Arts grantee, 1972. Office: Art in America Brant Publications 575 Broadway Fl 5 New York NY 10012-3230*

BAKER, EMILY LIND, editor, digital library specialist; b. Washington, Jan. 22, 1944; d. David and Elizabeth R. Delman; m. D. James Baker, Sept. 7, 1968. BA cum laude, Harvard U., 1965; MA, U. Wash., 1979. Reference libr. Mus. Fine Arts, Boston, 1965-68; program mgr. Coun. on the Arts and Humanities, Boston, 1969-73; teaching asst. U. Wash., Seattle, 1977; editor Jackson Sch. Internat. Studies, U. Wash., Seattle, 1980; cons. editor Seattle, 1980-82; devel. dir. A Contemporary Theater and Seattle Children's Theater, 1982-83; cons. editor Nat. Acad. Scis., Washington, 1984-85, Am. Petroleum Inst., others, Washington, 1985-88; mgmt. cons. The Oceanography Soc., Washington, 1988-92, UN Devel. Fund for Women, N.Y.C., 1990-92; cons. editor NSF, Embassy of France, Washington, 1992; cons. editing and prodn. Am. Memory Libr. of Congress, Washington, 1993-95, digital conversion specialist Nat. Digital Libr. Program, 1996—; bd. dirs. Nat. Aquarium Soc., Washington. Editor numerous reports and articles. Mem. Forest Hills Tree Com., Washington, 1990-94; majority coun. mem. EMILY'S List, Washington, 1996—. Mem. Am. Hist. Assn., Asia Soc., Women's Aquatic Network, Nat. Mus. Women in the Arts (charter mem.). Office: Libr of Congress Nat Digital Libr Program 101 Independence Ave SE Washington DC 20540-1310

BAKER, ERNEST WALDO, JR., advertising executive; b. Sedalia, Mo., Oct. 20, 1926; s. Ernest Waldo and Sara Elizabeth (Staples) B.; m. Joan Elaine Bauman, Sept. 4, 1948; children: Robert E., Michael E. BJ, U. Mo., 1948; D in Bus. Sci., Cleary Coll., 1972. Copywriter Zimmer-Keller Advt. Agy., Detroit, 1948-51; account exec. Denman & Baker, Inc., Detroit, 1951-63; chmn. Baker, Abbs, Cunningham & Klepinger, Birmingham, Mich., 1964-90, DDB Needham Worldwide, Troy, Mich., 1990-93; exec. v.p. BBDO Detroit, 1993—. Bd. visitors Sch. Nursing, Oakland U., Rochester Hills, Mich., 1987—. With U.S. Army, 1944-45, PTO. Mem. Adcraft Club Detroit. Republican. Methodist. Office: BBDO Detroit 2600 W Big Beaver Rd Ste 500 Troy MI 48084-3337

BAKER, FLOYD WILMER, surgeon, retired army officer; b. Leavenworth, Kans., May 25, 1927; s. Floyd Winfield and Lolita Clare (Somers) B.; m. Darlene Marie Fulk, Apr. 10, 1949; children: Linda Marie, Diane Louise, Barbara Jayne. B.A., U. Kans., 1950, M.D., 1953; grad., Army Command and Gen. Staff Coll., 1964, Indsl. Coll. Armed Forces, 1967. Diplomate: Am. Bd. Surgery. Commd. 1st lt. U.S. Army, 1953, advanced through grades to maj. gen., 1980; intern Madigan Gen. Hosp., Tacoma, 1953-54; resident in gen. surgery Fitzsimons Army Hosp., Denver, 1955-59; dir. personnel and tng. Office of Surgeon Gen., 1970-71; comdg. gen. Brooke Army Med. Center, Ft. Sam Houston, Tex., 1974-78; Letterman Army Med Center, Presidio of San Francisco, 1978-81; chief surgeon U.S. Army, Europe; comdg. gen. U.S. Army 7th Med. Command,, 1981-83, U.S. Army Health Services Command, Ft. Sam Houston, 1983-86; retired U.S. Army, 1986. Served with USNR, 1945-46. Decorated Legion of Merit (2), Meritorious Service medal, Army Commendation medal (3), Air medal (2), Disting. Service medal. Fellow Am. Coll. Physician Execs.; mem. AMA, Soc. U.S. Army Flight Surgeons. Republican. Baptist. Home and Office: 1413 Wiltshire Ave San Antonio TX 78209-6050

BAKER, FRANK C. (BUZZ BAKER), advertising executive; m. Terry Baker; 1 child, Scott. BA in History and Econs., Harvard U., postgrad. With Fletcher/Mayo Assocs., St. Joseph, Mo., 1976-81; pres. & mng. dir. Cedar Rapids unit, dir. acct. mgmt. Creswel Munsell Fultz & Zirbel, Cedar Rapids, Iowa, 1981-90, pres., CEO, 1990—. Bd. dirs. United Way, Hugh O'Brien Found., March of Dimes, Young Parent's Network. Named to Ad Fed Hall of Fame, 1991. Mem. Nat. AgriMktg. Assn., Cedar Rapids Advt. Fedn. Avocation: sports. Office: Creswell Munsell Fultz & Zirbel 4211 Signal Ridge Rd NE Cedar Rapids IA 52406-2879*

BAKER, FREDERICK MILTON, JR., lawyer; b. Flint, Mich., Nov. 2, 1949; s. Frederick Milton Baker and Mary Jean (Hallitt) Rarig; m. Irene Taylor; children: Jessica, Jordan. BA, U. Mich., 1971; JD, Washington U., St. Louis, 1975. Bar: Mich. 1975, U.S. Dist. Ct. (we. dist.) Mich. 1980, U.S. Dist. Ct. (ea. dist.) Mich. 1981, U.S. Ct. Appeals (6th cir.) 1983, U.S. Supreme Ct. 1986. Instr. law Wayne State U., Detroit, 1975-76; research atty. Mich. Ct. Appeals, Lansing, 1976-77, law clk. to chief judge, 1977; asst. prof. T.M. Cooley Law Sch., Lansing, Mich., 1978-80; ptnr. Willingham & Cote, Lansing, 1980-86, Honigman, Miller, Schwartz & Cohn, Lansing, 1986—. Author: Michigan Bar Appeal Manual, 1982; editor Mich. Bar Jour., 1984-89; contbr. articles to profl. jours. Founder, pres. Sixty Plus Law Ctr., Lansing, 1978-87, bd. dirs., 1987—; mem. community adv. bd. Lansing Jr. League, 1983-90; co-founder, dir., sec.-treas. John D. Voelker Found., 1989—; bd. dirs. Lansing chpt. ACLU, 1997—, bd. dirs. Greater Lansing chpt., 1997—; treas. Kehillat Israel, 1996-98. Fellow Mich. State Bar Found.; mem. ABA (Outstanding Single Project award 1980, Disting. brief award 1988), Mich. Bar Assn. (vice chmn. jour. adv. bd. 1984-87, chmn. jour. adv. bd. 1987—, young lawyers sect. coun. 1980-84, grievance com. 1982-84, John W. Cummiskey award 1984), Ingham County Bar Assn. Unitarian. Club: Big Oak (Baldwin, Mich.). Avocations: photography, fishing, running, frisbee, squash. Home: 640 Oakwood Dr East Lansing MI 48823-3101 Office: Honigman Miller Schwartz & Cohn 222 N Washington Sq Ste 400 Lansing MI 48933-1800

BAKER, GAIL DYER, lawyer; b. West Point, N.Y, Mar. 16, 1954; s. Hillier Locke Jr. and Miriam Jane (Dyer) B. BA magna cum laude, U. Minn., 1978; JD, Suffolk U., 1981. Bar: Minn. 1981, U.S. Dist. Ct. Minn. 1981. Assoc. R.C. Ploetz & Assocs., Mpls., 1981-82; exec. dir., staff atty. Legal Assistance of Olmsted County, Rochester, Minn., 1982-85; assoc. Steward, Perry, Mahler & Bird, P.A., Rochester, 1985-87, Ryan & VanDerHeyden, Rochester, 1987-88, Ryan & Grinde Ltd., Rochester, 1988-89; ptnr. Baker Law Offices, Rochester, 1989—. Class agt. Suffolk U. Law Sch.; mem. task force on adoption and foster care Minn. Supreme Ct., 1996-97; co-chair Children in Need of Protection and Svcs. Rules Commn., 1997-99. Mem. ABA (young lawyers divsn. dist. rep. 1985-87, publs. chmn. 1987-90, child adv. vice chmn. 1985-90, family law sect. pub. devel. bd. 1989—, mediation com. 1989-90, children and law task force 1989—, task force devel. standards of practice for attys. representing children in dependency and neglect cases 1994-96), Minn. Bar Assn. (family law sect., coahc h.s. mock trials 1990—), Olmsted County Bar Assn. (treas. 1984-86, chair law day 1983-84, chair Bicentennial of Const. 1988, v.p. 1996-97, pres. 1997-98), U. Minn. Alumni Assn., Phi Beta Kappa, Phi Delta Phi. Republican. Presbyterian. Home: 1412 Berkman Ct SE Rochester MN 55904-4934 Office: Baker Law Offices 2212 2nd St SW Rochester MN 55902-0824

BAKER, GEORGE BRIAN, principal; b. Clintwood, Va., Sept. 14, 1954; s. Charles Dewey and Margaret Linkous Baker; m. Brenda Gaye Dolinger, Jan. 26, 1977; children: Lydia, Charles. BS, Va. Poly. Inst. and State U., 1977, Master's degree, 1991. Cert. prin., elem., mid. and h.s. Classroom tchr. Dickenseon County Pub. Sch., Clintwood, 1977-92, prin., 1992—; reading tutor Reading Pals, Clintwood, 1998-99; action plan adviser Dickenson County Pub. Schs., 1997—. Vol. Clintwood High Athletics, 1996; mem., coach Little League, Clintwood, 1985-90; leader Boy Scouts Am., Clintwood, 1985-91. Mem. NEA, Va. Edn. Assn., Dickenson Edn. Assn., Kiwanis. Methodist. Avocations: fishing, hunting, sports, walking. Home: PO Box 399 Clintwood VA 24228 Office: Longs Fork Elem RR 2 Box 60 Clintwood VA 24228

BAKER, GEORGE CHISHOLM, engineering executive, consultant; b. Dartmouth, N.S., Can., Oct. 29, 1918; s. Clifford Lyall and Edith (Chisholm) B.; m. Ethel Marie Suzanne Humbert, Jan. 2, 1942; children: Alison Marie, Catherine Ann. Diploma, Royal Mil. Coll. Can., 1939, D Engrng. (hon.), 1988; BA in Sci., Toronto U., 1946; D Engrng. (hon.), Tech. Coll. N.S., 1987; DCL, Acadia U., 1993. Registered profl engr., Can. Pres. Kentville (N.S.) Pub. Co. Ltd., 1948-77; engr. Kentville Electric Commn., 1960-81; exec. v.p. Tidal Power Corp., Halifax, N.S., 1971-89; pres. G.C. Baker Engrng. Ltd., Kentville, 1977—; chmn. Cam Pubs. Ltd., New Glasgow, N.S., 1978—. Contbr. numerous articles to profl. pubs. Chmn. Acadia U. Inst., Wolfville, N.S., 1968-70; gov. Acadia U., Wolfville, 1979-92. Maj. Signal Corps Royal Can. Army, 1939-46. Decorated Order of Brit. Empire. Fellow Engring. Inst. Can., Can. Acad. Engring.; mem. IEEE (Centennial Gold medal), Can. Soc. Elec. Engrs. Office: G C Baker Engring Ltd, 536 Main St, Kentville, NS Canada B4N 1L3

BAKER, GEORGE HAROLD, III, physicist; b. Cheverly, Md., Mar. 23, 1949; s. George Harold Jr. and Betty (Fost) B.; m. Donna Prillaman, Jun 21, 1975; children: Matthew C., Jeffrey P., Virginia E. BA, Western Md. Coll., 1971; MS, U. Va., 1974; PhD, USAF Inst. Tech., Dayton, Ohio, 1987. Teaching asst. U. Va., Charlottesville, 1971-73; physicist Harry Diamond Labs., Adelphi, Md., 1973-77; physicist Def. Nuclear Agy., Alexandria, 1977-87, group leader, 1987-89, asst. for program devel., 1989-94; chief innovative concepts divsn., 1994-96; dir. Springfield (Va.) Rsch. Facility, 1996-99; sr. scientist Logicon, Alexandria, Va., 1999—. Contbr. articles to profl. jours. Tchr. Agape Christian Fellowship, Chantilly, Va., 1974—, elder, 1994—; music and youth leader New Life Fellowship, Annandale, Va., 1979-83; canvasser Citizens for Sensible County Planning, Fairfax County, Va., 1989—. Fellow Nuclear Electromagnetic Soc. (chmn. program com. 1984, session chair 1996, 98, co-chair non-proliferation and arms control underground focus group 1996-99; chmn. nat. HPM conf. steering group 1999); mem. IEEE (session chmn. 1987, 92), N.Y. Acad Sci., Forum for Mil. Application of Directed Energy, Phi Delta Theta. Achievements include patent for optically coupled differential voltage sensor, 1976; co-developer sea-going nuclear EMP simulator concept, 1979; initiated Def. Nuclear Agy. EMP underground test program, 1983, High Power Microwave program, 1984, space nuclear power, 1994. Office: Logicon South Kings Hwy Alexandria VA 22310

BAKER, GILBERT JENS, management consultant; b. Clinton, Iowa, Nov. 15, 1946; s. Gilbert LeRoy and Jenis Marie (Willardsen) B.; children: Courtenay, Kirstie, Gilbert, Geoffrey. Student. U. Iowa, 1965-68; BA, U. No. Iowa, 1970; postgrad., Mankato State U., 1971-72; BA in Acctg., Mt. St. Clare Coll., 1991. Tchr. History Lake Mills (Iowa) Community Schs., 1970-74; underwriter Am. Family Ins. Co., Madison, Wis., 1974-76; owner, dir. G. Baker Dist. Ins., Clinton, Iowa, 1976—, Gateway Vending Co., Clinton, 1977—, G.B. Systems Ltd., Clinton, 1979—, Bacor Ltd., Clinton, 1982—; bd. dirs. Gateway Home Health Care, Clinton, Clinton Area Devel. Corp., River City Ventures, Merc. Bank; mem. fin. com. Samaritan Health Systems, 1989—. Bd. dirs. River City Ventures, Clinton, 1987-88, 91, sec., 1987-88, Clinton Area Devel. Corp., 1991, v.p., 1994, chmn. bd., 1996; trustee Mt. St. Clara Coll., Clinton, 1995—, chmn. athletic com.; mem. ctrl. com. Clinton County Rep. Com., 1986-88; v.p. Clinton County Gaming Commn.; pres. Clinton County Gaming Assn., 1993—; v.p. Gateway YMCA, 1988—. Mem. River City C. of C. (pres. 1986-87), Rotary (pres. 1988—), Clinton County Club (dir. 1988, pres.-elect., pres. 1990-91). Avocations: basketball, golf, reading. Office: Bacor Ltd PO Box 3044 Clinton IA 52732-3104

BAKER, GRANT CODY, civil engineering educator; b. Eugene, Oreg., May 16, 1956; s. Irwin Gerald and Louise (Powell) B.; m. Tina Louise Denton, Apr. 9, 1988; children: Jessica, Calvin, Benjamin. BSChemE, U. Wash., 1978; MS in Mining Engring., U. Alaska, 1983, PhD in Geophysics, 1987. Chem. engr. UOP, Chgo., 1978-79; comml. fisherman F/V Patricia Sue, Anchorage, 1979-80; asst. prof. mech. engrng. U. Alaska, Fairbanks, 1988-94; asst. prof. civil engring. U. Alaska, Anchorage, 1994—; author, pub. Edutech, Anchorage, 1992—. Author: Bridge to Engineering, 1993, FORTRAN Reference Programs, 1995, ANSI C Reference Programs, 1996, BASIC Reference Programs, 1996, ANSI C Reference Programs, 1998. Named Engring. Prof. of Yr., 1993, 94, 96, 97, U. Alaska student chpt. ASME, ASCE. Republican. Baptist. Avocation: walking with family. Home: PO Box 240986 Anchorage AK 99524-0986 Office: U Alaska 3211 Providence Dr Anchorage AK 99508-4614

BAKER, GREGORY RICHARD, mathematician; b. Johannesburg, Transvaal, Republic South Africa, Nov. 9, 1947; came to U.S., 1972; s. Mervyn Colin and Valerie Rita (Deary) B.; M. Joanne Broker, Nov. 5, 1971 (div. Apr. 1978); 1 child, Kim; m. MaryEllen Asgeirsson, Oct. 7, 1979; 1 child, Kathryn Anne. BS, U. Natal, Durban, Republic South Africa, 1970, MS, 1973; PhD, Calif. Inst. Tech., 1977. Rsch. fellow Calif. Inst. Tech., Pasadena, 1976-77; instr. MIT, Cambridge, 1977-79, asst. prof., 1979-81; assoc. prof. U. Ariz., Tucson, 1981-86; rsch. math. Exxon Rsch. and Engrng. Co., Annondale, N.J., 1986-88; eminent scholar Ohio State U., Columbus, 1988—; cons. Cambridge Hydrodynamics Inc., Princeton, N.J., 1976-86, Inst. for Computer Applications in Sci. and Engring., NASA-Langley, 1980-81; mem. applied math. rev. panel for Dept. Energy, 1993; mem. NSF Small Bus. Innovation Rsch. Rev. Panel, 1993; mem. NSF/NRC Convocation on Sci., Math., Engrng. and Tech. Edn., 1995, NSF Review Panel on Fluid Mechanics, 1997, 98. Contbr. articles to profl. jours. including Physics of Fluids, Jour. Fluid Mechanics. Recipient Presdl. Young Investigator award, NSF, 1984. Mem. Soc. Indsl. and Applied Math., Am. Physics Soc. Achievements include development of reliable numerical methods for studies of evolution of free-surfaces in incompressible fluid flow. Office: Ohio State Univ Math Dept Columbus OH 43210

BAKER, GUY, coach; children: Samantha, Christen. BA in English Lit., Long Beach State U., 1987. Asst. coach water polo Long Beach (Calif.) State U., 1985-90; coach water polo UCLA, 1991—; coach women's water polo UCLA, 1995—. Recipient Gold medal Olympic Sports Festivals, 1985, 91, 89 as coach. Office: UCLA Morgan Ctr 325 Westwood Plz Los Angeles CA 90095-8356*

BAKER, HAROLD ALBERT, federal judge; b. Mt. Kisco, N.Y., Oct. 4, 1929; s. John Shirley and Ruth (Sarmiento) B.; m. Dorothy Ida Armstrong, June 24, 1951; children: Emily, Nancy, Peter. A.B., U. Ill., 1951, J.D., 1956. Bar: Ill. bar 1956. Practiced in Champaign, Ill., 1956-78; partner firm Hatch & Baker, 1960-78; chief judge U.S. Dist. Ct. (cen. dist.) Ill., Danville, 1978-94, sr. judge, 1994—; adj. mem. faculty Coll. Law, U. Ill., 1972-78; sr. counsel Presdl. Commn. on CIA Activities within U.S., 1975. Pres. Champaign Bd. Edn., 1967-76, pres., 1967-76. Served to lt. j.g. USN, 1951-53. Mem. ABA, Ill. Bar Assn. Democrat. Episcopalian. Office: US Dist Ct 201 S Vine St Rm 338 Urbana IL 61801*

BAKER, HAROLD WAYNE, retired news editor, anchor; b. June 14, 1916. BA in Journalism, U. Okla., 1938. News dir., anchor various radio stas., Enid, Muskogee, Okla., 1939-41; news editor WOW Radio-TV, Omaha, 1946-51; news editor/anchor WSM Radio-TV, Nashville, 1951-57; affairs dir., anchor WTLV, Jacksonville, Fla., 1957-76; mgr., exec. prodr. Fla. Pub. TV Network, 1976-81; lectr., govt. rschr. Author of genealogical and nostalgia books including The Royal and Historic Lineage of the Tabb/Lampton Families, 1988, From the Rear View Mirror, 1995, Miles and Miles and Kilometers, Too, 1996, The Spawn of Hessian John, 1999. With USN, 1942-45. Home: 4240 Coastal Hwy Saint Augustine FL 32095

BAKER, HARRISON SCOTT, computer consultant; b. Marion, Ohio, Mar. 12, 1950; s. Stanley Wallace and Starling (Dixon) B. BA, BS, Fla. State U., 1972, 80; MBA, Embry-Riddle Aeronaut. U., 1986. A&P rating, FAA; cert. product specialist, Microsoft; cert. computing technology, Computing Technology Industry Assn.; radiotelephone lic. with radar enforcement FCC. Mgr. Vincent Auto Parts, Inc., Marathon, Fla., 1972-78; maintenance supr. Ea. Air Lines, Inc., Miami, 1980-92; computer cons. Upper Sandusky, Ohio, 1992—. Author: Index to the Muster Rolls of PA in War of 1812, 1995, Early Settlers of Wyandot County, 1995; indexer: Obituaries in Upper Sandusky newspapers 1868-1911, 1994, Obituaries in Upper Sandusky newspapers 1912-1937, 1996, Obituaries in Upper Sandusky newspaper 1938-1958, 1997, Obituaries in Upper Sandusky newspapers 1959-1979, 1997, Journal of William Kennedy Beall, 1999. trustee Wyandot County Geneaol. Soc., 1995—. Mem. SAR (pres. Hancock chpt. 1995-96), IEEE Computer Soc., Assn. Computing Machinery, Soc. War of 1812 (Ohio pres. 1996-99), Sons of Union Vets. (camp sec. 1994-98). Avocations: electronics, genealogy. Home: PO Box 411 Upper Sandusky OH 43351-0411

BAKER, HELEN DOYLE PEIL, realtor; b. Los Angeles, June 26, 1943; d. James Cyril and Jacqueline (White) Doyle; m. Gary Edward Peil, Aug. 5, 1967 (dec. May 6, 1969); children: Andrea Christine, Kevin Doyle; m. Nathaniel W. Baker, Jr., Jan. 1, 1971 (div. July 23, 1983). AA, Santa Monica Coll., 1963; postgrad., U. Wash., 1963-64. Licensed real estate agent; cert. domestic violence counselor. Sales, mgmt. trainee Saks Fifth Ave., Beverly Hills, Calif., 1958-63; flight attendant Am. Airlines, Los Angeles, 1964-67; realtor, assoc. Stapleton Assocs., Honolulu, 1978-80; realtor Dolman Assocs. Inc., Kailua, Hawaii, 1980-87; loan rep. Honolulu Mortgage Co., Kailua, 1986-87; pres., owner, realtor Helen Baker Properties, Inc., Honolulu, 1987-93; v.p. Internat. Property Investment, Inc., Honolulu, 1993-94; owner Property Investment Internat., 1994—; loan officer Western Pacific Mortgage, Inc., 1999—; pres. Global Listing Svc. Hawaii Inc., 1990-96. Dir. Kailua Community Coun., 1987-91; pres., v.p., sec. Aikahi Community Assn., Kailua, 1980-85; vol. Am. Cancer Soc., Heart Assn. Schs., Kailua, 1971-86; adv. spouse abuse shelter, 1995-98. Mem. C. of C., Windward Spouse Abuse Coalition, Rotary. Avocations: tennis, fitness workout, reading, travel, music. Office: Property Investment Internat PO Box 37066 Honolulu HI 96837-0066

BAKER, HELEN MARIE, health services executive; b. Tulsa, Oct. 12, 1946; d. Joseph Donald and Caroline Emma (Nelson) Waldhelm; m. Lewis Edward Browder, 1964 (div. 1966); m. Lawrence Selden Baker, Nov. 23, 1978; children: Lawrence Nelson, Marjorie Lyn. Student, U. Tex., 1965-66. Staff asst. to pres. White House, Washington, 1970-73; v.p. Mgmt., Systems, Sales, Inc., Washington, 1973-74, Inter-Am. Svcs., Inc., Washington and Tex., 1974-83; v.p. Med. Diversified Svcs. Inc., San Antonio, 1983-90, exec. v.p., 1990-92, also bd. dirs., pres., CEO, 1992—. Editor newsletter Physician and Family, 1983-86. Elder St. Andrew Presbyn Ch., San Antonio, 1986-89; sponsor San Antonio Symphony, McNay Mus. of Art. Mem. San Antonio Mus. Assn. (sponsor), Club of Sonterra. Republican. Avocations: reading, singing, walking. Office: Med Diversified Svcs 15600 San Pedro Ave Ste 107 San Antonio TX 78232-3738

BAKER, HENRY S., JR., retired banker; b. Balt., June 10, 1926; s. Henry S. and Frances (Robinson) B.; m. Marian Stockton Towsend, June 12, 1948; children—Frances, Sandra, Stockton. B.A., Johns Hopkins U., 1950; grad. with honors, Grad. Sch. Banking, Rutgers U., 1957. With Md. Nat. Bank, Balt., 1950-86; sr. exec. v.p. Md. Nat. Bank, 1973-86; chmn. Redwood Capital Mgmt. Co., AAA Md., Ins. Agy. Inc., 1983—, Ind. Coll. Fund Md., 1984-89; v.p., bd. dirs. Manab Properties; bd. dirs. Md. Nat. Bank, Md. Nat. Corp., AAA MidAtlantic, Keystone Ins. Co., Mason Dixon Bankshares, Bank Md., chmn., 1995—. Chmn. Md. chpt. Nature Conservancy, 1984-90; chmn. investment com. Kennedy Inst. for Handicapped Children, 1985-88, Episcopal Diocese Md., 1974-80; trustee, treas. Garrison Forest Sch., 1962-88, St. Paul's Sch. for Girls, 1968-77; pres. Jr. Achievement Met. Balt., 1971, Florence Crittenden Home, 1964-66; bd. dirs. Keswick, Home for Incurables, 1965, pres., 1979; gen. campaign chmn. United Way Cen. Md., 1979. With USNR, 1944-46. Mem. Assn. Res. City Bankers, Md. Bankers Assn. (pres.), Md. State C. of C. (treas., dir.). Republican.

BAKER, HERMAN, medical educator, author; b. N.Y.C., Jan. 22, 1926; s. Harry and Fannie Baker; m. Shirley Levitz, Nov. 15, 1952; children: Elliott Robert, Joel Martin. BS, CCNY, 1946; MS, Emory U., 1948; PhD, NYU, 1956. Cert. specialist human nutrition Am. Bd. Nutrition. Research asst. Columbia U., N.Y.C., 1949-50; research assoc. Mt. Sinai Hosp., N.Y.C., 1950-60; assoc. prof. medicine N.J. Med. Sch., Jersey City, 1960-70; prof. medicine and preventive medicine N.J. Med. Sch., Newark, 1970—. Contbr. over 280 articles on metabolic imbalances to profl. jours.; author: Clinical Vitaminology: Methods and Interpretation. Fellow Am. Coll. Nutrition. Avocation: music. Home: 27 Wilk Rd Edison NJ 08837-2726 Office: NJ Med Sch Martland GB 159 65 Bergen St Newark NJ 07107-3001

BAKER, HOLLIS MACLURE, furniture manufacturing company executive; b. Allegan, Mich., Apr. 27, 1916; s. Hollis Siebe and Ruth (MacClure) B.; m. Betty Jane Brown, Aug. 2, 1947; children: Tomelyn Ann, Susan MacClure. Student, U. Va., 1935-37. With Baker Furniture, Inc., Holland, Mich., 1938-40, 45-73; v.p., treas. Baker Furniture, Inc., 1959-61, pres., 1961-70, chmn. bd., 1970-73; v.p., gen. mgr. Grand Rapids Chair Co., Mich., 1959-61; pres. Grand Rapids Chair Co., 1961-70; v.p., dir. Manor House, Inc., N.Y.C., 1958-70; pres. Boyne City R.R. Co., Mich., 400 Bldg. Corp., Palm Beach, Fla.; dir. Mich. Nat. Bank, Lansing, 1968-83, Am. Seating Co., Grand Rapids, 1973-83, Mich. Nat. Bank, Grand Rapids, 1959-84, Norton Gallery, Palm Beach, 1984-91. Author: A Brief History of Schloss Branzoll, 1975, A History of the Chateau de Caussade, 1980, A History of the Chateau de la Roque, 1985, Five Castles Are Enough, 1989. Bd. dirs. USCG Found., 1981-91. Lt. (s.g.) USNR, 1941-45. Mem. Nat. Assn. Furniture Mfrs. (dir.), Furniture Mfrs. Assn. Grand Rapids (dir., past pres 1970-84), Zeta Psi. Episcopalian. Clubs: Brook (N.Y.C.), River (N.Y.C.), New York Yacht (N.Y.C.), Leash (N.Y.C.); Kent Country (Grand Rapids), University (Grand Rapids), Indian (Grand Rapids), Peninsular (Grand Rapids); Everglades (Palm Beach), Bath and Tennis (Palm Beach); Buck's (London). Home: 301 Chapel Hill Rd Palm Beach FL 33480-4124 Office: 900 McKay Tower Grand Rapids MI 49502

BAKER, HOWARD HENRY, JR., former senator, lawyer; b. Huntsville, Tenn., Nov. 15, 1925; s. Howard Henry and Dora (Ladd) B.; m. Joy Dirksen, Dec. 22, 1951 (dec. 1993); children: Darek Dirksen, Cynthia; m. Nancy Landon Kassebaum, Dec. 7, 1996. Student, U. of South, Tulane U.; LLB, U. Tenn., 1949. U.S. senator from Tenn., 1967-85; minority leader, 1977-81, majority leader, 1981-85; ptnr. Vinson & Elkins, Washington, 1985-87; chief of staff Office of the Pres. U.S., Washington, 1987-88; ptnr. Baker, Worthington, Crossley, Stansberry & Woolf, Knoxville, Tenn., 1985-87, 88-95, Baker, Donelson, Bearman & Caldwell, Washington, 1995—; bd. dirs. Pennzoil Co.; chmn. bd. dirs. Cherokee Aviations, Newstar, Inc.; internat. adv. bd. Barrick Gold Corp. Bd. regents Smithsonian Instn.

BAKER, IAN ARCHBALD, explorer, educator, writer, photographer; b. N.Y.C., Dec. 10, 1957; s. John Milnes and Virginia Lea Busser Baker. BA in Art History cum laude, Middlebury Coll., 1980; MA in English Lit., Oxford U., 1985; postgrad., Columbia U. Field work Explorer's Club N.Y., India, Sikkim, and Nepal, 1981-82; acad. dir. semester abroad programs Sch. Internat. Tng., Brattleboro, Vt., 1983-90; freelance writer, photographer, 1993—; tour leader Smithsonian Instn., Boston Mus. Fine Arts, Distant Horizons; rsch. assoc. Found. Shamanic Studies; acad. advisor U. Wis., 1985-93; cons. Tibetan and Himalayan art Togendo Collection, Kyoto, Japan, 1990-92; founder Red Panda Expdns., Ltd., 1993—; leader rsch. expdns. in Namche Barwa-Tsangpo gorge region of Tibet, 1993-98. Author: The Tibetan Art of Healing with foreward by Dalai Lama, 1997, The Dalai Lamas' Secret Temple: Wall Paintings from the Lukhang, 1999; co-author: Tibet: Reflections from the Wheel of Life with foreword by Dalai Lama, 1993; co-prodr. (documentary film) Buddhist Hunters of Tsangpo Gorge, 1998; contbr. writings and photography to mags., books in Holland, France, Germany, U.S., Britain. Nat. Merit fellow Columbia U., 1990; Presdl. scholar Bread Loaf Sch. English, Lincoln Coll., Oxford U., 1985; selected by Rolex Awards for Enterprise for explorator rsch. in field of Himalayan sacred geography, 1990, named one of seven eoploreres for the millennium, Natl. Geographic Soc., 1999. Mem. The St. Nicholas Soc. N.Y., The Explorers Club (Internat. fellow 1997, Rsch. grantee 1980). Led Natl. Geographic Soc. expedition into Tsangpo Gorge's previously unexplored section and documented and measured 110' high talls that had previously been only subject of speculation. Named it Hidden Falls of Dorje Phagmo, 1998. Fax: 914-232-7306; 9771-423391. E-mail: ianbaker@mos.com.np. Home: GPO Box 1373, Kathmandu Nepal Address: 85 Girdle Ridge Rd Katonah NY 10536-3814

BAKER, J. A., II, management consultant, monetary architect, financial engineer; b. N.Y.C., Dec. 12, 1944; s. Leonard Ernest and Miriam Violet (Roché) B. Postgrad. in fin. svcs. mgmt., The Am. Coll., 1994—. ChFC, CLU, fin. planning advisor, assoc. registered investment advisor, property/casualty/liability field underwriter, comml. and personal lines; cert. instr., Monitor continuing and profl. edn.; cert. in advanced mgmt. Cons. mgr. Life Ins., N.Y.C., 1964-79; supr. Physician's Planning Group, Atty.'s Planning Svc., Bus. Planning Svcs., Profl. Svc. Corp., N.Y.C., 1979-81; CEO J A L B Enterprises, East Garden City, N.Y., 1980—; monitor N.Y. State continuing edn. program, 1996—, instr. continuing profl. edn. program, 1996—, licensing courses, 1996—. Bd. dirs. Medic Alert, Nassau County, N.Y., 1985-87; rep. The Living Bank; nominated mem.: Citizen Ambassador Program Internat. Fellow Life Underwriters Coun. (Bethesda, Md.); mem. Nat. Assn. Life Underwriters D.C. (emeritus mem., pres. Cortland chpt. 1974-75, legis. chair 1972-74, v.p. pub. info. Nassau County 1980-87, instr. Bklyn. 1987-90, Queens 1991-92), Am. Automobile Assn. (Spokane, Wash.), Am. Coun. Ind. Life Underwriters, Soc. Fin. Svc. Profls. (Bryn Mawr, Pa.), N.Y.C. Life Underwriters Assn., Profl. Ins. Agts. Fraternal Order of Police, N.Y. Civil Svc. Ret. Employee Assn. (N.Y.C.) Gen. Agts. Mgrs. Assn. Internat. (D.C., charter mem.), United Assn. of Entrepreneurs, N.Y. Jaycees (past dir.), Sovereign Mil. Order of Malta (pilgrim 1999), Am. Assn. Office: J A L B Enterprises Box 2053 630 Old Country Rd East Garden City NY 11531-2053

BAKER, JACK SHERMAN, architect, designer, educator; b. Champaign, Ill., Aug. 8, 1920; s. Clyde Lee and Jane Cecilia (Walker) B. BA with honors, U Ill., 1943, MS, 1949; cert., N.Y. Beaux Art Inst. Design, 1943. Aero engr., designer Boeing Aircraft, Seattle, 1943-44; assoc. Atkins, Barrow & Lasswith, Urbana, 1947-50; pvt. practice architecture Champaign, 1947—; mem. faculty U. Ill., Urbana, 1947—, prof. architecture, 1950-90, acting prof. emeritus, 1990—; former mem. exec. com. Sch. Architecture, U. Ill.; hon. bd. dirs. Gerhart Music Festival, Guntersville, Ala., Stravinsky awards, Champaign, Conservatory of Cen. Ill.; hon. bd. dirs. Ruth Hindman Found., Huntsville, Ala.; dir., performer personal performance loft space for Interaction of the Arts and Architecture, 1960—; participant U. Ill. Exploring the Arts course (Act-NCEA award), 1970—, campus honors program, 1995—; former mem. Chancellor's com. on graphic design and art acquisition and installation, former mem. adv. bd., designer of exhbn., Krannert Mus., U. Ill., engr. basic, Ft. Leonard Wood, MO., topog. engr., Ft. Blevoir, VA. Exhibitor water colors, arch. drawings, and photography; contbr. numerous jours. and profl. confs.; exhibited Monograft's Retrospective Arch. Exhibit, 1997, Krannert Art Mus. U. Japan, 1998. Mem. U. Ill. Pres.'s Coun., U. Ill. Bronze Cir., 1986; mem. mus. bd. and affiliate World Heritage Mus.; former mem. adv. bd. Krannert Ctr. for Performing Arts, Assembly Hall U. Ill.; exhbn. designer World Heritage Mus., U. Ill. Served with U.S. Army, 1945-46, Caserta, Italy, ETO. Recipient Excellence in Tchg. awards U. Ill., "prix d'Emulation Societe des Architectes Diplomes par le Gouvernment" Beaux-Arts medal, 1942, cert. for dedicated and disting. svc. Nat. AIA Com. on Environ. and Design, 1955, Decade of Achievement award World Heritage Mus., 1992, Heritage award PACA, 1997, numerous other honors and design excellence awards in field. Fellow AIA (medal 1977), Excellence in Edn. award and medal IC/AIA 1989; mem. Ill. Coun./AIA, Soc. Archtl. Historians, Nat. Coun. Archtl. Registration Bds. (cert.), Gargoyle, Scarab, Cliff Dwellers Club (Chgo.), Nat. Resources Def. Coun., The Nature Conservancy, Alpha Rho Chi. Home: 71 1/2 E Chester St Champaign IL 61820-4149 Office: U Ill 117 Temple Hoyne Buell Hall 611 Taft Dr MC-621 Champaign IL 61820-6922

BAKER, JAMES A., state supreme court justice; b. Evansville, Ind., Mar. 30, 1931. BBA, So. Meth. U., 1953, LLB, 1958. Bar: Tex. 1958, U.S. Dist. Ct. (no. dist.) Tex. 1958, U.S. Ct. Appeals (5th cir.) 1961, U.S. Ct. Appeals (11th cir.) 1981, U.S. Supreme Ct. 1980. Atty. Goldberg, Alexander and Baker, 1958-72, Weber, Baker and Allums, 1972-79; prin. Law Office of James A. Baker, 1979-86; judge U.S. Ct. Appeals (5th cir.), Dallas, 1986-95; justice Supreme Ct. of Tex., Austin, 1995—; lectr. State Bar of Tex. Profl. Devel. Program; guest lectr. So. Meth. U. Sch. Law, Dallas Bar Assn., El Centro Dalls C.C. Contbg. author Tex. Collection Manual, 1980. Fellow Tex. Bar Found., Dallas Bar Found.; mem. ABA (mem. task force on appellate delay reduction 1991-92), State Bar Tex., Dallas Bar Assn. (former chair bankruptcy and comml. law sect. 1974, bd. dirs. 1995), Coll. of State Bar Tex., Am. Judicature Soc., Inst. Judicial Adminstrn., William Mac Taylor Jr. Inn of Ct. Office: Supreme Ct Bldg 201 W 14th Rm 104 PO Box 12248 Austin TX 78711-2248

BAKER, JAMES BARNES, architect; b. N.Y.C., Feb. 18, 1933; s. William Edgar and Violet (Twachtman) B.; children: Mary Morgan, James Edgar, Catriona Griswold, Frederick Alden; m. Rosemary Burgis, June 14, 1997. A.B., Princeton U., 1954; M.Arch., Yale U., 1960. With firms Blake & Neski, N.Y.C., 1960-62, George Lewis, N.Y.C., 1962-63, Kahn & Jacobs, N.Y.C., 1963-64; ptnr. firm Baker & Blake, N.Y.C., 1964-72, Baker/Grinnell, N.Y.C., 1972-74; cons., 1974-77; dir. Llewelyn Davies Assocs., N.Y.C., 1976-78; pres. Tower Devel. Group Inc., Ohio, 1978-83, Park-Tower Devel. Co., Ltd., Bermuda, 1978-83, Springland Assocs. Inc., 1983-90; prin. Baker & Baker, Architects, N.Y.C., 1990—; pres. Tech. Panel Systems, 1992-93; mng. dir. William McDonough Archs., 1993-94, Forge Co., N.Y.C., London, 1994—; vis. prof. Sch. Architecture, CUNY. Trustee Darrow Sch., Mt. Lebanon Shaker Village. Recipient design awards HUD, others. Fellow AIA (bd. dirs., design awards); mem. Am. Arbitration Assn., Holland Soc., St. Nicholas Soc. Home: North Family Forge PO Box 98 New Lebanon NY 12125 also: 105-109 Strand, London WC2R 0AA, England

BAKER, JAMES EDWARD SPROUL, retired lawyer; b. Evanston, Ill., May 23, 1912; s. John Clark and Hester (Sproul) B.; m. Eleanor Lee Dodgson, Oct. 2, 1937 (dec. Sept. 1972); children: John Lee, Edward Graham (dec. Aug. 1988). A.B., Northwestern U., 1933, J.D., 1936. Bar: Ill. 1936, U.S. Supreme Ct. 1957. Practice in Chgo., 1936—; assoc. Sidley & Austin, and predecessors, 1936-48, ptnr., 1948-81; of counsel Sidley & Austin, 1981-93; lectr. Northwestern U. Law Sch., 1951-52; nat. chmn. Stanford U. Parents Com., 1970-75; mem. vis. com. Stanford Law Sch., 1976-79, 82-84, Northwestern U. Law Sch., 1980-89, DePaul U. Law Sch., 1982-87. Served to comdr. USNR, 1941-46. Fellow Am. Coll. Trial Lawyers (regent 1974-81, sec. 1977-79, pres. 1979-80); mem. ABA, Bar Assn. 7th Fed. Circuit, Ill. State Bar Assn., Chgo. Bar Assn., Soc. Trial Lawyers Ill., Northwestern U. Law Alumni Assn. (past pres.), Order of Coif, Phi Lambda Upsilon, Sigma Nu. Republican. Methodist. Clubs: John Evans (Northwestern U.) (chmn. 1982-85); University (Chgo.); John Henry Wigmore (past pres.); Midday (Chgo.), Legal (Chgo.), Law (Chgo.) (pres. 1983-85); Westmoreland Country (Wilmette, Ill.), Pauma Valley Country (Calif.). Home: 1300 N Lake Shore Dr Chicago IL 60610-2157 Office: Sidley & Austin 1 First Natl Plz Chicago IL 60603-2003

BAKER, JAMES ESTES, foreign service officer; b. Suffolk, Va., Jan. 21, 1935; s. Percy H. and Helen Mae Baker. B.A., Haverford Coll., 1956; M.A., Fletcher Sch. Law and Diplomacy, 1957; postgrad., U. Calif., 1970-71. Fgn. service officer Dept. State, 1960; minister counselor U.S. Mission to UN, N.Y.C.; prin. officer Office of Dir. Gen. of UN, 1980-84; dir. spl. econ. assistance programmes UN, 1984-86, dir. office of dir. gen., 1987-90, dir. spl. emergency programs, 1990-92, dir. dept. humanitarian affairs, 1992-95; adj. prof. L.I. U., N.Y., 1995—; sr. assoc. Carnegie Endowment for Internat. Peace, 1978. Served with U.S. Army, 1957-58. Mem. NAACP, Am. Fgn. Svc. Assn., Coun. Fgn. Rels., Am. Polit. Sci. Assn. Home: 4 E 8th St New York NY 10003-5913

BAKER, JAMES L., judge; b. Asheville, N.C., Sept. 15, 1954; s. J. Leonard and Elizabeth C. (Gahagan) B.; m. Karen Lynne Massey, Oct. 25, 1980; children: Anne Elizabeth, Sarah Catherine. BA, Mars Hill Coll., 1977; JD, Mercer U., 1980. Bar: N.C. 1982, U.S. Dist. Ct. (we. dist.) N.C. 1982, U.S. Dist. Ct. (mid. dist.) N.C. 1982, U.S. Ct. Appeals (4th, 5th and 11th cirs.) 1984, U.S. Supreme Ct. 1990. Atty. Marshall, N.C., 1982-83; asst. dist. atty. 24th Jud. Dist., N.C., 1983-94; sr. resident superior ct. judge 24th Jud. Dist., Marshall, N.C., 1995—; mem. Jud. Stds. Commn., Raleigh, N.C., 1997—. Mem., chmn. Madison County Bd. Edn., Marshall, 1987-90. Home: PO Box 397 Marshall NC 28753-0397 Office: Superior Ct 24th Jud Dist PO Box 940 Marshall NC 28753-0940

BAKER, JAMES ROBERT, federal agency administrator; m. Linda Nelson; children: Monica, Jason. Degree in agribus., So. State Coll. Mgr. Lewis Livestock Co., Conway, Ark., 1983-94; adminstr. Grain Inspection, Packers, & Stockyards Adminstrn. USDA, Washington, 1994—; chmn. Ark. Livestock and Poultry Commn., 1989—. Bd. dirs. Faulkner County Farm Bus., 1973—, pres., 1986; bd. dirs. Ark. Farm Bur., 1989—, nat. voting del., 1981, 96; mem. Faulkner County Ext. Adv. Bd.; charter bd. dirs. Faulkner County 4-H Found. Bd., 1985—, pres., 1979, 80; advisor Future Farmers Am. Recipient gold award Ark. Prodn. Credit Assn., Agr. Alumni award So. State Coll. Office: Grain Inspection Packers and Stockyard Adminstrn Dept Agr 1400 Independence Ave SW Washington DC 20250-0002

BAKER, JANICE MARIE, special education educator, researcher; b. Connellsville, Pa., May 8, 1949; d. Clarence Edward and Pauline (Walker) B.; 1 child, Charles James. BS, U. Pitts., 1971, PhD, 1990; MA, W.Va. U., 1975. Cert. spl. edn. tchr., Pa. Program supr. Pressley Ridge Sch., Pitts., 1975-79; tchr. spl. edn. Allegheny Intermediate Unit, Pitts., 1980-83; demonstration tchr. Falk Lab. Sch., U. Pitts., 1984-85, rsch. asst. Adaptive Learning Environ. Model unit, 1983-84, 85-86, grad. rsch. asst. spl. edn. program, 1986-87, rsch. assoc. Inst. for Practice and Rsch. in Edn., 1987-89, co-dir. project Mainstreaming Experiences Learning Disabled, 1989-91; asst. prof. spl. edn. program Vanderbilt U., Nashville, 1991-98, Indiana U. Pa., 1998—; coord. Saturday suspension program Fox Chapel Sch. Dist., Pitts., 1980-83; site coord. verbal problem solving in arithmetic SUNY-Buffalo, Pitts., 1988-90; adj. asst. prof. dept. instruction and learning U. Pitts., 1990-91; presenter in field. Contbr. articles to profl. jours. Mem. ASCD, Coun. for Exceptional Children, Am. Edn1. Rsch. Assn. Avocations: biking, walking, crocheting. Office: Indiana U Pa 203 Davis Hall Indiana PA 15705

BAKER, JEAN HARVEY, history educator; b. Balt., Feb. 9, 1933; d. F. Barton and Rose (Lindsay) Hopkins Harvey; m. R. Robinson Baker, Sept. 12, 1953; children—Susan Dixon, Robinson Scott, Robert W., Jean Harvey. A.B., Goucher Coll., Towson, Md., 1961; M.A., Johns Hopkins U., Balt., 1965, Ph.D., 1971. Lectr., instr. history Notre Dame Coll., Balt., 1967-69; instr. history Goucher Coll., Balt., 1969, asst. prof. history, 1969-75, assoc. prof. history, 1975-78, prof. history, 1979-82, Elizabeth Todd prof. history, 1981—. Author: The Politics of Continuity, 1973, Ambivalent Americans, 1976, Affairs of Party, 1983 (Berkshire prize in history), Maryland: A History, Mary Todd Lincoln: A Biography, 1986, The Stevensons: A Family Biography, 1995; editor Md. Hist. Mag., 1979. Am. Coun. Learned Socs. fellow, 1976, NEH fellow, 1982, Newberry Libr. fellow, 1991, Rockefeller Ctr. fellow, 1998; recipient Faculty Teaching prize Goucher Coll., 1979, Willie Lee Rose prize in Southern history, 1989. Mem. Orgn. Am. Historians, Am. Hist. Assn., Berkshire Conf. Women Historians, Phi Beta Kappa. Democrat. Home: 8717 Mcdonogh Rd Baltimore MD 21208-1021 Office: Goucher Coll History Dept Towson MD 21204

BAKER, JEFFREY CHARLES, telecommunications executive; b. Springfield, Ohio, Feb. 23, 1952; s. Robert Jones and Elizabeth (Hunt) B.; m. Linnea Liane Strehlow, May 14, 1977 (div. Mar. 1985); m. Maryanne Elise Lubresky, Mar. 24, 1986; children: Megan Elisabeth, Kelle Marie. BFA in Comms., U. Cin., 1976. Acct. exec., sta. mgr. Continental Cablevision, Springfield, 1976-78; spl. projects mgr. Tele-Communications, Inc., Middletown, Ohio, 1978; dir. mktg. Viacom Inc., Dayton, Ohio, 1978-80, gen. mgr., 1980-82; gen. mgr. Viacom Inc., Everett, Wash., 1982-86, v.p., bus. & mktg. ops., 1986; v.p., gen. mgr. Viacom Inc., Tacoma, Wash., 1986-90; pres. Sound Comms., Inc., Sky Comms., Inc., Bellevue, Wash., 1991-; v.p., gen. mgr. Supershuttle, Phoenix, 1994-95; v.p. S.W. region Cornell Bokelmann, Phoenix, 1995-97; pres. ICS of Ariz., Phoenix, 1997—; mem. bd. dirs. Wash. State Cable Comms. Assn., Seattle, 1985-90; mem. Women in Cable, Seattle, 1984-90; com. chair Ohio Cable TV Assn., Columbus, Ohio, 1976-80. Republican. Presbyterian. Avocations: collecting vintage American-made electric guitars from 1950's and 60's. Home: 10417 E Texas Sage Ln Scottsdale AZ 85259 Office: Gainey Ranch Town Ctr Ste 300 7702 E Doubletree Ranch Rd Scottsdale AZ 85258-2132

BAKER, JENNIFER L., secondary education educator; b. Poughkeepsie, N.Y., Oct. 19, 1971; d. John Walter and Linda Mae (Disbrow) B. BA in Spanish, SUNY, Geneseo, 1993. Tchr. Spanish leave replacement various H.S., N.Y., 1993-94; tchr. Spanish, Chatham (N.Y.) H.S., 1994-96, F.D. Roosevelt H.S., Hyde Park, N.Y., 1996—; acquired daily living specialist Cardinal Hayes Home for Children, Pleasant Valley, N.Y., 1989-93; lifeguard Anderson Sch., Staatsburg, N.Y., 1992-94; ski instr. Belleayre Mountain Ski Ctr., Highmount, N.Y., 1993—. Jenkins Mem. Teaching schollar N.Y. State PTA, 1989. Mem. N.Y. State Assoc. Fgn. Lang. Tchrs. Avocations: skiing, theatre, acting, sports. Home: 706 Violet Ave Lot 4 Hyde Park NY 12538-1718 Office: FD Roosevelt HS South Cross Rd Hyde Park NY 12538

BAKER, JENNIFER L., strategic communications consultant; b. Mar. 4, 1973. BA in Polit. Sci., U. S.C., 1995. Project mgr. DecisionQuest-EIM, Washington, 1995—. E-mail: jbaker@eimcom.com. Office: 1401 I St NW Ste 505 Washington DC 20005

BAKER, JERRY HERBERT, executive search consultant; b. Concord, N.C., Aug. 16, 1946; s. Herbert Junius and Doylen Walsh (Lowe) B.; m. Cassandra Jo Martin, June 28, 1969; children: Josephine D., Martin M. BA, Wake Forest U., 1968; MDiv, Harvard U., 1971. Min. Congl. Ch., N.J. and Fla., 1971-73; human resources specialist Am. Thread Co., Stamford, Conn., 1974; exec. recruiter Miller Brewing Co., Milw., 1974-76; exec. search cons. B.F. & E., Atlanta, 1976-79, MSL Internat., Atlanta, 1979-83; ptnr. Lamalie Assocs, Inc., Atlanta, 1983-91, Baker & Parker Inc., Atlanta, 1991—. Trustee Wake Forest U., Winston-Salem, N.C., 1997—; bd. visitors Harvard Div. Sch., 1997—. Mem. Assn. Exec. Search Cons. (sec.-treas. 1986-91), Harvard Divinity Sch. Alumni Assn. (pres. 1995-97). Republican. Home: 375 Dogwood Trl SE Marietta GA 30067-4643 Office: Baker & Parker Inc 5 Concourse Pkwy Ste 2440 Atlanta GA 30328-5347

BAKER, JILL WITHROW, artist, writer; b. Ilion, N.Y., Oct. 12, 1942; d. Alfred Seiders and Rosalee (Wilson) Withrow; m. James T. Baker, Aug. 23, 1963 (div. June 1978); children: Virginia, Elizabeth; m. Patrick Halvorson, Oct. 18, 1981 (div. June 1986). BFA, Baylor U., 1964; MFA, Pratt Inst., 1981. One-woman shows include U.S. Embassy, Seoul, Korea, 1978, Palazzo Strozzi, Florence, Italy, 1975, and others. Mem. Nat. Artists Equity Assn. (v.p. 1985-95, pres. N.Y. chpt. 1995—), Women's Caucus for the Arts, N.Y. Arts Equity, L.A. Artists Equity (pres. 1983-85). Democrat. Episcopalian. Home: 552 Broadway Apt 4B New York NY 10012-3948

BAKER, JOE DON, actor; b. Groesbeck, Tex., Feb. 12, 1936; s. Doyle Charles and Edna (McDonald) B.; m. Maria Dolores Rivero-Torres, Dec. 25, 1969 (div. 1978). B.B.A., North Tex. State Coll., Denton, 1958. Appeared in: New York stage plays Marathon 33, 1963, Blues for Mr. Charlie, 1964; appeared in: TV movies Mongo's Back in Town, 1971, To Kill a Cop, 1978; star: TV series Eischied, 1979; guest star numerous television series, 1966-72 including Gunsmoke, Bonanza, The Big Valley, The F.B.I., The High Chaparral, Mission: Impossible, The Streets of San Francisco; actor, exec. producer: TV movie Mongo's Back in Town, 1971, To Kill a Cop, 1978; appeared in: motion pictures Cool Hand Luke, 1967, Guns of the Magnificent Seven, 1969, Adam at 6 A.M., 1969, Junior Bonner, 1971, Walking Tall, 1972, Charlie Varrick, 1972, The Outfit, 1973, The Natural, 1984, Fletch, 1985, Edge of Darkness (BBC Mini-Series), 1985, The Living Daylights, 1987, Cape Fear, 1991, Citizen Cohn, 1992, Reality Bites, 1994, The Grass Harp, 1996, Golden Eye, 1995, Ruby Ridge, 1996, Mars Attack, 1996, Tomorrow Never Dies, 1997, Forces of Nature, 1999, others, (TV movies) George Wallace, 1997, To Dance with Olivia, 1997; actor (TV mini-series) Too Rich: The Secret Life of Doris Duke, 1999. Served with AUS, 1958-60. Mem. Actors Studio, N.Y.C. and Los Angeles, Sigma Phi Epsilon. Home: 23339 Hatteras St Woodland Hills CA 91367-3107*

BAKER, JOHN, director engineering; b. Portland, Oreg., Nov. 5, 1961. BS, U. Mo., Bolla Rolla, 1983. Registered profl. engr., Tex. Sr. project engr. City of Garland, Tex., dir. engrng. dept., 1996—. Mem. Am. Soc. Civil Engrs., Am. Soc. Profl. Engrs. Office: City of Garland Engineering Dept PO Box 469002 Garland TX 75046-9002*

BAKER, JOHN, electronics executive. Pres. Micro Electronics, Columbus, Ohio. Office: Micro Electronics PO Box 18177 Columbus OH 43218-0177*

BAKER, JOHN EDWARD, cardiac biochemist, educator; b. London, Dec. 12, 1954; came to U.S., 1984; s. Edward D. and Florence I. (Dobson) B.; m. Mary E. Zurawski, Oct. 29, 1988; children: David J., Elizabeth A. BSc, Poly. Wolverhampton, Eng., 1977; PhD, St. Thomas' Med. Sch., London, 1984. Sr. biochemist Cen. Pathology Labs., London, 1977-78; rsch. asst. St. Thomas' Hosp. Med. Sch., London, 1978-84; rsch. fellow Med. Coll. Wis., Milw., 1984-86, vis. prof., 1986-87, asst. prof. cardiothoracic surgery, 1987-92; assoc. prof., 1992—; bd. dirs. Adelaido Banazynski Sch. for Piano Studies. Contbr. rsch. med. articles on cardiovascular diseases to profl. jours.; patentee method for sealing blood vessel puncture sites and method for coating intraluminal stents. Bd. dirs. Adelaide Banaszynski Sch. for Piano Studies; founder Heart Sci. Found., Ltd. Grantee NIH, 1989, 90, 93, 97, Culpeper Found., 1987, Ronald McDonald Children's Charities, 1989, 91, Children's Hosp. Found., 1995. Mem. Am. Heart Assn. (mem. coun. on basic sci., mem. peer rev. rsch. com. Wis. affiliate 1989-93). Methodist. Avocation: walking, music. Office: Med Coll Wis 8701 W Watertown Plank Rd Milwaukee WI 53226-3548

BAKER, JOHN MILNES, architect; b. Port Jefferson, N.Y., Oct. 15, 1932; s. Alan Griffin and Lucy Hayden (Milnes) B.; m. Virginia Lea Busser (div. 1969); children: Ian Archbald, Jennifer Lea (Mrs. Christopher Warren); m. Elizabeth Jennings Morrison, Jan. 17, 1970; children: James Morrison, Hayden Sheffield. BA, Middlebury Coll., 1955; MArch, Columbia U., 1960. Designer, draftsman Sir Basil Spence, London, 1960-61; project mgr., later project architect Rogers & Butler, N.Y.C., 1962-64; project architect John A. Pruyn, AIA, N.Y.C., 1965-66; pvt. practice architecture N.Y.C., 1967-68, 75-79; ptnr. Manice & Baker, N.Y.C., 1968-74; pvt. practice architecture specializing in residential design Katonah, N.Y., 1979—; pres. J.M. Baker Houses Inc.; lectr. New Sch. for Social Rsch., N.Y.C. Author: How to Build a House with an Architect, 1977, rev. edit., 1988, The Baker Family and the Edgar Family of Rahway, N.J. and New York City, 1972, American House Styles: A Concise Guide, 1994. Trustee N.Y. Revels Inc.; past trustee Bedford Free Libr.; mem. Katonah Hist. Dist. Adv. Commn., Town of Bedford. Home designs included among Better Homes and Garden Top Ten Homes Plans, 1982; 3 designs selected by USIA for Design U.S.A., a traveling exhibit in USSR, 1989-90. Mem. AIA, Nat. Coun. Archtl. Registration Bds., Am. Arbitration Assn. (panel mem.), Soc. Archtl. Hists., St. Nicholas Soc. (pres.), Holland Soc. N.Y. (past trustee), St. Andrews Soc., Colonial Lords of Manors in Am., New Eng. Soc., Order Founders and Patriots, Soc. Colonial Wars, Pilgrims, Corinthians. Clubs: Coffee House, Squadron A, Century Assn. (N.Y.C.); Bellport Bay Yacht (past trustee) (N.Y.); Bedford Golf and Tennis; Norwalk Yacht (Conn.). Home: Rivendell Girdle Ridge Rd Katonah NY 10536 Office: 85 Girdle Ridge Rd Katonah NY 10536-3814

BAKER, JOHN RUSSELL, utilities executive; b. Lexington, Mo., July 21, 1926; s. William Frederick and Flora Anne (Dunford) B.; m. Elizabeth Jane Torrence, June 16, 1948; children—John Russell, Burton T. B.S., U. Mo., 1948, M.B.A., 1962. With Mo. Public Service Co., Kansas City, 1948—; treas. Mo. Public Service Co., 1966-68, v.p. fin., 1968-71, sr. v.p., 1971-73, exec. v.p., 1973—, also dir.; lectr. fin. U. Mo.; vice-chmn. Utilicorp United, 1991—. Vice-pres. Mid-Continent council Girls Scouts, U.S., 1981; adv. council Sch. Acctg., U. Mo., Columbia. Recipient Outstanding alumnus award Sch. Adminstrn. U. Mo., Kansas City, 1965; citation of merit U. Mo., 1995. Mem. Tax Execs. Inst. (pres. Kansas City 1968), U. Mo. Sch. Adminstrn. Alumni Assn. (pres. 1965). Republican. Methodist. Clubs: Kansas City, Blue Hills Country. Home: 205 NW Oxford Ln Lees Summit MO 64063-2118 Office: Utilicorp United Inc 20 W 9th St Kansas City MO 64105-1704

BAKER, JOHN STEVENSON (MICHAEL DYREGROV), writer; b. Mpls., June 18, 1931; s. Everette Barrette and Ione May (Kadletz) B. BA cum laude, Pomona Coll., Claremont Colls., 1953; MD, U. Calif. at Berkeley and San Francisco, 1957. Writer, 1958—; book cataloger Walker Art Center, Mpls., 1958-59; editor, writer neurol. rsch. articles Louis E. Phillips Psychobiol. Rsch. Fund, Mpls., 1960-61. Contbr. articles and poetry to various publs. in Eng. and U.S.; author 65 pub. poems, 21 short essays and 10 sets of aphorisms. Donor numerous species of native plants and seeds to Minn. Landscape Arboretum, U.S. Nat. Arboretum and Arnold Arboretum, Harvard U., papers of LeRoi Jones and Hart Crane to Yale U., Brahms recs. to Bennington Coll., several others. Recipient Disting. Service award Minn. State Hort. Soc., 1976; Cert. of Appreciation U.S. Nat. Arboretum, 1978; property registered as a Minn. Natural Area Minn. chpt. Nature Conservancy, 1990. Mem. Nu Sigma Nu. Office: PO Box 16007 Minneapolis MN 55416-0007

BAKER, JOSEPH RODERICK, III, aviculturist; b. Middletown, Ohio, Sept. 26, 1947; s. Joseph Roderick and Lois Patricia (Barnhart) B. BS in Math., Rensselaer Poly. Tech., 1969. Systems rep. Burroughs Corp., Honolulu, 1973-80; mgr. data processing Kenault Inc., Honolulu, 1980-81; v.p. Software Solutions Inc., Honolulu, 1982-83; br. mgr. DataPhase Corp., Honolulu, 1983-88; pres. Birds of Paradise, Kurtistown, Hawaii, 1987—. Lt. (j.g.) USN, 1969-73. Mem. Am. Fedn. Aviculture, Nat. Cockatoo Soc., Macaw Soc. Am., Eclectus Soc., Am. Contract Bridge League, Pionus Breeders Assn., Amazona Soc. Avocation: bridge.

BAKER, JUDITH J., nurse manager; b. Augusta, Ga., Oct. 30, 1955; D. Glenn and Mattie (Roberson) Beard. AD, U. S.C., Aiken, 1978, BSN, 1988; MS in Nursing Adminstrn., Med. Coll. Ga., 1992. Staff and charge nurse Med. Coll. Ga., Augusta, 1977; sr. nurse Ga. Regional Hosp., Augusta, 1978, lead nurse, 1980, nurse mgr. adult psychiat. unit, 1987, temporary staffing coord., 1992; part-time nurse adminstr., 1994, acting nurse mgr. child and adolescent program, 1996; sr. staff nurse III Med. Coll. Ga., 1998; grad. Dept. Human Resources Leadership Program, 1991.

BAKER, KATHERINE H., federal judge; b. 1941. JD, U. Houston, 1981. Pvt. practice, 1981—; apptd. part-time magistrate judge we. dist. U.S. Dist. Ct. Tex., 1988. Fax: (915) 837-9231. Office: 803 N 2d St Alpine TX 79830

BAKER, KATHY WHITTON, actress; b. Midland, Tex., June 8, 1950. Appearances include (theatre) Fool for Love, 1983 (Obie award 1983, Theatre World award 1984), Desire Under the Elms, 1984, Aunt Dan and Lemon, 1986, (films) The Right Stuff, 1983, Street Smart, 1987 (Nat. Soc. Film Critics Best Supporting Actress award 1987), Permanent Record, 1988, A Killing Affair, 1988, Clean and Sober, 1988, Jacknife, 1989, Dad, 1989, Mr. Frost, 1989, Edward Scissorhands, 1990, Article 99, 1992, Jennifer 8, 1992, Mad Dog and Glory, 1993, To Gillian on Her 37th Birthday, 1996, Inventing the Abbotts, 1997, (TV movies) Nobody's Child, 1986, The Image, 1990, One Special Victory, 1991, Weapons of Mass Distraction, 1997, (TV series) Picket Fences, 1992— (Emmy award Outstanding Lead Actress in a Drama Series, 1993, 1995, Golden Globe award, Best Actress in a TV Drama Series, 1994), Oklahoma City: A Survivor's Story, 1998, Lush Life, 1993, Not in This Town, 1997, ATF, 1998, Cider House Rules, 1999. Office: ICM 8942 Wilshire Blvd Beverly Hills CA 90211-1934*

BAKER, KEITH MICHAEL, history educator; b. Swindon, Eng., Aug. 7, 1938; came to U.S., 1964; s. Raymond Eric and Winifred Evelyn (Shepherd) B.; m. Therese Louise Elzas, Oct. 25, 1961; children—Julian, Felix. BA, Cambridge U., 1960, MA, 1963; postgrad., Cornell U., 1960-61; PhD, U. London, 1964. Instr. history and humanities Reed Coll., 1964-65; asst. prof. European history U. Chgo., 1965-71, assoc. prof., 1971-76, prof., 1977-89, master collegiate div. social scis., 1975-78, assoc. dean coll., 1975-78, assoc. dean div. social scis., 1975-78, chmn. commn. grad. edn., 1980-82; chmn. Council Advanced Studies in Humanities and Social Scis., 1982-86; prof. European history Stanford U., 1989—, J.E. Wallace Sterling prof. in humanities, 1992—, chair dept. history, 1994-95; Anthony P. Meier family prof. humanities, dir. Stanford Humanities Ctr., 1995—; vis. assoc. prof. history Yale U., 1974; mem. Inst. Advanced Study, Princeton (N.J.), 1979-80; vis. prof., dir. studies Ecole des Hautes Etudes en Scis. Sociales, Paris, 1982, 84, 91; fellow Ctr. for Advanced Study in Behavioral Scis., Stanford (Calif.) U., 1986-87; vis. prof. UCLA, 1989; vis. fellow Clare Hall, Cambridge (Eng.) U., 1994; chair scholars com. Am. Com. on the French Revolution, 1989. Author: Condorcet: From Natural Philosophy to Social Mathematics, 1975, Inventing the French Revolution, 1990; prin. author: Report Commission on Graduate Education, U. Chgo., 1982; editor: Condorcet: Selected Writings, 1977, The Political Culture of the Old Regime: The Old Regime and the French Revolution, 1987, The Terror, 1994; co-editor Jour. Modern History, 1980-89. Decorated chevalier Ordre des Palmes Académiques, 1988; elect. fellow, AAAS, 1991; elect. mem. Am. Philos. Soc., 1997, NEH fellow, 1967-68, Am. Coun. Learned Soc. Study fellow, 1972-73, Guggenheim fellow, 1979. Mem. Am. Hist. Assn. (com. on coms. 1991-94), Soc. French History Studies,Am. Soc. for 18th Century Studies. Office: Stanford U Dept History Stanford CA 94305

BAKER, KENDALL L., academic administrator; b. Clearwater, Fla., Nov. 1, 1942; s. Robert B. and Anne E. Baker; m. Tobin Ratliff McGough, Apr. 12, 1981; children: Kraig, Kris, Shannon, Brian. BA with honors, U. Md., 1963; MA, Georgetown U., 1967, PhD, 1969. Instr., Dept. Polit. Sci. U. Wyo., Laramie, 1967-69, asst. prof., 1969-73, assoc. prof., 1973-77, prof., 1977-82, chmn., 1979-82, asst. v.p. for Acad. Affairs, 1976-77; dean, Coll. Arts & Scis., Bowling Green State U., Ohio, 1982-87; v.p., provost No. Ill. U., DeKalb, 1987-92; pres. U. N. D., 1992—; cons. on survey research to various agys. and polit. candidates, 1967—; panel chmn. Rocky Mt. Social Sci. Conv. 1973, We. Social Sci. Conv., 1975, Council Colls. Arts and Scis., 1983, 86; guest participant study trip to Fed. Republic of Germany, 1977; election observer Fed. Republic of Germany, 1980. Author: The Wyoming Legislature: Lawmakers, the Public, and the Press, 1973; (with R. Dalton and K. Hildebrandt) Germany Transformed: Political Culture and the New Politics, 1981; contbr. articles on polit. sci. to profl. jours. Coach Laramie Soccer Assn., 1978-81. Mem. Am. Polit. Sci. Assn. (chmn. panel ann. conv. 1983), Midwest Polit. Sci. Assn. (chmn. panel ann. conv. 1985, 86), Conf. Group on German Politics (exec. com. 1984-87, co-editor newsletter 1985-91), Phi Kappa Phi, Omicron Delta Kappa, Pi Sigma Alpha. Home: Yale Dr Grand Forks ND 58201 Office: U ND Presidents Office Grand Forks ND 58202

BAKER, KENNETH, art critic, writer; b. Weymouth, Mass., May 3, 1946; s. Granville and Katherine B.; m. Tonia Aminoff, July 26, 1975. BA, Bucknell U., 1968. Freelance writer Boston, Providence, N.Y.C., 1969-84; art critic The Boston Phoenix, 1972-84; adj. faculty Boston Coll., Chestnut Hill, 1979-84; art critic San Francisco Chronicle, 1985—; mem. adj. faculty Stanford U., 1994, 97. Author: Minimalism, 1989, reprinted 1997. Recipient Mfrs. Hanover Trust-Art World award for newspaper criticism, 1985; Critic's fellow Nat. Endowment for Arts, 1975, 78; Critics' Workshop grantee Am. Fedn. Arts, 1970. Mem. PEN, Nat. Book Critics Cir., Internat. Assn. Art Critics. Avocation: aikido. Office: San Francisco Chronicle 901 Mission St San Francisco CA 94103-2905

BAKER, KENT ALFRED, broadcasting company executive; b. Sioux City, Iowa, Mar. 22, 1948; s. Carl Edmund Baker and Miriam M. (Hawthorn) Baker Nye. Student, Iowa State U., 1966-70. Editor Iowa State Daily, 1969-70; mem. U.S. Peace Corps., 1971-72; editor The Glidden (Iowa) Graphic, 1973-75; bureau chief The Waterloo (Iowa) Courier, Iowa, 1975; state editor The Des Moines Register, 1976-77; news dir. Sta. WQAD-TV, Moline, Ill., 1978; Sunday editor The Des Moines Sunday Register, 1979; news dir. Sta. KHON-TV, Honolulu, 1980-95; v.p., gen. mgr. KHON-TV, Honolulu, 1996—; chmn. Hawaii Freedom of Info. Coun., 1992-94. Recipient news writing awards Iowa Press Assn., 1973-74. Mem. Radio and TV News Dirs. Assn., Bishop Mus. Assn., Hoover Libr. Assn., Iowa State U. Alumni Assn. Office: Sta KHON-TV 1170 Auahi St Honolulu HI 96814-4917

BAKER, KERRY ALLEN, management consultant; b. Selmer, Tenn., Sept. 21, 1949; s. Austin Clark and Betty Ann (Brooks) B.; m. Ellen Fleming. BIE, Ga. Inst. Tech., 1971; MBA, Ga. State U., 1973; JD, Memphis State U., 1987. With dept. law State of Ga., 1971-73; div. engr. N.W. Ga. div. Gold Kist Inc., Ellijay, 1977-80; sr. mfg. engr. Plough, Inc., Memphis, 1980-82; mgr. indsl. engring. Plough, Inc., 1983-86, supr. mfg. engr., 1986-90; plant bus. mgr. Clorox Co., Dyersburg, Tenn., 1990-95; ops. mgr. Huish Detergents, Inc., Dyersburg, Tenn., 1995; pres. Rock Ridge Ventures, Inc., Dyersburg, 1997—; mgr. adminstrn. Gabriel Ride Products, Pulaski, Tenn., 1998-99; exec. dir. Mgmt. Recruiters of Dyersburg (Tenn.), 1996-97. Decorated Order of St. Barbara. Mem. Inst. Indsl. Engrs., Am. Prodn. and Inventory Control Soc., Nat. Fire Protection Assn., Scabbard and Blade, Rotary, Masons. Methodist. Home: PO Box 1178 Pulaski TN 38478-1178

BAKER, LAURENCE HOWARD, oncology educator; b. Bklyn., Jan. 14, 1943; s. Jacob and Sylvia (Tannenbaum) B.; m. Maxine V. Friedman, July 25, 1964; children: Mindy, Jennifer. BA, Bklyn. Coll. of CUNY, 1962; DO, U. Osteo. Medicine and Surgery, Des Moines, 1966. Diplomate Am. Bd. Internal Medicine. Rotating intern Flint Osteo. Hosp., Flint, Mich., 1966-67; med. resident Detroit Osteo. Hosp., 1967-69; fellow in oncology Wayne State U., Detroit, 1970-72; asst. prof. medicine, dept. oncology Wayne State U. Sch. Medicine, Detroit, 1972-76, assoc. prof. medicine, dept. oncology, 1976-79, prof. medicine, dept. oncology, 1979-82, assoc. chmn., dept. oncology, 1980-82, prof. medicine, dir. div. med. oncology, dept. internal medicine, 1982-86, prof. medicine, dir. div. hematology and oncology, dept. internal medicine, 1986-93, asst. dean for cancer programs, 1988-94; dir. Meyer L. Prentis Comprehensive Ctr. Met. Detroit; now prof. internal med. U. Mich. Sch. Medicine, Ann Arbor, dep., dir. clin. rsch. Comprehensive Cancer Ctr., 1994—; bd. dirs. Mich. Cancer Consortium, Dept. Pub. Health, Mich. Cancer Found., U.S. Bioscis. Sci. Bd.; assoc. chmn. S.W. Oncology Group; presenter in field. Author or co-author over 150 articles, 28 books, 15 case reports, over 90 abstracts in field; mem. editl. adv. bd. Primary Care and Cancer; assoc. editor New Agents and Pharmacology; reviewer Cancer Rsch., Cancer Treatment Reports, Cancer, Am. Jour. Clin. Oncology, JAMA, Investigational New Drugs. Major U.S. Army, 1968-70, Vietnam; USAR, 1970-74. Recipient Faculty Ednl. Devel. award bur. Health Manpower NIH, 1973; grantee S.W. Oncology Group, 1974—, Intergroup Sarcoma Contract, 1986-89, Cancer Ctr., 1989-90, Clin. Therapeutics, Kasle Trust, 1988-89, Marilyn J. Smith Breast Cancer Rsch. Fund, 1986—, Program Project, New Drug Devel., 1989-94. Mem. Am. Soc. Cancer Rsch., Am. Soc. Clin. Oncology, Am. Soc. for Clin. Pharmacology and Therapeutics, Am. Assn. Clin. Rsch., Am. Assn. Cancer Edn., Am. Coll. Osteo. Internists, Cen. Soc. Clin. Rsch. Office: 7216CCGD 1500 E Medical Center Dr Ann Arbor MI 48109-0940*

BAKER, LEE EDWARD, biomedical engineering educator; b. Springfield, Mo., Aug. 31, 1924; s. Edward Fielding and Oneita Geneva (Patton) B.; m. Jeanne Carolyn Ferbrache, June 20, 1948; children: Carson Phillips, Carolyn Patton. BEE, U. Kans., 1945; MEE, Rice U., 1960; PhD in Physiology, Baylor U., 1965. Registered profl. engr., Tex. Asst. prof. electrical engring. Rice U., Houston, 1960-64; asst. prof. physiology Baylor U. Coll. Medicine, Houston, 1965-69, assoc. prof., 1969-75; prof. biomed. engring. U. Tex., 1975-82; Robert L. Parker Sr. Centennial Prof. Engring. U. Tex., Austin, 1982—. Co-author: Principles of Applied Biomedical Engineering, 1968, 3d edit., 1989; author, co-author scientific papers. Served to lt. USN, 1943-46, PTO, 1951-53. Spl. research fellow NIH, 1964-65. Fellow Am. Inst. Med. and Biol. Engring., Royal Soc. Medicine; mem. IEEE (sr.), Biomed. Engring. Soc. (sr.), Am. Physiol. Soc. Avocation: gardening. Office: Univ Tex ENS 610 Biomed Engring Program Austin TX 78712

BAKER, LEONARD MORTON, manufacturing company executive; b. Medford, Mass., Oct. 2, 1934; s. Abraham and Sarah B.; m. Ruth Lee Edelstein, June 15, 1958; children: Charles Harold, Andrew Mark, Douglas Jon. BS in Chemistry, Harvard U., 1956; PhD in Phys.-Organic Chemistry, MIT, 1960. With Union Carbide Corp., 1959-92, assoc. dir., then dir. rsch. and devel., 1969-77; v.p. rsch. and devel. Union Carbide Corp., N.Y.C., 1977-80; v.p., gen. mgr. coatings materials div. Union Carbide Corp., 1980-82, v.p. splty. chems. div., 1982-84, corporate dir. tech., 1984-86, v.p. splty. and services Bus. Group., 1986, corp. v.p. tech., 1986; v.p. tech. Praxair, Inc., Danbury, Conn., 1992—; bd. dirs. Rogers (Conn.) Corp. Exec. bd. Cornell Inst. Biotech.; mem. sci. adv. com. MIT; mem. materials sci. adv. bd., vis. com. U. Conn.; industry rep. Nat. Acad.-Industry Program, NRC; industry adv. panel NSF; mem. industry adv. bd. Presdl. Sci. Adv. Commn.; mem. sci. adv. bd. Conn. Coll.; active Nat. Industry Coun. for Sci. Edn., R&D 2000 Com., adv. bd. Coun. for Competitiveness Rsch. Devel. MIT fellow, 1956-57; NSF fellow, 1957-58; Sun Oil Corp. fellow, 1958-59. Mem. AICE, N.Y. Acad. Scis. (sci. policy com.), Am. Chem. Soc., Indsl. Rsch. Inst. (fed. sci. and tech. com., pre-coll. edn. com., rsch. com.), Council Chem. Rsch. (gov. bd., univ./industry liaison com.), Soc. Chem. Industry, Dirs. Indsl. Rsch., Am. Mgmt. Assn. (rsch. and devel. council), Conn. Acad. Sci. and Engring., Sigma Xi. Home: 60 Lyons Plains Rd Westport CT 06880-1305 Office: Praxair Inc Old Ridgebury Rd Danbury CT 06817

BAKER, LESLIE MAYO, JR., banker; b. Brunswick, Md., May 22, 1942; s. Leslie Mayo Sr. and Betty Jane (Rinker) B.; m. Suzanne Baldwin Borum, Dec. 19, 1964; children: Leslie Roderic, Benjamin Spencer, Leslie Margaret Cecil. BA in English Lit., U. Richmond, 1964; MBA, U. Va., 1969. With Wachovia Bank and Trust Co., Winston-Salem, N.C., 1969—, asst. v.p., 1972-73, v.p. gen. loan adminstrn. office, then v.p. loan adminstrn. office, 1973-74, v.p., mgr. internat. dept., 1974-77, sr. v.p., mgr. internat. dept., 1977-80, exec. v.p. div. exec. adminstrn., 1980-90, pres., chief exec. officer, 1990-98; pres., CEO Wachovia Corp., Winston-Salem, N.C., 1998—. Trustee Southeastern Ctr. Contemporary Art, Winston-Salem, 1988; trustee Colgate Darden Grad. Sch., Charlottesville, 1982—; bd. visitors U. N.C. Grad. Sch., Chapel Hill, 1988; trustee Summit Sch., Winston-Salem, 1988. Capt. USMC, 1964-67, Vietnam. Mem. Robert Morris Assocs. (sr. assoc. Phila. 1980—). Episcopalian. Office: Wachovia Corporation 100 N Main St Winston Salem NC 27101-4047*

BAKER, LESTER, physician, educator, research administrator; b. S.I., N.Y., June 30, 1930; s. Samuel Baker; m. Liesel Gutman, July 10, 1960; children: Deborah Ann, Herbert Phillip. AB, Columbia Coll., N.Y.C., 1951; MA, U. Paris, 1952; MD, Columbia U., 1959. Diplomate: Am. Bd. Pediatrics. From inst. to prof. pediatrics U. Pa. Med. Sch., Phila., 1962—, prof., 1976—; dir. clin. rsch. ctr. Children's Hosp. Phila., 1970-94, sr. physician, 1971—, dir. div. endocrinology and diabetes, 1978—; co-dir. diabetes rsch. ctr. Sch. of Medicine U. Pa., 1985-90; mem. Nat. Diabetes Adv. Bd., 1986-90; dir. diabetes ctr. for children Childrens Hosp., 1993—. Author: Psychosomatic Families: Anorexia Nervosa in Context, 1978; mem. ed. bd. Diabetes 1974-76, Diabetes Care 1977-80. With U.S. Army, 1952-54. Mem. Am. Pediatric Soc., Soc. for Pediatric Rsch., Am. Diabetes Assn., John Morgan Soc. of U. Pa., Lawson Wilkins Pediatric Endocrine Soc. Home: 4625 Larchwood Ave Philadelphia PA 19143-2107 Office: Children's Hosp Phila Divsn of Endocrinology 34th and Civic Center Blvd Philadelphia PA 19104

BAKER, LLOYD HARVEY, retired lawyer; b. Sept. 17, 1927; s. George William and Marion (Souville) B.; m. Barbara I. Gustafson, Sept. 4, 1955; children: Laurie, Jeffrey. Student, Colgate U., 1945-48; LLB, NYU, 1951. Bar: N.Y. 1951, U.S. Dist. Ct. (so. and ea. dists.) N.Y. 1953, U.S. Ct. Appeals (2d cir.) 1970. Assoc. Milligan, Reilly, Lake & Schneider, Babylon, N.Y., 1952-53; staff Fgn. Claims Commn., Washington, 1954; spl. attorney windfall investigations FHA, Washington, 1955; asst. U.S. atty. for Ea. Dist. N.Y., 1955-59; sole practice Bayshore and Islip, N.Y., 1959-67; atty. Suffolk County (N.Y.) Legal Aid Soc., 1967-69; dep. chief civil div. U.S. Atty.'s Office for Ea. Dist. N.Y., 1969-74; asst. counsel met. region Penn Central R.R. and Conrail, N.Y.C., 1975-81; ptnr. Bleakley, Platt, Remsen, Millham and Curran, N.Y.C., 1982-87; asst. town atty. Town of Islip, N.Y., 1987-97, retired, 1997—. Mem. Suffolk County Republican Com., 1963-71. Mem. Suffolk County Bar Assn. (chmn. fed. ct. com.), Bay Shore (N.Y.) Yacht Club. Episcopalian. Home: 5 Mulberry Rd Islip NY 11751-3707 Office: Town Hall of Islip Main St Islip NY 11751

BAKER, LYNNE RUDDER, philosophy educator; b. Atlanta, Feb. 14, 1944; d. James Maclin and Virginia (Bennett) Rudder; m. Thomas B. Baker III, Feb. 1, 1969. BA, Vanderbilt U., 1966, MA, 1971, PhD, 1972; student, Johns Hopkins U., 1967-68. Asst. prof. philosophy Mary Baldwin Coll., Staunton, Va., 1972-76; asst. prof. philosophy Middlebury (Vt.) Coll., 1976-79, assoc. prof., 1979-84, prof., 1984-94, acting dean arts and humanities, 1982, chairperson humanities divsn., 1982-85, acting chairperson philosophy, 1986-87; prof. U. Mass., Amherst, 1989—, dir. philosophy grad. program, 1994—; mem. panel to select summer seminars NEH, Washington, 1982, mem. panel to select fellows, 1989-90. Author: Saving Belief: A Critique of Physicalism, 1988, Explaining Attitudes: A Practical Approach to the Mind, 1995; contbr. scholarly articles to profl. jours. Trustee Vanderbilt U., Nashville, 1969-70, mem. alumni bd. dirs., 1985-89. Mellon fellow, 1974, NEH fellow, 1983-84, Nat. Humanities Ctr. fellow, 1982-83, Woodrow Wilson Internat. Ctr. for Scholars fellow, 1988-89. Mem. Am. Philos. Assn. (program com. 1983, exec. com. 1992-95), Soc. for Philosophy and Psychology, Soc. Christian Philosophers (exec. com. 1992-95), Soc. Women in Philosophy, Phi Beta Kappa. Democrat. Episcopalian. Office: U Mass Dept Philosophy Amherst MA 01003

BAKER, MALCOLM, marketing executive. Pres. BRS Group Inc., Calif. Office: BRS Group Inc Ste B-325 100 Shoreline Hwy Mill Valley CA 94941-3645

BAKER, MARK ALLEN, author, historian, consultant; b. Binghamton, N.Y., Mar. 27, 1957; s. Ford William and Marilyn A. (Allen) B.; divorced; children: Aaron Anthony, Elizabeth Margaret, Rebecca Jeanne. BA, SUNY, Oswego, 1979. Computer operator Gen. Electric Corp., Liverpool, N.Y., 1980-81, tng. specialist, 1981-82; art dir. Genigraphics Corp., Liverpool, 1982-83, mgr. market research, 1983-85, exec. asst. to pres. and chief exec. officer, 1985-86, corp. bus. planner, 1986-90; pvt. rschr., 1986—; historian Internat. Boxing Hall Fame. Author: Baseball Autograph Handbook, I and II, 1990, Team Baseballs, All Sport Autograph Guide, 1994, Complete Guide to Boxing Collectibles, 1995, Auto Racing, 1995, Collector's Guide to Celebrity Autographs, 1996, Rock and Roll Memorabilia, 1997, The Standard Guide to Collecting Autographs, 1999, Advanced Autograph Collecting, 1999, Collector's Guide to Celebrity Autographs, 2000; contbr. articles to profl. jours. Lifetime donor mem. Baseball Hall Fame, Historian Internat. Boxing Hall of Fame. Mem. Am. Mgmt. Assn. (pres. 1985—), Assn. Computer Mfrs. (pres. 1985—), Assn. Med. Illustrators (corp. rep., pres. 1986—), Am. Assn. Individual Investors (pres. 1987—), Siggraph (pres. 1985—). Avocations: sports, literature, finance. Address: 166 Ridings Way Lancaster PA 17601-2715

BAKER, MARTHA KAYE, writer, editor; b. St. Louis, Dec. 6, 1946; d. Harold Benjamin and Clara Marigold (Harman) B.; m. Robert Riels, Nov. 25, 1970 (div. Nov. 1977); m. John E. Clifford, May 19, 1990. BS in Edn., Cen. Mo. State U., 1967, MA, 1968. Tchr. Lakeland Coll., Sheboygan, Wis., 1968-71; counselor Clergy Consultation Svc., St. Louis, 1971-73; tchr. U. Mo., St. Louis, 1976-81; reporter St. Louis Bus. Jour., 1981-87; freelance writer St. Louis, 1987—. Author: (guidebook) Missouri Botanical Garden; contbr. articles, revs. and essays to newspapers and popular mags. Mem. St. Louis Ind. Journalists Assn. Democrat. Episcopalian. Avocations: embroidery, gardening. Home: 3050 Hatherly Dr Saint Louis MO 63121-4534

BAKER, MARY EVELYN, church librarian, retired academic librarian; b. Columbus, Ohio, May 8, 1912; d. Abram Jackson and Martha Maria (Dailey) Shoemaker; m. Richard Heinley Baker, Sept. 18, 1937 (dec.); children: Richard Shoemaker, David Guy. BA, Ohio State U., 1934; BS in Libr. Sci., Western Res. U., Cleve., 1935. Mem. staff libr. Ohio State U., Columbus, 1935-37, 38-44, 1955-74, part-time libr., 1955-66, adminstrv. asst., 1958, serial cataloger, 1958-67, asst. reviser, sr. cataloger, 1967-68, head serial div. catalog dept., 1968-71, head catalog dept., 1971-74; libr. com. First Congl. Ch., Columbus, 1941-97, libr. co-chmn., 1962-65, 74-75, libr. chmn., 1976-97; past mem. ALA, sec. serials sect., resources and tech. div., 1970-73. Den mother Boy Scouts Am., Columbus, 1953-58; libr. co-chmn. Friendship Village, Dublin, Ohio, 1981-97, chmn., 1997—. Mem. Ohioana Libr. Assn. (past chmn. various coms., life mem.), PEO (telephone chmn. chpt. V 1987—), DAR (Indians com.), Ohio State Univ. Women's Club (past pres.), Agrl. Circle (past pres.), Franklin Co-Ret.ses Tchrs. Assn. (life mem.), Ohio Ret.ses Tchrs. Assn. (life mem.), Ohio State Alumni Assn. (life mem.), Polar Bear Alumni Assn. Columbus North H.S. (life), Alumni Assn. Univ. Sch. (life), Ohio State U. Retirees Assn. (life, bridge chmn. 1984—), Ohio Hist. Soc., Worthington Hist. Soc., Columbus Hist. Soc., Ch. Women United of Columbus and Franklin County, Columbus Mus. art, Columbus Zoo, Gypsies Travel Club, Motts Mil. Mus. (charter), Phi Mu (various offices including pres. active and alumni chpts.). Republican. Home: 6000 Riverside Dr Apt 233A Dublin OH 43017-1494

BAKER, MATTHEW EDWARD, state legislator; b. Westfield, Pa., Jan. 24, 1957; m. Brenda Fitzsimmons, Nov. 17, 1990. AAS in Parlegal Studies, Corning C.C.; BS in Polit. Sci. and Law, Elmira Coll.; student, Mansfield U. Dist. legis. polit. aide 68th legis. dist. Pa. Ho. of Reps., 1979-91; mem. 68th legis. dist. Pa. Ho. of Reps., Harrisburg, 1992—. Past trustee and Sunday sch. tchr. 1st Bapt. Ch., Wellsboro, Pa.; mem. adv. bd. Pa. Coll.; past mem. adv. bd. paralegal program Corning C.C.; vice chmn. Pa. Gov.'s Com. on Employment People with Disabilities; mem. Tioga County Job Task Force, Pine Creek Hdqs. Protection Group; past pres. Wellsboro Area Food Pantry; trustee Guthrie Healthcare Sys.; chmn. Laurel Health Devel. Coun.; committeeman 2d ward Wellsboro Rep. Com. Recipient Vol. of Yr. award Gov. of Pa., 1991, Rural Health Legis. of Yr. award, 1998; named Legislator of Yr., Ctr. Rural Health Pa. State Coll. Mem. Pa. Farmers Assn., Tioga County Farmers Assn., Charleston Valley Grange, Rotary. Avocations: hunting, fishing, basketball, tennis, reading. Home: 60 American St Wellsboro PA 16901-1305 Office: 74 Main St Wellsboro PA 16901-1504

BAKER, MERL, engineering educator; b. Cadiz, Ky., July 11, 1924; s. Jesse F. and Argie (Coyle) B.; m. Emily Wilson, Sept. 14, 1946; children: Merl Wilson, Marilyn Ruth. B.S. in Mech. Engring., U. Ky., 1945; M.S., Purdue U., 1948, Ph.D., 1952. Grad. asst. Purdue U., 1946-48; mem. faculty U. Ky., 1948-63, prof. mech. engring., 1955-63; exec. dir. Ky. Research Found., 1953-63; coordinator, dir. U. Ky. coop. programs with AID, 1956-63, exec. dir. research and relations with industry, 1957-63; dean U. Mo. Sch. Mines and Metallurgy, 1963; chancellor U. Mo., Rolla, 1964-73; spl. asst. to pres. statewide system U. Mo., 1973-77; coordinator energy conservation program Oak Ridge Nat. Lab., 1977-79, energy mgmt. specialist, 1979-82; provost U. Tenn.-Chattanooga, 1982-85, prof. engring., 1985-97, dir. Ctr. for Career Enhancement, 1985-97. Recipient Disting. Alumnus award U. Ky., 1965, Disting. Engring. Alumnus award Purdue U., 1968. Fellow Am. Soc. Engring. Mgmt. (bd. dirs.), Am. Soc. Engring. Edn.; mem. AIME, ASHRAE (award of merit tchg. 1959, chmn. edn. com. 1960-61, Disting. Svc. award 1971), NSPE (pres. Tenn. chpt. 1995-96), Ky. Acad. Sci., Newcomen Soc. N.Am., Cosmos Club (Washington), Blue Key, Scabbard and Blade, Sigma

Xi, Phi Kappa Phi, Phi Eta Sigma, Tau Beta Pi, Pi Tau Sigma, Sigma Pi Sigma, Omicron Delta Kappa, Chi Epsilon. Home and Office: 1973 Blairmore Rd Lexington KY 40502-2432

BAKER, MICHAEL HOWARD, sales executive; b. Saginaw, Mich., July 16, 1960; s. Howard Arnold Baker and Carol Lucille (Cochran) Whitman; m. Rene Beth Stanloski, Oct. 15, 1983 (div. Sept. 1986); m. Katrina Louise Shoemaker, Apr. 1, 1993; children: Alexander, Christian. Lic. FCC radiotelephone operator, Washington. Engr. WIOS AM/WKJC FM, Tawascity, Mich., 1982-84; gen. mgr. WJEB AM/WGMM FM, Gladwin, Mich., 1984-86, WBMB AM/WBMI FM, West Branch, Mich., 1986-89; sys. engr. BMS/AEI Caribbean, St Thomas, V.I., 1989; owner, mgr. Moonlight Prodns., West Branch, Mich., 1989-92; reg. sales mgr. Taylor Bldg. Products, West Branch, 1990-95; mgr. detail Saturn of Wausau, Wis., 1996-97; with Advanced Sys. and Designs, Troy, Mich., 1997—. Republican. Home: 2330 W Jefferson Ave Trenton MI 48183-2706 Office: Advanced Systems and Designs 1208 E Maple Rd Troy MI 48083-2817

BAKER, MICHAEL LYNDON, minister; b. Lancaster, S.C., June 25, 1949; s. Robert Lynn and Ruby Arretta (Shelton) B.; m. Sharon Elaine Sibbett, Apr. 9, 1971; 1 child, Kysha Lyn. B in Music Edn., Lee Coll., 1971; MusM, U. N.C., Greensboro, 1978, postgrad., 1979-84; LHD, East Coast Bible Coll., 1994. Ordained to ministry Ch. of God (Cleveland, Tenn.), 1971; cert. elem., high sch. tchr., N.C. Min. Randleman (N.C.) Ch. of God, 1971-80, sr. pastor, 1989-92; prof. East Coast Bible Coll., Charlotte, N.C., 1980-84; adminstrv. asst. media dept. internat. offices Ch. of God, Cleveland, Tenn., 1984-88; dir. comms. Ch. of God, Cleveland, 1996—; mem. ch. music com. Ch. of God, Cleve., 1984-92; bd. dirs. Gen. Assembly, Ch. of God., 1991, dir. comm., 1992—; coord. Pentecostal World Conf., Israel, Korea, 1992—. Contbr. articles to religious publs.; author various musical works to Pathway Music, 1978—. Chmn. March of Dimes, Randleman, 1978; chmn. bd. dirs. Randleman Housing Authority, 1991-92. Republican. Home: 1501 17th St NW Cleveland TN 37311-1510 Office: Ch of God Internat Offices PO Box 2430 Cleveland TN 37320-2430*

BAKER, NADINE LOIS, medical technician; b. Balt., Apr. 16, 1955; d. David and Elizabeth Baker. Sr. cardiology technician U. Md. Med. Sys., Balt., 1989-95; cardiovasc. technician Md. Gen. Hosp., Balt., 1997—; assisted living care provider, 1999—. Sabbath sch. supt. Sharon Seventh-Day Adventist Ch., Balt., 1996.

BAKER, NANCY KASSEBAUM (NANCY KASSEBAUM), former senator, foundation official; b. Topeka, July 29, 1932; d. Alfred M. and Theo Landon; children: John Philip, Linda Josephine, Richard Landon, William Alfred; m. Howard Baker, 1996. BA in Polit. Sci, U. Kans., 1954; MA in Diplomatic History, U. Mich., 1956. Mem. Maize (Kans.) Sch. Bd., 1972-75; mem. Washington staff Sen. James B. Pearson of Kans., 1975-76; mem. U.S. Senate from Kans., 1979-96, mem. fgn. relations com., labor and human resources com., Indian Affairs com.; mem. com. fgn. rels., subcom. African affairs, 1980-96, mem. subcom. arts, edn. Arts & Humanities, mem. com. banking, housing & urban affairs, subcom. internat. fin. & monetary policy; chmn., bd. trustees Robert Wood Johnson Found., 1997—. Mem. Kans. Press Women's Assn., Women's Assn. Instnl. Logopedics. Republican. Episcopalian. Office: Robert Wood Johnson Found Coll Rd East PO Box 2316 Princeton NJ 08543-2316*

BAKER, NANNETTE A., lawyer, city official; b. Tuscaloosa, Ala., Oct. 3, 1957. BS, U. Tenn., 1978; JD, St. Louis U., 1994. Bar: Mo., Ill. TV journalist St. Louis, Memphis, Knoxville; law clk. to Odell Horton, U.S. Dist. Judge, Memphis, 1994-95; with firm Lashley & Baer, P.C., 1995-96; assoc. firm Schlichter, Bogard & Denton, St. Louis, 1996—; chair Bd. Election Commrs. for City of St. Louis, 1997—. Bd. dirs. St. Patrick's Ctr., Nat. Mus. Transport, Coll. for Living; mem. adv. bd. SSM Rehab. Inst. Mem. ABA, ATLA, Mo. Trial Lawyer Orgn., Ill. Trial Lawyer Orgn., Nat. Bar Assn., Mound City Bar Assn. Office: 100 S 4th St Ste 900 Saint Louis MO 63102-1823

BAKER, PAMELA, lawyer; b. Detroit, Apr. 6, 1951; d. William D. and Lois (Tukey) Baker; m. Jay R. Franke, June 10, 1972; children: Baker Eugene, Alexandra Britell. AB, Smith Coll., 1972; JD, U. Wis. Madison, 1976. Bar: Ill. 1976, Wis. 1976. Ptnr. Sonnenschein, Nath & Rosenthal, Chgo. Contbr. articles to profl. jours. Mem. ABA (mem. employee benefits com. 1994—, chair-elect 1998-99, chair 1999—, mem. plan mergers and acquisitions com. 1985— mem. fed. regulation of securities com. 1989—, chair 1989-95), Ill. State Bar Assn. (sec. employee benefits sect. coun. 1989-90, vice chair 1990-91, chair 1991-92), Chgo. Bar Assn. (employee benefits com. 1978—, sec. 1984-85, vice chair 1985-86, chair 1986-87, fed. taxation com. 1980—, exec. coun. 1982-85). Office: Sonnenschein Nath & Rosenthal Sears Tower 233 S Wacker Dr Ste 8000 Chicago IL 60606-6342

BAKER, PAMELA W., accountant; b. Welch, W.Va., Dec. 24, 1957; d. Frederick E. and Betty I. (Hatmaker) Willis; m. Gary S. Adams, Aug. 10, 1085 (div. Apr. 1991); M. Grey C. Baker, Nov. 1, 1991; children: Grey S., Barrett C. BA, Lynchburg (Va.) Coll., 1980. CPA. Sr. auditor pub. accounts Roanoke, Va., 1980-84; mgr. Johnson, Burgess & Co., Nags Head, N.C., 1984-88; audit ptnr. Barbacane, Thornton & Co., Wilmington, Del., 1988—. Active St. Anthony Padua PTO, Wilmington, 1994—. Mem. AICPA, Del. Soc. CPAs, N.C. Assn. CPAs, Pa. Assn. Sch. Bus. Ofcls. Baptist. Avocations: reading, jogging, cycling. Office: Barbacane Thornton & Co 202 Bancroft Bldg 3411 Silverside Rd Wilmington DE 19810-4812

BAKER, PATRICIA ANN, publishing executive; b. Englewood, N.J., Apr. 3, 1939. BA, St. Mary's Coll., 1961. Prodn. designer Little, Brown Pubs., 1961-63; mktg. & promotion dir. Sunset Books, 1963-68; design & prodn. mgr. Hoover Instn. Press, Stanford, Calif., 1981-89; exec. editor Hoover Instn. Press, Stanford, 1989—. Office: Hoover Instn Press Stanford U Stanford CA 94305-6010

BAKER, PAUL RAYMOND, history educator; b. Everett, Wash., Sept. 28, 1927; s. Loren Robbins and Alma Irene (Ball) B.; m. Elizabeth O. Kemp, Feb. 11, 1972; 1 dau., Alice Elizabeth. AB, Stanford U., 1949; MA, Columbia U., 1951; PhD, Harvard U., 1960. Staff editor Ency. Americana, N.Y.C., 1952-55; instr., asst. prof. Calif. Inst. Tech., Pasadena, 1960-63; lectr. U. Calif.-Riverside, 1963-64, U. Oreg., Eugene, 1964-65; assoc. prof., then prof. history NYU, N.Y.C., 1965—, dir. Am. Civilization Program, 1972-92. Editor: Views of Society and Manners in America, 1963; gen. editor: American Problem Studies series, 40 vols., 1968—; author: The Fortunate Pilgrims, 1964, Richard Morris Hunt, 1980, Stanny: the Gilded Life of Stanford White, 1989; compiler: The Atomic Bomb, 1968, The Atomic Bomb, rev. edit., 1976; co-author: The American Experience, 5 vols., 1976, 79, (Spanish translation) Nueva Historia de los Estados Unidos, 1986; (with others) Master Builders, 1985, The Architecture of Richard Morris Hunt, 1986, (French translation) Richard Morris Hunt Architecte, The Italian Presence in American Art, 1860-1920, 1992, Henry Adams and His World, 1993, La Virtù e la Libertà, 1995. Kennedy traveling fellow Harvard U., 1958-59; NEH fellow, 1982. Mem. Am. Studies Assn. (pres. met. N.Y. chpt. 1968-69, Mary C. Turpie prize for outstanding contbns. to tchg. advisement and program devel. 1994), Soc. Archtl. Historians, Orgn. Am. Historians, Victorian Soc. in Am., Phi Beta Kappa (v.p., pres. Beta of N.Y. 1966-70). Home: 90 Hillside Ave Glen Ridge NJ 07028-2212 Office: NYU Dept History 53 Washington Square South New York NY 10012-1098

BAKER, PAUL THORNELL, anthropology educator; b. Burlington, Iowa, Feb. 28, 1927; s. Palmer Ward Baker and Viola Isabelle (Thornell) Loughlin; m. Thelma Marion Shoher, Feb. 21, 1949; children: Deborah C., Amy L., Joshua S., Felicia B. Student, U. Miami, 1947-49; BA, U. N.Mex., 1951; PhD, Harvard U., 1956. Rsch. U.S. Army Q.M., Natick, Mass., 1952-57; asst. prof. anthropology Pa. State U., University Park, 1957-61, assoc. prof., 1961-65, prof., 1965-81, Evan Pugh prof. anthropology, 1981-87, Evan Pugh prof. emeritus, 1987—, head dept., 1980-85; sci. advisor Wenner-Gren Found., N.Y.C., 1980-83; mem. U.S. Commn. for UNESCO 1982-84, exec. commn. 1983-84. Editor: Biology of Human Adaptability, 1966, Man in the Andes, 1976, Biology of High Altitude Peoples, 1978, The Changing Samoans, 1986; co-author: (with G.A. Harrison, J.M. Tanner, D.R. Pilbeam) Human Biology, 1988. Served with U.S. Army, 1945-47. Recipient Huxley medal Royal Anthrop. Inst. Gt. Brit., 1982; decorated Yugoslavian Order of the Golden Star with Necklace, 1988; Fulbright research scholar, 1962; Guggenheim Found. fellow, 1974-75. Fellow Am. Anthrop. Assn. (assoc. editor jour. 1973-76); mem. NAS, Am. Assn. Phys. Anthropologists (pres. 1969-71, Charles R. Darwin Lifetime Achievement award 1993), Human Biology Coun. (pres. 1974-77), Internat. Assn. Human Biologists (pres. 1980-89), Internat. Union Anthropol. and Ethnol. Scis. (hon. life., v.p. 1988-93, sr. v.p. 1993-98). Address: 45113 Pawnee Dr Fremont CA 94539-6663

BAKER, PEGGY MACLACHLAN, cultural organization administrator. BA in Classics, History, Edn., U. Mich., 1969, MA in Latin, History, 1972; MLS, Wayne State U., 1979. Dir., libr. Pilgrim Soc., Plymouth, Mass., 1995—; curator (exhibits) Harvest Home, 1993, Thanksgiving by the (Cook)book, 1996, Thanksgiving "Over There", 1997; gov.'s spl. commn. 375th Anniversary Landing of Pilgrims at Plymouth, 1995. Co-author, editor: Thanksgiving by the (Cook)book, 1976. Mem. Plymouth Hist. Alliance (sec. 1996—), Mass. Hist. Soc., Colonial Soc. Mass. Office: Pilgrim Soc 75 Court St Plymouth MA 02360-3823*

BAKER, PETER MITCHELL, laser scientist and executive, educator; b. London, July 18, 1939; s. George Edward and Clarice (Griffiths) B.; m. Sunny Baker, Oct. 15, 1988; 1 child, Scott George. BSc in Physics with honors, London U., 1963. Sr. physicist Itek Corp., Lexington, Mass., 1966-69; sr. v.p. Micronetic Systems, Burlington, Mass., 1969-74; tchr. physics Hillcrest Sch., Nairobi, Kenya, 1975-77; pres. Quantrad Corp., Torrance, Calif., 1977-84, Ebtec of Calif., Huntington Beach, 1985-88; exec. dir. Laser Inst. Am., Orlando, Fla., 1988—; lectr. lasers UCLA extension, 1986-88. Contbr. various articles on lasers and optics to profl. jours. Recipient Chief Exec. Officer award for Outstanding Small Bus., 1982. Fellow Laser Inst. Am. (pres. 1987, Pres.' award 1991). Avocations: walking, tennis. Office: Laser Inst Am 12424 Rsch Pkwy Ste 125 Orlando FL 32826 *My guiding principle is "Do What You Say."*

BAKER, PHILIP DOUGLAS, consultant, retired investment banker; b. Los Angeles, Mar. 19, 1922; s. J. Douglas and Alice (Brown) B.; m. Cornelia Draves, July 16, 1955; children: Brinton, Todd, Claudia, Samuel Baker. BS, UCLA, 1947; MBA, U. Calif., Berkeley, 1948. Assoc. Marshall Plan, Germany, 1948-52; with White, Weld & Co., Inc., N.Y.C., 1952-76, ptnr., 1960-72, sr. v.p., 1972-76; pres. Insts. of Religion and Health, 1978-81; cons. Nat. Exec. Service Corps, 1978—; chmn. bd. Found. Religion and Health, 1982-86; adj. assoc. prof. Grad. Sch. Bus. Adminstrn., NYU, 1964-66. Trustee Valley Hosp., 1972-83, West Bergen Mental Health, 1998—; pres. Valley Health Services, 1987-94; pres.'s coun. Berea Coll., 1988—. Capt. USMCR, 1943-46. Decorated Purple Heart. Mem. Investment Bankers Assn. Am. (pres. 1971-72), Securities Industry Assn. (vice chmn. bd. 1972), Bond Club N.Y. Home: 293 Greenridge Rd Franklin Lakes NJ 07417-2011

BAKER, R. ROBINSON, surgeon; b. Balt., Dec. 30, 1928; s. Henry Scott and Frances (Robinson) B.; m. Jean Harvey, Sept. 12, 1953; children: Susan, Scott, Robert, Jean. AB, Johns Hopkins U., 1950, MD, 1954. Diplomate: Am. Bd. Surgery and Bd. Thoracic Surgery. Intern Johns Hopkins U., 1954-55; sr. asst. surgeon Nat. Heart Inst., 1955-57; asst. resident Johns Hopkins Hosp., 1957-58, resident, 1958-61, chief surg. resident, 1961-62; surgeon-in-charge Johns Hopkins Hosp. (Breast Clinic), 1970—, Johns Hopkins Hosp. (Oncology Center), 1976; prof. surgery Johns Hopkins U., 1967—, prof. oncology, 1975—, Warfield M. Firor porf. surgery, 1991—; mem. (Coop. Lung Cancer Detection Group), 1971—. Recipient grants Am. Cancer Soc., 1966-71, grants John A. Hartford Found., 1968-73, grants Upjohn Co., 1973, grants Sterling-Winthrop Rsch. Inst., 1975—; named hon. fellow Royal Coll. Surgeons of Ireland. Fellow ACS, Royal Coll. Surgeons (hon.); mem. Soc. Univ. Surgeons, Am. Assn. Thoracic Surgery, So. Thoracic Surg. Assn., Soc. Head and Neck Surgeons, AMA, Am., So. Surg. Assns., Elkridge (Balt.) Club, Fishers Island (N.Y.) Club, Hay Harbor Club (Fishers Island). Home: 8717 McDonogh Rd Baltimore MD 21208-1021 Office: 600 N Wolfe St 634 Blalock Baltimore MD 21287

BAKER, REBECCA LOUISE, musician, music educator, consultant; b. Covina, Calif., Apr. 12, 1951; d. Allan Herman and Hazel Margaret (Maki) Flaten; m. Jerry Wayne Baker, Dec. 22, 1972; children: Jared Wesley, Rachelle LaDawn, Shannon Faith. Grad. high sch., Park River, N.D.; student, Trinity Bible Inst., 1968-69. Sec. Agrl. Stblzn. & Conservation Svc. Office, Park River, N.D., 1969; pianist, singer Paul Clark Singers & Vic Coburn Evangelistic Assn., Portland, Oreg., 1969-72; musician, singer Restoration Ministries Evangelistic Assn., Richland, Wash., 1972-80; musician, pvt. instr. Calvary Temple Ch., Shawnee, Okla., 1980-81; organist, choirmaster St. Francis Episcopal Ch., Tyler, 1984-87; co-founder, owner Psalmist Sch. of Music & Recording Studio, Whitehouse, 1983—; pianist/entertainer Willowbrook Country Club, Tyler, Tex., 1991—; pianist, vocalist Mario's Italian Restaurant, Tyler, 1994—; pianist Garner Ted Armstrong, Tyler, 1986—; pianist, dir. Children's Choir, Calvary Bapt. Ch., Tyler, 1987—; pianist, entertainer Ramada Hotel, Tyler, 1988-90; pianist Whitehouse (Tex.) Sch. Dist. choirs, 1988—; accompanist Tyler Area Children's Chorale, 1988-90, Univ. Interscholastic League; pvt. instr. keyboard and vocal. Composer: Religious Songs (12 on albums), 1979; pianist, arranger, prodr., rec. artist 6 albums; editor, arranger: Texas Women's Aglow Songbook, 1987; editor Shekinah Glory mag., 1989—; developer improvisational piano course; star, prodr. weekly, nationally syndicated mus. religious spls. for TV, 1995, 96, Proclaim His Glory, 1997—; played for receptions honoring Gov. George Bush, Tex. Senator Phil Gramm and Congressman John Bryant. Performer, spkr. many charitable, civic and religious orgns., Tex. and U.S. including AAUW, Kiwanis Clubs; co-founder Psalmist Mins. Internat., 1988—; founder, pres. Christian Music Tchr.'s Assn., 1991; worship leader Mayor's Prayer Breakfast, Tyler, 1994. Mem. Women's Aglow Fellowship (music dir., spkr., performer at retreats and tng. seminars). Republican. Full Gospel. Avocations: travel, reading, interior decorating, collecting. Home and Office: Psalmist Music & Recording PO Box 961 Whitehouse TX 75791-0961

BAKER, RICHARD EUGENE, corporate executive; b. Sioux City, Iowa, Aug. 9, 1939; s. Andrew A. J. and Betty J. (Wise) B.; m. Johanna Garbatscheck, Aug. 8, 1973. BA in Bus. Adminstrn., Calif. State U., Long Beach, 1961. Audit supr. Coopers & Lybrand, L.A., 1961-66; with Universal Studios Inc., Universal City, Calif., 1966-74; corp. contr. Universal Studios Inc., Universal City, 1974-86, v.p. and contrr., 1986-91, v.p., CFO, 1991-95, sr. v.p. reengring. value creation, 1995-97, cons., 1997—; bd. dirs. Motion Picture Industry Pension Plan, Studio City, Calif., Rsch. to Prevent Blindness, N.Y.C., St. Joseph Med. Ctr. Found., Burbank, Calif. Mem. AICPA, Calif. Soc. CPAs, Fin. Execs. Inst., Acad. Motion Picture Arts and Scis. Republican. Avocation: skiing. Office: Universal Studios Inc 507/4B 100 Universal City Plz Universal City CA 91608-1002*

BAKER, RICHARD GRAVES, geology educator, palynologist; b. Merrill, Wis., June 12, 1938; s. Dillon James and Miriam (Hinckley) B.; m. Debby J.Z. Baker; children: Kristina Kae, James Dillon, Charity Ann. BA, U. Wis., 1960; MS, U. Minn., 1964; PhD, U. Colo., 1969. Asst. prof. geology U. Iowa, Iowa City, 1970-75, assoc. prof., 1975-81, prof., 1981—, chmn. dept., 1992-95, prof. botany, 1988-92, prof. biol. scis., 1992—. Contbr. articles and chpts. to profl. publs. Chmn. Iowa chpt. Nature Conservancy, Des Moines, 1981-82. Grantee NSF, 1984-86, 88-90, 94-97, NOAA, 1992-93. Fellow Geol. Soc. Am., Iowa Acad. Sci.; mem. Am. Assn. Stratigraphic Palynologists, Am. Quaternary Assn., Ecol. Soc. Am. Office: Univ Iowa 121 Trowbridge Hall Dept Geology Iowa City IA 52242-1319

BAKER, RICHARD H., retired geneticist, educator; b. Hayfield, Minn., Sept. 14, 1936; married; two children. BS, U. Ill., 1959, MS, 1962, PhD in Zoology and Genetics, 1965. Rsch. assoc. mosquito genetics U. Ill., 1965, rsch. assoc., 1965-66, asst. prof. mosquito genetics, 1966-69; assoc. prof. internal medicine Sch. Medicine U. Md., Balt., prof., dir. Internat. Health Program, 1979-82; dir. Pakistan Med. Rsch., Lahore, 1969-79; with Fla. Med. Entomol. Lab, Inst. Food and Agr. Scis. U. Fla., Vero Beach, 1982—, dir. Fla. Med. Entomol. Lab., Inst. Food and Agr. Scis., 1998; cons. WHO, 1965. Mem. Genetics Soc. Am., Entom. Soc. Am., Am. Soc. Tropical Med. and Hygiene, Am. Genetic Assn., Am. Mosquito Control Assn., Sigma Xi. Office: U Fla Med Entom Lab Inst Food and Agr Scis 200 9th St SE Vero Beach FL 32962-4657*

BAKER, RICHARD HUGH, congressman; b. New Orleans, LA, May 22, 1948; m. Karen Carpenter; children: Brandon, Julie. BA, La. State U. State rep. La. Dist. 64, former chmn. com. on transp., hwys. and pub. works, 1981-82, state rep.; mem. La. Ho. of Reps., 100th-103rd Congresses from 6th La. Dist., 1987—; mem. transp. and infrastructure com. and vets. affs. com., chmn. Banking & Fin. Svcs. subcom. on Capital Mkts., Securities and Govt. Sponsored Enterprises, also real estate broker. Methodist. Office: US Ho of Reps 434 Cannon House Offc Bldg Washington DC 20515-1806

BAKER, RICHARD SOUTHWORTH, lawyer; b. Lansing, Mich., Dec. 18, 1929; s. Paul Julius and Florence (Schmid) B.; m. Kathleen E. Yull, 1956 (dec. 1964); m. Marina J. Vidoli, 1965 (div. 1989); children: Garrick Richard, Lydia Joy; m. Barbara J. Walker, 1997. Student, DePauw U., 1947-49; A.B. cum laude, Harvard, 1951; J.D., U. Mich., 1954. Bar: Ohio 1957, U.S. Dist. Ct. (no. dist.) Ohio 1958, U.S. Tax Ct. 1960, U.S. Supreme Ct. 1971, U.S. Ct. Appeals (6th cir.) 1972. Since practiced in Toledo; mem. firm Fuller & Henry, and predecessors, 1956-91; pvt. practice Toledo, 1991—; Chmn. nat. com. region IV Mich. Law Sch. Fund, 1967-69, mem.-at-large, 1970-85. Bd. dirs. Asso. Harvard Alumni, 1970-73; mem. Epworth Assembly, Ludington, Mich.. Served with AUS, 1954-56. Fellow Am. Coll. Trial Lawyers; mem. ABA, Ohio Bar Assn., Toledo Bar Assn., Lawyer-Pilots Bar Assn., Toledo Club, Harvard Club (pres. Toledo chpt. 1968-77), Capital Club, Phi Delta Theta, Phi Delta Phi. Office: 2819 Falmouth Rd Toledo OH 43615-2215

BAKER, RICK, make-up artist; b. Binghamton, N.Y., Dec. 8, 1950; s. Ralph B. and Doris (Hamlin) B.; m. Elaine Parkyn (div. 1984); m. Silvia Abascal, Nov. 10, 1987. Spl. effects makeup artist on the following films: Octaman, 1971, The Thing With Two Heads, 1972, Pirahna, 1972, Bone, 1972, The Exorcist, 1973, Schlock, 1973, Live and Let Die, 1973, Hell Up in Harlem, 1973, It's Alive, 1974, Death Race 2000, 1975, Black Caesar, 1975, Squirm, 1976, Food of the Gods, 1976, King Kong, 1976, Track of the Moonbest, 1976, Zebra Force, 1976, Kentucky Fried Movie, 1977, Star Wars, 1977, The Incredible Melting Man, 1978, It's Alive 2, 1978, The Fury, 1978 Tanya's Island, 1980, The Funhouse, 1980, The Incredible Shrinking Woman, 1981, An American Werewolf in London, 1981 (Acad. award Best Makeup), Videodrome, 1983, Greystoke: The Legend of Tarzan, Lord of the Apes, 1984, Starman, 1984, My Science Project, 1985, Cocoon, 1985, Ratboy, 1986, Captain Eo, 1986, Harry and the Hendersons, 1987 (Acad. award Best Makeup), Summer School, 1987, Missing Link, 1988, Coming to America, 1988, Gorillas in the Mist, 1988 (also assoc. prodr.), Gremlins 2; The New Batch, 1990 (also co-prodr.), The Rocketeer, 1991, Ed Wood, 1994 (Acad. award Best Makeup), Wolf, 1994, Batman Forever, 1995, The Amazing Panda Adventure, 1995, Just Cause, 1995, The Nutty Professor, 1996, The Frighteners, 1996, Escape from L.A., 1996, Men in Black, 1997, Mighty Joe Young, 1998, Life, 1999; TV work includes (movies): The Autobiography of Miss Jane Pittman, 1974 (Emmy award Best Makeup), An American Christmas Carol, 1979, Something Is Out There, 1988, Body Bags, 1993; (series) Davey and Goliath, 1960-65, Werewolf, 1987-88, Beauty and the Beast, 1987-90; designed spl. makeup effects for Michael Jackson's Thriller, 1983. Office: IATSE Local 706 11519 Chandler Blvd North Hollywood CA 91601-2618*

BAKER, ROBERT EDWARD, lawyer, retired financial corporation executive; b. Albion, Mich., May 6, 1930; s. Robert Charles and Loretto A. (Barrett) B.; m. Mary Anne Mulcahy, Feb. 20, 1965. B.B.A., U. Mich., 1952, LL.B., 1955. Bar: Mich. 1956. Atty. legal dept. Chrysler Corp., Detroit, 1955-64; with Chrysler Fin. Corp., Troy, Mich., 1964-90, also bd. dirs., v.p. corp. fin., 1970-80, v.p. fin., gen. counsel, 1980-85, vice chmn. bd., 1985-90; trustee Independence One Mut. Funds, Farmington Hills, Mich., 1990—. Trustee Comprehensive Health Svcs., Inc., 1972—, chmn. bd., 1977—; trustee, sec. Rose Hill Ctr., Inc., Holly, Mich.; trustee Sacred Heart Major Sem., Detroit, 1996—. With CIC, AUS, 1955-57. Recipient Disting. Service award Am. Fin. Services Assn., 1981. Mem. ABA, State Bar of Mich., Fin. Execs. Inst., Am. Assn. Sovereign Mil. Order of Malta, Orchard Lake Country Club. Roman Catholic. Home: 4327 Stoneleigh Rd Bloomfield Hills MI 48302-2157

BAKER, ROBERT ERNEST, JR., retired foundation executive; b. Tuscaloosa, Ala., Oct. 17, 1916; s. Robert Ernest and Faye (Whitson) B.; m. Billye Louise Driskell, June 25, 1947; 1 son, Brent Driskell. BS in Indsl. Engring, U. Ala., 1939. Registered profl. engr., Tex. Indsl. engring., mgmt. and fin. cons., 1939-62; exec. adminstr., sec. Moody Found., Galveston, Tex., 1962-97; ret., 1997. Presbyterian. Club: Arty. (Galveston). Home: 6 Adler Cir Galveston TX 77551-5828

BAKER, ROBERT FRANK, molecular biologist, educator; b. Weiser, Idaho, Apr. 9, 1936; s. Robert Clarence and Beulah (Hulet) B.; m. Mary Margaret Murphy, May 29, 1965; children: Allison Leslie, Steven Mark. B.S., Stanford U., 1959; Ph.D., Brown U., 1966. Postdoctoral rsch. assoc. Stanford (Calif.) U., 1966-68; asst. prof. dept. biol. scis. U. So. Calif., L.A., 1968-72, assoc. prof., 1972-83, prof., 1983—, dir. molecular biology div., 1978-80, mem. Comprehensive Cancer Ctr., 1984—; vis. assoc. prof. Harvard U. Med. Sch., Boston 1975-76; mem. genetic study sect. NIH, Bethesda, Md., 1977-79, 82. Contbr. articles to profl. jours. Grantee NIH, NSF, 1968—. Mem. Am. Soc. Zoologists, Am. Soc. Microbiology, Sigma Xi. Avocations: amateur radio, electronics. Home: 607 Almar Ave Pacific Palisades CA 90272-4208 Office: U So Calif Dept Molecular Biology MC 1340 Los Angeles CA 90089

BAKER, ROBERT I., business executive; b. Bridgeport, Conn., Sept. 28, 1940; s. Irwin Henry and Anna (Keane) B.; m. Patricia Turoczi, Nov. 28, 1968; children: Scott Allen, Christopher Keane. BA, U. Conn., 1962; postgrad., Syracuse U., 1975, U. Pa., 1978. With U.S. Electric Motors div. Emerson, Milford, Conn., 1963-66; with Henry G. Thompson div. Vt. Am., Branford, Conn., 1966-75; pres., gen. mgr. Magna div. Vt. Am., Elizabethtown, Ky., 1977-84, corp. v.p., 1982-84; pres., CEO, Vt. Am., Louisville, 1984-91; pres., owner Distbrs. Source, Portsmouth, N.H., 1991-92; CEO The Chamberlain Group, Inc., Elmhurst, Ill., 1992-96, The Chamberlain Group, Elmhurst, 1996—; mem. President's Roundtable, Martinsville, Ind., 1993—. Mem. Medinah Country Club, Abenaqui Country Club. Avocations: snow skiing, golf, woodworking. Home: 845 N Larch Ave Elmhurst IL 60126-1114 Office: The Chamberlain Group Inc 845 N Larch Ave Elmhurst IL 60126-1114*

BAKER, ROBERT J., medical academic dean, surgeon; b. Chgo., Feb. 17, 1927; s. Max and Rae Baker; m. Juanita Joan Anger, Apr. 20,1 958; children: Mark, Brian, Julie Ann. AB, Miami U., Oxford, Ohio, 1946; BS, MD, U. Ill., Chgo., 1950. Diplomate Am. Bd. Surgery. Intern Cook County Hosp., Chgo., 1950-51, resident in gen. surgery, 1953-58, assoc. chmn. dept. surgery, 1959-67, chmn. dept. surgery, 1967-69; prof. surgery U. Ill. Coll. Medicine, Chgo., 1967-88, chief gen. surgery, 1974-88; chmn. dept. surgery Med. Ctr. Del., Wilmington, 1988-93; prof. surgery U. Chgo. Sch. Medicine, 1993—, vice-chmn. dept. surgery, —; dean, bd. dirs. Nat. Ctr. Advanced Med. Edn., Chgo., 1974—. Editor: Mastery of Surgery, 1984, 2d edit., 1992; contbr. numerous articles to surg. publs. 1st lt. U.S. Army, 1951-53, Korea. Decorated Silver Star, Purple Heart. Fellow ACS; mem. Am. Assn. for the Surgery of Trauma, Am. Gastroent. Assn., Am. Surg. Assn., Cen. Surg. Assn., Chgo. Surg. Soc., Collegium Internationale de Chirurgie Digestivae, Ill. Surg. Soc., Shock Soc., Societe Internationale de Chirurgie, Soc. for Surgery of the Alimentary Tract, Soc. Univ. Surgeons, Western Surg. Assn. Avocations: sailing, skiing, jogging, antique clock collecting. Office: U Chgo Dept Surgery MC 5093 5841 S Maryland Ave Chicago IL 60637-1463

BAKER, ROBERT J(OHN), hospital administrator; b. Detroit, Feb. 2, 1944; s. Wesley Ries and Irma Louise (Richards) B.; m. Priscilla Horschak, Sept. 10, 1966; children: Scott, Katherine. B.A., Kalamazoo Coll., 1966; M.B.A., U. Chgo., 1968. Adminstr. Indian Hosp., Sells, Ariz., 1968-70; asst. dir. U. Minn. Hosp., Mpls., 1970-73, assoc. dir., 1973-74, assoc. dir. ops., 1974-77, sr. assoc. dir., 1977; dir. U. Nebr. Hosp. and Clinic, Omaha, 1977-86; pres., chief exec. officer U. Health Sys. Consortium, Oak Brook, Ill., 1986—. Served with USPHS, 1968-70. Recipient Mary H. Bachmeyer award U. Chgo., 1968; Carl A. Erickson fellow, 1966. Mem. Council Teaching Hosps., Omaha-Council Bluffs Hosp. Assn. (pres. 1983). Office: U Health Systems Consortium 2001 Spring Rd Ste 700 Oak Brook IL 60523-1890

BAKER, ROBERT LEON, naval medical officer; b. Oak, Nebr., Feb. 7, 1925; s. Oscar E. and Ada Veru (Davis) B.; m. Rebecca Chandler, Dec. 12, 1956; children: Rebecca Ann, Jay Milton, Betsy Jean, Robert Leon, Bruce Chandler, Brenda Carole. BS in Liberal Arts, La. Poly. Inst., 1945; BS in Medicine, U. Ark., 1949, MD with highest honors, 1949; grad. program health systems mgmt., Harvard U. Grad. Sch. Bus., 1972. Diplomate: Am. Bd. Obstetrics and Gynecology. Apprentice seaman U.S. Navy, 1943, commd. lt. (j.g.), M.C., 1949, advanced through grades to rear adm., 1973; rotating intern Tripler Gen. Hosp., Honolulu, 1949-50; resident in obstetrics and gynecology U.S. Naval Hosp., Oakland, Calif., 1954; assigned U.S. and overseas as obstetrician-gynecologist; chmn. dept. obstetrics and gynecology Naval Hosp., Portsmouth, Va., 1969-72; med. aide Office Comdr. in chief, NATO, 1970-72; dir. grad. tng. and chmn. dept. ob-gyn. Naval Regional Med. Center, Oakland, 1973-75; comdg. officer Naval Regional Med. Center, Phila., 1975-77, Naval Aerospace and Regional Med. Center, Pensacola, Fla., 1977-79; chief ob-gyn. service Baxter Gen. Hosp., Mountain Home, Ark., 1980-82; clin. prof. Va. Commonwealth U. Med. Sch., 1971—; med. dir. Hospice of Ozarks, 1984-96 . Contbr. articles to med. jours. Bd. dirs. Phila. YWCA, 1975-77, USO, Phila., 1976-77, Pensacola, Fla., 1978-80, Baxter County Regional Hosp., 1985-87, also various bds. tng. insts., 1980—; bd. dirs. Ctrl. Ark. Radiation Therapy Inst., 1990-96, chmn. adv. bd. Mountain Home, 1990-99; pres. Baxter County chpt. Am. Cancer Soc., 1995-96; founding mem. Internat. Coll. Hospice/Palliative Care, 1995; mem. Make A Wish Found.; bd. dirs. Internat. Hospice Inst. and Coll., 1996—. Decorated Legion of Merit, Meritorious Service medal, Navy Commendation medal; recipient Letters of Commendation Comdr. in Chief NATO, Sec. Navy; recipient Wish Team award for Ark., Make A Wish Found., 1996. Fellow Am. Coll. Obstetricians and Gynecologists (asst. sec. 1977-79, chmn. armed forces dist. Navy sect. 1967-69, vice-chmn. armed forces dist. 1971-74); mem. AMA (del. 1976-77), Assn. Mil. Surgeons U.S. (chpt. pres. 1973-74), Baxter County Med. Soc. (pres. 1982-84), Ark. Med. Soc. (del. 1985—), Acad. Hospice Physicians (founding mem.), Alpha Omega Alpha, Phi Chi. Mem. Christian Ch. (Disciples of Christ). Club: Union League (Phila.). Home: PO Box 44 Mountain Home AR 72654-0044 Office: 3763 Highway 5 S Mountain Home AR 72653-5944 *Time is critical for top management. It is divided into People time and Paper time. People time, almost invariably, must take precedence at any moment, but paper time still demands and must be accomplished. People time demonstrates concern. This perception by people of concern by management is the essential element of true leadership, and the essence of morale. One who can follow this precept while, at the same time completing paper work, is a top manager. This takes time.*

BAKER, ROBERT STEVENS, organist, educator; b. Pontiac, Ill., July 7, 1916; s. Stevens R. and Hattie (Thrasher) B.; m. Mary F. Depler, June 27, 1943; children: James S., Martha Faye. B.Mus., Ill. Wesleyan U., 1938, Mus.D., 1960; Sacred Mus.M., Union Theol. Sem., 1940, Sacred Mus.D., 1944; L.H.D., Bradley U., 1964; D.F.I., Westminster Choir Coll., 1966; D. Mus. A., Susquehanna U., 1967; M.A., Yale U., 1973. Dean Sch. Sacred Music, Union Theol. Sem., 1961-72; dir. Yale U. Inst. Music and Worship, 1973-75, prof. organ, 1973-87, prof. emeritus music, 1987—; Bd. dirs. Union Theol. Sem., 1959-61; trustee Westminster Choir Coll., 1968-72; chmn. organ award com. Inst. Internat. Edn., 1957-59, 63, 65, 66, 75. Organist, choirmaster, 1st Presbyn. Ch., Bklyn., 1941-53, Temple Emanu-El, N.Y.C., 1945-61, Fifth Ave. Presbyn. Ch., N.Y.C., 1953-61, St. James Episcopal Ch., N.Y.C., 1972-74, 1st Presbyn. Ch., N.Y.C., 1975-88, concert organist, 1945-88, recitalist, Westminster Abbey, 900th Anniversary, 1966, organ bldg. cons. Mem. Am. Guild Organists (dean N.Y.C. chpt. 1955-57, nat. councillor 1950-57, 72-75, chmn. nat. conv. 1956, rep., opening recitalist 1st Internat. Congress Organists, London 1957, recitalist nat. convs. 1947, 56), Hymn Soc. Am. (dir. 1961-75), Bohemians, St. Wilfrid Soc., Oratorio Soc. N.Y. (dir.), Coll. Ch. Musicians (dir.). Home: 84 Jesswig Dr Hamden CT 06517-2135 Office: 409 Prospect St New Haven CT 06511-2167

BAKER, ROBERT THOMAS, interior designer; b. Kansas City, Mo., Mar. 23, 1932; s. Robert Blume and Justina (Early) B. B.A. in Art, U. Mo., Columbia, 1954, M.A. in Interior Design, 1962; cert., Parsons Sch. Design, N.Y.C., 1958. Interior designer Edward Keith, Inc., Kansas City, Mo., 1958-60, 63-71, Nereoux Interiors, New Iberia, La., 1960-61, Bloomingdales, N.Y.C., 1962-63, Thomas Price Interiors, Kansas City, Mo., 1971-78; owner Robert Baker Interiors Inc., Kansas City, 1978-89; chmn. interior design dept. Au Marché, Inc., Kansas City, 1989; pres. Baker Design, Inc., Kansas City, 1989—; mem. guidance com. Found. Interior Designer Edn. Research, 1972-82 Bd. visitors Found. Interior Design Edn. Research, 1984-90. Mem. adv. bd. Toy & Miniature Mus. Kansas City, 1985—; bd. govs., chmn. adv. bd. Hand-in-Hand, 1995—. With USAAF, 1954-57. award of merit Mo.W./Kans. chpt., 1971. Fellow Am. Soc. Interior Designers (pres. Mo.W./Kans. chpt. 1966-72, 73-74, regional v.p. 1969-71, nat. gov. 1969-74). Presbyterian. Home and Office: 12801 Cherry St Kansas City MO 64145-1308 *As corn ball as it may sound in this day and age, I have always tried my best to treat my clients, my suppliers, my peers, and whomever I come in contact with, in the same manner that I hope they would treat me. Professionally, I have always tried to project my clients personality and interests so that the completed job reflects them and not me. To me, an interior is not a success if it winds up looking like the designer rather than the person, or persons, for whom it was designed.*

BAKER, ROBERT VERNON, JR., retired military officer, military trainer; b. Barberton, Ohio, Mar. 4, 1948; s. Robert Vernon Sr.; m. Mildred J. Benier; 3 children, 2 stepchildren. BS in Social Sci., Troy State U., 1977, MS in Personal Counseling, 1980. Apprentice machinist Firestone Tire & Rubber Co., Akron, 1966; enlisted U.S. Army, 1966, advanced through grades to col., 1990, ret., 1993; dir. mus. security Jacksonville (Ala.) State U., 1993-95; v.p. Inst. for Spl. Tng., Anniston, Ala., 1995-97; dir. tng. Ctr. for Domestic Preparedness, Ft. McClellan, Ala., 1998—; domestic violence instr. mil. police sch. U.S. Army, Ft. McClellan, 1994-98, anti-terrorism instr. Bur. Alcohol, Tobacco and Firearms, 1993-97; leadership cons. Jacksonville State U., 1994-98. Mem. DAV (life), Am. Legion (vice comdr. post 1994-96, county comdr. 1995-96, dist. comdr. 1997-98), Mil. Order of Purple Heart (life). Republican. Avocation: golf. Home: 1521 Valley Brook Dr SW Jacksonville AL 36265-3310 Office: Ctr Domestic Preparedness Bldg # 65 Fort Mc Clellan AL 36205

BAKER, ROBERT WOODWARD, airline executive; b. Bronxville, N.Y., Sept. 3, 1944; s. Richard Woodward and Dorothy Marilyn (Garett) B.; m. Martha Jane Hauschild, June 11, 1966; children: Richard Woodward, Robert Woodward, William Garrett, Suzanne. B.A., Trinity Coll., 1966; M.B.A., U. Pa., 1968. Dir. ramp services Am. Airlines, Inc., N.Y.C., 1973-76; asst. v.p. mktg. adminstrn. Am. Airlines, Inc., 1976-77; v.p. so. div. Am. airlines, Inc., Dallas, 1977-79; v.p. freight mktg. Am. Airlines, Inc., Dallas-Ft. Worth Airport, 1979-80; v.p. sales and advt. Am. Airlines, Inc., 1980-82, v.p. mktg. automation systems, 1982-85, sr. v.p. info. systems, 1985, sr. v.p. ops., 1985-89; sr. v.p. AMR Corp., 1985-89; exec. v.p. ops. Am. Airlines, Inc., 1989—. Office: Am Airlines Inc PO Box 619616 Dallas TX 75261-9616

BAKER, ROLAND JERALD, trade association administrator; b. Pendleton, Oreg., Feb. 27, 1938; s. Roland E. and Theresa Helen (Forest) B.; m. Judy Lynn Murphy, Nov. 24, 1973; children: Kristen L., Kurt F., Brian H. BA, Western Wash. U., 1961; MBA, U. Mich., 1968. Cert. purchasing mgr.; cert. profl. contract mgr. Asst. dir. purchasing and stores U. Wash., Seattle, 1970-75; mgr. purchasing and material control Foss Launch & Tug Co., Seattle, 1975-79; mem. faculty Shoreline Community Coll., 1972-79, Pacific Luth. U., 1977-79, Edmonds Community Coll., 1974-79; chmn. educators group Nat. Assn. Purchasing Mgmt., Tempe, Ariz., 1976-79, exec. v.p., 1979-98; pres. Nat. Assn. Purchasing Mgmt. Svcs., Tempe, Ariz., 1989-95; mem. faculty Ariz. State U., Tempe, 1988-91; mem. world bus. adv. Coun. Am. Grad. Sch. of Internat. Mgmt., Glendale, Ariz., 1994-98; mem. faculty Shoreline C.C., Seattle, 1998—. Author: Purchasing Factomatic, 1977, Inventory System Factomatic, 1978, Policies and Procedures for Purchasing and Material Control, 1980, rev. edit., 1992. With USN, 1961-70, comdr. Res., 1969-91. Recipient Disting. Achievement award Ariz. State U. Coll. Bus., 1997; U.S. Navy postgrad. fellow, 1967. Mem. Purchasing Mgmt. Assn. Wash. (pres. 1978-79), Nat. Minority Supplier Devel. Coun. (bd. dirs.), Am. Prodn. and Inventory Control Soc., Nat. Assn. Purchasing Mgmt. (exec. v.p. 1979-97), Nat. Contract Mgmt. Assn., Internat. Fedn. Purchasing and Materials Mgmt. (exec. com. 1984-87, exec. adv. com. 1991-98), Am. Soc. Assn. Execs. Office: Shoreline CC 16101 Greenwood Ave N Seattle WA 98133-5696

BAKER, RONALD DALE, dental educator, surgeon, university administrator; b. Pitts., Oct. 20, 1932; s. Dale and Bessie (Lyons) B.; m. Dorothy Sue Casper, Sept. 9, 1967; children: Brian Dale, Bradley Drew. D.D.S. summa cum laude, U. Pitts., 1956; M.A. in Edn., George Washington U., 1974. Diplomate: Am. Bd. Oral and Maxillofacial Surgery. Oral surgeon U.S.S. Sanctuary, Vietnam, 1969-70; dir. oral and maxillofacial surgery residency St. Albans Naval Hosp., N.Y., 1970-71; chmn. oral and maxillofacial surgery dept. Nat. Naval Dental Sch., Bethesda, Md., 1971-74; chmn. oral and maxillofacial surgery dept. Nat. Naval Med. Ctr., Bethesda, Md., 1974-76; prof., chmn. dept. oral and maxillofacial surgery U. N.C. Sch. Dentistry, Chapel Hill, N.C., 1978-94, dir. Clin. Dental Implant Program, 1986-97; cons. Nat. Naval Med. Ctr., Bethesda, Md., 1977-86, Naval Regional Med. Ctr., Camp Lejeune, N.C., 1977-86, Dorothea Dix Hosp., Raleigh, N.C., 1976-97, VA Hosp., Fayetteville, N.C., 1976-97. Served to capt. USN, 1956-76. Fellow Am. Coll. Dentistry, Am. Assn. Oral and Maxillofacial Surgeons (del. 1972-74, 84-86), Internat. Assn. Oral and Maxillofacial Surgeons, Pierre Fauchard Acad.; mem. ADA, N.C. Dental Soc., Southeastern Soc. Oral and Maxillofacial Surgeons, Omicron Kappa Upsilon, Phi Eta Sigma, Alpha Omega (scholarship award), Dental Sigma Delta. Home: 622 Wells Ct Chapel Hill NC 27514-6725

BAKER, RONALD JAMES, English language educator, university administrator; b. London, Aug. 24, 1924; s. James Herbert Walter and Ethel Frances (Miller) B.; m. Helen Gillespie Elder, Sept. 3, 1949; children: Ann, Lynn, Ian, Sarah, Katherine; m. Frances Marilyn Frazer; 1 son, Ralph Edward. BA, U. B.C., Can., 1951, MA, 1953; LLD (hon.), U. N.B., Can., 1970, Mt. Allison U., 1977, U. P.E.I., 1989, Simon Fraser U., 1990. Lectr. U. B.C., 1951-53, instr., 1953-54, 56-57, asst. prof., 1957-62, sec. Senate Com. Acad. Orgn., 1961-62, assoc. prof., 1962-63; prof. English Simon Fraser U., 1964-69, dir. acad. planning, 1964-65, head dept. English, 1964-68; first pres. U. P.E.I., Charlottetown, Can., 1969-78; univ. prof. U. P.E.I., 1979-91; dir. Inst. Dept. Leadership, U. P.E.I., David MacDonald Stewart prof. Can. studies, 1988-91; disting. vis. prof. U. New Eng., Australia, 1984; mem. Acad. Bd. B.C., 1963-69, Joint Bd. Tchr. Edn. B.C., 1964-66; mem., chmn. various selection coms., Can. Coun., 1971-77, Social Sci. and Humanities Rsch. Coun. Can. Nat. Def. Dept., 1981-98, Can. Radio-TV and Telecomm. Commn., 1982-87; bd. govs. N.S. Tech. Coll., Holland Coll., 1968-78, Killam Prize Com., 1984-87, Molson Prize Com., 1987-88; chair mil. and strategic studies com. Nat. Def. Can., 1989-98. Editor: The Faculty Handbook, 1960; author (with W. G. Hardwick): North Shore Regional College Study, 1965, Regional College Study: Delta, Langley, Richmond, Surrey, 1966; contbr. articles to profl. jours. Mem. interim coun. U. No. B.C., 1989-90; presiding officer Can. Citizen Ct., 199—. Served with RAF, 1943-47. Decorated Officer Order of Can., 1978; recipient Can. Centennial medal, 1967, Jubilee medal, 1977, Disting. Mem. award Can. Soc. Study of H.E., 1988, Can. 125 medal, 1992; Humanities Rsch. Coun. Can. fellow, 1954, 55, grantee, 1968; Royal Soc. Can. fellow, 1954-56; Can. Coun. rsch. grantee, 1969. Mem. Assn. Univs. and Colls. Can. (dir. 1972-78), Assn. Atlantic Univs. (pres. 1976-78), Can. Soc. for Study Higher Edn. (v.p. 1974, pres. 1975-76, named Disting. Mem. 1988), Assn. Can. Univ. Tchrs. English (pres. 1967-68), Can. Linguistic Assn. (exec. 1966-67).

BAKER, RONALD LEE, English educator; b. Indpls., June 30, 1937; m. Catherine Anne Neal, Oct. 21, 1960; children: Susannah Jill, Jonathan Kemp. B.S., Ind. State U., Terre Haute, 1960; M.A., Ind. State U., 1961; postgrad., U. Ill., 1963-65; Ph.D., Ind U., 1969. Instr. English U. Ill., Urbana, 1963-65; teaching assoc. Ind. U., Ft. Wayne, 1965-66; prof. English Ind State U., Terre Haute, 1966—; chmn. dept. Ind State U., 1980—; vis. lectr. U. Ill., 1972-73; vis. assoc. prof. Ind. U., Bloomington, 1975; vis. prof. Ind. U., 1978, 84. Author: Folklore in the Writings of Rowland E. Robinson, 1973, Hoosier Folk Legends, 1982, Jokelore, 1986, French Folklife in Old Vincennes, 1989, The Study of Place Names, 1991, From Needmore to Prosperity: Hoosier Place Names in Folklore and History, 1995; (with others) Indiana Place Names, 1975. Fellow Am. Folklore Soc.; mem. MLA, Am. Name Soc. (v.p. 1981-82), Hoosier Folklore Soc. (pres. 1970-79, exec. sec.-treas. 1988—). Home: 3688 N Randall St Terre Haute IN 47805-9736 Office: Indiana State University Terre Haute IN 47809

BAKER, RONALD PHILLIP, service company executive; b. Kansas City, Mo., Feb. 15, 1942; s. Harry and Ruth Sarah (Bornstein) B.; m. Marilyn Gitterman, Dec. 27, 1964 (div. Dec. 1993); children: Kevin, Corey; m. Dierdre Christensen, May 8, 1994. Student, U. Okla., 1960-63; BA in Sociology and Govt., U. Mo., Kansas City, 1965, postgrad., 1965. Acct. rep. Am. House and Window Cleaning Co., Kansas City, 1965-69; dist. ops. mgr. Am. Bldg. Services, Kansas City, 1969-72; pres. BG Maintenance Mgmt., Kansas City, 1972-86; chmn. bd. dirs. BGM Industries, Kansas City, 1987—; bd. dirs. Flo Harris Supporting Found., Village Shalom. V.p. Jewish Community Ctr., Kansas City, 1985-88, pres., 1989-90; pres. Jewish Vocat. Svcs., Kansas City, 1979-81; bd. dirs. Beth Shalom Synagogue, Kansas City, 1985-89, Jewish Community Ctrs. Assn., 1989-93, exec. com., 1990-91; co-chmn. Jewish Fedn. Greater Kansas City, 1986-92, v.p., 1992-93; bd. dirs. Jewish Community Found. Greater Kansas City, 1991-94, strategic planning com., 1997. Mem. Bldg. Svc. Contractors Assn. Internat. (bd. dirs., chmn. seminars, conv. speaker, pres. club 1981-93, mem. edn. com. 1981-90, chmn. edn. com. 1989—, info. ctrl. com. 1985-93, chmn. ann. conv. 1988, exec. com. 1988—, treas. 1989, v.p. 1990-92, pres. 1994, chmn. fin. com. 1990, mem. exec. com., chair strategic planning task force 1989-90, chmn., CEO seminar com. 1997-99, strategic planning com. 1996—, govt. affairs com. 1996—), Bldg. Owners and Mgrs. Assn. Kansas City, Jewish Fedn. Kansas City (v.p. 1986-87, 91-93, co-chmn. fin. resources planning com., Young Leadership award 1981), Menninger Found. (pres. Topeka chpt. 1986—), Hallbrook Country Club, Sigma Alpha Mu, Delta Sigma Pi. Republican. Avocations: water sports, boating, snow skiing, running, reading. Office: BGM Industries 1225 E 18th St Kansas City MO 64108-1605

BAKER, ROSALYN HESTER, economic development administrator; b. El Campo, Tex., Sept. 20, 1946. BA, Southwest Tex. State U., 1968; student, U. Southwestern La., 1969. Lobbyist, asst. dir. Govt. Rels. Nat. Edn. Assn., Washington, 1969-80; owner, retail sporting goods store Maui, Hawaii, 1980-87; legis. aide to Hon. Karen Honita Hawaii Ho. of Reps., Honolulu, 1987, mem., 1989-93, house majority leader, 1993, state senator Hawaii, 1993-98, majority leader, 1995-96; dir. office econ. devel. County of Maui, Hawaii, 1999—; co-chair ways and means com., 1998; mem. econ. devel. com., water, land and Hawaiian affairs com.; co-chair rules com. Hawaii State Dem. Conv., 1990, resolutions com. 1994. Del.-at-large Dem. Nat. Conv., 1984, 92, 96; mem. exec. com. Maui County Dem. Com., 1986-88; vice chmn. Maui Svc. Area Bd. om Mental Health and Substance Abuse; unit pres. Am. Cancer Soc. Democrat. Home: 2180 Vineyard Wailuku HI 96793 Office: 200 S High St # 612 Wailuku HI 96793

BAKER, ROSS KENNETH, political science educator, columnist; b. June 26, 1938. BA, U. Pa., 1960, PhD, 1967. Rsch. assoc. The Brookings Instn., Washington, 1967-68; prof. polit. sci. Rutgers U., New Brunswick, N.J., 1968—; staff mem. U.S. Senate, 1975-76, U.S. Ho. of Reps., 1982-83. E-mail: rosbaker@rci.rutgers.edu. Address: 316 S 1st Ave Highland Park NJ 08904-2120

BAKER, ROY E., accountant, retired educator; b. Kansas City, Mo., Dec. 6, 1927; s. Roy E. and Gladys (Cramer) B.; m. Doris Younger, May 16, 1976; 1 child, Susan. BS, U. Kans., 1956, MBA, 1957; DBA, Harvard U., 1962. CPA, Kans. Instr. U. Kans., 1957-59; asst. prof. Cornell U., 1962-67; program dir. acctg. U. Mo., Kansas City, 1967-71, dir. rsch., 1971-72, prof. acctg., 1970-90, chmn. dept., 1972-77; cons. in health care; seminar leader in acctg. field. Author: Cases in Auditing, 1969, Budgeting for Hospitals, 1971; contbg. editor: Accountants Handbook; contbr. articles to profl. jours. With USN, 1944-48, 50-52. Mem. AICPA, Am. Acctg. Assn., Fin. Execs. Inst., Inst. Mgmt. Accts., Mo. Soc. CPAs, Mo. Assn. Acctg. Educators, Optimists (life), Beta Gamma Sigma, Beta Alpha Psi. Mem. Ch. Nazarene. Home: 11701 Wornall Rd Kansas City MO 64114-5626

BAKER, RUSS, executive search firm owner; b. Phoenix, Sept. 30, 1950; s. Earl Russel and Thelma (Livingston) B.; m. Vicki Rose Skulley, Dec. 3, 1977; 1 child, Katherine Maureen. BS in BA, David Lipscomb Coll., Nashville, 1973; MBA, U. W. Fla., 1975. Ops. supr. Roadway Express, Inc., Nashville, 1976-77; terminal ops. mgr. Roadway Express, Inc., 1978-79; terminal mgr. Roadway Express, Inc., Florence, Ala., 1979-80; corp. transp. analyst Gulf & Western Natural Resources Group, Nashville, 1980; asst. corp. distbn. mgr. Gulf & Western Natural Resources Group, Nashville, 1980-81; corp. distbn. mgr. Gulf & Western Natural Resources Group, 1981-82; dir. transp. svcs. Ea. div. Gulf Atlantic Distbn. Svcs., Inc., Forest Park, Ga., 1982-83; dir. of ops. Har-Bet, Inc., Morrow, Ga., 1983-84; v.p. ops. Har-Bet, Inc., 1985-86; exec. recruiter Dotson Benefield & Assocs., Inc., Atlanta, 1986-87; owner Distbn. Recruiters, Atlanta, 1987—. Chmn. cmty. adv. panel Adamson Mid. Sch., 1993—, v.p. PTA, 1992-94; hon. life mem. Ga. PTA. at. Champion 56 pound weight throw, 1993. Mem. Internat. Platform Assn., Atheltics Congress/U.S.A. Republican. Ch. of Christ. Avocations: weightlifting, stamp collecting, track and field competition. Home: 2173 Danver Ct Jonesboro GA 30236-2619 Office: Distbn Recruiters 2256 Fellowship Rd # 160 Tucker GA 30084-4618

BAKER, RUSSELL PIERCE, archivist; b. Little Rock, Sept. 16, 1943; s. Pierce Russell Baker and Magdalene V. Goodman. BA, U. Ark., 1967; MA in Pub. History, U. Ark., Little Rock, 1985. Archival mgr. Ark. History Commn. and State Archives, Little Rock, 1970—; chmn. history and archives com. Am. Bapt. Assn., Little Rock, 1974-87. Author: Marriages and Obituaries from the Tennessee Baptist 1844-1862, 1979, Arkansas Township Atlas, 1984, A Historical Directory of Arkansas Post Offices 1832-1971, 1988. Bd. mem. Royal Oaks Property Owners Assn., Mabelvale, Ark., 1997—. Mem. Acad. Cert. Archivists (cert. archivist), Soc. Am. Archivists, Ark. Geneal. Soc. (bd. mem.). Avocations: genealogy, family history. Office: Ark History Commn & State Archives One Capitol Mall Little Rock AR 72201

BAKER, RUSSELL WAYNE, columnist, author; b. Loudoun County, Va., Aug. 14, 1925; s. Benjamin Rex and Lucy Elizabeth (Robinson) B.; m. Miriam Emily Nash, Mar. 11, 1950; children: Kathleen Leland, Allen Nash, Michael Lee. B.A., Johns Hopkins U., 1947, L.H.D.; L.H.D., Hamilton Coll., Franklin Pierce Coll., Princeton U., Yale U., Long Island U., Conn. Coll.; LL.D., Union Coll.; D.Litt., Wake Forest U., U. Miami, Rutgers U., Columbia U.; H.H.D., Hood Coll. With Balt. Sun, 1947-54; mem. Washington bur. N.Y. Times, 1954-62; columnist editorial page N.Y. Times, 1962—; column Observer nationally syndicated N.Y. Times News Svc. Author: City on the Potomac, 1958, American in Washington, 1961, No Cause for Panic, 1964, All Things Considered, 1965, Our Next President, 1968, Poor Russell's Almanac, 1972, The Upside Down Man, 1977, So This Is Depravity, 1980, (with others) Home Again, Home Again, 1979, Growing Up, 1982, The Rescue of Miss Yaskell and Other Pipe Dreams, 1983, The Good Times, 1989, There's a Country in My Cellar, 1990; editor The Norton Book of Light Verse, 1986, Russell Baker's Book of American Humor, 1993. Served with USNR, 1943-45. Recipient Frank Sullivan Meml. award, 1976, George Polk award for commentary, 1979, Pulitzer prize for disting. commentary, 1979, Pulitzer prize for biography, 1983, Elmer Holmes Bobst prize for nonfiction, 1983, Howland Meml. prize Yale U., 1989, Fourth Estate award Nat. Press Club, 1989. Mem. Am. Acad. and Inst. Arts and Letters (elected 1984), Am. Acad. Arts and Scis. (fellow 1993). Office: NY Times 229 W 43rd St New York NY 10036-3959*

BAKER, RUTH HOLMES, retired secondary education educator; b. Tewksbury, Mass., July 8, 1922; d. William Angus and Anna Martha (Lynch) MacIntyre; m. William Otis Baker; children: Leigh Holmes Flannery, Bruce William, Christopher Doty, Douglas MacIntyre, Deborah Woodbury Black. BA, Tufts U., 1944; postgrad., U. Wyo., 1944-45, Union Theol. Sch., 1947-48, Columbia U., 1947-48. Cert. water safety instr. Instr. swimming ARC, Manchester-by-the-Sea, Mass., 1937-54, Wenham, Mass., 1954—; tchr., athletic dir. Shore Country Day Sch., Beverly, Mass., 1960-71, Gov. Dummer Acad., Byfield, Mass., 1972-79; tchr., coach Manchester-by-the-Sea H.S., Mass., 1980-83; bookstore and snack bar mgr. Pingree Sch., Hamilton, Mass., 1984—. Republican. Episcopalian. Home: 40 Cherry St Wenham MA 01984-1313

BAKER, RUTH SHARON, nurse; b. Providence, Nov. 20, 1950; d. Benjamin and Sadie (Horowitz) B. ADN, R.I. Jr. Coll., 1972; BA in Psychology, R.I. Coll., 1986; MS in Health Svcs. Adminstrn., Salve Regina Coll., 1988. Cert. ACLS. Nurse cons. med. malpractice rsch., long term care Frank Caprio Esq., Providence; charge nurse Providence VA Med. Ctr., Davis Park; mem. long term care coord. coun. State R.I., 1987—. Capt. ARNC, 1988—. Mem. Am. Heart Assn., Jewish War Vets. of U.S. Home: 1904 Pinewood Dr Smithfield RI 02917-3141

BAKER, SAMUEL GARRARD, advertising agency executive; b. Austin, Tex., Nov. 20, 1950; s. Norman Linwood and Clara Stuart (Bierbower) B.; divorced; children: Jamie, Jack, Angela, Christopher. AA in Journalism, De Anza Coll., Cupertino, Calif., 1979; BA in Radio/TV journalism, San Jose State U., 1983. Advt. exec. Sta. KCEN-TV, Killeen, Tex., 1986-95, prodr. TV promotion, 1988; pres., CEO NSB Advt., 1995—, Svc. Ctrl., San Angelo, Tex., 1996—. Pres. Ft. Hood area United Way, Killeen, Tex., 1991, Killeen Vol. Fire Dept., 1991; chmn. bd. dirs. Killeen Crimestoppers, 1988; arts commr. City of Killeen, 1990-98; chmn. Arts Commn., 1992-93; bd. dirs. Cen. Tex. Better Bus. Bur., 1993-98. Recipient Addy award, 1989, 92, 94, 95, 96. Mem. 1st Cav. Divn. Assn., Ctrl. Tex. Homebuilders Assn. (bd. dirs. 1992-98, treas. 1995), Ctrl. Tex. Advt. League (founder, pres. 1988-89, 94-95), Killeen C. of C. (mil. affairs com. 1988-98, govt. affairs com. 1987-98, chmn. ambs. 1990-91), Exch. Club (pres. 1989-91), Hell on Wheels Assn. Methodist. Avocation: gardening. Home and Office: NSB Advt 7 Danube Rd San Angelo TX 76903-9490

BAKER, SAUL PHILLIP, geriatrician, cardiologist, internist; b. Cleve., Dec. 7, 1924; s. Barnet and Florence (Kleinman) B. B.S. in Physics, Case Inst. Tech., 1945; postgrad., Western Res. U., 1946-47; M.Sc. in Physiology, Ohio State U., 1949, M.D., 1953, Ph.D. in Physiology, 1957; J.D., Case Western Res. U., 1981. Intern Cleve. Met. Gen. Hosp., 1953-54; sr. asst. surgeon Gerontology Br. Nat. Heart Inst, NIH, now Gerontology Research Ctr., Nat. Inst. Aging, 1954-56; asst. vis. staff physician dept. medicine Balt. City Hosps. (now Francis Scott Key Hosp.) and Johns Hopkins Hosp., 1954-56; sr. asst. resident in internal medicine U. Chgo. Hosps., 1956-57; asst. prof. internal medicine Chgo. Med. Sch., 1957-62; assoc. prof. internal medicine Cook County Hosp. Grad. Sch. Medicine, Chgo., 1958-62; assoc. attending physician Cook County Hosp., 1957-62; practice medicine specializing in geriatrics, cardiology, internal medicine Cleve., 1962-70, 72-93, cons., 1993—; head dept. geriatrics St. Vincent Charity Hosp., Cleve., 1964-67; cons. internal medicine and cardiology Bur. Disability Determination, Old-Age and Survivors Ins., Social Security Adminstrn., 1963—; cons. internal medicine City of Cleve., 1964—; medicare med. cons. Gen. Am. Life Ins. Co., St. Louis, 1970-71; cons. internal medicine and cardiology Ohio Bur. Worker's Compensation, 1964—; cons. cardiovascular disease FAA, 1973—; cons. internal medicine and cardiology State of Ohio, 1974—. Contbr. articles to profl. and sci. jours. Mem. sci. coun. Northeastern Ohio affiliate Am. Heart Assn.; former mem. adv. com. Sr. Adult div. Jewish Community Ctr. Cleve.; mem. vis. com. colls. Case Western Res. U.; former mem. com. older people Fedn. Community Planning Cleve. Fellow AAAS, Am. Coll. Cardiology, Gerontol. Soc. Am. (former Ohio regent), Am. Geriatrics Soc., Cleve. Med. Library Assn. (life); mem. Am. Physiol. Soc., AMA, Ohio Med. Assn., N.Y. Acad. Scis., Chgo. Soc. Internal Medicine, Am. Fedn. Clin. Research, Soc. Exptl. Biology and Medicine, Am. Diabetes Assn., Diabetes Assn. Greater Cleve. (profl. sect.), Am. Heart Assn. (fellow council arteriosclerosis), Nat. Assn. Disability Examiners, Nat. Rehab. Assn., Am. Pub. Health Assn., Acad. Medicine Cleve., Internat. Soc. Cardiology (council epidemiology and prevention), Am. Soc. Law and Medicine, Sigma Xi, Phi Delta Epsilon, Sigma Alpha Mu (past pres. Cleve. alumni club). Club: Cleve. Clinical (past sec.). Lodges: Masons (32 degree), Shriners. Home: PO Box 24246 Cleveland OH 44124-0246

BAKER, SHERIDAN, English educator, author; b. Santa Rosa, Calif., July 10, 1918; s. Sheridan Warner and Juliet (Shaw) B.; m. Helen Elizabeth Barker, Apr. 6, 1946 (div. Aug. 1954); m. Sally Baubie Sandwick, June 17, 1955; children: Elizabeth C. Walton, Elizabeth Abbe, William S. Student, Santa Rosa Jr. Coll., 1935-37; AB, U. Calif., Berkeley, 1939, MA, 1946, PhD, 1950. Teaching fellow U. Calif.-Berkeley, 1946-49, lectr., 1949-50, vis. prof., 1970; instr. U. Mich., 1950-57, asst. prof., 1957-61, assoc. prof., 1961-64, prof., 1964-84, emeritus prof., 1984—; Fulbright lectr. U. Nagoya, Japan, 1961-62; vis. scholar U. Newcastle, Australia, 1986; mem. usage panel Am. Heritage Dictionary, 1964—. Author: The Practical Stylist, 1962, 8th edit.,

1998, The Essayist, 1963, The Complete Stylist, 1966, 3d edit., 1984, Ernest Hemingway: An Introduction and Interpretation, 1967, (with I.A. Richards and Jacques Barzun) The Written Word, 1971, (with Northrop Frye and George Perkins) The Practical Imagination, 1980, The Harper Handbook to Literature, 1985, 2d edit., 1996; editor: Mich. Quar. Rev., 1964-71, Henry Fielding's Writings, one vol., Fielding's Works, Wesleyan, Norton Critical Edit. Tom Jones, 1973, 96; contbr.: poems to New Yorker and other mags.; also articles on 18th century and modern lit. Bd. judges, ann. Explicator mag. prize, 1965-75; Donor Fund for Ann. Clarence D. Thorpe Dissertation prize, also Louis I. Bredvold Publn. prize U. Mich., 1967. Served to lt. comdr. USNR, 1940-46. Recipient Disting. Svc. award U. Mich., 1960, award of distinction Mich. Coll. English Assn., 1987; named in Top Fifty Living Am. Poets, Epoch 15, 1966; Rockefeller Found. fellow, Bellagio, Italy, 1978. Mem. AAUP (pres. Mich. Conf. 1959-60, pres. Mich. chpt. 1972-73), Mich. Acad. Sci., Arts and Letters (pres. 1963-64, editor papers 1954-61), Johnson Soc. Central Region (pres. 1975-76), Soc. Study of Narrative Lit. (pres. 1986-87), Phi Gamma Delta. Republican. Episcopalian (vestryman 1966-69, 74-77). Clubs: Flounders (U. Mich.), Racquet, Huron Valley Tennis. Home: 2866 Provincial Dr Ann Arbor MI 48104-4114

BAKER, SHIRLEY KISTLER, university administrator; b. Lehighton, Pa., Mar. 16, 1943; d. Harvey Daniel and Miriam Grace (Osenbach) Kistler; m. Richard Christopher Baker, Oct. 22, 1966; children: Nicholas Christopher, India Jane. BA, Muhlenberg Coll., 1965; MA, MALS, U. Chgo., 1974. Undergrad. libr. Northwestern U., Evanston, Ill., 1974-76; access libr. Johns Hopkins U., Balt., 1976-82; assoc. dir. librs. MIT, Cambridge, 1982-89; dean univ. librs. Washington U., St. Louis, 1989-95, vice chancellor for info. tech., dean univ. librs., 1995—. Contbr. articles to profl. jours. Mem. ALA, Nat. Info. Standards Orgn. (bd. dirs. 1990-94), Assn. Rsch. Librs. (bd. dirs. 1996—), Coalition for Networked Info., Mo. Libr. Network Corp. (bd. dirs. 1990—). Democrat. Avocations: reading, travel. Home: 6310 Alexander Dr Saint Louis MO 63105-2223 Office: Washington U Campus Box 1061 1 Brookings Dr Saint Louis MO 63130-4899*

BAKER, STEPHEN, advertising executive, author; b. Vienna, Austria, Apr. 17, 1923; s. Oscar and Renee (Lavesky) Bacher; 1 child, Stephen Scott. BA, William Jewell Coll.; postgrad., NYU, Art Students League. V.p., creative dir. Cunningham and Walsh, 1951-62; pres. Baker and Byrne, 1962-65; pres., dir. Mogul, Baker, Byrne & Weiss, N.Y.C., 1965-69, Baker Hartel, N.Y.C., 1969-72; pres. Stephen Baker Assocs., N.Y.C., 1974—; prof. NYU, 1982-84, N.Y. Sch. Visual Arts, 1982-93. Creator "Let Your Fingers Do The Walking" for AT&T; columnist Advertising Age mag., Art Direction mag.; author 23 books including How to Live with a Neurotic Wife, How to Play Golf in the Low 120's, How to Live with a Neurotic Husband, How to Be Analyzed by a Neurotic Psychoanalyst, How to Get a Job Without Asking for It, Games Dogs Play, I Hate Meetings, 5001 Names for Cats, The Executive Mother Goose, How to Live with a Neurotic Cat, 1985, How To Live With A Neurotic Dog, How To Look Like Somebody In Business Without Being Anybody, Advertising Layout and Art Direction, Visual Persuasion: Effect Of Pictures On The Subconscious, An Art Director's Viewpoint, Systematic Approach To Advertising Creativity, 1979, Get-Around Guide To New York City, 1982, Advertiser's Manual, 1988, How to Live with a Neurotic Cat Owner, 1992, Me & My Cat, 1993. Nominated Art Dir. of Yr. Nat. Soc. Art Dirs., 1961, 63. Home: 5 Tudor City Penthouse 5 New York NY 10017-6853

BAKER, STEPHEN DENIO, physics educator; b. Durham, N.C., Nov. 30, 1936; s. Roger Denio and Eleanor Elizabeth (Ussher) B.; m. Paula Eisenstein, June 24, 1962; children: Hannah Hitzhusen, Sarah Topper. BS, Duke U., 1957; MS, Yale U., 1959, PhD, 1963. Lectr. physics Rice U., Houston, 1963-66, asst. prof., 1966-69, assoc. prof., 1969-73, prof., 1973—. Office: Rice Univ Dept Physics-MS 61 6100 Main St Houston TX 77005-1892

BAKER, STEPHEN H., career officer; b. W. Stewartstown, N.H.. Grad., Hofstra U. Commd. 2d lt. USN, 1969, advanced through grades to rear admiral; various assignments include exec. officer to comdr. Attack Squadron 65/USN, Attack Squadron 42, 1985-88, 88-89; asst. chief of staff for opers./ USS Theodore Roosevelt Comdr. Carrier Group Eight, 1989-94; chief of staff for comdr. Naval Forces Cen. Command/U.S. Fifth Fleet, Bahrain, 1994-95; comdr. oper. test evaluation force Naval Forces Cen. Command/U.S. Fifth Fleet, Norfolk, Va., 1995—. Decorated Legion of Merit with gold star, Bronze Star, Meritorious Svc. medal with two gold stars, Navy Commendation medal, Navy Achievement medal, others. Office: 7970 Diven St Norfolk VA 23505-1461*

BAKER, STEPHEN MONROE, school system administrator. BA, Roanoke Coll.; MS, Radford U.; EdD, U. Va. Supt. Hanover County Pub. Schs., Ashland, Va., 1980-95; exec. dir. elem. and mid. sch. commn. So. Assn. Colls. & Schs., Decatur, Ga., 1995—. Named state finalist Nat. Supt. of Yr. award. Office: So Assn Colls & Schs 1866 Southern Ln Decatur GA 30033-4033

BAKER, STEVE J., airport executive. Mgr., pres., CEO London (Ont., Can.) Airport. Office: London Internat Airport, 1750 Crumlin Rd, London, ON Canada N5V 3B6*

BAKER, STUART DAVID, lawyer; b. N.Y.C., July 2, 1935; s. Stuart and Edith (Kennelly) B.; m. Alixandra Fitzwilliam-Tate Collins, June 16, 1980; children from previous marriage—Stuart Richard, David Michael, Elisabeth Kendall. BA, Hamilton Coll., 1957; LLB, Columbia U. Bar: N.Y. 1960. Assoc. Chadbourne, Parke, Whiteside & Wolff, N.Y.C., 1960-69, ptnr., 1969-85; ptnr. Chadbourne & Parke, N.Y.C., 1985—, mem. mgmt. com., 1985-95, 96—; corp. v.p. Purdue Frederick Co.; dir. Napp Pharm. Group Ltd. (UK), Mundipharma Labs. GmbH, Mundipharma AG (Switzerland); mem. supervisory bd. Mundipharma GmbH, Germany, 1994—. Vestryman St. Mary's Ch., Scarborough-on-Hudson, N.Y., 1967-76, sr. warden, 1974-76; chmn. zoning bd. appeals Town of Ossining, N.Y., 1968-78; mem. Coun. of Diocese of N.Y., 1974-79; dir. Legal Aid Soc., 1993—. Mem. N.Y. State Bar Assn., Conn. Bar Assn., Westchester County Bar Assn., Assn. Bar City of N.Y., Suffolk County Bar Assn., Internat. Bar Assn. (rapporteur), Inter-Am. Bar Assn., Union Internat. des Avocats, Swiss Am. C. of C., SAR, Sleepy Hollow Country Club, River Club (N.Y.C.), Netherlands Club (N.Y.C.), Les Ambassadeurs Club (London), Water Mill Beach (N.Y.) Club (pres. 1991-96). Episcopalian. Avocations: tennis; golf; windsurfing. Home: 16 Sutton Pl New York NY 10022-3057 Office: Chadbourne & Parke 30 Rockefeller Plz New York NY 10112-0002

BAKER, SUSAN LOWELL, psychologist; b. New Delhi, India, Nov. 14, 1956; d. Timothy Danforth and Susan (Pardee) B. BA, Cornell U., 1979; MEd, Boston U., 1982; PsyD, Mass. Sch. Profl. Psych., Boston, 1986. Lic. clin. psychologist; cert. health svc. provider, Mass. Rschr. L.E.A.A., Albany, N.Y., 1980; counselor, house mgr. Alternative Home, Inc., Newton, Mass., 1979-81; intern Tri-City Mental Health Ctr., Malden, Mass., 1981-82, Greater Lawrence Mental Health Ctr., Lawrence, Mass., 1982-84, North Shore Children's Hosp., Salem, Mass., 1984-85; outpatient psychologist North Shore Children's Hosp., Salem, 1985-86; intern Hampstead (N.H.) Hosp. - Sleep Disorders, 1985-86; dir. of tng./outpatient psychologist Melrose Wakefield Hosp., Mass., 1986-95; clin. psychologist Melrose, Mass., 1995—; supervision/cons., Melrose, 1995—. Author: (play) Portraits of Our Grandmothers, 1979. Vol. Shelter, Inc., Cambridge, 1994-95. Avocations: Kung Fu, gardening. Home: 9 Fairfield St Apt 3R Cambridge MA 02140-1919

BAKER, SUSAN MARIE VICTORIA, REV., writer, artist; b. Phila., Pa., Aug. 30, 1961; d. John Joseph and Dorothy Phyllis (Dispensiere) Erdlen. BA in Liberal Arts/Comm., Rowan U., 1983; postgrad., U. of Arts, Phila. Ordained priestess. Asst. editor Jersey Woman mag., Marlton, 1983-85; advt. and edit. asst. Regal Comm., Moorestown, N.J., 1987-88, Adams and Braverman Advt. Inc., Phila., 1989-90; adminstrv. asst. Rosanio, Bailets & Talamo Inc., Cherry Hill, N.J., 1990-92; pub. rels. and publs. cons. Roger Williams U., Providence; art critic, columnist Star of Isis; jeweler-crafter and healing artist. Author 3 books; songwriter (performed and published under name Chelsea Mann); art editor Avant mag., 1981; contbr. poetry to various publs.; composer numerous songs. Active animal rights and environ. activities; mem. Newport Cultural Arts Alliance. Recipient awards for poetry, creative writing.

BAKER, SUSAN P., public health educator; b. Atlanta, May 31, 1930; d. Charles Laban and Susan (Lowell) Pardee; m. Timothy Danforth Baker, June 23, 1951; children—Timothy D., David C., Susan L. A.B., Cornell U., Ithaca, N.Y., 1951; M.P.H., Johns Hopkins U., Balt., 1968; ScD (hon.), U. N.C., 1998. Rsch. assoc. Office of Chief Med. Examiner, Balt., 1968-81; rsch. assoc. Sch. Hygiene and Pub. Health, Johns Hopkins U., Balt., 1968-71, asst. prof., 1971-74, assoc. prof., 1974-83, prof. health policy and mgmt., 1983—, assoc. chmn. dept. health policy and mgmt., 1997—, joint appointment in environ. health scis., 1975—, joint appointment in pediatrics, 1983—, dir. Injury Prevention Ctr., 1987-88, co-dir., 1988—, acting head div. pub. health, 1988-90, joint appointment pediat. emergency medicine Sch. Medicine, 1991—; vis. prof. U. Minn. Sch. Pub. Health, 1975-87; chmn. nat. rev. panel for nat. accident sampling sys. Dept. Transp., Washington, 1976-81; vice chmn. com. on trauma rsch. Nat. Rsch. Coun., Washington, 1984-85; mem. adv. com. on injury control CDC, 1989—; mem. Armed Forces Epidemiol. Bd.; commr. West Latir Ditch Assn., N.Mex., 1990—; vis. lectr. in injury prevention Harvard Sch. Pub. Health, 1984-87; John T. Law meml. lectr. U. Calgary, Alta., 1984; expert panel Age 60 rule FAA, 1991-93; cons. and lectr. in field. Author: (monograph) Fatally Injured Drivers, 1970 (Prince Bernhard medal 1974), The Injury Fact Book, 1984, 2d edit., 1992, Saving Children: A Guide to Injury Prevention, 1991, Injury Prevention: An International Perspective, 1998; contbr. articles to books and articles to profl. jours. Recipient Charles A. Dana award for pioneering achievements in health, 1989, Johns Hopkins U. Disting. Alumnus award, 1996. Fellow Am. Assn. Automotive Medicine (bd. dirs. 1971-76, pres. 1974-75, award of merit 1985), Wing (assoc., hon.); mem. APHA (governing coun. 1975-77, jour. bd. 1983-87), Am. Trauma Soc. (bd. dirs., Disting. Achievement award 1981, Stone lectr. 1985), Aerospace Med. Assn. (editl. bd. 1994-97), Am.. Assn. for Surgery of Trauma (hon., Fitts oration award 1996), Phi Beta Kappa, Delta Omega. Office: Johns Hopkins U Sch Hygiene & Pub Health 624 N Broadway Baltimore MD 21205-1900

BAKER, SUZON LYNNE, secondary education mathematics educator; b. Sacramento, Calif., Mar. 29, 1943; d. Thomas Kestell and Dorothy (Espinosa) Lockart; m. Carl Leroy Baker, June 13, 1966; children: Michele, Eric. BA, Sacramento State U., 1965; MS, St. Francis Coll., Ft. Wayne, Ind., 1974. Cert. tchr., Ind. Math. tchr. Richland-Bean Blossom Sch., Ellettsville, Ind., 1966-68, Ft. Wayne Community Schs., 1968-70, Garrett-Keyser-Butler (Ind.) Schs., 1977—. Mem. Nat. Coun. Tchrs. Math., Ind. Tchrs. Math. Methodist. Avocations: sewing, yard work. Home: 4 Pinetree Rd Garrett IN 46738-9772 Office: Garrett High Sch 801 E Houston St Garrett IN 46738-1662

BAKER, THURBERT E., state attorney general; b. Rocky Mount, N.C., Dec. 16, 1952; m. Catherine Baker; children: Jocelyn, Chelsea. BA in Polit. Sci., U. N.C.; JD, Emory U., 1979. Mem. Ga. Ho. of Reps., 1988-90, asst. adminstrn. floor leader, 1990-93, adminstrn. floor leader, 1993-97; atty. gen. State of Ga., 1997—. Trustee DeKalb County (Ga.) Libr. Bd.; vice chmn. DeKalb County Bd. of Appeals; trustee Statewide Ga. Diabetes Bd.; trustee Ebenezer Bapt. Ch., Atlanta, DeKalb Coll. Found. Mem. DeKalb County C. of C. (bd. dirs.), Nat. Med. Soc.-Emory U. Office: Atty Gen Law Dept 40 Capitol Sq SW Atlanta GA 30334-9003

BAKER, TIMOTHY ALAN, healthcare administrator, educator, consultant; b. Myrtle Point, Oreg., July 30, 1954; s. Farris D. and Billie G. (Bradford) B.; 1 child, Amanda Susann. BS in Mgmt. with honors, Linfield Coll., McMinnville, Oreg., 1988; MPA in Health Adminstrn. with distinction, Portland State U., 1989, PhD in Pub. Adminstrn. and Policy, 1992. Registered emergency med. technician. Gen. mgr. Pennington's, Inc., Coos Bay, Oreg., 1974-83; dep. dir. Internat. Airport Projects Med. Svcs., Riyadh, Saudi Arabia, 1983-87; adminstrv. intern Kaiser Sunnyside Hosp., Portland, Oreg., 1988-89; grant mgr. Oreg. Health Sci. U., Portland, 1989-90; dir. health sci. program Linfield Coll., Portland, Oreg., 1992—, asst. prof. health scis.; rsch. assoc. Portland State U., 1990—; instr. S.W. Oreg. C.C., Coos Bay, 1980-83; pres. Intermed. Inc., Portland, 1987—; sr. rschr. small area analysis Oreg. Health Sci. U., 1990, The Oreg. Health Plan Project, 1990-91; developer, planner, prin. author trauma sys. devel. S.W. EMS and Trauma Sys., 1991-93, regional adminstr., Vancouver, 1990—; cons. ednl. def. Min. Civil Def., Riyadh, Saudi Arabia, 1992. Author: TQ:EMS: Total Quality Emergency Medical Services, 1996, TQ-EMS: The Tools of Total Quality, 1996; pub. Jour. Family Practice, Internat. Jour. Pub. Adminstrn., Internat. Jour. Emergency Med. Svcs., 1997. Planner mass disaster plan King Khaled Internat. Airport, 1983; EMS planner Emergency Med. Plan, Province of Cholburi, Thailand, 1985; bd. dirs. Coos County Kidney Assn., 1982, Coos Bay Kiwanis Club, 1979; regional adv. com. EMS and Trauma, State Wash. Dept. Health, 1990—. Recipient Pub. Svc. award Am. Radio and Relay League, 1969, Med. Excellence award KKIA Hosp., 1985; named Fireman of Yr. Eastside Fire Dept., 1982, Adminstr. of Yr., Wash. Dept. Health, 1993. Mem. Am. Mgmt. Assn., Am. Soc. Pub. Adminstrn. (doctoral rep. to faculty senate Portland State U. 1990), Am. Pub. Health Assn., Am. Coll. Healthcare Execs. Avocations: flying, scuba diving, photography, racquetball, amateur radio. Home: 608 N Hayden Bay Dr Portland OR 97217-7964 Office: Linfield Coll Portland Campus 2255 NW Northrup St Portland OR 97210-2952

BAKER, TIMOTHY DANFORTH, physician, educator; b. Balt., July 4, 1925; s. Frank and Alice Elizabeth (Chandler) B.; m. Susan Lowell Pardee, June 23, 1951; children: Timothy, David, Susan. BA, Johns Hopkins U., 1948, MPH, 1954; MD, U. Md., 1952. Intern U. Md. Hosp., Balt., 1952-53; resident pub. health N.Y. State Dept. Pub. Health, N.Y.C., 1953-56; health officer Syracuse, N.Y., 1958-59; asst. and acting chief health USAID, India, 1956-58; assoc. prof. Johns Hopkins U. Sch. Pub. Health, Balt., 1959-67, asst. dean, 1959-77, prof. internat. health, health svcs. adminstrn., and environ. health, 1967—, pres. faculty gen. assembly, 1987—; dir. Hubert H. Humphrey scholars program Johns Hopkins U. Sch. Pub. Health, 1987—; v.p., dir. Univ. Assocs., 1973-77; vis. prof. epidemiology U. Minn., 1976; dir. Intermed., 1982—; cons. health planning, med. edn., Brazil, Burma, India, Indonesia, Taiwan, Saudi Arabia, Kuwait, Ukraine, Viet Nam, Yunnan, China, Md., Calif., D.C.; external examiner U. Singapore. Author: Health Manpower in a Developing Economy, Assessment of Health Status and Needs, International Health Perspectives; contbr. articles to profl. publs. First vice chmn. Balt. com. Republican party; del., nominating com. Republican party; bd. dirs., treas. Pan Am. Health Edn. Found. Served with USAF, 1943-45; USPHS, 1956-58. Recipient Disting. Grad. award Balt. Polytechnic Inst. Fellow AAAS (govs. commn. on minority health, task force on violence); mem. Am. Pub. Health Assn. (chmn. epidemiology sect., internat. health sect., Lifetime Achievement award 1994), Md. Med. Soc. (chmn. health manpower com., ho. of dels.), Md. Pub. Health Assn. (pres.), Balt. Med. Soc. (chmn. med. care com.), Omicron Delta Kappa, Delta Omega. Republican. Home: 4705 Keswick Rd Baltimore MD 21210-2322 Office: Johns Hopkins U Sch Hygiene 615 N Wolfe St Baltimore MD 21205-2103

BAKER, VINCENT LAMONT, basketball player; b. Lake Wales, Fla., Nov. 23, 1971. Grad., Hartford U., 1993. Player Milw. Bucks, 1993-97, Seattle Supersonics, 1997—. Named to NBA All-Rookie First Team, 1994, All-NBA Third Team, 1996-97, All-NBA Second Team, 1997-98, NBA All Star, 1995-97. Avocation: singing. Office: c/o Seattle Supersonics 190 Queen Anne Ave N Ste 200 Seattle WA 98109-9711*

BAKER, WALTER ARNOLD, lawyer; b. Columbia, Ky., Feb. 20, 1937; s. Herschel T. and Mattie B. (Barger) B.; m. Jane Stark Helm, Apr. 24, 1965; children: Thomas Herschel, Ann Tate. AB magna cum laude, Harvard U., 1958, LLB, 1961. Assoc. Brown, Ardery, Todd & Dudley, Louisville, 1961-63; ptnr. Wilson, Baker, Herbert and Garmon, Glasgow, Ky., 1963-67; pvt. practice Glasgow, 1967-81, 83—; asst. gen. counsel Office Sec. Def., Washington, 1981-83; justice Supreme Ct. of Ky., Frankfort, 1996. Rep. Ky. Ho. of Reps., 1968-71, senator State of Ky., 1972-81, 89-96; active Ky. Coun. on Postsecondary Edn., 1997—. Lt. col. USAFR. Mem. Ky. Bar Assn., Barren County Bar Assn., Glasgow Rotary, Glasgow Golf and Country Club. Republican. Presbyterian. Address: 917 S Green St Glasgow KY 42141-2086 Office: 213 S Green St Glasgow KY 42141-2643

BAKER, WALTER LOUIS, retired engineering company executive; b. Earlton, N.Y., Aug. 7, 1924; s. Alberti and Louise (Schmidt) B.; m. Janet Katherine Sprague, Sept. 7, 1944 (dec.); children: Walter Kent (dec.), Lawrence Albert, Linda Louise, Louis Milton; m. Marion M. King, July 1, 1976 (dec.); stepchildren: Vinton P. King, John S. King; m. Shirley E. Lindsay, Mar. 30, 1985; stepchildren: Thomas M. Lindsay, Christopher J. Lindsay, Margaret S. Lindsay, Janet Lindsay Keeble, William D. Lindsay. B.E.E. (N.Y. State scholar, Coll. scholar), Clarkson Coll., 1944; M.S., Pa. State U., 1954. Registered profl. engr., Pa. Tech. supr. Tenn. Eastman Corp., 1944-45; sr. engr. Philco Corp., 1945-49; research asso. Pa. State U., State Coll., from 1949, prof., sr. mem. grad. faculty, 1965-82, prof. emeritus engrng. dept.; pres. Baker Engrng. Co., Portsmouth, R.I., 1981-92; cons. Spartan Electric Corp., 1960-61, U.S. Marine Corps, 1965, John I. Thompson & Co., 1952-68, HRB-Singer Co., 1958-67, Vitro Corp., 1981, Woods Hole Oceanography Inst., 1981-83, Dynamic Systems, Inc., 1980-84, Systems Resource Mgmt., 1984-86, BB&N, Inc., 1986-93. Co-author: Acoustic Performance Handbook, 1974; contbr. articles to profl. jours. Recipient U.S. Navy Meritorious Public Service citation. Mem. IEEE (sr., chmn., sec.-treas. Central Pa. sect.), Acoustical Soc. Am., N.Y. Acad. Scis., Sigma Xi. Republican. Methodist. Lodges: Elks, Lions. Address: Baker Engrng Co 6404 21st Ave W Apt H202 Bradenton FL 34209-7813

BAKER, WARREN J(OSEPH), university president; b. Fitchburg, Mass., Sept. 5, 1938; s. Preston A. and Grace F. (Jarvis) B.; m. Carol Ann Fitzsimons, Apr. 28, 1962; children: Carrie Ann, Kristin Robin, Christopher, Brian. B.S., U. Notre Dame, 1960, M.S., 1962; Ph.D., U. N.Mex., 1966. Research assoc., lectr. E. H. Wang Civil Engring. Research Facility, U. N.Mex., 1962-66; assoc. prof. civil engring. U. Detroit, 1966-71, prof., 1972-79, Chrysler prof., dean engring., 1973-78, acad. v.p., 1976-79; NSF faculty fellow M.I.T., 1971-72; pres. Calif. Poly. State U., San Luis Obispo, 1979—; mem. Bd. Internat. Food and Agrl. Devel., USAID, 1983-85; mem. Nat. Sci. Bd., 1985-94, Calif. Bus. Higher Edn. Forum, 1993-98; founding mem. Calif. Coun. on Sci. and Tech., 1989—; trustee Amigos of E.A.R.T.H. Coll., 1991-96; bd. dirs. John Wiley & Sons, Inc., 1993—; bd. regents The Am. Archtl. Found., 1995-97; co-chair Joint Policy Coun. on Agr. and Higher Edn., 1995—. Contbr. articles to profl. jours. Mem. Detroit Mayor's Mgmt. Adv. Com., 1975-76; mem. engrng. adv. bd. U. Calif., Berkeley, 1984-96; bd. dirs. Calif. Coun. for Environ. and Econ. Balance, 1980-85; trustee Nat. Coop. Edn. Assn.; chmn. bd. dirs. Civil Engring. Rsch. Found., 1989-91, bd. dirs., 1991-94. Fellow Engring. Soc. Detroit; mem. ASCE (chmn. geotech. div. com. on reliability 1976-78, civil engring. edn. and rsch. policy com. 1985-89), NSPE (pres. Detroit chpt. 1976-77), Am. Soc. Engring. Edn., Am. Assn. State Colls. and Univs. (bd. dirs. 1982-84). Office: Calif Poly State U Office of Pres San Luis Obispo CA 93407

BAKER, WILLIAM, British literature educator; b. Shipston-on-Stour, Warwicks, Eng., July 6, 1944; came to U.S., 1989; s. Stanley and Mabel (Woolf) Baker; m. Rivka Frank, Oct. 16, 1969; children: Sharon, Karen. BA in English Studies with honors, U. Sussex, Brighton, Eng., 1966; MPhil in English, U. London, 1970, PhD in English, 1974. Cert. MLS/ Loughborough U., Eng. Lectr. City Literary Inst., London, 1967-71, Ben Gurion U., Beer-Sheva, Israel, 1971-77, U. Kent, Canterbury, Kent, U.K., 1977-78; sr. lectr. West Midlands Coll., Walsall, U.K., 1978-85; housemaster Clifton Coll., Bristol, U.K., 1986-89; prof. No. Ill. U., DeKalb, 1989—; vis. prof. Pitzer Coll., Claremont Coll., Calif., 1981-82; mem. exec. com. Bibliography and Textual Studies, MLA, N.Y., 1996-99. Author: (book) Literary Theories, 1996; author/editor: (book) Scott: History of France, 1996; editor: (books) G.H. Lewes Letters, 1995, 99, British Book Collectors, 3 vols., 1998-99, Letters of Wilkie Collins, 2 vols., 1999, others; editor: George Eliot - G.H. Lewes Studies, 1981—; adv. editor: New Dictionary National Biography, U.K. and Oxford, 1995—. Rsch. fellow Am. Philos. Soc., 1997, Bibliograph. Soc. Am., 1995-96, Brit. Acad., 1979, 82. Office: No Ill Univ Dekalb IL 60115

BAKER, WILLIAM DUNLAP, lawyer; b. St. Louis, June 17, 1932; s. Harold Griffith and Bernice (Kraft) B.; m. Kay Stokes, May 23, 1955; children: Mark William, Kathryn X., Beth Kristie, Frederick Martin. AB, Colgate U., 1954; JD, U. Calif., Berkeley, 1960. Bar: Calif. 1961, Ariz. 1961, U.S. Supreme Ct. 1969. Practice in Coolidge, 1961, Florence, 1961-63, Phoenix, 1963—; law clk. Stokes & Moring, 1960; spl. investigator Office Pinal County Atty., 1960-61, dep. county atty., 1961-63; partner McBryde, Vincent, Brumage & Baker, 1961-63; assoc. atty. Rawlins, Ellis, Burrus & Kiewit, 1963-65, partner, 1965-81; pres., atty. Ellis & Baker, P.C., 1981-84, Ellis, Baker, Lynch, Clark & Porter P.C., 1984-86, Ellis, Baker, Clark & Porter, P.C., 1986-89, Ellis, Baker & Porter, P.C., 1989-92, Ellis Baker & Porter Ltd., Phoenix, 1992-95, Ellis, Baker & Porter, P.C., Phoenix, 1995-99; prin. William D. Baker, P.C., 1999—; referee Juvenile Ct. Maricopa County Superior Ct., 1966-85. Contbr. articles to profl. jours. Mem. Gov.'s Adv. Coun., Phoenix, 1969-71, Ariz. Environ. Planning Commn., 1974-75; bd. dirs. Agri-Bus. Coun., 1978—, sec., 1978-82; pub. mem. State Bd. Accountancy, 1995—, sec., 1998-99, treas., 1999—; spl. legal counsel Ariz. Com. Rep. Party, 1965-69, mem. exec. com., 1972-78; vice-chmn. Maricopa County Rep. Com., 1968-69, chmn., 1969-71; bd. dirs. San Pablo Home for Youth, 1964-72, pres., 1971; bd. dirs. Maricopa County chpt. Nat. Found. March of Dimes, 1966-71, campaign chmn., 1970; trustee St. Luke's Hosp., 1976-85, sec., 1978-82, chmn., 1982-85; bd. dirs. Luke's Men, 1971-80, pres., 1976-77; bd. dirs. Combined Health Resources, 1982-85, St. Luke's Health Sys., 1985-95, chmn., 1985-89; bd. dirs. St. Luke's Charitable Health Trust, 1995—; bd. dirs., v.p. Ariz. Anglican Cursillo Movement, 1982-86; Western dist. layman rep. Nat. Episcopal Cursillo Com., 1996-98; regional v.p. Colgate Alumni Corp., 1977-82; vice chancellor Episcopal Diocese Ariz., 1970-96; sr. warden Christ Ch. of Ascension, 1983-86; ch. atty. Episc. Diocese Ariz., 1996—. Served to 1st lt. USAF, 1954-57. Mem. ABA, Nat. Water Resources Assn. (co-chmn. task force on reclamation law 1990-97, resolutions com. 1990-93, chmn. state caucus 1993—), Ariz. Bar Assn., Calif. Bar Assn., State C. of C. (bd. dirs. 1988-92), Maricopa County Bar Assn., Flagstaff Golf Assn. (bd. dirs. 1992-93, 94-96, pres. 1994-95), Phoenix Country Club, Sigma Chi, Phi Delta Phi. Episcopalian. Home: 5309 N 34th St Phoenix AZ 85018-1416 Office: 2111 E Highland Ave Ste 355 Phoenix AZ 85016-4734

BAKER, WILLIAM FRANKLIN, public broadcasting company executive; b. Cleve., Sept. 20, 1942; s. William Franklin and Rita Marie (Huebner) B.; m. Jeannemarie Gelin, June 22, 1968; children: Christiane, Angela. BA in Comms. and Organizational Behavior, Case Western Res. U., 1965, MA in Comms. and Organizational Behavior, 1968, PhD, 1972; DSC (hon.), St. John's U., N.Y., 1981; LLD (hon.), St. Elizabeth Coll., 1995. Exec. producer Sta. WEWS-TV, Cleve., 1971-75; asst gen. mgr. Sta. WEWS-TV, 1975-77; v.p., gen. mgr. Sta. WJZ-TV, Balt., 1977-78; pres. Group W. Productions, Hollywood, Calif., 1978-79, Group W-TV, N.Y.C., 1979-81; chmn. Group W-TV Satellite Communications, N.Y.C., 1981-87; pres., chief exec. officer Sta. WNET/Channel 13, N.Y.C., 1987—; bd. dirs. Playhouse Pictures, Internat., Pub. Broadcast Svc., Leitch Video Ltd., The Consumers Union; owner Rudder Mag., Schneier Vineyards. Author: Down the Tube: An Insider's View of American Television, 1998. Bd. trustee St. Elizabeth Coll., Intrepid Air-Space Mus.; vice chmn. N.Y. Arts; bd. dirs., exec. com. PBS, Ea. Ednl. Network; bd. dirs. Lowell Obs., Liberty Sci. Ctr., Lamont-Doherty Earth Obs., Ctr. for Econ. Devel.; vice chmn. N.Y. Arts '97. Recipient 5 Emmy awards, 2 Twyla M. Conway awards, Trustees' award Nat. Acad. TV Arts and Scis., Dupont Columbia Journalism award, Triscort award, 1991, Modern Lang. award Iona Coll., 1991, Silver Circle award N.Y. TV Acad., Humanitarian award So. Manhattan Arts Coun. Fellow Explorers Club (North Pole expdn. 1983, South Pole expdn. 1974, 84, 88, 96); mem. NATAS (exec. com., bd. internat. coun., pres. N.Y. chpt., Gabriel award for outstanding broadcaster 1998), Nat. Assn. TV Program Execs., Nat. Assn. Broadcasters, Advt. Rsch. Found. (TV audience measurement coun.), Internat. Radio-TV Soc., Bd. Ctr. for Comm., Lighthouse Preservation Soc. (bd. dirs.), N.Y. Yacht Club. Roman Catholic. Home: 2 Highgate Rd Riverside CT 06878-2611 Office: 450 W 33rd St New York NY 10001

BAKER, WILLIAM MORRIS, cultural organization administrator; m. Robin Baker. BA in History, U. Va., 1961. With FBI, 1965-87-89-91, asst. dir. criminal investigative divsn., ret., 1991; dir. pub. affairs CIA, 1987-89; sr. v.p., dir. worldwide anti-piracy Motion Picture Assn., Encino, Calif., 1991-94, pres., COO, 1994—; spkr. in field; guest lectr. Ctr. for Internat. Affairs Harvard U., Fed. Exec. Inst. U. Va. 1st lt. USAF, 1962-65. Named Disting. Exec. by U.S. Pres. George Bush, 1990; recipient Disting. Intelligence medal CIA, 1989, Edmund J. Randolph award U.S. Atty. Gen.'s 40th Ann. Awards Ceremony, 1992, U.S. Marshals Star for lifetime achievement in law enforcement, 1992. Avocations: reading, running, sailing, skiing, cooking. Office: Motion Picture Assn 15503 Ventura Blvd Encino CA 91436-3103

BAKER, WILLIAM P. (BILL BAKER), former congressman; b. Oakland, Calif., June 14, 1940; m. Joanne Atack; children: Todd, Mary, Billy, Robby. Grad. in Bus. and Indsl. Mgmt., San Jose State Coll. Budget analyst State Dept. Fin., Calif.; assemblyman 15th dist. State of Calif., 1980-92; mem. of Congress from 10th Calif. dist., 1993-96; vice chmn. budget writing Ways and Means Com., 1984-91. Exec. v.p. Contra Costa Taxpayers Assn.; active Contra Costa County Farm Bur. With USCG Res., 1958-65. Republican. Address: 3189 Danville Blvd Ste 200 Alamo CA 94507*

BAKER, WILLIAM THOMPSON, JR., lawyer; b. N.Y.C., Jan. 19, 1944; s. William Thompson and Elizabeth (Baird) B.; children: Alice Whetherly, Richard Cass, Heather Thompson. BA cum laude, Yale U., 1965; JD, U. Va., 1968. Bar: N.Y. 1968, U.S. Dist. Ct. (so. and ea. dists.) N.Y. 1969, U.S. Supreme Ct. 1990, U.S. Ct. Appeals (D.C. cir.), 1992. Assoc. Thelen, Reid & Priest (formerly known as Reid & Priest), N.Y.C., 1968-74, ptnr, 1975—, mng. ptnr., 1986-87, mem. exec. com., 1980-82, 86-91, chmn. exec. com., 1990-91; chmn. Utility/Energy Svcs. Group, 1991—; chmn. legal com. Edison Electric Inst., 1997—. Trustee Episcopal Sch. in City of N.Y., 1969-71. Mem. ABA (chmn. subcommittee pub. utility law 1990—), New York County Lawyers Assn., Assn. Bar City N.Y., Union Club N.Y.C., Yale Club N.Y.C., N.Y. Anglers Club. Republican. Episcopalian. Avocations: fishing, fly tying, rod building, wood working.

BAKER, ZACHARY MOSHE, librarian; b. Mpls., June 8, 1950; s. Michael Harry and Margaret Esther (Zanger) B. BA, U. Chgo., 1972; MA, Brandeis U., 1974; MA in LS, UU. Minn., 1975. Head tech. svcs. Jewish Pub. Libr., Montreal, Que., Can., 1981-87; asst. libr. Yivo Inst. for Jewish Rsch., N.Y.C., 1976-80, assoc. libr., 1980-81, head libr., 1987-99; Reinhard family curator Judaica & Hebraics collections Stanford U. Librs., 1999—; hist. cons. Que. Inst. Rsch. on Culture, Montreal, 1983; libr. cons. U.S. Holocaust Meml. Coun., Washington, 1984-85, Fla. Atlantic U., Boca Raton, 1994, Ariz. State U., Tempe, 1998. Contbg. author: From a Ruined Garden, 1983, 98; author, contbg. editor Toledot, 1978-82, Judaica Librarianship, 1983—; editor: Yiddish Catalog and Authority File of the Yivo Library, 1990. Crown fellow Brandeis U., 1973-74; travel and rsch. grantee Andrew W. Mellon Found., 1997, Lucius N. Littauer Found., 1990, 94, 96, 98/. Mem. ALA, Assn. Jewish Librs. (pres. 1994-96), Assn. for Jewish Studies, Coun. Archives and Rsch. Libr. in Jewish Studies (pres. 1998—), Phi Beta Kappa, Beta Phi Mu. Avocations: map and atlas collecting, current events, travel.

BAKER-BRANTON, CAMILLE, counselor, educator; b. Greenwood, Miss., Aug. 30, 1950; d. Don Otho and Sarah (Goodpasture) Baker; children: Irene, Sarah. BS, MS, Miss. State U., 1972, PhD, 1989; MEd, MS, Delta State U., Cleveland, Miss., 1987. Lic. counselor, Miss.; cer. counselor; Diplomate Am. Bd. Med. Psychotherapists. Assoc. prof. behavioral scis. Delta State U., Cleveland, Miss., 1989—; mem. Job Tng. Placement Act Rev. Bd. Author: Coercive Sexual Behavior among College Students: A Causal Model, Coercive Sexual Behavior Rating Scale. Mem. AACD, DAR, Nat. Bd. Cert. Counselors, Coun. Exceptional Children, Assn. Children Learning Disabilities, Am. Mental Health Counselors Assn., Miss. Counseling Assn., Exch. Club, Phi Delta Kappa, Kappa Delta Pi, Delta Gamma. Home: 305 E Gresham St Indianola MS 38751-2426 Office: Delta State U PO Box 3142 Cleveland MS 38733

BAKER-GARDNER, JEWELLE, business executive, interior designer; b. Ayden, N.C., May 23, 1925; d. Roland Ray and Helen Wingate (Jackson) Cannon; m. Paul Thomas Baker, July 25, 1956 (dec. 1963); children: Paula Jewelle Baker Bryan, Paul Thomas; 1 stepchild, Blanche Baker Miller; m. Fred Calvin Gardner, Apr. 19, 1969 (dec. May 1983); 1 stepchild, Angela Gardner Jones Hollowell. Student Woods Bus. Sch., New Bern, N.C., 1942-45; BA, Am. Sch. Design, N.Y.C., 1948; BFA, U. N.C., Greensboro, 1950. Dept. head Navy Supply, Cherry Point, N.C., 1941-45; ptnr. Cannons Paint & Wallpaper Co., Ayden, 1945-70; exec. v.p. Baker Furniture Co., Kinston, N.C., 1950-63; operator Cannon Farms, Ayden, 1956—; pres., treas. Baker Furniture Co., Kinston, 1963-69; with consumer program Drexel Co., 1965-66; owner Jewelle Baker Cons., Kinston, 1969—; v.p. Gardner Homes, Elizabeth City, N.C., 1972-81; bus. cons. Gardner Constrn. Co., Kinston, 1975-81; bus. cons. Lenoir Plumbing & Heating Co., Kinston, 1975-81; chief exec. officer Gardner Homes, Elizabeth City, 1982—; chmn. bd., chief exec. officer Lenoir Plumbing & Heating Co., 1982—, Gardner Constrn. Co., 1982—; cons. Carolina Power & Light, 1963-65, N.C. Solar Energy Assn., 1977-79, Nutritional Therapy, Durham, 1979-81; lectr., 1950-63; del. U.S.-China Joint Session on Industry, Trade, and Econ. Devel., Beijing, 1988. Mem. Devel. Auth. of Neuse River Council of Govts., 1984-85. Columnist, Ayden Dispatch and Greenville News Leader, 1940-56; producer Performer Baker's Commls., 1960-69. Mem. C. of C. Kinston (bd. dirs., v.p., chmn. retail mchts. div.), So. Retail Furniture Assn., Nat. Retail Furniture Assn., N.C. Mchts. Assn., N.C. Farm Assn., Assoc. Gen. Contractors Am., Community Council for the Arts, Internat. Platform Assn., N.C. Zool. Assn., N.C. Art Soc., Kinston Country Club, Coral Bay Club, Pineknoll Golf and Country Club, Sea Water Marina Club. Democrat. Mem. Ch. Disciples of Christ. Home: 1708 Elizabeth Dr Kinston NC 28504-3416 Office: Gardner Constrn Co PO Box 856 Kinston NC 28502-0856

BAKER-RIKER, MARGERY, television executive; b. N.Y.C., May 5, 1948; d. Robert Charles and Elizabeth Madeline (Schiro) B.; m. Stephen J. Riker; stepchildren: Howard, Katherine, David. AB, Barnard Coll., 1970; MS, Columbia U., 1971. Assoc. producer CBS News, N.Y.C., 1971-73; field producer CBS News, Los Angeles, 1973-76; broadcast producer CBS News, N.Y.C., 1976-78, v.p. public affairs broadcasts, 1978-82, sr. broadcast producer, 1982-86, spl. events producer, 1986-93, nat. editor, 1993-95; exec. prodr. CBS News Prodns., N.Y.C., 1995—. Trustee The Brearley Sch., N.Y.C.; bd. dirs. The Cancer Inst. N.J. Club: Quaker Ridge Golf (Scarsdale, N.Y.). Office: CBS News 524 W 57th St New York NY 10019-2924

BAKER-ROELOFS, MINA MARIE, retired home economics educator; b. Holland, Mich., Mar. 1, 1920; d. Thomas and Fannie (DeBoer) Baker; m. Harold Eugene Roelofs, Aug. 16, 1985; children: Howard, Donald, Ann. BS, Iowa State U., 1942, MS, 1946; postgrad., Ariz. State U., 1965, Ind. State U., 1968, 76. Dietitian Annville (Ky.) Inst., 1942-45; chmn., tchr. home econs. Cen. Coll., Pella, Iowa, 1946-85, ret., 1985; mem. dean's grad. adv. coun. Iowa State U., Ames, 1955-56, coord. coop. plan, 1967-85. Editor: Dandy Dutch Recipes, 1991; co-editor: Pella Collectors Cookbook, 1982, A Taste of the World, 1992. Mem. com. Pell Hist. Soc. Grantee Govt. Cross-Cultural, 1974, NEH, 1980. Mem. AAUW, Am. Assn. Family and Consumer Sci. (life), Iowa Assn. Family and Consumer Sci. (pres. 1953-55, sec. 1979-81, Disting. Svc. award 1985), Iowa Elder Hostel Tchr. Ctrl. Coll. Aux., PEO Sisterhood, Women's Social and Literary Club (pres. 1990-92). Republican. Mem. Reformed Ch. Avocations: photography, reading, crafts. Home: 229 Main St Pella IA 50219-2024

BAKHT, BAIDAR, civil engineer, researcher, educator; b. Delhi, India, Sept. 4, 1940; arrived in Can., 1973; s. Mukhtar and Anwar Jehan Chishti; m. Anita Das, Sept. 11, 1968; children: Natasha, Sacha. BSc in Engring. Aligarh (India) U., 1962; MSc, Imperial Coll., London, 1972; DSc, London U., 1990. Registered profl. engr., Ont., Can. Asst. engr. Heavy Engring. Corp., Ranchi, India, 1962-66; engr. Dept. Environ., London, 1967-73; prin. rsch. engr. Ministry Transp. Ont., 1974-97; v.p. JMBT Stuctures Rsch., Inc., Toronto, Ont., 1997—; adj. prof. civil engring. U. Toronto, 1991—, Dalhousie U. Nova Scotia; chmn. Can. Hwy. Bridge Design Code. Co-author: Bridge Analysis Simplified, 1985, Bridge Analysis by Microcomputer, 1988, Soil-steel Bridges: Design and Construction, 1993, Bridge Engineering, Recent Innovations, 1994; Bridge Superstructures, New Developments, 1996; translator 14 books of Urdu poetry to English, 1985—; contbr. over 190 articles on structural engring. and Urdu Lit.; co-inventor unique deck slab of bridges, inventor of stressed-log bridge. Recipient Moisseif award ASCE, 1982, President's medal Road and Transp. Assn. Can., 1985, Profl. Engrs. Ont. Engring. medal, 1997. Fellow Instn. Engrs. (India) (cert. of merit 1990), Can. Soc. for Civil Engring. (Pratley award 1988, 94, Vance award 1996), Engring. Inst. Can. (Gzowski medal 1983), Profl. Engrs. Ont. (Engring. medal 1996). Avocation: translating Urdu poetry into English.

BAKINOWSKI, CAROL ANN, journalist; b. Waterbury, Conn., Apr. 8, 1949; m. John McCormick. BA in English, U. Conn., 1971; MS in Journalism, Columbia U., 1975. Stringer UPI, Hartford, Conn., 1968-71; copy editor Hartford Courant, 1971-74, Wall St. Jour., N.Y.C., 1975-76, Louisville Times, 1976-80; news design editor N.Y. Times, 1980—. Mem. Soc. News Design, Soc. Profl. Journalists. E-mail: carolbak@nytimes.com. Office: NY Times 229 W 43d St New York NY 10036

BAKKEN, EARL ELMER, electrical engineer, bioengineering company executive; b. Mpls., Jan. 10, 1924; s. Osval Elmer and Florence (Hendricks) B.; m. Constance L. Olson, Sept. 11, 1948 (div. May 1979); children: Wendy, Jeff, Brad, Pam; m. Doris Jane Marshall, Oct. 21, 1982. BEE, U. Minn., 1948, postgrad. in elec. engring., DSc (hon.), 1988; DSc (hon.), Tulane U., 1988. Ptnr. Medtronic, Inc., Mpls., 1949-57, pres., 1957-74, chmn., chief exec. officer, 1974-76, founder, sr. chmn., 1976-85, sr. chmn., 1985-89; dir. Medtronic, Inc., 1989-94. Contbr. articles to profl. jours.; developer first wearable, external, battery-powered heart pacemaker. Pres., bd. dirs. Bakken Libr. and Mus. Electricity in Life, Mpls., 1975-94, v.p., 1994—; pres. North Hawaii Cmty. Hosp., 1990—, Five Mtn. Med. Cmty., Waimea, Hawaii, 1997—; vice chmn. Pavek Mus. Broadcasting, Mpls., 1989—; chmn. bd. dirs. Archaeus Project, Waimea, Hawaii, 1985—. Staff sgt. USAAF, 1942-46. Decorated royal officer Order of Orange-Nassau (Netherlands); recipient Minn. Bus. Hall of Fame award, 1978, Outstanding Achievement award U. Minn., Mpls., 1981, Med.-Tech. Outstanding Achievement award Wale Securities, 1984, Engring. for Gold award NASPE, 1984, Achievement award Sci. Mus. Minn., 1988, Govs. award Minn. Med. Alley Assn., 1988, Centennial medal Coll. St. Thomas, 1986; named Outstanding Minnesotan of Yr. Minn. Broadcasters Assn., 1988, Lifetime Achievement award Entrepreneur of the Yr. program, 1991, Entrepreneur of Yr. award Minn. Entrepreneur's Club, 1993, Spl. Svc. award Richard Smart Big Island Cmty. Achievement, Waimea, Hawaii, 1995, Am. Creativity Assn. Lifetime Creative Achievement award, 1996, Lifetime Achievement award Minn. High Tech. Coun., 1996, Am. Heart Assn. Heart Ball honoree, Hawaii, 1996, Found. Laufman-Greatbatch prize, 1998, Spl. award Cardiostim 98 XX Anniversary for Engrs. and Industry Founders, 1998, Honpa Hongwanji Mission of Hawaii Living Treasure of Hawaii award, 1998, Heart Inst. Innovator award, 1998; named to Minn. Inventors Hall of Fame, 1995, Am. Heart Assn. West Hawaii Hall of Fame, 1998. Fellow IEEE (Centennial medal 1984, Eli Lilly award in med. and biol. engring. 1994), Bakken Soc., Instrument soc. Am., Am. Coll. Cardiology (hon.), Internat. Coll. Surgeons (hon.); mem. N.Am. Soc. Pacing and Electrophysiology (assoc., Disting. Svc. award 1985), Assn. Advancement Med. Instrumentation (Tex. Heart Inst. Innovator award 1998), Am. Antiquarian Soc., Minn. Med. Alley Assn. (bd. dirs. 1985-94). Lutheran. Avocations: history of medical electrical technology, future studies, ballroom dancing. Office: Medtronic Inc 7000 Central Ave NE Minneapolis MN 55432-3576

BAKKEN, GORDON MORRIS, law educator; b. Madison, Wis., Jan. 10, 1943; s. Elwood S. and Evelyn A. H. (Anderson) B.; m. Erika Reinhardt, Mar. 24, 1943; children: Angela E., Jeffrey E. BS, U. Wis., 1966, MS, 1967, PhD, 1970, JD, 1973. From asst. to assoc. prof. history Calif. State U., Fullerton, 1969-74, prof. history, 1974—, dir. faculty affairs, 1974-86; cons. Calif. Sch. Employees Assn., 1976-78, Calif. Bar Commn. Hist. Law., 1985—; mem. mgmt. task force on acad. grievance procedures Calif. State Univ. and Colls. Systems, 1975; mem. Calif. Jud. Coun. Com. Trial Ct. Records Mgmt., 1992—. Author 5 books on Am. legal history; contbr. articles to profl. jours. Placentia Jusa referee coord., 1983. Russell Sag resident fellow law, 1971-72, Am. Bar Found. fellow in legal history, 1979-80, 84-85; Am. Coun. Learned Socs. grantee-in-ai d, 1979-80. Mem. Orgn. Am. Historians, Am. Soc. Legal History, Law and Soc. Assn., Western History Assn., Calif. Supreme Ct. Hist. Soc. (v.p.), Phi Alpha Theta (v.p. 1994-95, pres. 1996-97). Democrat. Lutheran. Office: Calif State U 800 N State College Blvd Fullerton CA 92834-6846

BAKKENSEN, JOHN RESER, lawyer; b. Pendleton, Oreg., Oct. 4, 1943; s. Manley John and Helen (Reser) B.; m. Ann Marie Dahlen, Sept. 30, 1978; children: Michael, Dana, Laura. AB magna cum laude, Harvard U., 1965; JD, Stanford U., 1968. Bar: Oreg. 1969, Calif. 1969, U.S. Dist. Ct. Oreg. 1969. Ptnr. Miller, Nash, Wiener, Hager & Carlsen, Portland, Oreg., 1968—; lawyer del. 9th Cir. Jud. Conf., San Francisco, 1980-82. Author: (with others) Advising Oregon Businesses, 1979. Past bd. dirs. Assn. for Retarded Citizens, Portland; advisor Portland Youth Shelter House; mem. and counsel to bd. dirs. Friends of Pine Mountain Observatory, Portland. Mem. ABA (forum on constrn. industry and sect. pub. contract law and sci. and tech.), Fed. Comm. Bar Assn., Oreg. State Bar, Oreg. Assoc. Gen. Contractors (legal com. 1991, counsel to bd. dirs. 1992), Multnomah Athletic Club. Avocation: astronomy. Office: Miller Nash Wiener Hager & Carlsen 111 SW 5th Ave Portland OR 97204-3699

BAKKER, CORNELIS B., psychiatrist, educator; b. Rotterdam, Holland, Jan. 6, 1929; came to U.S., 1953, naturalized, 1963; s. Willem and Poulina J. (Reiff) B.; m. Marianne K. Rabdau, June 11, 1955; children: Paul, James, Gabrielle. M.D. with honors, U. Utrecht, Holland, 1952. Intern Clinics of Rotterdam, 1952-53, Sacred Heart Hosp., Spokane, 1953-54; resident in psychiatry Eastern State Hosp., Medical Lake, Wash., 1954-56, U. Utrecht, 1956-57, U. Mich. Med. Sch., 1957-59; instr., research asso. psychiatry U. Mich., Ann Arbor, 1959-60; instr. psychiatry U. Wash., Seattle, 1960-63; asst. prof. U. Wash., 1963-67, assoc. prof., 1967-72, prof. psychiatry, 1972-79, dir. Adult Psychiat. Inpatient Service, 1961-68; dir. Adult Devel. Program, 1968-79; prof., head dept. psychiatry U. Ill. Coll. Medicine, Peoria, 1979-84; med. dir. dept. psychiatry Sacred Heart Med. Ctr., Spokane, 1984—; clin. prof. dept. psychiatry and behavioral scis. U. Wash. Sch. Medicine, Seattle, 1985—; med. dir. Spokane Mental Health, 1999—; psychiat. cons. Soc. Sec. Hearings and Appeals, 1963-79, Ketchikan Community Mental Health Center, 1972-77; assoc. residency tng. dir. dept. psychiatry and behavioral scis. U. Wash., Seattle, 1991—. Contbr. articles to profl. jours.; author: (with M.K. Bakker Rabdau) No Trespassing! - Explorations in Human Territoriality, 1973. Dutch Govt. scholar, 1951-52, 52-53; Fulbright grantee, 1953; Fogarty Sr. fellow U. Leuven, Belgium, 1977-78; recipient Significant Achievement award Am. Psychiatric Assn., 1975. Fellow Am. Psychiatric Assn., Am. Coll. Psychiatrists. E-mail: bakkerc@inhs.org. Office: Sacred Heart Med Ctr Dept Psychiatry PO Box 2555 Spokane WA 99220-2555

BAKKER, THOMAS GORDON, lawyer; b. San Gabriel, Calif., Aug. 18, 1947; s. Gordon and Eva Marie (Hoekstra) B.; m. Charlotte Anne Kamstra, Aug. 1, 1969; children: Sarah, Jonathan. AB in History, Calvin Coll., Grand Rapids, Mich., 1969; JD, U. Mich., 1973. Bar: Ariz. 1973, U.S. Dist. Ct. Ariz. 1973, U.S. Ct. Appeals (9th cir.) 1973. Staff reporter Ariz. Criminal Code Revision Com., Phoenix, 1973-75; asst. atty. gen. State of Ariz., Phoenix, 1975-77; staff atty. div. 1 Ariz. Ct. Appeals, Phoenix, 1977-79; assoc. Burch, Cracchiolo et al, Phoenix, 1979-80; from assoc. to ptnr. Olson, Jantsch, Bakker & Blakey, Phoenix, 1980—; vice chmn. tort and ins. practice sect. Appellate Advocacy Commn., 1982-83; judge pro tem div. 1 Ariz. Ct. Appeals, 1985, 92. Served with U.S. Army, 1969-71. Fellow Ariz. Bar Found. (founding fellow); mem. Ariz. Bar Assn., Maricopa County Bar Assn., Am. Judicature Soc., Am. Acad. Health Care Attys., Def. Rsch. Inst., Ariz. Assn. Def. Counsel (bd. dirs.). Mem. Christian Reformed Ch. Avocations: reading, golf, aerobics, salt water fishing. E-mail: TGB@OJBB.com . Office: Olson Jantsch Bakker & Blakey 7243 N 16th St Phoenix AZ 85020-5203

BAKKO, ORVILLE EDWIN, retired health care executive, consultant; b. Kenyon, Minn., Oct. 10, 1919; s. Marcus and Caroline (Leding) B.; m. Norma Evelyn Cronquist, Sept. 25, 1951; children: Sandra Karen, Kristi Camille. BA, St. Olaf Coll., Northfield, Minn., 1941; M. in Hosp. Adminstrn., Northwestern U., 1948. Adminstrv. intern, resident U. Iowa Hosps., 1947-49; adminstrv. asst. Kadlec Hosp., Richland, Wash., 1949-50, asst. adminstr., then adminstr., 1950-56; asst. supt. Arroyo Del Valle Sanatorium, Livermore, Calif., 1956-60, Highland Hosp., Oakland, Calif., 1958-60; adminstr. Fairmont Hosp., San Leandro, Calif., 1960-82; vis. scholar Agder Coll., Kristiansand, Norway, 1983-84. Author: The Administrative Internship—What Can the Field Contribute to the Program?, 1948, Administration of Group Clinics, 1949, Employee Safety Program, 1970, Survey of Medical Rehabilitation in Norway, 1984. Mem. Alameda County Work Safety Com., 1959-72; mem. med. svcs. adv. com. Chabot Coll., San Leandro, 1962-72; mem. dis. svcs. adv. com. area 1 Regional Med. Program, 1970-72; 2d v.p., bd. dirs. Wash. State Hosp. Assn., 1954-55; pres. S.E. Wash. Hosp. Coun., 1953-54; chmn. Tri-City Hosp. Coun., 1954-56; trustee Commn. on Accreditation Rehab. Facilities, 1974-76; mem. Internat. Hosp. Fedn., 1982-88. Capt. Med. Adminstrv. Corps, AUS, 1942-46, NATOUSA. Decorated officer Ordre du Nichan-Iftikhar (Tunisia). Fellow Am. Coll. Healthcare Execs. (life); mem. Am. Hosp. Assn. (life, governing coun. rehab. and chronic disease hosp. sect. 1972-77, chmn. 1976), Calif. Hosp. Assn. (mem. com. on continuing care and rehab. 1967-70), Assn. Western Hosps., Health Care Execs. No. Calif., East Bay Hosp. Conf. (exec. com. 1971-72), Richland Toastmasters Club (officer 1949-56), Los Rios Homeowners Assn. (bd. dirs., chmn. landscape com. 1994-96), Rotary (charter). Mem. Emmanuel Faith Comm. Ch. Home: 11887 Caminito Corriente San Diego CA 92128-4552

BAKLANOFF, ERIC NICHOLAS, economist, educator; b. Graz, Austria, Dec. 9, 1925; came to U.S., 1937, naturalized, 1943; s. Nicolas W. and Lucille (King) B.; m. H. Christina Janes, June 17, 1956 (div. June 1973); children: Nicholas, Tanya, Ana-Maria; m. Joy Driskell, June 6, 1982. Student, Antioch Coll., 1943-44; A.B., Ohio State U., 1949, M.A., 1950, Ph.D., 1958; postgrad. (Fulbright scholar), U. Chile, 1957, Harvard Grad. Sch. Bus. Adminstrn., 1959; postgrad. (NDEA postdoctoral fellow), U. Tex., summer 1963. Instr. econs. Ohio State U., 1957-58; asst. prof. La. State U., 1958-61, assoc. prof., 1961-62; prof. econs., dir. Latin Am. Studies Inst., 1965-68; assoc. prof. econs., dir. Grad. Center for Latin Am. Studies, Vanderbilt U., 1962-65; prof. econs., dean for internat. studies and programs U. Ala., 1969-73, bd. visitors rsch. prof. econs., 1974-92, rsch. prof. econs. emeritus, 1992—; Disting. vis. prof. Luther Coll. summer 1965; cons. Am. Council on Edn., USAF Inst., Pres.'s Southeastern Council on Latin Am. Studies, 1963-64, U.S. Dept. Edn., Centro de Estudios y Communicacion Economica, Am. Enterprise Inst. Pub. Policy Rsch., Fed. Rsch. divsn., Hispanic divsn. Libr. of Congress. Author: Expropriation of U.S Investments in Cuba, Mexico and Chile, 1975, The Economic Transformation of Spain and Portugal, 1978, La Transformation Economica de Espana y Portugal: La economia del Fanquismo y de del Salazarismo, 1980; (with Jeffrey Brannon) Agrarian Reform and Public Enterprise in Mexico: The Political Economy of Yucatan's Henequen Industry, 1987; contbg. author: Revolutionary Change in Cuba, 1971, Modern Brazil: New Patterns and Development, 1971, Background to Revolution: The Development of Modern Cuba, 1979, Yucatan: A World Apart, 1980, The Iberian-Latin America Connection: Implications for U.S. Foreign Policy, 1986, State Shrinking: A Comparative Analysis of Privatization, 1987, The Alabama Economy: Issues for the 1990s, 1990, Portugal: Ancient Country, Young Democracy, 1990, Portugal: A Country Study, 1994, Cuba in Transition, 1998, others; editor, contbg. author: The Shaping of Modern Brazil, 1969, New Perspectives of Brazil, 1966, Mediterranean Europe and the Common Market, 1976, Competing for Latin American Markets: A Business Perspective on the Spanish American War Centennial, 1999; contbr. articles to profl. jours. Active Boy Scouts Am. Served with USNR, 1944-46, PTO. Decorated Knight of Grace, Hospitaler and Mil. Order St. Lazarus of Jerusalem, Malta obedience; named Outstanding Scholar U. Ala., 1980-81; fellow Ctr. Advanced Study Behavioral Scis., 1964-65; grantee U.S. Dept. State, Spain, 1974; rsch. fellow Andrew W. Mellon Found., 1987. Mem. Delta Chi, Beta Gamma Sigma, Sigma Delta Pi, Omicron Delta Epsilon, Phi Beta Delta. Eastern Orthodox. Office: U Ala PO Box 870224 Tuscaloosa AL 35487-0154

BAKROW, WILLIAM JOHN, college president emeritus; b. Parson, Kans., Apr. 22, 1924; s. Leonard A. and Edith (Strasberg) B.; children: Bruce Wrigley, Caren Edith, Lance. BA, Brown U., 1948; MS, Ind. U., 1958, EdD, 1960; LLD (hon.), St. Mary Coll., Omaha, St. Ambrose U. Reporter Providence Jour., 1948-51; legis. corr. U.P., Albany, N.Y., 1951-56; dir. devel. U. Buffalo, 1956-59, Canisius (N.Y.) Coll., 1961-66; pres. Motorola Exec. Inst., Oracle, Ariz., 1966-73, St. Ambrose U., Davenport, Iowa, 1973-87, Montserrat Coll. Art, Beverly, Mass., 1988-89; dir. Southeast Nat. Bank Moline, Ill., Sears Mfg. Co., Davenport., Mercy Hosp., Davenport, Handicapped Devel. Ctr., Davenport; Mem. Scott County Govtl. Study Commn., 1974—. Mem. Illowa Council exec. bd. Boy Scouts Am., 1975—; trustee Palmer Jr. Coll., Davenport, St. Katherine's-St. Mark's Sch., Bettendorf, Iowa, Endicott Coll., Beverly, Mass., Montserrat Coll. of Art, Beverly. Served with USNR, 1942-46. Home and Office: 4 Bayridge Ln Rockport MA 01966-1353

BAKULA, SCOTT, actor; b. St. Louis, Oct. 9. Student, Kans. U. Appearances include roles in regional prodns. of Godspell, Fiddler on the Roof, Joseph and the Amazing Technicolor Dreamcoat, Shenandoah, Off-Broadway prodns. of Accentuate the Positive, Three Guys Naked from the Waist Down, Broadway prodns. of Marilyn: An American Fable, Romance, Romance (Tony award nominee 1988); starred in TV series Eisenhower and Lutz, 1988, Gung Ho, 1986, Quantum Leap, 1989-93 (Emmy award nominee, Golden Globe award), Mr. & Mrs. Smith, 1996; guest appearances include (TV series) Matlock, Designing Women, My Sister Sam, Murphy Brown, Dream On; (TV movies) The Last Fling, The Infiltrator, I-Man, An Eye for an Eye, In the Shadow of a Killer, The Bachelor's Baby, 1996; (TV mini series) The Invaders, 1995, Mr. and Mrs. Smith, 1996, Netforce, 1999; appeared in films Sibling Rivalry, 1990, L.A. Story, 1991, Necessary Roughness, 1991, The Color of Night, 1994, Lord of Illusions, 1995, My Family, 1995, Cats Don't Dance, 1997, Major League: Back to the Minors, 1998, Luminarias, 1999, American Beauty, 1999; dir. Quantum Leap. Office: 15300 Ventura Blvd Ste 315 Sherman Oaks CA 91403-5870*

BAKWIN, EDWARD MORRIS, banker; b. N.Y.C., May 13, 1928; s. Harry and Ruth (Morris) B. BA, Hamilton Coll., 1950; MBA, U. Chgo., 1961. With Nat. Stock Yards Nat. Bank, National City, Ill., 1953-55; with Mid-City Nat. Bank Chgo., 1955—, asst. cashier, 1957-60, v.p., 1960-62, pres., 1962-72, chmn. bd., CEO, 1967—; chmn. bd., CEO Darling-Del. Corp., Chgo., 1972-86, MidCity Fin. Corp., 1982—, Nat. Stock Yards Co., 1985-93. Mem. Chgo. Crime Commn. Adv. bd. U. Chgo., 1967—; bd. dirs. Duncan-Med. YMCA, 1963-72, Northwestern Meml. Hosp., 1980-88; bd. dirs. West Cen. Assn., 1962-67, pres., 1962-65. Served with AUS, 1951-52. Mem. Am. Bankers Assn., Ill. Bankers Assn. (bd. govs. 1966-69), Explorers Club, Adventurers Club (Chgo.), Chgo. Yacht Club, Mid-Am. Club, N.Y. Yacht Club. Home: 175 E Delaware Pl Chicago IL 60611-1756 Office: Mid-City Nat Bank Chgo 2 Mid-City Pla Madison & Halsted Sts Chicago IL 60607

BAL, MIEKE, literature educator, cultural critic and theorist. PhD, U. Utrecht, The Netherlands. Susan B. Anthony prof. comparative lit. U. Rochester, N.Y., 1987-91; adj. vis. prof. visual and cultural studies U. Rochester, 1991-96; A.D. White prof.-at-large Cornell U., Ithaca, N.Y., 1998—; founding dir. Amsterdam Sch. for Cultural Analysis. Office: U Amsterdam, ALW/Spuistraat 210, 1012 VT Amsterdam The Netherlands

BALABAN, BOB, actor, director; b. Chgo., Aug. 16, 1945; s. Elmer and Elenore (Pottasch) B.; m. Lynn Grossman, Apr. 1, 1977; children: Mariah, Hazel. BA, NYU; studied with Uta Hagen, Viola Spolin. Studied with Second City comedy troupe, Chgo.; theatrical appearances include (off-Broadway) You're a Good Man Charlie Brown, 1967, Up Eden, 1968, The Basic Training of Pavlo Hummel, 1971, The Children, 1972, Marie and Bruce, 1980, The Three Sisters, 1982, Some Americans Abroad, 1991, (Broadway) Plaza Suite, 1968, The White House Murder Case, 1970, Some of My Best Friends, 1977, The Inspector General, 1978 (Best Featured Actor in Play Tony award nominee 1979), Speed the Plow, 1991, (regional theatre) The Boys Next Door, 1986, Who Wants to be The Lone Ranger?, 1971; dir. play: Girls, Girls, Girls, 1980; film debut in Midnight Cowboy, 1969; film appearences include Me Natalie, 1969, The Strawberry Statement, 1970, Catch-22, 1970, Making It, 1971, Bank Shot, 1974, Report to the Commissioner, 1975, Close Encounters of the Third Kind, 1977, Girlfriends 1978, Altered States, 1980, Absense of Malice, 1981, Prince of the City, 1981, Whose Life Is It Anyway?, 1981, 2010, 1984, In Our Hands, 1984, End of the Line, 1987, Dead Bang, 1989, Alice, 1990, Little Man Tate, 1991, Bob Roberts, 1992, Greedy, 1994, City Slickers Two, 1994, Waiting for Guffman, 1996, Deconstructing Harry, 1996, Clockwatchers, 1997, Natural Selcetion, 1998, Jakob the Liar, 1999; dir. films: Parents, 1989, My Boyfriend's Back, 1993, The Last Good Time, 1996, Subway Stories, 1997; TV debut in The Mod Squad; TV appearences include (film) Marriage: Year One, 1971, The Face of Fear, 1990, Giving up the Ghost, 1998, Swing Vote, 1999 (series episodes) Seinfeld, 1993; dir. TV: Tales from the Darkside, 1983, Amazing

Stories, 1985, Penn and Teller's Invisible Thread, 1987 Eerrie Indiana, 1991, Legend, 1995; writer: CE2K Diary, 1977. Mem. AEA, SAG, AFTRA, Astoria Found. (bd. dirs.). *

BALABAN, JOHN, poet, educator in English, translator; b. Phila., Dec. 2, 1943; m. Lana Flanagan, 1970; 1 child, Alexandra. BA in English with highest hons., Pa. State U., 1966; AM in English Lit., Harvard U., 1967. Instr. Internat. Voluntary Svcs. U. Can Tho, S. Vietnam, 1967-68; field rep., mgr. field office Com. of Responsibility to Save War-Injured Children, Saigon, Vietnam, 1968-69; instr. dept. English Pa. State U., Univ. Park, 1970-73, asst. prof. English, 1973-76, assoc. prof., 1976-82, prof. of English, 1982-92; prof. of English U. Miami, Fla., 1992—; dir. M of Fine Arts Program, Dept. English, Pa. State U., 1990-92, U. Miami, 1992—; speaker on Vietnamese lit. to many groups including The Asia Soc., N.Y.C., Harvard U. Am., Literary Translators Assn., Freer Gallery, Shakespeare Theatre and gave more than 100 poetry readings in U.S., Can. and Europe. Author: (books of poetry) After Our War (Lamont prize, nat. book award nomination), 1974, Letters from Across the Sea, 1978, Ca Dao Vietnam: A Bilingual Anthology of Vietnamese Folk Poetry, 1980, Blue Mountain, 1982, (novel) Coming Down Again, 1985, 2d edit. 1989, (novel for children) The Hawk's Tale, 1988, Vietnam: The Land We Never Knew, 1989, Words for My Daughter, 1991 (Nat. Poetry Series selection), (memoir) Remembering Heaven's Face, 1992, Locusts at the Edge of Summer: New and Selected Poems, 1997 (William Carlos Williams award, Nat. Book Award nomination); editor (with N.Q. Duc) Vietnam: A Traveler's Literary Companion, 1996; translator Vietnam Poems, 1970, editor, translator: Vietnamese Folk Poetry, 1974; contbr. articles, short stories, poetry to literary publs. and newspapers including The Hudson Rev., N.Y. Times, Translation, Prairie Schooner, Am. Scholar, Chelsea, Sewanee Rev., So. Rev., New Eng. Rev., Ploughshares, Harper's, Am. Poetry Rev. and others; cons. in translation Nat. Endowment for Humanities. Recipient Woodrow Wilson fellowship, Harvard U., 1966-67, Chris award (with Peter Wolff, M.D., 1969,, Lang. Study fellowship, Assn. Asian Scholars, 1971, translation fellowship Am. P.E.N. and Columbia U., 1974, Translation award, Translation Ctr. Columbia U., 1977, Fulbright-Hayes Sr. lectureship, Romania, 1976-77, The Steaua prize Romanian Writers Union, 1978, Fulbright Disting. Vis. lectureship, Romania, 1979, Vaptsarov medal Union of Bulgarian Writers, 1980, Creative Writing fellowship, Pa. Coun. on Arts, 1983-84, 89, Nat. Endowment Arts fellowship 1978, 85, Nat. Poetry Series Book Selection, 1990, Pushcart prize XV, 1990, Witter Bynner Translation fellowship, 1997; named NEH Younger Humanist fellow, 1971-72, fellow Inst. for Arts and Humanities, Pa. State U., 1991-92. Mem. Am. Literary Translators Assn. (past pres.). E-mail: jbalaban@Umiami.tr.miami.edu. Office: U Miami Dept English PO Box 248145 Coral Gables FL 33124-8145

BALABANIAN, NORMAN, electrical engineering educator; b. New London, Conn., Aug. 13, 1922; s. Adam B. and Elizabeth (Seklemian) B.; m. Jean Tajerian, Aug. 16, 1947 (div. 1977); children: Karen J., Doris R., Gary N., Linda C.; m. 2d, Rosemary Lynch, Jan. 19, 1979. BSEE, Syracuse U., 1949, MSEE, 1951, PhD, 1954. From instr. to prof. Syracuse U., 1949-91, prof. emeritus, 1991—; mem. tech. staff Bell Labs., Murray Hill, N.J., 1956, IBM Devel. Lab, Poughkeepsie, N.Y., 1962; vis. prof. U. Calif., Berkeley, 1965-66; mem. UNESCO field staff Inst. Politecnico Nacional, Mexico City, 1969-70; Fulbright fellow U. Zagreb, Zagreb, Jugoslavia, 1974-75; acad. advisor Inst. Nat. d'Elec. et d'Elec., Boumerdes, Algeria, 1977-78; chmn. Dept. of Elec. & Computer Engring. Syracuse U., 1983-90; vis. scholar MIT, 1990-95, Tufts U., 1990-95; courtesy prof. U. Fla., 1995—. Author: Network Synthesis, 1958, Fundamentals of Circuit Theory, 1961, Fourier Series, 1976, Ensenanza Programada en la Education Activa (in Spanish), 1974, Activne RC Mreze (in Serbo-Croatian), 1977, Electric Circuits, 1994; co-author: Linear Network Analysis, 1959, Electrical Network Theory, 1969, Electrical Science: Resistive Networks, 1970, Electrical Science: Dynamic Networks, 1973, Linear Network Theory, 1981; editor: Undergraduate Physics and Mathematics in Electrical Engineering, 1960, Electrical Engineering Education, 1961; editor (jour.) IEEE Transactions on Circuit Theory, 1963-65, (mag.) IEEE Technology and Society, 1979-86, 1993-95. Dist. commr. Dem. Party, Syracuse, N.Y., 1959-61; pres. Cen. N.Y. Civil Liberties Union, Syracuse, 1963-64, 79-80 (Civil Liberties award 1966); congl. candidate Liberal Party, People's Peace Party, Syracuse, N.Y., 1966. S/Sgt. Army AC, 1943-46. Recipient peace award Syracuse Peace Coun., 1966. Fellow IEEE (life mem., Centennial award 1984), IEEE Soc. Implications Tech. (v.p., pres. 1988-91), AAAS; mem. Am. Soc. for Engring. Edn. (life mem., pres. EE div. 1966-67), AAUP (pres. Syracuse U. chpt. 1964-65). Office: U Fla ECE Dept Gainesville FL 32611-6200

BALADA, LEONARDO, composer, educator; b. Barcelona, Spain, Sept. 22, 1933; s. Jose and Lucia (Ibanez) B.; m. Monica McCormack, July 3, 1962 (div. 1977); 1 child, Dylan; m. Joan Winer, July 28, 1979. Profesorado de Teoria, Conservatory del Liceu, 1953; Profesorado de Piano, Conservatory Liceu, Barcelona, Spain, 1954; diploma in composition, Juilliard Sch. Music, 1960; postgrad., Mannes Coll. Music, 1961-62. Instr. Walden Sch., N.Y.C., 1962-63; head dept. music UN Internat. Sch., N.Y.C., 1963-70; prof. composition Carnegie-Mellon U., Pitts., 1970—; Univ. prof. Carnegie-Melon U., Pitts., 1990—; mem. faculty Torroella de Montgri Internat. Music Course and Festival, Spain, 1991—. Composer-in-residence, Aspen (Colo.) Inst., 1970; guest composer, U. Tel Aviv, Israel, 1975, guest condr. various orchs.; collaborated with painter Salvador Dali, Nobel Prize laureate writer Camilo José Cela; composer numerous compositions including Guernica (premiered New Orleans Philharmonic), 1966, Sinfonia en Negro-Homenaje a Martin Luther King; commd. and premiered, Spanish Radio TV Symphony Orch., 1968; Maria Sabina; oratorio, premiered, Carnegie Hall, 1970; Cumbres; premiered at Carnegie Hall, 1971; Steel Symphony; premiered, Pitts. Symphony, 1972 (recorded by Lorin Maazel and Pitts. Symphony, New World Records); composer: commd. and premiered by Nat. Orch. Spain Auroris, 1973; Ponce de Leon, for narrator and orch., 1973, premiered by Jose Ferrer and, New Orleans Philharm. Symphony Orch., 1973, Concerto for Piano, Winds and Percussion, 1974; commd. by, Carnegie-Mellon U. Alumni Assn., premiered at, Carnegie Hall, 1974, Homage to Casals and Homage to Sarasate, 1975, premiered by Pitts. Symphony, 1976, Cantata NO-RES premiered by Barcelona Symphony Orch., Nat. Chorus of Spain, 1975 (City of Barcelona Composition prize 1976), Concertino for Castanets and Orch., world premier Philharmonia Orch. London, 1980, U.S. premiere Phila. Orch., 1987; Fantasias Sonoras, commd. by Pitts. Symphony Orch., 1987; composer chamber works Voces 1, for mixed chorus a capella, Tresis, 1971; commd. for guitar, flute and cello Composers Theatre Inc., premiered at, May Festival in N.Y.C., 1973; composer Apuntes for guitar quartet, 1974 (Internat. Composition prize Ciudad de Zaragoza), premiered Zaragoza, 1974; solo compositions include Analogias, for guitar, 1968 (premiered by Narciso Yepes at Besançon Music Festival Elementalis), for organ, 1972 (premiered by Pitts. Symphony, 1982 Sardana), 1979; commd. by Nat. Endowment Arts, premiered by N.Y. Philharm., 1982 Quasi un Pasodoble, 1981; premiered at Carnegie Hall, 1982 Concerto for Violin and Orch., 1982; commd. and premiered by Internat. Barcelona Music Festival, 1982 Hangman, Hangman (opera), 1982; grand opera in 2 acts, commd. by San Diego Opera Zapata, 1984; composer 2 act opera Christopher Columbus, commd. for 5th centennial of discovery of Am., premiere 1989, Teatro del Liceo, Barcelona, performed by tenor Jose Carreras and soprano Monserrat Caballé; composer Sinfonia Concertante for amplified guitar and orch., premiered by Narcisco Yepes and Nat. Orch. Spain, 1987, Zapata: Images for Orch., world premier by Nat. Orch. Spain, Am. premier by Pitts. Symphony, 1987, music for strings and flute, premiered by Atlanta Virtuosi, 1987, Torquemada, 1980, Columbus: Images for Orch., 1992, Symphony #4 premiere Lausanne Chamber Orch., 1992, Celebration premiere Prague Symphony, 1992, Escenas Borrascosas premiere by Nat. Orch. and Chorus of Spain, 1992, Music for Oboe and Orchestra premiered by Lorin Maazel and the Pitts. Symphony, 1993 (recorded), Line and Thunder premiere by Pitts. Symphony Orch., 1998, Shadows premiere by Cin. Symphony Orch., 1995, Morning Music premiere by Julius Baker and CMU Philharmonic, 1995, Concerto Magico for guitar and orchestra premiered by Angel Romero and Cin. Symphony Orch., 1997; also composer several ballets and songs; composer works for many soloists, including, Andrés Segovia, Nicanor Zabaleta, Alicia de Larrocha, Angel Romero, Narciso Yepes, music played by numerous orchs. at numerous festivals in U.S. and abroad, music recorded by Serenus Records, Louisville Orch. First Edit. Records, Deutsche Grammophon, BASF, New World Records, over 50 works pub. by Gen. Music and G. Schirmer. Recipient B. Martinu prize in composition Mannes Coll. Music, 1962, Internat. Composition prize Cuidad de Zaragoza, 1974, Internat. prize City of Barcelona, 1975, 80, Nat. Music prize of Catalonia, 1993; Fundacion March fellow. Mem. ASCAP (awards), Am. Music Center, Hispanic Soc. Am. (corr.). Office: Carnegie-Mellon U Sch Music Pittsburgh PA 15213

BALADI, NAOUM ABBOUD, surgeon; b. Aleppo, Syria, May 26, 1956; came to U.S., 1979; s. Abboud and Nadia Baladi; m. Houda Leon, Sept. 19, 1979; children: Carine, Christina, Stephanie. BA, Coll. Champagnat, Aleppo, Syria, 1973; MD, Aleppo U., 1979. Diplomate Am. Bd. Gen. Surgery, Am. Bd. Thoracic Surgery. Surgeon in tng. U. Mass., Worcester, 1980-85; cardiac surgeon in tng. U. N.Mex., Albuquerque, 1985-87; fellow heart and lung transplantation U. Pitts., 1987-88; cardiac surgeon St. Mary's Hosp., San Francisco, 1988—; pres. Pacific Cardiovasc. Surgeons, Daly City, Calif., 1993—; med. dir. Cardio Med. Solutions, Fountain Valley, Calif., 1996—. Fellow ACS, Internat. Soc. Heart and lung Transplantation, Soc. Thoracic Surgeons. Avocations: painting, soccer, swimming, travel. E-mail: nbaladi@prodigy.net. Office: Pacific Cardiovasc Surgeons 1500 Southgate # 209 Daly City CA 94015

BALAKIAN, PETER, English educator; b. Teaneck, N.J., June 13, 1951; s. Gerard and Arax Aroosian Balakian; m. Helen Jane Kebabian, Aug. 16, 1980; children: Sophia, Ann, James, Gerard. BA in History cum laude, Bucknell U., 1973; PhD in Am. Civiilization, Brown U., 1980. English prof. Colgate U., Hamilton, N.Y., 1980—. Author: Black Dog of Fate, 1997 (Pen/Albrand prize 1998), Dyer's Thustle, 1992, Reply From Wilderness, 1988, Sad Days of Light, 1983. Freedom to write com. PEN Am. Ctr., 1998—. Recipient Bood award N.J. Coun. for the Humanities, 1998, Anrahit Literary prize Columbia U., 1990. Mem. PEN, Authors Guild, Armenian Nat. Inst. (bd. dirs. 1997—). E-mail: pbalakian@Center.Colgate.edu. Home: 10 Hamilton St Hamilton NY 13346 Office: Dept of English Colgate U Hamilton NY 13346

BALANIS, CONSTANTINE APOSTLE, electrical engineering educator; b. Trikala, Thessaly, Greece, Oct. 29, 1938; came to U.S., 1955; s. Apostolos G. and Erini (Vlahocostas) B.; m. Helen Jovaras, May 21, 1972; children: Erini, Stephanie. BSEE, Va. Poly. Inst., 1964; MEE, U. Va., 1966; PhDEE, Ohio State U., 1969. Electronics engr. NASA, Hampton, Va., 1964-70; asst. professorial lectr. George Washington U. Extension, Hampton, 1968-70; vis. assoc. prof. dept. elec. engring. W.Va. U., Morgantown, 1970-72, assoc. prof., 1972-76, prof., 1976-83; prof. dept. elec. engring. Ariz. State U., Tempe, 1983-91, Regents' prof., 1991—, dir. Telecommunications Rsch. Ctr., 1988-99; cons. Motorola Inc., Scottsdale, Ariz., 1984-94, Loral Def. Systems, Litchfield Park, Ariz., 1986-88, Gen. Dynamics, Pomona, Calif., 1986-87, Naval Air Warfare Ctr., Patuxent River, Md., 1977-90, Naval Surface Warfare Ctr., Dahlgren, Va., 1985-86, Nat. Radio Astronomy Observatory, Green Bank, W.Va., 1972-74; Boeing, Seattle, 1996, Rockwell Internat., Cedar Rapids, Iowa, 1997. Author: Antenna Theory: Analysis and Design, 1982, 2d edit., 1997, Advanced Engineering Electromagnetics, 1989; patentee in field. Recipient Halliburton Best Researcher award W.Va. U., 1983, Russ award for Rsch., Ohio U., 1984, Teaching Excellence award Ariz. State U., 1988, also Outstanding Grad. Mentor award, 1996-97; grantee and contracts NASA, Army Rsch. Office, NSF, Office Naval Rsch., Dept. of Energy, Dept. of Transp., Naval Air Warfare Ctr., Naval Surface Warfare Ctr., Motorola Inc., Gen. Dynamics, McDonnell Douglas Helicopter, Sikorsky Aircraft, Rockwell Internat., Boeing Helicopters, IBM, 1972—. Fellow IEEE (Individual Achievement award region 6, 1989, Spl. Engring. Professionalism award Phoenix sect. 1992); mem. Am. Soc. Engring. Edn., Sigma Xi, Phi Kappa Phi, Eta Kappa Nu, Tau Beta Pi. Avocations: golf, jogging, tennis, bowling. Home: 3154 E Encanto St Mesa AZ 85213-6110 Office: Ariz State U Dept Elec Engring Tempe AZ 85287-7206

BALARAJAN, YOGARAJAH, electrophysiologist, cardiologist; b. Jaffna, Sri Lanka, May 1, 9162; came to the U.S., 1991; s. Thambimuthu and Valambighai Yogarajah; m. Poonkothai Sathasivam, June 8, 1995; 1 child, Abirami. MB, BChir, U. Colombo, Sri Lanka. Diplomate internal medicine, cardiology and electrophysiology Am. Bd. Internal Medicine. Intern house officer Srijayanardana Pura Gen. Hosp., Nugegoda, Sri Lanka, 1986-88; sr. house officer medicine St. Andrew's-Newham Gen. Hosp., London, 1989-91; resident internal medicine D.C. Gen. Hosp., Washington, 1991-95; cardiology fellow Luth. Gen. Hosp., Park Ridge, Ill., 1995-97; electrophysiology fellow U. Mass. Med. Ctr., Worcester, 1997-98; electrophysiologist, cardiologist Heart Ctr. Nev., North Las Vegas, 1999—. Mem. Am. Coll. Cardiology (affiliate), Royal Coll. Physicians. Avocations: playing racketball, basketball, watching movies. Home: Apt 217 501 Plantation St Worcester MA 01605

BALAS, EGON, applied mathematician, educator; b. Cluj, Romania, June 7, 1922; came to U.S., 1967, naturalized, 1973; s. Ignat and Boriska B.; m. Edith Lovi, 1948; children: Anna, Vera. Diploma licenciae, Bolyai U., Cluj, 1949; D.Sc.Ec. summa cum laude, U. Brussels; D.U. in Math., U. Paris. Asso. prof. econs. Inst. Econ. Sci., Bucharest, 1949-58; analyst Designing Inst. Forestry and Timber Industry, Bucharest, 1959-64; head math. programming sector Center Math. Stats. of Romanian Acad., 1964-66; research mathematician Internat. Computation Centre, Rome, 1966; vis. prof. ops. research U. Toronto, 1967, Stanford U., 1967; Ford disting. research prof. Carnegie Mellon U., 1967-68; prof. indsl. adminstrn. and applied math. Carnegie-Mellon U., 1968—, univ. prof., 1990—, holder GSIA alumni chair, 1980—; Thomas Lord Prof. Ops. Rsch., 1997—; vis. ops. rsch. analyst Fed. Energy Adminstrn., 1976; cons. NSF grantee, 1972—; vis. prof. Maths. Inst. Köln, 1980-81. Assoc. editor: Ops. Rsch., 1967-96, Zeitschrift für Operations Research; adv. editor: Discrete Applied Math., Jour. Combinatorial Optimization; mem. editorial bd. Computational Optimization and Applications, Revue Française d'Automatique et Recherche Operationelle, Annals of Operations Research; editorial assoc.: European Jour. Operational Research; contbr. over 180 articles to profl. jours. Recipient Alexander von Humboldt Sr. U.S. Scientist award, 1980-81, John von Neumann Theory award, 1995, Citation Classic, Current Contents, 1982. Mem. SIAM, Math. Programming Soc. (coun. 1989-92), Inst. Mgmt. Scis. (coun. 1972-75), Oper. Rsch. Soc. Research on math. programming, especially integer and disjunctive programming, combinatorial optimization, graphs, networks, crew scheduling, machine sequencing, energy models; developer of scheduling system for steel rolling. Home: 136 Beechwood Ln Pittsburgh PA 15206-4526 Office: Graduate School of Industrial Adm Carnegie Mellon Univ Pittsburgh PA 15213

BALÁS, IRENE BARBARA, artist; b. Budapest, Hungary, Feb. 28, 1928; came to U.S., 1973; d. Sandor and Ilona (Udvardy) B.; m. Tom Elliot, July 30, 1974 (dec. May. 1980). Studies with Karl Kaufmann and Hans Hoff, Vienna, Austria; B Degree, Budapest, 1943; MA in Art Therapy and Psychology, KunstAkad./Sigmund Freud Inst., Vienna, 1948. Cert. art therapist, psychoanalyst. Artist, 1974—. One-woman shows in Vienna, Paris, Munich, Madrid, Chile, Bolivia, Peru, Venezuela, Colombia, Haiti, N.Y., San Francisco, Miami and L.A.; represented in permanent collections Vatican, Mus. Atelier, other museums, and pvt. collections of Rockefeller, Henry Ford, Olga, Bruce Walker and others; commd. to paint History of Cuba in 7 paintings, 1990, Hungarian Hang Gliding Expdn. Around the World in 7 paintings for Mil. Mus. in Budapest, 1993; TV show hostess, 1977-78. Recipient Nat. prize of Austrian Painters, 1948. Home and Office: 1621 Collins Ave Apt 907 Miami FL 33139-3142

BALASA, MARK EDWARD, investment consultant; b. Petoskey, Mich., July 2, 1958; s. Edward S. and Mary N. (Wiklanski) B.; m. Laurel Marie Monaco, July 6, 1985; children: Bryant, Brett. AS, North Cen. Mich. Coll., Petoskey, 1978; BSBA, Cen. Mich. U., Mt. Pleasant, 1980; MA, Coll. Fin. Planning, Denver, 1992. CPA, Ill.; cert. fin. planner. Contr. Perfection Machinery Sales, Wheeling, Ill., 1981-87; investment cons. Elite Adv. Svcs., Schaumburg, Ill., 1987-89; investment cons., ptnr. Burton Investment Mgmt., Schaumburg, 1989—, Balasa & Hoffman, Inc., 1998—; tchr. Mundelein Coll., Chgo., 1988; pres. Balasa & Hoffman, Inc. Named One of the 200 Best Fin. Advisors in the Country Worth mag., 1996, 97, 98, One of Best 120 Planners for Physicians, Med. Econs. mag., 1998. Mem. AICPA, Internat. Assn. Fin. Planners (v.p. 1990-91, pres. 1991-92, exec. com. 1992-93), Internat. Assn. Fin. Planning (pres. Chgo. chpt. 1992-93). Roman Catholic. Avocations: running, racquetball, chess. Home: 1219 N Lakeview Ct Palatine IL 60067-2086 Office: Balasa & Hoffman Inc 1920 Thoreau Dr N Ste 174 Schaumburg IL 60173-4151

BALASI, MARK GEOFFREY, architect; b. Chgo., Feb. 29, 1952; s. Alfred Victor and Betty Lou (Biggs) B.; m. Barbara Jane Ritt, May 25, 1985; children: Geoffrey Adam, Maria Elizabeth. Student, Ecole-des-Beaux-Arts, Versailles, France, 1974-75; BS in Archtl. Studies, U. Ill., 1975; postgrad., U. Wis., 1986, 89, 92. Lic. architect, Ill., Mich., Ohio. Architect Davy McKee, Chgo., 1976-80, Perkins & Will, Chgo., 1980-82; prin. Hansen Lind Meyer Inc., Chgo., 1982-95; v.p. Phillips Swager Assocs., Naperville, Ill., 1995—; lectr. Italian Nat. Ctr. Hosp. Bldg. and Technique. Editor Balasi Archives, U. Iowa Librs. Spl. Collections; author: Balasic Family Vaudeville Album, 1994; important works include Villa Schaefer, Mattoon, Ill., Nunamaker House, Mattoon. Mem. Hist. Preservation Commn., McHenry County, Ill. Mem. AIA (Nat. Coun. Archel. Registration Bds. cert.), Am. Soc. Hosp. Engring., Acad. Architecture for Health, Health Facility Inst., PB4Y Assn., U. Ill. Alumni Assn. Avocations: genealogy, entomology, travel. Office: Phillips Swager Assocs 40 Shuman Blvd Ste 175 Naperville IL 60563-8464

BALAY, ROBERT ELMORE, editor, reference librarian; b. Wichita, Kans., Oct. 6, 1930; s. Loren Elmore and Gladys Lois (Crites) B.; m. Harriette Shirley Anderson, Dec. 23, 1961; children—Christopher Loren, Anne Gladys, Jean Mary. BA, Macalester Coll., 1952; MA, U. Minn., 1954; MS in Libr. Sci., Columbia U., 1959. Tech. writer Beech Aircraft Corp., Wichita, 1956-58; asst. librarian Grumman Aircraft Corp., Bethpage, N.Y., 1959-62, Gen. Precision, Little Falls, N.J., 1962-64; asst. sci. librarian Wayne State U., Detroit, 1964-68, adj. instr. library sci., 1966-67; head reference dept. Yale U. Library, New Haven, 1968-86; reference editor Choice mag., Middletown, Conn., 1986—. Editor: Guide to Reference Books, 11th edit., 1996; contbr. articles to profl. jours. Served with U.S. Army, 1954-56. Democrat. Home: 97 Livingston St New Haven CT 06511-2411 Office: Choice Mag 100 Riverview Ctr Middletown CT 06457-3445

BALAZ, BEVERLY ANN, publishing executive; b. Danbury, Conn., Dec. 15, 1949; d. William Charles and Loretta (Bielaczyc) B. BS in Edn., Western Conn. State U., 1972. Exec. sec., jr. copywriter Grolier Enterprises, Inc., Danbury, 1973-75; tchr. English and reading Brookfield (Conn.) Jr. H.S., 1975-76; trainee advt. and sales promotion Grolier Ednl. Corp., Danbury, 1977-78, coord. advt. and sales promotion, 1978-79, mgr. advt. and sales promotion prodn., 1979-81, mgr. advt. and sales promotion, 1981-83, mgr. mktg. adminstrn., 1983-88, dir. direct mktg., 1988-90, v.p. mktg., 1991-95; pres. Facts on File Pub., N.Y.C., 1996-97, William Charles & Assocs., Danbury, 1997-98; pub. Macmillan Libr. Reference USA, N.Y.C., 1998—. Vol. Danbury chpt. Am. Heart Assn.; bd. dirs. Arrowood Condominium Assn., 1989; officer exec. com., 1st v.p., dir. spl. events Keynotes, The Charles Ives Ctr. for the Arts. Mem. Direct Mktg. Assn., Women's Direct Response Group, Direct Mktg. Club N.Y.C. Democrat. Roman Catholic. Avocations: skiing, racquetball, boating. Home: 20 E Pembroke Rd Unit 73 Danbury CT 06811-3705 Office: Macmillan Libr Reference USA 1633 Broadway New York NY 10019-6708

BALBACH, GEORGE CHARLES, technology company executive; b. Waukegan, Ill., June 29, 1931; s. George Jacob and Martha Patterson (Shewmaker) B.; m. Elaine Barbara Davis, Dec. 15; children: Vanessa Anne, Melissa Lynn, George F. BS in Econs., U. Pa., 1953. Asst. controller Hills McCanna, Chgo., 1955-58; dir. mktg. Imperial-Eastman, Chgo., 1958-68; exec. v.p. Keltec, Inc., Elkhart, Ind., 1968-70; pres., CEO Hubbell Corp., Mundelein, Ill., 1970-74; pres., CEO, owner ASI Techs., Inc., Milw., 1974—. Inventor in field. Mem. Internat. Assn. Refrigerated Warehouses, Refrigeration Rsch. Found., Exec. Com. (adv. bd. 1991). Republican. Presbyterian. Avocations: vintage racing cars, skiing, sailing, reading. Home: 321 W Onwentsia Rd Lake Forest IL 60045-2828 Office: ASI Techs Inc 5848 N 95th Ct Milwaukee WI 53225-2613

BALBACH, STANLEY BYRON, lawyer; b. Normal, Ill., Dec. 26, 1919; s. Nyle Jacob and Gertrude (Cory) B.; m. Sarah Troutt Witherspoon, May 22, 1944; children: Stanley Byron Jr., Nancy Ann Fehr, Barbara, Edith. BS, U. Ill., 1940, LLD, 1942. Bar: Ill. 1942, Fla. 1980, U.S. Ct. Appeals (7th cir.) 1961, U.S. Supreme Ct. 1950. Ptnr. Couchman & Balbach, Hoopeston, Ill., 1945-48, Webber & Balbach, Urbana, 1948-81, Balbach & Fehr, Urbana, 1981—; nat. chmn. Jr. Bar Conf., 1955; bd. dirs. Atty.'s Title Guaranty Fund, Champaign, Ill. Author: Reverse Mortgages, 1997, The Lawyers Guide to Retirement: Serving a New Clientele in a Second Career in Real Estate, 1998. Mem. East Ctl. Ill. Area Agy. on Aging Bd. Capt. USAAF, 1942-45. Mem. ABA (ho. of dels. 1956, 65, chmn. spl. com. lawyers title guaranty funds 1962-70, liaison to lawyer title guaranty fund com., past mem. coun. law office practice and real property, probate and trust law sects.), LWV (bd.dirs.), Ill. State Bar Assn. (elder law coun., chmn. real estate com.), Am. Judicature Soc., Masons, Rotary, Phi Delta Phi, Alpha Kappa Lambda. Home: 1009 Douglas Ave Urbana IL 61801-4933 Office: Balbach & Fehr Box 217 102 N Broadway Ave Urbana IL 61801-2705

BALBI, KENNETH EMILIO, environmental lead specialist, researcher; b. N.Y.C., Apr. 13, 1963; s. George Emilio and Blanca Amelia (Fonseca) B.; m. Julie Ann Lopez, Feb. 19, 1989; children: Danielle Elizabeth, Joshua Emilio. MD, U. Ctrl. del Este, Dominican Republic, 1985; BS, SUNY, Albany, 1989. Rsch. assoc. Montefiore Med. Ctr., N.Y.C., 1988-94; govtl. case cons. SCITEC Corp., Kennewick, Wash., 1994-95; dir. tng. and profl. svcs. U.S. Lead, Oyster Bay, N.Y., 1995-97; v.p., co-founder ANDO Internat., Bklyn., 1995—; dir. franchise ops. PRO-TECT Franchising Inc., Oyster Bay, N.Y., 1996-97; v.p. rsch. & design AIA Environ. Corp., Astoria, N.Y., 1997-99. Contbr. articles to profl. jours. Mem. St. Michael's Hispanic Assn., Flushing, N.Y., 1991—, Cuban-Am. Assocs., Flushing, 1988—, Alliance to End Childhood Lead Poisoning, Washington, 1992—. Mem. AAAS, ASTM, Nat. Assn. Lead Inspectors, Nat. Lead Abatement Coun., Interam. Coll. Physicans and Surgeons, N.Y. Acad. Sci., United Internat. Med. Grads., Am. Indsl. Hygiene Assn., Steel Structure Painting Coun. Roman Catholic. Home: 24015B Oak Park Dr Douglaston NY 11362-2608 Office: ANDO Internat 861 Manhattan Ave Brooklyn NY 11222-2585

BALBOA, MARCELO, soccer player; b. Cerritos, Calif., Aug. 8, 1967; s. Luis B.; m. Cindy Balboa. Grad., San Diego State U., 1988. Player U.S. Nat. Team, 1988—, San Diego Nomads, APSL, 1989, San Francisco Blackhawks, APSL, 1990-91, Colo. Foxes, APSL, 1992, Leon, Mex. 1st Divsn., 1995-96, Colo. Rapids, 1996—; Mem. U.S. World Cup Team, 1994—. Named MVP World Cup, 1994, Colo. Rapids, 1997. Office: c/o Colo Rapids 555 17th St Ste 3350 Denver CO 80202-3909 also: US Soccer Fedn 1801 S Prairie Ave # 1811 Chicago IL 60616-1357*

BALCER, CHARLES LOUIS, college president emeritus, educator; b. McGregor, Iowa, May 23, 1921; s. Ludwig Frank and Iva (Vaughan) B.; m. Martha Elizabeth Belgum, Jan. 6, 1944; children—Mary Elizabeth, Mark Lewis, Beth Louise, Brian Charles. B.S., Winona (Minn.) State Tchrs. Coll., 1942; M.A., State U. Iowa, 1949, Ph.D., 1954. Tchr. Minn. and Iowa high schs., 1942-43, 46-47; instr. State U. Iowa, 1947-50; high sch. prin. Detroit Lakes, Minn., 1950-54; assoc. prof. speech St. Cloud (Minn.) State Coll., 1954-56, prof., acad. dean, 1958-64; prof. speech SUNY-Oswego, 1956-57; pres. Augustana Coll., Sioux Falls, S.D., 1965-80; pres. emeritus Augustana Coll., Sioux Falls, 1980—; Disting. Service prof. Augustana Coll., 1980-95; interim pres., CEO Good Samaritan Soc., 1997-98. Author: (with H. F. Seabury) Teaching Speech. Mem., bd. dirs. Evang. Luth. Good Samaritan Soc.; mem. Marquette Bank of S.D., Sioux Falls Symphony Assn. Served with AUS, 1943-46. Decorated knight 1st class Royal Order St. Olav, Norway). Mem. Speech Communication Assn. Am., Central States Speech Assn. (pres. 1954), NEA, Assn. Higher Edn., Delta Sigma Rho, Kappa Delta Pi, Phi Delta Kappa. Democrat. Home: 2501 S Kiwanis Ave Apt 201 Sioux Falls SD 57105-0160 *I have learned that the purpose of this earthly life is not happiness. It is to be useful, to be honorable, to be compassionate. It is to matter—to have it made some difference that you lived at all.*

BALCH, GLENN MCCLAIN, JR., academic administrator, minister, author; b. Shattuck, Okla., Nov. 1, 1937; s. Glenn McClain and Marjorie (Daily) B.; student Panhandle State U., 1958-60, So. Meth. U., summers 1962-64; BA, S.W. State U. Okla., 1962; B.D., Phillips U., 1965; MA, Chapman Coll., 1973, MA in Edn., 1975, M.A. in Psychology, 1975; PhD, U.S. Internat. U., 1978; postgrad. Claremont Grad. Sch., 1968-70, U. Okla., 1965-66; m. Diana Gale Seeley, Oct. 15, 1970; children: Bryan, Gayle, Wesley, Johnny. Ordained to ministry Meth. Ch., 1962; sr. minister First Meth. Ch., Eakly, Okla., 1960-63, First Meth. Ch., Calumet, Okla., 1963-65,

Goodrich Meml. Ch., Norman, Okla., 1965-66, First Meth. Ch., Barstow, Calif., 1966-70; asst. dean Chapman Coll., Orange, Calif., 1970-76; v.p. Pacific Christian Coll., Fullerton, Calif., 1976-79; sr. pastor Brea United Meth. Ch., 1978-89; pres., CEO So. Calif. Inst., 1988-95; pres. Westmar U., Le Mars, Iowa, 1995-96; exec. v.p. Advance Cons. Network (name now Synergistics, Inc.), Rochester, N.Y., 1996—; edn. cons. USAF, 1974-75; mental health cons. U.S. Army, 1969; bd. dirs. FINCA, 1989-95. Bd. dirs. Found. Internat. Community Assistance. With USMC, 1956-57. Recipient Eastern Star Religious Tng. award, 1963, 64; named Man of Year, Jr. C. of C., Barstow, 1969; Broadhurst fellow, 1963-65. Mem. Calif. Assn. Marriage and Family Therapists, Am. Assn. Marriage and Family Therapist, Rotary (pres. 1969-70, 83-84, 99—, dist. gov. 1987-88, 88-89), Masons, Shriners, Elks. Home: 39 Bowen Rd Churchville NY 14428 Office: Synergistics Inc 1200A Scottsville Rd Rochester NY 14624-5703

BALCH, STEPHEN HOWARD, professional society administrator; b. Bklyn., Jan. 31, 1944; s. Harry and Florence (Frey) B.; m. Maria Weston Schelz, Aug. 31, 1979; children: Leah, Daniel. BA magna cum laude, Bklyn. Coll., 1964; MA, U. Calif., Berkeley, 1967, PhD, 1972. Lectr. U. San Francisco, 1969-70; acting instr. U. Calif., Berkeley, 1970-71; vis. instr. Rutgers U., New Brunswick, N.J., 1971-72; asst. prof. urban policy Grad. Ctr. CUNY, N.Y.c., 1973-74, asst. prof. govt. John Jay Coll. Criminal Justice, 1974-79, assoc. prof. govt., 1979-92; pres. Nat. Assn. Scholars, Princeton, N.J., 1987—; bd. dirs. Nat. Alumni Forum, Washington, 1993—. Sr. editor Acad. Questions, 1987-91. Chmn. N.J. State adv. com. U.s. Civil Rights Commn., 1985-91, mem., 1991—. Am. Polit. Sci. Assn. congl. fellow, 1972. Mem. Phi Beta Kappa. Office: Nat Assn Scholars 575 Ewing St Princeton NJ 08540-2741*

BALCOM, ORVILLE, engineer; b. Inglewood, Calif., Apr. 20, 1937; s. Orville R. and Rose Mae (Argo) B.; B.S. in Math., Calif. State U., Long Beach, 1958, postgrad., 1958-59; postgrad. UCLA, 1959-62; m. Gloria Stadtmiller, July 23, 1971; children—Cynthia, Steven. Engr., AiResearch Mfg. Co., 1959-62, 64-65; chief engr. Meditron, El Monte, Calif., 1962-64; chief engr. Astro Metrics, Burbank, Calif., 1965-67; chief engr., gen. mgr. Varadyne Power Systems, Van Nuys, Calif., 1968-71; owner, chief engr. Brown Dog Engring., Lomita, Calif., 1971—. Mem. IEEE Computer Group, Independent Computer Cons. Assn. Patentee in field. Club: Torrance Athletic. Home: 24521 Walnut St Lomita CA 90717-1260 Office: PO Box 427 Lomita CA 90717-0427

BALCOMB, SCOTT HULL, mathematics educator; b. Ganado, Ariz., Jan. 18, 1953; s. George Spencer and Donna Jean (Hull) B.; m. Abigail Sanborn, Aug. 23, 1980; children: Theo Wilson, Hallie Spencer. BS, Bates Coll., 1975; MS, Oreg. State U., 1978. Instr. Boise (Idaho) State U., 1977-78, Phillips Exeter (N.H.) Acad., 1978-89; asst. prof. math. St. Joseph's Coll., Standish, Maine, 1989—. Author/co-author study guides: Elementary Statistics, 1992, Social Inquiry, 1995, Scientific Inquiry, 1996. Avocation: dairy farming. Office: St Josephs Coll 278 Whites Bridge Rd Standish ME 04084-5236

BALDACCI, JOHN ELIAS, congressman; b. Bangor, Maine, Jan. 30, 1955; m. Karen Weston; 1 child, Jack. BA in History, U. Maine, 1986. With Momma Baldacci's Restaurant, Bangor; mem. Bangor City Coun., 1978-82, Maine State Senate, 1982-94, 104th-105th Congress from 2nd dist., 1994—; Mem. agr. com. Maine State Senate, transp. com., regional whip North East. Democrat. Office: US House Reps 1740 Longworth Bldg Washington DC 20515-1902*

BALDASSARE, LOUIS J., school superintendent. Supt. Highlands Sch. Dist., Natrona Heights, Pa., 1986—; designer early childhood/early intervention program. Recipient Leadership for Learning award Am. Assn. Sch. Adminstrs., 1995. Office: Highlands Sch Dist California at 11th Ave PO Box 288 Natrona Heights PA 15065-0288*

BALDASSARI, ROBERT GENE, accountant; b. Springfield, Ill., Feb. 7, 1949; s. George John and Celesta Doreen (Combs) B.; m. Robyn Lynda Copeland (div. Mar. 1982); 1 child, Brandon; m. Susan Rae Smetzer, Oct. 6, 1984; children: Stephen, Amanda. BS in Acctg., Strayer Coll., 1975; MS in Taxation, Southeastern U., 1980. Tax mgr. Berlin, Karam & Ramos, Silver Spring, Md., 1981-86; tax ptnr. Brown, Dakes & Wannall, Fairfax, Va., 1986-96; ptnr. Matthews, Carter & Boyce, McLean, Va., 1996—; internat. liaison Ptnr. for DFK Internat., chmn. 1995-96; lectr. in field; adj. prof. taxation. Contbr. articles to profl. jours. Mem. planned giving com. Alexandria (Va.) Hosp. Found., Inova Fairfax Hosp.; mem. curriculum adv. bd. Strayer Univ., Washington. Recipient Outstanding Leadership award Strayer Coll., Washington. Mem. Va. Soc. CPAs (chmn. state tax com. 1989-91, mem. profl. ethics com. 1995-97, no. chpt. treas. 1991-92, sec. 1992-93, v.p. 1993-94, pres. 1994-95, Pres.'s award 1990-91, bd. dirs. 1996-99). Avocation: magic. Home: 9221 Dellwood Dr Vienna VA 22180-6122 Office: Matthews Carter & Boyce 8200 Greensboro Dr Ste 1000 Mc Lean VA 22102-3864

BALDASSARRO, ANTHONY, human resources professional; b. Deliceto, Italy, Oct. 2, 1960; came to U.S., 1981; s. Rocco and Carmela (D'Innocenzio) B. BS in Computer Sci., Montclair State U., 1990. Cert. compensation profl. Overseas Assignments Inventory. Supr. Servometer Corp., Cedar Grove, N.J., 1984-86; adminstr. internat. pers. Prudential Ins. Co., Newark, 1986-91, cons. internat. svcs., 1991-94, mgr. internat. human resources, 1994-97, dir. internat. human resources, 1997—. Vol. Prudential Cares, 1996-97, Jersey Cares, Morristown, N.J., 1997. Mem. Nat. Fgn. Trade Coun. (chmn. expatriate mgmt. com. 1997-98), Soc. for Internat. Human Resources, Am. Compensation Assn., Internat. Pers. Assn. Avocations: music, soccer, photography, travel. Office: Prudential Ins Co 751 Broad St Newark NJ 07102-3714

BALDASSIN, MICHAEL ROBERT, secondary school educator; b. Tacoma, Wash., July 26, 1955; s. Robert Allen and Mary Lee (Hager) B.; Mary Katherine Hartman, Oct. 10, 1981; children: Jessica, Corrine, Beau, Kaylee. BS in Sociology, U. Wash., 1980. Profl. football player San Francisco 49ers, 1977-80; police officer Seattle Police dept., 1980-83, Oakland (Calif.) Police Dept., 1983-91; Wash. state dir. drug and alcohol Fellowship of Christian Athletes, Kansas City, Mo., 1991-92; tchr., head football coach Bellarmine Prep, Tacoma, 1992—. Bd. dirs. youth adv. Sparrow Found., Seattle, 1995—. Decorated Medal of Valor, Oakland Police Dept., 1985; named Coach of Yr. Nat. Football Found., 1996. Avocation: horseback riding. Office: Bellarmine Preparatory High Sch 2300 S Washington St Tacoma WA 98405-1304

BALDAUF, KENT EDWARD, lawyer; b. Pitts., Feb. 6, 1943; s. Walter William and Esther (Burr) B.; m. Kathleen Dian Abels, June 10, 1967; children: Kent Edward Jr., Krista K., Kara K. BS in Metall. Engring., Carnegie Mellon U., 1964; JD, Cleve. State U., 1970. Bar: Pa. 1970, U.S. Patent and Trademark Office 1971, U.S. Ct. Appeals (Fed. cir.) 1990, U.S. Supreme Ct. 1977. Shareholder, v.p., dir. Webb Law Firm, Pitts., 1988—. Editor Cleve. State U. Law Rev., 1969-70. Mem. ABA, Pa. Bar Assn., Allegheny County Bar Assn., Am. Intellectual Property Law Assn. (pres. 1998-99), Pitts. Intellectual Property Law Ass n., Engrs. Soc. Western Pa., Valley Brook Country Club, Duquesne Club. Home: 480 Clubview Dr McMurray PA 15317-3023 Office: The Webb Law Firm 436 7th Ave Pittsburgh PA 15219-1826

BALDER, JAMES ELLSWORTH, infosystems specialist; b. Foley, Minn.; s. Ellsworth Edward and Alvina Mary (Rau) B.; m. Alberta M. Milton, Oct. 20, 1956; children: Cindy, James W., Timothy W., Rene Ann, Richard E. Student, U. Minn., 1956-57. Lead programmer Honeywell, Mpls., 1954-60; data processing mgr. North Am. Life and Casualty, Mpls., 1961-66; ops. mgr. Pullman, Inc., Hammond, Ind., 1966-69; operations mgr. Sci. Computers Inc., Mpls., 1969-76; v.p. ops. Warrington Assocs., Hopkins, Minn., 1977-86; v.p. mgmt. info. systems Dataserv, Inc., Eden Prairie, Minn., 1986-89; v.p. ops. Image Integration Inc., Eden Prairie, Minn., 1990-91; tech. svc. rep. Digital Solutions, Inc., Bloomington, Minn., 1992-95; ret., 1995; systems cons. Computer Related Mpls., 1956-95. With U.S. Army, 1951-54. Mem. Data Processing Mgrs. Assn. Republican. Roman Catholic.

BALDERSTON, WILLIAM, III, retired banker; b. Madison, Wis., Dec. 10, 1927; s. William and Susan (Ramsay) B.; m. Ruth McKinney; children: William IV, David M., Peter R., Mary M. Grad., Dartmouth Coll., 1950. With Philco Corp., 1951-64; with Lincoln First Banks, Inc. (various locations), 1966-84; pres., chief exec. officer Chase Lincoln First Bank, N.A., Rochester, N.Y., 1984-91, vice chmn., 1991-92; exec. v.p. Chase Manhattan Corp., 1991-93; ret., 1993; bd. dirs. Rochester Gas & Electric Corp., Bausch & Lomb, Inc., Home Properties of N.Y. Trustee U. Rochester. With USNR, 1945. Mem. Country Club Rochester, Genesee Valley Club. *

BALDESCHWIELER, JOHN DICKSON, chemist, educator; b. Elizabeth, N.J., Nov. 14, 1933; s. Emile L. and Isobel (Dickson) B.; m. Marlene R. Konnar, Apr. 15, 1991; children from previous marriage: John Eric, Karen Anne, David Russell. B. Chem. Engring., Cornell U., 1956; Ph.D., U. Calif. at Berkeley, 1959. From instr. to asso. prof. chemistry Harvard U., 1960-65; faculty Stanford (Calif.) U., 1965-71, prof. chemistry, 1967-71; chmn. adv. bd. Synchrotron Radiation Project, 1972-75; vis. scientist Synchrotron Radiation Lab., 1977; dep. dir. Office Sci. and Tech., Exec. Office Pres., Washington, 1971-73; prof. chemistry Calif. Inst. Tech., Pasadena, 1973—; chmn. div. chemistry and chem. engring. Calif. Inst. Tech., 1973-78; OAS vis. lectr. U. Chile, 1969; spl. lectr. in chemistry U. London, Queen Mary Coll., 1970; vis. scientist Bell Labs., 1978; mem. Pres.'s Sci. Adv. Com., 1969—, vice chmn., 1970-71; mem. Def. Sci. Bd., 1973-80, vice chmn., 1974-76; mem. carcinogenesis adv. panel Nat. Cancer Inst., 1973—; mem. com. planning and instl. affairs NSF, 1973-77; adv. com. Arms Control and Disarmament Agy., 1974-76; mem. NAS Bd. Sci. and Tech. for Internat. Devel., 1974-76, ad hoc com. on fed. sci. policy, 1979, task force on synfuels, 1979, Com. Internat. Security and Arms Control, 1992-95—; mem. Pres.'s Com. on Nat. Medal of Sci., 1974-76, pres., 1986-88, Pres.'s Adv. Group on Sci. and Tech., 1975-76; mem. governing bd. Reza Shah Kabir U., 1975-79; mem. Sloan Commn. on Govt. and Higher Edn., 1977-79, U.S.-USSR Joint Commn. on Sci. and Tech. Coop., 1977-79; vice chmn. del. on pure and applied chemistry to China, 1978; mem. com. on scholarly communication with China, 1978-84; chmn. com. on comml. aviation security NAS, 1988—, mem. def. sci. bd. task force on 'operation desert shield', 1990-91, mem. com. on internat. security and arms control, 1991-94—; mem. rsch. adv. coun. Ford Motor Co., 1979-94—, mem. chem. and engring. adv. bd., 1981-83; vis. lectr. Rand Afrikaans U., Johannesburg, South Africa, 1987, Found. Rsch. and Devel., Pretoria, South Africa, 1989. Mem. editorial adv. bd. Chem. Physics Letters, 1979-83, Jour. Liposome Rsch., 1986—. Served to 1st lt. AUS, 1959-60. Sloan Found. fellow, 1962-64, 64-65; recipient Fresenius award Phi Lambda Upsilon, 1968, Tolman award ACS, 1989. Mem. NAS, Am. Chem. Soc. (award in pure chemistry 1967, William H. Nichols medal 1990), Council on Sci. and Tech. for Devel., Am. Acad. Arts and Scis., Am. Philos. Soc. Home: PO Box 50065 Pasadena CA 91115-0065 Office: Divsn Chemistry & Chem Engring Calif Inst Tech # 127-72 Pasadena CA 91125*

BALDINE, JOANNE, academic administrator, researcher; b. Youngstown, Ohio, Dec. 5, 1950; d. Joseph James and Mary (Balash) B.; m. Robert Scanlan, June 4, 1983; 1 child, Robert Harris. BA, St. Louis U., 1972; MA, U. Hawaii, 1975, PhD, 1993. Rsch. intern East-West Ctr., Honolulu, 1980-81; rsch. asst. Harvard Law Sch., Cambridge, Mass., 1989-90, asst. dir. East Asian Legal Studies, 1994—; rsch. assoc. Am. Repertory Theatre, Cambridge, Mass., 1991-94. Asst. dir. (play) Crimes of the Heart, 1988. Mem. Poets Theatre, Cambridge, 1990—. Grantee NDEA, 1972, MIT, 1988. Mem. Soc. Philosophy and Tech., Am. Philos. Assn., Assn. Asian Studies, Japan Soc. Boston. Office: Harvard Law School Pound Hall 420 1563 Massachusetts Ave Cambridge MA 02138-2996

BALDING, BRUCE EDWARD, investment executive; b. Chgo., Oct. 15, 1931; s. John Barnard Balding and Dorothy (Davis) Jackson; m. Barbara Whitney, Feb. 25, 1955 (div.); 1 child, Elizabeth Balding Ruprecht. AB, Harvard Coll., 1953; MA, Harvard U., 1954. Pres. Van Cleef Jordan & Wood, N.Y.C., 1970-71, Controlled Equities, Inc., N.Y.C., 1970-80; v.p. Hamilton Gregg Capital, N.Y.C., 1977-80, pres., 1980-84; pres. Balding & Co., N.Y.C., 1983—; dir. Power Constrn. Co., Thomas, W.Va., 1990—. Bd. dirs. Davis & Elkins Coll., 1980-90; vis. bd. mem. Walnut Hill Sch., Natick, Mass., 1992—; pres. Nat. Inst. Social Scis., N.Y.C., 1994. Lt. U.S. Army, 1955-57, Korea. Recipient Citation, Republic of Korea, 1957. Mem. N.Y. Soc. Security Analysts, New Eng. Soc., The Pilgrims, Links Club, Piping Rock Club, Harvard Club N.Y., Harvard Club Mass. Republican. Episcopalian. Avocations: golf, tennis. Home: 549 Sagamore St Tidewatch 54 Portsmouth NH 03802

BALDINO-GLOSTER, TARA, critical coronary care nurse; b. Phila., Apr. 17, 1971; d. Louis and Jean (Cannavo) B.; married, Sept. 5, 1998. BSN, Thomas Jefferson U., 1994, postgrad., 1995—. RN, Pa. State RN intermediate coronary care unit Thomas Jefferson U., Phila., 1994-96, surg. coronary care RN, 1996—. Nursing Edn. grant Thomas Jefferson U., 1992, 93. Mem. Advanced Assn. of Critical Care Nurses, Sigma Theta Tau. Roman Catholic. Avocations: playing piano, family and friends. Office: Thomas Jefferson Univ Hosp 11th and Chestnut Sts Philadelphia PA 19107

BALDOCK, BOBBY RAY, federal judge; b. Rocky, Okla., Jan. 24, 1936; s. W. Jay and S. Golden (Farrell) B.; m. Mary Jane (Spunky) Holt, June 2, 1956; children: Robert Jennings, Christopher Guy. Grad., N.Mex. Mil. Inst., 1956; JD, U. Ariz., 1960. Bar: Ariz. 1960, N.Mex. 1961, U.S. Dist. Ct. N.Mex., 1965. Ptnr. Sanders, Bruin & Baldock, Roswell, N.Mex., 1960-83; adj. prof. Eastern N.Mex. U., 1962-81; judge U.S. Dist. Ct. N.Mex., Albuquerque, 1983-86, U.S. Ct. Appeals (10th cir.), 1986—. Mem. N.Mex. Bar Assn., Chaves County Bar Assn., Ariz. Bar Assn., Phi Alpha Delta. Office: US Ct Appeals PO Box 2388 Roswell NM 88202-2388

BALDRIDGE, MELINDA E., psychiatric nurse specialist; b. Newport News, Va., Dec. 18, 1957; d. Richard Kemp and Genevieve (Carlisle) Easley. BSN, Pittsburg (Kans.) State U., 1979; MA, Webster U., 1987; MS in Nursing Adminstrn., Georgetown U., 1991. RN, Kans, ANCC. Commd. 2d lt. U.S. Army, advanced through grades to lt. col.; clin. staff nurse medicine U.S. Army, Ft. Leonard Wood, Mo., 1979-80; clin. staff nurse psychiatry and orthopedic units U.S. Army, Bad Canstatt, Germany, 1980-81; clin. staff nurse psychiatry unit U.S. Army, Frankfurt, Germany; from asst. head nurse to head nurse psychiatry unit Womack Army Community Hosp. U.S. Army, Ft. Bragg, N.C., 1983-85; from clin. staff nurse to ward head nurse Walter Reed Army Med. Ctr., Washington, 1987-89; quality assessment dir. and edn. dir. Nat. Naval Med. Ctr., Bethesda, Md., 1991—; dept. head TRISARD, NNMC, 1992-95; chief psychiat. nursing svc. Tripler Med. Ctr., Hawaii, 1995—; adj. faculty dept. psychiatry Uniformed Svcs. U. Health Scis., Bethesda, Md. Mem. AAUW, ANA, Nat. Nurses Soc. Addictions, Am. Coun. Nursing Adminstrn., Assn.Mil. Surgeons U.S. (sect. nursing), Va. Nurses Assn., Washington Soc. Eating Disorders, Sigma Theta Tau. Home: 51-278 Kamehameha Hwy Kaaawa HI 96730

BALDRIGE, LETITIA, writer, management training consultant; b. Miami Beach, Fla.; d. Howard Malcolm and Regina (Connell) B.; m. Robert Hollensteiner; children: Clare, Malcolm. BA, Vassar Coll., 1946; postgrad., U. Geneva, 1946-48; D.H.L. (hon.), Creighton U., 1979, Mt. St. Mary's Coll., 1980, Bryant Coll., 1987, Kenyon Coll., 1990. Personal-social sec. to amb. Am. Embassy, Paris, 1948-51; intelligence officer Washington, 1951-53; asst. to amb. Am. Embassy, Rome, 1953-56; dir. pub. rels. Tiffany & Co., 1956-60; social sec. The White House, 1961-63; pres. Letitia Baldrige Enterprises, Chgo., 1964-69; dir. consumer affairs Burlington Industries, 1969-71; pres. Letitia Baldrige Enterprises, Inc., N.Y.C. and Washington, 1972—. Author: Roman Candle, 1956, Tiffany Table Settings, 1958, Of Diamonds and Diplomats, 1968, Home, 1972, Juggling, 1976, Amy Vanderbilt's Complete Book of Etiquette, 1978, Amy Vanderbilt's Everyday Etiquette, 1979, Entertainers, 1981, Letitia Baldrige's Complete Guide to Executive Manners, 1985, Letitia Baldrige's Complete Guide to a Great Social Life, 1987, Complete Guide to the New Manners for the '90s, 1990, New Complete Guide to Executive Manners, 1993, (novel) Public Affairs Private Relations, 1990, More Than Manners! Raising Today's Kids to Have Kind Manners and Good Hearts, 1997, In the Kennedy Style, 1998; columnist Copley News Syndicate; editor Exec. Advantage Newsletter; contbg. editor Town & Country Mag. Adv. bd. Woodrow Wilson House, Washington, Reading Is Fundamental, ARC Mus. Republican.

BALDUCCI, CAROLYN FELEPPA, writer; b. Feb. 13, 1946. BA, Manhattanville Coll., 1967. Mem. creative writing faculty U. Mich., Ann Arbor, 1977—. Author various novels, screenplays, poetry and translations. E-mail: balducci@umich.edu. Office: 624 5th St Ann Arbor MI 48103-4877

BALDWIN, ALEC (ALEXANDER RAE BALDWIN, III), actor; b. Massapequa, N.Y., Apr. 3, 1958; s. Alexander Rae Jr. and Carol (Martineau) B.; m. Kim Basinger, August 19, 1993,1995, daughter Ireland Eliesse. Student, George Washington U., 1976-79, NYU, 1979-80; studies with Marcia Haufrecht, Lee Strasberg Theater Inst., N.Y.C., 1979-80; studies with Mira Rostova, N.Y.C., 1982, 87, studies with Elaine Aiken. Ind. actor, 1980—. actor: (TV series) Cutter to Houston, 1982, The Doctors, 1980-82, Knot's Landing, 1984-85; TV movies Love on The Run, 1985, A Streetcar Named Desire, 1995, Dress Gray (miniseries), 1986, The Alamo: 13 Days to Glory, 1986, Sweet Revenge, 1990; (films) Forever Lulu, 1987, She's Having a Baby, 1987, Beetlejuice, 1988, Married to the Mob, 1988, Great Balls of Fire, 1989, Talk Radio, 1988, Working Girl, 1988, The Hunt for Red October, 1990, Miami Blues, 1990, Alice, 1990, The Marrying Man, 1991, Prelude to a Kiss, 1992, Glengarry Glen Ross, 1992, Malice, 1993, The Getaway, 1994, The Shadow, 1994, Heaven's Prisoners, 1995, Looking For Richard, 1996, The Juror, 1996, Heaven's Prisoners, 1996, Ghosts of Mississippi, 1996, Bookworm, 1997, The Edge, 1997, Thick as Thieves, 1998, Outside Providence, 1998, Mercury Rising, 1998, (also prodr.) The Confession, 1999, Notting Hill, 1999; (on Broadway) Loot (Theatre world award 1986),1986, Serious Money, 1988, Prelude to a Kiss (Obie Award), 1990, A Streetcar Named Desire, 1992; guest appearances include The Simpsons (voice), Larry Sanders Show, Inside the Actors Studio. Recipient Theater World award Theater World Pubs., 1986; named Outstanding New Talent on Broadway. Mem. SAG, AFTRA, Actors Equity Assn. Democrat. Roman Catholic. *

BALDWIN, ALLAN OLIVER, information scientist, higher education executive; b. Chgo., Apr. 10, 1948; s. Albert Oliver and Virginia Josephine (Stack) B.; m. Suzanne Balasty, Nov. 28, 1969 (div.); m. Janice Louise DiVito, Jan. 25, 1992; children: Steven, Jennifer, Jeremy, Matthew, Katherine. BS, U. Ill., Chgo., 1969; MBA, Keller Grad. Sch. Mgmt., 1982. Asst. systems mgr. U. Ill., Chgo., 1970-76, asst. dir. info. systems svcs., 1976-79, dir. hosp. info. svcs., 1979-86; dir. systems devel. Loyola U. Chgo., Maywood, Ill., 1986-88, asst. v.p. info. systems, 1988-90, acting v.p. info. tech., 1990-92, v.p. info. tech., 1992—. Chmn. parent human rels. com. Oak Park (Ill.)-River Forest High Sch., 1991. Mem. Coll. and Univ. Systems Engrs., Healthcare Info. Mgmt. Systems Soc., Med. Info. System Assn. Home: 1100 N East Ave Oak Park IL 60302-1230 Office: Loyola Univ Chicago 2160 S 1st Ave Bldg 201 Maywood IL 60153-3304

BALDWIN, ALLEN ADAIL, lawyer, writer; b. St. Augustine, Fla., July 15, 1939; s. Larrie Paul and Bertha Mae (Capallia) B. BA, Brigham Young U., 1969; JD, So. U., Baton Rouge, 1975. Bar: Fla. 1975. Tchr. Putnam County Sch. Bd., Palatka, Fla., 1969-71; pvt. practice Palatka, 1975—. Author: Tricks to Make the Angels Weep, 1986, Call It Not Heaven, 1991, Redeem Us From Virtue, 1992. Mem. Latter-day Saints Ch. Avocations: reading, swimming, hiking. Office: 308 Saint Johns Ave Palatka FL 32177-4723

BALDWIN, ANTHONY BLAIR, systems theoretician, agricultural executive; b. Pontiac, Mich., June 15, 1928; s. Dwight Clare and Naomi Joyce (Clark) B.; m. Erma Lu Moore, June 1952 (div. July 1953); m. Ann Joering Doyen, Sept. 25, 1955 (div. Jan. 1980); children: Kimberly Claire, Laura Brooks, Barron Todd. Student, Western Mich. U., 1948-50, U. Detroit, 1952, Cleve. State U., 1954-56, Case Western Res. U., 1960, U. Nebr., 1967, Edinboro U., 1985-87. Lic. realtor. Dir. fin. City of Euclid, Ohio, 1957-65; v.p., bd. dirs. Grand Traverse Corp., Farmington, Mich., 1969-76; bus. mgr. Cleve. State U., 1965-70; assoc. Donald W. Gropp & Assocs., Cleve., 1970-71; borough mgr. Borough of Grove City, Pa., 1971-72, Borough of Wilkinsburg, Pa., 1972-73; city mgr. City of Forest Grove, Oreg., 1973-74; owner A.B. Baldwin Devel. Enterprises, Sunnyside, Wash., 1974-84, Property Prospectors, Cochranton, Pa., 1988—; pres., founder The LIVING Inst. and Highland Hills Farms AgriTech. Ctr., Cochranton, Pa., 1988—, also bd. dirs. Author: The General Theory of Equilibration and the Universal Fairshare System; contbr. articles to profl. jours. and poetry to Am. Poetry Anthology, The Nat. Libr. of Poetry; presenter in field. Leader various Rep. orgns., Ohio, 1953-71, various civic orgns., Ohio, Pa., Oreg. and Wash., 1953-97; chair task force for devel. Cleve. State U. Urban Renewal Project Plan, 1965-66; leader various presdl. campaigns, 1955-92; chmn. Planning and Zoning Commn., Granger, Wash., 1977; candidate for treas. State of Ohio, 1970. With U.S. Army, 1946-48, Japan. Recipient Gold medal-Louisville award Mcpl. Fin. Officers Assn. U.S. and Can., Phila., 1965, Buckeye award Mcpl. Fin. Officers Assn. Ohio, 1964, Disting. Svc. award Jr. C. of C., Euclid, 1962, scholarship Pa. State System Higher Edn. Honors Program, Shippensburg U., 1987, others. Mem. Am. Assn. Ret. Persons, SCORE, "We the people..." (founder, pres. 1994-96), Internat. Platform Assn., Environ. Alliance for Sr. Involvement, Inst. Noetic Scis., HALT Ams. for Legal Reform, N.Am. Assn. for Environ. Edn. (WS chmn. 1993), Nat. Resources Def. Coun., Earth Island Inst., Granger C. of C. (pres. 1976-77), Chautauqua Network, Internat. Soc. Poets, Planners Network, Ocean Reef Yacht Club, El Dorado Ranch, Thousand Trails, Masons, Sigma Tau Gamma. Unitarian. Avocations: politics, writing, poetry, painting, sailing. Office: Highland Hills Farms AgriTech Ctr 8274 DeVillars Rd Cochranton PA 16314-9219

BALDWIN, BETTY JO, computer specialist; b. Fresno, Calif., May 28, 1925; d. Charles Monroe and Irma Blanche (Law) Inks; m. Barrett Stone Baldwin Jr. (dec. 1998); two daughters. AB, U. Calif., Berkeley, 1945. With NASA Ames Rsch. Ctr., Moffett Field, Calif., 1951-53, math tech. 14' Wind Tunnel, 1954-55, math analyst 14' Wind Tunnel, 1956-63, supr. math analyst structural dynamics, 1963-68, supervisory computer programmer structural dynamics, 1968-71, computer programmer theoretical studies, 1971-82, adminstrv. specialist astrophys. experiments, 1982-85, computer specialist, resource mgr. astrophysics br., 1985—; v.p. B&B Baldwin Farms, Bakersfield, Calif., 1978-98. Mem. IEEE, Assn. for Computing Machinery, Am. Geophys. Union, Am. Bus. Womens Assn. (pres., v.p. 1967, one of Top 10 Women of Yr. 1971). Presbyterian. Avocations: reading, bridge, hiking. Office: NASA Ames Rsch Ctr Mail Stop 245-6 Moffett Field CA 94035-1000

BALDWIN, BRUCE GREGG, botany educator, researcher; b. San Luis Obispo, Calif., Oct. 24, 1957; s. Robert Lee and Sally Louise (Elrod) B. BA in Biol. Scis. with honors, U. Calif., Santa Barbara, 1981; MS in Botany, U. Calif., Davis, 1985, PhD in Botany, 1989. NSF postdoctoral fellow U. Ariz., Tucson, 1990-92; asst. prof. dept. botany Duke U., 1992-94; curator Jepson Herbarium, asst. prof. in residence dept. integrative biology U. Calif., Berkeley, 1994-98, assoc. prof. residence dept. integrative biology, 1998—; Mellon vis. scholar Rancho Santa Ana Botanic Garden, 1994; rare plant cons. U.S. Fish & Wildlife Svc., Calif. Dept. Fish & Game, Calif. Native Plant Soc. Spl. Pub.; sci. cons. D.C. Health and Co., 2d edit. Biology: Discovering Life, TV series The Secret of Life, PBS, 1993, TV prodn. The Silversword Alliance BBC, 1990; lectr. in field. Contbr. articles to profl. jours. and books, reviewer; chief editor Jepson Flora project, 1994—. Recipient NSF Nat. Young Investigator award, 1994; Jastro-Shields grad. rsch. scholar, 1986-87, 87-88; Henry A. Jastro fellow, 1986-87, Dupont Summer rsch. fellow, 1987, Regents fellow, 1987-88; NSF dissertation improvement grantee, 1987-89, Duke U. Arts and Scis. Rsch. Coun. grantee, 1993-94, NSF Divsn. Environ. Biology rsch. grantee, 1994-97. Mem. Am. Soc. Plant Taxonomists (publicity com. 1993—, George R. Cooley award 1993). Achievements include research in plant systematics, phylogenetics, plant cytogenetics and chromosome evolution, plant speciation, California floristics, phytogeography, insular evolution. Avocations: backpacking, canoeing, fly fishing, traveling. Home: 2408 Parker St Berkeley CA 94704-2812 Office: U Calif Berkeley Jepson Herbarium Dept Integrative Biology 1001 Valley Life Scis Bldg 2465 Berkeley CA 94720-2465

BALDWIN, CALVIN BENHAM, JR., retired medical research administrator; b. Radford, Va., Dec. 22, 1925; s. Calvin Benham and Louise (Delp) B.; m. Elizabeth Buell, Mar. 10, 1951; children: Susan B., Sally C., Ann H. AB, U. N.C., 1949; postgrad., N.C., 1949-51; MPA, Harvard U., 1961. Research asst. Inst. Research Social Scis., Chapel Hill, N.C., 1949-50; methods examiner NIH, Bethesda, Md., 1953-55, budget examiner, 1955-57, adminstrv. officer, 1957-58, adminstrv. officer div. gen. med. sci., 1958-61;

exec. officer Divsn. Gen. Med. Scis., Bethesda, Md., 1961-62, Nat. Inst. Child Health, Bethesda, Md., 1963-70, Nat. Cancer Inst., Bethesda, Md., 1970-80; assoc. dir. adminstrn. NIH, Bethesda, 1980-86. Mem. Montgomery County Econ. Coun., Rockville, Md., 1982-85, Bethany Beach (Del.) Town Coun., 1991-92, 94-96. With U.S. Army, 1944-46, ETO. Recipient W.A. Jump meritorious award HEW, 1960; recipient Superior Service award HEW, 1973. Mem. NIH Alumni Assn. (pres. 1995-97), Phi Beta Kappa. Democrat. Unitarian. Home: 10705 Weymouth St Garrett Park MD 20896-0017

BALDWIN, CARLA SUZANN, psychologist; b. Bristol, Tenn., Sept. 21, 1954; d. Carl E. and Carolyn R. (Broce) B.; m. Thomas E. May, June 29, 1986; 1 child, Hannah Baldwin-May. BA in Psychology summa cum laude, Cleve. State U., 1983, MA in Psychology, 1985. Lic. psychologist, Pa. Psychologist PSI, Cleve., 1986-89, Shaler Area Sch. Dist., Glenshaw, Pa., 1990-95, Seneca Valley Sch. Dist., Harmony, Pa., 1995—. Contbr. articles to psychol. reports. Bd. dirs. Children's Meml. Fund, Pitts., 1997. Mem. Nat. Assn. Sch. Psychologists (cert.), Gaia Circle, Psi Chi. Office: Seneca Valley Sch Dist 124 Seneca School Rd Harmony PA 16037-9101

BALDWIN, CHARLES FRANKLIN, JR., automotive executive; b. Aberdeen, Md., May 15, 1916; s. Charles Franklin and Ruby Hood (Arthur) B.; m. Margaret Anne Forster, Apr. 1, 1940; Margot Ann, John Thomas, James Douglas. BA in Econs., George Washington U., 1941, postgrad., 1942-43. Asst. to chief ordnance officer U.S. Army, Washington, 1940-46; asst. to dir. Reconstruction Fin. Corp., Washington, 1946-48; chief stats. and reports Marshall Plan ECA, Washington, 1948-49; successively mgr. profit analysis, comptr., asst. plant. mgr. tractor plant, truck planning mgr., special projects mgr. Ford Motor Co., Dearborn, Mich., 1949-60, dir. internat. product planning, 1961-62; v.p. truck ops. Europe Ford Motor Co., London, 1963-72; chmn., pres. Zenith Time, LeLock, Switzerland, 1973-75; chief procurement and prodn. tank automotive command U.S. Army, Warren, Mich., 1976-88; cons. on tank design and prodn. various fgn. govts. Trustee First Presbyn. Ch., Dearborn; deacon Southfield United Presbyn. Ch., Southfield, Mich.; active arts couns. Southfield, Petoskey (Mich.), others. Mem. Soc. Automotive Engrs., Assn. Govt. Accountants, Detroit Inst. Arts (founders soc.), Bay View Assn., U. S. Yacht Racing Union, Petoskey Arts Coun. Republican. Methodist. Avocations: golf, boating, travel. Home and Office: 15101 Ford Rd Ste 410 CC Dearborn MI 48126-4611

BALDWIN, CLARENCE JONES, JR., electrical engineer, manufacturing company executive; b. San Antonio, Aug. 8, 1929; s. Clarence Jones and Viola Laura Baldwin; m. Audrey Jean Dayen, June 9, 1957; children: Elizabeth, Theodore, Laura, Barbara. BS in Elec. Engring., U. Tex., 1951, MS in Elec. Engring., 1952; EE, MIT, 1957; PMD, Harvard U. Bus. Sch., 1969. Regisered profl. engr., Pa. Elec. engr. Westinghouse Electric Corp., Pitts., 1952-62, engring. mgr., 1962-80, 89, divsn. mgr., 1980-88; engring. mgr. Asea Brown Boveri, inc., Pitts., 1990, Muncie, Ind., 1991-94; cons. Baldwin Assocs., Pitts., 1994—; mem. Engring. Accreditation Commn., N.Y.C., 1979-84. Contbr. numerous articles to profl. publs. Mem. exec. bd. Greater Pitts. coun. Boy Scouts Am., 1967-91, 97—, v.p., 1985-87, 89-91, pres., 1987-89. Named Outstanding Young Elec. Engr., Eta Kappa Nu, 1961, Disting. Engring. Grad., U. Tex., 1967; Am. Inst. Elec. Engrs. Fortescue fellow, 1951; Westinghouse Electric Corp. Lamme scholar, 1956. Fellow IEEE (life), Edgewood Country Club (Pitts.). Repubican. Methodist. Office: Baldwin Assocs 552 10th Ave New Brighton PA 15066-0276

BALDWIN, DANIEL, actor; b. Massapequa, N.Y., Oct. 5, 1960; s. Alexander Rae and Carol Newcomb (Martineau) B. BS Psych., Ball State U. film appearances include: Born on the Fourth of July, 1989, Harley Davidson and the Marlboro Man, 1991, Knight Moves, 1992, Lone Justice, 1994, Dead on Sight, 1994, Car 54, Where Are You?, 1994, Bodily Harm, 1995, Yesterday's Target, 1996, Twisted Desire, 1996, Trees Lounge, 1996, Mulholland Falls, 1996, The Invader, 1997, The Treat, 1998, On the Border, 1998, Love Kills, 1998, Vampires, 1998, Phoenix, 1998, Water Damage, 1999, Net Worth, 1999, Killing Moon, 1999; TV movies include: Too Good to Be True, 1988, L.A. Takedown, 1989, The Heroes of Desert Storm, 1991, Ned Blessing: The True Story of My Life, 1992, Attack of the 50-Foot Woman, 1993, Family of Cops, 1995; TV series include: Sydney, 1990, Homicide: Life on the Streets, 1993—. Address: Reeves Entertainment PO Box 16258 Beverly Hills CA 90209-2258*

BALDWIN, DANIEL FLANAGAN, mechanical engineer, researcher, educator; b. Fort Collins, Colo., Jan. 4, 1965; s. Lionel Vernon and Kathleen Baldwin; m. Kristen Jean Schamberger, Aug., 1989; children: Kelsey Rae, Patrick Flanagan, Christopher Glenn. BS in Engring. summa cum laude, Ariz. State U., 1988; MS, MIT, 1990, PhD, 1994. Engr. in tng., Ariz. Software analyst Colo. State U., Fort Collins, 1984, 85, rsch. asst., 1986; engring. intern Mitsubishi Electric Corp., Kamakura, Japan, 1987; Draper fellow C.S. Draper Lab., Cambridge, Mass., 1988-90; rsch. mgr. MIT, Cambridge, 1990-94; mem. tech. staff AT&T Bell Labs., Princeton, N.J., 1994-95; asst. prof. George W. Woodruff Sch. Mech. Engring. Ga. Inst. Tech., Atlanta, 1994—; gen. chair 3d Internat. Advanced Tech. Workshop; tech. program chair for the 2d internat. advanced tech. workshop on low cost flip chip tech., Internat. Microelectronics and Packaging Soc., 1998; symposium organizer The Pacific RIM/ASME Internat. Intersoc. Electronic and Photonic Packaging Conf., 1997, 99; co-chair Pacific RIM/ASME Internat. Intersoc. Electronic and Photonic Packing Conf., 1999. Referee Robotics and Computer-Integrated Mfg., 1992-94, ASME Jour. Sys. Dynamics and Control, 1996, Internat. Jour. Engring. Design and Automation, 1996, IEEE Transactions on Components, Packaging and Mfg. Tech., 1996—, Polymer Engring. and Sci.; contbr.: Computer-Aided Mechanical Assembly Planning, 1991; contbr. articles to IEEE Transactions in Robotics and Automation, Jour. Engring. Materials and Tech., Polymer Engring. and Sci., Jour. Japan Soc. of Polymer Processing, Rsch. in Engring. Design, Biomaterials, Internat. Jour. Microcircuits and Electronic Packaging, among others. Recipient Outstanding Rsch. Faculty of Yr. award, NSF Engring. Rsch. Ctr., 1996, 98, Milton C. Shaw Outstanding Young Mfg. Engring. award Soc. Mfg. Engrs. Mem. ASME (electric and electronic packaging divsn. Outstanding Young Engr. award 1998), IEEE, Am. Soc. Engring. Edn., Internat. Microelectronics and Packaging Soc., Surface Mount Tech. Assn., Soc. Mfg. Engrs., Soc. Plastics Engrs., Sigma Xi, Pi Tau Sigma, Tau Beta Pi, Phi Kappa Phi. Achievements include patent for microcellular foamed materials using supercritical fluids; patent for processing microcellular/supermicrocellular plastics; patents pending for injection molding of microcellular plastics; sheet extrusion of microcellular plastics; low-cost materials and processes for metallizing and bumping semiconductor devices; snap cure of underfill and flip chip interconnect of high I/O devices; research in advanced electronics packaging; materials processing, manufacturing system design; polymer processing, microelectronics manufacturing and assembly. Office: Ga Inst Tech George W Woodruff Sch Mech Engring Atlanta GA 30332-0405

BALDWIN, DAVID ALLEN, political science educator; b. Indpls., July 28, 1936; s. James Howell and Pearl Mabel (Fisher) B.; m. Marilyn Claire Austin, Aug. 10, 1957 (div. Sept. 1990); children: Sarah, Rebecca, Emily; m. Helen Virginia Milner, May 24, 1991. AB, Ind. U., 1958; MA, Princeton U., 1961, PhD, 1965; MA (hon.), Dartmouth Coll., 1978. Asst. prof. govt. Dartmouth Coll., Hanover, N.H., 1965-70, assoc. prof. govt., 1970-75, John S. Dickey Prof., 1975-80, prof. govt., 1980-85; prof. polit. sci. Columbia U., N.Y.C., 1985-89, Ira Wallach Prof., 1989—; dir. Inst. of War and Peace Studies, Columbia U., 1987-94. Author: Foreign Aid, 1966, Economic Statecraft, 1985 (Kammerer award 1986), Paradoxes of Power, 1989, Economic Development and Foreign Policy, 1966; editl. bd. Internat. Orgn., 1984-97, Polit. Sci. quar., N.Y.C., 1989-94, Jour. Internat. Affairs, 1988—. Mem. Coun. on Fgn. Rels., N.Y.C., 1986—. 1st lt. U.S. Army, 1962-63. Recipient Moffat Econs. prize Ind. U., Bloomington, 1958, fellowships German Marshall Fund, Washington, 1982-83, Brookings Instn., Washington, 1964-65, Danforth Found., St. Louis, 1958-64. Mem. Am. Polit. Sci. Assn. (recipient Kammerer award 1986), Internat. Polit. Sci. Assn., Internat. Studies Assn., British Internat. Studies Assn., Acad. Polit. Sci., Phi Beta Kappa. Home: 450 Riverside Dr New York NY 10027-6801 Office: Inst of War & Peace Studies Columbia University 420 W 118th St New York NY 10027-7213

BALDWIN, DAVID GREGORY, technical support representative; b. Ft. Lauderdale, Fla., Dec. 9, 1966. BA in History, Whitman Coll., Walla Walla, Wash., 1989. Auto Doc DOS developer Corbel, Jacksonville, Fla., 1994-97, Auto Doc certifier, 1997-98, tech. support rep., 1998—. Bd. dirs., editor newsletter Stewards St. Johns River, Jacksonville, 1992, 93, bd. dirs. , 1995, 96. Mem. N.E. Fla. Anthropol. Soc., Sierra Club. Democrat. Avocations: environmentalist, photographer. Home: PO Box 16653 Jacksonville FL 32245-6653

BALDWIN, DAVID RAWSON, retired university administrator; b. New Haven, Nov. 2, 1923; s. Albert A. and Hilda (Rawson) B.; m. Dorothy Elizabeth Sonstrom, June 19, 1948; children: Dwight Rawson, Brian Mark, James Albert. B.S. in Govt., U. Conn., 1947; M.P.A. (Volker fellow 1948-49), Wayne State U., 1949. Research asst. Conn. Pub. Expenditure Council, Hartford, 1948-50; exec. sec. Fayette County br. Pa. Economy League, Uniontown, 1950-51; chief assessor Fayette County, 1952-56; fiscal adviser to Pa. gov.-elect George Leader, 1954; research asso. Pa. Economy League, Pitts., 1956-59; budget sec. State of Pa., 1959-64, exec. asst. to treas., 1964-65; asst. sec. U.S. Dept. Commerce, 1965-69; v.p. bus. and finance Wayne State U., Detroit, 1969-71; assoc. v.p. for fin. affairs, asst. treas. Temple U., Phila., 1972-85; ret. Temple U., 1985; N.E. regional dir. Nat. Assn. State Budget Officers, 1962-64; cons. HEW, 1964. Served to lt. (j.g.) USNR, 1944-46. Mem. Am. Soc. Pub. Adminstrn., Nat. Assn. Coll. and U. Bus. Officers (chmn. com. on ins. 1970-72), Theta Xi (pres. 1947). Presbyn. (ruling elder). Home: 85 Runnymede Ave Jenkintown PA 19046-2016

BALDWIN, DAVID SHEPARD, physician; b. Rochester, N.Y., Sept. 5, 1921; s. Jacob and Anna B.; m. Halee Morris, June 24, 1945; children—Neil, Andrew, Daniel, James. B.A., U. Rochester, 1943, M.D., 1945. Intern Barnes Hosp., St. Louis, 1945-46; resident in medicine Bellevue Hosp., N.Y.C., 1946-48; renal fellow in medicine and physiology N.Y. U. Sch. Medicine, 1948-50, mem. faculty, 1950—, prof. medicine, co-dir. nephrology div., 1972—; attending physician Bellevue Hosp.; attending physician N.Y. U. Hosp.; cons. nephrology VA Hosp., N.Y.C.; mem. med. adv. bd. council high blood pressure research Am. Heart Assn. Author papers in med. jours., chpts. in books. Served as officer M.C. AUS, 1953-55. Mem. Am. Fedn. Clin. Research, Harvey Soc., Am. Heart Assn., Am. Soc. Nephrology, Am. Soc. Clin. Investigation, Internat. Soc. Nephrology, N.Y. Soc. Nephrology (pres. 1974-75), N.Y. Heart Assn. Home: 333 E 69th St New York NY 10021-5549 Office: 550 1st Ave New York NY 10016-6481 also: 20 E 68th St New York NY 10021-5844

BALDWIN, DEANNA LOUISE, dietitian; b. Oklahoma City, Okla., Jan. 14, 1946; d. Jesse Burlin and Celena Mae (Robison) Smith; m. James Stephen Baldwin, Apr. 7, 1989; 1 child, Melissa. BS, Stephen F. Austin, 1985. Dietetic tech. Pasadena (Tex.) Bayshore Hosp., 1969-70; payroll clk. Seismic Computing Corp., Houston, 1971-72; restaurant mgr., mgr. trainer H. Salt Fish n' Chips, Pasadena, 1972-75; asst. food svc. dir. East Tex. Med. Ctr. Hosp., Tyler, 1990-92; profl. network marketer, 1992—; sales woman Mary Kay Cosmetics, 1995—. Avocations: singing, sewing, cooking, crafts.

BALDWIN, DEWITT CLAIR, JR., physician, educator; b. Bangor, Maine, July 19, 1922; s. DeWitt Clair and Edna Frances (Aikin) B.; m. Michele Albre, Dec. 27, 1957; children: Lisa Anne, Mireille Diane. BA, Swarthmore Coll., 1943; postgrad. Div. Sch., Yale U., 1943-45, MD, 1949. Diplomate Am. Bd. Med. Examiners, Am. Bd. Pediatrics, Am. Bd. Family Practice. Intern, then resident in pediatrics U. Minn. Hosps., Mpls., 1949-51; rsch. fellow Yale Child Study Ctr., New Haven, Conn., 1951-52; instr., asst. prof. pediatrics U. Washington Sch. Medicine, Seattle, 1952-57; resident in psychiatry Met. State Hosp., Waltham, Mass., 1957-58; chief resident in psychiatry Mass. Meml. Hosps., Boston, 1958-59; fellow in child psychiatry Boston City Hosp., 1959-61; asst. prof. pediatrics Harvard Med. Sch., Boston, 1961-67; prof., chmn. behavioral scis. and community health U. Conn. Health Ctr., Farmington, 1967-71; prof. chmn. behavioral scis. U. Nev. Sch. Medicine, Reno, 1971-73, dir. health scis. program, 1971-81, prof. psychiatry and behavioral scis., 1971-83, asst. dean rural health, 1977-83, prof. emeritus psychiatry and behavioral scis., 1983—; pres. Earlham Coll. and Earlham Sch. Religion, Richmond, Ind., 1983-84; pres. Connor Prairie Pioneer Settlement Mus., Noblesville, Ind., 1983-84, dir. office edn. research, 1985-88, dir. divsn. med. edn., rsch., info., 1988-91, scholar-in-residence, 1991—; adj. prof. psychiatry and behavioral scis. Northwestern U. Med. Sch., Chgo., 1986—, 1986—; adj. prof. med. edn. U. Ill. Coll. Medicine, Chgo., 1988-93; pres. Med. Edn. and Rsch. Assocs., Inc., Chgo., 1992—; trustee Friends World Coll., Huntington, N.Y., 1980-83; bd. dirs. Nat. League Nursing, N.Y.C., 1981-83, Gt. Lakes Colls. Assn., 1983-84, Am. Rural Health Assn., 1985-87; mem. Nat. Bd. Med. Examiners, 1979-88, Nat. Adv. Coun. Nursing Tng., 1978-82; mem. coun. acad. socs. AAMC, Washington, 1987-94. Author: (with others) Behavioral Sciences and Medical Education, 1983, other books; author, editor: (with others) Interdisciplinary Health Care Teams in Teaching and Practice, 1981, Interdisciplinary Health Team Training, 1978; contbr. over 150 articles to scholarly publs. Recipient Rsch. Career Devel. award USPHS, 1961-67, Louis Gorin award in rural health, 1991, John P. McGovern award Health Scis., 1997; Commonwealth Fund fellow, 1951-52, Milbank Fund fellow, 1968, Rural Health fellow WHO, 1976. Mem. Assn. Behavioral Scis. and Med. Edn. (pres. 1978-79, 90-91), Nev. Bd. Oriental Medicine (pres. 1976-83). Democrat. Mem. Soc. of Friends.

BALDWIN, DONALD JAMES, II, software developer; b. Montgomery, Ala., July 1, 1963; s. Donald James and Sharon Ann Baldwin; m. Rachel Ann Dickerson, Sept. 5, 1998. BS in Info. Sys., U. Tex., Arlington, 1998. Dir. engring. support ASR Strategic Resources, Arlington, 1990—. Mem. Assn. Info. Tech. Profls. (pres. U. Tex. Arlington chpt. 1997, 98, local coord. 1999 nat. collegiate conf. 1999, java contest coord. nat. collegiate conf. com. 1999—, 1st place visual basic regional collegiate programming competition 1998, 3rd place visual basic nat. collegiate programming competition 1998), U.S. Naval Inst., Navy League U.S., Beta Gamma Sigma. Republican. Episcopalian. E-mail: don.baldwin@pobox.com. Fax: 817-557-5535. Office: ASR Strategic Resources 3307 Cambridge Dr Arlington TX 76013

BALDWIN, ED, coach; b. Mar. 21, 1954; m. Terri Baldwin; children: Shandia, Stevon. Grad., N.C. Ctrl. U., 1976. Asst. coach N.C. State U., 1985-88; head coach girls basketball U. N.C., Charlotte, 1988—; asst. coach U.S.A. Women's Basketball Select team, 1996, U.S.A. Basketball's World U. Games Gold Medal Team, 1997, U.S.A. Basketball's Olympic Festival North Team, 1993; ct. coach U.S. Women's Olympic Team Trials, 1988, Inaugural Women's NBA Tryout Camp, 1997. Named Raleigh Times and Raleigh Sports Club Coach of Yr.; recipient gold medal World U. Gamess Team, Italy, 1997. Office: U NC Charlotte Athletics 9201 University City Blvd Charlotte NC 28223*

BALDWIN, EDWIN STEEDMAN, lawyer; b. St. Louis, May 5, 1932; s. Richard and Almira (Steedman) B.; m. Margaret Kirkham, July 1, 1958; children: Margaret B. Dozler, Edwin S. Jr., Harold K. AB, Princeton U., 1954; LLM, Harvard U., 1957. Bar: Mo. 1957, U.S. Dist. Ct. (ea. dist.) Mo. 1957. Assoc. Teasdale, Kramer & Vaughan, St. Louis, 1957-64; ptnr. Armstrong, Teasdale, Schlafly & Davis, St. Louis, 1965-97, of counsel, 1998—. Fellow Am. Coll. Trust and Estate Counsel, St. Louis Country Club, Noonday Club. Republican. Episcopalian. Avocations: golf, hunting, sailing. Office: Armstrong Teasdale LLP 1 Metropolitan Sq Ste 2600 Saint Louis MO 63102-2740

BALDWIN, FRANK BRUCE, III, lawyer; b. Phila., Oct. 18, 1939; s. Frank Bruce and Eleanor Elizabeth (Dutton) B.; m. Joan L. Crowell, June 23, 1962; children: Elisa Rose, Bruce Andrew, Christopher Dutton. AB cum laude, Harvard U., 1961; LLB magna cum laude, U. Pa., 1964; LLM, U. London, 1965. Bar: Pa. 1966, Calif. 1967, U.S. Ct. Appeals (3d cir.) 1982. Vis. asst. prof. law U. Pa., 1965-66; acting assoc. prof. law U. Calif.-Davis, 1966-69; assoc. Morgan, Lewis & Bockius, Phila., 1969-72, 73-74; v.p., gen. counsel A.V.C. Corp., Phila., 1972-73; asst. gen. counsel IU Internat. Corp., Phila., 1974-82; ptnr. Saul, Ewing, Remick & Saul, Phila., 1982-83, Ehmann & Baldwin, 1983-85, Obermayer, Rebmann, Maxwell & Hippel, 1985-90; shareholder, dir. Baldwin Renner Clark & Buckwalter, PC, 1990—; stated clk. Presbytery of Phila. Gowen fellow, 1964-65. Mem. ABA, Pa. Bar Assn., Phila. Bar Assn., State Bar Calif., Order of Coif. Republican. Presbyterian. Club: Union League of Phila., Rittenhouse. Reporter Del. Criminal Code, Proposed Ofcl. Draft, 1967. Office: 987 Old Eagle School Rd Ste 705 Wayne PA 19087-1708

BALDWIN, FREDERICK STEPHEN, priest; b. Syracuse, N.Y., Aug. 11, 1946; s. Robert Frederick and Elizabeth (Thompson) B.; m. Elizabeth Carter, July 14, 1972 (div.); 1 child, Elizabeth Thompson. AB, Georgetown U., 1968; MDiv, Episcopal Div. Sch., 1976. Ordained as priest Episcopal Ch., 1977. Curate Holy Trinity Ch., N.Y.C., 1976-79; dir. pub. rels. Assn. Episcopal Colls., Nat. Hdqrs. Episcopal Ch., N.Y.C., 1979-82; assoc. rector St. James' Ch., N.Y.C., 1982-85; rector St. Bernard's Ch., Bernardsville, N.J., 1985—; chaplain Ch. Ctr. of UN, N.Y.C., 1979—, Episcopal cons., 1978—; pres. St. Martin's Retreat House, Bernardsville, 1985—. Bd. dirs. YMCA, Somerset Hills, 1987—, Harlem Sch. of Arts, N.Y.C., 1976-85, Lead Poison Control, Onondaga County, N.Y., 1971-73; mem. staff Office of Senator Robert F. Kennedy, Washington and Syracuse, 1965-68; capt. Police Dept. Lt. USN, 1968-73. Mem. Coll. of Preachers, Holland Lodge (chaplain). Home: The Rectory 29 Stevens St Bernardsville NJ 07924 Office: St Bernard's Ch Claremont Rd Bernardsville NJ 07924-2226

BALDWIN, GARZA, JR., lawyer, manufacturing company executive; b. Litchfield, Ill., Mar. 10, 1921; s. Garza and Hazel (Satterlee) B.; m. Margaret Jean Skinner, Sept. 7, 1946; children: Deborah Baldwin Lyman, Garza III, Beth Baldwin Johnson, Daniel David, Benjamin Willis. Student, Vincennes U., 1938-39; BS, Ind. U., 1942, JD with high distinction, 1948. Bar: Ind. 1948, U.S. Supreme Ct. 1956, N.C. 1959. Practiced in Indpls., Sullivan, Ind., 1948-57; city atty. Sullivan, 1951-55; asso. counsel Olin Corp., Pisgah Forest, N.C., 1957-58; div. counsel Olin Corp., 1958-63, sr. counsel, 1963-69, v.p., counsel fine paper and film group, 1969, v.p. corp. group fine paper and film, 1969-71, pres. group, 1971-85, v.p. parent co., 1969-85; pres., chief exec. officer Ecusta Corp., 1985-87; bd. mgrs. Wachovia Bank & Trust Co., Asheville, N .C., 1969-90; mem. Gov.'s Council for Econ. Devel., 1967-68, Gov.'s Efficiency Study Commn., 1973-74, N.C. Council on State Policies and Goals, 1974-78; mem. Gov.'s Bus. Council on Arts and Humanities, 1981-89; bd. dirs. N.C. Citizens for Bus. and Industry, 1970-92, v.p., 1972-73, chmn., 1974-75; bd. dirs. Ednl. Found. Commerce and Industry N.C., 1965-73, U. N.C. at Asheville Found., 1971-90, N.C. Engring. Found. Trustee Transylvania Cmty. Hosp., Brevard, N.C., 1969-83, Brevard Coll., 1978-86, St. Andrews Presbyn. Coll., Laurinburg, N.C., 1978-81, U. N.C., Asheville, 1974-77, N.C. Sch. Sci. and Math., 1985-91; chmn. bd. dirs. Mem. Mission Med. Ctr., Asheville, 1986, treas., 1989-93, bd. dirs., 1981-95; mem. adv. coun. to dean Sch. Bus. Ind. U.; mem. acad. alumni fellows Ind. U.; bd. dirs. Cmty. Found. Western N.C., 1990-96, Asheville chpt. ARC, 1990-95. Lt. (j.g.) USNR, 1942-45. Mem. ABA, Ind. Bar Assn., N.C. Bar Assn., Western Carolina Mfrs. Assn. (pres. 1962-71), N.C. Indsl. Coun. (pres. 1966-67), Am. Judicature Soc., Am. Legion, Order of Coif, Masons (32 degree), Elks, Biltmore Forest Country Club, Colleton River Country Club (Bluffton, S.C.), Country Club of N.C. (Pinehurst). Republican. Presbyterian. Home: 422 Crowfields Dr Asheville NC 28803-3276

BALDWIN, GEORGE CURRIDEN, physicist, educator; b. Denver, May 5, 1917; s. Harry Lewis and Elizabeth (Watson) B.; m. Winifred M. Gould, Apr. 27, 1952; children—George T., John E., Celia M. BA, Kalamazoo Coll., 1939; MA, U. Ill., 1941, PhD, 1943. Instr. physics U. Ill., Urbana, 1943-44; rsch. assoc. GE, Schenectady, N.Y., 1944-55; nuclear engr. GE, Cin., 1955-57; reactor mgr. Argonne (Ill.) Nat. Lab., 1957-58; physicist Gen. Engring. Lab. GE, Schenectady, 1958-67; adj. prof. nuclear engring. and sci. Rensselaer Poly. Inst., Troy, N.Y., 1964-67, prof., 1967-77, prof. emeritus, 1977—; staff mem. Los Alamos (N.Mex.) Nat. Lab., 1975-87; vis. scientist, 1987-99, ret., 1992. Author: An Introduction to Nonlinear Optics, 1969; contbr. articles on nuclear and radiation physics to sci. publs. Councilman, Niskayuna, N.Y., 1965-69; mem. Zoning Bd., 1969-77. Recipient Disting. Alumnus award Kalamazoo Coll., 1987. Fellow Am. Phys. Soc.; mem. AAAS, Phi Beta Kappa, Sigma Xi, Phi Kappa Phi, Gamma Alpha. Achievements include discovery of nuclear giant dipole resonance; research on gamma-ray lasers; discovery of 1776 Escalante inscription.

BALDWIN, GEORGE KOEHLER, retail executive; b. Cedar Rapids, Iowa, Nov. 17, 1919; s. Nathan and Ada Lillian (Kohler) B. BBA, State U. Iowa, 1942. From office mgr. to mgr. Wapsie Valley Creamery, Cedar Rapids, Iowa, 1946-60; treas., head payroll, accounts payable, sales audit dept. Armstrong's Inc., Cedar Rapids, 1960-87; also bd. dirs., treas. Armstrong's of Dubuque, Iowa, 1960-87; ret., 1987. Composed and copyrighted for band Kinnick Stadium band march, 1992. Mem. Cedar Rapids Performing Arts Commn.; bd. dirs., pres. Cedar Rapids Cmty. Concert Assn.; pres. State U. of Iowa Concert Band, 1941-42; sec., treas., asst. conductor El Kahir Shrine Band of Cedar Rapids; bd. dirs. Cedar Rapids Stamp Club; chmn. adminstrv. bd. Trinity United Meth. Ch., 1987-92, head usher and staff parish rels. com.; apptd. by mayor to Cedar Rapids Mcpl. Band Commn., 1994, vice chmn. 1998-2000. With U.S. Army, 1942-46, ETO. Decorated Bronze Star medal; named hon. Ky. Col.; George K. Baldwin day proclamation in his honor, Mayor of Cedar Rapids, Apr. 16, 1987. Mem. VFW, Cedar Rapids Consumer Credit Assn. (pres. 1968-69), Am. Theatre Organ Soc. (bd. dirs., treas. Cedar Rapids chpt.), Am. Legion, Rotary, Masons, Shrineres (past pres. uniformed units), Rotary Svc. Club (chmn. fellowship com., sgt. of arms), State U. Iowa Pres.'s Club. Methodist. Home: 1017 F Ave NW Cedar Rapids IA 52405-2724

BALDWIN, GORDON BREWSTER, lawyer, educator; b. Binghamton, N.Y., Sept. 3, 1929; s. Schuyler Forbes and Doris Ambeline (Hawkins) B.; m. Helen Louise Hochgraf, Feb., 1958; children: Schuyler, Mary Page. LLB, Cornell U., 1953; BA, Haverford Coll., 1950. Bar: N.Y. 1953, Wis. 1965. Pvt. practice Rochester and Rome, N.Y., 1953-57; prof. law U. Wis., Madison, 1957-99, Evjue-Bascom profl. law, 1991-99; emeritus prof. U. Wis., Masidon, 1999—; assoc. dean law U. Wis., Madison, 1968-70; dir. officer edn. U. Wis., 1972-99; of counsel Murphy & Desmond, S.C., Madison, Wis., 1986-95; chmn. internat. law U.S. Naval War Coll., 1963-64; Fulbright prof., Cairo, 1966-67, Tehran, Iran, 1970-71; lectr. State Dept., Cyprus, 1967, 1969, 1971; counselor internat. law U.S. Dept. State, Washington, 1975-76, cons., 1976-77; vis. prof. Chuo U., Tokyo, 1984, Giessen U., Fed. Republic Germany, 1987, 92, Thommasat U., Thailand, 1997; cons. U.S. Naval War Coll., 1961-65; chmn. screening com. on law Fulbright Program, 1974; mem. constl. law com. Multi-State Bar Exam, 1972-82; chmn. State Pub. Def. Bd., 1980-83, Wis. Elections Bd., 1991-96; cons., rep. Marshall Island Constn. Conv., 1990. Mem. Wis. Bd. Elections, 1991-95, Wis. head coun., 1998—. Ford Found. fellow, 1962-63. Fellow Am. Bar Found.; mem. AAUP (nat. coun. 1975-78, pres. Wis. conf. 1986-87), Bar Assn. (vice chmn. sect. on individual rights 1973-75), Fulbright Alumni Assn. (dir. 1979-82), Am. Law Inst., Order of Coif, Madison Club, Madison Lit. Club (pres. 1985-86), Univ. Club, Rotary (pres. Madison 1980), Phi Beta Kappa. Home: 3958 Plymouth Cir Madison WI 53705-5212 Office: U Wis 975 Bascom Mall Sch Law Madison WI 53706-1399

BALDWIN, HAROLD SCOTT, pediatrician; b. Honolulu, Md., Dec. 22, 1954. MD, U. Va. Sch. Medicine, 1981. Diplomate Am. Bd. Pediatrics. Intern U. Rochester/Strong Meml. Hosp., N.Y., 1982-86, resident in pediatrics; asst. prof. Children's Hosp., Phila.; fellow in pediatric cardiology U. Iowa Coll. Med., Iowa City, 1986-90. Recipient Established Investigator award Am. Heart Assn., 1995. Office: Children's Hosp Phila 3516 Civic Center Blvd Philadelphia PA 19104-4318*

BALDWIN, HENRY FURLONG, banker; b. Balt., Jan. 15, 1932; s. Henry du Pont and Margaret (Taylor) B.; div.; children: Mary Stevenson, Severn Eyre. AB, Princeton U., 1954. With Merc.-Safe Deposit & Trust Co., Balt., 1956—, v.p., 1963-65, sr. v.p., 1965, exec. v.p., 1965-70, pres., 1970-76, chmn. bd., CEO, 1976—; pres. Merc. Bankshares Corp., 1970-84, CEO, 1976—, also chmn. bd. dirs.; bd. dirs. Constellation Energy Group, Inc., CSX Corp., Merc. Safe Deposit & Trust Co., GRC Internat., Offitbank, Wills Group, Inc., St. Paul Cos.; mem. bd. dirs. Nat. Assn. Securities Dealers, Inc. Bd. trustee Johns Hopkins Hosp., chmn., 1989-94; bd. trustees Johns Hopkins U. With USMC, 1954-56. Office: Merc Bankshares Corp PO Box 1477 Baltimore MD 21203-1477

BALDWIN, IRA LAWRENCE, retired bacteriologist, educator; b. 1895. BS in Agrl. Chemistry, Purdue U., 1919, MS in Agrl. Chemistry, 1921, DSc (hon.), 1945; PhD in Bacteriology, U. Wis., 1926, DSc (hon.), 1972. Instr. bacteriology Purdue U., Lafayette, Ind., 1919-24; asst. prof. bacteriology Purdue U., Lafayette, 1924-25, assoc. prof. physiology Experiment Sta., 1926; asst. prof. bacteriology U. Wis., Madison, 1927-29, assoc. prof. bacteriology, 1929-32, asst. dean Coll. Agr., prof. bacteriology, 1932-

42, chmn. dept. bacteriology, 1941-44, dean Grad. Sch., 1944-45, dean Coll. Agr., dir. Agrl. Experiment Sta., 1945-48, dir. agrl. ext. svcs., 1945-48, v.p., 1948-58, spl. asst. to the pres., 1958-66, v.p. emeritus, prof. bacteriology emeritus, 1966—; under contract svc. agy. internat. devel. U. Wis. and U.S. Dept. State, 1966-76. Contbr. articles to profl. jours. Mem. NEA (emeritus), AAAS (emeritus), Am. Soc. for Microbiology (hon., sec.-treas. 1935-42, v.p. 1943, pres. 1944), Agrl. History Soc. (emeritus), Am. Forestry Assn. (emeritus), Am. Inst. Biol. Scis. (emeritus), Am. Phytopathol. Soc. (emeritus), Am. Soc. Plant Physiology (emeritus), Ind. Acad. Sci. (emeritus), Royal Soc. Arts-Eng. (emeritus), Soc. for Exptl. Biology and Medicine (emeritus), Soc. for Internat. Devel. (emeritus), Soil Conservation Soc. Am. (emeritus), Alpha Zeta, Phi Lambda Upsilon, Sigma Xi, Phi Beta Kappa, Phi Eta Sigma, Phi Kappa Phi. Home: 5026 E South Regency Cir Tucson AZ 85711-3040

BALDWIN, IRENE S., corporate executive, real estate investor; b. Dodge City, Kans., Sept. 8, 1939; d. Albert A. McMichael and Eleanor L. (Johnson) McMichael McGrath; m. Miles Edward Baldwin, June 30, 1961. BS, Friends U., 1961. Dress designer, Wichita, 1959-61; social worker Sedgwick County, Kans., 1963-65; owner motel chain, Kans., 1965—; comml. and agrl. real estate investor, 1971—; corp. sec.-treas. Baldwin, Inc., Kans., 1970—, fin. advisor, 1970—; pvt. practice fin. cons., Colby, Kans., 1975—; founder, advisor Charitable Found., Kans., 1980—. Fundraiser various charitable orgns., 1982—; pvt. placement of homeless animals, Kans. and Nebr., 1965—. Helped develop 1st artificial front leg for canines, 1985. Avocations: horseback riding, hiking, travel, sewing, drawing. Home and Office: 2320 S Range Ave Colby KS 67701-9056

BALDWIN, JAMES EDWIN, civil engineer, land development executive; b. Naylor, Ga., Jan. 22, 1924; s. Camillus Edwin and I. Elizabeth (Ledford) B.; m. Janet Smith, 1950 (div. 1981); children: Gary E., Janet C. BSCE, Ga. Inst. Tech., 1949. Registered profl. engr., Ga., S.C. Prin. Baldwin Engring. Co., Augusta, Ga., 1953-68; pres. Baldwin & Cranston Assocs., Inc., Cons. Engrs., Augusta, 1968-81, Columbia Land Corp., Augusta, 1964—; arbitrator Am. Arbitration Assn., Charlotte, N.C., 1981—; chmn. Augusta-Richmond County Planning and Zoning Commn., 1968-81. Mem. Richmond County Bd. Equalization, Augusta, 1978. Lt. (j.g.) USN, 1942-45. Mem. ASCE (past chpt. pres.), Ga. Soc. Profl. Engrs. (past state dir.), Augusta Country Club. Presbyterian. Avocations: hunting, fishing, golf. Home and Office: 4900 Columbia Rd Grovetown GA 30813-5208

BALDWIN, JAMES WILLIAM, lawyer; b. Inglewood, Calif., Dec. 4, 1923; s. Carl H. and Mary Agnes (Roberds) B.; married, June 1950; children: Carl, James, Mary, John, Linda. BA, Whittier Coll., 1949; LLB, UCLA, 1952. Bar: Calif. 1953. Dep. atty. gen. State of Calif., L.A., 1952-53; assoc. Thelen, Marrin, Johnson & Bridges, L.A., 1953-62, mng. ptnr., 1962—. With USMC, 1943-45, PTO. Mem. Calif. Bar Assn. Clubs: Calif. (L.A.); Newport Harbor Yacht (Newport Beach, Calif.). Home: 1368 Wilbury Rd San Marino CA 91108-2129*

BALDWIN, JANICE MURPHY, lawyer; b. Bridgeport, Conn., July 16, 1926; d. William Henry and Josephone Gertrude (McKenna) Murphy; m. Robert Edward Baldwin, July 31, 1954; children: Jean Margaret, Robert William, Richard Edward, Nancy Josephine. AB, U. Conn., 1948; MA, Mt. Holyoke Coll., 1950; postgrad., U. Manchester, Eng., 1950-51; MA, Tufts U., 1952; JD, U. Wis., 1971. Bar: Wis. 1971, U.S. Dist. Ct. (we. dist.) Wis. 1971. Staff atty. legis. coun. State of Wis., Madison, 1971-74, sr. staff atty., 1975-94; pvt. practice, Madison, 1994—; atty. adviser HUD, Washington, 1974-75, 78-79. Mem. AAUW, NOW, LWV (sec., bd. dirs. Dane County 1996—, exec. com. 1997—), U.S. and Wis. Women's Polit. Caucus, Legal Assn. for Women (chmn. Marygold Meili award com. 1997—), Wis. Bar Assn. (pres. govt. lawyers divsn. 1985-87, bd. govs. 1985-89, treas. 1987-89, participation of women in bar com. 1987-98, professionalism com. 1990-97, bd. bar examiners rev. 1990-94, law-related edn. com. 1992-95, govt. lawyers divsn. 1981—), Dane County Bar Assn. (legis. com. 1980-81, long range planning com. 1990-97, law for the pub. com. 1993-94), Wis. Women's Network, U. Wis. Univ. League, Older Women's League. Home and Office: 125 Nautilus Dr Madison WI 53705-4329

BALDWIN, JEFFREY KENTON, lawyer, educator; b. Palestine, Ill., Aug. 8, 1954; s. Howard Keith and Annabelle Lee (Kirts) B.; m. Patricia Ann Mathews, Aug. 23, 1975; children: Matthew, Katy, Timothy, Philip R. BS summa cum laude, Ball State U., 1976; JD cum laude, Ind. U., 1979. Bar: Ind. 1979, U.S. Dist. Ct. (so. dist.) Ind. 1979, U.S. Ct. Appeals (7th cir.) 1979, U.S. Dist. Ct. (no. dist.) Ind. 1984. Mem. majority leader's staff Ind. Senate, Indpls., 1976; instr. Beer Sch. Real Estate, Indpls., 1977-78, Am. Inst. Paralegal Studies, Indpls., 1987—; dep. Office Atty. Gen., Indpls., 1979-81; mng. ptnr. Baldwin & Baldwin, Danville, Ind., 1979—; agt. Nat. Attys. Title Assurance Fund, Vevay, Ind., 1983—; officer, bd. dirs. Baldwin Realty, Inc., Danville; conf. participant White House Conf. on Small Bus. (Ind. meeting 1994), congl. appointee, 1995; bd. dirs. Small Bus. Coun. Bd. dirs. Hendricks Civic Theatre, Inc.; organizer, Hendricks County Young Republicans, 1972; sec. Hendricks County Rep. Com., 1978-84; bd. dirs. Hendricks County Assn. for Retarded Citizens, Danville, 1982-86; cons. Hendricks County Right for Life, Brownsburg, Ind., 1984—; mem. philanthropy adv. com. Ball State U., Muncie, Ind., 1987—; judge Hendricks County unit Am. Cancer Soc., 1987; coordinator region 2 Young Leaders for Mutz, Indpls., 1987-88; cubmaster WaPaPh dist. Boy Scouts Am., 1988, S.M.E. chmn., 1988-89; steering com. Ind. Lawyers Bush/Quayle; founder, chmn. Christians for Positive Reform; candidate for Congress 7th Congl. Dist. of Ind.; del. to Annual Conf. South Ind. Conf. of United Meth. Ch., 1993, 95-98; host com. Midwest Rep. Leadership Conf., 1997; dist. coord. Hoosier Families for John Price for U.S. Senate. Recipient Presdl. award of honor Danville Jaycees, 1980; named hon. sec. State Ind., 1980. Mem. ABA, Ind. Bar Assn., Hendricks County Bar Assn., Indpls. Bar Assn., Internat. Platform Assn., Nat. Assn. Realtors, Ind. Assn. Realtors, Met. Indpls. Bd. Realtors (Hendricks County div.), Federalist Soc., Ind. Farm Bur., Nat. Fedn. Ind. Bus., Ind. C. of C., Danville C. of C. (sec. 1986), Moot Ct. Soc., Blue Key, Phi Soc. Methodist. Home: PO Box 63 Danville IN 46122-0063

BALDWIN, JEFFREY NATHAN, pharmacy educator; b. Sidney, N.Y., Dec. 20, 1947; s. Reverdy Ernest and Helen Elizabeth (Humphrey) B.; m. Suzanne Marie Smith, Dec. 27, 1969; children: Paul Kevin, Gregory Michael. AS, Jamestown C.C., 1967; BS in Pharmacy summa cum laude, SUNY, Buffalo, 1970; DPharm, U. Ky., 1973. Lic. pharmacist, Ky., Nebr. Resident in pharmacy U. Ky.-A.B. Chandler Med. Ctr., Lexington, 1970-73; pharmacy faculty U. Nebr. Med. Ctr., Coll. Pharmacy, Omaha, 1973—; med. faculty U. Nebr. Med. Ctr., Coll. Medicine, Omaha, 1977—; pres., co-founder Nebr. Coun. for Continuing Pharm. Edn., Inc., Omaha, 1980-82. Author: (chpts.) Points of Light: A Guide for Assisting Chemically Dependent Health Professional Students, 1996; sect. editor: Applied Therapeutics: The Clinical Use of Drugs, 1995; author 15 chpts. to books and over 20 articles to profl. jours. Chmn. Nebr. Pharmacist Recovery Network, Lincoln, Nebr., 1988—; chair tng. com. Mid Am. Coun., Boy Scouts, Omaha, 1997-98, scout leader, 1983—; counselor Camp CoHoLo, Gretna, Nebr., 1985-98. Recipient Leadership award McKesson, 1995. Fellow Am. Pharm. Assn. (Merit award 1995), Am. Soc. Health-Sys. Pharmacists (chair pediatric pharmacy spl. interest group 1977-78), Am. Assn. Colls. Pharmacy (chair substance abuse spl. interest group 1988-97, chair pharmacy practice sect. 1998-99), Nebr. Pharmacists Assn. (pres.-elect 1994-95, pres. 1995-96, chmn. bd. 1996-97, NARD Leadership award 1995). Avocations: travel, bicycling, backpacking, camping, whitewater rafting. Office: 982135 Nebr Med Ctr Omaha NE 68198-2135

BALDWIN, JOHN ASHBY, JR., retired naval officer; b. Balt., Apr. 20, 1933; s. John Ashby and Laura (Hanson) B.; m. Leslie Hall, Dec. 30, 1961; children: Charles Gambrill, Dorothy Sewell. B.S., U.S. Naval Acad., 1955; postgrad., U. Wash., 1962-64. Commd. ensign U.S. Navy, 1955, advanced through grades to vice adm., 1987; comdr. Destroyer Squadron 33, Pearl Harbor, Hawaii, 1975-77; dep. dir. Office of Program Appraisal, Office of Sec. of Navy, Washington, 1977-79; mil. asst. to Dep. Sec. Def., Washington, 1979-81; dir. Systems Analysis Div., Office of Chief of Naval Ops., Washington, 1980-82; comdr. Cruiser-Destroyer Group 3, 1982-84; dep. chief of staff for ops. and plans comdr. in chief U.S. Pacific Fleet, 1984-86; pres. Naval War Coll., Newport, R.I., 1986-87; dir. strategic plans and policy Joint Staff, Washington, 1987-89; pres. Nat. Def. U., Washington, 1989-92, retired, 1992. Decorated Def. D.S.M., Navy D.S.M., Legion of Merit, Bronze Star with combat V, Meritorious Service medal. Mem. U.S. Naval Inst. Episcopalian. Clubs: Nantucket Yacht, Wharf Rat, Metropolitan Club (Washington). Home: 2032 Ferry Farms Rd Annapolis MD 21402-1002

BALDWIN, JOHN CHARLES, surgeon, researcher; b. Ft. Worth, Sept. 23, 1948. BA summa cum laude, Harvard U., 1971; MD, Stanford U., 1975; MA Privatim (hon.), Yale U., 1989. Diplomate Am. Bd. Internal Medicine, Am. Bd. Surgery, Am. Bd. Thoracic Surgery. Fellow in medicine Harvard Med. Sch., Boston, 1975-77; fellow in surgery, resident in surgery Mass. Gen. Hosp., 1977-81; resident in cardiothoracic surgery Stanford (Calif.) U., 1981-82, chief resident cardiothoracic surgery, 1983, asst. prof., 1984-87; dir. heart-lung transplantation transplant rsch. lab. Stanford U., 1986-87; prof. surgery and chief cardiothoracic surgery Yale U., New Haven, 1988-94; cardiothoracic-surgeon-in chief Yale-New Haven Hosp.; DeBakey/Bard prof., chmn. Baylor Coll. Medicine, Houston, 1994-98; sr. attending physician, chief surg. svcs. Meth. Hosp., Houston, 1994-98; sr. attending physician, surgeon in chief Ben Taub Gen. Hosp., Houston, 1994; dean med. sch., v.p. health affairs Dartmouth U., 1998—; bd. dirs. United Network Organ Sharing, 1984-87; mem. clin. rsch. com. ad hoc rsch. grant rev. Cystic Fibrosis Found.; trustee New Eng. Organ Bank, 1988; mem. solid organ transplant com. Blue Cross & Blue Shield of Conn., 1990-94; mem. sci. adv. bd. Alexion Pharms., Inc., 1991-94; bd. dirs. Baylor Coll. Medicine Healthcare, Inc.; mem. adv. bd. Donate Life Found.; mem. exec. faculty Baylor Coll. of Medicine, pres.'s coun.; bd. dirs. New England chpt. Transplant Recipients Internat. Orgn., 1992-94. Co-editor: Thoracic Surgery, Oxford Textbook of Surgery, 1989—; assoc. editor Jour. Applied Cardiology, 1985-92; editorial bd. Jour. Thoracic and Cardiovascular Surgery, 1990-97, Transplantation, 1990—, Transplantation Sci., 1992-95, Andromeda Interactive Ltd., The Cardiovasc. System Interactive Teaching Program, 1993—; contbr. numerous articles and book chpts. in field. Mem. Harvard Club Schs. Com., Harvard Coll. Fund, Harvard U. Undergrad. Admissions Interview Com.; fellow Timothy Dwight Coll. Yale U., Yale U. Art Gallery Assocs.; mem. appointments and promotions com. Sch. Medicine, Yale U., 1991-94, bd. dirs. Neighborhood Music Sch. New Haven., 1989-92; bd. overseers Harvard U., 1995—; bd. permanent officers Yale U., 1988-94. John Harvard scholar, 1969, 70, Wendell scholar Harvard U., 1969, Rhodes scholar Oxford U., 1971, Alumni scholar Stanford Sch. Medicine, 1974 ; medalist Gothenburg (Sweden) Thoracic Soc., 1985; recipient Medaille de la Ville de Bordeaux French Thoracic Soc., 1987, travelling lectureship, 1988, Master Tchr. award Cardiovascular Revs. & Reports, 1990; travelling fellow Australia and New Zealand chpt., ACS, 1989; traveling lectureship, 1989. Fellow ACP, ACS, Royal Coll. Surgeons (Eng., traveling lectr. 1989), Am. Coll. Angiology, Am. Coll. Cardiology (mem. transplantation com. 1991-94, chmn. task force cardiac donor procurement Bethesda Conf. 1992), Am. Coll. Surgeons (bd. govs. 1993-97), Am. Coll. Chest Physicians, Mass. Med. Soc.; mem. AMA, AAAS, Am. Assn. Thoracic Surgery (mem. com. grad. edn. thoracic surgery 1992-97, chmn. Evarts A. Graham Meml. Traveling Fellowship com. 1993-99), Am. Soc. Transplant Surgeons (com. on heart transplantation 1986-89, adv. com. in issues 1989—, chmn. subcom. on heart transplantation, physician payment reform commn. 1989-92), Nat. Heart, Lung and Blood Inst. (cons. divsn. extramural affairs rev. br. 1990—), Assn. Acad. Surgery, Am. Physiol. Soc., Am. Heart Assn. (mem. rsch. grant peer rev. subcom 1984-87, coun. circulation, cert. of appreciation for outstanding svc. 1986), Am. Surg. Assn., Am. Thoracic Soc., Am. Soc. Artificial Internal Organs, Am. Soc. Extracorporeal Tech., Am. Assn. Lab. Animal Sci., Am. Organ Transplant Assn., Am. Venous Forum, Internat. Soc. Heart and Lung Transplantation (chmn. program com. 1988), Internat. Assn. Cardiac Biol. Implants, Internat. Fedn. Surg. Colls., Internat. Soc. Cardiovasc. Surgery, Internat. Soc. Cardio-Thoracic Surgeons (pres. 1999), Internat. Soc. for Heart Rsch. (mem. Am. sect.), Internat. Soc. for Artificial Organs, Mediterranean Assn. for Cardiology and Cardiac Surgery, New Century Soc., Thoracic Surgery Found. for Rsch. and Edn., Norman E. Shumway Surg. Soc., New Eng. Surg. Soc., Pan Am. Med. Assn. (coun. on organ transplantation), North Am. Soc. Pacing and Electrophysiology, Societe Internat. de Chirurgie, Royal Soc. Medicine, Soc. Univ. Surgeons, Thoracic Surgery Dirs. Assn. (chmn. curriculum com. transplantation 1993-94), Transplantation Soc., Assn. Alumni of Magdalen Coll. Oxford U., Assn. Rhodes Scholars, Acad. Surg. Rsch., Assn. Surg. Edn., Assn. Program Dirs. in Surgery, Conn. Thoracic Soc., Harris County Med. Soc., Calif. Med. Assn., Calif. Thoracic Soc., Calif. Thoracic Soc. Respiratory Care Assembly, No. Calif. Cystic Fibrosis Found., So. Calif. Transplant Soc., Conn. Med. Soc., Conn. Soc. Am. Bd. Surgeons, Mass. Med. Soc., N.Y. Soc. Thoracic Surgery, Harvard Med. Alumni Assn. (assoc.), Soc. Crit. Care Medicine, Soc. Thoracic Surgeons, Southeastern Surg. Congress, Southern Surg. Assn., Southwestern Surg. Congress, Tex. Surg. Soc., Halsted Soc., Houston Surg. Soc. Soc. for Organ Sharing, San Francisco Surg. Soc., Santa Clara Med. Soc., Stanford Med. Alumni Assn., Stanford Club Conn., Harvard Clubs San Francisco, Peninsula, N.Y.C., So. Conn., Houston, Boston, Mory's Assn., New Haven Lawn Club, Inner Quad Stanford U., The Hasty Pudding Club - Inst. 1770, Quinnipiack Club, Forum World Affairs, Ambs. Roundtable, Oxford Soc., Phi Beta Kappa, others. Office: Dartmouth U Office of the Dean Dartmouth Med Sch Hanover NH 03755

BALDWIN, JOHN EDWIN, chemistry educator; b. Berwyn, Ill., Sept. 10, 1937; s. Francis Miller and Irville (Miller) B.; m. Anne Kruesi Nordlander, Sept. 23, 1961; children—Claire Miller, John Nordlander, Wesley Hale. A.B. summa cum laude, Dartmouth Coll., 1959; Ph.D., Calif. Inst. Tech., 1963. Mem. chemistry faculty U. Ill., 1962-68; prof. chemistry U. Oreg., Eugene, 1968-84; dean Coll. Arts and Scis., 1975-80; prof. chemistry Syracuse U., N.Y., 1984—; cons. Stauffer Chem. Co., Office Sci. and Tech., NIH; 150th anniversary vis. prof. Chalmers U., 1990. Author: Experimental Organic Chemistry, 1965, also articles.; Adv. bd.: Organic Reactions. Guggenheim fellow, 1967; Sloan fellow, 1966-68; recipient Sr. U.S. Scientist award Alexander von Humboldt Found., 1974-75, Syracuse Sect. award Am. Chem. Soc., 1997. Home: 103 Burlingame Rd Syracuse NY 13203-1604

BALDWIN, JOHN WESLEY, history educator; b. Chicago, Ill., July 13, 1929; s. Edward N. and H. Gladys (McDaniel) B.; m. Jenny Jochens, Dec. 24, 1954; children: Peter, Ian, Birgit (dec.), Christopher. B.A., Wheaton Coll., 1950; M.A., Pa. State U., 1951; Ph.D., Johns Hopkins, 1956. Instr., then asst. prof. U. Mich., Ann Arbor, 1956-61; mem. faculty Johns Hopkins U., Balt., 1961—; prof. history Johns Hopkins U., 1966—, Charles Homer Haskins prof. history, 1986—; prof. e'tranger Coll. de France, 1984, 95. Author: The Medieval Theories of the Just Price, 1959, Masters, Princes and Merchants, 2 vols, 1970, The Scholastic Culture of the Middle Ages, 1971, City on the Seine: Paris under Louis IX, 1226-1270, 1975, The Government of Philip Augustus, 1986 (French transl. 1991), Les Registres de Philippe Auguste, 1992, The Language of Sex: Five Voices from Northern France Around 1200, 1994, (French translation) Les Languages de l'amour, 1997; editor (with Richard Goldthwaite) Universities in Politics: Case Studies from the Late Middle Ages and Early Modern Period, 1972. Decorated Chevalier Ordre des Arts et des Lettres (France); Prix Litteraire Etats-Unis-France, 1992; Guggenheim fellow, 1960-61, 83-84, Howard fellow, 1960-61, Fulbright fellow, 1953-55, 65-66; grantee Am. Coun. Learned Socs., 1965-66; sr. fellow NEH, 1972-73, 90-91. Fellow Medieval Acad. Am. (v.p. 1994, pres. 1996-97, Charles Homer Haskins medal 1990), Am. Acad. Arts and Scis., Brit. Acad. (corr.); mem. Soc. for French Hist. Studies, Royal Danish Acad. Scis. and Letters (fgn.), Am. Hist. Assn., Commn. Internat. de Diplomatique (hon.). Office: Johns Hopkins U Dept Of History Baltimore MD 21218

BALDWIN, JUDY, critical care nurse; b. Redfield, S.D., Oct. 20, 1942; d. Clifford Raymond and Helen Ethel (Schmidt) Becker; m. Howard Baldwin, Aug. 6, 1965; children: Rhonda, Steven. Diploma, Meth. Kahler Sch. Nursing, Rochester, Minn., 1963. Cert. advanced cardiac life support. Staff nurse Northern Hills Gen. Hosp., Deadwood, S.D., Homestake Hosp., Lead, S.D.; Meade County Medicare nurse S.D. State Health Dept., Sturgis, S.D.; primary care nurse intensive care unit Ft. Meade (S.D.) VA Hosp.; staff nurse Lookout Meml. Hosp., Spearfish, S.D., Community Meml. Hosp., Redfield, S.D.; clin. nurse Massa Berry Clinic, Sturgis. Home: HC 55 Box 112 Sturgis SD 57785-9195

BALDWIN, LEROY FRANKLIN, minister; b. Marion, Va., May 21, 1934; s. Charles Lee and Florence Lorene (Parks) B.; m. Betty Lou Mason, Feb. 24, 1953; children: Dennis Ray, Sandra Kay. BA, Wade Hampton Coll., 1962, M of Ministry, 1964; DD, Am. Bible Inst., 1971. Ordained to ministry Ch. of God, 1963. Evangelist Ch. of God, 1964-69; pastor Ch. of God, Va., N.C., S.C., 1969-90, Orangeburg, S.C., 1990-91; chaplain CAP, 1971-81; chmn., tchr. Ch. of God Ministerial Enrichment for Advancement of Mins.' Edn.; state chmn. World Missions Bd., Ch. of God., N.C., 1980-85; mem. Ministerial Examining-Licensing Bd. for Ch. of God, S.C., 1986-91; guest speaker orgns. and schs.; tchr. coll. extension courses. Capt. Aux. USAF, CAP. Home: 571 Perry Rd Greer SC 29651

BALDWIN, MILES ARNOLD, air force officer; b. Louisville, Oct. 14, 1946; s. Robert and Olivia Money Baldwin; m. Shirley Ann Jessee, June 8, 1968; 1 child, Jeffrey Matthew. BME, U. Louisville, 1969, MS, 1970, MME, 1973; MBA, Auburn U., 1994. Commd. 2d. lt. USAF, 1970, advanced through grades to col., 1992; F-4 aircrew mem. 44th Tactical Fighter Squadron, Kadena AB, Japan, 1975-76; chief radar sys. divsn. 81st Tactical Fighter Wing, USAFE RAF, Bentwaters, U.K., 1976-79; chief nuclear strike br. 474th tactical fighter wing Tactical Air Command, Nellis AFB, Nev., 1979-83; action officer strategy divsn. Air Staff The Pentagon, Washington, 1983-87, exec. officer joint staff J-8, 1988-92; dep. head Air War Coll., Air U., Maxwell AFB, Ala., 1992-97; dir. war gaming and simulation ctr. Nat. Def. U., Washington, 1997—. Pres. Oakton Glen Homeowners' Assn., Vienna, Va., 1988-92; ops. officer CAP, Mt. Vernon, Va., 1997—; house capt. Christmas in April Project, Montgomery, Ala., 1995-97. Methodist. Avocations: jogging, classic cars, stamps. E-mail: baldwinm@ndu.edu.

BALDWIN, PETER ARTHUR, psychologist, educator, author, minister; b. Andover, Mass., Apr. 7, 1932; s. Alfred Graham and Katherine (Ashworth) B.; m. Carolyn Whitmore, Sept. 3, 1955; children: Sarah MacDonald Baldwin-Welcome, Judith Helen Baldwin-Gleason, Robert Henry. B.A., Middlebury Coll., 1955; S.T.B., Boston U., 1959, Ph.D., 1964; student, New Coll., U. London, 1957-58. Certified psychologist, N.H. lic. psychologist Nat. Register Health Providers in Psychology; approved cons. in clin. hypnosis. Ordained to ministry Unitarian-Universalist Ch., 1959; pastor 2d Ch., Boston, 1955-57, in Dighton, Mass., 1958-62; religious counselor M.I.T., 1959-63; exec. dir. Liberal Religious Youth, Unitarian Universalist Assn., 1963-66; asst. prof. Crane Theol. Sch., Tufts U., 1965-67, Meadville Theol. Sch., U. Chgo., 1967-73; pastor All Souls 1st Universalist Soc., Chgo., 1971-73; assoc. prof. psychology New Eng. Coll., Henniker, N.H., 1973-74; vis. assoc. prof. psychology Colby-Sawyer Coll., New London, N.H., 1974-76; assoc. prof. dept. clin. psychology Antioch-New Eng. Grad. Sch., Keene, N.H., 1976—; pvt. practice, 1976—; assoc. faculty Ga. Sch. Profl. Psychology, Atlanta, 1993—; dir. Sr. High and Family Insts., Rowe, Mass., 1967-74; Nat. Edn. Conf. lectr. Williston Acad., 1967; Judy lectr., Omaha, 1970; invited speaker 5th Internat. Congress on Gestalt Therapy, Valencia, Spain, 1993. Recipient; Disting. Svc. Antioch New Eng. Grad. Sch., 1994, New Hampshire Psychological Assn., Margaret M. Riggs Disting. Contribution award, 1995. Fellow N.H. Psychol. Assn. (pres. 1980-81, 88-90); mem. APA, Liberal Religious Youth (life), Unitarian-Universalists Mins. Assn. Democrat. Home: RR 3 Pittsfield NH 03263-9803 Office: Univ Assocs in Psychology 222 West St Keene NH 03431-2455 also: Pancake Hill Rd Lower Gilmanton Pittsfield NH 03263

BALDWIN, RALPH BELKNAP, retired manufacturing company executive, astronomer; b. Grand Rapids, Mich., June 6, 1912; s. Melvin D. and Julie (Belknap) B.; m. Lois Virginia Johnston, Aug. 3, 1940; children: Melvin Dana II, Pamela, Bruce Belknap. B.S., U. Mich., 1934, M.S., 1935, PhD, 1937, LLD (hon.), 1975; ScD (hon.), Grand Valley State U., 1989, Aquinas Coll., 1999. Asst. dept. astronomy U. Mich., 1935-36, U. Pa., 1937-38; instr. dept. astronomy Northwestern U., 1938-42; lectr. Adler Planetarium, Chgo., 1940-42; sr. physicist Applied Physics Lab. Johns Hopkins, Silver Spring, Md., 1942-46; cons. Johns Hopkins, East Grand Rapids, Mich., 1946-47; acting supt. schs. East Grand Rapids, 1947; prodn. mgr. Oliver Machinery Co., Grand Rapids, 1947-56; dir. Oliver Machinery Co., 1948-87, successively personnel dir., prodn. mgr., sec., 1949-56, v.p., 1956-70, pres., 1970-84, chmn. bd., 1984-87; Chmn. bd. Internat. Woodworking Machinery and Furniture Supply Fair-U.S.A., 1969-70, 77-78. Author: The Face of the Moon, 1949, The Measure of the Moon, 1963, The Moon—A Fundamental Survey, 1966, The Deadly Fuze: Secret Weapon of World War II, 1980, They Never Knew What Hit Them, 1999; contbr. articles to profl. jours. Recipient Presdl. Cert. of Merit, 1947, U.S. Naval Bur. Ordnance award, 1945, U.S. Army Chief of Ordnance award, 1945, Disting. Alumnus award U. Mich., 1967, Woodworking and Furniture Digest award Forest Products Rsch. Soc., 1973, J. Lawrence Smith medal Nat. Acad. Scis., 1979, G.K. Gilbert award Geol. Soc. Am., 1986, Disting. Alumni award Ctrl. H.S., Grand Rapids, Mich., 1997. Fellow AAAS, Am. Geophys. Union, Meteoritical Soc. (Leonard medal 1986), Am. Acad. Arts and Scis.; mem. Am. Astron. Soc., Royal Astron. Soc. Can. (hon.), Grand Rapids Mus. Assn., NAM (dir. 1963-64), Employers Assn. Grand Rapids (pres. 1960-64), Woodworking Machinery Mfrs. Assn. (pres. 1964-68). Home: 4401 Gulf Shore Blvd N Apt 702 Naples FL 34103-3451

BALDWIN, RANSOM LELAND, animal science educator; b. Meriden, Conn., Sept. 21, 1935; s. Ransom Leland and Edna (Thurrot) B.; m. Mary Ellen Burns, June 1, 1957; children: Ransom Leland VI, Cheryl Lee, Robert Ryan. BS, U. Conn., 1957; MS, Mich State U., 1958, PhD, 1963. Research asst. Mich. State U., East Lansing, 1957-61; from asst. to assoc. prof. U. Calif., Davis, 1963-70, prof., 1970—. Assoc. editor Jour. Nutrition, 1971-73, 83—; contbr. research articles to profl. jours. Gugenheim fellow, Fulbright fellow, NSF fellow, U.S. NAS fellow, 1993; recipient Borden award, 1980, Am. Feed Mfrs. Assn. award, 1970. Fellow AAAS; mem. Am. Inst. Nutrition, Am. Diary Sci. Assn., Soc. Animal Sci., Sigma Xi. Home: 2101 Amador Ave Davis CA 95616-3014 Office: U Calif Dept Animal Sci Davis CA 95616

BALDWIN, ROBERT EDWARD, economics educator; b. Niagara Falls, N.Y., July 12, 1924; s. Gilbert and Margaret (Ostman) B.; m. Janice Murphy, July 31, 1954; children: Jean, Robert, Richard, Nancy. A.B., U. Buffalo, 1945; Ph.D., Harvard U., 1950. Instr., then asst. prof. econs. Harvard, 1950-57; asso. prof., then prof. econs. UCLA, 1957-64; prof. econs. U. Wis. at Madison, 1964-97, F.W. Taussig research prof., 1974-97, Hilldale prof., 1982-97, prof. emeritus, 1997—, chmn. econ. dept., 1975-79; chief economist Office Spl. Trade Rep., Exec. Office of President, 1963-64; vis. prof. Brookings Instn., Washington, 1967-68, U.S. Dept. Labor, 1975-76, World Bank, 1978-79; mem. adv. bd. Inst. Internat. Econs., chmn. social systems Rsch. Inst., 1986-89; rsch. assoc. Nat. Bur. Econ. Rsch., 1982—, Ctr. Econ. Policy Rsch., 1994—; chair panel on fgn. trade stats. NAS, 1989-91. Author: Economic Development and Export Growth, 1966, Nontariff Distortions of International Trade, 1970, Foreign Trade Regimes and Economic Development: The Philippines, 1975, The Inefficiency of Trade Policy, 1982, Polit. Econ. U.S. Import Policy, 1985, Trade Policy in a Changing World Economy, 1988; co-author: Economic Development, 1957, Disease and Economic Development, 1973; mem. bd. editors: Econs. and Politics, Jour. Asian Econs., Malaysia, Jour. Econ. Studies, Pakistan Devel. Rev, World Economy, Studies in Internat. Trade Policy, Series on Political Economy of Global Interdependence; editor: Trade Policy and Empirical Analysis, 1984, Empirical Studies of Commercial Policy, 1991; co-editor: The Structure and Evolution of U.S. Trade Policy, 1984, Current U.S. Trade Policy Analysis, Agenda and Administration, 1986, Issues in US-European Community Trade Relations, 1988, The Uruguay Round and Beyond, 1991. Written in his honor: (Ronald Jones and Anne Krueger, eds.) The Political Economy of International Trade, 1990. Fellow Am. Acad. Arts and Scis.; mem. Am. Econ. Assn., Internat. Trade and Fin. Assn. (pres. 1992), Midwest Econ. Assn. (pres. 1994), Coun. on Fgn. Rels., Conf. on Rsch. in Income and Wealth. Home: 125 Nautilus Dr Madison WI 53705-4329

BALDWIN, ROBERT LESH, biochemist, educator; b. Madison, Wis., Sept. 30, 1927; s. Ira Lawrence and Mary (Lesh) B.; m. Anne Theodora Norris, Aug. 28, 1965; children—David Norris, Eric Lawrence. B.A., U. Wis., 1950; D.Phil. (Rhodes scholar), Oxford (Eng.) U., 1954. Asst. prof., then asso. prof. biochemistry U. Wis., 1955-59; mem. faculty Stanford, 1959—, prof. biochemistry, 1964-98, prof. emeritus, 1998—, chmn. dept., 1989-94; vis. prof. Collège de France, Paris, 1972; mem. adv. panel biochemistry and biophysics NSF, 1974-76, NIH study sect. molecular and cellular biophysics, 1984-88. Assoc. editor Jour. Molecular Biology, 1964-68, 75-79; mem. editorial bd. Trends Biochem. Sci., 1977-84, Biochemistry, 1984—, Protein Sci., 1992-97. Mem. Searle Scholars award panel, 1993-96, 1997-98; mem. adv. panel in biophysics Burroughs-Wellcome, 1995—. Recipient Wheland award in chemistry U. Chgo., 1995; Guggenheim fellow, 1958-59. Mem.

NAS, Am. Soc. Biol. Chemists (Merck award 1999), Am. Chem. Soc., Am. Biophysics Soc. (coun. 1977-81, Cole award 1999), Am. Acad. Arts and Scis., Protein Soc. (coun. 1993-95, Stein and Moore award 1992). Home: 1243 Los Trancos Rd Portola Valley CA 94028-8125 Office: Stanford Med Sch Dept Biochemistry Beckman Ctr Stanford CA 94305-5307

BALDWIN, SHAUN MCPARLAND, lawyer; b. Chgo., Oct. 19, 1954; married James P. Baldwin, Sept. 17, 1988. BS, No. Ill. U., 1976; JD with distinction, John Marshall Law Sch., 1980. Bar: Ill. 1980, U.S. Dist. Ct. (no. dist.) Ill. 1980, U.S. Ct. Appeals (7th cir.) 1981. Assoc. McKenna, Storer, Rowe, White & Farrug, Chgo., 1980-86; assoc. Tressler, Soderstrom, Maloney & Priess, Chgo., 1986-87, ptnr., 1987—. Mem. ABA, Ill. Bar Assn., Def. Rsch. Inst. (chair ins. law com. 1996-98), Ill. Assn. Def. Trial Counsel (bd. dirs. 1996, amicus com. chair 1992—), Ill. Appel late Lawyers Assn. (bd. dirs. 1987-89), John Marshall Alumni Assn. (bd. dirs. 1982-86), Internat. Assn. Def. Trial Counsel (chair membership com. 1996-97, chair casualty ins. com. 1995-96). Office: Tressler Soderstrom Maloney & Priess 233 S Wacker Dr Ste 2200 Chicago IL 60606-6399

BALDWIN, STEPHEN, actor; b. Massapequa, N.Y., May 12, 1966; s. Alexander Rae and Carol Newcomb (Martineau) B.; m. Kennya, June, 1990, 1 daughter. film appearances include: The Beast, 1988, Homeboy, 1989, Last Exit to Brooklyn, 1989, Born on the Fourth of July, 1989, Crossing the Bridge, 1992, Bitter Harvest, 1993, Posse, 1993, New Eden, 1993, Eight Seconds, 1994, Threesome, 1994, A Simple Twist of Fate, 1994, Fall Time, 1994, The Usual Suspects, 1995, Under the Hula Moon, 1995, Fall Time, 1995, Fled, 1996, Crimetime, 1996, Bio Dome, 1996, Sub Down, 1997, Scar City, 1998, Friends and Lovers, 1998, Cross Country, 1998, Half Baked, 1998; TV series include: The Young Riders, 1989-92; TV movies include: Jury Duty: The Comedy, 1990, Dead Weekend, 1995; TV mini-series include Mr. Murder, 1998. Office: Schiffman Ekman Morris 22 W 19th St Fl 8 New York NY 10011-4204 also: IFA Talent Agy 8730 W Sunset Blvd Ste 490 Los Angeles CA 90069-2277*

BALDWIN, TAMMY, congresswoman; b. Madison, Wis., Feb. 11, 1962. BA, Smith Coll.; JD, U. Wis. Pvt. practice as atty., 1989-92; Dane Country supr. Board of Supervisors, 1986-1994; mem. 78th dist. Wis. State Assembly, 1993-99; mem. Wis. 2nd dist. 106th US Congress, Washington, DC, 1999—. Former supr. Dane County; mem. Nat. Women's Polit. Caucus, 1993—; state assemblywoman dist. 78 State of Wis., 1993—. Mem. NOW, ACLU, Wis. State Bar Assn., Internat. Network Lesbian and Gay Ofcls. Democrat. Home: 525 Riverside Dr Madison WI 53704-5529*

BALDWIN, WILLIAM, actor; b. Massapequa, N.Y.; s. Alexander Rae and Carol Newcomb (Martineau) B. BS in Polit. Sci., SUNY, Binghamton. Films include Born on the Fourth of July, 1989, Internal Affairs, 1990, Flatliners, 1990, Backdraft, 1991, Three of Hearts, 1993, Sliver, 1993, Pyromaniacs: A Love Story, 1995, Fair Game, 1995, Curdled, 1996, Virus, 1997, Fetishes, 1996, Shattered Image, 1998, Bulworth, 1998, Box, 1999, Virus, 1999; TV movie The Preppie Murder, 1989. Office: ICM 8942 Wilshire Blvd Beverly Hills CA 90211-1934*

BALDWIN, WILLIAM HOWARD, lawyer, retired foundation executive; b. Detroit, Feb. 21, 1916; s. Howard Charles and Ruth E. (Jensen) B.; m. Carol Lees, May 24, 1947; children: Susan, Jeffrey (dec.), Julie, Deborah. B.A., Williams Coll., 1938; J.D., U. Mich., 1941. Bar: Mich. 1941. Ptnr. Dykema Gossett, Detroit, 1970-77, of counsel, 1977—; chmn., trustee Kresge Found., Troy, Mich., 1963-87; asst. U.S. prosecutor Nuremburg Trials, 1946. Served with USAAF, 1942-45, lt. col. (ret.). Mem. ABA, Mich. Bar Assn., Lake Sunapee Golf Club (N.H.), Lake Sunapee Yacht Club, Gasparilla Golf Club (Fla.). Republican. Episcopalian. Home: PO Box 966 Boca Grande FL 33921-0966 also: PO Box 1308 New London NH 03257-1308

BALDWIN, WILLIAM RUSSELL, optometrist, foundation executive; b. Danville, Ind., July 29, 1926; s. Edward Claire and Letha Verona (Russell) B.; m. Honey Esther Fisher, Aug. 16, 1947; children: Linda Marie Smith (dec.), Leslie Ann Baldwin Bloom. BS, Pacific U., 1949, OD, 1951, ScD (hon.), 1991; MS, Ind. U., 1956, PhD, 1964; LHD (hon.), New Eng. Coll., 1982, D.S. (hon.), SUNY, 1998. Practice optometry, Beech Grove, Ind., 1951-54; dir. optometry clinic Ind. U., Bloomington, 1959-63; dean Coll. Optometry, Pacific U., Forest Grove, Oreg., 1963-69; pres. New Eng. Coll. Optometry, Boston, 1969-79; dean Coll. Optometry, U. Houston, 1979-90; pres. River Blindness Found., 1990-96, chmn. bd. dirs., 1996—. Author: (with C.R. Schick) Corneal Contact Lenses, Fitting Procedures, 1962; (with others) The Refractive State of the Eye, 1969, (with others) Pediatric Optometry, 1988; editor Vision Science Symposium, Ind. U., 1988, (with others) Refractive Anomolies, 1991. Mem. exec. com. Rep. Cen. Com., Washington County, Oreg., 1963-69; chmn. arts, scis. div. Ind. Reps., 1962-63; chmn. Vellore India Hosp. Fund Drive, 1959-61 chmn. bd. River Blindness Found., 1996—; mem. men's adv. coun. Bloomington Hosp., 1959-63. Recipient Disting. Alumni Svc. award Ind. U., 1977, Pacific U., 1995, Gold Medal award Beta Sigma Kappa, 1968, Pres.'s medal New Eng. Coll. Optometry, 1977; named Man of Vision Prevent Blindness Mass.,1994,Lifetime Achievement award Prevent Blindness Am., 1995; Disting. scholar Nat. Acad. Practice, 1994. Fellow AAAS; mem. working group Nat. Rsch. Coun. Com. Vision of NAS, Am. Optometric Assn. (chmn. com. on rsch., chmn. task force on manpower, Disting. Svc. award 1992), Assn. Schs. Colls. Optometry (pres. 1974-76, chmn. internat. optometric edn.), Am. Acad. Optometry (chmn. sect. on edn. 1984-87), Tex. Soc. to Prevent Blindness (v.p. 1985-90), Nat. Soc. to Prevent Blindness (bd. dirs. 1988-96, chmn. 1st World Conf. on Optometric Edn. 1990), Optometric Rsch. Inst. (bd. dirs. 1995—), Rotary, Sigma Xi, Sigma Nu, Kappa Kappa Sigma.

BALDWIN-HALVORSEN, LISA ROGENE, community health and critical care nurse; b. Silverton, Oreg., Aug. 17, 1960; d. Roger W. Baldwin and Udene L. Allen. BSN, Walla Walla Coll., 1982; MS in Nursing, Oreg. Health Scis. U., 1991, post Masters cert. Cmty. Health Nursing, 1993, postgrad., 1993—. RN, Oreg. Staff nurse Providence Med. Ctr., Portland, Oreg., 1982-96; asst. clin. mgr. ICU VA Med. Ctr., Portland, 1991-93, nurse educator critical care, 1994-95; nurse mgr. Providence Med. Ctr., 1996—; tchg. asst. Oreg. Health Scis. U., Portland, 1992-94, 95-96, rsch. asst., 1994-96; mem. logical job analysis panel Nat. Coun. State Bds., Chgo., 1993, item writer, Princeton, N.J., 1993. U. Club Found. fellow, Portland, 1994. Mem. ACCN, Oreg. Health Decisions. Avocations: cooking, ranching, reading. Office: Cardiac Intensive Care Unit 4805 NE Glisan St Portland OR 97213-2933

BALDYGA, LEONARD J., retired diplomat, international consultant; b. Chgo., Mar. 19, 1932; s. Stanislaw J. and Frances T. (Gorzynski) B.; m. Joyce Brinkley, June 25, 1960; children: Natalya M., Sarah E. AA, J. Sterling Morton Coll., 1954; BS, So. Ill. U., 1959; M Internat. Affairs, Columbia U., 1962. City editor Marion (Ill.) Daily Rep., 1958-59; fin. writer Am. Banker, N.Y.C., 1959-61; overseas, 1963-78; dep. dir. Europe U.S. Info. Agy., Washington, 1979-81, dir., 1981-83, 92-94; minister, counselor Am. Embassy, Rome, 1983-88, New Delhi, 1988-91; sr. rsch. assoc. Washington, 1994—; acting dir. Murrow Ctr. Tufts U. Fletcher Sch. Law and Diplomacy, Medford, Mass., 1991-92, adj. prof., 1991-92. Mem. editl. bd. Polish Ency. Britannica. Bd. trustees St. Stephen's Sch., Rome, 1984-88; bd. dirs. Ptnrs. for Dem. Change, San Francisco, Pub. Diplomacy Found. Decorated Polish Order of Merit Republic of Poland, 1994; recipient Presdl. Disting. Svc. award White House, 1984, Edward R. Murrow award Tufts U., 1988, Presdl. Merit award White House, 1988. Home: 3622 Vacation Ln Arlington VA 22207-3820 Office: Internat Rsch/Exchs Bd 1616 H St NW Washington DC 20006-4903

BALÉE, WILLIAM L., anthropology educator; b. Ft. Lauderdale, Fla., Oct. 12, 1954; s. William Lockert Balée and Lorraine Kathryn Monahan; m. Pamela Van Rees, May 24, 1980 (div. Dec. 1986); m. Maria da Conceição Bezerra, Mar. 9, 1987; children: Nicholas, Isabel. BA with high honors, U. Fla., 1975; MA, Columbia U., 1979, MPhil, 1980, PhD, 1984. Assoc. rschr. ecology Museu Paraense Emílio Goeldi, Belém, Brazil, 1988-91; chair ecology Museu Paraense Emílio Goeldi, Belém, Brazil, 1990-91; assoc. prof. anthropology Tulane U., New Orleans, 1991-98, prof., chair dept. anthropology, 1998—; adj. prof. anthropology CUNY, 1983, 84, SUNY, Purchase, 1982; adj. prof. social scis. CUNY, 1983; adj. prof. sociology and anthropology Rutgers U., 1984; vis. assoc. prof. Ctr. for L.Am. Studies, U. Fla., 1990; extensive fieldwork with forest peoples in Amazon of Brazil and Bolivia, 1980-97. Author: Footprints of the Forest: Ka'apor Ethnobotany, 1994 (award Soc. Econ. Botany 1996); editor: Advances in Historical Ecology, 1998; co-editor: Resource Management in Amazonia: Indigenous and Folk Strategies, Advances in Economic Botany, Vol. 7, 1989; mem. editl. bd. Ethnobotany; contbr. articles to profl. jours. and chpts. to books. Decorated officer Order of the Golden Ark (Netherlands); N.Y. Bot. Garden fellow, 1984-88, Fulbright-Hays fellow, 1980-81, Newcomb Coll. fellow, 1992-94, Conselho Nacional de Desenvolvimento Tecnológico e Cientifico fellow, 1988-91; grantee OAS, 1981-82, Ford Found., 1989-90, Jessie Smith Noyes Found., 1990-91, World Wildlife Fund, 1991-92, Tulane U., 1992, Wenner-Gren Found., 1993-94 ; apptd. to 60th and 61st Coll. Disting. Lectrs., Sigma Xi, 1997—; recipient Outstanding Book of Yr. award Soc. Econ. Botany. Fellow Am. Anthrop. Assn.; mem. Internat. Soc. Ethnobiology, Soc. Ethnobotanists (India), Soc. Ethnobiology, Soc. Ethnobotanists, Phi Beta Kappa (pres. Alpha of La. 1997-98), Phi Kappa Phi, Sigma Xi (Disting. Lectr. 1997—). Office: Tulane U Dept Anthropology 1021 Audubon St New Orleans LA 70118-5238

BALENTINE, WILLIAM (RAY), civil engineer; b. Kosciusko, Miss., Sept. 25, 1956; s. William Burl and Ora Mae (Ray) B.; m. Cynthia Diane Hastings, July 20, 1985; children: Carrie Diane, William Ryan. BSCE, Miss. State U., 1978. Registered profl. engr. and land surveyor, Miss. Engr., leader design squad Miss. Hwy. Dept., Jackson, 1978-85; project engr. Neel-Schaffer, Inc., Jackson, 1985-86; civil engr. design and planning U.S. Army C.E., Vicksburg, Miss., 1986-90; preconstrn. engr. U.S. Forst Svc., Jackson, 1990; engr. design sect. Miss. Dept. Transp., Jackson, 1990-97, roadway design engr., 1997-98, asst. roadway design divsn. engr., 1998-99, state planning engr., 1999—. Ordained deacon Northside Bapt. Ch., Clinton, Miss., 1993-96. Mem. Civitan (bd. dirs., v.p., pres.-elect, pres. Clinton 1994-97); Am. Assn. State Hwy. and Transp. Ofcls., Transp. Rsch. Bd. Avocations: golf, coaching baseball, basketball and soccer, travel. Home: 412 Harriette Holw Madison MS 39110-8344 Office: Miss Dept Transp PO Box 1850 Jackson MS 39215-1850

BALES, AVARY, nurse; b. Atlanta, July 22, 1940; d. Eugene Carlston and Florence Elizabeth (Cox) B. Diploma, Ga. Bapt. Hosp. Sch. Nursing, Atlanta; BS in Allied Health, Coll. of St. Francis, Joliet, Ill.; M in Health Care Adminstrn, Ctr. Mich. U., 1994. RN, Ga. Asst. dept. head Ga. Bapt. Hosp., Atlanta, 1961-72; house supr. Clayton Gen. Hosp., Riverdale, Ga., 1972-76; capt. emergency med. svcs. tng. div. Clayton County Fire Dept., Jonesboro, Ga., 1976-78; dir. info. svcs. West Paces Med. Ctr., Atlanta, 1976-97; dir. info. sys. Northlake Regional Med. Ctr., Tucker, Ga., 1997—. Home: 3281 Rock Creek Dr Rex GA 30273-2456

BALES, EDWARD WAGNER, consultant, former manufacturing executive; b. Chgo., Jan. 30, 1939; s. Edward Joseph and Esther (Wagner) B.; m. Barbara LaVarre, Nov. 26, 1960; children: Edward Joseph, Karen Mary, Kathryn Mary, Timothy Joseph. BEE, Ill. Inst. Tech., 1960; MBA, U. Chgo., 1969. Elec. engr. Motorola, Inc., Chgo., 1963-69, sales mgr., 1969-80, mgr. mktg. and client services, 1980-85; founder, dir. ops., chief of staff Motorola Univ., Chgo., 1985-90, dir. edn., external systems, 1990-97; pres. LTE Consulting Firm, 1997—. Mem. editorial bd. U.S. Gen. Acct. Office Jour. Mem. edn. coun. NSF; mem. edn. com. Nat. Conf. Bd.; vice chmn. edn. com. Bus. Industry Adv. Coun. to Orgn. Econ. Corp. and Devel.; pres. Mary Seat of Wisdom Ch. Bd., Park Ridge, Ill., 1980-83; trustee Nat. Sch. Bd. Assn. Found., Ray Graham Assn. for People with Disabilities; mem. Nat. Rsch. Coun. Commn. on Work, Learning and Assessment. Lt. USN, 1960-63. Mem. Nat. Alliance of Bus. (mem. edn. com., bus./policy com.), Soc. Actuaries Found. (bd. trustees), Nat. Sch. Bd. Found. (bd. trustees). Republican. Roman Catholic. Avocations: photography, automobile repair. Office: LTE 916 S Lincoln Park Ridge IL 60068-4513

BALES, JOHN FOSTER, III, lawyer; b. Springfield, Mass., July 17, 1940; s. John Foster II and Jean (Torrence) B.; m. Jane Lee Black, Sept. 11, 1965; children: Patricia, Elizabeth, Susan. BS in Enring., Princeton U., 1962; LLB, U. Va., 1965; LLM, Georgetown U., 1972. Bar: U.S. Supreme Ct. 1972. Staff atty. U.S. SEC, Washington, 1970-72; assoc. Morgan, Lewis & Bockius, Phila., 1972-76, ptnr., 1976—; bd. dirs. Independent Publs., Inc., Phila. Vice chmn. bd. trustees Presbyn. Med. Ctr., Phila., 1988-95; trustee Acad. Natural Scis., Phila, 1995—, The Presbyn. Found. Phila., 1995-96, Immigration Refugee Svcs. Am., 1998—, U.S. com. refugees, 1998—. Mem. ABA, Va. Bar Assn., Pa. Bar Assn., Phila. Bar Assn., Colo. Bar Assn. Republican. Office: Morgan Lewis & Bockius 1701 Market St Philadelphia PA 19103-2921

BALES, KENT ROSLYN, English language educator; b. Anthony, Kans., June 19, 1936; s. Roslyn Francis and Irene E. (Brinkman) B.; m. Maria Gyorei, Aug. 25, 1958; children—Thomas Imre, Elizabeth Irene. B.A., Yale U., 1958; M.A., San Jose State U., 1963; Ph.D., U. Calif., Berkeley, 1967. Instr. Menlo Sch., Menlo Park, Calif., 1958-63; acting instr. U. Calif., Berkeley, 1967; asst. prof. English U. Minn., Mpls., 1967-71, assoc. prof. English, 1971-82, prof. English, 1982—, chmn. dept. English, 1983-88; vis. fellow Literary Studies Inst., Budapest, Hungary, 1973-74, 80-81, 88-89. Contbr. chpts. to books and articles to profl. jours. Fulbright lectr., Budapest, 1980, Fulbright Research fellow, Budapest, 1988-89. Mem. MLA, Am. Studies Assn., Am. Comparative Lit. Assn., Midwest Modern Lang. Assn. Home: 2700 Irving Ave S Minneapolis MN 55408-1049 Office: Univ Minn Dept English 207 Church St SE Minneapolis MN 55455-0134

BALES, ROBERT FREED, social psychologist, educator; b. Ellington, Mo., Mar. 9, 1916; s. Columbus Lee and Ada Lois (Sloan) B.; m. Dorothy Louise Johnson, Sept. 14, 1941. B.A., U. Oreg., 1938, M.S., 1941; M.A., Harvard U., 1943, Ph.D., 1945. Research assoc. sect. on alcohol studies Yale U., 1944-45; instr. sociology Harvard U., Cambridge, Mass., 1945-47, asst. prof. sociology, research assoc. Lab. Social Relations, 1947-51, lectr. sociology, research assoc., 1951-55, assoc. prof., 1955-57, prof. social relations, 1957-86, prof. emeritus, 1986—, dir. Lab. Social Rels., 1960-67, chmn. social psychology program, dept. psychology and social rels., 1970-82; cons. psychology Harvard U. Health Svcs., 1970-82; vis. lectr. sociology and social psychology U. Mich., summer 1949, Columbia U., summer 1950; lectr. Salzberg Austria Seminar of Am. Studies, summer 1952, 56; Mem. bd. sci. counsellors NIMH, 1957-60. Author: Interaction Process Analysis: A Method for the Study of Small Groups, 1950, The Fixation Factor in Alcohol Addiction, 1980, (with Talcott Parsons, Edward A. Shils) Working Papers in the Theory of Action, 1953, (with Talcott Parsons, et al) Family, Socialization, and Interaction Process, 1955, (with Stephen P. Cohen and Stephen A. Williamson) SYMLOG, A System for the Multiple Level Observation of Groups, 1979, SYMLOG Case Study Kit and Instructions for a Group Self Study, 1980; contbr. to Group Dynamics, Research and Theory, 1953, The SYMLOG Practitioner, 1988, Social Interaction Systems, Theory and measurement, 1999, several other compilations; editor: (with A. Paul Hare and Edgar F. Borgatta) Small Groups, Studies in Social Interaction, 1955; author various instruments and booklets, sr. rsch., cons. SYMLOG Cons. Group, 1983—. Trustee Ella L. Cabot Trust. Mem. APA, Am. Sociol. Assn., Eastern Sociol. Soc. (pres. 1962-63), Am. Acad. Arts and Scis., Am. Psychol. Soc., Soc. Exptl. Social Psychology, Boston Psychoanalytic Soc. (affiliate). Home and Office: 17990 Bernardo Trails Pl San Diego CA 92128-1505

BALES, ROYAL EUGENE, philosophy educator; b. Pratt, Kans., Sept. 23, 1934; s. Harold Thomas and Gladys (German) B.; m. Flossie Kathleen O'Reilly, Apr. 16, 1960; children—David Scott, Elizabeth Laurel. B.Music Edn. cum laude, U. Wichita, 1956, M.A., 1960; Ph.D., Stanford U., 1968. Tchr. music Kans. Pub. Schs., 1956-57, 59-60; instr. philosophy Menlo Coll., Atherton, Calif., 1962-69, prof., 1970—, chmn. social scis. and humanities, 1971-74, dean liberal arts, 1974-79, provost, 1979-87, standing mem. president's adv. council, 1971-87; vis. fellow Harris-Manchester Coll., Oxford U., 1994, 98; Wong vis. prof. Guangdong U. of Law and Bus., Guangzhou, China, 1999. Contbr. articles to profl. jours. Pres. El Camino Youth Symphony Assn., 1985-87; bd. of govs. Manchester Coll., Oxford, 1994—. Scholar and fellow U. Wichita, 1952-60, Stanford U., 1966-67; prin. investigator NSF, Menlo Coll./Stanford, 1971-72; research grantee Stanford-Warsaw Exchange, Poland, 1969-70. Mem. Am. Philos. Assn., Soc. for Bus. Ethics, Save San Francisco Bay Assn., Phi Mu Alpha Sinfonia. Democrat. Avocations: classical music, designing and constructing furniture. Home: 1255 Sherman Ave Menlo Park CA 94025-6012 Office: Menlo Coll Florence Moore Bldg 1000 El Camino Real Atherton CA 94027-4300

BALES, RUBY JONES, retired elementary school educator and principal; b. Fayetteville, Tenn., Aug. 17, 1933; d. Albin O. and Jenny Katharine (Pickett) Jones; m. Emory H. Bales, Nov. 25, 1954; children: N. Katharine (dec.), David Emory, Evelyn Ann, Patrick Lee. BS in Biology, Tenn. Technol. U., 1956; MA in Supervision, Human Rels., George Washington U., 1975; EdD in Curriculum Instrn. and Reading, U. Md., 1984. Cert. tchr. grades 1-6, prin., supr., elem., middle sch. reading tchr. K-12. Tchr. gen. sci., math. Niceville (Fla.) Elem. Sch., 1956-57, Ruckel Jr. H.S., Niceville, 1957-59; tchr. biology, physical sci. Leon H.S., Tallahassee, 1959-60; tchr. 5th grade Potomac Elem. Sch., Dahlgren, Va., 1960-61, Charles County Pub. Schs., La Plata, Md., 1965-73; acting adminstrv. asst. Charles County Middle Pub. Sch.s, La Plata, Md., 1973-74; program coord. Mitchell Elem. Sch., Charles County, La Plata, 1974-75, adminstrv. asst., 1975-77; prin. Dr. James Craik Elem. Sch., Pomfret, Md., 1977-84, Eva Turner Elem. Sch., Waldorf, Md., 1984-86; instrnl. supr. elem. schs. Charles County Sch. Dist., La Plata, 1986-94; retired. Supt. Charles County Fair Sch. Exhibit, County Fair Bd., 1986-94. NSF scholar Fla. State U., 1958. Republican. Avocations: music, gardening. Home: PO Box 373 Dahlgren VA 22448-0373

BALES, VIRGINIA SHANKLE, health administrator. BA in Chemistry, Emory U., Atlanta, MPH. Dep. dir. Ctr. for Chronic Disease, 1970—, Ctr. for Chronic Disease Prevention and Health Promotion, 1988; dep. dir. program mgmt. CDC, 1998—. Office: CDC DHHS Mailstop D14 1600 Clifton Rd NE Atlanta GA 30333

BALES, WILLIAM JOSEPH, academic administrator; b. Morristown, Tenn., June 14, 1959; s. William W. and Mary Lynn (Shaver) B.; m. Valerie Michelle Cook, Oct. 25, 1997. BS, U. Tenn., Knoxville, 1981, MS, 1986. Instr. U. Tenn. Inst. Agr., Knoxville, 1986, assoc. dir. instnl. advancement, 1987-90, assoc. dir. alumni and devel., 1990-92, dir. alumni and devel., 1992-93; dir. devel. U. Tenn., Knoxville, 1993-96, asst. vice chancellor, 1996—; presenter in field. Coach, mgr. league softball Knoxville Parks and Recreation Dept., 1990-94; bd. dirs. Tenn. 4-H Alumni Assn., Knoxville, 1992-94; adv. rep. Tenn. 4-H Found., Knoxville, 1990-94. Mem. Coun. for Advancement and Support of Edn. Presbyterian. Avocations: golf, antiques. Home: 8117 Meadowood Ln Knoxville TN 37919-8730 Office: U Tenn 405C Andy Holt Tower Knoxville TN 37996

BALFE, JUDITH O'HARA, marketing professional, educator; b. New Rochelle, N.Y., Sept. 3, 1943; d. Joseph James and Helen Dorothy (Buderman) O'Hara; m. Joseph Balfe, Aug. 3, 1989; 1 child, Christopher. BA in Humanities, Coll. New Rochelle, 1989, MS in Career and Life Devel., 1991, MS in Comm. Arts, 1997. Owner, operator Miller Stripping/Antiques, Myrtle Beach, S.C., 1974-84; adminstrv. asst. Sch. of New Resources, Coll. New Rochelle, 1987-91, coord. acad. support, 1991-97, dir. mktg., 1997—. Scholar Mamaroneck Bus. Women, 1987. Mem. Am. Counseling Assn., Nat. Writers Union, Coll. New Rochelle Alumni Assn., Coll. New Rochelle Alumni Club (pres. 1989-92). Roman Catholic. Avocations: reading, writing, traveling. Home: 116 Cooper Dr New Rochelle NY 10801 Office: Coll of New Rochelle 29 Castle Pl New Rochelle NY 10805

BALFOUR, ANA MARIA, office manager; b. Buenos Aires, Dec. 16, 1942; came to the U.S., 1962; d. Alfredo Hector and Luisa (Zagnoni) Malaccorto; m. Guillermo Aylmer Balfour, July 10, 1964; children: Michele, Valeria, Alexandra. Student, U. Buenos Aires, 1961-62; BA, Am. U., 1964. Tchr. Ft. Rucker (Ala.) Middle Sch., 1964-65; med. asst. F.R. Leyva & G.A. Balfour, M.D., P.C., Washington, 1968-73, office mgr., 1973-88, adminstr., 1988—. Contbr. articles to profl. jours. Fundraiser Operation Smile, Stone Ridge Country Day Sch.-Sacred Heart; docent The Kreeger Mus., Washington, 1996—. Mem. Comisión Esperanza Damas Argentinas, So Others May Eat, Ivy Found., Com. Hispanic Designers, Com. Am.'s Film Festival. Roman Catholic. Avocations: gardening, Latin American art, reading. Office: FR Leyva GA Balfour MD PC 3301 New Mexico Ave NW Washington DC 20016-3622

BALFOUR, REGINALD JAMES, retired lawyer; b. Regina, Sask., Can., May 22, 1928; s. Reginald Mcleod and Martha (McElmoyle) B.; m. Beverly Jane Davidson, June 6, 1951 (dec. Sept. 1994); children: John Alan, James Roberts, Reginald William (dec.), Beverly Ann. Student, Luther Coll., 1946-48; LL.B., U. Saskatchewan, 1950. Bar: Sask. province bar 1952, appointed Queen's Counsel 1969. Sr. ptnr. Balfour, Moss, Regina, 1952—. Apptd. to Senate of Can., 1979—. Served to lt. Royal Can. Arty., 1950-54. Mem. Can. Bar Assn., Regina Bar Assn. (pres. 1956-57), Law Soc. Sask., United Services Inst. Progressive Conservative. Home: 175 Lansdowne Rd S, Ottawa, ON Canada K1M 0N8 Office: 700-2103 11th Ave, Regina, SK Canada also: Senate of Canada, Senate Bldg, Ottawa, ON Canada K1A 0A4*

BALFOUR, STEPHEN PAUL, educational analyst; b. L.A., Mar. 6, 1967; s. Richard Balfour and Linda Lindberg. BS, Tex. A&M U., 1990, MS, 1992, PhD, 1998. Asst. mgr. Kaplan Ednl. Svcs., College Station, Tex., 1993-94; advisor, program asst. Tex. A&M U., College Station, 1994—; lectr. dept. psychology Tex. A&M U., 1998. Tex. A&M U. Regents' fellow, 1990; recipient Hon. Mention award NSF, 1991. Mem. APA, Midwestern Psychol. Assn., Camarilla (v.p. 1994—, trustee 1998, pres. 1999), Phi Kappa Phi. Avocations: writing, cycling. Fax: (409) 862-4938. E-mail: balfour@tamu.edu. Office: Tex A&M U Coll Liberal Arts College Station TX 77843-4223

BALGEMAN, RICHARD VERNON, radiology administrator, alcoholism counselor; b. Berwyn, Ill., Dec. 25, 1929; s. Vernon Ernest and Regina Marie (Fitzgerald) B.; m. Wauneta Frances Laird, Nov. 15, 1952; children: Marcia, Kathleen, Barbara, Daniel. Radiology technician, Cook County Grad. Sch. of Med., 1951; BA in Health Svc., Governor State U., 1976, MA in Sci., 1978. Cert. technologist; ordained Deacon Roman Cath. Ch., 1997. Radiology adminstr. Manteno (Ill.) Mental Health Ctr., 1951-84; adminstrv. asst. bus. office Shapiro Devel. Ctr., Kankakee, Ill., 1984-88; with St. James Hosp., Chicago Heights, Ill., 1990-99. Inventor DuPont Cronex Tech. Aid, 1965. Village trustee Village of Manteno, 1969-72, chmn. planning commn., 1985-93; pres. Village View TV, Channel 10. With USNG, 1948-56. Gov.'s award Ill. Dept. Mental Health, Manteno, 1971; named Citizen of Yr. Manteno Hist. Soc., 1996. Mem. Am. Legion, Rotary. Roman Catholic. Avocations: camping, making miniature furniture, writing short stories. Home: 555 Park St Manteno IL 60950-1045

BALI, AJAY KUMAR, cardiologist; b. 1948; s. Ram Lal and Sarla (Lattha) B. MD, Med. Coll. Amritsar, India, 1972. Diplomate Am. Bd. Internal Medicine, added qualifications in geriatric medicine; diplomate Am. Bd. Cardiovascular Diseases. Intern Bronx (N.Y.) Lebanon Hosp., 1979-80, resident in medicine, 1980-82, fellow in cardiology, 1982-84; staff physician VA Hosp., Batavia, N.Y., 1984-86; staff cardiologist VA Hosp., Wilkes-Barre, Pa., 1986—. Fellow ACP, Am. Coll. Cardiology, Am. Coll. Chest Physicians; mem. AMA (Physician Recognition award 1992, 95), Am. Heart Assn. Democrat. Hindu. Office: VA Hosp 306 Indian Creek Dr Wilkes Barre PA 18702-7826

BALICK, HELEN SHAFFER, retired judge; b. Bloomsburg, Pa.; d. Walter W. and Clarissa K. (Bennett) Shaffer; m. Bernard Balick, June 29, 1967. JD, Dickinson Sch. Law, 1966, LLD, 1997. Bar: Pa. 1967, Del. 1969. Probate adminstr. Girard Trust Bank, Phila., 1966-68; pvt. practice law Wilmington, Del., 1969-74; staff atty. Legal Aid Soc. Del., Wilmington, 1969-71; master Family Ct. Del., New Castle County, 1971-74; bankruptcy judge, U.S. magistrate Dist. Del., Wilmington, 1974-90, chief judge, 1994-98; guest lectr. Dickinson Sch. Law, 1981-87; lectr. Dickinson Forum, 1982. Pres. bd. trustees Cmty. Legal Aid Soc., Inc., 1972-74; truste Dickinson Sch. Law, 1985—; mem. Citizens Adv. Com., Wilmington, 1973-74, Wilmington Bd. Edn., 1974. Recipient Women's Leadership award Del. State Bar Assn., 1997; named to Hall of Fame of Del. Women, 1994. Mem. Del. Bar Assn., Fed. Bar Assn., Nat. Conf. Bankruptcy Judges (bd. dirs. 1986), Nat. Assn. Women Lawyers, Del. Alliance Profl. Women (Trailblazer award 1984), Nat. Assn. Women Judges, Wilmington Women in Bus. (bd. dirs. 1080-83), Am. Judges Assn., Am. Coll. Bankruptcy, Am. Bankruptcy Inst., Turnaround

Mgmt. Assn. (bd. dirs. 1995-97), Dickinson Sch. Law Gen. Alumni Assn. (exec. bd. 1977-80, 87—, v.p. 1981-84, pres. 1984-87, Outstanding Alumni award 1991, Career Achievement award 1998), Phi Alpha Delta. Home: 2319 W 17th St Wilmington DE 19806-1330

BALICK, KENNETH D., international real estate finance executive; b. Albany, N.Y., Nov. 27, 1960; s. Sidney M. and Carole (Kaufmann) B. BS in Indsl. and Labor Rels., Cornell U., 1983; MPA, Harvard U., 1986. Legis. aide to Y. Seki Japan Parliament, Tokyo, 1983-84; dir. Asian programs Carnegie Coun. on Ethics and Internat. Affairs, N.Y.C., 1986-90; founder, pres. Trans-Pacific Consulting Group, N.Y.C., 1990-94; asst. to pres. Nomura Securities Internat., Inc., N.Y.C., 1994-97, dir. internat. bus. devel., 1997—; dir. internat. bus. devel. Capital Co. of Am., N.Y.C., 1998—; pub. spkr. in field. Am. Mensa scholar, Henry Luce scholar. Mem. Coun. on Fgn. Rels.

BALIGA, BANTVAL JAYANT, electrical engineering educator, research administrator; b. Madras, India, Apr. 28, 1948; came to U.S., 1969; s. Bantval Vittal and Sanjivi (Rao) B.; m. Pratima Nayak, Dec. 25, 1975; children: Avinash, Vinay. B in Tech., Indian Inst. Tech., Madras, 1969; MS, Rensselaer Poly. Inst., 1971, PhD, 1974. Mem. staff GE Rsch. Ctr., Schenectady, N.Y., 1974-78, program mgr., 1979-88, Coolidge fellow, 1983-88; prof. N.C. State U., Raleigh, 1988—, dir. power semiconductor rsch. ctr., 1991—; cons. power semiconductor industry, 1988—, EPRI, Palo Alto, Calif., 1989-92. Author: Power Semiconductor Devices, 1995, Modern Power Devices, 1987; author, editor: Epitaxial Silicon Tech, 1986; editor: Power Transistors, 1984, High Voltage ICs, 1988; contbr. over 450 articles to profl. jours.; holds over 90 patents. Recipient Dushman award GE, 1983; named among 100 Brightest Scientists in Am., Science Digest, 1984, Disting. Scientist, Asian Indians in N.Am., 1984. Fellow IEEE (assoc. editor Transactions on Electron Devices 1984-89, William Newell award 1991, Morris Liebman award 1993, J.J. Ebers award 1998, Lamme medal 1999); mem. Nat. Acad. Engring. Avocations: tennis, stamp collecting, travel. Office: NC State U Power Semiconductor Rsch Ctr Box 7924 Ctrl Campus Raleigh NC 27695

BALIGAR, VIRUPAX C., research soil scientist; b. Dharwar, Karnatak, India, June 1, 1942; s. Chanabasappa and Veeramma Baligar; m. Pampa V. Magadi, July 7, 1973; children: Sanjeev, Jenny. BS with honors, Karnatak U., Dharwar, 1965, MS with distinction, 1967; MS, Utah State U., 1971; PhD, Miss. State U., 1975. Faculty mem. U. Guelph, Ont., Can., 1977-79; rsch. soil scientist Purdue U., West Lafayette, Ind., 1979; rsch. advisor Inst. Interamericano Ciencias Agricolas/Embrapa World Bank, Sete Lagoas, Brazil, 1979-81; rsch. agriculturist Allied Corp., Morristown, N.J., 1981-83; vis. prof. USDA/W.Va. U., Beckley, 1983-84; rsch. soil scientist, supervisory scientist USDA-Agrl. Rsch. Svc., Beckley, 1984—; adj. prof. Va. Poly. and State U., Blacksburg. Author: Growth and Mineral Nutrition of Field Crops, 1991, 2d edit., 1997; editor: Crops as Enhancers of Nutrient Use, 1990, Plant-Soil Interaction at Low PH, 1991, Adaptation of Plants to Soil Stresses, 1994; author more than 190 rsch. publs. Fellow Am. Soc. Agronomy, Am. Soc. Soil Sci.; mem. Internat. Soc. Soil Sci. Office: USDA Agrl Rsch Svc 1224 Airport Rd Beaver WV 25813-0400

BALILES, GERALD L., lawyer, former governor; b. Stuart, Va., July 8, 1940. BA, Wesleyan U., 1963; JD, U. Va., 1967. Bar: Va. 1967, U.S. Supreme Ct. 1971. Asst. atty. gen. Commonwealth of Va., 1967-72, dep. atty. gen., 1972-75, atty. gen., 1982-85, gov., 1986-90; now with Hunton & Williams, Richmond, Va.; mem. Va. Ho. of Dels., 1976-82, mem. appropriations com., 1978-82, com. corp. ins. and banking, 1976-82, com. conservation and natural resources, 1979-82; formerly ptnr. Lacy and Baliles, Richmond; chmn. Joint House-Senate Ins. Study Com., 1977-79; Legal Drafting Sub-Com., State Water Study Commn., 1977-81; vice chmn. Joint House-Senate Com. on Nuclear Power Generation Facilities, 1977-79; chmn. Nat. Commn. Ensure Strong Competitive Airline Industry, 1993. Chmn. PBS; chmn. so. regional edn. bd. Commn. Ednl. Quality. Mem. Richmond Bar Assn., Va. Bar Assn. (exec. com. 1979), ABA (environ. quality com., natural resources law sect. 1973—, environ. control com., corp., banking and bus. law sect. 1974—), Va. State Bar (chmn. environ. quality com. 1975-77). Office: Hunton & Williams Riverfront Plz E Tower PO Box 1535 Richmond VA 23218-1535

BALIN, MARTY (MARTYN JEREL BUCHWALD), musician; b. Cin., Jan. 30, 1942; s. Joseph and Catherine E. Buchwald; children: Jennifer Ann, Delaney Mariah Skye. PhD, San Francisco State U. Founder, vocalist Jefferson Airplane, 1965-71, 75-80, 90—; also musician, vocalist Jefferson Starship, solo artist. Film appearances include Gimme Shelter, 1970; composer popular songs, including Volunteers, It's No Secret, Plastic Fantastic Lover, Young Girl Blues, Miracles, Sunday Blues, Atlanta Lady, Summer of Love, Solidarity; vocalist Hearts, Atlanta Lady; albums include Balin, KBC Band, Lucky, Bodacious D.F., Jefferson Airplane Reunion; recorded CD on Rhino Records, GWF Records, Trove Records, also video, CD Jefferson Starship. Address: care Joseph Buchwald PO Box 170040 San Francisco CA 94117-0040

BALIS, MOSES EARL, biochemist, educator; b. Phila., June 19, 1921; s. Harry and Frances (Spector) B.; m. Bernice M. Lamborg, Dec. 30, 1945; children—Frances Andrea, Ellen Joyce. B.A., Temple U., 1943; M.S., U. Pa., 1947, Ph.D., 1949. With Sloan-Kettering Inst., 1949-87, head nucleoprotein metabolism sect., 1957—, asso. mem., 1960-65, mem., 1965-87, chief div. cell metabolism, 1970-87; chair inst. senate, 1981-83; cons. Sloan-Kettering Inst., 1987-91; asso. prof. Med. Coll. Cornell U., 1954-66, prof. biochemistry, 1966-87, chmn. biochemistry unit, 1969-74; owner M.E. Balis, Inc., Fla.; vis. lectr. Adelphi U., 1963-64; cons. chemistry dept. Manhattan Coll., 1981-86; mem. study sects. Am. Cancer Soc., NIH.; mem. planning com. Nat. Cancer Plan; mem. rev. com. Nat. Large Bowel Cancer Program, 1977-81; pres. Med. Research Investment Fund, 1984-89. Mem. editorial bd. Cancer Rsch., 1969-73; assoc. editor, 1974-82. Served to lt. (j.g.) USNR, 1944-46. Recipient Research Career award USPHS, 1963. Mem. Am. Chem. Soc. (past sect. chmn.), AAAS, Am. Cancer Soc., Am. Soc. Biol Chemistry and Molecular Biology, Harvey Soc., Am. Assn. Cancer Rsch., Sigma Xi. Research, numerous publs. on metabolism of purines in normal and malignant tissues; determined biochem. action of anti-cancer drugs, biochemical nature of genetic defects. Home and Office: 11587 Pathway Ln Boynton Beach FL 33437-4932

BALK, CHRISTIANNE EVE, writer; b. Johnson City, N.Y., Aug. 25, 1952; d. Walter and Ann Balk; m. Karl Fiaccus, Aug. 24, 1985; 1 child, Elizabeth. BA in Biology, Grinnell Coll., 1974; M in English, U. Iowa, 1979, MFA, 1984. Author: (books) Bindweed, 1986 (Walt Whitman award Acad. Am. Poets 1985), Desiring Flight, 1995 (Verna Emery prize Purdue U. Press 1995). Office: PO Box 15633 Seattle WA 98115

BALK, ROBERT A., medical educator. BA, U. Mo., Kansas City, 1976, MD, 1978. Resident internal medicine U. Mo., Kansas City, 1978-81; fellow pulmonary and critical care medicine U. Ark., Little Rock, 1981-83, instr. medicine, 1981-83, asst. prof. medicine, 1983-85; staff physician Little Rock VA Med. Ctr., 1983-85; asst. prof. medicine Rush-Presbyn.-St. Luke's Med. Ctr., Chgo., 1985-88, assoc. prof., 1988-95, prof. medicine, 1995—, asst. dir. sect. pulmonary medicine, 1985-90, med. dir. respiratory care svcs., 1985-93, med. dir. noninvasive respiratory care unit, 1985-87, co-dir. med. intensive care unit, 1986-88, dir. med. intensive care unit, 1988-95, assoc. dir. sect. pulmonary & crit. care medicine, 1993—, assoc. dir. sect. critical care medicine, 1995—; dir. pulmonary & critical care medicine fellowship tng. program Rush-Presbyn.-St. Luke's Med. Ctr., dir. sect. Pulmonay CCC, Chgo., 1994-97, 97—. Contbr. articles to profl. jours. Recipient Dedicated Svc. & Superior Individual Effort in Patient Care Alice Sachs Meml. award, 1991, Alfred Soffer Rsch. award Am. Coll. Chest Physicians, 1995. Office: Rush-Presbyn St Luke's Med Ctr 1653 W Congress Pkwy Chicago IL 60612-3809

BALKA, SIGMUND RONELL, lawyer; b. Phila., Aug. 1, 1935; s. I. Edwin and Jane (Chernicoff) B.; m. Elinor Bernstein, May 29, 1966. AB, Williams Coll., 1956; JD, Harvard U., 1959. Bar: Pa. and D.C. 1961, N.Y. 1969, U.S. Supreme Ct. 1966. Sr. atty. Lilco, Mineola, N.Y., 1969-70; v.p., gen. counsel Brown Boveri Corp., North Brunswick, N.J., 1970-75; asst. gen. counsel Power Authority State N.Y., N.Y.C., 1975-80; gen. counsel Krasdale Foods, Inc., N.Y.C., 1980—; pres. Graphic Arts Coun. N.Y., 1980—. Chmn. Hunts Point Environ. Protection Coun., N.Y.C., 1980—; chmn. law com. N.Y.C. Community Bd. 6, Queens, 1980-88, chmn. econ. devel. com., 1988—; chmn. Soc. for a Better Bronx, 1985—; bd. dirs. Bronx Arts Coun., 1981—, Greater N.Y. Met. Food Coun., 1986—, Jewish Repertory Theatre, 1987—; chmn. Bronx Borough Pres.'s Adv. Com. on Resource Recovery, 1988-90; chair fellows, mem. vis. com. Williams Coll. Mus. of Art, 1996—. Fellow Am. Bar Found.; mem. ABA (co-chmn. pro bono project corp. law dept. 1986-88, chmn. 1988-90, com. of corp. gen. counsel 1974—, planning chmn. 1994-96, membership chmn. 1996-98), FBA, Am. Corp. Counsel Assn. (bd. dirs. Met. N.Y. chpt., bd. dirs. Found. 1992—), Assn. Bar City N.Y. Office: Krasdale Foods Inc 400 Food Center Dr Bronx NY 10474-7098

BALKCOM, CAROL ANN, insurance agent; b. Newport, R.I., June 20, 1952; d. Robert Terrence and Barbara Ruth (Hilton) Hannaway; m. Richard Roger Balkcom, Oct., 1981; children: Richard Robert, Geoffrey Adam. BA, R.I. Coll., 1974, MA in Teaching, 1981; Cert. Life Underwriter, Am. Coll., 1984, CHFC, 1986. CLU, ChFC. Tchr. Lincoln (R.I.) Jr. High Sch., 1974-78; sales agt. Met. Life Ins. Co., Pawtucket, R.I., 1978-80; mgr., agt. Phoenix Mut. Life Ins. Co., Providence, 1980-94; instr. R.I. Lic. Sch., Providence, 1986-93; dist. mgr. New Eng. Fin., New Port Richey, 1994—. Mem. industry com., membership com. Com. 100; mem. Jr. Svc. League, treas. 1999—. Mem. R.I. Life Underwriters (bd. dirs. 1981-84, 90—, 1st v.p. 1983-84), Soc. of Fin. Svc. Profls. (bd. dirs., edn. chmn. Tampa chpt. 1999—). Avocations: cooking, entertaining.

BALKE, ROBERT ROY, architect; b. Madison, Wis., Apr. 25, 1950; s. Roy Leonard and Elizabeth Katherine (Behling) B.; m. Margaret Miriam Cowles, June 11, 1949; children: Sarah Margaret, Andrew Robert. B in Environ. Studies summa cum laude, U. Detroit, 1972, MArch, 1974. With John Portman & Assoc., Atlanta, 1973-74; architect, prin. Thompson, Ventulett, Stainback & Assocs., Inc. Architects, Atlanta, 1974—. Co-author: A Case Study, The Influence of Energy on Building Design, 1976; prin. works include Buckhead Plz. Tower, Atlanta, Cornerstone Office Bldg. (Best Office Bldg. Nat. Design award P.C.I. 1993), Charlotte Carillon Tower and Parking Deck (Best Parking Nat. Design award P.C.I. 1993). Pres. pro life com. Sacred Heart, Atlanta, 1990-93; mem. property com. Zoo Atlanta. Recipient Alpha Rho Chi medal U. Detroit, 1974. Mem. AIA (Ga. exec. com. Atlanta 1990-92, design com. 1990-91, membership com. 1991-92, found. bd. 1993-95), St. Vincent DePaul Soc. (pres. Sacred Heart conf. 1994—), Atlanta Coffee House Club, Alpha Sigma Nu. Roman Catholic. Avocations: sailing, skiing, fishing, camping.

BALKE, VICTOR H., bishop; b. Meppen, Ill., Sept. 29, 1931; s. Bernard H. and Elizabeth A. (Knese) B. B.A. in Philosophy, St. Mary of Lake Sem., Mundelein, Ill., 1954, S.T.B. in Theology, 1956, M.A. in Religion, 1957, S.T.L. in Theology, 1958; M.A. in English, St. Louis U., 1964, Ph.D., 1973. Ordained priest Roman Catholic Ch., 1958; asst. pastor Springfield, Ill., 1958-62; chaplain St. Joseph Home Aged, Springfield, 1962-63; procurator, instr. Diocesan Sem., Springfield, 1963-70; rector, instr. Diocesan Sem., 1970-76; ordained, installed 6th bishop of Crookston, Minn., 1976—. Clubs: K.C, Lions. Office: Chancery Office PO Box 610 Crookston MN 56716-0610*

BALL, ARMAND BAER, former association executive, consultant; b. Dubach, La., Sept. 30, 1930; s. Armand Baer and Lovera (Sanderson) B.; m. Beverly Jane Hodges, Sept. 15, 1957; children—Kathryn Lynn, Robin Armand. BA, La. Coll., 1951; MRE, Southwestern Bapt. Theol. Sem., 1953; MS, George Williams Coll., 1960. Royal Ambassador dir. Fla. Bapt. Conv., Jacksonville, 1953-57; program dir. Woodlawn Boys' Club, Chgo., 1957-58; camp/youth dir. YMCA, Nashville, 1958-62; exec. dir. YMCA Camps Widjiwagan/duNord, St. Paul YMCA, 1962-74; exec. v.p. Am. Camping Assn., Martinsville, Ind., 1974-88; cons., 1988—; assoc. Campaign Assocs., Phila., 1989—. Author: (with Beverly H. Ball) Basic Camp Management, 1999; editor: A Cost Study of Resident Camps, 1985; Internat. Camping Fellowship newsletter, 1987-97; co-editor: Business and Finance, Site and Facilities; Trendlines newsletter. Cons. Ctr. for Disease Control, St. Petersburg (Russia) Children's Camps, Malaysian Tourist Bd., Pan-Am. Inst. of Phys. Edn. (Venezuela), Heritage Conservation and Recreation Svc., Project Reach, Boy Scouts Am., United Ch. of Christ, YMCA, Episcopal Ch.; mem. steering com. Internat. Camping Fellowship. Recipient Disting. Svc. award Am. Camping Assn., 1989; named Citizen of the Yr., Sanibel, Fla., 1999. Mem. Am. Soc. Assn. Execs. (cert. assoc. exec. life), World Future Soc., Audubon Soc., Canadian Camping Assn., Kiwanis. Home and Office: 1351 Middle Gulf Dr Apt 2A Sanibel FL 33957-4631

BALL, CARROLL RAYBOURNE, anatomist, medical educator, researcher; b. Leakesville, Miss., Oct. 11, 1925; s. Marvin Hugh and Elizabeth (Hillman) B.; m. Jannie Vee Brooks, Sept. 5, 1947 (dec. 1954); children: Hugh Brooks, Peter Stephen; m. Sally Ann Montgomery, Mar. 22, 1963 (div. 1976); 1 child, Lou Ellen. BA, U. Miss., 1947, MS, 1948, PhD, 1963. Grad. asst. in zoology U. Miss., Oxford, 1946-48; instr. Duke U., 1948-51; instr. anatomy Med. Sch. W.Va. U., 1951-57; asst. prof. biology U. So. Miss., 1957-60; asst. prof. U. Miss. Med. Ctr., Jackson, 1963-66, assoc. prof., 1966-71, prof., 1971—. Contbr. numerous articles to profl. jours. Pres. Jackson Civil War Round Table, 1983-84; chmn. Hist. Coker House Restoration Project, 1984—; v.p. Magnolia chpt. Nat. Assn. Watch and Clock Collectors, 1980-82; bd. dirs. Miss. Hist. Soc., 1976-79, 85-88, 93-96. Lt. comdr. USNR, 1944-71, PTO. NIH predoctoral trainee, 1960-63; Miss. Heart Assn. grantee, 1963-66. Mem. Am. Assn. Anatomists, Soc. Exptl. Biology and Medicine, Am. Assn. Pathology, So. Assn. Anatomy, Miss. Acad. Sci., Hattiesburg Jr. C. of C. (sec. 1959-60), Order of First Families of Miss., Sigma Xi, Alpha Epsilon Delta, Theta Nu Sigma, Beta Beta Beta (pres. 1947-48), Omicron Delta Kappa, Pi Kappa Alpha (sec. 1943-44). Methodist. Home: 905 Pinehurst Pl Jackson MS 39202-1742 Office: U Miss Med Ctr Dept Anatomy 2500 N State St Jackson MS 39216-4500

BALL, DAMON HOWARD, investment management executive; b. N.Y.C., May 7, 1957; s. Dayton Ball and Margaret (Howard) Ball Haskell; m. Sally Cates, Sept. 20, 1986; 1 child, Amanda Cates. BA, U. Pa., 1979; MBA, Harvard U., 1983. Assoc. Mfrs. Hanover, Boston, 1979-81; v.p. Winthrop Fin. Assocs., Boston, 1983-86, Needham & Co., N.Y.C., 1986-88; sr. v.p. Desai Captial Mgmt., N.Y.C., 1988—; bd. dirs. Finlay Enterprises, N.Y.C., Garden Botanika, Seattle; chmn. bd. dirs. Northstar TV Group, Grand Rapids, Mich. Mem. Union Club (N.Y.C.), Am. Yacht Club (Rye, N.Y.), Ea. Yacht Club (Marblehead, Mass.), Seawanhaka Yacht Club (Oyster Bay, N.Y.). Republican. Episcopalian. Avocations: sailing, tennis. Office: Desai Capital Mgmt 540 Madison Ave Fl 36 New York NY 10022-3271

BALL, DONALD EDMON, architect; b. Evansville, Ind., July 18, 1942; s. Harvey and Myrl (Norris) B. BA in Design, So. Ill. U., 1967. Registred architect Ariz., Calif., Colo., Nev.; cert. Nat. Coun. Archtl. Registration Bd. With design dept. Leo A. Daly Co., Architects and Engrs., Omaha, 1968; project mgr. Buetow & Assocs., St. Paul, 1969-70; ptnr. Comprehensive Design, Mpls., 1971-73; with Caudill Assocs., Aspen, Colo., 1973-76, Hagman Yaw, Ltd., Aspen, 1977; project mgr. Hauter Assocs., Aspen, 1978; pres. Jacobs, Ball & Assocs., Architects, Aspen and Denver, 1978-85; project mgr. Moshe Safdie & Assocs., Boston, 1985-87; dir. design Dwayne Lewis Architects, Inc., Phoenix, 1987-88; prin. Donald Ball and Assocs., Scottsdale, Ariz., 1988—. Mem. Aspen Bldg. Insp. Selection Com., 1982, Pitkin County Housing Authority Bd., Aspen, 1984. Mem. AIA (chmn. Colo. West chpt., documents com.), Ariz. Soc. Architects (profl. practice com.). Avocations: golf, old cars. Home and Office: 7702 E Sutton Dr Scottsdale AZ 85260-4031

BALL, DONALD LEWIS, retired English language educator; b. Balt., Oct. 25, 1922; s. Ambrose Markley and Daisy Gertrude (Anderson) B.; stepmother Thelma (Bonneville) B.; m. Barbara Jean Stevens, May 3, 1950; children: Helen Ball Williams, Ann S., Allison Ball Miller, Markley Ball Rizzi. BA, U. Richmond, 1948; MA, U. Del., 1951; PhD, U. N.C., 1965. Asst. mgr. resort hotels in Md. and Fla., 1948-53; instr. English Va. Mil. Inst., Lexington, 1953-57; part-time instr. U. N.C., Chapel Hill, 1957-60; faculty Coll. William and Mary, Williamsburg, Va., 1960-89, prof., 1976-89; vis. prof. English U.S. Mil. Acad., West Point, N.Y., 1984-85. Author: Samuel Richardson's Theory of Fiction, 1971, Fighting Amphibs-The LCS(L) in World War II, 1997; contbr. articles to profl. publs. Served to lt. (j.g.) USNR, 1943-46, PTO. Research grantee Coll. William and Mary, 1978. Mem. MLA. Democrat. Episcopalian. Avocations: genealogy, history, music. Home: 1 Cole Ln Williamsburg VA 23185-3313

BALL, DONALD MAURY, agronomist, consultant; b. Owensboro, Ky., Aug. 5, 1945; s. William Alonzo and Mary Ruth (Waltrip) B.; Vonda Lee Hatcher, June 3, 1967; children: Kelly Wayne, Allison Lee. BS, Western Ky. U., 1968; MS, Auburn U., 1973, PhD, 1976. Cert. profl. agronomist. Extension agronomist Auburn (Ala.) U., 1976-88, extension agronomist/prof., 1988-97, alumni prof., 1997—; mem. nat. adv. com. Alfalfa Seed Coun., Davis, Calif., 1983—; tech. advisor Oregon Tall Fescue Commn., Salem, Oreg., 1990—; tech. liaison Oreg. Clover Commn., Salem, 1994—; del. Internat. Grassland Congress, Nice, France, 1989; speaker in field. Author: Southern Forages, 1991, Practical Forage Concepts, 1999; contbr. over 300 articles to profl. and applied jours. and trade mags. Elder First Presbyn. Ch., Auburn, 1982-85. With U.S. Army, 1968-71. Recipient Superior Svc. award USDA, Washington, 1986, Extension Excellence award Auburn Univ. Alumni Assn., 1988, Alumnus of Yr. award Western Ky. Univ. Dept. Agrl., Bowling Green, 1990. Fellow Am. Soc. Agronomy (Crops and Soils award 1984, ext. Agronomy Edn. award 1993), Crop Sci. Soc. Am.; mem. Am. Forage and Grassland Coun. (pres. 1990-91, Merit award 1984, Medallion award 1993), So. Pasture and Forage Crop Improvement Conf. (chair 1987-88). Democrat. Office: Auburn Univ Dept Agronomy & Soils Auburn AL 36849

BALL, HOWARD GUY, education specialist educator; b. Lancaster, Ohio, Aug. 4, 1930; s. Howard Emitt and Edith Mildred (Clark) B.; married; children: Brian, Maryla. B.S., Ohio State U., 1952, M.S., 1969, Ph.D., 1972. Edn. specialist Ohio Dept. Edn., Columbus, 1964-71; assoc. prof. N.C. State U., 1971-74; mem. faculty Ala. A&M U., Normal, 1974—; prof. emeritus Ala. A&M U. (Sch. Library Media); chmn. bd. Communicon, Inc., Huntsville, Ala.; chmn. Media Svcs., Inc.; pres. Higby Inc.; dir. So. Inst. for Black Studies, 19956. Mem. editorial bd. Library Scene, 1979-80, Media and Methods: Early Years, 1984-85; contbr. articles to profl. jours.; authored, directed: Training of Librarians in CATV, 1975. Mem. Ala. Council Human Relations, 1978—, Ala. Democratic Council, 1978—; sec. Orgn. Inner City Govts., 1977—. Recipient NAACP Community award, 1976, Raleigh C. of C. educator's award, 1973. Mem. ALA, Assn. Educators Communication and Tech., Assn. Ednl. Research (regional v.p. 1985-86), Phi Beta Kappa, Phi Delta Kappa, Kappa Alpha Psi. Presbyterian. Club: Masons.

BALL, JAMES S., orchestra conductor, educator, musician; b. Chgo., Sept. 6, 1951; s. John Miller Ball and Audrey Mae Scott Roddy; m. Ami Yamori, Sept. 28, 1981; children: Jun Y., Ken Y. BMus, Oberlin Coll., 1974; MMus, Ga. State U., 1982; MMus in Conducting, Northwestern U., 1983; D of Mus. Arts, U. Mo., Kansas City, 1992. Vol. U.S. Peace Corps, San Jose, Costa Rica, 1975-77; prin. trombonist Nat. Symphony Orch. of Costa Rica, San Jose, 1975-80; prof. Nat. Youth Orch. of Costa Rica, San Jose, 1975-80; dir. bands Pensacola (Fla.) Jr. Coll./U. West Fla., 1984-87; assoc. condr. Kansas City (Mo.) Civic Orch., 1987-90; asst. condr. Mo. Chamber Orch., Columbia, 1990-92; performance mgr. U. Mo., Kansas City, 1991-94; music dir./condr. Lawrence (Kans.) Symphony Orch., 1993-94, Danville (Ill.) Symphony Orch., 1994—; guest condr. Lawrence Chamber Players, 1990, Kingsport (Tenn.) Symphony Orch., 1991, Oaxaca (Mex.) Symphony Orch., 1996; contestant Internat. Conducting Competition, Pescara, Italy, 1997. Founder advanced wind ensemble Nat. Youth Orch. Costa Rica, 1977, Sandy Springs (Ga.) Chamber Orch., 1984, Ann. H.S. Jazz Band Festival, Pensacola, 1986, New Ear, Contemporary Music Ensemble, Kansas City, Mo., 1993. Bd. dirs. Vermilion Heritage Found., Danville, 1995—; mem. steering com. Downtown Concert Series, Danville, 1997, chair steering com., 1998. Recipient Chancellor's Merit Scholarship award U. Mo., Kansas City, 1987-89; Eckstein grantee Northwestern U., 1982-83. Mem. Condrs. Guild (regional chair Latin Am., Am. Symphony Orch. League, Coll. Music Soc., Rotary Internat. (Paul harris fellow 1997), Pi Kappa Lambda. Home: 301 E Winter Ave Danville IL 61832-1857 Office: Danville Symphony Orch 1021 N Vermilion St Danville IL 61832-3074

BALL, JAMES WILLIAM, check cashing company executive; b. Tacoma, June 23, 1942; s. Montgomery McKinley and Ann Marie Ball; m. Patricia Miller, July 29, 1977; children: Katherine Kendall, Molly Elizabeth. Student, St. Martin's Coll., Lacy, Wash., 1960-61, San Jose City Coll., 1966-68; BA, San Jose State U., 1970, MA, 1971; postgrad., U. Calif., Irvine, 1971-72. Store mgr. Food Villa Inc., San Jose, Calif., 1972-76; asst. mgr. Ralph's Inc., San Jose, 1976-78; pres., owner Ball Liquors Inc., San Jose, 1978-88; pres. Fast Cash Inc., San Jose, 1984—. Mem. Nat. Check Cashers Assn., Inc. (dir. 1994—, sec. 1998), Calif. Check Cashers Assn. (v.p. 1988-97, pres., 1997). Office: Fast Cash Inc 2270 Quimby Rd San Jose CA 95122-1355

BALL, JENNIFER LEIGH, writer, editor; b. South Charleston, W.Va., Aug. 6, 1961; d. Robert Lee Ball and Lois Jean (Sovine) White. BA, Marshall U., Huntington, W.Va., 1983; MA, U. Colo., Colorado Springs, 1997. Copy writer Klausner Cooperage, Louisville, 1986; staff writer Ky. Power Co., Ashland, 1987-91; print buyer Focus on the Family, Colorado Springs, 1992-94; publs. mgr. Compassion Internat., Colorado Springs, 1994-96; editor Internat. Bible Soc., Colorado Springs, 1996—. Editor; Discerning the Times, 1999, Light Inside, 1998; co-produced video/acad. rsch., Ethnic Minority Diversity at University of Colorado: Perceptions and Communication Processes, 1997. Avocations: equine sports, volleyball, camping, hiking. Home: 231 Elmwood Dr Colorado Springs CO 80907-4355

BALL, JOHN FLEMING, advertising and film production executive; b. Evanston, Ill., Apr. 26, 1930; s. Edward Hyde and Kathleen (Fleming) B.; m. Anne Idabelle Firestone, Nov. 9, 1957; children—John Fleming, Jr., David Firestone, Sheila Anne. B.A., Princeton, 1952. Assoc. producer, progam exec. CBS, N.Y.C., 1955-59; with J. Walter Thompson Co., N.Y.C., 1959—; v.p. J. Walter Thompson Co., 1965—, dir. programs, 1965-67, dir. broadcasting, 1967—, pres., dir. Survival Anglia Ltd. div., 1972—; pres. Trident Anglia Inc., 1976—; chmn. John F. Ball Prodns., John F. Ball Co., 1984. Trustee Found. Am. Dance; chmn. instructional TV, Archidiocese of N.Y. With USN, 1952-54. Named to Knights of Holy Sepulchre of Jerusalem, 1991, Knights of Sovereign Mil. Order of Malta, 1992. Mem. Cap and Gown Club of Princeton U. (N.Y.C.), River Club, Links Club, Round Hill Club of Greenwich, Nassau Club (Princeton), Am. Club (London), Princeton Triangle Club (chmn. emeritus grad. bd.). Home: Deer Park Greenwich CT 06830 also: 110 Northport Point MI 49670 Office: 4 Woodside Rd Greenwich CT 06830-3819

BALL, JOHN H., construction executive; b. 1931; married. BS, Pa. State U., 1955. With R.M. Shoemaker Co. Inc., 1955—, pres., chief exec. officer, 1967—, also bd. dirs. Served with USMC, 1950-52. Office: R M Shoemaker Holdings Inc. PO Box 888 West Conshohocken PA 19428

BALL, JOHN H(ANSTEIN), lawyer; b. N.Y.C., Dec. 14, 1919; s. Nathan and Hattie (Hanstein) B.; m. Alice Wolf, June 12, 1946 (dec. Oct. 1989); children: Joan, Jean; m. Eleanor Shaw Ball, 1992. B.S., N.Y. U., 1941; LL.B., Columbia U., 1944. Bar: N.Y. State bar 1945, So. and Eastern dist. fed. ct. bars 1947. Assoc. firm Kaye, Scholer, Flerman, Hays & Handler, N.Y.C., 1944-56; counsel Kaye, Scholer, Flerman, Hays & Handler, 1977-81; counsel firm Robinson, Silverman, Pearce, Aronsohn & Berman, N.Y.C., 1981-89; ptnr. firm Borden & Ball, N.Y.C., 1981-89; counsel Tenzer, Greenblatt, Fallon & Kaplan, N.Y.C., 1989-97, Kramer, Levin, Naftahs & Frankel, N.Y.C., 1997—. Pres. Ctrl. Synagogue, N.Y.C., 1979-85; bd. overseers Hebrew Union Coll., 1985-90. Mem. Am., N.Y. State, N.Y.C., N.Y. County bar assns. Home: 737 Park Ave New York NY 10021-4256 Office: 919 3d Ave New York NY 10022

BALL, JOHN PAUL, publishing company executive; b. N.Y.C., Dec. 15, 1946; s. William Emil and Else (Schmidt) B.; m. Jayne Barbara Irwin, Jan. 30, 1970 (div. 1991); m. Eileen M. Mitchell, Oct. 25, 1997. Student, N.Y. Sch. Printing, 1964. Prodn. assoc. Macmillan Co., N.Y.C., 1964-65; asst. to pres. Frederick Fell, Inc., N.Y.C., 1965-69; v.p., dir. prodn. William Morrow & Co., Inc., N.Y.C., 1969-86; sr. v.p. mfg. and paper purchasing Macmillan Pub. Co., N.Y.C., 1986-94; pub. and graphic arts cons., chmn. bd. Electronic Pub. Svcs. Inc., N.Y.C., 1994—; exec. v.p., sec. IDG Books, Foster City, Calif., 1996—. Recipient Comet Press award graphic arts, 1964, Columbia

Scholastic Press Assn. Best Editorial Writing award, 1965. Office: IDG Books Worldwide Inc 919 E Hillsdale Blvd Foster City CA 94404-4247

BALL, JOHN ROBERT, healthcare executive; b. Opelika, Ala., July 16, 1944; s. John Cooper Jr. and Ellen Beverly (Williams) B.; m. Cornelia Anne Phillips, Aug. 13, 1966 (div. 1983); children: Kristen Anne, John Robert; m. Pamela Preston Reynolds, Jan. 9, 1988. AB, Emory U., 1966; JD, Duke U., 1971, MD, 1972. Research assoc. Duke U. Sch. Medicine, Durham, N.C., 1971-72, resident in medicine, 1972-74; asst. to dir. office asst. sec. for health USPHS, Rockville, Md., 1974-76; chief med. audit br. bur. quality assurance HEW, Rockville, 1976-77; sr. policy analyst Office Sci. and Tech. Policy Exec. Office of Pres., Washington, 1978-81; assoc. exec. v.p. ACP, Phila., 1981-86, exec. v.p., 1986-94, also master; sr. scholar Assn. Acad. Health Ctrs., Washington, 1994-95; exec. v.p., acting pres., CEO Pa. Hosp., Phila., 1995-96, pres., CEO, 1996-99; Robert Wood Johnson clin. scholar George Washington U., Washington, 1977-79; bd. mgrs. Pa. Hosp.; bd. dirs. Milbank Meml. Fund. Assoc. editor Jour. Am. Geriatrics Soc., 1984-86; mem. editorial bd. Internat. Jour. Tech. Assessment in Health Care, 1986-89, European Jour. Internal Medicine, 1988-94, Duke U. Law Jour., 1969-71; contbr. articles to profl. jours. Sr. surgeon USPHS, 1974-77. John Gordon Stipe scholar, Nat. Merit scholar, Emory U., 1962. Mem. Inst. Medicine of NAS, N.Y. Acad. Medicine, N.C. Bar Assn., Internat. Soc. for Tech. Assessment in Health Care, Am. Clin. and Climatol. Assn., Soc. Med. Adminstrs. Democrat.

BALL, KENNETH LEON, manufacturing company executive, organizational development consultant; b. N.Y.C., Aug. 11, 1932; s. Oscar and Elvira (Klein) B.; m. Patricia Ann Whitley; children: David B., Dana K. BA, Antioch Coll., Yellow Springs, Ohio, 1954; PhD, Washington U., St. Louis, 1958. Lic. psychologist, Mo. Gen. mgr. Pacific Coast div. Orchard Corp. Am., 1960-62; indsl. rels. dir. Orchard Corp. Am., St. Louis, 1963-64; v.p. indsl. rels. Orchard Corp. Am., 1965-66, v.p., dir., 1967-72, exec. v.p., dir., 1972-75, pres., dir., 1976-88; pres. Orchard Decorative Products div. Borden, Inc., St. Louis, 1988-92, Ken Ball Mgmt. Resources, St. Louis, 1993—; adj. prof. Washington U., 1978-79. Contbg. author: Humanizing Organizational Behavior, 1976, Making Organizatios Humane and Productive, 1981; contbr. articles to publs. Trust Antioch U., 1980-85, 89—; dir. Met. Employment and Rehab. Svc., St. Louis, 1975—, chair, 1985-86; dir. St. Louis chpt. Young Audiences, 1990, Narcotic Svc. Coun., 1976. Human Rels. Rsch. Found. fellow, 1955-58. Mem. APA, Inst. Mgmt. Cons., Nat. Spkrs. Assn., Acad. Mgmt., Soc. Psychologists in Mgmt. (dir. 1989—, pres. 1992-93). Home: 9875 Northbridge Rd Saint Louis MO 63124-1025 Office: Ken Ball Mgmt Resources 165 N Meramec Ave Ste 430 Clayton MO 63105-3772

BALL, LILLIAN, sculptor, educator; b. Augusta, Maine, Jan. 6, 1955; d. Kinsley Allen Jr. and Joanne (Haskell) B.; m. David Frederick Reed III, June 28, 1986. Student, Instituto Bellas Artes, San Miguel de Allende, Mexico, 1971, Nordenfiords Verdens U., Copenhagen, 1972-73, Harvard U., 1975-76, Parsons Sch. Design, N.Y.C., 1978, Columbia U., 1984-85, New Sch. Social Rsch., 1985. Mem. faculty sculpture N.Y. Feminist Art Inst., N.Y.C., 1989-92; guest lectr. Boston U. Program in Arts, 1978; vis. artist R.I. Sch. Design, Providence, 1987; invited artist Garner Tullis Monoprints, Santa Barbara, Calif., 1987; ajudicator Conn. State Sculpture Grants, Hartford, Conn., 1988; invited artist Urdla Print Pubs., Villeubanne, France, 1991,Internat. Contemporary Art Cruise, France,Spain, Italy, 1991; panelist The Ecstasy Panel, Dooley le Cappelaine Gallery, N.Y.C., 1992, Arts Link-Citizens Exch. Coun., N.Y.C., 1993; guest lectr. sculpture dept. NYU, N.Y.C., 1992, Academie der Kunst, Berlin, 1992; vis. artist Sch. Visual Arts Grad. Dept., N.Y.C., 1993, Vt. Studio Ctr., Johnson, 1993. One-woman shows at Snug Harbor Cultural Ctr., Staten Island, N.Y., 1989, Socrates Sculpture Park, L.I. City, N.Y., 1989, Hudson River Mus., Westchester, N.Y., 1990, Rubin Spangle Gallery, N.Y.C., 1992, Sculpture Ctr., N.Y.C., 1995, Queens Mus.; exhibited in group shows at Fla. Internat. U., Miami, 1980, Soho Ctr. Visual Arts, N.Y.C., 1980, Aldrich Mus., Ridgefield, Conn., 1980, Thorpe Intermedia Gallery, Sparkill, N.Y., 1985, The Sculpture Ctr., N.Y.C., 1986, 87, Richard Green, N.Y.C., 1986, White Columns, N.Y.C., 1986, Addison Ripley Gallery, Washington, 1987, Artists Space, N.Y.C., 1987, Sala Uno Galleria, Rome, 1987, Henry Feiwell Gallery, N.Y.C., 1988, Weatherspoon Art Gallery, Greensboro, N.C., 1988, Bard Coll., Annandale-on-Hudson, N.Y., 1988, Barbara Toll Fine Arts, N.Y.C., 1988, Ruggerio Henis, N.Y.C., 1989, Mott Ives Gallery, N.Y.C., 1991, Shoshana Wayne Gallery, Santa Monica, Calif., 1991, Urdla, Villeurbanne, Lyons, France, 1992, Nouvel Espace de Venissieux, France, 1992, Hawkins Gallery, N.Y.C., 1992, Dooley le Cappelaine Gallery, N.Y.C., 1992, Kunstlerhaus Bethanien, Berlin, 1992, John Post Lee Gallery, N.Y.C., 1993, Stephanie Theodore Gallery, N.Y.C., 1993, Art Finds, Easthampton, N.Y., 1993, Exit Art, N.Y.C., 1993, UCLA Wight Gallery, 1994, New Mus., N.Y.C., 1994, Jersey City, 1999: group shows (Chromaform) around the country; contbr. articles to profl. jours. Recipient Nat. Heritage Trust Grant, Artpark, Lewiston, N.Y., 1979, Nat. Endowment Arts fellowship in sculpture, 1986-87, fellowship printmaking N.Y. Found. Arts, 1991, Guggenheim Found. fellowship in visual arts, 1999. Avocations: sailing, cinema. Home and Office: 7 Harrison St New York NY 10013-2832

BALL, LINDA ANN, educator; b. Des Moines, Aug. 10, 1942; d. Vern Ray and Orletha Ann Carmichael; student Iowa State U., 1960-62; BS in Edn., Drake U., 1964; MS in Edn., Ill. State U., 1981; m. Robert Ray Ball, Aug. 15, 1964; children: Lindsay, Ryan, Justin. Tchr., Marshalltown, Iowa, 1964-68; TV tchr. Sta. WAND-TV, Decatur, Ill., 1969-71; tchr. Des Moines Public Schs., 1973-79; adv. Ill. State U. Panhellenic, Normal, 1979-80; tchr., faculty assoc. Metcalf Lab. Sch., Ill. State U., Normal, 1980—; presenter workshops and confs. Past mem. Jr. Women's Club, Assn. Advocacy and Edn. Disabled Citizens, Mid-Central Planning Commn. for Handicapped, Friends of the Arts; past pres. JayceeEttes, Campfire Girls Council; bd. dirs. United Cerebral Palsy. Co-author: Kaleidoscope, Language-Based Activities for Young Children, 1988, Look, Look I Wrote a Book, 1997. Cert. reading specialist, early childhood specialist. named finalist for Ill. Tchr. of Yr., 1997. Mem. Ill. Reading Council, Ill. State Kindergarten Conf. Commn. (chair), Early Childhood Edn. Assn., Ill. Edn. Assn., Ill. Assn. Supervision and Curriculum Devel. (Outstanding Early Childhood Educator 1992), Delta Zeta (collegiate province dir.), Delta Kappa Gamma. Democrat. Home: 3409 Windmill Rd Bloomington IL 61704 Office: Metcalf Lab Sch Ill State U Normal IL 61761

BALL, LOUIS ALVIN, insurance company executive; b. Oct. 25, 1921; s. George Rhodom and Frances Mariam (Beals) B.; m. Norma Jane Laudenberger, Jan. 17, 1947. BA in Bus. Adminstrn., Kans. State U., 1947. Asst. purchasing agt. Kansas City (Mo.) br. Ford Motor Co., 1942-46; with Farm Bur. Mut. Ins. Co., Inc., Manhattan, Kans., 1947—, claims underwriting mgr., 1956-61, sys. and procedures mgr., 1961—, asst. sec., 1977-81, corp. sec., 1981-90; ret., 1990. Mem. Nat. Ind. Insurers, Conf. Casualty Cos., Assn. Sys. Mgmt. (Internat. Merit award 1971, Internat. Achievement award 1978, Kansas City chpt. Merit award 1970, Kansas City chpt. Diamond Merit award 1977, chmn. ann. conf. 1982), Manhattan Country Club. Home: 1101 Pioneer Ln Manhattan KS 66502-4624

BALL, MARGIE BARBER, elementary school educator; b. San Antonio, Tex., June 28, 1943; d. Truman Joseph and Margaret Evelyn (Norman) Barber; m. Flamen Ball Jr., Aug. 20, 1966; children: Michael David, Matthew Joseph, Marissa Anne. BS, U. Houston, 1963; MS, Stephen F. Austin State U., 1985. Texas Tchr. Cert. Spanish tchr. Spring Branch Ind. Sch. Dist., Houston, Tex., 1964-66, tchr., 1966-68; dir. mother's day out Holy Spirit Episcopal, Tex., 1977-78; tchr. Nacogdoches (Tex.) Ind. Sch. Dist., 1979-82; kindergarten tchr. Christ Episc. Sch., 1982-87; early childhood tchr. Hudson Ind. Sch. Dist., Lufkin, Tex., 1987-94; tchr. pre-kindergarten/bilingual Lufkin Ind. Sch. Dist., 1994-95, tchr. pre-kindergarten/multi-age, 1995-96; tchr. kindergarten Hudson ISD, Lufkin, 1996-97; supr. student tchrs., adj. faculty Stephen F. Austin State U., Nacogdoches, 1997—. Mem. Tex. State Tchr. Assn., East Tex. Assn. Educators Young Children, Nacogdoches, Med. Wives Auxillary, Phi Delta Kappa. Republican. Presbyterian. Avocations: gardening, reading, travelling. Office: Stephen F Austin State U Box 13017 SFA Sta Nacogdoches TX 75962-3017

BALL, MARION J., health information professional. BA, U. Ky., 1961, MA, 1965; EdD, Temple U., 1978. Programmer, instr. behavioral sci. U. Ky. Med. Ctr., 1965-68; from asst. dir. to dir. health sci. ctr. Temple U., Phila., 1968-85; from dir. acad. computing to prof. dept. epidemiology U. Md., Balt., 1985-97; dir. WHO Collaborating Ctr. Health Informatics, Balt., 1993-97; adj. prof. U. Md. Sch. Nursing, Balt., 1986—, Johns Hopkins U., Balt., 1997—; rsch. prof. divsn. dental informatics U. Md. Coll. Dental Surgery/Dental Sch., 1989-93; v.p. First Cons. Group, 1997—. Assoc. editor Internat. Jour. Biomed. Computing, 1989-96; co-editor: Health Informatics series. Recipient pioneer award for computing in healthcare, 1992, pres.'s award Am. Med. Informatics Assn. Fellow Inst. of Medicine; mem. NAS Inst. Medicine, Internat. Med. Informatics Assn., Med. Libr. Assn., Am. Acad. Med. Adminstrs., Am. Assn. Med. Sys. & Informatics, Am. Hosp. Assn., Assn. Computing Machinery. Office: First Cons Group 2 Hamill Rd # W Baltimore MD 21210-1806

BALL, (ROBERT) MARKHAM, lawyer; b. Wilmington, Del., Mar. 24, 1934; s. Robert William and Helen (Slepicka) B.; m. Harriet Laura Janney, July 6, 1957; children: Laurence Markham, Richard Janney, Martha Harriet, Julia Helen. BA magna cum laude, Amherst Coll., 1956; BA with honors, Oxford (Eng.) U., 1958, MA, 1973; LLB, Harvard U., 1960. Bar: D.C. 1961, U.S. Supreme Ct. 1968. Law clk. U.S. Supreme Ct., Washington, 1960-61; assoc. Covington and Burling, Washington, 1961-64; asst. gen. counsel U.S. Office Econ. Opportunity, Washington, 1964-66; staff dir. U.S. Peace Corps, Washington, 1966-67; from assoc. to ptnr. Leva, Hawes, Symington, Martin and Oppenheimer, Washington, 1967-77; gen. counsel U.S. Agy. for Internat. Devel., Washington, 1977-79, mem. adv. com. on vol. fgn. aid, 1981-88; ptnr. Wald, Harkrader and Ross, Washington, 1980-85, Morgan, Lewis and Bockius, Washington, 1986-98, Holland and Knight, Washington, 1998—; adj. faculty Internat. Law Inst., Washington, 1985—; lectr. Law Sch., U. Va., 1991—. Council mem. Friends of the Amherst (Mass.) Coll. Library, 1981—; sec. Brasenose Coll. Charitable Found., Oxford, 1988—. Rhodes scholar Phi Beta Kappa, 1956-58. Mem. ABA, Internat. Bar Assn., Am. Soc. Internat. Law, Am. Arbitration Assn. (mem. arbitration panel 1986—, mem. corp. counsel com., 1987—), Alexandria Literary Soc. (sec. 1981—). Home: 7223 Stafford Rd Alexandria VA 22307-1806 Office: Holland & Knight LLP 2100 Pennsylvania Ave NW Washington DC 20037

BALL, MILLICENT JOAN (PENNY BALL), multimedia developer; b. Buffalo, Sept. 15, 1939; m. Neil Baggett, Aug. 9, 1965 (div. Nov. 1991). BS, Antioch Coll., 1961; PhD, U. Md., 1969. Rsch. assoc. Inst. Hochenergiephysik, Heidelberg, Germany, 1969-71; sr. programmer Imperial Coll., London, 1971-73; asst. prof. Purdue U., West Lafayette, Ind., 1973-77; systems analyst Calculon Corp., Germantown, Md., 1978-80; computer analyst Brookhaven Nat. Lab., Upton, N.Y., 1980-90; data mgmt. group leader Super Collider Lab., Dallas, 1990-94; pres.;project dir. MJB Cons., DeSoto, Tex., 1994-97; pres. MJB Plus, Inc., DeSoto, Tex., 1998—. Recipient SBIR award Dept. Energy, 1994. Mem. AAUW, Assn. Computing Machinery, Assn. for Women in Sci. Avocations: square dancing, travel. Home and Office: 1415 Country Ridge Dr De Soto TX 75115-7423

BALL, MILLIE (MILDRED PORTEOUS BALL), editor, journalist; b. New Orleans, Nov. 15, 1945; d. Harold Curtis and Mildred (Porteous) B.; m. Keith Cooper Marshall, Oct. 17, 1981. BA, Fla. State U., 1967. Editor young people's page The Times-Picayune, New Orleans, 1967-71, city desk reporter, 1971-79, staff writer Dixie Mag., 1979-82, staff writer living sect., 1982-89, travel editor, 1990—. Author: (with others) Fodor's New Orleans, 1990, Gault Millau New Orleans, 1991. Recipient various writing awards AP, La. Press Assn., Press Club New Orleans, Odyssey House, 1970-90, Lowell Thomas award Soc. Am. Travel Writers Found., 1992, Bronze Travel Journalist of Yr. award, 1994, Silver-Best Self-Illustrated Story award, 1994, Best Fgn. Story in Newspaper award, 1992, Best Newspaper Travel Sect., 1994, 95. Mem. Chi Omega. Presbyterian. Home: 530 Chartres St New Orleans LA 70130-2110 Office: The Times-Picayune 3800 Howard Ave New Orleans LA 70125-1429

BALL, NEAL, management consultant, philanthropist; b. Chgo., Oct. 7, 1935; s. Clyde E. and Alice Julia (Shillin) Ball. BS, U. Ill., 1959; cert. advanced mgmt., Northwestern U., 1963. Pub. affairs asst. Am. Hosp. Supply Corp., Evanston, Ill., 1960-63, dir. pub. affairs, 1965-71; cons. N. Ball Assocs., Chgo., 1963-65; dep. press sec. The White House, Washington, 1971-73; v.p. Am. Hosp. Corp., Evanston, 1973-86; advisor Neal Ball Co., Chgo., 1986—; dir. Nat. Med. Fellow, N.Y.C., 1984-97; mem. adv. com. Johns Hopkins Sch. Pub. Health, Balt., 1990-96; chmn. vis. com. Ctr. East Asian Studies U. Chgo., 1990-96. dir. Internat. Vistors Ctr. Chgo., 1982—; vice-chmn. com. on Africa and the Ams. Art Inst. Chgo., 1986—; founder, hon. chair Am. Refugee Comm., Mpls., 1982—; bd. govs. Internat. House U. Chgo., 1986—; pres. Friends of the Windows, Chgo., 1994—; mem. nat. adv. com. U.S. Comm. for UNICEF, N.Y.C., 1996—, dir. nat. adv. com., 1998—. Recipient World of Children award UNICEF, 1980. Mem. Univ. Club, The Casino. Home and Office: 1335 N Astor St Chicago IL 60610-2152

BALL, OWEN KEITH, JR., lawyer; b. Louisville, Feb. 19, 1950; s. Owen Keith and Martha Katherine (Guntherberg) B.; m. Shirley Marie Galinski, Sept. 16, 1972. BSCE, U. Kans., 1972, JD, 1980. Bar: Mo. 1980, U.S. Dist. Ct. (we. dist.) Mo. 1980, Kans. 1988, U.S. Dist. Ct., Kans., 1988. Ptnr. Smith, Gill, Fisher & Butts P.C., Kansas City, Mo., 1980-87; pvt. practice as a loan broker Lawrence, 1987-88, pvt. practice, 1988-91; legal counsel Marian Merrell Dow Inc., Kansas City, Mo., 1991-92; corp. counsel Marion Merrell Dow Inc., Kansas City, Mo., 1992-95, Hoechst Marion Roussel, Inc., Kansas City, Mo., 1995—. Mem. staff Hyatt Regency Hotel com. to investigate safety of the Hyatt Regency Hotel, Kansas City C. of C., 1981. Lt. USN, 1972-77. Mem. Am. Corp. Counsel Assn., Mo. Bar Assn., Kansas City Met. Bar Assn. Avocation: classical music. Office: 10236 Marion Park Dr Kansas City MO 64137-1405

BALL, RANDALL, physician assistant, medical technologist; b. Cleve., July 10, 1969; s. John Jr. and Garlene (Francis) B.; m. Mary Ann Hatfield, Aug. 5, 1995. Cert. in med. tech., Pikeville (Ky.) Meth. Hosp., 1991; BS, Pikeville Coll., 1991; B in Health Scis., U. Ky., 1994. Cert. physician asst. in surgery and primary care Nat. Commn. Cert. Physician Assts., Inc. Lab. aid, phlebotomist Pikeville Meth. Hosp., 1990-91; generalist med. technologist St. Joseph Hosp., Lexington, Ky., 1991-93; physician asst. PrimeCare, P.S.C., Elizabethtown, Ky., 1994-97, AcuteCare, LLC, Elizabethtown, 1997—. Named Physician Asst. Preceptor of Yr. U. Ky., 1995. Mem. Am. Soc. Clin. Pathologists (cert. med. technologist), Am. Acad. Physician Assts., Ky. Acad. Physician Assts. Democrat. Avocations: golf, swimming, tennis. Fax: 502-763-0051. E-mail: acutecre@ne.infi.net. Office: AcuteCare LLC 1239 Woodland Dr Elizabethtown KY 42701-2770

BALL, REX MARTIN, urban designer, architect; b. Oklahoma City, June 14, 1934; s. Ralph Martin and Sarah Mae (Kellner) B. BArch, Okla. State U., 1956; MArch, MIT, 1958. Lic. arch. Nat. Coun. Arch. Registration Bd.; cert. planner Am. Inst. Cert. Planners. With HTB Inc. (archtl., engrng., interior planning firm), Oklahoma City, 1958-94; chmn. emeritus HTB Inc., SD; founder, pres. Planning Assocs. Inc., 1960—; founder, pres., chmn., CEO Mid Continent Design Group, 1968—; presdl. appt. to U.S. Commn. of Fine Arts, 1994-97. Exhibitor U.S./USSR exhibit "The Socially Responsible Environment, 1980-90; contbr. articles to profl. jours. Commr. Tulsa Preservation Com., 1997—; bd. dirs. Price Tower Mus., 1998—. Capt. U.S. Army Corps of Engrs., 1957; ret., res., 1958-75. Recipient Bus. in the Arts award, 1988, 5 Who Care Corp. Humanitarian award, Gannett Found., 1988, Curt Schwartz Bus. in the Arts award, 1989, Phoenix award/ Downtown Now, 1992, Cityscape award City of Oklahoma City, 1992, Disting. Alumni award Okla. State U., 1995. Fellow AIA (mem. nat. com. on design); mem. Eastern Okla. AIA (past pres., cert. of appreciation 1997, 98), Tulsa C. of C. (past bd. dirs.), Urban Land Inst. (retiree assoc.), Oklahoma City C. of C. (forner v.p., bd. dirs. 1980-90), Nat. Trust for Hist. Preservation, Nat. Bldg. Mus., Okla. Heritage Assn., Soc. Am. Mil. Engrs. (former sustaining mem.), Am. Planning Assn., Okla. State U. Alumni Assn. (life mem., past bd. dirs., Tulsa and Okla. counties pres.), MIT Alumni Assn. (past Okla. pres.), Air Force Assn. (past pres. Gerrity chpt.), Urban League of Greater Oklahoma City (past bd. dirs.), Blue Key Club, Sigma Nu, Alpha Rho Chi. Fax: 918-748-9688. E-mail: ballrexm@aol.com. Home: 2203 E 20th St Tulsa OK 74104-5628

BALL, ROBERT JEROME, classics educator; b. N.Y.C., Nov. 4, 1941; s. William and Pauline Ball. BA, Queens Coll., 1962; MA, Tufts U., 1963; PhD, Columbia U., 1971. Asst. prof. classics U. Hawaii, Honolulu, 1971-76, assoc. prof., 1976-83, prof., 1983—. Author: Tibullus The Elegist: A Critical Survey, 1983, Reading Classical Latin: A Reasonable Approach, 1987, 2d edit., 1997, Reading Classical Latin: The Second Year, 1990, 2d edit., 1998; editor: The Classical Papers of Gilbert Highet, 1983, The Unpublished Lectures of Gilbert Highet, 1998. Recipient Excellence in Teaching award U. Hawaii, 1979; Presdl. scholar U. Hawaii, 1985. Mem. Am. Philol. Assn. (Excellence in Teaching award 1981). E-mail: Rball@hawaii.edu. Office: U Hawaii Dept European Langs Honolulu HI 96822

BALL, ROBERT M(YERS), social security, welfare and health policy specialist, writer, lecturer; b. N.Y.C., Mar. 28, 1914; s. Archey Decatur and Laura Elizabeth (Crump) B.; m. Doris Jacqueline McCord, June 30, 1936; children: Robert Jonathan, Jacqueline Ball Smith. AB, Wesleyan U., 1935, MA, 1936; hon. degree, U Md., Wesleyan U., Yale U. With Bur. Old Age and Survivors Ins., Social Security Bd., 1939-46, asst. dir., 1949-52, acting dir., 1953, dep. dir., 1953-62, commr. of social security, 1962-73; sr. scholar Inst. Medicine, Nat. Acad. Scis., 1973-81; writer, lectr., cons., 1981—; asst. dir. com. on edn. and social security Am. Coun. on Edn., 1946-49; staff dir. pension study Nat. Planning Assn., 1950-52; staff dir. adv. coun. Social Security, 1948-49, chmn. 1965, mem. 1979, 91, 96; mem. Nat. Commn. on Social Security Reform, 1982-83, White House Conf. on Social Security, 1998. *Robert Ball was one of the most influential participants in the development of Social Security and Medicare. He was the U.S. Commissioner of Social Security, 1962-73 and top Civil Servant at Social Security prior to his appointment by President Kennedy, with a total of thirty years service at the Social Security Administration. As Commissioner, he was in charge of setting up Medicare and administering it for the first seven years. Since leaving government in 1973, he continues to serve on official advisory councils. Consultant to labor, senior citizen groups and other organizations, Senators and Reps., and Presidential staff. Continues activity at 85.* Author: Pensions in the United States, 1952, Social Security Today and Tomorrow, 1978, (with Thomas N. Bethell) Because We're All in This Together, 1989, (with Thomas N. Bethell) Bridging the Centuries, The Case for Traditional Social Security, 1997, (with Thomas N. Bethell) Straight Talk about Social Security, 1998; also articles on social security, welfare, health care and nat. health ins. Recipient Disting. Svc. award Nat. Civil Svc. League, 1958, Rockefeller Pub. Svc. award, 1961, Arthur J. Altmeyer award, 1968, Clarence A. Kulp award Am. Soc. Risk and Ins., 1980, Elizur Wright award, 1990, Presdl. award Am. Soc. on Aging, 1988, Arthur S. Fleming award, 1989, Andrus award AARP, 1990, Cruikshank award Nat. Coun. Sr. Citizens, 199, others; named to Health Care Hall of Fame, 1999. Mem. Inst. Medicine (Lienhard award 1991), Nat. Acad. Pub. Adminstrn., Nat. Coun. on Aging (Ollie Randall award 1983), Gerontol. Soc. Am. (awrd 1996), Nat. Acad. Social Ins. (founding chmn. bd.), Phi Beta Kappa, Delta Kappa Epsilon. Home and Office: 7217 Park Terrace Dr Alexandria VA 22307-2036

BALL, SUSAN, arts association administrator, art historian; b. Pasadena, Calif., May 25, 1947; d. Charles Russell and Catherine (Piller) B.; m. Edward Kaufman, Mar. 19, 1983; 1 child, Emily Catherine. Student French art history, Ecole Du Louvre, Paris, 1967; BA in European Thought and Culture, Scripps Coll., 1969; MA in Art History, U. Calif., Riverside, 1974; M of Philosophy, Yale U., 1976, PhD, 1978; postgrad., U. Chgo., 1984-86; cert. in careers in bus. program, Columbia U., 1981. Rsch. asst. U. Calif., Riverside, 1972-74; rsch. asst. Yale U., 1974-75, teaching fellow, 1974-76; asst. prof. art history U. Del., Newark, 1978-81; rsch. assoc. Real Estate Bd. N.Y., 1981-82; asst. treas. Chase Manhattan Bank, N.Y.C. and Chgo., 1982-85; dir. govt. found. affairs Art Inst. Chgo., 1985-86; exec. dir. Coll. Art Assn., N.Y.C., 1986—; sr. honors examiner Swarthmore Coll., 1981; panelist women's admission PhD program Yale U., 1992, arts. svc. orgns. N.Y. State Coun. Arts, 1989-91, Del. State Arts Coun., 1980; planning cons. Del. Humanities Forum, 1978-81; juror Congl. Arts Caucus Art Competition, 1993; mem. adv. com. culture and arts 8th Congl. Dist., 1993—, creative caucus Scripps Coll., 1993-96, adv. bd. Coun. Am. Overseas Rsch. Ctrs., 1996—; spkr. in field. Author: Ozenfant and Purism, 1982; contbr. articles to art catalogs; editl. advisor Renaissance Soc. Newsletter, 1984-86; revs. editor Art Jour., 1986-87, mem. editl. bd., 1986-92; editor-in-chief, columnist From the Executive Director CAA News, 1986—. Bd. dirs. Nat. Cultural Alliance, 1989—, N.Y. Found. Arts, 1996—, v.p., 1997—; bd. dirs., chmn. exhbns. and gallery com. Del. Ctr. Contemporary Art, 1978-81; invited participant adv. panel art history NEH, 1988; mem. U.S. civil soc. observer del. to 50th anniversary of UNESCO constn. Ams. Universality UNESCO, Paris, 1995. Mem. Nat. Humanities Alliance (bd. dirs. 1988—, chmn. com. policy and planning 1994), Nat. Cultural Alliance (founding mem., bd. dirs. 1989—), Am. Coun. Learned Socs. (bd. dirs., rep. com. Conf. Adminstrv. Officers 1986—, exec. com. 1989-92, mem. numerous other coms.). Democrat. Office: c/o Coll Art Assn 275 7th Ave Fl 18 New York NY 10001-6708*

BALL, TRAVIS, JR., educational consultant, editor; b. Newport, Tenn., July 13, 1942; s. Travis and Ruth Annette (Duyck) B.; BA, Carson Newman Coll., 1964; MA, Purdue U., 1966. Instr., then asst. prof. English, Ill. Wesleyan U., Bloomington, 1966-69; vis. prof. English edn. Millikin U., 1969; asst. headmaster, chmn. English dept. Brewster Acad., Wolfeboro, N.H., 1969-72; dir. admissions, asst. to headmaster Park Tudor Sch., Indpls., 1972-88; cons. to Selwyn Sch., Denton, Tex., 1988-89; pres. Travis Ball & Assos., 1980-88; dir. comm. Verde Valley Sch., Sedona, Ariz., 1988-91; editor Projects in Enrollment Mgmt., 1992—; mem. commn. on curriculum and grad. requirements Ind. Dept. Public Instrn., 1974-76; mem. adv. council Ednl. Records Bur.; reviewer Nat. Stds. Project in Sci., Civics and Govt., 1994-95; ednl. cons., 1992—. Mem. Indiana Non-Public Edn. Assn. (treas., dir., vice chmn.), Independent Schs. Assn. Central States (conf. chmn.), Nat. Council Tchrs. English, Assn. Supervision and Curriculum Devel., Council Advancement and Support Edn. (adv. com. on ind. schs.), Nat. Assn. Ind. Schs. (workshop faculty 1986, 87), Sigma Tau Delta, Pi Kappa Delta, Phi Delta Kappa. Baptist. Editor, Tchrs. Service Com. Newsletter for English Tchrs., 1977-82; dept. editor English Jour., 1976-82; editor/pub. Contact: Newsletter for Admissions Mgmt., 1980-88. Office: 1739 Log Church Rd Newport TN 37821-5535

BALL, VIRGINIA BEALL, investor; b. Jacksonville, Tex., Jan. 1; d. John A. and DeLouise (McClelland) Beall; m. Edmund F. Ball, June 28, 1952; children: Robert, Nancy. Student, Lon Morris Jr. Coll., 1936-37; AB, Baylor U., 1940; grad. student, Tex. Christian U., 1942-43, Ball State U., 1952-54; HHD (hon.), Wabash Coll., 1975; hon. degree, Ball State U., 1986; Hon. degree, Keuka Coll., 1994. V.p. Muncie (Ind.) Airport, Inc., 1992—, B.B.S. Properties, Muncie, 1992—; trustee, chmn. Nat. Wildlife Fed. Endowment, Washington, 1980-93. Bd. dirs. Minnetrista Cultural Found., Muncie Ind. Com. Humanities, 1973-79, Ind. Youth Inst., Indpls.; former mem. adv. bd. Connor Prairie Settlement, Fishers, Ind., Interlochen (Mich.) Ctr. for Arts, Muncie Children's Mus., Human Genetics and Engrng. Lab., Ball State U., Muncie. Recipient Civic award Woman of Influence, Muncie, 1980; Old Main Tower award Baylor U., 1981, Sagamore of Wabash award Gov. of Ind., Indpls., 1984, Baylor Woman of Merit award Omicron Delta Kappa, 1989, Distinction award Ind. Humanities Coun., Indpls., 1990, VIVA award Muncie C. of C., Rotary Club, 1993, Huckins medal Baylor U., Pres.'s medal of distinction Ball State U., 1999; named Disting. Alumni, Lon Morris Jr. Coll., 1983. Mem. The Ninety-nines, Explorer's Club, Soc. Woman Geographers, Internat. Woman's Forum, Rotary Club. Republican. Avocations: travel, education. Home: 1707 W Riverside Ave Muncie IN 47303-3548 Office: Ball Assocs PO Box 1408 222 S Mulberry St Muncie IN 47305-2802

BALL, WILLIAM AUSTIN, health facility director, researcher; b. L.A., Feb. 16, 1948; s. Joe Martin and Norma Lou (Schouweiler) B.; m. Rachel Yvette Jeanne Tullier, July 21, 1972. BA summa cum laude, Harvard Coll., 1970; student, Ecole Normale Supérieure, Paris, 1970-71; PhD, U. Mich., 1976; MD, U. Pa., 1983. Diplomate Am. Bd. Psychiatry. Asst. prof. psychology Swarthmore (Pa.) Coll., 1976-80; assoc. prof. psychiatry U. Pa., Phila., 1988-89, 1989-96; dir. emergency svc. Hosp. U. Pa., Phila., 1994-98, med. dir. inpatient psychiatry svc., 1989-96; clin. monitor Merck Rsch. Labs., West Point, Pa., 1998—. Assoc. editor Jour. Genetic Psychology; contbr. articles to profl. jours. Recipient Rsch. Svc. award NIH, 1987, Earl Bond Teaching award 1991. Mem. Soc. for Neuroscience, Phi Beta Kappa. Avocations: tennis, running, French literature. Office: Merck Rsch Labs PO

Box 4 BL 2-5 West Point PA 19486 also: Hosp U Pa Dept Psychiatry 3400 Spruce St Philadelphia PA 19104-4204

BALL, WILLIAM JAMES, pediatrician; b. Charleston, S.C., Apr. 16, 1910; s. Elias and Mary (Cain) B.; BS, U. of South, 1930; MD, Med. Coll. S.C., 1934; m. Doris Hallowell Mason, July 9, 1938. Intern, Roper Hosp., Charleston, 1934-35; resident dept. pediatrics U. Chgo. Clinics, 1935-37; instr. pediatrics Med. Coll. S.C., 1938-42; practice medicine specializing in pediatrics, Charleston, 1938-42, Northwest Clinic, Minot N.D., 1946-51, Aurora, Ill., 1951-70; physician student Health Svc. No. Ill. U., 1970-72; mem. staff Copley Meml., Mercy Ctr. Health Care Svcs.; assoc. prof. Sch. Nursing, No. Ill. U., 1971-72. Mem. Bd. Health, Aurora, Ill., 1958-62; pediatrician, divsn. svcs. for crippled children U. Ill., 1952-86; pediatric cons. sch. dists. 129 and 131, Aurora, 1972-85, DeKalb County Spl. Edn. Assn., 1972-81, Sch. Assn. Spl. Edn. Dupage County, 1980-83, Mooseheart, Ill., 1970-83, Northwestern Ill. Assn. Handicapped Children; chmn. adv. com. Kane County Health Dept., 1986-95; pres. Kane County sub-area coun. Health Sys. Agy., Kane, Lake, McHenry Counties, 1977-78, sec., 1978-79. Served as capt. M.C., AUS, 1942-46; maj., 1946 to col., 1963, ret. 1970. Diplomate Am. Bd. Pediatrics. Recipient Golden Apple award Ill. Sch. Dist. 129, 1983, Shimkus award Aurora Vis. Nurses Assn., 1993. Fellow Am. Acad. Pediatrics; mem. AMA, Kane County Med. Soc. (pres. 1962), Am. Heart Assn., Am. Cancer Soc., Juvenile Protective Assn. of Aurora , The Ret. Officers Assn. (west suburban Chgo. chpt.), Phi Beta Kappa, Phi Chi, Pi Kappa Phi. Rotarian. Address: 309 S Bailey St Hobart OK 73651-3831

BALL, WILLIAM KENNETH, lawyer; b. DeQueen, Ark., Jan. 15, 1927; s. William P. and Lucille (Jeter) B.; m. Ella Hubbard Scaife, Dec. 28, 1950; children—Lucy Jane, William Ramsay, Charles Scaife. JD, U. Ark., 1953. Bar: Ark 1953, U. S. Supreme Ct., 1971. Law clk. to assoc. justice Ark. Supreme Ct., 1953-54; practice in Monticello, 1954—; ptnr. Ball, Barton & Hoffman, 1958-99; city atty. Monticello, 1961-93; of counsel Ball, Barton & Hoffman, 1999—; spl. justice Supreme Ct. Ark., 1975. Served with AUS, 1945-47, 50-52. Mem. Fellow Ark. Bar Found.; mem. Ark. Bar Assn., S.E. Ark. Bar Assn. (pres. 1957-58), Rotary (pres. 1962-63), Kappa Sigma, Delta Theta Phi. Presbyterian. Home: 104 Westminster Dr Monticello AR 71655-4814 Office: Ball Barton & Hoffman 106 W Oakland Ave Monticello AR 71655-4114

BALL, WILLIAM PAUL, physicist, engineer; b. San Diego, Nov. 16, 1913; s. John and Mary (Kajla) B.; m. Edith Lucile March, June 28, 1941 (dec. 1976); children: Lura Irene Ball Raplee, Roy Ernest. AB, UCLA, 1940; PhD, U. Calif., Berkeley, 1952. Registered profl. engr. Calif. Projectionist, sound technician studios and theatres in Los Angeles, 1932-41; tchr. high sch. Montebello, Calif., 1941-42; instr. math. and physics Santa Ana (Calif.) Army Air Base, 1942-43; physicist U. Calif. Radiation Lab., Berkeley and Livermore, 1943-58; mem. tech. staff Ramo-Wooldridge Corp., Los Angeles, 1958-59; sr. scientist Hughes Aircraft Co., Culver City, Calif., 1959-64; sr. staff engr. TRW-Def. Systems Group, Redondo Beach, Calif., 1964-83, Hughes Aircraft Co., 1983-86; cons. Redondo Beach, 1986—. Contbr. articles to profl. jours.; patentee in field. Bd. dirs. So. Dist. Los Angeles chpt. ARC, 1979-86. Recipient Manhattan Project award for contbn. to 1st atomic bomb, 1945. Mem. AAAS, Am. Phys. Soc., Am. Nuclear Soc., N.Y. Acad. Scis., Torrance (Calif.) Area C. of C. (bd. dirs. 1978-84), Sigma Xi. Home and Office: 209 Via El Toro Redondo Beach CA 90277-6561

BALLAM, SAMUEL HUMES, JR., retired corporate director; b. Phila., Apr. 12, 1919; s. Samuel Humes and Mary (McGarvey) B.; m. Dorothy Meadowcroft, May 1, 1943; children—Barbara J. Ballam Stephens, Samuel H., III. A.B., U. Pa., 1950; A.M.P., Harvard Bus. Sch., 1959. Fin. analyst Fidelity Bank, Phila., 1936-41, 46-48; investment officer Fidelity Bank, 1948-55, asst. to pres., 1955-56, v.p. br. system, 1956-60, sr. v.p. trust dept., 1960-66, exec. v.p. comml. dept., 1966-71; pres. Fidelcor, Inc., Phila., 1971-78; chief exec. officer Fidelcor, Inc., 1975-78; chmn. Am. Water Works Co., Inc., 1985-88; dir. numerous corps. Emeritus trustee U. Pa., Phila., 1970—; chmn. bd. dirs. Hosp. U. Pa., 1972-87; bd. dirs. Zool. Soc. Phila., 1978—, Balch Inst. for Ethnic Studies, Phila., 1964—, Geog. Soc. Phila., 1976-79. Capt. USAF, 1951-52. Republican. Episcopalian. Clubs: Union League (v.p., dir.), Merion Cricket. Avocations: tennis, photography. Home: 74 Middle Rd Bryn Mawr PA 19010-1756

BALLANFANT, KATHLEEN GAMBER, newspaper executive, public relations company executive; b. Horton, Kans., July 11, 1945; d. Ralph Hayes and Audrey Lavon (Heryford) G.; children: Andrea, Benjamin. BA, Trinity U., 1967; postgrad. NYU, 1976, Am. Mgmt. Inst., 1977, Belhaven Coll., 1985. Pub. info. dir. Tex. Dept. Community Affairs, Austin, 1972-74; pub. affairs mgr. Cameron Iron Works, Houston, 1975-77, Assoc. Builders and Contractors, Houston, 1982-84; pres. Ballanfant & Assoc., Houston, 1977-82, 84—; pres. Village Life Inc., 1985—; pres., chief exec. officer Village Life Publs.; owner Village Life newspaper, Southwest News newspaper, Houston Observer/Times newspaper, Village Life Printing & Typesetting, South Post Oak newspaper; mem. adv. council on Construction Edn., Tex. So. U., Houston, 1984—; mem. task force on ednl. excellence Houston Ind. Sch. Dist., 1983—; mem. devel. bd. Inter First Fannin Bank, 1986-88; bd. dirs. Bellaire Hosp., Westbury-Southwest Assn., Westland YMCA. Author: Something Special-You, 1972, Prevailing Wage History in Houston, 1983; editor newspaper Bellaire Texan, 1981-82, Austin Times, 1971. Vice pres. West Univ. Republic Women's Club, Houston, 1984—; fgn. vis. chmn. Internat. Inst. Edn., Houston, 1980—; docent Houston Zoo, 1982; bd. dirs. Westland YMCA. Named Tex. Woman of Achievement Tex. Womans Hosp., 1986; recipient Apollo IX Medal of Honor Gov. Preston Smith, 1970, Child Abuse Prevention award Gov. Dolph Briscoe, 1974, Tex. Community Newspaper Assn. (pres. 1988-89, bd. dirs. 1987-96). Mem. Bellaire C. of C. (bd. dirs. 1987-90, sec., treas. 1988), Rotary. Republican. Presbyterian. Avocations: traveling, racquetball, reading. Office: Village Life Inc 5160 Spruce St Bellaire TX 77401-3309

BALLANTINE, JOHN TILDEN, lawyer; b. Louisville, Feb. 26, 1931; s. Thomas Austin and Anna Marie (Pfeiffer) B.; m. Mary January Strode, May 15, 1954 (div. 1964); children: John T. Jr., William Clayton, Douglas C.; m. Beverley Jo Hackley, Dec. 8, 1967; 1 child, Susan Marie. BA with high distinction, U. Ky., 1952; JD, Harvard U., 1957. Bar: Ky. 1957, U.S. Ct. Appeals (6th cir.) 1958, U.S. Supreme Ct. 1982. Law clk. to presiding judge U.S. Dist Ct. (we. dist.) Ky., 1957-58; assoc. then ptnr. Ogden Newell & Welch, Louisville, 1958—; mem. civil rules com. Ky. Supreme Ct., 1988-96. Bd. dirs. Family and Children Agy., Louisville, 1965-75, pres., 1971-74; bd. dirs. Our Lady of Peace Hosp., Louisville, 1966-73, 88—, chmn., 1968-69, 91-93; bd. dirs. Met. United Way, Louisville, 1975-81; mem. Hist. Landmarks and Preservation Dists. Commn., Louisville, 1976-88; bd. dirs. Ky. Derby Festival, Louisville, 1975-81, v.p., 1975. 1st lt. USAF, 1952-54. Recipient Outstanding Young Man in Field of Law award Louisville Jaycees, 1966. Fellow Am. Coll. Trial Lawyers; mem. ABA, Ky. Bar Assn. (bd. govs. 1996—, ho. of dels. 1985-86, 89—, clients' security fund 1993-96, Ky. evidence rules rev. commn. 1995—), Louisville Bar Assn. (bd. dirs. 1969-71, 88, 89, 92, 93, 96—, pres. 1970, profl. responsibility com. 1988-93, past chmn. physician-atty. com.), U.S. 6th Cir. Ct. Appeals Jud. Conf. (life), Am. Bd. Trial Advs., Fed. Ins. and Corp. Counsel, Ky. Def. Counsel (pres. 1981-82), Louis D. Brandeis Am. Inn of Ct., Supreme Ct. Civil Rules Com., Ky. Character and Fitness Com., Pendennis Club, The Law Club, Lawyers Club. Office: Ogden Newell & Welch 1700 Citizens Plaza 500 W Jefferson St Ste 1700 Louisville KY 40202-2874

BALLANTINE, JOHN WALLIS, retired banker; b. Youngstown, Ohio, Feb. 16, 1946; s. George Woods and Elizabeth (Wallis) B.; m. Caroline Brummel, Oct. 21, 1973. BA, Washington & Lee U., 1968; MBA, U. Mich., 1970. Sr. v.p., head internat. asset mgmt. 1st Chgo. Corp., 1984-85, sr. v.p., head Latin Am. divsn., 1985-87, sr. v.p., head asset mgmt. group, 1987-88, sr. v.p., head N.Y. bank/NA banking, 1988-92, exec. v.p., 1992-95; exec. v.p., head internat. banking 1st Chgo. NBD Corp., 1995-96; exec. v.p. 1st Chgo. Corp. NBD Corp., 1996-98; ret., 1998. Trustee Lake Forest (Ill.) Coll., 1994—, Mus. Contemporary Art, Chgo., 1996—, Music and Dance Theater Chgo., 1996—, WTTW Comm., Inc., Chgo., 1993—, Kemper Mut. Funds, 1999—; bd. dirs. Hubbard St. Dance Chgo., 1993—.

BALLANTINE, MORLEY COWLES (MRS. ARTHUR ATWOOD BALLANTINE), newspaper editor; b. Des Moines, May 21, 1925; d. John and Elizabeth (Bates) Cowles; m. Arthur Atwood Ballantine, July 26, 1947 (dec. 1975); children—Richard, Elizabeth Ballantine Leavitt, William, Helen Ballantine Healy. AB, Ft. Lewis Coll., 1975; LHD (hon.), Simpson Coll., Indianola, Iowa, 1980. Pub. Durango (Colo.) Herald, 1952-83, editor, pub., 1975-83, editor, chmn. bd., 1983—; dir. 1st Nat. Bank, Durango, 1976—, Des Moines Register & Tribune, 1977-85, Cowles Media Co., 1982-86. Mem. Colo. Land Use Commn., 1975-81, Supreme Ct. Nominating Commn., 1984-90; mem. Colo. Forum, 1985—; trustee Choate/Rosemary Hall, Wallingford, Conn., 1973-81, Simpson Coll., Indianola, Iowa, 1981—, U. Denver, 1984—, Fountain Valley Sch., Colorado Springs, 1976-89, trustee emerita, 1993—; mem. exec. com. Ft. Lewis Coll. Found., 1991—. Recipient 1st place award for editorial writing Nat. Fedn. Press Women, 1955, Outstanding Alumna award Rosemary Hall, Greenwich, Conn., 1969, Outstanding Journalism award U. Colo. Sch. Journalism, 1967, Disting. Svc. award Ft. Lewis Coll., Durango, 1970, named to Colo. Cmty. Journalism Hall of Fame, 1987; named Citizen of Yr. Durango Area Chamber Resort Assn., 1990, Athena award Female Cmty. Leader, 1997. Mem. Nat. Soc. Colonial Dames, Colo. Press Assn. (bd. dirs. 1978-79), Colo. AP Assn. (chmn. 1966-67), Federated Women's Club Durango, Mill Reef Club (Antigua, W.I.) (bd. govs. 1985-91). Episcopalian. Address: care Durango Herald PO Drawer A Durango CO 81302

BALLANTINE, TODD H., environmental scientist; b. Washington, Aug. 9, 1946. BA in Econs., Colo. Coll., 1968; MS in Environ. Sci., U. Oxford, Eng., 1981. Pres., environ. scientist Ballantine Environ. Resources, Inc., Hilton Head Island, S.C., 1968—; produced prototype concept for San Jose River Watershed trust, Baja, Mex.; created prototype Wetland Evaluation Program, Hilton Head Island; planned and monitored 3 prototype systems for application of advanced-treated wastewater into wetlands, Hilton Head Island; designed and constructed programs for beach and dune stblzn., Hilton Head Island; chmn. Beaufort County Coun. Victoria Bluff Task Force; assessed and delineated more than 75 "404" wetlands in U.S. Author: Woodland Walks, 1978, Tideland Treasure, 1983; writer, illustrator 20 interpretive guides and exhibits for nature preserves, hist. parks and wildlife refuges. Recipient Harry Hampton Conservation Journalism award S.C. Wildlife Fedn., 1988; faculty fellow Leadership Hilton Head Island. Mem. Southeastern Ecol. Inst. Office: Ballantine Environ Resource 19 Evergreen Ln Hilton Head Island SC 29928-3113

BALLANTYNE, CHRISTIE MITCHELL, medical educator; b. Houston, Sept. 13, 1955; m. Yasmine Attie, June 21, 1980; children: Maria Leyla, Christina, Katina. BA magna cum laude, U. Tex., 1977; postgrad., NYU, Madrid, Spain, 1977; MD cum laude, Baylor Coll. Medicine, 1982. Diplomate Am. Bd. Internal Medicine, Am. Bd. Internal Medicine subspecialty Cardiovascular Disease; cert. ACLS instr. Resident in internal medicine U. Tex. Southwestern Med. Sch., Dallas, 1982-85; fellowship in cardiology Baylor Coll. Medicine, Houston, 1985-87, instr. sect. atherosclerosis and cardiology dept. medicine, 1988-89, asst. prof. atherosclerosis & cardiology dept. medicine, 1989-95, assoc. prof. dept. medicine, 1996—, assoc. chief and clin. dir. sect. atherosclerosis, 1997, dir. lipid and atherosclerosis lab., 1999—; attending Ben Taub Gen. Hosp. Cardiac Catherterization Lab., Houston, 1988—, Lipid Metabolism and Atherosclerosis Clinic, The Meth. Hosp., Houston, 1988—, Ben Taub Coronary Care Unit, Houston, 1989—; faculty mem. Am. Heart Assn./Squibb Tng. Ctr. for Clin. Mgmt. of Lipid Disorders, Baylor Coll. Medicine, 1990; co-investigator Lipoprotein and Coronary Atherosclerosis Study, 1990; sci. grant rev. com. Am. Heart Assn. Tex. Affiliate, 1991-96; pharmacy and therapeutics com. The Meth. Hosp., 1992-95. Assoc. editor Circulation, Jour. Cardiovasc. Risk; contbr. chpts. to books and articles to profl. jours. Recipient Mosby scholarship award, Grant-in-Aid awards Am. Heart Assn. Tex. Affiliate, 1989, 91, Sanofi-Winthrop Grant-in-Aid award, 1994, Established Investigator award, 1996, Clin. Investigator award Nat. Heart Lung and Blood Inst., NIH, 1990, Caroline Wiess Law award in Molecular Medicine, 1992; named fellow Am. Heart Assn./Bugher Found. Ctr. for Molecular Biology in the Cardiovascular Sys., 1987-89. Fellow ACP, Am. Coll. Cardiology (sec. Tex. chpt.), Coun. on Clin. Cardiology Am. Heart Assn., Coun. on Arteriosclerosis; mem. Am. Fedn. Clin. Rsch. (sch. rep. for Baylor 1992), Tex. Med. Assn., Harris County Med. Soc., Houston Cardiology Soc. (pres. 1996), Am. Heart Assn. (pres. Houston chpt. 1999), Phi Kappa Phi, Phi Beta Kappa, Alpha Omega Alpha. Office: Baylor Coll Medicine Sect Atherosclerosis 6565 Fannin St # A601 Houston TX 77030-2704

BALLANTYNE, MAREE ANNE CANINE, artist; b. Sydney, NSW, Australia, Oct. 22, 1945; came to U.S., 1946; d. Charles Venice and Yvonne Mavis (McSeperin) Canine; m. Kent McFarlane Ballantyne, Apr. 22, 1967; children: Christopher Kent, Joel Sokson. AA, Del Mar Coll., 1966; BA in English, U. Tex., 1971; postgrad., U. South Ala., 1974, U. Houston, 1981, Sonoma State U., 1982, 84, 85. Exhibited paintings in Mass., Tex., Ala.; creator logo for Gulf Coast Area Childbirth Edn. Assn., 1972, logo for Calif. Health Resources, 1985; contbr. articles to profl. jours. Charter mem. Gulf Coast Area Childbirth Edn. Assn., Mobile, Ala., 1971-76; mem. Mus. Guild, Corpus Christi, 1978-80, Art Mus., Mobile, 1972-76, Nat. Trust for Hist. Preservation, 1977-80. Recipient Cert. Appreciation, USCG, 1993, Letter of Appreciation USCG, 1993. Mem. Nat. Mus. Women in Arts (charter), Coast Guard Officers Spouses's Club. Avocations: reading about poet and artist William Blake, women artists and literature, raising tropical plants, creating hand-painted greeting cards. Home: 1920 SW 56th Ave Plantation FL 33317-5938

BALLANTYNE, RICHARD LEE, lawyer; b. Evanston, Ill., Dec. 10, 1939; s. Frank and Grace (Bowles) B.; children: Richard L. Jr., Brant. BS in Engring., U. Conn., 1965, MBA, 1967; JD with honors, George Washington U., 1969. Bar: Mass., 1970, Fla. 1994, U.S. Dist. Ct. Mass. 1976, U.S. Patent Office 1982. Dir. corp. devel. Itek Corp., Lexington, Mass., 1969-73, assoc. counsel, 1973-75; corp. counsel, sec. Goodhope Industries, Springfield, Mass., 1975-77; gen. counsel, asst. treas., sec. Compugraphic Corp., Wilmington, Mass., 1977-82; v.p., gen. counsel, sec. Prime Computer Inc., Natick, Mass., 1982-89, Harris Corp., Melbourne, Fla., 1989—. Served with U.S. Army, 1958-61. Mem. ABA, N.E. Corp. Counsel Assn. Inc. (pres. 1984-86), Licensing Execs. Soc., Am. Soc. Corp. Secs, Computer Law Forum. Republican. Avocations: jogging, golf. Office: Harris Corp 1025 W Nasa Blvd Melbourne FL 32919-0002

BALLARD, BARBARA W., state legislator; m. Albert L. Ballard. Rep. dist. 44 State of Kansas, 1993—; adminstr., dir. U. Kans. Democrat. Home: 1532 Alvamar Dr Lawrence KS 66047-1605*

BALLARD, CARRIE, artist; b. Crockett, Tex., Oct. 22, 1930; d. Rufus Lee and Lillie Lee Turner; m. Travis Ballard, July 4, 1952; children: David Girard Ballard, Melanie Ballard Fahey. AB, Baylor U., 1951; MEd, U. Houston, 1967; student, Houston Mus. Fine Arts. Cert. tchr., Tex. Elem. tchr. Ector Co. Sch., Odessa, Tex., 1951-52, Waco Schs., Tex., 1952-53; tchr. Pasadena (Tex.) Sch. Dist., 1954-68, Deer Park (Tex.) Sch., 1969-84. One-woman shows include Archway Gallery, Houston, 1990, U. Houston O'Kane Gallery, 1990, 94, Spicewood Gallery, Austin, Tex., 1991, 93, 94, 95, 96, Lampros Gallery, Woodlands, Tex., 1993, Buchanan Gallery, Galveston, Tex., 1998, Tex. Trails Gallery, San Antonio, 1998; represented in numerous pvt. and corp. collections. Recipient Hon. Mention, Pasadena Art League, 1988, 2d Pl. award, 1989, 1st Pl. award Deer Park Juried Art Show, 1987, Hon. Mention, Houston Civic Arts Assn., 1992, 97, 2d. Pl. award Houston Civic Arts Assn., 1997, Tex. Star award KLRU, 1992, Tex. Treasure award KLRU, 1993. Mem. Oil Painters Am., Allied Artists Am., Houston Civic Arts Assn., Soc. Outdoor Painters, Alla Prima Internat., Houston Art League. Avocations: gardening, travelling, reading. Home: 2816 Huckleberry Ln Pasadena TX 77502

BALLARD, CARROLL, film director, cinematographer; b. L.A., Nov. 14, 1937. Motion picture dir., prodr., cinematographer. Dir. films The Black Stallion, 1979, Never Cry Wolf, 1983, Nutcracker: The Motion Picture, 1986, Wind, 1992, Fly Away Home, 1996; mem. film crew The Duel, 1962, Star Wars, 1977; cinematographer T.V. movies Surfin', 1964, San Francisco Summer 1967, 1967. Office: c/o DGA 7920 Sunset Blvd Los Angeles CA 90046

BALLARD, CHARLES ALAN, investment banker; b. St. Louis; s. Fred William and Fern Ann (Markham) B. B.B.A., So. Meth. U., 1963. V.p. fin. Systems Capital Corp., Phila., 1967-69; exec. v.p., dir. Vanderbilt Corp., Phila., 1969-71; assoc. Dillon, Read & Co. Inc., N.Y.C., 1971-72; v.p. Dillon, Read & Co. Inc., 1972-78, sr. v.p., 1979-80, mng. dir., 1980-90, sr. advisor, dir., 1990—; chmn., dir. Ballard Properties Inc., Phila., 1982—; pres., dir. Ballard Marine, Inc., 1986—. Mem. council Nat. Municipal League, N.Y.C., 1981-85; mem. adv. bd. Nat. Entrepreneurship Found., Bloomington, Ind., 1983—, The Energy Bur., N.Y.C., 1981—. Recipient Merit award U. Wis.-La Crosse, 1975; recipient Achievement award Lions Club, Houston, 1963. Mem. N.Y. Stock Exchange (assoc.), Securities Industry Assn. (vice chmn. 1980-81, exec. com., bd. dirs. 1984-85), Investment Banking Com. (steering com. 1981—, vice chmn. 1981, 83, 86, 87, chmn. 1985). Clubs: Union League (Phila.); The Links (N.Y.C.); Merion Golf (Ardmore, Pa.); India House; Lighthouse Point (Fla.) Yacht and Racquet. Office: Warburg Dillon Read 299 Park Ave New York NY 10171-0002

BALLARD, CLYDE, state legislator; b. Batesville, Ark., June 8, 1936; s. Jeffery C. and Monnie F. Ballard; m. Ruth L. Guthrie, Feb. 6, 1955; children: Jeff, Shawn, Scott. Store mgr., gen. mgr. Peter Rabbit Stores, Wenachee, Wash., 1955-66; owner Ballard Svcs., Wenachee, 1967-87; caucus chmn., minority leader Wash. Ho. of Reps., Olympia, 1985-94, spkr. house, 1995-98, co-speaker house, 1999—. Republican. Methodist. Home: 1790 N Baker Ave East Wenatchee WA 98802-4157 Office: PO Box 40600 Olympia WA 98504-0600

BALLARD, DIANE E., nursing administrator; b. Manchester, N.H., May 17, 1957; d. Arthur A. and Georgianne (Beaulieu) B.; 1 child, Sarah Ann. Diploma, Cath. Med. Ctr. Sch. Nursing, Manchester, 1978; AS in Paralegal Studies, Hesser Coll., 1995; BSN, U. N.H., 1999. RN, Md., Tex., N.H. Staff relief nurse Circulating Nurses, Boston; nurse operating room Holy Cross Hosp., Silver Spring, Md.; staff relief nurse NE Staffing, Manchester; owner, adminstr. Staffing Agy., Manchester, 1986-91; nurse paralegal Sulloway & Hollis, PLLC, 1994—. Mem. Small Bus. Assn.

BALLARD, EDWARD BROOKS, landscape architect; b. Lexington, Mass., Jan. 25, 1906; s. Walter Clark and Clara Abbie (Bigelow) B.; m. Mina Louise McCormick, Dec. 20, 1947 (dec. Nov. 1994); 1 child, Robert Clark. A.B., Harvard U., 1927, M.L.A., 1933. Asst. to editor Horticulture mag., Boston, 1930; landscape architect, asso. field coordinator Nat. Park Service, 1933-39; exec. sec. Nat. Parks Assn., Washington, 1940-42; spl. rep. Nat. Recreation Assn., 1946-47; asst. dir. Md. Dept. Forest and Parks, Annapolis, 1947-48; supt. Cumberland Falls State Park, Corbin, Ky., 1948-49; prin. landscape architect Pa. Bur. Parks, Harrisburg, 1949-52; landscape architect Office Chief of Engrs., Dept. Army, 1952-58; chief mil. constrn. site planning Dept. Army, 1958-74; mng. landscape architect Miller, Wihry & Lee, Inc. (landscape architects and engrs.), Washington, 1975-80; U.S. coord. rep. com. on translation tech. terms, Internat. Fedn. Landscape Architects, 1979—; cons. mktg. profl. services to govt. agys. 1982-84, cons., editor Internat. Inst. of Site Planning, 1997—, bd. dirs. Pres. Fairlington Civic Assn., Arlington, Va., 1954-55; pres. Broyhill Crest Citizens Assn., Annandale, Va., 1961-62; sec. Annandale Community Council, 1959-60, chmn., 1963-65. Served to capt. U.S. Army, 1942-46, PTO. Emeritus fellow Am. Soc. Landscape Architects (pres. Potomac chpt. 1961-62, trustee 1964-67, nat. sec.-treas. 1967-71, nat. archivist 1972-76, sec.-treas. Coun. of Fellows 1976-78); mem. Harvard Sch. Design Assn., Va. Native Plant Soc. (chmn., nominating com. 1984-85, pres. Potowmack chpt. 1985-87), No. Va. Cmty. Appearance Alliance (sec.-treas. 1987-88, vice chmn. ops. 1989, exec. sec. 1990-91, bd. dirs. 1992-94), Washington House Residents Coun. v.p. 1996-97, pres. 1997-99), Delta Upsilon. Address: 5100 Fillmore Ave Apt 604 Alexandria VA 22311-5043 *To make Planet Earth livable for all people in harmony with Nature is to me the highest, though never completely attainable, goal of human existence. In this brief span of life it is enough reward to provide a better world for our posterity.*

BALLARD, FREDERIC LYMAN, JR., lawyer; b. Phila., Sept. 12, 1941; s. Frederic L. Sr. and Ernesta (Drinker) B.; m. Marion Scattergood, Dec. 20 1974; 1 child, Anne A.; stepchildren: William S. Dunning, Robert L. Dunning. BA, Harvard U., 1963, LLB, 1966. Bar: Pa. 1966, D.C. 1978. Assoc. Ballard Spahr Andrews & Ingersoll LLP, Phila., 1966-73, ptnr., 1973-78; ptnr. Ballard Spahr Andrews & Ingersoll LLP, Washington, 1978—. *Frederic L. Ballard, Jr. is a fourth generation partner in a law firm founded byhis great-grandfather Ellis Ames Ballard in Philadelphia in 1886.* Author: ABCs of Arbitrage, 1998. Mem. ABA (sect. of taxation, vice chair 1994-97). Home: 4413 Chalfont Pl Bethesda MD 20816-1812 Office: Ballard Spahr Andrews & Ingersoll 601 13th St NW Washington DC 20005-3807

BALLARD, GLEN, composer; b. Natchez, Miss., 1953. Grad. with honors, U. Miss., 1975. Recs. include Glen Ballard; co-writer, prodr. for Jagged Little Pill (Grammy award for Best Rock Album 1996, Grammy award for Album of Yr. 1996), Hold On, Release Me, Shadows and Light; composer: You Oughta Know (Grammy award for Best Rock Song 1996), The Places You Find Love, One Step, What's On Your Mind, Why is This Girl Giving Me Fever, Dance Electric, Try Your Love Again, All I Need, You Look So Good in Love (Country Song of Yr. 1986), Man in the Mirror, Nightline, State of Attraction, Keep the Faith, I Wonder Why, The Places You Find Love, others; composer for various artists including Al Jarreau, Earth, Wind & Fire, Sheena Easton, Celine Dion, Philip Bailey, K.T. Oslin, Jack Wagner, Michael Jackson, Wilson Phillips, Curtis Stigers, others. Office: Chasen & Co 8899 Beverly Blvd Los Angeles CA 90048-2431*

BALLARD, JOE N., career officer; b. Mar. 27, 1942. Commd. U.S. Army, advanced through grades to lt. gen., 1996; with U.S. Corp. Engrs., Washington. Office: US Corp Engrs 20 Massachusetts Ave NW Washington DC 20314-1000

BALLARD, JOHN STUART, retired educator, former mayor, former lawyer; b. Akron, Ohio, Sept. 30, 1922; s. Irby S. and Sarah (McCormick) B.; m. Ruth Frances Holden, Oct. 22, 1949; children: Susan, Karen, John H., Mark, Ward; m. 2d, Patricia D. Whittenberger, Oct. 20, 1990. A.B., U. Akron, 1943; LL.B., U. Mich., 1948. Bar: Mich. 1948, Ohio 1949. Spl. agt. FBI, 1949-52; practice law Akron, 1952-56, 64-65; pros. atty. Summit County, Ohio, 1957-64; mayor of Akron, 1966-80; adj. assoc. prof. dept. pub. adminstrn. and urban studies U. Akron, 1980-95; ret., 1995. Candidate for U.S. senator from Ohio, 1962. Served with inf. AUS, 1943-46. Recipient Distinguished Service award Akron Jr. C. of C., 1957. Episcopalian. Home: 171 Granger Rd Unit 144 Medina OH 44256-7312 *It is true that in giving we receive.*

BALLARD, JOHN WILLIAM, JR., banker; b. Kingston, Ont., Can., Mar. 8, 1922; came to U.S., 1922; s. John William and Evelyn Mary (Toohill) B.; m. Imogen Dean Billings, Dec. 29, 1947; children—John William III, Paul Billings, Jenny Evelyn. B.S., U. Kans., 1947. With Safety Fed. Savs. and Loan Assn., Kansas City, Mo., 1947-88; asst. v.p. Safety Fed. Savs. and Loan Assn., 1949-58, treas., 1958-62, pres., 1962-88, chmn. bd., 1968-88; vice chmn bd. Home Savs. Assn. Kansas City, F.A. (formerly Safety Fed. Savs. and Loan Assn.), 1988-91; ret., 1991; trustee Kansas City Blue Cross, sec., 1960-61, treas., 1961-71, chmn. bd., 1971-83; pres. Safety Ins. Agy., 1962-88; mem. thrift adv. bd. Fed. Res. Bank Kansas City, 1990-93; bd. dirs. Blue Ventures. Vice pres. Jr. C. of C., 1950, C. of C.; dir. Downtown Inc., 1967-88; trustee Savs. and Loan Found., Inc., 1966-70, mem. futures com. 1983-88; bd. dirs. Armour Meml. Home, Women's Christian Assn. Served with AUS, 1942-45. Decorated Bronze Star. Mem. Am. Royal Assn. (gov. 1962-88), Real Estate Bd. (dir. 1964-65, 71-74), Mo. Savs. and Loan League (pres. 1964-65), Kansas City Savs. and Loan League (pres. 1966-67), Mission Hills Country Club (Shawnee Mission, Kans.), Kansas City (bd. dirs. 1981-86, pres. 1985-86), Rotary (past v.p., bd. dirs.), Sigma Alpha Epsilon. Episcopalian. Home: 4306 W 112th St Leawood KS 66211-1725 *In our organization no one works for me, but with me. A man seldom becomes a success without the help of others.*

BALLARD, LINDA C., director financial aid; b. Houston, Aug. 19, 1959; d. Roosevelt Larue Sr. and Helen Ruth B.; 1 child, Alexandria Nickole Ballard-Demming. BBA, U. Houston, 1982. Data control supr. U. Houston, 1982-85, data entry supr., 1985-87, fin. aid. counselor, 1987-92; fin. aid. counselor U. St. Thomas, Houston, 1992-93, dir. fin. aid, 1993—. Asst. dir. youth dept. Greater True Vine Ch. Mem. Nat. Assn. Fin. Aid Adminstrs., Tex. Assn. Fin. Aid Adminstrs. Avocations: high school awareness programs, travel. Home: 8829 Woodlyn Houston TX 77078 Office: U St Thomas Fin Aid Dept 3800 Montrose Blvd Houston TX 77006-4626

BALLARD, LOUIS WAYNE, composer; b. Miami, Okla., July 8, 1931; s. Charles Guthrie and Leona Mae (Quapaw) B.; m. Ruth Sands, Dec. 6, 1965; children by previous marriage: Louis Anthony, Anne Marie, Charles Christopher. B.Mus. and Music Edn., U. Tulsa, 1954; M.Mus., 1962; D.Mus. (hon.), Coll. Santa Fe, 1973. Dir. vocal and instrumental music Nelagoney (Okla.) Public Sch., 1954-56; dir. vocal music Webster High Sch., Tulsa, 1956-58; pvt. music tchr., 1959-62; music dir. Inst. Am. Indian Arts, Santa Fe, 1962-65; dir. performing arts Inst. Am. Indian Arts, 1965-69; nat. dir. music edn. curriculum and rev. Bur. Indian Affairs, Washington, 1969-79; lectr., clinician, 1960—; pres. First Am. Indian Films, Inc., 1969—. Composer, Santa Fe, 1979—; guest composer West German Music Festival, Saarbrü, 1986, Musik im 20 Jahrhundert, Ariz. State U., 1992, U. Ill. at Champagne, 1992, Ea. Music Festival, Greensboro, N.C., 1994, 95, 96; gala concert Carnegie Hall, 1992; full concert in Beethoven Chamber Music Hall, Bonn (first Am. composer), 1989; (ballet) Koshare, 1964, The Four Moons, 1967, Maid of the Mist and the Thunderbeings, 1991; (orchl. music) Fantasay Aborigine, Nos. I, II, III, IV, V; (chamber music) Rhapsody for Four Bassoons, Incident at Wounded Knee, Desert Trilogy, Ritmo Indio, Katcina Dances for cello-piano suite; (choral cantatas) The Gods Will Hear, Portrait of Will Rogers, Thus Spake Abraham; (oratorio) Dialogue Differentia text in Latin, Lakota-Sioux, English, Live On, Heart of My Nation (choral cantate with native Am. dialect), Manitoo, Gitche Manitoo (Am. Indian Doxology); (band works) Nighthawk Keetowa; (percussion) Cecega Ayuwipi, Music for the Earth and the Sky; (guitar) Quetzalcoatl's Coattails, 1992, The Lonely Sentinel, 1993, The Fire Moon (string quartet), A City of Silver, A City of Fire, A City of Light (piano concert pieces), numerous others.; commd. writer Lila Wallace Reader's Digest Arts Ptnrs./Meet the Composer, 1991; commd. writer (opera) Ministry Lower Saxony (Germany), 1993-94; author: The American Indian Sings, Book 1, 1970, Book 2, 1991, American Indian Chants for the Classroom, Oklahoma Indian Chants for the Classroom, also articles. Recipient 1st Marion Nevins MacDowell award chamber music, 1969, Nat. Indian Achievement award, 1972, Catlin Peace Pipe award Nat. Indian Lore Assn., 1976, ASCAP award, 1966-88, Lifetime Music Achievement award First Americans in Arts, 1997; F.B. Parriott grad. fellow, 1969; grantee Ford Found., 1970; grantee Nat. Endowment Arts, 1967, 69, 76, 79; commd. by Martha B. Rockefeller Found., 1969, Am. Composers Orch., 1982, commd. by Ministry Lower Saxony for Opera in Norden Gymnasium, West Germany, 1994. Mem. ASCAP, Music Educators Nat. Conf. (chmn. minority concerns com. for N.Mex. 1976), Am. Symphony Orch. League, Internat. Soc. for Polyaesthetic Music Edn. and Performance (lectr.), Phi Beta Kappa (alumni mem. Beta chpt. Okla. 1999). Lodge: Masons, Scottish Rite (32d degree). Office: PO Box 2072 Santa Fe NM 87504-2072

BALLARD, MARY MELINDA, financial communications and investment banking firm executive, consumer advocate; b. Sikeston, Mo., Apr. 21, 1958; d. Claude M. and Mary (Birnbach) B.; m. Emil Pena, Jan. 1, 1989 (div. July 1990); m. Ronald C. Allison, Oct. 1994; 1 child, Reese Colton Allison. BA, Monmouth Coll., 1976; MBA, NYU, 1980; postgrad., Columbia U. V.p. corp. comm. United Brands Co., N.Y.C., 1976-79; v.p. mktg. Oscar de la Renta Ltd., 1979-81; pres., chief exec. officer Ficom Internat., Inc., N.Y.C., 1981—; exec. v.p. Ruder Finn Inc., N.Y.C., 1989—; dir., CEO MBP Interests Inc., 1989—; ptnr. Kamero Ptnrs., 1994—; officer, dir. Tex. Interlock Corp., 1995-96; exec. v.p., CFO Millenium Tech. Transfer, Inc., 1996—; officer dir. Capital Bank, 1997—; bd. dirs. Reese Colton Enterprises, Inc., Millenium Tech. Transfer, Inc., Nat. Coun. Real Estate Investment Fiduciaries, Tex. Interlock Corp.; cons. to fgn. govts. and major corps. Contbr. articles to profl. jours. Trustee Ballard Family Found., Children's Aid Soc.; exec. mem. Tex. Dem. Roundtable, 1994—. Recipient CLIO Ann. Report award Fin. World, 1984, 86. Mem. Internat. Assn. Bus. Communicators (Golden Quill 1984), Pub. Investor Relsa. Inst. Methodist. Avocations: collecting art, thoroughbred race horses, ranching. Home and Office: PO Box 746 Dripping Springs TX 78620-0746

BALLARD, MELVIN RUSSELL, JR., investment executive, church official; b. Salt Lake City, Oct. 8, 1928; s. Melvin Russell and Geraldine (Smith) B.; m. Barbara Bowen, Aug. 28, 1951; children: Clark, Holly, Meleea, Tamara, Stacey, Brynn, Craig. Student, U. Utah, 1946, 50-52. Sales mgr. Ballard Motor Co., Salt Lake City, 1950-54; investment counselor Salt Lake City, 1954-56; founder, owner, mgr. Russ Ballard Auto, Inc., Salt Lake City, 1956-58, Ballard-Wade Co., 1958-67; owner, mgr. Ballard Investment Co., Salt Lake City, 1962—; mem. Quorum of Twelve, 1979—; gen. authority LDS Ch., Salt Lake City, 1976—; bd. dirs. Nate-Wade, Inc., Salt Lake City, Silver King Mines, Inc., Salt Lake City, Huntsmand Chem. Co., Salt Lake City; chmn. bd. dirs. Deseret Book Co., Salt Lake City; gen. ptnr. N & R Investment, Salt Lake City, 1958—, Ballard Investment Co., Salt Lake City, 1955—. Bd. dirs. Salt Lake Jr. Achievement, 1978-80; bd. dirs. Freedoms Found., 1978—, David O. McKay Inst. Edn., 1979—; active Coun. Twelve Apostles, 1979. 1st lt. USAR, 1950-57. Mem. Salt Lake Area C. of C. (gov. 1979—). Republican. Office: LDS Church 50 E North Temple Salt Lake City UT 84150-0002*

BALLARD, MICHAEL EUGENE, lawyer; b. Mobile, Ala., Jan. 24, 1953; s. John T. and Dolores (Hall) B. BS, U. Ala., 1975, MBA, 1977, JD, 1978; LLM in Taxation, Emory U., 1980. Bar: Ala. 1978. Assoc. Stokes, Clark & McAtee, Mobile, 1978-80, Hamilton, Butler, Riddick, Tarlton & Sullivan, Mobile, 1981-86; atty. Cooper & Worsham, CPA's, Atlanta, 1980; pvt. practice law Mobile, 1986-90; mem. firm Drinkard, Ulmer, Hicks & Leon, Mobile, 1990-93, Drinkard, Ulmer & Hicks, Mobile, 1993-94, Whitfield & McAlpine, P.C., Mobile, 1994-98, Ulmer, Hillman & Ballard, Mobile, 1998—; lectr. U. So. Ala., 1986—. Mem. Ala. Bar Assn. (client security fund com. 1985—, vice chmn. 1995-98), Mobile Bar Assn. (vice chmn. constrn. com. 1990, probate com. 1985-87, 89-90, 96—, constrn. and bylaws com. 1983-86, 89—, bankruptcy sect. 1996—), Estate Planning Coun. Mobile (exec. bd. 1987-89), Athelstan Club. Episcopalian. Office: 63 S Royal St Ste 1107 Mobile AL 36602

BALLARD, WILEY PERRY III, hematologist, oncologist; b. Atlanta, Mar. 30, 1952; s. Wiley Perry Jr. and Anne Sykes (Equen) B.; m. Jane Elliot Roberts, Aug. 15, 1992; children: Wiley Perry IV, William Roberts. AB with high honors, Dartmouth Coll., 1974; MD, Emory U., 1978. Diplomate Am. Bd. Internal Medicine, Am. Bd. Med. Oncology, Am. Bd. Hematology. Intern in medicine N.Y. Hosp.- Cornell Med. Ctr., N.Y.C., 1978-79, resident in medicine, 1979-81, asst. chief resident in medicine, 1981, fellow in hematology-oncology, 1983-84, chief clin. fellow in hematology-oncology, 1984-85, asst. attending physician, 1985-87; fellow in infectious disease Tufts-New England Med. Ctr., Boston, 1981-82; fellow in gen. internal medicine Cornell U. Sch. of Medicine, N.Y.C., 1982-83; instr. in medicine Cornell U. Med. Coll., N.Y.C., 1984-86, asst. prof. medicine, 1986-87; attending physician Piedmont Hosp., Atlanta, 1987—; pvt. practice Atlanta, 1987—; mem. adv. bd. Am. Cancer Soc., Atlanta, 1990-92, v.p. med. affairs, 1992—, bd. dirs., 1993—, exec. com., 1993—. Contbr. articles to profl. jours. Bd. dirs. CHRIS Homes, 1991—. Clin. fellow Am. Cancer Soc., 1983-85, Kate Rosenberg fellow N.Y. Hosp.- Cornell Med. Ctr. Mem. ACP, Am. Soc. Clin. Oncology, Am. Soc. Hematology, Piedmont Driving Club, Peachtree Golf Club, Phi Beta Kappa, Alpha Omega Alpha. Episcopalian. Avocations: golf, tennis, skiing, squash. Home: 562 Arden Oaks Ct NW Atlanta GA 30305-1955 Office: Peachtree Hematology-Oncology 95 Collier Rd NW Ste 5015 Atlanta GA 30309-1721

BALLAS, NADIA S., writer, poet; b. Phila., Dec. 27, 1971; d. Samir K. and Nida (Abdo) B. BA in English Lit., Rosemont (Pa.) Coll., 1994; postgrad., Suffolk U., 1996—. Cons. image and writer cons. Cherry Hill, N.J., 1991-94; legis. intern Senator Edward M. Kennedy, 1997-98; intern pub. policy Mass. Children's Legis. Caucus, 1998; asst. legal counsel Sen. Magnani Mass. Legislature; law clk. Children's Legal Svcs., 1999; mem. So. Poverty Law Ctr. Author: (poetry anthologies/collections): Beyond the Stars, 1995, Best Poets of 1996, 1996. Congl. aide Congressman Andrews, Somerdale, N.J., 1995; intern Camden County Dem. Com., Cherry Hill, 1995; vol. West Jersey Hosp., Voorhees, 1988; friend John F. Kennedy Libr.; mem. N.J. Dem. Victory Fund, Dem. Nat. Com.; vol. Children's Def. Fund; vol. congl. aide. Named Best Poet of 1996, Nat. Libr. of Poetry, Ohio. Mem. ABA (student divsn.), Internat. Platform Assn., So. Poverty Law Ctr., Internat. Alliance of Holistic Lawyers. Avocations: reading, exercising, travel, politics, volunteerism. Office: 117 Farmington Rd Cherry Hill NJ 08034

BALLDIN, ULF INGEMAR, medical researcher; b. Malmö, Sweden, Apr. 5, 1939; came to U.S., 1992; s. Anton and Ebba T. (Engholm) B.; m. Susanne Ploman, June 29, 1974; children: Carl H., B. Christian, Fredrik J. BA, U. Lund, Sweden, 1959, MD, 1967, PhD, 1973; D (hon.), State Scientific Rsch. Inst., Moscow, 1995. Lic. physician, Sweden. Instr. physiology U. Lund, Sweden, 1964-67, rsch. physician, 1968-73; resident U. Hosp., Lund, Sweden, 1974; acting assoc. prof. U. Lund, 1975; rsch. flight surgeon Nat. Defense Rsch., Linköping, Sweden, 1976; sr. rsch. med. officer Nat. Defense Rsch. Establishment, Stockholm, 1977-86; rsch. dir. Nat. Def. Rsch. Establishment, Stockholm, 1987—; dir. Inst. Aviation Medicine Nat. Def. Rsch. Establishment, Sweden, 1987-92; adj. prof., head dept. aerospace medicine Karolinska Inst. Med. Sch., Stockholm, 1982-91; liaison scientist Brooks AFB, USAF, San Antonio, 1992-98; clin. asst. prof. U. Tex. Med. Br., Galveston, 1997—. Co-author: (chpt.) Textbook of Military Medicine, 1998; contbr. articles to profl. jours. Surgeon Lt. comdr. Swedish Air Force, 1976-99. Fellow Aerospace Med. Assn. (v.p., coun. mem.); mem. Royal Swedish Acad. War Scis., Internat. Acad. Aviation and Space Medicine (dir. 1993-97, 2d v.p. 1997-99, 1st v.p. 1999—). Achievements include improving inert gas elimination for decreasing risk of decompression sickness in divers and during extravehicular space activity, improved G-tolerance in fighter pilots with balanced pressure breathing during G and extended coverage anti-G suit. Avocations: flying, sailing, diving, music, jogging. Home: 14227 Parkhurst St San Antonio TX 78232-4733 Office: USAF Rsch Lab AFRL/HEP 2504 Gillingham Dr Ste 25 Brooks AFB TX 78235-5100

BALLENGEE, JAMES MCMORROW, lawyer; b. Charleston, W.Va., Jan. 10, 1923; s. Lanty Ernest and Marie Vivian (McMorrow) B.; m. Jo McIlhattan, June 7, 1947; children: James M., Elizabeth Ann, Sarah Jo. A.B., Morris Harvey Coll., 1946, LL.D. (hon.), 1972; J.D., Washington and Lee U., 1948. Bar: W.Va. 1948, Pa. 1962. Assoc. firm Mohler, Peters & Snyder, Charleston, W.Va., 1948-53, Dayton, Campbell & Love, Charleston, 1953-57; assoc. counsel Sears, Roebuck & Co., Phila., 1957-61; ptnr. Morgan, Lewis & Bockius, Phila., 1962, counsel, 1986—; pres., chmn. Phila. Suburban Water Co., Bryn Mawr, Pa., 1962-76, Phila. Suburban Corp., Radnor, Pa., 1968-81, Enterra Corp., 1981-86. Bd. dirs. Bryn Mawr Hosp.; past pres. met. bd. Phila. area YMCA; past pres. Fairmount Park Council for Historic Sites; past chmn. Ea. Pa. chpt. Arthritis Found.; trustee Phila. Mus. Art, Arthritis Found., George C. Marshall Found.; rector emeritus bd. trustees Washington and Lee U.; v.p., treas. Devon Horse Show and Country Fair; pres. Devon Horse Show Found. Served to 1st lt. U.S. Army, 1943-46, 50-52, Korea. Decorated Bronze Star. Mem. ABA, Pa. Bar Assn., W.Va. Bar Assn., Greater Phila. C. of C. (bd. dirs., past chmn.), Order of Coif, Phi Beta Kappa. Democrat. Presbyterian. Clubs: Philadelphia, Merion Golf. Home: 711 Williamson Rd Bryn Mawr PA 19010-1830 Office: 1701 Market St Philadelphia PA 19103

BALLENGER, HURLEY RENÉ, electrical engineer; b. Jacksonville, Ill., Nov. 26, 1946; s. Leonard Hurley and Katherine Natalie (Daniel) B.; m. Sandra Ann Rubley, Dec. 9, 1986. Student, Ill. Coll., 1964-65, 75. Technician electronics div. Hughs Aircraft, Inc., Tucson, 1973; maintenance supr. Fiatallis N.Am., Springfield, Ill., 1973-75, project engr., 1975-83, plant engr., 1983-86; tech. advisor CNC/CAM Fiatallis Europe, Lecce, Italy, 1986-87; plant engr. Illini Tech., Inc., Springfield, Ill., 1988, plant and mfg. engr., 1988-98; facilities engr. Phoenix Internat. (formerly Illini Tech., Inc.), Springfield, Ill., 1998—. Mem. career adv. bd. Lincoln Land Community Coll., Springfield, 1983-85. Served to staff sgt. USAF, 1965-72, Vietnam. Lutheran. Avocations: photography, home computing. Office: Phoenix Internat 5300 Rising Moon Rd Springfield IL 62707-6228

BALLENGER, THOMAS CASS, congressman; b. Hickory, N.C., Dec. 6, 1926; s. Richard E. and Dorothy (Collins) B.; m. Donna Davis, June 14, 1952; children: Cindy Ballenger Brinkley, Melissa Ballenger Jordan, Dorothy Davis Weaver. Student, U. N.C., 1944-45; BA, Amherst Coll., 1948. Pres. Plastic Packaging, Hickory, 1957-86, chmn. bd., 1986—; pres. Hickory Paper Box Co., 1961-80; mem. 100th-105th Congresses from 10th N.C. dist., 1987—; mem. oversight & investigations, worker protections, internat. econ. policy & trade and western hemisphere, edn. and workplace, internat. rels. coms. County commr. Catawba County, N.C., 1966-74, chmn. commn., 1970-74; mem. N.C. Ho. of Reps., Raleigh, 1974-76, N.C. Senate, Raleigh, 1976-86, U.S. Congress, 10th Dist., 1986. Mem. Hickory C. of C. Republican. Episcopalian. Lodge: Rotary (pres. Hickory club). Avocations: golf, swimming. Office: 2182 Rayburn House Office B Washington DC 20515-3310

BALLENTINE, J. GREGORY, economist; b. Buffalo, July 21, 1948; s. Richard Erwin and Maryalice (Callanan) B.; m. Martha Elizabeth Scott, Sept. 16, 1967; children: Greta K., Dorothy E. Student, Georgetown U., 1966-67; BS, Springhill Coll., 1970; PhD, Rice U., 1974. Asst. prof. Wayne State U., Detroit, 1974-77, assoc. prof., 1977-79; assoc. prof. U. Fla., Gainesville, 1979-81, prof., 1981-83; dep. asst. sec. U.S. Dept. Treasury, Washington, 1981-83; assoc. dir. Office of Mgmt. and Budget, Washington, 1983-85; prin. KPMG Peat Marwick, Washington, 1985-97, Pricewaterhouse Coopers, Washington, 1997—; cons. GAO, Washington, 1979-81; dir. grad program Wayne State U., Detroit, 1977-79. Co-editor: Pub. Fin. Quar., 1981-83. Mem. Am. Econ. Assn., Nat. Tax Assn. (bd. dirs.), Nat. Assn. Bus. Economists. Office: Pricewaterhouse Coopers Ste 800W 1301 K St NW Washington DC 20005-3333

BALLER, WILLIAM WARREN, school psychologist; b. Lincoln, Nebr., June 12, 1943; s. Warren Robert and Dorothy Gwendolyn (Jensen) B.; m. Janet Elizabeth Thomsen, June 19, 1979; children: William Carter, Candice Elizabeth. BS in Edn., U. Nebr., 1965; MA in Edn., U. Mo., 1967, PhD in Psychology, 1969. Lic. sch. psychologist, N.Y. Tchg. asst. spl. edn. U. Nebr., Lincoln, 1964-65; tchg. asst. spl. edn. U. Mo., Columbia, 1965-68, instr. psychology and edn., 1968-69; asst. prof. psychology and edn. Idaho State U., Pocatello, 1969-73, assoc. prof., 1973-79, prof., 1980-86; prof. human behavior Disting. U.S. Internat. U., San Diego, 1979; sch. psychologist Utica (N.Y.) City Sch. Dist., 1986—; neuropsychologist hosps., Utica, 1988—. Contbr. articles to profl. jours. Elder 1st Presbyn. Ch., Utica, 1994—. Nebr. career scholar Ford Found., Lincoln, 1963; NDEA tchg. fellow U.S. Office Edn., U. Mo., 1965-68. Mem. Am. Acad. Polit. and Social Scientists, Am. Legion, Phi Beta Kappa, Phi Delta Kappa. Avocations: woodwork/home improvement, camping, reading. Office: Utica City Sch Dist 1115 Mohawk St Utica NY 13501-3700

BALLESTEROS, JUVENTINO RAY, JR., minister; b. L.A., June 27, 1953; s. Juventino Ray and Esther Marie (Mendoza) B.; m. Rebecca Ann Williamson, Dec. 30, 1978. BA, Birmingham South Coll., 1977; MA, Presbyn. Sch. Christian Edn., 1979; D Ministry, Union Theol. Sem., 1982. Intern minister Crystal Cathedral, Garden Grove, Calif., 1978, Philippi Presbyn. Ch., Raeford, N.C., 1980-81; assoc. minister 1st Presbyn. Ch., Fayetteville, N.C., 1982-84, Orlando, Fla., 1984-92; pastor, Christian Edn. Crystal Cathedral, Garden Grove, Calif., 1992—; chmn. Div. Edn., Fayetteville, 1982-84, Nat. Tchr. Edn. Program, Fayetteville, 1983-84. Bd. dirs. Cumberland County Clean Community Council, Fayetteville, 1982-84, Nat. Tchr. Ednl. Program, Durham, N.C.; bd. advisors Jr. League, Fayetteville, 1983-84; v.p. Spouse Abuse Inc., Orlando, 1984-86; bd. trustees Union Theol. Sem./Presbyn. Sch. Christian Edn., 1996—. Mem. Religious Educators Assn., Assn. Presbyn. Ch. Educators. Republican. Avocation: all sports. Office: Crystal Cathedral 12141 Lewis St Garden Grove CA 92840-4699

BALLESTEROS, PAULA M., nurse; b. Jonesport, Me., Oct. 18, 1950; d. Paul Frederick and Janice Madeline (Beal) Mitchell; m. Ernesto Gascon Ballesteros, Apr. 4, 1981; children: Christopher, Jonathan. BS in Profl. Arts, St. Joseph's Coll., 1984; BSN, Husson/Ea. Me. Med. Ctr. Baccalaureate Sch. Nursing, 1994. Cert. Nursing Administrn. Patient care mgr. Ea. Me. Med. Ctr., Bangor, 1974—, bd. trustees, 1993-95; chairperson adv. bd. Ea. Maine Tech. Coll., Bangor, Me., 1993-94; pres. Me. Coun. Nurse Mgrs., 1991-93, Ea. Me. Med. Ctr. auxiliary, Bangor, Me., 1993-95. Contbr. articles to profl. jours. Mem. St. Joseph Hosp. Auxiliary. Mem. Am. Orgn. Nurse Execs., Penobscot Med. Soc. Auxiliary, Me. Assn. Hosp. Auxiliaries (pres. 1994—). Democrat. Protestant. Avocations: skiing, tennis, reading. Home: 78 Packard Dr Bangor ME 04401-2531 Office: Ea Maine Med Ctr 489 State St Bangor ME 04401-6616

BALLESTEROS, SEVERIANO, professional golfer; b. Pedrena, Spain, Apr. 9, 1957; s. Baldomero and Carmen (Sota) B.; m. Carmen Botin O'Shea; children: Javier, Miguel, Carmen. Chmn. Fairway, S.A., Madrid, 1981; main victories include Under 25 Nat. Championship, Vizcaya Open, 1974, Under 25 Nat. Championship, 1975, Profl. Championship Catalonia, Profl. Championship Tenerife, Dutch Open, Lancome Trophy, Donald Swaelens Meml., World Cup, 1976, French Open, Braun Internat., UniRoyal Internat., Swiss Open, Japanese Open, Dunlop-Phoenix (Japan), Otago Charity (New Zealand), World Cup, 1977, Kenia Open, Under 25 Nat. Open Championship, Greensboro Open, Martini Internat., German Open, Scandinavian Open, Swiss Open, 1978, Lada English Golf Classic, Brit. Open, El Prat Open (Spain), 1979, Masters, 1980, 83, Madrid Open, Martini Internat., Dutch Open, 1980, Scandinavian Open, Spanish Open, Suntory World Match Play, Australian PGA Championship, Dunlop-Phoenix, 1981, San Remo Masters, Madrid Open, French Open, Suntory World Match Play, 1982, M.H.T. Westchester Classic, Irish Open, Lancome Trophy, Sun City Challenge, Sun Alliance Championship, 1983, Brit. Open, 1984, 88, Suntory WMP, Sun City Challenge, 1984, USF&G Classic, World Match Play Championship, Irish Open, French Open, Sanyo Open, Spanish Open, Ryder Cup (mem. winning team), 1985, Dunhill Brit. Masters, Carrolls Irish Open, Johnnie Walker Montecarlo Open, Peugeot French Open, KLM Dutch Open, Lancome Trophy, 1986, Suze Open, APG Larios, Ryder Cup winning team, 1987, A.P.G. Larios, Mallorca Open de Baleares, Westchester Classic Scandinavian Enterprise Open, German Open, Lancome Trophee British Open, Visa Taiheiyo Club Masters, 1988, Epson Gran Prix, Cepsa Madrid Open, Swiss Open/Ebel European Masters, Ryder Cup (tied), 1989, Open Baleares, 1990, Volvo PGA Championship, Dunhill Brit. Masters, Chunichi Crowns, Toyota World Match Play, 1991, Turespaña Open de Baleares, Dubal Desert Classic, 1992, Benson and Hedges Internat. Open Mercedes (German) Masters, 1994; Capt. European Ryder Cup Team, 1997. Recipient Prince of Asturias award, 1989, Olympic Order, 1998. Roman Catholic. Office: Fairway SA, Pasaje de Pena 2-4, 39008 Santander Spain also: PGA 100 Ave of the Champions Palm Beach Gardens FL 33410*

BALLHAUS, WILLIAM FRANCIS, JR., aerospace industry executive, research scientist; b. L.A., Jan. 28, 1945; s. William Francis Sr. and Edna A. Ballhaus; m. Jane Kerber; children from previous marriage: William Louis, Michael Frederick; stepchildren: Benjamin Joel, Jennifer Angela. BSME with honors, U. Calif., Berkeley, 1967, MS in Mech. Engring., 1968, PhD in Engring., 1971. Rsch. scientist U.S. Army Aviation R & D, Ames Rsch. Ctr., Moffett Field, Calif., 1971-79; chief applied computation aeronautics br. NASA-Ames Rsch. Ctr., Moffett Field, 1979-80, dir. astronautics, 1980-84, dir., 1984-89; acting assoc. adminstr. NASA Hdqrs., Washington, 1988-89; v.p. rsch. tech. Martin Marietta Astronautics Group, Denver, 1989-90, v.p., dir. Centaur program, 1990; pres. Civil Space and Communications, Denver, 1990-93, Aero & Naval Sys., 1993-94; v.p. sci. & engring. Lockheed Martin Corp., Bethesda, Md., 1995—; co-chmn. Air Force Scientific adv. bd., 1996—. Contbr. articles on computational fluid dynamics to profl. jours. Mem. sci. and acad. adv. bd. U. Calif., 1987-92; mem. engring. adv. bd. U. Calif., Berkeley and Davis, U. Md., MIT Aero and Astro Dept.; chmn. govt. and edn. div. United Way of Santa Clara County, Calif., 1987; mem. Air Force Sci. Adv. Bd., 1994—. Capt USAR. Decorated Presdl. Rank of Disting. Exec., 1985; recipient H. Julian Allen award NASA-Ames Rsch. Ctr., 1977, Arthur S. Flemming award Jaycees, Washington, 1980, Disting. Profl. Engring. Sci. and Tech. award NSPE, 1986, Disting. Exec. Svc. award Sr. Execs. Assn., 1989, Disting. Svc. medal NASA, 1989, Disting. Engring. Alumnus award U. Calif., Berkeley, 1989. Fellow AIAA (pres. 1988-89, Lawrence Sperry award 1980), Royal Aero. Soc.; mem. NAE, Internat. Acad. Astronautics, Tau Beta Pi (named Eminent Engr. Berkeley chpt.). Roman Catholic. Home: 7735 Greentree Rd Bethesda MD 20817-1420 Office: Lockheed Martin Corp 6801 Rockledge Dr Bethesda MD 20817-1877

BALLIETT, JOHN WILLIAM, entrepreneur, real estate executive; b. Rochester, N.Y., Sept. 10, 1947; s. Charles Garrison and Burnetta Elizabeth (Purtell) B.; BS in Physics, Grove City Coll., 1969; postgrad. U. Rochester, 1969-71; m. Betsy Jane Van Patten, Jan. 25, 1969; 1 child, Noelle Elizabeth. Devel. engr. Eastman Kodak Co., 1969-70; scientist Tropel Inc., 1970, mgr. applied optics, 1971-72, mktg. mgr., 1972-73; exec. v.p., dir. Quality Measurement Systems Inc., Penfield, N.Y., 1973-77; pres. QMS Internat., Inc., Penfield, 1974-77, Balliett Assocs., Sarasota, Fla., 1978—, Shore Lane Devel. Corp. subs. (merger Sandbar Devel. Corp. 1990), 1981—, pres., 1990—; pres., pub. Suncoast TV Facts, Inc., Sarasota, 1979-81; pres. Charter One, Inc., Sarasota, 1981—, Palma Sola Enterprises, Inc., 1990—; chmn., chief exec. officer Charter One Hotels & Resorts, Inc., 1989—; pres. Alacho Inc., 1992—; pres. Servus Hotel Group, Inc., N.Y.C., 1997—; spkr. at nat. and internat. timesharing confs. Founding dir. Internat. Found. for Timesharing. Mem. Fla. Bar (citizen mem. greivance com.), U.S. C. of C., Sarasota County C. of C., Am. Land Devel. Assn., Nat. Timeshare Council, Fla. Hotel-Motel Assn. Contbr. articles on timesharing to profl. publs. Patentee optical systems. Home: 1404 Westbrook Dr Sarasota FL 34231-3549 Office: 2032 Hillview St Sarasota FL 34239-2334

BALLIETT, WHITNEY, writer, critic; b. N.Y.C., Apr. 17, 1926; s. Fargo and Dorothy (Lyon) B.; m. Elizabeth Hurley King, 1951; children: Julia, Elizabeth, Will; m. Nancy Kraemer, 1965; children: Whitney, Jamie. BA with honors, Cornell U., 1951. Mem. editl. staff New Yorker mag., N.Y.C., 1951—, successively collator, proofreader, reporter, 1951-57, staff writer, 1957—; columnist on jazz, book, movie, theater and art reviewer, reporter. Author: The Sound of Surprise, 1959, Dinosaurs in the Morning, 1962, Such Sweet Thunder, 1966, Super-Drummer: A Profile of Buddy Rich, 1968, Ecstasy at the Onion, 1971, Alec Wilder and His Friends, 1974, New York Notes, 1976, Improvising, 1977, Night Creature, 1981, Jelly Roll, Jabbo, and Fats, 1983, American Musicians: Fifty-Six Portraits in Jazz, 1986, American Singers: Twenty-Seven Portraits in Song, 1988, Barney, Bradley and Max: Sixteen Portraits in Jazz, 1989, Goodbyes and Other Messages: A Journal of Jazz, 1981-90, 91, American Musicians II: Seventy Two Portraits in Jazz, 1996; contbr. to N.Y. Rev. Books, 1998—. Served as sgt. USAAF, 1946-47. Recipient Acad. award in lit. Am. Acad. Arts and Letters, 1996. Mem. Century Assn. Office: 114 E 90th St New York NY 10128-1550

BALLINGER, CHARLES KENNETH, information specialist; b. Johnstown, Pa., July 28, 1950; s. Delores Jean (Cool) B.; m. Deb C. Delger, Sept. 14, 1985. Programmer analyst Cowles Pub. Co., Spokane, Wash., 1975-78; systems analyst Old Nat. Bank, Spokane, 1978-82; software engr. ISC System, Spokane, 1982; micro computer analyst Acme Bus. Computers, Spokane, 1982-85; info. ctr. analyst Wash. Water Power Co., Spokane, 1985-92; office automation analyst EDS Corp., Spokane, 1992-96, software engr.-mini/micro, 1996-98, info. analyst for client-server human resources info. sys., 1998—; cons. IDP Co., Spokane, 1978—. Contbr. articles to profl. jours. Served with Signal Corps, U.S. Army, 1968-71. Mem. IEEE (assoc.), Spokane Health Users Group (pres. 1979-83). Avocations: software development, motorcycling, boating, shooting, amateur radio. Home: 3810 S Havana St Spokane WA 99223-6006 Office: EDS-I/S Avista Corp 1411 E Mission Ave Spokane WA 99202-2617

BALLINGER, ROYCE EUGENE, academic administrator, educator; b. Burkburnett, Tex., Feb. 21, 1942; s. Royce and Luceil Evelyn (Tucker) B.; m. Ruth Ann Hamshar, May 15, 1976. BA, U. Tex., 1964; MS, Tex. Tech U., 1967; PhD, Tex. A&M U., 1971. Asst. prof. biology Angelo State U., San Angelo, Tex., 1971-74, assoc. prof., 1974-76; assoc. prof. U. Nebr., Lincoln, 1976-82, dir. biol. scis., 1982-90, prof., 1982—, assoc. vice chancellor rsch., 1993—; dir. Nebr. EPSCoR, Lincoln, 1993—; bd. govs. Ctr. Gt. Plains Studies U. Nebr., Lincoln, 1981-88; internat. adv. panel Chinese U. Devel. Project, World Bank, Montreal, Can., 1988; nat. adv. coun. BIOCOM, S.C., 1992-96. Author: How to Know Amphibians and Reptile, 1983; contbr. 110 articles to profl. jours. Governing bd. mem. Nat. EPSCoR Coalition, Washington, 1995-98. Rsch. grantee NSF, 1968-80, 93—, Dept. Energy, 1993, Dept. Def., 1993, NASA, 1993. Mem. Am. Soc. Ichthyologists & Herpetologists (bd. govs. 1985-87), Sigma Xi. Office: Nebr EPSCoR UNL Campus 203 Whittier Bldg Lincoln NE 68583-0848

BALLINGER, WALTER FRANCIS, surgeon, educator; b. Phila., May 16, 1925; s. Robert I. and Frances (Taylor) B.; children: Walter Francis, Christopher Bardin, David Gordon; m. Mary Randolph Gordon Dickson, Oct. 4, 1980. Student, Cornell U., 1942-44; M.D., U. Pa., 1948. Intern 1st Surg. Div., Bellevue Hosp., N.Y.C., 1948-49; asst. resident surgery 1st Surg. Div., Bellevue Hosp., 1949-50, chief resident surgery, 1955-56; asst. resident surgery Columbia-Presbyn. Med. Center, 1953-55; from instr. to assoc. prof. Jefferson Med. Coll., Phila., 1956-63; assoc. prof. surgery Johns Hopkins Sch. Medicine, 1964-67; Bixby prof., head dept. surgery Washington U. Sch. Medicine, St. Louis, 1967-78; prof. surgery Washington U. Sch. Medicine, 1978-92, prof. emeritus surgery, 1992—; med. dir. health adminstrn. program Wash. U. Sch. Medicine, 1993—. Editor: Research Methods in Surgery, 1964, The Management of Trauma, 1968, 4th edit., 1985, (with T. Drapanas) Practice of Surgery: Current Review, 1972, 2d edit., 1974; editor-in-chief (with G. Zuidema) Surgery, 1971-97, (with J. Hepner) Best Practices and Benchmarking in Healthcare; mem. editl. bd. Brit. Jour. Surgery, 1989-94. Served to capt. U.S. Army, 1950-52. Markle scholar med. sci., 1961-66. Mem. Am. Surg. Assn., Soc. Clin. Surgery, Soc. Univ. Surgeons, A.C.S., James IV Assn., Halsted Soc. Home: 1203 Log Cabin Ln Saint Louis MO 63124-1528

BALLMAN, DONNA MARIE, lawyer; b. Mansfield, Ohio, July 23, 1959; d. Earl J. and Florine (Hansel) B. BA, Wellesley (Mass.) Coll., 1981; JD, U. Miami, 1986. Bar: Fla. 1986, U.S. Dist. Ct. (so. and mid. dists.) Fla.; cert. mediator. Assoc. William B. Cagney III PA, Miami, Fla., 1986-87, Hornsby & Whisenand, Miami, Fla., 1987-90; prin. Donna M. Ballman, PA, North Miami Beach, Fla., 1990—; bd. dirs. Grand Jury Assn. Fla.; councilwoman Cmty. Coun. Two Dade County, 1997-98. Producer, dir., host Legalvision (TV talk show), Miami, 1985-86, (radio talk show) Law Beat, Miami, 1984-86. Paul B. Anton scholar U. Miami Sch. Law, 1985-86, Fla. Assn. Women Lawyers scholar, 1985. Mem. Assn. Trial Lawyers Am., Am. Arbitration Assn., Nat. Coun. Jewish Women (life), Nat. Assn. Women's Bus. Owner's (mem. bd. dirs., co-chair govt. affairs com. 1991-92), Fla. Bar, Fla. Assn. for Women Lawyers (mem. bd. dirs. 1992-95, chair legis. com. 1991-92, chair gender bias com. 1992-95), Grand Jury Assn. Fla. (Woman of Distinction award 1995), Dade County Bar Assn. (sr. citizens handbook com., young lawyers sect. 1988, vol. lawyers 1988-89), Downtown Bus. and Profl. Women (Woman of Yr. award 1991-92, 1st v.p. 1992-94), Omicron Delta Kappa. Office: Donna M Ballman PA 13899 Biscayne Blvd Ste 154 North Miami Beach FL 33181-1650

BALLMER, STEVE, software company executive. Degree in applied math. and econs., Harvard U.; postgrad., Stanford U. Asst. product mgr. Procter and Gamble; v.p. mktg., v.p. corp. staffs, sr. v.p. syss. software Microsoft Corp., Redmond, Wash., 1980—, now exec. v.p. sales and support; mem. exec. com. Microsoft. Active bd. overseers Harvard U., adv. coun. Stanford Bus. Sch. Avocations: exercise, jogging, playing basketball. Office: Microsoft Corp 1 Microsoft Way Redmond WA 98052-6399*

BALLOU, CHARLES HERBERT, financial executive; b. Columbus, Ohio, Aug. 21, 1945; s. Herbert W. Jr. and Esther Louise (Varner) B.; m. Lois Marie Orlando, Nov. 12, 1967; children: Christina, Michael, Gregg. BS, Ohio State U., 1967. CFP. Mfr. rep. Will Ross Inc., Indpls., 1970-72; asst. v.p. Merrill Lynch, Columbus, 1972-84; pres., CEO Asset Planning Mgmt. and Rsch., Columbus, 1984—. Co-author: Standard of Living Analysis, 1988; author (newspaper column) Chuck Ballou, 1990. Capt. U.S. Army, 1967-70. Mem. Inst. Cert. Fin. Planners, Cen. Ohio Soc., Internat. Assn. Fin. Planning, Kiwanis. Roman Catholic. Home: 3104 Wareham Rd Columbus OH 43221-2246 Office: Asset Planning Mgmt & Rsch 3100 Tremont Rd Ste 102 Columbus OH 43221-2013

BALLOU, HOWARD BURGESS, commercial plumbing designer; b. New Haven, Feb. 12, 1938; s. Raymond Cotton and Edith Yale (Ballou) B.; m. Elizabeth Capacite Flores, June 27, 1987; children from previous marriage: Jeffrey Howard, Scott Raymond, Rachel Cotton. Assocs. in Constrn. Mgmt. with honors, Richland Coll., Dallas, 1979; student in acctg. and econs., U. Tex., Dallas, 1980. Lic. gen. contractor, Va.; cert. sr. engring. tech.; cert. master plumber, Tex. Constrn. trades, draftsman, 1958-68; sr. designer, resident engr. ICI Am., Stamford, Conn., 1968-70; sr. designer Connell Assocs. and J.M. Montgomery, Miami and Ft. Lauderdale, Fla., 1970-74; pvt. practice Va., Tex., 1975-77; project engr. Continental Mech., Dallas, 1977-85; sr. plumbing designer Purdy-McGuire, Dallas, 1977-85; mech. coord. Tech. Constrn. Svc., Nashville, 1986; project mgr. J.K. Johnson Mech. Contractors, Sheffield, Ala., 1987-88; designer Kimberly Clark, Memphis, 1988-94; plumbing designer Shappley Design Cons., Memphis, 1994-95; pvt. practice Memphis, 1995—; instr., head drafting dept. Elkins Inst., Dallas, 1977-85; columnist Contractor Mag., 1984-85. Co-author: Beth Howard Associates Guide Book, 1989, Beth Howard Associates Fiancee Visa Guide, 1990; contbr. articles to profl. jours. Chmn. plumbing and mech. bd. City of Plano, Tex., 1980-84; scoutmaster Boy Scouts Am., Conn., Fla., 1950-69; officer, instr. CAP, New Haven; eucharistic min. Holy Rosary Cath. Ch., Memphis, 1995—. Mem. Am. Soc. Plumbing Engrs. (v.p. tech. 1981-82), Nat. Writers Club (profl., founder, pres. North Tex. chpt. 1984-85), St. Vincent DePaul Soc., Philippine-Am. Club, KC (3d degree). Republican. Avocations: writing, cooking, gardening, travel. Home: 503 Chalmers Rd Memphis TN 38120-1516

BALLOU, JANICE DONELON, research director; b. New Brunswick, N.J., May 13, 1944; s. Peter and Kathryn (Koval) Donelon; m. Donald Thomas Ballou, Nov. 12, 1966 (div. 1984); children: Peter, David. BA, Douglas Coll., 1966; MA, Rutgers U., 1977. Tchr. Sayreville (N.J.) Jr. High Sch., 1966-71; dir. field ops. Eagleton Inst., Rutgers U., New Brunswick, N.J., 1977-80, assoc. dir., 1980-82, dir., 1989—; v.p. divsn. head Louis Harris & Assocs., N.Y.C., 1982-86; v.p. group head Response Analysis, Princeton, N.J., 1986-89; bd. dirs. Inst. Rsch. on Aging and Health Fin., Princeton, N.J., Essex C.C. Found. Co-founder Parents Drug and Alcohol Coun., Highland Park, N.J., 1991; bd. dirs. Rutgers Substance Abuse Task Force, New Brunswick, 1990-93, The Citizen's Com. on Biomed. Ethics, Summit, N.J., 1993-98; chair Pathways to Participation Civic Edn. Program com., New Brunswick, 1992; grad. bd. Leadership N.J., 1991-99; pres. Bd. Leadership N.J. Grad. Orgn., 1995; mayor Highland Park Econ. Devel. Com., 1999. Leadership N.J. fellow Partnership for N.J., 1990, Ford Found. fellow, 1990; named Alumnae of Yr. by Highland Park High Sch., 1992. Mem. Am. Assn. Pub. Opinion Rsch. (pubs. chair 1988-90, sec.-treas. 1991-93), Nat. Network State Polls (mem. exec. coun. 1989—), Nat. Coun. Pub. Polls (mem. exec. coun. 1993—), N.J. Internat. Forum Women (sec.), Douglass Coll. Associate Alumnae Douglass Soc. Avocations: raising Christmas trees, travelling, hiking, outdoor activities, reading. Office: Rutgers U Eagleton Inst Politics New Brunswick NJ 08901

BALLOU, JEFFREY PIERRE, producer; b. Pitts., Aug. 2, 1967; s. Kasib Rashid and Geneva (Williams) B. BA in Journalism and African American Studies, Pa. State U., 1990; MA in Journalism and Pub. Policy, Am. Un., 1992; grad., Howard U., 1992. Hearst news prodr. fellow-in-residence Sta. WCVB-TV, Boston, 1990-91; freelance newswriter WTTG-TV, Washington, 1992; assignment editor C-SPAN, Washington, 1992; freelance corr. Sta. WAMU-FM, Washington, 1990-92; asst. editor Sta. WTOP-AM, Washington, 1992-93; asst. prodr. Nat. Pub. Radio, Washington, 1990-93; White House prodr. CONUS Comm., Washington, 1993-95; prodr., 1995—, White House prodr., 1996—. Author selected op-ed columns and feature stories. Named One of Outstanding Young Men of Am., 1989. Mem. Nat. Press Club, Radio and TV News Dirs. Assn. (mem. diversity task force), Soc. Profl. Journalists (bd. dirs. D.C. chpt. 1993-95, Taishoff Broadcast fellow 1994), Nat. Assn. Black Journalists, Washington Assn. Black Journalists (v.p. 1993, pres. 1994), Capital Press Club, Pa. State Alumni Assn. Coll. Comm. (bd. dirs. 1993-95), Pa. State U. Alumni Coun. (bd. dirs. 1993-96), Nat. INROADS Alumni Assn., White House Corrs. Assn., Radio and TV Corrs. Assn., Nat. Eagle Scout Assn., Alpha Phi Alpha, Free and Accepted Masons (Prince Hall affiliation). Baptist. Avocations: reading, dancing, writing, community service, travel. Home: 1011 Independence Ave SE Washington DC 20003-3921 Office: CONUS Communications 9th Fl 1825 K St NW Ste 9 Washington DC 20006-1202

BALLOU, KENNETH WALTER, retired transportation executive, university dean; b. Boston, June 6, 1930; s. Thomas Walter and Anne M. (Blanck) A.; m. Ann Dysart, Aug. 14, 1954; children—Stephen K., Jeffrey S., Laura A., Ellen S. A.B., Tufts U., 1953, Ed.M., 1954; postgrad., Rutgers U., 1955-56, UCLA, 1978, Wharton Sch., U. Pa., 1979, NYU, 1980. Tchr. pub. schs. Verona, N.J., 1954-56; asst. dir. admissions Northeastern U., Boston, 1954-59, dir. admissions, 1959-65, dean univ. relations, 1965-69, dean Univ. Coll., 1969-74, dean adult edn., 1974-78; pres. Wellesley Motor Coach Co., Mass., 1978-88; v.p., gen. mgr. Waters Bus. Systems, Inc., Framingham, Mass., 1978-88; cons. U.S. Office of Edn., various colls.; corporator Framingham Savs. Bank, 1980-85; mem. Spl. Legis. Commn. on Sch. Transp. Safety; sr. lectr. in mngt. Northeastern U., 1979—. Author monographs in field of adult edn. and sch. transp. Chmn. Framingham Sch. Com., 1962-68; corporator Framingham Union Hosp., 1969—; corporator Northeastern U., 1986—, mem. nat. coun., bd. overseers, 1989-98, mem. long range planning com., life mem. President's Club; bd. dirs. Mass. Osteo Hosp., 1970-72; life mem. Danforth Mus. Art, Framingham Hist. Assn.; mem. Sudbury Valley Trustees; past mem. bd. assessors 1st Parish, Framingham. Mem. AAUP, Assn. Higher Edn., Am. Mgmt. Assn., Adult Edn. Assn., Am. Assn. Continuing Edn., Coun. Advancement of Edn., Am. Pers. and Guidance Asn., Mass. Sch. Transp. Assn. (pres. 1988—), Nat. Sch. Transp. Assn. (Golden Merit award 1988), Nat. Pupil Transp. Assn., Mass. Sch. Bus. Ofcls. Assn., Mass. Audubon Soc., Ariz. Hist. Soc., Zeta Psi, Ventana Canyon Golf and Racquet Club, Sudbury River Tennis Club. Democrat. Home: 5325 N Strade De Rubino Tucson AZ 85750

BALLOWE, JAMES, English educator, author; b. Carbondale, Ill., Nov. 28, 1933; s. Frank Charles and Wilma Ruth (Maynard) B.; children: Jeffrey, Mary; m. Ruth Ganchiff. BA, Millikin U., 1954; MA, U. Ill., 1956, PhD, 1963. Tchr. pub. schs. Decatur, Ill., 1954-55; grad. asst. U. Ill., 1955-61; asst. prof. English Millikin U., 1961-63; mem. faculty dept. English Bradley U., Peoria, Ill., 1963—, prof., chmn., 1971-74, dean Grad. Sch., 1974-86, assoc. provost, 1979-86, dean communications and fine arts, 1986-90, disting. univ. prof., 1999; chmn. Commn. Instns. Higher Edn., North Central Assn., 1985-86; narrator Herrin Massacre, Nat. Pub. Radio, 1997. Author: poetry The Coal Miners, 1979; editor: George Santayana's America, 1967, Anglo-Welsh Poetry, 1989. Mem. Ill. Arts Coun., 1975-83, Ill. State Mus. Bd., 1977—, Ill. Humanities Coun., 1997—. Recipient Poetry award Ill. Arts Coun., 1975, 78, Creative Non-fiction award Ill. Arts Coun., 1993. Mem. Ill. Assn. Grad. Schs. (pres. 1979-80), Midwestern Assn. Grad. Schs. (pres. 1978-79). Home: Bradley U 2554 Cherie Ln Ottawa IL 61350 Office: Bradley U 1501 W Bradley Ave Peoria IL 61625

BALLWEG, MARY LOU, nonprofit association administrator and founder, writer, consultant. BA in Comparative Lit. with honors, U. Wis., 1971. Staff writer Investor, Wis.' Bus. mag., Milw., 1972, mng. editor, 1973-74; scriptwriter, film dir. Moynihan Assocs., Milw., 1975; cons. communication, film making Milw. and Washington, 1976-81; co-founder Internat. Endometriosis Assn., Milw., 1980-82, exec. dir., pres., 1980—; lectr. in field. Author/editor: The Endometriosis Sourcebook, 1995, Overcoming Endometriosis, 1987; scriptwriter, dir.: (films) Domestic Violence: All-American Crime; contbr. articles to profl. jours., chpts. to books. Helped to found Margaret Sanger Cmty. Health Clinic, Milw., 1971-72, and endometriosis rsch. program Dartmouth Med. Sch., 1994—, Vanderbilt U. Sch. Medicine, 1998—. Mem. Am. Soc. Reproductive Medicine, Am. Assn. Gynecologic Laparoscopists, Am. Women in Sci., Nat. Asian Women's Orgn., Internat. Women's Health Coalition, European Soc. Human Reproduction and Embryology, Soc. Ob-Gyns. Can., Soc. Advancement Women's Health Rsch., Reproductive Immunology Spl. Interest Group, Women in Communications (bd. dirs. southeast Wis. chpt. 1976-77, editor newsletter), NOW. Office: Internat Endometriosis Assn 8585 N 76th Pl Milwaukee WI 53223-2633

BALMAIN, KEITH GEORGE, electrical engineering educator, researcher; b. London, Ont., Can., Aug. 7, 1933; s. William and Laeta Marguerite (Whaley) B.; m. Joan Shirley Ebbutt, Aug. 16, 1958. B Applied Sci. in Engring. Physics, U. Toronto, 1957; MSEE, U. Ill., 1959, PhDEE, 1963. Profl. engr., Ont. Rsch. assoc. dept. elec. engring. U. Ill., Urbana, 1963-64, asst. prof. elec. engring., 1964-66; asst. prof. U. Toronto, 1966-67, assoc. prof., 1967-73, prof., 1973—, chmn. div. engring. sci., 1985-87, chmn. rsch. bd., 1987-90; sr. chairholder indsl. rsch. chair in electromagnetics NSERC/Bell Can./Nortel, 1991—. Author: (with E.C. Jordan) Electromagnetic Waves and Radiating Systems, 2d edit., 1968. Recipient Best Paper of Yr. award Antennas and Propagation Soc., 1970; co-recipient NASA Group Achievement award, 1992. Life fellow IEEE. Office: U Toronto Dept Elec & Comp Engring, 10 Kings College Rd, Toronto, ON Canada M5S 3G4*

BALMASEDA, LIZ, columnist; b. Puerto Padre, Cuba, 1959. AA, Miami-Dade (Fla.) C.C., 1979; BS Comm., Fla. Internat. U., 1981. Intern Miami Herald, Fla., 1980, with Spanish lang. publ., 1981, gen. assignment reporter, feature writer, 1987, with Sunday Mag. tropic, 1990, local columnist, 1991; ctrl. Am. bur. chief Newsweek, El Salvador, 1985; freelance columnist NBC News, Honduras. Appeared on NBC Today Show, Oprah show. Recipient 2d place Ernie Pyle award Scripps Howard Found, 1984, 3d place feature writing Fla. Soc. Newspaper Editors, 1st prize Guillermo Martinez-Marquez contest Nat. Assn. Hispanic Journalists., 1989, Pulitzer Prize for commentary, 1993, 1st prize commentary Fla. Soc. Newspaper editors. Office: The Miami Herald One Herald Plaza Miami FL 33132*

BALMER, THOMAS ANCIL, lawyer; b. Longview, Wash., Jan. 31, 1952; s. Donald Gordon and Elisabeth Clare (Hill) B.; m. Mary Louise McClintock, Aug. 25, 1984; children: Rebecca Louise, Paul McClintock. AB, Oberlin Coll., 1974; JD, U. Chgo., 1977. Bar: Mass. 1977, D.C. 1981, U.S. Dist. Ct. Mass. 1977, Oreg. 1982, U.S. Dist. Ct. Oreg. 1982, U.S. Ct. Appeals (9th cir.) 1982, U.S. Ct. Appeals (D.C. cir.) 1983, U.S. Supreme Ct. 1987. Assoc. Choate, Hall & Stewart, Boston, 1977-79, Wald, Harkrader & Ross, Washington, 1980-82; trial atty. antitrust div. U.S. Dept. Justice, Washington, 1979-80; assoc. Lindsay, Hart, Neil & Weigler, Portland, Oreg., 1982-84; ptnr. Lindsay, Hart, Neil & Weigler, Portland, 1985-90, Ater Wynne LLP, Portland, 1990-93, 97—; dep. atty. gen. State of Oregon, Salem, 1993-97; adj. prof. of law Northwestern Sch. Law Lewis and Clark Coll., 1983-84, 90-92. Contbr. articles to law jours. Active mission and outreach com. United Ch. of Christ, Portland, 1984-87, Met. Svc. Dist. Budget Com., Portland, 1988-90; bd. dirs. Multnomah County Legal Aid Svc., Inc., 1989-93, chair 1992-93; bd. dirs. Chamber Music Northwest, 1997—. Mem. ABA, Oreg. Bar Assn. (chmn. antitrust sect. 1986-87). Democrat. Home: 2521 NE 24th Ave Portland OR 97212-4831 Office: 222 SW Columbia St Ste 1800 Portland OR 97201-6618

BALMUTH, BERNARD ALLEN, retired film editor; b. Youngstown, Ohio, May 19, 1918; s. Joseph and Sadie (Stein) B.; m. Rosa June Bergman, Mar. 2, 1952; children: Mary Susan, Sharon Nancy. BA in English, UCLA, 1942. Postal clk. U.S. Postal Svc., L.A., 1946-55; asst. and apprentice film editor, film editor L.A., 1955-90; ret., 1990; instr. film editing dept. of the arts UCLA Extension, 1979—; film editing cons. Am. Film Inst., L.A., 1982-92. Author: (manual) The Language of the Cutting Room, 1979, (text) Introduction to Film Editing, 1989. Initiator petition STOP Save TV Original Programming and Stop Excessive Reruns, 1971-75. Sgt. U.S. Army, 1942-46. Recipient Honor Cert. for Contribution Acad. TV Arts and Scis., 1974, Emmy nomination Best Editing, 1982. Mem. Am. Cinema Editors (life, bd. dirs. 1982-85, 97—, sec. 1985-87, v.p. 1987-91, chmn. spl. awards com. 1988—, hon. historian 1993—), Hollywood Film and Labor Coun. (rep. for Editors Guild 1972—), Stage Soc. (bd. dirs., sec. 1949-54). Democrat. Jewish. Avocations: cinema, theatre, dancing, cinema books, tennis. Address: care Rosallen Publs PO Box 927 North Hollywood CA 91603-0927

BALOG, GEORGE G., city director of public works. BS in Civil Engring., Va. Mil. Inst., 1964; JD, U. Balt., 1973; postgrad. sr. execs. program, Harvard U., 1989. Dir. dept. pub. works City of Balt.; mem. City of Balt. Bd. Estimates; chair Northeast Waste Authority, and Archtl. and Engring. Awards Commn.; disting. visitor and rep. Japan, Germany, Belgium, France, China, Russia. Recipient Pub. Svc. citation Gov. Md., 1996, citation of Merit Mayor Balt., 1996, Pub. Svc. award Md. Minority Contractors Assn., 1996; named one of Top Ten Pub. Works Leaders of Yr. for U.S. and Can., Am Pub. Works Assn., 1996. Mem. Am. Pub. Works Assn. (Founder's award 1997, Presdl. award 1997), Engring. Soc. Balt. (Civic Achievement award, Elijah E. Cummings Svc. award). Office: City of Baltimore Dept Pub Works 600 Abel Wolman Mcpl Bldg Baltimore MD 21202*

BALOG, IBOLYA, accountant; b. Subotica, Yugoslavia, July 11, 1953; came to U.S., 1969; d. Balint and Adela (Dohocki) B. B.A., Lehigh U., 1975; M.B.A., Temple U., 1980. CPA. Adminstrv. asst. Chain Bike Corp., Allentown, Pa., 1975-77; controller Bicycle Corp. Am., Allentown, 1982-87; acct. Cohen & Rogozinski, CPA's, Allentown, 1987-92; mgr. Parente, Randolph, Orlando, Carey & Assocs., CPA's, 1992—. Bd. dirs. YWCA, Allentown, 1986-95, treas. 1993, pres. 1994, trustee 1995—. Mem. AAUW (treas. 1984 85, Outstanding Woman 1985), AICPA, Pa. Inst. CPAs (pres. Lehigh Valley chpt. 1998-99), Inst. Mgmt. Accts. (v.p. Lehigh Valley chpt. 1997—), Am. Women's Soc. CPAs (pres. Lehigh Valley affiliate, 1993-94), Allentown Rotary Club. Democrat. Home: 1522 1/2 W Chew St Allentown PA 18102-3645 Office: Parente Randolph Orlando Carey & Assocs 1427 W Chew St Allentown PA 18102-3658

BALOG, RITA JEAN, retired librarian; b. Ashtabula, Ohio, Sept. 24, 1930; d. Frederick Carroll and Marguerite Ethel (White) Grady; m. Richard Francis Balog, Oct. 16, 1949; children: Rebecca Kay, Richard Francis Jr., Ronald Frank, Robert Henry. AA, Kent State U., 1977, BA in Gen. Studies, 1978, MLS, 1980. Clk., typist Harbor Pub. Libr., Ashtabula, 1973-75, children's libr., 1975-80; libr., dir. Harbor-Topky Meml. Libr., Ashtabula, 1980-97; ret., 1997; vol. libr. Thomas Jefferson Elem. Sch., Harbor Spl. Sch., Ashtabula, 1972-75. Sec., mem. Ashtabula Archtl. Restoration and Rev. Bd., 1975—; vol. leader Lake River coun. Girl Scouts U.S., Niles, 1958-73, mem. nominating com., 1989-91, bd. dirs., 1991-95, child camp dir.; trustee Coun. Ashtabula County Librs., chair, 1994-96. Mem. ALA, AAUW, Ohio Libr. Assn., N.E. Ohio Libr. Assn. (regional adv. bd. 1984-86), Coun. Ashtabula County Librs. (pres. 1985-86), Ashtabula Area Mus. and Hist. Soc. (trustee 1992-98), Zonta (pres. 1987-89). Democrat. Avocations: collecting rocks, wild flowers, swimming, needlecraft.

BALOGUN, JOSEPH A., physical therapist, educator, researcher; b. Idofin-Isanlu, Kogi, Nigeria, Jan. 1, 1955; came to U.S., 1980; s. Ezra and Abiba Rhoda (Eniamo) B.; m. Adetutu Olusola, Dec. 23, 1989; children: Omotade, Omotayo, Omotola. BSc in Physiotherapy, U. Ibadan, Nigeria, 1977; MS, U. Pitts., 1981, PhD, 1985. Phys. therapist Gen. Hosp., Mubi and Ilorin, Nigeria, 1977-80; asst. prof. Russell Sage Coll., Troy, N.Y., 1984-86; sr. lectr., cons. Obafemi Awolowo U., Ile-Ife, 1986-90; vice dean health scis. Obafemi Awolowo U., Ile-Ife, 1990-91; assoc. prof., dir. indsl. rehab. lab. Tex. Woman's U., Houston, 1991-93; prof., chmn. SUNY Health Sci. Ctr., Bklyn., 1993—, assoc. dean students acad. affairs, 1994—; vis. rsch. scholar U. Fla., Gainesville, 1988; adj. assoc. prof. Baylor Coll. Medicine, Houston, 1992-93; cons. program evaluator Kingsborough C.C., Bklyn., 1995-96; reviewer Women's Health Jour., 1993, Perceptual and Motor Skills, 1993; external examiner U. Lagos, Nigeria, 1989-91; program evaluator Nat. U. Commn., Lagos, 1990-91; editl. cons. Jour. Nigeria Assn. Phys. Therapy Students, 1986-91; vis. prof. Barry U., Miami Shores, Fla., 1996-98; abstractor, reviewer Phys. Therapy, 1984—; reviewer Jour. of Allied Health, 1998—; grant reviewer Found. for the Long Term Care, Albany, 1997—; reviewer Jour. Allied Health, 1998—. Author: (with others) Prevention of Musculoskeletal Injuries, 1990; mem. editl. bd. Internat. Jour. Physiotherapy Theory and Practice, 1995-96; assoc. editor Jour. Nigeria Soc. Phys. Therapy, 1986-94, Jour. of Human Muscle Performance, 1991-93, Internat. Jour. Physiotherapy Theory and Practice, 1997—; contbr. over 70 articles to profl. jours. Recipient scholarship Fed. Govt. Nigeria, 1974-77, 80-84, Alumni Scholarship award U. Pitts., 1984, Acad. Instn. program award Isotechnologies, Inc., 1992; grantee Russell Sage Coll., 1985, Obafemi Awolowo U. Ile-Ife, Nigeria, 1988, Tex. Woman's U., 1992, Found. for Long Term Care, 1995, SUNY, Bklyn., 1995, 98; hon. fellow Inst. Pub. Health Obafemi Awolowo U., Ile-Ife, Nigeria, 1997—. Fellow Am. Coll. Sports Medicine; mem. Am. Phys. Therapy Assn. (Minority Initiatives award 1996), Nigeria Soc. Physiotherapy (jour. reviewer 1984-86), Am. Phys. Therapy Assn. (sect. edn. cons. pool 1996—, com. for screening proposals/abstracts for ann. sci. exposition 1997—). Avocations: reading, soccer. Home: 8708 Glenwood Rd Brooklyn NY 11236-3412 Office: SUNY Health Scis Ctr Box 16 450 Clarkson Ave Brooklyn NY 11203-2056

BALON, THOMAS WILLIAM, exercise physiologist; b. Albany, N.Y., Mar. 3, 1952. BS, SUNY, Brockport, 1975; MS, Ball State U., 1976; PhD, U. Toledo, 1983. Postdoctoral fellow Boston U. Sch. Medicine, 1983-86; asst. prof. U. Iowa, Iowa City, 1986-92; assoc. rsch. scientist City of Hope Nat. Med. Ctr., Duarte, Calif., 1992—; book reviewer MacMillan Pub. Co., N.Y.C., 1988, W. C. Brown Co., Madison, Wis., 1990; guest reviewer Jour. of Applied Physiology, Bethesda, Md., 1987-91; prin. investigator NIH, 1990—, Am. Diabetes Assn., 1987. Contbr. articles to Jour. of Applied Psychology, Biochem. Jour., Am. Jour. Physiology, Jour. of Biol. Chemistry, also chpt. to book. Fellow Am. Coll. Sports Medicine; mem. Am. Diabetes Assn. (grantee), Am. Physiol. Soc. Office: City of Hope Nat Med Ctr Dept Diabetes Endocrin/Met Duarte CA 91010

BALOUN, JOHN CHARLES, wholesale grocery company executive, retired; b. Chgo., May 1, 1934; s. John Nicholas and Anne (Giera) B.; m. Lynette Anne Jehs, July 27, 1963 (dec. Apr. 1998); children: John Christopher, Michael Warren. BSC, DePaul U., 1956. CPA, Ill. Mem. audit staff Arthur Andersen & Co., Chgo., 1956-63; contr., asst. sec. Super Food Svcs., Inc., Chgo., 1963-67; treas. Super Food Svcs., Inc., 1967-68, Dog'N Suds, Inc., Champaign, Ill., 1968-69; dir. planning and control distbn. div. Champion Internat., Inc., Chgo., 1969-74; treas. IGA, Inc., Chgo., 1974-77, v.p., 1977-80; v.p. fin. IGA Inc., Chgo., 1986-93, contr., 1993-96; ret. IGA, Inc., 1996; v.p. fin. Allied Van Lines, Inc., Broadview, Ill., 1980-83; contr., dir. corp. devel. Altair Corp., Northbrook, Ill., 1984-86. Pres. bd. dirs. Bethlehem Ctr. Food Bank, Carol Stream, Ill., 1990-91, bd. dirs., 1988-93, 96—. 2d lt. AUS, 1957. Republican. Home: 610 Western Ave Glen Ellyn IL 60137-4058

BALOW, IRVING HENRY, retired education educator; b. Wabasha, Minn., Jan. 19, 1927; s. Laurence Christian and Katherine (Yost) B.; m. Joyce Elizabeth Binner, June 8, 1950 (dec. 1980); children: Mary, Thomas, Michael, Robert, Ann.; m. Alta Sitton, June 27, 1981. B.S., U. Minn., 1951, M.A., 1957, Ph.D., 1959. Elementary sch. tchr. Theilmann, Minn., 1951-53; tchr. elem. sch. Wabasha, 1953-54, 56-57; instr. U. Minn., 1957-59; mem. faculty U. Calif., Riverside, 1959—, prof. edn., 1968—, chmn. dept., 1963-70, assoc. dean, 1970-71, acting dean, 1971-72, dean, 1972-87, acting dean Grad. Sch. Mgmt., 1990-92; retired, 1992; reading cons., 1959—. Contbr. articles to profl. jours. Served with USAAF, 1945-47. Home: 138 Green Oaks Dr Riverside CA 92507-4005

BALOWS, ALBERT, microbiologist, educator; b. Denver, Jan. 3, 1921; s. Lazerus and Anna (Kleiner) B.; m. Patricia Ann Barker, Oct. 7, 1956; children: Eve Ellen, Daniel Scott. BA in Biology (Lowell scholar), Colo. Coll., 1942; MS in Microbiology, Syracuse U., 1948; PhD (Haggin fellow), U. Ky., 1952. Diplomate: Am. Bd. Med. Microbiology. Microbiologist St. Joseph Hosp., Lexington (Ky.) Clinic, 1952-69; dir. bacteriology div. Ctrs. Disease Control, USPHS, Atlanta, 1969-81; asst. dir. lab. sci. Ctrs. Disease Control, USPHS (Ctr. Infectious Diseases), 1981-88; dir. emeritus Ctr. Disease Control, USPHS (Ctr. Infectious Diseases), 1988; asst. prof. medicine U. ky. Med. Ctr., Lexington, 1960-63, assoc. prof. medicine and cell biology, 1963-69; prof. lab. medicine Emory U. Sch. Medicine, 1970-98, prof. lab. medicine emeritus, 1998—; prof. biology Ga. State U., Atlanta, 1970—; lectr. Am. Soc. Microbiology Found., 1974-76; cons. clin. microbiology VA Hosp., Good Samaritan Hosp., Lexington, 1965-69; Med. Svc. Corps Dept. Army, 1973-79; bd. dirs. WHO Internat. Collaborating Ctr. for Rsch. Syphilis Serology and Immunology, 1974-82, WHO Internat. Collaborating Ctr. for Rsch. and Ref. in Antibiotic Susceptibility Testing, 1975-82, WHO Internat. Collaborating Ctr. for Rsch. and Ref. in Diagnostic Methods and Materials, 1985-88; mem. expert panels bacterial diseases, biol. standardization, lab. sci. WHO, Geneva, 1977-88. Founding editor-in-chief Jour. Clin. Microbiology, 1974-79, Current Microbiology, 1982—; editor Applied Microbiology, 1965-74, Ann. Rev. Microbiology, 1979—, C.C. Thomas med. microbiology series, 1964-90; author, editor over 75 books on microbiology and infectious disease; mem. editorial bds. 6 sci. jours.; editor: The Prokaryotes, 1981, sr. editor: The Prokaryotes, 2d edit., 1991; gen. editor: Topley & Wilson's Microbiology & Microbal Infections, 9th edit., 1998 (winner Advanced Edited Book category Med. Soc. London 1998); contbr. articles to profl. jours. Bd. dirs. Lexington chpt. NCCJ, 1960-64. With M.C. AUS, 1943-46. Named Lab World Microbiologist of Yr., 1980; recipient Becton-Dickinson award in clin.

microbiology, 1981, Silver medallion for outstanding contbns. to clin. microbiology Italian Soc. Microbiology, 1983, Louis T. Benezet Disting. Alumni award Colorado Coll., 1988, Abbott Labs. award for devel. of rapid lab. diagnostic techs., 1990, Disting. Profl. Recognition award, Am. bd. Med. Microbiology, 1997, bioMerieux Sonnenwirth award for exemplary leadership in clin. microbiology, 1999. Fellow Am. Acad. Microbiology (bd. govs. 1973-77, 89-95, chmn. 1975-76), N.Y. Acad. Scis., AAAS, Am. Pub. Health Assn., Infectious Disease Soc. Am., Am. Acad. Lab. Physicians and Scientists; mem. Am. Soc. Microbiology (now emeritus, pres.-elect 1979-80, pres. 1980-81, council, also mem. council policy com. 1974-82, P.R. Edwards award for outstanding service furthering high profl. ideals and standards in microbiology from S.E. br. 1987, elected hon. mem. 1988), Am. Soc. Clin. Pathology, Soc. Gen. Microbiology, AAUP, Med. Mycol. Soc. Am., Soc. Applied Bacteriology, Am. Veneral Disease Assn., South Ctrl. Assn. Clin. Microbiology (hon.), Assn. State & Territorial Pub. Health Lab. Dirs. (hon.), Sci. Writers Guild, Sigma Xi, Blue Key, Omicron Delta Kappa, Tau Kappa Alpha, Zeta Beta Tau, B'nai B'rith. Home and Office: 105 Bay Colt Rd Alpharetta GA 30004-3531 *Self esteem, good will and understanding are achieved by effective communication. Regrettably we fail because we do not listen. I have patterned my life after an ancient Chinese proverb: "First you must learn to listen well; then you will know that you have talked too much.".*

BALSAM, THEODORE, physician; b. N.Y.C., Apr. 11, 1931; s. Abraham and Esther (Golden) B.; m. Barbara Korn, Dec. 25, 1952; children: Hugh, Adrienne, Lisbeth. BA, NYU, 1952; MD, Chgo. Med. Sch., 1957; MPH, Johns Hopkins U., 1959. Diplomate Am. Bd. Internal Medicine. Intern Charity Hosp., New Orleans, 1957-58; fellow Johns Hopkins U., Balt., 1958-59; resident in medicine Bklyn. Hosp., 1959-61, fellow in gastroenterology, 1961-62; physician USPHS, S.I., 1962-64; pvt. practice Founders Med. Group, Chgo., 1964—; pres. med. staff Louis A. Weiss Meml. Hosp., Chgo., 1976-78, 93-95, dir. patient hosp. orgn., 1996—. Mem. Sch. Bd., Lincolnwood, Ill., 1970-72. Fellow Am. Coll. Gastroenterology; mem. AMA, Ill. State Med. Soc., Chgo. Med. Soc. Avocation: travel. Office: Weiss Meml Hosp 4640 N Marine Dr Chicago IL 60640-5719*

BALSAMELLO, JOSEPH VINCENT, information services manager; b. Bronx, N.Y., Feb. 8, 1956; s. Joseph and Marie (Fariello) B.; m. Carmela Totaro, Aug. 22, 1981; children: Nicholas, Sarah, Alyssa, Jenna, Stephen (dec.). BA in Psychology, William Paterson Coll., 1980. Inside salesperson Gen. Sportcraft Co. Ltd., Bergenfield, N.J., 1978-84, MIS mgr., 1984-88; sr. programmer, analyst UPS, Mahwah, N.J., 1988-93, MIS project leader, 1993—; bus. adv. coun. CPI Bus. Schs., Paramus, N.J., 1986-89. Coord. St. Mary's Ch., Pt. Jervis, N.Y., 1990-91; vol. Expectant/New Father Resource, Mothers of Supertwins, 1998—. Roman Catholic. Avocations: reading, music, theater, hiking, swimming.

BALSAMO, SALVATORE ANTHONY, technical and temporary employment companies executive; b. Boston, May 30, 1933; s. Anthony and Rosalia (Giambanco) B.; m. Yvonne Mollomo, Nov. 23, 1952; children: Anthony Joseph, Linda Marie Balsamo Wirta, Vicki Christine. Grad. high sch., Boston, 1951. Restranteur, 1955-61; asst. br. mgr. John Hancock, Boston, 1961-66; v.p. TAD Temporaries, Inc., Cambridge, Mass., 1966-69; chmn. bd., chief exec. officer, treas. Tech. Aid Corp. (now TAC Worldwide Cos.), Newton, Mass., 1969-99, chmn. bd., 1999—, also bd. dirs.; bd. dirs. Tech/Aid, TAC/Temps Inc., EDP/Temps and Contract Services, MicroTemps Systems and Programming, TAC/Medical Services Inc., Systems Mgmt. and Devel. Inc., Computer Enterprise Inc., Agy. for Personnel, TAC/Profl. Recruiters. Mem. fundraising com. Cath. Charitable Bur. Boston; founder, trustee Balsamo Meml. Charitable Found. Served to sgt. U.S. Army, 1953-55. Recipient award USAFR, 1977, Enterpreneurship Key to City of Cin., Mayor Charlie Luken, 1986. Mem. Nat. Assn. Temporary Services (1st v.p. 1987, 2d v.p. 1986-87, treas. 1985-86, exec. com. 1985—, bd. dirs. 1984—, govt. relations com.), Nat. Tech. Services Assn. (pres. New Eng. chpt. 1978-80, pres. 1983-84, exec. com., bd. dirs.), Mass. Assn. Temporary Services (v.p. tech. services 1982—, pres. 1979-81), New Eng. Design and Drafting Assn., Nat. Assn. Corp. Treas. Club: 100 of Mass. Avocation: tennis. Office: TAC Worldwide Cos 109 Oak St Newton MA 02464-1441*

BALSEIRO GONZALEZ, MANUEL, management executive, consultant; b. Coruna, Galicia, Spain, July 4, 1940; s. Manuel and Benjamina (Gonzalez) Balseiro; m. Emilia Lopez, Sept. 16, 1962; children: Cristina, Manuel, Cesar, Emilia, Jorge. Diploma in Mgmt., Deusto U., Bilbao, Spain, 1972, Navarra U., Barcelona, Spain, 1983. Sales adminstr. Montaner y Simon, S.A., Coruná, 1957-65; systems and sales person N.C.R., Oviedo, Bilbao, 1965-74; fin. mgr. Atlantica, S.A., Pontevedra, 1974-79; econs. com. mgr. H.J. Barreras, S.A., Vigo, 1979-81; gen. mgr. Feuga, Santiago De Compostela, Coruná, 1982—; bd. dirs. Talleres Reunidos, S.A., Coruná, 1988—; ID Norconsult, S.A., Madrid, 1990—, ID Umaiberica, S.A., Orense, 1994; pres., CEO CEEI, S.A., Santiago De Compostela, 1991—. Fellow Internat. Assn. Cons. in Higher Edn. (regional dir. 1991); mem. N.Y. Acad. Scis., European Assn. for T. Transfers (bd. dirs. 1990—), Lyon's Internat. (charter), Order of St. John of Jerusalem (Knight of Justice award 1992, Grand Hospitaller, Grand Cross 1996), Ordo Supremus Templi Hierosolymitani (Commdr./Prior award 1992, Magnus Oficialis 1995, Magnus Prior Spain 1996), Oxford Club, Club of Rome (Spanish chpt.). Roman Catholic. Office: Fundacion Empresa Universidad Gallega, Conga 1 Coruná Galicia, 15704 Santiago de Compostela Spain

BALSER, ROBERT EDWARD, animation film producer, director; b. Rochester, N.Y., Mar. 25, 1927; s. Syrel Jesse and Goldie (Weisenberg) B.; m. Cima Diane Feinberg, June 25, 1950; 1 child, Trevel Morley. BA, UCLA, 1950. Dir. animation TVC, London, 1967-68, WorldWide Prodn., Barcelona, Spain, 1969-70, Halas and Batcheler, London, 1971-72; owner, dir. Pegbar Prodns., Barcelona, 1972-93; dir. TV series Cromosoma, Barcelona, 1994-95; retired cons. Barcelona, 1995; animation cons. Egypt, 1996, Turkey, 1996-99; pres. "CARTOON" (media program), 1988—; v.p. ASIFA Internat., 1979-94, pres. Spain, 1980-93; animation cons., Egypt, 1996, Turkey, 1996. Co-dir. The Yellow Submarine, 1967-68; supv. dir. The Jackson 5, 1971; producer numerous ednl. and TV series. V.p. Benjamin Franklin Found., Barcelona, 1986—, Am. Soc. Barcelona, 1986-90; pres. Benjamin Franklin Sch. Bd., Barcelona, 1986-95. With USN, 1945-46. Recipient EMMY award NATAS, 1980; 1st prize publicity Venice and Annecy Festivals, Italy and France, 1964, Acad. Motion Picture Arts Scis. Democrat. Jewish. Avocations: film, collecting stamps and coins.

BALSIGER, DAVID WAYNE, television-video director, researcher, producer, writer; b. Monroe, Wis., Dec. 14, 1945; s. Leon C. and Dorothy May (Meythaler) B.; m. Nancy Marie Dixon, Oct. 12, 1991; children from previous marriages: Jennifer Anne, Lisa Atalie, Lori Faith. Student, Pepperdine U., Malibu, Calif., 1964-66, Cypress Jr. Coll., 1966, Chapman Coll. World Campus Afloat, Orange, Calif., 1967-68, Internat. Coll., Copenhagen, 1968; BA, Nat. U., San Diego, 1977; LHD (hon.), Lincoln Meml. U., Harrogate, Tenn., 1978. Chief photographer, feature writer Anaheim (Calif.) Bull., 1968-69; pub., editor Money Doctor, consumer mag., Anaheim, 1969-70; media dir. World Evangelism, San Diego, 1970-72; dir. mktg. Logos Internat. Christian Book Pubs., Plainfield, N.J., 1972-73; pres., dir. Master Media, advt. agy., Costa Mesa, Calif., 1973-75; pres. Balsiger Lit. Svc., Costa Mesa, 1973-78; v.p. communications Donald S. Smith Assocs., Anaheim, Calif., 1975-78; dir. creative devel. Sunn Classic Pictures, L.A., Salt Lake City, 1976-78; owner Writeway Lit. Assocs., Costa Mesa, 1978-92, Balsiger Enterprises, Costa Mesa, 1978-92, Bibl. News Svc., 1980-90; v.p. Donald S. Smith Assocs., Anaheim, 1982-86; owner BNS Publs., 1986-92; v.p. Am. Portrait Films Internat., Anaheim, 1990-91; chief rschr., field prodr., dir. Sun Internat. Pictures, Salt Lake City, 1992-94; exec. producer, dir. audio-video-media divsn. Group Pub., Loveland, Colo., 1994-98; prodr., rights mgr. Grizzly Adams Prodns., Loveland, Colo., 1998—; vis. prof. Nat. U., San Diego, 1977-80. Author: The Satan Seller, 1972, The Back Side of Satan, 1973, Noah's Ark: I Touched It, 1974, One More Time, 1974, It's Good to Know, 1975, In Search of Noah's Ark, 1976, The Lincoln Conspiracy, 1977, Beyond Defeat, 1978, On the Other Side, 1978, 8 Mini Guide Books (travel series), 1979, Presidential Biblical Scoreboard, 1980, 84, 88, Family Protection Scoreboard, South Africa, 1987, 88 (terorism), 89 (liberation theology), Candidates Biblical Scoreboard, 1986, Scoreboard Alert, 1989, Face in the Mirror, 1993, Ancient Secrets of the Bible, 1994, The Incredible Dicovery of Noah's Ark, 1995, The Incredible Power of Prayer, 1996; director, field producer, writer, researcher: TV and motion pictures including Operation Thanks, 1965, The Life and Times of Grizzly Adams, 1976-77, In Search of Noah's Ark, 1976, The Lincoln Conspiracy, 1977, The Bermuda Triangle, 1977, The Incredible Power of Prayer, 1997 (Dove Family Approved Seal award, Film Adv. Bd. Excellence award 1997, Freedom's Found. George Washington medal, 3 Telly awards, Worldfest Charleston award); (CBS Network specials) Ancient Secrets of the Bible, 1992, The Incredible Discovery of Noah's Ark, 1993, Ancient Secrets of the Bible II, 1993, Mysteries of the Ancient World, 1994, (13 TV shows and videos) Ancient Secrets of the Bible Collectors Series, 1995 (Covenant awards, Telly awards, WorldFest Charleston award, Religion in Media Angel awards, Film Adv. Bd. Excellence award, Communicator awards, Dove Family Approved Seal award, Dove Silver Sales Achievement award 1995); chier rschr., prodr. (6 TV shows and videos) Angels Sent On Assignment, 1996 (Communicator Crystal awards, Dove Family Approval Seal award, Film Adv. Bd. Excellence award 1997); exec. prodr. (video) Chadder's Stowaway Adventure, 1996 (Dove Family Approved Seal award, Film Adv. Bd. Excellence award), Sing and Play Music Video, 1996 (Dove Family Approved Seal award, Communicator award, Film Adv. Bd. Excellence award), Sing and Play Music Jamboree, 1997 (Dove Family Approved Seal award, Film Adv. Bd. Excellence award), Chadder's Wild Frontier Adventure, 1997 (Dove Family Approved Seal award, Film Adv. Bd. Excellence award), pub. editor Christian Singles Connection, 1991-92; frequent debate page columnist USA Today, 1987-94; prodr. (TV spls.) Secrets of the Bible Code Revealed, 1998, The Bible Code: Future and Beyond, 1999, Millennium Fears: Fact or Fiction, 1999; chief rschr. (TV spls.) The Quest for Noah's Ark, 1999, Secrets of the Bible Code Revealed II, 1999, Bible's Greatest Miracles, 1999, Bible's Greatest Secrets Revealed, 1999; prodr. (videos) Family 911: What to do Until Help Arrives, 1999, How to Prepare Your Family for Y2K and Other Disasters, 1999; author numerous law enforcement publs. Press agt. John G. Schmitz congl. campaign, 1972, Gordon Bishop supr. campaign, Orange County, 1970; press agt. asst. Ronald Reagan for Gov., statewide, 1966; statewide campaign mgr. James E. Johnson for U.S. Senate, 1974; campaign mgr. Dave Gubler Congl. campaign, 1974; candidate Costa Mesa City Coun., 1980; Rep. candidate for Congress from 38th Dist. Calif., 1978; mem. Calif. Rep. Assembly, 1975-78, 81-84, Rep. Assocs. Orange County, 1977-79; mem. World Affairs Coun. Orange County and San Diego, 1969-70; assoc.mem. Calif. Rep. Cen. Com., 1969-70; bd. dirs. Chapman Coll. World Campus Afloat, 1967, Chrisma Ministries, Orange, Calif., 1969-73; founder Ban the Soviets Coalition, 1983-84; exec. com. Anatole Fellowship, 1983-87; founder, pres. Nat. Citizens Action Network, 1984-95; bd. dirs. Internat. Ch. Relief Fund, 1987-92. Recipient Vietnam appreciation citation Am. Soldiers in Vietnam, 1966, George Washington Honor medal Freedoms Found., 1978, 79, Religion in Media Angel trophy, 1981, 85, 87, 88, 89, 92, 93, 94, 95, 5 Telly awards for Ancient Secrets series, 1996; named Writer of Month Calif. Writer, 1967; grand winner Mercury award for Pub. Affairs, 1987, Gold Mercury award for Pub. Affairs Mag., 1987, Silver Mercury award for affairs video script, 1988, Nat. Faith and Freedom award Religious Heritage of Am., 1994; named to Lit. Hall of Fame, 1977; hon. tourism amb. Rep. of South Africa, 1991. Mem. Nat. Univ. Pres. Assocs., Coun. on Nat. Policy, Internat. Christian Visual Media Assn. (bd. mem.), Nat. Religious Broadcasters, Internat. Bible Reading Assn. (adv. bd.), Evang. Press Assn., Christian Action Network (adv. bd.). Address: PO Box 1987 Loveland CO 80539-1987 *I believe successful people have a God given purpose strong enough to make them form the habit of doing things they don't like to do in order to accomplish their purpose. Every single qualification for success is acquired through habit. People form habits and habits form futures.*

BALSLEY, PHILIP ELWOOD, entertainer; b. Augusta County, Va., Aug. 8, 1939; s. Henry Elwood and Marjorie Walden (Fielding) B.; m. Wilma Lee Kincaid, July 21, 1962; children—Gregory, Mark, Leah. Grad. high sch. With group Statler Bros., 1961—; treas. Statler Bros. Prodns., 1973—. Bd. dirs. Happy Birthday U.S.A. Recipient numerous Grammy awards, Country Music Assn. awards. Presbyn. Office: PO Box 2703 Staunton VA 24402-2703

BALSTER, ROBERT LOUIS, pharmacologist; b. St. Cloud, Minn., Oct. 12, 1944; s. Louis and Marion Mae (Vandergon) B.; m. Sandra Kay Herwig, June 25, 1966; 1 child, Sarah Elizabeth Balster. BS, U. Minn., 1966; PhD, U. Houston, 1970. Postdoctoral fellow in psychiatry and pharmacology U. Chgo., 1970-72; rsch. assoc. in psychiatry Duke U., Durham, N.C., 1972-73; asst. prof. pharmacology Med. Coll. Va., Richmond, 1973-78; assoc. prof. Med. Coll. Va., 1978-84, prof. pharmacology, 1984—; dir. Inst. for Drug and Alcohol Studies, 1993—; chair Drug Abuse Adv. Com., FDA, Rockville, Md., 1983-84. Editor-in-chief Drug Alcohol Dependence; contbr. more than 250 articles to profl. jours. Recipient NIH Merit award, 1993—. Fellow Coll. on Problems of Drug Dependence (charter fellow, pres. 1995-96), Am. Coll. Neuropsychopharmacology, Am. Psychol. Assn. (pres. psychopharmacology divsn. 1989-90, chair bd. sci. affairs 1995-96); mem. European Behavioral Pharmacology Soc. (coun. mem. 1986-94). Achievements include development of lab. methods for studying the behavioral effects of drugs of abuse and procedures for drug abuse potential evaluation. Office: Va Commonwealth U PO Box 980310 Richmond VA 23298-0310

BALT, CHRISTINE ANN, family nurse practitioner; b. Gary, Ind., July 24, 1962; d. Casimir and Barbara Ann (Sohaney) B. AAS in Nursing, Purdue U., 1982; BSN, Ind. U., Indpls., 1986, MSW, 1992; MS in Primary Care Nursing, Ind. Wesleyan U., Marion, 1996. RN, Ind.; cert. family nurse practitioner; AIDS cert. RN. Staff nurse St. Catherine Hosp., East Chicago, Ind., 1983-84, Riley Hosp. for Children, Indpls., 1983-84, St. Francis Hosp., Beech Grove, Ind., 1984-85; pvt. duty nurse St. Vincent Stress Ctr., Indpls., 1985-86; staff nurse St. Joseph Hosp., Chgo., 1986-87, VA Med. Ctr., Indpls., 1987-96; family nurse practitioner St. Francis Med. Group, Indpls., 1996-98; nurse practitioner divsn. infectious diseases Ind. U. Dept. Medicine, Indpls., 1999—; mem. adv. bd. Midwest AIDS Tng. and Edn. Ctr., Indpls., 1998—. Chair Marion County HIV/AIDS Coalition, Indpls., 1993; bd. dirs. Friends of Walther Cancer Rsch. Ctr., Indpls., 1990-91. Mem. Assn. Nurses in AIDS Care (chair nat. membership com. 1998, pub. rels. com. 1998-99), Ind. State Nurses Assn., Sigma Theta Tau. Avocations: music, cross stitch, golf. Office: Ind U Dept Medicine Wishard Meml Hosp 1001 W 10th St OPW430 Indianapolis IN 46202

BALTAKE, JOE, film critic; b. Camden, N.J., Sept. 16; s. Joseph John and Rose Clara (Bearint) B.; m. Susan Shapiro Hale. BA, Rutgers U., 1967. Film critic Gannett Newspapers (suburban), 1969, Phila. Daily News, 1970-85; movie editor Inside Phila., 1986—; film critic The Sacramento Bee, 1987—; leader criticism workshop Phila. Writer's Conf., 1977-79; film critic. Contbg. editor: Screen World, 1973-87 ; author: The Films of Jack Lemmon, 1977, updated, 1986; contbr. articles to Films in Rev., 1969—, broadcast criticism for Prism Cable TV, 1985; cons. Jack Lemmon: American Film Institute Life Achievement Award, 1987, Jack Lemmon: A Life in the Movies, 1990. Recipient Motion Picture Preview Group award for criticism, 1986, citation Phila. Mag., 1985, First Pl. commentary award Soc. of Profl. Journalists, 1995. Mem. Nat. Soc. Film Critics. Office: Sacramento Bee 2100 Q St Sacramento CA 95816-6899 *Life's philosophy: "Living well is the best revenge."*

BALTAKIS, PAUL ANTANAS, bishop; b. Troškunai, Panevezys, Lithuania, Jan. 1, 1925; s. Juozas and Apolonia (Lauzikaite) B. PhD, Franciscan Sem., Rekem, Belgium, 1949; ThD, Franciscan Sem., St. Truidem, Belgium, 1955. Assoc. pastor Roman Cath. Parish of Resurrection, Toronto, Ont., Can., 1953-69; councilman Lithuanian Franciscan Vicariate, Kennebunkport, Maine, 1967-79, provincial superior, 1979-84; Roman Cath. bishop Lithuanian Catholics, Bklyn., 1984—. Spiritual adviser Lithuanian Boy Scouts Assn., Bklyn., 1964-84, Lithuanian Vets., Bklyn., 1970-79. Recipient For the Merits award Lithuanian Boy Scouts Assn., 1988, For the Merits award Lithuanian Vets., 1977, Ellis Island Medal of Honor, 1993, Merits award Lithanian Republic, 1994. Mem. Knights of Lithuania (hon.), Nat. Conf. Bishops & U.S. Cath. Conf. Home and Office: 361 Highland Blvd Brooklyn NY 11207-1910

BALTAZZI, EVAN SERGE, engineering research consulting company executive; b. Izmir, Turkey, Apr. 11, 1921; came to U.S., 1959, naturalized, 1964; s. Phocion George and Agnes Zoe (Varda) B.; m. Nellie Despina (Biorlaro), July 17, 1945; children—Agnes, James, Maria. D.Phys. Scis., Sorbonne U., Paris, 1949; D.Phil. in Chemistry, Oxford (Eng.) U., 1954. Research dir. French Nat. Research Ctr., Paris, 1947-59; group leader organic chemistry research Nat. Aluminate Corp., Chgo., 1959-61; mgr. organic chemistry sect. IIT Research Inst., Chgo., 1961-63; dir. research lab. Addressograph-Multigraph Corp., Chgo. and Cleve., 1963-77; pres. Evanel Assocs., Sagamore Hills, Ohio, 1977—; mem. com. on U.S. currency NRC, 1985-86. Author: Basic American Self-Protection, 1972, Kickboxing, 1976, Stickfighting, 1977, Self-Protection at Close Quarters, 1981, Self-Protection Complete: The A.S.P. System, 1992, Dog Gone West: A Western for Dog Lovers, 1994, Plato and Socrates Trial, 1995; patentee in field; originator Am. Self-Protection System. Mem. judo com. U.S. Olympic Com., 1967-74. Recipient Citizen of Yr. award Citizenship Coun. Met. Chgo., 1964; Outstanding Achievement award in sci. Immigrants Service League, 1965, citation, 1965; Outstanding Program award YMCA, 1967; recognition award Gordon Rsch. Confs., 1976; Ohio Spl. Olympics Gold medal volunteering award, 1999; NRC Can. fellow, 1955, Brit. Coun. fellow, 1952-54. Fellow Am. Inst. Chemists (vice chmn. Chgo. chpt. 1970), Am. Chem. Soc. (sr.), Royal Chem. Soc. U.K., Am. Inst. Chem., Soc. Photog. Scientists and Engrs. (pres., bd. dirs. Cleve. chpt. 1975-82), Am. Self-Protection Assn. (pres. 1965—), N.Y. Acad. Scis. Avocations: fencing, judo, aikido, Am. self-protection originator.

BALTER, ALAN, conductor, music director. Music dir. Memphis Symphony Orch., Akron Symphony Orch.

BALTER, BERNICE, religious organization administrator. Exec. dir. Women's League for Conservative Judaism, N.Y.C., 1978. Office: 48 E 74th St New York NY 10021-2735

BALTER, FRANCES SUNSTEIN, civic worker; b. Pitts.; d. Elias and Gertrude Susntein; m. James Stone Balter, May 15, 1948; children: Katherine (Mrs. Ross Anthony), Julia Frances, Constance Cantor, Daniel Elias. Student, Sarah Lawrence Coll., 1939-43, New Sch. Social Rsch., 1941-43; cert. Inst. Arts Adminstrn., Harvard U., 1973. Adminstrv. asst., assoc. prodr. Ednl. TV Sta. WQED-TV, Pitts., 1963-67; prodr., mng. dir. Freedom Readers, 1964-67; co-founder, incorporator, sec. bd. dirs. Pitts. Coun. Arts, 1967-70; cultural cons. Mayor's Office Dir. Office Cultural Affairs, Pitts., 1968; initiator Three Rivers Arts Festival 1960; co-dir. Ohio and Miss. River Valley Art Festival, 1961-62; mem. Pa. Coun. Arts, 1972-78; cofounder Pioneer Crafts Coun., Mill Run, Pa., 1972; exec. dir. Poetry on the Buses, 1974—. Bd. dirs. Coun. for Arts MIT, 1985-93, Palm Beach Festival, 1987-89. Named Woman of Yr. Art Post-Gazette, 1969. Mem. Assn. Couns. on Arts, Nat. Soc. Arts and Leteters, Nat. League Am. PEN Woemn (assoc., Pitts. chpt.).

BALTER, LESLIE MARVIN, business communications educator; b. N.Y.C., Feb. 27, 1920; s. Harry and Rose B.; m. Frances Hughes; 1 son by previous marriage, Kenneth Robert (dec. 1979); 1 dau. by previous marriage, Sheila Beth. BSEE, Columbia U., 1941; postgrad., Rutgers U.; MA, NYU, 1969. Civilian radio engr. Signal Corps Devel. Lab., Ft. Monmouth, N.J., 1941-45, in ETO, 1942; chief engr. Masters Crystal Co., quartz crystal prodn., 1945-46; founder Jersey City Tech. Inst., dir., 1947—, founder br. operation as Paterson (N.J.) Inst., 1956—; founder Sch. Bus. Machines, teaching IBM machines, Plaza Sch., Paramus, N.J., 1958—; cons. test engr. Consumers Rsch., Washington, N.J. Contbr. articles to Electronic Design Mag., Bus. Edn. World, Tech. Edn. News. Mem. N.J. Vocat. Edn. Master Plan Com. Comm. chmn. Jersey City CD Coun., 1950-53; pres. Ferncroft Park Coop. Mem. IEEE (life, participant Legacies 1994), N.J. Assn. Pvt. Career Schs. (pres. 1971), N.J. Bus. Edn. Assn., Columbia Club N.Y., Delta Pi Epsilon. Home: 41 Ferncroft Park Ramsey NJ 07446-2575 Office: Plaza Sch Bergen Mall Paramus NJ 07652

BALTHASER, LINDA IRENE, academic administrator; b. Kokomo, Ind., Feb. 25, 1939; d. Earl Isaac and Evelyn Pauline (Troyer) Showalter; m. Kenneth James Balthaser, June 1, 1963. BS magna cum laude, U. Ind., 1961; MS, Ind. U., 1962. Tchr. bus. edn. Southport H.S., Indpls., 1962-63; sec. administrv. sec. office of pres. Ind. U., Bloomington, 1963-66; with Ind. U.-Purdue U. Fort Wayne, Ind., 1969—; asst. to dean arts and letters, 1970-86, asst. dean arts and letters, 1986-87, asst. dean arts and scis., 1987—; founding co-dir. Weekend Coll., 1979-80; bd. dirs. Associated Chs. Fort Wayne, 1980; mem. Ind. com. Nat. Mus. Women in Arts. Ind. Conf. N. Evang. United Brethren Ch. scholar, 1957-61. Recipient Women of Achievement award YWCA, 1990. Mem. Fort Wayne-Allen County Hist. Assn., Embassy Theatre Found., Fort Wayne Mus. Art, Fort Wayne Zool., Soc. Nat. Assn. Women Edn., Am. Assn. Univ. Administr. Internat. Platform Assn., AAUW (trustee 1995-97, Nat. grantee Fort Wayne br. 1995), Delta Pi Epsilon, Phi Alpha Epsilon, Alpha Chi, Kappa Delta Pi, Phi Kappa Phi, Mensa, United Ch. of Christ (trustee 1994-97); club: Univ. Women's (pres. 1967-68). E-mail: balthase@ipfw.edu. Home: 2917 Hazelwood Ave Fort Wayne IN 46805-2403 Office: 2101 E Coliseum Blvd Fort Wayne IN 46805-1445

BALTIC, SCOTT MICHAEL, magazine editor; b. Oak Park, Ill., Nov. 10, 1952; s. Michael Baltic and Charlotte Leona (Peterson) Rydberg; m. MarShelle Marie Peterson Jacobs, May 18, 1974 (div. Dec. 1980). BA, North Park Coll., 1974; MS in Journalism, Northwestern U., 1988. Realty specialist VA, Chgo., 1977-87; editor Midwest Real Estate News, Argus Bus. (now Intertec Pub.), Chgo., 1989-91, editor Fire Chief Mag., 1991—. Contbr. articles to profl. jours. and newspapers, including Chgo. Tribune, Chgo. Sun-Times, Chgo. Reader, Chgo. Enterprise, Crain's Chgo. Bus., Crain's Small Bus., Columbia Journalism Rev., others. Avocations: typography, genealogy. Home: 5934 N Washtenaw Ave Chicago IL 60659-3914 Office: Intertec Pub 35 E Wacker Dr Ste 700 Chicago IL 60601-2107

BALTIMORE, DAVID, academic administrator, microbiologist, educator; b. N.Y.C., N.Y., Mar. 7, 1938; s. Richard I. and Gertrude (Lipschitz) B.; m. Alice S. Huang, Oct. 5, 1968; 1 dau., Teak. BA with high honors in Chemistry, Swarthmore Coll., 1960; postgrad., MIT, 1960-61; PhD, Rockefeller U., 1964. Research assoc. Salk Inst. Biol. Studies, La Jolla, Calif., 1965-68; assoc. prof. microbiology MIT, Cambridge, 1968-72, prof. biology, 1972-95; Ivan R. Cottrell prof. molecular biology and immunology MIT, 1994-97; inst. prof. MIT, Cambridge, 1995-97, Am. Cancer Soc. prof. microbiology, 1973-83, 94-97, dir. Whitehead Inst. Biomed. Rsch., 1982-90; pres. Rockefeller U., N.Y.C., 1990-91, prof., 1990-94; pres. Calif. Inst. Tech., Pasadena, 1997—. Mem. editorial bd. Jour. Molecular Biology, 1971-73, Jour. Virology, 1969-90, Sci., 1986-98, New Eng. Jour. Medicine, 1989-94. Bd. govs. Weizmann Inst. Sci., Israel; bd. dirs. Life Sci. Rsch. Found.; cochmn. Commn. on a Nat. Strategy of AIDS; ad hoc program adv. com. on complex genome, NIH; mem. office AIDS rsch. adv. coun. NIH, chair vaccine adv. com., 1997—. Recipient Gustav Stern award in virology, 1970; Warren Triennial prize Mass. Gen. Hosp., 1971; Eli Lilly and Co. award in microbiology and immunology, 1971; Nat. Acad. Scis. U.S. Steel award in molecular biology, 1974; Gairdner Found. ann. award, 1974; Nobel prize in physiology or medicine, 1975. Fellow AAAS, Am. Med. Writers Assn. (hon.), Am. Acad. Microbiology; mem. NAS, Am. Acad. Arts and Scis., Inst. Medicine, Pontifical Acad. Scis., Royal Soc. (Eng.) (fgn.). Office: Calif Inst Tech 1200 E California Blvd Pasadena CA 91125-0001

BALTIMORE, RICHARD LEWIS, III, foreign service officer; b. N.Y.C., Dec. 31, 1947; s. Richard Lewis Jr. and Lois Marcella (Madison) B.; m. Eszter Ekue, Dec. 4, 1993; children: Krisztina Eva, Josephine Lois. Student, MacMurray Coll., 1965-67; BS in Internat. Affairs, George Washington U., 1969; JD, Harvard U., 1972. Polit./econ. officer Am. Embassy, Lisbon, Portugal, 1973-75, Pretoria, South Africa, 1976-79; spl. asst. to Secs. of State Vance, Muskie and Haig Dept. of State, Washington, 1979-81; polit. officer Am. Embassy, Cairo, 1981-83; polit. chief Am. Embassy, Budapest, Hungary, 1984-87; deputy dir. regional affairs Bur. Near Eastern and South Asian Affairs, Washington, 1987-88, dir. regional affairs, 1988-90; dep. chief of mission Am. Embassy, Budapest, 1990-94; sr. policy adviser to asst. sec. for European-Can. affairs Dept. State, Washington, 1994-95; pres. 38th class of Sr. Seminar, Nat. Fgn. Affairs Tng. Ctr. Fgn. Svc. Inst., Dept. State, Washington, 1995-96; dep. chief mission Am. Embassy, San Jose, Costa Rica, 1996-99; consul gen. Jeddah, Saudi Arabia, 1999—. Avocations: hiking, whitewater rafting, archaeology, scuba diving, bungee jumping. Office: Am Embassy Unit 2501 APO AA 34020-9501

BALTZ, ANTONE EDWARD, III, journalist, writer, academic administrator; b. Memphis, Aug. 23, 1965; s. Antone Edward Jr. and Mary (Tobin) B.; m. Kristine Lynn Harrison, Mar. 16, 1996. BA, U. Notre Dame, 1987; M in Liberal Studies, U. Denver, 1997. News editor The Observer, Notre Dame, Ind., 1986-87; intern Notre Dame Mag., 1987; reporter City News Bur., Chgo., 1987-88; legal writer DuPage Press Svc., Wheaton, Ill., 1988-90; staff writer Chgo. Daily Law Bull., 1990-92; staff corr. Bur. Nat. Affairs, Washington, 1992—; dir. liberal studies dept. U. Coll. U. Denver; instr. Coll. DuPage, Glen Ellyn, Ill., 1990-92; freelance writer Chgo. Sun-Times, 1990-92, DuPage Press, Elmhurst, Ill., 1990-91. Contbr. articles to legal jours. Mem. student adv. bd. U. Denver, 1994-96; pres. St. Vincent's Single Adults, Denver, 1994. Recipient Media award for sensitivity to Asian Americans, Asian-Am. Bar Assn., 1991, Achievement award Chgo. Bar Assn., 1992. Mem. Soc. Profl. Journalists. Roman Catholic. Avocations: rock climbing, backpacking, skiing, fly fishing, harmonica.

BALTZ, PATRICIA ANN (PANN BALTZ), elementary education educator; b. Dallas, June 20, 1949; d. Richard Parks and Ruth Eileen (Hartschuh) Langford; m. William Monroe Baltz, Sept. 6, 1969; 1 childm Kenneth Chandler. Student, U. Redlands, 1967-68; BA in English Lit. cum laude, UCLA, 1971. Cert. tchr. K-8, Calif. Tchr. 4th grade Arcadia (Calif.) Unified Sch. Dist., 1972-74, 92—, substitute tchr., 1983-85, tchr. 3dr grade, 1985-87, tchr. 6th grade, 1987-90, tchr. 4th and 5th grade multiage, 1990—; sci. mentor tchr. Arcadia Unified Sch. Dist., 1991-94; mentor Tech. Ctr. Silicon Valley, San Jose, Calif., 1991. Tchr. rep. PTA, Arcadia, 1980-93; mem. choir, children's sermon team, elder Arcadia Presbyn. Ch., 1980-93; chaperone, vol. Pasadena (Calif.) Youth Symphony Orch., 1988-90; vol. Am. Heart Assn., 1990-92. Recipient Outstanding Gen. Elem. Tchr. award, Outstanding Tchr. of the Yr. award Disney's Am. Tchr. Awards, 1993, Calif. Tchr. of Yr. award Calif. State Dept. Edn., 1993, Georgie award Girl Scouts of Am., 1993, The Self Esteem Task Force award L.A. County Task Force to Promote Self-Esteem & Personal & Social Responsibility, 1993, Profl. Achievement award UCLA Alumni Assn.; apptd. to Nat. Edn. Rsch. Policies & Priorities Bd., U.S. Sec. Edn. Richard Riley; Pann Baltz Mission Possible Scholar named in her honor. Mem. NEA, Nat. Sci. Tchrs. Assn., Calif. Tchr. Assn., Arcadia Tchrs. Assn. Avocations: reading, singing, calligraphy, book-making, computers. Home: 1215 S 3rd Ave Arcadia CA 91006-4205 Office: Arcadia Unified Sch Dist Camino Grove Elem Sch 700 Camino Grove Ave Arcadia CA 91006-4438

BALTZ, RICHARD ARTHUR, chemical engineer; b. Red Bud, Ill., Aug. 1, 1959; s. Arthur A. and Arlou M. (McDonald) B. BSChemE, U. Mo., Rolla, 1981. Process design engr. corp. engring. dept. Monsanto, St. Louis, 1981-83; process engr. Nitro Plant Monsanto, Nitro, W.Va., 1983-89; process engring. specialist W.G. Krummrich Plant Monsanto, Sauget, Ill., 1989-97; process engring. specialist W.G. Krummrich Plant, Solutia, Inc., Sauget, Ill., 1997—. Mem. AIChE. Roman Catholic. Home: Apt J 3749 Huntington Valley Dr Saint Louis MO 63129-2267 Office: Solutia Inc 500 Monsanto Ave Sauget IL 62206-1198

BALTZ, RICHARD JAY, health care company executive; b. Kingston, N.Y., June 6, 1952; s. Harold H. and Virginia K. (Luedtke) B.; m. Mary Melissa White, May 26, 1974; 1 child, Christopher Jay. BS, St. Lawrence U., 1974; MA, George Washington U., 1978. Lic. nursing home adminstr. Adminstr. Hudson Valley Sr. Residence, Kingston, N.Y., 1974-76; adminstr. resident/asst. Buffalo VA Med. Ctr., 1977-80, asst. chief Med. Adminstrv. Svc., 1980-83; chief Med. Adminstrv. Svc. Syracuse (N.Y.) VA Med. Ctr., 1984-86; assoc. dir. trainee Albany (N.Y.) VA Med. Ctr., 1987; assoc. med. ctr. dir. Togus (Maine) VA Med. Ctr., 1988-90, VA Med. Ctr., Jackson, Miss., 1990-97; dir. VA Med. Ctr., Fayetteville, N.C., 1997—; adj. prof. dept. health care adminstrn. U. Ala., Birmingham, 1990-94. Bd. dirs. Kennebec, Maine unit Am. Cancer Soc., 1988-90, pres., 1989, 90, Maine divsn., 1988-90. Fellow Am. Coll. Healthcare Execs. Home: 442 Shawcroft Rd Fayetteville NC 28311-2945 Office: VA Med Ctr 2300 Ramsey St Fayetteville NC 28301

BALTZER, PATRICIA GERMAINE, elementary school educator; b. Johnstown, Pa., May 16, 1951; d. Harry and Doris Mae Findley; m. Dennis Duane Baltzer, Jan. 5, 1985; 1 child, Kourtney Noelle. BS, U. Pitts., Johnstown, 1973; cert. prin., Ind. U. Pa., 1994. Cert. prin., Pa. Tchr. Windber (Pa.) Area Sch. Dist., 1973—, chairperson sci. com.; coord. Project Hugs and Kisses, Windber, 1993-98. Mem. Assn. for Childhood Edn. Internat. (Successful Teaching award 1993), Keystone State Reading Assn., Laurel Highlands Math. Alliance, Pa. Assn. Elem. Sch. Prins. (student), Bus. and Profl. Women's Orgn. (Young Careerist chairperson). Avocations: reading, theater, writing, travel. Office: Windber Area Sch Dist Windber PA 15963

BALUTIS, ALAN, federal agency administrator. Fellow Nat. Assn. Schs. Pub. Affairs and Adminstrn., 1975-79; asst. prof. polit. sci. SUNY, Buffalo; sr. analyst Office Program Evaluation Dept. Commerce, Washington, 1979-82, chief policy and sys. staff, 1982-83, dir. Office Sys. ad Spl. Projects, 1983-84, dir. Office Mgmt. and Orgn., 1984-87, dir. Budget, Planning, and Orgn., 1987-94, dir. Budget, Mgmt., and Info., 1994—. Author 4 books; contbr. more than 100 articles to profl. jours. Office: Dept Commerce Budget Mgmt and Info 14th & Constitution Ave NW Washington DC 20230

BALZ, DANIEL JOHN, newspaper editor, journalist; b. Freeport, Ill., May 5, 1946; s. Charles Edward and Phyllis Victoria (Irion) B.; m. Nancy Jean Johnson, June 14, 1969; 1 child, John Paul. B.S. in Journalism, U. Ill., Champaign, 1968, M.S. in Communications, 1972. Reporter Phila. Inquirer, 1972; reporter Nat. Jour., Washington, 1972-76, dep. editor, 1976-78; reporter, editor Washington Post, 1978-85, nat. editor, 1985-89, reporter, 1989—. Served with U.S. Army, 1968-71. Office: Washington Post 1150 15th St NW Washington DC 20071-0002*

BALZEKAS, STANLEY, JR., museum director; b. Chgo., Oct. 8, 1924; s. Stanley and Emily B.; (widower); children—Stanley, III, Robert, Carole Rene. B.S., DePaul U., Chgo., 1950, M.A., 1951. Pres. Balzekas Mus. Lithuanian Culture, Chgo., 1966—, Balzekas Motor Sales, Chgo., 1952—. Trustee Lincoln Acad., Cath. Charities, Ukrainian Inst. Modern Art, Am.-Lithuanian Coun.; chmn. Sister Cities/Chgo.-Vilnius Friendship Com.; mem. Human Rels. Commn. Chgo.; mem. adv. bd. Chgo. Cultural Affairs. Served with AUS, 1942-45, ETO. Decorated Bronze Star; decorated 3d degree order Grand Duke Gediminas, Pres. Lithuania; recipient Wigilia medal Polish Geneal. Soc. Am. Mem. Ethnic Cultural Preservation Coun. (pres. 1977—), Press Club (Chgo.), Literary Club (Chgo.), City Club (Chgo., ethnic chmn.), Exec. Club (Chgo.). Office: 4030 S Archer Ave Chicago IL 60632-1140

BALZHISER, RICHARD EARL, research and development company executive; b. Wheaton, Ill., May 27, 1932; s. Frank E. and Esther K. (Merrill Werner) B.; m. Christine Karnuth, 1951; children: Gary, Robert, Patricia, Michelle. B.S. in Chem. Engring., U. Mich., 1955, M.S. in Nuclear Engring., 1956, Ph.D. in Chem. Engring., 1961. Mem. faculty U. Mich., Ann Arbor, 1961-67; White House fellow, spl. asst. to sec. Dept. Def., Washington, 1967-68; chmn. dept. chem. engring. U. Mich., 1970-71; assoc. dir. energy, environ. and natural resources White House Office of Sci. and Tech., Washington, 1971-73; dir. fossil fuel and advanced systems Electric Power Rsch. Inst., Palo Alto, Calif., 1973-79, sr. v.p. R&D, 1979-87, exec. v.p. R&D, 1987-88, pres., chief exec. officer, 1988-96, pres. emeritus, 1996—; bd. dirs. Houston Ind., Electrsource, Aerospace Corp., Mobil, Pacific Northwest Nat. Lab., Lawrence Livermore Lab., Nat. Renewable Energy Lab. Coauthor: Chemical Engineering Thermodynamics, 1972, Engineering Thermodynamics, 1977. Mem. Ann Arbor City Coun., 1965-67, mayor pro tem, 1967. Mem. Nat. Acad. Engring. Lutheran. Fax: 650-855-2090. E-mail: rbalzhis@epri.com. Office: Electric Power Rsch Inst 3412 Hillview Ave Palo Alto CA 94304-1344

BAM, FOSTER, lawyer; b. Bridgeport, Conn., Jan. 11, 1927; s. Frederick and Alma (Foster) B.; m. Sallie A. Baldwin; children: Sylvia Carol, Sheila Catherine, Eric Foster. Grad., Loomis Sch., 1944; AB, Yale U., 1950, LLB, 1953. Bar: N.Y. 1954, Conn. 1968. Mem. faculty acctg. Yale, 1952-53; with Spence & Hotchkiss, N.Y.C., 1954-55; asst. U.S. dist. atty. So. Dist. N.Y., 1955-58; ptnr. Kramer, Levin, Naftalis & Frankel (formerly Feldman, Kramer, Bam, Nessen), N.Y.C., 1958-67, Cummings & Lockwood, 1968—; bd. dirs. The Evergreen Funds. Trustee Phoenix Sci. Ctr.; chmn. Am. Mus. Fly Fishing, Calif. Acad. Sci.; trustee Bermuda Biol. Sta. for Rsch. Recipient Johnny Foyle Meml. award, 1969. Mem. ABA, Conn. Bar Assn., Greenwich Bar Assn., Exptl. Aircraft Assn., Phi Beta Kappa. Home: 51 Londonderry Dr Greenwich CT 06830-3508 Office: Cummings & Lockwood 2 Greenwich Plz Ste 3 Greenwich CT 06830-6390

BAMBACE, ROBERT SHELLY, lawyer; b. Spokane, Wash., Sept. 23, 1930; s. Felix Shelly and Constance Marion (Vandervert) B.; m. Madelyn Constance Saxer, May 11, 1957; children: Michelle Suzanne, Mark Shelly, Robert Sean, Peter Joseph, Constance Diane. BS, Georgetown U., 1953; LLB, St. Mary's U., San Antonio, 1961. Bar: Tex. 1961, U.S. Dist. Ct. (so. dist.) Tex. 1967, U.S. Ct. Appeals (5th cir.) 1967, U.S. Ct. Appeals (11th cir.), 1981, U.S. Supreme Ct. 1983; cert. labor law specialist, Tex. Trial atty. NLRB Region 23, Houston, 1961-63; assoc. Fulbright & Jaworski, Houston, 1963-71, ptnr., 1971—, chmn. labor sect., 1974—; panelist profl. seminars; spkr. on devels. in labor law for law students and mgmt. groups. Contbr. numerous articles to profl. jours. Fellow Tex. Bar Found. (life), Tex. Bar Assn. (life); mem. ABA, Houston Bar Assn., Houston Mgmt. Lawyers forum, State Bar Tex., Tex. State Bar (labor law com. 1970-71), S.W. Found. Rsch. and Edn., Argyle Club (San Antonio), Houstonian Club, Tex. Tech. U. Dad's Club. Republican. Roman Catholic. Office: Fulbright & Jaworski 1301 Mckinney St Ste 5100 Houston TX 77010-3031

BAMBAKIDIS, PETER, neurologist, educator; b. Akron, Ohio, Nov. 2, 1948; s. Nicholas and Zopigi (Dragoumanou) B.; m. Anna Savaris, Aug. 18, 1974; children: Athe, John A., Theodore. Student, U. Akron, 1966-67; BMus, Cleve. Inst. Mus., 1971, MMus, 1973; postgrad., U. Pitts., 1974-75, Ohio State U., 1978-80; MD, Case Western Res. U., 1984. Diplomate Am. Bd. Psychiatry and Neurology, Am. Bd. Clin. Neurophysiology. Resident in neurology Mayo Grad. Sch. Medicine, Rochester, Minn., 1984-88; fellow EEG Mayo Grad. Sch. Medicine, Rochester, 1988-89; pvt. practice Cleve., 1989-92; asst. prof. neurology Case Western Res. U., Cleve., 1992—; neurologist Fairview Med. Group, 1994—; violinist Akron Symphony Orch., 1966-67, Richmond (Va.) Sinfonia, Richmond Symphony Orch., 1973-74, West Australian Symphony Orch., Perth, 1976-78, Columbus (Ohio) Symphony Orch., 1978-80; freelance musician, 1967-73; tchg. asst. Cleve. Inst. Music, 1971-73; tchg. fellow dept. music U. Pitts., 1974-75; follow-up asst. regional pediat. intensive care transport sys. Rainbow Babies and Children's Hosp., Cleve., 1981-82; hosp. affiliations Fairview Gen. Hosp., Cleve., U. Hosps. Cleve., St. John & Westshore Hosp., Westlake, Ohio, Luth. Med. Ctr., Cleve., S.W. Gen. Hosp., Middleburgh Hts., Ohio. Tuesday Musical Club scholar, 1968, Ranney Found. scholar, 1968, Hellenic U. Club scholar, 1983. Mem. Am. Acad. Neurology, Am. Clin. Neurophysiology Soc., U.S. Weight-lifting Fedn., Phi Kappa Lambda. Avocations: weight lifting, near/middle eastern music and mysticism, writings of early church fathers. Office: 18099 Lorain Ave # 145 Cleveland OH 44111-5611

BAMBER, LINDA SMITH, accounting educator; b. Columbus, Ohio, Jan. 4, 1954; d. Charles Randall and Martha Jo (Wise) Smith; m. Edward Michael Bamber, Mar. 13, 1981. BS summa cum laude, Wake Forest U, 1976; MBA, Ariz. State U., 1980; PhD, Ohio State U., 1983. Cost acct. RJ Reynolds, Winston-Salem, N.C., 1975-76, gen. acct., 1976-77; tutor, rsch. asst. Ariz. State U., Tempe, 1977-78; teaching asst. Ohio State U., Columbus, 1978-82; asst. prof. U. Fla., Gainesville, 1983-88, assoc. prof., 1988-90; assoc. prof. U. Ga., Athens, 1990-96, prof., 1996—; vis. assoc. prof. Ind. U., Bloomington, 1989-90. Author: Annotated Instructor's Edition of Cost Accounting: A Managerial Emphasis, 1990, 93, 96, assoc. editor: Acctg. Horizon, 1993-97; mem. editl. bd. The Acctg. Rev., 1987-89, 93—, Advances in Acctg., 1992—; contbr. articles to profl. jours. Selig fellow U. Ga., 1991, Terry fellow U. Ga., 1994, 95, 96, 97; recipient Rsch. Devel. award U. Fla., 1985, Tchg. award Ohio State U., U. Fla., U. Ga., 1981-94. Mem. Am. Acctg. Assn. (S.E. dir. fin. reporting sect. 1993-94, group leader, panelist, chmn. New Faculty Consortium 1991-95, rsch. adv. com. 1996-98, mem. coun. 1995-97, mgmt. acctg. sect. chmn. membership outreach com. 1995-97, Wildman medal award com. 1996-97, nominations com. 1996-97, corp. acctg. policy seminar com. 1997-98), Phi Beta Kappa, Phi Kappa Phi, Beta Gamma Sigma. Avocations: swimming, water skiing, travel. Office: U Ga JM Tull Sch Acctg Athens GA 30602

BAMBERGER, DAVID, opera executive; b. Albany, N.Y., Oct. 14, 1940; s. Bernard J. and Ethel K. Bamberger; m. Carola Beral, June 8, 1965; 1 son, Steven B. B.A., Swarthmore Coll., 1962; postgrad., U. Paris, 1961, Yale U., 1963. Mem. directing staff N.Y.C. Opera, 1966-70; guest dir. Nat. Opera Chile, 1970, Cin. Opera, 1968, Augusta Opera (Ga.), 1970, Pitts. Opera, 1971, 76, 81, Columbus Opera (Ohio); gen. dir. Cleve. Opera, 1976—; artistic dir. Toledo Opera Assn., 1983-85. Bd. dirs. Opera Am., Nat. Alliance Musical Theater Producers. Author Jewish history textbooks; contbr. articles to Opera News. Office: Cleveland Opera 1422 Euclid Ave Ste 1052 Cleveland OH 44115-2063*

BAMBERGER, GERALD FRANCIS, plastics marketing consultant; b. Hannover, Germany, Sept. 20, 1920; came to U.S., 1938, naturalized, 1943; m. Ursula Friede, Mar. 27, 1946; children—Gale, Richard, Annette, Peter. Comml. diploma, Ecole Supérieure de Commerce, Neuchatel, Switzerland, 1938. Pres. A. Bamberger Corp., Bklyn., 1938-54, Interplastics Corp., N.Y.C., 1955-62; prodn. mgr. plastics div. Cities Service Corp., Hicksville, N.Y., 1963-67; pres. Bamberger Polymers, Inc., New Hyde Park, N.Y., 1967-85; plastics mktg. cons., 1985—. Served with M.I. AUS, 1943-46. Decorated Bronze Star. Mem. Soc. Plastics Industry, Soc. Plastics Engrs., Plastics Pioneers Assn.

BAMBERGER, JOSEPH ALEXANDER, mechanical engineer, educator; b. Hamburg, Germany, Nov. 21, 1927; came to U.S., 1940; s. Seligman and Else (Buxbaum) B.; m. Dorothy Frank, Dec. 24, 1950; children: David, Michael. BME, CUNY, 1949; MME, NYU, 1954. R & D engr. Kramer Trenton Co., Trenton, N.J., 1949-59; mech. engr., scientific staff Brookhaven Nat. Lab., Upton, N.Y., 1959-82; prof. mech. tech. Suffolk Community Coll., Selden, N.Y., 1982-95; mem. staff R&D objects conservation Met. Mus. Art, N.Y.C., 1996—; cons. Typhoon Air Conditioning, Div. Hupp Corp., Bklyn., 1952-59. Contbr. articles to ASHRAE Jour., Advances in Cryogenic Engring., Cryogenics, ASME Transactions, Jour. Vacuum Sci. and Tech., Nuclear Instruments and Methods, Studies in Conservation. Dir. Temple Beth El, Patchogue, N.Y., 1962-84; chmn. Cryogenic Safety Com., Brookhaven Lab., 1980-82. Mem. N.Y. Acad. Sci., AAAS, ASHRAE. Achievements include patent for Electrically Insulating Feedthrough for Cryogenic Applications; research in low temperature cooling systems for superconducting magnets, cryogenic pumping systems, liquid hydrogen bubble chamber design and operation.

BAMBERGER, MICHAEL ALBERT, lawyer; b. Berlin, Feb. 29, 1936; s. Fritz and Kate (Schwabe) B.; m. Phylis Skloot, Dec. 19, 1965; children—Kenneth A., Richard A. AB magna cum laude, Harvard U., 1957, LLB magna cum laude, 1960. Bar: N.Y. 1960, D.C. 1982. Assoc. Proskauer Rose Goetz & Mendelsohn, N.Y.C., 1960-69; assoc. Finley, Kumble, Wagner, Heine, Underberg, Manley, Myerson & Casey, N.Y.C., 1970, ptnr., 1971-87; ptnr. Sonnenschein Nath & Rosenthal, N.Y.C., 1987—; mem. faculty various legal seminars and insts.; mem. joint editl. bd. on uninc. orgn. acts. ABA/Nat. Conf. Commrs. on Uniform State Laws, 1994—; chmn. bd. Transcontinental Music Publs., New Jewish Music Press. Co-editor: State Limited Partnership Laws, 7 vols. and supplements, 1987—, State Limited Liability Company and Partnership Laws, 5 vols. and supplements, 1993—; editor Harvard Law Rev., 1958-60; contbr. articles to profl. jours. Vice chair bd. overseers Hebrew Union Coll.-Jewish Inst. Religion, N.Y.C.,; v.p., bd. dirs. Leo Baeck Inst., Selfhelp Cmty. Svcs.; bd. dirs. Ctr. Jewish History. Mem. ABA (com. on ltd. partnerships 1980—, chair com. on tech. and intellectual property 1992-95, chair, ad hoc com. on security interests in intellectual property 1990-98), First Amendment Lawyers Assn., N.Y. State Bar Assn. (exec. com. comml. and fed. litigation sect. 1989-93), Assn. Bar City N.Y. (com. on fed. legislation 1979-82, com. on civil rights 1982-86, chmn. 1983-86), N.Y. County Lawyers Assn. (securities com. 1980-82). Jewish. Home: 172 E 93rd St New York NY 10128-3711 Office: Sonnenschein Nath & Rosenthal Ste 2401 1221 Avenue Of The Americas New York NY 10020-1089

BAMBERGER, RICHARD H., lawyer; b. Cleve., Sept. 18, 1945. BA, Bowdoin Coll., 1967; JD, Case Western Res. U., 1972. Bar: Ohio 1972. Law clk. to Hon. William K. Thomas U.S. Dist. Ct. (no. dist.), Ohio, 1972-74; ptnr. Baker & Hostetler, Cleve.; adj. prof. law Case Western Res. U., 1996—. Mem. ABA (mem. employee benefits com.), Ohio State, Cleve. Bar Assn. Office: Baker & Hostetler 3200 Nat City Ctr 1900 E 9th St Ste 3200 Cleveland OH 44114-3475

BAMBERGER-HERRMANN, JULIA KATHRYN, social worker; b. Phila., Dec. 23, 1960; d. William Thomas and Julia Kathryn (O'Brien) B; m. Robert F. Herrmann Jr., Nov.22, 1997. BA in Social Work, Holy Family Coll., Phila., 1983. Cert. social worker. Recreational therapy asst., physical therapy asst. Ashton Hall Nursing Home, Phila., 1979-83; hairdresser asst. St. John Neumann Nursing Home, Phila., 1982-83; recreational therapy asst. Evangelical Manor, Phila., 1983; social worker The Consortium/Southwest Sr. Citizens Ctr., Phila., 1983-90; resource specialist Phila. Corp. for Aging, 1990-92, case mgr. Family Caregiver Support program, 1992—. Mem., chair Alzheimer's Disease and Related Disorders Assn., Phila., 1983—; vol. Ashton Hall Nursing Home, Phila., 1983-89; V.I.P. blood donor ARC, 1978—; solicitor Cath. Charities Appeal, 1979-92; mem. Pro Life Coalition of Southeastern Pa., 1986—; soprano singer guitar Mass group Maternity Blessed Virgin Mary Roman Cath. Ch., Phila., 1977—; vol. Perpetual Adoration Soc. Our Lady of Fatima Roman Cath. Ch., 1988-97; majority inspector Election Bd., 1992—; mem. Gloria Dei Ch. Womens Ministries. Recipient Cert. of Appreciation Alzheimer's Disease and Related Disorders Assn., 1985, 91, 95; named one of Outstanding Young Women Am., 1985, 86, 88. Mem. Social Svc. Workers Assn. Nursing Homes, Archbishop Ryan H.S. for Girls ALumnae Assn. (corr. sec. 1985-95), Holy Family Coll. Alumni Assn. (rec. sec. 1985-90, cert. of appreciation 1984, 90, bd. dirs., class rep. 1983—, Disting. Alumni Svc. award 1992), Assn. Ch. Musician in Phila., Classic Thunderbird Club (bd. dirs. 1994-95), Epsilon Nu Cath. Adult Club, Phi Chi. Democrat. Avocations: tennis, bowling, singing, dining out, movies. Home: 9207 Rising Sun Ave Philadelphia PA 19115 Office: Phila Corp for Aging 642 N Broad St Philadelphia PA 19130-3409

BAMBRICK, JAMES JOSEPH, labor economist, labor relations executive; b. N.Y.C., Apr. 26, 1917; s. James Joseph and Mae (Murphy) B.; m. Margaret Mary Donlan, June 26, 1948; children: Patricia Bambrick Benek (dec.), Thomas G., Mary Alice Bambrick Schneider, Kathleen, James Joseph Jr. BS, NYU, 1940, MBA, 1942; BS, U.S. Mcht. Marine Acad., 1946. Exec. dir. Labor Bur., N.Y.C., 1940-42; personnel dir. Allegheny Airlines, Wilmington, Del., 1942-44; mgr. labor relations research The Conf. Bd., N.Y.C., 1947-58; corp. labor economist Standard Oil Co., Cleve., 1958-81; exec. dir. Labor Econ. Inst., Cleveland Heights, Ohio, 1981—; mem. bus. adv. council U.S. Bur. Labor Stats., Washington, 1971—, chmn. wages and indsl. relations com., 1980-85; instr. NYU, 1946-53, John Carroll U., University Heights, Ohio, 1968-71; lectr. Cleve. State U., 1963-68. Author: Preparing for Collective Bargaining, 1959, Handbook of Modern Personnel Administration, 1972; contbr. chpts. to The Foreman/Supervisor's Handbook, 1984; contbr. articles to profl. jours. Chmn. Ohio Rep. Fin. Com., Cuyahoga County, Cleve., 1963—; pres. Cath. Interracial Council, Cleve., 1965-68, bd. dirs. 1969—; v.p. Navy League of U.S., Cleve., 1984—. Served to lt. USNR, 1944-46. Named Hibernian Man of the Yr. Ancient Order of Hibernians, 1974. Fellow Soc. for Advancement of Mgmt. (pres. 1955-58); mem. Am. Econ. Assn., Indsl. Relations Research Assn., U.S. Mcht. Marine Acad. Alumni Assn. (pres., bd. dirs. N.E. Ohio, 1965—). Republican. Clubs: City (Cleve.) (trustee 1972-75, v.p. Forum Found. 1981—). Lodge: K.C. Avocations: fencing, sailing, golf.

BAMBURG, JAMES ROBERT, biochemistry educator; b. Chgo., Aug. 20, 1943; s. Leslie H. and Rose A. (Abrahams) B.; m. Alma Y. Vigo, June 7, 1970 (div. Dec. 1984); children: Eric Gregory, Leslie Ann; m. Laurie S. Minamide, June 22, 1985. BS in Chemistry, U. Ill., 1965; PhD, U. Wis., 1969. Project assoc. U. Wis., Madison, 1968-69; postdoctoral fellow Stanford U., Palo Alto, Calif., 1969-71; from asst. to full prof. Colo. State U., Ft. Collins, 1971—, acad. coordinator cell and molecular biol. program, 1975-78, interim chmn. dept. biochemistry, 1982-85, 88-89, assoc. dir. neuronal growth and devel., 1986-90, dir. neuronal growth and devel., 1990-96, assoc. chmn., 1996—; vis. prof. MRC Molecular Biol. Lab., Cambridge, Eng., 1978-79, MRC Cell Biophysics Unit, London, 1985-86, Children's Med. Rsch. Inst., U. Sydney, Australia, 1992-93, U. Calif. San Diego, 1999—; mem., chmn. NIH Biomed. Scis. Study Sect., Bethesda, Md., 1980-85; ad hoc mem. Physiol. Chem. Study Sec., 1997, Molecular Devel. Cell Neurosci., 1998-99. Contbr. articles to sci. jours. Fellow NSF, 1964-65, Nat. Multiple Sclerosis Soc., 1969-71, J.S. Guggenheim Found., 1978-79, Fogarty Ctr., 1985-86, 92-93, W. Evans Vis. scholar U. Otago, N.Z., 1991; recipient Disting. Svc. award Colo. State U. 1989, Outstanding Adviser award, 1996. Mem. Am. Chem. Soc., Am. Soc. Cell Biology, Am. Soc. Biochem. Mol. Biol., Internat. Neurochem. Soc., Sigma Xi (pres. CSU chpt. 1989). Home: 2125 Sandstone Dr Fort Collins CO 80524-1825 Office: Colo State U Dept Biochemistry MRB Rm 235 Fort Collins CO 80523

BAMFORD, CAROL MARIE, marketing executive; b. Des Moines, May 18, 1948; d. Harry C. and Ellen T. (Andersen) Jensen; m. Bruce S. Nesbit, June 8, 1968 (div. Jan. 1978); m. Paul J. Bamford, June 9, 1979 (div. Dec. 1984); m. John V. Florian, Apr. 6, 1991. BA, Drake U., 1969, MA, 1972. Lic. tchr., Iowa. Tchr. English Des Moines Pub. Schs., 1969-79; mgr. product and promotional publs. Comshare, Inc., Ann Arbor, Mich., 1979-83; mgr. advt. and sales promotion Univ. Microfilms, Inc. subs. Bell and Howell Co., Ann Arbor, 1983-88, mktg. mgr., 1988-92, v.p. mktg., 1992-95; v.p. mktg. Briggs Corp., Des Moines, 1995—, Briggs Tech., Des Moines, 1997—. Recipient awards Soc. for Tech. Communication, 1980-86, Award of Excellence, Internat. TV Assn., 1988, Crystal Addy award Am. Advt. Fedn., 1988. Mem. Info. Industry Assn. (Mktg. Achievement award 1986-91, vice-chmn. mktg. com. 1991, chmn. mktg. com. 1992), Phi Beta Kappa. Democrat. Lutheran. Office: Briggs Corp 7300 Westown Pkwy West Des Moines IA 50266-2525

BAMFORD, JOSEPH CHARLES, JR., gynecologist, obstetrician, educator, medical missionary; b. Paterson, N.J., Oct. 23, 1930; s. Joseph Charles and Luise (Whitehead) B.; m. Susan Jane Hall, Apr. 13, 1951; children: Joseph Charles III, Elizabeth Ann. BS, Rutgers U., 1952; MD, N.Y. Med. Coll., 1956. Diplomate Am. Bd. Ob-Gyn. Intern, U. Vt., 1956-57; resident in ob-gyn N.Y. Med. Coll., N.Y.C., 1957-60, asst. clin. instr. dept. ob-gyn, 1960-64, clin. instr., 1964-65, asst. prof., 1965-70, asso. prof., 1970-72, asst. dean, 1966-68, asso. dean, 1968-72, acting v.p. hosp. affairs, 1971-72; sect. chief psychosomatic ob-gyn Met. Hosp. Center, N.Y.C., 1963-72, chief svc., 1971-72; practice medicine specializing in ob-gyn, Paterson, N.J., 1962-66, St. Johnsbury, Vt., 1972-76; asst. obstetrician and gynecologist Flower and Fifth Ave. hosps., N.Y.C., 1960-66, asst. attending, 1966-70, attending, 1970-72; asst. vis. obstetrician and gynecologist Met. Hosp. Center, N.Y.C., 1960-66, asso., 1968-70, vis., 1970-72, vis. ob-gyn, Indian Health Svc. Hosp., Fort Difiance, Ariz., 1981; clin. asst. ob-gyn Paterson Gen. Hosp., 1962-64, asso. attending, 1964-66, attending, 1966-67, cons., 1967—; attending obstetrician and gynecologist Northeastern Vt. Regional Hosp., St. Johnsburg, 1972-76, cons., 1976—; vis. obstetrician and gynecologist St. Jude Missions Hosp., St. Lucia, 1986; med. officer Tumutumu Mission Hosp., Kenya, 1987-88; cons. Beatrice D. Weeks Meml. Hosp., Lancaster, N.H., 1972-80, vol. program, Vermont Medical Soc. Steering Com. for retired physician, 1996—; chmn. subcom. for fact finding Mayor's Com. for Hosp. Facilities Planning, Paterson, 1964-66; chmn. med. adv. com. Passaic County (N.J.) Com. for Planned Parenthood, 1965-67; mem. N.J. Com. on Med. Edn., 1965-66; trustee Greater Paterson Gen. Hosp., 1966—, So. Vt. Art Ctr., 1997—. Pres. Lyndon State Coll. Found., 1980-84. Lt. comdr. USNR, 1960-62. Fellow Am. Coll. Obstetricians and Gynecologists (mem. com. on course coordination 1977-79); mem. No. New Eng. Acad. Medicine, Obstet. and Gynecol. Soc. N.Y. Med. Coll. (mem. exec. com. 1963-66), Vt. (mem. judicial com. 1975-77), Caledonia County (v.p. 1974-75) med. socs. Contbr. articles to profl. jours. Home: Box 724 Myrickview Vlg Dorset VT 05251

BAN, STEPHEN DENNIS, natural gas industry research institute executive; b. Hammond, Ind., Dec. 16, 1940; s. Stephen and Mary Veronica (Holecsko) B.; m. Margie Cahill, Aug. 17, 1963; children: Stephen, Mary Beth, Brian. BSME, Rose Hulman Inst. Tech., 1962; MS in Engring. Sci., Case Inst. Tech., 1964, PhD in Engring., 1967. Chief div. fluid and chem. processes Battelle Columbus (Ohio) Labs., 1970-72, chief div. emission systems, 1972-76, corp. coord. engring. scis. program, 1972-76; v.p. R & D, Bituminous Materials, Inc., Terre Haute, Ind., 1976-81; v.p. R & D, Gas

Rsch. Inst., Chgo., 1981-83, sr. v.p. R & D ops., 1983-86, exec. v.p., chief oper. officer, 1986-87, pres., chief exec. officer, 1987—; bd. dirs. UGI Corp., Valley Forge, Pa., Energen Corp., Birmingham, Ala.; mem. indsl. adv. bd. U. Ill., Chgo., 1983—; mem. energy rsch. adv. bd. U.S. Dept. Energy, Washington, 1987-90, mem. adv. com. on renewable energy and energy efficiency joint ventures, 1992-95; mem. Coun. Energy Engring. Rsch., Washington, 1983-87; mem. bd. on energy and environ. sys. NRC, 1993-96; mem. Natural Gas Coun., 1993-97. Fellow NDEA, 1962-65, NSF, 1965-67. Mem. U.S. Energy Assn. (bd. dirs. 1992—), Chgo. Econs. Club, Sigma Xi, Tau Beta Pi. Office: Gas Rsch Inst 8600 W Bryn Mawr Ave Ste 1100S Chicago IL 60631-3562

BANACH, ART JOHN, graphic artist; b. Chgo., May 22, 1931; s. Vincent and Anna (Zajac) B. Grad. Art. Inst. of Chgo., 1955; pupil painting studies Mrs. Melin, Chgo.; m. Loretta A. Nolan, Oct. 15, 1966; children: Heather Anne, Lynnea Joan. Owner, dir. Art J. Banach Studios, 1949—, cartoon syndicate for newspapers, house organs and advt. functions, 1954—, owner and operater advt. agy., 1954-56, feature news and picture syndicate, distbn. U.S. and fgn. countries. Dir. Speculators S Fund. Recipient award 1st Easter Seal contest Ill. Assn. Crippled, Inc., 1949. Chgo. Pub. Sch. Art Soc. Scholar. Mem. Artist's Guild Chgo., Am Mgmt. Assn., Chgo. Assn. of Commerce and Industry, Chgo. Federated Advt. Club, Am. Mktg. Assn., Internat. Platform Assn., Chgo. Advt. Club, Chgo. Soc. Communicating Arts, Am. Ctr. For Design, Chgo. Calligraphy Collective, Columbia Yacht Club, Advt. Execs. Club, Art Dirs. Club (Chgo.). Home: 1076 Leahy Cir East Des Plaines IL 60016-6050

BANAS, C. LESLIE, lawyer; b. Swindon, Wiltshire, Eng., Oct. 29, 1951; came to U.S. 1957; d. Stanley M. and Helena Ann (Boryn) B.; m. Dale J. Buras, May 1, 1976; children: Eric, Andrea. BA magna cum laude, U. Detroit, 1973; JD cum laude, Wayne State U., 1975. Bar: Mich. 1976, U.S. Supreme Ct. 1980. Atty. Hyman & Rice, Southfield, Mich., 1976-77; atty. Hyman, Gurwin, Nachman, Friedman & Winkelman, Southfield, 1977-82, ptnr., 1982-87; ptnr. Honigman Miller Schwartz and Cohn, Detroit, 1987—. Contbr. articles to profl. jours. Trustee Karmanos Cancer Inst., Oakland region. Mem. ABA, State Bar Mich. (chair real estate ownership and investment entities, real property sect.), Fed. Bar Assn., Nat. Assn. Women Bus. Owners (greater Detroit chpt.), Detroit Bar Assn., Oakland County Bar, Women's Econ. Club (trustee, v.p.), Birmingham Athletic Club. Roman Catholic. Avocations: photography, skiing, golf. Office: Honigman Miller Schwartz and Cohn 2290 1st National Bldg Detroit MI 48226

BANAS, CONRAD MARTIN, mechanical engineer, chief scientist; b. Warren, Mass., Nov. 27, 1927; s. Martin and Caroline (Krupska) B.; m. Erna Maier, Sept. 19, 1949 (div. Nov. 1970); children: Stephen, Richard, Susan, Patricia, Pamela; m. Gene Tomaiuolo Banas, July 19, 1974; children: Jonathan, Jeremy. BSME, Worcester Poly., 1953; MSME, U. Conn., 1957, MS in Physics, 1965. Registered profl. engr., Conn. Asst. rsch. engr. United Technologies Rsch. Ctr., East Hartford, Conn., 1953-57, rsch. engr., 1957-61, sr. rsch. engr., 1961-76, mgr. indsl. laser processing, 1976-90; chief scientist United Technologies Indsl. Lasers, South Windsor, Conn., 1990-93; cons. Laser Materials Processing, 1993—; adj. asst. prof. U. Hartford, 1957-62; lectr. U. Conn., Storrs, 1963-67. Patentee in field; contbr. articles to profl. jours. Sgt. U.S. Army, 1945-48. Recipient Adams Lecture award Am. Welding Soc., 1988, Co. Excellence awards United Technologies, 1983, 87, 89, Outstanding Achievement award Pa. State Applied Rsch. Lab., 1996. Fellow Laser Inst. of Am. (Arthur L. Schawlow award 1997); mem. Am. Welding Soc., Am. Soc. Metals, Tau Beta Pi, Sigma Xi. Avocations: skiing, softball, cycling, sailing. Home: 56 Volpi Rd Bolton CT 06043-7547

BANAS, SUZANNE, middle school educator; b. Miami, Fla., Mar. 28, 1959; d. Frank and Norma (Eliscu) B. BA in Sci., U. Miami, 1981, MS in Edn., 1986; PhD, Union Inst., 1994. Cert. tchr. sci., Fla.; nat. bd. cert. tchr. early adolescence generalist Nat. Bd. Profl. Tchg. Stds. Tchr. Dade County Pub. Schs., Miami, 1988—; curriculum writer Gender Equity Network, Miami, 1993-97, Arise Found., Miami, 1995-97; tchr., chairperson dept. sci., team leader Cutler Ridge Mid. Sch., Miami, 1990—; adj. prof. Fla. Internat. U., Miami, 1996—; advisor Acad. for Instrnl. Leadership, Miami, 1994-96, Annenberg Challenge Grant, Miami, 1995-96; cons. Urban Sys. Initiative, 1995-98; Internet tchr. trainer/mentor, 1998—. Recipient Fla. Explores! award Fla. State U./TDRA, 1993, Tchyr. of Yr. award Cutler Ridge Mid. Sch., 1996. Mem. Dade County Sci. Tchrs. Assn. (pres. 1994—), Fla. Assn. Sci. Tchrs. (bd. dirs. 1998—), Nat. Sci. Tchrs. Assn. Office: Cutler Ridge Mid Sch 19400 Gulfstream Rd Miami FL 33157-8658

BANASCHEWSKI, BERNHARD, mathematics educator; b. Munich, Germany, Mar. 22, 1926; arrived in Can., 1955; s. Adalbert Schremmer and Anna Magdalena Banaschewski; m. Barbara R. Harrison, Feb. 8, 1965 (div. Feb. 1969); 1 child Bernhard Francis Harrison; m. Angela M. Gensey, June 7, 1993. Diploma in math., Hamburg (Fed. Republic Germany) U., 1952, Dr. rer. nat., 1953. Asst. Hamburg U., 1953-55; asst. prof. McMaster U., Hamilton, Ont., Can., 1955-57, assoc. prof., 1957-59, prof., 1959-64, McKay prof. math., 1964-91, prof. emeritus, 1991—, chmn. dept., 1961-67, 82-87; vis. prof. Tulane U., New Orleans, 1959-60, 67-68, 70, U. Cape Town, South Africa, 1979, 88, 90, 93; mem. Natural Scis. and Engring. Rsch. Coun., Ottawa, Ont., 1981-88. Editor: Categorical Aspects of Topology and Analysis, 1982; co-editor: Continuous Lattices, 1981; assoc. editor Can. Jour. Math., 1969-79; mem. editl. bd. Topology and Its Applications, 1971-93, Quaestiones Mathematicae, 1987; contbr. articles to profl. jours. With German Army, 1944-45. Fellow Royal Soc. Can.; mem. Can. Math. Soc. (v.p. 1983-85). Avocations: literature, art, cooking. Office: McMaster U, Dept Math and Stats, Hamilton, ON Canada L8S 4K1

BANASIK, ROBERT C., ; s. Barbara Jean Willows; children: Robert John, Marcus Alan, Jason Andrew. BSME, Wayne State U., 1965; MS in Indsl. Engring., Tex. Tech. Coll., 1967; MBA, Ohio State U., 1973, PhD, 1974. Registered profl. negr., Ohio; lic. nursing home adminstr.; lic. pilot. Test and devel. engr. Ford Motor Co., Dearborn, Mich., summer 1964; indsl. engr. Chrysler Corp., Highland Park, Mich., summer 1965; corp. rsch. staff Nationwide Ins. Co., Columbus, Ohio, summer 1968; mgmt. sys. engr. Riverside Meth., Columbus, Ohio, 1970-71; owner, mgmt. sys. cons. Banasik Assocs., Columbus, Ohio, 1971—; dir. mgmt. sys. engr. Grant Hosp., Columbus, 1973-78; owner, real estate investment co. RMJ Investment Enterprises, Columbus, 1975-85, pres., 1983-85; pres. Banasik and Strayer Archs. & Engrs., Inc., Columbus, 1988-93; tchg. asst. Tech. Tech. Coll., Lubbock, Tex., 1965-67, mem. industry adv. bd., 1987—, dept. indsl. engring., 1987-88; rsch. assoc. Ohio State U., Columbus, 1967-69, tchg. assoc., 1972; asst. prof. bus. Grad. Sch. Adminstrn. Capital U., Columbus, 1973-79, assoc. prof. bus., 1979—; editor topics in hosp. material mgmt. Aspen Sys. Corp., Germantown, Md., 1978-84; presenter IEEE Ergonomics Symposium, Cambridge, Eng., 1969, Nat. Human Factors Soc., Phila., 1969, 40th Ops. Rsch. Conv., Anaheim, Calif., 1971, Ohio State U., 1977, Fin. Execs. Inst., Columbus, 1977, Ohio Hosp. Assn., Cin., 1977, 83; spkr. Marion County chpt. Am. Inst. Indsl. Engrs., 1979, Toledo chpt., 1983, German Village Kiwanis, Columbus, 1985, Tex. Tech. student chpt., Lubbock, 1987; expert witness on numerous bills related to health care industry, 1979—, Creasey, Ohio Dept. Human Svcs. vs. Ethicare, Franklin County Common Please Ct., 1984, Ohio Dept. Human Svcs. vs. Discount Drug Mart, 1985, vs. Discount Drug Mart, 1985, vs. Rene Baldrich, Md., 1987, Ohio Dept. Health Cert. Need Bd. vs. Comprehensive Mgmt. Svcs., 1987-88, Crestvie Nursing Home vs. Threshold Data Sys., 1989, Edgewood Nursing Home vs. the State of Ohio, 1990, Robin Redden vs. U. Cin., 1990, Eaglewood Nursing Home vs. State of Ohio, 1990, Debbie Zeech vs. Kroger, 1990. Contbr. articles to profl. jours. including Hosp. Adminstrn. Currents, Purchasing Adminstrn., Resident and Staff Physician, among others. Pres., bd. dirs. Franklin County chpt., United Cerebral Palsy, Columbus, 1975-80; bd. dirs. Asset Data Sys., Columbus, 1977-84, Transp. Resources, Inc., Columbus, 1979-80; founder, bd. dirs. Support Resources, Inc., Columbus, 1978-85; pres. Omnilife Sys., Inc., Columbus, 1979—; pres., adminstr. Patterson Health Ctr., Columbus, 1979—, Bryant Health Ctr., Ironton, Ohio, 1983—; pres. Equity Mgmt., Inc., Columbus, 1985—; owner Omnivend, Columbus, 1985—; cons. dir. Ketcham Nursing Home, Crooksville, Ohio, 1985-86; bd. dirs. Ohio Acad. Nursing Homes, Columbus, 1985—, bd. pres., 1986-89; pres. Shelby Manor Health Ctr., Inc., Shelbyville, Ky., 1986—, Hamilton Health Ctr., Inc., 1986—, Samaritan Health Ctr., Medina, Ohio, 1988—; bd. sec. Clintonville Family Practice, Columbus, 1987—. Mem. NSPE, Am. Coll. Health Care Adminstrn., Aircraft Owners and Pilots Assn., Am. Inst. Indsl. Engrs., Alpha Kappa Psi, Phi Kappa Phi, Alpha Phi Mu, Sigma Xi, Beta Gamma Sigma.

BANASZYNSKI, CAROL JEAN, educator; b. Hawkins, Wis., Jan. 3, 1951. BS in Biology, U. Wis., LaCrosse, 1973; MS in Profl. Devel., U. Wis., Whitewater, 1987. Tchr. Deerfield Cmty. Schs., 1973—. Coach Youth T-ball/softball; co-chairperson Adopt-A-Highway; group leader 4-H Club; counselor Boy Scout Environtl. Merit Badge program;. Recipient Wis. H.S. Tchr. of Yr., 1997-98, Wis. Tchr. of Yr. 1998, Award of Excellence Wis. Assn. of Sch. Bds., 1997, Wis. Dept. of Instrn., 1997, Wis. Edn. Assn. Coun., 1997, Wis. Legis. Citation for Tchg. Excellence, 1997-98; named Educator of Yr. Nat. H.S. Assn., 1998, Outstanding Tchr. Radioshack/Tandy, 1999; Kohl fellowship, 1997. Mem. Wis. H.S. Assn., Nat. Biology Tchrs. Assn., Nat. Sci. Tchrs. Assn., Nat. Parks and Conservation Assn., Wis. Secondary Sci. Tchrs. (state conf. presenter), Wis. Elem. Sci. Tchrs., BioNet, DEA (scholarship com. chairperson), Wis. Edn. Assn. Coun., Dane County Talented and Gifted Coords. Assn. (vision com., dist. math meet coord.), Wis. Ctr. for Academically Talented Youth. Office: Deerfield Cmty Sch Dist Deerfield WI 53559

BANCEL, MARILYN, fund raising management consultant; b. Glen Ridge, N.J., June 15, 1947; d. Paul and Joan Marie (Spangler) B.; m. Rik Myslewski, Nov. 20, 1983; children: Carolyn, Roxanne. BA in English with distinction, Ind. U., 1969. Cert. fund raising exec. Ptnr. The Sultan's Shirt Tail, Gemlik, Turkey, 1969-72; prodn. mgr. High Country Co., San Francisco, 1973-74; pub. Bay Arts Rev., Berkeley, Calif., 1976-79; dir. devel. Oakland (Calif.) Symphony Orch., 1979-81; assoc. dir. devel. Exploratorium, San Francisco, 1981-86, dir. devel., 1986-91; prin. Fund Devel. Counsel, San Francisco, 1991-93; v.p. The Oram Group, Inc., San Francisco, 1993—; co-chmn. capital campaign com. Synergy Sch., San Francisco, 1995-99; adj. prof. U. San Francisco, 1993—. Mem. adv. bd. Mus. City of San Francisco, 1995—, San Francisco Bot. Gardens, 1998—. Fellow U. Strasberg, France, 1968. Mem. Nat. Soc. Fund Raising Execs. (bd. mem. Golden Gate chpt.), Am. Assn. Fund Raising Counsel, Devel. Execs. Roundtable, Phi Beta Kappa. Democrat. Avocation: gardening. Office: The Oram Group 44 Page St Ste 604C San Francisco CA 94102-5972

BANCHOFF, THOMAS FRANCIS, mathematics educator; b. Trenton, N.J., Apr. 7, 1938; s. Thomas Francis and Ann Maria (Scarborough) B.; m. Lynore Wilhelmina Gause, July 6, 1963 (div. Aug. 1998); children: Thomas Francis III, Ann Wilhelmina, Mary Lynn. A.B., U. Notre Dame, 1960; M.A., U. Calif., Berkeley, 1962, Ph.D., 1964; M.A. ad eundem, Brown U., 1970; DSc (hon.), Fairfield U., 1998. Benjamin Peirce Instr. Harvard U., Cambridge, Mass., 1964-66; research assoc. Universiteit van Amsterdam, The Netherlands, 1966-67; asst. prof. Brown U., Providence, R.I., 1967-70, assoc. prof., 1970-75, prof. math., 1975—, acting dean student affairs, 1970-71; W.H. Annenberg Disting. prof. Brown U., Providence, 1998-99; vis. prof. I.H.E.S., Bures-sur-Yvette, France, 1980-81, U. Notre Dame, 1994; vis. assoc. prof. UCLA, 1974; pres. Banchoff-Strauss Prodns., Providence, 1977-83, Thomas Banchoff Prodns., Providence, 1983—; editl. cons. Springer-Verlag; G. Leonard Baker vis. prof. Yale U., 1998. Author: Linear Algebra through Geometry, 1983, 2d edit., 1991, Cusps of Gauss Mappings, 1983, Beyond the Third Dimension, 1990, 2d edit., 1996, Flatland: A New Introduction, 1991; assoc. editor Math. Mag., 1979-81, Am. Math. Monthly, 1981-86, Geometricae Dedicata, 1985-96; editor: Communications in Visual Mathematics, 1997—; writer, dir. computer animated films: The Hypercube: Projections and Slicing, 1978 (Prix de la Recherche Fondamentale, Brussels), The Hypercube: Foliation and Projections, 1985, Fronts and Centers, 1988. Woodrow Wilson fellow, 1959, Danforth Found. fellow, 1960, NSF rsch. fellow, 1967, Office Naval Rsch. fellow, 1983-87; recipient sr. citation Brown U., 1976, Lester Ford award for Math. Exposition, 1978, Joseph Priestly award, 1987, Philip Bray award for tchg. excellence, 1993, New Eng. Soc. of Math. Assn. Am. award for Disting. Coll. of Univ. Tchg. of Math., 1995, Deborah and Franklin Tepper Haimo Nat. award for Disting. Coll. or Univ. Tchg. of Math., 1996; named Carnegie Found. R.I. Prof. of Yr., 1998. Mem. Am. Math. Soc., Math. Assn. Am. (pres.-elect 1998-99, pres. 1999-2001), Nat. Coun. Tchrs. of Math., Soc. Values in Higher Edn. (bd. dirs. 1978-84), Common Cause R.I. (state governing bd. 1992-94, pub. svc. achievement jud. reform award 1994). Democrat. Roman Catholic. Club: Art (Providence) (bd. mgrs. 1979-80). Home: 18 Colonial Rd Providence RI 02906-2525 Office: Brown U Math Dept Providence RI 02912 *One idea, the fourth dimension, has provided me the most challenge and fascination and has introduced me and my students to remarkable people and their creations, from Edwin Abbott and his Flatland to Salvador Dali and his Corpus Hypercubicus. Our own computer graphics films are contributions in the same spirit, to challenge all to see in new ways.*

BANCIK, STEVEN CHARLES, information specialist, researcher; b. Cleve., Apr. 23, 1958; s. Paul Milan and Geraldine (Everstine) B. BA in Sociology, Psychology, Anthropology, Kent (Ohio) State U., 1994, M in Libr. & Info. Sci., 1999. Asst. mgr. Waldenbooks, Akron, Ohio, 1983-88; mgr. without portfolio Waldenbooks, Northern, Ohio, 1988; mgr. divsn. reader's mkt. Waldenbooks, Akron, Ohio, 1988-90; scheduling advisor Dept. Undergrad. Studies Kent State U., computer lab. mgr., 1994-97, tchg. asst. dept. history, 1999; bd. trustees Kent State U., 1996-98; senator rep. The Sch. of Libr. and Info. Sci. in Grad Student Senate; tchg. asst. Kent State U., 1999. Tech. design cons. Kent State Historian, 1998-99. Mem. Am. Libr. Assn. (rep. Kent State U. 1996, exec. officer student chpt. 1995-96), Libr. Adminstrn. Mgmt. Assn., Assoc. Libr. Student Svc. Orgn. (treas. 1996, newsletter cartoonist 1994-97), Phi Alpha Theta (newsletter editor 1999—). Republican. Avocations: museum studies, ancient antiquities, rare books, applied CD-ROM technologies, commercial art. E-mail: sbancik@wordlnet.att.net. Home: PO Box 706 Kent OH 44240-0013

BANCROFT, ALEXANDER CLERIHEW, lawyer; b. N.Y.C., Feb. 6, 1938; s. Harding F. and Jane (Northrop) B.; m. Margaret A. Armstrong, Mar. 14, 1964; 1 dau., Elizabeth. A.B., Harvard U., 1960, LL.B., 1963. Mem. Shearman & Sterling, N.Y.C., 1964—, ptnr., 1973—. Home: 15 E 91st St New York NY 10128-0648 Office: 599 Lexington Ave Fl C2 New York NY 10022-6030

BANCROFT, ANN, polar explorer; b. 1956; d. Dick and Debbie B. Former tchr., coach, wilderness instr. St. Paul, Minn.; mem. Steger Internat. Polar Expedition, 1986 (first woman to reach the North Pole by dogsled); leader Am. Women's Trans-Antartic Expedition, 1993 (first women's team to reach the South Pole on skis). Subject of corp. video Vison of Teams, 1998; featured in Remarkable Women of the 20th Century, 1998. Founder Am. Women's Expedition Foun. Named Ms. Mag. Woman of Yr., 1987; inductee Girls and Women in Sport Hall of Fame, 1992, Nat. Women's Hall of Fame, 1995; recipient Women First award YWCA, 1993. Fax: 612-333-1325. E-mail: kristi@basecamp1.com. Office: Base Camp Promotions 119 N 4th St Ste 406 Minneapolis MN 55401-1709*

BANCROFT, ANNE (MRS. MEL BROOKS), actress; b. N.Y.C., Sept. 17, 1931; d. Michael and Mildred (DiNapoli) Italiano; m. Mel Brooks, 1964; 1 son. Broadway stage appearances include Two for the Seesaw, 1957 (Tony award 1957), The Miracle Worker, 1959-60 (Tony award 1960), Devils, 1977, Golda, 1977-78, Duet for One, 1981; stage appearances include Mystery of the Rose Bouquet, 1989; motion pictures include Treasure of the Golden Condor, 1952, Don't Bother to Knock, 1952, Tonight We Sing, 1953, The Kid from Left Field, 1953, Demetrius and the Gladiators, 1954, Gorilla at Large, 1954, The Raid, 1954, A Life in the Balance, 1954, The Brass Ring, 1954, Naked Street, 1955, New York Confidential, 1955, The Last Frontier, 1955, Girl in the Black Stockings, 1957, Restless Breed, 1957, The Pumpkin Eater, 1964, Seven Women, 1966, Slender Thread, 1966, The Graduate, 1967, Young Winston, 1972, The Prisoner of 2nd Avenue, 1975, The Hindenburg, 1975, Lipstick, 1976, Silent Movie, 1976, The Turning Point, 1977, Fatso, 1979, The Elephant Man, 1980, To Be or Not to Be, 1983, Garbo Talks, 1984, Agnes of God, 1985, 'Night, Mother, 1986, 84 Charing Cross Road (Brit. Acad. award 1987), Torch Song Trilogy, 1988, Bert Rigby You're a Fool, 1989, Honeymoon in Vegas, 1992, Love Potion #9, 1992, Point of No Return, 1993, Mr. Jones, 1993, Malice, 1993, How to Make an American Quilt, 1995, Home for the Holidays, 1995, Dracula, Dead and Loving It, 1995, GI Jane, 1997, Critical Care, 1997, Great Expectations, 1998, Antz, 1998, Mark Twain's America in 3D, 1998, Up at the Villa, 1999 ; TV appearances include Kraft Music Hall, Jesus of Nazareth, 1977, Marco Polo, 1982, Broadway Bound, 1992, Mrs. Cage, PBS, 1992, Oldest Living Confederate Widow Tells All, 1994, The Homecoming, 1996, Sunchasers, 1997, AFI's 100 years ... 100 Movies, 1998, Deep in My Heart, 1999, A Salute to Dustin Hoffman, 1999; dir., writer, star: (TV spl.) Annie-The Woman in the Life of Men, 1970 (Emmy award 1970). Recipient Acad. award for performance in The Miracle Worker, 1962, Best Actress award Cannes Internat. Film Festival for performance in Pumpkin Eater, 1964, Lifetime Achievement in Comedy award Am. Comedy Awards, 1996. Address: c/o The Culver Studios 9336 Washington Blvd Culver City CA 90232-2628*

BANCROFT, GEORGE MICHAEL, chemical physicist, educator; b. Saskatoon, Sask., Can., Apr. 3, 1942; s. Fred and Florence Jean B.; m. Joan Marion MacFarlane, Sept. 16, 1967; children: David Kenneth, Catherine Jean. B.Sc., U. Man., 1963; M.Sc., 1964; Ph.D., Cambridge (Eng.) U., 1967, M.A., 1970, Sc.D. (E.W. Staecie fellow), 1979. Univ. demonstrator Cambridge U.; then teaching fellow Christ Coll.; mem. faculty U. Western Ont., London, now prof. dept. chemistry; pres. Can. Inst. for Synchrotron Radiation. Author: Mössbauer Spectroscopy, 1973; also articles in photoelectron spectroscopy, synchrotron radiation studies; revs. Mössbauer Spectroscopy. Recipient Harrison Meml. prize, 1972, Meldola medal, 1972, Rutherford Meml. medal, 1980, Alcan award, 1990, Herzberg award, 1991, Can. Inst. of Chemistry Palladium medal, 1996, Morley medal Am. Chem. Soc., 1998; Guggenheim fellow, 1982-83. Fellow Royal Soc. Can.; mem. Royal Soc. Chemistry, Can. Chem. Soc., Can. Geol. Soc., Can. Physics Soc. Mem. United Ch. Can. Clubs: Curling, Tennis (London). Office: U Western Ont, Chemistry Dept, London, ON Canada N6A 5B7

BANCROFT, JAMES RAMSEY, lawyer, business executive; b. Ponca City, Okla., Nov. 13, 1919; s. Charles Ramsey and Maude (Viersen) B.; m. Jane Marguerite Oberfell, May 28, 1944; children: John Ramsey, Paul Marshall, Sara Jane Bancroft Clair. AB, U. Calif., Berkeley, 1940, MBA, 1941; JD, Hastings Coll. Law, 1949. Bar: Calif. 1950; CPA, Calif. With McLaren, Goode, West & Co., CPAs, San Francisco, 1946-50; ptnr. Bancroft, Avery & McAlister, San Francisco, 1950-86, of counsel, 1986-92; owner, mgr. Bancroft Vineyard, 1982—; of counsel Bancroft & McAlister, San Francisco, 1992—; mng. ptnr. Bancroft Investments, San Francisco, 1980—; pres. Madison Properties, Inc., San Francisco, 1967-98, Adams Properties, Inc., 1969-79, Adams-Western Inc., 1969-78; chmn. bd. Adams Capital Mgmt. Co., 1987-88, pres., 1988—; chmn. bd. UNC Resources, 1978-82, dir., 1984-85; chmn. bd. United Nuclear Corp., Falls Church, Va., 1972-82, Madison Capital Inc., San Francisco, 1986-93. Former pres. Suisun Conservation Fund; former dir. Suisun Resource Conservation Dist.; former trustee Dean Witter Found., 1952-94; pres. Harvey L. Sorensen Found.; bd. dirs. Calif. Urology Found.; former dir. San Francisco Found for Rsch. and Edn. Orthopedic Surgery; chmn. Pacific Vascular Rsch. Found.. Lt. USNR, 1942-46. Mem. ABA, Confrérie des Chevaliers du Tastevin, Bohemian Club, Pacific Union Club, Order of Coif, Phi Beta Kappa. Office: 221 Main St Ste 440 San Francisco CA 94105

BANCROFT, MARGARET ARMSTRONG, lawyer; b. Mpls., May 9, 1938; d. Wallace David and Mary Elizabeth (Garland) Armstrong; m. Alexander Clerihew Bancroft, Mar. 14, 1964; 1 child, Elizabeth. BA magna cum laude, Radcliffe Coll.-Harvard U., 1960; JD cum laude, NYU, 1969. Bar: N.Y. 1971. Reporter Mpls. Star and Tribune, 1960-61, UPI, N.Y. and N.J., 1961-66; mem. Dechert Price & Rhoads, N.Y.C.; adj. prof. law NYU Sch. Law. Bd. dirs., mem. exec. com. Vis. Nurse Svc. N.Y.; pres. Vis. Nurse Svc. N.Y. Home Care, Inc. Mem. Am. Law Inst. Office: Dechert Price & Rhoads 30 Rockefeller Plz Fl 22 New York NY 10112-2200

BANCROFT, PAUL, III, investment company executive; b. N.Y.C., Feb. 27, 1930; s. Paul and Rita (Manning) B.; m. Monica M. Devine, Jan. 2, 1977; children by previous marriage: Bradford, Kimberly, Stephen, Gregory. BA, Yale U., 1951; postgrad., Georgetown Fgn. Svc. Inst., 1952. Account exec. Merrill Lynch Pierce Fenner & Smith, N.Y.C., 1956-57; assoc. corp. fin. dept. F. Eberstadt & Co., N.Y.C., 1957-62; ptnr. Draper, Gaither & Anderson, Palo Alto, Calif., 1962-67; with Bessemer Securities Corp., Palo Alto, Calif., 1967-92; ind. venture capitalist N.Y.C., 1988—; v.p. Venture Capital Investments, 1967-74, sr. v.p. securities investments, 1974-76, pres., CEO, dir., 1976-87; cons. Bessemer Securities Corp., 1988-92; bd. dirs. Unova, Inc., Scudder Securities Trust, Scudder Value Equity Trust, Scudder Internat. Fund, Scudder Global/Internat. Fund, Scudder New Asia Fund, Scudder New Europe Fund, Inc.; founder, past pres. and chmn. Nat. Venture Capital Assn. 1st lt. USAF 1952-56.. Mem. Yale Club, Pacific Union Club, Bohemian Club. Home and Office: PO Box 6639 Snowmass Village CO 81615

BANDA, GERALDINE MARIE, chiropractic physician; b. Orange, N.J., Oct. 15, 1951; d. Albert Joseph and Maria Grace B.; 1 child, Gabriele Grace. BA, Seton Hall U., 1974; D of Chiropractic, N.Y. Chiropractic Coll., 1984. Cert. scoliosis mgmt. specialist. Staff writer The Herald News, Passaic, N.J., 1974-77; tchr. St. Genevieve's Roman Cath. Sch., Elizabeth, N.J., 1977-80; chiropractic physician Banda Chiropractic Office, Cranford, N.J., 1984—, 1996—. Contbr. articles to profl. jours. and newspapers. Activist community svc. projects and scoliosis screenings, Cranford, 1984—; founding mem. Queen City Acad. Charter Sch., Plainfield, N.J. Named Outstanding Young Woman of Am., 1981. Mem. Am. Chiropractic Assn. (mem. coun. on diagnostic imaging), N.J. Chiropractic Soc., Cranford C. of C., N.J. Women's Bus. Owners Assn. Avocations: old movies, reading, swimming, golf, travel. Office: Banda Chiropractic Office 623 N Wood Ave Linden NJ 07036-4151

BANDEEN, ROBERT ANGUS, management corporation executive; b. Rodney, Ont., Can., Oct. 29, 1930; s. John Robert and Jessie Marie (Thomson) B.; m. Mona Helen Blair, May 31, 1958; children: Ian Blair, Mark Everett, Robert Derek, Adam Drummond. B.A., U. Western Ont., 1952; Ph.D., Duke U., 1959; LL.D. (hon.), U. Western Ont., 1975, Dalhousie U., 1978, Queens U., 1982; D.C.L. (hon.), Bishop's U., 1978. Asst. economist Can. Nat. Rys., Montreal, Que., 1955-56, research statistician, 1956-58, staff officer planning, 1958-60, chief costs and stats., 1960, chief devel. planning, 1960-66, dir. corp. planning, 1966-68, v.p. corp. planning and fin., 1968-71, v.p. Great Lakes region, 1971-72, exec. v.p. fin. and adminstrn., 1972-74, pres., chief exec. officer, 1974-82; chmn., pres., chief exec. officer Crown Life Ins. Co., 1982-84, chmn.. chief exec. officer, 1984-85; chmn., pres., chief exec. officer Cluny Corp., Toronto, Ont., 1986—; bd. dirs. Talisman Energy, Inc., Greyvest Fin. Svcs. Inc., Grevest, Inc., Clarke Inc., Greater Toronto Airports Authority, Inc., Nat. Challenge Systems, Inc.; former chancellor Bishop's U. Senator Stratford Shakespearean Festival Found.; gov. Participation, Can. Olympic Trust; mem. Isle Maligne Soc., Duke U.; bd. visitors Fuqua Sch. Bus., Duke U.; bd. dirs. Nat. Aboriginal Achievement Found. Decorated knight Order St. John; officer Order of Can.; recipient Salzberg medal Syracuse U., 1982. Mem. Delta Upsilon. Clubs: Mount Royal (Montreal); York, Cambridge (Toronto). Home and Office: Cluny Corp, 305-1166 Bay St, Toronto, ON Canada M5S 2X8

BANDEEN, WILLIAM REID, retired meteorologist; b. Escanaba, Mich., Oct. 11, 1926; s. Orren I. and Jean (Guthrie) B.; m. Joan Sleeper, Dec. 17, 1960; children: Kevin Orren, Karen Jean, Keith Morse. BS, U.S. Mil. Acad., 1948; MS, NYU, 1955. Commd. 2d lt. U.S. Army, 1948, advanced through grades to capt., 1959, ret., 1959; with NASA, Goddard Space Flight Ctr., Greenbelt, Md., 1959-89, assoc. dir. space and earth scis. for ops., 1986-89, ret., 1989. Contbr. articles to profl. jours. Fellow AAAS, Am. Geophys. Union, Am. Meteorol. Soc.

BANDEL, DAVID BRIAN, accountant; b. Chgo., Aug. 18, 1951; s. Frank John and Lorraine Mary (Buzinski) B. BA in Psychology, So. Ill. U., 1974, BS in Acctg., 1977. CPA, Ill. Staff acct. Porte Brown LLC, Elk Grove Village, Ill., 1977-83, mgr., 1984-86, ptnr., 1987—; dir. Harris Bank, Elk Grove, Ill., 1996—. Treas. United Way, Elk Grove Village, 1990-96; bd. dirs. Greater O'Hare Assn., Elk Grove Village, 1994—, amb., 1979-86, treas., 1998—. Recipient Paul Harris fellow. Mem. AICPA, Ill. CPA Soc. (dir. pub. rels. O'Hare chpt. 1990), Rotary (pres. 1988-89). Roman Catholic. Avocations: sports, investing, community fundraising. Home: 553 Birch St Itasca IL 60143-1646 Office: Porte Brown LLC 845 Oakton St Elk Grove Village IL 60007-1904

BANDEMER, NORMAN JOHN, healthcare consulting executive; b. Detroit, Sept. 13, 1949; s. Marvin Gustave and Helen Theresa (Jashinski) B.; m. Elaine Ellen Massie, Sept. 4, 1971; children: Norman John II, Marisa Nikol. BBA, Eastern Mich. U., 1971; MBA, Mich. State U., 1977. Field auditor Blue Cross and Blue Shield of Mich., Detroit, 1971-72; supr. State of Mich. Medicaid Program, Lansing, 1972-77; asst. dir. Mich. Hosp. Assn. Svc. Corp., Lansing, 1977-83; v.p. of operation Bronson/Beaumont Mgmt. Svcs., Kalamazoo, Mich., 1983-86; exec. dir. The Travelers Health Network, Grand Rapids, 1986-88; regional dir. Coopers & Lybrand, Detroit, 1988-90; mng. ptnr. ADA Consulting Group-Healthcare Consulting, Grand Rapids, 1990—; guest speaker Health Care Benefits, Direct Contracting, 1992. Author: Health Care Costs in Michigan, 1991, Medicaid Program in Mich., 1992. Hon. coach Mich. State U. Athletic Booster Club, East Lansing, 1987. Mem. Lansing City Club, Healthcare Fin. Mgmt. Assn., Mich. Assn. CPAs Healthcare Com., Mich. State U. Alumni Club. Roman Catholic. Avocations: golf, travel, watching sporting events. Office: ADA Consulting Group 7705 Tobemory Ct SE Ste 100 Ada MI 49301-9362

BANDER, MYRON, physics educator, university dean; b. Belzyce, Poland, Dec. 11, 1937; came to U.S., 1949, naturalized, 1955; s. Elias and Regina (Zielonka) B.; m. Carol Heimberg, Aug. 20, 1967. B.A., Columbia U., 1958, M.A., 1959, Ph.D., 1962. Postdoctoral fellow CERN, 1962-63; research assoc. Stanford Linear Accelerator Center, 1963-66; mem. faculty U. Calif., Irvine, 1966—, prof. physics, 1974—, dean phys. scis., 1980-86; chair dept. physics, 1992-95. Sloan Found. fellow, 1967-69. Fellow Am. Phys. Soc. Office: U Calif Irvine CA 92697-4575

BANDER, THOMAS SAMUEL, dentist; b. Grand Rapids, Mich., Mar. 3, 1924; s. Samuel and Jennie (David) B.; m. DoLores Abraham, Sept. 7, 1947; children: Samuel T., Jacquelyn Marie. AS, Grand Rapids Jr. Coll., 1944; DDS, U. Mich., 1948. Pvt. practice dentistry Grand Rapids, Mich., 1948—. Pres. St. Nicholas Orthodox Ch., Grand Rapids, 1965. Served with U.S. Army, 1941-44, to capt. USAF, 1955-57. Fellow Am. Coll. Dentists, Internat. Coll. of Dentists, ADA, Acad. Operative Dentistry; mem. West Mich. Dental Soc. (pres. 1978), Mich. Dental Assn. (chmn. sci. program 1977-78), Kent County Dental Soc. (pres. 1965), Cascade Hills Country Club. Republican. Eastern Orthodox. Avocations: golfing, traveling, tennis. Home: 616 Manhattan Rd SE Grand Rapids MI 49506-2077 Office: 2426 Burton St SE Grand Rapids MI 49546-4806

BANDERAS, ANTONIO, actor; b. Malaga, Spain, Aug. 10, 1960. Films include: Labyrinth of Passion, 1982, Y del sefuro...Ilbranos señor!, 1983, El Caso Almeria, 1983, The Stilts, 1984, La corte de Faraon, 1985, Requiem por un campesino espanol, 1985, The Puzzle, 1986, 27 Hours, 1986, Matador, 1986, Delirios de amor, 1986, The Way They Were, 1987, Law of Desire, 1987, The Pleasure of Killing, 1988, Baton Rouge, 1988, Women on the Verge of a Nervous Breakdown, 1988, Going South Shopping, 1988, Si que dicen que cai, 1989, The White Dove, 1989, Tie Me Up! Tie Me Down!, 1990, Against the Wind, 1990, New Land, 1991, Woman in the Rain, 1991, Madonna: Truth or Dare, 1991, Borges Tales, Part I, 1991, The Mambo Kings, 1992, Shoot!, 1993, Outrage, 1993, Philadelphia, 1993, The House of the Spirits, 1993, Of Love and Shadows, 1994, Interview With the Vampire, 1994, Never Talk to Strangers, 1995, Miami Rhapsody, 1995, Four Rooms, 1995, Desperado, 1995, Assassins, 1995, Two Much, 1996, Evita, 1996, The Mask of Zorro, 1997, Crazy in Alabama, 1998, The 13th Warrior, 1999; dir. Crazy in Alabama, 1999; prodr. White River Kid, 1999. Office: care CAA 9830 Wilshire Blvd Beverly Hills CA 90212-1804 also: Agents Associes, 201 Rue du fauborg, Saint Honore Paris 75008, France*

BANDES, SUSAN JANE, museum director, educator; b. N.Y.C., Oct. 18, 1951; d. Ralph and Bessie (Gordon) B. BA, NYU, 1971; MA, Bryn Mawr Coll., 1973, PhD, 1978; postgrad., Mus. Mgmt. Inst., Berkeley, Calif., 1990. Asst. prof. Sweet Briar (Va.) Coll., 1978-83; project dir. Am. Assn. Mus., Washington, 1983-84; program officer J. Paul Getty Trust Grant Program, L.A., 1984-86; prof., dir. Kresge Art Mus. Mich. State U., East Lansing, 1986—. Author, editor: Caring for Collections, 1984, Affordable Dreams: The Goetsch-Winckler House and Frank Lloyd Wright, 1991; author: Abraham Rattner, The Tampa Museum of Art Collection, 1997; editor: The Prints of John S. de Martelly, 1903-1979. Recipient award Am. Philos. Soc., 1981, publ. award AIA, 1990; Samuel H. Kress fellow, 1972-73, 75-76, Whiting fellow, 1976-77; Fulbright-Hayes grant, 1974-75. Mem. Nat. Inst. for Conservation (treas. 1986-90), Mich. Alliance for Conservation (treas. 1994-95, sec. 1996-97, treas. 1997-98, pres. 1998—), Mich. Mus. Assn. (bd. dirs. 1987-92), Mich. Coun. for Humanities (coun. 1988-92), Midwest Art History Soc. (bd. dirs. 1997—). Avocations: sailing, collecting oriental rugs. Office: Mich State U Kresge Art Mus East Lansing MI 48824

BANDLER, JOHN WILLIAM, electrical engineering educator, consultant; b. Jerusalem, Nov. 9, 1941; m. Beth; children: Lydia, Zoe. B.Sc., Imperial Coll. Sci. and Tech., London, 1963, Ph.D., 1967; D.Sc., U. London, 1976. With Mullard Research Labs., Eng., 1966-67; postdoctoral fellow, sessional lectr. U. Man., Can., 1967-69; asst. prof. McMaster U., Hamilton, Ont., Can., 1969-71; assoc. prof. McMaster U., 1971-74, prof. elec. engring., 1974—, chmn. dept., 1978-79, dean faculty, 1979-81, coordinator group on simulation, optimization and control, 1973-83, dir. research in simulation optimization systems research lab., 1983—; pres. Optimization Systems Assocs., Inc., 1983-97, Bandler Corp., Inc., 1997—. Author more than 300 tech. papers. Recipient Automated Measurements Career award Automatic Radio Frequency Techniques Group, 1994. Fellow IEEE, Inst. Elec. Engrs. U.K., Royal Soc. Can.; mem. Electromagnetics Acad., Assn. Profl. Engrs. Province of Ont. Office: McMaster U, Dept Elec & Comp Engring, Hamilton, ON Canada L8S 4L7 *Proceeding in a direction not sanctioned by my peers has always proved tough, but the results achieved have almost always been worth the effort.*

BANDLER, RICHARD, advertising executive; b. N.Y.C., July 12, 1917; s. Maurice and Edna (Lee) B.; m. Eleanor Slater Trenholm, Jan. 7, 1966; children—Judith Finch, Patricia Hornblower, Elise, Tatiana. Dir. purchasing B. T. Babbitt Co., N.Y.C., 1939-42; nat. program sales mgr. Reuben H. Donnelley Corp., N.Y.C., 1946-49; founder, pres. Richard Bandler Co. Inc., directory advt., N.Y.C., 1949-87. Served with U.S. Army, 1942-45. Decorated Purple Heart with three battle stars. Mem. Masters of Foxhounds Assn. Unitarian. Home: 5266 Fisher Island Dr Fisher Island FL 33109-0280

BANDOW, DOUGLAS LEIGHTON, editor, columnist, policy consultant; b. Washington, Apr. 15, 1957; s. Donald E. and Donna J. (Losh) B. A.A., Okaloosa-Walton Jr. Coll., Niceville, Fla., 1974; B.S. in Econs., Fla. State U., 1976; J.D., Stanford U., 1979. Bar: Calif. 1979 D.C. 1984. Sr. policy analyst Reagan for Pres. Com., Los Angeles, 1979-80, Arlington, Va., 1980; sr. policy analyst Office of Pres. Elect, Washington, 1980-81; spl. asst. to the Pres. for policy devel. White House, Washington, 1981-82; editor Inquiry Mag., Washington, 1982-84; sr. fellow Cato Inst., Washington, 1984—; nat. syndicated columnist Copley News Svc., San Diego, 1983—. Author: Unquestioned Allegiance, 1986, Beyond Good Intentions: A Biblical View of Politics, 1988, Human Resources and Defense Manpower, 1989, The Politics of Plunder: Misgovernment in Washington, 1990, The Politics of Envy: Statism as Theology, 1994, Tripwire: Korea and U.S. Foreign Policy in a Changed World, 1996; editor: U.S. Aid to the Developing World, 1985, Protecting the Environment, 1986; co-editor: The U.S.-South Korean Alliance, 1992, Perpetuating Poverty, 1994; contbr. articles to periodicals. Recipient Freedom Leadership award Freedoms Found., Valley Forge, Pa., 1977; recipient cert. for polit. and journalistic activities Freedoms Found., Valley Forge, Pa., 1979; named Man of Yr. N.Y. State Coll. Reps., 1982; recipient Nat. Young Am. award Boy Scouts Am., 1977. Mem. Calif. Bar Assn., ABA, D.C. Bar Assn., Washington Ind. Writers. Office: Cato Inst 1000 Massachusetts Ave NW Washington DC 20001-5400

BANDSTRA, TED E., federal judge; b. 1948. BA, Calvin Coll., Grand Rapids, Mich.; JD, U. Miami. Magistrate judge U.S. Dist. Ct. (so. dist.) Fla., Miami, 1990—. Office: 105 US Courthouse 300 NE 1st Ave Miami FL 33132-2126

BANDURA, ALBERT, psychologist; b. Mundare, Alta., Can., Dec. 4, 1925; came to U.S., 1949, naturalized, 1956; m. Virginia Varns; 2 children. B.A., U. B.C., 1949, D.Sc. (hon.), 1979; M.A. in Psychology, U. Iowa, 1951, Ph.D. in Psychology, 1952. Prof. psychology Stanford U., 1953—, David Starr Jordan prof. social sci. in psychology, 1973—. Author: (with R.H. Walters) Adolescent Aggression, 1959, (with R.H. Walters) Social Learning and Personality Development, 1963, Principles of Behavior Modification, 1969, Aggression, 1973, Social Learning Theory, 1977, Social Foundations of Thought and Action: A Social Cognitive Theory, 1986; editor: Psychological Modeling: Conflicting Theories, 1971, Self-Efficacy in Changing Societies, 1995, Self-Efficacy: The Exercise of Control, 1997. Guggenheim fellow, 1972. Fellow Am. Acad. Arts and Scis., Ctr. Adv. Study in Behavioral Sci.; mem. Am. Psychol. Soc. (William James award 1989), Inst. Medicine NAS, Am. Psychol. Assn. (Disting. Scientist award divsn. 12, 1972, Disting. Sci. Contbn. award 1980, pres. 1974), Calif. Psychol. Assn. (Disting. Scientist award 1973, Lifetime Disting. Contbr. award 1998), Western Psychol. Assn. (pres. 1980), Internat. Soc. Research on Aggression (Disting. Contbn. award 1980), Soc. Child Devel., Inst. of Medicine. Office: Stanford U Dept Psychology Stanford CA 94305-2130

BANDURRAGA, PETER LOUIS, museum director, historian; b. Los Angeles, Apr. 2, 1944; s. Luis Cipriano and E. Lillian (Slingsby) B.; m. Diane Elizabeth Nassir, Mar. 4 , 1979. B.A., Stanford U., 1966; M.A., U. Calif.-Santa Barbara, 1968; Ph.D., U. Calif.Santa Barbara, 1977. Instr. Chapman Coll., Orange, Calif., 1977-78; research librarian Ventura County Hist. Mus., Ventura, Calif., 1978-81; dir. Nev. Hist. Soc., Reno, 1981—; mem. Nev. State Adv. Council on Libraries, 1981-86, adv. bd. State Hist. Records, 1981—; adj. prof. U. Nev., Reno, 1981—. Co-author: Ventura County's Yesterdays today, 1980, Neon Nights, 1990. Mem. Am. Assn. State and Local History, Western Mus. Council, Soc. Calif. Archivists, Nev. Mus. Assn. Democrat. Methodist. Office: Nev Hist Soc 1650 N Virginia St Reno NV 89503-1738

BANDY, JACK D., lawyer; b. Galesburg, Ill., June 19, 1932; s. Homer O. and Gladys L. (Van Winkle) B.; m. Betty McMillan, Feb. 18, 1956; children: Jean A. Bandy Abramson, D. Michael, Jeffery K. *Great-great grandparents, Reuben and Sibby Adkisson Bandy were among the first settlers of Knox County, Illinois in 1837. They bought 160 acres near Galesburg, and started the family farm. After Reuben's death (1861), it was operated by their son, George, and his wife, Narcissa Holland Bandy. When George retired, his son, George Albert "Burt" and his wife Mattie Mears Bandy, continued the farm until 1907 when they sold it and moved to Galesburg. Their son, Homer Oliver, married Gladys Lillian Van Winkle Bandy. They were parents of Jack D. Bandy, subject of this biography.* BA, Knox Coll., 1954; LLB, U. La Verne, 1967. Bar: Calif. 1972. Safety engr. Indsl. Indemnity Co., L.A., 1960-65, sr. safety engr., 1965-69, resident safety engr., 1969-72; trial atty. Employers Ins. of Wausau, L.A., 1972-79; mng. atty. Wausau Ins. Cos., L.A., 1979-92; arbitrator, mediator L.A. Superior Mcpl. Ct., 1992—. Contbr. articles to profl. jours. Youth leader YMCA, Mission Hills, Calif., 1965-72. Served with U.S. Army, 1954-56. Mem. Calif. State Bar, Am. Soc. Safety Engrs. (cert. safety profl.).

BANDY, MARY LEA, museum official; b. Evanston, Ill., June 16, 1943; d. DeWitt Clinton and Ruth (Coale) Gibson; m. Gary Bandy, June 3, 1967. B.A., Stanford U., 1965. Asst. editor Harry N. Abrams, Inc., N.Y.C., 1966-73; asso. editor publs. Mus. Modern Art, N.Y.C., 1973-76, asso. coordinator exhbns., 1976-78, dir. dept. film, 1980-93, chief curator dept. film and video, 1993—. Office: Mus Modern Art 11 W 53rd St New York NY 10019-5498*

BANE, BERNARD MAURICE, publishing company executive; b. Salem, Mass., Nov. 23, 1924; s. Julius and Rhoda (Trop) B. Student Northeastern U., 1946-48, law sch., 1948-49. Various sales and merchandising positions, 1949-55; with The Ivy League Enterprise, Boston, 1955-65; with BMB Pub. Co., Boston, 1965—, pub., 1965—. Author, pub.: The Bane in Kennedy's Existence, 1967, Is President John F. Kennedy Alive... and Well?, 1973, 16th edit., 1997, On the Impact of Morality in Our Times, 1985, Vatican "One": The Fault Line of Vatican II, 1986; producer, and host: The Fringe Voice, 1989—. Chmn. local Miss Am. Pageant, 1961. Mem. Nat. Notary Assn., Am. Soc. Notaries. Home: 854 Massachusetts Ave Cambridge MA 02139-3024 Office: PO Box 390931 Cambridge MA 02139-0021

BANE, MARY JO, political science educator; b. Princeville, Ill., Feb. 24, 1942; d. Fred W. and Helen (Callery) B.; m. Kenneth Winston, May 31, 1975. BS in Internat. Rels., Georgetown U., 1963; MAT, Harvard U., 1966, DEd, 1972. Tchr. English U.S. Peace Corps, Liberia, 1963-65; tchr. social studies Arlington (Mass.) Pub. Schs., 1966-67; tchr. English and social studies Brookline (Mass.) Pub. Schs., 1968-71; rsch. assoc. Ctr. Ednl. Policy Rsch. and Huron Inst. Harvard U., Cambridge, Mass., 1971-72, project co-dir. Ctr. Study of Pub. Policy, 1972-75, assoc. prof. edn., lectr. in sociology, 1977-80, assoc. prof. pub. policy, 1981-86, dir. Malcolm Wiener Ctr. for Social Policy, 1987-92, prof. pub. policy, 1986-90; Malcolm Wiener Prof. of Social Policy Kennedy Sch. of Govt., Harvard U., Cambridge, Mass., 1990-92; lectr. in Sociology U. Mass., Boston, 1972-75; assoc. dir. Ctr. Rsch. on Women, asst. prof. edn., lectr. in sociology Wellesley (Mass.) Coll., 1975-77; dep. asst. sec. for program planning and budget analyst Office Planning and Budget U.S. Dept. Edn., Washington, 1980-81; exec. dep. commr. N.Y. State Dept. Social Svcs., 1984-86, commr., 1992-93; asst. sec. Adminstrn. for Children and Families Dept. Health and Human Svcs., Washington, 1993-96; Prof. Pub. Policy Harvard U., Cambridge, Mass., 1997—; Ida Bean vis. prof. U. Iowa, 1980; chair bd. overseers panel study income dynamics Inst. Rsch. U. Mich., 1982-86; regents lectr. U. Calif., Berkeley, 1987; mem. adv. com. urban poverty NAS, 1986-90, chair com. child devel. rsch. and pub. policy, 1987-90; mem. pres. adv. coun. Columbia U. Tchrs. Coll., N.Y.C., 1988-92; mem. grants adv. coun. Smith Richardson Found., 1989-92; bd. dirs. Manpower Demonstration Rsch. Coun., 1989-92, 97—; active William T. Grant Found. Commn. on Work, Family and Citizenship, 1987-88. Author: (with others) Inequality: A Reassessment of the Effects of Family and Schooling in America, 1972, Here to Stay: American Families in the Twentieth Century, 1974, Japanese translation, 1981, (with George Masnick) The Nation's Families 1960-90, 1980; editor: (with Donald Levine) The Inequality Controversy, 1975, (with Manuel Carballo) The State and the Poor in the 1980s, 1984, (with Kenneth I. Winston) Gender and Public Policy: Cases and Comments, 1993, (with David Ellwood) Welfare Realities: From Rhetoric to Reform, 1994; contbr. articles to profl. jours. Fellow Nat. Acad. Pub. Adminstrn.; mem. Am. Sociol. Assn., Population Assn. Asm., Assn. Pub. Policy Analysis and Mgmt. Office: Harvard Univ Kennedy Sch Govt 79 John F Kennedy St Cambridge MA 02138-5801*

BANEGAS, ESTEVAN BROWN, environmental biotechnology executive; b. Hatch, N.Mex., May 10, 1941; s. Estevan Vera Banegas and Josephine (Brown) Crew; m. Amanda Martin, Sept. 5, 1970. BS, N.Mex. U., 1964; MBA, Wake Forest U., 1978. Sales mgr. agr. divsn. Ciba-Geigy Corp., San Juan, P.R., 1968-73; mktg. mgr. agr. divsn. Ciba-Geigy Corp., Greensboro, N.C., 1974-80; dir. corp. planning Ciba-Geigy Corp., Ardsley, N.Y., 1980-81; dir. product mgmt. agr. divsn. Ciba-Geigy Corp., Greensboro, 1981-83, dir. strategic planning agr. divsn., 1983-85; pres. joint venture Union Carbide Corp. and DNA Plant Tech. Agri-Diagnostics Assocs., Cinnaminson, N.J., 1985-92, also bd. dirs.; pres. Techshare, Inc, Greensboro, 1992—; pres., CEO Dominion BioScis., Inc., Blacksburg, Va., 1993—, also bd. dirs.; spkr. mktg. biotech. products Agbio Conf., 1989; vis. faculty joint ventures and strategic partnering Internation Rsch. Inst., 1992; bd. advisors U. Minn., St. Paul, 1985-88, N.Mex. State U. Hispanic Leadership Project, 1993-96, Radford Coll. for Global Studies, 1994; bd. dirs. Va. Tech. Intellectual Properties, Inc., 1994—; mem. adv. bd. The Egg Factory, 1998—; bd. dirs. agrl. devel. bd. Ohio State U., Columbus, 1987-93; mem. Coun. Entrepreneural Devel., spkr., 1995; spkr on biopesticides BioIndustry Conf., 1997. Capt. USMC, 1964-67, Vietnam. Decorated Cross of Gallantry with silver star (South Vietnam). Mem. Am. Chem. Soc. (speaker mktg. strategies 1988), Biotech. Industry Orgn. (spkr. 1997), Am. Phytopathology Soc., Golf Course Supts. Am., Coun. for Entrepreneurial Devel. Republican. Roman Catholic. Avocations: golf, gardening, hiking, church activities. Office: Techshare Inc 3558 Old Onslow Rd Greensboro NC 27407-7826

BANERJEE, (BIMAL), artist, educator; b. Calcutta, India, Sept. 4, 1939; naturalized, 1978; s. Dashurathee and Madhabilata B. Baccalaureate with 1st class honors, Indian Coll. Art, Calcutta, 1960; student, Coll. Art, New Delhi, 1965-67, Atelier 17, Paris, 1967-69, Ecole des Beaux-Arts, Paris, 1967-70, Pratt Inst., N.Y.C., 1969-72; studies with H.W. Jensen, NYU, 1976; Ed.M., M.A., Columbia U., 1978, Ed.D., 1988. Lectr. NAD, N.Y.C., 1969, Bloomfield (N.J.) Coll., 1980-81; lectr. Parsons Sch. Design/New Sch., N.Y.C, 1979, faculty, 1983-88; art therapist St. John's Episc. Hosp., Queens, N.Y., 1981-83; tchr., art cons. N.Y.C. Pub. Schs., 1984—; art tchr. Cath. High Sch., N.Y.C., 1987; lectr. Columbia U. Tchrs. Coll., N.Y.C., 1988—; guest lectr. Tchrs. Coll., Columbia U., 1984. Multi-media performance artist shows include Parsons Sch. Design/New Sch., 1986, Columbia U., 1978, 79, 84, Hofstra U., 1979, Just Above Midtown Gallery, N.Y.C., 1977, 78, Bertha Urdang Gallery, N.Y.C., 1976, Fremar Gallery, L.I., N.Y., 1974, Galerie du Haut Pave, Paris, 1968-69, Mcpl. Galeria, Levanto, Italy, 1968, Kumar Gallery, New Delhi, 1970, Arts & Prints Gallery, Calcutta, 1963, 64, Art Heritage Gallery, New Delhi, 1990, Chitrakoot Gallery, Calcutta, 1990, Bertha Urdang Gallery, N.Y.C., 1991, Chemould Gallery, Calcutta, 1993, Cite Internationale des Arts, Paris, 1994, 99, numerous others; internat. biennials in Paris, Tokyo, Rejika, Miami, Hawaii, Bradford, Eng., Biella, Ibiza, Triennale-India, Berlin Triennale, Joan Miro Drawing prize, Barcelona, Ljubljana, others; exhibited in 28 one-man shows, U.S., Europe and India; introduced new media Fumage and Carbontransfer; represented in permanent collections Mus. Modern Art, Paris, Mus. Modern Art, Barcelona, Spain, Mus. Fine Arts, Boston, Mus. Art, Iowa City, Mus. Modern Art de la Ville de Paris, Mus. Internat. of Electrography Art, Cuenca, Spain, Ctr. National d'Art Contemporain, Paris, Ministry Cultural Affairs, France, Neil Sack Gallery, Johannesburg, South Africa, Nat. Gallery Modern Art, New Delhi, Nat. Acad. Art, New Delhi, Essex Libr., London, The Pallas Gallery, London, Bibliothèque Nat., Paris, Honolulu Acad. Art, Rockefeller Bros. Found., N.Y.C., N.Y. Pub. Libr. Art Collection, N.Y.C., Bklyn. Mus., others; represented in pub. collections Mus. Modern Art, Paris, Mus. Modern Art, Barcelona, Mus. Fine Arts, Boston, Mus. Art, Iowa City, Mus. Modern Art de la Ville de Paris, Mus. Internat. Electrography Art, Cuenca, Spain, Centre National d'Art Contemporain, Paris, Min. Cultural Affairs, France, Neil Sack Gallery, Johannesburg, Nat. Gallery Modern Art, New Delhi, Nat. Acad. Art, New Delhi, Essex Libr., London, Pallas Gallery, London, Bibliotechque Nationale, Paris, Honolulu Acad. Art, Rockefeller Bros. Fund, N.Y.C., N.Y. Pub. Libr., N.Y.C., Bklyn. Mus. Inst. Arts and Scis., Bklyn., Bklyn. Mus., others; contbr. articles, poetry, short stories, children's lit. to profl. jours. Recipient awards Hawaii Biennial, 1971, 73, 79, Arthur Kaplan award, 1978, award Painters and Sculptors Soc., 1972, Culturelle Internat. award, Paris, 1968, Nat. award Nat. Art Acad., India, 1967, 70, State Acad. award Bengal State, and Punjab State, 1967, Statue of Victory world cultural prize Nat. Ctr. Study and Rsch., Salsomiggiore, Italy, 1984, also others; grantee Govt. of India, 1965-67, Govt. of France, 1967-70, Adolph and Esther Gottlieb Found., 1989. Mem. Mus. Modern Art, Found. for Community of Artists of N.Y.C., Coll. Art Assn. of Am., Print Club Philadelphia, World Print Council, Smithsonian Instn., Ancient Art—Paris. Home: Loft 2C 106 Ridge St New York NY 10002-2554 Office: Bertha Urdang Gallery 23 E 74th St New York NY 10021-2617

BANERJEE, AJOY KUMAR, engineer, constructor, consultant; b. Dacca, Bangladesh, Apr. 23, 1945; came to U.S., 1966; s. Kalidas and Anjali (Mukherjee) B.; m. Marjorie Burren; children: Shonali Misha, Monisha Jenni. B Tech. in Civil Engring. with honors, Indian Inst. Tech., Kharagpur, 1966; M of Engring., U. Detroit, 1967; PhD in Structural Engring., Cornell U., 1973. Registered profl. engr., N.Y., Mass., Va., Mo. V.p. Stone & Webster Internat., Boston, 1973-99; pres. Banerjee Cons. Inc., 1999—; dir. expansion Ariz. Pub. Svcs., 1999—; mem. Presdl. Del. to India and China. Contbr. articles to Nuclear Safety Jour., Nuclear Engring. and Design Jour., Jour. Structural Div. ASCE, Am. Nuclear Soc. Proceedings, ASME Proceedings. Fellow ASCE, ASME; mem. IEEE (com. on probabilistic risk assessment 1981-82), Am. Nuclear Soc. (power divsn. program com., vice chmn. tech. and pub. issues com.), Internat. Assn. Structural Mechanics in Reactor Tech., Nuclear Mgmt. and Resources Coun. (utility tech. group on life extension, alt. com. on design basis documentation). Achievements include development of programs and methodologies for nuclear power plant life extension and increasing power rating. Office: Ariz Pub Svcs PO Box 53999 Mail Sta 8983 Phoenix AZ 85072-1127

BANERJEE, MARIANNE HEAFIELD, systems analyst; b. Mt. Clemens, Mich., Sept. 14, 1967; d. David Edward and Patricia Ann (Kurth) H.; m. Aaron Nath Banerjee, July 21, 1990. BA in Math., Earlham Coll., 1989; MS in Math., So. Ill. U., Carbondale, 1992. Tchg. asst. So. Ill. U., Carbondale, 1990-91; part-time instr. math. Essex C.C., Balt., 1993-94; tutor advancement via individual determinatin Fairfax (Va.) County Pub. Schs., 1994-95, substitute tchr., 1997-98; tech. support specialist Computech, Bethesda, Md., 1995-96; sys. analyst AMI (Advanced Mgmt., Inc.), McLean, Va., 1997; quality control splst. The Assn. Software Co., Falls Church, Va., 1998; sys. analyst Marconi Systems Techs., Dahlgren, Va., 1998—. Home: 7620 Willow Point Dr Falls Church VA 22042-7530 Office: Marconi Systems Techs PO Box 381 Dahlgren VA 22448

BANERJEE, PRASHANT, industrial engineering educator; b. Calcutta, West Bengal, India, Apr. 15, 1962; came to U.S., 1986; s. Prabhat K. and Bani Banerjee; m. Madhumita Banerjee, Dec. 11, 1987; children: Jay, Ann. BSME, Indian Inst. Tech., Kanpur, India, 1984; MS in Indsl. Engring., Purdue U., 1987, PhD, 1990. Indsl. engr. Tata Steel Co., Jamshedpur, India, 1984-85; asst. prof. U. Ill., Chgo., 1990-96, assoc. prof., 1996—; cons. Caterpillar Inc., Peoria, Ill., 1992, Motorola Inc., 1994-97, Monsanto, Inc., 1996—. Author: Automation and Control of Manufacturing Systems, 1991, Object-oriented Technology in Manufacturing, 1992; contbr. articles to profl. jours. NSF rsch. grantee, 1992, 95, Nat. Inst. Standards and Tech. rsch. grantee, 1995. Mem. ASME, Inst. Indsl. Engrs., Inst. Mgmt. Scis., Soc. Mfg. Engrs. Avocations: sports, current events, religious discussions. Home: 197 Brookwood Ln W Bolingbrook IL 60440-5508 Office: Univ Ill Engring Dept Chicago IL 60607-7022

BANERJEE, SUJATA, telecommunications educator; b. Manchester, Eng., Sept. 11, 1966; parents Sanat K. and Debi Banerjee; m. Vibhu O. Mittal. BTech in Elec. Engring., Indian Inst. Tech., Bombay, 1987, MTech in Elec. Engring., 1988; PhD in Elec. Engring.-Sys., U. So. Calif., L.A., 1993. Asst. prof. U. Pitts., 1993—. Contbr. articles to profl. jours. Recipient Early Faculty Career award NSF, 1997. Mem. IEEE (assoc. editor Transactions on Reliability 1994—). Fax: (412) 624-2788. E-mail: sujata@tele.pitt.edu. Office: U Pitts SIS Bldg Rm 702 Pittsburgh PA 15260

BANERJI, RANAN BIHARI, mathematics and computer science educator; b. Calcutta, India, May 5, 1928; came to U.S., 1961, naturalized, 1969; s. Bijan Bihari and Setabja (Chatterji) B.; m. Purnima Purkayastha, July 8, 1954; children: Anindita Banerji Spielberg, Sunandita Banerji Ogawa. B.S., Patna U., 1947; M.S., Calcutta U., 1949, D.Phil., 1956. Research scholar Calcutta U., 1950-53, lectr., 1956; vis. asst. prof. Pa. State U., 1953-55; maintenance engr. Indian Statis. Inst., 1956-58; mem. faculty Case Western Res. U., 1958-74, prof. computer sci., 1968-74; prof. computer sci. Temple U., Phila., 1974-82; prof. math. and computer sci. St. Joseph's U., Phila., 1983-92; prof. emeritus St. Joseph's U., 5, 1993—; vis. prof. U. Paris, U. Vienna, U. Calcutta, Czech Tech. U.; asst. prof. engring. U. N.B., Can., 1959-61; cons. in field. Author: Theory of Problem Solving, 1969, Artificial Intelligence, 1980; (with M. Mesarovic) Non-numerical Problem Solving, 1969; (with A. Elithorn) Artificial and Human Intelligence, 1986, Formal Techniques in Artificial Intelligence, 1989;assoc. editor Elsevier Sci. Pubs., Amsterdam; reviewer computing, mathematics reviews; contbr. articles to profl. jours. Gold medalist univs. Patna and Calcutta. Fellow Am. Assn. Artificial Intelligence; mem. ACLU, Common Cause, Sci. within Consciousnes. Hindu Quaker. Home: N409 Haddon View Apts 1 MacArthur Blvd Westmont NJ 08108 Office: St Joseph's U Dept Math and Computer Sci 5600 City Ave Philadelphia PA 19131-1308 *It is my belief that the only successful actions by men and women are those done in selfless service to God. The rest, however laudable, are risky at best.*

BANET, CHARLES HENRY, academic administrator, clergyman; b. Ft. Wayne, Ind., Dec. 8, 1922; s. Henry Alexander and Cecilia Marie (Henry) B. Student, St. Charles Sem., 1949; BA, St. Joseph's Coll., 1950, LLD (hon.), 1991; AMLS, U. Mich., 1951; LittD (hon.), Calumet Coll. of St. Joseph, 1970; LLD (hon.), St. Joseph's Coll., 1991. Joined Soc. of Precious Blood, 1943; ordained priest Roman Cath. Ch., 1949. Librarian St. Joseph's Coll., Rensselaer, Ind., 1952-65, exec. v.p., 1964-65, pres., 1965-93, pres. emeritus, 1993—, also bd. dirs.; parochial vicar Holy Rosary Ch., Galveston, Tex., 1994—; vice provincial Soc. Precious Blood, 1965-69. Assoc. editor: Philosophy Today, 1957-88; author: Our Lady of Precious Blood in Art,

1961. Bd. dirs. Ind. Colls. Ind. Found., sec.-treas., 1973, pres. 1980-82, exec. com.; bd. dirs. Ind. Colls. Ind., pres. 1975-76, 77-78; pres. Ind. Conf. Higher Edn., 1978-79; dist. chair Boy Scouts of Am., 1981; Ind. Bicentennial Commr., 1973-79. Recipient Sparks-Jones award, 1977; named Sagamore of the Wabash, 1979, 85, 93, Ky. Col., 1985. Mem. Ind. Acad., Blue Key, Phi Beta Kappa, Beta Phi Mu, Alpha Lambda Delta. Home: Holy Rosary Church 1420 31st St Galveston TX 77550-4321

BANEY, JOHN EDWARD, insurance company executive; b. Pitts., May 27, 1934; s. James V. and Mathilda M. (McGary) B.; m. Joan A. McGrath, June 14, 1958; children: Jay E., Diane L., Timothy J. B.A., U. Pa., 1957; grad. Advanced Mgmt. Program, Harvard U., 1980. With trust dept. First Pa. Bank & Trust, Phila., 1957-58, Remington Rand, Phila., 1958-62; brokerage cons. Conn. Gen. Life Ins. Co., Phila., 1962-68; brokerage mgr. Conn. Gen. Life Ins. Co., Detroit, 1968-72; dir. agys. Conn. Gen. Life Ins. Co., Hartford, 1972-73; v.p. brokerage div. Hartford, 1973-77, v.p. career agts. div., 1977-82; pres. bd. dirs. CG Equity Sales Co., Bloomfield, Conn., 1973, 82; sr. v.p. adminstrv. services Employee Benefits Group, 1982-83; pres. broker div. INA a CIGNA Co., Phila., 1983-85, pres. Internat. & Broker div., 1985-90; pres. J.E. Baney Holdings, Phila., 1990—; exec.-in-residence Baylor U., 1976; CEO, chmn. Underwriters Capital (Merrett) Ltd., 1993-95; bd. dirs. Montgomery and Collins, Inc., Boston, United Nat. Ins. Group; pres. Am. Excess Inc. Assn., 1987-88. Mem. exec. com. Hartford Whalers Hockey Team, 1976-78; bd. dirs. Birmingham (Mich.) YMCA, 1970-71, Found. New Am. Music, 1982—; trustee Hartford Grad. Ctr., 1981-83; trustee, chmn. bd. mgrs. Moore Coll. Art, 1988—. With U.S. Army Res., 1958-64. Mem. Am. Coun. Life Ins., CLU Assn., Quechee Club, Union League, Phila. Country Club, Merion Cricket Club, Ocean Reef Club. Republican. Roman Catholic. Home: PO Box 1122 Quechee VT 05059-1122

BANEY, RICHARD NEIL, physician, internist; b. Phila., Apr. 13, 1937; s. Robert Emmet and Mary Elizabeth (Hedges) B.; m. Carolyn Vern Kurey, Feb. 17, 1962; children: Richard N. Jr., Michael D., Marisa V., Brian E. BS, Georgetown U., 1958; MD, U. Pitts., 1963. Diplomate Am. Bd. Internal Medicine, Am. Bd. Rheumatology. Intern VA & Parkland Hosp., Dallas, 1963-64; resident U. Pitts., 1967-70; internist Jess Parrish Hosp., Titusville, Fla., 1971-76; chief med. staff Jess Parrish Hosp., Titusville, 1974-76; internist Melbourne (Fla.) Internal Med. Assocs., Holmes Regional Med Ctr., 1976-95; sr. v.p. med. affairs Holmes Regional Med. Ctr., Melbourne, Fla., 1995-96; CEO Health First Physicians, 1995-98; ret., 1998; trustee Holmes Regional Med. Ctr., Melbourne, 1984-95; founding dir., chmn. bd. dirs. Reliance Bank Fla., Melbourne, 1985-95; founding dir., chmn. bd. Bank Brevard, 1996—. Trustee Fla. Inst. Tech., Melbourne, 1989—, mem. exec. com., 1987—, vice chmn. bd. trustees, 1991—; pres. Canaveral chpt. Am. Heart Assn., Rockledge, Fla., 1973-74; chmn. bd. trustees Sea Pines Rehab. Hosp., Melbourne, 1992-94. Med. officer, lt. comdr. USN, 1964-67. Fellow ACP; mem. Am. Coll. Rheumatology, Am. Coll. Physicians Execs., Brevard County Med. Soc. (pres. 1977-78), Navy League U.S., Eau Gallie Yacht Club (commodore 1985-86), Coast Club (bd. dirs. 1985-91, chmn. bd. 1989-91). Republican. Avocations: jogging, bicycling, travel, collecting antique maps, golf.

BANG, MARY JO, poet; b. Oct. 22, 1946. BA in Sociology, Northwestern U., Evanston, Ill., 1971, MA, 1975; BA in Photography, Westminster U., London, 1989; MFA, Columbia U., 1998. Poetry co-editor Boston Rev., 1995—; contbr. poerty to lit. publs. Recipient Bakeless prize, 1996, New Writers award Gt. Lakes Colls. Assn., 1998. E-mail: maryjobang@aol.com.

BANGASSER, RONALD PAUL, physician; b. Freeport, Ill., Jan. 25, 1950; s. Paul Francis and Florence (Ihm) B.; m. Susan Marie Andretta, June 19, 1971; children: Debra, Sandi. BA, Northwestern U., Chgo., 1971; MD, Chgo. Med. Sch., 1975. Physician Valley Family Med., Yucaipa, Calif., 1978-93; physician Beaver Med. Group, Redlands, 1993—, med. dir., 1997—; med. dir. San Bernardino Found. for Med. Care, 1984-89, Redlands Med. Group, Redlands, Calif., 1986-92, Calif. Found. for Med. Care, San Francisco, 1991-94, Beaver Med., Redlands, 1997—; com. mem. CMA, San Francisco, 1991-95, LOPAC, San Bernardino, 1992-99, Leg Affairs Commn., San Francisco, 1994—; bd. dirs. CAL PAC, San Francisco, 1990-96. Bd. dirs. Blue Shield of Calif., 1998—. Mem. Calif. Med. Assn. (bd. dirs. 1995—, vice spkr. 1999—, exec. com. 1999—). Republican. Roman Catholic. Avocations: scuba diving, skiing, swimming, hiking. Home: 12724 Valley View Ln Redlands CA 92373-7632 Office: Beaver Med Group 242 Cajon St Redlands CA 92373-5202

BANGEL, HERBERT K., lawyer; b. Norfolk, Va., May 29, 1928; m. Carolyn Kroskin; children: Nancy Jo, Brad J. BS in Commerce, U. Va., 1947, JD, 1950. Bar: Va. 1949, U.S. Dist. Ct. (ea. dist.) Va., U.S. Ct. Appeals (4th cir.), U.S. Tax Ct., U.S. Bd. Immigration Appeals, D.C., U.S. Supreme Ct. Ptnr. Bangel, Bangel & Bangel, Portsmouth, Va., 1950—; bd. dirs. Portsmouth Enterprises, Inc., Dominion Bank Greater Hampton Roads, Tidewater Profl. Sports Inc.; substitute judge Portsmouth Gen. Dist. Ct., 1979-84; mem. U.S. Ct. Appeals (4th cir.) Jud. Conf. Commr. Eastern Va. Med. Authority (named changed to Med. coll of Hampton Rds.), 1983-91, vice chmn., 1987-88; pres., chmn. Portsmouth Area United Fund, 1971-73; bd. dirs. Portsmouth Indsl. Found., 1968-90, bd. dirs. Urban League Tidewater (Va.), 1978-79, Tidewater chpt. Am. Heart Assn., 1983-84, Portsmouth Community Trust Distbn. Com., 1977-87, chmn., 1985-86; bd. dirs. Maryview Hosp., 1969-87; trustee Portsmouth-Chesapeake Area Found., 1968-72, United Community Funds and Councils Va., 1970-71, others; chmn. Portsmouth Redevel. and Housing Authority, 1977-83. Named First Citizen, City of Portsmouth, 1974. Mem. ABA, Va. Bar Assn., Portsmouth Bar Assn. (pres. 1964), Norfolk Bar Assn., Tidewater Trial Lawyers Assn. (bd. dirs. 1968-73), Va. Trial Lawyers Assn. (bd. govs. 1970), Assn. Trial Lawyers Am., Suburban Country Club (pres. 1961-62), Oceans Club (bd. dirs. 1973-76), Town Point Club (bd. govs. 1983—), Portsmouth Sports Club, Moose, Elks, B'nai B'rith. Democrat. Jewish. Home: 1 Crawford Pkwy Apt 1702 Portsmouth VA 23704-2613 Office: Bangel Bangel & Bangel PO Box 760 Portsmouth VA 23705-0760

BANGERTER, VERN, secondary education educator. Physics tchr. Timpview High Sch., Provo, Utah, 1978—. Named Utah State Tchr. of Yr., 1993. Office: Timpview High Sch 3570 N 650 E Provo UT 84604-4675

BANGS, CATE (CATHRYN MARGARET BANGS), film production designer, interior designer; b. Tacoma, Mar. 16, 1951; d. Henry Horan and Belva Virginia (Grandstaff) B.; m. Steve Gobin, Nov. 1, 1986 (div. 1999). Student, Hammersmith Coll Art and Bldg., London, 1971; BA cum laude, Pitzer Coll., 1973; MFA, NYU, 1978. Owner Flying Pencil Design, L.A., 1981—. Prodn. designer: Lucky Day, 1990; (TV series) My So Called Life, 1994, Fudge-A-Mania, 1994; set designer: (TV series) Picket Fences, 1995-96, (film) Home Alone 3, 1997, Midnight in the Garden of Good and Evil, 1997; art dir.: (film) Volcano, 1997; (TV) The Notorious, 1997, Nothing Sacred, 1997-98 (Emmy and SMPTAD nomination 1998), Charmed, 1998-99. Bd. dirs. Hollywood Heights Assn., 1985-87, Cahuenga Pass Property Owners Assn.,1990; 1st v.p. Friends of the Highland-Camrose Bungalow Village, 1985-97. Recipient Dramalogue Critics award, 1983. Mem. Soc. Motion Picture and TV Art Dirs. (cert.; exec. bd. 1997-99), Set Designers and Model Makers (cert., exec. bd. 1980-99, v.p. 1989-91, pres. 1991-99), United Scenic Artists. Democrat. Buddhist. Home: 3180 Oakshire Dr Los Angeles CA 90068-1743

BANGS, F(RANK) KENDRICK, former business educator; b. Lostant, Ill., May 17, 1914; s. Mark Howard and Mary Hay (Henning) B.; m. Elizabeth Jane Paisley, May 19, 1944; children—John Kendrick, James Paisley. B.E., Ill. State Normal U., 1936; M.P.S., U. Colo., 1946; Ed.D., Ind. U., 1952. Tchr. bus. Rosiclare (Ill.) High Sch., 1936-37, Carmi (Ill.) High Sch., 1937-42; asst. prof. bus. adminstrn. U. Colo., Boulder, 1946-58; assoc. prof. U. Colo., 1958-64, prof., 1964-81, chmn. gen. bus. div., 1964-79; vis. prof. Coll. Bus., Ill. State U., Normal, 1979-80, 84, U. Tex-Austin, 1982, Southwestern La U., Lafayette, 1983, 85, 86, 87, U. Colo., 1987-88; cons. adminstrv. mgmt., small bus. Chmn. fin. stability bd. Colo. Pvt. Schs. Assn., 1977—. Contbr.: articles to Jour. Bus. Edn. Served with inf. U.S. Army, 1942-46. Decorated Bronze Star; recipient Robert L. Stearns award U. Colo. Alumni, 1976; John Robert Gregg award Gregg div. McGraw-Hill Pub. Co., 1978. Mem. Mountain-Plains Bus. Edn. Assn. (pres. 1958-59, Leadership award 1967-68), Nat. Bus. Edn. Assn. (co-editor yearbook 1975, nat. pres. 1967-68), Adminstrv. Mgmt. Soc. (pres. Denver chpt. 1963-64, Diamond Merit award 1967), Colo. Bus. Edn. Assn. (pres. 1956-57), Beta Gamma Sigma, Delta Pi Epsilon (nat. pres. 1968-69, pres. Research Found. 1979—). Presbyterian. Club: Rotary (Boulder). Home: 4840 Thunderbird Dr Apt 188 Boulder CO 80303-3829

BANGS, JOHN KENDRICK, lawyer, foundation executive, former chemical company executive; b. Fairfield, Iowa, Nov. 7, 1920; s. William Henry and Edna (Weller) B.; m. Elizabeth Harlow, Dec. 16, 1944; children—John Harlow, Amy Elizabeth, Gregory William. A.B., U. Iowa, 1942; JD, Columbia, 1948. Bar: N.J. 1948, U.S. Supreme Ct. 1968. Assoc. firm Crummy & Consodine, Newark, 1948-52; atty. W.R. Grace & Co., N.Y.C., 1952-59, asst. sec., 1956-59; atty. Shulton, Inc., Clifton, N.J., 1959-73, sec., gen. counsel, 1963-73, v.p., 1967-73; also dir.; sec. exec. com., asst. sec. Am. Cyanamid Co., Wayne, N.J., 1973-78, sec., 1978-85; trustee, counsel The Schultz Found., Verona, N.J., 1985-91. Served to lt. USNR, 1942-45. Mem. Sigma Nu. Republican. Methodist.

BANGS, JOHN WESLEY, III, law enforcement administrator; b. Phila., Dec. 26, 1941; s. John Wesley Jr. and Sarah Emily (Morcom) B.; m. Donna Louise McClanahan, June 1, 1963; children: Louis M., Terry M., John W. IV. AA summa cum laude, E. Los Angeles Coll., 1976. Calif. Commn. on Peace Officer Standards and Training: Basic, Intermediate, Advanced, Supervisory, Mgmt. Police officer Los Angeles Police Dept., 1964-70, sgt., 1970-74, lt., 1974-84; chief spl. officer I L.A. World Airports, Airport Police Bur., 1988—, L.A. Internat. Airport, 1988—; lectr. U. So. Calif., 1978-79. Author: Narcotics Overview, 1983, Psychological Evaluation for Police Candidates, 1969. Cub master Cub Scouts Am., Ontario, Calif., 1968; scout master Boy Scouts Am., Ontario, 1971; explorer leader Explorer Scouts Am., Los Angeles, 1976; mem. Greater Los Angeles Scouting Council, 1976. Sgt. U.S. Army, 1959-62. Mem. Internat. Assn. Chiefs of Police, Calif. Peace Officers Assn., Calif. Narcotics Officers, Los Angeles Police Protective League, Los Angeles Police Relief Assn. Republican. Episcopalian. Avocations: fishing, boating, breeding German shepherd dogs. Office: LA Airport Police 1 World Way Los Angeles CA 90045-5803

BANGS, WILL JOHNSTON, lawyer; b. N.Y.C., Oct. 7, 1923; s. Lawrence Cutler and Alma Elizabeth (Johnston) B.; m. Judith Esther Lindhal, July 27, 1957; children: Marjorie Elizabeth, Martha Ellen Alice. BA, Middlebury Coll., 1948; LLB, U. Mich., 1953. Bar: Mass. 1953, U.S. Dist. Ct. (Mass. dist.) 1955, U.S. Supreme Ct. 1973. Staff atty. Liberty-Mut. Ins. Co., Boston, 1953-56; sr. ptnr. Choate, Hall & Stewart, Boston, 1956—. Mem. fin. com., Concord, Mass., 1968-70; mem. Carlisle (Mass.) Conservation Commn., 1972-78, Carlisle Town Rep. Com., 1982-89. With U.S. Army, 1943-46. Fellow Am. Coll. Trial Lawyers; mem. ABA, Boston Bar Assn., Somerset Club, Concord Country Club. Home: 119 Bingham Rd Carlisle MA 01741-1537 Office: Exchange Pl 53 State St Boston MA 02109-2804

BANGSUND, EDWARD LEE, former aerospace company executive, consultant; b. Two Harbors, Minn., July 16, 1935; s. Ilo Henry and Hildur Margaret (Holter) B.; m. Caryl Ann Billingsley, Oct. 10, 1956; children: Julie Ann, Trina Lee, John Kirk, Edward Eric. BME, U. Wash., 1959. With Boeing Co., 1956-71; engr. Apollo program Boeing Co., Cape Kennedy, Fla., 1967-69, Houston, 1969-71; mgr. space vehicle design Space Systems div. Boeing Aerospace, Seattle, 1971-76, mgr. Inertial Upper Stage Futures, 1976-85, mgr. space transp., 1985-87, dir. strategic planning, 1987-90, dir. space mktg., 1990-95; pres., CEO BCA Enterprises, 1995—; cons. engring. Orbital Techs. Corp., 1995—. Contbr. articles to profl. publs.; patentee in field. Pres. Springbrook Parents Adv. Com., 1972-75; chmn. Citizens Budget Rev. Com., 1973-75, 76-78, Citizens Facility Planning Com., 1977-78, Citizens for Kent (Wash.) Schs. Levy, 1974, 76; bd. dirs. Kent Youth Ctr., 1980-83; pres. Kent Sch. Bd., 1978-84. Named to Apollo-Saturn Roll of Honor, NASA, 1969; recipient Golden Acorn award Wash. Congress PTA, 1977, Vol. of Yr. award Kent Sch. Dist., 1977, 78. Fellow AIAA (assoc., mem. space systems tech. com. 1985-87, dep. dir. region VI 1986-89, chmn. space transp. tech. com. 1987-90, pub. policy com. 1989-94); mem. Internat. Acad. Astronautics, Internat. Astronautical Fedn. (chmn. space transp. exec. com. 1991-94), Nat. Space Found., Aerospace Industries Assn. (mem. space com. 1987-94, chmn. 1990-94), Space Bus. Roundtable (pres. Seattle chpt., bd. dirs. 1988-95), Boeing Mgmt. Assn. (vice chmn. 1990-91, chmn. 1993-94). Republican. Lutheran. Home and Office: 13611 SE 251st St Kent WA 98042-6631

BANIAK, SHEILA MARY, accountant; b. Chgo., Feb. 26, 1953; d. DeLoy N. and Ann (Pasko) Slade; m. Mark A. Baniak, Oct. 7, 1972 (div. Feb. 1994); 1 child, Heather Ann. Assocs. in Acctg., Oakton Community Coll., 1986; student, Roosevelt U., 1986—; MBA, North Park Coll., Chgo., 1995. Cert. enrolled agt. IRS; accredited tax adviser Accreditation Coun. Accountancy and Taxation. Owner, mgr. Baniak and Assocs., Chgo., Ill., 1984—; acct. Otto & Snyder, Park Ridge, 1984-87; spl. projects coordinator, supplemental instr. Oakton Community Coll., Des Plaines, Ill., 1986—; acctg. computer instr. Oakton Community Coll., Des Plaines, 1987—; adm. mem. acctg. Oakton C.C., Des Plaines, 1986—, cons., mem. Edn. Found., 1986—; instr. Ray Coll. Design, 1987—, dir. evening sch., 1994, fin. aid officer, Chgo. and Woodfield, 1994; mem. rsch. bd. advisors Am. Biog. Inst., Inc., 1988; tchr. fin. mgmt., retail math., bus. math., bus. computers, strategic retail mgmt. and econs.; part time coll. instr. commerce dept. Northwestern Bus. Coll., 1995—; asst. to interim fin. dir. Art Inst. Ill., 1995-96; acctg. and credit mgr. Fragomen, Delrey & Bernsen, P.C., 1996—. Author: A Small Business Collection Cycle Primer for Accountants, 1985, The Mathematics of Business, 1989. Ill. CPA Soc. scholar, 1984, Roosevelt U. scholar, 1986, Nat. Assn. Accts. scholar, 1985. Mem. Nat. Assn. Accts. (dir. community responsibility suburban Chgo. chpt. 1986—, speaker 1988, dir. profl. devel. seminars 1988, dir. communications 1989—), Nat. Assn. Tax Practitioners, Nat. Assn. Enrolled Agts., Ill. Soc. Enrolled Agts. (pres.; pres. N.W. Chgo. chpt. 1992, chmn. edn. 1990—). Home: 5718 W Cullom Ave Chicago IL 60634-1718

BANICH, MARIE T., psychology educator; b. N.Y.C., Aug. 6, 1957; d. John and Serafina (Fiore) B. BA, Tufts U., 1978; PhD, U. Chgo., 1985. From asst. prof. to assoc. prof. psychology dept. U. Ill., Champaign-Urbana, 1985-98, prof. psychology dept., 1998—; co-chair biol. intelligence maj. rsch. theme Beckman Inst., U. Ill., Urbana, 1994—. Author: (book) Neuropsychology, 1997. Beckman fellow Ctr. for Advanced Study, U. Ill., 1989; univ. scholar U. Ill., 1996. Avocations: tennis, hiking. Office: U Ill 2161 Beckman Inst 405 N Mathews Ave Urbana IL 61801-2325

BANIK, DOUGLAS HEIL, marketing executive; b. Camden, N.J., May 21, 1947; s. Wilmer Harry and Marie Grace (Heil) B.; m. Marcia Lynne Knotts, Jan. 31, 1981 (div. June 1986); children: Shannon Danae Vezina, Corey Jamison Vezina; m. Lauren Clark Abbe, Oct. 4, 1986; 1 child, Mark Mitchell Banik. AB, Harvard U., 1969; MA, U. Pa., 1970, PhD, 1973. Asst. prof. psychology Wellesley (Mass.) Coll., 1973-76; assoc. dir. rsch. Benton & Bowles, N.Y.C., 1976-79; v.p. rsch. Advt. Rsch. Found., N.Y.C., 1979-81; v.p., assoc. dir. rsch. Saatchi & Saatchi Compton, N.Y.C., 1981-83; v.p., dir. mktg. rsch. Ogilvy & Mather, L.A., 1983-86; sr. v.p., dir. rsch. and strategic planning D'Arcy Masius Benton & Bowles, Chgo., 1987-90, dir. strategic svcs., 1990-93, dir. strategy, 1993-94; ind. cons. mktg. strategy, 1995-96; program mgr. Worldwide Comm. Rsch. IBM Corp., 1996—; cons. Med. Ctr., U. Calif., Davis, 1986, Columbia Pictures, Inc., Studio City, Calif., 1987; mem. gov.'s task force on telecomm., 1992. Editor: Jour. Advt. Rsch., 1979-80. Pres. Roosevelt Island Resident's Assn., N.Y.C., 1979-81; mem. com. infants, children, pregnant and lactating mothers White House Conf. on Nutrition Edn., 1979; pres. Garibaldi Sq. Homeowners Assn., Chgo., 1991. Merit scholar Harvard U., 1965-69; Nat. Sci. Found. fellow U. Pa., 1969-73. Avocations: motorcycling, sailing, photography, marine biology. Office: IBM Corp Rt 100 Somers NY 10589

BANIK, SAMBHU NATH, psychologist; b. Joypara, India, Nov. 7, 1935; s. Padma L. and Kadambini B.; BSc, Calcutta U., 1956, MSc, 1958; PhD, Bristol U., 1964; m. Promila Roy, Nov. 16, 1968; children: Sharmila, Kakali. Staff psychologist Des Moines Child Guidance Center, 1965; sr. psychologist, dir. internship tng. Univ. Hosp. Saskatoon, Sask., Can., 1965-69; dir. psychol. services, 1969-71; asst. chief mental health svcs. Glenn Dale Hosp. and D.C. Village, 1971-81; chief South Cmty. Mental Health Center, Washington, 1981-84, chief child and youth svcs., 1984-88, clin. adminstr. NE/SE Family Ctr., Washington, 1988—; pres. Family Diagnostic and Therapeutic Ctr., Washington, 1993—; exec. dir. Pres.'s Com. on Mental Retardation HHS, Washington, 1990-93, cons. psychologist, 1993—; pres. Banik and Assocs. Family Diagnostic and Therapeutic Ctr., 1993—; v.p. devel., chmn. Third World Found., 1993—; asst. prof. U. Sask., 1965-71; vis. prof. Bowie State Coll. (Md.), 1972-81, Thakur Hariprasad Inst., India, 1994. Mem. nat. adv. coun. drug abuse, 1987-90; mem. advisory bd. ARC, Washington, 1987-90; founder, pres. Prabashi, Inc., 1974-78, Assn. Indians in Am., 1980-84; pres. U.S.-Asia Found., 1995—; v.p. India Cultural Coordinating Com., 1979-80; sec. gen. Asian Pacific Am. Cultural Heritage Council, 1981-82; treas. Asian Pacific Am. Heritage Council, 1982-84; mem. spl. com. 3d Conv. Asian Indians in N.Am., 1984, chmn. Indian Am. Forum Polit. Edn., Md., 1986-88, 94—; chmn. Third World Found. 1993—; advisory bd. Ednl. India Found., Inc., 1993—, Commonwealth Assn. for the Mentally Handcapped and Developmental Dis., 1992—; chmn. Internat. Cooperation and Coordinating Com. 11th World Congress on Mental Retardation, 1993-94, Bd. Trustees, Woodley House, Wash. D.C., Pub. Mem, Svc., Personel, Review Bd., Wash. D.C., 1996; commr. Commn. People with Disabilities, Montgomery County. Recipient Dept. Humanitarian Svcs. award D.C., 1986, Cmty. Svcs. award Assn. Indians in Am., 1987, Citizen award Mayor of Balt., Ramkamal Sinha Meml. Gold medal, 1994, Excellence in Human Svc. award Bangalore 1994, Cmty. Svc. award U.S. Asia Found., 1995. Mem. APA, Am. Group Psychotherapy Assn., D.C. Psychol. Assn., Internat. Acad. Forensic Psychology, Nat. Health Svcs. Providers in Psychology. Contbr. articles to profl. jours.ticles to profl. jours. Home: 8606 Bradmoor Dr Bethesda MD 20817-3633

BANISTER, JUDITH, demographer, educator; b. Washington, Sept. 10, 1943; d. William Price and Helen Barbara (Myers) B.; m. Kim Woodard, Dec. 17, 1966; children: Adrian Banard, Dawn Banard. BA in History, Swarthmore Coll., 1965; PhD in Demography, Stanford U., 1978. Postdoctoral rsch. fellow East-West Population Inst., Honolulu, 1978-80; statistician/demographer U.S. Bur. of Census, Washington, 1980-82; chief China br. Ctr. for Internat. Rsch., 1982-92, Washington, 1992-94; part-time prof. George Washington U., Washington, 1981-92; prof. demography divsn. social sci. Hong Kong U. Sci. and Tech., 1997—. *Judith Banister and her husband began studying China and Chinese language in thelate 1960s during China's "Cultural Revolution". In 1971 they joined the first U.S. student group to visit China in decades. The delegation met Premier Chou Enlai, who explained the Chinese Government's decision to invite President Nixon. Banister subsequently focused on the demography of China and Asia in her Stanford University Ph.D. program, at the U.S. Census Bureau International Programs Center, and now at the Hong Kong University of Science & Technology. Her current research is about migration, mortality, population and environment in China including Hong Kong.* Author: China's Changing Population, 1987, Vietnam Population Dynamics and Prospects, 1993; co-author: The Population of North Korea, 1992, Human Dimensions of Asian Security, 1996; contbr. articles to profl. jours. Mem. Population Assn. Am., Internat. Union for Sci. Study of Population, Assn. Asian Studies, Hong Kong Sociol. Assn. Fax: (852) 2335 0014. E-mail: SOJB@UST.HK. Office: Hong Kong U Sci & Tech, Rm 3385 Acad Bldg, Clear Water Bay Kowloon Hong Kong

BANJOKO, ALIMI AJIMON, financial planner; b. Mona, St. Andrew, Jamaica, Nov. 11, 1954; came to U.S., 1980; s. Alton Alex and Martha Naomi (Needham) Harvey; m. Garnett Marlene St. Clair Clarke, Jan. 19, 1980; children: Che Lafianu, Pryha Krist-Loyé, Mikal Alaiye. BA (hons.), U. of the West Indies, Mona, 1978; MA, Bklyn. Coll., 1992; diploma law, U. Wolverhampton, 1997. CFP; registered investment advisor. Adminstrv. officer Ministry of Fgn. Affairs, Kingston, Jamaica, 1979; account exec., registered rep. John Hancock Cos., Boston, 1981-83; pres. PFS Group Inc., Bklyn., 1983—. Author: The Theory of Organic Capital Formation, 1996; host It's Your Money, 1993-94. Co-prodr. (video) The Way to Wealth, 1998. Organizer 6th Congl. Dist. Rainbow Coalition, Far Rockaway, N.Y., 1984; chmn. Capital Investment Plan, First Ch. of God, Far Rockaway, 1986-90, trustee, 1985-87; mem. Allen AME, Jamaica, N.Y., 1990—; co-founder Lignum Vitae Soc., 1992—. Mem. Inst. Cert. Fin. Planners, N.Y. Civil Air Patrol. Avocations: internat. politics, swimming, nature walking, flying. Office: PFS Group Inc 5306 Church Ave Brooklyn NY 11203-3609

BANK, MARJI D., actress; b. Dallas, Sept. 22, 1923; d. John and Rose (Kaufman) Doctoroff; m. Harvey Stuart Bank, Feb. 14, 1954 (dec. Dec. 1980); children: Roanne Bank, Heidi Sue Cairns. AA, U. Chgo., 1940; BS, Northwestern U., 1944. Performed at 24 theatres, including Kennedy Ctr., The Alley, Mo. Rep., Purdue U., Ind. Rep., Goodman Theater, Royal George Theatre, Ivanhoe Theatre, Peninsula Players, Northlight, Candlelight, Forum; lead actress in plays including Plaza Suite, 1973, Gingerbread Lady, 1973, Never Too Late, 1973, Promenade All, 1973, Man-in-the-Moon Marigolds, 1974, One Flew Over the Cuckoo's Nest, 1975, Saturday, Sunday, Monday, 1977, On Golden Pond, 1981, Driving Miss Daisy, 1988, Social Security, 1989, Lost in Yonkers, 1993; supporting credits include Shear Madness, 1982-99, The Perfect Ganesh, 1995, Uncle Vanya, 1990, Steel Magnolias, 1988, She Always Said Pablo, 1987, All My Sons, 1987, Les Belles Soeurs, 1982, Buried Child, 1980, The Big Knife, 1977, Hot L Balt., 1975, Streetcar named Desire, 1973, Our Town, 1973, Prisoner of 2d Ave, 1974, House of Blue Leaves, 1972, Cat on a Hot Tin Roof, 1970. Recipient Joseph Jefferson Best Prin. Actress award, 1993. Mem. SAG, AFTRA, Actor's Equity Assn., The Arts Club. Democrat. Jewish.

BANK, RON, principal. Prin. Jacoby Creek Elem. Sch., Bayside, Calif., 1982—. Recipient Elem. Sch. Recognition award U.S. Dept. Edn., 1989-90. Office: Jacoby Creek Elem Sch 1617 Old Arcata Rd Bayside CA 95524-9301*

BANKER, GILBERT STEPHEN, industrial and physical pharmacy educator, administrator; b. Tuxedo Park, N.Y., Sept. 12, 1931; s. Gilbert Miller and Mary Edna (Gladstone) B.; m. Gwenivere May Hughes, Mar. 31, 1956; children: Stephen, Susan, David, William. BS in Pharmacy, Union Coll., Albany, N.Y., 1953; MS, Purdue U., 1955, PhD, 1957. Research found. fellow Purdue U., West Lafayette, Ind., 1955-57, asst. prof. pharmacy, 1957-61, assoc. prof., 1961-64, prof., 1964-67, head indsl. and phys. pharmacy dept., from 1967; dean, prof. pharmacy U. Minn., Mpls., 1985-92; dean emeritus, disting. prof. drug delivery U. Iowa, Iowa City, 1992; in coop. tng. program Upjohn Co., Kalamazoo, 1958. Editor: Modern Pharmaceutics, 1970, 90, Pharmaceuticals and Pharmacy Practice, 1980, Pharmaceutical Dosage Forms: Dispense Systems, 1988, 2d edit., 1994; contbr. articles to profl. jours.; patentee in field. Recipient Outstanding Alumnus of Yr. award Albany Coll. Pharmacy-Union U., 1977, Disting. Alumni award Sch. Pharmacy and Pharmacal Scis. Purdue U., 1989. Fellow Acad. Pharm. Scis. (v.p. 1971-72), Am. Pharm. Assn. (Indsl. Pharmacy award 1971, ho. dels. 1977-80), Am. Assn. Advancement of Scis., Am. Assn. Pharm. Scis. (chair 1993-94); mem. Sigma Xi (pres. Purdue chpt. 1971-72), Rho Chi. Office: Univ of Iowa Coll of Pharmacy Iowa City IA 52242

BANKO, RUTH CAROLINE, retired library director; b. Phillipsburg, N.J., Mar. 28, 1931; d. Arthur William and Virginia Miller (Wilson) Osborn; m. Marvin Kenneth Banko (dec.); children: David, Sallie, Susan, Joseph, Elisabeth. Cert. libr. tech. asst., Northampton AreaC.C. Salesman Stanley Home Products, 1958-95; dir. Riegelsville (Pa.) Pub. Libr., 1974-97. Social ambudsman County Agy. on Aging, Doylestown, Pa.; asst. dir. Pearl Buck Found., Dublin, Pa.; mem. Riegelsville Fire Aux., 1992—; councilman, Planning Commn., Riegelsville Borough Coun., 1972-89; mem. States Legis. Com., 1972-88; mayor Borough of Riegelsville, 1990-97; disaster chmn., blood chmn., bd. mem. ARC, Doylestown, 1966-86; pres. jr. high and area coun. PTA, Easton, 1966-74; pres. Boro Coun., 1980-81; v.p., trustee Riegelsville Pub. Libr. Recipient award for svc. ARC, Doylestown. Mem. Pa. Boroughs Assn. (legis. com. 1972-97), Pa. Mayors Assn., Easton Area Coun. PTAs (life). Democrat. Lutheran. Home: 449 Easton Rd Riegelsville PA 18077-0223

BANKOFF, JOSEPH R., lawyer; b. Newark, Dec. 22, 1945. BS, Purdue U., 1967; JD, U. Ill., 1971. Bar: Ill. 1971, Ga. 1972. Law clk. to Hon. Walter P. Gewin U.S. Ct. Appeals (5th cir.), 1971-72; ptnr. King & Spalding, Atlanta. Asst. editor U. Ill. Law Forum, 1969-70. Mem. ABA, Ill. State Bar Assn., State Bar Ga., Atlanta Bar Assn., Nat. Inst. Trial Advocacy (trustee 1995—), Am. Law Inst., Order of Coif, Omicron Delta Kappa. Office: King & Spalding 191 Peachtree St NE Atlanta GA 30303-1740

BANKOFF, SEYMOUR GEORGE, chemical engineer, educator; b. N.Y.C., Oct. 7, 1921; s. Jacob and Sarah (Rashkin) B.; m. Elaine K. Forgash; children—Joseph, Elizabeth, Laura, Jay. BS, Columbia U., 1940, MS, 1941; PhD in Chem. Engring., Purdue U., 1952. Research engr. Sinclair Refining Co., East Chicago, Ind., 1941-42; process engr. du Pont Manhattan project U. Chgo., Richland, Wash., Arlington, N.J., 1942-48; asst. prof. dept. chem. engring. Rose Poly. Inst., Terre Haute, Ind., 1948-52; assoc. prof. Rose Poly. Inst., 1952-54, prof., chmn. dept. chem. engring., 1954-58; NSF sci. faculty fellow Calif. Inst. Tech., Pasadena, 1958-59; prof. chem. engring. Northwestern U., Evanston, Ill., 1959—; Walter P. Murphy prof. chem., mech. and nuclear engring. Northwestern U., 1971-92; prof. emeritus, 1992—; chmn. energy engring. council Northwestern U., 1975-80, chmn. Ctr. for Multiphase Flow and Transport, 1988—; vis. scientist Centre d'Etudes Nucléaires, Commissariat d'Energie Atomique, Grenoble, France, 1980; vis. prof. Imperial Coll. Sci. and Tech., London, 1985; cons. to U.S. Nuclear Regulatory Commn., 1974-87, Los Alamos Sci. Lab., 1974-89, Electric Power Research Inst., 1984-86, Westinghouse, 1984—, Savannah River Lab., duPont, 1987—, Korea Atomic Energy Research Inst., 1988; mem. adv. council Ams. for Energy Independence, Washington, 1978—; chmn. vis. com. Brookhaven Nat. Lab., 1984, engring. tech. div. Oak Ridge Nat. Lab., 1986; pres. SGB Assocs. Inc., 1986—. Mem. editl. adv. bd.: Internat. Jour. Multiphase Flow, 1975—, Nuc. Engring. and Design, 1984—; editor 6 vols. on heat transfer; contbr. 200 articles on rsch. in heat transfer and control theory to profl. jours. Recipient Max Jakob Meml. award AICE and ASME, 1987, Donald Q. Kern award AIChE, 1996, Outstanding Chem. Engr. award Purdue U., 1994; named Disting. Engring. Alumnus, 1971; Guggenheim fellow, 1966, Fulbright fellow, 1967, Internat. Ctr. Health and Mass Transfer, Yugoslavia. Fellow AICE (chmn. edn. com. 1968-71, chmn. heat transfer and energy conversion divsn. 1987, Robert E. Wilson Nuc. Chem. Engring. award 1994, Heat Transfer and Energy Conversion Divsn. award 1995), ASME; mem. Am. Nuclear Soc. (co-chmn. U.S. Sci. com., 9th Internat. Heat Transfer Conf., U.S. del. Internat. Heat Transfer Assembly), Nat. Acad. Engring. Achievements include co-invention of resistivity probe for void fraction measurement in gas-liquid flows; contbn. to theory of boiling heat transfer, vapor explosions, stratified condensing flows, stability of thin liquid films. Office: Northwestern Univ Chem Engring Dept Evanston IL 60208

BANKOWSKY, RICHARD JAMES, English educator; b. Wallington, N.J., Nov. 25, 1928. BA, Yale U., 1952; MA, Columbia U., 1954. Prof. English Calif. State U., Sacramento, 1959—. Author: A Glass Rose, 1958, After Penetcost, 1961, On a Dark Night, 1964, The Pale Criminals, 1967, The Barbarians at the Gates, 1972. Grantee Nat. Inst. Arts and Letters, 1964, Rockefeller Found., 1967. Office: Calif State U English Dept 6000 J St Sacramento CA 95819-2605

BANKS, ALBERT VICTOR, JR., government administrator; b. Harrisburg, Pa., Apr. 9, 1956; s. Albert Victor Sr. and Virginia Lee (Harris) B.; m. Judy Ann Williams, Jan. 22, 1984; children: Simóne Janae, Asha Victoria. AA in Psychology, Harrisburg Area C.C., 1976; BA in Urban Studies, Temple U., 1978; cert., Tufts U., 1986; MS, N.H. Coll., 1987. Lic. in real estate sales, Pa. From intern to devel. planner Adv. Cmty. Devel. Corp., Phila., 1976-80; housing program coordinator II Office Housing and Cmty. Devel., Phila., 1980-83; dir. cmty. devel. Livingston/Rosenwinkel, P.C. Architects & Planners, Phila., 1983-85; specialist econ. devel. Phila. Urban Coalition, 1985-87; program planning analyst II Phila. Housing Authority, 1987-91; dep. dir. cmty. and econ. devel. dept. City of Harrisburg, 1991-92; housing and devel. analyst Commonwealth of Pa., Harrisburg, 1992-94, planner econ. devel., 1994-96, mgmt. analyst, 1996—; realtor Coldwell-Banker, 1994-98, Howard Hanna/Detweiler, 1999—; cons. Phila. Comml. Devel. Corp., 1984-86, GMB Assocs., Phila., 1987, PGM Assocs., 1987, Phila. Care, 1988, Keating Constrn. Co., 1989, A.V. Banks Enterprises, 1990-91, Coleman Group, 1992, YMCA, Germantown; franchise owner Market Am., 1998; guest speaker Pa. State U. Author: (anthology) Voices, 1981. Vol. rschr. Phila. Unemployment Project, 1979; mem. bd. advisors Point Breeze Neighborhood Adv. Com. Phila., 1983; vol. instr. gen. equivalency diploma program Temple U., Phila., 1985; mem. Leadership Harrisburg, 1992—; pres. Edgmont Recreation Assn., 1992; bd. dirs. Harrisburg Multicultural Coalition, 1993-95; bd. mem. Harrisburg Area C.C. Alumni, 1994, v.p., 1997; bd. dirs. NAACP, 1994, chairperson Harrisburg chpt., 1995; fund distbn. vol. United Way, 1997-98. Recipient Liberty Bell award Mayor of Phila., 1982. Mem. Am. Planning Assn. (sec. 1982-85, co-chmn. program com. 1985-88, sec. nat. com. 1985-88), Am. Soc. Notaries, Inst. for Coop. Housing (bd. dirs., com. chmn. 1986-88), Nat. Assn. Redevel. Ofcls. (bd. dirs. 1982-83), Harrisburg Area C.C. Alumni Assn. (bd. dirs. 1994—, v.p. 1998—), Chapel of Four Chaplains (hon.), Alpha Phi Alpha. Methodist. Avocations: writing, hiking, biking, tennis, photography. Home: 6551 Lyters Harrisburg PA 17111-4626

BANKS, ALLAN RICHARD, artist, art historian, researcher; b. Dearborn, Mich., Feb. 15, 1948; s. Henry Selman and Lillian Margaret (Radovic) B.; children: Christine Marie, Aaron Richard; m. Holly Hope Tumblin, Jan. 1997. Ind. pvt. study, Soc. Arts and Crafts, Detroit, 1966-69; student, Atelier Lack, Inc., Mpls., 1970-73, R.H. Ives Gammell Studio, Williamstown, Mass., 1976. Artist, with studio in Newburg, N.Y., 1979-81, Huron, Ohio, 1981-87; portrait artist, with studio in Spring Hill, Fla., 1987-93; dir. Atelier of Plein Air, Safety Harbor, Fla., 1993—; lectr./demonstrator Portraits South, Inc., Raleigh, N.C., 1993, Atelier LeSueur, Mpls., 1995. Exhibited in group shows Sotheby's, N.Y.C., 1997, Guild of Boston Artists, 1996, 20th Century Exhbn., Amarillo Tex.-Springville, Utah, 1982, Butler Inst. Am. Art, Vixseboxse Art Galleries, Cleve., Salmagundi Club, Amarillo (Tex.) Art Ctr., Maryhill Mus. Art, Goldendale, Wash., Historic East-West Russia Exhibit, 1996, others; represented in collections at Wadsworth Athenaeum, Newark Art Mus., Montclair (N.J.) Mus., Hamilton Fish Meml. Libr., Nat. Portrait Gallery/Smithsonian. Trustee Mus. Natural History, Safety Harbor, 1995—; mem. Downtown Bus. Assn., Inc., Safety Harbor, 1994—. Elizabeth T. Greenshields Found. fellow, Montreal, 1972, 73; John and Anna Stacey Found. grantee, N.Mex., 1979, Ohio Arts Coun. grantee. Mem. Am. Soc. Classical Realism (pres. 1997—), Met. Mus. Art, Appleton Mus. Art (Ocala, Fla.), Salmagundi Club, New Am. Acad. Ard. Lutheran. Avocations: travel, museums. Home: PO Box 233 Safety Harbor FL 34695-0233

BANKS, AUBREY, architect, educator; b. Chgo., July 30, 1926; s. William James Sr. and Marguerite (Crooks) B.; m. Barbara Ann Every. BA in Architecture, U. Ill., 1950. Designer Edwin Bruno, Architect, Skokie, Ill., 1950; asst. dept. architecture U. Ill., Chgo., 1951-52; apprentice Frank Lloyd Wright, Spring Green, Wis., 1952-59; mem. architecture faculty Frank Lloyd Wright Sch. Architecture, Spring Green, Wis., 1959-88; architect E. John Kapp & Assocs., Madison, Wis., 1988-95; self-employed architect Madison, 1995—. Bd. mem. Friends of Monona Terrace, Madison, 1955-98. Mem. AIA, Internat. Solar Energy Soc., Am. Solar Energy Soc. Office: Architecture Network Inc 116 E Dayton St Madison WI 53703-2114

BANKS, CHARLES AUGUSTUS, III, manufacturing executive; b. 1940. BA in Internat. Rels., Brown U., 1962. With Cameron Brown Co., 1965-67; with Ferguson Enterprises Inc., Newport News, Va., 1967—, pres., COO, 1989-93, pres., CEO, 1993—. Office: Ferguson Enterprises Inc 12500 Jefferson Ave Newport News VA 23602-4314*

BANKS, CHERRY ANN MCGEE, education educator; b. Benton Harbor, Mich., Oct. 11, 1945; d. Kelly and Geneva (Smith) McGee; m. James A. Banks, Feb. 15, 1969; children: Angela Marie, Patricia Ann. BS, Mich. State U., 1968; MA, Seattle U., 1977, EdD, 1991. Tchr. Benton Harbor Pub. Sch., 1968; staff assoc. Citizens Edn. Ctr. N.W., Seattle, 1984-85; edn. specialist Seattle Pub. Schs., Seattle, 1985-87; pres. Edn. Material and Svcs. Ctr., Edmonds, Wash., 1987—; asst. prof. edn. U. Wash., Bothell, 1992-96, assoc. prof. edn., 1996—; cons. Jackson (Miss.) Pub. Schs., 1988, Seattle Pub. Schs., 1988-90, Little Rock Pub. Schs., 1989, Scott Foreman Pub. Co., Glenview, Ill., 1992—; vis. asst. prof. Seattle U., 1991-92. Co-author: March Toward Freedom, 1978, Teaching Strategies for the Social Studies, 1999; co-editor: Multicultural Education: Issues and Perspectives, 1989, rev. edits., 1993, 97; assoc. editor Handbook of Rsch. on Multicultural Edn.; contbr. chpts. to books. Mem. Jack and Jill Am., Seattle, 1978-94, First AME Headstart Bd., Seattle, 1981-83; trustee Shoreline C.C., Seattle, 1983-95; bd. dirs. King County Campfire, Seattle, 1985-88. Recipient Outstanding Commitment and Leadership of C.C. award Western Region Nat. Coun. on Black Am. Affairs, 1989. Mem. ASCD, Nat. Coun. for Social Studies Programs Com. (vice chairperson Carter G. Woodson Book award com. 1991-92, chair person 1992-93, mem. nominating com.), Am. Rsch. Assn., The Links, Inc., Phi Delta Kappa (founding, Seattle U. chpt.), Alpha Kappa Alpha. Avocations: tennis, swimming, reading, traveling. Office: U Wash Edn Program 22011 26th Ave SE Bothell WA 98021-4900

BANKS, DAVID R., health products executive; b. Harrison, Ark.. BA, U. Ark. CEO Leisure Lodges, Inc., also chmn. bd. dirs.; pres. Beverly Enterprises, Inc., Ft. Smith, Ark., 1979-89, CEO, 1989, also chmn. bd. dirs.; Bd. dirs. Ralston-Purina Co., Wellpoint Health Networks, Nationwide Health Properties, Inc. Office: 1200 S Waldron Rd Fort Smith AR 72903

BANKS, DAVID RUSSELL, health care executive; b. Arcadia, Wis., Feb. 15, 1937; s. J.R. and Cleone B.; married; children: Melissa, Michael. B.A., U. Ark., 1959. Vice pres. Dabbs, Sullivan, Trulock, Ark., 1963-74; chmn., chief exec. officer Leisure Lodges, Ft. Smith, Ark., 1974-77; registered rep. Stephens Inc., Little Rock, 1974-79; pres., CEO Beverly Enterprises, Ft. Smith, Ark., 1979—, chmn. bd., dir., 1990-99, pres., CEO, 1999—; dir. Nat. Council Health Centers, Pulaski Bank, Little Rock. Served with U.S. Army. Office: Beverly Enterprises Inc 5111 Rogers Ave Ste 40-a Fort Smith AR 72919-9002*

BANKS, DEIRDRE MARGARET, church organization administrator; b. Melbourne, Australia, May 9, 1934; came to U.S., 1975; d. Haldane Stuart and Vera Avice (Fisher) B. MA, Simpson Coll., 1980. Missionary nurse Leprosy Mission, Kathmandu, Nepal, 1960-69; dean of women Melbourne Bible Inst., 1970-75; asst. to dir. Bible Study Fellowship, Oakland, Calif., 1975-79; dir. adult ministries First Covenant Ch., Oakland, 1980-87; assoc. pastor for adults, First Covenant Ch., St. Paul, 1987-89; exec. dir. Covenant Women Ministries, Chgo., 1989-99. Chairperson ch. edn. bd. Pacific S.W. Conf. Evang. Ch., 1985-87, Gilead Group, Oakland, 1985-87; bd. dirs., chairperson Gilead Group Housing for Abused and Homeless Women and Children; bd. chmn. Barnabas Project for Abused and Homeless Women and Children, 1990-93; mem. bd. world mission Evang. Covenant Ch., 1986-89; bd. Covenant Enabling Residences Inc. for Developmentally Disabled Adults, pres., 1996-98. Mem. Evangel. Covenant Ch. Office: Evang Covenant Ch 5101 N Francisco Ave Chicago IL 60625-3611

BANKS, ERIC KENDALL, lawyer; b. St. Louis, Aug. 21, 1955; s. Willie James Banks Jr. and Grace (Kendall) Palmer; children: Brittany Renee, Bryson Kendall. BSBA, U. Mo., St. Louis, 1977; JD, U. Mo., Columbia, 1980. Bar: Mo. 1980, Ill. 1988, U.S. Dist. Ct. (we. dist.) Mo. 1980, U.S. Dist. Ct. (ea. dist.) Mo. 1984, U.S. Ct. Appeals (8th cir.) 1984, U.S. Ct. Appeals (D.C. cir.) 1998, U.S. Tax Ct. 1988, U.S. Supreme Ct. 1996. Asst. gen. counsel Mo. Pub. Svc. Commn., Jefferson City, 1980-84; asst. atty. Office Circuit Atty., St. Louis, 1984-87; pvt. practice, St. Louis, 1987-91, Clayton, Mo., 1991-92; corp. counsel Siegel-Robert, St. Louis, 1992-97; city counselor City of St. Louis, 1997-99; ptnr. Thompson, Coburn, 1999—, Thompson Coburn, St. Louis, 1999—; adj. prof. civil law St. Louis U. Law Sch., 1987-92, Washington U. Sch. law, 1991; sec. bd. dirs. Black Leadership Tng. Program, St. Louis, 1975-77. Sec. bd. dirs. Wesley House Assn.; bd. trustees Mo. U. Law Sch. Found. St. Louis Met. Leadership Program fellow, 1975-77. Mem. ABA (labor and employment com.), Nat. Bar Assn., Bar Assn. Met. St. Louis, Mo. Bar Assn. (adminstrv. law com., com. counsel), Mound City Bar Assn., Bar Assn. Met. St. Louis. Lutheran. Club: Toastmasters Internat. (adminstrv. v.p. 1983, William Tellman award 1982). Avocations: karate, reading, photography, public speaking, community work. Fax: (314) 552-7256. E-mail: ebanks@thompsoncoburn.com. Home: 2755 Russell Blvd Saint Louis MO 63104-2137 Office: Thompson Coburn One Mercantile Ctr Saint Louis MO 63101

BANKS, ERNEST (ERNIE BANKS), retired professional baseball player; b. Dallas, Jan. 31, 1931; s. Eddie B. Student, Northwestern U. Baseball player Kansas City Monarchs (Negro Am. League), 1950-51, 53; baseball player Chgo. Cubs, 1953-71, mgr. group sales, to 1982, 1st base coach, to 1989; spokesperson New World Van Lines, 1984—; now ret.; formerly co-owner, v.p. Bob Nelson-Ernie Banks Ford, Inc., Chgo.; with Associated Films Promotions, L.A., 1982-84. Author: (with Jim Enright) Mr. Cub. Past mem. bd. Chgo. Transit Authority; active Boy Scouts Am., YMCA. Served with AUS, 1951-53, Europe. Named most valuable player Nat. League, 1958, 59; recipient awards from Fans, 1969, awards from Press Club, 1969, awards from Jr. C. of C., 1971; inducted into Tex. Sports Hall Fame, 1971, Baseball Hall of Fame, 1977; mem. Nat. League All-Star Team, 1957-70; hold major league record for most career grand slam home runs. Office: Ernie Banks Internat Inc 520 Washington Blvd Ste 284 Marina Del Rey CA 90292*

BANKS, EVELYN YVONNE, middle school educator; b. Houston, Sept. 7, 1951; d. Fred, Sr. and Mary Killings. BS, U. North Tex., 1974; M degree, Tex. So. U., 1993. Dean of instrn. North Forest Ind. Sch. Dist., Houston, 1976—. Counselor/coord. youth coun. N.W. Cmty. Bapt. Ch., 1989-96, dir. Sch. for Christian Living; bd. dirs. N.W. Cmty. Acad., 1996-99. Named Secondary Tchr. of Yr., North Forest Ind. Sch. Dist., Houston, 1992. Mem. Greater Houston Area Reading Coun., Tex. State Tchrs. of English, Delta Sigma Theta, Phi Delta Kappa (adv. 1992). Avocations: reading, participating in church activities, sewing. Home: 8530 Tilgham St Houston TX 77016

BANKS, HALBERT JAY, real estate executive; b. Austin, Tex., Feb. 21, 1955; s. William Halbert and Mildred Shipley B.; m. Helen Elizabeth Mendiola, Apr. 16, 1983. Pub. affairs analyst Western Co. N.Am., Ft. Worth, 1980-82; dir. mktg., investor rels. Gulf Nuclear, Inc., Houston, 1982-84; sr. v.p. leasing & asset mgmt. Alliance Comml. Investments, Inc., Houston, 1984-87; CFO Tex. Internat. Cons., Inc., Houston, 1984—; real estate cons. Lewis Cos., Houston, 1995-97; dir. real estate svcs. Am. Retirement Corp., Brentwood, Tenn., 1997—. Peer leader Alvin (Tex.) C.C., 1991; bd. dirs. Samaritan Counseling Ctr. Bay Area, Inc., Houston, 1988-89. Presdl. scholar, 1991. Mem. Rotary, Phi Theta Kappa. Republican. Episcopalian. Office: Am Retirement Corp 111 Westwood Pl Ste 402 Brentwood TN 37027

BANKS, HELEN AUGUSTA, singer, actress; b. Petersburg, Va., Sept. 8, 1922; d. Robert Augustus and Helen (Fisher) B. Student, Victoria Sch. of Music, N.Y.C., 1940-43. Singer and actress. Mem. pub. safety com. Cmty. Bd. No. 9, 1983—. Recipient Svc. award The Bd. Christian Edn., St. John Bapt. Ch., N.Y.C., 1989. Mem. Am. Guild Variety Artists, Am. Assn. Ret. Persons, Sickle Cell Found., U.S. Ski Team Found., Internat. Skiing History Assn. Democrat. Baptist. Avocations: skiing, in line skating, tennis. Home: 408 W 150th St Apt 6 New York NY 10031-2828

BANKS, HENRY H., academic dean, physician; b. Boston, Mar. 9, 1921; s. Isaac and Bessie B.; m. Judith Epstein, June 1945; children: Nancy (Mrs. Curt Civin), Betsy (Mrs. David Epstein), Steven. AB cum laude, Harvard U., 1942; MD, Tufts U., 1945. Diplomate Am. Bd. Orthopedic Surgery (pres. 1978-79, exec. dir. 1979-86). Surg. intern Beth Israel Hosp., Boston, 1945-46; asst. resident in surgery Beth Israel Hosp., 1947-49; asst. resident orthopedic lab. and pathology Children's Hosp., Boston, 1949-50; asst. resident orthopedic surgery Children's Hosp., 1950-51, Mass. Gen. Hosp., Boston, 1951-52; chief resident orthopedic surgery Peter Bent Brigham Hosp., Boston, 1952, Children's Hosp. Med. Center, Boston, 1952-53; practice medicine, specializing in orthopedic surgery Boston, 1953—; prof. Tufts U. Sch. Medicine, 1970-90, prof. emeritus, 1990—, chmn. dept. orthopedic surgery, 1970-84, assoc. dean, 1972-82, sr. assoc. dean med. affairs, 1982, acting med. dean, then med. dean, 1983-90, dean emeritus, 1990—; dir. orthopedic surgery Boston City Hosp., 1970-74; orthopedic surgeon-in-chief New Eng. Med. Center Hosps., 1970-84; orthopedic surgeon children's Hosp. Med. Ctr., 1953-70, Peter Bent Brigham Hosp., 1953-70, chief orthopedic surgery, 1968-70. Author: A Century of Excellence: The History of Tufts University School of Medicine, 1893-1993, 1993, Orthopaedic Surgery at Tufts University School of Medicine, 1893-1998, 1998; editor: The Pediatric Clinics of North America-Musculoskeletal Disorder I, 1967; guest editor: Clinical Orthopedics and Related Research, 1968, Orthopedic Clinics of North America, 1976, 78; contbr. articles to profl. jours. With M.C. AUS, 1945-47. Mem. AMA, ACS, Am. Orthopedic Assn. (v.p. 1986-87), Am. Acad. Orthopedic Surgeons, Am. Acad. Cerebral Palsy (pres.), Eastern Orthopedic Assn., Mass. Med. Soc., Internat. Soc. Orthopedic Surgery and Traumatology, Boston Orthopedic Club (pres.), Pediatric Orthopedic Soc., Am. Bd. Orthopedic Surgery (sec., pres. 1973-79, exec. dir. 1979-86), Univ. Club (Boston). Home: 54 Commonwealth Ave Boston MA 02116-3043 Office: 136 Harrison Ave Boston MA 02111-1817

BANKS, HOLLY HOPE, artist; b. Columbus, Ohio, Apr. 16, 1957; d. Harold Russell and Ramona Faye (Corder) Tumblin; m. Allan R. Banks, Jan. 7, 1997. BA, U. Toledo, 1981; student, Atelier Plein-Air Studios, 1994. Artist, 1981—; instr. gifted children program Toledo Mus. Art, 1980-81; copyist Nat. Gallery Art, Washington, 1982-86; asst. instr. Atelier Plein-Air Studios, Safety Harbor, Fla., 1994-96. Cover artist Masterpieces, 1997; exhibited in group shows Union Russian Artists, Moscow, 1996, Kolomna, Russia, 1996, Top 10 Emerging Artist Exhbn., Pasadena, Calif., 1998; featured emerging artist Am. Artist Mag., Oct. 1998; contbr. poetry to jours.; contbr. The Best of Portrait Painting, 1998. Recipient Renee and Stephen McNeely award for best representational oil, 1998. Mem. Am. Soc. Classical Realism, Am. Artist Profl. League, Audubon Artists, Portrait Soc. Am., Inc. Avocations: gourmet cooking, gardening. Office: PO Box 233 Safety Harbor FL 34695-0233

BANKS, JAMES ALBERT, educational research director, educator; b. Marianna, Ark., Sept. 24, 1941; s. Matthew and Lula (Holt) B.; m. Cherry Ann McGee, Feb. 15, 1969; children: Angela Marie, Patricia Ann. A.A., Chgo. City Coll., 1963; B.E., Chgo. State U., 1964; M.A. (NDEA fellow 1966-69), Mich. State U., 1967, Ph.D., 1969; LHD, Bank St. Coll. Edn., 1993. Tchr. elementary sch. Joliet, Ill., 1965, Francis W. Parker Sch., Chgo., 1965-66; asst. prof. edn. U. Wash., Seattle, 1969-71; assoc. prof. U. Wash., 1971-73, prof., 1973—, chmn. curriculum and instrn., 1982-87; dir. Ctr. for Multicultural Edn., 1991—; vis. prof. edn. U. Mich., 1975, Monash U., Australia, 1985, U. Warwick, Eng., 1988, U. Minn., 1991; vis. lectr. U. Southampton, Eng., 1989, Harry F. and Alva K. Ganders disting. lectr. Syracuse U., 1989; disting. scholar lectr. Kent State U., 1978, U. Ariz., 1979, Ind. U., 1983; vis. scholar Brit. Acad., 1983; Sachs lectr. Tchrs. Coll. Columbia U., 1996; Tyler eminent scholar chair Fla. State U., 1998; Carl and Alice Daeufer lectr. U. Hawaii, Manoa, 1999; com. examiners Edn. Testing Svc., 1974-77; nat. adv. coun. on ethnic heritage studies, U.S. Office Edn., 1975-78; com. on fed. role in ednl. rsch. NAS, 1991-92, mem. com. on developing a rsch. agenda on edn. of ltd. proficient and bilingual students, 1995-97. Author: Teaching Strategies for Ethnic Studies, 1975, 6th edit., 1997, Teaching Strategies for the Social Studies, 1973, 5th edit., 1999, Teaching the Black Experience, 1970, Multiethnic Education: Practices and Promises, 1977, An Introduction to Multicultural Education, 1994, 2d edit., 1999, Educating Citizens in A Multicultural Soc., 1997, (with Cherry Ann Banks) March Toward Freedom: A History of Black Americans, 1970, 2d edit., 1974, rev. 2nd edit., 1978, Multiethnic Education: Theory and Practice, 1981, 3rd edit., 1994, (with others) Curriculum Guidlines for Multicultural Education, 1976, rev. edit., 1992, We Americans: Our History and People, 2 vols., 1982; contbg. author Internat. Ency. of Edn., 1985, Handbook of Research on Teacher Education, 1990, Handbook of Research on Social Studies Teaching and Learning, 1991, Encyclopedia of Ednl. Rsch., 1992, Handbook of Research on the Education of Young Children, 1993, Review of Research in Education, vol. 19, 1993; editor: Black Self Concept, 1972, Teaching Ethnic Studies: Concepts and Strategies, 1973, (with William W. Joyce) Teaching Social Studies to Culturally Different Children, 1971, Teaching the Language Arts to Culturally Different Children, 1971, Education in the 80's: Multiethnic Education, 1981, (with James Lynch) Multicultural Education in Western Societies, 1986, (with C. Banks) Multicultural Education: Issues and Perspectives, 1989, 3d edit., 1997, Handbook of Research on Multicultural Education, 1995, Multicultural Education, Transformative Knowledge, and Action, 1996; editorial bd. Jour. of Tch. Edn., 1985-89, Coun. Interracial Books for Children Bull., 1982-92, Urban Edn., 1991-96; contbr. articles to profl. jours. Recipient Outstanding Young Man award Wash. State Jaycees, 1975, Outstanding Service in Edn. award Seattle U. Black Student Union, 1985, Pres.'s award TESOL, 1998; Spencer fellow Nat. Acad. Edn., 1973-76; Kellogg fellow, 1980-83; Rockefeller Found. fellow, 1980. Mem. ASCD (bd dirs. 1976-79, Disting. lectr. 1986, Disting. scholar, lectr. 1994, 97), Nat. Coun. Social Studies (bd. dirs. 1973-74, 80-85, pres. 1982), Internat. Assn. Intercultural Edn. (editl. bd.), Social Sci. Edn. Consortium (bd. dirs. 1976-79), Am. Ednl. Rsch. Assn. (Disting. scholar/rschr. on minority edn. 1986, Rsch. Review award 1994, com. on role and status of minorities in edn. rsch. 1992-94, mem. publs. com. 1995-96; Disting. Career Contbn. award, 1996; pres.-elect 1996-97, pres. 1997-98, exec. bd. 1998-99), Phi Delta Kappa, Phi Kappa Phi, Golden Key Nat. Honor Soc., Kappa Delta Pi (laureate chpt.). Office: U Wash 110 Miller Hall Box 353600 Seattle WA 98195-3600 *One of the greatest strengths of our nation is its tremendous ethnic, racial, and cultural diversity. A major goal of my career is to increase understanding and communication across different ethnic, cultural and racial groups and to make it possible for each ethnic, cultural and racial group to make its greatest contribution to the nation. My belief that educational institutions can play a major role in improving race relations in our nation has greatly influenced my life and career.*

BANKS, LISA JEAN, government official; b. Dec. 19, 1956; d. Bruce H. and Jean P. (Como) Banks. BSBA, Northeastern U., Boston, 1979. Coop. trainee IRS, Boston, 1975-79; revenue officer IRS, Reno, 1979-81; spl. agt. Houston, 1981-84, Anchorage, 1984-90; spl. agt. Office Inspector Gen. procurement fraud task force DVA, Boston, 1990-92; spl. agt. Office Inspector Gen. NASA, Kennedy Space Center, Fla., 1992—; fed. womens program mgr., 1980-81. Pres. Make-A-Wish Found. of Cen. Fla., 1994-96, 99—, v.p. wish granting, 1996-99. Mem. Nat. Assn. Treasury Agts., Fed. Law Enforcement Officers Assn. Roman Catholic. Office: NASA Office of Inspector Gen PO Box 21066 Kennedy Space Center FL 32815

BANKS, MCRAE CAVE, II, management educator, consultant; b. Portsmouth, Va., May 8, 1950; s James W. and Martha Ann (Nemec) B.; m. Lucy D. Hawk, Dec. 22, 1980; children: Caroline D., Margaret S., Elizabeth M., Michael C., Katherine C., John H. BA, Va. Poly. Inst. and State U., 1972, PhD, 1987; MA, Northwestern U., 1973. Owner, mgr. Banks Enterprises, Evanston, Ill., 1973-74; registered rep. IDS, Glenview, Ill., 1974-75; asst. v.p. mktg. Singer Safety Products, Chgo., 1975-78; gen. mgr. Britton Enterprises, Fredericksburg, Va., 1978-79; women's track coach Va. Poly. Inst. and State U., Blacksburg, 1979-82; asst. prof. mgmt. Radford (Va.) U., 1982-87; asst. prof. Miss. State U., Starkville, 1987-90, assoc. prof., 1990-94, prof., 1994-95, acting dir. Agribus. Inst., 1994-95; Harry G. Stoddard prof. mgmt. and dept. head Worcester (Mass.) Poly. Inst., 1995—; cons., trainer to over 100 orgns. Editor FOCUS on Mgmt., 1987-97; contbr. articles to profl. jours., also monographs. Mem. com. Va. Gov.'s Conf. on Small Bus., 1986; judge Blue Chip Enterprise Initiative, 1991-93; bd. deacons United Ch. of Christ, 1997—. Named Va. Tech Sports Hall of Fame 1999. Fellow Soc. for Advancement Mgmt. (bd. dirs. 1984-99, pres. 1993-94, President's Merit award 1989, Gold Meml. award 1990), Acad. Mgmt. (assoc. dir. placement 1989-92, dir. 1992-95, asst. program chmn. entrepreneurship divsn. 1994-95, program chmn. 1995-96, divsn. chair 1997-98, sponsorship chair 1996-99), So. Mgmt. Assn. (track chmn. 1993-94), Va. C. of C. (chmn. region II task force on small bus. 1985-87, Coalition for Venture Support 1996—, exec. com. WPI Venture forum 1996—), U.S. Assn. Small Bus. and Entrepreneurship, Phi Kappa Phi. Republican. Office: Worcester Poly Inst Dept Mgmt 100 Institute Rd Worcester MA 01609-2247

BANKS, MELISSA RICHARDSON, fund raising professional; b. Corpus Christi, Tex., June 5, 1962; d. Henry Gary and Patricia Lou (Kurth) Richardson; m. Steven Matisons Banks, Nov. 25, 1987 (div. Oct. 2, 1998). BA, Southwest Tex. State U., 1986; MS, Tex. A&M U., 1992. Devel. coord. Tex. A&M U., College Station, 1990-93; dir. devel. Autry Mus. Western Heritage, L.A., 1993-98; dir. corp. sponsorships and mktg. Libr. Found. of Los Angeles, 1999—. Mem. Am. Assn. Museums, Am. Prospect Rsch. Assn., Nat. Soc. Fund Raising Execs., Planned Giving Roundtable, Phi Beta Delta. Home: 923 E 3rd St Ste 203 Los Angeles CA 90013-1846 Office: Libr Found of Los Angeles c/o Los Angeles Pub Libr 630 W 5th St Los Angeles CA 90071

BANKS, PETER MORGAN, enviromental research business executive; b. San Diego, May 21, 1937; s. George Willard and Mary Margaret (Morgan)

B.; m. Paulett M. Behanna, May 21, 1983; children by previous marriage: Kevin, Michael, Steven, David. M.S. in E.E, Stanford U., 1960; Ph.D. in Physics, Pa. State U., 1965. Postdoctoral fellow Institut d'Aeronomie Spatiale de Belgigue, Brussels, Belgium, 1965-66; prof. applied physics U. Calif., San Diego, 1966-76; prof. physics Utah State U., 1976-81, head dept. physics, 1976-81; vis. assoc. prof. Stanford U., 1972-73, prof. elec. engring., 1981-90, dir. space, telecommunications and radiosci. lab., 1982-90, dir. ctr. for aeronautics and space info. systems, 1983-90; prof. atmospheres, oceans, and space sci. U. Mich., 1990-95, adj. prof., 1996—; dean Coll. Engring., U. Mich., 1990-95; pres. Earth Data Corp., 1985-86; pres., CEO Environ. Rsch. Inst. Mich., 1995-97, ERIM Internat., Inc., 1997—; vis. scientist Max Planck Inst. for Aeronomie, Germany, 1975; pres. La Jolla Scis., Inc. 1973-77, Upper Atmosphere Rsch. Corp., 1978-82; chmn. NASA adv. com. on sci. uses of space sta., 1985-87, prin. investigator space shuttle experiments 1982, 85, 91; mem. Jason Group, 1983-97; bd. dirs. Indsl. Tech. Inst., Ann Arbor, Mich., 1990-98, Tecumseh Products Corp., X-Rite Corp., Consortium for Internat. Earth Sci. Data Networking, Saginaw, Mich., 1990-97, Rsch. Environ. IndustriesInc.; chmn. bd. trustees, Consortium Internat. Earth Sci. Info. Networks, 1991-94; chmn. bd. dirs. Corp. for Studies and Analysis, Chantilly, 1998—; co-chmn. NRC Commn. on Phys. Scis., Math. and Applications, 1998—. Author: (with G. Kockarts) Aeronomy, 1973, (with J.R. Doupnik) Introduction to Computer Science, 1976; assoc. editor: Jour. Geophys. Research, 1974-77; assoc. editor: Planetary and Space Sci, 1977-83, regional editor, 1983-86; contbr. numerous articles in field to profl. jours. Mem. space sci. adv. council NASA, 1976-80. Served with U.S. Navy, 1960-63. Recipient Appleton prize Royal Soc. London, 1978, Space Sci. award AIAA, 1981, NASA Disting. Service medal, 1986; Alumni fellow Pa. State U., 1982. Fellow Internat. Acad. Astronautics, Am. Geophys. Union; mem. Internat. Union Radio Sci., Nat. Acad. Engring., Cosmos Club. Episcopalian. Home: 3485 Narrow Gauge Way Ann Arbor MI 48105-2576 Office: ERIM Internat Inc 2023 Plyouth Rd Ann Arbor MI 48105-2554

BANKS, RELA, sculptor; b. Yaroslav, Poland, Oct. 8, 1933; came to U.S., 1947; d. Jacob and Frieda (Weintraub) Heuberg; m. Stanley Frederic Banks, Aug. 9, 1953; children: Andrew Howard, J. Monica, Gary Mitchell. Student, Mus. Modern Art, 1957, Art Students League, N.Y.C. and Woodstock, N.Y., 1958-61, Summit (N.J.) Art Ctr., 1966-75. Chmn. nat. juried exhibit Summit Art Ctr., 1976, mem. adminstrv. com., 1977-79, chmn. standing com. spl. events, trustee; mem. exec. com. Phoenix Gallery, N.Y.C., 1983; chmn. membership com. Stone Sculpture Soc. N.Y., 1980-82. One-woman shows include Robins Art Gallery, South Orange, N.J., 1973, Montclair (N.J.) Coll., 1974, Caldwell (N.J.) Coll., 1974, 83, Summit Art Ctr., 1976, Newark Acad., Livingston, N.J., 1976, Douglas Coll., New Brunswick, N.J., 1978, First Women's Bank, N.Y.C., 1979, Phoenix Gallery, 1979, 81, 83, Morris Mus. Arts and Scis., Morristown, N.J., 1983, Ann Leonard Gallery, Woodstock, 1983, NECCA Mus., Bklyn., Conn., 1985, Schiller-Wapner Galleries, N.Y.C., 1985, 87, Ann Norton Sculpture Galleries, West Palm Beach, Fla., 1987, David Gary Ltd, Millburn, N.J., 1988; exhibited in group shows at Phoenix Gallery, 1979, 83, Morris Mus. Art, 1979, 83, Invitational Woodstock Artists Assn., 1980, 84, Eilaine Benson Gallery, Bridgehampton, N.Y., 1980, Searles Art Ctr., Great Barrington, Mass., 1980, Nabisco Art Gallery, 1981, Summit Art Ctr., 1981, First Womens Bank, 1981, Fairleigh Dickinson U., Madison, N.J., 1983, NYU Grad. Sch. Bus., 1983, AT&T Gallery, Basking Ridge, N.J., 1984, Shering Plough Gallery, N.J., 1984, New Orleans Mus. Art, 1986, Gallery Contemporary Art at U. Colorado Springs, Colo., 1986, Schiller-Wapner Galleries, 1986, Lever House, N.Y.C., 1986, Aldrich Mus. Contemporary Art, Ridgefield, Conn., 1986, Okla. Art Ctr., Oklahoma City, 1987, "After Henry Moore", Emily Lowe Mus., Hofstra U., Hempstead, N.Y., 1988, group exhibition , Poland; represented in permanent collections New Orleans Mus. Art, Everson Mus., Syracuse, N.Y., Morris Mus. Sci. and Art, Okla. Art Ctr., Vassar Coll. Gallery, Poughkeepsie, N.Y., Millburn (N.J.) Pub. Library, Minn. Mus. Art, Mpls., Woodstock Hist. Soc., Fordham U., Lincoln Ctr., N.Y.C., Aldrich Mus. Contemporary Art, Warsaw Mus., Poland, various pvt. and corp. collections. Mem. Woodstock Artists Assn. Office: Rela Banks Studio Mink Hollow Rd Woodstock NY 12498

BANKS, ROBERT J., bishop; b. Winthrop, Mass., Feb. 26, 1928; s. Robert Joseph and Rita Katherine (Sullivan) B. AB, St. John's Sem., Brighton, Mass., 1949; STL, Gregorian U., Rome, 1953; JCD, Lateran U., Rome, 1957. Ordained priest Roman Cath. Ch., 1952, ordained titular bishop of Taraqua, 1985. Prof. canon law St. John Sem., Brighton, Mass., 1959-71, acad. dean, 1967-71; rector St. John's Sem., 1971-81; vicar gen. Boston Archdiocese, 1984; aux. bishop Boston, 1985-90; bishop Diocese of Green Bay, Wis., 1990—. Office: Diocese of Green Bay PO Box 23825 Green Bay WI 54305-3825

BANKS, ROBERT SHERWOOD, lawyer; b. Newark, Mar. 28, 1934; s. Howard Douglas and Amelia Violet (Del Bagno) B.; m. Judith Lee Henry; children—Teri, William; children by previous marriage—Robert, Paul, Stephen, Roger, Gregory, Catherine. A.B., Cornell U., 1956, LL.B., 1958. Bar: N.J. 1959, N.Y. 1968. Practice law Newark, 1958-61; atty. E.I. duPont, Wilmington, Del., 1961-67; with Xerox Corp., Stamford, Conn., 1967-88; v.p., gen. counsel Xerox Corp., 1975-88; sr. counsel Latham & Watkins, N.Y.C., 1988-89; gen. counsel Keystone Holdings, 1989-92; bd. dirs. Cornell U. Found.; mem. panel of mediators, neutral advisors Ctr. for Pub. Resources. Mem. adv. coun. Cornell Law Sch.; past trustee U.S. Supreme Ct. Hist. Soc.; past bd. dirs. Ctr. for Pub. Resources. Mem. ABA, N.Y. Bar Assn., Am. Arbitration Assn. (panel arbitrators), Am. Judicature Soc. (exec. com., bd. dirs., pres. 1989-91), Cornell Law Assn., Am. Corp. Counsel Assn. (bd. dirs., chmn. 1982-83), Atlantic Athletic Club, Jonathan's Landing Club.

BANKS, RUSSELL, financial planner, consultant; b. N.Y.C., Aug. 2, 1919; s. Thomas and Fay (Cowen) B.; m. Janice Reed, June 19, 1949; 1 son, Gordon L. BBA, CCNY, 1936-40; JD, N.Y. Law Sch., 1960. Bar: N.Y. 1961. Sr. acct. Selverne, Davis Co., N.Y.C., 1940-45; pvt. practice N.Y.C., 1945-61; exec. v.p. Met. Telecomm. Corp., Plainview, N.Y., 1961-62; pres., former CEO Grow Group, Inc. (formerly Grow Chem. Corp.), N.Y.C., 1962-95; also dir. Grow Group, Inc. (formerly Grow Chem. Corp.), 1962-95; pres. Russell Banks & Co. Ltd., 1995—; cons. Imperial Chem. Industries, PLC., 1995-96; adj. prof. bus. adminstrn. Baruch Coll., 1996-98. Editor: Managing the Small Company. Recipient award of achievement Sch. of Bus. Alumni Soc. of CCNY, 1977; Winthrop-Sears medal Chem. Industry Assn., 1980. Mem. Nat. Paint and Coatings Assn. (past pres.), Am. Mgmt. Assn. (gen. mgmt. planning coun. 1966—, former trustee, exec. com.), Met. Club, Annabel's Club, Sky Club. Home: 14 E 75th St New York NY 10021-2657 Office: 1114 Ave of the Americas New York NY 10036

BANKS, THERESA ANN, retired elementary education educator; b. Camden, N.J., Apr. 5, 1946; d. Frederick Douglas and Betty Mae (Norman) Clarke; m. James Donald Banks, Feb. 14, 1987; 1 child, Elizabeth Pearl Banks. BS, Cheyney U., 1968. Third grade tchr. Loudenslager Elem. Sch., Paulsboro, N.J., 1968-81, tchr. basic skills, 1981-86; tchr. basic skills Billingsport Elem. Sch., Paulsboro, 1986-98; ret., 1998; tchr. art activities Enrichment Prog., Paulsboro, 1988-98, Sunshine Club Billingsport Sch., 1990-98. Chmn. youth program ARC for Paulsboro Sch. System, 1970-80, Sunshine Club/Billingsport Sch., 1990—, Billingsport Sch. Store, 1992-95; active Aluminum Tab Program, Camden, 1991-98. Mem. NEA, N.J. Edn. Assn., Paulsboro Edn. Assn., Nat. Coun. Tchrs. Math. Baptist. Avocations: reading, cooking, sewing, art, horses. Home: 253 Deptford Ave Woodbury NJ 08096-3508

BANKS, VIRGINIA ANNE (GINGER BANKS), association administrator; b. Dallas, Mar. 19, 1949; d. James Houston and Mary Virginia (Bussey) B. B of Journalism, U. Tex., 1971. Traveling cons. Alpha Omicron Pi Fraternity, Indpls., 1971-73; adminstrv. asst. Alpha Omicron Pi Fraternity, Nashville, 1973-74; pub. info. officer Tex. Dept. of Community Affairs, Austin, 1974-76; asst. dir. of comm. State Bar of Tex., Austin, 1976-78, assoc. editor Tex. Bar Jour., 1977-79, mng. editor Tex. Bar Jour, 1979-91, comm. dir., 1991-99, dir. pub. svcs. divsn., 1992-99, dir. info. tech. divsn., 1999—; internat. rush chmn. Alpha Omicron Pi, Nashville, 1976-77, internat. v.p. ops., 1977-81, internat. pres., 1981-85, v.p. found., 1985-90, mem. fraternity devel. com., 1985-89, pres. Pi Kappa Corp., 1991-95, mem. Austin Alumnae chpt., 1973—, alumnae adv. com. network specialist, 1996-98, del. nat. panhellenic Conf., 1987-93, chmn. Perry award com., 1992-98, mem. rituals, traditions and jewelry com., 1998—, chair rituals, traditions and jewelry com., 1998—; com. to devel. relationship statement, Nat. Panhellenic Conf., 1983, del., 1987-93, area advisor coll. Panhellenics com., 1985-88, chmn. liaison com., 1987-88, mem. Project Future collegiate concerns com., 1987-89, field cons. seminar com., 1987, chmn., 1988, resolutions com., 1988, chmn. pub. rels. com., 1991-93, mem. ednl. devel. com., 1991-93. Editor Alpha Omicron Pi Centennial History Book, 1995-97; contbr. articles to mags. Bd. dirs. Lone Star Girl Scout Coun., Austin, 1973-75, Nat. Interfraternity Found., 1986-89, M.L. Roller scholarship com., 1988-89, nominations com., 1988-89; mem. Humane Soc. Austin, 1981—; chmn. mag. adv. com. Ex-Students Assn., U. Tex., Austin, 1989-95; mem. Tarrytown United Meth. Ch. Recipient presdl. citation State Bar of Tex., 1981, 90, 94, presdl. citation Alpha Omicron Pi, 1988, 97, Rose award Alpha Omicron Pi, 1991, Adele K. Hinton award, 1997. Mem. Am. Soc. Assn. Execs., Assn. Fraternity Advisors, Internat. Assn. Bus. Communicators, Nat. Assn. Bar Execs. (mem. pub. svcs. activities com. 1995-98, vice-chair pub. svc. activities com. 1996-97, chair pub. svcs. activities com. 1997-98, chair awards com. 1995-96, mem. pub. rels. and comms. sect. 1991—, mem. sect.'s comms. audit com. 1994-95, chair sect.'s comms. audit com. 1995-98, mem. sect.'s coun., 1997—, mem. sect.'s program com. 1995-98, co-chair sect.'s program com. 1996-98, sect.'s sec. 1998—), Women in Comms., PEO Sisterhood, Alpha Omicron Pi (Austin alumnae chpt.). Avocations: gardening, sailing, cooking. Home: 3108 W Terrace Dr Austin TX 78757-4332 Office: State Bar of Tex PO Box 12487 Austin TX 78711-2487

BANKS, WILLIAM ASHTON, librarian; b. Beckley, W.Va., Apr. 24, 1943; s. William Smith and Mary Frances (File) B.; m. Grace Wallace Powars, Aug. 9, 1969; children: Michele, Elizabeth, Nancy, Kathryn. BA in Music, Am. U., 1970; ThM in English Bible, Capital Bible Sem., 1980; MA in Music, Am. U., 1988; MLS, Cath. U., 1989. Pvt. music instr., musician Alexandria, Va., 1961—; adj. prof. Religion Washington Bible Coll., Lanham, Md., 1976-85; music libr. Am. U., Washington, 1985-88; libr. Notre Dame Acad., Middleburg, Va., 1988-94, Washington Bible Coll., Lanham, Md., 1994—. Co-author: Old Testament Parsing Guide, vol. 1, 1985, vol. 2, 1990; author: Justin Holland: The Guitar's Black Pioneer, 1989. Mem. Conservative Club, Alexandria, 1987—. Mem. Am. Fedn. Musicians, Va. Cath. Edn. Assn., Phi Mu Alpha Sinfonia. Republican. Presbyterian. Avocation: photography. Home: 2601 Londonderry Rd Alexandria VA 22308-2334 Office: Washington Bible Coll 6511 Princess Garden Pkwy Lanham Seabrook MD 20706-3538

BANKS, WILLIAM J. P., alderman; b. July 28, 1949; m. Shirley A. Mader; children: Lisa Marie, Joseph William. BA, De Pauw U., 1971, JD, 1975. Adminstrv. aide to Congressman Morgan Murphy, 1976-78, asst. corp. counsel, 1978-83; alderman City of Chgo., 1983—; chmn. Land Acquisition Disposition and Leases Com.; former mem. Com. on Zoning; mem. Aging and Disabled Com., Budget and Govt. Ops. Com., Capital Devel. Com., Health Com., Housing Com., Local Transp. Com., Aviation Com.; mem. Chgo. City Coun.; commr. Home Equity Commn., 1989—; atty. Recipient Ray Switzer Cmty. Svc. award N.W. Neighborhood Fedn., Outstanding Pub. Svc. award 25th Police Dist., Pres.'s award North River Commn., 1979. Mem. Ital. Am. Police Assn. (Man of Yr.), Justinian Soc. Lawyers (Award of Excellence), Polish Nat. Alliance, Emerald Soc., Fraternal Order of Police, Montclare C. of C., Elmwood Park C. of C., Belmont Ctrl. C. of C. Office: 6839 W Belmont Ave Chicago IL 60634-4646*

BANKS, WILLIE J., orthopaedic surgeon, educator; b. July 4, 1944. MD, Howard U., 1970. Chief orthopaedic surgery Washington VA Med. Ctr.; assoc. prof. orthopaedic surgery Howard U., Washington. Mem. VA Orthopaedic Surgeons Assn. (pres.). Home: 2300 24th Rd Apt 65Y Arlington VA 22206

BANKSON, MARJORY, religious association administrator; m. Peter Bankson. BA in Govt. and Econs., Radcliffe Coll., 1961; M in Am. History, U. Alaska, 1961; postgrad., Va. Episcopal Sem., 1985; LLD, Va. Theol. Sem., 1999. H.S. history and English tchr.; counselor Dartmouth Coll., 1969-70; profl. potter, 1970-80; pres. Faith at Work, Falls Church, Va., 1985—. Author: Briaded Streams: Esther and a Woman's Way of Growing, Seasons of Friendship: Naomi and Ruth as a Pattern, This Is My Body...Clay, Creativity and Change, (videos) The Potter and Clay, With Tongues of Fire (Five Women from the Book of Acts), The Call to the Soul, 1999. Mem. Ch. of the Saviour. Office: 106-B East Broad St Falls Church VA 22046-4501*

BANKSTON, ARCHIE MOORE, JR., lawyer; b. Memphis, Oct. 12, 1937; s. Archie M. and Elsie Bernice (Shaw) B.; m. Emma Ann Dejan, Apr. 16, 1966; children—Louis, Alice. BA, Fisk U., 1959; LLB, Washington U., St. Louis, 1962, MBA, 1964. Bar: Mo. 1963, N.Y. 1966. Asst. divsn. counsel Gen. Foods Corp., White Plains, N.Y., 1964-67, product mgr. Maxwell House divsn., 1967-69; asst. sec. and corp. counsel PepsiCo, Inc., Purchase, N.Y., 1969-72; divsn. counsel Xerox Corp., Stamford, Conn., 1973; sec. and asst. gen. counsel Consol. Edison Co. of N.Y. Inc., N.Y.C., 1974-89, sec., assoc. gen. counsel, 1989—; sec. Consolidated Edison, Inc., N.Y.C., 1998—. Trustee Beth Israel Med. Ctr., Coll. New Rochelle, Hoff-Barthelson Music Sch., Scarsdale, N.Y.; mem. Westchester County African Am. Adv. Bd.; former bd. dirs. Urban League of Westchester County, Associated Black Charities, Mental Health Assn. Westchester County; mem. 100 Black Men, Inc., N.Y.C. Recipient Black Achievers in Industry award Harlem br. YMCA, 1971, Merit award Black Exec. Exchange Progam Nat. Urban League, 1974, Disting. Svc. Commendation awards Mental Health Assn., 1987, 92. Mem. ABA, Am. Soc. Corp. Secs. (past chmn. membership com., 50th anniversary nat. conf. com., corp. practices com., audit com., past bd. dirs., chmn. budget com., edn. com., securities industry com.), Stockholder Rels. Soc. N.Y. (past pres.), Westchester Clubmen (past pres.), Phi Delta Phi, Sigma Pi Phi, Alpha Phi Alpha. Office: Consol Edison Co NY Inc 4 Irving Pl New York NY 10003-3502

BANKSTON, NATHANIEL D., city registrar; b. Baton Rouge, Oct. 4, 1948. Student, Southeastern La. U., 1966-72. Registrar of voters East Baton Rouge Parish, La., 1969—; mem., past pres. East Baton Rouge Parish Bd. Election Suprs.; mem. State of La. Bd. Election Suprs.; mem. La. Election Code Commn.; mem., bd. trustees La. Registrars of Voters Retirement Sys.; past mem. exec. bd. Greater Baton Rouge Postal Customer Coun. Mem. Nat. Assn. County Recorders, Election Ofcls., & Clks., La. Registrars of Voters Assn. (past pres., past bd. dirds., chmn. legis. and conv. coms.). Avocations: ham radio (advance class operator), airplane piloting (instrument rated and commercial). Office: Office of City Registrar 222 Saint Louis St Baton Rouge LA 70802-5817*

BANNAN, PATRICIA MARY, nutrition specialist, public relations consultant; b. Mar. 17, 1972; d. William Glenn and Joanne (Cass) B. BS in Nutrition and Dietetics cum laude, U. Del., 1994; MS in Nutrition Comm., Tufts U., 1999. rsch. investigator U. Del., Newark, 1993; mem. adv. bd. D.C. Food Bank, Washington, 1995-96; co-host nutrition program Stas. WBIG-WTEM, Rockville, Md., 1996-97; freelance prodr. CNN Med. News, Atlanta, 1998—; asst. prodr. The Dollars and $ense of Eating Right, Lemon-Aid Films, Inc., 1997, website designer, 1998; workshop tchr. phys. edn. dept. Harvard U., 1997. Nutrient rsch., computer analyst Campbell Soup Co., Newark, Del., 1992-94; nutrition specialist food and nutrition corp. practice group Porter Novelli, pub. rels., Washington, 1995—. Author, prodr. video tape What's Cooking—A Guide for Food Shopping for International Students, 1994; author, photographer: A Training Guide for Portioning and Plating of Salads, Cold Plates, and Deserts, 1995; also articles. Recipient Woman of Promise award for acad. excellence, 1993; scholar Am. Restaurant Assn., 1992-94, U. Del., 1992-94, E.V. McCollum scholar Md. Dietetic Assn., 1995, scholar Tufts U., 1997-98, Dietitians in Bus. and Comm., 1997. Mem. Am. Dietetic Assn. (Edith Jones scholar 1994, recognized Young Dietitian of Yr. 1997), Soc. for Nutrition Edn. (chmn. comm. divsn., scholar Delaware Valley chpt. 1993), Radio and TV News Dirs. Assn., Mass. Dietetic Assn. (scholar 1998), D.C. Met. Dietetic Assn. (editor newsletter 1995-97, past scholarship co-chmn.), Mortar Bd. (historian 1994), Golden Key, Order of Omega, Kappa Omicron Nu, Chi Omega. Roman Catholic. Avocations: acting, photography, travel. E-mail: pbannan@porternovelli.com. Home: 139 Charles St Apt 2 Boston MA 02114 Office: Porter Novelli 855 Boylston St Boston MA 02116

BANNARD, ANN, sculptor; b. Nov. 19, 1927. BA, Sweet Briar Coll., 1949; grad., Am. Acad. Art, Chgo., 1951; student, Pima C.C., Tucson, 1988. Grant writer, coord. Davidson Elem. Sch., Tucson, 1978-80; resource coord. Doolen Jr. H.S., Tucson, 1982. One-man shows include Los Llanos Gallery, Santa Fe, 1981, Eleanor Jeck Galleries, Tucson, 1982; group shows include City Ct. Bldg., Tucson, 1989, Tucson Convention Ctr., 1990, Rosequist Gallery, Tuscon, 1992, Learning Connection, Green Valley, Ariz., 1993, Obsidian Gallery, Tucson, 1996, Tucson Botanical Garden, 1996, 97; represented in permanent collections Tucson Mus. Art, Milestone Oil Co., Denver, Coventry (Eng.) Cathedral, Hadley Sch. Blind, Winnetka, Ill., Chgo. Bulls Exec. Offices, Pvt. Sculpture Garden, L.A., Sweet Briar Coll., others. Grantee Richey Sch., 1989-90; named Disting. Alumna, Sweet Briar Coll., 1992. E-mail: ybannard@aol.com. Home and Office: 4556 N Trocha Alegre Tucson AZ 85750

BANNARD, WALTER DARBY, artist, art critic; b. New Haven, Sept. 23, 1934; s. Homes and Janet (Darby) B. B.A., Princeton U., 1956. Chmn. dept. art and art history U. Miami, Fla., 1989-97; Lectr. in field, 1969—; vis. prof. Princeton (N.J.) U., 1974, also other univs.; mem. grad. faculty Sch. Visual Arts, N.Y.C., 1984-89; curator Hans Hoffman Hirshorn Mus., 1976; mem. internat. exhbn. com., 1976-78; co-chmn. internat. panel for visual arts Nat. Endowment for Arts, 1979-81. Contbr. articles and revs. on modern painting to profl. jours.; contbg. editor: Artforum, 1973-74; 75 one-man shows internat. galleries and mus. include retrospective Balt. Mus. Art, 1973, retrospective U. Tampa, 1997; numerous internat. group shows; represented in permanent collections at Mus. Modern Art, N.Y.C., Whitney Mus. Am. Art, Met. Mus. Art, N.Y.C., Guggenheim Mus., N.Y.C., others; juror numerous competitions, 1969—; sole juror Australian Bi-Centenary Art Competition, 1988. Recipient Nat. Found. Arts award, 1968-69; Francis J. Greenburger Found. award, 1986; John Simon Guggenheim Meml. Found. fellow, 1968; Richard A. Florsheim Art Fund grantee, 1991. E-mail: wbannard@aol.com. Office: 1300 Campo Sano Ave Coral Gables FL 33146-1171

BANNATYNE, MARK WILLIAM MCKENZIE, technical graphics educator; b. West Chester, Pa., May 22, 1952; s. Isobel Steel B.; m. Tatiana Yurievna Shcherbakova, Sept. 2, 1990; children: Yuri Markovich, Kirill Markovich. AAS, B.C. Inst. Tech., Burnaby, Can., 1982; BS, Utah State U., 1988, MS, 1991; PhD, Purdue U., 1994. Staff tchr. indsl. tech. and edn. dept. Utah State U., Logan, 1986-89, lectr. indsl. tech. and edn. dept., 1990, grad. prof. indsl. tech. and edn. dept., 1990-92; grad. instr. Purdue U., West Lafayette, Ind., 1992-94; asst. prof. dept. instnl. and curricular studies Coll. Edn. U. Nev., Las Vegas, 1995-97; assoc. prof. tech. graphics dept. Purdue U., West Lafayette, 1997—; instr. Bridgerland Applied Tech. Ctr., Logan, 1988-92; mem. Engring. State Com., Logan, 1990-92, Gov.'s Coun. on Fgn. Exch., Salt Lake City, 1991-92; presenter Far West Popular Am. Culture Conf., 1996, 97, Rocky Mountain States Conf., Moscow, 1992, Tech. Edn. Assn., Kansas City, Mo., 1994, Jistec '96, Jerusalem, 1996, Far West Popular and Am. Culture Conf., 1996, 97, ASEE Conf., Seattle, 1998, IV'98 Conf., London, 1998; dir. Focus 1996, Moscow, 1996; presenter Winter Sch. Computer Graphics '99 Conf., Plzen, Czech Republic, 1999. Author: (book review) Tech. Tchr., 1989, ERIC Document, 1996, Popular Culture Rev., 1997; editl. bd. Jour. Tech. Studies; contbr. articles to profl. jours. Leader Boy Scouts of Am., Logan, 1984-86. Mem. Internat. Tech. Edn. Assn. (conf. chair fgn. and internat. programs 1991), Am. Soc. Engring. Edn. (vice chmn. internat. divsn.), Assn. for Computing Machinery-Spl. Interest Group for Graphics, Am. Vocat. Assn. (presenter conf. 1991), Phi Kappa Phi, Epsilon Pi Tau. Mem. LDS Ch. Avocations: ice hockey, opera, art, foreign travel, history. Office: Purdue U Tech Graphics Dept 1419 Knoy Hall Rm 363 Purdue University IN 47907

BANNEN, JOHN T., lawyer; b. LaCrosse, Wis., Oct. 29, 1951; s. James J. and Ruth J. (Frisch) B.; m. Carol A. Swanson, Aug. 16, 1975; children: Ryan M., Kelly A., Erin C. BA summa cum laude, Coll. of St. Thomas, 1973; JD, Marquette U., 1976; LLM in Taxation, DePaul U., 1989. Bar: Wis. 1976, U.S. Dist. Ct. (ea. and we. dists.) Wis. 1976, U.S. Tax Ct. 1979, U.S. Claims Ct. 1983, U.S. Supreme Ct. 1984. Shareholder Charne, Clancy & Taitelman, S.C., Milw., 1976-91; ptnr. Quarles & Brady, Milw., 1991—. Mem. coun. Christ the King Parish, Wauwatosa, Wis., 1989-93, trustee, 1996-98; bd. dirs. Guardianship Svcs. for Indigents, Milw., 1983-87; mem. adv. bd. Sch. Sisters of Notre Dame, 1993-98, pres., 1995-98. Fellow Am. Coll. Trust and Estate Counsel (state law coord. for Wis. 1990-95); mem. ABA, Assn. Advanced Life Underwater, Wis. Bar Assn. (bd. dirs. real property, probate and trust law sect. 1990-93), Milw. Bar Assn. (chmn. delivery of legal svcs. to the elderly com. 1984-86, chmn. probate practice and procedure sect. 1986-88), Greater Milw. Benefits Coun., Wis. Retirement Plan Profls. Ltd. (bd. dirs. 1988-91), Am. Soc. CLUs and Cert. Fin. Cons. (bd. dirs. Milw. chpt. 1996-98), KC (bd. dirs. Wauwatosa chpt. 1983—). Avocations: reading, gardening, Spanish language, cooking. Office: Quarles & Brady 411 E Wisconsin Ave Ste 2550 Milwaukee WI 53202-4497

BANNER, BURTON, pediatrician; b. N.Y.C., Aug. 29, 1948. BA cum laude, CUNY, 1970; MD, SUNY, Bklyn., 1974. Diplomate Nat. Bd. Med. Examiners, Am. Bd. Pediatrics. Intern Nassau County Med. Ctr., 1974-75; resident in pediatrics Montefiore Med. Ctr., Bronx, N.Y., 1975-77; fellow in pediatric endocrinology NYU Med. Ctr., 1977-78; pvt. practice in pediatrics Staten Island, N.Y., 1981—; clin. asst. prof. N.Y.U. Med. Sch., N.Y.C., 1986—. Mem. Med. Soc. of the State of N.Y., Richmond County Med. Soc. Office: 2281 Victory Blvd Staten Island NY 10314-6625

BANNER, MARILYN RUTH, artist, educator; b. St. Louis, Mar. 30, 1945; d. Harry Bromberg and Edna Davis; m. Carl David Banner, May 9, 1974; 1 child, Gabe. BFA, Washington U., 1968; cert. art tchr. grades K-12, U. Md., 1975; MS in Edn., Mass. Coll. Art, 1982. Art tchr. Green Acres Sch., Rockville, Md., 1974-76, 83-93, Montgomery County Alternative Schs., Wheaton, Md., 1996—. Group leader, cmty. coord. No Limits for Women in the Arts, Washington; bd. mem., treas. Washington Musica Viva, Kensington, Md. Residency fellow Va. Ctr. for the Creative Arts, Sweet Briar, 1992, 93, 95, 99. Democrat. Jewish. Avocations: swing dancing, folk dancing. E-mail: BannerArts@aol.com. Home: 9925 Dickens Ave Bethesda MD 20814-2105 Office: BannerArts 4233C Howard Ave Kensington MD 20895

BANNICK, JANICE CAROL, automotive dealerships executive; b. Clinton, Iowa, Oct. 12, 1938; d. Claus John and Irma Jeanne (Switzer) Greve; m. Robert T. Gallagher, May 21, 1958 (div. Apr. 1967); children: Angela Jeanne, Carol Ellen; m. Mearl G. Bannick, June 24, 1967 (dec. Aug. 1991). Student, Old Dominion Coll., Norfolk, Va., 1956-58, U. Wis., Milw., 1980-83, U. Tex., Arlington, 1983-86, Bradley U., 1992-94. Contr. Kimberly Chrysler-Plymouth, Inc., Davenport, Iowa, 1974-79; cons. Davenport and Milw., 1979-80; contr. Stark Oldsmobile, Inc., Menomonee Falls, Wis., 1980-83; bus. mgr., field rep. Motors Holding divsn. Gen. Motors Corp., Detroit, 1986-89; contr., CFO S&K Chevrolet Pontiac and Oldsmobile, Peoria, Ill., 1989-96; automotive cons. Peoria and Springfield, Ill., 1996-97; contr., dealer acctg. Gen. Acceptance Corp., Bloomington, Ind., 1997-98; CFO Anthony Pontiac, Gurnee, Ill., 1998—. Bd. dirs., treas. St. Marks Luth. Ch., Chillicothe, Ill., 1994-96, Peoria Art Gild, 1995-96. Republican. Avocations: watercolor painting, reading, running, walking, antique refinishing, gourmet cooking, golf. Home: 2608 N Augusta Dr Wadsworth IL 60083-8910

BANNING, LANCE GILBERT, historian, educator; b. Kansas City, Jan. 24, 1942; s. E. Willis and Marie G. B.; m. Lana J. Sampson, July 11, 1964; 1 child, Clinton E. BA, U. Mo., Kansas City, 1964; MA, PhD, Washington U., St. Louis, 1971. Prof. history U. Ky., Lexington, 1973—; John Adams prof. U. Groningen, The Netherlands, 1997. Author: The Jeffersonian Persuation, 1978, The Sacred Fire of Liberty, 1995, Jefferson and Madison, 1995. Fellow Guggenheim Found., Fullbright, Nat. Humanities Ctr.; recipient Internat. Book award Phi Alpha Theta, 1979, 1996, Merle Curti award Orgn. Am. Historians, 1996. Address: 604 Cromwell Way Lexington KY 40503

BANNISTER, BRIAN, retired organic chemist; b. Gateshead, Durham, England, Mar. 10, 1926; came to U.S., 1952; s. Arthur and Margaret Ethel (Spencer) B.; m. Mary Josephine Shea, Dec. 31, 1957. BA with 1st class hons., U. Oxford, Eng., 1947, BSc., MA, PhD, 1952. Sr. scientist Upjohn Co., Kalamazoo, Mich., 1954-92. Inventor with numerous patents; contbr. articles to Jour. of Am. Chem. Soc., The Chem. Soc. (Brit.), 1953-92.

Recipient Sr. Govett scholarship, New Coll., Oxford, 1947,. Mem. Am. Chem. Soc., The Chem. Soc. (Brit.), Sigma Xi. Home: 4150 E Hillandale Dr Kalamazoo MI 49008-3138

BANNISTER, DAN R., professional and technical services company executive; b. Detroit, 1930; married. With Grand Cen. Aircraft Co., 1952-53; with Dynaelectron Corp. (name changed to Dyncorp), Reston, Va., 1952—, v.p., 1962-72, group v.p., 1972-77, sr. v.p. tech. svc. and staff, 1977-83, exec. v.p. tech. svc. and staff, 1983-85, pres., CEO, 1985—, also bd. dirs.; chmn. of the bd. Dynaelectron Corp. (name changed to Dyncorp), 1997—; chmn. Combined Health Appeal, 1993-94, Profl. Svcs. Coun., 1993-94. Bd. Dirs. Fairfax Symphony Orch., Reston Bd. Commerce, Washington Airports Task Force. Served with USAF, 1948-52. Mem. Nat. Def. Exec. Rsch., Am. Def. Preparedness Assn., Am. Mgmt. Assn. (bd. dirs.), Electronic Industries Assn., Easter Seal Soc. (chmn.), Fairfax County C. of C. (bd. dirs.), Employee Stock Ownership Plan Assn. (sec., vice chair), Nat. Contract Mgmt. Assn., Tower Club. *

BANNISTER, GEOFFREY, university president, geographer; b. Manchester, Eng., Sept. 19, 1945; came to U.S., 1973; s. Leslie and Doris (Shankland) B.; m. Margaret Janet Sheridan, Jan. 28, 1968; children: Katherine, Janet. BA, U. Otago, New Zealand, 1967, MA with honors, 1969; PhD, U. Toronto, Can., 1974. Asst. prof. Boston U., 1973-77, acting chmn. geography, 1977-78, dean liberal arts, grad. sch., 1978-87; exec. v.p. Butler U., Indpls., 1987-89, pres., 1989—; cons. Urban Affairs Ministry of State, Can., 1973; legal cons. U.S. Dept. of State 1982-84; bd. dirs. Somerset Group, Ind. Nat. Bank. Co-author atlas Spatial Dynamics of Postwar County Economic Change, 1977; contbr. articles to profl. jours. Chmn. bd. trustees Cambridge (Mass.) Montessori Sch., 1979-80; mem. corp. Sea Edn. Assn., Woods Hole, Mass., 1979-87; bd. dirs. United Way of Cen. Ind., 1990—, chmn. 1992 Premeire Campaign, edn. chmn.; bd. dirs. Greater Indpls. Progress Com., 1988—; pres. Midwest Collegiate Cons; chmn. World Rowing Championship, 1994. Fellow U. Toronto, 1970-71, Can. Council, 1972. Mem. Nat. Labor/Higher Edn. Coun., Nat. Assn. Scholars, Indpls. Bus. Jour. Blue Ribbon Panel, Indpls. Commn. on African-Am. Males, C. of C., Econ. Club, English Speaking Union U.S. (Indpls. br.), Coun. Urban Coll. of Arts, Letter and Scis., Kiwanis, Phi Beta Kappa. Avocations: bicycling, golf, skiing. Office: Butler U 4600 Sunset Ave Indianapolis IN 46208-3487*

BANNISTER, LOIS ANN, library director; b. Lawton, Okla., Mar. 17, 1940; d. Earl A. and Vera Mary Ellen Wilkerson; m. Wesley Eugene Bannister, Aug. 18, 1967; children: Makala Sue, Cody Traver. BA, U. Sci. and Arts Okla., Chickasha, Okla., 1961. Tchr. Amber (Okla.) Pub. Schs., 1961-67, Chickasha Pub. Schs., 1967-69; libr. dir. Marlow (Okla.) Pub. Libr., 1993—. Mem. Okla. Libr. Assn., Marlow C. of C., Marlow Friends of Libr. Baptist. Avocations: needlework, handicrafts, reverse glass painting. E-mail: marlowlc@starcomm.net. Office: Marlow Pub Libr 407 W Seminole St Marlow OK 73055

BANNISTER, RICHARD D, sculptor; b. Buffalo, Apr. 16, 1944; s. Leroy and Doris Elizabeth (Nesbitt) Dickerson; m. Mary Jane Overall, Nov. 12, 1969 (div.); 1 child, Adrian Richard; m. Mary Francis Mager, Jan. 16, 1981; children: Victoria Elizabeth, Elisha Richard. AAS in Agrl. Engring., Cornell U., 1964; student, SUNY, Alfred, 1966-67, SUNY, Brockport, 1970-72; BFA, Instituto Allende, San Miguel de Allende, Mexico, 1974, MFA, 1977. Owner Diamond Internat., Richard's Sta.; ptnr. RDB Properties; owner, operator Oak Orchard Lodge; instr. sculpture Instituto Allende, San Miguel de Allenda, asst. dir. foundry, asst. gallery dir., juror, asst. to head sculpture dept., 1972-77. Elder Barre Ctr. Presbyn. Ch. With U.S. Army, 1966-68. Recipient Her Honor Pauline M. McGibbon award Can. Agr. Internat. Wood Carving Exhbn., 1977. Office: Richards Sta 13579 Maple St Albion NY 14411-9402

BANNISTER, ROBERT CORWIN, JR., history educator; b. Bklyn., June 4, 1935; s. Robert C. and Ruth (Allen) B.; m. Joan Turner, June 8, 1958; children: Robert Stanley, Emily E., Paul Andrew, James Peter. BA, Yale U., 1955; BA, MA, Oxford U., Eng., 1957, 61; PhD, Yale U., 1961. Instr. history Yale U., New Haven, 1960-62; asst. to full prof. Swarthmore Coll., Pa., 1962-98; Bicentennial prof. U. Helsinki, 1977-78; Fulbright prof. U. Rome, 1985, U. Leiden, Netherlands, 1992; mem. advanced placement program Ednl. Testing Service, Princeton, N.J., 1963-79; vis. prof. U. Queensland, Australia, 1988. Author: Ray Stannard Baker, 1966, Social Darwinism: Science and Myth, 1978, Sociology and Scientism, 1987, Jessie Bernard: The Making of a Feminist, 1991; editor: American Values in Transition, 1972, On Liberty, Society and Politics: The Essential Essays of William Graham Sumner, 1992. Mem. Am. Studies Assn., Am. Hist. Assn., Orgn. Am. Historians. Democrat. Office: Swarthmore College Ave Swarthmore PA 19081-1390

BANNON, ANTHONY LEO, museum director; b. Hanover, N.H., Dec. 6, 1942; s. Robert E. and Frances Ann (Cacioppo) B.; children: Nicholas, Brendan. BS, St. Bonaventure, 1964; MA, SUNY, Buffalo, 1974, PhD, 1996. Tchr. sci. and English Father Baker High Sch., Lackawanna, N.Y., 1964-66; critic Buffalo News, 1966-85; dir. Burchfield-Penney Art Ctr., asst. v.p. cultural affairs SUNY Coll. at Buffalo, 1985-96; dir. George Eastman House Internat. Mus. Photography and Film, Rochester, N.Y., 1996—; chmn. visual arts program N.Y. State Coun. on Arts, N.Y.C., 1986-88; co-chmn. arts programming com. World Univ. Games, Buffalo, 1991-93; vice chmn. Empire State Craft Alliance, Saratoga Springs, N.Y., 1988-93; chmn. bd. Quick Fine Arts Ctr., St. Bonaventure U., 1996—. Author: The Photo-Pictorialists of Buffalo, 1981, The Taking of Niagara, 1983, Arcadia Revisited, 1989. Mem., vestry Ch. Good Shepard, Buffalo, 1986-89; bd. dirs. Greater Rochester Visitors Assn., 1996-97, Rochester Arts and Cultural Coun., 1997—; trustee N.Y. State Alliance of Arts Orgns., 1998—, Rochester Sch. for the Deaf, 1998—. Recipient Excellence in Writing about Deafness award Gallaudet Coll., 1985, Merit award Am. Photog. Hist. Soc., 1982; Profl. Study Leave grantee N.Y. State/United Univ. Professions, 1993, Outstanding Arts Adminstr. award The Buffalo Partnership, 1995. Mem. Am. Assn. Mus., Mus. Assn. N.Y. State (counselor 1994—), Gallery Assn. N.Y. State (trustee 1997—), Buffalo State Coll. Found. (trustee 1985-91), Soc. Photog. Edn., Am. Assn. Mus. Dirs. Office: George Eastman House 900 East Ave Rochester NY 14607-2298

BANNON, GEORGE, retired economics educator, department chairman; b. Phila., May 25, 1925; s. Joseph Aloysius and Violet May (McCartney) B.; m. Rosemary Ann Chirico, Aug. 19, 1950; children: Patricia Ann, Christina Ann, Terence George. Student, U. Ga., 1944, N.C. State U., 1944; AB, Muhlenberg Coll., 1947; MBA, Lehigh U., 1967. Contr. Overseas Underwriters Ltd., Nassau, Bahamas, 1957-61; internal auditor Bethlehem (Pa.) Steel Corp., 1961-68, sr. systems and procedure analyst, 1968-72, adminstrv. asst., 1972-81; vis. assoc. prof. Moravian Coll., Bethlehem, 1981-85; asst. prof. Muhlenberg Coll., Allentown, Pa., 1985-88; chmn. dept. econs. Muhlenberg Coll., Allentown, 1988-96; ret., 1996; official Ea. Collegiate Football Officials Assn., Princeton, N.J., 1955-65; Pa. Interscholastic Football Officials Assn., Harrisburg, Pa., 1952-71. Organizer Allentown Area Luth. Parish, Luth. Ch. in Am., 1964-67; bd. dirs. Allentown Area Luth. Parish, 1984-87. Recipient Outstanding Official award Pa. Interscholastic Football Officials Assn., 1971. Mem. Nat. Assn. Accts. (rsch. com. 1979-84, mktg. com. 1985-86, bd. dirs. 1987-93, v.p. 1995-96, mem. nat. exec. com. 1995-96), Am. Mgmt. Assn., Fin. Exec. Inst., Allentown C. of C., Am. Assn. Collegiate Schs. Bus., West Allentown Kiwanis Club (pres. 1986-87). Avocations: photography, coin collecting, gardening. Home: 9 W Sycamore Pl Lewisburg PA 17837-9229

BANOFF, SHELDON IRWIN, lawyer; b. Chgo., July 10, 1949. BSBA in Acctg., U. Ill., 1971; JD, U. Chgo., 1974. Bar: Ill. 1974, U.S. Tax Ct. 1974. Ptnr. Katten Muchin & Zavis, Chgo., 1974—; chmn. tax conf. planning com. U. Chgo. Law Sch., 1993-94. Co-editor Jour. of Taxation, 1984—; contbr. articles to profl. jours. Mem. ABA, Chgo. Bar Assn. (fec. taxation com., mem. exec. coun. 1980—), Chgo. Fed. Tax Forum, Am. Coll. Tax Counsel. Office: Katten Muchin & Zavis 525 W Monroe St Ste 1600 Chicago IL 60661-3693

BANOVETZ, JAMES M., public administration educator, consultant. P-rof., dir. divsn. pub. adminstrn. No. Ill. U., DeKalb, 1979-97, prof., dir. emeritus divsn. pub. adminstrn., 1998—, sr. rsch. assoc. Ctr. for Govtl. Studies, 1998—. Editor: Managing Local Government Finance, 1996. Fellow Nat. Acad. Pub. Adminstrn.; mem. Ill. City Mgmt. Assn. (Lifetime Achievement award 1997). Address: 7 Miller Ct Dekalb IL 60115-2311

BANS, PHIL, retired corporate security professional; b. Ft. Lewis, Wash., Feb. 28, 1962; s. Phil Sr. and Rebecca Martinez Bans; m. Esperanza Marquez, Nov. 7, 1978; 1 child, Phil III. AA in Gen. Edn., Hartnell Coll., 1995. Maintence offcl. So. Pacific RR, Salinas, Calif., 1983-86; corp. security officer Electronic Data Systems, Salinas, 1986-95; tng. officer EDS (GM), L.A., Plano, Tex.; tng. officer Corp. Security Officer Disaster Preparedness, 1992-94. Treas. honors club Hartnell Coll., 1994-95; v.p. Salinas Youth Football, 1998; exec. v.p. Salinas Colts/Broncos Youth Football, Salinas, 1999—, bd. dirs. 1998—; sec., exec. bd. Monterey Bay Youth Football League, Salinas, 1999—; vol. Palma H.S., basketball/baseball concession chair 1998-99. Democrat. Avocations: sports memorbilla, card collecting, coca cola collector. Fax: 831-771-1750. E-mail: philbans@prodigy.net. Office: Phils Collectibles PO Box 56 Salinas CA 93902

BANSAK, STEPHEN A., JR., investment banker, financial consultant; b. Bridgeport, Conn., Sept. 19, 1939; s. Stephen A. and Genevieve Bansak; m. Susan Jean Dizon, July 20, 1984; children: Cynthia A., Thomas S., Stephen A. III, Kirk C. BS, Yale U., 1961; MBA, U. Pa., 1968. With Kidder, Peabody & Co., Inc., N.Y.C., 1968-89, v.p., 1971-75, co-mgr. dept. corpl fin., 1975-84; vice chmn. Kidder, PEabody Internat., N.Y.C., 1984—; bd. dirs. Kidder Peabody P.R., KP Realty Advisers; sr. cons. Concord Internat. Ptnrs., 1990—, bentley Assocs., 1990-92; vice chmn. Myers, Craig, Vallone, Francois, Inc., 1992-93; sr. advisor Universal Tech. inst., 1995-97, Motay Electronics, Inc., 1993-97, Buenavenjura Filamor Echuas (Manila), 1991-94; vis. lectr. Wharton Grad. Sch., U. Pa., 1989; bd. dirs. Filbrin, Inc., Lighthouse Ptnrs., Troy Bioscis., Inc.; bd. dirs., vice chmn. Computerized Med. Sys., Inc.; mem. adv. bd. Global Health Care Ptnrs. (DLJ Mcht. Banking); adv. com. Manschot Opportunity Fund. Past trustee, v.p. Rumson (N.J.) Country Day Sch. Lt. USN, 1962-66, Vietnam. Mem. Philippine-Am. C. of C. (bd. dirs.), U.S.-Asia inst. (past bd. dirs.), India House (past pres. Broad St. Club), Navesink Country Club, Yale Club N.Y.C., Troon Golf and Country Club, Securities Industry Assn. (chmn. corp. fin. com., rule 415 com.), Am. Stock Exch. (ofcl.).

BANSE, KARL, retired oceanography educator; b. Koenigsberg Pr., East Prussia, Germany, Feb. 20, 1929; came to U.S., 1960, naturalized; s. Karl and Wally B. PhD in Oceanography, U. Kiel, Fed. Republic Germany, 1955; Dr. honoris causa, U. Kiel, Germany, 1995. Postdoctoral fellow in marine sci. U. Kiel, 1955-57; Govt. India scholar Central Marine Fish Research Sta., India, 1958-60; asst. prof. oceanography U. Wash., Seattle, 1960-63, assoc. prof. oceanography, 1963-66, prof. oceanography, 1966-95, retired, 1995. Recipient Lifetime Achievement award ASLO, 1998. Fellow Marine Biology Assn. India. Office: U Wash Sch Oceanography Box 357940 Seattle WA 98195-7940

BANSEMER, RICHARD FREDERICK, bishop; b. Oswego, N.Y., May 26, 1940; s. Reinhold Mathias and Oralee Ann (Brierly) B.; m. Barbara Anne Gallmeier, June 9, 1962 (dec. Feb. 1968); 1 child, John David.; m. Mary Ann Troutman, July 18, 1971; children: Aaron Richard, Andrew Christopher. BA, Newberry (S.C.) Coll., 1962; BD, Luth. Theol. So. Sem., 1966; DD (hon.), Newberry Coll., 1988, Roanoke Coll., 1988. Ordained to ministry Evang. Luth. Ch. in Am., 1966. Assoc. pastor Univ. Luth. Ch., Gainesville, Fla., 1966-68; pastor St. John Luth. Ch., Roanoke, 1968-73, Lord of the Mountains Luth. Ch., Dillon, Colo., 1973-78, Rural Retreat (Va.) Luth. Parish, 1978-87; bishop Va. Synod Evang. Luth. Ch. in Am., Salem, 1988—. Author: People Prayers, 1976, The Chosen and the Changed, 1977, Grace and the Grave, 1981, Risen Indeed, 1982, In Plain Sight, 1982, Day Full of Grace, 1987, O Lord, Teach Me to Pray, 1995, Praying on the Journey with Christ, 1997, We Believe, 1999. Trustee Roanoke Coll., 1988—. Office: Evang Luth Ch in Am Va Synod PO Box 70 Salem VA 24153-0070

BANSTETTER, ROBERT J., lawyer; b. 1940. BS, St Louis U., 1963; JD, U. Ill., 1966. Bar: Mo. 1967, Ill. 1966. Atty. Labor Rels. Internat. Shoe, 1966-70; v.p., gen. coun. & sec. Gen. Am. Life Ins. Co., 1992—. Office: Gen Am Life Ins Co 700 Market St Saint Louis MO 63101-1829*

BANTA, HENRY DAVID, physician, researcher; b. Electra, Tex., Mar. 3, 1938; arrived in The Netherlands, 1985; s. Henry Eugene and Hazel (Rippy) B.; divorced; children: Elizabeth Christian, Barbara Shawn, Michael David, Heather Alexandra; m. Ellen Hoen, June 19, 1998. Student, Duke U., 1956-59, MD, 1963; MPH, Harvard U., 1968, MS, 1969. Diplomate Am. Bd. Preventive Medicine. Intern King County Hosp., Seattle, 1963-64; resident U. Wash. Hosps., Seattle, 1964-65, Health Services Adminstrn. Harvard Sch. Pub. Health, 1968-69; from asst. to assoc. prof. community medicine Mt. Sinai Sch. Medicine, N.Y.C., 1969-75; from researcher to asst. dir. office tech. assessment U.S. Congress, Washington, 1975-83; dep. dir. Pan Am. Health Orgn., Washington, 1983-85; prof. tech. assessment U. Limburg, Maastricht, The Netherlands, 1987-91; sr. rschr. The Netherlands Orgn. for Applied Rsch., Leiden, 1992—; adj. prof. Cmty. Med., Mt. Sinai Sch. Med., N.Y.C., 1996—, vis. prof. Internat. Health, Boston U. Sch. Public Health, 1996—; cons. WHO, The Hague, The Netherlands and Copenhagen, 1985-92, European Commn., Brussels, 1986—, World Bank, Washington, 1987—, The Netherlands Ministry Health,The Hague, 1987—, Swedish Coun. on Health Care Tech. Assessment, 1989—, U.S. Office Tech. Assessment, 1993-95. Author: (with others) Toward Rational Technology in Medicine, 1981, Anticipating and Assessing Health Care Technology, 1987, Lasers in Health Care, 1991, Health Care Technology and Its Assessment, 1993, Health Care Technology and Its Assessment in Eight Countries, 1994; also articles. Served to lt. comdr. USPHS, 1965-67. Milbank Fund fellow, 1970-73, Robert Wood Johnson Health Policy fellow, 1974, Ctr. Advanced Study Behavioral Sci. fellow, 1986. Mem. Internat. Soc. Tech. Assessment in Health Care (bd. dirs. 1985-90, 92—, editor newsletter 1988—, v.p. 1997—, pres. 1999—). Avocations: wine tasting and buying, ballet. Office: PG/TNO, PO Box 2215, 2301 CE Leiden The Netherlands

BANTA, JAMES ELMER, physician, epidemiologist, university dean; b. Tucumcari, N.Mex., July 1, 1927; s. James Elmer and Edna Mae (Murnahan) B. M.D., Marquette U., 1950; M.P.H., Johns Hopkins U., 1954; diploma, U.S. Naval Med. Sch., 1952. Med. officer USN, 1950-60; capt. med. officer USPHS, 1960-69; dir. med. program Peace Corps, 1963-65; dir. Office Internat. Health, HEW, 1967-68; med. officer WHO, 1968-70; prof. public health U. Hawaii, 1970-73; dep. dir. Office Health, AID, State Dept., Washington, 1973-75; dean, prof. Sch. Public Health and Tropical Medicine, Tulane U., New Orleans, 1975-87; prof. Sch. Pub. Health U. Hawaii, Honolulu, 1987-88; clin. prof. dept. community and family medicine Georgetown U., Washington, 1990—; adj. prof. dept. health care scis. George Washington U., Washington, 1992—. Co-author: How to Travel the World and Stay Healthy, 1969, Year-round Travelers' Health Guide, 1978; Contbr. articles on epidemiology, microbiology and health to profl. jours. Served with USN, 1944-46. Recipient Outstanding Service award Georgetown U., 1965. Fellow AAAS, Am. Coll. Preventive Medicine, Am. Public Health Assn., Am. Heart Assn., Am. Coll. Epidemiology, Coll. Phys. Phila.; mem. ACLU, Common Cause, Environ. Action, Assn. Schs. Public Health (pres. 1979-81), Sigma Xi, Phi Sigma, Delta Omega. Office: George Washington U Med Ctr 2300 I St NW Washington DC 20037-2336

BANTEL, LINDA MAE, museum curatorial consultant; b. King City, Calif., May 30, 1943; d. Clifford Burnett and Helen Vernelle (Mallicotte) Bantel; m. David Hollenberg, June 15, 1980; 1 child, Matthew Bantel Hollenberg. M.A., NYU, 1973. Research cons. N.Y. Hist. Soc., N.Y.C., 1975-76; guest co-curator Art Mus. of South Tex., Corpus Christi, Tex., 1977-79; research assoc. Met. Mus. Art, N.Y.C., 1978-80; curator, dir. of mus. Pa. Acad. Fine Arts, Phila., 1980-95. Co-author: (with James Thomas Flexner) The Face of Liberty: Founders of the U.S., 1975; author: The Alice M. Kaplan Collection, 1980; William Rush, American Sculptor, 1982; (with Marcus Burke) Spain and New Spain: Mexican Colonial Arts in Their European Context, 1979; contbr. to American Paintings in the Metropolitan Museum of Art Vol. II: A Catalogue of Works by Artists Born Between 1816-1845, 1985, (with others) Searching Out the Best, 1988, Raphaelle Peale Still Lifes, 1988; contbr. to Antiques mag., 1989. Mem. Coll. Art Assn., Am. Assn. Mus. Home: 703 W Phil Ellena St Philadelphia PA 19119-3513

BANTJES, ADRIAN ALEXANDER, history educator; b. Kingston, Ont., Can., Sept. 19, 1959; s. Adrian and Aida Mercedes (Aróstegui) B.; m. Mary Margaret Henning, May 14, 1994. MA in History, Rijksuniversiteit Leiden, The Netherlands; PhD in L.Am. History, U. Tex., 1991. Asst. prof. L.Am. history U. Wyo., Laramie, 1991-97, assoc. prof. L.Am. history, 1997—. Author: As If Jesus Walked on Earth Cardenismo, Sonora and the Mexican Revolution, 1998; contbr. articles to profl. jours. NEH grantee, 1991, ACLS/SSRC grantee, 1999. Office: U Wyo Dept History Laramie WY 82071-3198

BANTRY, BRYAN, entrepreneur, producer, director; b. Jacksonville, Fla., Oct. 12, 1956. Owner, operator dog-walking svc., 1969-73; photographer's agt. Patrick Demarchelier, 1973—; owner Bryan Bantry Hair-Makeup Agy., N.Y.C., 1973—, Bryan Bantry Celebrity Model Mgmt., N.Y.C., 1992—; chmn., chief exec. officer Royal Atlantic Airways, N.Y.C., 1991—. Co-prodr. (Broadway plays) You Can't Take it With You, 1983, Aren't We All, 1985, (off-Broadway plays) Greater Tuna, 1982, Hey Ma...Kaye Ballard, 1984; creator TV pilot Man's Best Friend, 1983; prodr. (feature documentary) The Cream Will Rise: The Sophie B. Hawkins Story, 1998, (feature film) Ladies Who Do, 1999; theatre prodr. (Broadway musical) Street Corner Symphony, 1997-98; prodr., co-dir. feature short film Eventual Wife, 1999. Chmn. Batoto Yetu inner-city youth program, N.Y.C., 1992—. Mem. League of Am. Theatres and Prodrs.

BANUELOS, BETTY LOU, rehabilitation nurse; b. Vandergrift, Pa., Nov. 28, 1930; d. Archibald and Bella Irene (George) McKinney; m. Raul, Nov. 1, 1986; children: Patrice, Michael. Diploma, U. Pitts., 1951; cert., Loma Linda U., 1960. RN, Calif.; cert. chem. dependency nurse. Cons. occupational health svcs. Bd. Registered Nurses, 1984—; lectr., cons. in field. Recipient Scholarship U. Pitts. Mem. Dirs. of Nursing, Calif. Assn. Nurses in Substance Abuse. Home and Office: 15 Oak Spring Ln Laguna Hills CA 92656-2980

BANUK, RONALD EDWARD (RON), mechanical engineer; b. Brockton, Mass., Oct. 22, 1944; s. Joseph John and Leocadia Marilyn (Gusciora) B.; m. Patricia Audrey Ryan, July 4, 1969; children: Kim, Lance. BSME, Northea. U., 1967; MSME, San Diego State U., 1971. Design and stress engr. in advanced systems Ryan Aero. Co., San Diego, 1967-76; sr. tech. specialist Northrop Corp., Pico Rivera, Calif., 1976-94, program mgr., 1987-89, structures tech. area mgr., 1991, prin. investigator in advanced structure and foam devel., 1986-93; prin. engr. structures Advt. Tech. Transit Bus, 1993—; tech. lead for Navy's Composite Destroyer Deck. Author: Papers on Foam and Composites: SAMPE, 1993, 97, 98, DOE & ASME, 1996, Mary: Past, Present and Future, 1997. Mem. Soc. Adv. Material and Process Engring. Avocation: writing on religion. Home: 6441 Ringo Cir Huntington Beach CA 92647-3323 Office: Adv Structural Design/Devel 9N10/W10 1 Hornet Way El Segundo CA 90245-2804

BANWART, GEORGE JUNIOR, food microbiology educator; b. Algona, Iowa, Sept. 15, 1926; s. George W. and Leah R. (Schneider) B.; m. Sally Jean Foss, Mar. 18, 1955; children—Deborah, Geoffrey. B.S., Iowa State U., 1950, Ph.D., 1955. Asst. prof. U. Ga., Athens, 1955-57; head egg products sect. U.S. Dept. Agr., Washington, 1957-62; research microbiologist U.S. Dept. Agr., Beltsville, Md., 1965-69; assoc. prof. Purdue U., Lafayette, Ind., 1962-65; prof. food microbiology Ohio State U., Columbus, 1969-88, prof. emeritus, 1988. Author: Basic Food Microbiology, 1979, 2d edit., 1989; contbr. numerous articles to profl. jours. Served with U.S. Army, World War II. Mem. Inst. Food Technologists. Developer Banwart salmonella flask. Home: 174 Brookside Ct Palm Harbor FL 34683-5322

BANWART, WAYNE LEE, agronomy, environmental science educator; b. West Bend, Iowa, Jan. 9, 1948; s. Albert R. and Betty R. (Zaugg) B.; m. Charlen Ann Schrock, Mar. 22, 1970; children: Krista, Kara, Neil. MS, Iowa State U., 1972, PhD, 1975. Asst. prof. U. Ill., Urbana, 1975-79, assoc. prof., 1979-84, prof., 1984-89, prof., assoc. head dept. agronomy, 1989-94, asst. dean, 1994—; vis. scientist Constrn. Engring. Lab., Champaign, 1985-86; chmn. Nat. Atmospheric Deposition Program, 1986. Co-author: (textbook) Soils and Their Environment, 1992. Mem. patient satisfaction com. HMO, Champaign, 1987-93; pres. citizen's adv. com. Mahomet-Seymour Schs., 1981. Nat. Coll. Tchrs. of Agr. fellow, 1987. Fellow Am. Soc. Agronomy (George D. Scarseth award 1973), Soil Sci. Soc. Am.; mem. Internat. Soil Sci. Soc., Gamma Sigma Delta (pres.). Achievements include discovery that agricultural crops subject to acid rain will suffer little or no yield reduction or physiological damage; discovery that plant uptake and translocation of TNT is very limited while RDX is readily taken up and concentrated in plant tissues; that organic amendments offer promise for bioremediation of soils contaminated with these explosives. Home: 504 N Division St Mahomet IL 61853-9536 Office: U Ill 1301 W Gregory Dr Urbana IL 61801-3608

BANZHAF, JOHN F., III, legal association executive, lawyer; b. N.Y.C., July 2, 1940; s. John F., Jr. and Olga (Mischenko) B.; m. Ursula Maag, 1971. B.S. in Elec. Engring, M.I.T., 1962; J.D. magna cum laude, Columbia U., 1965. Civilian research asst. Signal Corps Engring. Labs., 1957; research engr., cons. Lear Siegler Corp., 1959-62; editor Columbia Law Rev., 1964-65; research fellow Nat. Municipal League, 1965; law clk. to U.S. Dist. Judge Spottswood W. Robinson III, 1965-66; assoc. firm Watson, Leavonworth, Kelton & Taggart, N.Y.C., 1967; founder, exec. dir. Action on Smoking and Health, Washington, 1968—, Nat. Inst. Legal Activism, 1980—; prof. law and legal activism Nat. Law Center, George Washington U., 1968—; exec. dir. Action on Safety and Health, 1971-80, Open America, 1975-80; founder Nat. Center for Law and the Deaf, 1975—; Bd. dirs. Consumers Union, 1971. Recipient 17th ann. Sat. Rev. award distinguished TV programming in pub. interest, 1969; Advt. Age award, 1967, 68; those who made advt. news, 1967, 68; Benjamin Franklin Lit. and Med. Soc. award, 1981. Mem. Sigma Xi, Eta Kappa Nu, Tau Beta Pi. Home: 2810 N Quebec St Arlington VA 22207-5215 Office: 2013 H St NW Washington DC 20006-4207 *Despite the increasing complexity of society, and the seemingly overwhelming power of large institutions both public and private, one determined individual can still have a significant and beneficial impact on society. (I was responsible, as an individual, for over 200 million dollars worth of free radio and television time for anti-smoking commercials which led to the ban on cigarette commercials.).*

BAPST, DONALD JOSEPH, JR., writer; b. Troy, Oct. 2, 1967; s. Donald and Barbara Bapst; life partner David Faulk, Aug. 15, 1990 (div. May 1993); life ptnr. Peter Gerhäuser, June 30, 1993. BA, Columbia Coll., 1989; MFA, Bklyn. Coll., 1991; French lang. cert., La Sorbonne, Paris, 1994. English tchr. Bklyn. Coll. and L.I. U., 1989-92; office asst. Southbank U., London, winter 1992, Bank of Am., San Francisco, 1992-93; writer, editor, translator Typeline France, Paris, 1993-95; travel counselor Coun. Travel and Maritz Travel, San Francisco, 1996-97; vol. instr. econs. English U.S. Peace Corps, U. Ouagadougou, Burkina Faso, 1997-98; mgr. media rels., publicist, writer Cmty. Mktg., Inc., San Francisco, 1998-99; freelance writer and editor San Francisco, 1999—. Editor, translator, writer The Connoisseur's France, 1995-97; author of poetry. Mgr. AIDS Awareness Week, Bklyn. Coll., 1990-91; vol. vaccine adv. Project Inform, San Francisco, 1992-93; protocol translator Act Up Paris, 1995; writer HIV treatment updates FACTS, Paris, 1995-96.

BAPTIST, ALLWYN J., health care consultant; b. India, July 10, 1943; came to U.S., 1971; s. Peter L.G. and Trescilla (Lobo) B.; m. Anita Lobo, Sept. 8, 1973; children: Alan, Andrew, Annabel, Arthur. B.Sc., U. Calcutta, India, 1962; cert. mgmt., U. Chgo., 1978. CPA, Ill; chartered acct., India. Divisional acct. Rallis India Ltd., Bombay, 1967-71; mgr. Chgo. Blue Cross, 1972-79; sr. mgr. Price Waterhouse, Chgo., 1979-84; v.p., dir. Truman Esmond and Assocs., Barrington, Ill., 1984-86; ptnr. Laventhol and Horwath, Chgo., 1986-90, BDO Seidman, Chgo., 1991—; mem. adv. bd. St. Mary of Nazareth Hosp., 1989—, mem. gov. bd., 1992-94, 96-98, lifetime trustee. Contbr. articles to profl. jours. Mem. fin. com. St. James Ch., Arlington Heights, Ill., 1987; mem. AICPA Health Care Com., 1991-94. Mem. Healthcare Fin. Mgmt. Assn. (dir., sec. 1983—, pres. 1988-89, recipient William J. Follmer award 1984, Reeves award 1989, Muncie Gold award 1992, founders medal of honor 1998), India Cath. Assn. Am. (treas. 1980, 87, pres. 1988). Avocations: travel, reading, tennis, golf. Office: BDO Seidman 205 N Michigan Ave Chicago IL 60601-5927

BAPTIST, ERROL CHRISTOPHER, pediatrician, educator; b. Colombo, Sri Lanka, Feb. 24, 1945; came to U.S., 1974; s. Egerton Cuthbert and Hyacinth Margaret (Colomb) B.; m. Christine Rosemary Francke, Aug. 7, 1976; children: Lauren Marianne, Erik Christopher; MB BS, Faculty of Medicine, U. Ceylon, 1969. Diplomate Am. Bd. Pediatrics. Intern, Colombo Gen. Hosp. and Children's Hosp., Colombo, Sri Lanka, 1969-70; resident house officer Dist. Hosp., Gampola, Sri Lanka, 1970-71; resident house officer Base Hosp., Kegalle, Sri Lanka, 1971-74; family practitioner, Marawila, Sri Lanka, 1974; resident physician in pediatrics Coll. Medicine and Dentistry N.J., Newark, 1975-77; practice medicine specializing in pediatrics, Rockford, Ill., 1977—; asst. prof. pediatrics U. Ill. Coll. Medicine, Rockford, 1977—, assoc. prof., 1994—; chmn. dept. pediatrics St. Anthony Med. Ctr., Rockford, 1986—. Recipient 10 Raymond B. Allen Instructorship awards U. Ill., Faculty Disting. Tchrs. award U. Ill. Coll. of Medicine at Rockford, 1997. Fellow Am. Acad. Pediatrics; mem. So. Med. Assn. Roman Catholic. Home: 5112 Parliament Pl Rockford IL 61107-5066 Office: Mulford Village Office Park 461 N Mulford Rd Rockford IL 61107-5165

BAPTIST, THOMAS R., association administrator; b. Chgo., Oct. 18, 1956. BS in Natural Resources Conservation, Conn. U., 1978; M in Environ. Sci., U. New Haven, 1997. Compliance officer Greenwich (Conn.) Inland Wetlands and Watercourses Agency, 1978-80; dir. Town of Greenwich, 1980-97; exec. dir. Nat. Audubon Soc., Greenwich, 1997; instr. landscape ecology N.Y. Botanical Garden Inst. Ecosystem Studies, 1984-94. Co-author: Connecticut Birds, 1989; contbr. articles to profl. jours. Bd. dirs., co-founder Land Conservation Coalition Conn., 1985—, Mianus River Watershed Coun., 1986—; appointee Long Island Sound Assembly, 1990—; mem. Redding Zoning Commn., 1987—, Redding Water Pollution Ctrl. Commn., 1989-92; chmn. Water Resources Rsch. Com., 1981-83. Recipient Conservation award Garden Club Am., 1996, Conservation Achievement award, 1988, Regional Best Birder Nat. Audubon Soc., 1981, 82; named Conservationist Yr. Conn. Assn. Conservation and Inland Wetland Commn., 1993. Mem. Conn. Ornithol. Assn. (pres. 1992-95). Office: Nat Audubon Soc 613 Riversville Rd Greenwich CT 06831-2624*

BAPTISTE, THOMAS L., career officer. BSBA in Fin., Calif. State U., 1973; student navigator tng., Mather AFB, Calif., 1973-74; student, MacDill AFB, Fla., 1974-75, 81-82, Williams AFB, Ariz., 1977-78, Squadron Officer Sch., 1977; student F-4 qualification tng., George AFB, Calif., 1978-79; student, Air Command and Staff Coll., 1986; MPA, Golden Gate U., 1987; student, Air War Coll., 1990, Johns Hopkins U., 1997. Commd. 2d lt. USAF, 1973, advanced through grades to brig. gen., 1997; weapons sys. officer and instr. 44th Tactical Fighter Squadron, Kadena Air Base, Japan, 1975-77; aircraft comdr., standardization and evaluation officer 334th Tactical Fighter Squadron, Seymour Johnson AFB, N.C., 1979-81; stationed at MacDill AFB, Fla., 1982-84, 85-89; F-16 instr. pilot and chief, standardization/evaluation div. 8th Tactical Fighter Wing, Kunsan Air Base, S. Korea, 1984-85; asst. dir. nuc. ops. Hdqs. Def. Nuc. Agy., Alexandria, Va., 1990-92; comdr. 52d Ops. Group, Spangdahlem Air Base, Germany, 1992-94; chief weapons tech. control div. Joint Staff, Pentagon, Washington, 1994-96, asst. dep. dir. internat. negotiations, 1994-96, directorate strategic plans and policy, 1994-96; dep. comdr. Can. N. Am. Aerospace Def. Command Region, Winnipeg, Manitoba, 1996-98; comdr. Cheyenne Mountain Ops. Ctr., Cheyenne Mountain Air Sta., Colorado Springs, Colo., 1998—. Decorated Air medal. Office: CMOC/CC 1 Norad Rd Ste 5 304 Cheyenne Mountain Air Station CO 80914-6064

BAQUET, CHARLES R., III, federal agency administrator; b. New Orleans, Dec. 24, 1941. BA, U. Xavier, 1963; MPA, Syracuse U., 1975. With Fgn. Svc., 1968; consular officer Fgn. Svc., Paris, 1969-71; gen. svcs. officer bldg. mgmt. Dept. of State, 1971, adminstrv. officer Bur. Adminstrn., 1971-75, spl. asst. to Asst. Sec. of Adminstrn., 1978-79; gen. svcs. officer U.S. Consulate Gen., Hong Kong, 1975-76; councillor adminstrv. affairs U.S. Embassy, Beirut, 1976-78; dep. Office of Ops., 1979-83; dir. regional mgmt. ctr. U.S. Embassy, Paris, 1983-87; sr. seminar Fgn. Svc. Inst., 1987-88; with U.S. Consul Gen., Cape Town, South Africa, 1988-91; U.S. amb. to Djibouti, 1991-93; dep. dir. Peace Corps, Washington, 1994—. Vol. Peace Corps, Somali Republic, 1965-67. Office: Peace Corps 1111 20th St NW Washington DC 20526-0002

BAQUET, DEAN PAUL, newspaper editor; b. New Orleans, Sept. 21, 1956; s. Edward Joseph and Myrtle (Romano) B.; m. Dylan Landis, Sept. 6, 1986; 1 child, Ari Theogene Landis. Student, Columbia U., 1974. Investigative reporter The Times Picayune/The States Item, New Orleans, 1978-84; investigative reporter Chgo. Tribune, 1984-87, assoc. met. editor for investigations, chief investigative reporter, 1987-90; investigative reporter N.Y. Times, 1990-92, projects editor, 1992-95, deputy met. editor, 1995, nat. editor, 1995—. Recipient Pulitzer prize for investigative reporting Columbia U., N.Y.C., 1988. Office: The New York Times 229 W 43rd St New York NY 10036-3959*

BARA, JEAN MARC, advertising executive; b. Roubaix, France, Aug. 22, 1946; came to U.S., 1970; s. Henri and Marie Antoinette (Dousseau) B.; m. Marian Yu, May 8, 1973; 1 child, Patrick Luc. B in Engring., Fed. U. Rio Grande do Sul, Brazil, 1969; MBA, Columbia U., 1972. With Chase Manhattan Bank, 1972-88, assigned Chase's Brazilian affiliate, Banco Lar Brasileiro, 1978-80, mng. dir., head corp. and retail mktg. planning and product mgmt., Rio de Janeiro, 1980, v.p., head Brazil/Argentina/Paraguay liaison office, N.Y.C., 1980-82, v.p. corp. banking team head, Latin Am. coordinator for mining and metals, N.Y.C., 1983; v.p. nat. Positioning Group N.Y.C., 1984; corp. fin. exec. Chase Investment Bank, 1985-88; with Young & Rubican, Inc., 1988—, v.p., corp. treas. 1988-89, sr. v.p., corp. treas., 1989-91, sr. v.p. fin., corp. treas., 1991; exec. dir., CFO Landor Assocs., 1992-94, chief worldwide ops., 1994-96, CFO Burson Marsteller, 1997—; pres. Ams.-Ea. Region, chief learning officer Landor Assocs., 1998—. Mem. Beta Gamma Sigma. Home: PO Box 4446 Greenwich CT 06831-0408 Office: Landor Assocs 230 Park Ave S New York NY 10003-1513

BARAB, MARVIN, financial consultant; b. Wilmington, Del., July 16, 1927; s. Jacob and Minnie (Press) B.; m. Gertrude Klein, June 13, 1951; children: Jordan, Neal, Caryn. BS with distinction, Ind. U., 1947, MBA, 1951. Dir. mktg. Edward Weiss & Co., Chgo., 1951-56; dir. bus. rsch. Parker Pen Co., Janesville, Wis., 1956-59; dir. mktg. rsch. packaging and graphics Mattel Inc., Hawthorne, Calif., 1959-65; pres. Barcam Pub. Co., Rolling Hills Estates, Calif., 1959-70, Rajo Publs., Rolling Hills Estates, 1967-70, So. Calif. Coll. Med. & Dental Careers, Anaheim, 1970-81, Barbrook, Inc., Rolling Hills Estates, 1981-86; cons. Marvin Barab & Assocs., Rolling Hills Estates, Calif., 1981—. Editor: Rand McNally Camping Guide, 1967-70; contbr. articles to various publs., 1982-87. Treas. Harbor Free Clinic, 1990-92; bd. dirs. So. Bay Contemporary Art Mus., 1993-94, sec., 1994. Mem. Nat. Assn. Trade and Tech. Schs. (hon. life, sec. 1977-79, pres. 1979-81, bd. dirs.), Calif. Assn. Paramed. Schs. (pres. 1973-77). Avocations: travel, music, art. Office: PMB 110 904 Silver Spur Rd Palo Verdes CA 90274-3800

BARABINO, WILLIAM ALBERT, science and technology researcher, inventor; b. Bay Shore, N.Y., Feb. 11, 1932; s. John Joseph and Anna Marie (Gates) B.; children: Susan Beth, Diane Marie, William John. Student, Fordham U., 1951; AS, SUNY, Farmingdale, 1952; student, St. Louis U., 1957; diploma, Alexander Hamilton Inst., N.Y.C., 1963. Dist. mgr. Piper Aircraft Corp., Ctrl. Am., Mex., 1960-62; application engr. Lab. for Electronics, Boston, 1962-63; mktg. mgr. spl. equipment divsn. Itek Corp., Waltham, Mass., 1963-65; bus. cons. North Reading, Mass., 1965-68; dir. Andover (Mass.) Inst. Bus., 1968-70; sci. and tech. rschr. North Reading, 1970—; founder, mng. gen. ptnr. Mass Light Internat. Group, Agoura Hills, Calif., 1992—; founder, CEO Brief Necessities, Agoura Hills, Calif., 1990; cons. CTS Corp., Proctor and Gamble, Scovill Corp., Am. Enviro Products, Inc., Plessey Co., Ltd., GM, Goodyear Aerospace, Ford Motor Co. Patentee tire pressure alarm and warning systems (6), brake wear warning system, fluid level and condition detection systems, personal, feminine and infant hygiene systems (7), treatment for causes of scalp diseases, based on theory then electron-microscopy capture of mitochrondia with dual set of double-walled membranes, liquid dispensing swab applicator, others; contbr. articles to profl. jours. Mem. 1996 Rep. Presdl. Task Force. Capt., rated pilot/rated navigator USAF, 1952-59. Mem. VFW, DAV, Am. Legion. Republican.

BARACSKAY, DANIEL JOHN, political scientist, educator; b. Parma, Ohio; s. Donald James and Jane Anne (Homer) B. BA, U. Akron, 1993, MA, 1995; MBA, Cleve. State U., 1994; MA, U. Cin., 1997, PhD, 1998. Office staff Kona-Kini Prodns., Inc., Medina, Ohio, 1987-93; tchg./rsch. asst. U. Akron, 1993-95; libr. asst. U. Cin., 1995-96, instr./tchg. asst., 1996-97, rsch. fellow, 1997—; rschr. U. Cin., 1995—, U. Akron, 1994-95. Author: The Modern Era of State Regulation, 1998; contbr. articles to profl. jours. Buchtel Coll. Arts and Scis. scholar, 1994-95, McMicken Coll. Arts and Scis. scholar, 1995-97, Charles Phelps Taft scholar, 1998. Mem. Am. Polit. Sci. Assn., Am. Soc. Pub. Adminstrn., Pi Sigma Alpha. Roman Catholic. Avocations: reading, family time, writing, exercising, walking. Home: 3696 Puritan Dr Brunswick OH 44212-4180 Office: Univ of Cincinnati Mail Location 0375 Cincinnati OH 45221-0375

BARAD, JILL ELIKANN, family products company executive; b. N.Y.C., May 23, 1951; d. Lawrence Stanley and Corinne (Schuman) Elikann; m. Thomas Kenneth Barad, Jan. 28, 1979; children: Alexander David, Justin Harris. BA English and Psychology, Queens Coll., 1973. Asst. prod. mgr. mktg. Coty Cosmetics, N.Y.C., 1976-77, prod. mgr. mktg., 1977; account exec. Wells Rich Greene Advt. Agy., L.A., 1978-79; product mgr. mktg. Mattel Toys, Inc., L.A., 1981-82, dir. mktg., 1982-83, v.p. mktg., 1983-85, sr. v.p. mktg., 1985-86, sr. v.p. product devel., 1986, exec. v.p. product design and devel., exec. v.p. mktg. and worldwide product devel., 1988-89; pres. girls and activity toys div. Mattel Toys, Inc. (name now Mattel, Inc.), L.A., 1989-90; pres. Mattel USA, El Segundo, Calif., 1990-92; pres., COO Mattel, Inc., El Segundo, Calif., 1992-97, pres., CEO, 1997, chmn., CEO, 1997—; former bd. dirs. Bank of Am., bd. dirs. Microsoft Corp., Mattel, Inc., Pixar Animation Studios; bd. fellows Claremont U. Ctr. and Grad. Sch. Bd. govs. Town Hall of Los Angeles; trustee emeritus Queens Coll. Found.; chair exec. adv. bd. Children Affected by AIDS Found., Mattel Found, bd. advs. Children's Scholarship Fund, Catalyst, The For All Kids Found., Inc. Exec. bd. Med. Scis. UCLA,. Office: Mattel Inc 333 Continental Blvd El Segundo CA 90245-5012

BARADAT, RAYMOND ALPHONSE, recording industry executive; b. Tulare, Calif., Aug. 14, 1942; s. Leon Pierre and Jeanne Elizabeth (Lasbareilles) B.; m. Dolores Jean Oliver, Aug. 1, 1964 (div. Jan., 1973); 1 child, Raymond Alphonse, Jr.; m. Sandra Gina Santiago, June 26, 1985. AA, Coll. of The Sequoia, 1980; BA, New Coll. of Calif., 1981. Sales mgr. Tulare Pipe and Electric, Tulare, Calif., 1969-74; pres. Charade Record Company, Tulare, Calif., 1974--; attendance supervisor Tulare Joint Union High School, Tulare, Calif., 1975--; rschr., cons. Motown Records, Rhino Records, Collectables Records, Polygram Records, Dionysus Records. Recording artist albums include The Charades, Into The 90's; producer albums include Tule Fog, Lipstick Traces, Looking Like Love, Please Be My Love Tonight, Rare Los Angeles Tracks. Mem. Nat. Acad. of Recording Arts and Sciences. Democrat. Roman Catholic. Avocation: record collecting. Home and Office: Charade Records 1384 E Sequoia Ave Tulare CA 93274-4536

BARAGWANATH, ALBERT KINGSMILL, curator; b. Lima, Peru, July 20, 1917; s. John Gordon and Leila Radcliff (Morris) B.; m. Eileen Mary Flanagan, Sept. 1, 1943; children—Joan Baragwanath Shaw, Janice, John Blackburn, Patricia. Grad., Hill Sch., Pottstown, Pa., 1936; B.A., Princeton, 1940; M.A. in Am. History, Columbia, 1952. With traffic and sales dept. Eastern Air Lines, N.Y.C., 1946-50; librarian Mus. City N.Y., 1952-58, curator prints and portraits, 1959—, sr. curator, 1963-79, sr. curator emeritus, 1980—; mem. N.Y.C. Mayor's Task Force on Municipal Archives, 1966; mem. adv. com. Mus. Am. Folk Art, 1969—. Author: More Than a Mirror to the Past: The First Fifty Years of the Museum of the City of New York, 1973, 50 Currier & Ives Favorites, 1978, 100 Currier & Ives Favorites, 1978; New York Life at the Turn of the Century in Photographs, 1985; contbr.: New York City Guide, 1964, Currier and Ives, Chronicles of America, 1968. Served from pvt. to capt. AUS, 1941-46, ETO; Served from pvt. to capt. AUS, PTO. Decorated Combat Inf. badge. Mem. Am. Hist. Print Collectors Soc. (dir.). Home: 20 Summit Ave Larchmont NY 10538-2930 Office: 1220 5th Ave New York NY 10029-5221

BARAJAS, FELIPE LARA, deacon; b. Poncitlan, Jalisco, Mexico, May 1, 1938; came to U.S., 1973; s. Filiberto Escoto and Antonia Velazquez (Lara) B.; m. Teresa Margarita Hernandez, Apr. 7, 1973; children: Felipe de Jesus, Alfred Joseph. BA, Instituto America, 1963; Physical Edn. degree, Educacion Audiovisual, 1964; Ednl. Puppetry degree, Secretaria E. Publica, 1971. Elem. tchr. Escuela Cervantes, Guadalajara, Mex., 1961-64; instr. puppetry Dirección de Edn. Audiovisual, Guadalajara, 1964-65; elem. tchr. Jalisco State Penitentiary, 1965-67; prin. parochial sch. San Joaquín, Mex., 1967-68, Las Fuentes Zapopan, Mex., 1969-71; tchr. physical edn. Colegio Augustin de Iturbide, Tamazula, Mex., 1971-72; vol. tchr. San Antonio Literacy Coun., 1976-77; instr. puppetry Mex. Cultural Inst., San Antonio, 1982; sec. Permanent Diaconal Community, San Antonio, 1986-90; deacon Holy Rosary Cath. Ch., San Antonio, 1986—; elem. tchr. Circle Sch., San Antonio, 1986—; instr. in field; promotor Small Christian Communities, 1986—. Tchr. San Antonio Literacy Coun., Inc., 1976-77; puppetry tchr. Mexican Cultural Inst., San Antonio, 1982. Democrat. Home: 239 Havana Dr San Antonio TX 78228-4759 Office: Holy Rosary Cath Ch 159 Camino Santa Maria St San Antonio TX 78228-4901

BARAL, LILLIAN, artist, retired educator; b. Perehinsko, Poland; d. Leon and Esther (Ludmer) B. BA, Hunter Coll., 1939, MA in Art, 1969. Cert. fine arts, secondary English, elem. tchr., N.Y. Sec., publicity asst. Coun. for Democracy, N.Y.C.; translator, radio script writer, announcer U.S. Office of War Info., Voice of Am., N.Y.C.; writer, publicity specialist Citizens Com. on Displaced Persons, N.Y.C., Consulate Gen. of Israel, N.Y.C.; publicity specialist Madison Books, Pub. House, N.Y.C., Brandeis U., Waltham, Mass.; pub. rels. dir. Israel Govt. Tourist Office, N.Y.C.; publicity asst. Huntington Hartford Gallery of Modern Art, N.Y.C.; fine arts tchr. Parsons Jr. H.S., Queens, N.Y., 1962-82; painter, sculptor, 1956—; art tour leader 92d St YMHA, 1985, 86. Exhbns. include N.Y. Pub. Libr., Little Gallery, 1966, Whitehouse Gallery, N.Y.C., 1967, Am. House, N.Y.C., 1968, Lord & Taylor, N.Y.C., 1970, Center Art Gallery, N.Y.C., 1971, Marie Pellicone Gallery, N.Y.C., 1979, Womanart Gallery, N.Y.C., 1979, BFM Gallery, N.Y.C., 1980, Bennett Gallery, Fairfield, Conn., 1981, Queens Mus., 1981, New Sch. for Social Rsch., N.Y.C., 1982, Lever House, N.Y.C., 1983, W.C. Post Coll., L.I., N.Y., 1984, Southhampton Coll., L.I., 1984, Queensborough C.C. Art Gallery, N.Y.C., 1985, 86, UAHC Gallery, N.Y.C., 1988, Mari Galleries, Mamaroneck, N.Y., 1989; represented in permanent collections Yad Vashem Mus., Jerusalem, Hebrew U., Jerusalem; shows at B'nai B'rith Klutznick Nat. Jewish Mus., Washington, Libr. Gallery, U. Maine, Augusta, Chaffee Ctr. Visual Arts, Rutland, Vt., Holocaust Mus. and Resource Ctr. Jewish Fedn., Scranton, Pa., 1995, Davidson and Daughters Gallery, Portland, Maine, 1998; also numerous pvt. collections; subject newspaper, mag. articles, TV interview. Mem. N.Y. Artists Equity (exec. bd. 1985-86), United Fedn. Tchrs., Mus. Modern Art (N.Y.C.). E-mail: bobblat@worldnet.att.net. Home: 98-50 67th Ave Forest Hills NY 11374-4965 Studio: 30 E 20th St New York NY 10003-1310 also: 149 Fort Rd Apt 5 S Portland ME 04106-1643

BARAL, RAM CHANDRA, educator, special education; b. Thanchaur, Nepal, July 15, 1951; came to U.S, 1987; s. Keshav Raj and Jamuna Devi (Paudel) B.; m. Kusum, May 11, 1975; children: Rubi, Susanna, Juotsana, Subas, Sudesna. MA in Polit. Sci., Tribhuwan U., Kathmandi, Nepal, 1984, U. Ariz., 1989; MA in Ednl. Psychology, U. Ariz., 1993, PhD in Spl. Edn., 1995; DD, Asian Acad. Christian Studies, Hyderabad, India, 1997. Asst. prof. Tribuwan U., Kathmandu, Nepal, 1976-86; rsch. assoc. U. Ariz., Tucson, 1987-95; prof. Miss. Valley State U., Itta Bena, 1995—; spl. edn. advisor Napalese Embassy in U.S., Washington, 1995—. Author: Delivery of Services in Special Education, 1998. Recipient Leadership award HAggai Inst., Singapore, 1985, Tech. award Miss. Inst. Higher Learning, JAckson, 1997, Educator award His Majesty King of Nepal, 1998. Mem. Coun. Exceptional Children. Avocation: writing. Home: 304 Church St Winona MS 38967 Office: Miss Valley State U Hwy 82 W 14000 S Itta Bena MS 38947

BARAN, JAN WITOLD, lawyer, educator; b. Ingolstadt, Germany, May 14, 1948; came to U.S., 1951; s. Jerzy Leopold and Leonce Sidonie (Vanden Bussche) B.; m. Kathryn Kavanagh, June 16, 1979; children: Brendan Jerzy, Maria Leonce, Elise Jett, Anna Margaret. BA, Ohio Wesleyan U., 1970; JD, Vanderbilt U., 1973. Bar: Tenn. 1973, D.C. 1976, U.S. Dist. Ct. D.C. 1980, U.S. Ct. Appeals D.C. 1980, U.S. Ct. Appeals (10th cir.) 1994, U.S. Supreme Ct. 1980. Legal counsel Nat. Rep. Congl. Com., Washington, 1975-77; exec. asst. Fed. Election Commn., Washington, 1977-79; assoc. Baker & Hostetler, Washington, 1979-81, ptnr., 1981-85; ptnr. Wiley, Rein & Fielding, Washington, 1985—; gen. counsel, George Bush for Pres., Inc., 1987-88; gen. counsel, Bush-Quayle, Inc., 1988; lectr. Practicing Law Inst., Washington, 1978—. Author: The Election Law Primer for Corporations, 1984, 88, 92, 99. Chmn. nat. adv. bd. Jour. of Law and Politics, 1983—; gen. counsel Am. bicentennial Presdl. Inaugural Inc., 1989, Rep. Nat. Com., 1989-92; mem. Pres. Commn. Fed. Ethics Law Reform; amb., head U.S. del. World Adminstrv. Radio Conf. WARC, Malaga, Spain, 1992; trustee Citizens Rsch. Found., 1995—; gen. counsel, dir. Bus.-Industry Polit. Action Com., 1996—. Patrick Wilson scholar, 1970-73. Mem. ABA (chmn. com. election law 1981—), D.C. Bar Assn., FBA (chmn. polit. campaign and election law com. 1981-83). Roman Catholic. Home: 1608 Walleston Ct Alexandria VA 22302-3928 Office: Wiley Rein & Fielding 1776 K St NW Ste 900 Washington DC 20006-2332

BARAN, PAUL, computer executive; b. Poland, Apr. 29, 1926; came to U.S., 1928; m. Evelyn Murphy, 1955; 1 child, David. BSEE, Drexel U., 1949; MS in Engring., UCLA, 1959; DSc in ENgring. (hon.), Drexel U., 1997. With Eckert Mauchly Computer Co., 1949, Rosen Engring. Products Co., 1950-54; systems group Hughes Aircraft Co., 1955-59; with RAND Corp., 1959-64; co-founder Inst. for Future, 1968; founder Cabledata Assocs., 1972; co-founder Equatorial Comm., 1978-80; founder Packet Techs., 1980, Telebit, 1980, Metricom, Inc., 1985; founder, chmn. bd. Com21, Inc., Milpitas, Calif., 1992—; pres.'s coun. RAND, 1997—. Recipient Edwin H. Armstrong award IEEE Comms. Soc., 1987, First Annual award ACM Spl. Interest Group in Comms., 1989, Fellowship award Marconi Internat., 1991, Centennial 100 medal Drexel U., 1992, Pioneer award Electronic Frontier Found., 1993, Computers and Comm. Found. award, 1996, award NAE, 1996. Fellow AAAS, IEEE (life, Alexander Graham Bell medal 1990),. Achievements include design of first doorway gun detector; inventor packet switching. Home: 83 James Ave Atherton CA 94027-2009

BARANDES, ROBERT, lawyer; b. Bklyn., May 15, 1947; s. Max and Helen (Berger) B.; m. Joan Noveck, May 28, 1970 (div. Jan. 1981); m. Kathleen Lindsey, Aug. 22, 1982 (div. Jan. 1986). Student, U. Coll., London, 1967-68; BA magna cum laude, Union Coll., Schenectady, N.Y., 1969; JD, Harvard U., 1972. Bar: N.Y. 1973, U.S. Dist. Ct. (so. and ea. dists.) N.Y. 1976. From assoc. to ptnr. Barandes, Rabbino & Arnold, N.Y.C., 1972-81; ptnr. Rober, Barandes & Fertel, LLP, N.Y.C., 1981-96; prodr. Broadway revival of Damn Yankees, 1994-96, (on Broadway) Epic Proportions, 1999—. Assoc. producer: (Broadway Play) On The Waterfront, 1995, Lyricist Musical Etched in Stone, 1984; writer, lyricist, musical Star Crossed Lovers, 1984; bookwriter, lyricist musical Almost Eden, 1990. Mem. ABA, League Am. Theatres and Producers, The Players Club, Phi Beta Kappa. Jewish. Avocations: writing, skiing, golf, tennis. Office: Roper Barandes & Fertel LLP 130 W 42nd St Ste 2600 New York NY 10036-7800

BARANOVA, ELENA, basketball player; b. Russia, Jan. 28, 1972; came to U.S., 1997; Ctr. Israel, 1992-94, CKSK, Russia, 1994-97, WNBA - Utah Starzz, Salt Lake City, 1997—. Recipient Gold medal European Championship, Soviet Nat. Team, 1991, Barcelona Olympics, 1992, Bronze medal, European Championship, 1995. Avocations: shopping, housekeeping, electric piano. Office: Utah Starzz Delta Ctr 301 W South Temple Salt Lake City UT 84101-1216*

BARANOVICH, DIANA LEA, music educator; b. New Orleans, Nov. 1, 1961; d. Walter Horace and Margaret (Rothman) B.; m. Robert Charles Shoup, June 12, 1982; children: Nadia Lea, Raymond Christopher. MusB, Loyola U., 1983, MEd, 1986; Dalcroze cert., Carnegie-Mellon U., 1993; postgrad., U. Houston, 1990-93. Cert. tchr. music, dance, drama, English, h.s. counselor, Tex. Tchr. music St. Tammany Schs., Slidell, La., 1983-84, Lynn Oaks Sch., Braithwaite, La., 1984-86; choir dir. Fort Bend Pub. Sch., Houston, 1990-93; tchr., cons. music and dance New Orleans, 1996—; prof. music edn. Normal U. Beijing, China, 1995-97; cons., trainer tchrs. music and dance Kinderland Learning Ctr., Singapore, 1996—; vol. tchr. dance, movement and Chinese studies Alice Harte Elem. Sch., New Orleans, 1996—; pvt. tchr. piano and movement, 1996—; tchr. tap dancing and choreography New Orleans Dance Acad., 1997—. Contbr. articles to profl. jours. Sponsor St. Joseph's Indian Sch., Childreach, Food for the Poor. Mem. Music Tchrs. Nat. Assn., Music for People, Dalcroze Soc. Am. (patron). Avocations: theater, ethnic dancing, creative writing, composing children's music, piano. Home: 2601 Hudson Pl New Orleans LA 70131-3853

BARANSKI, CHRISTINE, actress; b. Buffalo, N.Y., May 2, 1952; d. Lucien and Virginia (Mazerowski) B.; m. Matthew Cowles, Oct. 15, 1983. BA, Juilliard Sch., 1974. Plays include 'Tis a Pity She's a Whore, The Real Thing (Antoinette Perry award 1984), Cat on a Hot Tin Roof, She Stoops to Conquer, Angel City, Blithe Spirit, Coming Attractions, The Undefeated Rumba Champ, Otherwise Engaged, A Midsummer Night's Dream (Obie award 1983), Rumors (Antoinette Perry award 1989), Nick and Nora, 1991, Lips Together Teeth Apart, 1992; (films) Soup for One, 1981, Lovesick, 1983, Crackers, 1985, 9 1/2 Weeks, 1986, Legal Eagles, 1986, The Pick-up Artist, 1987, Reversal of Fortune, 1990, Life with Mikey, 1993, Addams Family Values, 1993, The War, 1994, The Ref, 1994, The Birdcage, 1996, Cruel Inventions, 1999, The Odd Couple II, 1998, Bulworth, 1998, Bow Finger, 1999; (TV series) Cybill, 1995— (Emmy award 1995, SAG award for Comedy Show); (TV movie) To Dance with the White Dog, 1993; (TV appearences) Playing for Time, Murder Ink, All My Children, Big Shots in America, Texas, Another World. *

BARANSKI, JOAN SULLIVAN, publisher; b. Andover, Mass., Apr. 6, 1933; d. Joseph Charles and Ruth G. (McCormack) Sullivan; m. Kenneth E. Baranski, Apr. 20, 1970. BS, U. Mass., Lowell, 1955. Tchr. Andover Public Schs., 1955-61; assoc. editor sci. and reading sch. dept. Holt, Rinehart and Winston, N.Y.C., 1961-65; promotion coord. sch. dept. Harcourt Brace Jovanovich, N.Y.C., 1965-74; mgr. div. verifiability and testing Harcourt Brace Jovanovich, 1974-75; editor-in-chief Teacher mag., Macmillan Co., Stamford, Conn., 1975-81; editor-in-chief sch. dept. Harper & Row Pubs., N.Y.C., 1981-84; v.p., editor-in-chief Globe Book Co., Simon and Schuster Edn. Group, 1984-88; pub. Joint Coun. Econ. Edn., N.Y.C., 1989-92; pub. Econs. Am., Nat. Coun. on Econ. Edn., N.Y.C., 1992-98; writer, editor, 1999—. Contbg. author: Winston Basic Reading Series, 1963, Little Owl Program, 1964. Home and Office: 250 E 87th St New York NY 10128-3115

BARANY, JAMES WALTER, industrial engineering educator; b. South Bend, Ind., Aug. 24, 1930; s. Emery Peter and Rose Anne (Kovacsics) B.; m. Judith Ann Flanigan, Aug. 6, 1960 (div. 1982); 1 child, Cynthia. BSME, Notre Dame U., 1953; MS in Indsl. Engring., Purdue U., 1958, PhD, 1961. Prodn. worker Studebaker Corp., 1949-52; prodn. liaison engr. Bendix Aviation Corp., 1955-56; mem. faculty Sch. Indsl. Engring. Purdue U., West Lafayette, Ind., 1958—, now prof., assoc. head indsl. engring. Sch. Indsl. Engring.; cons. Taiwan Productivity Ctr., Western Electric, Gleason Gear Works, Am. Oil Co., Timken Co. Served with U.S. Army, 1954-55. Recipient Best Counselor award Purdue U., 1978, Best Engring. Tchr. award, 1983, 89, Outstanding Indsl. Engring. Tchr. award, 1983, 87, 89, Outstanding Tchr. award Purdue U., 1989, Marion Scott Faculty Exemplary Character award Purdue U., 1993; NSF and Easter Seal Found. rsch. grantee, 1961, 63, 64, 65; Perdue Tchg. Acad. founding fellow, 1997, Indiana Gov.'s Sagamore of the Wabash award, 1998. Mem. Inst. Indsl. Engring. (life, Fellows award 1982, Disting. Educator award 1989, Disting. Svc. award 1992, Cert. of Svc. Appreciation 1994), Soc. Mfg. Engr., Am. Soc. Engring. Edn., Methods Time Measurement Rsch. Assn., Human Factors Soc., Order of Engr., Sigma Xi, Alpha Pi Mu, Tau Beta Pi (Eminent Engr. award 1982), founding fell. Purdue U. Teaching Acad., 1997. Home: 101 Andrew Pl Apt 201 West Lafayette IN 47906-3928 Office: Purdue U Dept Indsl Engring West Lafayette IN 47907-1287

BARASCH, CLARENCE SYLVAN, lawyer; b. N.Y.C., May 20, 1912; s. Morris and Bertha Lydia (Herschdorfer) B.; m. Naomi Bosniak, July 1, 1957; children: Lionel, Jonathan. AB, Columbia U., 1933, JD, 1935. Bar: N.Y. 1936, U.S. Dist. Ct. (so., ea. and no. dists.) N.Y. 1936, U.S. Ct. Appeals (2d cir.) 1936. Pvt. practice N.Y.C., 1935—; lectr. law of real estate brokerage at various real estate bds.; faculty of N.Y. Real Estate Bd. on courses for lic. renewals required by the Dept. of State of N.Y.; chmn. Columbia U. Law Sch. Class of 1935 Ann. Fund 1965—, Columbia Coll. Class of 1933 Ann. Fund, 1977-79; decade chmn. Columbia Coll. Ann. Fund; pres. Jewish Campus Life Fund, Inc. of Columbia U., 1970-87. Author: (with Elliot L. Biskind) The Law of Real Estate Brokers, 1969; also cumulative supplements, 1971-83; contbr. articles to profl. jours. Capt. Signal Corps AUS, 1942-46. Recipient cert. of appreciation Columbia U., 1981, medal for conspicuous svc. Columbia U., 1984. Mem. ABA, N.Y. State Bar Assn. (real property com.), N.Y. County Lawyers Assn. (com. on real estate brokerage matters), Real Estate Bd. N.Y. (mem. legis and law cms., 1970—, mem. arbitration panel 1989—, rev. ann. diary and manual and author of summary of real estate brokerage law and related legal matters 1991— edits.), Am. Arbitration Assn. (arbitration panel 1986—), Men's Club (bd. dirs. 1972-80), Columbia U. Law Sch. Alumni Assn. (bd. dirs. 1985-89). Jewish (mem. adv. bd. to chaplain Columbia 1950-70). Home: 1016 5th Ave New York NY 10028-0132 Office: 425 Park Ave New York NY 10022-3506

BARASCH, DAVID M., prosecutor. U.S. atty. U.S. Dist. Ct. (mid. dist.) Pa. Office: US Attorney Mid District of PA Federal Bldg PO Box 11754 Harrisburg PA 17108-1754

BARASCH, MAL LIVINGSTON, lawyer; b. N.Y.C., May 14, 1929; s. Joseph and Ernestine (Livingston) B.; m. S. Ann Beckley, May 19, 1962; children: Amy Pitcairn Barasch, Jody Taylor Barasch. B.S. in Econs. with distinction, U. Pa., 1951; LL.B., Yale U., 1954. Bar: N.Y. 1957, U.S. Dist. Ct. (so. dist.) N.Y. 1960, U.S. Tax Ct. 1960. Assoc. Mudge Rose Guthrie Alexander & Ferdon, N.Y.C., 1957-62; assoc. Rosenman & Colin, N.Y.C., 1962-67; ptnr. Rosenman & Colin, 1968—; mem. exec. com., 2d v.p. library N.Y. Law Inst., 1979—. Dist. leader, mem. exec. com. N.Y. County Dem. Com., 1961-65; treas., bd. dirs. Lenox Hill Neighborhood House; bd. dirs. Visions, Svcs. for the Blind and Visually Impaired. With U.S. Army, 1954-56. Fellow N.Y. Bar Found., Am. Coll. Trust and Estate Counsel; mem. ABA, N.Y. State Bar Assn., Assn. of Bar of City of N.Y., Internat. Acad. Estate and Trust Law (academician), Beta Gamma Sigma. Club: University (N.Y.C.). Home: 1088 Park Ave New York NY 10128-1132

BARASH, ANTHONY HARLAN, lawyer; b. Galesburg, Ill., Mar. 18, 1943; s. Burrel B. and Rosalyne J. (Silver) B.; m. Jean Anderson, May 17, 1965; children: Elizabeth, Matthew, Katherine, Andrew. AB cum laude, Harvard U., 1965; JD, U. Chgo., 1968. Bar: Calif. 1969, S.C. Assoc. Irell & Manella, L.A., 1968-71; assoc. Cox, Castle & Nicholson, L.A., 1971-74, ptnr., 1975-80; ptnr. Barash & Hill, L.A., 1980-84, Wildman, Harrold, Allen, Dixon, Barash & Hill, L.A., 1984-87, Barash & Hill, L.A., 1988-93, Seyfarth, Shaw, Fairweather & Geraldson, L.A., 1993-96; sr. v.p. corp. affairs, gen. counsel Bowater, Inc., Greenville, S.C., 1996—; bd. dirs. Deauville Restaurants, Inc. Trustee Pitzer Coll., 1981-98, vice-chmn., 1984-96; pres., bd. dirs. Beverly Hills Bar Assn. Found., 1983-96; bd. dirs. Nat. Equal Justice Libr., Urban League of the Upstate, Peace Ctr. for the Performing Arts. Fellow Am. Bar Found. (life); mem. ABA, S.C. Bar, State Bar Assn. Calif., Greenville County Bar Assn., Beverly Hills Bar Assn. (bd. govs. 1979-81, 88-94, pres. 1992-93), Harvard Club N.Y. Home: 1212 Shadow Way Greenville SC 29615-3843 Office: Bowater Inc 55 E Camperdown Way Greenville SC 29601-3597

BARASH, PAUL GEORGE, anesthesiologist, educator; b. Bklyn., Feb. 22, 1942; s. Abraham Malcolm and Rose (Shenker) B.; m. Norma Ellen Bernard, Aug. 19, 1967; children: David, Daniel, Jed. BA, CCNY, 1963; MD, U. Ky., 1967; MA (hon.), Yale U., 1982. Diplomate Am. Bd. Anesthesiology. Intern SUNY Kings County Hosp., Bklyn., 1967-68; resident Yale-New Haven Hosp., 1970-72, chief resident, 1972-73; asst. prof. anesthesiology Yale U., New Haven, 1973-78, assoc. prof., 1978-82, prof., 1982—, assoc. dean clin. affairs, 1991-94; chmn. dept. anesthesiology, Yale U., New Haven, 1983-94. Assoc. editor: Advances in Anesthesia, 1984; assoc. editor Jour. Clin. Monitoring, 1984. Surgeon USPHS, 1968-70. Fellow Am. Coll. Anesthesiology, Am. Coll. Chest Physicians; mem. Soc. Cardiovasc. Anesthesiologists (pres. 1984-86), Conn. Soc. Anesthesiologists (pres. 1982-83), Internat. Anesthesia Rsch. Soc., Am. Soc. Anesthesiologists (editor-in-chief Anesthesia Refresher Courses 1985-96). Home: 867 Robert Treat Ext Orange CT 06477-1649 Office: Yale U Sch Medicine 333 Cedar St New Haven CT 06510-3289

BARASHKOV, NICKOLAY NICKOLAYEVICH, polymer chemist, researcher; b. Kimry, Russia, May 11, 1952; came to U.S., 1993; s. Nikolay A. and Klavdia A. (Gorshkova) B.; m. Irina I. Barashkova, Jan. 11, 1975; 1 child, Andrew N. MS, Lomonosov Inst. Chem. Tech., Moscow, 1975; 1st PhD, Karpov Inst. Phys. Chemistry, Moscow, 1978, sr. scientist, 1983, 2d PhD (DSc), 1990. Head chemistry group Karpov Inst. Phys. Chemistry, 1989-93; vis. scientist Fermi Nat. Lab., Batavia, Ill., 1993; vis. assoc. prof. Tex. Tech. U., Lubbock, 1993-94; rsch. scientist U. Tex., Dallas, 1994-97; sr. rsch. chemist Radiant Color, Richmond, Calif., 1997—; mgr. internat. (U.S.-Russian) project, Internat. Sci. and Tech. Ctr., Batavia and Moscow, 1995-96. Adv. bd. Jour. Chemistry and Life, Moscow, 1994-97; author: Polymer Composites, 1984, Structurally-Colored Polymers, 1987, Optically Transparent Polymers, 1992, Fluorescent Polymers, 1994, 2 other books. Recipient 1st prize Mendeleev's Chem. Soc., 1983. mem. Am. Chem. Soc., N.Y. Acad. Scis. Achievements include 25 patents in field of colored and fluorescent polymers. Office: Radiant Color Co 2800 Radiant Ave Richmond CA 94804

BARAYON, RAMON SENDER, writer; b. Madrid, Oct. 29, 1924; came to U.S., 1939; s. Ramon Jose and Amparo B.; m. Judith Levy, Feb. 14, 1982; children: Jonathan, Andres, Sol, Xaveire Elna. MusB, San Francisco Conservatory, 1963; MA, Mills Coll., 1966. Co-founder, co-dir. San Francisco Tape Music Ctr., 1963-66, Morning Star Ranch, Occidental, Calif., 1966-70; exec. dir. Ahimsa Ch., Occidental, Calif., 1970-71; freelance writer Occidental, Calif., 1971-76; exec. dir. Friends Morning Star, Occidental, Calif., 1976-80; freelance writer San Francisco, 1980-92; exec. dir. Peregrine Found., San Francisco, 1992—. Contbr. articles to profl. jours. Avocations: divination, Jack Russell terriers. Office: Peregrine Found PO Box 94146 San Francisco CA 94146-0141

BARAZZONE, ESTHER LYNN, academic administrator, educator; b. Bluefield, W.Va., Mar. 7, 1946; d. Vincent and Alma Gladys (Wilson) B.; m. Jay Reise, Aug. 25, 1977; children: Matthew, Nicholas. BA, New Coll., 1967; MA, Columbia U., 1969, PhD, 1982; cert. bus. adminstrn., U. Pa., 1981; D (hon.), Doshisha Women's Coll., 1999. Mem. faculty Hamilton and Kirkland Coll., Clinton, N.Y., 1974-81; assoc. dir. corp. and found. rels. U. Pa., Phila., 1982-83; assoc. provost, dir. corp. and found. rels. Swarthmore (Pa.) Coll., 1983-87; v.p., acad. affairs, dean Phila. Coll. Textiles, 1987-92; pres. Chatham Coll., Pitts., 1992—; bd. dirs. Dollar Bank, Deloitte Touche, Pitts. Author: (with others) To Beijing and Beyond, 1998. Bd. dirs. The Carnegie, Pitts., 1993, Hist. Soc. Western Pa., 1993, World Affairs Coun., Pitts., 1994; mem. adv. bd. Pitts. Symphony Orch., 1993. Grantee Am. Coun. Edn.-Nat. Identification Program Forum, 1992, YWCA, 1996; fellow Columbia U., 1968-72; Fulbright scholar Fulbright Internat. Scholar Exch., 1967-68; named Woman of Yr., Vectors, 1999. Mem. Internat. Women's Forum (founding mem.), Coun. Ind. Colls. (bd. dirs., exec. com.), Duquesne Club, Longue Vue Club. E-mail: barazzone@chatham.edu. Office: Chatham Coll Woodland Rd Pittsburgh PA 15232

BARBA, HARRY, author, educator, publisher; b. Bristol, Conn., June 17, 1922; s. Michael Hovanessian and Sultone (Mnatsignanian) B.; m. Roberta Ashburn Riley, 1955 (div. 1963); 1 child, Gregory Robert; m. Marian Andrea Homelson, Oct. 29, 1965. AB, Bates Coll., 1944; MA, Harvard U., 1951; MFA, U. Iowa, 1960, PhD with honors, 1963; postgrad., NYU, 1955-56, Boston U., 1950-51, NYU, 1955-56, CCNY, 1956-57, Columbia U., 1957-58, U. Middlebury, 1945. Stringer, feature writer Bristol (Conn.) Press, 1944-45; file clk. supr. new departure GM Corp., 1944-45; instr. English & writing Wilkes Coll., 1947, U. Conn., Hartford, 1947-49; tchr. English Seward Park H.S., N.Y.C., 1955-59; instr. U. Iowa, 1959-63; asst. prof. Skidmore Coll., 1963-68; prof. English, dir. writing Marshall U., Huntington, W.Va., 1968-70; title I writing arts dir. Skidmore Coll., W.Va., 1969-70; comml. & pub. svcs. radio-TV interviewee, reader, lectr. Damascus U., W.Va., 1961—; prof. English, dir. writing Marshall U., Huntington, W.Va., 1968-70; Title I Writing Arts dir. W.Va., 1969-70; vis. Am. specialist Damascus U., 1963-64; disting. vis. lectr. contemporary lit., cons. SUNY, Albany, 1977-78; reader, lectr. USIS Libr., Damascus, Syria, 1963-64; innovator, dir., devel. writers confs. for creative growth in several nat., regional and urban contexts, 1964—; pres., pub., exec. dir. Harian Creative Books, Gallston Spa, N.Y., 1967—; cons. Bantam Books, Random House, 1967, 69-70, Nat. Found. for Arts, Nat. Found. for Humanities, U.S. Dept. Edn., N.Y. State Coun. Arts, N.Y. State Edn. Dept., Poets & Writers, Inc., Harvard U., others. *Harry Barba's main accomplishments are as follows: securing a functionally creative education; serving as a creative and innovative educator in academia and the civic community, teaching, lecturing, T.V. and radio interviewers, writing; founding and development of Harian Creative Books and "The Workshop Under the Sky" locally, nationally & internationally ("One World is Better Than Home"); development of career as a writer of social function fiction, 1950—; dialogue with administrators locally and nationally, development of the creative arts in the North Country; support in recovering son of a first marriage who is now "creatively functioned".* Author: For the Grape Season, 1960, 3 By Harry Barba, 1967 3 X 3, 1969, The Case for Socially Functional Education, Art and Culture, 1970-74, One of A Kind, (The Many Faces and Voices of America), 1976, The Day the World Went Sane, 1979, series What's Cooking in Congress? A Congressional Smorgasbord of Recipes, 1979 (compiled and co-editor with Marian Barba), 1982; Gospel According to Everyman, 1981, Round Trip to Byzantium, 1985 (Pulitzer prize nominee 1985), A Pretty Girl (PEN Sunducated Fiction award 1985), Mona Lisa Smiles (co-published with Princeton U. Press), 1993. Founder, dir. Skidmore Coll. Writers and Educators Conf., 1967, Adirondack-Metroland Writers and Educators Conf., 1967—. Recipient cert. of merit Dictionary Internat. Biography, 1974, Internat. Man of Yr. award Cambridge (Eng.) Internat. Biographical Ctr., 1991-92; grad. fellow U. Iowa, 1961-62, Yaddo residence fellow, 1950, Macdowell Colony residence fellow, 1970, World's Hall of Fame, 1992—, Guggenheim fellow, 93-94; Skidmore rsch. grantee, 1965-68, N.Y. State coun. Arts grantee, 1971, U. Benedeum grantee, 1969; established Harian Creative awards for fiction, poetry, essays, mus. compositions, photography and graphic arts, 1973. Mem. MLA, Coll. English Assn., Authors Guild, Writers Union PEN, Com. Small Press Editors and Pubs., Harvard Grad. Soc. Advanced Study and Rsch., Harvard Alumni Assn., HArvard Club Ea. N.Y. (dir. 1975-79). Home and Office: 47 Hyde Blvd Ballston Spa NY 12020-1607

BARBA, ROBERTA ASHBURN, retired social worker; b. Morgantown, W.Va., June 23, 1931; d. Robert Russell and Mary Belle (Rogers) Ashburn; m. Harry C. Barba, Jan. 28, 1956 (div. June 1963); 1 child, Gregory Robert; m. Robert Franklin Church, May 10, 1972. BSSW, W.Va. U., 1953; postgrad., U. Conn., Hartford, 1953-54; MSSW, NYU, 1957. Diplomate in Am. Bd. Examiners; lic. N.Y., W.Va. Pvt. practice W.Va., 1968—; evaluator P.A.C.E., Star City, W.Va., 1973-74; social worker Family Svc. Assn., Morgantown, W.Va., 1974-75, 85-87; human resources asst., social worker Sundale Rest Home, Morgantown, 1977-79; cons., residential svcs. specialist Coordinating Coun. for Ind. Living, Morgantown, 1983-88; provider W.Va. Dept. Welfare, Human Svcs., Morgantown, 1980-87; social worker maternity svcs. Monongalia County Health Dept., Morgantown, 1985-87; social worker Hospice of Preston County, Kingwood, W.Va., 1988-89; shelter worker, field work instr. Bartlett House W.Va. Sch. Social Work, Morgantown, 1986-90; case mgr. Region VI Area Agy. on Aging, Fairmont, W.Va., 1990-92; case mgr. geriatric program W.Va. U., Morgantown, 1992-95; ret., 1995. Author: (with others) Working with Terminally Ill, 1990, (short fiction) Kids Know, 1992; freedom writer Amnesty Internat., 1987—. George Davis Bivens Found. grantee, 1953-54. Mem. NASW (charter mem., cert. diplomate), ACLU, NOW, Acad. Cert. Social Workers, W.Va. Human Resources Assn., W.Va. Child Care Assn., Monongalia County Coun. Social Agys, Phi Beta Kappa. Avocations: gardening, reading, dogs, cats, travel. Home: 429 Fairmont Rd Morgantown WV 26501-4244

BARBADORO, PAUL J., federal judge; b. Providence, June 4, 1955; s. Donald James and Elizabeth B.; m. Inez E. McDermott, Aug. 16, 1986; children: Katherine E., John James. BA cum laude, Gettysburg Coll., 1977; JD magna cum laude, Boston Coll., 1980. Bar: N.H. 1980. Asst. atty. gen. N.H. Atty. Gen., Concord, 1980-84; legal counsel U.S. Sen. Warren B. Rudman, Washington, 1984-86, Orr & Reno, Concord, 1986-87; dep. chief counsel U.S. Senate Iran-Contra Com., Washington, 1987; dir. Rath, Young, Pignatelli and Oyer, Concord, 1987-92; judge U.S. Dist. Ct., Concord, 1992-97, chief judge, 1997—; mem. adv. group for dist. of N.H., Civil Justice Reform Act, Concord, 1992-94; mem. long range planning com. N.H. Supreme Ct., 1989-90; mem. 1st Cir. Jud. Coun., 1994-96; adj. prof. Franklin Pierce Law Ctr., 1997-98. Mem. N.H. Bar Assn. (chmn. unauthorized practice of law com. 1982-84, jud. conf. com. on automation and tech. 1996—, com. on cooperation with the cts. 1997—), U.S. Dist. Ct. N.H. Bar, 1st Cir. Ct. Appeals Bar, Order of Coif. Office: WB Rudman Courthouse Rm 409 55 Pleasant St Concord NH 03301-3954

BARBAGELATA, ROBERT DOMINIC, lawyer; b. San Francisco, Jan. 9, 1925; s. Dominic Joseph and Jane Zeffra (Frugoli) B.; m. Doris V. Chatfield, June 8, 1956; children: Patricia Victoria, Robert Norman, Michael Alan. B.S., U. San Francisco, 1947, J.D., 1950. Bar: Calif. bar 1950, U.S. Supreme Ct. bar 1964. Pvt. practice San Francisco, 1950—; judge pro-tem San Francisco County Superior Ct., 1992-95; lectr. U. San Francisco Law Sch., Pacific Med. Center. Contbr. to legal jours. Served with USNR, 1943-46. Mem. Calif. State Bar, Calif. Trial Lawyers Assn. (lect., v.p.), Am. Bd. Trial Advocates (nat. pres. 1981-82, Trial Lawyer of Yr. 1986-87), Assn. Trial Lawyers Am., Am. Coll. Trial Lawyers, Internat. Soc. Barristers, San Francisco Lawyers Club,. Roman Catholic. Home: 819 Holly Rd Belmont CA 94002-2214 Office: 109 Geary St San Francisco CA 94108-5632

BARBAKOW, JEFFREY, health facility administrator; b. 1944. BS, San Jose U.; MBA, U. So. Calif. With Merrill Lynch Capital Mkts. and several additional affiliates, 1972-88, MGM/UA Communications Inc., 1988-91, Donaldson, Lufkin & Jenrette Securities Corp., 1991; dir. Tenet Healthcare, Santa Barbara, Calif., 1990—, chmn. bd., CEO, 1993—. Office: Tenet Healthcare Inc 3820 State St Santa Barbara CA 93105-3112

BARBAN, ARNOLD MELVIN, advertising educator; b. San Antonio, Sept. 17, 1932; s. Sam and Ida Dollie (Wolfson) B.; m. Barbara Marie Fox, June 2, 1955; children: Polly Gwen, Pamela Florence. BBA, U. Tex., 1955, MBA, 1959, PhD, 1964. Asst. to v.p. Joske's of Tex., San Antonio, 1955-56; asst. prof. U. Houston, 1959-64; from asst. prof. to prof. in communications U. Ill., Urbana, 1964-83; prof. U. Tex., Austin, 1983-87; prof. advt. U. Ala., Tuscaloosa, 1987—, chmn. advt. and pub. rels. dept., 1992-97; rsch. prof. communications dept. U. Ill., 1972-83, head advt. dept., 1978-83; cons. Gulf Oil Corp., Houston, 1962, 64, Farm Rsch. Inst., Urbana, 1965-83, Dept. Def., Ft. Sheridan, Ill., 1984; cons. editor Grid Pub. Co., Columbus, Ohio, 1974-84. Author: Readings in Advertising and Promotion Strategy, 1968, Essentials of Media Planning, 1987, 3d edit., 1993, Advertising Media Sourcebook, 4th edit., 1997, Advertising: Its Role in Modern Marketing, 8th edit., 1994, Advertising Media: Strategy and Tactics, 1992, Advertising Campaign Strategy, 1996; editor U. Houston Bus. Rev., 1962-64; cons. editor Jour. Advt., 1979-81; mem. editl. rev. bd. Jour. Current Issues and Rsch. in Advt., 1980—, Jour. Advt., 1983-88, 91-94; contbr. articles to profl. jours. Cons. Democratic congl. campaign, Champaign, Ill., 1972. Sgt. U.S. Army, 1956-58. Recipient Outstanding Svc. award Houston Advt. Club, 1964, disting. svc. award Dicionary Internat. Biography, Cambridge, England; fellow U. Tex., Austin, 1960, 1962, Am. Acad. Advt., 1986. Fellow Am. Acad. Advt. (pres. 1981-82, Sandy award 1997). Jewish. Avocations: gardening, reading, listening to classical music. Home: 11485 April Sound Dr Northport AL 35475-3334 Office: U Ala PO Box 870172 Tuscaloosa AL 35487-0154

BARBANTI, SERGIO, diplomat; b. Milan, Italy, Aug. 28, 1957; came to U.S., 1994; s. Bruno and Francesca (Boga) B. LLB magna cum laude, Rome U., 1977-85. Cert. lawyer, Rome, 1985. Atty., 1985-86; dep. head Africa Desk, Gen. Directorate Econ. Affairs Ministry Fgn. Affairs, Rome, 1987-90; head Italian Delegation Paris Club, 1988-90; dep. chief mission Embassy of Italy, Harare, Zimbabwe, 1990-94; counselor, dep. head Press and Info. Office Embassy of Italy, Washington, 1994-98; dep. head NATO, 1998—; gen. directorate polit. affairs Ministry Fgn. Affairs, Rome, 1998—; rep. Italian Govt. Orgn. Am. States, Washington, 1995-98. Mem. Harare Club, Cosmos Club. Roman Catholic. Avocations: poetry, literature, philosophy. Home: via Sardegna 29, 00187 Rome Italy Office: Ministry Fgn Affairs, Piazza Farnesina 1, 00100 Rome Italy also: Embassy of Italy 1601 Fuller St NW Washington DC 20009

BARBARIN, OSCAR ANTHONY, psychologist; b. New Orleans, July 25, 1945; s. Oscar Anthony and Inez M. (Molison) B. AB, St. Joseph's Sem., Washington, 1968; MA, NYU, 1971; PhD in Psychology, Rutgers U., 1975. Dir. community field sta. U. Md., College Park, 1974-79; asst. prof. U. Mich., Ann Arbor, 1979-83, dir. family devel. project, 1981-96, prof. psychology and social work, 1990—, dir. ctr. for the child and the family, 1992—, exec. dir. South Africa Initiative, 1996—. Author: Childhood Cancer and the Family, 1986. Fellow APA, Am. Orthopsychiat. Assn. (bd. dirs.); mem. Assn. of Black Psychologists (life). Office: Dept Psychology U Mich East Engring Bldg 525 E University Ave Ann Arbor MI 48109-1109

BARBARITO, GERALD MICHAEL, bishop; b. Bklyn., Jan. 4, 1950. BA, Cathedral Coll., Douglaston, N.Y., 1971; MDiv, Immaculate Conception Sem., Huntington, N.Y., 1975; licentiate, Cath. U. Am., Washington. Ordained priest Roman Cath. Ch., 1976. Deacon St. Francis Assisi; with St. Helen's Ch., Howard Beach, N.Y., 1976-81; asst. chancellor Diocese of Bklyn., vice chancellor, 1984-92, sec. to Bishop Daily, 1992—; titular bishop Diocese of Gisipa, 1994—; auxiliary bishop Diocese of Bklyn., 1994—; regional bishop Bklyn. Vicariate East; vicar for ministry Diocese of Bklyn.; master of ceremonies for Aux. Bishop Joseph P. Denning, 1984-90; cons. canonical affairs com. Nat. Conf. Cath. Bishops. Mem. Cath. Biblical Assn., Canon Law Soc. Am. Office: 1956 Betchelder St Brooklyn NY 11229*

BARBARO, SALVATORE, educator; b. Oct. 13, 1933. BA, NYU, 1955; MS, L.I. U., 1976; MA, CUNY, 1984; PhD, Columbia State U., 1997. Assoc. dir. SUNY Coll., Purchase, 1970-75; tchr.-adminstr. Peekskill (N.Y.) City Sch. Dist., 1980-87; adj. prof. Mercy Coll., Dobbs Ferry, N.Y., 1987-97; trainer Phoenix Acad., Shrub Oak, N.Y., 1996—; adj. prof. Marist Coll., Poughkeepsie, N.Y., 1986-87. Chief adminstrn. USAF 552d Band, Stewart AFB, 1973-93; condr., concert master No. Westchester Symphony Orch., Westchester, N.Y., 1968-90. E-mail: salbar@vh.net. Home: 73 Harmony Hill Rd Pawling NY 12564-2025

BARBAROSH, MILTON HARVEY, merchant banking executive; b. Montreal, Que., Can., Apr. 22, 1955; came to U.S., 1986; s. William and Ethel Barbarosh; m. Ricki Tucker, June 1, 1980; children: Marli, Lori, Liana. BCom with honours in Acctg., Concordia U., Montreal, 1976; Can. Chartered Acct., McGill U., Montreal, 1977; MBA, York U., Toronto, Ont., Can., 1980. Sr. staff acct. Thorne, Ernst & Whinney/KPMG Peat Marwick, Montreal, 1976-79; mgr. merger and acquisitions Clarkson Gordon/Ernst Young, Toronto, 1980-84, Royal Bank of Can., Toronto, 1984-86; pres. JW Charles Group, Inc., Boca Raton, Fla., 1987-88, JW Charles Capital Corp., Boca Raton, 1986-89; pres. Stenton Leigh Capital Corp., Boca Raton, 1989—. Author: (with others) The Acquisition Decision; editor M&A in Canada for Harris-Bentley Ltd. Fellow Can. Inst. Chartered Bankers; mem. The Can. Inst. of Chartered Bus. Valuators, Am. soc. Appraisers (sr.), Inst. Chartered Accts. Ont., Quebec Order Chartered Accts., McGill U. Alumni, U. Toronto Alumni, Concordia U. Alumni, York U. Alumni, Pres.'s Club Fla. Atlantic U., Boca Raton Golf and Country Club. Office: 1900 Corporate Blvd NW Boca Raton FL 33431-8502

BARBATO, JOSEPH ALLEN, writer; b. N.Y.C., Feb. 23, 1944; s. Joseph Michael and Florence (Kelly) B.; m. Augusta Ann DeLait, Oct. 23, 1965; children: Louise, Joseph. BA, NYU, 1964, MA, 1969. Newswriter NYU, N.Y.C., 1964-68, dir. alumni comms., 1969-74, sr. devel. writer, 1974-78; staff writer Shell Oil Co., N.Y.C., 1968-69; ind. writer N.Y.C., 1978-90; editl. dir. The Nature Conservancy, Arlington, Va., 1990-98; pres. Barbato Assocs., Alexandria, Va., 1999—; mem. edit. bd. Small Press mag., N.Y.C., 1984-86; communications cons. univs., hosps., etc., 1978-90. Co-author: You Are What You Drink, 1989; editor: What We Really Know About Mind-Body Health, 1991; co-editor: Heart of the Land, 1995, Patchwork of Dreams, 1996, Off the Beaten Path: Stories of Place; contbg. author: The Book of the Month, 1986; columnist edn., health, lit. numerous mags. and newspapers including Smithsonian, N.Y. Times, Village Voice, Christian Sci. Monitor, others. Mem. Authors Guild, Nat. Book Critics Cir., Soc. Profl. Journalists. Office: Barbato Assocs 5420 Gary Pl Alexandria VA 22311-1505

BARBE, DAVID FRANKLIN, electrical engineer, educator; b. Webster Springs, W.Va., May 26, 1939; . Damon and Mary K. (Cooper) B.; m. Irene Theresa Barbe; children: John David, Jane Suzanne. BS with high honors in Elec. Engring., W.Va. U., 1962, MSEE, 1964; PhD in Elec. Engring., Johns Hopkins U., 1969. Instr. elec. engring. W.Va. U., Morgantown, 1962-65; fellow engr. Westinghouse Advanced Tech. Lab, Balt., 1965-71; head functional devices sect. Electronics Div., Naval Research Lab., Washington, 1971-74; head microelectronics br. Electronics Div., Naval Research Lab., 1974-79, asst. for electronics and phys. scis., 1979-83; dir. Submarine and ASW Programs Submarine and ASW Systems, Office of Sec. of Navy, 1983-85; prof. elec. engring U. Md., College Park, 1985—, assoc. dir. Engring. Research Ctr., 1985-87, exec. dir. Engring. Research Ctr., 1987—; mem. adv. group on electron devices Dept. Def., 1971-79, 87-90; IEEE Nat. lectr. on electron devices, 1987-88; mem. steering com. Internat. Conf. on Charge-Coupled Devices, Edinburgh, 1974, 76, San Diego, 1975; lectr. 1st Internat. NATO Congress on Charge-Coupled Devices, U. Louvain-La Neuve, Belgium, 1975; mem. program com. Internat. Solid State Circuits Conf., 1993—; pres. Elec. Engring. Acad. W.Va. U., 1995-97. Contbr. numerous articles on electronics to profl. publs. Recipient Naval Rsch. Lab. Publ. award, 1975, Dept. Def. award, 1979, Very High Speed Integrated Circuits Pioneer award, 1987, Disting. Alumni award Elec. and Engring. Acad., W.Va. U., 1990. Fellow IEEE (assoc. editor Electron Devices Newsletter 1975-79, adminstrv. com. Electron Device Soc. 1977-83, nat. lectr. 1987-88, awards bd. 1990-94); mem. Am. Phys. Soc., Sigma Xi, Tau Beta Pi, Eta Kappa Nu (charter mem. sr. exec. svc.). Home: 6532 Burgundy Ln Clarksville MD 21029-2600 Office: U Md Engring Rsch Ctr Potomac Bldg College Park MD 20742

BARBE, WALTER BURKE, education educator; b. Miami, Fla., Oct. 30, 1926; s. Victor Elza and Edith (Burris) B.; m. Marilyn E. Wood, Feb. 7, 1967; 1 child, Frederick Walter. BS, Northwestern U., 1949, MA, 1950, PhD, 1953. Tchr. Dade County Bd. Pub. Instrn., 1947; asst. Psycho-Ednl. Clinic Northwestern U., 1949-50; instr. psychology, dir. reading clinic Baylor U., 1950; asst. prof. elementary edn. Kent State U., 1952-53, prof., head spl. edn. dept., 1960-64; adj. prof. U. Pitts., 1964-72, Ohio State U., 1972-89; pub. Modern Learning Press, 1997—; editor Highlights for Children, 1964—, bd. dir.; prof. edn., bd. dir. Jr. League Reading Center, U. Chattanooga, 1953-59; bd. dir. Zaner-Bloser; bd. dirs. internat. council Improvement of Reading Inst. Author: Reading Clinic Directory, 1955, (with Ralph Roberts) Teenage Tales, 1957, (with Dorothy Hinman) We Build Our Words, 1957, Educators Guide to Personalized Reading, 1961, Helping Children Read Better, 1970; sr. author: (with Paul Witty) Creative Growth with Handwriting Series, 1975, Personalized Reading Instruction: New Techniques that Increase Reading Skill and Comprehension, 1975, (with Jerry Abbott) Barbe Reading Skills Check Lists, 1975, (with Swassing and Milone) Teaching through Modality Strengths: Concepts and Practices, 1979; sr. editor: (with Joseph Renzulli) Psychology and Education of the Gifted: Readings, 3d edit, 1980, Basic Skills in Kindergarten, 1980, Resource Book for Kindergarten Teachers, 1980; editor: Teaching of Reading; Selections, 1965, (with Edward Frierson) Educating Children with Learning Disabilities, 1967, Compass Points in Literature, Searchlights in Literature, 1969, Helping Children with Special Needs Series, 1974; author: (with Francis, Braun) Spelling: Basic Skills for Effective Communication, 1982, (with Lucas, Wasylyk) Basic Skills for Effective Communication, 1984, (with others) Handwriting: Basic Skills and Application Series, 1984, Growing Up Learning, 1985, (with Francis, Gentry, San Jose) Spelling Connections: Words Into Language, 1988, (with others) Reading and Study Skills Mastery, 1996, (with others) Vocabulary, Word Analysis and Comprehension, 1996. With AUS, 1944-46. Fellow Am. Psychol. Assn.; mem. Nat. Assn. Gifted Children (pres. 1958), Touchstone Applied Sci. Assn. (bd. dirs.

1997—), Internat. Reading Assn. (Disting. Svc. award 1992). Democrat. Presbyterian. Home: RR 2 Box 2476 Beach Lake PA 18405-9735 Office: 910 Church St Honesdale PA 18431-1921

BARBEE, GEORGE E. L., financial services and business executive; b. Washington, Jan. 26, 1943; s. H. Randolph and Grace Lunt (Davenport) B.; m. Molly Morse Johnson, May 21, 1977; children: Gregory, John, Scott, Jefferson. AB, Brown U., 1965; MBA, U. Va., 1967. Fin. analyst W. R. Grace & Co., N.Y.C., 1968; product mgr. Wilkinson Sword Inc., Mountainside, N.J., 1968-70; mgr. new products Noxell divsn. Procter & Gamble, Balt., 1970-74; sr. mktg. exec. Gillette Corp., Boston, 1974-79; co-founder, exec. dir. Consumer Fin. Inst., Newton, Mass., 1979-86; ptnr., exec. dir. personal fin. svcs. PricewaterhouseCoopers LLP, Waltham, Mass., 1986-91; ptnr., exec. dir. client svcs. nat. office PricewaterhouseCoopers LLP, N.Y.C., 1991-92; ptnr. Worldwide Client Svc., 1992—; dir. Victory Van Internat., Washington; TV commentator fin. and bus. news NBC, CNN, PBS, ABC, CBS, 1981—. Author fin. and bus. articles. Republican. also: PricewaterhouseCoopers LLP 160 Federal St Boston MA 02110-1700

BARBEE, LINTON E., lawyer; b. Big Spring, Tex., Sept. 1, 1938; m. Sharon Casey, June 13, 1981; children: Lindsay, Blake, Stacey, Michael, Angela. Grad., No. Tex. State U., 1996, BA with high honors, 1996; JD with honors, U. Tex., 1966. Bar: Tex. 1966. Partner Fulbright & Jaworski, Dallas, 1990—; adj. prof. law U. Tex. Sch. Law. Pres. U. Tex. Sch. Law Alumni Assn.; bd. visitors U. Tex. Sch. Law. Mem. ABA (real property, internat. law sect., bus. law sect.), State Bar Tex. (bus. law sect.), Dallas Bar. Assn. (oil and gas sect., corp. counsel sect.), Order of Coif, Tex. Law Rev. Office: Fulbright & Jaworski 2200 Ross Ave Ste 2800 Dallas TX 75201-2784*

BARBEE, LLOYD AUGUSTUS, lawyer; b. Memphis, Aug. 17, 1925; s. Ernest A. and Adlena G. B.; m. Roudaba Bunting-Thacher, Sept. 5, 1954 (div.); children: Finn T., Daphne E., Rustam A. B.A., LeMoyne Coll., 1949; J.D., U. Wis., Madison, 1955. Bar: Wis. 1956, U.S. Dist. Ct. (we. dist.) Wis. 1956, U.S. Dist. Ct. (ea. dist.) Wis. 1962, U.S. Ct. Appeals (7th cir.) 1969, U.S. Dist. Ct. (ea. dist.) Ill. 1982 N.Y. 1984, U.S. Dist. Ct. (so. dist.) N.Y. 1984, U.S. Dist. Ct. (ea. dist.) N.Y. 1984, U.S. Ct. Appeals (2d cir.) 1985, U.S. Ct. Appeals (D.C. cir.) 1986, U.S. Supreme Ct. 1965. Assoc. Riley, Riley & Pierce, Madison, 1955-57; examiner Indsl. Commn. Wis., Madison, 1957-62; legal cons. Wis. Gov.'s Commn. Human Rights, Madison, 1959; sole practice Milw., 1962—; mem. Wis. Ho. of Reps., 1965-77; chief legal counsel Social Devel. Commn., Milw., 1993-96; lectr. U. Wis., Milw., 1976-80, adj. prof., 1980—; adj. assoc. prof. Bronx C.C., CUNY, 1990-94; tutor East Harlem Tutorial Program, 1991-92. Chmn. City of Madison Mayor's Commn. Human Rights; chmn. legal redress and Milw. United Sch. Integration Com.; chmn. 6th ward Milw. Dem. Party, 1967-68; chmn. Affirmative Action del. selection Dem. Conv., 1972-76; chmn. Wis. Black Polit. Caucus, 1972-76, Nat. Rainbow Coalition, 1986-87; bd. dirs. Milw. Symphony Orch., 1994-97; vice-chair Elders of Color Project Wis. Coun. Sr. Citizens, 1999. Served with USN, 1943-46. Named Man of Yr. Alpha Phi Alpha, 1965; recipient Sch. Integration award Sherman Park Assn., 1976, Rufus King award, 1989, Humanities and law award Milw. Cmty. Jour., 1980, Legal and Cmty. Leadership award Milw. Theol. Inst., 1981, award Mil. Black Adminstrs. and Educators, 1980, Frontiers Cmty. Svc. award, 1978, 1st African Ams. award, 1984, award for commitment to human rights Wis. Equal Rights Coun., 1985, Faculty award U. Wis-Milw., 1985, Svc. to Bd. Visitors award U. Wis. Sch. Law, 1985, West High Human Rels. Coun. award, 1986, Disting. Black Attys. award Miller's Wis., 1989, award for Inspirational Leadership and Outstanding Dedication Wis. Assn. Minority Attys., 1993, Civil Libertarian award for Struggle to Attain Reproductive Rights in Wis., African Ams. for Choice, 1993, Wis. Assn. of Minority Attys. award, 1993, Milw. Homeless Project Inc. award 1993, Black Excellence award Milw. Times newspaper, 1994, Eunice Z. Edgar award for Lifetime Libertarian Achievement award ACLU-Wis., 1995, seventh ann. James H. Baker award Cmty. Brainstorming Conf., Milw., 1996, Malcolm X Commemoration Mt. Freedom award, 1997; Proclamation of Lloyd A. Barbee Day by Mayor John O. Norquist, 1997; Barbee St., City of Milw. named for him, dedicated 1997, award for career svc. to people of Milw. Wis. Assn. Minority Attys., 1999. Mem. Nat. Assn. Afro-Am. Studies, NAACP (pres. Wis. state, Medgar Evers award 1968), Wis. N.Y., Fed. bar assns., Wis. Black Lawyers Assn., Bar Assn. 7th Fed. Circuit (chmn. Wis. Adminstrn. Justice com.), State Hist. Soc. Wis., Nat. Conf. Black Lawyers. Home: 726 W Rock Pl Milwaukee WI 53209-6528

BARBEE, ROBERT D., state official; married; three children. BS, MS, Colo. State U. Former park ranger Big Bend Nat. Park, Point Reyes Nat. Seashore, others; former supt. Cape Hatteras Nat. Seashore, Hawaii Volcanoes Nat. Park, Redwood Nat. Park, Yellowstone Nat. Park; field dir. Alaska Field Office. Office: Alaska Field Office Nat Park Service Anchorage AK 99501*

BARBEOSCH, WILLIAM PETER, banker, lawyer; b. N.Y.C., Nov. 25, 1954; s. Peter Joseph and Marie Delores (Slesiona) B.; m. Marta B. Varela, Sept. 6, 1986. AB magna cum laude, Brown U., 1976; JD, Columbia U., 1979; MBA, Yale U., 1989. Bar: N.Y. 1980, U.S. Tax Ct. 1985. Atty. Casey, Lane and Mittendorf (and successor firms), N.Y.C., 1979-86, Milbank, Tweed, Hadley and McCloy, N.Y.C., 1986-87; mgmt. assoc. Swiss Bank Corp., N.Y.C., 1989-90; v.p. The Chase Manhattan Pvt. Bank, N.Y.C., 1990-99, mng. dir., 1999—. Mem. N.Y. State Bar Assn., Assn. of the Bar of City of N.Y., Stone House Club, R.I. Alpha, Phi Kappa Psi (sec. 1974-75). Republican. Roman Catholic. Club: Brown U. (N.Y.C.), Stone House. Avocations: swimming, history, politics. Home: 545 W 111th St Apt 7E New York NY 10025-1965 Office: The Chase Manhattan Bank 1211 Ave of the Ams New York NY 10036-8890

BARBER, ANN MCDONALD, physician; b. Washington, Jan. 14, 1951; d. Charles Finch and Lois Helen (LaCroix) B. MS in Math., BS in Math., Stanford U., 1974; MD, Northwestern U., Chgo., 1981. Diplomate Am. Bd. Internal Medicine. Mathematician NIH, Bethesda, Md., 1974-76; program analyst engr. II Mass. Gen. Hosp., Boston, 1976-77; resident in internal medicine Northwestern U. Med. Ctr., Chgo., 1981-84; med. staff fellow NIH, Bethesda, 1984-87; sr. staff fellow Nat. Cancer Inst., Bethesda, 1987-91; computer scientist DOE, 1991-92; attending physician Providence Hosp., Washington, 1992-96; v.p. investments Reliance Group Holdings, N.Y.C., 1996—; peer reviewer Annals Of Internal Medicne, ACP, Phila., 1986-96; cons. Inst. for New Generation Computer Tech., Tokyo, 1991. Contbr. articles to profl. jours. Vol. Zacchaeus Free Med. Clinic, Washington, 1990-96. Recipient Physician's Recognition award AMA. Fellow ACP; mem. AAAS, Am. Med. Info. Assn. Office: Reliance Group Holdings 55 E 52nd St New York NY 10055

BARBER, BEN BERNARD ANDREW, journalist; b. Warwick, Eng., May 2, 1944; came to U.S., 1948; s. Stephen S. and Miriam (Idler) B.; m. Risa Richman (div. Apr. 1982); children: Karen Cloud, Forest; m. Nognoy Pinsanoa, Apr. 23, 1983; children: Stephanie, Natalie. Cert. in French lang. and civilization, Sorbonne U., Paris, 1964; BA, Trinity Coll., Hartford, Conn., 1964; cert. in Asian studies, Gannett fellow, U. Hawaii, 1987; MJ, Boston U., 1979. Reporter Middlesex News, Framingham, Mass., 1979; free-lance reporter Miami (Fla.) Herald, Boston Globe, Balt. Sun, Toledo Blade, San Francisco Examiner, London Observer, Newsweek, Network News Svc., San Diego Union, Omni mag., MacLean's mag., L'Actualite, Atlantic mag.; Miami corr. USA Today, 1983-86; internat. desk editor United Press Internat., 1989-90; policy analyst Refugee Policy Group, 1991-92; correspondent Sunday Age, Melbourne, Australia; state dept. corr. The Washington Times, 1994—; trainer journalism workshops U.S. Info. Agy., Africa. Contbr. articles to profl. jours. Jewish. Avocation: international travel. Office: The Washington Times Fgn Desk 3600 New York Ave NE Washington DC 20002-1996

BARBER, CHARLES EDWARD, newspaper executive, journalist; b. Miami, Fla., Oct. 30, 1939; s. James Plemon and Margaret Katherine (Grimes) B. m. Judith Margaret Tuck, May 28, 1960; children: Janet Lynn Wood, Christopher Edward. AA, Santa Fe Community Coll., 1971. Prodn. mgr. dept. student publs. U. Fla., Gainesville, 1966-68, ops. mgr., 1968-70, asst. dir., 1970-72, dir. div. publs., 1974; prodn. mgr. State Univ. System Press, Gainesville, 1975-76; pres., gen. mgr. Campus Communications, Inc., Gainesville, 1976—; pres. The Herald Pub. Co., Inc., 1990—, Tuck Barber & Assocs., 1995—; pub. The High Springs Herald, 1990—; dir. Campus Press; cons. in field. Co-author: (with Judy Barber) screenplay This Small Island, 1989; adv. editor Fla. Quar., 1973-74; contbr. articles to profl. jours. Mem. citizens adv. coun. Stephen Foster Elem. Sch., Gainesville, 1976-77, Santa Fe H.S., 1991, Spring Hill Mid. Sch., 1992; mem. Friends of Five, 1975-77, Friends of Libr., 1975-77; Fla. Census 2000 (complete count com.); mem. Fla. Newspaper Oral History Project, 1996—; chmn. book com. Fla. State Prison, 1973-85, 89-94; bd. dirs. Gainesville H.S. Band Boosters, 1978-79, 83-84, treas., 1984; key communicator Alachua County Sch. Bd., 1980-91; spl. registered dep. sheriff Alachua County Sheriff's Dept., 1979-92; mem. gifted students boosters Howard Bishop Mid. Sch., 1980-82; dir. Howard Bishop Band Boosters, 1980-82; mem. pres.'s coun. U. Fla., 1978—; mem. Leadership Gainesville, 1979, Leadership Fla., 1997; mem. steering com. Fla. Alliance for Better Campaigns; mem. Fla. Correct Ct. Com. for 2000 Census; pack com. chmn. Cub Scouts Am., 1977-78; dir. The Prevention Partnership, 1992-94, Hippodrome State Theatre, 1992-95. With USCGR, 1957-65. Recipient Nat. 1st pl. for Editl. Writing Hearst Found., 1965, Svc. award Santa Fe C.C., 1982, Cert. of Appreciation Big Bros. and Big Sisters of Gainesville, 1984, Vols. for Internat. Student Affairs, 1986, 88, 89, 90, Fla. Track Club, 1988, U. Fla. Divsn. Housing, 1990, 91, Addy award Gainesville Advt. Fedn., 1986, 87; named to Ind. Fla. Alligator Hall of Fame, 1996. Mem. Am. Collegiate Network (adv. com. 1989-91), Am. Advt. Fedn., 1978-88, Nat. Press Club, Assn. for Edn. in Journalism and Mass Communication, Coll. Newspaper Bus. and Advt. Mgrs. (bd. dirs. 1980-81), Fla. Alliance for Better Campaigns, Steering Com., Fla. Scholastic Press Assn. (newspaper judge 1981-85), Fla. Newspaper Advt. and Mktg. Execs. (chmn. edn. com. 1984-87), Fla. Press Club, Fla. Press Assn. (bd. dirs. 1992—, v.p. 1997, pres. 1998, chmn. continuing edn. com. 1992—, award for weekly newspaper advt. 1993, 1st pl. award for editl. writing 1994, 1st pl. award for newspaper promotion 1992, 1st pl. award weekly newspaper advt. 1994, Best of Show award weekly newspaper advt. 1994, 1st pl. award weekly newspaper promotion 1995, 1st pl. award for weekly newspaper cmty. svc., 1995, 3rd pl. award weekly newspaper advt. 1996, 3d pl. weekly newspaper promotion 1997), Gainesville Advt. Fedn. (bd. dirs. 1979-80), Internat. Newspaper Fin. Execs., Internat. Newspaper Mktg. Assn., Coll. Media Advisers, Nat. Newspaper Assn. (H.M. for weekly newspaper promotion, 1996), Newspaper Assn. Am., New Media Fedn., Soc. of News Design, So. Univ. Newspapers (bd. dirs. 1980-89), High Springs Hist. Soc., First Amendment Found., Alachua C. of C., Gainesville Area C. of C., High Springs C. of C., Alligator Alumni Assn. (bd. dirs. 1980—, named Mr. Alligator 1986, Hall of Fame, 1996), U. Fla. Nat. Alumni Assn., Soc. Profl. Journalists (treas. No. Fla. chpt. 1972-75, 86-91, pres.'s club 1994-95), Substance Abuse Prevention Partnership (coun. 1992-95), Leadership Gainesville Alumni Assn., Red Herring Club, Rotary (sustaining, sec. 1993-94), The Heritage Club, Alpha Phi Gamma. Office: Campus Comm Inc PO Box 14257 Gainesville FL 32604-2257

BARBER, CHARLES FINCH, retired metals company executive, financial services company executive; b. Chgo., Feb. 26, 1917; s. Henri Newton and Lillian (Wanner) B.; m. Lois Helen LaCroix, Aug. 30, 1947; children: Charles Bradford, Ann McDonald, Robin Goodhue, Elizabeth Barber Siegler. B.S., Northwestern U., 1939; LL.B., Harvard, 1942; M.Phil. (Rhodes scholar), Oxford U., 1948; LL.D. (hon.), Mont. Tech., 1976; D.Eng. (hon.), Colo. Sch. Mines, 1981. Bar: D.C. bar 1942, N.Y. State bar 1956, U.S. Supreme Ct 1946. Assoc. Covington & Burling, Washington, 1948-54; asst. solicitor gen. U.S., 1954-56; gen. counsel Asarco, Inc. (formerly Am. Smelting & Refining Co.), N.Y.C., 1956-63, v.p., 1959-63, exec. v.p., 1963-69, pres., 1969-71, chmn., chief exec. officer, 1971-82, chmn. fin. com., 1982-84; bd. dirs. Salomon Bros. Fund Inc., Salomon Bros. Investors Fund Inc., Salomon Bros. Capital Fund Inc., Salomon Bros. Series Funds Inc., The Emerging Markets Income Fund Inc., The Asia Tigers Fund Inc., The India Fund Inc.; chmn. Regulatory Adv. Com., N.Y. Stock Exch.; mem. Fin. and Operational Surviellance Com. Bd. mgr. Swarthmore Coll., 1966-74; bd. dirs., treas. Soc. Ams., 1982-98; mem. coun. Rockefeller U., Woodrow Wilson Internat. Ctr. for Scholars. Lt. comdr. USNR, 1941-46. Decorated Legion of Merit with combat V. Mem. ABA, Am. Soc. Internat. Law, AIME (assoc.), Council Fgn. Relations; mem. Conf. Bd. (sr. mem.), Copper Devel. Assn. (chmn. 1977-79, dir. 1971-82), Internat. Copper Rsch. Assn. (dir. 1971-82), Nat. Mining Assn. (hon. dir., chmn. 1980-83), Am. Mining congress, Pilgrims, Phi Beta Kappa. Clubs: Harvard (N.Y.C.); Met. (Washington); Belle Haven (Greenwich). Home: 66 Glenwood Dr Greenwich CT 06830-7015*

BARBER, CLARENCE LYLE, economics educator; b. Wolseley, Sask., Can., May 5, 1917; s. Richard Edward and Lulu Pearl (Lyons) B.; m. Barbara Anne Patchet, May 10, 1947; children—Paul Edward, Richard Stephen, David Stuart, Alan Gordon. BA, U. Sask., 1939; MA, Clark U., 1941; postgrad., U. Minn., 1941-43, PhD, 1952; LLD (hon.), U. Guelph, 1988. With Stats. Can., 1945-48; mem. faculty McMaster U., 1948-49, U. Man., Winnipeg, Can., 1949-85; prof. econs. U. Man., 1956-85, disting. prof., 1982-85, emeritus, 1985—, head dept., 1963-72; vis. prof. Queen's U., 1954-55, McGill U., 1964-65; Commr. Royal Commn. on Farm Machinery, 1966-71; spl. adviser on nat. income Phillipines Govt., 1959-60; commr. for study welfare policy in Man., 1972; mem. Nat. Commn. on Inflation, 1979, Royal Commn. Econ. Union and Devel. Prospects for Can., 1982-85. Author: Inventories and the Business Cycle, 1958, The Theory of Fiscal Policy as Applied to a Province, 1966, (with others) Inflation and Unemployment: The Canadian Experience, 1980, Controlling Inflation: Learning from Experience in Canada, Europe and Japan, 1982, False Promises: The Failure of Conservative Economics, 1993. Served with RCAF, 1943-45. Named Officer in Order of Can., 1987; Can. Coun. Profl. Leave fellow, 1970-71. Fellow Royal Soc. Can.; mem. Canadian Assn. U. Tchrs. (pres. 1958-59), Canadian Econ. Assn. (pres. 1971-72), Am. Econ. Assn., Royal Econ. Soc., Social Sci. Research Council Can. (mem. exec. 1972-73), U. Victoria Faculty Club. Home: 766 Richmond Ave, Victoria, BC Canada V8S 3Z1

BARBER, EARL EUGENE, consulting firm executive; b. Dayton, Ohio, Dec. 8, 1939; s. Earl Garnet and Mary Helen (Brown) B.; m. Sandra Kay Reese, Mar. 11, 1960; children: Steven, Amy, Dana. BS, Ball State U., 1963; MDiv., Asbury Theol. Sem., Wilmore, Ky., 1977. Tchr. Muncie (Ind.) Community Schs, 1963-65; exec. mem. Gen. Motors, Muncie, 1965-73; pres. Barber Electric, Wilmore, 1973-77; sr. pastor Calvary Temple, Plainview, Tex., 1977-79; exec. Borg Warner Corp., Muncie, 1979-84; chief ops. officer Barber Cons. Resources, Muncie, 1984—. Author: Statistical Process Control for the Worker, 1985, Statistical Process Control: The Basic Tools, 1986, Team Leader Training, 1989, Problem Solving, 1992, 96, Understanding SPC for Short Production Runs, 1990, Total Quality Management, 1991, Team Building, 1992, Problem Solving, 1994, Time Management, 1995. Mem Mayor's Task Force, Muncie 1980. Mem. Am. Soc. Quality Control (Ptnrs. award for quality 1989, sustaining mem.), Delaware County Ministerial Assn., Epsilon Pi Tau. Republican. Methodist. Avocations: writing, music, boating. Office: Barber Cons Resources Inc 4900 N Wheeling Ave Muncie IN 47304-5843

BARBER, EDWARD BRUCE, medical products executive; b. Chgo., Mar. 11, 1937; s. Edward Vanrennsaler and Alice (Reinertsen) B.; m. Louise Joy Griebler, May 23, 1964. BS, Lake Forest (Ill.) Coll., 1957; MBA, U. Chgo., 1958. Market rsch. cons. Container Corp. of Am., Chgo., 1959-61; pres. Christiansen & Barber Assoc. Ltd., Chgo., 1961—; chmn., CEO Odyssey Travel Ltd., Chgo., 1974—; founder, chmn. M.E. Team, Inc., South Plainfield, N.J., 1980—, also bd. dirs.; pres. Colts Necks Farms, Inc. 1990—; cons. Lab. Supply Co., Louisville, 1990—, Graham-Field Surg., Inc., Hauppage, N.Y., 1990—; ptnr. Wynne Med./Statco Med., 1996—, Sci. Supply Co., Schiller Park, Ill., 1990—; bd. dirs. Golden Eagle Travel, Huntington Beach, Calif. Mem. Internat. Assn. of Travel Agys., Health Industries Distbr. Assn., Masons. Republican. Lutheran. Avocations: travel, coin collector. Office: Christiansen Barber Assocs Ltd Ste 310 6800 W Raven St Chicago IL 60631-2528

BARBER, JAMES ALDEN, military officer; b. Poplar Bluff, Mo., May 6, 1934; s. James Alden and Ellamay (Morris) B.; m. Beverly June Kingsbury, June 12, 1955; children: Judith Lynn Barber Joyce, Steven Alden, Susan Barber Blackwell. BA in Econs., U. So. Calif., 1955; MA in Econs., Vanderbilt U., 1960; MA in Internat. Rels., Stanford U., 1964, PhD in Polit. Sci., 1965. Commd. ensign USN, 1955, advanced through grades to capt., 1975; commanding officer USS Hissem, 7th Fleet, Vietnam, 1966-68; Stephen B. Luce Prof. of Naval Strategy U.S. Naval War Coll., Newport, R.I., 1968-71; commanding officer USS Schofield, 7th Fleet, Vietnam, 1971-72; exec. asst. to under sec. of Navy Washington, 1975-76; commanding officer USS Horne, 7th Fleet, 1977-79; dep. dir. Politico-Mil. Affairs, Navy Dept., Washington, 1979-82; dep. dir., sr. fellow Strategic Concepts Devel. Ctr., Washington, 1982-84; CEO, pub. U.S. Naval Inst., Annapolis, Md., 1984—. Author: Social Mobility and Voting Behaviour; co-author: Military and American Society; contbr. articles to encys. and profl. jours. Recipient Alfred Thayer Mahan award, U.S. Navy League, 1971; decorated Bronze Star with Combat "V", Def. Superior Svc. medal, Legion of Merit and others. Mem. Coun. on Fgn. Rels., U.S. Naval Inst., Interuniv. Seminar on Armed Forces and Soc., Naval Inst. Found., U.S. Naval Acad. Found., N.Y. Yacht Club, Army and Navy Club. Democrat. Presbyterian. Avocations: gardening, book collecting, sailing. Office: US Naval Inst 291 Wood Rd Annapolis MD 21402-1254

BARBER, JAMES DAVID, political scientist, retired educator; b. Charleston, W.Va., July 31, 1930; s. Daniel Newman and Edith (Naismith) B.; m. Amanda Joan Mackay Smith, Nov. 25, 1972; children: Sara Naismith, Jane Lewis, Luke David, Silas Higginson. BA, U. Chgo., 1950, MA, 1955; PhD, Yale U., 1960. Mem. rsch. staff U. Chgo. Indsl. Relations Center, 1951-53, 55; asst. prof. polit. sci. Stetson U., DeLand, Fla., 1955-57; instr. to prof. Yale U., 1960-72, dir. grad. studies in polit. sci., 1965-67; dir. Office for Advanced Polit. Studies, 1967-68; prof. chmn. dept. polit. sci. Duke U., Durham, N.C., 1972-77, James B. Duke prof., 1977-95, ret., 1995; dir. Harvard-Yale-Columbia Intensive Summer Studies Program, 1966-67; series editor Harcourt Brace Jovanovich, 1970—; cons. Nat. Indsl. Conf. Bd., Com. on Econ. Devel., Center for Information on Am., Commn. on Year 2000, Twentieth Century Fund.; guest scholar Brookings Instn., 1964-65, 71-72. Author: The Lawmakers: Recruitment and Adaptation to Legislative Life, 1965, Power in Committees: An Experiment in the Governmental Process, 1966, Citizen Politics, 1969, The Presidential Character: Predicting Performance in the White House, 1972, 77, 85, 92, The Pulse of Politics: Electing Presidents in the Media Age, 1980, 92, Erasmus: A Play on Words, 1981, Politics by Humans: Research in American Leadership, 1988, The Book of Democracy, 1995; editor: Political Leadership in American Government, 1964, Power to the Citizen, 1971, Race for the Presidency, 1977, (with others) Women Leaders in American Politics, 1985; chmn. editorial bd. Polit. Sci., 1969-71; contbr. articles to profl. jours. Mem. Charter Commn., Wallingford, Conn., 1959-61, mem. Bd. Fin., 1960-61; chmn. Nat. Coalition for a Responsible Congress, 1970; bd. dirs. Univs. Nat. Anti-war Fund, 1970; bd. dirs. Amnesty Internat., USA, 1981-85, chmn., 1984-86; bd. dirs. Ctr. for Pub. Integrity, 1990—; chair Com. to Rescue Liberian Children, 1993—. Served with U.S. Army, 1953-55. Samuel S. Fels fellow Yale U., 1957-60; NSF fellow, 1961-63; fellow Ctr. for Advanced Studies in Behavioral Scis., 1968-69; scholar in residence Rockefeller Found. Study and Conf. Ctr., Bellagio, Italy, 1975. Mem. AAUP, Am. Polit. Sci. Assn. (coun. 1976-77), Assn. to Unite the Democracies (bd. dirs. 1992—), Nat. Assn. Scholars (bd. dirs. 1991—). Democrat. *

BARBER, JAMES P., lawyer; b. Berkeley, Calif., Nov. 11, 1944. BA, U. Calif., Santa Barbara, 1967; JD, U. Calif., 1973. Bar: Calif. 1973. Ptnr. Hancock, Rothert & Bunshoft LLP, San Francisco, 1980—. Articles editor Hastings Law Jour., 1972-73. Mem. ABA, State Bar Calif., Bar Assn. San Francisco, Def. Rsch. Inst., Thurston Soc., Order of the Coif. Office: Hancock Rothert & Bunshoft LLP 4 Embarcadero Ctr Ste 300 San Francisco CA 94111-4106

BARBER, JAMES RICHARD, mechanical engineering educator; b. High Wycombe, U.K., Apr. 15, 1942; came to U.S., 1981; s. Ernest and Clara Barber; m. Anne Stephanie Leech (div. Aug. 1984); children: Andrew Graham, Audrey Madeleine; m. Maria Comninou, Sept. 15, 1984. BA, Cambridge (Eng.) U., 1963, MA, 1967, PhD, 1968, ScD, 1992. Chartered engr., U.K. Tech. asst. Brit. Rail, U.K., 1963-69; lectr. mech. engring. U. Newcastle upon Tyne, U.K., 1969-81, reader solid mechanics, 1981; assoc. prof. mech. engring and applied mechanics U. Mich., Ann Arbor, 1981-84, prof. mech. engring. and applied mechanics, 1984—. Author: Elasticity, 1992; mem. editl. bd. Jour. Thermal Stresses, 1994; mem. editl. adv. bd. Internat. Jour. Mech. Scis.; contbr. over 150 articles to profl. jours. Recipient Rsch. grants NSF, Aluminum Co. Am., Ford Motor Co., Raybestos Products Co., GM and others. Fellow Instn. Mech. Engrs. (U.K.); mem. ASME (assoc. editor Jour. Applied Mechanics 1997—). Avocation: amateur chamber music player (piano, viola, clarinet). E-mail: jbarber@umich.edu. FAX: 734-647-3170. Office: Univ Mich 2350 Hayward Ann Arbor MI 48109-2125

BARBER, JERRY RANDEL, medical device company executive; b. Killarney, W.Va., Sept. 23, 1940; s. Edward Clay and Nora (Mullins) B.; m. Carrolyn Rae Acree, June 9, 1964; 1 child, Alyssa Rae. BSChemE, W.Va. U., 1962; MSChemE, Ohio State U., 1964, PhD, 1968. Rsch. engr. Union Carbide Corp., South Charleston, W.Va., 1968-73, group leader rsch., 1973-77, assoc. dir. rsch., 1977-81; dir. rsch. Union Carbide Corp., Tarrytown, N.Y., 1981-89; dir. new bus. and tech. devel. Union Carbide Corp., Danbury, Conn., 1989-93; gen. mgr. Medisyn Techs., Corp., Las Vegas, Nev., 1993-94; mng. dir. Medisyn Techs. Ltd., Arklow, Ireland, 1994-97; exec. v.p. techs. McGhan Med. Corp., Santa Barbara, Calif., 1997-98; v.p. R & D Mentor Corp., Irving, Tex., 1998—. Mem. AIChE, Am. Acad. Sci., Sigma Xi. Democrat. Methodist. Home: 2785 Poli St Ventura CA 93003-1556 Office: Mentor Corp 3041 Skyway Cir N Irving TX 75038-3540

BARBER, JOSEPH CLIFFORD, college administrator; b. Hartford, Conn., July 19, 1971; s. Joseph Charles and Frances Martha Barber. BA, U. Conn., 1992, MPA, 1994. Rsch. intern Conn. Peace Action, Hartford, 1992; tchg. asst. dept. polit. sci. U. Conn., Storrs, 1992, tchg./rsch. asst. Inst. Pub. and Urban Affairs,, 1993-94; adminstrv./mgmt. intern Office of Town Mgr., Mansfield, Conn., 1993; environ. organizer/AmeriCorps mem. Conn. Pub. Interest Rsch. Group/Neighborhood Green Corps, Hartford, 1995-96; asst. dir. Office Cmty. Svc. and Civic Engagement/Trinity Coll., Hartford, 1996—. Founding mem. Inter-Neighborhood Collaborative, Hartford, 1997—; charter bd. dirs. Hartford Preservation Alliance, 1997—; mem. Hartford Neighborhood Environ. Project Grant Adv. Com., 1997—; tenant rep. Maple Ave. Revitalization Group, Hartford, 1996—. Mem. ASPA, Phi Beta Kappa. E-mail: jbarber@mail.trincoll.edu. FAX: 860-987-6229. Office: Trinity Coll 300 Summit St # 702574 Hartford CT 06106

BARBER, KENNETH W., funeral director; b. Binghamton, N.Y., Nov. 18, 1952; s. Robert W. and Hawthorne (Corey) B.; m. Cynthia J. Cable, Sept. 20, 1975; children: Jocelyn C., Kyla D., Drew K. BBA, MusB, Lycoming Coll., Williamsport, Pa., 1974; grad. mortuary sci., Simmons Sch., Syracuse, N.Y., 1975. Pres. Barber Meml. Home, Inc., Johnson City, N.Y., 1975—; treas. Broome County Funeral Svc., Inc., Binghamton, N.Y., 1976—. Bd. dirs. Johnson City YMCA, 1986-89, Our Lady of Lourdes Hospice, Binghamton, 1978-81, 96—; chmn. United Health Svcs. Found., Johnson City, 1991-93, mem.-at-large exec. com., 1993-95; mem. Wyo. Conf. Found. bd. United Meth. Ch., 1988-93. Broome County Coun. Chs., Binghamton, 1977—; bd. dirs. United Health Svcs., Inc., Diabetes Assn. of So. Tier; chmn. adminstrv. bd. Blvd. United Meth. Ch., 1993—. Mem. Broome County Funeral Dirs. Assn. (pres. 1986-87), N.Y. State Funeral Dirs. Assn.(regional gov., 1994-97), Nat. Funeral Dirs. Assn., Trust 100, Internat. Order of Golden Rule, Rotary (bd. dirs. 1978-81, v.p. Johnson City 1994—, pres. 1995—). Republican. Methodist. Avocations: golf, tennis, racquetball, softball, basketball. Home: 708 Princeton Dr Vestal NY 13850-2936 Office: Barber Meml Home Inc 428 Main St Johnson City NY 13790-1916

BARBER, KIMBERLY LISANBY, elementary education educator; b. Oak Park, Ill., Sept. 3, 1955; d. Donald Ross Lisanby and Mary (MacInnes) Walker; m. Gary F. Barber, Aug. 6, 1977; children: Kati Jean, Kari Elizabeth. AA, Moraine Valley Community Coll., 1975; BA cum laude, North Cen. Coll., 1977; postgrad., Roosevelt U., Chgo.; MSEd summa cum laude, No. Ill. U., 1991, postgrad., 1996. Cert. tchr., Ill. Tchr. kindergarten Horizon Day Care, Northbrook, Ill., 1977-80; dir. Mom's Day Out/Des Plaines (Ill.) United Meth. Ch., 1980-88, Mom-Tots/Des Plaines United Meth. Ch., 1988-97; tchr., gifted edn. coord., asst. prin., grantwriter Ohio (Ill.) Cmty. Consol. Grade Sch., 1997—; prin. Lincoln Elem. Sch., Spring Valley, Ill., 1997—; prof. dept. edn. Aurora (Ill.) U., 1997—. Co-author:

Small, Rural, Broke and Gifted. Edn. cons., insvc. tng., chair Bd. of Ch. and Soc., United Meth. Ch.; conf. coord. Christian Social Involvement.

BARBER, LARRY EUGENE, financial planner; b. Sabetha, Kans., Aug. 4, 1931; s. Paul W. and Nellie C. (Nicholas) B.; m. Norma J. Schroeder, Sept. 9, 1951; children: Mark E., Gary P., Jay D., Craig A., Kirk N. BSBA, U. Nebr., Omaha, 1952; M in Fin. Svcs., Am. Coll., 1981. CLU; CFP; accredited estate planner, tax preparer. Inst. agt. Conn. Gen., Omaha, 1970-77; tax and fin. planning, cons. Colo. Agy. State Mut. Life (now Allmerica Fin. Svcs.), Denver, 1977—; v.p. Bus. and Personal Fin. Planning Ltd., Denver, 1985—; pres. Barco Enterprises, Inc., 1996—. Lt. col. USAFR, 1951-52. Mem. Nat. Assn. Life Underwriting, Am. Soc. CLUs, Internat. Assn. Fin. Planners, Optimists. Home: 1030 S Garrison St Lakewood CO 80226-4129 Office: 720 S Colorado Blvd 800 So Denver CO 80246-1904

BARBER, LAURA ELIZABETH, medical/surgical nurse; b. Cherry Point, N.C., Mar. 2, 1969; d. Ted Eugene and Nanette Elaine (Lambert) B. BS in Nursing, Roberts Wesleyan Coll., Rochester, N.Y., 1992. RN, N.C.; cert. ACLS, BLS Am. Heart Assn. Nurses aide Bertrand Chaffee Hosp., Springville, N.Y., 1989; tchrs. aide Presch. Learning Ctr./League for Handicap, Springville, 1988, 89, 90; nurse extern Strong Meml. Hosp., Rochester, 1991-92; staff nurse N.C. Bapt. Hosp., Winston-Salem, 1992-95, Star Med. Staffing, L.P., 1995-96; sch. nurse Lake Hills Sch., Eustis, Fla., 1997-98, profoundly mental handicap tchr, 1998—. Mem. Dolphin Rsch. Ctr. Republican. Baptist.

BARBER, LLOYD INGRAM, retired university president; b. Regina, Sask., Can., Mar. 8, 1932; s. Lewis Muir and Hildred (Ingram) B.; m. Muriel Pauline MacBean, May 12, 1956; children: Muir, Brian, Kathleen, David, Susan, Patricia. BA, U. Sask., 1953, BComm, 1954; MBA, U. Calif., Berkeley, 1955; PhD, U. Wash., 1964; LLD (hon.), U. Alta., 1983, Concordia U., 1984; postgrad., U. Regina, 1993. Hon. chartered acct. Instr. commerce U. Sask., 1955-57, asst. prof., 1957-64, assoc. prof., 1964-65, prof., 1965-68, 74-76, dean commerce, 1965-68, v.p., 1968-74; pres. U. Regina, Sask., prof. adminstrn., 1976-90; Indian claims commr. Govt. of Can., 1969-76, hon. lt. col.; spl. inquirer for Elder Indian Testimony, 1977-81; bd. dirs. Bank of N.S., The Molson Cos., Cominco, CP Ltd., Working Ventures, Inc., N.W. Co. Ltd., Can. West Global Comm. Corp., Greystone Capital Mgmt. Inc.; cons. to bus. and govt.; hon. prof. Shandong U. Trustee Inst. Rsch. on Public Policy, 1972-79; bd. dirs. Indian Equity Found., 1978-79, Can. Scholarship Trust Fund, Regina United Way, 1977-79; past bd. dirs. Wascana Centre Authority; bd. dirs. Nat. Mus. Nature, Inst. Saskatchewan Enterprise, Can. Polar Commn.; bd. dirs., past trustee Can. Scheneley Football Awards; adv. com. to Rector on pub. affairs award Concordia U., 1983; past mem. Northwest Territories Legis. Coun., 1967-70, Natural Sci. and Engring. Rsch. Coun. Officer Aboriginal Order of Can.; recipient Vanier medal, 1978; named hon. Sask. Indian Chief Little Eagle. Mem. Am. Inst. Pub. Adminstrn., Nat. Stats. Coun., Assn. Univs. and Colls. Can. (past pres.), Am. Econ. Assn., Can. Econ. Assn., Order of Can. (companion), Sask. Order of Merit, Assn. Commonwealth Univs. (coun.), Assiniobia Club, Regina Beach Yacht Club, Masons. Mem. United Ch. Office: PO Box 510, Regina Beach, SK Canada S0G 4C0

BARBER, MARSHA, company executive; b. Peoria, Ill., Dec. 7, 1946; d. Jack R. and Dorothy M. (Zeine) Hursey; m. Thomas L. Barber, June 15, 1968; 1 child, Brett A. BS, So. Ill. U., Carbondale, 1968; postgrad., So. Ill. U., Edwardsville. Now pres. Plus 1 Exec. Stes, Columbus; instr. elem. edn., Alton, Ill.; regional coun. rep. Ill. Edn. Assn.; mem. So. Ill. U. Edn. Adv. Coun.; mem. Ohi Bd. Realtors, Columbus Bd. Realtors. Mem. Women's Bus. Bd., Columbus, Ohio. Mem. NEA, Columbus Area C. of C. (small bus. adv. coun., exec. com., chair N.W. Area Bus. Coun.), Sports Car Club Am., Nat. Assn. of Women Bus. Owners, Nat. Assn. Watch and Clock Collectors, Exec. Suite Assn., Dublin C. of C.

BARBER, MICHELE A., title one educator; b. Titusville, Pa., Jan. 18, 1964; d. Robert R. Averill and Carol A. (Fish) Covell; m. Timothy M. Barber, July 12, 1986. BS in Elem. Edn., U. of Pa., Clarion, 1985; MEd in Reading, U. of Pa., Slippery Rock, 1990. Substitute tchr. Warren County Sch. Dist., 1985-86; head tchr. Happy Hours Children's Ctr., Vienna, Va., 1986; substitute tchr. Fairfax County Sch. Dist., Springfield, Va., 1987; substitute tchr. various suburban schs., New Castle, Pa., 1987-90, Pitts., 1990-91; ESL tchr. Allegheny Intermediate Unit, Pitts., 1991, 92-93; reading specialist Woodland Hills Sch. Dist., Pitts., 1991-92, 93-94, New Brighton (Pa.) Sch. Dist., 1993, Oil City (Pa.) Sch. Dist., 1994-95, Erie City (Pa.) Sch. Dist., 1997-98; fed. programs monitor Pa. Dept. Edn., Harrisburg, 1993-94; mem. early childhood task force, Woodland Hills Sch. Dist., 1994. Mem. Sch. Improvement Coun.; asst. troop leader Girl Scouts U.S.; Ophelia Project leader. Recipient scholarship Dr. Barbara Barnes, Titusville, Pa., 1981; Title I Parent Involvement grantee. Mem. NEA, ASCD, Three Rivers Reading Coun., Internat. Reading Assn. Nat. Coun. Tchrs. Math., Pa. Assn. Fed. Programs Coords., Erie Reading Coun. Avocations: reading, travel, volleyball, skating, swimming. Home: 2963 Holman Dr Erie PA 16509-6005

BARBER, NICHOLAS CARL, tax specialist, real estate executive; b. Schenectady, N.Y.; s. Joseph F. and Philomena (Savignano) B.; m. Laura A. Sherak, Mar. 20, 1987; children: Courtney, Robyn. AAS, SUNY, Cobleskill, 1966; student, Rochester Inst. Tech., 1967-68; BS in Mgmt., Empire State Coll., 1998. Cert. county dir., N.Y. Claims rep. Hartford Ins. Group, Albany, N.Y., 1968-76; owner, prin. N.C. Barber Agy., Schenectady, 1978—; account exec. Jardine Ins. Brokers, Schenectady, 1981-82; v.p. Complete Coverage Ins., Schenectady, 1982-84; county dir. Real Property Tax Agy., Schenectady, 1991—; real estate cons., ins. cons. Schenectady County Govt., 1991-97. Mem. Schenectady County Legislature, 1980-91, majority leader, 1982-84, 90-91; bd. mem. City-County Youth Bd., Schenectady, 1980-91, Schenectady Boys Club, 1980-82, Aeroscis. Mus., Schenectady, 1982-85; bd. dirs. County Econ. Devel. Corp., Schenectady, 1986-91. Sgt. USNG, 1967-73. Mem. Sons of Italy in Am. (trustee 1980-82), Masons, Elks. Republican. Avocations: public speaking, acting. Home: 905 Nott St Schenectady NY 12308-2318

BARBER, PHILLIP MARK, lawyer; b. Pitts., Apr. 7, 1944; s. Armour G. and Irene Estelle (Doyle) B.; m. Barbara Jean Jennings, Aug. 6, 1966 (div. Dec. 1981); children: Heather C., Jessica L., Melissa A.; m. Penelope Louise Constantikes, Apr. 15, 1989 (div. Nov. 1991). BA, U. Mich., 1966; JD, Harvard U., 1969. Bar: Idaho 1969, Calif. 1971, U.S. Ct. Appeals (9th cir.) 1974, U.S. Supreme Ct. 1977. Law clk. Supreme Ct. Idaho, Boise, 1969-70; assoc. Nossaman, Waters, Scott, Krueger & Riordan, L.A., 1970-71; asst. atty. gen. State of Idaho, Boise, 1971-72; assoc. Elam, Burke, Jeppesen, Evans & Boyd, Boise, 1972-76, ptnr., 1977-81; ptnr. Hawley, Troxell, Ennis & Hawley, Boise, 1981—; mem. select com. on bar examination Idaho Supreme Ct., 1973-74, select com. on appellate rules, 1976-77, standing com. 1977-84; mem. Idaho Code Commn., 1978-96. Contbr. articles to profl. jours. Chmn. rules com. Idaho Dem. Comm., 1976; chmn. Boise Area Econ. Devel. Coun., 1985-88; leadership coun., N.W. Policy Ctr., 1988-97; vice chmn. N.W. Bus. Coalition, 1987-89; mem. exec. com. Idaho Bus. Coun., 1986-94. Recipient Disting. Citizen award Idaho Stateman Newspapers, 1985. Mem. ABA, Idaho State Bar (exam. com. 1983-85), State Bar Calif., Boise Bar Assn., Boise Area C. of C. (bd. dirs. 1980-81, 83-88, pres., chmn. bd. 1985). Roman Catholic. Avocations: golf, skiing, photography. Home: 262 S Mobley Ln Boise ID 83712-8329 Office: Hawley Troxell Ennis & Hawley 877 Main St Ste 1000 Boise ID 83702-5884

BARBER, ROBERT CHARLES, physics educator; b. Sarnia, Ont., Can., Apr. 20, 1936; s. Alexander Sinclair and Emma Violet (Jackson) B.; m. Carole Holland, Sept. 15, 1962; children: Anne Margaret Barber-Somers, Ruth Elizabeth Barber-Dueck, Keith Robert Watson-Barber. BSc, McMaster U., 1958, PhD, 1962. Postdoctoral fellow McMaster U., Hamilton, Ont., 1962-65; asst. prof. physics U. Man., Winnipeg, Can., 1965-68, assoc. prof., 1968-75, prof., 1975—, acting head dept., 1984, head dept., 1987—; vis. prof. U. Minn., Mpls., 1971-72; chmn. grad. and postdoctoral fellowships com. 3, Nat. Scis. and Engring. Rsch. Coun., 1988, 89, mem. postdoctoral fellowship grant selection com., 1987, mem. adv. com. tenure abroad, 1988; mem. Internat. Postdoctoral Com., 1991-93, chmn., 1993. Bd. dirs. Alcohol and Drug Edn. Svcs., Inc., Man., 1976-79; asst. leader 135th Winnipeg Cub Pack, Boy Scouts Can., 1977-80; mem. Winnipeg S. Foster Parents Assn., foster parent, 1983-84, 85, 87, 88; bd. deacons Broadway-First Bapt. Ch., 1966-68, 73-74, chmn. bd. 1968, 1986-88, chmn. Christian edn. com., 1969-71, 82-83, 85-86; bd. dirs. Bapt. Union of Western Can., 1981-84, chmn. task force on Bapt. Leadership Tng. Sch., Calgary, 1982-83, mem. Man. exec. bd., 1981-84. Nat. Scis. Engring. Rsch. Coun. grantee. Mem. Internat. Union Pure and Applied Physics (assoc. sec.-gen. 1993—, sec. commn. symbols, units, nomenclature atomic masses and fundamental constants 1978-81, 81-84, chmn. commn. 1984-87, 87-91, head Can. del. to gen. assembly 1981, 84, active other coms.), Internat. Union Pure and Applied Chemistry (assoc., titular 1979-91, mem. commn. atomic weights and isotope abundances 1987—), Can. Assn. Physicists (dir. full mems. 1988—, councillor Man. sect. 1974-76), Can. Assn. Univ. Tchrs. Office: U Man Dept Phys & Astronomy, 301 Allen Bldg, Winnipeg MB Canada R3T 2N2

BARBER, ROBERT OWEN, village administrator; b. Evanston, Ill., Mar. 7, 1964; s. Robert Eugene and Elaine Shirley (Glauner) B.; m. Donna Mae Meyer, June 15, 1991; children: Steven, Michael. BS in Polit. Sci., Econs., No. Ill. U., 1986, MA in Pub. Adminstrn., 1988. Adminstrv. aide Village of Palatine, Ill., 1986-88; adminstr. Village of Beecher, Ill., 1988—. Mem. Will County Local Emergency Planning Com., Joliet, Ill., 1994—; treas. Zion Luth. Ch., Beecher, 1989-95, chmn. bd. trustees, 1995—; v.p. Beecher Susquicentennial Commn., 1993-96. Named to Outstanding Yong Men of Am., 1989; No. Ill. U. scholar, 1986. Mem. Internat. City/County Mgmt. Assn., Ill. City/County Mgmt. Assn., Met. Mgrs. of Chgo., Am. Pub. Wks. Assn., Beecher C. of C., Golden Key. Lutheran. Home: PO Box 1507 Beecher IL 60401-1507 Office: Village of Beecher PO Box 1154 724 Penfield St Beecher IL 60401

BARBER, RUSSELL BROOKS BUTLER, television producer; b. Nov. 11, 1934; s. Russell Brooks and Verga Merrill (Lesher) Butler. BA, U. Puget Sound, 1957; AM, Stanford U., 1959; PhD, Northwestern U., 1963. Exec. prodr. Sta. WCBS-TV, N.Y.C., 1964-71; religion editor Sta. WNBC-TV, N.Y.C., 1973-90, media lectr., 1993—. Author: Among First Patriots, 1976. Advisor Templeton Found., London, 1976—; dir. Coun. Chs. N.Y.C., 1979—; mem. comms. com. Am. Cancer Soc. N.Y., N.Y.C., 1978—, N.Y.C. Mission Soc., 1979—, Laymen's Nat. Bible Com., N.Y.C., 1983—, Conn. Diocese Episcopal Ch., Hartford, 1984—, media cons., prodr., host Diocese Armenian Ch. of Am., 1992—; established Barber Scholars, U. Puget Sound, Tacoma, 1978—, Nat. Lecture Tours on Media. Recipient Faith and Freedom award Religious Heritage Am., St. Louis, 1982, Emmy awards NATAS, N.Y.C., 1984, 85, 88, U. Thant Peace award UN Peace Meditation, 1986, Gabriel award Nat. Cath. Assn. for Broadcasters and Communicators, 1987, Triscort award Roman Cath. Ch., 1988; named Knight Comdr. Order St. John of Jerusalem, N.Y.C., 1985. Mem. NATAS, World Assn. Christian Comms. E-mail: rbbb2@aol.com. Home: Scout Farm 6 Hard Hill Rd Bethlehem CT 06751 Office: Enlightenment Enterprises Inc 419 E 57th St Ste 8F New York NY 10022-3060

BARBERA, ANTHONY THOMAS, accountant, educator; b. Bklyn., Oct. 5, 1955; s. Thomas Anthony and Rachelle Regina (Crocitto) B. BS summa cum laude, St. John's U., Jamaica, N.Y., 1977, MBA, 1987. CPA, N.Y. Staff acct. Price Waterhouse, N.Y.C., 1977-80, sr. acct., 1980-83, audit mgr., 1983-84; grad. asst. St. John's U., Jamaica, N.Y., 1985-87, asst. prof., 1987-96; vis. asst. prof. SUNY-Old Westbury, 1996—, dir. internships and placement, 1998—; mem. com. on fin. acctg. Savs. Banks Assn. N.Y. State, N.Y.C., 1983-84. Contbr. articles to profl. jours. Recipient William R. Donaldson award Catholic Accts. Guild, Diocese of Bklyn., 1977; N.Y. State Regents scholar, 1973-77; Robert E. Gilleece doctoral fellow CUNY Grad. Sch., 1989-93; AICPA Doctoral fellow, 1989-92. Mem. AICPA, N.Y. State Soc. CPAs (profl. conduct com., recruitment com. CPA careers, cooperation com. with ednl. instns.), Am. Acctg. Assn., Securities Industry Assn., Decision Scis. Inst., Beta Alpha Psi, Beta Gamma Sigma, Omicron Delta Epsilon. Republican. Roman Catholic. Lodge: KC. Home: 32 Northcote Rd Westbury NY 11590-1504 Office: SUNY-Old Westbury Bus and Mgmt Dept Old Westbury NY 11568

BARBERA, JOSE EDUARDO, international trade professional; b. Cordoba, Argentina, Aug. 8, 1950; came to U.S., 1988; s. Antonio and Petrona (Moreno) B. Lic. Bus. Adminstrn., U. Cordoba, Argentina, 1979; MBA, U. Wis., 1984; postgrad., U. Cordoba, 1985—. CPA, Argentina. Gen. mgr. Bertolina S.A., Cordoba, 1972-82; advisor Govt. of Cordoba, 1985-87; undersec. Ministry of Fgn. Trade, Cordoba, 1987—; dir. Cordoba Trade Ctr., N.Y.C., 1989—; prof. U. Cordoba, 1982-90, Cath. U., Cordoba, 1984-85, U. Rio IV, Argentina, 1984; U.S. rep. Banco de la Prov. de Cordoba in N.Y., 1987. Mem. Am. Soc., Argentine Am. C. of C. Avocations: hiking, tennis, camping. Home: 52 E End Ave # 7A New York NY 10028-7954 Office: Cordoba Trade Ctr 1 World Trade Ctr Ste 4547 New York NY 10048-4508

BARBERI, MATTHEW, physical education and health educator; b. New Haven, Nov. 12, 1916; m. Maryhannah Slingerland, Sept. 22, 1941; children: Robert, Richard, Susan, Marnie, Tom. BS, Arnold Coll., 1938; MS, NYU, 1949; postgrad., Yale U., 1953. Recreation dir. Children's Ctr., Hamden, Conn., 1938-40; tchr. phys. edn. New Haven Pub. Schs., 1940-41, tchr. health and phys. edn., 1945-46; asst. supr. phys. edn. dept. Hamden (Conn.) Pub. Schs., 1947-54, dir. health and phys. edn., 1955-81; adj. prof. So. Conn. State U., New Haven, 1956-98; mem. Conn. Gov.'s Fitness Com., Hartford, 1968-75. Contbr. articles to profl. jours. Instr. water safety and first aid ARC, New Haven, 1945-81. Lt. USNR, 1941-45, PTO. Recipient cert. of achievement ARC, 1960; named Adminstr. of Yr. City Dirs. Coun. of AAHPERD. Mem. Conn. Assn. Health, Phys. Edn. and Recreation (pres. 1958-59, Profl. Honor award), Hamden Edn. Assn. (pres. 1952-53). Roman Catholic. Avocations: farming, fishing. Home: 42 Thornton St Hamden CT 06517-1320

BARBETTA, MARIA ANN, health information management consultant; b. Bristol, Pa., Mar. 20, 1956; d. Eugene Charles and Anna Barbetta. AA, Bucks County C.C., 1976; BS, Coll. Allied Health Professions, Temple U., 1978. Dir. med. records Cumberland Regional Health Plan, Vineland, N.J., 1978; dir. health info. mgmt. St. Mary Hosp., Langhorne, Pa., 1978—; cons. med. records St. Joseph's Home for Aged, Holland, Pa., 1983-94; spkr., cons. in field. Mem. Am. Mgmt. Assn., Nat. Med. Records Imaging Users Group (sec. 1992-93, chair 1994-95, past chair 1995-98), Am. Health Info. Mgmt. Assn. (contbg. author jour. 1992, 93), Pa. Health Info. Mgmt. Assn. (chairperson credentials com. 1999—, edn. com. 1985-87, 91-92, project mgr. strategic plan 1987-89, sec. 1990-91, edn. com. 1991-92), RTAS Med. Record Users Group (co-chair 1993-94, 94-95), Southeastern Pa. Health Info. Mgmt. Assn. (chmn. membership com. 1987-88, membership com. 1988-89, chmn. program and edn. 1989-90, sec. 1992-93, pres.-elect 1996-97, pres. 1997-98). Avocations: volunteer work, reading, travel, independent cons. for Longaberger Baskets and Pottery. Home: 4707 Grandview Ave Bensalem PA 19020-1011 Office: St Mary Med Ctr Langhorne-Newtown Rd Langhorne PA 19047

BARBI, JOSEF WALTER, engineering, manufacturing and export companies executive; b. Melk, Noe, Austria, Sept. 26, 1949; s. Walter and Hermine (Mayr) B.; 1 child, Anna Katherina. Student, U. Saskatoon, Sask., Can., 1974, Kans. State U., 1982. Mech. engr. Zizala Metalwarenfabriken, Melk, 1963-65, Austrian Farmers Coop., Pochlarn, Austria, 1970-72; area mgr. Internat. Systems & Controls Corp., Regina, Sask., Can., 1974-75; mng. dir. Bakem Agro-Indsl. C.A., Caracas, Venezuela; gen. mgr. Intercon. Agro Indsl. Devel. Inc., Hialeah, Fla., 1977-81; internat. mktg. mgr. MEC Co., Kans., 1982-84; adviser internat. ops. Calif. Pellet Mill Co., I.R., San Francisco, 1984-91; CEO ASIMA Corp., Independence, Kans., 1984-97, Internat. Nutrition Techs., Independence, 1987—; pres. Engineered Systems & Equipment, Inc., Caney, Kans., 1988—; v.p. Sunflower Aquaculture LLC, DeSoto, KS, 1997-98; owner Royal Farms, Independence, 1989—; CEO Midland Ind. Group L.C., 1998; cons. govts. of Venezuela, 1976-77, fish farm coops., Europe, 1987; spkr. in field. Contbr. articles to profl. jours. Bd. dirs. Internat. Independence C.C., 1987-89, Jr. Achievement, Independence, 1987-90. Mem. World Aquaculture Soc., Am. Feed Industries Assn. (bd. dirs. 1993—), C. of C., Rotary Internat. Home: PO Box 250 Caney KS 67333

BARBIERI, ARTHUR ROBERT, insurance agent, former chemical company official; b. Paterson, N.J., June 10, 1926; s. Otto Arthur and Sadie (Maxwell) B.; children: Elaine, Debra, Donna; m. Carole Jones, Dec. 26, 1979. Student, Rutgers U., 1957-58, Utah State U., 1962-69, Weber Coll., 1980—. Asst. buyer Allen B. Dumont Labs., Clifton, N.J., 1947-54; field supr. Housing Guild, Inc., Smithtown, N.Y., 1954-56; buyer Thiokol Corp., Danville, N.J., 1956-60; sr. buyer Thiokol Corp., Brigham City, Utah, 1960-72, purchasing agt., 1972-85, sr. buyer, 1985-88, ret., 1988; propr. Arts Tax Svc., 1990; income tax preparer, 1990—, ins. sales, 1994—; life and health ins. agt. for leading cons., 1992—. Bd. dirs. Brigham City Cmty. Theatre, Thiokol Credit Union; precinct capt. Dem. Party, 1973; mem. Lake Havasu City C. of C.; mem. fin. bd. St. Michaels Meth. Ch.; agt. Colo. River Front for AEX, Inc.; vol. mediator Mohave Supreme Ct., 1991—. With USN, 1944-46, PTO. Mem. Elks, Masons (past master, chmn. Grand Lodge youth com. 1979), Shriners (No. Utah pres. 1974-75), Jobs Daus. (assoc. grand guardian 1978), Kiwanis. Home: 3044 Jennie Ln Lake Havasu City AZ 86404

BARBIERI, CHRISTOPHER GEORGE, professional society administrator; b. Bklyn., Jan. 9, 1941; s. Nicholas Joseph and Marie Anne (Bacigalupo) B.; m. Joanne Lee Barnett, Jan. 30, 1965 (div. 1980); children—Matthew, Deborah, Lisa; m. Laurel E. Praet, July 6, 1985. B.S., Cornell U., 1962; M.S., U. Vt., 1964. Adminstrv. asst., asst. new products mgr., new products mgr., retail sales mgr. H.P. Hood & Sons, Boston, 1964-69; pres. Vt. C. of C., Montpelier, 1969—. Past mem. adv. bd. Congl. Travel and Tourism Caucus; bd. dirs. Union 32 H.S., 1977-80; del. White House Conf. on Better Librs., 1979; mem. Vt. Travel and Recreation Coun., 1988-91; chmn. Vt. Metric Coordinating Coun., past chair Vt. Employer Support for Guard and Res. Com.; past bd. dirs. New Eng. Trade Adjustment Assistance Ctr.; past chmn. New Eng.-USA Found., 1990-92; adv. coun. U. Vt.; former mem. Washington County Rep. Com.; past bd. dirs. Vt. Employers Health Alliance; trustee Est. States Expdn.; active Vt. State Rep. Exec. Com. With Air N.G., 1964-70. Mem. Vt. Assn. Execs. (pres. 1972), Vt. Assn. Chamber Execs. (pres. 1971), Small Bus. Adv. Coun. (past chmn.), Vt. Auto Enthusiasts (dirs.), Coun. State C. of C. (chair 1996-98). Roman Catholic. Lodge: Kiwanis (pres. Burlington 1972-73). Office: PO Box 37 Montpelier VT 05601-0037

BARBO, BEVERLY ANN, printing and publishing company executive; b. Cambridge, Minn., May 9, 1933; d. Bennett Harrington and Irene Anna-Catherine (Torell) Foote; m. David William Barbo, Sept. 4, 1953; children: Pamela Carlson, Mical, Timothy (dec.). BA in Elem. Edn., Bethany Coll., 1985; postgrad., Kans. U. Receptionist Cambridge State Hosp.; salesperson, dist. mgr. Avon, Mpls.; with pers. dept. Snelling & Snelling, Denver; decorator, salesperson Sears, Denver; wetworker for health products Health-Tech Enterprises, Lindsborg, Kans.; co-owner Barbo-Carlson Enterprises, Lindsborg; workshop and seminar leader; active planning confs. for various orgns. Author: (book) The Walking Wounded, 1987. Councilwoman Lindsborg City Coun., 1997-2001; bd. dirs. McPherson County Humane Soc.; mem. So. Poverty Law Ctr., People for the Am. Way, The Compassionate Friends. Mem. AAUW (mem.-at-large, past chpt. pres.), Parents, Friends and Families of Lesbians and Gays. Democrat. Avocations: art, music, reading, photography. Home: 108 N Main St Lindsborg KS 67456-2227 Office: Barbo-Carlson Enterprises 108 N Main St Lindsborg KS 67456-2227

BARBOR, JOHN HOWARD, lawyer; b. Pitts., Mar. 4, 1952; s. Thomas Sharp and Irene (Park) B.; m. Gretchen Suzanne Kunst, Mar. 20, 1982; children: Peter Howard, Katherine Suzanne. AB, Dartmouth Coll., 1974; JD, Boston Coll., 1977. Bar: Pa. 1977. Ptnr. Barbor and Barbor, Indiana, Pa., 1978-89, Barbor & Cicola, Indiana, 1989-93; Barbor & Vaporis, Indiana, 1993—. Bd. dirs., solicitor Indiana County YMCA, 1985-94; solicitor Indiana County Red Cross, 1979—; bd. dirs. Indiana Arts Coun., 1986-89; bd. dirs. Indiana County Zoning Appeals Bd., 1995—, chmn., 1998—. Mem. ABA, Pa. Bar Assn., Pa. Bar Inst. (bd. govs. 1995-97), Ind. County Bar Assn. (exec. bd. 1988, 95), Ind. Country Club, Phi Beta Kappa. Republican. Lutheran. Home: 18 Daugherty Dr Indiana PA 15701-2222 Office: Barbor and Vaporis 917 Philadelphia St Indiana PA 15701-3911

BARBOUR, BLAIR ALLEN, electro-optical engineer, researcher; b. Huntington, W.Va., Aug. 12, 1962; s. James Alfred and Carolyn Louise (Meadows) B.; m. Susan Lynne Bird, June 30, 1984; children: Amanda Nicole, Jenna Elyse, Brett Allen, Scott Adam. BS of Engring. Physics, Marshall U., 1984; MS in Electro-Optics, U. Dayton, 1986. Registered profl. engr., Ala. Lab. mgr. Fillite USA Inc., Huntington, 1980-84; rsch. physicist UDRI, Dayton, Ohio, 1984-86; sr. optical engr. The Boeing Co., Huntsville, 1986-92; divsn. dir. Nichols Rsch. Corp., Huntsville, 1992—; pres. Photon-X Inc., Huntsville, 1999—; bd. dirs., gov. U. Ala., Huntsville, 1992—, mem. optical alliance, 1992—; divsn. dir. Nichols Rsch. Corp., Huntsville, 1992—; optical cons. The Boeing Co., Huntsville, 1988-94; bd. dirs., chmn. AVMC. Contbr. papers to profl. jours. Sunday sch. tchr. 1st Bapt. Ch., Huntsville, 1988-92; youth softball coach Westco League, Madison, Ala., 1992—; youth soccer coach Nat. Youth Soccer Orgn., Madison, Ala., 1993-94; boys youth leader Royal Ambs.-FBC, Huntsville, 1993—. Mem. Soc. Photo-Instrumentation Engrs., Optical Soc. Am., Sigma Xi. Achievements include patent for ice monitoring and detection system; patent pending for spatial phase sensor, for achromatic waveplate, for phase measuring RF/MMW sensor; development of revolutionary spatial phase measurement technology that will change and improve standard amplitude measurement sensor, wave measurement sensor, system for receiving and enhancing electromagnetic radiation input signals. E-mail: barb5609@aol.com. Office: Photon X Inc MS 913 115 Chad Ln Madison AL 35758

BARBOUR, CHARLENE, management firm executive; b. Smithfield, N.C., Aug. 23, 1949; d. Charles Ray and Charlotte June (Langdon) B.; m. Phil Barbour, Apr. 14, 1968; 1 child, Phillip Shaun. AA in Bus., Hardbarger Jr. Coll., 1968. Adminstrv. asst. N.C. Dept. Human Resources, Raleigh, 1970-80; account exec. Olson Mgmt. Group, Raleigh, 1980-86; pres., CEO Mgmt. Concepts, Inc., Garner, N.C., 1986—; founder, ptnr. Wall St. Mortgage Corp., 1996. State campaign mgr. Ruby Hooper for Gov., 1992. Mem. Assn. Execs. N.C. (CEO conf. chmn. 1992-93, program com. 1992-93, trade show com. 1992-93), Garner C. of C. (comm. chmn. 1989, bd. dirs. 1995-98, vice chmn. membership and comm. 1989-92, chair pub. rels. 1996-97, vice chairwoman 1997-98, chairwoman 1998-99), Buena Vista Hospitality Group (coun. advisors 1992), Nat. Assn. of RV Parks and Campgrounds (Exec. Dir. of Yr. award 1994), Campground Assn. Mgmt. Profls. (founder), Cardinal Club (founder). Democrat. Baptist. Avocations: boating, golf, water activities. E-mail: cbarbour@ntwrks.com. Home: 2320 Amelia Rd Clayton NC 27520-8307 Office: Mgmt Concepts Inc 893 US Hwy 70 W Garner NC 27529-4547

BARBOUR, CLAUDE MARIE, minister; b. Brussels, Oct. 2, 1935; came to U.S., 1969; Diploma d'État d'Infirmières, École d'Infirmières, Paris, 1956; diploma d'Études Religieuses, Faculté Libre de Théolog, Paris, 1958; MST, N.Y. Theol. Sem., 1970; DST, Garrett Evang. Theol. Sem., 1973. Ordained to ministry Presbyn. Ch., 1974. Youth counselor Young Women's Christian Assn., Geneva, 1959-61, Edinburgh, 1965-67; missionary Paris Evang. Missionary Soc., So. Africa, 1962-64; deaconess Ch. of Scotland, Edinburgh, 1967-69; from asst. to assoc. pastor First United Presbyn. Ch., Gary, Ind., 1974-80; from asst. to assoc. prof. Cath. Theol. Union, Chgo., 1976-86, prof., 1986—; prof. McCormick Theol. Sem., Chgo., 1990-96; founder, dir. Shalom Ministries and Community, Chgo., 1975—; parish assoc. First Presbyn. Ch., Evanston, Ill., 1983—. World Coun. Chs. scholar, Geneva, 1969, United Presbyn. Ch. Commn. on Ecumenical Mission and Rels., N.Y., 1972; recipient Laskey award United Meth. Ch. Womens Div. the Bd. Global Ministries, N.Y., 1972, Civic award Ind. Women's Coun., 1976, Challenge of Peace award Chgo. Ctr. for Peace Studies, 1991, Martin P. Wolf O.F.M. award Justice, Peace and Integrity of Creation Coun. of the English-Speaking Conf. of the Order of Friars Minor, 1996. Mem. AAUW, Internat. Assn. for Mission Studies, Nat. Assn. Presbyn. Clergywomen, Am. Soc. Missiology, Assn. Prof. Mission, Midwest Fellowship Prof. Mission, Assn. Presbyn. in Cross-Cultural Mission. Home: 1649 E 50th St Apt 21A Chicago IL 60615-6110 Office: Catholic Theological Union 5401 S Cornell Ave Chicago IL 60615-5664

BARBOUR, MICHAEL G(EORGE), botany educator, ecological consultant; b. Jackson, Mich., Feb. 24, 1942; s. George Jerome and Mae (Dater) B.; m. Norma Jean Yourist, Sept. 30, 1963 (div. 1981); m. Valerie Ann Whitworth, Jan. 25, 1987; children: Julie Ann, Alan Benjamin, Steven Allan Whitworth. B.S. in Botany, Mich. State U., 1963; Ph.D. in Botany, Duke

U., 1967. Asst. prof. botany U. Calif., Davis, 1967-71, assoc. prof., 1971-76, prof., 1976—, chmn., 1982-85; prof. environ. horticulture U. Calif., Davis, 1993—; ptnr. Ecolabs Cons., Davis, 1969—; vis. prof. botany dept. Hebrew U., Jerusalem, 1979-81; vis. prof. marine scis. dept. La. State U., Baton Rouge, 1984. Co-author: Coastal Ecology, Bodega Head, 1973, Botany, 6th edit., 1982, Terrestrial Vegetation of California, 1977, 2d edit., 1988, Terrestrial Plant Ecology, 1980, 3d edit., 1998, North American Terrestrial Vegetation, 1988, 2d edit., 1999, California's Changing Landscapes, 1993, Plant Biology, 1998. Fulbright Found. fellow Adelaide, Australia 1964; Guggenheim Found. fellow, 1978; NSF rsch. grantee, 1968-78, MAB/NSF rsch. grantee, 1989-92, USDA rsch. grantee, 1992—. Mem. Ecol. Soc. Am., Brit. Ecol. Soc., Sigma Xi. Democrat. Jewish. Office: U Calif Environ Horticulture Dept U Calif Davis CA 95616

BARBOUR, WILLIAM H., JR., federal judge; b. 1941. BA, Princeton U., 1963; JD, U. Miss., 1966; postgrad, NYU, 1966. Bar: Miss. Ptnr. Henry, Barbour & DeCell, Yazoo City, Miss., 1966-83; judge U.S. Dist. Ct. (so. dist.) Miss., 1983—, chief judge, 1989-96, judge, 1996—. Youth counselor Yazoo City, 1971-82. Office: US Dist Ct 245 E Capitol St Ste 430 Jackson MS 39201-2414*

BARBOUR, WILLIAM RINEHART, JR., retired book publisher; b. N.Y.C., Mar. 2, 1922; s. William Rinehart and Mary (McKelvey) B.; m. Mary Munsell, Nov. 17, 1951; children: Bruce R., Elizabeth M., Alan W. Student, Mich. State Coll., 1941-42. With Fleming H. Revell Co., 1944-83, pres., 1968-80, chmn., 1980-83. Co-author: (with wife) Trading Places, 1991, Home Exchange Vacationing, 1996. Served with USAAF, 1942-44. Named Pub. of Year Religious Heritage Am., 1974. Home: Shell Point Village 6809 Turban Ct Fort Myers FL 33908-1669

BARBOZA, ANTHONY, photographer, artist; b. New Bedford, Mass., May 10, 1944; s. Anthony Canto and Lillian (Barros) B.; m. Laura Carrington, June 15, 1985; children: Danica Chizu-Alita, Alexio Kyoshi-Tuari, Lien Orianna; children by previous marriage: Leticia, Laryssa. Grad. high sch., New Bedford. Lectr. Internat. Ctr. Photography, 1975, 83, Mass. State Coun. of Arts, 1982, Columbia Coll. Photography, Chgo., 1983, Oberlin (Ohio) Coll., 1984, Ohio U., Athens, 1986, Mus. Sch. Fine Arts, Boston, 1989, Lowell (Mass.) U., 1989, Rochester (N.Y.) Inst. Tech., 1991; freelance photographer for advt. campaigns including Clairol, Hanes, Coca-Cola, Pepsi-Cola, United Negro Coll. Fund., Burger King, Soft Sheen Products, Kodak, McDonalds, Anheiser Busch, AT&T, Coors, Universal Pictures, Spike Lee Prodns., numerous others; panelist, judge Mass. State Coun. of Arts, 1978, Nat. Endowment Arts, 1981. Solo exhbns. include Pensacola (Fla.) Art Mus., 1966, Jacksonville (Fla.) Art Mus., 1969, Light Impressions Gallery, Rochester, N.Y., 1973, Friends Gallery of N.Y., 1974, Studio Mus. Harlem, N.Y.C., 1982; group shows include Addison Gallery Am. Arts, Andover, Mass., 1971, Mus. Modern Art, N.Y.C., 1978, Photokina, Germany, 1982, 84, City of Munich, 1985, Washington Project for Arts, 1989; in permanent collections Mus. Modern Art, N.Y.C., Newark Art Mus., U. Ghana, U. Mex., others; contbr. to books A Day in the Life of Hollywood, 1992, Color of Fashion, 1992, Songs of My People, 1992, The African Americans, 1993, A Day in the Life of Israel, 1994. Grantee N.Y. State Coun. of Arts, 1974, 76, Nat. Endowment Arts, 1980. Avocations: painting, writing, gardening, design, literature. Home: 915 Gloucester Ct Westbury NY 11590-5301 Studio: 13 Laight St # 17 New York NY 10013-2119

BARBRE, ERWIN S., publishing company executive. BA, Washington U., JD. Pvt. practice law; editor-in-chief Rsch. Inst. Am. subs. Thomson Profl. Pub., Washington; mng. editor, v.p. Lawyers Coop. Pub. Co. subs. Thomson Profl. Pub.; pres., gen. mgr. Bancroft-Whitney subs. Thomson Profl. Pub.; v.p., gen. mgr. topical pub. business unit Shepard's, Colorado Springs, 1992, with citations bus. unit, 1993, sr. v.p., gen. mgr. citations bus. unit, 1996; COO Shepard's, 1996—. Mem. Washington U. Law Rev. Office: Shepards 555 Middle Creek Pwky Colorado Springs CO 80921*

BARCA, JAMES JOSEPH, fire department administrative services executive; b. New London, Conn., Feb. 20, 1944; s. Mariano and Angeline (Curzio) B.; m. Elizabeth Drake Garrison, Mar. 28, 1969 (div. Jan. 1983); m. Janet Louise Shields, Jan. 14, 1984. BSE in Indsl. Engring., U. Cen. Fla., 1972. Launch tech. IBM Corp., Cape Canaveral, Fla., 1968-69; indsl. engr. Honeywell, Inc., St. Petersburg, Fla., 1972-75, Tampa, Fla., 1975; mgr. mgmt. div., budget & mgmt. dept. City of St. Petersburg, 1975-81; mgr. fire adminstrv. svcs. St. Petersburg Fire and Rescue Dept., 1981—; exec. mem. Pinellas County (Fla.) Disaster Adv. Com., 1981—; mem. ARC Disaster Com., St. Petersburg, 1985-94, adv. coun., Pinellas, 1994—. Author: Disaster Planning for Adult Congregate Living Facilities, 1985, St. Petersburg Disaster Operations Plan, 1986—. Guest speaker representing St. Petersburg Emergency Mgmt. program at various civic assn. mtgs., 1981—. With USN, 1962-66. Recipient NASA Apollo Achievement award for Apollo 11 Moon landing participation. Republican. Roman Catholic. Avocations: computers, photography, home video. Office: Saint Petersburg Fire & Rescue Dept 400 ML King St S Saint Petersburg FL 33701-4472

BARCEL, ELLEN NORA, secondary school educator, free-lance writer, editor; b. N.Y.C., Jan. 25, 1945; d. Oliver Vincent and Anna (Goss) B. BA, SUNY, Stony Brook, 1967, MA, 1969. Cert. elem. and secondary tchr., N.Y. Tchr. Patchogue (N.Y.)-Medford Sch. Dist., 1967-96; dir., cataloguer Southold Indian Mus., 1985—, editor 1986—. Contbr. articles to profl. jours. Grantee N.Y. State Coun. on Arts, Mus. Aid Program 1987, 88, 89, 90. Mem. Nat. Coun. for Social Studies, Am. Philatelic Soc., Am. Tropical Assn., Am. Soc. for Philatelic Pages and Panels (bd. dirs., sec. 1992-95), Mesoam. Archaeol. Study Unit, N.Y. State Coun. for Social Studies, L.I. Coun. for Social Studies (grant 1991), Soc. for Am. Archaeology, Ea. States Archaeol. Fedn., N.Y. State Archaeol. Assn. (L.I. chpt., trustee 1986-89, v.p. 1989—), Archaeol. Soc. Ohio, Suffolk County Archaeol. Assn., Delta Kappa Gamma (v.p. Beta Psi chpt. of Pi state 1997-98, chpt. pres. 1998—). Avocations: genealogy, photography, philately. Home and Office: PO Box 39 East Setauket NY 11733-0039

BARCELO, JOHN JAMES, III, law educator; b. New Orleans, Sept. 23, 1940; s. John James Jr. and Elfrida Margaret (Bisso) B.; m. Lucy L. Wood, July 14, 1974; children—Lisa, Amy, Steven. B.A., Tulane U., 1962, J.D., 1966; S.J.D., Harvard U., 1977. Bar: La. 1967, D.C. 1974, U.S. Supreme Ct. 1974, N.Y. 1975. Fulbright scholar U. Bonn, Fed. Republic Germany, 1966-67; research assoc. Harvard U. Law Sch., Cambridge, Mass., 1968-69; prof. law Cornell U. Law Sch., Ithaca, N.Y., 1969—, A. Robert Noll. prof. of law, 1984-96, dir internat. legal studies, 1972-88, 90—, William Nelson Cromwell prof. internat. and comprative law, 1996—; cons. Import Trade Adminstrn., Dept. Commerce. Author: (with others) Law: Its Nature, Functions and Limits, 3rd edit., 1986, International Commercial Arbitration, 1999; contbr. articles to profl. jours. Mem. Am. Assn. for Comparative Study of Law (bd. dirs.), Am. Soc. Internat. Law, Soc. Comprative Law, Maritime Law Assn. U.S. Office: Cornell U Law Sch Myron Taylor Hall Ithaca NY 14853

BARCELÓ, NANCY VIRGINIA (RUSTY BARCELÓ), academic administrator; b. Merced, Calif., June 5, 1946; d. Gilbert Barcelo and Virginia Lucero Barceló. BA, Chico State Coll., 1969; MA, U. Iowa, 1972, PhD, 1980. Coord. U. Oreg., Eugene, 1973-75; various adminstrv. positions U. Iowa, Iowa City, 1975-81, dir. summer session, 1981-87, acting dir. affirmative action, 1982-83, assoc. dir., 1987-91, asst. dean, 1991-95, asst. provost, 1994-96; assoc. v.p. U. Minn., Mpls., 1996—; adj. asst. prof. U. Iowa, Iowa City, 1981-96, U. Minn., Mpls., 1996—. Bd. dirs. Midwest Consortium Latino Rsch., 1985—, Minn. Minority Encouragement Project, 1996—, Casa de Esperanza, 1997—, Youth Trust, 1997—, Children, Youth and Family Consortium, 1997—, El Fondo de la Comunidad, 1999. Avocations: music, hiking, biking, jogging. E-mail: barcelo@mailbox.mail.umn.edu. Office: U Minn 432 Morrill 100 Church St SE Minneapolis MN 55455

BARCEY, HAROLD EDWARD DEAN (HAL BARCEY), real estate counselor; b. Flint, Mich., Sept. 11, 1949; s. Glen Edward and Joyce Paulene (Dean) B.; children: Allen, David, Richard, Jackson, Joseph, Chris, Andrew, Steve. BA, U. Fla., 1971, postgrad., 1971-76. Cert. residential mktg. specialist, cert. residential brokerage mgr., cert. residential appraiser, accredited buyer rep., cert. buyer rep. Activist, lectr., fundraiser various environ. orgns. and projects, Fla., Ga., 1970-75; advt. mgr., salesman Towne & Suburban Realty, Salem, Ohio, 1977-87; broker-mgr. Seasons Real Estate Counselors, Salem, 1987—; Artist "Man in Balance with Nature" symbol, 1969. Campaign worker McCarty for Pres., Youngstown, 1967; bd. dirs. adult edn. program Alachua County, Fla., 1969; bd. dirs. Balance Fund Found., Balt., 1970-73, Good Earthkeeping, Inc., Gainesville, Fla., 1971-73; del. Conf. on Population Explosion and the Devel. Profl., Airlie, Va., 1969; solicitor LifeBanc of Ohio, Salem, 1989—; campaign worker Morris Udall for Pres., Gainesville, 1975. Named for Outstanding Citizen Contbn., Village of Canfield, Ohio, 1967. Mem. Nat. Assn. Realtors, Am. Assn. Cert. Appraiser, Realtors Nat. Mktg. Inst., Alpha Gamma Sigma. Democrat. Roman Catholic. Avocations: travel, writing, music. Home and Office: 1288 W Perry St Salem OH 44460-3550

BARCHAS, JACK DAVID, psychiatrist, educator; b. Los Angeles, Nov. 2, 1935; s. Samuel Isaac and Cecile Margaret (Pasarow) B.; m. Patricia Ruth Corbitt, Feb. 9, 1957; 1 son, Isaac Doherty. B.A., Pomona Coll., 1956; M.D., Yale U., 1961. Intern Pritzker Sch. Medicine, U. Chgo., 1961-62; postdoctoral fellow in biochemistry and pharmacology NIH, 1962-64; resident in psychiatry Stanford Med. Sch., 1964-67, instr., 1966-67, asst. prof., 1967-71, assoc. prof., 1971-76, prof., 1976—, Nancy Friend Pritzker prof. psychiatry and behavioral scis., 1976—; now prof. psychiatry, chmn. dept. psychiatry Cornell U. Med. Campus, N.Y.C.; dir. Nancy Pritzker Lab. of Behavioral Neurochemistry, 1976—. Editor; author: Serotonin and Behavior, 1973, Neuroregulators and Psychiatric Disorders, 1977, Psychopharmacology from Theory to Practice, 1977, Catecholamines - Basic and Clinical Frontiers, 1979, Isoquinolines and Beta-Carbolines, 1981, Research on Mental Illness and Addictive Disorders: Progress and Prospects, 1984, Neuropeptides in Neurology and Psychiatry, 1986, In Situ Hybridization in Neurobiology, 1987, Perspectives in Psychopharmacology, 1988, Biological Rhythms and Mental Illness, 1988; contbr. articles to profl. jours. Served with USPHS, 1962-64. Recipient Psychopharmacology award Am. Psychol. Assn., 1970, Research Scientist award NIMH, 1980—. Fellow Am. Psychiat. Assn., Am. Coll. Neuropsychopharmacology; mem. Soc. Neurosci., Am. Coll. Neuropsychopharmacology (Daniel Efron award 1978), Am. Soc. Pharmacology and Exptl. Therapeutics, Am. Physiol. Soc., Am. Soc. Neurochemistry, Am. Chem. Soc., Am. Psychosomatic Soc., Psychiat. Research Soc., Soc. Biol. Psychiatry (A.E. Bennett award 1968), Am. Psychopathol. Assn., Inst. Medicine Nat. Acad. Scis. (chmn. bd. Mental Health and Behavioral Medicine). Office: Cornell U Med Campus 1300 York Ave New York NY 10021-4896*

BARCHET, STEPHEN, physician, former naval officer; b. Annapolis, Md., Oct. 25, 1932; s. Stephen George and Louise (Lankford) B.; m. Marguerite Joan Racek, Aug. 9, 1965. Student, Brown U., 1949-52; MD, U. Md., 1956. Diplomate Am. Bd. Ob-Gyn.; cert. physician exec. Commd. ensign M.C. U.S. Navy, 1955, advanced through grades to rear adm., 1978; intern Naval Hosp., Chelsea, Mass., 1956-57; resident in ob-gyn Naval Hosp., 1958-61; resident in gen. surgery Naval Hosp., Portsmouth, Va., 1957-58; fellow Harvard Med. Sch., 1959-60; obstetrician-gynecologist Naval Hosp., Naples, Italy, 1961-63, Portsmouth, N.H., 1963-64, Beaufort, S.C., 1964-66, Bremerton, Wash., 1967-70; chief ob-gyn Naval Hosp., Boston, 1970-73; asst. head, tng. br. Bur. Medicine and Surgery, Washington, 1973; head Bur. Medicine and Surgery, 1973-75; dep. spl. asst. to surgeon gen. Navy, 1975; assoc. dean Sch. Medicine, Uniformed Services U. Health Scis., Bethesda, Md., 1976-77; exec. sec. bd. regents Sch. Medicine, Uniformed Services U. Health Scis., 1976-77; spl. asst. to surgeon gen. for med. dept. edn. and tng. Bur. Medicine and Surgery, Navy Dept., Washington, 1977-79; insp. gen. Bur. Medicine and Surgery, Navy Dept., 1979-80; comdg. officer Naval Health Scis. and Edn. and Tng. Command, Nat. Naval Med. Center, Bethesda, 1977-79; asst. chief planning, resources BUMED, 1980-82; dep. surg. gen., dep. dir. naval medicine Dept. Navy, 1982-83; ret., 1983; with Pacific Med. Ctr., Seattle, 1985-91; cons. Mil. Health Care, Seattle, 1987—; prin. MSA Programs, Seattle, 1995—; mng. ptnr. Benefit Payment Solutions, 1998—; clin. asst. prof. Boston U. Sch. Medicine, 1971—; alt. regent Nat. Libr. Medicine, Bethesda, 1977-79; adj. prof. health care scis. George Washington U. Sch. Medicine and Health Scis., Washington, 1978—; ex officio mem. grad. med. edn. nat. adv. com. HEW, 1978-79; chmn. med.-dental com. Intersvc. Tng. Rev. Orgn., Washington, 1977-79; chmn. Washington Med. Savs. Accounts Project, 1994. Contbr. articles to med. jours. Sec. The Rainier Club, 1992-93; bd. dirs. North Seattle C.C. Found., 1992-95. Decorated Bronze star, others. Fellow Am. Coll. Obstetricians and Gynecologists, Am. Coll. Physician Execs.; mem. AMA, Md. Med. Soc., Assn. Mil. Surgeons U.S., Soc. Med. Cons. Armed Forces, Wash. State Med. Assn., King County Med. Assn., N.W. Mil. Health Benefit Assn. (exec. dir. 1991-94). Home and Office: 18601 SE 64th Way Issaquah WA 98027-8616 *Lastings achievements depend not only upon Knowledge well applied, but also upon doing what ought to be done.*

BARCHI, BARBARA ANN, education and training services consultant; b. Detroit, Feb. 11, 1940; d. John and Ann (Kovachevich) B.; m. Alan L. McBroom, Oct. 1, 1960 (div. Nov. 1976). BS, Wayne State U., 1961, MEd, 1967; PhD, U. Mich., 1975. Permanent cert. in teaching, Mich. Tchr. Detroit Pub. Schs., 1961-62, Garden City (Mich.) Sch. Dist., 1962-65, Livonia (Mich.) Pub. Schs., 1965-73; asst. prof. elem. edn. Ill. State U., Normal, 1975-78; nat. coord., dir. Nat. Diffusion Network Project U.S. Dept. Edn., LaSalle, Ill., 1978-82; coord. edn. project U.S. Dept. Edn., Ill., 1985-86; 1st edn. specialist Nat. PTA, Chgo., 1984-85; pres., dir. Ednl. Renewal Assocs. Inc., Chgo., 1982-86; assoc. prof. sci., tech. and soc. Pa. State U., University Park, 1986-90, dir., prin. co-investigator nationwide STS project for NSF, 1987-90; pres. Barchi & Assocs., Edn.and Tng. Svcs., Fullerton, Calif., 1991—; cons., program evaluator Future Scientists and Engrs. Am., NSF, Anaheim, Calif., 1993-95; presenter in field. Author: (support manual) Looking in on Your School: To Improve Public Education, 1985; creator curriculum materials; contbr. articles to profl. jours. Grantee NSF, 1987-90, U.S. Dept. Edn., 1979-81. Mem. Nat. Coun. Social Studies (adv. coms. tchr. edn. and cert. 1977-80, sci. and soc. 1981-84, citizenship edn. 1985-88), Nat. Diffusion Network (elec. adv. com. 1982-84), Am. Ednl. Rsch. Assn., Phi Delta Kappa. Home and Office: Barchi and Assocs 2851 Rolling Hills Dr Spc 222 Fullerton CA 92835-2375

BARCHI, ROBERT LAWRENCE, clinical neurologist, neuroscientist, educator; b. Phila., Nov. 23, 1946; s. Henry John and Elizabeth (Pesci) B.; m. Joan E. Mollman, Sept. 20, 1976; children: Jonathan Robert, Jennifer Elizabeth. BS, Georgetown U., 1968, MS, 1969; PhD, U. Pa., 1972, MD, 1973. Diplomate Am. Bd. Neurology and Psychiatry, Am. Bd. Med. Examiners. Resident in neurology U. Pa. Hosp., 1973-75; asst. prof. biochemistry U. Pa. Med. Sch., Phila., 1974-75, asst. prof. neurology and biochemistry, 1975-78, assoc. prof., 1978-81, prof., 1981—, David Mahoney prof. neurosci., 1985—, chmn. neurosci. grad. program, 1983-89, dir. Mahoney Inst. Neurol. Scis., 1983-96; vice-dean rsch. sch. medicine U. Pa. Med. Sch., 1989-91, chmn. dept. neurosci., 1992-95, chmn. depts. neurology and neurosci., 1995-99; provost and chief acad. officer U. Pa., 1999—; mem. med. adv. bd. Muscular Dystrophy Assn., 1982-94; mem. adv. bd. Cephalon Inc., 1992—, chmn., 1996—; mem. sci. adv. bd. Phila. Ventures Inc., 1992-95, TransMolecular, Inc., 1996—; pres. Penn NeuroCare, 1996-99. Author: (with Rosenberg, Prusiner, DiMauro) Molecular and Genetic Basis of Neurological Disease, 2 edits.; mem. editorial bd. Muscle and Nerve Jour., 1981-82, 95—, Jour. Neurochemistry, 1981-90, Jour. Neurosci., 1988-91, Ion Channels, 1988—, Current Opinion Neurology and Neurosurgery, 1992—, The Neuroscientist, 1993—, Neurobiology of Disease, 1994—; contbr. chpts. to textbooks, numerous articles to profl. jours. Recipient Lindback award U. Pa., 1979, Javits award NIH, 1985, Scientific Achievement award Am. Heart Assn., 1997. Fellow AAAS, Am. Acad. Neurology, Am. Neurol. Assn. (bd. councillors 1992-94); mem. Inst. Medicine of the NAS, Biophys. Soc., Soc. for Neurosci. (pub. lectr. 1985), Am. Soc. Clin. Investigation, Assn. Am. Physicians, Phila. Coll. Physicians, Phi Beta Kappa, Alpha Omega Alpha. Avocation: antiquarian horology. Office: U Pa Depts Neurology & Neurosci 215 Stemmler Hall Philadelphia PA 19104

BARCHILON, JACQUES, foreign language educator, researcher, writer; b. Casablanca, Morocco, Apr. 8, 1923; came to U.S., 1947; s. Jaime and Perla (Bendavid) B.; m. Judith S. Merrill, 1999; children from previous marriage: Nicole Andrée, Paul Émile. BA in History, U. Rochester, 1950; MA in Comparative Lit., Harvard U., 1951, PhD in Romance Langs., 1956. Tchg. fellow Harvard U., Cambridge, Mass., 1953-55; instr. Smith Coll., Northampton, Mass., 1955-56, Brown U., Providence, 1956-59; asst. prof. U. Colo., Boulder, 1959-65; assoc. prof. U. Colo., 1965-71, prof., 1971-91, prof. emeritus, 1991—; dir. study abroad program, U. Bordeaux, France, 1966-67; exch. prof. French and comparative lit. Ctr. Univ. de Savoie, Chambéry, France, 1978-79; dir. internat. colloquium on Conte merveilleux Ctr. Culturel Internat., Cerisy-La-Salle, France, 1983; lectr. in field. Author: Perrault's Tales of Mother Goose, The Dedication Manuscript of 1695, 1956, The Authentic Mother Goose Fairy Tales and Nursery Rhymes, 1960, Le Conte merveilleux français de 1690 à 1790, cent ans de féerie et de poésie ignorées de l'histoire littéraire, 1975, Le Nouveau Cabinet des Fées, 18 vols., 1978, Contes de Perrault, 1980, Charles Perrault, 1981; co-editor: (with E.E. Flinders and J. Anne Foreman) A Concordance to Charles Perrault's Tales, Vol. I Contes de Ma mère l'Oye, 1977, Vol. II, The Verse Tales, Griselidis, Peau d'Ane and Les Souhaits ridicules, 1979, Charles Perrault, a Critical Biography, 1981, (with Catherine Velay-Vallantin and J. Anne Foreman) Pensées chrétiennes, 1987, (with R. Holman) Concordance to La Rochefoucauld's Maximes, 1995, (with P. Hourcade) Contes de Madame d'Aulnoy, vol. I and vol. II, 1998; editor Cermeil, 1984-86, Marvels and Tales, 1987—; contbr. numerous articles to profl. jours. With Free French Forces, 1943-45. Grantee Am. Philos. Soc., 1962, 63, 71, 79, 93; travel Am. Coun. Learned Socs., 1983, Coun. Internat. Exch. Scholars, 1978-79, Fulbright Found., 1978-79. Mem. MLA, Am. Assn. Tchrs. of French, Soc. d'Études du 17ème Siècle, N.Am. Soc. 17th Century French Lit. Democrat. Mem. Soc. of Friends. Avocations: skiing, hiking, camping, travel, writing. Office: U Colo Dept French & Italian Box 238 Boulder CO 80309-0238

BARCIA, JAMES A., congressman; b. Bay City, Mich., Feb. 25, 1952. Grad., Saginaw Valley State U., 1974. Staff asst. to U.S. Senator Philip Hart, 1971; cmty. svc. coord. Mich. Cmty. Blood Ctr., Bay City, 1974-75; mem. Ho. of Reps. from 101st Mich. Dist., 1977-82, mem. edn. com., 1977-82, chmn. pub. works com., 1979-82, majority whip, 1979-82; mem. Mich. Senate, 1983-92; mem. 103rd Congress from 5th Mich. dist. U.S. Ho. of Reps., 1993—, mem. sci. and transp. and infrastructure coms.; mem. UAW Local 688, 1970-71, Saginaw Valley Univ. Bd. Control, 1973-74. Recipient disting. svc. award Saginaw Valley State U. Alumni Assn., 1977, Golden Eagle award Am. Fedn. Police; named Fed. Legislator of Yr., Mich. Credit Union League, Legislator of Yr., Satari Club Internat.; elected to Bay City Ctrl. Hall of Fame, 1981. Mem. NRA, Bay Area C. of C., Mich. Assn. Osteopathic Physicians and Surgeons (hon. lay mem.), Bay City Jaycees (Disting. Svc. award 1982), United Conservation clubs, Elks, Bay City Lions. Home: 915 E Harbor Vw Bay City MI 48706-3996 Office: US Ho of Reps 2419 Rayburn Bldg Washington DC 20515-2205*

BARCLAY, H(UGH) DOUGLAS, lawyer, former state senator; b. N.Y.C., July 5, 1932; s. Hugh and Dorothy Barclay; m. Sara Seiter, Aug. 15, 1959; children: Kathryn D., David H., Dorothy G., Susan M., William A. BA, Yale U., 1955; JD, Syracuse U., 1961; DSc (hon.), St. Lawrence U., 1985; LLD, SUNY, 1990. Bar: N.Y. 1962. Ptnr. Hiscock & Barclay and predecessors, Syracuse, N.Y., 1961—; sec., gen. counsel KeyCorp and subs., Albany, N.Y., 1971-89; mem. N.Y. State Senate, 1965-84, chmn. Judiciary com., chmn. Select Task Force on Ct. Reorgn., chmn. senate codes com.; dir., chmn. bd. Syracuse Supply Co; chmn. bd. Eagle Media, Inc. Mem. N.Y. State Econ. Power Allocation Bd., N.Y. Racing Assn., bd. trustees; pres. Met. Devel. Assn.; trustee, former chmn. Syracuse U., chair chancellor search com.; vice chmn. N.Y. State George Bush for Pres., 1988; chmn. N.Y. State Bush-Quayle campaign, 1992; mem. policy coun. Gov. Pataki's Transition Team; bd. visitors Syracuse U. Coll. Law; mem. Onondaga C.C. Found. Lt. arty. U.S. Army, 1955-57, Korea. Mem. ABA, N.Y. State Bar Assn. Office: Hiscock & Barclay PO Box 4878 221 S Warren St Syracuse NY 13202-1633

BARCLAY, JAMES RALPH, psychologist, educator; b. Grand Rapids, Mich., May 6, 1926; s. Gordon William and Ruth Margaret (Christensen) B.; m. Lisa Kurcz, Dec. 29, 1954; children: Anne, Robert, Gregory, Christopher. A.B., Sacred Heart Sem., Detroit, 1947; M.A., U. Mich., 1956, Ph.D., 1959. Diplomate: Am. Bd. Profl. Examiners in Psychology. Tchr. Boy's Republic, Detroit, 1952-53; child welfare worker State of Minn., 1953-54; instr. dept. edn. U. Detroit, 1955-58; sch. psychologist Redford Univ. Schs., Detroit, 1956-59; vis. lectr. U. Mich., 1959; asst. prof., assoc. prof., prof., dir. U. Counseling Center, Idaho State U., 1959-64; prof., coordinator Sch. Psychology Program, Calif. State Coll. at Hayward, 1964-69; prof., chmn. dept. ednl. psychology and counseling U. Ky., Lexington, 1969-91; pvt. practice Charleston, S.C., 1991—; cons. Idaho Dept. Edn., Oakland Schs., Louisville, U.S. Office Edn. Proposal Rev. Mem. Bd. Psychol. Examiners Idaho, 1962-64. Author: Counseling Psychology and Philosophy, 1968, Controversial Issues in Testing, 1968, Foundations of Counseling Strategies, 1971, Psychological Assessment, 1991; editor: Personnel and Guidance Jour., 1978-84; editorial cons.: Measurement and Evaluation in Guidance, 1969-73, Sch. Psychology Digest, Jour. Sch. Psychology; Contbr. articles to profl. jours. Fellow APA (diplomate). Home: 330 Concord St 5 F-G Charleston SC 29401-1549

BARCLAY, ROBERT, JR., chemist; b. Mt. Vernon, N.Y., Apr. 1, 1928; s. Robert and Emma Josephina (Neher) B. AB, Cornell U., 1948; PhD, U. Md., 1957. Chemist Barrett Div. Allied Chem. Corp., Edgewater, N.J., 1948-51, Am. Cyanamid Co, Linden, N.J., 1951-52; project scientist Union Carbide Corp., Bound Brook, N.J., 1956-69; sr. rsch. scientist Chem. Div. Morton Thiokol, Trenton, N.J., 1969-79; sect. head Hydrocarbon Rsch. Inc., Lawrenceville, N.J., 1979-86; cons. Amoco Performance Products Inc., Bound Brook, 1986-90. Contbr. chpt. to book Condensation Monomers, 1972. Fellow Am. Inst. Chemists (emeritus); mem. Am. Chem. Soc. (sec. Trenton sect. 1979-81, alt. councillor 1983-84). Roman Catholic. Achievements include 13 patents for synthesis of high performance condensation polymers and ultraviolet cured urethane acrylate polymers, and others. Home: 6 Berrywood Dr Hamilton NJ 08619-1906

BAR-COHEN, AVRAM, mechanical engineering educator; b. Bklyn., Jan. 19, 1946; s. Simon and Dorothy (Halperin) Markowitz; m. Annette Pavony, Sept. 11, 1966; children: Barak, Raanan, Talia Dvora. SB, MIT, 1968, SM, 1968, PhD, 1971. Sr. engr. Raytheon Co., Bedford, Mass., 1968-73; lectr. dept. mech. engring. Ben Gurion U., Beer Sheva, Israel, 1973-75, sr. lectr., 1975-77, 79-81; assoc. prof. Ben Gurion U. of the Negev, Beer Sheva, Israel, 1981-84, prof., 1988; vis. assoc. prof. U. Minn., 1984-85, adj. prof., 1985-87, 89, assoc. prof., 1989-91, prof. dept. mech. engring., 1992—, dir. Thermodynamics and Heat Transfer divsn., 1992-98, James J. Renier vis. chair Tech. Leadership, 1996—, exec. dir. Ctr. Devel. Tech. Leadership, 1998—; vis. assoc. prof. MIT, Cambridge, 1977-78; adj. prof. Naval Postgrad. Sch., Monterey, Calif., 1982; exec. cons. Control Data Corp., Mpls., 1985-89. Author: (with A.D. Kraus) Thermal Analysis and Control of Electronic Equipment, 1983, Design and Analysis of Heat Sinks, 1995; editor: (with A.D. Kraus) Advances in Thermal Modeling of Electronic Components and Systems, vol. I, 1988, vol. II, 1990, vol. III, 1992, vol. IV, 1998; contbr. articles to profl. jours. Recipient Edwin F. Church medal Am. Soc. of Mechanical Engineers, 1994. Fellow ASME (v.p. rsch. 1998—), IEEE (editor-in-chief Transaction on Components and Packaging Technologies 1995), N.Y. Acad. Scis., Sigma Xi, Pi Tau Sigma, Tau Beta Pi.

BARCOME, MARIGAIL, special education educator; b. Green Bay, Wis., July 7, 1945; d. Elvin and Helen (Pecor) B.; m. Peter J. Serlemitsos, Mar. 27, 1978. BS, U. Wis., Oshkosh, 1969; MEd, U. Md., 1976. Spl. edn. tchr. Eisenhower Jr. H.S., Laurel, Md., 1969-83; learning disabilities mainstreaming support tchr. Laurel H.S., 1983—. Recipient Exceptional Tchrs. award St. Mary's Coll., 1985. Mem. Coun. Exceptional Children, Md. Student Asst. Program, Learning Disability Assn. of Am., Learning Disability Assn. of Montgomery County, Am. Culinary Fedn., Inc. Avocations: ikebana, pottery, fiber and textile arts, culinary arts, pastry arts. Office: Laurel High Sch 8000 Cherry Ln Laurel MD 20707-9264

BARCUS, GILBERT MARTIN, medical products executive, business educator; b. N.Y.C., Sept. 20, 1937; s. Leon A. and Dorothy (Brownstein) B.; m. Sondra Ettin, May 6, 1961; children: David A., Ruth A. Barcus Feinberg. BS, NYU, 1959; MBA, L.I. U., 1969. Stock broker Ernst & Co., N.Y.C., 1962-65, Johnson & Johnson, 1965-80; sales mgr. McNeil Labs., Ft. Washington, Pa., 1965-75; mktg. mgr. USA Devices Ltd., New Brunswick, N.J., 1976-77; dir. product mgmt. TENS div. Stimtech, Inc., Mpls., 1977-78; products dir. Critikon, Inc., Raritan, N.J., 1979-80; v.p. mktg. Electro Biology, Inc., Fairfield, N.J., 1980-82; dir. sales, mktg. Medtronic/Med. Data Systems, Ann Arbor, Mich., 1982-85; v.p. corp. devel. Am. Biomaterials

Corp., Princeton, N.J., 1985-86, sr. v.p., 1986-88; pres. Sandar Assocs. L.L.C., North Brunswick, N.J., 1980—, Rsch. Resources Internat. L.L.C., North Brunswick, 1998—; gen. mgr. Creative Care Sys., Maplewood, N.J., 1986-88; sales and mktg. staff Life Scis., Inc., Lebanon, N.H., 1988-90, Healthwatch, Inc., Vista, Calif., 1990-95, Lunar Corp., Madison, Wis., 1992-95, Norland Med. Systems, Fort Atkinson, Wis., 1995-97, Norland Med. Sys.; exec. dir. Clinsites, Charlotte, N.C., 1997—; pres., CEO Rsch. Resources Internat., North Brunswick, N.J., 1998—; exec. dir. Clinsites, Charlotte, N.C., 1997; pres. Rsch. Resources Internat., North Brunswick, N.J., 1998—; lectr. Bus. Week Mktg. Seminars, 1988, UN Soviet Econs. Mission, 1992; prof. mktg. Coll. S.I., CUNY, 1990—, chmn. bus. dept. curriculum adv. bd., 1995—, dir. internship program, 1994—; vis. prof. mktg. Montclair (N.J.) State U., 1992-94; vis. prof. Kingsborough Coll., 1995—; adj. prof. Middlesex Coll., Edison, N.J., 1987—; lectr. dept. bus. Brookdale C.C. Author books; contbr. articles to profl. jours. Chmn. Marlboro (N.J.) Fire Commn., 1970-76; dir. Small Bus. Devel. Ctr. Middlesex County, 1988-91. Students in Free Enterprise fellow Walmart Found., 1992-95. Fellow Assn. Advancement Med. Instrumentation, Internat. Assn. Study of Pain; mem. Ann Arbor C. of C. (legis. com. 1981-84), NYU Alumni Assn. (dir. 1987-92), Accts. for Pub. Interest N.J. (chmn. golf com. 1995-97), Travis Pointe County Club (Mich.), Princeton Club of N.Y. (program com. 1993-96), NYU Club, Forsgate Country Club (v.p. 1986-91, house com. 1993—), Pi Lambda Phi. Home: 421A Andover Dr Cranbury NJ 08512

BARCUS, ROBERT GENE, educational association administrator; b. Monticello, Ind., Oct. 22, 1937; s. Harold Eugene and Marjorie Irene (Dilling) B.; BPE (Alumni scholar 1957), Purdue U., 1959; MA, Ball State U., 1963; postgrad. Ind. U., summer 1966; supts. license Butler U., 1967; m. Mary Evelyn Shull, Aug. 9, 1959; children: Jennifer Sue, Debra Lynn. Tchr., coach Wabash (Ind.) Jr. H.S., 1959-63; tchr. Wabash H.S., 1963-64; tchr., coach North Central H.S., Indpls., 1964-65; salary cons. Ind. State Tchrs. Assn., Indpls., 1965-67, asst. dir. rsch., 1967-68, dir. spl. services, 1968-70, exec. asst., 1971-72, adminstrv. asst., 1972-73, asst. exec. dir. spl. services and tchr. rights, 1973-82, asst. exec. dir. adminstrn., personnel and governance, 1982-85, asst. exec. dir. labor rels. and adminstrn., 1985-93, assoc. exec. dir. labor rels and adminstrn., 1993—. Mem. NEA, Wabash City (past pres.), Washington Twp. (past pres.) tchrs. assns., Kappa Delta Pi, Pi Delta Kappa. Mem. Ch. of the Brethren (clk. 1966-74, chmn. 1979-83, 87, 92-96, 97-98, 98-99). Clubs: Indpls. Press, Columbia, Ind. Schoolmen's. Home: 2230 Brewster Rd Indianapolis IN 46260-1521 Office: 150 W Market St Indianapolis IN 46204-2875

BARD, ALLEN JOSEPH, chemist, educator; b. Dec. 18, 1933; m. Fran; children: Eddie, Sara. BSc in Chemistry summa cum laude, CCNY, 1955; MA in Chemistry, Harvard U., 1956, PhD in Chemistry, 1958. Instr. chemistry The U. Tex., Austin, 1958-60, asst. prof., 1960-62, assoc. prof., 1962-67, prof., 1967—, Jack S. Josey Professorship Energy Studies, 1980-82, Norman Hackerman Prof. Chemistry, 1982-85, Hackerman-Welch Regents Chair Chemistry, 1985—; lectr. numerous univs., 1969-96; mem. U.S. nat. com. Internat. Union Pure and Applied Chemistry-Nat. Rsch. Coun., 1983—, chair, 1988-89, bd. energy and environ. sys., 1983-86, 93—, bd. chem. scis. tech., 1982-87, co-chair, 1985-87, nat. materials adv. bd. com. on electrochem. aspects of energy conservation and prodn., 1985, com. on chem. scis. and ad hoc panel on DOE rsch., 1980-84, NAS, NRC liaison com. on high temp. sci. and tech,. 1984; pres. Internat. Union Pure and Applied Chemistry, 1991-93; mem. adv. bd. Dept. Energy and Energy Rsch., panel on Cold Fusion, 1989; chem. adv. com. NSF, 1981-84; mem. external adv. com. Beckman Inst., 1989—; bd. govs. Weizmann Inst., 1995—, sci. & acad. adv. com., 1995—. Author: Chemical Equilibrium, 1966, Integrated Chemical Systems, 1994; co-author: Electrochemical Methods, 1980; editor Electroanalytical Chemistry, 19 vols., 1966—, Encyclopedia of the Electrochemistry of the Elements, 16 vols., 1973—, (with others) Standard Potentials in Aqueous Solution; mem. editl. and adv. bds. Jour. Am. Chem. Soc., editor-in-chief, 1982—; mem. editl. bd. Electrochimica Acta, divsn. editor, 1978-80; mem. editl. and adv. bds. Dictionary of Modern Sci. and Tech., 1989—, Ency. of Sci. Instrumentation, 1990—, Ency. of Phys. Sci. and Tech., 1984—, Ency. of Sci. and Tech., 1992—, Analytical Letters, 1967—, Analytical Scis., 1985—, Catalysis Letters, 1988—, Chem. Instrumentation, 1967-77, Chem. Physics Letters, 1992—, Critical Revs. in Analytical Chemistry, 1985-91, Jour. Photoacoustics, 1982-84, New Jour. Chemistry, 1978-93, Jour. Supercritical Fluids, 1988—, Organic Thin Films and Surfaces, 1991—, Heterogeneous Chemistry Revs., 1993—, Accounts of Chem. Rsch., 1993—, Russian Chem. Bull., 1995—; contbr. over 600 articles to profl. jours. Recipient Outstanding Achievement in Fields of Analytical Chemistry award Eastern Analytical Symposium, 1990, Townsend Harris medal City Coll. N.Y., 1989, Edward Mack award Ohio State U., 1989, Math. and Phys. Scis. award N.Y. Acad. Scis., 1986, Docteur Honoris Causa award U. de Paris-VII, 1986, Bruno Breyer Meml. award Royal Australian Chem. Inst., 1984, Scientific Achievement award City Coll. N.Y., 1983, Sherman Mills Fairchild scholar Calif. Inst. Tech., 1977, Ward Medal in Chemistry, 1955, Luigi Galvani medal Societa Chimica Italiana, 1992, Sigillum Magnum di Bologna, 1996. Fellow Electrochem. Soc. (Olin-Palladium medal 1987, Henry Linford award 1986, Carl Wagner Meml. award 1981); mem. AAAS (coun. del. 1992-95, chair-elect chemistry sect. 1996), Am. Chem. Soc. (G.M. Kosolapoff award 1992, Oesper award Cin. sect. 1989, Analytical Chemistry award 1988, Willard Gibbs award Chgo. sect. 1987, Fisher award in Analytical Chemistry 1984, Harrison Howe award Rochester sect. 1980), Nat. Acad. Scis. (chmn. chemistry sect. 1996-99, award in chem. scis. 1998), Am. Acad. Arts and Scis. (award 1990), Internat. Soc. Electrochemists (Linus Pauling award 1998), Am. Philos. Soc., Assn. Harvard Chemists, Sigma Xi. Achievements include research involving application of electrochemical methods to study of chemical problems and include investigations in electroanalytical chemistry, electron spin resonance, electro-organic chemistry, high resolution electrochemistry, electrogenerated chemiluminescence and photoelectrochemistry. Office: U Tex Lab Electrochem Dept Chemsitry Austin TX 78712*

BARD, JAMES F., JR., information systems professional; b. Hagerstown, Md., Feb. 19, 1937; s. James F. and Mary Catherine (Hoffman) B.; m. Nancy Lee Van Schoyck, May 4, 1957 (div. Sept. 1971); children: Susan L. Widick, James W. Bard, Mary-Jo L. Woods; m. Ruth Mary Grabowsky, July 31, 1972; children: Barbara J. Savage, James A. McKeown, Jeffrey L. Eby. AA, Yuba Coll., 1968; B in Gen. Studies, U. Nebr., 1969. Enlisted USAF, 1954, commd. 2d lt., 1969, advanced through grades to capt., ret., 1980; with logistics mgmt. divsn. Air Force Plant Rep. Office Westinghouse, Balt., 1981-89; info. systems mgr. U.S. Army Corps Engrs., Balt., 1989—; pres. bd. dirs. Beale AFB (Calif.) Credit Union, 1966-68; info. tech. validation authority North Atlantic divsn. U.S. Army Corps Engrs., N.Y.C., 1997—. Soccer coach PG County Boys' Club, Camp Springs, Md., 1970-72. Mem. U. Nebr. Alumni Assn., Buccanneers Pleasure Club, Republican Club, Elks, Moose. Republican. Baptist. Avocations: coin collecting, gardening. Home: 3424 Nottingham Rd Westminster MD 21157-8304 Office: CENAB-IM PO Box 1715 Baltimore MD 21203-1715

BARD, JOHN FRANKLIN, consumer products executive; b. Owatonna, Minn., Mar. 1, 1941; s. Franklin Spencer and Nina Carolyn (Geyer) B.; m. Barbara Ann Bowers, Aug. 1, 1964; children: Steven George, Kristin Elizabeth Taylor. BS in Bus., Northwestern U., 1963; MBA, U. Cin., 1972. Internat. contr. Procter & Gamble Co., Cin., 1963-78; group v.p. Clorox Co., Oakland, Calif., k1978-84, dir., 1979-84; exec. v.p., pres., chief oper. officer Tambrands Inc., Lake Success, N.Y., 1985-90, dir., 1986-89; sr. v.p. Wm. Wrigley Jr. Co., Chgo., 1990—. Bd. dirs. Alameda County YMCA, Oakland, 1979-87, L.I. United Way, 1989-90, Greater N. Mich. Ave. Assn., Chgo., 1991—; dir., vice-chmn. Keep Am. Beautiful, Inc. Mem. Tax Found. (policy com.), 410 Club, Econ. Club Chgo., Fin. Execs. Inst., Sea Pines Country Club (S.C.),. Office: Wm Wrigley Jr Co 410 N Michigan Ave Chicago IL 60611-4213

BARD, JUDY KAY, librarian; b. Topeka, Kans., May 10, 1943; d. Wilbur Dean and Kathryn Lucille (Bauer) White; m. Nelson Parker Bard Jr., June 20, 1965; children: Daniel Oliver, Nathaniel Arthur. BA in English cum laude, Hiram (Ohio) Coll., 1965; MA, U. Va., 1968; MLS in Libr. Sci., Ind. U., 1984. Cert. tchr., Ohio, W.Va., Pa. Prof. ESL Internat. Lang. Inst., Elkins, W.Va., 1974-84; prof. English Davis & Elkins Coll., Elkins, 1975-86; sch. libr. Harman (W.Va.) Sch., 1986-87; libr. Lancaster (Pa.) County Libr., 1988-92; libr. Lebanon (Pa.) Campus Harrisburg Area C.C., 1992—, sec. mid-states faculty coun., 1996, sec. faculty coun., 1997-98, mem. exec. com. faculty coun., 1997—; exec. com. mem. Middle States Re-Accreditation Self-Study, 1996-97; sec. faculty coun. Harrisburg Area C.C., 1997-98, mem. strategic planning com., 1998. Complier, editor Historic Beverly booklet, 1970. Charter mem., sec., Randolph County Creative Arts Coun., Elkins, 1969-86, Beverly (W.Va.) Cmty. Action, 1969-86; delivery person Randolph County Meals on Wheels, Elkins, 1970-85; deacon Elizabethtown Ch. of Brethren, 1986—. Mem. Pa. Libr Assn. (past preservation round table chair, co-chair ann. conf. bookstore 1998, past regional sec., chairperson South Ctrl. chpt.). Avocations: kayaking, biking, needlework, modern dance. Office: Pushnik Family Libr 735 Cumberland St Lebanon PA 17042-5235

BARD, TERRY ROSS, rabbi; b. Chgo., Jan. 17, 1944; s. Bernard David and Lillian (Terry) B.; m. Kay Elsa Bard, Aug. 6, 1966 (dec. 1974); children: Michael Aaron, Amy Shira; m. Linda Faye Bard, Dec. 18, 1975; 1 child, Rachel Joy. AB with distinction, Brown U., 1966; BHL, Hebrew Union Coll., 1968; MAHL, Hebrew Union Coll., Cin., 1971; postgrad., Harvard U., 1975; DD, Hebrew Union Coll., 1996. Ordained rabbi, 1971; bd. cert. chaplain APC, 1998; cert. chaplain AMHC, 1978, NAJC, 94. Asst./assoc. rabbi Temple Shalom, Newton, Mass., 1971-76; rabbi Congregation Shalom, Chelmsford, Mass., 1976-98, rabbi emeritus, 1998—; dir. dept. pastoral care and edn. Beth Israel Deaconess Med. Ctr., Boston, 1984—, coord. med. ethics program, 1985-98; dir. dept. pastoral care and edn. Mass. Mental Health Ctr., Boston, 1976-96; dir., psychotherapist Rabbinic Counseling Ctr., Newton, Mass., 1976—; bd. dirs. Jewish Cmty. Coun., Boston, 1976-84; v.p. Interfaith Counseling Svcs., Inc., Newton, 1988-93; lectr., cons. in field. Author: Medical Ethics in Practice, 1990; editor, Cura Animarum, 1987-94; editl. adv. com. Jour. Health Care, 1987—, Jour. Pastoral Care, 1984—, chmn. bd. mgrs., 1991-97; abstract and book rev. editor Jour. of Assn. Mental Health Clergy, 1980-87; contbr. articles to profl. jours. Adv. bd. Health Decisions USA, The Boston Experience, 1990-96, Mass. Health Decision, 1990-98, New Eng. Organ Bank, 1990—; mem. devel. com. Beth Israel Hosp., 1986-95, resuscitation com., 1995—, pharmacy com., 1993—, pub. affairs com., 1985-96, com. clin. investigations, 1985—, originator ethics adv. group, coord. clin. ethics program, 1984—, human subjects com. Harvard Pilgrim Health Plan, 1991-97, others; inst. rev. bd. Havard Med. Sch., 1975-90, 99—, faculty divsn. med. ethics, 1993—; mem. Cath.-Jewish Com., Archdiocese of Boston, 1973—. Recipient Nat. Conf. Christians and Jews, spl. recognition, 1971, Farband Labor Zionist award for excellence in field of religious studies, 1966, Founder's award Hebrew Union Coll.-Jewish Inst. Religion, 1996. Mem. Am. Psychiat. Assn. (ex-officio mem. com. on religion and psychiatry), Assn. Mental Health Clergy (pres. 1982-84, Anton T. Boisen award 1994), Mass. Bd. Rabbis (pres. 1980-82), Ctrl. Conf. Am. Rabbis, Chelmsford Clergy Assn., Assn. Clin. Pastoral Edn., Nat. Assn. Jewish Chaplains. Office: Beth Israel Deaconess Med Ctr East Campus 330 Brookline Ave Boston MA 02215-5400

BARDACH, JOAN LUCILE, clinical psychologist; b. Albany, N.Y., Oct. 3, 1919; d. Monroe Lederer and Lucile May (Lowenberg) B. AB, Cornell U., 1940; AM in Psychology, NYU, 1951; PhD in Clin. Psychology, 1957; cert. in psychoanalysis and psychotherapy, NYU, 1970. Supr. clin. psychologist NYU Rusk Inst. Rehab. Medicine, 1959-61; asst. chief and acting chief psychologist Rusk Inst. Rehab. Medicine, 1962-65, dir. psychol. services, 1965-82; research psychologist, mem. faculty N.Y. Med. Coll., 1961-62, clin. prof. rehab. medicine (psychology), 1976—; supr. postdoctoral program psychoanalysis and psychotherapy NYU, 1978—; pvt. practice clin. psychology and psychoanalysis N.Y.C., 1957—; non-govtl. orgn. rep. to UN Internat. Ctr. Sociol., Penal and Penitentiary Rsch. and Studies, Messina, Italy, 1985—; prin. investigator NIMH, 1976-81; mem. adv. bd. Coalition Sexuality and Disability, Planned Parenthood, 1983-89; cons. in field. Contbr. articles to profl. jours., chpt. to books. Recipient 3 awards for ednl. film, Choices: In Sexuality With Physical Disability, Internat. Film Festivals, Pioneer award for Sexual Attitude Reassessment Workshops The Coalition on Sexuality and Disability, 1989; NIMH fellow Inst. Sex Rsch., U. Ind., 1976. Fellow Am. Orthopsychiat. Assn.; mem. Am. Psychol. Assn., Am. Congress Rehab. Medicine, Sex Info. and Edn. Council U.S., Nat. Register Health Service Providers in Psychology, Eastern Psychol. Assn., N.Y. State Psychol. Assn. Home and Office: 50 E 10th St New York NY 10003-6221

BARDACK, PAUL ROITMAN, lawyer, consultant; b. N.Y.C., Nov. 13, 1953; s. Lawrence Stanley and Charlotte (Sebold) B.; m. Esther Roitman, May 27, 1979; children: David, Avi, Daniella. BA, Yale U., 1975; JD, Am. U., 1978. Bar: D.C. 1980. Atty. U.S. Dept. HUD, Washington, 1978-79; gen. counsel to U.S. congressman Robert Garcia, Washington, 1979-81; atty. Barrett Smith Schapiro Simon & Armstrong, N.Y.C., 1981-83; mgr. econ. devel. dept. City of Cleve., 1983-84; chief exec. officer, gen. counsel Econ. Devel. Resources, Inc., Phila. and Washington, 1984-86; sr. policy advisor Gov. Thomas Kean, Trenton, N.J., 1986-89; dep. asst. sec. for econ. devel. HUD, Washington, 1989-93; v.p. Nat. Mentoring Partnership, Washington, 1993-99; cons. Booz Allen & Hamilton, McLean, Va., 1999—. Mem. ABA, D.C. Bar Assn. Jewish. Home: 14833 Melfordshire Way Silver Spring MD 20906-5745 Office: Booz Allen & Hamilton 8251 Greensboro Dr Mc Lean VA 22102

BARDACKE, PAUL GREGORY, lawyer, former attorney general; b. Oakland, Calif., Dec. 16, 1944; s. Theodore Joseph and Frances (Woodward) B.; children: Julie, Brynn, Francheska, Chloe. BA cum laude, U. Calif.-Santa Barbara, 1966; JD, U. Calif.-Berkeley, 1969. Bar: Calif. 1969, N.Mex. 1970. Lawyer Legal Aid Soc., Albuquerque, 1969; assoc. firm Sutin, Thayer & Browne, Albuquerque, 1970-82; atty. gen. State of N.Mex., Santa Fe, 1982-86; ptnr. Sutin, Thayer & Browne, 1987-90, Eaves, Bardacke, Baugh, Kierst & Kiernan, P.A., 1991—; adj. prof. N.Mex. Law Sch., Albuquerque, 1973—; mem. faculty Nat. Inst. Trial Lawyers Advocacy, 1978—. Bd. dirs. All Faiths Receiving Home, Albuquerque; bd. dirs. Friends of Art, 1974, Artspace Mag., 1979-80, Legal Aid Soc., 1970-74. Reginald Heber Smith fellow, 1969. Fellow Am. Coll. Trial Lawyers; mem. ABA, Calif. Bar Assn., N.Mex. Bar Assn., Am. Bd. Trial Advocates (pres. N.Mex. chpt. 1992-93). Democrat. Office: PO Box 35670 Albuquerque NM 87176-5670

BARDAGLIO, PETER WINTHROP, humanities educator; b. Hartford, Conn., Apr. 25, 1953; s. George William and Mary Frances (White) B.; m. Wrexie Anne Lainson, Dec. 21, 1983; children: Sarah Jennings Agan, Jesse Barrett Agan, Anne Winthrop. BA, Brown U., 1975; MA, Stanford U., 1978, PhD, 1987. Vis. lectr. U. Md., College Park, 1981-83; instr. Goucher Coll., Balt., 1983-87; asst. prof. Goucher Coll., 1987-93, assoc. prof., 1993-95, Elizabeth Conolly Todd disting. assoc. prof., 1995-99, prof., 1999—, Elizabeth Connolly Todd disting. prof., 1999—, chair History Dept., 1996-98; spkr. Md. Humanities Coun. Spkrs. Bur., 1996—;. Author: Reconstructing the Household: Families, Sex, and the Law in the Nineteenth Century South, 1995 (Orgn. Am. Historians James A. Rawley prize for best book on history of race rels. in the U.S., 1996); contbr. essays, articles to profl. jours. Elder Catonsville (Md.) Presbyn. Ch., 1992—. Fellow Nat. Humanities Ctr.; mem. Am. Hist. Assn. (Littleton-Griswold rsch. grant 1989), Orgn. Am. Historians, Am. Studies Assn., So. Hist. Assn. (membership com. 1991-92), Am. Soc. for Legal History. Home: 9 Dutton Ct Catonsville MD 21228-4922 Office: Goucher Coll 1021 Dulaney Valley Rd Baltimore MD 21204-2753

BARDEEN, WILLIAM ALLAN, research physicist; b. Washington, Pa., Sept. 15, 1941; s. John and F. Jane (Maxwell) B.; m. Marjorie Ann Gaylord; children: Charles Gaylord, Karen Gail. AB in Physics, Cornell U., 1962; PhD in Physics, U. Minn., 1968. Rsch. assoc. SUNY, Stony Brook, 1966-68; mem. Inst. for Advanced Study, Princeton, N.J., 1968-69; asst. prof. Stanford (Calif.) U., 1969-72, assoc. prof., 1972-75; scientist Fermilab, Batavia, Ill., 1975-93, head theoretical physics, 1987-93, scientist, 1994—; head theoretical physics SSC Lab., Dallas, 1993-94; vis. scientist CERN, Geneva, Switzerland, 1971-72, Max Planck Inst. for Physics, Munich, 1977, 86. Author: Barden-Bardeen Genealogy, 1993; editor: Symp. on Anomalies, Geometry, Topology, 1985; mem. editl. bd. Phys. Rev., 1981-84, 92-94, Jour. Math. Physics, 1986-90, European Physics Jour. C, 1997—; contbr. numerous articles to profl. jours. Trustee Aspen Ctr. for Physics, 1987-91. Fellowship Alfred P. Sloan Found., 1971-74, John Simon Guggenheim Found., 1985-86; recipient sr. scientist award Alexander von Humboldt Found., 1977. Fellow Am. Phys. Soc. (exec. com. divsn. of particles and fields 1988-90, J. J. Sajurai prize for theoretical particle physics 1996); mem. Am. Acad. Arts and Scis., NAS. Avocations: genealogy, basketball. Office: Fermilab MS 106 PO Box 500 Batavia IL 60510-0500

BARDELAS, JOSE ANTONIO, allergist; b. Havana, Cuba, Feb. 3, 1948; came to U.S., 1961; s. Jose A. and Georgina (Leyva) B.; m. Sallie Young, July 3, 1971; children: Joseph, Mary. BA in Human Biology, Johns Hopkins U., 1970, MD, 1973. Intern, then resident in pediats. Johns Hopkins Hosp., Balt., 1973-75; fellow in allergy and immunology Nat. Jewish Ctr., Denver, 1975-77; pvt. practice Greensboro, N.C., 1977—; asst. clin. prof. pediats. U. N.C., Chapel Hill, 1979—. Fellow Am. Acad. Allergy and Immunology; mem. AMA, N.C. Soc. Allergy and Immunology (pres. 1982), N.C. Med. Soc. (mem. exec. coun. 1990, 91), High Point Med. Soc. (pres. 1989). Roman Catholic. Avocations: golf, reading. Home: 400 Edgedale High Point NC 27262-3607 Office: 100 Westwood Ave High Point NC 27262-4320

BARDELL, PAUL HAROLD, JR., electrical engineer; b. Casper, Wyo., Feb. 2, 1935; s. Paul Harold and Grace Adalee (Hooser) B.; m. Dorothy Estelle Chandler, June 9, 1956 (div. 1974); children: Paul Harold III, Renée Grace; m. Adrienne Marie Pati, Jan. 10, 1976. BSEE, U. Colo., 1956; MSEE, Stanford U., 1962, PhD, 1965. With IBM, 1956-93; sr. tech. staff mem. IBM, Poughkeepsie, N.Y., 1982-91, fellow, 1991-93; chief scientist Va. Laser Tech., Inc., Carmel, N.Y., 1993-95; mem. indsl. adv. bd. elec. and computer engrng. dept. U. Mass., Amherst, 1987-90; mem. curriculum coun. on elec. engrng. Nat. Tech. U., 1990-92; ind. cons., 1993—. Co-author: Built-In Test for VSLI, 1987; contbr. articles to IEEE Transactions on Computers; contbr. articles, mem. editorial bd. Jour. Electronic Testing, Theory and Applications. Lt. USNR, 1956-58. Fellow IEEE; mem. AAAS, Am. Phys. Soc., N.Y. Acad. Scis. Achievements include patents for Industrial Circuits; for Built-In Self Test. Home and Office: 46 Wellington Dr Carmel NY 10512-3817

BARDEN, DON H., communications executive; b. Detroit, Dec. 20, 1943; s. Milton Sr. and Hortense (Hamilton) B; m. Bella Marshall, May 14, 1988; 1 child, Keenan. Student, Ctrl. State U., 1963-64. Councilman City of Lorain, 1972-75; owner, pres. Don H. Barden Co., 1976-81; talk show host WKYC-TV NBC, Cleve., 1977-80; chmn., pres. Barden Comm., Inc., Detroit, 1981—; pres. Urban Action Inc.; del. White House Conf. on Small Bus.; pres. Lorain City Com. Action Agy.; bd. dirs. Nat. Cable TV Assn. IOB, MI Cable TV Assn., 1st Independence Nat. Bank, Met. Detroit Conv. Bur. Mem. exec. com. Dem. Party; mem. Edn. Task Force; dir. Detroit Symphony Orch., 1986—. Office: Barden Cablevision 12775 Lyndon St Detroit MI 48227-3982

BARDEN, JANICE KINDLER, personnel company executive; b. Cleve.; d. Norman Allen and Bessie G. (Black) Kindler; m. Hal Barden, Nov. 12, 1944 (dec. Jan. 1985) 1 child, Sheryl Andrea Barden Coholan. BBA, Miami U., Oxford, Ohio, 1947; M in Indsl. Psychology, Kent State U., 1948. Asst. dir. admissions Fairleigh Dickinson U., Teaneck, N.J., 1950-53; gen. mgr. Pilots Employment Assocs., Teterboro, N.J., 1953-71; founder, pres. Aviation Pers. Internat., New Orleans, 1971—; commr. jury U.S. Dist. Ct. (ea. dist.) La., New Orleans, 1965—; lectr. in field. Chmn. History of Aviation Collection U. Tex., Dallas, 1980—; served on Pres. Com. Rehab. Vietnam POW Pilots; mem. FAA's Blue Ribbon Panel. Recipient Disting. Alumnus award Kent State U., 1986, Cuyahoga Falls H.S., 1988, Doswell award Nat. Bus. Aircraft Assn., 1994. Mem. AAUW, Nat. Bus. Aircraft Assn. (chmn. conf. 1975, 85, 87, 90, 94), Flight Safety Found. (chmn. corp. seminar), Profl. Aircraft Maint. Assn., Bus. and Profl. Women's Club, Kent State Alumni Assn. (bd. dirs. 1976-82), Women in Aviation, Order of Rainbow (grand coord. 1973-84), Psi Chi. Republican. Episcopalian. Office: Aviation Pers Internat PO Box 6846 New Orleans LA 70174-6846

BARDEN, KENNETH EUGENE, lawyer, educator; b. Espanola, N.Mex., Nov. 21, 1955; s. Lloyd C. and Beverly A. (Coverdale) B. BA cum laude, Ind. Ctrl. U., 1977; JD, Ind. U., 1977; cert., Harvard U., 1983. Bar: Ind. 1981, U.S. Dist. Ct. (so. dist.) Ind. 1981, U.S. Tax Ct. 1983, U.S. Ct. Mil. Appeals 1983, U.S. Ct. Appeals (6th and 7th cirs.) 1983, U.S. Ct. Internat. Trade 1983, U.S. Ct. Claims Ohio 1990, Rep. of Palau, 1998. Law clk. Marion County Prosecutor's Office, Ind., 1976-78, Krieg Devault Alexander & Capehart, Indpls., 1978-79; baliff Marion County Mcpl. Ct. 7, 1979-81, commr.-judge pro tem, 1981; pub. defender criminal divsn. 1 Marion County Superior Ct., 1981; asst. to U.S. magistrate U.S. Dist. Ct. (so. dist.) Ind., Indpls., 1982-84; city atty. City of Richmond, Ind., 1984-89; pres. Bd. Pub. Works and Safety, 1988-89; corp. counsel Richmond Power & Light Co., 1984-89; pres. City of Richmond Bd. Pub. Works and Safety, Ohio, 1988-89; chief gen. counsel City of Dayton, Ohio, 1989-98; tax atty., asst. atty. gen. Rep. of Palau, 1998—; adj. prof. law Ind. Ctrl. U., Indpls., 1983. Contbr. articles to profl. jours. Nat. v.p. Coll. Dems. of Am., 1979-82; ward chmn. Marion County Dems., 1977-81; precinct committeeman Wayne County Dems., 1985-89, treas. 2d dist., 1986-89; del to NATO European Youth Leadership Conf., 1980; co-founder Hubert H. Humphrey Tng. Inst. for Campaign Politics, 1980; treas. Perry Twp. Dem. Club, 1980-83; alt. del. Dem. Nat. Conv., 1980; del. White House forum on Domestic and Econ. Policy, 1975; del Youth Conf. on Nat. Security and the Atlantic Alliance, Mt. Vernon Coll., Washington, 1976, Am. Coun. Young Polit. Leaders Fgn. Policy Conf., 1987; mem. U.S. Youth Coun. under Pres. Carter, 1980; mem. Ind. Gov.'s Cmty. Corrections Com., 1973-75; mem. adv. coun. Friends of the Battered, 1985-88; mem. pers. policies forum Bur. Nat. Affairs, 1985-88; mem. Dem. Leadership Coun., 1987—, Am. Coun. of Young Polit. Leaders, 1986—; founding mem., bd. dirs. Richmond (Ind.) Cmty. Devel. Corp., 1986-89; legal counsel Richmond Greater Progress Com., 1987-89. Recipient Youth in Govt. award Optimist Club, 1972; named one of Outstanding Young Men in Am., 1986. Mem. ABA (com. on industry regulation, Young lawyers divsn. labor law com., urban, state and local govt. sect., vice chair Town Hall com. 1985-87, chair 1987-88, vice chair citizenship edn. com. 1987-88, victims com. sect. of criminal justice 1985—, lawyers and arts com., chmn. town hall com. 1987-91, vice chmn. citizenship edn. com. 1987-94, chair Arson Law Project 1993-94, contbr. editor Arson Law Reporter), Fed. Bar Assn., Ind. State Bar Assn., Indpls. Bar Assn., Wayne County Bar Assn., Ind. Coun. on World Affairs, Fed. Energy Bar Assn., Ind. Assn. Cities and Towns, Nat. League of Cities, Am. Soc. Pub. Adminstrs., Athenaeum Club (Indpls.), World Trade of Ind. Club, Kiwanis, Phi Alpha Delta, Epsilon Sigma Alpha, Alpha Phi Omega. Methodist. E-mail: kbarden@palaunet.com. Home: PO Box 6011 Palau PW 96940-0841 Office: Tax Counsel Rep of Palau PO Box 6011 Palau PW 96940

BARDEN, ROBERT CHRISTOPHER, lawyer, psychologist, educator, analyst, author; b. Richmond, Va., June 7, 1954; s. Elliott Hatcher and Jane Elizabeth Cole (Ferris) B.; m. Robin Jones, Nov. 14, 1987. BA summa cum laude, U. Minn., 1976, PhD in Clin. Psychology, 1982; postgrad., U. Calif., Berkeley, 1977; JD cum laude, Harvard U., 1992. Lic. cons. psychologist, Minn., Tex.; diplomate Am. Bd. Forensic Examiners. Project asst. NSF, 1978-79; intern in psychology VA Med. Ctr., Stanford Med. Ctr., Palo Alto, Calif., 1979-80; dir. psychology Internat. Craniofacial Surg. Inst., Dallas, 1980-87; corp., civil litigation, family and health law atty. Lindquist and Vennum, Mpls., 1992-96; psychologist, lawyer, expert witness, pub. policy analyst R.C. Barden & Assocs., 1996—; asst. prof. psychology So. Meth. U., Dallas, 1980-84; asst. prof., dir. child clin. psychology U. Utah, Salt Lake City, 1984-87, rsch. faculty dept. surgery, 1987-93; vis. faculty, asst. prof. psychology Gustavus Adolphus Coll., St. Peter, Minn., 1988; pres. Optimal Performance Sys., Inc., Cambridge, 1989—; mem. Minn. Bd. Psychology, 1993-97; adj. prof. law U. Minn. Law Sch., 1995—; cons. and spkr. in field. Consulting editor Devel. Psychology, 1989; editor Harvard Jour. Law and Pub. Policy, 1990-91; contbr. to profl. pubs. Project dir. ch. cmty. svc. projects, Mpls. and Cambridge, 1988—; mem. Minn. Bd. Psychology, 1993-97, Higher Edn. Coordinating Bd., 1993-94; rep. Minn. Sixth Congl. Dist. Recipient Young Scholar award Found. for Child Devel., Faculty Scholar award W.T. Grant Found., 1987-89; NSF fellow, 1978, NIMH fellow, 1976, 77. Mem. ABA, APA, Soc. for Rsch. in Child Devel., Internat. Soc. Clin. Hypnosis, Harvard Law Sch. Soc. Law and Medicine, Lowell House Commons Rm. Harvard U., Nat.Assn. for Consumer Protection in Mental Health Practices (pres. 1995—), Sigma Xi, Phi Beta Kappa. Avocations: church and service work, tennis, martial arts, mountain climbing, music. Home and Office: RC Barden and Assocs 1093 Duffer Ln North Salt Lake UT 84054-3313

BARDEN, THOMAS EARL, English literature educator; b. Richmond, Va., Aug. 5, 1946; s. Chester Earl and Lucy Virginia (Duling) B.; m. Rayna Claire Zacharias, June 21, 1981; children: Zacharias, Matthias, Daniel. BA,

U. Va., 1968, MA, 1972, PhD, 1975. Acting asst. prof. U. Va., Charlottesville, 1975-76; prof. English U. Toledo, Ohio, 1976—, dir. Am. studies program, 1991-97, dir. grad. English studies, 1997—; panelist, traditional arts panel The Ohio Arts Coun., Columbus, 1978-82; Fulbright sr. lectr. U. Wales, Swansea, 1993-94. Editor: (oral histories)Weavils in the Wheat: Interviews with Virginia Ex-slaves, 1976, 2d edit., 1980, The Travels of Peter Woodhouse, 1981, (folk narratives) Virginia Folk Legends, 1991 (Am. Folklore Soc. publ. award). 1st lt., arty. U.S. Army, 1968-71. Democrat. Avocations: guitar, boating. Home: 2841 Kenwood Blvd Toledo OH 43606-3226 Office: U Toledo Dept English Toledo OH 43606

BARDIN, CLYDE WAYNE, biomedical researcher; b. McCamey, Tex., Sept. 18, 1934; s. James A. and Nora Irene (Barnett) B.; m. Bonnie Lambdin, June 24, 1958 (div.); m. Dorothy Kreiger, Aug. 11, 1978 (dec. Apr. 1985); m. Beatrice MacDonald, June 12, 1987; children: Charlotte E., Stephanie F. BA in Biology, Rice U., 1957; MS with honors, Baylor U., 1962, MD with honors, 1962; Docteur (hon.), Universtes de Caen, France, 1990, U. Pierre et Murie Curie, Paris, 1997. Cert., licensed MD, Tex., Pa., N.Y. Resident in medicine N.Y. Hosp., N.Y.C., 1962-64; clin. assoc. NIH, Bethesda, Md., 1964-67, sr. investigator, 1967-70; assoc. prof. Milton S. Hershey Med. Ctr., Pa. State U., Hershey, 1970-72, prof. medicine, 1972-78; v.p. The Population Coun., N.Y.C., 1978-95; pres. Bardin LLC, N.Y.C., 1996—, Thyreos Corp., 1997—; adj. prof. Rockefeller U., N.Y.C., 1978—, Cornell Med. Ctr., N.Y.C., 1985—; cons. WHO, 1972-73; chmn. bd. sci. counselors Nat. Inst. Child Health and Human Devel., Bethesda, 1982-83; chmn. endocrine study sect. NIH, Bethesda, 1977-79; mem. nat. prostate cancer task force Nat. Cancer Inst., 1973-78; endocrinologist Nat. Inst. Child Health and Human Devel., NIH, 1996-97. Editor 18 books on medicine and endocrinology; mem. editl. bd. 16 sci. jours.; contbr. over 500 articles to sci. jours. Advisor internat. divsn. Ford Found., N.Y.C., 1975-79; bd. dirs. Harris and Harris Group, Inc., 1994—; chmn. bd. dirs. The Hormone Found., 1997-98. Decorated Order of Comdr. of Lion (Finland), 1983; recipient Transatlantic medal Brit. Endocrine Socs., 1988; named fellow Josiah Macy Jr. Found., 1976-77, Disting. Alumnus Rice U., 1994, Disting. Alumnus N.Y. Hosp.-Cornell Med. Ctr., 1992. Mem. Am. Assn. Physicians, Am. Soc. Clin. Investigation, Am. Soc. Andrology (coun., v.p., pres. 1984-89, Serono award 1984, Disting. Andrologist award 1992), Endocrine Soc. (coun. 1976-79, pres. 1993-94, Sidney H. Ingbar Disting. Svc. award 1996), Internat. Soc. Andrology (exec. coun. 1981-85), Internat. Assn. Axel Munthe Awards (bd. dirs. 1982-92), Internat. Com. Contraception Rsch. (chmn. 1978-95), Inst. Medicine. Democrat. Achievements include direction of a team of scientists that developed seven contraceptives as well as treatments for menopause and cancer.

BARDIN, DAVID J., lawyer; b. N.Y.C., June 2, 1933; s. Shlomo and Ruth (Jonas) B.; m. Livia Goldeen, Mar. 12, 1961; children: Jacob, Matthew, Joseph, Sarah. AB, Columbia U., 1954, JD, 1956. Bar: N.Y. 1956, D.C. 1966, Israel 1970. Atty., dep. gen. counsel FPC, Washington, 1958-69; asst. to atty. gen. Jerusalem, 1970-72; counsel Environ. Protection Service, Jerusalem, 1973; commr. N.J. Dept. Environ. Protection, Trenton, 1974-77; dep. adminstr. FEA, Washington, 1977; adminstr. Econ. Regulatory Adminstrn., Dept. Energy, Washington, 1977-80; counsel, mem. Arent Fox Kintner Plotkin & Kahn LLPC, Washington, 1980—; lectr. law Bar-Ilan U., Tel Aviv U., U. Va. Extension. Co-author: AGA Select Gas Use Handbook: Natural Gas for Environmental Control, 1985; contbr. chpts. on internat. energy trade and U.S. regulation of internat. trade in energy law and transactions, (treatise) Matthew Bender, 1990, Psychological Coercion and Human Rights, 1994. Trustee Liberty State Pk. Devel. Corp., 1990—, The Found. Jewish Studies, 1991—, Pinelands Preservation Alliance, 1991—, Nat. Assn. of Atty. Gen., Moot Ct. Panel, 1992—, Mental Health Liaison Group, 1993—; bd. mgrs. Adas Israel Congregation, 1998—; adv. neighborhood commr. of D.C., 1999—. With U.S. Army, 1956-58. Mem. ABA, Fed. Bar Assn., Fed. Energy Bar Assn. (bd. dirs. 1985-87), Found. for Energy Law Jour. (bd. dirs. 1987-90). Democrat. Jewish. Office: Arent Fox Kintner Plotkin & Kahn LLPC 1050 Connecticut Ave NW Washington DC 20036-5339 *Combine careful thought with timely action: rely on oneself, work with others, and procrastinate only if there's a very strong reason. Finally, apply this test: How will I explain my acts and omissions to a grandchild?.*

BARDIN, ROLLIN EDMOND, electrical engineering executive; b. Greensburg, Ky., Apr. 2, 1932; s. Tolbert Edward and Mary Margaret (Wise) B.; m. Patricia Lou Ott, Dec. 20, 1953 (div. June 1956); 1 child, Rollin Edmond Jr.; m. Lillian Patricia Sweeney, Jan. 20, 1958; 1 child, Susan Lynn. AA in Engring., Miami Dade Jr. Coll., 1963; BSEE, U. Miami, 1965. Cert. master electrician. Stock clk. Margaret Ann Stores, Miami Shores, Fla., 1950-51; meter reader Fla. Power & Light, Miami, Fla., 1951-56, svc. rep., 1956-61; engr. Hughes & Weaver, Miami, 1965-68, E. R. Brownell, Miami, 1968-70; bldg. inspector FHA, Miami, 1970-73; elec. contractor Bison Electric, Inc., Miami, 1973-80; prin. R. E. Bardin Elec. Contractor, Inc., Miami, 1980—. Chief petty officer, USCGR, 1951-92, ret. Recipient presdl. citation John F. Kennedy, 1961, Ronald Regan, 1981. Mem. NRA, Smithsonian Assocs., U.S. Ski Assn., Moose, Miami Dolphin Club, PGA Tour Ptnrs., Am. Legion, Miami Springs Golf and Country Club. Democrat. Avocations: golf, snow skiing, target shooting, music, Miami Dolphins football.

BARDLIVING, CLIFFORD LEE, JR., graphic designer; b. Stamford, Conn., Mar. 15, 1953; s. Clifford Lee and Jane Elizabeth B.; m. Tanya Lynn Morris, Oct. 24, 1981; children: Cameron Lee, Amber Rose. Student in graphic design, U. Conn., 1971-76. Mech. artist Hyer/Smith, Inc., Stamford, 1976-78, Redington, Inc., Stamford, 1978-79; asst. art dir. TCI Advt., Greenwich, Conn., 1979-81; graphic coord. Xerox Learning Systems, Stamford, 1981-82; studio mgr. F. Scott Kimmich & Co., Norwalk, Conn., 1983-89; v.p., dir. graphic svcs. Kallir, Philips, Ross, Inc., N.Y.C., 1989-92; dir. studio svcs. Bryan, Brown, Maynard, Edelman, New Haven, Conn., 1993-94; sr. graphic designer Cage Graphic Arts, Inc., Phila., 1995—; Afro-Am. art cons. Lockwood/Mathews Mansion Mus., Norwalk, 1993—. Artist: (pencil drawings) Heritage, 1974 (Best Portrait New Canaan Art Show 1978); logo designs include Stamford Sickle Cell Counseling Svc., 1980, Respect Your School logo Columbus Magnet Sch., 1994, Bend Don't Break musical play, 1995; designer st. banner for town of Willow Grove, Pa. Second v.p. Columbus Magnet Sch. PTO Coun., Norwalk, 1993—; trustee Miracle Temple Ch., Norwalk, 1993—, deacon, 1985—, pres. men's fellowship, 1992—, Sunday sch. supt., 1985-89; sponsor C.L.A.S.S. Scholarship Program, Norwalk, 1990—; treas. Stamford Sickle Cell Counseling Svc., 1980-82; chmn. pers. com. Mt. Airy Ch., Phila., 1996, vice chmn. bd. trustees, 1999. Recipient Pres.'s award Kallir, Philips, Ross Inc., 1991. Democrat. Pentecostal. Avocations: painting and drawing, jogging and exercising, Bible study. Home: 8907 Cheltenham Ave Glenside PA 19038-5207

BARDO, JOHN WILLIAM, university administrator; b. Cin., Oct. 28, 1948; s. John Thomas and Grace Roberta (Day) B.; m. Deborah Joan Davis, Aug. 8, 1975; 1 child, Christopher. Student, U. Southampton, Eng., 1968-69; BA in Econs., U. Cin., 1970; MA in Sociology, Ohio U., 1971; PhD in Sociology, Ohio State U., 1973. Asst. prof. Wichita (Kans.) State U., 1973-79, assoc. prof., 1979-83, chmn. dept. sociology, 1978-83; prof. Southwest Tex. State U., San Marcos, 1983-86, dean Sch. Liberal Arts, 1983-86; prof. U. N. Fla., Jacksonville, 1986-90, provost, v.p., 1986-89; prof. dept. sociology and anthropology Bridgewater (Mass.) State Coll., 1990-95, v.p. acad. affairs, 1990-95, provost, 1993-95; chancellor Western Carolina U., Cullowhee, N.C., 1995—; vis. lectr. Monash U., Clayton, Australia, 1977; vis. prof. Univ. Coll. Wales, Swansea, 1981; cons. various orgns. and govt. agys. Co-author: Urban Sociology: An Integrated Approach, 1982; editor: Defining the Mission of AASCU Institutions, 1990; contbr. articles to profl. jours. and books chpts. Co-chair N.C./Estern Band of Cherokee Indians Econ. Devel. Task Force, 1996—; bd. dirs. N.C. Arboretum, 1995—; trustee N.C. Ctr. for the Advancement of Teaching, 1995—. Recipient Humanities award Kans. Com. for Humanities, 1978; named one of Outstanding Young Men in Am., Jaycees, 1979. Mem. Am. Sociol. Assn., Assn. for Consumer Rsch., Mid-South Sociol. Assn., Am. Assn. Higher Edn., Am. Assn. State Colls. and Univs. (coll. rep. resource ctr.), Soc. Applied Multivariate Rsch. (pres.-elect 1993—), Alpha Kappa Delta, Phi Kappa Phi. Greek Orthodox. Avocations: photography, golf. Home: 10 Chancellor Dr Cullowhee NC 28723-6874 Office: W Carolina Univ Chancellor Cullowhee NC 28723

BARDOLPH, RICHARD, historian, educator; b. Chgo., Feb. 18, 1915; s. Mark and Anna (Veldman) B.; m. Dorothy Corlett, July 28, 1945; children: Virginia Ann (Mrs. George Haskett), Mark III, Richard. B.A., U. Ill., 1940, M.A., 1941, Ph.D., 1944; Litt.D., Concordia Coll., 1968; LL.D., Concordia Theol. Sem., 1983. Mem. faculty dept. history U. N.C. at Greensboro, 1944-80, head dept., 1960-80, Jefferson Standard prof., 1970-80; Fulbright lectr. Denmark, 1953-54; Mem. regional selection com. Woodrow Wilson Nat. Fellowship Found.; mem. commn. theology and ch. relations Luth. Ch.-Mo. Synod. Author: Agricultural Literature and Illinois Farmer, 1948, Negro Vanguard, 1959 (Mayflower award 1960), Civil Rights Record, 1849-1970, 1970; Mem. bd. editors: Jour. So. History; Contbr. articles to profl. jours. and encys. Active ACLU, NAACP. Recipient Max O. Gardner award for Outstanding Contbns. to Welfare of Human Race U. N.C., 1979; Ford Found. fellow HArvard U., 1952-53, Guggenheim fellow, 1956-57, sr. fellow NEH, 1971-72. Mem. ACLU, NAACP, Am. Hist. Assn., Orgn. Am. Historians, So. Hist. Assn., Phi Beta Kappa. Home: 207 Tate St Greensboro NC 27403-1838

BARDON, JANE ELIAS, economist; b. Athens, Greece, Sept. 5, 1951; came to U.S., 1971, naturalized, 1977; d. Elias Theophanes and Apollonia (Jafetis) Bardouniotis; student (scholar) Bologna Center, Johns Hopkins U., 1974-75; B.A. (Pres.'s scholar), Temple U., 1974, M.A., 1977, Ph.D., 1982. Instr., Greek, German, English as fgn. lang., Athens, Greece, 1969; in charge deposits Nea Ionia br. Nat. Bank of Greece, 1970; research asst. econs. dept. Temple U., Phila., 1975-78, lectr. econs., 1979-80, supr. part-time faculty, econs. dept., 1979-80; economist div. internat. prices Bur. Labor Stats., U.S. Dept. Labor, Washington, 1980-81; economist Internat. Trade Adminstrn., U.S. Dept. Commerce, 1981-84, Dept. Treasury, 1984-90, Dept. of State, Agy. Internat. Devel., 1990-96, writer, cons. 1996-98, Fgn. Agrl. Svc. USDA, 1998—. Mem. Am. Econ. Assn., Western Econ. Assn., Assn. Grad. Students in Econs. Temple U. (past pres.), Soc. Govt. Economists. Phi Beta Kappa, Omicron Delta Epsilon. Home: 604 Dale Dr Silver Spring MD 20910-4214

BARDOS, KAROLY, television and film educator, writer, director; b. Budapest, Pest, Hungary, Dec. 31, 1942; came to U.S., 1970; s. Laszlo and Klara (Weisz) B.; m. Eva Beres, 1964 (div. 1967); m. Gizella Viczko, 1970 (div. 1987); 1 child, Melinda. BA, U. Budapest, 1963, MA, 1966, postgrad., 1969; postgrad., NYU, 1970; postgrad., dir. fellow, Am. Film Inst. Ctr. Advanced Film Studies, 1972-75. Lectr. film adult audiences Hungarian Film Inst., 1966-69; asst. dir., writer Hungarian TV, Budapest, 1966-69; prodr., dir. Am.-Hungarian TV Channel 68-60, NJ, 1978-80, Am.-Hungarian TV Channel 25, NY, 1992—, Am.-Hungarian TV Channel 17, Miami, 1992—, Ctr. for the Media Arts, N.Y.C., 1980-85; asst. prof. St. John's U., Jamaica, N.Y., 1985-93; master tchr. Dept. Film & TV NYU, 1998—; dir., editor The World of Films PBS, 1990-91; cons., lectr. Am. Film Inst. Ctr. for Advanced Film Studies, 1972-73; tech. cons. N.Y. Ctr. For Visual History, N.Y.C., 1983; sr. lectr. CMA, 1980-85; blue ribbon panel judge Nat. Emmy TV awards, 1981—. Author: (screenplays) Father of the Moving Picture, 1975, The Crown, 1980, Forced March, 1987, The Containment, 1989-90; dir. Backstage at the Tony Awards, 1997, (live webcasting) Tony Awards Online; co-prodr. Fallen Nest, 1998-99; exec. prodr. Static, 1998-99, Millenium Gala TV Show. Recipient 1st prize Internat. Ednl. Film Festival, Tokyo, 1968, Best Am. Short Feature award U.S. Am. Film Festival, 1977, 1st prize Internat. Rehab. Film Festival, N.Y.C., 1981, Blue Ribbon award, 1st prize Am. Film Festival, N.Y.C., 1985, 2d prize Nat. Coll. Advt. awards, 1991. Mem. AAUP, Univ. Film and TV Assn., Nat. Acad. TV Arts and Scis., Am. Film Inst. Alumni Assn., Writers Guild of Am. Jewish. Office: NYU Dept Film & TV 721 Broadway Fl 9 New York NY 10003-6862

BARDOS, THOMAS JOSEPH, chemist, educator; b. Budapest, Hungary, July 20, 1915; came to U.S., 1946, naturalized, 1952; s. Arthur and Vilma (Brachfeld) B.; m. Mary Jane Choate, Mar. 24, 1951. Diploma in chem. engring., Royal Hungarian Tech. U., Budapest, 1938; PhD in Chemistry, U. Notre Dame, 1949. Chem. engr. Vacuum Oil Co., Budapest, 1938-46; rsch. assoc. U. Tex., Austin, 1948-51; sect. head Armour & Co., Chgo., 1951-60; prof. med. chemistry and biochem. pharmacology SUNY, Buffalo, 1960-94, prof. emeritus, 1994—. Contbr. articles sci. jours. Recipient Ebert prize Acad. Pharm. Scis., 1971. Fellow AAAS, N.Y. Acad. Scis.; mem. Am. Chem. Soc. (Schoellkopf medal Western N.Y. sect. 1974), Chem. Soc. (London), Hungarian Acad. Scis. (hon.), Am. Soc. Biol. Chemists, Am. Assn. Cancer Rsch., Am. Pharm. Assn., Cosmos Club (Washington), Sigma Xi, Rho Chi. Achievements include isolation and first synthesis of folinic acid (leukovorin); design and synthesis of antifolates, nucleoside analogs, dual antagonists (phosphoraziridines) and antitemplates (modified DNA, RNA and oligonucleotides) as anticancer and antiviral agents. Home: 131 Burbank Dr Buffalo NY 14226-3935

BARDSLEY, KAY, historian, archivist, dance professional; b. Port Said, Egypt, Apr. 17, 1921; came to U.S., 1929; d. Chris and Helen (Jones) Lanitis; m. James Calvert Bardsley, May 30, 1947 (wid. Sept. 1978); children: Wendy Jane, Amy Kim; m. Donald Marshall Kuhn, Feb. 25, 1990. Student, Duncan Dance Tng./Carnegie, Hall, Steinway Hall Studios, N.Y.C., 1931-42; BA cum laude, Hunter Coll., 1942. Dance debut Maria-Theresa Duncan, N.Y.C., 1934; soloist Maria-Theresa Heliconiades, N.Y.C., 1936-42; Duncan tchr. Maria-Theresa Sch., N.Y.C., 1937-46; tchr. Creative Dance for Children, N.Y.C., 1960-66, Isadora Duncan-Maria-Theresa Heritage Group, N.Y.C., 1977-81; fashion editor Woman's Day, N.Y.C., 1943-45; TV work WPIX Gloria Swanson Hour, 1948-49; writer TV Guide, 1949; writer/prodr. ABC Network/Don Ameche Langford Show, 1949-50; syndicated film series prodr., 1950-60; prodr. video documentation of Duncan Repertory, 1976-80. Writer, lectr. in field; prodr.: (documentary) The Last Isadorable, 1988, reissued, 1997; contbr. articles to profl. dance jours. and publs. including Dance Scope, 1977, Ballet Rev., 1991, 94; most recent works in field include ReAnimations of Duncan Masterworks, A Four-year Project, presented at Dance ReConstructed Conf., Rutgers U., 1992, numerous conf. presentations and documentation of Isadora Duncan's 1st sch.; pub. by Congress for Rsch. in Dance Ann., 1979; resident dancer scholar U. Oreg., Eugene, 1997-98. Trustee Coun. for the Arts in Westchester, N.Y., 1973-76; bd. dirs. Bicentennial Com., Chappaqua, N.Y., 1973-76; co-chmn. Community Day, 1973, 75. Grantee NEA, N.Y.C., 1980; pioneer NYU/Master Tchr. Dance Tng. Inst., 1987; recipient 1997-98 Creativity award in Dance U. Oreg. Mem. Soc. Dance History Scholars, Am. Dance Guild, World Dance Alliance, Dance Critics Assn. (bd. dirs. 1997—), Isadora Duncan Internat. Inst. (dir., founder 1978-99). Office: Isadora Duncan Internat Inst 6305 S Geneva Cir Englewood CO 80111-5437

BARDWICK, JUDITH MARCIA, management consultant; b. N.Y.C., Jan. 16, 1933; d. Abraham and Ethel (Krinsky) Hardis; m. John Bardwick, III, Dec. 18, 1954 (div.); children: Jennifer, Peter, Deborah; m. Allen Armstrong, Feb. 10, 1984. BS, Purdue U., 1954; MS, Cornell U., 1955; PhD, U. Mich., 1964. Lectr. U. Mich., Ann Arbor, 1964-67; asst. prof. psychology U. Mich., 1967-71, assoc. prof., 1971-75, prof., 1975-83, assoc. dean, 1977-83; clin. prof. psychiatry U. Calif., San Diego, 1984—; pres. In Transition, Inc. (name changed to Judith M. Bardwick, PhD, Inc., 1991), 1983—; mem. population research study group NIH, 1971-75. Author: Psychology of Women, 1971, In Transition, 1979, The Plateauing Trap, 1986, Danger in The Comfort Zone, 1991, In Praise of Good Business, 1998; co-author: Feminine Personality and Conflict, 1970; editor: Readings in the Psychology of Women, 1972; coauthor Feminine Personality and Conflict, 1970; mem. editorial bd. Women's Studies, 1973—, Psychology of Women Quar., 1975—; contbr. articles to profl. jours. Mem. social sci. adv. com. Planned Parenthood Am., 1973. Fellow APA; mem. Midwest Psychol. Assn., N.Y. Acad. Scis., Am. Psychosomatic Soc., Phi Beta Kappa. Home and Office: 1389 Caminito Halago La Jolla CA 92037-7165 *I am particularly grateful to the principle of academic freedom which has allowed me to pursue intellectual questions that I considered important. No other institution would have supported my pursuit of the answers to questions that seemed significant for theoretical or applied reasons before those issues were obviously important to society.*

BARDWIL, JOSEPH ANTHONY, investments consultant; b. Bklyn., Oct. 29, 1928; s. Najeb B. and Malvina (Galaini) B.; m. Valerie Pavilonis, Feb. 11, 1961; children: Anita, James, David, Joanna. BS in Econs, U. Pa., 1950; MBA, NYU, 1956. Reporter, mgr. Dun & Bradstreet, Inc., N.Y.C., 1950-57; gen. investment mgr. Prudential Ins. Co., 1957-69; v.p. Hartz Mountain Corp., Harrison, N.J., 1969-88; prin. Bardwil Assocs., Cranford, N.J., 1989—. Mem. Assn. Investment Mgmt. & Rsch., N.Y. Soc. Security Analysts. Republican. Roman Catholic. Home and Office: 321 North Ave E Unit 128 Cranford NJ 07016-2451

BARDYGUINE, PATRICIA WILDE, ballerina, ballet theatre executive; b. Ottawa, Ont., Can., July 16, 1928; came to U.S., 1943; d. John Herbert and Eileen Lucy (Simpson) White; m. George Bardyguine, Dec. 14, 1953; children: Anya, Youri. Student, Profl. Children's Sch., N.Y.C. Dancer Am. Concert Ballet, N.Y.C., 1943-44, Marquis De Queras Ballet Internat., N.Y.C., 1944-45, Ballet Russe De Monte Carlo, tours nationwide, 1945-49; guest artist Roland Petit Ballet De Paris, 1949; prin. ballerina Met. Ballet, touring throughout Europe, 1950, N.Y.C. Ballet, 1950-65; dir. Harkness House, N.Y.C., 1965-67; ballet mistress Am. Ballet Theater, N.Y.C., 1969-82; ret. artistic dir. Pitts. Ballet Theatre, 1997—, advisor, tchr., 1997—; dir. Am. Ballet Theater Sch., 1979-82; dance panelist Nat. Endowment for Arts, N.Y. State Coun. for the Arts; judge Lausanne Internat. Competition; guest tchr., coach N.Y.C. Ballet, Joffrey Ballet, Dance Theater of Harlem, The Royal Ballet of Stockholm, Internat. Summer Seminar, Cologne, Germany, Heinz Bosl Found., Munich, St. Moritz, Japan, Australia, Republic of Korea. Soloist six European tours, also tour of Orient; numerous TV appearances; commd. by N.Y. Philharm. to choreograph ballets Festival, 1964, At the Ball, 1965, Viennese Evening, 1966, Petite Suite, 1967. Adminstr. scholar fund Sch. A. Ballet Group; mem. Nat. Bd. Regional Ballet; Fulbright panelist. Recipient YWCA award for Leadership in Arts and Letters, 1990, Cultural award for Extraordinary Contbns. to Cultural Life in Region, Pitts. Ctr. for Arts, 1997, Cultural award for outstanding contbns. to cultural climate of the region Pitts. Ctr. for Arts, 1997; named Pitts. Woman of Yr. in Arts and Music, 1994. Mem. Am. Guild Mus. Artists, AFTRA, Dance/USA (bd. dirs.). Office: Pitts Ballet Theatre 2900 Liberty Ave Pittsburgh PA 15201-1511

BARDZELL, JEFFREY SCOTT, graphics designer; b. Fairfax, Va., Feb. 23, 1970; s. Richard B. and Delia Grace (Bradley) Jennings; m. Shaowen Lu, Nov. 26, 1994. BA in English, Mary Washington Coll., 1992; MA in Comparative Lit., Ind. U., 1994, postgrd. in comparative lit., 1997—. Assoc. instr. dept. comparative lit. Ind. U., Bloomington, 1993-96, editl. asst. East Asian Studies Ctr., 1996-97; graphic designer East Asian Studies Ctr. Ind. Edn. Policy Ctr., 1997—; dir. publs., comms. Ind. Edn. Policy Ctr., Bloomington, 1997—. Editor: (literary mag.) Aubade, 1989-92, East Asian Newsletter, 1996-97, (newsletter) Policy News and Notes; asst. editor: (jour.) Taoist Resources, 1996-97; webmaster: Yearbook of Comparative and Gen. Lit., 1997—; co-author: Indiana's Early Literacy Intervention Grant Program Implementation Study, 1998. Mem. Mortar Bd., Fredericksburg, Va., 1991-92. Mem. MLA, Edn. Writers Assn., Phi Beta Kappa. Avocations: graphic design, internet design. Home: 922 Woodbridge Dr Bloomington IN 47408-2786 Office: Ind Edn Policy Ctr Smith Rsch Ctr Ste 170 Bloomington IN 47405

BARE, BRUCE, retired life insurance company executive; b. Pierson, Iowa, May 26, 1914; s. Edward E. and Myrtle Viola (Sloan) B.; m. Adaline Light, June 14, 1936; children: Bruce Jr., Barbara Bare Spaulding, John. B.A., Grinnell (Iowa) Coll., 1935; LL.D. (hon.), Westmont Coll., Santa Barbara, Calif., 1971. C.L.U. With New Eng. Mut. Life Ins. Co., 1935—; gen. agt. New Eng. Mut. Life Ins. Co., Los Angeles, 1946-80, field v.p., 1979-82; Trustee Westmont Coll., 1947—, chmn., 1965; past pres. Fuller Evangelistic Found., Pasadena, Calif.; chmn. bd. trustees African Enterprise Internat., 1979-84. Recipient Farrell award Los Angeles C. of C., 1968; named to Hall of Fame Gen. Agts. and Mgrs. Assn., 1977. Mem. Am. Soc. C.L.U.'s (pres. 1964, trustee 1974), Life Underwriters Assn. (past pres. Los Angeles chpt.), Los Angeles Life Ins. Mgrs. Assn. (past pres.). Presbyterian. *The important thing is to establish goals a step at a time as you go through life. College diploma, proper job with opportunity, careful discharge of all responsibilities assumed, proper marriage and complete commitment to the Christian way of life. A periodic check on goal and accomplishments should provide incentive for greater goals. Success will be a result of never turning aside from Christian principles in all aspects of life.*

BARE, CHARLES LAMBERT, education director; b. Lakenheath, U.K., Aug. 29, 1970; s. Merle Monroe and Betty Gloria Bare; m. Jo Ellen Auld, Aug. 10, 1996. BA in Legal Adminstrn., U. West Fla., 1992, MPA, 1994. Instnl. rev. specialist U.S. Dept. Edn., Atlanta, 1994-96; spl. agt. U.S. Dept. Edn. Office Inspector Gen., Atlanta, 1996-97; asst. dir. govtl. rels. U. West Fla., Pensacola, 1997—. Participant Leadership Santa Rosa, Santa Rose County, Fla., 1998—; sea turtle monitor Nat. Pk. Svc., Pensacola Beach, Fla., 1998—. Mem. ASPA, Gulf Breeze C. of C. (univ. rep. 1998—). Methodist. Avocations: softball, biking, web design. E-mail: twobares@bigfoot.com and cbare@uwf.edu. Fax: 850-474-3131. Home: 3882 Bay Wind Dr Gulf Breeze FL 32561 Office: Univ West Fla 11000 University Pkwy Pensacola FL 32561

BAREFOOT, HYRAN EUVENE, academic administrator, educator, minister; b. Mantee, Miss., Jan. 14, 1928; s. James Lee and Martha Caroline (Martin) B.; m. Joyce Lynn Camp, Nov. 24, 1949; children—Judy Barefoot Thomas, June Barefoot Dark, Jane Barefoot Hunter. B.A., Miss. Coll., 1949; B.D., New Orleans Bapt. Theol. Sem., 1952, Th.D., 1955; postdoctoral U. N.Mex., 1965-66, Bapt. Theol. Sem., 1971. Asst. prof. religion Union U., Jackson, Tenn., 1957-60; asst. prof. N.T., So. Bapt. Theol. Sem., Louisville, 1960-62; prof. religion Union U., 1962—, chmn. dept. religion, 1966-75, chmn. div. humanities, 1972-75, v.p. acad. affairs, 1975-87, acad. dean; pres. 1987-96, chancellor, 1996—; pastor Liberty Bapt. Ch., Calhoun, La., 1946-49, Goss Bapt. Ch., Miss., 1949-52, Hebron Bapt. Ch., New Hebron, Miss., 1952-55, First Bapt. Ch., Crowley, La., 1955-57, Woodland Bapt. Ch., Brownsville, Tenn., 1957-60, 66-75. Recipient Tchr. of Yr. award Union U., 1967, Disting. Faculty award, 1973; named Jackson Tenn. Man of the Yr., 1993. Mem. Assn. So. Bapt. Colls. (sec. 1984-85). Club: Jackson Rotary. Avocations: antique furniture refinishing; hunting; fishing. Home: 120 Redfield Dr Jackson TN 38305-8526 Office: Union U Office of Chancellor Jackson TN 38305

BAREFORD, WILLIAM JOHN, chemical engineer; b. Plainfield, N.J., Oct. 7, 1940; s. Harold Shaw and Harriett Grace (Hine) B.; m. Barbara DeMott, June 23, 1962; children: Katherine A., Jessica L. Bareford Krawitt. B Chem. Engring., Cornell U., 1964, M Chem. Engring., 1988. R&D engr. E.I. duPont de Nemours & Co., Wilmington, Del., 1966-68; prodn. engr. E.I. duPont de Nemours & Co., Orange, Tex., 1968-71; mfg. engr. E.I. duPont de Nemours & Co., Memphis, 1971-80; materials and logistics cons. E.I. duPont de Nemours & Co., Wilmington, 1980-86; sr. environ. cons. E.I. duPont de Nemours & Co., Deepwater, N.J., 1986-93; mgr. facilities, safety, health and environ. affairs Holman Enterprises, Pennsauken, N.J., 1994—; prin. cons. Condux, Newark, Del., 1998—. Author: Platinum Metal Uses, 1983, Early Reduction Credit, 1992. Treas., Centreville, Del., 1986-92; pres. Meadows Civic Assn., Centreville, 1989-93; dir. Cornell Alumni Assn. Ambs. Network, 1988—. Capt. U.S. Army, 1964-66. Fellow Internat. Precious Metal Inst.; mem. AIChE, Cornell Club Del. (pres. 1989-90), Sigma Xi, Alpha Chi Rho. Achievements include patents for regeneration of hydrogen peroxide catalyst; creation of DuPont precious metal recovery program, creation and implementation of DuPont environmental data system. Office: Condux Ste 9 1201 Possom Park Rd Newark DE 19711

BAREIS, DONNA LYNN, biochemist, pharmacologist; b. Abington, Pa., May 1, 1954; d. Walter Charles and Doris (Cameron) B.; m. Paul Joseph Amico, Jan. 24, 1981. BS in Biochemistry, Pa. State U., 1975; PhD in Pharmacology, Duke U., 1979. Staff fellow NIH, Bethesda, Md., 1979-81; pharmacologist U.S. Army Med. Rsch. Inst. Chem. Def., Aberdeen Proving Ground, Md., 1981-82; program mgr. U.S. Army C.E., Washington, 1982-83; sr. scientist Sci. Applications Internat. Corp., Joppa, Md., 1983-87; div. mgr. Sci. Applications Internat. Corp., Joppa, 1987-89; asst. v.p. Sci. Applications Internat. Corp., Frederick, Md., 1989-94, v.p., 1994-97, corp. v.p., 1997—; bd. dirs. High Tech. Coun. Md. Contbr. articles to sci. jours. Lighting designer Rockville (Md.) Musical Theater, 1980—; pres. Swan Point Condominium Assn., Columbia, Md., 1982-84. Mem. AAAS, Soc. for Risk Analysis, Potomac Region Porsche Club of Am. (tech. chmn. 1998—), Cattail Creek Country Club (bd. dirs. 1995-96), Sigma Xi. Home: 8805 Blue Sea Columbia MD 21046-1412

BAREISS, ERWIN HANS, computer scientist, mathematician, nuclear engineer, educator; b. Schaffhausen, Switzerland, May 10, 1922; came to U.S., 1951, naturalized, 1957; s. Karl Johann and Helene Fredericke (Kraft) B.; m. Doris Lilly Wicky, June 4, 1960; children: John Frederick, Peter Andrew. Diploma in Math., Physics and Chemistry, U. Zurich, 1949, Ph.D. in Math, 1951; M.S. in Applied Mechanics, Lehigh U., 1952. Mathematician U.S. Navy Taylor Research and Devel. Ctr., Washington, 1952-56; cons. U.S. Navy Taylor Research and Devel. Ctr., 1956-57; analyst Argonne Nat. Lab., Ill., 1957-63, sr. mathematician, 1963-76; sci. lectr. Harvard U., 1964; prof. computer sci. Northwestern U., Evanston, Ill., 1970-71, prof. computer sci. and engring. sci., 1971-76; prof. elec. engring. and computer sci., engring. sci. and applied math. and nuclear engring. Northwestern U., 1976-92; prof. emeritus Northwestern U., Evanston, Ill., 1992—, chmn. computer sci. program, 1978-88, dir. tech. computing; bd. dirs. Swiss Benevolent Soc., Chgo., pres., 1969-77, hon. mem., 1980—. Contbr. articles on sci. computation to profl. publs. Janggen-Poehn fellow, 1950-51; K.C. Baldwin research fellow, 1951-52. Mem. Am. Math. Soc., Soc. Indsl. and Applied Maths., Swiss Math. Soc., Swiss Soc. Natural History, Sigma Xi. Home: 3400 Lake Knoll Dr Northbrook IL 60062-6318 Office: Northwestern U McCormick Sch Engring & Applied Sci Evanston IL 60208

BARELA, BERTHA CICCI, elementary education educator, artist; b. McKeesport, Pa., June 13, 1913; d. James and Julia (Kolesar) Faix; m. John Slebodnik, June 23, 1934 (dec. 1967); children: Dolores S. Garvis, James, John, Judith Greene, Jane Minda, William, Cyrilla Lombardi, Rosemary Lewis, Martha Williams; m. Amerigo Cicci, May 25, 1974 (dec. 1975); m. Abran Barela, Dec. 8, 1984 (div. Nov. 1992). BA, Seton Hill Coll., 1970. Elem. tchr. Blessed Sacrament Sch., Greensburg, Pa., 1967-74; ind. artist, clown Phoenix, 1985—; asst. pre-sch. tchr. Sunnyslope Ctr.; guest art tchr. various schs., 1980-90; Westmoreland (Pa.) County Girl Scout Leader; internat. del. St. Louis; tchrs. aide, 1996-98. Formerly news and mag. writer; numerous commissioned art works. Dep. registrar Maricopa County, Phoenix, 1983-86, election bd. worker, 1980-97; Dem. committeewoman, election worker, Pa., 1960-73, Phoenix, 1980—. Mem. Sunnyslope Recreation Ctr. (adv. bd. 1998). Avocation: performing as Lollipop the Clown. Home: 841 E Cinnabar Ave Phoenix AZ 85020-1732

BARENBOIM, DANIEL, conductor, pianist; b. Buenos Aires, Nov. 15, 1942; s. Enrique and Aida (Schuster) B.; m. Jacqueline DuPre, June 15, 1967 (dec.); m. Elena Bashkirova, Nov. 28, 1988; 2 children. Student, Mozarteum, Salzburg, Austria, Accademia Chigiana, Siena, Italy; grad., Santa Cecilia Acad., Rome, 1956. Music dir. Chgo. Symphony Orch., 1991—. Debut with Israel Philharm. Orch., 1953, Royal Philharm. Orch., Eng., 1953, debut as pianist, Carnegie Hall, N.Y.C., 1957, Berlin Philharm. Orch., 1963, N.Y. Philharm. Orch., 1964, 1st U.S. solo recital, N.Y.C., 1958, as pianist performed in N.Am., South Am., Europe, Soviet Union, Australia, New Zealand, Near East; condr., 1962—, conducted English Chamber Orch., London Symphony Orch., Israel Philharm. Orch., N.Y. Philharm. Orch., Phila. Symphony, Boston Symphony, Chgo. Symphony Orch., others; mus. dir., Orchestre de Paris, 1975-89, Chgo. Symphony Orch., 1991—, Staatsoper Berlin, 1992—; artistic adviser, Israel Festival, 1971-74, over 100 recordings as pianist and condr.; debut as pianist at age 7, Buenos Aires. Recipient Beethoven medal, 1958; Harriet Cohen Paderewski Centenary prize, 1963, Legion of Honor, France, 1987. Office: 29 rue de la Coulouvreniere, 1204 Geneva Switzerland also: Chgo Symphony Orch 220 S Michigan Ave Chicago IL 60604-2501

BARFIELD, BILLY JOE, agricultural engineer, educator; b. Logansport, La., Oct. 8, 1938; s. William Merrell and Eva Ida (Horn) B.; m. Annette Kathryn Grider; children: Michelle, William. BS in Agrl. Engring., Tex. A&M U., 1961, BS in Civil Engring., 1961, PhD in Agrl. Engring., 1968. Registered profl. engr., Okla. Rsch. asst. in agrl. engring. Tex. A&M U., College Station, Tex., 1964-68; prof. agri. engring. U. Ky., Lexington, 1968-92; dept. head biosys. and agrl. engring. Okla. State U., Stillwater, 1992—. Author: Design Hydrology & Sedimentology, 1980, 94; editor: Modification of Aerial Environ. of Crops, 1978. Active Ky. River Authority, Frankfort, Ky., 1990-92, Maxey Flats Mgmt. Com., Frankfort, Ky., 1990. Maj. USAFR, 1961-78. Fellow Am. Soc. Agrl. Engrs. (Outstanding Young Prof. 1978, Hancor award 1993). Office: Okla State U Biosys and Agrl Engring Stillwater OK 74078

BARFIELD, ROBERT F., retired mechanical engineer, educator, dean; b. Thomaston, Ga., Feb. 8, 1933; s. Jason Malcome and Nettie Lee Barfield; m. Marion Janelle Neill, June 25, 1953 (div. Jan. 1980); children: Kimberly Faith, Robert Frederick Jr.; m. Sara de Saussure Davis, Nov. 27, 1981 (div. Jan. 1984); m. Leonette Walker, May 1990 (div. June 1994). B.M.E., Ga. Inst. Tech., 1956, M.S.M.E., 1958, Ph.D., 1965. Diplomate: registered profl. engr. Preliminary design engr. AiResearch Corp., Los Angeles, 1957-59; asst. prof. mech. engring. Ga. Inst. Tech., Atlanta, 1959-65; corp. mech. engr. Thomaston Mills Corp., Ga., 1965-67; prof. mech. engring. U. Ala., Tuscaloosa, 1967-94, prof. emeritus, 1994, dean of engring., 1982-94, dean emeritus, 1994; dir., sr. adv. Shiraz Tech. Int., Iran, 1975-77; gen. bd. Assn. Internt. practical Tng., 1980-85; dir. Capstone Engring. Soc., 1982-94; head mech. engring. program, dir. Oil Testing Ctr., U. Petroleum and Minerals, Dhahran, Saudi Arabia, 1971-73; advisor King Saud U., Riyhad, Saudi Arabia, 1982-89, U. Jordan, 1984, Yarmouk U., Jordan, 1986, Birzeit U., Isarael, 1985, Kabul U., Afghanistan, 1963; mem. Accreditation Bd. for Engring. and Tech., visitor in Mech. engring.; mem. Ala. Commn. High Tech. Bd. dirs. Salvation Army Ala., 1996—, Turning Point, Inc., 1995—. Recipient Disting. Service award Inperial Orgn. for Social Services, Tehran, Iran, 1977, U. Ala. Faculty Senate, 1980, Engr. of Yr. award Ala. Soc. Profl. Engrs., 1987, Liberty Bell award Ala. Law Assn., 1987; inductee Engring. Hall of Fame, 1998. Fellow ASME; mem. Am. Soc. Engring. Edn., Nat. Soc. Profl. Engrs., Ala. Acad. Sci., Tuscaloosa C. of C., Sigma Xi, Tau Beta Pi, Pi Tau Sigma, Phi Kappa Phi, Upsilon Pi Epsilon, Tau Alpha Pi. Presbyterian. Home: Ste 120 1655 N McFarland Blvd Tuscaloosa AL 35406 Office: Univ Ala PO Box 870200 Tuscaloosa AL 35487-0154

BARFIELD, W. LEON, federal judge; b. 1947. JD, U. Ga., 1977. Law clk. Hon. Elie L. Horton Ga. Superior Ct., Waycross, 1976-77; asst. dist. atty. City of Augusta, Ga., 1979-81; asst. U.S. atty. So. Dist. Ga., 1981-93; magistrate judge U.S. Dist. Ct. (so. dist.) Ga., Augusta, 1993—. Served with U.S. Army, 1967-69. Office: 500 Ford St E Augusta GA 30901-2358

BARGAR, NANCY GAY, real estate company executive; b. Jamestown, N.Y., Apr. 2, 1950; d. Robert Sellstrom and Mabel Je'Anne (Griffin) B. BA in Am. Studies, Kirkland Coll., Clinton, N.Y., 1972; 5th yr. cert. in edn., U. Vt., 1972. Mktg. asst. Spaulding & Slye, Boston, 1973; tchr. Wasatch Acad., Mt. Pleasant, Utah, 1975; reporter The Post-Jour., Jamestown, 1976-77; staff journalist N.Y. State Assembly, Albany, 1978-79; nat. mktg. dir. IDBI (Indsl. Devel. Bond Ins.) Mgrs., Inc., N.Y.C., 1982-85; dir. major gifts Chautauqua (N.Y.) Instn., 1985-87; pers. Fluvanna Realty Corp., Jamestown, 1988—; minority leader Chautauqua County Legislature, Mayville, 1997, majority leader, 1998—; presiding ptnr. Discriminating Investors, Jamestown, 1991-94. Co-author: Patients Handbook, 1981. Grad. Chautauqua Leadership Network; campaign mgr. Congressman Stan Lundine, Jamestown, 1982; mem. Chautauqua County Human Svcs. Com., 1998—; del. 31st Congl. Dist., Dem. Nat. Conv., Chgo., 1996; Dem. candidate for N.Y. State Senate, 1992-94; bd. dirs. Chautauqua County Visitors Bur., 1992—, South and Ctr. Chautauqua Lake Sewer Dist., 1992—; charter bd. dirs. Lakewood (N.Y.) Devel. Corp., 1992—; mem. fin. com. 1st Presbyn. Ch., Jamestown; bd. trustees Jamestown C.C., 1999—. Rotary Found. ambassadorial scholar Stockholm Journalism Sch., 1979-80. Mem. Chautauqua County Women's Polit. Caucus (charter), Am. Scandinavian Heritage Found., Chautauqua Lake Yacht Club, Rotary (bd. dirs. Jamestown 1990-91, Paul Harris fellow 1994). Home: 11 W Terrace Ave Lakewood NY 14750-1160 Office: Fluvanna Realty Corp 15 E 4th St Rm 10 Jamestown NY 14701-5055

BARGAR, ROBERT SELLSTROM, investor; b. Jamestown, N.Y., Aug. 8, 1919; s. Crawford Nathaniel and May Eugenia (Sellstrom) B.; m. JeAnne Griffin, Apr. 9, 1949; children: Nancy Gay, David Griffin, Alison May Churchill, Douglas Crawford. BS in Econs., U. Pa., 1941; prodn. mgmt. cert., Grad. Sch. Engring., U. Pa., 1941. Mgmt. trainee S.M. Flickinger Co. Inc., Jamestown, 1946-52, v.p., 1952-70, pres., 1970-81; cons., asst. to chmn. bd. S.M. Flickinger Co. Inc., Buffalo, 1981-82; chmn. bd. Fluvanna Realty Corp., Jamestown, 1961—. Bd. dirs. Chautauqua (N.Y.) Found., 1976-94, Lakeview Cemetery Assn., 1971-96; trustee Chautauqua Instn., 1974-82. Lt. comdr. USNR, 1942-46, PTO. Recipient Man of Yr. award Jamestown chpt. NCCJ, 1979. Mem. Sportsman's Club (bd. dirs. 1986-95, pres. 1992-94; Stowe, N.Y.). Home: 304 Arlington Ave Jamestown NY 14701-2108 Office: JBC CO 4th and Pine Bldg Jamestown NY 14701

BARGELLINI, PIER LUIGI, electrical engineer; b. Florence, Italy, Feb. 7, 1914; came to U.S., 1948, naturalized, 1956; s. Angelo and Giovanna (Cecchi) B.; m. Anna Cioni, Sept. 8, 1941; children: Clara, Angela, Leonard M. Grad., U. Florence, 1933; DEng, Poly. Inst., Turin, 1937; MSEE, Cornell U., 1949. Engr. Italo Radio Co., Rome, 1937-41; head spl. tests lab. Fivre Co., Florence, 1941-44; researcher microwave physics Inst. Italian Nat. Research Council, 1945-50; mem. faculty U. Pa., Phila., 1950-68; sr. scientist COMSAT Labs., Clarksburg, Md., 1968-83, cons., 1984—; mem. adv. engring. faculty Montgomery County C.C., 1970-75, trustee nominating com., 1975-82; adj. prof. elec. engring. U. Pa., 1987-89. Editor: Communications Satellite Systems and Communications Satellite Technology, 1974; contbr. articles to profl. jours.; lectr. internat. univs. Recipient City of Columbus (Ohio) award Inst. Internat. Communications, 1975, Columbus Gold medal City of Genoa, Italy, 1987; Inst. Internat. Edn. fellow, 1948. Fellow IEEE (life), AIAA (assoc.); mem. Internat. Acad. Astronautics. Democrat. Home and Office: PO Box 517 South Wellfleet MA 02663-0517

BARGER, JAMES EDWIN, physicist; b. Manhattan, Kans., Dec. 28, 1934; s. Edgar Lee and Carolyn Marie (Grantham) B.; m. Mary Elizabeth Rupp, Aug. 24, 1957; children: Elaine Marie Fleckenstein, Carolyn Ruth Hanson, James Rupp, Corinne Elizabeth Noordzij. B.S., U. Mich., 1957; M.S., U. Conn., 1960; Ph.D., Harvard U., 1964. Teaching asst. Harvard U., Cambridge, 1961-64; v.p. BBN Techs. (formerly Bolt Beranek & Newman, Inc.), Cambridge, Mass., 1965-75; chief scientist BBN Techs. (formerly Bolt Beranek & Newman, Inc.), 1975—; trustee Winchester Savs. Bank. Mem. Methods and Procedures Com., Town of Winchester, 1967-71; trustee Winchester Hosp., 1972—; corp. mem. Mt. Vernon House, 1979—. Served with USNR, 1957-63. NSF fellowship, 1960-64. Fellow AAAS, Acoustical Soc. Am.; mem. Marine Tech. Soc., Indsl. Noise Control Engring., Winchester Country Club, Cosmos Club, Tau Beta Pi, Pi Tau Sigma. Congregationalist (deacon). Home: 3 Lakeview Rd Winchester MA 01890-3801 Office: BBN Techs 70 Fawcett St Cambridge MA 02138-1110

BARGER, LOUISE BALDWIN, religious organization administrator; b. Mexia, Tex., Nov. 7, 1938; d. Curtis Arthur and Vada Irene (Barker) Baldwin; m. Billy Joe Barger, June 15, 1957; children: Kenneth Gene, Keith Dean, Kimberly Ann Barger Moeller. BS, Tex. Woman's U., 1961; MS in Nursing, St. Louis U., 1974, PhD in Higher Edn., 1981; MRE, So. Bapt. Theol. Sem., 1982. Ordained to ministry Am. Bapt. Chs. in U.S.A., 1986. Faculty Mo. Bapt. Hosp. Sch. Nursing, 1973, St. Louis U., 1974-80; min. Christian edn., mem. pastoral staff 3d Bapt. Ch., St. Louis, 1980-86; dir. leader devel. Am. Bapt. Chs. Pa. and Del., Valley Forge, Pa., 1986-93; interim dir. evangelism and social concern Am. Bapt. Chs. Pa. and Del., Valley Forge, 1989-91; exec. min. Am. Bapt. Chs. of the Rocky Mountains, 1993—; mem. Christian edn. com., Area V, Gt. Rivers region, Am. Bapt. Chs. Mo., and Am. Bapt. Chs. U.S.A., 1981-86; Handicapped Ministry, Home Mission Bd. So. Bapt. Conv., 1983; mem. Mins. Coun., Am. Bapt. Conv., U.S.A., Am. Bapt. Chs., U.S.A. Author: Growing through the Sunday School: A Sourcebook for Sunday School Growth, 1988; co-author: New and Renewed Churches: A Time of Prayer and Preparation for Invitation to New Life, 1991, New and Renewed Churches; A Time of Invitation ti New Life, 1992; contbr. Bapt. Leader. Mem. Handicapped Ministry Home Mission Bd., So. Bapt. Conv., 1983. Recipient Richard Hoiland citation Am. Bapt. Chs. U.S.A.; grantee Fund of Renewal Am. Bapt. Chs. U.S.A., 1980, Hazle Fund, 1984. Mem. Religious Edn. Assn., Assn. Profs. and Researchers in Religious Edn. Office: Am Bapt Ch Rocky Mts 3900 S Wadsworth Blvd Ste 365 Denver CO 80235-2220 *As Christians we are called first to BE the persons we were intended to become. All of our DOING is to be an expression of our BEING.*

BARGER, RICHARD WILSON, hotel executive; b. Cleve., Aug. 16, 1934; s. Harold Wilson and Blanche (Smith) B.; m. Barbara K. Schroeder, July 20, 1963; children—Scott Wilson, Christopher Armon. B.S., Cornell U., Ithaca, N.Y., 1956. Resident mgr. Sheraton Cleve. Hotel, 1964-67; gen. mgr. Sheraton Biltmore Hotel, Providence, 1967-68, Sheraton Peabody Hotel, Memphis, 1968-69, Sheraton Boston Hotel, 1969-72; v.p., regional mgr. Sheraton Corp., Boston, 1972-79; chmn. Barger Hotel Corp., Boston, 1979—, Conf. Planning Assoc., 1987—; cons., lectr. hotel adminstrs. Mem. coun. Cornell U., Ithaca, N.Y. Mem. Boston C. of C., Boston Conv. Bur. (dir.), Cornell U. Alumni Fund, Sigma Chi. Republican. Episcopalian. Home: 63 Neptune St Beverly MA 01915-4746 Office: Barger Hotel Corp 63 Neptune St # A Beverly MA 01915-4746

BARGER, VERNON DUANE, physicist, educator; b. Curllsville, Pa., June 5, 1938; s. Joseph F. and Olive (McCall) B.; m. Annetta McLeod, 1967; children: Victor A., Amy J., Andrew V. B.S., Pa. State U., 1960, Ph.D., 1963. Rsch. assoc. U. Wis., Madison, 1963-65, asst. prof., then assoc. prof. physics, 1965-68, prof. physics, 1968—, J.H. Van Vleck prof., 1983—, dir. Inst. Elem. Particle Physics Rsch., 1984—, Hilldale prof., 1987-91, Vilas prof., 1991—; vis. prof. U. Hawaii, 1970, 79, 82, U. Durham, 1983, 84; vis. scientist CERN, 1972, Rutherford Lab., 1972, SLAC, 1975. Co-author: Phenomenological Theories of High Energy Scattering; Classical Mechanics; Classical Electricity and Magnetism; Collider Physics. Recipient Alumni Fellow award Pa. State U., 1974; Guggenheim fellow, 1972; Fermilab Frontier fellow, 1999. Fellow Am. Phys. Soc. Methodist. Research in elementary particle theory and phenomenology; achievements include classification of hadrons as Regee recurrences; analysis of neutrino scattering and oscillations; weak boson, Higgs boson and heavy quark production; electroweak models; supersymmetry and grand unification; future collider physics. Office: U Wis Dept Physics 1150 University Ave Madison WI 53706-1302

BARGER, WILLIAM JAMES, management consultant, educator; b. Los Angeles, Nov. 1, 1944; s. James Ray and Aylene M. (Skinner) B.; m. Jane A. Cox, Jan. 30, 1988. BA, U. So. Calif., 1966; MA, Harvard U., 1970, PhD, 1972. Asst. prof econs. U. So. Calif., Los Angeles, 1971-76; v.p. Bank Am., Los Angeles, 1976-81; sr. v.p. Gibraltar Savs. Co., Beverly Hills, Calif., 1981-84, exec. v.p., 1984-88; pres. High Point Acad., Pasadena, Calif., 1995—. Mem. Phi Beta Kappa.

BARHAM, CHARLES DEWEY, JR., electric utility executive, lawyer; b. Goldsboro, N.C., July 7, 1930; s. Charles Dewey and Helen Wilkinson (Douglass) Barham Hughes; m. Margaret Wright Crow, June 17, 1960; children: Margaret Douglass, Charles Dewey III. B.S., Wake Forest U., 1952, J.D., 1954. Bar: N.C. 1954. Asst. atty. gen. N.C. Dept. Justice, Raleigh, 1958-66; assoc. gen. counsel Carolina Power & Light Co., Raleigh, N.C., 1966-73; ptnr. Douglass & Barham, Raleigh, 1974-80; v.p., sr. counsel Carolina Power & Light Co., Raleigh, 1981-82, sr. v.p., gen. counsel, 1982-87, sr. v.p., 1982-90, exec. v.p, 1990-95; ptnr. Douglass & Barham, 1995—; chmn. bd., pres. Nuclear Mut., Ltd., Hamilton, Bermuda, 1981-86, bd. dirs. 1973-95; bd. dirs. Nuclear Elec. Ins. Ltd., 1987-95 Hamilton; gen. counsel World Nuclear Fuel Mkt., Atlanta, 1974-80; gen. counsel Meredith Coll., Raleigh, 1977-80, trustee, 1984-87, 90-93, 95—; mem. regional bd. dirs. Wachovia Bank of N.C., 1990-95. Pres. Raleigh YMCA, 1982-92; bd. vis. Sch. Law Wake Forest U., 1998—. Capt. USNR, 1955-77. Mem. ABA, N.C. Bar Assn. Democrat. Baptist. Clubs: Raleigh Civitan (dir. 1974-77), Glen Forest (pres. 1977).

BARHAM, MACK ELWIN, lawyer, educator; b. Bastrop, La., June 18, 1924; s. Henry Alfred and Lockie Izorie (Harper) B.; m. Ann LeVois, June 3, 1946; children: Bret L., Megan. J.D., La. State U., 1946; postgrad., U. Colo., 1964-65. Judge City Ct., Bastrop, 1948-61, 4th Jud. Dist. Ct., Parishes of Ouachita and Morehouse, 1961-67, 2d Circuit Ct. of Appeal, 1967-68; assoc. justice La. Supreme Ct., 1968-75; prof. Sch. Law, Tulane, 1975-78; counsel Lemle, Kelleher, Kohlmeyer & Matthews, 1975-78; pres. Barham & Churchill, 1979-88; founder Barham & Arceneaux, New Orleans, 1988—; mem. faculty Am. Acad. Jud. Edn., U. Ala., 1968-73. Chmn. Ouachita Valley council Boy Scouts Am. Recipient award Freedoms Found. at, Valley Forge, 1969; Outstanding Service award ACLU, 1976; Creative Intelligence award Am. Found. Sci., 1976. Mem. La. Juvenile Judges Assn. (past pres.), La. Law Inst. (council), Internat. Acad. Estate and Trust Law, Scribes, Kiwanis, Blue Key, Order of Coif, Omicron Delta Kappa, Lambda Chi Alpha, Phi Delta Phi, Phi Alpha Delta. Home: 5837 Bellaire Dr New Orleans LA 70124-1103 Office: Barham & Arceneaux 650 Poydras St Ste 2700 New Orleans LA 70130-6126

BARHAM, STEVEN GARY, public radio station executive; b. Jan. 12, 1954. BA in English and Philosophy, U. Ark., Fayetteville, 1980; MPA, U. Ark., Little Rock, 1998. Sports editor Baxter Bull., Mountain Home, Ark., 1984-89; project analyst Ark. Crime Info. Ctr., Little Rock, 1989-92; dir. comm. and devel. Ark. Advocates, Little Rock, 1992-94; dir. devel. Sta. UALR, pub. radio, Little Rock, 1994—. E-mail: sgbarham@ualr.edu. Home: 330 N Summit St Little Rock AR 72205

BARHYDT, SALLY J., publishing company executive; b. Kansas City, Mo., Aug. 22, 1940; d. Frank Giles and Dorothy Evelyn (Watson) B.; m. Peter R. Karsten, Apr. 12, 1980. BSN, U. Kans., 1962. RN, N.Y. Staff nurse N.Y. Hosp./Payne Whitney Clin., N.Y.C., 1962-63, McGraw-Hill Book Co., N.Y.C., 1964-67, 68-78; sr. editor, nursing McGraw-Hill, Inc., N.Y.C., 1985-89; staff nurse Lenox Hill Hosp., N.Y.C., 1967; exec. dir. Plymouth Ch. of the Pilgrims, Bklyn., 1979-84; asst. v.p. NLN, N.Y.C., 1989-92; editor-in-chief, nursing Appleton & Lange, Inc., Norwalk and Stamford, Conn., 1992—. mem. ANA. Democrat. Presbyterian. Avocations: reading mysteries, aerobics, photography, hiking. *

BARHYTE, DONALD JAMES, retired newspaper executive; b. Poughkeepsie, N.Y., May 16, 1937; m. Patricia E. Dressler (dec. 1989), Dec. 27, 1958; children: Mark, Leslie; m. Karin Bianchi, June 20, 1992. Student, U. Ky. Data processing mktg. rep. IBM, 1962-68; with Multimedia, Inc., Greenville, S.C., 1968—, asst. treas., then treas., 1971-73, v.p. fin., treas., 1973-77, v.p. fin. and adminstrn., treas., 1977-84, treas., chief fin. officer, 1985-87; pres. Multimedia Newspaper Co., 1987-89; ret., 1989. Trustee, pres., St. Francis Community Hosp., 1979-80; bd. dirs., pres. United Way, 1985. Mem. Am. Mgmt. Assn., Am. Newspaper Pubs. Assn., So. Newspaper Pubs. Assn., Greenville C. of C. (v.p. cmty. devel., bd. dirs.), Poinsett Club., Jonathan's Landing Golf Club. Roman Catholic. Home: 3128 Casseekey Island Rd Jupiter FL 33477-1357

BARICH, DEWEY FREDERICK, emeritus educational administrator; b. Chisholm, Minn., Feb. 19, 1911; s. Eli and Angelia (Erro) B.; m. Verna Arling Eddy, Dec. 29, 1934; children—Judy, Dewey, Barbara, Wendy. Student, Jr. Coll., Hibbing, Minn., 1929-31; BS in Indsl. Edn., Stout Inst., Menomonie, Wis., 1933; MA in Edn., U. Mich., 1939; EdD, Wayne State U., Detroit, 1961; LLD (hon.), Western New Eng. Coll.; LHD (hon.), Detroit Inst. Tech., 1977. Tchr. indsl. arts Public Schs. Flint, Mich.; also dept. chmn. Longfellow Jr. High Sch.; chmn. Indsl. Survey Com. on Flint Industries and; mem. Indsl. Arts Supr.'s Council, 1936-38; instr. metal trades Trenton (Mich.) High Sch., 1938-39; instr. indsl. arts Central Mich. Coll. Edn., Mt. Pleasant, 1939-40; state supr. Nat. Def. (later War Prodn.) Tng., Mich. State Bd. Control for Vocat. Edn., 1940-42; prof., head indsl. arts dept. Kent State U., 1942; (on mil. leave 1943-45), univ. coordinator vets. affairs, 1945-51; mgr. ednl. affairs dept. Ford Motor Co., 1951-58; pres. Detroit Inst. Tech., 1958-76, chancellor emeritus, 1976—. Co-author: Applied Drawing and Sketching; Metal Work for Industrial Arts Shops; Contbr. articles to profl. jours. Mem. Pres. Truman's Conf. Occupational Safety, Pres. Eisenhower's Conf. Occupational Safety; chmn. bd. dirs. Nat. Safety Council, 1973-76; chmn. occupational safety standards commn. Mich. Dept. Labor, 1969-70; chmn. Mich. Occupational Standards Commn., 1975-76, Dept. State cons. Internat. Adv. Com. on Medium Level Manpower, Ibadan, Nigeria, 1969; mem. State Bd. Control Vocat. Edn.; chmn. adv. bd. Ariz. Ctr. Occupational Safety and Health; pres. bd. dirs. Pima Community Coll. Found. Served as lt. (j.g.) USNR; engring. officer LCI, (L) Flotilla 24 Staff 1943-45; engring. officer LCI, (L) Flotilla 24 Staff 21 mos, PTO. Awarded commendation for service by flotilla comdr.; recipient Indsl. Vocat. Edn. Laureate award. Mem. NEA, Am. Vocat. Assn. (speaker; mem. nat. policies and planning com. for indsl. arts edn.), Am., Ohio indsl. arts assns., Soc. Automotive Engrs., Mich. Indsl. Edn. Assn. (speaker), Nat. Assn. Indsl. Tchr. Educators, Engring. Soc. Detroit, Am. Soc. Engring. Edn., Miss. Valley Indsl. Arts Conf., Southwest Safety Conf. (pres. 1981—), So. Ariz. Safety Council (pres.), Epsilon Pi Tau, Phi Delta Kappa, Iota Lambda Sigma. Episcopalian. Clubs: Economic, Detroit Athletic, Rotary. Home: 685 S La Posada Cir Apt 802 Green Valley AZ 85614-5138 *Like so many of my contemporaries, I am a son of immigrant parents who instilled in their children a deep conviction that the United States was, indeed, the land of opportunity. I lived my early years on the "Iron Range" of northern Minnesota, sometimes called the "melting pot of America", where hard work was accepted as a positive way of life, and where there prevailed an atmosphere of high motivation and expectation.*

BARICKMAN, RICHARD BRUCE, English educator, writer; b. St. Louis, Oct. 20, 1942; s. Albert Melvin and Evelyn Beatrice (Hickman) B.; m. Joan Estes, July 13, 1963; children: Christopher, Julia. BA, Wash. U., 1964; MA, Yale U., 1966, PhD, 1970. Asst. prof. English Yale Univ., New Haven, Conn., 1968-73; assoc. prof. English (dept. chair) Hunter Coll., CUNY, 1973—; cons. on sexual harassment Wm. Paterson Coll., Paterson, N.Y., 1991. Author: Corrupt Relations, 1982, Sexual Harassment: A Resource Manual, 1992; contbr. articles. to profl. jours. Bd. dirs. Learning Cmty. Sch., Wilton, Conn., 1975-79. Dem. Avocations: clarinet performance, cycling, cooking, gardening. Office: Hunter Coll Dept English 695 Park Ave New York NY 10021-5024

BARIE, PHILIP STEVEN, surgeon, educator; b. Buffalo, Aug. 18, 1953; s. Kenneth George and Eleanor Lucille (Davis) B.; m. Elaine Catherine Dash, May 31, 1981; children: Catherine, Steven, Alexandra. AB cum laude, MD, Boston U., 1977. Diplomate and surgical critical care cert. Am. Bd. Surgery. Jr. resident in surgery N.Y. Hosp.-Cornell Med. Ctr., N.Y.C., 1977-79; fellow in surgery and physiology Albany (N.Y.) Med. Coll., 1979-81; sr. resident in surgery N.Y. Hosp.-Cornell Med. Ctr., 1981-83, adminstrv. chief resident surgery, 1983-84; asst. prof. surgery Cornell U. Med. Coll., N.Y.C., 1984-89, assoc. prof., 1989—, chief divsn. trauma and critical care dept. surgery, 1998—; attending surgeon, dir. surg ICU, N.Y. Hosp., N.Y.C., 1984—; cons. in surgery Cath. Med. Ctr., N.Y.C., 1985—; chmn. inst. rev. bd. Med. Coll. Cornell U., N.Y.C., 1988-92; cons. specialist, mem. med. control bd. Health Ins. Plan Greater N.Y., 1990-98; cons. in critical care therapeutics U.S. Pharmacopeial Conv., 1991—; mem. med. adv. bd. N.Y. Blood Ctr. Editor-in-chief Surg. Infections; mem. editl. bd.: Jour. of Surg. Infections: Index and Revs., 1993—, Shock, 1996—, Contemporary Surgery, 1996—, Air Med. Jour., 1997—, Jour. of Surg. Outcomes, 1997—, Jour. of Trauma, 1998—, Critical Care Medicine, 1998—; editor Surgical Infections, 1999—; co-editor: Surgical Intensive Care, 1993 (Best New Book in Med Scis. Assn. Am. Pubs. 1994); contbr. articles to profl. jours. Mem. med. adv. bd. N.Y. Blood Ctr., 1999—. Fellow ACS, Am. Coll. Critical Care Medicine, Am. Surg. Assn.; mem. N.Y. Acad. Medicine (sec. surg. sect. 1991-92), N.Y. Surg. Soc. (coun. mem.-at-large 1995—), Soc. Critical Care Medicine (sec.-treas. surg. sect. 1995-96, chair-elect surg. sect. 1996-97, mem. coun. 1997—, chair surg. sect. 1997-98), Am. Thoracic Soc., Am. Assn. for Surgery of Trauma (Peter C. Canizaro award 1992), Internat. Surg. Soc., Am. Physiol. Soc., Soc. Univ. Surgeons, N.Y. State Soc. Surgeons (bd. dirs. 1992—, sec. 1995-97, pres.-elect 1997-99, pres. 1999—), N.Y. Acad. Scis., Surg. Infection Soc. (mem. coun. 1994-97, treas. 1998—), Soc. Civil War Surgeons, Assn. for Acad. Surgery, Shock Soc., Ea. Assn. for Surgery of Trauma (bd. dirs. 1996-99), Am. Med. Writers Assn., Halsted Soc., Surg. Infection Soc. Found. (trustee 1998—, treas. 1998—). Office: NY Hosp-Cornell Med Ctr Dept Surgery 525 E 68th St Dept Surgery New York NY 10021-4885

BARIK, SUDHAKAR, microbiologist, research scientist; b. Sainkula, Orissa, India, Aug. 14, 1949; came to U.S., 1980; s. Ananda Chandra and Sakhamani (Behera) B.; m. Dharashri Behera, Mar. 4, 1979; children: Santwana, Sambit. BSc, Utkal U., Orissa, 1972, MSc, 1974, PhD, 1979. Postdoctoral fellow U. Okla., 1980-82; rsch. assoc. U. Ill., Urbana, 1982-84, U. Ark., Fayetteville, 1984-87; asst. prin. scientist Atlantic Rsch. Corp., Alexandria, Va., 1987-88; prin. scientist, group leader ARCTECH, Inc., Chantilly, Va., 1988-92; sr. devel. microbiologist Lederle Labs. Am. Cyanamid Co., Pearl River, N.Y., 1992-94; group leader process devel. Wyeth-

Lederle Vaccines and Pediat. Am. Home Products, Inc., Pearl River, 1994-98; mgr. vaccines devel. Wyeth-Lederle Vaccines, Am. Home Products, Inc., Pearl River, 1998—. Contbr. articles to profl. jours., chpts. to books. Fund raiser PTA, Annandale, Va., 1987-92; sci. fair judge for high schs., Annandale and Alexandria, 1987-92. Mem. Am. Soc. Microbiology, Soc. Indsl. Microbiology. Avocations: reading, outdoor activities, community service, travel, collecting stamps. Home: 8 Ambrey Ln Thiells NY 10984-1608 Office: Lederle Labs 401 N Middletown Rd Pearl River NY 10965-1299

BARIL, MAURICE, career officer; b. Saint-Albert de Warwick, Que., Can., Sept. 22, 1943; m. Huguette Desjardins; children: François, Hélène. Student, U. Ottawa, 1961-64; cert., Officer Tng. Corps, 1964, École Supérieure de Guerre, Paris, 1977. Commd. 2nd lt. Royal 22nd Regiment, 1963, advanced through ranks to lt. gen., 1995; with 1st Commando Airborne Rgt., Valcartier and Edmonton, Can., 1968-71; comdr. tng. co. Recruit Sch.; ops. officer, adjutant 3d Bn., Valcartier, Can., and Cyprus; comdr. 2d Bn., La Citadelle, Québec, 1980; comdt. inf. sch. Combat Tng. Ctr., Gagetown, N.B., Can., 1982, comdr., 1990; dir. land studies Can. Forces Command and Staff Coll., 1984, dep. commdt., 1985; dir. land ops., tng., and resources, dir. inf. Nat. Def. Hdqs., Ottawa, Can., 1986, dir. gen. land doctrine ops., 1989; mil. advisor UN Dept. Peacekeeping Ops., 1992; comdr. Land Force Que. Area, Montréal, 1995, Land Force Command, 1995-97; chief of def. Govt. of Canada, 1997—. Avocations: fishing, hunting, marksmanship, golf, skiing. Office: Chief Def Staff Nat Def Hdqs, 101 Colonel By Dr, Ottawa, ON Canada K1A 0K2

BARIL, NANCY ANN, gerontological nurse practitioner, consultant; b. Paterson, N.J., May 10, 1952; d. Kenneth Gerald and Jeanette Elenore (Girodet) Keiser; m. Joel Mark Baril, Apr. 15, 1984; children: Jason Kenneth, Jennifer Jean. AA, Gulf Coast C.C., 1976; BS in Nursing, Fla. State U., 1978; M in Nursing, UCLA, 1983. Registered pub. health nurse, Calif.; ANA cert. gerontol. nurse practitioner. Charge nurse, nurse preceptor Cedar Sinai Med. Ctr., L.A., 1979-83; RN Nursing Svcs. Incorp., Sherman Oaks, Calif., 1980-83; nurse practitioner Santa Monica Peer Counseling Ctr., Santa Monica, Calif., 1983; nurse cons., gerontol. nurse practioner Summit Health Ltd., Burbank, Calif., 1983-85; nurse cons. Geriatric Assocs., Granada Hills, Calif., 1983-85; nurse cons., gerontol. nurse practitioner Care Enterprises West, Burbank, 1985-86; patient svcs. coord., gerontol. nurse practitioner ARA Living Ctrs., Glendale, Calif., 1986-87; DON, gerontol. nurse practitioner Astoria Convalescent Hosp. Sign of the Dove, Sylmar, Calif., 1988-91; gerontol. nurse practitioner Balboa Plz. Med. Group, 1991-98, Absolute Health Care, Mission Hills, Calif., 1998—. Mem. PTA, Granada Hills, 1985. Mem. ANA, Calif. Coalition of Nurse Practioners, Calif. Nursing Assn., Gerontol. Soc., Sigma Theta Tau (rec. sec. 1983-85). Democrat. Episcopalian. Avocations: reading, crossword puzzles, gardening, jet-skiing. Home: 11513 Woodley Ave Granada Hills CA 91344 Office: Absolute Health Care 11046 Sepulveda Blvd Mission Hills CA 91345-1414

BARISH, CHARLES FRANKLIN, internist, gastroenterologist, educator; b. Franklin, N.J., Jan. 5, 1955; s. Philip and Laura (Freedman) B.; m. Debrah Lee Kaufman, Aug. 13, 1977; children: Philip, Stefanie, Jacob. BS in Chemistry with honors, U. Fla., 1976, MD, 1980. Diplomate Am. Bd. Internal Medicine with qualifications in gastroenterology. Resident, fellow Wake Forest U. Sch. Medicine, Winston-Salem, N.C., 1980-85; physician Wake Internal Medicine Cons., Raleigh, N.C., 1985—; pres., founder Wake Rsch. Assocs., Raleigh, 1985—; clin. asst., prof. medicine U. N.C. Sch. Medicine, Chapel Hill, 1985—; co-founder Peak Rsch., 1998; chmn. nutritional care com. Rex Hosp., Raleigh, 1987-97. Co-author: Gastroesophageal Reflux Disease, 1985; contbr. articles to profl. jours. Pres. Jewish Comty. Ctr., Raleigh, 1995-97; v.p. Jewish Fedn. Greater Raleigh, 1993-97, bd. dirs., 1989—; bd. dirs. Crohn's and Colitis Found., 1997—. Fellow ACP, Am. Coll. Gastroenterology; mem. AMA, Am. Gastroenterol. Assn., Am. Coll. Physician Execs., Am. Soc. Gastrointestinal Endoscopy, N.C. Med. Socs., Wake County Med. Socs., Crohn's and Colitis Found. Am., Am. Liver Found., B'nai Brith, Alpha Omega Alpha, Phi Kappa Phi, Alpha Epsilon Delta. Avocations: golf, skiing, gardening. Office: Wake Internal Medicine Cons 3100 Blue Ridge Rd Ste 300 Raleigh NC 27612-8035

BARISH, JULIAN I., psychiatrist; b. Sault Ste Marie, Mich., Mar. 12, 1917; s. Max and Nancy Barish; m. Judith Sophian, June 7, 1941; children: Richard K., Patricia L. Speckert. AB, U. Mich., 1938, MD, 1941, MS, 1948; cert. in psychoanalysis, Columbia U., 1955. Diplomate Am. Bd. Psychiatry and Neurology. Intern Bridgeport Hosp., Bridgeport, Conn., 1941-42; resident psychiatry Neuropsychiat. Inst., U. Mich. Med. Ctr., Ann Arbor, 1946-48; fellow in psychiatry, instr. psychiatry N.Y. Hosp.-Cornell Med. Ctr., N.Y.C., 1948-56; pvt. practice psychiatry and psychoanalysis N.Y.C., Larchmont, N.Y., 1949—; candidate, preceptor, collaborating psychoanalyst Columbia U. Psychoanalytic Ctr., N.Y.C., 1949-57, 72-77; asst. prof. psychiatry Grad. Sch. Psychiatry, Downstate Med. Ctr., Bklyn., 1956-58; co-founder, co-dir. The Psychiat. Treatment Ctr., N.Y.C., 1961-68; chief adolescent svc. Four Winds Hosp., Katonah, N.Y., 1968-70; assoc. clin. prof. psychiatry Mt. Sinai Med. Ctr., N.Y.C., 1974—; mem. nat. bd. Soc. for Sci. Study of Sex, N.Y.C., 1978-80; councillor Westchester Psychiat. Soc., White Plains, N.Y., 1971-73; chmn. com. on adolescent care Nat. Assn. Pvt. Psychiat. Hosps., Washington, 1965-68. Contbr. articles to profl. jours. Panelist youth conf. Westchester Citizens Com., Nat. Coun. on Crime & Delinquency Jr. Leagues, Scarsdale, N.Y., 1967; del. White House Conf. on Youth, Estes Park, Colo., 1971; participant Spl. Action Office for Drug Abuse Prevention, Conf. on Youth Oriented Drug Programs, Washington, 1972; prin. speaker Riveredge Hosp. Conf. on Hosp. Treatment Adolescents, Forest Park, Ill., 1968. Major Med. Corps, U.S. Army, 1942-46, ETO. Recipient Richard L. Frank M.D. Meml. award for Disting. Leadership in Adolescent Psychiatry, 1996. Fellow Am. Soc. Adolescent Psychiatry (life, pres. 1975-76), Am. Psychiat. Assn. (life, vice chmn. coun. on nat. affairs and social issues 1972-74); mem. AMA (life), Am. Psychoanalytic Assn. (life, cert.), Am. Acad. Psychoanalysis (life). Home and Office: 17 E 93rd St New York NY 10128-0609

BARISH, LAWRENCE STEPHEN, nonpartisan legislative staff administrator; b. Bklyn., Nov. 30, 1945; s. Louis C. and Anna (Sanders) B.; m. Sharon Lee Shapiro, July 2, 1967; 1 child, Lauren. BS in Polit. sci., U. Wis.-Madison, Wis., 1967; MA in Govt., U. Ariz., 1970. Legis. analyst Legis. Reference Bur., Madison, Wis., 1971-87, dir. of Reference and libr. svcs., 1987—; chmn. rsch., comm. staff sec. Nat. Conf. State Legislatures, Denver, 1995-97; redistricting cons. Wis. Legis. and Local Govt. units, 1980—. Editor State Almanac, 1987—; contbr. articles to profl. jours. Home: 1429 W Skyline Dr Madison WI 53705-1134 Office: Wis Legis Reference Bur 100 N Hamilton St Madison WI 53703-2116

BARIST, JEFFREY A., lawyer; b. Jersey City, Dec. 29, 1941; s. Irving and Lillian (Finkelstein) B.; m. Joan Elaine Travers, Feb. 19, 1967; children: Jessica, Alexis. AB, Rutgers U., 1963; JD, Harvard U., 1966. Bar: N.Y. 1967, U.S. Ct. Appeals (2d cir.) 1968, U.S. Dist. Ct. (so. dist.) N.Y. 1969, U.S. Supreme Ct. 1975. Law sec. U.S. Dist. Judge Irving Ben Cooper, N.Y.C., 1966-67; ptnr., chmn. nat. litigation group Milbank, Tweed, Hadley & McCloy, N.Y.C., 1996—. Author: Commercial Arbitration Law and Clauses, 1994; contbr. articles to profl. jours. Bd. dirs. N.Y. Assn. for New Ams.; trustee Rutgers U. Fellow Am. Coll. Trial Lawyers; mem. Am. Law Inst. Office: Milbank Tweed Hadley McCloy 1 Chase Manhattan Plz Fl 47 New York NY 10005-1413

BARITZ, LOREN, history educator; b. Chgo., Dec. 26, 1928; s. Joseph Harry and Helen (Garland) B.; m. Phyllis L. Handelsman, Dec. 26, 1948; children: Tony, Joseph. BA, Roosevelt U., 1953; MA, U. Wis., 1954, PhD, 1956. Asst. prof. history Wesleyan U., Middletown, Conn., 1956-62; assoc. prof. Roosevelt U., Chgo., 1962-63; prof. U. Rochester, 1963-69, chmn. dept. history, 1964-67; leading prof. SUNY, Albany, 1969-71; exec. v.p. Empire State Coll., exec. dir. univ. comm. on purposes and priorities, 1975-76; from exec. v.p. to provost SUNY, 1971-79; dir. N.Y. Inst. Humanities; prof. history NYU, 1979-80; provost, vice chancellor for acad. affairs U. Mass., Amherst, 1980-83; prof. history U. Mass., 1980-91, prof. emeritus, 1991—; vis. lectr. U. Wis.-Madison, 1959-60; cultural cons. to UNESCO, Paris, 1968-71; mgmt. cons. Balykchy Inst. of Bus. and Law, Kyrgyzstan, 1997, Slovak U. of Tech., Bratislava, Slovak Republic, 1997, Comenius U., Bratislava, 1998. Author: City on a Hill, 1964, Servants of Power, 1960, Sources of the American Mind, 2 vols., 1966, The Culture of the Twenties, 1970, The American Left, 1971, Backfire, 1985, 98, The Good Life, 1989. Co-chmn. policy coun. rsch. and svc. Assembly Univ. Goals, Am. Acad. Arts and Scis., 1969-70; del. Dem. Nat. Conv., 1968; bd. govs. chmn. com. on acad. affairs Haifa U., 1975-92; mem. exec. bd. Nat. Com. for Labor, Israel, 1984-94; mgmt. cons. Am. Stock Exchange, 1994-95, 97. Rsch. Tng. fellow Social Sci. Rsch. Coun., 1955-56, grantee, 1960; grantee Am. Council Learned Socs., 1963. Home: 51 Forest Ave Apt 133 Old Greenwich CT 06870-1529

BARKAI, ORNIT, television producer, broadcast journalist; b. Gesher Haziv, Israel, May 8, 1956; came to U.S., 1983; d. Elimelech and Yona (Mendel) B.; m. Nachum Sandberg Sadan, June 16, 1983; children: Shir, Ron. BA in Social Work, Hebrew U., Jerusalem, 1979; MA in Mass Comm., Emerson Coll., 1986. Lic. radio sta. operator FCC. News asst. WGBH-TV, Boston, 1984-85; host/prodr./dir. WERS-FM, Boston, 1983-86, WUNR-AM, WTTP-AM, Boston, 1986-87; TV prodr. Brookline, Mass., 1986-87; news asst. WBZ-TV, Boston, 1988; reporter/prodr./editor Israel Army Radio, Tel Aviv, 1988-89; assoc. prodr. Monitor Cable News, Boston, 1992; TV prodr. Carlisle, Mass., 1993—; moderator, interviewer The Zionist House, Boston, 1984; mem. programming com. New Eng. chpt. Women in Film and Video, Boston, 1993-94. Prodr./dir. (TV documentary) Past Forward, 1994—; prodr./dir./editor/videographer (TV documentary) Let Them Fly..., 1986; prodr./editor/photographer (multi-media) Emerson Coll. Libr., 1985; artist/desiger, 1992—. Tutor (for immigrant children) The Jewish Agy., Jerusalem, 1976-79; participant Peace Now Movement, Tel Aviv, 1982-83. Lt. Israel Def. Forces, 1974-76, 79-81. Mem. Women in Film and Video Programming Com., Boston Film and Video Found., Ctr. Ind. Documentary, Am. Craft Coun. Jewish. Avocations: silversmithing, design, outdoor sports, music. E-mail: ornit@aol.com. FAX: 978-371-7855.

BARKAN, JOEL DAVID, political science educator, consultant; b. Toledo, Apr. 28, 1941; s. Manuel and Toby (Wolfe) B.; m. Sandra Lynn Hackman, Sept. 9, 1962; children: Bronwyn Michelle, Joshua Manuel. AB, Cornell U., 1963; MA, UCLA, 1965, PhD, 1970. Asst. prof. polit. sci. U. Calif., Irvine, 1969-72; asst. prof. polit. sci. U. Iowa, Iowa City, 1972-76; assoc. prof. U. Iowa, 1976-81, prof., 1981—, chmn. dept. polit. sci., 1985-87, dir. ctr. internat. and comparative studies, 1981-83; vis. rsch. fellow Makerere U., Uganda, 1966-67, U. Dar es Salaam, Tanzania, 1973-74, Fondation Nationale des Sciences Politiques, Paris, 1978-79, U. Nairobi, Kenya, 1979, 80, Ctr. Study of Developing Socs., New Delhi, 1984, Cornell U., 1990; regional governance adviser for Ea. and So. Africa, U.S. Agy. Internat. Devel., 1992-94; sr. fellow U.S. Inst. Peace, 1997-98. Co-author, editor: Politics and Public Policy in Kenya and Tanzania, 1979, rev. edit., 1984, Beyond Capitalism Versus Socialism in Kenya and Tanzania, 1994; co-author: The Legislative Connection, 1984; author: An African Dilemma, 1975; contbr. articles to profl. jours. Mem. Iowa City Fgn. Rels. Coun., pres. 1989-90. Social Sci. Rsch. Coun. fellow, 1966-68; Fulbright fellow, 1978-79; Indo-Am. fellow, 1984; Randolph fellow, 1997-98; Rockefeller Found. grantee, 1973-74; U.S. AID grantee, 1978-81; Ford Found. grantee, 1992-98. Mem. Am. Polit. Sci. Assn., African Studies Assn. (bd. dirs. 1990-93), Coun. Fgn. Rels. E-mail: joel-barkan@uiowa.edu. Office: U Iowa Dept Polit Sci Iowa City IA 52242

BARKAN, LEONARD, humanities educator; b. N.Y.C., Oct. 6, 1944; s. Benjamin Barkan and Frances Katz. BA, Swarthmore Coll., 1965; AM, Harvard U., 1967; PhD, Yale U., 1971. Dir. dramatic assn. Yale U., New Haven, 1969-71; asst. prof. English U. Calif., San Diego, 1971-74; assoc. prof., then prof. English and art history Northwestern U., Evanston, Ill., 1974-88, F.B. Snyder prof. English, 1988-90; prof. English and fine art U. Mich., Ann Arbor, 1990-94; Samuel Rudin Univ. prof. humanities NYU, N.Y.C., 1994—. Author: Nature's Work of Art, 1975, The Gods Made Flesh, 1986, Transuming Passion, 1991, Unearthing the Past, 1999. Fellow Am. Acad. Arts and Scis., N.Y. Inst. for Humanities (bd. dirs. 1997—), Phi Beta Kappa. Avocation: writing on food and wine. E-mail: lb2@is.nyu.edu. Office: NYU Dept English 19 University Pl New York NY 10003

BARKEMEYER, MARSHA D., artist, educator; b. Shreveport, La., Nov. 25, 1949; d. Robert H. Davenport and Elizabeth R. Rabourn; m. Charles A. Barkemeyer, 1969; children: Henry, Carl. BA, U. New Orleans, 1975; postgrad., La. State U., 1985-86. Owner, dir. North St. Gallery, Baton Rouge, 1989-90; art tchr. La. State U. Lagniappe, Baton Rouge, 1998-99. One-woman shows include North St. Gallery, Baton Rouge, 1989-90, Morin Miller Gallery, N.Y.C., 1990, Fair Hope, Ala., 1990, Caffery Gallery, Baton Rouge, 1998. Roman Catholic. Home: 4527 Highland Rd Baton Rouge LA 70808

BARKEN, BERNARD ALLEN, lawyer; b. St. Louis, July 20, 1924; s. Gottlieb and Hattie E. (Rubin) B.; m. Jocelyn Moss Kopman, Sept. 1, 1948; children: Thomas L., Dale Susan. JD, Washington U., 1947. Bar: Mo. 1947, U.S. Dist. Ct. (ea. dist.) Mo. 1947, U.S. Ct. Appeals (8th cir.) 1954, U.S. Tax Ct. 1966, U.S. Ct. Appeals 2nd cir.) 1985, U.S. Supreme Ct. 1984. Sole practice St. Louis, 1947-80; ptnr. Shifrin & Treiman, St. Louis, 1980-88; pres. Bernard A. Barken, St. Louis, 1988-91; ptnr. Barken & Bakewell L.L.P., St. Louis, 1991—. With USAAF, 1943-44. Mem. ABA, Bar Assn. Met. St. Louis (v.p. 1958, chmn. young lawyers 1953). Jewish. Avocations: piano, tennis, gardening. Home: 30 Vouga Ln Saint Louis MO 63131-2628 Office: 500 N Broadway Ste 2000 Saint Louis MO 63102-2130

BARKER, BARBARA, real estate professional; b. Pulaski, Tenn., July 18, 1938; d. Dan and Anna (Butler) Ingram; m. Emmet Barker, Nov. 25, 1960; children: Melanie, Lynn, Harvey, Dan. BS, U. Tenn., 1960. Home economist Knoxville (Tenn.) Utilities Bd.; tchr. Arlington High Sch., Arlington Heights, Ill.; pres. Barbara Barker and Assocs., Brownsville, Tenn., Deerfield (Ill.) Ptnrs.; also owner, mgr. Re/Max Deerfield, Coldwell Banker, Deerfield, Ill. Exec. bd., treas. Arden Shore Sch.; Wome's Bd. Union League Club. Mem. Nat. Assn. Realtors, Ill. Assn. Realtors, Women's Coun. Realtors (pres. 1993-94, exec. bd., North Shore Mem. of Yr. 1997), North Shore Bd. Realtors, Tenn. Home Econs. Assn. (v.p.). Home: 1050 Meadowbrook Ln Deerfield IL 60015-3459 Office: Purdential Burnet Realty 734 Waukegan Rd Deerfield IL 60015-4304

BARKER, BARBARA ANN, ophthalmologist; b. Paterson, N.J., Nov. 10, 1943; d. Earle Louis and Dorothy Louise (Williamson) Barker; m. Joel Ira Papernik, July 28, 1972. BA magna cum laude, Conn. Coll., 1965; BS, Yale U., 1967; MA, Rutgers Med. Sch., 1974; MD, Mt. Sinai Sch. Medicine, 1976. Diplomate Am. Bd. Ophthalmology. Intern, Beth Israel Med. Center, 1977; resident Mt. Sinai Sch. Medicine/Beth Israel Med. Center, 1980, fellow in glaucoma, 1980-81, fellow cornea, refractive surgery, 1981-82, now mem. staff; rsch. technician The Rockefeller U., N.Y.C., 1965-66; tchr. Riverdale Country Sch., N.Y.C., 1967-68; rsch. asst. Sloan Kettering Inst., N.Y.C., 1969-72; assoc. clin. prof. Mt. Sinai Sch. Medicine, N.Y.C., 1982—; pvt. practice medicine specializing in ophthalmology, N.Y.C., 1983—; mem. staff N.Y. Eye and Ear Hosp., Cabrini Hosp. Recipient Resident Paper award Beth Israel Med. Center, 1989, Honor award Am. Acad. Ophthalmology, 1995; Beth Israel Research grantee, 1983; NSF grantee, 1966. Mem. Internat. Soc. Refractive Keratoplasty, AMA, Am. Med. Women's Assn., Women's Med. Soc. N.Y.C., N.Y. County Med. Assn. (mem. com.), Phi Beta Kappa. Home and Office: 11 E 86th St New York NY 10028-0501

BARKER, BARBARA YVONNE, nursing home administrator; b. Whittier, Calif., Apr. 19, 1951; d. Donald Wayne and Ruth Berta (Hagen) Schutt; m. Jimmy D.W. McWilson, Feb. 23, 1974 (div. Sept. 1980); m. Richard Alexander Barker, Aug. 01, 1987; 1 child, Christina Nicole. AS in Respiratory Therapy, Mt. San Antonio Coll., Walnut, Calif., 1971; BSBA, U. Redlands, 1989; MPA, Marist Coll., 1996. Lic. nursing home adminstr., Calif., Iowa; registered respiratory therapist; lic. respiratory care practitioner. Neonatal respiratory therapist U. Calif.-San Diego Med. Ctr., 1971-74; respiratory therapy supr. Hillside Hosp., 1974-75; asst. dir. ops. J.D.W. McWilson and Assocs., 1975-77; sales rep. Baxter-Travenol Home Respiratory Therapy, 1984-86; clin. application specialist Infrasonics, Inc., 1987-88; respiratory therapist/clin. coord., nursing home adminstr. Sharp Health Care, 1977-84, 88-90; nursing home adminstr. Care West Anza, 1990, Brighton Pl. Spring Valley, San Diego, 1990-91; dir. respiratory care No. Dutchess Hosp., Rhinebeck, N.Y., 1991-98; adminstr. Dubuque (Iowa) Nursing and Rehab Ctr, 1998—; cons. health care delivery sys. various acute and long-term care orgns., Dutchess County, N.Y., 1991—; developer quality assurance program long-term care facility, San Diego, 1990; med. products rschr. devel. neonatal ventilator device FDA, San Diego, 1988; coord. regional healthcare seminar, Dutchess County, Marist Coll. Author quality assurance protocol durable med. equipment cos., San Diego Am. Lung Assn., 1989; developer instrnl. manuals for patients with chronic lung disease and asthma, San Diego, 1990. Bd. mem. San Diego chpt. Calif. Assn. Health Facilities, 1990-91; participant Christmas in April civic rebldg. program, Poughkeepsie, N.Y., 1992-93. Mem. Am. Assn. Respiratory Therapy, Calif. Soc. Respiratory Therapy (treas., bd. mem., ednl. developer 1986-90), Calif. Assn. Health Facilities, Mid Hudson Repiratory Care Dirs. Assn. Democrat. Lutheran. Avocations: boating, cross-country skiing. Office: Dubuque Nursing and Rehab Ctr 2935 Kaufmann Ave Dubuque IA 52001

BARKER, BEN DALE, dentist, educator; b. Burlington, N.C., Dec. 19, 1931; married; 3 children. BS, Davidson Coll., 1954; DDS, U. N.C., 1958; MEd, Duke U., 1962. From instr. to assoc. prof. fixed prosthodontics U. N.C., Chapel Hill, 1958-65, assoc. prof. preventive dentistry and dental sci., 1965-69, asst. dean, 1968-69, prof., assoc. dean, 1969-75, prof., dean Sch. Dentistry, 1981-89, prof. dept. dental ecol. Sch. Dentistry, 1989—; program dir. W.K. Kellogg Found., 1975-81; mem. Coun. Internat. Rels., 1979-83, Bd. Health Care Svc., Inst. Medicine, NAS, 1987—, Comty. Estate Rsch. Agenda Aging and Comty. Health Prom. & Disability Rev., 1988-90; vis. prof. New Cross Hosp., London, 1972-73. Fellow Am. Coll. Dentists, Internat. Coll. Dentists; mem. ADA (mem. coun. dental edn. 1986-92, chmn., 1990-92), Inst. Medicine-NAS. Office: Univ NC Sheps Ctr Health Svcs Rsch 725 Airport Rd Chapel Hill NC 27514-5714*

BARKER, CHARLES, conductor. Music dir., condr. Am. Chamber Orch., 1981-87, John Curry Skating Co., 1983; music dir. State Ballet of Mo., 1985-87; prin. condr. Am. Ballet Theatre, 1987—; music dir., prin. condr. Australian Ballet, 1997—; prin. guest condr. Nat. Symphony of London. Condr. numerous orchs. including The Royal Philharm., New Symphony of London, New Japan Philharm., San Francisco Ballet, Pa. Ballet, La Compania Nat. de Danza, Mexico City, Pacific Symphony, others; appeared at Met. Opera House, Kennedy Ctr., Carnegie Hall; condr. summer arts festival L.I. Univ., 1987-92; musical dir., condr. The Second Hurricane, New Fed. Theater, N.Y.C.; music dir. summer music festival, East Hampton, N.Y.; TV includes TV Asahi, BBC, PBS, ABC. Office: Am Ballet Theatre 890 Broadway New York NY 10003-1211*

BARKER, CHARLES OLIVER, military officer; b. Waycross, Ga., Oct. 7, 1945; s. Gilbert Harrison and Lucy Jay Barker; m. Mary Conoly Lemon, Dec. 22, 1968; children: Emma Suzanne, Thomas Harrison, Lucy Anne. BA, Emory U., 1967, MD, 1971; MPH, Johns Hopkins U., 1994. Diplomate Am. Bd. Family Practice, Am. Bd. Preventive Medicine. Commd. ensign USN, 1972, advanced through grades to capt., flight surgeon, 1972-75; pvt. practice South Ga. Med. Ctr., Valdosta, 1975-90; flight surgeon South Ga. Med. Ctr., Norfolk, Va., 1991-93; resident in aerospace medicine South Ga. Med. Ctr., Balt., Pensacola, Fla., 1993-96; sr. med. officer USS Enterprise South Ga. Med. Ctr., Norfolk, 1996-98; asst. dir. aerospace medicine South Ga. Med. Ctr., Washington, 1998—. Contbr. articles to profl. publs. Recipient Vol. of Yr. award Am. Diabetes Assn., Patient Edn. award, Spl. Humanitarian award 1990, Hon. Life Bd. Mem. 1990; decorated S.W. Asia campaign medal with two bronze stars and Marine Corps; Kuwait Liberation medal, Kuwait Liberation medal (Saudi Arabia). Mem. Am. Acad. Family Physicians, Aerospace Med. Assn., Am. Coll. of Healthcare Execs., Ga. Acad. of Family Physicians (bd. dirs. ednl. found. 1983-88, various coms. 1978-82). Avocations: running (Boston marathon), swimming, biking, triathlon. E-mail: cobarker@us.med.navy.mil. Home: 6354 Brampton Ct Alexandria VA 22304

BARKER, CLIVE, artist, screenwriter, director, producer, writer; b. Liverpool, Eng., 1952; s. Len and Joan B. Student, U. Liverpool, Eng. Author: (plays) Incarnations (Frankenstein in Love, History of the Devil, Colossus), Forms of Heaven (Paradise Street, Subtle Bodies, Crazyface); (short story collection) Books of Blood I-VI (books IV, V, and VI released in U.S. as The Inhuman Condition, 1986, In the Flesh, 1986, Cabal; (novels) The Damnation Game, 1985, Weaveworld, 1987, Cabal, 1988, The Great and Secret Show, 1989, Imajica, 1991, The Thief of Always, 1992, Everville, 1994, Sacrament, 1996, A-Z of Horror, 1997, Galiee, 1998; prodr. Hellraiser II: Hellbound, 1990, Candyman, 1992, Hellraiser III: Hell on Earth, 1992, Candyman II: Farewell to the Flesh, 1995, Hellraiser: Bloodline, 1996, Gods & Monsters, 1997, (Fox TV) Spirits and Shadows, 1997; (writer and dir. screenplays) Hellraiser, 1987, Nightbreed, 1990, Lord of Illusions, 1995, Art Exhibition, 1998.

BARKER, CLYDE FREDERICK, surgeon, educator; b. Salt Lake City, Aug. 16, 1932; s. Frederick George and Jennetta Elizabeth (Stephens) B.; m. Dorothy Joan Bieler, Aug. 11, 1956; children: Frederick George II, John Randolph, William Stephens, Elizabeth Dell. BA, Cornell U., 1954, MD, 1958. Diplomate Am. Bd. Surgery. Intern Hosp. U. Pa., Phila., 1958-59, resident in surgery, 1959-64, fellow in vascular surgery, 1964-65; fellow in med. genetics U. Pa. Sch. Medicine, Phila., 1965-66, assoc. in surgery, 1964-68, assoc. in med. genetics, 1966-72; attending surgeon Hosp. U. Pa., Phila., 1966—; chief div. transplantation U. Pa. Sch. Medicine, Phila., 1966—, asst. prof. surgery, 1968-69, assoc. prof. surgery, 1969-73, prof. surgery, 1973—, J. William White prof. surg. research, 1978-82, chief div. vascular surgery, 1982—, Guthrie prof. surgery, 1982—, John Rhea Barton prof. surgery, 1983—, chmn. dept. surgery, 1983—; chief surgery Hosp. U. Pa., Phila., 1983—; dir. Harrison Dept. Surgery research U. Pa., Phila., 1983—; mem. immunobiology study sect. NIH; chmn. clin. practices U. Pa., 1987-89. Mem. editl. bd. Jour. Transplantation, 1977—, Clin. Transplantation, 1988—, Jour. Surg. Rsch., 1979-85, Jour. Diabetes, 1981-86, Archives of Surgery, 1987—, Transplantation Procs., 1990—, Surgery, 1991-95, Cell Transplantation, 1991—, Postgrad. Gen. Surgery, 1991-95, Jour. ACS, 1994—, Annals of Surgery, 1995—; contbr. articles to profl. jours. and textbooks. Markle Found. Scholar, 1968-74; NIH grantee, 1974—; recipient Merit award NIH, 1987-95. Fellow AOA, NAS (Inst. Medicine), ACS (com. Forum on Fundamental Surg. Problems 1983-88, vice chmn. 1987-88, bd. govs. 1994—, pres. Phila. chpt. 1991-92), Coll. Physicians Phila., Royal Coll. Surgeons Eng. (hon.); mem. AMA, Assn. Acad. Surgery, Am. Diabetes Assn., Am. Soc. Artificial Internal Organs, Am. Fedn. Clin. Rsch., Juvenile Diabetes Found., Soc. Univ. Surgeons, Am. Surg. Assn. (recorder 1991-96, pres. 1996-97), Soc. Clin. Surgery (chmn. membership 1984-85), Halsted Soc. (chmn. membership 1984-85, v.p. 1985-86, pres. 1986-87), Surg. Biology Club II, Soc. Vascular Surgery, Internat. Cardiovascular Soc., Internat. Surg. Group (treas. 1988-94, pres. 1994-95), Internat. Soc. Surgery (v.p. U.S. chpt. 1995-97, pres. 1997—), Transplantation Soc. (councilman 1978-84, 94—), Am. Soc. Transplant Surgeons (chmn. membership 1980-81, treas. 1988-91, pres. 1992-93), Am. Acad. Arts and Scis., Assn. Am. Physicians, Phila. Acad. Surgery (program chmn. 1984-86, v.p. 1986-88, pres. 1988-89), Greater Del. Valley Soc. Transplant Surgeons (pres. 1978-80), Am. Philos. Soc. Home: 3 Coopertown Rd Haverford PA 19041-1012 Office: Hosp Univ Pa Dept Surgery 3400 Spruce St Philadelphia PA 19104-4204

BARKER, DOUGLAS ALAN, lawyer; b. Martinsville, Va., Oct. 25, 1957; s. Cecil Ray and Virginia Adeline (Bryant) B.; children: Daryn Ruth, Dylan Victoria. BS, Va. Tech., 1981; MBA, The Citadel, 1988; JD cum laude, Pepperdine U., 1993. Bar: Calif. 1993, U.S. Dist. Ct. (ctrl. dist.) Calif. 1993, S.C. 1996, U.S. Dist. Ct. S.C. 1996. Assoc. Haight, Brown & Bonesteel, Santa Monica, Calif., 1993-96, Young Clement Rivers & Tisdale, Charleston, S.C., 1996-97; individual practice law Charleston, 1997—. Lt. comdr. USN, 1981-87. Decorated Expeditionary medal USN, Beirut, Lebanon, 1983. Mem. ABA, L.A. Bar Assn., Charleston County Bar Assn., Assn. Bus. Trial Lawyers, L.A. JD/MBA Assn., Phi Delta Phi (magister 1992-93). Avocation: military history. Home: 1253 Sam Snead Dr Mount Pleasant SC 29464-6923 Office: 3 Broad St Charleston SC 29401-2973

BARKER, EDWIN BOGUE, musician; b. Tucson, Apr. 14, 1954; s. Francis Hustis and Mary Jeanne (Austin) B.; m. Pamela Paikin, 1980; children: Rachel Leigh, Ilana Michelle. Studies with Henry Portnoi, Peter Mercurio, Angelo LaMariana, Richard Stephan, 1965-76; MusB with honors, New Eng. Conservatory Music, 1976. Prin. bass Lake George Opera Orch., N.Y., 1971-72; mem. Chgo. Symphony Orch., 1976-77; prin. bass Boston Symphony, 1977—; mem. Boston Symphony Chamber Players, 1977—; instr. double bass New Eng. Conservatory Music, 1977-90, 98—, Boston Conservatory Music, 1980-83; instr. double bass and chamber music Berkshire

Music Ctr. (Tanglewood), 1978—; prof. double bass Boston U., 1980—; substitute mem. N.Y. Philharm., 1976; bass and string clinics Am. String Tchrs. Assn. and U. Mich., Ann Arbor, 1982, 83; instr. double bass Teton Orchestral Tng. Seminar, Wyo., 1984-86; mem. player's com. Boston Symphony Orch., 1989-93; prin. bass and faculty mem. Georg Solti Orchestral Tng. Project, Carnegie Hall, 1994—; prin. bass UN Orchestra Musicians of the World, Geneva, 1995—; master classes U. Ga., 1997, Juilliard Sch., 1999. Solo appearances with Boston Symphony Orch., Tanglewood, New England Conservatory Symphony Orch., Bergen (Norway) Music Festival, others; concerto performance with Boston Symphony, Madrid, 1993; other performances include: Concerto for Double Bass and Chamber Orchestra by Gunther Schuller, Boston premiere, 1987, Concerto for Double Bass and Chamber Orchestra by James Yannatos, premiere performance, 1986, Concerto for Double Bass and Orchestra by Edward Tubin, with Boston Symphony Orchestra, Boston premiere, 1994, Juilliard Quartet, Libr. of Congress, 1992, Muir Quartet, 1998, 99; recs. include Three Sonatas for Double Bass, 1998. Recipient Benjamin H. Delson award Berkshire Music Ctr., 1975; named one of Outstanding Young Men of Am., 1986, Most Outstanding Alumni New Eng. Conservatory of Music, 1993. Mem. Am. Fedn. Musicians., Internat. Soc. Bassists (dir. 1983). Office: CAMI Foster Division 165 W 57th St New York NY 10019-2201

BARKER, EMMETT WILSON, JR., trade association executive; b. Humboldt, Tenn., Aug. 30, 1937; s. Emmett Wilson and Rebecca Evelyn (Coble) B.; m. Barbara Anne Ingram, Nov. 25, 1960; children: Melanie Lynn, Emmett Daniel. B.S. in Agr, U. Tenn., Knoxville, 1960. Advt. and sales promotion mgr. Security Mills, Inc., Knoxville, 1960-62; dir. pub. rels. Am. Feed Mfrs. Assn., Chgo., 1962-67; pres. Agrl. Services Assn., Bells, Tenn., 1967-72; spl. asst. to pres. United Foods, Inc., Bells, 1972-73; exec. sec. Equipment Mfrs. Inst. (formerly Farm and Indsl. Equipment Inst.), Chgo., 1973-79, pres., 1979—; nat. chmn. Farm-City Coun., 1970, bd. dirs., 1981; mem. adv. com. Found. Am. Agr., 1981, Alliance to Save Energy, 1980; mem. exec. com. nat. Indsl. Coun. Mfg. Trade Group, 1981; chmn. Found. Found., 1996; chmn. Bennet Agrl. Roundtable, 1987. Pub.: Directory of Communicators in Agriculture, 1968. Chmn. Nat. Endowment for Soil and Water Conservation, 1982—; bd. dirs. Am. Nat. Standards Inst., 1982—. Served with U.S. Army, 1958-64. Recipient Disting. Service award and Hon. Am. Farmers degree Future Farmers Am., 1967, Meritorious Service award Nat. Assn. Farm Broadcasters, 1968; named Man of Year Memphis Agr. Club, 1970. Mem. Am. Soc. Assn. Execs., Nat. Assn. Mfrs. (chmn. coun., bd. dirs. 1987), Pub. Rels. Soc. Am., Agrl. Rels. Coun., Chgo. Soc. Assn. Execs., Nat. Agrl. Mktg. Assn., Agrl. Electronics Assn. (chmn. 1995—), Am. Soc. Agrl. Engrs., Rotary, Union League (Chgo.). Republican. Mem. Ch. Good Earth. Coun. Office: Equipment Mfrs Inst 10 S Riverside Plz Chicago IL 60606-3708

BARKER, FRED, research geologist, scientific editor; b. Seekonk, Mass., Nov. 4, 1928; s. Reuben and Eleanor Regina (Mead) B.; m. Margaret Walsh, May 7, 1961; children: Matthew F., Thomas A., Aileen M. BS, MIT, 1950; MS, Calif. Inst. Tech., 1952, PhD, 1954; postgrad., Harvard U., 1956-57. Rsch. geologist U.S. Geol. Survey, Juneau, Alaska, 1954-55, Menlo Park, Calif., 1955-56, Washington, 1957-62; rsch. geologist U.S. Geol. Survey, Denver, 1962-93, geologist emeritus, 1993—; editl. adviser Elsevier Pub. Co., Amsterdam, The Netherlands, 1974-93. Author: Trondhjemites, Dacites, and Related Rocks, 1979; contbr. articles to profl. publs. Vis. rsch. fellow U. Witwatersrand, Johannesburg, South Africa, 1974; rsch. grantee Nat. Geog. Soc., Swaziland, 1972, Mariana Islands, 1976. Fellow Geol. Soc. Am. (editl. advisor, 1974-78), Mineral Soc. Am.; mem. Am. Geophys. Union (guest editor 1981). Avocations: nontechnical writing, photography, skiing, rifle shooting. Home: 14155 W 21st Pl Golden CO 80401-2001 Office: US Geol Survey PO Box 25046 Denver CO 80225-0046

BARKER, GARRY GENE, art center administrator; b. Nov. 26, 1943. BA in English, Berea Coll., 1965; postgrad., Morehead State U., 1984-85. Asst. dir. So. Highland Craft Guild, Asheville, N.C., 1965-70; dir. Ky. Guild of Artists and Craftsment, Berea, 1971-80; dir. student crafts Berea Coll., 1985-96; dir. Ky. Folk Art Ctr. Morehead State U., 1997—. Author: Fire on the Mountain, 1983, Copperhead Summer, 1985, Mountain Passage and Other Stories, 1986, All Night Dog, 1988, Bitter Creek Breakdown, 1989, The Handcraft Revival in Southern Appalachia, 1930-1990, 1991, Mitchell Tolle: American Artist, 1992, Notes from a Native Son, 1995, Berea Hospital: The First Century, 1997. E-mail: g.barker@morehead-st.edu. Office: 102 W First St Morehead KY 40351-9616

BARKER, HAROLD GRANT, surgeon, educator; b. Salt Lake City, June 10, 1917; s. Frederick George and Jennetta (Stephens) B.; m. Kathleen Butler, July 29, 1949; children: Janet Stephens, Douglas Reid. A.B., U. Utah, 1939, postgrad., 1939-41; M.D., U. Pa., 1943. Diplomate Am. Bd. Surgery. Intern. Hosp. U. Pa., 1943-44, asst. resident in surgery, 1947-51, sr. resident in surgery, 1951-52, asst. attending surgeon, 1952-53; also asst. instr., research fellow U. Pa., 1946-51, instr., research fellow, 1951-52, assoc. in surgery, 1952-53; asst. prof. surgery Columbia U., 1953-57, assoc. prof., 1957-68, prof., 1968-82, prof. emeritus, 1982—; asst. attending surgeon Presbyn. Hosp., 1953-57, assoc. attending surgeon, 1957-69, attending surgeon, 1969-89, cons. surgeon, 1989—, dir. med. affairs, 1974-82; pvt. practice, Phila., 1952-53, N.Y.C., 1953-88. Contbr. articles med. jours. Served from 1st lt. to capt., M.C. AUS, 1944-46, ETO. Fellow ACS; mem. Soc. U. Surgeons, N.Y. Surg. Soc., Am. Physiol. Soc., Soc. Exptl. Biology and Medicine, AMA, Halsted Soc., N.Y. State (chmn. surg. sect. 1961-62), N.Y. County med. socs., Am. Surg. Assn., N.Y. Gastroent. Assn., Société Internationale de Chirurgie, Soc. Surgery Alimentary Tract, Allen O. Whipple Surg. Soc., Am. Assn. History Medicine, Collegium Internationale Chirurgiae Digestivae, Century Assn., Manursing Island Club, Am. Yacht Club. Home: 1 Forest Ave Rye NY 10580-4209

BARKER, HAROLD KENNETH, former university dean; b. Louisville, Apr. 14, 1922; s. J.M. and Fannie Mae (Elliott) B.; m. Elizabeth Johns, Mar. 11, 1948 (dec.); children: Leslie Ann, Glenn Lewis.; m. Beverly Williams, Feb. 28, 1984. A.B., U. Louisville, 1948, M.A., 1949; Ph.D., U. Mich., 1959. Instr. Gunfire Prep. Sch., Hanau, Germany, 1946; sch. psychologist, vis. tchr. Bay City (Mich.) Pub. Schs., 1949-52; also instr. Bay City Jr. Coll.; sch. psychologist Ypsilanti (Mich.) Pub. Schs., 1952-53; instr. Eastern Mich. U., 1954-58; asst. dir. Bur. Appointments and Occupational Info., U. Mich., 1954-59; assoc. exec. sec. Am. Assn. Colls. Tchr. Edn., Washington, 1959-66; dir. Am. Assn. Colls. Tchr. Edn., 1972—; dean Coll. Edn., U. Akron, 1966-85, asst. to pres., 1985-87, dean emeritus, 1987; Bd. dirs. World U., San Juan, P.R., 1966—, Joint Council Econ. Edn., 1979. Editor: AACTE Handbook of International Education Programs, 1963; contbr. articles to profl. jours. and periodicals. Chmn. bd. dirs. Edwin Shaw Hosp., 1989; trustee U. Akron Found., 1994—. Recipient award outstanding profl. svc. Am. Assn. Colls. Tchr. Edn., 1966; named Hon. Alumni U. Akron, 1992. Mem. Phi Delta Kappa (internat. commn. 1962-69). Home: 1811 Brookwood Dr Akron OH 44313-5061

BARKER, HORACE ALBERT, biochemist, microbiologist; b. Oakland, Calif., Nov. 29, 1907; s. Albert Charles and Nettie (Hindry) B.; m. Margaret McDowell, Aug. 29, 1933; children—Barbara B. Friede, Elizabeth B. Mark, Robert H. A.B., Stanford U., 1929, Ph.D., 1933; Sc.D. (hon.), Case-Western Res. U., 1964; Dr. honoris causa, U. München, Fed. Republic Germany, 1990. NRC fellow Hopkins Marine Station, Pacific Grove, Calif., 1933-35; gen. edn. bd. fellow Tech. U., Delft, Holland, 1935-36; Guggenheim fellow Mass. Gen. Hosp., Boston, 1941-42; instr. soil microbiology U. Calif., Berkeley, 1936-40, asst. prof. soil microbiology, 1940-45, assoc. prof. microbiology, 1945-46, prof. microbiology, soil microbiologist, 1946-59, prof. biochemistry, microbiologist, 1959-75; Guggenheim fellow, vis. prof. microbiology NYU Med. Sch., 1962; vis. prof. biochemistry Stanford Med. Sch., 1962; chmn. dept. plant nutrition U. Calif., Berkeley, 1949-50, chmn. dept. plant biochemistry, 1950-53, chmn. dept. biochemistry, 1962-64; dir. Ann. Reviews Inc., Palo Alto, Calif., 1946-62. Author: Bacterial Fermentations, 1956; contbr. articles to profl. jours.; patentee in field. Named Calif. Scientist of Yr., Calif. Mus. Sci. and Industry, 1965; recipient Sugar Research award NAS, 1945, Carl Neuberg medal Am. Soc. European Chemists and Pharmacologists, 1959, Hopkins Meml. medal Biochem. Soc., 1967, Nat. Sci. medal U.S. Pres., 1969. Mem. NAS, AAAS, Am. Acad. Arts and Scis., Am. Soc. Biochemistry and Molecular Biology, Am. Soc. Microbiology. Office: U Calif Barker Hall Berkeley CA 94720

BARKER, JAMES REX, water transportation executive; b. Cleve., Aug. 3, 1935; s. William Wardel and Elizabeth Ranghild (Wandler) B.; m. Kaye Elizabeth Schumacher, Aug. 3, 1957; children: James Arthur, Karen Elizabeth, Mark William. BA, Columbia U., 1957; MBA with distinction, Harvard U., 1963; DSc (hon.), Maine Maritime Acad., 1978. Planning exec. Pickands Mather & Co., Cleve., 1963-67; v.p. Harbridge House, Boston, 1967-69; founder, exec. v.p. Temple, Barker & Sloane, Wellesley, Mass., 1970-71; chmn. bd. Moore McCormack Resources, Inc., Stamford, Conn., 1971-87; chief exec. officer Moore McCormack Resources, Inc., 1971-87; vice chmn., founder, co-owner Mormac Marine Group Inc., Stamford, Conn., 1987—; chmn., prin. Interlake Steamship Co., Stamford, 1987—; prin., dir. Meridian Aggregates, 1992—; vice chmn., prin. owner Moran Towing Co.; bd. dirs. Pittston Co., GTE, Eastern Enterprises, Skuld, Oslo, Norway. Trustee, chmn. Stamford Hosp. Lt. (j.g.) USCG, 1975-61. Mem. Am. Bur. Shipping (bd. mgrs.). Episcopalian. Clubs: Wee Burn Country, Noroton Yacht, N.Y. Yacht, Landmark, Rolling Rock, Union, Links. Home: 180 Long Neck Point Rd Darien CT 06820-5816 Office: Mormac Marine Group Inc 3 Landmark Sq Ste 300 Stamford CT 06901-2599

BARKER, JEANNE WILSON, principal, computer educational consultant; b. Columbus, Ohio, Mar. 10, 1939; d. Robert Sydney and Marjorie Helen (McQuillen) Wilson; m. Larry L. Barker, June 11, 1961 (div. June 1974); children: Theodore Allen, Robert Milford. BS in Edn., Ohio U., 1960, MS, 1963. Cert. edn. specialist, Fla. Music tchr. Newark (Ohio) City Schs., 1960-61; elem. tchr. Logan (Ohio) City Schs., 1962-63, aast. prin. East Elem. Sch., 1963-65; supervising tchr. Ohio U., Logan, 1964-65; dir. R&D Dept. Grant, State of Fla., Tallahassee, 1972-74; pre-sch. tchr. Temple Israel, Tallahassee, 1974-75; elem. tchr. Maclay Sch., Tallahassee, 1975-79, prin., 1980—; dir. Fla. Microcomputer project Fla. State U., Tallahassee, 1983-86, adj. instr., 1988—; computer cons. Jefferson/Wakulla County Schs., 1985—. Contbr. articles to profl. jours.; presenter in field. DeWitt Hooker fellow Fla. Coun. Ind. Schs., Tampa, 1987. Mem. Internat. Reading Assn., Alpha Delta Kappa. Democrat. Methodist. Avocations: fishing, travel, golf, reading. Office: Maclay Sch 3737 N Meridian Rd Tallahassee FL 32312-1199

BARKER, JUDY, foundation executive; b. Burlington, N.C., Feb. 5, 1941; d. Thelma Ferguson; children: Lesa, Lori. Student, Ohio State U., Franklin U.; HHD, Xavier U., 1986. Administrv. asst. Children's Hosp., Columbus, Ohio, 1963-68, Mount Carmel Hosps., Inc., Columbus, 1969-72; administr. Borden Found., Borden, Inc., Columbus, 1973-75, exec. dir., 1975-83, dir. civic affairs, 1977-79, pres., 1983—, v.p. social responsibility, 1979-98; pres. Avon Products Found., N.Y.C., 1998—; Bd. dirs. Ohio State U. Hosps.; mem. Columbus Commn. on Ethics and Values; mem. adv. bd. Ohio State U. Sch. Home Econs.; mem. found. ctr. adv. nat. Nat. Directory Corp. Giving; active N.Y. Contbns. Adv. Group; mem. corp. adv. bd. Philanthropic Adv. Svc.; bd. dirs. Coun. Better Bus. Bur. Found., Greater Columbus Art Coun.; mem. Afro.-Am. adv. bd. Columbus Mus. Art. Bd. dirs. Pub./Pvt. Ventures, Ohio State U. Hosps., Columbus Commn. on Ethics and Values; mem. Sch. Home Econs. adv. bd. Ohio State U.; mem found. ctr. adv. bd. nat. Directory Corporate Giving; active N.Y. Contributions Adv. Group; mem. corp. adv. com. Philanthropic Adv. Svc.; mem., bd. dirs. Coun. Better Bus. Bur. Founds., Greater Columbus Arts Coun.; mem. Afro-Am. adv. bd. Columbus Mus. of Art; bd. dirs Columbus Airport Authority. Recipient award to women achievers YWCA, 1982, 84, 91, named Woman of Yr. YMCA Columbus, Ohio; recipient cmty. svc. award United Negro Coll. Fund, 1981. *

BARKER, KEITH RENE, investment banker; b. Elkhart, Ind., July 28, 1928; s. Clifford C. and Edith (Hausmna) B.; children by previous marriage: Bruce C., Lynn K.; m. Elizabeth S. Arrington, Nov. 24, 1965; 1 child, Jennifer Scott. AB, Wabash Coll., 1950; MBA, Ind. U., 1952. Sales rep. Fulton, Reid & Co., Inc., Ft. Wayne, Ind., 1951-55, office, 1955-59, asst. v.p. then v.p., 1960, dir., 1961, asst. sales mgr., 1963, sales mgr., 1964, dir. Ind. ops.; sr. v.p. Fulton, Reid & Co., 1966-75; pres., CEO Fulton, Reid & Staples, Inc., 1975-77; ptnr. William C. Roney & Co., 1977-79; exec. com. Cascade Industries, Inc.; assoc. A.G. Edwards & Sons, Inc., 1984-89, v.p. investments, 1989—; dir. Fulton, Reid & Staples, Inc., Craft House Corp., Nobility Homes, Inc. Pres. Historic Ft. Wayne, Inc.; cons. to Mus. Historic Ft. Wayne; nominee, trustee Ohio Hist. Soc.; mem. Smithsonian Assocs.; mem. fin. com. E. Tenn. Hist. Soc.; v.p. Ft. Wayne Hist. Soc.; bd. dirs. Ft. Wayne YMCA, 1963-64. Recipient Achievement cert. Inst. Investment Banking, U. Pa., 1959. Mem. Alliance Française, VFW (past comdr.), Co. Mil. Historians, Cleve. Grays, Am. Soc. Arms Collectors, 1st Cleve. Cavalry Assn., Nat. Assn. Securities Dealers (bus. conduct com.), Beaver Creek Hunt Club, Cleve. Athletic Club, Rockwell Springs Club, Hill and Dale Club, Masons, Phi Beta Kappa. Episcopalian. Home: 170 Cheskogili Way Loudon TN 37774-7811 Office: AG Edwards & Sons Inc 8848 Cedar Springs Ln Knoxville TN 37923-5408

BARKER, KENNETH NEIL, pharmacy administration educator; b. Spring Valley, Ohio, Mar. 25, 1937; s. Kenneth Clyde and Marjorie Dorothy (Smith) Barker; m. Louise Arlene Ferguson, Aug. 17, 1957; children: Bradford Neil, Linda Louise, Douglas Adams. B.S., U. Fla., 1959, M.S., 1961; Ph.D., U. Miss., 1971. Mgr. sterile products pharmacy svc. U. Ark. Med. Center-Little Rock, 1961-62, project dir. drug systems rsch., 1962-66; projects coord. Sch. Pharmacy, U. Miss., 1966-70; dir. adminstrv. rsch. U.S. Pharmacopeia, 1970-72; assoc. prof. pharmacy adminstrn., assoc. dir. Rsch. Inst. Sch. Pharmacy, N.E. La. U., 1972-75; Sterling prof., dir. Ctr. Pharmacy Opers. Design Sch. Pharmacy, Auburn U., Ala., 1975—; pres. K.N.B. Inc., Auburn, Ala., 1980—. Co-inventor unit dose dispensing concept for hosps., 1959. Recipient commendation HEW, 1974, Harvey A.K. Whitney award Am. Assn. Hosp. Pharmacists, 1981, A. Richard Bliss, Jr. citation of appreciation Nat. Kappa Psi Pharm. Fraternity, 1998; named Outstanding Grad. prof. Auburn U., 1992-93. Mem. Am. Pharm. Assn. (Remington Honor medal 1998), Acad. Pharm. Scis., Am. Soc. Hosp. Pharmacists (research award 1973, 85, 87), Am. Assn. Colls. Pharmacy, Ala. Pharm. Assn., Am. Assn. Pharm. Sci., Ala. Soc. Hosp. Pharmacists, Rho Chi. Presbyterian. Home: 412 Blake St Auburn AL 36830-6102 Office: Auburn U Pharmacy Dept Auburn AL 36849

BARKER, LARRY LEE, communications educator; b. Wilmington, Ohio, Nov. 22, 1941; s. Milford and Ruth Maxine (Garringer) B.; children: Theodore Allen., Robert Milford. B.A., Ohio U., 1962, M.A., 1963, Ph. D, 1965. Asst. prof. So. Ill. U., Carbondale, 1965-66, Purdue U., West Lafayette, Ind., 1966-69; assoc. prof. Fla. State U., Tallahassee, 1969-71, prof., 1971-75; prof. emeritus Auburn (Ala.) U., 1995—; pres. Spectra Inc., New Orleans, 1979—. Author: (with R. Kibler) Conceptual Frontiers in Speech Communication, 1969, Behavioral Objectives and Instruction, 1970, Listening Behavior, 1971, Speech Communication Behavior, 1971, Communication Vibrations, 1974, Speech—Interpersonal Communication, 1974, (with R. Edward) Intrapersonal Communication, 1980, (with R. Kibler) Objectives for Instruction and Evaluation, 1981, Communication, 1982, Communication in the Classroom, 1982, (with others) Effective Listening, 1982, (with L. Malandro) Nonverbal Communication, 1983, (with K. Wahlers) Groups in Process, 1983, (with others) Intrapersonal Communication Processes, 1987, (with K. Watson) Interpersonal and Relational Communications, 1989; contbr. articles to profl. jours. Recipient outstanding award in discussion Tau Kappa Alpha, 1962, outstanding tchr. award Central States Speech Assn., 1969. Mem. APA, ASTD, Speech Comm. Assn. (Robert J. Kibler Meml. award 1986), Internat. Comm. Assn. (v.p. 1972-74), Internat. Listening Assn. (chmn. rsch. com. 1979-82, pres. 1986-87). Methodist. Home: 77 Audubon Blvd New Orleans LA 70118-5537

BARKER, LISA ANN, aerospace engineer; b. Lompoc, Calif., Feb. 1, 1965; d. Robert Andrew and Donna Jean (Eden) B. BS in Aerospace, Purdue U., 1987. Aerospace engr. NASA Marshall Space Flight Ctr., Huntsville, Ala., 1987—. Mem. AIAA. Avocations: crafts, reading.

BARKER, LLYLE JAMES, JR., management consultant, journalism educator, public relations executive; former army officer; b. Columbus, Ohio, July 28, 1932; s. Llyle James and Mabel Lucile (Johnson) B.; B.S., Ohio State U., 1954; postgrad. U. Wis., 1961; M.S. in Mass Communication, Shippensburg State Coll., 1975; m. Maxine Ruth Metcalf, Jan. 15, 1956; children—Llyle J., Daryl Alan Commd. officer U.S. Army, advanced through grades to maj. gen.; served in Korea, Vietnam, Thailand and W.Ger.; pub. affairs officer, Hawaii, 1957-59, NORAD, 1961-63, Dept. Army, 1966-69, 7th Army, 1969-71, Joint Casualty Resolution Ctr., 1974, European Command, 1975-77, U.S. Army Europe, 1979-80; dep. chief info. Dept. Army, 1980-81, chief pub. affairs, 1981-84; prof. Sch. Journalism, Ohio State U., Columbus, 1984-98; cons. mgmt. comm.; assoc. Gannett Ctr. Media Studies (now Freedom Forum Media Studies Ctr.), Columbia U. Decorated D.S.M., Legion of Merit, others. Mem. World Future Soc. Pub. Relations Soc. Am., Assn. Edn. in Journalism and Mass Communications. Contbr. articles to mil. and journalism jours. Home: 6844 Chateau Chase Dr Columbus OH 43235-3942 Office: Ohio State U Sch Journalism 242 W 18th Ave Columbus OH 43210-1107

BARKER, NANCY LEPARD, university official; b. Owosso, Mich., Jan. 22, 1936; d. Cecil L. and Mary Elizabeth (Stuart) Lepard; m. J. Daniel Cline, June 6, 1956 (div. 1971); m. R. William Barker, Nov. 18, 1972; children: Mary Georgia Harker, Mark L. Cline, Richard E., Daniel P., Melissa B. Van Arsdel, John C. Cline, Helen Grace Garrett, Wiley D., James G. BSc, U. Mich., Ann Arbor, 1957. Spl. edn. instr. Univ. Hosp. U. Mich., Ann Arbor, 1958-61; v.p. Med. Educator, Chgo., 1967-69; asst. to chmn., dir. careers for women Northwood U., Midland, Mich., 1970-77, asst. prof., chmn. dept. fashion mktg. and merchandising, 1972-77, dir. arts programs and external affairs, 1972-77, v.p., 1978—; cons. and lectr. in field. Co-author: (children's books) Wendy Well Series, 1970-72; contbr. chpts. to books, articles to profl. jours. Advisor Mich. Child Study Assn., 1972—; chmn. Matrix: Midland Festival, 1978; bd. dirs. Nat. Coun. of Women, 1971—, pres., 1983-85, chmn. centennial com., 1988; bd. dirs. ArtServe, Mich., Family and Children's Svcs., Internat. Coun. Women, Paris. Recipient Hon. award Ukrainian Nat. Women's League, 1983, Disting. Woman award Northwood U., 1970, Outstanding Young Woman award Jr. C. of C., 1974; named one of Outstanding Young Women in U.S. and Mich., 1974; nominee (2) Mich. Women's Hall of Fame. Mem. Internat. Coun. Women (bd. dirs. Paris 1991—), The Fashion Group, Internat. Furnishings and Design Assn. (pres. Mich. chpt. 1974-77), Mich. Women's Studies Assn. (founding mem.), Arts Midland Coun. (pres. 2 terms, 25th Anniversary award), Internat. Women's Forum, Mich. Women's Forum, Contemporary Rev. Club, Midland County Lawyers' Wives, Zonta, Phi Beta Kappa, Phi Kappa Phi, Alpha Lambda Delta, Phi Lambda Theta, Phi Gamma Nu, Delta Delta Delta. Republican. Episcopalian. Home: 209 Revere St Midland MI 48640-4255 Office: Northwood Univ VP Univ Rels Midland MI 48640-2398

BARKER, OREL O'BRIEN, retired activity and social service director; b. Wis., June 6, 1918; d. Otto Fahrenkrug and Margaret (Berg) Machenske; m. Wilbert Ervin O'Brien, Sept. 20, 1935 (dec. Aug. 1965); children: Marilyn, Maureen, Marleen, Merridith, Wilbert Jr., Margaret. Lic. activity dir., activity dir. coord., social svc. coord., Ind. U., 1975. Occupl. therapy asst. Westview Nursing Home, Racine, Wis., 1971-73; occupl. therapist asst. Pine Manor Nursing Home, Clintonville, Wis., 1973-75; activity dir. Rynard Ent., Indpls., 1975-85; ret., 1985. Author, poet: Echo' of the Heart, 1990, Sunshine and Shadows, 1995; contbr. poetry to various publs. Active St. Stephen's Luth. Ch. Named Activity Dir. of the Yr., Ind. Health Care, 1985. Mem. Wis. Fellowship Poets, Westview Retirement Club. Home: 1628 N Auburn St Indianapolis IN 46224-5709

BARKER, RICHARD ALEXANDER, organizational psychologist; b. San Diego, Aug. 11, 1947; s. Alexander Markewich and Donna Lee Barker; m. Barbara Yvonne Schutt, Aug. 1, 1987; children: Jaime Lynn, Cory Richard. AB in Psychology, San Diego State U., 1974, MS in Indsl. and Organizational Psychology, 1976; EdD, U. San Diego, 1990. Statis. analyst U.S. Navy Pers. R & D Center, San Diego, 1974-75; pers. and testing analyst City of San Diego, San Diego, 1976, cons. various orgns., 1976-78; employment mgr. Computer Scis. Corp., San Diego, 1978; indsl. psychologist Gen. Dynamics Corp., San Diego, 1978-91; instr. music San Diego City Coll., 1976-91; lectr. psychology, mgmt. sci., stats., orgnl. behavior U. Redlands, 1978-91; asst. prof. bus., chair mgmt. dept. Marist Coll., Poughkeepsie, N.Y., 1991-98; chair dept. mgmt. Sch. Mgmt., assoc. prof. bus. Clarke Coll., Dubuque, Iowa, 1998—. Mem. editorial bd. Jour. Leadership Studies, 1994—; contbr. articles to profl. jours. Bd. dirs. San Diego Youth Svcs., Inc., chmn. pers. com., 1978-81. Served with USNR, 1968-69. Mem. APA, Computer Automated Systems Assn./Soc. Mfg. Engrs., Nat. Mgmt. Assn., Am. Fedn. Musicians, Psi Chi. Office: Clarke Coll Bus Dept 1550 Clarke Dr Dubuque IA 52001

BARKER, RICHARD GORDON, corporate research and development executive; b. Rochester, N.Y., Feb. 8, 1937; s. Richard I. and Laura (Gordon) B.; m. Nancy Heiligman, Sept. 7, 1957 (dec.); children: Laurie Frances, Richard, Jonathan David; m. Mary Kathryne Simpson, Sept. 16, 1995. A.B., Hamilton Coll., 1958; M.S., Inst. Paper Chemistry, 1960, Ph.D., 1963. Research scientist Union Camp Corp., Princeton, N.J., 1962-69, group leader, 1969-71, sect. leader, 1971-74, dir. research and devel. projects, 1974-79, lab. dir., then corp. dir. research and devel., 1979—; rep., trustee Pulp and Paper Found., Maine, pres., Miami, U. Pulp Paper Found. Contbr. articles to profl. jours.; patentee in field. Mem. Empire State Paper Rsch. Assn. (chmn. rsch. steering com. 1975-82, v.p. N.Am. chpt. 1982-90, pres. 1990-96), TAPPI (bd. dirs., chmn. bd. dirs. publs, com., chmn. rsch. mgmt. com.; v.p. 1997—), Inst. of Paper Chemistry (past chmn., exec. council, past chmn. pulping and bleaching subcom. rsch. adv. com.), Princeton C. of C., Am. Chem. Soc., Soc. Rsch. Adminstrs., R & D Coun. N.J. (bd. dirs.). TAPPI Rsch. Mission Com. (chmn.). Home: 7 Quaker Rd Princeton Junction NJ 08550-1615 Office: Union Camp Corp Rsch & Devel Div PO Box 3301 Princeton NJ 08543-3301

BARKER, ROBERT JEFFERY, financial executive; b. Glendale, Calif., Feb. 22, 1946; s. Albert and Margaret E. (Windle) B.; m. Ildiko Barker, Jan. 1, 1989; 1 child, Alexander A. BSEE, UCLA, 1968, MBA, 1970. Cert. mgmt. acctg. Cost analyst Lockheed, Sunnyvale, Calif., 1976-78; from cost acctg. supr. to fin. systems mgr. Monolithic Memories Inc., Sunnyvale, 1976-84; dir. fin. Waferscale Integration, Inc., Fremont, Calif., 1984-88, v.p. fin., chief fin. officer, 1988-94; cfo Micrel, San Jose, CA, 1994; bd. dirs., treas. Am. Electronics Assn. Credit Union, Santa Clara, Calif., 1988—, bd. chmn., 1991; dir. Monolithic Memories Integration Fed. Credit Union, Sunnyvale, 1977-84, pres. 1983-84. Dir. Vets. Task Force, Palo Alto, Calif., 1980-87, pres. 1987. Capt. USAF, 1970-74. Mem. Nat. Assn. Accts., Fin. Execs. Inst., Toastmasters (pres. 1986-87). Republican. Methodist. Avocations: beach doubles volleyball, jogging, sports. Home: 1 Winchester Dr Atherton CA 94027-4040

BARKER, ROBERT WILLIAM, television personality; b. Darrington, Wash., Dec. 12, 1923; s. Byron John and Matilda Kent (Tarleton) B.; m. Dorothy Jo Gideon, Jan. 12, 1945 (dec. Oct. 1981). BA in Econs. summa cum laude, Drury Coll., 1947. Master of ceremonies: Truth or Consequences, Hollywood, Calif., 1957-75, Price is Right, 1972—, Miss Universe Beauty Pageant, 1966-87, Miss U.S.A. Beauty Pageant, 1966-87, Pillsbury Bake-Off, 1969-85, Bob Barker Fun and Games Show, 1978—; host: Rose Parade, CBS, 1969-88; appeared in (feature film) Happy Gilmore, 1996. Served to lt. (j.g.) USNR, 1943-45. Recipient Emmy award for Best Audience Participation Host, 1981-82, 82-83, 86-87, 87-88, 89-90, 90-91, 91-92, 93-94, 94-95, 95-96. Mem. AGVA, AFTRA, Screen Actors Guild. Office: The Price is Right care CBS TV 7800 Beverly Blvd Los Angeles CA 90036-2112*

BARKER, SARAH EVANS, judge; b. Mishawaka, Ind., June 10, 1943; d. James McCall and Sarah (Yarbrough) Evans; m. Kenneth R. Barker, Nov. 25, 1972. BS, Ind. U., 1965; JD, Am. U., 1969; LLD (hon.) U. Indpls., 1984; Doctor Pub. Svc. (hon.) Butler U., 1987; LLD (hon.) Marian Coll., 1991; LHD U. Evansville, 1993. Bar: Ind., 1969, U.S. Dist. Ct. (so. dist.) Ind., 1969, U.S. Ct. Appeals (7th cir.), 1973, U.S. Supreme Ct., 1978. Legal asst. to senator U.S. Senate, 1969-71, spl. counsel to minority, govt. ops. com., permanent investigations subcom., 1971-72; dir. rsch., scheduling and advance Senator Percy Re-election Campaign, 1972; asst. U.S. atty. So. Dist. Ind., 1972-76, 1st asst. U.S. atty., 1976-77, U.S. atty., 1981-84; judge U.S. Dist. Ct. (so. dist.) Ind., 1984-94, chief judge, 1994—; assoc., then ptnr. Bose, McKinney & Evans, Indpls., 1977-81; mem. long range planning com. Jud. Conf. U.S., 1991-96, exec. com., 1989-91, standing com. fed. rules of practice and procedure, 1987-91, dist. judge rep., 1988-91; mem. jud. coun. 7th cir. Ct. Appeals, 1988—, jud. fellows commn. U.S. Supreme Ct., 1993-98; jud. adv. com., sentencing commn., 1995-97, bd. advisors, Ind. U.,

Purdue U., Indpls.; mem. pres.'s cabinet Ind. U.; bd. visitors Ind. U. Sch. of Law, Bloomington. Mem. Ind. Hist. Soc.; bd. dirs. Clarian Health Ptnrs. Recipient Peck award Wabash Coll., 1989, Touchstone award Girls Club of Greater Indpls., 1989, Leach Centennial 1st Woman award Valparaiso Law Sch., 1993, Most Influential Women award Indpls. Bus. Jour., 1996, Paul Buchanan award of excellence Indpls. Bar Found., 1998; named Ind. Woman of Yr., Women in Comm., 1986, Ind. Univ. Disting. Alumni, 1996. Mem. ABA, Ind. Bar Assn., Indpls. Bar Assn. (Antoinette Dakin Leach award 1993), Fed. Judges Assn., Nat. Assn. Former U.S. Attys., Am. Judicature Soc., Lawyers Club, Kiwanis. Republican. Methodist. Office: US Dist Ct 210 US Courthouse 46 E Ohio St Indianapolis IN 46204-1903

BARKER, SYLVIA MARGARET, nurse; b. Glens Falls, N.Y., Sept. 11, 1914; d. Victor Howell and Julia Helen (Lansing) B. Student, Green Mountain Coll., 1933; diploma, Mt. Sinai Hosp. Sch. Nursing, 1936; BS, Columbia U., 1947, MA, 1951. RN, N.Y. Staff nurse Mt. Sinai Hosp., N.Y.C., 1936-37, gynecology head nurse, 1937-40, nursing arts asst. instr., 1940-41, nursing of children instr., 1941-45, nursing arts instr.-in-charge, 1945-48; instr. in charge nursing arts Michael Reese Hosp., Chgo., 1948-50; nursing of children supr. Mt. Sinai Hosp., N.Y.C., 1951-66, asst. dir. insvc. edn., 1966-72, assoc. dir. nursing, 1972-77, acting dir. nursing, assoc. dir. nursing, 1972, assoc. dir. nursing affairs, 1977-86, cons. nursing adminstrn., 1986-94; hon. clin. assoc. faculty CUNY, 1984-87, 89-91; presenter SUNY, Downstate, 1982, N.Y. State Nurses Assn., 1982, Mt. Sinai Hosp., N.Y.C., 1983, 91, 92, United Hosp. Fund and Office of Profl. Discipline, N.Y.C., 1983, Cornell Med. Ctr., 1984, CCNY, 1984-91, Charleston W.Va. Eye, Ear, Nose and Throat Clinic, 1986, Hunter-Bellevue Sch. Nursing, 1987-91. Contbr. articles to profl. jours. Bd. dirs. Nurses House, 1991-95, sec., 1995-97, pres., 1997—. Recipient Alumni Achievement award Nursing Edn. Alumni Assn. Tchrs. Coll., 1994, Leadership in Profl. and Allied Orgns. Achievement award, 1999; writings and papers in Archives of Found. N.Y. State Nurses Assn., 1993; Guggenheim scholar Mt. Sinai Hosp. Sch. Nursing, 1936. Mem. ANA (Coun. Nursing Adminstrn. Membership award 1998, Disting. Membership award 1998), Nat. League for Nursing, So. N.Y. League for Nursing, N.Y. State Nurses Assn. (bylaws com. 1982-85, nominating com. 1995, Jane Delano Disting. Svc. award 1982, Nursing Svc. Adminstrn. award 1984, Recognition 50 Yr. Membership award 1986, Hon. Recognition award 1992), N.Y. Counties RNs Assn. (search com., exec. dir. 1993-94, chair bylaws com. dist. 13 1983-91, bd. dirs. 1983-85, Recognition 50 Yr. Membership award 1989), Alumnae Assn. of Mt. Sinai Hosp. Sch. Nursing (bd. dirs. 1981-84, pres. 1987-91, treas. 1991-95, sec. 1995—), Sigma Theta Tau. Avocations: ballet, philharmonic orchestra, reading, writing, collecting owls. Home and Office: 788 Columbus Ave Apt 6K New York NY 10025-5942

BARKER, THOMAS CARL, retired health care administration educator, executive; b. Cedar Rapids, Iowa, May 25, 1931; s. Carl Edward and Bertha Olive (Simons) B.; m. Mary Irene Beorkrem, Sept. 1, 1952 (dec. 1995); children: Cheryl Lynn, Thomas Carl Jr. (dec.), Laura Ann, David Edward; m. Patricia Blount Moore, May 2, 1998. Student, Loras Coll., 1949-50, Coe Coll., 1950-51; BS, U. Iowa, 1954, MA, 1960, PhD, 1963. Acct. Wilson & Co., Cedar Rapids, Iowa, 1951-54; contract adminstr. Collins Radio Co., Cedar Rapids, 1956-57; with customer rels. The Cryovac Co., Cedar Rapids, 1957-58; bus. officer Mercy Hosp., Iowa City, Iowa, 1958-59; rsch. asst. U. Iowa, 1959-60, tchg. asst., 1961-63, asst. prof., 1963-64; adminstrv. assoc. U. Iowa Hosp., 1960-62; rsch. assoc. UAW Internat. Union, Detroit, 1964-67; dir. Mich. Health and Social Security Rsch. Inst., Detroit, 1964-67; adj. assoc. prof. health econs. Wayne State U., Detroit, 1966-67; Arthur Graham Glasgow prof., dir. Sch. Hosp. Adminstrn. Med. Coll. Va., Richmond, 1967-71; prof., dean and CEO Sch. Allied Health Professions Va. Commonwealth U., Richmond, 1969-96, dean emeritus, prof. emeritus, 1996—; mem. com. on allied health edn. and accreditation AMA, chmn. com., 1988-91; served as mem. or cons. to various pub. health svcs., including NIH, Health Resources Adminstrn., VA, HEW agys.; mem. dean's com. VA Med. Ctr., Richmond, 1974—; mem. Ctrl. Va. Health Sys. Agy., 1976-88, pres., 1979-80; mem. Va. Health Coord. Coun., 1986-88. Contbr. articles to profl. jours. With USN, 1949-56; capt. Res., ret. Named Hon. Alumni, Med. Coll. Va. Fellow APHA, Am. Soc. Allied Health Professions (pres. 1975-76); mem. Am. Health Planning Assn., Assn. Univ. Programs in Health Adminstrn., Soc. Sons. Revolution in State of Va., Va. Assn. Allied Health Professions, Va. Hosp. Assn., Rotary (pres. Richmond club 1991-92), Phi Kappa Phi. Roman Catholic. E-mail: tcbarker@hsc.vcu.edu. Fax: 804-828-1894. Home: 2251 Winterfield Rd Midlothian VA 23113-4145 Office: The Grant House PO Box 980203 Richmond VA 23298-0203

BARKER, THOMAS WATSON, JR., energy company executive; b. Atlanta, Nov. 8, 1944; s. Thomas Watson Sr. and Nancy (Blackwell) B.; m. Patricia Tate, June 18, 1966 (div. Aug. 1984); children: Virginia Tate Barker, Thomas Watson III; m. Mitzi Riddle, Oct. 19, 1985. BS in Indsl. Engring., Ga. Inst. Tech., 1966; MBA, U. Ala., 1969; AMP, Harvard Bus. Sch., 1982. Sales engr. The Trane Co., LaCrosse, Wis., 1966-68; mem. fin. staff So. Natural Gas Co., Birmingham, Ala., 1969-76, v.p. gas supply dept., 1982-84; asst. treas. Sonat, Inc., Birmingham, 1976-81, treas., 1981-82, v.p. fin., 1984—; bd. dirs. Workshops Inc. Bd. dirs. Better Bus. Bur., Birmingham, 1989—, Leadership Birmingham, 1989—, Boys and Girls Club, Ala. Ballet; mem. adv. bd. St. Vincent's Hosp.; mem. Norton bd. advisors Birmingham-So. Coll.; mem. MBA adv. com. U. Ala. Mem. Fin. Exec. Inst. (bd. dirs. 1980-82), Country Club Birmingham, Summit Club, Newcomen Soc., Kiwanis, Beta Gamma Sigma. Avocations: golf, jogging. Office: Sonat Inc 1900 5th Ave N Birmingham AL 35203-2610

BARKER, VERLYN LLOYD, retired minister, educator; b. Auburn, Nebr., July 25, 1931; s. Jack Lloyd and Olive Clara (Bollman) B. AB, Doane Coll., 1952, DD, 1977; BD, Yale U., 1956, STM, 1960; postgrad., U. Chgo., 1960-61; PhD, St. Louis U., 1970. Ordained to ministry United Ch. of Christ, 1956. Instr. history, chaplain Doane Coll., Crete, Nebr., 1954-55; pastor U. Nebr., 1956-59; sec. ministry higher edn. United Ch. Bd. Homeland Ministries, N.Y.C., 1961-96; ret. United Ch. Bd. Homeland Ministries, Cleve., 1996. Author: Health and Human Values: A Ministry of Theological Inquiry and Moral Discourse, 1987; editor: The Church and the Public School, 1980, Science, Technology and the Christian Faith, 1990; contbg. author: Campus Ministry, 1964; mem. editorial adv. com. Jour. Current Social Issues; contbr. articles to various publs. Pres. United Ministries in Higher Edn., N.Y.C., 1971-77. Mem. AAAS, ACLU, Am. Assn. Higher Edn., Am. Studies Assn., Acad. Polit. Sci., Am. Acad. Polit. and Social Sci., Soc. Health and Human Values, Doane Coll. Alumni Assn. (pres. 1957-58), Nat. Assn. for Sci., Tech. and Soc., Yale Club.

BARKER, VIRGINIA LEE, nursing educator. Diploma, Ind. U. Sch. Nursing, 1952, BS, 1955, MS, 1961, EdD, 1969. Dean sch. nursing, prof. Alfred (N.Y.) U., 1969-78; prof., dean nursing U. Louisville, 1978-81; dean Mary Black Sch. Nursing, prof. U. S.C., Spartanburg, 1981-90; dean profl. studies, prof. nursing SUNY, Plattsburg, 1990-98; cons. N.Y. Regents Coll. Nursing Program, 1972-91; project dir. federally funded telenursing project for rural upstate N.Y., 1993-98; dir. project to develop virtual reality simulations for edn. physicians, nurses, allied health pers., 1995—. Contbr. articles to profl. jours. Mem. ARC. Recipient N.Y. State Nurses Assn. Soc. Disting. Practitioners Grants. Mem. ANA, N.Y. Nurses Assn. (pres.), Nat. League for Nursing (com. mem.), S.C. League for Nursing, Am. Assn. Higher Edn., AAUW, Ind. U. Sch. Nursing Alumni Assn. (pres.), S.C. Deans and Dirs. Nursing Fedn. (chair), Sigma Theta Tau, Phi Kappa Phi, Kappa Delta Pi.

BARKER, WALTER LEE, thoracic surgeon; b. Chgo., Sept. 9, 1928; s. Samuel Robert, M.D., and Esther (Meyerovitz) B.; m. Betty Ruth Wood, Apr. 4, 1967. A.B. cum laude, Harvard U., 1949, M.D., 1953. Diplomate Am. Bd. Surgery, Am. Bd. Thoracic Surgery. Intern, resident in gen. and thoracic surgery Cook County Hosp. and Presbyn. St. Luke's Med. Ctr. and affiliated hosps., Chgo., 1953-62; practice medicine specializing in thoracic surgery Chgo., 1962-95; clin. prof. surgery U. Ill.; prof. emeritus, 1998; head sect. thoracic surgery Cook County Hosp., 1972-93, cons. sect., 1993-98; chmn. dept. surgery St. Joseph Hosp., Chgo., 1982-97; researcher on tuberculosis, pleural infections, lung cancer. Author: The Post Operative Chest, 1977; editl. bd. Chest, 1984-89; cons. to editor, 1989—; contbr. articles to profl. jours. Served with M.C., USNR, 1955-57. Fellow Am. Coll. Chest Physicians (credentials com. 1984-89), ACS; mem. Am. Assn. Thoracic Surgery, AMA (rep. to HS of dels. 1988-94), Boylston Med. Soc., Chgo. Med. Soc., Ill. Med. Soc., Chest Club, Chgo. Surg. Soc. (v.p. 1990-91, chmn. membership com. 1991-92), Ill. Surg. Soc., Central Surg. Soc., Inst. Medicine, Soc. Thoracic Surgeons (founding mem., cons. editor Ann. Thoracic Surgery), Sigma Xi. Home: 2912 N Commonwealth Ave Apt 11C Chicago IL 60657-6215

BARKER, WALTER WILLIAM, JR., artist, educator; b. Coblenz, Germany, Aug. 8, 1921; s. Walter William and Selma Rosalie (Zinke) B.; children: Emily Croy, Michael Brendan. B.F.A., Washington U., 1948; M.F.A., Ind. U., 1950. Mem. faculty Sch. Art, Washington U., St. Louis, 1950-63, Bklyn. Mus. Sch., 1963-66; mem. faculty dept. art U. N.C., Greensboro, 1966—, prof., 1984-92, prof. emeritus, 1992—, lectr. on art, 1992—; Chmn. Venice Com., N.C., 1969-75. One-man shows include Otto Gerson Gallery, N.Y.C., 1959, Albert Landry Gallery, N.Y.C., 1963, Betty Parsons Gallery, N.Y.C., 1966, 69, Webster Coll., St. Louis, 1991, Weatherspoon Gallery U. N.C., Greensboro, 1994; represented in permanent collections U. Tex., Austin, Mus. Modern Art, N.Y.C., City Art Mus. of St. Louis, Washington U., St. Louis, L.A. County Mus., Phila. Mus. Fine Art, Boston Mus. Fine Art, Corcoran Gallery Art, Ark. Art Ctr., Little Rock, U. Minn., Mpls., U. Mass., Amherst, Hirschorn Mus., Washington, Libr. of Congress, Washington, St. Louis U., U. Mo., Columbia, Swan Hill Art Mus., Victoria, Australia; columnist on art St. Louis Post Dispatch, 1962-78. Served with AUS, 1942-45. Recipient Disting. Alumni citation Washington U., St. Louis, 1972. Episcopalian. Home: 1606 Walker Ave Greensboro NC 27403-2319 also: Dogfish Head Rd West Southport ME 04576 Office: 1000 Spring Garden St Greensboro NC 27412-0001 *As an artist I have found that search for self can only be undertaken successfully if there is deep respect for the visual world.*

BARKER, WILLIAM ALFRED, physics educator; b. Los Angeles, May 9, 1919; s. Lawrence and Natalie (Cole) B.; m. Mary Louise Miller, June 25, 1941 (dec.); children: Gail (Mrs. Michael Kahle), Patrick Cole, Claire Stewart, Louisa Lawrene (dec.), Michael Lawrence; m. Jean Hyun Lee, Jan. 19, 1985. B.A., Yale, 1941; M.S., Calif. Inst. Tech., 1949; Ph.D., St. Louis U., 1952. Mem. faculty St. Louis U., 1949-64, Swiss Fed. Inst. Tech., 1953-55; prof. physics U. Santa Clara, 1964-88; cons. Argonne Nat. Lab., 1958-64, industry. Contbr. articles to profl. jours. Served with USNR, 1941-45, PTO. Mem. Am. Phys. Soc., Am. Assn. Physics Tchrs., Phi Beta Kappa, Sigma Xi, Pi Mu Epsilon, Alpha Sigma Nu. Roman Catholic. Research on quantum mechs., relativity, statis. physics, nuclear orientation, planetary atmospheres, quantum electronics, cosmology, exclusive interaction, accelerating alpha decay. Home: 185 N El Monte Ave Los Altos CA 94022-3126

BARKER, WILLIAM DANIEL, hospital administrator; b. New Orleans, July 21, 1926; s. William Daniel and Ada (Will) B.; m. Nancy Pool, Sept. 23, 1949; children: Nancy Louise, Julia Ann, William Daniel III, Marion DeVilbiss. B in Bus. Adminstrn., Emory U., 1949; M in Hosp. Adminstrn., Ga. State U., 1966. Bus. office mgr. Emory U. Hosp., Atlanta, 1949-50; asst. adminstr. Griffin (Ga.) Spalding County Hosp., 1950-51; adminstr. Winder-Barrow (Ga.) Hosp., 1951-52; hosp. field rep. Ga. Dept. Pub. Health, Atlanta, 1952-54, hosp. cons., 1954-55; asst. adminstr. Tri-County Hosp., Ft. Oglethorpe, Ga., 1955-60; asst. dir. Crawford Long Hosp. Emory U., Atlanta, 1960-73, adminstr., 1973-84, dir. hosps., 1984-90, exec. dir. hosp., 1987-90; ret., 1991; prof. Emory U., Atlanta, 1988-93; bd. dirs. Ga. Fed. Bank, Atlanta, Blue Cross Blue Shield Ga., Inc.; provider affairs com. Blue Cross Blue Shield Assn., United Network for Organ Sharing, bd. dirs., 1991—; bd. govs. SunHealth, Charlotte, N.C., chmn., 1988-89; bd. commrs. Joint Commn. on Accreditation of Healthcare Orgns., 1981-86; v.p. Greater Atlanta Coalition on Health Care, 1983-84; mem. Gov.'s Coun. Malpractice Ins., 1975-83, Medicaid Adv. Com. Ga. Dept. Human Resources, 1973-77, Health Facilities Planning Com. Met. Atlanta Coun. for Health, 1971-74, Atlanta Regional Commn. Emergency Med. Task Force 1969-73, Gov.'s Commn. on Nursing, 1970-71, adv. commn. Internat. Implant Registry, 1989—, vice-chmn., 1991, chmn., 1992; pres. Health Careers of Ga., Inc., 1969-70, Ga. Coun. Paramed. Edn., 1968. Contbr. articles to profl. jours. With U.S. Army, 1944-46. Recipient R.C. Williams award Ga. State U., 1966, Disting. Alumni award, Ga. State U., 1979, Disting. Svc. award, Ga. Med. Assn. Atlanta, 1980; Disting. Guest Lectr. Ga. State U., 1978. Fellow Am. Coll. Healthcare Execs. (regent 1972-75); mem. Am. Hosp. Assn. (chmn. 1979, Speaker of Ho. 1980, Disting. Svc. award 1987), Ga. Hosp. Assn. (pres. 1966-79, Gold Honor award of Excellence 1980), Ansley Golf Club. Baptist. Home: 50 S Prado St NE Atlanta GA 30309-3309

BARKER, WILLIAM THOMAS, lawyer; b. Pitts., Feb. 28, 1947; s. V. Wayne and Cordelia (Whitten) B.; m. June K. Robinson, Jan. 30, 1981. BS, Mich. State U., 1969, MS, 1969; JD, U. Calif.-Berkeley, 1974. Bar: Calif. 1975, Ill. 1976. Assoc. programmer-analyst Control Data Corp., Sunnyvale, Calif., 1969-71; law clk. Pa. Supreme Ct., Erie, 1974-75; assoc. Sonnenschein Carlin Nath & Rosenthal, Chgo., 1975-82, ptnr., 1982—; moderator Ill. Ins. Law Forum, Counsel Connect, 1994—; co-moderator Nat. Ins. Law gen. forum, 1996—. Bd. editors Def. Counsel Jour., 1987—; contbg. editor Bad Faith Law Report, 1990—; mem. editl. bd. Ins. Litigation Reporter, 1987—; editor Covered Events, 1995-96, editor emeritus, 1996—; ins. law publs. bd. Def. Rsch. Inst., 1992-97; contbr. articles to profl. jours. Fellow Am. Bar Found.; mem. ABA (chair-elect com. on appellate advocacy, tort and ins. practice sect., 1994-95, chair 1995-96, chair gen. comm. bd. 1996-97), Internat. Assn. Def. Counsel (Yancey Meml. award for best article 1995, chair spl. com. on Amicus Curie 1996-97), Chgo. Council Lawyers (sec. 1987-88, bd. gov. 1989-91, chair com. prof. resp. 1990-95), Chgo. Bar Assn. (chmn. com. constl. law 1984-85), Def. Rsch. Inst., Am. Law Inst., Ill. Assn. Def. Trial Coun. Home: 132 E Delaware Pl Apt 5806 Chicago IL 60611-4951 Office: Sonnenschein Nath Et Al 8000 Sears Tower 233 S Wacker Dr Ste 8000 Chicago IL 60606-6342

BARKER-NUNN, JEANNE BEVERLY, English educator; b. Mpls., Nov. 24, 1946; d. Paul Barker and Beverly Jeanne (Nunn) Johnson; m. Lee Gordon Hesselroth, Nov. 26, 1982; children: Tyler Hesselroth, Andrew Hesselroth. BS in English, U. Minn., 1968; MA in English, E. Carolina U., 1977; PhD in Am. Studies, U. Minn., 1985. Instr. U. Minn., Mpls., 1977-85, E. Carolina U., Greenville, N.C., 1974-76; asst. prof. Mich. State U., East Lansing, 1985-91; mng. editor Signs: Jour. of Women in Culture and Soc., Mpls., 1991-95; dir. J.B. Barker-Nunn & Assocs., St. Paul, Minn., 1996—; adj. prof. dept. English, U. Minn., Mpls., 1995—; cons. editor various bus. and univs., 1992—. Editor: (book) History and Theory, 1996; contbr. articles to profl. jours. Adv. bd. dirs. Linwood A Sch., St. Paul, 1995—, Groveland Park Elem. Sch., St. Paul, 1994-95; ministry mem. spiritual devel. Unity Unitarian Universalist Ch., St. Paul, 1997—. Rsch. grantee Mich. State U., 1987, 89, 90; recipient Presdl. Svc. award U. Minn., 1985, Dissertation fellowship U. Minn., 1983-84. Mem. Am. Studies Assn., Nat. Coun. Tchrs. of English, MLA. Avocation: attending arts performances and events. Home and Office: JB Barker-Nunn & Assocs 1833 Berkeley Ave Saint Paul MN 55105-1659

BARKETT, ROSEMARY, federal judge; b. Ciudad Victoria, Tamaulipas, Mex., Aug. 29, 1939; came to U.S., 1946, naturalized, 1958; BS summa cum laude, Spring Hill Coll., 1967; JD, U. Fla., 1970. Bar: Fla., U.S. Dist. Ct. (so. dist.) Fla., U.S. Ct. Appeals (5th cir.), U.S. Supreme Ct. Pvt. practice West Palm Beach, Fla., 1971-79; judge 15th Jud. Cir. Ct., Palm Beach County, Fla., 1979-84, 4th Dist. Ct. Appeal, West Palm Beach, Fla., 1984-85; assoc. justice Supreme Ct. Fla., Tallahassee, Fla., 1985-92, chief justice, 1992-94; judge U.S. Ct. of Appeals (11th cir.) Fla., Miami, 1994—; mem. faculty U. Nev., Reno, Fla. Jud. Coll. Mem. editorial bd. The Florida Judges Manual. Mem. vis. com. Miami U. Law Sch.; mem. bd. visitors St. Thomas U. Recipient Woman of Achievement award Palm Beach County Commn. on Status of Women, 1985; named to Fla. Women's Hall of Fame, 1986. Fellow Acad. Matrimonial Lawyers; mem. ABA, Fla. Bar Assn. (family law sect., chairperson ct. stats. and workload com. and study commn. on guardianship law, lectr. on matrimonial media and criminal law continuing legal edn.), Palm Beach County Bar Assn., Am. Acad. Matrimonial Lawyers (award 1984), Fla. Assn. Women Lawyers (Palm Beach chpt.), Nat. Assn. Women Judges, Palm Beach Marine Inst. (former chairperson, bd. trustees), Acad. Fla. Trial lawyers (Achievement award 1988), Assn. Trial Lawyers Am. (Achievement award 1986). Office: 99 NE 4th St Rm 1223 Miami FL 33132-2140*

BARKEY, BRENDA, technical writer, publications manager; b. Hawthorne, Calif., Dec. 22, 1959; d. Greta E. B.; 1 child, Tiffany. BSCE, Comm., U. Washington, 1983. Cert. aerobics instr., Am. Coun. on Exercise. Tech. writer, editor Care Computer Sys., Bellevue, Wash., 1983-87, tech. writing supr., 1987-88; tech. writer Municipality of Met. Seattle, 1988-91; project mgr. West Point Treatment Plant Ops. Documentation, King County, Seattle, 1991-96; pvt. practice Edmonds, Wash., 1997—; presenter in field. Co-author: A Team Approach to Training and Documentation in a Changing Organization, 1993, Putting Operations and Maintenance Manuals to Work for You, 1991; author: West Point Treatment Plant Operations and Maintenance Manual. Bd. dirs., sec. Edmonds (Wash.) Greenery Assn., 1996—. Recipient Merit awards, Soc. Tech. Communication, Seattle, 1989, 91. Avocations: swimming, bicycling, running, aerobics.

BARKIN, ELLEN, actress; b. N.Y.C., Apr. 16, 1955; m. Gabriel Byrne, 1988; 1 son, Jack. Student, CUNY; grad., Hunter Coll. Ind. theatrical, film actress, 1980—. Theatrical prodns. include Shout Across the River, 1980, Killings on the Last Line, 1980, Extremities, 1982; appeared on TV soap Search for Tomorrow; TV films include Kent State, 1981, We're Fighting Back, 1981, Terrible Joe Moran starring James Cagney, 1984, Act of Vengence, 1986, Clinton and Nadine, 1988; film appearances include Diner, 1982, Daniel, 1983, Tender Mercies, 1983, Eddie and the Cruisers, 1983, The Adventures of Buckaroo Banzai, 1984, Harry and Son, 1984, Enormous Changes at the Last Minute, 1985, Down by Law, 1986, Desert Bloom, 1986, The Big Easy, 1987, Siesta, 1987, Made in Heaven, 1987, Sea of Love, 1989, Johnny Handsome, 1989, Switch, 1991, Man Trouble, 1992, Mac, 1993, This Boy's Life, 1993, Into the West, 1993, Bad Company, 1995, Wild Bill, 1995, Mad Dog Time, 1996, The Fan, 1996. Office: care CAA 9830 Wilshire Blvd Beverly Hills CA 90212-1804

BARKIN, MARTIN, pharmaceutical company executive, physician; b. Toronto, Ont., Can., July 20, 1936; s. Jack and Freda (Spivak) B.; m. Lillian Carol Kohm, June 9, 1957; children: Tim, Jeff, Risa Beth, Robbie. M.D., U. Toronto, 1960, B.Sc. in Medicine, 1962, M.A., 1963. Cert. in surgery, urology, Can. Chief urologist Sunnybrook Hosp., Toronto, 1970-83; chmn. Sunnybrook Clinics, Toronto, 1982-83; prof. surgery U. Toronto, 1980—; pres., chief exec. officer Sunnybrook Med. Ctr., Toronto, 1984-87; dep. minister of health Province of Ont., 1987-91; health care cons. Peat Marwick, 1991-92; pres., CEO Draxis Health Inc., 1992—; chmn. Deprenyl Animal Health, Kans., Sunnybrook & Women's Coll. Health Scis. Ctr.; sec. Premier's Coun. on Health Strategy, 1987-91; bd. dirs. Novopharm Biotech., Inc., Bone Care Internat., Inc., Draxis Health, Inc. Contbr. articles to profl. jours. Decorated Queen Elizabeth II Silver Jubilee medal, Can., 1976. Fellow R.C.S.; mem. Am. Urology Assn. (pres. Northeast sect. 1984-85), Can. Urol. Assn. (exec. 1980-83), Soc. Pelvic Surgeons. Jewish. Clubs: Granite, Goodwood. Avocation: hunting. Home: 54 Old Forest Hill Rd, Toronto, ON Canada M5P 2P9 Office: Draxis Health Inc, 6870 Goreway Dr, Mississauga, ON Canada L4V 1P1

BARKIN, MARVIN E., lawyer; b. Winter Haven, Fla., Nov. 9, 1933; s. Isadore and Jean (Epstein) B.; m. Gertrude Parnes, Sept. 20, 1959; children: Thomas I., Michael A., Pamela L. AB, Emory U., 1955; LLB cum laude, Harvard U., 1958. Bar: Fla. 1958, U.S. Dist. Ct. (mid. and so. dists.) Fla., U.S. Ct. Appeals (5th and 11th cirs.), U.S. Supreme Ct. Research aide Dist. Ct. Appeal Fla., Third Dist., Miami, 1958-60; assoc., then ptnr. Fowler, White, Collins, Gillen, Humkey & Trenam, Tampa, 1960-69; ptnr. Trenam, Kemker, Scharf, Barkin, Frye, O'Neill & Mullis, Tampa, 1970—; mem. Fla. Bd. Bar Examiners, 1979-84, chmn., 1982-83; chmn. corp., banking and bus. law sect. Fla. Bar, 1974-75, chmn. appellate ct. rules subcom., 1972-73. Mem. Am. Law Inst., Am. Bar Found., Nat. Conf. Bar Examiners (bd. mgrs. 1985-95, chmn. 1993-94, 11th cir. ct. appeal com. on lawyer qualifications and conduct), Fla. Bar, Omicron Delta Kappa. Democrat. Jewish. Home: 1605 Culbreath Isles Dr Tampa FL 33629-4824 Office: Trenam Kemker Scharf Barkin Frye O'Neill & Mullis 101 E Kennedy Blvd Tampa FL 33602-5179

BARKIN, ROBERT ALLAN, graphic designer, newspaper executive, consultant; b. Toronto, Ont., Can., Sept. 2, 1939; came to U.S., 1940, naturalized, 1950; s. Jacob and Mildred Barkin; m. Susan Davis, Jan. 23, 1987; children: Craig, Robin, Richard, Jamie. B.A., George Washington U., 1960. From artist to advt. and sales promotion dir. Giant Food Inc., Washington, 1960-69; freelance artist, designer Washington, 1969-72; v.p. Lawrence Dobrow & Assos., Washington, 1972-73, Taft Communications Corp., Washington and N.Y.C., 1973-74; cons. MacHarmans Assos., Auckland, N.Z., 1975; Freelance cons., Washington, 1976-77; art dir. Washington Post mag., 1977-78; asst. mng. editor Washington Post, 1978-85; cons. Barkin & Davis Inc., 1986—; tchr. life drawing and anatomy Georgetown U., 1973-76; inst. D.C. St. Acad., 1970. Exhbns. in, Washington, Phila. and Auckland; rep. pvt. and pub. collections. Recipient Silver Lions award Venice, Italy, 1975, also awards N.Y.C. Art Dirs. Club, Print Mag., Soc. Newspaper Design, Communications Art Assn., Ad Club Washington, Am. Inst. Graphic Arts, Printing Industry Am., Beckett Paper Co. Mem. Art Dirs. Club Washington (Gold medal 1979), Soc. Publ. Designers, Soc. Newspaper Designers. Home and Office: 1107 Notley Rd Silver Spring MD 20904-6243

BARKIN, SOLOMON, economist; b. N.Y.C., Dec. 2, 1907; s. Julius and Lillian (Kroll) B.; m. Elaine N. Rappaport, Apr. 21, 1940; children: David Peter, Roger Michael, Amy Claire. BS, CCNY, 1928; MA, Columbia U., 1929. Instr. CCNY, 1929-31; asst. dir. N.Y. State Commn. on Old Age Security, 1929-33, NRA Labor Adv. Bd., 1933-36; chief labor sect., divsn. indsl. econs. U.S. Dept. Commerce, 1936-37; dir. research Textile Workers Union Am., 1937-63; dep. dir. manpower and social affairs directorate, chief social affairs divsn. OECD, 1963-68; prof. econs. U. Mass., Amherst, 1968-78; prof. emeritus U. Mass., 1978—; vis. prof. econs. Erasmus U., Rotterdam, The Netherlands, 1979; adj. prof. indsl. relations, Columbia, 1959-63; labor cons. WPB.; mem. Am. standard textile safety code, standing adv. com. U.S. Bur. Labor Statistics; vice chmn. com. on research Pres.'s Conf. on Indsl. Safety; chmn. bd. Interunion Inst., Inc.; textile cons. U.K. Mission of ECA.; Specialist Internat. Information Service, U.S. Dept. State; mem. Sec. Labor's Com. on Automation; chmn. com. on job redesign Nat. Com. on the Aging; v.p. Joint Council on Econ. Edn.; mem. AFL-CIO Standing Com. on Research; Am. del. Inter-Am. Statis. Congress, to European Productivity Agy. Conf. on Human Relations, Rome, 1956, OEEC Internat. Textile Conf., Milan, 1957; del. ILO, 1961; econ. adviser Internat. Fedn. Textile and Clothing Workers Assn., 1960. Author: The Older Worker in Industry, 1933, Toward Fairer Labor Standards, 1948, The Decline of the Labor Movement, 1961, Worker Militancy and Its Consequences, 2d edit. 1983; co-author: Work Duty Charts for Textile Operations, 1951, Textile Workers Job Primer, 1953, Forms for Calculating the Frequency for Periodic Work Duties, Manpower Policies and Problems in the Netherlands, 1967, Workers' Negotiated Savings Plans for Capital Formation, Manpower Policy in Norway, 1972; editor: Technical Change and Manpower Planning: Coordination Enterprise Level, 1967; co-editor Arbitration Jour., 1954-59, Internat. Labor, 1968; mem. editl. bd. Jour. Econ. Issues, 1981-85, Relations Industrielles, 1986-91. Recipient Spl. Lifetime Achievement award Jour. Polit. Economy, 1972; subject of book by Donald Stabile: Activist Unionism: The Institutional Economics of Solomon Barkin, 1993; Columbia U. fellow, 1932-33, Wertheim fellow Indsl. Rels. Harvard U., 1948-49; Fulbright scholar, New Zealand, 1981. Fellow div. psychol. and social scis. Gerontol. Soc., Inc.; mem. Indsl. Relations Research Assn. (past pres.), Am. Statis. Assn., Council on Fgn. Relations, Am. Econ. Assn., Nat. Planning Assn. (trustee), Assn. Evolutionary Econs. (Instl. policy adv. com. 1984—), Phi Beta Kappa (assocs.). Home: 49 Long Hill Rd Leverett MA 01054-9749*

BARKLEY, BRIAN EVAN, lawyer, political consultant; b. Teaneck, N.J., Jan. 30, 1945; s. Henry E. and Alice M. (Schultz) B.; m. Pamela A. Martin, May 5, 1979; children: Leigh Elizabeth, Christine Elizabeth, Brett Evan. BA, U. Md., 1967; JD with honors, George Washington U., 1970. Bar: Md. 1970, D.C. 1976, U.S. Dist. Ct. Md. 1973. Assoc., Everngam & Goldstein, Silver Spring, Md., 1970-72; pvt. practice law, Silver Spring, 1972-80, Rockville, Md., 1980-86; spl. asst. Rep. Michael Barnes, Washington, 1981-84; sr. ptnr. Barkley and Kennedy, Chartered 1987—. Vice chmn. Nat. Capital chpt. Nat. Multiple Sclerosis Com., Washington, 1980-86, 1998—, chmn. chpt. svcs. com., 1985—; chmn. Montgomery County Multiple Sclerosis Com., Rockville, Md., 1980; major gifts chmn. Shady Grove Hosp., 1980; campaign mgr. Barnes for Congress, Rockville, 1980, campaign chmn.,

1982-84; campaign mgr. Montgomery County for Mondale, 1984; del. Dem. Nat. Conv., 1984; vice chmn. Montgomery County for Dukakis, 1988. Recipient Humanitarian award Nat. Multiple Sclerosis Soc., 1989. Mem. Md. Bar Assn., Rockville C. of C. (pres. 1996-97), Montgomery County Bar Assn., Bethesda Country Club, Masons. Democrat. Home: 12405 Copenhaver Ter Potomac MD 20854-3028 Office: 51 Monroe St Ste 1407 Rockville MD 20850-2408

BARKLEY, CHARLES WADE, professional basketball player; b. Leeds, Ala., Feb. 20, 1963. Student, Auburn U., 1981-84. mem. U.S. Olympic Basketball Team, 1992. With Phila. 76ers, 1984-92, Phoenix Suns, 1992-96; now with Houston Rockets, 1996—; mem. U.S. Olympic team, 1992, 1996. Author: (with Roy S. Johnson) Outrageous! The Fine Life and Flagrant Good Times of Basketball's Irresistible Force, 1992; film appearances include: Forget Paris, 1995. Recipient NBA All-Star Game Most Valuable Player award, 1991, Schick Pivotal Player award, 1986-88, NBA Most Valuable Player Award, 1993, IMB award, 1986-88; named to NBA All-Star team, 1988-93. Named to All-Rooki Team, 1985. Holds single game records for most offensive rebounds in one quarter-11, and most offensive rebounds in one half-13, 1987. Office: Houston Rockets Two Greenway Plz Ste 400 Houston TX 77046-3865*

BARKLEY, HENRY BROCK, JR., research and development executive; b. Raleigh, N.C., Apr. 5, 1927; s. Henry Brock and Thelma Maurine (Dutt) B.; m. Edith Sumner Stowe, June 24, 1950; children: Margaret Susan, Henry Brock III, Jane Stowe. Student U. N.C., 1944-45; BS, U.S. Naval Acad., 1949; BSEE, U.S. Naval Postgrad. Sch., 1954, MSEE, 1955. Supr. space power sect. Bendix, Ann Arbor, Mich., 1962-63; chief reactor div. Lewis Research Center, NASA, Sandusky, Ohio, 1963-73; asst. gen. mgr., dir. power reactors EG&G Idaho, Inc., Idaho Falls, 1973-81; mgr. internat. bus. Babcock & Wilcox Co., Lynchburg, Va., 1981-83, mgr. 205 plant project services, 1983-87, mgr. space power and propulsion, 1987-89, dir. space and def. systems, 1989-92; cons., 1992—; dir. Devel. Workshop, Inc., Idaho Falls., 1977-81; IEEE Disting. lectr. in S.Am. and C.Am., 1984. Bd. dirs. Sandusky (Ohio) Concert Assn., 1965-73; chmn. Huron (Ohio) sch. levy campaigns, 1970. Served to lt. comdr. USN, 1949-61. Mem. IEEE, Am. Nuclear Soc., Am. Guild Organists. Presbyterian. Home: 1216 Norvell House Ct Lynchburg VA 24503-1940

BARKLEY, MARLENE A. NYHUIS, nursing administrator; b. Waupun, Wis., Aug. 31, 1934; d. Fred and Esther Elsie (Leu) Nyhuis; m. Peter Don Barkley, Sept. 1, 1956; children: Peter Scott, John Fredric. Dipl. nursing, Milw. County Hosp., 1955; cert. nurse practitioner, U. Miami, Fla., 1976; AA, Miami Dade C.C., Fla., 1983; BSN cum laude, U. Miami, 1985; MSN, Barry U., 1996. RN, Fla. Nurse Waupun (Wis.) Meml. Hosp., 1956-57; nurse coord. Courtland Med. Ctr., Milw., 1958-61, Planned Parenthood, Bloomington, Ind., 1971-74; nurse practitioner Miami VA Med. Ctr., 1976-83, program dir., 1983-98; adj. prof. Barry U., Miami Shores, Fla., 1997; cons. on home care, 1997—. Mem. ANA (cert.), Am. Acad. Nurse Practitioners, Advanced Practice Coun., Fla. Nurses Assn., So. Pain Soc., U. Miami Alumni Assn., Sigma Theta Tau. Presbyterian. Avocations: rollerblading, bicycling. Home: 321 31st St NW Naples FL 34120-1705

BARKLEY, MONIKA JOHANNA, general contracting professional; b. Lexington, Ky., Feb. 22, 1961; d. Ellis Leon McCollum and Doris Leni (vonderLippe) Hutson; m. Samuel Custer Barkley II, Feb. 14, 1986. Cert. in acctg., Fayette City Vocat.-Tech Coll., 1982. Claims processor Western Ins., Lexington, 1979-82; constrn. sec. Price, Inc.-Neal, Inc., Lexington, 1982-84; quality control adminstr. Jacobs Builders, Inc., Jacksonville, N.C., 1984-90; pres. Unicorn Constrn., Goldsboro, N.C., 1984—; quality control adminstr. Flynn Co., Inc., Dubuque, Iowa, 1988-89; sec. to pres. Wooten Oil Co., Goldsboro, N.C., 1990-91; contract adminstr. Colejon Corp., Cleve., 1991-95; office mgr.-adminstr. JC&B Constrn. Co., Goldsboro, N.C., 1995-97; pres. Phoenix Constrn. Assocs., Inc., Goldsboro, 1995—. Rep. dist. chair, Lexington, 1979; county coord. Dole for Pres., Hayes for Gov., Jones for Congress, 1996, 98; alt. del. to Rep. Nat. Conv., 1996; sec. exec. com. Wayne County Rep. Com., 1997-99, media dir., Winders for Sheriff, 1998. Recipient Contractor Safety award U.S. Army Corp Engrs., Seymour Johnson AFB, N.C., 1988, Contractor of Yr. award, 1988. Fellow VFW Aux. (Outstanding Svc. award 1985), Order of Ea. Star; mem. Vets. United for Strong Am. (nat. sec. 1985-89), Pearl Harbor Commemorative Assn. (nat. sec. 1989—, Wayne County Rep. Women's Club (v.p. 1995, 99), Wayne County C. of C. (amb. 1999), Wayne County Citizen s For Better Tax Control (sec. 1995), Wayne County Rep. Women's Club (v.p. 1999). Baptist. Avocations: political campaigns, writing cookbooks, gardening, painting. Home and Office: PO Box 10627 Goldsboro NC 27532-0627

BARKLEY, PAUL HALEY, JR., architect; b. Washington, Sept. 24, 1937; Paul Haley Sr. and Mary Barrett (Brewer) B.; m. Jeanette Frances Nickerson, Dec. 20, 1975. Student, Ecole D'Art Americaines, Fontainebleau, France, 1959; BArch, U. Va., 1960. Registered architect, Va., Md., D.C. Archtl. designer Strang & Childers Architects, Annandale, Va., 1960-61; project designer Alan J. Lockman Architect, Washington, 1962-63; design assoc. D.G. Chase & Assocs., Alexandria, Va., 1964; pres. Barkley Pierce Assocs., Falls Church, Va., 1965-94; sole practice Paul H. Barkley, FAIA, Architect, Falls Church, Va., 1994—; bd. dirs. Hist. Falls Church; lectr. archtl. divsn. continuing edn., 1966-91; mng. ptnr. Village Ctr. Assocs., Falls Church, 1983—. Prin. works include Falls Ch. Community Ctr., 1967, Vega Precision Labs., 1972, 1st Va. Bank, Arlington, 1979, Sullyfield Commerce Ctr., 1986, Rigg's Nat. Bank, McLean, Va., 1988; contbr. articles to profl. jours. Chmn. Falls Church Bus. Devel. Comm., 1987-93; exec. com. Citizens for a Better City, Falls Church, 1987-92; mem. Falls Church Pvt. Pub. Partnership, 1991-98, pres., 1993-94, bd. dirs., 1991-98. With USAF, 1960-63. Recipient excellence in design award Falls Church Village Preservation and Improvement Soc., 1979, Indsl. Devel. Vol. of Yr. award So. Indsl. Devel. Coun., 1982, Bus. Person of Yr. award City of Falls Church, 1988; Margaret Thompson Biddle fellow U. Va., 1959. Fellow AIA (bd. dirs. 1986-89, pres. Va. Soc. 1984, regional rep. Coll. of Fellows 1993-95, numerous other offices, Disting. Svc. award 1983, Outstanding Svc. award No. Va. chpt. 1982, award of recognition of outstanding achievement 1988, Noland award 1991)); mem. Falls Church C. of C. (bd. dirs. 1973-75, 99, pres. 1976, 3d v.p. 1977-79), Va. Found. for Arch. (pres. 1988-89, trustee 1993-99). Avocations: photography, travel, collecting art. Home and Office: 311 Chestnut St Falls Church VA 22046-2404

BARKLEY, RICHARD CLARK, ambassador; b. Chgo., Dec. 23, 1932; s. Harold Clark and Chrystal Leone (Boddiger) B.; m. Nina Margretha Schultz, Feb. 27, 1954; children: Katharina Lynn, Crystal Nina. BA, Mich. State U., 1954; MA, Wayne State U., 1958; postgrad., U. Frieburg, Germany, 1961. Joined Fgn. Svc., Dept. State, Washington, 1962; 2d sec. Am. Embassy, Helsinki, Finland, 1963-65; vice consul Am. Consulate, Santiago, Dominican Republic, 1965-67; 1st sec. U.S. Mission, Berlin, 1972-74; dep. chief mission Am. Embassy, Oslo, 1979-82; polit. counselor Am. Embassy, Bonn, Fed. Republic Germany, 1982-85; dep. chief mission Am. Embassy, Pretoria, Republic of South Africa, 1985-88; amb. to German Dem. Republic Berlin, 1988-90; amb. to Turkey Ankara, 1991-94. Bd. dirs. Inst. for Turkish Studies; chmn. Palace Arts Found. Inc., 1998—. Capt. U.S. Army, 1955-57. Recipient Disting. Alumni award Wayne State U., 1991, Disting. Honor award Dept. State, 1991. Mem. Am. Fgn. Svc. Assn., Alpha Tau Omega.

BARKLEY, WILLIAM DONALD, museum executive; b. New Westminster, B.C., Can., Apr. 4, 1941; s. Donald MacMillan and Ethel Margaret (Mines) B.; m. Helen Gayle Alanson, Aug. 29, 1964; children: Warren Vincent, Colleen Michelle. BS, U. B.C., 1964, MA, 1971. Cert. tchr. Can. Tchr. Salmon Arm (B.C.) Sr. Secondary Sch., 1965-68; wildlife biologist Wye Marsh Wildlife Ctr., Midland, Ont., Can., 1968-72; chief interpretation Can. Wildlife Svc., Ottawa, Ont., 1972-77; asst. dir. B.C. Provincial Mus., Victoria, 1977-84; CEO Royal BC Mus., Victoria, 1984—; advisor cultural resource mgmt. program U. Victoria, 1985—; lectr. univs. Contbr. articles to Nat. History Interpretation mag., 1965—. Bd. dirs. Tourism Victoria, 1985—. Recipient Disting. Svc. award Interpretation Can., Ottawa, 1983, Can. 125 award for svc. to mus. cmty. Fellow Can. Mus. Assn.; mem. Can. Mus. Assn. (pres. 1987-89), B.C. Mus. Assn., Internat. Coun. of Mus.-Can., Can. Pks. and Wilderness Soc., Can. Nature Fedn., Victoria A.M. Tourism Svcs. Assn. (treas.). Mem. United Ch. Can. Avocations: design and production stained glass, backpacking, skiing, wind surfing, numismatics. Office: 675 Belleville St., Victoria, BC Canada V8V 1X4

BARKLEY-LUEDERS, ELAINE KAY, production art manager; b. Alameda, Calif., July 11, 1960; d. William Gene and Mary Jane (Riggs) B.; m. Robert C. Lueders, Jan. 23, 1998. AA in Liberal Arts, Johnson County Cmty. Coll., 1992; BS in Journalism, U. Kans., 1994. Copychecker, editor Gill Studios, Inc., Lenexa, Kans., 1980-85; prodn. artist, corp. photographer Susan Crane, Inc., Dallas, 1986-89; 4 color process stripper, camera operator Lithographics, Inc., Overland Park, Kans., 1989-94; markets reporter Vance Publishing, Lenexa, 1994-95; prodn. asst. Marketshare Publs., Overland Park, 1995; graphic designer, 4 color process stripper Meseraull Printing, Inc., Lawrence, Kans., 1995-97; prodn. art mgr. Sandy Inc., Lenexa, 1997—. Newsletter editor Lawrence Photo Alliance, 1995; contbr. articles to profl. jours. Journalism scholarship U. Kans., 1993, 94. Mem. Soc. of Profl. Journalists, Kans. Alumni Assn., Aircraft Owners and Pilots Assn. Roman Catholic. Avocations: sailing, flying. Office: Sandy Inc 16201 W 110th St Lenexa KS 66219-1313

BARKMAN, ANNETTE SHAULIS, real estate management executive; b. Somerset, Pa., Oct. 18, 1948; d. Norman Albert and Janice Lorraine (Robbins) S.; m. Jon A. Barkman, Dec. 1, 1983; children: Caitlin Elizabeth, Meredith Elizabeth. BA, Dickinson Coll., 1969; MA, Indiana U. of Pa., 1975. Psychol. svcs. asso. II Bedford/Somerset Mental Health Clinic, Somerset, 1972-78, Somerset State Hosp., 1978-79; pvt. practice hypnosis cons., Somerset, 1976—; pres. Habitability, Inc., real estate mgmt., Somerset, 1978—; exec. mgr. Gt. N.E. Land & Cattle Co., Somerset, 1980-82; owner, mgr. Somerset Credit and Collection Bur., 1981—; realtor James F. Custer Real Estate, 1980-87; Barkman Realty Inc., 1988—; cons. Somerset County Headstart Program, 1977, 78; mem., bd. dirs. Children's Aid Soc. Somerset, 1986—. Squadron comdr. CAP, Somerset, 1977-78, recipient Meritorious Service award, 1977. Mem. Somerset Welfare League (pres. 1991), Chi Omega. Home: 388 High St Somerset PA 15501-1301 Office: 116 N Center Ave Somerset PA 15501-2029

BARKMAN, DEBRA RAE, nephrology nurse; b. Winfield, Kans., Aug. 18, 1954; d. Raymond O. and Gloria Mae (Stangle) B. Diploma, Wesley Sch. Nursing, Wichita, Kans., 1975; BS in Health Arts, Coll. St. Francis, Joliet, Ill., 1985. RN, Kans.; cert. nephrology nurse. Staff nurse, surg. gynecology Wesley Med. Ctr., Wichita, 1975-78, staff nurse, acute dialysis, 1978-79, head nurse, acute dialysis, 1979-86; head nurse, acute dialysis svcs. Wichita Dialysis Ctr., 1986-88, edn. and quality coord., 1988-92, quality, risk mgmt., satellite supr., 1992-94; ops. area mgr. Renal Mgmt. Inc., 1995—; mem. early intervention prevention steering com. Nat. Kidney Found., N.Y.C., 1993-95, mem. key person legis. com., 1992—; mem. Nat. Task Force on Technician Practice Del., 1995-96; elected mem. ESRD Network # 12 Med. Rev. Bd., 1994-97. Nursing editor Family Focus Patient Jour. of Nat. Kidney Found., 1995; author abstracts. Mem. quality of dialysis steering com. Nat. Kidney Found., 1995-97, bd. dirs., 1995-97. Recipient cert. for meritorious svc. Big Bros.-Big Sisters, Sedgwick County, Kans., 1982, 83, NKF Disting. Svc. award, 1996, NKF Leadership award, 1998; Am. Nephrology Nurses Assn. Nurse in Washington internship grantee, 1992. Mem. Am. Nephrology Nurses Assn. (chpt. pres.-elect 1992, chpt. chair 1993), Assn. Practitioners in Infection Control (chpt. legis. rep. 1992-95), Coun. Nephrology Nurses and Technicians (program chair ann. meeting 1992-93, nat. coun. chair 1994-96, rsch. chair 1997-98, chair 1999 spring clin. meeting, Outstanding Contbn. award 1992), Delta Sigma Chi. Republican. Roman Catholic. Avocations: cooking, travel, needlework, pian. Home: 11834 Chgo Plz # 6 Omaha NE 68154 Office: Renal Mgmt Inc 600 S Cherry St Ste 900 Denver CO 80246-1710

BARKMAN, JON ALBERT, lawyer; b. Somerset, Pa., Oct. 8, 1947; s. Blair Albert and Billie (Dietz) B.; m. Annette E. Shaulis, Dec. 1, 1983. BA, Washington and Jefferson U., 1969; JD, Duquesne U., 1975. Bar: Pa. 1975, U.S. Dist. Ct. (we. dist.) Pa. 1975, U.S. Supreme Ct. 1984, U.S. Ct. Appeals (3rd cir.) 1989. Mem. claims dept. Liberty Mut. Ins. Co., Pitts., 1969-71; dist. justice Commonwealth of Pa., Somerset, 1973-93; pvt. practice Somerset, 1975—; pres. Barkman Realty, Inc., Somerset County Settlement and Abstract Co. Inc. Advisor Com. Against Sexual Assault, Somerset, Pa., 1984; Pa. del. Nat. Spl. Ct. Judges Conv., Honolulu, 1989, Atlanta, 1991. Paul Harris fellow, 1989. Mem. ABA, ATLA, Pa. Trial Lawyers Assn., Somerset County Bar Assn. (pres. 1990—), Allegheny County Bar Assn., Elks, Rotary. Republican. Methodist. Home: 388 High St Somerset PA 15501-1301 Office: 116-118 N Center Ave Somerset PA 15501-2027

BARKOCY, ANDREW BERNARD, executive search firm executive; b. McAdoo, Pa., Feb. 22, 1932; s. John Michael and Margaret Ann (Kutchera) B.; m. Frances Rita Zaremba, May 19, 1956; children: Andrea, Allen, Gary. BS Commerce in Acctg., Rider Coll., 1963, postgrad., 1969-70. Cert. personnel cons. Acctg. mgr. McGraw Hill, Inc., N.Y.C., 1963-69; asst. contr. Transamerica DeLaval, Trenton, N.J., 1969-71; contr. glass div. Combustion Engring., Pennsauken, N.J., 1971-73; pres., owner Snelling & Snelling, Trenton, 1973-82, Princeton (N.J.) Exec. Search, 1982—; prin. Andrew B. Barkocy, Inc. Acctg. Svc., Princeton, 1963—; bd. dirs., v.p. Chambersburg Savs. and Loan, Trenton, 1976—; ethics dir. Midlantic Assn. Personnel Cons., 1995—. With USN, 1950-54, Korea. Mem. Inst. Mgmt. Accts. (pres. Trenton chpt. 1991-92, nat. dir. 1995—). Republican. Roman Catholic. Avocations: cruising, gardening, associations. Home: 49 Canal Run W Washington Crossing PA 18977-1155 Office: Princeton Exec Search PO Box 7373 Princeton NJ 08543-7373

BARKOFF, RUPERT MITCHELL, lawyer; b. New Orleans, May 7, 1948; s. Samuel and Martha (Lewis) B.; m. Susan Joyce Levitt, May 31, 1970; children: Stuart, Jeffrey, Lisa. BA in Econs. with high distinction, U. Mich., 1970, JD magna cum laude, 1973. Bar: Ga. 1973. Assoc. Kilpatrick Stockton LLP, Atlanta, 1973-80, ptnr., 1980—. Contbr. articles to profl. jours. Mem. ABA (bus. law sect., antitrust sect., forum on franchising, panelist ann. forums 1980-92, chmn. 1989-92, assoc. editor Franchise Law Jour. 1981-86), Ga. Bar Assn. (corp. and banking sect.), Atlanta Bar Assn., Phi Beta Kappa. Democrat. Jewish. Home: 5215 Vernon Springs Trl NW Atlanta GA 30327-4511 Office: Kilpatrick Stockton LLP 1100 Peachtree St NE Ste 2800 Atlanta GA 30309-4501

BARKSDALE, BARRY W., career officer. BS in History, USAF Acad., 1972; student pilot tng., Columbus AFB, Miss., 1972-73, Davis-Monthan AFB, Ariz., 1973, 81, 86; student, Squadron Officer Sch., 1981, USMC Command and Staff Coll., 1984, Air Command and Staff Coll., 1985, Air War Coll., 1988; MA in Mgmt., U. Phoenix, 1989, Army War Coll., 1991; student Phase II, Joint Profl. Mil. Edn., 1992. Commd. 2d lt. USAF, 1972, advanced through grades to brig. gen., 1997; aircraft comdr. 75th Tactical Fighter Squadron, England AFB, La., 1973-76; forward air controller tng. Patrick AFB, Fla., 1976-77; wing scheduler 51st Composite Wing, Osan Air Base, S. Korea, 1977-78; chief weapons and tactics then asst. ops. officer 549th Tactical Air Support Tng. Squadron, Patrick AFB, 1978-81; flight comdr. 355th Tactical Fighter Squadron, Myrtle Beach AFB, S.C., 1981-83; action officer then exec. officer to dep. chief plans Hdqs. Tactical Air Command, Langley AFB, Va., 1983-86; various positions Davis-Monthan AFB, 1986-90, 95-97; chief detection and monitoring br., counternarcotics ops. Joint Staff, Pentagon, Washington, 1991-93; comdr. 554th Support Group, Nellis AFB, Nev., 1993-94, 57th Ops. Group, Nellis AFB, Nev., 1994-95, 37th Tng. Wing, Lackland AFB, Tex., 1997—. Decorated Legion of Merit. Office: 37 TRW/CC 1701 Kenly Ave Ste 242 Lackland AFB TX 78236-5155

BARKSDALE, CLARENCE CAULFIELD, banker; b. St. Louis, June 4, 1932; s. Clarence M. and Elizabeth (Caulfield) B.; m. Emily Catlin Keyes, Apr. 4, 1959; children: John Keyes, Emily Shepley. AB, Brown U., 1954; postgrad., Washington U. Law Sch., St. Louis, 1957-58, Stonier Grad. Sch. Banking, Rutgers U., 1964, Columbia U. Grad. Sch. Bus., 1968; LLD (hon.), Maryville Coll., St. Louis, 1976, Westminster Coll., Fulton, Mo., 1982, St. Louis U., 1989. With Centerre Bank NA (formerly 1st Nat. Bank), St. Louis, 1958-89, asst. cashier, 1960-62, asst. v.p., 1962-64, v.p., 1964, exec. v.p., 1968-70, pres., 1970-76, chief operating officer, 1974-88, chmn. bd., chief exec. officer, 1976-88; vice chmn. Boatmen's Bancshares, Inc., St. Louis, 1988-89; vice chmn. bd. dirs. Washington U., St. Louis, 1989—; bd. dirs. SBC Comms., Inc., Bus. Response, Inc. Bd. dirs. Mo. Bot. Gardens, Alzheimers Assn., Grand Ctr. Inc., St. Louis Cmty. Found. With M.I., U.S. Army, 1954-57. Mem. St. Louis Club, St. Louis Country Club, Noonday Club, Bogey Club of St. Louis, Harbor Point Golf Club, Little Harbor Club), Wequetosing Golf Club (Harbor Springs, Mich.), Ocean Club, Gulfstream Golf Club (Delray Beach, Fla.), Alpha Delta Phi. Office: Washington U 7425 Forsyth Blvd Saint Louis MO 63105-2161

BARKSDALE, JAMES LOVE, communications company executive; b. Jackson, Miss., 1943; married. Grad., U. Miss., 1965. V.p. Cook Industries, Inc., 1973-79; former pres. ISD, Inc.; sr. v.p. info. systems, chief info. officer Fed. Express Corp., Memphis, 1979-83, exec. v.p., COO, 1983-92, also dir.; pres., COO McCaw Cellular Commns.; CEO AT&T Wireless Svcs. (merger McCaw Cellular Comms. and AT&T Wireless Svcs.); pres., CEO Netscape Comms. Corp., Mountain View, Calif., 1995—, also bd. dirs.; bd. dirs. 3Com Corp., @Home, Harrah's Entertainment, Robert Mondavi Winery. Office: Netscape Comms Corp 501 E Middlefield Rd Mountain View CA 94043-4042*

BARKSDALE, RHESA HAWKINS, federal judge; b. Jackson, Miss., Aug. 8, 1944; s. John Woodson Jr. and Mary Bryan (Saunders) B. BS, U.S. Mil. Acad., 1966; JD, U. Miss., 1972. Law clk. to Hon. Byron R. White U.S. Supreme Ct., 1972-73; assoc., then ptnr. Butler, Snow, O'Mara, Stevens & Cannada, Jackson, 1973-90; judge U.S. Ct. Appeals (5th cir.), Jackson, 1990—; instr. U. Miss. Sch. Law, Jackson, 1975-76, Miss. Coll. Sch. Law, Jackson, 1976. Chmn. Miss. Vietnam Vets. Leadership Program, Jackson, 1982-85; del. Rep. Nat. Conv., New Orleans, 1988; elector election of Pres. of U.S., Jackson, 1988. Capt. U.S. Army, 1966-70, Vietnam. Decorated Silver Star, Bronze Star for Valor, Purple Heart; Cross of Gallantry with silver star (Republic of Vietnam). Mem. Am. Inn of Ct. (Charles Clark chpt.), Phi Delta Phi (Nat. Grad. of Yr. 1972). Episcopalian. Office: US Ct Appeals 5th Cir James O Eastland Courthouse 245 E Capitol St Rm 200 Jackson MS 39201-2414*

BARKSDALE, RICHARD DILLON, civil engineer, educator; b. Orlando, Fla., May 2, 1938; s. William Spruill and Lucile Dillon B.; m. Bonnie Alice McClung, Nov. 16, 1962; children—Cheryl Lynn, Richelle Denise. A.S., So. Tech. Inst., Marietta, Ga., 1958; B.C.E., Ga. Inst. Tech., 1962, M.S., 1963; Ph.D., Purdue U., 1966. Registered profl. engr., Fla., Ga., S.C., N.C., Ala., Tenn., La. Asst. prof. civil engring. Ga. Inst. Tech., 1965-69, asso. prof., 1969-75, prof., 1975-95, prof. emeritus, 1995—; v.p. Soil Systems, Inc., Marietta, 1972-79, Soil Systems of the Carolina, 1976-79; spl. lectr. So. Tech. Inst., 1958-60; mem. com. longterm pavement performance Strategic Hwy. Rsch. Program. Contbr. articles in field to profl. jours. Co-pres. Briarcliff High Sch. Booster Club, 1983-84, Briarcliff High Sch. PTA, 1985-86. Recipient Ga. Engring. Soc. award, 1961; co-recipient Croda prize Instn. Highway Engrs., 1989; NSF grantee, 1966-67; rsch. fellow Brit. Sci. and Engring. Rsch. Coun., 1988. Mem. ASCE (Norman medal 1978, pres. Ga. sect. 1975-76, chmn. nat. com. structural design of roadways), Nat. Stone Assn. (prof. of yr. 1996), Appalachee Sportsman Club (pres. 1974-95), Phi Kappa Phi (pres. Ga. Tech. chpt. 1979). Republican. Baptist. Office: Ga Tech Institute Sch Civil Engring Atlanta GA 30332*

BARKSDALE-LADD, MARY ALICE, education educator; b. Roanoke, Va., Feb. 12, 1954; d. Byrd H. and Mary Anne (St. Clair) Barksdale; m. Frank L. Ladd, July 28, 1990. BA in Elem. Edn., Clemson U., 1976, MEd in Reading Edn., 1979; EdD in Curriculum and Instrn., Va. Tech., 1988. Tchr. Greenville (S.C.) Schs., 1976-81, Bedford (Va.) County Schs., 1981-83; grad. asst. Va. Tech., Blacksburg, 1983-88; prof. W.Va. U., Morgantown, 1988-94, U. South Fla., Tampa, 1994—; presenter in field. Co-editor: Jour. of Computing in Childhood Edn., 1995-97; contbr. articles to profl. jours.; reviewer publs. in field. Fulbright scholar 1995. Mem. Internat. Reading Assn. (Albert J. Harris award 1995), Fla. Reading Assn., Nat. Reading Conf., Coll. Reading Assn., Ea. Ednl. Rsch. Assn., Fulbright Assn., Phi Delta Kappa. Office: Univ South Fla Childhood/Lang Arts/Reading Dept 4202 E Fowler Ave Tampa FL 33620-9951

BARLASCINI, CORNELIUS OTTAVIO, JR., physician; b. Richmond, Va., Oct. 5, 1956; s. Cornelio O. Sr. and Gloria Stella (Massucco) B.; m. Laura Amelia Petrelli, June 22, 1991; 1 child, Louis Ernest. BA, U. Va., 1979, MD, 1983. Intern, resident and fellow Med. Coll. Va., Richmond, 1983-88; assoc. dir. Diabetes Treatment Ctr., Columbus, Ga., 1988-95; chief endocrinology sect. South Ga. Med. Ctr. Contbr.: (textbook) Drug Therapy in Emergency Medicine, 1990; contbr. articles to profl. jours.; inventor in field. Recipient Sandra Tate Russell award Va. chpt. Am. Diabetes Assn., 1988. Fellow ACP; mem. The Endocrine Soc., Phi Beta Kappa. Home: Via S Vittoria 156, 16039 Sestri Levante Levonte, Italy

BARLEY, JOHN E., state legislator; b. Lancaster, Pa., Dec. 6, 1945; m. Jane L. Reeder, 1966; children: Robert, Thomas, Susan, Cindy. Hon. doctoral degree, Thaddeus Stevens State Sch., 1997. Ptnr. Star Rock Farms, 1963—; mem. from dist. 100 Pa. Ho. of Reps., 1984—, past mem. local govt. com., agr. and rural affairs com., consumer affairs com., conservation com., chmn. house rep. campaign com., caucus sec., 1990—, chmn. majority appropriations, 1997—; chmn. Pa. Ag Reps., 1988-91; chief fundraiser House Rep. Campaign Com.; mem. Commonwealth Nat. Bank, Lancaster Ctr. Adv. Bd., 1986—, bd. dirs. agrl. loan divsn., 1982-85. Mem. Lancaster County Rep. Com., 1976—; mem. Pa. Agr. Rep., 1978, chmn., 1988; trustee Evangelical Sch. Theology, 1985—, Heritage Ctr. Mus. Lancaster County, Heart to Heart Pregnancy Ctr. Recipient Master Farmer award Pa. Agrl. Extension Svc., 1978, Guardian of Small Bus. award Nat. Fedn. Ind. Bus., 1997; Named Outstanding Young Farmer Am. Jaycees, 1979. Mem. Lancaster C. of C. and Industry, Quarryville Area C. of C. Address: Po Box 202020 Harrisburg PA 17120-2020*

BARLEY, LINDA R., health education and gerontology educator; b. Chgo., Apr. 16, 1947; d. Richard Theodore Swindell and Susanne Viviane Hedges; m. Kohen-Iraqui, May 10, 1975 (div. July 1979). BA, St. Francis Coll., Bklyn., 1973; MS, Hunter Coll., 1975; EdD, Columbia U., 1980. Elem. tchr. Sacred Hearts Jesus/Mary, Bklyn., 1968-72; dept. head Queens (N.Y.) Hosp. Ctr., 1972-74, Governeur Hosp., N.Y.C., 1974-76; clin. adminstr. Mary Immaculate Hosp., Queens, 1976-81; prof. York Coll., Queens, 1981-96, acad. dean, 1991-96, prof, dept. chair, 1996—; mem. adv. bd. Mary Immaculate Hosp., Queens, 1981-90; pres. SEQCOAS, Inc., Queens, 1974-81. Co-author, editor SAGE Newsletter, 1986-88; contbr. articles to profl. jours. Bd. dirs. AIDS Ctr. Queens, Forest Hills, N.Y., 1990-96. Mem. APHA, Nat. Coun. Aging, Am. Alliance. Democrat. Roman Catholic. Avocations: Aikido, science fiction and fantasy, opera, dance. E-mail: barley@ycvax.york.cuny.edu. Office: York Coll CUNY 94-20 Guy R Brewer Blvd Jamaica NY 11451

BARLIANT, RONALD, federal judge; b. Chgo., Aug. 25, 1945; s. Lois I. Barliant; children: Claire, Anne. BA in History, Roosevelt U., Chgo., 1966; postgrad., Northwestern U., Chgo., 1966-67; JD, Stanford U., 1969. Bar: Ill. 1969, U.S. Dist. Ct. (no. dist.) Ill., U.S. Ct. Appeals (7th cir.). VISTA vol., staff atty. Cook County Legal Assistance Found., Chgo., 1969-72; assoc. Miller, Shakman, Hamilton and Kurtzon, Chgo., 1972-76, ptnr., 1976-88; judge U.S. Bankruptcy Ct. (no. dist.) Ill., Chgo., 1988—; adj. prof. debtor-creditor rels. John Marshall Law Sch., 1991-92; bd. dirs. Cook County Legal Assistance Found., 1975-82; gen. counsel Chgo. Coun. Lawyers, 1983-86. Mem. Fed. Bar Assn. (bd. dirs. 1992-94), Nat. Conf. Bankruptcy Judges (bd. govs. 1997—). Avocations: opera, theatre, golf, Cubs baseball. Office: US Bankruptcy Ct 219 S Dearborn St Rm 738 Chicago IL 60604-1702*

BARLOW, ANNE LOUISE, pediatrician, medical research administrator; b. Skipton-in-Craven, Eng., Jan. 28, 1925; came to U.S., 1951, naturalized, 1954; m. Howard Cadwell, May 19, 1951; children: Barbara Anne, John James Stewart; m. Alastair Ramsay, Dec. 19, 1969. MB BS, London (Royal Free Hosp.) Sch. Medicine for Women, U. London, 1948; diploma in child health, Royal Colls. Eng., 1950; MPH with honors, Yale U., 1952. House physician North Lonsdale Hosp., Barrow-in-Furness, Lancashire, Eng., 1948-49; house surgeon Royal Infirmary (Glasgow), Scotland, 1949; resident to profl. unit of child health Royal Hosp. for Sick Children, Glasgow, 1949-50; jr. hosp. med. officer Knightswood Infectious Diseases Hosp., Glasgow, 1950; Rotary Found. Internat. fellow U. Toronto Med. Sch., Ont., Can., 1950-51; research asst. Yale U. Sch. Pub. Health, New Haven, 1952-53; clinic physician in cancer prevention Arlington, Va., part-time 1953-54; resident, staff physician William H. Maybury Tb Sanatorium, Northville, Mich., 1954-

56; research dir. Detroit Feeding Study with the Detroit City Health Dept., 1954-56; research asst., instr. sch. health U. Pitts. Grad. Sch. Pub. Health, 1957-62; pvt. practice medicine specializing in pediatrics Pitts., 1959-62; mem. courtesy staff St. Margaret Hosp., Pitts., 1959-62; research assoc. Tice Lab for Tb research, Cook County Hosp., Chgo., Ill., 1962; med. writer product info. Abbott Labs., North Chicago, Ill., 1963-66, med. specialist antibiotic medicine, 1966-68; mgr. clin. devel. pharm. products div. Abbott Lab., North Chicago, Ill., 1968-71, asst. med. dir., 1971-72, mgr. parenteral nutrition hosp. products div., 1972-73, med. dir., 1973-80, v.p. med. affairs hosp. products div., 1980-84; pres. Albamed, Inc., 1985—; asst. clin. prof. Med.Coll. Pa., 1988; cons. maternal, child and sch. health, dir. well baby clinic Lake County (Ill.) Health Dept., 1963-76; pres. Tb Sanatorium Bd. Lake County Health Dept., Ill., 1976-79; dir., pres. Lake County Bd. Health, 1979-82; health officer Village of North Barrington, Ill., 1964-67; physician-adviser Head Start Lake County Community Action Project, 1970-84; chmn. profl. adv. com. Lake County Health Dept., 1972-84; preceptor Pediatric Nurse Assoc. Program. Contbr. articles on maternal and infant care, pediatrics and nutrition; patentee high calorie solution of low molecular weight glucose polymer mixtures useful for intravenous adminstrn. Bd. dirs. Heart Assn. of Lake County, 1979-84, chmn. nutrition com. 1980-82, v.p. 1982-83, pres., 1983-84; mem. sch. bd. Grant Twp. Cmty. H.S. (Ill. Dist. 124), 1973-79; sec. to governing bd. Spl. Edn. Dist. of Lake County, 1977-79; assoc. Nat. Coll. Edn., Evanston, Ill., 1976-84; chmn. Am. Women's Hosp. Svc., 1986-95; vol. Guardian ad Litem, 1989—. Recipient Charlotte Danstrom award for excellence Women in Mgmt., 1984, award of merit for outstanding contns. to pub. health Ill. Pub. Health Assn., 1975; recipient award of merit for outstanding community service to Lake County Community Action Project, 1976, award for outstanding and dedicated service as pres Lake County TB Sanatorium Bd., 1979, TWIN award YWCA, 1983. Mem. AAAS, NOW, LWV, AMA (chair sr. physician adv. com. 1996—), Am. Med. Women's Assn. (councilor for orgn. and mgmt. 1977-79, treas. 1980, 1st v.p. 1981, pres. 1983, chair found. 1992-95, Elizabeth Blackwell medal 1992), Fla. Med. Assn. (vice chair Internat. Med. Grad. sect. 1998—), Med. Women's Internat. Assn. (v.p. N. Am. 1993-95). Home and Office: 20 S 19th St Fernandina Beach FL 32034-2767

BARLOW, AUGUST RALPH, JR., minister; b. Sewickley, Pa., Oct. 9, 1934; s. August Ralph and Kathryn Viola (Adams) B.; m. Elizabeth Evone Anderson, Aug. 27, 1960; children: Paul Martin, Andrew Ralph, Ann Kathryn. BA, Haverford Coll., 1956; BD, Yale U., 1959, STM, 1964. Ordained to ministry Meth. Ch., 1959. Pastor Fox Chapel Meth. Ch., Pitts., 1959-60, Butler St. Meth. Ch., Pitts., 1961-62, Lawrenceville Cmty. Ch., Pitts., 1962-63; intern Cleve. Inner City Protestant Parish, 1960-61; from tchg. min. to pastor Beneficent Congl. Ch., Providence, 1964-97, pastor emeritus, 1997—; bd. govs. Beneficent House, 1970-97, Beneficent Commons Housing, Providence, sr. min., devel. team, 1991-95; bd. dirs. Pastoral Counseling Ctr., Greater Providence, v.p., 1984-86, pres., 1995-97; pres. Steere House, Providence, 1983-86, past bd. dirs.; bd. dirs. Home Health Svcs. of R.I., 1986-93, chmn. ch. in soc. com., 1985-86; mem. R.I. Conf., United Ch. of Christ, 1964—, mem. com. on ministry, 1981-83, past bd. dirs.; mem. urban divsn. R.I. Coun. Chs., 1979-82. Editor-in-chief: (jour.) Expanding Horizons, 1996—; contbr. articles to Christian Century, editorials, commentaries to Providence Jour.-Bull., The East Bay Window, Expanding Horizons, Religious Broadcasting Sta. WEAN, 1964-87. Adv. coun. Providence Pub. Libr., 1968-71; bd. dirs. Mouthpiece Coffee House, Providence, 1969-75, pres., 1974-75; bd. dirs. Citizens United Renewal Enterprises, 1972-77; alumni class agt. for scholarship funds Haverford Coll. and Yale U. Div. Sch., 1979-95; active R.I. Hosp. Corp., 1980-95. Rsch. fellow Yale U. Div. Sch., 1979; recipient Alumnal Bd. award Yale U. Div. Sch., 1997. Mem. Providence Intown Chs. Assn., Mins. Assn. R.I. Conf. United Ch. of Christ, Dodeka Symposium, Rotary (trustee Rotary Charities Found. 1977-82, Paul Harris fellow), Beneficent Order of Spike, Phi Beta Kappa. Democrat. Home and Office: 103 Angell Rd Lincoln RI 02865-4710

BARLOW, F(RANK) JOHN, mechanical contracting company executive; b. Milw., July 12, 1914; s. Ernest A. and Alice E. (Norton) B.; m. Dorothy M. Marx, Oct. 13, 1935; children: Joyce D., Bonnie M., Joan C., Grace M., Jacqueline S., Wendy J., Terri L., Alice M. BS in Mech. Engring., U. Wis., 1937; DSc (hon.), 1994. Engr. Buffalo Forge Co., 1937-40; sales engr. Buffalo Forge Co., Chgo., 1940-42; plant engr. A.O. Smith Corp., Milw., 1942-44; chief mech. engr. Western Condensing Co., Appleton, Wis., 1944-46, profl. mgr., 1946-53; owner Azco, Inc., Appleton, Wis., 1953—, pres., 1959-80, chmn. bd., 1959—; chmn. bd. Azco Group Ltd., 1982—; pres. Sanco, Ltd., Appleton, 1959—, Baldwin Barlow Corp., Appleton, 1965-83, The Downey Co., Milw.; pres. Ave. Dept. Inc., Appleton, Inc.; treas. Winagamie Corp., 1965-88; bd. dirs. Beta Color Inc., First Nat. Bank Appleton; dir., mem. exec. com. Air Wis., 1965-92; chmn. bd. dirs. Transpace Carriers, 1986-88. County chmn. March of Dimes, 1957—, state co-chmn., 1958; industry chmn. com. fund dir., 1968-69; bd. dirs. Nat. Cert. Pipe Welding Bur., Cmty. Found., 1986—, Beth Color Inc., 1991—, Bergstrom-Mahler Mus., 1993-95 (also pres. 1995); trustee Azco Employees Profit Sharing Trust, Wis. Acad. Scis., Arts & Letters, 1988—; pres. Appleton Devel. Coun., 1983-86; mem. adv. bd. Mich. Tech. U. Seaman Mus., 1995. Recipient Industry award Wis. Soc. Profl. Engrs., 1967, Cert. Commendation Gov. Tommy Thompson, 1998. Mem. CAP, ASCE, Mech. Contractors Assn. Am. (nat. dir., pres. 1974-75, disting. service award 1982), Mech. Contractors Assn. Wis. (pres.), Wis. Soc. Profl. Engrs. (chpt. pres. 1968—), Am. Soc. Heating, Refrigerations and Airconditioning Engrs., Appleton C. of C., Flying Engrs., Nat. Soc. Profl. Engrs. Clubs: Butte Des Morts Golf (dir., pres. 1961, 62). Lodges: Masons, Shriners, Rotary, Elks (past exalted ruler). Home: 178 River Dr Appleton WI 54915-1213 Address: PO Box 177 Appleton WI 54912-0177

BARLOW, JEAN, art educator, artist; b. L.A., Dec. 13, 1940; d. Sydney R. and Rose (Ballen) Barlow; m. Gordon M. Nunes, Sept. 21, 1973 (dec. Dec. 1991). BA cum laude, UCLA, 1963, MA, 1965, MFA, 1968. Tchg. assoc. UCLA, 1964-68; instr. Univ. Adult Sch., L.A., 1966-70; lectr. Calif. State U., Long beach, 1967-69; instr. Beverly Hills (Calif.) Adult Edn., 1969, East L.A. Jr. Coll., 1969-70; lectr. UCLA, 1986, instr. ext. divsn., 1969-96; instr. Santa Monica (Calif.) City Coll., 1969—; mentor program mem. Santa Monica City Coll., 1989-90; pvt. art tchr., L.A., 1970-96; cons. in field. One woman shows include Jenet Gallery, L.A., 1965, Santa Monica City Coll., 1974; exhibited in group shows at So. Calif., 1965, Orlando Gallery, L.A., 1967, 68, Santa Monica City Coll., 1974, 78, 80, 87, 88, 91, 94, 95, Living Room Gallery, 1997, Bergemot Station T2, 1999; invitational pastel drawing Scripps Coll., So. Calif., 1965. Avocations: photography, home landscape and decoration, creative cooking, writing.

BARLOW, JIM B., newspaper columnist; b. Port Arthur, Tex., Aug. 19, 1936; s. Joseph B. and Goldie (Johnson) B.; m. Karleen Ann Smith, Aug. 24, 1968 (div. Jan. 1974); 1 child, Samantha Lynn; m. Susan Ann Bischoff, June 20, 1975. BA, U. North Tex., Denton, 1972. Newsman KPAC-TV, Port Arthur, Tex., 1959-61; news dir. KPNG-Radio, Port Neches, Tex., 1962-63; reporter Beaumont (Tex.) Enterprise, 1963-64, Denton Record-Chronicle, 1964-66; asst. city mgr. City of Denton, 1967; staff writer U. North Tex., Denton, 1968; newsman AP, Dallas-Houston, 1968-75; dir. info. svcs. Houston Ind. Sch. Dist., 1975-77; reporter Houston Chronicle, 1977-87, columnist, 1987—. Co-author: Big Town, Big Money, 1974. With U.S. Army, 1956-59. Mem. Soc. Am. Bus. Editors and Writers. Avocations: reading, cooking, exercise. Home: # 112 2929 Buffalo Speedway Houston TX 77098 Office: 801 Texas Ave Houston TX 77002-2906

BARLOW, JOHN PERRY, writer; b. Wyo., 1947; m. Elaine Parker (div. 1996); children: Leah Justine, Anna Winter, Amelia. Degree in comparative religion with honors, Wesleyan U., 1969. Mgr. Bar Cross Land and Livestock Co., Cora, Wyo., 1971-88; co-founder, vice chmn. Electronic Frontier Found., 1990—; bd. dirs. WELL; cons. Vanguard Group of CSC, Global Bus. Network. Contbg. editor numerous publs. including Comm. of the ACM, Microtimes, Mondo 2000; contbg. writer Wired; co-writer songs for The Grateful Dead, 1971—. Berkman fellow Harvard Law Sch., 1998—; named Thomas Jefferson of Cyberspace, Yahoo Mag. Internet Life, 1996, one of 25 Most Influential People in Fin. Svcs., Future Banker Mag., 1999,. E-mail: Barlow@EFF.org. Office: Electronic Frontier Foundation 168 S Franklin Pinedale WY 82941-1009*

BARLOW, JOHN SUTTON, neurophysiologist, electroencephalographer, lexicographer; b. Raleigh, N.C., June 10, 1925; s. David Henry and Anne Mary (Sutton) B.; m. Sibylle E. Jahrreiss, Aug. 5, 1950; children: Thomas Walter, Robert Sutton, Lisa Katharine. BS, U. N.C., 1944, MS, 1948; MD, Harvard U., 1953. Diplomate Am. Bd. Cert. EEG. Clin. and rsch. fellow, asst. resident in neurology Mass. Gen. Hosp., Boston, 1953-57; clin. and rsch. fellow Harvard Med. Sch., Boston, 1953-57; rsch. assoc. in elec. engring. MIT, Cambridge, 1954-64, rsch. affiliate Rsch. Lab. of Electronics, 1964—; asst. neurology Mass. Gen. Hosp., Boston, 1957-61, neurophysiologist neurology svc., 1961—; rsch. assoc. neurology Harvard Med. Sch., Boston, 1961-69, prin. rsch. assoc., 1969-78, sr. rsch. assoc. neurophysiology, 1979—; mem. neurology study sect. NIH, Bethesda, Md., 1966-70; mem. rev. panel on neurol. devices FDA, Washington, 1974-76; cons. dept. neurology VA Med. Ctr., Boston, 1979-89, part-time staff, 1989-98; cons. dept. neurology New Eng. Med. Ctr., Boston, 1979—. Author: The Electroencephalogram: Its Patterns and Origins, 1993, A Chinese-Russian-English Dictionary, 1995; editor: (with Karenina Kollmar-Paulenz) Otto Ottonovich Rosenberg and his Contribution to Buddhology in Russia, 1998; cons. editor EEG Clin. Neurophysiology, 1970-86; translator/editor books from the Russian, Czech and Chinese; contbr. articles and revs. to profl. jours. Served from ensign to lt. (j.g.) USN, 1944-46. Recipient Rsch. Career Devel. award NIH, 1962-71, Sr. Scientist award Alexander von Humboldt Found., Göttingen, Germany, 1979, Sr. Scientist Exch. award NAS, U.S.A./USSR Acad. Scis., Moscow, 1982, 83, 88; rsch. grantee NIH, 1962-88; Fogarty Internat. fellow, 1979. Mem. Internat. Brain Rsch. Orgn., Am. EEG Soc. (pres. 1975-76), Am. Neurol. Assn., Am. Acad. Neurology, Soc. Neurosci., Am. Geophys. Union, Ea. Assn. EEG (pres. 1971-72), Assn. Asian Studies, European Assn. Chinese Studies, Dictionary Soc. North Am. Avocations: music, rail travel, foreign languages, international relations.

BARLOW, KENNETH JAMES, management consultant; b. St. Catherines, Ont., Can., July 18, 1932; s. Percy Joseph and Alice Maude (Metcalf) B.; m. Iris Isabel Isnor, Dec. 21, 1957 (div. 1990); children: Richard, Catherine, Brian. BSc, U. B.C., Vancouver, Can., 1962; MBA, U. Western Ont., 1964. Constrn. supr. to dir. various orgns., Eng. and Can., 1947-58; sr. cons. Urwick Currie and Ptnrs., Toronto, Ont., 1964-69; pres. Barlow Assocs. Inc., Toronto, 1969—; keynote spkr., lectr., seminar leader N.Am., Africa, Europe, Australasia. Author: Professional Management for Consulting Engineers, 1972, Internal Transfer of Ownership, 1986; cons. editor Can. Cons. Engr. mag., 1982-91; contbr. numerous articles to profl. jours. Mem. ASCE, Assn. Profl. Engrs. Ont., Inst. Cert. Mgmt. Cons. Ont., Profl. Services Mgmt. Assn. Office: Barlow Assocs Inc 1155 North Service Rd W Ste 11, Oakville, ON Canada L6M 3E3

BARLOW, LARRY S., federal agency administrator; b. San Diego, Oct. 2, 1948. BA, U. Puget Sound, 1970; MBA, Troy State U., 1975. Dir. adminstrn. Dept. Def., Washington, 1998—. Office: Dept Def Under Sec Acquisition and Tech 3000 Defense Pentagon Washington DC 20301

BARLOW, MATTHEW BLAISE JOSEPH, merchant banker; b. Carlisle, Eng., Jan. 30, 1935; s. John Barlow and Elsie (Butler) Corner-Barlow; m. Mary Alice Jenkins, Aug. 15, 1964; 1 child, Mark Gerard. BA, Ealing Coll.; BSc, U. Petroleum and Minerals Dharan, Saudi Arabia, 1978; BS, U. Oriental Africa Studies, Lagos, Nigeria, 1981; MSc, Aston U., Birmingham, Eng., 1986. FBIM, FAAI. Dep. mng. dir. fin. and adminstrn. Nat. Bank of Nigeria, Lagos, 1979-82; project mgr. Chemsult, Sacramento, Calif., and Johannesburg, Republic of South Africa, 1978-91; loss leaders rep. Arabian Oil, Saudi Arabia, 1977-97; from asst. supt. to supt. Complant Internat., Saudi Arabia, 1989—; assoc. asst. Life Ins. Pension Svc., Gloucester, Eng., 1979—; gen. mgr. Western Exec., Cheltenham, Eng., 1986—; acct. marine aviation Tops, Gloucester, 1988—; tech. mgr. Wescott Freight, Gloucestershire, 1990—; chartered act. PES Middlesbrough, Lucern, Switzerland and Dhahran, Boston, 1977-97. With U.K. mil., 1953-55. Fellow Inst. Acctg., Inst. Cost and Mgmt. Acctg., Am. Inst. Cost and Consulting Engrs., British Inst. Mgmt., Royal Inst. British Architects, Inst. Internat. Accts.; mem. N.Y. Acad. Scis. Home: 10 Vectis Close Tudor Park Estates, Lincoln Hills Rd, Ross on Wye Herefordshire HR9 5LR, England also: Savoi Arabea Social Inv 360 B St PO Box 500 Biggs CA 95917

BARLOW, NADINE GAIL, planetary geoscientist; b. La Jolla, Calif., Nov. 9, 1958; d. Nathan Dale and Marcella Isabel (Menken) B. BS, U. Ariz., 1980, PhD, 1987. Instr., planetarium lectr. Palomar Coll., San Marcos, Calif., 1982; grad. rsch. asst. U. Ariz., Tucson, 1982-87; postdoctoral fellow Lunar and Planetary Inst., Houston, 1987-89; NRC assoc. NASA/Johnson Space Ctr., Houston, 1989-91, vis. scientist, 1991-92, support scientist exploration programs office, 1992; vis. scientist Lunar and Planetary Inst., Houston, 1992-95; assoc. prof. U. Houston, Clear Lake, 1991-95; pres. Minerva Rsch. Enterprises, 1995—; asst. prof. astronomy, dir. Robinson Obs. U. Ctrl. Fla., Orlando, 1996—; co-dir. intern program Lunar and Planetary Inst., 1988-89. Editor (slide set) A Guide to Martian Impact Craters, 1988; assoc. editor Encyclopedia of Earth Sciences, 1996; contbr. articles to profl. jours. Named among Outstanding Women and Ethnic Minorities Engaged in Sci. and Engring., Lawrence Livermore Nat. Lab., 1991. Mem. AAUW (pres. Clear Lake chpt. 1991-93, program v.p. 1993-95, v.p. interbr. coun. 1990-91, chmn. Tex. task force on women and girls in sci. and math. 1991-92, dir. state pub. ploicy 1991-94, Tex. Woman of Yr. 1992, mem. pub. policy com. 1994-95, chmn. steering com. Tex. edln. equity 1994-95), Am. Astron. Soc. (pres. officer divsn. planetary scis. 1993—, status of women in astronomy com. 1987-90, 1995-98), Meteoritical Soc., Am. Geophys. Union, Geol. Soc. Am. (planetary geology divsn. nominating com. 1996-97). Achievements include research and compilation of primary data source on 42,283 impact craters on Mars; identification of possible source craters for Martian meteorites. Office: U Ctrl Fla Dept of Physics Orlando FL 32816

BARLOW, WALTER GREENWOOD, public opinion analyst, management consultant; b. Liverpool, Eng., Sept. 10, 1917; came to U.S., 1920, naturalized, 1928; s. Walter and Sarah Ellen (Greenwood); m. Hanna Hansen, 1951 (dec. 1974); children: Eric, Francine, Deborah, Alison; m. Joan K. Frahm, June 21, 1980 (div. 1989). B.A., Cornell U., 1939. Reporter Washington Daily News, 1940; mem. editorial staff Time mag., 1941; with Opinion Rsch. Corp., 1946-65, pres., 1960-65; pres. Howard Chase Assocs., Inc., N.Y.C., 1965-68; founder Rsch. Strategies Corp., N.Y.C., 1965, pres., 1966—; bd. dirs. A.D. Publs. (formerly Presbyn. Life Mag.), 1968-72, pres., 1970-72; pres. Crawford House, Inc., 1988-90. Mem. N.J. Bd. Pub. Welfare, 1966-80, vice chmn., 1973-80; mem. adv. coun. Electric Power Rsch. Inst., 1977-81; trustee Cornell U., 1968-75, univ. coun., 1968—; bd. dirs. support agy. United Presbyn. Ch. in U.S.A., 1973-80; bd. dirs. Renewal Found., 1990—, pres., 1995; bd. dirs. Family Svc. Assn. Am., 1958-69, v.p., 1964-67, pres., 1967-69; commr. Middle States Assn. Colls. and Schs., 1982-88. Maj. AUS, 1941-46, ETO. Decorated Bronze Star. Mem. Am. Assn. Pub. Opinion Rsch., Phi Beta Kappa, Phi Kappa Phi. Presbyterian. Clubs: Cornell of N.Y., Nassau (Princeton, N.J.). Office: 217 Wall St Princeton NJ 08540-1512

BARLOW, WALTER JOHN, JR., utilities executive, consultant; b. Bayonne, N.J., Dec. 9, 1948; s. Walter John and Stasia Mary (Ryngiewicz) B.; m. Rebecca Louise Gay, Mar. 19, 1977; children: Jessica, Jennifer, Jan-Michael, Jarrod. BA, St. Anselm's Coll., 1970. Tech. dir. A.C. Lawrence Leather Co., South Paris, Maine, 1970-85, Pownal Tanning, North Pownal, Vt., 1985-88, Engring. Industries, Norway, Maine, 1988-91; gen. mgr. Paris Utility Dept., South Paris, 1991—. Chmn. Paris Budget Commn., South Paris, Maine, 1993—; vice chmn. Paris Planning Bd., South Paris, 1994—; chair bd. trustees Paris Utility Dist., South Paris, 1976-79. Mem. Am. Waterworks Assn., Maine Rural Water Assn. (Best Tasting Drinking Water 1993, 97, Merit of Honor 1996), Maine Water Utilities Assn., Maine Backflow Prevention Assn. (pres. 1997-98), New Eng. Tanners Club (pres. 1982), New Eng. Waterworks Assn., KC (grand knight 1968, award 1974). Republican. Roman Catholic. Avocations: fishing, gardening, youth basketball, lector, hiking. Office: Paris Utility Dist 65 Park St PO Box 154 South Paris ME 04281-0154

BARLOW, WILLIAM PUSEY, JR., accountant; b. Oakland, Calif., Feb. 11, 1934; s. William P. and Muriel (Block) B.; student Calif. Inst. Tech., 1952-54. AB in Econs., U. Calif.-Berkeley, 1956. CPA, Calif. Acct. Barlow, Davis & Wood, San Francisco, 1960-72, ptnr., 1964-72; ptnr., J.K. Lasser & Co., 1972-77, Touche Ross & Co., San Francisco, 1977-78; self employed acct., 1978-89; ptnr. Barlow & Hughan, 1990—. Co-author: Collectible Books: Some New Paths, 1979, The Grolier Club, 1884-1984, 1984; editor: Book Catalogues: Their Varieties and Uses, 2d edit., 1986, Officially Sealed Notes, 1996—; contbr. articles to profl. jours. Fellow Gleeson Libr. Assocs., 1969, pres., 1971-74; mem. Coun. Friends Bancroft Libr., 1971-98, chmn., 1974-79; bd. dirs. Oakland Ballet, 1982—, pres. 1986-89, chmn. 1995-98. Recipient Sir Thomas More medal Gleeson Libr. Assocs., 1989; named to Water Ski Hall of Fame, 1993. Mem. Am. Water Ski Assn. (bd. dirs., regional chmn. 1959-63, pres. 1963-66, chmn. bd. 1966-69, 77-79, hon. v.p. 1969—), Internat. Water Ski Fedn. (exec. bd. 1961-71, 75-78), Bibliog. Soc. Am. (coun. 1986-92, pres. 1992-96), Grolier Club (N.Y.C.), Roxburghe Club (San Francisco), Book of Calif. Club (bd. dirs. 1963-76, pres. 1968-69, treas. 1971-83). Home: 1474 Hampel St Oakland CA 94602-1346 Office: 449 15th St Oakland CA 94612-2821

BARMACK, NEAL HERBERT, neuroscientist; b. N.Y.C., Aug. 23, 1942; married, 1964; 2 children. BS, U. Mich., 1963; PhD, U. Rochester, 1970. Asst. lectr. psychology U. Rochester, 1968-69, rsch. assoc. to sr. rsch. assoc. neurophysiology dept ophthalmology, 1969-75, assoc. scientist, 1975-80; sr. scientist Neurol. Sci. Inst., Good Samaritan Hosp. and Med. Ctr., Portland, 1980-81; assoc. prof. biol. sci. U. Conn., 1981-82; sr. scientist, chmn. R.S. Dow Neurol. Sci. Inst., 1990-96; sr. scientist Neurol. Sci. Inst. Neurol. Sci. Inst., Portland, 1998—. Mem. Soc. Neurosci., Am. Physiol. Soc., Internat. Brain Rsch. Orgn., Nat. Eye Inst. Achievements include research in Neural control of eye movements; plasticity of reflexive eye movements; the cellular and biochemical basis of cerebellar modulation of reflex function. Office: Neurol Sci Inst 1120 NW 20th Ave Portland OR 97209*

BARMAN, ROBERT JOHN, home electronics company executive; b. Glendale, Calif.; s. Robert Grant and Geraldine (Howe) B.; m. Jean Ann Crane, June 19, 1965; children: John Robert, Jeffrey Wynn. BS in Mktg., Calif. State U., L.A., 1965. Sales coord. Teledyne Packard Bell, L.A., 1965-67; dist. mgr. Teledyne Packard Bell, Fresno, L.A., 1968-71; regional sales mgr. Teledyne Packard Bell, Boston, 1971-73; major accounts sales mgr. Quasar Co., L.A., 1973-75, regional sales mgr., 1975-76, sales mgr., 1976-77, zone mgr., 1985—; v.p., br. mgr. Quasar Co., Seattle, 1977-84; gen. mgr. Matsushita, L.A., 1985-95; mem. mgmt. com. Matsushita Elec. Corp. of Am. West; mem. distbg. coun. Quasar Co., Chgo.; mgr. spl. markets, region mgr., gen. mgr. Panasonic Co. West, 1995—. Bd. dirs. Irvine (Calif.) Aquatics Swim Team, Bellevue (Wash.) Athletic Club Swim Team. Office: Panasonic Co W 6550 Katella Ave Cypress CA 90630-5102

BARMANN, BERNARD CHARLES, SR., lawyer; b. Maryville, Mo., Aug. 5, 1932; s. Charles Anselm and Veronica Rose (Fisher) B.; m. Beatrice Margaret Murphy, Sept. 27, 1965; children: Bernard Charles Jr., Brigit. PhD, Stanford U., 1966; JD, U. San Diego, 1974; MPA, Calif. State U., Bakersfield. Bar: Calif. 1974, U.S. Dist. Ct. (so. dist.) Calif. 1974, U.S. Dist. Ct. (ea. dist.) Calif. 1978, U.S. Ct. Appeals (9th cir.) 1984, U.S. Supreme Ct. Asst. prof. Ohio State U., Columbus, 1966-69, U. Toronto, Ont., Can., 1969-71; dep. county counsel Kern County, Bakersfield, Calif., 1974-85; county counsel Kern County, Bakersfield, 1985—; adj. prof. Calif. State U., Bakersfield, 1986—. Editor: The Bottom Line, 1991-93, contbr. articles to profl. jours. Mem. exec. bd. So. Sierra coun. Boy Scouts Am., Bakersfield, 1986—; bd. dirs. Kern County Acad. Decathlon, Bakersfield, 1988—. Danforth Found. fellow, 1963-65; grantee Fulbright Found., 1963-65. Mem. Calif. Bar Assn. (law practice mgmt. sect. exec. com.), County Counsel Assn. Calif. (bd. dirs. 1990—, chair 1993-94), Rotary. Avocations: golf, skiing, travel, photography. Office: Kern County Office of County Counsel 1115 Truxtun Ave Bakersfield CA 93301-4639

BARMANN, LAWRENCE FRANCIS, history educator; b. Maryville, Mo., June 9, 1932; s. Francis Lawrence and Clary Weber (LaMar) B. B.A., St. Louis U., 1956, Ph.L., 1957, S.T.L., 1964; M.A., Fordham U., 1960; post-grad., Princeton, 1965-66; Ph.D., Cambridge U., Eng., 1970. Tchr. history St. Louis U. High Sch., 1957-59; asst. prof. history St. Louis U., 1970-73, asso. prof., 1973-78, prof., 1978—, asst. dir. Am. Studies Program, 1981-83; dir. Am. Studies Program, 1983-88; prof. theol. studies St. Louis U., 1996—. Author: Newman at St. Mary's, 1962, Baron Friedrich von Hügel and the Modernist Crisis in England, 1972, The Letters of Baron Friedrich von Hügel and Professor Norman Kemp Smith, 1982; contbr. articles profl. jours. Recipient award Mellon Faculty Devel. Fund, 1987, 92, 94; rsch. grantee Am. Philos. Soc. PHila., 1971, Beaumont Fund, 1977, 82; Danforth assoc., 1978—. Mem. Am. Acad. Religion, Cambridge Soc. (founding 1977), Am. Cath. Hist. Assn., Phi Beta Kappa. Home: The Lindell Ter 12-A 4501 Lindell Blvd Saint Louis MO 63108-2038 Office: 221 N Grand Blvd Saint Louis MO 63103-2006 *I have found for myself that the meaning of life is the joy of continuous discovery in unending intellectual, emotional and spiritual growth, and the satisfaction which comes from sharing my vision and concerns with the young people who will lead the next generation.*

BARMETTLER, JOSEPH JOHN, lawyer; b. Omaha, Sept. 10, 1933; s. William Thomas and Dorothy Lucy (Flynn) B.; m. Jeanne Waller, June 21, 1958; children: Joseph Jr., Gregory, Richard, Katie, Peggy Carbullido, Timothy, Michael. BSC, Creighton U., 1956, JD, 1959. Bar: Nebr. 1959, U.S. Dist. Ct. Nebr. 1959, U.S. Ct. Appeals (8th cir.) 1963, U.S. Ct. Claims 1963. Assoc. Fitzgerald, Hamer, Brown & Leahy, Omaha, 1959-64; ptnr. Fitzgerald, Schorr, Barmettler & Brennan, Omaha, 1964—, CEO, 1988—; gen. counsel Metro. Community Coll., Omaha, 1974—, Village of Boys Town, Nebr., 1991—, City of La Vista, Nebr., 1963—. Mem. devel. coun. Omaha Legal Aid Soc., 1989—; pres.'s coun. Creighton U., Omaha, 1990—. Fellow Nebr. Bar Found.; mem. Nebr. Bar Assn. (chmn. ways, means and planning com. 1993-94, ho. of dels. 1986—, chmn. budget and adminstrn. com. 1993-94), Omaha Bar Assn., Omaha Downtown Rotary (dir. 1986-89, Paul Harris fellow). Republican. Avocations: boating, golf, photography. Office: Fitzgerald Schorr Barmettler & Brennan PC Ste #1100 Woodmen Tower Omaha NE 68102

BARMORE, LEON, head basketball coach; b. Ruston, La., June 3, 1944; m. Rachel Clark; 1 child, Shannon. BS in Health and Phys. Edn., La. Tech U., 1967, MA, 1971. Head basketball coach Bastrop (La.) H.S., 1967-71, Ruston (La.) H.S., 1971-77; asst. basketball coach, assoc. head coach La. Tech U., Ruston, 1977-82, co-head basketball coach, 1982-85, head basketball coach, 1985—. Named Sun Belt Conf. Coach of Yr., 1994, Am. South Conf. Coach of Yr., 1990, Nat. Coach of Yr. U.S. Basketball Writer's Assn., 1990, State Coach of Yr. La. Sports Writer's Assn., 1990, 88, Naismith Nat. Coach of Yr., 1988, Sugar Bowl State Coach of Yr., 1988. Office: Louisiana Tech Univ Off of Head Basketball Coach Ruston LA 71272*

BARNA, ARPAD ALEX, electrical engineering consultant; b. Budapest, Hungary, Apr. 3, 1933; came to U.S., 1957; s. Sandor and Erzsebet (Markus) B. Diploma of Elec. Engring., Tech. U. Budapest, 1956; Degree of Engr., Stanford U., 1966, PhD in Elec. Engring., 1968; BA in Lit., U. Calif., Santa Cruz, 1986. Part-time grad. asst. Poly. U. Budapest, 1954-56; with Ctrl. Rsch. Inst. for Physics, Hungarian Acad. Scis., Budapest, 1956, Calif. Inst. Tech., Pasadena, 1957-61, Ransom Systems, San Pedro, Calif., 1961, U. Chgo., 1961-63, Stanford Linear Accelerator Ctr., 1963-69; assoc. prof. elec. engring. U. Hawaii, Honolulu, 1969-72; with Hewlett-Packard Labs., Palo Alto, Calif., 1972-83; pvt. elec. engring. cons. Capitola, Calif., 1966—; cons. Harshaw Chem. Co., Cleve., 1966-69, Cintra, Inc., Mountain View, Calif., 1969, Avantek, Inc., Santa Clara, 1969-72, W.W. Hansen Labs. of Physics, Stanford U., 1972-83, Audio Devel., Inc., Palo Alto, 1977, Monolithic Microsystems, Inc., Santa Cruz, Calif., 1982-84, SiScan Corp., Campbell, Calif., 1982-86, IMEC, Berkeley, Calif., 1990—; mem. faculty Calif. State U., Sacramento, 1972, UCLA, 1977, 81, Stanford U., 1981, U. Calif., Santa Cruz, 1984, 87. Reviewer IEEE Jour. Solid State Circuits, IEEE Transactions on Info. Theory, Jour. Optical Soc. Am., IEEE Electron Devices Letters, IEEE Proceedings, Jour. Applied Physics; contbr. articles to profl. jours.; author: High Speed Pulse Circuits, 1970, Operational Amplifiers, 1971, 2d edit. 1989, High Speed Pulse and Digital Techniques, 1980, VHSIC Technologies and Tradeoffs, 1981; co-author: Integrated Circuits in Digital Electronics, 1973, 2d edit. 1987, others. Mem. IEEE (sr.). Jewish. Avocation: bridge. E-mail: drarpad@aol.com. Home and Office: 750 Bay Ave Apt 305 Capitola CA 95010-2741

BARNA, DOUGLAS PETER, collection agency executive; b. Passaic, N.J., Nov. 28, 1945; s. Peter Richard and Marie (Saltamachia) B.; m. Nancy M. Viverito, Oct. 1971 (div. Oct. 1974); m. Norma Rae Hudson Fitzsimmons, July 3, 1983; stepchildren: Sherry, Michael, Gail, Laura, Kelly, Kenneth. BS in Bus. Mgmt., Fairleigh Dickinson U., 1968. Product control and accounts receivable specialist IBM Corp., Franklin Lakes, N.J., 1964-72; credit mgr. Star Graphic Sys., Clifton, N.J., 1972-74; corp. credit mgr. The Harvey Group, Woodbury, N.Y., 1975; sales exec. Contract Equity Corp., Melville, N.Y., 1976, Media Coords. Ltd., Levittown, N.Y., 1976-78; v.p. sales Valer Enterprises Inc., Bohemia, N.Y., 1978-84; pres. Douglas Equity Enterprises Ltd., Medford, N.Y., 1985—; owner Douglas Enterprises, Medford, 1985—; pres. Bulldog Devel. Inc., Patchogue, 1988-94. Mem. Comml. Law League Am., Comml. Agy. Sect., Greater Patchogue C. of C. (dir. 1987-96, treas. 1994-96), Kiwanis (bd. dirs. 1994-97, Kiwanian of Yr. 1996), Phi Gamma Pi (pres. 1967-68). Avocations: swimming, traveling, reading, gourmet foods. Home: 100 Pine Ave Flanders NY 11901-4027 Office: Nat Recovery Svcs 3241 Route 112 Bldg 2 Medford NY 11763-1411

BARNA, RICHARD ALLEN, lighting company executive, broadcasting executive; b. N.Y.C., Oct. 7, 1948; s. Raymond Alexander and Miriam (Friedman) B.; m. Eileen Maisel; children: Ross, Hayley. BA, Brown U., 1970; OPM degree, Harvard U., 1985. Program dir. WHCN Concert Network, Inc., Hartford, Conn., 1970-71; pres. ProMedia, Inc., Northvale, N.J., 1971-96; v.p. RAB Electric Mfg., Inc., Bronx, N.Y., 1976-78; pres., CEO RAB Electric Mfg., Inc., Northvale, N.J., 1978—; COO Zy Doc Techs., Happaughe, N.Y., 1997—; cons. Harvard Bus. Sch. Cmty. Ptnrs., N.Y.C., 1998—; Internet tech. cons. N.Y. Pub. Libr., 1998—. Vice pres. Banksville Fire Dept., Bedford, N.Y., 1987-94; trustee, treas. North Castle Pub. Libr., Armonk, 1991-96. With U.S. Army, 1971-77. Avocations: sailing, skiing. Office: RAB Electric Mfg 170 Ludlow Ave Northvale NJ 07647-2306

BARNABEO, SUSAN PATRICIA, lawyer; b. Plainfield, N.J., July 27, 1960; d. Austin E. and Patricia F. B. BA magna cum laude, Bucknell U., 1982; JD magna cum laude, U. Mich., 1985. Bar: N.Y. 1986, N.J. 1986. Assoc. Milbank, Tweed, Hadley & McCloy, N.Y.C., 1985-90; assoc. counsel film programming HBO, N.Y.C., 1990-93, sr. counsel film programming, 1993-95; v.p., sr. counsel film programming, 1995—. Mem. ABA, Assn. of Bar of City of N.Y. Office: 1100 Ave Of The Americas New York NY 10036-6712

BARNARD, ALLEN DONALD, lawyer; b. Williston, N.D., Feb. 22, 1944; s. Donald J. and Ruth E. (Franklin) B.; m. Andra Lynn Lebsock, Nov. 24, 1962; children: Alana, Aaron. BA in Social Scis., U. N.D., 1965; JD, U. Notre Dame, 1968. Bar: Minn. 1968, U.S. Dist. Ct. Minn. 1968, U.S. Ct. Appeals (8th cir.) 1971, U.S. Supreme Ct. 1973. Assoc. Best & Flanagan, Mpls., 1968-72, ptnr., 1972—, mng. ptnr., 1991-93; city atty. City of Golden Valley, Minn., 1988—, housing and redevel. authority atty., 1978—. Mem. ABA, Hennepin County Bar Assn., Mpls. Athletic Club, Madeline Island Yacht Club (bd. dirs. 1991-97). Avocations: sailing, skiing. Office: Best & Flanagan 4000 US Bank Pl 601 2nd Ave S Ste 4000 Minneapolis MN 55402-4331

BARNARD, ANNETTE WILLIAMSON, elementary school principal; b. Phoenix, Nov. 29, 1948; d. Water Albert and Geraldine Williamson; m. Richard W. Heinrich, Sept. 1969 (div.); 1 child, Jennifer Anne; m. Charles Jay Barnard, June 6, 1981. AA, Mesa C.C., 1979; BA in Spl. Edn., Elem. Edn., Ariz. State U., 1981, postgrad., 1989; M in Edn. Leadership, 1996, No. Ariz. U., 1996. Cert. tchr., prin., Ariz. Tchr. spl. edn. Tempe (Ariz.) Sch. Dist., 1981-83, tchr. Indian community, 1983-84; tchr. elem. sch. Kyrene Sch. Dist., Tempe, 1984-97; sch. dist. mentor coord., 1994-96; tchr. Chandler (Ariz.) Sch. Dist., 1986-89; v.p. Pendergast Elem. Sch., Phoenix, 1997-98; prin. Arredondo Elem. Sch., Tempe Sch. Dist., 1999—; chair profl. stds. and cert. com. Ariz. Bd. Edn., Phoenix, 1990-94; chair facilitator Kyrene Legis. Action Community, 1991-94; mentor Kyrene Sch. dist., 1990—; commencement spkr. Ariz. State U., 1981; design. team. mem. Quality Cert. Employee Appraisal System; speaker in field. Contbg. author: Environmental Education Compendium for Energy Resources, 1991, System of Personnel Development, 1989; contbr. articles to profl. jours. Bd. dirs. Ariz. State Rep. Caucus, Phoenix, 1990-93, precinct committeewoman, Tempe, 1990-92. Recipient Profl. Leadership award Kiwanis Club Am., Tempe, 1984; nominee to talent bank Coun. on Women's Edn. Programs U.S. Dept. Edn., 1982; named Tchr. of Yr., local newspaper, 1993. Mem. ASCD, Kyrene Edn. Assn. (chair legis. com. 1990-94), Kappa Delta Pi, Phi Kappa Phi, Phi Theta Kappa, Pi Lambda Theta. Featured in PBS Cornerstones video, 1994. Home: 3221 W Jasper Dr Chandler AZ 85226-1421

BARNARD, ARLENE, retired secondary education educator; b. Red Lion, Pa., Apr. 7, 1922; d. W. Collins and Nettie Ellen (Curran) Workinger; 1 child, Tiffany West. BS, Indiana U. of Pa., 1942; MA, San Diego State U., 1979; postgrad., Stanford U., 1983. Cert. secondary tchr., computer ctr. dir., Calif. Tchr. S.W. Jr. H.S., Sweetwater H.S. Dist., San Diego, 1968-76, tchr. 12th grade English and English lit., 1976-94; chair English dept.; gifted/talented edn. coord., 1979-83; microcomputer instr., summer 1983; Stanford U. intern, summer 1984. Recipient scholarship Stanford U. Mem. NEA, Calif. Tchrs. Assn., Sweetwater Edn. Assn., Calif. Scholarship Fedn. (advisor), Phi Delta Kappa. Home: 3334 Rio Vista Dr Bonita CA 91902-1039

BARNARD, BRUCE K., academic administrator; b. Glendale, Calif., Feb. 5, 1959; s. Thomas E. and Madelyn Newcomer B.; m. Amy Jayce Watkins, Oct. 6, 1984; children: Elizabeth, David. BA, So. Nazarene U., 1982; MEd, Boston U., 1984. Prof. Ea. Nazarene Coll., Quincy, Mass., 1985-87; dir. Colby Coll., Waterville, Maine, 1986—. Councilor City of Waterville, 1994, planner, 1999—; mem. exec. bd. Kennebec Valley Coun. Govts., Fairfield, Maine, 1999—; bd. trustees Ea. Nazarene Coll., 1997—. Republican. Avocations: skiing, golf, fly fishing. Home: 8 Park Pl Waterville ME 04901 Office: Colby Coll 5400 Mayflower Hhill Waterville ME 04901

BARNARD, CHARLES NELSON, editorial consultant, author; b. Arlington, Mass., Oct. 5, 1924; s. Charles Nelson and Mae E. (Johnson) B.; m. Diana Lee Pattison, Aug. 6, 1949 (div. Aug. 1970); children: Jennifer Lee, Rebecca, Charles Nelson, Patrick; m. Karen Louise Zakrison, Apr. 18, 1971 (div. Jan. 1987). B.J., U. Mo., 1949. Editor Dell Pub. Co., N.Y.C., 1949; assoc. editor True mag., Fawcett Publs., N.Y.C., 1949-54, mng. editor, 1954-63; sr. editor Sat. Evening Post, N.Y.C., 1964-65; exec. editor True Mag., 1965-67, editor, 1968-70; travel editor Modern Maturity, publ. of Am. Assn. Ret. Persons; editorial cons., freelance writer, 1971—. Author: The Winter People, 1973, 20,000 Alarms, 1974, I Drank the Water Everywhere, 1975, The Money Pit, 1976, It Was a Wonderful Summer for Running Away, 1977; editor: A Treasury of True, 1957, Official Automobile Handbook, 1959, Anthology of True, 1962; contbr. to: Ency. Brit., Readers Digest, Smithsonian mag., Nat. Geographic, Travel and Leisure, Nat. Wildlife. Served from pvt. to sgt. AUS, 1944-46; war corr. Mem. Alpha Tau Omega, Sigma Delta Chi, Kappa Tau Alpha. Home: 225 Valley Rd Cos Cob CT 06807-2213

BARNARD, DRUIE DOUGLAS, JR., former congressman, former bank executive; b. Augusta, Ga., Mar. 20, 1922; s. Druie Douglas and Lucy (Burns) B.; m. Betty Lee Blanchard; children: Pamela Barnard Chafee, Lucy Barnard Bard, D. Douglas III. AB, Mercer U., 1943, JD, 1948; LLD, Augusta Law Sch., 1980. Asst. examiner Fed. Reserve Bank of Atlanta, 1949-50; asst. v.p. Ga. R.R. Bank, Augusta, 1950-62, exec. v.p., 1967-76; exec. sec. State of Ga., Atlanta, 1963-66; mem. U.S. Ho. of Reps., Washington, 1977-92; chmn. subcom. of Govt. Ops. Com.; mem. bd. trustees Mercer U., Macon, Ga., 1978. Chmn. Dem. com. Richmond County, Augusta, 1960-62; mem. exec. com. Ga. Dem. Party, Atlanta, 1963-66; bd. dirs. State Dept. Transp., Atlanta, 1967-76. With U.S. Army, 1943-45, ETO. Recipient Young Man of Yr. award Augusta C. of C., 1957, Man of Yr. award Area Planning and Devel. Commn., 1980. Baptist. Home: 3555 Granite Way Augusta GA 30907-8972

BARNARD, GEOFFREY W., federal judge; b. 1945. Magistrate judge for V.I., U.S. Magistrate Ct., Charlotte Amalie, St. Thomas, 1986—. Office: US Magistrate Ct 345 US Courthouse 5500 Veterans Dr Charlotte Amalie VI 00802-6424

BARNARD, GEORGE SMITH, lawyer, former federal agency official; b. Opelika, Ala.; s. George Smith and Caroline Elizabeth (Dowdell) B.; m. Muriel Elaine Outlaw, July 26, 1945; children: Elizabeth Elaine Barnard Crutcher, Charles Dowling, Beverly Laura Barnard Parker, Andrew Carey. BA, U. Ala., 1948, LLB, 1950. Bar: Fla. 1978, Ala. 1950, U.S. Tax Ct. 1950, U.S. Dist. Ct. Ala. 1950, U.S. Dist. Ct. Fla. 1978, U.S. Dist Ct. (so. dist. trial bar) Fla. 1995, U.S. Supreme Ct. 1965, U.S. Ct. Claims 1979, U.S. Ct. Appeals (Fed. cir.) 1984, U.S. Ct. Appeals (11th cir.) 1985. Pvt. practice, Opelika, 1950-51; with IRS, 1951-78; attache, revenue service rep., Sao Paulo Brazil, 1965-71, Mexico City, 1971-77; ptnr. Barnard, P.A., Miami, Fla., 1978-87, of counsel, 1987-91; lectr. taxation U. Ala., 1958-60. Pres. Rocky Ridge Vol. Fire Dept., 1956-58, Rocky Ridge Civic Club, 1959, Ala. chpt. Nat. Assn. Internal Revenue Employees, 1962; commr. Rocky Ridge Civic Water Works, 1960-62; bd. dirs. S.E. Pompano Homeowners Assn., 1996—. With USAAF, 1942-46. Recipient Albert Gallatin award U.S. Treasury Dept., 1978; named Hon. Citizen of Tex., 1979, Hon. Admiral in Tex. Navy, 1979. Mem. Fgn. Svc. Retirees Assn. of Fla. (advisor/dir. for S.E. Fla. 1987-98, dir. emeritus 1998—, original incumbent historian 1998—), Kappa Sigma. Republican. Home: 2761 SE 9th St Pompano Beach FL 33062-6712 Office: 3940 N Andrews Ave Fort Lauderdale FL 33309-5240

BARNARD, KATHRYN ELAINE, nursing educator, researcher; b. Omaha, Apr. 16, 1938; d. Paul and Elsa Elizabeth (Anderson) B. BS in Nursing, U. Nebr., Omaha, 1960; MS in Nursing, Boston U., 1962; PhD, U. Wash., Seattle, 1972; DSc (hon.), U. Nebr., 1990. Acting instr. U. Nebr., Omaha, 1960-61; acting instr. U. Wash., Seattle, 1963-65, asst. prof., 1965-69, prof. nursing, 1972—, assoc. dean, 1987-92; bd. dirs. Nat. Ctr. for Clin. Infant Programs, Washington, 1980—. Chmn. rsch. com. Bur. of Community Health Svcs., MCH, 1987-89. Recipient Lucille Petry award Nat. League for Nursing, 1968, Martha Mae Eliot award Am. Assn. Pub. Health, 1983, Professorship award U. Wash., 1985. Fellow Am. Acad. Nursing (bd. dirs. 1980-82); mem. Inst. Medicine; mem. Am. Nurses Assn. (chmn. com. 1980-82, Jessie Scott award 1982, Nurse of Yr. award 1984), Soc. Research in Child Devel. (bd. dirs. 1981-87), Sigma Theta Tau (founders award in research 1987). Democrat. Presbyterian. Home: 11508 Durland Ave NE Seattle WA 98125-5904 Office: University of Washington Family & Child Nursing Box 357920 Seattle WA 98195-7920*

BARNARD, KURT, retail trend/consumer spending forecaster, publisher; b. Hamburg, Germany, Apr. 16, 1927; s. León and Senta (Künstlinger) Barnard-Jeserski; m. Wendy Holly Love, Dec. 9, 1979; 1 child, Lance Jonathan. Student, NYU, 1948, N.Y. State U., 1953; grad., New Sch. for Social Research, 1957. N.Y. corr. European and Japanese bus. publs., 1957-60; dir. Latin Am., Far Eastern pub. relations Anglo-Affiliated Corp., N.Y.C., 1955-60; mktg. dir. Am. Research Merchandising Inst., Chgo., 1960-67; exec. dir. Internat. Mass Retail Assn., N.Y.C., 1967-69; exec. v.p. Internat. Mass Retailing Assn., N.Y.C., 1969-74, pres., 1974-76; exec. dir. Fedn. Apparel Mfrs., N.Y.C., 1976-86; launched Barnard's Retail Cons. Group and Barnard's Retail Mktg. Report, 1984; launched Barnard's Retail Cons. Group and Barnard's Retail Mktg. Report, 1984 (now Barnard's Retail Trend Report); cons. on wage-price freeze to dir. U.S. Office Emergency Preparedness, 1971-72; condr. retailing seminars in Europe, U.S.; frequent commentator on retailing and consumer spending issues on TV, Radio, including McNeil-Lehrer Newshour, CBS Evening News, NBC's Today Show, ABC's Good Morning Am. show, CNN, CNBC, Wall Street Journal Radio; organizer Nat. Loss Prevention Coun., 1972, Store Thieves and Their Impact, A Study, 1973; named mem. U.S. Govt. Industry Sector Adv. Com., 1978; mem. U.S. Govt. Exporters Adv. Com., 1979; chmn. bd. N.Y. Internat. Fashion Fair, 1980; leader nat. campaign against fair trade laws. Author: Cargo of Death, 1966, An Untapped Source of Store Profits, 1974, Picture of a Tragedy, 1974, How Chains Succeed With Non-Foods, 1974, Can Supermarkets Capture Non-Food Sales?, 1974, In Retailing: Future Shock is Now, 1975, Guidelines to Effective Marketing Strategies for Self-Service Retailers, 1975; co-author: Mass Merchandisers Guide to Sales and Expense Reporting, 1969, Marketing: Key to Retail Prosperity, 1985; contbr. articles to mags. and profl. jours. Recipient Disting. Service award U.S.O., 1965, Am. Soc. Assn. Execs. award, 1965; commd. Ky. col., 1975; DuPont Co. grantee, 1971-75. Mem. Nat. Assn. Bus. Economists, Mus. Modern Art. Office: 17 Kenneth Rd Montclair NJ 07043-2541

BARNARD, MORTON JOHN, lawyer; b. Chgo., Mar. 22, 1905; s. Julius and Martha (Wittman) B.; m. Eleanor Spivak, Aug. 16, 1936; 1 child, James W. PhB, U. Chgo., 1926, JD, 1927. Bar: Ill. 1927, U.S. Supreme Ct. 1949, U.S. Ct. Mil. Appeals 1954, U.S. Dist. Ct. (no. dist.) Ill., U.S. Ct. Appeals (7th cir.). Ptnr. Barnard and Barnard, Chgo., 1934-41, 46-84, Foss, Schuman, Drake & Barnard, Chgo., 1985-88; ptnr. Gottlieb & Schwartz, Chgo., 1989-90, of counsel, 1990-93; of counsel Miller, Shakman, Hamilton, Kurtzon & Schlifke, Chgo., 1993-97; adj. prof. John Marshall Law Sch., Chgo., 1947-64; pres. Ill. State Bar Assn., 1971-72; lectr. in field. Author: Contested Estates, 1985, 93; contbr. articles to profl. jours. Life mem. Chgo. Hist. Soc. Lt. col. U.S. Army, 1942-46. Recipient Certs. of Appreciation Ill. State Bar Assn., 1972, Chgo. Bar Assn., 1986, Bd. Govs.' award Ill. State Bar Assn., 1988, Austin Fleming Disting. Svc. award Chgo. Estate Planning Coun., 1993, Addis E. Hull award Ill. Inst. for Continuing Legal Edn., 1996. Fellow Am. Coll. Trust and Estate Counsel (bd. regents 1968-74), Am. Bar Found., Am. Bar Assn. (life), Ill. Bar Found., Chgo. Bar Found.; mem. Union League Club (Chgo.). Republican. Avocations: singing and acting in Bar Assn. Christmas Spirits, 1932-95. Home: 228 Woodlawn Ave Winnetka IL 60093-1553

BARNARD, ROBERT N., lawyer; b. Madison, Wis., Dec. 15, 1947; s. Robert Julian and Dorothy Jane (Nichol) B.; m. Katherine Elaine Chott, Mar. 1, 1980; children: Suzanna Katherine, Sarah Elizabeth. AB, Harvard U., 1969; JD, Stanford U., 1975. Bar: Ill. 1975, U.S. Dist. Ct. (no. dist.) Ill. 1975. Assoc. Mayer, Brown & Platt, Chgo., 1975-81; ptnr. Mayer, Brown & Platt, London, Eng., 1982-88, Chgo., 1988—. Trustee U. Notre Dame, London, 1986-88. Lt. U.S. Army, 1969-72. Mem. Union League Club. Office: Mayer Brown & Platt 190 S La Salle St Chicago IL 60603-3441

BARNARD, ROLLIN DWIGHT, retired financial executive; b. Denver, Apr. 14, 1922; s. George Cooper and Emma (Riggs) B.; m. Patricia Reynolds Bierkamp, Sept. 15, 1943; children: Michael Dana, Rebecca Susan (Mrs. Paul C. Wulfestieg), Laurie Beth (Mrs. Kenneth J. Kostelecky). B.A., Pomona Coll., 1943. Clk. Morey Merc. Co., Denver, 1937-40; ptnr George C. Barnard & Co. (gen. real estate and ins.), Denver, 1946-47; v.p. Foster & Barnard, Inc., 1947-53; instr. Denver U., 1949-53; dir. real estate U.S. P.O. Dept., Washington, 1953-55, dep. asst. postmaster gen., bur. facilities, 1955-59, asst. postmaster gen., 1959-61; pres., dir. Midland Fed. Savs. & Loan Assn., Denver, 1962-84; vice chmn. Bank Western Fed. Savs. Bank, 1984-87; vice chmn., pres. Western Capital Investment Corp., 1985-87. Mayor City of Greenwood Village, Colo., 1989-93, chmn. Planning and Zoning Commn., 1969-73, mem. coun., 1975-77; pres. Denver Area coun. Boy Scouts Am., 1970-71, mem. exec. bd., 1962-73; mem. adv. bd. Denver Area coun. Boy Scouts Am., 1973—; bd. dirs. Downtown Denver Improvement Assn., pres., 1965; bd. dirs. Bethesda Found., Inc., 1973-82, Children's Hosp., 1979-84, treas., 1983-84; bd. dirs. Children's Health Corp., Inc., 1982-93; trustee Mile High United Fund, 1969-72, Denver Symphony Assn., 1973-74; bd. dirs. Colo. Coun. Econ. Edn., 1971-80, chmn. 1971-76; trustee, v.p., treas. Morris Animal Found., 1969-81, pres., chmn. 1974-78, trustee emeritus, 1981—; trustee Denver Zool. Found., 1994—, exec. v.p. 1996—; mem. acquisitions com. Friends Found. Denver Pub. Libr., 1994—; mem. dir. Wings over the Rockies Air & Space Mus. Found., 1998—. Nominated One of Ten Outstanding Young Men in Am., U.S. Jaycees, 1955, 57; recipient Disting. Svc. award Postmaster Gen. U.S., 1960; Silver Beaver award Boy Scouts Am., 1969; named Outstanding Citizen of Yr., Sertoma, 1982, Colo. Citizen of Yr., Colo. Assn. Realtors, 1982, Citizen of West, Nat. Western Stockshow, 1994. Mem. Greater Denver C. of C. (pres. 1966-67), U.S. League Savs. Instns. (bd. dirs. 1972-77, vice chmn. 1979-80, chmn. 1980-81, mem. nat. legis. com., exec. com. 1974-77), Savs. League Colo. (exec. com. 1969-73, pres. 1971-72), Colo. Assn. Commerce and Industry (dir. 1971-76), Fellowship Christian Athletes (Denver area dir. 1963-76), Western Stock Show Assn. (dir. 1971—, exec. com. 1982-94, 1st v.p. 1985-94), Mountain and Plains Appaloosa Horse Club (pres. 1970-71), Roundup Riders of the Rockies (bd. dirs. 1979—, treas. 1980-87, v.p. 1987-89, pres.-elect 1989-91, pres. 1991-93). Republican. Presbyterian. Home: 3151 E Long Rd Greenwood Village CO 80121-1716

BARNARD, WILLIAM MARION, psychiatrist; b. Mt. Pleasant, Tex., Dec. 17, 1949; s. Marion Jaggers and Med (Cody) B. BA, Yale U., 1972; MD, Baylor U., 1976. Diplomate Am. Bd. Psychiatry and Neurology. Resident NYU/Bellevue Med. Ctr., 1976-79; liaison, consultation fellow L.I. Jewish/Hillside Med. Ctr., 1979-80; chief, liaison, consultation psychiatrist Queens (N.Y.) Med. Ctr., 1980-83; liaison, consultation psychiatrist Mt. Sinai Med. Ctr., N.Y.C., 1983-84; clin. asst. prof. NYU Med. Sch., N.Y.C., 1984-87; emergency psychiatrist VA Med. Ctr., N.Y.C., 1984-87; pvt. practice Pasadena, Calif., 1987—; chief psychiat. svc. Las Encinas Hosp., Pasadena, 1989, chief staff, 1990, med. dir. gen. adult. psychiat. svc., 1990-92, asst. med. dir., 1992; med. dir. BHC Alhambra Hosp., Rosemead, Calif., 1992—. Chmn. mental health com. All Saints AIDS Svc. Ctr., Pasadena, 1990-94, bd. dirs., 1991-94; bd. dirs. Pasadena Symphony, 1989-97, v.p., 1996-97; bd. dirs. Whiffenpoof Alumni, New Haven, 1991—, haberdasher, 1995—. Wilson scholar Yale U., 1973. Mem. NYU-Bellevue Psychiat. Assn., Am. Soc. Addiction Medicine, Calif. Med. Assn., So. Calif. Psychiat. Soc., Acad. Psychosomatic Medicine, L.A. County Med. Assn., Amateur Comedy Club N.Y.C., Met. Opera Club, Yale Club N.Y.C., Univ. Glee Club of N.Y.C., Order of St. John (knight). Republican. Episcopalian. Office: 2810 E Del Mar Blvd Ste 11B Pasadena CA 91107-4323

BARNEA, URI N., music director, conductor, composer, violinist; b. Petah-Tikvah, Israel, May 29, 1943; came to U.S., 1971; s. Shimon and Miriam Burstein; m. Lizbeth A. Lund, Dec. 15, 1977; 2 children. Tchg. cert., Oranim Music Inst., Israel, 1966; postgrad., Hebrew U., Israel, 1969-71; MusB, Rubin Acad. Music, Israel, 1971; MA, U. Minn., 1974, PhD, 1977; D (hon.), Rocky Mountain Coll., 1999. Music dir. Jewish Cmty. Ctr., Mpls., 1971-73; condr. Youval Chamber Orch., Mpls., 1971-73; asst. condr. U. Minn. Orchs., Mpls., 1972-77; music dir., condr. Unitarian Soc., Mpls., 1973-78, Kenwood Chamber Orch., Mpls., 1974-78, Knox-Galesburg Symphony, 1978-83, Billings (Mont.) Symphony Soc., 1984—; asst. prof. Knox Coll., Galesburg, Ill., 1978-83; violinist, violist Yellowstone Chamber players, Billings, 1984—; violist Tri-City Symphony, Quad-Cities, Ill., Iowa, 1983-84; condr. Cedar Arts Forum String Camp, Cedar Falls, Iowa, 1981, 82. European conducting debut, London, Neuchatel and Fribourg, Switzerland, 1986; Can. conducting debut No. Music Festival, North Bay, Ont., 1989; Violin Concerto, 1990; Russian conducting debut Symphony Orch., Kuzbass, Kemerovo, 1993; recordings include: W. Piston's Flute and Clarinet Concertos, Mario Lombardo's Oboe Concerto, two compact discs of Am. music; composer numerous compositions including String Quartet (1st prize Aspen Composition Competition 1976), Sonata for Flute and Piano, 1975 (Diploma of Distinction 26th Viotti Internat. Competition, Italy 1975), Ruth, a ballet, 1974 (1st prize Oberhoffer Composition Contest 1976). Active in music adv. panel Ill. Arts Coun., 1980-83; v.p. Cmty. Concert Assn., Galesburg, 1980-83; bd. dirs. Knox Coll. Credit Union, Galesburg, 1982-83, Sta. KEMC Pub. Radio, Billings, 1984—, Fox Theater Corp., Billings, 1984-86. Recipient Friend of the Arts title Sigma Alpha Iota, 1982; Ill. Arts Coun. grantee, 1979; Hebrew U. Jerusalem scholar, 1972-74, Hebrew U. and Rubin Acad. Mus. scholar, 1969, 70; Individual Artist fellow Mont. Arts Coun., 1986. Mem. NEA (music adv. panel 1990-95), ASCAP, Am. Composers Forum, Condrs. Gukld, Am. String Tchrs. Assn. Office: Billings Symphony Soc 201 N Broadway Ste 350 Billings MT 59101-1936

BARNEBEY, KENNETH ALAN, food company executive; b. Fremont, Nebr., Apr. 16, 1931; s. Hoyt F. and Mae S. (Mott) B.; m. Faith Price, May 10, 1969; children: Robert, Mark, Holiday, Cindy, Kendra, Valerie, Bonnie, Laurel, Susan. Student, U. Md., 1950, U. Tampa, 1951; BA in Transp., U. Wash., Seattle, 1953; grad. advanced mgmt. program, Harvard U., 1977. With Tropicana Products, Inc., Bradenton, Fla., 1955-80, gen. sales mgr., then v.p. mktg. and sales, 1957-77, exec. v.p., 1977, pres., chief adminstrv. officer, 1977-79, chmn. bd., chief exec. officer, 1979-81, also dir.; corp. v.p. Beatrice Foods, Inc., 1979-81; pres., dir., dep. chmn. Am. Agronomics Corp., Tampa, Fla., 1981-86; bus. acquisition cons. Bradenton, Fla., 1981—; bd. dirs. Dependable Ins. Group Inc. Am., Exmart, Cmty. Bank Holding Co.; mem. sch. mktg. program Fla. Citrus Dept., 1973—; dir. First Union Bank. Bd. dirs., pres. Am. Acad. Achievement; bd. dirs. Manatee Jr. Coll., Asolo State Theatre, Blowing Rock (N.C.) Hosp., Blowing Rock Stage Co. Theater; mem. Fla. Coun. of 100; adv. coun. Fla. State U.; exec. svc. corp. pres. Manasota Basin Bd. Served with U.S. Army, 1953-55. Mem. Am. Mgmt. Assn. (lectr.), NAM (mktg. adv. com., dir.), Fla. Canners Assn. (mktg. adv. com.), Manatee County C. of C. (dir., chmn. econ. devel. com.). Clubs: Manatee County Exchange (past pres.), Bradenton Country, Blowing Rock Country (past pres.), State of Fla. Govs. Coun. of 100. Home and Office: PO Box 2490 Blowing Rock NC 28605-2490

BARNER, JOHN L., radiologist; b. Webster City, Iowa, Nov. 25, 1907; s. George Stewart and Rumayne Hertzler (Brennaman) B.; m. Margaret Graham Wallace, Oct. 19, 1935; children: John L. II, Diane Wallace, L. Lemuel. AB, Grinnell U., 1929; MD, Jefferson Med. Coll., 1933. Cert. in radiology. Intern Med. Ctr., Jersey City, 1933-34, resident in oncology, 1935-37; resident in oncology Meml. Hosp. Cancer, N.Y.C., 1937-39; resident in radiol. oncology Cin. Gen. Hosp., 1939-40; dir. Athens (Ga.) Cancer Clinic, 1947-72, Am. Cancer Soc. State of Ga., Atlanta, 1950-72. Contbr. articles to med. jours. Fellow Am. Coll. Radiology; mem. Am. Radium Soc., Inter-Am. Coll. Radiology, Radiol. Soc. N.Am., Mil. Order Loyal Legion of U.S. (commdr. 1982-99), Caledonian Soc. of Fla. West (chmn.), Knight Templar, Masons, Shriners, Sarasota Yacht Club (fleet surgeon), Oaks Country Club. Republican. Episcopalian.

BARNES, A. JAMES, academic dean; b. Napoleon, Ohio, Aug. 30, 1942; s. Albert James and Mary Elizabeth (Morey) B.; m. Sarah Jane Hughes, June 19, 1976; children: Morey Elizabeth, Laura LeHardy, Catherine Farrell. BA with high honors, Mich. State U., 1964; JD cum laude, Harvard U., 1967. Asst. prof. bus. adminstrn. Ind. U., 1967-69; trial atty. Dept. Justice, 1969-70, asst. to dep. atty. gen., 1973; asst. to adminstr. EPA, 1970-73; campaign mgr. for Gov. Milliken of Mich., 1974; ptnr. Beveridge, Fairbanks & Diamond, Washington, 1975-81; gen. counsel Dept. Agr., 1981-83; adj. prof. Georgetown U. Sch. Bus. Adminstrn., Washington, 1978-80; gen. counsel EPA, 1983-85, dep. adminstr., 1985-88; dean Sch. Pub. Environ. Adminstrn., prof. pub. and environ. affairs Ind. U., 1988—; spl. counsel Beveridge, Fairbanks & Diamond, Washington, 1988-97. Co-author: Law for Business, 7th edit., 1999, Business Law and the Regulatory Environment, 10th edit., 1997, Essentials of Business Law, 1994, Law of Commercial Transactions and Business Associations, 1995. Del. Ind. Republican Conv., 1968, Mich. Rep. Conv., 1974. Recipient Outstanding Teaching award Ind. U., 1969. Mem. Met. Club (Washington), Skyline Club (Indpls.), Edgartown (Mass.) Yacht Club. Office: Ind U SPEA # 300 Bloomington IN 47405

BARNES, A. KEITH, management educator; b. Peterborough, Eng., July 5, 1934; came to U.S., 1975; s. Archibald and Constance Louise (Snart) B.; m. Judith Anne Lamplugh, Dec. 26, 1955; children: Warren, Douglas, Lisa. BSc in Engring., Nene Univ., 1955; MBA in Mgmt., Pepperdine U., 1980, EdD in Adminstrn., 1984. Engr., designer Perkins Diesel, Eng. and Can., 1954-57; various positions Blackwood Hodge, Toronto, Can., 1957-70; various mgmt. positions J.I. Case Co. (Tenneco), Toronto, Can., 1970-81; from asst. to assoc. prof. U. La Verne, Calif., 1981-84; from assoc. prof. to Hunsaker prof. mgmt. U. Redlands, Calif., 1984—; spkr. numerous orgns., 1974—. Author: Management Maturity: Prerequisite to Total Quality, 1994; editor Jour. Applied Bus. Rsch., 1988-93; mem. editl. bd. Jour. Mgmt. Sys., 1986—. Bd. dirs. San Gorgonio Meml. Hosp., 1993-94. Republican. Avocations: carpentry, tennis, chess, computer programming, writing fiction. Home: PO Box 439016 San Diego CA 92143-9016 Office: U Redlands Box 3080 1200 E Colton Ave Redlands CA 92374-3755

BARNES, ANDREW EARL, newspaper editor; b. Torrington, Conn., May 15, 1939; s. Joseph and Elizabeth (Brown) B.; m. Marion Otis, Aug. 26, 1960; children: Christopher Joseph, Benjamin Brooks, Elizabeth Cheney. B.A., Harvard U., 1961. Reporter, bur. chief Providence Jour., 1961-63; from reporter to edn. editor Washington Post, 1965-73; met. editor, asst. mng. editor St Petersburg Times, Fla., 1973-75, mng. editor, 1975-84; editor, pres. St. Petersburg (Fla.) Times, 1984—, chief exec. officer, 1988—; chmn. bd. dirs. Congl. Quar., Times Pub. Co., Poynter Inst.; mem. Pulitzer prize bd. Mem. Fla. Coun. of 100. With USAR, 1963-65. Alicia Patterson fellow, 1969-70. Mem. Newspaper Assn. Am. (vice-chair), Am. Soc. Newspaper Editors, Fla. Soc. Newspaper Editors (pres. 1980-81), Internat. Press Inst. Home: 15724 Puckett Rd Dade City FL 33525-7066 Office: Saint

Petersburg Times 490 1st Ave S PO Box 1121 Saint Petersburg FL 33731-1121

BARNES, BEN BLAIR, company executive, electrical engineer; b. Gadsden, Ala., Mar. 7, 1935; s. Newton Eldridge Jr. and Sara Aileen (Roach) B.; m. Pat Harris, June 3, 1956 (div. 1989); 1 child, Douglas Harris; m. Elba Crowe Clarke, Feb. 25, 1991. BEE, Ala. Poly. Inst., 1956; MSEE, U. Ala., 1962; PhD, Auburn U., 1965. Registered profl. engr., Ala., Tenn. Instrument engr. E.I. du Pont de Nemours & Co., Aiken, S.C., 1957-59; computer engr. NASA Marshall Space Flight Ctr., Huntsville, Ala., 1959-63; mem. faculty elec. engring. dept. Va. Poly. Inst. and State U., Blacksburg, 1965-66; dept. mgr. Computer Scis. Corp., Huntsville, 1966-67; asst. dean engring. U. Tenn., Knoxville, 1967-70; dir. Computer Ctr. Auburn (Ala.) U., 1970-80; head computer sci. Calif. State Coll. Stanislaus, Turlock, 1981; prin. Ben Barnes & Assocs., Auburn, 1981-87; chief exec. officer Ala. Supercomputer Authority, Huntsville, 1987-98; v.p. SilverTech Assocs., Dadeville, Ala., 1998—. 2d lt. U.S. Army, 1956-57. Mem. IEEE, Assn. for Computing Machinery. Home: 1622 Sandstone Ct Montgomery AL 36117-1704 Office: SilverTech Assocs 13 Eagle Peak Dadeville AL 36853

BARNES, BETTY RAE, counselor; b. Wichita, Kans., June 24, 1932; d. Henry Charles and Vivian Augusta (Lamberth) Archer; m. Orland Eugene Barnes, Mar. 18, 1953; children: Terry Lee, Steven Gregory. BA, Our Lady of the Lake, San Antonio, 1986, MS in Counseling Psychology, 1989. Cert. profl. sec.; lic. profl. counselor; lic. marriage and family therapist, registered sex offender treatment provider; Am. Assn. for Marriage and Family Therapy approved supr. Info. specialist S.W. Rsch. Inst., San Antonio, 1975-96; ret., 1996; counselor Community Clinic, Inc., San Antonio, 1989—, counselor/counseling coord., 1991—; counselor Community Counseling Ctr., Our Lady of the Lake U., San Antonio, 1989-91. Co-chmn. Life After Loss com. Am. Cancer Soc. Recipient Outstanding Achievement award Sch. Bus. and Pub. Adminstrn., Our Lady of the Lake U., 1984. Mem. Am. Assn. Marriage and Family Therapists (clin.), Am. Cancer Soc. (co-chmn. life after loss com.), Tex. Assn. Marriage and Family Therapists (bd. mem.), Tex. Counseling Assn., Internat. Assn. for Addictions and Offender Counselors, San Antonio Assn. for Marriage and Family Therapy (past pres.), San Antonio Mus. Assn., Delta Mu Delta. Avocations: piano, reading, collecting pewter. Office: Community Clinic Inc 210 W Olmos Dr San Antonio TX 78212-1956

BARNES, CARLYLE FULLER, manufacturing executive; b. Bristol, Conn., Feb. 16, 1924; s. Fuller Forbes and Myrtle (Ives) B.; m. Elizabeth Anne May, Oct. 1, 1949; children: Lynne Elizabeth, Janis Lee, Joan Wells, Fuller Forbes. A.B., Wesleyan U., 1948. Staff asst. Wallace Barnes Co. div. Barnes Group Inc., 1948-50, gen. mgr., 1951-53, dir., 1951-92, pres., 1953-64, chmn. bd., 1964-77, chmn. exec. com., 1977-94, ret., 1994. Bd. dirs. Bushnell Meml. Hall. Home: Peacedale St Bristol CT 06010

BARNES, CHARLES ANDREW, physicist, educator; b. Toronto, Ont., Can., Dec. 12, 1921; came to U.S., 1953, naturalized, 1961; m. Phyllis Malcolm, Sept., 1950. BA, McMaster U., 1943; MA, U. Toronto, 1944; PhD, Cambridge U., 1950. Physicist Joint Brit.-Canadian Atomic Energy Project, 1944-46; instr. physics U. B.C., 1950-53, 55-56; mem. faculty Calif. Inst. Tech., 1953-55, 56—, prof. physics, 1962-92; prof. emeritus physics, 1992—; guest prof. Niels Bohr Inst., Copenhagen, 1973-74. Editor, contbr. to profl. books and jours. Recipient medal Inst. d'Astrophysique de Paris, 1986, Alexander von Humboldt U.S. Sr. Scientist award, Fed. Republic of Germany, 1986; NSF sr. fellow Denmark, 1962-63. Fellow AAAS, Am. Phys. Soc. Office: Calif Inst Tech 1201 E California Blvd Pasadena CA 91125-0001

BARNES, CHRISTOPHER RICHARD, geologist; b. Nottingham, Eng., Apr. 20, 1940; m. Susan Miller, Aug. 19, 1961; children: Penny, Joanne, Allison. B.S., U. Birmingham, Eng., 1961; Ph.D., U. Ottawa, 1964. Asst. prof. U. Waterloo, Ont., Can., 1965-70, assoc. prof., 1970-76, prof., chmn. dept., 1976-81; prof., head dept. earth scis. Meml. U. Nfld., St. John's, Can., 1981-87; dir. gen. sedimentary and marine geosci. Geol. Survey Can., Ottawa, Ont., 1987-89; dir. Centre for Earth and Ocean Rsch. U. Victoria, BC., Can., 1989—, dir. Sch. Earth and Ocean Sci., 1991—; sr. research fellow U. Southampton, Eng., 1971-72. Fellow Royal Soc. Can. (pres. Acad. Sci. 1990-93, Bancroft award 1982); mem. Geol. Assn. Can. (pres. 1983, past pres. medal 1977, Ambrose medal 1991), Can. Geol. Found., Can. Geosci. Coun. (pres. 1979), Coun. of Chairs Can. Earth Sci. Depts. (chair 1983-85, 95-97, 97-99), Internat. Union Geol. Sci. (mem. com. on stratigraphy, chair subcom. on ordovician stratigraphy 1982-89), Natural Sci. and Engring. Rsch. Coun. Can. (group chmn. earth sci. and interdisciplinary 1987-90), Atomic Energy Control Bd., Assn. Profl. Engrs. and Geoscientists of B.C., Order of Can. Office: SEOS U Victoria, PO Box 3055, Victoria, BC Canada V8W 3P6

BARNES, DAVID BENTON, school psychologist; m. Cheryle Kirkland; children: David, Matthew, Bryan. BSc with honors, Springfield Coll., 1958; MEd, U. Maine, 1962; EdD, Rutgers U., 1970. Cert. tchr., Maine. Asst. football coach Boston U., 1964-66; dir. Counselling Ctr., asst. prof. edn. Acadia U., Wolfville, N.S., Can., 1966-71, acting dean Sch. Edn., 1969-70, assoc. prof., 1970; chief psychologist Fundy Med. Health Ctr., Wolfville, 1971-73; psychologist Atlantic Child Guidance Ctr., 1974-77; supr. spl. svcs. Cape Breton County Sch. Bd., 1977-82, Lunenburg County Dist. Bd., 1982-87; sch. psychologist, spl. edn. adminstr. Bennington-Rutland Supervisory Union, Vt., 1987-90; psychologist N.W. Psycho-Ednl. Program, Rome, Ga., 1990-92, Chattahoochee-Flint RESA, Ellaville, Ga., 1991-97, Dougherty County Sch. Sys., Albany, Ga., 1998—; mem. adminstrv. task force for spl. edn. N.S. Dept. Edn.; mem. N.S. Adv. Coun. on Tchr. Edn.; mem. Met. Mental Health Planning Bd.; mem. Aqua Percept Nat. Adv. Bd.; founder Camp Recskill; founder, bd. dirs. Cape Breton Child Guidance Ctr.; adj. faculty mem. U. Coll. of Cape Breton, Acadia U., Walden U. Co-author: Special Educator's Survival Guide: Practical Techniques and Materials for Supervision and Instruction. Grantee Can. Govt., 1978-87, Province of N.S., 1978-79, N.S. Tchrs. Union, 1980-81, Internat. Youth Yr., 1985, Donner Found., Laidlaw Found., Windsor Found. Mem. Can. Univ. Counselors Assn., Atlantic Inst. Edn. (steering com. for counselor edn.), Assn. Profl. Staffs of Community Mental Ctrs. (sec.-treas.), Can. Assn. for Children With Learning Disabilties (v.p.), Provincial Assn. for Children with Learning Disabilities (bd. dirs.), N.S. Mental Health Assn. (bd. dirs.), Dartmouth Mental Health Assn. (v.p.), Cape Breton Mental Health Assn. (bd. dirs.), Coun. Exceptional Children, Assn. Psychologists N.C., Nat. Assn. Sch. Psychologists. Office: Dougherty County Sch Sys PO Box 1470 Albany GA 31702-1470

BARNES, DENNIS NORMAN, lawyer; b. Kingston, Pa., Feb. 10, 1940; s. Leslie Orland and Mary Whitney (Brown) B.; m. Ingrid Daubitz, Oct. 5, 1961; children: Richard, Kendra. AB, Dartmouth Coll., 1962; JD, Georgetown U., 1965. Bar: D.C. 1966, U.S. Ct. Appeals (D.C. cir.) 1966, U.S. Supreme Ct. 1995. Assoc. Morgan, Lewis & Bockius LLP, Washington, 1970-75, ptnr., 1975—. Capt. JAGC, U.S. Army, 1966-70. Mem. ABA, D.C. Bar Assn., Maritime Adminstrv. Bar Assn. (pres. 1991), Assn. Transp. Practitioners. Office: Morgan Lewis & Bockius LLP 1800 M St NW Washington DC 20036-5802

BARNES, DONALD MICHAEL, lawyer; b. Hazleton, Pa., June 15, 1943; s. Donald A. and Margaret (Resuta) B.; m. Mary Catherine Gibbons, June 3, 1967; children: Donald M., Stephanie A., Susan E. BS in Indsl. Engring., Pa. State U., 1965; JD cum laude, George Washington U., 1970. Bar: D.C. 1970, U.S. Dist. Ct. D.C. 1970, U.S. Ct. Appeals (D.C. cir.) 1970, U.S. Ct. Appeals (5th cir.) 1975, U.S. Ct. Appeals (4th cir.) 1980, U.S. Ct. Appeals (8th cir.) 1981, U.S. Ct. Appeals (6th cir.) 1993, U.S. Supreme Ct. 1975. Assoc. Arent, Fox, Kintner, Plotkin & Kahn, Washington, 1970-78; ptnr. Arent, Fox, Kintner, Plotkin & Kahn, 1978-97; mng. shareholder Jenkens & Gilchrist, Washington, 1997—. Notes editor George Washington Law Rev., 1969-70. Mem. ABA (criminial justice, antitrust, litigation and adminstrv. law sects.), Fed. Bar Assn., D.C. Bar Assn., Order of Coif, Phi Delta Phi. Office: Jenkens & Gilchrist 1919 Pennsylvania Ave NW Washington DC 20006-3404

BARNES, DONALD RAY, writer, genealogical researcher; b. Washington, June 15, 1946; s. Ernest Ray Barnes and Evelyn (Raley) B.; children: Alexandra, Philippa, Christian. BA in Bus., Strayer Coll., 1973, MA in Bus., 1976. Cert. genealogist. Appraiser D.C. Govt., Washington, 1972-91. Author: Write it Right: A Manual for Writing Family Histories and Genealogies, 1983, 2d edit., 1988; contbr. articles to profl. jours. Mem. Nat. Geneal. Soc. (life), Md. Geneal. Soc. (life). Roman Catholic. Office: DR Barnes Assocs PO Box 50741 Albuquerque NM 87181

BARNES, DONALD WINFREE, financial services executive; b. Newport News, Va., Aug. 14, 1943; s. Robert Winfree and Mary Linda (Riley) B.; m. Sandra Kay Steward, Apr. 30, 1966; children: April Kathleen, Summer Marie, Steven Edward. AA, Miami Dade Community Coll., 1968; BS, Fla. Atlantic U., 1970, MBA, 1988. Lic. life, health and variable annuity agt, NASD series 7. Item processor S.E. Bank Corp., Miami, Fla., 1962-68, rsch. analyst, 1971-74, securities salesman, 1974-78; asst. revenue collector Broward County Bd. County Commrs., Ft. Lauderdale, Fla., 1978-83; treas. Coral Gables (Fla.) Fed. Savs. & Loan, 1983-95; agt. MassMutual DBS FIN Group, Ft. Lauderdale, 1995-96; sr. v.p., cashier Boca Raton (Fla.) First Nat. Bank, 1996-99. Treas. Boca Glades Bapt. Ch., Boca Raton, 1984-95; coach little league baseball and flag football. Mem. Miami Bond Club (bd. dirs., v.p., pres.). Republican. Avocations: softball, golf, fishing. Office: Boca Raton First Nat Bank Ste 100B 7301A W Palmetto Park Rd Boca Raton FL 33433-3473

BARNES, DUNCAN, magazine editor, writer; b. New Rochelle, N.Y., Nov. 15, 1935; s. Francis Duncan and Christine Sinclair (Lawther) B.; m. Anne E. Fiske, May 27, 1961; children—Lesley Thorp, Jason Coleman. B.A. in English, Dartmouth Coll., 1957. Staff writer St. Petersburg Times, Fla., 1958-61; staff writer Sports Illustrated, N.Y.C., 1961-68; dir. pub. relations, Winchester Group Olin Corp., N.Y.C., 1968-80; editorial dir. Winchester Press, N.Y.C., 1972-80; editor Field & Stream, N.Y.C., 1981-99, editor-at-large, 1999—. Editor: History of Winchester Firearms, 1980, AKC's World of the Pure-Bred Dog, 1984; contbg. editor: The Random House Dictionary of the English Language, 1966. Mem. Sportfishing and Boating Partnership Coun., U.S. Fish and Wildlife Svc. Mem. Outdoor Writers Assn. Am., Boone and Crockett Club. Office: Field & Stream 2 Park Ave New York NY 10016-5675*

BARNES, EDWARD DEAN, lawyer; b. Frankfort, Ky., Feb. 23, 1944; children: Jessica Marie Oliverio, Stefan Edward, Elena Ruxandra. BA, East Carolina U., 1966; JD, U. Richmond, 1971. Bar: Va. 1971. Law clk. to Chief Justice Carrico Supreme Ct. of Va., 1971-72; adj. faculty J. Sargeant Reynolds C.C., Richmond, Va., 1972-78, U. Richmond Law Sch., 1991-96; ptnr. Bremner, Baber & Janus, 1977-78, Edward D. Barnes & Assocs., 1978-96; pres., CEO Barnes & Batzli, P.C., Chesterfield County, Va., 1996—; bd. dirs., gen. counsel Old Dominion Eye Bank, Eye Assocs. Am. Contbr. articles to profl. jours. Bd. dirs. Va. Head Found., 1987-90; active YMCA Indian Guides and Indian Princess Programs, Chesterfield County, 1995—; youth soccer coach, 1995—. Fellow Am. Acad. Matrimonial Lawyers; mem. Internat. Soc. for Philos. Enquiry, Mensa, Chesterfield Bar Assn. (pres. 1998—), Richmond Metro Bar Assn. (pres. 1998—). E-mail: EBarnes@BarnesBatzli.com. Office: Barnes & Batzli PC 9401 Courthouse Rd Chesterfield VA 23832-6666

BARNES, EDWARD LARRABEE, architect; b. Chgo., Apr. 22, 1915; s. Cecil and Margaret Helen (Ayer) B.; m. Mary Elizabeth Coss, Mar. 4, 1944; 1 child, John Cecil. B.S. cum laude, Harvard U., 1938, M.Arch. (Sheldon Travelling fellow), 1942; D. Fine Arts (hon.), R.I. Sch. Design, 1983; L.H.D. (hon.), Amherst Coll., 1984. Architect N.Y.C., 1949—; practice includes pre-fabricated house, pvt. houses, camps, acad. bldgs. & master plans, office bldgs. and corp. headquarters, museums, bot. gardens; archtl. design critic, lectr. Pratt Inst., Bklyn., 1954-59; design critic, lectr. Yale U., New Haven, Conn., 1957-64; Eliot Noyes critic Harvard U., 1979; Thomas Jefferson prof. architecture U. Va., 1980; mem. Westchester Council of Arts, 1967-71, Urban Design Council of N.Y.C., 1972-76; trustee Am. Acad., Rome, 1963-78, 1st v.p., 1973, 1st vice chmn., 1975; vis. com. MIT, 1965-68, Harvard Grad. Sch. Design. 1978-88; assoc. Nat. Acad. Design, 1969, academician, 1974—; bd. dirs. Municipal Art Soc., 1960, treas., 1961; trustee Mus. Modern Art, N.Y.C., 1975-93, life trustee, 1993—; mem. adv. council Trust for Pub. Land, 1984-90; mem. Westchester County Planning Bd., 1976-88. Work exhibited Mus. Modern Art., N.Y.C., Sarah Scaife Gallery, Pitts., Whitney Mus., N.Y.C., Nat. Bldg. Mus., Washington; work pub. in archtl. mags. Recipient award for distinction in arts Yale, 1959, Arnold Brunner prize Nat. Inst. Arts and Letters, 1959, Silver medal Archtl. League N.Y., 1960, Harleston Parker medal Boston Soc. Architects, 1972, Bard award for Excellence in Archtl. and Urban Design, 1978, 85, Louis Sullivan award, 1979, Honor award Conn. Soc. Architects, 1980, award of Honor for Art and Culture Mayor of N.Y.C., 1982, Honor award N.Mex. Soc. Architects, 1983, Excellence in Design award N.Y. State Assn. Architects, 1984, Thomas Jefferson medal U. Va., 1981, Harvard U. 350th Anniversary medal, 1986, Alumni Lifetime Achievement award Harvard U. Grad. Sch. Design, 1993, Am. Craft Coun. award of distinction for Haystack Sch., 1998. Fellow AIA (Medal of Honor N.Y. chpt. 1971, collaborative achievement in architecture 1972, Honor award 1972, 77, 86, Firm award 1980, 25 Yr. award 1994, Pres. award N.Y. chpt.), Am. Acad. Arts and Scis.; mem. Am. Acad. and Inst. Arts and Letters, Century Assn. Home: 975 Memorial Dr Cambridge MA 02138-5753 Office: 320 W 13th St New York NY 10014-1200

BARNES, ERIC RANDOLPH, Olympic athlete; b. Charleston, W.Va., June 16, 1966. Ranked 3rd in U.S. in shot put, Track & Field News, 1986, 1st place Southwest Conf., 1987, Silver medal, track and field, shot put, Olympic Games, Seoul, 1988, 1st place indoor title USA/Mobil Championship, 1990, Gold medal Goodwill Games, 1990, 1st place outdoor title USATF, 1993, 2nd place World Championships, 1993, Gold medal, track and field, shotput, Olympic Games, Atlanta, 1996; holder shot put world record at 75 feet 10 1/4 inches. Office: USA Track & Field 1 REA Dome Ste 140 Indianapolis IN 46206-0120*

BARNES, FRANK STEPHENSON, electrical engineer, educator; b. Pasadena, Calif., July 31, 1932; s. Donald Porter and Thedia (Schellenberg) B.; m. Gay Dirstine, Dec. 17, 1955; children: Stephen, Amy. BS, Princeton U., 1954; MS, Stanford U., 1955, PhD, 1958. Fulbright prof. Coll. Engring., Baghdad, Iraq, 1957-58; rsch. assoc. Colo. Rsch. Corp., Broomfield, 1958-59; assoc. prof. U. Colo., Boulder, 1959-65, prof. dept. elec. engring., 1965—; chmn. dept. U. Colo., 1964-81, faculty rsch. lectr., 1965, acting dean Coll. Engring. and Applied Sci., 1980-81, disting. prof., 1997—, dir. interdisciplinary telecom. program, 1971-75, 88-89, 1996—; disting. lectr. IEEE Elec. Device Soc., 1994-97. Regional editor Electronics Letters of Brit. Instn. Elec.Engrs., 1970-75; exec. editor Ann. Rev. Telecom. Bd. dirs. Accreditation Bd. Engring. and Tech., 1980-82. Recipient cert. of merit Internat. Comm. Assn., 1989, Meritorious Svc. award IEEE Edn. Soc., 1993, Leon Montgomery award Internat. Comm. Assn., 1994, Univ. Colo. Centennial Celebration Engring. Recognition award, 1994; fellow Internat. Engring. Consortium, 1995. Fellow AAAS, IEEE (editor Student Jour. 1967-70, mem. G-Ed Adcom 1970-77, v.p. publ. activities 1974-75, pres. device soc. 1974-75, mem. ednl. activities bd. 1976-82, editor IEEE Transactions on Edn. 1988-94, mem. press bd. 1989-90, ednl. activities bd., cert. of merit, Centennial medal), Soc. Lasers in Medicine, Engrs. Coun. Profl. Devel. (dir. 1976-82, chmn. com. on advanced level accreditation 1976-78), Bioelectromagnetics Soc. (bd. dirs. 1982-84, 96-98), Engring. Info. (bd. dirs. 1984-90). Home: 225 Continental View Dr Boulder CO 80303-4516 *There are always more interesting problems to solve than time to solve them. The trick is to find important problems which can be solved with an effort which is small compared to the value of the results and where one can have a good time learning new ideas at the same time.*

BARNES, FREDERIC WOOD, JR., journalist; b. West Point, N.Y., Feb. 1, 1943; s. Frederic W. and Rosa (Miller) B.; m. Barbara Beatty, Sept. 2, 1967; children: Karen, Sarah, Grace, Frederic W. III. BA in History, U. Va., 1965. Reporter Charleston (S.C.) News Courier, 1965-67, Washington (D.C.) Star, 1967-77, 78-79, Balt. Sun, 1979-85; sr. editor The New Republic, Washington, 1985-95; exec. editor The Weekly Std., Washington, 1995—; Nieman fellow Harvard U., 1977-78; panelist Presdl. debate, Louisville, 1984; regular panelist The McLaughlin Group (TV), Washington, 1988-98; moderator Issues in the News Voice of America, Washington, 1988—; polit. analyst (TV) CBS This Morning, 1990—; host (TV) Beltway Boys, Fox News Channel, 1998—. Editor: A Cartoon History of the Reagan Years, 1988; host (syndicated radio show) What's the Story?, 1992—. With U.S. Army, 1960-62. Named Father of Yr., Father's Day Com., 1994. Office: The Weekly Standard 1150 17th St NW Ste 505 Washington DC 20036-4617

BARNES, GERALD R., bishop; b. Phoenix, Ariz., June 22, 1945. Grad., St. Leonard Sem., Dayton, Ohio; student, Assumption-St. John's Sem., San Antonio. Ordained priest Roman Cath. Ch., 1975, titular bishop of Monte Fiascone. Aux. bishop San Bernardino, Calif., 1992-95, bishop, 1996—; Chmn. com. Hispanic affairs Nat. Conf. Cath. Bishops. Office: 1201 E Highland Ave San Bernardino CA 92404-4607*

BARNES, GRANT ALAN, book publisher; b. Ukiah, Calif., Aug. 24, 1932; s. Walter Joseph and Hazel Marie (Brown) B.; m. Irina Valentina Morozoff, Aug. 29, 1954; children—Theodore Alan, Walter Scott, Marian June. AB, U. Calif., Berkeley, 1961. Exec. editor U. Calif. Press, Berkeley, 1965-83; dir. Stanford U. Press, Calif., 1983-93, dir. emeritus, 1993—; bd. dirs. Wilderness Press. Contbr. articles to profl. jours., and reviews for jours. Mem. Soc. Pub. Sci. and Scholarship (bd. dirs.), Phi Beta Kappa. Avocations: lic. pvt. pilot. Home: 2193 Bloomfield Rd Sebastopol CA 95472-5409

BARNES, HARPER HENDERSON, movie critic, editor; b. Greensboro, N.C., July 2, 1937; s. Bennett Harper and Cora Emmaline (HEnderson) B.; m. Janice Stauffacher, May 10, 1961 (div. 1985); m. Roseann Marie Weiss, May 31, 1986. Critic, reporter St. Louis Post-Dispatch, 1965-70, editor, critic, 1973-97; editor The Phoenix, Boston, 1970-72, St. Louis mag., 1997—; instr. Washington U., St. Louis, 1990, 94. Author: Blue Monday, 1991. With U.S. Army, 1959-62. Avocations: bicycling, fishing. Office: St Louis Mag 6358 Delmar Blvd Saint Louis MO 63130-4719

BARNES, HARRY F., federal judge; b. 1932. Student, Vanderbilt U., 1950-52; BS, U.S. Naval Academy, 1956; LLB, U. Ark., 1964. With Pryor & Barnes, Camden, Ark., 1964-66, Barnes & Roberts, Camden, 1966-68, Gaughan, Laney, Barnes & Roberts, Camden, 1968-78, Gaughan, Laney & Barnes, Camden, 1978-82; mcpl. judge Camden and Ouachita Counties, 1975-82; circuit judge 13th jud. dist. State of Ark., 1982-93; judge U.S. Dist. Ct. (we. dist.) Ark., 1993—; mem. Ark. Jud. Discipline and Disability Commn. With USMC, 1956-86, col. res. ret. Named Outstanding Trial Judge in Ark., Ark. Trial Lawyers Assn., 1986. Mem. ABA, Ark. Bar Assn., Ark. Jud. Coun. (bd. dirs.). Office: PO Box 1735 El Dorado AR 71731-1735

BARNES, HARRY G., JR., human rights activist, conflict resolution specialist, retired ambassador; b. St. Paul, June 5, 1926; s. Harry George and Bertha Pauline (Blaul) B.; m. Elizabeth Ann Sibley; children: Pauline, Adrienne, Douglas, Sibley. BA summa cum laude, Amherst Coll., 1949, LLD (hon.), 1984; MA in History, Columbia U., 1968; PhD in Engring. (hon.), Stevens Inst., 1985; LLD (hon.), Monterey Inst. Internat. Studies, 1989. With fgn. service U.S. Dept. State, 1951-88; vice-consul Bombay, India, 1951-53; vice consul, 2d sec. Prague, Czechoslovakia, 1953-55, Moscow, 1957-59; polit. officer Office of Soviet affairs, Dept. State, Washington, 1959-62; dep. chief mission Kathmandu, Nepal, 1963-67; dep. chief of mission Bucharest, Romania, 1968-71; chief jr. officer program Dept. State, Washington, 1971-72, dep. exec. sec., 1972-74; amb. to Romania Bucharest, 1974-77; dir. gen. fgn. service, dir. pers. Dept. State, Washington, 1977-81; amb. to India, New Delhi, 1981-85, Chile, Santiago, 1985-88, ret.; exec. dir. Critical Langs. and Area Studies Consortium, 1989-94; dir. conflict resolution and human rights programs The Carter Ctr., Atlanta, 1994—; Cyrus Vance vis. prof. internat. rels. Mt. Holyoke Coll., spring 1990; Sol Linowitz vis. prof. internat. rels. Hamilton Coll., fall 1990; James and Joan Warburg vis. prof. internat. rels. Simmons Coll., fall 1991-spring 1993; sr. fellow World Wild Life Fund-Conservation Found., 1989—; interim dir. Human Rights Program Career Ctr., 1993-94; chmn. bd. dirs. Romanian-Am. Enterprise Fund, 1996—. With U.S.Army, 1944-46. Decorated Grand Cross, Order of Bernardo O'Higgins (Chile), 1990; recipient Pres.' Meritorious Svc. award, 1983, 88, Pres.' Disting. Svc. award, 1987. Presbyterian. Avocation: trekking. Home: PO Box 73 Peacham VT 05862-0073 Office: Carter Ctr One Copenhill Atlanta GA 30307*

BARNES, HOWARD G., communications executive, film and video producer; b. N.Y.C., Dec. 27, 1913; m. Joan Lesavoy, Jan. 9, 1949 (div. Nov. 1957); foster children: Marshall Alan (dec.), Denis Joy; m. Mary Ellena Mock, Dec. 7, 1958 (div.); children: Christie Ann, Paul Louis Lloyd; m. Patricia Lee Sills, August 4, 1965 (div.); children: Paxton Louise, Gillian Leigh. A.B., U. Mich., 1935. Announcer radio sta. WIP, Phila., 1935, KYW, Phila., WHN, N.Y.C., 1936; producer WOR Mut., 1936-38; exec. producer MCA, 1938; producer, writer, exec. CBS, N.Y.C., 1938-46; v.p. in charge network programs CBS Radio, 1955-60; dir. programs CBS-TV, Hollywood, 1960-63; producing independently, 1946-48; v.p. in charge radio and TV Dorland, Inc., N.Y.C., 1948-51; pres. Gen. Entertainment Corp., 1949-60; TV exec. Ashley Famous Agy., Inc., 1963-66; dir. film prodn. Westinghouse Broadcasting Co., N.Y.C., 1966-67; exec. v.p. Group W Films Westinghouse Broadcasting Co., 1967-73, also dir. parent co.; ind. producer, 1973-89; gen. mgr., dir. advt. The Walking Ctr., Beverly Hills, Calif., 1989-91; pres. Ragazza Inc., Washington, Conn., 1980-81; bd. govs. Dramalites, Washington, Conn., 1979-89; dir. Trio Films, Ltd., London, 1973-79; ptnr. The Barnes/Sabinson Partnership, 1976-84; exec. dir. Entertainment Hall of Fame Found., 1974-77; cons. film and video Conn. State Dept. Edn., 1985-89; lectr. Sch. Comm., San Diego State U., 1996-97. Lt. USNR, 1942-45. Home: 1930 W San Marcos Blvd Spc 358 San Marcos CA 92069-3930

BARNES, HUBERT LLOYD, geochemistry educator; b. Chelsea, Mass., July 20, 1928; s. George Lloyd and Mary Ellen (MacPherson) B.; m. Mary Talbot Westergaard; children: Roy Malcolm, Catherine Patricia. BS, MIT, 1950; PhD, Columbia U., 1958. Resident geologist Peru Mining Co., Hanover, N.Mex., 1950-52; lectr. geology Columbia U., N.Y.C., 1952-54; postdoctoral fellow Geophys. Lab. Carnegie Inst., Washington, 1956-60; prof. Pa. State U., University Park, 1960-96, dir. ore deposits rsch. sect., 1969-96, emeritus, 1997; vis. prof. Mineralogy-Petrology Inst., Heidelberg, 1974, Academia Sinica, 1983, U. Sydney, 1987, U. Witwatersrand, 1990; Crosby lectr. MIT, Cambridge, 1983, mem. geophysics rsch. bd. NRC, 1976-80; mem. U.S. Nat. Com. on Geology, 1983-86; cons. numerous corps.; dir. NATO Advanced Study Inst., Salamanca, 1987; gen. chmn. 1st Goldschmidt Conf., Balt., 1988, co-chmn. PA. State U., 1995; chmn., sec. Internat. Symposium on Hydrothermal Reactions, Pa. State U., 1985; guest prof. Nanjing U., People's Republic of China, 1996; Air-India disting. lectr. Indian Inst. Tech., Bombay, 1996; hon. prof., disting. vis. fellow U. Wales, 1996—; pres. Applied Rsch. & Exploration, 1994—. Author: Uranium Prospecting, 1956. Editor: Geochemistry of Hydrothermal Ore Deposits, 1967, 79, 97; co-editor: Hydrothermal Experimental Techniques, 1987; consulting editor Internat. Geol. Rev., 1999—. Vice-pres. Pa. chpt. Humboldt Found., 1996—. N.L. Britton scholar, 1955-56; Guggenheim fellow, 1966-67, Japan Soc. Promotion Sci. fellow, 1997; recipient Sr. Humboldt prize Humboldt Found. Germany, 1988; named Disting. Prof. Geochemistry Pa. State U., 1990; Can. Inst. Mining and Metallurgy lectr., 1969, C.F. Davidson lectr., St. Andrews, Scotland, 1971. Fellow Mineral Soc. Am., Geol. Soc. Am., Geochem. Soc. (councillor 1970-73, v.p. 1983, pres. 1984-85); mem. Soc. Econ. Geologists (councilor 1981-84, Thayer Lindsley lectr. 1980-81), Am. Geologic Inst. (governing bd. 1981-83), U.S. Nat. Geochemistry Com. (chmn. 1976-78). Home: 213 E Mitchell Ave State College PA 16803-3655 Office: Pa State U Ore Deposits Rsch Sect 235 Deike Bldg University Park PA 16802-2711

BARNES, ISABEL JANET, microbiology educator, college dean; b. Union City, N.J., Sept. 22, 1936; d. Carl Robert and Isabel Sarah (Cappelletti) B.; m. John D. Bowman, June 15, 1978 (dec. Nov. 1986). BS, Pa. State U., 1958; MS, Cornell U., 1960; PhD, Hahnemann Med. Coll., 1969; postgrad., Inst. Ednl. Mgmt. Harvard U., 1991. Asst. prof. microbiology Hershey Med. Ctr., Pa. State U., 1968-73; asst. prof., then assoc. prof. Sangamon State U., Springfield, Ill., 1973-76; assoc. prof. med. tech. U. Wis., Madison, 1976-85; interim dean Sch. Allied Health Professions, 1981-84; prof. med. tech. Ferris State U., Big Rapids, Mich., 1985—; dean Coll. Applied Health Scis., 1985—, acting v.p. Acad. Affairs, 1992-93. Bd. dirs. Mecosta County Gen. Hosp., 1988—, sec. 1991-94, pres., 1996-97, v.p. 1997-99, Alliance for Health, 1993—, Mich. Hemophilia Found., 1989-95, 97—, sec. 1991-94. Mem. AAUP, Assn. of Schs. of Allied Health Professions (bd. dirs. 1989-91), Coll. Health Deans (pres. 1988-90), Am. Assn. Higher Edn., Nat. Assn.

Women in Edn., Mich. Bd. Podiatric Medicine and Surgery. Office: Ferris State U Coll Allied Health Scis Big Rapids MI 49307

BARNES, JAMES A., journalist. BA in Russia Area Studies, Washington and Lee U., 1978. Rsch. assoc. Am. Enterprise Inst.; chief speechwriter U.S. Sec. Treasury James Baker; polit. corr. Nat. Jour., 1987—. Office: Nat Jour 1501 M St NW Ste 300 Washington DC 20005-1700*

BARNES, JAMES BYRON, university president; b. Akron, Ohio, Apr. 4, 1942; s. Roy and Kathleen (Elrod) B.; m. Tommie Schade, Aug. 14, 1965. AB in Social Sci., Ind. Wesleyan U., 1965; MEd in History, Kent State U., 1969; Ed.S. in History and Social Sci., Vanderbilt U., 1972; EdD in Social Sci. Edn., U. Ga., 1976. Assoc. prof. Cen. (S.C.) Wesleyan Coll., 1970-76; assoc. prof. Ind. Wesleyan U., Marion, 1976-81, dean of coll., 1981-84; asst. gen sec. Dept. Edn. and Ministry Wesleyan Ch., Marion, 1984-85; v.p. acad. affairs Houghton (N.Y.) Coll., 1985-87; pres. Ind. Wesleyan U., Marion, 1987—. Mem. Grant Co. Community Found., Marion, 1987—; mem. adv. bd. Salvation Army, 1989—. Grantee NEH, 1987. Mem. Rotary, Marion/Grant County C. of C. Mem. Wesleyan Ch. Office: Ind Wesleyan U 4201 S Washington St Marion IN 46953-4990*

BARNES, JAMES GARLAND, JR., lawyer; b. Ga., Mar. 3, 1940; s. James Garland Sr. and Carolyn L. (Stewart) B.; m. Lucy Curtis Ferguson, Nov. 1976; children: Susan Whitney, David Lawrence, Matthew Martin. BA, Yale U., 1961; LLB, U. Mich., 1966. Bar: Ill. 1967. With firm Baker & McKenzie, Chgo., 1966—, ptnr., 1973—. Co-author: The ABCs of the UCC Article 5: Letters of Credit. Mem. adv. com. Ill. Sec. of State's Corp. Acts, 1981-95; U.S. del. to UNCITRAL, 1993-95, ICC Banking Com., 1998. Mem. ABA (chmn. letter of credit subcom. 1991-96), Ill. Bar Assn. (chmn. corp. and security law sect. 1977-78), Chgo. Bar Assn. (chmn. corp. law com. 1982-83, chmn. profl. responsibility com. 1983-84), Legal Club Chgo. Office: Baker & McKenzie 1 Prudential Pla 130 E Randolph St Ste 3700 Chicago IL 60601-6342

BARNES, JAMES JOHN, history educator; b. St. Paul, Nov. 16, 1931; s. Harry George and Bertha (Blaul) B.; m. Patience Rogers Plummer, July 9, 1955; children—Jennifer Chase, Geoffrey Prescott. BA, Amherst Coll., 1954; B.A., New Coll., Oxford, 1956, MA, 1961; PhD, Harvard U., 1960; DHL, Coll. of Wooster, 1976. Instr. history Amherst Coll., 1959-62; asst. prof. history Wabash Coll., Crawfordsville, Ind., 1962-67, assoc. prof. history, 1967-76, prof. history, 1976—, chmn. dept. history, Hadley prof., 1979-97. Author: Free Trade in Books: A Study of the London Book Trade since 1800, 1964, Authors, Publishers and Politicians: The Quest for an Anglo-American Copyright Agreement 1815-54, 1974, (with Patience P. Barnes) Hitler's Mein Kampf in Britain and America 1930-39, 1980, (with Patience P. Barnes) James Vincent Murphy: Translator and Interpreter of Fascist Europe, 1880-1946, 1987, (with Patience P. Barnes) Private and Confidential Letters from British Ministers in Washington to the Foreign Secretaries in London, 1849-67, 1993; contbr. articles to profl. jours. Mem. Rhodes Scholar Selection Com. for Ind., 1965-89, Crawfordsville Community Action Coun., 1966-69, Crawfordsville Community Day Care Com., 1966-67; mem. vestry St. John's Episcopal Ch., 1966-69; mem. Ind. Adv. Com. State Rehab. Svcs. for Blind, 1979-81; trustee Ind. Hist. Soc., 1982—. Recipient Disting. Alumni award St. Paul Acad. and Summit Sch., 1989; Rhodes scholar, 1954-56, Fulbright scholar, 1978; Woodrow Wilson fellow, 1956-57, Kent fellow, 1958, Great Lakes Colls. Assn. Teaching fellow, 1958, Great Lakes Colls. Assn. Teaching fellow, 1975; rsch. grantee Amherst Coll., 1960-61, Social Sci. Rsch. Coun., 1962, 70, Wabash Coll., 1962—, Am. Coun. Learned Socs., 1964-65, 80, Am. Philos. Soc., 1964, 68, 76, 91; named Hon. Alumnus, Wabash Coll., 1994. Mem. Am. Hist. Assn., Ouiatenon Literary Soc., Conf. Brit. Studies, Rsch. Soc. Victorian Periodicals, Am. Rhodes Scholars, Soc. Historians Am. Fgn. Rels., Ind. Hist. Soc., Montgomery County Hist. Soc., Midwest Victorian Studies Assn. (pres. 1989-91), Ind. Assn. Historians, N.E. Victorian Studies Assn., Nat. Book League, U.S. Chess Fedn., Bibliog. Soc. U.K., Soc. for History of Authorship, Reading and Pub., Am. Coun. of Blind, United Oxford and Cambridge Club of London, Phi Beta Kappa. Home: 7 Locust Hl Crawfordsville IN 47933-3347 Office: Wabash Coll History Dept Crawfordsville IN 47933

BARNES, JAMES MILTON, physics and astronomy educator; b. Ypsilanti, Mich., July 5, 1923; s. J. Milton and Elsie (Fischer) B.; m. Marjorie Ruth Petersen, Dec. 17, 1949. B.S., Eastern Mich. U., 1948; M.S., Mich. State U., 1950, Ph.D., 1955. Asst. prof. Eastern Mich. U., Ypsilanti, 1955-58, asso. prof., 1958-61, prof., 1961-88, prof. emeritus, 1988—, head dept. physics and astronomy, 1961-74. Served with AUS, 1942-46. Mem. A.A.A.S. (life), Nat. Sci. Tchrs. Assn. (life), Am. Assn. Physics Tchrs., Sigma Xi, Sigma Pi Sigma, Pi Mu Epsilon. Club: Ann Arbor (Mich.) Country. Home: 4872 Whitman Cir Ann Arbor MI 48103-9774 Office: Eastern Mich U Physics Dept Ypsilanti MI 48197

BARNES, JAMES RANDAL, state official; b. El Dorado, Ark., May 1, 1951; s. James William and Nelda Faye (Brooks) B.; m. Angela Alvilda Pick, Apr. 24, 1982; children: Alexandra Brooks, Andrew August. BBA, Baylor U., 1973; MPA, SW Tex State U., 1998. Employment interviewer Employment Commn. State of Tex., Sulphur Springs, 1973-75, statistician, 1983-92; labor market analyst Employment Commn. State of Tex., Austin, 1975-83; planner Employment Commn., State of Tex., Austin, 1992-94, asst. dir. Labor Market Info. Workforce Commn., 1994—; broker First Pick Realty, Temple, Tex., 1986-95. Alderman City of Pflugerville, Tex., 1992-94, mem. libr. bd., 1994, co-chmn. Deutschen Pfest, 1990, vice chmn. parks and recreation commn., 1991-92; co-chmn. ch. advance bldg fund dr., St. Elizabeth Ch., Pflugerville, 1995. Mem. Tex. Pub. Employees Assn. (pres. 1993), Amer. Soc. for Pub. Administration, Pi Alpha-Natl. Hon. Soc. for Pub. Affairs and Administration. Avocations: reading, walking, youth soccer coach. Office: State Tex Workforce Commn 101 E 15th St Austin TX 78701-1442

BARNES, JAMES THOMAS, JR., aquarium director; b. Southport, N.C., June 28, 1958; s. James Thomas Sr. and Kathleen Hall B.; m. Robin Antoinette Sluder, June 1, 1991; children: Heather Michelle Leonard, Lindsey Kathleen Barnes. B Environ. Product Design, N.C State U., 1980; MFA in Advt. Design, Syracuse U., 1988. Designer Wittkamp Design Assocs., Raleigh, N.C., 1980; exhibits curator N.C. Aquarium, Pine Knoll Shores, N.C., 1980-87, exhibit, design cons., 1987-89, dir., 1989—. Author: North Carolina's Hurricane History, 1994 (Book award N.C. Soc. Historians 1995), Florida's Hurricane History, 1998. Recipient Design award Am. Soc. Tech. Comm., Nat. Frisbee Design award, 1986, ADDY Design award, 1989, Charlton Tebeau Book award Fla. Hist. Soc., 1999. Mem. Am. Assn. Zool. Parks and Aquariums, Lions. Democrat. Methodist. Avocations: photography, music, surfing, basketball, writing. Office: North Carolina Aquarium PO Box 580 Atlantic Beach NC 28512

BARNES, JANICE BRYANT, elementary educator; b. Texarkana, Ark., Oct. 18, 1945; d. Willard T. and Lorene (Combs) B.; m. William Howard Barnes, Feb. 17, 1973; children: Wendy, Bill. BS in Edn., Henderson State U., 1967, MS in Edn., 1969; MS, Memphis State U., 1984, cert. in adminstrn. and supervision, 1987. Tchr. Texarkana Pub. Schs., 1967-70; tchr. Hamilton Elem. Sch. Memphis City Schs., 1970-73, tchr. A.B. Hill Elem. Sch., 1973-77, tchr. Sharpe Elem. Sch., 1977-91, tchr. Knight Rd. Elem. Sch., 1991-92, instrnl. facilitator Knight Rd. Elem. Sch., 1992—. Co-author curriculum materials in field. Bd. dirs. Mountain Tenn. Outreach Project, Nashville, 1992-97, Memphis Chrysalis Cmty., 1997—; pastor parish rels. com. Asbury United Meth. Ch., Memphis, 1996—, youth dir., 1989-94. Mem. ASCD, Internat. Reading Assn., Nat. Assn. for Year-Round Edn. Methodist. Fax: 901-366-2516. Office: Knight Rd Elem Sch 3237 Knight Rd Memphis TN 38118-4200

BARNES, JAY WILLIAM, JR., architect, rancher; b. Austin, Tex., Aug. 26, 1924; s. Jay William Sr. and Helen Vera (Colvin) B.; m. Eva Hoop, Apr. 12, 1952; children: Jay William III, Sherrill Ann. BS in Civil Engring., U. Tex., 1950. Registered architect, Ariz., Nev., La., Okla., Mont., N.Mex.; registered structural engr., Tex. Draftsman Preston Geren, Architect, Ft. Worth, 1950-55; architect, ptnr. Barnes, Landes & Goodman, Austin, 1955-58, Barnes Landes Goodman Youngblood, Austin, 1958-83; owner, rancher J Bar E Investments, Austin, 1983—; chmn., trustee Tex. Archtl. Found., Austin, 1973-83; chmn. Am. Inst. Archtl. Rsch., Washington, 1978; lectr. U. Tex., Austin, 1988-91. prin. works include Austin H.S., First Bapt. Ch., Brackenridge Hosp., Jr. Sr. H.S. Hopi Nation, Second Mesa, Ariz. Mem. Performance Certification Bd., Tex., 1972-73; vice-chmn. Conv. Ctr. Com., Austin. Sgt. U.S. Army, 1943-46, ETO, Asia. Fellow AIA (treas., dir. 1974-78); mem. Tex. Soc. Architects (pres., dir. 1961-92, Llewelyn W. Pitts award 1986), Austing C. of C. (bd. dirs., v.p., 1972-74), Nat. Coun. Architects Registration Bd., Austin Country Club, Lions (pres. 1955-80), Masons, U. Tex. Ex-Students Assn., Littlefield Soc. Republican. Baptist. Avocations: golf, fly fishing. Home: 3905 Belmont Park Dr Apt A Austin TX 78746-1168*

BARNES, JHANE ELIZABETH, fashion design company executive, designer; b. Balt., Mar. 4, 1954; d. Richard Amos and Muriel Florence (Chase) B.; m. Howard Ralph Feinberg, Dec. 12, 1981 (div.); m. 2d, Katsuhiko Kawasaki, Feb. 12, 1988. A.S., Fashion Inst. Tech., 1975. Pres., designer Jhane Barnes for ME, N.Y.C., 1976-78; pres., designer, owner Jhane Barnes Inc., N.Y.C., 1978—; owner Jhane Barnes Textiles, LLC. Recipient Coty award Menswear Am. Fashion Critics, 1980, 1984, Contract Textile award Am. Soc. Interior Designers, 1983, 84, Product Design awards Inst. Bus. Designers and Contract Mag., 1983-86, 94, Outstanding Am. Menswear Designer award Woolmark, 1990, Dalmore, 1990, Good Design award Best of Neo Con award. I.D. 40, 1996, 97; named Most Promising Designer Cutty Sark, 1980, Outstanding Designer, 1982, Outstanding Menswear Designer, Coun. of Fashion Designers Am., 1982, Design Resources Coun., 1989, 94, Designer of Yr., Neckwear Assn. Am., 1997. Office: Jhane Barnes Inc 119 W 40th St Fl 20 New York NY 10018-3904

BARNES, JOANNA, author, actress; b. Boston, Nov. 15, 1934; d. John Pindar and Alice Weston (Mutch) B. BA, Smith Coll., 1956. Actress appearing in motion pictures: Auntie Mame, 1958, B.S. I Love You, 1971, Spartacus, 1963, The Parent Trap, 1961, The War Wagon, 1971, The Parent Trap, 1998; TV appearances include What's My Line, The Tonight Show with Johnny Carson, Merv Griffin Show, Trials of O'Brien, Dateline: Hollywood, Murder She Wrote; book reviewer L. A. Times, syndicated columnist Chgo. Tribune, N.Y. News Syndicate, 1963-65; author: Starting from Scratch, 1968, The Deceivers, 1970, Who Is Carla Hart, 1973, Pastora, 1980, Silverwood, 1985. Mem. Phi Beta Kappa.

BARNES, JOHN WADSWORTH, director, writer; b. Belford, N.J., Mar. 25, 1920; s. Edward Crosby and Dorothy M. (Leek) B.; m. Joan Waddell, Sept. 5, 1942 (div. Jan. 1952); m. Jeanne Leah Weinstein, June 6, 1953; children: Joshua Edward, Judith Ann, Ezra David. *Wife Jean Weinstein, MM, American Conservatory of Music, Chicago, 1954. Violinist Bloomingdale House of Music, Manhattan. Concert Master, The Brooklyn Height Symphony Orchestra. Son Joshua Edward, BA in Astronomy and Astrophysics, Harvard 1979; PhD in Astronomy, University of California, Berkely 1984. Member of Institute for Advanced Study, Princeton, 1984-89. Associate professor, Institute of Astronomy, University of Hawaii. Daughter Judith, New York Studio School, Paris; Art Student's League. Apprenticed to sculptor Jose De Creeft. Mezzo soprano: Shelter Island Friends of Music, Dame Myra Hess Concert Series, Chicago. Son Ezra David, BA in English and theatre Amherst 1984; MFA in acting, National Theatre Conservatory. Leading actor Off-Broadway and regional, 1989.* Diploma, Monmouth Jr. Coll., Long Branch, N.J., 1939; student, U. Chgo., 1939-42. Editor Trend, a literary mag., Chgo., 1941-42; writer, dir. Columbia Broadcasting System, Chgo., 1942-46; editor Together The Urban League, Chgo., 1947; freelance writer, 1948-50; writer, dir., producer Ency. Britannica Films, Wilmette, Ill., 1951-55, London, 1955-63, Rome, 1963-65; exec. producer N.Y. Film Unit, Ency. Britannica Ednl. Corp., N.Y.C., 1965-73; pres. John Barnes Prodns., N.Y.C., 1973—; bd. dirs. Nat. Shakespeare Co., N.Y.C.; Shakespeare adv. bd. Colonial Theatre, Westerly, R.I. *From reviews of Barnes' films: Howard Thompson, New York Times: "Comes the revolution to the tired, assembly-line format of educational films: the accomplishment primarily of the brilliant young director-producer, John Barnes." Cecille Starr, Saturday Review of Literature: "Here we are, quite suddenly and unexpectedly, faced with two educational films by writer-director-producer John Barnes which any adult could sit through with pleasure." David Shone, Media and Methods: "This was a difficult film to realize, but Barnes brings it off with a subtle grace and power that are remarkable."* Writer, dir., prodr.: (films) To Live Together, 1950, The Baltimore Plan (Edinburgh Film Festival) 1952, American Revolution (Boston Film Festival) 1954, The Living City (Oscar nomination 1953), Eng.: William Shakespeare, 1954, The Pilgrims, 1954, Michelangelo (Am. Film Festival award 1966); writer, co-dir.: (with Gordon Weisenborn) People of the Mississippi (Edinburgh Film Festival), 1952; prodr., co-dir. Can. Oedipus Rex, 1959, Hamlet, 1959, Eng.: Great Expectations, 1960, Greece: Athens, The Golden Age, 1961, Eng.: Magna Carta, parts I and II, 1960 (Scholastic Nat. Film award), France: Art of the Middle Ages and Chartres Cathedral, 1962, Eng: Macbeth, 1964, John Keats, His Life and Death, 1973; author: (book for musical) The Beautiful Dream of Ilya Ilich Oblomov, 1983 (TV serial) Rape of the Fair Country, BBC-TV, 1982; writer play Kidnapped, 1989, Kembles of the Garden, 1990, Huck and Jim, 1990, Alice James, 1991. Bd. of govs. St. Ann's Sch., Bklyn., 1970-75; pres. Bklyn. Heights Music Soc., Bklyn., 1985-88, pres. emeritus, 1988—. John Barnes week long showing of films Institutio Mexicano Norte Americano De Relaciones Culturales, 1966, series of weekly screenings of films Ciné 16, San Jose, Calif., 1997-98; several films named to Nat. Archives. Mem. The Dramatists Guild, Inc. Democrat. Home: 144 Columbia Hts Brooklyn NY 11201-1690

BARNES, JOSEPH CURTIS, aircraft development executive; b. Ashland, Oreg., Jan. 1, 1913; s. Joseph Curtis and Flora Ellis (Bushong) B.; m. Janet A. Eames, Nov. 1, 1942; children: Joseph Curtis III, Robin Bushong, Bonnie McLean. AB, Stanford U., 1935, MA, 1938; student V-7 program, USN Acad., 1940. Artist Walt Disney Studio, Burbank, Calif., 1938-40; with Barnes Bros., Medford, Orgn., 1940-80; chief exec. officer Tipsy Bee Rsch., Medford, 1980-86. Patentee vertical lift by flettner rotor; inventor silent lift vehicle, vehicle for vertical flight and ground transport. Served to lt. comdr. USNR, 1940-46, PTO. Mem. Am. Helicopter Soc. Republican. Avocation: application of man power for vertical flight. Home and Office: 4455 Fern Valley Rd Medford OR 97504-9405

BARNES, JUDITH ANNE, communications executive; b. Rochester, N.Y., Feb. 28, 1948; d. Robert William and Louise (Marriott) B. BA in English, Russell Sage Coll., 1970; MS in Tech. Communication, Rensselaer Polytechnic Inst., 1971, PhD in Communications, 1984. Asst. dir. admissions Russell Sage Coll., Troy, N.Y., 1971-72; spl. cons. communications The Rensselaerville (N.Y.) Inst., 1973-77; dir. advt. The Mayfair Group Stores, Albany, N.Y., 1977-82; dir., communications Cohoes (N.Y.) Specialty Stores, 1984-86, v.p., mktg., advt., and communications, 1986-89; prin. J.A. Barnes & Co., 1989—; adj. instr., lectr. various univs. and orgns. and tech. comm. seminars for industry, 1971—; comm. and advt. cons. for numerous bus., health, profl., comml. and civic orgns., 1971—. Author: Understanding Freedom of Speech in America, 1976. Co-founder, v.p. mktg. and programming, bd. dirs. Troy Music Hall Assn., 1979-82; co-founder, bd. dirs. Capitol Chamber Artists, Troy; bd. dirs. Capital Regional Mag., Albany, Troy Econ. Devel. Commn., Cowan and Lobel Gourmet Marketplace, Friends of Chamber Music, Troy Chromatic Concerts, Heritage Artists, Cohoes Music Hall, Historic Albany Found., Hudson-Mohawk Urban Cultural Park Commn., Samaritan Hosp. Found., Upper Hudson Planned Parenthood, Ctr. Gallery; chair bd. trustees The Sage Colls. Mem. Rensselaer Poly. Inst. Alumni Assn. Democrat. Avocations: gardening, historic preservation, art, symphonies, dance.

BARNES, JUDITH P., nursing administrator; b. Hornsby, Tenn., Mar. 2, 1946; d. Jack Clayton and Ethyl (Tate) Parsons; m. Jesse C. Barnes, Sr., Nov. 11, 1967; children: Jessika, Jesse Jr., Jason, Jennifer, Jeremiah, Janey. Student, Memphis State U., 1964-65; diploma, Bapt. Coll. Nursing, Memphis, 1967; AS, Meridian (Miss.) Jr. Coll., 1975; student, Tidewater Community Coll., Chesapeake, Va., 1983-84, 87-88. Cert. CPR instr., first aide instr., battlefield medic instr. Charge nurse Bapt. Meml. Hosp., 1967-68; air-evac nurse Trippler Army Hosp., Honolulu, 1968-69; lamaze instr., midwifery, labor and delivery Camp Kue Army Hosp., Naha, Okinawa, 1970-73; staff nurse, charge nurse, nurse mgr. Jeff Anderson Meml. Hosp., Meridian, 1973-76; supr., nurse mgr. Maryview Med. Ctr., Portsmouth, Va., 1981-89; ER trauma nurse, charge Norfolk Gen. Hosp., 1981-88; hemodialysis nurse, charge Hampton Gen., Hope, Hampton, Va.; DON Autumn Care, Suffolk, Va., 1981-82; DON, supr. Newport News Gen. Hosp., Newport News, Va., 1989-97; med. officer 801st Airborne and 81st MP Divsn., Fort Story, Va., 1993-96; mgr. Anthem Alliance for Healthcare Inc., Portsmouth, Va., 1998—; mem. alcohol abuse team Kaiser Meml. Found., Honolulu, 1968-70; tchr., instr. Suffolk Christian Sch., 1977-81; inservice edn., staff devel. Childrens Hosp. of the Kings Daughters, Childrens Health Line, 1997—. Capt. U.S. Army, 1968-73, USAR, 1988—. Decorated Commendation Medal U.S. Army. Mem. Res. Officers Assn., Assn. Mil. Surgeons U.S., Tenn. Nurses Assn., Res. Officers Assn., Emergency Nurses Assn., VFW, ROA, AARP, Va. Nurses Assn. Home: 617 Brunswick Rd Portsmouth VA 23701-2222

BARNES, KAREN KAY, lawyer; b. Independence, Iowa, June 22, 1950; s. Walter William and Vashti (Greenlee) Sessler; m. James Alan Barnes, Feb. 12, 1972; children: Timothy Matthew, Christopher Michael. BA, Valparaiso U., 1971; JD, DePaul U., 1978, LLM in Taxation, 1980. Bar: Ill. 1978, U.S. Dist. Ct. (no. dist.) Ill. 1978. Ptnr. McDermott, Will & Emery, Chgo., 1978-88; prin. William M. Mercer, Inc. and predecessor firm, Chgo., 1989-93; staff dir. legal dept. McDonald's Corp., Oak Brook, Ill., 1993-95, home office dir. legal dept., 1995-97, regulatory practice group leader and mng. counsel, 1998—; instr. John Marshall Grad. Sch. Law, Chgo., 1986-87; mem. adv. bd. John Marshall Sch. Law, 1996—. Contbr. case note to DePaul Law Rev., 1976, note and comment editor DePaul Law Rev., 1976-77, editor Taxation For Lawyers, 1986-88. Mem. Chgo. Bar Assn. (chair employee benefits com. 1991-92), Midwest Pension Conf. (name chnged to Midwest Benefits Coun.), WEB (pres. Chgo. chpt. 1986-88, v.p. nat. bd. 1988, pres, 1989-90), Profit Sharing Coun. Am. (legal and legis. com. 1994—, bd. dirs. 1997—, 2d vice chair 1997-98, 1st vice chair 1998-99). Lutheran. Home: 3 S 102 Black Cherry Ln Glen Ellyn IL 60137 Office: McDonald's Corp McDonald's Plz Oak Brook IL 60523-1900

BARNES, KATE, poet; b. Apr. 9, 1932. BA, Scripps Coll., 1952. appt. first poet laureate, State of Maine, 1997—. Author: (poetry collections) Crossing the Field, 1995, Where the Deer Were, 1995; contbr. to numerous lit. mags., including Harpers and The New Yorker.

BARNES, KAY, mayor of Kansas City, Missouri. BS in Secondary Edn., U. Kans.; MS in Secondary Edn. and Pub. Adminstrn., U. Mo., Kansas City. Staff mem. Westport area Cross-Lines Coop. Coun.; pres. Kay Waldo, Inc., human resources devel. co., Kansas City, Mo.; Mayor City of Kansas City, Mo., 1999—; condr. over 400 pub. seminars Nat. Seminars, Inc.; cons., keynote spkr. 14 reginal confs. through U.S., Am. Bus. Women's Assn.; former co-host, prodr. cable TV show Let's Talk; former instr. U. Mo., Kansas City, U. Kans., Ctrl. Mich. U. Author: About Time! A Woman's Guide to Time Management. Co-founder Ctrl. Exch.; vol. Cross-Lines Coop. Coun.; a founder women's resource svc. U. Mo., Kansas City; developer multicultural women's speaking panels through western U.S.; mem. Jackson County (Mo.) Legislature, from 1974; mem. Kansas City City Coun., from 1979; chmn. Tax Increment Financing Commn., 1993-97; pres. bd. dirs. Women's Employment Network; mem. or dir. numerous other orgns., including Women's Found. Greater Kansas City, Greater Kansas City Sports Commn.; mem. chancellor's adv. bd. of Women's Ctr., U. Mo., Kansas City. Named One of 7 Outstanding Women in Kansas City, 1977. Mem. Greater Kansas City C. of C. (com.). Office: Mayor's Office City Hall 29th Fl 414 E 12th St Kansas City MO 64106*

BARNES, KEITH LEE, electronics executive; b. San Francisco, Sept. 14, 1951; s. Arch Lee and Charlotte Mae (Sanborn) B.; m. Sharon Ann Tosaw, June 9, 1976; children: Allecia, Alexandra, Wyatt. BS, Calif. State U., San Jose, 1976. Mgr. engring. and mktg. Gould, Inc., Rolling Meadow, Ill., 1976-79; v.p., gen. mgr. Kontron Electronics, Mountain View, Calif., 1979-85; v.p. Valley Data Scis., Mountain View, 1985-86; pres., CEO Integrated Measurement Sys., Beaverton, Oreg., 1986—; bd. dirs. Data Io Corp., VXI Electronics. Patentee in field. Bd. dirs. Lintner Ctr. for Higher Edn., Portland, 1993-94, Eclipse Tech., Beaverton, 1994-95, Am. Electronics Assn., 1992-93, chmn. Oreg. bd., 1993; bd. trustees Oreg. Grad. Inst. for Sci. and Industry, 1996—. Mem. IEEE, PGC. Republican. Roman Catholic. Office: Integrated Measurement Systems 9525 SW Gemini Dr Beaverton OR 97008-7149

BARNES, LARRY GLEN, journalist, editor, educator; b. Louisville, July 10, 1947; s. Roy Glen and Phyllis Jane (Dunn) B.; m. Susan Gayle Morrow, Dec. 27, 1969 (dec. July, 1973); 1 child, Brian; m. Mary Frances Meiman, July 14, 1979. Student, Murray State U., 1965-68, 71-73, Def. Info. Sch., 1968. Journalist, editor various locations Dept. of the Army, 1968-71; staff writer Louisville Courier-Jour., 1972-75, Lexington (Ky.) Herald-Leader, 1975; mng. editor Corydon (Ind.) Harrison County Press, 1976-77; assoc. editor Ky. Sports World, Louisville, 1977-81; editor Publs. Divsn., Ft. Knox, Ky., 1981-82, Inside the Turret, Ft. Knox, 1982—. With U.S. Army, 1968-71. Recipient Naismith citation Atlanta Tipoff Club, 1981, Journalist award Dept. Army, Washington, 1986, 1st pl. commentary writing Tng. & Doctrine Command. Ft. Monroe, Va., 1985, 87, 88, 89, 90, Thomas Jefferson award Dept. Def., Washington, 1982, 86; named Editor of Yr., Army Tng & Doctrine Command, 1982. Mem. Soc. Profl. Journalists, Am. Fedn. Govt. Employees. Democrat. Baptist. Avocations: photography, watching movies, collecting, 45 r.p.m. records, reading. Home: 2220 Manchester Rd Louisville KY 40205-3044 Office: Pub Affairs Office PO Box 995 Fort Knox KY 40121

BARNES, LYNNE HANAWALT, nurse, educator; b. Williamsport, Pa., Nov. 30, 1943; d. Donald R. and Rita K. (Kohllepp) Hanawalt; m. William C. Barnes, Nov. 1, 1975; children: Daniel R. Pierce, Wendy L. Mohr, Christopher, Geoffrey. Diploma, Riverside White Cross Sch. Nursing, 1964. Charge nurse Drs. Hosp., Columbus, Ohio, 1964-66; office nurse Dr. Ben Cohen, 1966-68; staff nurse Ohio State U. Hosp., Columbus; head nurse orthopedics unit S.W. Wash. Med. Ctr., Vancouver, 1971-73; head nurse urology and gen. surgery units Emanuel Hosp., Portland, Oreg., 1974-79; office nurse Columbia Family Physicians, Vancouver, 1980-94; nurse mgr. Vancouver Clinic-Battle Ground Satellite, 1994-96, Columbia Family Physicians, Vancouver, 1997-98, Olsten Health Svcs., Portland, 1999—; chmn. bd. diabetes edn. S.W. Wash. Health Dept.; founder, chair. regional seminar for continuing edn. office nurses, Oreg., Wash. Bd. mem. CDM Home Care Svcs., Vancouver. Mem. Am. Assn. Office Nurses (past nat. bd. dirs., past nat. sec.), Am. Assn. Urology Allied (past pres. Portland chpt., Chpt. of the Yr.), Oreg. Nurse's Assn., Columbia River Assn. Office Nurses (founder, pres.). Home: 3317 NE 103rd Ave Vancouver WA 98662-7565 Office: Olsten Health Svcs 825 NE 20th Ste 310 Portland OR 97232

BARNES, MARGARET ANDERSON, business consultant; b. Johnston County, N.C.; m. Benjamin Barnes, Dec. 26, 1959. BS, N.C. Ctrl. U., 1958; MA, U. Md., 1975; PhD, Columbia Pacific U., 1986. Lic. ins. agt., Md.; ordained Christian min. and elder in World Evangelism, 1992. Math. tchr. Tarboro (N.C.) Sch. Sys., 1959-61; math. statistician Bur. of Census, Suitland, Md., 1962-67, 69-70, Govt. of D.C., 1967-68; cons. NIH, Bethesda, Md., 1970-72; chief of data stds. Nat. Insts. of Health, Bethesda, Md., 1972-73; with exec. clearance office HEW, Rockville, Md., 1973-77; founder, pres. MABarnes Cons. Assoc., Lanham, Md., 1978-95; commr. State of Md. Accident Fund, Balt., 1979-89; mem. adv. bd. Universal Bank, Lanham, 1980-83, Interstate Gen. Corp., St. Charles, Md., 1981-83; founder Christian Ministries, 1983—, Christ Centered Ministries Esprit, 1995—, Mleecole Pub., 1997—; profiled for First Record: "Women of Achievement in Prince George's County History", 1994. Chairwoman Glenwood Park Civic Assn., Lanham, 1967-80. Democrat. Avocations: piano, sewing, reading, prose writing, artistic designing. Home: PO Box 586 Lanham Seabrook MD 20703-0586 Office: Christ Centered Ministries Esprit PO Box 802 Lanham Seabrook MD 20703-0802

BARNES, MARK JAMES, lawyer; b. Oak Park, Ill., Jan. 10, 1957; s. James W. and Lorraine (Brady) B. BS in Polit. Sci. summa cum laude, Ariz. State U., 1978; JD, UCLA, 1981. Staff atty. Senator Ted Stevens U.S. Senate, Washington, 1981-83, chief counsel Senator Ted Stevens, 1983-84; assoc. Davis, Wright & Jones, Anchorage, 1984-86; dep. gen. counsel U.S. Office of Personnel Mgmt., Washington, 1986-87; assoc. dir. adminstrn. U.S. Office Personnel Mgmt., Washington, 1988-89; counsel to sec. for drug abuse policy HHS, Washington, 1989-93; pvt. practice Washington, 1993—. Alaska ambassador organizing com. Anchorage Olympics, 1986; mem. exec. com.,

World Forum on Future of Sport Shooting Activities, 1998—. Mem. ABA, Alaska Bar Assn., Ariz. Bar Assn., D.C. Bar Assn., Phi Beta Kappa. Republican. Roman Catholic. Avocations: travel, movies, stamps. Office: 1350 Eye St NW Ste 1255 Washington DC 20005-3390

BARNES, MARTIN MCRAE, entomologist; b. Calgary, Alta., Can., Aug. 3, 1920; s. Harry Olan and Vida (Killian) B.; m. Julia Butts, Aug. 31, 1946; children—Wayne, Martin, Delia, Brian. B.S., U. Calif., Berkeley, 1941; Ph.D., Cornell U., 1946. Mem. faculty U. Calif., Riverside, 1946—, prof. entomology, 1962-91, prof. emeritus, 1991—, chmn. dept. entomology, 1988, entomologist agrl. rsch. expt. sta., 1946-91. Contbr. articles to profl. jours. Fellow AAAS, Entomol. Soc. Am. (hon., pres. Pacific br. 1976-77); mem. Sigma Xi. Democrat. Research in deciduous orchard and vineyard entomology, conservation of invertebrates. Home: 1946 Prince Albert Dr Riverside CA 92507-5836 Office: U Calif Dept Entomology Riverside CA 92521*

BARNES, MELVER RAYMOND, retired chemist; b. nr. Salisbury, N.C., Nov. 15, 1917; s. Oscar Lester and Sarah Albertine (Rowe) B. AB in Chemistry, U. N.C., 1947; D of Physics (hon.), World U., 1983; DSc in Chemistry (hon.), Assoc. Univs., 1987, PhD in Chemistry (hon.), 1990; PhD in Chemistry (hon.), Albert Einstein Internat. Acad. Found. and Associated Univs., 1990. Chemist Pitts. Testing Labs., Greensboro, N.C., 1948-49, N.C. State Hwy. and Pub. Works Commn., Raleigh, 1949-51, Edgewood (Md.) Arsenal, 1951-61, Dugway (Utah) Proving Ground, 1961-70. Recipient Albert Einstein Bronze medal, 1988, Alfred Nobel Medal award Albert Einstein Internat. Acad. Found., 1991, Albert Einstein Acad. Found. Cross of Merit, 1992. Mem. AAAS, Am. Statis. Assn., Am. Chem. Soc., Am. Phys. Soc. Home and Office: 1486 Swicegood Rd Linwood NC 27299-9386

BARNES, MICHAEL DARR, lawyer, think tank executive; b. Washington, Sept. 3, 1943; s. John P. and Vernon (Smith) B.; m. Claudia Fangboner, June 13, 1970; children—Sarah Dillon, Garrett Hatton. BA in Eng. Lit., U. N.C., 1965; postgrad., Inst. of Higher Internat. Studies, Switzerland, 1965-66; J.D. with honors, George Washington U., 1972. Bar: D.C. 1973. Spl. asst. to Sen. Edmund S. Muskie, Muskie for Pres. Com., 1970-72; atty. Covington & Burling, Washington, 1972-75; exec. dir. Nat. Democratic Platform Com., Dem. Nat. Conv., 1975-76; commr. Pub. Service Commn. of Md., 1975-78; mem. 96th-99th Congresses from 8th Md. Dist., mem. fgn. affairs com., chmn. met. affairs subcom., chmn. Western Hemisphere subcom., mem. budget com.; chmn. Fed. Govt. Service Task Force; ptnr. Arent, Fox, Kintner, Plotkin & Kahn, Washington, 1987-93, Hogan & Hartson, Washington, 1993—; chmn. Ctr. for Nat. Policy, 1993—; co-chmn. U.S.-Panama Bus. Coun.; bd. dirs. Washington Gas Light Co., Overseas Devel. Coun., Internat. Human Rights Law Group, Ctr. for Internat. Policy; sr. adv. com. Nat. Dem. Inst. foir Internat. Affairs; chmn. Commn. on U.S.-L.Am. Rels.; lectr. in field; provider regular commentary Fox TV, WMAL Radio, Washington. Co-author: Third World Stability: Central America as a European-American Issue; editor George Washington Law Rev.; asst. editor Dem. Rev. mag., 1974-78; contbr. articles to profl. jours. Vice chmn. Washington Met. Area Transit Commn., 1976-78, Md. Dem. Com., 1992—; bd. dirs. U. Md. Found., Md. Edn. Coalition, U.S. Com. for UNICEF; mem. Inter-Am. Dialogue, Coun. on Fgn. Rels.; chmn. Md. Campaign for Clinton-Gore, 1992; chmn. Md. Commn. on Growth in Chesapeake Bay Region; mem. Met. Washington Airports Authority; trustee fed. polit. action com. Greater Washington Bd. of Trade. Named One of the Two Dozen Most Influential Mems. of the House, Almanac of Am. Politics, Most Influential Mem. of Congress from Md. or Va., Washington Post, Best Pub. Ofcl., Washingtonian Mag., 1983, 84, 85, 86; recipient Children's Champion award U.S. Com. for UNICEF, 1988; listed among 100 Most Powerful People in Private Washington, Regardie's Mag. to date; Barnes House, a 13-story dormitory for refugees in Israel was dedicated in his honor in 1987 for his role in Operation Moses. Mem. U.S. Assn. Former Mems. of Congress (bd. dirs.). Office: Hogan & Hartson 555 13th St NW Ste 7 West Washington DC 20004-1161

BARNES, MYRTLE SUE SNYDER, editor; b. Farmville, Va., July 14, 1933; d. George McClure and Alma White (Hillsman) Snyder; m. Shelton W. Barnes, Dec. 23, 1954 (dec. Aug. 1979); children: Donna Barnes Boulter, David Brian. BJ, Northwestern U., 1955. Reporter Times-Herald, Newport News, Va., 1956-60, 67-72, city editor, 1972-75, asst. mng. editor, 1975-82; mng. editor Daily Press & Times Herald, Newport News, 1982-87; adminstrv. editor Daily Press, Newport News, Va., 1987-95, reader editor, 1995-96, ret., 1996; mem. jury for Pulitzer prize Columbia U., 1977, 78; mem. Accreditation Coun. on Edn. in Journalism and Mass Comm., 1986-91. Pres. Newport News Libr. Friends; v.p. Va. Coalition on Open Govt. Named to Va. Comm. Hall of Fame, 1993. Mem. AP Mng. Editors (chmn. com. 1986-88, bd. dirs. 1988-91, Meritorious Svc. award 1993), Va. AP Newspapers (chmn. 1987), Nat. Fedn. Press Women (bd. dirs. 1972-74, numerous awards for writing and editing), Va. Press Women (pres. 1970-72, Press Woman of Yr. 1973, numerous awards for writing and editing), Soc. Profl. Journalists (pres. Tidewater chpt. 1978, George Mason award Richmond chpt. 1986), Nat. Congress Parents and Tchrs. (life). Avocations: reading, traveling, theater, handwork. Home: 19 Rose Briar Pl Hampton VA 23666-6818

BARNES, PATRICIA ANN, art teacher; b. San Antonio, Sept. 26, 1942; d. John Homer and Dorothy Bernice (Foster) Sanders; m. Henry Franklin Snodgrass, Oct. 31, 1960 (div. 1967); children: William Franklin, George Huston II, John Charles Joseph; m. Joseph LeRoy Barnes Jr., Aug. 18, 1969; children: Shana Lynn, Janna Lee, Joseph Leroy III. AAS, Bee County Coll., 1986; BFA, Corpus Christi State U., 1988; MA, Tex. A&M U., 1990. Art tchr. J.T.P.A. Summer Youth Program, Beeville, Tex., 1990; adj. art tchr. St. Philips Coll., San Antonio, 1991-93; art tchr. Runge (Tex.) Ind. Sch. Dist., 1993-96; art tchr., dept. head Skidmore (Tex.)-Tynan Ind. Sch. Dist., 1996—; owner Patty's Pyrographics, Three Rivers, Tex., 1995—; Delphi forum mgr. Poly's Clay Castle. Mem. Nat. Art Edn. Assn., Nat. Polymer Clay Guild, Tex. Art Edn. Assn., Coastal Bend Art Edn. Assn., South Tex. Silk Artists Guild. Avocations: glass fusing, polymer clay jewelry, reading, fishing, sewing. Home: RR 1 Box 497 Three Rivers TX 78071-9711 Office: Skidmore-Tynan Ind Sch Dist PO Box 409 Skidmore TX 78389-0409

BARNES, PAUL MCCLUNG, lawyer; b. Phila., June 27, 1914; s. Andrew Wallace and Luella Hope (Andrew) B.; m. Elizabeth McClenahan, Dec. 28, 1940 (dec.); children: Andrew M., Margaret L. Lenart, James D., John R. (dec.). B.A., Monmouth (Ill.) Coll., 1936; J.D., U. Chgo., 1939. Bar: Colo. bar 1939. Assoc. Bannister & Bannister, Denver, 1939-40; assoc. Foley & Lardner, Milw., 1940-47, ptnr., 1948-88, of counsel, 1988—; dir. Wis. Public Service Corp., 1974-77, Kickhaefer Mfg. Co., 1965-85, Attys. Liability Assurance Soc., Ltd., 1979-87; sec. Sta-Rite Industries, Inc., 1965-73. Mem. adv. bd. Milw. Protestant Home, 1975-87. Served with USNR, 1942-45. Mem. ABA, Wis. Bar Assn., Order of Coif. Office: Foley & Lardner 777 E Wisconsin Ave Ste 3800 Milwaukee WI 53202-5367

BARNES, PETER, lawyer; b. Cambridge, Mass., Apr. 13, 1940; s. C. Tracy Barnes and Janet (White) Lawrence; children: K. Tracy, John E.; m. Jan Adair. BA magna cum laude, Yale U., 1962; LLB cum laude, Harvard U., 1965. Bar: D.C. 1966, Md. 1984. Assoc. Leva, Hawes, Symington, Martin & Oppenheimer, Washington, 1965-71, ptnr., 1972-83; ptnr. Venable, Baetjer & Howard, Balt., 1983-86; mem., shareholder Swidler & Berlin, Chtd., Washington, 1987-98; ptnr. Swidler Berlin Sheriff Friedman, LLP, Washington, 1998—; bd. dirs. Walker & Dunlop, Inc., Washington. Mem. The Met. Club, The Elkridge Club. Home: 4 Deep Run Ct Cockeysville MD 21030-1600 Office: Swidler Berlin Shereff Friedman LLP 3000 K St NW Ste 300 Washington DC 20007-5116

BARNES, PRISCILLA, actress. Appeared in films The Last Married Couple In America, 1980, The Wild Women of Chastity Gulch, 1982, Perfect People, 1988, Licence To Kill, 1989, Erotique, 1993, Mallrats, 1995, The Crossing Guard, 1995. Office: HWA Talent Reps 1964 Westwood Blvd Ste 400 Los Angeles CA 90025-4651

BARNES, RAYMOND EDWARD, fire department official; b. Denver, Colo., May 1, 1950; s. Carroll E. and Margaret A. (Minckler) B.; m. Katherine Michele Sanchez, Jan. 3, 1970; 1 child, Tamara Adrienne. BS in Aerospace Tech., Bus., Edn., Met. State Coll., 1971; postgrad., Red Rocks C.C., 1974-75, U. No. Colo., 1976; grad. exec. fire officer program, Nat. Fire Acad., 1990; MPA, U. Colo., 1991. With City of Aurora (Colo.) Fire Dept., 1971—, paramedic and rescue technician, 1976-79, lt., 1979-82, capt., 1982-85, battalion chief, suppression, 1985-87, dir. tng., 1987-91, fire chief, 1991—; adj. instr. Nat. Fire Acad., Md., 1987—; co-dir. Rocky Mountain Fire Acad.; metro co-chair Region VIII Tng. Resources and Data Exch. Active Aurora Gang Task Force; past committeeman, del. to county, state polit. assemblies;. Mem. Internat. Assn. Fire Chiefs (com. on terrorism), Internat. Assn. Metro Fire Chiefs (bd. mem.), Internat. Soc. Fire Svc. Instrs., Internat. Assn. Firefighters (occupl. safety and health com.), Instn. Fire Engrs., Soc. Nat. Fire Acad. Instrs., Soc. Exec. Fire Officers, Fire Dept. Safety Officers Orgn., State Fire Chiefs, Denver Metro Fire Chiefs, Aurora C. of C. (bd. dirs. leadership forum), Homeowners Assn. (past pres. bd. dirs.). Avocations: whitewater rafting, mountain biking, world travel, skiing, golf. Home: 3966 S Sable Cir Aurora CO 80014-5176 Office: City of Aurora Fire Dept 1470 S Havana St Aurora CO 80012-4090*

BARNES, REBECCA MARIE, assistant principal; b. Jackson, Tenn., Nov. 5, 1942; d. Hewitt C. and Willette (Atwater) Johnson; m. Timothy Barnes; children: Mark, Michael, Matthew. BA in Edn., Harris Tchrs. Coll., 1965; MA, Webster U., 1983. Cert. tchr. elem. and mid. sch., reading, gifted/talented. Tchr. St. Louis Pub. Schs., 1965-95; asst. prin. Compton-Drew ILC Middle Sch. at the Sci. Ctr., 1996—. Vol. Habitat for Humanity, St. Louis, Berea House, Black Repertory Theater. Named Tchr. of Yr. Iota Phi Lambda; recipient Outstanding Svc. award United Negro Coll. Fund. Mem. ASCD, Internat. Reading Assn., Nat. Mid. Schs. Assn., Gifted Assn. Mo., Mo. Botanical Gardens, St. Louis Sci. Ctr., Delta Sigma Theta. Avocations: reading, gardening, computers, The Arts. Home: 2655 Wedgwood Dr Florissant MO 63033-1429

BARNES, RICHARD GEORGE, physicist, educator; b. Milw., Dec. 19, 1922; s. George Richard and Irma (Ott) B.; m. Mildred A. Jachens, Sept. 9, 1950; children: Jeffrey R., David G., Christina E., Douglas A. B.A., U. Wis., 1948; M.A., Dartmouth Coll., 1949; Ph.D., Harvard U., 1952. Teaching fellow Harvard, 1950-52; asst. prof. U. Del., 1952-55, asso. prof., 1955-56; asso. prof. Iowa State U., 1956-60, prof., 1960-88, chmn. dept. physics, 1971-75, prof. emeritus, 1988—; sr. physicist Ames Lab., U.S. Dept. Energy, 1960-88; chief physics div. Ames Lab., AEC, 1971-75; vis. rsch. prof. Calif. Inst. Tech., 1962-63; guest profl. Tech. U. Darmstadt, Germany, 1975-76; vis. prof. Cornell U., 1982-83; program dir. solid state physics NSF, 1988-89, condensed matter physics NSF, 1995; chmn. Metal Hydrides Gordon Rsch. Conf., 1987. Served with USAAF, 1942-43; C.E. AUS, 1944-46. Recipient U.S. Sr. Scientist award Alexander von Humboldt Found., 1975-76. Fellow Am. Phys. Soc. Home: 8 Lockwood Dr Kennebunk ME 04043-7705 Office: Iowa State U Physics Dept Ames IA 50011

BARNES, RICHARD GORDON, English literature educator, poet; b. San Bernardino, Calif., Nov. 5, 1932; s. Harold Maxwell and Kathleen Mary B.; m. Kate Beston, Aug. 17, 1953 (div. 1970); children: Elizabeth, Harold, Henry, Jean; m. Mary Twiss (div. 1980); children: Sarah, Richard; m. Patricia Casey, July 30, 1982; children: Paul, Ellen, Louis. BA, Pomona Coll., 1954; MA, Harvard U., 1955; PhD, Claremont Grad. Sch., 1960. Instr. Pomona Coll., Claremont, Calif., 1956-58, asst. prof. English,, 1962-67, assoc. prof., 1967-70, prof., 1973-98, prof. emeritus, 1998—; acting instr. U. Calif.-Riverside, 1958-59. Author: (plays) Nacho, 1964, The Death of Buster Quinine, 1972, Purple, 1973, Tenebrae, 1979, A New Death of Buster Quinine, 1994, The Sand Mirror, 1998; (poetry) A Lake On The Earth, 1982, A Pentacostal, 1985, Few and Far Between, 1994; (song lyrics, poems and stories) The Real Time Jazz Band Songbook, 1990; translator: Three Spanish Sacramental Plays, 1968, An Anglo-Saxon Gnomic Poem, 1968; editor: Episodes in Five Poetic Traditions, 1972; The Psalms of David and Others, 1977, A Moral Fabletalk, 1987; writer, dir. films: Another Movie, 1968, XING, 1968, Two Poems of the T'ang, 1970; vocalist, washboard player Real Time Jazz Band 1967—; rec. The Rub Board Tutor, 1985, Alive in Little Bridges, 1990; actor (film) Rancho California, 1989, Kobayashi Maru, 1994. Recipient Wig award Pomona Coll., 1963; Mellon grantee, 1975. Mem. Medieval Assn. Pacific, Assn. Lit. Scholars and Critics, Phi Beta Kappa. Democrat. Episcopalian. Home: 434 W 7th St Claremont CA 91711-4204 Office: Pomona Coll Dept English 140 W 6th St Claremont CA 91711-4301

BARNES, ROBERT F., agronomist; b. Estherville, Iowa, Feb. 6, 1933; s. Chester Arthur and Pearl Adella (Stoelting) B.; m. Bettye Jeanne Burrell, June 25, 1955; children: Bradley R., Rebecca L. Reinalda, Roberta K. Nixon, Brian L. AA, Estherville Jr. Coll., 1953; BS, Iowa State U., 1957; MS, Rutgers U., 1959; PhD, Purdue U., 1963. Rsch. agronomist USDA-Agrl. Rsch. Svc., West Lafayette, Ind., 1959-70; lab. dir. USDA-Agrl. Rsch. Svc., University Park, Pa., 1970-75; staff scientist nat. program staff USDA-Agrl. Rsch. Svc., Beltsville, Md., 1975-79; assoc. dep. adminstr. So. region USDA-Agrl. Rsch. Svc., New Orleans, 1979-84, dep. adminstr. So. region, 1984-86; exec. v.p. Am. Soc. of Agronomy, Madison, Wis., 1986-99, also fellow; asst. prof. Purdue U., West Lafayette, 1963-66; assoc. prof., 1966-70; adj. prof. Pa. State U., University Park, 1966-70; adj. prof. agronomy U. Wis., Madison, 1986-99; pres. Internat. Grassland Congress, Lexington, Ky., 1981. Editor: Forages, 1995; contbr. articles to profl. jours. With U.S. Army, 1953-55, Germany. Recipient H.S. Stubbs Meml. Lecture award Tropical Grassland Soc., Brisbane, Australia, 1984, Henry A. Wallace award Iowa State U., 1991. Fellow AAAS, Crop Sci. Soc. Am. (pres. 1984-85); mem. Am. Forage and Grassland Coun. (medallion 1981), Grazing Lands Forum (pres. 1986-87), Forage and Grassland Found. (pres. 1993-97). Avocations: walking, reading. Office: Am Soc of Agronomy 677 S Segoe Rd Madison WI 53711-1048

BARNES, ROBERT VERTREESE, JR., masonry contractor executive; b. Dallas, Oct. 7, 1946; s. Robert Vertreese and Doris Corinne (Haffen) B.; m. Deborah Dee Brown, May 31, 1968; children: Robert V. III, John David, Leslie Shannon. BS in Indsl. Tech., Tex. A&M U., 1976. Registered bldg. contractor, Ariz.; registered and cert. bldg. contractor, Fla. Salesman Sears, Roebuck and Co., Dallas, 1965-66, dept. mgr., 1967-69; estimator Dee Brown Masonry, Inc., Dallas, 1970-75, contract adminstr., 1976-77; v.p. Cardinal Masonry Co., Houston, 1978-79; v.p. Dee Brown Masonry, Inc., Houston, 1980-85, exec. v.p., 1985-89; exec. v.p. Dee Brown, Inc., Houston, 1985-89, pres., COO, 1990—; v.p., sec./treas., dir. Shiloh Investment Co., 1974—, Stone Erectors, Inc., 1989-93; exec. v.p. Dee Brown Masonry/Hatch, Inc., 1989-90; pres., CEO, dir. Masonry Tech., Inc., 1993—; dir. Stone Anchor, Inc., 1993—, Pacific Water Jet LLC, 1996, Skinner Marble and Granite LLC, 1997, Salesmanship Club Dallas, 1997—; trustee, chmn. bricklayers health and welfare Bricklayer's Pension Fund, 1983-85. Pres. Katy Youth Soccer Assn., 1980-81; mgr. Solar "74" Soccer Club, 1986-88, Diggers Soccer Club, 1989-92; dir. Whiterock Ch.'s Athletic Assn., 1972-77; bishop warden St. Cuthbert's Episcopal Ch., 1985-86; bd. dirs. St. John's Episc. Sch., 1987-93, v.p., 1988-89, sch. fin. com., health, safety and ins. com., bldg. facility com., chmn. bldg. and grounds com., 1988-90, co-chmn. devel. com., vestry mem., fin. com., athletic dir., 1999—; exec. com. Constrn. Rsch. Ctr., U. Tex., Arlington, 1992-94, vice chmn., 1994, chmn. elect, 1995, chmn., 1995-96. Mem. ASTM (C12, C15, C18 coms. 1990—), Mason Contractors Assn. Am. (contract rsch. com. 1982-83, chmn. labor com., codes and stds. com.), Marble Inst. Am., Constrn. Specification Inst., Associated Gen. Contractors Dallas (subcontractor rels. com. 1988-89, AGC mktg. com. 1990-93, co-chmn. gencontractor/subcontractor rels. com. 1993-94, bd. dirs. 1995-98, transition com. AGC/ABC 1995-96, nat. assn. bd. dirs. assoc. mem. AGC 1995-98), Masonry Alliance Codes and Stds. (treas. 1996—), Constrn. Edn. Found. (trustee 1996-98), Baylor Inst. Rehab. (trustee 1997—, vice chmn. 1998—), Assn. Masonry Contractors Tex. (pres. 1983, sec./treas. 1981-82, v.p. 1990-91), So. Bldg. Congress, Nat. Bldg. Environment and Thermal Envelope Counsel, Assn. Masonry Contractors Houston (pres. 1982-84, v.p. 1981), Am. Subcontractor Assn. (v.p. 1982-83, bd. dirs. Houston 1982-85, also mem. nat. coms., dir. north Tex. chpt. 1995-97), United Masonry Contractors Dallas (dir. constrn. edn. found. 1996-98, mem. program com. 1996-98), Dallas Exec. Assn., Houston C. of C., N.W. Houston C. of C., Dallas C. of C., East Dallas Younglife (bd. dirs. 1990—), Tex. A&M U. Blue and Gold Alumni Assn., Tex. A&M U.-Commerce Mayo Found., Tex. A&M U. Commerce Amb., John Brown U. Parents Cabinet (founder, pres. 1989-93), Dallas Pioneer Assn., Pine Forest Country Club (Houston), Dallas Athletic Club, Baylor Health Club, Tom Landry Ctr., Delta Sigma Pi. Republican. Office: Dee Brown Inc PO Box 28335 Dallas TX 75228-0335

BARNES, ROBERT VINCENT, elementary and secondary school art educator; b. Flint, Mich., May 27, 1948; s. Albert J. and Mary Elizabeth (Morey) B.; m. Sandra E. Mathews-Barnes, Dec. 20, 1986; 1 child, Kathryn R. BA, Adrian Coll., 1970; postgrad., U. Mich., 1973-75, Ctrl. Mich. U., 1976-80, Getty Ctr. Edn. Arts, Cin. Art Mus., Cranbrook Acad. Art, Marygrove Coll., Cranbrook Acad. Art, 1995—; MA, Marygrove Coll., 1997. Cert. tchr. art grades kindergarten through 12, Mich. Tchr. art Flushing (Mich.) Community Schs., 1971—; instr. Flint Inst. Arts, 1975-76; tchr. genealogy adult edn. program Mott C.C., Flushing, Fenton and Grand Blanc, Mich., 1976-84. Author: Flushing Area Families, 1981, Fenton Area Families, 1984; editor Flint Geneal. Quar., 1981. Past pres. Flint Geneal. Soc., Fenton Hist. Soc.; bd. dirs., past pres. Flushing Area Hist. Soc.; pres. Fenton Mus. Bd., 1984-86; chmn. Fenton 150th Com., 1984; co-chmn. Fenton Civic Com. for New Mus., 1985-86; com. mem. Genesee County Sesquicentennial, Flint, 1986. Recipient 1st prize Flushing Art Fair, Flushing Jr. Women's League, 1975, 78, Orren Hart award Flushing Area Hist. Soc., 1983. Mem. NEA, Mich. Edn. Assn., Nat. Art Edn. Assn., Mich. Art Edn. Assn., Flushing Edn. Assn., Ohio Geneal. Soc., Ohio Hist. Soc. Methodist. Avocations: pottery, painting, family history research. Office: Springview Elem Sch 2033 Springview Dr Flushing MI 48433-1447

BARNES, ROSEMARY LOIS, minister; b. Grand Rapids, Mich., Sept. 17, 1946; d. Floyd Herman and Cora Agnes (Beukema) Herms; m. Louis Herbert Adams, Feb. 22, 1969 (div. Oct. 1976); 1 child, Louis Herbert Jr.; m. Robert Jearold Barnes, Oct. 8, 1976. BA, Calvin Coll., 1968. Ordained to ministry Home Ministry Fellowship, 1980; cert. social worker. Group worker Kent County Juvenile Ct., Grand Rapids, Mich., 1966-68; tchr. Sheldon Elem. Sch., Grand Rapids, 1968-69; social worker Kent Dept. Social Services, Grand Rapids, 1969-75, 75-84; tchr., mission worker Emmanuel House, San Diego, 1975; co-pastor, founder River of Life Ministries, Grand Rapids, 1980—; instr. Gt. Lakes Inst. Bible Studies, Grand Rapids, 1988; tchr., founder River of Life Sch. Christian Leadership, Grand Rapids, 1981—; v.p. Aglow, Grand Rapids, 1982-83; sec., treas. Western Mich. Full Gospel Ministers Fellowship, Grand Rapids, 1984-85; mem. bd. chaplains Dunes Correctional Facility, Saugatuck, Mich., 1986-91; coord. 1988 Washington for Jesus March, One Nation Under God, Inc.; co-pastor Gun Lake River of Life, 1988; prof. Great Lakes Inst., 1988; county coord. Grand Rapids Full Gospel Ministers Fellowship, 1990-92; co-pastor Defiance, Ohio River of Life, 1992-93; bd. dirs. Wyo. Cmty. Cable Access TV. Participant TV show Ask the Pastor, 1993—; dir., producer TV show River Reflections, 1994—; Mich. women's coord. Let The Redeemed of the Lord Say So, 1994; sponsor Grand Rapids cable TV Jewish Jewels, 1995—. Bd. dirs. Alcohol Incentive Ladder, Grand Rapids, 1979. Mem. Women in Leadership. Republican. Mem. Ind. Charismatic Ch. Avocation: playing the trumpet. Fax: (616) 454-6525. E-mail: rbarnesrol@aol.com. *My passion to see the Lord's church grow into Him, mature and spotless, is the force that motivates me to teach the Word of God. I believe that when His Bride is fully mature He will come to her and together they will rule and reign forever.*

BARNES, ROY EUGENE, lawyer; b. Atlanta, Mar. 11, 1948; m. Marie Dobbs Barnes; children—Harlan, Allison, Alyssa. A.B., U. Ga., 1969, J.D. cum laude, 1972. Bar: U.S. Ct. Appeals 1972, Ga. 1972, U.S. Dist. Ct. 1973, U.S. Ct. Appeals (5th cir.) 1973, U.S. Supreme Ct. 1979, U.S. Ct. Appeals (11th cir.) 1983. Ptnr. Barnes & Browning, Marietta, Ga., 1975—; mem. Ga. Senate, 1974—, chmn. com. on spl. judiciary, 1978-80, chmn. com. on judiciary, 1980-82, chmn. com. on constl. revision, 1981, adminstrn. floor leader, 1983—. Mem. Am. Judicature Soc., Assn. Trial Lawyers Am., ABA, State Bar Ga., Ga. Trial Lawyers Assn., Inc., Cobb County Bar Assn. Office: Barnes & Browning 166 Anderson St SW Ste 225 Marietta GA 30060-8603 Also: Office of the Governor State Capitol, Rm 111 Atlanta GA 30334*

BARNES, SANDRA HENLEY, publishing company executive; b. Seymour, Ind., Jan. 15, 1943; d. Ray C. and Barbara (Cockerham) Henley; m. Ronald D. Barnes, Sept. 3, 1961; children: Laura Winkler, Barrett and Garrett (twins). Student, Ind. State U., 1962-63. Asst. sales mgr. Marquis Who's Who, Indpls., 1973-79, sales, svc. mgr., 1979-82, mktg. ops. mgr., 1982-84; mktg. mgr. Marquis Who's Who, Chgo., 1984-86; dir. mktg. Marquis Who's Who, Wilmette, Ill., 1986-87; v.p. mktg. Macmillan Directory Div., Wilmette, 1987-88; group v.p. product mgmt. Marquis Who's Who, Wilmette, 1988-89; pres. Marquis Who's Who, 1989-92; v.p. Reed Reference Pub., New Providence, N.J., 1992-96; v.p., fulfillment Reed Elsevier-New Providence, 1996-97, LEXIS-NEXIS, Dayton, Ohio, 1997-98, Lexis Law Pub., Charlottesville, Va., 1997-98, Congrl. Info. Svc., Bethesda, Md., 1997-98; sr. v.p. Ednl. Comms., Inc., Lake Forest, Ill., 1998—. Republican. Avocation: reading. Office: Ednl Comm Inc 721 N McKinley Rd Lake Forest IL 60045

BARNES, SHIRLEY ELIZABETH, foreign service officer; b. St. Augustine, Fla., Apr. 5, 1938; d. James Albert and Evelyn (Findley) B. Student, Boston U., 1959-60; BBA, CUNY, 1959; MBA, Columbia U., 1970; student, Nat. Def. U., 1990. Adminstrv. assoc. Ford Found. Ecole Nat. de Droit et d'Adminstrn., Kinshasa, Zaire, 1962-65; program asst. African Am. Inst., N.Y.C., 1965-66; adminstrv. asst. U.S. Info. Svc. English Lang. Sch., Kinshasa, 1966-68; account exec. J. Walter Thompson Advt., N.Y.C., 1970-73; v.p., account supr. John F. Small Advt., N.Y.C., 1973-76, Uniworld Advt., N.Y.C., 1976-79; Norman, Craig & Kummel, 1979-80; owner, pres. Barnes Findley Internat., N.Y.C., 1980-83; sr. fgn. svc. officer U.S. Dept. State, Washington and abroad, 1983—; amb. to Madagascar U.S. Govt., 1998—; cons. Richard K. Manoff Advt., U.S. Agy. for Internat. Devel., Kinshasa, Port-au-Prince, Haiti, 1981-83. Mem. nat. adv. bd. Hampshire Coll., Amherst, Mass., 1972-74; bd. dirs. Cinque Gallery, N.Y.C., 1974—. Mem. Delta Sigma Theta. Avocations: art of African diaspora, African and African-American history, jazz, opera. Office: DOS-Antananarivo Washington DC 20521-2040

BARNES, STEPHEN PAUL, financial planner; b. Corsicana, Tex., July 30, 1957; s. Paul Gordon and Barbara Jewell (Hawkins) B.; m. Tina Marie Dacus, Dec. 20, 1980 (div. 1985); m. Kathie Jo Beck, Feb. 20, 1988; 1 child, Stephanie Kathryn. BS, Grand Canyon U., 1982. CFA, CFP. Sales rep. Phil Bramsen Distbrs., Mesa, Ariz., 1978-81, credit mgr., 1981-82; registered rep. John Hancock Fin. Svcs., Phoenix, 1983-86; mktg. mgmt. assoc. John Hancock Fin. Svcs., Boston, 1986-87; sales mgr. John Hancock Fin. Svcs., Phoenix, 1987-90; portfolio mgr. Barnes Investment Adv., Phoenix, 1990—; bd. dirs. Desert Schs. Fed. Credit Union, 1990-98, vice chmn. bd. dirs., 1995, chmn. bd. dirs., 1995-97. Editor Ariz. Stock Analysis Newsletter, 1996-98. Pub. address announcer home basketball games Grand Canyon Coll., 1977-96; dir. United Way capital dr. Western region John Hancock Fin. Svcs., 1988, 89; com. chair capital dr. John C. Lincoln Day Care Ctr., Phoenix, 1987. Named one of 200 Best Fin. Advisors, Worth Mag., 1996, 97, 98. Mem. Inst. CFPs (nat. dir., chair pub. rels. com., past pres., dir. Phoenix soc.), Assn. for Investment Mmgt. and Rsch., Phoenix Soc. of Fin. Analysts, Ariz. Assn. of Inst. CFPs (chmn. 1993-96). Republican. Methodist. Avocations: fine wines and foods, baseball, music. E-mail: Stephen@Barnesinvest.com. Home: 7515 North 21st Pl Phoenix AZ 85020-4751 Office: 5225 N Central Ave Ste 208 Phoenix AZ 85012-1461

BARNES, STEVE JAMES, elementary education educator; b. Spokane, Wash., Feb. 17, 1960; s. Roy Martin and Janette Marta (Schlicting) B.; m. Peggy Louis Stretch, June 23, 1984; children: Brandon James, Brittney Nicole. BA in Edn., Ea. Wash. U., 1982, M in Curriculum, 1989, adminstrv. cert., 1991. Profl. edn. cert. in tchg. and adminstrn. Wash. Tchr. 7th and 9th grade math and social studies Ctrl. Valley Sch. Dist. #356, Spokane, 1983; tchr. 6th grade Nine Mile Falls (Wash.) Sch. Dist., 1983-86; tchr. 6th grade Spokane Pub. Schs., 1986-95, title 1 facilitator, 1995-96; large sch. facilitator/instrnl. facilitator Holmes Elem. Sch., Spokane Pub. Schs., 1996—. Soccer, baseball, basketball coach YMCA and Spokane Youth Sports, 1991—. Mem. ASCD, NEA, Internat. Reading Assn., Wash. Edn. Assn., Wash. Sci. Tchrs. Assn. Avocations: football, basketball, softball, golf, gardening. Home: 3921 S Sunderland Dr Spokane WA 99206-8629 Office: Spokane Pub Schs Dist #81 200 N Bernard St Spokane WA 99201-0206

BARNES, SUSAN CAROL, member of parliament; b. Malta, Sept. 8, 1952; m. John Barnes, 1974; children: Devon, John Anthony, Amanda. BA in English Lit. and Lang., U. Western Ont., 1974, LLB, 1977. Bar: Law Soc. of Upper Can. Instr. bus. law, banking law U. Western Ont., 1982-86; pvt.

practice London, Ont., 1986-93; mem. Can. Parliament for London West, 1993—; arliamentary sec. to Minister of Nat. Revenue, 1996-98; mem. pub. accounts com., 9196-98, industry com., 1998—; govt. vice chair standi ng com. on justice and legal affairs, 1994-96; part-time mem. Ont. Criminal Code Rev. Bd., 1986-93; part-time instr. Law Soc. Bar Admissions Course, London; participant 46th seminar Commonwealth Parliamentary Assn., London, 1997, 37th Can. Regional Conf., Toronto, 1998, 44th Plenary Conf., Wellington, New Zealand 1998; participant Commonwealth Joint Colloquium on Parliamentary Supremacy and Jud. Independence, Burkinghamshire, Eng., 1998. Chair Fed. Ont. Liberal Caucus, 1995-96; mem. exec. com. Can. Inter-Parliamentary Union Group, 1994-96, mem. working group on revision of statutes; chair drafting com. on corruption 94th Inter-Parliamentary Union Conf., Bucharest, Romania, 1995; participant Parliamentary Bus. and Labour Trust, B.C. Tel., 1994, Bank of Montreal, 1995, Fish, Food and Allied Workers, 1996; mem. Fed. Ont. Caucus Task Force, 1994; organizer, worker all fed. and provincial election campaigns, 1979—; mem. exec. bd., bd. dirs. London West Liberal Assn., 1979—; mem. adv. bd. Orch. London; past mem. London-St. Thomas adv. bd. Can. Nat. Inst. for Blind; past bd. dirs. Brain Tumor Found. of Can.; moderator All Candidates Meeting for Mayor and Bd. of Control, Project Control, 1991; v.p., pres. United Ch. Women, Calvary United Ch., London, 1981-83; mem. legal bd. London Girl Guides, 1979-82. Office: Ho of Commons, Rm 26 W Block, Ottawa, ON Canada K1A 0A6

BARNES, SUSAN LEWIS, lawyer; b. Palo Alto, Calif., June 11, 1943; d. Prof. and Mrs. L.J. Lewis; m. Sanford C. Barnes; 1 child, Jason Bullard Barnes. BS, Stanford U., 1965; JD, U. Wash., 1968. Law clk. Ariz. Ct. Appeals, Tucson, 1968-71; law clk. U.S. Atty.'s Office, Seattle, 1971-96, 1st asst. U.S. atty., 1994-96, interim U.S. Atty., 1993, 1st asst. U.S. Atty., 1991-93, chief civil divsn., 1982-91; ptnr. McKay Chadwell PLLC, Seattle, 1996—; pres. Fed. Bar WDWN, 1995; lawyer's rep. 9th cir. Office: McKay Chadwell PLLC 701 5th Ave Seattle WA 98104-7016

BARNES, THOMAS JOHN, lawyer; b. Grand Rapids, Mich., Apr. 1, 1943; s. James and Adeline (Molenda) B.; m. Lynn Marie Owens, Aug. 19, 1967; children: Nicolle, Cynthia. BA in Acctg., Mich. State U., 1965, BA in Polit. Sci., 1966; JD, Wayne State U., 1972. Bar: Mich. 1972, U.S. Dsit. Ct. (ea. and we. dists.) Mich. 1972, U.S. Ct. Appeals (6th cir.) 1974, U.S. Dist. Ct. (hno. dist.) Ind. 1994, U.S. Ct. Appeals (7th cir.) 1995. Ptnr. Varnum, Riddering, Schmidt & Howlett, Grand Rapids, 1972—; arbitrator Mich. Employment Rels. Commn.; speaker in field. Editor-in-chief Wayne Law Rev.; contbr. articles to profl. jours. Mem. ABA (nat. labor rels. bd. practice and procedures com.), Mich. Bar Assn. (labor coun., sec., treas. 1987-88, chmn. 1989-90). Roman Catholic. Avocations: reading, horse racing, sports. Office: Varnum Riddering Schmidt & Howlett 333 Bridge St NW Grand Rapids MI 49504-5369

BARNES, THOMAS JOSEPH, migration program administrator; b. St. Paul, June 18, 1930; s. Ralph Weikert and Helen (O'Connor) B.; m. Mai Tang; children: An, Kim, Kevin; children by previous marriage: Christopher, Ross, Karen, Shannon. *Life has favored him with a marriage that is a true partnership, and with children who have evolved into adults able to prosper by their own wits and wiles. A subsidiary pleasure has been the ability to communicate, however imperfectly but in their own language, with Chinese, French, Lao, Thai, and Vietnamese. Slipping into the rhythm of a different culture proves the thesis ofthe Arab proverb: "Each new language is a new soul."* BA, U. Minn., 1950, MA, 1951. With fgn. service, 1957-80; vice consul Saigon, Vietnam, 1958-60; prin. officer Am. consulate, Hue, Viet Nam, 1960-61; polit. officer Bangkok, Thailand, 1962-64, Vientiane, Laos, 1964-67; province sr. adviser Binh Long, Vietnam, 1967-68; country officer for Laos State Dept., 1968-70; prin. officer Am. Consulate, Udorn, Thailand, 1970-71; assoc. dir. AID, Nhatrang, Vietnam, 1971-72; consul gen. Tangier, Morocco, 1972-73, Can Tho, Vietnam, 1973; polit. counselor Bangkok, 1973-75; sr. staff mem. for East Asia Nat. Security Council, 1975-76; student Sr. Seminar in Fgn. Policy, State Dept., 1976-77; regional refugee coordinator Bangkok, 1977-78; diplomat-in-residence U. Hawaii, 1978-79; dir. Interagy. Working Group on Kampuchea, Dept. State, Washington, 1979-80; with UN High Commn. for Refugees, 1980-90; dep. rep. UN High Commn. for Refugees, Somalia, 1980-81; chief S.W. Asia sect. UN High Commn. for Refugees, Geneva, 1982-86; head supplies and food aid service UN High Commn. for Refugees, 1986-87, head orgn. and mgmt., 1987-90; coord. for ops. and program devel. Internat. Cath. Migration Commn., Geneva, 1991-95. Author: (monograph) Of All the 36 Alternatives; Indochinese Resettlement In America, 1977; author: (short story) Fall of the Trinh, 1998. Served to capt. AUS, 1951-56. Decorated UN Svc medal, Korean Svc. medal, Bronze Star with 2 oak leaf clusters, Nat. Def. Svc. medal. Recipient Award for Valor, Meritorious Honor award State Dept., Superior Honor awards State Dept, AID. Home: 5910 Upvalley Run Austin TX 78731-3669

BARNES, VIRGIL EVERETT, II, physics educator; b. Galveston, Tex., Nov. 2, 1935; s. Virgil Everett and Mildred Louise (Adlof) B.; m. Barbara Ann Green, 1957 (dec. 1964); 1 son, Virgil Everett III; m. Linda Dwight Taylor, 1970; children—Christopher Richard Dwight, Charles Jeffrey, Daniel Woodbridge. AB magna cum laude with highest honors, Harvard U., 1957; PhD, Cambridge (Eng.) U., 1962. Rsch. assoc. Brookhaven Nat. Lab., Upton, N.Y., 1962-64, asst. physicist, 1964-66, assoc. physicist, 1966-69; mem. faculty Purdue U., 1969—, prof. physics, 1979—; asst. dean Purdue U. (Sch. Sci.), 1974-78; cons. in field. Author papers on exptl. high energy particle physics. NSF predoctoral fellow Gonville and Caius Coll., Cambridge U., 1959-62; Marshall scholar Cambridge U., 1957-59; recipient Perkin Elmer prize Harvard U., 1956. Mem. AAAS, AAUP, Am. Phys. Soc., N.Y. Acad. Scis., Phi Beta Kappa, Sigma Xi. Home: 801 N Salisbury St West Lafayette IN 47906-2715 Office: Purdue U Dept Physics West Lafayette IN 47907

BARNES, WALLACE, manufacturing executive; b. Bristol, Conn., Mar. 22, 1926; s. Harry Clarke and Lillian (Houbertz) B.; m. Audrey Kent, June 14, 1947 (div. Aug. 1962); children: Thomas Oliver, Jarre Ann; m. Mrs. Frederick B. Hollister, Jr. (div. Feb. 1973); 1 adopted son, Frederick Hollister; m. Joan C. Fierri, Mar. 3, 1973 (div. May 1985); m. Barbara Hackman Franklin, Nov. 29, 1986. BA, Williams Coll., 1949; LLB, Yale U., 1952; grad., Advanced Mgmt. Program, Harvard, 1973; LLD (hon.), U. Hartford, 1988. Bar: Conn. 1952. Pres. Nutmeg Air Trans. Inc., 1949-55; asst. to treas. Northeast Airlines Inc., Boston, 1951; assoc. firm Beach, Calder & Barnes (and predecessor), Bristol, 1952-55; partner Beach, Calder & Barnes (and predecessor), 1956-62; exec. v.p. Assoc. Spring Corp. (name changed to Barnes Group Inc.), 1960-64, pres., 1964-77, chmn., chief exec. officer, 1977-91, chmn. bd., 1991-95, ret., 1995; chmn. bd. Rohr Inc., Chula Vista, Calif., 1995-98; chmn. Coun. Employment and Tng. Commn. State of Conn., Bristol, 1997—; sr. ptnr. Sky Bight Ptnrs.; dir. Aetna Life and Casualty Co., 1971-96, Barnes Group Inc., 1954-96, DeMaria ElectroOptics Systems Inc., 1996—, Loctite Corp., 1990-96, Rogers Corp., 1983-98, Rohr Inc., 1988-98; chmn. bd. Tradewind Turbines Corp., 1994—; ptnr. Green Acres Farm, 1986—. Pres. Bristol Cmty. Chest, 1956; bd. dirs., mem. exec. com. Bristol Boys Club, pres., 1965-68; bd. regents U. Hartford, 1961-94, lifetime regent, 1995, chmn., 1988-93; trustee Bristol Girls' Club Assn.; bd. dirs. New Eng. Legal Found., 1986-90, New Eng. Coun., 1980-83, Jr. Achievement North Ctrl. Conn., 1980-90; nominee for Congress, 1st Congl. Dist. Conn., 1954; Rep. town chmn. Bristol, 1953-55; mem. Conn. Senate from 5th Dist., 1958-62, 8th Dist., 1966-70, minority leader, 1969; Gov.'s Clean Water Task Force, 1966-67; bd. dirs. Cmty. Coun. of Capital Region, 1975-77, Hartford Symphony Soc., 1971-78, Coun. on Employment and Fair Taxation, 1978-80, Bus. Coalition on Health, 1983-88, Conn. Pub. Expenditure Coun., 1979-85; trustee Am. Clock and Watch Mus., Bristol Regional Environ. Ctr.; bd. trustees New Eng. Air Mus.; corporator Inst. of Living, Hartford, Bristol Hosp., St. Francis Hosp., Hartford Hosp.; co-chair Conn. Children's Med. Cap. Campaign, chmn. CBIA, 1982-93; bd. dirs. Conn. Econ. Devel. Corp. Served as aviation cadet USAAF, 1944-45. Recipient Disting. Svc. award Bristol Jaycees, Keystone award Boys Clubs Am., 1967, Humanitarian award Tunxis C.C., 1982, Human Rels. award Nat. Conf. Christians and Jews, 1985, Hon. Alumnus award U. Hartford, 1985, Salute to Wallace Barnes Bristol C. of C., 1991, Hall of Fame award Jr. Achievement North Ctrl. Conn., 1996, Exec. Philanthropist of Yr. Nat. Soc. Fund Raising Exec., 1996; Bartels fellow U. New Haven, 1992. Mem. ABA, Conn. Bar Assn., Am. Judicature Soc., Am. Arbitration Assn., Bristol Hist. Soc., Newcomen Soc., Conn. Bus. and Industry Assn. (past chmn., dir.), Greater Hartford C. of C. (bd. dirs., exec. com. 1991—), Am. Legion, Elks, Econ. Club, Yale Club, Williams Club, Farmington Country Club, Chippanee Golf Club. Home and Office: Sky Bight 1875 Perkins St Bristol CT 06010-8910

BARNES, WALLACE RAY, retired lawyer; b. Easton, Pa., Nov. 7, 1928; s. Charles Hicks and Erma (Saylor) B.; m. Helen Honey Bartley, July 2, 1958; children: Charles Calvin, Elizabeth McKee, Douglas Wittmer. A.B., Duke U., 1950; LL.B., Harvard U., 1957. Bar: Pa. 1958, Ohio 1973. Atty. Allegheny Ludlum Steel, Pitts., 1957-62; atty. Columbia Gas, Md., N.Y., Pa., Pitts., 1962-73; sec., gen. counsel Columbia Gas, Ky., Md., N.Y., Ohio, Pa., Va., W.Va., Columbus, Ohio, 1973-78; sr. counsel Columbia Gas, 1978-81, assoc. gen. counsel, 1981-88, dep. gen. counsel, 1988-96, ret., 1996; corp. dir. Columbia Gas Ohio, 1973-78, N.Y., 1973-78. Bd. dirs. Pitts. Better Bus. Bur., 1972-74. Served with USN, 1951-54. Mem. Fed. Bar Assn. (pres. chpt. 1961), ABA, Ohio Bar Assn., Phi Beta Kappa, Fox Chapel Racquet Club, Racquet Club of Columbus, Gowmill Athletic Club, Wikertree Tennis Club. Home: 2438 Sandover Rd Columbus OH 43220-2845

BARNES, WALTER C., JR., physician; b. May 28, 1931. MD, Northwe. U., 1957; MPH, Harvard U., 1962; PhD, U. Calif., Berkeley, 1980. Diplomate Am. Bd. Preventative Medicine in aerospace medicine. Flight surgeon USAF, 1958-80, advanced through grades to col., ret., 1980; sr. physician Occupl. Medicine Monsanto, 1980-85; asst. prof. U. Tex. Health Sci. Ctr., San Antonio, 1985-88; physician various positions, Mo., Ill., 1988—. Address: 1580 N Woodlawn Warson Woods MO 63122

BARNES, WESLEY EDWARD, energy and environmental executive; b. Chgo., Sept. 11, 1937; s. Donald Edson and Helen Mary (Popovich) B.; m. Constance Arlene Simpson, Nov. 9, 1957; children: Dawn Ellen, Wesley Edward II. Grad., Indsl. Coll. of Armed Forces, 1973; BS, Cen. Mich. U., 1976, MBA, 1981. Chief warrant officer USN, 1955-68; sr. mktg. rep. UNIVAC, Washington, 1968-70; regional mgr. Weismantel Assocs. Inc., Washington, 1970-71; dir. computer ops. U.S. SBA, Washington, 1971-75; asst. dir. legis. affairs U.S. ERDA, Washington, 1975-77; dir. bus. rels. U.S. Dept. Energy, 1977-80, dir. major projects, 1980-83; chief exec. officer Western Rsch. Inst., Laramie, Wyo., 1983-90; pres., chief exec. officer Mktg. Bus. Assocs., Ltd., Washington, 1990-94; project mgr. Dept. of Energy, Yucca Mountain Project, 1995-97; energy and environ. cons. Dagsboro, Del., 1997—; bd. dirs. Econ. Devel. Corp., Laramie, 1986-90. Mem. Rep. Nat. Com. Mem. Am. Mgmt. Assn. (pres.'s assn.), Cripple Creek Country Club, K. of C. (lector 1981-82). Roman Catholic.

BARNES, WILLIAM DOUGLAS, advertising executive; b. Washington, Sept. 1, 1953; s. Berry Carter and Virgina Mae (Keeler) B. BBA, U. Miami, Fla., 1980, MBA, 1984. Staff acct. Arthur Andersen & Co., Miami, 1980-81; sr. acct. Storer Comm., Miami, 1981-84; pres., personnel cons. Profl. Resources, Miami, 1984-86; acct. exec. Miami Herald, 1986-90; pres. Barnes & Assoc. Advt., Ft. Lauderdale, 1990-97; gen. mgr. Strategic Resource Group, Inc., Ft. Lauderdale, 1997—. Mem. Beta Alpha Psi (chmn. alumni com. 1980). Republican. Office: Strategic Resource Group Inc 11080 SW 11th Pl Fort Lauderdale FL 33324-4116

BARNES-BROWN, PETER NEWTON, lawyer; b. Rutland, Vt., Aug. 22, 1948; s. Rufus Enoch and Julia Pottwin (Morgan) Brown; m. Susan Linda Barnes, Aug. 11, 1974; children: Diana Morgan, David Alexander, Julia Elizabeth. AB, Brown U., 1970; JD, U. Pa., 1976. Bar: Ga. 1978, N.Y. 1979, Mass. 1985. Law clk. Assoc. Justice Alfred H. Joslin R.I. Supreme Ct., Providence, 1977-78; assoc. Olwine, Connelly, Chase, O'Donnell & Weyher, N.Y.C., 1978-84, Goodwin, Procter & Hoar, Boston, 1984-86; internat. counsel Cullinet Software, Inc., Westwood, Mass., 1986-89; prin. Van Wert & Zimmer, P.C., Lexington, Mass., 1989-93; co-founder, mem. Morse, Barnes-Brown & Pendleton, P.C., Waltham, Mass., 1993—; dir., clk. New England-Latin Am. Bus. Council, Inc., Boston, 1992—. Contbr. articles to profl. jours. Mem. ABA, Mass. Bar Assn., N.Y. State Bar Assn., State Bar Ga., Boston Bar Assn. Office: Morse Barnes-Brown & Pendleton PC Reservoir Place 1601 Trapelo Rd Waltham MA 02451-7333

BARNES-GUZMAN, BETH YVETTE, grants administrator; b. Decorah, Iowa, Dec. 22, 1962; d. Kenneth Earl and Yvonne Karen (Barth) Barnes; m. Julio Guzman, Aug. 26, 1989; children: Cassandra, Amanda; stepchildren: Julio, Michael. BA in Bus. Mgmt., Ctrl. Coll., Pella, Iowa, 1985. Svc. analyst Equitable of the U.S., West Des Moines, Iowa, 1985-87; adminstrv. asst. Affiliated Bank Group, Waukegan, Ill., 1987, Lorimar Film Entertainment, Des Plaines, Ill., 1987-88, Prestige Linen, Des Plaines, 1988-89, Hemdale Releasing, Des Plaines, 1989-90, Helping Svcs. for N.E. Iowa, Decorah, 1990-93; grant adminstr., writter Upper Explorerland Regional Planning Commn., Postville, Iowa, 1993-98; fiscal and human resources dir. Northland Agy. on Aging, 1998—; creator bylaws and articles of incorporation Upper Explorerland Regional Planning Commn. Housing Inc., Postville, 1996. Bd. mem. United Way, Decorah, 1991-93; fgn. exch. coord. EF Found., Decorah, 1993-94; Sunday sch. tchr. Decorah Luth. Ch., 1996—. Records Mgmt. grantee Iowa State Hist. Soc., Winneshiek County, 1995, Housing grantee Iowa Dept. Econ. Devel., Cities of Monona, Oelwein, Strawberry Point, Cresco, 1996, Iowa Dept. Econ. Devel., Strawberry Leisure Homes, 1996, Housing Needs Assessment grantee Iowa Dept. Econ. Devel., Clayton, Fayette and Howard Counties, 1997. Mem. Iowa Assn. Housing Ofcls. (cert. housing inspector). Avocations: volleyball, swimming, gardening. Home: 701 W Main St Decorah IA 52101-1625

BARNESS, LEWIS ABRAHAM, physician; b. Atlantic City, N.J., July 31, 1921; s. Joseph and Mary (Silverstein) B.; m. Elaine Berger, June 14, 1953 (dec. Jan. 1985); children: Carol, Laura, Joseph; m. Enid May Fischer Gilbert, July 5, 1987; stepchildren: Mary, Elizabeth, Jennifer, Rebecca. A.B., Harvard U., 1941, M.D., 1944; M.A. (hon.), U. Pa., 1971. Intern Phila. Gen. Hosp., 1944-45; resident Children's Med. Center, Boston, 1947-50; asst. chief, then chief dept. pediatrics Phila. Gen. Hosp., 1951-72; vis. physician U. Pa. Hosp., 1952-57, acting chief, then chief, 1957-72; mem. faculty U. Pa. Sch. Medicine, 1951-72, prof. pediatrics, 1964-72; chmn. dept. U. So. Fla. Med. Sch., Tampa, 1972-88, prof. pediatrics, 1988—; vis. prof. Univ. Wis., 1987-92, prof. emeritus, 1993—. Author: Pediatric Physical Diagnosis Yearbook, edits. 1-6, 1957—; editor: Advances in Pediatrics, 1976—, Pediatric Nutrition Handbook, 3d edit., 1991; asst. editor Pediatric Gastroenterology and Nutrition, 1981-91; editl. bd. Cons., 1960-84, Pediatrics, 1978-83, Core Jour. Pediatrics, 1980—, Contemporary Pediatrics, 1984—, Jour. Clin. Medicine and Nutrition, 1985-95, Nutrition Rev., 1985-87. Mem. dietary guidelines adv. com. USDA. Served to capt. AUS, 1945-46. Recipient Lindback Teaching award U. Pa., 1963; Borden award nutrition, 1972; Noer Disting. Prof. award, 1980, Joseph B. Goldberger award in clin. nutrition, 1984, Joseph St. Geme Leadership award 7 pediatric socs., 1991, U. So. Fla. Svc. award, 1997; inductee Phila. Pediat. Soc. Hall of Fame, 1996. Fellow Am. Inst. Nutrition; mem. AAAS, Am. Pediatric Soc. (recorder-editor 1964-75, pres. 1985-86, John Howland award 1993), Soc. Pediatric Rsch., Am. Acad. Pediatrics (chmn. com. on nutrition 1974-81, Abraham Jacobi award 1991, Med. Edn. Lifetime Achievment award 1995), Dietary Guidelines Adv. Commn., USDA, Sigma Xi, Alpha Omega Alpha. Home: 1115 W Virginia Ave Tampa FL 33603-4538 Office: U South Fla Dept Pediat 12901 Bruce B Downs Blvd Tampa FL 33612-4742 *Most people, when given the opportunity, try to be unselfish and prefer to do good. The human brain is a fantastic instrument, which when exercised, can solve most problems.*

BAR-NESS, YEHESKEL, electrical engineer, educator; b. Baghdad, Iraq, Apr. 28, 1932; arrived in Israel, 1950; came to U.S., 1978; m. Varda Bar-Ness, Aug. 21, 1952; children: Yael, Yaron, Yegal. BEE, Technion U., Haifa, Israel, 1958, MEE, 1963; PhD, Brown U., 1969. Chief engr. Elscint Inc., Haifa, 1971-75; assoc. prof. Tel-Aviv U., 1973-78; vis. prof. Brown U., 1978-79, U. Pa., Phila., 1979-81; prof. elec. engring. Drexel U., Phila., 1981-83; tech. staff mem. AT&T Bell Lab., Holmdel, N.J., 1983-85; disting. prof. elec. and computer engring. N.J. Inst. Tech., Newark, 1985—, dir. ctr. communication and signal processing rsch., 1985—; vis. prof. elec. engring. Tech. U. Delft, The Netherlands, 1993-94. Recipient Kaplan Price award Gov. of Israel, 1974. Fellow IEEE; mem. Communication Soc. of IEEE (sec. communications systems engring. com. 1985-87, vice chmn., 1987-89, chmn. 1990-91, editor IEEE transaction on comm., editor-in-chief IEEE Comm. Letters). Home: 2 Etna Ct Marlboro NJ 07746-1307 Office: NJ Inst of Tech 323 King Blvd Newark NJ 07102-1824

BARNET, BRUCE, publishing executive. Pres., CEO Reed Pub. USA (named changed to Cahners Bus. Info.), Newton, Mass., 1996—. Office: Reed Elsevier Inc 275 Washington St Newton MA 02458-1646*

BARNET, RICHARD JACKSON, author, educator; b. Boston, May 7, 1929; s. Carl J. and Margaret L. (Block) B.; m. Ann Birnbaum, Apr. 10, 1953; children: Juliana, Beth, Michael. AB summa cum laude, Harvard U., 1951, LLB cum laude, 1954. Bar: Mass. bar 1954. Rsch. fellow Am. Law Inst., 1957-58; assoc. Choate, Hall & Stewart, Boston; fellow Russian Rsch. Ctr. Harvard U., 1959-60; spl. asst. Dept. State, 1961; dep. dir. Office of Polit. Rsch. U.S. ACDA, 1961-62; fellow Ctr. for Internat. Studies Princeton U., 1963; co-dir. Inst. for Policy Studies, Washington, 1963-77, 90—; sr. fellow Inst. for Policy Studies, 1977—; vis. prof. Yale U., 1970, Nat. U. Mexico, 1973, U. Paris, 1982; vis. com. Harvard U. Author: Who Wants Disarmament, 1960, (with Marcus Raskin) After Twenty Years, 1965, (with Richard Falk) Security in Disarmament, 1965, Intervention and Revolution, 1968, The Economy of Death, 1969, (with Marcus Raskin) An American Manifesto, 1970, Roots of War, 1972, (with Ronald Muller) Global Reach, 1974, The Giants, 1977, The Lean Years, 1980, Real Security, 1981, The Alliance, 1983, The Rockets' Red Glare, 1990, (with John Cavanagh) Global Dreams, 1994, (with Ann Barnet) The Youngest Minds, 1998; contbg. editor: Sojourners mag., 1979—. 1st lt. JAGC U.S. Army, 1955-57. Recipient Sidney Hillman prize Amalgamated Clothing Workers Am., 1975, U. Mo. Sch. Journalism award, 1981. Mem. World Peacemakers, Coun. on Fgn. Rels. Home: 1716 Portal Dr NW Washington DC 20012-1116

BARNET, ROBERT JOSEPH, cardiologist, ethicist; b. Port Huron, Mich., Apr. 27, 1929; s. John A. and Ruth Elizabeth (Wittliff) B.; m. Helen Kresoja, Dec. 8, 1969; children: Benedict, Maria, Antonia, Peter, Elizabeth, Rebecca, Christina, Jacqueline, Ann. Student, Port Huron Jr. Coll., summers 1947, 49; MD, Loyola U., Chgo., 1951; BS in Chemistry magna cum laude, U. Notre Dame, 1954; MA in History, U. of Nev., 1986; MA in Philosophy, U. Notre Dame, 1988. Diplomate Am. Bd. Internal Medicine, Nat. Bd. Med. Examiners. Med. intern Boston City Hosp., 1954-55; rotating intern Mercy Hosp., Chgo., 1955; asst. resident in medicine Boston City Hosp., 1958-59; clin. and research fellow in cardiology Children's Med. Center and House of the Good Samaritan, Boston, 1959-60; cons. fellow in rheumatic fever pediatric service Boston City Hosp., 1959-60; acamedician Cath. Acad. Sci., Washington, 1995—; research fellow in pediatrics Harvard U., Boston, 1959-60; clin. fellow in cardiology Mass. Meml. Hosps., Boston, 1960-61; physician-in-charge St. Francis Mission Hosp., Solwezi, No. Rhodesia, 1961-62; vis. physician Solwezi Boma Rural Hosp., No. Rhodesia, 1961-62; dir. clinics, assoc. in medicine Stritch Sch. Medicine, Loyola U., Chgo., 1962-65; physician-in-charge Cardiac Clinic, Loyola U., Chgo., Fantus Outpatient dept. Cook County Hosp., Chgo., 1962-65, Hypertension Clinic, Fantus Outpatient dept. Cook County Hosp., 1962-65; lectr. in electrocardiography and cardiology Loyola U., Chgo., 1962-65; assoc. attending physician dept. medicine Cook County Hosp., 1962-63, attending physician, 1963-65; practice medicine specializing in cardiology Reno, 1965-87; med. staff Washoe Med. Center, 1965—, St. Mary's Hosp., 1965—; assoc. clin. prof. cardiology U. Nev.; also assoc. dir. Lab. Environ. Patho-Physiology, Desert Research Inst., U. Nev., Reno, 1965-68; dir. Cardiac Care unit Washoe Med. Center, 1965-83, exec. com., 1967-71, 73-77, vice chief dept. medicine, 1969, chief, 1970-71, 78, chief dept. emergency services, 1973-77; cons. in cardiology disability determination unit State of Nev., 1966-87, Crippled Children's Svc., 1966-76, Reno VA Hosp., 1967-80; asst. clin. prof. med. edn. U. Utah, 1968-71; cons. Churchill Pub. Hosp., Fallon, Nev., 1969-87, Pershing Gen. Hosp., Lovelock, Nev., 1969-87; clin. assoc. U. Nev., Reno, 1971-72, assoc. clin. prof. medicine, 1973-77, prof., 1978—; vis. scholar U. Notre Dame, 1989-90, 96-97; prof. med. ethics St. Louis U., 1993-95; mem. rev. bd. Nev. State Bd. Med. Ethics, 1994—. Contbr. articles to med. jours. Served with U.S. Army, 1955-58. Recipient Clin. Faculty Honor award for outstanding tchr. Loyola U., 1963-64; Acemedician Catholic Acad. of Sci. Fellow A.C.P. (bd. govs. 1980-85), Am. Coll. Cardiology (bd. govs. 1974-77), Am. Coll. Chest Physicians; mem. Nev., Washoe County med. socs., Am. Fedn. Clin. Research, Nev. Heart Assn. (bd. dirs., exec. com., pres. 1974-75). Home: 166 Greenridge Dr Reno NV 89509-3927 *I have tried to dedicate my life to the service of all and the betterment of the community while striving for professional excellence without compromise of my moral and religious principles.*

BARNET, WILL, artist, educator; b. Beverly, Mass., May 25, 1911; s. Noah and Sarah (Toahnich) B.; m. Mary Sinclair, Feb., 1935 (div.); children: Peter George, Richard Sinclair, Todd Williams; m. Elena Ona Ciurlys, Mar. 4, 1953; 1 dau., Ona Willa. Student, Boston Mus. Fine Arts Sch., 1927-30, Art Students League, N.Y.C., 1930-33; DFA (hon.), Mass. Coll. Art, 1989. Instr. painting Art Students League, N.Y.C., 1946—; faculty Cooper Union, N.Y.C., 1945—; prof. Cooper Union, 1965—; instr., critic Pa. Acad., Phila., 1967—; faculty Famous Artists Painting Course, Westport, Conn., 1954—, Mont. State Coll., summer 1951, Summer Artists Workshop, Regina Coll., U. Sask., Can., 1957; instr. advanced painting U. Minn. at Duluth, summer 1959, Wash. State U., Spokane, summer 1963, Pa. State U., summer 1965, Des Moines Art Center, summer 1965; distinguished vis. prof. Pa. State U., 1965-66; vis. critic Yale, 1952-53; vis. prof. Cornell U., 1968-69; condr. grand art tour of, Europe, April, 1959, Ford Found. artist in residence program, 1964. Contbr. to: Art Students League Mag; one-man shows, Hudson D. Walker Gallery, 1938, Galerie St. Etienne, 1943, Berthe Schaefer Gallery, Arthur Harlow & Co., Inc., all N.Y.C., 1946, U.S. Nat. Mus., Washington, 1946, Bertha Schaefer Gallery, N.Y.C., 1947, 48, Krasner Gallery, N.Y.C., Gallery Trastevere, Rome, 1960, Terry Dintenfass Gallery, N.Y.C., 1982, Kennedy Galleries, N.Y.C., 1984, 86, 88, retrospective, Inst. Contemporary Art, Boston, 1961, Mary Harriman Gallery, Boston, 1963, 64, Va. Mus., Richmond, 1964, Waddell Gallery, N.Y.C., 1965, 66, 68, 70, Des Moines Art Center, 1965, Pa. Acad. Phila., 1969, Fairweather Hardin Gallery, Chgo., 1971, David and David, Phila., 1972, print retrospective, Asso. Am. Artists, N.Y.C., 1972-79, Hirschl & Adler Galleries, Inc., 1973, 76, 81, Essex Inst., Salem, Mass., 1980, painting retrospective, Neuberger Mus., Purchase, N.Y., 1979, 94, Ringling Mus., Sarasota, Fla., 1980, Wichita Art Mus., Wichita, Kans., 1983, traveling mus. retrospective, Currier Gallery Art, Manchester, N.H., 1984, Huntsville Mus. Art, Ala., 1984, Minn. Mus. Art, St. Paul, 1984-5, Art Gallery of Hamilton, Ont., Can., 1985, Farnsworth Libr. and Art Mus., Maine, 1985, Meek-Harmon Gallery, Naples, Fla., 1990, Terry Dintenfass Gallery, 1991, 94, Butler Inst., Youngstown, Ohio, 1992, Philharm. Ctr. Arts, Naples, Fla., 1994, Ogonquit Mus. Am. Art, Maine, 1994, Worcester Art Mus, Mass., 1995, Nat. Mus. Am. Art, Washington, 1995, Terry Dintenfars Gallery, 1996; drawing retrospective Ark. Art Ctr., Little Rock, 1991—; exhibited, Art U.S.A., 1959, Glenn Horowitz Bookseller, inc., East Hampton, N.Y., 1997, Nat. Acad. Mus., N.Y.C., 1997, Maine Coast Artists, 1998, Tabor De Nagy Gallery, N.Y.C., 1998; represented in permanent collections, Minn. Inst. Arts, Met., N.Y.C., Fogg Art Mus., Library of Congress, Art Gallery, U. N.D., U. Art Gallery, Berkeley, Calif., Cin. Art Mus., Duncan Phillip Meml. Mus., Washington, Phila. Art Mus., Honolulu Acad., Mus. Modern Art, Bklyn. Mus., Mont. State Coll., Whitney Mus. Am. Art, Mus. Fine Arts, Boston, Guggenheim Mus., N.Y.C., Farnsworth Mus. Maine, Butler Inst., Ohio, Ashmolean Mus., Oxford, Eng., Brit. Mus., London; exhibited in museums throughout, U. S., including, Art Inst. Chgo., Los Angeles Mus., Portland Mus., John Herron Inst., Carnegie Inst., Virginia Mus. Fine Arts, Columbia (S.C.) Mus. Art (1st Biennial); pub. Will Barnet 27 Master Prints, 1982; illustrator The World in a Frame; subject of Robert Doty work: Will Barnet, 1984. Recipient Bronze medal, 3d prize Corcoran Biennial, 1961, Benjamin Altman 1st prize NAD, 1977, Medal of Honor, Nat. Arts Club, 1990, The Winthrop Rockefeller Meml. award, 1992, The Butler Medal for Life Achievement in Am. Art award Butler Inst. of Am. Art, 1992; name to Gallery of Honors, Art World Mag., 1990. Fellow Royal Soc. Arts; mem. Art Students League (life), NAD (life), Am. Abstract Artists, Soc. Am. Graphic Artists, Inc., Fedn. Modern Painters and Sculptors, Century Assn. Liberal, Am. Acad. and Inst. Arts and Letters, Tibor DeNagy Gallery. Unitarian. Home and Studio: 15 Gramercy Park S New York NY 10003-1705

BARNETT, ARTHUR DOAK, political scientist, educator; b. Shanghai, China, Oct. 8, 1921; s. Eugene Epperson and Bertha Mae (Smith) B.; m. Jeanne Hathaway Badeau, Mar. 22, 1954; children: Katherine Hathaway, Stewart Doak, Martha Jeanne. BA summa cum laude, Yale U., 1942, MA, 1947, cert. Chinese, 1947; LLD, Franklin and Marshall Coll., 1967; LittD, Washington Coll., 1985; DHL, Monmouth Coll., 1990. Fellow Inst. Current World Affairs in China and S.E. Asia, 1947-50, 52-53; corr. Chgo. Daily

News, 1947-50, 52-53, 53-55; cons. ECA, 1950-51; consul, pub. affairs officer Am. consulate-gen. Hong Kong, 1951-52; assoc. Am. Univs. Field Staff, 1953-55; head dept. fgn. area studies Fgn. Service Inst., Dept. State, 1956-57; rsch. fellow Coun. Fgn. Relations, 1958-59; program assoc. Ford Found., 1959-61; prof. polit. sci. Columbia U., 1961-69; sr. fellow Brookings Instn., 1969-82, sr. fellow emeritus, 1982—; prof. Chinese studies Johns Hopkins U. Sch. Advanced Internat. Studies, Washington, 1982-89; prof. emeritus Johns Hopkins U. Sch. Advanced Internat. Studies, 1989—; sr. fellow East-West Center Hawaii, 1976-77, 86; mem. joint com. Contemporary China Social Sci. Research Council and Am. Council Learned Socs., 1963-64, 65-67, 80-81, chmn., 1963-64; sub-com. Chinese govt., 1965-71, mem. steering com. Chinese fgn. policy, 1974-76; exec. com. Internat. Com. Chinese Studies, 1963-65; bd. dirs. Nat. Com. on U.S.-China Relations, 1966-93, 94—, chmn. bd. dirs., 1968-69; mem. adv. panel on China Dept. State, 1966-69; vis. com. East Asian civilizations Harvard U., 1962-64; chmn. contemporary China studies com. Columbia U., 1961-67; mem. Inst. Current World Affairs, 1958-60, 66-71, bd. govs., 1960-66, 73-79, vice chmn., 1973-74, hon. trustee, 1992—; mem. Liaison Com. Study Contemporary China, 1965-70, Atlantic Council China Study Group, 1982-83; mem. com. on scholarly communication with People's Republic of China, Nat. Acad. Scis.-Am. Council Learned Socs.-Social Sci. Research Council, 1970-76, vice chmn., 1972-75; co-chmn. China council Asia Soc., 1976-79; mem. U.S.-People's Republic of China Joint Commn. on Sci. and Tech. Cooperaton, 1979-81; mem. Internat. Rsch. Coun. Ctr. for Strategic and Internat. Studies, 1990—, sr. advisor Rsch. Ctr. for Contemporary China, Peking U., 1991—; counselor United Bd. for Christian Higher Edn. in Asia, 1992—; mem. Washington Coun. on Non-Proliferation, 1992—; mem. com. on U.S.-China policy Atlanta Coun. Nat. Com. on U.S.-China Rels., 1992-93. Author: Communist Economic Strategy: The Rise of Mainland China, 1959, Communist China and Asia: Challenge to American Policy, 1960, Communist China in Perspective, 1962, China on the Eve of Communist Takeover, 1963, Communist China: The Early Years, 1964, Cadres, Bureaucracy and Political Power in Communist China, 1967, China after Mao, 1967, A New U.S. Policy Toward China, 1970, Uncertain Passage: China's Transition to the Post—Mao Era, 1974, China Policy: Old Problems and New Challenges, 1977, China and the Major Powers in East Asia, 1977, China and the World Food System, 1979, China's Economy in Global Perspective, 1981, The FX Decision, 1981, U.S. Arms Sales: The China-Taiwan Tangle, 1982, The Making of Foreign Policy in China: Structure and Process, 1985, After Deng, What? Will China Follow the USSR?, 1991, China's Far West: Four Decades of Change, 1993; co-author: The United States, China, and Arms Control, 1975; editor: Communist Strategies in Asia: A Comparative Analysis of Governments and Parties, 1963, United States and China in World Affairs, 1966, Chinese Communist Politics in Action, 1969, (with Edwin O. Reischauer) The United States and China: The Next Decade, 1970; (with Ralph N. Clough) Modernizing China: Post-Mao Reform and Development, 1983; editorial adv. bd. Fgn. Affairs, 1972-92; mem. editorial bd. China Quar., 1967-81, Asian Survey, 1967-92; adv. com. Washington Jour. Modern China, 1992-95. Served to capt. USMCR, 1942-46. Mem. Am. Polit. Sci. Assn. (chmn. Conf. Communist Studies 1965-66), Assn. Asian Studies (dir. 1962-65), Asia Soc. (council Chinese affairs 1966-71, co-chmn. China council 1976-79), Council Fgn. Relations (steering com. Project on U.S. and China in World Affairs 1962-66), UN Assn. (China panels 1966-67 70-71, 79-80, Japan panel 1973), Phi Beta Kappa. Office: Johns Hopkins Sch Advanced Internat Studies 1740 Massachusetts Ave NW Washington DC 20036-1903

BARNETT, BENJAMIN LEWIS, JR., physician; b. Woodruff, S.C., July 22, 1926; s. Benjamin Lewis and Mattie Bernice (Skinner) B.; m. Annalyne Louise Hall, Oct. 25, 1958; children: Benjamin Lewis III, Jane Kristen. BS, Furman U., 1946, LLD, 1978; MD, Med. U. S.C., 1949. Diplomate Am. Bd. Family Practice (mem. exam. bd. 1975-81, dir. 1976-81, exec. com. 1979-81, pres. 1980-81). Intern Protestant Episcopal Hosp., Phila., 1949-50; pvt. practice Woodruff, 1950-70; assoc. prof. family practice Med. U. S.C., Charleston, 1970-74; prof. family practice Med. U. S.C., 1974-77, asst. dir. family practice residency program, 1970-75, chief undergrad. curriculum, 1970-77, vice-chmn. dept. family practice, 1973-77, asst. dean for student affairs, 1975-77; clin. staff Med. U. Hosp., Charleston County Hosp., 1970-77; Walter M. Seward prof. U. Va. Med. Sch., 1977, chmn. dept. family medicine, 1977-96, baccalaureate, 1986, faculty senate, 1988-92, 1988-92; family medicine physician-in-chief U. Va. Med. Center Hosp., 1977-96; admissions com. U. Va. Med. Sch., 1997—; Stoneburner lectr. Med. Coll. Va., 1975; Daniel Drake lectr. U. Cin., 1976; Robert P. Walton lectr. Med. U. S.C., 1978; Goodlark prof. U. Tenn., 1979; Roy J. Gerard lectr. Mich. State U., 1992; vis. scholar U. Mich. Med. Sch., 1984; vis. prof. Med. Coll. of Ga., 1982, Case Western Res. Sch. Medicine, 1984, U. Vt., 1988, U. N.Mex., 1991, U. S.C. Sch. Medicine, 1999; Mack Lipkin vis. prof. U. Oreg., 1987, U. Utah, 1989; Donald J. Welter Meml. lectr. Med. Coll. Wis., 1989; Frederick Lytel Meml. lectr., Abington, Pa., 1989; Bradford Strock lectr. Harrisburg (Pa.) Gen. Hosp., 1989; 7th Leland Blanchard Meml. lectr. Soc. Tchrs. Family Medicine ann. meeting, Nashville, 1985; health officer, Town of Woodruff, 1950-54; keynote speaker Assn. Depts. Family Medicine, Clearwater, Fla., 1991; commencement speaker U. Va. Med. Sch., 1992, 97; Grand Prof. Rounds St. Margaret's Hosp., Pitts., 1993; Julian Keith lectr. Bowman Gray Sch. Medicine, 1993; keynote speaker leadership conf. Fla. Med. Assn., Ponta Vedra, 1994, AHEC conf. S.C. Family Practice, Myrtle Beach, 1994; B. Leslie Huffman lectr. Med. Coll. of Ohio, Toledo, 1994; grad. speaker McLennan County Med. Edn. and Rsch. Found., Waco, Tex., 1995; lectr. and cons. in field. Author: Between the Lines, 1989; editor: S.C. Family Physician, 1973-74; contbr. articles to med. jours. and chpts. to textbooks. Mem. Spartanburg County Bd. Edn., 1968-70, sec. 1969-70; trustee Bethea Bapt. Home for Aged, Darlington, S.C., 1972-73; mem. bd. trustees Furman U., 1994—. Named Citizen of Year Woodmen of World, 1968; recipient Golden Apple award for clin. teaching Student AMA, 1973; Thomas W. Johnson award Am. Acad. Family Physicians, 1976, Disting. Alumnus award Med. U. S.C., 1993; Barnett Professorship in Family Medicine established U. Va. Bd. Visitors, 1997; Thomas Jefferson award U. Va., 1997. Mem. AMA (mem. residency rev. com. for family practice 1974-79), Va., Albemarle County med. socs., Soc. Tchrs. Family Medicine (v.p. 1974, sec.-treas. 1975, dir. 1981-85, cert. of excellence 1983, F. Marian Bishop award 1996), Am. Acad. Family Physicians, S.C. Acad. Family Physicians (v.p. 1973, pres. 1975-76), Spartanburg County Med. Soc. (v.p. 1968), Am. Philatelic Soc., Coun. Acad. Socs., Furman U. Alumni Assn. (dir. 1972-77), U. Va. Raven Soc., Alpha Omega Alpha (faculty councilor, vis. prof. U. S.C. Sch. Medicine 1999), Alpha Kappa Kappa (pres. 1948), Kappa Alpha (v.p. 1944). Baptist (deacon, chmn. bd.). Home: 2406 Northfields Rd Charlottesville VA 22901-1728

BARNETT, BERNARD, accountant; b. N.Y.C., Oct. 14, 1920; s. Abraham L. and Rose (Albert) B.; m. Helen Salla, July 9, 1953; children: Susan Christensen, Douglas (dec.). BBA magna cum laude, CCNY, 1941. CPA, N.Y., Mich., La., N.C., Va. Ptnr. Apfel & Englander, CPAs, N.Y.C., 1941-69; ptnr. Seidman & Seidman, CPAs, N.Y.C., 1970, sr. ptnr., nat. dir. tax practice, 1971-86; sr. cons. BDO Seidman, LLP, N.Y.C., 1987—; pres. Found. Acctg. Edn., 1977-78; exec. dir. Fiduciary Income Tax Inst., 1986—; adv. commn. to commr. IRC; mem. N.Y. State Bd. Pub. Accountancy; mem. faculty, mem. adv. com. Inst. Estate Planning, U. Miami (Fla.) Law Sch., 1972—; mem. adv. bd. Tax Mgmt. Inc.; mem. faculty Am. Law Inst/ABA Estate Planning Course, 1978-91, Nat. Trust Sch. of Am. Bankers Assn.; cons. CBS News Ann. Income Tax Program, 1977-90; pres. N.Y.C. Estate Planning Coun., 1967-68. Co-author: Estate Planning and the CPA, 1958, Attorneys Handbook of Accounting, 2d edit., 1979, 3d edit., 1991, Analysis of the Tax Reform Act of 1969, 1970; mem. editorial bd. Trusts and Estates, 1979—, Tax Adviser, 1970-94, emeritus, 1994—, Taxation for Accts., 1973-98, Practical Tax Strategies, 1999—. Served with AUS, 1942-46; to maj. USAF, 1951-52. Mem. AICPA (gov. coun. 1971-80, chmn. task force on estate and gift tax reform 1979-83, chmn. joint disciplinary trial bd. 1982-84, chmn. task force on income taxation of trusts and estates 1983-87, v.p. 1985-86, bd. dirs. 1985-86, chmn. joint trial bd. divsn. 1984-93, mem. nat. rev. bd. 1984-88, trustee benevolent fund 1983-86, AICPA Disting. Svc. award for CPA in tax practice 1984, chmn. liaison AICPA tax divsn. with ABA tax sect., mem. faculty ann. adv. estate planning conf.), N.Y. State Soc. CPAs (pres. 1976-77), Nat. Conf. Lawyers and CPAs (co-chmn. 1978-81), Accts. Club Am. (pres. 1977-80), Berkshire Golf Club (res., Ascot, Eng.). Office: BDO Seidman LLP 330 Madison Ave New York NY 10017-5001

BARNETT, CRAWFORD FANNIN, JR., internist, educator, cardiologist, travel medicine specialist; b. Atlanta, May 11, 1938; s. Crawford Fannin and Penelope Hollinshead (Brown) B.; m. Elizabeth McCarthy Hale, June 6, 1964; children: Crawford Fannin III, Robert Hale. Student Taft Sch., 1953-56, U. Minn., 1957; AB magna cum laude, Yale U., 1960; postgrad. (Davison scholar) Oxford (Eng.) U., 1963; MD (Trent scholar), Duke, 1964. Intern internal medicine Duke U. Med. Center, Durham, N.C., 1964-65, resident, 1965; resident internal medicine Wilmington (Del.) Med. Ctr., 1965-66; dir. Tenn. Heart Disease Control Program, Nashville, 1966-68; pvt. practice medicine specializing in internal medicine and travel medicine, Atlanta, 1968—; dir. Travel Immunization Ctr., Atlanta; mem. staff Crawford Long, Northside, Grady Meml., West Paces, North Fulton, hosps. (all Atlanta); mem. teaching staff Vanderbilt Med. Ctr., Nashville, 1966-68, Crawford Long Meml. Hosp., 1969—; clin. instr. internal medicine, dept. medicine Emory U. Med. Sch., Atlanta, 1969—. Bd. govs. Doctors Meml. Hosp., 1971-80; bd. dirs. Atlanta Speech Sch., 1976-80, 92—, Historic Oakland Cemetery, 1976-86, So. Turf Nurseries, 1977-92, Tech Industries, 1978-92; bd. dirs. Am. Chestnut Found., 1990, bd. trustees Mary Brown Found. of Atlanta, 1998—. Served as surgeon USPHS, 1966-68. Fellow Am. Geog. Soc., Royal Soc. of Tropical Medicine and Hygiene, Royal Geog. Soc., Royal Soc. Medicine, Explorers Club (life, N.Y.C.); mem. Am. Soc. Tropical Medicine and Hygiene, Am. Fedn. Clin. Rsch., Coun. Clin. Cardiology, AMA, Ga. Med. Assn., Atlanta Med. Assn., Am. Heart Assn., Ga. Heart Assn., Am. Soc. Internal Medicine, Am. Coll. Physicians, Ga. Soc. Internal Medicine, Am. Assn. History Medicine, Ga. Hist. Soc., Atlanta Hist. Soc. (bd. govs. 1976-84), Ga. Trust for Hist. Preservation, Nat. Trust Hist. Preservation, Internat. Hippocratic Found. Soc. (Greece), Faculty of History of Medicine and Pharmacy Worshipful Soc. Apothecaries of London, Atlanta Com. on Fgn. Relations (chmn. exec. com. 1972-88), So. Council Internat. and Public Affairs, Newcomen Soc., Atlanta Clin. Soc., Wilderness Med. Soc., Internat. Soc. Travel Medicine (founding), Travelers Century Club, Circumnavigators Club, South Am. Explorers Club, Victorian Soc. Am. (bd. advisers Atlanta chpt. 1971-86), Mensa, Gridiron, Piedmont Driving Club, Yale Club (dir. 1970-74), Nine O'Clocks Club, Pan Am. Doctors Club, Phi Beta Kappa. Episcopalian. Contbr. articles to profl. publs. Home: 2739 Ramsgate Ct NW Atlanta GA 30305-2817 Office: 3250 Howell Mill Rd NW Ste 205 Atlanta GA 30327-4108

BARNETT, DAVID HUGHES, software engineer, computer systems architect; b. Rockville Centre, N.Y., Oct. 9, 1947; s. Paul Wilson Jr. and Patricia (Hughes) B.; m. Rosemary Friday, July 9, 1979 (div. 1983); m. Demery Culum, Apr. 10, 1996. BA, Drew U., 1970. Cert. software quality engineer, cert. quality engr. Program analyst So. Nev. Drug Abuse Coun., Las Vegas, 1974-75; project supr. Treatment Alternatives to Street Crime, Las Vegas, 1975-78; sr. project assoc. Helix Group, Berkeley, Calif., 1978-81; cons. Pacific Inst. for Rsch. and Evaluation, Berkeley, 1979-80; rsch. tech. Sonoma State U., Rohnert Park, Calif., 1981-82; system mgr. Database Minicomputers, San Francisco, 1982-84; cons. sys. programmer Wells Fargo Bank, San Francisco, 1984-89; messaging architect Kaiser Permanente, Walnut Creek, Calif., 1989-96; info. tech. architect IBM, San Ramone, Calif., 1996; info. tech. arch. Digital Equipment Corp., Walnut Creek, 1996-98; sys. arch. Kaiser Permanente, Walnut Creek, 1998—. Contbr. articles to profl. jours. Mem. IEEE, Am. Soc. for Quality Control (cert. software quality engr.). Office: 25 N Via Monte SH80 Walnut Creek CA 94598-1317

BARNETT, DOROTHY PRINCE, retired university dean; b. Charlotte, N.C., Aug. 18, 1931; d. Abraham Hamilton and Susan (Peacock) Prince; m. Isaac Barnett, Dec. 27, 1977. AB, Oberlin Coll., 1953; MA, Syracuse U., 1954; EdD, Ind. U., 1962. Instr. Alcorn Coll., Lorman, Miss., summer 1954, So. U., Baton Rouge, 1954-55; asst. prof. N.C. Agrl. and Tech. State U., Greensboro, 1955-62, prof., 1962-94, chairperson dept. edn., 1966-77, chairperson dept. secondary edn. and curriculum, 1977-89, asst. dean, dir. tchr. edn. Sch. Edn., 1983-90, dean Sch. Edn., 1991-94, ret., 1994; educator, reader U.S. Dept. Edn., Washington, 1968-94; mem. multicultural com. Met. project Am. Assn. Colls. for Tchr. Edn., Washington, 1990-92; cons. initiative conf. Phelps State Consortium, N.Y.C., 1971-73, Norfolk State U., Washington, 1981-89; reader Corp. for Pub. Broadcast, Washington, 1982; mem. bd. examiners Nat. Coun. for Accreditation of Tchr. Edn.; presenter state, nat. and local tchr. edn. confs., 1970-94; bd. dirs. Holmes Group. Contbr. articles to ednl. publs. Bd. dirs. Charlotte Hawkins Brown Hist. Found., Sedalia, N.C., Holmes Group, 1991-94. Recipient Honored Alumnus award Sch. Edn. Syracuse (N.Y.) U., 1992; John Hay Whitney Found. fellow, N.Y., 1961-62; Ellis L. Phillips Found. intern, N.Y., 1964-65. Mem. Phi Delta Kappa, Pi Lambda Theta, Kappa Delta Pi. Democrat. Presbyterian. Avocations: reading, music, walking, bridge. Home: 4702 Royalshire Rd Greensboro NC 27406-8705

BARNETT, EDWARD WILLIAM, lawyer; b. New Orleans, Jan. 2, 1933; s. Phillip Nelson and Katherine (Wilkinson) B.; m. Margaret Mauk, Apr. 3, 1933; children: Margaret Ann Stern Edward William. B.A., Rice U., 1955; LL.B., U. Tex.-Austin, 1958. Bar: Tex. 1958. Mem. Baker & Botts, Houston, 1958—, mng. ptnr., 1984-98; bd. dirs. Tex. Commerce Bancshares; bd. dirs., chmn. Cen. Houston, Inc., 1989-91. Trustee Rice U., Houston, 1991—, chmn. bd. trustees, 1996—; trustee Baylor Coll. Medicine, St. Luke's Episcopal Health System; life trustee U. Tex. Law Sch. Found.; bd. dirs. Tex. Rsch. League, Tex. Assn. Taxpayers; chmn. Greater Houston Partnership, 1992. Fellow Am. Coll. Trial Lawyers; mem. ABA (chmn. sect. antitrust law 1981-82), State Bar Tex., Houston Bar Assn., Coronado Club (pres. 1989), Houston Country Club, Old Baldy Club. Office: Baker & Botts 3000 One Shell Plaza Houston TX 77002*

BARNETT, ELIZABETH LUCINDA (LUCY), television news producer; b. Bryn Mawr, Pa., Mar. 16, 1975; d. Samuel Treutlen and Elizabeth Newbold Barnett. BA, Washington and Lee U., 1997. News prodr. WDBJ, Roanoke, Va., 1996-98, WGAL, Lancaster, Pa., 1998—. Vol. Devon (Pa.) Horse Show and Country Fair, 1989—. Mem. Soc. Profl. Journalists (pres. coll. chpt.), Omicron Delta Kappa. Republican. Episcopalian. Avocation: cooking. E-mail: LucyBarnett@hotmail.com. Home: Apt A 1728 Judie Ln Lancaster PA 17603

BARNETT, GENE HENRY, neurosurgeon; b. Phila., Feb. 2, 1955; s. Edgar Tyron and Anne Shirley (Wenner) B.; m. Kathleen Marie Seng, May 9, 1984 (div. Sept. 1990); 1 child, Alexander; m. Cathy Ann Sila, Apr. 21, 1995; children: Austin, Addison. BA summa cum laude, Case Western Res. U., 1976, MD, 1980. Dir. gamma knife ctr. Cleve. Clinic Health sys., 1997—; intern Cleve. Clinic Found., 1980-81, neurosurgery resident, 1981-86, staff neurosurgery, 1987—, co-dir. residency program, 1992-95, vice chmn. dept. neurosurgery, 1993—, program dir. dept. neurosurgery, 1995—, dir. brain tumor ctr., 1995—; hon. registrar U. Edinburgh, Scotland, 1985; fellow Harvard Med. Sch., Mass. Gen. Hosp., 1986-87; cons. in field. Editor: Image Guided Neurosurgery: Clinical Applications of Surgical Navigation Systems, 1998; contbr. 95 articles to profl. jours., 26 chpts. to books. Grantee Epilesy Found. Am., 1979, NINDS, 1995; clin. & rsch. fellow Harvard Med. Sch., Mass. Gen. Hosp., Boston, 1986-87. Office: Cleve Clinic Found 580 9500 Euclid Ave Cleveland OH 44195-0001

BARNETT, GUY OCTO, physician, educator; b. Chula Vista, Calif., Sept. 18, 1930; married, 1958; three children. BA, Vanderbilt U., 1952; MD, Harvard U., 1956. Resident Peter Bent Brigham Hosp., 1956-61; clin. assoc. Nat. Heart Inst., 1958-60; investigator Am. Heart Assn., 1961-67; physician, prof. medicine, dir. computer sci. lab Mass. Gen. Hosp., 1979—; prof. medicine Harvard U., 1980—; lectr. elec. engr. MIT, 1972—. Fellow Inst. Medicine-NAS; mem. IEEE, Assn. Computing Machinery, Biomed. Engring. Soc., ACP, Am. Med. Informatics Assn. (bd. dirs. 1984—). Office: Mass Gen Hosp Lab Computer Sci 50 Staniford St Boston MA 02114*

BARNETT, HAROLD THOMAS, school system superintendent; b. Pasadena, Tex., Dec. 8, 1948; s. Herbert G. and Nettie Mae (Sanders) B.; m. Erin Lynn McCommon, Dec. 28, 1971; children: Erin Averyl, Benjamin T. MusB in Edn., Baylor U., 1971; MEd, U. Ga., 1974, EdD, 1983. Cert. tchr., adminstr., Ga. Tchr. St. Albans Episc. Elem. Sch., Waco, Tex., 1972-73; tchr. North Clayton Jr. High Sch., College Park, Ga., 1973-75, asst. prin., 1975-82; prin. Griffin (Ga.) High Sch., 1982-90; supt. of schs. Cartersville (Ga.) City Sch. System, 1990—. Trustee Etowah Found., Cartersville; bd. dirs. Cartersville-Bartow County United Way, Christian Counseling Svc., ARC of Bartow County; bd. control Northwest Ga. Regional Edn. Svcs. Agy. Mem. Ga. Sch. Bd. Assn., Ga. Assn. Ednl. Leaders, Profl. Assn. Ga. Educators, Am. Assn. Sch. Adminstrs., Ga. Sch. Supts. Assn., Cartersville-Bartow County C. of C., Cartersville Rotary Club. Baptist. Avocations: fishing, hunting, reading. Office: Cartersville City Schs 310 Old Mill Rd Cartersville GA 30120-4027

BARNETT, HENRY LEWIS, pediatrician, medical educator; b. Detroit, June 25, 1914; s. Lewis and Florence (Marx) B.; m. Shirley Blanchard, Oct. 19, 1940; children—Judith Florence, Martin David. Student, Dartmouth Coll., 1931-32; B.S., Washington U., St. Louis, 1938, M.D., 1938; DSc (hon.), Yeshiva U., 1995. Instr. dept. pediatrics Washington U. Sch. Medicine, 1941-43; asst. prof. dept. pediatrics Cornell U. Med. Coll., 1946-50; asso. prof., 1950-55; prof., chmn. dept. pediatrics Albert Einstein Coll. Medicine, 1955-72, asso. dean clin. affairs, 1970-72, Univ. prof., 1972-81, prof. emeritus, 1981—; dir. pediatric service Bronx Municipal Hosp. Center, 1955-64; dir. Internat. Study Kidney Disease in Children, 1967-81; med. dir. Children's Aid Soc., 1981-97; cons. Appleton-Century-Crofts, 1981-83; Mem. WHO Infant Metabolism Team to, Netherlands and Sweden, 1950, WHO Sci. Group Pediatric Rsch., 1967; adv. bd. Internat. Pediatric Assn., 1969-74; cons. Cento Meeting Pediatric Edn. and Family Planning, Ankara, Turkey, 1972, Nat.Inst. Child Health and Human Devel., 1974-85; mem. bd. on maternal, child, and family health rsch. NRC, 1974-82; mem. coun. Found. for Child Devel., 1966—; chmn. med. adv. bd. Am. Council for Emigrees in Professions, 1974-83; trustee, mem. med. adv. com. Children's Aid Soc., 1977-81, recipient trustee award 1992; Felton Bequests vis. prof. Royal Children's Hosp., Melbourne, Australia, 1978; cons. Asian Study Renal Disease in Children, 1978-81. Contbr. articles to profl. jours.; Editor: Pediatrics, 13th-17th edits. Served to capt. M.C. AUS, 1943-46. Fellow Am. Acad. Pediatrics (E. Mead Johnson award 1949, Kidney award 1992); mem. N.Y. Acad. Sci., Inst. Medicine NAS, AAAS, Soc. Pediatric Rsch. (pres. 1959-60), Soc. Exptl. Biology and Medicine, Harvey Soc., Am. Pediatric Soc. (pres. 1981-82, John Howland award and medal 1984), Am. Soc. Clin. Investigation, Assn. Am. Physicians, Am. Soc. Nephrology (John P. Peters award 1988), Brit. Pediatric Soc. (hon.), Am. Physiol. Soc., N.Y. Acad. Medicine, Nat. Turkish Pediatric Assn. (hon.), Societe Francaise de Pediatre (corr.), Royal Coll. Pediatrics and Child Health (hon.), Sigma Xi, Alpha Omega Alpha. Home: 118 W 79th St New York NY 10024-6445 Office: Children's Aid Soc 150 E 45th St New York NY 10017-3115

BARNETT, JAMES F., JR., historic properties and archives administrator; b. Batesville, Ark., Mar. 25, 1950. BA, Hendrix Coll., 1972; MA, U. Ark., 1982. Profl. musician, 1972-77; adminstrv. positions area bank, 1974-78; dir. divsn. hist. properties Miss. Dept. Archives and History, Natchez, 1981—. Mem. Internat. Soc. Bassists, Sigma Psi. Office: Miss Divsn Hist Prop Grand Village Natchez Indns 400 Jefferson Davis Blvd Natchez MS 39120-5110*

BARNETT, JAMES MONROE, rector, author; b. Baton Rouge, La., Oct. 21, 1925; s. James Monroe Sr. and Egeria Overton (Brooks) B.; m. Marian Jean Scofield, Aug. 15, 1956; children: James Mark, John Michael, Thomas Overton, Paul Winston. BA, La. State U., 1946; MDiv., Seabury-Western Theol. Sem., 1951; D Ministry, U. of South, 1979. Ordained priest Episcopal Ch., 1952. Rector Trinity Ch., Norfolk, Nebr., 1958-92; lectr. theol. seminaries, U.S. and Eng. Author: The Diaconate: A Full and Equal Order, 1979, rev. edit., 1995. Chmn. Nebr. Liturgical Commn., Omaha, 1970—; mem. exec. council Diocese of Nebr., Omaha, 1969-70, 76-88; mem. Comm. on Ministry, Omaha, 1982-86. Mem. N.Am. Assn. for Diaconate (bd. trustees), Associated Parishes, Assn. of Liturgy and Music Commns. Avocations: woodworking, antique furniture restoration, gardening.

BARNETT, JANICE ELAINE, critical care nurse; b. Flagstaff, Ariz., Jan. 3, 1951; d. Garland and Evelyn Rose (Benson) Downum; m. Joe Edwin Barnett, Aug. 9, 1972; children: Analie Rose, Daniel Joseph. BA, U. Okla., 1972; BSN summa cum laude, Tex. Woman's U., 1989. Staff nurse in ICU Decatur (Tex.) Community Hosp. Mem. Mortar Board, Phi Beta Kappa, Sigma Theta Tau, Alpha Chi. Home: RR 1 Box 137 Ponder TX 76259-9601

BARNETT, JOEY VICTOR, pharmacologist, educator, researcher; b. Evansville, Ind., June 18, 1958; s. Victor Alan and Judy Kay (Kohlmeyer) B. BS in Biology, U. So. Ind., 1980; PhD in Pharmacology, Vanderbilt U., 1986. Rsch. intern Argonne (Ill.) Nat. Lab., U.S. Dept. Energy, 1981; rsch. fellow Brigham & Women's Hosp., Harvard Med. Sch., Boston, 1986-89, instr. medicine, 1989-92; asst. prof. medicine and pharmacology Vanderbilt U., Nashville, 1992—; rsch. investigator Tenn. affiliate Am. Heart Assn., 1993-95, established investigator Am. Heart Assn., 1996—; mem. devel. mechanisms panel NSF, 1995-98. Co-author: Heart Failure: Basic Science and Clinical Aspects, 1993; contbr. articles and abstracts to profl. jours. Founding bd. dirs. Dismas House in Ctrl. Mass., Worcester, 1987-90; co-chair cardiovasc. devel. panel Nat. Am. Heart Assn., 1997—. Mass. affiliate Am. Heart Assn. fellow, 1986-88; recipient Nat. Rsch. Svc. award Nat. Heart Lung and Blood Inst./NIH, Boston, 1988-90, Disting. Alumni award U. So. Ind., 1991. em. AAAS, N.Y. Acad. Scis., Ind. Acad. Sci., Basic Rsch. Coun. Am. Heart Assn., Sigma Zeta, Sigma Xi. Roman Catholic. Achievements include research on the molecular mechanisms that regulate development of the cardiovascular system. Office: Vanderbilt U Divsn Cardiology 315 Med Rsch Bldg II 2220 Pierce Ave Nashville TN 37212-3163

BARNETT, JONATHAN, architect, city planner; b. Boston, Jan. 6, 1937; s. David and Josephine Barnett; m. Nory Miller, Mar. 19, 1983. BA magna cum laude, Yale U., 1958, MArch, 1963; MA Mellon fellow, U. Cambridge, Eng., 1960. Designer Haines, Lundberg & Waehler, Archts., N.Y.C., 1963, 64; assoc. editor Archtl. Record, N.Y.C., 1964-67; cons. New City Exhbn. at Mus. Modern Art, 1966, 67; prin. urban designer N.Y.C. Planning Dept., 1967-68, dir. urban design group, 1969-71; prof., dir. grad. program in urban design CCNY, 1971-98; prof. of city and regional planning U. Pa., Phila., 1998—; vis. prof. U. Wis., Milw., 1981; William Henry Bishop prof. Yale U., 1983; Kea disting. vis. prof. U. Md., 1988, 89; Sam Gibbons eminent scholar U. South Fla., 1991-94; planning cons., 1971—; cons. AIA, South Street Seaport Mus., Nat. Park Svc., Louisville, Kansas City, Cleve., Charleston, S.C., Norfolk, Va., Pitts., Salt Lake City, Sioux City, Iowa, Wildwood, Mo., N.Y.C., Miami, Fla., Brookfield, Wis., also others; lectr. in field; mem. vis. com. Harvard U. Grad. Sch. Design, 1976-81, Yale U. Sch. Architecture, 1974-80, UCLA, 1990. Author: Urban Design as Public Policy, 1974, (with John C. Portman, Jr.) The Architect as Developer, 1976, Introduction to Urban Design, 1982, The Elusive City, 1986, The Fractured Metropolis, 1995; editor: Perspecta 8, 1962; contbr.: New Zoning, 1970, Collaborations: Artists and Architects, 1981, The Practice of Local Government Planning, 1988, Cities in Our Future, 1997; editorial cons.: Archtl. Record, 1968-90; mem. adv. bd. Jour. Urban Design, 1996—, Process: Architecture, 1977—; contbr. articles to profl. jours. Mem. adv. bd. Environment and Behavior, 1968-78; bd. dirs. D.C. Preservation League, 1996—; mem. Com. of 100 on Fed. City. Fellow AIA; mem. Am. Inst. Cert. Planners, Archl. League N.Y. (v.p. 1968-70, dir. 1975-98, pres. 1977-81), Mcpl. Art Soc. (bd. dirs. 1970-78, 81-86), Inst. for Urban Design (bd. dirs. 1989—), Berzelius Soc., N.Y. Landmark Conservancy (bd. dirs. 1972-97), Congress New Urbanism (bd. dirs. 1995—), Yale Club, Century Assn., Elizabethan Club of Yale. Unitarian. Home: 2800 University Ter NW Washington DC 20016-3459 Office: Dept of City and Regional Planning Univ Pa Philadelphia PA 19104

BARNETT, KERRY EVAN, state business administrator. BA, U. Rochester, N.Y., 1978; JD, Yale U., 1987. Attorney Lindsey, Hart, Neil and Weigler, Oreg., 1987-89; asst. to Gov., Office of the Gov., Oreg., of counsel, sr. policy advisor, 1991-93; dir., ins. commr., supt. banks Oreg. Dept. Consumer and Business Svcs., Salem, 1993—; mem. Oreg. Med. Ins. Pool Bd., 1993—, Small Employer Reins. Pool, 1993—; mem. Oreg. Health Coun., 1993-96, Oreg. Health Reform Implementation Group, 1993-95. Office: Dept Consumer & Bus Svcs 350 Winter St NE Salem OR 97310-0220

BARNETT, LARRY R., umpire; b. W.Va., Jan. 3, 1945; married; 2 children. Grad., Al Somers Sch.; doctorate (hon.), Bowling Green State U. Former umpire Midwest League, Tex. League; umpire maj. league baseball Am. League, N.Y.C., 1967—; with Umpires Union, Phila. With Ohio NG. Office: Am League 350 Park Ave New York NY 10022 also: Umpires Union 1735 Market St Philadelphia PA 19103

BARNETT, LESTER ALFRED, surgeon; b. N.Y.C., Mar. 11, 1915; s. Benjamin and Rae Viola (Marcus) B.; m. Jean Wolfe, Apr. 16, 1939; children: Barbara Jane Barnett Grossman, James A. Student, Ohio State U., 1932-35; B.A. with spl. honors, George Washington U., 1936, M.D., 1939. Diplomate: Am. Bd. Surgery. Intern Gallinger Mcpl. Hosp., Washington, 1939-40; resident St. Peter's Gen. Hosp., New Brunswick, N.J., 1940-41, Walter Reed Gen. Hosp., Washington, 1942-43, Grasslands Hosp., Valhalla, N.Y., 1944-46; practice medicine specializing in surgery Long Branch, N.J., 1945-92, specializing in diseases of the breast, 1985-95; mem. staff Monmouth Med. Center, 1946-95, surgeon emeritus, 1995, ret., 1995, dir. dept. surgery, 1961-71, pres. med. staff, 1970-73, trustee, 1975-96; bd. mgrs. Monmouth Meml. Sch. Nursing, 1953-65; clin. prof. surgery emeritus Hahnemann U.-Med. Coll. of Pa., 1970-96; assoc. in surgery U. Pa. Sch. Medicine; cons. surgery Jersey Shore Med. Ctr., Neptune; sr. attending in surgery Monmouth Med. Ctr., 1993; chmn. adv. bd. to cancer ctr. Monmouth Med. Ctr., 1993—; trustee, dir. donor rels. Monmouth Health Care Found., 1995—. Author sci. articles. Trustee Monmouth Coll., 1971-78. Served to 1st lt. M.C. AUS, 1942-43. Recipient Pinnacle award Monmouth Med. Ctr., 1990. Fellow Am. Coll. Gastroenterology, A.C.S.; mem. N.J. Med. Soc. (Golden Merit award 1989), Monmouth County Med. Soc. (pres. 1959-60). Jewish. Clubs: Hollywood Golf (Deal, N.J.); Ocean Beach (Elberon, N.J.); Masons, B'nai B'rith (past lodge pres.). Home: 675 Ocean Ave Apt 9C Long Branch NJ 07740-5155

BARNETT, LINDA KAY SMITH, vocational guidance counselor; b. Booneville, Miss., Nov. 20, 1955; d. John Thomas and Clara Vernell (Brown) Smith; m. William Wayne Barnett, June 26, 1982; 1 child, John William. AA, N.E. Miss. C.C., Booneville, 1975; BS, Miss. State U., 1977, MEd, 1978, EdS, 1982. Vocat. guidance counselor, dist. test coord. Iuka (Miss.) City Schs., 1979-91; vocat. guidance counselor Tishomingo County Schs., Iuka, 1991—. Treas. Iuka H.S. PTA, 1984-85. Mem. Miss. Sch. Counselors Assn. (state v.p. secondary divsn. 1992-94), N.E. Counseling Assn. (pres. 1989-90, pres.-elect 1987-88, 88-89, sec.-treas. 1982-83, 96-99), Nat. Bd. for Cert. Counselors (nat. cert. counselor, nat. cert. sch. counselor). Ch. of Christ. Avocations: travel, sports, meeting people.

BARNETT, MARGARET EDWINA, nephrologist, researcher, business consultant; b. Ft. Benning, Ga., July 28, 1949; d. Eddie Lee and Margaret Thomas (Herndon) B. BS magna cum laude with distinction in Zoology, Ohio State U., 1969; MD, Johns Hopkins U., 1973; PhD in Cellular and Molecular Biology, Case Western Res. U., 1984; postgrad. Purdue U., 1992; postgrad. in med. acupuncture UCLA, 1996, cert. exec. MBA program, 1999. Med. technologist blood bank Johns Hopkins Hosp., Balt., 1971-73; intern Greater Balt. Med. Ctr., Towson, Md., 1973-74; med. resident Cleve. Clinic Ednl. Found., 1974-75, Univ. Hosps. Cleve., 1975-76; nephrology fellow, 1976-78, med. teaching fellow, 1978-84; nephrology rounding physician Cmty. Dialysis Ctr., Cleve. and Mentor, Ohio, 1978-83; rsch. assoc. Case Western Res. U., Cleve., 1978-79, 83-84; physician emergency medicine Huron Regional Urgent Care Ctrs., Inc., Cleve., 1983-84; preceptor renal correlation conf., Case Western Res. Sch. Medicine, 1980-81, lectr. anatomy and histology 1979-83; asst. prof. medicine/nephrology Milton S. Hershey Med. Ctr. Pa. State U., Hershey, 1984-87, acting chief renal and electrolyte divsn., 1985, dir. peritoneal, 1986-87, assoc. dir. hypertension, 1986-87; pvt. practice medicine specializing in nephrology and hypertension Arnett Clinic, Lafayette, Ind., 1987-93; dir. outpatient dialysis St. Elizabeth Hosp. Med. Ctr., Lafayette; clin. assoc. faculty of Lafayette Ctr. Sch. Medicine Ind. U., 1987-93; clin. asst. prof. of medicine, Ind. U. Sch. Medicine, 1989-94, pharmacology clin. preceptor Purdue U., 1988-93; spl. guest lectr. hypertension Drug Cos., Ill., Ind., S.D., Ky., Ohio, Pa., 1988-94, Calif., 1995—; assoc. dean rsch. and grad. studies Sch. Allied Health Scis. Ind. U., 1993-94, vis. prof. medicine dept. health info. adminstrn. Allied Health Scis., Ind., U., 1994, medicine dept. phys. therapy Nat. Inst. Fitness & Sport, 1993-94; dir. dialysis svcs. King/Drew Med. Ctr., L.A., 1994—; asst. prof. medicine Charles R. Drew U., 1994—, asst. dir. nephrology fellowship program, 1995—; faculty mem. Nat. Bur. Info. on Coronary Heart Disease Risk, 1991-94, mem. cardiorenal subcom., 1995-97; rep. rsch. and grad. studies alumni adv. coun. Ohio State U., 1990-93. Del. in nephrology and hypertension citizen amb. program People to People Internat. to Russia, Belarus and Lithuania, 1994, Chinese Med. Assn. 80th Anniversary, Beijing, 1995, Johannesburg and Capetown, South Africa, 1996, active, 1994—; active nat. speaker's program Pfizer Pharm. Co., 1994—; rep. So. Calif. regional quality coun. GAMBRO Healthcare, Inc., Lakewood, Colo., 1998—. Scholar GM, Leo Yassinoff, Alpha Epsilon Delta, Beanie Drake, Am. Heart Assn., 1977; recipient NIH-Nat. Rsch. Svc. award, 1979-82; Ohio div. Am. Heart Assn. grantee, 1980-81; Ohio Kidney Found. grantee, 1977-78; Pres.'s Scholarship award, 1967-69; AMA Physician Recognition award, 1984-87, various medals for slalom racing. Fellow ACP; mem. John Hopkins Med. and Surg. Soc., AMA (physician rsch. evaluation panel 1981-83), Internat. Soc. of Nephrology, Assn. Black Cardiologists, Inc., Am. Soc. Hypertension, Nat. Kidney Found., Am. Acad. Med. Acupuncture (assoc.), World Tae Kwon Do Fedn., Seoul, Korea, Mensa, Am. Film Inst., Phi Beta Kappa, Alpha Epsilon Delta, Alpha Kappa Alpha. Democrat. Avocations: slalom racing, Tae Kwon Do (2d degree black belt). E-mail: mbarnett@anderson.ucla.edu.

BARNETT, MARILYN, advertising agency executive; b. Detroit; d. Henry and Kate (Boesky) Schiff; BA, Wayne State U.; children: Rhona, Ken. Founder, part-owner, pres. Mars Advt. Co., Southfield, Mich. Bd. dirs. Mich. Strategic Fund. Appointed to Mich. bi-lateral trade team with Germany, Named Outstanding Retail Woman of Yr., Outstanding Retail Mktg. Exec., Bd. Dirs. Oakland U., Mich.'s Top 25 Women Bus. Owner's List, Entrepreneur of Yr., Oakland Exec. of Yr., 1997. Mem. AFTRA (dir.), SAG, Exec. Women Am., Am. Women in Radio & TV (Top Agy. Mgmt. award, Outstanding Woman of Yr.), Internat. Women Forum, Women's Forum Club, Com. of 200, Women's Econ. Club (Ad Woman of Yr.), Adcraft. Office: MARS Advt 23999 Northwestern Hwy Southfield MI 48075-2528 also: MARS Advt Co 6671 W Sunset Blvd Ste 1591 Los Angeles CA 90028-7123

BARNETT, MARK WILLIAM, state attorney general; b. Sioux Falls, S.D., Sept. 6, 1954; s. Thomas C. and Dorothy Ann (Lievrance) B.; m. Deborah Ann Barnett, July 14, 1979. BS in Govt., U. S.D., 1976, JD, 1978. Bar: S.D. Pvt. practice law Sioux Falls, 1978-80; asst. atty. gen. State of S.D., Pierre, 1980-83, spl. prosecutor, 1984-90, atty. gen., 1990—; ptnr. Schmidt, Schroyer, Colwill and Barnett, Pierre, 1984-90; mem. S.D. Law Enforcement Tng. Commn., 1987—; mem. S.D. Bar Commn., 1986-88, 89-92, S.D. Corrections Commn., 1987. Bd. dirs. D.A.R.E., S.D. drug prevention prog., 1987—. Mem. S.D. Bar Assn. (pres. young lawyers' sect. 1985), Am. Judicature Soc. (nat. bd. dirs. 1984-88), State's Atty. Assn. (bd. dirs. 1987-90). Republican. Avocations: golf, weight lifting, snowmobiling. Office: Office Atty Gen 500 E Capitol Ave Pierre SD 57501-5070*

BARNETT, MARTHA WALTERS, lawyer; b. Dade City, Fla., June 1, 1947; d. William Haywood and Helen (Hancock) Walters; m. Richard Rawls Barnett, Jan. 4, 1969; children: Richard Rawls, Sarah Walters. BA cum laude, Tulane U., 1969; JD cum laude, U. Fla., 1973. Bar: Fla. 1973, U.S. Dist. Ct. (mid. and so. dists.) Fla. 1973, U.S. Ct. Appeals (3d, 4th and 11th cirs.) 1975, D.C. 1989. Assoc. Holland & Knight LLP, Tallahassee, Fla., 1973-78, ptnr., 1979—; bd. dirs., v.p. Fla. Lawyers Prepaid Legal Svc. Corp., 1978-80, pres., 1980-82, legis. com., 1983-84, mem. commn. on access to justice, 1984-86, exec. coun. tax sect., 1987-88, exec. coun. pub. interest sect., 1989-91; active Fla. Commn. Ethics, 1984-87, chairperson, 1986-87, Fla. Taxation and Budget Reform Commn., 1989—; Legal adv. bd. Martindale-Hubbell, 1990—; chair Ho. of Dels., 1994-96. Mem. Fla. Coun. Econ. Edn., Fla. Edn. Found.; bd. dirs. Lawyers Com. Civil Rights Under Law. Nominated candidate for pres. elect of the Amer. Bar Assn., 1999—. Fellow Am. Bar Found. (life); mem. ABA (exec. coun. sect. on individual rights and responsibility 1974-86, bd. govs. 1986-89, task force on minorities in profession 1984-86, commn. on women in profession 1987-90, long range planning com. 1988-91, chair bd. govs. fin. com. 1988-89, bd. editors ABA Jour. 1990-94, exec. coun. sect. legal edn. and admission to bar 1990-94, chairperson commn. on pub. understanding about the law 1990-93, others), Nat. Inst. Dispute Resolution (sec.-treas. 1988-94, bd. dirs. 1988-94, Gov. appt. Fla. Constitution revision Commn., 1997-98), Am. Law Inst., Fla. Bar Assn. (exec. coun. pub. interest law sect. 1989-91), Tallahassee Bar Assn. Office: Holland & Knight LLP PO Drawer 810 Tallahassee FL 32302-0810

BARNETT, MARY LOUISE, elementary education educator; b. Exeter, Calif., May 1, 1941; d. Raymond Edgar Noble and Nena Lavere (Huckaby) Hope; m. Gary Allen Barnett, Aug. 9, 1969; children: Alice Marie, Virginia Lynn. BA, U. of Pacific, 1963; postgrad., U. Mont., 1979-82, U. Idaho, 1984—. Cert. life elem. tchr., Calif.; standard elem. credential, Idaho; elem. tchr., Mont. Tchr. Colegio Americano de Torrean, Torreon, Coahuila, Mexico, 1962-63, Summer Sch. Primary Grades South San Francisco, 1963-66, Visalia (Calif.) Unified Sch. Dist., 1966-69, Sch. Dist. # 1, Missoula, Mont., 1969-73, Fort Shaw-Simms Sch. Dist., Fort Shaw, Mont., 1976-83, Sch. Dist. #25, Pocatello, Idaho, 1983-93, Greenacres Elem., Pocatello, 1993-94; tchr. 2d grade Bonneville Elem., Pocatello, 1994-95; tchr. Windsong Presch., Missoula, Mont., 1995-98, Headstart of Missoula, 1998—. Foster mom Ednl. Found. Fgn. Students, Pocatello, Idaho, 1986-89; vol. Am. Heart Assn., Am. Cancer Soc., Pocatello, 1986-88, Bannock March of Dimes, Pocatello, 1988, Pocatello Laubach Lit. Tutoring, 1989; state v.p. membership, del. to P.W. Australian Mission Study; vice moderator Kendall Presbyn. Women, moderator, 1991—; moderator Kendall P.W. 1990-92; dean, treas. Presbyn. Ch., 1997—. Recipient scholarship Mont. Delta Kappa Gamma Edn. Soc., Great Falls, Mont., 1976, Great Falls AAUW, 1980, Great Falls Scottish Rite, 1981, Five Valleys Reading Assn., Missoula, Mont., 1982. Mem. AAUW (v.p., mem. com. Idaho divsn. 1990-92, book chair 1995—), ASCD, NEA, Nat. Coun. Tchrs. English, Internat. Reading Assn., Assn. Childhood Edn. Internat., Laubach Literacy Tutors (sec. 1993—), Bus. and Profl. Women Pocatello (sec. 1993—), Mortar Bd., Alpha Lambda Delta, Delta Kappa Gamma (state fellowship chmn., corr. sec. Pocatello chpt. 1986-88, 2d v.p. 1994-96), Moose (musician 1981-82), Order Eastern Star (musician 1984-85), Gamma Phi Beta (sec. Laubach Tutors 1993-95), Delta Kappa Gamma (2d v.p. Phi chpt. 1996—). Democrat. Presbyterian. Avocations: music, aquacise, aerobics, crafts, cross stitch. Home: 103 E Crestline Dr Missoula MT 59803-2412 Office: Edu-Care Presch 408 Stephens Missoula MT 59801

BARNETT, MICHAEL, sports agent, business manager; b. Olds, Alta., Can., Oct. 9, 1948; came to U.S., 1988; s. Terence R. and Mary M. Barnett; m. Dalyce M. Giordano, Apr. 2, 1988; children: Jesse, Joey, Justin, Janie, Jenna. Student, St. Lawrence U., 1968-70; BS in Health and Phys. Edn., U. Calgary, 1973. Registered agent Nat. Hockey League Players Assn., Sports Lawyers Assn. Profl. hockey player, 1973-75; founder, CEO Corpsport Internat.; agent, bus. mgr. Wayne Gretzky, 1981—; internat. v.p. Internat. Mgmt. Group; gen. mgr. Ninety-Nine All Stars; pres. Internat. Mgmt. Group Hockey, 1990. Active H.E.L.P., L.A. Named one of Top 100 Most Powerful in Sports, The Sporting News, 1994, 95, 96, 98, One of Twelve Most Powerful in Hockey, Hockey News, 1995. Mem. U.S.A. Hockey, U.S. Golf Assn. Avocations: golfing, running. Home: PO Box 50 Lake Arrowhead CA 92352-0050 Office: PO Box 565 Ste 01-270 28200 Hwy 189 Lake Arrowhead CA 92352

BARNETT, PETER JOHN, property development executive, educator; b. Rockville Ctr., N.Y., Dec. 11, 1944; s. Arnold Peter and Rita Marie (Peters) B. BA in Philosophy, Cathedral Coll., Huntington, N.Y., 1966; STB in Theology, Cath. U., 1970; MA in Theology, St. John's U., Jamaica, N.Y., 1970. Dir. religious edn. St. Margaret of Scotland, Selden, N.Y., 1970-71, Holy Name of Mary, Valley Stream, N.Y., 1971-74, St. Patricks, Bay Shore, N.Y., 1974-86; exec. dir. Wyandanch (N.Y.) Homes & Property Devel. Corp., 1986—; prof. religious studies St. Joseph's Coll., Patchogue, N.Y., 1985—; cons. Silver, Burett, Ginn, N.J., 1976—. Cons.: (textbook) This is Our Faith, 1986. Chairperson Nassau/Suffolk Coalition for Homeless, N.Y., 1993, 95, 96. Democratic. Roman Catholic. Avocations: ski, sail, travel, explore, tennis. Office: Wyandanch Homes & Property Devel Corp 1434 Straight Path Wyandanch NY 11798-3909

BARNETT, PETER RALPH, health science facility administrator, dentist; b. Bklyn., Oct. 21, 1951; s. Seymour and Betty Natalie (Cobbs) B.; m. Susan Clay, Jan. 27, 1990; children: Regina, Alexis, Alana. AB, Colgate U., 1973; DMD, U. Pa., 1977, MBA, 1979. Lic. dentist, Pa., N.J., N.Y. Dir. mgmt. sys. U. Pa. Sch. Dental Med., Phila., 1979-81, asst. dir. clinic mgmt., 1981-84; dir. profl. affairs Pearle Dental, Inc., Dallas, 1984-86, v.p. and dir. dental ops., 1986-87; dir. vision benefits Pearle Health Svcs., Inc., Dallas, 1987-88, v.p. managed vision care, 1988-91, sr. v.p. franchising and sales, 1991-92, sr. v.p. quality and franchising, 1992-93; assoc. Healthcare Venture Assocs., Irving, Tex., 1993-94; exec. dir. Prudential DMO, Atlanta, 1994-95; sr. v.p., COO United Dental Care, Dallas, 1995-98; pres. Protective Dental Care, Managed Care, 1999—; pres. United Dental Care, 1998—; bd. dirs. CollaGenex Pharms., Inc., Newtown, Pa. Author and co-author several profl. articles on health care mgmt., fin., and mktg. Bd. dirs. PTA Brinker Elementary Sch. Plano, Tex. 1988-89. Mem. ADA, Nat. Assn. Dental Plans (bd. dirs., chmn. bd. 1998—). Democrat. Jewish. Avocations: running, reading, tennis, karate, gardening. Home: 1304 Chippewa Dr Plano TX 75093-5021 Office: Protective Dental Care Ste 500 East 1301 Perston Rd Dallas TX 75240-4911

BARNETT, RALPH LIPSEY, engineering educator; b. Chgo., July 15, 1933; B.C.E., Ill. Inst. Tech., 1955, M.S. in Mechanics, 1958; married; 2 children. Assoc. rsch. engr. structural mechanics Armour Rshc. Found., Chgo., 1955-60; evening instr. civil engring. Ill. Inst. Tech.; structural rsch. engr. R & D dept. Stanray Corp., Chgo., 1960-62; sr. rsch. engr., group leader Ill. Inst. Tech. Rsch. Inst., Chgo., 1962-68, evening instr. mech. and aerospace engring., 1967-69, full time faculty mem., 1969—, prof. mech. and aerospace engring., 1969—; dir. R & D, dir. rubber lab., dir. indsl. chemistry lab. Felt Products Mfg. Co., Skokie, Ill., 1968-69; chmn. bd. Triodyne, Inc., Niles, Ill., cons. engr. Triodyne Environ. Engrs. Inc., Niles, Ill., 1972—, Alliance Tool Co., Maywood, Ill., 1984—, Inst. Advanced Safety Studies, Niles, 1984—, Tryodyne Fire & Explosion, Oakbrook, Ill., Triodyne-Wangler Constrn. Co., Inc., Niles, Triodyne Recreation, Inc., Niles, Triodyne Safety Systems LLC, 1999. CECO Steel Co. scholar, 1953; Armour Rsch. Found. fellow, 1955. Mem. ASCE (Collingwood prize 1960), ASME (Prize paper Chgo. sect. 1962), ASTM, AAUP, Am. Acad. Mechanics, Am. Concrete Inst., Am. Soc. Safety Engrs., Nat. Safety Coun., Am. Soc. Agrl. Engrs., Nat. Fire Protection Assn., Graphic Arts Tech. Found., Am. Soc. Metals, Am. Nat. Standards Inst. (sec.), Am. Soc. Engring. Edn., Sigma Xi, Chi Epsilon, Pi Tau Sigma, Tau Beta Pi. Author papers, chpts. in books. Home: 2721 Alison Ln Wilmette IL 60091-2101 *Indebtedness to the past, dedication to the present, and obligation to the future: can success fail to follow such an outline?.*

BARNETT, R(ALPH) MICHAEL, theoretical physicist, educational agency administrator; b. Gulfport, Miss., Jan. 25, 1944; s. Herbert Chester and Lisa Margaret (Kielley) B.; m. Suzanne Hamilton, Feb. 10, 1980; children: Leilani Pinho, Julia Alexandra, Russell Alan. BS, Antioch Coll., 1966; PhD, U. Chgo., 1971. Postdoctoral fellow U. Calif., Irvine, 1972-74; rsch. fellow Harvard U., Cambridge, Mass., 1974-76; rsch. assoc. Stanford (Calif.) Linear Accelerator Ctr., 1976-83; vis. physicist Inst. Theoretical Physics U. Calif., Santa Barbara, 1983-84; staff scientist Lawrence Berkeley Nat. Lab., 1984-89, sr. scientist and head particle data group, 1990—; co-dir. QuarkNet Ednl. Project, 1999—; v.p. Contemporary Physics Edn. Project, 1987-98, pub. info. coor. Am. Phys. Soc. Dvsn. of Particles and Fields, 1994-97; edn. coord. ATLAS experiment at CERN, Geneva. Author: Teachers' Resource Book on Fundamental Particles and Interactions, 1988, Review of Particle Physics, 1990, 92, 94, 96, 98, Particle Physics—One Hundred Years of Discoveries, 1996, Guide to Experimental Particle Physics Literature, 1993, 96, (chart) Fundamental Particles and Interactions, 1987, 90, 95, 99, World-Wide Web features, The Particle Adventure, 1995, The Quark Adventure, 1999. Fellow Am. Phys. Soc. (pub. info. coord. divsn. particles and fields 1994-97, taskforce on informing the public). Achievements include research on the Standard Model and its extensions, including studies of nature and validity of quantum chromodynamics; analyses of neutral current couplings; calculations of the production of heavy quarks; predictions of properties and decays of supersymmetric particles and higgs bosons. Office: Lawrence Berkeley Nat Lab MS-50-308 1 Cyclotron Rd Berkeley CA 94720

BARNETT, RICHARD CHAMBERS, historian, educator; b. Davenport, Fla., Apr. 27, 1932; s. Jones Richard and Helen June (Chambers) B.; m. Betty May Tribble, Oct. 18, 1957; children—Amelia Carlton, Colin Warwick. B.A., Wake Forest Coll., 1953; M.Ed., U. N.C., 1954, Ph.D., 1963. Instr., acting chmn. dept. social sci. Gardner-Webb Coll., 1956-58; instr. history Wake Forest U., Winston-Salem, N.C., 1961-62, asst. prof., 1962-67, assoc. prof., 1967-76; prof. Wake Forest U., Winston-Salem, N.C., 1976-94; chmn. dept. history Wake Forest U., Winston-Salem, N.C., 1968-75, 83-87, acting dean Grad. Sch., 1979; retired. Contbg. author history and polit. sci. vols., also articles and book revs. Pres Winston-Salem-Forsyth PTA, 1969-71; bd. mgrs. N.C. PTA, 1971-73, exec. com., 1972-73, life mem.; adv. com. N.C. Bd. Edn., 1973-76. Served with CIC, AUS, 1954-56. Southeastern Inst. Medieval and Renaissance Studies fellow, summer 1974. Mem. Am. Hist. Assn. (pres. elect N.C. conf. 1991-92, pres. 1992-93), AAUP, Carolinas Symposium Brit. Studies (pres. 1979-80), So. Conf. Brit. Studies (pres. 1990-92), N.Am. Conf. Brit. Studies (coun. 1990-92), Danforth Assocs. Home: 2130 Royall Dr Winston Salem NC 27106-5234

BARNETT, ROBERT BRUCE, lawyer; b. Waukegan, Ill., Aug. 26, 1946; s. Bernard and Betty Jane (Simon) B.; m. Rita Lynn Braver, Apr. 10, 1972; 1 child, Meredith Jane. BA, U. Wis., 1968; JD, U. Chgo., 1971. Bar: D.C. 1971. Law clk. to Hon. John Minor Wisdom U.S. Ct. Appeals (5th cir.), 1971-72; law clk. to assoc. justice Byron R. White U.S. Supreme Ct., Washington, 1972-73; legis. asst. Sen. Walter F. Mondale, Washington, 1973-75; assoc. Williams & Connolly, Washington, 1975-78, ptnr., 1979—; adj. prof. Georgetown Law Sch., 1973-80. Bd. trustees John F. Kennedy Ctr. for Performing Arts, 1994—; bd. visitors Sanford Inst. of Pub. Policy, Duke U., 1998—. Democrat. Office: Williams & Connolly 725 12th St NW Washington DC 20005-5901

BARNETT, ROBERT GLENN, lawyer; b. Oxford, Miss., July 30, 1933; s. Arden and Vera (Turner) B.; m. Rae Ragsdale, Apr. 21, 1962; children: Laura Lee, Mary Melissa. BA, U. Miss., 1959, JD, 1961. Ptnr. Houston & Barnett, Southaven, Miss., 1961-63, Neal, Houston, Elliott & Barnett, Jackson, Miss., 1963-65, Barnett & Barnett, Jackson, Miss., 1965-70; legal counsel Deposit Guaranty Nat. Bank, Jackson, 1970-79, gen. counsel, sec. to bd., 1979-95; counsel Butler, Snow, O'Mara, Stevens and Cannada, Jackson, 1996—; vis. prof. U. Miss. Law Sch., Oxford, Miss., 1978-79, 85; banking law course coord., lectr. Sch. Banking of the South, Baton Rouge, 1978-79. Pres. Family Services Assn., Jackson, 1970-71; bd. dirs. Community Services Assn., 1968-70; bd. govs. Jackson Symphony Orch. Assn., 1981-85. Lt. (j.g.) USNR, 1954-58; capt. USNR, 1979. Fellow Young Lawyers of Miss. Bar (pres. 1995-96); mem. ABA (banking law com. 1982—), Miss. Bar Assn. (2d v.p. 1968-69), Jackson Legal Aid Bd. Trustees (pres. 1965-67), Miss. Bankers Assn. (chmn. bank lawyers com.), Miss. Jr. Bar Assn. (pres. 1967-68), Miss. Corp. Counsel Assn. (pres. 1988), So. Conf. Bank House Counsel (chmn. 1989), Lions (pres. North Jackson chpt. 1967-68), River Hills Tennis Club (dir. 1979-82, Lake Caroline Golf Club. Baptist. Office: PO Box 22567 Jackson MS 39225-2567

BARNETT, SAMUEL TREUTLEN, international company executive; children: Elizabeth L., Katharine T., Emily R., Alexander W. BA, Wesleyan U., 1969; MEd, Temple U., 1973, EdD, 1975. Tchr. The Haverford Sch., 1969-74; leadership devel. specialist Phila. Sch. Dist., 1974-75; freelance cons., 1971-76; tng. cons. U.S. Office Personnel Mgmt., Pa., 1976-79; founder, chief cons. Barnett Internat. a subsidiary PAREXEL Internat., Media, Pa., 1979-99; ptnr. Pricewaterhouse Coopers, Phila., 1999—; spkr. in field. Contbr. articles to profl. jours. Mem. ASTD, Drug Info. Assn. Office: Pricewaterhouse Coopers 2400 Eleven Penn Ctr Philadelphia PA 19103

BARNETT, SUZANNE WILSON, history educator; b. Columbus, Ohio, June 1, 1940; d. George Leedom and Dorothy May (Macklin) Wilson; m. Redmond James Barnett, June 7, 1969. BA, Muskingum Coll., New Concord, Ohio, 1961; AM, Harvard U., 1963, PhD, 1973. Lectr. Suffolk U., Boston, 1970-72, Boston U., 1971-72; instr. Wellesley (Mass.) Coll., 1972-73; asst. prof. U. Puget Sound, Tacoma, 1973-79, assoc. prof., 1979-85, prof., 1985—, Robert G. Albertson prof., 1998—; vis. asst. prof. U. Va., Charlottesville, 1973. Author, co-editor: Christianity in China: Early Protestant Missionary Writings, 1985; contbr. articles to profl. jours. Bd. dirs. Chinese Reconciliation Project Found., Tacoma, 1994—. Fulbright-Hays Grad. fellow U.S. Office Edn., Taiwan, Japan, 1967-68, Lang. and Rsch. fellow Inter-Univ. Program and Academia Sinica, Taipei, Taiwan, 1986-87, Postdoctoral fellow History of Christianity in China Project, 1990. Mem. Am. Hist. Assn. (coun., tchg. divsn. 1992-95), Assn. Asian Studies (bd. dirs., China and Inner Asia coun. 1979-82, program com. 1998—, chair 1999—), ASIANetwork (bd. dirs. 1996—, chair 1998-99), Soc. History Edn. (nat. adv. coun. 1996—). Democrat. Avocations: jogging, dining, opera. Home: 3401 N 29th St Tacoma WA 98407-6250 Office: U Puget Sound Dept History 1500 N Warner St Dept History Tacoma WA 98416-0033

BARNETT, VIVIAN ENDICOTT, curator; b. Putnam, Conn., July 8, 1944; d. George and Vivian (Wood) Endicott; m. Peter Herbert Barnett, July 1, 1967; children: Sarah, Alexander. AB magna cum laude, Vassar Coll., 1965; MA, NYU, 1971; postgrad., CUNY, 1979-81. Research asst. Solomon R. Guggenheim Mus., N.Y.C., 1973-77, curatorial assoc., 1978-79, assoc. curator, 1980-81, rsch. curator, 1981-82, curator, 1982-91; dir. Roethel Benjamin Archive at Guggenheim Mus., N.Y.C., 1991—. Author: The Guggenheim Museum: Justin K. Thannhauser Collection, 1978, The Guggenheim Museum Collection 1900-1980, Kandinsky at the Guggenheim, 1983, 100 Works by Modern Masters from the Guggenheim Museum, 1984, Works by Robert Barry, Sol LeWitt, Robert Mangold, Richard Tuttle from the Collection of Dorothy and Herbert Vogel, 1987, Kandinsky and Sweden, 1989, Kandinsky in Major Collections in the West, 1989, Kandinsky Watercolours: Catalogue Raisonné, vol. I 1900-1921, 1992, vol. II 1922-44, 1994, Kleine Freuden, 1992, Das bunte Leben: Kandinsky in Lenbachhaus, 1995, The Blue Four: Feininger, Jawlensky Kandinsky, Klee in the New World, 1997; also articles; contbr. to Kandinsky in Paris: 1934-44, 1985, Exiles and Emigre's: 1933-1945, 1997. John Simon Guggenheim fellow, 1990. Mem. Am. Assn. Museums, Internat. Coun. Museums, Coll. Art Assn. Am., Soc. Kandinsky (sec. 1992—). Office: Solomon R Guggenheim Mus 1071 5th Ave New York NY 10128-0112

BARNETT, WILLIAM ARNOLD, economics educator; b. Boston, Oct. 30, 1941; s. Marcus Jack and Elizabeth Leah (Forman) B.; m. Melinda Gentry, Sept. 1, 1991. BS, MIT, 1963; MBA, U. Calif., Berkeley, 1965; MS, Carnegie Mellon U., 1972, PhD, 1974. System devel. engr., Apollo Project, Rocketdyne div. Rockwell Internat. Corp., Canoga Park, Calif., 1963-67; research econometrician Bd. Govs., Fed. Reserve System, Washington, 1973-81; Stuart Centennial prof. econs. U. Tex., Austin, 1981-90; prof. econs. Washington U., St. Louis, 1990—; vis. prof. econs. U. Aix-Marseille, Aix-en-Provence, France, 1979, Duke U., Durham, N.C., 1987-88; organizer ann. symposia in econ. theory and econometrics; assoc. dir. Ctr. for Econ. Rsch., U. Tex., Austin, 1981-90. Author: Consumer Demand and Labor Supply, 1981; editor three spl. edts. Jour. of Econometrics, 1979, 80, 85, Cambrige U. Press Monograph series, 1985—, Cambridge U. Press Jour. Macroeconomic Dynamics, 1997—; assoc. editor Jour. of Bus. and Econ. Stats., 1982-97; contbr. approx. 75 articles to profl. jours. Contract selection panel mem. NIH, Washington, 1983; cons. World Bank, Washington, 1985. R.K. Mellon Found. fellow, 1971-73; rsch. grantee NSF, Washington, 1977-89, Hogg Found., Houston, 1983. Fellow ICC Inst. (sr., editor 1983—), Am. Statis. Assn. (assoc. editor 1982—, fellow 1989—, program chair 1992—), Jour. Econometrics (charter fellow 1989—); mem. Inst. Math. Stats., Econometric Soc. (contbr. to jour.), Am. Econ. Assn., MIT Club (St. Louis). Home: 11030 Wellsley Ct Saint Louis MO 63146-5529 Office: Washington U Dept Econs Saint Louis MO 63130

BARNETTE, CURTIS HANDLEY, steel company executive, lawyer; b. St. Albans, W.Va., Jan. 9, 1935; s. Curtis Franklin and Garnett Drucella (Robinson) B.; m. Lois Joan Harner, Dec. 28, 1957; children: Curtis Kevin, James David. AB with High Honors, W.Va. U., 1956; postgrad. (Fulbright scholar), U. Manchester, 1956-57; J.D., Yale U., 1962; grad. advanced mgmt. program, Harvard U., 1974-75; LLD (hon.), W.Va. U., 1995, Allentown Coll., 1996, U. Charleston, 1998, Lehigh U., 1999. Bar: Conn. 1962, Pa. 1968, D.C. 1988, W.Va. 1990. Atty. Wiggin & Dana, New Haven, Conn., 1962-67; atty. Bethlehem (Pa.) Steel Corp., 1967-92, sec., 1976-92, gen. counsel, 1977-92, sr. v.p., 1985-92, chmn., chief exec. officer, 1992—, also bd. dirs., 1986—; lectr. U. Md., 1958-59; law tutor Yale U., 1962-67; chmn., bd. dirs. Am. Iron and Steel Inst., 1997, dir., 1992—; bd. dirs. Met. Life Ins. Co., Owens Corning, Lehigh Valley Partnership; chmn. Internat. Iron and Steel Inst., 1994-95, dir. 1992—. Trustee Lehigh U., 1993—, Pa. Soc., 1993—; mem. Adminstrv. Conf. U.S., 1988-89; dir. W.Va. U. Found.,

1982—, chair, 1987-88; mem. adv. com. on Trade Policy and Negotiations, 1989—, Coal Commn., 1990. With U.S. Army Counterintelligence Corps, 1957-59; major USAR, 1959-67. Mem. ABA, Fed. Bar Assn., Pa. Bar Assn., Conn. Bar Assn., Northampton County Bar Assn., D.C. Bar Assn., W.Va. Bar Assn., Assn. Gen. Counsel (pres. 1988-90), Am. Soc. Corp. Secs. (chmn. 1986), Am. Law Inst., Pa. Chamber Bus. and Industry (dir. 1985-93), Bus. Coun., Bus. Roundtable (policy com. 1992—), Pa. Bus. Roundtable (dir. 1986—, chmn. 1994-95, Loblolly Bay and Loblolly Pines, Links, Saucon Valley Country Club, Bet hlehem Club, Blooming Grove Hunting and Fishing Club, Yale Club of N.Y.C., Univ. Club of Washington, Phi Beta Kappa, Beta Theta Pi, Phi Alpha Theta, Phi Delta Phi. Home: 1112 Prospect Ave Bethlehem PA 18018-4914 Office: 1170 8th Ave Bethlehem PA 18016-7600

BARNEVIK, PERCY NILS, electrical company executive; b. Simrishamn, Sweden, Feb. 13, 1941; s. Einar and Anna Barnevik; m. Aina Orvarsson, 1963; 3 children. MBA, Gothenburg Sch. Econs., Sweden, 1964; postgrad., Stanford U., 1965-66; TechnDr honoris causa, U. Linkoping, Sweden, 1989; Econ. Dr. honoris causa, U. Gothenburg, Sweden, 1991; JD (hon.), Babson Coll., 1995; Sci. Dr. honoris causa, Cranfield U., 1998. With The Johnson Group, Sweden, 1966-69; with Sandvik AB, Sandviken, Sweden, 1969-80, group controller, 1969-75; pres. U.S. affiliate, 1975-79; exec. v.p. Sandvik, Sweden, 1979-80; pres., chief exec. officer ASEA, 1980-87; chmn. Sandvik AB, 1983—; pres., CEO Asea Brown Boveri Ltd., 1988-96, chmn., CEO, 1996-97; chmn. Investor AB, Sweden, 1997—, Asea Brown Boveri Ltd., 1997—, AstraZeneca PLC, 1999—; bd. dirs. GM, Detroit; chmn. AstraZeneca PLC, U.K., 1999—. Office: Asea Brown Boveri Hldg Ltd, PO Box 8131, CH-8050 Zurich Switzerland also: Investor AB, S-10332 Stockholm Sweden

BARNEY, AUSTIN DUNHAM, II, estate planner; b. Hartford, Conn., Apr. 27, 1945; s. Philip Cushman and Elizabeth Cole (Freeman) B.; m. Susan C. Rumney, Aug. 26, 1976; children: Austin C. D. III, Amanda Brandegee. BA in Polit. Sci., Yale U., 1967; MPA, Syracuse U., 1969. Lic. real estate broker, Conn., N.Y., Mass.; lic. life/health ins., securities, Conn. Mgmt. asst. U. Hartford, Conn., 1967-68; jr./sr. planner Hartford Police Dept., 1969-70; sr. planner Commn. on City Plan City of Hartford, 1970; sr. adminstrv. analyst fin. dept. City of Hartford Budget and Rsch. Divsn., 1970-71, prin. adminstrv. analyst fin. dept., 1971-72; dir. land use policy planning State of Conn., Dept. Environ. Protection, 1972-73; exec. dir. Environ. Ctrs. Inc., 1973-75; pvt. practice cons., 1975-76; dir. natural resources mgmt. and community design Westledge Ctr. for Edn., 1976-78; sr. cons. corp. citizenship Cigna Corp. (Conn. Gen. Ins. Corp.), 1979-82; dir. contbns. and civic affairs Cigna Corp., Conn. Gen. Ins. Corp., 1982-84; pres., founder Farmvest, Inc., 1984—; prin. Bus. Planning Assocs., 1991-96; pres. Life Legacy Advisors, LLC, Avon, Conn., 1996—; dir. Spiritus Wines, Inc., Aid to Artesans; ptnr. Folly Farm Assocs., 1983-90; pres. Folly Farm, Inc., 1983-90. Zoning commr. Town of Simsbury, Conn., 1976—; del. People's Republic China, Yale-China Assn., fall 1979, 80; corporator Hartford Pub. Libr., 1981—; corporator The Ctr. Families and Children, 1996—; bd. dirs., exec. com. Riverfront Recapture, Inc., 1981-90; bd. trustees Hartford Art Sch., 1969—, pres. 1984-86, 96—; bd. dirs. Conn. Trust for Hist. Preservation, 1982-85, The Nature Conservancy, treas. 1986-89, vice-chmn., 1989—, Oak Leaf award, 1995; bd. dirs. U. Conn. Found., 1988-92, Ensign-Bickford Found., 1987-93, v.p., 1989-93; bd. dirs. Ea. States Expo.; chmn. Conn. trustees 1993—; elector Wadsworth Atheneum, 1983—; bd. dirs., chmn. fin. com. Conn. Earth Day 20, Inc., 1990; regent U. Hartford, 1980-86, 90—. Recipient Oak Leaf award Nature Conservancy, 1995. Mem. Nat. Assn. Life Underwriters, Am. Assn. Life Underwriters, Conn. Assn. Life Underwriters, Hartford Assn. Life Underwriters, Conn. Life Leaders.

BARNEY, CAROL ROSS, architect; b. Chgo., Apr. 12, 1949; d. Chester Albert and Dorothy Valeria (Dusiewicz) Ross; m. Alan Fredrick Barney, Mar. 22, 1970; children: Ross Fredrick, Adam Shafer, John Ross. BArch, U. Ill., 1971. Registered architect, Ill. Assoc. architect Holabird & Root, Chgo., 1972-79; prin. architect Orput Assoc., Inc., Wilmette, Ill., 1979-81; prin. architect, pres. Ross Barney & Jankowski, Inc., Chgo., 1981—, also bd. dirs.; studio prof. Ill. Inst. Tech., Chgo., 1993-94; asst. prof. U. Ill., Chgo., 1976-78. Prin. works include Cesar Chavez Elem. Sch., Chgo., Glendale Heights (Ill.) Post Office (Disting. Bldg. award Chgo. chpt. AIA 1989). Plan commr. Village of Wilmette, 1986-88, mem. Econ. Devel. Commn., 1988-90, chmn. Appearance Rev. Commn., 1990—; trustee Children's Home and Aid Soc. Ill., Chgo., 1986—; mem. adv. bd. Small Bus. Ctr. for Women, Chgo., 1985—, Loop Coll., Chgo., 1986. Recipient Fed. Design Achievement award, 1992, Firm award AIA Chgo., 1995; Francis J. Plym travelling fellow, 1983. Fellow AIA (bd. dirs. Chgo. chpt. 1978-80, v.p. 1981-82, Disting. Svc. award Chgo. chpt. 1978, Ill. Coun. 1978, Honor award 1991, 94); mem. Nat. Coun. Archtl. Registration Bds. (cert.), Chgo. Women in Architecture (founding pres. 1978-79), Chgo. Network, Cliff Dwellers Club (bd. dirs. 1995). Home: 601 Linden Ave Wilmette IL 60091-2819 Office: Ross Barney & Jankowski Inc 30 W Monroe St Chicago IL 60603-2401

BARNEY, CHARLES RICHARD, transportation company executive; b. Battle Creek, Mich., June 7, 1935; s. Charles Ross and Helena Ruth (Croose) B.; m. Grace Leone Nightingale, Aug. 16, 1958; children: Richard Nolan, Patricia Lynn. B.A., Mich. State U., 1957; M.B.A., Wayne State U., 1961. Fin. analyst Ford Motor Co., Dearborn, Mich., 1958-65; gen. mgr. RentCo div. Fruehauf Corp., Detroit, 1965-72; pres. Evans Trailer Leasing, Des Plaines, Ill., 1973-77; v.p., gen. mgr. U.S. Rwy. Equipment Co., Des Plaines, 1972-77; pres. Evans Railcar div. Evans Trans. Co., 1978-84; pres. W.H. Miner div. Miner Enterprises, Geneva, Ill., 1985—; mem exec. com. Ry. Progress Inst., 1984—, chmn., 1990—. Served to 1st lt., inf. U.S. Army, 1958. Mem. Ry. Supply Assn. (dir. 1977-80). Congregationalist. Club: St. Charles Country (Ill.). Home: 1903 Shoreline Dr Saint Charles IL 60174-5563 Office: 1200 E State St Geneva IL 60134-2440

BARNEY, CHRISTINE ANNE, psychiatrist, educator; b. Rochester, N.Y., July 11, 1959. BS with honors and distinction, Cornell U., 1980, MS, 1985; MD, U. Rochester, 1986. Diplomate Am. Bd. Psychiatry and Neurology, Am. Bd. Forensic Medicine; lic. physician, N.H. Resident in psychiatry Dartmouth Med. Sch., 1986-90; co-leader med. intern's support group Dartmouth Hitchcock Med. Sch., 1987-88.; on-call psychiatrist Nashua Brookside Hosp., 1988-90; chief resident, instr. clin. psychiatry Dartmouth Med. Sch., 1989-90; pvt. practice outpatient psychiatrist, 1990—; group leader yr. 1 interviewing course Dartmouth Med. Sch., 1987-88, sect. coleader 4th yr. course, 1992, adj. asst. prof. psychiatry, 1992—; lectr. med. aspects of AIDS, Vt. Law Sch., 1987; presenter, orgnl. com. mem. ann. seminar Psychobiology of Women, 1990—; supr. to psychiat. residents, 1991—; co-leader incest survivors support group West Ctrl. Svcs., Lebanon, Newport, N.H., 1989-90. Trustee, chair Fairlee Libr. Mem. AMA, Am. Psychiat. Soc. (practice rsch. network 1998—), N.H. Psychiat. Soc. (councillor on N.H. psychiat . soc. exec. coun. 1992—, sec.-treas. 1995-97, pres. 1998—, del. from N.H. to Carrier Advis 1992—), N.H. Med. Soc., N.Y. State Coll. Agrs. Honor Soc., Alpha Zeta, Alpha Omega Alpha. Avocations: board sailing, snorkeling, nature photography, quilting. Office: The Carriage House 6 S Park St Lebanon NH 03766-1300

BARNEY, JOHN CHARLES, lawyer; b. N.Y.C., Nov. 18, 1939; s. Harold Lamont and Sara Eleanor (Johnston) B.; m. Joyce Marie Ebbinge; children—John C., Karen E., William L. BA, Wesleyan U., 1961; LLB, Columbia U., 1964. Bar: N.Y. 1964, U.S. Dist. Ct. (so. and ea. dists.) N.Y. 1966, U.S. Dist. Ct. (no. and we. dists.) N.Y. 1977, U.S. Ct. Appeals (2d cir.) 1973, U.S. Supreme Ct. 1979. Assoc. Donovan, Leisure, Newton and Irvine, N.Y.C., 1964-66; staff atty. N.Y. State Law Revision Commn., Ithaca, 1966-68; ptnr. Barney, Grossman, Dubow & Marcus, Ithaca, 1968—; asst. dist. atty. Tompkins County, N.Y., 1968-70; mem. N.Y. State Com. on Profl. Standards, 3d Jud. Dept., 1984-90, chmn. 1989-90 . Chmn. Bd. Zoning Appeals, Lansing, N.Y., 1975-92; mem. Bd. Edn., Lansing, 1981-96, v.p., 1983-89, pres., 1989-96; bd. edn. Tompkins-Seneca-Tioga Bd. Coop. Ednl. Svcs., 1997—; bd. dirs. Challenge Industries (sheltered workshop), Ithaca, 1970-80. Mem. Tompkins County Bar Assn. (pres. 1983-84), N.Y. State Bar Assn. Republican. Unitarian. Home: 12 Stormy View Rd Ithaca NY 14850-9774 Office: Barney Grossman Dubow & Marcus 119 E Seneca St Ithaca NY 14850-4352

BARNEY, KELLEE, university athletics coach; b. Leavenworth, Wash., May 12, 1961; m. Michael Barney, Aug. 12, 1995; 1 child, Jarryd Michael. Student, Wenatchee Valley Coll., 1979-81; BS in Sociology, U. Idaho, 1983. Asst. women's coach, recruiting coord. Portland (Oreg.) State U., 1983-85; asst. women's coach, recruiting coord. Wash. State U., Pullman, 1985-93, assoc. women's head coach, personnel dir., 1993-94; head coach women's basketball Gonzaga U., Spokane, Wash., 1994—. Office: Gonzaga U Women's Athletics Dept 502 E Boone Ave Spokane WA 99258-0001

BARNEY, KLINE PORTER, JR., retired engineering company executive, consultant; b. Dec. 16, 1934; s. Kline Porter and Doris (Nielsen) B.; m. Cheryl Kathleen Taylor, June 14, 1957; children: Peter, Suzanne, Cathleen, Patrick, Andrew. BS, U. Utah, 1957; MPA, San Diego State U , 1971. Registered profl. engr., 14 states. Asst. engr. Fallbrook (Calif.) Pub. Utility Dist., 1960-63; pres. Engring. Sci., Inc., Arcadia, Calif., 1963-85, Parsons Mcpl. Svcs., Inc., Pasadena, Calif., 1985-89; sr. v.p. Parsons Engring. Sci., Inc., Pasadena, 1989-97; cons., 1997—; mgr. Kline Barney Engrs., 1999—; presenter on field of privatization, 1983—; environ. cons. Contbr. articles to profl. jours. Mem. exec. bd. San Gabriel coun. Boy Scouts Am., 1981-96. Capt. USMC, 1957-60. Mem. ASCE, Am. Acad. Environ. Engrs. (diplomate), Am. Waterworks Assn., Water Environ. Fedn., Tau Beta Pi, Chi Epsilon, Phi Eta Sigma. Republican. Mem. LDS Ch. Avocations: hiking, astronomy. Home: 800 Juniperpoint Dr Salt Lake City UT 84103-3331

BARNEY, LINDA SUSAN, manufacturing specialist; b. Latrobe, Pa., Mar. 31, 1948; d. William Kramer and Kathryn (Voytilla) B. BS in Edn., Ind. U. of Pa., 1970; BBA, Tampa (Fla.) Coll., 1983; MBA, Fla. Met. U., Tampa, 1996. Tchr. Greater Latrobe (Pa.) Sch. Dist., 1970-81; from staff acct. to acctg. supr. Systems and Simulation, Tampa, Fla., 1986-89; project acct. Olin Ordnance, St. Petersburg, Fla., 1989-96; mfg. specialist BIC Spl. Mkts. Divsn., Clearwater, Fla., 1997-98; cost acctg. mgr. HIT Promotional Products, Largo, Fla., 1998—. Recipient Small Bus. award, 1993. Mem. NAFE, AAUW, Internat. Platform Assn., Women's Inner Cir. of Achievement, Am. Biographical Inst. (dep. gov.). Democrat. Lutheran. Avocations travel, golf, hiking, studies. Home: 9100 9th St N Apt 710 Saint Petersburg FL 33702-3078

BARNEY, STEVEN MATTHEW, human resources executive; b. Kansas City, Mo., June 8, 1943; s. Robert Matthew and Kathryn (Patterson) B.; m. Karen Frank, July 3, 1965; children: Matthew, Alicon, Heather, Robert. BJ, U. Wis., 1965, MHA, 1978. Editorial writer, polit. reporter Wis. State Jour., Madison, 1965-73; assoc. exec. dir. St. Marys Hosp. Med. Ctr., Madison, 1973-84; commr. Wis. Hosp. Rate Setting Commn., Madison, 1984-86; exec. dir., CEO HealthWise of Ky., Lexington, 1986-88; sr. v.p. human resources SSM Health Care, St. Louis, 1988—; v.p. ACMG, Inc., Dayton, Ohio, 1987-88; instr. U. Wis., Madison, 1980-86; bd. dirs. Dean HMO, Madison. Contbr. articles to profl. jours. Chair, mem. Funeral Dirs. Lic. Bd., Madison, 1975-79; mem. Ins. Adv. Coun., Madison, 1980-81; bd. dirs. Urban League of Met., St. Louis, 1998—. Recipient Svc. award South Cen. Wis. EMS Assn., Madison, 1981-82. Fellow Am. Coll. Health Care Execs. Democrat. Methodist. Home: 336 S Spoede Rd Saint Louis MO 63141-8436 Office: SSM Health Care 477 N Lindbergh Blvd Saint Louis MO 63141-7832

BARNEY, SUSAN LESLIE, academic administrator; b. Quantico, Va., Oct. 7, 1945; d. Duane Edwin and Joan Clarice (Long) B. BA, Ohio State U., 1972; JD, Capital U., 1977. Bar: Ohio 1979. With acctg. dept. Golden Gate U., San Francisco, 1977-80, dir. acctg., 1980-83, v.p. adminstrn., 1983-94, emerita v.p. adminstrn., 1994—; asst. sec. bd. trustees Golden Gate U., 1983-94. Mem. ABA. Methodist. Home: 25819 Eaton Way Bay Village OH 44140-2537

BARNEY, THOMAS MCNAMEE, lawyer; b. Indpls., Mar. 14, 1938; s. John R. and Helen (Adams) B.; m. Marjorie Joan Eckhert, Sept. 9, 1961; children: Lynn M., Thomas M. Jr., Katherine J. BA, Cornell U., 1960; JD, Ind. U., 1966; LLM in Taxation, NYU, 1967. Bar: Ind. 1966, N.Y. 1967, Fla. 1977. Assoc. Barney & Hughes, Indpls., 1966-67, Dewey, Ballantine, Bushby, Palmer & Wood, N.Y.C., 1967-69; assoc. Phillips, Lytle, Hitchcock, Blaine & Huber, Buffalo, 1969-74, ptnr., 1975—; lectr. in taxation SUNY, Buffalo, 1969-82, mem. adv. bd. grad. tax. cert. program, 1981—. Author: Major Changes in Estate Tax, 1981. Sec. Upstate N.Y. Synod. Evang. Luth. Ch. Am., Syracuse, 1987-96; bd. dirs. Luth. Theol. Sem., Phila., 1988-91, Niagara Luth. Home Found., 1988—. Lt. (j.g.) USN, 1960-63. Mem. Erie County Bar Assn. (chmn. tax com. 1981-84), Fla. Bar Assn., Ind. Bar Assn., Am. Coll. Trust and Estate Counsel. Office: Phillips Lytle Hitchcock Blaine & Huber 3400 Marine Midland Ctr Buffalo NY 14203-2887

BARNHARDT, ZEB ELONZO, JR., lawyer, independent consultant; b. Winston-Salem, N.C., Dec. 28, 1941; s. Zeb Elonzo and Katie Sue (Taylor) B.; m. Pam Hall; children: Daniel Black, Kathleen Martin. AB, Duke U., 1964; JD, Vanderbilt U., 1969. Bar: N.C. 1969. Assoc. Womble Carlyle Sandridge & Rice, PLLC, Winston-Salem, 1969-75, mem., 1975-97, of counsel, 1997-98; owner, mgr., cons. Barnhardt & Assocs., Inc., Winston-Salem, 1998—; pvt. practice law, Winston-Salem, 1998—. Alumni admissions adv. com. Duke U., 1970-72; bd. dirs. Industries for Blind, Winston-Salem, 1973-85, vice chmn., 1983-84, chmn., 1985; bd. dirs. Goodwill Industries, Winston-Salem, 1973-80; bd. dirs. The Little Theatre, Winston-Salem, 1979-85, asst. treas., 1980, treas., 1981-82, v.p., 1983-84, pres., 1984-85; adv. bd. Salvation Army, Winston-Salem, 1973-85, chmn., 1979-80; bd. dirs. Leadership Winston-Salem, 1984-92, v.p. adminstrn., 1988-89, pres. 1989-90; com. mem. Winston-Salem Found., 1975-84, vice chmn., 1978-80, chmn., 1983-84; trustee High Point U., 1984-96. With USN, 1964-66. Recipient Disting. Service award as Young Man of Yr. Winston-Salem Jaycees, 1974; Disting. Alumni award Duke U., 1979. Mem. ABA (fed. regulation securities laws com., law firms com., com. on law and accounting, bus. law sect.), N.C. Bar Assn. (chmn. securities regulation com. 1985-87, vice chmn. bus. law sect. 1987-89, chmn. bus. law sect. 1989-91, bd. govs. 1991-94, chmn. membership recruitment and retention com. 1997—), Forsyth County Bar Assn., Winston-Salem Jaycees (life, pres. 1973-74), N.C. Jaycees (regional dir. 1974-75, legal counsel 1975-77), Greater Winston-Salem C. of C. (bd. dirs. 1973-74), Forsyth Country Club, Rotary. Democrat. Methodist. Home: 4389 Winterberry Ridge Ct Winston Salem NC 27103 Office: Barnhardt & Assocs Inc 4389 Winterberry Ridge Ct Winston-Salem NC 27103-9738

BARNHART, CHARLES ELMER, animal sciences educator; b. Windsor, Ill., Jan. 25, 1923; s. Elmer and Irma (Smysor) B.; m. Norma McCarty, Dec. 28, 1946 (dec. Dec. 25, 1970); children: John D., Charles E., Norman R.; m. Jean M. Hutton, Jan. 12, 1973; stepchildren: Mark, David, Bonnie, Beth Hutton. B.S. in Agr., Purdue U., 1945; M.S., Ia. State U., 1948, Ph.D., 1954. Mem. faculty U. Ky., Lexington, from 1948, assoc. prof. animal sci., 1955-57, prof., 1957-88, prof. emeritus, 1988—, dean, dir. exptl. sta. and coop. extension service, 1969-88, dean emeritus, 1988—; pres. So. Assn. Agrl. Scientist, 1982-83. Bd. dirs. Ky. Bd. Agr., 1966-88, Ky. State Fair and Expn. Ctr., 1969-88, Ky. Tobacco Rsch. Bd., Farm Credit Svcs. Mid Am., 1988-93, Ky. Farm Bur., 1969-76; mem. Gov.'s Coun. on Agrl., 1971-80. Named Man of Yr. in Ky. Agr. Progressive Farmer, 1962, Man of Yr. for Ky. Agr. Ky. Agrl. Communicators, 1979; elected to Saddle and Sirloin Portrait Gallery, 1987. Mem. Am. Soc. Animal Sci., Ky. Hist. Soc., Farmhouse Fraternity, Masons (32 deg.), Shriners, Epsilon Sigma Phi, Gamma Sigma Delta., Omicron Delta Kappa, Sigma Xi. Methodist. Patentee in field. Home: 1017 Turkey Foot Rd Lexington KY 40502-2712

BARNHART, DOUGLAS E., construction company executive; b. Tex., Dec. 15, 1946. BS in Civil Engring., Tex. Tech. U. V.p. C.E. Wylie Constrn. Co., San Diego; CEO Douglas E. Barnhart, Inc., San Diego; chmn. Calif. Contractor's State Lic. Bd.; commr. Calif. Uniform Pub. Constrn. Cost Acctg. Commn.; bd. dirs. San Diego Nat. Bank. Recipient Small Bus. Award for Excellence, Bus./Industry award Greater San Diego Industry-Edn. Coun., 1994. Mem. Am. Arbitration Assn., Associated Gen. Contractors Am. (chmn., dir. Constrn. Apprenticeship Trust, dir. Constrn. Pension Trust, chmn. naval engring. com., vice chmn. heavy indsl. divsn.), Associated Builders and Contractors, Lincoln Club San Diego, Soc. Mil. Engrs., San Diego Associated Gen. Contractors (pres. 1994), Greater San Diego C. of C. (bd. dirs.). Office: Douglas E Barnhart 16981 Via Tazon Ste H San Diego CA 92127-1645

BARNHART, FORREST GREGORY, lawyer; b. Alpine, Tex., Sept. 11, 1951; s. F. Neil and Jody (Ogg) B. AB, Vassar Coll., 1973; JD, Cornell U., 1976. Bar: Fla. 1976, U.S. Dist. Ct. (so. dist.) Fla. 1977, U.S. Ct. Appeals (5th and 11th cirs.) 1977; cert. civil trial lawyer. Assoc. Levy, Plisco, Perry, Shapiro, Kneen & Kincade, West Palm Beach, Fla., 1976-78; assoc. Montgomery Searcy & Denney, P.A., West Palm Beach, 1978-81, ptnr., 1981-89; ptnr. Searcy, Denney, Scarola, Barnhart & Shipley, P.A., West Palm Beach, 1989—; lectr. in field; moderator TV show Call the Lawyer, 1983-85; dir. WXEL-TV and FM, Pub. Radio and TV, West Palm Beach. Contbr. chpt. to The Advocates Primer, 1991. Spkr., com. mem. Floridians Against Constnl. Tampering, 1984; mem. Jud. Nominating Commn., 1986-90; trustee Fla. Lawyers Action Group; bd. dirs. 1000 Friends of Fla., Legal Aid Soc. Palm Beach County. Recipient Al J. Cone award; mem. Eagle Hall of Fame, 1991. Fellow ATKA, ABA, FBA (treas. 1983-84, sec., v.p. 1984-85, pres. 1986-87), Fla. Bar, Palm Beach County Bar Assn. (vice chmn. fed. ct. practice com. 1981-82, media law com. 1981-82, bench bar com. 1980-81, chmn. pub. rels. com. 1983-84, TV com. 1984—), Palm Beach Trial Lawyers Assn. (founding dir.), Acad. Fla. Trial Lawyers (sec. 1990-91, treas. 1991-92, pres.-elect 1992-93, pres. 1993—, bd. dirs. 1986-90, chmn., key man legis. com. 1986—, mem. coll. of diplomates, steering counsel continuing edn. com., Eagle Benefactor, Disting. Lectr. in Jurisprudence 1988, sec. 1990-91), Fla. Lawyers Action Group (chair bd. trustees), Cornell Club. Home: 236 Miraflores Dr Palm Beach FL 33480-3618 Office: Searcy Denney Scarola Barnhart & Shipley 2139 Palm Beach Lakes Blvd West Palm Beach FL 33409-6601

BARNHART, JO ANNE B., government official; b. Memphis, Aug. 26, 1950; d. Nelson Alexander and Betty Jane (Fitzpatrick) Bryant; m. David Lee Ross, Feb. 14, 1976 (div. June 1983); m. David Ray Barnhart, May 24, 1986. Student U. Tenn., 1968-70; B.A., U. Del., 1975. Space and time buyer deMartin-Marona & Assocs., Wilmington, Del., 1970-73; adminstrv. asst. Mental Health Assn. Wilmington, 1973-75; dir. SERVE nutrition program Wilmington Sr. Ctr., 1975-77; legis. asst. to Senator William V Roth, Jr., Washington, 1977-81; dep. assoc. commr. Office Family Assistance, HHS, Washington, 1981-83, assoc. commr., 1983-86; Rep. staff dir. U.S. Senate Govt. Affairs Com., 1987-90; asst. sec. family support HHS, Washington, 1990-91, asst. sec. for children and families, 1991-92; staff U.S. Sen. William V. Roth, 1993—; mem. adv. bd. on welfare indicators U.S. Dept. HHS, 1996—. Campaign mgr. U.S. Senator William V. Roth, 1988, 1994; polit. dir. Nat. Rep. Senatorial Com., 1995-97; polit. and pub. policy cons., 1997—; mem. Social Security adv. bd., 1997—. Republican. Methodist.

BARNHART, NIKKI LYNN CLARK, elementary school educator; b. Terre Haute, Ind., Mar. 14, 1940; d. Wilbur Ellis and Margaret Jane (Cork) Clark; m. James Walter Barnhart; children: Tracey Lynn, Kelly Jean, Darby Jane, Holly Anne. BEd, Shippensburg U., 1961, MEd, 1964; cert. reading specialist, Western Md. U., 1979; EdD, U. Md., 1984. Cert. elem. tchr., English tchr., guidance counselor, Pa.; cert. Reading Recovery. Tchr. Chambersburg (Pa.) Schs., 1961-62, Spring Grove (Pa.) Area Schs., 1963-66, Hanover (Pa.) Pub. Schs., 1967—; presenter profl. conf. and convs. Author: Hanover through History, 1976. Mem. Hanover Borough Coun., 1993—; consistory mem. Emmanuel Ch., Hanover, 1984-92. Chpt. I parent minigrantee Pa. Dept. Edn., 1996; recipient Outstanding Elem. Educator award Phi Delta Theta, 1999. Mem. Internat. Reading Assn. (exemplary program award for bldg. 1997), South Ctrl. Reading Coun. (various offices, Celebrate Literacy award 1996), Delta Kappa Gamma (Eta chpt., Alpha Alpha State Golden Anniversary award 1980, Alpha Alpha State Founder's award 1982). Republican. Mem. United Ch. of Christ. Avocations: reading, cooking. Office: Clearview Sch 100 W Clearview Rd Hanover PA 17331-1615

BARNHART, ROBERT KNOX, writer, editor; b. Chgo., Oct. 17, 1933; s. Clarence L. and Frances (Knox) B.; m. Cynthia Ann Rogers, Sept. 16, 1955; children: Michael, John, David, Rebecca, Katherine. BA, U. of the South, 1956. Editor Clarence L. Barnhart, Bronxville, N.Y., 1956-75, editor-in-chief, 1976-79; pres. Clarence L. Barnhart, Inc., Bronxville and Briarcliff, N.Y., 1979-92; pres., editor-in-chief Rogers Knox & Barnhart, Garrison, N.Y., 1992—. Author: Barnhart Dictionary of Etymology, 1988, Barnhart Dictionary of New English, I, 1973, II, 1980, III, 1990, Dictionary of Science, 1986, American Heritage, The Barhart Abbreviations Dictionary, 1995, The Barnhart Concise Dictionary of Etymology, 1995; co-author: Let's Read, 1960-66, World Book Dictionary, 1976-99; contbr. World Book Ency., Dictionaries, Internat. Ency. of Lexicography. Recipient Outstanding Book in Art, Lit., and Lang. award Assn. Am. Pubs., 1988. Mem. MLA, Am. Dialect Soc., Dictionary Soc. N.Am., Nat. Coun. Tchrs. English. Office: Barnhart Books 11 Bridle Path Garrison NY 10524-0042

BARNHILL, CHARLES JOSEPH, JR., lawyer; b. Indpls., May 22, 1943; s. Charles J. and Phyllis (Landis) B.; m. Elizabeth Louise Hayek, Aug. 14, 1971; children: Eric Charles, Colin Landis. B.S. in Econs., U. Pa., 1965; J.D., U. Mich., 1968. Bar: Ill. 1968, U.S. Dist. Ct. (no. dist.) Ill. 1968, U.S. Ct. Appeals (7th cir.) 1969, U.S. Supreme Ct. 1972. Assoc. Kirkland & Ellis, Chgo., 1968; Reginald Heber Smith fellow Chgo. Legal Aid, 1968-69; assoc. Katz & Friedman, Chgo., 1969-72; ptnr. Davis, Miner, Barnhill, & Galland, P.C. (now Miner, Barnhill & Galland), Madison, Wis., 1972—; spl. master Fed. Dist. Ct. (no. dist.) Ill.; bd. dirs. Combined Health Appeal; chair Wis. Ctr. for Tobacco Rsch. and Intervention, 1996; asst. editor Mich. Law Rev., 1968. Bd. dirs. Legal Assistance Found., Chgo., 1972-74, Old Town Triangle Assn., Chgo., 1972-75. Mem. ABA (chmn. employment litigation of litigation sect. 1975-78), Chgo. Council Lawyers (bd. dirs. 1974-76), Barristers Soc., Order of Coif. Office: Miner Barnhill & Galland 44 E Mifflin St Ste 803 Madison WI 53703-2800

BARNHILL, DAVID STAN, lawyer; b. Washington, N.C., May 10, 1949; s. Arthur David and Ida Bea (Cox) B.; m. Katherine C. Felger, July 26, 1975; children: Hannah Katherine, Mary Rachel. BS, Va. Poly. Inst., 1971, MS, 1973; doctoral studies, U. Va., 1976-79; JD magna cum laude, Washington and Lee U., 1983. Bar: Va. 1983, U.S. Ct. Appeals (4th cir.) 1983, U.S. Supreme Ct. 1990, Federal Ct. Claims 1994. Asst. prof. social sci. Va. Intermont Coll., Bristol, Va., 1973-76; soc. sci. researcher U. Va., Charlottesville, Va., 1979-80; assoc. Woods, Rogers & Hazlegrove, Roanoke, Va., 1983-88, ptnr., 1989—. Author of several profl. articles. Bd. dirs. Total Action Against Poverty, Roanoke, 1987-90, DePaul Children's Svcs., Roanoke, 1985-95, Legal Aid Roanoke Valley, 1990-92. Sgt. USNG, 1972-78. Named Lead Articles Editor Washington & Lee Law Review, 1982-83. Mem. ABA (forum on constrn. industry, civil litigation sect.), Va. State Bar (chmn. 6th dist. ethics com. 1990-91, bd. govs. constrn. law sect. 1991—, chair, 1998, state bar coun. 1995—, state bar disciplinary bd. 1995—, vice chair bench-bar and media rels. com. 1996—), Va. Bar Assn. (constrn. law coun., civil litigation coun.), Roanoke Bar Assn. (bd. dirs. 1992-94), Va. Assoc. Gen. Contractors (legal affairs and contract documents coms. 1992—), Va. Tech. Alumni Assn., Order of the Coif. Democrat. Baptist. Avocations: middle distance running, writing. Home: 5145 Falcon Ridge Rd Roanoke VA 24014-5720 Office: Woods Rogers & Hazlegrove 10 S Jefferson St Ste 1201 Roanoke VA 24011-1319

BARNHILL, HENRY GRADY, JR., lawyer; b. Buena Vista, Ga., Aug. 24, 1930; s. Henry Grady and Imogene (Hogg) B.; m. Sarah Carolyn Haire, Oct. 29, 1953; children: Grady Michael, Stephen Drew, Kevin Scott, Carol Kelly. JD, Wake Forest U., Winston-Salem, N.C., 1958. Bar: N.C. 1958, U.S. Dist. Ct. (ea., mid. and we. dists.) N.C. 1958, U.S. Ct. Appeals (4th cir.) 1961, U.S. Supreme Ct. 1983, U.S. Ct. Appeals (fed. cir.) 1985. Assoc. Womble Carlyle Sandridge & Rice, Winston-Salem, 1958-61, ptnr., 1961—. Mem. bd. visitors Sch. of Law Wake Forest U. Lt. USAF, 1951-55. Fellow Am. Coll. Trial Lawyers (state chmn. 1986-88); mem. Am. Bd. Trial Advs., N.C. Assn. Def. Attys., N.C. Bar Assn. (litigation sect.), 4th Cir. Jud. Conf., Forsyth County Bar (pres. 1979-80), Inns of Ct. (Chief Justice Joseph Branch). Democrat. Presbyterian. Avocation: tennis. Home: 3121 Robinhood Rd Winston Salem NC 27106-5610 Office: Womble Carlyle Sandridge & Rice PLLC PO Drawer 84 1600 BB&T Financial Ctr Winston Salem NC 27102

BARNHILL, HOWARD EUGENE, insurance company executive; b. Nankin, Ohio, Oct. 2, 1923; s. William Wallace and Juliaette (Garver) B.; m. Evelyn Lucille Poorman, Aug. 24, 1944; children: Eric Stephen, Phillip William. B.A., Ashland (Ohio) Coll., 1946; grad., Advanced Mgmt. Program, Harvard U., 1967. C.L.U. With Mut. Ins. Co. N.Y., 1946-72, sr. v.p., 1969-

72; pres., chief exec. officer N.Am. Life & Casualty Co., Mpls., 1972-79, chmn. bd., pres., chief exec. officer, 1979-85, chmn. bd., chief exec. officer, 1985-88, ret., 1989; owner Barnhill & Assocs., Cons., 1989—; former bd. dirs. Nat. City Bank, Mpls., Preferred Life Ins. Co. of N.Y. Former bd. dirs. North Am. Life & Casualty Allianz of Am. Served to lt. USNR, 1943-46, 50-52. Mem. Life Ins. Mktg. Research Assn. (past chmn.), Greater Mpls. Area C. of C. (past chmn.), Comty. Ch. Club, Lafayette Club. Home (winter): 3726 Rachel Ln Naples FL 34103-3725

BARNHILL, JAMES ORRIS, theater educator; b. Sumner, Miss., May 23, 1922; s. James Arthur and Louise (Sullivan) B. BA, Yale U., 1947, MFA, 1954; MA, NYU, 1949; MA (hon.), Brown U. Instr. in English Brown U., Providence, 1954-56, from asst. prof. to assoc. prof., 1956-70, prof., 1970-78, prof. in theater arts, 1978-86, prof. emeritus, 1986—; vis. prof. English R.I. Sch. Design, Providence, 1987-88, 90-94, Tougaloo (Miss.) Coll., 1989; actor Trinity Square Repertory Theatre, Providence, 1971-73. Lt. (j.g.) USNR, 1943-46, PTO. Fulbright prof. English M.S. U. Baroda, India, 1984-85, St. Xavier Coll., Ahmedabad, India, 1988-89, Am. Lit. Univ. Punjab, Pakistan, 1994-96. mem. Univ. Club, Players Club. Baptist. Avocations: hobbies, calligraphy, sculpture. Home: 81 Transit St Providence RI 02906-1022 Office: Brown U Dept Theatre Arts PO Box 1897 Providence RI 02912-1897

BARNHOLDT, TERRY JOSEPH, chemical, industrial, and general engineer; b. Wiota, Iowa, Sept. 22, 1921; s. Claus Edward and Leona (Consaul) B.; m. Martha Francis Cannon, 1946 (dec. 1975); children: Martha Jane, Terry (Ted) Joseph Jr. BChE, Clarkson Coll. Tech., 1943; postgrad. degree in chem. engring. and adminstrn. engring., Cornell U., 1947; MBA (hon.), U. N.C., Charlotte, 1967; JD, Atlanta Law Sch., 1981. Project, process engr. Std. Oil Co., Richmond, Calif., 1947-49; Perth Amboy, N.J., 1949-51; br. mgr. The Clorox Co., Charlotte, N.C., 1949-51; pres., gen. mgr. Allied Prodrs. Supply Co., Charlotte, 1959-66; mgr. mfg. and engring. BASF Wyandotte, Charlotte, 1966-68; sales mgr. Detrex Chem. Industries, Charlotte, 1969-70; chem. mfg. sales rep. Valchem Chem. United Mchts., Charlotte, 1970-74; sales, mfg. rep. Star Chemicals Co., Macon, Ga., 1976-78; mgr. shipping Pepsi-Cola Beverage Corp., Atlanta, 1979; project engr. Metro Atlanta Rapid Transit Authority, 1981-84; comml. real estate specialist Gen. Svc. Adminstrn., Atlanta, 1984-85; gen., indsl. engr. Def. Logistics Agy., Manassas, Alexandria and Ft. Belvoir, Va., 1986—. 1st lt. U.S. Army, 1943-46. Mem. NSPE, AIChE, ATLA, Am. Chem. Soc., Assn. Energy Engrs., Def. Acquisition Corps, Alpha Chi Sigma. Republican. Presbyterian. Avocations: running, handball, free weights, golf. Home: 12301 Strong Ct Fairfax VA 22033-2846 Office: Def Logistics Agy DLIS BIS 8725 John J Kingman Rd Ste 2533 Fort Belvoir VA 22060-6217

BARNHOUSE, ROBERT BOLON, lawyer; b. Marietta, Ohio, July 18, 1937; s. C. Bolon and Enid Marie (Keith) B.; m. Carolyn Miller, June 3, 1961 (div.); 1 child, Lauren Dudley; m. Elizabeth Ann Bailey, July 15, 1977. BA, Ohio Wesleyan U., 1959; LLB, NYU, 1962. Bar: Md. 1962, U.S. Supreme Ct. 1970. Assoc. Piper & Marbury, Balt., 1962-69, ptnr., 1970-94; pvt. practice Law Offices of Robert B. Barnhouse, Balt., 1995—. Mem. Vol. Coun. Equal Opportunity, Balt., 1984—, chmn., 1993-94; counsel, bd. dirs. Am. Cancer Soc., Md., 1969-83; mem. bus. adv. bd. DAV, Balt., 1992-95. Root-Tilden scholar NYU, 1962. Fellow Am. Coll. Trial Lawyers; mem. ABA, Md. State Bar Assn., Md. Assn. Def. Trial Counsel (past pres.), Bar Assn. Balt. City. Avocations: photography, art, history. Office: 111 S Calvert St Ste 2700 Baltimore MD 21202-6143

BARNICK, HELEN, retired judicial clerk; b. Max, N.D., Mar. 24, 1925; d. John K. and Stacy (Kankovsky) B. BS in Music cum laude, Minot State Coll., 1954; postgrad., Am. Conservatory of Music, Chgo., 1975-76. With Epton, Bohling & Druth, Chgo., 1968-69; sec. Wildman, Harrold, Allen & Dixon, Chgo., 1969-75; part-time assignments for temporary agy. Chgo., 1975-77; sec. Friedman & Koven, Chgo., 1977-78; with Lawrence, Lawrence, Kamin & Saunders, Chgo., 1978-81; sec. Hinshaw, Culbertson et al., Chgo., 1982; sec. to magistrate judge U.S. Dist. Ct. (we. dist.) Wis., Madison, 1985-91; dep. clk., case adminstr. U.S. Bankruptcy Ct. (we. dist.) Wis., Madison, 1992-94; ret., 1994. Mem. chancel choir 1st Bapt. Ch., Mpls.; mem. choir, dir. sr. high choir Moody Ch., Chgo.; mem. chancel choir Fourth Presbyn. Ch., Chgo., Covenant Presbyn. Ch., Madison; dir. chancel choir 1st Bapt. Ch., Minot, N.D.; bd. dirs., sec.-treas. Peppertree at Tamarack Owners Assn., Inc., Wisconsin Dells, Wis.; mem. Festival Choir, Madison. Mem. Christian Bus. and Profl. Women (chmn.), Bus. and Profl. Women Assn., Participatory Learning and Tchg. Orgn., Sigma Sigma Sigma. Home: 7364 Old Sauk Rd Madison WI 53717-1213

BARNIDGE, LEROY, JR., military officer. BSME, La. Tech. U., 1971; grad., Squadron Officer Sch., 1976; M in Logistics Mgmt., Air Force Inst. Tech., 1978; grad., Air Command and Staff Coll., 1983, Indsl. Coll. of Armed Forces, 1989; program for sr. ofcls. in nat. security, Harvard U., 1990; seminar on fgn. polit. & internat. rels., MIT, 1991. Commd. 2d lt. USAF, 1971, advanced through grades to brigadier gen., 1997; maintenance supr. 55th Orgnl. Maintenance Squadron Offutt AFB, Nebr., 1978-80; reconnaissance sys. officer Hdqs. Strategic Air Command, Offutt AFB, 1980-82; dir. acads. B-1B Combat Crew Tng. Squadron Dyess AFB, Tex., 1985-86; comdr. 338th Combat Crew tng. Squadron, dep. comdr. 96th Combat Support Group, Dyess AFB, 1986-88; chief force design divsn. Joint Chiefs of Staff J-8, Washington, 1989-91; asst. dep. comdr. for maintenance 28th Bomb Wing, Ellsworth AFB, S.D., 1991-92; comdr. 28th Logistics Group Ellsworth AFB, 1992-93; comdr. 319th Ops. group, dep. comdr. for ops. 319th Bomb Group, Grand Forks AFB, N.D., 1993-94; comdr. Coll. Aerospace Doctrine, Rsch. and Edn. Air U., Maxwell AFB, Ala., 1994-95; comdr. 28th Bomb Wing, Ellsworth AFB, 1995-97; vice comdr. San Antonio Air Logistics Ctr., Kelly AFB, Tex., 1997-98; comdr. 509th Bomb Wing, Whiteman AFB, Mo., 1998—. Decorated Def. Superior Svc. medal, Legion of Merit, D.F.C., Meritorious Svc. medal with 4 oak leaf clusters. Office: Ste 009 509 BW/CC 509 Spirit Blvd Whiteman AFB MO 65305-5055

BARNOFF, ROBERT MARK, civil engineering educator; b. Punxsutawney, Pa., Aug. 28, 1926; s. Joseph A. and Ruth A. (Morris) B.; m. Norma Gugliemi; children: Joni, Janice, Mark, Joseph. B.S., Pa. State U., 1951, M.S., 1956; Ph.D., Carnegie Inst. Tech., 1966. Steel detailer Am. Bridge Co., 1951-52; constrn. engr. John Mohr & Sons, 1952-53; bridge designer Gannett Fleming Corddry & Capenter, 1953-55; from instr. to prof. civil engring. Pa. State U., University Park, 1955-79, prof., chmn. dept. civil engring., 1979-85; vis. prof. Bucknell U. Contbr. articles on civil engring. to profl. jours. Served with USNR, 1944-46. NSF sci faculty fellow, 1965-66. Mem. ASTM, ASCE, Am. Concrete Inst., Sigma Xi, Tau Beta Pi, Chi Epsilon. Achievements include patents on concrete testing device and bridge deck systems. Home and Office: 606 Nimitz Ave State College PA 16801-6415

BARNOUW, ERIK, broadcasting educator, writer; b. The Hague, Holland, June 23, 1908; came to U.S., 1919, naturalized, 1928; s. Adriaan Jacob and Anne Eliza (Midgley) B.; m. Dorothy Maybelle Beach, June 3, 1939 (dec. 1987); children: Jeffrey, Susanna, Karen; m. Elizabeth Prince, Apr. 28, 1989. A.B., Princeton U., 1929. Writer and dir. radio advt. Erwin Wasey & Co., 1931-35, Arthur Kudner, 1935-37; writer, editor CBS, N.Y.C., 1939-40; script editor NBC, N.Y.C., 1942-44; commentator overseas br. OWI, 1943-44; supr. edn. unit Armed Forces Radio Service, War Dept., 1944-45; mem. faculty Columbia U., N.Y.C., 1946—, prof. dramatic arts in charge film, radio and TV, 1964-69, editor Ctr. for Mass Communication, 1948-72; chief motion picture, broadcasting and recorded sound div. Library of Congress, Washington, 1978-81; fellow Woodrow Wilson Center for Scholars, 1976; cons. communications USPHS, 1947-50. Occasional writer, adapter: (radio and TV series) Theatre Guild, 1945-61; writer, producer: (TV series) Decision, 1957-59; producer (film) Hiroshima-Nagasaki, August 1945, 1970 (Spl. award Vt. Film Festival 1972); director, writer (film) Fable Safe, 1971 (Silver Dragon award Cracow Film Festival 1972); author: (3 act play) Open Collars, 1928, Handbook of Radio Writing, 2d edit, 1947, Handbook of Radio Production, 1949, Mass Communication, 1956, The Television Writer, 1962, (with S. Krishnaswamy) Indian Film, 1963, 2d edit., 1980, A History of Broadcasting in The U.S.: A Tower in Babel, vol. 1, 1966, The Golden Web, vol. 2, 1968, The Image Empire, vol. 3, 1970 (Bancroft prize 1971), Documentary: A History of the Nonfiction Film, 1974, rev. edit., 1983, 93, Tube of Plenty: The Evolution of American Television, 1975, rev. edit., 1982, 1990, The Sponsor: Notes on a Modern Potentate, 1978, The Magician and the Cinema, 1981, House with a Past, 1992, Media Marathon: A Twentieth century Memoir, 1996; co-author: Conglomerates and the Media, 1997; editor: Radio Drama in Action, 1945; editor in chief International Encyclopedia of Communications, 4 vols., 1989; co-editor: The flaherty - four Decades in the cause of Independent Cinema, 1996. Recipient Gavel award for Decision films Am. Bar Assn., 1959, Eastman-Kodak gold medal, 1982; Fulbright Research fellow India, 1961-62; Guggenheim fellow, 1969; JDR 3d fellow, 1972; Indo-Am. fellow, 1978-79. Mem. Authors League Am. (sec. 1949-53), Radio Writers Guild (pres. 1947-49), Writers Guild Am. (chmn. 1957-59), Acad. TV Arts and Scis. (bd. govs. 1966-68), Internat. Film Seminars (pres. 1960-68), Soc. Am. Historians, Phi Beta Kappa. Address: PO Box 25 Fair Haven VT 05743

BARNSTONE, WILLIS (ROBERT BARNSTONE), language literature educator, poet, scholar; b. Lewiston, Maine, Nov. 13, 1927; s. Robert Carl and Dora E. (Lempert) B.; m. Helle Phaedra Tzalopoulou, June 1, 1949; children: Akiki Dora, Robert Vassilios, Anthony Dimitrios. BA cum laude, Bowdoin Coll., 1948, DLitt (hon.), 1981; MA with high honors, Columbia U., 1956; PhD with distinction, Yale U., 1958. Tchr. Anavrita Acad., Athens, Greece, 1949; instr. French overseas program U. Md., Perigueux, France, 1955-56; asst. prof. Spanish Wesleyan U., Middletown, Conn., 1958-62; mem. faculty Ind. U., Bloomington, 1962—, prof. comparative lit., Spanish, Portuguese,, 1968—, prof. comparative lit. and Latin Am. studies, 1972-75, Disting. prof. comparative lit., Spanish and Portuguese, 1975-94; Dist. prof. emeritus Ind. U., 1995—; vis. prof. U. Mass., Amherst, summer 1965, U. Calif., Riverside, 1968-69; O'Conner prof. lit. Colgate U., spring 1971; Fulbright lectr. Professorado de Avenida de Mayo, Buenos Aires, 1975-76, Fgn. Studies U., Peking, 1984-85; vis. prof. Summer Inst. Lit., U. Tex., Austin, summer 1977. Author: Poems of Exchange, 1951, Notes for a Bible, 1952, From This White Island, 1959 (Pulitzer prize nomination 1960), Sappho, 1965, A Sky of Days, 1967, A Day in the Country, 1971, Antijournal, 1971, New Faces of China, 1973, The Unknown Light: The Poems of Fray Luis de Leon, 1979, Overheard, 1979, A Snow Salmon Reached The Andes Lake, 1980, Borges at Eighty: Conversations, 1982, A Bird of Paper: Poems of Vicente Aleixandre, 1982, The Poetics of Ecstasy: Variaties of Ekstasis from Sappho to Borges, 1983, Borges, Poet of Ecstasy, 1985, Five A.M. in Beijing: Poems of China, 1987, Sappho and the Greek Poets, 1988, others; editor: Rinconete y Cortadillo, 1960, Soledades, 1965, Modern European Poetry, 1966, New Spoon River, 1968, Concrete Poetry: A World View, 1969, Spanish Poetry From the Beginning Through the Nineteenth Century, 1970, Eighteen Texts: Writings by Contemporary Greek Authors, 1972, The Other Bible: Jewish Psuedepigrapha, Christian Apocrypha, Gnostic Scriptures, 1984, Laughing Lost in the Mountains: Selected Poems of Wang Wei, 1989, Six Masters of the Spanish Sonnet: Quevedo, Sor Juana Inés de la Cruz, Antonio Machado, Federico García Lorca, Jorge Luis Borges, Miguel Hernández, 1993, With Borges on an Ordinary Evening in Buenos Aires, A Memoir, 1992, The Poetics of Translation: History, Theory, Practice, 1993, The Secret Reader, 1996, (with Aliki Barnstone) A Book of Women Poets from Antiquity to Nos, 1992, Funny Ways of Staying Alive, 1993, Sunday Morning in Fascist Spain: 1948-1953, 1994; translator: Eighty Poems of Antonio Machado, 1959, The Other Alexander, 1959, Mexico Before Cortez: Art, History and Legend, 1963, Physiologus Theobaldi Episcopi de Naturis Duodecim Animalium, 1964, The Song of Songs, 1970, The Poems of Mao Tse-tung, 1972, My Voice Because of You, 1975; editor, translator: Greek Lyric Poetry, 1962, The Poems of Saint John of the Cross, 1967; contbg. editor: Books Abroad. Served with U.S. Army, 1954-56. Guggenheim fellow, 1961-62; Am. Council Learned Socs. fellow, 1969-70; NEH fellow, 1979-80; recipient Cecil Hemley Meml. award Poetry Soc. Am., 1969, Lucille Medwick Meml. award, 1978, Emily Dickinson award Poetry Soc. Am., 1985, W.H. Auden award N.Y. State Council on the Arts, 1986. Mem. PEN. Democrat. Address: Ind Univ Western European Studies Bloomington IN 47405-6630*

BARNUM, ALEXANDER STONE, journalist; b. N.Y.C., May 15, 1960; s. John Wallace and Nancy (Grinnell) B. BA, Antioch Coll., Yellow Springs, Ohio, 1983; MS, Columbia U., 1987. Editl. asst. Washington Post, 1983-86; staff writer San Jose Mercury News, 1987-91, San Francisco Chronicle, 1991—; mem. exec. com. Global Edn. Partnership, 1997—; mentor, San Francisco State U., 1992-94; High County Inst. fellow U. Mont., Missoula, 1996. Vol. Project Open Hand, San Francisco, 1992-94, Tsongas for Pres., San Francisco, 1992. Knight Sci. Journalism fellow MIT, Cambridge, 1994-95; recipient awards Best of the West, 1997, Calif. Newspaper Pubs. Assn., 1997, San Francisco Peninsula Press Club, 1987, 97, East Bay Press Club, 1997. Mem. Soc. for Profl. Journalists, Soc. for Environ. Journalists. Office: San Francisco Chronicle 901 Mission St San Francisco CA 94103-2905

BARNUM, BARBARA STEVENS, retired nursing educator; b. Johnstown, Pa., Sept. 2, 1937; d. William C. and Freda Inzes (Claycomb) Burkett; m. H. James Barnum (dec.); children: Lauren, Elizabeth, Catherine, Anne, Shauna, Sallee, David. AA in Nursing, St. Petersburg Jr. Coll., 1958; BPh, Northwestern U., 1967; MA, DePaul U., 1971; PhD, U. Chgo., 1976. RN, Ill., N.Y. Dir. nursing svcs. Augustana Hosp. and Health Care Ctr., Chgo., 1970-71; dir. staff edn. U. Chgo. Hosps. and Clinics, 1971-73; prof. U. Ill., Chgo., 1973-79; dir. div. health svcs., sci. and edn. Columbia U. Tchrs. Coll., N.Y.C., 1979-87; editor Nursing & Health Care Nat. League for Nursing, N.Y.C., 1989-91; editor div. nursing Columbia-Presbyn. Med. Ctr., Columbia U., N.Y.C., 1991-95; prof. Sch. Nursing Columbia U., N.Y.C., 1995-98; ret., 1998; chmn. bd. Barnum & Souza, N.Y.C., 1989-92; civilian cons. to surgeon gen. USAF, 1980-87. Author: Nursing Theory, Analysis, Application and Evaluation, 4th edit., 1994, Writing for Publication: A Primer for Nurses, 1995, (with K. Kerfoot) The Nurse as Executive, 4th edit., 1995, Spirituality and Nursing: From Traditional to New Age, 1996; editor: Nursing Leadership Forum, 1994-98. Mem. governing bd. Nurses House, 1979-86, Nat. Health Coun., 1981-90, others. Fellow Am. Acad. Nursing (governing bd. 1982-84); mem. Sigma Theta Tau (Founders' award 1979). Home: 80 Park Ave Apt 15G New York NY 10016-2547*

BARNUM, JOHN WALLACE, lawyer; b. N.Y.C., Aug. 25, 1928; s. Walter and Frances (Long) B.; m. Nancy Russell Grinnell, Sept. 13, 1958; children: Alexander Stone, Sarah Kip, Cameron Long. BA, Yale U., 1949, LLB, 1957. Bar: Conn. 1957, N.Y. 1958, D.C. 1977; on Brussels fgn. lawyer list, 1995. Analyst 1st Banking Corp., Tangier, Morocco, 1950; reg. rep. Bache & Co., London and Paris, 1951-52; assoc. Cravath, Swaine & Moore, N.Y.C., 1957-62, ptnr., 1963-71; gen. counsel U.S. Dept. Transp., Washington, 1971-73, undersec., 1973-74, dep. sec., 1974-77; resident fellow Am. Enterprise Inst. for Pub. Policy Rsch., Washington, 1977-78, vis. fellow, 1978-86; ptnr. White & Case, Washington, 1978-94, McGuire Woods Battle & Boothe, LLP, Brussels, 1995—; lectr. Practising Law Inst.; U.S. del. Inter-Am. Comml. Arbitration Commn., 1969-71; adv. mem. Coun. on Wage and Price Stability, 1974-77; mem. Coun. Adminstrv. Conf. U.S., 1973-77; bd. dirs. Palmer Nat. Bank, 1983-94, George Mason Bank, N.A., Washington (formerly Palmer Nat. Bank), 1994-97. Bd. editors Regulation: AEI Jour. on Govt. and Soc., 1977-86. Chmn. bd. Internat. Play Group, 1962-77; bd. dirs., mem. exec. com. N.Y C. Ctr. Music and Drama, 1969-75; trustee Washington Drama Soc. (Arena Stage), 1983-93; bd. overseers Corcoran Gallery of Art, Washington, 1994—. Mem. Internat. Bar Assn., N.Y. State Bar Assn. (exec. com., chmn. antitrust law sect. 1979-80), D.C. Bar Assn., Am. Bar Found., Nat. Def. Transp. Assn. (chmn. mil. airlift com. 1983-94, bd. dirs. 1988-94), Am. Arbitration Assn. (bd. dirs. 1968-98, exec. com. 1968-72), Cercle Royal Gaulois Artistique et Litteraire, Watersportvereniging Noord Beveland, Met. Club, Chevy Chase Club, Amateur Ski Club, N.Y. Yacht Club. Home: 182 Ave Franklin Roosevelt, 1050 Brussels Belgium also: 2029 Connecticut Ave NW Washington DC 20008 Office: McGuire Woods, 250 Ave Louise, Bte 64, 1050 Brussels Belgium

BARNUM, ROBERT LYLE, artist, art educator; b. Edmonton, Alberta, Can., Sept. 5, 1951; s. Fredrick Joshua and Ouida C. (Bohrer) B.; m. Cheryl A. Nelson, June, 1978 (div. Aug., 1985); children: Kelda Elizabeth, Holly Lorraine; m. Lisa Marie Arnold, June 8, 1986; children: Tobias Robert, Skyler Chance. AA, Oregon Coll. of Art, Ashland, 1974; BS, So. Oreg. State, 1978; MFA, Idaho State U., 1980. Faculty replacement Idaho State U., Pocatello, 1979-80; instr. St. Francis Coll., Fort Wayne, Ind., 1980-82; asst. prof. St. Francis Coll., Fort Wayne, 1982-85; full time faculty mem. Columbia Coll., Chgo., 1985-88, permanent contract faculty mem., 1989; faculty mem. Ferris State U., Big Rapids, Mich., 1989-94, tenured faculty mem., 1994-95; assoc. prof. Ferris State U., Big Rapids, 1995—; dir. Rankin Gallery Ferris State U., Big Rapids, Mich., 1993-95; presenter slide presentations, lectures, workshops, 1989—; including pub. lecture series Sara Roby collection Fort Wayne Mus. of Arts, 1989, slide presentation and lecture, Watercolor USA Honor Soc. Meeting, Houston, 1990, slide presentation and painting demonstration, Mich. Watercolor Soc., Detroit, 1994, Arrowmot Sch. of Arts and Crafts, Gatlinburg, Tenn., 1995, slide presentation, workshop West Riverside, Calif., 1995; proposed Walk of Art to Ferris State U., presidential art collection,1st piece unveiled Nov., 1996; proposed Inst. of Tech. Aesthetic Study, now under consideration by Ferris State U. adminstrn. Artist: exhibited in juried competitions Nat. Watercolor Mems. Exhibit Brand. Calif., 1990 (hon. mention), 29th ann invitational, New Orleans, 1990, (hon. mention), Adirondack Nat. Exhibit of Am. Watercolors, Old Forge, N.Y., 1991 (traveling Exhibit), 1992, 45th ann. Juried Fine Art Show, Colorado Springs, 1991 (3d Pl. award), 9th ann. juried Art Rsch. Ctr., Mt. Pleasant, Mich. 1992, (1st pl. award), Watercolor West XXIX Brea (Calif.) Civic Ctr., 1992 (Signature Membership award), 30th ann. juried art show, Ctrl. Mich U., Mt. Pleasant, (1st pl. water colors), 1993, Watercolor W. 27th ann. juried exhbit, 1995 (St. Cuthberts Mill and Bockingford Paper award), Mich. Watercolor 50th exhibit Detroit Inst. Arts, 1996, (Travelling Exhbit Merit award), Watercolor USA, Springield (Mo.) Art Mus., 1997, (Travelling Exhbit Merit award); 1-man shows: Beverly (Ill.) Art Ctr., 1988,Stone House Gallery, Fredonia, Kans., 1990, JCCA Gallery, St. Louis, 1994, Miller Gallery, Cin., 1996, Prarie Brooke Arts, Overland Park, Kans., 1998; group exhbits include: Art Traders Internat., Chgo., 1989, Starry-Sheets Fine Arts Gallery, Irvine, Calif., 1990, Perception Gallery, Grand Rapids, Mich., 1992, Mystery, Metaphores, Memory, Krasl Art Ctr., St. Joseph, Mich. 1995, The New Realism, Detroit Artist Market, 1996, River Gallery, Chattanooga, Tenn., 1997, Joyce Petter Gallery, Saugatuck, Mich., 1999, others; contbr. articles to Am. Artist Mag., 1989, 98, The Artist Mag., 1994. Fine Arts acad. award 27th Internat. Exhibit LWS, New Orleans, 1997. Purchase award 1997 Watercolor U.S.A., Springfield, Mo. Art Mus., 1997. Mem. Am. Watercolor Soc. (signature mem.), Watercolor USA Honor Soc. (signature mem.). Home: 9739 S Calgary Dr Stanwood MI 49346-9796 Office: Ferris State U 1408 Bond Cir Big Rapids MI 49307-2700

BARNUM, WILLIAM MILO, architect; b. N.Y.C., June 17, 1927; s. Phelps and Catharine (Davis) B. Student Phillips Andover Acad., 1942-45; B.A., Yale, 1950; M.Arch., U. Pa., 1952; m. Katharine Miller, Aug. 10, 1971; children: Anne Lyttleton, Catharine Hollerith, William Milo, Nathaniel Phelps, Caleb Townsend. Archtl. asst. job capt. Eggers & Higgins, 1952-54; job capt. W. Stuart Thompson & Phelps Barnum, architects, 1954-58, jr. ptnr., 1958-60; sr. ptnr. Phelps Barnum & Son, N.Y.C., 1960-68; pres. William Milo Barnum Assocs., Inc., N.Y.C., 1968—. Chmn. Archtl. Rev. Bd., Greenwich, Conn. Mem. selectmen's com. High Sch. Property, Greenwich, 1964-68; bd. dirs. Community Chest, Greenwich, 1964-68. Mem. alumni coun. Phillips Acad., Andover, Mass., 1965-68; v.p. bd. trustees Putnam Indian Field Sch., vice chmn.; bd. dirs. Episcopal Ch. at Yale; bd. dirs. Episcopal Ch. Bldg. Fund. With USNR, 1945-46, PTO. Mem. Concrete Industry Bd. (bd. dir.), AIA (N.Y. chpt. office practices com.), Met. Builders Assn., (liaison com.), Andover Alumni Assn. N.Y.C. (pres. 1964-65), Hist. Soc. Greenwich (v.p.), Soc. Colonial Wars, Yale Club (coun. 1958-79, pres. 1970-72) (N.Y.C.), Acoaxet Club, Hollenbeck Club, Spindle Rock Club. Prin. works include Westminster Sch. Chapel, 1961, Westminster Sch. Acad. Ctr., 1964, Howmet Office Bldg., Greenwich, Mfrs. Hanover Bank, Bklyn., Pickwick Pla., Greenwich, R.T. Vanderbilt Corp. Hdqrs., Norwalk, Conn., Union Trust Sq., Greenwich, Gen. Host Corp. Hdqrs., Stamford, Conn., Gateway Ctr., Greenwich, The Boatyard Condominium, City Island, N.Y., Gorham Island Office Bldg., Westport, Conn., N.Y. Offices Scudder Stevens and Clark, Mason Place Mixed Use Hist. Restoration, Greenwich, Shawmut Bank offices and Br. Landmark Sq. Bldg., Stamford, Shawmut br., New Canaan, St. Andrews by the Sea Episcopal Ch. Renovation and Reconstruction, Little Compton, R.I.; cons. to judges com., decorator new U.S. Courthouse Ho., 500 Pearl St., N.Y.C., Scudders Stevens & Clark 5 Fls.; cons. judges com. new U.S. Ct. House, White Plains, N.Y. Office: 32 Custom House St Providence RI 02903-2614

BARNWELL, FRANKLIN HERSHEL, zoology educator; b. Chattanooga, Oct. 4, 1937; s. Columbus Hershel and Esther Bernice (Ireland) B.; m. Adrienne Kay Knox, June 13, 1959; 1 child, Elizabeth Brooks. BA, Northwestern U., 1959, PhD, 1965. Instr. biol. sci. Northwestern U., Evanston, Ill., 1964, research assoc., 1965-67; asst. prof. U. Chgo., 1967-70; from asst. prof. to prof. zoology, ecology and behavioral biology U. Minn., Mpls., 1970—, head dept. ecology, evolution and behavior, 1986-93; mem. adv. panel NASA, 1963-67, NSF, Washington, 1980; faculty Orgn. for Tropical Studies, San Jose, Costa Rica, 1966-85, bd. dirs.; Nat. Confs. on Underground Rsch., bd. dirs., treas., 1990-96; investigator rsch. R/V Alpha Helix, various locations, 1979, vis. scientist. Contbr. articles on zoology to profl. jours. NSF fellow, 1965; named Minn. Coll. Sci. Tchr. of Yr., Minn. Acad. Sci. and Minn. Sci. Tchrs. Assn., 1997. Fellow Linnean Soc. London, AAAS; mem. Soc. Intergrative and Comparative Biology, Internat. Soc. for Chronobiology, Assocs. Orgn. for Tropical Studies, Crustacean Soc. (founding and sustaining mem., bd. dirs., sec. 1991-98), Phi Beta Kappa, Sigma Xi. Office: U Minn Dept Ecology Evol & Behav 1987 Upper Buford Cir Saint Paul MN 55108-6097

BARO, SUSAN MARIE, surgeon; b. Pottstown, Pa., Aug. 15, 1966; d. Lawrence Dominick and Gloria June (Poncheri) B. BS, Albright Coll., 1988; DO, Phila. Coll. Osteo. Medicine, 1992. Intern Phila. Coll. Osteo. Medicine, 1992-93, surg. resident, 1993-97, fellow in trauma/critical care, 1997-98. Mem. Pa. Osteo. Med. Assn., AMA, ACOS. Episcoplaian. Avocations: musician (piano, flute, vocals). Home: 389 Deuce Dr Wall NJ 07719-9475 Office: Jersey Shore Med Ctr 1945 Route 33 PO Box 397 Neptune NJ 07754

BAROFF, GEORGE STANLEY, psychologist, educator; b. Bronx, N.Y., Nov. 27, 1924; s. Irving and Ida (Herman) B.; m. Rose Kislin, June 15, 1952 (dec. May 1992); children: Marina Binet, Roy James. BS in Zoology, George Washington U., 1948, MA in Clin. Psychology, 1950; PhD in Clin. Psychology, NYU, 1955. Research psychologist dept. med. genetics N.Y. State Psychiat. Inst., 1952-60; chief clin. psychologist Vineland (N.J.) Tng. Sch., 1960-63; asso. prof. psychology U. N.C., Chapel Hill, 1963-67; prof. U. N.C., 1967—, dir. devel. disabilties tng. inst., 1964—; forensic psychologist with criminal defendants who may be mentally retarded, 1987—. Author: Mental Retardation: Nature, Cause and Management, 1974, 3d edit., 1999, Developmental Disabilities: Psychosocial Aspects, 1991; contbr. articles to profl. jours. Served with U.S. Army, 1943-45. Mem. Am. Psychol. Assn., Am. Assn. Mental Retardation, N.C. Psychol. Assn. Jewish. Home: 417 Granville Rd Chapel Hill NC 27514-2723 Office: Dev Disabilities Tng Inst Univ NC-Chapel Hill Chapel Hill NC 27599-3370

BAROLINI, TEODOLINDA, literary critic; b. Syracuse, N.Y., Dec. 19, 1951; d. Antonio and Helen (Molony) B.; m. Douglas Gardner Caverly, June 21, 1980 (dec. Nov. 1993); 1 child: William Douglas. BA, Sarah Lawrence Coll., 1972; MA, Columbia U., 1973, PhD, 1978. Asst. prof. Italian U. Calif., Berkeley, 1978-83; assoc. prof. Italian NYU, 1983-89; prof., 1989-92; prof. Italian, chmn. dept. Italian Columbia U., N.Y.C., 1992—. Author: Dante's Poets, 1984 (Howard R. Marraro prize MLA 1986, John Nicholas Brown prize Medieval Acad. Am. 1988, transl. into Italian as Il miglior fabbro 1993), The Undivine Comedy, 1992; contbr. articles to profl. jours. Guggenheim fellow, 1998. Mem. MLA, Dante Soc. Am. (v.p. 1983-86, 91-94, 95-97, pres., 1997—), Medieval Acad. Am., Renaissance Soc. Am. Office: Columbia U Dept Italian 510 Hamilton Hall New York NY 10027

BAROLSKY, PAUL, art history educator; b. Paterson, N.J., July 13, 1941; s. Benjamin and Eva (Keizer) B.; m. Ruth H. Lassow, Aug. 12, 1966; children: Deborah Eve, Daniel G. BA, Middlebury (Vt.) Coll., 1963; PhD, Harvard U., 1969. Commonwealth prof. art history, McIntire Dept. Art U. Va., Charlottesville, 1969—. Author: Infinite Jest, 1978, Daniele da Volterra, 1979, Walter Pater's Renaissance, 1987, Michelangelo's Nose, 1990, Why Mona Lisa Smiles, 1991, Giotto's Father, 1992, The Faun in the Garden, 1994. Office: U Va McIntire Dept Art Fayerweather Hall Charlottesville VA 22903*

BARON, ALMA FAY S., management educator; b. Pitts., July 26, 1923; d. Max J. and Emma C. (Aronson) Spann; m. Lee A. Baron, Dec. 23, 1944; children—Ellen J., Michael A., Jill S. B.A., U. Pitts., 1943; Ph.D., U. Wis-Madison, 1974. Advt. mgr. Kaufmann's, Pitts., 1943; head copywriter Levy Bros., Houston, 1945; fashion coordinator Baron's, Madison, Wis., 1946-54;

host TV Talent, Sta. WMTV, Madison, Wis., 1953-54, Sta. WQED, Pitts., 1954-58, Sta. KORN, Mitchell, S.D., 1958-66, Sta. KELO, Sioux Falls, S.D., 1959-66; co-owner Lee Baron's Women's Store, Madison, 1966-71; instr. U. Wis. Mgmt. Inst., Madison, 1974-77, assoc. prof. mgmt., 1978-81, prof. mgmt., 1981-88, prof. emeritus, 1988—; mem. internat. bd. Inst. Cert. Profl. Secs., 1977-81; vis. faculty La. State U., Baton Rouge, Pa. State U., Univ. Park, U. Okla., Norman, Purdue U., W. Lafayette; lectr. in Scandanavia, U.K., India; started Sr. Class TV progam in Madison, Wis., 1996, now statewide. Author: Assertiveness in the Business Environment, 1979, Nonverbal Communication, 1981, Women in Management: Strategies for Success, 1995; contbr. articles to profl. jours. Pres., Madison Civic Music Assn., 1971-73; v.p. YWCA, Madison, 1973-76; pres. Madison Civics Club, 1985-86; chmn. bd. advisers St. Mary's Hosp., 1986—. Recipient Woman of Achievement award This is Madison, 1977, Outstanding Women award Select mag., 1976, Madisonian award Wis. State Jour., 1975, Sales and Mktg. award Sales Mktg. Execs., 1977, Meritorious Ind. Study Course award Nat. Univ. Extension Assn., 1980, Disting. Service award U. Wis. Extension, 1982, Outstanding Prof. award U. Wis.-Madison, 1985, Robert A. Jerred award U. Wis. Sch. Bus., 1988, Women of Distinction award YWCA, 1993, U. Wis. Disting. Alumni award, 1995, Jean Harris Rotary Dist. award, 1998. Mem. AAUW, Am. Bus. Comm. Assn., Am. Soc. Tng. and Devel. (mem. sr. faculty symposium 1980), Wis. Internat. Women's Forum (initiator 1987—), Gen. Semantics Assn., Wis. Acad. Arts and Scis., Assn. Platform Speakers, Nat. Telemedia Coun. (Journalist award 1996), U. Wis. Ret. Faculty Assn. (incoming chair 1999—), B'nai B'rith, Blackhawk Country Club, Zeta Phi Eta. Home: 3 Honeylocust Trl Madison WI 53717-1507

BARON, CAROLYN, editor, author, publishing executive; b. Detroit, Jan. 25, 1940; d. Gabriel and Viola Cohn; m. Richard W. Baron, Nov. 14, 1975. B.A. in Liberal Arts, U. Mich., 1961. Editor, editorial prodn. dir. Holt, Rinehart & Winston, N.Y.C., 1965-71; mng. editor E.P. Dutton Co., Inc., N.Y.C., 1971-74; exec. editor E.P. Dutton Co., Inc., 1974-75; adminstrv. editor Pocket Books, Simon & Schuster, N.Y.C., 1975-78; v.p., editor-in-chief Pocket Books, Simon & Schuster, 1978-79, Crown Pubs., N.Y.C., 1979-81; v.p., pub. Dell Pub. Co., N.Y.C., 1981-86, pres., pub., 1986—; sr. v.p. Bantam, Doubleday, Dell, N.Y.C., 1989—. Office: Dell Pub Co Inc 1540 Broadway New York NY 10036-4039*

BARON, CHARLES HILLEL, lawyer, educator; b. Phila., Aug. 18, 1936; s. Samuel A. and Rose (Bailinky) B.; m. Irma Elaine Frankel, June 15, 1958 (dec. 1985); children: Jessica Susan, Ira Benjamin, David Hume; m. Dianne M. Quartarone, Sept. 9, 1988; 1 child, Samuel Guy. AB in Philosophy with honors, U. Pa., 1958, PhD in Philosophy, 1972; LLB, Harvard U., 1961. Bar: Pa. bar 1967, U.S. Supreme Ct. bar 1970, Mass. bar 1972. Asst. prof. law U. Pa., 1965-66; assoc. firm Blank Rome Klaus & Comisky, Phila., 1966-68; chief law reform, consumer's adv. Community Legal Svcs., Inc., Phila., 1968-70; assoc. prof. law Boston Coll., 1970-74, prof., 1974—, assoc. dean, 1972-74; exec. dir. Resource Ctr. Consumers Legal Svcs., 1975-77. Author: (with M. Saks) The Use, Nonuse, and Misuse of Applied Social Research, 1980, Droit Constitutionnel et Bioéthique: L'Expérience Americaine, 1997; contbr. articles to profl. jours. Chmn. Cheltenham Twp. (Pa.) Dem. Party, 1966-68; mem. Mass. Health Facilities Appeals Bd., 1974-75; chmn. Mass. Gov.'s Adv. Com. on Prepaid Legal Svcs., 1978-86; bd. dirs. CEPA Found.; mem. bd. overseers Mass. Supreme Jud. Ct. Hist. Soc., 1999—. Recipient various community awards; U. Pa. fellow, 1961-63. Mem. ABA, Am. Assn. Law Schs., Soc. Am. Law Tchrs., Am. Soc. Law and Medicine (bd. editors Am. Jour. Law and Medicine 1978—, bd. dirs.), Civil Liberties Union Mass. (bd. dirs., pres. 1989-91, trustee Mass. Civil Liberties Found.), ACLU. Jewish. Home: 60 Grove Hill Ave Newton MA 02460-2335 Office: Boston Coll Law Sch 885 Centre St Newton MA 02459-1154

BARON, JAMES NEAL, organizational behavior and human resources educator, researcher; b. L.A., June 24, 1955; s. Robert Filger and Lila Jean (Lederer) B.; m. Mary Theresa Dumont, Dec. 20, 1980; children: Isaac, Nina. BA in Sociology, Reed Coll., 1976; MS in Sociology, U. Wis., 1977; PhD in Sociology, U. Calif., Santa Barbara, 1982. Instr. dept. sociology U. Calif., Santa Barbara, 1981-82; from asst. prof. to prof. orgnl. behavior Stanford (Calif.) U., 1982-92, Walter Kenneth Kilpatrick prof. orgnl. behavior and human resources, 1992—, assoc. dean acad. affairs, 1994-97; asst. prof. sociology Stanford U., 1982-86, assoc. prof., 1986-90, prof., 1990-94; co-dir. Human Resources Rsch. Initiative, 1992-94; affiliate faculty mem. Stanford Ctr. Orgns. Rsch., Pub. Mgmt. Program, Inst. Rsch. on Women and Gender, Orgns. and Mental Health Rsch. Tng. Program, 1982-89, Orgns. and Aging Rsch. Tng. Program, 1985-88; researcher and presenter in field. Mem. editorial bd. Rsch. in Social Stratification and Mobility, 1983-89, Adminstrv. Sci. Quar., 1984-90, Indsl. Rels., 1993—; contbr. articles to profl. jours. Mem. policy bd. Ctr. Rsch. on Women, Stanford U., 1983-85, steering com. Stanford Ctr. Orgns. Rsch., 1989-90, 92-94, com. on performance appraisal for merit pay Nat. Rsch. Coun., 1989-91, adv. com. Grad. Mgmt. Admissions Coun. Rsch. Program on Test Registrants and Minority Students, 1989-96, com. acad. policy, planning and mgmt., bd. trustees, Stanford U., 1990-93; bd. dirs. Las Lomitas Found., Found. Ednl. Excellence, Menlo Park, 1993-95; educator various nat. and internat. orgns; adv. bd. Citicorp Behavioral Scis. Rsch. Coun., 1994—; adv. com. Indsl. Rels. Ctr., Carlson Sch. Mgmt., U. Minn., 1997—. Bus. Sch. Trust Faculty fellow Stanford U., 1990-92, Bass Faculty fellow, 1989-90, fellow Ctr. Advanced Study in Behavioral Scis., 1988-89, Marvin Bower fellow Harvard Bus. Sch., 1997-98, Jacdicke faculty fellow Stanford, 1998-99; Disting. Rsch. vis. Nat. U. Singapore, 1991. Mem. Am. Sociol. Assn. (coun. sect. orgns. and occupations 1988-91, chair nominations com. sect. on orgns. and occupations 1993-94, EGOS prize 1985), Acad. Mgmt. Office: Stanford University Grad Sch of Bus Stanford CA 94305-5015

BARON, JEFFREY, pharmacologist, educator; b. Bklyn., July 10, 1942; s. Harry Leo and Terry (Goldstein) B.; m. Judith Carol Rothberg, June 27, 1965; children: Stephanie Ann, Leslie Beth, Melissa Leigh. B.S. in Pharmacy, U. Conn., 1965; Ph.D. in Pharmacology, U. Mich., 1969. Rsch. fellow in biochemistry U. Tex. Southwestern Med. Sch., Dallas, 1969-71, rsch. asst. prof. biochemistry and pharmacology, 1971-72; asst. prof. pharmacology U. Iowa, Iowa City, 1972-75, assoc. prof. pharmacology, 1975-80, prof. pharmacology, 1980—; mem. chem. pathology study sect. NIH, Bethesda, Md., 1983-87, environ. health scis. rev. com. NIH, Nat. Inst. Environ. Health Scis., Research Triangle Park, N.C., 1990-94. Contbr. numerous articles to profl. jours., chpts. to books. Recipient Rsch. Career Devel. award NIH, 1975-80, numerous rsch. grants NIH. Mem. Am. Soc. for Pharmacology and Exptl. Therapeutics, Am. Soc. Biochem. and Molecular Biology, Am. Assn. for Cancer Rsch., Soc. Toxicology, Internat. Soc. for Study Xenobiotics. Achievements include discovery of the role of heme synthesis in regulating the induction of cytochrome P450 in liver; participation in the discovery of oxygenated cytochrome P450; immunohistochemical localization of cytochromes P450 and other xenobiotic-metabolizing enzymes in liver and extrahepatic tissues. Office: U Iowa Dept Pharmacology Rm 1-376 Bowen Sci Bldg Iowa City IA 52242

BARON, JUDSON RICHARD, aerospace educator; b. N.Y.C., July 28, 1924; s. Louis and Leah (Berzin) B.; m. Selma Francine Wasserman, Sept. 4, 1949; children—Jason Roberts, Jeffrey Scott. B.Aero. Engring., NYU, 1947; SM, MIT, 1948, ScD, 1956. Registered profl. engr., Mass. Stress analyst Chance Vought Aircraft Co., 1947; mem. research staff MIT, 1948-54, research asst., 1954-56, mem. faculty, 1957—, prof. aeros. and astronautics, 1957-89, prof. emeritus, sr. lectr., 1989-98; cons. in field, 1957—. Mem. Air Force Sci. Adv. Bd., 1987-91. With AUS, 1943-46. Decorated Bronze Star; recipient Exceptional Civilian Svc. award. Dept. Air Force, 1991. Fellow AIAA (assoc. editor jour. 1989-96), Sigma Xi, Tau Beta Pi, Gamma Alpha Rho. Home: 7 Gould Rd Lexington MA 02420-1003 Office: 77 Massachusetts Ave Cambridge MA 02139-4307

BARON, MARTIN RAYMOND, psychology educator; b. Stamford, Conn., Oct. 27, 1922; s. Harry Isaac and Gertrude (Sondak) B.; m. Shirley Elaine Thalberg, July 28, 1945 (dec. Feb. 26, 1989); children: Carol Ann Baron Burch, Cynthia Ellen Baron Keohane, Marcia Wendy; m. Joy Gray Bennett, Sept. 29, 1992. B.A., Yale U., 1943, M.A., State U. Iowa, 1948, Ph.D., 1949. Asst. prof. psychology Kent (O.) State U., 1949-53, assoc. prof., 1953-58, prof., 1958-71; prof. psychology U. Louisville, 1971-86, prof. emeritus, 1986—, chmn. dept., 1971-72; acting dean U. Louisville (Coll. Arts and Scis.), 1972-73, asst. v.p. for acad. affairs, 1973-76, asst. exec. v.p. planning, 1976-81. Assoc. editor: Behavioral Sci, 1973-92; contbr. articles to psychol. publs. Bd. dirs. Coalition for Homeless of Louisville and Jefferson County, Ky., 1986-94, Seven Counties Svcs. Inc., Louisville, 1989-95, chmn., 1990-92. With AUS, 1943-46. Mem. Am. Psychol. Assn., Midwestern Psychol. Assn., Southeastern Psychol. Assn., So. Soc. Philosophy and Psychology, Sigma Xi. Home: 1611 Spring Dr Apt 5C Louisville KY 40205-1341

BARON, MELVIN FARRELL, pharmacy educator; b. L.A., July 29, 1932; s. Leo Ben and Sadie (Bauchman) B.; m. Lorraine Ross, Dec. 20, 1953; children: Lynn Baron Friedman, Ross David. PharmD, U. So. Calif., 1957, MPA, 1973. Lic. pharmacist, Calif. Pres. Shield Health Care Ctrs., Van Nuys, Calif., 1957-83; dir. externship program U. So. Calif., L.A., 1981; v.p. Shield Health Care Ctrs., Inc. (C.R. Bard, Inc. subsidiary), 1983-86; pres. Merit Coll., 1988-92, PharmCom., L.A., 1990—; asst. prof. clin. pharmacy U. So. Calif., L.A., 1991—, asst. dean pharm. care programs, 1995—, dir. PharmD/MBA program, asst. dean programmatic advancment, 1998; prin. New Horizon Pharmacy Cons.; adj. asst. prof. U. Without Walls, Shaw U., Raleigh, N.C., 1973; project dir. Hayne Found. Drug Rsch. Ctr. U. So. Calif., L.A., 1973; assoc. dir. Calif. Alcoholism Found., 1973-75; adj. asst. prof. clin. pharmacy Sch. of Pharmacy U. So. Calif., L.A., 1981-91; cons. Topanga Terr. Convalescent Hosp., 1970-80, Calif. Labor Mgmt. Plan for alcoholism programs and coords., 1974, Office of Alcoholism, State of Calif., Nat. In-Home Health Svc., 1975, Continuity of Life Team, 1975, Triad Med., Longs Drug Stores, HealthTek, others; vis. prof. Tokyo Coll. Pharmacy, 1994, Sandoz Pharm Co., 1995; lectr. Meijo U., Nagoya U., Japan, 1994; presenter Nat. Pharmacy Dir. Conf., 1995; cons., mem. sci. adv. bd. Leiner Health Products, 1998; cons. Prime Care Pharmacy, 1998—, Jackson Meml. Hosp., 1998, New Horizon Pharmacy; chairperson nominating com. CPHA, 1998; co-developer Trends in Healthcare Svcs. Adv. bd. Pharmacist Newsletter, 1980—. Chmn. Friends of Operation Bootstrap, 1967-77; svc. chmn. tng. coord. Am. Cancer Soc., San Fernando Valley, Calif., 1980; mem. adv. bd. L.A. VNA, 1982; bd. dirs. pres. QSAD, 1987-88; pres. bd. Everywoman's Village, 1988-89; bd. dirs. Life Svcs., 1988—; pres. bd. counselors, U. So. Calif., 1988-92, mem. Calif. State Bd. Pharmacy Com. on Student/Preceptor Manual, 1991-93. Named Disting. Alumnus of Yr., U. So. Calif., Sch. of Pharmacy Alumni Assn., 1979, U. So. Calif. Torchbearer, 1990-91, Hon. Tchr. of Yr. U. So. Calif. Sch. Pharmacy, 1997. Fellow Am. Coll. Apothecaries; mem. Am. Pharm. Assn., Am. Soc. Health Sys. Pharmacists, Calif. Pharmacist Assn. (chair edn. com.), Am. Soc. Pub. Adminstrn., Am. Assn. Colls. of Pharmacy, Phi Kappa Phi, Rho Chi Lambda Sigma (hon., faculty advisor), Rho Chi. Home: 323 San Vicente Santa Monica CA 90402-1629 Office: U So Calif 1985 Zonal Ave Los Angeles CA 90033-1039

BARON, ROBERT, folklorist; b. N.Y.C., Jan. 27, 1951; s. Charles and Helen Esther (Suss) B.; m. Lise May Korson, Jan. 2, 1982; 1 child, Violet. BA, U. Chgo., 1972; MA, U. Pa., 1976, PhD, 1994. Sr. rsch. specialist Bklyn. Mus., 1977-79; folk arts coord. N.Y. State Coun. on Arts, N.Y.C., 1980-84, mus. program assoc., 1984-85, dir. folk arts program, 1985—; dir. museum program, 1996—; presenter in field; cons. Artpart, 1979, Bklyn. Rediscovery, 1978-79; adj. lectr. Am. Studies dept. Rutgers U., Newark, 1979-80; bd. dirs. Mid Atlantic Arts Found., 1995-96, also chair, mem. traditional arts com., 1996—, mem. performing arts com., 1995-96. Co-editor: Public Folklore, 1992; contbr. articles to profl. publs. Pres. U. Chgo. Folklore Soc., 1970-71; mem. N.J. Folklife adv. coun. N.J. Hist. Commn., 1979-80; field researcher, presenter Festival Am. Folklife, Smithsonian Instn., 1974; mem. multi-disciplinary panel N.J. State Coun. on Arts, 1984, mem. presenting orgns. panel, 1994; mem. traditional arts adv. com. New Eng. Found. for Arts, 1990-93; mem. nat. adv. com. Fund for Folk Culture, 1991-95; coord. ethnic folklife festival Caribbean traditions Internat. House of Phila., 1978; mem. panel N.J. Folk Arts Apprenticeships, 1995, Folk Arts Orgn., 1997, 99; mem. orgn. granting panel Conn. Commn. on Arts, 1995. U. Pa. teaching fellow, 1976-77; Wenner-Gren Found. grantee, 1976. Mem. Am. Folklore Soc. (state of profession com. 1992-94, nominating com. 1996-98), nat. Coun. for Traditional Arts (bd. dirs. 1992—), Mid. Atlantic Folklife Assn. (v.p. 1991-93, pres. 1993—, bd. dirs. 1995—). Jewish. E-mail: rbaron@nyscar.org. Home: 211 8th Ave Brooklyn NY 11215-2658 Office: NY State Coun on Arts 915 Broadway New York NY 10010-7108

BARON, SAMUEL HASKELL, historian; b. N.Y.C., May 24, 1921; s. James and Dinah (Bader) B.; m. Virginia Wilson, Dec. 22, 1949; children—Sheila, Carla, Laura. BS, Cornell U., 1942; MA, Columbia U., 1948; PhD, 1952. Instr. history U. Tenn., 1948-53; vis. lectr. Northwestern U., 1953-54, U. Mo., 1954-55, U. Nebr., 1955-56; from asst. prof. to prof. Grinnell (Iowa) Coll., 1956-66; prof. U. Calif.-San Diego, 1966-72; Alumni Disting. prof. history U. N.C., Chapel Hill, 1972-91, prof. emeritus, 1991—; chmn. Conf. Slavic and Ea. European History, 1976. Author: Plekhanov: The Father of Russian Marxism, 1963, The Travels of Olearius in Seventeenth Century Russia, 1967, Muscovite Russia: Collected Essays, 1980, Explorations in Muscovite History, 1991, Plekhanov in Russian History and Soviet Historiography, 1994; co-editor: Windows on The Russian Past: Essays on Soviet Historiography since Stalin, 1977, Introspection in Biography: The Biographer's Quest for Self-Awareness, 1985, Religion and Culture in Early Modern Russia and Ukraine, 1997. Served from pvt. to capt. AUS, 1942-46. Ford Found. fellow, 1958-59, Guggenheim Found. fellow, 1970-71, Nat. Endowment Humanities fellow, 1976; chair named in his honor U. N.C., 1994. Mem. AAUP (council 1962-65), Am. Hist. Assn., Am. Assn. Advancement Slavic Studies, Early Slavic Studies Assn. (pres. 1991). Home: 5 Marilyn Ln Chapel Hill NC 27514-5958 Office: U NC Dept History Chapel Hill NC 27599-3195

BARON, SEYMOUR, engineering and research executive; b. N.Y.C., Apr. 5, 1923; s. Benjamin and Tillie (Schuster) B.; m. Florence Chill, Aug. 27, 1950; children: Richard Mark, Paul Lawrence. B.S. in Engring., Johns Hopkins U., 1944, M.S., 1947; Ph.D., Columbia U., 1950. Lab. researcher U.S. Indsl. Chem. Co., 1944-47; research asst. Columbia U., N.Y.C., 1947-50; chief engr. Burns and Roe, Inc., Oradell, N.J., 1950-64; v.p. Burns and Roe, Inc., 1964-75, sr. v.p., 1975-76, sr. corp. v.p., 1976-84, dir., 1967—; assoc. dir. Brookhaven Nat. Lab., Upton, N.Y., 1984-94; dir. S.C. nuclear waste program Med. U. S.C., Charleston, 1994—; bd. dirs. Argonne Univs. Assn., also mem. exec. com., spl. com. for reactor devel., reactor devel. and safety div., 1976-82; mem. adv. com., engring. tech. div. Oak Ridge Nat. Lab.; mem. N.J. Commn. on Radiation Protection; mem. rev. com. on fusion and rev. com. on chem. tech. div. U. Chgo., 1983—; adj. prof. Columbia U., Poly. Inst. N.Y. Fellow ASME, Am. Nuclear Soc., AAAS; mem. Am. Inst. Chem. Engrs., Nat. Acad. Engring., Sigma Xi, Phi Lambda Upsilon. Club: Lions (Oradell). Office: Med U SC 159 1/2 Rutledge Ave Charleston SC 29403-5831

BARON, SHELDON, research and development company executive; b. Bklyn., May 13, 1934; s. Harry and Edna (Schleifer) B.; m. Doris Earl Rudd, Aug. 11, 1961; 1 son, David. BS, Bklyn. Coll., 1955; MA, Coll. William and Mary, 1961; PhD, Harvard U., 1966. Simulation engr. USAF-NACA, Hampton, Va., 1955-57; aerospace technologist NASA, Hampton, 1958-65, Cambridge, Mass., 1965-67; mgr., researcher Bolt Beranek & Newman, Cambridge, 1967-71, mgr., prin. scientist, 1971-79, v.p., 1979-94, sr. v.p., 1994-98; ind. cons. Cambridge, 1999—; mem. sci. adv. bd. U.S. Army Missile Command, Huntsville, Ala., 1975-77; mem. working group on simulation, 1982-84; chmn. working group on human performance modelling Nat. Acad. Scis.-NRC, 1983-87. Assoc. editor: Jour. Cybernetics and Info. Scis., Washington, 1976-81. Served to 1st lt. USAF, 1955-57. Fellow IEEE; mem. Control Systems Soc. (sec., treas. 1982-84), AIAA, Harvard Soc. Engrs. and Scientists (pres. 1976-78). Home: 7 Birch Hill Ln Lexington MA 02421-7445 Office: BBN Techs GTE Internetwkg 10 Moulton St Cambridge MA 02138-1119

BARON, SHERI, advertising agency executive; b. Bklyn., Sept. 3, 1955; d. Irwin Murray Glaser and Rosalind (Mendelson) Krasik; m. Peter T. Colonel, Sept. 20, 1981 (dec.); m. Alan R. Baron, Dec. 14, 1996. B.A. in Psychology, SUNY-Cortland, 1977. Account exec. Ted Bates Co., N.Y.C., 1978-80; account exec. SSC&B Advt. (name now Ammirati & Puris/LINTAS), Inc., N.Y.C., 1980-82, v.p. account supr., 1982-83, v.p. mgmt. supr., 1983-84, sr. v.p. mgmt. supr., 1984-88, exec. v.p., 1988—, bd. dirs. 1990-94; pres. Gotham Inc., 1994—. Named to Am. Advt. Fedn. Hall of Achievement, 1993, 40 Under 40 List, Crain's N.Y. Bus., 1994. Mem. Advt. Women N.Y., Cosmetic Exec. Women, Fashion Group Internat. Home: 11 W 20th St New York NY 10011-3704 Office: Gotham Inc 100 5th Ave New York NY 10011-6903

BARONAS, JEAN MARIE, computer systems engineer, educator; b. Bath, N.Y., Feb. 27, 1954; d. Albert Alizas and Justine Julian (Statsaitis) Baronas; m. Henry Benard Freedman, Apr. 22, 1976 (div. Mar. 1987). AAS, Rochester Inst. Tech., 1974, BS, 1976; MS, Johns Hopkins U., 1993; post-grad., George Washington U., 1997—. Plant mgr. Stephenson, Inc., Washington, 1976-78; lab. mgr. Les Etronics Corp., Springfield, Va., 1978-80; sales rep. Seimens Corp., Port Washington, N.Y., 1980-81; owner, pub. Technology Watch, Springfield, 1981-85; computer sys. analyst U.S. Dept. Commerce, Gaithersburg, Md., 1983-90; sr. mgr. standards Assn. for Info. and Image Mgmt., Silver Spring, Md., 1990-95; mgr. comm. standards Xerox Corp., Washington, 1995—; adj. prof. Johns Hopkins U., Balt., 1994—; presenter in field. Student mentor Johns Hopkins U., 1994—; mem. com. Montgomery Village Found., Gaithersburg, 1993—; vol. J.F. Kennedy Ctr., Washington, 1994-95. Recipient Superior Performance award U.S. Dept. Commerce, 1985. Mem. The Internet Soc., Standards Engring. Soc. Republican. Roman Catholic. Avocations: swimming, opera. Home: 20521 Strath Haven Dr Gaithersburg MD 20886-4055 Office: Xerox Corp 1401 H St NW Ste 200 Washington DC 20005-2193

BARONDES, SAMUEL HERBERT, psychiatrist, educator; b. Bklyn., Dec. 21, 1933; s. Solomon and Yetta (Kaplow) B.; m. Ellen Slater, Sept. 1, 1963 (dec. Nov. 22, 1971); children: Elizabeth Francesca, Jessica Gabrielle. AB, Columbia U., 1954, MD, 1958. Intern, then asst. resident in medicine Peter Bent Brigham Hosp., Boston, 1958-60; sr. asst. surgeon USPHS, NIH, Bethesda, Md., 1960-63; resident in psychiatry McLean and Mass. Gen. hosps., Boston, 1963-66; asst. prof., then assoc. prof. psychiatry and molecular biology Albert Einstein Coll. Medicine., Bronx, N.Y., 1966-69; prof. psychiatry U. Calif., San Diego, 1969-86; prof., chmn. dept. psychiatry, dir. Langley Porter Psychiat. Inst. U. Calif., San Francisco, 1986-94, dir. Ctr. Neurobiology and Psychiatry, 1994—, Jeanne and Sanford Robertson Prof. Neurobiol. and Psychiatry, 1996—; pres. McKnight Endowment Fund for Neurosci., 1989—; mem. sci. adv. com. Rsch. Am.; mem. governing coun. Internat. Brain Rsch. Orgn., 1994—; mem. bd. scientific couns., NIMH, 1997—. Author: Molecules and Mental Illness, 1993, Mood Genes, 1998; mem. editorial bds. profl. jours.; contbr. numerous articles to profl. publs. Recipient Rsch. Career Devel. award USPHS, 1967, Elliott Royer award, 1989, P.H. Stillmark medal Estonia, 1989; Fogarty Internat. scholar NIH, 1979. Fellow AAAS, Am. Psychiat. Assn., Am. Coll. Neuropsychopharmacology; mem. Inst. Medicine Nat. Acad. Sci. E-mail: barondes@socrates.ucsf.edu. Office: U Calif-San Francisco Langley Porter Psychiat Ins 401 Parnassus Ave San Francisco CA 94143-0984

BARONDESS, JEREMIAH ABRAHAM, physician; b. N.Y.C., June 6, 1924; s. Benjamin and Dora (Greenberg) B.; m. Sue Kaufman, Nov. 22, 1953 (dec. 1977); 1 child, James Joseph; m. Linda Hiddemen, Dec. 10, 1982. MD, Johns Hopkins U., 1949; DSc (hon.), Albany Med. Coll., Union U., 1978; LittD (hon.), N.Y. Inst. Tech., 1992; DMedSci (hon.), Med. Coll. Pa., 1993; DSc (hon.), N.Y. Med. Coll., 1998. Diplomate Am. Bd. Internal Medicine (bd. govs., council gen. internal medicine 1975-81). Intern, then asst. resident in medicine Osler Med. Svc. Johns Hopkins Hosp., 1949-51; asst. medicine Johns Hopkins U. Med. Sch., 1950-51; mem. virology sect., research div. Children's Hosp., Phila., also; rsch. fellow virology U. Pa. Med. Sch., 1951-53; asst. resident, then chief resident in medicine N.Y. Hosp.-Cornell U. Med. Center, 1953-55; mem. faculty Cornell U. Med. Coll., 1953—, clin. prof. medicine, 1971-78, prof. clin. medicine, 1978-87, Irene F. and I. Roy Psaty Disting. Prof. Clin. Medicine, 1987-89, William T. Foley Disting. Prof. in Clin. Medicine, 1989-90, adj. prof. clin. medicine, 1990, prof. emeritus, 1993—; mem. staff N.Y. Hosp., 1953—, attending physician, 1971—; chief pvt. med. svc., 1971-92; hon. staff mem. N.Y. Hosp., 1992—; assoc. chmn. dept. medicine, 1983-90; asst. vis. physician Bellevue Hosp., 1960-67; cons. medicine Meml. Hosp. Cancer and Allied Diseases, 1972-90; Alpha Omega Alpha vis. prof. U. P.R. Med. Sch., 1972; Meyerowitz meml. lectr. U. Rochester Sch. Medicine, 1980; disting. lectr. U. N.C., 1982; vis. prof. medicine U. Ill. Med. Sch., 1974, U. Va. Med. Sch., 1976, Mayo Clinic and Med. Sch., 1978, U. Iowa Sch. Medicine, 1979, U. Tex. Med. Ctr., 1986, 90, U. Pa., 1986, U. Va., 1989, N.Y. Med. Coll., 1990, SUNY Health Sci. Ctr., Bklyn., 1992; mem. nat. resources com. Johns Hopkins U., 1965—, trustee, 1977-94, trustee emeritus, 1994—, chmn. vis. com. Sch. Medicine, 1978-92. Author: (with A.M. Harvey and J. Bordley) Differential Diagnosis, (with J. McGovern and C. Roland) The Persisting Osler, 1985, (with C. Roland) The Persisting Osler II, 1994, (with A.H. Samiy and R.G. Douglas) Textbook of Diagnostic Medicine, 1987; editor: Diagnostic Approaches to Presenting Syndromes, 1971; co-editor Differential Diagnosis, 1994; mem. editl. bd. Forum on Medicine, Pharos, Internat. Jour. Technol. Assessment in Health Care, Jour. Royal Soc. Med.; contbr. articles to profl. jours. Bd. dirs. Am. Fedn. Aging Rsch., 1996—. Served with AUS, 1943-46; Served with USPHS, 1951-53. Recipient Wiggers award Albany Med. Coll. Union U., 1978, Alfred Stengel award ACP, 1983; named Hon. Alumnus Cornell U. Med. Coll., 1974. Fellow AAAS, Royal Coll. Physicians London, ACP (chmn. bd. govs. 1973-75, bd. regents 1975—, pres.-elect 1977-78, pres. 1978-79, pres. emeritus 1988), Federated Coun. Internal Medicine, Royal Soc. Medicine, Royal Soc. Health, Royal Coll. Physicians Ireland (hon.); mem. Am. Clin. and Climatol. Assn. (coun. 1975-78, pres. 1994), Am. Osler Soc. (pres. 1983-84), Am. Fedn. Clin. Rsch., APHA, Assn. Am. Physicians, Harvey Soc., N.Y. Heart Assn., Inst. Medicine NAS (coun. 1979-81, co-chair coun. on health care tech., chair com. on managed care and chronic disease 1996), N.Y. Acad. Scis., N.Y. Acad. Medicine (pres. 1990—), Internat. Soc. Internal Medicine, Phi Beta Kappa, Alpha Omega Alpha (dir. 1978-79, pres. 1987-89), Century Club (N.Y.C.), Cosmos Club (Washington). Jewish. Home: 544 E 86th St New York NY 10028-7536 Office: NY Acad Medicine 1216 5th Ave New York NY 10029-5202

BARONE, ANGELA MARIA, artist, researcher; b. Concesio, Brescia, Italy, June 29, 1957; came to U.S., 1983; d. Giuseppe and Adelmina (D'Ercole) B. Laurea cum laude in geol. scis., U. Bologna, Italy, 1981; PhD in Marine Geology, Columbia U., 1989. Cert. in profl. photography, N.Y. Inst. Photography, N.Y.C., 1992; cert. in the fine art of painting and drawing North Light Art Sch., Cin., 1993. Collaborative asst. Marine Geology Inst., Bologna, 1981-83, Inst. Geology and Paleontology, Florence, Italy, 1982-83, Sta. de Geodynamique, Villefranche, France, 1982; grad. rsch. asst. Lamont-Doherty Geol. Obs., Palisades, N.Y., 1983-89; postdoctoral rsch. asst. Lamont-Doherty Geol. Obs., Palisades, 1989; postgrad. rschr. Scripps Instn. of Oceanography, La Jolla, Calif., 1990-92; artist San Diego, 1993—. Contbr. articles to profl. jours. Mem. Am. Geophys. Union (co-pres. meeting session 1990), Nat. Mus. Women in Arts (assoc.). Home: 7540 Charmant Dr Apt 1222 San Diego CA 92122-5044

BARONE, JANINE MASON, foundation administrator; b. Fullerton, Calif., Apr. 18, 1964; d. Guy T. and Helen M. Mason; m. John J. Barone, Aug. 15, 1992; 1 child, Alexander Mason Barone. BA, U. San Diego, 1986. Sales assoc. Mutual of Omaha, San Diego, 1986-87; regional mgr. Fieldstone Found., San Diego, 1988—; mem. steering panel Union Inst., Washington, 1995-97. Mem. adv. bd. Ptnrs. in Edn., San Diego, 1988-94, Eureka Cmtys., San Diego, 1995—; mem. San Diego Grantmakers, 1990—, chair, 1993-96; bd. dirs. San Diego Children's Initiative, 1992-97, San Diego Blood Bank Found., 1994—; mem. com. United Way, San Diego, 1993-97; chair, capt. Neighborhood Watch, City of Del Mar, Calif., 1993—, mem. mediation com., 1998—. Mem. Nat. Soc. Fund Raising Execs. (bd. 1998—, co-chair San Diego Philanthropy Day 1998), LEAD San Diego (Alumni of Yr. 1995), Univ. San Diego Class of '86 Alumni Group.

BARONE, JOHN ANTHONY, university provost emeritus; b. Dunkirk, N.Y., Aug. 30, 1924; s. John A. and Josephine (Audino) B.; m. Rose Marie Pace, Aug. 23, 1947. BA, U. Buffalo, 1944; MS, Purdue U., 1948, PhD, 1950; ScD (hon.), Fairfield U., 1992. Research fellow Purdue U., 1948-50; instr. Fairfield (Conn.) U., 1950-51, asst. prof., 1951-56, assoc. prof., 1956-62, prof. chemistry, 1962-92, dir. research and grants, 1963-66, v.p. planning, 1966-70, provost, 1970-92, emeritus, 1992—; mem. rev. and evaluation com. Conn. Regional Med. Program, 1970-76; dir. NSF In-Service Inst., 1961-69; mem. steering com. comprehensive health planning United Community Services; bd. dirs., mem. Corp. Conn. Blue Cross, 1973-77; bd. dirs., mem. exec. com. Blue Cross-Blue Shield Conn., 1977-94; project mgr. HUD New Rural Soc. contract, 1972-76; mem. adv. com. on fed. matters Conn. Commn. for

Higher Edn., 1974-77; pres. UN Assn. Conn., 1970-72; mem. Conn. Health and Edn. Facilities Authority, 1987—, vice-chmn., 1988—; mem. adv. com. Conn. Dept. Health Svcs., 1987-93. Contbr. articles profl. jours. Trustee Conn. Coun. for Sci. Edn., Hall-Brooke Found., St. Vincent's Coll., Ctr. for Fin. Studies, vice chmn., 1977-94; bd. dirs. Jesuit Rsch. Coun. Am., chmn., 1968-70; bd. dirs. Higher Edn. Ctr. for Urban Studies, Health Systems Agy. S.W. Conn., 1977-84; mem. Conn. Statewide Health Coordinating Coun., 1979-87, chmn., 1984-87. Served with AUS, 1944-46. Barone Campus Ctr. at Fairfield U., Barone Resource Ctr. at St. Vincent's Coll. named in his honor, 1992; cancer rsch. grantee NIH, dir. NSF undergrad. rsch. program, 1961-67. Fellow AAAS; mem. Am. Chem. Soc. (chmn. western Conn. sect. 1966), AAUP (1st pres. Fairfield U. chpt.), Newcomen Soc., Phi Beta Kappa, Sigma Xi, Phi Lambda Upsilon. Democrat. Roman Catholic. Club: Algonquin.

BARONE, ROSE MARIE PACE, writer, retired educator, entertainer; b. Buffalo, Apr. 26, 1920; d. Dominic and Jennie (Zagara) Pace; m. John Barone, Aug. 23, 1947. BA, U. Buffalo, 1943; MS, U. So. Cal., 1950; cert. advanced study, Fairfield (Conn.) U., 1963. Tchr. Angola (N.Y.) High Sch., 1943-46, Puente (Calif.) High Sch., 1946-47, Jefferson High Sch., Lafayette, Ind., 1947-50; dir. Warren Inst., Bridgeport, Conn., 1951-53; instr. U. Bridgeport, 1953-54; tchr. bus. subjects Bassick H.S., Bridgeport, 1954-74, Harding H.S., Bridgeport, 1974-80; instr. Fairfield U., Conn., 1969; freelance writer, 1980—; chair State Poetry Festival, 1987. Founder Pet Rescue; chmn. cmty. affairs com. Area Coun. Cath. Women, 1988-90, sec., 1990-91, chmn. family affairs com., 1991, v.p., 1992-93; chmn. cmty. affairs Ch. Women United, 1992—, state area chmn., 1995-97, state UN chair, 1997—. Pace-Barone Minority yearly scholar Fairfield U., Auerbach Found. scholar, 1956; recipient Playwriting prize Conn. Federated Women's Clubs, 1955, 1st prize for poetry, 1985, Short Story award Federated Women Conn., 1987, 88, 90, Citizen award Bridgeport Dental Assn., 1982, State/Town Hero award, 1986, Anniversary medal and marble statuette Fairfield U., Cmty. Care Successful Aging award, 1992, Salute to Women award YWCA, 1993, Woman of Substance award, 1994, Woman Distinction Girl Scout award, 1998, craft and flower awards. mem. NEA, AAUW (treas. 1957-58, named gift grant 1989, cultural and poetry chair 1992—, rec. sec. 1992-93, internat. rels. 1993-94, v.p. program 1995-97, contest chair 1995—, Conf. of Women award 1997), Am. Assn. Ret. People (v.p. 1987-88, pres. 1988-89, 94-95, instr. 55 Alive, cmty. affairs chair 1990-94, 95—), Owl (sec. 1987-89, pres. 1989-90), Nat. League Am. PEN Women (Bridgeport historian 1966-84, state historian 1983—, treas. br. 1985-88, state pres. 1986-88, state lit. chair 1988—, br. membership chair 1990, Nat. Historian award 1976, 88), Fairfield Area Poets (founder, pres. 1990—, editor 5 vols. Conn. poets), UN Assn. USA (pres. Bridgeport 1964-66, 68-70, v.p. 1988—, chmn. area UN Days 1960—, pres. Conn. chpt. 1971—, state chmn. UNICEF to 1984, area UNICEF Ctr. 1984—, state historian 1984—), Conn. Bus. Tchrs., Bridgeport Edn. Assn. (sec. 1966-68), VFW (aux. 1989), Am. Legion (aux. contest chair 1989—, historian 1993-95, Aux. Nat. Cmty. Svc. award 1993), Fairfield Arts Coun., Fairfield Philatelic Soc. (sec. 1971-78, founder advisor Philatelic Jrs. 1972-80), Fairfield U. Women's Club (founder, pres. 1950, 74—, v.p. 1973-74), Southport Women's Club (garden dept. sec. 1981-85, chmn. 1985-87), John & Rose Marie Barone Resource Ctr. St. Vincent's Coll., Pi Omega Pi. Home: 1283 Round Hill Rd Fairfield CT 06430-7329

BARONE, STEPHANIE LYNN, academic administrator, psychology researcher; b. Harrisburg, Pa., Aug. 15, 1965; d. Gary Andrew and Michaelene Ann (Verotsky) B. BS in Indsl. Psychology, Bus., Pa. State U., 1987, MS in Counselor Edn., Student Pers., 1990, postgrad., 1990—. Intern govt. svcs. Commonwealth of Pa., Harrisburg, 1986-88; coord. residence hall programs Pa. State U., University Park, 1988-90, asst. dir. office conduct standards, 1990—; counselor, trainer Oasis Counseling and Crisis Intervention Ctr., State College, Pa., 1984-86; co-instr. Pa. State U., University Park, 1987—; interviewer Dickinson Sch. Law, Carlisle, Mass., 1985—; lectr. Newman Ctr. Pa. State U., University Park. Mem. AACD, Pa. Assn. for Specialists in Group Work, Assn. for Specialists in Group Work, Assn. for Student Jud. Adminstrs., Sr. HAT Soc., Phi Beta Kappa, Chi Sigma Iota. Democrat. Roman Catholic. Avocations: swimming, biking, jet skiing, parasailing, scuba diving.

BAROODY, ALBERT JOSEPH, JR., pastoral counselor; b. Columbia, S.C., Sept. 8, 1952; s. Albert Joseph and Hazel (Haskin) B.; m. Nancy Dell Weatherford, Jan. 3, 1976; children: Joseph McKinley, Blakely Adelle. BS in Sociology, U. S.C., 1974; MDiv, S.E. Bapt. Theol. Sem., Wake Forest, N.C., 1978, D of Ministry, 1984. Ordained to ministry Bapt. Ch., 1977; lic. profl. counselor, S.C., 1992; cert. pastoral counselor. Chaplain intern and resident Bapt. Med. Ctr., Columbia, S.C., 1977-79; dir. pastoral svcs. Easley (S.C.) Bapt. Hosp., 1979-80, McLeod Regional Med. Ctr., Florence, 1980-91; pastoral counselor McLeod Counseling Svcs., Florence, 1991-94, Cmty. Care and Counseling, Florence, 1994—; chaplain Lions Club, Florence, 1980-83; interim pastor various local chs., S.C., 1981—; pastoral cons. Tuomey Hosp., Sumter, S.C., 1983, Conway (S.C.) Hosp., 1985-86, 92-94, Williamsburg County Hosp., Kingstree, S.C., 1986-88. Author: (with others) Ministry to Youth in Crisis, 1988; contbr. articles to profl. jours. including The Care Giver Jour., Bereavement mag., Jour. Pastoral Care. Continuing edn. state rep. Coll. Chaplains, 1983-92; adv. bd. Salvation Army, Florence, 1987-92, Hospice, Florence, 1988-94, chmn., 1993-94; chmn. Devel. Com. of S.E. Region Assn. for Clin. Pastoral Edn., 1986-90; liason coun. S.C. Organ Procurement Assn., 1988-91; mem. Pee Dee Coalition Against Domestic and Sexual Assault cmty. svcs. adv. coun., 1996—. Fellow Am. Assn. Pastoral Counselors (cert., S.E. region fin. com. 1996-99); mem. Assn. Profl. Chaplains (cert. chaplain). Avocations: traveling, reading, water skiing. Office: Cmty Care & Counseling St John's Episcopal Ch 252 S Dargan St Florence SC 29506-2534

BAROODY, MICHAEL ELIAS, trade association executive; b. Washington, Sept. 14, 1946; s. William J. and Nabeeha (Ashooh) B.; m. Mary Cecilia Patton, Dec. 16, 1967; children—Michael Elias, Timothy, Catherine, Matthew, Peter, Meghan. B.A. in Polit. Sci., U. Notre Dame, 1968. Legis. asst. Senator Roman Hruska, Washington, 1970-71; exec. asst. Senator Bob Dole, Washington, 1972-75; congl. liaison FEA, Washington, 1975-77; dir. pub. affairs Republican Nat. Com., Washington, 1977-81; exec. asst. to U.S. trade rep. William Brock, Washington, 1981; dep. asst. to Pres., dir. pub. affairs The White House, Washington, 1981-85; asst. sec. for policy Dept. Labor, Washington, 1985-89; sr. v.p. for policy and comms. Nat. Assn. Mfrs., 1990-93; pres. nat. policy forum A Rep. Ctr. for Exch. of Ideas, 1993-94; v.p. pub. affairs Nat. Assn. Mfrs., Washington, 1994-96, sr. v.p. pub. affairs, 1997-99, sr. v.p. policy comm. and pub. affairs, 1999—. Editor-in-chief: Commonsense: A Republican Jour. Thought and Opinion, 1978-80, 94, Rep. Platform, 1980. Chmn. bd. Nat. Ctr. for Neighborhood Enterprise, 1997—. Lt. (j.g.) USN, 1968-70. Greek Catholic. Home: 4628 Newcomb Pl Alexandria VA 22304-1505

BARPAL, ISAAC RUBEN, retired technology and operations executive; b. Argentina, Feb. 21, 1940; came to U.S., 1964; s. David and Gala Barpal; children: David, Daniel, Donna. BSEE, BS in Math., Calif. State Poly. U., 1967; MSEE, PhDEE, U. Calif., Santa Barbara, 1970. Registered profl. engr., Pa., Calif., N.J., Fla., Brazil. Engring. and project mgr. transp. div. Westinghouse Electric Co., Pitts., 1971-74; exec. mgr. transp. div. Westinghouse Electric Co., Brazil, 1974-80; pres., country mgr. Westinghouse Electric Co., Venezuela, 1980-83; pres., regional mgr. for L.Am., Westinghouse Electric Co., Pitts., 1983-87, corp. v.p. sci. and tech., 1987-93; sr. v.p., chief tech. officer AlliedSignal Inc., Morristown, N.J., 1993-98; ret., 1998, exec. cons. in sci., tech. and engring.; mem. adv. coun. Calif. Poly. State U. Sch. Engring., San Luis Obispo, 1989-95. Bd. dirs. Ben Franklin Advanced Tech. Ctr., Pitts., 1987-93, Carnegie Sci. Ctr., Pitts., 1987-93, Pitts. Symphony Soc., 1989-93. Recipient Honored Alumnus award Calif. Poly. State U., 1988. Fellow IEEE; mem. IEEE Engring. Mgmt. Soc. (Engring. Mgr. of Yr. award 1991), NSPE. E-mail: ibarpal@amp94.hbs.edu. Home: 25 Glimpsewood Ln Morristown NJ 07960-3767*

BARQUÍN, RAMÓN CARLOS, III, political scientist, consultant; b. Boston, June 26, 1973; s. Ramón Carlos II and Rebecca (Torres) B. BA in L.Am. Studies, BA in Econs., BS in Politics, Brandeis U., 1996; student in law, U. P.R., Guaynabo, 1997—, Interam. U. P.R., 1997—. Pres. B&B Importers, Inc., Lexington, Mass., 1993-97; law intern Castro, Delgado-Cadilla & Assocs., Hato Rey, P.R., 1994; exec. dir. Instituto de Formación Democrática, Guaynabo, 1994—; bus. cons. and ethnic program dir. New Eng. Ethnic Prodn., Chelsea, Mass., 1996-97; bus. cons. OPPED, Inc.-Compare Supermarkets, Mass., 1997; founder, CEO, BGR Computer Learning Ctr., Inc., Millennium Technologies Assocs. Corp., 1997—; dir. pub. affairs Instituto de Formación Democrática, Guaynabo, P.R., 1993—; sales dir. Rodrigues Wholesale Distbrs., Chelsea, 1996-97; pub. affairs and polit. cons. Hispanic Am. C. of C., Boston, 1996—, Latino, Boston, 1996, La Coperativa-Promotions 2000, Chelsea, Mass., 1997; ind. polit. analyst WUNR-1600 AM Radio Adv. Bd., Boston, 1997; founder Inst. Internat. Trade and Fgn. Policy, 1997—. Author: Think Tanks and Governance, 1995, Cuba in Transition: Comparison of IMF and World Bank Conditionalities and Cuba's Econ Reforms, 1996, Governance and Latin America, 1997, The Castro Regime Under the Bretton Woods Economic System, Cuban Communism 9th edit., 1998; contbr. to San Juan Star newspaper, 1998. Avocations: judo, sailing, poetry, reading, dancing. Fax: (787) 789-1720. E-mail: RBarquin3@worldnet.att.net. Home: Inst de Formacion Democratica PO Box 3595 Guaynabo PR 00970-3595 Office: Am Mil Acad The 4th R Ste Carr 177 Km 6.8 Guaynabo PR 00969

BARR, CARLOS HARVEY, lawyer; b. Greeley, Colo., Oct. 12, 1936; s. Charles Allen B. and Zelma Arvilla (Sechler) Turner; m. Martha Lucia Sánchez-Morales, May 10, 1985. BA in Polit. Sci., U. Wash., 1959, MA in Polit. Sci., 1967; JD, George Wash. U., 1971. Bar: Wash. 1971, U.S. Dist. Ct. (ea. dist.) Wash. 1972, U.S. Dist. Ct. (we. dist.) Wash. 1979, U.S. Ct. Appeals (9th cir.) 1973, U.S. Supreme Ct. 1981, U.S. Tax Ct. 1985; cert. Spanish-English interpreter, Wash. Mgmt. intern U.S. Dept of Army, Ft. Lewis, Wash., 1960; joined Fgn. Svc., Dept. State, 1960, officer, 1960-61; vice consul U.S. Consulate Gen., Monterrey, Mex., 1961-64; consular officer, third sec. Am. Embassy, Khartoum, Sudan, 1964-66; analyst Latin Am. Bur., Washington, 1967-68; personnel officer Washington, 1968-70, consular affairs officer, 1970-71, resigned; dir. legal svcs. Community Action Com. OEO, Pasco, Wash., 1971-72; lawyer Spokane (Wash.) County Legal Svc., 1972-73; pvt. practice Kennewick, Wash., 1973-75, Richland, Wash., 1975—. Mem. ABA, ATLA, Wash. Bar Assn., Wash. Trial Lawyers Assn., Fed. Bar Assn., Hispanic Bar Assn. Wash., Inter-Am. Bar Assn., Nat. Hispanic Bar Assn., Acad. Polit. Sci. Avocation: Spanish literature. Office: 1207 George Washington Way Richland WA 99352-3411

BARR, CHARLES F., lawyer, reinsurance company executive. BA, Boston Coll., 1972; JD, Suffolk U., 1976. Bar: Mass. 1977, Conn. 1993; CPCU. Counsel Comml. Union Ins. Cos., 1977-81; asst. gen. counsel Reliance Ins. Cos., 1981-87; v.p., gen. counsel United Pacific Life Ins. Co., 1984-87, Gen. Accident Ins. Co., 1987-89; asst. gen. counsel Gen. Reins. Corp., Stamford, Conn., 1989-90, v.p., asst. gen. counsel, 1990-94, sr. v.p., gen. counsel, sec., 1994—. Office: Gen Reins Corp 695 Main St Stamford CT 06901-2141

BARR, DAVID JOHN, civil, geological engineering educator; b. Evansville, Ind., Mar. 5, 1939; s. Ralph Emerson and Selma Louise (Sander) B.; m. Kay Arlene Porter, Jan. 23, 1965; 1 child, John Matthew. C.E., U. Cin., 1962; MSCE, Purdue U., 1964, PhD, 1968. Registered profl. engr., Ohio. Asst. prof. civil engring. U. Cin., 1968-72; prof. geol. engring. U. Mo., Rolla, 1972—, chmn. dept. geol. and petroleum engring., 1987-92, dir. Mo. Mining and Mineral Resources Rsch. Inst., 1980-87, asst. to vice chancellor for acad. computing, 1986-87; cons. in field. Author: (with others) Remote Sensing for Resource Managemnt, 1983; contbr. Ency. Applied Geology, 1984. Bd. dirs., fireman Rolla Rural Fire Protection Assn., 1975-88. Recipient New Tech. award NASA, 1973-74; NASA rsch. fellow Manned Spacecraft Ctr., Houston, 1969, 70. Mem. NSPE, ASCE (chmn. aerospace div. 1977), Mo. Soc. Profl. Engrs. (Rolla chpt. pres. 1992-93), Am. Soc. Photogrammetry (pres. Rolla region 1975), Soc. Mining Engrs., Assn. Engring. Geologists, Am. Soc. for Engring. Edn., Nat. Assn. Mineral Inst. Dirs. (nat. chmn. 1987-88). Avocations: hunting, fishing. Office: U Mo-Rolla Dept Geol and Petroleum Engring 129 McNutt Rolla MO 65401-0249

BARR, DAVID JOHN, artist, educator; b. Detroit, Oct. 10, 1939; s. John A. and Phyllis E. (Prince) B.; m. Elizabeth Margaret Dwaihy, June 19, 1982; children: Heather, Gillian. BFA, Wayne State U., 1962, MFA, 1965. Prof. art Macomb C.C., Warren, Mich., 1965—; founder, artistic dir. Mich. Legacy Art Park, Thompsonville, Mich., 1995—. One-man shows Hanamura Gallery, Detroit, 1965, Kazimir Gallery, Chgo., 1968, 69, 71, 72, Evanston (Ill.) Art Ctr., 1969, Donald Morris Gallery, Detroit, 1973, Art Rsch. Ctr., Kansas City, Mo., 1974, Marianne Friedland Gallery, Toronto, Ont., Can., 1975, Richard Gray Gallery, Chgo., 1975, 86, U. Pitts., 1975, Donald Morris Gallery, Birmingham, Mich., 1976, 79, 81, 84, 87, 89, 92, San Jose (Calif.) Mus. Art, 1978, Kent (Ohio) State U., 1979, Meadowbrook Art Gallery, Oakland U., Rochester, Minn., 1982, Mot Coll., Flint, Mich., 1985, Momentum Gallery, Mpls., 1986, Swords into Plowshares Gallery, Detroit, 1990, Washtenaw Coll., Ann Arbor, Mich., 1993; exhibited in numerous group shows, 1966—, latest being Flint Inst. Art, 1990, Pontiac (Mich.) Art Ctr., 1992; commns. include Structurist Transformation, Fairlane Town Ctr., Dearborn, Mich., 1976, Crystal Transformation, Macomb C.C., 1976, Sunset Cube, Meadowbrook Festival Ground, Oakland U., 1981, Strata, Lakeview Square, Battle Creek, Mich., 1983, Polaris Ring, Mich. Hist. Mus., Lansing, 1988, Blue Arc, Hoffman Corp., Appleton, Wis., 1989, Soaring, Bishop Internat. Airport, Flint, 1994, Source, Detroit Zoo Wildlife Interpretive Ctr. Butterfly-Hummingbird Garden, 1995, Revolution, Chrysler World Hdqrs., Auburn Hills, Mich., 1996, Revolution II, Brussels, 1998; represented in permanent collections Dennos Mus. Ctr., Northwestern Mich. Coll., Traverse City, Detroit Inst. Arts, Flint Inst. Arts, Ft. Lauderdale Mus., Oakland U., Portland (Oreg.) Art Mus., U. Mich., also corp. collections; contbr. articles to profl. jours. Recipient Mich. Arts award Arts Found. Mich., 1977, Disting. Alumni award Wayne State U., 1983, Gov. of Mich.'s artist award Concerned Citizens for Arts in Mich., 1988, Humanity in the Arts award Wayne State U., 1998. Home: 22600 Napier Rd Novi MI 48374-3202 Office: Macomb CC 14500 12th St Warren MI 48092

BARR, DIXIE LOU, geriatrics nurse; b. Butler, Ohio, Mar. 11, 1934; d. Gerald Edward and Aldine Marie (Barre) Beam; children: Daniel, Dennis, Denise. Lic. practical nurse, Timken-Mercy Hosp., Canton, Ohio, 1971; ADN, Walsh Coll., Canton, 1990. Cert. geriatric nurse, gerontol. nurse. Charge nurse Wyandot County Nursing Home, 1994-95; DON Hospitality House, Massillon, Ohio, 1995-96, with, 1996-98; dir. nursing The Pines, Canton, Ohio, 1998—. Home: 2614 10th St NW Canton OH 44708-4274 Office: The Pines 3015 17th St NW Canton OH 44708

BARR, DONALD ROY, statistics and operations research educator, statistician; b. Durango, Colo., Dec. 10, 1938; s. Russell Wesely and Elizabeth Joanette B.; m. Loudean Suttle, June 14, 1958; children: Mark Edward, Bryan Michael. B.A., Whittier Coll., 1960; MS, Colo. State U., 1962, Ph.D., 1965. Instr. Colo. State U., 1964-65; asst. prof. math. U. Wis.-Oshkosh, 1965-66; prof. stats. and ops. rsch. Naval Postgrad. Sch., Monterey, Calif., 1966-87; v.p. Evaluation Tech. Inc., 1987-88; pres. Evaluation Tech. Inc., Monterey, 1988-89; v.p. VRC Corp., Monterey, 1988-89; prof. math. Naval Postgrad. Sch., Monterey, CA, 1990-93; prof. systems engring. U.S. Mil. Acad., West Point, N.Y., 1993—; liaison scientist London br. Office Naval Rsch., 1982-83; vis. prof. systems engring., U.S. Mil. Acad., West Point, N.Y., 1992-93. Author: College and University Mathematics, 1968, Finite Statistics, 1968, Probability, 1971, Analytic Geometry: A Vector Approach, 1971, Probability: Modeling Uncertainty, 1981, Statistics by Calculator, 1983; contbr. articles to profl. jours. Recipient Rist prize for best paper in mil. ops. rsch. Mil. Ops. Rsch. Soc., 1996, Payne award for ops. rsch. U.S. Army, 1997. Mem. Am. Stat. Assn., Ops. Research Soc. Am., Internat. Test and Evaluation Assn., Sigma Xi. Home: PO Box 2071 Paradise CA 95967-2071 Office: US Mil Acad Dept Systems Engring West Point NY 10996

BARR, EMILY, television station executive. BA in Film Studies, Carleton Coll., 1980; MBA in Mktg., George Washington U., 1986. News editor KSTP-TV, St. Paul, Minn., 1980-81, news promotion specialist, 1981-82; writer, prodr. WJLA-TV, Washington, 1983-85; advtg. & promotion mgr. KHOU-TV, Houston, 1985-87, dir. creative svcs., 1987-88; dir. broadcast ops. WMAR-TV, Balt., 1988-93, acting gen. mgr., 1993, asst. gen. mgr., 1993-94; pres., gen. mgr. Sta. WTVD, Raleigh, N.C., 1994-97, Sta. WLS-TV, Chgo., 1997—; grad. leadership program Greater Balt. Com., 1990; active NAPTE, 1988—, BPME, 1983-93, CBS Promotion Caucus, 1987-88. Vol. Mus. Broadcast Comms.; bd. dirs. United Cerebral Palsy-Chgo., Children's Meml. Hosp. Found.; commr. Chgo. State St. Commn. Recipient Dante award Joint Civic com. for Italian Americans, 1998. Mem. Ill. Broadcast Assn., Chgo./Midwest TV Acad., Chgo. C. of C. (bd. dirs.), Chgo. Cen. Area Com. (bd. dirs.). Office: 190 N State St Chicago IL 60601-3302

BARR, HOWARD RAYMOND, architect; b. Pitts., Feb. 15, 1910; s. Robert Wesley and Myrtle (Hockensmith) B.; m. Margaret Claire Pressler, Apr. 30, 1938; children: Richard Stuart, Alan Robert. BArch., U. Tex., 1934. Gen. practice architecture Austin, Tex., 1939-42, 46; assoc. Giesecke, Kuehne & Brooks, Architects, 1946-50; ptnr. Kuehne, Brooks & Barr, 1950-60, Brooks & Barr, 1960-65; ptnr. Brooks, Barr, Graeber & White, 1965-73, pres., 1973-77; sr. v.p., dir. 3D/Internat. Inc., 1973-78; prin. Howard R. Barr, Architect-Cons., 1978—. Works include: U.S. Embassy Bldg., Mexico, Manned Spacecraft Ctr., Houston, Lyndon B. Johnson Libr. and Sid Richardson Hall, Austin, U.S. Dept. Labor Bldg., Washington, U. Tex. Med. Sch. and Hermann Teaching Hosp., Houston, S.W. Tex. Med. Sch., U. Tex., San Antonio, FAA Communication Bldgs., San Juan, P.R. and Balboa, C.Z. Assoc. dir. Lifetime Learning Inst., Austin, Tex., 1985-89, dir. 1989-93; mem. City of Austin Parks and Recreation Bd., 1966-70; commr. Tex. Urban Devel. Commn., 1970-72; trustee Tex. Archtl. Found., 1969-75. Lt. comdr. USNR, 1942-46. Fellow AIA (dir. 1974-76); mem. Tex. Soc. Architects (pres. 1969, Llewllyn W. Pitts. award for disting. service to profession 1979), Sphinx, Tau Sigma Delta, Phi Kappa Psi, Headliners Club. Methodist. Home: 4602 Ridge Oak Dr Austin TX 78731-5212 Office: 504 Congress Ave Ste 302 Austin TX 78701-3502

BARR, IRWIN ROBERT, retired aeronautical engineer; b. Newburgh, N.Y., May 16, 1920; s. Abraham Herman and Esther (Reibel) B.; m. Florence Lenore Skliar, Oct. 19, 1941 (dec. Feb. 1957); children: Mary Barr Megee, Betty Barr Mackey, Joan Barr Blanco, Alan Howard; m. Dorothy Friendly Weeks, Sept. 20, 1958. Cert. aero. engring., Inst. Aeros., 1940. Registered profl. engr., Md. Design group engr. Glenn L. Martin Co., Balt., 1940-50; chief ordnance engr., then pres. and chief exec. officer AAI Corp., Hunt Valley, Md., 1950-89; chmn. bd. emeritus AAI Corp., Hunt Valley, 1989—. Patentee rocket stblzn. and control sys., aircraft, weapons, wheels, suspensions, bearings, solar energy collectors, med. catheter, heart pump, aluminum-powered batteries. Served with USAAF, 1944-46. Named to Ordnance Hall of Fame, Aberdeen Proving Ground, Md., 1985. Home: 13801 York Rd Apt C7 Cockeysville Hunt Valley MD 21030-1826

BARR, JAMES, III, telecommunications company executive; b. Oak Park, Ill., Mar. 2, 1940; s. James Jr. and Florence Marie (Erichsen) B.; m. Joan Benning, Aug. 12, 1961; children: James IV, Brett Christopher, Heather Kathryn, Stephanie Alexandra. BS in Engring., Iowa State U., 1962; MBA, U. Chgo., 1967. Engr. Ill. Bell Tel. Co., Chgo., 1962-66, staff mgr. for regulatory affairs, 1966-69; dist. mgr. for planning AT&T, N.Y.C., 1969-72, dir. regulatory affairs, 1975-80; dir. product mgmt. AT&T, Basking Ridge, N.J., 1980-85; sales v.p. AT&T, N.Y.C., 1985-90; gen. mktg. mgr. Bell Can., Ottawa, Ont., 1972-75; pres., CEO, TDS TELECOM, Madison, Wis., 1990—; exec. v.p., bd. dirs. N.Y. Bd. Trade, 1985-90; bd. dirs. Tel. and Data Sys., Chgo., Ctr. for Telecom. Mgmt., L.A., Nat. Rural Tel. Assn., Washington, Aerial Comms., Chgo., TDS TELECOM, Madison, Wis. Mem. dean's adv. coun. Bus. Sch. U. Wis., 1997—. Republican. Roman Catholic. Office: TDS TELECOM 301 S Westfield Rd Madison WI 53717-1799

BARR, JAMES HOUSTON, III, lawyer; b. Louisville, Nov. 2, 1941; s. James Houston Jr. and Elizabeth Hamilton (Pope) B.; m. Sarah Jane Todd, Apr. 16, 1970 (div.); 1 child, Lynn Jamison, m. Cindy Ann Jeffries, May 31, 1997, one child, Worden Washington. Student, U. Va., 1960-63, U. Tenn., 1963-64; BSL, JD, U. Louisville, 1966. Bar: Ky. 1966, U.S. Ct. Appeals (6th cir.) 1969, U.S. Supreme Ct. 1971, U.S. Ct. Mil. Appeals 1978. Law clk. Ky. Ct. Appeals, Frankfort, 1966-67; asst. atty. gen. Ky. Frankfort, 1967-71, 79-82; asst. U.S. atty. U.S. Dept. Justice, Louisville, 1971-79, 83—; 1st asst. U.S. Atty., 1978-79; asst. dir. counsel U.S. Army C.E., Louisville, 1982-83. Lt. comdr. USNR, 1967-81, lt. col. USAR, 1981-91. Mem. Fed. Bar Assn. (pres. Louisville chpt. 1975-76, Younger Fed. Lawyer award 1975), Ky. Bar Assn., Louisville Bar Assn., Soc. Colonial Wars, SAR, Soc. Ky. Pioneers, Pendennis Club, Louisville Boat Club, Filson (Louisville) Club, Delta Upsilon. Republican. Episcopalian. Home: 100 Westwind Rd Louisville KY 40207-1520 Office: US Atty 510 W Broadway Ste 1000 Louisville KY 40202-2281

BARR, JAMES NORMAN, federal judge; b. Kewanee, Ill, Oct. 21, 1940; s. James Cecil and Dorothy Evelyn (Dorsey) B.; m. Trilla Anne Reeves, Oct. 31, 1964 (div. 1979); 1 child, James N. Jr.; m. Phyllis L. DeMent, May 30, 1986; children: Renae, Michele. BS, Ill. Wesleyan U., 1962; JD, Ill. Inst. Tech., 1971. Bar: Ill. 1972, Calif. 1977. Assoc. Pretzel, Stouffer, Nolan & Rooney, Chgo., 1974-76; claims counsel Safeco Title Ins. Co., L.A., 1977-78; assoc. Kamph & Jackman, Santa Ana, Calif., 1978-80; lawyer pvt. practice Law Offices of James N. Barr, Santa Ana, 1980-86; judge U.S Bankruptcy Ct. Ctrl. Dist. Calif., Santa Ana, 1987—; adj. prof. Chapman U. Sch. Law, 1996—. Lt. (s.g.) USN, 1962-67, Vietnam. Mem. Fed. Bar Assn. (Orange County chpt. bd. dirs. 1996—), Orange County Bar Assn. (cmty. outreach com.), Nat. Conf. Bankruptcy Judges, Orange County Bankruptcy Forum (bd. dirs. 1989—), Peter M. Elliott Inn Ct. (founder, first pres. 1990-91). Office: US Bankruptcy Ct 411 West 4th St Santa Ana CA 92701-4593

BARR, JOHN BALDWIN, chemist, research scientist; b. Niagara Falls, N.Y., Nov. 8, 1932; s. Lorne Haworth and Myra (Baldwin) B.; m. Patricia Jane Kromer, Sept. 18, 1954; children: Mark Kromer, John Robert, Kathryn Jean, Karen Patricia. BA, U. Buffalo, 1954; MS, U. Mich., 1956; PhD, Pa. State U., 1961. Rsch. chemist Corning Glass Works (N.Y.), 1961-62; sr. rsch. chemist Union Carbide Corp., Parma, Ohio, 1962-71; rsch. scientist Union Carbide Corp., Parma, 1971-82, sr. rsch. scientist, 1982-86; sr. rsch. scientist Amoco Performance Products, Parma, 1986-90, Alpharetta, Ga., 1990-91; assoc. rsch. scientist Amoco Performance Products, Alpharetta, 1991-95; cons. Rsch. Opportunities, Inc., Torrance, Calif., 1996—. Contbr. articles to profl. jours.; patentee in field. Shell Oil Co. fellow, 1959. Mem. Am. Chem. Soc., Am. Carbon Soc., N.Am. Thermal Analysis Soc., Sigma Xi, Phi Lambda Upsilon. Republican. Episcopalian.

BARR, JOHN MICHAEL, investor, training and management consultant; b. Columbus, Ohio, May 13, 1957; s. William Harvey and Mary Louise (Chesser) B.; m. Mary Elizabeth Mudd, Sept. 4, 1982. BA in History, Polit. Sci., Ohio Dominican Coll., 1979; MA in Polit. Sci., Ohio State U., 1980. Tchr. pub. schs., 1981-88; secondary edn. educator Whitehall City Schs., 1981-83, South Western City Schs., 1983-88; profl. investor, speaker, cons., mediator/arbitrator Westerville, Ohio, 1988—. Mem. Rep. Nat. 500 Club, Washington, 1991, Franklin County Reps., Columbus, 1990, Rep. Nat. Campaign Coun., 1988—, Ohio Rep. Party, 1993—; mem. Rep. Presdl. Task Force. Mem. ASTD, Am. Assn. Individual Investors (life), NRA (life, chmn. second amend. task force 1993—), Internat. Platform Assn., Mkt. Technicians Assn., soc. for Profls. in Dispute Resolution, Japan Aikido Assn. (life), Internat. Listening Assn. Methodist. Avocations: shooting, aikido, travel, poetry. Office: PO Box 506 Westerville OH 43086-0506

BARR, JOHN MONTE, lawyer; b. Mt. Clemens, Mich., Jan. 1, 1935; s. Merle James and Wilhelmina Marie (Monte) B.; student Mexico City Coll., 1955; BA, Mich. State U., 1956; JD, U. Mich., 1959; m. Marlene Joy Bielenberg, Dec. 17, 1954; children: John Monte, Karl Alexander, Elizabeth Marie. Admitted to Mich. bar, 1959, since practiced in Ypsilanti; mem. Ellis B. Freatman, Jr., 1959-61; ptnr., chief trial atty. Freatman, Barr, Anhut & Moir and predecessor firm, 1961-63; pres. Barr, Anhut, Assoc. PC, 1963-94; pres. Barr, Anhut & Assocs., 1994—; city atty. City of Ypsilanti, 1981. Lectr. bus. law Eastern Mich. U., 1968-70. Pres., Ypsilanti Family Service, 1967; mem. Ypsilanti Public Housing Com., 1980-84; sr. adviser Explorer law post Portage Trail council Boy Scouts Am., 1969-71, commr. Potawatomi dist., 1973-74, commr. Washtenong dist., 1974-75, dist. committeeman, 1984, wolverine coun. v.p., 1992, v.p. Great Saulk Trail coun., 1995—; bd. dirs. Mich. Mcpl. League Legal Def. Fund., pres. 1989-90. Served with USAF, 1959-60. Recipient Silver Beaver award Boy Scouts Am., 1992, Mich. Mcpl. League award of Merit Mcpl. League Legal Def., 1992. Mem. State Bar Mich. (grievance bd. hearing panel 1969-97, state rep. assembly 1977-82, bd. commrs. 1993—), Am., Ypsilanti, Washtenaw County (pres. 1975-76, Profl. and Civility award 1998) Bar Assns., Washtenaw County Trial Lawyers Assns., Mich. Mcpl. Attys. Assn. (pres. 1989-90, MAMA dist. mcpl. atty. award, 1993), U.S. (instr. piloting, seamanship, sail), Ann Arbor (comdr. 1972-73) power squadrons. Lutheran. Club: Washtenaw Country. Contbr. articles to boating mags. Home: 1200 Whittier Rd Ypsilanti MI 48197-2152 Office: 105 Pearl St Ypsilanti MI 48197-2611

BARR, JOHN ROBERT, lawyer; b. Gary, Ind., Apr. 10, 1936; s. John Andrew and Louise (Stentz) B.; m. Patricia A. Ferris, July 30, 1988; children: Mary Louise, John Mills, Jennifer Susan. BA, Grinnell Coll., 1957; LL.B. cum laude, Harvard U., 1960. Bar: Ill. 1960. Assoc. Sidley & Austin, Chgo., 1960-69, ptnr., 1970—; mem. Ill. Ho. of Reps., 1981-83, Commn. on Presdl. Scholars, Washington, 1975-77; mem. Ill. Electric Utility Property Assessment Task Force, 1998-99. Chmn. Ill. Bd. Regents, 1971-77; mem. Ill. Bd. Higher Edn., 1971-77, 87—; chmn. Ill. Student Assistance Commn., 1985—; chmn. Rep. Ctrl. Com. of Cook County, Chgo., 1978-85; mem. Rep. state ctrl. com. 9th Congl. Dist. Ill., 1986-93; trustee Grinnell Coll., 1996—; bd. dirs. Steppenwolf Theatre Co., Chgo., 1992—; vestry mem. St. Mark's Ch. Mem. ABA (chmn. task force on utility deregulation of state and local tax coms.), Ill. State Bar Assn. (chmn. state tax sect. coun. 1986-87), Chgo. Bar Assn. (chmn. com. on state and mcpl. taxation 1974-75), Taxpayers' Fedn. Ill. (treas. 1990-92, vice chmn. 1992-95, chmn. 1995-97), The Civic Fedn. (bd. dirs. 1993-97), Selden Soc., Nat. Assn. State Bar Tax Sects. (sec.-treas. 1989-90, vice chmn. 1990-91, chmn. 1991-92), Inst. Profls. in Taxation, Emil Verban Soc., Law Club, Legal Club Chgo., Chgo. Club, Phi Beta Kappa. Episcopalian. Home: 1144 Asbury Ave Evanston IL 60202-1137 Office: Sidley & Austin 1 First Natl Plz Chicago IL 60603-2003

BARR, KENNETH L., mayor; b. Fort Worth, TX, 1942; s. Willard B.; married; 1 daughter. BBA, Tex. Christian U., postgrad. With The Barr Printers, now pres., CEO; mem. Ft. Worth Transp. Authority, chair, 1992-93; mem. City Coun. for the Near South Side Coun. Dist.; mayor City of Ft. Worth, 1996—. Mem., elder Univ. Christian Ch.; bd. dirs. Dallas-Ft. Worth Internat. Airport, Casa Manana Theater, The Gladney Fund; chair Work Force Devel. Bd., Strategy 2000 Bd.; former bd. dirs. Lena Pope Home Bd., Child Study Ctr. Bd. Recipient Rotary Found. Paul Harris fellow. Mem. Printing Industry Assn.-Tex. CEO Roundtable (organizing mem., bd. rep.). Address: Office of the Mayor 1000 Throckmorton St Fort Worth TX 76102-6311*

BARR, KEVIN CURTIS, poet; b. Cin., Sept. 26, 1963; s. Fred Curtis Sutton and Betty Jane B. Pvt. security officer Pinkerton Security Co., Cin., 1994—. Author: (poetry books) My Love Is, 1997, Once Sprinkled By A Saintly Tear, 1997, Oh Chaka Fame Tonite, 1998, The Red Eagle Soars from Heaven, 1998. Recipient Cert. of achievement Talent Search Am., Nashville, 1994, Cert. of merit Nashville Newsletter, 1996. Avocations: creating comic book characters, dancing, beginning novelist. Home: 1111 Elm St Apt 520 Cincinnati OH 45210-2257

BARR, MARI R., federal agency administrator. BS, U. Wis., Stevens Point, 1975; Master's degree, U. Wis., Oshkosh, 1976. Various positions, ending with chancellor's office U. Wis., Green Bay, 1979-93; sr. advisor to sec. U.S. Dept. HUD, Washington, 1993-97, dep. asst. sec. human resources, 1997—. Office: Dept of the Interior Human Resources Dept 1849 C St NW Washington DC 20240

BARR, MARTIN, health care and higher education administrator; b. Phila., Nov. 11, 1925; s. Louis and Bella (Moskowitz) B.; m. Nancy Lipschutz, July 15, 1951; children: Lawrence Allen, Richard Andrew, Debra Ann, Steven Bruce. B.Sc. in Pharmacy, Temple U., 1946; M.Sc. in Pharmacy, Phila. Coll. Pharmacy and Scis., 1947; Ph.D., Ohio State U., 1950. Grad. asst., then instr. Ohio State U. Coll. Pharmacy, 1947-50; from asst. prof. pharmacy to prof. phys. pharmacy and pharm. research Phila. Coll. Pharmacy and Sci., 1950-61; prof. pharmaceutics Wayne State U. Coll. Pharmacy, 1961-87, prof. emeritus, 1987—, chmn. dept., 1961-63, dean, 1963-72, v.p. spl. assignments, 1972-76, v.p., sec. to bd. govs., 1976-78, sec. to bd. govs., acting v.p. for health affairs, 1978-80, v.p., dep. provost, 1980-82, dean Coll. Pharmacy and Allied Health Professions, 1982-87; exec. v.p. corp. bus. and med. devel. Mich. Health Care Corp., Detroit, 1987-90, v.p. bd., profl. rels., 1990-92, v.p. continuous quality improvement, 1992-95; cons. HEW, 1964-69. Contbg. author: Pharmacy, Compounding and Dispensing, 2d edit, 1956, Remington's Practice of Pharmacy, 11th edit, 1956, 12th edit., 1965; Profl. editor: Mid-Atlantic Apothecary, 1953-64, Apothecary, 1953-64, Central Pharm. Jour, 1961-64. Chmn. Mayor's Com. for Narcotics Rehab., Detroit, 1971-73; pres. Oakland County unit Mich. Heart Assn., 1970-72. Recipient Disting. Service award, Disitng. Alumnus award Alumni Assn. Coll. Pharmacy, Temple U., 1957, Disting. Alumnus award Temple U., 1964, Alpha Zeta Omega award, 1979, Meritorious Service award Wayne State U. Pharm. Alumni Assn., Ann. Alumus award Phila. Coll. Pharmacy and Sci., 1983, John H. Webster award Met. Detroit Pharmacist Assn., 1985, Disting. alumnus award Pharmacy Alumni Assn., 1987, Jack L. Beal Postbaccalaureate award Ohio State U. Coll. Pharmacy Alumni Assn., 1989, Disting. Svc. award Wayne State U. Pharmacy Alumni Assn., 1993. Fellow Am. Coll. Apothecaries, Acad. Pharm. Scis.; mem. Am. Pharm. Assn. (pres. Phila. 1954-55, chmn. sci. sect. 1959-60, Ebert medal 1956), Am. Soc. Hosp. Pharmacists, Mich. State Pharm. Assn. (pharmacist of yr. 1971), Am. Assn. Colls. Pharmacy (chmn. sect. tchrs. pharmacy 1959-60, chmn. conf. tchrs. pharmacy 1961-62), Detroit Occupational Therapy Assn. (advocate award 1995), Sigma Xi, Rho Chi. Home: 7430 Tall Timbers West Bloomfield MI 48322-1082

BARR, MAURICE ALAN, elementary education educator; b. Hazelhurst, Miss., Dec. 31, 1951; s. Robert Guiton and Mavis (Mitchem) B.; m. Marcella Isabel Palma, Dec. 19, 1981; 1 child, Alan Maurice. AS, Modesto (Calif.) Jr. Coll., 1978; BS, Calif. Christian Coll., 1981; MDiv, Mennonite Brethren Bibl. Sem., 1988. Mid. sch. tchr. Reef-Sunset Unified Sch. Dist., Avenal, Calif., 1992—, coach mid. sch., 1993-95, mem. curriculum and instrn. coun., dist. math. chmn., 1994-96, opportunity tchr., 1997-99. Elder Presbyn. Ch., 1999-01. Mem. West Kings County Tchrs. Assn. (pres. 1995-96, negotiator 1995-96), Mariners (chaplain 1995-96). Avocations: gardening, computing, golfing, chaplain, deacon. Office: Reef-Sunset Middle Sch 608 N 1st Ave Avenal CA 93204-1071

BARR, M.E. See BIGELOW, MARGARET ELIZABETH BARR

BARR, MICHAEL BLANTON, lawyer; b. Freeport, N.Y., July 24, 1948; s. Harry Kyle and Rosemary (Blanton) B.; m. Nancy Nickeson, Aug. 11, 1979; children: Nicholas Upton, Jessica Nickeson, Alice Primrose. B.S., Georgetown U., 1970; J.D., George Washington U., 1973. Bar: D.C. 1973. U.S. Dist. Ct. D.C. 1973, U.S. Ct. Appeals (D.C. cir.) 1974, U.S. Ct. Appeals (3d cir.) 1979, U.S. Ct. Appeals, (4th cir.) 1976, U.S. Ct. Appeals (6th cir.) 1981, U.S. Supreme Ct. 1980. Assoc. LeBoeuf, Lamb, Lieby & McRae, Washington, 1973-76, Hunton & Williams, Washington, 1976-80; ptnr. Hunton & Williams, Washington, 1980—, mng. ptnr. Washington office, 1985—. Contbr. articles to profl. jours. Bd. trustees Georgetown Day Sch.; bd. dirs. Am. Sch. of Tangier, Morocco, 1989—. Mem. ABA, Internat. Bar Assn., D.C. Bar Assn. Clubs: City Tavern (Washington), Union League (N.Y.). Home: 8004 Glendale Rd Chevy Chase MD 20815-5903 Office: Hunton & Williams 1900 K St NW Washington DC 20006

BARR, MICHAEL CHARLES, securities trader; b. White Plains, N.Y., Nov. 2, 1947; s. Charles Yerger and Joan Tames (Biggar) B.; m. Helen June Rumsey, Mar. 17, 1973. Student, Washington and Lee U.; BA summa cum laude, Rutgers Coll., 1969; JD, Columbia U., 1972, MBA, 1980. Bar: N.J. 1976, N.Y. 1978, U.S. Supreme Ct. 1976. Assoc. McCarter & English, Newark, 1976-77, Conboy, Hewitt, O'Brien & Boardman, N.Y.C., 1977-78; investment banker Kidder, Peabody & Co., Inc., N.Y.C., 1980-82; v.p. Mfrs. Hanover Trust Co., N.Y.C., 1982-90, A-L Assocs., N.Y.C., 1990-92; corp. sec., dir. H. Rivkin & Co., Inc., N.Y.C., 1992-93; securities analyst Standard & Poor's Corp., N.Y.C., 1993-98; Russian securities specialist H. Rivkin & Co., Inc., N.Y.C., 1998-99; emerging markets specialist HP Capital Mkts. Group, N.Y.C., 1999—. Adv. bd. Washington and Lee Alumni Coll., 1996-98. Lt. USN, 1972-76. Recipient Loyal Son award Rutgers Alumni Assn., 1976. Mem. U.S. Polo Assn., Phi Beta Kappa. Office: HP Capital Mkts Group 100 Wall St New York NY 10005

BARR, RICHARD STUART, computer science and management science educator; b. Austin, Tex., Sept. 3, 1943; s. Howard Raymond and Margaret (Pressler) B.; m. Mary Shipp Sanders, Mar. 10, 1990; 1 child, Jonathan Austin. BSEE, U. Tex., 1966, MBA, 1972, PhD, 1978. Assoc. dir. Coll. of Bus. Computer Ctr. U. Tex., Austin, 1968-72; exec. v.p. Analysis, Rsch. & Computation, Inc., Austin, 1975-76; asst. prof. mgmt. info. scis. So. Meth. U., Dallas, 1976-80, assoc. prof., 1980-84, assoc. prof. ops. rsch. and engring. mgmt., 1984-89, assoc. prof. computer sci. and engring., 1989—, dir. parallel processing lab., 1989-97, dir. telecomm. mgmt. rsch. lab., 1997—; pres. Telsoft Techs., Inc., Dallas, 1996—; cons. Dept. Treas., Dept. Agr., Dept. Health and Human Svcs.; vis. fellow Dept. Treas., 1977-78; vis. scholar, Princeton (N.J.) U., 1984, U. Colo., Boulder, 1992. Assoc. editor Jour. of Heuristics, Jour. on Computing; contbr. articles to profl. jours. Recipient Rsch. Excellence award So. Meth. U. Sch. Bus., 1980, Outstanding Grad. Instr. award, 1983; named Outstanding Instr., Nat. Tech. U., 1991, 92, 93, 94, 95, 96, 97, 98.; grantee NSF, 1993—. Mem. Inst. for Ops. Rsch. and Mgmt. Scis., INFORMS (assoc. editor jour.), Computing Soc. (chmn.). Home: 6812 Velasco Ave Dallas TX 75214-3763 Office: So Meth U Sch Engring and Applied Scis Dallas TX 75275

BARR, ROBERT LAURENCE, JR., congressman, lawyer; b. Iowa City, Iowa, Nov. 5, 1948; s. Robert Laurence and Beatrice Emily (Radenhausen) B.; children: Adrian Robert, Derek Ryan; m. Jerilyn Dobbin, Dec. 31, 1986. BA in Internat. Rels., U. So. Calif., 1972; JD, Georgetown U., 1977. Bar: Ga. 1977, Fla. 1979. Analyst, atty., chief legis. staff CIA, Washington, 1970-78; assoc. Law Offices of Edwin Marger, Atlanta, 1979-81; pvt. practice Marietta, Ga., 1981-85, 91-94; ptnr. Brock & Barr, Marietta, 1985-86; U.S. atty. for No. Ga., 1986-90; mem. 104th Congresses from 7th Ga. dist. U.S. Ho. of Reps., Washington, 1995—; mem. banking and fin. svcs., govt. reform and oversight, judiciary and vets. affairs coms.; gen. counsel Cobb County Republican Com., 1981-83, 1st vice-chmn., 1983-85, chmn. 85-86; pres. Southeastern Legal Found., Atlanta, 1990-91; bd. dirs. Met. Atlanta Coun. Alcohol and Drugs, 1989-91. Mem. editl. staff Am. Criminal Law Rev., 1974-77. Mem. Ga. Bar Assn., Fla. Bar Assn., Cobb County Bar Assn., Atlanta Bar Assn., Kiwanis, Phi Alpha Delta, Delta Phi Epsilon. Methodist. Home: 631 Concord Rd SW Smyrna GA 30082-4409 Office: US Ho of Reps 1130 Longworth Bldg Washington DC 20515-1007*

BARR, ROGER TERRY, sculptor; b. Milw., Sept. 17, 1921; s. Clinton Marion and Helen Inez (Barry) B.; m. Helena Brinton May, 1947 (div. 1953); m. Beryl Sharrar, July 4, 1959 (div. 1970); m. Elizabeth Gunn Quandt, Dec. 23, 1971 (dec. Dec. 1994). Student, U. Wis., 1939-41, 42, Nat. U. Mexico, 1941; B.A., Pomona Coll., 1947; M.F.A., Claremont Grad. Sch., 1949; postgrad., Jepson Art Inst., L.A., 1949-50, Atelier 17, Paris, 1957, Sorbonne, 1962-63. Instr. UCLA, 1950-52, San Francisco Art Inst., 1954-56; founding dir. Coll. Art Study Abroad, Paris, 1959-69; prof. Am. Coll. in Paris, 1962-69; prof., chmn. dept. art Calif. State U., Hayward, 1969-70. Represented in collections at, Hirshhorn Mus. and Sculpture Garden, Smithsonian Instn., Washington, Mus. Fine Arts, Boston, Nat. Art Mus., Goteborg, Sweden, San Francisco Mus. Modern Art, Mus. Fine Art, Sao Paulo, Brazil, Mus. Art Richmond, Va., U.S. Steel Corp., Pitts., other public and pvt. collections.; Important works include monumental sculpture in marble, Symposium Forma Viva, Portoroz, Yugoslavia, 1968, fountain/sculpture in welded bronze, Chamber of Commerce Plaza, Santa Rosa, 1975, Arch/Flight One, state office bldg., Redding, Calif.; commn. by Art in Pub. Bldgs. Program, Office State Architect Calif., 1978-79; stainless steel sculpture, commn. by State Printing Facility, Salem, Oreg., 1981, wind kinetic sculpture, Santa Rosa Bus. Park, Calif., 1981, fountain/sculpture, Civic/Conv. Ctr., Anchorage, Alaska, wind kinetic 12-piece sculpture, Ravenwood Sch., Eagle River, Alaska, 1983-84, two story stainless steel waterfront sculpture, San Francisco, 1985, Union Bank, San Ramon, 1986; solo exhbn. Victor Fischer Gallery, Oakland, 1984, San Francisco, 1988, Gallery 30, Burlingame, Calif., 1990, Bay Area Rapid Transit ctrl. station, Oakland, Calif., 1988, Chapman U. Collection, 1987, Kaiser-Permanente Med. Ctr., Petaluma, Calif., 1988, Cen. Corp. Ctr., Riverside, Calif., 1989, Catellus Corp., Santa Fe Springs, Calif., 1991, Santa Rosa Jr. Coll., 1994, Pomona Coll., 1997; Phoenix Trio, 3-part 18' windwands private collection Beaulieu-Sur-Mer, France, illustrator: Answer in the Affirmative and the Oldest Man (M.F.K. Fisher) 1963, The Conversion of the Jews (Philip Roth), Epstein (Philip Roth), The Peacocks of Avignon (Harvey Swados), Fernand le Flic; illustrator: (book) Memoirs of a Tourist (Stendahl); lectr., numerous univs., colls. and schs. art. Served to lt. USNR, 1942-46. Catherwood Found. fellow in Europe, 1956; Djerassi Found. fellow, 1984. Home and Office: 52720 Avenida Carranza La Quinta CA 92253-3128*

BARR, RONALD JEFFREY, dermatologist, pathologist; b. Mpls., Jan. 5, 1945; s. Maxwell Michael and Ethel Deana (Ring) B.; m. Ulla Elisabet Edstam; children: Anna, Jessica, Sara. BA, Johns Hopkins U., 1967, MD, 1970. Diplomate Am. Bd. Pathology, Am. Bd. Dermatology. Intern U. Calif., San Diego, 1970-71, resident in pathology, 1971-75; resident in dermatology U. Calif., Irvine, 1975-78, fellow in dermatopathology, 1975-78, asst. prof. dermatology, 1977-83, assoc. prof. dermatology and pathology, 1983-86, prof. dermatology and pathology, 1987—, dir. Dermatopathology Lab., 1979—; prof., chmn. dept. dermatology U. Calif., Davis, 1986-87; bd. dirs. Am. Bd. Dermatology, 1989—, pres., 1997. Contbr. more than 10 chpts. to books. more than 100 articles to profl. jours. Lt. USN, 1971-73. Fellow Am. Soc. Dermatopathology (pres. 1988-89); mem. Internat. Soc. Dermatopathology (exec. com.), Internat. Com. for Dermatopathology (sec.-treas. 1987-91, pres. 1992-93). Office: U Calif Irvine Med Ctr Dermatopathology Lab 101 The City Dr S Orange CA 92868-3201

BARR, SANFORD LEE, dentist; b. Chgo., Jan. 18, 1952; s. Mike and Bernice (Kaplan) B.; m. Randy Joyce Briskman, Dec. 24, 1973; children: Shelby Paige, Blake Jared, Taylor Ashley. BS, U. Ill., 1972; DDS, Northwestern U., 1976. Resident gen. practice VA Hosp., Chgo., 1976-77; gen. practice dentistry Chgo., 1977—; attending dentist Rush Med. Coll., Chgo., 1977—; asst. prof. Presbyn.-St. Luke's Hosp., Chgo., 1977—, Northwestern U. Sch. Dentistry, Chgo., 1977-83; cons. VA Hosp., Chgo., 1978—. Mem. adv. bd. Homehealth of Ill. Chgo., 1984—. Fellow Acad. Gen. Dentistry, Acad. Facial Aesthetics; mem. ADA, Acad. Hosp. Dentistry, Chgo. Dental Soc., Alpha Omega (treas. 1984, pres. elect 1988), Tau Delta Phi. Jewish. Lodge: B'nai B'rith (v.p. Chgo. chpt. 1984—). Avocations: computers, photography, golf, baseball. Home: 632 Dauphine Ct Northbrook IL 60062-2256 Office: 25 E Washington St Chicago IL 60602-1708

BARR, SOLOMON EFREM, allergist; b. Washington, Mar. 24, 1929; s. Barney and Jennie Florence (Brickman) B.; B.A. (Emma K. Carr scholar 1948-49; Maria M. Carter scholar), George Washington U., 1951, M.D., 1954; m. Rita Zeasla Cohan, June 20, 1954; children—Linda, Steven, Carol, Sharon. Intern, Phila. Gen. Hosp., 1954-55; resident D.C. Gen. Hosp., 1957-58, George Washington U., 1959-60; practice medicine specializing in allergies, Silver Spring, Md., 1960-78, Rockville, Md., 1978—; mem. staff Holy Cross Hosp., George Washington U.; asso. clin. prof. medicine George Washington U. Sch. Medicine. Served as capt. M.C., U.S. Army, 1955-57. Recipient Freshman award in chemistry Alpha Chi Sigma, 1948, award in Chemistry, Sigma Kappa, 1948, John Ordronaux award in medicine George Washington U., 1954; diplomate Am. Bd. Internal Medicine, Am. Bd. Allergy and Immunology. Fellow Am. Acad. Allergy, A.C.P., Am. Coll. Allergists, Am. Assn. Cert. Allergists; mem. Washington Allergy Soc., Montgomery County, Md. State med. socs., AMA (Physician's Recognition award 1974-77, 77-80), Smith-Reed-Russell, William Beaumont, Jacobi Med. Soc. Washington, Phi Beta Kappa, Alpha Omega Alpha. Club: Phi Delta Epsilon Grad. of Washington (pres. 1971-72). Contbr. articles to med. publs., most recent on insect sting allergy. Home: 5713 Magic Mountain Dr Rockville MD 20852-3233 Office: 121 Congressional Ln Rockville MD 20852-1542

BARR, THOMAS D., lawyer; b. Kansas City, Mo., Jan. 23, 1931; m. Cornelia Harrington, Sept. 26, 1953; children: Daniel C., Phoebe Anne Hotz, Robert A., Sara E. B.A., U. Mo., Kansas City, 1953; LL.B., Yale U., 1958. Bar: N.Y. State 1959, U.S. Supreme Ct. 1964. Assoc. firm Cravath, Swaine, & Moore, N.Y.C., 1958-65; ptnr. firm Cravath, Swaine, & Moore, 1965—; bd. dirs. Salzburg Seminar. Dep. dir. Nat. Commn. on Causes and Prevention of Violence, 1968-70; mem. exec. com. Lawyers' Com. for Civil Rights Under Law, nat. co-chmn., 1977-79; trustee Milton S. Eisenhower Found. Served to lt. USMC, 1953-55. Mem. Am., N.Y. State Bar Assn., Assn. Bar of City of N.Y., Am. Coll. Trial Lawyers, Internat. Acad. Trial Lawyers, Am. Bar Found., Am. Law Inst., Coun. Fgn. Rels. Home: 18 Meadowcroft Ln Greenwich CT 06830-3823 Office: Cravath Swaine & Moore Worldwide Pla 825 8th Ave Fl 38 New York NY 10019-7475

BARR, WILLIAM PELHAM, lawyer, former attorney general of United States; b. N.Y.C., May 23, 1950; s. Donald and Mary (Ahern) B.; m. Christine Moynihan, June 23, 1973; 3 children. AB, Columbia U., 1971, MA, 1973; JD, George Washington U., 1977. Bar: Va. 1977, D.C. 1978. Staff officer CIA, Washington, 1973-77; law clk. to presiding judge Cir. Ct., Washington, 1977-78; assoc. Shaw, Pittman, Potts & Trowbridge, Washington, 1978-82, 83-84, ptnr., 1985-89, 93—; dep. asst. dir. domestic policy staff The White House, Washington, 1982-83; asst. atty. gen. Office Legal Counsel, U.S. Dept. Justice, Washington, 1989-90, dep. atty. gen., 1990-91, atty. gen., 1991-93; exec. v.p., gen. counsel G.T.E. Corp., Washington, 1994—. Mem. ABA, Va. State Bar Assn., D.C. Bar Assn., KC. Republican. Roman Catholic. Office: GTE Corp 1850 M St NW 1200 Washington DC 20036*

BARR, WILLIAM ROBERT, industrial engineer, consultant; b. Detroit, Oct. 25, 1947; s. Robert Webb and Marion (Squire) B.; m. Diane Gayle Buddemeier, June 25, 1988 (dec.). BSIE, U. Mich., 1970, MSIE, 1974; MBA, Western Mich. U., 1977. Registered profl. engr., Mich. Indsl. engr. Upjohn Co., Kalamazoo, 1974-82; program mgr. Kellogg Co., Battle Creek, Mich., 1982-91; pres. William Barr Assoc. Inc., Augusta, 1991—; instr. Western Mich. U., Kalamazoo, 1980-92. Contbr. articles to profl. jours. Active ordinance com. Ross Twp., Mich., 1987, chmn. road improvement com., 1989, active zoning bd., 1995-99. With U.S. Army, 1972-73. Mem. NSPE, Inst. Indsl. Engrs. (chpt. officer 1995—), Indsl. and Ops. Engring. Acad. U. Mich., Alpha Pi Mu, Tau Beta Pi. Achievements include the development of computer model for the analysis of capacity in production facilities. Avocations: backpacking, tennis, cross-country skiing. Office: William Barr Assoc Inc PO Box 507 Augusta MI 49012-0507

BARRACANO, HENRY RALPH, retired oil company executive, consultant; b. Bklyn., Apr. 8, 1926; s. Ralph Henry and Josephine (Chianese) B.; m. Dorothy Sue Bartlow, Aug. 19, 1945; children: Ralph Robert, Susan Jo Barracano Ratterree, Linda Joyce Barracano Swartz. BSEE, Pa. State U., 1948. Registered profl. engr., Okla. Distbn. engr. Pub. Svc. Co. Okla., Tulsa, 1948-51; elec. engr. W.R. Holway & Assocs., Tulsa, 1951-56; from staff engr. to asst. to sr. v.p. engring. and constrn. Arabian Am. Oil Co., 1956-83; ind. cons., 1983-89; sr. project mgr. Hudson Engring. and Project Mgmt. Corp., 1990-91; ind. cons., 1992—; mem. grievance com. State Bar Tex., 1994-99; arbitrator NASD, 1994—. Precinct chair Dem. Party, Harris County, Tex., 1984-98; precinct judge Harris County, 1984-90. 1st Lt. Signal Corps U.S. Army, 1943-59. Named Outstanding Engring. Alumnus, Pa. State U., 1993, Alumni Fellow award, 1997, Pa. State Pioneer, 1998. Mem. IEEE (life sr. mem., various offices held), Petroleum Club Houston (resident mem.), Northgate Country Club. Avocations: tennis, traveling. Home and Office: 7723 Allegro Dr Houston TX 77040-2508

BARRACK, WILLIAM SAMPLE, JR., petroleum company executive; b. Pitts., July 26, 1929; s. William Sample and Edna Mae (Henderson) B. B.S., U. Pitts., 1950; postgrad., Dartmouth Coll. With Texaco, Inc., N.Y., 1953—; mktg. mgr. Northeast Texaco, Inc., 1953-62; dist. mgr. Texaco, Inc., Portland, Maine, 1962-65; asst. mgr. distbn. and devel. Texaco, Inc., N.Y., 1965-66, asst. mgr. mktg. research and project devel., 1966-67; asst. div. mgr. Texaco, Inc., Norfolk, Va., 1967-68; area dir. Texaco, Inc., Brussels, Belgium, 1968-70; v.p. Texaco Europe Ltd., N.Y., 1970; asst. to chmn. bd. Texaco, Inc., N.Y.C., 1971; v.p. internat. Europe Texaco, Inc., 1971-76, v.p. producing Eastern hemisphere, 1976-77; v.p. personnel and corp. services Texaco, Inc., White Plains, N.Y., 1977-80; chmn., chief exec. officer Texaco Ltd., London, Eng., 1980-83; sr. v.p. Texaco Inc., White Plains, N.Y., 1983-92, ret., 1992; bd. dirs. Standard Comml. Corp., Wilson, N.C., Consol. Natural Gas Co., Pitts.; mem. Naval War Coll. Found., Newport, R.I.; bd. vis. U. Pitts. Sch. Engring.; dir. Arabian Am. Oil Co., 1977-78; sr. dir. Caltex Petroleum Corp., 1983-92. Trustee Manhattanville Coll.; bd. dirs. Texaco Found. Inc., Mary Rose Soc., Disting. Alumni U. Pitts., Internat. Exec. Svc. Corps. Comdr. USNR, 1951-53. Mem. Fgn. Policy Assn. N.Y. (gov.). Clubs: N.Y. Yacht; Ida Lewis Yacht; North Sea Yacht (Belgium); Woodway Country, Ox Ridge Hunt; Clambake (Newport, R.I.); Australian (Sydney), 25 Yr. Club of The Petroleum Industry; The Pa. Soc.

BARRAGÁN, CELIA SILGUERO, elementary education educator; b. Corcoran, Calif., Feb. 4, 1955; d. Frutoso Silguero and Olinda Gonzalez S.; m. Mario Barragan Jr., Nov. 12, 1977; children: Maricela Aimé, Mario Armando. BS, S.W. Tex. State U., 1976, MA, 1977. 3d grade tchr. Crockett Elem. Sch., San Marcos, Tex., 1977-78; 3 grade tchr. Bowie Elem. Sch., San Marcos, 1978-84; 5th grade tchr. Travis Elem. Sch., San Marcos, 1984-85, 86-94, Hernandez Intermediate Sch., San Marcos, 1994—; asst. prin., bilingual coord. Bonham Elem. Sch., San Marcos, 1985-86, title I reading tchr., trainer, cons., 1995-96; cons., trainer Language Circle, Minn.; Winter High ability program tchr. S.W. Tex. State U.; project read trainer Spanish Translator San Marcos Consolidated Schs., project math trainer; migrant tchr., Princeville, Ill. S.W. Tex. State U. grant, 1998-99; recipient Latino award for cmty. recognition S.W. Tex. State U. Mem. Internat. Reading Assn., Tex. Reading Assn., Tex. State Tchrs. Assn., Tex. Assn. Bilingual Edn., Tex. Classroom Tchrs. Assn., San Marcos (Tex.) Assn. Bilingual Edn. (v.p. 1990-91, 94—, pres. 1995—, Bilingual Tchr. of Yr. 1991, Travis Elem. Tchr. of Yr. 1993, Hernandez Intermediate Tchr. of Yr. 1995, Secondary Tchr. of Yr. 1995), Orton Dyslexia Soc., Nat. Coun. Tchrs. Math., Tex. Assn. Bilingual Educators. Roman Catholic. Home: 301 N Edward Gary St # 255 San Marcos TX 78666-5707 Office: Hernandez Intermediate 333 Stagecoach Trl San Marcos TX 78666-5028

BARRAGE, BILLY MICHAEL, judge; b. Durant, Okla., June 9, 1950. BSBA, Southeastern State U., 1971. Bar: Okla. 1980, U.S. Dist. Ct. (ea. dist.) Okla. 1980, U.S. Ct. Appeals (10th cir.) 1980, U.S. Supreme Ct. 1982, U.S. Dist. Ct. (no. dist.) Okla. 1993. Legal intern, 1974-75; assoc. Stamper & Otis, 1975-93; ptnr. Stamper, Otis & Burrage, 1982-94. Contbr. articles to profl. jours. Fellow Okla. Bar Found. (trustee); mem. ABA, Okla. Bar Assn. (v.p., pres. 1990), Pushmataha County Bar Assn. Office: US Courthouse 5th & Okmulgee St PO Box 2999 Muskogee OK 74402-2999*

BARRAM, DAVID J., federal agency administrator. BA, Wheaton Coll., 1965; MBA, Santa Clara U., 1973. Staff acct. Price Waterhouse & Co., Boston, 1965-66; various fin. and mktg. positions Hewlett-Packard, 1970-83, contr. computer products group; v.p. fin. and adminstrn., CFO Silicon Graphics, Inc., 1983-85; v.p. fin., CFO, then v.p. corp. comm. Apple Computer, Inc., 1985-93; dep. sec. Dept. Commerce, Washington, 1993-95; adminstr. GSA, Washington, 1996—. Chair Calif. Commn. Pub. Sch. Adminstrs. and Leadership; bd. dirs. Nat. Ctr. Edn. and Economy. With USN, 1966-69. Recipient Disting. Svc. award Assn. Calif. Sch. Adminstrs. Office: General Services Administration Office of the Administrator 1800 F St NW Washington DC 20405-0002

BARRAT, MARTINE, photographer, videographer, filmmaker. lectr. Internat. Ctr. Photography, N.Y.C. Author: Do or Die, 1993; filmmaker, photographer video series You Do the Crime, You Do the Time, 1978; photography appeared in N.Y. Times Mag., Life, Vanity Fair, Village Voice, French Vogue, Paris Match, Le Monde Libération, Switch, Merian, Die Zeit, Süddeutsche Zeitung (Germany); one-woman shows include 9 city exhbn.. throughout Germany; exhibited in group shows at Nat. Mus. Lyon, 1994, Mus. City N.Y., 1995, Nat. Mus. Copenhagen, 1998, High Mus., Atlanta, 1993, Mus. Fine Arts, Springfield, Mass., Mairie du 18ème, Paris, 1997; represented in permanent collections at Mus. Modern Art, Whitney Mus. Am. Art, Bklyn. Mus., Mus. City N.Y., Bibliothèque Nat., La Maison Européenne de la Photographie, Pompidou Ctr. Grantee Nat. Endowment for Arts, Ministry Cultural Affairs, Ministry Fgn. Affairs, France. Home: 222 W 23rd St New York NY 10011-2301

BARRAT-GORDON, RENE, social worker; b. Utica, N.Y., May 9, 1955; d. Joseph and Helen (Korman) B.; m. Armand Grunberger, July 9, 1979 (div. Feb. 1990); 1 child, Monique Jacqueline; m. Lawrence Gordon, June 23, 1991; 1 child, Jenna Michelle. Student, Miami U., Oxford, Ohio, 1973-75; BSW, Ohio State U., 1976; M Social Sci. Adminstrn., Case Western Res. U., 1979. Lic. ind. social worker, Ohio. Social worker neurosurg and trauma units Cleve. Met. Gen. Hosp., 1979-87; social worker neuro-oncology unit Cleve. Clin. Found., 1987-93, social worker out-patient oncology, 1993—; adj. prof. Case We. Res. U. Sch. Applied Social Sci., Cleve., 1980—, instr. continuing edn., 1988; active Cleve. Area Head Injury Found., 1980-90; cons., Cleve., 1987-89; presenter in field. Contbr. articles to profl. jours. Vice pres. Pioneer Women, Cleve., 1985-87, fundraiser, 1986-88. Bruce H. Stewart fellow, 1994-95. Mem. NASW (chmn. practice and knowledge com. 1983-85), Acad. Cert. Social Workers, Nat. Orgn. Oncology Social Work. Avocations: jogging, biking, singing. Home: 2155 Halcyon Rd Beachwood OH 44122-1301 Office: Cleveland Clinic Found 9500 Euclid Ave Cleveland OH 44195-0002

BARRATT, CYNTHIA LOUISE, pharmaceutical company executive; b. El Paso, Tex., Feb. 13, 1953; d. John Edward and Louise Joy (Lacy) B.; m. Nat G. Adkins, Jr., Oct. 5, 1980. BJ, U. Tex., 1975. Buyer Joske's of Tex., San Antonio, 1975-80, Craigs of Tex., Houston, 1981-83; v.p. sales ops. Akorn, Inc., Abita Springs, La., 1980-86; CEO, chmn. bd. dirs. NGLC Corp., Richmond, Tex., 1983—; pres., CEO, bd. dirs. CynaCon/Ocusoft, Richmond, 1986—. Mem. NAFE, Rosenberg/Richmond C. of C., DAR, Ft. Bend County Mus. Assn. Avocations: golf, snorkeling, skiing. Office: OcuSoft Inc PO Box 429 Richmond TX 77406-0429

BARRATT, DONNA LEE, elementary school educator; b. Westwood, N.J., Nov. 23, 1965; d. Robert Roy B. and Arlene Rose (Solar) Landwehr. BA in English Edn. cum laude, Trenton St. Coll., 1988; MA in Edn., Georgian Ct. Coll., 1998. Tchr. English, N.J., Pa.; elem. tchr., N.J. Tchr. English St. Mary H.S., South Amboy, N.J., 1989-92; mid. sch. lang. arts tchr. Joyce Kilmer Sch., Milltown, N.J., 1992-94, Manalapan-Englishtown (N.J.) Mid. Sch., 1994—; Presenter inservice writing workshop Manalapan-Englishtown Bd. Edn., Manalapan, N.J., 1997. Mem. Nat. Coun. Tchrs. English, Kappa Delta Pi Edn. Honor Soc.. Roman Catholic. Avocations: reading, music, bike riding, hiking. Office: Manalapan Englishtown Middle Sch 155 Millhurst Rd Manalapan NJ 07726-4002

BARRATT, ERNEST STOELTING, psychologist, educator; b. North Charleroi, Pa., Mar. 31, 1925; s. Robert Duff and Marie Agnes (Stoelting) B.; m. Karen Marie Creel, Dec. 18, 1968; 1 son, Christopher Robert; 1 dau. by previous marriage, Robin Rhein. BA, Tex. Christian U., 1947, MA, 1949; PhD, U. Tex., 1952. Asst. prof. U. Del., Newark, 1951-57; prof. Tex. Christian U., Fort Worth, 1957-62; prof., chief psychophysiology lab. and psychology sect. U. Tex. Med. Br., Galveston, 1962—; Marie B. Gale Centennial prof. psychiatry U. Tex. Med. Br., 1998—. Contbr. articles to profl. jours. Trustee Galveston Ind. Sch. Dist., 1971-89. Served with USN, 1943-46. Spl. fellow UCLA Brain Research Inst., 1961-62. Fellow APA, Am. EEG Soc., Soc. for Personality Assessment, Am. Psychol. Soc., Internat. Orgn. Psychophysiology; mem. Soc. for Neurosci., Soc. Psychophysiol. Rsch., Soc. Biol. Psychiatry, Internat. Soc. for Study Individual Differences (pres. 1989-91). Roman Catholic. Home: 2641 Gerol Dr Galveston TX 77551-1529 Office: U Tex Med Br Dept Psychiatry & Behavioral Sci Galveston TX 77550

BARRATT, RAYMOND WILLIAM, biologist, educator; b. Holyoke, Mass., May 4, 1920; s. George A. and Elizabeth (Bretschneider) B.; m. Helen Ruggles, July 1943 (div. 1968); children: Marguerite E., William R.; m. Barbara H. Kellerup, Oct. 16, 1971. B.Sc., Rutgers U., 1941; M.Sc., U. N.H., 1943; Ph.D., Yale, 1948; M.A. (hon.), Dartmouth, 1958. Asst. plant pathology and horticulture U. N.H., 1943-44; rsch. assoc., asst. plant pathologist Conn. Agrl. Expt. Sta., 1944-45; rsch. assoc. biology Stanford (Calif.) U., 1948-53, rsch. biologist, acting asst. prof., 1953-54; mem. faculty Dartmouth Coll., 1954-70, prof. botany, 1958-62, prof. biology, 1962-70, chmn. dept., 1965-69, lectr. microbiology Med. Sch., 1962-70; prof. biology Humboldt State U., 1970-92, dean sci., 1970-84; mem. vis. staff Vt. Environ. Center, Ripton, summers 1970, 71; dir. Fungal Genetics Stock Ctr., 1970-85. Mem. Hanover Sch. Bd., 1964-68; mem. Dresden (N.H.) Sch. Bd., 1964-68, chmn., 1968. Mem. Genetics Soc. Am. (chmn. com. maintenance genetic stocks 1964-68), Sigma Xi, Alpha Zeta, Phi Sigma, Kappa Sigma. Achievements include research on microbial genetics. Home: 6949 Fickle Hill Rd Arcata CA 95521-9040

BARRECA, CHRISTOPHER ANTHONY, lawyer; b. Pittsfield, Mass., Sept. 15, 1928; s. Christopher Joseph and Jennie (Cannici) B.; m. Alice Hazlehurst, Sept. 5, 1953; children—Christopher, Alice, Jennifer. A.A., Boston U., 1950, J.D., 1953; LL.M., Northwestern U., 1968. Bar: Mass. 1954, Ky. 1969, U.S. Dist. Ct. (we. dist.) Ky. 1970, Mass. 1995, U.S. Ct. Appeals (6th cir.) 1970, Conn. 1988. With Gen. Electric Co., Fairfield, Conn., 1953-93, labor arbitration and litigation counsel., 1971-80, sr. labor and employment law counsel., 1980-93, ptnr., office chair Paul, Hastings, Janolsky & Walker LLP, Stamford, Conn., 1993—; mem. arbitration services adv. com. Fed Mediation and Conciliation Service, 1973—; adj. prof. U. Louisville, 1970-71, U. Bridgeport (Conn.) Sch. of Law, 1986—; selectman Weston, 1997—. Chmn., Weston (Conn.) Bd. Edn., 1977-82; trustee, vice chair exec. com., chmn. com. legal affairs Boston U., 1977—. Served with AUS, 1946-47. Mem. ABA (chmn. labor and employment law sect. com. labor arbitration advocacy, elected to governing council of labor and employment law sect. 1986—, chair 1996-97), Boston U. Sch. Law Alumni Assn. (Silver Shingle award 1982). Club: Aspetuck Valley Country (Weston, pres. 1995-96). Co-author, editor: Labor Arbitrator Development, 1983, A Practical Guide for Advocates 1990; contbr. articles to profl. jours. Home: 6 Aspetuck Hill Ln Weston CT 06883-2601 Office: 1055 Washington Blvd Stamford CT 06901-2216

BARREDO, RITA M., auditor; b. Torrington, Conn., June 24, 1953; d. Avelino and Josephine (DiNoia) B. BA, U. Conn., 1975; BS, Post Coll., 1981; MS in Acctg., U. Hartford, 1984, MBA, 1990. CPA, Conn.; cert. info. sys. auditor, cert. internal auditor; cert. mgmt. acct.; diplomate Am. Bd. Forensic Accts., Am. Bd. Forensic Examiners. Timekeeper Timex Corp., Waterbury, Conn., 1976-85; auditor Def. Contract Audit Agy., Lowell, Mass., 1985—. Mem. AICPA, Am. Coll. Forensic Examiners, Am. Womens Soc. CPAs, Conn. Soc. CPA (continuing profl. edn. com. 1989-95, 97— social and recreation com. 1996-97), Inst. Mgmt. Accts. (sec. Waterbury chpt. 1994—), Inst. Internal Auditors, Info. Sys. Audit and Control Assn. Home: 130 Dawes Ave Torrington CT 06790-3627 Office: Def Contract Audit Agy 400 Main St East Hartford CT 06108-0968

BARREIRA, BRIAN ERNEST, lawyer; b. Fall River, Mass., Sept. 1, 1958; s. Ernest R. and Lillian (Rego) B. BS in Ops. Mgmt., Boston Coll., 1980; JD, Boston U., 1984, LLM in Taxation, 1990. Bar: Mass. 1985. Estate settlement specialist State Street Bank and Trust Co., Boston, 1985-87; assoc. Barron & Stadfeld, Boston, 1987-88, Winokur, Winokur, Serkey, Rosenberg, & Hingham, P.C., Plymouth, 1988-96; sole practice Plymouth, Mass., 1996—. Contbr. articles to profl. jours. Mem. ABA (chmn. elder law com. 1990-95, chmn. long-term health care issues com. 1992-96), Nat. Acad. Elder Law Attys., Mass. Bar Assn. (mem. probate sect. coun. 1993-94, 95-97). Home: 1525 Tremont St Duxbury MA 02332-3313 Office: 225 Water St Ste 212 Plymouth MA 02360-4026

BARREN, BRUCE WILLARD, merchant banker; b. Olean, N.Y., Jan. 28, 1942; s. James Lee and Marion Frances (Willard) B.; children from previous marriage: James Lee, Christina Roseanne. Student, The Hun Sch. of Princeton, 1959; BS, Babson Coll., 1962; MS, Bucknell U., 1963; grad. cert., Harvard U., 1967, Cambridge U., England, 1968. CPA, Pa., FCA, England. Sr. cons. Price Waterhouse, N.Y., 1963-67; v.p. Walston & Co., Inc., N.Y., 1967-70; sr. v.p. Delafield Childs, Inc., N.Y., 1970-71; chmn. The EMCO/Hanover Group, L.A., 1971—; sr. v.p. Goodway, Inc., 1972-73; pres. Park West Med. Group, Inc., 1980-81; CEO First Pacific Bank, 1984-85; exec. editor The Mgmt. Gazette, 1988-98; chmn., mem. exec. adv. com. Vitafort Internat. Corp., L.A., 1996-97; vice-chmn. Four Winds Enterprises Inc., San Diego 1985-87, F.W. Myers & Co., Rouses Point, N.Y., 1990-91; vice chmn., CEO Hydro-Mill Co., Chatsworth, Calif., 1996-98; CEO Potomak Worldwide Ltd., 1998—; bd. dirs. various U.S. and internat. cos., 1978-95; author, instr. CPA, CPE courses, Tex., Calif. and N.Y.; U.S. rep. Transatlantic Bio-scis. Fund, London, 1988-91; instr. loan documentation and valuation procedures Sanwa Bank, 1995-96. Contbr. over 100 articles to profl. jours. including CFO and Contr. Alert. Recipient Disting. Svc. awards Calif. State Senate and State Assembly, Office of the Gov., Office of State Treas., Counties of L.A. and Orange, Calif., San Diego, City of L.A., Congl. Tribute, U.S. Senate, 1986, U.S. Ho. of Reps., 1988, 89, Mayor L.A., 1987, 90-91; named to Athletic Hall of Fame, Princeton U. Mem. Am. Mgmt. Assn. (author, instr.). Roman Catholic. Avocation: writing. Home: 11099 W Sunset Blvd Los Angeles CA 90049-3224 Office: The EMCO/Hanover Group Inc, Standbrook House 2-5 Old Bond St, London W1H 3TB, England

BARRERA, EDUARDO, Spanish language and literature educator; b. Rio Grande City, Tex., May 29, 1921; s. Bonifacio and Antonia (Rodrígues) B.; m. Maria Ninfa Cárdenas, Aug. 13, 1944; children: Maria Elena, Eduardo Ubil, David. BS, Tex. A&I Coll., 1952, MS, 1953; PhD, U. Tex., 1976. Cert. elem. and secondary sch. tchr., Tex. Tchr. grade 5 Ringgold Annex, Rio Grande City, 1952-53; tchr. Spanish Rio Grande H.S., Rio Grande City, 1956-63; cons. Tex. Edn. Agy., Austin, 1964, 65; tchr. Spanish Pan Am. U., Edinburgh, Tex., 1966-83, chmn. dept. fgn. langs., 1983-86; lectr. U. Tex. Pan Am., Edinburgh, 1987—; evaluator in bilingual proficiency Tex. Edn. Agy., Austin and Edinburgh, 1978-86. With U.S. Signal Corps, 1941-45. Mem. Tex. Assn. Coll. Tchrs. (life, pres. local chpt. 1966—), KC (grand knight 1988-89). Roman Catholic. Avocations: violin, church choir, fishing. Home: 1007 W Samano St Edinburg TX 78539-4052 Office: Univ Tex Pan Am 1201 University Dr Edinburg TX 78539

BARRERE, CLEM ADOLPH, business brokerage company executive; b. Bradford, Pa., Jan. 5, 1939; s. Clem A. and Ruth Eleanore (Brauner) B.; m. Jamie Elizabeth Newton, Aug. 30, 1969; 1 child, John Coleman Barrere. B Engring., Yale U., 1960; PhD in Chem. Engring., Rice U., 1965; postgrad., Emory U., 1975. Registered profl. engr., Tex., Okla.; bd. cert. broker; cert. bus. intermediary. Group leader rsch. dept. Conoco, Inc., Ponca City, Okla., 1965-69; dir. gas engring. Conoco, Inc., Houston, 1969-72, dir. gas ops., 1972-77, mgr. loss control, 1977-81; mgr. Dupont-Transp. Svc., Houston, 1981-87, Dupont-Safety and Environ., Houston, 1987-89; pres. Barrere & Co. Ventures, Houston, 1989—; dir. Barrere & Co. Realtors, Houston, 1978—. Contbr. articles to profl. jours.; 7 patents in field. Mem. Mus. Fine Arts, Houston, Zool. Soc., Houston, Mus. Natural Sci., Houston, 1970-96. Recipient Citations for Svc., Am. Petroleum Inst., 1988, Gas Processors Assn., 1989; NSF rsch. grantee, 1963-65. Fellow Internat. Bus. Brokers Assn. (dir. 1998—); mem. Tex. Bus. Brokers Assn., Houston Gas Processors Assn. (pres. 1981-82), Tex. Rolls-Royce Assn. (dir. 1987-96, Spl. award 1991), Houston Gun Collectors (pres. 1964), Houston Area Realtors, Petroleum Club, Lakeside Country Club, Phi Lambda Upsilon. Republican. Methodist. Avocations: car restorations, travel, sailing, genealogy. Home: 5652 Doliver Dr Houston TX 77056-2322 Office: Barrere & Co Ventures 7500 San Felipe St Ste 600 Houston TX 77063-1790

BARRERE, JAMIE NEWTON, real estate executive; b. Russellville, Ark., June 7, 1946; d. James Edward Jr. and Martha (Spillers) Newton; m. Clement Adolph Barrere Jr., Aug. 30, 1969; 1 child, John Coleman. BA in Math., U. Ark., 1968; graduate, Realtor Inst., 1984. Cert. real estate brokerage mgr.; grad. Realtor Inst.; accredited relocation coord. Asst. programmer, analyst Conoco, Ponca City, Okla., 1968-69; programmer, analyst Bonner & Moore Assocs., Houston, 1969-70; tchr. math. Lamar Consol. H.S., Rosenberg, Tex., 1970-72; assoc. broker Betty James, Realtors, Houston, 1972-78; pres. Barrere & Co., Realtors, Houston, 1978-96, Barrere Relocation affiliate Heritage Tex. Properties, Houston, 1996—; mem. adv. bd. Western Bank-Westheimer, Houston, 1986; mem. Employee Relocation Coun. Mem. Harris County Heritage Soc., Houston, 1970—, Houston Jr. Forum, 1980—, Am. Heart Assn. Guild, Houston Zool. Soc.; guild mem. Mus. Fine Arts, Houston, 1978—, Covenant House; trustee St. Luke's United Meth. Ch.; bd. dirs., children's dept. vol. Moores Sch. Music Soc. U. Houston, 1992—; life mem. Tex. Real Estate Polit. Action Com.; former cub scout leader Boy Scouts Am. Mem. Nat. Assn. Realtors (mem. Equal Opportunity Com. 1985), Tex. Assn. Realtors (bd. dirs. 1989-98, mem. Multiple Listing Svc. com. 1985-90), Houston Assn. Realtors (bd. dirs. 1986-89, 93-95, v.p. 1993, mem. and chmn. various coms.), Houston C. of C. (amb. 1986), DAR, U. Ark. Alumnae Assn. (life, v.p. Houston chpt. 1985-88), RELO Internat. Relocation Network, Lakeside Country Club, Petroleum Club, Tanglewood Garden Club (bd. dirs. 1973-86, 93-95), Delta Delta Delta (past pres. Houston alumnea). Avocations: swimming, travel, music, genealogy, historical preservation. Office: Barrere & Co 4295 San Felipe St Ste 300 Houston TX 77027-2915

BARRETT, ARCHIE DON, consultant , former federal official; b. Paris, Tex., Aug. 13, 1935; s. Archie Lafayette and Mabel Clara (Dickinson) B.; m. Miriam Meda Rowell, Aug. 31, 1958; children: Julie Ann, Cynthia Dawn, Archie Don Jr. BS, U.S. Mil. Acad., 1957; MPA, Harvard U., 1962, PhD in Polit. Economy and Govt., 1971. Commd. 2d lt. USAF, 1957, advanced through grades to col., 1979, ret., 1981; instr. to asst. prof. USAF Acad., Colo., 1965-67, assoc. prof., 1969-71; fighter pilot 13th Tactical Fighter Squadron, Thailand, 1968-69; instr. NATO-Weapons Sys. Sch., Ober Ammergau, Germany, 1971-73; plans officer 86th Tactical Fighter Wing, Ramstein, Germany, 1973-75; air staff USAF Hdqrs. Pentagon, Washington, 1975-79; rsch. assoc. Nat. Def. U., Ft. McNair, Washington, 1979-81; legis. staff House Armed Svcs. Com., Washington, 1981-94; prin. dep. asst. sec. Army, Manpower and Res. Affairs, Washington, 1994-97; vis. lectr., Naval Postgraduate Schl. Author: Reappraising Defense Organization, 1983; contbr. chpts. to books and articles to profl. jours. Mem. Assn. of the U.S. Army, Am. Legion, Ret. Officers Assn., Order of Daedalians, Air Force Assn., Phi Kappa Phi. Democrat. Methodist. E-mail: archbarret@gcsx.net. Address: PO Box 8627 Monterey CA 93943-8627

BARRETT, BARBARA MCCONNELL, ranch owner, community leader, lawyer; b. Indiana County, Pa., Dec. 26, 1950; d. Robert Harvey and Betty (Dornheim) McC.; m. Craig R. Barrett, Jan. 19, 1985. BS, Ariz. State U., 1972, MPA, 1975, JD, 1978. Bar: Ariz. 1978, U.S. Dist. Ct. Ariz. 1979, U.S. Supreme Ct. Ariz. 1979. Atty. The Dial Corp., Phoenix, 1976-80; assoc. gen. counsel, asst. sec. Southwest Forest Industries, Inc., Phoenix, 1980-82; vice chmn. CAB, Washington, 1982-83, mem., 1983-84, vice chmn., 1984-85; ptnr. Evans, Kitchel & Jenckes, P.C., Phoenix, 1985-88, 1989; dep. adminstr. FAA, Washington, 1988-89; pvt. practice internat. bus. and aviation law Paradise Valley, Ariz., 1989—; pres./c.e.o. American Mngmt. Assn., N.Y.C., 1997-98; pres. Triple Creek Ranch, Mont.; chmn. bd. dirs. Valley Bank Ariz.; chmn. nominating com. The Lovelace Inst.; treas. Asia-Pacific Econ. Cooperation Edn. Found., 1995-99; mem. exec. com., vice chairperson career opportunities subcom. U.S. Dept. Def., 1989-93; mem. adv. com. Gov.'s Regional Airport, Pres.'s Adv. Com. on Trade Negotiations; mem. Adminstrv. Coun. U.S., 1982-85; chmn. U.S. Sec. of Commerce Export Leaders Conf., 1988, Transp. Cluster Gov.'s Strategic Partnership for Econ. Devel., 1992-94; mem. Ariz. Disease Control Rsch. Commn., 1993-95; v.p. East Valley Partnership, 1992-94; v.p. Internat. Women's Forum, 1991-99, pres., 1999—, mem. coun. fgn. rels.; mem. Phoenix Coun. Fgn. Rels., 1979—; mem. steering com. Thunderbird Internat. Symposium, 1992—; bd. dirs. Raytheon Co., Exponent, Inc.; mem. adv. bd. China Mist Tea Co. Chmn. Ariz. Dist. Export Coun., 1985-91, Ronald W. Reagan Scholarship Program, 1987-90, Airshow Can. Symposium, 1989, 91; chmn. World Trade Ctr. Ariz., 1992-94, chmn. emerita; bd. dirs. Nat. Air and Space Mus. Smithsonian Inst., 1988-89, Palms Clinic and Hosp. Corp., 1985—, Goldwater Inst., 1991—; trustee, devel. com., chairperson Thunderbird Am. Grad. Sch. Internat. Mgmt., Glendale, Ariz., Embry-Riddle Aeronaut. U., Prescott, Ariz., Daytona Beach, Fla., 1989-96; pres. World Affairs Ariz., 1987-88; vice chmn. Kid's Voting USA, 1989-94; trustee Lovelace Inst., 1995-99; bd. dirs., chairperson nominating com. Ctrl. Ariz. chpt. ARC, 1993-99; bd. dirs. Ctr. Internat. Pvt. Enterprise, 1998; mem. Gov.'s Task Force Canamex Corridor, 1998; pres. bd. Maricopa Colls. Found., 1997-98. Fellow Inst. Harvard U., 1999; named Woman of Yr., Ariz. State U., 1971, named to Hall of Fame, Coll. Pub. Programs, 1989, Coll. Liberal Arts, 1995; recipient Disting. Achievement award Ariz. State U., 1987, Coll. Bus., 1994, Woman Who Made a Difference award Internat. Women's Forum, 1988, Dick Cheney citation U.S. Sec. of Def., 1992, FAA Adminstr.'s award, 1989, Woman of the Yr. Network of Women in Hospitality, 1998, Horatio Alger award, 1999; Dubois scholar, 1977. Mem. Am. Mgmt. Assn. (truste, chmn. exec. com., pres. N.Y.C. 1997-98), Nat. Assn. Corp. Dirs., Ariz. State U. Law Soc. (bd. govs. 1991-94), Ariz. State U. Found. (bd. dirs., program chair), Ariz. Women in Internat. Trade (bd. dirs., exec. com. 1989-94), Phoenix C. of C. (bd. dirs. 1989-95), Reagan Alumni Assn., Nat. Policy Forum, Econ. Club of Phoenix (past pres.).

BARRETT, BERNARD MORRIS, JR., plastic and reconstructive surgeon; b. Pensacola, Fla., May 3, 1944; s. Bernard Morris and Blanche (Lischkoff) B.; m. Julia Mae Prokop, Nov. 26, 1972; children: Beverly Frances, Julie Blaine, Audrey Blake, Bernard Joseph. BS, Tulane U., 1965; MD, U. Miami, 1969. Diplomate Am. Bd. Plastic Surgery. Surg. intern Meth. Hosp. and Ben Taub Hosp., Houston, 1969-70; resident in gen. surgery Baylor Coll. Medicine, Houston, 1970-71, UCLA, 1971-73; resident in plastic surgery U. Miami (Fla.) Affiliated Hosps., 1973-75, chief resident in plastic surgery, 1975; fellow in plastic surgery Clinica Ivo Pitanguy, Rio de Janeiro, 1973; instr. surgery Baylor Coll. Medicine, 1970-71, clin. instr. plastic surgery, 1977-80, clin. asst. prof., 1980-90, clin. assoc. prof., 1991-97, clin. prof. surgery, 1997—; instr. surg. emergecies L.A. County Paramedics, 1972-73; plastic surgery coord. for jr. med. students Sch. Medicine U. Miami, 1975; practice medicine specializing in plastic and reconstructive surgery Houston, 1976—; pres., chmn. bd. dirs. Plastic and Reconstructive Surgeons, P.A., 1978—; chmn. Tex. Inst. Plastic Surgery, Houston; assoc. chief plastic surgery St. Luke's Episcopal Hosp., Houston, 1991—; attending physician Jr. League Clinic, Tex. Children's Hosp., Houston, 1977—; active staff St. Luke's Hosp., Houston, Meth. Hosp., Houston; clin. assoc. in plastic surgery U. Tex. Med. Sch., Houston, 1976—; instr. surg. emergencies Harris County C.C.; dir. Am. Physicians ins. Exch., Austin, vice chmn., bd. dirs., 1995—; past chief of staff, chief plastic surgery Travis Centre Hosp., Houston, 1985—; dir. Physicians for Peace, Norfolk, Va., 1991—; cons. physician Houston Oilers, 1978-97; attending physician Ontario Motor Speedway, Calif., 1972-73. Author: Patient Care in Plastic Surgery, 1982, 2d edit., 1996, Manuel de Ciudados en Cirugia Plastica, 1985, Atencion al Paciente de Cirugia Plastica, 1998; contbr. articles to med. publs., presentations to profl. confs.; inventor Barrett sterling surgigrip. Bd. dirs. Plastic Surgery Ednl. Found., Chgo.; mem. Fed. Coun. on Aging, Washington, 1991-93, Pres.'s Coun. U. Miami, 1997—; adv. bd. Johnson & Johnson, New Brunswick, N.J. Lt. comdr. M.C., USNR, 1969-74. Surg. exch. scholar to Royal Coll. Surgeons, London, 1968; hon. dep. sheriff Harris County, Tex. (Houston). Fellow ACS; mem. Am. Assn. Plastic Surgery, Am. Soc. Plastic and Reconstructive Surgeons, Royal Soc. Medicine, Michael E. DeBakey Internat. Cardiovascular Surg. Soc., Am. soc. for Aesthetic Plastic Surgery, Denton A. Cooley Cardiovascular Surg. Soc., Tex. Med. Assn., Tex. Soc. Plastic Surgery, Harris County Med. Assn., Lipoplasty Soc. N.Am., Houston Soc. Plastic Surgery, D. Ralph Millard Plastic Surg. Soc. (pres. 1993-94, v.p. 1977-79, sec., treas. 1975-77, historian 1980—), U. Miami Sch. Medicine Nat. Alumni Assn. (bd. dirs. 1975-77, pres. coun. 1997—), Houston City Club, Houstonian Club, Royal Biscayne Racquet Club. commodore Club, Coral Beach and Tennis Club, Sweetwater Country Club, Alpha Kappa Kappa (pres. 1968-69). Office: 6624 Fannin St Ste 2200 Houston TX 77030-2334

BARRETT, BILL, sculptor; b. L.A., Dec. 21, 1934; s. H. Stanford and Theodora (Rogers) B.; children: Kevin Stanford, Alexander, Shannon; m. Debora Hicks. B.S. in Design, U. Mich., 1958, M.S. in Design, 1959, M.F.A., 1960. Instr. Cleve. Inst. Art, 1963-64; assoc. prof. Eastern Mich. U., Ypsilanti, 1960-68; lectr. CCNY, 1970-78; lectr. sculpture Columbia U., N.Y.C., 1979-85; vis. artist Vt. Studio Sch., summers 1987, 88. One-man shows Hanamura Galleries, Detroit, 1964, Eastern Mich. U. Gallery, 1965, Kalamazoo Art Ctr., 1966, 10 Downtown Show, N.Y.C., 1969, Benson Gallery, L.I., N.Y., 1969, 70, 72, 74, 77, 80, 81, Lantern Gallery, Ann Arbor, Mich., 1970, James Yu Gallery, N.Y.C., 1973, Katonah Art Gallery, 1974, County Exec. Bldgs. Show, White Plains, N.Y., 1975, CUNY Grad. Mall, 1976, Bklyn. Boro Hall, 1976-77, Sarah Y. Rentschler Gallery, N.Y.C., 1978, DeGraaf Forsythe Galleries, Ann Arbor, 1982, 87, Sculpture Ctr., N.Y.C., 1983, Kouros Gallery, N.Y.C., 1985, 87, 94, 96, Bellevue Hosp. Garden, 1985-86, Benkert Gallery, Zurich, 1984, 85, 90, 94, DeGraaf Galleries, Chgo., 1987, 89, Shidoni Gallery, 1990, Cline gallery, Santa Fe, 1993, 94, 96, Nardin Gallery, N.Y.C., 1998, JJ Brookings Gallery, San Francisco, 1998; group shows include Gen. Electric Sculpture Show, Fairfield, Conn., 1978, Alexander Milliken Gallery, N.Y.C., 1978, Am. Mission Bldg. UN, N.Y.C., 1978-80, Guild Hall Mus., East Hampton, L.I., N.Y., 1980, Sculpture Ctr., 69th St., N.Y.C., 1980, Canton Art Ctr., Ohio, 1981, Bot. Gardens outdoor show, Sculptor's Guild, Bronx, N.Y.C., 1981, Sculptural Arts Mus., Atlanta, 1982, Kouros Gallery, N.Y.C., 1987, Lever House, N.Y.C., 1982, Phoenix Bot. Gardens, 1982-83, Sid Deutsch Gallery, N.Y.C., 1983, Shidoni, Tesuque, N.Mex., 1989-90, Santa Fe Mus. Art, 1990-91, Hakone Biennial Competition, Tokyo, 1992, Turner Carroll Gallery, Sante Fe, 1992, Cline Gallery, Sante Fe, 1993, 94, Bologna Landi Gallery, East Hampton, N.Y., 1992, 93, Eve Mannes Gallery, Atlanta, 1992, 93, 94, La Quinta (Calif.) Sculpture Garden, 1994, Mongerson-Wunderlich Gallery, Chgo., 1994, Kouros Gallery, N.Y.C., 1996, 97, Century Assn., N.Y.C., 1997, Mongerson-Winderleck Gallery, Chgo., 1996, J.J. Brookings Gallery, San Francisco, 1996, Cline Fine Art, Santa Fe, 1996, Thomas McCormick Works of Art, Chgo., 1997, Freedman Gallery Albright Coll., Reading, Pa., 1998; represented in permanent collections Cleve. Mus. Art, Norfolk (Va.) Mus. Art, Henry Ford C.C., Dearborn, Mich., U. Mich. Mus. Art, Ann Arbor, Guild Hall Mus. Art, Scotsdale (Ariz.) Ctr. for the Arts, Knoxville (Tenn.) Mus. Art, Santa Fe Mus. Art, Albuquerque Mus. Art, Neuberger Mus. Art, Purchase, N.Y., U. Hartford, Conn., Hitachi Corp., Kyushu Plant, Kanda, Japan; represented in books Outdoor Sculpture Object and Environment, Whiteney Library of Design, N.Y. Art Yearbook, 1975-76, Vol. 1, The Process of Sculpture; sculpture commd. for N.Y.C. Hari IV, 1982, Criminal Cts. Bldg., Hartford, Conn., 1986, Goddard Ctr. for Arts, Ardmor, Okla., 1986, Hakone Open Air Mus., Tokyo, 1987, Portman Corp., Embarcadaro, San Francisco, 1989, Portman Corp., Atlanta, 1989, Pacific Enterprises, L.A., 1989, West Group One Bunkerhill, L.A., 1992, Bishop Ranch, San Ramon, Calif., 1998. Recipient R.J. Reynolds Meml. award, 1986, Audubon Artists Gold Medal award sculpture, 1990, Chaim Gross award, 1992. Mem. Sculptors Guild of N.Y. (pres. 1983-88), Century Club (N.Y.C.). Home: 11 Worth St New York NY 10013-2922 also: 11 Worth St New York NY 10013-2922*

BARRETT, BRUCE RICHARD, physics educator; b. Kansas City, Kans., Aug. 19, 1939; s. Buford Russell and Miriam Aileen (Adams) B.; m. Gail Louise Geiger, Sept. 3, 1961 (div. Aug. 1969); m. Joan Frances Livermore, May 21, 1979. BS, U. Kans., 1961; postgrad., Swiss Poly., Zurich, 1961-62; MS, Stanford U., 1964, PhD, 1967. Research fellow Weizmann Inst. Sci., Rehovot, Israel, 1967-68; postdoctoral research fellow, research assoc. U. Pitts., 1968-70; asst. prof. physics U. Ariz., Tucson, 1970-72, assoc. prof., 1972-76, prof., 1976—, assoc. chmn. dept., 1977-83, mem. faculty senate, 1979-83, 88-90, 91-97, program dir. theoretical physics NSF, 1985-87, mem. tech. transfer com., 1996-97, 98—, mem. grad. coun., 1998—; chmn. adv. com. Internat. Scholars, Tucson, 1985-96; chmn. rsch. policy com. U. Ariz. Faculty Senate, 1993-94, 95-96. Woodrow Wilson fellow, 1961-62; NSF fellow, 1962-66; Weizmann Inst. fellow, 1967-68; Andrew Mellon fellow, 1968-69; Alfred P. Sloan Found. research fellow, 1972-74; Alexander von Humboldt fellow, 1976-77; Japanese Soc. for Promotion of Sci. rsch. fellow, 1998; NSF grantee, 1971-85, 87—; Netherlands F.O.M. research fellow Groningen, 1980; recipient sr. U.S. scientist award (Humboldt prize) Alexander von Humboldt Found., 1983-85. Fellow Am. Phys. Soc. (publs. com. divsn. nuclear physics 1983-86, program com. 1993-94, chmn. steering com. for Nuclear Physics Summer Sch. 1996-98, mem. exec. com. four corners sect. 1998—), Phi Beta Kappa (pres. Alpha Ariz. chpt. 1992), Sigma Xi, Sigma Pi Sigma, Omicron Delta Kappa, Beta Theta Pi. Office: U Ariz Dept Physics PO Box 210081 Tucson AZ 85721

BARRETT, BRYAN EDWARD, prosecutor; b. Lafayette, Ind., Sept. 11, 1960; s. Donald Edward and Eva Rose (Schroeder) B.; m. Michelle Ann Gerstle, July 10, 1990; children: Jacob Edward Gerstle, Nathan Edward Gerstle, Lucas Donald Gerstle. BA, Purdue U., 1982; JD, Ind. U., 1985. Bar: S.C., Ind. Dep. prosecutor Shelby County Prosecutor, Shelbyville, Ind., 1985-91; pvt. practice Shelbyville, 1991-94; prosecutor Shelby County Prosecutor, Shelbyville, 1995-98; asst. U.S. atty. U.S. Dist. Ct. (so. dist.) Tex., Laredo, 1999—; pres. Local Drug-Free Coalition, Shelbyville, 1997, Shelby County Youth Shelter Bd., Shelbyville, 1993. Named one of Outstanding Young Men of Am., 1986. Mem. Nat. DA Assn., Ind. Pros. Atty. Assn., S.C. Bar Assn., Shelby County Bar Assn., Shelby County Babe Ruth Baseball, Shelbyville Boy's Club, Fraternal Order Police. Republican. Roman Catholic. Avocations: reading, writing, golf, volunteer coaching, politics. Home: 1618 Eagle Crest Loop Laredo TX 78045 Office: US Attys Office So Dist Tex Laredo Divsn 1501 Matamoros St Laredo TX 78040

BARRETT, CAROLYN HERNLY, paralegal; b. Geneva, Ill., Jan. 17, 1954; d. Wayne Francis and Genevieve (Moyer) Hernly; m. Bradley Clayton Barrett, June 20, 1976; children: Heather Hernly, Lance Clayton, Colin Courtney. Grad., Moser Bus. Coll., 1975; BS in Bus. Mgmt., Nat.-Louis U., 1996. Legal sec. Rathje, Woodward, Dyer & Burt, Wheaton, Ill., 1975-77; paralegal Chadwell, Kayser, Ruggles, McGee & Hastings, Chgo., 1978-80, Patrick James Perretti, Glen Ellyn, Ill., 1992-95; adminstrv. asst. Charles C. Snyder, PC, Oak Brook, Ill., 1996—; adminstr. Bedrava, Lyman & Van Epps, Oak Brook, Ill., 1998—. Pres. Forest Glen PTA, Glen Ellyn, 1988-90; mem. Rep. Senatorial Innter Cir., Washington, 1991—, Nat. Trust for Hist. Preservation; chair ways and means com. Glen Ellyn Hist. Soc., 3d v.p., 1992—. Recipient Medal of Freedom, Rep. Senatorial Inner Cir., 1994. Mem. DAR, Nat. Fedn. Rep. Women, Women in Arts (charter). Presbyterian. Avocations: collecting antiques, travel, scuba, restoring homes. Home: 675 N Main St Glen Ellyn IL 60137-4045

BARRETT, CHRISTINE KHAN, engineering project management coordinator; b. Tewksbury, Mass., Oct. 17, 1955; d. Jeanne (Rousseau) Khan; m. William E. Barrett, Jr., Oct. 11, 1986; children: Antonia, James, Winora. BA in Sociology magna cum laude, Boston Coll., 1977; MS in Pub. Mgmt. and Policy, Carnegie-Mellon U., 1979. Park aide Minuteman Nat. Hist. Park, Concord, Mass., 1976-77; rsch. policy analyst U.S. Dept. Labor, Washington, 1978; sr. bus. sys. analyst, analyst/task mgr. Am. Mgmt. Sys., Inc., Arlington, Va., 1979-86; comm. support mgr. Las Vegas Valley Water Dist., 1986-94, sr. projects analyst, 1994—; liason Nev./Calif. region underground svc. alert Las Vegas Valley Water Dist., 1989-91, mem. strategic planning team, corp. culture task force, pilot empowerment tng. and amb., field and office coordination com., 1991-95. Crisis phone vol. Temporary Asst. Domestic Crisis, 1988-90; parent vol., CCD instr. Our Lady Las Vegas Sch., 1989—; career day speaker Clark County High Schs., 1996—. Recipient Certs. Appreciation, Temporary Asst. Domestic Crisis, 1990-95. Mem. ASPA (Nev. chpt.), Project Mgmt. Inst., Am. Pub. Works Assn., Am. Water Works Assn.. Avocations: family activities, jazzercise, music, theatre, travel.

BARRETT, CRAIG R., computer company executive; b. 1939. Assoc. prof. Stanford U., 1965-74; with Intel Corp., Chandler, Ariz., 1974—, v.p. components tech. and mfg. group, sr. v.p., gen. mgr. components tech. and mfg. group, exec. v.p., mgr. components tech., now pres., COO. Office: Intel Corp 5000 W Chandler Blvd Chandler AZ 85226-3699*

BARRETT, CYNTHIA TOWNSEND, neonatologist; b. Santa Barbara, Calif., Sept. 8, 1937; d. George Barker and Elizabeth Louise (Magee) B. AB, Vassar Coll., 1958; MD, Harvard U., 1962. Diplomate. Am. Bd. Pediats. Intern, resident in pediats., pediat. chief resident U. Wash., 1962-66, fellow in physiology & biophysics, 1966-67; fellow in fetal cardiovascular physiology U. Calif., San Francisco, 1967-70; chief divsn. neonatology, assoc. prof. pediats. UCLA Sch. Medicine, 1970—. Mem. Internat. Newborn Intensive Care Soc., European Soc. Perinatal Rsch., Western Soc. Pediat. Rsch., Am. Thoracic Soc., Soc. Pediat. Rsch., Perinatal Rsch. Soc. Republican. Episcopalian. Home: 6778 Shearwater Ln Malibu CA 90265-4144 Office: UCLA Sch Medicine Dept Pediats Rm B2-369 Los Angeles CA 90095-1752

BARRETT, DAVID EUGENE, judge; b. Hiawassee, Ga., June 25, 1955; s. Homer and Laura Arispah (Wilson) B.; children: Laura Elizabeth, Thomas Jeffrey. BA summa cum laude, U. Ga., 1977, JD cum laude, 1980. Assoc. Erwin, Epting, et al, Athens, Ga., 1980-84, Blasingame, Burch, et al, Athens, 1984; pvt. practice Hiawassee, 1984-92; judge Recorders Ct., 1986-92, Superior Ct., Enotah Cir., 1992—; counsel Towns County Humane Soc., Hiawassee, 1985-92; counselor Alzheimer Support, Hiawassee, 1985. Mem. ABA, Ga. Bar Assn., Mountain Bar Assn. (sec. 1987-88, v.p. 1988-89, pres. 1989-90), Western Bar Assn. (sec. 1983-84), Trial Lawyers Assn. Am., Towns County C. of C. (bd. dirs. 1986-87, 90-92, pres. 1988), Demosthenian Lit. Soc. (bd. dirs., sec. bd. trustees 1978-89, chmn. bd. 1986-89), Athens Jaycees (v.p. 1983-84). Home: 924 Mining Gap Lane Young Harris GA 30582 Office: 59 S Main St Ste K Cleveland GA 30528-1376

BARRETT, DAVID J., broadcast company executive. Formerly v.p., gen. mgr. WBAL-AM, Balt.; v.p., dep. gen. mgr. Hearst Broadcasting, N.Y.C.; exec. v.p., COO Hearst Broadcasting Group & Argyle TV Inc., N.Y.C., 1990—. Office: Hearst Broadcasting Group and Argyle TV 888 7th Ave New York NY 10106*

BARRETT, ELIZABETH ANN MANHART, nursing educator, psychotherapist, consultant; b. Hume, Ill., July 11, 1934; d. Francis J. and Grace C. (Manhart) Fridy; children: Joseph B., Jeffrey F., Paula G. Brown, Pamela M. Temple, Scott D. BS in Nursing summa cum laude, U. Evansville, 1970, MA, 1973, MS in Nursing, 1976; grad. Gestalt Assocs. for Psychotherapy, 1982; PhD in Nursing, NYU, 1983; grad. Am. Inst. for Mental Imagery, 1995. Instr. nursing U. Evansville, Ind., 1970-73, asst. prof., 1973-76; staff nurse Welborn Bapt. Hosp., Evansville, 1975-76; staff nurse Bellevue Psychiat. Hosp., N.Y.C., 1976-79; clin. tchr. CUNY, 1977-82; asst. prof. Adelphi U., 1979-80; group practice Nurse Healers, 1979-82; pvt. practice psychotherapy, 1980—; nurse researcher Mt. Sinai Med. Ctr., N.Y.C., 1982-86, asst. dir. nursing, 1983-86; assoc. prof. Hunter Coll., N.Y.C., 1986-89, prof., 1994—, dir. grad. studies, 1989-92, coord. Ctr. for Nursing Rsch., 1993—; cons. Internat. Soc. Univ. Nurses; co-chair adv. com. Martha E. Rogers Ctr. for Study of Nursing Svc., 1994-96. Mem. com. Regional Health Planning Council, Evansville, 1974-77. Mem. editl. bd. Alt. Therapies in Health and Medicine, 1995—. Recipient Disting. Nursing Alumnus award NYU, 1994, Disting Nurse Rschr. award Found. N.Y. State Nurses Assn., 1995. Fellow Am. Acad. Nursing; mem. Am. Nurses Assn. (cert. psychiat.-mental health), Nat. League Nursing, Ea. Nursing Rsch. Assn. (charter), Ea. Nursing Rsch. Soc., Soc. Rogerian Scholars (co-founder, 1st pres. 1988-90), NOW, Phi Kappa Phi, Sigma Theta Tau (Upsilon chpt. pres. 1986-88), Alpha Tau Delta, Sigma Xi. Home: 415 E 85th St Apt 9E New York NY 10028-6358 Office: Hunter Coll 425 E 25th St New York NY 10010-2547

BARRETT, ELLEN COLBY, magazine editor; b. Chgo., Ill., Jan. 20, 1945. BA in Jounalism, Calif. State U., Long Beach. From staff reporter to bureau chief U.S. News & World Report, L.A., Denver; dir. pub. rels. The Colo. Historical Soc.; feature reporter food and dining NBC TV, Denver; radio talk show host The Food and Restaurant Show, Denver; travel writer L.A. Times/Washington Post syndicate; exec. editor Southern Living Mag.; foods editor Southern Living Mag., Birmingham, Ala., 1996—; exec. editor Cooking Light Mag. Mem. Internat. Assn. Culinary Profls., Am. Inst. Wine and Food, Assn. Food Journalists. Office: Time, Warner, Inc. Southern Living Magazine 2100 Lakeshore Dr Birmingham AL 35209-6721*

BARRETT, EVELYN CAROL, retired secondary education educator; b. Ocean Springs, Miss., Feb. 6, 1928; d. Charles Edward and Irene Effie (Hopkins) Engbarth; m. Arthur James Barrett, June 10, 1951; children: George Stanley, Ruth Anne, James Sidney, Carolyn Jean. Diploma with honors, Jr. Coll. (now Miss. Coast Coll.), Perkinston, Miss., 1945; BS in Commerce with high honors, Miss. So. Coll. (now U. So. Miss.), 1947; MBA in Acctg., La. State U., 1950; also numerous continuing edn. courses, 1950-82. Bookkeeper-sec. Non-Commn. Officers Club, Kessler AFB, Miss., summer 1947; asst., secretarial practice office and divsn. rsch.; instr. in typing Coll. Commerce, La. State U., 1947-50; instr. Miss. So. Coll., summer 1950; clk.-stenographer dept. physics U. Ill., Urbana, 1951-52; instr. in shorthand Ill. Comml. Coll., 1951-52; tchr. Milford (N.H.) H.S., 1957-58; tchr. bus. edn. Merrimack (N.H.) H.S., 1958-90, head dept. bus. edn., 1971-81; ret., 1990; grad. asst. La. State U., 1947-50; instr. auditing Rivier Coll., 1982; registered rep. R. Danais Investment Co., Manchester, N.H.; account exec. John, Edward & Co., Lebanon, N.H.; ind. beauty cons. Mary Kay Cosmetics, Merrimack; tutor in shorthand, acctg.; cons. acctg. sys. Organizer, 1st pres. Merrimack Group Hillsborough County Ext. Svc., 1957-58; active Girl Scouts U.S.A., including Cadette leader, 1959-63, sr. troop leader Switwater coun., 1970-72, adult vol. trainer, 1964-66, troop program cons., 1963-64. Mem. AAUW, NEA, N.H. Edn. Assn., N.H. Bus. Educators Assn. (v.p. 1964-65, pres. 1965-67, rep. to N.H. Vocat. Assn. 1986-87, sec. 1967-68, treas. 1973-75, historian 1986-87), N.H. Supervisory Union 27 (sec.-treas. 1961-62), Merrimack Tchrs. Assn. (sec. 1984-85, Disting. Educator award 1980, Excellence in Edn. award 1985), New Eng. Bus. Educators Assn., Am. Vocat. Assn., N.H. Assn. Computer Edn. Statewide, Ea. Bus. Edn. Assn., Nat. Bus. Edn. Assn., Delta Zeta, Phi Theta Kappa, Pi Omega Pi, Delta Pi Epsilon, Alpha Delta Kappa (chpt. award of appreciation 1980, historian N.E. region 1981-83, sec. N.E. region 1995-97, v.p. N.H. Alpha chpt. 1978-79, pres. N.H. Alpha chpt. 1979-82, N.H. state sgt.-at-arms 1982-84, N.H. state treas. 1984-88, state membership chmn. 1988-92, state chaplain 1992-94, N.H. state pres. elect 1994-96, N.H. state pres. 1996-98, N.H. state immediate past pres. 1998), Audubon Soc. N.H., Delta Sigma Epsilon (chpt. corr. sec.), Gen. Electric Women's Club, Reeds Ferry Women's Club, Manchester Coll. Women's Club, Our Lady of Mercy Ladies Guild, Merrimack Sr. Citizen Club, Manchester Area Ret. Educators Assn., Nashua Area Ret. Educators Assn., N.H. Ret. Educators Assn. Roman Catholic.

BARRETT, FRANK JOSEPH, insurance company executive; b. Greeley, Nebr., Mar. 2, 1932; s. Patrick J. and Irene L. (Printy) B.; m. Ruth Ann Nealon, Aug. 20, 1956; children: Patrick, Mary, Anne, Karen, Thomas. BS in Law, U. Nebr., 1957; LLB, Nebr. Coll. Law, 1959. Bar: Nebr. 1959, U.S. Supreme Ct. 1976. Asst. gen. counsel, asst. sec. Nebr. Nat. Life Co., 1957-61; dir. ins. State of Nebr., Lincoln, 1961-67; exec. v.p., sec., gen. counsel Ctrl. Nat. Ins. Group of Omaha, 1967-75; exec. v.p., chief counsel Mut. of Omaha (and Affiliates), 1975-81; pres., CEO Ctrl. Nat. Ins. Co. of Omaha, 1981-89, Ins. Rsch. Svc. Co., Omaha, 1989—; of counsel Lamson, Dugan & Murray, Omaha, 1990—; bd. dirs. Underwriters Ins. Co., Risk Capital Reins. Co.; mem. fin. com. Preferred Profl. Ins. Co.; chmn. Gov.'s Blue Ribbon Coalition on Health Care Reform. State organizational chmn. 3 Nebr. gubernatorial campaigns. Served in U.S. Army, 1953-55, Korea. Recipient service citation Am. Nat. Red Cross, 1964, 65. Mem. Nebr. Bar Assn., Omaha Bar Assn., Am. Arbitration Assn., Fedn. Ins. Counsels, Consumer Credit Ins. Assn. (past pres. and dir.), Nat. Assn. Ind. Insurers (gov., past chmn.), Nat. Assn. Ins. Commrs. (past pres.), Am. Legion, Irish-Am. Cultural Soc., K.C., ARIAS-U.S. (cert.). Democrat. Roman Catholic. Fax: (402) 333-2341. Home: 516 S 119th St Omaha NE 68154-3115

BARRETT, HERBERT, artists management executive; b. N.Y.C., May 31, 1910; s. John and Mollie (Pike) B.; m. Betty Palash, May 29, 1937; children: Nancy, Katherine. B.A., Cornell U., 1930. Pub. rels. counsel Cadillac Car Co., N.Y.C., 1934—, GM, N.Y.C., 1935—; mgr., pres. Herbert Barrett Mgmt. (artists mgmt. assn.), N.Y.C., 1940—; mgr. inaugural Great Performers series Avery Fisher Hall, Lincoln Center for Performing Arts, N.Y.C., 1965; mem. adv. com. Town Hall, N.Y.C., 1970—; mem. recommendation bd. Avery Fisher Artist Program, Lincoln Center Performing Arts; mem. nat. adv. bd. Van Cliburn Internat. Quadrennial Piano Competition. Recipient Patrick Hayes award for outstanding svc. to Internat. Soc. for the Performing Arts Found., 1997. Mem. Little Orch. Soc. (treas. 1970—, mgr. 1967—), Internat. Assn. Festival and Concert Mgrs. (exec. bd. 1969—), Phi Beta Kappa. Home: 15 W 72nd St New York NY 10023-3402 Office: 1776 Broadway Ste 1610 New York NY 10019-2083

BARRETT, IZADORE, retired fisheries research administrator; b. Vancouver, B.C., Can., Oct. 4, 1926; came to U.S., 1956; s. Samuel Barrett and Rose (Hyatt) Gordon; m. Fulvia Mercedes Quesada, July 5, 1958; children: Marcus, Byron, Norman, Dora. BA, U. B.C., 1947, MA, 1949; postgrad., U. Toronto, 1949-52; PhD, U. Wash., 1980. Chief hatchery biologist B.C. Game Commn., Vancouver, 1952-56; scientist Inter-Am. Tropical Tuna Commn., La Jolla, 1956-67; chief biologist UNDP Fisheries Devel. Project, Santiago, Chile, 1967-69; fisheries advisor FAO, Santiago, 1969-70; dep. dir. S.W. Fisheries Ctr., La Jolla, 1970-77, dir., 1977-88; sci. and research dir. S.W. region, Nat. Marine Fisheries Svc., 1988-92; ret., 1992; rsch. assoc. Scripps Inst. Oceanography, La Jolla, 1977—; mem. sci. and statis. com. Pacific Fisheries Mgmt. Coun., Portland, Oreg., 1977-90; chmn. sci. and statis. com. Western Pacific Fisheries Mgmt. Coun., Honolulu, 1976-79. Contbr. articles to profl. jours. Bd. govs. San Diego Oceans Found., 1985-95; chmn. Mayor's San Diego/La Jolla Underwater Park Com., 1978-92; mem. adv. coun. Inst. Marine Resources U. Calif., La Jolla, 1979-85; bd. govs. San Diego Sci. Fair, 1984-92. Fellow Am. Inst. Fisheries Rsch. Biologists (v.p. 1973-76).

BARRETT, J. CARL, cancer researcher, molecular biologist; b. Portsmouth, Va., Dec. 28, 1946; s. Jacob Weaver and Dixie Wike (Ring) B.; m. Roberta Mick, June 8, 1968; children: James, Paul, Lia. BS in Chemistry, Coll. of William and Mary, 1969; PhD in Biophysical Chemistry, Johns Hopkins U., 1974. Postdoctoral fellow divsn. biophysics Johns Hopkins U., Balt., 1974-77; sr. staff fellow lab. pulmonary function and toxicology Nat. Inst. Environ. Health Scis., Rsch. Triangle Park, N.C., 1977-82, group leader environ. carcinogenesis group, 1977-87, rsch. chemist, 1982-87, chief lab. molecular carcinogenesis, 1987—, dir. program environ. carcinogenesis div. intramural rsch., 1992-96, sci. dir., 1995—; adj. prof. dept. pathology U. N.C., 1978—, dept. epidemiology, 1992—; adj. mem. genetics curriculum U. N.C., 1979—, toxicology curriculum, 1985—; adj. sr. fellow Ctr. Study of Aging and Human Devel. Duke U. Med. Ctr., 1993—; mem. study sections NIH, Nat. Cancer Inst., Nat. Cancer Inst. Can.; ad hoc reviewer; vis. prof. Sun Yat-Sen U., People's Rep. China, 1987, Inst. Zoology Academia Sinica, Taiwan, 1992, NYU, 1992; keynote speaker, organizer, chair numerous symposia, conferences, workshops; invited speaker more than 75 symposia, conferences, univs. worldwide, 1986—; mem. Task Force Health Effects of Synthetic Fuels Dept. Energy, 1980; mem. workshop Internat. Program Chem. Safety, 1982; mem. working group WHO, 1983, Internat. Agy. Rsch. Cancer, France, 1985, 86, peer rev. com. sci. coun., 1988; mem. adv. panel Calif. Biotech., Inc., 1990, Greenwall Found., 1989; mem. various adv. bds., coms. Nat. Coun. Radiation Protection & Measurements, Am. Health Found., Nat. Cancer Inst., U.S. EPA, Health Effects Inst.-Asbestos Rsch. Com., Chem. Industry Inst. Toxicology, also external expert, ad hoc mem.; cons. Abbott Labs., 1989-91, Chem. Industry Inst. Toxicology, 1991-92; chmn. sci. coun. Internat. Agy. for Rsch. on Cancer, 1998. Author: Mechanisms of Environmental Carcinogenesis: Volume I-Role of Genetic and Epigenetic Changes, 1987, Vol. II-Multistep Models of Carcinogenesis, 1987; co-author: Carcinogenesis-A Comprehensive Survey: Volume 9, Mammalian Cell Transformation: Mechanisms of Carcinogenesis and Assays for Carcinogens, 1985, Comparative Molecular Carcinogenesis: Volume 376-Progress in Clinical and Biological Research, 1992; editor-in-chief Molecular Carcinogenesis, 1992—, mem. editl. bd., 1988—; assoc. editor Cancer Rsch., 1984—, Mutagenesis, 1985-88, Toxicology in Vitro, 1986-90; mem. editl. bds. profl. jours., 1988—; contbr. over 365 articles to profl. jours. Recipient merit awards NIH, 1989, 94, 97, Dir.'s award, 1995, 96, Ramazzini award Collegium Ramazzini, Italy, 1995, Secretary's award for Disting. Svc., Dept. Health and Human Svcs., 1996; NSF grantee, 1966; Dow Chem. Co. fellow, 1968. Mem. AAAS, Am. Chem. Soc., Am. Assn. Cancer Rsch. (program com., Rhodes award com., chair spl. membership com., bd. dirs. 1998—), Internat. Soc. Diffrentiation (bd. dirs. 1998—). Office: Nat Inst Environmental Hlth Scis PO Box 12233 Research Triangle Park NC 27709*

BARRETT, JAMES EDWARD, JR., management consultant; b. Lowell, Mass., Dec. 9, 1929; s. James E. and Margaret A. (Holland) B.; A.B., Harvard U., 1951; postgrad. Air Command and Staff Coll., 1953; m. Dorothy G. Walle; children—James Edward III, Dorothy Anne, William H., M. Stephen. Asst. prof. Harvard U., 1955-58; systems analyst, mgr. Raytheon Co., 1958-62; mktg. mgr. Kepner-Tregoe, Inc., Princeton, N.J., 1963-65; mgr., dir. K-T Europe, 1966-67; pres. AAI, 1967-68; pres. Cresheim Co., Inc., Phila., 1968—, chmn. Cresheim, Ltd. (U.K.), 1979-95, Cresheim do Brasil, Sao Paulo, 1980-99. bd. dirs. Swansea Press, Inc. 1986-95. Pres., Wyndmoor (Pa.) Community Assn., 1977-79; dir. Alzheimer's Assn. of Southeastern Pa., 1995—, v.p., 1996—. Served to capt. USAF, 1951-55. Mem. Am. Assn. Small Research Cos. (pres. Phila. chpt. 1977-80), Inst. Mgmt. Cons. (v.p. chpt. 1977-81, nat. dir. 1981-87, nat. v.p. 1983-86). Clubs: Harvard (N.Y.C., Phila.). Author: Managing Your Distributors; contbr. num erous articles to profl. jours. Home: 8315 Flourtown Ave Wyndmoor PA 19038-7924 Office: Cresheim Management Cons PO Box 27785 Philadelphia PA 19118-0785

BARRETT, JAMES EMMETT, federal judge; b. Lusk, Wyo., Apr. 8, 1922; s. Frank A. and Alice C. (Donoghue) B.; m. Carmel Ann Martinez, Oct. 8, 1949; children: Ann Catherine Barrett Sandahl, Richard James, John Donoghue. Student, U. Wyo., 1940-42, LLB, 1949; student, St. Catherine's Coll., Oxford, Eng., 1945, Cath. U. Am., 1946. Bar: Wyo. 1949. Mem. firm Barrett and Barrett, Lusk, 1949-67; atty. Niobrara Sch. Dist., 1950-64; county and pros. atty. Niobrara County, Wyo., 1951-62; atty. Town of Lusk, 1952-54; atty. gen. State of Wyo., 1967-71; judge U.S. Circuit Ct. Appeals (10th cir.), 1971—, now sr. judge. Active Boy Scouts Am.; sec.-treas. Niobrara County Republican Central Com.; trustee St. Joseph's Children's Home, Torrington, Wyo., 1971-85. Served as cpl. AUS, 1942-45, ETO. Recipient Distinguished Alumni award U. Wyo., 1973. Mem. VFW, Am. Legion, Order of Coif (hon. mem. Wyo. Coll. Law/U. Wyo. chpt.). Office: US Ct Appeals PO Box 1288 Cheyenne WY 82003-1288

BARRETT, JAMES THOMAS, immunologist, educator; b. Centerville, Iowa, May 20, 1927; s. Alfred Wesley and Mary Marjorie (Taylor) B.; m. Barbro Anna-Lill Nilsson, July 31, 1967; children—Sara, Robert, Annika, Nina. BA, State U. Iowa, 1950, MS, 1951, PhD, 1953. Asst. prof. bacteriology and parasitology U. Ark. Sch. Medicine, Little Rock, 1953-57; asst. prof. microbiology U. Mo. Sch. Medicine, Columbia, 1957-59, assoc. prof., 1959-67, prof., 1967-94; prof. St. George's (Grenada, W.I.) U. Sch. Medicine, 1994—; exchange prof. U.S. and Romanian Acads. Sci., 1971; vis. scientist Spanish Ministry Edn. and Sci., 1986. Author: Textbook of Immunology, 5th edit., 1988, Basic Immunology and Its Medical Application 2d edit., 1980, Medical Immunology, 1991, Microbiology and Immunology Casebook, 1995, Microbiology and Immunology Concepts, 1998; editor: Contemporary Classics in the Life Scienes, 1986, Contemporary Classics in Clinical Medicine, 1986, Contemporary Classics in Plant, Animal and Environmental Sciences, 1986. Served with USN, 1944-45. NIH Fogarty sr. fellow, 1977-78; Fulbright scholar, 1984. Mem. Am. Assn. Immunology, Am. Soc. Microbiology, Sigma Xi. Home: 901 Westport Dr Columbia MO 65203-0741 Office: Saint Georges U Sch Medicine, Saint George's Grenada

BARRETT, JANE HAYES, lawyer; b. Dayton, Ohio, Dec. 13, 1947; d. Walter J. and Jane H. Barrett. BA, Calif. State U.-Long Beach, 1969; JD, U. So. Calif., 1972. Bar: Calif. 1972, U.S. Dist. Ct. (cen. dist.) Calif. 1972, U.S. Ct. Appeals (9th cir.) 1982, U.S. Supreme Ct. Assoc. Arter, Hadden, Lawler, Felix & Hall, L.A., 1972-79, ptnr., 1979-94, mng. ptnr., 1984-93; ptnr. Preston, Gates & Ellis, 1994—; mng. ptnr. Preston, Gates & Ellis, L.A., 1994—; lectr. bus. law Calif. State U., 1973-75. Mem. adv. bd. Harriet Buhai Legal Aid Ctr., 1991-96, mem. bd. pub. counsel, 1996-98; pres. Pilgrim Parents Orgn. 1990-91. Named Outstanding Grad. Calif. State U., Long Beach, 1988, Outstanding Alumnae Polit. Sci., 1993. Fellow Am. Bar Found.; mem. ABA (bd. govs. 1980-84, chmn. young lawyers divsn. 1980-81, com. on delivery of legal svcs. 1985-89, exec. coun. legal edn. and admissions sects. 1985-89, fin. sec. torts and ins. practice 1982-83, adv. mem. fed. judiciary com. 1994-96, v.p. 1997—, v.p. Am. Bar Endowment 1984-90, bd. dirs. 1990—, sec. 1993-95, v.p. 1998-99, pres., 1999—, bd. fellows young lawyers divsn. 1992—), Calif. State Bar (com. adminstrn. of justice, editl. bd. Calif. Lawyers 1981-84), Legion Lex (bd. dirs. 1990-93), Los Feliz Homeowners Assn. (bd. dirs.). Democrat. Office: Preston Gates & Ellis 725 S Figueroa St Ste 2100 Los Angeles CA 90017-5421

BARRETT, JANET TIDD, academic administrator; b. Crystal City, Mo., Nov. 29, 1939; d. Lewis Samuel and Mamie Lou (Hulvey) Tidd; m. David Clark Barrett, June 3, 1961; children: Barbara, Pam. Diploma in nursing, St. Lukes Hosp. Sch. Nursing, 1960; BSN with honors, Washington U., St. Louis, 1964, MS in Nursing, 1979; PhD, St. Louis U., St. Louis, 1987. Assoc. prof. Maryville Coll., St. Louis, 1979-89; academic dean Barnes Coll., St. Louis, 1989-91; dir. BSN program Deaconess Coll. of Nursing, 1991—. Contbn. author to Beare and Meyers: Principles of Medical-Surgical Nursing. St. Lukes Hosp. scholar; recipient Sister Agnita Claire Day Rsch. award St. Louis U. Mem. Nat League Nursing, Mo. League Nursing, St. Luke's Alumni Assn., N. Am. Nursing Diagnosis Assn., Sigma Theta Tau, Pi Lambda Theta, Phi Delta Kappa.

BARRETT, JEFFREY SCOTT, real estate company executive; b. Elgin, Ill., Dec. 12, 1949; s. Charles Clayton and Dorothy Grace (Smith) B.; m. Mary Ferriss Vincent, July 24, 1971; children: Elizabeth Towne, Chad Brayton. BS, Drake U., 1971. Loan officer, v.p. Greenebaum Mortgage Co., Chgo., 1971-76; with CB Richard Ellis Inc., Chgo., 1976—; real estate fin. officer Richard Ellis Inc., Chgo., sales mgr., v.p., resident mgr.; 1st v.p., resident mgr. Richard Ellis Inc.; sr. v.p., sr. mng. officer, mng. dir. CB Richard Ellis Inc., Chgo. Mem. Chgo. Real Estate Coun. (pres. 1982), Chgo. Office Leasing Brokers Assn. (pres. 1994), Meadow Club, Glen Oak County Club. Republican. Presbyterian. Avocations: basketball, coach, sports, golf. Home: 1114 Irving St Wheaton IL 60187-3843 Office: CB Richard Ellis Inc 1900 E Golf Rd Schaumburg IL 60173-5834

BARRETT, JOHN ANTHONY, publishing and printing company financial executive; b. Phila., Aug. 12, 1942; s. Stephen Francis and Margaret (Walsh) B.; m. Joan Victoria Lyncheski, Oct. 21, 1967; children: John Anthony Jr., Stephanie Lea. BSBA, Mt. St. Mary's Coll., Emmitsburg, Md., 1964; postgrad., Drexel U., 1980. Mgr. mfg. acctg. Scott Paper Co., Phila., 1968-77; contr. W.B. Saunders Co. div. CBS Inc., Phila., 1977-82; v.p., contr., chief fin. officer Diversified Printing Corp., Atglen, Pa., 1982-87; v.p. sales ops. Maxwell Communication Corp., Greenwich, Conn., 1987-89; v.p. fin. planning and control Arcata Graphics Co., Balt., 1989-94; bus. cons. Washington, 1994-95; sr. v.p., CFO Univ. Press Am., Inc., Lanham, Md., 1995-97, Nat. Book Network, Inc., 1995-97; bus. cons., 1997—; v.p., CFO BDP Internat., Inc. Global Logistics and Transp., Phila., 1997—. Lt. USN, 1964-68; Vietnam. Mem. Fin. Execs. Inst. Roman Catholic. Home: 1405 Stockton Ct Arnold MD 21012-2470

BARRETT, JOHN J(AMES), JR., lawyer; b. Phila., May 19, 1948; s. John J. and Carmela (DiJohn) B.; m. Rosemary A. Campagna, Aug. 23, 1969; children: Jeffrey, Kristin, Jacqueline. BA, Temple U., 1970, JD, 1973. Bar: Pa. 1973, N.J. 1987, U.S. Dist. Ct. (ea. dist.) Pa. 1973, U.S. Ct. Appeals (3rd cir.) 1975, U.S. Dist. Ct. (mid. dist.) Pa. 1986, U.S. Supreme Ct. 1986, U.S. Dist. Ct. N.J. 1987. Assoc. Saul, Ewing, Remick & Saul, Phila., 1973-80; ptnr. Saul, Ewing, Remick & Saul, 1980—. Mem. Nat. Assn. R.R. Trial Counsel, Phila. Assn. Def. Counsel. Office: Saul Ewing Remick & Saul 3800 Centre Sq W Philadelphia PA 19102

BARRETT, KATHERINE, writer, multimedia producer; b. N.Y.C., May 24, 1954; d. Herbert and Betty (Palash) B.; m. Richard H. Greene, Feb. 21, 1982; children: Benjamin, Sandra. BS in Journalism, Northwestern U., 1976. Reporter Comml. Appeal, Memphis, 1976-78; assoc. editor, sr. writer, sr. editor Ladies' Home Jour., N.Y.C., 1980-84, contbg. editor, 1984-98; freelance writer, columnist numerous publs., 1984—; prodr. Walt Disney Family Edn. Found., San Francisco, 1996—; v.p. Barrett & Greene, N.Y.C., 1996—; spl. project editor Governing mag., Washington, 1997—; spkr. on state and city mgmt., 1992—; cons. Maxwell Sch., Syracuse (N.Y.) U , 1996—; mem. adv. bd. Govtl. Acctg. Stds. Bd., Norwalk, Conn., 1996—, Urban Inst., Washington, 1996—. Author: The Man Behind the Magic, 1991, Frankly, My Dear, 1996; co-prodr. (CD-ROM) Walt Disney: An Intimate History, 1998; contbr. numerous articles to Newsweek, Reader's Digest, Glamour, Ladies Home Jour., Fin. World, also others. Recipient award for excellence N.Y. Soc. CPA's, 1991, Children's Choice award Internat. Reading Assn., 1992, Washington Monthly Journalism award, 1999.

BARRETT, KATHLEEN ANNE, assistant principal; b. Jersey City, Aug. 16, 1954; d. Judson Bernard and Patricia Mary Ann (Conlon) B. BA, Iowa Wesleyan Coll., 1976; MA, Jersey City State Coll., 1993. Tchr. elem. Jersey City Pub. Schs., 1976-90, tchr. spl. edn., 1990-97, asst. prin., 1997—. Vol. oper. rm. Riverview Hosp., Red Bank, N.J. Mem. ASCD, NEA, Caucus for Educators Exceptional Children, Jersey City Edn. Assn., Phi Delta Kappa. Roman Catholic. Avocations: reading, needlework, arts and crafts. Office: PS 28 167 Hancock Ave Jersey City NJ 07307

BARRETT, LAKE H., energy industry executive; b. New London, Conn., Dec. 9, 1945; s. Hildreth Ernest and Maryllia (houston) B.; m. Lynn Buckley Mar. 5, 1966; children: Lake Hildreth, Lawrence Davis. BSME, U. Conn., 1967, MSME, 1971. Nuclear project engr. Gen. Dynamics, Groton, Conn., 1967-73; sr. nuclear engr. Bechtel Power Corp., Gaithersburg, Md., 1973-74; section leader Nuclear Regulatory Commn., Washington, 1974-80, site dir. Three Mile Island, 1980-84, engring branch chief, 1984-85; dir. trans. and waste systems Dept. Energy, Washington, 1985-88, dir. quality assurance, 1988-90, dir. Rocky Flats prog. office, 1990-93, acting dir., 1993—. Avocations: vol. community svc., skiing. Office: Dept of Energy Civilian Radioactive Waste Mgmnt 1000 Independence Ave SW Washington DC 20585-0002

BARRETT, LAURENCE IRWIN, public relations executive, writer; b. N.Y.C., Sept. 6, 1935; s. Harold and Ruth (Gaier) B.; m. Paulette Singer, Mar. 9, 1957 (div. 1983); children: Paul M., David A., Adam S.; m. Martha Priddy Patterson, July 24, 1988. BA, NYU, 1956; MS in Journalism, Columbia U., 1957. Polit. reporter and columnist N.Y. Herald Tribune, N.Y.C., 1958-62; Washington correspondent N.Y. Herald Tribune, Washington, 1962-65; assoc. editor Time Inc., N.Y.C., 1965-69; sr. editor Time Inc., 1970-75, N.Y. regional bur. chief, 1975-78, sr. White House correspondent, 1978-85, nat. polit. correspondent, 1986-92, contbr., 1993-97; Washington dep. bur. chief, 1989-91; v.p. Powell Tate, Washington, 1998—; panelist various TV and radio talk shows; asst. prof. sch. comm. Am. U., 1995-97. Co-author: The Winning of the White House, 1988, 89; author: Gambling with History: Reagan in the White House, 1983, The Mayor of New York, 1965; contbr. articles to mags., newspapers, profl. jours. With U.S. Army, 1957. Mem. Nat. Press Club, Soc. of the Silurians. Jewish. Office: Powell Tate 700 13th St NW Ste 1000 Washington DC 20005-5926

BARRETT, LIDA KITTRELL, mathematics educator; b. Houston, May 21, 1927; d. Pleasant Williams and Maidel (Baker) Kittrell; m. John Herbert Barrett, June 2, 1950 (dec. Jan. 1969); children: John Kittrell, Maidel Horn, Mary Louise. BA, Rice U., 1946; MA, U. Tex., Austin, 1949; PhD, U. Pa., 1954. Instr. math. U. Conn., Waterbury, 1955-56; vis. appointment U. Wis., Madison, 1959-60; lectr. U. Utah, Salt Lake City, 1956-61; assoc. prof. U. Tenn., Knoxville, 1961-70, prof., 1970-80, head math. dept., 1973-80; assoc. provost No. Ill. U., DeKalb, 1980-87; dean, arts and scis. Miss. State U., Mississippi State, 1987-91; sr. assoc. Edn. and Human Resources Directorate NSF, Washington, 1991-95; prof. math. U.S. Mil. Acad., West Point, N.Y., 1995-98; adj. prof. U. Tenn., 1998—; ind. math. cons., Knoxville, Tenn., 1964-80, 98—. Contbr. articles on topology, applied math. and math. edn. to profl. jours. Mem. Math. Assn. Am. (pres. 1989, 90), Am. Math. Soc., Soc. Indsl. and Applied Math., Nat. Coun. Tchrs. Math., Am. Assn. Higher Edn., Phi Kappa Phi, Sigma Xi. Episcopalian. Office: U Tenn Dept Math Ayres Hall-Rm 121 Knoxville TN 37996-1300*

BARRETT, LINDA L., real estate executive; b. Hudson, Mich., Aug. 16, 1948; d. David John and Georgia Elizabeth (Spengler) B.; 1 dau., Toni. Student, U. Mich., 1970-73. Cert. residential brokerage mgr. Sales mgr. Collins Real Estate, Hudson, Mich., 1973-79; owner, broker Homeland Real Estate, Lake Leann, Mich., 1979-82; mgr. broker Mid-Mich. Real Estate, Jackson, Mich., 1982-85; exec. v.p. Michael Saunders & Co., Sarasota, Fla., 1986-95, cons., 1995—; mem. adv. bd. Sotheby's Internat. Mem. Econ. Devel. Coun., Com. of 100. Mem. AAUW, NAFE, Internat. Real Estate Fedn., Nat. Mktg. Inst., Nat. Assn. Realtors, Fla. Assn. Realtors, Sarasota C. of C., Global Travel Internat. Network, 2000 Notable Am. Women (profl. stds. com. woman's coun.), Econ. Devel. Coun., CRB, Profl.'s Network Investment Orgn. Avocations: gardening, bonsai, golfing, snorkling, travel.

BARRETT, LISA MARIE, acupuncture physician, herbologist; b. Hudson, Mich., Feb. 26, 1954; d. David John and Georgia Elizabeth (Spengler) B. Grad., Lansing Bus. U., Mich., 1973, Sch. Natural Healing Arts, Sarasota, Fla., 1997. Diplomate acupuncture, Chinese herbology, Nat. Certification Commn. for Acupuncture & Oriental Medicine; cert. herbologist, Nambudripad's allergy elimination technique practitioner. Pvt. practice acupuncture Sarasota, Fla., 1997—. Mem. MENSA, Am. Assn. Oriental Medicine, Fla. State Oriental Med. Assn. Avocations: Feng Shui, Qigong, reading, horseback riding, walking. E-mail: lotushealth@earthlink.net.

BARRETT, LORETTA ANNE, publishing executive; b. Mt. Vernon, N.Y., July 1, 1941; d. Edward Vincent and Irene Marie (Wynne) B. Student, Rosemont (Pa.) Coll., 1958-60; BA cum laude, U. Pa., 1962, MAT, 1965. Editor Doubleday & Co. Anchor Press, N.Y.C., 1965-67; editorial dir. Doubleday & Co. Special Projects, N.Y.C., 1967-72; exec. editor, publisher Anchor Press, Doubleday & Co., N.Y.C., 1972-83; exec. editorial v.p. Doubleday & Co., N.Y.C., 1983-90; pres. Loretta Barrett Books, Lit. Agy., 1990—; bd. dirs. Reading is Fundamental, Washington, 1967—, Through the Flower, Santa Fe, N.Mex., 1986—. Assoc., trustee Coun. Pa. Women U. Pa., 1989; bd. dirs. Athena Inst., Haverford, Pa., 1987—, Grandparenting Found., Lake Placid, N.Y., 1987, Nathan Wharton Found., 1998. Mem. Women in the Media, Assn. of Author's Reps., Inc. Democrat. Roman Catholic. Avocations: skiing, tennis, travel. Office: Loretta Barrett Books 101 5th Ave New York NY 10003-1008*

BARRETT, MARTIN JAY, financial executive; b. N.Y.C., Mar. 12, 1949; s. Nat and Pearl Barrett; m. Bette Sue Levy, Sept. 9, 1984. BS in Acctg., Lehmann Coll., CUNY, 1976. Assoc. exec. dir. for ops. Hetrick-Martin Inst., N.Y.C., 1998—; CFO Ackerman Inst. for Family Therapy, N.Y.C., 1992-98; assoc. exec. dir. for ops. Hetrick-Martin Inst., N.Y.C., 1998-99; pres. Forty Plus of N.Y., N.Y.C., 1999—; pres. 40 Plus of N.Y., N.Y.C., 1992; chief auditor N.Y.C. Carpenters Benefit Funds, N.Y.C., 1972-92; mgr. pension and med. benefits Nat. Health and Welfare Assn., N.Y.C., 1967-72. Editor: (newsletter) The Good News Is ... The Bad News Is ..., 1993-98. Chmn. community planning bd. #6, Manhattan, 1998—, parks and landmarks com. Cmty. Bd. 6, N.Y.C., 1994-96, chmn. pub. safety com., 1992-94, vice chmn. planning bd., 1996-98, chmn. budget and legis. affairs, 1996-98; mem. Sutton Area Com., 1993—; pres. Phipps Plz. West Tenant's Assn., N.Y.C., 1989-92; v.p., trustee Belleview South Pk. Assn., N.Y.C., 1991—; chmn. pub. safety Ams. for Dem. Action, N.Y.C., 1995-96; campaign treas. various local and state elected ofcls. and judges, N.Y.C., 1978-94; mem. Nat. Trust Hist. Preservation Soc., 1990—, Wildlife Conservation Soc., 1992—; commr. of deeds N.Y.C., 1984—; bd. trustees 14th St. Bus. Improvement Dist. Mem. Am. Mgmt. Assn., Inst. Mgmt. Accts., Knights of Pythias (Hubert H. Humphrey chancellor comdr. 1995-97, fin. sec. 1997—). Avocations: literature, performing arts, fine arts, travel, civil affairs. Office: 40 Plus of New York 15 Maiden Ln New York NY 10038

BARRETT, MATTHEW W., banker; b. County Kerry, Ireland, Sept. 20, 1944; arrived in Can., 1967.; Grad. advanced mgmt. program, Harvard Bus. Sch.; LLD (hon.), St. Mary's U., Halifax, 1992, York U., North York, 1993, Concordia U., Montreal, U. Waterloo; DCL (hon.), Bishop's U., Lenoxville, 1993; DLitt (hon.), U. N.B.; LLD (hon.), Acadia U., 1997, DLitt, 1997. Clerk Bank of Montreal, London br., 1962-67; teller Bank of Montreal, 1967-68, support svcs., 1968-78, v.p. mgmt. svcs., 1978—, v.p. B.C. divsn., 1979-80, sr. v.p. ea. and no. Ont., 1980-85, exec. v.p. and group exec. personal banking, 1985-87, bd. dirs., 1987—, pres. and COO, 1987-89, CEO, 1989—, chmn. bd. dirs., 1990—; bd. dirs. Molson Cos. Ltd., The Seagram Co. Ltd., Conf. Bd. Can., Nesbitt Burns Inc.; dir. U. Western Ont. Program Adv. Com. Bd. dirs. Montreal Bd. of Trade Heritage Found., Can. Coun. for Nat. Unity, dir. bus. coun. on nat. issues; founding dir. Harvard Bus. Sch. Alumni, Ottawa chpt.; mem. dean's adv. coun. Schulich Sch. Bus., York U.; trustee, mem. fin. com. Toronto Hosp.; dir. Asia Pacific Found; bd. govs. Jr. Achievement of Can. Decorated officer Order of Can.; recipient Golden Plate award Am. Acad. Achievement, 1993; named Sales and Mktg. Exec. of Yr., Sales and Mktg. Assn. Toronto, 1994, Outstanding CEO of Yr., Fin. Post mag., 1995. Avocations: fly fishing, tennis, reading. Office: Bank Montreal, PO Box 1 First Canada Pl, Toronto, ON Canada M5X 1A1*

BARRETT, MICHAEL HENRY, civil engineer; b. Dove Creek, Colo., June 20, 1932; s. Frank Ace and Carrie Ethel (Snyder) B.; m. Barbara Jane Kreutz, Aug. 7, 1954; children: Robert, Mary, Bonnie, William. B.S. in Civil Engring, U. Colo., 1955, postgrad., 1955-64; M.B.A., U. Denver, 1979. Registered profl. engr., Colo., Calif., Fla., Wis., N.C., Minn., N.Mex., Utah. Design engr., then partner Ketchum & Konkel, Denver, 1955-69; pres. Ketchum, Konkel, Barrett, Nickel, Austin, Denver, 1969-79; chmn. bd. Ketchum, Konkel, Barrett, Nickel, Austin, 1979-85, pres., chmn., 1986-88; prin., cons. Martin/Martin, 1988—; dir. Testing Cons., Inc., Martin Assoc. Group; mem. faculty U. Colo., 1963-64, U. Denver, 1968-69; lectr. Civil Def., 1962-68. Patentee in field. Exec. bd. Denver Area council Boy Scouts Am., 1970—, pres., 1974-75, area v.p., 1976-82, area pres., 1982; mem. Westminster (Colo.) Planning Comm., 1971-72; chmn. bd. dirs. Denver Boys, Inc. Served with USNR, 1951-54, USAR, 1955-63. Recipient Lincoln Arc Welding award, 1966, 68, award Am. Inst. Steel Constrn., 1969, Disting. Engring. Alumnus award U. Colo., 1984, Honor award Colo. Engring. Coun., 1984, Silver Beaver award Boy Scouts Am., 1977, Silver Antelope award, 1983. Fellow ASCE (life); mem. Nat. Soc. Profl. Engrs., Am. Concrete Inst., Soc. Exptl. Stress Analysis, Profl. Engrs. Colo. (pres. 1970), Am. Cons. Engrs. Coun. (1st place award 1973, pres. Colo. chpt. 1982, Orley Phillips award 1992, com. of fellows 1993, peer reviewer 1984—, George Washington Leadership award 1998), Structural Engrs. Assn. Colo., Am. Arbitration Assn., Harvard Bus. Sch. Club, Denver C. of C., Rotary (dir. 1976-78). Office: Martin & Martin Inc 4251 Kipling St Wheat Ridge CO 80033-2896

BARRETT, MICHAEL JOHN, anesthesiologist; b. Milw., Feb. 27, 1954; s. Walter Joseph and Valerie Clara (Wisniewski) Baclawski; m. Joan Marie Rowley, May 28, 1983; children: Michael J. Jr., Jessica Marie, Monica Jane. BS in Math. with honors, U. Wis., 1974; MD, Med. Coll. Wis., 1981; MBA, U. Toledo, 1998. Diplomate Am. Bd. Anesthesiology, Nat. Bd. Medicine and Surgery, Nat. Bd. Med. Examiners, Am. Acad. Pain Mgmt., Am. Bd. Anesthesiology Pain Mgmt. Intern Med. Coll. Wis. Affiliated Hosps., Milw., 1981, resident in anesthesiology, 1982-84; dir. anesthesiology Putnam Community Hosp., Palatka, Fla., 1984-92, dir. Putnam Pain Ctr., 1985-92; pres. Putnam Anesthesia Assocs., Palatka, 1985-92; staff anesthesiologist St. Vincent Med. Ctr., Toledo, 1992—, dir. Pain Mgmt. Ctr., 1994—. Bd. dirs. Round Lake Park Homeowners Assn., Palatka, 1986-88. Walter Zeit fellow; recipient St. Vincents Physician Excellence award, 1996. Mem. AMA, Internat. Anesthesia Rsch. Soc., Am. Soc. Anesthesiologists, Am. Soc. Regional Anesthesiologists, Ohio Med. Assn., Acad. Medicine of Toledo and Lucas County, Am. Neuromodulation Soc., Ohio Soc. Anesthesiologists, Putnam County Med. Soc. (pres. 1989-91), Phi Beta Kappa, Phi Kappa Phi. Republican. Roman Catholic. Avocations: boating, private pilot, swimming. Home: 8646 Plum Hollow Pt Holland OH 43528-8487 Office: Assoc Anesthesiologists 2409 Cherry St Ste 4 Toledo OH 43608-2600

BARRETT, MICHAEL JOSEPH, priest; b. N.Y.C., Oct. 6, 1952; s. Patrick Joseph and Margaret Mary (Rogan) B. BA, Columbia Coll., 1974; STD, Pontifical Atheneum Holy Cross, Rome, 1987. Ordained priest by Pope John Paul II, Rome, 1985. Sales rep. Gulf Oil Chems. Co., N.Y.C., 1974-76; acct. exec. Merrill Lynch & Co., N.Y.C., 1976-78; dir. devel. The Heights Found., Inc., N.Y.C., 1978-83; asst. prof. Roman Coll. of Holy Cross, Rome, 1985-88; del. vicar for Tex. Opus Dei Prelature, Houston, 1988—; retreat master Featherock Conf. Ctr., Schulenburg, Tex., 1988—; chaplain Southgate Cultural Ctr., Houston, 1988—; co-host (radio talk show) Faith Matters, 1997-98. Alumnus advisor Columbia U. Secondary Schs. Com., N.Y.C., 1981-83. Roman Catholic. Avocations: tennis, jogging, classical music, reading. Home and Office: 5505 Chaucer Dr Houston TX 77005-2631

BARRETT, NANCY SMITH, university administrator; b. Balt., Sept. 12, 1942; d. James Brady and Katherine (Pollard) Smith; children: Clark, Christopher. BA, Goucher Coll., 1963; MA, Harvard U., 1965, PhD, 1968; PhD, Harvard U., 1968. Dep. asst. dir. Congl. Budget Office, Washington, 1975-76; sr. staff Council of Econ. Advisors, Washington, 1977; prin. research assoc. The Urban Inst., Washington, 1977-79; dep. asst. sec. U.S. Dept. Labor, Washington, 1979-81; instr. Am. U., Washington, 1966-67, asst. prof. econs., 1967-70, assoc. prof., 1970-74, prof., 1974-89; dean Coll. of Bus. Adminstrn. Fairleigh Dickinson U., Teaneck, N.J., 1989-91; provost, v.p. acad. affairs Western Mich. U., Kalamazoo, 1991-96, U. Ala., Tuscaloosa, 1996—. Author: Theory of Macroeconomic Policy, 1972, 2d rev. edit., 1975, Theory of Microeconomic Policy, 1974, (with G. Gerardi and T. Hart) Prices and Wages in U.S., 1974; contbr. articles on econs. of mfg. to profl. jours. Woodrow Wilson fellow, 1963-64; Fulbright scholar, 1973. Mem. Am. Econs. Assn., Phi Beta Kappa. Home: 3957 Gaineswood Ln Tuscaloosa AL 35406-3568 Office: U Ala Office Acad Affairs Box 870114 Tuscaloosa AL 35487

BARRETT, PATRICIA RUTH, government official; b. Sioux Falls, S.D., Mar. 31, 1954; d. Donald Abraham and Ruth Irene (Miller) Haggar; m. Clancy Erik Barrett, Aug. 7, 1976; children: Elizabeth Brooke, Leia Lynn. BSBA, U. North Colo., 1979; postgrad., Iowa State U., 1991—. Real estate salesperson Haggar's Action Realty, Pierre, S.D., 1973-76; real estate broker Patricia Barrett Real Estate, Rapid City, S.D., 1987-89; asst. mgr. for adminstrn. Census Bur., U.S. Dept. Commerce, Waterloo, Iowa, 1989-90; fed. warehouse examiner USDA, Kansas City, Mo., 1990—. Leader Girl Scouts U.S.A. Aurelia, Iowa, 1991-94; bd. dirs. sch. bd. Aurelia Cmty. Sch. Dist., 1994=97; bd. dirs. Cherokee (Iowa) Area Econ. Devel. Corp., 1995-97. Republican. Lutheran. Avocations: martial arts, gardening, painting, reading. Home: 46422 160th Ave Laurens IA 50554-8631

BARRETT, PAUL, journalist; b. N.Y., 1961. Degree in Am. history, Harvard U., 1983. Reporter Phila. bur. Wall St. Jour., 1987-88, Washington, U.S. Dept. Justice reporter, U.S. Supreme Ct. reporter, 1991-96, dep. legal editor, 1997—. Home: Wall St Jour 200 Liberty St New York NY 10281*

BARRETT, PAUL J., pharmacist; b. Pryor, Okla., July 14, 1962; s. Joe C. and Lenna M. (McMillen) B.; m. Susan G. Cartier, Feb. 14, 1990; 1 child, Drew Phillip. BS in Pharmacy, Purdue U., 1985, PharmD, 1986; MPA, U. Maine, 1992. Registered pharmacist, Ind., Maine; bd. cert. pharmacotherapy specialist. Staff pharmacist Ind. U. Hosp., Indpls., 1985-86, R.I. Hosp., Providence, 1986-87; clin. pharmacist Aroostook Med. Ctr., Presque Isle, Maine, 1987—; cons. pharmacist Aroostook Residential Ctr., Presque Isle, 1991—, So. Acres Boarding Home, Westfield, Maine, 1998—. Bd. dirs. Maine Sch. Adminstrn. Dist. #1, Presque Isle, 1993-96. Fellow Am. Soc. Cons. Pharmacists; mem. Am. Coll. Clin. Pharmacists, Am. Soc. Health Sys. Pharmacists, Maine Soc. Health Sys. Pharmacists (dir. 1992-96, pres. 1996-98). Republican. Congregationalist. Home: 132 Canterbury St Presque Isle ME 04769-3021 Office: Aroostook Med Ctr 140 Academy St Presque Isle ME 04769-3171

BARRETT, PAULETTE SINGER, public relations executive; b. Paris, Dec. 20, 1937; came to U.S., 1947; d. Andrew M. and Agatha (Kinsbrunner) Singer; m. Laurence I. Barrett, Mar. 9, 1957 (div. 1983); children: Paul Meyer, David Allen, Adam Singer. BA, NYU, 1957; MS in Journalism, Columbia U., 1958. News dir. Yardney Electric Corp., N.Y.C., 1958-61; freelance writer newspapers and pub. relations orgns., N.Y.C. and Washington, 1961-73; assoc. dir. pub. info. Columbia U., N.Y.C., 1973-77; from account exec. to v.p., then sr. v.p. Edelman Pub. Rels. Worldwide, N.Y.C., 1977-80, sr. v.p. and gen. mgr., 1980, exec. v.p., gen. mgr., 1986-88, exec. v.p., dir. corp. affairs div., 1988-89; exec. v.p. Rowland Co., N.Y.C., 1980-82; exec. dir. communications UJA-Fedn./N.Y., N.Y.C., 1982-86; sr. v.p., mng. dir. Hill and Knowlton, Chgo., 1989-90; pres. Barrett Comm., Chgo. and N.Y.C., 1990—. Office: Barrett Comms 310 W 56th St 9F New York NY 10019

BARRETT, REGINALD HAUGHTON, biology educator, wildlife management educator; b. San Francisco, June 11, 1942; s. Paul Hutchison and Mary Lambert (Hodgkin) B.; m. Katharine Lawrence Ditmars, July 15, 1967; children: Wade Lawrence, Heather Elizabeth. BS in Game Mgmt., Humboldt State U., 1965; MS in Wildlife Mgmt., U. Mich., 1966; PhD in Zoology, U. Calif., Berkeley, 1971. Rsch. biologist U. Calif., Berkeley, 1970-71, acting asst. prof., 1971-72; rsch. scientist div. wildlife rsch. Commonwealth Scientific and Indsl. Rsch. Orgn., Darwin, Australia, 1972-75; from asst. prof. to prof. U. Calif., Berkeley, 1975—. Author: (with others) Report on the Use of Fire in National Parks and Reserves, 1977, Research and Management of Wild Hog Populations, Proceedings of a Symposium, 1977, Sitka Deer Symposium, 1979, Symposium on Ecology and Management of Barbary Sheep, 1980, Handbook of Census Methods for Birds and Mammals, 1981, Wildlife 2000: Modeling Habitat Relationships of Terrestrial Vertebrates, 1986, Translocation of Wild Animals, 1988, Wildlife 2001: Populations, 1992; contbr. articles, abstracts, reports to profl. jours. Recipient Outstanding Profl. Achievement award Humboldt State U. Alumni Assn., 1986, Bruce R. Dodd award, 1965, Howard M. Wight award, 1966; Undergrad. scholar Nat. Wildlife Fedn., 1964, NSF grad. fellow, 1965-70; Union found. Wildlife Rsch. grantee, 1968-70. Mem. The Wildlife Soc. (pres. Bay Area chpt. 1978-79, pres. western sect. 1997-98, cert. wildlife biologist, R.F. Dasmann Profl. of Yr. award western sect. 1989), Am. Soc. Mammalogists (life), Soc. for Range Mgmt. (life), Ecol. Soc. Am. (cert. sr. ecologist), Soc. Am. Foresters, Australian Mammal Soc., Am. Inst. Biol. Scis., AAAS, Calif. Acad. Scis., Internat. Union for the Conservation of Nature (life), Calif. Bot. Soc., Orgn. Wildlife Planners, Sigma Xi, Xi Sigma Pi. Episcopalian. Avocations: hunting, fishing, photography, camping, backpacking. Office: U Calif 151 Hilgard Hall Berkeley CA 94720-3110

BARRETT, RICHARD DAVID, university director, consultant, bank executive; b. Cin., Sept. 27, 1931; s. Oscar Slack and Helen Rust (Kaiper) B.; m. Pamela P. Soldwedel, Feb. 25, 1971; children: David, Kimball, Randall. Grad., Choate Sch.; BA, Yale U., 1953; postgrad., George Washington U., NYU. Prodn. control Reynolds Metals Co., 1954-56; v.p. ops. Nat. Bank Washington, 1956-66; officer Irving Trust Co., N.Y.C., 1966-70; v.p. mktg. First Am. Bank, N.A., Washington, 1970-74; sr. v.p. First Am. Bank, N.A., 1974—, head internat. div., head retail ops. and mktg. group, v.p. internat. and pvt. banking group, exec. v.p. mktg. and community rels.; dir. planned giving Georgetown U., Washington; pres. Barrett Planned Giving, Inc., Washington; past mem. Bankers Assn. Fgn. Trade, Greater Washington Area Bd. Trade Internat. Com. Author: (with Molly E. Ware) Planned Giving Essentials: A Step-by-Step Guide to Success, 1997. Past trustee Meridian House Internat.; past bd. dirs., treas. Hospice Care of D.C., Watergate South Inc.; past trustee Washington Hosp. Ctr.; past chmn., past mem. bd. dirs. Nat. Capitol Area Health Care Coalition, Hospice Care of D.C. Lt. (j.g.) USNR, 1953-54. Mem. Nat. Soc. Fund Raising Execs., Nat. Com. on Planned Giving, Yale Club, Met. Club, Chevy Chase Club (Md.). Home: 700 New Hampshire Ave NW # 906 Washington DC 20037-2406

BARRETT, ROBERT MATTHEW, lawyer, law educator; b. Bronx, N.Y., Mar. 18, 1948; s. Harry and Rosalind B. AB summa cum laude, Georgetown U., 1976, MS in Fgn. Service, JD, 1980. Bar: Calif. 1981. Assoc. Latham & Watkins, L.A., 1980-82, Morgan, Lewis & Bockius, L.A., 1982-84, Skadden, Arps, Slate, Meagher & Flom, L.A., 1984-86, Shea & Gould, L.A., 1986-87, Donovan, Leisure, Newton & Irvine, L.A., 1988-90; ptnr. Barrett & Zipser, L.A., Calif., 1991-93; prof. law U. LaVerne Law Sch., Woodland Hills, Calif., 1993—. Civilian vol. L.A. Sheriff's Dept., 1997—. Mem. State Bar Calif. (standing com. on profl. responsibility and conduct 1995—, chair 1997-98, spl. advisor 1998-99), L.A. Bar Assn. (bd. advisors vols. in parole com. 1981—). Fax: 818-883-8142. Address: Univ La Verne Coll Law 21300 Oxnard St Woodland Hills CA 91367-5016

BARRETT, ROBERT MITCHELL, electrical engineer; b. San Diego, Dec. 7, 1943; s. William Francis and Dorothy Lillian (Noll) B.; m. Darleene Frances Fuller, Aug. 8, 1971; children: Katherine Louise, Michelle Frances. BSEE, N.Mex. State U., 1967; MBA, U. So. Calif., L.A., 1973. Commd. 2d lt. USAF, 1967, advanced through grades to maj., 1981, ret., 1987; sys. engr. Air Force Ballistics Missile Office, Norton AFB, Calif., 1978-82, chief launch control sys., 1982-83; sys. engr. GPS user equipment Air Force Space Divsn., L.A., 1983-85, chief, IONS sys. engring., 1985-87; self-employed engr. Mentone, Calif., 1987-89; mem. tech. staff Jet Propulsion Lab., Pasadena, Calif., 1989-93, stds. engr., 1993—. Decorated Air Force Commendation medal, Meritorious Svc. medal. Mem. IEEE, Soc. Automotive Engrs. Avocations: gardening, fishing, horse breeding. Office: Jet Propulsion Lab 4800 Oak Grove Dr Pasadena CA 91109-8001

BARRETT, ROGER WATSON, lawyer; b. Chgo., June 26, 1915; s. Oliver R. and Pauline S. B.; m. Nancy N. Braun, June 20, 1940; children—Victoria Barrett Bell, Holly, Oliver. A.B., Princeton U., 1937; J.D., Northwestern U., 1940. Bar: Ill. 1940. Mem. firm Poppenhusen, Johnson, Thompson & Raymond, Chgo., 1940-43; 45-50; charge documentary evidence Nuremberg Trial, 1944-45; regional counsel Econ. Stablzn. Agy., Chgo., 1951-52; ptnr. Mayer, Brown & Platt, Chgo., 1952-91, of counsel, 1991—. Life trustee Mus. Contemporary Art, Chgo. With AUS, 1943-45. Mem. ABA, Ill. Bar Assn., Chgo. Bar Assn., Am. Coll. Trial Lawyers, Indian Hill Club (Winnetka), Old Elm Club, Commonwealth Club (Chgo.), Caxton Club (Chgo.). Home: 84 Indian Hill Rd Winnetka IL 60093-3934 Office: Mayer Platt & Brown 190 S La Salle St Chicago IL 60603-3410

BARRETT, STEPHEN MICHAEL, editor; b. Urbana, Ill., June 6, 1968; s. Carl Lee and Lynn Morine (Winship) B.; m. Michele Elizabeth Rose Barrett, Oct. 1, 1994; children: Gabriella, Stephen Jr., Julia. BA in Comms., U. Wis., 1990. Videographer Sta. WSAW-TV, Wausau, Wis., 1987-91, Sta. WPTV-TV, West Palm Beach, Fla., 1991-92; special projects prodr. Sta. WTVT-TV, Tampa, 1992-97; mng. editor Sta. WFTS-TV, Tampa, 1997—. Recipient Best Videography award AP, 1991, Best Documentary Internat. TV and Video Assn., 1996. Mem. NATAS (Emmy 1998), Soc. of Profl. Journalists (exec. bd. 1997—, 8 Awards of Excellence 1995, 96, 97, 98). Avocations: scuba diving, skiing. E-mail: barrettstephen@hotmail.com. Office: WFTS TV 4045 N Himes Ave Tampa FL 33607

BARRETT, THOMAS JOSEPH, sales executive, computer systems consultant; b. Montclair, N.J., June 18, 1955; s. Joseph Thomas and Marion Helen (Staples) B.; m. Wendy Irene Stout, Mar. 15, 1980; children: John, Christopher. Student, Syracuse U., 1973-74; BS in Agronomy and Plant Genetics, U. Ariz., 1979. Asst. supt. Skyline Country Club, Tucson, 1979-81, USN, China Lake, Calif., 1981-83; supt. Palos Verdes Golf Club, Palos Verdes Estates, Calif., 1983-87; dist. mgr. Rain Bird Sales, Glendora, Calif., 1987-92, regional sales mgr., 1992-97, mtkg. mgr., 1997—; v.p., dir. Tucson Women's Hockey Club, 1978-81. Author software Estimator, 1992. Mem. Am. Soc. Landscape Architects. Home: 104 Ash Cir Noblesville IN 46060-9101 Office: Rain Bird Sales 145 N Grand Ave Glendora CA 91741-2469

BARRETT, THOMAS LEON FRANCIS, information technology software executive; b. Shenandoah, Pa., July 19, 1938; s. Thomas Francis and Leocadia Modesta (Pietkiewicz) B.; m. Helene Elizabeth Ryan, June 29, 1963; children: Kathleen Theresa, Maureen Patricia, Thomas Leon Francis, Jr. Student, Bloomsburg State Tchrs. Coll., 1956-57, Pa. State Inst. Tech., 1964-66, Villanova U., 1966-70; BS in Computer Scis., Pacific Western U., 1982, MS, 1994, PhD, 1995. Profl. safe cracker Mosler Safe Co., Phila., 1958-66; programmer, mathematician Missile and Space divsn. GE, Valley Forge, Pa., 1966-69, software engr., 1972-73; chief programmer reentry systems divsn. GE, Phila., 1973-78; supr. software engring. GE, Valley Forge, 1978-81, mgr. software engring. reentry sys. dept., 1981-86, mgr. info. tech. software engring. reentry-enrviron systems dept., 1986-88, sr. sys. engr. Space Def. Initiative, 1988-93; software cons. Programming Methods Inc., N.Y.C., 1969-70; programmer analyst GTE Data Svcs., Mt. Laurel, N.J., 1970-72; sr. sys. software engr. for strategic def. Martin Marietta, Blue Bell, Pa., 1994; software configuration mgmt. and systems engring sr. cons. Lockheed Martin Missiles and Space, East Windsor, N.J. Valley, Forge, Pa., 1995—. V.p. Intra County Swim League, Delaware County, Pa., 1980-81, treas., 1982-88; basketball coach Cath. youth orgn. Sacred Heart Parish, Clifton Heights, 1975-85, track coach Cath. youth orgn., 1977-82, chmn. Cath. charities dr., 1980-81, gen. chair Cath. Life 2000, 1992, pres. parish coun., 1992, 93, 94, 95, vice chmn. parish coun. 1987-91, 94; basketball ofcl. Pa. Interscholastic Athletic Assn., 1982-93. Named Man of Yr. Sacred Heart Parish Clifton Hts., 1988. Mem. Holy Name Soc., Cath. Youth Orgn. (chief advisor 1972-85), Clifton Heights Swim Club (pres. 1987-90, dir. swim team 1976-81), Elks, KC (3 degree). Republican. Roman Catholic. Home: 18 Glenwood Cir Aldan PA 19018-3112 Office: Lockheed Martin Astrospace 2101 PO Box 800 Philadelphia PA 19105-0800

BARRETT, THOMAS M., congressman; b. Milwaukee, Wis., Dec. 8, 1953; m. Kristine Barrett; children: Thomas John, Anne Elizabeth. BA in Economics, U. Wis., 1976, JD with honors, 1980. Atty. Smith & O'Neill, Milw., 1982-84; mem. Wis. State Assembly, 1984-89, Wis. State Senate from 5th Dist., 1989-92, 105th Congress from 5th Wis. dist., Washington, D.C., 1993—; chmn. Com. on Elections, 1987, Com. on Health, 1988-89, Devel. Disabilities Law Legislative Coun. Com., 1988, Long Term Health Care Ins. Legislative Coun. Com., 1988; chmn. Trial Court System Funding Legislative Coun. Com., 1990; mem. Banking & Fin. Svcs. Com., Govt. Reform & Oversight Com. Bd. dirs. Sojourner Truth House, Shalom High Sch., Transcenter Home for Youth. Recipient Circle of Friends award Milw. Advocates for Retarded Citizens, 1989, Health Leadership award State Med. Soc., Govt. Leadership award Rehab. for Wis.; named to Clean Sixteen list for environ. voting record by Wis. Environ. Decade, 1987, 89, 90. Mem. Wis. Bar Assn., Phi Beta Kappa. Office: US Ho Reps 1214 Longworth Office Bldg Washington DC 20515-4905*

BARRETT, TINA, professional golfer; b. Balt., Md., June 5, 1966; d. Barbara Smith; m. Dan Friedman, Nov. 27, 1993. BA cum laude, Longwood Coll., 1988. Winner Eastern Amateur, 1987, Md. State Amateur, 1988; golfer Ladies Pro Golf Assn., 1988—. Avocations: Balt. Orioles and Pheonix Suns fan. *

BARRETT, WILLIAM E., congressman; b. Lexington, Nebr., Feb. 9, 1929; s. Harold O. and Helen Stuckey B.; m. Elsie L. Carlson, 1952; children: William C., Elizabeth A., David H., Jane M. AB, Hastings (Nebr.) Coll., 1951; grad., Nebr. Realtors Inst. Cert. real estate broker, Nebr. Admissions counselor Hastings Coll., 1952-54, asst. dir. admissions, 1954-56; ptnr. Barrett Agy., Lexington, 1956-59; pres. Barrett-Housel & Assocs., Inc., 1970-90; former pres. Dawson County Young Rep.; del. Rep. Co. Conv., from 1958; mem. Nebr. Rep. State Exec. Com., 1964-66; chmn., formerly mem. Rep. Nat. Com., state coord. Mobilization of Rep. Enterprise Programs, 1965-66; del. Rep. Nat. Conv., 1968; mem. Nebr. Legislature, 1979-90, speaker, 1987-90; mem. 102nd-105th Congresses from 3rd Nebr. Dist., 1991—; work in campaigns for various rep. candidate, 1960; officer Barrett-Housel & Assocs., Inc., 1969—; dir. Farmers State Bank; chmn. Agr. subcom. on Gen. Farm Commodities, mem. forestry, resource conservation & rsch. coms.; mem. oversight & investigations, worker protections, agr., edn. and workplace coms.; mem. Econ. & Ednl. Opportunity Com. Trustee, co-founder Nebr. Real Estate Polit. Edn. Com.; elder First Presbyn. Ch., Lexington; moderator Presbytery of Platte, 1972-73, chmn. gen. coun., 1973, mem. staff nominating com. Synod of Lakes and Prairies, from 1973. With USN, 1951-52. Named Legislator of Yr. Nat. Rep. Legislators Assn., 1990. Mem. Nebr. Assn. Ins. Agts., Nat. Assn. Ins. Agts., Dawson Co. Bd. Realtors, Nebr. Assn. Realtors, Nat. Assn. Realtors, Nebr. Jaycees (named one of three outstanding young men of Nebr. 1962), Rotary (Lexington). Office: Offices of House Mems US Ho of Reps 2458 Rayburn Bldg Washington DC 20515-2703*

BARRETT, WILLIAM GARY, advertising executive; b. N.Y.C., Oct. 24, 1943; s. Herbert Mark and Toni Eileen (Craig) B.; m. Christina Louise Sjogren, Sept. 11, 1977 (div. 1980); m. Donna Lou Gault, May 11, 1984; 1 child, Daniel Martin. BA, U. Buffalo, 1964. Sr. media planner Grey Advt., N.Y.C., 1966-69; supr. network rels. Batten, Barton, Durstine & Osborn Advt., N.Y.C., 1969-71; v.p., media dir. Martin Landey, Arlow, N.Y.C., 1971-74; v.p. media and mktg. Shaller-Rubin Assocs., N.Y.C., 1974-77; sr. v.p., dir. media and mktg. svcs. Young & Rubicam and Dentsu, Young & Rubicam, N.Y.C., 1977-86; exec. v.p., dir. communications svcs. Earle Palmer Brown, Washington, 1986-88; exec. v.p., dir. client svcs. S.F.M. Media/MPG, LLC, N.Y.C., 1988—. Lt. U.S. Army, 1964-65. Avocations: skiing, photography, scuba diving, wine collecting. Home: 400 W End Ave New York NY 10024-5750 Office: SFM Media Corp 1180 Ave Of The Americas New York NY 10036-8401

BARRETT, WILLIAM JOEL, investment banker; b. Darien, Conn., Aug. 26, 1939; s. William J. and Virginia Barrett; m. Sara Schrock, Sept. 1, 1962; children: William, Brian, Christopher, Peter. BA, DePauw U., Greencastle, Ind., 1961; MBA, NYU, 1963. Investment analyst Met. Life Ins. Co., 1961-66; v.p. Gregory & Sons, investment bankers, 1966-69, G.A. Saxton, investment bankers, 1969-74; sr. v.p. Janney Montgomery Scott, Inc., N.Y.C., 1974—; bd. dirs. Supreme Industries, Inc., Shelter Components Corp., Esmor Correctional Svc., Inc., Fredericks of Hollywood, Inc., TGC Industries, Inc., Am. Country Ins. Co. Inc. Bd. trustees De Pauw U., Diocesan Investment Trust N.J. Mem. Univ. Club, India House Club, Bond of N.Y. Club, Shrewsbury Sailing and Yacht Club, Sea Bright Lawn Tennis Club, Seabright Beach Club, Rumson Country Club. Republican. Episcopalian. *

BARRETT, YVONNE LAUGHLIN, retail manager; b. Newark, N.J., July 24, 1943; d. Marion and Ola D. (Johnson) Laughlin; m. Jesse Moore, Sept. 23, 1984 (div. 1996); children: Durand, Anthony, Yvette; m. Frederick A. Barrett, Apr. 6, 1997. Student, Essex County Coll., 1978, 91—. Lic. life ins. producer. Store mgr. Lerner Ltd., N.Y.C., N.J., 1961-87, A & E Stores, Ridgefield, N.J., 1987-88; entrepreneur sponsoring social affairs Oldie But Goodies, N.J., 1990—. Writer of poetry. Mem. NAFE, NAACP, DAV (life aux.).

BARRETTA-KEYSER, JOLIE, professional athletics coach, author, film and TV casting director; b. Phila., Aug. 17, 1954; d. Philip Francis and Norma Roberta (Podoszek) Barretta; m. Joel D. Keyser; children: Evan Barrett, Kyra Lani. Student, U. Calif., Long Beach, 1972-76, U. Florence, Italy, 1974-75. Tchr. gymnastics Los Angeles City Sch. Dist., 1973-77, judge, 1976-82; coach, choregrapher Kips Gymnastic Club, Long Beach, Calif., 1976-78, So. Calif. Acrobatics Team, Huntington Beach, Calif., 1979-81, UCLA, 1980-82; pres. West Coast Waves Rhythmic Gymnastics, Rolling Hills Estates, Calif., 1980—; mem. coaching staff U.S. Nat. Rhythmic Gymnastics Team, 1983—; exec. Cell Tech Health Corp., 1996—; coach Centro Olimpico Nazionale Italia, Rome, 1974-76; lectr. dance, phys. edn. Calif. State U., Dominguez Hills, Carson, 1981-92; French lang. mistress of ceremonies rhythmic gymnastics event U.S. Olympic Games, L.A., 1984; invited observer Inst. Phys. Culture, Bejing, 1985, Bulgarian Gymnastics Fedn., Sophia, 1982-90; meet dir. state and regional championships, L.A. County, 1984, '86; internat. lectr. body alignment; pres. Rhythymic Gymnasts Devel. Program, 1984—; developer RIGOR (Rhythmic Gymnastics Outreach) for U.S.A. recreation programs; mem. rhythmic gymnastics adv. com. & bd. Internat. Spl. Olympics, 1990—. Author: Body Alignment, 1985; columnist Internat. Gymnast Mag., 1987-90; contbg. columnist The Crayon Report, 1996—. Tour leader Acad. Tours Inc. U.S./Bulgaria Friendship Through Sports Ann. Tour, N.Y. and Bulgaria, 1987. Recipient recognition plaque U.S. Womens Sports Awards Banquet, 1984-89. Mem. U.S. Rhythmic Gymnastics Coaches Assn. (pres. 1984—), U.S. Gymnastics Fedn. (bd. dirs. 1985—, nat. team coach 1984-93, appointed to ethics com., mem. del., coach internat. competitions U.S., Mex., Hungary, Bulgaria, Belgium, Can. 1984—, choreographer age group devel. compulsory div. 1987, staff Olympic Tng. Ctr. 1984—, charter mem. ethics com. 1991-94), Inst. Noetic Scis., Internat. Spl. Olympics (adv. bd. rhythmic gymnastics), Womans Sports Found. Republican. Avocations: dance, skiing, languages, singing, composing. Office: West Coast Waves 11661 San Vicente Blvd Ste 609 Los Angeles CA 90049-5114

BARRETT-CONNOR, ELIZABETH LOUISE, epidemiologist, educator; b. Evanston, Ill., Apr. 8, 1935; m. James D. Connor; 3 children. BA, Mt. Holyoke Coll., 1956, DSc (hon.), 1985; MD, Cornell U., 1960; MD (hon.), U. Utrecht, The Netherlands, 1996, U. Bergen, Norway, 1996. Diplomate Am. Bd. Internal Medicine, Nat. Bd. Med. Examiners. Instr. medicine U. Miami, Fla., 1965-68, asst. prof. medicine, 1968-70; asst. prof. community and family medicine U. Calif., San Diego, 1970-74, assoc. prof. community and family medicine, 1974-81, prof. community and family medicine, 1981—, acting chair dept. community and family medicine, 1981-82, chmn. dept. family and preventative medicine, 1982-97; mem. hosp. infection control com. VA Med. Ctr., San Diego, 1971-81; Kelly West Meml. lectr. Am. Diabetes Assn., Indpls. 1987; vis. prof.Royal Soc. Medicine, London, 1989; John Rankin lectr. U. Wis., 1989; Don McLeod Meml. lectr., Halifax, N.S., Can., 1990; Elizabeth Blackwell lectr., Rochester, Minn., 1991; Lila Wallace vis. prof. N.Y. Hosp.-Cornell Med. Ctr., N.Y.C., 1992; Donald P. Shiley vis. lectr. Scripps Clinic and Rsch. Found., La Jolla, Calif., 1993; Leonard M. Schuman lectr. U. Mich., 1993; disting. vis. U. Western Australia, 1997; disting. lectr. geriatrics Duke U. Med. Ctr., Durham, N.C., 1998. Contbr. articles to profl. jours. Recipient Frederick Murgatroyd prize, 1965, Kaiser award for excellence in tchg., 1982, Dr. of Yr. award San Diego Health Care Assn., 1987, merit award Nat. Inst. Aging, 1987, Making a Difference for Women's Health award Soroptimists, La Jolla, 9195, clin. svc. award Soc. for Advancement Women's Health Rsch., 1997; NIH grantee, 1970—. Fellow ACP (James D. Bruce Meml. award 1994), Am. Heart Assn. (chmn. budget com. coun. on epidemiology 1987-88, chmn. coun. on epidemiology 1988-89m Ancel Keys lectr. 1995, Elizabeth Barrett-Connor rsch. award 1995, Merit award 1998), Royal Soc. Health, Am. Coll. Preventive Medicine (Katharine Boucot Sturgis lectr. 1986, Am. Coll. Nutrition, Royal Soc. Medicine; mem. APHA (chmn. epidemiology sect. 1989-90, Wade Hampton Frost lectr. 1993), Assn. Tchrs. Preventive Medicine (bd. dirs. 1987-92, Outstanding Educator award 1992), Inst. Medicine, Soc. Epidemiol. Rsch. (pres. 1983, John Cassell Meml. lectr. 1997), Phi Beta Kappa. Office: U Calif San Diego Family and Preventative Medicine 9500 Gilman Dr # Mc607 La Jolla CA 92093-5003*

BARRICK, WILLIAM HENRY, lawyer; b. Byron, Ill., May 10, 1916; s. William B. and Georgia (Bishop) B.; m. Elizabeth Norton, Nov. 1, 1941 (dec. Dec. 1995); children: W. Boyd II, Nancy Barrick Carlin. AB, U. Ill., 1936, LLB, 1938, JD, 1958; postgrad., Judge Adv. Sch., U. Mich., 1945. Bar: Ill. 1938, U.S. Supreme Ct. 1945, Fla. 1969. Sec. to presiding justice Ill. Supreme Ct., 1942-52; ptnr. Andrews, Essington & Barrick, Rockford, Ill., 1938-50; ptnr. Barrick & Switzer, Rockford, 1950—, Naples, Fla., 1969—; asst. exec. Office JAG, U.S. Army, Washington, 1945-46; city atty., Rockford, 1941; justice of peace, Oglecty, Ill., 1937-41. editor: Synopsis of Ill. Laws, Rand McNally & Co., Bankers Directory, 1950-70. Trustee Rockford Coll., 1970—; chmn. coun. advisors U. Dubuque Theol. Sem., 1985-91; gov. Regent's Coll., London, 1987-90. Decorated Legion of Merit. Fellow Am. Coll. Trust and Estate Counsel, Am. Bar Found.; mem. Winnebago County Bar Assn. (pres. 1966-67), Chgo. Bar Assn., Fed. Bar Assn., Am. Fed. Comm. Bar Assn., Bar Assn. 7th Fed. Cir., Fla. Bar Assn., Am. Judicature Soc., Soc. Dorset Men (life). Office: Barrick Switzer 1 Madison St Rockford IL 61104-1100*

BARRICKMAN, LES L., psychiatrist; b. Centerville, Iowa, Nov. 2, 1953; s. Bob and Margie (Gorden) B. BA, William Penn Coll., 1976; DO, Kirksville Coll. Osteopathic, 1982. Diplomate Am. Bd. Psychiatry and Neurology, Am. Bd. Adult Psychiatry, Am. Bd. Adolescent Psychiatry. Intern Des Moines Gen. Hosp., 1982-83; resident adult psychiatry U. Iowa Coll. Medicine, Iowa City, 1983-86, resident child/adolescent psychiatry, 1986-88, assoc. faculty, 1989-90, instr., 1990-93, asst. prof., 1991-93; clin. asst. prof. U. N.Mex., Iowa City, 1995; dir. child/adolescent edn. tng. program U. Iowa, 1991-93; assoc. prof. U. Hawaii, Honolulu, 1996-98; clin. assoc. prof. dept. psychiatry Coll. Medicine, 1999—; pvt. practice Honolulu, 1998—. Mem. AMA, Am. Psychiat. Assn., Am. Acad. Child/Adolescent Psychiatry.

BARRICKS, MICHAEL ELI, retinal surgeon; b. Chgo., Feb. 22, 1940; s. Arthur Goetz and Ruth (Zuckerman) B.; m. Zondra Dell Natman, Jan. 18, 1992; 1 child, Charleigh Ruth. BA, Harvard Coll., 1961; MD, U. Chgo., 1965; PhD, Stanford U., 1973. Diplomate Nat. Bd. Med. Examiners; lic. physician, Calif. Intern then resident in surgery Stanford (Calif.) U., 1965-67, postdoctoral fellow, 1967-72; resident, fellow in ophthalmology Bascom Palmer Eye Inst., Miami, Fla., 1972-76; fellow in retinal surgery U. Calif., San Francisco, 1976-77; asst. prof., dir. retina svc. U. Tex., San Antonio, 1977-78; retinal surgeon, dir. retina svc. Permanente Med. Group., Oakland, Calif., 1979—; asst. clin. prof. U. Calif., San Francisco, 1980-92, assoc. clin. prof., 1993—; bd. dirs. Barricks Mfg. Co., Gadsden, Ala. Contbr. articles to profl. jours. Recipient Gold award Am. Acad. Pediatrics, Outstanding Physician award Kaiser Hosp., 1982, Cert. of Appreciation for Outstanding Teaching, U. Calif, San Francisco; ; Nat. scholar Fisher Body Craftsmans Guild; USPHS fellow Stanford U., 1967-70, Atholl McBean fellow Stanford Rsch. Inst., 1970-71. Fellow Am. Acad. Ophthalmology; mem. Permanente Ophthalmologic Soc. (pres. 1981), Vitreous Soc., Harvard Varsity Club, Crimson Key Soc.

BARRIE, BARBARA, actress; b. Chgo., May 23, 1931; d. Louis and Frances Rose (Boruszak) Berman; m. Jay Malcolm Harnick, July 23, 1964; children: Jane Caroline Harnick, Aaron Louis Harnick. BFA, U. Tex., 1953. Appeared with N.Y. Shakespeare Festival, 1960, 65, 69, Am. Shakespeare Festival, 1958-59; appeared on Broadway in: Wooden Dish, 1955, Beau Stratagem, 1959, Company, 1970, Prisoner of Second Ave., 1972, Selling of the President, 1971, California Suite, 1976, The Killdeer, 1974 (Obie award, Drama Desk award 1974), Big and Little Phoenix Theatre, N.Y.C., 1979, Isn't it Romantic, 1984, Fugue, Long Wharf Playhouse, 1986, After-Play, 1995; numerous TV appearances including Barney Miller, Two of a Kind, 1982, Barefoot in the Park, 1982, Double Trouble (series), 1984-85, as Mamie Eisenhower in Backstairs at the White House, Family Ties, 1987, Mr. President, 1987, TV movies include: The Execution, My Breast; appeared in films One Potato, Two Potato, 1964 (Cannes Festival Acting award 1964), The Caretakers, 1963, Breaking Away, 1979 (Oscar nomination), Private Benjamin, 1980, Real Men, 1986, The Passage, End of the Line, 1986, (TV series) Suddenly Susan, 1996, (TV mini series) Scarlett, 1994, (voice) Hercules, 1997. Active ERA. Mem. AFTRA, SAG, Actors Equity Assn., Acad. Motion Picture Arts and Scis. Address: c/o Liebman & Resnick 159 W 53d New York NY 10023

BARRIENTOS, JANE ELLEN, art educator; b. Agawam, Mass., July 20, 1953; d. John Carleton and Madeline (Ploof) Bitgood; m. Moises Jonas Barrientos, June 25, 1973. BA in Econs., Westfield State Coll., 1978; cert., Paier Coll. Fine Art, 1995. Owner Agawam Arts & Crafts Shop, 1973-85; instr. art Am. Decorative Arts Studio, West Springfield, Mass., 1985—. Author: The Art of Deception Vol. I, 1997, Vol. II, 1998; contbr. articles to profl. jours. Mem. Nat. Soc. Decorative Painters, Acad. Artists Assn., Springfield Mus. and Libr. Assn., Friends of West Springfield Libr., PTA. Avocations: sailing, travel, hiking. Office: Am Decorative Arts Studio 33 Cooper St West Springfield MA 01089-2807

BARRIER, JOHN WAYNE, engineer, management consultant; b. Savannah, Tenn., June 17, 1949; s. John H. and Evelyn (Williams) B.; m. Janet Putnam, Aug. 21, 1969; children: Jennifer, James, Joseph, Jeremy. BS in Chem. Engring., U. Tenn., 1972, MS in Adminstrn., 1975. Chem. engr. Monsanto Co., Decatur, Ala., 1972-76; chem. engr. TVA, Muscle Shoals, Ala., 1976-82, process devel. leader, 1982-85, project mgr., 1985-86, program mgr., 1986—; instr. mgmt. Faulkner U., Florence, Ala., 1980—. Contbr. articles to profl. jours. Named one of Outstanding Young Men in Am., 1979; recipient Tech. Achievement award U.S. Dept. Energy, 1985, Jump Meml. award U.S. Dept Commerce, 1986. Mem. Nat. Mgmt. Assn. Avocations: travel, sports, hiking. Home: 3000 County Road 10 Florence AL 35633-2942 Office: TVA 435 CEB Muscle Shoals AL 35633

BARRIGER, JOHN WALKER, IV, transportation executive; b. St. Louis, Aug. 3, 1927; s. John Walker and Elizabeth chambers (Thatcher) B.; m. Evelyn Dobson, Dec. 29, 1955; children: John Walker V., Catherine B. Dunsby. BS, MIT, 1949; CT, Yale U., 1950. With Santa Fe Railway, 1950-58, 70-83, GTE Sylvania Info. Sys., 1968-70, Santa Fe Pacific Corp., 1983-85, Chgo., Mo. and We. Railway, 1986-90; v.p. Derson Group Ltd., 1990—. Trustee John W. Barriger Ill. Nat. R.R. Libr., St. Louis; bd. dirs. St. Louis Merc. Libr. Served with USN, 1946. Recipient Bronze Beaver award MIT, 1975. Mem. Newcomen Soc., Econ. Club. Chgo., Exec. Club Chgo., MIT Club Chgo., Kenilworth Club, Union League Chgo., Sheridan Shores Yacht Club, Delta Kappa Epsilon. Republican. Roman Catholic. Home: 155 Melrose Ave Kenilworth IL 60043-1248 Office: 332 S Michigan Ave Ste 700 Chicago IL 60604-4303

BARRINGER, PAUL BRANDON, II, lumber company executive; b. Sumter, S.C., Aug. 22, 1930; s. Victor Clay and Gertrude (Hampton) B.; m. Merrill Underwood, May 27, 1957; children: Merrill U., Victor Clay, Ann Hampton. B.S., U. Va., 1952; postgrad., George Washington U., 1954. With Human Relations Lab., Washington, 1954; with Coastal Lumber Co., Weldon, N.C., 1954—; chmn. bd., CEO Coastal Lumber Co., 1967—; bd. dirs. BB&T Corp., Sea Pines Co., Inc.; mem. Pres.'s Task Force on Internat. Pvt. Enterprise, Industry Policy Adv. Com. for trade policy matters; mem. U. Va. Exec. Com. Capital Fund Campaign, 1994—. With USAD, 1952-54. Mem. NAM (bd. dirs.), Chief Execs. Orgn. (dir.), Zeta Psi, Sigma Delta Psi, Lambda Chi. Episcopalian. Clubs: Sea Pines Country, Summitt, Chockoyotte Country, Farmington Country. Home: 14 S Calibogue Cay Hilton Head Island SC 29928-2912 Office: Coastal Lumber Co PO Box 829 Weldon NC 27890-0829

BARRINGER, PHILIP E., retired government official; b. Haverford, Pa., Oct. 2, 1916; s. D. Moreau and Margaret (Bennett) B.; m. Sophia F. Hazard, Aug. 10, 1946 (dec. Apr. 1979); children: Thomas H., C. Frances, Paul M.; m. Bettyanne Rusen, Oct. 15, 1988. Student, Heidelberg (Germany) Coll., 1934; A.B. cum laude in European History, Princeton U., 1938; LL.B., U. Pa., 1948; grad., Nat. War Coll., 1952. Bar: Pa. 1949. U.S. sec. Legal Directorate, Allied Control Council for Germany, 1945-46; with Office Sec. Def., 1949-64; dep. dir. European region Office Asst. Sec. for internat. security affairs, 1956-64; attaché, politico-mil. affairs Am. embassy, London, Eng., 1964-66; dep. dir. Near East and South Asia region Office Asst. Sec. Def. for internat. security affairs, Washington, 1966-67; dir. fgn. mil. rights Dept. Def., 1967-99; ret., 1999; mem. numerous U.S. dels.; dir. Barringer Crater Co., Phila. Pres. Alexandria (Va.) Civic Orch., 1950-52; co-founder, mem. Cleveland Park Chamber Music Group, 1957—; trustee All Souls Unitarian Ch., Washington, 1964, 67-70, chmn., 1969-70; del. to Unitarian-Universalist Gen. Assemblies, 1968-80, Internat. Assn. for Religious Freedom meetings, 1975, 84, 87. Mem. Pa. N.G., 1937-40; served to lt. col., arty. AUS, 1941-46, ETO. Decorated Army Commendation medal; recipient Meritorious Civilian Svc. medal Sec. Def., 1975, 81, Disting. Civilian Svc. award, 1989; Meritorious Exec. award Sr. Exec. Svc., 1990. Mem. Am. Soc. Internat. Law, Internat. Inst. Strategic Studies (London), Am. Hiking Soc. (bd. dirs. 1988-94), Cosmos Club, Princeton Club, Cleveland Park Club, Potomac Appalachian Trail Club (pres. 1990-91), Appalachian Trail Conf. (bd. mgrs. 1991-97). Home: 4609 38th St NW Washington DC 20016-1803 Office: Office Asst Sec Def (ISA) Washington DC 20301-2400

BARRIOS, RICHARD (JOHN), writer, film historian; b. Houma, La., July 2, 1954; s. Manny Clement and Gladne Marie (Thibodeaux) B. MusB in Music History magna cum laude, Loyola U., New Orleans, 1980; MusM in Music History and Lit., U. Houston, 1984; MA in Cinema Studies, NYU, 1986. Fin. asst. Houston Grand Opera, 1981-82; opera promotion staff Boosey & Hawkes, Inc., N.Y.C., 1986-91; freelance writer, rschr. N.Y.C., 1991—; cons., program annotator Kino Video, N.Y.C., 1997—; film programmer, lectr. Am. Film Inst., Washington, 1996, Film Forum, N.Y.C., 1996; lectr. Smithsonian Inst., Washington, 1995, U.S. Army Band, Ft. Myer, Va., 1998. Author: A Song in the Dark: The Birth of the Musical Film, 1995 (Theatre Libr. Assn. prize 1996); contbr. articles to profl. jours.; appeared in and narrator: (film) Busby Berkeley: Going Through the Roof, 1997. Co-chmn. reconciling congregation com. Ch. of St. Paul and St. Andrew, N.Y.C., 1996—, staff-parish com., 1994-98, lay del. to ann. conf., 1998—. Mem. Met. Opera Guild, Soc. for Cinephiles, Lesbian and Gay Cmty. Svcs. Ctr. (advocate). Democrat. Methodist. Avocations: travel, opera, fitness, cooking. Home: Apt 3K 159-00 Riverside Dr W New York NY 10032

BARRISKILL, MAUDANNE KIDD, primary school educator; b. Balt., Apr. 2, 1932; d. John Graydon and Maudine (Adams) Kidd; m. Peter Herbert Barriskill, Nov. 30, 1957; children: John, Michael. BA, So. Meth. U., 1954; student early childhood edn., Old Dominion U., 1970; student, Katharine Gibbs Sch., N.Y.C., 1954-55, Juilliard Sch. Music, N.Y.C., 1948-50. Exec. sec., copywriter trainee J. Walter Thompson Advt. Agy., N.Y.C., 1955-59; founder Maude Barry Interior Design, Virginia Beach, 1970-73; founder, dir. The Home Sch., Virginia Beach, 1975—; tchr. Ea. Shore Chapel Presch., Virginia Beach, 1970-75, Montessori Child Devel. Ctr., Virginia Beach. Author children's books and workbooks. Tchr. Sunday sch. Home: 4721 Newgate Ct Virginia Beach VA 23455-4033

BARRITT, EVELYN RUTH BERRYMAN, nurse, educator, university dean; b. Detroit, Sept. 4, 1929; d. George C. and Ruby (Mathews) Berryman; m. Ward LeRoy Barritt, Oct. 28, 1951; 1 dau., Kelli Jo. A.A., Graceland Coll., 1949; diploma, Independence (Mo.) Sanitarium and Hosp. Sch. Nursing, 1952; B.S.N., Ohio State U., 1956, M.A., 1962, Ph.D., 1971. Asst. instr. nursing Atlantic City Hosp., 1952-53; staff nurse Shore Meml. Hosp., Somers Point, N.J., 1953-54, Ohio State U. Hosp., Columbus, 1954-55; instr. White Cross Hosp., Columbus, 1955-57; asso. dir. nursing service Riverside Meth. Hosp., Columbus, 1957-64; asst. exec. dir. Ohio Nurses Assn., Columbus, 1964-65; dean Capital U. Sch. Nursing, Columbus, 1965-72, Coll. Nursing, U. Iowa, Iowa City, 1972-79; prof. nursing Coll. Nursing, U. Iowa, 1972-80; prof. Sch. Nursing U. Miami, Fla., 1980—, dean, 1980-85; bd. dirs. Health Coun. South Fla., 1988—, pres., 1990-92; bd. dirs. So. Fla. Perinatal Network, Inc., 1980-89, pres., 1984-86; mem. Fla. Bd. Ind. and Pvt. Colls. and Univs., 1980; co-chmn. Dade County Indigent Care Task Force, 1991-93. Author: Florence Nightingale: Her Wit and Wisdom, 1975; author, editor: Thoughts on CareGiving, 1998; contbr. articles to profl. jours. Mem. Am. Nurses Assn., Ohio Nurses Assn. (pres. dist. 1966-68), Iowa Nurses Assn., Fla. Nurses Assn., Graceland Coll. Alumni Assn., Am. Assn. Higher Edn., Am. Assn. Colls. Nursing (pres. 1976-78), Independence Hosp. Sch. Nursing Alumnae Assn. Home: 416 Park Blvd N Venice FL 34285-1332

BARR-KUMAR, RAJ, architect; b. Colombo, Ceylon, Feb. 5, 1946; came to U.S., 1974; s. Alexander Hamilton Barr-Kumarakulasinghe and Francesca ThangaRanee (Winslow) Barr-Kumar; m. Athina Kambouri, Feb. 14, 1975 (dec. Feb. 1977); m. Bernadette Dipica Wikramanayake, Jan. 29, 1994. BS, U. Ceylon, Colombo, 1971; grad. diploma in architecture, U. London, 1974; MArch, U. Kans., 1975; postgrad., Harvard U., 1978. Lic. architect Washington, N.Y., Va., Md., Fla., Kans.; cert. Nat. Coun. Archtl. Registration Bds. Designer Panditaratna & Adithiya RIBA, Ceylon, 1967-71, Jon Prescott RIBA, Hong Kong, 1971-72, NE Met. Regional Hosp. Bd./Watkins Gray Internat., London, 1972-73, Llewellyn-Davies Assocs., London, 1973-74, Patty Berkebile Nelson Assocs./Seligson Assocs., Kansas City, Mo., 1975-78; sr. designer Barret Daffin & Carlan, Tallahassee, Fla., 1979-80; mgr. computer aided design Wolfberg, Alvarez, Taracido Assocs., Rosslyn, Va., 1982-83; pres. Barr-Kumar Architects Engrs., Washington, 1981—; asst. prof. U. Kans., Lawrence, 1975-79; assoc. prof. Fla. A&M U., Tallahassee, 1979-85; dir., assoc. prof. Fla. A&M Architecture Ctr., Washington, 1981-84; vis. prof. Washington Alexandria Ctr. Va. Polytech. Inst., 1984-86; assoc. prof. Howard U., Washington, 1986-94; vis. prof. Washington Alexandria Ctr., Va. Polytech. Inst., 1998, Emens Disting. vis. prof. Ball State U., 1999; spkr., panelist Smithsonian Inst., Washington, 1982—, Nat. Bldg. Mus., Washington, 1985—, Corcoran Art Gallery, 1998—, Lambda Alpha Internat., 1994—; mem. adv. coun. on architecture No. Va. C.Cs., 1983—; apptd. mem. FIDER Nat. Interior Design Accrediting Bd., 1986-92; chair Anne Arundel County Devel. Design Awards, Md., 1985-90; examiner Nat. Coun. Archtl. Registration Bd., 1990; lectr. in field. Chair archtl. group Luther Pl. Shelter for Homeless, Washington, 1990—; co-chair DC-HOME Housing Assistance Team, Washington, 1990—; pres. Sri Lanka Assn., Washington, 1991-93; mem. bldg. and preservation coms. Washington nat. Cathedral, 1995—. Recipient County Exec. Appreciation cert. Anne Arundel County, Md., 1990. Fellow AIA (bd. dirs. Washington chpt. 1984-97, pres. 1990, host chpt. chair nat. conv. 1988-91, nat. bd. dirs. 1991-97, nat. v.p. 1994, nat. pres. 1997, Outstanding Svc. award Washington chpt. 1990, Walter Wagner fellow 1992, Richard Upjohn fellow 1994, Nat. citation for exceptional svc. 1997), Bahamian Inst. Architects, Japan Inst. Architects (hon.), Philippine Inst. Architects (hon.), United Architects of Philippines (hon.), Sri Lanka Inst. Architects (hon.); mem. Royal Inst. Brit. Architects, Royal Archtl. Inst. Can. (hon.), Mex. Soc. Architects (hon.). Office: Barr-Kumar Architects Engrs PC 1825 I St NW Ste 400 Washington DC 20006-5415

BARRON, ALMEN LEO, microbiologist; b. Toronto, Ont., Can., Jan. 19, 1926; came to U.S., 1954, naturalized, 1963; s. Max and Bena (Sussman) B.; m. Shirley Brovender, Sept. 14, 1949; 1 child, Joshua Charles. BSA, Ont. Agrl. Coll., U. Toronto, 1948, MSA, 1949; PhD, Queen's U., Kingston, Ont., 1953. Mem. faculty SUNY, Buffalo, 1954-74; prof. microbiology SUNY, 1968-74; dir. Erie County (N.Y.) Virology Lab., 1968-74; prof. microbiology, chmn. dept. microbiology and immunology U. Ark. Med. Sci., Little Rock, 1974-91, prof. emeritus, 1991—; cons. Little Rock VA Med. Ctr., 1974-91; vis. prof. Hadassah Med. Sch., Hebrew U., Jerusalem, 1972, Kaohsiung Med. Coll., (Taiwan), 1982. Co-editor: Microbiology: Basic Principles and Clinical Applications, 1983; editor: Microbiology of Chlamydia, 1988. Recipient Commonwealth Fund travel award, 1964, Golden Apple award Student AMA, 1975, 77, Disting. Faculty award Ark. Caduceus Club, 1990; Fulbright rsch. scholar Israel, 1964. Mem. Am. Acad. Microbiology (emeritus 1991—), Am. Soc. Microbiology (pres. South Central br. 1980), Infectious Diseases Soc. Am. (emeritus 1991—), Am. Assn. Immunologists. Research on Chlamydia organisms. Home (winter): 1421 N University Ave Apt N318 Little Rock AR 72207-5161 Home (summer): 165 Ontario St Unit 302, Kingston, ON Canada K7L 2Y6

BARRON, ANDREW ROSS, chemistry educator, consultant; b. Eng., May 20, 1962; came to U.S., 1986; BSc, ARCS, Imperial Coll., London, 1983, DIC, PhD, 1986. Prof. chemistry Harvard U., Cambridge, Mass., 1987-95, Rice U., Houston, 1995—; team owner Ross Racing; founder Gallia Inc., Cambridge, 1992=97; pres. Aluminum Rsch. Bd., Cambridge, 1991-98; sci. advisor to Nat. Sci. Resource Ctr., Washington, 1992—. N.Am. regional editor Advanced Materials for Optics and Electronics, 1992—; mem. editl. bd. Advanced Materials, 1985—, Chemistry Materials, 1996—; contbr. numerous articles to sci. jours.; patentee in field. Sci. advisor, lectr. Cambridge Fire Dept., 1990-95, Houston Fire Dept., 1995—; sci. advisor Cambridge Sch. Com., 1990-95. Recipient Humboldt rsch. award Humboldt Found., Germany, 1997. Fellow Royal Soc. Chemistry; mem. Am. Chem. Soc., Materials Rsch. Soc., Am. Ceramics Soc., Royal Soc. Chemistry (Meldola medal and prize 1991, Corday Morgan medal and prize 1995).

Avocations: Lotus cars, cooking, opera, theatre. E-mail: arb@ruf.rice.edu. Office: Rice U Dept Chemistry 6100 Main St Houston TX 77005-1827

BARRON, CHARLES ELLIOTT, retired electronics executive; b. Midland, Tex., Feb. 17, 1928; s. Thomas Paul and Hollie Belle (Pickerill) B. ; m. Sarah Alice Crawford, July 18, 1950; children: Thomas, Sarah, Robert. BSEE, Vanderbilt U., 1949; BD, Southwestern Bapt. Theol. Sem., 1958. Geophysicist Shell Oil Co., various locations, 1949-54, Tex. Pacific Coal and Oil Co., Ft. Worth, 1954-59; engring. mgr. then gen. mgr. Gen. Electric Co., Utica, Syracuse and Binghamton, N.Y., 1959-87; pres. ops. Eaton Corp., Melville, N.Y., 1987-88; pres., chief exec. officer AIL Systems, Inc. (sub. of Eaton Corp.), Deer Park, N.Y., 1989-91, also bd. dirs., 1989-93. Bd. dirs. Roberson Ctr., Binghamton, N.Y., 1981-84, United Way L.I., 1991; chmn. major firms drive Broome County (N.Y.) United Way, 1981-83, bd. dirs.; mem. engring. adv. bd. Syracuse U., 1986-91; mem. engring. sch. council SUNY, Binghamton, 1982-83. Mem. Nat. Security Indsl. Assn. (Comcac com. 1986-88, trustee 1989-91), L.I. Assn. (bd. dirs. 1988-91), Security Affairs Support Assn. (bd. dirs. 1989-91). Republican. Baptist.

BARRON, CHARLES THOMAS, psychiatrist; b. Hattiesburg, Miss., May 2, 1950; s. Palmer H. and Eleanor Clarice (Sherman) B. BS, U. So. Miss., 1972; MD, U. Miss., 1976. Diplomate Am. Bd. Psychiatry and Neurology. Resident psychiatry St. Vincent's Hosp. and Med. Ctr. N.Y., N.Y.C., 1976-79; fellow inpatient psychiatry St. Vincent's Hosp. and Med. Ctr. N.Y., 1979-80; physician-in-charge psychiatry/substance abuse Beth Israel Med. Ctr., N.Y.C., 1980-84; physician-in-charge inpatient svcs. (psychiatry) Beth Israel Med. Ctr., 1984-88; instr. Mt. Sinai Sch. Medicine, N.Y.C., 1980-87; asst. clin. prof. psychiatry Mt. Sinai Sch. Medicine, 1987-88, 91—; assoc. dir. psychiatry Gouverneur Hosp., N.Y.C., 1988-90; clin. asst. prof. psychiatry NYU, 1989-90; dir. inpatient svcs. (psychiatry), assoc. dir. psychiatry Mt. Sinai Svcs., Elmhurst, N.Y., 1990-96; dir. inpatient/emergency svcs., dep. dir. psychiatry Elmhurst Hosp. Ctr. Mt. Sinai Svcs., Elmhurst, N.Y., 1996—; author/presenter presentation World Psychiat. Assn., 1981; presenter Ottawa Child & Adolescent Conf., 1988. Mem. Am. Psychiat. Assn. (presenter 1986, 90, 94), Internat. AIDS Soc., Am. Orthopsychiat. Assn., Am. Pub. Health Assn. Office: D10-34 79-01 Broadway Elmhurst NY 11373-1329

BARRON, ERIC, earth scientist; b. Lafayette, Ind., Oct. 26, 1951; married; 2 children. BS, Fla. State U., 1973; MS, U. Miami, 1976, PhD in Geophysics, 1980. Fellow Nat. Ctr. Admospheric Rsch., 1980-81; assoc. prof. marine geology and geophysics U. Miami, 1985-86; EMS Environ. Inst. Pa. State U., State College, 1986—. Editor-in-chief Earth Interactions. Mem. Am. Geophys. Union, Geol. Soc. Am., Soc. Econ. Paleontologists and Mineralogists, Am. Meteorol. Soc., Assn. Am. Geographers. Office: Pa State U EMS Environ Inst 248 Deike Bldg University Park PA 16802-2711*

BARRON, HAROLD SHELDON, lawyer; b. Detroit, July 4, 1936; s. George Leslie and Rose (Weinstein) B.; m. Roberta Yellin, Nov. 17, 1963; children: Lawrence Ira, Jean Louise. A.B., U. Mich., 1958, J.D., 1961. Bar: N.Y. 1963, Mich. 1961, Ill. 1983, Pa. 1992. Pvt. practice N.Y.C., 1962-68; practice in Southfield, Mich., 1968-83, Chgo., 1983-93, Pa., 1991—; atty. Hughes Hubbard & Reed, 1962-68; corp. counsel Bendix Corp., 1968-69, sec., assoc. gen. counsel, 1969-72, sec., gen. counsel, 1972-83, v.p., 1974-83; ptnr. Arnstein, Gluck, Lehr, Barron & Milligan, Chgo., 1983-86, Seyfarth, Shaw, Fairweather & Geraldson, Chgo., 1986-91; v.p., gen. counsel Unisys Corp., Blue Bell, Pa., 1991-92, sr. v.p., gen. counsel, 1992-94; sr. v.p., gen. counsel, sec., 1994—; mem. nat. adv. coun. and faculty Practising Law Inst., N.Y.C.; bd. dirs. Royal Maccabees Life Ins. Co., Southfield, 1983-94; chmn. bd. F.A. Tucker Group, Inc., 1991-95. Com. visitors U. Mich. Law Sch.; trustee Children's Hosp. Mich., Detroit, 1976-84; mem. Census Adv. Com. on Privacy and Confidentiality, 1975-76; mem. governing bd., adv. coun. Purdue U. Info. Privacy Rsch. Ctr.; bd. dirs. Citizens Rsch. Coun. of Mich., 1982-83, Greater Phila. Econ. Devel. Coalition. Served with USA, 1961-62. Mem. ABA (coun. bus. law sect., sec. bus. law sect., chmn. com. of corp. gen. counsel, sect. bus. law coun., com. corp. law and taxation, internat. bus. law com., com. devels. in investment svcs., com. long-range issues affecting bus. law practice, com. on corp. laws), Am. Arbitration Assn., Am. Soc. Corp. Secs. (securities law com.), Mich. Bar Assn., Assn. Bar City N.Y. (com. corp. law depts.), Carlton Club, Chgo. Club, Bryn Mawr Country Club (Chgo.), Green Valley Country Club (Phila.). Office: Unisys Corp PO Box 500 Blue Bell PA 19424-0001

BARRON, HOWARD ROBERT, lawyer; b. Chgo., Feb. 17, 1930; s. Irwin P. and Ada (Astrahan) B.; m. Marjorie Shapira, Aug. 12, 1953; children: Ellen Barron Feldman, Laurie A. PhB, U. Chgo., 1948; BA, Stanford U., 1950; LLB, Yale U., 1953. Bar: Ill. 1953. Assoc. Jenner & Block, Chgo., 1957-63, ptnr., 1964-97; assoc. Schiff Hardin & Waite, Chgo., 1953, of counsel, 1997—. Contbr. articles to profl. jours. and books. Mem., then pres. Lake County Sch. Dist. 107 Bd. Edn., Highland Park, 1964-71; pres. Lake County Sch. Bd. Assn., 1970-71; mem. Lake County High Sch. Dist. 113 Bd. Edn., Highland Park, 1973-77; mem. Highland Park Zoning Bd. Appeals, 1984-89. Lt. (j.g.) USNR, 1953-57. Mem. ABA (co-chmn. sub-com. labor and employment law, com. corp. counsel litigation sect. 1983—), Ill. State Bar Assn. (chmn. antitrust sect. 1968-69), Fed. Bar Assn., Chgo. Bar Assn., Yale Law Sch. Assn. (v.p. 1978-81), Yale Law Sch. Assn. Ill. (pres. 1962), Internat. Bar Assn., Standard Club, Metro. Club, Yale Club (N.Y.C.). Democrat. Home: 1366 Sheridan Rd Highland Park IL 60035-3407 Office: Schiff Hardin & Waite 6600 Sears Tower Chicago IL 60606

BARRON, JAMES TURMAN, journalist; b. Washington, Dec. 25, 1954; s. James Pressley and Leirona Faith (Turman) B.; m. Jane-Iris Farhi, Apr. 1, 1995. AB cum laude, Princeton U., 1977. Copy person N.Y. Times, N.Y.C., 1977-78, rsch. asst., 1978-79, reporter, 1979—; acting editor, The Living Sect. N.Y. Times, 1996-97; broadcast corespondent Sta. WQXR-FM, N.Y.C., 1987—, Sta. WQEW-AM, N.Y.C., 1992-98; writer Pub. Lives column N.Y. Times, 1998—. Contbr. to books. Mem. Princeton Club, Deadline Club N.Y. (asst. treas. 1993-95, v.p. 1995—). Methodist. Office: NY Times 229 W 43rd St New York NY 10036-3959

BARRON, JEROME AURE, law educator; b. Tewksbury, Mass., Sept. 25, 1933; s. Henry and Sadie (Shafmaster) B.; m. Myra Hymovich, June 18, 1961; children—Jonathan Nathaniel, David Jeremiah, Jennifer Leah. A.B. magna cum laude, Tufts Coll., 1955; JD, Yale U., 1958; LL.M., George Washington U., 1960. Bar: Mass. 1959, D.C. 1960. Law clk. to chief judge U.S. Ct. Claims, Washington, 1960-61; assoc. firm Cross, Murphy & Smith, Washington, 1961-62; asst. prof. law U. N.D., Grand Forks, 1962-64; vis. assoc. prof. U. N.Mex., Albuquerque, 1964-65; assoc. prof. George Washington U., from 1965, prof., 1973—, dean, 1979-88, Lyle T. Alverson prof. law, 1987—; dean Syracuse U. Coll. Law, 1972-73. Author: (with Donald Gillmor and Todd Simon) Mass Communication Law, Cases and Comment, 6th edit., 1997, First Amendment in a Nutshell, 1993, Constitutional Law: Principles and Policy, 5th edit., 1996, (with C. Thomas Dienes) Constitutional Law In A Nutshell, 4th edit., 1998; contbr. articles, chpts. to profl. publs. Served with U.S. Army, 1959-60. Mem. ABA, D.C. Bar, Cosmos Club, Phi Beta Kappa. Office: George Washington U 2000 H St NW Washington DC 20006-4234

BARRON, KEVIN DELGADO, physician, educator; b. St. John's, Nfld., Can., Apr. 21, 1929; s. S. John Augustine and Mercedes (Delgado) B.; m. Elizabeth E. Grossmann, June 14, 1956; children—Kevin Lawrence, Sheila Christine. Student, Meml. Univ. Coll., St. John's, 1945-47; M.D., C.M., Dalhousie U., Halifax, N.S., Can., 1947-52. Diplomate: Am. Bd. Psychiatry and Neurology. Intern Victoria Gen. Hosp., Halifax, 1951-52; asst. resident in internal medicine Victoria Gen. Hosp., 1952-53, Queen Mary Vets. Hosp., Montreal, Que., Can., 1953-54; asst. resident in neurology Montefiore Hosp., N.Y.C., 1954-55; chief resident in neurology Montefiore Hosp., 1955-56, fellow in neuropathology, 1956-59, adj. attending physician dept. neurology, 1956-59; instr. neurology Columbia U., N.Y.C., 1957-59; asso. in neurology and psychiatry Northwestern U. Med. Sch., Chgo., 1959-61; asst. prof. Northwestern U. Med. Sch., 1961-63, asso. prof., 1964-67, prof., 1968-69; prof., chmn. dept. neurology, prof. pathology Albany, N.Y., 1969-93; clin. prof. neurology and adj. prof. pathology Albany, 1993—; cons. neurologist Beth Abraham Home, N.Y.C., 1957-59; asst. attending neurologist Morrisania City Hosp., N.Y.C., 1958-59; attending neurologist, neuropathologist VA Hosp., Hines, Ill., 1960-62, sect. chief neurology service, dir. electron microscope lab., 1962-64, chief neurology service, dir. neuropathology research service, 1964-69; neurologist-in-chief Albany Med. Center Hosp., 1969-93; dir. neuropathology research sect. research service VA Hosp., Albany, 1969-93; cons. to numerous hosps.; chmn. medicine search com. Albany Med. Coll., 1980-81, mem. med. bd., 1980-81, bd. govs., 1980-82. Contbr. articles to various publs. Fulbright fellow, 1976; sr. U.S. Sci. Humboldt Found., 1976-77. Fellow Am. Acad. Neurology; mem. Am. Neurol. Assn. (councillor), Am. Assn. Neuropathologists, Assn. Univ. Profs. Neurology, Soc. Neurosci., Chgo. Neurol. Soc. (v.p. 1967). Office: Ste 900 251 New Karner Rd Albany NY 12205

BARRON, PATRICK KENNETH, bank executive; b. Atlanta, Aug. 10, 1945; s. Seward Golden and Azzie Lee (Wilson) B.; m. Martha Ann Morgan, Sept. 3, 1965; children: Christina Lee, Deborah Ann, John Patrick. BBA cum laude, U. Miami (Fla.), 1975; postgrad., Harvard U., 1984. Supr. Fed. Res. Bank, Atlanta, 1967-71; mgr. br. Fed. Res. Bank, Miami, 1971-88, asst. v.p. br., 1974, asst. br. mgr., 1981, v.p., br. mgr., 1982, sr. v.p., 1987; sr. v.p. Fed. Res. Bank, Atlanta, 1988, 1st v.p., 1991. Mem. adv. coun. Fla. Internat. U., Miami, 1988-89; vice chmn., exec. com. Greater Miami C. of C., 1985-88; mem. fin. com. United Way of Dade County, Miami, 1984-88; rep. United Way, Atlanta, 1989; mem. Leadership Atlanta, 1989-90; mem. pres.'s coun. U. Miami, 1992—. Mem. Am. Inst. Banking, Beta Gamma Sigma. Republican. Lutheran. Avocations: tennis, running, gardening, reading. Home: 2654 Nutwood Trce Duluth GA 30097-7476 Office: Fed Res Bank 104 Marietta St NW Atlanta GA 30303-2706*

BARRON, PEGGY PENNISI, management consultant; b. Chgo., Jan. 27, 1958; d. Louis Legendre and Jane Harriet (Peters) Pennisi; m. Stan Barron, May 3, 1986; children: Brian Alexander, Christine Deanna. BS with honors, U. Ill., Chgo., 1979. Data processing mgr. Oasis Aviation, Inc., L.A., 1980-87; pres. Millennium Enterprises, L.A., Calif., 1987—. Author: Broken Bloodlines, 1997, The Big Daddy, 1999. Mem. NAFE, Phi Beta Kappa, Phi Kappa Phi. Avocations: scuba diving, sky diving, cooking and travel.

BARRON, PURIFICACION CAPULONG, nursing administrator, educator; b. Pampanga, The Philippines, Jan. 24, 1932; d. Alfonso E. and Lucia N. (Nabong) Capulong; m. Rodrigo I. Barron, July 7, 1968; 1 child, Joseph Rodney. Diploma, St. Luke's Hosp., Manila, 1951; student, St. Louis U., 1954-55; BSN, Columbia U., 1960; MA, Philippine Women's U., 1966. Sch. nurse Manila City Schs., 1951-54; staff nurse Mt. Sinai Hosp., N.Y. Polyclinic, St. Clare Hosp., St. Luke's Hosp., 1954-60; prin., chief nurse, instr. Ortanez Gen. Hosp. and Sch. Nursing, Quezon City, Philippines, 1960-64; chief nurse Am. Hosp. and St. Catherine Hosp., Manila, 1964-65; instr. Lorraine Sch. Nursing, Ont., Can., 1965-66; lectr. Ottawa (Ont.) U. Sch. Nursing, 1966-71; asst. prof. Ind. State U. Sch. Nursing, Terre Haute, 1971-74; DON Holiday Home, Clinton, Ind., 1974-75; pvt. duty nurse, 1975-90; dir. Countryside Health Ctr., Buchanan, Ga., 1991-92; co. nurse SAHA Union Internat., Ga., 1992—; dir. nursing Pine Knoll Nursing, Carrollton, Ga., 1992-93; medicare and nursing care plan coord. Meadowbrook Manor of Carrollton, 1993-95; dir. profl. svcs. Higgins Gen. Hosp., Bremen, Ga., 1996; asst. dir. nursing Bagwell Nursing Home, Carrollton, Ga., 1997—; instr. Cen. Luzon Sch. Nursing, Martinez Sch. Nursing, The Philippines, Lorrain Sch. Nursing, Pembroke, Ont., Can.; paramed. examiner ins. applicants, 1982-90; nurse Camp McIntosh, summer 1987. Mem. ANA, Philippine Nursing Assn. (life), St. Luke's Hosp. Alumni Assn. (life.). Home: 103 Kristy Ln Carrollton GA 30117-2527

BARRON, RANDALL FRANKLIN, mechanical engineer, educator, consultant; b. Many, La., May 16, 1936; s. Benjamin Franklin and Inez (Norsworthy) B.; m. Shirley Estelle McDuffie, Mar. 14, 1958; children: Randall Franklin Jr., Donna Carol, Steven Dale, Brian Richard. BS, La. Tech U., 1958; MS, Ohio State U., 1961, PhD, 1964. Registered profl. engr., La. Instr. mech. engring. Ohio State U., Columbus, 1958-64, asst. prof., 1965; assoc. prof. La. Tech U., Ruston, 1965-70, prof., 1970-97, prof. emeritus, 1997—; engring. cons. Riley-Beaird, Inc., Shreveport, La., 1966-86; mem. La. State Bd. Registration for Profl. Engrs. and Land Surveyors, 1989-94, chmn. bd., 1992-93. Author: Cryogenic Systems, 1985, Cryogenic Heat Transfer, 1999; contbr. articles to nat. and internat. jours. Recipient Engring. and Sci. Coun. Profl. Achievement award, 1981; Phi Kappa Phi scholar, 1982. Fellow ASME (Nat. Profl. Devel. lectr. in cryogenics 1988-99); mem. Cryogenic Soc. Am., Am. Soc. for Engring. Edn., Kiwanis, Sigma Xi, Tau Beta Pi, Pi Tau Sigma (Gold medal 1968). Republican. Methodist. E-mail: rbarron@bayou.com. Office: La Tech U Mech Engring Dept PO Box 10348 Ruston LA 71272

BARRON, ROS, artist; b. Boston, July 4, 1933; d. Louis and Ida (Titel) Myers; m. Harris Barron, Apr. 19, 1953; children: Matt Lewis, Nina Rebecca. B.F.A., Mass. Coll. Art, 1954. Fellow Bunting Inst., Harvard U., 1966-68; co-dir. Zone Visual Theater Co., 1970; assoc. prof. art U. Mass.-Harbor Campus, Boston, 1974—; vis. artist U. Colo., Boulder, 1983; presenter Arts at the Bunting, 1997. Producer numerous video performance tapes.; one-woman shows include North Hall Gallery, Mass. Coll. Art, Boston, 1988, Watson Gallery, Wheaton Coll., Norton, Mass., 1989, Harbor Gallery U. Mass., Boston, 1990, Mobius, Boston, 1993, Brick Bottom Gallery, Boston, 1996; exhbns. include Whitney Mus. Am. Art, 1967-68, Helen Shlien Gallery, Boston, 1979, 82, Mus. Modern Art, N.Y.C., 1980, 84, Le Nouveau Musee, Lyon, France, 1979, Montevideo Gallery, Amsterdam, Holland, 1979, World Wide Video Festival, Kijkhuis, Holland, 1984, Hirschhorn Mus., Washington, 1984, North Hall Gallery; travelling group exhbns. include Project Rembrandt Biennial, 1991-92, Women's Caucus for Art, 1992; represented in permanent collections Mus. Fine Arts, Boston, Harvard U., Smith Coll. Collection, Worcester Art Mus., Addison Gallery Am. Art., Inst. Contemporary Art, Boston, Samuel P. Harn Mus. Art, U. Fla., Gainesville, Mus. of Modern Art, N.Y.C., Mus. Modern Art, N.Y.C.; performance Art: (with Harris Barron) Mr. & Mrs. Zone: Art Life Art, Mobius Theatre, Boston, 1987, Performance Art: (with Harris Barron) Mr. & Mrs. Zone Again, Mobius Theatre, Boston, 1997, Eartheart and other video works, Mobius Theatre, Boston, 1999. Bd. dirs. Boston Performance Artists. Recipient Design award HUD, 1968; N.Y. Found. for Arts grantee, 1972; Guggenheim Found. grantee, 1972; Nat. Endowment Arts grantee, 1975; Rockefeller Found. grantee, 1978-80; Mass. Council Arts grantee, 1981-82, 83. Address: 30 Webster Pl Brookline MA 02445-7337 *I am a visual artist. As a painter and video artist, my work involves how I see and transform reality. My life force feels the ontological mystery, an intense state of wonder, and the endlessness of seeing. Strategies of surrealism and the transformational process provide emotional, intellectual, and metaphysical coherence to my work.*

BARRON, SARA, nurse manager; b. Albuquerque, May 13, 1955; d. Fred C. and Martha (Clark) B.; m. Robert Lowy, Oct. 4, 1982; children: Jeremy, Haley, Rachel. BSN, U. N.Mex., 1980, MS, 1988. RN. Dir. rehab. and transitional care units Lourdes Med. Ctr., Pasco, Wash., 1993—. Mem. Am. Orgn. Nurse Execs., Wash. Orgn. Nurse Execs.

BARRON, STEPHANIE, museum curator. AB, Columbia U., 1972; student, Harvard Inst. Arts Adminstrn., 1973; MA, Columbia U., 1974; postgrad., CUNY, 1975-76. Intern, curatorial asst. Solomon R. Guggenheim Mus., 1971-72; Nat. Endowment Arts intern in edn. Toledo Mus. Art, 1973-74; exhbn. coord. Jewish Mus., N.Y.C., 1975-76; assoc. curator modern art L.A. County Mus. Art, 1976-80, curator Twentieth Century Art, 1980-94, coord. curatorial affairs, 1993-96, sr. curator Twentieth Century art, 1995—, v.p. edn. and pub. programs, 1996—; mem. search com. for chair dept. art history UCLA, 1993; lectr., panelist in field. Contbr. articles to profl. jours. Mem. art adv. panel IRS, 1996—; advisor U.S. Holocaust Mus., 1996—; mem. bd. trustees Scripps Coll., 1996—; mem. steering com. Villa Aurora, 1994—. Recipient George L. Wittenborn award ARLIS, 1991, award for best Am. exhbn. of yr. Assn. Internat. Critics Art, 1991, Theo Wormland Kunstpreis, 1992, George L. Wittenborn award, 1992, Alfred H. Barr Jr. award Coll. Art Assn., 1991, 92, E.L. Kirchner prize, Switzerland, 1997, award for best exhbn. catalogue Assn. Internat. Art Critics Art, First Pl. award Am. Assn. Art Mus., 1998, Hon. Mention, Art Librariana Assn., 1998; named Woman of Yr., Bus. and Profl. Women of UJA, Jewish Fedn., 1991, Friends of Tel Hashomer, 1991; named to Order of Merit, 1984; fellow Nat. Endowment of Arts, 1986-87; John J. McCloy fellow in art, 1981. Fellow Am. Acad. Arts and Scis.; mem. Art Table. Office: LA County Mus Art 5905 Wilshire Blvd Los Angeles CA 90036

BARRON, SUSAN, clinical psychologist; b. Chgo., May 13, 1940; d. Earl and Trixie (Chernoff) B.; m. Eugene Pratt, Jan. 18, 1975 (div. 1983). BBA, CCNY, 1960, MA, 1963; PhD, CUNY, 1973. Lic. psychologist; diplomate Am. Bd. Psychol. Specialties. Intern psychologist Bellevue Psychiat. Hosp., N.Y.C., 1964-65, psychologist, 1966-67; thcg. fellow CUNY, 1965-66; staff psychologist Lighthouse, N.Y. Assn. for the Blind, N.Y.C., 1968-71, sr. clin. psychologist, 1971-74; dir. psychol. counseling svcs. Peninsula Ctr. for the Blind, Palo Alto, Calif., 1974-75; cons. psychologist N.Y. State Commn. for Blind and Visually Handicapped, N.Y.C., 1975-78, 86—; dir. psychol. svcs. Thoms Rehab. Hosp., Asheville, N.C., 1978-79; state coord. psychol. svcs. N.Y. State Office Vocat. Rehab., Albany, 1979-85; founder, dir. Family Support Program ICU N.Y. Infirmary-Beekman Downtown Hosp., N.Y.C., 1982-84; cons. clin. psychologist N.Y. Hosp. Cornell U. Med. Ctr., 1987—; pvt. practice, 1987—; behavioral scientist diabetes control/complications trial NIH Cornell U. Med. Ctr., N.Y.C., 1987—; cons. clin. psychologist Joslin Ctr. for Diabetes St. Luke's-Roosevelt Hosp. Ctr./Columbia U. Phys. and Surg., N.Y.C., 1994-95; cons. clin. psychologist Joslin Ctr. Diabetes, St. Lukes-Roosevelt Hosp. Ctr., U. Hosp. of Columbia U. Coll. of Physicians and Surgeons, N.Y.C., 1994-95, Health Psychology Assocs., Calif., 1997—, N.Y.C., 1997—; mem. Nat. Human Svcs. Adv. Bd.-Retinitis Pigmentosa Found., Balt., 1975-82; cons. Del. State Commn. for Blind, 1975-78, Am. Found. Blind, 1974-82, Calif. Dept. Rehab., 1974-82, Hawaii State Svcs. Blind, 1974-82, Ariz. State Svcs. Blind, 1974-82, Nev. State Svcs. Blind, 1974-82; spkr. Nat. Multiple Disabilities Conf., 1982, NAS, 1981; mem. adv. bd. doctoral psychology internship program Rusk Inst. of Rehab. Medicine, NYU Med. Ctr., 1979-84; behavioral scientist Diabetes Control and Complications Trial NIH-Cornell U. Med. Ctr., 1987—; mem. mended hearts NYU Med. Ctr., Cardiac Prevention and Rehab. Ctr. Contbr. articles to profl. jours. Recipient Leadership award Alumni Assn. CCNY, 1960, 62, Rsch. award Retinal Dystrophy Soc., Australia, 1975, Charles H. Best medal for disting. svc. Am. Diabetes Assn., 1994. Fellow Am. Orthopsychiat. Assn. (life); mem. APA, AAAS, Am. Coll. Forensic Examiners, Calif. State Psychol. Assn., Am. Coll. Advanced Psychologists (bd. cert. founding fellow), N.Y. Acad. Scis., Mended Hearts. Office: 347 5th Ave Rm 603 New York NY 10016-5010

BARROS, NÉLIO BAPTISTA, biological oceanographer; b. Vila Velha, Brazil, Jan. 23, 1960; s. Amylton and Celeste (Cavalieri) B. BSc in Oceanology, U. Rio Grande (Brazil), 1982; MSc in Biol. Oceanography, U. Miami (Fla.), 1987, PhD in Marine Biology and Fisheries, 1993. Rsch. biologist Hubbs Sea World Rsch. Inst., Orlando, Fla., 1994—; corp. cons. Sea World Inc., Orlando, 1991—. Author (book chpt.) The Bottlenose Dolphin, 1990. Mem. The Soc. Marine Mammalogy, The Oceanography Soc., Am. Soc. Mammalogists. Roman Catholic. Avocations: foreign languages, traveling, tennis, swimming, theater. Office: Hubbs Sea World Rsch Inst 6295 Sea Harbor Dr Orlando FL 32821-8043

BARROSO, EDUARDO GUILLERMO, surgeon, educator; b. N.Y.C., June 8, 1962. MD, U. Miami, 1988. Diplomate Am. Bd. Surgery, Am. Bd. Plastic Surgery. Intern Rush Presbyn. St. Luke's Med. Ctr., Chgo., 1988-89, resident in gen. surgery, 1989-93; fellow in plastic surgery Northwestern U., Chgo., 1993-96; house staff Rush Presbyn. St. Luke's Hosp., 1988-93, Northwestern Meml. Hosp., Chgo., 1993-96; pvt. practice plastic surgery; clin. instr. Rush Presbyn. St. Luke's Hosp., 1988-93, Northwestern Meml. Hosp., 1993-96, U. Miami, 1996—. Office: 400 Arthur Godfrey Rd 305 Miami Beach FL 33140

BARROW, CHARLES HERBERT, investment banker; b. Evanston, Ill., July 23, 1930; s. Franklin and Ardis (Mozingo) B.; m. Patricia Wandelt, Dec. 27, 1952; children: Paula, Carla, Barbara. A.B., Princeton U., 1952; M.B.A., U. Chgo., 1956. With No. Trust Co., Chgo., 1952-86, v.p., 1962-68, sr. v.p., 1968-74, exec. v.p., 1974-78, sr. exec. v.p., 1978-81, pres., 1981-86, also dir.; with Blunt Ellis & Loewi, Inc. Kemper Securities, Inc., Chgo., 1987—, sr. dir., 1987-91; mng. dir. Everen Securities, Inc. (formerly Kemper Securities, Inc.), 1991—; sr. advisor Sumitomo Trust and Banking Co., 1989-93; life mem. adv. coun. J.L. Kellogg Grad. Sch. of Mgmt., Northwestern U. Bd. dirs. Planned Parenthood Assn., Chgo., 1965-81, pres., 1972-73; bd. dirs. Rehab. Inst. Chgo., 1974—, chmn., 1982-83; trustee McCormick Theol. Sem., Chgo., 1984-95, treas., 1988-92, chmn., 1992-95, nat. trustee, 1995-96, trustee, 1996—. Mem. Chgo. Club, Comml. Club, Univ. Club, Commonwealth Club, Econ. Club, Bankers Club (pres. 1979-80), Bond Club, Glen View Club (Ill.), Michigan Shores Club (Wilmette, Ill.), Ocean Reef Club (Key Largo, Fla.). Presbyterian. Office: Everen Securities Inc 77 W Wacker Dr Fl 31 Chicago IL 60601-1694

BARROW, CLYDE WAYNE, political scientist, educator; b. Alice, Tex., Feb. 15, 1956; s. Floyd Smith and Wanda Ruth (Conner) B.; m. Trini Jean Lewis, Dec. 20, 1981. BA in Polit. Sci., Tex. A&I U., 1977; MA in Polit. Sci., UCLA, 1979, PhD in Polit. Sci., 1984. Teaching fellow UCLA, 1978-82, dir. instrnl. devel., 1982-84; vis. asst. prof. U. Tex., San Antonio, 1984-85, Tex. A&M U., College Station, 1985-87; from asst. prof. to prof. polit. sci. U. Mass. at Dartmouth, North Dartmouth, 1987-96, prof., 1996—, acting chmn. dept., 1992-93, 95, sr. rsch. assoc. Ctr. for Policy Analysis, 1993-94, dir. Ctr. for Policy Analysis, 1994—; mem. adv. bd. Arnold Dubin Labor Edn. Ctr., North Dartmouth, 1988—; policy cons. Office of Mayor, City of Fall River, Mass., 1993—, New Bedford CEO Club, 1994—, Fall River Sch. Dept., 1995—, Sandwich Sch. Dept., 1996—, Fall River Housing Auth., 1997; exec. staff analyst Gov.'s Commn. on Commonwealth Pt. Devel., Mass., 1994, Gov.'s Regional Econ. Devel. Strategies Project, 1996; regional analyst Mass. Benchmark Initiative, 1997—. Author: Universities and the Capitalist State, 1990, Critical Theories of the State, 1993; mem. bd. editors Sociol. Inquiry, 1992-95, Jour. Politics, 1993-97; mng. editor New England Jour. Pub. Policy, 1994-97; also articles. Recipient Fontera Meml. award Arnold Dubin Labor Edn. Ctr., 1991. Mem. Am. Polit. Sci. Assn., Western Polit. Sci. Assn., Conf. for Study Polit. Thought, U. Mass. Faculty Fedn. (treas. 1991-96, pres. 1998—). Office: U Mass Ctr Policy Analysis 285 Old Westport Rd North Dartmouth MA 02747-2356

BARROW, LIONEL CEON, JR., communications and marketing consultant; b. N.Y.C., Dec. 17, 1926; s. Lionel Ceon and Wilhelmina Barrow; m. Frederica Harrison; children: Lea, Kirsten Erin; stepchildren: Brenda Marie, Aurea Nellie, Rhonda Patricia, Emily Harrison Smith, Laura Harrison. BA in English, Morehouse Coll., 1948; MA in Journalism, U. Wis., 1958, PhD in Mass Communications, 1960. Reporter Richmond Afro-Am., Va., 1953-54; teaching and research asst. U. Wis., Madison, 1954-60; asst. prof. dept. communication Mich. State U., Lansing, 1960-61; research project dir. Bur. Advt., N.Y.C., 1961-63; research project supr. Kenyon & Eckhardt Advt. Agy., N.Y.C., 1963-64; research group head Foote Cone & Belding, N.Y.C., 1964-68, assoc. research dir., v.p., 1968-71; chmn. dept. Afro-Am. studies U. Wis., Milw., 1971-72, 74-75, prof. mass comms. and Afro-Am. studies, 1971-75; dean Sch. Communications Howard U., Washington, 1975-85, prof. communications, 1975-86; pres. The Barrow Info. Group, Columbia, Md., 1986—; vis. prof. Stanford U., 1971, Ohio State U., 1986; bd. dirs. Journalism Coun. Inc., 1970, pres., 1971-79; mem. Higher Edn. Group Washington; sec. elected advs. Md. Conf. on Small Bus., 1987-89. Author contbr. articles in field. Served with AUS, 1945-47, 50-53. Recipient media citation Journalism Edn. Assn., 1974; recipient radio pioneer award Medgar Evers Coll., 1979. Mem. Assn. for Edn. in Journalism and Mass Communications (founder, first head minorities and comm. divsn.), Nat. Assn. Black Journalists, Capitol Press Club, NAACP (life mem.), 24th Infantry Regimental Combat Team Assn. (Combat Infantry badge). Office: The Barrow Info Group PO Box 606 Columbia MD 21045-0606*

BARROW, MARIE ANTONETTE, elementary school educator; b. Jamaica, Nov. 2, 1952; d. Edward Emmanuel and Mildred Pancheta (Brown) Rerrie; children: Melissa Alicia, Matthew Andre. BA, Coll. of New Rochelle, 1976; MA, Bank St. Coll. Edn., 1982. Tchr. spl. edn. Ossining (N.Y.) Pub. Schs., 1978-91, tchr. 2d grade, 1991—; presenter Brookside Sch., Ossining, 1994, Staff Devel. Ctr., White Plains, N.Y., 1992; mem. study group to examine elem. sch. gifted/talented programs, Ossining Union Free Sch. Dist., 1993-94. Nominee N.Y. State Tchr. Yr., 1997. Mem. Assn. for Supervision and Curriculum Devel., Tchrs.s for Child Centered Learning, Brookside Sch. Behavior Com. (chmn. 1990-92). Avocations: reading, writing, dancing, singing, tennis. Home: PO Box 24 White Plains NY 10603-0024

BARROW, RICHARD EDWARD, architect; b. Birmingham, Ala., Feb. 3, 1940; s. Ralph A. and Hazel C. (McElroy) B.; m. Sylvia Ann Scherl, Sept. 28, 1963; children: Lisa Dawn, Kathryn Heather. BArch, Auburn U., 1963; postgrad., U. Utah, 1967-69. Reg. architect Ala., Utah. Draftsman Edward M. Paul Architects, Birmingham, 1960-63, Paul Lemoine Architects, Salt Lake City, 1967-68, Dean Gustavson, FAIA, Salt Lake City, 1968-69; project mgr. Marcellous Wright & Ptnrs., Richmond, Va., 1969-71; project architect Cobb, Adams, & Benton, Birmingham, 1971-77; ptnr. Arnold & Barrow Architects, Birmingham, 1977-84, Waters, Barrow & Assocs., Birmingham, 1984-89; pvt. practice Birmingham, 1989-93; pres. Richard E. Barrow Architects, Inc., Birmingham, 1994—; mem. Ala. Bd. for Registration of Architects, Birmingham, 1988—; mem. archtl. adv. com. Auburn U., 1982-89, chair, 1995-96; bldg. com. Wesley Student Ctr. Jacksonville (Ala.) State U., 1991; R&D subcom. Nat. Coun. Archtl. Registration Bds., Washington, 1992-95, coord. graphics, 1995, ARE subcom., 1996-98, coord., 1997; renovations include Women's Pavillion, U. Ala. Hosp., 1985, Cahaba Heights United Meth. Ch., 1989; architect new facilities including Asbury United Meth. Ch., 1986, Sumatanga Retreat Ctr., 1992. Bd. dirs. So. region Nat. Coun. Archtl. Registration Bds., 1996—, New Life Harvest Mission, Birmingham, 1990-96, Blue Lake (Ala.) Emmaus Cmty., 1990-91, Ala. Young Adult Chrysalis, treas. 1995-97; mem. adv. bd. WBHM Pub. Radio, 1996—. Capt. USAF, 1963-67. NIH fellow, 1967. Fellow AIA (Richard Upjohn fellow 1992, Pres.'s award 1979, 81, 82, Henry Adams Book award). Republican. Methodist. Avocations: flying, golf. Office: 2820 Columbiana Rd Ste 210 Birmingham AL 35216-2565

BARROW, ROBERT EARL, retired agricultural organization administrator; b. Swansea, Mass., Jan. 30, 1930; s. Charles H. and Etta (Campbell) B.; m. Dolores A. Pannoni, Jan. 30, 1954; children: Kyle A. Kawa, Susan E. Gregory. Grad. high sch., Swansea, 1948. Sr. v.p. 1st Fed. Savs. & Loan Assn., Providence, 1949-77; mgr. Old Red Bank, Fall River, Mass., 1978-79; mgr. bookkeeping Uncle Matty's Tropical Gardens, Warwick, R.I., 1980-87; sec. Nat. Grange, Washington, 1983-85, lectr., program dir., 1985-87, pres., 1987-95; master Swansea Grange #148, 1959-60, Bay State Pomona #33, 1965-66, Mass. State, 1981-85. Mem. Bretton Woods Com., 1988—, Agrl. Policy Adv. Com., 1988-94, transp. alternatives group Transp. 2020, 1988, 4-H Coun., 1988—, Bd. Hwy. Users Fedn., 1988—, Nat. Farm Coalition, 1988—, Coalition for Fiscal Restraint, 1988—. With U.S. Army, 1951-53. Avocations: profl. singer, gardening, bell collecting. Office: Nat Grange 1616 H St NW Washington DC 20006-4999

BARROW, THOMAS DAVIES, oil and mining company executive; b. San Antonio, Dec. 27, 1924; s. Leonidas Theodore and Laura Editha (Thomson) B.; m. Janice Meredith Hood, Sept. 16, 1950; children: Theodore Hood, Kenneth Thomson, Barbara Loyd, Elizabeth Ann. BS, U. Tex., 1945, MA, 1948; PhD, Stanford U., 1953; grad. advanced mgmt. program, Harvard U., 1963. With Humble Oil & Refining Co., 1951-72; regional exploration mgr. Humble Oil & Refining Co., New Orleans, 1962-64, sr. v.p., 1967-70, pres., 1970-72, also bd. dirs.; exec. v.p. Esso Exploration, Inc., 1964-65; sr. v.p. Exxon Corp., N.Y.C., 1972-78; chmn., CEO Kennecott Corp., Stamford, Conn., 1978-81; vice chmn. Standard Oil Co., 1981-85; investment cons. Houston, 1985-89; chmn. GX Tech., Houston, 1990—; pres. Thomson-Barrow, 1989—; sr. chmn., bd. dir. GeoQuest Internat. Holdings, Inc., Houston, 1990-97; pres. Tecolotita, Inc., 1991—, T-BAR-X, Houston, 1995—; chmn. bd. dirs. GPS Tech. Corp., Houston, 1986-98, Tobin Internat., 1998—; mem. commn. on natural resources NRC, 1973-78, commn. on ph ys. sci., math. and natural resources, 1984-87, bd. on earth scis., 1982-84; trustee Woods Hole Oceanographic Instn., 20th Century Fund-Task Force on U.S. Energy Policy; chmn. bd. dirs. Petroleum Info./Dwights, 1994-97. Pres. Houston Grand Opera, 1985-87, chmn., 1987-91; trustee Am. Mus. Natural History, Stanford U., 1980-90, Tex. Med. Ctr., 1983—, Geol. Soc. Am. Found., 1982-87; trustee Baylor Coll. Medicine, 1984—, vice chmn bd. trustees, 1991—. Served to ensign USNR, 1943-46. Recipient Disting. Achievement award Offshore Tech. Conf., 1973, Disting. Engring. Grad. award U. Tex., 1970, Disting. Alumnus, 1982, Disting. Geology Grad., 1985, Disting. Natural Sci. Grad., 1990; named Chief Exec. of Yr. in Mining Industry, Fin. World, 1979. Fellow N.Y. Acad. Scis.; mem. Nat. Acad. Engring., Am. Mining Congress (bd. dirs. 1979-85, vice chmn. 1983-85), Am. Assn. Petroleum Geologists, Geol. Soc. Am., Internat. Copper Research Assn. (bd. dirs. 1979-85), Nat. Ocean Industry Assn. (bd. dirs. 1982-85), AAAS, Am. Soc. Oceanography (pres. 1970-71), Am. Geophys. Union, Am. Petroleum Inst., Am. Geog. Soc., Houston Country Club, The Hills Club, Petroleum Club, River Oaks Country Club, Houston Club, Sigma Xi, Tau Beta Pi, Sigma Gamma Epsilon, Phi Eta Sigma, Alpha Tau Omega. Episcopalian. Office: 5847 San Felipe St Ste 3830 Houston TX 77057-3011

BARROW, THOMAS FRANCIS, artist, educator; b. Kansas City, Mo., Sept. 24, 1938; s. Luther Hopkins and Cleo Naomi (Francis) B.; m. Laurie Anderson, Nov. 30, 1974; children—Melissa, Timothy, Andrew. B.F.A., Kansas City Art Inst., 1963; M.S., Ill. Inst. Tech., 1965. With George Eastman House, Rochester, N.Y., 1966-72; asst. dir. George Eastman House, 1971-72; assoc. dir. Art Mus., U. N. Mex., Albuquerque, 1973-76; assoc. prof. U. N.Mex., 1976-81, prof., 1981—, Presdl. prof., 1985-90. Author: The Art of Photography, 1971; sr. editor: Reading into Photography, 1982; contbr. to Brit. Ency. Am. Art, 1973, A Hundred Years of Photographic History: Essays in Honor of Beaumont Newhall, 1975, Experimental Vision, 1994; forward The Valiant Knights of Daguerre, 1978; contbr. articles to profl. jours.; one-man shows include Light Gallery, N.Y.C., 1974-76, 79, 82, Amarillo Art Ctr., 1990, Andrew Smith Gallery, Santa Fe, 1992, Laurence Miller Gallery, N.Y.C., 1996, U. N.Mex. Art Mus., 1997; exhibited in group shows including Pace Gallery, N.Y.C., 1973, Hudson River Mus., Yonkers, N.Y., 1973, Internat. Mus. Photography, Rochester, 1975, Seattle Art Mus., 1976, Mus. Fine Arts, Houston, 1977, Retrospective exhbn. L.A. County Mus. Art, 1987—; represented in permanent collections Nat. Gallery Can., Mus. Modern Art, Getty Ctr. for Arts and Humanities. Nat. Endowment for Arts fellow, 1971, 78. Office: U NMex Dept Art Albuquerque NM 87131

BARROWMAN, MIKE, Olympic athlete, swimmer. Olympic swimmer Barcelona, Spain, 1992. Recipient 200m Breaststroke Gold medal Olympics, Barcelona, 1992; holder world record for 200m breaststroke. Office: US Swimming One Olympic Plz Colorado Springs CO 80909 also: Internat Swimming Hall of Fame One Hall of Fame Dr Fort Lauderdale FL 33316*

BARROWS, FRANK CLEMENCE, newspaper editor; b. Lewes, Del., Nov. 2, 1946; m. Mary S. Newsom, Nov. 16, 1985; 1 child, Margaret S. BA, St. Andrews Coll., 1968. Reporter, columnist Charlotte Observer, 1969-72, 76-81, asst. sports editor, 1981-82, asst. met. editor, 1982-83, exec. sports editor, 1983-84, 86, dep. features editor, 1985, dep. met. editor, 1986-87, asst. mng. editor, 1987-88, dep. mng. editor, 1988-92, mng. editor, 1992—. Contbr. numerous articles to mags. Mem. Am. Soc. Newspaper Editors, Soc. Newspaper Design, Investigative Reporters and Editors. Home: 1810 Shoreham Dr Charlotte NC 28211-2134 Office: Charlotte Observer 600 S Tryon St Charlotte NC 28202-1842

BARROWS, RICHARD LEE, economics educator, academic administrator; b. Columbus, Ohio, Sept. 21, 1945; s. Neil Proctor and Audrey Anne (Winning) B.; m. Linda Kathryn Jenkins,June 17, 1967; children: Brienne Ellen, Shannon Lynne. Student, UCLA, 1965; BA, Ohio State U., 1967; MA, U. Wis., 1971, PhD, 1972. Vol. U.S. Peace Corps, Sierra Leone, 1967-69; asst., then assoc. prof. U. Wis., Madison, 1972-78, prof. agrl. econs., 1978—, assoc. vice chancellor, 1988-93, acting dean internat. studies, 1989-90; interim vice-chancellor acad. affairs, 1992-94; interim dean coop. extension U. Wis. Extension, Madison, 1988, assoc. dean and dir. Coll. Agriculture and Life Scis., 1994—; dir. farmland preservation programm Wis. Dept. Agr., Trade and Consumer Protection, Madison, 1977-78; exec. dir. Wisconsin Rural Leadership Inc., Madison, 1983-86; dir. Wis. Ctr. Demand-side Rsch. Inc., Madison, 1989-92; chair, bd. dirs. Midwest Univs. Consortium for Internat. Activities Inc., Columbus, Ohio, 1989—; bd. dirs. MUCIA Global, Inc., 1995-98, Parent Share/Oreg. Contbr. articles to profl. jours. Trustee Village Bd., Deerfield, Wis., 1986-88; chmn. Dane County, Wis. Lakes and Watershed Commn., 1988-95; elder 1st Presbyn. Ch., Oregon, Wis., 1990-95. Recipient Superior Svc. award U.S. Dept. Agr., 1982, Wis. Idea award U. Wis., 1987. Mem. Am. Agrl. Econs. Assn. (Outstanding Extension Program award 1981), Soil Conservation Soc. Am., Rotary, Lions (chpt. pres. 1986), Kiwanis, Phi Beta Kappa. Avocations: hiking, cross country skiing. Home: 1540 Woodvale Dr Oregon WI 53575-1735 Office: U Wis Coll Agrl & Life Scis 116 Agriculture Hall 1450 Linden Dr Madison WI 53706-1522

BARROWS, RONALD THOMAS, lawyer; b. Detroit, Jan. 19, 1954; s. Harland Wayne and Jeanette Edith (Authier) B. BA in English and Polit. Sci. magna cum laude, Oakland U., 1976; JD, Wayne State U., 1979. Bar: Mich. 1979, U.S. Dist. Ct. (ea. dist.) Mich. 1979, U.S. Ct. Appeals (6th cir.) 1983, U.S. Tax Ct. 1986; lic. real estate broker, Mich; cert. comml. investment mem. Realtors Nat. Mktg. Inst. Assoc. Abbott, Nicholson, Quilter, Esshaki & Youngblood, P.C., Detroit, 1979-80; counsel Lindon Land Co., Inc., Harper Woods, Mich., 1980-82; pvt. practice St. Clair Shores, Mich., 1981-87; ptnr. Barrows & Alt, P.C., Troy, Mich., 1987-90; sole practice Grosse Pointe, Mich., 1990—; cons./counselor to corp. and pvt. real estate investors and developers; adj. prof. Oakland U. Paralegal Program, 1989-90. Contbr. articles to profl. jours. Mem. Mich. Comml. Investment Coun.; chmn. adv. com. Mich. chpt. Nat. Multiple Sclerosis Soc., co-chair coun. adv. com., mem. client programs com. Mem. ABA, ATLA, Mich. Bar Assn. (title stds. com. 1985—, real property coun. 1987-97, treas. 1994-97, chmn. water law com. 1985-90), Nat. Assn. Realtors, Mich. Assn. Realtors (sr. instr. 1980-91), Macomb County Assn. Realtors (lawyer realtor com. 1984-88), Nat. Order Barristers. Republican. Presbyterian. Avocations: sailing, billiards, theater, photography. Office: PO Box 36958 Grosse Pointe MI 48236-0958

BARRS, JAMES THOMAS, linguistics educator; b. Danville, Ga., Sept. 2, 1904; s. Andrew Robert and Dollie Lee (Brown) B.; m. Vida Fitz Randolph, Sept. 2, 1931; children: Dorothy Caroline, Ann Radcliffe, Andrew Fitz-randolph. *With his AM half-finished, Mr. Barrs married Vida, who had just received her MS in medical science at Harvard Medical School. From her weekly $32 as technician in Boston City Hospital, she uncomplainingly financed the rest of his AM and all of his PhD. Next year their family began, resulting in 3 children, 9 grandchildren, and already 7 great-grandchildren. She died in 1973, at age 70. In 1952, Nathaniel Fritz Randolph of her family gave the land for Princeton University's campus.* AB summa cum laude, U. Ga., 1927; AM, Harvard U., 1932, PhD, 1936; student, Mercer U., 1928. Registrar, tchr. English South Ga. Coll., Douglas, 1937-42, dean, 1940-42; asst. prof. English Washington Coll., Chestertown, Md., 1943-45; from asst. prof. to prof. English Northea. U., Boston, 1945-71, prof. emeritus, 1971—; lectr. Sta. WAYX, Waycross, Ga., 1940-42, Sta. WBZ-WBZA, Boston and Springfield, Mass., 1959-60, Stas. WEEI, WCRB, WILD, Boston, and Concert Network, 1960s, Sta. WGBH-TV, Boston, 1958-59. Contbr. to scholarly publs. Mem. MLA, N.E. MLA (chmn. linguistics sect. 1972-73), Nat. Coun. Tchrs. of English (bd. dirs. 1969-70, chmn. semantics sect. 1972, mem. com. on pub. and profl. rels. 1967-70, mem. com. on semantics in sch. programs 1960-71), N.Y. Acad. Scis., Coll. English Assn. (bd. dirs. 1962-65), Conf. on Coll. Composition and Comm., New England Assn. Tchrs. of English (adv. mem. exec. bd. 1960-70, chmn. sch. and coll. liaison com. 1962-65, chmn. nominating com. 1966-69), Phi Beta Kappa (sec. Newton com. 1972-97, pres. Northea. U. assocs. 1965-68), Phi Kappa Phi (copy editor nat. forum). Home and Office: 4 Bay Rd Milford MA 01757-2819

BARRY, A. L., church official; b. Woodbine, Iowa, Aug. 4, 1931; s. Thomas A. and Helen Barry; m. Jean Heim, Aug. 24, 1952; children: Kristin Becker, Beth Miko, Keith. Student, Bethany Luth. Coll., 1951, Concordia Theol. Sem., Luth. Sem., 1956; ThM, Luther Northwestern Sem., 1968; DD, Concordia Theological Sem., 1986. Pastor Pilgrim Luth., Mpls., 1956-60, St. John & Peace, Claremont, Minn., 1960-62, Trinity, Trimont, Minn., 1962-67; mission and stewardship counselor Iowa Dist. West, Ft. Dodge, 1967-75; exec. sec. bd. for missions Luth. Ch.-Mo. Synod, St. Louis, 1975-77; exec. for missions Iowa Dist. East, Cedar Rapids, 1977-82, pres., 1982-92; pres. Luth. Ch.-Mo. Synod, St. Louis, 1992—; active world missionaries, overseas ptnr. chs. in 28 countries. Author numerous stewardship, mission and evangelism booklets and materials for congregations. Office: The Luthern Ch Mo Synod Internat 1333 S Kirkwood Rd Saint Louis MO 63122-7295*

BARRY, ANNE M., public health officer. BA in Occupl. Therapy, Coll. St. Catherine; JD, William Mitchell Coll. Law; MPH, U. Minn. Dep. commr. health Minn. Dept. Health, Mpls., commr. health, 1995—. Office: Minn Dept Health 121 7th Pl E Ste 450 Saint Paul MN 55101-2117

BARRY, CAMILLE T., health and human services director. BS in Nursing, U. Akron; MS in Mgmt., George Mason U., PhD in Health Policy and Adminstrn. Staff nurse, nurse mgr. various acute care ctr. hosps.; sr. program analyst Sec.'s Commn. on Nursing, 1988; program analyst former Nat. Ctr. for Nursing Rsch. at NIH, Bethesda, Md.; spl. asst. for health policy Sec., Dept. Vets. Affairs; sr. drug policy advisor, counselor to Sec. Shalala U.S. Dept. Health and Human Svcs., Rockville, Md., now dep. dir. Ctr. for Substance Abuse Treatment; adj. asst. prof. George Mason U., Fairfax, Va.; ofcl. del. to UN Commn. on Narcotic Drugs, Vienna; US. del. to Internat. Fedn. Non-Govt. Orgns., Malaysia; cons. divsn. govtl. affairs Am. Nurses' Assn. Author: Redesigning Patient Care Delivery, 1990; contbr. articles to profl. jours. *

BARRY, DAVE, columnist, author; b. Armonk, N.Y., July 3, 1947; 1 child, Robert; m. Michelle Kaufman, 1996. Grad., Haverford Coll., 1969. Reporter, editor Daily Local News, West Chester, Pa., 1971-75; with AP, instr. bus. writing Phila., 1975-83; columnist The Miami (Fla.) Herald, 1983—. Author: Taming of the Screw: Several Million Homeowner's Problems Sidestepped, 1983, Babies and Other Hazards of Sex, 1984, Bad Habits: A One Hundred Percent Fact Free Book, 1985, Stay Fit and Healthy Until You're Dead, 1985, Dave Barry's Guide to Marriage and/or Sex, 1987, Claw Your Way to the Top, 1987, Dave Barry's Greatest Hits, 1988, Dave Barry Slept Here, 1989, Dave Barry Turns 40, 1990, Dave Barry Talks Back, 1991, Dave Barry's Only Travel Guide You'll Ever Need, 1991, Dave Barry Does Japan, 1992, Dave Barry Is Not Making This Up, 1994, Dave Barry's Complete Guide to Guys, 1995, Dave Barry in Cyberspace, 1996, Dave Barry is from Mars and Venus, 1997, Dave Barry Turns 50, 1998. Recipient Disting. Writing award Soc. Newspaper Editors, 1987, Pulitzer prize for commentary, 1988. Office: Miami Herald 1 Herald Plz Miami FL 33132-1693

BARRY, DAVID EARL, lawyer; b. N.Y.C., Nov. 25, 1945; s. David J. Barry and Beatrice A. Richtmyer; m. Teresa M. Anderson, July 26, 1969; children: Andrea, David R., Kristin. BA, Coll. Holy Cross, Worcester, Mass., 1966; JD, Harvard U., 1969. Bar: N.Y. 1969, Conn. 1978. Ptnr. Kelley Drye & Warren, N.Y.C., 1969—. Mem. ABA, Univ. Club, Apawamis Club. Roman Catholic. Home: 1 Oneida St Rye NY 10580-1717 Office: Kelley Daye & Warren 101 Park Ave New York NY 10017-5530

BARRY, DAVID WALTER, infectious diseases physician, researcher; b. Nashua, N.H., July 19, 1943; s. Walter and Claire B.; m. Gracia Chin; children: Christopher, Jennifer. BA in French literature with highest honors magna cum laude, Yale Coll., 1965; student, Sorbonne, Paris, 1963-64; MD, Yale U., 1969. Cert. State of Conn. Med. Examining Bd., State of Md. Med. Examining Bd., State of N.C. Bd. Med. Examiners; diplomate Nat. Bd. Med. Examiners, Am. Bd. Internal Medicine, Am. Bd. Infectious Diseases. Intern, then resident Yale-New Haven Hosp., 1969-72; staff assoc., dir., acting dep. dir. divsn. virology, bur. biologics FDA, 1972-77; head anti-infectives sect., dept. clin. investigation, med. divsn. Burroughs Wellcome Co., Research Triangle Park, N.C., 1977-78, head dept. clin. investigation, med. divsn., 1978-85, head dept. virology, Wellcome rsch. labs., 1983-89, dir. divsn. clin. investigation, 1985-86, v.p. rsch. Wellcome rsch. labs., 1986-89, v.p. rsch., devel. and med. affairs, Wellcome rsch. labs., 1989-95, pres. Wellcom rsch. labs., 1994-95, also bd. dirs.; chmn., CEO Triangle Pharms. Inc., Durham, N.C., 1995—; chmn., bd. participants inter-co. collaboration on AIDS Drug Devel., 1998—; dir. influenza vaccine task force, bur. biologics FDA, 1976-77, mem. rsch. human subjects com.; adj. prof. sch. medicine Duke U., 1977-92; mem. com. pub.-pvt. sector rels. vaccine innovation, inst. medicine NAS, 1983, roundtable drugs and vaccines against AIDS, 1989, industry liaison panel, 1992; mem. AIDS task force NIH, 1986, AIDS program adv. com., 1988; deans coun. Yale Sch. Medicine, 1989-96; cons., lectr. in field; bd. dirs., Wellcome Found., Family Health Internat. Mem. editorial bd. AIDS rsch. and Human Retroviruses, AIDS Patient Care; contbr. articles to profl. jours. Active N.C. Indsl. (Vaccine) Commn. Sr. surgeon USPHS, 1972-77. Vis. fellow U. Md., 1975-76. Fellow ACP, Infectious Diseases Soc. Am., Royal Soc. Medicine; mem. AAAS, AMA, Am. Soc. Virology, Am. Soc. Microbiology, Am. Fedn. Clin. Rsch., Pharm. Mfrs. Assn. (med. and sci. sect., com. AIDS 1989, AIDS task force 1989, R & D steering com. 1990, commn. treatment drug dependence and abuse 1990-95), N.C. Med. Soc., Durham-Orange Counties Med. Soc., Venezuelan Soc. Internal Medicine (hon.), Alpha Omega Alpha. Achievements include 15 patents for treatment of viral infections, patent for the Use of Azidothymidine to Treat AIDS and ARC, for the Treatment of Idiopathic Thrombocytopaenic Purpura. Office: Triangle Pharms Inc 4 University Pl 4611 University Dr Durham NC 27707-3458

BARRY, DESMOND THOMAS, JR., lawyer; b. N.Y.C., Mar. 26, 1945; s. Desmond Thomas and Kathryn (O'Connor) B.; m. Patricia Mellicker, Aug. 28, 1971; children: Kathryn, Desmond Todd. AB, Princeton U., 1967; JD, Fordham U., 1973. Bar: N.Y. 1974, U.S. Dist. Ct. (so. and ea. dist.) N.Y. 1974, U.S. Ct. Appeals (2d cir.) 1974, U.S. Ct. Appeals (9th cir.) 1980, U.S. Ct. Appeals (5th cir.) 1983, U.S. Ct. Appeals (3d cir.) 1984, U.S. Supreme Ct. 1985. Assoc. Condon & Forsyth, N.Y.C., 1973-79, ptnr., 1979—. Trustee Canterbury Sch., New Milford, Conn., 1970-80. Capt. USMC, 1967-70, Vietnam. Decorated Navy Commendation medal with combat V, Combat Action medal, 1969, Vietnamese Cross of Gallantry, 1969. Mem. ABA (chmn. aviation & space law com. 1996-97), N.Y. State Bar Assn., Assn. of Bar of City of N.Y., Internat. Assn. Def. Counsel (exec. com. mem.), Univ. Club N.Y.C., Winged Foot Golf Club. Republican. Roman Catholic. Home: 9 Thomas Pl Norwalk CT 06853-1500 Office: Condon & Forsyth LLP Ste 1750 685 Third Ave New York NY 10017

BARRY, DONALD J., government official. BS in Am. Instns. with distinction, U. Wis., 1971, LLB cum laude, 1974. Solicitor's Office honors program participant U.S. Dept. Interior, 1974-75, atty. advisor Solicitor's Office, 1975-80, asst. solicitor br. fish and wildlife, 1980-85; majority gen. counsel for fisheries and wildlife Mcht. Marine and Fisheries Com., U.S. Ho. of Reps., 1985-91; v.p. U.S. Land and Wildlife, World Wildlife Fund, 1991-93; U.S. commr. Gt. Lakes Fishery Commn., U.S. Dept. Interior, Washington, 1993-97, asst. sec., 1997—. Office: US Dept Interior 1849 C St NW Rm 3156 Washington DC 20240-0001*

BARRY, DONALD JAMES, government official; b. Madison, Wis., Oct. 19, 1949. BA, U. Wis., 1971, JD, 1974. Bar: Wis. 1974. With Solicitor's Office, Dept. Interior, Washington, 1974-75, staff atty. U.S. Fish and Wildlife Svc., 1975-80, chief counsel of Svc., 1980-85; gen. counsel for fisheries and wildlife U.S. Ho. of Reps. Com. on Mcht. Marine and Fisheries, Washington, 1985-91; v.p. for US. land and wildlife World Wildlife Fund, Washington, 1991-93; counselor to asst. sec. for fish and wildlife and parks Dept. Interior, Washington, 1993-96, dep. asst. sec. for fish and wildlife and parks, 1996—, acting asst. sec. for fish, wildlife and parks, 1997-98, asst. sec. for fish, wildlife and parks, 1998—. Home: 1717 Hollinwood Dr Alexandria VA 22307-1927 Office: Dept Interior Office Asst Sec for Fish Wildlife-Parks 1849 C St NW Rm 3156 Washington DC 20240-0002*

BARRY, DONALD LEE, investment broker; b. Ft. Gordon, Ga., Sept. 1, 1953; s. C. Donald and Della (Newman) B.; m. Peggy Summerfield, Aug. 8, 1980 (div. June 1983); m. Lora Fankhauser, Oct. 6, 1990. Student, Wichita State U., 1974-1981. Lic. stocks and commodity trader, life ins. agt. Instr. Cyr's Driving Sch., Wichita, Kans., 1974-78, v.p., 1978-81; investment broker A.G. Edwards & Sons, Wichita, 1981-85, v.p. investments, 1985-96, sr. v.p. investments, 1996—; chmn.,coun. mem. A.G. Edwards & Sons, 1990; bd. dirs. Exploration Place, 1999—. Bd. dirs. Wichita Pub. libr., 1980, 93—, treas., 1981-83, 1st. v.p., 1996; bd. dirs. Interfaith Ministries Exec. Com., Wichita, 1983—, St. Francis Hosp. Found., 1991-95, Wichita chpt. NCCJ, 1991, Via Christi Hosp. Found., 1996-98, Exploration Place, 1998—; bd. dirs. Goodwill Industries, 1994—, treas., 1995-97; pres. Wichita Pub. Libr., 1997-99. Recipient Outstanding Citizen award Interfaith Ministries, 1991. Mem. Am. Mensa Ltd., Rotary Internat., Wichita Com. on Fgn. Rels. Republican. Episcopalian. Home: 7715 Oneida Ct Wichita KS 67206-3850 Office: AG Edwards & Sons 201 N Main St Wichita KS 67202-1500

BARRY, EDWARD WILLIAM, publisher; b. Stamford, Conn., Nov. 24, 1937; s. Edward and Elizabeth (Cosgrove) B.; m. Barbara Helen Walker, Sept. 14, 1963; children—Wendy Elizabeth, Neil Edward. B.A. with honors, U. Conn., 1960. Pres. The Free Press, N.Y.C., 1972-82, Oxford U. Press Inc., N.Y.C., 1982—; sr. v.p. Macmillan Pub. Co., N.Y.C., 1973-82; exec. coun. mem. Profl. and Scholarly Pubs., 1993; adv. bd. Pace U. Grad. Program in Pub., 1990—; bd. dirs. Rsch. Lib. Group. Mem. Assn. Am. Pubs. (bd. dirs. 1995—), Am. Assn. Higher Edn. (bd. dirs. 1995—), Phi Alpha Theta. Home: 62 High Rock Rd Stamford CT 06903-2012 Office: Oxford U Press Inc 198 Madison Ave Fl 9 New York NY 10016-4341

BARRY, FRANCIS JULIAN, JR., lawyer; b. New Orleans, Oct. 7, 1949; s. Francis Julian and Bertha Anna (Lion) B.; m. Janice Leigh Gonzales, May 8, 1976; children: Francis III, Maria. BA, Tulane U., 1970, JD, 1973. Bar: La. 1973, U.S. Dist. Ct. (ea. dist.) La. 1973, U.S. Ct. Appeals (5th cir.) 1973, U.S. Dist. Ct. (we. dist.) La. 1978, U.S. Ct. Appeals (11th cir.) 1982, U.S. Supreme Ct. 1991. Assoc. Deutsch, Kerrigan & Stiles, New Orleans, 1973-78, ptnr., 1978—; Editor Admiralty Law Inst. Symposium Tulane U., New Orleans, 1973. Adv. editor Tulane Maritime Law Jour. (formerly The Maritime Lawyer), 1975—. Served to capt. USAR. Mem. Fed. Bar Assn., La. Bar Assn., New Orleans Bar Assn., Maritime Law Assn. U.S. (proctor, carriage of goods com. 1982-87, transp. hazardous substances com. 1987—), Admiralty Law Inst. New Orleans (mem. planning com. 1998—), U.S. Naval Inst., Southeastern Admiralty Law Inst., La. Assn. Def. Counsel, Assn. Average Adjusters London, Am. Legion, Navy League U.S., Army-Navy Club (Washington), La. Landmarks Soc., Bienville Club, Univ. Club (N.Y.C.), Empire Club, Iris Club, Azalea Club, Lotus Club, Plimsoll Club, Mariners Club, The Round Table Club. Republican. Roman Catholic. Home: 4301 Dumaine St New Orleans LA 70119-3617 Office: Deutsch Kerrigan & Stiles 755 Magazine St New Orleans LA 70130-3672

BARRY, GENE, actor; b. N.Y.C., June 14, 1919; s. Martin and Eva Klass; m. Betty Claire Kalb, Oct. 22, 1944; children: Michael Lewis, Fredric James, Elizabeth. Actor on Broadway; plays include Rosalinda, 1942, Movers, (directed by Max Rheinhardt), 1945, The Would Be Gentleman, Catherine Was Great, The Perfect Setup, 1962, La Cage Aux Folles (nominee Tony award), 1983; nightclub performer; motion pictures include Thunder Road, The War of the Worlds, 1953, Soldier of Fortune, 1955, Houston Story, 1958, C*na Gate, 1957, 27th Day, 1957, Maroc 7, 1968; star TV series Bat Masterson, NBC, 1959-61, Burke's Law, 1963-66, 94-95, The Name of the Game, 1968-71; TV movies include Prescription Murder, 1968, Istanbul Express, 1968, Do You Take This Stranger, 1971, Aspen, 1977, A Cry for Love, 1980, The Girl, the Gold Watch and Dynamite, 1981, The Adventures of Nelly Bly, 1981, Perry Mason: The Case of the Lost Cove, 1987, Turn Back the Clock, 1989, The Gambler Returns: The Luck of the Draw, 1991; co-starred with Clark Gable and Susan Hayward. Recipient Golden Globe award, 1964, ADL Man of Yr. award, 1986. Mem. Screen Actors Guild (past 1st v.p.). Office: 10390 Santa Monica Blvd Los Angeles CA 90025

BARRY, HERBERT, III, psychologist; b. N.Y.C., June 2, 1930; s. Herbert and Lucy Manning (Brown) B. BA, Harvard U., 1952; MS, Yale U., 1953, PhD, 1957. USPHS-NIMH rsch. fellow Yale U., 1957-59, asst. prof. psychology, 1960-61; asst. prof. psychology U. Conn., Storrs, 1961-63; rsch. assoc. prof. pharmacology U. Pitts. Sch. Pharmacy, 1963-70, prof., 1970-87; prof. pharmacology and physiology U. Pitts. Sch. Dental Medicine, 1987-94; prof. pharm. scis. U. Pitts. Sch. Pharmacy, 1995—; mem. alcohol rsch. rev. com. Nat. Inst. Alcohol Abuse and Alcoholism, 1972-76; mem. sociobehavioral subcom. AIDS rsch. rev. com. Nat. Inst. Drug Abuse, 1988-89; trustee Ctr. for the Study of Econ., 1988—. Author: (with H. Wallgren) Actions of Alcohol, 1970, (with A. Schlegel) Adolescence; An Anthropological Inquiry, 1991; field editor Psychopharmacology, 1974-91; contbr. articles to profl. jours. Mem. Allegheny County Dem. Com., 1984—. Recipient NIMH Research Scientist Devel. award, 1967-77. Fellow Am. Psychol. Assn. (council reps. 1975-76, pres. div. psychopharmacology 1980-81), Am. Assn. Pharm. Scientists, AAAS; mem. Am. Soc. Pharm. Exptl. Therapeutics, Psychonomic Soc., Am. Coll. Neuropsychopharmacology, Schalkenbach Found. (bd. dirs. 1997—), Phi Beta Kappa, Sigma Xi. Episcopalian. Home: 552 N Neville St Apt 83 Pittsburgh PA 15213-2830 Office:

U Pitts 512 Salk Hall Pittsburgh PA 15261-1905 *I believe that the contrasting behaviors of persistence and innovation both contribute to effective learning and creativity. Awareness of the need for both contrasting behaviors may help people to avoid the failures caused by overemphasis of either one.*

BARRY, JAMES P(OTVIN), writer, editor; b. Alton, Ill., Oct. 23, 1918; s. Paul Augustine and Elder (Potvin) B.; m. Anne Elizabeth Jackson, Apr. 16, 1966. BA cum laude, Ohio State U., 1940. Commd. 2d. lt. Arty. U.S. Army, 1940, advanced through grades to col., served ETO, 1944-46; adviser to Turkish Army, 1951-53; detailed Army Gen. Staff, Washington, 1953-56; ret., 1966; adminstr. Capital U., Columbus, Ohio, 1967-71; freelance writer, editor Columbus, 1971-77; dir. Ohioana Library Assn., 1977-88; editor Ohioana Quar., 1977-88; sr. editor Inland Seas, 1984—; photographer, documentary and book illustrator, 1968—. Author: Georgian Bay: The Sixth Great Lake, 1968, 3rd edit., 1995, The Battle of Lake Erie, 1970, Bloody Kansas, 1972, The Noble Experiment, 1972, The Fate of the Lakes, 1972, The Louisiana Purchase, 1973, Henry Ford and Mass Production, 1973, Ships of the Great Lakes, 1973 (Dolphin Book Club selection), Ships of the Great Lakes, rev. edit., 1996, The Berlin Olympics, 1975, The Great Lakes: A First Book, 1976, Wrecks and Rescues of the Great Lakes, 1981 (Dolphin Book Club selection), Georgian Bay: An Illustrated History, 1992, Old Forts of the Great Lakes, 1994, also booklet on Lake Erie for Ohio EPA, 1980; contbr. articles to mags. and jours.; over 300 photographs accepted for permanent collection Inst. Gt. Lakes Rsch. Recipient award Am. Soc. State and Local History, 1974, Nonfiction History award Soc. Midland Authors, 1982; named Gt. Lakes Historian of Yr., Marine Hist. Soc. Detroit, 1995. Mem. Internat. Assn. Gt. Lakes Rsch., Assn. Gt. Lakes Maritime History, Can. Nautical Rsch. Soc., Gt. Lakes Hist. Soc., Marine Hist. Soc., Ohio Hist. Soc., World Ship Soc., Royal Can. Yacht Club, Columbus Country Club, Capital Club, Phi Beta Kappa. Home: 353 Fairway Blvd Columbus OH 43213-2507

BARRY, JOHN J., labor union leader. Pres. Internat. Brotherhood Elec. Workers, Washington. Office: Internat Brotherhood Elec Workers 1125 15th St NW Washington DC 20005-2707*

BARRY, JOHN L., military officer. BS in Internat. Affairs & Polit. Sci., USAF Acad., 1973; grad., Squadron Officer Sch., 1977; M in Pub. Adminstrn., U. Okla., 1980; grad., Armed Forces Staff Coll., 1984, Harvard U., 1994. Commd. 2d lt. USAF, 1973, advanced through grades to brigadier gen., 1997; air staff tng. officer Office of Inspector Gen. Hdqs. USAF, Washington, 1979-80; aide to comdr. 12th Air Force, Bergstrom AFB, Tex., 1983-84; action officer for fighter programs Dep. Chief Staff for Pers. Resources, Hdqs. USAF, Bergstrom AFB, 1985; White House fellow, exec. officer, liaison to NASA adminstr. NASA, Washington, 1985-86; chief of safety 8th Tactical Fighter Wing, Kunsan Air Base, South Korea, 1987-88; ops. officer 421st Tactical Fighter Squadron, Hill AFB, Utah, 1988-89; comdr. 34th Tactical Fighter Squadron, Hill AFB, 1989-90; mil. asst. to sec. of def. The Pentagon, Washington, 1990-92; comdr. 56th Ops. Group, MacDill AFB, Fla., 1992-93, 39th Wing and 7440th Composite Wing, Incirlik Air Base, Turkey, 1994-96; dir. plans and programs Hdqs. U.S. Air Forces in Europe, Ramstein Air Base, Germany, 1996-98; comdr. 56th Fighter Wing, Luke AFB, Ariz., 1998—. Decorated Def. Superior Svc. medal, Legion of Merit, Meritorious Svc. medal with 3 oak leaf clusters; Nat. Security fellow Harvard U., 1994. Office: 56 FWICC 7224 N 139th Dr Luke AFB AZ 85309-1420

BARRY, LEI, medical equipment manufacturing executive; b. Fitchburg, Mass., May 27, 1941; d. Leo Isaacson and Irene Helen (Melanson) Isaacson Godbout; m. Delbert M. Berry (div.); children: David M., Susan L.; m. Frank H. Mahan III, June 25, 1976; stepchildren: Jodi L., Sarah C., Amy S., Frank H. IV. Grad. high sch., Waltham, Mass. Advt. salesperson, broadcaster various radio and TV stas., N.C. and Tex., 1961-67; New Eng. sales rep. Hollister, Inc., Chgo., 1967-71, Northeastern sales mgr., 1971-76; v.p., ptnr. Mahan Assocs., Blue Bell, Pa., 1976—; pres. Blue Bell Bio-Med., Inc., 1982-98. Bd. mgrs. YMCA, Ambler, 1989-95. Mem. Whitpain Twp. Planning Commn., 1986-91; bd. dirs. Interfaith of Ambler, 1988—, pres., 1988-98; mem. affordable housing adv. coun. Fed. Home Loan Bank, Pitts, 1993-97. Mem. Healthcare Mfrs. Mktg. Coun. (bd. dirs.), Blue Bell Rotary, Wissahickon Valley C. of C. (bd. dirs. 1987-92), Wissahickon Valley Hist. Soc. (past bd. dirs.). Republican. Avocations: tennis, skiing, gourmet cooking. Office: 1399 Blue Bell Rd Blue Bell PA 19422-0455

BARRY, MARYANNE TRUMP, federal judge; b. N.Y.C., Apr. 5, 1937; d. Fred C. and Mary Trump; m. John J. Barry, Dec. 26, 1982; 1 child, David W. Desmond. BA, Mt. Holyoke Coll., 1958; MA, Columbia U., 1962; JD, Hofstra U., 1974, LLD (hon.); LLD (hon.), Seton Hall U., Caldwell Coll. Bar: N.J. 1974, N.Y. 1975, U.S. Ct. Appeals (3d cir.), U.S. Supreme Ct. Asst. U.S. Atty., 1974-75, dep. chief appeals div., 1976-77, chief appeals div., 1977-82, exec. asst. U.S. Atty., 1981-82, 1st asst., 1981-83; judge U.S. Dist. Ct., N.J., 1983—; chmn. Com. on Criminal Law Jud. Conf. of U.S., 1994-96. Fellow Am. Bar Found.; mem. ABA, N.J. Bar Assn., Am. Judicature Soc. (bd. dirs.), Assn. Fed. Bar State of N.Y. (pres. 1982-83). Office: US Dist Ct PO & Courthouse Bldg Rm 333 PO Box 999 Newark NJ 07101-0999*

BARRY, NADA DAVIES, retail business owner; b. London, Dec. 2, 1930; d. Ernest Albert J. and Natalie Emma (Rossin) Davies; m. Jacob J. Ebeling-Koning, Aug. 1952 (div. 1962); m. Robert I Barry, 1963 (div. 1976); children: Natasha E.-K. Sigmund, Derek B. Ebeling-Koning, Gwen E.-K. Waddington, Trebor C. Barry. Student, Mills Coll., 1948-50; BA, Barnard Coll., 1952. Owner The Wharf Shop, Sag Harbor, N.Y., 1968—; founder Sag Harbor Youth Com. Bd. dirs. The Hampton Day Sch., Bridgehampton, N.Y., 1966-74; active Noyac Civic Coun., Ladies Village Improvement Soc., Sag Harbor, LWV of The Hamptons; founder Sag Harbor Youth Com. Mem. AAUW, Sag Harbor C. of C. (bd. dirs.), Nat. Trust Historic Preservation, Nature Conservancy, Sanibel-Captiva Conservation Found., Sag Harbor Hist. Soc., Sag Harbor Whaling Museum, Bailey-Matthews Shell Mu., Barnard Coll. Club. Avocations: gardening, photogrphy, traveling, shelling, theatre. Office: The Wharf Shop PO Box 922 Sag Harbor NY 11963-0025

BARRY, NORMAN J., JR., lawyer; b. Chgo., Apr. 1, 1950. BA, U. Notre Dame, 1972, JD, 1975. Bar: Ill. 1975. Ptnr. Donohue, Brown, Mathewson, & Smyth, Chgo. Office: Donohue Brown Mathewson & Smyth 140 S Dearborn St Ste 700 Chicago IL 60603*

BARRY, RICHARD A., public relations executive; b. Chgo., Ill., Nov. 11, 1934. BS in Polit. Sci., Loyola U., 1956; cert. in publ. and graphics, U. Chgo., 1958. Asst. editor No. Ind. Pub. Svc. Co., Hammond, 1956-58; dir. pub. rels. Loyola U., Chgo., 1958-66; dir. devel. and pub. rels. St. Xavier Coll., Chgo., 1966-68; sr. v.p. Daniel J. Edelman, Inc., Chgo., 1968-70; exec. v.p. PCI, Chgo., 1970-72; pres. Pub. Comms., Inc., Chgo., 1972—. Office: Public Communications Inc 35 E Wacker Dr Ste 1254 Chicago IL 60601-2109*

BARRY, RICHARD FRANCIS, retired life insurance company executive; b. N.Y.C., Aug. 28, 1917; s. Thomas Francis and Gertrude Mary (Spillane) B.; m. Irene Patricia Schulties, July 24, 1948. B.B.A., St. John's U., Bklyn., 1948; J.D., Fordham U., 1953. Bar: N.Y. 1954. With Met. Life Ins. Co., N.Y.C., 1937-82; v.p., office of pres., then v.p. human resources Met. Life Ins. Co., 1979-80, sr. v.p. human resources, 1980-81, sr. v.p. office of chmn., 1981-82, ret. 1982; mem. faculty St. John's U., 1955-60. Bd. dirs. Urban Acad. for Mgmt., Inc., 1979-82, Met. Life Found., 1981-82; sec. Nat. Assn. Drug Abuse Problems, N.Y.C., 1979-82; mem. Coop. Edn. Commn. N.Y.C., 1979-82. Served with AUS, 1943-45. Mem. Adminstrv. Mgmt. Soc. (pres. N.Y.C. chpt. 1972-73), Life Office Mgmt. Assn., Bar Assn. State N.Y., N.Y. C. of C. and Industry. Republican. Roman Catholic. Home: 237 Berry Hill Rd Syosset NY 11791-2105

BARRY, RICHARD FRANCIS, III, publishing executive; b. Norfolk, Va., Jan. 18, 1943; s. Richard F. and Mary Margaret (Perry) B.; m. Carolyn Ann Kennett, Aug. 7, 1965; children: Carolyn Michelle, Christopher David. B.A., LaSalle Coll., 1964; J.D., U. Va., 1967. Bar: Va. 1967. Assoc. Kaufman, Oberndorfer & Spainhour (now Kaufman and Canoles), Norfolk, 1967-71, ptnr., 1972-73; corp. sec. Landmark Comm., Inc., Norfolk, 1973-74; pres. Roanoke Times & World-News, Va., 1974-76; pres. The Virginian-Pilot and The Ledger-Star, Norfolk, 1976-78, pub., 1983-90; pres., COO, dir. Landmark Comm., Inc., Norfolk, 1978—, CEO, 1984-91; vice chmn. Landmark Comm., Inc., 1991—; bd. dirs. The Weather Channel, Greensboro News and Record, Inc., Times World Corp., Trader Pub. Co., Capital Gazette Newspapers Inc., InfiNet Co. Trustee or past trustee Norfolk Acad., Chrysler Mus., U. Va. Colgate Darden Bus. Sch. Found., Cath. H.S. Found., Old Dominion Univ. Ednl. Found.; bd. dirs., past pres., campaign chmn. United Way of South Hampton Rds.; bd. visitors, past rector Old Dominion U., co-chmn. capital campaign. Office: Landmark Comm Inc 150 W Brambleton Ave Norfolk VA 23510-2018

BARRY, STEVE, sculptor, educator; b. Jersey City, June 22, 1956; s. Thomas Daniel and Lorraine (Lowery) B. BFA, Sch. Visual Arts, N.Y.C., 1980; MFA, Hunter Coll., N.Y.C., 1984. Adj. lectr. Hunter Coll., 1984-89; assoc. prof. U. N.Mex., Albuquerque, 1989—; Kohler Arts and Industry Residency, 1996. Exhbns. include Bklyn. Army Terminal, N.Y.C., 1983, City Gallery, N.Y.C., 1986, 90, Storefront for Art and Architecture, 1988, Artists Space, N.Y.C., 1989, Santa Barbara Art Mus., 1990, Kohler Arts Ctr., Sheboygan, Wis., 1991, Hirshhorn Mus., Washington, 1990, Fla. State U., 1992, Contemporary Art Mus., Houston, 1992, CAFE Gallery, Albuquerque, 1993, Charolette Jackson, Santa Fe, 1993, Ctr. for Contemporary Arts, Santa Fe, 1994, U. Wyo. Art Mus., 1995, Site Santa Fe, 1996, Sheldon Art Mus., Lincoln, Nebr., 1997, U. N.Mex. Art Mus., Albuquerque, 1997, Cedar Rapids (Iowa) Mus. of Art, 1998. Grantee Clocktower Nat. Studio, 1985, NEA, 1986, 88, 90, N.Y. State Coun. for the Arts, 1987, N.Y. Found. for the Arts, 1988; recipient AVA award, 1990. Home: PO Box 1046 Corrales NM 87048-1046 Office: U NMex Dept Art & Art History Albuquerque NM 87131-1401

BARRY, THOMAS CORCORAN, investment counsellor; b. Cleve., Feb. 9, 1944; s. Willard Corcoran and Harriet (Mullin) B.; m. Patricia Ryan, Feb. 14, 1976; children: Oliver Mullin, Lillian Nicholson, Michael Corcoran. B.A. in Latin Am. Studies, Yale U., 1966; M.B.A., Harvard U., 1969. Chartered Fin. Analyst. Market research analyst Corning Glass Works, Brazil and Japan, 1966-67; investment analyst T. Rowe Price Assocs., Inc., Balt., 1969-70; partner Cole, Thompson and Barry, Inc., Cleve., 1971-73; pres. Rowe Price New Horizons Fund, Balt., 1973-81, Saratoga Assocs., 1981-83; pres., CEO Rockefeller and Co. Inc., 1983-93; pres. Zephyr Mgmt., L.P., 1994—; dir. numerous cos. Trustee William T. Grant Found., 1989—l, Univ. Sch., Cleve., 1998—. Office: 320 Park Ave New York NY 10022-6815

BARRY, WILLIAM ANTHONY, priest, writer; b. Worcester, Mass., Nov. 22, 1930; s. William and Catherine (McKenna) B. AB, Boston Coll., 1956, STL, 1963; MA, Fordham U., 1960; PhD, U. Mich., 1968. Joined S.J., Roman Cath. Ch., 1950, ordained priest, 1962. Tchr. high sch. Fairfield (Conn.) Prep., 1956-58; lectr. U. Mich., Ann Arbor, 1968-69; from asst. to assoc. prof. Weston Jesuit Sch. of Theology, Cambridge, Mass., 1969-78; rector Jesuit community Boston Coll., Chestnut Hill, Mass., 1988-91; vice provincial S.J. of New Eng., Boston, 1978-84, asst. novice dir., 1985-88, provincial, 1991-97; co-dir. S.J. Tertianship, 1997—; dir. staff Ctr. for Religious Devel., Cambridge, 1971-78; trustee Boston Coll., Chestnut Hill, 1988-91, adj. assoc. prof., 1989-91. Co-author: Communication, Conflict, Marriage, 1974, The Practice of Spiritual Direction, 1982; author: God and You, 1987, Seek My Face, 1989, Now Choose Life, 1990, Paying Attention to God, 1990, Finding God in All Things, 1991, Spiritual Direction and the Encounter with God, 1992, God's Passionate Desire and Our Response, 1993, Allowing the Creator to Deal with the Creature, 1994, What Do I Want in Prayer?, 1994, Who Do You Say I Am?, 1996, Our Way of Proceeding, 1997, With an Everlasting Love, 1999. Mem. Phi Beta Kappa, Phi Kappa Phi. Democrat. Roman Catholic. Avocations: reading, writing. Home and Office: Campion Ctr 393 Concord Rd Weston MA 02493-1398

BARRY, WILLIAM HENRY, JR., federal judge; b. Nashua, N.H., Feb. 3, 1930; s. William H. and Mabel Sidney (Monica) B.; m. Nancy Collins, Aug. 10, 1958; children: William, Julia, Maura. BS, Holy Cross Coll., Worcester, Mass., 1956; JD, Suffolk U., Boston, 1961. Bar: N.H., 1961. Adjuster Liberty Mutual Ins., Worcester, 1956-61; atty. Harkaway, Barry & Gall, Nashua, 1961-65, Small Bus. Adminstrn., Concord, N.H., 1965-66; asst. U.S. atty. U.S. Dept. Justice, Concord, 1966-68; clerk U.S. Dist. Ct., Concord, 1968-72, U.S. magistrate judge, 1972-95; of counsel Barry Law Office, Nashua, 1995—. Candidate 2d dist. U.S. Congress, N.H., 1966; dir. Big Bros./Big Sisters, Nashua, 1990-97. Sgt. U.S. Army, 1950-52, Korea. Fellow N.H. Bar Assn. Democrat. Roman Catholic. Office: 255 Main St Nashua NH 03060-2929

BARRY, WILLIAM PATRICK, military officer; b. Boston, Aug. 1, 1957; s. John Joseph III and Esther Marie (Doherty) B.; m. Monica Marie Fournier. BS, U.S. Air Force Acad., 1979; MA in Polit. Sci., Stanford U., 1987; DPhil in Politics, Oxford (U.K.) U., 1996. Commd. 2d lt. USAF, 1979, advanced through grades to lt. col., 1995; student pilot USAF, Williams AFB, Ariz., 1979-80; aircraft comdr. 42d Air Refueling Squadron USAF, Loring AFB, Maine, 1980-84; instr. pilot, exec. officer 509th Air Refueling Squadron USAF, Pease AFB, N.H., 1984-86; flight examiner 380th Air Refueling Wing, Plattsburgh AFB, N.Y., 1990-92; instr. dept. polit. sci. USAF Acad., Colorado Springs, Colo., 1987-89, asst. prof. polit. sci., 1995-98; politico military affairs officer Hdqs. U.S. European Command, Stuttgart, Germany, 1998—. Named one of Outstanding Young Men of Am., Montgomery, Ala., 1986. Mem. Am. Assn. Advancement of Slavic Studies. Avocations: gardening, cross-country skiing, flying. Address: HQ Useucom Unit 30400 Box 2388 APO AE 09128

BARRY(BRANKS), DIANE DOLORES, podiatrist; b. Cornwall, Ont., Can., Apr. 3, 1958; d. George Henry and Dolores Angeline (Latulippe) Barry; m. Paul Lloyd Branks, Sept. 19, 1987; children: Katherine Ann Branks, Andrew Joseph Branks, Annemarie Elizabeth Branks. BS, U. San Diego, 1980; B in Med. Sci., Calif. Coll. Podiatric Medicine, 1983, D in Podiatric Medicine, 1985. Lab technician Scripps Rsch. Inst., La Jolla, Calif., 1980, Salk Inst., La Jolla, 1981, Quidel Labs., La Jolla, 1982; dry waller Barry Drywall, San Diego, 1985; med. office mgr. Bay Harbor Podiatry Group, Harbor City, Calif., 1985; podiatry resident VA West L.A., 1986; podiatrist Bay Harbor Podiatry Group, 1987-88, Southeast Med. Ctr., Huntington Park, Calif., 1987-88; podiatrist Kaiser Permanente, Fontana, Calif., 1988-97, Baldwin Park, Calif., 1997—. NIH grantee, 1997. Fellow Am. Coll. Foot and Ankle Surgeons, Am. Coll. Foot and Ankle Orthops.; mem. Am. Podiatric Med. Soc., Am. Diabetic Assn., Calif. Podiatric Med. Soc. (alt. 1994, 96, del. 1995), So. Calif. HMO Podiatric Med. Soc. (founder, pres. 1989-91, 97-98), vice pres., 1999—. Republican. Roman Catholic. Avocation: weight lifting. Office: Kaiser Permanente Med Ctr 1011 Baldwin Park Blvd Baldwin Park CA 91706-5806

BARRYMORE, DREW, actress; b. L.A., Feb. 22, 1975; d. John Jr. and Jaid Barrymore. Appearances include (films) Altered States, 1980, E.T.: The Extra-Terrestrial, 1982, Irreconcilable Differences, 1984, Firestarter, 1984, Cat's Eye, 1985, Poison Ivy, 1992, Bad Girls, 1994, Boys on the Side, 1995, Batman Forever, 1995, Mad Love, 1995, Wishful Thinking, 1996, Scream, 1996, Like a Lady, 1996, Everyone Says I Love You, 1996, All She Wanted, 1997, Best Men, 1997, Never Been Kissed, 1998 (also prodr.), Home Fries, 1998, The Wedding Singer, 1998, Ever After: A Cinderella Story, 1998, Never Been Kissed, 1999; (TV episodes) Amazing Stories, 1985, Con Sawyer and Hucklemary Finn, 1985, 2000 Malibu Road, 1992; (host) Hansel and Gretel, 1986; (TV movies) Suddenly Love, 1978, Bogie, 1980, The Screaming Woman, 1986, Babes in Toyland, 1986, Conspiracy of Love, 1987, Beyond Control: The Amy Fisher Story, 1993; (TV spls.) Screen Actors Guild 50th Anniversary, 1984, Night of 100 Stars II, 1985, Happy Birthday, Hollywood, 1987, Disney's 30th Anniversary, 1987. Office: 1122 S Robertson Blvd Ste 15 Los Angeles CA 90035-1432*

BARSALONA, FRANK SAMUEL, theatrical agent; b. S.I., N.Y., Mar. 31, 1938; s. Peter and Mary (Rotunno) B.; m. June Harris, Sept. 1, 1966; 1 dau., Nicole. BA, Wagner Coll., S.I., 1958; postgrad., Herbert Berghof Sch., N.Y.C., 1959-60. Agt. Gen. Artists Corp., N.Y.C., 1960-64; founder, since pres. Premier Talent Agy., N.Y.C., 1964—; co-founder, pres. Phila. Fury, 1977-80; lectr., moderator music industry; founding ptnr. Precision Media Corp., 1984-97; bd. dirs. Paradigm Music Group; ptnr. SVC Network. Bd. govs., trustee Rock & Roll Hall of Fame Mus., Cleve. Recipient numerous awards Billboard Publs., cover subject spl. issue, 1984; named to Performance Mag. Hall of Fame, 1988. Mem. Mus. Am. Folk Art. (internat. adv. bd.). Office: Premier Talent Agy 17 E 76th St New York NY 10021

BARSAM, JOYCE LORNA, language educator, classicist; b. Lawrence, Mass., Feb. 12, 1941; d. Arthur Armenag and Helen Hermine (Zorigian) Shushan; m. Paul Charles Barsam, Sept. 26, 1966; children: Julie Roxanne, Charles Arthur, Ara Paul. BA magna cum laude, Tufts U., 1962, PhD, 1989; MA, Stanford U., 1964. Cert. secondary tchr., Mass. Instr., chair acting dept. Cardinal Cushing Coll., Brookline, Mass., 1964-67; lectr., instr. Northeastern Univ., Boston, 1989—; bd. trustee Tufts Univ., Medford, Ma., 1994—, bd. overseers humanities, 1989—. V.P. Nat. Ctr. Genocide Studies, Boston, 1980-85, founder; bd. dirs. Zoryan Inst. Rsch., Cambridge, Mass., 1985-90, founder; bd. trustees Armenian Assembly Am., Washington, 1984—; pub. sch. adv. com Town of Belmont, Mass., 1987-96. Mem. Am. Assn. Tchrs. French, Belmont Hill Club (bd. dirs. 1982-84), Alpha Omicron Pi (chpt. pres. 1961-62). Democrat. Avocations: community service, armenian cultural & philanthropic activities, tennis. Home: 170 Rutledge Rd Belmont MA 02478-2634

BARSAMIAN, J(OHN) ALBERT, lawyer, lecturer, educator, criminologist, arbitrator; b. Troy, N.Y., May 1, 1934; s. John and Virginia (Tachdjian) B.;m. Alice Missirilan, Apr. 21, 1963; children: Bonnie, Tamara. BS in Psychology with honors, Union Coll., 1956; JD, 1968; LLB, Albany Law Sch., 1959; postgrad., Nat. Jud. Coll., 1997. Bar: N.Y. 1961, U.S. Dist. Ct. (no. dist.) N.Y. 1961, U.S. Supreme Ct. 1967; fire tng. cert. N.Y. State Exec. Dept. Pvt. practice, 1961—; dir. criminal sci., chmn. dept. Russell Sage Coll., 1970-88, assoc. prof. criminal sci., 1977-82, prof., 1982-87; lectr. office local govt. divsn. criminal justice svcs. State N.Y., 1964-72, N.Y. State Police Acad., 1970; judge adminstrv. law N.Y. State Pub. Employment Rels. Bd., 1996—; faculty pub. affairs and policy pub. svc. tng. program Nelson A. Rockefeller Coll., 1986-91, Sch. Labor Rels. Extension divsn. Cornell U., 1986; gaming cons. Gov.'s Office Indian Rels., N.Y., 1991-92; spl. counsel Office of Police Chief, Cohoes, N.Y., 1986—, to city mgr., Troy, N.Y., 1993; counsel Watervliet Police Assn., 1967-74, Cohoes Police Assn., 1967-74, Colonie Police Assn., 1977-80, Troy Police Command Officers Assn., 1981-85, North Greenbush Police Assn., 1985-90, Office of the Police Chief, Syracuse, N.Y., 1985-90, Fire Dept. Union, Albany, N.Y., 1986, Schenectady Fire Fighters Union, 1992-95; gen. counsel Internat. Narcotic Enforcement Officers Assn., 1982-84, Troy Uniformed Firefighters Assn., 1977-97; spl. investigator Rensselaer County Dist. Atty., 1959-61; mem. law guardian panel N.Y. State Family Ct., 1967-77; mem. mediation panel N.Y. State Pub. Employment Rels. Bd., 1968-73. Founder, chmn. dept. police sci. Hudson Valley C.C., 1961-69; mem. adv. bd. History Ctr. Skidmore Coll., 1993—; bd. dirs. Rensselaer County ARC, 1966-70; memm. alumni coun. Union Coll., 1981-86; mem. parish coun. St. Peter Armenian Ch., Watervliet, N.Y., 1979-83, chmn., 1981-83, vice chmn., 1984; evaluator office of non-collegiate programs N.Y. State Dept. Edn., 1985—; hon. dep. sheriff St. Mary Parish (La.). Tarzian scholar Union Coll., 1952-56, Porter scholar, 1956-59; decorated chavalier, knight comdr. Sovereign Order of Cyprus; recipient Police Sci. Students' award Hudson Valley C.C., 1968, award for meritorious svc. to law enforcement Law Enforcement Officers Soc., 1969, Archbishop's cert. merit Armenian Ch. Am., 1973, Lawyers Coop. Pub. Co. prize in cirminal law, 1957. Mem. ABA (com. on police selection and tng. 1967-69, mem. Rensselaer county criminal justice coord. coun., 1976-78), N.Y. Bar Assn. (chmn. com. on police 1970-72, trial lawyers sect. com. cont. legal edn. 1977-97), Assn. Trial Lawyers Am., Nat. Assn. Adminstrv. Law Judges, Am. Arbitration Assn., Acad. Criminal Justice Scis., Am. Assn. Criminology, Union Coll. Alumni Assn. (Silver medal 1956), Les Amis d'Escoffier Soc., Masonic Vet. Assn. Troy (life), N.Y. State Trial Lawyers Assn., N.Y. Vet. Police Assn. (life, hon., counsel), Royal Order of Jesters, Shriners, Rose Croix (most wise master Delta chpt. 1986), Phi Delta Theta, Alpha Phi Sigma, Lambda Epsilon Chi. Home and Office: 5 Sage Hill Ln Albany NY 12204-1315

BARSAMIAN, KHAJAG SARKIS, primate; b. Arapkir, Turkey, July 4, 1951; came to U.S., 1977; s. Ohannes and Bulbul Borsumoglu. Student, Sem. of Armenian Patriarchate, Jerusalem, 1971; MDiv, Gen. Theol. Sem., N.Y., 1980, DD (hon.), 1991; MA, Oriental Inst. of Gregorian U., Rome, 1984, postgrad., 1984—. Ordained to ministry Armenian Ch., 1971. Asst. dean Sem. of Patriarchate of Jerusalem, 1971-74; canon sacrist Diocese of Armenian Ch., N.Y.C., 1977-80, vicar gen., dir. ecumenical office, 1984-90, primate, 1990—; mem. N.C.C. Governing Bd., N.Y.C. Contbr. articles to ednl. and scholarly jours. Mem. Internat. Soc. Liturgical Studies, Religion in Am. Life (bd. dirs., v.p.), Appeal of Conscience Found. (bd. dirs.), Am. Bible Soc. (bd. dirs.). Office: Diocese of the Armenian Ch 630 2nd Ave New York NY 10016-4806*

BARSAN, ROBERT BLAKE, dentist; b. Akron, Ohio, Apr. 7, 1948; s. Emil O. and Letitia (Dobrin) B.; m. Cheryl Lee Adams, Dec. 16, 1972; children: Erin Lee, Kathleen Letitia. BS, U. Cin., 1970; DDS, Ohio State U., 1974. Resident U. Chgo., 1976; gen. practice dentistry Cuyahoga Falls, Ohio, 1976—. Contbr. editor Modern Dental mag., 1984-89. Fellow Acad. Gen. Dentistry; mem. ADA (chmn. CPR 1984-90), Am. Endodontic Soc., Akron Gnathological Soc. (pres. 1986), Am. Acad. Cosmetic Dentistry, Fedn. Dentaire Internat., Canton Akron Cleve. Orthodontic Study Club (pres. 1994-98). Home: 3084 Silver Lake Blvd Silver Lake OH 44224-3033 Office: 330 Stow Ave Cuyahoga Falls OH 44221-2516

BARSANO, CHARLES P., medical educator, dean. BS in Biology, Loyola U., Chgo., 1969; PhD in Pathology, U. Chgo., 1974, MD, 1975. Diplomate Am. Bd. Internal Medicine. Resident internal medicine Barnes Hosp./Washington U., St. Louis, 1975-77; fellow endocrinology U. Chgo. Sch. Medicine, 1977-79, rsch. assoc. endocrinology, 1979-80; asst. prof. medicine Northwestern U. and Lakeside VA Med. Ctr., 1980-85; asst. prof. medicine U. Health Scis./Chgo. Med. Sch. and North Chgo. VA Med. Ctr., 1985-87, assoc. prof., 1987-92, prof. medicine, 1992-98, assoc. prof. pharmacology and molecular biology, 1992-94, prof. pharmacology and molecular biology, 1994-98, acting dean Med. Sch., assoc. dean for clin. affairs, vice-chmn. dept. medicine; staff physician med. svc./endocrinology sect. North Chgo. VA Med. Ctr. Mem. editl. bd. Thyroid, 1990-95; mem. adv. bd. Toxic Substance Mechanisms, 1993—. Recipient Bausch and Lomb Nat. Sci. award, 1965, Individual Nat. Rsch. Svc. award, 1979-80. Mem. Internat. Coun. for Control of Iodine Deficiency Disorders, Assn. Am. Med. Colls. (group on ednl. affairs sect. on resident edn.), Am. Assn. Clin. Endocrinologists, Am. Thyroid Assn. (fiscal com. 1982-85, pub. health com. 1986-88, membership com. 1990-93, chmn. membership com. 1993, local organizing com. 1994, bylaws com. 1995—), Endocrine Soc., Chgo. Endocrine Club (pres. 1984-85), Sigma Xi, Alpha Omega Alpha. E-mail: barsanoc@mis.finchems.edu. Fax: 847-578-3320. Office: Office Clin Affairs Finch Univ Health Scis Chgo Med Sch North Chicago IL 60064

BARSELOU, PAUL EDGAR, actor, writer; b. Cohoes, N.Y., May 31, 1922; s. Alfred William and Lydia Nancy (Hebert) B. B.A., SUNY, Albany, 1947, M.A., 1948; postgrad., U. Florence, Italy. Tchr. drama, speech, English Schenectady and Ft. Plain, N.Y., 1948-52; radio-TV actor-writer Troy, N.Y., 1952-54, Santa Monica, Calif., 1954-57; editorial supr. Aerospace, 1957-80; freelance actor-writer, 1954—; cons. identification neotropical butterflies. Appeared in numerous TV shows and motion pictures. Author: Identification Guide to the Genus Agrias. Served with USAAF, 1943-45. Decorated Air medal with oak leaf cluster. Mem. AFTRA, Screen Actors Guild. Roman Catholic. *Perseverence, tenacity, and a touch of blissful ignorance have helped me achieve success. I seem to do the impossible sometimes, but only because I don't know that what I'm doing can't be done.*

BARSHAI, RUDOLF BORISOVICH, conductor; b. Labinskaya, USSR, Sept. 28, 1924. Grad., Moscow Conservatory, 1948; student conducting with Ilya Musin, Leningrad; MusD (hon.), U. Southhampton. Founder Moscow Chamber Orch., 1955; led New Israel Orch., 1977-79; prin. condr., artistic advisor Bournemouth Symphony Orch., Eng., 1982-88; music dir., prin. condr. Vancouver Symphony Orch., B.C., Can., 1985-88; prin. guest condr. Orchestra National de France, 1987-89; guest condr. in Europe, U.S., Japan; compiler, instrumentalist Bach's Art of Fugue, 1972, 85; decoder, instrumentalist Bach's Das Musikalische Opfer, 1970; transcriber Prokofiev's Visions Fugitive, 1960, Shostakovich's Chamber Symphonies No. 1 and 2,

1968, Symphony for wind and strings, 1988, Chamber Symphony opus 83a, 1989, Chamber Symphony Opus 49a, 1995; numerous recs. for Melodia, Decca, EMI, Deutsche Grammophon; pres. jury, dir. condrs'. course Arturo Toscanini Internat. Condrs. Competition, Parma, Italy, 1990. Address: care Lies Askonas Ltd, 6 Henrietta St, London WC2E 8LA, England

BARSHEFSKY, CHARLENE, diplomat. BA with honors, U. Wis.; JD, Catholic U. Ptnr. Steptoe & Johnson, Washington, 1975-93; dep. U.S. trade rep. Exec. Office of the Pres. of the U.S., Washington, 1993-96, U.S. trade rep., 1996-97, 1997—. Office: Exec Office of the President US Trade Rep 600 17th St NW Washington DC 20508-0001

BARSNESS, RICHARD WEBSTER, management educator, administrator; b. Elbow Lake, Minn., Apr. 26, 1935; s. Russel E. and Joanna (Warga) B.; m. Dorothea L. Gother, Aug. 22, 1964; children: Karen Louise, Erik Richard. B.S., U. Minn., 1957, M.A., 1958, M.A.P.A., 1960, Ph.D., 1963. Budget analyst U.S. Bur. Budget, Washington, 1960-61; instr., asst. prof. Northwestern U., Evanston, Ill., 1962-69, assoc. prof., 1969-78, assoc. dean, 1972-78; dean, prof. Lehigh U., Bethlehem, Pa., 1978-92, prof., 1978—, Iacocca prof. bus., 1992-93, exec. dir. Iacocca Inst., 1992-95, Univ. disting. svc. prof., 1995—; pres. Lexington Group, Inc., 1997—; exec. sec. Lexington Group in Transport History, 1969-89; pres. Bus. History Conf., 1981-82; lectr. Transp. Ctr., Evanston, Ill., 1964-84; editl. cons. Various pubs. Contbr.: articles to profl. jours.; editor: Lexington Newsletter. Mem. Gov.'s Adv. Council State of Ill., 1969-72; gen. chmn. United Way Lehigh U., 1981. Recipient R.R. and E.C. Hillman award Lehigh U., 1991. Mem. Acad. Mgmt., Transp. Rsch. Forum, Bus. History Conf. (trustee 1978-81, pres. 1981-82), Internat. Assn. for Bus. and Society, Acad. Internat. Bus., Phi Beta Kappa, Beta Gamma Sigma, Phi Beta Delta. Republican. Episcopalian. Home: 769 Apollo Dr Bethlehem PA 18017-2556 Office: Lehigh U Coll Bus 621 Taylor St Bethlehem PA 18015-3117

BART, POLLY TURNER, real estate developer; b. Peterborough, N.H., Feb. 28, 1944; 1 child, Greta Rose Bart. BAcl, Radcliffe Coll., 1965; PhD in City Planning, U. Calif., Berkeley, 1979, PhD, 1979. Contbr. President's Nat. Urban Policy Report to Congress, Washington, 1980; asst. prof. U. Md., College Park, 1981-84; real estate salesperson Coldwell Banker Comml. Real Estate Services, Balt., 1984-87; pres. Investment Properties Brokerage, Inc., Balt., 1988-98; faculty Goucher Coll., 1998—; faculty Johns Hopkins U., Berman Real Estate Inst., 1993—. Fellow Danforth Found., 1975-79, Ford Found., 1981. Mem. Comml. Real Estate Women (co-founder). Avocations: writing poetry and music, swing and country dancing. Home and Office: Investment Properties Brokerage Inc 1902 Western Run Rd Cockeysville MD 21030-1123

BART, ROGER, actor. Actor with Broadway/first nat. tour credits including: Triumph of Love, London's West End, U.S. Tour, German prodns. of: The Who's Tommy, King David, How to Succeed in BusinessS, The Secret Garden, Big River; off-broadway includes: Henry IV, Parts I and II, Up Against It; role of Whizzer in Falsettos; singing voice for title role of Walt Disney's animated feature, Hercules; other canine credits include singing voice of Scamp in Disney's Lady and the Tramp Part II; acting role in The George Carlin Show, Fox TV. Winner 1999 Tony for best featured actor in Good Man Charlie Brown. Office: c/o SAG 1515 Broadway 44th Flr New York NY 10036*

BARTA, JAMES JOSEPH, judge; b. St. Louis, Nov. 5, 1940; BA, St. Mary's U., 1963; JD, St. Louis U., 1966. Bar: Mo. 1966, U.S. Supreme Ct. 1969. Spl. agt. FBI, Washington, Cleve. and N.Y.C., 1966-70; chief trial atty. St. Louis Circuit Atty., 1970-76; assoc. Guilfoil, Symington & Petzall, St. Louis, 1976-77; asst. U.S. atty. Eastern Dist. Mo., 1977-78; lectr. Greater St. Louis Police Acad., 1970-76; spl. asst. atty. gen. Mo., St. Louis, 1974-75; spl. asst. atty. (circuit), St. Louis, 1976-78; judge bankruptcy ct. U.S. Dist. Ct. for Eastern Dist. Mo., 1978—, chief judge bankruptcy ct., 1986-89, 95—; mem. U.S. Supreme Ct. Adv. Com. on Bankruptcy Rules, 1987-94, chmn. tech. subcom., 1990-94, style subcom., 1992-94; mem. tech. adv. com. St. Louis Council on Criminal Justice, 1972-74; dir. Organized Crime Task Force, St. Louis, 1972-74; project dir. St. Louis Crime Commn., 1975-77. Fellow Am. Coll. Bankruptcy (cir. chmn. 1990-94, bd. dirs. 1994-97, sec. bd. dirs. 1995-97); mem. ABA, Am. Bankruptcy Inst. (bd. dirs. 1989-94), Am. Judicature Soc., Mo. Bar Assn., St. Louis Bar Assn., St. Louis Bar Assn. CLE Inst. (at large 1989-93), Former Spl. Agts. FBI. Office: US Bankruptcy Ct 1 Met Sq 211 N Broadway Fl 7 Saint Louis MO 63102-2733

BARTA, JAMES OMER, priest, psychology educator, church administrator; b. Fairfax, Iowa, Oct. 22, 1931; s. Omer J. and Bertha (Brecht) B. BA, Loras Coll., 1952; Sacrae Theologiae Licentiatus, Gregorian U., Rome, 1956; PhD, Fordham U., 1962. Ordained priest Roman Cath. Ch., 1955. Prof. psychology Loras Coll., Dubuque, Iowa, 1957-94, v.p. acad. affairs, 1977-87; pres. Loras Coll., Dubuque, 1987-94; archbishop's vicar Cedar Rapids (Iowa) region, 1994-99; vicar Gen. Archdiocese of Dubuque, 1999—. Office: Archdiocesan Chancery 1229 Mt Loretta Ave Dubuque IA 52003-7800

BARTALINI, C. RICHARD, judge; b. Kincaid, Ill., Sept. 25, 1931; s. Chester Richard and Florinda (Galli) B.; m. Anne M. Evanoff, June 4, 1955; children: Robert Charles, Denise Anne, David Chester. BA, U. Calif., Berkeley, 1954; JD, U. Calif, San Francisco, 1957. Bar: Calif. 1957. Practice law Oakland, 1957-66, Alameda, 1966-77; dep. dist. atty. Alameda County, 1957-59; chief def. counsel Transit Casualty Co., 1959-60; chief trial atty. Alameda/Contra Costa Transit Co., 1960-61; asso. Nichols, Williams, Morgan & Digardi, 1961-66; partner Davis, Craig & Bartalini, 1966-77; judge Superior Ct. Calif., 1977-93; ret., 1993; atty., counselor Supreme Ct. U.S.; del. Calif. Bar Conf., 1963-68; cons. U.S. Dept. Justice, U.S. Dept. Edn.; faculty Nat. Inst. for Trial Advocacy, Ctr. for Trial and Appellate Advocacy, Hastings Coll. Law, Calif. Ctr. for Jud. Edn. and Rsch. Chmn. Alameda Youth Activities Com., 1958-63, Nat. Coun. on Mental Health and Retardation, 1965-69; mem. President's Coun. on Youth Opportunity, 1965-70; pres. Alameda Bd. Edn.; pres., v.p., bd. dirs. Alameda Boys Club; mem. exec. com. Nat. Found. March of Dimes; chmn. No. Calif. Area coun., mem. Nat. Commn. for Constl. Revision and mem. nat. area coun. com. Boys Clubs Am.; chmn. bd. dirs. Moreau High Sch., Hayward, Calif., Alameda Hosp. Found.; mem. adv. bd. Partners Program, The Close-Up Found.; mem. civil svc. bd. City of Alameda, 1992-96, mem. housing authority, 1996—; mem. Alameda County Grand Jury, 1997-98. Recipient Service award Nat. Congress Parents and Tchrs., 1972, Disting. Svc. award Alameda Unified Sch. Dist., 1972, Man and Boy award Boys Clubs Am., 1975; Bronze Keystone award Boys Club Am., 1979, Bronze Keystone and Svc. Bar awards Boys and Girls Clubs of Am., 1989; named Young Man of Yr. City of Alameda, 1965, Outstanding Civic Leader of Am., 1967. Mem. ATLA, ABA, Calif. Bar Assn., Alameda County Bar Assn. (dir.), Criminal Cts. Bar Assn., Com. for Advancement and Support of Edn., Nat. Assn. Ind. Schs., Alameda Collaborative for Children, Youth and Their Families, Alameda County Lawyers Club (past pres.), Calif. C. of C. (past dir.), Alameda Jaycees (past pres.), U.S. Jaycees (past legal counsel), Elks, Eagles, Kiwanis, Alameda Rod and Gun Club, Commonwealth Club, Chabot Gun Club, Phi Alpha Delta. Home: 1224 Bay St Alameda CA 94501-3914

BARTEAU, MARK ALAN, chemical engineering and chemistry educator; b. St. Louis, Sept. 8, 1956; s. Dallas Frank and Charlotte Jean (Shelker) B.; m. Diane Viola Jorgensen, June 25, 1983; children: Katherine Pearl, Alexander Bradford. BSChemE, Washington U., 1976; MSChemE, Stanford U., 1977, PhD, 1981. Postdoctoral fellow Tech. U. Munich, 1981-82; asst. prof. U. Del., Newark, 1982-87, assoc. prof., 1987-90, prof. chem. engring. and chemistry, 1990-94, Robert L. Pigford prof., 1994—, dir. Ctr. for Catalytic Sci. and Tech., 1996—. NSF Postdoctoral fellow, 1981; recipient Presdl. Young Investigator award NSF, 1985, Ipatieff prize Am. Chem. Soc., 1995, Internat. Catalysis award Internat. Assn. Catalysis Socs., 1998. Mem. AAAS, AIChE (Allan P. Colburn award 1991, assoc. editor jour.), Am. Chem. Soc. (Ipatieff prize 1994, Victor K. LaMer award 1982), Catalysis Soc. (Paul H. Emmett award 1993), Materials Rsch. Soc. Democrat. Office: Univ of Del Dept Chem Engring Newark DE 19716

BARTEE, ROBERTA P., nursing educator; b. Gulfport, Miss., Oct. 16, 1945; d. Vaughn Eugene and Blanche Marie (Phillips) Purvis; m. James H. Bartee, Sept. 4, 1971. Diploma, Charity Hosp. Sch. Nursing, 1966; BS, Northwestern State U., 1968; MS, U. Colo., 1971; postgrad., U. Hawaii, 1981-82. RN, La. Acting head nurse surg. unit Charity Hosp. New Orleans; asst. prof. La. State U. Med. Ctr., New Orleans, U. Hawaii, Honolulu, Linfield Coll., Portland, Oreg. Mem. ANA, AACN, Nat. League for Nursing, New Orleans Dist. Nurses Assn., Nat. Nursing Staff Devel. Orgn., Sigma Theta Tau. Home: 7015 Longvue Dr Mandeville LA 70448-7043

BARTEE, THOMAS CRESON, computer scientist, educator; b. Moberly, Mo., Dec. 18, 1926; s. Thomas Monroe and Verna Miller (Tippett) B.; m. Mildred Higdon, Sept. 5, 1953; 1 child, Thomas Quentin. B.A., Westminster Coll., 1949. Mem. staff computer research M.I.T.-Lincoln Lab., Lexington, Mass., 1955-63; Gordon MacKay lectr. in computer engring. Harvard U., Cambridge, Mass., 1963-69; dir. electronic design center Harvard U., 1969-72, Gordon MacKay prof. computer engring., 1970—; cons. Nat. Acad. Scis., IDA, IBM, Honeywell, Raytheon; IEEE disting. computer sci. lectr., 1972-74. Author: (with G. Birkhoff) Modern Applied Algebra, 1971, Introduction to Computer Science, 1972, Digital Computer Fundamentals, 7th edit., 1989, Basic Computer Programming, 1981, 2d edit., 1985, Data Communications, Networks and Systems, 1985, 2d edit., 1992, Digital Communications, 1986, Expert Systems in AI, 1987, ISDN, SNA AND DECNET, 1989; editor: IEEE-IRE Computer Jour., 1963-66. Recipient Disting. contbn. in computer sci. award Westminster Coll., 1980. Mem. IEEE (chmn. N.E. computer group 1973-74), Am. Math. Soc. Office: Aiken Computation Lab Harvard Univ Cambridge MA 02138 Home: 2534 S Walter Reed Dr Apt A Arlington VA 22206-1287

BARTEK, GORDON LUKE, radiologist; b. Valparaiso, Nebr., Dec. 27, 1925; s. Luke Victor and Sylvia (Buner) B.; m. Ruth Evelyn Rowley, Sept. 10, 1949; children: John, David, James. BSc, U. Nebr., 1948, MD, 1949. Diplomate Am. Bd. Radiology. Intern Bishop Clarkson Hosp., Omaha, 1949-50; resident in medicine Henry Ford Hosp., Detroit, 1952-53, resident in radiology, 1953-56; staff radiologist Ferguson Hosp., Grand Rapids, Mich., 1956-76, Holland City Hosp., Mich., 1956-76, Logan Hosp., Utah, 1976-78, St. Lawrence Hosp., Lansing, Mich., 1978-97, Spectrum Health, Grand Rapids, 1997—; asst. clin. prof. dept. radiology Mich. State Univ. Coll. Medicine, 1977-93, asst. prof. radiology, 1993-97; organizer Care Choices HMO, Lansing, 1983, bd. dirs., 1983-93. Served to lt. USN, 1949-52. Fellow Am. Coll. Radiology (councilor 1972-76, emeritus); mem. Mich. Radiology Practice Assn. (bd. dirs. 1984-97, chmn. western Mich. sect. 1970-71), Peninsular Club, Terravita Country Club. Republican. Roman Catholic. Avocations: flying, photography, skiing, snorkeling. Home and Office: 1350 Briarcliff Dr SE Grand Rapids MI 49546-9679

BARTEL, ARTHUR GABRIEL, educational administrator, city official; b. San Francisco, Oct. 20, 1934; s. Irving Peter and Elian Leah (Barker) B.; m. Dottie Lu Smith, Dec. 14, 1963 (dec. Apr. 1972); children: Brian Blake, Scott Michael; m. Suzane M. Loftis, Feb. 14, 1989. Student, San Jose State Coll., 1952-54; BS, U. Calif., Berkeley, 1957; postgrad., U. So. Calif., 1968-70; MA, Pepperdine U., 1973, Calif. State U., Fresno, 1995. Cert. FAA air traffic controller, 1957-77, naval flight officer, 1965; lic. standard tchr., life standard svc., life cmty. coll. life chief coll. adminstrv. officer, life cmty. coll. supr., life comty. coll. instr., spl. edn. svcs. credential, Calif. Enlisted USMC, 1954, commd. 2d lt., 1957, advanced through grades to maj., 1967; comdg. officer VMFA-314 Fighter-Attack Squadron USMC, El Toro, Calif., 1970-72; ret. USMC, 1977; gen. mgr. Nieuport 17 Restaurant, Santa Ana, Calif., 1977-78; pres., chief exec. officer High Flight Inc., Hanford, San Diego, Calif., 1978-81; teaching vice prin. Armona (Calif.) Union Elem. Sch., 1982-84, tchr. sci. and lang. arts., 1981-84; curriculum cons. Kings County Office Edn., Hanford, 1984-86; program specialist Kings County Supt. Schs., Hanford, 1986-91; prin. Kings County Cmty. Sch., Hanford, 1994-98, ret., 1998; councilman City of Hanford, 1986-90, mayor, 1988-90; mem. adv. bd. San Joaquin Valley Writing Project, 1984-86, 92—. Vice chmn. Hanford Planning Commn., 1982-86; vice chmn. bd. trustees Sacred Heart Hosp., 1987-93; bd. dirs. Navy League, 1992—. Decorated Air medal, Vietnam Cross of Gallantry; fellow internat. writing project U. Calif., Irvine, 1985. Mem. Assn. Calif. Sch. Adminstrs., Calif. Soc. Program Specialists, Hanford C. of C., DAV (life), Ret. Officers Assn., Navy League (v.p. 1993-95), Delta Upsilon (life). Avocations: hunting, fishing, coin collecting, gun and knife collecting, domestic and foreign traveling, antiques.

BARTEL, FRED FRANK, consulting engineer executive; b. Milw., Nov. 4, 1917; s. Fred F. and Alma O. (Koppelmeyer) B.; m. Ann E. Staudacher, Oct. 23, 1943; children—Betty Jo, Susan, Mary Jo, Robert. B.S. in Civil Engring., U. Wis., 1940; M.S., U. Md., 1942. Engring. aide Wis. Hwy. Dept., 1936-40; asst. dir. engring. Nat. Ready Mixed Concrete Assn., Silver Spring, Md., 1942-49; chief engr., sales mgr. Tews Lime and Cement Co., Milw., 1949-75, pres., chief exec. officer, 1975-83; cons. engr. on concrete and concrete aggregates Milw., 1983-89; ret., 1989; trustee in bankruptcy, 4X Corp., Neenah, Wis., 1985. Contbr. to books and other tech. publs. Served to capt. USAAF, 1942-46. Stanton Walker research fellow U. Md., 1942. Fellow ASCE; mem. ASTM, Am. Concrete Inst., Nat. Ready Mixed Concrete Assn. (chmn. bd. dirs. 1979), Wis. Ready Mixed Concrete Assn. (pres. 1969), Builders Exchange Milw. (pres. 1966-67). Republican. Roman Catholic. Lodge: Rotary. Home and Office: 5421 N Shoreland Ave Milwaukee WI 53217-5132

BARTELL, ERNEST, economist, educator, priest; b. Chgo., Jan. 22, 1932. PhB, U. Notre Dame, 1953; AM, U. Chgo., 1954; MA, Coll. Holy Cross, 1961; PhD, Princeton U., 1966; LLD (hon.), China Acad., Taipei, Taiwan, 1975, St. Joseph's Coll., 1983, King's Coll., 1984, Stonehill Coll., 1992. Ordained priest Roman Cath. Ch., 1961. Instr. econs. Princeton (N.J.) U., 1965-66; asst. prof. econs. U. Notre Dame, Ind., 1966-68, assoc. prof., 1968-71, chmn. dept. econs., 1968-71, dir. Ctr. Study of Man in Contemporary Soc., 1969-71, prof. econs., 1981—, exec. dir. Helen Kellogg Inst. Internat. Studies, 1981-97; pres. Stonehill Coll., North Easton, Mass., 1971-77; dir. Fund for Improvement Post Secondary Edn. U.S. Dept. Health, Edn. and Welfare, Washington, 1977-79; dir. Project 80 Assn. Cath. Colls. and Univs., Washington, 1979-80; overseas mission coord. Priests of Holy Cross, Ind. Province, 1980-84, assoc. dir. Holy Cross Mission Ctr., 1984-95; asst. to pastor St. Anthony Ch., Ft. Lauderdale, Fla., 1993—; bd. dirs. Inst. Ctrl. Am. Studies, Washington Office on Latin Am., 1988-93; active Inst. East-West Securities Studies Working Group on Sources in Instability, 1989-90, Internat. Ctr. Devel. Policy Commn. on U.S.-Soviet Rels., 1988-89, Overseas Devel. Coun., 1988—, The Bretton Woods Com., 1992—; mem. policy planning commn. Nat. Inst. Ind. Colls. and Univs., 1982-85. Author: Costs and Benefits of Catholic Elementary and Secondary schools, 1969; co-editor: Business and Democracy in Latin America, 1995; contbr. articles to profl. jours. Bd. regents U. Portland, Oreg., 1984—; bd. dirs. Missionary Vehicle Assn. Am., 1981-88, Big Bros. and Big Sisters Am., 1978-80, Brockton Community Housing Corp., 1974-77, The Brighter Day, 1974-77, Brockton Hosp., 1973-77, King's Coll., Wilkes-Barre, Pa., 1969-82; bd. trustees Emmanuel Coll., 1977-78, U. Notre Dame, 1974—, bd. fellows, 1974—; mem. adv. bd. Brockton Art Ctr., 1974-77; mem. exec. com. Opera New Eng., 1977; parochial vicar St. Anthony's Ch., Ft. Lauderdale, 1993—. Recipient Fenwick Alumni Recognition award, 1974; named Fenwick Hall of Fame, 1990. Fellow Soc. Values in Higher Edn.; mem. Am. Econ. Assn., Am. Assn. Higher Edn., Nat. Cath. Ednl. Assn. (chmn. govtl. rels. com. 1976-77, vice chmn. exec. com. 1976-77, chmn. mgmt. and planning com. 1974-76), Assn. Soc. Econs., Latin Am. Studies Assn., Young Pres. Orgn. (sec. 1974-77), Delta Mu Delta (hon.). Home: 227 Corby Hall Notre Dame IN 46556-5680 Office: U Notre Dame Kellogg Inst 211 Hesburgh Ctr Notre Dame IN 46556-5677

BARTELL, JEFFREY BRUCE, lawyer; b. Madison, Wis., Jan. 29, 1943; s. Gerald Aaron and Joyce Meta (Jaeger) B.; m. Angela Gina Baldi, Aug. 31, 1968; children: Jessica, Carey, Chad, Nicholas, Dana. BS in Econs., U. Wis., 1965, JD cum laude, 1968. Bar: Wis. 1968, U.S. Dist. Ct. (we. dist.) 1968, U.S. Dist. Ct. (ea. dist.) 1969, U.S. Ct. Appeals (7th cir.) 1970, U.S. Supreme Ct. 1971. Asst. atty. gen. State of Wis., Madison, 1968-71; counsel Wis. Citizens Study Com. on Jud. Orgn., Madison, 1971-72; commr. securities State of Wis., Madison, 1972-79; pres. N.Am. Securities Administrators Assn., 1978-79; ptnr. Michael, Best & Friedrich, Madison, 1979-83; mng. ptnr. Quarles & Brady, Madison, 1983—; lectr. on securities regulation U. Wis. Law Sch., Madison, 1982, 86, 92; mem. adv. com. on tender offers SEC, 1983. Pres. Madison Repertory Theatre, 1978-80; trustee Wis. Meml. Union, Madison, 1984—; bd. dirs. Madison Civic Ctr. Found., 1985-95, Friends of WHA-TV, 1996—, Ten Chimneys Found., 1997—, Overture Cultural Arts Project, 1998—; chair Madison Civic Ctr. Endowment Fund, 1988-91, Wis. Found. for Arts, 1990—; officer, bd. dirs. Forward Wis., Inc., 1984—. Capt. JAGC, USAR, ret. Mem. ABA (gavel awards com. 1992—), State Bar Wis. (dir. bus. law sect. 1983-91, chmn. sect. 1990-91, mem. bus. corp. law com. 1989-96), Dane County Bar, Wis. Law Alumni Assn. (pres. 1989-91), Rotary (bd. dirs. Madison 1987-88). Avocations: skiing, biking, music. Office: Quarles & Brady 1st Wis Plz PO Box 2113 Madison WI 53701-2113

BARTELL, LAWRENCE SIMS, chemist, educator; b. Ann Arbor, Mich., Feb. 23, 1923; s. Floyd Earl and Lawrence (Sims) B.; m. Joy Hilda Keer, Aug. 16, 1952; 1 son, Michael Keer. B.S., U. Mich., 1944, M.S., 1947, Ph.D., 1951. Research asst. Manhattan project U. Chgo., 1944-45; mem. faculty Iowa State U., 1953-65, prof. chemistry, 1959-65; prof. chemistry U. Mich., 1965—, Philip J. Elving prof. chemistry, 1987-94, prof. emeritus, 1994—; vis. prof. Moscow (USSR) State U., 1972, U. Paris XI, Orsay, France, 1973, U. Tex., 1978, 86; cons. Gillette Co., Chgo., 1956-62, Mobil Oil Corp., Paulsboro, N.J., 1960-84; mem. commn. on electron diffraction Internat. Union Crystallography, 1966-75. Assoc. editor: Jour. Chem. Physics, 1963-66; mem. editorial bd.: Jour. Computational Chemistry, 1979-90, Chem. Physics Letters, 1981-84. Served with USNR, 1945. Recipient Disting. Faculty Achievement award U. Mich., 1981, Disting. Faculty award Mich. Assn. Governing Bds., 1982, Creativity award NSF, 1982. Mem. Am. Chem. Soc. (petroleum research fund adv. bd. 1970-73), Am. Phys. Soc. (chmn. div. chem. physics 1977-78), Am. Crystallographic Assn., AAAS, Phi Beta Kappa, Sigma Xi, Phi Kappa Phi, Phi Lambda Upsilon, Alpha Chi Sigma. Home: 381 Riverview Dr Ann Arbor MI 48104-1847

BARTELLS, JAMES L., lawyer; b. Portage, Wis., Mar. 7, 1949; s. Elmer E. and Lucile E. (Peterson) B.; m. Rose M. McWilliams, Dec. 15, 1973; children: Carey, Jamie. BBA with honors, U. Wis., 1971, JD, 1974. Assoc. Ervin Johnson Law Office, Darlington, Wis., 1974; dist. atty. Lafayette County, Darlington, 1974-77; trial atty. Wausau (Wis.) Ins., 1977-84; ptnr. Ament, Wulf & Bartells, Merrill, Wis., 1984-86; assoc. Jerome Maeder, S.C., Wausau, 1986-90; pvt. practice Wausau, 1990—. Sec. Woman's Cmty., Wausau, 1993-97. Mem. Wis. State Bar, Marathon County Bar. Office: 613 Forest St Wausau WI 54403-5524

BARTELS, BETTY J., nurse; b. Cin., Mar. 7, 1925; d. William Charles and Irene Agnes (McLean) Roth; m. Donald Arthur Bartels Sr.; children: Donald A. Jr., Virginia, Frederick, Bernadette. Nursing diploma RN, Good Samaritan Hosp., 1946; student in libr. sci., Barry Coll., 1966-70. RN Sun Ray Health Resort, Miami, Fla., 1949-51; vol. libr. St. James Cath. Sch., Miami, 1966-70; RN North Shore Med. Ctr., Miami, 1970-72; charge RN Villa Maria Rehab. Ctr., Miami, 1972-76; pvt. duty RN Miami, 1976-80; staff RN North Shore Med. Ctr., Miami, 1979-91. Author: Amotrophic Lateral Sclerosis: Helping the Patient with Lou Gehrigs Disease, 1979, RN Mag., 1979. Vol. Bon Secours Hosp./Villa Marla Nursing Ctr., 1990—. Mem. Third Order of St. Dominic (pres., prioress 1974-80, 92—). Democrat. Roman Catholic. Avocations: do-it-yourself projects, fishing.

BARTELS, BRUCE MICHAEL, health care executive; b. Chgo., Oct. 13, 1946; s. John Phillip Frederick and Margaret Florine (Michael) B.; m. Patricia Kate Newman, Apr. 10, 1970; children: Sarah, Jennifer, Rebecca. BA, U. Wis., 1969; MBA, U. Chgo., 1975. Adminstrv. asst. U. Chgo. Hosp., 1975-77; asst. adminstr. Meth. Hosp., Indpls., 1977-81; exec. v.p. Med. Ctr. Hosp. Vt., Burlington, 1981-88; pres. York (Pa.) Hosp. and Found., 1988-95, York Health Sys., 1995-99, S. Ctrl. Cmty. Health, York, 1999—. Contbr. articles to profl. jours. Bd. dirs. YMCA, York, 1989-98, chmn., 1994-96; bd. dirs. ARC, 1990-96, United Way, 1991-96, WITF, Inc., Ctrl. Pa. Pub. Broadcasting, 1994—; bd. dirs. Pa. Trauma Systems Found., Mechanicsburg, 1990—, chmn., 1997-99. With U.S. Army, Korea. Fellow Am. Coll. Healthcare Execs. (membership com. 1990-93); mem. Am. Hosp. Assn., Hosp. Assn. Pa. (bd. dirs., chmn.), York C. of C., U. Chgo. Health Adminstrn. Alumni Assn. (exec. com. 1991-95), Rotary. Avocations: reading, running, travel. Office: S Ctrl Cmty Health 1001 S George St York PA 17403-3676

BARTELS, JUERGEN E., hotel company executive; b. Swinemuende, Germany, Sept. 14, 1940; s. Herbert and Lilli E. (Wendland) B.; m. Rachel M.P. Villemaire, Mar. 14, 1951. Final, Verner V. Siemens Sch., Hanover, Germany, 1956. V.p. Commonwealth Holiday Inns Can. Ltd., 1971-76; exec. v.p. Ramada Internat., Brussels, Belgium, 1976-77; pres. Ramada Hotel Group, Phoenix, 1978-83; exec. v.p. Ramada Inns, Inc.; mem. Ramada Mgmt. Com.; pres., CEO Carlson Hospitality Group, Carlson Cos., Inc., Mpls., 1983-95, 95-98; CEO, dir. Starwood Hotels and Resorts Worldwide, Inc., Greenwich, Conn., 1998—; hotel company executive; b. Swinemuende, Ger., Sept. 14, 1940; s. Herbert and Lilli E. (Wendland) B.; m. Rachel M.P. Villemaire, Mar. 14, 1951. Final, Werner V. Siemens Sch., Hanover, W. Germany, 1956. Vice pres. Commonwealth Holiday Inns Can. Ltd., Can., 1971-76; exec. v.p. Ramada Internat., Brussels, Belgium, 1976-77; pres. Ramada Hotel Group, Phoenix, 1978-83; exec. v.p. Ramada Inns, Inc.; mem. Ramada Mgmt. Com.; pres., CEO Carlson Hospitality Group, Carlson Cos., Inc., Mpls., 1983-95, 95-98, CEO, dir. Starwood Hotels and Resorts Worldwide, Inc., Greenwich, Conn., 1998—. Office: Starwood Hotels and Resorts Worldwide Inc 777 Westchester Ave White Plains NY 10604*

BARTELS, ROBERT EDWIN, aerospace engineer; b. Des Moines, May 24, 1955; s. Everett M. and Iola J. (Van Wyck) B. BS, Iowa State U., 1977; MDiv cum laude, N.W. Baptist Sem., Tacoma, Wash., 1983; MS, Iowa State U., 1992, PhD, 1994. Sr. engr. Boeing Comml. Airplane Co., Seattle, 1984-87; teaching asst. Iowa State U., Ames, 1987-92; grad. rsch. fellow NASA Iowa State U., 1992-94; NRC rsch. assoc. NASA Langley Rsch. Ctr., Hampton, Va., 1994-97, aerospace engr., 1997—; adj. prof. Tidewater C.C., 1998. Bd. dirs., treas. Second Wind Contemporary Dance Co., 1996-98. Recipient Grad. Student Tchg. Excellence award Iowa State U., 1991. Mem. AIAA (sr.), Phi Kappa Phi. Home: 519 W 20th St Apt 305 Norfolk VA 23517-1941 Office: NASA Langley Rsch Ctr Hampton VA 23361

BARTELS, STANLEY LEONARD, investment banker; b. N.Y.C., Sept. 1, 1927; s. Abraham and Anna (Schultz) B.; m. Linda Lauretz; children: Jonathan Scott, Nancy Merrill, Diane Brooke, Elizabeth Cara. BS, NYU, 1954, MBA, 1956; grad., N.Y. State Maritime Acad., 1947. Examiner Mfrs. Hanover Bank, N.Y.C., 1948-50; security analyst Standard & Poor's Corp., N.Y.C., 1950-53; sr. financial analyst internat. div. Ford Motor Co., N.Y.C., 1953-56; asst. treas. W.R. Grace, Inc., N.Y.C., 1956-57; v.p. Tex. McCrary, Inc.; also controller, asst. to pres. N.Y.C., 1957-60; gen. partner, mem. mgmt. com. J.R. Williston & Beane, N.Y.C., 1960-63; pres., dir. Electrocopy Corp., 1963-66; sr. v.p., dir. Shaskan & Co., Inc.; mem. N.Y. Stock Exchange, 1966-73; pres. J.D. Winer & Co., Inc.; mem. N.Y. Stock Exchange, 1973-74; v.p. L.M. Rosenthal & Co., Inc.; mem. N.Y. Stock Exchange, 1974-75; dir. Digital Optronics Corp., 1986-89; sr. v.p. Weinrich Zitzmann Whitehead, St. Louis, 1981-82, Laidlaw Adams & Peck, Inc., N.Y.C., 1982-84; exec. v.p., founding dir. Yorke McCarter Owen & Bartels, Inc., N.Y.C., 1984-91; exec. v.p. Hampshire Securities Corp., N.Y.C., 1991-94, also dir.; exec. v.p. Coleman and Co. Securities, Inc., 1995—; mem. N.Y. Stock Exchange, 1995—. Trustee Maritime Industry Mus. N.Y. State Maritime Coll., 1994—. Served to lt. comdr. USNR. Mem. Securities Industry Assn. (mem. nat. investment banking com. 1993—), N.Y. Soc. Security Analysts, Bond Club of N.Y., Naval Order of the U.S., Phi Alpha Kappa. Club: Univ. of N.Y. Home: Farley Rd Short Hills NJ 07078 *Only those projects that are of a beneficial nature to society have the tendency to survive.*

BARTELSTONE, RONA SUE, gerontologist; b. Bklyn., Jan. 10, 1951; d. Herbert and Hazel (Mittman) Canarick; m. Alan Joel Markowitz. BS in Social Welfare, SUNY, Buffalo, 1972; MSW, Ind. U., 1974. Lic. clin. social worker, Fla.; diplomate in social work; cert. care mgr. Social worker YM-YWHA of Greater N.Y., 1974-75; dist. supr. N.Y.C. Housing Authority, Bklyn., 1975-77; field instr. Barry U. Sch. Social Work, 1980-81; project dir. United Family & Children's Svcs., 1977-81; faculty Miami Dade Community Coll., 1981-82; adult educator Sch. Bd. Dade County, 1981-82; med. social worker Mederi Home Health Agy., 1979-82; mem. adj. faculty Nova U., 1986-88; pvt. practice Rona Bartelstone Assocs., Inc., Ft. Lauderdale, Fla., 1981—; adj. faculty Fla. Internat. U., S.E. Ctr. on Aging, 1996; cons. and trainer in field. Contbr. articles to various mags. Bd. dirs. Jewish Vocat. Svcs., Miami, 1985-92; mem. funding panel Area Agy. on Aging, Miami,

1985-89; active Friends of the Family Counseling Svcs., Miami, 1983-88; adv. bd., chair internship subcom. Lynn U., 1993-97; exec. bd. Fla. Geriatric Care Mgrs., 1993—, pres.-elect 1998—; chair tng. com., exec. v.p. Alzheimer's Assn., Miami, 1994-97, bd. dirs., 1999; co-chair Nat. Acad. Cert. Care Mgrs., 1994-97, v.p., 1997—; trustee Fla. Coun. on Aging, 1996—. Recipient Dade County Citizen of the Yr. award, 1982, NASW Social Worker of the Yr. award, 1982-83, Trail Blazer award, 1984, Up & Comers award in health care Price Waterhouse and So. Fla. Bus. Jour., 1990. Mem. NASW (treas. 1987-89), NICLC (del. coun. 1999—), Gerontology Soc. Am., Am. Soc. on Aging, Nat. Coun. on Aging, Assn. Profl. Geriatric Care Mgrs. (pres. 1988-94, chmn. credential com. 1993—), Nat. Acad. Cert. Care Mgrs. (co-chmn. 1994-97, v.p. 1997-2001), Fla. Geriatric Care Mgrs. Assn. (exec. bd. 1993—, pres.-elect 1998—), Fla. Coun. on Aging (bd. trustees 1996—). Democrat. Jewish. Home: 5342 SW 33rd Way Fort Lauderdale FL 33312-5574 Office: 2699 Stirling Rd Ste C304 Fort Lauderdale FL 33312-6592

BARTER, ROBERT HENRY, physician, retired educator; b. Harvard, Ill., Mar. 15, 1913; s. Francis Albert and Lula Mae (Rowbottom) B.; m. Joanne Rae Blied, Dec. 29, 1948; children: Robert Raymond, James Francis, Mary Joanne. BS, U. Wis., 1937, MD, 1940. Intern Cleve. City Hosp., 1940-41; resident Chgo. Lying-In Hosp., 1941-42, Wis. Gen. Hosp., Madison, 1946-48; chief med. officer obstetrics and gynecology Galinger Municipal Hosp., Washington, 1948-50; faculty George Washington U. Sch. Medicine, 1950—, prof., 1958-83, prof. emeritus, 1983—, chmn. dept. obstetrics and gynecology, 1958-67; cons. emeritus surgeon gen. USAF; sr. cons. emeritus Walter Reed Army Med. Center. Maj., M.C. AUS, 1942-46. Mem. AMA, ACS, Am. Gynecol. and Obstet. Soc., Am. Coll. Obstetricians and Gynecologists, Soc. Gynecol. Surgeons, N.Am. Ob-Gyn Soc., So. Gynecol. and Obstet. Soc., Gynecol. Vis. Soc. Gt. Brit. and Ireland (hon.), Naples Yacht Club, Sigma Xi, Alpha Omega Alpha, Nu Sigma Nu, Kappa Sigma. Clubs: Burning Tree, Congressional Country; Hole in the Wall Golf (Naples, Fla.), Port Royal (Naples, Fla., Royal Poinciana Golf (Naples, Fla.); Rehoboth Beach (Del.) Country. Home: 2905 Gulf Shore Blvd N Apt 503 Naples FL 34103-3902 also (winter): 2905 GSBN Apt 503 Naples FL 34103-3902 *Died Feb. 16, 1999.*

BARTGES, HANS, investment company executive. Pres. International Nederlanden, N.Y.C., BHF German Bank, N.Y.C. Office: BHF Bank Inc 590 Madison Ave Fl 28 New York NY 10022-2524*

BARTH, ALVIN LUDWIG, JR., state legislator; b. Phila., May 12, 1936; s. Alvin Ludwig Sr. and Margaret Howe (Strader) Ellis; m. Jane Grieg, June 18, 1962 (dec. Nov. 1983); children: Karl Johann, Bruce Norman; stepchildren: Marcy Johanson Voelker, Todd Johanson; m. Lee Marcy Johanson, Mar. 23, 1985. BS, Pa. State U., 1958; MBA, U. Utah, 1960; MST, Colby Coll., 1967. Sci. tchr., adminstr. Gould Acad., Bethel, Maine, 1960-88; dir. community rels. and devel. Stephens Meml. Hosp., Norway, Maine, 1988-90; mem. Maine Ho. of Reps., Augusta, 1990—. Bd. dirs. Maine Sch. Adminstrv. Dist. #44, Bethel, 1984-88; pres. Lakes Assn. Norway, Maine, 1974-80; sec. Bethel C. of C., 1964-66, cubmaster Boy Scouts Am., Bethel, 1978-82; bd. dirs. Oxford County United Way, Norway, 1990-92; vol., bd. dirs., past chmn. bd. dirs. Maine affiliate Am. Diabetes Assn., 1989-94; vol., sec. bd. dirs. Maine Conservation Edn. Found., 1987-94; vol. bd. dirs. Mahoosuc Land Trust; bd. dirs. Mahoosuc Arts Coun., 1996—. Internat. teaching fellow State of Victoria, 1971-72. Mem. Rotary (pres. 1997—), Masons (past master, past dist. dep. grand master). Republican. Episcopalian. Avocations: golf, philately. Office: Maine Ho of Reps 2 State St Augusta ME 04330-4508*

BARTH, DAVID KECK, industrial distribution industry consultant; b. Springfield, Ill., Dec. 7, 1943; s. David Klenk and Edna Margaret (Keck) B.; m. Dian Oldemeyer, Nov. 21, 1970; children—David, Michael, John. B.A. cum laude, Knox Coll., Galesburg, Ill., 1965; M.B.A., U. Calif., Berkeley, 1971. With data processing div. IBM Corp., Chgo., 1966; with No. Trust Co., Chgo., 1971-72; mgr. treasury ops., then treas. fin. services group Borg-Warner Corp., Chgo., 1972-79; treas. W.W. Grainger, Inc., Skokie, Ill., 1979-83, v.p., 1984-90; pres. Barth Smith Co., 1991—; mem. faculty Lake Forest (Ill.) Grad. Sch. Mgmt., 1994—; bd. dirs. Travis Internat., Inc., Houston; dir. Indsl. Distbn. Group Inc., Atlanta. Served to lt. USNR, 1966-69. Mem. Econ. Club Chgo., Univ. Club of Chgo., Beta Gamma Sigma, Phi Delta Theta. Lutheran. Office: 1000 Skokie Blvd Wilmette IL 60091-1161

BARTH, ELMER ERNEST, wire and cable company executive; b. Phila., May 15, 1922; s. Paul Adolph and Anna (Miller) B.; m. Ruth Bradstreet Stone, Sept. 18, 1943 (dec. Aug. 1990); 1 dau., Rebecca Barth Gallucci; m. Barbara E. Burbridge, Jan. 25, 1992. Ed., Bentley Sch. Accounting, 1947-51; B.B.A., Northeastern U., 1956. Asst. treas. Hayward Hosiery Co., Ipswich, Mass., 1945-56; v.p. ops. Rockbestos Co.; Mem. Marmon Group, New Haven, 1956-86; sec., treas., dir. Applied Data, Inc., North Haven, 1961-97; trustee Ipswich Savs. Bank, 1947-56. Bd. govs., vice chmn. fin. com. Children's Center, Hamden, Conn., 1965-68. Served with USNR, 1942-45. Recipient Charles D. Scott Disting. Career award New Eng. Wire & Cable Club. Club: Branford Yacht (commodore 1976), Ipswich Outboard, Inc. (sec., bd. dirs. Commodore 1988-89). Home: 1 Riverside Dr Ipswich MA 01938-2427

BARTH, FRANCES DOROTHY, artist; b. N.Y.C., July 31, 1946; d. Frank and Helen (Henning) B. BFA, Hunter Coll., 1968, MA, 1970. Instr. Princeton U., 1975-79, Sarah Lawrence Coll., Bronxville, N.Y., 1979-85, Yale U., 1986—. Exhibited various one-woman shows N.Y.C., 1974—, Chgo., 1981, 85, U. Mass. Amherst, 1994, E.M. Donahue Gallery, N.Y.C., 1994, 97, Millersville Coll., Pa., 1995, Marcia Wood Gallery, Atlanta, 1998; group shows Moore Coll. Art, 1970, Whitney Mus. Am. Art, N.Y.C., 1972-73, Houston Mus. Contemporary Art, 1972, Corcoran Gallery Art, Washington, Bard Coll., Annandale-on-Hudson, N.Y.C., 1973, Trenton State Coll., 1974, Princeton U. Art Mus., 1975, High Mus. Art, Atlanta, 1976, Bennington Coll., 1976, San Francisco Art Inst., 1978, U. Pa., 1978, MIT, 1978, Jan Cicero, CHI, 1995, Moravia Coll., Pa., 1999,; (group shows), William Patterson Coll., Wayne, N.J., 1979, group shows, NYU, 1979, Va. Commonwealth U., Richmond, 1980, Sarah Lawrence Coll., 1981, Mus. Modern Art, 1981, Cleve. Mus. Art, 1983, Indpls. Mus., 1984, 85, Princeton U., 1985, Hunter Coll., 1986, Yale U., 1987, Bennington Coll., 1991, Am. Acad. Arts and Letters, 1988, Met. Mus. Art, 1990, Andre Emmerich Gallery, 1991, La Vigie, Nimes, France, 1995, Charles Cowles Gallery, N.Y.C., 1996, Amer. Acad. of Arts and Letters, NYC, 1999, others; represented in permanent collections New 20th Century Wing, Met. Mus. Art, N.Y.C., 1987, Mus. Modern Art, N.Y.C., Akron Art Inst., Albright-Knox Gallery, Am. Can Co., Greenwich, Conn., Amerada Hess Corp., N.Y.C., Chase Manhattan Bank, N.Y.C., Cornell U., IBM Corp., N.Y.C., Mobil Oil Corp., N.Y.C., Prudential Inst. Co., N.J., Whitney Mus. Am. Art, Lehman Bros., N.Y.C. and Chgo., Isham, Lincoln & Beale, Chgo., Security Pacific Nat. Bank, Los Angeles, Swiss Bank Corp., N.Y.C., Cameron Iron Works, Houston, Mus. Modern Art, N.Y.C., Paul Haim Found., Paris, Humana, Inc., Louisville, Coudert Bros., N.Y.C., Dallas Mus. Art. Grantee Creative Artists Pub. Svc., 1973, NEA, 1974, 82, N.J. State Coun. on Arts, 1987, Adolph and Esther Gottlieb Ind. Support, 1993; John Guggenheim fellow, 1977; recipient Joan Mitchell Found. award, 1995.

BARTH, JOHN ROBERT, English educator, priest; b. Buffalo, Feb. 23, 1931; s. Philip C. and Mary K. (Eustace) B. A.B., Fordham U., 1954, M.A., 1956; Ph.L., Bellarmine Coll., 1955; S.T.B., Woodstock Coll., 1961, S.T.L., 1962; Ph.D., Harvard U., 1967. Joined Society of Jesus, Roman Catholic Ch., 1948; tchr. English, French, Latin (Canisius High Sch.), Buffalo, 1955-58; asst. prof. English Canisius Coll., Buffalo, 1967-70, Harvard U., Cambridge, Mass., 1970-74; assoc. prof. English U. Mo.-Columbia, 1974-77, prof., 1977-79, Catherine Paine Middlebush prof. English, 1979-82, prof. English, chmn. dept., 1980-83, prof. English, 1983-85; Thomas I. Gasson prof. English Boston Coll., 1985-86; prof. English U. Mo.-Columbia, 1986-88; dean Coll. Arts and Scis., Boston Coll., 1988—. Author: Coleridge and Christian Doctrine, 1969, 2d edit., 1987, The Symbolic Imagination: Coleridge and the Romantic Tradition, 1977 (Book of Yr. award, Conf. on Christianity and Lit. 1977), Coleridge and the Power of Love, 1988 (U. Mo. Curators Publ. award 1989); editor: Religious Perspectives in Faulkner's Fiction, 1972; co-editor: Marginalia in Collected Works of Samuel Taylor Coleridge, 1984—, Coleridge, Keats and the Imagination: Romanticism and Adam's Dream, 1990; mem. bd. advisors Wordsworth Circle, Phila., 1976—; mem. editl. bd. cons. Thought, 1980-93, mem. adv. bd. Studies in Romanticism, 1981—, European Romantic Rev., 1990—, Renascence, 1993—; mem. editl. adv. bd. Christianity and Literature, 1989—; mem. editl. planning bd. Religion and the Arts, 1996—. Trustee St. Louis U., 1974-79, St. Peter's Coll., 1985-91, Coll. of the Holy Cross, 1989-93, Canisius Coll., 1992-98. Recipient Howard Mumford Jones prize Harvard U., 1967; Dexter fellow, 1967; NEH summer grantee, 1969; Am. Council Learned Socs. grantee, 1970; Harvard U. research grantee, 1973. Mem. AAUP, Conf. on Christianity and Lit. (dir. 1980-83), MLA (del. assembly 1979-83, exec. com. romantic divsn. 1975-79, exec. com. religious approaches 1983-87), Wordsworth-Coleridge Assn. (v.p. 1978, pres. 1979), Keats-Shelley Assn. Address: St Mary's Hall Boston College Chestnut Hill MA 02167 Office: Boston Coll Office Dean Coll Arts and Scis Gasson Hall 103 Chestnut Hill MA 02167*

BARTH, JOHN SIMMONS, writer, educator; b. Cambridge, Md., May 27, 1930; s. John Jacob and Georgia (Simmons) B.; m. Harriette Anne Strickland, Jan. 11, 1950 (div. 1969); children: Christine Anne, John Strickland, Daniel Stephen; m. Shelly I. Rosenberg, Dec. 27, 1970. BA, Johns Hopkins U., 1951, MA, 1952; LittD (hon.), Univ. Md., 1969. Instr. English Pa. State U., 1953-56, asst. prof. English, 1957-60, assoc. prof. English, 1960-65; prof. English SUNY, Buffalo, 1965-73; prof. creative writing Johns Hopkins U., Balt., 1973-91, prof. emeritus creative writing, 1991—. Author: The Floating Opera, 1956 (Nat. Book award nomination 1956), The End of the Road, 1958, The Sot-Weed Factor, 1960, Giles Goat-Boy, 1966, Lost in the Funhouse, 1968 (Nat. Book award nomination 1968), Chimera, 1972 (Nat. Book award 1973), Letters, 1979, Sabbatical: A Romance, 1982, The Literature of Exhaustion, and The Literature of Replenishment, 1982, The Friday Book: Essays and Other Nonfiction, 1984, Don't Count on It: A Note on the Number of the 1001 Nights, 1984, The Tidewater Tales: A Novel, 1987, The Last Voyage of Somebody the Sailor, 1991, Once Upon a Time: A Floating Opera, 1994, Further Fridays: Essays, Lectures, and Other Non-fiction, 1984-94, 1995, On with the Story, 1996. Recipient Brandeis Univ. Creative Arts award, 1965, F. Scott Fitzgerald award, 1997, PEN/Malamud award, 1998, Lifetime Achievement award Lannan Found., 1998; Rockefeller Found. grantee, 1965-66, Nat. Inst. Arts and Letters grantee, 1966. Mem. AAAL, Am. Acad. Arts and Scis. Office: Writing Seminars Johns Hopkins U Baltimore MD 21218

BARTH, KARL LUTHER, retired seminary president; b. Milw., Nov. 7, 1924; s. G. Christian and Louise A. (Schneeman) B.; m. Jean L. Kelly, June 8, 1947; children: Linda, Karl, Laurel, Kurt, Lisa. *Grandfather, Gustav Adolph Barth, came to this country from Germany to complete his education for the Lutheran Ministry. He graduated from Concordia Seminary, St. Louis, in 1864. He and his wife, Margaretha, lost all four children to diphtheria in 1880, but were blessed later with four more children. Father, G. Christian Barth, was president of Concordia Theological Seminary in Springfield, Illinois. He also served as vice-president of The Lutheran Church-Missouri Synod. Maternal grandmother, Margaretha Schneemann, emigrated from Germany in 1892 with four young children after death of her husband Karl, and settled in St. Louis where oldest child, Louise, married G. Christian Barth in 1906.* B.A., Concordia Sem., 1945, M.Div., 1947; D.D. (hon.), Concordia Theol. Sem., 1975. Ordained to ministry, Lutheran Ch., 1947. Asst. pastor First English Lutheran Ch., New Orleans, 1947-50; pastor Trinity Evan. Lutheran Ch., Centralia, Ill., 1950-52, St. Paul's Lutheran Ch., West Allis, Wis., 1956-70; pres. So. Wis. Dist. Luth. Ch. Mo. Synod, Milw., 1970-82, bd. for mission svcs., 1982-90, bd. dirs., 1992—; pres. Concordia Sem., St. Louis, 1982-90; exec. dir. 150th Anniversary Luth. Ch. Mo. Synod. Contbr. articles to profl. jours. Vice pres. So. Wis. dist. Lutheran Ch., Mo. Synod, 1966-70; chmn. Com. on Theology and Ch. Relations, St. Louis, 1974-82; denominational rep. Div. Theol. Studies Lutheran Council U.S.A., N.Y.C., 1975-81; mem. adv. bd. Wis. Citizens Concerned for Life, 1976-82. Republican. Home: 13330 W Bluemound Rd Elm Grove WI 53122-2536

BARTH, MARK HAROLD, lawyer; b. Lincoln, Ill., June 22, 1951; s. Harold Julius and Maxine Virginia (Schroeppel) B.; m. Jannette Morgan Berg, June 29, 1974; children: Katherine, Erica. BA, The Johns Hopkins U., 1973; JD, Georgetown U., 1977. Bar: N.Y. 1978. Assoc. Curtis, Mallet-Prevost, Colt & Mosle, N.Y.C., 1977-86, ptnr., 1986—; resident London office, 1988-92. Mem. ABA, Internat. Bar Assn., Assn. Bar City N.Y. Office: Curtis Mallet-Prevost Colt & Mosle 101 Park Ave New York NY 10178

BARTH, MICHAEL CARL, economist; b. Newark, Apr. 3, 1941; s. Abe and Frances (Keller) B.; m. Marilyn Levy, Dec. 11, 1966; children: Christopher Jay, Karen Rebecca. B.A., Harpur Coll., Binghamton, N.Y., 1962; M.A., U. Ill., Champaign, 1963; Ph.D., CUNY, 1971. Rsch. assoc. CCNY Rsch. Found., N.Y.C., 1965-67; lectr. econs. CCNY, 1966-68; economist Pres's. Commn. on Income Maintenance, Washington, 1968-69, Office Econ. Opportunity, Washington, 1969-73; dir. income sec. policy/analysis U.S. Dept. HEW, Washington, 1973-75; vis. assoc. prof. econs. U. Wis., Madison, 1975-76; dep. asst. sec. U.S. Dept. HHS, Washington, 1976-80; prin. ICF Inc., Washington, 1980-87, sr. v.p., 1987—; pres. ICF Info. Tech. Inc., Washington, 1992-95; exec. v.p. ICF Kaiser Internat. Consulting Group, Fairfax, Va., 1995—; bd. dirs. ICF Info. Tech., Inc, ICF Resources. Author: (with G. Carcagno and J. Palmer) Toward an Effective Income Support System: Problems, Prospects and Choices, 1974; editor: Greenhouse Effect and Sea Level Rise, 1984 contbr. articles to profl. jours. Recipient Sec.'s Spl. citation HEW, 1975, Sec.'s Outstanding Achievement award, 1977. Mem. Am. Econ. Assn., Indsl. Relations Research Assn. Home: 3818 Military Rd NW Washington DC 20015-2704 Office: ICF Kaiser Internat Inc 9300 Lee Hwy Fairfax VA 22031-1200

BARTH, RICHARD, pharmaceutical executive; b. N.Y.C., May 23, 1931; s. Alexander Haddon and Georgina (Grant) B.; m. Mary Elizabeth McAnaney, June 13, 1959; children: Leanore, Jennifer, Richard, Michele, Alexander. AB cum laude, Wesleyan U., 1952; LLB, Columbia U., 1955; postgrad., NYU, 1959-62. Bar: N.Y. 1958, N.J. 1966. Assoc. firm Burke & Burke, 1957-65; gen. counsel, sec., mem. mgmt. com. Ciba, 1965-70; dir. Radio Shack Corp., 1964-65; v.p., gen. counsel, mem. mng. com., dir. Ciba-Geigy Corp., Ardsley, N.Y., 1971-86; chmn., pres., chief exec. officer, dir. CIBA-GEIGY Corp., Ardsley, N.Y., 1986-96; dir. Novartis Corp., 1997—; bd. dirs. Bank of N.Y., Bowater, Inc., Imclone Systems Inc.; trustee Wesleyan U., Middletown, Conn., 1987-90, N.Y. Med. Coll., 1990—, chmn. bd., 1994—. Contbr. articles to profl. jours. Mem. substandard housing bd., Summit, N.J., 1968-70; mem. Pres. Clinton's Coun. Sustainable Devel. Mem. ABA, N.Y. Bar Assn., N.J. Bar Assn., Phi Delta Phi, Psi Upsilon. Home and Office: 470 West End Ave # 15A New York NY 10024-4933

BARTH, ROBERT HENRY, nephrologist, educator; b. Newark, Oct. 31, 1944; s. Robert Henry and Wilma Elizabeth (Van Ness) B.; m. Elettra Nerbosi, May 10, 1976. BA in Chemistry, Cornell U., 1967; MD cum laude, U. Bologna, Italy, 1976. Diplomate Am. Bd. Internal Medicine, Am. Bd. Nephrology. Chemist Sandoz, Inc., Hanover, Basel, N.J., Switzerland, 1967-68, 70, Internat. Flavors and Fragrances, Union Beach, N.J., 1968-69; resident Berkshire Med. Ctr., Pittsfield, Mass., 1976-80; fellow, rsch. assoc. Rogosin Kidney Ctr. N.Y. Hosp.-Cornell U. Med. Ctr., 1980-83; assoc. dir. Baumritter Kidney Ctr. Albert Einstein Coll. Medicine, Bronx, N.Y., 1983-86; physician, chief nephrology, chief dialysis VA Med. Ctr., Bklyn., 1986—; instr., asst. prof. Albert Einstein Coll. Medicine, Bronx, 1983-86, attending physician, 1983-86; asst. prof., assoc. prof. SUNY Health Sci. Ctr., Bklyn., 1986—; attending physician Bronx Mcpl. Hosp. Ctr., 1983-86. Contbr. chpts. in books and articles to profl. jours.; software program developer. Pres. Bklyn. VA Med. Ctr. Med. Soc., 1996—. Mem. Am. Soc. for Artificial Internal Organs (bd. trustees 1996-99, program chmn. 1998, ann. meeting), Am. Soc. Nephrology (abstract reviewer 1993 ann. meeting session chmn.), Internat. Soc. Peritoneal Dialysis, Internat. Soc. Nephrology, Nat. Kidney Found. (exec. bd., coun. on Dialysis 1990-94), N.Y. Soc. Nephrology, Physicians for Nat. Health Program, Adirondack Mountain Club. Avocations: hiking, skiing, photography, jazz. Home: 187 E 4th St New York NY 10009-7201 Office: VA Med Ctr 800 Poly Pl Brooklyn NY 11209-7104

BARTH, ROLF FREDERICK, pathologist, educator; b. N.Y.C., Apr. 4, 1937; s. Rolf L. and Josephine Barth; m. Christine Ferguson, Oct. 30, 1965; children: Suzie, Alison, Rolf, Christofer. AB, Cornell U., 1959; MD, Columbia U., 1964. Diplomate Am. Bd. Pathology. Surg. intern Columbia-Presbyn. Med. Ctr., N.Y.C., 1964-65; postdoctoral fellow Karolinska Inst., Stockholm, 1965-66; rsch. assoc. Nat. Inst. Allergy and Infectious Diseases, NIH, Bethesda, Md., 1966-68; resident pathology br. Nat. Cancer Inst., 1966-68, Nat. Inst. Health, 1968-70; Prof. dept. pathology and oncology U. Kans. Med. Ctr., Kansas City, 1970-77; clin. prof. dept. pathology Med. Coll. Wis. and U. Wis., Madison, 1977-79; prof. dept. pathology Ohio State U., Columbus, 1979—. Contbr. articles to profl. jours. Sr. asst. surgeon USPHS, 1966-70, inactive Res., 1970—. Grantee Dept. Energy, NIH. Mem. Am. Assn. Exptl. Pathology, Am. Assn. Immunologists, Am. Assn. Cancer Rsch., Internat. Soc. for Neutron Capture Therapy, Sigma Xi, Phi Kappa Phi. Office: Ohio State U Dept Pathology 165 Hamilton Hall 1645 Neil Ave Columbus OH 43210-1218

BARTH, SHARON LYNN, nurse; b. Stamford, Conn., Oct. 27, 1948; d. Donald Eric and Jane Dolores (Fabrizio) Walker; m. James Leander Barth Jr., June 8, 1967 (divorced); children: Kristen Lynne, Jennifer Leigh, Shannon Lynlee. AA summa cum laude, Coll. of Albermarle, Elizabeth City, N.C., 1974; BSN cum laude, Calif. State U., Sacramento, 1991; postgrad., U. Phoenix, Sacramento, 1997—. RN, Calif.; Neonatal Advanced Life Support, Calif.; cert. lactation educator. Staff nurse Kaiser Permanente, Sacramento, 1991-93, charge nurse, 1993-97, asst. clin. nurse mgr., 1997—; guest lectr. Teen Parenting classes, Maternal-Child classes CSUS. Mem. Assn. Women's Health, Assn. Obstetric and Neonatal Nurses, Phi Kappa Phi, Sigma Theta Tau, Golden Key. Avocations: swimming, reading. Home: 8142 Bonnie Oak Way Citrus Heights CA 95610-0726

BARTH, UTA, artist, educator; b. Berlin, Jan. 29, 1958. BA, U. Calif., Davis, 1982; MFA, UCLA, 1985. From asst. prof. to assoc. prof. art dept. U. Calif., Riverside, 1990—. One-woman shows include Howard Yezersky Gallery, Boston, 1990, Rochester (N.Y.) Inst. Tech., 1993, Calif. Mus. Photography, Riverside, 1993, Wooster Gardens, N.Y.C., 1994, Mus. Contemporary Art, L.A., 1995, ACME, Santa Monica, Calif., 1995, 98, Tanya Bonakdar Gallery, N.Y.C., 1996, London Projects, London, 1996, 98, S.L. Simpson Gallery, Toronto, Ont., Can., 1996, Mus. Contemporary Art, Chgo., 1997, Andrehn-Schiptjenko, Stockholm, 1997, 99, Tanya Bonakdar Gallery, N.Y., 1998, Lawing, Houston, 1998, Bonakdar Jancou Gallery, N.Y., 1998, 99, Rena Branston Gallery, San Francisco, 1999, Galerie Camargo Vilaça, São Paulo, 1999, Lannan Found., Santa Fe, N. Mex., 1999; group shows include Tom Solomon's Garage, L.A., 1994, Long Beach (Calif.) Mus. Art, 1994, Mus. De Beyard, Netherlands, 1994, L.A. County Mus. Art, 1994, San Bernardino County Mus., 1994, The New Mus., N.Y.C., 1995, Mus. Modern Art, N.Y.C., 1995, Rooseum-Ctr. for Contemporary Art, Malmo, Sweden, 1996, Magasin 3 Stockholm Konsthall, 1996, Wexner Ctr. for Art, Columbus, Ohio, 1997, Mus. Contemporary Art, Miami, 1997, Whitney Mus. Art, N.Y.C., 1997, 98, Mus. Contemporary Art, L.A., 1998, Matthew Marks Gallery, N.Y.C., 1997, Parco Gallery, 1997, De Appel Found., Amsterdam, The Netherlands, 1997, IKON Gallery, Birmingham, Eng., 1998., Mus. Fine Arts, Houston, 1998, Worcester (Mass.) Art Mus., 1999, Laband Art Gallery, L.A., 1999; featured in Photography at Princeton, TimeOut, Flash Art, Arforum, Art in Am., Art Monthly, Art & Text, The Birmingham Post, Jour. of Contemporary Art, L.A. Times, Paper Mag., others. Grantee NEA, 1990-91, 94-95, Art Matters Inc., 1992-93, 95. Home and Office: 3411 Colbert Ave Los Angeles CA 90066-1234

BARTHEL, WILLIAM FREDERICK, JR., engineer, electronics company executive; b. Washington, July 14, 1940; s. William Frederick and Eva (Buday) B.; m. Barbara Joan Adams, Nov. 18, 1961; 1 son, William Frederick III. BS, McNeese State U., 1972. Shop mgr. Electronic Unlimited, Lake Charles, La., 1968; quality control engr. Rockwell Internat., Cedar Rapids, Iowa, 1974-79, mgr. quality assurance, 1979, sr. engring. scientist, process control devel., 1980-81; engring. mgr. process reliability Digital Equipment Corp., Andover, Mass., 1981-87, engring. mgr. performance assurance, 1987-91; dir. quality Gables Engring., Inc., Coral Gables, Fla., 1991-93, v.p. ops., 1993—. Served with USAF, 1958-62. Mem. Am. Chem. Soc., Am. Inst. Chemists. Republican. Home: 745 SE 25th Ln Homestead FL 33033-5234 Office: Gables Engring Inc 247 Greco Ave Miami FL 33146-1808

BARTHELMAS, NED KELTON, investment and commercial real estate banker; b. Circleville, Ohio, Oct. 22, 1927; s. Arthur and Mary Bernice (Riffel) B.; m. Marjorie Jane Livezey, May 23, 1953; children: Brooke Ann, Richard Thomas. B.S. in Bus. Adminstrn., Ohio State U., 1950. Stockbroker Ohio Co., Columbus, 1953-58; pres. First Columbus Securities Corp., 1958—; pres., dir. Ohio Fin. Corp., Columbus, 1960—; pres. Thwirs, Inc., Columbus, 1986—; trustee, chmn. Am. Guardian Fin., Republic Fin.; bd. dirs. Nat. Foods, Midwest Capital Corp., Capital Equity Corp., Midwest Nat. Corp., 1st Columbus Realty Corp., Dublin Nat. Corp. (all Columbus). Served with Adj. Gen.'s Dept., AUS, 1944-47. Mem. Nat. Assn. Securities Dealers (past vice chmn. dist. bd. govs.), Investment Bankers Assn. Am. (exec. com. 1973), Investment Dealers Ohio (sec., treas. 1956-72, pres. 1973), Nat. Stock Traders Assn., Young Pres.'s Orgn. (pres. 1971), World Bus. Coun., Columbus Pres.'s Assn., Nat. Investment Bankers (pres. 1973), Internat. Real Estate Inst., Exec. Hall Fame, Columbus Jr. C. of C. (pres. 1956), Ohio C. of C. (trustee 1957-58), World's Pres.'s Assn. (Exec. Hall of Fame award 1993), Columbus Area C. of C. (dir. 1956, named an Outstanding Young Man of Columbus 1962), Newcomen Soc., Coun. for Ethics in Econs., Coun. of Orgn. of Am. States, Wisdom Hall of Fame, Internat. Soc. Financiers, Oxford Club, Execs. Club, Pres.' Club (Ohio State U.), Internat. Platform Assn., Stock and Bond Club (past pres.), named top 25 corp. Dirs. (1984-90), Columbus Club, Scioto Country Club, Crystal Downs Country Club, Ohio State U. Faculty Club, Kiwanis (legion of honor 1992), Am. Legion, Admirals Club, Alpha Kappa Psi, Phi Delta Theta (Golden Legion award). Office: 1241 Dublin Rd Columbus OH 43215-7000

BARTHELME, STEVEN, English educator; b. July 7, 1952. BA in English, U. Tex., Austin, 1973; MA in Writing, Johns Hopkins U., 1984. Prof. dept. English U. So. Miss., Hattiesburg, 1986—. Author: And He Tells the Little Horse the Whole Story, 1987; co-author: Double Down, 1999; author more than 100 essays, short stories and articles in profl. jours. and newspapers. Office: U So Miss Dept English PO Box 5144 Hattiesburg MS 39406-1000

BARTHOLD, CLEMENTINE B., retired judge; b. Odessa, Russia, Jan. 11, 1921; came to U.S., 1925; d. Joseph Anton and Magdalene (Richter) Schwan; m. Edward Brendel Barthold, July 5, 1941 (dec.); children: Judith Anne Barthold DeSomone, John Edward. Student, Aberdeen Bus. Coll., 1940; BGS, Ind. U. S.E., 1978; JD, Ind. U., Indpls., 1980. Bar: Ind. 1980, U.S. Dist. Ct. (so. dist.) Ind. 1980. Sec., asst. to mgr. Clark County C. of C., Ind., 1959-60; chief probation officer Clark Cir. Ct. and Superior Cts., Jeffersonville, 1960-72; rsch. cons. Pub. Action Correctional Effort, Clark and Floyd Counties, 1972-75; instl. parole officer Ind. Women's Prison, Indpls., 1975-80; atty. State of Ind., 1980-83; judge Clark Superior Ct. No. 1, Jeffersonville, 1983-95; ret., 1995; ptnr. Barthold & De Simone Attys. at Law, 1998—. Councilwoman Clark County, Jefferson, 1997—. Recipient Good Govt. award Jeffersonville Jaycees, 1966, Good Citizenship award, 1967, Wonder Woman award, 1984, Robert J. Kinsey award, 1986, Sagamore of Wabash award, 1986, Outstanding Cmty. Svc. award Social Concerns League, 1966, Disting. Svc. award, Outstanding Contbn. to Field of Correction award, Women of Achievement award, Jeff BPW Appreciation award, Juvenile Justice award, Disting. Contemporary Women in History award, Disting. Leadership award, Women of Achievement award, 1982-83, Appreciation award VIPO, 1983, Children and Youth Recognition award, 1984, Gov.'s Exemplary award, 1984, 88, 89, 92, Commitment to Youth award, 1987, Warren W. Martin award, 1973, 87, Outstanding Child Advocacy in Ind. award, 1987, Cmty. Svc. award, 1988, Orgnl. Renewal award, 1988, Parents Without Ptnrs. award, 1989, Ind. Youth Investment award, 1992, Excellence in Pub. Info. and Edn. award, 1992. Mem. LWV, Ind. Bar Assn., Clark County Bar Assn., Ind. Correctional Assn. (pres. 1971, Disting. Svc. award 1967, 85), Ind. Judges Assn., Ind. Juvenile Justice Task Force, Ind. U. Alumni Assn., Howard Steamboat Mus., Bus. Profl. Women's Club, Ladies Elks Aux. Roman Catholic. Home: 948 E 7th St Jeffersonville IN 47130-4106

BARTHOLD, LIONEL OLAV, engineering executive; b. Gt. Barrington, Mass., Mar. 20, 1926; s. Walter Jensen and Josephine (Salmon) B.; children by previous marriage: Floyd F., Walter Scott; m. Deborah Kline, Aug. 12, 1989; 1 child, Julian. BS in Physics, Northwestern U., 1950. Registered profl. engr., N.Y. Mgr. transmission engring. Gen. Electric, Schenectady, 1960-69; pres. Power Technologies Inc., Schenectady, 1969-86, chmn., 1986-98; bd. dirs. Trustco Bank Corp.; bd. dirs., chmn. Cellutech, llc, Everett, Mass.; pres. Adirondack Conservancy, Adirondack Land Trust, 1988-92. Patentee in field; author numerous tech. papers. Bd. dirs. Proctors Theatre, Schenectady, 1983—. Recipient Cigre Philip Sporn award, 1993. Fellow IEEE (1st prize paper 1962); mem. NAE, Power Engring Soc. IEEE (pres. 1980-83, Power Life award 1989), C. of C. (bd. dirs. 1983), Lake George Club. Republican. Methodist. Avocations: sailing; skiing; backpacking. Office: Power Technologies Inc 1482 Erie Blvd Schenectady NY 12305-1000

BARTHOLOMAUS, BRETT WILLIAM, small business owner; b. Milw., Jan. 19, 1944; s. Weber and Beatrice (Elmergreen) B.; m. Joan Anne Cavosi, Feb. 19, 1977; children: Laura, Thomas, Eric. Student, Milw. tech. Coll. Lic. pvt. security Wis. Motorcycle sales rep. Vic Panetti & Sons, Milw., 1963-75; maint. supr. U. Wis., Milw., 1977; owner North Trail Inn Supper Club, Tigerton, Wis., 1978-82; security supr. Sentinal Detective agy., Wausau, Wis., 1988—. Author: (poetry book) Moments Beautiful, Moments Bright, 1993, (novel) Reflection of Evil, 1998; poetry pub. various pubs.; numerous poetry readings. Vol. numerous charitable orgns. Recipient Golden Poets award World of Poetry, 1988, 89, 90, 92.. Democrat. Roman Catholic. Avocations: motorcycling, backpacking, weight lifting, family. Home and Office: 209 Kirkwood St Hatley WI 54440-9711

BARTHOLOMAY, WILLIAM C., insurance brokerage company executive, professional baseball team executive; b. Evanston, Ill., Aug. 11, 1928; s. Henry C. and Virginia (Graves) B.; m. Sara Taylor, 1950, (div. 1964); children: Virginia, William T., Jamie, Elizabeth, Sara; m. Gail Dillingham, May 1968 (div. Apr. 1980). Student, Oberlin Coll., 1946-49, Northwestern U., 1949-50; BA, Lake Forest Coll., 1955. Ptnr. Bartholomay & Clarkson, Chgo., 1951-63; v.p. Alexander & Alexander, Chgo., 1963-65; pres. Olson & Bartholomay, Chgo. and Atlanta, 1965-69; sr. v.p. Frank B. Hall & Co. Inc., N.Y.C. and Chgo., 1969-72, exec. v.p., 1972-73, pres., 1973-74, vice chmn., 1974-90; chmn. bd., dir. Atlanta Braves, 1966—; pvt. practice cons. Chgo., 1990-91; pres. Near North Nat. Group, 1991—; vice chmn. Turner Broadcasting System, Inc., Atlanta; bd. dirs. WMS Industries Inc., Chgo., Midway Games, Inc., Exec. Coun. Maj. League Baseball, Maj. League Baseball Players Pension Plan; bd. govs. Arlington Internat. Racecourse, Ltd. Commr. Chgo. Park Dist., 1980—, Chgo. Pub. Bldg. Commn., 1989—; bd. dirs. Chgo. Maternity Ctr., Lincoln Park Zool. Soc.; trustee Adler Planetarium, Mus. Sci. and Industry, Roosevelt U., Chgo.; former trustee Lake Forest (Ill.) Coll., Ogelthorpe Coll., Atlanta, Marymount Manhattan Coll., N.Y. With USNR, 1951-54. Mem. Chief Execs. Orgn., World Pres.'s Orgn., Chgo. Pres.'s Orgn., Nat. Assn. CLU, Chgo. Assn. CLU, Chgo. Club, Racquet Club, Saddle and Cycle Club, Econ. Club, Onwentsia Club, Shoreacres Club (Lake Forest), Brook Club, Links Club, Racquet & Tennis Club, Doubles Club (N.Y.C.), Piedmont Driving Club, Atlanta Country Club, Peachtree Golf Club, Commerce Club. Episcopalian. Home: 180 E Pearson St Chicago IL 60611-2130 Office: Near North Nat Group 875 N Michigan Ave Ste 2000 Chicago IL 60611-1954 also: Atlanta Braves PO Box 4064 Atlanta GA 30302-4064

BARTHOLOMEW, ARTHUR PECK, JR., accountant; b. Rochester, N.Y., Nov. 20, 1918; s. Arthur Peck and Abbie West (Dawson) B.; m. Mary Elizabeth Meyer, Oct. 4, 1941(wid. Oct. 1992); children: Susan B. Hall, Arthur Peck III, James M., Virginia B. Keyser. AB, U. Mich., 1939, MBA, 1940. With Ernst & Whinney (name now Ernst & Young), 1940-79, successively jr. accountant, partner charge Eastern dist., Detroit office, 1940-64; nat. office, Cleve. Ernst & Whinney, 1964-65, N.Y. office, 1965-79, also mem. mng. com.; instr. accounting U. Mich., 1940, George Washington U., 1945-46. Mem. Mich. Gov.'s Task Force for Expenditure Mgmt., 1963-64; mem. 2d Regional Plan Commn. N.Y.; Bd. dirs. Detroit League for Handicapped, 1952-64; treas. Grosse Pointe War Meml. Assn., 1961; bd. dirs., v.p. Greater N.Y. council Boy Scouts Am. Served from pvt. to capt. AUS, 1942-46. Mem. AICPA, Inst. Mgmt. Accts. (pres. Detroit 1963-64, nat. pres. 1974-75), The Conf. Bd., Mich. Soc. CPAs, N.Y. Soc. CPAs, Detroit Country Club, Gulf Stream Golf Club, Wall St. Club (pres. 1976-78), Ocean Club Fla. (pres. 1993-94), Phi Beta Kappa, Phi Kappa Phi, Beta Gamma Sigma, Phi Eta Sigma, Beta Alpha Psi, Phi Kappa Sigma. Republican. Presbyterian. Home: 6665 N Ocean Blvd Boynton Beach FL 33435-3329

BARTHOLOMEW, CHARLES R., advertising executive. Vice chmn., client svcs. dir., dir. Evans Group, Denver. *

BARTHOLOMEW, GILBERT ALFRED, retired physicist; b. Nelson, C., Can., Apr. 8, 1922; s. Alfred and Anna (Lenzman) B.; m. Rosalie May Dinzey, Apr. 19, 1952 (dec. Dec. 10, 1990); m. Anna Lubicz-Luba, July 24, 1992. B.A., U. B.C., 1943; Ph.D., McGill U., 1948. With Atomic Energy of Can., Ltd., 1948-83, head neutron physics br., 1962-71, dir. physics div., 1971-83. Contbr. articles to profl. jours. Fellow AAAS, Royal Soc. Can., Am. Phys. Soc.; mem. Can. Assn. Physicists, Can. Nuclear Soc., Assn. for Baha'i Studies, Sigma Xi. Home: PO Box 150, Lions Bay, ON Canada V0N 2E0

BARTHOLOMEW, JOHN NILES, church administrator; b. Rochester, N.Y., Dec. 30, 1934; s. Donald Hague and Adair (Wellington) B.; m. Mary Townsend, June 18, 1955; children: David Malcolm, Jean Elizabeth Bartholomew Parker. BA, Cornell U., 1955; BD, Princeton Theol. Sem., 1958, ThD, 1971. Sunday sch. missionary Presbyn. Bd. Nat. Missions, Tok, Alaska, 1958-61; pastor First Presbyn. Ch., Sayre, Pa., 1962-66; instr. Princeton (N.J.) Theol. Sem., 1968-69; asst. to assoc. prof. sociology, dean The Lindenwood Colls., St. Charles, Mo., 1969-82; mem. office of rev. & evaluation Presbyn. Ch. (U.S.), Atlanta, 1982-87; synod exec., stated clk. Presbyn. Ch. (U.S.A.), Jacksonville, Fla., 1988—; hon. assoc. rector Trinity Episcopal Ch., St. Charles, 1972-80; vis. asst. min. Ch. of Scotland, Glasgow, 1980; stated clk. Presbytery of Elijah Parish Lovejoy, St. Louis, 1980-82; con. Evang. Presbyn. Ch., Ghana, 1988. Author: (with others) Administration in the Church, 1969; contbr. articles and revs. to profl. jours. Mem. City Coun., St. Charles, 1971-75. Fellow Soc. Sci. Study of Religion; mem. Am. Sociol. Assn., Religious Rsch. Assn. Avocations: sailing, woodturning and working. Home: 930 River Rd Orange Park FL 32073-4130 Office: Synod of South Atlantic 118 E Monroe St Jacksonville FL 32202-3214

BARTHOLOMEW, LLOYD GIBSON, physician; b. Whitehall, N.Y., Sept. 15, 1921; s. Emerson F. and Minnie (Swinton) B.; m. Elisabeth Thrall, Dec. 27, 1943; children: Suzanne, Lynne, Lloyd Gibson, Deborah, Douglass Thrall. AA, Green Mountain Jr. Coll., 1939; BA, Union Coll., Schenectady, 1941; MD, U. Vt., 1944; MS in Internal Medicine (fellow), U. Minn., 1952; LHD (hon.), Green Mountain Coll., 1984. Diplomate Am. Bd. Internal Medicine, subsplty. bd. gastroenterology. Intern Mary Hitchcock Meml. Hosp., Hanover, N.H., 1944-45; resident Mary Hitchcock Meml. Hosp., 1945-46, 48-49; asst. internal medicine Dartmouth, 1948-49; 1st asst. div. internal medicine Mayo Clinic, Rochester, Minn., 1949-52; asst. to staff div. internal medicine Mayo Clinic, 1952-53; practice medicine, specializing in gastroenterology Rochester, 1952—; instr. internal medicine Mayo Found., U. Minn., 1952-58, asst. prof., 1958-63, assoc. prof. internal medicine, 1963-67, prof. medicine, 1967—; prof. medicine Mayo Med. Sch., 1973—; attending physician St. Mary's, Meth. hosps., Rochester, 1952; mem. adv. bd. to surgeons gen. of armed forces and asst. sec. def., 1978-86; mem. policy bd. Bush Found., 1978-87. Contbr. articles profl. pubs. Trustee Green Mountain Coll. Poultney, Vt., 1991—, chmn. bd. trustees, 1997—. Capt. M.C. AUS, 1946-47; col. M.C., 1960-86, ret. Recipient Woodbury prize in medicine, 1944, Carbee prize in obstetrics, 1994, disting. svc. award U. Vt. Coll. Medicine, 1977, Henry J. Plummer disting. clinician award Mayo Dept. Inst. Internat. Medicine, 1992, disting. svc. award Green Mtn. Coll. Alumni Assn., 1995. Mem. AMA (sec. gastroenterology sect. 1962-68, vice chmn. gastroenterlogy sect. 1968-69, chmn. 1969-70, mem. council sci. assembly 1969, chmn. program planning com. 1971-75, chmn. council sci. assembly 1974-76, chmn. council continuing physician edn. 1976-77), Minn. Med. Assn. (del. ho. dels. 1964—, chmn. scholarship and loan com. 1967—, alt. del. to AMA 1974-77, 85—, del. to AMA 1978-83, Pres.'s award 1983, Disting. Service award 1987), So. Minn. Med. Assn. (pres. 1963-64), Zumbro Valley Med. Soc. (sec.-treas. 1969-70, v.p. 1970-71, pres. 1971-72), Soc. Med. Cons. to Armed Forces (mem. governing council 1980-86, pres. 1984, del. to AMA 1984-92), Am. Gastroent. Assn. (com. on procedures 1970-72, presdl. commn. on future of assn. 1973-74, com. on constn. and by-laws 1980-85), Minn. Soc. Internal Medicine, Sigma Xi. Home: 1201 6th St SW Rochester MN 55902-1918 Office: Mayo Med Sch 200 1st St SW Rochester MN 55905-0001

BARTHOLOMEW, REGINALD, diplomat; b. Portland, Maine, Feb. 17, 1936; m. Rose-Anne Dognin; children: Sylvie, Christian, Damien, Jonathan. B.A., Dartmouth Coll., 1958; M.A., U. Chgo., 1960. Instr. U. Chgo., 1961-64; instr. Wesleyan U., Conn., 1964-68; dep. dir. Policy Planning Staff Dept. State, 1974-77, dep. dir. Bur. Politico-Mil. Affairs, 1977, dir. Bur. Politico-Mil. Affairs, 1979-81; with NSC, 1977-79; spl. Cyprus coordinator Dept. State, 1981-82, spl. negotiator for U.S.-Greek def. and econ. cooperation negotiations, 1982-83, U.S. amb. to Lebanon, 1983-86; with NSC, 1977-79; U.S. amb. to Spain, 1986-89; with Sec. State Internat. Security Affairs, 1989-92; U.S. perm. rep. to NATO, 1992-93; U.S. amb. to Italy, 1993-97; vice-chmn., mng. dir. Merrill Lynch Europe Holdings Ltd, London, 1997—; chmn. Merrill Lynch, Italy. Mem. Council on Fgn. Relations (internat. inst. for strategic studies). Office: Merrill Lynch Europe Holdin 25 Ropemaker St London AE 09624-9998*

BARTHOLOMEW, SHIRLEY KATHLEEN, municipal official; b. Marysville, Wash., Jan. 26, 1924; d. Clarence E. and Mary (Hall) B. Grad. high sch., Marysville, 1943. Sec. Everett (Wash.) Broadcasting Corp. Inc., 1960-77, 1st Pacific Broadcasting, Everett, 1977-80; news dir. Sta. KRKO, Everett, 1943-80. Mem. coun. COunty of Snohomish, Everett, 1980-89, chmn., 1987-88; mem. Marysville City Coun., 1994—. Named to Edward R. Morrow Broadcast Hall of Fame, 1980; recipient Mng. Editors Citation AP, 1958-73. Republican. Avocations: opera, symphony. Office: City of Marysville 4822 Grove St Marysville WA 98270-4456

BARTILUCCI, ANDREW JOSEPH, university administrator; b. N.Y.C., Nov. 29, 1922; s. Rocco and Philomena (Innello) B.; m. Lucy Ann Fulvio, June 10, 1950; children—Mary Ann, Phyllis, Eugenie. BS, St. John's U., 1944; MS, Rutgers U., 1949; PhD, U. Md., 1953. Analytical chemist Armed Services Med. Procurement Lab., War Dept., 1947-48; assoc. research pharmacist, research and devel. div. Merck & Co., 1949-50; prof. pharmacy, asst. dean Coll. Pharmacy St. John's U., 1952-56, dean, 1956-88, v.p. for health professions, clin. svc. and rsch., 1979-91; acting dean St. John's Coll. Liberal Arts & Scis., 1989-91, exec. v.p., 1991-96, spl. asst. to pres., 1996—; Fellow Am. Found. Pharm. Edn., 1950-52. Served as pharmacist's mate USNR, 1944-46; ensign 1949-57; Pharmacist dir. USPHS(R), 1957-98. Fellow AAAS; mem. Am. Coll. Apothecaries, N.Y. Acad. Scis., N.Y. Acad. Pharmacy, Am. Pharm. Assn., N.Y. State Bd. Pharmacy, Sigma Xi, Rho Chi, Phi Delta Chi. Home: 115 Roosevelt St Garden City NY 11530-2309 Office: Saint Johns Univ 8000 Utopia Pkwy Jamaica NY 11432-1343

BARTIZAL, ROBERT GEORGE, computer systems company executive, business consultant; b. Oak Park, Ill., Aug. 24, 1932; s. George Frank and Mildred (Hoffman) B.; m. Kathleen Elizabeth Dougherty, Apr. 9, 1960 (dec. Feb. 1993); children: Jeffrey Robert, Julia Ann, John Joseph; m. Barbara Foote Bell, May 18, 1996. B.S.B.A., U. Nebr., 1954; postgrad. Advanced Mgmt. Program, Northeastern U., 1973. With IBM, 1954-65; sales rep. IBM, Omaha, 1958-63; mktg. mgr. IBM, St. Paul, 1963-65; asst. dist. mgr. IBM, Mpls., 1965; with Control Data Corp., 1965-75, Pacific Rim regional mgr., 1967-68; Central and East European regional mgr. Control Data Corp., Frankfurt, W. Ger., 1968-71; v.p. edn. services Control Data Corp., 1972-73; v.p. govt. bus. mgmt. office Control Data Corp., Mpls., 1974-75; with Dataproducts Corp., Woodland Hills, Calif., 1975-80; sr. v.p., sales and mktg. Dataproducts Corp., 1975-77, exec. v.p., dir., 1977-80; pres., chief exec. officer, chmn. Logisticon, Inc., Santa Clara, Calif., 1980-85; gen. ptnr. Bartizal and Sherby and RGB Assocs., 1986—; chmn. Datavision Techs., Inc., San Francisco, Eltron Internat., Camarillo, Calif. Validyne Engring. Corp., Northridge, Calif., Work Place Sys., Pasadena, Calif.; bd. counselors UCLA Sch. Dentistry, Westwood, Calif. Mem. Woodland Hills Community Ch. Served with U.S. Army, 1954-56. Mem. Sigma Alpha Epsilon. Republican. Congregationalist.

BARTKUS, RICHARD ANTHONY, magazine publisher; b. Chgo., Mar. 14, 1931; s. Anthony J. and Mary (Petraitis) B.; m. Betty Ann Luetke, Jan. 2, 1954; children: Susan Kimberly, David Richard. Student, U. Ill., 1949-55. Circulation trainee Chgo. Tribune, 1955-58; asst. advt. mgr. Kilner Pub. Co., Chgo., 1958-59; advt. mgr. Cox Publs., Arcadia, Calif., 1959-60; advt. mgr. Bond Pub. Co., 1960, western advt. mgr., advt. dir., 1969-75; pub. Road & Track mag., Newport Beach, Calif., 1975-91; v.p. CBS Publs., 1977-91. With USMC, 1951-53. Mem. Univ. Athletic Club. Home: 18681 Via Torino Irvine CA 92612-3438

BARTKUS, ROBERT EDWARD, lawyer; b. Kearny, N.J., Sept. 30, 1946; s. Edward Charles and Dorothy Agnes (Konschott) B.; m. Mary Bartkus. BA with honors, Swarthmore Coll, 1968; JD, Stanford U., 1976. Bar: Calif. 1976, N.J. 1977, N.Y. 1977, U.S. Supreme Ct (3d, 2d cirs.), U.S. Dist. Ct. N.J., U.S. Dist. Ct. (so. and ea. dist.) N.Y. Spl. counsel Schulte, Roth & Zabel, N.Y.C., 1985-88; teaching asst. Stanford U. Law Sch., 1976; mem. Dist. X Ethics Com., 1992—; lectr. N.J. Inst. for Continuing Edn., 1988—; master John J. Gibbons Intellectual Property Inn of Ct. Articles coeditor Stanford Law Rev., 1974-76; author Innovation Competition 28 Stanford Law Rev. 1976; author, editor: New Jersey Federal Civil Practice, 1992, N.J. Federal Civil Procedure, 1999; mem. editl. bd. N.J. Law Jour. (Alfred C. Clapp award 1995). Atty. Community Law Offfice, 1976-79, Legal Aid Soc., 1979-87; mem. alumni coun. Swarthmore Coll., 1977-78. Lt. USNR, 1968-73. Mem. ABA (ethics com. Dist. X), NASD (arbitrator), Nat. Assn. Securities Dealers, N.J. Bar Assn. (chair fed. practice com.), Assn. Fed. Bar of State of N.J., Morris County Bar Assn., Am. Arbitration Assn. (arbitrator), Delta Upsilon. Home: 6 Terrill Dr Califon NJ 07830 Office: Profl Corp 90 Maple Ave Morristown NJ 07960-5221

BARTLE, HARVEY, III, federal judge; b. Bryn Mawr, Pa., June 6, 1941; s. Harvey Jr. and Dorothy L. (Baker) B.; m. Nathalie Akin Vanderpool, June 12, 1993; children: Elizabeth Louisa Masterson, Harvey IV, Peter Dixon Baker. AB in History, Princeton U., 1962; LLB, U. Pa., 1965. Bar: Pa. 1965, U.S. Dist. Ct. (ea. dist.) Pa. 1965, U.S. Ct. Appeals (3d cir.) 1969, U.S. Supreme Ct. 1978. Law clk. to Hon. John Morgan Davis U.S. Dist. Ct. (ea. dist.) Pa., 1965-67; assoc. Dechert, Price & Rhoads, 1967-73, ptnr., 1973-79, 81-91; Pa. Ins. Commr., 1979-80, Pa. Atty. Gen., 1980-81; judge U.S. Dist. Ct. (ea. dist.) Pa., 1991—. Editor Law Review U. Pa. Capt. U.S. Army Res. Mem. ABA, Phila. Bar Assn., Am. Law Inst. Episcopalian. Office: US Dist Ct US Courthouse Rm 16614 601 Market St Philadelphia PA 19106

BARTLE, ROBERT GARDNER, retired mathematics educator; b. Kansas City, Mo., Nov. 20, 1927; s. Glenn Gardner and Wanda (Mittank) B.; m. Doris Marie Sponenberg, Oct. 6, 1951; children—James, John; m. Carolyn June Bloemker, Apr. 1, 1982. B.A. with highest honors, Swarthmore Coll., 1947; S.M., U. Chgo., 1948, Ph.D., 1951. Postdoctoral fellow Yale U., New Haven, 1951-52, instr., 1952-55; from asst. prof. to prof. math. U. Ill., Urbana, 1955-90, prof. emeritus, 1990—; prof. math Ea. Mich. U., Ypsilanti, 1990-97. Exec. editor Math. Revs., 1976-78, 1986-90; mem. editorial bds. various math. jours.; contbr. articles to profl. jours. and books. Mem. Am. Math. Soc., Math. Assn. Am., London Math. Soc. Home: 3340 Alpine St Ann Arbor MI 48108-1704

BARTLETT, ALEX, lawyer; b. Warrensburg, Mo., Aug. 7, 1937; s. George Vest and May (Woolery) B.; m. Sue Gloyd, June 5, 1961 (div. June 1978); children: Ashley R., Nathan G.; m. Eleanor M. Veltrop, Oct. 27, 1978. BA, Cen. Mo. State U., 1959; LLB, U. Mo., 1961. Bar: Mo. 1961, U.S. Ct. Mil. Appeals 1963, U.S. Supreme Ct. 1965, U.S. Dist. Ct. (we. dist.) Mo. 1966, U.S. Ct. Appeals (8th cir.) 1968. From assoc. to ptnr. Hendren & Andrae, Jefferson City, Mo., 1965-79; mem. Bartlett, Venters, Pletz & Toppins, P.C., Jefferson City, 1980-87; pvt. practice Jefferson City, 1987-90; mem. Husch & Eppenberger, LLC, Jefferson City, 1990—; with Transit Casualty Co. Receivership, 1986-90, commr. claims, 1986-87, spl. claims counsel, 1987-89, dir. legal affairs dept., 1989-90; lectr. law U. Mo., Columbia, 1965-66. Contbr. editor Mo. Law Rev., 1960-61. Served to capt. JAGC, U.S. Army, 1962-65. Mem. ABA, FBA, Mo. Bar Assn. (chmn. young lawyers sect. 1972-73, ct. modernization com. 1972-74, jud. reform com. 1974-76, chmn. cts. and jud. com. 1978-79, legis. com. 1981-84, President's award 1976, Smithson award 1976), Cole County Bar Assn., Am. Coll. Trial Lawyers (chmn. Mo. 1994-96), Order of Coif. Democrat. Office: Husch and Eppenberger PO Box 1251 235 E High St Jefferson City MO 65102-3236

BARTLETT, ALLEN LYMAN, JR., retired bishop; b. Birmingham, Ala., Sept. 22, 1929; s. Allen Lyman and Edith Buell (West) B.; m. Jerriette L. Kohlmeier, Dec. 28, 1957; children: Christopher, Stephen, Catherine. BA, U. of South, 1951, D.D. (hon.), 1988; M.Div., Va. Theol. Sem., 1958, D.Min., 1980, D.D. (hon.), 1986. Ordained to ministry Episcopal Ch. 1958, ordained priest 1959. Vicar St. James' Ch., Alexander City, Ala., 1958-61, St. Barnabas Ch., Roanoke, Ala., 1958-61; rector Zion Ch., Charles Town, W.Va., 1961-70; dean Christ Ch. Cathedral, Louisville, 1970-85; ordained bishop, 1986; bishop coadjutor Diocese of Pa., Phila., 1986-87, bishop, 1987-98; ret.; dep. Episcopal Gen. Convention, 1964-67, 73-85; mem. exec. coun. Episcopal Ch., 1979-85. Lt. (j.g.) USN, 1952-55. Mem. Union League, Phi Beta Kappa. Democrat. Avocations: tennis, hiking. Home: 316 S 10th St Philadelphia PA 19107-6149

BARTLETT, ARTHUR EUGENE, franchise executive; b. Glens Falls, N.Y., Nov. 26, 1933; s. Raymond Ernest and Thelma (Williams) B.; m. Collette R. Bartlett, Jan. 9, 1955; 1 dau., Stacy Lynn. Sales mgr. Forest E. Olson, Inc., 1960-64; co-founder, v.p. Four Star Realty, Inc., Santa Ana, Calif., 1964-71, v.p., sec., 1964-71; founder, pres. Comps, Inc., Tustin, Calif., 1971-81; co-founder, chmn. of bd., pres., CEO Century 21 Real Estate Corp., Tustin, 1980—; pres. Larwin Sq. LLC Shopping Ctr, Tustin, Calif., 1979—. Chmn. bd. United Western Med. Ctrs., 1981-87. Named to Internat. Franchise Assn. Hall of Fame, 1987. Mem. Internat. Franchise Assn. (v.p., bd. dirs. 1975-80). Lodge: Masons. Office: 275 Centennial Way Ste 209 Tustin CA 92780-3709

BARTLETT, BEATRICE STURGIS, modern China historian, educator; b. New Haven; d. Russell Sturgis Bartlett and Emilie Jeanette (Daggett) Reynolds. MA, Columbia U., 1966; MPhil, Yale U., 1970, PhD, 1980. Tchr. history, chair history dept., asst. head of sch. The Brearley Sch., N.Y.C., 1953-66; rschr. Palace Mus., Taipei, Taiwan, 1970-79; rsch. scholar Ming-Qing Archives, Beijing, 1980-81; postdoctoral Harvard U., Fairbank Ctr., Cambridge, Mass., 1981-83; asst. prof. history Yale U., New Haven, 1983-89, assoc. prof. history, 1989-93, prof. history, 1993—; co-organizer 15th Yale Conf. on Tchg.: Asia at the Secondary Level, 1969; organizer 1st Internat. Ch'ing Archives Symposium, Palace Mus., Taipei, 1978; mem. subcom. on librs. and archives in China Am. Coun. Learned Socs., 1981-83; mem. com. East Asian Librarians. Author: Monarchs and Ministers, The Grand Council in Mid-Ch'ing China, 1723-1820, 1991, paperback edit., 1994; co-author: Reading Documents: The Rebellion of Chung Jen-Chieh, 1986, revised edit., 1993. Fulbright-Hays fellow, 1970-71, 95, Commn. on Scholarly Comm. with China fellow, 1980-81, 95, NEH fellow, 1990. Mem. Assn. Asian Studies. Home: 311 Saint Ronan St Apt B-3 New Haven CT 06511-2328 Office: Yale U Dept History PO Box 208324 320 York St New Haven CT 06520-8324

BARTLETT, BYRON ROBERT, consumer products company marketing executive; b. Phoenix, May 15, 1952; s. Gordon Arthur and Frances Rita (Bishop) B.; m. Sheila Gaye Rouse, June 14, 1975; children: Kara Michele, Kristen Marie, Kevin Michael, Katelyn Maura. BS, Purdue U., 1974. Brand asst. Procter & Gamble Co., Cin., 1974-75, asst. brand mgr., 1975-77; product dir. The Nestle Co., White Plains, N.Y., 1977-79, group product dir., 1979-82; group product dir. McNeil Consumer Products div. Johnson & Johnson, Fort Washington, Pa., 1982-86; mktg. mgr. Binney & Smith div. Hallmark Cards Inc., Easton, Pa., 1986-88; dir. brand mgmt. SmithKline Beecham Consumer Brands, Pitts., 1988-92, dir. bus. devel., 1992—. Mem. Am. Mgmt. Assn., Licensing Execs. Soc. Republican. Lutheran. Avocations: golf, tennis, music, reading, the stock market. Home: 1889 Springmont Dr Pittsburgh PA 15241-2158 Office: SmithKline Beecham Consumer Brands PO Box 1479 Pittsburgh PA 15230-1479

BARTLETT, CHARLES LEFFINGWELL, foundation executive, former newspaperman; b. Chgo., Aug. 14, 1921; s. Valentine C. and Marie (Frost) B.; m. Josephine Martha Buck, Dec. 16, 1950; children: Peter B., Michael V., Robert S., Helen B. Student, St. Mark's Sch., Southboro, Mass., 1934-39; A.B., Yale U., 1943. Reporter Chattanooga Times, 1946-62, Washington corr., 1948-63; editor News Focus Service, 1958-63; columnist Field Syndicate, 1962-80, Chgo. Sun-Times, 1963-75, Chgo. Daily News, 1975-78, Field Syndicate, 1978-81; pres. Jefferson Found., 1982—; editor Coleman/Bartlett's Washington Focus, 1988—. Author: (with Edward Weintal) Facing the Brink, 1957. Served as lt. USNR, 1943-46. Recipient Pulitzer prize for nat. reporting, 1955. Roman Catholic. Clubs: Gridiron, Federal City. Home: 4615 W St NW Washington DC 20007-1515 Office: The Jefferson Found 1529 18th St NW Washington DC 20036-1358*

BARTLETT, CHERYL ANN, public health service administrator; b. Norwich, Conn., June 28, 1954; d. William Jr. and Frances (Fredette) B.; m. Rogers Washburn Cabot Jr., June 5, 1982 (div. July 1995); m. Bruce Templin Miller, Sept. 10, 1995. ASN, Quinnipiac Coll., 1979; student healthcare adminstrn., Stonehill Coll. Cert. Infection Control, dialysis nursing, HIV/AIDS nursing. Nursing supr. Nantucket (Mass.) Cottage Hosp., 1981-95, interim dir. nursing, 1995, dir. clin. svcs., 1995-97; public health officer Public Health Assocs. of Nantucket, Southeastern, Mass., 1989—; exec. dir. Nantucket AIDS Network, 1989—; spkr. in field. Bd. dirs. Nantucket Housing Authority Properties Inc., Nantucket, 1997—; apptd. pres. Cmty. Action Com., Cape Cod and Islands, 1993—; selectman Town of Nantucket, 1993-96, county commr., 1993-96, chmn. Nantucket Bd. Health, 1992-94, Coun. for Health and Human Svcs., 1990-93, 96—. Recipient Cmty. Recognition award AIDS Action Com. of Mass., 1996, Outstanding Cmty. Health Program, U.S. Dept. of Health and Human Svcs., 1993, Outstanding Citizens award Nantucket Rotary Club, 1992, Recognition for Dedication and Commitment for the Care of AIDS Patients, Mass. State Senate, 1991, Mass. House of Reps., 1991. Mem. ANA, Assn. of Nurses in AIDS Care (govt. rels. com. 1997), Assn. of Infection Control Practitioners (nominating com. 1991-92, bd. dirs. 1997—), Mass. Nurses Assn. Avocations: reading, gourmet cooking, 3rd world travel, public health volunteer work. E-mail: msbart@nantucket.net. Home: PO Box 1248 Nantucket MA 02554-1248 Office: Nantucket AIDS Network 35 Old South Rd Nantucket MA 02554-2895

BARTLETT, CLIFFORD ADAMS, JR., lawyer; b. N.Y.C., Mar. 17, 1937; s. Clifford Adams and Frances (Burke) B.; m. Eileen Marie McCarthy; children: Elizabeth, Kathleen, Clifford III, Christopher, Karen, Charles, Eileen, Kevin, Jamison. BA, St. Francis Coll., N.Y.C., 1959; JD, St. John's U., N.Y., 1962. Bar: N.Y. 1963, U.S. Dist. Ct. (so. dist.) N.Y. 1964, U.S. Supreme Ct. 1966. Ptnr. Bartlett, McDonough, Bastone & Monaghan, Mineola, N.Y., 1992—; mem. faculty Practicing Law Inst., N.Y., 1980—, Nassau Acad. Law, Mineola, N.Y. & N.Y.C., 1984—, Law Jour. Seminars, N.Y.C., 1985. Mem. ABA, N.Y. State Bar Assn., Nassau County Bar Assn., Nassau-Suffolk Trial Lawyers Assn., Suffolk County Bar Assn., Med. Def. Lawyers Assn. (v.p. 1982—). Avocations: golf, skiing, swimming. Office: 300 Old Country Rd Mineola NY 11501-4198 also: 237 Park Ave New York NY 10017-3140 also: 81 Main St White Plains NY 10601-1711

BARTLETT, CODY BLAKE, lawyer, educator; b. Syracuse, N.Y., Apr. 21, 1939; s. Stanley Jay and Izora Elizabeth (Blake) B.; m. Claudine Germaine Bouthillette, Dec. 27, 1968; 1 child, Cody Blake. AAS, Auburn C.C., 1960; BA with high honors, Mich. State U., 1963; JD, Harvard U., 1966. Bar: Mich. 1967, N.Y. 1967, Colo. 1993, U.S. Dist. Ct. (no. dist.) N.Y. 1967, U.S. Dist. Ct. (ea. dist.) Mich. 1967, U.S. Supreme Ct. 1984, U.S. Dist. Ct. (we. dist.) N.Y. 1985, Colo. 1993; cert. strength and conditioning specialist. Law clk. Onondaga County Dist. Atty.'s Office, Syracuse, N.Y., 1965; assoc. atty. Touche, Ross, Bailey & Smart, Detroit, 1966; law clk. Onondaga County Family Ct., Syracuse, 1967; assoc. atty. Melvin & Melvin, Syracuse, 1967; budget and accounts officer Appellate Div., 4th Dept., Rochester, N.Y., 1967-69, dep. dir. adminstrn., 1969-72, dir. adminstrn., 1972-80; chief atty. State Commn. on Jud. Conduct, 1980-84; ptnr. Newman, Kehoe, Wunder and Bartlett, Lyons, N.Y., 1984-91, Kehoe, Bartlett & Kehoe, Wolcott, N.Y., 1992-94, Bartlett Law Offices, 1994—; spl. adminstr. N.Y. State Dangerous Drug Program, Western N.Y., 1973-75; adj. prof. polit. sci. dept. SUNY-Brockport, 1983-85, Grad. Sch. Pub. Adminstrn., SUNY-Brockport,

1985-90; adj. prof. Syracuse U. Coll. Law, 1980-84, Coll. Criminal Justice, Rochester Inst. Tech., 1979-80; grad. asst. polit. sci. dept. Mich. State U., 1962-63; lectr. jud. ethics and discipline Office Ct. Adminstrn., 1990. Author: Staying Fit Past Fifty, 1992; contbr. articles on legal issues and sports and fitness to publs.; drafter numerous legis. bills that became law. Mem. adv. com. Regional Criminal Justice Edn. and Tng. Ctr., Monroe Community Coll., Rochester, N.Y., 1974-80; div. leader YMCA, Midtown Rochester Membership drive, 1976; mem. East Bloomfield Planning Bd., 1984-87, chmn., 1985-87; trustee Village of East Bloomfield, 1985-87; mem. Zoning Bd. of Appeals, Village of Sodus Point, 1986-87; adv. bd. Sodus Bay Hist. Soc., 1992; justice Sodus Point Village, 1994-95; adv. bd. Wolcott C. of C., 1993; mem. Circuit of Reebok Profls. and Specialists, 1992-94. Recipient Disting. Alumni award Assn. Bds. Trustees of SUNY, 1980; Nat., regional, and state powerlifting and bench press champion, 1982, 83, 96-97; N.Y. State and Am., nat. and world Bench Press Record Holder, 1996, 97. Mem. N.Y. State Bar Assn. (spl. com. on jud. conduct 1984-90, profl. sports com. 1988-90), Wayne County Bar Assn., Onondaga County Bar Assn. (chmn. Syracuse City Ct. com. 1968-72), Nat. Strength and Conditioning Assn. (cert. specialist, bd. dirs., lectr. 1989-96), Phi Kappa Phi, Pi Sigma Alpha. Home: 7094 Overlook Dr Sodus Point NY 14555-9620 Office: 12032 E Main St Wolcott NY 14590-1022

BARTLETT, D. BROOK, federal judge; b. 1937. BA, Princeton U., 1959; LLB, Stanford U., 1962. Assoc. Stinson, Mag, Thomson, McEvers & Fizzell, 1962-67, ptnr., 1967-69; asst. atty. gen. State of Mo., 1969-73, 1st asst. atty. gen., 1973-77; assoc. Blackwell, Sanders, Matheny, Weary & Lombardi, 1977-78, ptnr., 1978-81; judge U.S. Dist. Ct. (we. dist.) Mo., Kansas City, 1981-95, chief judge, 1995—. Office: US Dist Ct 400 E 9th St Rm 8552 Kansas City MO 64106

BARTLETT, DAVID, journalist; b. Bethlehem, Pa., Mar. 23, 1946; s. Bertram Francis and Sally Caroline (Lewis) B.; m. Joan Carol Benevelli, Dec. 27, 1975. BA, Trinity Coll., Hartford, Conn., 1969. News dir. WRC Radio, Washington, 1979-81; mng. editor Metromedia TV news, Washington, 1981-83; dir. news and English broadcasts Voice of Am., Washington, 1984-85; program dir. NBC Radio Networks, N.Y.C., 1986-88, v.p., 1988-89; pres., COO Radio-TV News Dirs. Assn., Washington, 1989-97; dir. global news svcs. Worldspace Corp., Washington, 1998—.

BARTLETT, DAVID CARSON, state legislator; b. New London, Conn., Feb. 2, 1944; s. Neil Riley and Susan Marion (Carson) B.; m. Barbara Hunting, July 14, 1973 (div. 1974); m. Janice Anne Wezelman, Feb. 11, 1979; children: Daniel Wezelman, Elizabeth Anne. Student, Wesleyan U., Middletown, Conn., 1962-64; BA, U. Ariz., 1966, MA, 1970; JD, Georgetown U., 1976. Teaching asst. U. Ariz., Tucson, 1967-69; program analyst U.S. Dept. Labor, Washington, 1970-76; assoc. Snell & Wilmer, Tucson, 1976-77; pvt. practice Tucson, 1976-79; assoc. Davis, Eppstein & Hall, Tucson, 1979-85; mem. Ariz. Ho. of Reps., Tucson, 1983-88, Ariz. State Senate, 1989-92; chief counsel for civil rights Ariz. Atty. Gen.'s Office, Tucson, 1993-99, spl. couns., 1999—. Democrat. Home: 3236 E Via Palos Verdes Tucson AZ 85716-5854 Office: Ariz Attorney Gen 400 W Congress St Ste 215 Tucson AZ 85701-1352

BARTLETT, DAVID FARNHAM, physics educator; b. N.Y.C., Dec. 13, 1938; s. Frederic Pearson and Margaret Mary (Boulton) B.; m. Roxana Ellen Stoessel, Nov. 19, 1960; children: Andrew, Susannah, Christopher, Jennifer. AB, Harvard U., 1959; AM, Columbia U., 1961, PhD, 1965. Instr. Princeton U., N.J., 1964-67, asst. prof., 1967-71; assoc. prof. physics U. Colo., Boulder, 1971-82, prof., 1982—. Editor: The Metric Debate, General Relativity and Gravitation, 1989; contbr. articles to profl. jours. Fellow Am. Phys. Soc.; mem. Am. Assn. Physics Tchrs., Am. Geophys. Union. Democrat. Home: 954 Lincoln Pl Boulder CO 80302-7234 Office: U Colo Dept Physics PO Box 390 Boulder CO 80309-0390

BARTLETT, DEDE THOMPSON, company executive; b. N.Y.C., Aug. 27, 1943; d. George Juul and Emilie Martha (Jones) Thompson; m. James Wesley Bartlett, Apr. 27, 1974; children: Katherine Morgan, John Eriksen. BA, Vassar Coll., 1965; MA, NYU, 1969. Pres., dir. Mobil Found., 1984-87; corp. sec. Mobil Corp. and Mobil Oil Corp., 1987-90; v.p., corp. sec. Philip Morris Cos. Inc., 1991-94, v.p. corp. affairs programs, 1995—. Trustee, vis. fellow Woodrow Wilson Nat. Fellowship Found., Princeton, N.J.; trustee Aldrich Mus. Recipient Woman of Yr. award YWCA, 1987, A Better Chance, 1987. Mem. N.Y. Women's Agenda, Internat. Alliance, Women's Econ. Round Table, Women's Execs. in Pub. Rels., Women's Forum, Fin. Women's Assn., Vassar Club (Fairfield County, Conn.). Home: 151 Woodridge Dr New Canaan CT 06840-3512

BARTLETT, DESMOND WILLIAM, engineering company executive; b. Southampton, Eng., Feb. 11, 1931; came to U.S., 1971; s. Walter Hayward and Gladys (Akerman) B.; m. Joan Margaret Mitchell, July 19, 1952; children: Jennie Claire. Grad. Marine Engring., U. Coll., Southampton, 1951; diploma, Shippingport Nuclear Sch., Pitts., 1961; exec. devel. diploma, Cornell U., 1978. Registered profl. engr., Europe; chartered engr. U.K.; lic. chief engr., U.K. Ministry of Transport, nuclear power plant operator, U.K. Ministry of Def. Engr. officer Cunard Steamship Co., Liverpool, Eng., 1952-57; engr. Vickers Armstrong Ltd., Southampton, 1957-59; project mgr. Rolls Royce & Assocs., Derby, Eng., 1959-65; chief engr. Cammell Laird Shipbuilders & Engrs., Birkenhead, Eng., 1965-71; cons. Gibbs & Hill, Inc., N.Y.C., 1971-72; project dir. Westinghouse Electric Co., Pitts., 1972-79; pres. Dravo Engrs. Inc., Pitts., 1979-85, C.F. Braun, Inc., Alhambra, Calif., 1986-89; v.p. bus. devel. Raytheon Engrs. and Constructors, Inc., Phila., 1991-95; v.p. Corp. Ventures Flour Daniel, Irvine, Calif., 1995-98, Bartlett Consulting Ltd., Sewickley, Pa., 1998—; bd. dirs. Dravotec spa, Milan, Italy, F.C. de Weger Bv, Rotterdam, Dravo-Still, Inc., Pitts., Worley Santa Fe Ltd., London, Santa Fe Braun (UK) Ltd, London, Biomechanics Corp. Am. Melville, N.Y., Badger Catlytic Ltd., New Malden, England, Catalytic Svcs., Caracas, Venequela, Cosa United C.A., Caracas, United Yemen, Sana Yemen. Decorated officer Order Brit. Empire (Eng.). Fellow Inst. Marine Engrs.; mem. ASME, Am. Nuclear Soc., Am. Mgmt. Assn., Project Mgmt. Inst., Am. Petroleum Inst., Coun. on Fgn. Rels. (L.A. com. on fgn. relations). Clubs: Duquesne.

BARTLETT, DIANE SUE, clinical mental health counselor, family therapist; b. Laconia, N.H., Dec. 6, 1947; d. Fred Elmer and Dorothy Pearl (Wakefield) Davis; m. Josiah Henry Bartlett, Aug. 23, 1980; 1 child by previous marriage, Fred Louis Hacker; 1 stepchild, Juliet. AA, Plymouth State Coll., 1982, MEd, 1988; B Gen. Studies summa cum laude, U. N.H., 1984. Lic. clin. mental health counselor. Mental health counselor Ossipee, N.H., 1995—; police comm. specialist Divsn. Motor Vehicles, Concord, N.H., 1970-76, br. office mgr., 1976-83, coord. motor vehicle registrations, 1983-84; tax collector City of Dover, N.H., 1984; intern Lakes Region Mental Health Divsn., Laconia, N.H., 1985; counselor Latchkey Pastoral Counseling, Laconia, 1984-87; family therapist Children's Best Interest, Laconia, 1988—; mental health counselor Carroll County Mental Health Svcs., Wolfeboro, N.H., 1988-95; participant N.H. Ann. Conf. on Status and Role of Women, Concord, 1985-87; mem. Carroll County Domestic Violence Coun., 1997—. Mem. Moultonboro (N.H.) Sch. Feasibility Study Commn., 1978; mem. adminstrv. bd. dirs., chmn. pastor-parish rels. com. United Meth. Ch., Moultonboro, 1983-94, N.H. ann. conf., 1986-88; mem. Friends of Families in Carroll County, 1995—. Grantee N.H. Charitable Found., 1985. Mem. ACA, Am. Mental Health Counselors Assn., Internat. Soc. for Study Dissociation. Avocations: skiing, swimming, reading, writing. Home: PO Box 14 Moultonborough NH 03254-0014 Office: Mountainside Bus Ctr 127 Route 28 Ossipee NH 03864-7300

BARTLETT, ELIZABETH SUSAN, audio-visual specialist; b. Bloomington, Ind., Sept. 11, 1927; d. Cecil Vernon and Nell (Helfrich) Bartlett; m. Frederick E. Sherman, July 8, 1955 (div. 1978). Student, Ind. U., 1946-48. Traffic-continuity dir. WTTS-Radio, Bloomington, Ind., 1947-48; program dir. WTTV-TV, Indpls., 1949-59; creative dir. Venus Advt. Agy., Indpls., 1960-68; prodn. mgr. Nat. TV News, Detroit, 1968-71; owner, producer Susan Sherman Prodns., Greenwich, Conn., 1971-73; audiovisual officer NSF, Washington, 1973—; lectr. in field. Concept writer/prodr. film: The Observatories, 1981; prodr.: Science: Woman's Work, 1982, Keyhole of Eternity, 1975, What About Tomorrow?, 1978, The American Island, 1970, The New Engineers, 1986, Discover Science, 1988, A Brain, Books and a Curiosity, 1992, others. Recipient Silver award Internat. Film and TV Festival of N.Y., 1970, 74, Gold medal Nat. Ednl. Film Festival, 1982, 89, Chris Bronze plaque Columbus Film Festival, 1982, Bronze award Internat. Film & TV Festival of N.Y., 1982, Gold award 1976, Gold Camera award U.S. Indsl. Film Festival, 1982, Silver Cindy award, Info. Film Producers Assn., 1982, award for creative excellence U.S. Indsl. Film Festival, 1975, Techfilm Festival award, 1979, 80, 88, Gold award Houston Internat. Film Festival, 1987, Art Direction Mag. Creativity award, 1988; named Outstanding Woman for Contbn. in Arts, Federally Employed Women, 1984. Mem. Am. Women in Radio and TV (chpt. pres. 1953-56, 69-70), Washington Film and Video Coun. (pres. 1978-79), Coun. on Internat. Non-Theatrical Events (adv. bd., Golden Eagle award 1970, 74, 76-79, 82, 87), Women in Film and Video, Radio/TV News Dirs. Assn. Home: 809 S Columbus St Alexandria VA 22314-4206 Office: NSF Pub Affairs Divsn 4201 Wilson Blvd Arlington VA 22230-0001

BARTLETT, GORDON E., state legislator; b. Springfield, Mass., Apr. 24, 1926; m. Martha Bartlett; 1 child. BS, Babson Coll., 1950. Exec. dir. Rep. State Com., 1975-78; N.H. state rep. Dist. 6, 1991—; mem. transp. com. N.H. Ho. of Reps. Mem. N.H. Police Assn. (assoc.), Gilford Police Relief Assn. Address: 40 Silkwood Ave Belmont NH 03220-3137*

BARTLETT, GRANT A., professional sports team executive; b. Riverside, Nova Scoti, Can.. BS with honors, Mount Allison, NYU; MS in Geology, Carleton U.; PhD, NYU. Chmn. emeritus Dominion Energy Can.; co-owner Calgary Flames; mng. dir. Apogee Capital Ltd., 1998—, pres., CEO. Mem. several Canadian and Am. profl. socs. relating to engring. and scientific rsch. Achievements include more than 25 years of diversified experience in the petroleum industry, govt. and academia. Office: Can Airlines Saddledome, PO Box 1540 Station M, Calgary, AB Canada T2P 3B9*

BARTLETT, JAMES LOWELL, III, investment company executive; b. Boston, May 26, 1945; s. James Lowell and Shirley Victoria (Wyatt) B.; m. Shannon Mara McMillion, May 4, 1979; children: James Lowell IV, Zachary Morgan, Matthew Wyatt. BS, U. Calif., Berkeley, 1967, MBA, 1968. Loan officer nat. div. Bank of Am., Los Angeles, 1968; fin. mgr. Psychology Today mag., Del Mar, Calif., 1969; pres. Forum Communications Corp.; pub. Cuisine, Politics Today, Volleyball mags., N.Y.C., 1970-82; pres. Bartlett & Co., Santa Barbara, Calif., 1982—. Commr. Internat. Volleyball Assn., 1977-80. Mem. LDS Ch. Office: 5662 Calle Real Santa Barbara CA 93117-2317

BARTLETT, JAMES WILLIAMS, psychiatrist, educator; b. Balt., Feb. 2, 1926; s. James Williams and Margaret Baylor (Alexander) B.; m. Nancy Bieszad, May 8, 1954; children: John Alexander, Anne Lee, Thomas Martin. B.A., Harvard U., 1948; M.D., Johns Hopkins U., 1952. Mem. faculty U. Rochester Med. Center, N.Y., 1957—, prof. psychiatry, 1968-96; prof. emeritus psychiatry U. Rochester Med. Ctr., N.Y., 1996—; prof. health services U. Rochester Med. Center, N.Y., 1968-85, assoc. dean Sch. Medicine and Dentistry, 1966-83; med. dir. Strong Meml. Hosp., 1967-83; prof. psychiatry, dean faculty health sci. Aga Khan U., Karachi, Pakistan, 1990-93; also acting rector Aga Khan U. Served with USNR, 1944-46. Fellow Am. Psychiat. Assn. (life); mem. Assn. Am. Med. Coll., Soc. Med. Adminstrs., Western N.Y. Psychoanalytic Soc., Rochester Acad. Medicine.

BARTLETT, JOHN BRUEN, financial executive; b. Salt Lake City, Oct. 14, 1941; s. John B. and Helen Smith (Partridge) B.; children: Alison, Brian. B in Engring., U. Rochester, 1963; MBA, Rutgers U., 1968. CPA, Calif., Mass. Engr. Aerojet Gen., Sacramento, 1963-65, Hamilton Standard, Windsor Locks, Conn., 1965-67; acct., CPA Arthur Andersen & Co., San Francisco, 1968-76, Hartford, 1976-77; chief fin. officer UniFirst Corp., Wilmington, Mass., 1977—. Mem. Fin. Exec. Inst., Texas. Club. Avocations: tennis, skiing. Office: UniFirst Corp 68 Jonspin Rd Wilmington MA 01887-1086*

BARTLETT, JOHN GILL, infectious disease physician; b. Syracuse, N.Y., Feb. 12, 1937; s. Kenneth Gill and Bernice (Kleinhaus) B.; m. Jean Scott; children: Valerie, Joshua, Scott. BS, Dartmouth Coll., 1959; MD, Upstate Med. Ctr. Internship Peter Bent Brigham Hosp., Boston, 1963-65; assoc. prof. U. Ala., Birmingham, 1967-68; residency UCLA-Wadsworth Hosp., L.A., 1968-70; asst. prof. medicine UCLA, Balt., 1970-75; assoc. prof. Tufts U. Sch. Medicine, Boston, 1975-80; prof., 1980; prof. Johns Hopkins U. Sch. Medicine, Balt., 1980—, chief of staff. Contbr. articles to profl. jours. and chpts. to books; author 10 books in field of infectious diseases. Mem. Assn. Am. Physicians, Am. Soc. Microbiology, A Thoracic Soc., Infectious Diseases Soc. Am., Am. Fedn. Clin. Rsch., AAAS, ACP, Interurban Club, Peripatetic Club, Assn. Subsplty. Profs., Assn. Profs. Medicine. Avocation: painting. Home: Johns Hopkins U Sch of Medicine 205 Wendover Rd Baltimore MD 21218*

BARTLETT, JOHN LAURENCE, lawyer; b. L.A., June 9, 1942; s. Oswald and Sarah Elisabeth (Caldwell) B.; m. Jane Helen Dormann, June 22, 1963; children: Jennifer Lynn, George Andrew. AB, UCLA, 1963; LLB, Stanford Law Sch., 1967. Bar: D.C. 1967, U.S. Dist. Ct. D.C. 1968, U.S. Ct. Appeals (D.C. cir.) 1969, U.S. Ct. Appeals (4th cir.) 1976, U.S. Supreme Ct. 1976, U.S. Ct. Appeals (2d cir.) 1977. Assoc. Kirkland & Ellis, Washington, 1967-72, ptnr., 1972-83; ptnr. Wiley, Rein & Fielding, Washington, 1983—; bd. dirs. Arinc Inc., Aeronautical Radio, Inc., Blacksmith Inc., Cmty. Residences Found., chmn. 1995—. Mem. ABA, Fed. Comm. Bar Assn., Computer Law Assn. Home: 2757 N Nelson St Arlington VA 22207-5033 Office: Wiley Rein & Fielding 1776 K St NW Washington DC 20006-2304

BARTLETT, JOHN WESLEY, consulting firm executive; b. Camden, N.J., Oct. 18, 1935; s. William W. and Naomi Verna (Snook) B.; m. Helen Barbara Boulas, Mar. 2, 1968 (dec. Feb. 1986); children: Larah, Tanya; m. Elaine Veronica Wepplo, Aug. 14, 1987; 1 child, Chris. BSChemE, U. Rochester, 1957; MChemE, Rensselaer Poly. Inst., 1959, PhD, 1962. Staff engr. Knolls Atomic Power Lab., Schenectady, N.Y., 1957-62; asst. prof. U. Rochester, N.Y., 1962-68; Fulbright prof. nuclear engring. Istanbul (Turkey) Tech. U., 1968-69; program mgr. Pacific N.W. Labs., Richland, Va., 1969-78; presdl. exch. exec. Nat. Bur. Standards, Washington, 1973-74; dir. energy and environment Analytic Scis. Corp., Reading, Mass., 1978-89; cons. to sec. U.S. Dept. Energy, Washington, 1989-90, dir. Office Civilian Radioactive Waste Mgmt., 1990—; pres. The Bartlett Co., Vienna, Va., 1993-96, SC&A, McLean, Va., 1996—. Contbr. articles to profl. jours. Mem. Sch. Bd., Richland, 1970-73; mem., mayor pro tem City Coun., Richland, 1974-78; vice chair Conservation Commn., Lynnfield, Mass., 1979-89. Rsch. grantee NSF, 1963-64, NIH, 1965-68, recipient Robert E. Wilson award, AIChE, 1993. Mem. AAAS, Am. Nuclear Soc. (exec. com. 1976-80, 86-90), Rotary (bd. dirs. Richland club 1976-78), Sigma Xi. Republican. Avocations: model shipwright, piano. Home: 1350 Beverly Rd Apt 707 McLean VA 22101 Office: SC&A Inc 1355 Beverly Rd Mc Lean VA 22101

BARTLETT, JOSEPH WARREN, lawyer; b. Boston, June 14, 1933; s. Charles W. and Barbara (Hastings) B.; m. May Parish, Apr. 28, 1956 (div.); children: Charles, Susan, Henry; m. Barbara Bemis, Sept. 20, 1980. AB, Harvard U., 1955; LLB, Stanford U., 1960. Bar: Mass. 1962, D.C. 1969, N.Y. 1981. Law clk. Chief Justice Warren, U.S. Supreme Ct., 1960-61; pvt. practice Boston, 1961-66; ptnr. Gaston & Snow, Boston, 1966-80; ptnr. Gaston & Snow (formerly Gaston Snow Beekman & Bogue), N.Y.C., 1980-90, of counsel, 1990-91; ptnr. Mayer, Brown & Platt, 1991-96, Morrison & Foerster, N.Y.C., 1996-; counsel Mass. Commn. Adminstrn., 1964-65; gen. counsel, under sec. Dept. Commerce, Washington, 1967-69; prin. adviser on universal social security coverage Sec. of HEW, Washington, 1978-79; acting prof. Stanford U., 1978; trustee, mem. fin. com. Montefiore Med. Ctr.; mem. Council on Fgn. Relations; adj. prof. NYU Law Sch. Served to 1st lt. U.S. Army, 1956-57. Fellow Am. Bar Found.; mem. Am. Law Inst., Am. Bar Assn., Boston Bar Assn. (pres. 1977-78). Democrat. Episcopalian. Home: 200 E 71st St Apt 16C New York NY 10021-5147 Office: Morrison & Foerster 1290 Avenue Of The Americas New York NY 10104

BARTLETT, KATHARINE TIFFANY, law educator; b. New Haven, Feb. 16, 1947; d. Edgar Parmelee and Elizabeth (Clark) B.; m. Christopher H. Schroeder, Aug. 13, 1975; children: Emily, Ted, Elizabeth. BA, Wheaton Coll., 1968; MA, Harvard U., 1969; JD, U. Calif., Berkeley, 1975. Bar: Calif. 1975, N.C. 1980, U.S. Dist. Ct. (no. dist.) Calif. 1975, U.S. Dist. Ct. (mid. dist.) N.C. Law clk. to presiding justice Calif. Supreme Ct., San Francisco, 1975-76; atty. Legal Aid Soc. of Alameda County, Oakland, Calif., 1976-79; professor of law Duke U., Durham, N.C., 1979—; vis. prof. UCLA, 1985-86, Boston U., 1990. Grad. prize fellow Harvard U., 1968-69, fellow Nat. Humanities Ctr., 1992-93. Mem. Am. Law Inst., Soc. Am. Law Tchrs., N.C. Women Attys., Am. Law Inst. (reporter for principles of family dissolution), Phi Beta Kappa. Democrat. Office: Duke Univ Law Sch Sci Dr and Towerview Rd PO Box 90389 Durham NC 27708-0360*

BARTLETT, LEONARD LEE, communications educator, retired advertising agency executive, advertising historian; b. Mountain Home, Idaho, May 31, 1930; s. Harold Roberts and Alma Martina (Nixon) B.; m. Sue Ann Kipfer, Nov. 5, 1966; children: Jennifer, Deborah; children by previous marriage: Linda Lee, Cynthia, Nancy, Pamela, William Charles. BA, Brigham Young U., Provo, Utah, 1957, MA, 1989. Advt. mgr. Steiner Co., Chgo., 1957-59; sr. v.p. Marsteller Inc., Chgo., 1959-67; vice chmn. Cole & Weber, Inc., Seattle, 1966-84; chmn. Cole & Weber Calif., San Francisco, 1984-86, Los Angeles, 1986-87; assoc. prof. communications Brigham Young U., Provo, 1987—; acting chmn. dept. comms. Brigham Young U., Provo, 1995-96, chmn. dept. comms., 1996—, asst. to pres. univ. comms., 1997—. Served with USAF, 1951-56. Mem. Am. Assn. Advt. Agys. (chmn. Western region 1980, nat. bd. 1980-81). Republican. Mem. Ch. Jesus Christ of Latter-day Saints. Home: 2060 Oak Ln Provo UT 84604-2123*

BARTLETT, LYNN CONANT, English literature educator; b. Bethlehem, Pa., Dec. 14, 1921; s. Fay Conant and Marie Agnes (McGuiness) B.; m. Margaret Emma Johnson, June 29, 1946; 1 dau., Anne Elston. B.A., Lehigh U., 1943; A.M., Harvard, 1947, Ph.D., 1957; B. Litt., Oxford U., Eng., 1952. Instr. English Lehigh U., 1946; teaching fellow Harvard, 1948-50; instr. Vassar Coll., 1952-57; asst. prof., 1957-62, asso. prof., 1962-70, prof., 1970-92, prof. emeritus, 1992—, asst. dean coll., 1958-61, sec. coll., 1966-76. Editor: (with W.R. Sherwood) The English Novel, Background Readings, 1967. Served with AUS, 1943-46. Decorated Bronze Star. Mem. Phi Beta Kappa, Sigma Phi Epsilon. Clubs: Harvard (N.Y.C.), Circumnavigators Club. Home: 170 College Ave Poughkeepsie NY 12603-2806

BARTLETT, MICHAEL JOHN, lawyer; b. Paterson, N.J., June 8, 1943; s. Ernest John and Alice Edith (Schrell) B.; children: Tara Christine, Jessica Simons, Darren Michael. BA cum laude, Amherst Coll., 1965; JD, U. Va., 1969. Bar: Va. 1969, D.C. 1971, U.S. Sup. Ct. 1976. Atty., Office Gen. Counsel, NLRB, Washington, 1969-71; atty. law offices Joseph C. Wells, Washington, 1971-74, assoc. Vedder, Price, Kaufman, Kammholz & Day, Washington, 1974-76, ptnr., 1976-80; prin. (Michael J. Bartlett, P.C.), Ogletree, Deakins, Nash, Smoak & Stewart, Washington, 1980-86; staff v.p. employee relations Eastern Airlines, Inc., 1986-87, shareholder Verner, Liipfert, Bernhard, Mc Pherson and Hand, Chartered, 1987-94; pvt. practice, 1994-98; mgr. labor law polity U.S. C. of C., 1998—. Mem. exec. bd. Arlington (Va.) YMCA, 1982-86, treas., 1984-86. Andrew D. Lawrie scholar, Amherst Coll., 1964-65; Am. Jurisprudence award in labor law Lawyer Coop. Pub. Co., 1969. Mem. Va. State Bar, D.C. Bar, Fed. Bar Assn., ABA (sect. on labor law). Contbr. articles to profl. jours. Home: 4650 Washington Blvd Apt 926 Arlington VA 22201-5746 Office: 1615 H St NW Washington DC 20062-2000

BARTLETT, NEIL, chemist, educator; b. Newcastle-upon-Tyne, Eng., Sept. 15, 1932; s. Norman and Ann Willins (Vock) B.; m. Christina Isabel Cross, Dec. 26, 1957; children: Jeremy John, Jane Ann, Christopher, Robin. B.Sc., Kings Coll., U. Durham, Eng., 1954; Ph.D. in Inorganic Chemistry, Kings Coll., U. Durham, 1957; D.Sc. (hon.), U. Waterloo, Can., 1968, Colby Coll., 1972, U. Newcastle-upon-Tyne, 1981, McMaster U., Can., 1992; D.Univ. (hon.), U. Bordeaux, France, 1976, U. Ljubljana, Slovenia, 1989, U. Nantes, France, 1990; LLD, Simon Fraser U., Can., 1993. Lectr. chemistry U. B.C., Vancouver, Can., 1958-63; prof. U. B.C., 1963-66; prof. chemistry Princeton U., N.J., 1966-69, U. Calif., Berkeley, 1969—; mem. adv. bd. on inorganic reactions and methods Verlag Chemie, 1978—; mem. adv. panel Nat. Measurement Lab., Nat. Bur. Stds., 1974-80; E.W.R. Steacie Meml. fellow NRC, Can., 1964-66; Miller vis. prof. U. Calif., Berkeley, 1967-68; 20th G.N. Lewis Meml. lectr., 1973; William Lloyd Evans Meml. lectr. Ohio State U., 1966; A.D. Little lectr. Northeastern U., 1969; Phi Beta Upsilon lectr. U. Nebr., 1975; Henry Werner lectr. U. Kans., 1977; Jeremy Musher Meml. lectr., Israel, 1980, Randolph T. Major Meml. lectr. U. Conn., 1985, J.C. Karcher lectr. U. Okla., 1988; Brotherton vis. prof. U. Leeds, Eng., 1981; Erskine vis. lectr. U. Canterbury, New Zealand, 1983; Wilsmore fellow Melbourne U., Australia, 1983; vis. fellow All Souls Coll., Oxford U., 1984; Miller prof. U. Calif.-Berkeley, 1986-87; George H. Cady lectr. U. Wash., Seattle, 1994; Leermakers lectr. Wesleyan U., 1995; Davis Meml. lectr. U. New Orleans, 1997, Pierre Duhem seminaires, U. Bordeaux, 1998. Bd. editors Inorganic Chemistry, 1967-79, Jour. Fluorine Chemistry, 1971-80, Synthetic Metals, Revue Chimie Minerale; mem. adv. bd. McGraw-Hill Ency. Sci. and Tech. Recipient Rsch. Corp. award; E.W.R. Steacie prize, 1965; Elliott Cresson medal Franklin Inst., 1968; Kirkwood medal Yale U. and Am. Chem. Soc. (New Haven sect.), 1969; Dannie-Heinemann prize The Gottingen acad. 1971; Robert A. Welch award in chemistry, 1987; Alexander von Humboldt Found. award, 1977; medal Jozef Stefan Inst., Slovenia, 1980; Moissan medal, 1986; Prix Moissan, Paris, 1988; fellow Alfred P. Sloan Found., 1964-66; Bonner Chemiepries, Bonn, 1991; Berkeley citation, 1993. Fellow Royal Soc., Am. Acad. Arts and Scis., Royal Inst. Chemistry, Chem. Inst. Can. (1st Noranda lectr. 1963); mem. NAS (fgn. assoc.), Leopoldina Acad. (Halle, Salle), Akademie der Wissenschaften in Gottingen, Associé Etranger, Academia Europaea, Académie des Sciences, Institut de France, Am. Chem. Soc. (chmn. divs. fluorine chemistry 1972, inorganic chemistry 1977, award in inorganic chemistry 1970, W.H. Nichols award N.Y. sect. 1983, Pauling medal of Pacific N.W. sects. 1989, Disting. Svc. award 1989, award for Creative Work in Flourine Chemistry 1992), Phi Lambda Upsilon (hon.). Home: 6 Oak Dr Orinda CA 94563-3912 Office: U Calif Dept Chemistry Berkeley CA 94720

BARTLETT, NORMA THYRA, retired administrative assistant; b. Raymond, S.D., June 7, 1922; d. Wilhelm Emil and Olga Sophie (Mailand) Claussen; m. Fred Otis Metcalf, Mar. 29, 1941 (dec. Apr. 1963); children: Linda E. Bucklin, Barry Otis; m. Francis Grindal Bartlett, Dec. 27, 1963. BA, U. Wash., 1969; Diploma, Inst. of Children's Lit., 1997. Cert. profl. sec. Office mgr. Fed. Old Line Ins. Co., Everett, Wash., 1949-55; supr. office svc. Scott Paper Co., Everett, Wash., 1958-63; tchr. bus. edn. Canyon Park Jr. H.S., Seattle, 1969, Bellevue (Wash.) C.C., 1969; exec. asst. Peoples Bank, Starkville, Miss., 1970-76; prin. Satellite Steno Svc., Starkville, Miss., 1976-77; office mgr. Donald Wiley & Assocs., Sydney, Australia, 1977-80; bd. dirs. United Cmty. Fund Snohomish County, Everett, Wash., 1961-62; pres. Scott Paper Co. Fellowship Fund, Everett, 1961. hon. life mem. United Luth. Ch. Women, Everett, Wash., 1958—; organizer, charter pres. Starkville Bus. and Profl. Women, 1972-74; pres. Welcome Wagon Club, Ocean Springs, Miss., 1982-83; tutor Jackson County Literacy, Ocean Springs, 1985-88; organizer Discourse, Ocean Springs, 1985-86. Norma T. Bartlett scholarship named in her honor Starkville Area Bus. and Profl. Women, 1978. Mem. AAUW, Intertel, U. Wash. Alumni Assn., Mensa (local sec. 1989-91, editor newsletter 1987-89). Democrat. Lutheran. Avocations: needlework, reading, writing, travel. Home: 5716 N 33d St #4 Tacoma WA 98407

BARTLETT, PAUL A., organic chemist; b. Trenton, N.J., Jan. 5, 1948. AB, AM, Harvard U., 1969; PhD in Organic Chemistry, Stanford U., 1972. Prof. chemistry U. Calif., Berkeley, 1973—, prof. emeritus, 1996—. Recipient Alexander von Humboldt Sr. Scientist award, 1988, Arthur C. Cope Scholar award ACS, 1990. Fellow AAAS. Office: U Calif Dept Chem MC1460 Berkeley CA 94720-1460

BARTLETT, PAUL DANA, JR., agribusiness executive; b. Kansas City, Mo., Sept. 16, 1919; s. Paul D. and Alice May (Hiestand) B.; m. Joan Jenkins, May 14, 1949; children—J. Alison Bartlett Jager, Marilyn Bartlett Hebenstreit, Paul Dana III, Frederick Jenkins. BA, Yale U., 1941. Chmn. Bartlett and Co., Kansas City, Mo., 1961-77; pres., chmn. bd. Bartlett and Co. (formerly Bartlett Agri Enterprises, Inc.), Kansas City, 1977—, chrm., dir.; bd. dir. United Mo. Bank, United Mo. Bancshares. Lt. USN, 1942-46. Office: Bartlett and Company 4800 Main St Ste 600 Kansas City MO 64112-2509

BARTLETT, PETER B., investment company executive. Gen. ptnr. Brown Bros. Harriman & Co., N.Y.C. Office: Brown Bros Harriman & Co 59 Wall St New York NY 10005-2808*

BARTLETT, PETER GREENOUGH, engineering company executive; b. Manchester, N.H., Apr. 22, 1930; s. Richard Cilley and Dorothy (Pillsbury) B.; Ph.B., Northwestern U., 1955; m. Jeanne Eddes, July 8, 1954 (dec. 1980); children: Peter G., Marta, Lauren, Karla, Richard E.; m. Kathleen Organ, July 21, 1984. Engr., Westinghouse Electric Co., Balt., 1955-58; mgr. mil. communications Motorola, Inc., Chgo., 1958-60; pres. Bartlett Labs., Inc., Indpls., 1960-63; assoc. prof. elec. engring. U. S.C., Columbia, 1963-64; dir. research Eagle Signal Co., Davenport, Iowa, 1964-67; div. mgr. Struthers-Dunn, Inc., Bettendorf, Iowa, 1967-74; pres. Automation Systems, Inc., Eldridge, Iowa, 1974-89; pres., chmn. Cybertronics, Inc., Davenport, 1989—. Mem. IEEE. Republican. Presbyterian. Patentee in field. Home and Office: 2336 E 11th St Davenport IA 52803-3701 Office: Cybertronics Inc Davenport IA 52803

BARTLETT, RICHARD CHALKLEY, business executive, writer, conservationist; b. L.A., May 23, 1935; s. Theodore Lester Bartlett and Maud Chalkley (Colley) Newsom; m. Joanne Krieger; children: Lisa, Christopher. BS in Communications, U. Fla., 1956. With advt. sales dept. The Miami (Fla.) Herald, 1958; internat. sales and mgmt. exec. for home parties div. Tupperware Inc., Orlando, 1959-65; v.p. advt. and sales promotion Vanda Beauty Counselor div. Dart Industries, Orlando, Fla., 1965-71; exec. v.p. mktg. Dynasty Industries Inc., Dallas, 1971-73; dir. mktg. svcs. Mary Kay Inc., Dallas, 1973-76, v.p. mktg., 1976-85, exec. v.p. mktg., 1986-87, pres., COO, 1987-93; vice-chmn. Mary Kay Holding Corp., Dallas, 1993—; CEO The Richmont Group, 1994-95, chmn., 1995—; bd. dirs. Armor Holding, Inc.; chmn. U.S. Direct Selling Assn., Washington, 1991-93, U.S. Direct Selling Edn. Found., Washington, 1993-94, bd. dirs., chmn. internat. grant com., 1997— ; vice chmn. edn. World Fedn. Direct Selling, 1997—; adv. bd. U. Fla. Ctr. for Retailing Edn. and Rsch., Gainesville, Tex. Corp. Recycling Coun., Austin; global adv. bd. The Economist Group, Cross-border Monitor; mem. emeritus adv. bd. Ctr. for Retailing Studies, Tex. A&M U., College Station; adv. coun., bd. dirs. Com. Nat. Inst. for Environment; mem. adv. coun. U. Tex. Press; mem. adv. com. Coll. Agrl. Sci. and Natural Resources, Tex. Tech. U.; bd. dirs. Nat. Environ. Edn. and Tng. Found. Author: The Direct Option, 1994, Saving the Best of Texas: A Partnership Approach to Conservation, 1995; co-author: The Sportsman's Guide to Texas, 1988. Bd. dirs. Dallas Mus. Natural History; co-vice chmn. Tex. Environ. Edn. Partnership Exec. Com.; bd. dirs. Better Bus. Bur. Met. Dallas, Dallas Arboretum and Botanical Soc., Heard Natural Sci. Mus. and Wildlife Sanctuary; chmn. ex-officio The Nature Conservancy of Tex. With U.S. Army, 1957. Named Outstanding Marketer to Yr., Southwestern Mktg. Assn., 1991, Chief of Exec. of Yr., Internat. TV Assn., 1992; named to U.S. Direct Selling Assn. Hall of Fame, 1994, U.S. Direct Selling Edn. Found. Circle of Honor, 1995, Pi Kappa Phi Nat. Hall of Fame, 1996; recipient Oak Leaf award Nature Conservancy, 1997. Mem. Acad. Mktg. Sci. (Disting. Marketer of Yr. 1995), World Econ. Forum, Nat. Ctr. for Policy Analysis, The Conf. Bd., Dallas Com. on Fgn. Rels. Avocations: conservation work, performing arts. Office: Mary Kay Holding Corp 4300 Westgrove Dr Dallas TX 75248-2447

BARTLETT, RICHARD JAMES, lawyer, former university dean; b. Glens Falls, N.Y., Feb. 15, 1926; s. George Willard and Kathryn M. (McCarthy) B.; m. Claire E. Kennedy, Aug. 18, 1951; children: Michael, Amy. BS, Georgetown U., 1945; LLB, Harvard U., 1949; LLD (hon.), Union Coll., 1974; ScD (hon.), Albany Med. Coll., 1986. Bar: N.Y. 1949. Pvt. practice Glens Falls, 1949-73; with Clark Bartlett & Caffry, 1962-73; justice N.Y. State Supreme Ct., 1973-79; chief adminstr. of courts N.Y. State, 1974-79; dean Albany Law Sch., Union U., Albany, 1979-86; mem. Bartlett, Pontiff, Stewart, & Rhodes P.C., Glens Falls, N.Y., 1986—; chmn. N.Y. Bd. Law Examiners, 1998—, N.Y. Jud. Commn. on Justice for Children, 1988-90; chmn., bd. trustees Nat. Conf. Bar Examiners, 1987-97; del. N.Y. Constl. Conv., 1967. Trustee Hyde Collection, Glens Falls, 1967—. Capt. USAF, 1951-53. Fellow Am. Bar Found.; mem. ABA (house dels. 1997—), N.Y. State Bar Assn., Assn. Bar City of N.Y., Warren County Bar, N.Y. Bar Found. (bd. dirs. 1989—, v.p. 1997—), Am. Law Inst. Republican. Roman Catholic. Office: 1 Washington St PO Box 2168 Glens Falls NY 12801-2963*

BARTLETT, RICHMOND JAY, soil chemistry educator, researcher; b. Columbus, Ohio, Sept. 23, 1927; s. Claude Jay and Cecil Jane (Richmond) R.; m. Martha Louise Harry, Feb. 16, 1952 (dec. Apr. 1987); children: Amy, Anne, Ellen, Samuel. BA, Ohio State U., 1949, PhD, 1958. Newspaper reporter Indpls. and Columbus, 1950-52; promotional writer Peoria (Ill.) and Columbus, 1952-55; asst. soils sect. Ohio State U., Columbus, 1955-58; from asst. prof. to assoc. prof. U. Vt., Burlington, 1958-67, prof. soil chemistry, 1967-97, prof. emeritus, 1997—; cons. chemistry environmental soil, water and plant nutrition. Contbr. articles to profl. jours., 1958—. Sgt. U.S. Army, 1946-48 Japan. Fellow AAAS, Am. Soc. Agronomy, Soil Sci. Soc. Am.; mem. Internat. Soil Sci. Soc., Phi Beta Kappa, Sigma Xi, Gamma Sigma Delta, Phi Lambda Upsilon. Progressive. Home: 410 North St Burlington VT 05401-1626 Office: U Vt Dept Plant and Soil Sci Burlington VT 05405

BARTLETT, ROBERT JAMES, principal. Prin. Robinwood Elem. sch., Florissant, Mo., 1985-98, dir. staff devel., 1998—. Recipient Elem. Sch. Recognition award U.S. Dept. Edn., 1989-90, St. Louis Prin. of Yr., 1994. Mem. St. Louis Suburban Prins. Assn. Office: 1005 Waterford Florissant MO 63033-5931*

BARTLETT, RODNEY J., chemistry and physics educator; b. Memphis, Mar. 31, 1944; s. Robert Henry and Sue Anne (Payne) B.; m. Beverly Jean Featherston, Aug. 17, 1966; children: Robert Darron and Ronald Eric. BS in Chemistry and Math., Millsaps Coll., 1966; PhD in Quantum Chemistry, U. Fla., 1971. NSF postdoctoral fellow Aarhus U., Denmark, 1971-72; assoc. rsch. scientist John Hopkins U., Balt., 1972-74; prin. rsch. scientist Battelle Pacific NW Labs., Richland, Wash., 1974-76; sr. rsch. scientist Battelle Pacific NW Labs., 1976-77, Battelle Meml. Inst., Richland, 1977-79; Chemistry, Physics group leader Battelle Meml. Inst., 1979-81; Chemistry, Physics prof. U. Fla. (Gainesville), 1981-87, grad. rsch. prof., 1988—; adv. bd. Theoretical Chimica Acta, 1989—; editl. bd. Internat. Jour. Quantum Chemistry, 1988-91, Jour. Chemical Physics, 1991-93, Molecular Physics, 1992—. Contbr. articles to profl. jours. Fellow Guggenheim Harvard, U. Calif. (Berkeley), 1986-87. Fellow Internat. Acad. Quantum Molecular Sci., Am. Physical Soc.; mem. Am. Chemical Soc. (chair, subdivision Theoretical Chemistry, 1985). Office: University of Florida Quantum Theory Project PO Box 118435 Gainesville FL 32611-8435

BARTLETT, ROGER DANFORTH, engineering executive; b. Brentwood, Mo., Dec. 19, 1949; s. Robert Danforth and Margaret Elizabeth (Gruber) B.; m. Cynthia A. Adkins, July 1, 1978; children: Rex Danforth, Ryan Andrew, Megan Leigh. BSEE, Bradley U., 1971. Engr., Revomat, Parkville, Mo., 1971-72; div. engr. Am. Multi-Cinema, Inc., Kansas City, Mo., 1972-75, project mgr., 1975-78, assoc. dir. corp. engring., 1978-82, dir. corp. engring., 1982-85; dir. constrn. Commonwealth Theatres, Inc., 1985-87, dir. purchasing/tech. svcs., 1987-88; dir. midwest constr. United Artist Theatre Cir., 1988-89; pres. Bartlett & Assocs., Inc., 1989—. Mem. IEEE, SMPTE, Constrn. Specifications Inst. Home and office: 8701 W 72nd St Shawnee Mission KS 66204-1132

BARTLETT, ROSCOE G., congressman; b. Ky., June 3, 1926; married; 10 children. BA, Columbia Union, 1947; MS, U. Md., 1948, PhD, 1952. Asst. prof. Loma Linda Med. Sch., 1952-54, Howard Med Sch., 1954-56; rschr. NIH, 1956-59; engr. Naval Aerospace Med. Inst., 1959-62, 62-67; dir. Space Life Scis. Divsn. Johns Hopkins U., 1968-74; dir. rsch. devel. IBM, 1975-87; owner Roscoe Bartlett & Assocs.; mem. 105th Congress 3rd term from 6th Md. Dist., 1993—, chmn. small bus. subcom. on govt. programs and oversight; mem. Nat. Security Com., Sci. Com., Small Bus. Republican. Office: US Ho of Reps 2412 Rayburn House Ofc Bldg Washington DC 20515-2006*

BARTLETT, SHIRLEY ANNE, accountant; b. Gladwin, Mich., Mar. 28, 1933; d. Dewey J. and Ruth Elizabeth (Wright) Frye; m. Charles Duane Bartlett, Aug. 16, 1952 (div. Sept. 1982); children: Jeanne, Michelle, John, Yvonne. Student, Mich. State U., 1952-53, Rutgers U., 1972-74. Auditor State of Mich., Lansing, 1951-66; cost acct. Templar Co., South River, N.J., 1968-75; staff acct. Franco Mfg. Co., Metuchen, N.J., 1975-78; controller Thomas Creative Apparel, New London, Ohio, 1978-80; mgr. gen. acctg. Ideal Electric Co., Mansfield, Ohio, 1980-85; staff acct. Logangate Homes, Inc., Girard, Ohio, 1985-88; pvt. practice acctg. Youngstown, 1985—; acct. Universal Devel. Enterprises, Liberty Twp., Ohio, 1987-88; v.p. Lang Industries, Inc., Youngstown, 1984-93. Author: (play) Our Bicentennial-A Celebration, 1976. Soloist various orchestras, Mich., Va.; mem. Human Relations Commn., Franklin Township, 1971-77, Friends of Am. Art; treas. Heritage Found., New Brunswick, N.J., 1973-74, New London Proceeds Corp., 1979-83; commr. Huron Park Commn., Ohio, 1979-83; elected Dem. com. mem., N.J., Ohio, 1970-82; vol. IRS for small bus., 1988-94; mem. planning com. Youngstown State U. Tax Insts., 1990-95, presenter, 1990—; bd. dirs., treas. Discovery Place, Inc., 1991-95. Mem. NAFE, NOW (treas. Youngstown chpt. 1986-93), Am. Soc. Women Accts. (bd. dirs. 1986-88, 96—, v.p. 1988-89, pres. 1989-91, bd. dirs., 1996—, scholarship com. 1991—, chair chpt. devel. 1995-96, chair program com. 1997—), Nat. Women's Polit. Caucus, Bus. and Profl. Women (v.p. 1980—), Am. Soc. Notaries, Women's Jour. Network, Citizen's League of Greater Youngstown, Internat. Platform Assn., Friends of Am. Art, Youngstown Opera Guild, Investment Club (pres. 1997-99, treas. 1999—). Democrat. Unitarian. Club: Franklin JFK (treas. 1970-72, v.p. 1973-78), Chataqua Literary, Scientific Circle (pres. 1979—). Avocations: music, knitting, needlecrafts. Home and Office: Bartlett Acctg Svcs 370 Goldie Rd Liberty Township OH 44505-1950

BARTLETT, THOMAS FOSTER, international management consultant; b. Oklahoma City, Nov. 28, 1918; s. Martin Johnson and Clara Nell (Mattingly) B. BS, Harvard U., 1943, MBA, 1948; cert., Sorbonne, Paris, 1987, Oxford (Eng.) U., 1988, Cambridge (Eng.) U., England, 1989, U. Salamanca, 1993, U. Genoa, 1994; grad., US Command and Gen. Staff Coll, Ft. Leavenworth, Kans., 1945. Asst. to pres. Am. Express Co., N.Y.C., 1948-50; export promotion specialist Dept. of State, Paris; mem. U.S. Mission to NATO Dept. Def., London and Paris; econ. cons. Am. Embassy, Rome, 1950-55; exec. asst. to pres. for internat. devel. Kaiser Industries, Oakland, Calif., 1955-56; mktg. specialist Bigelow-Sanford Inc., N.Y.C., 1957-59; pres. Internat. Mgmt. Cons. Thomas F. Bartlett & Assocs., N.Y.C., 1959—; cons. for UN, U.S. and fgn. govts. corps., other orgns. Capt. U.S. Army, 1943-46, maj. USAF Res. Mem. Am. Soc. Profl. Cons., Am. Mgmt. Assn., Am. Mktg. Assn., Harvard Club. Avocations: travel, photography, lecturing. Office: Thomas F Bartlett & Assoc 330 E 52nd St New York NY 10022-6718

BARTLETT ABOOD, KATHLEEN GENE, artist, educator; b. Detroit, Jan. 31, 1949; d. William Jacob and Anne Myrtle Bartlett; m. George Thomas Abood, Aug. 21, 1981; children: Thomas Michael Bartlett, Jessica Cody, Lily Brook. Student, Wayne State U., Detroit, 1967-69; cert. in graphic arts, U. Calif., Santa Cruz, 1986, BFA in Studio Art, 1988. Multimedia artist Primal Visions Studio, Santa Cruz, 1980—; project coord. Santa Cruz Lifeyard Project, 1982-84; artist in residence William James Assn., Santa Cruz, 1984—; program dir. West Hawaii Arts Guild, Kailua-Kona, 1990-91; program designer Art Mus. Santa Cruz County, 1992-93; project dir., artist in residence 1st Night Santa Cruz, 1994—; lead artist in residence Cmty. Youth Arts Project, Santa Cruz, 1994—; artist facilitator Santa Cruz County Detention Facilities, 1984—; dir. vis. artists West Hawaii Arts Guild, 1990-91; Youth Arts Project, 1994-96; artist in the cmty. Cultural Coun. Santa Cruz Cou; cons. edn. program Mus. Santa Cruz County, 1991-92. One-woman shows include The Poet and Patriot, Santa Cruz, 1983, Cafe Riva at Santa Cruz Mcpl. Wharf, 1985, 320 Gallery, Santa Cruz, 1986, Santa Cruz Art Ctr., 1986, Pearl Alley Bistro, Santa Cruz, 1987, U. Calif. Santa Cruz Women's Ctr., 1988, Santa Cruz Art Ctr., 1998; exhibited in group shows at Lifeyards Cmty. Arts Project at San Lorenzo Pk., Santa Cruz, 1982, Cooper House Gallery, Santa Cruz, 1983, Mt. St. Mary's Coll., L.A., 1986, L.A. Printmaking Soc. Invitational, 1987, William James Gallery, Santa Cruz, 1988, Eloise Pickard Smith Gallery, 1988, 89, 94, West Hawaii Gallery, Kailua-Kona, 1991, Wailoa Art Ctr., Hilo, Hawaii, 1991, Kona Village Resort, Kaupulehu, Hawaii, 1991, Santa Cruz Art League, 1991, Nordstrom, San Francisco and San Jose, Calif., 1991, L.A. Printmaking Soc./Honolulu Printmakers Traveling Exhbn., 1991, Stevenson Libr. U. Calif. Santa Cruz, 1992, Galeria Museo, San Francisco, 1992, Current Santa Cruz County Open Studios Tour, 1992, Many Hands Gallery at Santa Cruz Art Ctr., 1993, New Women's Art Gallery, Santa Cruz, 1993, Pajaro Valley Gallery, Watsonville and Gavilan Coll., Gilroy, Calif., 1993, Art Mus. of Santa Cruz Palomar Annex and Rental Gallery, 1993, Galeria Tonantzin, San Juan Batista, Calif., 1994, 95, Fresno (Calif.) Arts Coun., 1994, Primal Visions Art Gallery, 1994, Chaminade Artists Series 22, Santa Cruz, 1995, 4th World Conf. of Women, Beijing, 1995, Nat. Mus. Women in the Arts, Washington, 1996, Made in Santa Cruz Gallery, 1997, Santa cruz Art League, 1997, Atelier Gallery, Santa Cruz, 1997-98, Mus. Art and History, Santa Cruz, 1998. Bd. dirs. 1st Night Santa Cruz, 1996—, coord. cmty. outreach, 1994-96; mem. arts edn. com. Art Mus. Santa Cruz County, 1991-93; mem. open studios steering com. Cultural Coun. Santa Cruz County, 1993-95; mem. adv. bd. William James Found., 1994-96; mem. adv. coms. social environment and children's issues, cmty. needs assessment United Way of Santa Cruz County, 1994-95; mem. Bay St. Art Wall rev. com. City of Santa Cruz Arts Commn., 1994-95. Artist in residence grantee Calif. Arts Coun., Sacramento, 1982—, Santa Cruz County Cmty. Found., 1994-96, City of Santa Cruz Arts Commn., 1982-84, 94, Cultural Coun. Santa Cruz County, 1995-96, Nat. Arts for Change award Bravo Network and TCI Cablevision, 1997, Discovery award Art Inst. Calif., Napa, 1994. Mem. Nat. Mus. Women in Arts, Calif. Wellness Found., L.A. Printmaking Soc., Art Mus. of Santa Cruz County. Avocations: water sports, travel. Home: 300 Plateau Ave Santa Cruz CA 95060-6457

BARTLEY, BURNETT GRAHAM, JR., oil company and manufacturing executive; b. Pitts., Nov. 10, 1924; s. Burnett Graham and Helen (McKee) McKenney B.; m. Mary Lou Gilbert, Aug. 7, 1947; children: Burnett III, Davison Wittmer, Richard McKenney, Parker Bowen, Heather Swinston, Tiffany Gilbert. BA, Yale U., 1949; grad. advanced mgmt. program, Harvard U., 1967. Rep. sales Koppers Co. Inc., Pitts., 1949-52, dist. mgr. sales, 1952-56, v.p. sales, 1956-58, v.p., gen. mgr. forest products, 1958-69, dep. chmn. bd., 1969-79, exec. v.p., 1979-88; chmn., chief exec. officer chems. and coatings Kop-coat, Inc., Pitts., 1988-90; chmn., chief exec. officer Anegada Group, Inc., Pitts., 1990—; chmn., CEO Ameritex Chem. and Coatings Co., Irving, Tex.; chmn. Bridgewater Steel Corp., N.J., Trans-Ocean Trading Corp., Ltd.; chmn. bd. Edgewater Marine Corp., Morgantown, W.Va. Dir. World Affairs Coun., Pitts., 1987; Trustee Rehab. Ctr. Pitts., 1989, Children's Hosp., Pitts., 1989, Mich. Inst. Tech., 1989; chmn. bd. trustees Point Park Coll., Pitts., 1989; bd. dirs. Penn. Economy League, 1989; pres. Health Rsch. and Svcs. Found., Pitts., 1989. Lt. inf. U.S. Army, 1943-45, ETO. Mem. Am. Wood Preserver's Inst. (pres. 1970), Am. Wood Preserver's Assn. (pres. 1975), So. Pressure Treaters Assn. (pres. 1974), Harvard-Yale-Princeton Club, Duquesne Club, Fox Chapel Golf Club, Annapolis Yacht Club, Buffalo Launch Club, Rolling Rock Club, Laurel Valley Golf Club, Pitts. Athletic Club, St. John (V.I.) Yacht Club, St. Thomas (V.I.) Yacht Club. Republican. Presbyterian. Avocations: hydroplanes, flying, sailing, fishing, motorcycling. Office: Anegada Group Inc 2335 Koppers Bldg Pittsburgh PA 15219 also: Fairwinds Estate PO Box 248 Mayville NY 14757-0248 also: Villa # 4113 Virgin Grand, Great Cruz Bay Cruz Bay VI 00830

BARTLEY, DAVID ANTHONY, electronics executive; b. Connellsville, Pa., Apr. 5, 1946; s. Anthony Eugene and Dorothy Charlotte (Hilliard) B.; m. Anna Luralene Smith, June 25, 1969 (div. Nov. 1977); 1 child, Marva Joanna. Student Alderson-Broaddus Coll., 1964-65, Fairmont State Coll., 1965-66. Mech. designer Tex. Instruments Co., Dallas, 1966-70; sales rep. Multi-Plate Co., Inc., Dallas, 1970-74, v.p., gen. mgr., 1974-81, pres., 1981—. Mem. Am. Electronics Assn. (chmn. membership com. Tex. council, 1987-88, vice chmn., chmn. program com. Tex. council, 1988—, nat. program steering com. 1988-89, nat. bd. dirs. 1988-89), Technology Exec. Roundtable, Dallas C. of C. Republican. Lutheran. Office: 2362 Lufield Dr Dallas TX 75229-2022

BARTLEY, LARRY DURAND, computer systems planner, mayor; b. Shreveport, La., Mar. 21, 1960; s. Larry Deavun Bartley and Zealia Janette (Scoggin) King; m. Kathleen Lucille Gunn, July 19, 1980. AS, City U., Bellevue, Wash., 1989; BTh, Jacksonville Theol. Sem., 1990, ThM, 1993. Dir., camera operator Sta. KFDM-TV, Beaumont, Tex., 1976-78; electronic warfare technician USN, Mayport, Fla., 1979-89; electronics technician Grumman Tech. Svcs., Titusville, Fla., 1989-91; electronics technician A Computer Scis. Raytheon, Patrick AFB, Fla., 1991-94; mayor, coun. mem. City of Titusville, 1992—; computer sys. contr. Computer Scis. Raytheon, Patrick AFB, 1994—; pres. Space Coast League Cities, Brevard County, Fla., 1997-98; mem. Space and Tech. Adv. Com., Viera, Fla., 1997-98; mem. Space Coast Bus. Roundtable, Viera, 1998. Mem. Tourist Devel. Coun., Cape Canaveral, Fla., 1997—; bd. dirs. Police Athletic League, Titusville, 1995—. Mem. DAV, Brevard Civic and Mil. Assn., Am. Legion. Avocations: reading, golfing, working out. Home: 160 N Williams Ave Titusville FL 32796-2524 Office: City Titusville 555 S Washington Ave Titusville FL 32796-3551

BARTLEY, ROBERT LEROY, newspaper editor; b. Marshall, Minn., Oct. 12, 1937; s. Theodore French and Iva Mae (Radach) B.; m. Edith Jean Lillie, Dec. 29, 1960; children: Edith Elizabeth, Susan Lillie, Katherine French. BS, Iowa State U., 1959; MS, U. Wis., 1962; LLD, Macalester Coll., 1982, Babson Coll., 1987; HHD, Adelphi U., 1992. Reporter Grinnell (Iowa) Herald-Register, 1959-60; staff reporter Wall Street Jour., Chgo., 1962-63, Phila., 1963-64; editorial writer Wall Street Jour., N.Y.C., 1964-70, Washington, 1970-71; editor editorial page Wall Street Jour., N.Y.C., 1972-78; editor Wall Street Jour., 1979—, v.p., 1983—. Author: The Seven Fat Years, 1992. Trustee emeritus Mayo Found. Served to 2d lt. USAR, 1960. Recipient Overseas Press Club citation, 1977, Gerald Loeb award, 1979, Pulitzer prize for editorial writing, 1980. Mem. Am. Soc. Newspaper Editors, Soc. Profl. Journalists, Nat. Conf. Editl. Writers, Am. Polit. Sci. Assn., Coun. on Fgn. Rels., Heights Casino Club. Office: The Wall Street Jour 200 Liberty St New York NY 10281-1003

BARTLEY, SCOTT ANDREW, genealogist, archivist; b. Springfield, Vt., Jan. 4, 1959; s. Leonard Maurice and Marjorie-Jean (Lamphere) B.; m. Christopher Todd Smith Norris, Oct. 26, 1988. AS, N.H. Vocat.-Tech. Coll., Claremont, 1979; student, U. Mass., Boston, 1988; MLS, Simmons Coll., 1994. Enging. technician Vt. Rsch. Corp., North Springfield, 1979-84; substitute tchr. high sch., Springfield, 1984-85; geneal. rschr. North Springfield, 1984-85; reference libr. New Eng. Hist. Geneal. Soc., Boston, 1985—, manuscripts curator, 1989—; lectr. archives and genealogy, nationally, 1985—; mem. adv. bd. Mass. Hist. Records, Boston, 1997—. Editor: Vermont Families in 1791, Vol. 1, 1992, Vol. 2, 1997; compiler: Transcription of the State copy of the 1850 Federal Census for Springfield and Baltimore, Vermont, 1993; editor several archival and geneal. newsletters, 1990-96. Mem. Soc. Am. Archivists (Roundtable chair 1990-92, editor Roundtable Newsletter 1990-94), New. Eng. Archivists, Geneal. Soc. Vt. (pres. 1993-96). Avocations: genealogy, travel, bowling, volleyball. Home: 258 Shawmut Ave Apt 4 Boston MA 02118-2143 Office: New Eng Hist Geneal Soc 99 Newbury St # 101 Boston MA 02116-3007

BARTLO, SAM D., lawyer; b. Cleve., Oct. 5, 1919. BBA, Case Western Res. U., 1941; JD, Cleve.-Marshall Law Sch., 1950. Bar: Ohio, 1950, U.S. Supreme Ct., 1958. Mem. firm Buckingham, Doolittle & Burroughs, Akron, Ohio, 1971-90. Capt. U.S. Army, 1942-46. Fellow Am. Bar Found. (life), Ohio Bar Found. (life, pres. 1981-82, trustee 1976-81); mem. ABA (bd. govs. 1989-92, ho. of dels. 1977-94, state del. 1981-89, exec. com. 1990-92, chair ops. com. 1991-92, trustee FJE resource coun. 1992-94), Akron Bar Assn. (pres. 1967-68, exec. com. 1968-7), Ohio State Bar Assn. (coun. dels. 1970-86, pres. 1977-78, exec. com. 1973-79), Am. Judicature Soc., Nat. Conf. Bar Presidents (trustee 1979-82), Ohio Legal Ctr. Inst. (pres. 1979-81, trustee 1977-81). Office: Buckingham Doolittle Burroughs PO Box 1500 Akron OH 44309-1500

BARTLOW, GENE STEVEN, association executive, retired air force officer; b. Alva, Okla., Dec. 19, 1939; s. C. Merle and Mildred Violet (Stevens) B.; m. Carolyn F. Strickland, Dec. 31, 1960 (div. Apr. 4, 1962); 1 child, Karie Jean Bartlow Parsons; m. Karin C. Jacobsen, Jan. 13, 1967; children: Christina K., Erik K. BA in Edn. Comm., N.W. Okla. State U., 1962; disting. grad., Indsl. Coll. Armed Forces, Washington, 1972; MPA, Ball State U., 1978; grad., Air War Coll., Maxwell AFB, Ala., 1984; MS in Computers and Info. Mgmt., Webster U., St. Louis, 1995. Cert. assn. exec., Am. Soc. Assn. Execs. Tchr. speech, debate coach Liberal (Kans.) Pub. H.S., 1962-63; commd. 2d lt. USAF, 1964, advanced through grades to full col.; chief logistics plans divsn. 68th tactical air support group Tactical Air Command, Shaw AFB, S.C., 1971-73; chief logistics plans inspection br. Hdqs. Tactical Air Command, Langley AFB, Va., 1973-76; chief NATO logistics plans br. Hdqs. USAF in Europe, Ramstein Air Base, Germany, 1976-80; dep. comdr. for resource mgmt. 474th tactical fighter wing Tactical Air Command, Nellis AFB, Nev., 1980-83; chief congl. activities divsn. Office Asst. Sec. Air Force (Acquisition), Washington, 1984-87; dean adminstrn., prof. sys. acquisition mgmt. Indsl. Coll. Armed Forces, Nat. Def. U., 1987-90; ret., 1990; asst. exec. dir., CFO, Assoc. Cath. Charities, Archdiocese of Washington, 1990-91; dep. exec. dir. Internat. Assn. for Dental Rsch.-Am. Assn. for Dental Rsch., Washington, 1991-94; pres., CEO, Am. Wood Preservers Inst., Fairfax, Va., 1995-97; adj. prof. mgmt. Nat.-Louis U., McLean, Va., 1989-97, U. Md. U. Coll., 1998—; sec., bd. dirs. Coalition for Oral Health, Washington, 1993-94; lectr. congl. liaison activities exec. mgmt. course Def. Sys. Mgmt. Coll., Ft. Belvoir, 1986-92. Contbr. articles to profl. jours. Decorated Legion of Merit, others. Mem. Ret. Officers Assn., Air Force Assn., Greater Washington Soc. Assn. Execs., Painting and Decorating Contractors of Am. (exec. v.p. 1998—). Republican. Congregationalist. Avocations: photography, music, American Civil War history and politics. Home: 6501 Tiburon Ct Springfield VA 22152-2824

BARTMAN, ROBERT E., state education official. Commdr. of edn., elem. and secondary edn. State of Mo. Office: State Dept Edn PO Box 480 Jefferson City MO 65102-0480*

BARTMANN, KATHRYN, collections management executive. Dir. Comml. Fin. Svcs., Tulsa. Office: Comml Fin Svcs 2448 E 81st St Tulsa OK 74137-4248

BARTNER, JAY B., school system administrator. Former prin. Old Orchard Beach (Maine) High Sch., 1986-91; supt. Old Orchard Beach Sch. Dist., 1991—. Recipient Blue Ribbon Sch. award U.S. Dept. Edn., 1990-91. Office: Old Orchard Beach Sch Dist 28 Jameson Old Orchard Beach ME 04064*

BARTNER, MARTIN, newspaper executive; b. Newark, Apr. 11, 1930; s. Joseph and Kate (Libman) B.; m. Audrey Mayer, May 20, 1956; children—Douglas, Lisa. B.S., NYU Sch. Commerce, N.Y.C. Classified ad mgr. Jersey Jour., Jersey City, 1955-65; advt. dir. Star-Ledger, Newark, 1965-80, assoc. pub., 1980-88, pub., 1988—. Bd. dirs. ARC, East Orange, N.J., 1980-82, Black Achievers, Newark, 1982-84, NCCJ, 1989—, N.J. Press Assn., 1986-88, N.J. Symphony, 1994—, Paper Mill Playhouse, Millburn, N.J.; mem. West Orange (N.J.) Jewish Ctr., treas., 1980-82. Served with U.S. Army, 1953-55. Mem. Advt. Club N.J. (bd. dirs. 1981-83), Greater Newark C. of C. (bd. dirs. 1986). Mem. KP (sec. 1975-77). Office: Newark Morning Ledger Co 1 Star Ledger Plz Newark NJ 07102-1200*

BARTNICKI-GARCIA, SALOMON, microbiologist, educator; b. Mexico City, May 18, 1935; came to U.S., 1957; s. Israel Bartnicki and Refugio Garcia; m. Ildiko Nagy, Aug. 10, 1975; children—Linda Laura, David Daniel. Bacteriological Chemist, Inst. Politecnico Nacional, Mexico City, 1957; Ph.D., Rutgers U., 1961. Rsch. assoc. microbiology Rutgers U., 1961-62; mem. faculty U. Calif., Riverside, 1962—, prof. plant pathology and microbiology, 1971-94, prof. emeritus, 1994, rsch. prof., 1994—, chmn. dept. plant pathology, 1989-92, dir. grad. program in microbiology, 1997—; vis. prof. Organic Chemistry Inst., U. Stockholm, 1969-70; selected faculty rsch. lectr. U. Calif., Riverside, 1989. Author research and rev. papers. Grantee NIH, 1963-96, NSF, 1971-96. Fellow AAAS, Am. Phytopathol. Soc. (Ruth Allen award 1983); mem. Am. Soc. Microbiology, Mycol. Soc. Am. (Disting. Mycologist award 1994), Brit. Soc. Gen. Microbiology, Brit. Mycol. Soc. (hon.), Am. Soc. Biol. Chemists. Home: 7030 Gaskin Pl Riverside CA 92506-5614 Office: U Calif Dept Plant Pathology Riverside CA 92521

BARTNIKAS, RAYMOND, electrical engineer, educator; b. Kaunas, Lithuania, Jan. 25, 1936; s. Andrius and Eugenia (Kanisauskas) B.; m.

Margaret McLachlan, Aug. 19, 1967; children: Andrea Marie, Thomas Benedict. BASc, U. Toronto, 1958; M in Engring., McGill U., Montreal, 1962, PhD, 1964. Rsch. engr. No. Electric Co. (now No. Telecom), Lachine, Que., Can., 1958-63; mem. sci. staff phys. scis. divsn. No. Electric R&D Labs. (now Bell-No. Rsch. Labs), Ottawa, Ont., 1963-68; research scientist, sci. dir. materials sci. research div., Disting. Sr. Scientist Hydro-Quebec Inst. Research, Varennes, Que., 1968—; adj. prof., lectr. theory of dielectrics McGill U., 1968-75; adj. prof. Fleming Found., visitor dept. elec. engring. U. Waterloo, Ont., 1969—; adj. prof. dept. engring. physics Ecole Poly. U. Montreal, 1992—; vis. prof. U. Rome, 1994—; cons. Cepel Inst. Rsch., Rio de Janeiro, 1973-84; mem. Task Force on Long Term Performance of Insulating Materials Nat. Acad. Scis., 1976-77; mem. elec. engring. com. Nat. Scis. and Engring. Rsch. Coun. Can., 1987-90; mem. Commn. de la recherche universitaire Conseil des Universites, Que., 1989-93. Author, editor: ASTM book series on Engring. Dielectrics, 1979, Elements of Cable Engineering, 1980, Power Cable Engineering, 1987; contbr. articles on dielectric and discharge loss mechanisms in elec. insulating systems to profl. jours. Decorated officer Order of Can. Fellow IEEE (mem. energy com. 1978—, mem. insulated condrs. com. 1966—, mem. awards and recognition com. 1984-88, IEEE Thomas Dakin Disting. Sci. Achievement award 1980, Centennial medal 1984, Whitehead Meml. award 1987, Morris Leeds award 1989, MacNaughton Gold medal 1993), ASTM (chmn. elec. insulation com. 1979-85, mem. editl. bd. Jour. Testing and Evaluation 1985—, award of merit 1985, Charles Dudley medal, appreciation award, Arnold Scott award), Can. Acad. of Engring., Inst. Elec. Engrs. Japan (Disting. hon. lectr. symposium on elec. insulating materials 1983), Inst. Physics (U.K.), Royal Soc. Can. Acad. Scis. (Thomas W. Eadie medal 1994); mem. Dielectrics and Elec. Insulation Soc. of IEEE (pres. 1976-78, mem. editl. bd. Elec. Insulation Mag. 1984-91), Internat. Electrotech. Commn. (mem. com. insulation materials, chmn. subcommittee on tests 1993—), Order Engrs. Que., Can. Stds. Assn. (Merit award, John Jenkins award), Can. Elec. Assn., Can. Stds. Coun. (J.P. Carrière award 1992), French-Can. Assn. for Advancement of Scis. (Urgel Archambault award 1993), U. Toronto Engring. Alumni Assn. (engring. medal 1993). Roman Catholic. Office: Hydro-Québec Inst Rsch, 1800 Boul Lionel-Boulet CP 1000, Varennes, PQ Canada J3X 1S1

BARTNOFF, JUDITH, judge; b. Boston, Apr. 14, 1949; d. Shepard and Irene F. (Tennenbaum) B.; m. Eugene F. Sofer, Sept. 10, 1978; 1 child, Nelson Bartnoff Sofer. BA magna cum laude, Radcliffe Coll., 1971; JD (Harlan Fiske Stone scholar), Columbia U., 1974; LLM, Georgetown U., 1975. Bar: D.C. 1975, U.S. Dist. Ct. D.C. 1975, U.S. Ct. Appeals (D.C. cir.) 1980, U.S. Ct. Appeals (fed. cir.) 1985, U.S. Ct. Appeals (11th cir.) 1988, U.S. Ct. Appeals (3d cir.) 1989, U.S. Claims Ct. 1991. Fellow Inst. Pub. Interest Representation, Georgetown Law Ctr., Washington, 1974-75; staff atty. Council Pub. Interest Law, Washington, 1975-77; spl. asst. to asst. atty. gen. criminal div. Dept. Justice, Washington, 1977-78; assoc. dep. atty. gen. Dept. Justice, 1978-80; spl. asst. U.S. atty. Office of U.S. Atty., Washington, 1980-81, asst. U.S. atty., 1982-85; assoc. firm Patton, Boggs & Blow, 1985-87, ptnr., 1988-94, assoc. ind. counsel, 1993-94; assoc. judge Superior Ct. of D.C., Washington, 1994—; mediator U.S. Dist. Ct. D.C., 1991-94; mem. com. on pro se litigation U.S Dist. Ct., 1991-94. Mem. D.C. Bar Task Force on Children at Risk, 1997—. Fellow Am. Bar Found.; mem. Nat. Assn. Women Judges, D.C. Bar, Women's Bar Assn. Office: 500 Indiana Ave NW Washington DC 20001-2131

BARTO, BRADLEY EDWARD, small business owner, educator; b. N.Y.C., Nov. 25, 1956; s. Kenneth William and Edna Ruth (Dalton) B.; m. Cheryl Annette Pray, Nov. 28, 1987; 1 child, David Bradley. B Engring., N.Y. Maritime Coll., 1982; M Gen. Adminstrn., U. Md., 1989; postgrad., U. Sarasota. Sr. engr. Advanced Tech., Inc., McLean, Va., 1982-85, Arinc Rsch., Inc., Annapolis, Md., 1985-87; pres., owner B Square Computing, Inc., Riva, Md., 1987—; pres. BCD Enterprises, Riva, Md., 1995—; prof. U. Md., College Park, 1990—, portfolio reviewer Excel program, 1995—. Inventor Chocks, 1995. Republican. Lutheran. Avocations: gofl, baseball, tennis, writing children's books. Home: 905 Malvern Hill Dr Davidsonville MD 21035-1242 Office: B Square Computing PO Box 606 Riva MD 21140-0606

BARTO, CHARLES O., JR., lawyer; b. Altoona, Pa., Aug. 12, 1946; s. Charles O. and Ernestine I. (Styers) B.; m. Marsha D. Packer, July 31, 1971; 1 child, Megan Suzanne. BA, Pa. State U., 1968; JD, Dickinson Sch. of Law, 1971. Bar: Pa. 1971, U.S. Dist. Ct. (mid. dist.) Pa. 1971, U.S. Supreme Ct. 1975, U.S. Ct. Appeals (3d cir.) 1979, U.S. Tax Ct. 1985. Asst. pub. defender Dauphin County Pub. Defender's Office, Harrisburg, Pa., 1971-73; assoc. Killian, Gephart & Snyder, Harrisburg, 1971-74; ptnr. Killian & Gephart, Harrisburg, 1975-83; prin. Charles O. Barto, Jr. & Assocs., Harrisburg, 1983—; gen. counsel Pa. Health Care Assn., Harrisburg, 1971—; conflicts counsel Hosp. Assn. Pa., Harrisburg, 1990—. Contbr. articles to books in field. V.p. St. Thomas Civic Assn., Linglestown, Pa., 1976-87; pres. consistory St. Thomas United Ch. of Christ, Linglestown, 1989, 92; chair constn. com. Pa. Coun. Chs., Harrisburg, 1990—, parliamentarian, 1990—; mem. Pa. Forestry Assn. Recipient Better Life award Pa. Health Care Assn., 1988, award of merit Health Care Facilities Assn. Pa., 1977, Boss of Yr. award Dauphin County Legal Secs. Assn., 1985-86. Mem. ABA, Pa. Bar Assn., Dauphin County Bar Assn., Assn. Trial Lawyers Am., Pa. Trial Lawyers Assn., Nat. Health Lawyers Assn. (bd. dirs. 1994—, pres. 1997-98), Kiwanis, Koons Pool and Swim Club (pres. 1994—). Democrat. Avocations: tennis, skiing, coaching softball, computer programming, collecting pens. Office: Charles O Barto Jr & Assocs 608 N 3rd St Harrisburg PA 17101-1102

BARTO, CHERYL, educational association administrator, researcher; b. Rochester, Minn., Apr. 26, 1962; d. Lawrence Richard and Elizabeth Ann (Ellingson) Pray; m. Bradley Edward Barto, Nov. 28, 1987; 1 child: David Bradley. BA, U. Minn., 1984; postgrad., St. Mary's U. Minn. Counselor March House, Mpls., 1984-86; sign language interpreter State of Ill., Chgo., 1986-87; coord. Nat. Info. Ctr. Deafness Gallaudet U., Washington, 1987-92, dir. advancement svcs., 1992—, dir. ann. giving, 1998—; cons., interpreter Nat. Aquarium, Washington, 1987-90. Mem., chmn. Better Hearing and Speech Month, Washington, 1992—; pres. RPI, 1996—. Mem. Assn. Profl. Rschrs. Advancement, Coun. Advancement and Support Edn. Home: 905 Malvern Hill Dr Davidsonville MD 21035-1242 Office: Gallaudet U 800 Florida Ave NE Washington DC 20002-3660

BARTO, DEBORAH ANN, physician; b. West Chester, Pa., July 27, 1948; d. Charles Guy and Jeannette Victoria (Golder) B. BA, Oberlin Coll., 1970; MD, Hahnemann U., 1974. Intern, resident Kaiser Permanente Hosp., San Francisco, 1974-77; dir. med. oncology Evergreen Hosp., Kirkland, Wash., 1980-85, head oncology quality assurance, 1992-94; med. dir. Cmty. Home Health Care Hospice, Seattle, 1981-84; hosp. ethics com. Evergreen Hosp., 1995-98. Mem. Evergreen Women's Physicians. Democrat. Buddhist. Avocation: horseback riding. Office: Evergreen Profl Plz 12911 120th Ave NE Ste E60 Kirkland WA 98034-3047

BARTO, SUSAN CAROL, writer; b. Bklyn., June 21, 1941; d. William O. and Eda (Birra) Forcellon; m. Harry W. Barto, Mar. 11, 1960; 1 child, William M. *Husband Harry W. was honorably discharged from the 50th Armored Division of the National Guard. He served on the New Providence, N.J. Borough Council. He retired after 35 years with AT&T. He is now a consultant with Lucent Technologies. Son William M. has an MA in Psychology from Seton Hall University, a PhD in History from Drew University. He is now member of the social science faculty at SUNY. The family has traveled to many countries, including England, Ireland, Germany, France, Italy, Egypt, and Israel.* Cert., Katherine Gibbs, 1960; student, Union Coll., 1979-82. Sec. dean of students Montclair (N.J.) State Coll., 1960; sec. Presbyn. Synod of N.J., East Orange, N.J., 1961-62; exec. sec. Union County Rep. Com., Westfield, N.J., 1971-79; legis. aide State Senator James Vreeland-Morris County, N.J., 1977-79. Author of short stories. County com. woman Union County Rep. Com., Westfield, 1970-82; active New Providence (N.J.) Libr. Bd., 1979-86. Recipient plaque of appreciation New Providence (N.J.) Libr. Bd., 1986. Mem. Friends of the Hunterdon Mus. of Art (pres. 1996—). Presbyterian. Home and Office: 1 Fisher Ct Lebanon NJ 08833-2107

BARTOK, MICHELLE, cosmetic company executive; b. Youngstown, Ohio, Feb. 18, 1961; d. Albert James and Judith Ann (Phillips) Bartok; m. John Anthony Garruto, Apr. 2, 1988 (div. 1997); children: Catherine Michelle, Gabrielle Bartok. BS in Physiol. Psychology, U. Calif., Santa Barbara, 1983. EMT, Calif. Asst. to phys. therapist Santa Barbara Phys. Therapy, 1983-84, Escondido (Calif.) Phys. Therapy, 1984-85; regional sales rep. Ft. Dodge Labs., San Francisco, 1985-87; owner North Coast Therapeutics, Oceanside, Calif., 1987-92; CEO, Innovative Bioscis. Corp., Carlsbad, Calif., 1992—. Mem. Nat. Women's Fitness Assn., Women's Enterprise Network, Soc. Cosmetic Chemists, Beauty Industry West (pub. rels. dir. 1991-92, chair symposium 1996), Internat. Spa and Fitness Assn. (sponsor Ironman competition 1989). Avocations: surfing, scuba diving, yoga. Home: 178 Grandview St Encinitas CA 92024-1009 Office: Innovative Bioscis Corp 2724 Loker Ave W Carlsbad CA 92008-6603

BARTOK, WILLIAM, environmental technologies consultant; b. Budapest, Hungary, May 1, 1930; s. Imre and Irma (Singer) B.; m. Susan V. Roth; Aug. 11, 1957; children: Michael F., Sylvia D., Richard E. BEng in Chem. Engring., McGill U., 1954, PhD in Phys. Chemistry, 1957. Research chemist Exxon Research & Engring. Co., Linden, N.J., 1957-61, sr. research chemist, 1961-66, research assoc., 1966-73, sr. research assoc., 1973-80; sci. advisor Exxon Research & Engring. Co., Clinton and Linden, N.J., 1980-86; sr. v.p. Energy and Environ. Research Corp., Irvine, Calif., 1986-91; sr. v.p. tech. Rsch.-Cottrell Cos., Somerville, N.J., 1991-92; cons., 1993—. Editor: Combustion of Synthetic Fuels, 1983; co-editor: Fossil Fuel Combustion, 1991; contbr. articles to profl. jours., chpts. to books. Mem. Combustion Inst. (bd. dirs. 1980-92), Am. Chem. Soc. (award in chemistry of contemporary tech. problems 1987), Am. Inst. Chem. Engrs. Avocations: music, reading, tennis, swimming, photography. Home and Office: 956 Wyandotte Trl Westfield NJ 07090-3733

BARTOLETTI, BARBARA MARIE, corporate secretary; b. Lynwood, Calif., Jan. 17, 1949; d. Tildo and Louise Maxine (Duff) Bartoletti; m. Hubert H. Hinds Jr., Apr. 16, 1976 (div. June 1989). Grad. high sch., South Gate, Calif. Various positions Atlantic Richfield Co., L.A., 1969-77, asst. corp. sec., 1977—. Mem. Am. Soc. Corp. Secs. Republican. Office: Atlantic Richfield Co 515 S Flower St Bldg 4589 Los Angeles CA 90071-2201

BARTOLI, CECILIA, coloratura soprano, mezzo soprano; b. Italy, 1967; d. Pietro Angelo and Silvana B. Attended, Academia de Santa Cecilia. Recording artist Decca/London, 1986—. Stage debut, Verona, 1987; appearances include La Scala, Opéra Bastille, Carnegie Hall, Berlin, Nantes, Warsaw, Naples, Orch. Hall, Chgo.; albums: Rossini Recitals, Mozart Arias, Rossini Heroines; #1 album If You Love Me (33 weeks Billboard charts, Grammy nomination, Best Classical album, 1994), 1992, Mozart Portraits, 1995, An Italian Songbook, 1997. Named Musical America's Vocalist of Yr., 1993; recipient Grammy award Best Classical Vocal, 1994. Office: c/o Edgar Vincent 157 W 57th St Ste 502 New York NY 10019*

BARTOLINI, ROBERT ALFRED, electrical engineer, researcher; b. Waterbury, Conn., Apr. 4, 1942; s. Alfred N. and Maria D. (Cartoceti) B.; m. Janice M. Daly, June 13, 1964; children: Jill C., Ellen G., Robin M. BSEE, Villanova U., 1964; MSEE, Case Western Res. U., 1966; PhD, U. Pa., 1972. Rsch. scientist RCA Labs., Princeton, N.J., 1966-79, leader optical sys., 1979-83, head optoelectronic rsch., 1983-87; head laser diode rsch. David Sarnoff Rsch. Ctr., Princeton, 1987-89, dir. integrated cir., 1989-96, sr. dir. integrated cir. lab., 1996-97; v.p. integrated cir. lab. Sarnoff Corp., Princeton, 1997—; chmn. elect. engring. dept. LaSalle U., 1982-90. Contbr. 35 articles to jours. in field; presenter 65 profl. presentations. Chmn. Sewer Oper. Com., West Windsor, N.J., 1974-82, chmn. assessment bd., West Windsor, N.J., 1984; vice chmn. Stony Brook Regional Sewerage Authority, Princeton, N.J., 1980-96, chmn., 1997—. Recipient 3 labs. achievement awards RCA Labs., 1970, 76, 80, Outstanding Paper award Soc. Internat. Display, 1979, Engring. Alumni award Villanova U., 1986, Sarnoff award RCA Corp., 1986. Fellow IEEE (Centennial medal 1984), Optical Soc. Am. (chmn. laser conf. 1987-91); mem. Sigma Xi (nat. lectr. 1983-84), Tau Beta Pi, Eta Kappa Nu. Achievements include 22 U.S. patents and research in embossable holographic development, optical data storage media development, optical data storage system development, surface emitting diode laser development. Office: Sarnoff Corp 201 Washington Rd Princeton NJ 08540

BARTOLOCCI, PAULETTE E MARIE, elementary school educator, aerobic instructor; b. Phillipsburg, Pa., Aug. 19, 1969; d. Anthony Thomas and Pauline Virginia (Leh) B. BS in Elem. Edn., St. Joseph U., Phila., 1991; MS in Bilingual, Bicultural Studies, Lehigh U., 1997. 6th grade tchr. Our Lady of Prepetual Help, Bethlehem, Pa., 1992-93; 1-4th grade lang. arts tchr. for ESOL children Allentown (Pa.) Sch. Dist., 1993-97, interim asst. to dir. instrl. support svcs., 1998, 6th grade lang. arts tchr., 1997—; fellow Pa. State Nat. Writing Project, Fogelsville, Pa., 1993—, outreach mem., 1995—; cheerleading coach S. Mountain Middle Sch., Allentown, 1998-99. Grantee Nat. Writing Project, Pa. State U., 1995-99. Mem. ASCD, Pa. Edn. Assn., Allentown Edn. Assn., Nat. Coun. Tchrs. of English, Aerobics and Fitness Assn. Am. (cert., instr. summer 1998). Republican. Roman Catholic. Avocations: aerobics, singing, jazz dancing, guitar. Home: 2 Dusty Rd Easton PA 18105

BARTOLOTTI, JOSSIF PETER See CARRINGTON, J(OSEPH) P(ETER)

BARTON, ALAN JOEL, lawyer; b. N.Y.C., Sept. 2, 1938; s. Sidney and Claire (Greenfield) B.; m. Ann Rena Beral, Jan. 29, 1961; children: Donna Frieda Olsen, Brian Joseph. AB, U. Calif., Berkeley, 1960, JD, 1963. Assoc. Nossaman, Krueger & Mash, Los Angeles, 1963-70, ptnr., 1970-80; ptnr. Paul, Hastings, Janofsky & Walker, Los Angeles, 1980—; lectr. corp. and securities law U. Calif. Continuing Edn. Bar, 1980—; lectr. venture capital and securities law Practicing Law Inst., 1986—. Assoc. editor U. Calif. Law Rev., 1963. Dir. Ctr. for Study of Young People in Groups, L.A., 1988—; trustee Dubnoff Ctr. for Ednl. Therapy, North Hollywood, Calif., 1976-80. Mem. ABA (com. on fed. regulation of securities), Calif. Bar Assn. (com. on corps.), Order of Coif, The Calif. Club. Republican. Jewish. Avocations: movies, contemporary art, tennis, travel. Office: Paul Hastings Janofsky & Walker 555 S Flower St Fl 23 Los Angeles CA 90071-2300*

BARTON, ALLEN HOISINGTON, sociologist; b. Greenwich, Conn., Oct. 7, 1924; s. Horace Allen and Elizabeth (Hoisington) B.; m. Judith Schneider, Mar. 11, 1949; children: Stephen, Hugh, Matthew, Julia. AB, Harvard U., 1947; PhD, Columbia U., 1957. Dir. Bur. Applied Social Rsch. Columbia U., N.Y.C., 1962-77, instr. sociology, 1953-54; rsch. assoc. Bur. Applied Social Rsch., Columbia U., N.Y.C., 1957-62; asst. prof. to prof. Columbia U., N.Y.C., 1957-90, chmn. sociology dept., 1989-90; lectr. sociology U. Oslo, Norway, 1948-49; adj. prof. sociology U. Fla., 1993-98. Author: Studying the Effects of College Education, 1959, Organizational Measurement, 1961, Communities in Disaster, 1969, Background Attitudes and Activities of American Elites, 1985; co-author: Opinion-Making Elites in Yugoslavia, 1973, Decentralizing City Government, 1977; co-editor: Making Bureaucracies Work, 1980. Del. Conn. Dem. Conv., 1968; mem. Dem. Town Com., Greenwich, 1971-90. With U.S. Army, 1943-46. Recipient Worcester prize for best pub. opinion article, 1996; Social Sci. Rsch. Coun. grantee, 1949-50, Carnegie Corp. grantee, 1968-71, Ford Found. grantee, 1970-74, grantee NIMH, NSF, 1972-75. Mem. AAAS, Am. Sociol. Assn., Am. Assn. Pub. Opinion Rsch., Internat. Sociol. Assn., Soc. For Study Social Problems. Avocations: travel, hiking, snorkeling, photography. Home: 118 Wolf's Trail Chapel Hill NC 27516-9060

BARTON, BABETTE B., lawyer, educator; b. Los Angeles, Apr. 30, 1930; d. Milton Vernon and Ruth (Schreiber) Barancik; children: Jeffrey B. Barton, David R. Barton, Baird R. Barton. B.S., U. Calif., Berkeley, 1951, LL.B., 1954. Bar: Calif., U.S. Dist. Ct., U.S. Ct. Appeals 1955. Law clk. to Chief Justice Phil S. Gibson, Calif. Supreme Ct., San Francisco, 1954-55; lectr., acting prof. Sch. of Law, U. Calif., Berkeley, 1961-72, prof. law, 1972—; Adrian A. Kragen chair U. Calif., Berkeley; cons. Calif. Inter Agy. Task Force on Electronic Funds Transfers, 1978-79, Dept. Treasury, 1963; mem. adv. com. Calif. Bd. Legal Specialization, 1980-83. Contbr. chpts. to books in field. Mem. adv. com. Alameda County Dir. Welfare, 1970-73; bd. dirs. Family Service Berkeley, 1967-74, Univ. Students' Coop. Assn., 1966-74. Recipient Citation award Boalt Hall Alumni Assn., 1997. Fellow Am. Law Inst., Am. Bar Found.; mem. ABA (taxation sect. chmn. tchg. tax. com. 1994-96, real property probate and trust sect. coun. 1977-79), Calif. State Bar (chmn. taxation sect. 1976-77, Joanne M. Garvey award taxation sect. 1997), Western Regional Bar Assn. (chmn. 1978-79), Am. Coll. Tax Counsel, San Francisco Tax Club, San Francisco Estate Planning Coun., Berkeley Tennis Club (bd. dirs. 1988-90, pres. 1990-91). Home: 16 Saint James Dr Piedmont CA 94611-3533 Office: U Calif Berkeley Sch Law 892 Simon Boalt Hall Berkeley CA 94720-7201

BARTON, BERNARD ALAN, JR., lawyer; b. Glens Falls, N.Y., Aug. 13, 1948; s. Bernard A. Sr. and Geraldine (Bushey) B.; children: Lindsey, Kylie. BA, U. Fla., 1969, JD, 1975, LLM, 1976. Bd. cert. tax lawyer. Ptnr. Holland & Knight, Tampa, Fla., 1976—. Editor, contbg. author Florida Taxation, State Taxation Series, 1994. Mem. ABA, Nat. Assn. Bond Attys., Fla. Bar Assn. (exec. coun. tax sect., chmn. various coms. 1980-99). Republican. Episcopalian. Office: Holland & Knight 400 N Ashley Dr PO Box 1288 Tampa FL 33601-1288

BARTON, BILLIE JO, artist, educator; b. Childress, Tex., June 23, 1926; d. Robert Douglas and Erma Ada (Collier) Perry; m. Hudson James Barton, June 28, 1947; 1 child, David Douglas. Student, Frank Wiggins Sch., 1944-45, ABC Sch. Dist., 1956-86; studied with Ken Decker, Mary Bugher. Art instr. Smithys Art Gallery, Orange, Calif., 1976-77, Internat. Studio, Cerritos, Calif., 1978-79, Lakewood, Calif., 1980—; juror Fine Art Commn., Buena Park, Calif., 1993-96. Author: The Guidebook for Oil Painters, 1993; work pub. in books: Artists of California, 1993, Encyclopedia of Living Artist, 1997; editor Buena Park Art Guild newsletter, 1993; group exhibits and juried shows include The La Mirada (Calif.) Art Gallery, 1993-94, Art Assocs. Gallery, Huntington Beach, Calif., 1994, Calif. Coun. Art League, 1992, 93, 94, Knott's Berry Farm Artist Round-Up, Buena Park, 1992, 93, 94, Fine Art Inst. San Bernadino County Mus., Redlands, Calif., 1992, 93, 94, Santa Barbara 6th Ann. Festival Art, 1994, Festival Whales Dana Point Harbor, Dana Point, Calif., 1995, Newport Beach Festival Art, Newport, Calif., 1995, Tall Ships Show, Dana Point, 1995, 21st Ann. Juried Art Exhibit, Cypress, Calif., 1996, Sunday Arts Delight, Cypress, 1996, Ann. Father's Day Celebration, Dana Point, 1996. Parent aide PTA, Lakewood, 1959-64; den mother Cub Scouts Am., Lakewood, 1961; precinct worker Los Angeles County Elections, Norwalk, Calif., 1949, Lakewood, 1965-86. Fellow Nat. Mus. Women in Arts, Niguel Art Assn., Nat. Assn. Fine Art, Buena Art Guild (recording sec. 1992-96, Best of Show award 1992), Ea. Star Lodge (hostess 1966-67); mem. La Palma Art Assn. (news editor, v.p. 1975-76, Artist of Yr. award 1976). Republican. Avocations: travel, gardening. Home and Studio: 11720 207th St Lakewood CA 90715-1331

BARTON, CHARLES DAVID, religious studies educator, author, researcher, historian; b. Austin, Tex., Jan. 28, 1954; s. Charles Grady and Hilda Rose (Seely) B.; m. Cheryl Edith Little, Mar. 18, 1978; children: Damaris Ann, Timothy David, Stephen Daniel. Degree in religious edn., Oral Roberts U., 1976; D.Litt (hon.), Pensacola Christian Coll., 1997. Dir. youth Aledo (Tex.) Christian Ctr., 1974-75, dir. Christian edn., dir. youth, 1977-87, dir. Christian edn., elder, 1987—; dir. youth Jenks (Okla.) 1st Assembly, 1975-76; dir. Christian edn., dir. youth Sheridan Christian Ctr., Tulsa, Okla., 1976-77; pres. Splty. Rsch. Assocs., Inc./WallBuilders, Aledo, 1987—. Author: America: To Pray or Not to Pray, 1987, The Myth of Separation, 1988, What Happened in Education?, 1989, The Bulletproof George Washington, 1990, Original Intent, 1995; prodr. (videos) America's Godly Heritage, Keys to Good Government, Edn. and the Founding Fathers, Spirit of the American Revolution, Foundations of American Government. Bd. dirs. Youth Leadership Coun., Cin., 1990, Tex. Christian Coalition, 1993—; mem. bd. advisors Released Time, Sacramento, 1987, Nat. Prayer Embassy, Washington, 1988; mem. coun. Nat. Policy Forum, 1994. Recipient Writing award Amy Found., 1989, 2 Angel awards Excellence in Media, 1995, George Washington medal Freedoms Found. at Valley Forge, Medal of Honor, DAR, 1998. Republican. Office: WallBuilders PO Box 397 Aledo TX 76008-0397

BARTON, DAWN KANANI, elementary school educator; b. Landstuhl, Germany, Mar. 6, 1971; came to U.S., 1971; d. Brian Leigh and Georgina Allyne (Plucker) Clevenger; m. Charles Raymond Barton II, Sept. 5, 1992. BS in Elem. Edn. cum laude, Towson U., 1994; MS in Sch. Adminstrn., Western Md. Coll., 1998. Camp leader Dept. Pks. and Recreation, City of Balt., 1990-93; substitute tchr. Baltimore County Pub. Schs., Owings Mills, Md., 1992, long-term substitute, 1994; substitute tchr. Harford County Pub. Schs., Jarrettsville, Md., 1993; tchr. 3rd grade Anne Arundel County Pub. Sch., Glen Burnie, Md., 1994-95, tchr. 5th grade, 1995—; team leader pub. sch. Glen Burnie, 1995-97, chairperson edn. mgmt. team, prin. designee, 1996-97; table leader Staff Devel. Ctr., Arnold, Md., 1996; instr. Md. Summer Ctr. Gifted & Talented, 1998; office mgr. Electronics Boutique, 1998— . Camp leader Baltimore County Renaissance Program, 1997; active PTA, liaison, 1995-96; tchr. Sunday sch. Baltimore County Bapt. Ch., Reisterstown, Md., 1994—, child care dir., 1998. Lions Club scholar, Reisterstown, 1989. Avocations: reading, writing, computers. Home: 1911 Powder Mill Rd York PA 17402

BARTON, FRITZ ENGEL, plastic surgeon, educator; b. Ft. Worth, Tex., Mar. 5, 1942. BS, So. Meth. U., 1963, MD, 1967. Diplomate Am. Bd. Surgery, Am. Bd. Plastic Surgery; lic. physician, Tex., Colo. Intern in internal medicine U. N.C., N.C. Meml. Hosp., Chapel Hill, 1967-68; resident in gen. surgery U. Tex. Southwestern Med. Sch./Affiliated Hosps., Dallas, 1970-74; resident in plastic surgery Inst. Reconstructive Plastic Surgery, NYU, N.Y.C., 1974-76; prof., chmn. divsn. plastic surgery dept. surgery U. Tex., Dallas; attending staff mem. Parkland Meml. Hosp., Baylor U. Med. Ctr., Children's Med. Ctr., Presbyn. Hosp. Dallas, VA Med. Ctr. Dallas, Zale Lipshy Univ. Hosp. Contbr. numerous articles to profl. jours. With U.S. Army, Vietnam, 1968-70. Recipient Tattinger award of distinction Susan G. Komen Found. for Breast Cancer Rsch., 1986. Mem. AMA, ACS, Am. Assn. Plastic Surgeons, Am. Soc. for Aesthetic Plastic Surgery (chmn. edn. commn. 1990-93, parliamentarian 1993, v.p. 1997-98, pres.-elect 1999-2000, Simon Fredricks award 1989, 98, Best Sci. Presentation 1991,), Am. Soc. Aesthetic Plastic Surgeons, Am. Soc. Plastic and Reconstructive Surgeons (chmn. strategic planning com. 1990, time and place com. 1991-92, fin. com. 1991-93, ops. com. 1991-93), Plastic Surgery Ednl. Found. (chmn. selected readings in plastic surgery com. 1983—, editor-in-chief selected readings in plastic surgery 1980—, pres.-elect 1991-92, pres. 1992-93), Assn. Acad. Chmn. Plastic Surgery, Tex. Soc. Plastic Surgery, Tex. Med. Assn., Dallas Soc. Plastic Surgeons, Alpha Omega Alpha. Office: Dallas Plastic Surgery Inst Ste 6000 LB 13 411 N Washington Ave Dallas TX 75246

BARTON, GAIL MELINDA, psychiatrist, educator; b. Worcester, Mass., Apr. 20, 1937; d. Walter Earl and Elsa Viola (Benson) B.; m. Duncan John Kretovich, Aug. 31, 1968 (div. 1986); 1 child, Mariah Lynne. AB, Jackson Coll., Medford, Mass., 1959; MD, Women's Med. Coll. Pa., 1966; MPH, U. Mich., 1971. Diplomate Am. Bd. Psychiatry and Neurology, Am. Bd. Forensic Examiners. Rotating intern St. Joseph Mercy Hosp., Ann Arbor, Mich., 1966-67; resident in psychiatry U. Mich., Ann Arbor, 1967-70, chief resident dept. psychiatry, 1970-71, asst. prof. psychiatry, dir. continuing care clinic psychiatry dept., 1971-77; assoc. prof., 1977-82; mem. outpatient staff dept. psychiatry U. Mich., Ann Arbor, 1979-82; dir. rsch. and devel. dept. mental health State of Mich., East Lansing, 1977-79; assoc. clin. prof. U. Vt., Burlington, 1982-84; med. dir. Howard Mental Health, Burlington, 1982-84; assoc. clin. prof. Dartmouth Coll., Hanover, N.H., 1984-88, clin. prof., 1988-91, prof., 1992—; dir. inpatient psychiatry VA Hosp., White River Junction, Vt., 1984-89; acting chief of psychiatry, 1989-90; dir. mental hygiene clinic VA Hosp., White River Junction, Vt., 1990—. Author: Mental Health Adminstration, 2 vols., 1983, Ethics and Law, 1984; co-editor: Handbook of Emergency Psychiatry, 1986; mem. editorial bd. Hosp. and Community Psychiatry Jour., 1984-93. Incorporator Mt. Ascutney Hosp., Windsor, Vt., 1987—; mem. search com. for police chief, Windsor, 1987; trustee 1st Congl. Ch., Hartland, Vt., 1987-91, 92—, chmn., 1990-91, 93—; bd. trustees Historic Windsor, 1995—, events com., 1994—. Fellow Am. Coll. Psychiatrists (program com. 1982-84, awards com. 1985-89, site com. 1990-95, nominating com. 1996—), Am. Coll. Mental Health Adminstrn. (pres. 1987-89), Am. Psychiat. Assn. (program com. 1976-82, task force on emergency care issues 1978-83, hosp. and cmty. psychiat. svc. 1990-93); mem. Am. Med. Women's Assn. (dir. med. students 1980, subcom. on mental health 1993—), Am. Coll. Emergency Physicians (behavioral com. 1978-81). Avocations: off-loom weaving, painting, needlepoint, canoeing, skiing. Office: VA Med Ctr N Hartland Rd White River Junction VT 05001

BARTON, GERALD LEE, farming company executive; b. Modesto, Calif., Feb. 24, 1934; s. Robert Paul and Alice Lee (Hall) B.; m. Janet Murray, June 24, 1955; children: Donald Lee, Gary Michael, Brent Richard. BA with distinction, Stanford U., 1955. Owner, pres. Barton Ranch, Escalon, Calif., 1961—; v.p. R.P. Barton Mfg. Co., Escalon, 1963-86; chmn. bd. Diamond Walnut Growers Inc., 1976-81, chmn. emeritus, 1981—, pres., 1986-90; chmn. Diamond-Sunsweet Co., Stockton, Calif., 1978-80, Sun Diamond Growers, Inc., 1980-81; bd. dirs. Calif. Fin. Holding Co., Stockton, Stockton Savs. Bank; vice chmn. Fed. Land Bank, Modesto, Calif., 1976-81; chmn. Growers Harvesting Com., Modesto, 1976-77; mem. pomology rsch. adv. bd. U. Calif., Davis, 1968-74, Walnut Mktg. Bd., San Francisco, 1971-73, 77—; mem. Calif. Walnut Commn., 1987—; mem. agribus. adv. bd. U. Santa Clara, 1979-89; dir. Ross Hort. Found.; mem. San Joaquin County U. Calif. Ext. Adv. Bd. Chmn. bd. edn. Escalon Unified Sch. Dist., 1963-75; vice chmn. San Joaquin County Sch. Bds. Assn., 1965; bd. dirs. St. Joseph's Healthcare Corp., 1991-95; trustee Yosemite Assn., 1999—. With AUS, 1956-58. Decorated Order of the Golden Walnut; named Outstanding Young Farmer in San Joaquin County C. of C., 1965, Farmer of Yr. Escalon C. of C.; recipient U. Calif. Friend of Extension award, 1992; named to San Joaquin County Agrl. Hall of Fame, 1993; recipient Disting. Svc. award Calif. Walnut Commn., 1998. Mem. Stanford U. Alumni Assn., Delta Chi. Republican. Presbyterian. Office: 22398 Mcbride Rd Escalon CA 95320-9637

BARTON, GLEN A., manufacturing company executive; b. Alton, Mo.. BS in Civil Engring., U. Mo., Columbia, 1961; grad. Exec. Program, Stanford U., 1977. With Caterpillar Inc., Peoria, Ill., 1961—, mgr. merchandising divsn. gen. offices, 1983-84, mgr. products control, 1984-86, v.p., 1987-89, exec. v.p., 1989-90, group pres., 1990-98, vice chmn., bd. dirs., 1998—; mem. adv. bd. Bank One, Peoria, Bradley U., Peoria, INCO Ltd. Mem. Nat. Mining Assn. (bd. dirs., chmn. mfrs. divsn. bd. govs.), Mineral Info. Inst. *

BARTON, GREGORY MARK, Olympic athlete, kayak racer; b. Jackson, Mich., Dec. 2, 1959. BS in Mech. Engring., U. Mich., 1983. Olympic kayak racer, 1000 meter singles L.A., 1984; Olympic kayak racer, 1000 meter singles and doubles Seoul, Korea, 1988; Olympic kayak racer, 1000 meter singles Barcelona, Spain, 1992. Recipient Bronze medal 1000 meter kayak singles Olympics, L.A., 1984, Gold medal 1000 meter kayak singles Olympics, Seoul, 1988, Gold medal 1000 meter kayak doubles Olympics, Seoul, 1988, Bronze medal 1000 meter kayak singles Olympics, Barcelona, 1992. Office: c/o US Olympic Com 1750 E Boulder St Colorado Springs CO 80909-5724

BARTON, HALBERT EVERETT, anthropology educator, consultant; b. Portland, Oreg., Dec. 18, 1963; s. John Selby and Irene Elizabeth (Brooks) B.; m. Mayra Pilar Santos-Febres, Aug. 17, 1991 (div. Jan. 1996). BA, U. Calif., Santa Cruz, 1987; MA, Cornell U., 1990, PhD, 1995. Vis. prof. English Met. U., Cuprey, P.R., 1992; vis. prof. anthropology U. Calif., Santa Cruz, 1995; artist-in-residence Miracle Theatre Group, Portland, 1996-97; asst. prof. anthropology L.I. U., Bklyn., 1998—; cultural cons. Lincoln H.S., Portland, 1996-97, El Puente Acad., Bklyn., 1997—, Bronx Pub. Schs., 1998; invited presenter Oreg. Coun. on Humanities, Portland, 1997; co-dir. CICRE, Carolina, P.R., 1998—. Youth advisor Lafayette (Calif.) Presbyn. Ch., 1995. Post-doctoral rsch. fellow Rockefeller Found., U. P.R., 1998. Mem. Am. Anthropology Assn., L.Am. Studies Assn., Soc. for Ethnomusicology, Nat. Assn. Practicing Anthropologists, Soc. for Cultural Anthropology, Dance Rsch. Congress. Democrat. Presbyterian. Avocations: basketball, tennis, folk music, dancing. Home: 17210 SE 32nd St Vancouver WA 98683 Office: LI Univ Dept Anthropology 1 University Plaza Brooklyn NY 11201

BARTON, JAMES CARY, lawyer; b. Raymondville, Tex., Sept. 1, 1940; s. Dewey Albert and Dorothy Marie (Keene) B.; m. Isabel Pattee Critz, Sept. 12, 1964 (div. June 1975); children: Hamilton Keene, James Albert, John Franklin; m. Carolyn Ann Cox, Dec. 20, 1975; stepchildren: Holly Ann Adams, Laura Lee Adams, Jennifer Lynn Adams. BA, Baylor U., 1962; LLB, Harvard U., 1965. Bar: Tex. 1965, U.S. Dist. Ct. (so. dist.) Tex. 1972, U.S. Tax Ct. 1977. Trial atty. FPC, Washington, 1965-67; atty.-advisor U.S. Tax Ct., Washington, 1967-68; assoc. to ptnr. Kleberg, Mobley, Lockett & Weil, Corpus Christi, Tex., 1969-75, Brown, Maroney, Rose, Baker & Barber, Austin, Tex., 1975-82; ptnr. to of counsel Johnson & Swanson, Austin and Dallas, 1982-88; dir. Smith, Barshop, Stoffer & Millsap, Inc., San Antonio, 1988-91; prin. J. Cary Barton, P.C., San Antonio, 1991-93; prin Barton & Schneider, L.L.P., San Antonio, 1993—; speaker in field. Sgt. USAF, 1968-69. Mem. ABA, State Bar Tex. (mem. coun. of real estate probate and trust law sect. 1982-85, mem. real estate forms com. 1986—), Am. Coll. Real Estate Lawyers, Tex. Bd. legal Specialization (cert. in comml. real estate law), Tex. Coll. Real Estate Attys. Democrat. Episcopalian. Office: One Riverwalk Pl 700 N Saint Marys St Ste 1825 San Antonio TX 78205-3596

BARTON, JAMES MILLER, lawyer, international business consultant; b. Scarsdale, N.Y., Apr. 13, 1942; s. Ralph Miller and Eleanor (LaRose) B.; m. Nancy Claudia Bishop, Aug. 7, 1965; children: James Miller Jr., Timothy Ralph, Allison Megen. BA, Yale U., 1964; LLB, U. Va., 1967. Bar: Conn. 1967, U.S. Tax Ct. 1971, U.S. Supreme Ct. 1971. Assoc. Cummings & Lockwood, Stamford, Conn., 1967-75, ptnr., 1975-96, mem. exec. and fin. coms., 1980-95; ptnr. Levett Rockwood & Sanders, Westport, Conn., 1996-99; legal cons. fgn. investment; active Ministry Privatization Czech Republic, Prague, 1992-93; v.p. Avian Farms, Inc., Waterville, Maine, 1996-99; sr. cons. internat. affairs Preferred Health Systems, LCC, Bethesda, Md., 1995-98; dir. corp. affairs Advanced Cell Tech., Inc., Worcester, Mass., 1996-99; CEO, Cyagra, LLC, Amherst, Mass., 1999—, Hematech, LLC, Amherst, 1999—. Contbr. articles to profl. jours. Trustee Greenwich Acad., 1988-96, chmn., 1993-96; bd. dirs. Greenwich Choral Soc., 1970's, Stamford Symphony, 1994—. Mem. ABA, Conn. Bar Assn., Greenwich (Conn.) Bar Assn., Stanwich Club (Greenwich), Yale Club (N.Y.); Yale Club (Greenwich) (bd. dirs. 1970s). Avocations: opera, theater, reading, tennis. Office: care Levett Rockwood Et Al PO Box 5116 33 Riverside Ave Westport CT 06881

BARTON, JANICE SWEENY, chemistry educator; b. Trenton, N.J., Mar. 22, 1939; d. Laurence U. and Lillian Mae (Fletcher) S.; m. Keith M. Barton, Dec. 20, 1967. BS, Butler U., 1962; PhD, Fla. State U., 1970. Postdoctoral fellow Johns Hopkins U., Balt., 1970-72; asst. prof. chemistry East Tex. State U., Commerce, 1972-78, Tex. Woman's U., Denton, 1978-81; assoc. prof. Washburn U., Topeka, 1982-88, prof., 1988—, chair chemistry dept., 1992—; mem. undergrad. faculty enhancement panel NSF, Washington, 1990; mem. NSF instr. lab. improvement panel, 1992, 96, 99. Contbr. articles to profl. jours. Active Household Hazardous Waste Collection, Topeka, 1991, Solid Waste Task Force, Shawnee County, Kans., 1990; mem. vol. com. YWCA, Topeka, 1984-87. Rsch. grantee Petroleum Rsch. Fund, Topeka, 1984-86, NIH, Topeka, 1985-88; instrument grantee NSF, Topeka, 1986, 95. Mem. Am. Chem. Soc. (sec. Dallas-Ft. Worth sect. 1981-82), Kans. Acad. Sci. (pres.-elect 1991, pres. 1992, treas. 1995—), Biophys. Soc., Sigma Xi (pres. TWU club 1980-81), Iota Sigma Pi (mem.-at-large coord. 1987-93). Home: 3401 SW Oak Pky Topeka KS 66614-3218 Office: Washburn U Dept Chemistry Topeka KS 66621

BARTON, JAY, university administrator, biologist; b. Chgo., June 22, 1922; s. Jay and Agnes (Heisler) B.; m. Ann Taylor, Aug. 1, 1946; children: Sarah, Elizabeth, Peter, Rachel, Matthew, Mary, Judith. A.B., U. Mo., 1947, M.A., 1948, Ph.D. in Zoology, 1951; D.Sc. (hon.), U. Alaska, 1984. Instr. zoology, then asst. prof. Columbia, 1950-55; from asst. prof. to prof. biology St. Joseph's Coll., Rensselaer, Ind., 1955-65; staff biologist commn. undergrad. edn. in biol. scis. George Washington U., 1965-67; prof. biology, chmn. dept. W.Va. U., 1967-69, provost for instrn., 1968-77, v.p. for acad. affairs, 1977-79; pres. U. Alaska, 1979-84; v.p. acad. affairs U. Mo., 1985-89; advisor Nat. Agrarian U., Peru, 1989-91; assoc. investigator Argonne Nat. Lab., 1958; bd. dirs., mem. exec. com. Biol. Scis. Curriculum Study, 1969-85, chmn. bd., 1978-85; mem. exec. com. Nat. Assn. State Univs. and Land-Grant Colls., 1982; bd. dirs. Public Svc. Satellite Corp., 1981-83; dir. Ott Water Engring., Redding, Calif., 1983-88. Mem. Mo. Opportunity 2000 Commn., 1985-87. Served with AUS, 1943-46. AEC fellow, 1949-50; Lalor fellow, 1951-52; NSF fellow and Fulbright scholar Copenhagen, Denmark, 1961-62. Mem. AAAS, Nat. Assn. Biology Tchrs. (bd. dirs., exec. com.), Am. Inst. Biol. Scis., Alaska C. of C. (dir. 1982), Sigma Xi, Phi Kappa Phi, Delta Epsilon Sigma. Home: 244 Holgerson Rd Sequim WA 98382-9536

BARTON, JOE LINUS, congressman; b. Waco, Tex., Sept. 15, 1949; s. Larry Linus and Bess Wynell (Buice) B.; m. Janet Sue Winslow, Jan. 31, 1970; children—Bradley Linus, Alison Renee, Kristin Elizabeth. BS in Indsl. Engring., Tex. A&M U., 1972; MS in Indsl. Adminstrn., Purdue U., 1973. Asst. to v.p. Ennis (Tex.) Bus. Forms, 1973-81; The White House fellow Washington, 1981-82; cost control cons. ARCO, Dallas, 1982-84; mem. 101st-105th Congresses from 6th Tex. dist., 1985—, mem. energy and commerce com., mem. sci. and tech. com., mem. commerce and sci. com., chmn. energy and power subcom. of commerce com., mem. Rep. steering com. Mem. Assn. Former Students Tex. A&M U. (councilman at large 1985—). Methodist.

BARTON, JOHN JOSEPH, obstetrician, gynecologist, educator, researcher; b. Rockford, Ill., Mar. 19, 1933; s. L. David and Helen M. (Fox) B.; m. Lois Maltby, 1959 (div. 1965); children: Mary Katherine, Karen Ann. BA in History, U. Ill., 1957; BS in Medicine, U. Ill., Chgo., 1959, MD, 1961; student Law, Loyola U., Chgo., 1966-69. Diplomate Am. Bd. Ob.-Gyn.; cert. Advanced Cardiac Life Support. Rotating intern Cook County Hosp., Chgo., 1961-62, resident in ob.-gyn., 1962-65; fellow gynecologic pathology Northwestern U., Chgo., 1963, clin. asst. ob.-gyn., 1963-64, clin. instr. ob.-gyn., 1964-65, assoc. in ob.-gyn., 1965-71; prof. ob.-gyn. Cook County Grad. Sch. of Medicine, Chgo., 1965—; dir. ob.-gyn. rsch. and edn. Cook County Hosp., Chgo., 1965-69; chmn. ob.-gyn. Ill. Masonic Med. Ctr., Chgo., 1970—; assoc. prof. ob.-gyn. U. Ill. Coll. Medicine, Chgo., 1971-83, prof., 1983-93, lectr. in ob.-gyn., 1993—; prof. ob.-gyn. Rush Med. Coll., Chgo., 1993—; clin. clerkship subcom. U. Ill. Coll. Medicine, 1974-90, acad. senate 1977-91, 85-87, perinatal steering com., 1977-92, admissions com. 1985-91, screening subcom. 1988-89; ad hoc com. on rules for governance, Rush Med. Coll., Chgo., 1993—, curriculum com. 1993, com. on student evaluation and promotions, 1994—, core ckerkship subcom. of curriculum com. 1995—; editl. bd. Jour. Obstetrics and Gynecology, Am. Jour. Obstetrics and Gynecology, Internat. Jour. Obstetrics and Gynecology. Contbr. numerous articles to profl. jours., chpts. to books, including Laparoscopy in Gynecologic Practice, 1972, Guidelines for Perinatal Care, 1983, Antepartum HIV Screenings: A Comparison of Methodologies, 1990. Vol. cons. Ob.-Gyn. Claremore (Okla.) Indian Hosp., 1979-80, 86, Fort Defiance (Ariz.) Indian Hosp., 1981, Red Crescent Soc., Heliopolis, Cairo, Egypt, 1987; vol. surgeon Internat. Red Cross and Red Crescent Soc. Vols., West Beirut, Lebanon, 1982; mem. Ill. Gov.'s AIDS adv. coun.; advisor, expert witness Atty. Gen. State of Ill. on Standards of Practice in Ob.-Gyn.; mem. com. formation of outcome-oriented surveillance systems for Ill. Dept. of Pub. Health, adv. com. to Health Planning Com. for Chgo., perinatal adv. com. Ill. Dept. Health, steering com. Mayor Washington's Infant Mortality Reduction Initiative and others. Sgt. U.S. Marine Corps, 1950-55. Fellow Am. Coll. Obstetricians and Gynecologists (adv. coun. 1977-81, adv. coun. dist. VI 1977-81, chmn. Ill. sect. 1977-78, com. on profl. liability 1989-92, Jr. Fellow Rsch. prize award 1991), Ctrl. Assn. Obstetricians nd Gynecologists (ctrl. travel club, sci. awards com. 1985-89. chmn. 1987-89, Ann. prize award 1988), Chgo. Gynecol. Soc. (exec. com. 1994—, pres. 1995-96), Am. Coll. Surgeons, Soc. Contemporary Medicine and Surgery, Am. Soc. Clin. Hypnosis, Chgo. Inst. Medicine, Royal Soc. Medicine (London); mem. Ill. Assn. Maternal and Child Health, Assn. Profs. Gynecology and Obstetrics, Am. Pub. Health Assn., Phi Kappa Phi, Nu Sigma Nu. Avocations: rancher quarter horses, exotic animals, hounds, harleys. Home: Bar T Ranch 20516 Bunker Hill Rd Marengo IL 60152-8003 Office: Ill Masonic Med Ctr 836 W Wellington Ave Chicago IL 60657-9224

BARTON, JOHN MURRAY, artist, appraiser, consultant, lecturer; b. N.Y.C., Feb. 8, 1921; s. Boris and Lena (Sirota) Silver; m. Irene Zevon, Dec. 15, 1945 (div. 1958); 1 child, Leonard Steven; m. Hilda, Jan. 21, 1966; 1 child, Erika Jane. Fine Art degree, Art Students League, 1936, 45; student, Tschacbasov Sch. Creative Art, 1955. Cert. Appraisal Studies in Fine and Decorative Arts, NYU, 1996. Pres. John Barton Assos., Inc., N.Y.C., 1966-85, J.M.B. Pub. Ltd., N.Y.C., 1968-85, Multiple Reprodns. Inc., N.Y.C., 1968-85; appraiser 19th and 20th century prints. One-man shows include Fantasy Gallery, Washington, Hudson Guild, N.Y., Highgate Gallery, N.J., Glassboro State Coll., N.J., Swain Art Gallery, N.J., Fromuth Gallery, Pa., J. Walter Thompson, N.Y.; executed murals Pub. Sch. 41, N.Y., Mid. Sch. 141, N.Y., Carolina State Bank, S.C., U.S. Rubber Co.; represented in collections in Bklyn. Mus., Met. Mus., N.Y., Butler Mus., Ohio, Fort Worth Art Ctr., Tex., Haifa Mus. of Modern Art, Israel, N.Y. Pub. Libr., Newark Pub. Libr., Phila. Mus. Art, Phila., Yale U. Mus., New Haven, N.C. Coll., Durham, U. N.C., Greensboro, Libr. Cong., Washington. Home: 45 Christopher St New York NY 10014-3533 Studio: 92 Grove St New York NY 10014-3548

BARTON, JONATHAN MILLER, clergyman; b. Elizabeth, N.J., June 26, 1952; s. Douglas William and Deborah (Gray) B.; m. Elizabeth Dora Rinehart, May 19, 1985 (div. June 1990); 1 child, Katherine Nicole; m. Elizabeth Wood Stark, July 17, 1994; stepchildren: Liza, Archer Blair. Student, Union Coll., 1970-72; BA in Psychology, Kean Coll., 1974; MDiv, Drew U, 1978. Ordained to ministry Presbyn. Ch., 1981. Asst. chaplain Drew U., Madison, N.J., 1976-78, resident dir., 1977-81; hunger action enabler Elizabeth, Newark, Newton presbyteries United Presbyn. Ch. U.S.A., 1978-82; cons. World Hunger Edn. Svc., Washington, 1983; assoc. regional dir. Ch. World Svc., Rocky Hill, N.J., 1983-85; regional dir. Ch. World Svc., Richmond, Va., 1985—; mem. Nat. IMPACT Briefings, Washington, 1978-84; mem. coord. com. N.J. State Food Conf., 1979; spl. asst. to coord. U.S. Nat. Com. for World Food Day, 1981-83; mem. 4th World Food Issues Conf., Cornell U., 1982; testifier Senate Subcom. on edn., ARts and Humanities, 1982; mem. NGO Com. for UN Internat. Conf. on Population Consultation, 1984, UN/NGO Com. on Food and Rural Devel. Food Forum, 1985, UN/NGO Consultation on African Crisis, 1985; mem. Summer Inst. in Devel. Edn., Tao, N.Mex., 1986; mem. prep. com. for visit Dir.-Gen. UN/FAO on FAO's 50th anniversary commemoration, Washington, 1993; attended US AID Conf. Global Edn., Williamsburg, Va., 1989; mem. Gov.'s Conf. Infant Mortality, Richmond, Va., 1986. Regional editor Va. Steps, Ch. World Svc., 1985—; contbr. articles to various publs. in field. Co-chair grant com. Va. Hands Across Am., 1986; co-founder, chair Madison, N.J. chpt. Amnesty Internat., 1976-80; chair program adv. com. Ch. World Svc., 1987-89; chair Divsn. Mission and Svc., Presbytery of James, 1992-93; bd. dirs. Va. Interfaith Ctr. Pub. Policy, 1987-93; bd. dirs. Direct Ministries, Va. Coun. Chs., 1986—, mem. Va. refugee adv. coun., 1992— ; co-founder, convener Va. Congress on Hunger, 1987—; founding mem. bd. dirs. Va. Hunger Found., 1992—. Recipient C.J. Helen svc. award Miquin Lodge #68, 1967, Virgil honor Order of the Arrow, 1968, Lighthouse award Foodbank S.E. Va., 1993. Mem. Internat. Platform Assn. Office: Church World Svc 1627 Monument Ave Richmond VA 23220-2906

BARTON, KAY G., state official. Student, U. Grenoble, France, 1972; BA in Social Work, U. Ark., 1975, JD, 1983; MSW, U. Ark., Little Rock, 1977, postgrad. Sch. of Law, 1980-82. Law clk. Pettus, Johnson and Gibson, Fayetteville, Ark., 1982-83; law clk. legal dept. Wal-Mart Stores, Inc., Bentonville, Ark., 1983-84; law clk. Davis & Assocs., P.A., Springdale, Ark., 1984, assoc., 1984-86; pvt. practice Springdale, 1986-91; asst. atty. gen. consumer protection divsn. Office of Atty. Gen., Little Rock, 1991-92, dep. atty. gen., consumer counsel of Ark. consumer protection divsn., 1992—, dep. atty. gen., acting dir. Medicaid fraud control unit, 1994, now sr. asst. atty. gen.; adj. prof. criminal justice dept. U. Ark., Little Rock. Recipient Arnold award for trial advocacy. Mem. ABA (Best Performance award), Nat. Assn. Attys. Gen., Ark. Trial Lawyers Assn., Ark. Bar Assn., Ark. Women Lawyers Assn., Phi Beta Kappa, Phi Beta Phi, Zeta Tau Alpha. Office: Attorney General Bldg 323 Center St Ste 200 Little Rock AR 72201-2605*

BARTON, LEWIS, consultant; b. N.Y.C., Mar. 9, 1940; s. Louis and Mary (Mosca) Bologna; m. Barbara Joan Hummell, Sept. 6, 1964; children: Glenn Scott, Gregory Jon. Student, Adelphi U., 1957-59. Sales rep. Olivetti Corp., N.Y.C., 1962-64, W. Ralston Co., Chgo., 1964-65, Milprint Co., N.Y.C., 1965-66; pres., founder Sigma Quality Foods, Farmingdale, N.Y., 1966-88, Sigma Star Food Corp., N.Y.C., 1993-98; pres. Drake & Di Lewis Inc. Consultants; ret.; lectr. various confs. Patentee several package design constructions and methods. With USAF, 1961-62. Named to Pres. Coun. for Ednl. Distinction, Adelphi U. Mem. Nat. Single Svc. Food Assn. (charter, chmn. 1977-79, Svc. award 1982), Assn. Dressings and Sauces, Dwight D. Eisenhower Soc. (founder), Columbus Citizen's Found., Internat. Orgn. Packaging Profls. Home: 45 Sutton Pl S New York NY 10022-2444

BARTON, NANCY SHOVER, nursing administrator; b. Harrisburg, Pa., May 31, 1951; d. Marlin Burd and Zelma Pearl (Schell) Shover; 1 child, Sandra Gehl. Diploma, Ga. Bapt. Hosp. Sch. Nursing, 1972; BSN, Med. Coll. of Ga., 1974, MSN, 1976; cert. in total quality mgmt., Xavier U., 1992. Asst. prof. nursing Hall Sch. of Nursing Brenau Coll., Gainesville, Ga., 1979-83; asst. prof., coord. ADN program Houston Bapt. U., 1984-88; gerontology clin. nurse specialist N.E. Ga. Med. Ctr., Gainesville, 1988-90, nursing quality assurance coord., dir. nursing, profl. practice, 1990-95; dir. clin. mgmt. sys. Med. Ctr. of Ctrl. Ga., Macon, 1995—. Mem. ANA, Ga. Nurses' Assn., Nat. Assn. Healthcare Quality, Nat. Assn. Quality Assurance Profls., Ga. Orgn. Nurse Execs., Sigma Theta Tau.

BARTON, NEAL, JR., meteorologist; b. Beaumont, Tex., May 15, 1959; m. Neal and Mildred(Smith) B.; m. Carra Jo Mathis, Feb. 9, 1985. BS in Comm., Lamar U., 1981. Disc jockey Beaumont, 1979-82; weathercaster KJAC-TV, Beaumont, 1982-84, KTBC-TV, Austin, Tex., 1985; chief weathercaster KTRE-TV, Lufkin, Tex., 1985-86, KTVE-TV, Monroe, La., 1986-89; weekend meteorologist WFAA-TV, Dallas, 1989-95; chief meteorologist KSTW-TV, Seattle, 1995-98; staff Sta. WSMV-TV, Nashville, 1998—. Mem. Am. Meteorol. Soc., Nat. Weather Assn. Republican. Baptist. Avocations: reading, horseback riding, boating, fishing. Office: WSMV-TV PO Box 4 Nashville TN 37202*

BARTON, PETER RICHARD, III, communications executive; b. Washington, Apr. 6, 1951; m. Laura Perry. BA, Columbia U., 1971, MS, 1972; postgrad., Harvard U., 1979, MBA, 1982. Mem. gov's staff State of N.Y., 1975-80; sr. v.p. Tele-Communications Inc., Englewood, Colo., 1982-86; pres. Cable Value Network, Mpls., 1986-88; sr. v.p. Tele-Communications Inc., Englewood, CO, 1988-90; pres. Liberty Media Corp, 1990-97, Barton and Assocs., 1997—.

BARTON, RAYBURN, educational administrator. Exec. dir. Bd. Edn., Boise, Idaho, 1997—. Office: Higher Education Commission 1333 Main St Ste 200 Columbia SC 29201-3201*

BARTON, RAYMOND OSCAR, III, concrete company executive; b. Augusta, Ga., Sept. 30, 1949; s. Raymond Oscar Jr. and Anne Wilcox (Claussen) B.; m. Jane Barbara Tilley, Dec. 28, 1972; 1 child, Todd Jeffrey. BS, USAF Acad., 1972; MS, Troy State U., 1984. Commd. instr. pilot USAF, 1973, advanced through grades to capt., 1984; pilot, instr. USAF, Nellis AFB, Nev., 1983-84; exec. v.p. Claussen Concrete Co., Inc., Augusta, Ga., 1985-88; pres. Claussen Concrete Co., Inc., 1988-89, also bd. dirs.; spl. agt. Northwestern Mut. Life Ins. Co., 1989-91; real estate agt. VIP Realty Svcs., Inc., Augusta, 1991-93; pres. Am. Concrete, Inc., Augusta, 1993—; concrete technologist Nat. Ready-Mixed Concrete Assn., 1986; bd. dirs. Ga. Concrete and Products Assn. Chmn. troop com. Boy Scouts Am., 1991, den leader Webelo coun., 1988-89. Lt. Col. Ga. Air N.G., until 1995. Decorated Commendation medal, Meritorious Svc. medal. Mem. Augusta Country Club. Republican. Episcopalian. Avocations: golf, fishing, hunting. Home: 754 Tripps Ct Augusta GA 30909-1816

BARTON, STANLEY FAULKNER, management consultant; b. Halesowen, Worcestershire, Eng., Dec. 30, 1927; came to U.S., 1957, naturalized, 1963; s. Lazarus and Alice (Faulkner) B.; m. Marion Brittain, Dec. 20, 1952; children: Carolyn Francesca, Andrea Elizabeth. B.Sc. (hons.), U. Birmingham, Eng., 1949; Ph.D., U. Birmingham, 1952. Group leader Naval Rsch. Establishment, Halifax, N.S., Can., 1953-56; project coord. Def. Rsch. Chem. Labs., Ottawa, Ont., Can., 1956-57; devel. engr. Procter & Gamble, Cin., 1957-58; R & D group leader Procter & Gamble, 1958-59, R & D sect. head, 1959-69; tech. dir. food products-natural resources ITT, N.Y.C., 1969-76; sr. v.p. tech. and quality ITT Rayonier, Inc., Stamford, Conn., 1976-90; v.p., dir. Spectrum Internat. Assocs., Inc., Tucson, 1990-92; pres. Catalina Cons., 1990—. Mem. Am. Theater Organ Soc. Home: 4051 N Circulo Manzanillo Tucson AZ 85750-1879 Office: Catalina Cons 4051 N Circulo Manzanillo Tucson AZ 85750-1879

BARTON, THOMAS JACKSON, chemistry educator, researcher; b. Dallas, Nov. 5, 1940; s. Ralph and Florence (Whitfield) B.; m. Elizabeth Burton, Oct. 1, 1966; children—Ralph, Brett. B.S., Lamar U., 1962; Ph.D., U. Fla., 1967. NIH fellow Ohio State U., 1967; mem. faculty Iowa State U., Ames, 1967—, prof. chemistry, 1978—, disting. prof., 1984—, program dir. Ames Lab., 1986-88, dir. Ames Lab, 1988—, dir. Inst. for Phys. Rsch. and Tech., 1998—; NAS exch. scientist USSR, 1975; assoc. prof. U. Montpellier, France, 1983; mem. coun. on materials scis. Dept. Energy, 1992-97. Contbr. research papers to profl. publs. Recipient Fredric Stanley Kipping award in organosilicon chemistry, 1982; Gov.'s Medal for sci. teaching, 1983, Excellence in Teaching faculty achievement award Burlington No. Found., 1988, Outstanding Sci. Accomplishment in Materials Chem., Dept. Energy Materials Scis. Divsn., 1989. Fellow Japan Soc. Promotion of Sci., 1981; mem. Am. Chem. Soc. (Midwest award 1995). Methodist. Home: 815 Onyx Cir Ames IA 50010-8429 Office: Iowa State Univ Dept Chemistry Ames IA 50011

BARTON, TINA ROXANNE, technical information specialist, writer; b. Palmer, Tenn., May 14, 1962; d. Kenneth Edward and Esther Irene Nunley; m. Gary Bryant Barton, Nov. 20, 1993; 1 child, Logan Elliot Haynes. AS magna cum laude, Motlow State C.C., 1995; BBA in Mktg./Mgmt. cum laude, Cumberland U., 1999. Cert. profl. sec. Elem. sch. tchr. Tracy City (Tenn.) Elem., 1984-90; teller, bookkeeper Franklin County Bank, Winchester, Tenn., 1989-90; sec. Otey Meml. Parish, Sewanee, Tenn., 1990, Tenn. Dept,. Human Svcs., Tracy City, 1990-92; admissions asst. U. South, Sewanee, 1992-93; tech. info. specialist Sverdrup Tech., Arnold AFB, 1993—; owner TTT Temp. Svcs., 1992-94. Area mgr., troop leader, vol. Moccasin Bend coun. Girl Scouts Am., Chattanooga, 1985-91; treas. Grundy County Dem. Party, Tracy City, Tenn., 1985-91; active Methodist Ch., pub. newsletter. Mem. NAFE, Soc. Profl. Journalists, Soc. Aerospace Communicators, Mountain Optimist Club (v.p., pres. 1989-92). Avocations: reading, music, outdoor recreation, photography. E-mail: Tina.Barton@arnold.af.mil.

BARTON, WILLIAM RUSSELL, government official; b. Detroit, Aug. 18, 1925; s. Richard and Dorothy (Miller) B.; m. Helen Ann Wilkes, Sept. 18, 1955; children: James Richard, Ann Elizabeth. B.A., Mich. State U., 1952. Spl. agt. U.S. Secret Service, 1953-64; spl. agt. in charge U.S. Secret Service, Milw., 1964-70; Hdqrs. mgr. U.S. Secret Service, Washington, 1970-78; spl. agt. in charge U.S. Secret Service, Los Angeles, 1978-79; asst. to dir. U.S. Secret Service, Washington, 1979-82, dep. dir., 1982-85; inspector gen. Gen. Services Adminstrn., 1985—. Served to sgt. USMC, 1943-45, PTO. Mem. Fed. Investigators Assn., Internat. Chiefs of Police, Fed. Exec. Inst. Alumni Assn., Nat. Sheriff's Assn. Republican. Methodist. Office: Gen Svcs Adminstrn 18th & F St NW Rm 5340 Washington DC 20405-0002

BARTON-COLLINGS, NELDA ANN, political activist, newspaper, bank and nursing home executive; b. Providence, Ky., May 12, 1929; m. Harold Bryan Barton, May 11, 1951 (dec. Nov. 1977); children: William Grant (dec.), Barbara Lynn, Harold Bryan, Stephen Lambert, Suzanne; m. Jack C. Collings, Mar. 28, 1992. Student, Western Ky. U., 1947-49; grad., Norton Meml. Infirmary Sch. Med. Tech., 1950; student, Cumberland Coll., 1978, LLD (hon.), 1991. Lic. nursing home adminstr.; registered med. technician. Pres. Barton & Assocs. Inc., Corbin, Ky., 1977—, Hazard Nursing Home Inc., Ky., 1977-97, Health Sys. Inc., Corbin, 1978-97, Corbin Nursing Home Inc., 1978-97, Williamsburg Nursing Home, Inc., 1978-98; pres. Key Distbg. Inc., 1980—, pres., chmn. bd., 1981-97; pres., chmn. bd. The Whitley Whiz Inc., Williamsburg, 1983-97; chmn. bd. dirs. Tri-County Nat. Bank., 1985-97, Harlan Nursing Home, Inc., 1986, Knott Co. Nursing Home, Inc., 1986; pres. Tri-County Bancorp, Inc., 1987—; chmn. bd. Instl. Pharmacy, Corbin, Ky., 1990—; pres., chmn. bd. Wolfe County Health Care Ctr., 1990; mem. exec. com. Corbin Deposit Bank, 1982-84; bd. dirs. Greensburg (Ky.) Deposit Bank, Williamsburg (Ky.) Nat. Bank, Campbellsville Nat. Bank,

McCreary Nat. Bank, Tri County Nat. Bank, Somerset Nat. Bank, Laurel Nat. Bank; chmn., organizer, dir. Green County Bancorp Inc., 1987—; organizer, dir. Laurel Nat. Bank, 1996—; mem. nat. adv. com. SBA, 1990-92; active Nat. Policy Forum, 1994—. Mem. Fedn. Coun. on Aging, 1982-87; bd. dirs. Leadership Ky., 1984-88, adv. com., 1987—; bd. dirs. Cumberland Coll. Found., 1995, mem. devel. bd., 1981—; v.p. Southeastern Ky. Rehab. Com., 1981-93; mem. Fair Housing Task Force, Corbin, 1981-84, Ky. Mansions Preservation Found. Inc., Corbin Comty. Devel. Com., 1970-83; cub scout den mother, 1965-67; pres. Corbin Cen. Elem PTA, 1963-65; vice chmn. 9th dist. PTA, 1958-59; Rep. nat. committeewoman for Ky., 1968-96, sec., 1993-96; vice-chmn. Rep. Nat. Com., 1984-93; sec.-treas. Nat. Rep. Inst. Internat. Affairs, 1984-86; active numerous other polit. orgns. Recipient Ky. Woman of Achievement award Ky. Bus. and Profl. Women, 1983, Recognition award Joint Rep. Leadership, U.S. Congress, Dwight David Eisenhower award, 1970, John Sherman Cooper Disting. Svc. award Ky. Young Reps. Fedn., 1987, Outstanding Layperson award Ky. Med. Assn., 1992, Nelda Barton Comty. Svc. award Ky. Assn. Health Care Facilities, 1992, 5th Dist. Rep. Party Recognition award, 1996, Tribute to Nelda Barton-Collings Rep. Party of Ky. and 5th Dist. Lincoln Club, 1997; Nelda Barton Collings Rep. internship award established by Rep. Party of Ky., 1997, Jefferson Co. Ky. Office for Women Hall of Fame, 1999, Ky. State Senate Cert. for Outstanding Women in Bus. and Leadership, 1999; named Ky. Col., 1968, Ky. Rep. Woman of Yr., Ky. Fedn. Rep. Women, 1969; named to 5th Dist. Lincoln Club Hall of Fame, 1996; Nelda Barton Day proclaimed by Mayor of Corbin, 1973; Western Ky. U. Acad. scholar, 1947-49. Mem. Am. Coll. Nursing Home Adminstrs., Ky. Assn. Health Care Facilities (legis. com. 1980-97), Ky. Assn. Nursing Home Adminstrs. (bd. dirs., polit. action com. 1979—), Ky. Med. Aux. (chmn. health edn. com. 1975-77), Ky. Commn. on Women, Women's Aux. So. Med. Assn. (Ky. counselor), Whitley County Med. Aux. (pres. 1959-60), Aux. Ky. Med. Assn., Ky. Mothers Assn. (parliamentarian 1970—, hon. Mother of Ky. award 1983), Ky. C. of C. (bd. dirs. 1983—, v.p. Region 5 1985—, 1st vice chmn. 1989, chmn. 1990-91). Avocations: fishing, oil painting. Home: 1311 7th Street Rd Corbin KY 40701-2207 Office: Health Systems Inc PO Box 1450 Corbin KY 40702-1450

BARTOO, RICHARD KIETH, chemical engineer, consultant; b. Potter County, Pa., June 3, 1938; s. Raymond Eldon and Norma Grace (Butler) B.; m. Nancy Jo Hoebler, Oct. 15, 1988 (div.); children: Scott Lee, Roy Keith; m. Barbara A. Wilber, Oct. 13, 1995. BS in Chem. Engring., Carnegie Inst. Tech., 1962; MS in Chem. Engring., Carnegie Mellon U., 1972. Process engr. Atlas Chem. Industries, Wilmington, Del., 1962-64, Central Romana By-Products Co., La Romana, Dominican Republic, 1964-66; process engr. rsch. div. Consol Coal Co., Library, Pa., 1966-68; pilot plant engr. The Benfield Corp., Mt. Lebanon, Pa., 1968-72, sr. process engr., 1972-81; sr. process engr. Union Carbide Corp. (now UOP), Tarrytown, N.Y., 1989-95; sr. process engr. Union Carbide Corp. (now UOP), Des Plaines, Ill., 1995-99, ret., 1999. Contbr. chpts. to books, articles to profl. jours. Mem. AIChE. Methodist. Achievements include design, consulting on operation and troubleshooting acid gas scrubbing processes, including a chemical process called "Hot Potassium Carbonate Process," or Benfield Process used for removal of CO2 and H2S from industrial gas streams.

BARTOS, JERRY GARLAND, corporate executive, mechanical engineer; b. Dallas, Feb. 5, 1933; s. Vladimir Thomas and Ella Marie (Rezek) B; m. Marlene Louise Buehrer, Sept. 25, 1954 (div. 1978); children: Marla Jeanette, Sara Jane, Julie Ann; m. Candye Laverna Gould, Feb. 24, 1979; 1 child, Mary Meghan. BSME, So. Meth. U., 1954. Registered profl. engr., Tex., Mont. Sales engr. Trane Co., Dallas, 1957-61; asst. v.p. Trane Co., LaCrosse, Wis., 1961-62; chief engr. Linskie Co., Dallas, 1962-64; pres. Bartos, Inc., Dallas, 1964—; Hon. Consul Czech Republic for North Tex., 1996—. Contbr. articles to profl. jours. Mem. Dallas City Coun., 1987—; chmn. Clean Dallas, Inc., 1974, Greater Dallas Planning Coun., 1986, pres., 1984-86; bd. dirs. Dallas Ind. Sch. Dist., 1979-81; pres. North Dallas C. of C., 1975-76; hon. consul Czech Republic for North Tex., 1995—. Recipient Speakers-Authors award Am. Air Filter Co., 1972, Svc. award Luth. Ch., 1975, Life Mem. award State PTA, 1976, Rotarian award, 1993; Paul Harris fellow, 1993. Mem. Am. Soc. HVAC Engrs. (life, chair com. Dallas chpt. 1957—), Tex. Soc. Profl. Engrs., U.S. C. of C. (founder, regional chair small bus. orgn. 1978-79), Dallas C. of C. (vice chmn. 1976-77), North Dallas C. of C. (pres. 1975-76, chmn. 1976), Small Businessmen Assn. (Small Businessman of Yr. award 1974). Republican. Office: Bartos Inc 3239 Oradell Ln Dallas TX 75220-6040

BARTOSIC, FLORIAN, lawyer, arbitrator, educator; b. Danville, Pa., Sept. 15, 1926; s. Florian W. and Elsie (Woodring) B.; m. Eileen M. Payne, 1952 (div. 1969); children: Florian, Ellen, Thomas, Stephen; m. Alberta C. Chew, 1990. B.A., Pontifical Coll., 1948; B.C.L., Coll. William and Mary, 1956; LL.M., Yale U., 1957. Bar: Va. 1956, U.S. Supreme Ct. 1959. Asst. instr. Yale U., 1956-57; assoc. prof. law Coll. William and Mary, 1957, Villanova U., 1957-59; atty. NLRB, Washington, 1956, 57, 59; counsel Internat. Brotherhood of Teamsters, Washington, 1959-71; prof. law Wayne State U., 1971-80, U. Calif., Davis, 1980-92; recalled to tchg., 1994—; prof. emeritus law U. Calif., Davis, 1993—, dean law, 1980-90; adj. prof. George Washington U., 1966-71, Cath. U. Am., 1960-71; mem. panel arbitrators Fed. Mediation and Conciliation Service, 1972—; hearing officer Mich. Employment Relations Commn., 1972-80, Mich. Civil Rights Commn., 1974-80; bd. dirs. Mich. Legal Services Corp., 1973-80, Inst. Labor and Indsl. Relations, U. Mich., Wayne State U., 1976-80; mem. steering com. Inst. on Global Conflict and Cooperation, 1982-83; mem. adv. bd. Assn. for Union Democracy Inc., 1980—, adv. coms. Calif. Jud. Council, 1984-85, 87; vis. scholar Harvard Law Sch., 1987, Stanford Law Sch., 1987; sr. rsch. scholar ILO, 1990-91; acad. visitor Oxford U., London Sch. Econs., 1991; mem. exec. bd. Pub. Interest Clearinghouse, 1988-90. Co-author: Labor Relations Law in the Private Sector, 1977, 2d edit., 1986; contbr. articles to law jours. Mem. ABA (sec. labor relations law sect. 1974-75), Fed. Bar Assn., Am. Law Inst. (acad. mem. labor law adv. com. on continuing profl. edn.), Soc. Profls. in Dispute Resolution (regional v.p. 1979-80), Indsl. Rels. Rsch. Assn., Internat. Soc. Labor Law and Social Legis., Internat. Indsl. Rels. Assn., Am. Arbitration Assn. (panel), Nat Lawyers Guild, ACLU (dir. Detroit chpt. 1976-77), Order of Coif (hon.), Scribes. Home: 235 Ipanema Pl Davis CA 95616-0253 Office: U Calif Sch Law Mrak Hall Dr Davis CA 95616

BARTOW, BARBARA JENÉ, university program administrator; b. Buffalo, June 26, 1950; d. Nicholas Michael Bojack and Lillian Lenore Bennett; m. Michael Hartzell Bartow; children: Barbara Simmons, Edward Michael Hagen. AA in Journalism, Miami Dade Jr. Coll., 1990; M. in Non-fiction Writing, USAF Air U., 1990, M. Adminstrn. Auto. mechanic Amoco, Miami, Fla., 1969-70; cargo dispatcher McKinley Transport Worldwide, Ont., Can., 1970-72; office adminstr. Modernage Furniture, Miami, 1972-74; social svc. rep. Vets. Adminstrn. and DAV and Am. Legion, 1976—; commdr. DAV and Am. Legion, 1985-86; deputy chief of staff DAV, 1986. Contbr. poetry to World of Poetry, Internat. Soc. Poets, Internat. Libr. of Poetry, Libr. of Congress, 1990—. Active crisis intervention CASA, Fla., 1984-86; foster parent DCFS, Ill.; Dem. polit. activist, Ill., Fla., N.Y., Pa., 1976—. Sgt USAF, 1974-82. Recipient citation of merit DAV, Fla., 1985. Roman Catholic. Avocations: writing, social work, wheelchair racing. Home: 1515 Lantern Ln Joliet IL 60433-2910

BARTRAM, RALPH HERBERT, physicist; b. N.Y.C., Aug. 16, 1929; s. Herbert L. and Grace L. Bartram; m. Ellen Anderson Devlin, Oct. 9, 1953; children: Ellen Ruth, Robert Arthur. Student, Northwestern U., 1948-49; BA cum laude, NYU, 1953, MS, 1956, PhD, 1960. Engr. Sylvania Electric Products Inc., Kew Gardens, N.Y., 1953-56; advanced rsch. physicist Gen. Telephone & Electronics Labs., Inc., Bayside, N.Y., 1956-61, cons., 1961-85; mem. faculty U. Conn., Storrs, 1961—, prof. physics, 1971-92, dept. head, 1986-92, prof. emeritus, 1992—; rsch. assoc. Atomic Energy Rsch. Establishment, Harwell, Eng., 1967-68; vis. prof. U. Oxford, Eng., 1978; sr. vis. fellow U. Strathclyde, Scotland, 1993; cons. U.S. Army, 1966-71, Am. Optical Co., 1966-78, Brookhaven Nat. Lab., 1971-85, Timex Corp., 1981-82, Polaroid Corp., 1987-88, Boston U., 1993—, ALEM Assocs., 1996—. Author: (with J.-M. Spaeth and J.R. Niklas) Structural Analysis of Point Defects in Solids, 1992; contbr. articles on physics to profl. jours.; patentee microwave devices. Served with USN, 1946-48. Grantee U.S. AEC, 1963-69, U.S. Army Rsch. Office, 1971-78, 82-92, NSF, 1974-77, 83-91, NATO, 1985-90. Fellow Am. Phys. Soc.; mem. Optical Soc. Am., AAAS, AAUP, Conn. Acad. Sci. Engring., Phi Beta Kappa, Sigma Xi, Phi Kappa Phi, Sigma Pi Sigma, Phi Eta Sigma. Home: 67 Independence Dr Mansfield Center CT 06250-1541 Office: U Conn Dept Physics Storrs Mansfield CT 06269

BARTREM, DUANE HARVEY, retired military officer, designer, building consultant; b. Lansing, Mich., June 4, 1928; s. Harvey Theodore and Ruby Leola (Thomas) B.; m. Frances Lillie Bushee, Sept. 12, 1948; children: Lawrence Duane, Jeffrey Earl. BA in Bus. Adminstrn., Columbia Coll., Mo., 1976. Enlisted U.S. Army N.G., Lansing, 1948, commd. 2d lt., 1951, advanced through grades to col., 1951-76, comdr. battery, 1956-60; facilities engr. Mich. Nat. Guard, Lansing, 1960-69; chief engr. Mich. Nat. Guard, Lansing, Mich., 1969-76; comdr. 119 FA Bn. Mich. Nat. Guard, Lansing, 1971-75, comdr. 46th Brigade, 1975-76, comptr., 1976-83, ret., 1983; prin. residential design office Lansing, 1955-60, Grand Ledge, Mich., 1967—. Chmn. congregation Bretton Woods Covenant Ch., 1986-89, vice chmn., 1995-97; scout leader local and regional levels Boy Scouts Am. With USNR, 1946-48. Decorated Army Commendation with 3 clusters, Meritorious Svc. medal with 2 clusters, Legion of Merit. Mem. Retired Officers Assn., Assn. of the U.S. Army (mem. resolutions com. 1973, 74, chair resolutions com. 1975, area v.p. 1976—, mem. adv. bd. 1978—, chair by-laws com. 1978—, past state pres., past region pres. 1988-92, coun. of trustees 1992-96, Pres.'s medal 1998), Grand Lodge Rotary (pres. 1989-90, Paul Harris award 1992), Chief Okemos Coun. Boy Scouts Am. (pres. 1973-79, exec. bd. 1970—; disting. Eagle Scout 1989, Silver Beaver award 1969, Silver Antelope 1983, God and Svc. award 1992, James E. West fellow). Protestant. Avocation: golf.

BARTTER, BRIT JEFFREY, investment banker; b. Berea, Ohio, Dec. 27, 1949; s. Lynn Martin Bartter and Scharlie Ellen (Watson) Handlan; m. Marilyn McCullough, Aug. 25, 1973; children: Bryndl Lynn and Blake McCullough (twins). AB in Econs., Duke U., 1972; MS in Fin., Cornell U., 1976, PhD in Fin., 1977. Asst. prof. computer sci. Grad. Sch. Bus. Cornell U., Ithaca, N.Y., 1976; asst. prof. fin. Grad. Sch. Mgmt. Kellogg Grad. Sch. Mgmt., Northwestern U., Evanston, Ill., 1977-79; assoc., then v.p. Merrill Lynch Capital Markets, Chgo., 1979-83; v.p. The First Boston Corp., Chgo., 1983-87, dir., 1988-89, mng. dir., 1989-94; mng. dir. Merrill, Lynch Investment Banking, Chgo., 1995—; bd. dirs. Coun. for Young Profls., Chgo., 1985-87. Contbr. articles to Jour. of Fin., Fin. Mgmt. Bd. dirs. Cornell Coun. Chgo., 1987-88, Duke Campaign Chgo., 1987-88; mem. governing bd. Chgo. Symphony Orch. Mem. Econ. Club Chgo., Northwestern U. Assocs., Glen View Golf Club, Chgo. Club. Home: 221 Apple Tree Rd Winnetka IL 60093-3703 Office: Merrill Lynch Investment Bkng 5500 Sears Tower Chicago IL 60606

BARTUNEK, JAMES SCOTT, psychiatrist; b. Flint, Mich., Oct. 20, 1962; s. Steven James and Frances Annabelle (Peters) B.; m. Carol Lynn Tobis, Feb. 26, 1994; 1 child, Rebecca. BS, U. Mich., Flint, 1985; MD, Wayne State U., 1989. Resident in psychiatry Sinai Hosp. Detroit, 1989-92; mem. staff Crittenton Hosp., Rochester, Mich., 1993—. Mem. Am. Psychiat. Assn., Founder's Soc. Detroit Inst. Arts, U. Mich. Club, Wayne State U. Med. Alumni Club. Avocations: reading, sports, travel, Shakespearean theater. Home: 3541 Hidden Forest Ct Orion MI 48359-1477 Office: 1460 Walton Blvd Ste 215 Rochester Hills MI 48309

BARTUNEK, KENNETH STEVEN, finance educator; b. Flint, Mich., May 11, 1965; s. Steven James and Frances Annabelle (Peters) B. Student, U.S. Naval Acad., 1983; BS in Math., U. Mich., Flint, 1987; PhD in Bus. Adminstrn., La. State U., 1991; MS in Fin. Math., U. Chgo., 1998. Chemistry rsch. asst. U. Mich., Flint, 1984; intern Mich. Bell Telephone, Detroit, 1987; instr. fin. La. State U., Baton Rouge, 1991; asst. prof. fin. Fla. Atlantic U., Boca Raton, 1991-97, assoc. prof. fin., 1997—. Mem. Art Inst. of Chgo. Branstrom scholar U. Mich., Ann Arbor, 1984, James B. Angell scholar, 1985-87; La. State U. Alumni Fedn. fellow, 1987-91; recipient Am. Legion award, 1983, Bausch and Lomb Sci. award, 1983, Best of Class award GM 1983. Mem. Internat. Platform Assn., Am. Fin. Assn., So. Fin. Assn., Ea. Fin. Assn., Phi Kappa Phi, Beta Gamma Sigma. Roman Catholic. Avocations: exercising, travel. Home: Apt 0-209 2950 Olivewood Ter Boca Raton FL 33431 Office: Fla Atlantic U Dept Fin PO Box 3091 Boca Raton FL 33431-0991

BARTUNEK, ROBERT R(ICHARD), JR., lawyer; b. Cleve., July 2, 1946; s. Robert Richard and Clare Elizabeth (Lonsway) B.; 1 child, Kathryn Elizabeth. BS, Bucknell U., 1968; MBA, Ohio State U., 1974, JD, 1975; LLM, U. Mo., Kansas City, 1986. Bar: Mo. 1975, Kans. 1997, U.S. Dist. Ct. (we. dist.) Mo. 1975, U.S. Tax Ct. 1981, U.S. Dist. Ct. Kans. 1997. Ptnr. Beckett, Lolli & Bartunek, Kansas City, 1975-96, Swanson, Midgley, Gangwere, Kitchin & McLarney, Kansas City, 1997—. Mem. Men's Sr. Baseball League. Decorated Bronze Star. Mem. ABA, Lawyers Assn. Greater Kansas City, Kansas City Met. Bar Assn. (chmn. tax law com.). Roman Catholic. Home: 608 W Dartmouth Rd Kansas City MO 64113-2029 Office: Swanson Midgley Gangwere Kitchin & McLarney 922 Walnut 1500 Commerce Trust Bldg Kansas City MO 64106

BARTUS, RAYMOND THOMAS, neuroscientist, pharmaceutical executive, writer; b. Chgo., May 19, 1947; s. Frank A. and Katherine (Bogus) B.; m. Cheryl Marie Gyure, Feb. 11, 1967; children: Raymond T., Kristin Marie. B.A., California State U. Pa., 1968; M.S., N.C. State U., 1970, Ph.D., 1972. NRC postdoctoral fellow, research assoc. Naval Med. Rsch. Lab., Groton, Conn., 1972; scientist Parke-Davis Rsch. Labs., Ann Arbor, Mich., 1973-75, sr. scientist, 1975-78; sr. scientist Lederle Labs., Am. Cyanamid Co., Pearl River, N.Y., 1978-79, group leader neuroscience, dir. geriatric discovery program, 1979-88; sr. v.p. R & D, chief sci. officer Cortex Pharms. Inc., Irvine, Calif., 1988-91, interim pres., 1990, exec. v.p., chief oper. officer, 1991-92; chief sci. officer Cortex Pharms. Inc., Irvine, 1988-92; also bd. dirs. Cortex Pharms. Inc., Irvine, Calif.; sr. v.p. neurobiology Alkermes Inc., Cambridge, Mass., 1992-96, sr. v.p. preclin. R&D, 1996—; prof. NYU Med. Ctr., 1979-94; adj. prof. U. Calif., Irvine, 1988-92, Tulane U., 1978-87, Tufts U., 1992—; cons. in field. Editor-in-chief, founder, Neurobiology of Aging, 1980-89; contbr. articles on neurosci. to profl. jours. Mem. Alzheimers Assn. (sci. med. bd. 1986-92), Soc. Neurosci., Am. Coll. Neuropsychopharm., N.Y. Acad. Sci., Brain Tumor Soc., Am. Assn. Pharm. Sci. E-mail: rtbartus@alkermes.com. Office: Alkermes Inc 64 Sidney St Cambridge MA 02139-4170

BARTZ, CAROL, software company executive; b. Alma, Wis., Aug. 29, 1948; m. William Marr; 1 child. BS in Computer Sci. with honors, U. Wis., 1971; DSc (hon.), Worcester Poly. Inst.; LittD (hon.), William Woods U. With sales mgmt. dept. 3M Corp., Digital Equipment Corp., 1976-83; mgr. customer mktg. Sun Microsys., 1983-84, v.p. mktg., 1984-87, v.p. customer svc., 1987-90, v.p. worldwide field ops., exec. officer, 1990-92; chmn. bd., CEO Autodesk, Inc., San Rafael, Calif., 1992—; pres. Sun Fed., from 1987; bd. dirs. AirTouch Comm., Bea Sys., Cadence Design Sys., Cisco Sys., Inc.; mem. President's Export Coun., 1994; adv. coun. bus. sch. Stanford U. Bd. dirs. U. Wis. Sch. Bus., Nat. Breast Cancer Rsch. Found., Found. for Nat. Medals Sci. and Tech.; mem. adv. coun. Stanford U. Bus. Sch.; mem. Com. of 200; adv. for women's health issues; former mem. Ark. of Gov.'s Econ. Summit, Little Rock. Recipient Donald C. Burnham Mfg. Mgmt. award Soc. Mfg. Engrs., 1994. Mem. Calif. C. of C. (bd. dirs.). Avocations: gardening, tennis. Office: Autodesk Inc 111 Mcinnis Pkwy San Rafael CA 94903-2700*

BARTZ, WILLIAM WALTER, musician; b. Huntsville, Ala., Aug. 9, 1959; s. Rudolph Carl and Marjorie Ann (Caddy) B. AA, Black Hawk, 1985; BA, St. Ambrose, 1988. Freelance copywriter Moline, Ill., 1987-89; copywriter WPXR/WKBF, Rock Island, Ill., 1988-89; creative svcs. dir. WOC/KUUL, Davenport, Iowa, 1989-95; mgr. Menards, Joliet, Ill., 1996-97; CEO Visions, Joliet, 199697, Walgreens, Joliet, Ill., 1997. Recipient Phi Theta Kappa nomination Black Hawk Coll., 1984. Mem. Greek Orthodox Ch. Avocations: reading, exercise, songwriting, writing. Address: PO Box 4012 Joliet IL 60434-4012 Office: 1514 Essington Rd Joliet IL 60435-2866

BARUCH, EDUARD, management consultant; b. Bklyn., Dec. 19, 1907; s. Emile and Grace (Willis) B.; m. Dorothy Hurd, Sept. 8, 1934 (dec. Aug. 1994); 1 child, Hurd; m. Malyn Crusius, Feb. 9, 1996. Student, Rhenania Coll., Switzerland, 1924-26; AB, Columbia U., 1930; postgrad., Law Sch., 1933. Trust adminstr. spl. loan div. Irving Trust Co., N.Y.C., 1933-39; sales exec. Bankers Life Co., Des Moines, 1939-42; v.p. charge sales James H. Rhodes & Co., 1942-47; nat. sales mgr. vending div. Pepsi Cola Co., 1947-49; v.p. Heli-Coil Corp., Danbury, Conn., 1949-55; exec. v.p. Heli-Coil Corp., 1955-56, pres., 1956-70; indsl. commr. State Conn., 1973-75; corp. cons., 1970—; exec. com., mem. bd. Barden Corp. (acquired by F.A.G. Schinefert Germany), Danbury, Conn.; bd. dirs. Savs. Bank, Danbury. Mem. Soc. Automotive Engrs., Rotary (past pres., Paul Harris fellow), Masons, Shriners, Jesters, KT (Bridgeport, Conn.), Princeton U. Club, Wings Club (N.Y.C.), Ridgewood Country Club (Danbury), Coral Ridge Yacht Club (gov.), Tower Club, Lago Mar Beach and Tennis Club, Navy League (Ft. Lauderdale), Danbury Hosp. Pres. Coun., Psi Upsilon, Phi Delta Phi. Presbyterian. Home (winter): 936 Intracoastal Dr Fort Lauderdale FL 33304-3640 also (summer): 936 Intracoastal Dr Fort Lauderdale FL 33304-3640 Office: 57 North St Danbury CT 06810-5660 *I learned from yesterday, it is past. Today is my gift to use - it is a present.Both will prepare me for tomorrow, the future.*

BARUCH, HURD, lawyer, arbitrator; b. N.Y.C., Nov. 29, 1937; s. Eduard and Dorothy (Hurd) B.; m. Mary Ellen Kinney, July 8, 1964; children: Edward, Michael, Amy. BA, Hamilton Coll., 1957; LLB, Yale U., 1960; MBA, Columbia U., 1961. Bar: Conn. 1960, N.Y. 1966, D.C. 1971, Pa. 1972, Ill. 1988, U.S. Supreme Ct. 1964. Ptnr. Winston & Strawn, Chgo.; spl. counsel divsn. trading and markets, SEC, 1969-72. Author: Wall Street Security Risk, 1971. Capt. USAFR, 1961-64. Mem. Ill. State Bar Assn., D.C. Bar, KM, Order of Coif, Phi Beta Kappa, Beta Gamma Sigma. Office: Winston & Strawn 35 W Wacker Dr Ste 4200 Chicago IL 60601-1695

BARUCH, JORDAN JAY, management consultant; b. N.Y.C., Aug. 21, 1923; s. Solomon L. and Minnie (Kessner) B.; m. Rhoda Wasserman, June 3, 1944; children: Roberta, Marjory, Lawrence. B.S., Mass. Inst. Tech., 1948, M.S., 1948, Sc.D., 1950. V.p., dir. Bolt, Beranek & Newman, Inc., Cambridge, Mass., 1949-66; dir. Bolt, Beranek & Newman, Inc., 1949-77, Boston Broadcasters, 1963-77, 81-83; dir. Inst. for Mental Health Initiatives, 1982—, treas., 1982-98; dir. Gould Corp., 1985-88, Baupost Group, 1984-98, Navigation Scis. Inc., 1984-86; asst. prof. elec. engring. MIT, 1950-53, lectr., 1954-70; lectr. bus. adminstrn. grad. sch. bus. adminstrn. Harvard U., 1970-74; prof. Amos Tuck Sch. Bus. Adminstrn., Thayer Sch. Engring., Dartmouth Coll., Hanover, N.H., 1974-77; asst. sec. sci. and tech. Dept. Commerce, 1977-81; pres. Jordan Baruch Assocs., 1981—; mem. bd. sci. and tech. for internat. devel. Nat. Rsch. Coun.; advisor to U.S./Israel Hightech Commn.; founder Nat. Ctr. Indsl. Sci. & Tech., Dalian, China; founder, U.S. advisor U.S./Israel Bianational Indsl. R&D Found., 1978—; regent Nat. Libr. Medicine, 1998—. Contbr. articles to books and profl. jours. Bd. dirs. Inst. Mental Health Initiatives. Served with AUS, 1942-46. Named Outstanding Young Elec. Engr. Eta Kappa Nu, 1956. Fellow Acoustical Soc. Am., IEEE, AAAS, Nat. Acad. Engring., Am. Acad. Arts and Scis. Patentee loudspeakers, acoustical treatments, automotive mufflers. Home and Office: 2700 Chesapeake St NW Washington DC 20008-1042

BARUCH, MONICA LOBO-FILHO, psychological counselor; b. Rio de Janeiro, Jan. 11, 1954; d. Max and Margot Lobo-Filho; m. Robert Karl Baruch, Dec. 30, 1973 (div. May 1985). BA in Psychology, U. Rochester, 1975; MA in Counseling Edn., U. Mo., Kansas City, 1978. Cert. Nat. Bd. Cert. Counselors. Tchr. curriculum devel. St. Patrick's Sch., Rio de Janeiro, 1974-76; tchr., soccer coach Pembroke Country Day Sch., Kansas City, Mo., 1977-78; tchr., trainer Berlitz Sch. Langs., Kansas City and Washington, 1976-79; counselor, cons. Youth Understanding, Washington, 1979-81; pvt. practice, 1981—; academic faculty counselor Georgetown U., Washington, 1982-90; newsletter editor, mem. exec. bd. Greater Washington Coalition of Mental Health Profls. and Consumers, 1996—. Co-author: Weight Control: A Guide for Counselors and Therapists, 1987. Named one of Outstanding Young Women in Am., 1981. Mem. ACA, Am. Mental Health Counselors Assn., Multiple Personality Study Group, Md. Mental Health Counselors Assn. (program chmn. 1989, exec. bd. 1993, sec. 1996—, chairperson profl. practice devel. 1996—), Md. Assn. Counseling and Devel. (ethics com. 1990). Avocations: tennis, studying, volunteering.

BARUCH, RALPH M., communications executive; came to U.S., 1940, naturalized, 1944; s. Bernard and Alice B.; m. Jean Ursell de Mountford, June 9, 1963; children by previous marriage: Eve, Renee, Alice, Michele. Student, Sorbonne, U. Paris. Account exec. SESAC, 1947-50, Dumont TV, 1950-54; Eastern Sales mgr. Enterprises, N.Y.C., 1954-59; v.p. internat. sales Eastern Sales mgr. Enterprises, 1959-67, v.p., gen. mgr., 1967-70; group pres. CBS, 1970-71; pres., chief exec. officer Viacom Internat. Inc., N.Y.C., 1971-78; chmn. bd., mem. office of chief exec. Viacom Internat. Inc., 1979-87; sr. fellow Gannett Ctr. for Media Studies Columbia U., 1988; bd. dirs. Orange and Rockland Utilities; cons. Adv. Commn. on Comm., USIA, 1979-86. Bd. dirs., mem. exec. com. Internat. Rescue Com., N.Y.C., 1975-88, vice chmn.; mem. President's Coun. for Internat. Youth Exch., 1982; trustee Mus. TV and Radio, Carnegie Hall, Lenox Hill Hosp., 1980—; advisor N.Y.C. Mayor's Coun. on Cultural Affairs, 1994. Bd. dirs. exec. com. Interant. Rescue Com., N.Y.C., 1975-88, vice chmn.; mem. Pres.'s Coun. for Internat. Youth Exchange, 1982; trustee Mus. of TV & Radio, Carnegie Hall, Lenox Hill Hosp., 1980-94, Thirteen-WNET; adv. Mayor's Coun. on Cultural Affairs, N.Y.C., 1994; vice-chmn. Carnegie Hall. Fellow Internat. Council TV Acad. Arts and Scis. (pres. 1973-76, 85-87, dir. 1976—); mem. Internat. Radio and TV Soc. (pres. co-chmn. minority placement com., pres., past pres. Found.), Nat. Acad. Cable Programming (chmn. emeritus), Nat. Assn. Broadcasters (task force on pub. broadcasting, chmn. program producers and distbrs. com.), Cable TV Edn. Found. (chmn.). Office: Viacom Inc 1633 Broadway New York NY 10019-6708

BARUSCH, LAWRENCE ROOS, lawyer; b. Oakland, Calif., Aug. 23, 1949; s. Maurice Radston and Phyllis (Roos) B.; m. Susan Amanda Smith, Aug. 7, 1983; children: Nathaniel M., Ariana G. BA summa cum laude, Harvard U., 1971, JD cum laude, 1975. Bar: Calif. 1975. Assoc. Cotton, Seligman & Ray, San Francisco, 1975-77; gen. counsel Jones & Guerrero Co., Inc., Agana, Guam, 1977-82; ptnr. Klemm, Blair & Barusch, P.C., Agana, Guam, 1982-85; assoc. Davis, Graham & Stubbs, Salt Lake City, 1986-87; counsel Parsons, Behl & Latimer, Salt Lake City, 1987-89, shareholder, 1989—; counsel Guam Tax Code Commn., 1990-94; adj. prof. U. Utah Coll. Law, 1998-99, vis. assoc. prof., 1999—; mem. com. U.S. activities of foreigners and tax treaties, tax sect. ABA, 1994—. Contbr. articles to Guam Bar Jour., Utah Bar Jour. and Tax Notes. Chmn Dem. Party, Davis County, Utah, 1997-99. Sheldon fellow Harvard U., 1971. Mem. Guam Bar Assn. (pres. 1982-84), No. Marianas Bar Assn., Utah Bar Assn. (chmn. tax sect. 1994-95), Calif. Bar Assn., Phi Beta Kappa. Office: Parsons Behle & Latimer 201 S Main St Ste 1800 Salt Lake City UT 84111-2218

BARUSCH, RONALD CHARLES, lawyer; b. Oakland, Calif., Sept. 6, 1953; s. Maurice Radston and Phyllis Rose (Roos) B.; m. Cynthia Jean Dahlin, May 28, 1977; children: Margaret Camilla Dahlin Barusch, Christopher Charles Barusch Dahlin, Julia Rose Barusch Dahlin. AB, Harvard U., 1974, JD, 1978; M in Pub. Policy, J.F. Kennedy Sch. Govt., 1978. Bar: Mass. 1978, U.S. Ct. Appeals (1st cir.) 1979, U.S. Dist. Ct. Mass. 1979, U.S. Ct. Appeals (D.C. cir.) 1981, U.S. Dist. Ct. D.C. 1982. From assoc. to ptnr. Skadden, Arps, Slate, Meagher & Flom, Boston, 1978-81, Washington, 1981-96; ptnr. Skadden, Arps, Slate, Meagher & Flom, Sydney, Australia, 1996—. Democrat. Home: 3 McLean Crescent Mosman VA 22207-5300*

BARVILLE, REBECCA PENELOPE, elementary school educator; b. Tulare, Calif., Nov. 7, 1936; m. David Leopold Barville, June 8, 1958; children: Mark, Becky, Curtis. BA, Simpson Coll., San Francisco, 1958; MA summa cum laude, Fresno State U., 1974. Cert. reading specialist, edn. adminstr., elem. tchr., Calif. Social worker Tulare County Welfare Dept., Porterville, Calif., 1961-63, San Bernadino Welfare, Ontario, Calif., 1963-65; tchr., reading specialist Pleasant View Sch., Porterville, 1969—; instr. Porterville Coll., 1993—. Pres. PTA, Lindsay, Calif., 1966-67. Fellow Delta Kappa Gamma; mem. AAUW (bd. dirs. 1974-83), Calif. Reading Assn. (sec. 1974), Pleasant View Educators Assn. (past pres., sec. 1985—). Republican. Presbyterian. Club: P.E.O. (v.p. 1986-87). Avocations: cross country skiing, swimming, hiking, biking, reading.

BARWIG, REGIS NORBERT JAMES, priest; b. Chgo., Jan. 16, 1932; s. Ladislas-Joseph and Josepha Agnes (Neugebauer) B. AB, St. Procopius Coll., 1954; postgrad., Georgetown U., 1957, Pontifical Lateran U., Rome, 1959-61. Ordained priest Roman Cath. Ch., 1959. Sec. to abbot of Lisle, 1955-61; sec. gen. Christian Unity Apostolate, 1961-64; founding prior Claremont Priory, Cedarburg, Wis., 1964-67; prior Community of Our Lady, Oshkosh, Wis., 1968—; co-chmn. 1st Festival Faith, Milw., 1966; chmn. Ecumenical Conf. Spiritual and Liturgical Renewal Religious Life, 1969—; mem. Green Bay Diocese Ecumenical Commn., 1970-73; theol. cons. Consortium Perfectae Caritatis, 1974—; preacher, U.S. and Europe; U.S. liaison for beatification of Pope Pius IX, 1975—; assoc. Wanda Landowska Music Ctr., Lakeville, Conn., 1969; bd. dirs. Inter-Cath. Press Agy., N.Y., 1967-72. Author: Changing Habits, 1971, Waiting for Rain, 1975, Reflections on Spiritual Life for Order of Malta, 1982; translator: His Will Alone, 1971, Wanda Landowska Diaries, 1971, Pius XI-A Close-up, 1975, Pius IX-More than a Prophet, 1977, Writings of Blessed Maximilian Maria Kolbe, 1977, Evaluations of the Possibility of Constructing a Christian Ethic on the Assumptions of the Philosophy of Max Scheler, 1982; editor: Conferences of Mother Mary of Jesus, 1968; contbr. articles to religious publs. Decorated Bruderschaft, Collegio Teutonico, Vatican City, Knight Comdr., Order Isabel la Catolica, Spain, Cross of Merit, Sovereign Mil. Order of Malta, Magistral Chaplain, Conventual Chaplain of Honor, Prelatial Councillor, Chief of Chaplains, Polish Assn., Sovereign Mil. Order of Malta, Knight Comdr. Ecclesiastical Grace, Gold Benemerenti medal Sacred Mil. Constantinian Order of St. George-Bourbon Two Sicilies, Chaplain Am. Del., Knight Equestrian Order Holy Sepulcher of Jerusalem, Grand Priory of Poland, Gold Cross Merit Primate of Poland, hon. Canon, Royal Coll. Chpt., Wilanow-Warsaw. Mem. Selden Soc., Queen Mary Coll., Polish-Am. Assn. Wis. (chaplain 1979—), Polish Arts Club. Home and Office: 2804 Oakwood Ln Oshkosh WI 54904-8406 *From my Roman Catholic faith and my Polish heritage I imbibed early a sense of the importance of Divine Providence in one's life. In this context, then, regret and disappointment are both futile and destructive emotions. Everything can be redeemed. Radical eternalism makes one look Above and Beyond.*

BARWINSKY, JAROSLAW, cardiac surgeon; b. Oct. 15, 1926. MD, U. Manitoba, 1955. Prof. U. Manitoba, Winnipeg, Can., 1963—. Home: 225 Handsart Blvd, Winnipeg, Canada R3P0CG

BARZ, RICHARD L., microbiologist; b. Rockford, Ill., Mar. 22, 1955; s. William Edward and Rosemary Alice (Easton) B.; m. Susan Jane Hennefent, May 12, 1989; children: Megan, Richard Jr. BS in Microbiology, Colo. State U., 1975. Microbiologist Leprino Foods, Denver, 1975-76, rsch. technician, 1976-78, mgr. quality assurance, 1978-82, dir. quality assurance, researcher, 1982-86, v.p., 1986-94, sr. v.p., 1994—. Achievements include patents in field in IQF Freezing Mozzarella Cheese; Coating Application of Mozzarella Cheese; Same Day Manufacture of Mozzarella Cheese. Home: 151 Equiwax Dr Catle Rock CO 80104 Office: Leprino Foods 1830 W 38th Ave Denver CO 80211-2200

BARZA, HAROLD A., lawyer; b. Montreal, Que., Can., July 28, 1952; came to U.S., 1969; s. Solomon A. and Evelyn (Elkin) B. BA, Boston U., 1973; JD, Columbia U., 1976. Bar: N.Y. 1977, Calif. 1978, U.S. Dist. Ct. (cen. dist.) Calif. 1978. Law clk. to judge U.S. Dist. Ct. (so. dist.) N.Y., 1976-77; assoc. Munger, Tolles & Rickershauser, L.A., 1978-81; ptnr. Gelles, Singer & Johnson, L.A., 1982-83, Gelles, Lawrence & Barza, L.A., 1983-87, Loeb & Loeb, 1987—; adj. prof. mass comm. law Southwestern U. Sch. Law, L.A., 1979-82; judge pro tem., L.A. Mcpl. Ct., 1985—. Mem. bd. editors Columbia Law Rev., 1975-76. Mem. steering com. Jewish Nat. Fund, L.A., 1983. James Kent scholar, 1974-76, Harlan Fiske Stone scholar, 1973-74. Mem. Los Angeles County Bar Assn. (trial lawyers, litigation and entertainment sects.), ABA (mem. antitrust com. on antitrust litigation). Office: Loeb & Loeb 1000 Wilshire Blvd Ste 1800 Los Angeles CA 90017-2475

BARZUN, JACQUES, author, literary consultant; b. Créteil, France, Nov. 30, 1907; came to U.S., 1920, naturalized, 1933; s. Henri Martin and Anna-Rose B.; m. Mariana Lowell, Aug. 1936 (dec. 1979); children: James Lowell, Roger Martin, Isabel; m. Marguerite Davenport, June 1980. Ed., Lycée Janson de Sailly, Paris; AB, Columbia U., 1927, MA, 1928, PhD, 1932. From lectr. history to assoc. prof. Columbia U., N.Y.C., 1927-45, prof., 1945, dean grad. faculties, 1955-58, dean faculties and provost, 1958-67, prof. emeritus, spl. adviser on arts, 1967-75; lit. adviser Scribner's, N.Y.C., 1975-93. Author: The French Race, 1932, Teacher in America, 1945, Berlioz and the Romantic Century, 1950, 3d edit., 1969, Pleasures of Music, 1951, 2d edit., 1977, God's Country and Mine, 1954, Music in American Life, 1956, Darwin, Marx, Wagner, 1941, The Energies of Art, 1956, Of Human Freedom, 2d edit, 1964, Race: A Study in Superstition, 1937, The Modern Researcher, 1957, 5th edit., 1993, The House of Intellect, 2d edit, 1975, Classic, Romantic and Modern, 1961, Science: The Glorious Entertainment, 1964, The American University, 1968, 2d edit., 1995, A Catalogue of Crime, 1971, 2d edit., 1986, On Writing, Editing and Publishing, 1971, The Use and Abuse of Art, 1974, Clio and the Doctors, 1974, Simple and Direct, 1975, 2d edit., 1993, Critical Questions, 1982, A Stroll With William James, 1983, A Word or Two Before You Go, 1986, The Culture We Deserve, 1989, Begin Here: On Teaching and Learning, 1990, An Essay on French Verse, 1991; mem. editl. bd. The American Scholar, 1946-76, Ency. Brit, 1979—; editor: Selected Letters of Lord Byron, 1953, Nouvelles Lettres de Berlioz, 1954, The Selected Writings of John Jay Chapman, 1957, Follett's Modern American Usage, 1966. Trustee N.Y. Soc. Libr., 1968-97; mem. adv. coun. Univ. Coll. at Buckingham. Decorated Legion of Honor; Extraordinary fellow Churchill Coll., U. Cambridge (Eng.). Fellow Royal Soc. Arts, Royal Soc. Lit.; mem. Soc. Am. Historians, Mass. Hist. Soc. (corr.), AAAL (pres. 1972-75, 77-78), Am. Philos. Soc., Am. Acad. for Liberal Edn., Acad. Delphinale (Grenoble), Century Assn., Phi Beta Kappa.

BASAR, TAMER, electrical engineering educator; b. Istanbul, Turkey, Jan. 19, 1946; came to U.S., 1969; s. Munir and Seniye (Pirilsu) B.; m. Tangul Unerdem, Dec. 27, 1975; children: Gozen, Elif. B.S. in Elec. Engring., Robert Coll., Istanbul, 1969; M.S., Yale U., 1970, M.Phil., 1971, Ph.D., 1972. Research fellow Harvard U., Cambridge, Mass., 1972-73; sr. researcher scientist Marmara Research Inst., Gebze, Kocaeli, Turkey, 1973-80; adj. assoc. prof. Bogazici U., Istanbul, 1974-80; assoc. prof. elec. engring. U. Ill., Urbana, 1980-83, prof., 1983—, disting. prof., 1998—. Co-author: Dynamic Noncooperative Game Theory, 1982, 2d edit., 1995, H-infinity Optimal Control and Related Minimax Design Problems, 1991, 3rd edit., 1999; editor: Dynamic Games and Applications in Econs., 1986; co-editor: Differential Games and Applications, 1989, Advances in Dynamic Games and Applications, 1994; contbr. articles to profl. jours.; editor 2 jours. in control theory; assoc. editor 1 jour. in econs. and 1 in control. Recipient Young Scientist award in Applied Math., Turkish Nat. Rsch. Coun., 1976, Sedat Simavi Found. award, 1979, Medal of Sci., Turkey, 1993. Fellow IEEE (v.p. Control Sys. Soc. 1997-98, pres.-elect 1999, Disting. Mem. award 1993, Best Paper award 1995); mem. Soc. for Indsl. Applied Math., Internat. Soc. Dynamic Games (pres. 1990-94), Game Theory Soc., Am. Math. Soc., Sigma Xi. Home: 2810 Valley Brook Dr Champaign IL 61822-7621 Office: U Ill 1308 W Main St Urbana IL 61801-2307

BASART, JOHN PHILIP, electrical engineering and radio astronomy researcher, educator; b. Des Moines, Feb. 26, 1938; s. Philip Edwin and Hildreth Pauline (Belden) B.; m. Luann Kay Stow, Mar. 2, 1960; children—Jill Eileen Urban, Ann Marie. B.S., Iowa State U., 1962, M.S., 1963, Ph.D. in Elec. Engring., 1967. Research assoc. Nat. Radio Astronomy Obs., Charlottesville, Va., 1967-69; system scientist Very Large Array, Socorro, N.Mex., 1979-81; asst. prof. Iowa State U., Ames, 1969-73, assoc. prof., 1973-80, prof., 1980—; rschr. in radio astronomy, non destructive evaluation, image processing, wave propagation; campus coord. Iowa Space Grant Consortium. Contbr. articles to profl. jours. Served with USAF, 1955-59. Recipient student award IRE, 1962. Mem. IEEE (sr. mem.), AIAA, Am. Geophys. Union, Am. Astron. Soc., Royal Astron. Soc., Internat. Astron. Union, Internat. Soc. for Optical Engring., Sigma Xi, Eta Kappa Nu, Tau Beta Pi, Phi Kappa Phi. Office: Durham Ctr Iowa State U Ames IA 50011

BASCH, DARLENE CHAKIN, clinical social worker; b. Bklyn., Oct. 12, 1954; d. Samuel Benedict and Vivian (Sidranski) Chakin; m. Loren Bernhardt Basch, May 31, 1982; children: Michael Oswald, Ethan Raphael. BS, Cornell U., 1976; M in Social Welfare, U. Calif., Berkeley, 1979. Lic. clin. social worker, Calif.; bd. cert. Diplomate Social Work. Cottage clin. supr. St. Vincent's Sch., San Rafael, Calif., 1979-83; program dir. Jewish Family and Children's Service, San Francisco, 1983-84, therapist, program dir. family life edn., 1985-87; pvt. practice therapist Los Angeles, Calif., 1982—; clin. soc. worker Family Friends UCLA Med. Ctr., 1988-95; lead interviewer trainer, interviewer resources advisor Spielberg's Survivors of the Shoah Visual History Found., L.A., 1994—; exec. dir. Descendants of Shoah, L.A., 1995—; tchr. Rosenberg's Integrative Body Psychotherapy, 1999—. Chmn. Generation-to-Generation, San Francisco, 1979-87; sec. Holocaust Library and Research Ctr., San Francisco, 1980-87; exec. com. mem. World Gathering of Holocaust Survivors, Jerusalem, 1980-81. Mem. NASW, Soc. Clin. Social Work, Internat. Soc. Traumatic Stress Studies, Internat. Assn. Body Psychotherapy (exec. dir. 1994-97), Soc. Clin. Social Work. Avocations: singing, guitar, reading, walking, spirituality. Office: 6310 San Vicente Blvd Ste 350 Los Angeles CA 90048-5499

BASCH, PAUL FREDERICK, international health educator, parasitologist; b. Vienna, Austria, Nov. 10, 1933; came to U.S, 1939; s. Richard and Anne Herta Basch; m. Maria Natalicia Mourão, Aug. 16, 1966; children: Richard Joseph, Daniel David. BS, CCNY, 1954; MS, U. Mich., 1956, PhD, 1958; M in Pub. Health, U. Calif., Berkeley, 1967. Asst. prof. biology Kans. State Tchrs. Coll., Emporia, 1959-62; from asst. to assoc. research zoologist U. Calif., San Francisco, 1962-70; assoc. prof. internat. health Stanford (Calif.) U., 1970-83, prof., 1983-97, prof. emeritus, 1997—; cons. WHO, Pan Am. Health Orgn., UN Indsl. Devel. Orgn., NIH, U.S. Agy. for Internat. Devel. Author: Textbook of International Health, 1990, Schistosome Biology, 1991, 2d edit., 1999, Vaccines and World Health, 1994, also numerous articles. Grantee USPHS, WHO, others. Fellow Royal Soc. Tropical Medicine and Hygiene; mem. APHA, Am. Soc. Parasitologists, Am. Soc. Tropical Medicine and Hygiene, Nat. Council Internat. Health. Democrat. Office: Stanford U Sch Medicine Dept Health Rsch and Policy Stanford CA 94305-5405

BASCH, REVA, information services company executive; b. Chgo., Aug. 1, 1947; d. Victor Hugo and Hertha (Levi) B.; m. Jerrald C. Shifman, Apr. 17, 1982. BA in English Lit. summa cum laude, U. Pa., 1969; MLS, U. Calif., Berkeley, 1971. Head libr. Cogswell Coll., San Francisco, 1971-72; tech. info. specialist Gilbert Assocs. Inc., Reading, Pa., 1973-79; tech. libr. NuTech, San Jose, Calif., 1980-81; rsch. assoc. Info. on Demand, Berkeley, Calif., 1981-82, asst. dir. rsch., 1982-83, dir. rsch., 1983-86, v.p., dir. rsch., 1985-86; software designer Mead Data Ctrl., Personal Computer Sys. Group, Menlo Park, Calif., 1986-88; pres. Aubergine Info. Svcs., The Sea Ranch, Calif., 1986—. Author: Secrets of the Super Searchers, 1993, Electronic Information Delivery: Ensuring Quality and Value, 1995, Secrets of the Super Net Searchers, 1996, Researching Online for Dummies, 1998; columnist Online mag., CyberSkeptic's Guide to Internet Rsch.; contbr. articles to profl. jours. Recipient award for best paper UMI/Data Courier, 1990, Online Champion award Dun & Bradstreet. Mem. Assn. of Ind. Info. Profl.(pres.1991-92), Spl. Librs. Assn. , Assn. Info. and Dissemination Ctrs., Info. Bay Area, So. Calif. Online Users Group. Avocations: online communications, reading, travel, cooking.

BASCH, RICHARD VENNARD, photographer, producer, writer, director; b. Inpls., Jan. 22, 1945; s. Richard and Helen Louise (Vennard) B.; m. Meredith Baker, Feb. 12, 1966; 1 child, Nicholas; m. Vicki Sylvester, Aug. 15, 1977. Cert., U. Fine Arts, Perugia, Italy, 1965, London Film Sch., 1966; BA, Antioch Coll., 1968; DFA, London Inst. for Applied Rsch., 1995. Dir. filmmaker tng. Am. Film Inst., Washington, 1968-69; instr. film history R.I. Sch. Design, Providence, 1970-73; cons. in theatre Antioch Coll., Yellow Springs, Ohio, 1976-77; prin., photographer Richard Basch Studio, Washington, 1979—; dir. film programs Brown U., 1972-73; cons. Smithsonian Instn., Washington, 1979—. Author: Faces of Fairmont Heights, 1970; producer (films) The Burning Issue, 1984, Notes from the Future, 1996. Mem. Am. Soc. Mag. Photographers. Episcopalian. Office: Richard Basch Studio 2627 Connecticut Ave NW Washington DC 20008-1545

BASCOM, C. PERRY, foundation administrator, lawyer; b. Boston, July 30, 1936; s. William Richardson and Jean Ames (Hall) B.; m. Sally Cissel Greenwood, July 18, 1995; children: Elisabeth Brooke, Heather Ames, Sarah Duff Greenwood, Amy McOrmond Greenwood. B.A., Yale U., 1958; LL.B., Harvard U., 1961. Bar: Mo. 1961. Assoc. Bryan Cave, St. Louis, 1962-72, ptnr., 1972-95; adminstr. Gateway Foundation, St. Louis, 1995—; judge St. Louis Night Housing Ct., 1970-72; lectr. on various topics, including truth in lending, Real Estate Settlement Procedures Act, techniques in comml. bank lending, devels. in Mo. banking law, electronic funds transfers. Sr. warden Trinity Ch., St. Louis, 1974-78. Served with USAR, 1961-68. Mem. Mo. Bar Assn. Home: 4650 Pershing Pl Saint Louis MO 63108-1908 Office: Gateway Foundation 720 Olive St Ste 1977 Saint Louis MO 63101-2338

BASCOM, RUTH F., retired mayor; b. Ames, Iowa, Feb. 4, 1926; d. Frederick Charles and Doris Hays Fenton; m. John U. Bascom, June 14, 1950; children: Lucinda, Rebecca, Ellen, Thomas, Paul, Mary. BS, Kans. State U., Manhattan, 1946; MA, Cornell U., 1949. Tchr. Dickinson County Cmty. H.S., Kans., 1946-48, Nat. Coll. Edn., Chgo., 1949-51; co-chair Cascadia High Speed Rail, 1995-98. Chair City and State Bicycle Com., 1971-83; mem., chair Met. Park Bd., Eugene, 1972-82; past bd. pres. Youth Symphony; city councilor City of Eugene, Oreg., 1984-92, coun. v.p., pres., 1988-90, mayor, 1993-97; v.p., pres. LWV, Eugene, 1967-69; adv. coun. Willamette Valley Passenger Rail, 1997—. Recipient Gold Leaf award Internat. Soc. Arboriculture, 1993. Democrat. Congregational. Avocations: music, tree farm, bicycling. Fax: 541-683-4717. Home: 2114 University St Eugene OR 97403-1542 Office: City of Eugene 777 Pearl St Ste 105 Eugene OR 97401-2720

BASCOM, WILLARD NEWELL, engineer, scientist, underwater archaeologist; b. N.Y.C., Nov. 7, 1916; s. Willard Newell and Pearle (Boyd) B.; m. Rhoda Nergaard, Apr. 15, 1946; children: Willard, Anitra. Student, Colo. Sch. Mines; D in Natural Scis. (hon.), U. Genoa, Italy, 1992. Registered profl. engr., Fla., D.C. Research engr. U. Calif., Berkeley, 1945-50, Scripps Inst. Oceanography, La Jolla, Calif., 1950-54; exec. sec., dir. Mohole Project Nat. Acad. Scis., Washington, 1954-62; pres. Ocean Sci. and Engring., Inc., Washington, 1962-72; dir. Coastal Water Research Project, Long Beach, Calif., 1973-85; mem. plowshre com. AEC, 1962-70; mem. Naval Rsch. Adv. Com., 1971-79; mem. coastal cons. bd. U.S. Army Engrs., 1980-85; mem. Sea Grant Coll. Bd., NOAA, 1979-88; mem. ocean scis. bd. NAS, 1978-81. Author: Waves and Beaches, 1964, rev. 2d edit., 1980, A Hole in the Bottom of the Sea, 1961, Deep Water, Ancient Ships, 1976, The Crest of the Wave, 1988, Endangered, 1995, Brother Jonathan's Gold, 1999; contbr. over 100 articles to sci. jours. Recipient Disting. Achievement medal Colo. Sch. Mines, 1979, Compass Disting. Achievement award Marine Tech. Soc., 1970, John Wiley Jones award, 1978, Rolex award, 1993. Mem. Explorers Club (Explorers medal 1980), Cosmos Club, Adventurers Club. Achievements include patent for deep ocean search-recovery system; inventor first dynamic positioning for holding ships in deepwater.

BASCONCILLO, LINDY, insurance and financial services company executive; b. Honolulu, Dec. 11, 1943; s. Catalino M. and Primitiva (Barientos) B.; children: Lisa M., Rod Alan. BA, Pacific Union Coll., 1965; MA, Azusa Pacific U., 1979. CLU. Tchr., vice prin. Santa Monica (Calif.) Jr. Acad., 1965-68; tchr. Temple City (Calif.) Unified Schs., 1968-79; sales agent N.Y. Life Ins. Co., Eugene, Oreg., 1980-81, tng. mgr., 1981-87; sales mgr. MONY Fin. Svcs., Eugene, 1987-88; sr. mktg. cons. Prudential Ins. and Fin. Svcs., Woodland Hills, Calif., 1988-89; sales mgr. Prudential Ins. and Fin. Svcs., Sacramento, 1989-91; bus., estate, retirement specialist John Deere Life Ins. Co., Calif. and Nev., 1991-94; dist. sales mgr. Mut. of Omaha, 1994-95; mng. dir. Elite Consulting, Lincoln, Calif., 1994—; brokerage dir. Nat. Life of Vt., 1995-96; reg. rep., agy. tng. dir. MassMutual, Sacramento, 1996—; bus. cons. Jr. Achievement, Eugene, 1986; pres.-elect Eugene Life Underwriters Assn., 1988, v.p., 1987; chairperson Life Underwriter Tng. Coun., 1987, moderator, 1984-86. Mem. coun. for minority edn. U. Oreg., Eugene, 1986-88; mem. Lane County Tng. and Devel. Com., Eugene, 1985-87. Mem. Sacramento Chpt. CLU's (bd. dirs.), Sacramento Life Underwriters Assn. Avocations: snow skiing, golfing. Home: 1812 5th St Lincoln CA 95648-2328 Office: 2180 Harvard St Ste 375 Sacramento CA 95815-3324

BASDEN, CAMERON, ballet mistress, dancer; b. Dallas. Scholarship student, The Joffrey Ballet Sch., 1976-77. Dancer Dallas Ballet, 1975-76, Joffrey II Dancers, N.Y.C., 1977-79; dancer The Joffrey Ballet, N.Y.C., 1979—, asst. ballet mistress, 1990-93; ballet mistress The Joffrey Ballet, N.Y.C., Chgo., 1993—; prof. dance Manhattanville Coll. Office: Joffrey Ballet 70 E Lake St Fl 1300 Chicago IL 60601-5913*

BASE, CAROL CUNNINGHAM, occupational health nurse, clinical research scientist; b. Darby, Pa., Nov. 28, 1949; d. Charles Thomas McIntyre and Helen Marie (Graham) Cunningham; m. Joseph Michael Base, Jr., Nov. 11, 1982. AAS in Nursing, Del. County Community Coll., Media, Pa., 1983; BSN, Widener U., Chester, Pa., 1990; MS in Health Edn., St. Joseph's U., 1993. RN, Pa.; cert. occupational health nurse and hearing conservationist; cert. case mgr.; cert. spirometry, Nat. Inst. Occupational Safety and Health. Staff nurse Met. Hosp., Springfield, Pa., 1983; charge nurse Taylor Hosp., Ridley Park, Pa., 1984-86; occupational health nurse PECO Energy Co., Berwyn, Pa., 1985-92, supr. nursing, 1992-95, mgr. clin. svcs., 1995-96; pres. C.C. Base Occpl. Health Enhancement Svcs., Berwyn, 1996—; clin. scientist Wyeth-Ayerst Pharms., Radnor, Pa., 1998—. Vice pres. bd. dirs. Delaware County Home Care. Recipient Wong Moss award for outstanding success in profession, extensive svc. to cmty. and commitment to edn. Delaware County C.C., 1995. Mem. NAFE, Am. Assn. Occupational Health Nurses, Am. Cancer Soc. (nurse's edn. com. 1988—), N.E. Assn. Occupational Health Nurses (nomination chair 1993-94, v.p. 1996-98), Del. Valley Pa. Assn. Occupational Health Nurses (1st v.p. 1993-97, pres. 1997—), Pa. Assn. Occupational Health Nurses (2d v.p. 1994-98—), Sigma Theta Tau. Home: 720 Heatherstone Dr Berwyn PA 19312-2503

BASE, GRAEME ROWLAND, illustrator, author; b. Amersham, Eng., Apr. 6, 1958; s. Geoffrey Donald and Elizabeth Enid (Philips) B.; m. Robyn Anne Paterson, Aug. 1, 1981; children: James Geoffrey, Katherine Gabrielle, William Alexander. Art diploma, Swinburne Inst. Tech., 1978. Author, illustrator: My Grandma Lived in Gooligulch, 1983, Animalia, 1986 (Australian Children's Book award Children's Book Coun. Australia 1987, Kids Own Australia Literature award 1988), The Eleventh Hour: A Curious Mystery, 1988 (Australian Children's Book award Children's Book Coun. Australia 1989, Book Design award Australian Book Pub. Assn. 1988, Young Australian Best Book award 1989, Kids Own Australia Literature award 1989), The Sign of the Seahorse, 1992, The Discovery of Dragons, 1996, The Worst Band in the Universe, 1999; illustrator: Adventures With My Best Worst Friend, 1982, The Island Bike Business, 1982, Jabberwocky From "Through the Looking Glass," 1985, Jabberwocky: A Book of Brillig Dioramas, 1996. Office: Penguin Books Australia Ltd, 487 Maroondah Hwy PO Box 257, Ringwood VIC 3134, Australia

BASFORD, JAMES ORLANDO, container manufacturing company executive; b. Akron, Ohio, Apr. 17, 1931; s. Napoleon Orlando and Hazel Martha (Fersner) B.; m. Mary Eleanor Hagmeyer, Mar. 16, 1957; children: Jeffrey James, Gregory Robert, Lisa Jean Cullity. Student, Kent State U., 1949-51, 55-58. Asst. sales mgr. San Hygene Mfg. Co., Akron, 1958-60; gen. sales mgr. Adjusta Post Mfg., Akron, 1960-64; area sales mgr. Gaylord Container, Columbus, Ohio, 1964-74; v.p. Buckeye Container Co., Wooster, Ohio, 1974-78, pres., 1978-95, chmn. bd. dirs., 1994-96; bd. dirs. Wayne County Nat. Bank, Wooster; chmn. bd. dirs. Pahaque Wilderness, Inc., San Diego; pres. Jelige LLC, Wooster, Ohio. Bd. dirs. Boys Village, Smithville, Ohio, 1985— (pres., 1998—); chmn. Wayne County Econ. Devel. Commn., 1995. With USAF, 1951-54, Korea. Mem. Wooster C. of C. (bd. dirs. 1977-80). Republican. Lutheran. Club: Wooster Country (pres. 1981-83). Lodge: Rotary (bd. dirs. Wooster club 1978-81). Avocations: golf, tennis, skiing. Home: 1097 Greens View Dr Wooster OH 44691-2659

BASFORD, ROBERT EUGENE, retired biochemistry educator, researcher; b. Montpelier, N.D., Aug. 21, 1923; s. Eugene M. and Bertha (Cudworth) B.; m. Carol Kaufman Phebus, Dec. 23, 1965; 1 child, Lee A. Phebus. B.S., U. Wash., 1951, Ph.D., 1954. Postdoctoral fellow U. Wis.-Madison, 1954-58; asst. prof. U. Pitts., 1958-63, assoc. prof., 1963-70, prof., 1970-93, prof. emeritus, 1993—; cons. Mine Safety Appliance Co., Pitts., 1966-69; mem. neurol. scis. study sect. NIH, Washington, 1977-80.

BASH, FRANK NESS, astronomer, educator; b. Medford, Oreg., May 3, 1937; s. Frank Cozad and Kathleen Jane (Ness) B.; m. Susan Martin Fay, Sept. 10, 1960; children—Kathryn Fay, Francis Lee. B.A., Willamette U., 1959; M.A. in Astronomy, Harvard U., 1962; Ph.D., U. Va., 1967. Staff scientist Lincoln Lab. MIT, 1962; assoc. astronomer Nat. Radio Astronomy Obs., Green Bank, W.Va., 1962-64; rsch. asst. U. Va., 1965-67; postdoctoral faculty assoc. U. Tex., Austin, 1967-69, asst. prof. astronomy, 1969-73, assoc. prof., 1973-81, prof., 1981—, Frank N. Edmonds Regents prof., 1985—; chmn. dept. astronomy U. Tex., 1983-86, dir. W.J. McDonald Obs., 1989—; mem. astronomy adv. panel NSF, 1988-91; chmn. vis. com. Nat. Radio Astronomy Obs., 1990, mem., 1990-93; mem. vis. com. Arecibo Obs., 1990-95, chmn., 1994; mem. planning com. NASA Astrophys. Data Systems, 1991-95; bd. dirs., mem. rep. Assoc. Univs. for Rsch. in Astronomy, 1995—. Author: (with Daniel Schiller and Dilip Balamore) Astronomy, 1977; contbr. articles to profl. jours. Grantee NSF, 1967—, The Netherlands NSF, 1979, W.M. Keck Found., 1988. Mem. Am. Astron. Soc. (councillor 1996—), Astron. Soc. Pacific (bd. dirs. 1995-97, v.p. 1997-99, pres. 1999—), Internat. Astron. Union, Internat. Sci. Radio Union, Tex. Assn. Coll. Tchrs. (pres. U. Tex. chpt. 1980-82), Tex. Philos. Soc., Town and Gown Club (Austin). Office: U Tex at McDonald Obs McDonald Obs Mail Code C1402 Austin TX 78712

BASH, LEE, educational administrator; b. Mishawaka, Ind., Dec. 4, 1941; s. Harry N. and Margaret (Welsher) B.; m. Sandra D. Halioris, June 28, 1986; 1 child, John Blackwood. BFA, SUNY, Buffalo, 1971, MFA, 1979, PhD, 1983. Chair dept. fine and performing arts Bellarmine Coll., Louisville, 1985—; dir. Ky. Gov.'s Sch. for Arts, Louisville, 1987—; cons. Ky. Ctr. for Arts, Louisville, 1986—. Author: Index of Jazz Educators Journal, 1989, Complete Guide to Jazz and Improvisation Instruction, 1984; contbr. to Jazziz Mag., 1990—. Mem. Internat. Assn. Jazz Educators (mem. adv. bd. 1986-88, assoc. editor 1986—), Ky. Arts Adminstrs. (pres. 1990—). Office: Bellarmine Coll Newburg Rd Louisville KY 40205

BASH, PHILIP EDWIN, publishing executive; b. Huntington, Ind., Aug. 13, 1921; s. Philip Purviance and Nell (Johnson) B.; m. Flora Wiley Oberg, Mar. 11, 1944; children: Barbara, Kingsley, Roger, Amy. B.A., DePauw U., 1943. Account exec. Leo Burnett Co., Inc., Chgo., 1947-54; account supr., v.p., sr. v.p. mktg. services Clinton E. Frank Inc., Chgo., 1954-64; pres. Clinton E. Frank Inc., 1964-72; pres. Barrington (Ill.) Press, Inc., 1972-86, also bd. dirs. Chmn. bd. trustees Shimer Coll., 1989—; trustee Garrett Theol. Sem., 1976—, chmn. bd., 1989—. Served to lt. (j.g.) USNR, 1943-46, PTO. Mem. Am. Assn. Advt. Agys. (bd. govs. Chgo. council), Am. Mktg. Assn., Sigma Chi. Methodist (trustee). Clubs: University (Chgo.), Economics (Chgo.); Barrington Hills Country. Office: 200 James St Barrington IL 60010-3328

BASHAM, W. RALPH, federal agency administrator; m. Judith A. O'Bryan; three children. BA in Bus. Adminstrn., Southeastern U. Various positions to deputy asst. dir. for trng. U.S. Secret Svc., spl. agt. in Charge of Vice Presdl. Protective Svc., spl. agt of Dignitary Protective Divsn., spl. agt. of Protective support Divsn., spl agt. of Fin. Mgmt. Divn. and Office of Inspection, asst. dir. for Adminstrn.; dir. Fed. Law Enforcement Tng. Ctr. U.S. Dept. Treasury, 1998—. Mem. Sr. Exec. Svc. Office: US Dept Treasury Fed Law Enforcement Tng Ctr Glynco GA 31524

BASHIRI, IRAJ, Central Asian studies educator; b. Behabahan, Iran, July 31, 1940; came to U.S., 1966; s. Muhammad and Robab Bashiri; m. Carol L. Sayers, Apr. 18, 1968; children: Mariam, Manuchehr, Mehrdad. BA cum laude, Pahlavi U., Shiraz, Iran, 1963; MA, U. Mich., 1968, PhD, 1972; D (hon.), Tajikstan State U., 1996. Coord., tchr. Peace Corps, Brattleboro, Vt., 1967-68; asst. prof. Iranian studies U. Minn., Mpls., 1972-77, coord. Middle East studies program, 1975-77, assoc. prof. Iranian studies, 1977-87, acting chair South Asian studies, 1981, assoc. chair Russian and Eastern European studies, 1987-90, acting chair Russian and Eastern European studies, 1990-91, assoc. prof. Cen. Asian studies, 1987-96, prof. Ctrl. Asian studies, 1996—; assoc. prof. Russian studies, 1997-98, 1998-, 1982, chair Slavic and Central Asia langs. and lit., 1997—; mem. rev. bd. Internat. Rsch. and

Exchs. Bd. for Tajikistan, Princeton, N.J., 1991—; editor bilingual series Mazda Pub., Encino, Calif., 1985-90; mem. selection com. MacArthur Found., Mpls., 1990-91, mem. internat. seminar, 1990; prof. internat. rels. Kyrgyz State Nat. U., 1998-99. Author: Fiction of Sadeq Hedayat, 1984, Firdowsi's Shahname: 1000 Years After, 1994, Kamal Khujandi: Epoch and its Importance in the History of Central Asian Civilization, 1996, The Samanids and the Revival of the Civilization of Iranian Peoples, 1998; editor: The Pearl Cannon, 1986; contbr. articles, essays to profl. publs. Internat. edn. travel grantee U. Minn., 1990-92; IREX resident scholar, Tajikistan, 1993-94. Fellow Middle East Studies Assn.; mem. Am. Inst. Iranian Studies (trustee 1975-79), Assn. for Cen. Asian Studies, Assn. Advancement Cen. Asian Rsch. (chair devel. com. 1990—), Am. Assn. Tchrs. of Slavic and Eastern European Langs., Acad. Scis. Tajikistan (hon. internat.). Avocations: writing realist fiction, fishing, travel. Home: 518 8th St SE Minneapolis MN 55414-1208

BASHKIN, LLOYD SCOTT, marketing and management consultant; b. Bridgeport, Conn., July 11, 1951; s. Jules Bernard and Luella (Kobre) B.; children: Marisa Elizabeth, Carly Michelle. BS in Fin., Syracuse U., 1973, MBA in Mktg. and Acctg., 1974; postgrad., Columbia U., 1975-78. Corp. staff mktg. cons. RCA, N.Y.C., 1974-77; mgr. entertainment, indsl. mktg. and nat. sales RCA, Cherry Hill, N.J., 1977-79; v.p. mktg. and sales CCA Electronics Corp. div. Singer Co., Cherry Hill, 1979-80; pres. Lloyd Scott & Co., Cherry Hill, 1980—, Sydex, Cherry Hill, 1987-88; adj. instr. Temple U. Grad. Sch., Phila., 1980-82; adj. prof. Drexel U. Grad. Sch., Phila., 1982—; speaker in field. Trustee, chmn. mktg. com. Food Bank South Jersey, 1985—; mem. Camden County Pvt. Industry Coun., 1989-90; mem. cabinet World Affairs Coun., 1989, Community Leaders Recognition Com., 1991—. Recipient Commendation award Gov. of N.J., 1981, SBA, 1983, Nat. Distbn. and Logistics Honorary award Delta Nu Alpha, 1973, Nat. Broadcasting Honorary award Alpha Epsilon Rho, 1979. Mem. Am. Mktg. Assn., C. of C. of So. N.J. (chmn. small bus. action com. 1982-85, strategic planning and mktg. com. 1985—, bd. dirs. 1984—, chmn. programming com. 1989-92), Greater Cherry Hill C. of C. (chmn. small bus. coun. 1982-83), Rotary (bd. dirs. Garden State club 1980-81). Avocations: skiing, photography, guitar. Office: Exec Mews 1930 Marlton Pike E Ste U-102 Cherry Hill NJ 08003-4211

BASHKOW, THEODORE ROBERT, electrical engineering consultant, former educator; b. St. Louis, Nov. 16, 1921; s. Maurice Louis and Caroline (Davidson) B.; m. Delphina Brownlee, Sept. 12, 1960; 1 stepdau., Lynn Michele. B.S., Washington U., St. Louis, 1943; M.S., Stanford U., 1947, Ph.D., 1950. Mem. tech. staff David Sarnoff Research Labs., RCA, 1950-52, Bell Telephone Labs., 1952-58; mem. faculty Columbia U., 1958-91, prof. elec. engring., 1967-79, prof. computer sci., 1979-91, chmn. dept. elec. engring., 1968-71, mgr. Sch. Engring. Computing Center, 1961-64; cons. to industry, 1959—; dir. MSI Inc., Woodside, N.Y., 1961—; chmn. tech. program 1968 Spring Joint Computer Conf.; chmn. sci. sect. Internat. Fedn. Info. Processing Congress, 1965. Author articles, chpts. in books. Served to 1st lt. USAAF, 1943-45. Mem. Assn. Computing Machinery, IEEE, Profl. Group Circuit Theory and Electronic Computers. Home: 92 Jay St Katonah NY 10536-3729

BASHLINE, ARYL ANN, photographer, fiber artist; b. Butler, Pa., Jan. 10, 1956; d. James Wade and Anna Heloise (LaBorde) B. BA in History, Edinboro U., 1977; BA in Art, Slippery Rock U., 1987; MA in Art, Bloomsburg U., 1993. Coord. exhibits, adminstr. Associated Artists Butler (Pa.) County Art Ctr., 1994—; freelance fiber artist, photographer Butler, 1987—; photographer Butler County Hist. Soc., 1987—; tchr. art and photography Butler Co. C.C., 1997—, Hoyt Inst. Fine Art, New Castle, Pa., 1994, C.C. Allegheny County, Pitts., 1995-96; tchr. photography Lenape Vo-Tech, Ford City, Pa., 1995-97. Photographs included in Pa. Mag., 1992, Bird Talk, 1989. Mem. Am. Assn. Mus., Nat. Audubon Soc. (We. Pa. chpt.). Democrat. Lutheran. Avocations: gardening, genealogy, music. Office: Associated Artists Butler County 344 S Main St PO Box 245 Butler PA 16003-0245

BASHOOK, PHILIP G., medical association executive, educator; b. Bklyn., Mar. 10, 1943; children: Jeremy, Amy. BS in Zoology, U. Calif., Santa Barbara, 1965; MSc in Biology, Calif. State U., Northridge, 1968; EdD, U. B.C., Can., 1971. From asst. to assoc. prof. Ctr. Ednl. Devel. Health Sci. Ctr. U. Ill., Chgo., 1971-74; assoc. dir. Michael Reese Hosp. and Med. Ctr., Chgo., 1975-80, dir., 1980-87; dir. Office Edn. Am. Psychiatric Assn., Washington, 1987-90; dir. evaluation and edn. Am. Bd. Med. Specialities, Evanston, Ill., 1991—; adj. assoc. prof. Dept. Med. Edn., U. Ill. Coll. Medicine, Chgo., 1975-87, 91—; adj. assoc. prof. dept. psychiatry and behavior scis. George Washington, 1988-91; mem. accreditation rev. com. Accreditation Coun. Continuing Med. Edn., 1980-87, vice chmn., 1982-87. Co-author: Construction and Use of Written Simulations, 1976; author 17 books; contbr. chpts. to books and articles to profl. jours. Bd. dirs. Pub. Sch. Dist. # 69 Cook County, Ill., 1980-87, bd. sec., 1985-87. Office: Am Bd of Med Specialties 1007 Church St Ste 404 Evanston IL 60201-5913

BASHORE, GEORGE WILLIS, bishop; b. Lancaster, Pa., Jan. 21, 1934; m. Carolyn Ruth Baumgartner, Sept. 20, 1957; children: Wanda Bashore Allison, John, Barbara Bashore Heagy. BA, Princeton U., 1955; MDiv, United Theol. Sem., Dayton, Ohio, 1958, D.Ministry, 1976; DD, Albright Coll., 1974. Ordained elder Evang. United Brethren Ch., 1958. Pastor Cen. Pk. Ch., Reading, Pa., 1959-73; supt. Lebanon-Reading Dist., Ea. Pa. Conf., 1973-79; sr. pastor 1st United Meth. Ch., Lancaster, Pa., 1979-80; elected bishop United Meth. Ch., Boston, 1980-88, bishop, Pitts., 1988—. Office: United Meth Ctr W Penn Conf PO Box 5002 1204 Freedom Rd Cranberry Township PA 16066-4914

BASHORE, IRENE SARAS, research institute administrator; b. San Jose, Calif.; d. John and Eva (Lionudakis) Saras; m. Vincent Bashore (div.); 1 child, Juliet Ann. BA, Pepperdine U., 1950; MA in Theatre Arts, Calif. State U., Fullerton, 1977. Founder, exec. dir. Inst. for Dramatic Rsch., Fullerton, Calif., 1967—.

BASHOUR, FOUAD ANIS, cardiology educator; b. Tripoli, Lebanon, Jan. 3, 1924; s. Anis E. and Mariana (Yazigi) B.; m. Val Imm, Sept. 28, 1978. BA, Am. U. of Beirut, Lebanon, 1944, MD, 1949; PhD, U. Minn., 1957. Intern Am. U. of Beirut Hosp., Beirut, 1949-50; med. officer UNRWA, 1950-51; resident in internal medicine U. Minn. Hosps., 1951-54; rsch. fellow U. Minn. Med. Schs., 1954-55; instr. in medicine U. Minn., 1955-57; rsch. assoc. Am. U. Med. Sch., Beirut, 1957, asst. prof. medicine cardiopulmonary lab. sect., 1957-59; instr. internal medicine U. Tex. Southwestern Med. Ctr., Dallas, 1959-60, assoc. prof. internal medicine, 1963-71, dir. Cardiovascular Inst., 1967-78, prof. medicine, 1971-85, prof. medicine and physiology, 1985—; mem. staff Parkland Meml. Hosp., Dallas; prof. emeritus of physiology and internal medicine, 1995—; mem. staff Zale-Lipshy Univ. Hosp., Dallas; founder, pres. Cardiology Fund, Inc., 1972-93; program dir. consultation agreement lectrs. Univ. Kuwait, U. Tex., 1977-85; mem. chancellor adv. coun. U. Tex., 1985—; mem. bd trustees of coms. on promotions and med. sch. Am. U. Beirut, 1996—; cons. in field. Mem. editorial bd. Chest, 1963-69, Lebanese Med. Jour., 1957-59, cited in the Warren Commn. Pub., 1963; contbr. more than 200 articles to profl. publs. Elder Christ Luth. Ch., Dallas. Recipient Americanism award DAR, 1970; named Knight Order of Holy Cross Jerusalem; Fouad Bashour ann. lectr. disting. physiologist in his honor, 1974—, Fouad Bashour distinguished chair in physiology in his honor, 1990, eminent scholar, Tex., 1985, Wisdom Hall of Fame, eminent Wisdom fellow, 1998. Fellow Am. Coll. Chest Physicians (emeritus), Am. Physiol. Soc. (circulation group), Am. Heart Assn. (coun. on basic sci., coun. on circulation); mem. Am. Fedn. Clin. Rsch. (emeritus), Ctrl. Soc. Clin. Rsch. (emeritus), So. Soc. Clin. Investigation (emeritus), Tex. Med. Assn., Dallas County Med. Assn., Am. Soc. Internal Medicine, Tex. Med. Found., Order of Cedars of Lebanon (officer 1971), cons. Tex. Bd. of Med. Examiners. Fax: (214) 648-9376. Office: U Tex Southwestern Med Ctr 5323 Harry Hines Blvd Dallas TX 75235-9040

BASHWINER, STEVEN LACELLE, lawyer; b. Cin., Aug. 3, 1941; s. Carl Thomas and Ruth Marie (Burlis) B.; m. Arden J. Lang, Apr. 24, 1966 (div. 1978); children: Heather, David; m. Donna Lee Gerber, Sept. 13, 1981; children: Margaret, Matthew. AB, Holy Cross Coll., 1963; JD, U. Chgo., 1966. Bar: Ill. 1966, U.S. Dist. Ct. Ill. 1967, U.S. Ct. Appeals (7th cir.) 1968, U.S. Supreme Ct. 1970. Assoc. Kirkland & Ellis, Chgo., 1966-72, ptnr., 1972-76; ptnr. Friedman & Koven, Chgo., 1976-86, Katten Muchin & Zavis, Chgo., 1986—. Served to sgt. USAFR, 1966-72. Mem. ABA, Fed. Bar Assn., Chgo. Bar Assn., Chgo. Inn of Ct., Legal Club Chgo., Law Club Chgo, Tavern Club. Home: 834 Green Bay Rd Highland Park IL 60035-4630 Office: Katten Muchin & Zavis 525 W Monroe St Ste 1600 Chicago IL 60661-3693

BASICHIS, GORDON ALLEN, author, screenwriter; b. Phila., Aug. 23, 1947; s. Martin and Ruth (Gordon) B.; m. Marcia Hammond; 1 child, Casey James. BS, Temple U., 1969. Reporter Phila. Bull., 1969; writer, reporter Santa Fe News, 1971-72; with advt., pub. relations Jay Bernstein Pub. Relations, Los Angeles, 1978-80; screenwriter Metro Goldwyn Mayer Feature Films, Culver City, Calif., 1982-83; ind. writer, 1983—; pres. Moonlight, Inc., L.a., 1982—; exec. v.p. Antigua Rd. Prodns., 1996. Author: Beautiful Bad Girl: The Vicki Morgan Story, 1985, (novel) Constant Travelers, 1978; producer, dir. (video documentary) Jerry: One Man's Triumph, 1980; coprodr. (TV series) Frank and Jesse; screenwriter Breach of Trust, 1994, Princess Pamela, 1999; co-writer Shysters, 1996; exec. prodr. Land of Dreams, 1999. Mem. Dem. Nat. Com. Mem. Writers Guild Am. West, Am. Film Inst., Simon Wiesenthal Inst., Statue of Liberty/Ellis Island Found. Office: PO Box 1511 Beverly Hills CA 90213-1511

BASIL, BRAD L., technology education educator. Middle sch. tchr. Mt. Logan Middle Sch., Chillicothe, Ohio; asst. prin. Mt. Logan Middle Sch., Chillicothe; middle sch. tchr. Smith Middle Sch., Chillicothe, 1988—. Recipient Tchr. Excellence for Ohio award Internat. Tech. Edn. Assn., 1992. Office: Smith Middle Sch 345 Arch St Chillicothe OH 45601-1519 also: Mt Logan Middle Sch 841 E Main St Chillicothe OH 45601-3509

BASIL, DOUGLAS CONSTANTINE, author, educator; b. Vancouver, C., Can., May 30, 1923; s. William and Christina (Findlay) B.; m. Evelyn Margaret Pitcairn, 1950; 1 dau., Wendy Patricia. B.Commerce, U. B.C., 1949; B.A., 1949; Ph.D., Northwestern U., 1954; postgrad., London Sch. Econs., 1950. Instr. Marquette U., 1951-54; asst. prof. Northwestern U., 1954-57; asso. prof. U. Minn., 1957-61; prof. mgmt. U. So. Calif., 1961-88, prof. emeritus, 1988—; cons. mgmt. devel.; lectr., Brussels, Caracas, Bogota, Paris, London, others. Author: Executive Development, 1964, (Paul Cone, John Fleming) Effective Decision Making Through Simulation, 1972, Organacao E Controls Da Pequena Empresa, 1968, La Direccion de la Pequena Empresa, 1969, Managerial Skills for Executive Action, 1970, Leadership Skills for Executive Action, 1971, Women in Management: Performance, Prejudice, Promotion, 1972, Autorite Personnelle et Efficacite des Cadres, 1972, Conduccion y Liderazgo, 1973, Developing Tomorrow's Managers, 1973, Management of Change, 1974, others.; Contbr. (Paul Cone, John Fleming) articles to profl. jours. Served to capt. Canadian Army, 1943-46. Home: 2201 Warmouth St San Pedro CA 90732-4532 Office: Grad Sch Bus Adminstrn Los Angeles CA 90007

BASILE, JOSEPH JOHN, art history educator, archaeologist; b. Bklyn., Dec. 25, 1965; s. Joseph and Lisa (Putzer) B.; m. Marrco L. Sylvester, Apr. 18, 1998. BA, Boston U., 1987; AM, Brown U., 1990, PhD, 1992. Instr. Boston U. Acad., 1993-94; asst. prof. Md. Inst., Balt., 1994—; excavator Petra, Jordan, Brown U., Providence, R.I., 1995, Corfu, Greece, 1988, Rome Am. Acad., 1991; assoc. dir. Brown U. Excavations, Petra, Jordan. Contbr. articles to profl. jours. Mem. AAUP, Am. Schs. Oriental Rsch., Archael. Inst. Am., Coll. Art Assn., Charles Village Civic Assn. Roman Catholic. Avocations: reading, music, movies, cooking, sports. Home: 44 E 26th St Baltimore MD 21218-4542 Office: Md Inst Coll Art 1300 W Mount Royal Ave Baltimore MD 21217-4134

BASILE, RICHARD EMANUEL, retired management consultant, educator; b. Buffalo, Dec. 24, 1921; s. Giustino Gregory and Minnie (Bailey) B.; m. Mariette Ruth Borocco, Oct. 12, 1946 (dec. Feb. 1994). B.A., Washington and Lee U., 1943; postgrad., U. Mo., 1947-48, Columbia U., 1965; L.H.D., Combs Coll., Phila., 1969. Geologist U.S. Geol. Survey, 1946-47; mgr. St. Clair Country Club, Belleville, Ill., Avelez Hotel, Biloxi, Miss., Carteret Club, Trenton, N.J., 1948-51; instr. U. Mo., 1948-49; head hotel mgmt. dept. Paul Smith's Coll., 1951-57, adminstrv. dean, 1961-66; mgr. Am. Mgmt. Assn. Acad., 1957-61; dir. devel. ARA, Inc., Phila., 1966-67; v.p. purchasing ARA Services, Inc., 1966-68, v.p., 1968-70; prof. U. Nev., Las Vegas, 1970-88, prof. emeritus, 1988—; pres. Univ. Assocs., Inc., Las Vegas, 1971-92; adv. bd. Paul Smith's (N.Y.) Coll., 1994—; cons. Indsl. Relations Counselors, Area Redevel. Act, U.S. Govt., XIX and XXI Olympiads, 1968, 76; mem. NRC, 1977-80; com. chmn. XI Internat. Congress on Nutrition, Rio de Janeiro, 1978; U.S. Dept. Commerce tech. rep. Cyprus Internat. Trade Show, Nicosia, 1982; mem. Nev. Employee-Mgmt. Relations Bd., 1981—; treas., bd. dirs. Marriott's Camelback Inn and Resort, Scottsdale, Ariz., 1987-91; cons. to hospitality industry. Cons. editor: Restaurant Hospitality Mag. Contbr. articles to profl. jours. Pres. Adirondock (N.Y.) Med. Ctr., 1960-66; sec. treas. Paradise Valley Physical Therapy Clinic, Las Vegas, 1987-89; bd. dirs. Saranac Lake chpt. ARC, Nat. Council on Hotel and Restaurant Edn., Washington; bd. mem. arbitration, mediation and fact finding bd. Los Angeles Employees Rels. Bd.; arbitrator Teamsters local 995, Nev. Resort Assn., Nat. Assn. Security Dealers Regulations, 1997—. Paul Harris fellow, 1980—; eminent fellow Wisdom Hall of Fame, 1998; Winston Churchill medal of wisdom and eminent Churchill fellow, 1999. Mem. Utility Shareholders Assn. Nev. (bd. dirs. 1994—, v.p. 1997-99), Am. Arbitration Assn. (panel arbitrators 1961—), Pa. Acad. Fine Arts, Vesper Club, Peale Club, Masons, K.T., Rotary (pres. 1962-63), Sigma Phi Epsilon, Alpha Kappa Psi. Home: 1800 S 14th St Las Vegas NV 89104-3124 Office: 4505 S Maryland Pky Las Vegas NV 89154-9900 *Success? Is it not in the eye of the beholder? A strong hero worship from childhood days of those selected educators, religious and business leaders who were honest, unselfish, and who enjoyed pure living—not solely materialistic gain. A family who exemplified the work ethic, and a wife who was almost psychic in her ability to keep me from wearing an oversized hat.*

BASILICO, CLAUDIO, molecular biologist, educator; b. Milan, Italy, Feb. 7, 1936; came to U.S., 1967; s. Vittorio and Enrica (Belloni) B.; m. Mariapia Casartelli, Oct. 7, 1961; children—Stefano, Francesca, Enrica. M.D., U. Milan, 1960. Vis. research fellow div. biology Calif. Inst. Tech., 1962; staff Internat. Lab. Genetics and Biophysics, Naples, Italy, 1963-66; research assoc. dept. cell biology Albert Einstein Coll. Medicine, 1966-67; vis. research scientist dept. pathology NYU Sch. Medicine, N.Y.C., 1967-69; research asst. prof. NYU Sch. Medicine, 1969, assoc. prof., 1970-75, prof. dept. pathology, 1975-89, prof., chmn. dept. microbiology, 1990—; mem. adv. com. on cellular and devel. biology, Am. Cancer Soc., 1979-83; dir. growth regulation program NYU Cancer Ctr., 1979—; assoc. dir. Skirball Inst. Biomolecular Medicine, 1998—. Contbr. articles to profl. jours. Trustee Cold Spring Harbor Lab., 1981-86. Mem. Am. Soc. Microbiology, Am. Assn. Cancer Research, Am. Soc. Virology. Office: Medical Science Bldg 550 1st Ave Rm 256 New York NY 10016-6481*

BASINGER, CHERYL KATHRYN RICKETTS, organizational development executive; b. Lancaster, Ohio, Aug. 6, 1955; d. John Thomas and Rita Joan (Bader) Ricketts; m. Ned Naden Basinger, July 26, 1980; children: Christopher, Kimberly. BS/MS with honors, Ohio State U., 1977. Mgmt. trainee Landmark, Inc., New Philadelphia, Ohio, 1978-79; personnel specialist Landmark, Inc., Columbus, Ohio, 1979-81; co-owner, mgr. Fairfield Mfg., Inc., Pickerington, Ohio, 1983-90; mgr. employment and devel. Countrymark, Inc., Delaware, Ohio, 1981-88; dir. devel. and mktg. Comprehensive Tng. and Devel. Inst., Worthington, Ohio, 1988-89; pres. Performance Dimensions, Inc., Pickerington, 1989-92; account exec. Franklin Quest Co., Inc., 1989-97; mem. Pres.'s Pyramid Club Franklin Internat. Inst., Inc., 1991-95, mem. adv. bd., 1992-94; area v.p. Franklin Covey Co., 1997—. Instr. new mem. class, Peace United Meth. Ch., Pickerington, 1982-90. Mem. ASTD (pres. cen. Ohio chpt. 1986, asst. regional dir. 1987-89, regional dir 1990-91, chair, Coun. Regions and Chpts. 1991, dir. nat. cons. network 1992, nat. awards com. 1993-95, Region III Contbr. of Yr. 1986, 91), Ohio State U. Agr. Alumni Coun. (v.p., sec.). Republican. Avocations: raising sheep, running. Office: Franklin Covey Co 8850 Chateau Dr NW Pickerington OH 43147-9713

BASINGER, KAREN LYNN, renal dietitian; b. Mechanicsville, Md., July 4, 1955; d. Leonard Marcus and Mary Jane (Harding) Brookbank; m. Joseph Andrew Basinger, Nov. 17, 1984; 1 child, James Marcus. BS, U. Md., 1977; MS, Hood Coll., 1987. Lic. nutritionist. Libr. technician Bowie (Md.) State Coll., 1973-79; instr. St. Mary's County Adult Edn., Leonardtown, Md., 1979-80; home economist Zamoiski Co., Balt., 1977-83; nutritionist/WIC coord. South County Health Plan, Prince Frederick, Md., 1979-80; nutritionist Walter Reed Army Med. Ctr., Washington, 1980-82; renal dietitian Mid Atlantic/BMA, Camp Springs, Md., 1982-87, Kidney Care Ctr., Landover, Md., 1987-99; instr. dietary intern program Andrews AFB, 1988-91; renal dietitian Silver Spring (Md.) Artificial Kindey Ctr., 1998—; outpatient dietitian Holy Cross Hosp., Silver Spring, 1999—; lectr. in field. Mem. profl. adv. bd. Nat. Kidney Found./NCA, 1989-94; chair coun. on renal nutrition Nat. Kidney Found., 1993-94, program chair, 1990-92. Recipient Spl. Recognition Nat. Kidney Found./NCA, 1990, 92, Recognized Renal Dietitian/NCA, 1991, 94. Mem. Am. Nutritionists Assn., Am. Home Econs. Assn., Md. Home Econs. Assn. (bylaws chair 1982-94), Am. Dietetic Assn., Washington Metro. Coun. on Renal Nutrition (chair 1986-91, 95-98, nutrition symposium chair 1989), U. Md. Alumni Assn. Democrat. Lutheran. Avocation: cross-stitch. Office: Holy Cross Hosp 1500 Forest Glen Rd Silver Spring MD 20910

BASINGER, LAWRENCE EDWIN, real estate executive; b. Riverside, Calif., Oct. 7, 1958; s. Billie Joe Basinger and Jorene Edna (Anderson) Murley; m. Stephanie L. Glover, June 10, 1995, 1 child: Morgan Alexis. Student, East Tex. State U., 1976-77, Dallas C.C., 1980-86, Tarleton State U., 1986-97. S.w. regional mgr. Southland Corp., Dallas, 1981-85; br. mgr. GE Capital, Dallas, 1985-92; exec. v.p. Golden Feather Realty, Dallas, 1992-98; CEO Freelance, Inc., Irving, Tex., 1999—. Writer (album) Basingers First, 1997. Spkr. seminars GE Capital, Dallas, 1990, Golden Feather Realty, Balt., 1997. Avocations: golf, tennis, songwriting. Home: 6223 Linden Ln Dallas TX 75230-1310 Office: Freelance Inc 1105 E Shady Grove Irving TX 76050

BASINGER, WILLIAM DANIEL, computer programmer; b. Washington, Feb. 14, 1952; s. James Samuel and Eleanor (Freeburger) B.; m. Martha Kecskes, July 1, 1978 (div. 1983); m. Mary Teresa Richardson, June 11, 1988. BA in Linguistics, U. Md., 1974; MS in Linguistics, Georgetown U., 1977; MS in Computer Sci., Johns Hopkins U., 1989. Programmer Evaluation Techs., Arlington, Va., 1977-78; programmer, analyst, cons. Vitro Corp., Silver Spring, Md., 1978-84, 87-88; programmer, analyst Tracor Applied Scis., Rockville, Md., 1984-88, PRC, Inc., McLean, Va., 1988-89; sr. programmer, analyst Systems & Computer Tech. group George Washington U., Washington, 1989-95; sr. programmer, statistician PRC, Inc., Reston, 1996-97; sr. systems analyst, Yr. 2000 Assessment Project M-Cubed Info. Systems, Rockville, Md., 1997—; cons. applications software dept. geology George Washington U., Washington, 1990-91, 93—. Contbr. articles to profl. jours. Contbr., sponsor Statue of Liberty/Ellis Island Found., N.Y.C., 1985—. Md. State Sen. scholar U. Md., 1970-74. Mem. Assn. Computing Machinery, Am. Geophys. Union, N.Y. Acad. Scis. Republican. Roman Catholic. Home: Apt 203 11342 Cherry Hill Rd Beltsville MD 20705-3735 Office: M-Cubed Info Systems 3206 Tower Oaks Blvd Ste 210 Rockville MD 20852-4220 also: 3700 E West Hwy Hyattsville MD 20782-2015

BASINSKI, ANTHONY JOSEPH, lawyer; b. Pitts., Apr. 11, 1947; s. Anthony F. and Emily C. (Klocko) B.; m. Elisabeth Fawcett, Oct. 4, 1980; children: Ann Elisabeth, Robert Anthony. BA, U. Pitts., 1969, JD, 1974. Bar: Pa. 1974, U.S. Dist. Ct. (we. dist.) Pa. 1974, U.S. Ct. Appeals (3d cir.) 1981, U.S. Ct. Appeals (4th cir.) 1992, U.S. Ct. Appeals (fed. cir.) 1995. Law clk. to presiding justice Pa. Supreme Ct., Pitts., 1974-76; ptnr. Reed, Smith, Shaw and McClay, Pitts., 1976—. Served with U.S. Army, 1969-71, Vietnam. Mem. Allegheny County Bar Assn., Am. Arbitration Assn. (arbitrator 1983—). Democratic. Roman Catholic. Home: 1749 Taper Dr Pittsburgh PA 15241-2623 Office: Reed Smith Shaw & McClay 435 6th Ave Ste 2 Pittsburgh PA 15219-1886

BASINSKI, ZBIGNIEW STANISLAW, metal physicist, educator; b. Wolkowysk, Poland, Apr. 28, 1928; emigrated to Can., 1956, naturalized, 1961; s. Antoni and Maria Zofia Anna (Hilferding) B.; m. Sylvia Joy Pugh, Apr. 1, 1952; children: Stefan Leon Hilferding, Antoni Stanislaw Hilferding. BA, Oxford (Eng.) U., 1951, BSc, 1952, MA, 1954, DPhil, 1954, DSc, 1966; D honoris causa, St. Staszic U. Acad. Mining and Metallurgy, Krakow, Poland, 1991. With div. indsl. cooperation Mass. Inst. Tech., 1954-55; mem. staff Nat. Research Council Can., 1956-87, prin. research officer, 1965-87; research prof. dept. material sci. and engring. McMaster U., Hamilton, Ont., Can., 1987-92, prof. emeritus, 1992—; Ford distinguished vis. prof. Carnegie Inst. Tech., 1963-64; Commonwealth vis. prof. and vis. fellow Wolfson Coll., Oxford U., 1969-70; vis. research scientist Cavendish Lab.; also overseas fellow Churchill Coll., both Cambridge (Eng.) U., 1980-81. Contbr. articles to sci. jours. Recipient Canadian Metal Physics medal, 1977; decorated officer Order of Can. Fellow Royal Soc. London, Royal Soc. Can. Home: 98 Bluebell Crescent, Ancaster, ON Canada L9K 1G1 Office: McMaster U, Dept Materials Sci and Engring, Hamilton, ON Canada L8S 4M1

BASKA, JAMES LOUIS, wholesale grocery company executive; b. Kansas City, Kans., Apr. 3, 1927; s. John James and Stella Marie (Wilson) B.; m. Juanita Louise Carlson, Oct. 14, 1950; children: Steven James, Scott David. BSBA, U. Kans., 1949; JD, U. Mo., 1960. Bar: Kans. 1960. Pres., chief exec. officer Baska Laundry Co., Kansas City, 1951-62; ptnr. Rice & Baska, Kansas City, 1962-76; corporate sec., gen. counsel Assoc. Wholesale Grocers Inc., Kansas City, 1976-77, v.p., sec., gen. counsel, 1977-79, exec. v.p., chief fin. officer, sec., gen. counsel, 1979-84, pres., chief exec. officer, 1984-92; pres. emeritus, 1992. Served as staff sgt. U.S. Army, 1944-46. Mem. Nat. Grocers Assn. (bd. dirs. 1980-89, chmn. 1987-88), Food Mktg. Inst. (bd. dirs. 1988-93). Republican. Roman Catholic. Avocations: hunting, golf. Office: Assoc Wholesale Grocers Inc PO Box 2932 5000 Kansas Ave Kansas City KS 66106-1135 *There is always room at the top and my objectives whatever they may be and no matter how big or wild, are always attainable. The only questions are—am I ready to make the move and willing to pay the price?.*

BASKE, C. ALAN, manufacturing company executive; b. Detroit, Apr. 19, 1927; s. Clarence A. and Alice Loraine (Severance) B.; m. Shirley Ann Duckworth, Feb. 24, 1945; children: Nance, Roger, Douglas, Brian. Radio officer, USCG Hoffmann Island, Bklyn., 1944. Radio officer U.S. Maritime Svc., Atlantic, Pacific, Caribbean, 1944-45; owner/mgr. Alan's Auto Svc., Dearborn, Mich., 1946; svc. parts mgr. Detherage-McDonald Auto Sales, Dearborn, Mich., 1946-48; field sales agt. Sun Electric Corp., Detroit/Jackson, 1948; asst. dir. Sun Electric Corp., Chgo., 1948-53; mfg. rep. Valley Bearing, Chgo., 1953-74, owner/pres., 1974-86; cons. Libertyville, Ill., 1986—. Advisor Boy Scouts Am. troop 80, Libertyville, 1954-65; vestryman St. Lawrence Ch., Libertyville, 1958-66; bd. dirs. Libertyville/Freemont High Sch. Dist., 1962-64; chmn. Condell Hosp., 1968-72, 84-86, bd. dirs., 1963-72, 77-86; trustee Lake Forest (Ill.) Acad., 1969-75; pres. Waukegan (Ill.) Symphony Chorus, 1984-88; founding mem. Coll. Lake County Found., pres., 1975-82. Mem. Libertyville Country Side Assn. (bd. dir./officer), Island Goat Sailing Soc., Waukegan Power Squadron (life), Waukegan Yacht Club (dir., past commodore), Libertyville Boat Club (founder dir.), U.S. Sailing Assn. (judge 1998—), Waukegan Yacht Club Jr. Found. (founder, pres. 1997—). Republican. Episcopalian. Avocations: sailing, flying, skiing, traveling. Home and Office: 15252 W Oak Spring Rd Libertyville IL 60048-1620

BASKERVILL, CHARLES THORNTON, lawyer; b. South Boston, Va., May 26, 1953; s. William Nelson and Julia Alice (Moore) B.; m. Pamela Temple Shell, July 17, 1976; children: Ann Cabell, Susannah Thornton. BA, Hampden-Sydney Coll., 1975; JD, U. Richmond, 1978. Bar: a. 1978, U.S. Dist. Ct. (ea. dist.) Va. 1978. Assoc. White, Hamilton, Wyche & Shell, P.C., Petersburg, Va., 1978-96; asst. commonwealth's atty Petersburg, 1985—; assoc. Shell, Johnson, Andrews, Baskervill & Baskervill, P.C., Petersburg, 1996—; commr. of accts. City of Petersburg, Va., 1996—. Former dir. Petersburg Crime Prevention Found. Named to Athletic Hall of Fame, Hampden-Sydney Coll., 1988. Mem. Prince George County Bar Assn. (sec.-treas. 1990-91, pres. 1991-92), Petersburg Bar Assn. Methodist. Avocations: golf, tennis. Office: Shell Johnson Andrews Baskervill & Baskervill PC 43 Rives Rd Petersburg VA 23805-9287

BASKERVILLE, CHARLES ALEXANDER, geologist, educator; b. Jamaica, N.Y., Aug. 19, 1928; s. Charles H. and Annie M. (Allen) B.; m. Susan Platt, July 5, 1979; children: Mark Dana, Shawn Allison, Charles Morris, Thomas Marshall. BS, CCNY, 1953; MS, NYU, 1958, PhD, 1965. Cert. geologist, Maine, Ind.; cert. profl. geologist. Asst. civil engr. N.Y. State Dept. Transp., Babylon, 1953-66; prof. engrng. geology CUNY, N.Y.C., 1966-79, dean sch. of gen. studies, 1970-79, prof. emeritus, 1979—; project rsch. geologist U.S. Geol. Survey, 1979-90; prof. geology Ctrl. Conn. State U., New Britain, 1990—, dept. chmn., 1992-94; Commonwealth vis. prof. George Mason U., Fairfax, Va., 1987-89; mem. U.S. Nat. Com. on Tunnelling Tech., NRC, chmn. subcom. on edn. and tng.; mem. Am. del Internat. Tunnelling Assn. to Internat. Colloquim of Tunnelling and Underground Works, Beijing, People's Republic of China, 1984; cons. in field; guest lectr. various colls., 1964—; geol. program evaluator for colls. seeking continued mid. states accreditation. Author numerous sci. papers. Mem. com. for minority participation in the geoscis. U.S. Dept. Interior, 1972-75; panelist Grad. Fellowship Program NRC; chmn. Minority Grad. Fellowship Program, 1979-80; mem. com. of visitors for edn. and human resources program divsn. earth scis. NSF, 1991; mem. N.Y. State Low Level Radioactive Waste Com. NAS, 1994-96. Recipient Founders Day award N.Y. U., 1966, 125th Anniversary medal The City Coll., 1973, award for excellence in engrng. geology Nat. Consortium Black Profl. Devel., 1978, Recognition award Nat. Assn. Black Geologists and Geophysicists, 1998. Fellow Geol. Soc. Am. (sr., com. on minorities in geoscis., chmn. com. on coms. 1989), N.Y. Acad. Scis., Geol. Soc. Washington, Am. Inst. Profl. Geologists, Assn. Engrng. Geologists (rep. to nat. bd. dirs. 1973-74, chmn. N.Y.-Phila. sect. 1973-74), Internat. Assn. Engrng. Geology, Yellowstone-Bighorn Rsch. Assn., Sigma Xi. Office: Ctrl Conn State U Dept Physics and Earth Scis 1615 Stanley St New Britain CT 06050-4010

BASKHARONE, ERIAN AZIZ, mechanical and aerospace engineering educator; b. Cairo, Egypt, Sept. 28, 1947; came to U.S. 1974; s. Aziz and Mofida (Khlil) B.; children: Richard, Robert, Daniel; m. Magda I. Saleeb, Jan. 14, 1995; 1 child, Christian. MS in Aerospace Engrng., U. Cin., 1975, PhD in Aerospace Engrng., 1979. Registered profl. engr., Tex. Asst. lectr. Coll. Engrng., U. Cairo, 1970-74; rsch. asst. U. Cin., 1974-79, postdoctoral fellow, 1979-80; sr. engr. Garrett Turbine Engine Co., Phoenix, 1980-85; assoc. prof. mech. and aerospace engrng. Tex. A&M U., College Station, 1985—; cons. Aux. Power Units div. Allied Signal Aerospace Co., Phoenix, 1989—. Contbr. articles to profl. jours. Recipient disting. teaching award Amoco Found., 1992, award of excellence in engrng. teaching, Gen. Dynamics Corp., 1991, cert. of recognition by the Inventions and Contbns. Bd., NASA Lewis Rsch. Ctr., 1983. Mem. AAUP, ASME, AIAA (sr.), Am. Soc. Engrng. Edn., Internat. Gas Turbine Inst. (mem. turbomachinery tech. com.), Sigma Gamma Tau. Democrat. Orthodox Christian. Achievements include patent for radial inboard pre-swirl system for turboprop engine cooling; research on turbomachinery flow fields and non-traditional perturbation models in the mathematical and application aspects of the finite-element method, turbomachinery aerodynamics, fluid-induced vibrations and rotordynamics. Home: 2706 Echo Glen Cir Bryan TX 77803-5183 Office: Tex A&M Univ Dept Mech Engrng College Station TX 77843-3123

BASKIN, C(HARLES) R(ICHARD), retired civil engineer, physical scientist; b. Houston, Mar. 6, 1926; s. Charles Todd and Bessie Emma (Heilig) B.; B.S. in Civil Engrng., La. State U., 1953; m. Peggy June Holden, Dec. 31, 1952; children: Richard Karl, Sheila Frances. Design engr. City-Parish Dept. Pub. Works, Baton Rouge, 1953-57; city engr. City of Plaquemine (La.), 1957-58; sect. head, asst. chief engr. Tex. Bd. Water Engrs., Austin, 1958-62; asst. chief engr. Tex. Water Commn., Austin, 1962-65; asst. chief engr. and chief engr. Tex. Water Devel. Bd., Austin, 1965-77; dir. data and engrng. services div. Tex. Dept. Water Resources, Austin, 1977-83; spl. asst. Office of Asst. Dir. Info. Systems, U.S. Geol. Survey, Reston, Va., 1983-92. Chmn., Tex. Mapping Adv. Com., 1968-83, Water Oriented Data Programs sect. Tex. Interagy. Council on Natural Resources and the Environment, 1968-72, Tex. Natural Resources Info. System Task Force, 1972-83; mem. Non-Fed. Adv. Com. on Water Data for Public Use, 1970-83; chmn. Water Data Coordination Task Force, Interstate Conf. on Water Problems, 1975-83. Served with U.S. Army, 1944-47; POW; Commd. Adm. Tex. Navy, 1961; recipient John Wesley Powell award U.S. Geol. Survey, 1972, Combat Inf. badge. Mem. Phi Kappa Phi, Tau Beta Pi (chpt. pres. 1950), Chi Epsilon, Phi Eta Sigma, Sigma Tau Sigma (pres. 1950). Adventist (elder). Avocations: photography, walking. Contbr. articles to profl. jours. Home: 304 N Woodlake Dr Columbia SC 29229-8932

BASKIN, DAVID STUART, neurosurgeon, educator; b. N.Y.C., Feb. 11, 1952; s. Norman and Selma (Schorr) B. BA with high honors, Swarthmore Coll., 1974; MD, Mt. Sinai Sch. Medicine, CUNY, 1978. Diplomate Am. Bd. Neurol. Surgery. Intern in surgery U. Calif., San Francisco, 1978-79, resident in neurosurgery, 1979-84; asst. prof. Baylor Coll. Medicine, Houston, 1984-89, assoc. prof., 1989-94, assoc. prof. anesthesiology, 1993-94; chief neurosurgery VA Hosp., Houston, 1984-92, attending neurosurgeon, 1992—; prof. neurosurgery Baylor Coll. Medicine, Houston, 1994—, prof. anesthesiology, 1994—; attending physician Meth. Hosp., Ben Taub Hosp., Tex. Children's Hosp., St. Luke's Episc. Hosp., Inst. for Rehab. and Rsch., Houston, 1984—, Tex. Orthopedic Hosp., 1994—. Contbr. numerous articles to profl. jours. Mem. Alzheimer's Exec. Coun. Recipient Acad. award Am. Acad. Neurol. Surgeons, 1983, Wakeman award for rsch. in neurosci., 1990, Disting. Alumni awadr Mt. Sinai Sch. Medicine, 1990. Fellow ACS, Stroke Coun. of Am. Heart Assn.; mem. AMA, AAAS, Congress Neurol. Surgeons, Joint Sect. on Spinal Disorders of Congress Neurol. Surgeons/Am. Assn. Neurol. Surgeons, Pituitary Found. Am., Soc. Univ. Neurosurgeons, Rocky Mountain Neurol. Soc., So. Med. Assn., Houston Neurol. Soc., Pituitary Soc. Houston, Tex. Med. Assn., Harris County Med. Soc., Phi Beta Kappa, Sigma Xi, Alpha Omega Alpha. Avocations: scuba diving, hunting, fishing, skiing. Office: Baylor Coll Medicine 6560 Fannin St Ste 944 Houston TX 77030-2706

BASKIN, LEONARD, sculptor, graphic artist; b. New Brunswick, N.J., Aug. 15, 1922; s. Samuel and May (Guss) B.; m. Esther Tane, Nov. 26, 1946; 1 child, Tobias Isaac; m. Lisa Unger, Oct. 1967; children—Hosea Thomas, Lucretia Manya. Student, Yale Sch. Art, 1941-43; A.B., New Sch., N.Y.C., 1949; D.F.A., New Sch., 1966; L.H.D., Clark U., 1966, Rutgers U., 1967; D.F.A., U. Mass., 1968; student Paris and Florence; honorary degree, Springfield Coll., 1997; LHD, Spertus Inst., Chgo., 1998. Prof. graphics Smith Coll., 1953-74; vis. prof. art Hampshire Coll., Amherst, Mass. One-man shows N.Y.C., 1954, 56, 57, 60-62, 65-76, 91-97, Boston, 1952, 55, 59, also London, Rotterdam, Paris, Gallery 68, Bselfast, Maine, 1991, Midtown Payson Gallery, N.Y. 1991, 95, Portland (Maine) Mus., 1992, Art Inst. Boston, 1992, Minn. Ctr. Book Arts, Mpls., 1992, Bridwell Libr. So. Meth. U., Dallas, 1992, Grolier Club, N.Y., 1992, Evelyn Siegel Gallery, Ft. Worth, 1993, Beamesdefer Gallery, Highland Park, N.J., 1993, Denenberg Fine Arts, San Francisco, 1993, Emory U., Atlanta, 1993, Dorothy McRae Gallery, Atlanta, 1993, 94, U. Del., 1993, John Hay Libr. Brown U., 1993, U. Mich., Ann Arbor, 1994, Libr. Congress, Washington, 1994, Conway Gallery, Georgetown, Ohio, Washington, 1994, Ann Arbor Art Assn., 1994, R. Michelson Gallery, Northampton, Mass., 1994, 95, Cove Gallery, Wellfleet, Mass., 1994, 95, Vered Gallery, Easthampton, N.Y., 1994, Bishop Gallery, Scottsdale, Ariz., 1994, Munson Galleries, Santa Fe, 1994, Beinecke Rare Book and Manuscript libr. Yale U., 1994, Princeton U., 1994, Wilshire Blvd. Temple, Beverly Hills, Calif., 1995, Mount Saint Joseph Coll. Art Mus., Cin., 1995, Callahan Gallery, Boston, 1995, Instituto Artes Graficas, Oaxaca, Mex., 1995, Islington Design Ctr., London, 1995, Oberlin Coll., 1995, U. Calif., San Diego, 1996, Corp. Ctr., 1996, Fresno (Calif.) Mus. Art, 1996, Bradley U., Peoria, Ill, 1996, Bowles Sorokko Galleries, San Francisco, 1996, U. San Francisco, 1996, S.F.A. Gallery Stephen F. Austin U., Nacogdoches, Tex., 1996, U. Wis., Madison, 1997, Serg Sorokko Galleries, San Francisco, 1997, Susan Conway Gallery, Washington, 1997, R. Michelson Galleries, Northampton, 1997, Dennenberg Fine Arts, San Francisco, 1997, Salander-O'Reilly Gallery, N.Y., 1997, Tyler (Tex.) Mus. Art, 1997, Washington U., 1997, Phoenix Pub. Libr., 1998, Hampshire Coll, Amherst, Mass., 1998, Hunter Mus. Art, Chattanooga, 1998, Woodrow Wilson Ctr., Washington, 1998, Wilson Libr. U. N.C., Chapel Hill, 1998; represented in permanent collections Met. Art., Mus. Modern Art, Library of Congress, Nat. Gallery Art, Art Inst. Chgo., museums Phila., Boston and Worchester, Fogg Mus. at Harvard, others. Served with USNR, 1943-46. Recipient 1st prize engraving São Paulo Biennial, 1962, medal Am. Inst. Graphic Arts, 1965, Cultural Achievement in the Arts award Nat. Found. Jewish Culture, 1995; Tiffany fellow, 1947; Guggenheim fellow, 1953; grantee Nat. Inst. Arts and Letters, 1961. Mem. Royal Acad. Belgium, Am. Acad. Arts and Letters, 1968 (medal of merit for graphic arts 1969), Am. Inst. Graphic Artists, Nat. Acad. of Design, 1994. Office: PO Box 314 Leeds MA 01053-0314

BASKIN, OTIS WAYNE, business educator; b. Houston, Oct. 26, 1945; s. Samuel and Ollie Estell (Key) B.; m. Maryan Kay Patrick, Dec. 26, 1970. BA, Okla. Christian Coll., 1968; MA, U. Houston, 1970; PhD, U. Tex., 1975. Asst. prof. Tex. Luth. Coll., Seguin, 1970-75; prof. U. Houston, 1975-87; prof., acad. dir. Ariz. State U., Phoenix, 1987-91; prof., dean Memphis State U., 1991-92, prof., dir. family bus., 1992-95; dean George L. Graziadio Sch. Bus. and Mgmt. Pepperdine U., Malibu, Calif., 1995—; vis. faculty U. Md., London, 1979, Oxford U., 1994; dir. Durham Found., Memphis, 1992-95; cons. Ministry Trade, Sophia, Bulgaria, 1990, Utara U., Malaysia, 1992. Author: Guidelines for Research in Business Communication, 1977, (With Craig Aronoff) Interpersonal Communication in Organizations, 1980, Getting Your Message Across, 1981, Public Relations: The Profession and the practice, 1983, (with Grover Starling) Issues in Business and Society: Capitalism and Public Purpose, 1985; contbr. articles to profl. jours. Bd. dirs. Jr. Achievement Memphis, 1991-92, Econ. Club Memphis, 1991-94, Theatre Memphis, 1992-95, Margurite Pizza Gala for St. Jude's Hosp., Memphis, 1992-95. Recipient Advancing Pub. Rels. Through Rsch. award Tex. Pub. Rels. Soc., Houston, 1983. Mem. Acad. Mgmt. (divsn. chair 1985), Rotary, Sigma Iota Epsilon (bd. dirs. 1986—), Beta Gamma Sigma. mem. Ch. of Christ. Avocations: reading, travel. Office: George L Graziadio Sch Bus & Mgmt Pepperdine Univ Malibu CA 90263

BASKIN, RONALD JOSEPH, cell biologist, physiologist, biophysicist educator, dean; b. Joliet, Ill., Nov. 25, 1935; s. Mack Robert and Evelyn Josephine (Rudzinski) B.; m. Lydia Olga Lendl, Mar. 29, 1957; children—Ronald James, Thomas William. A.B., UCLA, 1957; M.A., 1959, Ph.D., 1960. Asst. prof. biology Rensselaer Poly. Inst., Troy, N.Y., 1961-64; asst. prof. zoology U. Calif., Davis, 1964-67; assoc. prof. U. Calif., 1967-71, prof., 1971—, chmn. dept. zoology, 1971-78, assoc. dean coll. letters and sci., 1986-90; mem. editorial bd. U. Calif. Press. Contbr. articles to sci. publs. Nat. Heart Inst. predoctoral fellow, 1957-60. Mem. Biophys. Soc., Soc. Cell Biology, Am. Physiol. Soc., N.Y. Acad. Scis., Sigma Xi. Office: Molecular & Cellular Biology Sect U Calif Davis CA 95616

BASKIN, SCOTT DAVID, lawyer; b. N.Y.C., Oct. 24, 1953; s. George and Anne (Strauss) B.; m. Sherry Nahmias, Mar. 13, 1982; children: Jonathan, Felicia. BA, Stanford U., 1975; JD, Yale U., 1978. Bar: Calif. 1978, U.S. Dist. Ct. (cen., ea., so. and no. dists.) Calif. 1979, U.. Appeals (9th cir.) 1979. Law clk. Hon. Herbert Choy, 9th Cir. Ct., Honolulu, 1978-79; ptnr. Irell & Manella, Newport Beach, Calif., 1979—; lectr. Calif. Continuing Edn. of the Bar, 1985—. Contbr. articles to profl. publs. Mem. ABA. Office: Irell & Manella 840 Newport Center Dr Ste 500 Newport Beach CA 92660-6324

BASKIN, STUART JAY, lawyer; b. Bklyn., Apr. 22, 1950; s. Joseph and Anne (Straus) B.; m. Linda D. Lennon, June 21, 1987; 1 child, Rebecca. BA, Stanford U., 1972, JD, 1975; JD, Stanford U., 1975. Bar: N.Y. 1976, U.S. Dist. Ct. (so. and ea. dists.) N.Y. 1982, U.S. Ct. Appeals (2d cir.) 1982, U.S. Ct. Appeals (1st cir.) 1990, U.S. Ct. Appeals (3d cir.) 1992, U.S. Ct. Appeals (5th and 7th cir.) 1993, U.S. Ct. Appeals (11th cir.) 1995, U.S. Supreme Ct. 1993. Law clk. to Walter R. Mansfield U.S. Ct. Appeals for 2d Cir., N.Y.C., 1975-76; to William J. Brennan, Jr., U.S. Supreme Ct., Washington, 1976-77; spl. asst. to dir. Office for Civil Rights, HEW, Washington, 1977-78; asst. U.S. Atty. for so. dist. N.Y., Dept. Justice, N.Y.C., 1978-82; ptnr. Kramer, Levin, Nessen, Kamin & Frankel, N.Y.C., 1982-89, Shearman & Sterling, N.Y.C., 1989—; adj. prof. trial practice NYU Sch. Law, N.Y.C., 1986-88. Contbg. author: U.S. Securities and Investment Regulation Handbook, 1992; pres. Stanford Law Rev., 1974-75; contbr. articles to legal jours. Recipient John Marshall award for best trial lawyer Dept. Justice, 1982. Mem. ABA, Assn. Bar City N.Y., Fed. Bar Coun.

BASKIN, WILLIAM GRESHAM, counselor, music educator, vocalist; b. Cameron, Tex., July 14, 1933; s. James Dollar and Ruth (McKinney) B.; m. Margaret Lee Williams, Mar. 26, 1959; 1 child, Susan Elizabeth. Student, U. Tex., 1951-54; B of Music Edn., S.W. Tex. State U., 1955; postgrad., Ea. Wash. U., 1956; MEd, S.W. Tex. State U., 1961. Cert. life elem. and secondary tchr., profl. music tchrs., provisional vis. techr., profl. counselor, profl. prin., Tex.; lic. profl. counselor, Tex.; nat. cert. counselor; nat. cert. career counselor; nat. cert. sch. counselor. Choral dir. San Marcos (Tex.) Bapt. Acad., 1957-58, Carrizo Springs (Tex.) Ind. Sch. Dist., 1958-62, Victoria (Tex.) High Sch., 1962-68; counselor Brazosport Ind. Sch. Dist., Freeport, Tex., 1968—; music dir. 1st Bapt. Ch., Carrizo Springs, 1958-62, Bapt. Temple, Victoria, 1962-64; interim music dir. 1st Bapt. ch., Victoria, 1965, Freeport, 1972-73, 87-88, 89, Lake Jackson, Tex., 1978-79, Temple Bapt. Ch., Clute, Tex., 1990; mem. Music Educators Nat. conf., 1958-68; del. Am. Mental Health Counselors Assn. and Citizen Amb. Program People to People Internat. to Chinese Assn. Mental Health and Chinese Assn. for Sci. and Tech. of People's Republic of China in Beijing, Shanghai and Kunming, 1994; del. from Am. Sch. Counselor's Assn. and Citizen Amb. Program of People to People Internat. to 1st U.S./Russia Joint Conf. on Edn., Moscow, 1994. Mem. Victoria Fine Arts Assn. (pres. 1964-66), 1963-68; mem. Brazosport Fine Arts Coun., Lake Jackson, 1970-73, Brazoria County Hist. Mus., Angleton, Tex., 1990—; del. Tex. Gov.'s Conf. on Arts, Austin, 1966-68; del. Dem. Precinct Conv., Lake Jackson, 1976, 77, 93, Brazoria County Dem. Conv., Angleton, 1977, Tex. Dem. Conv., San Antonio, 1977; deacon 1st Bapt. Ch., Lake Jackson, 1989, also youth worker. Scholar PTA, Victoria, 1966. Mem. Music Educator's Nat. Conf., NEA (del. 1977-79), Am. Sch. Counselors Assn., Nat. Career Devel. Assn., Assn. for Specialists in Group Work, Assn. for Measurement and Evaluation in Counseling and Devel., Tex. Assn. for Measurement and Evaluation in Counseling and Devel., Tex. Career Guidance Assn., Tex. Sch. Counselors Assn., Tex. Assn. for Counseling and Devel. (senator 1979-82, legis. com. 1984-87), Tex. Music Educators Assn. (state bd. dirs. 1964-68, dist. choral chmn. 1964-68), Tex. State Schrs. Assn., Brazosport Edn. Assn. (pres. 1977-78), Brazoria County Assn. Counseling and Devel. (legis. chmn. 1984—), Rotary (Brazosport club, Paul Harris fellow 1988). Avocations: gardening, flying. Home: 111 Oyster Bend Ln Lake Jackson TX 77566-3105 Office: Brazosport Ind Sch Dist PO Drawer Z Freeport TX 77541

BASLER, RICHARD ALAN, medical consultant; b. San Francisco, Sept. 12, 1939; s. Henry Edwin and Margaret Henrietta (Cooper) B.; m. Carol Audrey Foster, Aug. 4, 1962; children: Rodney Giles, Eric Richard. BA, U. Calif., Berkeley, 1960; MBA, U. Phoenix, Irvine, Calif., 1983. Indsl. engr., prodn. supr. Standard Register, Oakland and Corcoran, Calif., 1967-72; knitting supt. Duplan Knits West, Carson, Calif., 1972-75; prodn. supr. Am. Edwards Labs., Irvine, 1976-78, chief indsl. engr., 1978-80, supr. mfg. engrng., 1980-86, with engrng. systems devel., 1986-87; mgr. quality assurance/quality control Cardiovascular Devices Inc., 1987-88; dir. quality assurance/quality control Applied Vascular Devices Inc., 1988-90, dir. compliance, 1990-94; dir. compliance Micro Therapeutics, Inc., 1994-96; v.p. ops. Laurus Med. Corp., Irvine, Calif., 1996-97; pres. Med-Visory Cons., Irvine, 1997—; owner Internat. Numismatics, Irvine, 1974—. Editor Calif. Engr. mag., 1959, ASQ Scope mag., 1998; contbr. articles to mags. Bd. dirs. UNCAP, Inc., L.A., 1980-82; pres. Colonnade of History, 1990—. Recipient Kenneth Brainard Meml. Literary award, George Bennett Meml. Literary award. Mem. Am. Soc. Quality, U.S. Kerry Blue Terrier Club (gov. 1983-85), Gt. Western Terrier (bd. dirs. 1979-92). Republican. Avocations: ancient numismatics, breeding show dogs. Office: Med-Visory Cons 15412 Verdun Cir Irvine CA 92604

BASLER, THOMAS G., librarian, administrator, educator; b. Cleve., Mar. 8, 1940; s. Gordon Fred and Bertha Elizabeth (Gerspacher) B.; m. Samille Jones, Nov. 25, 1986; children from previous marriage: William T., Elizabeth E., Charles G. BEd, U. Miami, Coral Gables, Fla., 1962; MS, Fla. State U., 1964; PhD, Laurence U., Santa Barbara, Calif., 1977. Intern Emory U., Atlanta, 1965; asst. prof., librarian Insts. Marine Scis., Miami, Fla., 1966-68; librarian Am. Mus. Natural History, N.Y.C., 1968-70, N.Y. Acad. Medicine, N.Y.C., 1970-72; prof., dir. library Med. Coll. Ga., Augusta, 1972-91; dir. libr. and learning resources ctrs. Med. U. S.C., Charleston, 1991—, dir. environ. hazards assessment program info. sys., 1994—, chair dept. of libr. sci. and informatics; cons. Abbott Pharm. Co., North Chicago, Ill., 1973-83; chmn. Regents Acad. Com. on Libraries, Univ. System Ga., 1984-85; mem. adv. council SE Atlantic Regional Med. Library, 1984—. Author: Health Science Librarianship, 1977, Medical School Library Directorship, 1977, also articles. Mem. Consortium So. Biomed. Libraries, Inc. (sec.-treas. 1983—). Home: 1205 Manor Ln Mount Pleasant SC 29464-5188 Office: Med U SC 171 Ashley Ave Charleston SC 29425-0001

BASMAJIAN, JOHN VAROUJAN, medical scientist, educator, physician; b. Constantinople, Turkey, June 21, 1921; came to Can., 1923, naturalized, 1927; s. Mihran and Mary (Evelian) B.; m. Dora Belle Lucas, Oct. 4, 1947; children: Haig, Nancy, Sally. MD with honors, U. Toronto, 1945; LLD (hon.), Queen's U., 1999. Intern Toronto Gen. Hosp., 1945; surg. resident Sunnybrook Hosp. and Hosp. for Sick Children, Toronto, 1946-48; from lectr. to prof. U. Toronto, 1949-57; prof. anatomy, chmn. dept. anatomy Queen's U., Kingston, Ont., 1957-69; prof., dir. regional rehab. rsch. and tng. ctr. Emory U., Atlanta, 1969-77; prof. medicine McMaster U., Hamilton, Ont., Can., 1977-86; prof. emeritus McMaster U., Hamilton, Ont., 1986—; dir. rehab. ctr. Chedoke-McMaster Hosps., Hamilton, 1977-86; exec. sec. Banting Rsch. Found., Toronto, 1954-57; chmn. rsch. com. Fitness Coun. Can., Ottawa, Ont., 1965-69; spl. cons. med. rsch. Ga. Inst. Tech., Atlanta, 1984—; dir. rsch. and tng. grants Ea. Seal Rsch. Inst., Toronto, 1990-95; bd. dirs. Can. Physiotherapy Found., Toronto, 1984-89; lectureships in Europe, Asia, South Am., Australia, Japan, others. Author 11 med. sci. and clin. books in multiple edits. and transls., 1953—; editor 9 med. clin. books in multiple edits. and transls., 1977—; series editor: Rehabilitation Medicine Library, 24 vols., 1977—; editl. bd. Am. Jour. Phys. Medicine, 1968-90, Am. Jour. Anatomy, 1971-74, Electromyography and Clin. Neurophysiology, 1966-85, Electro-diagnostic-therapy, Physiotherapy Can., 1979-84, Jour. Motor Behavior, 1980—, Med Post; assoc. editor Anat. Record, 1970-73, 77—, BMA Audiotape Series, 1970-77; contbr. articles to profl. jours.; prodr. several motion pictures; inventor sci. and med. devices and techniques. Mem. and chmn. Bd. Edn., Kingston, Ont., 1960-68; founding chmn. bd. govs. St. Lawrence Coll. Applied Arts and Tech., Ont., 1964-69. Served to capt. M.C., Can. Army, 1943-46. Decorated officer Order of Ont., officer Order of Can.; recipient awards including Starr Gold medal U. Toronto, 1957, Kabakjian award Armenian Youth Fedn., 1967; NRC (Can.) vis. scientist Soviet Acad. Scis., 1963, Henry Gray Laureate, 1991,. Fellow Am. Acad. Angiology, Royal Coll. Physicians (Can.), Royal Coll. Physicians and Surgeons (Glasgow, hon.), Royal Coll. Physicians (Edinburgh, hon.), Physicians Coll. Rehabilitative Medicine (Australia, hon., Edinburgh, hon.); mem. Am. Assn. Anatomists (pres. 1985-86, Henry Gray Laureate award 1991), Can. Assn. Anatomists (founding, sec. 1965-69, J.C.B. Grant award 1985), Am. Congress Rehab. Medicine (Gold Key award 1977, Coulter lectr. 1988), Biofeedback Soc. Am. (founding, pres. 1978-79), Internat. Soc. Electromyographic Kinesiology (founding, pres. 1955-60), Order St. John of Jerusalem (hon. life mem.), Am. Orthopedic Foot Soc. (hon. life), Australian Biofeedback Soc. (hon. life), Venezuelan Biofeedback Soc. (hon. life), Mex. Soc. Anatomy (hon. life), Columbian Assn. Phys. Medicine (hon. life), Physiotherapy Assn. North Greece (hon. pres. 1995—). Avocations: travel; music; gardening; writing. Office: McMaster U Med Sch, Box 2000, Hamilton, ON Canada L8N 3Z5

BASNETT, C. JAN, English educator; b. Mt. Carmel, Ill., May 19, 1956; d. W.C. and Joanne Mae (Mix) Bridges; m. Terry Allen Basnett, Mar. 5, 1977; children: T. Aaron, Cara M. BS, U. So. Ind., 1978; MS, U. Evansville, 1981; BA, Oakland City Coll., 1989. Cert. tchr. Ill. Evaluator W.A.V.E., Inc., Mt. Carmel, 1978-80; instr. Wabash Valley Coll., Mt. Carmel, 1981-89, Salem (Ill.) Cmty. H.S., 1989—; social worker Welborn Hosp., Evansville, Ind., 1988-89. Avocations: reading, cooking, boating, music. Home: 3941 Hester Ln Salem IL 62881-6657

BASNIGHT, ARVIN ODELL, public administrator, aviation consultant; b. Manteo, N.C., Sept. 14, 1915; s. Thomas Allen and Mary Meekins Basnight; m. Marjorie Jane Gauthier, Dec. 6, 1941; children: Mary Ann Basnight Wolf, William Gaylord, Michael André. Student in Mech. Engrng., N.C. State U., 1932-35; student in Pub. Adminstrn., Am. Univ., 1936-42. Park ranger U.S. Nat. Parks, Kitty Hawk, N.C. and Mesa Verde, Colo., 1938-40; pers. adminstr. CAA, Washington, 1940-42; fin., budget accounts FAA, Washington, 1945-62; adminstr. Washington, Atlanta, L.A., 1962-74; bd. dir., chmn. bd. Palos Verdes (Calif.) Nat. Bank, 1982-92; aviation cons., L.A., 1974-92. Co-chmn. Salute to Doolittle Raiders, Santa Monica, Calif., 1991; pres. Palos Verdes Breakfast Club, 1990. Maj. USAF, 1942-45. Decorated D.F.C.; recipient Disting. Svc. medal U.S. Fed. Aviation, 1966. Mem. Nat. Aeros. Assn. (Honor award 1991), Aero Club So. Calif. (pres., bd. dirs. 1974-97). Achievements include development of air safety programs and certification for Lockheed C-141 and 1011, MacDonald Douglas MD-10, Boeing 737 and 747. Home: 1536 Paseo Del Mar Palos Verdes Estates CA 90274

BASOLO, FRED, chemistry educator; b. Coello, Ill., Feb. 11, 1920; s. John and Catherine (Marino) B.; m. Mary P. Nutley, June 14, 1947; children: Mary Catherine, Freddie, Margaret-Ann, Elizabeth Rose. BE, So. Ill. U., 1940, DSc (hon.), 1984; MS, U. Ill., 1942, PhD in Inorganic Chemistry, 1943; LLD (hon.), U. Turin, 1988; Laurea Honoris Causa, U. Palermo, Italy, 1997. Rsch. chemist Rohm & Haas Chem. Co., Phila., 1943-46; mem. faculty Northwestern U., Evanston, Ill., 1946—, prof. chemistry, 1958—, Morrison prof. chemistry, 1980-90, chmn. dept. chemistry, 1969-72; Charles E. and Emma H. Morrison prof. emeritus Nortwestern U., Evanston, Ill., 1990—; guest lectr. NSF summer insts.; chmn. bd. trustees Gordon Rsch. Conf., 1976; pres. Inorganic Syntheses, Inc., 1979-81; mem. bd. chem. scis. and tech. NRC-Nat. Acad. Scis.; adv. bd. Who's Who in Am., 1983; cons. in field. Author: (with R.G. Pearson) Mechanisms of Inorganic Reactions, 1958, (with R.C. Johnson) Coordination Chemistry, 1964; assoc. editor Chem. Revs., 1960-65, Inorganica Chemica Acta, 1967—, Inorganica Chemica Acta Letters, 1977—; editorial bd. Jour. Inorganic and Nuclear Chemistry, 1959—, Jour. Molecular Catalysis, Chem. Revs.; co-editor Catalysis, Transition Metal Chemistry; editor Inorganic Syntheses XVI; contbr. articles to profl. jours. Recipient Ballar medal, 1972, So. Ill. U. Alumni Achievement award, 1974, Dwyer medal, 1976, James Flack Norris award for Outstanding Achievement in Teaching of Chemistry, 1981, Oesper Meml. award, 1983, IX Century medal Bologna U., 1988, Mosher award, 1990, Padova U. medal, 1991, Chinese Chem. Soc. medal, 1991, G.C. Pimental award, 1992, Chemical Pioneer award, 1992, Gold medal Am. Inst. Chemists, 1993, Joseph Chatt medal Royal Soc. Chemistry, 1996; Guggenheim fellow, 1954-55; NSF fellow, 1961-62; NATO sr. scientist fellow Italy, 1981; Sr. Humboldt fellow, 1992; Inauguration mem. Hall of Fame Chem. Dept. So. Ill. U., 1996. Fellow NAS, AAAS (chmn. chemistry sect. 1979), Am. Acad. Arts and Scis.; mem. Am. Chem. Soc. (asst. editor jour. 1961-64, chmn. divsn. inorganic chemistry 1970, pres. 1983, bd. dirs. 1982-84, award for rsch. in inorganic chemistry 1964, Disting. Svc. award in inorganic chemistry 1975, N.E. regional award 1971, award in chem. edn. 1992, Chem. Pioneer award 1992, Gold Medal award 1993, Willard Gibbs medal 1996), Royal Soc. Chemistry (Joseph Chatt medal 1996), Italian Chem. Soc. (hon.), Acad. Nat. dei Lincei (Italy), Sigma Xi (Monie A. Ferst medal 1992), Phi Lambda Upsilon, Alpha Chi Sigma, Phi Kappa Phi, Kappa Delta Phi, Phi Lambda Theta (hon.). Office: Northwestern U Chemistry Dept 2145 Sheridan Rd Evanston IL 60208-0834*

BASOLS, JOSE ANDRES, school director, priest; b. Sariñena, Huesca, Spain, Sept. 15, 1941; came to U.S., 1966; s. Manuel and Maria Cruz (Torres) B. B in Philosophy, Colegio Central PP, Escolapios, Irache, Spain, 1963; degree in Theology, S.O.L.A. Niagara U., 1968; MA in Guidance and Counseling, Villanova U., 1969. Nat. cert. counselor; nat. sch. cert. counselor; ordained priest Roman Cath. Ch., 1968. Boarders' dir. Devon Prep Sch., Pa., 1968-69; guidance dir. Colegio Ponceño, Ponce, P.R., 1969-83; dir., high sch. prin. Colegio Ponceño, 1983-95; dir. Colegio Calasanz, San Juan, P.R., 1995—; dir. spiritual retreats Cursillos de Cristiandad; marriage and family counselor; supr. ATP Ctr., TOEFL Ctr., NCC test Ctr.; guest speaker Annual Convs. Counselors, Schs. P.R.; mem. vis. com. Mid. States Assn. Colls. Schs.; vice-chmn. adv. coun. P.R. Office Coll. Bd., 1990-93; pres. P.R. Assn. Pvt. Edn., 1991-93; mem. P.R. State Com. Goals 2000, P.R. State Commn. on Cmty. Svc. and Social Action, P.R. State Scholarship Coun. Author: Estudios en las Instituciones Postsecundarias y Universitarias de Puerto Rico, 1998; editor: Semillas, Calin; contbr. articles to profl. jours. Recipient P.R. Counselor of Yr. award, 1983, P.R. Counselor of Yr. Most Disting. Human Svcs. award, 1986, P.R. Counselor of Yr. Most Disting. Rsch., 1987, Outstanding Sch. of Nation award U.S. Dept. Edn., 1991, 92, Educator of Yr. award Cámara de Comercio de Ponce y Sur de P.R., 1991,

Disting. Exec. of Yr. in Edn. award Assn. de Ejecutivos de Ventas y Mercadeo de Ponce y Sur de P.R., 1992. Mem. ASCD, Nat. Assn. Secondary Sch. Prins. (Cert. Recognition 1991), Am. Counseling Assn., P.R. Assn. Counseling and Devel. (pres. 1982-83), Caribbean Counselors' Assn. (pres. 1989-90), Assn. Religious Values and Counseling. Avocation: photography. Office: Colegio Calasanz PO Box 29067 San Juan PR 00929-0067

BASON, GEORGE R., JR., lawyer; b. N.Y.C., 1954. ABmagna cum laude, Harvard U., 1975, JDcum laude, 1978. Bar: N.Y. 1979, U.S. Dist. Ct. (so. and ea. dists.) N.Y. 1979; cert. Avocat à la Cour de Paris 1992. Assoc. Davis Polk & Wardwell, N.Y.C., 1978-85, ptnr., 1986—. Mem. ABA, Bar Assn. City N.Y., Phi Beta Kappa (alpha of Mass. chpt.). Office: Davis Polk & Wardwell 450 Lexington Ave New York NY 10017-3911

BASORA, ADRIAN ANTHONY, ambassador; b. N.Y.C., July 18, 1938; married; 1 child. AB, Fordham U., 1960; MPA, Princeton U., 1962. With Fgn. Svc., 1962-95; polit. counselor U.S. Embassy, Paris, 1983-86; dep. chief mission U.S. Embassy, Madrid, 1986-89; dir. European and Soviet affairs Nat. Security Coun., Washington, 1989-91; sr. rsch. fellow Ctr. Study Fgn. Affairs, Arlington, Va., 1991-92; U.S. amb. to Czech republic, 1992-95; pres. Eisenhower Exch. Fellowships, Phila., 1996—. Office: 256 S 16th St Philadelphia PA 19102-3334

BASOV, NIKOLAI GENNADIEVICH, physicist; b. Usman, nr. Voronezh, USSR, Dec. 14, 1922; s. Gennadiy Fedorovich and Zinaida Andreevna (Molchanova) B.; m. Ksenia Tikhonova, Feb. 15, 1927; children: Gennadiy, Dmitriy. Grad., Moscow Mech. Inst., 1950, Can. Phys. Math. Sci., 1953, D. Phys. Math. Sci., 1956; LL.D. (hon.), Polish-Mil.-Tech. Acad., 1972, Jena U., 1974, Prague Poly. Inst., 1975, U. Pavia, Italy, 1977, Madrid Poly. U., 1985; Karl Marx Stadt Tech. U., 1988. With P. N. Lebedev Phys. Inst., USSR Acad. Sci., 1948—, vice dir. for sci. work, 1958-73, head lab. quantum radio physics, 1963—; prof. solid state physics Moscow Inst. Phys. Engrs., 1963—; dir. P. N. Lebedev Phys. Inst., 1973-89, dir. quantum radiophysics div., 1989-98; scientific leader Inst. Quantum Radiophysics, 1998—; mem. expert coun. of prime-minister of Russian Govt., 1991—. Author over 500 works. Research on principle of molecular generator, 1952, realized molecular generator on molecular beam of ammonia, 1955, 3-level system for receiving states with inversal population suggested, 1955, proposed use of semicondrs. for creation lasers, 1958, realized various types of semicondr. lasers with excitation through p-n junctions, electronic and optical pumping, 1960-65, research on obtaining short powerful pulses of coherent light; proposed thermal and chem. methods for laser pumping, 1962, gas dynamic lasers, 1966; research optical data processing, 1965—; proposed, 1961, realized thermonuclear reactions by using powerful lasers, 1968; developed main trends in optical frequency standards, 1967-68; inventor electron-beam pumped semicondr. laser projection TV, 1968; proposed, 1966, realized eximer lasers, 1970; realized stimulation of chem. reactions by infrared laser radiation, 1970; proposed and realized electro-ionization laser, 1971; proposed concept of low-entropy compression of high-aspect ratio multilayer thermonuclear targets, 1974, showed possibility of their stable compression, 1983; realized lasers with long-time stability of 2.10-14, 1982; chief editor Priroda, 1967-90, Kvantovaya Elektronika, 1971—. Chmn. bd. All-Union Soc., Znanie, 1978-90, hon. chmn., 1990—; dep. USSR Supreme Soviet, 1974-89; mem. presidium Supreme Soviet, 1982-89; v.p. exec. coun. World Fedn. Sci. Workers, 1976-83; v.p. WFSW, 1983-90, hon. mem., 1990—. Decorated Order Lenin (5), Order of Patriotic War hero twice Socialist Labour; recipient Lenin prize, 1959, Nobel prize for fundamental rsch. in quantum electronics resulting in creation of masers and lasers, 1964, Gold medal Czechoslovakian Acad. Scis., 1975, A. Volta's Gold medal, 1977, Order of Kirill and Mephodii (Bulgaria), 1981, E. Henkel Gold medal German Dem. Rep., 1986, Commodor's cross Order of Merit, Poland, 1986, Kalinga prize UNESCO, 1986, Gold medal Slovakian Acad. Scis., 1988, M.V. Lomonosov Gold medal USSR Acad. Scis., 1989, State prize of USSR, 1989, Edward Teller medal, 1991. Fellow Optical Soc. Am., Indian Nat. Sci. Acad., Amer. Phys. Soc., 1998; mem. European Acad. Scis. and Arts (Salzburg chpt.), Internat. Acad. Scis. (hon.), USSR Acad. Scis. (presidium 1967-90, advisor 1990—), Acad. Natural Scis. of Russian Fedn. (hon.) Acad. Scis. German Dem. Rep., Polish and Czechoslovakian Acad. Scis., German Acad. Natural Scis. Leopoldina, Bulgarian Acad. Scis., Royal Swedish Acad. Engring., European Acad. Arts, Scis. and Humanities (Paris chpt.), Acad. Scis. Ga., Acad. Scis. Belorussia, fell., Amer. Physical Soc., 1998. Office: PN Lebedev Phys Inst, 53 Leninsky Prospekt, Moscow Russia

BASQUIN, MARY SMYTH (KIT BASQUIN), independent curator, writer; b. N.Y.C., July 3, 1941; d. Joseph Percy and Virginia Sandford (Gibbs) Smyth; m. Maurice Hanson Basquin, Feb. 4, 1967 (div. Feb. 1984); children: Susan, Peter Lee, William. BA, Goucher Coll., Balt., 1963; MA, Ind. U., 1970. Asst. dir. pub. rels. Indpls. Mus. Art, 1971-72; dir. Kit Basquin Gallery, Frankfort, Ind., 1972-79, Indpls., 1977-79, Milw., 1981-83; curator edn. Haggerty Mus. Marquette U., Milw., 1988-95; dir. outreach Milw. Wis. Humanities Coun., 1995-98; curator Marvin Lowe Retrospective, Ind. U. Art Mus., 1998; instr. art history Concordia U., Mequon, Wis., 1991, instr. Marquette U., Gaza, 1996; pres. contemporary art soc. Milw. Art Mus., 1986-87, prints and drawings subcom., 1991—, pres. Print Forum, 1996-97; mem. program com. Midwest Mus. conf., Milw., 1992. Wis. editor New Art Examiner, Chgo., 1980-81; contbr. articles to profl. jours. Bd. trustees Ten Chimneys Found., Genesee Depot, Wis., 1997—. Mem. Univ. Club N.Y., Univ. Club Milw. Episcopalian. Avocations: fashion, theater, concerts, swimming, biking. Home & Office: 925 E Wells St Apt 625 Milwaukee WI 53202-3953

BASS, CAROL ANN (MITZI BASS), English language educator; b. Dallas, Aug. 29, 1951; d. Charles Eugene and Lucy (Patrick) Watson; m. Harold F. Bass, Jr., Jan. 8, 1972; children: Jessica, Franklin. BA with honors, George Peabody Coll. Tchrs., Nashville, 1973; MA, George Peabody Coll. Tchrs., 1974. Tchr. Battle Ground Acad., Franklin, Tenn., 1974-77; adj. instr. Henderson State U., Arkadelphia, Ark., 1985-94; instr. Henderson State U., 1994—. Deacon 1st Bapt. Ch., Arkadelphia, 1993—; vol. Clark County Election Com., Arkadelphia, 1996, Am. Cancer Soc., Arkadelphia, 1985—; bd. dirs. Group Living, Inc., Arkadelphia, 1995—. Mem. AAUP, Nat. Coun. Tchrs. English, Sigma Tau Delta, Pi Beta Phi. Democrat. Avocations: reading, gardening. Office: Henderson State U 1100 Henderson St Arkadelphia AR 71999-0001

BASS, CHARLES F., congressman; b. Jan. 8, 1952; s. Perkins and Katharine J. Bass; m. Lisa L.; children: Lucy, Jonathan. AB, Dartmouth Coll., 1974. Field worker Congressman William S. Cohen, 1974; legis. asst. Congressman David F. Emery, 1975-76, chief of staff, 1976-79; v.p. High Std., Inc., Dublin, N.H., 1980-94; chmn. Columbia Archtl. Products, Beltsville, Md., 1980-94; mem. 105th Congress from N.H. 2nd dist., 1994—; mem. ho. budget com. on nat. security, govt. reform and mgmt., working groups on nat. security and govt. reform, vice chmn. subcom. on civil svc., subcom. on govt. mgmt., info. and tech. Trustee N.H. Higher Edn. Assistance Found., Monadnock Conservancy, N.H. Humanities Coun. Mem. Monadnock Rotary (pres. 1992-93), Amoskeag Vets., Masons. Office: US Ho of Reps 218 Cannon Bldg Washington DC 20515-2902 also: 142 N Main St Concord NH 03301-4917 also: 170 Main St Nashua NH 03060-2731 also: 78 Main St Littleton NH 03561-4012*

BASS, CHARLES MORRIS, financial and systems consultant; b. Miami, Fla., Sept. 21, 1949; s. Benjamin and Ellen Lucille (Williams) B; children: Cheryl Ellen, Benjamin Charles. BA, U. Md., 1972; MS, Am. Coll., 1982. CLU; chartered fin. cons. Group rep. Monumental Life Ins. Co., 1972-73; agt. Equitable Life Ins. Co., N.Y., 1973-76; ptnr. Bass, Bridge and Assocs., Columbia, Md., 1976-81; pres. Multi-Fin Svc., Inc., Balt., 1981-83; gen. mgr. Mfrs. Fin. Group, Denver, 1983-85; ptnr. Regency Econometrics Group, Denver, 1985—; speaker in field. Chmn. United Way Howard County, 1977-78; mem. Econ. Devel. Adv. Coun. Howard County, 1979-83. Served with USAF, 1968-71. Mem. Million Dollar Round Table, Nat. Assn. Life Underwriters, Am. Soc. C.L.U.s, Gen. Agts. and Mgrs. Assn., Columbia Life Underwriters Assn. (pres. 1982), Estate Planning Coun., Howard County C. of C., Howard County Bus. Club, Columbia Bus. Exchange. Methodist. Home and Office: 5690 W Coal Mine Ave Littleton CO 80123-3903

BASS, DANIEL THOMAS, banker; b. Houston, May 31, 1964; s. Tom and Mary Ann (King) B.; m. Michele Bass, Nov. 3, 1990. BBA in Fin., U. Tex., 1986; MS in Info. Mgmt., Marymount U., 1994. Sr. fin. analyst Sheshunoff Info. Mgmt. Svc., Austin, 1986-91, F.D.I.C., Washington, 1991-94; assoc. Alex Sheshunoff Investment Banking, Austin, 1994-96; sr. mgr. KPMG Peat Marwick, Houston, 1996-97; v.p. acquisitions Compass Banks of Tex., Houston, 1998—. Office: Compass Banks of Texas Inc 24 E Greenway Plz Ste 1401 Houston TX 77046-2486

BASS, GEORGE FLETCHER, archaeology educator; b. Columbia, S.C., Dec. 9, 1932; s. Robert Duncan and Virginia (Wauchope) B.; m. Ann Singletary, Mar. 19, 1960; children: Gordon Wauchope, Alan Joseph. MA, Johns Hopkins U., 1955; PhD, U. Pa., 1964; PhD (hon.), Bogazici U., Istanbul, Turkey, 1987, U. Liverpool, 1998. Asst. prof. U. Pa., Phila., 1964-68, assoc. prof., 1968-73; prof. archaeology Tex. A&M U., College Sta., 1976-80, Disting. prof., 1980—, George T. and Gladys H. Abell prof. nautical archaeology, 1986—; Yamini Family prof., 1994—; dir. excavations of ancient shipwrecks off Turkish coast, 1960—; pres. Inst. Nautical Archaeology, 1972-82, 96—. Author: Archaeology Under Water, 1966, Cape Gelidonya, 1967, History of Seafaring, 1972, Archaeology Beneath the Sea, 1975, Yassi Ada I, 1982, Ships and Shipwrecks of the Americas, 1988; adv. editor Am. Jour. Archaeology, 1987-99, Archaeology, 1987—, Internat. Jour. Nautical Archaeology, 1987—, Nat. Geog. Rsch., 1987-94. Lt. U.S. Army, 1957-59, Korea. Recipient Centennial award Nat. Geog. Soc., 1988, La. Gorce Gold medal, 1979, Lowell Thomas award Explorers Club, 1986; named one of Outstanding Young Men of Yr., Jaycees, 1967. Mem. Inst. Nautical Archaeology (pres. 1973-82), Archaeol. Inst. Am. (Gold medal for disting. archaeol. achievement 1986), Soc. for Hist. Archaeology (J.C. Harrington medal 1999), Nat. Maritime Hist. Soc., Mothers Against Drunk Driving. Presbyterian. Avocation: classical music. Home: 1600 Dominik Dr College Station TX 77840-3623 Office: Tex A&M U Nautical Archaeology College Station TX 77843-4352

BASS, HYMAN, mathematician, educator; b. Houston, Oct. 5, 1932; s. Isador and Fanny (Weiss) B.; m. Mary Ellen Popkin, June 9, 1957 (div. 1978); children: Anne Ruth, Ivan Philip; m. Dorothea Henriette Goldys, Nov. 1, 1979; 1 dau., Gabriella Sierra. B.A., Princeton U., 1955; M.S., U. Chgo., 1956, Ph.D. (NSF grad. fellow), 1959. Ritt instr. math. Columbia U., 1959-62, asst. prof., 1963-64, chmn. dept. math., 1975—; asso. prof., chmn. at Barnard Coll., 1964-65, prof., 1965—; Vis. mem. Inst. Advanced Study, Princeton, 1964, 65-66, Inst. de Hautes Etudes Scientifiques, Paris, 1968-69; vis. prof. Universidad Nacional Autónoma de Mex., 1965, Tata Inst. Fundamental Research, Bombay, 1965-66, 69, 76, 80, U. Paris, 1968, 73, 81, Cambridge U., 1973, Instituto de Matematica Pura e Applicada, Rio de Janeiro, 1977, Bar Ilan U., Israel, 1980; chmn. adv. com. pure math. NRC, 1970-71; adv. panel, div. math. NSF, 1973-75; vis. coms. various math. depts. colls., univs.; disting. lectr. Kans. State U., U. Ind., 1982; Karcher lectr. U. Okla., 1979; Barrett Meml. lectr. U. Tenn., 1978, others; spkr. in field. Editorial bd.: Jour. Indian Math. Soc, 1968—, Cambridge Tracts in Pure and Applied Math.; 968: Jour. Pure and Applied Algebra, 1970—, Am. Jour. Mathematics, 1971—, North-Holland Math. Library, 1971—, Acad. Press Series in Pure and Applied Math, 1974—. NSF fellow Coll. de France, 1962-63; Sloan fellow, 1964-66; Guggenheim fellow, 1968-69; recipient Van Amridge book prize Columbia, 1969, Cole prize Am. Math. Soc., 1975; Phi Beta Kappa Nat. Vis. scholar, 1991-92. Fellow AAAS; mem. NAS (chair math. scis. edn. bd. 1992—), Am. Math Soc. (editorial bd. 1969—, coun. 1969-72), London Math. Socs., Société Mathématique de France, Soc. Collaborateurs N. Bourbaki, Math. Assn. Am., Am. Acad. Arts and Scis. Home: 435 Riverside Dr New York NY 10025-7743 Office: Columbia U 605 Math Broadway & 116th St New York NY 10027

BASS, JACK, journalism educator; b. Columbia, S.C., June 24, 1934; s. Nathan and Esther (Cohen) B.; m. Carolyn E. McClung, Mar. 3, 1957 (div. June 1984); children: Kenneth, David, Elizabeth; m. Nathalie Dupree, Apr. 10, 1994. AB, U. S.C., 1956, MA, 1976. Copy editor The News and Courier, Charleston, S.C., 1960-61; editor, pub. West Ashley Jour., Charleston, 1961-63; govtl. affairs reporter, editor Columbia Newspapers, 1963-66; bur. chief The Charlotte Observer, Columbia, 1966-73; rsch. scholar Duke U., Durham, N.C., 1973-75; writer-in-residence S.C. State Coll., Orangeburg, 1975-78; rsch. fellow/project dir. U. S.C., Columbia, 1979-85; prof. journalism U. Miss., Oxford, 1987—; sec.-treas. Nathalie Dupree Enterprises, Atlanta, 1994—. Co-author: The Orangeburg Massacre, 1970, The Transformation of Southern Politics, 1976; author: Porgy Comes Home, 1972, Unlikely Heroes, 1980, Taming The Storm, 1993 (Robert Kennedy Book award Grand Prize 1994); co-editor: The American South Comes of Age, 1987. Dir. So. Edn. Found., Atlanta, 1980-88; Dem. candidate U.S. Ho. of Reps., Columbia, 1978. Lt. (j.g.) USNR, 1956-60. Named S.C. Journalist of the Yr. Soc. Profl. Journalists, 1968, 70; recipient 1st Disting. Alumnus award Coll. Journalism, U. S.C., 1984; Nieman fellow, 1965-66. Mem. Authors Guild. Avocation: tennis. Home: 601 S 8th St Oxford MS 38655-4303 Office: University of Mississippi Dept Journalism University MS 38077

BASS, JAMES ORIN, lawyer; b. Sumner County, Tenn., July 12, 1910; s. Francis Marion and Sadie (Dunn) B.; m. Susanne Warner, June 9, 1937; children: James Orin, Edwin Warner, Francis Marion II, Susan Richardson. B.A., U. of South, 1931; LL.B., Harvard, 1934. Bar: Tenn. 1934. Ptnr. Bass, Berry & Sims, Nashville, 1937—. Mem. Tenn. Ho. of Reps. from Davidson County, 1936-38, Tenn. Senate, 1940-42. Served to lt. col. AUS, 1942-45, ETO. Mem. ABA, Tenn. Bar Assn., Nashville Bar Assn. (pres. 1951), Am. Coll. Trial Lawyers. Presbyterian. Home: 4412 Georgian Pl Nashville TN 37215-4528 Office: Bass Berry & Sims 2700 First American Ctr Nashville TN 37238

BASS, JONATHAN, dermatologist; b. Cleve., July 2, 1953; m. Stephany Schatel. AB, Washington U., St. Louis, 1975; MD, U. Cin., 1979. Intern in internal medicine Mt. Sinai Med. Ctr., Cleve., 1979-80, resident in internal medicine, 1980-81; resident in dermatology MetroHealth Med. Ctr., Cleve., 1981-84, staff dermatologist, dermatopathologist, 1986—; fellow in dermatopathology Cleve. Clinic Found., 1985-86; asst. prof. dermatology, sr. instr. pathology Case Western Res. U. Sch. Medicine, Cleve., 1986—. Fellow Am. Soc. Dermatopathology, Am. Acad. Dermatology, Ohio Dermatological Assn., Cleve. Dermatological Soc.; mem. AMA. Office: MetroHealth Med Ctr Dept Dermatology 2500 MetroHealth Dr Cleveland OH 44109-1900*

BASS, JOSEPH OSCAR, minister; b. Vicksburg, Miss., Jan. 23, 1933; s. Sylvester and Jeanette (Sims) B.; m. Charline Delores Sanders, June 5, 1955; children: Karen Sue, Julie Yvette. BRE, Western Bapt. Coll., Kansas City, Mo., 1956; BA, Nat. Coll., Kansas City, 1958; MRE, Cen. Bapt. Sem., Kansas City, Kans., 1959; MA, U. Mo., 1969, postgrad., 1975-76; MDiv, Mo. Sch. Religion, Columbia, 1971; LHD (hon.), Va. Coll., Lynchburg, 1974; PhD, Walden U., Naples, Fla., 1976. Ordained to ministry Am. Bapt. Chs. in U.S.A., 1954. Pastor chs., Kans., Mo., 1955-62; indsl. missionary to Thailand Am. Bapt. Conv., 1962-69, assoc. exec. dir. world mission support, 1969-72; nat. dir. fund of renewal Progressive Nat. Bapt. Conv., Am. Bapt. Conv., Valley Forge, Pa., 1972-74; exec. dir. home mission bd. Progressive Bapts.; pastor, founder Alpha Bapt. Ch., Alpha Acad. Christian Growth, Willingboro, N.J., 1977—; mem. adv. coun. internat. affairs Nat. Coun. Chs., Washington, 1974-81; mem. exec. coun. Am. Bapt. Chs., mem. gen. bd.; founder Bankok's Inter-racial Coun. Author: These Are They, 1970, The History of the Progressive National Baptist Convention, 1976; co-author: One in Nine Americans Is Black, 1973, The Black American Experience, 1974. Mem. men's com. Japan Internat. Christian U., 1972; pres. Burlington County (N.J.) Cmty. Action Program, 1972-73, pres. 1973—; bd. dirs. Burlington County United Way Campaign; vice-chmn. N.J. Chaplaincy Cons. Com.; founder Ptnrs. in Edn.; gen. bd. A.B.C. Ch.; chaplain Family Svcs. Burlington County. Mem. Am. Sociol. Assn., Nat. Doctoral Assn. Educators, World Wide Acad. Scholars., Willingboro Clergy Assn. (pres. 1987—), Congress of Willingboro (chair), Willingboro Hall of Fame (pres.), Rotary Internat. Achievements include youngest Am. to become pres. of AFL-CIO Local 221 at age 16; first Am. to meet PhD lang. requirements in Thai; instituted international director school to work program, 1998; graduate Leadership N.J., 1998. Home: 2 Normont Ln Willingboro NJ 08046-1321 Office: 15 Rose St Willingboro NJ 08046-2537 *Since nothing in this life is forever, I have made a quality decision to accept every moment of life I have left as an unearned gift from God the Creator-giver and translate it into service to humanity.*

BASS, LEE MARSHALL, food products company executive; b. 1950. With Bass Enterprises Prodn. Co., Ft. Worth, 1970—; chmn. bd. Nat. Farms, Inc., Kansas City, Mo., 1992—, also bd. dirs.; pres. Lee M. Bass Inc., Ft. Worth. Office: Nat Farms Inc 4800 Main St Kansas City MO 64112-2510 also: Modern Art Mus 1309 Montgomery St Fort Worth TX 76107-3015 also: Bass Bros Enterprises 201 Main St Fort Worth TX 76102-3105 also: Lee M Bass Inc 201 Main St Fort Worth TX 76102-3105*

BASS, LYNDA D., medical/surgical nurse, educator; b. Suffolk, Va.; d. H.M. and Katie Lea Bass. BSN, N.C. Agrl. and Tech. State U., Greensboro, 1968; MS in Nursing, Cath. U. Am., 1974; Gen. Surgery Clin. Specialist, George Washington U. Hosp., Washington. Cert. BCLS instr., CPR instr.-trainer. Clin. instr. Suburban Hosp., Bethesda, Md.; edn./tng. quality assurance coord. Howard U. Hosp., Washington; clin. educator Providence Hosp., Washington; edn. specialist VA Md. Healthcare Sys., Balt.; coord. clin. staff Devel. Mount Vernon Hosp., Alexandria, Va. Capt. U.S. Army, 1968-71, Vietnam. Mem. Nat. Nursing Staff Devel. Assn., Chi Eta Phi.

BASS, NANCY AGNES, airport executive; b. Beaver Falls, Pa., Feb. 26, 1937; d. John Joseph and Kathleen Lillian (Retzer) Paff; m. Lee Herbert Bass, Jan. 10, 1959; children: Thomas Andrew, Marilee, Laura Kathleen. Student, Clarion State Coll., 1954-56. Purchasing clk. Orange County Purchasing Dept., Santa Ana, Calif., 1957-60; bookkeeper Cal Gas, Ridgecrest, Calif., 1975-78; interline mgr. C and M Airlines, Inyokern, Calif., 1978-82; mgr. CLC Engring and Surveying, Ridgecrest, Calif., 1982-86; gen. mgr. Indian Wells Valley Airport Dist., Inyokern, Calif., 1985—, Ridgecrest (Calif.) Redevel. Agy., 1989-90; chair Kern County Aviation Transp. Tech. Adv. Com., Bakerfield, Calif., 1989, 92; mem. tech. adv. com. for aeronautics State of Calif. Transp. Commn., 1994—. Bd. dirs. Ridgecrest Bd. of Appeals, 1986-90, dir. High Desert Child Abuse Prevention Coun., Ridgecrest, 1985-87, Am. Cancer Soc., Ridgecrest, 1988—, sec. Airport Dist. Formation Com., Ridgecrest, 1983-85; planning commr. City of Ridgecrest, 1990—, vice-chair, 1992-94, chair 1995—; dir., treas. Ridgecrest Area Conv. & Visitor Bur., 1992-94, chair., 1995—. Mem. Calif. Assn. Airport Execs., Am. Assn. Airport Execs. (cert.), Altrusa. Home: 600 W Coral Ave Ridgecrest CA 93555-5214 Office: IWV Airport Dist PO Box 634 Inyokern CA 93527-0634

BASS, NORMAN HERBERT, physician, scientist, university and hospital administrator, health care executive; b. N.Y.C., July 10, 1936; s. Julius and Celia (Annex) B.; m. Kathleen Bass; children: Joel Martin, Rebecca Pier, Robert Farrell. BS (Ford Found. scholar 1953, N.Y. State Regents scholar 1954), Swarthmore (Pa.) Coll., 1958; MD, Yale U., 1962. Diplomate: Am. Bd. Psychiatry and Neurology. Intern Med. U. Wash. Hosp., Seattle, 1962-63; resident in neurology U. Va. Hosp., Charlottesville, 1963-65; clin. fellow in neurology Mass. Gen. Hosp., Boston, 1965-67; NIH fellow Harvard U. Med. Sch., 1965-67; from asst. prof. to prof. neurology U. Va. Med. Sch., Charlottesville, 1967-79, dir. Clinic Neurosci. Rsch. Ctr., 1973-79; prof. neurology, chmn. dept. Albert B. Chandler Med. Center, U. Ky., Lexington, 1979-85; neurologist in chief Univ. Hosp., 1979-85; dir. lab. neurochemistry Sanders-Brown Ky. Rsch. Ctr. Aging, 1979-85; dean Sch. Medicine, prof. dept. Neurology Med. Coll. Ga., 1985-86; prof. neurology, rehab. medicine, chief div. rehab. medicine U. Md. Sch. Medicine, Balt., 1986-89; prof. neurology, rehab. medicine U. Pitts., 1989-92; sr. v.p., chief med. officer Harmarville Rehab. Ctr. Inc., Pitts., 1989-92; prof. pediatrics and neurology Sch. Medicine, Boston U., 1992—; sr. v.p. med. affairs Franciscan Childrens Hosp. and Rehab Ctr., 1992-94; pvt. practice Cape and Islands, 1994—; cons. neurology VA Med. Ctr., Lexington, Augusta, Balt., Pitts., Boston; chmn. nat. rsch. program merit rev. bd. in neurobiology VA, 1978-81; mem. bd. sci. advisers Delta Regional Primate Ctr., Tulane U., 1978-81, chmn., 1979-81; chmn. profl. adv. bd. Epilepsy Assn. VA Ky., 1978-82; chmn. study sect. Nat. Inst. Disability and Rehab. Rsch., 1986-89; program surveyor Commn. on Accreditation of Rehab. Facilities, 1987-92; mem. panel co-chari Task Force Med. Rehab. Rsch. Office Sci. Policy, NIH, 1990; vis. prof. pharmacology U. Goteborg, Sweden, 1972-73. Assoc. editor Neurochem. Rsch. Jour., Jour. Neurol. Rehab.; mem. editorial bd. Stroke jour.; contbr. numerous articles to med. jours. Served to maj. M.C. USAR, 1963-69. Recipient Rsch. Career Devel. award NIH, 1971-75, Nat. Inst. Neurologic Disease rsch. fellow in neurochemistry, 1965-67; Markle scholar in acad. medicine, 1969-74. Fellow Am. Acad. Neurology (S. Weir Mitchell rsch. award 1967, chmn. sect. on geriatrics 1986, sect. on neurol. rehab. 1987), AAAS, Stroke Coun. of Am. Heart Assn., Am. Acad. Cerebral Palsy and Devel. Medicine; mem. Am. Assn. U. Profs. Neurology (v.p. 1980-81), Am. Assn. Anatomists, Am. Soc. Neurochemistry, Am. Soc. Neuro. Rehab., Soc. Neurosci., Internat. Soc. Neurochemistry, Child Neurology Soc., Am. Neurol. Assn., Assn. Rsch. Nervous and Mental Disease, Nat. Head Injury Found., Inc., AMA, Am. Congress Rehab. Medicine, Nat. Assn. Rehab. Facilities Inc., Nat. Multiple Sclerosis Soc., Nat. Head Injury Found., Alpha Omega Alpha. Office: 107B County Rd North Falmouth MA 02556-2019

BASS, PAUL, pharmacology educator; b. Winnipeg, Man., Can., Aug. 12, 1928; came to U.S., 1958; s. Benjamin and Sarah B.; m. Ruth Zipursky, May 31, 1953; children: Stuart, Susan. B.S. in Pharmacy, U. B.C., 1953, M.A. in Pharmacology, 1955; Ph.D. in Pharmacology, McGill U., 1957, fellow in Biochemistry, 1957-58; fellow in Physiology, Mayo Found., 1958-60. Research asst. Ayerst, McKenna & Harrison, Can., 1956; assoc. lab. dir. Parke, Davis & Co., 1960-70; prof. pharmacology Sch. Pharmacy and Sch. Medicine, U. Wis., Madison, 1970—. Mem. editorial bd.: Am. Jour. Physiology, 1976-79, 81-92, Jour. Pharmacology and Exptl. Therapeutics, 1980—; contbr. chpts. to books, articles to profl. jours. Mem. Am. Soc. Pharmacology and Exptl. Therapeutics, Am. Gastroent. Assn. Home: 153 Nautilus Dr Madison WI 53705-4329 Office: 425 N Charter St Madison WI 53706-1508

BASS, PERRY RICHARDSON, oil company executive; b. Wichita Falls, Tex., Nov. 11, 1914; s. E. Perry and Annie (Richardson) B.; m. Nancy Lee Muse, June 28, 1941; children: Sid R., Edward P., Robert M., Lee M. B.S. in Geology, Yale U., 1937; D. Humanitarian Service (hon.), Tex. Christian U., 1983; LHD (hon.), Yale U., 1993. Chmn. Sid Richardson Carbon & Gas, Ft. Worth, 1959—; pres. Perry R. Bass, Inc., Ft. Worth, 1941—, also dir.; pres. Sid Richardson Found., Ft. Worth, 1960—, also dir.; dir. Bass Enterprises Prodn. Co., Ft. Worth; mem. ad hoc com. Tex. Energy and Natural Resources Adv. Com.; mem. exec. com. Nat. Petroleum Council, 1961-75, Nat. Oil Policy Commn. on Possible Future Petroleum Problems, 1965; designer, builder fireboats for U.S. Navy. Chmn. Tex. Parks and Wildlife Commn., 1977-83, chmn. emeritus, 1988—; mem. adv. com. bd. visitors Univ. Cancer Found. of M.D. Andersen Hosp. and Tumor Inst. Recipient Silver Beaver award Boy Scouts Am., 1965, Silver Antelope award, 1969, Silver Buffalo award, 1976; Baden-Powell World fellow World Scout Found., 1988; Golden Deed award Ft. Worth Exchange Club, 1967; Disting. Civic Service award Dallas/Ft. Worth Hosp. Council, 1983, Conservation award Chevron, 1988, Bus. Hall of Fame Tex., 1989, Charles Goodnight award Star-Telegram & Nat. Cutting Horse Assn., 1991, Conservationist of the Yr. Tex. Outdoor Writers, 1992, Humanitarian Newsmaker of the Yr. Ft. Worth Chpt. Soc. Profl. Journalist and Tex. Gridiron Club, 1992, Citizen Conservationist of the Yr. Sportsmen Conservationists of Tex., 1992, medal of honor DAR, 1994, disting. bus. leadership award U. Tex., Arlington, 1994, Chuck Yeager award Nat. Fish & Wildlife Found., 1995. Mem. Am. Assn. Petroleum Geologists, Am. Petroleum Inst. (exec. com.), All Am. Wildcatters, Ind. Petroleum Assn. Am., Tex. Mid-Continent Oil and Gas Assn. (exec. com., City Club of Ft. Worth, Ft. Worth Boat Club, River Crest Country Club (Ft. Worth), Petroleum Club of Ft. Worth, N.Y. Yacht Club, Royal Ocean Racing Club (London), Ft. Worth Club. Office: Richardson Sid Carbon & Gas Co 201 Main St Fort Worth TX 76102-3105

BASS, ROBERT OLIN, manufacturing executive; b. Denver, July 22, 1917; s. Olin R. and Cora (Durham) B.; m. Isabelle Cantrell, Mar. 22, 1941; 1 dau., Susan. B.S. in Bus. Adminstrn., U. Denver, 1941. Pres. Eberhardt-Denver Co., 1956; exec. v.p., asst. gen. mgr. Morse Chain Co., Ithaca, N.Y., 1956-58; pres. Morse Chain Co., 1958-66; group v.p. indsl. Borg-Warner Corp., 1966-68, exec. v.p., 1968-75, pres., 1975-79, vice chmn., 1979-82, chief oper. officer, 1975-80, dir., 1973-83; ret. Chmn. metals and machinery sect. Chgo. Met. Crusade of Mercy, 1968; mem. bus. adv. council Coll. Bus. Adminstrn., U. Denver, 1976-89; trustee Field Mus. Natural History, Chgo.

Mem. Am. Mgmt. Assn. (v.p., chmn. gen. mgmt. planning council 1976-79, trustee 1979-82).

BASS, RONALD, screenwriter. Screenplays include Code Name: Emerald, 1985, Black Widow, 1987, Gardens of Stone, 1987, (with Barry Morrow) Rainman, 1988 (Academy award best original screenplay 1988), Sleeping with the Enemy, 1991, (with Amy Tan) The Joy Luck Club, 1993; screenwriter, exec. prodr.: (with Al Franken) When a Man Loves a Woman, 1994, Dangerous Minds, 1995, (with Terry McMillan) Waiting to Exhale, 1995, My Best Friend's Wedding, 1997, What Dreams May Come, 1998, Stepmom, 1998, How Stella Got Her Groove Back, 1998, Entrapment, 1999, Snow Falling on Cedars, 1999, Passion of Mind, 1999. Office: Creative Artists Agency care Jay Moloney 9830 Wilshire Blvd Beverly Hills CA 90212-1825*

BASS, STEVEN CRAIG, computer science educator; b. Indpls., July 29, 1943; s. Leland Ellsworth and Isabelle Frances (Ross) B.; m. Sara Ann Hiday, Sept. 4, 1965 (div. Apr. 1988); children: Leland Kai, Marshall Lynn; m. Kevyn Anne Salsburg, Jan. 2, 1989. BSEE, Purdue U., 1966, MSEE, 1968, PhD in Elec. Engring., 1971. Prof. elec. engring. Purdue U., Lafayette, Ind., 1971-88; prof. elec. and computer engring. George Mason U., Fairfax, Va., 1988-91; prin. engr. Mitre Corp., McLean, Va., 1988-91; prof. computer sci. and engring., chmn. dept. U. Notre Dame, Notre Dame, Ind., 1991—; cons. Magnovox Co., Ft. Wayne, Ind., 1971-73, Admiral Corp., Chgo., 1973-76, Kimball Internat., Jasper, Ind., 1978-84, Tektronix Corp., Wilsonville, Oreg., 1987-88. contbr. over 25 articles to profl. jours., delievered over 35 papers at sci. confs. Rescue officer Stockwell (Ind.) Vol. Fire Dept., 1985-88. Recipient numerous grants from NSF, USAF, IBM, Mitre Corp., others. Fellow IEEE (v.p. circuits and sys. soc. 1981, 91-93, mem. audio engring. soc.); mem. Tau Beta Pi. Roman Catholic. Achievements include 3 U.S. and 6 fgn. patents in the field of digital signal processing. Office: U Notre Dame Dept Computer Sci & Engring 384 Fitzpatrick Hl Engrng Notre Dame IN 46556-5637

BASSECHES, ROBERT TREINIS, lawyer; b. N.Y.C., Jan. 24, 1934; s. Jacob Thomas and Paula (Treinis) B.; m. Harriet Itkin, July 6, 1958; children: K.B., Joshua, Jessica. BA, Amherst Coll., 1955; LLB, Yale U., 1958. Bar: D.C. 1962, U.S. Ct. Appeals (D.C. cir.) 1962, U.S. Ct. Appeals (2d cir.) 1978, U.S. Ct. Appeals (4th cir.) 1998. Law clk. to judge David L. Bazelon U.S. Ct. Appeals (D.C. cir.), Washington, 1958-59; law clk. to justice Hugo L. Black U.S. Supreme Ct., Washington, 1959; assoc. Shea & Gardner, Washington, 1959-63, ptnr., 1963—, adminstrv. ptnr., 1980-86, chmn., exec. com., 1988-93. Trustee Green Acres Sch., Rockville, Md., 1971-76, pres., chmn. bd. trustees, 1973-75; pres. Chevy Chase (Md.) Village Citizens Assn., 1976. Mem. Maritime Adminstrv. Bar Assn. (pres. 1969-71, sec. 1967-69), Phi Beta Kappa. Office: Shea & Gardner Ste 800 1800 Massachusetts Ave NW Washington DC 20036-1872

BASSEN, NED HENRY, lawyer; b. N.Y.C., June 8, 1948; s. Harold Russell and Annette (Frankfeldt) B.; m. Susan Millington Campbell, July 2, 1999; children: Amanda Lee, Susannah Spence. BS, Cornell U., 1970, JD, 1973. Bar: N.Y. 1974, U.S. Dist. Ct. (so. and ea. dists.) N.Y. 1974, U.S. Ct. Appeals (11th cir.) 1984, U.S. Dist. Ct. (ea. dist.) Mich 1990. Assoc. Baer Marks & Upham, N.Y.C., 1975-80; assoc. Kelley Drye & Warren, N.Y.C., 1973-75, 80-83, ptnr., 1983-92; ptnr. and labor group head Mudge Rose Guthrie Alexander & Ferdon, N.Y.C., 1993-95; ptnr., co-chair labor and employment group Hughes Hubbard & Reed LLP, N.Y.C., 1995—. Note and comment editor Cornell Law Rev., 1972-73. V.p. local condominium assn., 1988-93. Mem. ABA (labor and employment law sect.), U.S. Coun. for Internat. Bus., Indsl. Rels. Com., Indsl. Rels. Rsch. Assn., N.Y. State Bar Assn. (labor law sect., com. on equal employment opportunity law), N.Y. State Mgmt. Attys. Conf. Office: Hughes Hubbard & Reed LLP 1 Battery Park Plz Fl 12 New York NY 10004-1482

BASSETT, ANGELA, actress; b. N.Y.C., Aug. 16, 1958. Appeared in (plays) Colored People's Time, 1982, The Mystery Plays, 1984-85, The Painful Adventures of Pericles, Prince of Tyre, 1986-87, Joe Turner's Come and Gone, 1986-87, (Broadway) Ma Rainey's Black Bottom, (Broadway) Joe Turner's Come and Gone, 1988, King Henry IV Part I, 1987; (TV movies) Line of Fire: The Morris Dees Story, 1991, The Jacksons: An American Dream, 1992, A Century of Women, 1994; (films) F/X, 1986, Kindergarten Cop, 1990, Boyz N the Hood, 1991, City of Hope, 1991, Innocent Blood, 1992, Malcolm X, 1992, Passion Fish, 1992, What's Love Got to Do with It, 1993 (Acad. award nominee for best actress 1993, Golden Globe award best actress in a musical or comedy 1994), Strange Days, 1995, Panther, 1995, Waiting to Exhale, 1995, A Vampire in Brooklyn, 1995, Contact, 1997, How Stella Got Her Groove Back, 1998, Wings Against the Wind, 1999, Cosm, 1999, 50 Violins, 1999. Address: ICM 8942 Wilshire Blvd Beverly Hills CA 90211-1934 Address: Krost-Chapin Management 9465 Wilshire Blvd Ste 430 Beverly Hills CA 90212-2613*

BASSETT, CAROL ANN, journalism educator, writer; b. Langley AFB, Va., Mar. 2, 1953; d. William Brainard and Genevieve (Rivaldo) B. BA summa cum laude in Humanities, Ariz. State U., 1977; MA in Journalism, U. Ariz., 1982. Ptnr. Desert West News, Tucson, 1985-90; freelance writer Tucson, 1980-95; freelance writer for mags. Missoula, Mont., 1995-98; mem. faculty Sch. Journalism U. Mont., Missoula, 1996-98; mem. faculty Sch. Journalism and Comm. U. Oreg., Eugene, 1998—. Editor Tucson Weekly, 1989-90; contbr. numerous articles to nat. and internat. mags. including N.Y. Times. Recipient 2d Place Gen. Reporting award Ariz. Press Club, 1987, Gold medal for best environ. documentary Houston Internat. Film Festival, 1990, 1st Place Gen. Reporting award Ariz. Press Club, 1992, Silver Medal for Energy Issues documentary, Houston Internat. Film Festival, 1992; co-recipient Alfred I. duPont Columbia award, 1984-85, First Place award Investigative Reporting, 1986, 1st Place Polit. Reporting, 1989, First Amendment Journalism award, 1986; grantee Fund for Investigative Journalism, 1985, 87, Corp. for Pub. Broadcasting, 1988, Oxfam Am., 1991. Address: 2569 Friendly St Eugene OR 97405-2265

BASSETT, CHARLES WALKER, English language educator; b. Aberdeen, S.D., July 7, 1932; s. Wilfred Walker and Angela (Jewett) B.; m. Carol Hoffer, Sept. 15, 1956 (dec. Feb. 5, 1995); children—David, Elizabeth. BA, U. S.D., 1954, MA, 1956; PhD, U. Kans., 1964. Asst. instr. English U. S.D., 1954-56; asst. instr. English U. Kans., 1958-64; instr. U. Pa., Phila., 1964-66, asst. prof., 1966-69; asst. prof. English Colby Coll., Waterville, Maine, 1969-74, assoc. prof., 1974-80, prof., 1980-83, Charles A. Dana prof. Am. studies and English, 1983-93; Lee Family prof. Am. studies and English Colby Coll., 1993—; dir. Am. studies Colby Coll., Waterville, Maine, 1971-87, 89-96, chmn. dept. English, 1987-89. Book rev. editor Am. Quar., 1983-91; assoc. editor: Ency. of Polit. Parties and Elections in the U.S., 1991; contbr. articles to profl. jours. Recipient Charles Bassett/Sr. Class Tchg. award, 1993, award for dedicated svc. Colby Alumni Assn., 1997; S.L. Whitcomb fellow, 1961-62, U. Kans. fellow, 1962-63; U. Pa. Faculty Rsch. grantee, 1966-68; Humanities and Mellon grantee, 1973-96. Mem. MLA (New Eng. rep. del. assembly), Am. Studies Assn. (Mary C. Turpie award 1994). Democrat. Roman Catholic. Home: 9 Martin Ave Waterville ME 04901-4625 Office: Colby Coll Dept English Waterville ME 04901

BASSETT, EDWARD CALDWELL, JR., lawyer; b. Newton, Mass., July 4, 1952; s. Edward C. and Marie A. (Querfurth) B.; m. Nancy A. Bassett, May 17, 1981; children: Andrew, Allison, Christopher. AB, Boston Coll., 1974, JD, 1977. Bar: Mass. Ptnr., mem. mgmt. com. Mirick, O'Connell DeMallie & Lougee, Worcester, Mass., 1977—. Editor: Benders UCC Reporter Digest, 1977; contbr. articles to profl. jours. Chmn. Southboro (Mass.) Bd. Appeals, 1985-94; exec. com., trustee Anna Maria Coll., Paxton, Mass., 1992-94. Avocation: tennis. Office: Mirick O'Connell et al 1700 Bank of Boston Twr Worcester MA 01608

BASSETT, ELIZABETH EWING (LIBBY BASSETT), writer, editor; b. Cleve., July 22, 1937; d. Ben and Eileen Grace (Ewing) B.; m. Robert Richter, Feb. 20, 1994. AA, Bradford Jr. Coll., Mass., 1957. Girl Friday Time-Life, animated film cos., others, 1957-63; asst. producer, stage mgr. N.Y. State Pavilion at N.Y. World's Fair, 1963-64; writer, reporter, editor AP, N.Y.C., 1965-72; free-lance corr. AP, Newsweek, Voice of America, UNICEF, ABC Radio, Africa, 1972-74; resident corr. ABC News, Cairo, 1974-77; dir. publs. and comm. World Environment Ctr., N.Y.C., 1978-85; cons. writer, editor, editorial designer Women's Environ. and Devel. Orgn., 1989-98, UN orgns. and others, 1985—; co-organizer Project on Religion and Human Rights, 1994-95; guest lectr. Am. U. Cairo, Rutgers U., Columbia U., L.I. U., Hunter Coll., CUNY; press officer Global Survival Conf., Oxford, Eng., 1988; press coord. Global Forum on Environ. and Devel., Moscow, 1990, Parliamentary Earth Summit, Rio de Janeiro, 1992; info. officer Internat. Green Cross/Global Forum, Kyoto, Japan, 1993; comm. coord. World Women's Congress for Healthy Planet, Miami, 1991; press. coord. WEDO Web, NGO Forum on Women, China, 1995. Author: The Growth of Environment in the World Bank, World Environment Center, 1982, UNEP N.Am. News, 1986-91, Shared Vision, 1988-92, The Global Forum Decade, 1995, also others. Mem. Soc. Profl. Journalists, Soc. Environ. Journalists, Internat. Sci. Writers Assn.

BASSETT, JOHN E., dean, English educator; b. Washington, May 12, 1942; s. J. Earl and Frances E. (Walker) B.; m. Kay E. Hobart, Sept. 5, 1964; children: Laura, Gregory. BA in History, Ohio Wesleyan U., 1963, MA in English, 1966; PhD in English, U. Rochester, 1970. Instr. U. Rochester, N.Y., 1969-70; asst. prof. Wayne State U., Detroit, 1970-75, assoc. prof., 1975-84; prof., head dept. English No. Carolina State U., Raleigh, 1984-93; dean Coll. Arts and Scis., prof. English Case Western Res. U., Cleve., 1993—. Author: William Faulkner: An Annotated Checklist of Criticism, 1972, Faulkner: The Critical Heritage, 1975, Faulkner: A Checklist of Recent Criticism, 1983, Vision and Revisions: Essays on Faulkner, 1989, Faulkner in the Nineties: A Bibliography of Criticism, 1991, A Heart of Ideality in My Realism and Other Essays on Howells and Twain, 1991, Harlem in Review: Critical Reactions to Black American Writers 1917-1939, 1992, Defining Southern Literature, 1997, Thomas Wolfe: An Annotated Bibliography of Criticism, 1996; contbr. articles to profl. jours. Mem. MLA, Mark Twain Soc., Thomas Wolfe Soc., Soc. for Study of So. Lit., Assn. Depts. of English (pres. 1990-91), Phi Beta Kappa, Phi Kappa Phi, Phi Alpha Theta. Office: Coll Arts and Scis Case Western Res U Cleveland OH 44106-7068

BASSETT, JOHN WALDEN, JR., lawyer; b. Roswell, N.Mex., Mar. 21, 1938; s. John Walden Sr. and Evelyn (Thompson) B.; m. Patricia Lubben, May 22, 1965 (dec. Apr. 22, 1995); children: John Walden III, Loren Patricia; m. Nolana Knight, May 2, 1998. AB in Econs., Stanford U., 1960; LLB with honors, U. Tex., 1964. Bar: Tex. 1964, N.Mex. 1964. Assoc. Atwood & Malone, Roswell, 1964-66; White House fellow, spl. asst. to U.S. atty. gen., Washington, 1966-67; ptnr. Atwood, Malone, Mann & Turner and predecessors, P.A., Roswell, 1967-95, Bassett & Copple, LLP, 1995—; bd. dirs. A.H. Belo Corp., Dallas, AMMA Found., Washington. Assoc. editor: U. Tex. Law Review, 1962; mem. N.Mex. State Bd. of Edn., 1987-91. Pres., chmn. bd. United Way of Chaves County, N.Mex., 1973; bd. dirs. Ednl. Achievement Found., Roswell, 1992—. 1st lt. U.S. Army, 1961-68. Mem. ABA, Tex. Bar Assn., N.Mex. Bar Assn., Chaves County Bar Assn., Order of Coif, Rotary (pres. 1976, Roswell), N.Mex. Amigos, Phi Delta Phi. Republican. Episcopalian. Home: 5060 Bright Sky Rd Roswell NM 88201-8800 Office: Bassett & Copple 400 N Pennsylvania Ave Ste 250 Roswell NM 88201-4788

BASSETT, LAWRENCE C, management consultant; b. N.Y.C., Dec. 11, 1931; s. David Isaac and Genia Esther Bassett; m. Charlotte Corinne Margolis, Jan. 24, 1960; children: Wendy Jill, Craig Henrid, Heidi Jill, Evan Henrid. BA, NYU, 1953, MBA, 1958. Pers. mgr. Republic Carloading & Distbg. Co., N.Y.C., 1956-61; dir. pers. Clay Adams Inc., N.Y.C., 1961-63; asst. dir. pers. Montefiore Hosp. and Med. Ctr., N.Y.C., 1963-65; dir. pers. Hosp. for Joint Diseases and Med. Ctr., N.Y.C., 1965-67; sr. cons. Orgn. Resources Counselors Inc., N.Y.C., 1967-76; pres. Applied Leadership Tech. Inc., Bloomfield, N.J., 1976-86, The Bassett Cons. Group Inc., Thornwood, N.Y., 1986—; adj. prof. NYU, 1978—, N.Y. Med. Coll., 1992, Fairleigh Dickenson U., Teaneck, N.J., 1964-86; instr. Helene Fuld Sch. for RN's, N.Y.C., 1966-67. Author: Achieving Excellence, 1986; producer & presenter audio & video tape tng. albums; contbr. articles to profl. jours. Pres., v.p. Mt. Pleasant Bd. Edn., Thornwood, N.Y., 1973-76, 81-87; docent Am. Mus. Natural History. With U.S. Army, 1953-55. Mem. Soc. Profl. Mgmt. Cons. (bd. dirs., v.p.), Inst. Mgmt. Cons. (cert. mgmt. cons.), Am. Soc. for Tng. and Devel., Am. Hosp. Assn., Am. Arbitration Assn., Nat. Speakers Assn., Masons. Avocations: clock making, baking, beekeeping, skiing, orchid growing. Home and Office: The Bassett Cons Group Inc 1 Ilana Ln Thornwood NY 10594-2001

BASSETT, LESLIE RAYMOND, composer, educator; b. Hanford, Calif., Jan. 22, 1923; s. Archibald Leslie and Vera (Starr) B.; m. Anita Elizabeth Denniston, Aug. 21, 1949; children—Wendy Lynn (Mrs. Lee Bratton), Noel Leslie, Ralph (dec.). B.A. in Music, Fresno State Coll., 1947; M.Music in Composition, U. Mich., 1949, A.Mus.D., 1956; student, Ecole Normale de Musique, Paris, France, 1950-51. Tchr. music pub. schs. Fresno, 1951-52; mem. faculty U. Mich., 1952—, prof. music, 1965—, Albert A. Stanley disting univ. prof., 1977—, chmn. composition dept., 1970, Henry Russel lectr., 1984, emeritus, 1992; guest composer Berkshire Music Center, Tanglewood, Mass., 1973. Served with AUS, 1942- 46. Fulbright fellow, 1950-51; recipient Rome prize Am. Acad. in Rome, 1961-63; grantee Soc. Pub. Am. Music, 1960, Nat. Inst. Arts and Letters, 1964, Nat. Council Arts, 1966; Guggenheim fellow, 1973-74, 80-81; recipient Pulitzer prize in music for Variations for Orch., 1966; citation U. Mich. regents, 1966; Walter Naumburg Found. rec. award for Sextet, 1974; Disting. Alumnus award Calif. State U., Fresno, 1978; Disting. Artist award Mich. Council Arts, 1981; Citation of Merit, U. Mich. Sch. Music Alumni, 1980. Mem. Am. Composers Alliance, Mich. Soc. Fellows, Am. Acad. of Arts and Letters, Pi Kappa Lambda, Phi Kappa Phi, Phi Mu Alpha. Methodist. Office: U Mich Sch Music Ann Arbor MI 48109

BASSETT, PETER Q., lawyer; b. Buenos Aires, Argentina; s. John Jewett and Helen (Gibbs) B.; m. Wendy O. Bassett, Sept. 2, 1972; children: Elisabeth E., Laura G. AB, Princeton U., 1971; JD, George Washington U., 1975. Assoc. Alston, Miller & Gaines, Atlanta, 1975-81; ptnr. Alston & Bird, Atlanta, 1981—. Mem. Ga. Bar Assn., Atlanta Bar Assn. Avocation: motorcycles. Office: Alston & Bird 1201 W Peachtree St NW Ste 4200 Atlanta GA 30309-3424*

BASSETT, TINA, communications executive; b. Detroit; m. Leland Kinsey Bassett; children: Joshua, Robert. Student, U. Mich., 1974, 76-78, 81, Wayne State U., 1979-80. Advt. dir. Greenfield's Restaurant, Mich. and Ohio, 1972-73; dir. advt. and pub. rels. Kresco, Inc., Detroit, 1973-74; pub's. rep. The Detroiter mag., 1974-75; pub. rels. dir. Detroit Bicentennial Commn., 1975-77; prin. Leland K. Bassett & Assocs., Detroit, 1976-86; intermediate job devel. specialist Detroit Coun. of the Arts, 1977; project dir. Detroit image campaign dept. pub. info. City of Detroit, 1975, spl. events dir., 1978, dep. dir. dept. pub. info., 1978-83, dir. dept. pub. info., 1983-86; pres., prin. Bassett & Bassett, Inc., Detroit, 1986—; bd. dirs. Diverse Steel Corp. Publicity chmn. Under the Stars IV, V, VI, VII, VIII, IX and X, Benefit Balls, Detroit Inst. of Arts Founders Soc., 1983-88, Detroit Inst. of Arts Founders Centennial Ball, 1985, publicity chmn. Mich. Opera Theater, Opera Ball, 1987; program lectr. Wayne County Close-Up Program, 1984; mem. ctrl. planning com. Am. Assn. Mus.; mem. Founders Soc., Detroit Inst. Arts, 1988—; mem., publicity chair Grand Prix Ball, 1989; co-chair, prodr. Mus. Hall Ctr. for Performing Arts; bd. dirs. arts coun. Detroit Inst. Arts, 1996, bd. dirs. cinema arts coun., 1996—; bd. dirs. Weizman Inst. Sci., 1996-97. Named Outstanding Woman in Agy. Top Mgmt., Detroit chpt. Am. Women in Radio and TV, 1989. Mem. AIA (hon., pub. dir. 1990-91, Richard Upjohn fellowship 1991), Detroit Hist. Soc., , Internat. Women's Forum, Music Hall Assn., Pub. Rels. Soc. Am. (Advt. Woman of Yr. 1989), Woman's Advt. Club Detroit, Cinematic Arts Coun., DIA Board of Dirs., 1996—. Home: 30751 Cedar Creek Dr Farmingtn Hls MI 48336-4989 Address: Bassett & Bassett 1502 Randolph St Ste 200 Detroit MI 48226-2299

BASSETT, WILLIAM AKERS, geologist, educator; b. Bklyn., Aug. 3, 1931; s. Preston Rogers and Jeanne Reed (Mordorf) B.; m. Jane Ann Kermes, Sept. 8, 1962; children—Kari Nicalo, Jeffrey Kermes, Penelope North. B.A., Amherst Coll., 1954; M.A., Columbia U., 1956, Ph.D., 1959. Research assoc. Brookhaven Nat. Lab., 1960-61; Asst. prof. U. Rochester, N.Y., 1961-65; asso. prof. U. Rochester, 1965-69, prof. geology, 1969-77; prof. geology Cornell U., Ithaca, N.Y., 1978—; vis. prof. Brigham Young U., 1967-68; Crosby vis. prof. MIT, 1974. Research, publs. on the devel. of techniques for investigation of properties of minerals at pressures and temperatures within the earth's interior. Recipient Bridgman award AIRAPT, 1997; NSF grantee; Guggenheim fellow, 1985. Fellow Geol. Soc. Am., Mineral. Soc. Am. (Roebling medal 1994, Bridgman award 1997), Am. Geophys. Union, AAAS; mem. Sigma Xi (pres. Rochester chpt. 1977-78). Home: 765 Bostwick Rd Ithaca NY 14850-9310 Office: Cornell U Dept Geol Scis Ithaca NY 14853

BASSETT, WOODSON WILLIAM, JR., lawyer; b. Okmulgee, Okla., Nov. 7, 1926; s. Woodson William and Bee Irene (Knerr) B.; m. Marynm Shaw, Dec. 16, 1950; children: Woodson William III, Beverly M., Tod Corbett. J.D., U. Ark., 1949. Bar: Ark. 1949. Employed in New Orleans and Monroe La., 1949-51; claims examiner Employers Group Ins. Cos., 1949-51; mgr. Light Adjustment Co., 1951-56; v.p. legal dept. Preferred Ins. Cos., 1957-62; sr. partner Bassett Law Firm, 1962—; spl. chief justice Ark. Supreme Ct., 1991—; mem. Ark. Bd. Law Examiners. Mem. editorial staff: Ark. Law Review, 9. Pres. Sherman Lollar Boys Baseball League, 1962; v.p. Babe Ruth Baseball Assn., 1968; chmn. bd. dirs. Fayetteville Public Library, 1975-79. Served with AUS, 1950-51. Fellow Am. Coll. Trial Lawyers; mem. ABA, Ark. Bar Assn., Washington County Bar Assn. (pres. 1973-74), Am. Bd. Trial Advs., Def. Law Inst., Am. Counsel Assn., Ark. Def. Counsel Assn., Am. Inns of Ct., Delta Theta Phi, Kappa Sigma. Home: 2210 Manor Dr Fayetteville AR 72701-2640 Office: Bassett Law Firm 221 N College Ave Fayetteville AR 72701-4238

BASSETTI, FRED FORDE, architect; b. Seattle, Jan. 31, 1917; s. Frederick Michael and Sophie Marie (Forde) B.; m. Mary Wilson, June 30, 1944 (div. 1969); children: Ann, Catherine, Margaret; m. Moira Feeney, June 29, 1971 (div. 1985); children: Megan, Michael; m. Gwenyth Piper Caldwell, Dec. 20, 1989; stepchildren: Megan, Ben, Piper, Sam. BArch, U. Wash., 1942; MArch, Harvard U., 1946. Registered architect, Alaska, Idaho, Mont., Oreg., Wash. Draftsman Paul Thiry, Seattle, 1944, Alvar Aalto, Cambridge, Mass., 1946; designer Naramore, Bain, Brady & Johanson, Seattle, 1946; prin. Bassetti & Morse, Seattle, 1947-62, Fred Bassetti & Co., Seattle, 1962-81, Bassetti, Norton, Metler, Seattle, 1981-85, Bassetti, Norton, Metler, Rekevics, Seattle, 1985-94, Bassetti Architects, Seattle, 1994—; bd. dirs. Discuren Found., Seattle. Prin. works include Coll. Engring. Bldgs., U. Wash., 1970, Fed. Office Bldg., Seattle, 1975, U.S. Embassy, Lisbon, Portugal, 1984, PACCAR Tech Ctr., Mt. Vernon, Wash., 1985, AT&T Gateway Tower, Seattle, 1990; patentee in field. Mem. Seattle Design Com., 1976-78, Seattle Landmarks Bd., 1978-79. Named Best Local Architect, Seattle Weekly poll, 1988. Fellow AIA (pres. Seattle chpt. 1967; 57 nat. or regional awards, Seattle chpt. medal 1988); mem. Nat. Acad. N.Y.C. (academician 1997), Allied Arts of Seattle and King County (pres. 1970-72). Avocations: tennis, skiing, bicycling, windsurfing. Office: Bassetti Architects 1011 Western Ave Seattle WA 98104-1040*

BASSIN, JULES, foreign service officer; b. N.Y.C., Apr. 16, 1914; s. Abe and Bessie (Brooks) B.; m. Beatrice M. Kellner, Dec. 25, 1938; children: Arthur Jay, Nelson Jay. B.S., CCNY, 1936; J.D., N.Y.U., 1938; student, Criminal Investigation Sch., U.S. Army, 1943, Security Intelligence Sch., 1944, Mil. Govt. Sch., U. Va., 1944, Far East Civil Affairs, Harvard, 1945; grad., Armed Forces Staff Coll., 1960. Bar: N.Y. bar 1939. Dir. law div. Gen. Hdqrs., Supreme Comdr. Allied Powers, Tokyo, Japan, 1945-51; legal attache Am. embassy, Tokyo, 1951-56; also spl. asst. to ambassador for politico-mil. affairs; spl. asst. to ambassador for mut. security affairs Am. Embassy, Karachi, 1956-59; State Dept. faculty adviser Armed Forces Staff Coll., Norfolk, Va., 1960-62; chief titles and rank br. Dept. State, 1962-63, chief functional assignments br., 1963-65, dir. functional personnel program, 1965-67, spl. asst. to dep. undersec. state for adminstrn., 1967-69, exec. sec. Bd. Fgn. Service, 1967-69; dep. rep. of U.S. to European office UN and other internat. orgns.; also dep. chief U.S. mission with personal rank of minister, Geneva, Switzerland, 1969-74; cons. on refugee and migration affairs Dept. State, 1974—; cons. USIA, 1975-76. Served from 2d lt. to maj., Judge Adv. Gen. Corps. AUS, 1942-46; col. Res. Mem. Am. Fgn. Service Assn. Club: American Internat. (Geneva) (exec. com.). Home: 2891 Audubon Ter NW Washington DC 20008-2309 Office: Dept of State Washington DC 20520

BASSINGTHWAIGHTE, JAMES BUCKLIN, physiologist, educator, medical researcher; b. Toronto, Sept. 10, 1929; s. Ewart MacQuarrie and Velma Emeline B.; m. Joan Elizabeth Graham, June 18, 1955; children: Elizabeth Anne, Mary, Alan, Sarah, Rebecca. BA, U. Toronto, 1951, MD, 1955; postgrad., Med. Sch. London, 1957-58; PhD, Mayo Grad. Sch. Medicine U. Minn., 1964. Intern Toronto Gen. Hosp., 1955-56; physician Internat. Nickel Co., Sudbury and Matheson, Ont., 1956-57; house physician Hammersmith Hosp., London; postgrad. Med. Sch. London, 1957-58; teaching asst. physiology U. Minn., Mpls., 1961-62; fellow Mayo Grad. Sch. Medicine, Rochester, Minn., 1958-64, instr., 1964-67, asst. prof., 1967-69, assoc. prof., 1969-72; vis. prof. Pharmacology Inst., U. Bern, Switzerland, 1970-71; asso. prof. bioengring. U. Minn., 1972-75; prof. physiology Mayo Grad. Sch. Medicine, 1973-75, prof. medicine, 1975; prof. bioengring., radiology and biomath U. Wash., Seattle, 1975—; dir. Ctr. for Bioengring., 1975-80; vis. prof. medicine and physiology McGill U., 1979-81; affiliate prof. physiology Limburg U., Maastricht, The Netherlands, 1990—; mem. study sect. NIH, 1970-74, 80-83; chmn. Biotech. Resources Adv. Com., 1977-79, chmn. 1st Gordon Rsch. Conf. on Water and Solute Transport in Microvasculature, 1976; chmn. workshop on metabolic imaging Nat. Heart, Lung and Blood Inst., 1985; Lewellen-Thomas lectr., U. Toronto, 1991; Coulter lectr. U. N.C., 1995; Oxford lectr. Internat. Soc. Magnetic Resonance Medicine, 1996. Author: (with L.S. Liebovitch and B.J. West) Fractal Physiology, 1994; contbr. over 200 articles to profl. publs. Recipient NIH Rsch. Career Devel. award, 1964-74, Louis and Artur Lucian award McGill U., 1979, Witzig award Cardiovasc. Sys. Dyamics Soc., 1982, Faculty Achievement award for outstanding rsch. U. Wash. Coll. Engring., 1993; Edmund Hustinx chair Maastricht U., 1999. Mem. AAAS, Am. Heart Assn. (coun. on circulation 1976—), Biophys. Soc. (assoc. editor Biophys. Jour. 1980-83), Biomed. Engring. Soc. (dir. 1971-74, pres. 1977-78, Alza award 1986, editor-in-chief Annals of Biomedical Engring. 1993—), Microcirculatory Soc. (mem. coun. 1975-78, 80-83, pres. 1990-91, Landis award 1995), Am. Physiol. Soc. (mem. circulation group, editorial bd. 1972-76, 79-83, mem. edn. com.), Internat. Union Physiol. Scis. (U.S.A. nat. com. 1978-86, U.S. del. to assembly 1980, 83, 86, chmn. 1983-86, chmn. Commn. on Bioengring. and Clin. Physiology 1986-97, chmn. satellite to 30th Congress on Endothelial Transport 1986, co-chmn. satellite on microvascular networks 1989, chmn. satellite on Physiome Project 1997). Achievements include research in cardiovascular physiology and bioengineering, biomathematics and computer simulation with emphasis on ion and substrate exchange in heart, fractals in physiology, integrative biology and originator of the Physiome Project. Home: 3150 E Laurelhurst Dr NE Seattle WA 98105-5333 Office: U Wash Ctr for Bioengring PO Box 35-7962 Seattle WA 98195-7962

BASSIOUNY, HISHAN SALAH, surgeon, educator; b. Cairo, Mar. 30, 1954; m. Sandra Bassiouny; children: Deenah, Faith-Iman. Mb. Bch. Diploma with honors, Cairo U., 1977. Diplomate Am. Bd. Surgery; lic. surgeon, Ill., Mich., Md. Intern Cairo U. Hosps., 1977-78; surg. externship Linz (Austria) Gen. Hosp., 1980-81; intern Md. Gen. Hosp., Balt., 1981-82; resident Henry Ford Hosp., Detroit, 1982-86, clin. vascular fellow, 1986-87; postdoctoral rsch. fellow, instr. surgery U. Chgo., 1987-89, asst. prof. surgery, 1989—, assoc. prof. surgery, 1996—, dir. non-invasive vascular lab.; mem. staff U. Chgo. Med. Ctr., Little Co. Mary Hosp., Weiss Meml. Hosp., dir. non-invasive vascular lab. Contbr. chpts. to books and numerous articles to profl. jours. Recipient Louis Block award, 1989; grantee W.L. Gore, 1987-89, NIH, 1988—, Mellon Found., 1990, U. Chgo., 1992-93, Washington Sqare Found., 1992, Am. Heart Assn., 1995—. Fellow ACS; mem. AAAS, AAS, Am. Heart Assn. (sci. coun. 1992—, coun. atherosclerosis, coun. cardio-thoracic and vascular surgery), Am. Venous Forum, Midwestern Vascular Soc., North Am. Vascular Biology Orgn., Internat. Soc. Cardiovascular Surgery, Chgo. Surg. Soc., Peripheral Vascular Surg. Soc., Soc. Vascular Surgery. Office: U Chgo Hosp # MC5028 5841 S Maryland Ave Chicago IL 60637-1435*

BASSIS, MICHAEL STEVEN, academic administrator; b. N.Y.C., Sept. 8, 1944; s. Lewis and Barbara (Fay) B.; m. Mary Suzanne Wilson, Dec. 27, 1977; children: Anne Elizabeth, Christina, Jessica, Nicholas. BA with honors, Brown U., 1967; MA, U. Chgo., 1968, PhD, 1974. Asst. dir. acad. potential project Brown U., 1966-67; rsch. assoc. Ctr. for the Study of the

Acts of Man U. Pa., 1968; instr., asst. prof.-assoc. prof. dept. sociology and anthropology U. R.I., 1971-81, acting asst. dean Coll. Arts and Scis., 1977-78; assoc. Harvard U. Grad. Sch. Edn., 1980-81; assoc. dean faculty U. Wis., Parkside, 1981-85, assoc. prof. sociology, 1981-86, interim asst. chancellor ednl. svcs., 1985-86; v.p. acad. affairs Ea. Conn. State U., 1986-89; exec. v.p., univ. provost Antioch U., Yellow Springs, Ohio, 1989-93; pres. Olivet (Mich.) Coll., 1993-98; dean, warden U. South Fla./New Coll., Sarasota, 1998—; presenter in field. Author (with W.R. Rosengren) The Social Organization of Nautical Education: The U.S., Great Britain and Spain, 1976, (with R.J. Gelles and A. Levine) Sociology: An Introduction, 4th edit., 1991, Social Problems, 1982; editor Teaching Sociology, 1982-85; contbr. articles to profl. jours. NIMH grantee, 1967-71, Exxon Edn. Found. grantee, N.Y.C., 1975, Fund for Improvement of Post-Secondary Edn. grantee, Washington, 1978. Mem. Am. Sociol. Assn. (undergrad. edn. sect., membership com. 1979-81, coun. 1980, 82, 86-89, teaching resources group 1984-86, publs. com. 1985, chair 1987-88), Am. Assn. Higher Edn., Nat. Soc. Experiential Edn. Home: 460 Pheasant Dr Sarasota FL 34236-1922 Office: USF/New Coll Sarasota FL 34243

BASSIST, DONALD HERBERT, retired academic administrator; b. Dallas, Oct. 28, 1923; s. Ellis and Adele (Gutz) B.; m. Norma Dale Andersen, Oct. 14, 1950; children: Matthew Perry, Bradford Beaumont. AB, Harvard U., 1948; MBA, Portland State U., 1975; grad., U.S. Army command and Gen. Staff Coll., 1967. Pres. Bassist Coll., Portland, Oreg., 1963-98; ret.; chmn. ednl. adv. bd. pvt. vocat. schs., Salem, Oreg., 1972-78; active Oreg. Ednl. Coordinating Coun., 1970-73. Writer, dir. (film) Fashion: The Career of Challenge, 1969 (N.Y. Internat. Bronze award). Lt. A.C., U.S. Army, 1943-46; lt. col. Corps of Engrs., ret., 1972. Mem. Nat. Assn. Scholars, Japanese Garden Soc. (bd. dirs. 1988-93), Portland Advt. Fedn. (bd. dirs. 1969-72). Avocations: gardening, travel.

BASSLER, ROBERT COVEY, artist, educator; b. N.Y.C., Nov. 9, 1935; s. Robert Stein and Joan (Covey) B.; m. Linda Marie Allen, June 14, 1964. BA, Bard Coll., 1957; MFA, U. So. Calif., 1960. Instr. sculpture Occidental Coll., 1960-64; prof. sculpture Calif. State U., Northridge, 1964-97, prof. emeritus, 1998—; artist in residence Calif. Inst. Tech., 1970-71; art film tour Arts Coun. Gt. Britain. Solo exhbns. include Comara Gallery, L.A., 1961, 63, Occidental Coll., L.A., 1961, 70, Calif. State U. Bakersfield, 1964, L.A. Mcpl. Art Gallery, Barnsdall Park, 1965, 81, Calif. State U., Northridge, 1965, Santa Barbara (Calif.) Mus. Art, 1968, Molly Barnes Gallery, L.A., 1969, Baxter Art Gallery, Calif. Inst. Tech., 1971, Galerie La Demeure, Paris, 1972, Amerika-Haus, West Berlin, 1972, Wenger Gallery, L.A., 1988, Security Pacific Pla., L.A., 1989-90, Calif. State U., Northridge, 1997, Orlando Gallery, Sherman Oaks, Calif., 1997; exhibited in group shows at Jewish Mus., N.Y.C., Milw. Art Ctr., San Francisco Mus. of Art, Los Angeles County Mus. of Art, Pasadena Mus. of Art, Long Beach (Calif.) Mus. of Art, LaJolla (Calif.) Mus. of Art, San Francisco Mus. of Art, Newport Harbor Art Mus., Oakland Mus. of Art, Esther Bear Gallery, Santa Barbara, Houston Mus. of Art, Ackland Meml. Art Ctr., Chapel Hill, N.C., Mus. Fine Arts, St. Petersburg, Fla., Jacksonville (Fla.) Art Mus., Musée d'Art Moderne, Paris, Galerie La Demeure, Paris, Redfern Gallery, London, U.S. Embassy, London, Wenger Gallery, L.A., Calif. Inst. Tech., Amerika Haus, Berlin, Sculpture in the City, Century City, Calif., Fine Arts Gallery, San Diego, Art Park, L.A., Design Ctr., L.A., Washington Sq., Washington, Fine Arts Bldg., L.A., Valerie Miller Gallery, Palm Desert, Calif., Tom Bradley Terminal, L.A. Internat. Airport; represented in permanent collections including Atlantic Richfield Corp., Container Corp. Am., Quinn & Assocs., L.A., Security Pacific Nat. Bank, Carter Hawley Hale Stores Inc., Home Savs. & Loan, The Ahmanson Collection, Chgo. Convention Ctr., Arts Coun. of Gt. Britain, U. So. Calif., Bard Coll., N.Y., Kirk O' The Valley, Reseda, Calif., Calif. State U., Northridge. With AUS, 1959-62. Recipient Pres.'s Creativity award Calif. State U., Northridge, 1978, Meritorious Performance award, 1989, 96. Developed technique for casting clear polyester resin. E-mail: robert.c.bassler@csun.edu. Address: 8329 Melvin Ave Northridge CA 91324-4132 *My current work explores visual phenomena created by light and structural juxtapositions and their resulting effects upon one's concept of reality. Most recently painted interpretations of NASA photographs of our planet have been incorporated as provocative elements of beauty, fragility, order and chaos. These phenomena represent to me a broader aspect of the limited realities normally perceived. It is my intention to expand awareness of these concerns through my art.*

BASSLER, WILLIAM G., federal judge; b. 1938. BA, Fordham Univ. Coll., 1960; JD, Georgetown U., 1963; LLM, NYU, 1969. Law sec. to Hon. Mark A. Sullivan N.J. Superior Ct., 1963-64; with Parsons, Canzona, Blair & Warren, 1964-70; ptnr. Labrecque, Parsons & Bassler, 1970-83, Evans, Koelzer, Osborne, Kreizman & Bassler, 1983-84, Carton, Nary, Witt & Arvantis, 1984-88; judge Superior Ct. State of N.J., 1988-91; fed. judge U.S. Dist. Ct. (N.J. dist.), Newark, 1991—. Mem. ABA, N.J. State Bar Assn., Monmouth County Bar Assn. Office: Martin Luther King Fed CourtHouse PO Box 999 50 Walnut St Rm 5060 Newark NJ 07101*

BASSNETT, PETER JAMES, retired librarian; b. Sutton Coldfield, Warwickshire, Eng., Nov. 16, 1933; emigrated to Can., 1966; s. Lionel and Phyllis (Mair) B.; m. Ann Gorham, Dec. 12, 1959; children: Madeline Jane, Sarah Catherine. A.Library Assn., N. Western Poly. Sch. Librarianship, London, 1963. Chartered librarian, U.K. Library asst. City of Westminster, London, 1958-61; tech. librarian Cement & Concrete Assn., London, 1963-64; librarian-in-charge London Borough of Haringey, 1964-66; adminstrv. asst. to dir. Calgary Pub. Library Bd., Alta., 1966-72; dir. systems and mgmt. North York Pub. Library Bd., Ont., 1972-75; CEO librs. Scarborough Pub. Library Bd., Ont., 1975-95; ret., 1995; exec. coordinator Ont. Pub. Libraries Programme Rev., Toronto, 1980-82. Contbr. articles to profl. jours. Chmn. adv. com. on library arts programme So. Alta. Inst. Tech., 1969-72. Fellow Libr. Assn. (U.K.); mem. Alta. Libr. Assn. (pres. 1969-70), Pvt. Librs. Assn., Powys Soc. Home: 29 Highbridge Pl, Scarborough, ON Canada M1V 4R7

BASSO, KEITH HAMILTON, cultural anthropologist, linguist, educator; b. Asheville, N.C., Mar. 15, 1940; s. Joseph Hamilton and Etolia (Simmons) B.; div. BA, Harvard U., 1962; MA, Stanford U., 1965, PhD, 1967. Asst. prof. anthropology U. Ariz.-Tucson, 1967-71, assoc. prof., 1972-76, prof., 1977-81; prof. anthropology Yale U., 1982-88, U. N.Mex., Albuquerque, 1988—; mem. Inst. Advanced Study, Princeton, N.J., 1975-76; Weatherhead fellow Sch. Am. Research, Santa Fe, N.M., 1977-78; cons. cultural and historical matters White Mountain and San Carlos Apache Tribes; mem. steering com. Nat. Coalition for Am. Indian Religious Freedom; bd. trustees Nat. Mus. of the Am. Indian, 1991-96. Author: Wisdom Sits in Places: Landscape and Language Among the Western Apache, 1996 (awarded Western States Book award 1996, Victor Turner prize for ethnographic writing 1997), Western Apache Language and Culture: Essays in Linguistic Anthropology, 1991, Portraits of the White Man, 1979, The Cibecue Apache, 1970; editor: Senses of Place, 1996, Meaning in Anthropology, 1976, Western Apache Witchcraft, 1969. Mem. AAAS, Assn. Am. Indian Affairs (bd. dirs. 1978-86), Am. Anthropol. Assn., Am. Ethnol. Soc. (pres. 1983-84), Linguistic Soc. Am. Democrat. Home: 12 Pool St NW Albuquerque NM 87120-1809 Office: U NMex Dept Anthropology Albuquerque NM 87131

BASSUK, ELLEN LINDA, psychiatrist; b. N.Y.C., Feb. 8, 1945; d. Irving and Molly (Pakarow) B.; children: Daniel, Sarah. BA, Brandeis U., 1964; MD, Tufts U., 1968; Dr.P.S. (hon.), Northeastern U., 1993. Diplomate Am. Bd. Psychiatry. Intern Mt. Auburn Hosp., Cambridge, Mass., 1968-69; resident psychiatry Univ. Hosp., Boston, 1969-70, Boston State Hosp., Boston, 1970-71; resident psychiatry Beth Israel Hosp., Boston, 1971-73, dir. psychiat. emergency svcs., 1974-82; fellow Bunting Inst., Cambridge, Mass., 1982-84; assoc. prof. psychiatry Harvard Med. Sch., Boston, 1983—; founder, pres. The Better Homes Fund, Newton, Mass., 1988—; mem. Com. on Health Care of Homeless Persons Inst. of Medicine, Washington, 1986-88. Editor: The Practitioners Guide to Psychoactive Drugs, 1977, 83, 91, 97; series editor Plenum Press; editor-in-chief Am. Jour. Orthopsychiatry, 1994-98; contbr. numerous articles to profl. jours. Fellow Am. Psychiat. Assn.; mem. Mass. Psychiat. Soc. Home: 20 Randolph Rd Chestnut Hill MA 02467-2338 Office: The Better Homes Fund 181 Wells Ave Newton MA 02459-3344

BAST, JAMES LOUIS, trade association executive; b. Balt., Apr. 19, 1936; s. Louis and Evelyn Frances (Alling) B.; m. Mary Margaret Griffin, June 13, 1959; children: Andrew Griffin, James Mark, Cynthia Elizabeth. B.A., Columbia U., 1958, B.S.M.E., 1959; M.B.A., NYU, 1968. With Pitney Bowes Inc., Stamford, Conn., 1963-72, 73-90, chief fin. officer, 1976-82, v.p. fin., contr., 1976-77, sr. v.p. fin. and adminstrn., 1977-82; pres. Pitney Bowes Bus. Systems, Stamford, Conn., 1987-90; pres., chief exec. officer Dictaphone Corp. subs. Pitney Bowes Inc., Rye, N.Y., 1982-87; CEO A. B. Dick Co., Chgo., 1990-92; CEO, pres. Presstek, Inc., Hudson, N.H., 1993; pres., CEO, Coun. Better Bus. Burs., Inc., Arlington, Va., 1994—; cons., contr. Bunker Ramo Corp., Trumbull, Conn., 1972-73. Served to lt. USN, 1959-63. Home: 1250 S Washington St # 503 Alexandria VA 22314-4455 Office: Coun Better Bus Burs Inc 4200 Wilson Blvd Arlington VA 22203-1800

BAST, KENNETH GEORGE, healthcare executive; b. Milw., Oct. 31, 1949; s. George H. and Genevieve (Zimmel) B.; m. Patricia A. Hogan, Nov. 17, 1973. BBA, Marquette U., 1971; MBA, U. Wis., 1977. Personnel asst. St. Joseph Hosp., Warren, Ohio, 1972-74; v.p. ops. Meml. Hosp., Burlington, Wis., 1974-80; pres. No. Ill. Med. Ctr., McHenry, Ill., 1980-82; v.p. TW3 Corp., Downer's Grove, Ill., 1982-84; v.p. health services John Knox Village, Lee's Summit, Mo., 1984-89; cons. Hamilton/KSA, Mpls., 1989-97; ind. cons. Burnsville, Minn., 1997-98; v.p. health care consulting Health Dimensions Consulting Group, St. Paul, 1998—; project dir. Mobile Intensive Care program Emergency Med. Services, McHenry, 1981-82; instr. Cen. Mo. State U., Kansas City, 1986—; adj. faculty Master of Healthcare Adminstrn. program U. Minn., 1995-97; mem. review bd. of Swedish long term care health facilities, Jonkoping, Sweden, 1987; bd. dirs. Multi Hosp. Mut. Ins., Hamilton, Bermuda. Mem. McHenry Econ. Commn., 1982, Govs. Adv. Council on Aging, Mo., 1985-88. Mem. Am. Hosp. Assn., Nat. Council on aging, Am. Coll. Health Care Adminstrs., Kansas City C. of C. (Pres. Club). Roman Catholic. Avocation: photography.

BAST, ROBERT CLINTON, JR., medical researcher, medical educator; b. Washington, Dec. 8, 1943; s. Robert Clinton and Ann Christine (Borland) B.; m. Blanche Amy Simpson, Oct. 21, 1972; 1 child, Elizabeth Simpson Bast. BA cum laude, Wesleyan U., Middletown, Conn., 1965; MD magna cum laude, Harvard U., 1971. Diplomate Am. Bd. Internal Medicine, Am. Bd. Med. Oncology, Am. Bd. Hematology. Predoctoral fellow dept. pathology Mass. Gen. Hosp., Boston, 1967-69; intern Johns Hopkins Hosp., Balt., 1971-72; rsch. assoc. biology br. Nat. Cancer Inst., NIH, Bethesda, Md., 1972-75; asst. resident Peter Bent Brigham Hosp., Boston, 1975-76; fellow med. oncology Sidney Farber Cancer Inst., Boston, 1976-77; asst. prof. medicine Harvard U. Med. Sch., Boston, 1977-83, assoc. prof., 1983-84; prof. Duke U. Med. Ctr., Durham, N.C., 1984-92, Wellcome clin. prof. medicine in honor of R. Wayne Rundles, 1992-94, co-dir. div. hematology-oncology, 1984-94; dir. clin. research programs Duke U. Comprehensive Cancer Ctr., Durham, 1984-87; dir., 1987-94; Harry Carothers Wiess chair cancer rsch. U. Tex. M.D. Anderson Cancer Ctr., 1994—, head divsn. med., 1994—; dir. divsn. med. oncology dept. medicine U. Tex. Health Sci. Ctr., Houston, 1994—; hosp. appointments include asst. in medicine Peter Bent Brigham Hosp., 1976-77; jr. assoc. in medicine Brigham and Women's Hosp., 1977-82; cons. oncologist Boston Hosp. Women, 1978-80; physician Duke U. Med. Ctr., 1984-94; internist M.D. Anderson Cancer Ctr., 1994—; mem. biol. response modifiers decision network com. Nat. Cancer Inst., 1984-87, exptl. immunology study sect., 1983-84, 90-92; mem. grant rev. com. Leukemia Soc. Am., 1985-87, adv. com. oncologic drugs FDA, 1985-89, chmn. 1988-89; bd. dirs. Cancer and Leukemia Group B., 1986-88, Am. Council Transplantation, 1985-87; mem. grant rev. com. Am. Cancer Soc., 1987; numerous other coms.; Edward G. Waters Meml. lectr., 1987; John Ohtani Meml. lectr., 1991; D. Nelson Henderson lectr., 1991; Stolte Meml. lectr., 1992; Arnold O. Beckman Disting. Lectureship, 1993; Robert C. Knapp lectr., 1996; Alan Dembo Meml. Keynote lectr., 1997. Contbr. numerous articles on tumor immunology, immunodiagnosis and immunotherapy of cancer and cellular immunology to profl. jours. Served as surgeon USPHS, 1972-75. Recipient Dominus award, 1984, Robert C. Knapp award, 1990, Recognition Outstanding Leadership and Advocacy award Nat. Coalition for Cancer Rsch., 1995, Smith Kline Beecham Clin. Labs. award Clin. Ligand Soc., 1996, award of Achievement, Ptnrs. in Courage, ACS, 1998; grantee Nat. Cancer Inst., NIH, HHS, 1978—; scholar Leukemia Soc. Am., 1978-83. Fellow ACP; mem. Internat. Gynecol. Cancer Soc. (coun. 1997—), The Reticuloendothelial Soc., Am. Soc. Microbiology, Am. Assn. Cancer Rsch., Am. Assn. Immunologists, Assn. Am. Physicians, Am. Soc. Clin. Oncology, Am. Fedn. Clin. Rsch., Am. Soc. Clin. Investigation, Internat. Soc. Immunopharmacology, Soc. Biol. Therapy (bd. dirs. 1984-86), Am. Soc. Hematology, Soc. Gynecol. Oncology (assoc.). Achievements include development of monoclonal antibodies to react with human ovarian cancer, leading to CA125 blood test; techniques for selective elimination of tumor cells from human bone marrow; identification of molecular changes associated with malignant transformation of ovarian epithelium. Office: U Tex MD Anderson Cancer Ctr 1515 Holcombe Blvd # 092 Houston TX 77030-4009

BASTIAANSE, GERARD C., lawyer; b. Holyoke, Mass., Oct. 21, 1935; s. Gerard C. and Margaret (Lally) B.; m. Paula E. Paliska, June 1, 1963; children: Elizabeth, Gerard. BSBA, Boston U., 1960; JD, U. Va., 1964. Bar: Mass. 1964, Calif. 1970. Assoc. Nutter, McClennen & Fish, Boston, 1964-65; counsel Campbell Soup Co., Camden, N.J., 1965-67; gen. counsel A&W Internat. (United Fruit Co.), Santa Monica, Calif., 1968-70; ptnr. Kindel & Anderson, Los Angeles, 1970—. Mem. ABA, Calif. Bar Assn., Mass. Bar Assn., Japan Am. Soc., Asia Soc., World Trade Ctr. Assn. Clubs: California (Los Angeles); Big Canyon Country (Newport Beach, Calif.). Home: 2 San Sebastian Newport Beach CA 92660-6828 Office: Kindel & Anderson 2030 Main St Ste 1300 Irvine CA 92614-7220

BASTIAN, DONALD NOEL, bishop, retired; b. Estevan, Sask., Can., Dec. 25, 1925; s. Josiah and Esther Jane (Millington) B.; m. Kathleen Grace Swallow, Dec. 20, 1947; children: Carolyn Dawn, Donald Gregory, Robert Wilfrid, John David. BA, Greenville Coll., 1953, STD (hon.), 1974; BD, Asbury Theol. Sem., 1956, DD (hon.), 1991; DD (hon.), Seattle Pacific U., 1965; DHL (hon.), Roberts Wesleyan Coll., 1990. Ordained to ministry Free Meth. Ch. N.Am., 1954; pastor chs. Lexington, Ky., 1953-56, New Westminster, B.C., Can., 1956-61; pastor College Free Meth. Ch., Greenville, Ill., 1961-74; bishop Free Meth. Ch. N.Am., Toronto, 1974-90, mem. bd. adminstrn., 1964-90; exec. editor Light and Life mag. Free Meth. Ch. N.Am., 1974-84, chmn. editorial adv. com. Light and Life mag., 1980-86; bishop Free Meth. Ch. in Can., 1990-93. Author: The Mature Church Member, 1960, Along the Way, 1974, Belonging, 1974; editor: The Joy of Christian Fathering: Five First Person Accounts, 1979, Counterfeit: The Lie of Living Together Unmarried, 1988. Recipient Disting. Service award Asbury Theol. Sem., 1974; Presdl. award Greenville Coll., 1972. Mem. Can. Holiness Fedn. (pres. 1977, 78), Christian Holiness Assn. (v.p. 1977-78), Evang. Fellowship of Can. (pres. 1989-91). Home: 63 Adirondack Cres, Brampton, ON Canada L6R 1E5 *I live by the conviction that, however durable it may seem, evil is by nature unstable. Righteousness, by contrast, gives stability to life in the long pull.*

BASTIAN, JAMES HAROLD, air transport company executive, lawyer; b. Hannibal, Mo., Nov. 26, 1927; s. Ira Russell and Opal (Maddox) B.; m. Mary Jean Zugel, Feb. 5, 1955; children: Raphael Maria, Marquette Maria, Bartholomew Barnabas, Boniface Benedict. BS, U. Mo., 1950; JD with honors, George Washington U., 1956. Bar: D.C., Va. 1956, U.S. Supreme Ct. 1960, Md. 1975. Assoc. Adair, Ulmer, Murchison, Kent & Ashby, 1956-61; v.p., sec. Pacific Corp., 1961-74; sec. Air Am., Inc., 1961-74, Air Asia Co. Ltd., 1973-74; ptnr. Howard, Poe & Bastian, 1965-84, Bastian and Bastian, 1984-95; sec., dir. Permawick Co., 1974-95; v.p., sec., dir. So. Air Transport, Inc., Columbus, Ohio, 1974-79, pres., chief exec. officer, 1979-83, chmn. bd., chief exec. officer, 1983—; chmn. bd., chief exec. officer SimuFlite Tng. Internat., 1991-98; mem. mil. airlift com. Nat. Def. Transp. Adminstrn., 1988—. Served with USNR, 1945-46. Mem. Va. Bar Assn., Md. Bar Assn., D.C. Bar Assn., Met. Club, Army and Navy Club (Washington), Riviera Country Club (Miami, Fla.), Congl. Country Club (Bethesda, Md.), Wings Club (N.Y.C.), Order of Colf. Home: 140 Arvida Pky Miami FL 33156-2313 also (summer): PO Box 11-114 Telluride CO 81435-4004

BASTIANELLO, SANDRA CREWS, therapist; b. Winston-Salem, N.C., Aug. 29, 1950; d. Howard Clarence and Rachel Gray (Gentry) Crews; m. Arthur George Bastianello, Aug. 4, 1973; children: Laura Michelle, Cynthia Marie. BA, U. N.C., 1972; MS, Old Dominion U., 1982; postgrad., Ga. State U., 1991-94. Lic. profl. counselor; nat. cert. counselor; nat. bd. cert. clin. hynotherapist. Tchr. Surry County Schs., Dobson, N.C., 1972-73, Chatham County Schs., Pittsboro, N.C., 1973-75, High Meadows Sch., Roswell, Ga., 1982-92; cons. Marietta, Ga., 1992-93; ednl. therapist Counseling and Assessment Ctr., Marietta, 1993-94; therapist Dr. Spencer Gelernter & Assocs., Marietta, 1994-99; intern The Wellness Inst., 1996-98; therpaist pvt. practice, Roswell, 1999—; tchr. in-svc. facilitator High Meadows Sch., Roswell, 1983-92; presenter Nat. Conf. Trichotillomania Learning Ctr. Evaluator: (tchr.'s guide) Free the Horses: A Self-Esteem Adventure, 1990. Grad. tuition grantee Sch. of Grad. Study, Old Dominion U., Norfolk, Va., 1980. Mem. Am. Counseling Assn., Play Therapy Assn. (vol. internat. conf. 1993), Am. Counselor Assn., Internat. Assn. Marriage and Family Counselors, Am. Mental Health Counselor Assn., Heart Centered Hypnotherapy Assn., Heart Centered Therapies Assn. (sec. adv. bd., co-chair internat. conv.), Chi Sigma Iota (steering com. 1993-94). Democrat. Home: 4280 Post Oak Tritt Rd Marietta GA 30062-5700 Office: Ste 150 Old Roswell Lakes Pky Roswell GA 30076

BASTIDAS, HUGO XAVIER, painter; b. Quito, Ecuador, Aug. 18, 1956; came to U.S., 1960; s. Hugo Enrique and Leonor (Jaramillo) B.; m. Susan Kay Bengtson, Nov. 22, 1989. BA, Rutgers U., 1979; Cert. in Sculpture, Bklyn. Mus. Sch. of Art, N.Y.C., 1979-80; MFA, Hunter Coll./CUNY, N.Y.C., 1987. bd. dirs. Aljira: A Ctr. for Contemporary Art, chair of artist advisory. One-person shows include: Nohra Haime Gallery, N.Y.C., 1994, 95, 96, 97, Aljira: A Ctr. for Contemporary Art, 1996, ETS Gallery, Princeton, N.J., 1989, others; group shows include: Nohra Haime Gallery, 1994-97, Ben Shahn Galleries, William Paterson Coll. of N.J., Wayne, 1996, Muscarelle Mus. of Art, Williamsburg, Va., 1996, Art Chgo./Nohra Haime Gallery, Chgo., 1996, Jersey City Mus., 1996, Kentler Internat. Drawing Space, N.Y.C., 1994, Matsuzakaya Art Gallery, Osaka, Japan, 1995, numerous others. Co-chair hist. preservation Weehawken Environ. Com., N.J., 1997. Recipient Robert Smithson Meml. scholarship, 1979-80, Schwartz and Hofflich CPA award Silvermine Artists' Guild, 1986, Fulbright fellowship, 1990, awards Colombian Ecuadorian Assn. of Am., 1995; grantee Pollock-Krasner Found., 1992. Mem. Ecuadorian House of Culture (bd. dirs. 1994-96). Home/Studio: 445 E 86th St Apt 10E New York NY 10028-6439

BASTIEN, JANE SMISOR, music educator; b. Hutchinson, Kans., Jan. 15, 1936; d. Herbert D. and Gladys I. (Haston) Smisor; m. James W. Bastien; children: Lisa Bastien Hanss, Lori Bastien Vickers. AA, Stephens Coll., 1955; BA, Barnard Coll., 1957; MA, Columbia U., 1958. Asst. prof. Tulane U., New Orleans, 1958-75; pvt. piano tchr., La Jolla, Calif., 1975—. Author/composer: Bastien Piano Books/Ednl. Piano Books for Children and Adults. Recipient Alumnae award Stephens Coll., 1960. Mem. Nat. Assn. Music Tchrs. (Lifetime Achievement award 1999), Music Tchrs. Assn. of Calif. (State Tchg. award 1996). Republican. Presbyterian. Avocations: gardening, collecting antiques. Home and Studio: 2431 Vallecitos Ct La Jolla CA 92037-3146

BASTRON, JAMES ARTHUR, retired neurologist; b. Ottumwa, Iowa; s. Alexander E. and Grayce Margaret Bastron; m. Louise Frances Lomas; children: Malcolm Dewitt, Mary Jo, James Arthur. BA, U. Iowa, 1941, MD, 1944; MS in Neurology, U. Minn., 1954. Rotating intern Wesley Meml. Hosp., Chgo., 1944-45; resident pathology Columbia U. Coll. Physicians and Surgeons, N.Y.C., 1947-48; fellw in surgery, internal medicine and neurology Mayo Found., Rochester, Minn., 1948-53; cons. in neurology and electromyography Mayo Clinic, Rochester, 1954-91, Jacksonville, Fla., 1954-91; head neurology dept. Mayo Clinic, Jacksonville, 1989-90; emeritus staff Mayo Clinic, 1990—; hosp. dir. Fed. Med. Ctr., Rochester, 1985-87. Elder First Presbyn. Ch., Rochester. Capt. U.S. Army, 1945-47, USAF, 1954. Mem. Alpha Omega Alpha. Avocations: golf, gardening, fishing. Home: 2220 Hillside Ln SW Rochester MN 55901-1147 Office: Mayo Clinic 200 First St SW Rochester MN 55905

BASU, ASIT PRAKAS, statistician; b. Bangladesh, Mar. 17, 1937; came to U.S., 1962, naturalized, 1979; m. Sandra Bergquist; children: Amit K., Shumit K. BS with honors, Calcutta U., 1956, MS, 1958; PhD, U. Minn., 1966. Asst. prof. stats. U. Wis., Madison, 1966-68; mem. research staff IBM Research Center, Yorktown Heights, N.Y., 1968-70; asst. prof. indsl. engrng. and mgmt. sci. Northwestern U., Evanston, Ill., 1970-71; asso. prof. math. U. Pitts., 1971-74; prof. stats. U. Mo., Columbia, 1974—; chmn. dept. U. Mo., 1976-83. Co-editor 4 books on reliability and quality control; contbr. articles to profl. jours. Fellow Royal Statis. Soc., Am. Statis. Assn., Inst. Math. Stats., AAAS; mem. Calcutta Statis. Assn., Internat. Statis. Inst., Am. Soc. Quality COntrol, Biometric Soc. Office: Univ Mo Dept Stats Columbia MO 65211

BASU, SUNANDA, scientific administrator, researcher in space physics; b. Calcutta, West Bengal, India, Dec. 9, 1940; d. Chunilal and Amita Chatterjee Ganguli; m. Santimay Basu, Apr. 5, 1961; 1 child, Susanto. BSc in Physics, Calcutta (India) U., 1960, PhD in Radio Physics, 1972; AM in Physics, Boston U., 1963. Rsch. assoc. Inst. Radio Physics, U. Calcutta, India, 1973-75; NAS resident rsch. assoc. Air Force Geophysics Lab., Hanscom AFB, Mass., 1975-78; sr. physicist Emmanuel Coll., Boston, 1978-89; sr. rsch. physicist Inst. Space Rsch., Boston Coll., 1989-92; program dir. aeronomy, atmospheric scis. divsn. NSF, Arlington, Va., 1992—; mem. com. Solar Terrestrial Rsch. Panel on Jicamarca Radio Obs., Peru, 1980-83; chairperson CEDAR Working Group on High Latitude Plasma Structure, 1987-92, STEP WG3 Project on Global Aspects of Plasma Structures, 1990-97, USNC/URSI Commm. G, 1994-96, mem. exec. com., 1988-90, vice chairperson, 1991-93; mem. adv. com. atmospheric scis. NSF, 1988-92; organizer CEDAR/HLPS & STEP/GAPS Workshop, Peaceful Valley, Colo., 1992; cons. Ctr. Space Rsch. MIT, Cambridge, Mass., 1991-92; mem. U.S. nat. del. to Internat. Sci. Radio Union Gen. Assemblies, 1981, 84, 87, 90, 93, 96; mem. steering com. S-RAMP/SCOSTEP, 1998—. Author chpts. to books; contbr. over 60 papers, articles to profl. jours. Mem. AAAS, Am. Geophy. Union, Internat. Sci. Radio Union (mem. commns. G and H), Sigma Xi (pres. Hanscom chpt. 1986-87). Office: NSF 4201 Wilson Blvd Rm 775 Arlington VA 22230-0001

BASUK, RICHARD, physician; b. N.Y.C., Sept. 27, 1951; s. Benjamin and Ruth B.; m. Philomena Perri, Nov. 26, 1978;1 child, Samantha. AB magna cum laude, Brown U., 1973; MS, NYU, 1977. Bd. cert. plastic surgeon. Resident NYU Med. Ctr., N.Y.C., 1977-81, 82-84, chief resident, 1981-82; plastic surgeon pvt. practice, N.Y.C., 1985—; chief sect. plastic surgery Good Samaritan Hosp., Sufferon, N.Y., 1992—, sec. med. exec. com., 1994—, chmn. by laws com., 1989—, co-chmn. 10k run, 1994—, mem. spring ball com., 1993—; lectr. in field. Mem. steering com. Mamonides Soc., Wayne, N.J., 1993—. Hand Surgery fellow NYU Med. Ctr., 1984-85. Mem. Am. Soc. Plastic & Reconstructive Surgery, Am. Coll. Surgeons, Northeastern Soc. Plastic Surgeons, N.Y. Regioal Soc. Plastic & Reconstructive Surgeons, Phi Beta Kappa, Sigma Xi. Avocations: reading, running, cooking, law. Office: 122 E Ridgewood Ave Paramus NJ 07652

BATA, RUDOLPH ANDREW, JR., lawyer; b. Akron, Ohio, Jan. 9, 1947; s. Rudolph Andrew and Margaret Eleanor (Ellis) B.; m. Genevieve Ruth Brannan, Aug. 25, 1968 (div. May 1985); 1 child, Seth Andrew; m. Linda Lee Waldo, May 7, 1985; 1 child, Sarah Ariel. BS, So. Coll., Collegedale, Tenn., 1969; JD, Emory U., 1972. Bar: D.C. 1973, N.C. 1978, U.S. Dist. Ct. N.C. 1991, U.S. Ct. Appeals (4th cir.) 1991; cert. mediator AOC. Assoc. ICC, Washington, 1972-73; in house counsel B.F. Saul Real Estate Investment Trust, Chevy Chase, Md., 1973-74; staff atty. Martha, Cafferky, Powers & Jordan, Washington, 1974-75; asst. corp. counsel Hardee's Food Systems, Inc., Rocky Mount, N.C., 1975-78; ptnr. Bata & Blomeley, Murphy, N.C., 1978-87, 88-90, Bata & Sumpter, Murphy, 1987-88; sole practice, 1990—. Bd. dirs. Cherokee County United Fund, Murphy, 1981-83. Mem. ABA, N.C. Bar Assn., D.C. Bar Assn., 30th Jud. Dist. Bar Assn., So. Soc. of Adventist Attys. (pres. 1984-85), Cherokee County C. of C. (bd. dirs. 1980-82). Avocations: golf, tennis, hiking. Office: 225 Valley River Ave Ste A Murphy NC 28906-2920

BATAILLE, GRETCHEN, academic administrator. B of English, Calif. Polytech. State U., M of English Edn.; D, Drake U. Chair dept. English

Ariz. State U., chair dept. English, assoc. dean acad. personnel, until 1994; provost U. Calif., Santa Barbara, 1994-97; provost, acad. v.p. Wash. State U., Pullman, 1997—. Author: Living the Dream in Arizona: The Legacy of Martin Luther King, Jr., 1992, Native American Women: A Biographical Dictionary, 1994, Ethnic Studies in the United States, 1998, others. Office: Wash State U French Adminstrn 422 Pullman WA 99164-1046

BATALDEN, PAUL BENNETT, pediatrician, health care educator; b. Mpls., Dec. 4, 1941; s. Abner Bennett and Martha (Bjornstad) B.; m. LaVonne Marie Olson; children: Maren, Sonja. BA, Augsburg Coll., 1963; MD, BS, U. Minn., 1967. Diplomate Am. Bd. Pediatrics. Clin. assoc. Nat. Cancer Inst., Bethesda, Md., 1969; med. dir. Job Corps, Washington, 1970-72; dir. Community Health Svc., Rockville, Md., 1972-73; dir., Bur. Community Health Svc., Rockville, 1973-75; pediatrician Park Nicollet Med. Ctr., Mpls., 1975-86, quality assurance dir., 1976-84, chief oper. officer, 1984-86; v.p. med. care, head quality resource group Hosp. Corp. of Am., Nashville, 1986-94; Breech chmn. Dept. Health Care Quality Improvement Edn. and Rsch. Henry Ford Health Sci. Ctr., 1990—; prof., dir. Ctr. Healthcare Improvement Leadership Devel. Dartmouth Med. Sch.; founding chmn. Inst. for Healthcare Improvement; bd. dirs. Allina Health Sys. Author: Quality Assurance in Ambulatory Care, 1980, Clinical Improvement Action Guide, 1998; contbr. articles on quality in healthcare and aspects of pediatric practice to profl. jours. Regent Augsburg Coll., Mpls., 1978-90. Recipient Guild of Honor, 1963, Pub. Svc. award Nat. Med. Assn., 1974, Disting. Alumnus award Augsburg Coll., 1984, Award of Honor, Am. Hosp. Assn., 1997, Codman award, 1998. Mem. Inst. of Medicine of NAS, Am. Acad. Pediatrics, Minn. Med. Assn., Tenn. Med. Assn., N.H. Med. Assn., Alpha Omega Alpha.

BATCHA, GEORGE, mechanical and nuclear engineer; b. Marblehead, Ohio, Oct. 24, 1928; s. John and Anna (Groholy) B.; m. Erika Voelker, Jan. 1, 1982; 1 child, Susan Kolodziejczyk. BA, Bowling Green State U., 1951; MS in Engring. Sci., U. Toledo, 1968; R&D test and evaluation program cert., U.S. Army Logistics Mgmt. Coll. and Assn. for Sys. Mgmt.; certs. numerous U.S. Army Tng. Schs. R&D test and evaluation program cert, U.S. Army Logistics Mgmt. Coll. and Assn. for Systems Mgmt.; certs. numerous U.S. Army tng. schs.; registered profl. engr., Ohio, Mich.; cert. nat. engring. examiners. With Standard Products Co., Port Clinton, Ohio, 1951, A.O. Smith Co. Landing Gear Divsn., Toledo, Ohio, 1951; army rep. Glenn L. Martin Co., Balt., 1952-54, Cleve. Pneumatic Tool Co., 1954-55, Hardware Stamping divsn. Ford Motor Co., Sandusky, Ohio, 1955-59; mech. design and test engr. Missile and Def. Engring. divsns. Chrysler Corp., Detroit, 1959-62; mech. and nuclear engr. NASA, Lewis Rsch. Ctr., Plum Brook Sta., Sandusky, 1962-74; mech. and system mgmt. engr. Armament Rsch. & Devel. Command, U.S. Army, Dover, N.J., 1974-81, Rock Island, Ill., 1974-81; mech. engr. Tank Automotive and Armaments Command, Warren, Mich., 1981—. Author numerous tech. reports. With U.S. Army, 1952-54. Recipient Apollo Achievement award, NASA, 1969, accomplishments awards, 1981, 82, Cost Reduction awards, 1971-74, Dept. Army Achievement award Tank Automotive and Armaments Command, 1985, Superior Performance award Spl. Act award, 1990-98; Bowling Green State U. scholar, 1948. Mem. NSPE, Order of Engr., Nat. Coun. engring. Examiners (cert.), Am. Acad. Environ. Engrs. (diplomate, radiation protection), Soc. Logistics Engrs. (cert. prof. logistician), U.S. Army Logistics Mgmt. Coll. and Assn. for Systems Mgmt. (cert. in R&D), Am. Legion. Byzantine Catholic. Achievements include serving as team leader of Logistics Engring. Team; research in technical assessment and guidance of developmental programs of all elements of integrated logistics support in tank-automotive weapon system and equipment; subspecialties include:mechanical engineering and nuclear engineering. Fax: 810-574-6323. E-mail: batchag@tacom.army.mil. Home: 12851 E Outer Dr Detroit MI 48224-2730

BATCHELDER, ALICE M., federal judge; b. 1944; m. William G. Batchelder III; children: William G. IV, Elisabeth. BA, Ohio Wesleyan U., 1964; JD, Akron U., 1971; LLM, U. Va., 1988. Tchr. Plain Local Sch. Dist., Franklin County, Ohio, 1965-66, Jones Jr. High Sch., 1966-67, Buckeye High Sch., Medina County, 1967-68; assoc. Williams & Batchelder, Medina, Ohio, 1971-83; judge U.S. Bankruptcy Ct., Ohio, 1983-85, U.S. Dist. Ct. (no. dist.) Ohio, Cleve., 1985-91, U.S. Ct. of Appeals (6th cir.), Cleveland, 1991—. Mem. ABA, Fed. Judge's Assn., Fed. Bar Assn., Medina County Bar Assn. Office: 143 W Liberty St Medina OH 44256-2215

BATCHELDER, ANNE STUART, former publisher, political party official; b. Lake Forest, Ill., Jan. 11, 1920; d. Robert Douglas and Harriet (McClure) Stuart; m. Clifton Brooks Batchelder, May 26, 1945; children: Edward, Anne Stuart, Mary Clifton, Lucia Brooks. Student Lake Forest Coll., 1941-43. Clubmobile driver ARC, Eng., Belgium, France, Holland and Germany, 1943-45; pub., editor Douglas County Gazette, 1970-75, 79-90; bd. dirs. Firstier Bank Omaha; dir., treas. U.S. Checkbook Com. Mem. Rep. Ctrl. Com. Nebr., 1955-62, 70-83, vice chmn. Ctrl. Com., 1959-64, chmn., 1975-79, mem. fin. com., 1957-64; chmn. women's sect. Douglas County Rep. Fin. Com., 1995, vice chmn. com., 1958-60; v.p. Omaha Woman's Rep. Club, 1957-58, pres., 1959-60; alt. del. Nat. Conv., 1956, 72, del., 1980, 84, 88; mem. Rep. Nat. Com. for Nebr., 1964-70; asst. chmn. Douglas County Rep. Ctrl. Com., 1971-74; 1st v.p. Nebr. Fedn. Rep. Women, 1971-72, pres., 1972-74; chmn. Nebr. Rep. Com., 1975-79; vice-chmn. Bundling Fedn. Rep. Women, 1998—; mem. Nebr. State Bldg. Commn., 1979-83; Rep. candidate for lt. gov., 1974. Sr. v.p. Nebr. Founders Day, 1958; trustee Hastings Coll., 1977—; bd. dirs. YWCA, 1983-89, Omaha Libr. Found., 1991—; past trustee Brownell Hall, Vis. Nurse Assn.; past pres. Nebr. chpt. Freedoms Found. at Valley Forge; chmn. fin. George Bush for Pres., Nebr., 1987-88; apptd. Kennedy Ctr. Performing Arts, 1989, 94, Pres.' Adv. Com. on the Arts, 1990-92, Nat. Com. for the Performing Arts, 1992—; mem. Nebr. Rep. State Fin. Com., 1990, Nat. Fin. Com. Bush-Quayle, 1992; active Omaha Meth. Hosp. Found., Brownell-Talbot Sch. Found. Elected to Nebr. Rep. Hall of Fame, 1984; named Citizen of the Yr. Midlands Coun. Boy Scouts Am., 1997. Mayflower Soc., Colonial Dames, P.E.O., Nat. League Pen Women Omaha Country, Omaha. Presbyterian. Home: 6875 State St Omaha NE 68152-1633

BATCHELDER, JENNIFER JO, legislative staff member; b. Reno, Sept. 14, 1973; d. William Joseph Raddatz and Andrea Elizabeth Clark; m. Gregory J. Batchelder, Mar. 22, 1997. BA, Smith Coll., 1996. Co-mgr. Limited Too, Reno, 1996; exec. dir. Washoe County Dem. Party, Reno, 1998; field coord. Nev. Dem. Party, Reno, 1998; com. sec. Nev. Assembly, Carson City, 1999. Roman Catholic.

BATCHELDER, SAMUEL LAWRENCE, JR., retired corporate lawyer; b. Boston, Apr. 3, 1932; s. Samuel L. and May W. (Read) B.; m. Jane B. Borden, 1955 (div. 1965); children: John H., Benjamin A.; m. Marion C. Thomas, 1967; children: Timothy C., Lily L. AB, Harvard U., 1954, LLB, 1960. Bar: Mass., 1960, U.S. Dist. Mass. 1961. Assoc. Goodwin, Procter & Hoar LLP, Boston, 1960-67, ptnr., 1968-97, of counsel, 1997—. Active ARC, bd. dirs. local orgns., Boston, 1966—, chmn. Mass. Bay unit, 1979-83, mem. various nat. coms., 1981—, chmn. resolutions com., 1998—, NE Blood Svcs., 1981-92; mem. grad. coun. Milton Acad., 1986-91, chmn., 1989-91, trustee, 1989-92; trustee Mass. Continuing Legal Edn., 1995—; dir. Exec. Svc. Corps. N.E., 1998—. Served to 1st lt. U.S. Army, 1954-57. Mem. ABA, Mass. Bar Assn., Boston Bar Assn. (chmn. corp. law com. 1985-88, mem. gov. coun. 1988-91, legal edn. com. 1995—), Brookline Friendly Soc. (trustee 1998—). Democrat. Club: The Country Club (Brookline, Mass.). Avocations: tennis, skiing, gardening, music, art. Office: 66 Laurel Rd Chestnut Hill MA 02467-2211 also: Goodwin Procter & Hoar Exchange Pl Boston MA 02109

BATCHELLER, JOSEPH ANN, entrepreneur; b. Jacksonville, Fla., Dec. 11, 1932; d. Osmer St. Clair and Lorena (Jones) Deming; m.David Springsteen Batcheller, Aug. 8, 1957; children: Elizabeth Batcheller Whalen, Osmer Deming, John Alden. AA, Stephens Coll., Columbia, Mo., 1952; BA, U. N.C., 1955. Sec. Seminole Oil Co., Miami, Fla., 1957-61, pres., bd. dirs., 1961-65; pres., chmn. Blue Water Mobile Home Sales, Inc., Tavernier, Fla., 1967-76; dir. Miami Heart Inst., Miami Beach, 1973—, v.p., 1975—, exec. v.p., 1986-89, pres., chief exec. officer, 1989-93; sec., bd. dirs. Bluegrass Plant Foods, Inc., Cynthiana, Ky., 1958-72; chmn. Superior Plant Foods, Inc., Lakeland, Fla., 1958-60; v.p., bd. dirs. Pensacola Petroleum Co., Inc., Miami, 1961-65, Top Power Stas., Miami, 1961-65, Atico Savs. Bank, Miami, 1987-88, Pan Am. Bank, Miami, 1984-87; bd. dirs. Intercontinental Bank; vice chmn. Miami Heart Rsch. Inst., Inc., 1993—. Bd. dirs. Am. Heart Assn., Miami, 1989-91; mem. adv. bd. Convent of Sacred Heart, Miami, 1973-77; mem. parents adv. bd. Furman U., Greenville, S.C., 1979-83. Mem. Surf Club on Miami Beach (pres. bd. govs. 1993-97, vice chmn. 1997—), Surf Club Debutante Com. (chmn. 1976-82, 86, 87), Bay Point Property Owners Assn. (pres. 1991-96), Young Patronesses of Opera, English Speaking Union, DAR. Episcopalian. Avocations: reading, boating, beaux arts. Home: 4595 Sabal Palm Rd Miami FL 33137-3363 Office: The Surf Club 9011 Collins Ave Miami FL 33154

BATCHELOR, BARRINGTON DE VERE, civil engineer, educator; b. Lucea, Jamaica, W.I., July 2, 1928; s. Reginald Augustus and Vera Louise (O'Connor) B.; m. Alison Yvonnie Johnston, Sept. 14, 1960; children: Roger, Nicola, Wayne. B.Sc. with honors (Elias Issa scholar), U. Edinburgh, 1956; Ph.D. (Commonwealth scholar), U. London, 1963; student, Nat. Def. Coll. Can., 1982-83. Registered profl. engr., Ont. Asst. engr. Sir William Halcrow & Partners, London, 1956-58; exec. engr. Ministry Edn., Jamaica, 1958-63; sr. exec. engr. Ministry Edn., 1963-64; ptnr. Franks & Batchelor, cons. engrs., Kingston, Jamaica, 1964-66; asst. prof. civil engring. Queen's U., Kingston, Ont., Can., 1966-68; assoc. prof. Queen's U., 1968-72, prof., 1972-93, prof. emeritus, 1993—. Bd. govs. Kingston Gen. Hosp. Fellow Engring. Inst. Can., Can. Soc. Civil Engrs.; mem. ASCE, Am. Concret Inst., Instn. Engrs. (Jamaica), Profl. Engrs. Ont. (councillor). Home: 150 Collingwood St, Kingston, ON Canada K7L 3X5 Office: Queen's U, Dept Civil Engring, Kingston, ON Canada K7L 3N6

BATCHELOR, DAVID HENRY LOWE, marketing consultant; b. Reading, Berkshire, Eng., May 2, 1940; s. Henry Vesci Batchelor and Marjorie Ellen McNeff; m. Sarah Ann Glasson, Aug. 4, 1991; children: Lancelot, Nicholas, Edward. BA with honors, Oxford (Eng.) U., 1961, MA with honors, 1963. Diploma in comm., advt. and mktg. Advt. Assn. and Inst. Practitioners in Advt. Mktg. dir. Lenthiric Morny Ltd. (subs. BAT Industries), London, 1967-73; v.p. internat. Germaine Monteil Cosmetiques Corp. (subs. BAT Industries), N.Y.C., 1973-77; pres., gen. mgr. Yardley of London Venezolana S.A. (subs. BAT Industries), Valencia, Venezuela, 1977-81; v.p. ops. Yardley Ams., Inc. (subs. BAT Industries), Ft. Lauderdale, Fla., 1981-85; pres. internat. Crystal Brands Jewelry Group, N.Y.C., 1985-92; v.p. sales and mktg. Andin Internat., Inc., N.Y.C., 1993; sr. v.p. product mktg. Playboy Enterprises, Inc., Chgo., 1994-97; mng. ptnr. McEvoy/Batchelor LLC, New Canaan, Conn., 1997—; interim pres. Alu, Inc., N.Y.C., 1997-98; cons. Alpha Investment, Inc., N.Y.C., 1998. Mem. U.K. Advt. Assn., U.K. Inst. Practitioners in Advt., Metro Hartford C. of C. (com. mem. internat. bus. coun.), Royal Yachting Assn. Avocations: current affairs, history, music, sailing. E-mail: dbatchelor@esslink.com and McEvoyBatchelor@email.com. Fax: 860-738-9403. Home: 134 Pinney St Winsted CT 06098-3920 Office: McEvoy/Batchelor Internat LLC Ste 7 66 Seminary St New Canaan CT 06840

BATCHELOR, J. CASEY, career military officer; b. Corsicana, Tex., Sept. 17, 1975; s. Patrick C. and Carolyn (Reynolds) B. BS in Econs., US Naval Acad., 1998. Ensign USN, Annapolis, Md., 1994—. Mem. Omicron Delta Epsilon. Presbyn. Avocation: golf. Home: 1824 Dartmouth Ln Corsicana TX 75110-2206

BATCHELOR, JAMES KENT, lawyer; b. Long Beach, Calif., Oct. 4, 1934; s. Jack Morrell and Edith Marie (Ottinger) B.; m. Jeanette Lou Dyer, Mar. 27, 1959; children: John, Suzanne; m. Susan Mary Leonard, Dec. 4, 1976. AA, Sacramento City Coll., 1954; BA, Calif. State U., Long Beach, 1956; JD, Hastings Coll. Law, U. Calif., 1959. Bar: Calif. 1960, U.S. Dist. Ct. (cen. dist.) Calif. 1960, U.S. Supreme Ct. 1968; cert. family law specialist Calif. Bd. Legal Specialization, 1980. Dep. dist. atty., Orange County, Calif., 1960-62; assoc. Miller, Nisson, Kogler & Wenke, Santa Ana, Calif., 1962-64; ptnr. Batchelor, Cohen & Oster, Santa Ana, 1964-67, Kurilich, Ballard, Batchelor, Fullerton, Calif., 1967-72; pres. James K. Batchelor, Inc.; tchr. paralegal sect. Santa Ana City Coll.; judge pro-tem Superior Ct., 1974—; lectr. family law Calif. Continuing Edn. of Bar, 1973—. Contbr. articles to profl. jours. Fellow Am. Acad. Matrimonial Lawyers (pres. So. Calif. chpt. 1989-90); mem. ABA, Calif. State Bar (placque chmn. family law sect. 1975-76, advisor 1976-78), Orange County Barristers (founder, pres., placque 1963), Calif. State Barristers (placque 1965, v.p.), Orange County Bar Assn. (plaque sec. 1977, pres. family law sect. 1968-71, Best Lawyers in Am. 1989-90, 91-92, 93-94, 95-96, 97-98, 99—). Republican. Methodist. Office: 765 The City Dr S Ste 270 Orange CA 92868-4942

BATCHELOR, JOSEPH BROOKLYN, JR., electronics engineer, consultant; b. Jersey, Ga., Apr. 11, 1922; s. Joseph Brooklyn and Mary Arlie (Reece) B.; m. Clara Owens, July 14, 1940; children: Joseph Brooklyn III, James Alfred, William Owens. Diploma, North Ga. Coll., 1940. Registered profl. engr., Ill., Ga. Owner, pres. JRS Electronics-Svc., Rsch. & Cons., Monroe, Ga., 1946-57; dir. rsch. and engring. Cen. Electronics, Inc., Chgo., 1957-61; rsch. engr. Hallicrafters Corp., Chgo., 1961-63; aircraft devel. engring. specialist Lockheed A/C Corp., Marietta, Ga., 1965-70; pres., chmn. BRECO Corp., Walnut Grove, Ga., 1972-75; cons. engr. Batchelor Labs., Libertyville, Ill., 1963-65; owner, mgr. Batchelor Labs., Walnut Grove, 1970-72, Jersey, 1975—; pres. PATRONIX-Patent Holding Corp., Chgo., 1958-61. Patentee in field; inventor radio-location device for lost student pilots WWII. Chmn. bd. Monroe Christian Ch., 1950-57. Sgt. USAF, 1945-46, World War II. Mem. AAAS, Citizens Adv. Coun. on Energy, Mensa. Avocations: amateur radio, classical music, reading. Home and Office: 101 Main St Jersey GA 30235

BATCHELOR, KAREN LEE, English language educator; b. Oregon City, Oreg., June 17, 1948; d. Jewel Elaine Durham; m. Luis Moncado, Mar. 17, 1978 (div. Aug. 1988); children: Virginia, Travis. BA in English, San Francisco State U., 1971, MA in English, 1980. Vol. U.S. Peace Corps, Andong, South Korea, 1972-74; tchr. English as second lang. City Coll. San Francisco, 1975—; tchr. trainer U. Calif., Berkeley, 1986—; acad. specialist USIA, 1991—; speaker in field. Co-author: (textbooks) Discovering English, 1981, In Plain English, 1985, More Plain English, 1986, The Writing Challenge, 1990, The English Zone, Books 1-4, 1998; contbr. articles to profl. jorus. Mem. Tchrs. English to Speakers of Other Langs., Calif. Tchrs. English to Speakers of Other Langs. Office: City Coll San Francisco 50 Phelan Ave San Francisco CA 94112-1821

BATCHVAROV, ALEXANDER IVANOV, financial analyst; b. Sofia, Bulgaria, June 5, 1961; came to the U.S., 1993; s. Ivan Anguelov and Dimka Petrova Batchvarov. MSc in Econs., Econs. Inst., Sofia, 1986; PhD, Acad. Scis., Sofia, 1991; MBA, U. Alta., Can., 1993. Sessional prof. U. Alta., Edmonton, 1992-93; mgr. fin. instns. Citibank, N.A., N.Y.C., 1993-94; asst. analyst structured fin. Moody's Investors Svc., London, 1994-95; v.p. structured fin. Moody's Investors Svc., N.Y.C., 1995-97, v.p. sovereign group, 1997-98; fixed income analyst, head internat. ABS rsch. Merrill Lynch, N.Y.C., London, Hong Kong, 1998—; cons. Maclab Enterprises, Edmonton, 1991, Moscow, 1992; trade specialist Intercomertz, Sofia, 1985-86. Author: Completion of the EC Market-Implications for Outside World, 1991; contbr. articles to profl. jours. Internat. sec. Nat. Student Coun., Sofia, 1987-89. Recipient Golden badge for acad. merit Ministry of Edn., Sofia, 1980, 84; Rector's and Dean's scholar Higher Inst. Econs., Sofia, 1981-85, Internat. scholar Bus. Sch. U. Alta., Edmonton, 1991-92. Mem. Assn. for Investment Mgmt. and Rsch. (affiliate), N.Y. Soc. Security Analysts (affiliate). Avocations: international travel, art. Office: Merrill Lynch World Fin Ctr North Tower New York NY 10281 also: Merrill Lynch Internat, 25 Ropenmaker St 2A, London EC2Y WK, England

BATDORF, LYNN ROBERT, horticulturist; b. Lebanon, Pa., Aug. 4, 1954; s. Robert LeVoy Smith Jr. and Rudella Louise (Brandt) Batdorf; m. Holly A. Hamilton, Oct. 24, 1998; children: Jessica Zischka, Theodore Robert. AA in Horticulture, Inst. of Applied Agrl., 1974; BSBA, U. Coll., 1984; BS in Ornamental Horticulture, U. Md., 1994. Cert. profl. horticulturist. Agrl. rsch. technician U.S. Nat. Arboretum, Washington, 1977-80, horticulturist, 1980—; horticultural cons. TJ Horticultural Svcs., Washington, 1989—; instr. water garden mgmt. course Montgomery Coll., Germantown, Md., 1996—. Author: Boxwood Handbook: A Practical Guide to Knowing and Growing Boxwood, 1995, revised 1997; contbr. National Arboretum Book of Outstanding Garden Plants, 1989, Time-Life Gardener's Guide, Perennials, 1988, The Washington Star Garden Book, 1988. Recipient Cert. of Merit U.S. Dept. Agrl., 1980, 89, 91, (2) 93, 96. Mem. Am. Boxwood Soc. (hon. life, bd. dirs.,) Internat. Registration Authority for Cultivated Boxwoods, Am. Hemerocallis Soc., Internat. Water Lily Soc., Internat. Soc. for Horticultural Sci., Am. Assn. of Botanic Gardens and Arboreta, Royal Horticulture Soc., European Boxwood and Topiary Soc. (hon. life),. Office: US Nat Arboretum 3501 New York Ave NE Washington DC 20002-1958

BATDORF, SAMUEL B(URBRIDGE), physicist; b. Jung Hsien, China, Mar. 31, 1914; s. Charles William and Nellie (Burbridge) B.; m. Carol Catherine Schweiss, July 19, 1940; children: Samuel Charles, Laura Ann. AB, U. Calif., Berkeley, 1934, AM, 1936, PhD, 1938. From instr. to assoc. prof. physics U. Nev., 1938-43; aero. rsch. scientist Langley Lab., NACA, 1943-51, chmn. advanced study com., 1946-51, mem. NACA subcom. on aircraft structural metals, 1946-51; from adv. physicist in rsch. lab. to dir. devel. Westinghouse Elec. Corp., Pitts., 1951-56; from asst. dir. rsch. to tech. dir. weapons sys. Lockheed Missile & Space Co., Palo Alto, Calif., 1956-58; mgr. comm. satellites Inst. Def. Analysis, Washington, 1958-59; from mgr. product planning to dir. rsch. in physics, electronics and bionics Aeronutronic, Newport Beach, Calif., 1959-62; from dir. office of rsch. to prin. staff scientist Aerospace Corp., El Segundo, Calif., 1962-77; mem. aeromechanics adv. com. Air Force Office Sci. RSch., 1965-71, tech. assessment panel Engrs. Joint Coun., 1968-71; cons. NSF, 1967-71; Sigma Xi lectr. communication satellites; Disting. prof. Tsing Hua U., Republic of China, 1969; adj. prof. engring. and applied sci. UCLA, 1973-86; vis. scholar Va. Poly. Inst. and State U., 1984. Contbr. articles to profl. jours. Pres. Engrs. Club Va. Peninsula, 1948. Fellow AIAA (edn., structures and materials coms.), ASME (hon., edn. materials and space structures coms., chmn. applied mechanics divsn. exec. com. materials and space structures com. 1960), Am. Phys. Soc., Am. Acad. Mechanics (pres. 1982-83); mem. Aerospace Club, Academia Club, Phi Beta Kappa, Phi Kappa Phi. Republican. Presbyterian. Home: 1106 Tower 1 24055 Paseo Del Lago Laguna Hills CA 92653-2678

BATE, BRIAN R., psychologist; b. Cleve., July 4, 1940; s. Paul A. and Claire N. B.; children: Jennifer A., Julia L. BA in English, Western Res. U., 1963, MS in Psychology, 1965; PhD in Psychology, Case Western Res. U., 1972. Lic. psychologist, Ohio. Instr. Cuyahoga C.C. Western Campus, Parma, Ohio, 1969, from asst. prof. to prof. of psychology, 1970—; pvt. practice, Cleve., 1972-96. Contbr. articles to profl. jours. Nat. Merit Scholar Princeton U., 1958-61, Western Res. U., 1962-63; USPHS fellow, 1963-67. Mem. APA, Am. Fedn. Musicians, Edelweiss Ski Club, Cleve. Buddhist Temple. Achievements include development and teaching of the first underclass-level behavior modification course in United States, 1970-77. Home: 6511 Mill Rd Cleveland OH 44141-1560 Office: Cuyahoga Cmty Coll Western Campus Parma OH 44130-5199

BATE, WALTER JACKSON, English literature educator; b. Mankato, Minn., May 23, 1918; s. William G. and Isabel (Melick) B. A.B., Harvard U., 1939, M.A., 1940, Ph.D., 1942; L.H.D., Ind. U., 1969, U. Chgo., 1973; Litt.D., Merrimack Coll., 1970, Boston Coll., 1971, Rutgers U., 1979, Colby Coll., 1979, Fordham U., 1982. Mem. faculty English Harvard, 1946—, prof., 1956—, chmn. dept. history and lit., 1955-56, chmn. dept. English, 1956-63, 66-68, Abbott Lawrence Lowell prof. humanities, 1962-79, Kingsley Porter Univ. prof., 1979—. Author: Negative Capability, 1939, The Stylistic Development of Keats, 1945, From Classic to Romantic, 1946, Criticism: the Major Texts, 1952, The Achievement of Samuel Johnson, 1955, Prefaces to Criticism, 1959, Writings of Edmund Burke, 1960, John Keats, 1963 (Pulitzer Prize 1964), Coleridge, 1968, The Burden of the Past and the English Poet, 1970, Samuel Johnson, 1977 (Pulitzer Prize 1978, Nat. Book Award 1978, Nat. Book Critics Circle award 1978); co-editor: Biographia Literaria for the Collected Works of Coleridge, 1982; British and American Poets, 1985, Harvard Scholars in English, 1991; Contbg. editor: Bollingen edit. of Collected Coleridge, Yale edit. of Johnson. Guggenheim fellow, 1956, 65. Mem. Am. Philos. Soc., Brit. Acad., Am. Acad. Arts and Scis., Phi Beta Kappa (Christian Gauss award lit. history and criticism 1956, 64, 70). Home: Harvard U Barker Ctr Cambridge MA 02138 Office: Widener Libr Harvard U Cambridge MA 02138

BATEMAN, C. BARRY, airport terminal executive. Airport dir. Gen. Mitchell Internat. Airport, Milw. Office: Gen Mitchell Internat Airport 5300 S Howell Ave Milwaukee WI 53207-6156*

BATEMAN, CAROL VAUGHAN, pharmacist; b. Richmond, Va., Dec. 23, 1941; d. Harold Benjamin and Verna Pearl (Vaughan) B. Student, Vanderbilt U., 1960-61; BS in Chemistry, U. Richmond, 1964; BS in Pharmacy, U. S.C., 1970. Registered pharmacist, S.C., Hawaii. Pharmacist Camden (S.C.) Walgreen Agy., 1970-74; pharmacist, IV supr. Providence Hosp., Columbia, S.C., 1974-81; asst. pharmacy dir. Hilton Head Hosp., Hilton Head Island, 1981-87; interim pharmacy dir. Hilton Head Hosp., 1987-88; asst. pharmacy mgr. Revco, 1988-90; pharmacist Self Meml. Hosp., Greenwood, S.C., 1990-93; kinetics pharmacist Self Meml. Hosp., 1993—; vice chmn. S.C. Bd. Pharmacy, 1996-97, chmn. 1997-98; clin. instr. U. S.C. Coll. Pharmacy, 1984—. Editor: Prescriptions for the Kitchen, 1987. Mem. S.C. Heart Assn. Task Force on Hypertension, 1975-81; bd. dirs. Planned Parenthood of Hilton Head, 1986-88; vol. Greenwood Free Clinic, 1997—, Vols. in Med. Missions,, 1993—; bd. dirs. Abbeville County Hist. Soc., 1993-96, v.p. 1997-98, pres., 1999—; mem. Rockcreek Homeowners Assn., 1991—; co-founder S.C. Recovery and Intervention Pharmacist Team, 1988-89. Mem. S.C. Pharm. Assn. (chmn. continuing edn. com. 1974-78, v.p. 1978-79, mem. awards com. 1982-84, chmn. conv. com. 1984-85, pres. 1988-89, S.C. Pharmacist of Yr. award 1976), Am. Pharm. Assn., S.C. Soc. Health-Sys. Pharmacists (ann. award 1975), 8th Dist. Pharm. Assn. (v.p. 1991-92), Nat. Assn. Bds. of Pharmacy (co-chmn. dist. III convention 1998), Am. Soc. Health-Sys. Pharmacists, Faculty House U. S.C., U. S.C. Alumni Assn., Phi Lambda Sigma. Republican. Methodist. Avocations: gardening, travel, collecting orientalia and pharmacy antiques, walking. Home: 401 Rock Creek Blvd Greenwood SC 29649-8918 Office: Self Meml Hosp 1325 Spring St Greenwood SC 29646-3875

BATEMAN, DAVID ALFRED, lawyer; b. Pitts., Jan. 28, 1946; s. Alfred V. and Ruth G. (Howe) B.; m. Trudy A. Heath, Mar. 13, 1948; children: Devin C., Mark C. A.B. in Geology, U. Calif.-Riverside, 1966; J.D., U. San Diego, 1969; LL.M., Georgetown U., 1978. Bar: Calif. 1970, U.S. Dist. Ct. (so. dist.) Calif. 1970, U.S. Ct. Mil. Appeals 1972, Wash. 1973, U.S. Dist. Ct. (we. dist.) Wash. 1973, U.S. Supreme Ct. 1974, D.C. 1976, U.S. Dist. Ct. D.C. 1977, U.S. Ct. Claims 1979, U.S. Ct. Appeals (9th cir.) 1981. Assoc. Daubney, Banche, Patterson and Nares, Oceanside, Calif., 1969-72; asst. atty. gen. State of Wash., Olympia, 1977-81; ptnr. Bateman & Woodring, Olympia, 1981-85, Woodring, Bateman & Westbrook, 1985-89, Hanemann & Bateman, 1989-92, Hanemann, Bateman & Jones, 1992—; instr. Am. Inst. Banking, San Diego, 1972, U. Puget Sound, Olympia campus, spring, 1979. Served to capt. JAGC, USAF, 1972-77; col. JAGC, USAFR, 1977-97. Mem. Calif. State Bar Assn., D.C. Bar Assn., Wash. State Bar Assn., Rotary (past chmn. internat. svcs. com.). Roman Catholic.

BATEMAN, GILES HIRST LITTON, finance executive; b. Rochdale, Eng., Nov. 13, 1944; came to U.S., 1976; s. Ralph Merton and Barbara Yvonne (Litton) B.; m. Jenny Margaret, Oct. 28, 1967 (div. 1986); children: Matthew, Lisa; m. Doña Maria Adler, Oct. 7, 1986; children: Stephanie, Melody. BA, Oxford U., Eng., 1966; MBA with high distinction, Harvard U., 1971. Mgmt. trainee, indsl. engr., regional indsl. engr. Metal Box Co., Eng., 1966-69; cons. McKinsey & Co., London, 1971-73; corp. planning mgr., divsn. mgr. Norcros Ltd., Witham, England, 1973-76; co-founder, CFO, exec. v.p., bd. dirs. The Price Co., San Diego, 1976-91; chmn. bd. CompUSA, Dallas; vis. prof. Sch. Bus. U. San Diego, 1991; bd. dirs., chmn. CompUSA, Inc., Dallas, Cross-Borders Inc., N.Y.C., Boatracs, Inc., San Diego. Bd. trustees San Diego Repertory Theater, 1992-97; mem. adv. bd. Ctr. Retail Studies, Tex. A&M U. Baker scholar Harvard U., 1971. Avocations: personal computers, exercise, science fiction, traveling, theater. Home: 251 Stratford Park Cir Del Mar CA 92014-3255 Office: CompUSA 14951 N Dallas Pkwy Dallas TX 75240-7570*

BATEMAN, HERBERT HARVELL, congressman; b. Elizabeth City, N.C., Aug. 7, 1928; m. Laura Yacobi; children: Herbert Harvell, Laura Margaret. B.A., Coll. William and Mary, 1949; J.D., Georgetown U., 1956.

Bar: Va. 1956. Practice law Newport News, Va., 1957-82; law clk. U.S. Ct. Appeals for D.C. Cir., 1956-57; mem. firm Jones, Blechman, Woltz & Kelly, 1957-82; mem. Va. Senate, 1968-82, chmn. consumer credit study commn., 1970-74, chmn. milk commn. study commn., 1973-75; mem. 98th-105th Congresses from 1st Va. dist., Washington, D.C.; mem. House com. on sci. and tech., 1982-84; mem. House merchant marine com., 1982-94; mem. House armed svcs. com. (name now nat. security com.), 1984—; co-chmn. Congrl. Space Caucus, 1984—; founder Va. Joint Legis. Audit and Rev. Commn., 1973; ranking Rep. Merchant Marine Subcom.; mem. House transp. and infrastructure com., 1995—; chmn. subcom. on mil. readiness, 1995—. Mem. adv. bd. Mary Immaculate Hosp. Newport News; pres. Peninsula United Fund, 1966-67; chmn. Peninsula Arena-Auditorium Authority, 1964-68; pres. Newport News Homeownership Assn., 1969-71; commr. Peninsula Ports Authority Va., 1969-74; bd. dirs. Peninsula Econ. Devel. Council, 1968—; coordinator Citizens for Rev. Constrn., 1970; chmn. Heart Fund campaign, Newport News, 1971. Served to 1st lt. USAF, 1951-53. Mem. Va. Jaycees (past pres.), U.S. Jaycees (gen. legal counsel 1962-63), Hampton Roads Jaycees (hon. pres. 1960-63), Peninsula C. of C. (chmn. legis. com. 1970-72), Newport News Propeller Club, Omicron Delta Kappa, Phi Delta Phi, Pi Kappa Alpha. Republican. Office: US Ho of Reps 2350 Rayburn HOB Washington DC 20515

BATEMAN, JEANNINE ANN, county official; b. Hillsboro, Kans., July 6, 1945; d. Forrest Edward and Alvina (Bernhardt) Skibbe; m. Rufus J. Bateman, Apr. 25, 1965; 1 child, Kristine Kay. AS in Bus., Butler County Cmty. Coll., El Dorado, Kans., 1996; student, Baker U., Baldwin City, Kans., 1963-64, Wichita State U., 1997—. Bookkeeper Marion County Coop., Marion, Kans., summer 1963; abstract asst. Hannaford Title Co., Marion, 1964-74, 79-84; clk., dep. Marion County Treas. Office, Marion, 1984-94, treas., 1994—. Treas. Marion Warrior Boosters, 1993, 1st Dist. Rep. Women, Kans., 1997—; bd. dirs. Leadership Marion County, 1994-95, sec., treas., 1995-96, v.p., 1996-97. Mem. North Ctrl. Kans. County Treasurers (sec., treas. 1996-97, v.p. 1997-98, pres. 1998-99), Kans. County Treasurer's Assn. (sec. 1999), Marion County Rep. Women, Marion County Rep. Party, Order of the Purple, Kiwanis Club Marion, Phi Theta Kappa. N.Am. Baptist. Avocations: walking, hiking, reading, basketball, football. Office: Marion County Treas PO Box 257 Marion KS 66861-0257

BATEMAN, JOHN JAY, classics educator; b. Elmira, N.Y., Feb. 17, 1931; s. Joseph Earl and Etha M. (Edwards) B.; m. Patricia Ann Hageman, July 5, 1952; children: Kristine M., Kathleen A., John Eric. BA, U. Toronto, 1953; MA, Cornell U., 1954, PhD, 1958. Lectr. Univ. Coll., U. Toronto, 1956-57; lectr., then asst. prof. U. Ottawa, 1957-60; mem. faculty U. Ill., Urbana, 1960—; prof. classics and speech U. Ill., 1968-93; prof. emeritus, 1993—; head dept. classics U. Ill., 1966-73, chmn., 1988-92, acting dir. Sch. Humanities, 1973-74. Author, editor books and articles. Dem. precinct committeeman, 1964-68; sec. Champaign Dem. Central Com., 1965-66. Mem. Am. Philol. Assn. (sec.-treas. 1968-73), Soc. Bibl. Lit., Renaissance Soc. Am. Home: 5508 41st Ave E Bradenton FL 34208-6835 Office: U Ill Fgn Lang Bldg 707 S Mathews Ave Urbana IL 61801-3625

BATEMAN, MERRILL JOSEPH, university president; b. Lehi, Utah, June 19, 1936; s. Joseph Fredric and Belva (Smith) B.; m. Marilyn Scholes, Mar. 23, 1959; children: Michael, Mark, Michele, Melisa, Merilee, Matthew, McKay. BA, U. Utah, 1960; PhD, MIT, 1965. Exec. Mars, Inc., 1971-75; dean Sch. Mgmt. Brigham Young U., Provo, Utah, 1975-79; pres. Brigham Young U., 1996—; mgmt. cons. Provo, 1979-92; mem. 2d Quorum of 70 LDS Ch., Salt Lake City, 1992-94, presiding bishop, 1994-95, mem. 1st Quorum of 70, 1996—; pres. Deseret Mgmt. Corp., Salt Lake City, 1993-95. 1st lt. USAF, 1964-67. Danforth fellow, 1960-64, Woodrow Wilson fellow, 1960-61. Mem. Am. Assn. Presidents of Colls. and Univs. (pres.), Mountain West Conf. Coun. of Presidents, Phi Kappa Phi, Beta Kappa. Office: Brigham Young U PO Box 21346 Provo UT 84602-1346

BATEMAN, MILDRED MITCHELL, psychiatrist; b. Cordele, Ga., Mar. 22, 1922; married; 2 children. BS, J.C. Smith U., 1941; MD, Woman's Med. Coll. Pa., 1946. Staff physician Larkin (W.Va.) State Hosp., 1947-48, clin. dir., 1951-52, 55-58, supt., 1958-60; supr. dir. profl. svcs. W.Va. Dept. Mental Health, 1960-62; dir. State Capital, 1962-77; prof., chmn. psychiat. Sch. Medicine Marshall U., Huntington, W.Va., 1977-82, prof. psychiatry, 1982—; staff psychiatrist Huntington VA Med. Ctr., 1986—; clin. dir. Huntington (W.Va.), 1996—; mem. com. mental illness and mental retardation Commn. Aging, W.Va. Commn. Mental Retardation, Govt. W.Va. Commn. Status of Women & Coop. Health Statis. Adv. Com., Nat. Ctr. Health Statis.; trustee Menninger Found. Mem. AMA, Inst. Medicine-NAS, Am. Psychiat. Assn. (v.p. 1973, Warren Williams Disting. award 1991). Office: Huntington Hospital PO Box 448 Huntington WV 25709-0448*

BATEMAN, PAUL WILLIAM, government official, business executive; b. Whittier, Calif., Feb. 28, 1957; s. John William and Glenus Bernice (Redman) B.; m. Marguerite Cameron; children: Ellen Ryan, Nancy Cameron, Greer Aidan. BA, Whittier Coll., 1979. Asst. to former pres. Office of Richard Nixon, N.Y.C. and San Clemente, Calif., 1979-81; dep. dir. adminstrv. ops. div. The White House, Washington, 1981-82; exec. asst. to asst. sec. for econ. devel. U.S. Dept. Commerce, Washington, 1982-84, dep. asst. sec. for econ. devel., 1984-85; dep. treas. of U.S. Dept. Treasury, 1985-88; sr. v.p. New Eng. Council, Inc., Boston, 1988-89; dep. asst. to Pres. The White House, 1989-93; dir. pub. affairs Gold Inst., Washington, 1994-95; exec. v.p. Gold Inst., 1995—; v.p. Klein & Saks, Inc., 1995-96; v.p. George Washington Boyhood Home Found., 1994-96; exec. dir. Silver Inst., 1996—; pres. Klein & Saks, 1996—. Republican. Episcopalian. Home: 490 Fort Williams Pky Alexandria VA 22304-1810 Office: 1112 16th St NW Ste 240 Washington DC 20036-4818

BATEMAN, ROBERT MCLELLAN, artist; b. Toronto, Ont., Can., May 24, 1930; s. Joseph Wilbur and Anne (McLellan) B.; m. Suzanne Bowermann, June 1961 (div. 1975); children: Alan, Sarah, John; m. Birgit Freybe, Aug. 1975; children: Christopher, Rob. BA in Geography with honors, U. Toronto, 1954; postgrad., Ont. Coll. Edn., 1955; DSc (hon.), Carleton U., Ottawa, 1982; LLD (hon.), Brock U., St. Catherine, Ont., 1982; D Letters for Fine Arts (hon.), McMaster U., Hamilton, Ont., Can., 1983; LLD (hon.), U. Guelph, Ont., 1984; LittD (hon.), Lakehead U., Thunder Bay, Ont., 1986; LLD (hon.), Laurentian U., Sudbury, Ont., 1987; DFA (hon.), Colby Coll., 1989, Northeastern U., 1991; DSc (hon.), McGill U., Montreal, 1995. Tchr. Nelson H.S., Burlington, Ont., 1958-63, 65-69; tchr. geography Nigeria, 1963-65; tchr. art Lord Elgin H.S., Burlington, Ont., 1970-76. One-man shows include Tryon Gallery, London, 1975, 79, Beckett Gallery, Hamilton, Ont., Can., 1978, 87, Smithsonian Instn., 1987, Nat. Mus. Natural Sci., Ottawa, 1981-82, also touring U.S. and Can., Can. Embassy, Tokyo, 1992; represented in permanent collections Govt. Ont. Art Collection, Toronto Bd. Trade, Hamilton Art Gallery, Leigh Yawkey Woodson Art Mus., Wausau, Wis., H.R.H. The Prince of Wales, H.R.H. Prince Phillip, The Late Princess of Monaco, Am. Artists Collection, Gilcrease Mus., Tulsa, Art Gallery of Greater Victoria; commd. World Wildlife Fund, 1971, Endangered Species Silver Bowl, 1971, Endangered Species Postage Stamp Series, 1976-81, "Northern Reflections - Loon Family", 1981, Govt. Can. wedding gift to Prince of Wales, 1981, Can. Post Office, Royal Can. Mint-Platinum Polar Bear series, 1990; subject of the Art of Robert Bateman, 1981, A Day in the Life of Robert Bateman, 1985, The World of Robert Bateman, 1985, Robert Bateman An Artist in Nature, 1990, Natural Worlds: Robert Bateman, 1996, The Life and Times of Robert Bateman, 1997. Bd. dirs. Elsa Wild Animal Appeal, Toronto, 1975—; commr. Niagara Escarpment Commn., Georgetown, Ont., 1973-85. Decorated Queen Elizabeth Silver Jubilee medal Govt. of Can., 1977, Officer of Order of Can., 1984; recipient award of excellence Soc. Animal Artists, 1979, 80, 86, 90, Excellence award in arts for contbn. to artist cmty. Hamilton-Wentworth, Ont., 1980, Gov. Gen. award for conservation, Quebec City, Can., 1987, Lescarbot award Can. Govt., 1992, Rachel Carson award, 1996, Golden Plate award Am. Acad. Achievement, 1998; named Artist of Yr., Am. Artist Collection, 1980, Master Artist, Leigh Yawkey Woodson Mus., Wausau, Wis., 1982, Environ. Hero, Nat. Aububon Soc., 1998, others.

BATEMAN, WILLIAM MAXWELL, retired construction company executive; b. Winnipeg, Man., Can., May 7, 1920; s. Norman Silver and Veda (Maxwell) B.; m. Gaye Marjorie, Oct. 22, 1949; children—Kathryn, Paul, Anne, Leslie. BASc, U. Toronto, Can., 1949. Project engr. C.A. Pitts Gen. Contractors, Toronto, Ont., Can., 1949-63, v.p., chief engr., 1963-67, sr. v.p., dir., 1967-71; pres. Lake Ont. Cement Ltd., Toronto, 1972-80, Genstar Constrn. Ltd., Toronto, 1980-81; pres., chief operating officer Banister Continental Ltd., Edmonton, Alta., Can., 1981-85; pres., chief exec. officer Banister Inc., 1990-91; pvt. practice engrng. Edmonton, 1985; dir. Banister Continental Ltd., 1981-86. Contbr. chpt. to book, articles to profl. jours. Flight lt. RCAF, 1941-45. Decorated D.F.C., RAF; Officer Royal Order of St. John. Mem. Assn. Profl. Engrs. Ont., Assn. Profl. Engrs. Geologists and Geophysicists of Alta., Alta. Arbitration and Mediation Soc., Mayfair Golf Club, Mississauga Golf Club (past pres.). Anglican. Home: 1320 Potter Greens Dr, Edmonton, AB Canada T5T 6A3

BATENIC, MARK K., manufacturing company executive. Sr. v.p. retail sales and mktg. Fleming Cos. Inc., Oklahoma City, Okla. Office: Fleming Cos Inc 6301 Waterford Blvd Oklahoma City OK 73118-1198*

BATES, BARBARA J. NEUNER, retired municipal official; b. Mt. Vernon, N.Y., Apr. 8, 1927; d. John Joseph William and Elsie May (Flint) Neuner; m. Herman Martin Bates, Jr., Mar. 25, 1950; children: Roberta Jean Bates Jamin, Herman Martin III, Jon Neuner. BA, Barnard Coll., 1947. Confidential clk. to supr. Town of Ossining, N.Y., 1960-63, receiver of taxes, 1971-90; ret.; pres. BNB Assocs., Briarcliff Manor, N.Y., 1963-83, Upper Nyack Realty Co., Inc., Briarcliff Manor, 1966-71. V.p. Ossining (N.Y.) Young Rep. Club, 1958; pres. Young Womens Rep. Club Westchester County (N.Y.), 1959-61; regional committeewoman N.Y. State Assn. Young Rep. Clubs, 1960-62; mem. Westchester County Rep. Com., 1963-95; mem. Ossining Women's Rep. Club, 1960-92, pres., 1984-85; mem. Westchester County Women's Rep. Club, 1957-92. Mem. DAR, Jr. League Westchester-on-Hudson, Receivers Taxes Assn. Westchester County (legis. liaison, v.p., pres. 1984-85), Hackley Sch. Mothers Assn. (pres. 1968), R.I. Hist. Soc., Ossining Hist. Soc., Westchester County Hist. Soc., Briarcliff-Scarborough Hist. Soc., Ossining Woman's Club. Congregationalist. Home: 78 Holbrook Ln Briarcliff Manor NY 10510-1122 also: 663 Reynolds Rd Chepachet RI 02814-1629

BATES, BARRY D., career officer; b. Norman, Okla., Jan. 26, 1947. Commd. U.S. Army, advanced through grades to maj. gen., 1998; comdg. gen. Army and Air Force Exchange Svc., Dallas, 1998—. Office: Army and Air Force Exchange Svc Dallas TX 75266

BATES, CHARLES BENJAMIN, elementary school administrator; b. Balt., Aug. 24, 1934; s. Charles Benjamin and Mary Elizabeth (Holden) B.; m. Martha Pearl Copenhaver, Apr. 9, 1960; children: Benjamin Madison, Lelia Ann, William Andrew. BS, Towson State Tchrs. Coll., 1961; MEd, Loyola Coll., Balt., 1968; PhD, Columbia Pacific U., 1982. Cert. tchr., Md. Tchr. Balt. County Pub. Schs., 1958-68, vice prin., 1968-77, prin., 1977-78, elem. adminstr., 1979-86; cons. edn. and history Joppa, Md., 1986—; adj. prof. Columbia Pacific, Balt., 1982-87; curriculum cons. Balt. County Pub. Schs., Towson, 1986; cons. history Am. History Workshop, N.Y.C., 1990. Editor: Edward Fenner (book); editor Bates Chronicles, 1981-93; contbr. articles to profl. jours. Exec. bd. PTA, 1961-86; bd. trustees Balt. Streetcar Mus., 1988-96, 98—; pres. The Bates Assn., 1993-96, past pres. exec. bd., 1996-98. Sgt. U.S. Army, 1957-63. Recipient Svc. to Cmty. award VFW, 1986, Katharine Lee Bates award, 1998. Mem. Orton Soc. (bd. dirs. 1974-77), Assn. Elem. Sch. Adminstrs. (exec. bd. 1974-77), Rwy. Hist. Soc. (exec. bd. 1986-88), New Eng. Hist. and Geneal. Soc., Nat. Hist. Soc., Md. Geneal. Soc., Md. Hist. Soc., NRHS (historian), BSM (dir. sch. tours, historian). Republican. Avocations: streetcars and trains, flags, civil war, genealogy. Home: 202 Frazier Ct Joppa MD 21085-4434

BATES, CHARLES CARPENTER, oceanographer; b. nr. Harrison, Ill., Nov. 4, 1918; s. Carl Albert and Vera Elizabeth (Carpenter) B.; m. Pauline Barta; children: Nancy Ann, Priscilla Jane, Sally Jean. Grad. (Rector scholar 1936-39), DePauw U., 1939; M.A., U. Calif. at Los Angeles, 1944; Ph.D. in Geol. Oceanography, Tex. A. and M. Coll., 1953; student, Cath. U., 1947-48, Johns Hopkins, 1951, George Washington U., 1954. Geophys. trainee Carter Oil Co., 1939-41; spl. asst. to pres. Am. Meteorol. Soc., 1945-46; mem. survey phys. and geol. environment Marshall Is. relative to pending Bikini atomic bomb tests, 1946; with div. oceanography U.S. Navy Hydrographic Office, 1946- 57, dept. dir. div., 1953-57; environmental surveillance coordinator Office Devel. Coordinator, Office Naval Research, 1957-60; chief underground nuclear test detection br. Advanced Research Projects Agy., Office Sec. Def., 1960-64; sci. and tech. dir. U.S. Naval Oceanographic Office, 1964-68; sci. adviser to comdt., also chief scientist Office Research and Devel., USCG, 1968-79; environ. cons., 1979—; v.p. Spectrum Internat. Assocs., 1986-88; mem. bd. experts Civil Service Examiners, 1954-60; mem. adv. com. postdoctoral awards for Fulbright grants NRC, 1957-60, chmn., 1959-60; vis. geoscientist Am. Geol. Inst., 1959-60; mem. meteorology panel, space sci. bd. Nat. Acad. Sci., 1959-61; mem. Mcht. Marine Council, 1968-71, Nat. Transp. Research Bd., 1968-71; mem. sea grant adv. council La. State U. System, 1968-79; co-chmn. U.S.-Japan panel marine facilities U.S.-Japan Natural Resource Program, 1969-71. Author: Geophysics in Affairs of Man, 1982, America's Weather Warriors, 1814-1985, 1986; numerous articles, reports in field. Served to capt. USAAF, 1941-45, lt. col. USAFR, 1941-65. Decorated Bronze Star; recipient U.S. Navy Meritorious Civilian award, 1962, U.S. Navy Superior Civilian Service award, 1969, U.S. Dept. Transp. Silver medal, 1973. Mem. Am. Geophys. Union (chmn. com. interaction sea and atmosphere 1950, mem. council 1964-67), Soc. Exploration Geophysicists (council 1963-67, v.p. 1965-66, hon. mem. 1981), Am. Meteorol. Soc. (chmn. com. indsl. bus. and agrl. meteorology 1946-48), Am. Assn. Petroleum Geologists (President's award 1954), Am. Mgmt. Assn. (research and devel. council 1970-79), Sigma Xi. Home and Office: 136 W La Pintura Green Valley AZ 85614-1927

BATES, CHARLES EMERSON, library administrator; b. L.A., Dec. 1, 1946; s. Willard Emerson Bates and Erica (Schmidt) Bates Beckwith; m. Mary Joan Genz, Aug. 7, 1971; children: Christopher, Noah, Colin. BA, Valparaiso U., 1968; MEd, Loyola U., Chgo., 1970; MLS, Rosary Coll., 1973. Head reference Decatur (Ill.) Pub. Libr., 1973-74; cons. Rolling Prairie Libr. Sys., Decatur, 1974-76; asst. dir. Fond du Lac (Wis.) Pub. Libr., 1976-81; dir. Pueblo (Colo.) Libr. Dist., 1981—. Bd. dirs. Pueblo United Way, 1982-86; pres., bd. dirs. Sangre de Cristo Arts and Conf. Ctr., Pueblo, 1990-96; pres. bd. dirs. Rosemount Victorian House Mus., Pueblo, 1984-90. Mem. ALA, Colo. Libr. Assn., Ark. Valley Libr. Sys. (pres. 1984-85, 89-90, 96-97, 97—), Rotary (pres. bd. dirs. 1981—). Lutheran. Office: Pueblo Libr Dist McClelland Libr 100 E Abriendo Ave Pueblo CO 81004-4232*

BATES, CHARLES TURNER, lawyer, educator; b. Tarrytown, N.Y., Jan. 3, 1932; s. Harry Cole and Helen Morris (Turner) B. A.B., Hamilton Coll., 1953; LL.B., Yale U., 1958. Bar: N.Y. 1958. Atty. firm Townley & Updike, N.Y.C., 1958-69; atty. CBS Inc., N.Y.C., 1969-71; asst. sec. CBS Inc., 1971-74, sec., asso. gen. counsel, 1974-88; instr. in history Hackley Sch., Tarrytown, N.Y., 1988—. Trustee Hackley Sch., Tarrytown, N.Y., 1972-76, 81-88, Hamilton Coll., 1975-79. With Ordnance Corps, U.S. Army, 1953-55. Mem. Am. Soc. Corp. Secs., Phi Beta Kappa, Sigma Phi. Republican. Episcopalian.

BATES, CHARLES WALTER, human resources executive, lawyer; b. Detroit, June 28, 1953; s. E. Frederick and Virginia Marion (Nunneley) B. BA in Psychology and Econs. cum laude, Mich. State U., 1975, M in Labor and Indsl. Rels., 1977; postgrad., DePaul U., 1979-80; JD, William Mitchell Coll. Law, 1984. Bar: Wash. 1990, U.S. Dist. Ct. (we. dist.) Wash. 1992; cert. sr. profl. in human resources. Vista vol., paralegal Ventura County Legal Aid Assn., Calif., 1975-76; job analyst Gen. Mills, Inc., Mpls., 1977-78; plant pers. asst. Gen. Mills, Inc., Chgo., 1978-80; plant asst. pers. mgr. Gen. Mills Inc., Chgo., 1980-81; pers. mgr. consumer foods mktg. Gen. Mills, Inc., Mpls., 1981-82; pers. mgr. consumer foods mktg. divns. Saluto Pizza, Mpls., 1982-84; human resources mgr. Western divsn. Godfather's Pizza, Inc., Costa Mesa, Calif., 1984-85; human resources mgr. western U.S. and Can. Godfather's Pizza, Inc., Bellevue, Wash., 1985-91; dir. human resources Royal Seafoods, Inc., Seattle, 1991-92, dir. human resources, employee rels. counsel, 1992-94, dir. human resources, counsel, 1994-95; sr. internal auditor PACCAR, Inc, Bellevue, Wash., 1995-97; dir. field human resources PACCAR Automotive, Inc., Renton, Wash., 1997, dir. human resources, 1997—; instr. employee labor rels. Lake Washington Tech. Coll., 1992-94. Mem. editl. adv. bd. Recruitment Today mag., 1990-91. Candidate for lt. gov. of Minn., 1982; asst. scoutmaster Boy Scouts Am., 1971—, asst. advisor activities Order of Arrow, 1989-92, 96-97; Sammamish Cmty. Councilmem., Bellevue, 1990-93; mem. East Bellevue Transp. Study Adv. Group, 1989-92; mem. Bellevue Civil Svc. Commn., 1997—, vice chair, 1999—. Recipient Scouter's Tng. award Boy Scouts Am., 1979, Dist. award of merit, 1991, VigilHonor, 1990. Mem. ABA (labor and employment law), Wash. State Bar Assn., King County Bar Assn. (labor law sect.), Nat. Eagle Scout Assn., N.W. Human Resources Mgmt. Assn. (Lake Washington chpt.), Soc. for Human Resources Mgmt. Home: 232 168th Ave NE Bellevue WA 98008-4522 Office: PACCAR Automotive Inc 1400 N 4th St Renton WA 98055-1535

BATES, DAVID VINCENT, physician, medical educator; b. Kent, Eng., May 20, 1922; s. John Vincent and Alice (Dickins) B.; m. Margaret Sutton, Mar. 24, 1948; children—Anne Elizabeth, Joanna Margaret, Andrew Vincent. M.B., B.Ch., Cambridge (Eng.) U., 1945, M.D., 1954. Intern, resident St. Bartholomew Hosp., 1944- 45; sr. lectr. medicine U. London Sch. Medicine, 1953-56; research fellow U. Pa., 1952; physician Royal Victoria Hosp., Montreal, Can., 1967-72; asst. prof. medicine McGill U. Sch. Medicine, 1956-72, prof. exptl. medicine, 1965-72, asso. dean grad. studies and research, 1964-67, chmn. dept. physiology, 1967-72; dean, faculty of medicine U. B.C., 1972-77, prof. physiology and medicine, 1972-87; dir. respiratory div., joint cardiorespiratory service Royal Victoria, Montreal Childrens hosps., 1957-67; mem. Sci. Council Can., 1973-79. Author: (with Christie) Respiratory Function in Disease, 1965, 3d edit., 1989, A Citizens Guide to Air Pollution, 1972, Environmental Health Risks and Public Policy, 1994, Five Minutes into the "Eroica", 1997, also articles. Recipient Robert Cooke medal Am. Acad. Allergy, 1966, Ramazzini medal, 87, Connaught award Can. Lung Assn., 1991, Trudeau Gold medal Am. Lung Assn., 1993, Coady medal, BCMA, 1996. Fellow Royal Coll. Physicians (London), Royal Coll. Physicians (Can.), Royal Soc. Can., A.C.P.; mem. Am., Canadian socs. clin. investigation, Am., Canadian physiol. socs., Physiol. Soc. London. Home: 4891 College Highroad, Vancouver, BC Canada V6T 1G6

BATES, DAVID VLIET, religious school administrator, minister; b. Cleve., Sept. 30, 1938; s. George Axford and Freda (Haines) B.; m. Charm Ann Kinney, June 10, 1960; children: Mark Kenneth, David Paul, Peter Jonathan. BTh, Bapt. Bible Sem., Clark's Summit, Pa., 1962; MS in Edn., So. Ill. U., 1970; cert. advanced studies in edn., No. Ill. U., 1977. Lic. to ministry Evang. Free Ch. Am., 1988; cert. tchr., supr., adminstr., Ill. Min. various chs. Evang. Free Ch. Am. chs., 1970-90; min. Rock Valley Chapel, Beloit, Wis., 1990-93; adminstr. Rockford (Ill.) Christian Elem. Sch., 1977—; interim pastor Maywood Free Ch., Rockford, 1985-87, Forest Hills Free Ch., Rockford, 1987-88, Congl. Christian Ch., Stillman Valley, Ill., 1988-90; bd. dirs. Christian Life Ctr. Sch., Rockford, 1990-92. Mem. Assn. Christian Sch. Internat. (regional com., state rep. 1988—). Republican. Office: Rockford Christian Sch 1401 N Bell School Rd Rockford IL 61107-2872

BATES, EDWARD BRILL, retired insurance company executive; b. Lexington, Mo., May 14, 1919; s. Worth and Faye Marvin (Brill) B.; m. Mary Louise Van Sickle (dec. Mar. 1999); children: Lynn Louise Bates Russell, Stephen Worth. BABA, U. Chgo., 1940; LLD (hon.), Trinity Coll., Hartford, Conn., 1974; LHD (hon.), U. Hartford, 1976. With Conn. Mut. Life Ins. Co., 1946—; gen. agt. Conn. Mut. Life Ins. Co., Kansas City, 1949-53, Los Angeles, 1953-59; 2d agy. v.p. Conn. Mut. Life Ins. Co., Hartford, 1960-61; v.p. Conn. Mut. Life Ins. Co., 1961-62, exec. v.p., 1962-67, pres., 1967-77, chmn., 1977-84, chmn. exec. com., 1985-87. Mem. Country Club Fla., Ocean Club. Home: 4 Pine Ln E Village Of Golf FL 33436

BATES, GEORGE WILLIAM, obstetrician, gynecologist, educator; b. Durham, N.C., Feb. 15, 1940; s. George W. and Lillian M. (Streete) B.; m. Susanne Rayburn, Oct. 18, 1969; children: Jonathan Rayburn, Jeffrey William, Robert Wiser. BS, U. N.C., 1962, MD, 1965; SM, MIT, 1984. Diplomate Am. Bd. Ob-Gyn. (examiner 1984-93). Intern U. Ala., Birmingham, 1965-66; resident ob-gyn U. N.C., Chapel Hill, 1966-70; prof., chmn. ob-gyn U. Tenn., Knoxville, 1972-76; fellow reproductive endocrinology U. Tex., Dallas, 1976-78; prof., dir. reproductive endocrinology U. Miss. Med. Ctr., Jackson, 1978-86; prof. ob.-gyn. Coll. Medicine Coll. Medicine, Med. U. S.C., Charleston, 1986-90, dean, 1986-89; v.p. med. edn. Greenville (S.C.) Hosp. System, 1990-96; exec. v.p., chief med. officer Prin.Care, Inc., Brentwood, Tenn., 1996-98; v.p. devel. Vanderbilt U. Med. Ctr., Nashville, 1998—; CEO Breathe Am., Inc. Co-author: Obstetrics and Gynecology for Medical Students, 1992, 95; editor: Manual of Clinical Problems in Obstetrics and Gynecology, 1982, 86, 90; contbr. numerous articles to profl. publs. Commr. coun. Boy Scouts Am., 1989-90, v.p. adminstrn., 1992, pres., 1993-94; elder Mt. Pleasant Presbyn. Ch., Westminster Presbyn. Ch.; mem. pres.'s adv. coun. Mars Hill Coll., Presbyn. Coll. Maj. USAF, 1970-72. Morehead scholar, 1958; NIH rsch. trainee, 1976-78; Sloan fellow, 1983; recipient Eagle Scout award, 1955, Henry Fordham award, 1966, Golden Apple award, 1987, Silver Beaver award, 1989, Hon. Alumnus award Med. U. S.C., 1990, Disting. Eagle Scout award, 1991; named Prof. of Yr., U. Miss., 1980. Mem. ACOG (chmn. fin. com. 1990-94, health care commn. 1994-97, Jr. Fellow Profl. of Y. award dist. IV 1991), AMA, AAAS, Assn. Profs. Ob-Gyn. Found. (bd. dirs 1993), Am. Gyn.-Ob. Soc., Nat. Bd. Med. Examiners, Gynecol. Investigation, Am. Fertility Soc. (bd. dirs. 1991-94, treas. 1994-96), Soc. Gynecol. Surgeons, Accreditation Coun. Grad. Med. Edn., So. Atlantic Assn. Obstetricians and Gynecologists, Ctrl. Assn. Obstetricians and Gynecologists, Endocrine Soc., Rotary, Alpha Omega Alpha. Office: Vanderbilt U Med Ctr 1211 22d Ave S Nashville TN 37232

BATES, GERALD EARL, bishop; b. Caldwell, Ohio, Sept. 12, 1933; s. Earl and Lillian Inez (Merritt) B.; m. Marlene Rachel Parsons, Aug. 21, 1954; children: David Earl, William Randall, Elizabeth Ann. AA, Spring Arbor Coll., 1953; AB, Greenville Coll., 1955; MDiv, Asbury Theol. Sem., 1958; ThM, Western Theol. Sem., 1964; PhD, Mich. State U., 1975; DD (hon.), Roberts Wesleyan Coll., 1986, Greenville Coll., 1998. Missionary with Gen. Missionary Bd. Free Meth. Ch. of N.Am., Winona Lake, Ind., 1957-85; area adminstrv. asst. for Cen. Africa Free Meth. Ch. of N.Am., 1973-85; bishop Free Meth. Ch. of N.Am., Indpls., 1985—. Author: Soul Afire, 1981, 2d edit., 1993; chmn. bd. editors: Book of Discipline, 1985. Trustee Ctrl. Coll., Kans., Asbury Theol. Sem., Wilmore, Ky., Spring Arbor Coll., Mich.; chmn ., bd. dirs. Free Meth. Ch. of N.Am., King Trust N.A.; bd. dirs. India Missionary Tng. Bd., Wesley Internat. Bible Sem., Nigeria, J. Wesley Bible Inst., Budapest, Hungary, Free Meth. Found.; pres. Free Meth. World Fellowship, 1989-95; mem. World Meth. Coun. Recipient Alumnus of Yr. award Spring Arbor Coll., 1974, Goodwill Amb. award Noble County C. of C., 1988, Alumnus of Yr. award Asbury Theol. Sem., 1991. Mem. Phi Kappa Phi. Republican. Avocations: reading, travel, photography. Home: 6715 Oak Lake Dr Indianapolis IN 46214-2038 Office: PO Box 535002 Indianapolis IN 46253-5002

BATES, GLADYS EDGERLY, sculptor; b. Hopewell, N.J., July 15, 1896; d. Webster and Edna Reid (Boyts) Edgerly; m. Kenneth Bates, July 12, 1923; children—Kenneth, David Dunlop, Thomas Edgerly. Student, Corcoran Gallery Sch. of Art, 1910-16, Pa. Acad. Fine Arts, 1916-21. Exhibited in one-man show, Pen and Brush Club, N.Y.C., 1945; exhibited in two-man shows, including, Woodmere Gallery, Phila., 1948, Lyman Allyn Mus., New London, Conn., 1952, Madison (Conn.) Art Gallery, 1958, Rowayton (Conn.) Art Gallery, 1961, Noank (Conn.) Arts Club, 1967, group shows including, Art Inst. Chgo., 1934, 39, Tex. Centennial, Dallas, 1936, Carnegie Inst., Pitts., 1938, Archtl. League, N.Y.C., 1941, Addison Gallery, Andover, Mass., 1941, 51, Phila. Mus., 1949, Phila. Art Alliance, 1950, N.J. State Mus., Trenton, 1953; represented in permanent collections including, Met. Mus. Art, N.Y.C., Pa. Acad. Fine Arts, Phila., N.J. State Mus. Recipient awards including Widener Gold medal Pa. Acad. Fine Arts, 1931; nat. assn. medal; Huntingdon prize Nat. Assn. Women Artists, 1934; Fellow Nat. Sculpture Soc. Home: 94 Brook St Noank CT 06340-5513

BATES, HAMPTON ROBERT, JR., pathologist; b. Roanoke, Va., Feb. 1, 1933; s. Hampton Robert and Mary Mildred (Crowder) B.; m. Carole Harrison Young, Apr. 12, 1958; children: Hampton Robert III, Catherine Louise Franck. BS in Chemistry, Roanoke Coll., 1953; MD, Med. Coll. Va., 1957. Diplomate Am. Bd. Pathology, Am. Bd. Nuc. Medicine, Nat. Bd. Med. Examiners. Intern Med. Coll. Va. Hosp., Richmond, 1957-58, resident in pathology, 1958-62, faculty, 1962-63; practice medicine specializing in pathology and nuc. medicine Richmond, 1963-95; ind. rschr., 1995—; pathologist Johnston-Willis Hosp., Chippenham Med. Ctr.; v.p. Clin. Lab. Consultants, Inc., Richmond, 1972-95; forensic pathologist Richmond Met. Area, 1959-95. Contbr. articles on descriptive, exptl. and forensic pathology to med. jours. Fellow Coll. Am. Pathologists (life); mem. AMA, AAAS, Med. Soc. Va., Richmond Acad. Medicine, Swedish Pathol. Soc. (corr.), Rokitansky Soc., Diogenes Club. Episcopalian. Home: 641 Mobrey Dr Richmond VA 23236-4148

BATES, HAROLD MARTIN, lawyer; b. Wise County, Va., Mar. 11, 1928; s. William Jennings and Reba (Williams) B.; m. Audrey Rose Doll, Nov. 1, 1952 (div. Mar. 1978); children—Linda, Carl. m. Judith Lee Farmer, June 23, 1978. B.A. in Econs., Coll. William and Mary, 1952; LL.B., Washington and Lee U., 1961. Bar: Va. 1961, Ky. 1961. Spl. agt. FBI, Newark and N.Y.C., 1952-56; tech. sales rep. Hercules Powder Co., Wilmington, Del., 1956-58; investigator U.S. Def. Dept., Lexington, Va., Louisville, 1959-62; practice law, Louisville, 1961-62; sec.-treas., dir., house counsel Life Ins. Co. of Ky., Louisville, 1962-66; practice law, Roanoke, Va., 1966—; sec., dir. James River Limestone Co., Buchanan, Va., 1970-96; sec. Eastern Ins. Co., Roanoke, 1984-87. Pres., Skil, Inc., orgn. for rehab. Vietnam vets., Salem, Va., 1972-75; freshman football coach Washington and Lee U., 1958-60. Served to cpl. U.S. Army Airborne, 1946-47, PTO. Mem. Va. Bar Assn., Roanoke Bar Assn., William and Mary Alumni Assn. (bd. dirs. 1972-76), Soc. Former Spl. Agts. of FBI (chmn. Blue Ridge chpt. 1971-72). Republican. Home: 2165 Laurel Woods Dr Salem VA 24153-1807 Office: 406 Professional Arts Bldg Roanoke VA 24011

BATES, JAMES EARL, academic administrator; b. Ligonier, Pa., Aug. 10, 1923; s. Earl Barrington and Margaret (Kinsey) B.; m. Lauralou Courtney, Apr. 15, 1950; children: Susan Bates Jaren, Sara Bates Hudson, James Barrington, Willa Laurens. DSc, Temple U., 1946; DPM, Pa. Coll. Podiatric Medicine, 1970; EdD (hon.), Franklin Pierce Coll., 1972; DSc (hon.), Calif. Coll. Podiatric Med., 1995; LLD, Barry U., 1995; LHD (hon.), Pa. Coll. Podiatric Medicine, 1996. Practice podiatric medicine Phila., 1946-71; assoc. prof. roentgenology Temple U., Phila., 1948-60; prof., pres. Pa. Coll. Podiatric Medicine, Phila., 1962-95, chancellor, 1995-96, chancellor, CEO, 1997-98; cons. to dean Sch. Podiatric Medicine Temple U., 1998—; cons. BHRD Region IX, HEW, San Francisco, 1973-74, Region V, Chgo., 1974-75; del. Nat. Commn. on Certifying Health Manpower; mem. health adv. com. HEW, 1972-73; adv. panel for podiatry Inst. Medicine, Nat. Acad. Scis., 1972-76; adv. council for comprehensive health planning Pa. Dept. Health, 1972-75, health manpower task force edn. com., 1976; mem. task force on health manpower distbn. Nat. Health Council, 1973, mem. com. on manpower, 1976-83; mem. Nat. Adv. Council on Health Professions Edn., 1983-87; cons. team So. Regional Ednl. Bd. Feasibility Study for So. Podiatry Sch., 1975-76; mem. Statewide Profl. Standards Rev. Council, 1976-82, Greater Phila. Com. for Med.-Pharm. Scis. Contbr. sci. articles to profl. jours. Trustee First United Meth. Ch. of Germantown, 1965-72, past chmn. fin. com.; v.p. bd. Germantown Businessmen's Assn., Disting. Service award, 1964; chmn. 277th and 278th Ann. Germantown Week, 1958-59; dep. service dir. Phila. CD Council, 1966-73; mem. Health Adv. Commn., Phila., 1976; past pres., bd. mgrs. Germantown YMCA; v.p. Phila. Boosters Assn.; trustee Univ. City Sci. Center, Phila. Served with M.C. AUS, World War II. Recipient citation Pa. Coll. Podiatric Medicine, 1970, citation Gov. Pa., 1973, lifetime achievement award Podiatric Mgmt. Mag., 1993. Fellow Internat. Acad. Preventive Medicine (dir. 1973-78), Brit. Soc. Podiatric Medicine (hon. 1991—), Royal Soc. Health (Eng.), Am. Coll. Foot Roentgenologists (pres. 1958-59), Coll. Physicians Phila.; mem. Am. Podiatry Assn. (Merit award 1962, gen. chmn. Region Three Ann. Conv. 1975—), Pa. Podiatry Assn. (pres. 1959-60, Man of Yr. award 1961, Spl. citation 1973), Greater Phila. Podiatry Soc. (pres. 1955-56), Fedn. Assns. Schs. of Health Professions (pres. 1975-76), Am. Assn. Colls. Podiatric Medicine (pres. 1969-72), Pyramid Club, Pi Epsilon Delta, Pi Delta. Republican. Clubs: Greate Bay Country, Union League, Pyramid Club. Office: Pa Coll Podiatric Medicine 810 N Race St Philadelphia PA 19107-2496

BATES, JAMES ROBERT, newspaper editor; b. Great Bend, Kans., Dec. 12, 1954; s. Robert Lane and Phyllis Fern (Koltermann) B.; m. Jennifer Petkus, Nov. 7, 1986. BS, U. Kans., 1977; postgrad., U. Colo., 1979-80. Copy editor Springfield (Mo.) Daily News, 1977-78; reporter Colo. Springs (Colo.) Sun, 1978-79, news editor, 1980-86; copy editor, asst. news editor Denver Post, 1986-87, news editor, 1987-89, exec. news editor, 1989—. Recipient design and editing awards Colo. Press Assn., Colo. AP, 1986—. Mem. Soc. Newspaper Design. Office: The Denver Post 1560 Broadway Denver CO 80202-5177*

BATES, JOHN CECIL, JR., lawyer; b. Buffalo, May 27, 1936; s. John C. and Geraldine K. Bates; m. Ellen Clare Eyler, June 28, 1964; children: Andrew, Jeremy, Eliot, Emily. AB magna cum laude, Harvard U., 1958; JD, U. Mich., 1961; LLM, NYU, 1962. Bar: N.Y. 1962, D.C. 1977. Assoc. Milbank, Tweed, Hadley & McCloy, N.Y.C., 1963-72; spl. asst. tax policy Treasury Dept., Washington, 1973-76; ptnr. Squire, Sanders & Dempsey, Washington, 1977-84, Reid & Priest, Washington, 1984-91, Foley & Lardner, Washington, 1992-94; tax policy advisor Dept. Treas. Tech. Assistance Program (Ctrl. and Eastern Europe), 1995—; tax and fin. cons. to state local and fgn. govts., also others, 1977—; adj. prof. Fordham U. Grad. Sch. Bus. Adminstrn., 1992. Co-author: Federal Law of Public Finance, 1988; contbr. numerous articles on tax and fin. to profl. jours. Founding mem. St. George (Maine) Hist. Soc. Mem. ABA (chmn. com. tax sect. 1981-83), D.C. Bar Assn., Fed. Bar Assn., Govt. Fin. Officers Assn., Assn. of Bar of City of N.Y., Coun. for Excellence in Govt., Harvard Club; sr. fellow Internat. Law Inst., 1997—. Avocations: archtl. preservation, environ. protection, music. Home: PO Box 11482 Washington DC 20008-0682 also: PO Box 293 Tenants Harbor ME 04860-0293

BATES, JOHN WYTHE, III, lawyer; b. Richmond, Aug. 22, 1941; s. John Wythe, Jr. and Virginia (Wellington) B.; m. Beverly Jane Estes, June 20, 1964; children: Elizabeth Puller, Kathryn Wellington. BS, Va. Tech., 1963; LLB, U. Va., 1966. Assoc. McGuire Woods Battle & Boothe, L.L.P., Richmond, 1966-71, pntr., 1971—, mng. ptnr., 1989-96; mem. Va. Racing Commn., 1997—. Chmn. United Way Gtr. Richmond, 1975-76; pres. Family and Children's Svc. Richmond, 1978-80; trustee St. Paul's Coll., 1989-96, Va. Found. Ind. Colls., 1994—; sr. warden St. Stephen's Ch., 1985-86. Va. Law Found. fellow, 1997. Mem. Am. Coll. Real Estate Lawyers, Richmond Real Estate Group, Forum Club, River Rd. Citizens Assn. (pres. 1983-84), Country Club Va. (pres. 1987-88), Bull and Bear Club (pres. 1980-81), Commonwealth Club. Episcopalian. Avocations: golf, waterfowl hunting. Office: McGuire Woods Battle & Boothe LLP One James Ctr 901 E Cary St Richmond VA 23219-4057

BATES, JOSEPH HENRY, physician, educator; b. Little Rock, Sept. 19, 1933; s. Henry Ermer and Susan Elizabeth (Wallis) B.; m. Patsy McGinnis, Aug. 6, 1955; children—Patricia, Susan Elizabeth, Joseph Henry, III, Elisabeth Lee. BS, U. Ark., 1957, MD, 1957, MS, 1963. Diplomate: Am. Bd. Internal Medicine (pulmonary disease; mem. exam. bd.). Med. intern U. Ark. Med. Center, 1957-58, resident in internal medicine, 1958-61, fellow in infectious diseases, 1961-63; clin. investigator Little Rock VA Med. Center, 1963-66; mem. faculty U. Ark. Med. Center, Little Rock, 1967—; prof. medicine U. Ark. Med. Center, 1973—, vice chmn. dept., 1978-98; chief med. service Little Rock VA Hosp., 1970-98, dep. state health officer, Ark. Dept. Health, 1998—; dir. Mercantile Bank Ark. Author research papers in field, chpts. in books. Chmn. Ark. chpt. NCCJ, 1980; chmn. biracial commn. Little Rock public schs., 1977-79; bd. dirs. Am. Lung Assn., 1972-90. Served as officer M.C. AUS, 1956-65. Grantee USPHS, 1961-63; Grantee NIH, VA, also pvt. founds. and corps., 1963—. Mem. ACP (gov.), Am. Coll. Chest Physicians (gov.), Am. Fedn. Clin. Rsch., Am. Thoracic Soc. (pres. 1988-89), Infectious Disease Soc., So. Soc. Clin. Rsch., Am. Lung Assn. (pres. 1994-95), Aassn. Am. Physicians, Assn. Profs. Medicine. Presbyterian. Home: 5 Glenridge Rd Little Rock AR 72227-2208 Office: 4300 W 7th St Little Rock AR 72205-5446

BATES, KATHY, actress; b. Memphis, June 28, 1948. BFA, So. Meth. U., 1969. Film appearances include Taking Off, 1971, Straight Time, Come Back to the Five and Dime, Jimmy Dean, Jimmy Dean, Summer Heat, Arthur 2: On the Rocks, Signs of Life, High Stakes, Men Don't Leave, Dick Tracy, White Palace, Misery, 1990 (Acad. award for Best Actress 1990, Golden Globe award), At Play in the Fields of the Lord, 1991, The Road to Mecca, Prelude to a Kiss, Fried Green Tomatoes, 1991 (Golden Globe nomination, BAFTA nomination), Used People, A Home of Our Own, North, Curse of the Starving Class, Dolores Claiborne, 1994, Angus, 1995, Diabolique, 1996, The War at Home, 1996, Primary Colors, 1998, Swept from the Sea, 1998, Titanic, 1998; stage appearances include Vanities, 1976, Semmelweiss, Crimes of the Heart, The Art of Dining, Goodbye Fidel, 1980, Chocolate Cake and Final Placement, 1981, 5th of July, Come Back to the 5 & Dime, Jimmy Dean, Jimmy Dean, 'night, Mother, 1983 (Tony nomination, Outer Critics Circle award), Two Masters: The Rain of Terror, 1985, Curse of the Starving Class, Frankie and Johnny in the Clair de Lune (OBIE award 1988), The Road to Mecca; TV appearances include (series) The Late Shift (Golden Globe award, Am. Comedy award, SAG award), The Love Boat, St. Elsewhere, Cagney & Lacey, L.A. Law, China Beach, Homicide, N.Y.P.D. Blue, (pilot) Fargo, (miniseries) Murder Ordained, The Stand, 1994, (movies of the week) Johnny Bull, No Place Like Home, Roe vs. Wade, Hostages, The West Side Waltz, 1995, The Late Shift, 1996; dir. Talking With, PBS Great Performances, (NBC). Office: Susan Smith & Assocs 121 N San Vicente Blvd Beverly Hills CA 90211-2303

BATES, MARCIA JEANNE, information scientist educator; b. Terre Haute, Ind., July 30, 1942; d. Robert Joseph and Martha Jane B. BA, Pomona Coll., 1963; MLS, U. Calif., Berkeley, 1967; PhD, U. Calif., 1972. Peace corps vol. Saraburi, Thailand, 1963-64, Nongkhai, Thailand, 1964-65; jr. specialist Inst. Libr. Rsch., U. Calif., Berkeley, 1968; acting instr. U. Calif., Berkeley, 1969-70; asst. prof. U. Md., College Park, 1972-76; asst. prof. U. Wash., Seattle, 1976-80, assoc. prof., 1980-81; assoc. prof. U. Calif., Los Angeles, 1981-91, prof., 1991—; prof. and dept. chmn. libr. and info. sci. U. Calif., Los Angeles, 1993-95; cons. U.S. Libr. Congress, Washington, 1986, 91, Getty Art His. Info. Program, Santa Monica, Calif., 1988-91, Info. Access Co., Foster City, Calif., 1992-95; mem. editl. bd. Jour. of Asis, 1989—, Libr. Quar., 1993—. Co-author: For Information Specialists, 1992; contbr. articles to profl. jours. Recipient Distinguished Lectureship award N.J. Am. Soc. for Info. Sci., New Brunswick, 1991. Fellow AAAS (sect. T electorate nominating com. 1980-84, chmn. 1983-84), mem. Am. Soc. Info. Sci. (bd. dirs. 1973-74, Best Jour. Article Yr. award, 1980, Rsch. award 1998), Assn. Records Mgrs. Adminstrs., Calif. Libr. Assn. (mem. task force on future of Libr. profession, 1993-95), Phi Beta Kappa. Design of info. sys. and interfaces for search and subject access in info. retrieval sys. Avocations: walking, photography, travel. Office: Grad Sch Edn & Info Studies UCLA 405 Hilgard Ave Los Angeles CA 90095-1520

BATES, MICHAEL, Olympic athlete, track and field. Olympic track and field participant Barcelona, Spain, 1992. Recipient 200m Track and Field Bronze medal Olympics, Barcelona, 1992. Office: USA Trace and Field 1 Rca Dome Ste 140 Indianapolis IN 46225-1023*

BATES, MICHAEL LAWRENCE, curator; b. Louisville, Ky., Oct. 14, 1941; s. Hugh Louis and Emily Stiles (Willyard) B.; m. Katalin Uzdi, 1996; 1 child, Andrew. AB, U. Chgo., 1963, PhD, 1975. Curator of Islamic coins Am. Numismatic Soc., N.Y.C., 1970—; numismatist Fustat Excavations, Cairo, Egypt, 1978-80; sec. Am. Inst. for Yemeni Studies, Chgo., 1978-81; mem. council Internat. Numismatic Commn., 1979-91, v.p., 1986-91; cons. curator Kuwait Nat. Mus., 1981-85. Author: Islamic Coins, 1982; co-author: Greek, Roman and Islamic Coins from Sardis, 1981; editor Internat. Numismatic Newsletter, 1986-90. Fellowship Nat. Endowment for the Arts, 1976, Am. Rsch. Ctr. in Egypt, 1981-82, Samir Shamma Vis. Islamic Numismatic fellow St. Cross Coll. Oxford U., 1994, Near East Ctr. fellow UCLA, 1996; Gen. Motors Nat. scholar, 1959-63. Fellow Am. Oriental Soc., Middle East Studies Assn., Middle East Medievalists (v.p. 1990-92). E-mail: bates@annumsoc.org. Home: 1334 River Rd Edgewater NJ 07020-1424 Office: Am Numismatic Soc 155th St And Broadway New York NY 10032-7598

BATES, PATTI JEAN, communications specialist in public safety; b. Cin., Apr. 19, 1959; d. Harold Lee and Emily (Cox) Blinkhorn; m. Michael Bates, Apr. 12, 1986. BS in Forestry Recreation, U. Wis., Stevens Point, 1982; MA in Pub. Adminstrn., No. Ky. U., 1997. Cert. pub. safety communicator Assn. Pub. Safety Comm. Officials, Fla. Groundskeeper Cinti Tech. Coll., Cin., 1984-86; comm. specialist Union Twp., Cin., 1986-99; dir. adminstrn. Kenton County (Ky.) Detention Ctr., 1999—. Named Outstanding Student Alumni Assn., No. Ky. U., 1997. Mem. Am. Soc. Pub. Adminstrn., Inter City-County Mgmt. Assn., Fraternal Order Police Assn., Alumni Assn. No. Ky. U. Avocations: environ. issues, hiking, softball, phys. fitness. Office: Kenton County Jail Court St Covington KY 41011

BATES, REITTA IONE, retired mental health nurse; b. Mazon, Ill., Dec. 9, 1924; d. Albert G. and Veda M. (Sutton) Frazer; m. Jesse Ray Bates, Feb. 16, 1947 (dec. Mar. 20, 1991); children: Cathy Ann, Marcus Ray, Cynthia Marie. Diploma, Silver Cross Hosp., Joliet, Ill., 1946; student, Olivet Nazarene Coll., Bourbonnais, Ill., Kankakee Community Coll. RN, Mo., Ill. Night house supr. Silver Cross Hosp., 1946-47, 48, 49-50; nurse Manteno State Hosp., 1953-78; med.-surg. staff nurse Skaggs Community Hosp., Branson, Mo., 1982-85; student nurse part-time Kankakee Community Coll., 1971-74, Olivet Nazarene Coll., 1967. Vol. Hospice Am., 1994-95. Nurse cadet World War II. Mem. Mo. State Nurses Assn. Home: 1203 Mill St Cassville MO 65625

BATES, RICHARD MATHER, dentist; b. May 21, 1932; s. Richard Mather and Virginia Susan (Brokaw) B.; m. Jean Frances Delk, June 27, 1959; children: Bruce H., Susan F. BS, Lewis and Clark Coll., 1954; DMD, U. Oreg., 1958. Gen. practice dentistry Portland, Oreg., 1958-98; pres., dir. Dentist Benefit Corp., Portland, 1981-90; past chmn. bd. dirs. Oregon Dental Svc., Dentists Benefit Ins. Co.; dental dir. Gentle Dental P.C. of Oreg., Portland, 1996-98; clin. assoc. Oreg. Health Sci. U., Portland, 1976-79; mem. dental staff Physicians and Surgeons Hosp., Portland, 1965-85. Pres. Pub. Affairs Forum of Washington County, Beaverton, Oreg., 1965-66; bd. dirs. Oreg. Trail chpt. ARC, Portland, 1970-76; pres., co-founder Dental Aid for Children, Hillsboro, Oreg., 1970; chmn. bd. Dentists Benefit Corp., 1981-90. Recipient Disting. Svc. award Beaverton Jaycees, 1965. Fellow Internat. Coll. Dentists, Am. Coll. Dentists, Acad. Gen. Dentistry (Dentist of Yr. award Oreg. unit 1972); mem. ADA, Oreg. Dental Assn. (pres. 1983-84), Washington County Dental Soc. (pres. 1967-68), Beaverton Area C. of C. (pres. 1976, J. Arthur Young award 1975), N.W. Regional Pony of Am. Club (pres. 1970-72), Oreg. Pony of Am. Club (Beaverton chpt. pres. 1977-78), Cedar Hills Lodge, Kiwanis (Beaverton chpt. pres. 1970). Presbyterian.

BATES, ROGER ALAN, entertainer; b. Attleboro, Mass., Sept. 2, 1951; s. George Weston and Dora Jean (Coffin) B.; m. Amy Hautman, Sept. 14, 1989; children: Britt, Tyler. Student, Bryant Coll., 1970-73, R.I. Sch. of Music, 1975-76. Musician Mpls., 1975-85; owner Bates Music, Mpls., 1982—; stand up comedian Mpls., 1987—; humor cons. Bates Music/Funnybiz, Mpls., Cary, N.C., 1995—. Author: How to Play by Ear-Guitar/Keys, 1983, How to be Funnier, 1995, Laugh Your Way Through Parenthood, 1997, (cassette) World's Greatest Joker Cassette, 1995. Mem. Am. Assn. of Therapeutic Humor, Carolina Health and Humor Assn. Home: 109 Barcliff Ter Cary NC 27511-8900

BATES, WALTER ALAN, former lawyer; b. Wadsworth, Ohio, Oct. 27, 1925; s. Edwin Clinton and Gertrude (Connor) B.; m. Aloise Grasselli O'Brien, Feb. 9, 1957; children: Charles, Aloise, Walter Alan Jr., Thomas, David. BS cum laude, Harvard U., 1945, LLB, 1950. Bar: Ohio 1950, U.S. Dist. Ct. (no. dist.) Ohio 1954, U.S. Ct. Appeals (6th cir.) 1965, U.S. Ct. Appeals (7th cir.) 1966, U.S. Dist. Ct. Conn. 1976, U.S. Ct. Appeals (2nd cir.) 1977, U.S. Dist. Ct. Minn. 1978, U.S. Ct. Appeals (8th cir.) 1980, U.S. Ct. Appeals (5th cir.) 1984, U.S. Dist. Ct. (no. dist.) Tex. 1988, U.S. Supreme Ct. 1989. Assoc. McKeehan, Merrick, Arter & Stewart, Cleve., 1950-60; ptnr. Arter & Hadden, Cleve., 1960-94; ret., 1994. Chmn. bd. trustees Cleve. Inst. Music, 1980-85, hon. trustee, 1985—; assoc. v.p., chmn. new programs com. United Way Svcs., Cleve., 1982-85, trustee, 1985-88; mem. Cleve. panel Ctr. for Pub. Resources; trustee Apollo's Fire, 1998—. Lt. USN, 1945-46, 51-53. Mem. ABA (antitrust sect.), Ohio State Bar Assn. (chmn. bd. govs. antitrust sect. 1987-91), Cleve. Bar Assn. (joint com. on bar admissions 1990-97, cert. grievance com. 1992-95). Republican. Roman Catholic. Clubs: Kirtland Country (sec., bd. dirs. 1981-86), Mentor Harbor Yachting (bd. dirs. 1980-89, commodore 1988), Tavern, Harvard (Cleve. pres. 1968-69). Avocations: sailing; traveling. Home: 18235 Shaker Blvd Cleveland OH 44120-1754 Office: Arter & Hadden 1100 Huntington Bldg Cleveland OH 44115

BATES, WILLIAM, III, lawyer; b. Phila., May 1, 1949; s. William and Elizabeth (Martin) B. BA, Yale U., 1971; JD, Stanford U., 1974. Bar: Calif. 1974, U.S. Dist. Ct. (no. dist.) Calif. 1976, U.S. Dist. Ct. (ea. dist.) Calif. 1978, U.S. Dist. Ct. (ctrl. dist.) Calif. 1984, U.S. Ct. Appeals (9th cir.) 1986, U.S. Dist. Ct. (so. dist.) Calif. 1987. Law clk. to chief judge U.S. Dist. Ct. Conn., Hartford, 1974-75; assoc. McCutchen, Doyle, Brown & Enersen, San Francisco, 1975-81, ptnr., 1981—. Mem. ABA (mem. bus. bankruptcy com.), State Bar Calif. (chair rules of ct. com. 1979-80, mem. uniform comml. code com. 1985-88, mem. debtor/creditor rels. com. 1989-92), San Francisco Bar Assn. (chair comml. law and bankruptcy sect. 1991-92). Democrat. Episcopalian. Avocations: wine tasting, golf, bicycling, travel. Office: McCutchen Doyle Brown & Enersen 3 Embarcadero Ctr San Francisco CA 94111-4003

BATES, WILLIAM HUBERT, lawyer; b. Lexington, Mo., Apr. 14, 1926; s. George Hubert and E. Norma (Comer) B.; m. Joy LoRue Godbehere, Oct. 20, 1956; children: William Brand, Joy Ann. BA, U. Mo., 1949; JD, U. Mich., 1952. Bar: Mo. 1952. With Lathrop & Gage L.C., Kansas City, Mo., 1952—, chmn., 1988-95; l. Mem., pres. bd. curators U. Mo. Multi-Campus U., 1983-89. Sgt. U.S. Army, 1943-46, ETO. Recipient Brotherhood award NCCJ, 1984; Disting. Alumni award U. Mo., 1989, Geyer award for pub. svc., 1991. Fellow Am. Bar Found. (state chmn. 1990-97); mem. ABA (ho. of dels. 1990-93), Mo. Bar Assn. (bd. dirs. 1982-91, v.p., pres. 1988-91), Kansas City Bar Assn. (pres. Found. 1985-87), Lawyers Assn. Kansas City (Charles Evans Whittaker award 1990), Mo. C. of C. (chmn., bd. dirs. 1983-85), Greater Kansas City C. of C. (bd. dirs., chmn. 1975-92), Van Guard Club, Mercury Club, Beta Theta Pi (Man of Yr. award Kansas City 1985, Oxford Cup 1996). Democrat. Methodist. Avocations: golf, swimming, music. Home: 310 W 49th St Apt 1002 Kansas City MO 64112-3400 Office: Lathrop & Gage L C 2345 Grand Blvd Ste 2600 Kansas City MO 64108-2617

BATESEL, BILLY PAUL, English language educator; b. Hocomo, Mo., June 25, 1938; s. Camby and Mary Clementine (Casto) B.; m. Sarah Margaret Dodge, Aug. 11, 1968. BS in Edn., Southwest Mo. State Coll., 1960; MA, U. Mo., 1968, PhD, 1973. Tchr. English John F. Kennedy Schule, West Berlin, Germany, 1976-78; instr. English Mo. Western State Coll., St. Joseph, 1978-79; asst. prof. English U. Ark., Fayetteville, 1979-81; tchr. English Am. Sch. in Aberdeen, Scotland, 1981-85, Verdala Internat. Sch., Cottonera, Malta, 1985-86; asst. prof. English Emporia (Kans.) State U., 1986-89; prof. English Mayville (N.D.) State U., 1989—; presenter lectures, workshops in field; coord. Bush Found. Faculty Devel. project, Mayville State U., 1992-95, 1997-98; discussion leader Gt. Books of the Gt. Plains, Fargo, N.D., 1996—; cons. for standards and benchmarks for N.D. English curriculum, Dept. Pub. Instrn. State of N.D., 1994—, panelist, Natl. Assesment of Ednl. Prog. (NAEP) in writing, 1998. Contbr. articles to profl. jours. Mem. NCTE, N.D. Coun. Tchrs. English, Am. Profl. Ptnrship for Lithuanian Edn., Assn. Am. Colls. and Univs., Soc. Am. Baseball Rschrs., M-300 Club, Comet Athletic. Democrat. Mem. United Ch. Christ. Avocation: running. Office: Mayville State U 330 3rd St NE Ste NE Mayville ND 58257-1299

BATEY, SHARYN REBECCA, clinical research scientist; b. Nashville, Apr. 19, 1946; d. Robert Thomas and Sue (Alred) B. BS in Pharmacy, U. Tenn., 1969, D of Pharmacy, 1975; MS in Pub. Health, U. S.C., 1984. Registered pharmacist, Tenn. Hosp. pharmacist Vanderbilt Hosp., Nashville, 1969-71, VA Hosp., Beckley, W.Va., 1971-72, Gainesville, Fla., 1972-73, Battle Creek, Mich., 1973-74; hosp. pharmacy resident VA Hosp., Memphis, 1974-76; psychopharmacy resident Menninger Found., Topeka, 1976-77; clin. pharmacist William S. Hall Psychiat. Inst., Columbia, S.C., 1977-82; asst. prof. U. S.C. Coll. Pharmacy, Columbia, 1977-83, asst. prof. Sch. Medicine, 1981-83, assoc. prof. Coll. Pharmacy and Sch. Medicine, 1983-89; prof., 1989; chief clin. pharmacy services and ednl. programs William S. Hall Psychiat. Inst., Columbia, 1982-89; clin. rsch. scientist Burroughs Wellcome Co., Research Triangle Park, N.C., 1989-95; clin. program head, Glaxo Wellcome, Inc., Research Triangle Park, 1995-97, sr. clin. rsch. program head, 1997—; clin. drug research/drug devel. fellow U. N.C. and Burroughs Wellcome, Research Triangle Park, 1983-84; pharmacist cons. NIMH, Bethesda, Md., 1983-84, Health Care Fin. Adminstrn., Balt., 1985-89. Author audio visual programs Psychotropic Medication Education Program for Adults, Adolescents and Children, 1978, 84, 88, 89; contbr. articles on psychopharmacology to profl. jours. Recipient Significant Achievement award Am. Psychiat. Assn., 1980, Sci. Exhibit award Am. Psychiat. Assn., 1981. Mem. Am. Coll. Clin. Pharmacy, Am. Soc. Hosp. Pharmacists (chmn. edn. and tng. working group of psychopharmacy spl. interest group 1983-85, chmn. elect 1985-86, chmn. 1986-87, past chmn. 1987-88, project leader psycopharmacy specialty recognition petition 1986-89, psychopharmacy fellow selection com. 1986-88, chmn. psychopharmacy spl. practice group 1989), S.C. Dementia Registry (pres. user policy coun. 1989). Avocations: travel, reading. Home: 4824 Highgate Dr Durham NC 27713-9417 Office: Glaxo Wellcome Inc Research Triangle Park NC 27709

BAT-HAEE, MOHAMMAD ALI, educational administrator, consultant; b. Sanandadj, Iran, June 19, 1935; came to U.S., 1964, naturalized, 1991; s. Mohammad Ameen and Khadeejeh (Esteefaee) B.; m. Aghdas Seyedalshohadaee, Aug. 16, 1961; children: Farzeen, Farshad, Neshat. BS, U. Tehran, Iran, 1962; MS in Edn., So. Ill. U., Carbondale, 1966, PhD, 1968. Cert. tchr. level G, N.C. Asst. prof. U. Mo., St. Louis, 1968-69; dean student Pahlavi U., Shiraz, Iran, 1969-70, chmn. dept. psychology, 1971-73, assoc. prof. psychology, assoc. dean Coll. Art and Scis., 1973-75, prof., 1976-84, dean Coll. Art and Scis., 1976-77; instrnl. supr. Wake Tech. C.C., Raleigh, N.C., 1985-87; tchr. O'Berry Ctr., Goldsboro, N.C., 1988-89, asst. dir. programs, 1990-91, cmty. employment dir. III, 1992-96, prof. outreach ordinator, 1996—. Author: Education, Aims and Techniques, 1970, Psychology of Management, 1971, Elementary Math for Elementary Statistics, 1972, Development of Knowledge and Logical Thinking in Children, 1997; also articles. Bd. dirs. Cmty. Sch., Shiraz, 1972-73, Kanoon-e-Iranian, Raleigh, 1986-88, 1989-94; mem. Kurdish Nat. Congress, N.Am., 1992-94. Rsch. grantee U. Mo., 1969, U. Shiraz, 1970, AID, 1975. Mem. Am. Assn. on Mental Retardation, Am. Psychol. Soc., Nat. Applied Behavior Analysis, N.C. Assn. on Mental Retardation (chmn. staff devel. 1992—, award for svcs. in leadership and rsch. 1996), N.C. Applied Behavior Analysis, Internat. Applied Behavior Analysis. Democrat. Avocations: woodcarving, calligraphy, poetry, jogging, gardening. Home: 919 Hampshire Ct Cary NC 27511-4100

BATISTA, ALBERTO A., editor; b. Tacajo, Oriente, Cuba, Mar. 4, 1945; came to the U.S., 1994; s. Aris A. Batista and Marina Reyes. BA in Spanish Lang. Lit., U. Havana, 1977, MA in Philosophy, 1984; postgrad., Inst. Internat. Politics, Havana, 1983, Inst. Book Pub., Moscow, 1984. Prof. social sci. H.S. level Oriente, 1963-68; prof. philosophy U. Havana, 1968; TV prodr. The Cuban Inst. Radio, Havana, 1969; journalist, film critic Adelante Jour., Camaguey, Cuba, 1970-71; journalist Monthly Rev. Bayardo, Camaguey, 1971-73; ednl. program cons. The Chem. Industry, Havana, 1973-76; journalist Monthly Mag. Quimica, Havana, 1977-79; cons. The Ministry of Culture, Havana, 1984-92; assoc. editor SIBI Pub. House, Miami, Fla., 1995-96; consulting editor Pipin Prodns., Miami, 1996-97. Author: (One of a Thousand Days, 1975, The New Conquerors, 1975, The Rifle's Edges, 1981, One of the Eleventh, 1981, Infidelities of Three Sisters, 1986, Relation Between Creation and Literary Investigation and Book Publishing, 1990. Mem. Nat. Trust Historic Preservation, Libr. Congress, Mus. of the Am. Indian, Mus. Natural Sci. E-mail: Abati55574@aol.com. Office: Tiempos del Mundo Newspaper 3rd Fl 401 5th Ave Fl 3 New York NY 10016-3317

BATISTA, ALBERTO ENTIMIO, marketing professional; b. Miami Beach, Fla., Apr. 25, 1968; s. Laureano F. and Adela M. (De la Campa) B. BA in Polit. Sci., So. Meth. U., 1990. Mgmt. trainee Johnson & Higgins, N.Y.C., 1991-92; fin. cons. Merrill Lynch, Miami, Fla., 1992-95; mktg. assoc. Coutts (USA) Inc., Miami, 1995-99; with Std. Chanered Bank, Miami, Fla., 1999—.

Big bro. United Way, Miami, 1994. Mem. Sigma Theta Epsilon. Roman Catholic. Avocations: soccer, tennis, snow skiing. Home: 2925 Bridgeport Ave Coconut Grove FL 33133-3607 Office: Std Chanered Bank 701 Brickell Ave Ste 1700 Miami FL 33131-2860

BATISTONI, RONALD, educational association administrator; b. Plainfield, N.J., Oct. 22, 1938; s. Atillio Raymond and Ann Agnes (Paznick) B.; children: Raymond, Jeanine, Melissa. BS in Secondary Edn., Seton Hall U., 1960, EdD in Ednl. Adminstrn., 1991; MA in English/Am. Lit., Montclair (N.J.) U., 1968. Tchr. English/Latin Bergenfield (N.J.) Pub. Schs., 1960-64; tchr. English West Morris Regional H.S. Dist., Chester, N.J., 1964-69, chmn. dept. English, 1969-70, supt., 1991-92, asst. supt., 1992-94; dir. nat. assessment programs N.J. Prins. and Suprs. Assn., Chester, 1995—; prin. West Morris Ctrl. Sch., Chester, 1979-91. Pres. Iron Hills Conf., Morris County, N.J., 1988-89; exec. sec. Washington Twp. Outreach, N.J., 1979-84. Recipient Presdl. Citation for Vol. Svc., Pres. Reagan, 1981. Mem. Am. Ednl. Rsch. Assn., Nat. Assn. Secondary Sch. Prins., N.J. Prins. and Suprs. Assn. Avocations: reading, computers travel, outdoors. Home: 1244 Mazetti Rd Stroudsburg PA 18360-8666

BATIUK, THOMAS MARTIN, cartoonist; b. Akron, Ohio, Mar. 14, 1947; s. Martin and Verna (Greskovics) B.; m. Catherine L. Wesemeyer, June 26, 1971; 1 child, Brian. B.F.A., Kent (Ohio) State U., 1969, cert. edn., 1969. Tchr. art Eastern Heights Jr. High Sch., 1969-72; syndicated cartoonist, 1972—. Cartoonist: comic strip Funky Winkerbean, 1972—, John Darling, 1979—, Crankshaft, 1987—; collections include Funky Winkerbean, 1973, Funky Winkerbean, Play It Again Funky, 1975, Funky Winkerbean, Closed Out, 1977, Yearbook, 1979, You Know You've Got Trouble When Your Mascot is a Scpaegoat, 1984, Football Fields are for Band Practice, 1986, Sunday Concert, 1987, Henry C. Dinkle-Live at Carnegie Hall, 1988, A Pizza Pilgrim's Progress, 1990, Funky Winkerbean: Gone with the Woodwinds, 1992, Would the Ushers Please Lock the Doors, 1994, Crankshaft: I've Still Got It, 1995; co-author: And One Slice With Anchovies!, 1993, Crankshaft, 1992; forward: A PArent's Guide to Band and ORchestra, 1991, Attack of the Band Moms, 1996. Recipient 46th Annual Ohio Gov.'s award-Journalism, 1995. Mem. Nat. Cartoonists Soc., Newspaper Features Coun. Office: care Universal Press Syndicate 4520 Main St Kansas City MO 64111*

BATLA, RAYMOND JOHN, JR., lawyer; b. Cameron, Tex., Sept. 1, 1947; s. Raymond John and Della Alvina (Jezek) B.; m. Susan Marie Clark, Oct. 1, 1983; children: Sara, Charles, Michael, Traci. BS with highest honors, U. Tex., 1970, JD with honors, 1973. Bar: Tex. 1973, D.C. 1973, U.S. Dist. Ct. (so. dist.) Tex. 1982, U.S. Ct. Appeals (D.C. cir.) 1974, U.S. Ct. Appeals (5th cir.) 1982, U.S. Ct. Appeals (10th cir.) 1978, U.S. Supreme Ct. 1977. Structural engr. Tex. Hwy. Dept., Austin, 1970; assoc. Hogan & Hatson, Washington, 1973-82, gen. ptrn., 1983—; mem. Am. Endowment for Democracy Internat. Observer Del. to Czechoslovakia, 1990; sec. Coun. on Alt. Fuels, 1987-97. Author: Petroleum Regulation Handbook, 1980, Natural Gas Yearbook, 1991; columnist, mem. editorial bd. Natural Gas mag., 1984-91, Energy Law Jour., 1991-93; contbr. articles to profl. jours. Mem. ABA (mem. spl. com. for energy fin., vice chmn. energy com. 1981, cen. and Ea. Europe law inst. internat. law com., spl. com on energy fin. 1989—), Fed. Energy Bar Assn. (chmn. internat. energy transactions com. 1993-94), Fed. Bar Assn., D.C. Bar Assn., State Bar Tex., City Club of Wash., London Capital Club, Order of Coif, Chi Epsilon, Tau Beta Pi. Home: 12406 Shari Hunt Grv Clifton VA 20124-2056 Home: 5 Half Moon St, London W1Y 7RA, England Office: 555 13th St NW Washington DC 20004-1109 Also: Hogan & Hartson, 21 Garlick Hill, London EC4V 2AU, England also: 5 Half Moon St, London W1Y 7RA, England

BATLIN, ROBERT ALFRED, editor; b. San Francisco, Aug. 24, 1930; S. Philip Alfred and Lavenia Mary (Barnes) B.; m. Diane Elise Giblin, July 4, 1956; children—Lisa, Philippa. B.A., Stanford U., 1952, M.A., 1954. Reporter San Bruno Herald, 1952-53; copy editor, then dept. editor San Francisco News, 1956-59; dept. editor San Francisco News-Call Bull., 1959-65; feature editor San Francisco Examiner, 1965-74, arts editor, 1974-85, asst. style editor, 1985—. Served with AUS, 1954-56. Mem. Soc. of Profl. Journalists. Home: 91 Fairway Dr Daly City CA 94015-1215 Office: 110 5th St San Francisco CA 94103-2918

BATLIVALA, ROBERT BOMI D., oil company executive, economics educator; b. Bombay, India, Feb. 17, 1940; came to U.S., 1962, naturalized, 1968; s. Dean Shaw and Rose (Engineer) B.; m. Carole Gretchen Feustel, May 9, 1964; children: Amy, Dina. BS in Geology, Chemistry, St. Xavier Coll., Bombay, Ind., 1960; MBA in Bus., Econs., Loyola U., Chgo., 1970; PHD in Bus., Econs., Ill. Inst. Tech., 1971; post-doctoral studies, U. Chgo., 1972-73. Rsch. chemist Reynolds Metals Co., McCook, Ill., 1962-64; from sales engr. to staff dir. econs. Amoco Corp., Chgo., 1964-1988, dir. antitrust econs., 1988-93; dir. regulatory econs., 1993—; adj. prof. bus. and econs. Rosary Coll., River Forest, Ill., 1976—, Graduate Sch. Bus., 1986-96; bd. dirs. Pvt. Bancorp, Inc., Chgo., Am. Ins. Exch. Contbr. articles to profl. jours., 1971-78. Bd. dirs. Ctr. for Conflict Resolution, 1990-96, Ill. Ins. Exch., 1997—. Recipient Stuart Tuition scholarship, Ill. Inst. Tech., 1970-71, Recognition award Rosary Coll. Grad. Sch. Bus. Alumni Assn., River Forest, 1986. Mem. ABA (assoc.), Nat. Assn. Mfrs. (corp. fin., mgmt. & competition com., regulation, transp. com. 1980—), Am. Econ. Assn., Assn. of Energy Economists, Loyola U. Grad. Bus. Alumni Assn. (pres., sr. v.p. 1971-73, Disting. Alumni award 1975), Oak Park Country Club. Avocations: ancient history, reading, writing, travel, languages. Home: 1106 Keystone Ave River Forest IL 60305-1326 Office: Amoco Corp 200 E Randolph St Ste 3500 Chicago IL 60601-7125

BATLLE, DANIEL, nephrologist; b. Barcelona, Spain, Feb. 11, 1950; came to U.S., 1975; s. Narciso and Francisca (Campi) B.; m. Joan Batlle, Mar. 11, 1983; children: Jordi, Nicholas, Natalie. MD, U. Barcelona, 1973. Diplomate Am. Bd. Internal Medicine and Nephrology. Resident Wayne State U., Detroit, 1975-77; nephrology fellow U. Ill., Chgo., 1977-79, asst. prof. medicine, 1980-85; assoc. prof. medicine Northwestern U., Chgo., 1985-89, prof. medicine, 1989—; chief divsn. nephrology, hypertension Northwestern U., 2d Northwest Meml. Hosp., Chgo., 1992—. Editorial bd. Seminars in Nephrology, 1987—, Am. Jour. of Kidney Diseases, 1988—, Hypertension, 1992—, The Kidney, 1992—. Fellow ACP, Am. Heart Assn. (high blood pressure coun.); mem. Nat. Kidney Found. (sci. adv. bd. 1987—, chmn. nominating com. sci. adv. bd. 1989-91, chmn. program com. clin. meeting 1993—), Am. Soc. for Clin. Investigation, Cen. Soc. for Clin. Rsch., Soc. Gen. Physiologists, Am. Physiol. Soc., Am. Soc. Nephrology, Internat. Soc. Nephrology, Am. Heart Assn., N.Y. Acad. Scis. Office: Northwestern U Med Sch 303 E Chicago Ave Chicago IL 60611-3072

BATRA, N.D., communications educator; b. Mar. 4, 1937. PhD, Gujarat U., 1980. Prof. comms., chair comms. dept. Norwich U., Northfield, Vt., 1986—; columnist The Statesman, Calcutta, 1995—. E-mail: batra@norwich.edu. Office: Norwich U Northfield VT 05664

BATRA, ROMESH CHANDER, engineering mechanics educator, researcher; b. Dherowal, Panjab, India, Aug. 16, 1947; came to U.S., 1969; s. Amir Chand and Dewki Bai (Dhamija) B.; m. Manju Dhamija, June 26, 1972; children: Monica, Meenakshi. BSME, Panjabi U., Patiala, India, 1968; MASc, U. Waterloo, Ont., Can., 1969; PhD, Johns Hopkins U., 1972. Postdoctoral rsch. assoc. Johns Hopkins U., Balt., 1972-73; rsch. assoc. McMaster U., Hamilton, Ont., 1973-74; asst. prof. U. Ala., Tuscaloosa, 1976-77; asst. prof. engring. mechanics U. Mo., Rolla, 1974-76, assoc. prof., 1977-81, prof., 1981-94; Clifton C. Garvin prof. Va. Polytech. Inst. & State U., Blacksburg, 1994—; mem. NRC Panel on Armaments, 1996—. Editor: Contemporary Research in Engineering Science, 1995; co-editor: Contemporary Research in the Mechanics and Mathematics of Materials, Internat. Ctr. for Numerical Methods in Engring., 1996, Constitutive Laws, Experiments and Numerical Implementation, Internat. Ctr. for Numerical Methods in Engring., 1995, Material Instabilities, Theory and Applications, 1994, Impact, Waves and Fracture, 1994; assoc. editor Jour. Engring. Materials and Tech., 1996—; mem. editl. bd. Internat. Jour. Plasticity, 1989—, Internat. Jour. Engring. Design and Analysis, 1992—, Continuum Mechanics and Thermodynamics, 1993—, Computational Mechanics, 1994-96; editor: Mathematics and Mechanics of Solids, 1995—; mng. editor Computational Mechanics, 1997—; reviewer for various jours. in field; contbr. numerous articles to profl. jours. Grantee NSF, 1980-83, 87—, Army Rsch. Office, 1985—, Office of Naval Rsch., 1994—; Alexander von Humboldt award for sr. scientists, 1992, Jai Krishna award Indian Geotech. Soc., 1994; inducted into Hopkins Soc. Scholars, 1993. Fellow ASME (chair elasticity com. 1995—, co-editor symposium procs. 1991, 94, 95, co-editor meeting procs. 1999, mem. awards nom. com. 1997—), Am. Acad. Mechanics, Am. Soc. Engring. Edn. (Centennial award 1993), Soc. Engring. Sci. (bd. dirs. 1991-96, editor meeting procs. 1982, v.p. 1995, pres. 1996); mem. Midwestern Mechanics Conf. (editor procs. 1991, bd. dirs. 1989-93), Soc. Natural Philosophy (treas. 1987-89, editor meeting procs. 1981). Office: Va Polytech Inst & State U Dept Engring Sci & Mechanic 220 Norris Hall Blacksburg VA 24061-0219

BATRA, TILAK RAJ, research scientist; b. Girotte, Sargodha, India, Dec. 11, 1936; came to U.S., 1964; s. Agya Ram and Jiwani Bai (Sachdeva) B.; m. Krishna Gulati, Sept. 9, 1962; children: Sanjay, Serena. B Vet. Sci., U. Jabalpur, India, 1959; M Vet. Sci., U. Agra, India, 1961; MS, U. Hawaii, 1966; PhD, U. Ill., 1968. Lectr. U. Jabalpur, India, 1961-64; rsch. asst. U. Ill., Urbana, 1966-68, rsch. assoc., 1968-69; rsch. programmer U. Guelph, Ont., Can., 1969-76; rsch. scientist Agr. Can., Ottawa, Ont., 1976—. Recipient East West Ctr. Scholarship, Honolulu, 1964-66, Japan Sci. and Tech. awad Japan Internat. Sci. and Tech. Ctr., Tokyo, 1990-91, excellence in genetics and physiology award Can. Animal Sci. Assn., Ottawa, Ont., 1993. Mem. Can. Soc. Animal Sci. (dir. 1986-88, sec.-treas. 1988-90), Am. Dairy Sci. Assn., Can. Animal Sci. Assn., Internat. Soc. Animal Genetics, Nat. Mastitis Coun. Avocations: reading, travel, hiking, swimming. Office: Centre Food & Animal Rsch, Agr. Can CEF, Ottawa, ON Canada

BATSAKIS, JOHN GEORGE, pathology educator; b. Petoskey, Mich., Aug. 14, 1929; s. George John and Stella (Vlahkis) B.; m. Mary Janet Savage, Dec. 28, 1957; children: Laura, Sharon, George. Student, Va. Mil. Inst., 1947, Albion Coll., Mich., 1948-50; M.D., U. Mich., 1954. Diplomate Am. Bd. Pathology. Intern George Washington Univ. Hosp., Washington, 1954-55; resident in pathology U. Mich. Hosp., Ann Arbor, 1955-59; prof. pathology U. Mich., Ann Arbor, 1969-79; chmn. dept. pathology M.D. Anderson Hosp. U. Tex., Houston, 1981-96; chm. and prof. emeritus dept pathology M.D. Anderson Hosp. U. Tex., 1996—; Ruth Legett Jones prof. U. Tex., Austin, 1982-96; adj. prof. oral pathology U. Tex. Dental Br., Houston; cons. Armed Forces Inst. Pathology, 1972—, VA Hosp., Ann Arbor, 1968-79; Hayes Martin lectr. Am. Soc. for Head and Neck Surgery, 1994; Gunnar Holmgren lectr. Swedish Nat. Ear, Nose, Throat Meeting, 1994; William Christopherson lectr. U. Louisville Dept. of Pathology, 1995; external examiner U. Hong Kong Dental Sch., 1995—; Francis A. Sooy lectr. dept. otolaryngology, head and neck surgery U. Calif., San Francisco, 1997; 2d Matthews lectr. dept. pathology Emory U., 1997; spkr. in field. Author: Tumors of the Head and Neck, 2d edit., 1979; editor Clin. Lab. Ann., 1981-86; co-editor Advances in Anatomic Pathology, 1994—; mem. editorial bd. 13 jours., 1974—; contbr. numerous articles to profl. jours. Bd. trustees, v.p. Mike Hogg Found., Houston, 1991—; trustee George C. Marshall Found., Lexington, Va., 1995—. Capt. U.S. Army, 1959-61. Recipient William H. Rorer award Am. Coll. Gastroenterology, 1972, Disting. Alumnus award Albion Coll., 1987, Reviewer of the Decade award AMA Archives Otolaryngology Head Neck Surgery, 1990, Presdl. award Am. Soc. Head and Neck Surgery, 1991, Harlan Spjut award Houston Soc. Clin. Pathologists, 1992, Honor award Am. Laryngologic Assn., 1995; Spl. Honored Guest of Am. Soc. for Head and Neck Surgery, 1993. Fellow ACP, Am. Soc. Clin. Pathologists, Am. Acad. Otolaryngology (assoc., honor award 1994), Coll. Am. Pathologists (chmn. commn. anatomic pathology), Royal Soc. Medicine. Republican. Episcopalian. Home: 1701 Hermann Dr Unit 3304 Houston TX 77004-7331 Office: 1452 W Bear Lake Rd NE Kalkaska MI 49646-9051

BATSCHA, ROBERT MICHAEL, museum executive; b. Rochester, N.Y., June 24, 1945; s. Theodor and Margaretha Batscha; 1 child, Eric T.G. BA, Queens Coll., 1967; M in Internat. Affairs, Columbia U., 1969, PhD in Internat. Relations, 1972. Sr. cons. OECD, Paris, 1972-76; assoc. prof. Queens Coll., N.Y.C., 1968-72, 75-81; adj. assoc. prof. Columbia U., N.Y.C., 1980-81; pres. Mus. of TV and Radio, N.Y.C., 1981—; chmn. faculty seminar in communication, Columbia U., 1977-85; pres. Population Resource Ctr., N.Y.C., 1976-81, bd. dirs. 1981—; with Ctr. for Communication, N.Y.C., 1979—; bd. dirs. Queens Coll. Author: Foreign Affairs News and the Broadcast Journalist, 1975, Dissemination of Social Science Research to Policy Makers, 1976. Mem. Century Assn. (N.Y.C.). Avocations: reading, horseback riding, travel. Office: The Mus of TV and Radio 25 W 52nd St New York NY 10019-6104

BATSELL, JACOB PAUL, journalist; b. Prescott, Ariz., June 4, 1974; s. Gary Alan Batsell and Linda Jane Dauwalder. BA in Journalism, Ariz. State U., 1996; postgrad., U. Tex., Austin, 1999—. Editor State Press, Ariz. State U., Tempe, 1994; corr. Ariz. Republic, Phoenix, 1992-96; reporting intern Chgo. Tribune, 1996, San Jose (Calif.) Mercury News, 1996-97; reporter Seattle Times, 1997-99. Flinn scholarship The Flinn Found., 1992-96. Mem. Soc. of Profl. Journalists, Investigative Reporters and Editors. Avocations: reading, bicycling, running. E-mail: jbatsell@aol.com.

BATSHAW, MARILYN SEIDNER, insurance professional; b. East Orange, N.J., Aug. 19, 1946; d. Gerald and Sylvia (Weinstein) Seidner; 1 child, Andrew Curt. BA, Newark State Coll., Union, N.J., 1968; MA, Kean Coll., Union, 1972, 0prin. cert., 1984. Cert. hearing aid dispenser, audiologist, elem. and deaf and hearing impaired tchr., supr., prin., N.J. Tchr. of deaf N.J. Dept. Edn., Trenton, 1972-74, audiologist, 1974-82, cons. in spl. edn., 1982-86; prin., dir. edn. Lakeview Sch., Cerebral Palsy Assn. Middlesex County, Edison, N.J., 1986-94; prin. ARC Essex Sch., Livingston, N.J., 1994-96; billing and eligibility case mgr. Prudential Health Care Group, Cranbury, N.J., 1997-99; dir. ESC Sch. West Amwell Campus Hunterdon County Edn. Svcs. Commn., Lambertville, N.J., 1999—. Officer Parents for Deaf Awareness. Mem. ASCD, N.J. ASCD, Ednl. Audiology Assn., Am. Speech-Lang. and Hearing Assn. (cert. clin. competence in audiology), N.J. Speech-Lang. and Hearing Assn., A.G. Bell Assn., Am. Auditory Soc., Am. Acad. Audiology, N.J. Acad. Audiology, Coun. Exceptional Children, N.J. Coun. Exceptional Children, Nat. Assn. Edn. Young Children. Home: 166 Westgate Dr Edison NJ 08820-1158 Office: ESC Sch West Amwell Campus 1422 Rt 179 Lambertville NJ 08530

BATSON, RICHARD NEAL, lawyer; b. Nashville, May 1, 1941; s. John H. and Mildred (Neal) B.; children: John Hayes, Richard Davis. BA cum laude, Vanderbilt U., 1963, JD, 1966. Bar: Ga. 1967. Law clk. to Judge Griffin B. Bell U.S. Ct. Appeals (5th cir.), Atlanta, 1966-67; assoc. Alston & Bird (formerly Alston, Miller & Gaines), Atlanta, 1967-71, ptnr., 1971—; spkr. Nat. Conf. Bankruptcy Judges, 1982, 86, 87, 88, 94, 96, Bank Lending Inst., 1986-87, also other instns. and assns.; adj. prof. Emory U. Sch. Law, 1994-95; co-lectr. Ga. State U., fall 1984; mem. bankruptcy rules com. Jud. Conf. U.S., 1993—. Co-author: Problem Loan Strategies, 1985, rev. 1998; contbg. author Bankruptcy Litigation Manual, 1990—; contbg. editor Norton Bankruptcy Law and Practice, 1990—. Sgt. USAF, 1967-73. Fellow Am. Coll. Trial Lawyers, Am. Coll. Bankruptcy (bd. dirs., pres. 1997—); mem. Atlanta Bar Assn. (pres. 1979-80), Am. Law Inst., Southeastern Bankruptcy Law Inst. (bd. dirs., pres. 1986-87), Nat. Bankruptcy Conf. (exec. com.). Avocations: hiking, outdoor activities. Office: Alston & Bird One Atlantic Ctr 1201 W Peachtree St NW Ste 4200 Atlanta GA 30309-3424

BATSTONE, JOANNA L., physicist. Computer scientist IBM Thomas J. Watson Rsch. Ctr., Hawthorne, N.Y. Recipient Robert Lansing Hardy Gold Medal award Minerals, Metals & Materials Soc., 1991, Cosslett award Microbeam Analysis Soc., 1989, Burton award Microscopy Soc. Am., 1995. Office: IBM Thomas J Watson Rsch Ctr 30 Saw Mill Rd Hawthorne NY 10532

BATT, ALYSE SCHWARTZ, technical officer; b. Bronx, N.Y., Aug. 8, 1960; d. Irwin Aaron and Beryl (Leff) Schwartz; m. David Charles Batt, Feb. 14, 1993; children: Shannon Paige, Megan Brooke. AAS in Data Processing, SUNY, Farmingdale, 1980; BBA in Bus. Computers, Hofstra U., 1987; MS in Mgmt. Engring., L.I. U., 1995. Programmer trainee State Ins. Fund, N.Y.C., 1980; programmer analyst cons. Bradford Nat. Corp., N.Y.C., 1981-83; programmer E.F. Hutton, N.Y.C., 1983; programmer analyst Chase Manhattan Bank, N.Y.C., 1983-87; sr. systems analyst Met. Life Ins. Co., N.Y.C., 1987-89; sr. programmer analyst Orion Pictures Corp., N.Y.C., 1989-91, Chase Manhattan Bank, N.Y.C., 1991—. Mem. Bayshore Skating Club, Commack Skating Club, Massapequa Road Runners Club, N.Y. Road Runners Club, Plainview-Old Bethpage Road Runners Club, Ladies Aux. Massapequa Fire Dept. (treas.). Republican. Jewish. Avocations: roller skating, running. Home: 153 Massachusetts Ave Massapequa NY 11758-4111

BATT, NICK, property and investment executive; b. Defiance, Ohio, May 6, 1952; s. Dan and Zenith (Dreher) B. BS, Purdue U., 1972; JD, U. Toledo, 1976. Asst. prosecutor Lucas County, Toledo, 1976-80, civil divsn. chief, 1980-83; village atty. Village of Holland, Ohio, 1980-91; law dir. City of Oregon, Ohio, 1984-91; spl. counsel State of Ohio, 1983-93; pres. Property & Mgmt. Connection, Inc., Toledo, 1993—. Mem. Maumee Valley Girl Scout Coun., Toledo, 1977-80; bd. mem. Bd. Cmty. Rels., Toledo, 1975-76; mem. Lucas County Dem. Exec. Com., 1981-83. Named One of Toledo's Outstanding Young Men, Toledo Jaycees, 1979. Mem. KC, Elks. Democrat. Roman Catholic. Office: 1732 Arlington Ave Toledo OH 43609-3050

BATT, PHILIP E., former governor; b. Wilder, Idaho, Mar. 4, 1927; m. Jacque Fallis, 1948; children: Bill, Rebecca, Leslie. Attended, U. Idaho, 1944-48. Elected mem. Idaho State Legislature, 1965-77; lt. gov. State of Idaho, 1978-82, gov., 1995-99. First pres. Idaho Food Producers; co-chmn. Wilder United Charity Auction; mem. Idaho Potato Growers Commn.; mem. bd. dirs. Wilder Farm Labor Com.; mem. bd. trustees Coll. Idaho; past pres. Idaho Hop Growers Assn., Hop Growers of Am., Homedale PTA.

BATT, RONALD ELMER, gynecologist, scientist; b. Buffalo, Sept. 24, 1933; s. Elmer Lawrence and Mary Catherine (Roll) B.; m. Carol Mary Schaab, Dec. 28, 1957; children: Paula, Douglas, Thomas, Neil, Jennifer, John; m. 2d, Kathleen Over Cansdale, May 19, 1982; stepchildren: William, James, Suzanne, Timothy, John, Mark. *Great, great, great grandfather Franz Joseph Batt and his wife Barbara Weber emigrated from Morschweiler, Alsace on October 20, 1836 aboard the Mary Ann, an American ship. Caught in a hurricane on November 29, Batt promised the Blessed Virgin to build a chapel in her honor if his family reached the U.S. safely. In 1853 he built the Maria Hilf Kapelle which immediately became a pilgrimage for all nationalities in Western New York. The Chapel of Our Lady Help of Christians was elevated to a Catholic parish in 1890 and was placed on the National Register of Historic Places at the Bicentennial of the U.S.A.* BS in Biology, Niagara U., 1954; MD, U. Buffalo, 1958. Intern Millard Fillmore Hosp., Buffalo, 1958-59; resident in ob-gyn SUNY, Buffalo, 1959-60, 62-66; rsch. fellow Harvard U. Med. Sch., 1963-64; asst. in surgery Peter Bent Brigham Hosp., Boston, 1963-64; fellow in gynecologic surgery Mayo Clinic, 1965; practice gynecology specializing in endometriosis and reproductive surgery Buffalo, 1966—; prof. clin. gynecology, clin. prof. social and preventive medicine SUNY Buffalo. *Dr. Batt's research has focused on endometriosis. His surgical studies include refinement of the operative technique for conservative surgery by laparoscopy and laparotomy; and extraluminal, wedge, segmental and low anterior resection for bowel endometriosis, published in Hunt's Atlas of Female Infertility Surgery, 1986, 92, 99. Original studies on pathophysiology include: Mullerianosis, the theory of a congenital form of endometriosis associated with pelvic peritoneal pockets; and the first observation of reversal of the secondary sex ratio in favor of female births following surgery for endometriosis. Other studies include: environmental toxins in patients with endometriosis and controls. Participated in genetic studies of endometriosis, Oxford University Oxegene study.* Co-author: Another Era: A Pictorial History of the School of Medicine and Biomedical Sciences, State University of New York at Buffalo 1846-1996; contbr. chpts. to books, articles to profl. jours. With M.C., USN, 1960-62. Fellow Royal Coll. Surgeons Can., Am. Coll. Obstetricians and Gynecologists, ACS; mem. Am. Soc. Reproductive Medicine, Soc. Reproductive Surgeons, Am. Assn. History Medicine, Internat. Soc. History Medicine. Office: Buffalo Children's Hosp 219 Bryant St Buffalo NY 14222

BATTAFARANO, DANIEL FRANCIS, rheumatologist; b. Darby, Pa., Jan. 17, 1956; s. Nicholas C. and Margaret Rose (Maguire) B.; m. Karen Susan Pietryka, Apr. 27, 1985; children: Margaret, Claire, Monica, Vincent. BS, U. Scranton, 1977; MA, Bryn Mawr Coll., 1979; DO, Phila. Coll. Osteo. Medicine, 1983. Diplomate Am. Bd. Internal Medicine, sub-bd. Rheumatology. Intern, resident Brooke Army Med. Ctr., San Antonio, 1983-87; internist, chief dept. medicine Nuernberg Hosp., West Germany, 1987-90; fellow in rheumatology, then rheumatologist Fitzsimmons Army Med. Ctr., Aurora, Colo., 1990-93; asst. chief rheumatology Brooke Army Med. Ctr., 1993-97, dir. Internal Med. resident rsch., 1994-97, dir., transitional year residency and intern coord., 1994-97; dep. dir. med. edn. U.S. Army Med. Command, Ft. Sam Houston, Tex., 1997-98; dir. continuing med. edn. U.S. Army, 1997-98; chief dept. med. sci. Acad. Health Scis., Ft. Sam Houston, Tex., 1998—; clin. asst. prof. medicine U. Tex. Health Sci. Ctr., San Antonio, 1993—; asst. prof. medicine Uniformed Svcs. U. Health Scis., Bethesda, Md., 1998-99; prof. medicine Uniformed Svcs. U. Health Scis., Bethesda, 1999—; affiliate clin. faculty, dept. medicine Brooke Army Med. Ctr., Ft. Sam Houston, Tex., 1997—, adj. prof. physical therapy Baylor U. Grad. Sch., Waco, Tex., 1998—. Reviewer of profl. jours.; mem. adv. bd. U.S. Army Med. Dept. Jour., 1998—. Med. adv. bd. Lupus Found. Am., San Antonio, 1994—. Col. U.S. Army, 1983—. Fellow ACP, Am. Coll. Rheumatology; mem. Assn. Mil. Surgeons U.S., Assn. Mil. Osteo. Physicians and Surgeons. Avocations: reading, travel, athletics, gardening, birding. Office: Acad Health Scis 3151 Scott Rd Fort Sam Houston TX 78234

BATTAGLIA, ANTHONY J., federal judge. Apptd. magistrate judge so. dist. U.S. Dist. Ct. Calif., 1993. Fax: (619) 702-9940. Office: 1145 US Courthouse 940 Front St San Diego CA 92101-8994

BATTAGLIA, ANTHONY SYLVESTER, lawyer; b. Binghamton, N.Y., Aug. 21, 1927; s. Sylvester Anthony and Helen B.; m. Catherine Jean, Oct. 1, 1972; children: Christina, Marc Anthony; children by previous marriage—Anthony, Sandra, Brian, Brenda Lee. A.A., U. Fla., 1948, B.A., 1949, LL.B., 1953, J.D., 1967. Bar: Fla. 1953, U.S. Dist. Ct. (mid. and so. dists.) Fla., U.S. Ct. Appeals (5th, 11th cirs.), U.S. Tax Ct., U.S. Ct. Appeals (D.C. cir.), U.S. Ct. Mil. Appeals; cert. ct. approved abritrator U.S. Dist. Ct., U.S. Supreme Ct. 1966. Asst. to U.S. dist. atty., So. Dist. Fla., 1953-56; ptnr. Parker, Parker & Battaglia, St. Petersburg, Fla., 1953-56, Parker, Battaglia & Ross, St. Petersburg, 1965-73, Parker, Battaglia, Parker, Ross & Ross, St. Petersburg, 1973-75, Battaglia, Parker, Ross, Parker & Stolba, St. Petersburg, 1975-76, Battaglia, Ross & Stolba, 1976-77, Battaglia, Ross, Stolba & Forlizzo, 1977-78, Battaglia, Ross & Forlizzo, 1978-80, Battaglia, Ross, Hastings, Dicus & Andrews, 1980-93, Battaglia, Ross, Dicus & Wein PA, 1993—; mem. Fla. Pub. Svc. Commn., 1971; chmn. bd. Metrocare, Inc., 1975-78; mem. grievance com. U.S. Dist. Ct., 1985-88; pres. Asst. U.S. Attys. Assn. for Mid. Dist. Fla., 1994; guest lectr. Stetson U., 1994; bd. dirs. Intervest Bank, 1st Bankers Tampa Bay, N.A., St. Petersburg, Nat. Bank Fla., St. Petersburg; chmn. adv. bd. 1st Union Nat. Bank, South Pinellas, Fla. Republican nat. committeeman, Fla., 1956-64, bd. dirs., Tampa div.; bd. dirs. San Carlo Opera Fla., 1972-74, pres., chmn. bd. dirs., Pinellas County div., 1974-76; bd. dirs. St. Petersburg Opera Co., 1976-77; chmn. bd. Pinellas County Arthritis Found., 1985; founding sponsor Civil Justice Found. Elected to U. Fla. Hall of Fame, 1951. Master Ferguson-White Am. Inn of Ct.; fellow Am. Coll. Mortgage Attys.; mem. ABA, ATLA (sustaining), Fla. Bar Assn. (bd. govs. 1993-99), St. Petersburg Bar Assn. (pres. 1990), Fed. Bar Assn. (v.p. Mid. Fla. dist.), Internat. Bar Assn., Hillsborough County Bar Assn., Acad. Fla. Trial Lawyers (judge student competition 1985), Am. Judicature Soc. (Supreme Ct. Hist. Soc. 1985-89), Nat. Assn. Criminal Def. Lawyers, Acad. Criminal Justice Scis., Fla. Criminal Def. Trial Lawyers, Criminal Def. Lawyers Hillsborough County, Pinellas County Trial Lawyers Assn. Roscoe Pound Am., Trial Lawyers Found. (judicial nominating com.), U. Fla. Nat. Alumni Assn., St. Petersburg C. of C. (gov.), Pinellas Inns Ct. (master bench), Fla. Bar Bd. of Govs. Roman Catholic. Clubs: Treasure Island Tennis and Yacht (bd. dirs.), Suncoast Tiger Bay, St. Petersburg Yacht, Nat. Italian Am. Found., Italian-Am. Unico Internat. Lodge: K.C. Home: 430 72nd St S Saint Petersburg FL 33707-1237 Office: 980 Tyrone Blvd N Saint Petersburg FL 33710-6333

BATTAGLIA, BASIL RICHARD, political party official, company executive; b. Wilmington, Del., Oct. 28, 1935; s. Bruno and Carmella (Cannatelli) B.; m. Sandra Battaglia; children: Lisa Maria, Michael Basil. AB, LaSalle Coll., 1959; LLB, Mt. Vernon Sch. Law, 1963. Owner title search firm, chmn. chmn. Rep. Eighth Councilman Dist., Wilmington; mem. Mayor's Citizens Adv. Com. Urban Renewal; v.p. Del. Fedn. Young Reps.; bd. dirs. Active Young Reps. Wilmington; mem. Rep. City Edn. Com.; chmn. Rep. Fund Raising Dinners; registrar in chancery New Castle County; chmn. Wilmington Rep. City Exec. Com.; fin. chmn. Del. State Rep. Party, 1993—; co-chmn. Presdl. Pers. Advt. Com.; mem. fin. com. George Bush for Pres. Campaign, 1988; chmn. Rep. Nat. Com. Northeastern Chmn. Com.; adminstr. Del. Mem Turnpike; mem. bd. Del. Visitors and Conv. Bur.; bd. dirs. Nat. Constn. Ctr. Named Outstanding Young Rep., Wilmington, 1969. Mem. Nat. Assn. County Officers. Roman Catholic. Office: PO Box 1955 Wilmington DE 19899-1955 also: Delaware State Republican Party 1401 Clinton St Wilmington DE 19806-1312

BATTAGLIA, BRIAN PETER, lawyer; b. St. Petersburg, Fla., Oct. 10, 1960; s. Anthony S. and Virginia A. (Knopick) B.; m. Nancy L. Pateras, Sept. 27, 1986; children: Jason Michael, Matthew Brian. BS in Criminology, Fla. State U., 1982; JD, Drake U., 1985; LLM in Health Law, Loyola U., Chgo. Bar: Fla. 1986, U.S. Dist. Ct. (mid. dist.) Fla. 1987, U.S. Ct. Appeals (11th cir.) 1992, U.S. Supreme Ct. 1993. Cert. mediator cir. and county ct., Fla., 1995—. Assoc. Battaglia, Ross, Dicus and Wein, P.A., Tampa, St. Petersburg, 1986-90, shareholder litigation dept., 1990—, chair health law practice group; adj. prof. St. Petersburg Jr. Coll. People's Law Sch., 1988-92, Stetson U. Coll. of Law, 1997-99; mem. 6th cir. unlicensed practice of law com. Fla. Supreme Ct., 1993-95, chmn., 1995. Contbr. articles to law jours. Bd. dirs. Pinellas Opportunity Coun., 1988-92, pres., 1990-92; bd. dirs. Head Start, 1989-91, Bay Area Legal Svcs., 1994-97; v.p. Comty. Law Program, 1990-92, pres., 1992-95. Recipient pro bono cert. of appreciation Cmty. Law Program, 1993. Mem. ABA (com. on condemnation, zoning and land use litigation 1991-95), Am. Health Lawyers Assn., Fla. Bar (vice chmn. eminent domain com. 1994-95, health law sect. 1996-99, Pres.'s Pro Bono Svc. award 6th jud. cir. 1994), Am. Judicature Soc., Hillsborough County Bar Assn., St. Petersburg Bar Assn. (exec. com. 1993-95, 99—, Pro Bono award 1990, chair law day com. 1999), Delta Theta Phi, Alpha Phi Sigma. BPBlaw@aol.com. Office: 980 Tyrone Blvd N Saint Petersburg FL 33710-6333

BATTAGLIA, FREDERICK CAMILLO, physician; b. Weehawken, N.J., Feb. 15, 1932; m. Jane B. Donohue; children—Susan Kate, Thomas Frederick. BA, Cornell U., 1953; MD, Yale U., 1957; DSc (hon.), U. Ind. Diplomate: Am. Bd. Pediatrics. Intern in pediatrics Johns Hopkins Hosp., 1957-58; USPHS postdoctoral fellow biochemistry Cambridge (Eng.) U., 1958-59; Josiah Macy Found. fellow in physiology Yale U. Med. Sch., 1959-60; asst. resident, fellow in pediatrics Johns Hopkins Hosp., 1960-61, resident, fellow, 1961-62; USPHS surgeon lab. perinatal physiology NIH, San Juan, P.R., 1962-64; asst. prof., Johns Hopkins Med. Sch., 1963-65; mem. faculty U. Colo. Med. Sch., Denver, 1965—; prof. pediatrics, prof. Ob-Gyn U. Colo. Med. Sch., 1969—, dir. div. perinatal medicine, 1970-74, chmn. dept. pediatrics, 1974-89; attending pediatrician Children's, Denver Gen., Fitzsimons Gen. hosps. Assoc. editor: Pediatrics, 15th edit; med. progress contbg. editor: Jour. Pediatrics, 1966-74; mem. editorial bd.: European Jour. Ob-Gyn, 1971—; assoc. J. Perinatal med. editor Biol. Neonate, 1979—; contbr. numerous articles med. jours. Mem. Assn. Am. Physicians, Am. Acad. Pediatrics (E. Mead Johns award 1969), Am. Gynecologic and Obstet. Soc., Soc. Pediatric Rsch. (pres. 1976-77), Perinatal Rsch. Soc. (pres. 1974-75), Western Soc. Pediatric Rsch. (pres. 1987—), Soc. Gynecol. Investigation, Am. Pediatric Soc. (pres. 1996), Internat. Congress Perinatal Medicine (pres. 1996), Soc. Gynecol. Investigation (coun. 1969-72), Soc. Exptl. Biology and Medicine, Inst. of Medicine, Phi Beta Kappa, Sigma Xi. Home: 2975 E Cedar Ave Denver CO 80209-3211 Office: Fitzsimons Bldg 260 Mail Stop F 441 PO Box 6508 Aurora CO 80045-0508

BATTAGLIA, LYNNE ANN, prosecutor. U.S. atty. Md., 1993—; chief of staff Office of U.S. Sen. Barbara A. Mikulski. Office: US Attys Office US Courthouse Rm 6625 101 W Lombard St Baltimore MD 21201-2626

BATTAT, EMILE A., management executive; b. Mar. 17, 1938; s. Abe N. and Marguerite (Elias) B.; m. Vivian L. Masri, Apr. 12, 1964; children: Lisa, David. BS, MIT, 1959, MS, 1960; MBA, Harvard U., 1962. Mktg. analyst Standard Oil Co., N.Y.C. and N.J., 1962-65; mgr. corp. diversification Kaiser Aluminum, Oakland, Calif., 1965-69; v.p., dir. Kaiser Internat., Oakland, 1969-78; pres., CEO, dir. Minemet Inc., Stamford, Conn., 1978-94; pres. Piedmont Enterprises Inc., Riverside, Conn., 1994—; chmn., CEO Atrion Corp., 1998—. Treas. Harbor Point Assn., 1987-97tax collector Harbor Point Tax Dist., 1987-97. Mem. Sigma Xi, Pi Tau Sigma, Tau Beta Pi. Office: 1117 E Putnam Ave Ste 200 Riverside CT 06878-1333

BATTEN, ALAN HENRY, astronomer; b. Tankerton, Kent, Eng., Jan. 21, 1933; emigrated to Can., 1959, naturalized, 1975; s. George Cuthbert and Gladys (Greenwood) B.; m. Lois Eleanor Dewis, July 30, 1960; children: Michael Henry John, Margaret Eleanor. BSc with 1st class honors, U. St. Andrews, Scotland, 1955, DSc, 1974; PhD, U. Manchester, Eng., 1958. Rsch. asst. in astronomy, jr. tutor St. Anselm Residence Hall, U. Manchester, 1958-59; postdoctoral fellow Dominion Astrophys. Obs., Victoria, B.C., Can., 1959-61; mem. staff Dominion Astrophys. Obs., 1961-91, assoc. rsch. officer, 1970-76, sr. rsch. officer, 1976-91, guest scientist, 1991—; part-time lectr. astronomy U. Victoria, 1961-64; guest investigator Vatican Obs., 1970, Inst. de Astronomia y Fisica del Espacio, Buenos Aires, 1972. Author: Binary and Multiple Systems of Stars, 1973, Resolute and Undertaking Characters: The Lives of Wilhelm and Otto Struve, 1988; editor: Extended Atmospheres and Circumstellar Matter in Spectroscoscopic Binary Systems, 1973, Algols, 1989; sr. author: Eighth Catalogue of the Orbital Elements of Spectroscopic Binary Systems, 1989; co-editor: The Determination of Radial Velocities and Their Applications, 1967; translator: L'Observation des Etoiles Doubles Visuelles par P. Couteau, 1981; contbr. articles to profl. jours. Pres. Willows Elem. Sch. PTA, Victoria, 1971-73; mem. Anglican Ch. Can. Diocesan Synod, B.C., 1966-68, 74; mem. adv. coun. Ctr. Advanced Studies in Religion and Soc., U. Victoria, 1993—, chmn., 1997—. Erskine Vis. fellow U. Canterbury, New Zealand, 1995; recipient Queen's Silver Jubilee medal Can., 1977. Fellow Royal Soc. Can. (convenor interdisciplinary sect. 1980-81, mem. coun. 1980-81), Royal Astron. Soc., Explorers Club; mem. Internat. Astron. Union (v.p. 1985-91, pres. commn. 30 1976-79, pres. commn. 42 1982-85, chmn. nat. orgn. com. XVII Gen. Assembly 1975-79), Royal Astron. Soc. Can. (pres. 1976-78, hon. pres. 1993-98, editor jour. 1981-88), Astron. Soc. Pacific (v.p. 1965-68), Can. Astron. Soc. (pres. 1972-74), Am. Astron. Socs., Ancient Soc. Coll. Youths. Home: 2987 Westdowne Rd, Victoria, BC Canada V8R 5G1 Office: Dominion Astrophys Obs, 5071 W Saanich Rd, Victoria, BC Canada V8X 4M6

BATTEN, FRANK, newspaper publisher, cable broadcaster; b. Norfolk, Va., Feb. 11, 1927; s. Frank and Dorothy (Martin) B.; m. Jane Neal Parke; children: Frank, Mary, Dorothy. Grad., Culver Mil. Acad., 1945; AB, U. Va., 1950; MBA, Harvard U., 1952; LittD (hon.), Washington and Lee U., 1996. Reporter The Norfolk Ledger-Star; with advt. and circulation depts. The Virginian-Pilot and Norfolk Ledger-Star newspapers; v.p. The Norfolk Virginian-Pilot and Norfolk Ledger-Star newspapers, 1953, pub., 1954—; chmn. bd. Landmark Comm., Norfolk, 1967-97, chmn. exec. com., 1998—; also chmn. Greensboro (N.C.) News & Record; chmn. Roanoke (Va.) Times, KLAS-TV; dir. Capital-Gazette Communications Inc., Annapolis, Md.; 2d vice chmn. AP, 1977-79, 1st vice chmn., 1979-81, chmn. bd., 1982-87; founder The Weather Channel, 1982; formerly chmn. AP Pension, Tech., Fgn. ops. coms.; past chmn. AP Nominating Com., Va. AP Members; former dir. So. Newspaper Pubs. Assn.; former chmn. bd. Newspaper Advt. Bur. Trustee Culver Ednl. Found., U.S. Naval Acad. Found., So. Newspaper Pubs. Found., U. Va. Grad. Bus. Sch. Sponsors, Hollins Coll.; past chmn. bd. Old Dominion U.; past vice chmn. State Coun. Higher Edn. for Va.; past pres. and campaign chmn. Norfolk Area United Fund; chmn. com. for Internat. Naval Rev., 1957; mem. bd. visitors Coll. William and Mary. With U.S. Merchant Marine, World War II, also USNR. Recipient Norfolk's First Citizen award, 1966, Alumni Achievement award Harvard Bus. Sch., 1998. Mem. Newspaper Assn. of Am. (dir.), Delta Kappa Epsilon. Episcopalian. Office: Landmark Communications Inc 150 W Brambleton Ave Norfolk VA 23510-2018*

BATTEN, JANE KIMBERLY, olympic athlete; b. McRae, Ga., Mar. 29, 1969. Grad., Fla. State U., 1991. Winner 2d place NCAA 400 meter hurdles, 1990, 3rd place 400 meter hurdles, 1991, 1st place 400 meter hurdles Mobil/USA Championships, 1991, 5th place World Championships, 1991, 4th place, 1992, Silver medal 400 meter hurdles Atlanta Olympics, 1996. Office: USA Track & Field PO Box 120 Indianapolis IN 46206-0120*

BATTENFELD, JOHN LEONARD, educator, journalist; b. Norwalk, Conn., Aug. 25, 1943; s. John Leonard and Mary Florence Fay B.; m. Meredith J. Charpentier, Apr. 16, 1968 (div. Sept. 1975); m. Yasuyo Aso, Apr. 23, 1977; children: John O., Sachiko C. BA, NYU, 1969; MFA, New Sch. Social Rsch., 1998. Journalist UPI, N.Y.C., 1969-76; asst. press sec. Mayor's Office, N.Y.C., 1976-81; editor UPI, N.Y.C., 1981-83; fgn. corr. UPI, Tokyo, 1983-85, Reuters Ltd., Hong Kong, New Delhi, & Seoul, 1985-95; lectr. NYU, N.Y.C., 1999—, Boston U., 1998—; mng. dir. CommuniKana, Inc., Westport, Conn., 1995—; freelance writer. With USNR, 1965-67. Mem. Soc. Profl. Journalists, Pub. Rels. Soc. Am., Assn. Edn. Mass Comm. & Journalism. Democrat. Roman Catholic. Office: PO Box 3324 Westport CT 06880

BATTERDEN, JAMES EDWARD, business executive; b. Balt., Dec. 25, 1925; s. James Edward and Mary Elizabeth (Noonan) B.; m. Berenice Brown, Apr. 22, 1950; children: James, Julia, Mark, Mary, Stephen, Margaret, John, Brigid. Student U. Md., 1946-47, U. Balt., 1947-48, Balt. Inst., 1948-50. Auditor, State of Md., Balt., 1947-52; salesman Uniroyal Corp., Balt., 1952-61, Comml. Envelope Co., Balt., 1961-63; salesman Oscar T. Smith Co., Balt., 1963-97, v.p., 1971-97, ret. 1997, also dir. With USN, 1944-46. Mem. VFW, Mt. St. Joseph Alumni Assn. (Hall of Fame 1987). Democrat. Roman Catholic. Lodge: K.C. Avocations: theatre, travel, cards, ping-pong, swimming.

BATTERMAN, BORIS WILLIAM, physicist, educator, academic director; b. N.Y.C., Aug. 25, 1930; children: Robert W., William E., Thomas A. Student, Cooper Union Coll., 1949-50, Technische Hochschule, Stuttgart, Germany; SB, MIT, 1952, PhD, 1956. Mem. tech. staff Bell Tel. Labs., Murray Hill, N.J., 1956-65; assoc. prof. Cornell U., Ithaca, N.Y., 1965-67, prof. applied and engring. physics, 1967—, dir. Sch. Applied and Engring. Physics,, 1974-78, dir. Synchrotron Radiation Lab. (CHESS),, 1978-97, Walter S. Carpenter Jr. prof. engring., 1985—; mem. U.S.A. Nat. Com. Crystallography, NAS, 1969-72. Assoc. editor Jour. Crystal Growth, 1964-74. Fulbright scholar, 1953-54; Guggenheim fellow, 1971, Fulbright Hayes fellow, 1971, Alexander von Humboldt fellow, 1983. Fellow AAAS, Am. Phys. Soc. Office: Cornell Univ Wilson Lab Ithaca NY 14853

BATTERMAN, STEVEN CHARLES, engineering mechanics and bioengineering educator, forensic engineering and biomechanics consultant; b. Bklyn., Aug. 15, 1937; s. Jacob and Anna (Abramowitz) B.; m. Judith Wilpon, Mar. 29, 1959; children: Scott David, Risa Karen, Daniel Adam. BCE, Cooper Union, 1959; ScM (NSF fellow), Brown U., 1961, PhD, 1964; MA (hon.), U. Pa., 1971. Mem. faculty U. Pa., 1964-97, prof. mech. engring. and applied mechanics, 1974-79; assoc. prof. orthopaedic surgery rsch. U. Pa. (Sch. Medicine), 1972-74, prof. orthopaedic surgery research, 1974-97; prof. biomechanics in vet. medicine U. Pa Sch. Vet Medicine, 1975-84, prof. bioengring., 1974-97; emeritus prof. Sch. Engring. and Applied Sci., Sch. Medicine U. Pa., 1997—; pres. Cons. Assocs., Inc., Cherry Hill, N.J.; forensic enring. and biomechanics cons. to govt., industry, ins. cos., attys. Contbr. numerous articles to profl. jours.; patentee apparatus for acoustically determining periodontal health. Recipient S.R. Warren Disting. Teaching award U. Pa., 1982. Mem. ASCE, ASME, Am. Acad. Mechanics, Am. Soc. Engring. Edn., Biomed. Engring. Soc., Soc. Exptl. Mech., Soc. Automotive Engrs., Am. Soc. Safety Engrs., Am. Acad. Forensic Scis. (Founder's award 1992, pres.-elect 1993-94, pres. 1994-95), Assn. for Advancement Automotive Medicine, Sigma Xi, Tau Beta Pi, Chi Epsilon. Jewish. Home: 109 Charlann Cir Cherry Hill NJ 08003-2906 Office: U Pa 120 Hayden Hall Philadelphia PA 19104

BATTERSBY, HAROLD RONALD, anthropologist, archaeologist, linguist; b. Guildford, Surrey, Eng., Nov. 16, 1922; came to U.S., 1960, naturalized, 1972; s. Eric and Lillian (Darnell) B.; m. Betty Yertchenig O'Hannesian, Apr. 22, 1944. BA in Modern Near Eastern Studies, U. Toronto, Can., 1960; Ph.D. in Altaic Studies-Anthropology Linguistics, Ind. U., 1969. Corr. Surrey Times, London-Guildford, 1947-55; adv. dir. Turkish Post, Istanbul, 1949-53; instr. English Istanbul Med. Faculty, 1948-49, Amerikan Lisan ve San'at Dersanesi, Istanbul, 1948-54, Pangalti Ermeni Orta Okulu, Istanbul, 1949-56; coordinator athletic events USO, Istanbul, 1948-54; asst. Royal Ont. Mus., Toronto, 1957-59; asst. mgr. City of Toronto, 1957-59; research asst. in med. anthropology U. Pitts., 1960-62; asst. Ind. U., Bloomington, 1962-69; assoc. prof. anthropology SUNY-Geneseo, 1970—, dir. linguistics program, 1978—; Author: Anatolian Archaeology: A Comprehensive Bibliograph, 2 vols., 1976; sect. editor: Altaic and Uralic Studies, Ultimate Reality and Meaning, 1982—; contbr. articles to profl. jours., translations, proofreading and editing of Biblical, religious beliefs, ethnographic and linguistic texts into Altaic langs. and from Altaic langs. into English. Author: Anatolian Archaeology: A Comprehensive Bibliograph, 2 vols., 1976; sect. editor: Altaic and Uralic Studies, Ultimate Reality and Meaning, 1982—; contbr. articles to profl. jours., translations, proofreading and editing of Biblical ethnographic and linguistic texts into Altaic langs. and from Altaic langs. into English. Served with RAF Vol. Res., 1939-46. NDEA fellow; Ind. U. grantee; Geneseo Found. grantee, 1973, 77, 78—. Fellow Royal Anthrop. Inst. Gt. Brit. and Ireland, Am. Anthrop. Assn., Royal Asiatic soc.; mem. Am. Oriental Soc., Royal Ctrl. Asian Soc., Royal Soc. Asian Affairs, Hakluyt Soc., Internat. Soc. Oriental Rsch., Middle East Inst., Chgo. Anthrop. Soc., Inst. Ency. of Human Ideas on Ultimate Reality and Meaning, Brit. Inst. Archaeology at Ankara, Am. Oriental Soc., Am. Soc. Study People of Ea. Europe and No. and Ctrl. Asia, Linguistic Soc. Am., Niagara Linguistic Soc., N.Y. State Coun. Linguistics, Soc. Armenian Studies, Zoryan Inst., Ind. U. Alumni Assn., The Smithsonian Assocs., The Wilson Ctr. Assocs., Lambda Alpha. Republican. Episcopalian. Club: Ind. U. Linguistics. Home: 7339 Groveland Station Rd Groveland NY 14462 Office: SUNY Anthropology Dept Sturges 13F Office and Lab Geneseo NY 14454*

BATTERSBY, JAMES LYONS, JR., English language educator; b. Pawtucket, R.I., Aug. 24, 1936; s. James Lyons and Hazel Irene (Deuel) B.; m. Lisa J. Kiser, Aug. 6, 1990; 1 child, Julie Ann. BS magna cum laude, U. Vt., 1961; MA, Cornell U., 1962, Ph.D., 1965. Asst. prof. U. Calif., Berkeley, 1965-70; assoc. prof. English Ohio State U., Columbus, 1970-82, prof., 1982—; cons. Ohio State U. Press, U. Ky. Press, U. Calif. Press, Prentice-Hall, McGraw Hill, Fairleigh Dickinson U. Press, U. Mich. Press, U. Ala. Press. Author: Typical Folly: Evaluating Student Performance in Higher Education, 1973, Rational Praise and Natural Lamentation: Johnson, Lycidas and Priciples of Criticism, 1980, Elder Olson: An Annotated Bibliography, 1983, Paradigms Regained: Pluralism and the Practice of Criticism, 1991, Reason and the Nature of Texts, 1996; contbg. author: Domestick Privacies: Samuel Johnson and the Art of Biography, 1987, Fresh Reflections on Samuel Johnson: Essays in Criticism, 1987, Criticism, History and Intertextuality, 1988, Beyond Poststructuralism: The Speculations of Theory and the Experience of Reading, 1996; also articles. With U.S. Army, 1954-57. Woodrow Wilson fellow, 1961-62, 64-65, Samuel S. Fels fellow, 1964-65, U. Calif. Summer Faculty fellow, 1966, Humanities Research fellow, 1969; recipient Kidder Medal U. Vt., 1961. Mem. MLA, Am. Soc. 18th Century Studies, Midwest Soc. 18th Century Studies, Royal Oak Found., Phi Beta Kappa, Phi Kappa Phi, Kappa Delta Pi. Home: 472 Clinton Heights Ave Columbus OH 43202-1277

BATTESTIN, MARTIN CAREY, English language educator; b. N.Y.C., Mar. 25, 1930; s. Martin Augustus and Marion (Kirkland) B.; m. Ruthe Rootes, June 14, 1963; children: David, Catherine. BA summa cum laude, Princeton U., 1952, PhD, 1958. English master Westminster Sch., Simsbury, Conn., 1952-53; instr. Wesleyan U., Middletown, Conn., 1956-58, asst. prof., 1958-61; asst. prof. U. Va., Charlottesville, 1961-63, assoc. prof., 1963-67, prof., 1967-75, William R. Kenan, Jr. prof. English, 1975-98, emeritus prof., 1998—, chmn. dept. English, 1983-86; vis. prof. Rice U., Houston, 1967-68; assoc. Clare Hall, Cambridge (Eng.) U., 1972. Author: The Moral Basis of Fielding's Art, 1959, 75, The Providence of Wit, 1974, 89, Henry Fielding: A Life, 1989, 2d edit., 1993, New Essays by Henry Fielding, 1989, 93; editor: Joseph Andrews (Henry Fielding), 1961, 67, Shamela (Henry Fielding), 1961, Tom Jones (Henry Fielding), 1974, 2d edit., 1975, Amelia (Henry Fielding), 1983, Tom Jones: A Collection of Critical Essays, 1968, British Novelists, 1660-1800, 1985; co-editor: The Correspondence of Henry and Sarah Fielding, 1993. Am. Coun. Learned Socs. fellow, 1960-61, 72; Guggenheim fellow, 1964-65; Sr. fellow Coun. Humanities, Princeton U., 1971; Ctr. for Advanced Studies fellow U. Va., 1974-75; NEH Bicentennial Rsch. fellow, 1975-76. Mem. MLA (chmn. sec. VII 1967, adv. editor publs. 1982-86), South Atlantic Modern Lang. Assn., Am. Soc. 18th Century Studies, Internat. Assn. Univ. Profs. English (chmn. sect. V 1990-92), Assn. of Lit. Scholars and Critics, The Johnsonians. Mem. Ch. of England. Home: 1832 Westview Rd Charlottesville VA 22903-1648 Office: U Va Dept English Bryan Hall Charlottesville VA 22903-3289

BATTEY, JAMES F., federal agency administrator. BS in Physics with honors, Calif. Inst. Tech.; MD, PhD, Stanford U. Mem. staff, then head molecular structure sect. lab. biol. chemistry Nat. Cancer Inst., NIH; chief molecular neurosci. sect. lab. neurochemistry Nat. Inst. Neurol. Disorders and Stroke; acting dir. divsn. intramural rsch. Nat. Inst. Deafness and Other Comm. Disorders, Bethesda, Md., 1995—, dir., 1998—; adj. prof. George Washington U. Sch. Medicine. Author: (with Leonard Davis and Michael Kuehl) Basic Methods in Molecular Biology; contbr., co-contbr. over 120 rsch. articles to profl. jours. Recipient Commendation medal Pub. Health Svc., 1990, Outstanding Svc. medal, 1994; postdoctoral fellow Harvard Med. Sch. Office: Nat Inst Deafness & Comm Disorders Bldg 31 31 Center Dr MSC 2320 Bethesda MD 20892-2320

BATTEY, RICHARD HOWARD, judge; b. Aberdeen, S.D., 1929; m. Shirley Ann Battey; children: David, Russell, Dianne. BA, U. S.D., 1950, JD, 1953. Bar: S.D. 1953. Atty. City of Redfield, S.D., 1956-63; state's atty. Spink County, S.D., 1959-65, 81-84; chief judge U.S. Dist. Ct. S.D., Rapid City, 1994—, sr. judge, 1999—; practicing atty., Redfield, 1956-85; mem. criminal laaw com. Jud. Conf. U.S., 1993-99; adj. prof. U. S.D., 1973-75. Served with AUS, 1953-55. Mem. Dist. Judges Assn. 8th Cir. Ct. Appeals (past pres.). Office: US Dist Ct 318 Fed Bldg 515 9th St Rapid City SD 57701-2626

BATTIN, RICHARD HORACE, astronautical engineer; b. Atlantic City, Mar. 3, 1925; s. Horace Leslie and Martha Esther (Scheu) B.; m. Margery Katheryn Milne, Aug. 25, 1947; children: Thomas, Pamela, Jeffrey. BS, MIT, 1945, PhD, 1951; DSc (hon.), Tex. A&M U., 1999. Instr. math. MIT, Cambridge, 1946-51, research mathematician Instrumentation Lab., 1951-56, adj. prof. aero. and astronautics, 1979-95, sr. lectr., 1995—; sr. staff mem. Ops. Research Group, Arthur D. Little, Inc., Cambridge, 1956-58; tech. dir. Apollo Mission Devel.; assoc. dir. Instrumentation Lab., 1958-73; assoc. head NASA program dept. Charles Stark Draper Lab., Inc., 1973-87, mem. aerospace safety adv. panel, 1980-86. Author: (with J.H. Laning, Jr.) Random Processes in Automatic Control, 1956, Astronautical Guidance, 1964, An Introduction to the Mathematics and Methods of Astrodynamics, 1987; Mem. editorial com.: Celestial Mechanics, 1968-74. Pres. Project Impact, 1981-90; Mem. Lexington (Mass.) Town Meeting, 1956—; mem. Lexington Appropriations Com., 1958-64. Lt. (j.g.) Supply Corps USNR, 1945-46. Recipient Louis W. Hill Space Transp. award AIAA, 1972, Mechanics and Control of Flight award, AIAA, 1978; Superior Achievement award Inst. of Navigation, 1980; Teaching award dept. aeros. and astronautics M.I.T., 1981, Pendray Aerospace Lit. award, AIAA, 1987, von Karman Disting. Lectureship award in astronautics AIAA, 1989. Fellow AIAA (hon., assoc. editor jour. 1967-87, chmn. astrodynamics tech. com. 1978-80, dir. tech. 1979-82), Am. Astronautical Soc. (Dirk Brouwer award 1996); mem. Nat. Acad. Engring., Internat. Acad. Astronautics, Celestial Mechanics Inst., Sigma Xi, Hancock Men's Club (pres. 1974-76). Home: 15 Paul Revere Rd Lexington MA 02421-6632 Office: MIT 77 Massachusetts Ave Cambridge MA 02139-4307

BATTIN, R(OSABELL) RAY (ROSABELL HARRIET RAY), audiologist, neuropsychologist; b. Rock Creek, Ohio; d. Harry Walter and Sophia (Boldt) Ray; A.B., U. Denver, 1948; M.S., U. Mich., 1950; Ph.D., U. Fla., 1959; postgrad. U. Miami (Fla.) Sch. of Medicine, 1957, U. Iowa, 1958; Diplomate Am. Bd. Profl. Disability Cons., Am. Bd. Forensic Examiners (cert. forensic examiner, cert. med. examiner); diplomate forensic neuropsychology; devel. psychology; diplomate psychol. assessment; m. Tom C. Battin, Aug. 24, 1949. Instr. in speech pathology U. Denver, 1949-50; audiologist Ann Arbor (Mich.) Sch., 1950-51; audiologist Houston (Tex.) Speech and Hearing Center, 1954-56; dir. speech pathology-psychology Hedgecroft Hosp. and Rehab. Center, Houston, 1956-59; audiologist with Drs. Guilford, Wright and Draper, Houston, 1959-63; pvt. practice in psychology, audiology and psycholinguistics, Houston, 1959—; clin. instr. dept. otolaryngology U. Tex. Sch. Medicine, Galveston, 1964-80; dir. of audiology vestibulography and speech pathology lab. Houston Ear Nose and Throat Hosp. Clinic, 1963-73; adj. clin. instr. U. Houston, 1981-86; lectr. The First Word program Sta. KUHT-TV, 1959; guest lectr. to various workshops and schs., 1959—; v.p. Behavioral Perceptual Ctr., 1986—; neuropsychol. cons. edn. div. Environ. Health Screening Lab., 1989—, mem. adv. bd., 1989—. Bd. dirs. Juvenile Ct. Vols., 1980-83, Children's Resource and Info. Ctr., 1981-85, Dyslexic Adult Support Services, 1986-90; bd. dirs. Music Fest, 1991—; mem. adv. bd. Life Choices, 1993—; bd. dirs. Houston Repretory Theater, 1993—. Lic. psychologist, Tex. Recipient Gold award for Ednl. Exhibit, Am. Acad. Pediatrics, 1969, Lifetime Achievement award Houston Psychol. Assn., 1996. Fellow Am. Speech and Hearing Assn. (profl. services bd. 1967-70, com. on pvt. practice 1971-74), World Acad. Inc.; mem. Am. Coll. Forensic Examiners, Acad. Pvt. Practice in Speech Pathology and Audiology (pres. 1968-70), Am. Psychol. Assn., Tex. Speech and Hearing Assn. (v.p. 1968), Cleft Palate Assn., Tex., Houston psychol. assns., Harris County Biofeedback Soc. (pres. 1984), Acad. of Aphasia, Internat. Assn. of Logopedics and Phoniatrics, Am. Auditory Soc., Orthopsychiat. Assn., Am. Biofeedback Soc., Tex. Biofeedback Soc., Sigma Alpha Eta. Author: (with C. Olaf Haug) Speech and Language Delay, 1964; Vestibulography, 1974; Private Practice: Guidelines for Speech Pathology and Audiology, 1971; editor (with Donna R. Fox) Private Practice in Audiology and Speech and Language Pathology, 1978; contbr. author: Seminars in Speech, Language, Hearing (Northern); Auditory Disorders in School Children (Roeser and Downs); Current Therapy of Communications Disorder (Perkins); editor Jour. Acad. Pvt. Practice in Speech Pathology and Audiology, 1981-84; contbr. articles in field to profl. jours.; author (with Irvin A. Kraft) The Dysynchronous Child (film), 1971; The Battin Clinic Language Learning Screening Test for Preschool Children, 1985., The Battin Scale of Parent's Attitude Toward Family Experience and Need for Child Cochlear Implant Candidates. Home: 3837 Meadow Lake Ln Houston TX 77027-4029 Office: Battin Clinic 3931 Essex Ln Houston TX 77027-5113

BATTINO, RUBIN, chemistry educator, retired; b. N.Y.C., June 22, 1931; s. Sadik and Anna (Decastro) B.; m. Charlotte Alice Ridinger, Jan. 30, 1960; children—David Rubin, Benjamin Sadik. B.A., CCNY, 1953; M.A., Duke U., 1954, Ph.D., 1957; M.S., Wright State U., 1978. Lic. profl. clin. counselor, Ohio. Research chemist Leeds & Northrup Co., Phila., 1956-57; asst. prof. Ill. Inst. Tech., Chgo., 1957-66; prof. Wright State U., Dayton, Ohio, 1966-95, ret., 1995, prof. emeritus, 1995—; vis. prof. U. Vienna, Austria, Oxford U., Eng., Hebrew U. Jerusalem, Ben Gurion U., U. New Eng., Australia, U. Canterbury, N.Z., Okayama U. Sci., Japan, Rhodes U., U. Turku, Finland. Author: (with S.E. Wood) Thermodynamics-An Introduction, 1968; Oxygen and Ozone, 1981, Nitrogen and Air, 1982, (with S.E. Wood) The Thermodynamics of Chemical Systems, 1990, (with T.L. South) Ericksonian Approaches, A Comprehensive Manual, 1997; mem. editorial bd. Solubility Data Series, Jour. Chem. and Engring. Data; contbr. tech. papers to profl. jours. Fulbright fellow, 1979; recipient Outstanding Tchr. award Wright State U., 1979, 93, Outstanding Engr. award Engring. and Sci. Found., Dayton, 1985, Bd. Trustees award Wright State U., 1985. Mem. AAAS, Am. Chem. Soc., Internat. Union Pure and Applied Chemistry (commn.), Sigma Xi, Phi Lambda Upsilon. Democrat. Jewish. Office: Wright State U Chemistry Dept Dayton OH 45435

BATTISTELLI, JOSEPH JOHN, electronics executive; b. Bridgeport, Conn., Oct. 22, 1930; s. Joseph John and Maria (Brunetti) B.; m. Helen Josephine Thompson, Apr. 5, 1961; children: Jay Dominick, Randall Victor. BSEE, U. Conn., 1958; MSEE, U. Ariz., 1960. Registered profl. engr., Ariz., Ohio. V.p. Electro Tech. Analysis Corp., Tucson, 1960-68; rsch. engr. Ohio U., Athens, 1968-72; sr. engr. Hughes Aircraft Co., Culver City, Calif., 1972-74; dir. engring. Lockheed Aircraft Co., Ont., Calif., 1974-80; dir. Riyadh area Litton Industries, Beverly Hills, Calif., 1980-91; v.p. Orion Ltd., Reston, Va., 1991—; cons. FAA, Washington, 1962-72, U.S. Army

Electronics Command, Ft. Monmouth, N.J., 1962-74, Lockheed Aircraft Co., Ont., 1980—, Nat. Airlines, 1998—; adj. prof. elec. engring. Embry-Riddle U., 1997—; adj. prof. math. Yavapi C.C., 1997—. Contbr. articles to profl. jours. With U.S. Army, 1952-54. Mem. IEEE, Sigma Xi, Tau Beta Pi, Eta Kappa Nu, Phi Kappa Phi.

BATTISTI, PAUL ORESTE, county supervisor; b. Herkimer, N.Y., Mar. 16, 1922; s. Oreste and Ida (Fiore) B.; m. Constance Muth Drais, May 18, 1985; children—Paul J., Cathy (Mrs. D. Capage), Deborah, Thomas, Daniel, Melora, Stephen. Student, Cornell U., Ithaca, N.Y., 1947-48, U. Neb., 1951-52. With VA, 1946-75; dir. VA Hosp., Martinez, Calif., 1969-73; western region dir. San Francisco, 1973-75; adminstr. State Vets. Home Calif., 1976-86; supr. County of Napa, 1989—; chmn., CEO Medam., Inc.; dir. Med. Am. Corp.; health care cons. 1975-88; chmn. Bay Area Air Quality Mgmt. Dist.; mem. exec. bd. Assoc. Bay Area Govts.; chmn. Bay Area Regional Planning Com.; mem. exec. bd. Bay Area Econ. Forum; chmn. Napa River Flood Control Dist. Fellow Am. Coll. Hosp. Adminstrs.; mem. Hosp. Conf. No. Calif. (pres.), Nat. Assn. State Vets. Homes (pres.). Home: Silverado Country Club 117 Milliken Creek Dr Napa CA 94558-1240

BATTLE, DOLORES ELAINE, speech, language pathologist, educator; b. Boston, July 10, 1941; d. William A. and Sylvia V. (Miles) Matthews; m. Charles Battle, Aug. 28, 1965; children: Clark, Leslie A. BA, U. Mass., 1963; MS in Edn., Buffalo State Coll., 1971, PhD, 1978. Speech, lang. pathologist Children's Hosp., Buffalo, 1965-70; speech and lang. pathologist Buffalo State Coll., 1970-72, prof. speech pathology, 1972—, sr. advisor to pres., 1996—; mem. bd. examiners N.Y. State Edn. Dept., Albany, 1986-97. Editor: Communication Disorders Multi-Cultural Popular, 1993, 98. Fellow Am. Speech and Hearing Assn. (legis. councilor 1980—, Recognition award, cert., Spl. Contbn. Multicultural Affairs award, fin. planning bd.); mem. Am. Speech-Lang.-Hearing Assn., N.Y. State Speech and Hearing Assn. (del. corr. 1985-86, Disting. Svc. award 1991, Honors award 1993), Speech and Hearing Assn. Western N.Y. (pres. 1974, Recognition award), Nat. Black Assn. for Speech and Hearing, Buffalo Hearing and Speech Assn. (bd. dirs. 1990-98), Internat. Assn. Logopedics & Phoniatrics (bd. dirs. 1995-98, 99—, sec. 1999—).

BATTLE, EMERY ALFORD, JR., sales executive; b. McComb, Miss., May 23, 1947; s. Emery Alford and Torrey Wofford (Copenhaver) B.; m. Martha Lee Kuntz, July 1971 (div. Jan. 29, 1985); children: Emery Alford III, Meredith Lindsay. BS in Pharmacy, U. Miss., 1971. Staff pharmacist Wilson-Quick, Super-X Foxall Pharmacy, Nashville, 1971-74; sales rep. Eli-Lilly and Co., Nashville, 1974-79, Deknatel Suture Co., Nashville, 1979-81, U.S.C.I. Inc., Nashville, 1981-84; mfr. rep. Cardiac Systems, Inc., Nashville, 1984-85; sales rep. Cordis Corp., Nashville, 1985-87; mgr. sales Cordis Corp., Dallas, 1987-91; mgr. sales Cordis Corp., Nashville, 1991-98, regional dir. sales, 1998—. Mem. Dallas Symphony Assn., 1990. Recipient Pres.'s Club award U.S.C.I. Inc. 1981-83, Pres.'s award Eli-Lilly, 1975-77. Mem. Mayflower Soc., Pilgrim Soc. Episcopalian. Avocations: golf, reading, jazz music, fitness and exercise.

BATTLE, FRANK VINCENT, JR., lawyer; b. Chgo., July 19, 1942; s. Frank V. and Dorothy (Foley) B.; m. Emily Nowak, June 25, 1966; children: Brian, John, Katherine. BS, Loyola U., Chgo., 1964; JD, DePaul U., 1968; LLM, NYU, 1969. Bar: Ill. 1969. Assoc. Sidley and Austin, Chgo., 1969-73; atty., advisor Office Tax Legis. Counsel U.S. Dept. Treasury, Washington, 1973-74; ptnr. Sidley and Austin, Chgo., 1974—. Mem. ABA, Ill. State Bar Assn., Chgo. Bar Assn. (fed. taxation sect., chmn. 1987-88), Skokie (Ill.) Country Club, Shoreacres Club (Ill.), Tamarack Country Club (Greenwich, Conn.) (bd. govs. 1995—), Chgo. Club, Mid-Day Club. Democrat. *

BATTLE, JEAN ALLEN, writer, educator; b. Talladega, Ala., June 15, 1914; s. William Raines and Lemerle McLemore (Allen) B.; m. Lucy Troxell, Aug. 25, 1940; 1 dau., Helen Carol Battle Salmon. Student, Birmingham So. Coll., 1932-33; B.S., Middle Tenn. State U., 1937; M.A., U. Ala., 1941; Ed.D., U. Fla., 1952; postgrad., Oxford U., 1980. Dept. chmn., dean students Fla. So. Coll., 1940-55, dean coll., 1956-59; dean Coll. Edn. U. South Fla., Tampa, 1959-71; prof. higher edn. U. South Fla., 1971; guest lectr. Rewley House, Oxford U., 1981; editor, pub. Tenn. Valley News.; Mem. Fla. Tchrs. Edn. Adv. Council, Fla. Continuing Edn. Council; mem. courses study com. Fla. Bd. Edn.; mem. Tampa Bay Com. on Fgn. Affairs; adv. com. Hillsborough County Hosp.; bd. dirs. Fla. Univ. System Honduras Program, World Trade Council, Tampa, Poynter Found., St. Petersburg, Fla., Harold Benjamin Found., U. Md.; bd. dirs., v.p. Southeastern Edn. Lab., Atlanta. Author: Culture and Education for the Contemporary World, 1969, (with others) The New Idea in Education, 1974, Choices for an Intelligent and Humane School and Society, 1981, Education: The Fate of Humanity, 1982, rev., 1983; Contbr. papers to tech. lit. Served to capt. USAAF, 1942-46. Recipient Disting. Service awards Fla. So. Coll., 1952, Disting. Service awards Fla. Citizenship Clearing House, 1957; Outstanding Alumnus award Middle Tenn. State U. Mem. SAR, Fla. Hist. Soc., Nat. Edn. Assn., Fla. Edn. Assn. (co-chmn. tchr. recruitment com.), Tampa C. of C. (edn. com.), Acad. Polit. Sci., Oxford Soc. (sec. Fla. br. 1990—), Omicron Delta Kappa, Pi Gamma Mu, Kappa Delta Pi, Phi Delta Kappa, Sigma Alpha Epsilon. Methodist. Club: Carrollwood Village Golf and Tennis. Home: 11011 Carrollwood Dr Tampa FL 33618-3905

BATTLE, JOE DAVID, engineer; b. Montgomery, Ala., Apr. 11, 1958; s. Marvin Andrew and Mary Della (Reynolds) B.; m. Margaret Carol Gillum, Jan. 18, 1980; children: Chloe Christine, John Edward. BS in Civil Engring. Tech., U. Ala., 1981. Coop. engr. Harbert Internat., Birmingham, Ala., 1977-78, B,E&K Inc., Birmingham, 1979-80; estimator Campbell & Assocs., Tuscaloosa, Ala., 1980-81; project coord. Pitts.-Desmoines Corp., Birmingham, 1981-83; staff project engr. VA, Dublin, Ga., 1983-85; asst. chief engr. VA, Indpls., 1985-88, chief engr., 1988—. Named Va. Fed. Engr. of Yr. Nat. Soc. Profl. Engrs. Mem. Fed. Exec. Assn., Am. Soc. Hosp. Engrs. Baptist. Lodge: Lions. Avocations: golf, outdoor sports. Office: VA Med Ctr 1481 W 10th St Indianapolis IN 46202-2803

BATTLE, LEONARD CARROLL, lawyer; b. Toronto, Ont., Can., Oct. 25, 1929; s. Leonard Conlon and Beatrice Hester B.; m. Marjory Estelle Holland, Dec. 28, 1953; children: David, Tracy, Thomas, Patricia, John, Mary. AB, U. Mich., 1950; JD, Ind. U., 1958. Bar: Mich. 1961, Ind. 1961, U.S. Ct. Mil. Appeals 1964, U.S. Supreme Ct. 1964. Claims adjuster State Farm Ins. Co., 1959-61; asst. pros. atty. Midland County (Mich.), 1961-67; sole practice, Midland, Mich., 1967—. Served to lt. col. JAG USAFR, 1950-84, USAFRR, 1984—. Mem. ATLA, Midland County Bar Assn. (pres.), Mich. State Bar Assn. (mil. law com.), Judge Advs. Assn. Clubs: Kiwassee Kiwanis, Elks (Midland). Home: 408 Harper Ln Midland MI 48640-7321 Office: 200 E Main St Midland MI 48640-6510

BATTLE, LUCIUS DURHAM, retired educational institution administrator, former diplomat; b. Dawson, Ga., June 1, 1918; s. Warren Lazarus and Jewel Beatrice (Durham) B.; m. Betty Jane Davis, Oct. 1, 1949; children: Lynne, John, Laura, Thomas. A.B., U. Fla., 1939, LL.B., 1946; LL.D.; L.H.D., Fla. State U. Mgr. student staff U. Fla. Library, 1940-42; assoc. adminstrv. analyst War Dept., 1942-43; fgn. affairs specialist Dept. State, Washington, 1946-49; spl. asst. to sec. of state Dept. State, 1949-53, 61-64, also exec. sec., 1961-62; asst. sec. of state for ednl. and cultural affairs, 1962-64; 1st sec. Am. Embassy, Copenhagen, 1953-55; dep. exec. sec. NATO, Paris, 1955-56; ambassador to UAR, 1964-67; asst. sec. state for Nr. Eastern and South Asian affairs Washington, 1967-68; v.p. corp. affairs Communications Satellite Corp., 1968-73, sr. v.p. corp. affairs, 1974-80; dir. COMSAT Gen. Corp., 1974-80; chmn. Fgn. Policy Inst., Sch. Advanced Internat. Studies, Johns Hopkins U., 1980-84; pres. Middle East Inst., Washington, 1973-74, 86-91, bd. dirs., 1973-81; chmn. UNESCO Gen. Conf., Paris, 1962; pres. Found. for Mid. East Peace, 1994—. V.p. Colonial Williamsburg, Inc., Williamsburg Restoration, Inc., 1956-61; chpt. mem. Protestant Episcopal Cathedral Found., Washington; chmn. bd. St. Albans Sch., 1973-76; vice chmn. Meridian House Internat., 1976-77; trustee George C. Marshall Research Found., Am. U., Cairo, 1970-79; chmn. vis. com. Ctr. for Middle Eastern Studies, Harvard, 1973-76; bd. dirs. Fgn. Policy Assn., 1974-84, Sch. Advanced Internat. Studies, 1975—, World Council of Washington, 1980, Smithsonian Assocs., 1981-85; Am. Near East Refugee Aid, 1985—; mem. fine arts com. Dept. State, 1973-77; mem. Nat. Study Comm. on Records and Documents Fed. Ofcls., 1975-76; pres. Bacon House Found., 1975-85, v.p. DACOR Bacon House Found. adv. bd. Ctr. for Contemporary Arab Studies, Georgetown U., 1976-86; mem. founders council Inst. for Study of Diplomacy, 1978-87; chmn. nat. com. to honor 14th centennial of Islam, 1979-84; chmn. Am. Inst. Islamic Affairs, 1984-87; pres. Found. for Middle Eastpeace, 1994. Served to lt. USNR, 1943-46. Decorated Order of Republic 1st class Egypt; recipient Fgn. Service Cup, Diplomatic and Consular Officers Ret., 1984, Founders award Sch. Advanced Internat. Studies. Mem. Am. Fgn. Service Assn. (pres. 1962-63), Order of Coif, Phi Beta Kappa, Alpha Tau Omega, Phi Delta Phi. Clubs: Met. (Washington); Alibi. Home: 4856 Rockwood Pky NW Washington DC 20016-3249

BATTLE, TIMOTHY JOSEPH, lawyer; b. San Francisco, May 20, 1953; s. Joseph Emmett and Mary Gertrude (McCarthy) B.; m. Lonnell Susan Freeman, Apr. 28, 1979; children: Ann, Megan, Mary Katharine. BA cum laude, U. Notre Dame, 1975; JD, U. Va., 1978. Bar: Va. 1979, D.C. 1980. Assoc. Miles & Stockbridge, Washington, 1986-87; ptnr. Krupin, Carr, Morris & Graeff, Washington, 1988-89, Carr, Morris & Graeff, Washington, 1990, Battle & Battle, Alexandria, Va., 1991—. Mem. Va. State Bar Assn. (lectr.), No. Va. Def. Lawyers. Home: 4400 Ferry Landing Rd Alexandria VA 22309-3150 Office: Battle & Battle PO Box 19631 112 S Alfred St Alexandria VA 22320-9631

BATTLE, WILLIAM ROBERT (BOB BATTLE), retired newspaper executive; b. Nolensville, Tenn., Dec. 25, 1927; s. William Robert and Cleo (Smith) B.; m. Elizabeth Ogilvie, Dec. 23, 1948; children: Valerie Elizabeth, William Robert III. Student, George Peabody Coll., 1946-49. Exec. offcl. Nashville Banner, 1943-98, police beat, county polit. beat, 1943-53, city editor, 1953-64, movie columnist, 1955-72, mng. editor, 1964-71, exec. editor, 1971-75, asst. to editor, 1975-78, regional editor, 1978-80, sr. editor, 1980-84, v.p., bus. editor, 1984-89, v.p., sr. bus. editor, 1989-98; staff writer Country Style mag. Appeared as newspaperman in: film Teacher's Pet, 1957, also in Country Music on Broadway, 1963; Contbr. numerous articles to nat. publs. Supt. gates and admissions Tenn. State Fair, 1953-64; pub. rels. chmn. Davidson County Coun. for Retarded Children, 1961-66; mem. exec. bd. Mid. Tenn. coun. Boy Scouts Am.; mem. 4-H Club Found.; exec. bd. dirs., past sec. Nashville Boys Club, now life mem. bd. dirs. Recipient Big Story award NBC-TV, 1956; named Man of Yr., 4-H Club, 1974, Man of Yr., Future Farmers Am., 1975, Silver Beaver award Boy Scouts Am., 1997; Robert Battle scholarship established in his honor Belmont U. Sch. Bus., By Opryland, U.S.A., 1989. Mem. Nashville Area C. of C., Tenn. Press Assn., Nat. Screen Coun., Country Music Assn., Nashville City Club, Masons (33d deg., knights commdr. ct. of honor), Shriners (potentate 1976), Royal Order of Jesters, Elks (former chmn. scholarship com.), Sigma Delta Chi (former chmn. scholarship com., former pres.). Methodist. Home: 4108 Crestridge Dr Nashville TN 37204-4243

BATTLES, LARA, counselor, psychotherapist; b. San Pedro, Calif., Oct. 13, 1949; d. Willis Ralph D. and Roxy Edith (Baker) B.; m. Thomas Leigh Morgan, Oct. 27, 1969 (div. Mar. 1973); m. Dennis Lindsay Lohof, Aug. 24, 1980; children: Jeremy Brant Lohof Burleigh, Jesse Quinn Lohof Burleigh, Darien Reed Will Lohof. BS in Psychology, Mont. State U., 1971; MA in Psychology of Counseling, Loyola-Marymount U., L.A., 1975. Cert. marriage, family and child counselor, Calif. Prevention specialist Straight Talk Clinic, Cypress, Calif., 1977, County Drug Abuse Program, San Luis Obispo, Calif., 1977-78; alcoholism counselor and program mgr. S.W. Mont. Regional Alcoholism Svcs., Helena, Mont., 1978-80; psychotherapist, counselor Arroyo Grande, Calif., 1981—; parenting educator Lucia Mar Adult Sch., Arroyo Grande, 1993—; clin. dir. Inst. for the Study of Family Co-Dependence, Arroyo Grande, 1988-90; counselor eating disorders aftercare, Pinecrest Hosp., Santa Maria, Calif., 1986-87. Vol. counselor Lucia Mar U.S. Dist., Arroyo Grande, 1990-93; vol. Dem. Party, South San Luis County, 1996—. Mem. Calif. Assn. Marriage and Family Therapists. Avocations: youth activities, gardening, astronomy, wilderness camping, myth collection. Office: 210B Traffic Way Arroyo Grande CA 93420-3335

BATTLES, ROXY EDITH, novelist, consultant, educator; b. Spokane, Wash., Mar. 29, 1921; d. Rosco Jirah and Lucile Zilpha (Jacques) Baker; m. Willis Ralph Dawe Battles, May 2, 1941; children: Margaret Battles Holmes, Ralph, Lara. AA, Bakersfield (Calif.) Coll., 1940; BA, Calif. State U., Long Beach, 1959; MA, Pepperdine U., 1976. Cert. tchr. English, adult basic edn. and elem. edn., Calif. Free-lance writer 50 nat. and regional mags., 1940—; tchr. elem. Torrance (Calif.) Unified Schs., 1959-85; tchr. adult edn. Pepperdine U., Torrance, 1969-79, 88-89; free-lance children's author, 1966—; mystery novelist Pinnacle Publs., N.Y.C., 1980; with Tex. A&M U., 1988; instr. Mary Mount Coll., Harbor Coll., 1995; author-in-residence Young Authors Festival, Am. Sch. Madrid, 1991; lectr. in field. Author: Over the Rickety Fence, 1967, The Terrible Trick or Treat, 1970, 501 Balloons Sail East, 1971, The Terrible Terrier, 1972, One to Teeter-Totter, 1973, 2d edit., 1975, Eddie Couldn't Find the Elephants, 1974, reprints, 1982, 84, 88, What Does the Rooster Say, Yoshio?, 1978, The Secret of Castle Drai, 1980, The Witch in Room 6, 1987, 3d edit., 1989 (nominee Garden State, Nene, and Hoosier awards), The Chemistry of Whispering Caves, 1988, rev. edit., 1997; playwright: The Lavender Castle, 1996, mus. version, 1997, Computer Encryptions in Whispering Caves, 1997. Active So. Calif. Coun. on Lit. for Children and Young People, 1973-80, 87—. Recipient Commendation UN, 1979; Hoosier award nominee, 1990; Garden State award nominee, 1990, Nene award nominee, 1992, 93. Mem. S.W. Manuscripters (founder), Surfwriters. Home: 560 S Helberta Ave Redondo Beach CA 90277-4353 *However I rail at prejudice, some prejudgment is inevitable and, except in extremity, foreseeable. Whether caused by neglect or studied plan, negatives are noticed. When the fixable remains unfixed, I deserve to be judged for my part, however I blame my adjudicator.*

BATTOCLETTI, ELIZABETH CARMEL, marketing executive; b. Santiago, Chile, July 16, 1962; came to U.S., 1963; d. Joseph Henry and Rosemary Theresa (Mashl) B. BA summa cum laude, U. Wis., 1988; MA, Georgetown U., 1990. Coder, keyer Milw. Ins. Co., 1985-86; claims examiner Am. Assn. Ret. Persons Prudential Ins. Co., Milw., 1986-88; claims analyst Gramm & Co., Inc., Vienna, Va., 1988-89; data entry operator CapitalCare, Inc., Tysons Corner, Va., 1989-91; freelance abstractor Delphic Assocs., Inc., Falls Ch., Va., 1990-91; med. claims examiner Claims Overload Sys., Arlington, Va., 1991-92; asst. to pres. for spl. projects The Citizens Network for Fgn. Affairs, Inc., Washington, 1992-97; internat. assoc. Bob Lawrence & Assocs., Inc., Alexandria, Va., 1997-98; sr. assoc. Bob Lawrence & Assocs., Inc., Alexandria, 1998—. Co-author: (workbook) Engineered Financing Plan and Feasibility Study Workbook for Russian Agri-enterprises, 1996; designer: (Web site) Rhapsody Acres Kennels, 1997; author: Geothermal Financing Workbook, 1998; Database of Geothermal Resources in Latin America and the Caribbean, 1999; contbr. abstracts to technol. publs.; contbr. poetry to anthologies. Wingspread fellow U. Wis., Milw., 1986; scholar Georgetown U., 1989. Mem. Women in Internat. Trade, Phi Beta Kappa. Avocations: horseback riding, reading, learning. Fax: (703) 836-6086. E-mail: ecbatto@aol.com. Office: Bob Lawrence & Assocs Inc 345 South Patrick St Alexandria VA 22314-2312

BATTOCLETTI, JOSEPH HENRY, electrical engineer, biomedical engineer, educator; b. Bridgeport, Ohio, Mar. 12, 1925; s. Joseph Matthew and Henrietta (Dzielski) B.; m. Rosemary Theresa Mashl, Aug. 25, 1951; children—Mary Rose, Theresa, Anne, Elizabeth, Mary Catherine, Timothy, James. B.E.E., U. Detroit, 1947; M.S. in Elec. Engring., Northwestern U., 1949; Ph.D., UCLA, 1961. Registered profl. engr., Wis. Radio engr. Motorola Inc., Chgo., 1949-51; assoc. prof. elec. engring. Loyola U., Los Angeles, 1951-62, chmn. dept. elec. engring., 1961-62; cons. Nat. Acad. Scis. to Chilean Univs., 1962-63; assoc. prof. Marquette U., Milw., 1963-66; mgr. applied research Badger Meter Co., Milw., 1966-70; prof. neurosurgery Med. Coll. Wis., 1970—; biomed. engr. VA Med. Ctr., Wood, Wis., 1978-95; adj. prof. Marquette U., 1989—. Mem. IEEE (Milw. sect. meml. award 1975, Centennial medal 1984). Roman Catholic. Home: 825 W Good Hope Rd River Hills WI 53217-3306 Office: 9200 W Wisconsin Ave Milwaukee WI 53226-3522*

BATTS, DEBORAH A., judge; b. Phila., Apr. 13, 1947; d. James A., Jr. and Ruth Violet (Silas) Batts; 2 children. BA, Radcliffe Coll., 1969; JD, Harvard U., 1972. Summer atty. Foley, Hoag & Eliot, Boston, Mass., 1970, Kaye, Scholer, Fierman, Hays & Handler, N.Y.C., 1971; law clerk to Hon. Lawrence W. Pierce U.S. Dist. Ct. (so. dist.) N.Y., N.Y.C., 1972-73; assoc. atty. Cravath, Swaine & Moore, N.Y.C., 1973-79; asst. U.S. atty. criminal divsn. U.S. Dist. Ct. (so. dist.) N.Y., N.Y.C., 1979-84; assoc. prof. law Fordham U., 1984-94, adj. prof. law, 1994—; spl. assoc. counsel dept. investigation N.Y.C., 1990-91; commr. law revision com. State of N.Y., 1990-94; judge U.S. Dist. Ct. (so. dist.) N.Y., N.Y.C., 1994—; Bd. trustees Cathedral Sch., N.Y.C., 1990-96; mem. faculty Corp. Counsel Trial Advocacy Program, 1988-94. Contbr. articles to legal jours. Trustee Spence Sch., 1987-95. Mem. Second Cir. Fed. Bar Coun., Assn. Bar. City N.Y., Lesbian and Gay Law Assn. Greater N.Y., Met. Black Bar Assn. Office: US Courthouse 500 Pearl St Rm 2510 New York NY 10007-1316*

BATTS, MICHAEL STANLEY, German language educator; b. Mitcham, Eng., Aug. 2, 1929; s. Stanley George and Alixe Kathleen (Watson) B.; m. Misao Yoshida, Mar. 19, 1959; 1 dau., Anna. BA, U. London, 1952, BA with honors, 1953, LittD, 1973; PhD, U. Freiburg, Germany, 1957; M.L.S., U. Toronto, 1974. Mem. faculty U. Mainz, Germany, 1953-54, U. Basel, Switzerland, 1954-56, U. Wurzburg, Germany, 1956-58; instr. German U. Calif., Berkeley, 1958-60; mem. faculty dept. German U. B.C., Can., 1960-91; prof. U. B.C., 1967-91, head dept., 1968-80. Author: Die Form der Aventiuren im Nibelungenlied, 1961, Bruder Hansens Marienlieder, 1964, Studien zu Bruder Hansens Marienliedern, 1964, Das Hohe Mittelalter, 1969, Das Nibelungenlied-Synoptische Ausgabe, 1971, Gottfried von Strasburg, 1971, A Checklist of German Literature, 1945-75, 1977, The Bibliography of German Literature: An Historical and Critical Survey, 1978, A History of Histories of German Literature, 1835-1914, 1993, Germanic Studies at Canadian Universities From the Beginning to 1995, 1998; editor: Seminar, 1970-80. Served with Brit. Army, 1947-49. Alexander von Humboldt fellow, 1964-65, 83; Can. Council sr. fellow, 1964-65, 71-72; Killam fellow, 1981-82. Fellow Royal Soc. Can.; mem. Canadian Assn. Univ. Tchrs. German (pres. 1982-84), Modern Humanities Rsch. Assn., Alcuin Soc. (exec. v.p. 1972-79, pres. 1979-80), Internat. Assn. for Germanic Studies (pres. 1990-95). Office: U Brit Columbia, German Dept, Vancouver, BC Canada V6T 1Z1

BATTS, WARREN LEIGHTON, retired diversified industry executive; b. Norfolk, Va., Sept. 4, 1932; s. John Leighton and Allie Belle (Johnson) B.; m. Eloise Pitts, Dec. 24, 1957; 1 dau., Terri Allison. BEE, Ga. Inst. Tech., 1961; MBA, Harvard U., 1963. With Kendall Co., Charlotte, N.C., 1963-64; exec. v.p. Fashion Devel. Co., Santa Paula, Calif., 1964-66; dir. mfg. Olga Co., Van Nuys, Calif., 1964-66; v.p. Douglas Williams Assocs., N.Y.C., 1966-67; co-founder Triangle Corp., Orangeburg, S.C., 1967; pres., chief exec. officer Triangle Corp., 1967-71; v.p. Mead Corp., Dayton, Ohio, 1971-73; pres. Mead Corp., Dayton, 1973-80, chief exec. officer, 1978-80; pres., chief operating officer Dart Industries, Inc., L.A., 1980-81, Dart & Kraft, Inc., Northbrook, Ill., 1981-86; chmn., chief exec. officer Premark Internat. Inc., Deerfield, 1986-96, chmn., 1996-97; chmn., CEO Tupperware Corp., Orlando, Fla., 1996-97. Trustee Children's Meml. Hosp., Chgo., 1984—, Northwestern U., 1989. *

BATTY, J. MICHAEL, geographer, educator; b. Liverpool, Eng., Jan. 11, 1945; s. Jack and Nellie (Marsden) B.; m. Susan Elizabeth Howell, Jan. 4, 1969; 1 child, Daniel Jack. BA, U. Manchester, Eng., 1966; PhD, U. Wales, 1984. Rsch. asst. U. Manchester, 1966-69; lectr. U. Reading, Eng., 1969-74; visiting asst. prof. U. Waterloo, Ontario, Can., 1974-75; reader U. Reading, 1975-79; prof. U. Wales, Cardiff, 1979-84, dean environ. design, 1984-87, chmn. planning, 1985-89; dir. Nat. Ctr. for Geog. Info. and Analysis SUNY, Buffalo, N.Y., 1991-95; dir. Ctr. Advanced Spatial Analysis Univ. Coll., London, 1995—. Author: Urban Modelling, 1976, Microcomputer Graphics, 1987, Fractal Cities, 1994; editor: Systems Analysis in Urban Policy-Making, 1983, Advances in Urban Systems Modelling, 1986, Cities of the 21st Century, 1991, Cities in Competition, 1995, Spatial Analysis, 1996. Recipient rsch. grants Econ. & Social Rsch. Coun., 1974-90, NSF, 1991-95, Joint Info. Syss. Com., 1996—, Office of Sci. and Tech., 1996—, Engring. and Physics Sci. Rsch. Coun., 1998—, award for tech. progress Assn. Geographic Info., 1998, Back award for contbns. for city design Royal Geographic Soc. Fellow Royal Town Planning Inst., Royal Soc. Arts, Chartered Inst. Transport. Avocations: travel, reading, drawing, China, America. Office: Univ Coll, 1-19 Torrington Pl, London WC1E 6BT, England

BATZLI, GEORGE OLIVER, ecology educator; b. Mpls., Sept. 23, 1936; s. Oscar H. and Bertha M. B.; m. Sandra Lou Scharf, Jan. 2, 1959; children—Jeffrey, Samuel. B.S. in Psychology, U. Minn., 1959; M.A. in Biology, San Francisco State U., 1965; Ph.D. in Zoology (Ecology), U. Calif., Berkeley, 1969. Research assoc. U. Calif., Davis, 1969-71; lectr. biology U. Calif., Santa Cruz, 1971; asst. prof. zoology U. Ill., Urbana, 1971-76, assoc. prof. ecology, 1976-80, prof. ecology, 1980—, head dept. ecology, ethology and evolution, 1983-88, 95-97; sr. scientist research in arctic environs., 1976-78, mem. ecology program adv. panel NSF, 1984-87; research scientist DSIR, N.Z., 1979; chmn. ecology program U. Ill., 1976-82. Contbr. articles on ecology to profl. jours.; spl. issue editor Arctic and Alpine Research, 1980, Oikos, 1983; mem. editorial bd. Ecology, Ecol. Monographs, 1981-84. Fellow NSF, 1962-63, NIH, 1967-69, 69-71, Zool. Inst. U. Oslo, Norway, 1982. Fellow AAAS; mem. Am. Inst. Biol. Scis., Am. Soc. Mammalogy, Ecol. Soc. Am., Brit. Ecol. Soc., Intecol, Am. Soc. Naturalists, Comp. Nutrition Soc. Office: U Ill Shelford Vivarium 606 E Healey St Champaign IL 61820-5502

BATZLI, TERRENCE RAYMOND, lawyer; b. Youngstown, Ohio, Dec. 28, 1946; s. Marion Raymond and Kathryn Velma (Hudran) B.; m. Sharon Lee Heinatz, Aug. 2, 1969; children—Catherine Barrett, Jonathan Raymond. B.S., U. Richmond, 1974, J.D., 1975. Bar: Va. 1975, U.S. Dist. Ct. (ea. dist.) Va. 1975, U.S. Dist. Ct. (we. dist.) Va. 1983, U.S. Ct. Appeals (4th cir.) 1984. Mem. Mays & Valentine and predecessor firms, Richmond, 1982-93; Durrette, Irvin & Bradshaw, Richmond, 1993-96; prin. Barnes & Batzli, PC, 1996—; mediator Access Family Mediation-McCammon Group; adj. prof. law Reynolds Community Coll., Richmond, 1980-82. Capt. U.S. Army, 1966-70. Mem. adv. bd. VA. Head Injury Found., 1990-91, Nat. Head Injury Found., 1988—. Fellow Am. Acad. of Matrimonial Lawyers; mem. Richmond Bar Assn. (chmn. family law sect. 1982-83, exec. com. 1982-83), Hanover County Bar Assn. (treas. 1997, sec. 1998), Metro Richmond Family Law Bar Assn. (founding pres.), Va. State Bar (bd. govs. family law sect. 1996—, sec. 1997), Hanover Assn. Bus. (pres. 1989, bd. dirs.). Republican. Methodist. Clubs: Ruritan (club pres., zone gov., dist. sec.), Burkwood (bd. dirs.). Lodge: Rotary (bd. dirs. 1980-84). Home: 10997 Sugarloaf Dr Mechanicsvlle VA 23116-4817 Office: Barnes & Batzli PC 4701 Cox Rd Ste 207 Glen Allen VA 23060-6802

BAUCCIO, LISA RUTH, obstetric nurse, high-risk perinatal nurse; b. Pitts., May 4, 1967; d. Raymond D. and Ruthann L. (Stevens) Valentine; m. Carmen J. Bauccio, May 12, 1990; children: Anthony M., Julia R. BSN, Carlow Coll., 1989; postgrad., U. Pitts. RN, Pitts. Asst. patient care Forbes Regional Health Ctr., Monroeville, Pa., 1987-89; clin. nurse II West Penn Hosp., Pitts., 1989—, instr. obstet. edn., 1991-94, mem. core com. critical care obstet. unit, 1992-97; speaker perinatal outreach program West Pa. Hosp., Pitts., 1993—. Fellow Nightingale Soc.; mem. AWHONN, Sigma Theta Tau, Delta Epsilon Sigma, Phi Eta Sigma, Alpha Lambda Delta. Home: 4037 Impala Dr Pittsburgh PA 15239-2705 Office: West Penn Hosp Unit E5DR Labor/Delivery 4800 Friendship Ave Pittsburgh PA 15224-1793

BAUCH, THOMAS JAY, lawyer, educator, former apparel company executive; b. Indpls., May 24, 1943; s. Thomas and Violet (Smith) B.; m. Ellen L. Burstein, Oct. 31, 1982; children: Chelsea Sara, Elizabeth Tree. BS with honors, U. Wis., 1964, JD with highest honors, 1966. Bar: Ill. 1966, Calif. 1978. Assoc. Lord, Bissell & Brook, Chgo., 1966-72; lawyer, asst. sec. Marcor-Montgomery Ward, Chgo., 1973-75; spl. asst. to solicitor Dept. Labor, Washington, 1975-77; dep. gen. counsel Levi Strauss & Co., San Francisco, 1977-81, sr. v.p., gen. counsel, 1981-96, counsel, 1996—; pvt. practice, Tiburon, Calif., 1996—; cons. prof. Stanford (Calif.) U. Law Sch., 1997—; ptnr. Ika Enterprises; mng. dir. Doughnet.com Inc.; mng. dir., gen. counsel Marine Desalinazation Corp. Mem. U. Wis. Law Rev., 1964-66. Bd. dirs. Urban Sch., San Francisco, 1986-91, San Francisco Psychoanalytic Inst., Gateway H.S., San Francisco, Charles Armstrong Sch., Belmont, Calif.; bd. visitors U. Wis. Law Sch., 1991-95. Mem. Am. Assn. Corp. Counsel (bd. dirs. 1984-87), Bay Area Gen. Counsel Assn. (chmn. 1994),

Univ. Club, Villa Taverna Club, Corrinthian Yacht Club, Order of Coif, San Francisco Yacht Club. Office: 49 Main St Tiburon CA 94920-2507

BAUCOM, SIDNEY GEORGE, lawyer; b. Salt Lake City, Oct. 21, 1930; s. Sidney and Nora (Palfreyman) B.; m. Mary B., Mar. 5, 1954; children: Sidney, George, John. JD, U. Utah, 1953. Bar: Utah 1953. Pvt. practice Salt Lake City, 1953-55; asst. city atty. Salt Lake City Corp., 1955-56; asst. atty. Utah Power and Light Co., Salt Lake City, 1956-60, asst. atty., asst. sec., 1960-62, atty., asst. sec., 1962-68, v.p., gen. counsel, 1968-75, sr. v.p., gen. counsel, 1975-79, exec. v.p., gen. counsel, 1979-89, dir., 1979-89; of counsel Jones, Waldo, Holbrook & McDonough, Salt Lake City, 1989—. Past chmn. Utah Coordinating Coun. Devel. Svcs., Utah Taxpayers Assn.; past pres. Utah State Fair Found.; past dir. Utah Power & Light Co., El Paso Electric Co., vice chmn. Mem. Alta Club, Lions, Phi Delta Phi. Mem. LDS Ch. Home: 2248 Logan Ave Salt Lake City UT 84108-2715 Office: Jones Waldo Holbrook & McDonough 1500 Wells Fargo Bank Bldg 170 S Main St Salt Lake City UT 84101-1605

BAUCUM, WILLIAM EMMETT, JR., electrical research engineer; b. Magnolia, Ark., July 8, 1945; s. William Emmett Sr. and Bronis Yvonne (Whittington) B.; m. Paulette Phillips, Mar. 21, 1965; children: William III, Rebecca. BA, David Lipscomb Coll., Nashville, 1966; postgrad., Ga. Inst. Tech., 1967; MS, U. Tenn., Knoxville, 1974; postgrad. space inst., U. Tenn., Tullahoma, 1978—. Physicist Y-12 plant Union Carbide Corp., Oak Ridge, Tenn., 1967-74, elec. engr. nat. lab., 1974-78; research engr. space inst. U. Tenn., Tullahoma, 1978-92; with WEBCOMM; cons. Tech. Engring. Services Co., Tullahoma, 1992—; adj. faculty Motlow State C.C., Tullahoma, 1987—. Contbr. chpt. to book, articles to profl. jours. Deacon Ch. of Christ; judge 4-H Club, Franklin County, Tenn., 1985; bd. dirs. Short Mountain Christian Camp, 1987. Mem. Internat. Microwave Power Inst. (v.p. bd. dirs. indsl., sci., med. instrumentation sect. 1987-89, pres. bd. dirs. 1989-92), Sigma Xi, Sigma Pi Sigma. Avocations: exercise walking, electronics, music. Home and Office: 1402 Harton Blvd Tullahoma TN 37388-5580

BAUCUS, MAX S., senator; b. Helena, Mont., Dec. 11, 1941; s. John and Jean (Sheriff) B.; m. Wanda Minge, Apr. 23, 1983. BA, Stanford U., 1964, LLB, 1967. Bar: D.C. 1969, Mont. 1972. Staff atty. CAB, Washington, 1967-68; lawyer SEC, Washington, 1968-71; legal asst. to chmn. SEC, 1970-71; sole practice Missoula, Mont., 1971-74; mem. Mont. Ho. of Reps., 1973-74; mem. 94th-95th congresses from 1st Dist. Mont., 1975-79, mem. com. appropriations; U.S. senator from Mont., 1979—, ranking minority mem., mem. environ. and pub. works com., mem. fin. subcom. on internat. trade, mem. health com., taxation and IRS oversight com., mem. agrl./nutrition and forestry coms., mem. intelligence/joint com. on taxation, mem. Senate Dem. steering and coordination com. Office: US Senate 511 Hart Senate Bldg Washington DC 20510-2602

BAUDOIN, LARRY ANTHONY, academic administrator; b. New Orleans, July 29, 1946; s. Louis Joseph Baudoin Sr. and Mildred Marie Bourgeois; m. Anna Marie Knobloch, May 29, 1968; children: Troy, Danica. BS, Nicholls State U., 1968; MBA, Nova Southeastern U., 1987. Acct. Union Carbide, Taft, La., 1968-70, Honeywell Aerospace, St. Petersburg, Fla., 1970-72; acct. U. South Fla., Tampa, 1972-75, assoc. bus. mgr., 1975-84, dir., 1984-86, asst. v.p., 1986-93; dean. fin. and adminstrn. Tulane U. Med. Sch., New Orleans, 1993—. Vol. Metro Ministries for the Homeless, Tampa, 1990-93, St. Feed for the Homeless, New Orleans, 1994-96; chmn. med. ctr. United Way, 1988-90; officer Homeowner's Assn., Tampa, 1981-92; sec.-treas., bd. dirs. New Villa Condo. Assn., 1995—; bd. dirs., v.p. Orlando Internat. Resort, 1996—. Recipient Svc. award Tulane Soc. Med. Students, 1994-95. Mem. Am. Mgmt. Assn., Assn. Am. Med. Coll. (prin. bus. officer, chmn.), Med. Group Mgmt. Assn., Inst. Mgmt. Accts. New Orleans (v.p. 1997—). Republican. Avocations: travel, photography, cooking. E-mail: lbaudoi@tmcpop.tmc.tulane.edu. Home: 29 Briarfield Dr Marrero LA 70072 Office: Tulane U Med Sch 1430 Tulane Ave New Orleans LA 70072

BAUDOIN, PETER, family business consultant; b. Breaux Bridge, La., Dec. 23, 1946; s. Roy Paul and Carrie (Broussard) B.; m. Donna Renz, Apr. 17, 1971; 1 child, Jonn Pierre. BS in BA, U. Southwestern La., 1968. CPA; cert. mgmt. acct. Ops. auditor Firestone Tire & Rubber Co., Akron, Ohio, 1969-71; sr. acct. Unishops of Clarkins, Inc., Akron, Ohio, 1972-73; cons. supr. Ernst & Young, Cleve., 1973-78; ptnr. Baudoin & Hamza CPAs, Lafayette, La., 1978-82; pres. Peter Baudoin Cons., Lafayette, La., 1982—; founder, mng. dir. Family Bus. Accts. and Advisors, Lafayette, La., 1990—; bd. dirs., treas., mem. body of knowledge task force Family Firm Inst., Boston, 1990—, chair 1997 internat. conf. in New Orleans; dir. programming Acadiana Family Bus. Forum, 1992—; spl. advisor Family Bus. Forum, La. State U., adj. prof. entrepreneurship and family bus.; vis. advisor Family Bus. Forum, Tex. A&M U. Contbr. numerous articles to profl. jours. Founding pres. Rocky River (Ohio) Jaycees, 1976; former chmn. adv. bd. Charity Depot, an agy. of Lafayette Cath. Svcs. Ctr., Inc. With USAR, 1968-75. Named hon. Paramount Chief Zokai of Liberia, bestowed by Mandingo Tribe, 1975. Mem. Fin. Execs. Inst., Inst. Mgmt. Accts. (nat. v.p. 1998-00, nat. bd. 1993-95, pres. Gulf South Coun. 1996-97, nat. v.p. 1998—), Serra Club of Lafayette (v.p. membership 1996-97, v.p. programming 1998—, pres.-elect 1998—), Secretariat of Fin. of Redemptorist Vice-Provincial New Orleans. Republican. Roman Catholic. Home: 101 Florida Ct Lafayette LA 70503-2005 Office: Peter Baudoin Cons 158 Industrial Pky Lafayette LA 70508-8309

BAUE, ARTHUR EDWARD, surgeon, educator, administrator; b. St. Louis, Oct. 7, 1929; s. Arthur Christian and Viola (Wegener) B.; m. Rosemary Dysart, Nov. 24, 1956; children: Patricia Sage Baue Nizen, Arthur Christian II, William Dysart, 6 grandchildren. AB summa cum laude, Westminster Coll., 1950; MD cum laude, Harvard, 1954; M Honoris Privatum, Yale U., 1975. Diplomate Am. Bd. Surgery (dir.), Am. Bd. Thoracic Surgery (dir.). cpt. asst. chief ops. surgery USAF, Philippine Islands, 1955-57; from intern to chief resident surgery Mass. Gen. Hosp., Boston, 1954-61; asst. prof. surgery U. Mo. Sch. Medicine, 1962-64; sr. registrar in thoracis surgery Bristol, Eng., 1965—; from asst. prof. to assoc. prof. surgery U. Pa. Sch. Medicine, Phila., 1964-67; Harry Edison prof. surgery Washington U. Sch. Medicine, St. Louis, 1967-75; surgeon-in-chief, dir. dept. surgery Jewish Hosp., St. Louis, 1967-75; chief of surgery Yale-New Haven Hosp., 1975-85; prof., chmn. dept. surgery Yale U., 1975-85, Donald Guthrie prof. surgery, 1977-85; assoc. dean for clin. affairs St. Louis U. Sch. Medicine, 1985-86; v.p. for the med. ctr. St. Louis U., 1986-90, prof. surgery, 1986-97, prof. emeritus, v.p. emeritus for the med. ctr., 1997; dir. surg. edn. St. Mary's Health Ctr., 1990-97; cons. surgery Nat. Bd. Med. Examiners; cons. to chief of staff VAMC, St. Louis, 1994-97; chmn. NIH surgery B study sect., 1978-82; bd. dirs., med. dir. Healthcare Mgmt., Inc.; vis. prof. various colls. Chief editor Archives of Surgery, 1977-88, sr. cons. editor, 1989-93' edptor Parameters of Health Care, 1986-90; mem. editl. bd. JAMA, 1977-88, Circulatory Shock, Am. Jour. Physiology, 1975-87, Post-grad. Gen. Surgery, Jour. Shock, 1994—; sr. editor: Glenn's Thoracic and Cardiovascular Surgery; contbr. over 580 articles to profl. jours. Life trustee Westminster Coll.; trustee Nat. Commn. for Quality Health Care, 1986-92, HEalth Care Leadership Coun.; bd. dirs. United Way. Capt. USAF, 1959, John and Mary R. Markle scholar acad. medicine, 1963; recipient Rsch. Career Devel. award USPHS, 1965-68, Scientist of Yr. award Sigma Xi, 1991. Mem. ACs, AMA (trustee jour., editl. bd. jour.), Assn. Am. Med. Colls. (coun. acad. socs.), Am. Assn. Thoracic Surgery, Am. Coll. Cardiology, Am. Coll. Chest Physicians, Assn. Acad. Surgery, New Eng. Surg. Soc., Internat. Cardiovasc. Soc., Soc. Thoracic Surgeons, Soc. Univ. Surgeons, Soc. Vascular Surgery, Shock Soc., Internat. Fedn. Shock Socs. (pres. 1992-95), Internat. Vascular Soc. Surgery, Am. Assn. for Surgery of Trauma, Am. Assn. Artificial Internal Organs, Organ Failur Acad. (Trieste, Italy, hon. pres. 1983—), Am. Physiol. Soc., Soc. Critical Care Medicine, Am. Surg. Assn., Ctrl. Surg. Assn., Halsted Soc. Societeé Internat. de Chirurgie, Soc. of Clin. Surgery, Surg. Inpectron Soc., James IV Assn. of Surgeons, Southern Thoracic Surg. Soc., Soc. for Surgery Alimentary Tract, St. Louis Surg. Soc. (hon.), Soc. Grad. Surgeons L.A. County-U. S.C. Med. Ctr. (hon.), Assn. VA Surgeons (hon.), Colombia Surg. Soc. (hon.), Chgo. Surg. Soc. (hon.), L.A. Surg. Soc. (hon.), Mpls. Surg. Soc. (hon.), Indonesian Shock Soc. (hon.), Alpha Omega Alpha. Office: St Louis U Hosp Saint Louis MO 63110-2539

BAUER, A(UGUST) ROBERT, JR., surgeon, educator; b. Phila., Dec. 23, 1928; s. A(ugust) Robert and Jessie Martha-Maynard (Monie) B.; BS, U. Mich., 1949, MS, 1950, MD, 1954; M Med. Sci.-Surgery, Ohio State U., 1960; m. Charmaine Louise Studer, June 28, 1957; children: Robert, John, William, Anne, Charles, James. Intern Walter Reed Army Med. Ctr., 1954-55; resident in surgery Univ. Hosp., Ohio State U., Columbus, also instr., 1957-61; pvt. practice medicine, specializing in surgery, Mt. Pleasant, Mich., 1962-74; chief surgery Ctrl. Mich. Community Hosp., Mt. Pleasant, 1964-65, vice chief of staff, 1967, chief of staff, 1968; clin. faculty Mich. State Med. Sch., East Lansing, 1974; mem. staff St. Mark's Hosp., Salt Lake City, 1974-91; pvt. practice surgery, Salt Lake City, 1974-91; clin. instr. surgery U. Utah, 1975-91. Trustee Rowland Hall, St. Mark's Sch., Salt Lake City, 1978-84; mem. Utah Health Planning Coun., 1979-81. Served with M.C., U.S. Army, 1954-57. Diplomate Am. Bd. Surgery. Fellow ACS, Southwestern Surg. Congress; mem. AMA, Salt Lake County Med. Soc., Utah Med. Assn. (various coms.), Utah Soc. Certified Surgeons, Salt Lake Surg. Soc., Pan Am. Med. Assn. (affiliate), AAAS (affiliate), Sigma Phi Epsilon, Phi Rho Sigma. Episcopalian. Club: Zollinger. Contbr. articles to profl. publs., researcher surg. immunology. Office: PO Box 17533 Salt Lake City UT 84117-0533

BAUER, BARBARA ANN, marketing consultant; b. Fairfield, Ohio, Dec. 4, 1944; d. Charles P. and Grace J. (Peteka) B.; m. Joseph J. Strojnowski. AA, So. Sem. Jr. Coll., Buena Vista, Va., 1964; BA, Am. U., 1966. Pub. relations, advt. specialist Sta. WOR-AM-FM-TV, N.Y.C., 1966-67; pub. relations mgr. Continental Corp., N.Y.C., 1967-68; dir. corp. communications Am. Internat. Group, N.Y.C., 1968-80; dir. mktg. mgmt. infos. CIGNA Corp., Phila., N.Y.C., 1980-83; asst. v.p. Citicorp Credit Services Inc., N.Y.C., 1983-87; v.p., dir. mktg. Skandia Am. Group, N.Y.C., 1987-88, v.p. corp. communications, 1988-89; pres. Bauer Mktg. and Communications, Goshen, N.Y., 1989—; mem. Reinsurance Cons. Network. Lifetime mem. Girl Scouts U.S. Mem. Pub. Rels. Soc. Am. (accredited, counselors' acad.), Assn. Profl Ins. Women (chair pub. rels., advisor bd. dirs.), Wed Pub. Rels. Group.

BAUER, BETSY (ELIZABETH BAUER), artist; b. Mt. Holly, N.J., Jan. 18, 1959; d. Richard Byram and Melvina Barnett (Miller) B. Student, MIT, 1979; BFA, Phila. Coll. Art, 1980; postgrad., Santa Fe Art Inst., 1995, Sch. Visual Arts, Parsons Sch. Design. One-woman shows include Hahn Ross Gallery, Santa Fe, 1996, 98, NAS, Washington, 1997, Bridgewater/Lustberg Gallery, N.Y.C., 1998, 99; exhibited in group shows at Visual Arts Mus., N.Y.C., 1984 , N.Y. Feminist Art Inst., N.Y.C., 1987, Hunter Mus., Chattanooga, 1996, Site Santa Fe, 1997, 98, 99, Bridgewater/Lustberg Gallery, N.Y.C., 1997, 98, Addison/Ripley Gallery, Washington, 1998, Nat. Mus. Women, 1999, N.Mex. Fine Arts, 1999—; represented in permanent collections at Hallmark Fine Art Collection, Kansas City, Mo., Rohm and Haas Corp., Phila. (award), U.S. State Dept.-Am. Embassy, Sarejevo, Nat. Acad. Scis., Washington; Poster and notecards designed for SFO, 1996, 98, 99; animator for advt. Fox-TV, 1993; contbr. articles to profl. jours.; included in New Am. Paintings, 1998, Women Artists in the Land of Enchantment Catalogue, 1999, N.Mex. 2000 Catalogue, 1999-2000. Mem. Santa Fe Coun. for Arts. Home: 66 Two Trails Rd Santa Fe NM 87505-9313 Office: Hahn Ross Gallery 409 Canyon Rd Santa Fe NM 87501-2717

BAUER, BRUCE F., aerospace engineer; b. Washington, Sept. 7, 1912; s. C. Max and Clara Z. Bauer; m. Myfanwy Rhys Bauer. Student, U. Colo., 1930-35; Aero. Engring. Degree, Curtiss-Wright Tech., 1937; Degree in Structural Engring., U. Calif., Long Beach, 1972. Design and devel. engr., flight test engr. XP-38 Lockheed Aircraft Co., Burbank, Calif., 1937-46; flight test engr. Lark Missile and B-36 and XF-92 Consolidated-Vultee, San Diego and Downey, Calif., 1947-48; design and devel. engr. for C-74 and C-124 Douglas Aircraft Co., 1948-50; design and devel. and flight test engr. on C-125, F-89, F-5 Air Conditioner Northrop Aircraft Co., 1950-64, design and devel. engr. Snark Missle and Polaris Navy Submarine Datico Surveillance Computer System, 1950-64; Apollo space, reliability and acceptance engr. N.Am. Space Div., 1964; Saturn S-IVB design, reliability and acceptance engr. Douglas Spare Div., 1964-68; DC-10 air-conditioning system design and devel. engr. Douglas Aircraft Co., 1968-72; contract specifications, reliability, and acceptance engr. for landing assault ships Litton Ships, Pasagoula, Miss., 1973; prin. engr. for final assembly and test facilities for Orbit Shuttle Rockwell Internat., 1973-79; cons. aerospace engr., 1978-84; math. and drafting instr. Curtiss-Wright Tech., Glendale, Calif., 1936-37; prefabricated housing engr., sales mgr. So. Calif. Homes, Inc., 1947-48. With USAAF, 1942-46, CBI, lt. col. USAFR, ret. Mem. AIAA (life, 7 awards 1980-88), Soc. Aeornautical W. Engrs. (charter), Inst. for Advance of Engring., Air Force Assn. (life, 3 meritorious awards, 3 state awards, nat. meritorious award, nat. exceptional svc. award), Res. Officers Assn. (life), Ret. Res. Officers Assn. (life), Phi Kappa Tau. Home: 18882 Parkview Ter Santa Ana CA 92705-1232

BAUER, CARL JONATHAN, public relations executive; b. Harrisburg, Pa., July 2, 1964; s. Carl Frederick and Beulah Katherine Bauer; m. Barbara Ann Esser, Sept. 23, 1989; children: Michael Jonathan, Carl Matthew. AA, Jefferson Coll., 1984; BS, So. Ill. U., 1987; postgrad., Fontbonne Coll., 1998—. News dir. Sta. KLPW-AM/FM, Washington, 1987-89; editor Union Missourian, Union, Mo., 1989-95; pub. rels. dir. East Ctrl. Coll., Union, 1995—; accreditation co-chair East Ctrl. Coll., 1997—; adv. bd. AP, Kansas City, Mo., 1989. Author: Continuing in Faith: St. Peter's Church 1844-1994, 1994. Past pres. St. Peter's United Ch. of Christ, Washington, 1995. Ed Brown scholarship So. Ill. U., 1986; recipient Profl. Devel. award, 1997. Mem. Nat. Coun. for Mktg. and Pub. Rels. (6 Medallion awards 1996—), Rotary Internat. (Paul Harris fellow 1997), Mo. C.C. Assn., Coun. for Advancement and Support for Edn., Phi Theta Kappa. Mem. United Ch. of Christ. Avocations: book collecting, reading, golf. Home: 302 East Lane Dr Washington MO 63090

BAUER, CAROLINE FELLER, author; m. Peter A. Bauer; 1 child, Hilary A. BA, Sarah Lawrence Coll., 1957; MLS, Columbia U., 1958; PhD, U. Oreg., 1971. Children's and reference libr. N.Y. Pub. Libr., N.Y.C., 1958-62; libr. Hewitt Sch., N.Y.C., 1960-61, Eron Prep. Sch., N.Y.C., 1962-63, Colo. Rocky Mountain Sch., Carbondale, 1963-65; art editor Pacific N.W. Libr. Assn. Quar., 1967-72; prodr., instr. Oreg. Edn. Pub. Broadcasting Sys., 1973-74; assoc. prof. Sch. Librarianship U. Oreg., 1966-79; cons. Ednl. Cons. Assocs., Denver, 1979-81; vis. storyteller N.Y. Pub. Libr., 1962-63; prodr., performer Caroline's Corner, Sta. KSNO, Aspen, Colo., 1964-66, Caroline: Folktales Around the World, NET affiliate, 1965-66, Caroline's Corner, Oreg. Ednl. Pub. Broadcasting Sys., 1972-80. Author: Children's Literature, 1973, Storytelling, 1974, Getting It Together with Books, 1974, Caroline's Corner, 1974, What's So Funny? Humor in Children's Literature (cassette), 1977, Handbook for Storytellers, 1977, This Way to Books, 1991, My Mom Travels Alot, 1981, Too Many Books! 1984, Celebrations, 1985, Presenting a Reader's Theater, 1987, Rainy Day, Windy Day, Snowy Day, 1988, Halloween, 1989, Read for the Fun of It, 1992, Leading Kids to Books Through Magic, 1996, Leading Kids to Books Through Puppets, 1997, Take a Poetry Break (video cassette) Creative Storytelling (video cassette), 1979, Valentine's Day, 1993, Putting on a Play, 1993, Caroline Feller Bauer's New Handbook for Storytellers, 1993, Thanksgiving Day, 1994, The Poetry Break, 1994, Leading Kids to Books Through Video, 1997, Leading Kids to Books Through Crafts, 1999; contbr. articles to profl. jours. Recipient Ersted award for disting. tchg. U. Oreg., 1968, Christopher award Jr. Literary Guild award of excellence Chgo. Woman in Pub., 1978, Dorothy McKenzie award for disting. contbn. to children's lit. So. Calif. Coun. on Lit. for Young People, 1986. Mem. ALA (notable books com. 1977-79, chmn. 1980, chmn. Laura Ingalls Wilder com. 1973-75, mem. Newbery-Caldecott com. 1972-78, bd. dirs. children's divsn. 1987-89), Pi Lambda Theta, Beta Phi Mu.

BAUER, CHRIS MICHAEL, banker; b. Milw., Sept. 2, 1948; s. Heinz Gerald and Maria (Weber) B.; m. Susan Marie Branton, June 28, 1969. BBA, U. Wis., 1970; MBA, Marquette U., 1976. Mgmt. trainee 1st Wis. Nat. Bank, Milw., 1970-72, spl. enterprise officer, 1972-74, asst. mgr., 1974-75; v.p. 1st Wis.-Racine, 1976-78; pres. 1st Wis.-Brookfield, 1978-84; 1st v.p. Firstar Corp. (formerly 1st Wis. Corp.), Milw., 1984-86, sr. v.p., 1986-89; pres., COO Firstar Bank Milw. (formerly 1st Wis. Nat. Bank), Milw., 1989-91; chmn., CEO Firstar Bank Milw. (formerly 1st Wis. Nat. Bank), 1991—, also bd. dirs. Bd. dirs. Aurora Health Care Metro Region, Milw., U. Wis.-Milw. Found., Milw. Pub. Libr. Found., Milw. World Festival Inc., J.A. of Wisconsin, Inc., Next Door Found., Siebert Lutheran Found., AAA Mich., AAA Wisconsin; mem. Greater Milw. Com. Mem. Bankers Roundtable, Milw. Country Club, Univ. Club, Westmoor Country Club. Lutheran. Office: Firstar Bank Milw 2640 Buckingham Pl Brookfield WI 53045

BAUER, DAVID CHRISTOPHER L., newspaper editor; b. Cin., Jan. 2, 1963; s. Keith N. and Sallie Ann Bauer; m. Angela Ann Garrett, Sept. 25, 1993; 1 child, Christopher G. BA, Morehead State U., 1985; grad., Citizens Police Acad., Bowling Green, 1998. Reporter Brown County Press, Mt. Orab, Ohio, 1985-86; editor Clermont Sun, Batavia, Ohio, 1986-87; adj. instr. Western Ky. U., Bowling Green, 1988-90, 92-94; mng. editor Ironton (Ohio) Tribune, 1990-91; various positions Daily News, Bowling Green, 1987-90, 91—, editor, 1995—; webmaster News Pub. LLC, Bowling Green, 1998—. Recipient 2d place investigation reporting award So. Newspaper Assn., 1992. Mem. Soc. Profl. Journalists. Methodist. Avocations: web page design, electronics. Fax: 502-783-3237. E-mail: dbauer@bgdailynews.com. Office: Daily News 813 College St Bowling Green KY 42102

BAUER, DIETRICH CHARLES, medical educator; b. Elgin, Ill., July 1, 1931; s. Karl. E. and Martha (Dietrich) B.; m. Lois L. Reed, Nov. 13, 1954. Student, Lake Forest (Ill.) Coll., 1949-51; BS, U. Ill., 1954; MS, Mich. State U., 1957, PhD, 1959; postgrad., Case Western Res. U., Cleve., 1959-61. Rsch. asst. dept. microbiology Mich. State U., East Lansing, 1957-59; asst. prof. dept. microbiology and immunology Ind. U. Sch. Medicine, Indpls., 1961-65, acting chmn. dept., 1964-65, 81, assoc. prof., 1965-68, prof., 1968-96, chmn. dept. microbiology/immunology, 1981-96; prof. emeritus Ind. U. Sch. Medicine; cons. Chas. Pfizer Co., 1968-71, John Wiley, Pub., 1979-80. Recipient Disting. Teaching award Ind. U., 1978, Faculty Colloquium on Excellence in Teaching award FACET, 1992. Mem. AAAS, Am. Soc. Microbiology, Am. Assn. Immunologists, Assn. Med. Sch. Microbiology and Immunology Chmn., Sigma Xi. Office: Indiana Univ Sch Medicine 635 Barnhill Dr Indianapolis IN 46202-5126*

BAUER, DOUGLAS F., lawyer; b. Lackawanna, N.Y., Nov. 20, 1942; s. Ellsworth W. and Gloria G. (Fakler) B. AB magna cum laude, Princeton U., 1964; JD cum laude, Harvard U., 1967. Bar: N.Y. 1967, D.C. 1979, U.S. Supreme Ct. 1979. Assoc. Chadbourne & Parke, N.Y.C., 1967-71; assoc. counsel Gulf & Western Industries, Inc. (Paramount Communications, Inc.), N.Y.C., 1971-75; gen. counsel Amerace Corp., N.Y.C., 1975-86; gen. counsel, corp. sec. Bowne & Co., Inc., N.Y.C., 1986—. Author: The Grolier Club 1884-1984, 1984; editor: The Bowne Family of Flushing, N.Y., 1987; contbr. articles to profl. jours. Mem. Fellows of the Pierpont Morgan Libr., N.Y.C., 1984—; trustee Bowne House Hist. Soc., Flushing, N.Y., 1986—, pres., 1996—; sec.-treas., trustee Robert Bowne Found., N.Y.C., 1986—; coun. Friends of the Princeton U. Libr., 1980—; chmn. bd. trustees Am. Printing History Assn., 1991-94. Mem. ABA, Assn. of Bar of City of N.Y. (non-profit com. 1997—), N.Y. State Bar Assn. (corp. law com. 1982—), Nat. Assn. Corp. Dirs., Am. Soc. Corp. Secs. Republican. Lutheran. Club: Princeton, Grolier. Home: 300 Rector Pl New York NY 10280-1416 Office: Bowne & Co Inc 345 Hudson St Fl 10 New York NY 10014-4589

BAUER, ELAINE LOUISE, ballet dancer; b. Indpls., July 18, 1949; d. Thomas Bryant and Elenita Mae (Bodwell) B.; m. D. David Brown, June 5, 1971. BA in Dance magna cum laude, Butler U., 1971, DFA (hon.), 1989. Registered fine arts craft artist. Mem. corps. de Ballet Boston Ballet Co., 1971; soloist Boston Ballet Co., Boston, 1972, principal ballerina, 1974-89; ret., 1989; ballet mistress Boston Ballet Co., 1990-95; tchr. Boston Conservatory, 1998—; tchr. dance divsn. Harvard Radcliffe U., 1998; artistic dir. Boston Ballet Sch's. Children's Summer Workshop, 1986-90; long range planning com. Walnut Hill Sch. for Performing Arts. Starred (with Rudolf Nureyev in) N.Y.C. debut of La Sylphide., 1980. Com. mem. Task Force on Future of Butler U. Fine Arts Coll., Indpls., 1986; co-organizer Glasnost Dance Medicine Conf., 1990; mem. bd. visitors Walnut Hill Sch. Fine Arts, 1991—, Butler U. Fine Arts Sch., 1996—. Recipient Alumni Achievement award, Butler U., 1987, Eliot Norton award for lifetime achievement in dance Boston Theater Dist. Orgn., 1990; named to North Cen. High Sch. Alumni Hall of Fame, 1991. Avocations: gardening, needlepoint, knitting, singing.

BAUER, ERNST GEORG, physicist, educator; b. Schoenberg, Germany, Feb. 27, 1928. MS, U. Munich, 1953, PhD in Physics, 1955. Rsch. asst. U. Munich, 1955-58; head crystal physics br. Michelson Lab., China Lake, Calif., 1958-69; prof. Tech. U. Clausthal, Germany, 1969-96; disting. rsch. prof. Ariz. State U., Tempe, 1993—. Author: Elektronenbeugung, 1958. Recipient Gaede prize German Vacuum Soc., 1988, Welch award Am. Vacuum Soc., 1992, Niedersachsenpreis, 1994. Fellow Am. Phys. Soc., Am. Vacuum Soc.; mem. Goettingen Acad. Sci., Materials Rsch. Soc., German Electron Microscopy Soc. Office: Ariz State Univ Dept Phys Astronomy Tempe AZ 85287-1504

BAUER, EUGENE ANDREW, dermatologist, educator; b. Mattoon, Ill., June 17, 1942; s. Eugene C. and Madge L. (Armer) B.; m. Gloria Anne Hehman, Feb. 19, 1966; children: Marc A., Christine A., J. Michael, Amanda F. BS, Northwestern U., 1964, MD, 1967. Diplomate Am. Bd. Dermatology, Nat. Bd. Med. Examiners. Intern Barnes Hosp., St. Louis, 1967-68; resident, fellow div. dermatology Washington U. Med. Ctr., 1968-70; instr. Washington U., St. Louis, 1971-72, asst. prof. dermatology, 1974-78, assoc. prof., 1978-82, prof., 1982-88; prof. chmn. Stanford U. Sch. Medicine, 1988-95; program dir. Gen. Clin. Rsch. Ctr., 1990-93; dean Stanford U. Sch. Medicine, 1995—; v.p. for med. affairs Stanford U., 1997—; mem. adv. coun. Nat. Inst. Arthritis and Musculoskeletal and Skin Diseases, 1997—; bd. dirs. Stanford Health Svcs., U. Calif. San Francisco-Stanford Health Care, Connetics Corp., Reconstructive Techs. Contbr. numerous articles to profl. jours. Served to lt. comdr. USNR, 1972-74. Fellow Am. Acad. Dermatology; mem. Am. Fedn. Clin. Research, Am. Soc. Clin. Investigation, Am. Dermatol. Assn., Soc. Investigative Dermatology (bd. dirs. 1981-86, assoc. editor Jour. Investigative Dermatology 1982-87, pres.-elect 1994-95, pres. 1995-96), Ctrl. Soc. Clin. Rsch., Assn. Am. Physicians, Inst. of Medicine of NAS, Am. Clin. and Climatological Assn. Office: Stanford U Sch Medicine Office of the Dean M121 Stanford CA 94305

BAUER, FREDERICK CHRISTIAN, motor carrier executive; b. Camden, N.J., Feb. 5, 1927; s. John Albert and Lillian (Saar) B.; m. Dorothy Jane Baker, Jan. 24, 1946; children: Susan, Joan, Scott, Christi. B.A., U. N.C., 1948, M.A., 1949, grad. exec. program, 1967. Tchr. R.J. Reynolds High Sch., Winston-Salem, N.C., 1949-51; sales rep. McLean Trucking Co., Winston-Salem, 1951-58; dist. sales mgr. McLean Trucking Co., Memphis, 1958-62; market research mgr. McLean Trucking Co., Winston-Salem, 1962-63; Western sales mgr. McLean Trucking Co., Indpls., 1963-67; v.p. sales McLean Trucking Co., Winston-Salem, 1967-74; exec. v.p. mktg. McLean Trucking Co., 1974-82; v.p. mktg. Kenan Transport Co., Chapel Hill, N.C., 1982—. Served with AUS, 1944-46. Mem. Research Inst. Am., Nat. Indsl. Conf. Bd., Am. Trucking Assn. (sales council 1963), Delta Nu Alpha, Sigma Chi. Presbyterian. Home: 150 Westhaven Cir Winston Salem NC 27104-1855 Office: Kenan Transport Co PO Box 2729 Chapel Hill NC 27515-2729

BAUER, HENRY HERMANN, chemistry and science educator; b. Vienna, Austria, Nov. 16, 1931; came to U.S., 1965, naturalized, 1969; s. Martin Josef and Anne (Rafael) B.; m. Barbara Bush, Aug. 25, 1986; children from previous marriage: Helen Suzanne, Judith Ann. B.Sc., U. Sydney, 1952, M.Sc., 1953, Ph.D., 1956. Rsch. assoc. U. Mich., 1956-58, vis. scientist, 1965-66; lectr., sr. lectr. U. Sydney, 1958-66; assoc. prof., prof. U. Ky., 1966-78; vis. prof. Southampton (Eng.) U., 1972-73; dean Coll. Arts and Scis. Va. Poly. Inst. and State U., Blacksburg, 1978-86, prof. chemistry and science studies Coll. Arts and Scis., 1986—. Author: Alternating Current Polarography and Tensammetry, 1963, Electrodics, 1973, Instrumental Analysis, 1978, Beyond Velikovsky, 1984, Enigma of Loch Ness, 1986, (under pseudonym Josef Martin) To Rise Above Principle, 1988, Scientific Literacy and the Myth of the Scientific Method, 1992. Fulbright fellow, 1956-58; Japan Soc. fellow for promotion of sci., 1974. Mem. Soc. Sci. Exploration (founding mem., councillor), Internat. Soc. Cryptozoology. Unitarian. Office: Va Poly Inst and State U Lane Hall Blacksburg VA 24061-0227

BAUER, JEAN MARIE, accountant; b. Morristown, N.J., Sept. 10, 1958; d. Earl F. and Patricia A. (O'Brien) W.; m. Ronald F. Bauer, Sr. AA in Acctg., County Coll. of Morris, 1978; BSBA, Coll. of St. Elizabeth, Convent

Station, N.J., 1986. Sec. to payroll supr. Monroe Calculator, Morris Plains, N.J., 1979-80; clk. typist Stewart Title, Morris Plains, 1980-81; with BASF Corp., Mount Olive, N.J., 1981—; credit rep. chems. div. BASF Corp., Parsippany, N.J., 1986-88; property acct. III BASF Corp., Mount Olive, N.J., 1988—. Co-leader folk group Sacred Heart Ch. of Dover, N.J., 1981, adult leader youth group, 1982, eucharistic minister, 1993—, vol. religious edn. chr. St. Jude Ch., Budd Lake, N.J., 1993; spl. dep. registrar boro Mountain Lakes, N.J., 1976. Named one of Outstanding Young Women in Am., U.S. Jaycees, 1985. Mem. Cath. Daughters Am. (treas. Dover chpt. 1987-89, regent 1989-91). Republican. Avocations: needlepoint, cooking, travel, gardening. Home: HC 1 Box 1896 Tafton PA 18464-9718 Office: BASF Corp Property Acctg 3000 Continental Dr N Budd Lake NJ 07828-1234

BAUER, JEROME LEO, JR., chemical engineer; b. Pitts., Oct. 12, 1938; s. Jerome L. and Anna Mae (Tucker) B.; children from previous marriage: children: Lori, Trish, Jeff. BSChemE, U. Dayton, 1960; MSChemE, Pa. State U., 1963; postgrad., Ohio State U., 1969. Registered profl. engr., Ohio. Asst. prof. chem. engring. U. Dayton, Ohio, 1963-67; mgr. advanced composites dept. Ferro Corp., Cleve., 1967-72; engring. material and process specifications mgr. Lockheed Missiles & Space Co., Inc., Sunnyvale, Calif., 1972-74; gen. dynamics design specialist Convair Div., San Diego, 1974-76, project devel. engr., 1976-77; dir. research Furane div. M&T Chems. Inc., Glendale, Calif., 1980-82; mem. tech. staff Jet Propulsion Lab., Calif. Inst. Tech., Pasadena, Calif., 1977-80, 82-90; mem. tech. staff mfg. engring. The Aerospace Corp., El Segundo, Calif., 1990—, engring. specialist, 1997—. Editor: Materials Sciences for Future, 1986, Moving Foreward With 50 Years of Leadership in Advanced Materials, 1994, Materials and Processes Challenges, 1996, Evolving & Revolutionary Technologies for the New Millennium, 1999; contbr. articles to profl. jours. Jr. warden St. Luke Episcopal Ch., La Crescenta, Calif., 1980, sr. warden 1981. Fellow Internat. Electronics Packaging Soc. (pres. L.A. chpt. 1982), Soc. Advancement of Material Process Engring. (membership chmn. no. Calif. sect. 1973-74, sec. San Diego sect. 1974-75, vice chmn. 1975-76, chmn. 1976, chmn. L.A. sect. 1977, nat. treas. 1978-82, gen. chmn. 31st internat. symposium exhbn., Las Vegas, Nev., 1986, Meritorious Achievement award 1983, internat. v.p. 1987-89, internat. pres. 1989-90); mem. Am. Inst. Chem. Engrs. (founder, chmn. Dayton sect. 1964-66, spl. projects chmn. Cleve. sect. 1968-69), Phi Lambda Upsilon, Delta Sigma Epsilon. Republican. Avocations: carpentry, photography, camping. Home: PO Box 3298 El Segundo CA 90245-8398 Office: The Aerospace Corp 2350 E El Segundo Blvd El Segundo CA 90245-4691

BAUER, JUDY MARIE, minister; b. South Bend, Ind., Aug. 24, 1947; d. Ernest Camiel and Marjorie Ann (Williams) Derho; m. Gary Dwane Bauer, Apr. 28, 1966; children: Christine Ann, Steven Dwane. Ordained to ministry Christian Ch., 1979. Sec. adminstrv. asst. Bethel Christian Ctr., Riverside, Calif., 1975-79; founder, pres. Kingdom Advancement Ministry, San Diego, 1979—, trainer, mgr. cons., Tex., Ariz., Calif., Oreg., Washington, Ala., Okla., Idaho and Republic of South Africa, Guam, Egypt, The Philippines, Australia, Can., Mozambique, Malarwie, Mex., Zimbabwe, Poland, Guatemala, Israel, Scotland, Ireland, Japan, Eng., Zambia, Botheswana, Holland, 1979—; pres. Witty Outerwear Distbrs. Internat., Inc., 1993-96 ; founder, co-pastor Bernardo Christian Ctr., San Diego, 1981-91; evangelism dir. Bethel Christian Ctr., 1978-81, undershepherd minister, 1975-79, adult tchr., 1973-81; chaplain La Mesa Fed. Penitentiary, Tijuana, Mex., 1998—; pres., founder Bethel Christian Ct r. of Rancho Bernardo, Calif., 1991—; condr. leadership tng. clinics, internat. speaker, lectr. in field. Author syllabus, booklet, tng. material packets. Pres., Bernardo Christian Ctr., San Diego, 1981-91. Mem. Internat. Conv. Faith Ministries, Inc. (area bd. dirs. 1983-88). *It's only in selling out to a cause worth dying for that we truly come alive and experience life to the fullest.*

BAUER, LOUIS EDWARD, retail bookstore executive, educator; b. Chgo., Mar. 11, 1937; s. Hermann Martin and Louise Eva (Winckler) B.; m. Inez Marie Gugel, Aug. 26, 1961; children: Erik Nathan, Ethan Joel, Elizabeth Marie, Elena Louise. Student, Valparaiso U., 1955-56; BS, No. State U., Aberdeen, S.D., 1961; MEd, Idaho State U., Pocatello, 1969. Asst. dir. student union No. State U., 1961-62; program dir. student union Idaho State U., 1962-67, dir. student union, 1967-69; dir. union and recreation U. Calif., Davis, 1969-74; dir. Stony Brook Union SUNY, Stony Brook, 1974-77; mng. dir. student union San Francisco State U., 1977-79; dir. aux. svcs. No. State U., 1979-87; pres., gen. mgr. Portland (Oreg.) State Bookstore, 1987—; adj. instr. Faculty of Bus., No. State U., 1979-87; maj. prof. Accelerated Degree program Concordia U., Portland, 1990—. Bd. dirs. Luth. Campus Coun., Portland, 1989-95. Mem. Optimists Internat. (lt. gov. 1985-86), Viking Athletic Club (bd. dirs. 1994—), City Club Portland. Democrat. Lutheran. Avocation: collecting old books. Home: 11845 NW Vaughn Ct Portland OR 97229-4859 Office: Portland State U Bookstore 1880 SW 6th Ave Portland OR 97201-5286

BAUER, MARION DANE, writer; b. Oglesby, Ill., Nov. 20, 1938; d. Chester and Elsie (Hempstead) Dane; m. Ronald C. Bauer, June 25, 1959 (div. Dec. 1988); children: Peter Dane, Elisabeth Alison. AA, LaSalle-Peru-Oglesby Jr. Coll., 1958; student, U. Mo., 1958-59; BA in Lang. Arts, U. Okla., 1961, postgrad., 1961-62. Author: Shelter from the Wind, 1976 (Notable Children's Book ALA, 1976), Foster Child (Golden Kite Honor Book award Soc. Children's Book Writers 1977), Tangled Butterfly, 1980, Rain of Fire, 1983 (Tchrs.' Choices award Nat. Coun. Tchrs. of English 1984, Revs. Choice award ALA Booklist 1983, Children's Book award Jane Addams Peace Assn. 1984), Like Mother, Like Daughter, 1985, On My Honor, 1986 (Newbery Honor Book 1987, Notable Children's Book ALA 1986, Best Books of 1986 Sch. Libr. Jour., Editors' Choice Booklist 1986, Pub.'s Weekly Choice The Yr.'s Best Books 1986, Flicker Tale Children's Book award, N.D., 1989, Golden Archer award, Wis. 1989, William Allen White Children's Book award, Kans., 1989, BBY, IRA selection for Janusc Korczak Lit. Competition Poland 1990), Touch the Moon, 1987, A Dream of Queens and Castles, 1990; (drama) God's Tears: A Woman's Journey, Face to Face, 1991 (Children's Book of Distinction, Hungry Mind Review, 1992), What's Your Story? A Young Person's Guide to Writing Fiction, 1992 (Notable Children's Book ALA 1992), Ghost Eye, 1992, A Taste of Smoke, 1993, A Question of Trust, 1994; editor: Am I Blue? Coming Out from the Silence, 1994, When I Go Camping With Grandma, 1995, A Writer's Story, From Life to Fiction, 1995, Alison's Wings, 1996, Our Stories, A Fiction Workshop for Young Authors, 1996, Alison's Puppy, 1997, If you Were Born a Kitten, 1997, Turtle Dreams, 1997, Alison's Fierce and Ugly Halloween, 1997, Bear's Hiccups, 1998, Christmas in the Forest, 1998, An Early Winter, 1999, Sleep, Little One, Sleep, 1999; contbr. articles, short stories to mags. and books in field. Mem. Authors Guild, Authors League Am., Soc. Children's Book Writers and Illustrators. Democrat. Avocations: camping, theater, raising Rex cats. Home: 8861 Basswood Rd Eden Prairie MN 55344-7407 Office: Clarion 215 Park Ave S New York NY 10003-1603 *Children are our future, of course, but they are also the touchstone for our present. To discover who we are and how we are doing we need only check our reflections in our children's eyes.*

BAUER, MARTY, talent agency execuive. Pres. The Bauer Co., Beverly Hills, Calif., 1978—. Office: The Bauer Co 9465 Wilshire Blvd Ste 620 Beverly Hills CA 90212-2612*

BAUER, MARY JANE, ; b. Scottsbluff, Nebr., May 11, 1955; d. Henry and Martha (Thompson) B.; m. Rodney Ray Pace, Sept. 11, 1997 (div.); children: John Ray Stauffer, Crystal Dawn Stauffer, Martha Jane Stauffer, David Andrew Stauffer. Grad. H.S., Bridgeport, Nebr. Songwriter, lyricist Is It True? and Our Beacon In The Night? on album The Songs of Praise, 1997, A Gift of Love, 1998. Mem. Nat. Environ. Soc., Nat. Childrens Cancer Fund, Disabled Am. Vets., Nat. Arbor Day Found., Colonial Williamsburg Found., Eagles. Avocations: singing, writing, fishing, art, beadwork. Home: PO Box 2183 North Platte NE 69103-2183

BAUER, MICHAEL, newspaper editor. Food and home editor San Francisco Chronicle. Office: San Francisco Chronicle 901 Mission St San Francisco CA 94103-2905*

BAUER, MICHAEL ANTHONY, computer scientist, educator; b. Dayton, Ohio, Feb. 18, 1948; married; 2 children. BSc, U. Dayton, 1970; MSc, U. Toronto, 1971, PhD in Computer Sci., 1978. Rschr. artificial intelligence Edinburgh U., 1974-75; prof. computer sci. U. Western Ont., 1975—, chmn. dept., 1991-96, sr. dir. ITS, 1996—; cons. Geac Computers Internat., 1984-88, IBM, 1991-94; advisor Internat. Bus. Machine Ctr. Advance Studies, 1990-91; vis. scientist IBM Ctr. for Advanced Studies, 1991-98. Mem. Can. Info. Processing Soc. (bd. dirs. 1984-88), Assn. Computing Machinery (bd. dirs. 1989-94). Achievements include research in distributed computing, especially distributed systems and applications management, distributed algorithms, correctness, languages for distributed computing, verification; software engineering, including methodologies, testing, formal specifications, development environments. Office: University of Western Ontario, Middlesex College Rm 355, London, ON Canada N6A 5B7

BAUER, OTTO FRANK, university official, communication educator; b. Elgin, Ill., Dec. 1, 1931; s. Otto Leland and Cora Dorothy (Berlin) B.; m. Jeanette L. Erickson, May 27, 1956; children: Steven Mark, Eric Paul. B.S., Northwestern U., 1953, M.A., 1955, Ph.D., 1959. Instr., then asst. prof. English USAF Acad., Colo., 1959-61, dir. debate, 1959-61; instr. to prof. Bowling Green State U., Ohio, 1961-71, dir. grad. admissions and fellowships, 1965-69; asst. dean Grad. Sch. Bowling Green State U., 1967-69, asst. v.p., 1970-71; ACE fellow U. Calif.-Berkeley, 1969-70; prof. communication U. Wis.-Parkside, Kenosha, 1971-79; vice chancellor U. Wis. -Parkside, Kenosha, 1971-76; acting chancellor U. Wis.-Parkside, 1974-75; vis. prof. communication, spl. asst. to chancellor U. Wis., Madison, 1976-77; vice chancellor for acad. affairs U. Nebr., Omaha, 1979-94, prof. communication, 1979—, vice chancellor emeritus, 1995; cons. Bishop Clarkson Coll. Nursing, Omaha, also 4 others, 1981—; mem. Commn. on Instns. Higher Edn., North Ctrl. Assn. Colls. and Schs., 1975-77, 84-88, cons., evaluator, 1976—, bd. dirs. 1989-94. Author: Fundamentals of Debate, 1966, rev. edit., 1999, Lower Moments in Higher Education, 1997; co-author: Guidebook for Student Speakers, 1966; editor: Introduction to Speech Communication, 1968. Bd. dirs. United Way Kenosha County, Wis., 1973-79, Kenosha County coun. Girl Scouts U.S., 1977-79; chmn. spkrs. bur. United Way Midlands, Omaha, 1983, mem. allocations coms., 1985-93, steering com., 1989-93; bd. dirs. Fontenelle Forest Assn., 1987-94, v.p., 1990-92; bd. dirs. Clarkson Coll., 1992—, vice-chair, 1995-97, chair, 1997—. Recipient Faculty Disting. Svc. award U. Wis., Parkside, 1978, Chancellor's medal U. Nebr., Omaha, 1994, Disting. Svc. award U. Nebr. Aviation Inst., Omaha, 1994; named Faculty Man of Yr., Bowling Green State U., 1967, Exec. of Yr., Nat. Secs. Assn., Omaha, 1980; Clarion DeWitt Hardy scholar, 1949-53. Mem. Am. Coun. on Edn. (exec. com. coun. of fellows 1982-85), Nat. Comm. Assn., Rotary. Office: U Nebr 6001 Dodge St Omaha NE 68182

BAUER, PETER, publishing executive. Pub. People Mag., 1998—. Office: People/Time Inc 1271 Ave of Americas New York NY 10020-1393*

BAUER, RALPH GLENN, lawyer, maritime arbitrator; b. Bellevue, Pa., May 22, 1925; m. Rosemary Larson. BS, Yale U., 1946; BSE, U. Mich., 1948, JD, 1951. Bar: Mich. 1951, N.Y. 1952. Assoc. Haight, Gardner, Poor & Havens, N.Y.C., 1951-69, ptnr., 1970-94; arbitrator, N.Y.C., 1973—; speaker Soc. Maritime Arbitrators, N.Y.C., 1978—; tchr. World Trade Inst., N.Y.C., 1986—; adj. prof. Cardozo Law Sch., 1992—, Hofstra Law Sch., 1995—. Author: Poor on Charter Parties, (supplement), 1974, Tiberg on Demurrage, 4th edit., 1995; contbr. articles to Tulane Law Rev., Lloyds Press, Congress Maritime Arbitrators and Jour. Maritime Law and Commerce. Ensign USN, 1943-46, PTO. Mem. ABA (chmn. com. 1986-88), Internat. Bar Assn., Maritime Law Assn. (chmn. com. 1993-95), London Maritime Arbitrators Assn. (supp.), Soc. Naval Architects (assoc.), Yale Club (N.Y.C.), Raritan Yacht Club (Perth Amboy, N.J.). Episcopalian. Avocation: boating. Office: Haight Gardner Holland & Knight 195 Broadway Rm 2400 New York NY 10007-3189

BAUER, RANDY MARK, management training firm executive; b. Cleve., Sept. 2, 1946; s. Ralph I. and Gloria P. Bauer; B.S. summa cum laude, Ohio State U., 1968; M.B.A., Kent State U., 1971; m. Sue Dellva, July 4, 1975; children—Sherri, Kevin. Mgmt. auditor Peat Marwick Mitchell & Co., Cleve., 1971-72; mgmt. devel. specialist GAO, Denver, 1972-80; adj. prof. mgmt. Columbia Coll., Denver, 1979—; pres. Leadership Tng. Assos., Denver, 1979—; condr. exec. devel. workshops U. Colo., Denver, 1979—. Recipient Best in 1976 award GAO. Mem. Am. Soc. for Tng. and Devel., Beta Gamma Sigma. Address: 10022 Oak Tree Ct Lone Tree CO 80124-9714

BAUER, RAYMOND GALE, sales professional; b. Merchantville, N.J., June 19, 1934; s. Robert Irwin and Florence Winifred (Guyer) B.; m. Jayne Whitehead, Feb. 15, 1955; 1 child, Linda Joan. AA, Monmouth Coll., West Long Branch, N.J., 1955; BBA, U. Miami, 1958. Divsn. mgr. R.J. Reynolds Tobacco Co., Winston-Salem, N.C., 1959-68; Mid. Atlantic mgr. U.S. Envelope Co., Springfield, Mass., 1968-74; divsn. sales mgr. Eastern Tablet Corp., Albany, N.Y., 1974-75; owner Ray Bauer Assos., mfrs. reps., Haddonfield, N.J., 1975—. With USAFR, 1959-64; officer Air Force Aux. Mem. Friends of Haddonfield (N.J.) Libr., Haddonfield Civic Assn., Smithsonian Assocs., Monmouth Coll., U. Miami Alumni Assn., Nat. Philatelic Soc., Am. Security Coun., Air Force Assn., Am. Conservative Union, Am. Mgmt. Assn., Internat. Platform Assn., Sch. and Home Office Products Assn., Am. Legion, Rep. Club (Haddonfield), U.S. Senatorial Club, Arrowhead Racquet Club, Iron Rock Swim and Country Club, Lambda Sigma Tau, Lambda Chi Alpha. Home and Office: 132 Maple Ave Haddonfield NJ 08033-1432

BAUER, RICHARD CARLTON, nuclear engineer; b. Batavia, N.Y., July 15, 1944; s. Willard Ronald and Ethel Ann (Roth) B.; B.S. in Chem. Engring. (Clarkson Trustee scholar), Clarkson Coll. Tech., 1966; M. in Engring., Cornell U., 1968; Ph.D. in Nuclear Sci., Engring. (Bettis Doctoral Program fellow), Carnegie-Mellon U., 1974; cert. in bus. mgmt. Am. Mgmt. Assn. Extension Inst., 1989; m. Madeline Joy Amreich, June 28, 1969; children: Jason Todd, Cheryl Robyn. Technician, Graham Mfg. Co., Batavia, N.Y., summer 1965; engr. Linde div. Union Carbide Corp., Tonawanda, N.Y., summer 1966; hot cell operator asst. Cornell U., Ithaca, N.Y., 1967; engr. Bettis Atomic Power Lab. div. Westinghouse Corp., West Mifflin, Pa., 1968-73, sr. engr., 1973-78, staff engr., 1978, mgr. AIW performance analysis, 1979-82, AIW/S5G performance analysis, 1982-86, mgr. centralized safety and plant analysis support, 1986-93, mgr. centralized thermal hydraulic devel. group, 1994—; employee tng. lectr. reactor safety, sec. lab. reactor ops. safety com. Chmn. Cornell Secondary Schs., Pitts.; chmn. P.E.I. Pitts. Regents fellow, 1962; AEC spl. fellow, 1967; registered profl. engr., Pa.; cert. fallout shelter analyst, multiprotection designer. Mem. Nat. Soc. Profl. Engrs., Pa. Soc. Profl. Engrs. (chmn. sustaining assocs. com., dir. chpt. 1981-83, 2d v.p. 1984, 1st v.p. 1985, chpt. pres. 1987, chpt. past pres. 1988, alt. state dir. 1989, state dir. 1990-94, Mathcounts com. 1984, chpt. award for meritorious service 1984, restructuring task force, 1992-93), Cornell Soc. Engrs. (regional v.p. 1970-83), Am. Nuclear Soc., Am. Mgmt. Assn., N.Y. Acad. Scis., Am. Inst. Chem. Engrs., Soc. Am. Mil. Engrs., Tau Beta Pi, Sigma Xi, Omega Chi Epsilon, Triangle Frat. Contbr. articles to sci. jours.

BAUER, ROBERT FOREST, petroleum engineer; b. Declo, Idaho, Jan. 10, 1918; m. 1940; 4 children. BS, So. Calif. U., 1942. From field rsch. engr. to chief field engr. Union Oil Co., Calif., 1942-52, chief field engr., 1952-54; mgr. offshore group Union, Continental, Shell & Super Oil Co., Calif., 1954-58; pres. Global Marine Exploration Co., 1958-66, chmn., 1966-83; prin. Bauer Land & Cattle Co., 1983—; lectr. Oreg. State U., 1969. Contbr. articles to profl. jours. Mem. UN Econ. Com. Asia & Far East, 1969. Mem. Nat. Acad. Engrs., Am. Inst. Mining, Metallurgy & Petroleum Engrs., Am. Petroleum Inst. Home: 800 Bauer Ranch Philipsburg MT 59858 also: 8570 Enramada Ave Whittier CA 90605-1142*

BAUER, ROGER DUANE, chemistry educator, science consultant; b. Oxford, Nebr., Jan. 17, 1932; s. Albert Carl and Minnie (Lueking) B.; m. Jacquelyn True, Aug. 10, 1956; children—Lisa, Scott, Robert. BS, Beloit Coll., 1953; MS, Kans. State U., 1957, PhD, 1959. Asst. prof. chemistry Calif. State U., Long Beach, 1959-64; assoc. prof. Calif. State U., 1964-69, prof., 1969-92; dean Calif. State U. (Sch. Natural Scis.), 1975-88. Served with U.S. Army, 1954-56. USPHS fellow, 1966; Am. Coun. on Edn. fellow, 1971. Mem. Am. Chem. Soc., Radiation Rsch. Soc., Sigma Xi, Phi Lambda Upsilon. Home: 6320 E Colorado St Long Beach CA 90803-2202 Office: Calif State U Coll Natural Sci Long Beach CA 90840

BAUER, SIMON HARVEY, chemistry educator; b. Kaunas, Lithuania, Oct. 12, 1911; came to U.S., 1921; BS, U. Chgo., 1931, PhD, 1935. Postdoctoral fellow Calif. Inst. Tech.; instr. fuel tech. Pa. State U.; mem. faculty Cornell U., Ithaca, N.Y., 1939—, prof. dept. chemistry, 1950—; fgn. adj. prof. Inst. Molecular Sci., Okazaki, Japan; cons. Los Alamos Nat. Lab., Argonne Nat. Lab., Calspan, Arco-Harvey Tech. Ctr., 1945-85, Lockheed Calic. Co.; lectr., tour speaker Am. Chem. Soc., 1975, 76, 77, 80, 89; Sievers lectr. U.S.C., 1974; Emerson lectr. Emory U., 1989; vis. prof. N.D. State U., 1974, U. Calif., Irvine, 1978, Riverside, 1978. Mem. editorial bd. Combustion and Flame; contbr. over 355 articles to profl. jours. Recipient Alexander von Humboldt award, 1979; Guggenheim fellow, 1949, NAS Interacad. Exch. fellow USSR, 1966. Fellow AAAS, Am. Phys. Soc., Am. Inst. Chemists; mem. Am. Chem. Soc., Sigma Xi, Phi Beta Kappa. Achievements include research in molecular structure determinations by diffraction, EXAFS and spectroscopic techniques, measurement of physical and thermochemical properties of boranes, kinetics of fast reactions and spectral emissions at high temperatures. Studies of condensation from supersaturated vapors. Office: Cornell U Dept Chemistry Baker Lab Ithaca NY 14853-5123

BAUER, STEVEN ALBERT, English educator, writer; b. Newark, Sept. 10, 1948; s. Albert Henry Bauer and Alice Marian Horrocks; m. Elizabeth Ann Arthur, June 19, 1982. BA in English, Trinity Coll., Hartford, Conn., 1970; MFA in English, U. Mass., 1975. Lectr. Colby Coll., Waterville, Maine, 1979-81, asst. prof., 1981-82; asst. prof. Miami U., Oxford, Ohio, 1982-86, assoc. prof., 1986-96, prof. English, 1996—; mem. adv. bd. Co. of Animals Fund, Columbus, Ohio, 1988—. Author: Satyrday, 1982 (ALA Book award 1982), Daylight Savings, 1989 (Peregrine Smith Poetry prize), The Strange and Wonderful Tale of Robert McDoodle, 1999. Fellow Fine Arts Work Ctr., 1978-79; Allan Collins fellow Bread Loaf Writers Conf., 1981, Master Artist fellow Ind. Arts Coun., 1988. Mem. Assoc. Writing Program (dir. member program 1986—), Poets and Writers. Democrat. E-mail: bauersa@muohio.edu. Home: 14100 Harmony Rd Bath IN 47010 Office: Miami U Dept English Oxford OH 45056

BAUER, STUART BARRY, urologist; b. Bklyn., Feb. 23, 1943. BA in Chemistry, Bklyn. Coll., 1964; MD, U. Rochester, 1968. Intern Harborview Hosp. U. Wash., Seattle, 1968-69; resident in surgery Tufts New Eng. Med. Ctr., Boston, 1971-72, resident in urology, 1972-75; assoc. in urology Children's Hosp., Boston, 1977-90; sr. assoc. urology Children's Hosp., 1990—; asst. prof. surgery/urology Harvard Med. Sch., Boston, 1977-90, assoc. prof. surgery/urology, 1990—. Contbr. 40 chpts. to books and numerous articles to profl. jours. Jonas E. Salk scholarship City of N.Y., 1954. Mem. Am. Acad. Pediatrics (chmn. sect. on urology 1994-95, sec. 1991-93, exec. com. mem. 1984-87, Rsch. awards 1998), Am. Urol. Assn., Urodynamics Soc., Internat. Continence Soc., Internat. Children's Contenence Soc. Avocations: skiing, sailing, hiking, bird watching, traveling. E-mail: bauerús@a1.tch.harvard.edu. Office: Dept Urology Children's Hosp 300 Longwood Ave Boston MA 02115

BAUER, THEODORE JAMES, physician; b. Iowa City, Nov. 18, 1909; s. Charles A. and Anna (Braun) B.; m. Helen Mattes, Sept. 1, 1938; children: Jane Helen Bauer Gray, Virginia Ann Bauer Biedron, Martha Jean Bauer. MD, U. Iowa, 1933, BS, 1934. Diplomate Am. Bd. Preventive Medicine and Pub. Health. Intern U.S. Marine Hosp., N.Y., 1933-34; resident in internal medicine U.S. Marine Hosp., Chgo., 1934-36; spl. tng. USPHS, 1936-37; regional cons. venereal disease control Dist. 5, San Francisco, 1938-41; veneral disease control officer Dist. 5, Kansas City, 1941-42; chief nat. div. venereal disease Washington, 1948-53; med. officer in charge Communicable Disease Ctr., Altanta, 1953-56; asst. surgeon gen., dep. chief Bur. State Svcs., Washington, 1956-60; chief Bur. State Services, 1960-62; veneral disease control officer Chgo. Health Dept.; also med. officer charge Chgo. Intensive Treatment Ctr., 1942-48; med. dir. Becton, Dickinson and Co., 1962-67, sr. v.p. rsch. and med. affairs, 1967-75, dir., 1965-85, cons., 1975—; dir. Med. Rsch. Mgmt. Group Inc., 1985-89; assoc. prof. bacteriology and immunology Emory U., 1954-58; mem. adv. com. Inst. Agrl. Medicine U. Iowa, 1954-72; spl. lectr. on venereal diseases Georgetown U. Sch. Medicine, Washington, Calif. U., Northwestern U.; mem. expert com. on venereal infections, trepinematoses WHO; bd. dirs. Nat. Council, 1972-76; mem. Surgeon Gen.'s Adv. Com. on Community Health Services, Adv. Council on the Chronic Sick of N.J., N.J. Health Care Adminstrn. Bd., 1975-86. Editor: Jour. Venereal Disease Info; mem. editorial bd.: Am. Jour. Syphilis, Gonorrhea and Other Venereal Diseases. Mem. gov's. adv. council Chronic Sick of N.J. Recipient Disting. Svc. award USPHS, 1962, Disting. Svc. medal Pub. Health Svc., Dept. Health, Edn., Welfare, 1962, Disting. Achievement award U. Iowa Alumni Assn., 1997. Fellow APHA (chmn. program area com. drugs), Am. Colls. Physicians; mem. AMA, Am. Veneral Disease Assn., Am. Soc. Hygiene Assn. (internat. adv. com.), Pharm. Mfrs. Assn. (med. sect.), Am. Venereal Disease Assn. (Disting. Achievement award 1934-35), Sci. Rsch. Soc. Am. (pres. Communicable Disease Ctr. Br. 1954), Am. Social Health Assn. (bd. dirs.), Nat. Adv. Cmty. Health Com., Bergen County Tuberculosis and Health Assn. (bd. dirs.), U.S.-Mex. Border Pub. Health Assn. (hon. life), Assn. Mil. Surgeons U.S., Bergen County Med. Soc., Med. Assn. N.J., Sigma Xi. Democrat. Roman Catholic. Avocations: golf, travel, investing. Home and Office: 451 Weymouth Dr Wyckoff NJ 07481-1216

BAUER, WILLIAM HENRY, musician; b. N.Y.C., Nov. 14, 1915; s. Charles Henry and Caroline (Schuessler) B.; m. Marion Veronica Costello, March 7, 1921; children: Pamela Ann, William Greig. Musician various bands, 1939-50; faculty N.Y. Conservatory Modern Music, 1946-49; staff musician NBC, N.Y.C., 1950-57; musician Benny Goodman, 1958—, Sherwood Inn, 1960-62, Ice Capades, 1963-67, Broadway Theatre, 1967-70; owner, tchr. Billy Bauer Guitar Sch., 1970—; Musician Woody Herman's First Herd, 1943-46. Author: (autobiography) Sideman, 1996; pub. The Guitar Instructor Reading Music; recorded jazz lines by Lennie Tristano, Lee Konitz and Warne Marsh, (with Lee Konitz) Duet for Saxophone and Guitar. With USO. Recipient Metronome Poll award, 1947-51, Down Beat Poll award, 1949-50. Mem. ASCAP. Avocations: writing mus. backgrounds and basic guitar studies. Office: Billy Bauer Guitar Sch 10 Harvard St Roslyn Heights NY 11577-2456 also: William H Bauer Inc PO Box 270 Albertson NY 11507-0270

BAUER, WILLIAM JOSEPH, federal judge; b. Chgo., Sept. 15, 1926; s. William Francis and Lucille (Gleason) B.; m. Mary Nicol, Jan. 28, 1950; children—Patricia, Linda. A.B., Elmhurst Coll., 1949, LLD, 1969; JD, DePaul U., 1952, LLD (hon.), 1993; John Marshall Law Sch., 1987; LLD (hon.), Roosevelt U., 1994. Bar: Ill. 1951. Ptnr. Erlenborn, Bauer & Hotte, Elmhurst, Ill., 1953-64; asst. state's atty. Du Page County, Ill., 1952-56; 1st asst. state's atty., 1956-58, state's atty., 1959-64; judge 18th Jud. Cir. Ct., 1964-70; U.S. dist. atty. No. Ill. Chgo., 1970-71; judge U.S. Dist. Ct. (no. dist.), Chgo., 1971-75; judge U.S. Ct. Appeals (7th cir.), 1975-86, chief judge, 1986-93; senior judge U.S. Ct. Appeals (7th cir.), Chicago, 1994-; instr. bus. law Elmhurst Coll., 1952-59; adj. prof. law DePaul U., 1978-91; former mem. Ill. Supreme Ct. Com. on Pattern Criminal Jury Instrns.; chmn. Fed. Criminal Jury Instrn. Com. 7th Cir. Trustee Elmhurst Coll., 1979—, De Paul U., 1984—, DuPage Meml. Hosp.; bd. advisors Mercy Hosp. Served with AUS, 1945-47. Mem. ABA, Ill. Bar Assn., Du Page County Bar Assn. (past pres.), Chgo. Bar Assn., Fed. Bar Assn. (former bd. dirs.). Roman Catholic. Clubs: Union League, Law, Legal (Chgo.). Office: US Ct Appeals 219 S Dearborn St Ste 2754 Chicago IL 60604-1803*

BAUERLY, RONALD JOHN, marketing educator; b. Monroe, Wis., Oct. 31, 1953; s. Jack Leroy and Josephine (Wiegel) B.; m. Robin Rochelle Kramer, Aug. 8, 1981; children: Shannon Marie, Thomas Joseph. BBA, U. Iowa, 1975, MBA, 1977; DBA, Southern Ill. U., Carbondale, 1989. Asst. mgr. K-Mart Corp., Racine, Wis., 1977-78; instr. Metropolitan Tech. Community Coll., Omaha, 1978, Loras Coll., Dubuque, Iowa, 1979-81, Northwest Mo. State U., Maryville, 1981-82; asst. prof. Brescia Coll., Owensboro, Ky., 1983-86; asst. prof. mktg. Western Ill. U., Macomb, 1987-91, assoc. prof., 1991-96, prof., 1996—. Editor Jour. of Contemporary Business Issues; contbr. articles to jours. Mem. Am. Acad. Advt., Am. Mktg. Assn., Assn. for Consumer Rsch., Acad. Mktg. Sci., Mktg. Mgmt. Assn., Phi Kappa Phi, Beta Gamma Sigma. Office: Western Ill U 424 Stipes Macomb IL 61455

BAUERSFELD, CARL FREDERICK, lawyer; b. Balt., June 9, 1916; s. Emil George and Irene Marie (Hulse) B.; m. Ann Yancey, Mar. 3, 1944 (div.); children: Elizabeth Bauersfeld Garnett, Carl F. Student, George Washington U., 1937-42; LLB, Am. U., 1937. Bar: D.C. 1937, U.S. Dist. Ct. D.C. 1937, U.S. Ct. Appeals (D.C. cir.) 1937, U.S. Supreme Ct. 1941, U.S. Ct. Claims 1946, U.S. Tax Ct. 1946, Md. 1957, U.S. Ct. Appeals (5th cir.) 1947, (9th cir.) 1956, (3d cir.) 1958, (8th cir.) 1960, (4th cir.) 1966, (2d cir.) 1970. Practiced in Washington, 1937—; now partner firm Bauersfeld, Burton, Hendricks & Vanderhoof, L.L.C.; lectr. on fed. taxation at various univs. Lt. comdr. USNR, 1942-46. Mem. ABA, Md. Bar Assn., Bar Assn. D.C., Congl. Country Club, Burning Tree Club, Sigma Nu Phi, Phi Sigma Kappa. Lutheran. Office: 7101 Wisconsin Ave Bethesda MD 20814-4871

BAUGH, CHARLES MILTON, biochemistry educator, college dean; b. Fayetteville, N.C., June 20, 1931; s. John Yewell and Dorothy Ann (Shaw) B.; m. Ebby O. Jonsdottir, Oct. 24, 1953; children: Dorothy Baugh Ledbetter, Barbara Baugh Baumer, Charis Baugh Spyridon, Lisa Baugh Eckert. BS in Biochemistry, U. Chgo., 1958; PhD in Biochemistry, Tulane U., 1962. Instr. Tulane U., New Orleans, 1963-64, asst. prof. biochemistry, 1964-65; asst. prof. medicine and pharmacology Washington U., St. Louis, 1965-66; assoc. prof. medicine and biochemistry U. Ala., Birmingham, 1966-70, prof. pediatrics, medicine and biochemistry, 1970-73; prof. biochemistry U. South Ala., Mobile, 1973—, chmn. dept., 1973-81, assoc. dean basic sci., 1976-87, dean Coll. Medicine to dean and v.p. med. affairs, 1987-92, 99—; extensive rsch. cons. Australian Nat. Health and Med. Rsch. Coun., 1975—, Med. Rsch. Coun. Can., 1976—; pres. South Ala. Med. Sci. Found., Mobile, 1982-92. Contbr. numerous articles, book chpts. to profl. publs. With USN, 1951-55. Predoctoral fellow NIH, Walter Libby Rsch. fellow Am. Heart Assn., La. chpt.; scholastic scholar U. Chgo.; recipient numerous grants NIH, Am. Cancer Soc., others. Fellow Royal Soc. Medicine (Eng.); mem. Soc. Exptl. Biology and Medicine, Am. Inst. Nutrition, Am. Soc. Biochemistry and Molecular Biology, Ala. Acad. Sci. (pres. 1982), So. Med. Assn. (hon.), Alpha Omega Alpha (hon.). Home and Office: 105 Deer Ct Daphne AL 36526-4012

BAUGH, COY FRANKLIN, corporate executive; b. Mt. Vernon, Ark., Feb. 7, 1946; s. Oather Lee Baugh and Eula Faye (Barnett) Baugh King; m. Cheryl Ann Linscott; 1 child, David F. AA, Glendale Coll., 1969; BS, Calif. State U., 1971; postgrad., Cornell U., 1978—; MBA, U. So. Calif., 1992. Sr. tax specialist Ernst & Young, 1971-74; audit supr. Amfac, Inc., San Francisco, 1974-77, v.p., treas., 1984-88; controller Fisher Cheese, Inc., Wapakoneta, Ohio, 1977-80, v.p. fin., 1980-84; v.p., treas. Furr's Inc., Lubbock, Tex., 1990-91, PacifiCare Health Sys., Inc., Cypress, Calif., 1993—. Clubs: L.A. Treasurers (pres. 1996). E-mail: baughúcf@exchang.phs.com. Office: Pacificare Health Sys PO Box 25186 Santa Ana CA 92799-5186*

BAUGH, JAMES A., mathematics educator, retired army officer; b. Lorain, Ohio, Aug. 17, 1950; s. Leslie G. and Louise K. Baugh; m. Debra J. Furr, June 7, 1973; children: Rachel M., Justin C. BS, U.S. Mil. Acad., 1973; M in Natural Sci., Ariz. State U., 1984; MBA, L.I. U., 1986. Major U.S. Army, 1968-92; math. instr. Maricopa C.C., Phoenix, 1994—. Chmn. scout com. Boy Scouts Am., Mesa, Ariz., 1997-99. Mem. Am. Assn. Math. Assn. Two-Year Colls., Faculty Assn. (senator, treas. 1994—). Republican. Mem. LDS Ch. Avocations: handball, tennis. Office: Gateway CC 108 N 40th St Phoenix AZ 85034

BAUGH, JERRY PHELPS, lawyer; b. Evansville, Ind., July 20, 1933; s. Emmanuel Henry and Elva Lorene (Winkler) B.; m. Mary Frances Jones, July 16, 1960; children: David E., Matthew K., Carolyn G. Student, Exeter (Eng.) U., 1953-54; AB, DePauw U., 1955; JD, U. Mich., 1958. Bar: Ind. 1958, U.S. Dist. Ct. (so. dist.) Ind. 1958, U.S. Supreme Ct. 1971. Fgn. service officer U.S. Dept. State, Washington, 1958-66; ptnr. Baugh & Baugh, Evansville, Ind., 1966-74; asst. city atty. City of Evansville, 1967-70, city atty., 1970-71; ptnr. Lacey, Terrell, Annakin, Heldt & Baugh, Evansville, 1974—, Terrell, Baugh, Salmon & Born LLP, Evansville, 1998—; asst. sec., dir. Cen. Ind., Evansville, 1982-91, sec., 1991-98. Mem. ABA, Ind. State Bar Assn., Evansville Estate Planning Coun. (pres. 1982-83), Evansville Bar Assn. (pres. 1983-84), Order of Coif. Democrat. Episcopalian. Home: 100 NW 1st St Apt 104 Evansville IN 47708-1223 Office: Terrell Baugh Salmon & Born 5011 Washington Ave Evansville IN 47715-4865

BAUGH, JOHN FRANK, wholesale company executive, retired; b. Waco, Tex., Feb. 28, 1916; s. John Frank and Nell (Turner) B.; m. Eula Mae Tharp, Oct. 3, 1936; 1 child, Barbara. Student, U. Houston, 1934-36. With A & P Food Stores, Houston, 1932-46; owner, operator Zero Foods Co., Houston, 1946-69; with Sysco Corp., Houston, 1969-98, chmn. bd., 1969-85, sr. chmn. bd., 1986-98, ret., 1998; bd. dirs. Bank of Houston. Founding trustee Houston Bapt. U.; chmn. deacons Bapt. Ch., Houston, 1954-55, chmn. bd. trustees, 1966-86; trustee, bd. regents Baylor U. Mem. Lakeside Country Club.

BAUGH, L. DARRELL, financial executive; b. Prairie Grove, Ark., Oct. 7, 1930; s. Lacey D. and Mary Grace (Brown) B.; m. Wileeta Claire Gray, June 15, 1958; children: Adrienne Leigh Calvo, John Grayson. BBA, U. Ark., 1954; MBA, U. Colo., 1960; CLU, Am. Coll., 1967. CLU, Am. Coll. 1967; chartered fin. cons.; cert. estate planner. With Penn Mutual Life Ins. Co., 1961-71; gen. agt. Penn Mut. Life Ins. Co., Sacramento, 1968-71; pres. Nat. Estate Planning Inst., Boulder, Colo., 1974—; faculty estate planning seminars Colo. State U.; dir. Nat. Assn. Estate Planner/Coun., 1992-95; cons. U. Colo. Center for Confs. Mgmt./Tech. Programs, 1975-80; sponsor ednl. programs for profl. estate planners and estate owners. Contbr. articles to profl. jours. Bd. dirs. Boulder Men's Christian Fellowship. With U.S. Army, 1954-56. Mem. Boulder C. of C., Soc. of Profl. Fin. Advisors, Boulder County Estate Planning Coun. (pres. 1972-73), Sacemento Estate Planning Coun., Soc. Fin. Svc. Profls., Nat. Registry Fin. Planners (interview com.), Nat. Assn. Estate Planners (planners accreditation com., mem. Denver study group), Student Venture (bd. dirs.), Flatirons Country. Office: 4770 Baseline Rd Boulder CO 80303-2666

BAUGHER, PETER V., lawyer; b. Chgo., Oct. 2, 1948; s. William and Marilyn (Sill) B.; m. Robin Stickney, Nov. 25, 1978; children: Julia Allison, Britton William Herbert. AB, Princeton U., 1970; JD, Yale U., 1973. Bar: Ill. 1974, U.S. Dist. Ct. (no. dist.) Ill. 1974, U.S. Ct. Appeals (7th cir.) 1974, U.S. Supreme Ct. 1987. Law clk. to judge U.S. Ct. Appeals (7th cir.), Chgo., 1973-74; from assoc. to ptnr. Schiff Hardin & Waite, Chgo., 1974-85; ptnr. Adams, Fox, Adelstein & Rosen, Chgo., 1985-89, Schopf & Weiss, Chgo., 1989—; pres. Chgo. Internat. Dispute Resolution Assn.; trustee Sta. WTTW Channel 11, Chgo., 1976-81, Kendall Coll., Evanston, Ill., 1980-92, WBEZ, Chgo. Pub. Radio, 1992-98, Ill. Humanities Coun., 1997—. Mem. adv. com. Rep. Nat. Com., Washington, 1976-81; alt. del. Rep. Nat. Conv., Detroit, 1980; pres. Chgo. Lincoln Inn of Ct., 1994-96. Mem. ABA, Chgo. Bar Assn. (chair internat. and fgn. law com.), Am. Law Inst., Chgo. Coun. Fgn. Rels., Am. Coun. Germany, Ripon Soc. (chmn. 1975-76), Univ. Club, Econ. Club Chgo., Michigan Shores Club. Republican. Home: 1310 Sheridan Rd Wilmette IL 60091-1834 Office: Schopf & Weiss 312 W Randolph St Chicago IL 60606-1764

BAUGHMAN, DENNIS JOHN, director of operations service; b. Lorain, Ohio, May 6, 1966. AS in Electronics, Lorain County C.C., Elyria, Ohio, 1987, AS in CAD, 1987; BS in Fin., Regis U., Denver, 1994. Field svc. engr. Reliance Comm./Tech., Orlando, Fla., 1988-90; regional svc. mgr. Reliance Comm./Tech., Denver, 1990-92, regional mktg. mgr., 1992-94; nat. svc. mgr. Reltec Svcs., North Ridgeville, Ohio, 1994-95; world wide ops. mgr. Reltec Svcs., North Ridgeville, 1995-97, dir. ops., 1997—, nat. account mgr., 1999—. Mem. Sales Execs. of Cleve., Assn. Field Svc. Mgrs. Office: Reltec 38683 Taylor Woods North Ridgeville OH 44039

BAUGHMAN, FRED HUBBARD, aeronautical engineer, former naval officer; b. Michigan City, Ind., Feb. 7, 1926; s. Palmer Hubbard and Mary Moore (Munson) B.; m. Marilyn Ann Weaver, June 20, 1947; children: Lynne Ann, Elizabeth Louise, Bruce Palmer, Laura Alice, Julia Ellen, Robert Alan. B.S., U.S. Naval Acad., 1947; B.S. in Aero. Engring., U.S. Naval Postgrad. Sch., 1956; M.S. in Nuclear Engring., Iowa State Coll., 1957; M.S. in Aeros. and Astronautics, MIT, 1967. Commd. ensign U.S. Navy, 1947, designated naval aviator, 1950, advanced through grades to rear adm., 1973; service in Korean conflict, 1950-53; S-3A project mgr. (Naval Air Systems Command Hdqrs.), Washington, 1968-73; force material officer staff (Naval Air Force, U.S. Pacific Fleet), San Diego, 1973-76; vice comdr. Naval Air Systems Command, 1976-79, comdr. Pacific Missile Test Center, 1979-82, ret., 1982; engr. cons. Aerospace Def. Mgmt. Decorated Legion of Merit with two stars, Air medal with star. Asso. fellow AIAA; mem. Internat. Test and Evaluation Assn. (charter sr. mem.), U.S. Naval Inst. (life), Naval Acad. Alumni Assn. (life), Sigma Xi. Episcopalian. Home and Office: 1600 Crump Farm Rd New Bern NC 28562-3653

BAUGHMAN, J. ROSS, photographer, writer, educator; b. Dearborn, Mich., May 7, 1953; s. Charles T. and Patricia Jane (Hill) B.; m. Jonalyn Sue Schuon, May 9, 1987 (div. 1995); 1 child, Henry Marshall. B.A. cum laude; B.A. (J. Winton Lemen Photojournalism scholar), Kent State U., 1975. Staff photographer, writer Lorain (Ohio) Jour., 1975-77; contract photographer, writer AP in Africa and Middle East AP in, 1977-78; co-founder Ind. Visions Internat., Inc., 1978; pres. Visions Photo Group, N.Y.C., 1978-97; dir. photography The Day Publ. Co., New London, Conn., 1997—; freelance editor, 1998—; mem. faculty New Sch. for Social Research, N.Y.C., 1979-97, NYU, 1980-82; co-founder, program dir. Focus Photography Symposiums, N.Y.C., 1981-88; adj. prof. U. Mo. Grad. Program in Journalism, N.Y.C., 1984-86. Author: Graven Images: a thematic portfolio, 1976, Forbidden Images: a secret portfolio, 1977, Some Ancestors of the Baughman Family in America: Tracing Back Twelve Generations from Switzerland through Virginia, 1989, Harvest Time, 1994, Apart From the World, 1997. Recipient Pulitzer prize in journalism for feature photography, 1978. Mem. Nat. Press Photographers Assn., Photographers Gallery, Am. Soc. Mag. Photographers (sustaining 1984—), Sigma Delta Chi. *

BAUGHMAN, JAMES CARROLL, information and communication educator; b. President Township, Pa., Nov. 13, 1941; s. Lewis Carroll and Viola Leah (Motter) B.; m. Carolyn England, Apr. 18, 1965; children: Sharon Elizabeth, Susan Carol. BS, Clarion U., 1963; MS, Drexel U., 1967; MA, Case We. Res. U., 1970, PhD, 1971. Tchr., media specialist Phillipsburg (N.J.) Pub. Schs., 1963-65, Weymouth (Mass.) Pub. Schs., 1965-66; supr. edn., demonstration ctr. coord. Mass. Dept. Edn., Boston, 1966-68; asst. prof., assoc. prof. Simmons Coll., Boston, 1971-87, prof., 1987—, dir. media program, 1980—; prin. cons. tchrs. ctr. project Boston Pub. Schs., 1975-78. Author: Trustees, Trusteeship and the Public Good, 1987, Policy Making for Public Library Trustees, 1993; editor: Trustee Voice Jour., 1994—; contbr. articles to profl. jours. Trustee Medfield (Mass.) Pub. Libr. Bd., 1989-94, vice-chair, 1991, chair, 1992. Grantee Whiting Found., 1978, Hollowell Rsch. Fund, 1987, 90. Mem. ALA (life, mem. chmn., 1998—, com. on accreditation 1995—, Rsch. Competition award 1976), Am. Libr. Trustee Assn. (bd. dirs.), Mass. Libr. Trustees Assn. Avocation: gardening,. Home: 101 Green St Medfield MA 02052-1924 Office: Simmons Coll 300 Fenway Boston MA 02115-5820

BAUGHMAN, KENNETH LEE, cardiologist, educator; b. Kansas City, Mo., Oct. 8, 1946; m. Cheryl Jean Cain, Aug. 10, 1968; children: Matthew Tyler, Christopher Rolle. AB in Chemistry, U. Mo., 1968, MD, 1972. Diplomate Am. Bd. Internal Medicine and Cardiology. Intern dept. internal medicine The Johns Hopkins Hosp., Balt., 1972-73, jr. and sr. asst. resident dept. internal medicine, 1973-75, asst. chief Osler Med. Svc., 1975-77; clin. and rsch. fellow div. Cardiology Mass. Gen. Hosp., Boston, 1977-79; asst. prof. Medicine div. Cardiology The Johns Hopkins Hosp., Balt., 1979-84, assoc. prof. Medicine div. Cardiology, 1984-94; prof. medicine clin. cardiology, 1994—; asst. dean postoctoral programs The Johns Hopkins Hosp., Balt., 1985-91, acting dir. div. Cardiology, 1991-92, dir. div. Cardiology, 1992—; chmn. joint com. on housestaff and postdoctoral program The Johns Hopkins U. Med. Hosp., 1985-91, resident, chmn. hours and supervision sub-com., 1989, chmn. maternity policy sub-com., 1990, mem. med. bd., 1985-91; lectr. in field. Contbr. 92 articles to profl. jours. Mem. Am. Heart Assn. (fellow coun. of clin. cardiology 1980—), Am. Coll. Cardiology (nat. program com. 1992-93, gov.-elect Med. chpt. 1993, gov., pres. 1995-96), Am. Fedn. Clin. Rsch., Paul Dudley White Soc., Internat. Soc. for Heart Transplantation. Home: 21 Dembeigh Hill Cir Baltimore MD 21210-1020 Office: The Johns Hopkins Med Inst Blalock 536 600 N Wolfe St Baltimore MD 21287-0005

BAUGHMAN, RAY HENRY, materials scientist; b. York, Pa., Jan. 14, 1943; s. Ray Henry and Ruth Marion (Beers) B.; m. Karen McCarthy, Apr. 30, 1989; children: Lara Crusan, Heather Leigh, Dana Marie, Rebecca Lynn, Alexander Murad. BS in Physics, Carnegie-Mellon U., 1964; MS in Materials Sci., Harvard U., 1966, PhD, 1971. Staff physicist Allied Signal, Inc., Morristown, N.J., 1970-73, group leader, 1974-78, mgr., 1978-90, rsch. fellow, 1990-97, aerospace fellow, 1997—; mem. adv. group for internat. confs. on synthetic materials, 1981—; advisor NATO, NSF, DOE, Japan Found. Mem. editl. bd. Synthetic Metals, 1978—; contbr. articles to profl. jours. Recipient Chem. Pioneer award Am. Inst. Chemists, 1995. Fellow Am. Phys. Soc. (mem. exec. com. forum on indsl. and applied physics 1995—); mem. AAAS, Am. Chem. Soc. (Coop. Rsch. award in Polymer Sci. and Egring, 1996), Materials Rsch. Soc., Russian Acad. Natural Scis. (elected academedian 1997). Achievements include discovery of new polymeric metals and non-linear optical materials, development of advances in understanding solid-state reactions, conducting polymer structure-property relationships and new carbon phases; invented electrochemical mechanical actuators, improved polymer batteries, improved switchable windows, new processes for the synthesis/fabrication of high temperature superconductors and improved sonar sensors; developed time-temperature indicators and new conducting polymers. Home: 411 Mountain Way Morris Plains NJ 07950-1103 Office: Alied Signal 101 Columbia Rd Morristown NJ 07960-4640

BAUGHMAN, R(OBERT) PATRICK, lawyer; b. Zanesville, Ohio, Nov. 18, 1938; s. Robert G. and Kathryn E. B.; m. Joyce Hall, June 17, 1959; 1 dau., Patricia. B.S., Ohio State U., 1960, J.D., 1963. Bar: Ohio 1963. Assoc. firm Sindell & Sindell, Cleve., 1964-71, Jones, Day, Reavis & Pogue, Cleve., 1972-73; asst. atty. gen. State of Ohio, Columbus, 1971-72; pres., prin. firm Baughman & Assocs., Cleve., 1973—. Mem. ABA, Ohio Bar Assn., Cuyahoga County Bar Assn., Nat. Council Self-Insurers, Internat. Assn. Indsl. Accident Bds. and Commns., Internat. Platform Assn. Episcopalian. Club: Columbia Hills Country. Office: 55 Public Sq Cleveland OH 44113-1901

BAUGHMAN, ROBERT PHILLIP, physician; b. Warren, Ohio, Oct. 31, 1951; s. George May and Ellyn (Van Huffel) B.; m. Elyse Ellen Lower, May 25, 1984. BS, Yale U., 1973; MD, Case Western Res. U., 1977. Intern, resident U. Cin., 1977-80, prof. Editor: Bronchoalveolar Lavage, 1990. Fellow ACP, Am. Coll. Chest Physicians; mem. Ctrl. Soc., Am. Thoracic Soc. Roman Catholic. Office: U Cin 231 Bethesda Ave # Ml564 Cincinnati OH 45229-2827

BAUGHMAN, VERNA LEE, anesthesiologist; b. Cokato, Minn., Feb. 14, 1946; d. Ernest T. and Esther M. (Bajari) B. BA, DePauw U., 1968; MD, Loyola U., 1981. Rsch. editor Ency. Britannica, Chgo., 1968-72; editl. coord. Michael Reese Hosp., Chgo., 1972, hosp. adminstr., 1973-79; assoc. prof. U. Chgo., 1985-89; asst. prof. U. Ill., Chgo., 1989-91, assoc. prof., 1991—. Mem. editl. bd. Jour. of Neurosurg. Anesthesiology; contbr. numerous articles to sci. jours. and chpts. to books. Named Outstanding House Staff Officer, 1985, Outstanding Clin. Instr., 1987, 91, 96, 98, 99. Fellow Stroke Coun.; mem. Am. Soc. Anesthesiologists (com. on sci. papers 1995—), Ill. Soc. Anesthesiologists, Internat. Anesthesia Rsch. Soc., Soc. for Neurosurg. Anesthesia and Critical Care. Home: 251 Marengo Ave Forest Park IL 60130-1680 Office: U Illinois at Chgo MC/515 1740 W Taylor St Chicago IL 60612-7232

BAUGHN, ROBERT ELROY, microbiology educator; b. Chanute, Kans., Jan. 31, 1940; s. Berryman Thomas and Oella Louise (Smith) B.; BS, The Citadel, 1963; MS (USPHS fellow), U. Tenn., 1966; PhD (NIH fellow), U. Cin., 1975; MBA, Houston Bapt. U., 1980; m. Myra Donell Phillips, Dec. 12, 1965; children—Heather Lynne, Brenna Gayle. Microbiologist, Hutcheson Meml. Tri-County Hosp., Ft. Oglethorpe, Ga., 1969-71, Parkridge Hosp., Chattanooga, 1971; instr. dept. dermatology and dept. microbiology and immunology Baylor Coll. Medicine, 1975-77, asst. prof., 1977-83, assoc. prof., 1983-93, prof., 1993—; with dept. med. tech. Sch. Allied Health Scis. U. Tex., Houston, clin. assoc. prof., 1985—; assoc. career rsch. scientist, VA, 1990—. Home: 11003 Atwell Dr Houston TX 77096-6129 Office: VA Hosp Bldg Dept Infectious Diseases 2002 Holcombe Blvd Houston TX 77030-4211

BAUGHN, WILLIAM HUBERT, former business educator and academic administrator; b. Marshall County, Ala., Aug. 27, 1918; s. J.W. and Beatrice (Jackson) B.; m. Mary Madiera Morris, Feb. 20, 1945; children: Charles Madiera, William Marsteller. BS, U. Ala., 1940; MA, U. Va, 1941, PhD, 1948. Instr. U. Va., 1942-43, asst. prof., 1946-48; assoc. prof., then prof. econs. and bus. adminstrn. La. State U., 1948-56; prof. U. Tex., 1956-62, chmn. fin. dept., 1958-60, assoc. dean Coll. Bus. Adminstrn., 1959-62; assoc. dir. Sch. Banking of South, 1952-66; dean Coll. Bus. and Pub. Adminstrn. U. Mo., 1962-64; dean Coll. Bus. and Adminstrn. U. Colo., 1964-84, pres., 1985, acting chancellor, 1986-87; pres. U. Colo. System, Boulder, 1990-91; pres. Am. Assembly Collegiate Schs. Bus., 1973-74; chmn. Big Eight Athletic Conf., 1970-71, 78-79, 86-87; dir. Stonier Grad. Sch. of Banking, Rutgers U., 1966-86; mem. council Nat. Collegiate Athletic Assn., 1983-86. Author: (with E.W. Walker) Financial Planning and Policy, 1961; editor: (with C.E. Walker) The Bankers' Handbook, 1966, (with C.E. Walker and T.I. Storrs) 3d rev. edit., 1988, (with D. R. Mandich) The International Banking Handbook, 1983. Served to 1st lt. USAAF, World War II; lt. col. Res. Home: 555 Baseline Rd Boulder CO 80302-7421 Office: U Colo System Boulder CO 80309

BAUKNIGHT, CLARENCE BROCK, consultant; b. Anderson, S.C., May 14, 1936; s. John Edward and Theodosia (Brock) B.; m. Harriet League, June 29, 1959; children: Harriet League, Clarence Brock. B.S., Ga. Inst. Tech., 1958. Dist. mgr. Wickes Corp., and predecessor, Atlanta, 1960-65; exec. v.p. Builder Marts Am., Inc., Greenville, S.C., 1965-87, pres., chief exec. officer, 1987-88, chmn. bd. dirs., 1987-88, now bd. dirs.; CEO, chmn. bd. dirs. Builderway, Inc., 1970-96; chmn. bd. dirs. Enterprise Computer Sys., Inc., 1970—; bd. dirs. Hambold, Inc. Mem. policy adv. bd. Joint Ctr. Urban Studies Harvard U., 1982-87; trustee Bumcombe St. United Meth. Ch., 1985-90, chmn., 1989-90, Greenville Hosp. System, 1987-93, chmn., 1991-92; bd. dirs. Greenville Health Corp., 1994-97. Mem. Chief Exec. Orgn., Greenville Country Club, Poinsett (Greenville), Cullasaja and Highlands, Wild Dunes, Masons, Shriners, Phi Delta Theta. Methodist. Home and Office: PO Box 2183 Greenville SC 29602-2183

BAUKOL, RONALD OLIVER, company executive; b. Chgo., Aug. 11, 1937; s. Oliver Peter and Clara Marie (Haugstad) B.; m. Gay Lynn Gollan, Aug. 29, 1959; children: David, Andrew, Kathlyn. BSChemE, Iowa State U., 1959; MSChemE, MIT, 1960. Engr., group leader Procter & Gamble, Cin., 1960-66; lab. supr. 3M Co., 1966-70; White House fellow, Washington, 1970-71; dir. regional offices EPA, Washington, 1971-72; dept. mgr. dental, new enterprises, diagnostic depts. Minn. Mining & Mfg. Co., St. Paul, 1972-82; v.p., gen. mgr. 3M/Riker Labs., 1982-86; mng. dir., CEO, 3M U.K. PLC, 1986-89; mng. dir. 3M Ireland, 1988-89; group v.p. Pharms. and Dental Products Group, 3M Co., St. Paul, 1989-90, Med. Products Group, 1990-91; v.p. Asia Pacific, 1991-94, v.p. Asia Pacific Can. and L.Am., 1994-95; exec. v.p. internat. ops., 1995—; bd. dirs. Graco, Inc., Mpls, 3M, The Toro Co. Chmn. bd. ARC St. Paul, 1979-81, dir. regional blood com., 1972-86; mem. alumni assn. bd. dirs. Iowa State U., 1974-76, gov. found., 1990—; trustee Minn. Med. Found., 1990-93, Children's Hosp., St. Paul, 1993-95, U.S. Coun. Internat. Bus., 1994—; mem. adv. coun. U. St. Thomas Ctr. Health and Med. Affairs, Minn., 1990-97, internat. programs adv. coun. Carlson Sch. Mgmt., U. Minn., 1998—; bd. dirs. Children's Health Care Found., St. Paul, 1995-97. Named Outstanding Young Alumnus, Iowa State U., 1969. Mem. Brit. Inst. Mgmt. (companion 1988-89), Exec. Coun. on Foreign Diplomacy (bd. overseers 1993—). Methodist. Avocation: tennis. Home: 70 Spruce St Saint Paul MN 55115-1947 Office: 3 M Ctr # 22014 Saint Paul MN 55144-0001

BAULE, STEVEN MICHAEL, secondary education educator, author; b. Southfield, Mich., Sept. 2, 1966; s. Chalres L. and Betty Ann (Lange) B.; m. Kathy Ann Schilling, June 13, 1992. BA, Loras Coll., Dubuque, Iowa, 1988; MALS, U. Iowa, 1991; EdD, No. Ill. U., 1997. Cert. tchr., adminstr., Ill., cert. tchr., Iowa. Tchr. Aquin Sch., Cascade, Iowa, 1989-90; libr. media specialist Haines Mid. Sch., St. Charles, Ill., 1991-94; coord. info. svcs. Glenbrook South H.S., Glenview, Ill., 1994-97; dir. info. tech. New Trier H.S. Dist., Winnetka, Ill., 1997—; editl. cons. Linworth Pub., Worthington, Ohio, 1995—; affiliate prof. No. Ill. U., DeKalb, 1994—. Author: Technology Planning, 1997; contbr. articles to profl. jours. Firefighter, St. Charles Fire Dept., 1992-96. Recipient Iowa Gov.'s Cup for Outstanding ROTC Grad., Gov. of Iowa, 1987; named Sch. Libr. of Yr., North Suburban Libr. Sys., Wheeling, Ill., 1997. Mem. Ill. Sch. Libr. Media Assn. (bd. dirs. 1997—, Highsmith Innovation award 1996), Am. Assn. Sch. Librs., Ill. Assn. Ednl. and Comms. Tech., Ill. Libr. Assn. (mem. technology task force 1997). Home: 3918 Carousel Dr Northbrook IL 60062-7535 Office: New Trier HS Dist # 203 385 Winnetka Ave Winnetka IL 60093-4238

BAUM, AXEL HELMUTH, lawyer; b. Berlin, Germany, July 14, 1930; came to U.S., 1933; s. Stefan H. and Gertrud (Goette) B.; m. Elisabeth K. Nordwall, Dec. 11, 1982; children—Nicholas S., Andreas S. B.A. cum laude, Amherst Coll., 1952; LL.B., Yale U., 1957. Bar: Conn. 1957, N.Y. 1958, U.S. Supreme Ct. 1976; Conseil Juridique, France, 1971; Avocat à la Cour (Paris) 1972. Assoc. Hughes, Hubbard & Reed, N.Y.C., 1957-64, ptnr., 1964—; ptnr.-in-charge European office Hughes, Hubbard & Reed, Paris, 1966—; fgn. atty. Lovell, White & King, London, 1959-60; lectr., spkr. various internat. forums and seminars, France, Germany, U.S., Middle East, 1970—; arbitrator, U.S. Del. to Arb. Comm. of Internat. Ct. of Arbitration of ICC, Paris, 1978—; Ctr. Pub. Resources Panel of Disting. Internatl. Mediators. Mng. editor Yale Law Jour., 1957; contbr. articles to profl. jours. Bd. dirs. Am. Aid Soc., France, 1981, chmn. 1995, Am. Ch. Com. France, 1991, World Monuments Fund France, 1989, Bd. trustees, AMer. Libr. of Paris, Served to lt. USNR, 1952-54. Mem. ABA, Internat. Bar Assn., Union Internat. des Avocats, Assn. Bar N.Y.C., London Ct. Internat. Arbitration, Amherst Assn. France (pres.), Amer. Arb. Assn., Polo Club (Paris), Yacht Club France, Swedish Cruising Club, Yale Club of N.Y.C. Avocations: sailing; tennis; swimming. Home: 8 Rue des Dames Augustines, 92200 Neuilly Seine France Office: Hughes Hubbard & Reed, 47 Ave Georges Mandel, 75116 Paris France

BAUM, BERNARD HELMUT, sociologist, educator; b. Giessen, Germany, Apr. 18, 1926; came to U.S., 1933, naturalized, 1934; s. Theodor and Beatrice (Klee) B.; m. Barbara B. Eisendrath, June 13, 1953; children: David Michael, Jonathan Klee, Victoria Lucille, Lisa Baum Kritz. PhB, U. Chgo., 1948, MA, 1953, PhD, 1959. Qualifications rating examiner, bd. adviser U.S. CSC, Chgo., 1952-54; instr. human relations, psychology Chgo. Police Officers' Coll. Edn. Program, 1955-59; dir. orgnl. analysis CNA Ins., Chgo., 1960-66; asso. prof. mgmt. and sociology U. Ill., Chgo., 1966-69; asso. dean U. Ill. (Coll. Bus. Adminstrn.), 1967-68; prof. mgmt. and sociology, 1969—; prof. health policy and adminstrn. Sch. Pub. Health U. Ill. at Chgo., 1973—, dir. health policy and adminstrn. Sch. Pub. Health, 1977-92; team leader joint evaluation mission of UN devel. program WHO primary health care and health mgmt. devel. projects in South Pacific, 1985; lectr. Roosevelt U., 1955-66, U. Chgo., 1961-68, Northwestern U., 1968-70, U. Colo., 1971-76; mem. speaker's bur. Adult Edn. Council Greater Chgo., 1963-76; vis. scholar Chiang Mai U., Thailand, 1988. Author: Decentralization of Authority in a Bureaucracy, 1961, (with others) Basics for Business, 1968; also articles; editor: (with others) Intervention: the Management Use of Organizational Research, 1975. Bd. dirs. Selfhelp Home for Aged, Chgo. With AUS, 1944-46; brig. gen. Ill. Army N.G., ret. Decorated Legion of Merit, Bronze Star; recipient Bus. Adminstrn. and Social Sci. Doctoral Dissertation award Ford Found., 1960. Mem. AAAS, Am. Sociol. Assn., Am. Acad. Polit. and Social Sci., Acad. Mgmt., Am. Pub. Health Assn., Sigma Xi. Home: 1405 Lincoln St Evanston IL 60201-2336 Office: U Ill Sch Pub Health M/C 923 Chicago IL 60680

BAUM, CARL EDWARD, electromagnetic theorist; b. Binghamton, N.Y., Feb. 6, 1940; s. George Theodore and Evelyn Monica (Bliven) B. BS with honors, Calif. Inst. Tech., 1962, MS, 1963, PhD, 1969. Commd. 2d lt. USAF, 1962, advanced through grades to capt., 1967, resigned, 1971; project officer Air Force Rsch. Lab. (formerly Phillips Lab.), Kirtland AFB, N.Mex., 1963-71, sr. scientist for electromagnetics, 1971—; pres. SUMMA Found.; U.S. del. to gen. assembly Internat. Union Radio Sci., Lima, Peru, 1975, Helsinki, Finland, 1978, Washington, 1981, Florence, Italy, 1984, Tel

Aviv, 1987, Prague, Czechoslovakia, 1990, Kyoto, Japan, 1993, Lille, France, 1996; mem. Commn. B U.S. Nat. Com., 1975—, Commn. E, 1982—, Commn. A, 1990—. Author: (with others) Transient Electromagnetic Fields, 1976, Electromagnetic Scattering, 1978, Acoustic, Electromagnetic and Elastic Wave Scattering, 1980, Fast Electrical and Optical Measurements, 1986, EMP Interaction: Principles, Techniques and Reference Data, 1986, Lightning Electromagnetics, 1990, Modern Radio Science, 1990, Recent Advances in Electromagnetic Theory, 1990, Direct and Inverse Methods in Radar Polarimetry, 1992, (with A.P. Stone) Transient Lens Synthesis: Differential Geometry in Electromagnetic Theory, 1991; editor: (with H.N. Kritikos) Electromagnetic Symmetry, 1995, (with L. Carin and A.P. Stone) Ultra-Wideband, Short-Pulse Electromagnetics 3, 1997, Detection and Identification of Visually Obscured Targets, 1998; contbr. articles to profl. jours. Recipient award Honeywell Corp., 1962, R&D award USAF, 1970, Harold Brown award Air Force Systems Command, 1990; Air Force Rsch. Lab. fellow, 1996; Electromagnetic pulse fellow. Fellow IEEE (Harry Diamond Meml. award, 1987, Richard R. Stoddart award, 1984); mem. Electromagnetics Soc. (pres. 1983-85), Electromagnetics Acad., Sigma Xi, Tau Beta Pi. Roman Catholic. Home: 5116 Eastern Ave SE Apt D Albuquerque NM 87108-5618 Office: AFRL/DEHP 3550 Aberdeen Ave SE Bldg 909 Albuquerque NM 87117-5748

BAUM, CAROL GROSSMAN, physician; b. N.Y.C., June 14, 1958; d. Jacob Joseph and Anita Pearl (Serbrinsky) Grossman; m. Michael Seth Baum, June 16, 1985; 1 child, Daniel Joseph. BS, CCNY, 1979; MD, NYU, 1983. Diplomate Nat. Bd. Med. Examiners, Am. Bd. Internal Medicine, Am. Bd. Allergy & Immunology. Resident in internal medicine St. Luke's Hosp., N.Y.C., 1983-86; fellow in allergy & clin. immunology Cornell U. Med. Coll., N.Y.C., 1986-88; pvt. practice internal medicine, allergy-clin. immunology N.Y.C., 1988-90; asst. attending allergy clinic N.Y. Hosp., N.Y.C., 1988—; dir. allergy clinic St. Luke's Hosp., N.Y.C., 1989-90, William F. Ryan Community Health Ctr., 1990; dir. dept. allergy and clin. immunology N.E. Permanente Med. Group, White Plains, N.Y., Stamford, Conn., 1990-98; med. dir. Hudson Valley Ind. Health, Tarrytown, N.Y., 1998—; clin. instr. medicine, Cornell U. Med. Coll., N.Y.C.; lectr., presenter in field. Contbr. articles to profl. jours. Fellow ACP, Am. Acad. Allergy, Asthma and Immunology; mem. AMA, Am. Med. Women's Assn., Westchester Med. Soc., N.Y. Acad. Scis., Am. Coll. Physician Execs., Phi Beta Kappa, Sigma Xi. Avocations: horseback riding, Hebrew studies, sailing, playing piano. Office: Ind Health 200 White Plains Rd Tarrytown NY 10591-5808

BAUM, CHRISTOPHER FREDERICK, economics educator, consultant; b. Chgo., Aug. 13, 1951; s. Clare Frederick and Olga Jean (Sturm) B.; m. Maryann Theresa Albertines, Aug. 9, 1975; children: Erik M., Elisabeth A., Christopher J., Jonathan A. BA, Kalamazoo Coll., 1972; MA, Fla. Atlantic U., 1973; PhD, U. Mich., 1977. Asst. prof. econs. Boston Coll., Chestnut Hill, Mass., 1977-83, assoc. prof. econs., 1983—; sec.-treas. Soc. Econ. Dynamics and Control, 1989-92; econ. cons., 1982—. Assoc. editor Computational Econs. Jour., 1990—; contbr. articles to profl. jours. Mem., vice chair, chair Sudbury (Mass.) Fin. Com., 1984-87; vol. Mass. Tech. Corps, Sudbury, 1995-97. Mem. Am. Econ. Assn., Econometric Soc., Soc. for Computational Econs. Office: Econs Dept Boston Coll Chestnut Hill MA 02467

BAUM, DWIGHT CROUSE, investment banking executive; b. Syracuse, N.Y., Nov. 21, 1912; s. Dwight James and Katharine Lucia (Crouse) B.; m. Hildagarde Engelhardt, Jan. 17, 1942; children: Dwight J., John E. E.E., Cornell U., 1936; M.B.A., Harvard U., 1938. Chartered fin. analyst. Asst. to v.p. Mine Safety Appliance Co., Pitts., 1938-40; armament supply officer Brit. Air Commn., Washington, 1940-46; asst. to partner Eastman Dillon & Co., Los Angeles, 1946-47; v.p. 1st Calif. Co., Los Angeles, 1947-56; gen. partner Eastman Dillon Union Securities & Co., Los Angeles, 1956-71; sr. v.p. Eastman Dillon Union Securities & Co., 1971-72; also dir. Eastman Dillon Union Securities & Co., Los Angeles, 1972-80; sr. v.p. Blyth Eastman Dillon & Co., Inc., adv. dir., 1980-83; sr. v.p. Paine Webber Inc, 1980—; bd. dirs. Dominguez Water Corp. (now Dominguez Svcs. Corp.). Trustee Alice Lloyd Coll.; bd. dirs. Planned Parenthood-World Population, Los Angeles. Decorated Order Brit. Empire. Mem. Nat. Assn. Securities Dealers (bd. govs. 1976-79), Los Angeles Soc. Fin. Analysts, IEEE, Pacific Stock Exch., Inc. (vice chmn. 1980-82), Phi Delta Theta. Clubs: Calif. (Los Angeles), Bond (Los Angeles). Home: 1011 Oak Grove Ave San Marino CA 91108-1025 Office: 200 S Los Robles Ave Pasadena CA 91101-2479

BAUM, E. HARRIS, lawyer; b. Phila., June 20, 1933; s. Albert I. and Rose Blanche (Nathanson) B.; m. Joyce L. Blumberg, June 24, 1957 (dec. Jan. 1981); children: Sharon, Susan, Lewis; m. Myrna Field, Mar. 25, 1983. BS, Temple U., 1954, LLB, 1957. Bar: Phila. 1958, Pa. 1958, U.S. Cir. Ct. (3rd cir.) 1958, U.S. Supreme Ct. Assoc. Harry Norman Ball, Esq., Phila., 1958-62; sr. ptnr. Zarwin, Prince & Baum, Phila., 1962-68, Zarwin & Baum, Phila., 1968-94; sr. ptnr., chief litigation dept. Zarwin, Baum, DeVito, Kaplan & O'Donnell, Phila., 1995—; lectr. in field. Pres. Keneseth Israel Synagogue, Elkins Park, Pa., 1996-98; exec. bd. Headhouse Conservancy, Phila., 1993—; adv. bd. Phila. Blind Assn.; active ASSIST Disabled Police Fire Fighters, Phila., 1994. With USAR, 1954-56. Mem. Pa. Trial Lawyers, Phila. Trial Lawyers, Athenaeum of Phila., Lawyer's Club, Bala Country Club, Million Dollar Adv. Forum. Avocations: cycling, traveling, sailing, golfing. Office: Zarwin Baum DeVito Kaplan & O'Donnell 1515 Market St Ste 1200 Philadelphia PA 19102-1981

BAUM, EDWARD, political science educator; b. N.Y.C., May 29, 1935; s. Edward S. and Rosalind (Fields) B.; 1 child, Sandra Martha Azancot; m. Anita C. James, Jan. 5, 1980 (div. Mar. 1999). BA, UCLA, 1957, PhD, 1964. Dep. chief party Advanced Tchrs. Coll., Kano, Nigeria, 1965-69; lectr. Calif. State U., Northridge, 1962-64; prof. Ohio U., Athens, 1964—; cons. Mgmt. Devel. Assocs., Athens, 1983—. Mem. city coun. City of Athens, 1996—; treas. Athens County Rep. Orgn., 1994—; dir. S.W. Ohio Sr. Olympics, Athens, 1991—. Mem. Civitan (treas. Athens chpt.). Republican. Avocations: golf, stamp collecting. E-mail: baum@ohiou.edu. Office: Ohio U Dept Polit Sci Bentley Hall Athens OH 45701-2979

BAUM, GORDON LEE, lawyer, non-profit organization administrator; b. St. Louis, Aug. 24, 1940; s. James Paul and Johnnie Thelma (Thompson) B.; m. Georgia Dee Thompson, Sept. 12, 1959 (div. 1977); children: Gordon Lee II, Mark Evans Sterling, Duane Russell Stuart; m. Linda Gaye Gulledge, Feb. 10, 1978; children: Laura Leigh, Renee Gabrielle. *Descended from Pennsylvania Dutch/German (Pennsylvaani Deitsch) pioneer Johann Theobald Baum (1693-1762), German Lutheran refugee from Elsass (Alsace), immigrated to America prior 1720. Among the first settlers in Reading, Pennsylvania area, he donated land and in 1738 helped establish Alsace Church and cemetery, now twin churches Alsace Lutheran and Grace Alsace (Reform). His son, Johannes (1725-1808), was a courtmartial man in Berks County militia during the Revolution. His son, Jonas (1765-1825), guard at Reading POW prison for captured British and Hessian soldiers. Henry Van Reed (1779-1829), founder of Van Reed Paper Mills in Reading.* Grad., U. Mo., 1965; JD, St. Louis U., 1969. Bar: Mo. 1969, U.S. Dist. Ct. Mo. 1969. Sr. inspection clk. Chevrolet Divsn. GM Corp., St. Louis, 1961-65, work standards engr., 1965-69; field dir. mid-west Citizens Coun. Am., Jackson, Miss., 1969-84; pvt. practice civil law St. Louis, 1969—; chief exec. officer, Coun. Conservative Citizens, St. Louis, 1985—, Conservative Citizens Found., St. Louis, 1985—; dir. St. Louis Met. Area Citizens Coun. Assoc. editor (newspaper) Citizens Informer, 1971—; talk show host WGNU Radio, St. Louis, 1995—. State Coord. Wallace Presdl. Campaign, Mo., 1972, 76; del. Dem. Party State Conv., 1976. Yeoman 2d class petty officer USN, 1958-61. Mem. Mo. Bar Assn., Phi Alpha Delta, MENSA, NRA, Sons of Confederate Vets., Hist. Soc. Berks County, Pa., Ger.-Am. Heritage Soc. Lutheran. Avocations: politics, history, hunting, gardening, travel. Home: 4219 Celburne Ln Bridgeton MO 63044-1502 Office: Coun of Conservative Citizens PO Box 221683 Saint Louis MO 63122-8683

BAUM, HERBERT MERRILL, toy company executive; b. Chgo., Dec. 6, 1936; s. Jack William and Ruth Frances (Ginsburg) B.; m. Diane Jean Kale, Nov. 1, 1975 (div. Sept. 1977); m. Karen Rochelle Oberman, Dec. 22, 1983. BSBA, Drake U., 1958. Account exec. Stern, Walters & Simmons, Chgo., 1962-66, Doyle, Dane & Bernbach, Chgo., 1966-69; v.p., account dir. Needham, Harper & Steers, Chgo., 1969-78; assoc. dir., dir. new products Campbell Soup Co., Camden, N.J., 1978, v.p. mktg., gen. mgr. soup div., 1978-84, exec. v.p. U.S. div., 1984-85; pres. Campbell USA, Camden, N.J., 1985-90, sr. v.p., 1986-89, exec. v.p., 1989-93; pres. Campbell N.Am., Camden, N.J., 1990-92, Campbell North & South Am., Camden, N.J., 1992-93; chmn., CEO Quaker State Corp., Irving, Tex., 1993-98; pres., COO Hasbro Inc., Providence, R.I., 1999—; bd. dirs. Am. Mktg. Assn., Meredith Corp., Whitman Corp., Dial Corp., Midas, Inc., Fleming Co., Inc., Hasbro, Inc. With U.S. Army, 1958-59. Mem. Am. Mktg. Assn. Home: 45 Loring Ave Providence RI 02906-5615 Office: Hasbro Inc 1011 Newport Ave Pawtucket RI 02861-2538

BAUM, JOHN, physician; b. N.Y.C., June 2, 1927; s. Louis Israel and Lilian (Treitman) B.; m. Erna Rose Bailis, Jan. 28, 1950; children: Nina, Jane, Carl, Antonia, Theodore. BA, NYU, 1949, MD, 1954. Intern Baltimore City Hosp., 1954-55; resident in medicine Lenox Hill Hosp., N.Y.C., 1955-56, VA Hosp., N.Y.C., 1956-57; NIH clin. trainee N.Y.U.-Bellevue Hosp., 1957-58; NIH research fellow Rheumatism Research Unit, Taplow, Eng., 1958-59; asst. prof. medicine U. Tex. Southwestern Med. Sch., 1962-68; dir. arthritis clinic Parkland Meml. Hosp., Dallas, 1959-68; dir. med. clinics Parkland Meml. Hosp., 1965-67; co-dir. pediatric arthritis clinic Scottish Rite Hosp., Dallas, 1960-68; mem. faculty U. Rochester (N.Y.) Med. Sch., 1968—, prof. medicine pediatrics and rehab., 1972-93, prof. medicine emeritus, 1993—, chmn. rsch. subjects rev. bd., 1987-96, prof. orthpedics (rehabilitation), 1991-93, prof. pediatrics, 1997—; vis. prof. rheumatology, hon. sr. rsch. fellow U. Birmingham, Eng., 1988-89; vis. prof. U. Kiev Med. Sch., 1995; dir. arthritis and clin. immunology unit Monroe Cmty. Hosp., 1968-93; dir. pediatric arthritis clinic Strong Meml. Hosp., 1970—; mem. drug efficacy panel NRC-NAS, 1960-65; mem. rsch. rev. bd. immunology VA, 1970-76; adv. panel U.S. Pharmacopeia, 1975—; coord. therapeutics U.S.-USSR Program Rheumatology, 1974—; mem. test com. for rheumatology Am. Bd. Internal Medicine, 1971-76. Mem. editl. bd. Clin. Rheumatology (Brussels), Jour. Rheumatology (Can.), Japanese Rheumatology, 1984-93; contbr. articles to profl. jours., chpts. to books. Served with AUS, 1944-46. Recipient award of merit Rochester Acad. Medicine, 1999; Fulbright scholar, 1958; clin. scholar rheumatology Arthritis Found., 1964-69. Mem. Am. Coll. Rheumatology (master 1993, coun. pediat. rheumatology 1975-80, 85—), Heberden Soc., Am. Fedn. Clin. Rsch., Am. Soc. Human Genetics, Am. Assn. Immunologists, Reticuloendothelial Soc., So. Soc. Clin. Investigation, Tex. Rheumatism Assn., Brit. Soc. Rheumatology, Midlands Rheumatology Soc. (Eng.), Polish Rheumatol. Soc. (hon.), La Found. Rheum Argentina (Dr. Oswaldo Carcia Morteo int. sci. com. 1997—), Great Lakes Interurban Club, Sigma Xi. Home: 1470 East Ave Rochester NY 14610-1619 Office: Strong Meml Hosp 601 Elmwood Ave Rochester NY 14642-0002 *If what I have achieved is called success, it is not because it has been my goal. As a clinician, teacher and researcher, I realize that success comes mostly with the latter, but my greatest satisfaction, which must have been my "secret goal," has been with the personal contacts that come through taking care of people and sharing my knowledge with students. The lagniappe of a supportive wife and fascinating children makes achieving the goals more worthwhile.*

BAUM, JULES LEONARD, ophthalmologist, educator; b. N.Y.C., Mar. 13, 1931; children from previous marriage: Jeffrey Stuart, Alison Rachel; m. Laura Klabin, 1990; stepchildren: Alexander Matthew, Samantha Merrill. AB, Dartmouth Coll., 1952; MD, Tufts U., 1956. NIH fellow in research in ophthalmology N.Y. U., 1958-59, researcher in ophthalmology, 1961-62; asst. prof. N.Y. U. (Med. Sch.), 1965-68; resident in ophthalmology Bellevue Hosp., N.Y.C., 1962-64; mem. faculty Tufts U. Med. Sch., 1968—, prof. ophthalmology, 1974-91; sr. surgeon New Eng. Med. Center Hosp., Boston, 1973-91; res. prof. Tufts U. Med. Sch., 1991—. Assoc. editor Ophthalmic Lit., 1967-85; mem. editl. bd. Investigative Ophthalmology and Vision Sci., 1978-82, Survey of Ophthalmology, 1970-79, Am. Jour. Ophthalmology, 1985-91, Ophthalmic Surgery, 1985-95, Cornea Jour., 1989—; contbr. articles to profl. jours. Served to capt. M.C. AUS, 1959-61. Recipient William Warner Hoppin award N.Y. Acad. Medicine; Alcon Rsch. Inst. award, 1991; NIH fellow, 1958-59, 64-65; Nat. Eye Inst. grantee. Fellow Royal Coll. Ophthalmologists; mem. Am. Acad. Ophthalmology (honor award 1979, sr. honor award 1990, bd. of councillors, 1981-83), Assn. Rsch. in Vision and Ophthalmology (trustee 1981-86, v.p. 1986), Castroviejo Soc. (exec. sec., treas. 1979-87, v.p. 1987-89, pres. 1989-91, Castroviejo Corneal Medalist 1997), Mass. Ophthalmology Soc. (sec. 1974-76), Ocular Microbiology Immunology Group (pres. 1990-91), Conferie des Chevaliers du Tastevin, Chaine des Rotisseur, Internat. Wine and Food Soc., Phi Beta Kappa. Jewish. Office: 1244 Boylston St Chestnut Hill MA 02467-2115

BAUM, LAURA, educator; b. N.Y.C., Jan. 3, 1948; d. Morton and Selma (Wallman) Berdy Roblin; children: Alexander Klabin, Samantha Klabin; m. Jules Baum, June 16, 1990. BS with distinction, Boston U., 1969, EdM, 1974; . Cert. spl. edn. adminstrn., moderate spl. needs children elem. edn., instr. perceptually handicapped, Mass. Tchr. spl. edn. middle and high schs. Wellesley (Mass.) Pub. Schs., 1969—; chmn. spl. svcs. dept. Wellesley Middle Sch., 1974-77; instr., supr. Lesley Coll., Cambridge, Mass., 1980-84, supr. spl. edn. student tchrs., 1980-84, instr., 1988-89, mentor Curry Coll., Milton, Mass., 1988; pvt. practice assessment, evaluation and diagnosis, Wellesley, 1969—; participant internship program Simmons Coll., 1992-96; spkr. in field; assoc. tchr. in edn. Wellesley Coll., 1993-94. Bd. dirs. Wellesley Cmty. Children's Ctr., 1979—; mem. children/youth com. Mass. Dept. Mental Health and Mental Retardation, 1979-81; chmn. mental retardation com. 1981-82, co-chmn. cmty. edn. com. 1982-84, bd. dirs., 1981-84; corr. sec. Wellesley Players, 1997-99. Mem. AAUW (1st v.p. Wellesley chpt. 1978-79), NEA, Mass. Tchr.'s Assn., Wellesley Tchr.'s Assn., Coun. Exceptional Children. Avocations: cooking, travel, computers, photography. Home: 81 Maugus Ave Wellesley MA 02481-7614 Office: Wellesley Mid Sch 50 Kingsbury St Wellesley MA 02481-4831

BAUM, MARSHA LYNN, law educator; b. Fulton, N.Y., Aug. 13, 1957; d. Warren J. and Shirley M. (Kenyon) B.; m. Neil M. Mayor, Nov. 21, 1992. BA in History, U. Rochester, 1979; MS in Libr. Sci. with honors, Columbia U., 1982; JD, SUNY, Buffalo, 1985. Bar: N.Y. Libr. asst. Ctr. for Govtl. Rsch., Rochester, N.Y., 1979-81; reference libr. SUNY-Buffalo Law Libr., 1984-85, U. Minn. Law Libr., Mpls., 1985-87; head pub. svcs. U. Conn. Law Libr., Hartford, 1987-89, dep. dir., 1989-92, acting dir., 1991; dir. law libr., assoc. prof. law U. S.C. Law Sch., Columbia, 1992-97, U. N.Mex. Law Sch., Albuquerque, 1997—. Mem. ALA, Am. Assn. Law Librs., N.Y. State Bar Assn. Office: U NMex Law Libr Albuquerque NM 87131

BAUM, MICHAEL LIN, lawyer; b. Clinton, Okla., Apr. 10, 1952; s. William Eldon and Patricia (Schumacher) B.; m. Colleen Margaret Condon, Apr. 6, 1991; children: Elizabeth, Alexandra, Kevin. BA summa cum laude, UCLA, 1982, JD, 1985. Bar: Calif. 1985, D.C. 1993, U.S. Dist. Ct. (ctrl. dist.) Calif. 1986, U.S. Dist. Ct. (ea. and no. dists.) Calif. 1989, U.S. Dist. Ct. (we. dist.) Mich. 1991, U.S. Dist. Ct. (no. dist.) Ohio 1993, U.S. Dist. Ct. (no. dist.) N.Y. 1996, U.S. Ct. Appeals (9th cir.) 1990, U.S. Ct. Appeals (4th cir.) 1996, U.S. Ct. Appeals (7th cir.) 1997, U.S. Supreme Ct. 1991. Assoc. Kananack, Murgatroyd, Baum & Hedlund (and predecessor firms), L.A., 1985-87; ptnr., shareholder Baum, Hedlund, Aristei, Guilford & Downey, L.A., 1987—; mem. discovery and trial teams MDL 817 United Airlines 1989 aircrash at Sioux City, Iowa, Chgo.; mem. plaintiffs' steering com. MDL 891 Northwest Airlines 1990 aircrash at Detroit Met. Airport, Ill. State Ct. procs. for USAir 427 crash near Aliquippa, Pa., 1994, MDL 1041 USAir 1994 crash at Charlotte, N.C. Mem. State Bar Calif., D.C. Bar, Bar Assn. D.C., Consumer Attys. Calif. Office: Baum Hedlund Aristei Guilford & Downey 12100 Wilshire Blvd Ste 950 Los Angeles CA 90025-7114

BAUM, PETER ALAN, lawyer; b. Jamaica, N.Y., Sept. 22, 1947; s. Morris and Elsa (Sturtz) B.; m. Barbara Hartman, Nov. 29, 1969; children: Benjamin, Lisa, Alexander. BA, Colgate U., 1969; JD, Syracuse U., 1972. Bar: N.Y. 1973, U.S. Dist. Ct. (no. dist.) N.Y. 1974. House counsel William Porter Real Estate Co., Syracuse, N.Y., 1972-73; pvt. practice Syracuse, 1973-82; ptnr. DiStefano and Baum, Syracuse, 1983-85, Baum and Woodard, Syracuse, 1985-90; prin. Peter A. Baum Law Offices, Chittenango, N.Y., 1990-96; ptnr. Iaconis, Iaconis and Baum, Chittenango, 1997—; lectr. Onondaga C.C., Syracuse, 1976-79. Chmn. bd. dirs. Syracuse Area Landmark Theater, 1982-83; bd. dirs. Syracuse Opera Co., 1979-85. Mem. N.Y. State Bar Assn. (ho. of dels. 1992-93), Madison County Bar Assn. (pres. 1993), Onondaga County Bar Assn. (continuing edn. chmn. 1977-78), Onondaga Title Assn. Office: Iaconis Iaconis & Baum 282 Genesee St Chittenango NY 13037-1705

BAUM, PHYLLIS GARDNER, travel management consultant; b. Ashtabula, Ohio, Dec. 13, 1930; d. Charles Edward Schneider and Stella Elizabeth (Schaefer) Gardner; m. Kenneth Walter Baum, Oct. 21, 1948 (div. July 1971); children: Deidre Adair, Cynthia Gail; m. Dennis Carl Marquardt, Sept. 22, 1979 (dec. 1991). Grad. high sch., Cleve. Am. Soc. Travel Agents. Travel cons. Fredo Travel Svc., Ashland, Ohio, 1960-66; sales mgr. Travelmart, Willoughby, Ohio, 1966-68; br. mgr. Travelmart, Mentor, Ohio, 1966-68, Diners Fugazy Travel, Sun City, Ariz., 1968-69; travel cons. Jarrett's Travel Svc., Phoenix, 1969-72; sr. cons. Loyal Travel, Phoenix, 1972-74; co-mgr. Phil Carr Travel, Sun City, 1974-77; tour ops. mgr. ASL Travel, Phoenix, 1978-79; owner, mgr. Travel Temporaries, Glendale, Ariz., 1979—; cons. and lectr. in field. Adv. bd. mem. Small Bus. Devel. Ctr., Phoenix, 1986—. Mem. Pacific Asia Travel Assn. Ariz. (bd. dirs. 1986—), Ariz. Women in Travel, NAFE, Altrusa. Republican. Avocations: music, travel, tatting, knitting, horseback riding. Home and Office: Travel Temps 10249 N 45th Ave Glendale AZ 85302-1901

BAUM, REDFIELD T., SR., federal judge. Apptd. bankruptcy judge U.S. Dist. Ct. Ariz., 1990. Fax: (602) 640-5844. Office: 9th Fl 2929 N Central Ave Fl 9 Phoenix AZ 85012-2752

BAUM, RICHARD THEODORE, engineering executive; b. N.Y.C., Oct. 3, 1919. BA, Columbia U., 1940, BS, 1941, MS, 1948. Registered profl. engr., N.Y., D.C., and 20 other states, Nat. Bur. Engring. Registration. Engr. Electric Boat Co., Groton, Conn., 1941-43; with Jaros, Baum & Bolles, N.Y.C., 1946—, ptnr., 1958-86, ptnr. emeritus, cons. to firm, 1986—; mem. adv. coun., faculty of engring. and applied sci. Columbia U., N.Y.C., 1972—. 1st lt. USAAF, 1943-46. Egleston medalist Columbia U., 1985. Fellow ASME, ASHRAE, Am. Cons. Engrs. Coun.; mem. NAE (mech. engring. peer com. 1991-93), NSPE, N.Y. Acad. Scis., Nat. Soc. Energy Engrs., NRC (chmn. bldg. rsch. bd. 1987-91), Am. Arbitration Assn. (panel arbitrators 1973—), Coun. on Tall Bldgs. and Urban Habitat (vice chmn. N.Am. chpt.), Univ. Club N.Y.C. Office: Jaros Baum & Bolles 80 Pine St New York NY 10005-1702

BAUM, ROBERT L., federal agency executive. BA with high distinction, Dartmouth Coll., 1977; JD, Washington U., St. Louis, 1981. Bar: D.C., Calif. Lawyer Hill, Farrer & Burrill, L.A., 1981-82, Reboul, MacMurray, Hewitt, Maynard & Kristol, L.A., 1982-84; atty. corp. rels. dept. L.A. Olympic Organizing Com., L.A., 1984; lawyer Dobrovir & Gebhardt, Washington, 1985-87, Arent Fox Kintner Plotkin & Kahn, Washington, 1987-93; assoc. solicitor for conservation and wildlife U.S. Dept. of the Interior, Washington, dir. Office of Hearings and Appeals, 1993—; v.p., sec. Windward Broadcasting, Inc., L.A., 1980-83. Author: Public Interest Law: Where Law Meets Social Policy, 1986; contbg. author: Treatise on Health Care Law, 1991, rev. edit., 1992; contbr. articles to law jours. Vol. VISTA, White River Junction, Vt., 1977-78; mem. health issues task force Clinton/Gore Campaign and Transition, 1992, co-chair environ. issues task force, 1992, mem. dept. justice transition team, 1992-93; vol. Dartmouth '77 Exec. Com., 1992—, Montgomery County Success!, 1995—, Md. Med. Adv. Commn. on Practice Parametersi, 1997—; mem. exec. com., chair legis. issues com. Montgomery County PTA, 1998. Fax: (703) 235-9014. E-mail: robertúbaum@ios.doi.gov. Office: Dept of the Interior Office of Hearings/Appeals 4015 Wilson Blvd Arlington VA 22203

BAUM, SELMA, customer relations consultant; b. Bklyn., Jan. 15, 1924; d. Samuel and Tillie (Bayer) Goldman; m. Milton W. Baum, Jan. 19, 1947; children: Victor C., Cynthia Baum-Baicker. Student, NYU New Sch. for Social Rsch. Communications mgr. Sobel & Goldman, Inc., N.Y.C., 1941-48; pub. rels. cons., 1948-65; comparison shopper Gimbels, Valley Stream, N.Y., 1965-67, mgr. comparison shopping office N.Y. div., N.Y.C., 1967-75, dir. consumer affairs East div., 1975-84; dir. corp. customer rels. Saks Fifth Ave., N.Y.C., 1984-89; cons. customer rels., Palm Beach, Fla., 1989—; lectr., writer in field. Arbitrator Met. N.Y. Better Bus. Bur. Mem. NAFE, Am. Mgmt. Assn. (industry panelist), N.Y. & N.J. Retail Mchts. Coun. (v.p.), Women in Communication (award N.Y. chpt. 1984), Nat. Retail Mchts. Assn. (consumer affairs com.), Fashion Group, Am. Coun. on Consumer Interests, Soc. Consumer Affairs Profls. in Bus. (chpt. pres. 1981-82, nat. dir. 1983-86, bd. dir. Found. 1985-89; nat. treas., fin. chmn., v.p. 1986-87, award N.Y. chpt. 1983), Greater N.Y. WINS (regional affairs com.), Direct Mktg. Assn. (customer rels. coun. 1987-88). Home and Office: 3460 S Ocean Blvd Apt 715 Palm Beach FL 33480-5969

BAUM, STANLEY, radiologist, educator; b. N.Y.C., Dec. 26, 1929; s. Herman and Fannie (Harris) B.; m. Jeanne Masch, June 29, 1958; children: Richard Arthur, Laura Dianne, Carol Lisa. BA, NYU, 1951; MD, U. Utrecht, Holland, 1957. Intern Kings County Hosp., N.Y.C., 1957-58; resident in radiology Grad. Hosp., U. Pa., Phila., 1958-61; trainee Nat. Cancer Inst., Bethesda, Md., 1958-61; fellow cardiovascular radiology Stanford (Calif.) U., 1961-62; instr. radiology U. Pa., Phila., 1962-63; asst. prof. U. Pa., 1963-66, assoc. prof., 1966-70, prof., 1970—, Eugene P. Pendergrass prof. radiology, 1977-96, chmn. dept. radiology, 1975-96; chmn. med. bd. Hosp. of U. Pa., 1983-86; chief cardiovascular radiology Mass. Gen. Hosp., Boston, 1971-75; prof. radiology Harvard Med. Sch., Boston, 1971-75; cons. Radiation Effects Research Found., Hiroshima, Japan, 1975-76; mem. cardiovasc. rev. bd. Am. Heart Assn., 1970-90. Editorial bd.: Investigative Radiology, 1970-80, New Eng. Jour. Medicine, 1975-76, Radiology, 1975-85, Gastrointestinal Radiology, 1975-79, Jour. Continuing Edn., 1978-80, Postgrad. Radiology, 1980-90. Fellow Am. Coll. Radiology, Am. Coll. Cardiology; mem. Inst. Medicine Nat. Acad. Sci., Soc. Cardiovascular Radiology (pres. 1974-76), Soc. Chmn. Acad. Radiology Depts. (pres. elect 1985-86, pres. 1986), Acad. Radiol. Rsch. (pres. 1997—). Home: 401 W Moreland Ave Philadelphia PA 19118-4207 Office: U Pa 3400 Spruce St Philadelphia PA 19104-4204

BAUM, STANLEY DAVID, lawyer; b. Bklyn., Feb. 22, 1954; s. Irwin and Muriel A. (Margolis) B.; m. Ilyne Rhona Fried, June 9, 1979; children: Andrew, Miranda. BS, U. Pa., 1976, JD, 1980; LLM, NYU, 1984. Bar: N.Y. 1981, U.S. Tax Ct. 1993. Assoc. Carter, Ledyard & Milburn, N.Y.C., 1988-98, Swidler, Berlin, Shereff, Friedman, LLP, N.Y.C., 1998—. Contbr. numerous articles to profl. jours. Mem. N.Y. State Bar Assn. (tax sect., com. on employee benefits), N.Y.C. Bar Assn.

BAUM, STANLEY M., lawyer; b. Bronx, N.Y., Mar. 6, 1944; s. Abraham S. and Mae (Weiner) B.; m. Louise Rae Iteld, Aug. 30, 1970; children: Rachel Jennifer, Lauren Amy. BS in Commerce, Rider Coll., 1966; JD summa cum laude, John Marshall Law Sch., 1969. Bar: Ga. 1970, U.S. Dist. Ct. (no. dist.) Ga. 1970, U.S. Ct. Appeals (5th cir.) 1970, U.S. Supreme Ct. 1973, U.S. Ct. Appeals (11th cir.) 1981, U.S. Tax Ct. 1983. Law clk. to U.S. atty. No. Dist. Ga., 1969; legal aide Ga. Gen. Assembly, 1970-71; asst. U.S. atty. No. Dist. Ga., 1971-74; ptnr. Bates & Baum, 1974—. Pres. Congregation Shearith Israel, 1976-78; chmn. Rep. Party of DeKalb County, 1983-85, 4th Dist. Rep. Party, 1985-89; pres. Resurgens, Atlanta, 1987-88, Electoral Coll., 1988; del. Rep. Nat. Conv., 1992; mem. DeKalb County Bd. Ethics, 1991—, chair 1993; mem. Met. Atlanta Rapid Transit Authority Bd. Ethics, 1993—. Mem. ABA (criminal justice sect. white collar com.), Ga. Bar Assn., Atlanta Bar Assn. (chmn. criminal law sect. 1985-86, bd. dirs. 1986-87), Fed. Bar Assn. (pres. Atlanta chpt. 1976-77, nat. council 1974-77), Dekalb Bar Assn. (pres. 1989-90), Am. Judicature Soc., Nat. Dist. Attys. Assn. Clubs: Atlanta Lawyers. Lodge: Masons. Office: 3151 Maple Dr NE Atlanta GA 30305-2503

BAUM, WERNER A., former academic administrator, meteorologist; b. Giessen, Germany, Apr. 10, 1923; came to U.S., 1933, naturalized, 1934; s. Theodor and Beatrice (Klee) B.; m. Shirley Bowman, Jan. 20, 1945; children: Janice Michelle, Sandra Roslyn. B.S., U. Chgo., 1943, M.S., 1944, Ph.D., 1948; D.Sc., Mt. St. Joseph Coll., 1971, U. R.I., 1974; D.P.A., Husson Coll., 1972. Cert. cons. meteorologist. Teaching asst. U. Chgo., 1943, instr., 1943-44, 1947, research asst., 1946; research assoc., asst. prof. U. Md., 1947-49; assoc. prof., head dept. meteorology Fla. State U., 1949-51, prof., head dept., 1951-58, dir. univ. research, 1957-60, dean Grad. Sch., 1958-60, dean faculties, 1960-63, v.p. for acad. affairs, 1963; v.p. acad. affairs U. Miami, 1963-65; v.p. sci. affairs NYU, N.Y.C., 1965-67; dep. adminstr. Environ. Sci.

Services Adminstrn., 1967-68; pres. U. R.I., Kingston, 1968-73; pres. emeritus U. R.I., 1984—; chancellor U. Wis., Milw., 1973-79; chancellor emeritus U. Wis., 1979—; dean Coll. Arts and Scis., Fla. State U., Tallahassee, 1979-90, dean emeritus, 1990—; treas. Assn. Urban Univs., 1976-77; pres. Com. Urban Program Univs., 1977-79, pres. emeritus, 1979—; cons. climatologist USAF, summer 1953; dir. Sta-Rite Industries, 1978-82; mem. exec. res. U.S. Weather Bur., 1958-62; councilor Oak Ridge Inst. Nuclear Studies, 1958-62; cons. NAS, 1962-64, mem. climate bd., 1980-87; mem. NRC com. on climatology; adv. to U.S. Weather Bur., 1955-57; mem. Nat. Adv. Com. on Oceans and Atmosphere, 1971-73, 76-77, 78-79; trustee Univ. Corp. Atmospheric Research, 1959-63, 65-67, 80-83, corp. sec., 1963-67; chmn. adv. com. edn. and manpower U.S. Weather Bur.; chmn. adv. panel atmospheric scis. program NSF, 1965-67; dir. Fund Overseas Research Grants and Edn., 1965-74; mem. sea grant adv. panel Commerce Dept., 1974-78; chmn. Nat. Climate Program Adv. Com., 1979-86. Author: Russian-English Dictionary of Meteorological Terms and Expressions, 1950; Contbr. articles to sci. jours. Served with USNR, 1944-46. Fellow AAAS (councilor 1955-56, acad. freedom and responsibility award 1985), Am. Geophys. Union, Am. Meteorol. Soc. (councilor 1956-59, 63-66, exec. com. 1976-79, pres. 1977-78, editor-in-chief periodicals 1957-61, spl. award for disting. svc. 1962, Charles Franklin Brooks award 1975, Cleveland Abbe award 1988, hon. mem. 1993); mem. Phi Beta Kappa, Sigma Xi, Phi Kappa Phi, Beta Gamma Sigma, Chi Epsilon Pi, Phi Sigma Delta. Home: 4436 Meandering Way # 207 Tallahassee FL 32308

BAUM, WILLIAM ALVIN, astronomer, educator; b. Toledo, Jan. 18, 1924; s. Earle Fayette and Mable (Teachout) B.; m. Ester Bru, June 27, 1961. B.A. summa cum laude, U. Rochester, 1943; Ph.D. magna cum laude, Calif. Inst. Tech., 1950. Physicist U.S. Naval Research Lab., Washington, 1946-49; astronomer Mt. Wilson and Palomar observatories, Pasadena, Calif., 1950-65; dir. Planetary Research Center, Lowell Obs., Flagstaff, Ariz., 1965-90; with astronomy dept. U. Wash., Seattle, 1990—; adj. prof. astronomy Ohio State U., 1969-91; adj. prof. physics No. Ariz. U., 1973-91; rsch. prof. astronomy U. Wash., Seattle, 1990-97, prof. emeritus, 1997—; cons. physics, astronomy, optics; cons. U.S. Army Research Office, Durham, N.C., 1967-74; vis. prof. Am. Astronomy Soc., 1961—; adv. com. Nat. Acad. Sci., 1958-67; mem. optical instrumentation panel adv. Air Force, 1967-76; coms. and panels NSF and NASA Office Space Scis., 1967-91; mem. NASA Viking Orbiter Imaging Team, 1970-79, Hubble Space Telescope Camera Team, 1977-96. Contbr. articles to tech. publs. Served to lt., jr. grade USNR, 1943-46. Guggenheim fellow, 1960-61. Mem. Am. Astron. Soc. (chmn. div. planetary scis. 1976-77), Royal Astron. Soc., Astron. Soc. Pacific, Internat. Astron. Union, Phi Beta Kappa, Sigma Xi, Theta Delta Chi. Home: 2124 NE Park Rd Seattle WA 98105-2422 Office: U Wash Dept Astronomy Seattle WA 98195

BAUM, WILLIAM WAKEFIELD CARDINAL, archbishop; b. Dallas, Nov. 21, 1926; s. Harold E. and Mary Leona (Hayes) W. Student, Kenrick Sem., St. Louis, 1947-51, U. St. Thomas Aquinas, Rome, 1956-58; STD, U. St. Thomas Aquinas, Rome, 1958; STL, Muhlenberg Coll., Allentown, Pa., 1957, DD, 1967; LLD, Georgetown U., St. John's U., Bklyn. Ordained priest Roman Cath. Ch., 1951. Assoc. pastor St. Aloysius Parish, St. Therese's Parish and St. Peter's Parish, Kansas City, Mo., 1951-56, 61-64, 67-68; adminstr. St. Cyril's Parish, Sugar Creek, Mo., 1960-61; pastor St. James Parish, Kansas City, 1968-70; chancellor Diocese Kansas City-St. Joseph, 1967-70; bishop of Springfield-Cape Girardeau, Mo., 1970-73; archbishop of Washington, 1973-80; elevated to cardinal Roman Cath. Ch., 1976; prefect Sacred Congregation for Cath. Edn., Rome, 1980-90; grand penitentiary cardinal Apostolic Penitentiary, Rome, 1990—; instr., then prof. Avila Coll., Kansas City, Mo., 1954-56, 58-63; Hon. chaplain of the Pope, 1961; peritus 2d Vatican Council, 1962-65; hon. prelate of the Pope, 1968; 1st exec. dir. Bishops' Commn. Ecumenical and Inter-religious Affairs, 1964-67; mem. Joint Working Group; reps. Cath. Ch. and World Council Chs., 1965-69; mem. Mixed Commn.; reps. Cath. Ch. and Lutheran World Fedn., 1965-66; mem. Vatican's Congregations Cath. Edn., Doctrine of Faith and Secretariat for Non Christians, Bishop's Welfare Emergency Relief Com. Author: The Teaching of Cardinal Cajetan on the Sacrifice of the Mass, 1958, Considerations Toward the Theology on the Presbyterate, 1961. Trustee, chancellor Cath. U. Am.; chmn. bd. trustees Nat. Shrine Immaculate Conception. Mem. Nat. Conf. Cath. Bishops (adminstrv. com.). Address: Via Rusticucci 13, Rusticucci 13, 00193 Rome Italy*

BAUMAN, DALE ELTON, nutritional biochemistry educator; b. Detroit, Dec. 26, 1942; s. Elton Blaine and Waneta Mary (Taylor) B.; m. L. Marie Vinande, Aug. 28, 1965; children: Rebecca, Todd, Jeffrey. B.S., Mich. State U., 1964, M.S., 1968; Ph.D., U. Ill., 1969. Asst. prof., assoc. prof. U. Ill.-Urbana, 1969-78; vis. prof. Mich. State U., East Lansing, 1978; assoc. prof., then prof. Cornell U., Ithaca, N.Y., 1979—, Liberty Hyde Bailey prof., 1987; chmn. NAS/NRC Bd. Agr. Contbr. articles to profl. jours. Leader and scoutmaster Boy Scouts Am., Mich., N.Y., 1978-83. Recipient N.Y. Farmers award, 1982, Alexander von Humboldt award, 1985, USDA Superior Svc. award, 1986, U. Ill. Alumni award, 1995. Mem. NAS (chmn. bd. on agr.), Am. Dairy Sci. Assn. (Nat. Student award 1967, Nutrition Rsch. award 1982, Biotech. award 1987, Physiology Rsch. award 1994), Am. Soc. Animal Sci. (Young Scientist award 1977, Growth Biology award 1996, Fellow Rsch. award 1999), Am. Inst. Nutrition, Nat. Acad. Sci., Coun. Agr. Sci. Tech. (Black award 1995). Methodist. Home: 2 Eagleshead Rd Ithaca NY 14850-9659 Office: Cornell U 262 Morrison Hall Ithaca NY 14853-4801

BAUMAN, EARL WILLIAM, accountant, government official; b. Arcadia, Nebr., Jan. 30, 1916; s. William A. and Gracia M. (Jones) B.; m. Margaret E. Blackman, Oct. 21, 1940 (dec. 1984); children: Carol Ann Bauman Ammerman. Earl William Jr.; m. Jessie C. Morgan, Dec. 23, 1990. BS with honors, U. Wyo., 1938; postgrad. Northwestern U., 1938-39. Acct., Haselmire, Cordle & Co., Casper, Wyo., 1939-42; asst. dir. fin. VA, Chgo., 1946-49, chief acctg. group VA, Washington, 1949-52, supr. systems acctg. GAO, Washington, 1952-55; supervising auditor GAO, Washington, 1955-58; dir. finance, asst. dir. Directorate Acctg. and Fin. Policy, Office Asst. Sec. Def., Washington, 1958-63; tech. asst. to comdr. AF Acctg. and Fin. Ctr., Denver, 1963-73; mem. investigations staff Ho. of Reps. Appropriations Com., 1953-54; prof. acctg. Benjamin Franklin U., 1960-63; mem. exec. council Army Finance, 1963-64; dir. Real Estate Investment Corp., 1962-64; sr. ptnr. EMB Enterprises, 1973—; chmn. Acctg. Careers Council Colo., 1969-71. Chmn. Aurora Citizens Adv. Budget Com., 1975-76; chmn. fin. and taxation com. Denver Met. Study, 1976-78. Served with AUS, 1942-46; col. Res., now ret. CPA. Mem. AICPA, Wyo. Assn. CPAs, Fed. Govt. Accts. Assn. (nat. v.p. 1972-73, pres. Denver 1973-74), Army Finance Assn., Am. Soc. Mil. Comptrollers, Denver Am. Soc. Mil. Comptrollers (pres. 1968-69), Citizens Band Radio Assn. (pres. 1963), Nat. Assn. Ret. Fed. Employees (Aurora 1072 pres. 1986-87), Alpha Kappa Psi, Beta Alpha Psi, Phi Kappa Phi. Club: Columbine Sertoma (pres. 1975-76). Avocations: photography, tennis, collector cars. Home: 536 Newark Ct Aurora CO 80010-4728

BAUMAN, GEORGE DUNCAN, former newspaper publisher; b. Humboldt, Iowa, Apr. 12, 1912; s. Peter William and Mae (Duncan) B.; m. Nora Kathleen Kelly, May 21, 1938 (dec. Feb. 13, 1990); m. Lucy H. Hume, Dec. 18, 1991. Student, Loyola U., Chgo., 1930-35; J.D., Washington U., St. Louis, 1948; Litt.D. (hon.), Central Meth. Coll.; LL.D. (hon.), Maryville Coll.; L.H.D. (hon.), Mo. Valley Coll., 1981, St. Louis Rabbinical Coll., 1981. Reporter Chgo. Herald Examiner, 1931-39; archtl. rep. Pratt & Lambert, Inc., St. Louis, 1939-43; reporter, rewriter, asst. city editor St. Louis Globe-Democrat, 1943-51, personnel mgr., 1951-59, bus. mgr., 1959-67, pub., 1967-84; adv. dir. Boatmen's Bank St. Louis. Bd. dirs. Boys Clubs Am., 1969-83, St. Louis YMCA, 1967-72, St. Louis City Welfare Commn., 1967-70, Better Bus. Bur., 1968-72, St. Louis Mcpl. Theatre Assn., 1968—, St. Louis Symphony Soc., 1968-86, Arts and Edn. Coun., 1972-83; mem. lay adv. bd. St. Vincent's Hosp., 1952-75, pres., 1957-58; mem. voting membership bd. Blue Shield, 1968-77; mem. nat. citizen's adv. com. Assn. Am. Med. Colls., 1975-84; mem. lay adv. bd. DePaul Cmty. Health Ctr., 1975-87; adv. bd. St. Louis Med. Soc., 1975-90; mem. exec. bd. St. Louis coun. Boy Scouts Am., 1967-86; mem. Pres.'s coun. St. Louis U., 1968-88; bd. visitors Mo. Mil. Acad., 1970-78; mem. adv. bd. Newman Chapel, 1964-89, pres., 1968; bd. dirs. Policemen and Firemen Fund, St. Louis, 1962-89, pres., 1968, 76-78; bd. dirs. United Way Greater St. Louis, 1964-1984, mem. exec. com., 1964, v.p., 1968-71; chmn. exec. com. and regional adv. com. Bi-State Regional Med. Program, 1968-75; bd. dirs. Health and Welfare Coun. Met. St. Louis, 1960-70, pres., 1965-67; sec. Bd. Election Commrs., St. Louis, 1957-61; bd. dirs. Catholic Charities, 1967-81, pres., 1969-70; bd. dirs. Child Ctr. Our Lady of Grace, 1965-80, pres., 1965-68; bd. dirs. Jr. Achievement Mississippi Valley, 1953-74, v.p., 1968, pres., 1978-80, nat. bd. dirs., 1979-84; mem. Conv. and Visitors Bur. of Greater St. Louis, 1968-77, v.p., 1974, pres., 1975-76; bd. dirs. Dismas House, 1964-73, pres., 1968; bd. dirs. Human Life Found., 1973-81, Downtown St. Louis, Inc., 1977-83; trustee Mo. Bapt. Hosp., 1970—, exec. com., 1974—, treas., 1978-79, sec. 1979—, vice chmn., 1981-84; trustee Jefferson Nat. Expansion Meml. Assn., 1968-84, Mo. Pub. Expenditure Survey, 2968-89, Freedoms Found. at VAlley Forge, 1968-75, David Ranken Jr. TEch. Inst., 1969—, Nat. Jewish Hosp. and Rsch. Ctr., 1970—; trustee Laclede Sch. Law, 1981-98, chmn., 1986-98; state chmn. Mo. Com. for Employer Support Guard and Res., 1982-90; chmn. Rejis Commn., 1983—. Decorated Knight of Malta; recipient Silver Beaver award, 1978, Disting. Alumnus citation Washington U., 1972, Bus. Leader of Yr. award Religious Heritage Am., 1973, citation Loyola U. Alumni Assn., 1973, Right Arm of St. Louis award St. Louis Regional Commerce and Growth Assn., 1980, Silver Crown award St. Louis Rabbinical Coll., 1983, Dept. Def. medal for Disting. Pub. Svc., 1983, Disting. Communal Svc. award B'nai Brith, 1983, St. Louis Dem. Man of Yr. award, 1984, Pres.'s award Loyola Acad., 1989; named to Loyola U. Athletic Hall of Fame, 1976. Mem. ABA, Newspaper Personnel Rels. Assn. (past pres.), Mo. C. of C. (dir. 1969-74), St. Louis C. of C. (exec. com. 1969-73, dir. 1969-73), Mo. Acad. Squires, Round Table (exec. com. 1975-84, v.p., treas. 1975-76, pres. 1977-79), Mo. Bar Assn., Bar Assn. St. Louis, Advt. Club of St. Louis (gov. 1972-75), Bogey Club (pres. 1980-82), St. Louis Club, Media Club (dir. 1968-84). Home: 37 Conway Close Rd Saint Louis MO 63124-1633

BAUMAN, JOHN ANDREW, law educator; b. 1921. BSL, U. Minn., 1942, LLB, 1947; JSD, Columbia U., 1958. Bar: Wis. 1947, Minn. 1948. Spl. fellow Columbia U., 1950-51; assoc. prof. U. N. Mex., 1947-54; assoc. prof. Ind. U., 1954-59, prof., 1959-60; prof. UCLA, 1960-91, prof. emeritus, 1991; exec. dir. Assn. Am. Law Schs., Washington, 1980-83, Mem. Order of Coif (sec.-treas. 1983-92). Author: (with York) Cases and Materials on Remedies, 1967, 5th edit., 1991. Office: UCLA Sch Law 405 Hilgard Ave Los Angeles CA 90095-9000

BAUMAN, JOHN DUANE, lawyer; b. Kaskaskia, Ill., Aug. 22, 1930; s. Louis Wells and Veronica Genevieve (Schmerbauch) B.; m. Avis Crysella Moore, Sept. 15, 1956; children: Mark Duane, Thomas Jon, Jeffery Paul. BA, S.E. Mo. U., 1952; JD, Washington U., St. Louis, 1957. Bar: Mo. 1957, Ill. 1957. Assoc. Baker, Kagy & Wagner, East Saint Louis, Ill., 1957-62; ptnr. Wagner, Bertrand, Bauman & Schmieder, Belleville, Ill., 1962-86, Hinshaw & Culbertson, Chgo. and Belleville, 1986—. Gen. counsel Okaw Valley coun. Boy Scouts Am., 1980-90. With U.S. Army, 1952-54. Mem. ABA, Ill. Bar Assn., Internat. Assn. Ins. Counsel (state membership chmn.), Assn. of Def. Trial Counsel (pres. 1975-76), St. Clair County Bar Assn. (pres. 1972-73), Horsemen's Benevolent and Protective Assn. (v.p. 1989-98), Ill. Thoroughbred Breeders and Owners Found. (bd. dirs. 1999—), Bradenton Country Club, St. Clair Country Club (pres. 1972-74), Paducah Country Club, Elks. Roman Catholic. Avocations: horse racing, golf. Office: Hinshaw & Culbertson PO Box 509 521 W Main St Belleville IL 62220-1533

BAUMAN, JOHN E., JR., chemistry educator; b. Kalamazoo, Jan. 18, 1933; s. John E. and Teresa A. (Wauchek) B.; m. Barbara Curry, June 6, 1964; children—John, Catherine, Amy. B.S., U. Mich., 1955, M.S., 1960, Ph.D., 1962. Chemist Midwest Research Inst., Kansas City, Mo., 1955-58; research assoc. U. Mich., Ann Arbor, 1958-61; prof. chemistry U. Mo., Columbia, 1961-97, prof. emeritus, 1997—. Active Mo. Symphony Soc. Recipient Faculty Alumni award, 1969, Amoco Teaching award, 1975, Purple Chalk award, 1980, all U. Mo. Mem. Am. Chem. Soc. (nat. lectr.), Mo. Acad. Sci., Kiwanis, Sigma Xi, Alpha Chi Sigma. Roman Catholic. Home: 3703 Woods Edge Rd Columbia MO 65203-6607 Office: Univ Mo 125 Chemistry Bldg Columbia MO 65211

BAUMAN, M. GARRETT, English educator; b. Paterson, N.J., Aug. 7, 1948; s. M. Garrett and Dorothy Otley Bauman; m. Carol Nobles, June 3, 1978; children: Cynthia J., Diana M., Amy E., Jeremy N. BA, Upsala Coll., 1969; MA, Binghamton U., 1971. Prof. English Monroe C.C., Rochester, N.Y., 1971—. Author: Ideas and Details, 1993; author, editor: The Shape of Ideas, 1995; contbr. articles to mags., newspapers, jours. Mem. founding com., steering com. Greenway Trail, Livingston County, N.Y., 1996—. Recipient Leavy award Freedom's Found., 1988, Creative Nonfiction award N.Y. Found. for Arts, 1995, Saltonstall Found., 1997. Avocations: nature studies, travel, tennis. Office: Monroe CC 1000 E Henrietta Rd Rochester NY 14623

BAUMAN, MARTIN HAROLD, executive search firm executive; b. N.Y.C., Dec. 26, 1929; s. Jack and Rose (Powsky) B.; m. Carol Weiner, Apr. 15, 1962 (dec. Feb. 1991); children: John Howard, Elizabeth Anne; m. Sherry Connor, July 1, 1995. BS in Mgmt., NYU, 1956, MBA in Mgmt., 1961, postgrad. in behavioral sci., 1961-67. Indsl. engr. Arch-Bilt Container, N.Y.C., 1956-59; tng. dir. S. Klein Dept. Stores, N.Y.C., 1959-61; v.p. personnel Br. Motor Express, N.Y.C., 1961-65; asst. personnel dir. United Mchts. & Mfrs., N.Y.C., 1965-68; pres. Martin H. Bauman Assocs., N.Y.C., 1968—; guest lectr. NYU, 1965-67; asst. adj. prof. Pace U., N.Y.C., 1967-69. Cpl. U.S. Army, 1951-53. Mem. Assn. Exec. Search Cons., Nat. Assn. Corp. and Profl. Recruiters, N.Y. Personnel Mgmt. Assn. Republican. Jewish. Avocations: sports, music, health club. Office: Martin H Bauman Assocs 375 Park Ave New York NY 10152*

BAUMAN, RICHARD ARNOLD, coast guard officer; b. Fitchburg, Mass., Aug. 16, 1924; s. Frederick Adams and Dorothy Arnold (Farnham) B.; m. Dorothy Helen Schmalz, June 5, 1948; children: Elizabeth Kay, Richard Arnold, Jr., Robert Arthur, William Lawrence. BS in Marine Transp., Mass. Maritime Acad., 1976, DPA (hon.), 1982; student, Armed Forces Staff Coll., Norfolk, Va., 1966-67, Nat. War Coll., Washington, 1974-75. Officer U.S. Mcht. Marine, 1944-57; commd. lt. U.S. Coast Guard, 1957, advanced through grades to rear admiral, 1980; liaison officer to comdr. in chief U.S. Atlantic Fleet, Norfolk, 1968-71; comdg. officer USCG Cutter Ingham, 1971-73; chief info. systems div. Coast Guard Hdqrs., Washington, 1973-74; chief port safety and law enforcement Coast Guard Hdqrs., 1975-78; ops. officer 9th Coast Guard Dist., Cleve., 1978-80; chief Office Navigation, Coast Guard Hdqrs., Washington, 1980-83; comdr. 1st Coast Guard Dist., Boston, 1983-85; U.S. commr. Permanent Internat. Assn. Navigation Congresses, 1980-84. Decorated Legion of Merit, Bronze Star Medal with combat V, Meritorious Service medal (2), Coast Guard Commendation medals (3), Joint Service Commendation medal, Navy Commendation medal with combat V, Vietnamese Gallantry Cross with Gold Star. Mem. Retired Officers Assn., Boston Marine Soc., Masons.

BAUMAN, ROBERT PATTEN, diversified company executive; b. Cleve., Mar. 27, 1931; s. John Nevin and Lucille (Patten) B.; m. Patricia H. Jones, June 15, 1961; children: John, Elizabeth. BA, Ohio Wesleyan U., 1953; MBA, Harvard U., 1955. Mktg. adminstrn. Maxwell House div. Gen. Foods, White Plains, N.Y., 1958-65, gen. mgr. Post div., 1967, corp. v.p., 1968, exec. v.p., 1968, pres., dir. internat. ops., 1973; dir. Avco Corp., Greenwich, Conn., 1980-85, chmn., CEO, 1981-85; vice chmn. Textron Inc., Providence, R.I., 1985-86; chmn. Beecham PLC, 1986-89; CEO SmithKline Beecham Plc., Brentford, Eng., 1989-94; chmn. Brit. Aerospace PLC, Farnborough, Eng., 1994-98, BTR plc, London, 1998-99; bd. dirs. Union Pacific Corp, CIGNA Corp., Reuters, Morgan Stanley, Russell Reynolds, Hathaway Holdings Inc., Panorama, Invensys plc. Author: Plants as Pets, 1982; co-author: From Promise to Performance, 1997. Mem. Conf. Bd. Clubs: Webhannet Golf (Kennebunk, Maine); Blind Brook (Port Chester, N.Y.), Wisley Golf (Surrey, Eng.), Pine Valley Golf.

BAUMAN, SUSAN JOAN MAYER, lawyer, mayor of Madison, Wisconsin; b. N.Y.C., Mar. 2, 1945; d. Curt H. J. and Carola (Rosenau) Mayer; m. Ellis A. Bauman, Dec. 29, 1968. BS, U. Wis., 1965, JD, MS, 1981; MS, U. Chgo., 1966. Bar: Wis. 1981, U.S. Dist. Ct. (we. dist.) Wis. 1981, U.S. Ct. Appeals (7th cir.) 1983, U.S. Dist. Ct. (ea. dist.) Wis. 1985. Tchr. Madison (Wis.) Pub. Sch., 1970-78; research asst. U. Wis. Law Sch., Madison, 1981; ptnr. Thomas, Parsons, Schaefer & Bauman, Madison, 1981-84; sole practice Madison, 1984-85; ptnr. Bauman & Massing, Madison, 1985-87; pvt. practice, Madison, 1987-97; mayor City of Madison, 1997—. Alderman Madison Common Coun., 1985-97, coun. pres., 1989-90; commr. equal opportunities com. City of Madison, 1985-89; mem. Econ. Devel. Commn., 1986-87, chmn. human resources com., 1987-90, mem. affirmative action com., 1988-93; mem. Cmty. Action Commn., 1988-97, pres., 1991-96; mem. Pub. Health Commn., 1991-97, Monona Terr. Conv. and Cmty. Ctr. Bd., 1993-97; pres. South Madison Health and Family Ctr., Inc., 1993-97; bd. visitors U. Wis. Coll. Letters and Scis., Madison, 1997—. Mem. Wis. Bar Assn., Dane County Bar Assn., Wis. Indsl. Rels. Alumni Assn. (pres. 1985-86), Madison Civics Club. Democrat. Avocations: knitting, reading, backpacking, cross-country skiing. Home: 4809 Hillview Ter Madison WI 53711-1201 Office: Office of the Mayor PO Box 551 Madison WI 53701-0551

BAUMAN, TATJANA, pathologist, consultant; b. Riga, Latvia, June 25, 1930; came to U.S., 1950; 1 child, Irene Bauman. BS, CCNY, 1961; PhD, Maximillian U, Munich, Germany, 1960, MD, 1960. Diplomate Am. Bd. Pathology, Am. Bd. Forensic Medicine. Resident in pathology VA Hosp., West Haven, 1961, Yale U., 1961; asst. prof. U. Conn., 1970; asst. clin. prof. U. So. Fla.; chief clin. pathology VA Hosp., 1976; pathologist VA Hosp., Bay Pines, Fla., 1979—. Republican. Lutheran. Home: 629 59th Ave Saint Pete Beach FL 33706

BAUMAN, WENDALL CARTER, JR., ophthalmologist, career officer; b. Oklahoma City, Nov. 7, 1956; s. Wendall C. and Donna M. (Kolzow) B. BS, Nebr. Wesleyan U., 1979; MD, Uniformed Svcs. U. Health Sci., 1983. Med. lic., Tex. Commd. USAF, 1979, advanced through grades to lt. col., 1995; resident in internal medicine Wright-Patterson Med. Ctr., Wright-Patterson AFB, Ohio, 1983-85; chief hosp. svc. USAF Hosp., Kunsan Air Base, Korea, 1985-86; staff physician USAF Clinic, Izmir, Turkey, 1986-87; resident in ophthalmology Wilford Hall Med. Sch., Lackland AFB, Tex., 1987-90; retina fellow Mass. Eye and Ear Infirmary Med. Sch. Harvard U., Cambridge, 1990-92, chief fellow retina svc., 1991-92; chief retina svc. Brooke Army Med. Ctr., Ft. Sam Houston, Tex., 1992—; asst. chief dept. surgery Brooke Army Med. Ctr., Ft. Sam Houston, 1996—. Contbr. articles to profl. jours. Recipient Investigators award Barcelona Med. Soc., 1991. Fellow Am. Acad. Ophthalmology; mem. AAAS, Tex. Med. Assn., Mass. Med. Assn. Methodist. Avocations: camping, hiking, fishing, gardening, stamp collecting. Home: 137 Primrose Pl San Antonio TX 78209-3832 Office: Ophthalmology Svc Brooke Army Med Ctr 2851 Roger Brooke Dr Fort Sam Houston TX 78234

BAUMAN, WILLIAM ALLEN, pediatrician, educator, health systems consultant; b. N.Y.C., Nov. 23, 1923; s. Louis and Stella (Kraus) B.; m. Joan Carlsen, June 28, 1952; children: William Carlsen, Phillip Allen, Pamela Joan. Student, Harvard U., 1942-43, 46; MD, Columbia U., 1947; postgrad. in biostats., Sch. Pub. Health, 1960-63. Intern L.I. divsn. Kings County Hosp., Bklyn., 1947-48; resident Babies Hosp., N.Y.C., 1948-50; chief pediatric clinic Vanderbilt Clinic, N.Y.C., 1954-65; practice medicine specializing in pediatrics N.Y.C., 1953-75; dir. med. data processing Presbyn. Hosp., N.Y.C., 1966-74, assoc. attending pediatrician, 1973-93, emeritus staff, 1994—; v.p. med. adminstrv. svcs. Group Health Inc., N.Y.C., 1974-77; chmn. bd. govs. Hillcrest Gen. Hosp.-Group Health Inc., 1975-79, attending pediatrician, 1975-79; sr. v.p. Health Svcs. Group Health Inc., 1977-79; v.p. med. affairs Danbury Hosp., Conn., 1979-90; mem. faculty dept. pediatrics Columbia U., 1952-73, assoc. clin. prof. pediatrics, 1973—; mem. med. bd. Maternity Ctr. Assn., 1969-95; chmn. faculty-student adv. bd. P&S Club, Coll. Physicians and Surgeons, Columbia U., 1970-90; chmn. com. on data processing N.Y. County Health Rev. Orgn., 1976-79. Contbr. articles to profl. jours. Mem. data protection rev. bd. N.Y. State Dept. Health, 1993—. With M.C. USAF, 1951-52. Fellow Am. Coll. Med. Informatics, N.Y. Acad. Medicine; mem. Am. Acad. Pediatrics, N.Y. County Med. Soc., AMA, Med. Soc. State N.Y. (chmn. com. info. tech. in medicine 1967-93), Assn. Ambulatory Pediatrics, Assn. Computing Machinery, Soc. Computer Medicine (bd. dirs.), Bioengring. Inst., Am. Soc. Info. Scis., N.Y. Acad. Scis., N.Y. State Assn. Professions, Am. Assn. Med. Systems and Infomatics (pres. 1983). Home and Office: 667 Heritage Hls Somers NY 10589-1927

BAUMANN, CAROL EDLER, retired political science educator; b. Plymouth, Wis., Aug. 11, 1932; d. Clarence Henry and Beulah Hanetta (Weinhold) E.; m. Richard Joseph Baumann, Feb. 28, 1959; children: Dawn Carol, Wendy Katherine. BA in Internat. Rels., U. Wis., 1954; PhD in Internat. Rels., London Sch. Econs./Polit. Sci., 1957. Chmn. Internat. Rels. Major U. Wis., Milw., 1962-79; dep. asst. sec. Bur. of Intelligence and Rsch./Dept. of State, Washington, 1979-81; prof. U. Wis., Milw., 1972-95, dir. internat. studies and programs, 1982-88, prof. emeritus, 1995—; dir. Inst. of World Affairs, Milw., 1964-97, dir. emeritus, 1997—. Author: Program Planning About World Affairs, 1991, The Diplomatic Kidnappings, 1973; editor: Europe in NATO: Deterrence, Defense, and Arms Control, 1987, Western Europe: What Path to Integration?, 1967. Active Gov.'s Commn. on the UN, 1964-79, 82-89; Dem. candidate 9th Congl. Dist., 1968; mem. World Affairs Coun. of Milw., 1964-75; bd. dirs. Wis. World Trade Ctr., 1987—, Wis. Dist. Export Coun., 1987—, Ea. Shores Libr. Sys., 1999—. Recipient pub. svc. achievement award Common Cause, Wis., 1991; Marshall scholar, 1954-57. Mem. China Coun. of Asia Soc., Coun. on Fgn. Rels., European Union's "Team Europe", Fgn. Policy Assn. (bd. dirs. 1990—, editl. adv. com. 1977-79, 82-88), Nat. Coun. World Affairs Orgns. (pres. 1977-79, bd. dirs. 1992-96), UN Assn. of USA (bd. dirs. 1977-79, 82-89), Soc. for Citizen Edn. in world Affairs (pres. 1977-79), Com. on Atlantic Studies, Internat. Studies Assn., Phi Kappa Phi, Phi Beta Kappa. Democrat. Lutheran. Avocations: walking, skiing, swimming, reading, travel. Home: W6248 Lake Ellen Dr Cascade WI 53011-1322

BAUMANN, CAROL KAY, clinical nurse specialist; b. Summersville, Mo., Dec. 12, 1946; d. Vern Underwood and Jean E. (Lay) Hines; children: Joell Christine, Richard Douglas. Diploma, Barnes Hosp., St. Louis, 1967; BS in Nursing, St. Louis U., 1981, MS in Nursing Rsch., 1989. Cert. oper. rm. nurse; cert. RN 1st asst.; cert. clin. nurse specialist. Staff nurse Barnes Hosp., St. Louis, 1967-68, head nurse neurosurgery, 1969-71; staff nurse St. John's Mercy Hosp., St. Louis, 1980-81, neurosurgery specialty nurse, 1981-85; surgery edn. coord. Mo. Bapt. Med. Ctr., St. Louis, 1985-90; asst. head nurse neuro/ophthalmology oper. rm. Barnes Hosp., St. Louis, 1990-92; clin. nurse specialist St. Louis U. Med. Ctr., 1992—; speaker in field. Contbr. articles to profl. jours. Mem. ANA, Assn. Oper. Rm. Nurses, Am. Assn. Neurosci. Nurses (Gateway City chpt. 1988—, charter sec.-treas. 1988-89, pres. 1989-91), Am. Assn. Neurol. Surgeons (assoc.), Mo. Assn. RN First Assts., Mo. Nurses Assn., Sigma Theta Tau. Home: 14515 Coeur Dalene Ct Chesterfield MO 63017-2401

BAUMANN, DANIEL E., newspaper executive; b. Milw., Apr. 10, 1937; s. Herbert F. and Agnes V. (Byrne) B.; m. Karen R. Weinkauf, Apr. 29, 1961; children: James W., Jennifer R., Colin D. BJ, U. Wis., 1958, MA in Polit. Sci., 1962, Cert. in Russian Area Studies, 1962. Reporter South Milwaukee (Wis.) Voice Jour., 1958-59, East St. Louis (Ill.) Jour., 1959-60; pub. relations rep. Credit Union Nat. Assn., Washington, 1962-64; reporter Paddock Publs., Inc., Arlington Heights, Ill., 1964-66, mng. editor, 1966-68, exec. editor, 1968-70, editor and pub. Paddock Circle newpapers, 1970-75, v.p., editor, 1975-83, sr. v.p., gen. mgr., editor, 1983-86, pres., editor, 1986-90, dir., 1986—; pres., chief operating officer Paddock Publs., Inc., Arlington Heights, 1990-98. Mem. High Tech. Corridors Coun., Palatine, Ill., 1986—; bd. dirs. Greater Woodfield Conv. and Visitors Bur., Schaumburg, Ill., 1985-93. With USNR. Recipient William Alan White award U. Kans., 1976. Mem. Newspaper Assn. Am., Am. Soc. Newspaper Editors, Internat. Newspaper Advt. and Mktg. Execs., Soc. Profl. Journalists, Chgo. Headline Club (Peter Lisagor award 1983), Chgo. Assn. Dir. Mktg., Sigma Delta Chi. Avocations: photography, travel. scuba diving. Office: Paddock Pubs Daily Herald 155 E Algonquin Rd Arlington Heights IL 60005-4617*

BAUMANN, EDWARD ROBERT, environmental engineering educator; b. Rochester, N.Y., May 12, 1921; s. John Carl and Lillie Minnie (Roth) B.; m. Mary A. Massey, June 15, 1946; children: Betsy Louise, Philip Robert. BSCE, U. Mich., 1944; BS in San. Engring, U. Ill., 1945, MS, 1947, PhD, 1954; NSF faculty fellow, U. Durham, Eng., 1959-60. Research assoc. U. Ill., 1947-53; assoc. prof. civil engring. Iowa State U., 1953-56, prof., 1956-91, Anson Marston Disting. prof. engring., 1972-91, emeritus Disting. prof., 1991—; cons. Water Quality Office of EPA, Culligan Internat., Lakeside Engring. Co., Bolton & Menk, many cities and industries. Author: Sewerage and Sewage Treatment, 1958; mem. editorial bd.: Internat. Jour.

Air and Water Pollution, London, 1960-67; asst. editor: San. Engr. Newsletter of ASCE, 1962-74; contbr. articles to profl. jours. V.p., treas. Water Found., Inc., 1978-83; mem. Iowa Bd. Health, 1975-76, Iowa State U. Rsch. Found., 1975-78, 83-91. With C.E., AUS, 1944-46. Recipient George B. Gascoigne medal Water Pollution Control Fedn., 1962, 80, Publs. award, 1963, Purification divsn. award Am. Water Works Assn., 1965, Anson Marston medal Iowa Engring. Soc., 1966, Disting. Svc. award, 1968, Gold medal Filtration Soc. Eng., 1970, Bedell award, 1977, Rsch. award, 1978, Philip F. Morgan award Water Pollution Control Fedn., 1986; named Water Works Man of Yr., 1972, Disting. Alumni award U. Ill. Alumni Assn., 1992. Fellow ASCE (life), Iowa Acad. Scis. (disting. sci. 1990), Am. Filtration Separations Soc. (F.M. Tiller award 1994); mem. NSPE (nat. bd. dirs.), AAUP, Am. Water Works Assn. (hon., life, internat. bd. dirs. 1978-80), Assn. Environ. Engring. Profs. (pres. 1967-70, 86-87, Nalco award, Founders award 1991), Am. Soc. Engring. Edn., Am. Inst. Chem. Engrs., Am. Acad. Environ. Engring. (diplomate), Filtration Soc. (Eng., bd. dirs., tech. editor, vice chmn. 1993, chmn. 1994, Fluid/Particle Separation Jour.), Rotary, Sigma Xi, Phi Kappa Phi (Centennial medal 1997), Chi Epsilon. Home: 1627 Crestwood Cir Ames IA 50010-5520 *It isn't enough to build a "big pie"; we must also protect its quality and learn how to cut it fairly.*

BAUMANN, ERNST FREDERICK, college president; b. N.Y.C., Oct. 4, 1943; s. Ernst and Grace (Crowley) B.; m. Kathleen Ann Brennan, June 17, 1967; children: Ernst Frederick Jr., Lori Ann, Macushla, Katrinka, Victoria, Greta. BA, Harvard U., 1967; postgrad., Colo. U. Observer, rsch. asst. High Altitude Obs., Nat. Ctr. for Atsmospheric Rsch., Boulder, Colo., 1967-69; uranium geologist, grade control engr. Kerr-McGee Corp., Casper, Wyo., 1969-71; mine geologist engr. Am. Smelting and Refining Co., Leadville, Colo., 1975; chief geologist, engr. Leadville (Colo.) Lead Corp., 1976-79; dir. adult basic edn. and gen. ednl. devel., counselor Upper Ark. Area Coun. Govts., Cañon City, Colo., 1987-96; corr. officer, supr. C.T.C.F./D.O.C., Cañon City, 1979-99; pres., chmn. Coll. of the Cañons, Cañon City, 1987-96; officer Colo. Territorial Correctional Facility, Dept. Corrections, Cañon City; recruiter Harvard U., Cañon City; pres., chmn. bd. Working in SETI Search for Extra-Terrestrial Intelligence. Co-author: Toward a New World: Powerful Proof of the Existence of God, 1995; editor: The Crucifixion; patentee mil. mountaineer's collapsible ski. Mayoral candidate City of Cañon City, 1983, 85. Maj. CAP, USAF Aux., 1980-99. Mem. K. of C. (scribe). Republican. Roman Catholic. Home: 1101 Phay Ave Canon City CO 81212-2248 Office: Coll of the Cañons Forge Rd/Indsl Park Canon City CO 81212

BAUMANN, GREGORY WILLIAM, physician, consultant; b. Detroit, June 20, 1947; s. Alfred Louis Baumann and Marian (Bartholomew) Martens. BS, U. Mich., 1968, MD cum laude, 1972, MA in Telecom. Arts, 1993. Diplomate Am. Bd. Emergency Medicine. Intern Albert Einstein Coll. Medicine, Bronx Mcpl. Dept. Surgery, 1972-73; resident in neurology U. Mich., 1973-74; staff physician Foote Hosp., Jackson, Mich., 1974—, chmn. emergency med. dept., 1979-89, med. dir. emergency med. svcs. project, 1981-86, dir. ambulatory care, 1982-90; pres. Abecdarian Prodns., Inc., Ann Arbor, Mich.; cons. emergency med. svcs., Jackson, 1982—; mem. adv. life support tech. com. Mich. Dept. Pub. Health, Lansing, 1985-87; med. dir. Mich. Internat. Speedway, Bklyn., 1986-96; chief med. examiner Jackson County, 1986-88; med. dir. Cleve. Indy Car Grand Prix. Bd. dirs. Hospice of Jackson, 1984-88; med. dir. Nazareth (Pa.) Speedway, 1987-96, Calif. Speedway, 1996; med. dir. Penske Motorsports, Inc., Brooklyn, Mich., 1997—. Recipient Merit award March of Dimes, 1970; rsch. grantee U. Mich. Med. Sch., 1972. Mem. AMA, Mich. Med. Soc., Jackson County Med. Soc., Kappa Tau Alpha. Lutheran. Avocations: computer applications in medicine, video production. Office: 12626 US 12 Brooklyn MI 49230

BAUMANN, HANS D., engineering executive. PhD, Columbia Pacific U. Registered profl. engr. Internat. cons., corp. v.p. Masoneilan Internat. Inc.; mgr. R&D Worthington S/A; dir. engring. CASHCO Inc.; chief engr. W & T Co.; founder H. D. Baumann Assoc. Ltd.; sr. v.p. Fisher Controls Internat., St. Louis; bd. dirs. E&J Cating Inc., H.D. Baumann Inc. Author 4 books; co-author 5 books; contbr. numerous articles to profl. jours.; patentee 140 patents in field. Bd. govs. Palm Beach Opera Co. Fellow ASME, ISA (life); mem. Abenaqui Country Club, Govs. Club (Palm Beach). Office: Fisher Controls Internat 35 Mirona Rd Portsmouth NH 03801-5344

BAUMANN, JULIAN HENRY, JR., lawyer; b. Ft. Leavenworth, Kans., Feb. 20, 1943; s. Julian Henry and Helene (Claiborne) B.; B.S., Clemson U., 1965; postgrad. U. Tenn., 1966; J.D., U. S.C., 1968; LL.M. in Taxation, N.Y. U., 1975; m. Karen Ann Hofmann, July 14, 1973; children—Andrew H., Allison C. Admitted to S.C. bar, 1968, Del. bar, 1976, assoc. firm Richards, Layton & Finger, Wilmington, Del., 1975-80, dir., 1980—. Served to capt., JAGC, U.S. Army, 1969-74. Fellow Am. Coll. Tax Counsel; mem. Am. Bar Assn., S.C. Bar Assn., Del. State Bar (chmn., sec. taxation 1990-91), Wilmington Tax Group (chmn. 1988-89), The Com. of 100 (pres. 1994-96); Bd. of Mgrs., The Nemours Found., Wilmington Club, Greenville Country Club. Democrat. Roman Catholic. Home: 8 Brendle Ln Wilmington DE 19807-1300 Office: Richards Layton & Finger One Rodney Sq 10th & King Sts Wilmington DE 19801

BAUMANN, MICHELLE RENAE, editor, writer; b. Walnut Creek, Calif., Aug. 17, 1970; d. Garry Benton and Beverly Ann (Harper) Miller; m. Brad Christopher Baumann, Oct. 19, 1996. BA, Calif. State U., Long Beach, 1992. Intern L.A. Mag., 1991-92; asst. editor Builder and Developer Mag., Newport Beach, Calif., 1992-93; mng. editor Indoor Comfort News, L.A., 1993-94; exec. editor Bobit Pub. Co., Redondo Beach, Calif., 1994-97; project mgr. Ctr. for Healthcare Info., Newport Beach, 1997—. Mem. emergency response team, Huntington Beach, Calif., 1996; vol. PAWS, Irvine, Calif., 1995, In Def. of Animals, Calif., 1996. Mem. Soc. Profl. Journalists (treas. Long Beach State chpt. 1992). Democrat. Methodist. Avocations: karate, running, crafts, reading, auto repair, travel.

BAUMANN, RICHARD GORDON, lawyer; b. Chgo., Apr. 7, 1938; s. Martin M. and Harriet May (Granof) B.; m. Terrie Bemel, Dec. 18, 1971; children: Michelle, Alison. BS cum laude, U. Wis., 1960, JD, 1964. Bar: Wis. 1964, Calif. 1970, U.S. Supreme Ct. 1973. Congressional intern U.S. Senator Hubert H. Humphrey, 1959; assoc. firm Kohner, Mann & Kailas, Milw., 1964-69, Sulmeyer, Kupetz & Alberts, L.A., 1969-73; mem. firm Sulmeyer, Kupetz, Baumann & Rothman, L.A., 1973—; judge pro tem L.A. Mcpl. Ct., 1980—; bd. dirs. Am. Bd. Cert. Assoc. editor Comml. Law Jour., 1991—. Fellow Comml. Law Found. (bd. dirs.); mem. Nat. Inst. on Credit Mgmt. (bd. dirs.), Acad. Comml. and Bankruptcy Law Specialists (bd. dirs.), Comml. Law League (pres. 1990-91, bd. govs. 1986-92, chmn. Western Region Mem. Assn. 1982-83). Office: 14th Fl 300 S Grand Ave Fl 14 Los Angeles CA 90071-3109

BAUMANN, ROBERT JAY, child neurology educator; b. Chgo., Oct. 22, 1940; s. Stephen S. and Evelyn (Hellerstein) B.; m. Judith Kravitz, Oct. 1964; children: Barbara, Stephen, Lauren. BS magna cum laude, Tufts U., 1961; MD, Western Res. U., 1964. Diplomate Am. Bd. Psychiatry and Neurology (examiner 1976—). Intern, resident in pediatrics and neurology U. Chgo. Hosps., 1965-69, fellow in child neurology, 1971-72; asst. prof. neurology U. Ky., Lexington, 1972-78, assoc. prof., 1987-92, prof., 1992—, assoc. prof. rehab., 1987—, assoc. prof. pediatrics, 1989-92, prof., 1992—, dir. regional neurology program, 1972—, dir. child neurology program, 1979—; cons. U.S. Commn. for Control Epilepsy, Washington, 1976; reviewer, cons. Nat. Inst. Neurol. Disease and Stroke, Bethesda, Md., 1979-95; neuroepidemiology cons. Ky.-Ecuador Ptnrs. of Ams., Quito, 1987-91, Am. Acad. Pediatrics, 1991—, Instituto de Investigaciones, Facultad de Ciencias Medicas, U. Ctrl. Del Ecuador, Quito. Chmn. United Jewish Appeal Campaign, Lexington, 1986-87; v.p. Cen. Ky. Jewish Fedn., Lexington, 1988-92. Capt. M.C., USAF, 1969-71. Mem. Child Neurology Soc., Am. Acad. Neurology, Am. Acad. Pediatrics (neuroepidemiologic cons. 1992—), Am. Coll. Epidemiology, Soc. for Epidemiologic Rsch., Profs. Child Neurology (bd. dirs. 1988-92). Office: U Ky Dept Neurology Ky Clinic 800 Rose St Dept Lexington KY 40536-0284

BAUMANN, THEODORE ROBERT, aerospace engineer, consultant, army officer; b. Bklyn., May 13, 1932; s. Emil Joseph and Sophie (Reiblein) B.; m. Patricia Louise Drake, Dec. 16, 1967; children: Veronica Ann, Robert Theodore, Joseph Edmund. B in Aerospace Engring., Poly. U., Bklyn., 1954; MS in Aerospace Engring., U. So. Calif., L.A., 1962; grad., US Army C&GS Coll., 1970, Indsl. Coll. of Armed Forces, 1970, US Army War Coll., 1979, Air War Coll., 1982. Structures engr. Glenn L. Martin Co., Balt., 1954-55; structural loads engr. N.Am. Rockwell, L.A., 1958-67; dynamics engr. TRW Systems Group, Redondo Beach, Calif., 1967-71, systems engr., 1971-75, project engr., 1975-84, sr. project engr., 1984-92; cons. SAAB-Scania Aerospace Div., Linkoping, Sweden, 1981-82; asst. dir. Dir. Weapons Systems, U.S. Army, Washington, 1981-85, staff officer Missile & Air Def. System div., 1975-81. Contbr. articles to Machine Design, tech. publs., tech. symposia. Asst. scoutmaster Boy Scouts Am., Downey, Calif., 1985-93; instr. Venice Judo Boys Club, 1966-86. Served from 2d lt. U.S. Army to col. USAR, 1954-88. Decorated Legion of Merit. Mem. AIAA; mem. Soc. Am. Mil. Engrs (life), Am. Legion, Res. Officers Assn. (life), U.S. Judo Fedn., Nat. Rifle Assn, Knights of Columbus. Republican. Roman Catholic. Achievements include developing a new method for the analysis and classification of random data; contbr. to air force ballistic missile program; devel. procedure for design of prestressed joints and fittings. Office: Theodore R Baumann & Assoc 7732 Brunache St Downey CA 90242-2206

BAUMANN-SINACORE, PATRICIA LYNN, nursing administrator; b. Carbondale, Pa., Jan. 30, 1962; d. John Frederick and Catherine Anne Hunt; married: children: Donnell Patricia and Taryn Frances Thorne. BSN, Wilkes Coll., 1987. Staff nurse, pulmonary and float Mercy Hosp., Scranton, Pa., 1987-88; asst. mgr. CMC Found., Scranton, 1988-89; mgr. CMCI Community Med. Ctr. Found., Scranton, 1989-90; dir. profl. svcs. Above All Home Health and Hospice, Taylor, Pa., 1991-93; surveyor, cons. Primary Care and Home Health divsn., Pa. Dept. Health, 1993-95; asst. adminstr. Interim Healthcare Svcs., Inc., Hughestown, Pa., 1995; quality assurance/risk management specialist Pa. Dept. Pub. Welfare, Clark Summit, 1997-98; risk mgr. dementia unit Mountain View Care Ctr., Scranton, 1998—; instr. DEPMED Power Distbn. 348th Gen. Hosp., Ashley, Pa. Capt. USAR, Desert Shield/Desert Storm, Saudi Arabia, 1990-91. Mem. Rotary (charter, v.p. 1994-95).

BAUMBERGER, CHARLES HENRY, lawyer; b. Port Huron, Mich., Sept. 13, 1941; s. Peter Julius and Evelyn Margaret (Jackson) B.; m. Martha Carolyn Megathlin, Aug. 8, 1969; children: Peter Scott, Charles Henry Jr. BA, Vanderbilt U., 1963; JD, U. Fla., 1966. Bar: Fla. 1966, U.S. Dist. Ct. (so. dist.) Fla. 1967; cert. civil trial lawyer. Atty. Stephens, Demos & Magill, Miami, Fla., 1967-68; ptnr. Hastings, Goldman & Baumberger, Miami, 1969-74; founding ptnr. Rossman & Baumberger P.A., Miami, 1974—; lectr. various continuing legal edn. programs; guest on numerous radio, TV talk shows, 1987—. Contbr. articles to profl. jours. Mem. Gov's. Task Force on Emergency Room and Trauma Care, 1987; So. Fla. Health Action Coalition, Inc., 1984; task force on trauma and trauma systems Dept. Transp., 1987—. Served to 1st lt. U.S. Army Res., 1966-72. Mem. ABA, ATLA (past chair of Profl. Negligence Sect.), Fed. Bar Assn., Dade County Bar Assn. (bd. dirs. 1977-88, pres. 1989-90), Fla. Bar (exec. coun. trial lawyers sect. 1983-89, chmn. 1990-91), Acad. Fla. Trial Lawyers (bd. dirs. 1980-89), Dade County Trial Lawyers Assn. (founding mem. bd. dirs. 1981-84), Am. Bd. Trial Advocates (Miami chpt. past pres.), Fla. Lawyers Action Group, So. Trial Lawyers Assn., Trial Lawyers for Pub. Justice (founding mem. 1982—), Am. Coll. Trial Lawyers, Coral Reef Yacht Club, Univ. Club. Democrat. Methodist. Home: 5755 Suncrest Dr Miami FL 33156-5704 Office: Rossman Baumberger & Reboso 44 W Flagler St Fl 23 Miami FL 33130-1808

BAUMEL, HERBERT, violinist, conductor; b. N.Y.C., Sept. 30, 1919; s. Leon and Fannie (Beckerman) B; m. Rachael Bail, Oct. 17, 1949 (div. Nov. 1970); children: Susan, Samuel, Mary Elizabeth (dec.); m. Joan Patricia French, July 11, 1971. Student, Mannes Sch. of Music, 1932-34; diploma, Curtis Inst. of Music, 1937-42; postgrad., Santa Cecilia, Accademia Chigiana, Rome and Siena, 1954-56. Violinist, concertmaster, conductor with orchs., chamber groups, Broadway shows, jazz ensembles, ballets, operas worldwide, 1939—; Baumel-Booth-Smith Trio (1st integrated classical trio to tour deep south), 1968-71; Baumel-Booth Duo, 1968-96; violinist/storyteller, 1970—, co-dir., Baumel Assocs., Yonkers, N.Y., 1984—; judge Fulbright Nat. Screening Com., 1965-67; guest artist Sponsors' Concerts of Dallas Chamber Music Soc., 1991, Internat. Piano Archives U. Md., College Park, Beveridge Webster Celebration Concert, 1991; lectr. and violinist with Dr. Joan French Baumel, 1991—, Yonkers Pub. Libr., 1992, Greenburgh (N.Y.) Pub. Libr., 1992, Waverly Heights, Gladwyne, Pa., 1993, 94, 95, Alliance Francaise, Westchester, N.Y., 1993, 94, 95, 96, 1st Unitarian Soc. Westchester, 1994, Workmen's Circle Lodge, Sylvan Lake, N.Y., 1994, Thomas Paine/Huguenot/New Rochelle (N.Y.) Hist. Soc., 1995, 96, others. Violinist Phila. Orch. with Ormandy, Toscanini, Walter, Monteux, Mitropoulos, Szell; first to play Samuel Barber's Violin Concerto with Curtis Symphony (Reiner), 1939 and Phila. Orch. (Ormandy); concert artist with: Stokowski, Stravinsky, Copland, Bernstein, Benny Goodman; concertmaster Phila. Opera, N.Y.C. Opera, N.Y.C. Ballet, Joe Bushkin Jazz Ensembles, (original Broadway musicals) New Girl in Town, Fiorello!, She Loves Me, Fiddler on the Roof, A Little Night Music, Rex, Dancin', also three Presdl. galas with Marilyn Monroe, Bill Cosby, Woody Allen, Jack Benny, Johnny Carson, Rudolph Nureyev, Margot Fonteyn; recs. with Heifetz, Horowitz, Rubinstein, Leonard Warren, Frank Sinatra, Edith Piaf, Tallulah Bankhead, many others; writer script and music ednl. audio-visual program The Art of Listening, 1972—; composer: Fiddlers Two, 1976, Caprice #48 1/2, 1978, Sentiment America, 1984, arranger 5 tunes from Fiddler on the Roof, 1971. Mem. adv. bd. Mark Brent Dolinsky Found., White Plains, N.Y., 1982—; played benefits for Westchester Assn. Retarded Citizens, 1982—, Coalition for the Homeless,Westchester County, N.Y., 1986—. Recipient Silver medal New York Music Week Assn., 1928, Gold medal New York Music Week Assn., 1929; 2-time Fulbright scholar to Rome, 1954-56; chosen for both Stokowski All-American Youth Orch. tours, S.Am., U.S., 1940, 41; chosen to organize, present and play concerts for U.S. Embassy and Cultural Offices throughout Italy with Anna Moffo, Ezio Flagello, Ivan Davis, Gimi Beni, and in honor of Queen Elisabeth of Belgium, 1954-56, Phila. Drama Guild Lectr. Series, 1978. Mem. Am. Fedn. Musicians, Curtis Inst. of Music Alumni Assn., Phila. Orch. Retirees and Friends. Democrat. Jewish. Avocations: tennis, gardening, reading, photography, chess. Home and Office: Baumel Assocs 86 Rosedale Rd Yonkers NY 10710-3033

BAUMEL, JOAN PATRICIA FRENCH, educator, writer, lecturer; b. Winona, Minn., Mar. 12, 1930; d. William Oswald and Gertrude Marie (Fitzgerald) French; m. Herbert Baumel, July 11, 1971. Student, l'Ecole du Louvre, France, 1950-51; student with high honors, Inst. Phonétique Sorbonne, Paris, 1950-51; BA magna cum laude, Douglass Coll., 1952; postgrad., U. Detroit, 1952-55, Case Western Reserve U., 1960, U. Akron, 1962, U. Notre Dame, 1963, Manhattanville Coll., 1971; MA in French, Rutgers U., 1965; PhD in Modern Langs., Fordham U., 1985. Tchr. French lang. and culture, elem. and coll. levels various schs. including Mother House of Religious of the Sacred Heart, Kenwood, Albany, N.Y., Ohio, Mich., 1955-66; tchr. French White Plains (N.Y.) Pub. High Sch., 1966-86; curricula creator Akron (Ohio) Pub. Schs., 1962-63; co-dir. Baumel Assocs., Yonkers, N.Y., 1984—, Concerts and Lectures with Herbert Baumel, 1991—, Words and Music Programs with Herbert Baumel, 1991—, Yonkers Pub. Libr., 1992, Waverly Heights, Gladwyne, Pa., 1993-95, Workmen's Circle Lodge, Sylvan Lake, N.Y., 1994, Thomas Paine/Huguenot Hist. Soc., New Rochelle, N.Y., 1995—; lectr. French lang. and culture Yonkers (N.Y.) Pub. Libr., 1992, Greenburgh (N.Y.) Pub. Libr., 1992, anti-semitism CUNY Grad. Ctr., B'nai B'rith Internat. Mus., Washington, 1st Unitarian Soc., Westchester, N.Y., Rockland (NY.) Ctr. for Holocaust Studies, Unitarian Ch. of All Souls, N.Y.C., Temple Beth Israel, Port Washington, N.Y., Holocaust Resource Ctr. and Archives, Queensborough C.C., CUNY, 1991, Women's Am. ORT, Midchester Jewish Ctr., Yonkers, 1992, Ctrl. Queens YM & YWCA, N.Y.C., 1992. Author: Paul Claudel and the Jews: A Study in Ambivalence, 1985; lectr. topics include French Anti-Semitism; The Gallic Road to the Concentration Camp; Klaus Barbie and the Children of Izieu, numerous others. Mem. adv. bd. Mark Brent Dolinsky Meml. Found. Recipient Woodrow Wilson fellowship, 1958-59, Yearbook Dedication award White Plains (N.Y.) Pub. H.S., 1980. Mem. Am. Assn. Tchrs. French, Nat. Writers Union, White Plains Tchrs. Assn., N.Y. State Assn. Fgn. Lang. Tchrs., French Inst./Alliance Francaise, Alliance Francaise Westchester, Phi Beta Kappa. Avocations: tennis, gardening, music, reading. Home and Office: Baumel Assocs 86 Rosedale Rd Yonkers NY 10710-3033

BAUMER, BEVERLY BELLE, journalist; b. Hays, Kans., Sept. 23, 1926; d. Charles Arthur and Mayme Mae (Lord) B.; BS, William Allen White Sch. Journalism, U. Kans., 1948. Summer intern reporter Hutchinson (Kans.) News, 1946-47; continuity writer, women's program dir. Sta. KWBW, Hutchinson, 1948-49; dist. editor Salina (Kans.) Jours., 1950-57; commd. writer State of Kans. Centennial Year, 1961; contbg. author: Ford Times, Kansas City Star, Wichita (Kans.) Eagle, Ojibway Publs., Billboard, Modern Jeweler, Floor Covering Weekly, other bus. mags., 1962-69; owner and mgr. apts., Hutchinson, 1970—; broadcaster Reading Radio Room, Sta. KHCC-FM, Hutchinson, 1982—, columnist The Hutchinson (Kans.) Record, 1983-86; info. officer, maj. Kans. Wing Hdqrs. CAP, 1969-72; participant People to People Citizen Ambassador program, People's Republic of China, summer 1988. Mem. Republican Presdl. Task Force. Recipient Human Interest Photo award Nat. Press Women, 1956, News Photo award AP, 1952. Mem. Fellows Menninger Found., Suffolk County Hist. Soc., Nat. Fedn. Press Women, Kans. Press Women (Comm. Contest award 1986), Am. Soc. Profl. and Exec. Women, Am. Film Inst., Nat. Soc. Magna Charta Dames, Nat. Soc. Daus. Founders and Patriots Am., Nat. Soc. Daus. Am. Colonists, Kans. Soc. Daus. Am. Colonists (organizing regent Dr. Thomas Lord chpt., state chmn. insignia com.), Nat. Soc. Sons and Daus. Pilgrims (elder Kans. br.), D.A.R., Ben Franklin Soc. (nat. adv. bd.), Daus. Colonial Wars, Order Descs. Colonial Physicians and Chirurgiens, Colonial Dames 17th Century (chaplain, charter mem. Henry Woodhouse chpt.), Plantagenet Soc., Internat. Platform Soc., U. Kans. Alumni Assn., Nat. Geneal. Soc. Author book of poems, 1941; editor: A Simple Bedside Book for People Who Are Kinda, Sorta Interested in Genealogy, 1983. Home and Office: 122 Downing Rd Hutchinson KS 67502-4453 *Kindness belongs in business, the professions and the trades. It is the most sincere form of good will and leaves no one uncomfortable.*

BAUMER, MARTHA ANN, minister; b. Cleve., Sept. 12, 1938; d. Harry William and Olga Erna (Zenk) B. BA, Lakeland Coll., 1960; MA, U. Wyo., 1963; MDiv, United Theol. Sem., 1973; D Ministry, Eden Theol. Sem., 1990. Parish minister Congl. United Ch. of Christ, Amery, Wis., 1973-79; organizing minister United Ch. of Santa Fe (N.Mex.), 1979-85; conf. minister Ill. South Conf. United Ch. of Christ, Highland, Ill., 1985-93; pastor Windsor (Wis.) United Ch. of Christ, 1993—; trustee pension bds. United Ch. of Christ, N.Y.C., 1983—, mem., chair exec. coun., 1977-83; del. World Coun. Chs., 1961, 83; trustee Eden Theol. Sem., St. Louis, 1990—. Contbr. articles to profl. publs. Mem. Coun. of Conf. Ministers United Ch. of Christ (sec.-treas. 1989-93). Office: Windsor United Ch of Christ PO Box 187 Windsor WI 53598-0187

BAUMGARDNER, BARBARA BORKE, publishing consultant; b. Harrisburg, Pa., Nov. 8, 1937; d. Otto Lockhart Borke and Margaretta Mildred (Feigley) Borke Traugh; m. E. Wayne Baumgardner, July 12, 1958; children: Brian Wayne, Bruce Edward. AB, Gettysburg (Pa.) Coll., 1959; MLA, Western Md. Coll., 1976, MEd, 1982. Cert. secondary tchr., Md. Sales promoter Scott, Foresman & Co., Chgo., 1959-60; tchr. Carroll County Pub. Schs., Westminster, Md., 1964-84; cons. McDougall, Littell & Co., Evanston, Ill., 1984-91; adj. prof. Western Md. Coll., Westminster, 1975. Mem. Savannah Symphony Women's Guild. Mem. Women's Assn. Hilton Head, Mensa, Fed. Garden Clubs of Md., Phi Mu. Republican. Presbyterian. Avocations: skiing, floral design, poetry, bridge, golf. Home: 64 Planters Row Hilton Head Island SC 29928-5504 also: PO Box 1642 6635 Silver Lake Dr Park City UT 84060

BAUMGARDNER, JAMES LEWIS, history educator; b. Bristol, Va., Jan. 26, 1938; s. John Richard and Roxie Katherine (Lewis) B.; children: Ellen Lorena, James Michael; m. Paula Louise Jones; stepchildren: Joseph Branscome, Sarah Elizabeth Brock. AA, Bluefield Jr. Coll., 1957; BA, Carson-Newman Coll., 1959; MA, U. Tenn.-Knoxville, 1964, PhD, 1968. Ordained to ministry Baptist Ch., 1955. Asst. prof. history Carson-Newman Coll., Jefferson City, Tenn., 1964-67, assoc. prof., 1967-73, prof., 1973—, chmn. history-polit. sci. dept., 1974-95. Contbr. articles to learned jours. Interim mem. Jefferson County (Tenn.) Bd. Sch. Commrs., 1978; mem. Anderson County (Tenn.) Bd. Edn., 1990-94; active interim, bivocation pastor. Served with U.S. Army, 1959-62. Named Bivocational Pastor of the Yr., Tenn. Bapt. Conv., 1997. Mem. Am. Hist. Assn., Acad. Polit. Sci., Orgn. Am. Historians, So. Hist. Assn., So. Bapt. Hist. Soc., Phi Alpha Theta. Office: Carson-Newman Coll PO Box 71929 Jefferson City TN 37760-7001

BAUMGARDNER, JOHN ELLWOOD, JR., lawyer; b. Balt., Jan. 6, 1951; s. John Ellwood and Nancy G. (Brandenburg) B.; m. Astrid Rehl, Sept. 7, 1974; children: Jeffrey Mark, Julia Alexis. Bar: N.Y. 1976. Assoc. Sullivan & Cromwell, N.Y.C., 1975-83, ptnr., 1983—; supervisory dir. The Turkish Pvt. Equity Investment Co., 1991-93; trustee JPM Advisor Funds, 1996. Mem. ABA, N.Y. State Bar Assn., Assn. of Bar of City of N.Y., Nat. Dance Inst. (bd. dirs. 1988-89), Princeton Club. Office: Sullivan & Cromwell 125 Broad St Fl 28 New York NY 10004-2489

BAUMGARDNER, MATTHEW CLAY, artist; b. Columbus, Ohio, Feb. 5, 1955; s. Alan Wirth and Mary Lou (Weidner) B.; m. Heather Evans; children: Zoe Klee, Eva Evans, Lila Joy. MFA, U. N.C., 1982. One-man shows include Presbyn. Coll., Clinton, S.C., 1980, Sumter (S.C.) Gallery, 1981, Wilkov/Goldfeder, N.Y.C., 1987, Wessel O'Connor Ltd., N.Y.C., 1988, 89, Howard Yezerski Gallery, Boston, 1992, Charles Cowles Gallery, N.Y.C., 1993, Gallery A, Chgo., 1995, Bentley Gallery, Scottsdale, Ariz., 1998, MD Modern, Houston, 1998; group exhbns. include Spartenburg (S.C.) Arts Ctr., 1979, Columbia (S.C.) Mus., 1979, Clemson (S.C.) U., 1980, Greenville (S.C.) County Mus., 1980, Greater Birmingham (Ala.) Arts Alliance, 1981, Gibbes Mus., Charleston, S.C., 1981, Mint Mus., Charlotte, N.C., 1981, Ackland Mus., Chapel Hill, N.C., 1982, Huntington (W.Va.) Mus., 1982, Edward Thorp Gallery, N.Y.C., 1985 Hudson Ctr. Gallery, N.Y.C., 1985, Edward Thorp Gallery, N.Y.C., 1985, Mokotoff Gallery, N.Y.C., 1985, 86, Wilkov/Goldfeder, N.Y.C., 1987, Trenton (N.J.) City Mus., 1988, Wessel O'Connor Ltd., N.Y.C., 1989, Stephanie Theodore Gallery, N.Y.C., 1991, Art Dealers Assn. Am., N.Y.C., 1993, New Mus. Contemporary Art, N.Y.C., 1993, Trans Hudson Gallery, Jersey City, 1993, N.Y.C., 1997, Gallery A, Chgo., 1994, 95, 98, Gallerie Marie-Louise Wirth, Zurich, Switzerland, 1995, Bentley Gallery, Scottsdale, Ariz., 1997, MD Modern, Houston, 1998. Recipient Purchase awards Mint Mus., Charlotte, N.C., 1981, Gibbes Mus., Charleston, S.C., 1981; Visual Artist fellow Nat. Endowment for the Arts, Washington, 1993. Episcopalian. Office: Baumgardner Studio 12 E 2nd St New York NY 10003-8906

BAUMGARDNER, RENEE ELAINE, urban planner; b. Johnstown, Pa., Aug. 21, 1971; d. Raymond Edward and Joyce Jean (Bowser) B. BA in geography, U. Pitts., Johnstown, 1993; MA in geography, Ohio U., 1995. Intern Somerset County (Pa.) Planning Commn., summers 1992-94; grad. asst. dept. geography Ohio U., Athens, 1993-95; planner Harford County Dept. Planning and Zoning, Bel Air, Md., 1996—. Social Sci. Divsn. scholar U. Pitts., 1993. Mem. Am. Planning Assn., Gamma theta Upsilon, Chi Lambda Tau. Methodist. Office: Harford County Dept Planning/Zoning 220 S Main St Bel Air MD 21014-3820

BAUMGARDT, BILLY RAY, university official, agriculturist; b. Lafayette, Ind., Jan. 17, 1933; s. Raymond P. and Mildred L. (Cordray) B.; m. D. Elaine Blain, June 8, 1952; children: Pamela K. Baumgardt Farley, Teresa Jo Baumgardt Adolfsen, Donald Ray. B.S. in Agr., Purdue U., 1955, M.S., 1956; Ph.D., Rutgers U., 1959. From asst. to assoc. prof. U. Wis., Madison, 1959-67; prof. animal nutrition Pa. State U., University Park, 1967-70, head dept. dairy and animal sci., 1970-79, assoc. dir. agrl. expt. sta., 1979-80; dir. agrl. research, assoc. dean Purdue U., West Lafayette, Ind., 1980-98; exec. v.p. Am. Registry Profl. Animal Scientists, Savoy, Ill., 1998—. Contbr. chpts. to books, articles to sci. jours. Recipient Wilkinson award Pa. State U., 1979. Fellow AAAS, Am. Dairy Sci. Assn. (Nutrition Rsch. award 1966, pres. 1984-85, award of Honor 1993); mem. Am. Inst. Nutrition, Am. Soc. Animal Sci., Nat. Agrl. Biotech. Coun. (chair 1993-94), Rotary, Sigma Xi. Home and Office: 2614 Trace 26 West Lafayette IN 47906-1888

BAUMGARDT, JUSTI MICHELLE, soccer player; b. Federal Way, Wash., July 22, 1975. Student in sociology, U. Portland. mem. U.S. Women's Nat. Soccer Team, 1993—, playing in Nike Victory Tour, St. Charles (Ill.), 1997, Nordic Cup, Denmark, 1993, Germany, 1994. Named Athlete of Yr. Seattle Times 1993, also Player of Yr. state of Wash.; 2-time

H.S. All-Am.; named Most Valuable Player, U. Portland, 1994; voted WCC Player of Yr., 1996. Office: US Soccer Fedn 1801-1811 S Prairie Ave Chicago IL 60616*

BAUMGARTEN, DIANA VIRGINIA, gerontological nurse; b. Bklyn., May 24, 1943; d. Francis and Leah (Cuoghi) DeMarco; married; children: Elizabeth Salonia, Matthew, Edward. AS, Broward C.C., 1991. RN, Fla. Pediats. staff nurse North Broward Med. Ctr., Pompano Beach, Fla., 1991; staff nurse Tamarac (Fla.) Convalescent Ctr., 1992; nursing supr. Tamarac (Fla.) Convalescent Ctr., Ft. Lauderdale, Fla., 1992-93; corp. nurse cons. HBA Health Mgmt. Corp., Ft. Lauderdale, Fla., 1993-94; acting DON Broward Convalescent Home, Ft. Lauderdale, 1994; acting asst. DON Springtree Walk Nursing Ctr., Sunrise, Fla., 1994; resident assessment coord., infection control officer Broward Convalescent Home, Ft. Lauderdale, 1994-95; asst. dir. nursing Adon Hillhaven Convalescent Ctr., Fla., 1995-97; dir. nursing Menorah House, 1997-98; legal nurse cons., case mgr. J.R. Health Mgmt., 1998—. Mem. ANA, Fla. Nurses' Assn., Phi Theta Kappa. Avocation: flute, classical music. Home: 11417 Little Bear Dr Boca Raton FL 33428-2609

BAUMGARTEN, PAUL ANTHONY, lawyer; b. N.Y.C., July 31, 1934; s. Louis S. and Margaret (Karol) B.; m. Susan T., Feb. 21, 1960; children—Stephen, Michael, Lisa, Deborah. BA, Swarthmore Coll., 1955; LLB, Harvard U., 1958. Bar: N.Y. Assoc. Otterbourg Steindler, Houston Rosen, N.Y.C., 1958-66; assoc. Halperin, Morris, Granett & Cowan, N.Y.C., 1960; with legal dept. Hill & Range Songs Inc., 1960-62, Warner Bros. Pictures Inc., 1962-64, Embassy Pictures Corp., 1964-70; ptnr. Krause, Hirsch & Gross, 1970-77, Rosenman & Colin, LLP, N.Y.C., 1977—; co-chmn. workshops on motion picture industry Practicing Law Inst.; trustee Copyright Soc. U.S., 1989-91. Co-author: Producing, Financing & Distributing Film (revised and expanded edition), 1992. Mem. Columbia Artists Mgmt. Inc. (dir.). Avocations: classical music; sailing; tennis. Home: 61 W Gate Blvd Plandome NY 11030-1452 Office: Rosenman & Colin LLP 575 Madison Ave Fl 26 New York NY 10022-2585

BAUMGARTEN, SIDNEY, lawyer, company executive; b. N.Y.C., July 30, 1933; s. Abraham and Doris (Kanarick) B.; children: Douglas, Frederick, Roger, Julia. AB, Brown U., 1954; JD, NYU, 1960. Bar: N.Y. 1961, U.S. Dist. Ct. (ea. and so. dists.) N.Y. 1961, U.S. Ct. Claims 1961, U.S. Ct. Appeals (2d cir.) 1961. Asst. mgmt., field underwriter Home Life Ins. Co., 1957-61; sole practice, 1961-67; asst. dist. atty. Queens County, N.Y., 1967-68; law sec. to presiding justice State of N.Y., Queens, 1968-73; asst. to Mayor City of N.Y., 1974-77; gen. counsel Phoenix House Found., 1978-80; sr. ptnr. Baumgarten, Swiedler & Waxman, N.Y.C., 1980-88; pvt. practice N.Y.C., 1989-94; pres., CEO Auragenics Inc., 1994—; lectr. various seminars, assns. and ednl. instns; adj. prof. law N.Y. Inst. Tech.; vis. prof. Found. U. Cardiology, Brazil, 1996. Co-chmn. area interviews alumni schs. program Brown U.; committeeman county Boy Scouts Am.; pres. N.Y.'s Finest Found., 1993; bd. dirs., chmn. N.Y. Therapeutic Communities, Inc.; trustee Lawrence Country Day Sch. (pres. 1985-87). Served with U.S. Army, 1954-56, with Res. 1956-73. Mem. Queens County Bar Assn., N.Y. Law Sch. Alumni Assn., East Side C. of C. (pres. 1983-86, chmn. 1987—), VFW, NRA (life), Am. Legion. Club: Brown U. (N.Y.C.). Office: 45 John St New York NY 10038-3706

BAUMGARTNER, ANTON EDWARD, automotive sales professional; b. N.Y.C., May 18, 1948; s. Hans and Carmen Maria (Figueroa) B.; m. Brenda Lee Lemmon, May 24, 1969 (div. 1990); 1 child, Anton Nicholaus; m. Virginia Thiele, 1992; 1 child, Bree Alexandra. BS, Woodbury U., 1970. Sales mgr. Maywood Bell Ford, Bell, Calif., 1966-69, O.R. Haan, Inc., Santa Ana, Calif., 1969-72; pres. Parkinson Volkswagen, Placentia, Calif., 1972-77; exec. v.p. United Moped, Fountain Valley, Calif., 1975-82; pres. Automobili Intermeccanica, Fountain Valley, 1975-82; gen. mgr. Bishop (Calif.) Volkswagen-Bishop Motors, 1982-85, Beach Imports-Irvine Imports, Newport Beach, Calif., 1985-88; chmn. bd. Stan and Ollie Ins. Co., Santa Ana, Calif., 1989—; exec. v.p. Asterism, Inc., 1992-96; chmn. Marich Acceptance Inland Empire, 1996—; mem. faculty, Automotive World Congress, Detroit, 1980. Contbr. articles to weekly serial publs. Mem. Coachbuilders Assn. N.Am. (sec. 1975-78). Office: Marich Acceptance 6 Satinbush Aliso Viejo CA 92656-1827

BAUMGARTNER, BRUCE, airport administrator. Mgr. aviation Denver Internat. Airport. Office: Denver Internat Airport Airport Office Bldg 8500 Pena Blvd Denver CO 80249-6340*

BAUMGARTNER, HOLLY LYNN, educator in English language and literature; b. Dec. 21, 1965. BA Eng. Lit, Classics magna cum laude, U. Toledo, 1992; MA, Bowling Green State U., 1995, postgrad. studies Rhetoric, Composition, 1996—. Pub. rels. dir. (children's) Thackeray's Books, Toledo, 1989-92; instr. U. Toledo Comty. and Tech. Coll., 1992-97; rsch. and refrence asst. Bowling Green State U., Bowling Green, Ohio, 1993-95; writing instr. Ohio State U., Toledo, 1996; instr. Owens C.C., Oregon, Ohio, 1995-97; h.s. tchr. Toledo Pub. Schs., 1997-98; instr. writing and humanities classes Mercy Coll of N.W. Ohio, Toledo, 1997—; participant in many coms. and sponsored many student activities at Bowling Green State, Toledo High Schs., Owens C.C. and U. Toledo; guest inst. divsn. continuing edn. Mercy Coll., Toledo, 1997; reader for children's radio. Presenter at many edn. and writing confs.; contbr. poetry to Jour. Lit. and Arts; essay to OADE newsletter; editor Contexts, Mercy Coll. lit. jour., 1999—. Camp counselor Ohio Forestry. Recipient Block scholarship U. Toledo, 1990-92; commendation from Lucas County commrs., 1998, Toledo mayor, 1998. Mem. MLA, Ohio Assn. Devel. Educators, Am. Fedn. Tchrs., Nat. Coun. Tchrs. English, Gold Key, Phi Kappa Phi. Home: 426 Eddington Ct Toledo OH 43615

BAUMGARTNER, JAMES EARL, mathematics educator; b. Wichita, Mar. 23, 1943; s. Earl Benjamin and Gertrude J. (Socolofsky) B.; m. Yolanda Yen-Hsu Loo, Jan. 29, 1966; children—Eric James, Jonathan David. AB, U. Calif., Berkeley, 1964, PhD, 1970; AM (hon.), Dartmouth Coll., 1981. J. W. Young rsch. instr. Dartmouth Coll., Hanover, N.H., 1969-71, asst. prof. math., 1971-76, assoc. prof., 1976-80, prof., 1980-83, J.G. Kemeny prof. math., 1983—; dept. chmn., 1995-98; vis. asst. prof. Calif. Inst. Tech. Pasadena 1971-72; cons. Coll. Bd., 1990—. Cons. editor Jour. Symbolic Logic, 1983-90; editor: Axiomatic Set Theory, 1984; contbr. articles to profl. jours., chpts. to books. Mem. Am. Math. Soc. (editor Transactions and Memoirs 1988-92, mng. editor 1992-94), Math. Assn. Am., Assn. Symbolic Logic (exec. coun. mem. 1993-95). Home: Lindy Ln Hanover NH 03755 Office: Dartmouth Coll Dept Math Hanover NH 03755

BAUMGARTNER, JOHN H., refining and petroleum products company executive; b. 1936; married. With Clark Oil & Refining Corp., Milw., 1956-82, retail sales rep., 1960-65, dist. mgr., 1965-72, regional mgr., 1972-74, v.p. retail mktg., asst. gen. sales mgr., 1974-75, sr. v.p. mktg., 1975-78, exec. v.p., 1978-82; pres. J.H. Baumgartner Enterprises, Brookfield, Wis., 1982—; v.p., owner Robert Kidd & Assocs. Inc., 1990—. Served with USMC, 1954-56.

BAUMGARTNER, ROBERT, consultant; b. Dallas, Aug. 20, 1934; s. Oren Floyd and Jessie Elizabeth (Seale) B.; m. Sabina Jumatayeva, Aug. 1, 1998; children: Janet, Cathy, Diane, Mitchell. BBA, So. Meth. U., 1956. V.p. Rep. Nat. Bank, Dallas, 1958-70, Bank of Southwest, Houston, 1970-71; v.p., treas. Marathon Mfg. Co., Inc., Houston, 1971-78; CEO Amistad Well Svc., Houston, 1978-79; treas. Anderson Clayton & Co., Inc., Houston, 1980-82; pres. Baumgartner Capital, Austin, Tex., 1982—. Mem. Assn. Corp. Growth, Fin. Execs. Inst., Beta Gamma Sigma. Republican. Methodist. Avocations: golf, travel. Home: 6474B Hart Ln Austin TX 78731-3140 Office: Tex Bus Svcs 2301 W Anderson Ln Ste 204 Austin TX 78757-1249

BAUMGARTNER, WILLIAM ANTHONY, cardiac surgeon; b. Covington, Ky., Apr. 18, 1947; s. Nicholas Raymond and Rosemary (Blank) B.; m. Betsy Reik; children: Bill Jr., Amy, Mark. BS, Xavier U., 1969; MD, U. Ky., 1973. Intern surgery Stanford (Calif.) U. Med. Ctr., 1973-74, asst. resident gen. surgery, 1974-75, asst. resident cardiothoracic surgery, 1975-76, asst. resident cardiovasc. surgery, 1976-77, chief resident cardiovasc. surgery, 1977-78, chief resident thoracic surgery, 1978, asst. resident gen. surgery, 1978-80, chief resident, 1980-81; cardiac surgeon-in-charge Johns Hopkins U. Sch. Medicine, Balt., 1993—. Editor: Heart and Heart Lung Transplantation, 1990. Grantee NIH, Bethesda, 1988, 92, 95. Mem. ACS, Am. Surg. Assn., Soc. Thoracic Surgeons, Internat. Soc. Heart and Lung Transplantation, Am. Soc. Transplant Surgeons, Am. Assn. Thoracic Surgery, Soc. Univ. Surgeons, Clin. Practice Assn. (pres., exec. vice dean clin. practice 1999—). Office: Johns Hopkins Hosp 600 N Wolfe St # 618 Baltimore MD 21287-0005*

BAUMHART, RAYMOND CHARLES, Roman Catholic church administrator; b. Chgo., Dec. 22, 1923; s. Emil and Florence (Weidner) B. BS, Northwestern U., 1945; PhL, Loyola U., 1952, STL, 1958; MBA, Harvard U., 1953; DBA, Harvard, 1963; LLD (hon.), Ill. Coll., 1977; DHL (hon.), Scholl Coll. Podiatric Medicine, 1983, Rush U., Chgo., 1987, Northwestern U., 1993, Xavier U., Cin., 1994; Ill. Benedictine Coll., 1994. Joined Jesuit Order, 1946; ordained priest Roman Cath. Ch., 1957. Asst. prof. mgmt. Loyola U., Chgo., 1962-64, dean Sch. Bus. Adminstrn., 1964-66, exec. v.p., acting v.p. Med. Ctr., 1968-70, pres., 1970-93; dir. evangelization and Christian life Cath. Archdiocese of Chgo., 1994—; Alfred Ring lectr. U. Fla., 1988; John and Mildred Wright lectr. Fairfield U., 1992; bd. dirs. Peer Food Products, Ceres Food Group, Inc. Author: An Honest Profit, 1968, (with Thomas Garrett) Cases in Business Ethics, 1968, (with Thomas McMahon) The Brewer-Wholesaler Relationship, 1969; corr. editor: America, 1965-70. Trustee St. Louis U., 1967-72, Boston Coll., 1968-71, Cristo Rey Prep. Sch.; bd. dirs. Coun. Better Bus. Burs., 1971-77, Cath. Health Alliance Met. Chgo., 1986-93; mem. U.S. Bishops and Pres.'s Com. on Higher Edn., 1980-84, Jobs for Met. Chgo., 1984-85, Chgo. Health Care Industry, 1990-94. Decorated cavalier Order of Merit, Italy, 1971, commendatore, 1994; recipient Rale medallion Boston Coll., 1976, Daniel Lord S.J. award Loyola Acad., Wilmette, Ill., 1992, Mary Potter Humanitarian award Little Company of Mary Hosp., Ill., 1993, Sword of Loyola Loyola U., Chgo., 1993, Theodore Hesburgh award Assn. Cath. Colls. and Univs., 1995; John W. Hill fellow Harvard U., 1961-62, Cambridge Ctr. for Social Studies Rsch. fellow, 1966-68. Mem. Comml. Club, Mid-Am. Club, Tavern Club. Home: 6525 N Sheridan Rd Chicago IL 60626-5344

BAUMHEFNER, CLARENCE HERMAN, banker; b. Lester Prairie, Minn., Apr. 1, 1912; s. Walter P. and Clare A. (Jacobs) B.; m. Virginia Haight, May 11, 1941; children—Robert, Bonnie. Grad., Am. Inst. Banking, 1940; student, Grad. Sch. Banking, Rutgers U., 1951. With Bank of Am., 1940—; With Bank of Am. (inspection dept.), 1940-43, insp., 1943-47, asst. chief insp., 1947-50, asst. to cashier, 1950-56, cashier and v.p., 1956-65, sr. v.p., cashier, 1965-66, exec. v.p., 1966-70, vice chmn. bd., 1970—. Clubs: Merchants Exchange (San Francisco), Bankers (San Francisco), Bohemian (San Francisco), Pacific Union (San Francisco). Home and Office: 555 California St Ste 1100 San Francisco CA 94104-1514

BAUMKEL, MARK S., lawyer; b. Flint, Mich., Feb. 17, 1951; s. Sherwood and Marilyn (Schiff) B.; m. Julie A. Kimbrell, Oct. 20, 1978; 1 child, Molly. BA cum laude, Oakland U., Rochester,Mich., 1973; JD cum laude, Wayne State U., 1977. Bar: Mich. 1977, U.S. Dist. Ct. Mich. 1977, U.S. Ct. Appeals (6th cir.) 1985. Assoc. dist. counsel U.S. SBA, Detroit, 1977-78; asst. pros. atty. Ingham County Prosecutor's Office, Lansing, Mich., 1978-79; assoc. atty. Shifman & Goodman, P.C., Southfield, Mich., 1979-81, Kaufman & Friedman, Southfield, 1981-84; sole practitioner Troy, Mich., 1984-94; ptnr. Provizer & Phillips, P.C., Southfield, 1994—. Mem. Assn. Trial Lawyers Am. (sustaining), Mich. Trial Lawyers Assn. (PAC contbr.), Oakland County Bar Assn., Wayne County Mediation Tribunal (mediator), Am. Arbitration Assn. (arbitrator), Oakland County Mediation (mediator). Avocations: long-distance running and biking, guitar. Home: 3826 Lakecrest Dr Bloomfield Hills MI 48304-3040 Office: 6785 Telegraph Rd # 400 Bloomfield Hills MI 48301-3135

BAUML, FRANZ HEINRICH, German language educator; b. Vienna, Austria, June 12, 1926; came to U.S., 1942, naturalized, 1945; s. Gustav Heinrich and Josefa B.; m. Betty Zeidner, Aug. 28, 1958; children—Carolyn, Mark, Deborah. B.S., Armstrong Coll., 1950; B.A., U. Calif., Berkeley, 1953, M.A., 1955, Ph.D., 1957. Prof. German U. Calif., Los Angeles, 1957—. Author: Rhetorical Devices and Structure in the Ackerman aus Bohmen, 1960, Kudrun: Die Handschrift, 1969, Medieval Civilization in Germany, 800-1273, 1969, A Dictionary of Gestures, 1975, A Concordance to the Nibelungenlied, 1976, Mittelalter, 1987, A Worldwide Dictionary of Gestures, 1997. Served with AUS, 1944-46; Served with U.S. Army, 1950-51. Fellow Netherlands Inst. for Advanced Study, 1991-92. Mem. Medieval Acad. Am. Office: U Calif Germanic Langs Los Angeles CA 90024

BAUMRIN, BERNARD STEFAN HERBERT, lawyer, educator; b. N.Y.C., Jan. 7, 1934; s. David and Regina (Zuckerburg) B.; m. Judith Anne Martin, Dec. 20, 1953; children: Seth, Jeanne, Rachel. Student, Marietta Coll., 1951-52, NYU, 1952-53; B.A., Ohio State U., 1956; Ph.D., Johns Hopkins U., 1960; postgrad., Washington U., St. Louis, 1965-67; J.D., Columbia U., 1970. Dir. forensics Johns Hopkins U., Balt., 1957-59; vis. asst. prof. philosophy Butler U., 1960-61, Antioch Coll., 1961; asst. prof. philosophy U. Del., Newark, 1961-64, Washington U., 1964-67; assoc. prof. philosophy Hunter Coll., CUNY, 1967-68, assoc. prof. philosophy Grad. Sch. and Lehman Coll., 1968-72, prof., 1972—, treas. univ. faculty senate, 1978-81, 90, exec. com., 1976-84, 87-91, 92-93, 98—, bd. dirs. Research Found., 1984-91; ptnr. Baumrin, Galub & Volkomer, 1979—; adj. prof. med. edn. Mt. Sinai Sch. of Medicine, 1988—; bd. dirs. CUNY Acad. for the Humanities and Scis. Author: Philosophy of Science, 2 vols., 1963, British Moralists, 1964, Hobbes's Leviathan, 1968, Moral Responsibility and the Professions, 1983; U.S. editor Jour. Applied Philosophy, 1986—; mem. adv. bd. Jour. Philosophy Psychiatry and Psychology, 1995—; cons. editor Metaphilosophy, 1968—; contbr. articles to profl. jours. AEC fellow, 1963, U. Del. fellow, 1962, Washington U. Forsyth fellow, 1964-67; CUNY grantee, 1968, 70, 89, 91, 93, N.Y. Council for Humanities grantee, 1976, NEH grantee, 1977-79, 91, Mellon Found. grantee, 1980-84, Am. Council Learned Socs. grantee, 1987. Mem. AAAS, AAUP, ACLU, N.Y. State Bar Assn. (chmn. ethics subcom., com. on legal edn. and admission to bar 1986—), Mind Assn., Am. Philos. Assn. (chmn. standing com. on philosophy and medicine 1988-92, chmn. standing com. on philosophy and law 1998—), Soc. for Philosophy and Pub. Affairs, Internat. Assn. Philosophy of Law and Social Philosophy, Conf. on Methods in Philosophy and the Scis. (chmn. 1988-90), Internat. Hobbes Assn. (exec. com. 1986—), Internat. Soc. Econs. and Philosophy (treas. 1994—). Office: CUNY Grad Sch 33 W 42nd St New York NY 10036-8099 also: Lehman Coll Philosophy Dept Bronx NY 10468

BAUNER, RUTH ELIZABETH, library administrator, reference librarian; b. Quincy, Ill.; d. John Carl and M. Irene (Nutt) B. BS in Edn., Western Ill. U., 1950; MS, U. Ill., 1956; postgrad., So. Ill. U., 1974, PhD, 1978. Asst. res. libr. Western Ill. U., Macomb, 1950; tchr., libr. Sandwich (Ill.) Twp. High Sch., 1950-54; circulation dept. asst. U. Ill. Libr., Urbana, 1955; asst. edn. libr. So. Ill. U., Carbondale, 1956-63, acting edn. libr., 1963-64, edn. and psychology libr., 1965-93, assoc. prof. curriculum and instrn. dept., 1971-93; coord. freshman yr. experience program, vis. assoc. prof. Coll. of Liberal Arts, Carbondale, 1994-96; dir. Grad. Residence Ctr. Librs., So. Ill. U., 1973-79; cons. in field; subject matter expert Learning Resources Svc. Interactive Video, Carbondale, 1990-91, also scriptwriter. Co-author: The Teacher's Library, 1966; contbr. articles to profl. jours. Pres. alumni constituency bd. Coll. Edn., Carbondale, 1988-89; bd. dirs. So. Ill. U. chpt. UN, 1985-86, 94-97; mem. Carbondale Bd. Ethics, 1989—; mem. bd. Jackson County AARP, 1997—; bd. dirs. So. Ill. Learning in Retirement, So. Ill. U. Emeritus Assn. Recipient Luck Has Nothing To Do With It award Oryx Press, 1993. Mem. ALA, AAUP (v.p. So. Ill. U. chpt. 1972-73), AAUW (univ. rep. Carbondale br. 1988-89), Assn. Coll. and Rsch. Librs. (chmn. edn. and behavioral scis. sect. 1976-77, Most Active Mem. award 1968-93), Ill. Libr. Assn., Phi Delta Kappa, Phi Kappa Phi, Delta Kappa Gamma. Office: 1206 W Freeman St Carbondale IL 62901-2351

BAURES, MARY MARGARET, psychotherapist, author; b. St. Petersburg, Fla., Sept. 13, 1947; d. Robert A. and Ruth S. Baures; divorced. BS, U. Fla., 1969; MA, Boston U., 1976, EdM, 1984; Cert. Advanced Grad. Study in Human Devel., Harvard U., 1986; D in Clin. Psychology, Antioch New Eng., 1994. Instr. Emerson Coll., Boston, 1981-86; counselor Beverly (Mass.) Hosp., 1984-86; emergency svc. clinician Ctr. for Mental Health, Waltham, Mass., 1987-91; psychotherapist Seacoast Counseling, Danvers, Mass., 1989—, Human Resource Inst., Brookline, Mass., 1993—; mem. neuropsychology intern Northshore Children's Hosp., Salem, Mass., 1990-91; founder, dir. Boycott Anorexic Mktg., 1993—. Author: Undaunted Spirits-Portraits of Recovery from Trauma, 1994; co-prodr. Strong at the Broken Places-Turning Trauma into Recovery, 1998, Letting Go of Bitterness and Hate Jour. of Humanistic Psychology, 1996. Office: Seacoast Counseling 85 Constitution Ln Danvers MA 01923-3658

BAUSCH, JAMES JOHN, foundation executive; b. New Brunswick, N.J., May 1, 1936; s. Charles John and Colette (Perdoni) B.; m. Janet Ellen Safer, May 22, 1970; children: Jennifer, David. Student, Fordham U., 1953-54; BS, St. Peter's Coll., 1955-58; postgrad., Emory U., 1958-61, Wharton Sch., U. Pa., 1977. Lectr. in social sci. Emory U., Ga. Inst. Tech., Atlanta, 1958-61; vol. U.S. Peace Corps, Bangladesh, 1961-63; chief U.S. Peace Corps South Asia div., Washington, 1965-69; dir. tng. Experiment in Internat. Living, Brattleboro, Vt., 1963-64; dir. edn. Coun. on Internat. Ednl. Exch., N.Y.C., 1964-65; program officer Ford Found., N.Y.C., 1969-71, 73-76; rep. Ford Found., Jakarta, Indonesia, 1971-73; v.p., sec. The Population Coun., N.Y.C., 1976-88; pres. Save the Children Fedn., Westport, Conn., 1988-92; vice chmn. A.T. Hudson & Co., Oradell, N.J., 1992-94; pres. J.J. Bausch Cons. Svcs., River Vale, N.J., 1992-94, Nat. Charities Info. Bur., N.Y.C., 1994-99; cons. in philanthropy, 1999—; trustee, mem. exec. com., chmn. fin. com., chmn. investment com., co-chmn. N.Y. Assocs. World Learning, Inc., Brattleboro, Vt., 1980-88; trustee, sec.-treas. Internat. Child Health Found., Columbia, Md., 1985-87, chmn. bd. trustees, 1987-94; mem. fin. com. Population Coun. 1976-88; trustee Ctr. Pvt. Vol. Orgns./Univ. Collaboration, N.C., 1990-92, Ind. Sector, Washington, 1991-93. Mem. Bretton Woods Com., Washington, 1991—; chmn. UNICEF Action for Children, N.Y.C., 1986-89. Mem. N.Y. Acad. Scis., Population Assn. Am., Am. Pub. Health Assn., Nat. Coun. Internat. Health (mem. exec. com. 1991-92), Carnegie Coun. on Ethics and Internat. Affairs, Nat. Peace Corps Assn. Democrat. Home: 4865 Featherbed Ln Sarasota FL 34242-1558

BAUSCH, RICHARD CARL, writer, educator; b. Ft. Benning, Ga., Apr. 18, 1945; s. Robert Carl and Helen (Simmons) B.; m. Karen Miller, May 3, 1969; children: Wesley, Emily, Paul, Maggie, Amanda. BA, George Mason U., 1973; MFA, U. Iowa, 1975. Instr. No. Va. C.C., Annandale, Va., 1975-80; prof., Heritage chair of creative writing George Mason U., Fairfax, Va., 1980—; vis. prof. U. Va., Charlottesville, 1985, 88, Wesleyan U., Middletown, Conn., 1986, 90, 92, 93; lectr., reader in field. Author: (stories) Spirits and Other Stories, 1987 (PEN/Faulkner award nomination 1988), The Fireman's Wife & Other Stories, 1990, Rare & Endangered Species, 1994, Modern Library Selected Stories, 1996, Someone to Watch Over Me, 1999; (novels) Real Presence, 1980, Take Me Back, 1981 (PEN/Faulkner award nomination 1982), The Last Good Time, 1984, Mr. Field's Daughter, 1989, Violence, 1992, Rebel Powers, 1993, Good Evening Mr. & Mrs. America and All the Ships At Sea, 1996, In the Night Season, 1998. Recipient Lila Wallace Reader's Best Writer's award Lila Wallace Fund, 1992, Acad. award in Lit. AAAL, 1993; grantee Nat. Endowment for the Arts, 1982; Guggenheim fellow John Simon Guggenheim Found., 1984. Fellow So. Writers; mem. PEN Am. Democrat. Roman Catholic. Avocations: songwriting, singing. Office: George Mason U English Dept 4400 University Dr Fairfax VA 22030-4444

BAUSE, GEORGE STEPHEN, anesthesiologist; b. Chester, Pa., Nov. 22, 1955. BS in Biophysics, Ursinus Coll., 1977; MPH in Epidemiology, MD, Johns Hopkins U., 1981. Diplomate Am. Bd. Anesthesiology with subspecialty in pain mgmt. Intern Johns Hopkins Hosp., Balt., 1981-82, resident in anesthesiology, 1982-84; fellow geriatric anesthesiology Johns Hopkins Hosp.-Nat. Inst. Aging, Balt., 1984-85; attending physician Yale-New Haven Hosp., 1985-92, dir. geriatric anesthesia, 1987-92; chief dept. anesthesia West Haven (Conn.) VA Med. Ctr., 1990-92; Whitacre dir. anesthesia edn. Meridia Health System, Ohio, 1992-96; asst. prof. Yale U., New Haven, 1985-91, assoc. prof., 1991-92; assoc. clin. prof. anesthesiology Case Western Res. U., Cleve., 1994—; hon. curator USA's Wood Libr.-Mus. of Anesthesiology, 1987—. Fellow Acad. Anesthesiology, Internat. Coll. Surgeons; mem. AMA, Am. Geriatric Soc., Am. Soc. Anesthesiologists, Am. Soc. Regional Anesthesia, Internat. Anesthesia Rsch. Soc., Soc. Cardiovascular Anesthesiologists. Office: PMB # 282 5247 Wilson Mills Cleveland OH 44143-3016

BAUSELL, R. BARKER, JR., research methodology educator; s. Rufus B. and Nellie (Bowman) B.; m. Carole R. Vinograd, Jan. 6, 1978; children: Jesse T., Rebecca B. BS in Edn., U. Del., 1968, PhD in Ednl. Rsch. and Evaluation, 1975. Rsch. methodologist Med. Coll. Pa., 1975-76; prof., coord. faculty rsch. U. Md., Balt., 1976-91, dir. office rsch. methodology, 1991-94, prof. rsch., 1994-98, dir. rsch. complementary medicine program, 1998—; sr. scientist Demarna Found. for Med. Care, 1994-98; cons., part-time dir. prevention rsch. ctr. Rodale Press, Inc.; presenter numberous seminars and confs. Author: (with C.R. Bausell and N.B. Bausell) The Bausell Home Learning Guide: Teach Your Child to Read, 1980, (with C.R. Bausell and N.B. Bausell) The Bausell Home Learning Guide: Teach Your Child to Write, 1980, (with C.F. Waltz) Nursing Research: Design, Statistics and Computer Analysis, 1981, (with C.R. Bausell and N.B. Bausell) The Bausell Home Learning Guide: Teach Your Child Math, A Practical Guide to Conducting Empirical Research, 1986, An Instructor's Manual for a Practical Guide to Conducting Empirical Research, 1986, (with C. Inlander and M. Rooney) How to Evaluate and Select a Nursing Home, 1988, Advanced Research Methodology: An Annotated Guide to Sources, 1991, Conducting Meaningful Experiments, 1994; editor: Evaluation and the Health Professions; author numerous monographs; contbr. numerous articles to profl. jours. Recipient Outstanding Rsch. award Nat. Wellness Conf., 1986, 87, Gov.'s award Meritorious Svc., 1992, award for Disting. Assessment Project Md. Assessment Resource Ctr., 1993. Achievements include research on documented effects of class size on student learning, effects of teacher experience on student learning, and determinants of health seeking (preventative) behavior. Home: 1311 Doves Cove Rd Baltimore MD 21286-1426 Office: U Md Complementary Med Program 2200 Kernan Dr Baltimore MD 21207-6697

BAUSHER, VERNE C(HARLES), banker; b. Reading, Pa.; s. La Verne H. and Helen M. (Dornes) B.; m. Sandra Stamm Bausher, May 22, 1965; children: Christopher S., Gretchen S., Samantha A., Andrew P. BS, Drexel U., 1961; MBA, Northwestern U., 1962. Asst. v.p. Cen. Nat. Bank of Cleve., 1962-69; v.p. Meridian Bank (formerly American Bank and Trust Co. of Pa.), Reading, 1969-83; exec. v.p. Penn Savs. Bank, Wyomissing, 1983-87; exec. v.p., chief lending officer Germantown Savs. Bank, Bala Cynwyd, Pa., 1987—. Trustee, v.p. Pub. Edn. Found. for Berks County, 1986—; bd. dirs. Wilson Sch. Dist., West Lawn, Pa., 1977—, pres., 1989-90; bd. dirs. Berks County Intermediate Unit, Reading, 1977—, YMCA of Reading, 1987-89. Republican. Lutheran. Avocations: reading, swimming, diving. Home: 4152 Hill Terrace Dr Sinking Spring PA 19608 Office: Germantown Savs Bank One Belmont Ave Bala Cynwyd PA 19004

BAUTISTA, ABRAHAM PARANA, immunologist; b. Davao, Philippines, Mar. 15, 1952; s. Eufronio Bernardo and Loreto (Parana) B. BS in Biology, Far Eastern U., Manila, Philippines, 1972; Diploma in Microbiology, U. Tokyo, 1978; MS, Aberdeen (Scotland) U., 1981, PhD in Immunology, 1984. Sr. rschr. lectr. U. Santo Tomas, Manila, 1976-81; rsch. scholar U. Aberdeen, 1979-84; rsch. assoc. East Carolina U., Greenville, N.C., 1984-89; asst. prof. La. State U. Med. Ctr., New Orleans, 1989-93, assoc. prof., 1993—; cons. Jefferson Trust/NationsBank, 1993—; reviewer, mem. NIH-Nat. Inst. Environ. Health Scis. Study Sect. for spl. program project, 1997—; mem. study sect. Alcohol and Toxicology #2, NIH, 1997—, adhoc mem. #1, 1997—; mem. study sect. molecular and cellular biology Am. Heart Assn., 1998—; mem. study sect. VA, reviewer, cons., 1998—. Guest editor, reviewer Jour. Leukocyte Biology, 1988—, Circulatory Shock, 1991—, Am. Jour. Physiology, 1991—, Alcohol, 1992—, Alcoholism Clin. and Exptl. Rsch., 1992—, Hepatology, 1993—, Gastroenterology, 1994—, Biochem. Pharmacol, 1995—, Internat. Jour. Cancer, 1995—, Alcohol Health & Rsch. World, 1997—; contbr. numerous articles to profl. jours. NIH-NIAAA grantee, 1995—; travel fellow Am. Assn. for Study Liver Disease, 1990; Internat. scholar Brit. Coun., 1979; recipient Rsch. award in Medicine, U. Aberdeen, 1981-84, F.I.R.S.T. award/Rsch. grantee NIH, 1991—; named Internat. UNESCO, 1978; named Philippine Med. Tech. Bd. Exam.

Topnotcher, 1972. Mem. AAAS, Internat. Cytokine Soc., Am. Assn. Immunology, N.Y. Acad. Scis., Inst. of Biology, Soc. for Leukocyte Biology, Rsch. Soc. of Alcoholism, Shock Soc., Sigma Xi. Achievements include first demonstration that endogenous or exogenous interleukin-1 regulates insulin biosynthesis in vivo and that hepatic immune response is suppressed in chronic alcoholics with hepatitis; first to demonstrate that chemokines (e.g. macrophage inflammatory protein-2) are involved in liver injury during alcohol intoxication. Home: 103 Hollow Rock Ct Slidell LA 70461-3422 Office: La State U Med Ctr 1901 Perdido St New Orleans LA 70112-1328

BAUTISTA, ANTHONY HERNANDEZ, biomedical company executive; b. Palo Alto, Calif., Sept. 19, 1955; s. Anthony Hernandez and Velma Rose (Morinan) B.; m. Jill Davis, June 17, 1978; children: Evan Thomas, Laura Anne. AA in Electronic Tech., Coll. of San Mateo, 1976; BSEE, San Jose (Calif.) State U., 1994. Elec. engr. Hewlett Packard, Palo Alto, Calif., 1976-86; mfg. engrng. mgr. Molecular Devices Corp., Menlo Park, Calif., 1986-91; ops. v.p. LJL Biosystems, Inc., Sunnyvale, Calif., 1991—. Mem. Toastmasters (adminstrv. v.p. 1990), Tau Beta Pi.

BAUTISTA, MICHAEL PHILLIP, school system administrator; b. Merced, Calif., June 15, 1952; s. Ynacio and Frances (Garcia) B.; m. Peggy Joyce Watkins, May 26, 1976; children: Michael P., Lisa M. B Music Edn., Emporia State U., 1974, MA, 1975; PhD, Tex. Tech U., 1981; adminstrv. cert., Okla. State U., 1986. Cert. adminstr., Colo., Supt., secondary prin., Okla., bldg. adminstr., Kans. Instr. U. Nebr., Lincoln, 1977-79; asst. prof. U. Tulsa, 1979-82; dir., adminstr. Jenks Pub. Schs., Tulsa, 1983-92; coord., adminstr. Denver Sch. of the Arts, Denver Pub. Schs., 1991-97, adminstrv. dir., 1997—; part-time instr. Tex. Tech U., Lubbock, 1975-77, Tulsa Jr. Coll., 1982-83; theatrical cons. MPB Assocs., Tulsa, 1983-91; v.p. internat. Network for Performing and Visual Arts Schs. Author: Ten Years of Stage Design at the Met (1966-1976); theatrical designer for various stage prodns. Bd. dirs. Carson-Brierly Dance Libr., Denver, 1992—, Friends of Chamber Music, Denver, 1992—; mem. steering com. Harwelden Inst., Tulsa, 1983-91; active Boy Scouts Am.; mem. Mayor's subcom. Arts Edn.; mem. exec. bd. Colo. Arts Assn. for Edn.; cantor Holy Family Cath. Ch. Recipient Svc. award St. Bernhards Parish, 1990, Amoco award for set design Am. Coll. Theatre Festival, 1989, Documentary citation Kansas City, Mo. Star, 1970. Mem. ASCD, U.S. Inst. Theatre Tech. Roman Catholic. Avocations: hiking, photography, music, design, painting, videography. Home: 4802 W 34th Ave Denver CO 80212-1819 Office: Denver Sch of Arts 150 S Pearl St Denver CO 80209-2016

BAUTZ, JEFFREY EMERSON, mechanical engineer, educator, researcher; b. Milw., Apr. 13, 1966; s. Thomas W. and Dona J. (Emerson) B.; m. Heather Sienkiewicz. BS in Math. and Engrng. Mechanics, U. Wis., 1988, MS in Engrng. Mechanics, 1989; postgrad., Stanford U., 1992—, Wayne State U., 1996—. Devel. engr. McDonnell Douglas Corp., St. Louis, 1989-90; rsch. engr. GE, Milw., 1990-91; engrng. project mgr., cons. on finite element method GM & Body Structure Design, Detroit, 1991—; project mgr. internat. experience GM-Opel Germany, 1997-99; instr. engrng. mechanics U. Wis., Madison, 1988-89; pres. PEB Profls.; instr. indsl. tech. and math. Macomb C.C., Warren, Mich., 1992—; part-time engrng. cons. Patentee in field. Mem. Rep. party, Macomb County, Mich. Mem. Am. Soc. Body Engrs., Engrng. Soc. Detroit. Avocations: basketball, volleyball, golf, racquetball. Home: 48550 Brittany Parc Dr Macomb Township MI 48044-2119 Office: GM Advanced Technology Vehicles PO Box 7083 1996 Technology Dr Troy MI 48083-4243

BAUTZ, LAURA PATRICIA, astronomer; b. Washington, Sept. 3, 1940; d. Charles Kothe and Laura Bautz. BA in Physics, Vanderbilt U., 1961; PhD in Astronomy, U. Wis., Madison, 197. From instr. to assoc. prof. astronomy Northwestern U., Evanston, Ill., 1965-75; program dir. astronomy sect. NSF, Washington, 1972-73, sr. staff assoc. NSF, 1975-79, dep. dir. physics divsn., 1979-81, dir. astronomy divsn., 1982-90; vis. researcher Lawrence Berkeley Lab., 1990-92, dep. dir. physics divsn. NSF, 1992-93, internat. programs divsn., 1994—. Fellow AAAS; mem. Internat. Astron. Union, Am. Phys. Soc., Phi Beta Kappa. Home: 1325 18th St NW Apt 506 Washington DC 20036-6510 Office: 4201 Wilson Blvd Arlington VA 22230-0001

BAUTZMANN, NANCY ANNETTE, artist; d. Edward Daniel and Marjorie Burton; m. Hermann August Bautzmann; children: Rachael Anne, Hermann August. BA in Fine Arts, Westminster Coll., 1974. tchr. Berkshire Mus., Pittsfield, 1985-94, My Studio, Pittsfield & Tucson, 1988—, Becket (Mass.) Arts Coun., 1989. Mem. Oil Painters Am. (signature), Ariz. Watercolor Assn., So. Ariz. Watercolor Assn. (signature), Acad. Artist Assn., Copley Soc. Boston (signature). Republican. Home: 7742 N Harelson Pl Tucson AZ 85704-4529

BAUZA, CHRISTINE DIANE, special education educator; b. Santa Monica, Calif., Sept. 16, 1961; d. William Gene and Dorothy Louise (Evans) Lough; m. Joseph Henry Bauza, July 26, 1986; 1 child, Crystal Marie. AA in Liberal Arts, Crafton Hills Coll., Yucaipa, Calif., 1981; BA in Liberal Studies, Calif. State U., Northridge, 1983, MA in Deaf Edn., 1986, multiple subjects-spl. edn. credentials, 1986. Tchr. comm. handicapped edn. San Bernardino County Supt. Schs., Rialto, Calif., 1986-98, Rialto Unified Sch. Dist., 1998—; tchr., cons. Cmty. Adv. Com., San Bernardino, Calif., 1990-91. Avocations: bowling, reading, crafts. Home: 1031 Cimarron Dr Redlands CA 92374-6335 Office: Bemis Elem Sch 774 E Etiwanda Ave Rialto CA 92376-4508

BAVASI, PETER JOSEPH, angling service executive; b. Bronxville, N.Y., Oct. 31, 1942; s. Emil Joseph and Evit E. (Rice) B.; m. Judith Marzonie, June 13, 1964; children: Patrick, Cristina. BA in Philosophy, St. Mary's Coll., Moraga, Calif., 1964. Minor league gen. mgr. Los Angeles Dodgers, 1964-68; dir. minor league ops. San Diego Padres, 1968-73, v.p., gen. mgr., 1973-76; pres., chief exec. officer Toronto Blue Jays, Ont., Can., 1976-81; pres. Peter Bavasi Sports, Inc., Tampa, Fla., 1981-84; pres., chief operating officer Cleve. Indians, 1984-87; pres., chief exec. officer Telerate Sports and SportsTicker, Jersey City, 1987-94; pres. ESPN/SportsTicker, Jersey City, 1995-96; owner, operator Masthope Guide Svc., Lackawaxen, Pa., 1996-97; pres. Masthope West Angling Svc., La Jolla, Calif., 1997—. Office: Masthope West Angling Svc 1001 Genter St Unit 3G La Jolla CA 92037-5531

BAVASI, WILLIAM JOSEPH, professional sports team executive; b. Bronxville, N.Y., Dec. 27, 1957; s. E.J. (Buzzie) B.; m. Tracy; children: Kyle, Katie. BA, U. San Diego, 1980. Minor league adminstr. Calif. Angels, 1980-84, dir. minor league ops., 1984-93; gen. mgr. Calif. Angels (renamed Anaheim Angels in 1997), 1993—. Office: Anaheim Angels Edison Internat Field 2000 E Gene Autry Way Anaheim CA 92806-6100*

BAVER, ROY LANE, retired protection services official, consultant; b. Dayton, Ohio, Sept. 20, 1942; s. Paul Vincent and Winifred (Korn) B.; m. Sandra Jean Stephen, Oct. 7, 1967; children: Dawn Maria, Denise Michele, Diana Melissa. AAS, Sinclair C.C., Dayton, 1979; BA in Urban Affairs, Wright State U., Dayton, 1985. Cert. state fire safety inspector, class IV automatic sprinkler inspector, fire inspector level I, sr. fire inspector, paramedic, CPR/first aid instr. Mechanic Casey's Union Oil, Centerville, Ohio, 1967-70; sales rep. Hauer Music, Dayton, Ohio, 1970-73; dep. fire marshal Washington Twp. Fire Dept., Centerville, 1973-96; ret., 1996; cons., RLB Consulting, Centerville, 1989—, R&S Enterprises, Centerville, 1997—; bd. dirs., treas. Americana Festival Inc. Bd. dirs. Far Hills Temple. Served in U.S. Army, 1964-66. Charter mem. Ohio Fire Off. Assn.; Mem. Bldg. Ofcls. and Code Adminstrs. Internat., S.W. Ohio Fire Safety Coun., Ohio Bldg. Ofcls. Assn. (Fire Ofcl. of Yr. 1993-94), Ohio Assn. Profl. Fire Fighters, Washington Twp. Fire Fighters Assn., Internat. Assn. Fire Fighters, Masons, Scottish Rite, Shriners, Order Ea. Star, Centerville HighTwelve Club, Internat. Shrine Clown Assn., Great Lakes Shrine Clown Unit Assn., Wright State Alumni Assn., City of Centerville Sister City Com. Assn., Phi Theta Kappa, Phi Alpha Alpha. Lutheran. Avocations: travel, collecting fire memorabilia, collecting stamps. Home: 145 Boyce Rd Centerville OH 45458-2475

BAWA, RUBINA, pharmacist; b. Chandigarh, India, July 21, 1971; d. Sukhdev Raj Bawa and Sudesh Bhalla. Degree, Albany Coll. Pharmacy, 1995. Pharmacist Eckerd Drugs, Guillerland, N.Y. Mem. PSCNY. Home: 1508 Vista Club Cir Apt 203 Santa Clara CA 95054-3707 Office: Eckerd Drugs 2080 Western Ave Guilderland NY 12084-9564

BAWA, SUKHDEV RAJ, biomedical researcher, educator, administrator; b. Lahore, Punjab, India, Dec. 25, 1929; came to U.S., 1958; s. Bhagat Ram and Lajwanti (Kaur) B.; m. Sudesh Bhalla, Nov. 29, 1954; children: Renu Kallianpur, Raj Bawa, Rubina Nitta. BSc with high honors, Panjab U., India, 1949, MSc with high honors, 1951, PhD, 1954. Lectr. dept. Zoology Panjab U., Chandigarh, India, 1954-58, founding chmn., prof. biophysics, 1964-93, dean, foreign students, 1985-87; lectr. dept. zoology Columbia U., N.Y.C., 1958-59, Boese postdoctoral rsch. fellow dept. zoology, 1959-60; population coun. rsch. fellow Rockefeller U., N.Y.C., 1960-61; biomedical rsch. fellow dept. anatomy Cornell U. Med. Coll., N.Y.C., 1960-61, instr. dept. anatomy, 1961-63; hon. rsch. fellow dept. zoology U. Wis., Madison, summer 1961; electronmicroscopist David Axelrod Inst. Wadsworth Ctr. for Labs. and Rsch., N.Y. State Dept. Health, Albany, N.Y., 1995—; prin. investigator Indian Coun. of Med. Rsch., 1967-69; vis. rsch. zoologist U. Calif., L.A., summer 1969; vis. rsch. scientist Inst. Zoology, U. Siena, Italy, 1972; vis. prof. Inst. Biophysics, U. Saarlandes, Homburg, Germany, 1976, 77, Downstate Med. Ctr., N.Y.C., 1979-80, U. Manitoba, Winnipeg, Can., summer 1986; vis. scientist Worcester Found. Exptl. Biology, Shrewsbury, Mass., 1980-81; hon. prof. U. Wis., Madison, summer 1981; mem. Standing Adv. Com. on Biophysics, Univ. Grants Commn., Govt. India, 1983-88, nat. lectr., 1985-86; guest prof. U. Saarlandes, Homburg, 1987; advisor electron microscope labs., Regional Sophisticated Instrumentation Ctr., Panjab U., India, 1983-88, coord. Biotechnology Ctr., 1986-88; adj. fac. Columbia Greene C.C., Hudson, N.Y., 1993; vis. instr. SUNY, Cobleskill, 1994. Mem. editorial bd. Jour. of Ultrastructure Rsch., 1969-85, Acta Anatomica, 1974-77; mem. sci. com. Jour. Submicroscopic Cytology, Bologna, Italy, 1970-77; mem. adv. editorial bd. Ultramicroscopy, 1986-95; mem. sci. editorial bd. Andrologia, 1993-95; contbr. numerous articles to profl. jours.; spkr. in field; contbr. workshops, symposia, internat. confs. Recipient U.S. Fulbright Travel award, 1958-63, U.S. Alumni Rsch. travel award, 1973-74, Project appreciation award USDA, Washington, 1975, Kazato Rsch. award XIth Internat. Congress for electron microscopy, Kyoto, Japan, 1986, Diatome award XII Internat. Congress of Electron Microscopy, Seattle, 1990; U.S. Alumni Rsch. travel grantee, 1968-69, 73-74; fellow Alexander von Humboldt Found., Bonn, Germany, 1972, 76, 77, 87, 92, 97. Mem. Electron Microscope Soc. of India (v.p. 1983-86, pres. 1986-93), Indian Biophysical Soc. (sec. 1986-88), No. India Sci. Assn. (founding sec. 1966-93). Achievements include research in ultrastructure of the Sertoli cell of the human testis, insect reproduction and sperm cells (Thermobia, Pyrilla, Dysdercus, honey bee, Pseudoscorpion, Callosobruchus), mammalian reproduction (hedgehog, rat, dog, human, goat, water buffalo etc.), effects of radiation on the rat testes. Avocations: reading, travel, photography, cooking, medical history. Office: David Axelrod Inst Wadsworth Ctr NY State Dept Health PO Box 22002 Albany NY 12201-2002

BAWDEN, JAMES WYATT, dental educator, dental scientist; b. St. Louis, Apr. 23, 1930; s. Leland Miller and Rose Helen (Watt) B.; children: Steven L., Michael J., Timothy C., David W. D.D.S., U. Iowa, 1954, M.S., 1960, Ph.D., 1961. Gen. practice dentistry Glenwood Springs, Colo., 1956-58; mem. faculty dept. pediatric dentistry Sch. Dentistry, U. N.C., Chapel Hill, 1961—, prof., 1965-77, Alumni disting. prof., 1977—, dean, 1966-74; mem. faculty Sch. Dentistry, U. Lund, Malmo, Sweden, 1974-75; vis. prof. Karlinska Inst., Stockholom, 1992-93; mem. med.-dental staff N.C. Univ. Hosp., Chapel Hill, 1975—, cons. various coms. NIH, Bethesda, Md., 1979—; mem. oral medicine and biology study sect. Nat. Inst. Dental Health, Bethesda, 1982-83; mem., past pres. So. Conf. Dental Deans and Examiners, 1966-74. Contbr. articles to profl. jours., dental textbooks and studies. Chmn. bd. dirs. United Fund, Chapel Hill, 1972. Served to lt. Dental Corps, USN, 1954-56. Recipient Disting. Svc. award Dental Found. N.C., 1974; named Disting. Educator, U. Iowa, 1985; USPHS postdoctoral fellow U. Iowa, 1958-61, Fogarty sr. internat. fellow NIH, 1992-93; grantee W.K. Kellogg Found., 1976-79, Nat. Inst. Dental Rsch., 1963-66, 75—. Fellow AAAS, Am. Acad. Pediatric Dentistry; mem. ADA (coun. dental edn. 1971-74), Inst. Medicine of NAS, Am. Assn. for Dental Rsch. (pres. 1984-85), N.C. Dental Soc. (Disting. Svc. award), Am. Assn. Dental Schs. (chmn. coun. of deans 1972-73), Internat. Assn. for Dental Rsch., Omicron Kappa Upsilon, Delta Sigma Delta. Avocation: tennis. Office: Univ NC Sch Dentistry Chapel Hill NC 27599*

BAWDEN, NINA (MARY), author; b. Eng., 1925. Author: Who Calls the Tune (in U.S. as Eyes of Green), 1953, The Odd Flamingo, 1954, Change Here for Babylon, 1955, The Solitary Child, 1956, Devil by the Sea, 1957, Just Like a Lady (in U.S. as Glass Slippers Always Pinch), 1960, In Honour Bound, 1961, Tortoise by Candlelight, 1963, The Secret Passage (in U.S. as The House of Secrets), 1963, On the Run (in U.S. as Three on the Run), 1964, Under the Skin, 1964, A Little Love, A Little Learning, 1966, The White Horse Gang, 1966, The Witch's Daughter, 1966, A Handful of Thieves, 1967, A Woman of My Age, 1967, The Grain of Truth, 1968, The Runaway Summer, 1969, The Birds on the Trees, 1970, Squib, 1971, Anna Apparent, 1972, Carrie's War, George Beneath a Paper Moon, 1974, The Peppermint Pig, 1975, Afternoon of a Good Woman, 1976, Rebel on a Rock, 1978, Familiar Passions, 1979, Walking Naked, 1981, Kept in the Dark, 1982, The Ice House, 1983, The Finding, 1985, Circles of Deceit, 1987, Keeping Henry, 1988, The Outside Child, 1989, Family Money, 1991, Humbug, 1992, The Real Plato Jones, 1993, In My Own Time, 1994, A Nice Change, 1997, Off the Road, 1999. Author: Who Calls the Tune (in U.S. as Eyes of Green), 1953, The Odd Flamingo, 1954, Change Here for Babylon, 1955, The Solitary Child, 1956, Devil by the Sea, 1957, Just Like a Lady (in U.S. as Glass Slippers Always Pinch), 1960, In Honour Bound, 1961, Tortoise by Candelight, 1963, The Secret Passage (in U.S. as The House of Secrets), 1963, On the Run (in U.S. as Three on the Run), 1964, Under the Skin, 1964, A Little Love, A Little Learning, 1966, The White Horse Gang, 1966, The Witch's Daughter, 1966, A Handful of Thieves, 1967, A Woman of My Age, 1967, The Grain of Truth, 1968, The Runaway Summer, 1969, The Birds on the Trees, 1970, Squib, 1971, Anna Apparent, 1972, Carrie's War, George Beneath a Paper Moon, 1974, The Peppermint Pig, 1975, Afternoon of a Good Woman, 1976, Rebel on a Rock, 1978, Familiar Passions, 1979, Walking Naked, 1981, Kept in the Dark, 1982, The Ice House, 1983, The Finding, 1985, Circle of Deceit, 1987, Keeping Henry, 1988, The Outside Child, 1989, Family Money, 1991, Humbug, 1992, The Real Plato Jones, 1993, In My Own Time, 1994, Granny the Pag, 1995, A Nice Change, 1997. Address: care Curtis Brown Ltd 10 Astor Pl New York NY 10003-6935 also: 22 Noel Rd, London N1 8HA, England also: 19, Kapodistriou, Nauplion 21100, Greece

BAWOROWSKY, JOHN MICHAEL, academic administrator; b. Chgo., June 17, 1959; s. Michael and Ida (Fixl) B.; m. Marjorie Sasso, July 31, 1982; children: Julie, Andrew, Christina. BS, Loyola U., Chgo., 1981; MS, U. Miami, 1982. Program coord. Ill. Inst. Tech., Chgo., 1982-84; coord. freshman recruitment Ill. Benedictine Coll., Lisle, 1984-88, dir. pub. info., 1988-90, dir. pub. rels., 1990-92; dir. pub. rels. Aurora U., 1992—; v.p. admission and fin. aid North Park U., Chgo.; treas. Assn. Chgo. Area Cath. Colls. and Univs., 1985-86; pres. Corridor Group, 1992; mem. St. James Sch. Bd., 1993—. Elected to St. James Elem Sch. Bd., 1993-96. Recipient Award of Excellence Nat. Sch. Pub. Rels. Assn., 1990, Pub. Rels. Campaign of the Yr. award Suburban Press Club of Chgo., 1991. Office: North Park University 3225 W Foster Ave Chicago IL 60625-4823

BAXENDELL, SIR PETER (BRIAN), petroleum engineer; b. Runcorn, Eng., Feb. 28, 1925; s. Leslie Wilfred Edward and Evelyn Mary (Gaskin) B.; m. Rosemary Lacey, 1949; children: Anne, Gillian, Peter, John. BSc, ARSM, Royal Sch. Mines, London; DSc (hon.), Heriot-Watt U., Queen's U. Belfast, U. London, U. Tech. Loughborough. With Royal Dutch/Shell Group, 1946-95, mng. dir. Shell-BP Nigeria, 1969-72, mng. dir. Royal Dutch/Shell Group, London, 1973-85, chmn. Shell U.K., 1974-79; chmn. Shell Transport & Trading Co. PLC, 1979-85, also bd. dirs.; chmn. Shell Can. Ltd., 1980-85, Hawker Siddeley Can., Inc., 1986-91; bd. dirs. Shell Oil Co., U.S.A., 1982-85, Shell Transport & Trading Co. PLC, 1973-95, Hawker Siddeley Group PLC, 1984-91, chmn. 1986-91, Inchcape PLC, 1986-93, Sun Life Assurance Co. Can., 1986-97. Decorated comdr. Order Brit. Empire, 1972, Knight bachelor, 1981, Comdr. Order Orange-Nassau, 1985; fellow Imperial Coll. Sci. and Tech. Fellow Inst. Petroleum, Royal Acad. Engring., Inst. Mining and Metallurgy. Address: 10 Upper Cheyne Row, London SW3 5JN, England

BAXT, WILLIAM G., medical educator; b. Mar. 31, 1941. BA, Brown U., 1963; MD, Yale U., 1967. Diplomate Am. Bd. Internal Medicine, Am. Bd. Emergency Medicine. Intern Columbia-Presbyn. Hosp., N.Y.C., 1967-68, resident in internal medicine, 1970-71, fellow in hematology, 1971-73; from asst. prof. medicine to prof. clin. medicine & surgery U. Calif., San Diego, 1973-94; prof., chmn. dept. emergency medicine U. Pa. Med. Ctr., Phila., 1994—; rsch. biologist U. Calif., La Jolla, 1976-77; med. dir. life flight aeromed. program U. Calif. Med. Ctr., San Diego, 1980-89, assoc. dir. divsn. emergency med. svcs., 1978-80, dir. dept. emergency medicine, 1980-94; chief emergency medicine svcs. U. Pa. Med. Ctr., 1994—. Co-author: (with others) Cellular Modifiction and Genetic Transformation by Exogenous Nucleic Acids, 1973, The Leukemia Cell, 1979, Systems Approach to Emergency Medical Care, 1983, Trauma: The First Hour, 1985; mem. editl. bd. Emergency Care Quar., Annals of Emergency Medicine; contbr. articles to profl. jours. Surgeon USPHS, 1968-70. Leukemia Soc. Am. scholar, 1976; recipient Physicians Recognition award AMA, 1985, Best Oral Clin. Sci. Paper U. Assn. for Emergency Medicine, 1988, Best Oral Methodology Paper Soc. for Acad. Emergency Medicine, 1990. Mem. Nat. Acad. Scis., Soc. for Acad. Emergency Medicine, Phi Beta Kappa. Home: 245 Maple Hill Rd Gladwyne PA 19035-1307 Office: Univ Pa Med Ctr 7 Silverstein Pavilion 3400 Spruce St Philadelphia PA 19104-4204*

BAXTER, BETTY CARPENTER, educational administrator; b. Sherman, Tex., 1937; d. Granville E. and Elizabeth (Caston) Carpenter; m. Cash Baxter; children: Stephen Barrington, Catherine Elaine. AA in Music, Christian Coll., Columbia, Mo., 1957; MusB in Voice and Piano, So. Meth. U., Dallas, 1959; MA in Early Childhood Edn., Tchrs. Coll., Columbia, 1972, MEd, 1979, EdD, 1988. Tchr. Riverside Ch. Day Sch., N.Y.C., 1966-71; headmistress Episcopal Sch., N.Y.C., 1972-87, headmistress emeritus, 1987—; founding head Presbyn. Sch., Houston, 1988-94; dir. Chadwick Village Sch., Palos Verdes Peninsula, Calif. Author: The Relationship of Early Tested Intelligence on the WPPSI to Later Tested Aptitude on the SAT. Mem. ASCD, Nat. Assn. Episcopal Schs. (former gov. bd., editor Network publ.), Nat. Assn. Elem. Sch. Prins., Ind. Schs. Assn. Admissions Greater N.Y. (former exec. bd.), Nat. Assn. for Edn. of Young Children, L.A. Assn. Sch. Heads, Nat. Assn. Elem. Sch. Prins., Assn. Supervision and Curriculum Devel., Kappa Delta Pi, Delta Kappa Gamma. Republican. Presbyterian. Home and Office: 26800 Academy Dr Palos Verdes Peninsula CA 90274-3980

BAXTER, CECIL WILLIAM, JR., retired college president; b. Stockton, Kans., Aug. 11, 1923; s. Cecil William and Marjorie LaVerne (Fitzpatrick) B.; m. Pat Ann Layman, June 6, 1951; children: Cecil William, Michael Kent, Patrick Alan. B.A., Kans. Wesleyan U., 1950; M.B.A., U. Denver, 1954; Ph.D., U. Tex., 1967. Secondary edn. tchr., then secondary sch. prin., 1951-60; bus. mgr. Cottey Coll., Nevada, Mo., 1960-65; dean instrn. Kansas City Community Jr. Coll., Kans., 1967-68, Forest Park Community Coll., St. Louis, 1968-70; pres. North Seattle Community Coll., 1970-85, pres. emeritus, 1985—; exec. dir. Coun. on Naturopathic Med. Edn., 1989-92; mem. faculty U. Wash., 1971; mem. Comm. on Colls. N.W. Assn. Schs. and Colls., 1981-85. Bd. dirs. Sr. Citizens Orgn., Seattle, 1972. Served with AUS, 1944-46. Ford Found. fellow U. Okla.; Kellogg Found. fellow U. Tex. Mem. Phi Delta Kappa. Lodge: Rotary.

BAXTER, DONALD WILLIAM, physician, educator, retired; b. Brockville, Ont., Can., Aug. 24, 1926; s. William Robert and Agnes B.; m. Anne Bieler, Aug. 20, 1988. M.D.C.M., Queens U., Kingston, Ont., 1951, M.Sc., 1953. Intern Kingston (Ont.) Gen. Hosp., 1951-52; resident Montreal (Que., Can.) Neurol. Inst., 1952-53, Boston City Hosp., 1953-57; asst. prof. medicine U. Sask., 1957-62; assoc. prof. neurology Temple U., Phila., 1962-63; prof. McGill U., Montreal, 1963-92, prof. emeritus, 1992—, chmn. dept. neurology and neurosurgery, 1979-86; dir. Montreal Neurol. Inst., 1984-92. Home: 1321 Sherbrooke St W #D71, Montreal, PQ Canada H3G 1J4

BAXTER, DUANE WILLARD, electrical engineer, consultant; b. Cleve., Apr. 20, 1928; s. James Bruce and Thelma Paulene Baxter; m. Elsie Lu Castner, May 14, 1955; children: Melody Susan, James Bruce. BSEE, Tri-State U., 1955. Elec. engr. IBM, Kingston, N.Y., 1955-62; rsch. mem. IBM, Yorktown Heights, N.Y., 1963-65; sr. engr. IBM, Rochester, Minn., 1965-87; cons. IBM, Rochester, 1987-95, Western Digital Corp., Rochester, 1995—. Patentee in field. Staff sgt. USMC, 1948-52. Mem. IEEE (sr.). Avocations: viticulture, wine making. E-mail: duane.baxter@worldnet.att.net. Home: 2212 SW 5th Ave Rochester MN 55902 Office: Western Digital Corp 1599 Broadway N Rochester MN 55906

BAXTER, JAMES WILLIAM, III, investment executive; b. New Albany, Ind., June 24, 1931; s. James William, Jr. and Beatrice F. (Diedrich) B.; m. Deborah Mary Smith, Nov. 26, 1980; 1 son, P. Andrew. B.S., Ind. U., 1953; postgrad., U. Louisville Sch. Bus. With Scudder, Stevens & Clark, 1963-89; office dir. Scudder, Stevens & Clark, Cin., 1972-78; chmn. bd., pres. Scudder, Stevens & Clark, Chgo., 1978-86; dir. Scudder, Stevens & Clark, N.Y.C., 1978-84; chmn., CEO, pres. Ky. Home Mut. Life, Louisville, 1992—; chmn., pres., CEO Ky. Home Capital Corp., Louisville, 1992—; dir. Keystone State Life Ins., Phila., 1994-98; chmn. bd. dirs. Southeastern Fin. Svcs., Louisville; vice chmn. bd. Ky. Home Trust Co., 1992—. Trustee Cin. Symphony Orch., 1975-78, Cin. Union Bethel, 1974-78; bd. dirs. United Cerebral Palsy, 1978-86; adv. council Episcopal Ch. Found., 1977-82. With U.S. Army, 1953-55. Mem. Tavern Club (Chgo.), Thoroughbred of Am. Club, Pendennis Club (Louisville). Home: 1715 Spring Dr Louisville KY 40205-1324 Office: Ky Mut Life 450 S 3rd St Louisville KY 40202-1440

BAXTER, JOHN LINCOLN, JR., manufacturing company executive; b. Brunswick, Maine, Mar. 11, 1920; s. John Lincoln and Constance (French) B.; m. Alice Preston Comee, June 1, 1942; children: John Randolph, Constance Baxter Marlow, Judith. B.A., Bowdoin Coll., 1942. Partner H. C. Baxter & Bros., Brunswick, 1942-65; v.p., dir. Snow Flake Canning Co., Brunswick, 1945-55; pres., dir. Snow Flake Canning Co., 1965-67; asst. gen. mgr., dir. Lamb-Weston, Inc., Portland, Oreg., 1965-67; exec. v.p., gen. mgr. Lamb-Weston, Inc., 1967-71, pres., 1971-73; v.p., food group chmn. Amfac, Inc., Honolulu, 1971-74; exec. v.p., food group chmn. Amfac, Inc., 1974-81; mgr. mergers and aquisitions Omnivest Inc., fin. co., Portland, Oreg., 1983-92; pres., chmn. bd. Zebron Corp., Tualatin, Oreg., 1981-83; bd. chmn. Reddicop Systems, Portland, 1980-81; dir. Black Butte Ranch Assn., 1981-84, chmn., 1982-84; pres., chmn. Black Butte Ranch Corp., 1987-88. Mem. Maine Ho. of Reps., 1955-92, majority leader, 1960-62, vice chmn. exec. coun., 1962-64; mem. New Eng. Interstate Water Pollution Control Commn., 1954-56; dir. Associated Oreg. Industries, 1977-81, Associated Industries Maine, 1955-57; pres., dir. Found. Oreg. Rsch. & Edn., 1977-79; dir. Oreg. Grad. Ctr.; trustee Lewis and Clark Coll., 1979-82, 88—; mem. Oreg. Ednl. Commn., 1982-86, chmn., 1983-85; chmn. Oreg. Task Force on Colls., 1988; chmn. budget com. Sisters (Oreg.) Sch. Dist., 1989-94. Mem. Nat. Canners Assn. (dir. 1954-56), Am. Frozen Food Inst. (dir. 1968-72), Frozen Potato Products Inst. (pres. 1970-71), Instant Potato Products Inst. (pres.), Maine Canners and Freezers (pres. 1960), N.W. Food Processors Assn. (pres. 1973-75), N.W. Packers and Growers Assn. (pres. 1971), Portland C. of C. (dir. 1978-81), University Club (N.Y.C.), University Club (Portland, Oreg.), Phi Beta Kappa. Republican. Office: PO Box 1539 Sisters OR 97759-1539

BAXTER, JOHN MICHAEL, editor; b. Upper Darby, Pa., Mar. 25, 1945; s. Allen and Judith Bryner (Bushey) B.; m. Carolyn Jane Johnson, Nov. 7, 1970 (div. May 1984); child: Jeffrey Michael, Wendy Beth. BA in English, Hobart Coll., 1967. Automotive editor Chilton Book Co., Radnor, Pa., 1971-79, mng. editor Specialist Mag., 1979-82, assoc. editor Automotive Industries Mag., 1982-83; automotive book editor Chilton Automotive Books, Radnor, Pa., 1983-89, sr. assoc. editor Owner-Operator Mag., 1989—. Author: Chilton's Auto Troubleshooting Guide, 1973; editor: About Sexual Abuse, 1989, Gas Turbine Engine, 1974. Dir. Gundaker Found. Inc., Wayne, Pa., 1984-90, 97—, treas., 1985-86; trustee Marple Presbyn. Ch., Broomall, Pa., 1993-98; bd. dirs. Huaguang Arts and Culture Ctr., 1998—. With U.S. Army, 1967-70, Vietnam. Decorated Army Commendation medal. Mem. Soc. Automotive Engrs. (treas. Phila. sect. 1998—), Truck Writers N.Am. (tech. achievement award com.), Fleet Maintenance Assn. Phila., Rotary Club (treas. Wayne chpt. 1990-98, sec. 1998—). Avocations: running, bicycling, rollerblading. Home: 3209 W Chester Pike Apt D-5 Newtown Square PA 19073-4260 Office: Cahners Bus Info Owner Operator Mag 201 King Of Prussia Rd Radnor PA 19087-5114

BAXTER, LAWRENCE GERALD, strategic analyst, law educator, business consultant; b. Pietermaritzburg, Republic of South Africa, Dec. 11, 1952; came to U.S. 1985; s. Gerald Robert and Renate Veronica (Volker) B.; children: Chantal, Imogen, Rochelle. B of Commerce, U. Natal, Pietermaritzburg, 1974, LLB, 1976; LLM, Cambridge U., 1977; PHD, U. Natal, 1985. Bar: Republic of South Africa 1978, N.C. 1988. Assoc. Livingston, Doull & Daly, Pietermaritzburg, 1978; sr. lectr. U. Natal, Pietermaritzburg, 1978-82, prof. law, 1982-86; prof. law Duke U., Durham, N.C., 1986-95; sr. v.p., spl. counsel for strategic devel. Wachovia Corp., Winston-Salem, N.C., 1995-96; exec. v.p., head emerging businesses Wachovia Corp., Winston-Salem, 1996—; adj. prof. law Bond U., Australia, 1990—; vis. prof. Duke U., 1986; vis. fellow Wolfson Coll., Cambridge, Eng., 1988; cons. Adminstrv. Conf. of U.S., Washington, 1987-88, 89-93. Author: Administrative Law, 1984; co-editor Natal and Kwazulu, 1980; contbr. articles to profl. jours. Mem. ABA (coun. sect. on adminstrv. law and regulatory practice, chmn. fin. svcs. com., reporter Working Group on Lawyers Representation of Regulated Clients 1992-93), N.C. Bar Assn. (task force on adminstrv. law and procedure 1987-88). Office: Wachovia Corp 101 N Cherry St Winston Salem NC 27102

BAXTER, LEO J., career officer; b. Apr. 19, 1946. Commd. U.S. Army, advanced through grades to maj. gen., 1997; with U.S. Army Field Artillery Ctr. and Ft. Sill, Ft. Sill, Okla. Office: US Army Field Artillery Ctr Fort Sill OK 73503

BAXTER, LOUISE T., educational administrator; b. N.Y.C., Mar. 14, 1944; d. John Prechtel and Tekla Chaykowsky. B of Edn., Empire State Coll., 1985; M of Edn., C.W. Post U., 1989. Vocat. tchr. Sewanhaka H.S., Floral Park, N.Y., 1976-79; vocat. tchr. BOCES 2/Eastern Suffolk BOCES, Patchogue, N.Y., 1980-89, program adminstr., 1989—; dir. L.I. Staff Deve. Consortium for Adult Edn., N.Y. State Dept. Edn., 1994-96; dir. GED Testing Svcs.-BOCES, N.Y. State Dept. Edn., 1994-96; access dir. adult svcs. BOCES, 1992-97. Named Outstanding Educator of Yr., Phi Delta Kappa, 1995. Mem. L.I. Vocat. Tchrs. Assn. (pres. 1982-84), Suffolk Assn. for Adult and Continuing Edn. (pres. 1995-97). Office: Ea Suffolk BOCES Brookhaven Tech Ctr 350 Martha Ave Bellport NY 11713-1525

BAXTER, MARVIN RAY, state supreme court justice; b. Fowler, Calif., Jan. 9, 1940; m. Jane Pippert, June 22, 1963; children: Laura, Brent. BA in Econs., Calif. State U., 1962; JD, U. Calif.-Hasting Coll. Law, 1966. Bar: Calif. 1966. Appointments sec. to Gov. George Deukmejian, 1983-88; dep. dist. atty. Fresno County, Calif., 1967-68; assoc. Andrews, Andrews, Thaxter & Jones, 1968-70, ptnr., 1971-82; apptd. sec. to Gov. George Deukmejian, 1983-88; assoc. justice Calif. Ct. Appeal (5th dist.), 1988-90, Calif. Supreme Ct., 1991—; mem. Jud. Coun. of Calif., chmn. policy coord. and liaison com., 1996—. Mem. Fresno County Bar Assn. (bd. dirs. 1977-82, pres. 1981), Calif. Young Lawyers Assn. (bd. gov. 1973-76, sec.-treas. 1974-75), Fresno County Young Lawyers Assn. (pres. 1973-74), Fresno County Legal Svcs., Inc. (bd. dirs. 1973-74), Fresno State U. Alumni Assn. (pres. 1970-71), Fresno State U. Alumni Trust Coun. (pres. 1970-75). Office: Calif Supreme Ct 350 McAllister St San Francisco CA 94102-3600

BAXTER, MEREDITH, actress; b. Los Angeles, June 21, 1947; d. Tom and Whitney (Blake) Baxter; m. David Birney, Apr. 10, 1974 (div. 1989); children: Ted, Eva, Kate, Peter and Mollie (twins). Student, Interlochen Arts Acad., Mich. Actress (films) including Ben, 1972, Stand Up and Be Counted, 1972, Bittersweet Love, 1976, All the President's Men, 1976, The November Plan, 1976, (TV movies) The Cat Creature, 1973, The Stranger Who Looks Like Me, 1974, The Imposter, 1975, The Night That Panicked America, 1975, Target Risk, 1975, Little Women, 1978, The Family Man, 1979, Beulah Land, 1980, The Two Lives of Carol Letner, 1981, Take Your Best Shot, 1982, Family Ties Vacation, 1985, The Rape of Richard Beck, 1985, Kate's Secret, 1986, The Long Journey Home, 1987, Winnie, 1988, She Knows Too Much, 1989, Jezebel's Kiss, 1990, The Kissing Place, 1990, Burning Bridges, 1990, A Bump in the Night, 1991, A Mother's Justice, 1991, A Woman Scorned: The Betty Broderick Story, 1992, The Betty Broderick Story: Part 2, 1992, (also exec. prodr.) Darkness Before Dawn, 1993, My Breast, 1994, One More Mountain, 1994, For the Love of Aaron, 1994, Betrayed: A Story of Three Women, 1995, After Jimmy, 1996, Inheritance, 1997; (plays) Guys and Dolls, Talley's Folley, Butterflies are Free, Varieties; star (TV series) Bridget Loves Bernie, 1972-73, Family, 1976-80, Family Ties, 1982-89, The Faculty, 1996; (TV spls.) Vanities, 1981, Missing...Have You Seen This Person?, 1985, Diabetes Update, 1986, Other Mothers, 1993, TV's Funniest Families, 1994, Miracle in the Woods, 1997, Let Me Call You Sweetheart, 1997; other TV appearances include The Interns, Police Woman, Medical Story, City of Angels, McMillan and Wife, The Streets of San Francisco. Mem. Am. Diabetes Assn. Office: William Morris Agency c/o John Kimble 151 S El Camino Dr Beverly Hills CA 90212-2775*

BAXTER, NEVINS DENNIS, bank consultant; b. N.Y.C., June 29, 1941; s. Sol and Beatrice B.; m. Anne Susan Hatow, July 30, 1972; children: S.J., Keith. BA, Columbia Coll., 1961; MA, Princeton U., 1962, PhD in Econs., 1964. Asst. prof. fin. U. Pa., 1965-69; v.p. Mathematica, Princeton, N.J., 1969-71; pres. Baxter & Co., Washington, 1971-75, Golembe Assocs., Inc., Washington, 1975-89; chmn. BEI Golembe Cons., Washington, 1989-90; vice chmn. BEI Holdings Ltd., Washington, 1990-93; prin. Baxter & Co., Washington. Contbr. articles to numerous profl. jours. Office: Baxter & Co Ste 308 1025 Thomas Jefferson St NW Washington DC 20007-5240

BAXTER, RALPH H., JR., lawyer; b. San Francisco, 1946. AB, Stanford U., 1968; MA, Cath. U. Am., 1970; JD, U. Va., 1974. Chmn. Orrick, Herrington & Sutcliffe LLP, San Francisco, 1990—; mem. adv. bd. nat. Employment Law Inst. Author: Sexual Harassment in the Workplace: A Guide to the Law, 1981, 2nd. rev. edit., 1989, 94, Manager's Guide to Lawful Terminations, 1983, rev. edit., 1991; mem. editorial bd. Va. Law Rev., 1973-74; mem. editorial adv. bd. Employee Rels. Law Jour. Mem. ABA (mgmt. co-chair com. on employment rights and responsibilities in workplace labor and employment law sect. 1987=90). Office: Orrick Herrington & Sutcliffe LLP Old Fed Res Bank Bldg 400 Sansome St San Francisco CA 94111-3143

BAXTER, RANDOLPH, judge; b. Columbia, Tenn., Aug. 15, 1946; s. Lenon Pillow and Willie Alexine (Hood) B.; m. Yvonne Marie Williams, Nov. 26, 1980; children: Mark, Melissa, Scott; m. Rebecca Terrell, Oct. 10, 1968; (div. Apr. 1976); 1 child, Kimberly Lynn. BS, Tuskegee Inst., 1967; JD, U. Akron, 1974. Bar: Ohio 1976, U.S. Dist. Ct. (no. dist.) Ohio 1978, U.S. Ct. Appeals (6th cir.) 1978, U.S. Supreme Ct. 1980. Salary analyst B.F. Goodrich Co., Akron, 1971-73; courts planner Criminal Justice Commn., Akron, 1973-76; dep. dir., pub. service dept. City Akron, 1976-78; asst. U.S. atty. U.S. Dept. Justice, Cleve., 1978-85, chief appellate litigation, 1982-85; judge U.S. Bankruptcy Court (no. dist.) Ohio, 1985-96, judge bankruptcy appellate panel U.S. Ct. Appeals for 6th Cir., 1996—; instr. real estate law Kent State U., 1974-78; adj. prof. U. Akron Coll. Law; v.p., dir. Alpha Phi Alpha Homes, Inc., Akron, 1971-85. Bd. dirs. Western Res. Hist. Soc., 1988-92, Christian Radio Fellowship, Tuskegee U., 1989—, Akron Auto Assn., 1990—, Children's Svcs. Inc., 1993—, Salvation Army, Akron, 1993—, Emmanuel Christian Acad., 1994—, Stan Hywet Found., 1995—, trustee, 1995—. Served to capt. AUS, 1968- 71, Vietnam. Named Man of Yr., Akron Jaycees, 1977; recipient Disting. Service award City Akron, 1978, Spl. Achievement award U.S. Dept. Justice, 1981, 82, Disting. Vets. award Fed. Exec. Bd. Cleve., 1982. Mem. ABA, Akron Barristers Club (pres. 1978-79), Fed. Bar Assn., Nat. Bar Assn., Akron Bar Assn., Nat. Conf. Bankruptcy Judges, Am. Bankruptcy Inst., Comml. Law League Am., Akron City Club, Alpha Phi Alpha. Home: 4133 Evergreen Ln Richfield OH 44286-9595 Office: US Bankruptcy Ct 127 Public Sq Ste 3205 Cleveland OH 44114-1216

BAXTER, RAOUL, meat packing company executive; b. 1950. BC, Centre Coll., 1970; MA, U. of Ky., 1974; LLB, Chase Coll. of Law, 1981. With Ind. Farm Bureau Co-op., 1976-78, Sara Lee Corp., 1978-87; with John Morrell & Co., 1987—, exec. v.p.; v.p. corp. devel. Smithfield (Va.) Foods Internat. Office: Smithfield Foods Internat 200 Commerce St Smithfield VA 23430-1204*

BAXTER, ROBERT BANNING, insurance company executive; b. Rochester, N.Y., Aug. 26, 1946; s. Robert Clarkson and Flora Corinne (Banning) B.; m. Sandra Anne Weber, Apr. 21, 1973; children: Matthew Hamilton, Darcy Colson, Jeffrey Ford. BA, U. Rochester, 1968. Chartered property casualty underwriter; cert. ins. counselor. Personal lines account underwriter Allstate Ins. Co., Rochester, 1973-77; asst. personal lines underwriting mgr. Reliance Ins. Co., Pitts., 1977-78; personal lines underwriting mgr. Reliance Ins. Co., Canandaigua, N.Y., 1978-79; regional personal lines underwriting mgr. Reliance Ins. Co., Cin., 1979-81, mktg. mgr., 1981-84; mktg. mgr. Hartford Ins. Group, Cleve., 1984-85; regional mktg. mgr. Nat. Grange Mut. Ins. Co., Syracuse, N.Y., 1985-88; asst. br. mgr., mktg. mgr. Gen. Accident Ins., Syracuse, 1988-90, br. mgr., 1990-93; CEO, gen. mgr. Dryden Mut. Ins. Co., Dryden, N.Y., 1994—. Capt. USAF, 1968-73, Thailand, also West Germany. Decorated Air Force Commendation medal (2). Mem. Soc. Chartered Property Casualty Underwriters, Soc. Cert. Ins. Counselors, Ins. Mgrs. Coun., Syracuse (sec.-treas. 1992, v.p. 1993, pres. 1994-95), Ind. Ins. Agts. Assn. N.Y. (assoc.), Profl. Ins. Agts. N.Y. (assoc.), Honorable Order of Blue Goose Internat., N.Y. Ins. Alliance (bd. dirs.). Republican. Unitarian. Avocation: numismatics. Home: 29 Forest Acres Dr Ithaca NY 14850-9782 Office: Dryden Mut Ins Co PO Box 635 12 Ellis Dr Dryden NY 13053

BAXTER, ROBERT HAMPTON, III, insurance executive; b. Glassport, Pa., Mar. 27, 1931; m. Barbara Miller, Aug. 4, 1956. Student, Carnegie Inst. Tech., 1949-50; A.B., U.S.C., 1954, J.D., 1958. Bar: S.C. bar 1959. Trust officer Citizens & So. Nat. Bank, Charleston, S.C., 1958-60, First Citizens Bank & Trust Co., Charlotte, N.C., 1960-68; with Aetna Life & Casualty Co., Atlanta, 1968-91; pres. The Resource Group, Atlanta, 1991—. Served to lt. (j.g.) USNR, 1954-57; comdr. USNR; ret. Mem. Bernardo Heights (Calif.) C.C., Phi Delta Phi. Republican. Presbyterian. Home: 12143 Caminito Corriente San Diego CA 92128-4569

BAXTER, ROBERT THEODORE STEWART, arts critic; b. Fresno, Calif., Oct. 15, 1940; s. Howard Dean and Lillian Gertrude (Reding) B. BA in Classics with honors, Stanford U., 1962, PhD in Classics, 1968. Tchg. asst. Stanford U., Palo Alto, Calif., 1964-65; instr. classical langs. and lit. Smith Coll., Northampton, Mass., 1966-68, asst. prof., 1968-75; freelance writer, 1975-79; arts critic Courier-Post, Camden County, N.J., 1979—. Contbr. articles and revs. to various publs., including Critic Opera Mag., Opera News, Opera Quar. Recipient 1st prize Critical Writing, N.J. Press Assn., 1984, 88, 2nd prize, 1989, 3d prize, 1997. Mem. Opera Club (pres. Phila. chpt. 1986—), Maria Callas Internat. Club, Schwarzkopf-Legge Soc. Home: 1218 Martin Ave Cherry Hill NJ 08002-2022 Office: Courier-Post 301 Cuthbert Blvd Cherry Hill NJ 08002-2998

BAXTER, STEPHEN BARTOW, retired history educator; b. Boston, Mar. 8, 1929; s. James Phinney 3d and Anne (Strang) B.; m. Ann Sweeney, Aug. 22, 1953; children: Clare, Persis Baxter Andrews, James, Nicholas, Stephen, Michael. AB in Econs. with honors, Harvard U., 1950; PhD, Cambridge U., 1955. Instr. history Dartmouth Coll., Hanover, N.H., 1954-57; asst. prof. U. N.C., Chapel Hill, 1958-62, assoc. prof., 1962-66, prof. history, 1966-91, Kenan prof. history, 1975-91; vis. asst. prof. U. Mo., Columbia, 1957-58; dir. post-doctoral summer seminars Clark Meml. Libr. UCLA, 1973, 88, Clark libr. prof., 1977-78; dir. summer seminars NEH, Chapel Hill, 1974, post-doctoral seminar, 1978-79. Author: The Development of the Treasury, 1660-1702, 1957, William III and the Defense of European Liberty, 1650-1702, 1966; (with Paul R. Sellin) Anglo-Dutch Cross Currents in the Seventeenth and Eighteenth Centuries, 1976; (with others) Major Crises in Western Civilization, vol. 1, 1965, Eighteenth Century Studies Presented to Arthur M. Wilson, 1973, The Revolution of 1688 and the Birth of the English Political Nation, 1973, Biography in the Eighteenth Century, 1980, Changing Views on British History, 1984; editor: Basic Documents of English History, 1968, England's Rise to Greatness, 1660-1763, 1983; mem. editorial bd. Jour. Modern. History, 1971-77, Albion, 1982-92. Guggenheim fellow, 1959-60, 73-74; Charles Henry Fiske III scholar Trinity Coll., 1950-51. Fellow Royal Hist. Soc.; mem. Conf. British Studies. Democrat. Roman Catholic.

BAXTER, SUSAN PARADISE, federal judge, lawyer; b. 1956. JD, Temple U., 1983. Bar: Pa. 1983. Ptnr. Cole, Raywid & Braverman, Erie, Pa., 1983-92; ct. solicitor Erie County, Erie, 1994; part-time magistrate judge for western dist. Pa., U.S. Magistrate Ct., Erie, 1995—. Office: US Magistrate Ct US PO and Courthouse Rm 227 617 State St Erie PA 16501-1127

BAXTER-SMITH, GREGORY JOHN, shareholder; b. Davenport, Iowa, Sept. 27, 1949; s. James Sanford Baxter and Doris Arlene (Olson) Smith; m. Carolyn Imes, June 10, 1975 (div. Oct. 1980); children: Bradley Imes, Brian McBride; m. Karen Ruth Thomas, Dec. 12, 1986. BA in English, Bucknell U., 1971; JD, U. Mo., 1974. Bar: Mo. 1974, U.S. Dist. Ct. (we. dist.) Mo. 1975, U.S. Tax Ct. 1975. Clk. Hon. Charles Shangler Mo. Ct. Appeals, Kansas City, 1974-75; assoc. Miller & Poole, Springfield, Mo., 1975-76; shareholder Poole & Smith, P.C., Springfield, 1976-78, Gregory J. Smith, P.C., Springfield, 1978-86, Poole, Smith & Wieland, P.C., Springfield, 1986-90, Smith & Fels, P.C., Springfield, 1990—. Mem. Springfield Met. Bar Assn., Greene County Estate Planning Coun., Elks. Republican. Lutheran. Avocation: golf.

BAY, MICHAEL BENJAMIN, film director; b. Feb. 17, 1964. Dir. films Bad Boys, 1995, The Rock, 1996, Armageddon, 1998; Producer Armageddon, 1998; Actor Vengence (TV), 1986, Armageddon, 1998. Office: Creative Artists Agy care Adam Krentzman 9830 Wilshire Blvd Beverly Hills CA 90212-1825*

BAY, PETER, orchestra conductor; b. Washington, Mar. 3, 1957; s. Pedro Matienzo and Hildegarde Clara (Maechler) B. BS, U. Md., 1978; MusM, Peabody Inst., Balt., 1980. Mem. faculty, artist Aspen (Colo.) Music Festival, 1980-90; asst. condr. Richmond (Va.) Symphony, 1982-85, assoc. condr., 1985-86, music advisor, 1986-87, prin. guest condr., 1987-88; music dir. Austin Symphony Orch., 1999—; music dir. Annapolis (Md.) Symphony Orch., 1983-90; assoc. condr. Rochester (N.Y.) Philharm. Orch., 1987-95; resident condr. St. Paul Chamber Orch., 1989-93; prin. guest condr. Rochester Philharm. Orch., 1995—; music dir. Erie (Pa.) Philharm., 1996-99, Britt Festival Orch., 1993—, Austin (Tex.) Symphony Orch., 1998—; instr. music Va. Commonwealth U., Richmond, 1984-87. Condr. (rec.) Benjamin Britten's The Sword in the Stone, 1985, Voices with Nexus. Recipient 1st prize Young Condrs. competition Balt. Symphony Orch., 1980; prize Leopold Stokowski Conducting competition, 1987. Office: Austin Symphony Orch 1101 Red River Austin TX 78701

BAY, RICHARD M., federal judge. Apptd. part-time magistrate judge ea. dist. U.S. Dist. Ct. Calif. Fax: (916) 246-5419. Office: 2986 Bechelli Ln Redding CA 96002-1903

BAYARD, RICHARD H., political party official. Chmn. Del. Democratic Party, Newport. Office: Delaware Democratic Party 240 N James St Ste 100A Newport DE 19804-3167*

BAYARD, SUSAN SHAPIRO, educator, small business owner; b. Boston, Dec. 26, 1942; d. Morris Arnold and Hester Muriel (Blatt) Shapiro; m. Edward Quint Bayard, Jan. 4, 1969; children: Jeffrey David, Lucy Quint. BA, Syracuse U., 1964; MA, U. Calif., Berkeley, 1966; Cert. Advanced Grad. Study, Boston U., 1984. Rsch. chemist Harvard Med. Sch., Boston, 1966; asst. scientist Polaroid Corp., Cambridge, Mass., 1966-67; instr. Boston U., 1968-70, Wheelock Coll., Boston, 1978-81; chmn. sci. dept. Tower Sch., Marblehead, Mass., 1981-85; dir., owner Bayard Learning Ctr., Marblehead, 1985-96; vis. lectr. Salem (Mass.) State Coll., 1994—, coord. Instrnl. Design Lab., 1995—, coord. PALMS presvc. program, 1998—, ednl. cons., workshop facilitator, 1986-91; ednl. cons., workshop facilitator Swampscott (Mass.) Pub. Schs., Lynn (Mass.) Pub. Schs.; instr., cons. N.E. Consortium, North Andover, Mass., 1986—. Mem. Town Mtg., Swampscott, 1988—, Supt. Screening Com., Swampscott, 1987, Mass. Ednl. TV Prog. Selection Com., 1979-87, Sch. Improvement Coun., Swampscott, 1988-89, Curriculum Evaluation Com., Swampscott, 1978-80. Grantee NSF, Syracuse U., 1962, 64; named Outstanding Woman Grad. Student, Boston U. Women's Guild, 1977. Mem. Nat. Sci. Tchrs.'s Assn., Pi Lambda Theta. Jewish. Avocations: tennis, reading, computers, piano.

BAYBAYAN, RONALD ALAN, lawyer; b. Paia, Hawaii, July 4, 1946; s. Celedonio Ladresa and Carlina (Domingo) B.; m. Dianne Lea, June 14, 1969 (div. June 1985); children: Alycia Kay, Amber Lea; m. Sharyn Dee Huckins, Dec. 31, 1985 (div. Oct. 1996). BA, Coe Coll., 1968; JD, Drake U., 1974. Bar: Iowa 1977, U.S. Dist. Ct. (so. dist.) Iowa 1977, U.S. Tax Ct. 1978, U.S. Dist. Ct. (no. dist.) Iowa 1980, U.S. Ct. Appeals (8th cir.) 1985, U.S. Supreme Ct. 1985, U.S. Dist. Ct. Hawaii 1986. Asst. law librarian Drake U., Des Moines, 1974-77; assoc. Law Office Mike Wilson, Des Moines, 1977-78; sole practice Des Moines, 1978—; bd. dirs. Berkley & Co. Amb.; presenter in field. Co-author: Paralegals in Family Law Practice in Iowa, 1995, How to Draft Wills and Trusts in Iowa, 1996, 99, A Practical Guide to Estate Administration in Iowa, 1997. Bd. dirs. Wakonda Christian Ch., 1989-90; dir. communique Victory Christian Ctr., 1991—; mem. bd. counselors Drake U. Law Sch., 1997—. Served with USAF, 1969-73. Mem. ABA, Iowa Bar Assn., Polk County Bar Assn., Am-Filipino Assn. Iowa (bd. dirs. 1986), Bass Anglers Sportsman Soc. (Iowa chpt. pres. 1979-82), Iowans for Better Fisheries (bd. dirs. 1991), Mid-Iowa Bassmasters (past pres., past v.p., past sec.). Republican. Home: 6217 Urbandale Ave Des Moines IA 50322-3541 Office: 4921 Douglas Ave Ste 3 Des Moines IA 50310-1802

BAYDA, EDWARD DMYTRO, judge; b. Alvena, Sask, Can., Sept. 9, 1931; s. Dmytro Andrew and Mary (Bilinski) B.; m. Marie-Thérèse Yvonne Gagné, May 28, 1953; children: Paula, Christopher, Margot, Marie-Thérèse, Sheila, Kathryn. BA, U. Sask., 1951, LLB cum laude, 1953; LLD (hon.), 1989. Bar: Sask. 1954; created Queen's Counsel, Exec. Br. of Govt., 1966. Barrister, solicitor Regina, Sask., 1953-72; sr. ptnr. Bayda, Halvorson, Scheibel & Thompson, 1966-72; justice Ct. Queen's Bench for Sask., Regina, 1972-74, Ct. Appeal for Sask., Regina, 1974-81; chief justice Sask., Regina, 1981—. Created Queen's Counsel. Roman Catholic. Home: 3000 Albert St, Regina, SK Canada S4S 3N7 Office: Ct Appeal Sask Courthouse, 2425 Victoria Ave, Regina, SK Canada S4P 3V7

BAYER, GARY RICHARD, advertising executive; b. St. Louis, Mar. 15, 1941; s. Kenneth Joseph and Ruth Margarite (Johnson) B.; m. Jeanette Marie Stis, July 13, 1963; children: Gregory Scott, Keith Russell, Kristen Holly. BA, Washington U., 1963. Copywriter Adult Edn. Council of Greater St. Louis, St. Louis, 1962, D'Arcy Advt. Co., St. Louis, 1963-67; from v.p. creative dir. to sr. v.p. exec. creative dir. D'Arcy MacManus & Masius, St. Louis, 1968-80; pres. Adcom. div. Quaker Oats Co., Chgo., 1980-85; pres., chief ops. officer Backer & Spielvogel Chgo., Inc., Chgo., 1985-87; chmn., CEO, chief creative officer Bayer Bess Vanderwarker Advt., Chgo., 1987-96; exec. v.p. devel. True North Comm., Chgo., 1996—. Chmn. Vols. Am., Ill. Mem. Am. Assn. Advt. Agys. (gov.-at-large 1988-95, sec.-treas. bd. dirs. 1991-92, bd. dirs. 1993-95, vice chair Ill. bd. govs.), Chgo. Advt. Fedn. (pres. 1990-93), Am. Advt. Fedn. (Hall of Fame judge 1994-95), Univ. Club, Met. Club, Phi Beta Kappa, Omicron Delta Kappa. Republican. Avocations: music, writing, travel, tennis, certified scuba diver. Home: 1010 E Illinois Rd Lake Forest IL 60045-2410 Office: True North Comms 101 E Erie St Chicago IL 60611-2812

BAYER, GREGORY D., historian, researcher; b. June 3, 1954. BA, St. John's Coll., 1978; PhD, U. Tex., 1995. Vis. fellow Inst. for Advanced Study, Princeton, N.J., 1998—.

BAYER, ROBERT EDWARD, retired defense department official, consultant; b. Cleve., Oct. 26, 1941; s. Charles and Pauline (Kamuf) B.; m. Mary Ellen Horrigan, Dec. 27, 1965 (div. 1981); m. Rozanne Deane Oliver, Jan. 29, 1983; children: Sylvia M., Laura A., Anne M., John C. BS in Social Sci. magna cum laude, John Carroll U., 1962; postgrad., Loyola U., 1962-63. Commd. 2nd lt. USAF, 1963, advanced through grades to lt. col., 1979, ret., 1983; mem. profl. staff Office of Sen. Sam Nunn U.S. Senate, Washington, 1983-86; mem. profl. staff Senate Com. on Armed Svcs., Washington, 1986-93; dep. asst. sec. of def. installations U.S. Dept. Def., Washington, 1993-97, ret., 1997. Pastor, spiritual dir. The Seeker Ch., Washington, 1989-93; co-chair Bridg Builders Fund. Nat. Def. fellow Loyola U., 1962-63. Mem. Parents, Families, Friends Lesbians Gays. Avocations: bicycling, swimming, travel. E-mail: roliver@erols.com.

BAYES, RONALD HOMER, English language educator, author; b. Freewater, Oreg., July 19, 1932; s. Floyd Edgar and Mildred Florence (Cochran) B. BS, East Oreg. State Coll., 1955, MS, 1956; postgrad., U. Pa., 1959-60; DDM, U. Delle Arti, Termi, Italy, 1982. Asst. prof. English Ea. Oreg. State Coll., LaGrande, 1955-56, assoc. prof. English, 1960-68; lectr. English U. Md., College Park, 1958-59, 66-67; prof. St. Andrews Presbyn. Coll., Laurinburg, N.C., 1968—; founder, exec. bd. St. Andrews Rev. & Press, Laurinburg, 1970-95; mem. N.C. State Arts Coun., Raleigh, 1987-89; master poet Atlantic Ctr. for Arts, New Smyrna Beach, Fla., 1988; cons. Nat. Coun. for Arts, Washington, 1969-71. Author: (poetry) Dust & Desire, 1961, Cages & Journeys, 1964, Child Outside My Window, 1965, History of the Turtle, 1970, The Casketmaker, 1972, Porpoise, 1974, Tokyo Annex, 1977, King of August, 1979, Fram, 1979, Beast in View, 1985, Guises, 1992; (fiction) Sister City, 1971. Chmn. Rep. Ctrl. Com., Union County, Oreg., 1967-68, Scotland County, N.C., 1980-81; bd. dirs. Scotland County Humane Soc., Laurinburg, 1993—. With U.S. Army, 1956-58. Woodrow Wilson Nat. fellow, 1959-60; named one of Outstanding Young Men of Am., 1960; recipient Outstanding Alumni award Ea. Oreg. State Coll., 1973; Roanoke-Chowan prize for poetry, 1973, N.C. Writers' Conf. award, 1987, master poet Atlana Ctr. for the Arts, 1988, N.C. arts grantee, 1988, N.C. award for Literature, 1989, cert. honor Poetry Coun. N.C., 1994; Disting. Prof. Creative Writing Chair named in his honor, 1999. Mem. Danforth Found. (assoc.), Internat. House Japan, Japan Soc., N.C. Poetry Soc. (life), Oregon Poetry Soc. (life), Mason. Republican. Episcopalian. Avocations: gardening, reading, jogging, travel. Home: PO Box 206 Laurinburg NC 28353-0206

BAYH, EVAN, senator, former governor; b. Terre Haute, Ind., Dec. 26, 1955; s. Birch Evans Jr. and Marvella (Hern) B.; married. BS in Bus. Econs., Ind. U., 1978; JD, U. Va., 1981. Atty. Bingham, Summers, Welsh & Spilman; sec. of state State of Ind., Indpls., 1987-89, gov., 1989-96; ptnr. Baker & Daniel Assocs., Indpls., 1997; U.S. senator from Ind., 1999—; chmn. State Recount Commn. & Corp. Law com.; mem. Nat. Edn. Goals Panel & Nat. Assessment Edn. Panel; chmn. Edn. Commn. States; vice chmn. Nat. Govs. Assn. Task Force Workforce Devel. Democrat. Address: US Senate 717 Hart Office Bldg Washington DC 20510 also: Ste 234 575 N Pennsylvania Ave Indianapolis IN 46204*

BAYLEN, JOSEPH O., retired history educator; b. Chgo., Feb. 12, 1920; s. Leo and Mary (Lakin) B.; m. Margaret Pringle, June 16, 1979; 1 son, James Leo; 1 stepdaughter, Julia. AA, Wright Jr. Coll., 1939; BE, No. Ill. U., 1941; MA, Emory U., 1947; PhD, U. N.Mex., 1949. Instr. history U. N.Mex., 1948-49; asst. prof. history N.Mex. Highlands U., Las Vegas, 1950-52; assoc. prof. N.Mex. Highlands U., 1952-54; prof. history, chmn. div. social sci. Delta State Tchrs. Coll., 1954-57; prof. history Miss. State U., 1957-61; prof. history U. Miss., 1961-66, chmn., 1963-66; chmn. dept. history Ga. State U., 1966-78, Regents' prof., 1969-83, emeritus Regents' prof. history, 1983—; lectr. in history Ctr. for Continuing Edn., U. Sussex, 1985-89; vis. asst. prof. U. Md. Overseas Program, Europe, 1952-53; vis. assoc. prof. Agnes Scott Coll., 1953; vis. prof. summers Emory U., 1952, U. Ala., 1960, Georgetown U., 1964, 65, Tulane U., 1966, 68, U. York, 1979; Fulbright-Hays lectr., U.K., 1961-62, 72-73; mem. Miss. Hist. Commn., 1954-57, 63-66; vice chmn. So. Humanities Conf., 1964-65, chmn., 1965-66; mem. Nat. Fulbright Adv. Screening Com., 1962-64, chmn., 1964-65; cons. NEH, 1969-83, BBC-TV, 1988—; mem. Fed. Govt. Regional Archives Com., 1971-74; chmn. adv. com. on history Univ. System of Ga., 1970-72, 76-78, British Libr., Consultative Group on Newspapers, 1990—; lectr. U. Sussex, City Univ., London. Author: monographs Mme. Juliette Adam, Gambetta, and the Idea of a Franco-Russian Alliance, 1960, Lord Kitchener and the Viceroyalty of India, 1910, 1965, Soldier-Surgeon; The Crimean War Letters of Dr. D.A. Reid, 1955-1856, 1968, W.T. Stead and the Russian Revolution of 1905, 1969; (with O.S. Pidhainy) East-European and Russian Studies in the American South, 1972; contbr.: (with others) Dictionary of Labour Biography, 1977, Biographical Dictionary of Internationalists, 1983, British Literary Magazines, 1984, Biographical Dictionary of Peace Leaders, 1985, Victorian Britain: An Encyclopedia, 1988, Papers for the Millions: The New Journalism in Britain..., 1988, Biographical Dictionary of American Journalism, 1989, Ency. of the British Press, 1992, Dictionary of Literary

Biography (British Publishing Houses 1881-1965), 1992; co-editor: (with N.J. Gossman) Biographical Dictionary of Modern British Radicals, 1770-1914, 3 vols., 1979-88, The 1890's An Encyclopedia of British Literature, Art and Culture, 1983, Twentieth Century Britain: An Encyclopedia, 1995, Shaping the Collective Memory, Government and International Historians through Two World Wars, 1996, A Journalism Reader, 1997; bd. editor: Encyclopedia of 1848 Revolutions; So. Humanities Rev.; mem. editl. adv. bd. Ency. of the World Press; contbr. over 150 articles to profl. jours., over 160 book revs. Capt. AUS, 1941-45. Guggenheim fellow, 1958-59, rsch. fellow Inst. Advanced Studies, Princeton U., 1966; summer fellowships and awards include So. Fellowship Found., 1955, Am. Philos. Soc., 1956, 65, Am. Coun. Learned Socs., 1961-62; English-Speaking Union, 1978; recipient Most Disting. Alumni award No. Ill. U., 1976, Disting. Prof. award Ga. State U., 1979, Disting. Prof. award Ga. State U. chpt. Omicron Delta Kappa, 1980, Hugh McCall award for disting. achievement in hist. studies, 1982. Fellow Royal Hist. Soc.; mem. Am. Hist. Assn. (exec. coun. 1972-75), So. Hist. Assn. (chmn. European history sect. 1972-73, exec. coun. 1983-86), N.Am. Conf. Brit. Studies (chmn. so. conf. 1977-79), European Movement, Travellers Club, London Press Club (bd. dirs.), Phi Kappa Phi, Omicron Delta Kappa, Phi Alpha Theta, Pi Gamma Mu, Kappa Delta Pi, Phi Kappa Tau. Home: 45 Saffrons Ct, Compton Place Rd, Eastbourne BN21 1DY, England

BAYLES, JENNIFER LUCENE, museum education curator; b. Tokyo, May 26, 1953; d. Lewis Allen Bayles and Rosemary (Buehler) Fraser; m. Robert Steinfeld, July 4, 1992; children: Noah Isaac, Ezra Milton. BA in Art History with honors, Ind. U., Bloomington, 1976; MA in Art History, cert. in mus. practice, U. Mich., 1984. Curatorial apprentice Indpls. Mus. Art, 1976; mus. apprentice Portland (Oreg.) Art Mus., 1976-78, asst. curator edn., 1978-81; asst. curator photographic collection dept. art history U. Mich., Ann Arbor, 1981-83, rsch. and editorial asst. Mus. Art, 1982-83; lectr. dept. mus. edn. Art Inst. Chgo., 1983-84; asst. curator edn. adult programs Albright-Knox Art Gallery, Buffalo, N.Y., 1984-85, curator edn., 1985—. Horace H. Rackman Grad. scholar, 1981-83; Acad. scholar U. Mich., 1982. Mem. Am. Assn. Mus. (regional rep. edn. com. 1979-81). Office: Albright-Knox Art Gallery 1285 Elmwood Ave Buffalo NY 14222-1096

BAYLESS, BETSEY, state official; b. Phoenix. BA in Latin Am. Studies and Spanish, U. Ariz., 1966; MPA, Ariz. State U., 1974. V.p. pub. fin. Peacock, Hislop, Staley & Given, Inc., Phoenix, Ariz.; asst. dir. Ariz. Bd. Regents; acting dir. dept. revenue State of Ariz., dir. dept. adminstrn., sec. of state, 1997—; bd. suprs. Maricopa County, 1989-97, chmn. bd., 1992, 94, vice chair, 1997. Nat. bd. advisors U. Ariz. Coll. Bus. & Pub. Adminstrn.; adv. bd. Ariz. State U. West; bd. dirs. Xavier Coll. Preparatory Found., Ariz. Ctr. for the Book; commr. Gov.'s Commn. Violence Against Women; mem. Ariz. Town Hall, Charter 100, Valley Leadership Class VI, Ariz. Rep. Caucus, Ariz. Women's Forum. Named to Hall of Fame, Ariz. State U. Coll. Pub. Programs; recipient Disting. Citizen award U. Ariz. Alumni Assn., Woman of Yr. award Capitol chpt. Bus. and Profl. Women, Disting. Achievement award NEH Fellowship, Achievement award Nat. Assn. Counties, 1993, Citizen award Bur. Reclamation, 1993, Woman of Achievement award Xavier Coll. Preparatory, 1995. Mem. Phi Beta Kappa (Freeman medal 1966). Office: State Capitol 1700 W Washington St 7th fl Phoenix AZ 85007

BAYLESS, RAYMOND GORDON, writer, artist, parapsychologist; b. Oakland, Calif., 1920. Author: The Enigma of the Poltergeist, 1967, Animal Ghosts, 1970, The Other Side of Death, 1971, Experiences of a Psychical Researcher, 1972, Apparitions and Survival of Death, 1973, Voices from Beyond?, 1976; co-author: Phone Calls from the Dead, 1979, The Case of Life After Death, 1981; contbr. articles to profl. jours., publs.; artist represented in permanent collections, including U.S. Dept. Air Force, U.S. Dept. Navy, U.S. Dept. State, Art in Embassies Program, Nat. Air and Space Mus., Internat. Aerospace Hall of Fame, San Diego, Kern Oil and Refining Co., Long Beach, Calif., Bank of Am., San Francisco, Weingart Found., L.A., Permanent Civil War Exhibit, Naval Hist. Ctr., D.C.; various paintings displayed in The Pentagon, Washington, 1974-76, 75-88, 91-98; exhibited in Air Force Art Collection, Pentagon, Washington, Washington Navy Mus., Vandenberg Air Force Base, Calif., U.S. Navy Art Collection, Naval Hist. Ctr., Washington Navy Yard; illustrator 6 book jackets Arkham House Pubs. Inc. Mem. Parapsychol. Assn., Brentwood (Calif.) Area C. of C. Address: 11348 Cashmere St Los Angeles CA 90049-3426

BAYLESS, THEODORE M(ORRIS), gastroenterologist, educator, researcher; b. Atlantic City, Apr. 14, 1931; s. David N. and Fan (Halpern) B.; m. Janet M. Nides, June 22, 1954; children: Jeffrey, Andrew, Neal. B.S., Bucknell U., 1953; M.D., Chgo. Med. Sch., 1957. Intern Cornell div. Bellevue Hosp., also Meml. Cancer Ctr., N.Y.C., 1957-58, 58-60; fellow gastroenterology Johns Hopkins U., Balt., 1960-62, prof., 1981—; physician Johns Hopkins Hosp., Balt., 1964—; clin. dir. Meyerhoff Digestive Disease-Inflammatory Bowel Disease Ctr. Johns Hopkins U.; Editor: Current Therapy-Gastroenterology, 1994, Current Management of Inflammatory Bowel Disease, 1989; co-editor: Lactose Digestion, 1980. Capt. USAR, 1962-64. Recipient Corson Nutrition medal Franklin Inst., Phila., 1987. Fellow ACP; mem. Am. Soc. Clin. Investigation, Am. Gastroenterology Assn. (dir. immunology, microbiology and inflammatory bowel disease 1991-96, Disting. Educator award 1987), Am. Coll. Phys. (Md. chpt. Clin. Investigation award, 1996, Janssen Disting. Clin. award, 1997), Alpha Omega Alpha. Jewish. Home: 2206 South Rd Baltimore MD 21209-4428 Office: Johns Hopkins Hosp 600 N Wolfe St Baltimore MD 21287-0005

BAYLEY, CHRISTOPHER T., public affairs consultant; b. Seattle, May 25, 1938; s. Emery P. and Dorothy (Dunn) B.; m. Cynthia Conroy, May 31, 1972; children—Elizabeth, Kathryn. AB magna cum laude, Harvard U., 1960, JD, 1966. Bar: Wash. 1967. Dep. atty. gen., chief consumer protection and antitrust div. Atty. Gens. Office, Seattle, 1969-70; pros. atty. King County, Seattle, 1971-79; of counsel Perkins Coie, Seattle, 1979-80, ptnr., 1980-82; sr. v.p. law Burlington Resources (formerly Burlington Northern Inc.), Seattle, 1983-86, corp. affairs, 1986-93; pres., CEO Glacier Park Co., Seattle, 1985-93; chmn. New Pacific Partners, Seattle, 1993—; bd. dirs. ADIC Corp., The Commerce Bank, Ballot Corp. Past. chmn. Seattle Found.; past mem. bd. overseers Harvard Coll.; trustee Discovery Inst., Scenic Am., E.B. Dunn Hist. Garden Trust; past mem. bd. govs. The Nature Conservancy. Served with USN, 1960-63, capt. Res. ret., 1985. Mem. Seattle Tennis Club. Home: 3702 E Prospect St Seattle WA 98112-4442 Office: 1411 4th Ave Ste 2300 Seattle WA 98101-2249

BAYLIS, ROBERT MONTAGUE, investment banker; b. N.Y.C., Aug. 20, 1938; s. Chester, Jr. and Dorothy Montague (Smith) B.; m. Lois Margaret Wells, Apr. 6, 1963; children: Robert Wells, David Martin, John Chester. A.B., Princeton U., 1960; M.B.A., Harvard U., 1962. CFA. Chartered fin. analyst CS First Boston, N.Y.C., 1963-96, vice chmn., 1992-96; chmn. CS First Boston Pacific, Hong Kong, 1993-94; dir. Covance, Inc., Host Marriott Corp., N.Y. Life Ins. Co., Gildan Activewear. Served with M.C. U.S. Army, 1962-63. Mem. N.Y. Soc. Security Analysts, Nat. Assn. Bus. Economists, Weeburn Country Club, Univ. Club, Nassau Club, Cap and Gown Club. Home: 116 Delafield Island Rd Darien CT 06820-6017 Office: 72 Cummings Point Rd Stamford CT 06902-7919

BAYLIS, WILLIAM THOMAS, systems engineering specialist; b. Bay Shore, N.Y., Oct. 21, 1952; s. William Wood and Viola Elaine (Burtis) B.; m. Milagros Marfisi, July 3, 1988; children: Christopher Thomas, Justin William Andrew. BSBA, U. Tenn., 1981; MBA in Mgmt., Dowling Coll., Oakdale, N.Y., 1984; PhD in Mgmt., Columbia Pacific U., San Raefel, Calif., 1986; postgrad., N.Y. Inst. Tech., 1987—. Asst. mgr. AIL div. Eaton Corp., Deer Park, N.Y., 1984-86, group leader, 1986-88; program mgr. Gen. Instrument Corp., Hicksville, N.Y., 1988-89, mgr. logistics engring., 1988-89; sr. logistics engr., logistics support analysis engring. lead McDonnell Douglas Space Systems Co., Kennedy Space Center, Fla., 1989-94; sys. engr. Avionics Rsch. Corp., Orlando, Fla., 1994—, systems engr., 1994—; engring. specialist, ILS, systems engr. Northrop Grumman, Melbourne, Fla., 1996—, lead assessor ISO 9001, 1996; Level II Integrated Database adminstr., security coord. for Space Sta. Freedom Program; pres. WTB Enterprises, Melbourne, Fla., 1990—; cons. in logistics and systems engring., systems devel. computer-based tng.; instr. space logistics tech. Brevard C.C. (adv. com. logistics systems tech. program), tchr. various logistics engring. courses; creator on-line college level courses; panel spkr. on space sta. group ops./logistics integration, Cocoa Beach, Fla., 1991, logistics support analysis spkr. Internat. Conf. and Tech. Exposition, Indpls., 1992; chmn. tech. adv. bd. SOLE Logistics Engring., 1992-94; chmn. tech. adv. bd. BCC's Multimedia Devel., 1994; spkr. in field. Author, editor: Starting a Retail Business, 1988, Trainer's Guide to Task Analysis, 1989, Logistics Engineer's Desk Reference, 1991, 2d edit., 92, LSA/LSAR Manual, 1992-94, Excel Manual, 1992-94, Word/Windows Manual, 1992-94; author: Training Requirements for Defense Contracts: A Practitioner's Desk Reference, 1989, Developing, Designing and Delivering Productive and Efficient Training, 1992; editor Training Issues column in Soletter, 1994; developer software course Lotus 123, 1989. With USN, 1974-78. Recipient Chmn. award SOLE, 1992, Guest Speaker award, 1992, Paper award, 1997, Space Congress Achievement award, 1992, Speaker award Fla. Conf. and Workshop, 1994, Cert. of Appreciation Air Force Jour. of Logistics, 1995, Brevard C.C. Outstanding Adjunct of Yr. award, 1994-95; named Coord. of Yr. Total Quality, 1994-99, Total Quality Facilitator of Yr., 1995. Mem. AIAA, Am. Mgmt. Assn., Soc. Logistics Engrs. (Splty. award in logistics support analysis 1991, 92, 93, Splty. award Logistics & Supportability Engring. Edn. 1996, Sole Paper award Logistics Edn. 1996, 97, Guest Spkr. award 1997), Internat. Soc. Philos. Enquiry, Assn. MBA Execs., Mensa, Intertel, Am. Legion, Phi Eta Sigma. Avocations: developing software, writing, photography, woodworking, reading. Home: 1988 Trevino Cir Melbourne FL 32935-4459 Office: Northip Grumman Corp Melbourne FL 32935

BAYLISS, SISTER MARY ROSINA, principal. Prin. Mt. De Sales Acad., Macon, Ga., 1996, pres., 1996—. Recipient Blue Ribbon Sch. award, 1990-91. Office: Mount De Sales Acad 851 Orange St Macon GA 31201-2164*

BAYLOR, DENIS ARISTIDE, neurobiology educator; b. Oskaloosa, Iowa, Jan. 30, 1940; s. Hugh Murray and Elisabeth Anne (Barbou) B.; m. Eileen Margaret Steele, Aug. 12, 1983; children: Denis Murray, Michael Randel; 1 stepchild, Michele Gonelli. BA in Chemistry magna cum laude, Knox Coll., 1961, DS (hon.), 1989; MD cum laude, Yale U., 1965. Post-doctoral fellow Yale Med. Sch., New Haven, Conn., 1965-68; staff assoc. Nat. Inst. Neurological Diseases and Stroke, Bethesda, 1968-70; spl. fellow USPSH Physiological Lab. Cambridge U., Eng., 1970-72; assoc. prof. physiology U. Colo. Med. Sch., Denver, 1972-74; assoc. prof. physiology Stanford U., Calif., 1974-75, assoc. prof. neurobiology, 1975-78, prof. neurobiology, 1978—, chmn. dept. neurobiology, 1992-95; First Annual W.S. Stiles lecturer U. Coll., London, England, 1989; Jonathan Magnes lecturer Hebrew U., Jerusalem, Israel, 1990; Woolsey lecturer U. Wis., 1992; E. Hille lectr. U. Washington, 1995; mem. NIH Visual Scis. Study Sect., 1984-88, chmn., 1986-88; vis. com. med. scis. Harvard U., 1987-93; chmn. Summer conf. on Vision FASEB, 1989; Wellcome vis. prof. U. Miami, 1995; mem. sci. adv. com. Alcon Rsch. Inst., 1994—; mem. HHMI Sci. adv. bd. 1997—, Med. adv. bd. 1998—; mem. sci. adv. bd. Found. Fighting Blindness, 1998—; trustee The Grass Found., 1995—. Mem. editorial bd. Jour. Physiology, 1977-84, Neuron, 1988-93, Jour. Neurophysiology, 1989—, Visual Neurosci., 1990-93, Jour. Neurosci., 1991—; contbr. articles to profl. jours. Recipient Sinsheimer Found. award, 1975, Mathilde Solowey award, 1978, Kayser Internat. award Retina Rsch. Found., 1988, Golden Brain award Minerva Found., 1988, Merit award Nat. Eye Inst., 1990, Alcon Rsch. Inst. award, 1991; Rank Optoelectronics prize Rank Orgn., Eng., 1980; Proctor medal Assn. Rsch. Vision & Ophthalmology, 1986, Von Sallman prize in eye rsch., 1998. Fellow Am. Acad. Arts and Scis.; mem. NAS, Phi Beta Kappa, Alpha Omega Alpha. Avocations: jogging, woodworking. Office: Stanford U Sch Med Neurobiology/Fairchild D237 299 Campus Dr Stanford CA 94305-5125

BAYLOR, DON EDWARD, professional baseball manager; b. Austin, Tex., June 28, 1949; s. George Edward and Lillian Joyce B.; m. Rebecca Giles, Dec. 12, 1987; 1 child by previous marriage, Don Edward. Student, Miami-Dade Jr. Coll., Miami, Fla., Blinn Jr. Coll., Brenham, Tex. With Balt. Orioles, 1970-76, Oakland Athletics, 1976, 88, California Angels, 1976-82, N.Y. Yankees, 1983-86, Boston Red Sox, 1986-87, Minnesota Twins, 1987; mem. World Series Championship Team, 1987; mgr. Colorado Rockies, Denver, CO, 1992-97—; hitting/batting coach Atlanta Braves, 1997—; Set new career record for hit by pitches; hit safely in 12 consecutive Am. League Championship Series games. Author: (with Claire Smith) Don Baylor, Nothing But the Truth: A Baseball Life, 1989. Chmn. nat. sports Cystic Fibrosis Found. Recipient Designated Hitter of Yr. award, 1985, 86, Roberto Clemente award, 1985; named Am. League's Most Valuable Player, 1979, Sporting News Player of Yr., 1979; player All-Star Game, 1979; named Nat. League Mgr. of Yr. Sporting News, 1995, Baseball Writers Assn. Am., 1995. Holder Am. League playoff record most RBI (10), 1982, Am. League single season record most times hit by pitch (35), 1986. Office: Atlanta Braves PO Box 4064 Atlanta GA 30302 Office: Major League Baseball Players Assn Players Assn 805 3d Ave New York NY 10022-7513*

BAYLOR, ELGIN GAY, professional basketball team executive; b. Washington, Sept. 16, 1934; m. Elaine; 1 dau., Krystle. Ed., Coll. Idaho, Seattle U. Profl. basketball player Los Angeles (formerly Minneapolis) Lakers, 1958-72; asst. coach New Orleans Jazz, NBA, 1974-76, coach, 1976-79; exec. v.p., gen. mgr. Los Angeles Clippers, 1986—, v.p. basketaballops. Most Valuable Player, NCAA Tournament, 1958; mem. NBA All-Star Team, 1959-65, 67-70; Rookie of the Yr., NBA, 1959; co-Most Valuable Player, NBA All-Star Game, 1959; named to NBA 35th Anniversary All-Time Team, 1980. Office: LA Clippers 3939 S Figueroa St Los Angeles CA 90037-1200*

BAYLOR, HARRY BROOKS, microbiologist; b. Hewitt, Minn., Mar. 30, 1914; s. George Brooks and Anna Elmira (Larsen) N.; m. Ellen Florence Haanela, Sept. 8, 1940; children—Lynn Brooks, Roy Allen, Gail Ann. B.S., U. Minn., 1938; Ph.D., Cornell U., 1943. Mem. tech. dept. Sheffield Farms Dairy, Inc., N.Y.C., 1946-47; mem. faculty dept. microbiology Cornell U., Ithaca, N.Y., 1947—; prof. emeritus Cornell U., 1977—; cons. Pasco Labs., Inc., Wheat Ridge, Colo., 1978-86; mem. grant review bd. USPHS, 1967-70; OAS lectr., Brazil, 1972, 73; teaching fellow Fed. U. of Rio de Janeiro, 1978. Contbr. articles to profl. jours. Served with USNR, 1943-46. Fulbright-Hayes fellow, 1966-67. Mem. Am. Soc. Microbiology, Am. Acad. Microbiology. Home: 61 Whitetail Dr Ithaca NY 14850-9458*

BAYLY, GEORGE V., manufacturing executive. CEO Ivex Packaging, Lincolnshire, Ill. Office: Ivex Packaging 100 Tri State Dr Lincolnshire IL 60069-4403*

BAYLY, JOHN HENRY, JR., judge; b. Washington, Jan. 26, 1944; s. John Henry and Salome Carole (Winters) B.; m. Barbara Jean Downey, Feb. 16, 1974 (dec. Jan. 1977); 1 child, Anne Louise; m. Katherine Bridget Kenny, Dec. 1, 1979; children: Johanna, Georgia. AB, Fordham U., 1966; JD, Harvard U., 1969. Bar: U.S. Dist. Ct. D.C. 1969, U.S. Ct. Appeals (D.C. cir.) 1969, D.C. 1971, U.S. Supreme Ct. 1974. Atty., advisor FCC, Washington, 1969-71; asst. atty. Office of U.S. Atty., Washington, 1971-75, 78-85; dep. minority counsel Senate Select Com. on Intelligence, Washington, 1975-76; acting asst. gen. counsel Corp. for Pub. Broadcasting, Washington, 1976-78; gen. counsel Legal Services Corp., Washington, 1985-87, pres., 1987-88; of counsel Stein, Mitchell & Mezines, Washington, 1988-90; judge D.C. Superior Ct., 1990—. Mem. D.C. Bar Assn., John Carroll Soc., Counsellors, Bryant Inn of Ct., Lawyers Club Washington, Phi Beta Kappa. Republican. Roman Catholic. Home: 3512 Runnymede Pl NW Washington DC 20015-2420 Office: DC Superior Ct 500 Indiana Ave NW Ste 1 Washington DC 20001-2191

BAYM, GORDON ALAN, physicist, educator; b. N.Y.C., July 1, 1935; s. Louis and Lillian B.; children—Nancy, Geoffrey, Michael, Carol. A.B., Cornell U., 1956; A.M., Harvard U., 1957, Ph.D., 1960. Fellow Universitetets Institut for Teoretisk Fysik, Copenhagen, Denmark, 1960-62; lectr. U. Calif., Berkeley, 1962-63; prof. physics U. Ill., Urbana, 1963—; vis. prof. U. Tokyo and U. Kyoto, 1968, Nordita, Copenhagen, 1970, 76, Niels Bohr Inst., Copenhagen, 1976, U. Nagoya, 1979; vis. scientist Academia Sinica, China, 1979; mem. adv. bd. Inst. Theoretical Physics, Santa Barbara, Calif., 1978-83; mem. subcom. theoretical physics, physics adv. com. NSF, 1980-81, mem. phys. adv. com., 1982-85; mem. nuclear sci. adv. com. Dept. of Energy/NSF, 1982-86, subcom. on theoretical physics; mem. adv. com. physics Los Alamos Nat. Lab., 1988; mem. nat. adv. com. Inst. Nuclear Theory. Author: Lectures on Quantum Mechanics, 1969, Neutron Stars, 1970, Neutron Stars and the Properties of Matter at High Density, 1977, (with L.P. Kadanoff) Quantum Statistical Mechanics, 1962, (with C.J. Pethick) Landau Fermi Liquid Theory: Concepts and Applications, 1991; assoc. editor Nuclear Physics; mem. editorial bd. Procs. Nat. Acad. Scis., 1986-92. Trustee Assoc. U. Inc., 1986-90. Recipient Alexander von Humboldt Found. Sr. U.S. Scientist award, 1983; fellow Am. Acad. Arts and Scis.; Alfred P. Sloan Found. research fellow, 1965-68; NSF postdoctoral fellow, 1960-62. Fellow AAAS, Am. Phys.Soc. (exec. com. div. history of physics 1986-88, 96-97, chair forum history of physics 1994-95, chair-elect 1995-96; mem. NAS (chair physics sect. 1995-98), Am. Astron. Soc., Internat. Astron. Union.

BAYM, NINA, English educator; b. Princeton, N.J., June 14, 1936; d. Leo and Frances (Levinson) Zippin; m. Gordon Baym, June 1, 1958; children—Nancy, Geoffrey; m. Jack Stillinger, May 21, 1971. B.A., Cornell U., 1957; M.A., Harvard U., 1958, Ph.D., 1963. Asst. U. Calif.-Berkeley, 1962-63; instr. U. Ill., Urbana, 1963-67, asst. prof. English, 1967-69, assoc. prof., 1969-72, prof., 1972—; Jubilee prof. liberal arts and scis. U. Ill., 1989—; dir. Sch. Humanities U. Ill., Urbana, 1976-87, sr. Univ. scholar, 1985; assoc. Ctr. Advanced Study U. Ill., 1989-90, permanent prof. Ctr. Advanced Study, 1997—, Swanlund Endowed chair, 1997—. Author: The Shape of Hawthorne's Career, 1976, Woman's Fiction: A Guide to Novels By and About Women in America, 1978, 2d rev. edit., 1993, Novels, Readers and Reviewers: Responses to Fiction in Antebellum America, 1984, The Scarlet Letter: A Reading, 1986, Feminism and American Literary History, 1992, American Women Writers and the Work of History, 1790-1860, 1995; gen. editor: Norton Anthology of American Literature; sr. editor Am. Nat. Biography; also author essays, edits., revs.; mem. editl. bd. Am. Quar., New Eng. Quar., Legacy, A Jour. of 19th Century Am. Women Writers, Jour. Aesthetic Edn. Am. Lit., Tulsa Studies in Women's Lit., Am. Studies, Studies Am. Fiction, Am. Periodicals, Hemingway Rev., Resources for Am. Lit. Study, Am. Lit. History, Cambridge U.P. Studies in Am. Lit. and Culture; mem. editl. adv. bd. PMLA. Guggenheim fellow, 1975-76, AAUW hon. fellow, 1975-76, NEH fellow, 1982-83; recipient Arnold O. Beckman award U. Ill., 1992-93. Mem. MLA (exec. com. 19th century Am. Lit. divsn., chmn. 1984, chmn. Am. Lit. sect. 1984), Am. Studies Assn. (exec. com. 1982-84, nominating com. 1991-93), Am. Lit. Assn., Am. Antiquarian Soc., Mass. Hist. Soc., Nathaniel Hawthorne Soc. (adv. bd.), Mortar Bd., Phi Kappa Phi, Phi Beta Kappa. Office: U Ill Dept English 608 S Wright St Urbana IL 61801-3613

BAYMILLER, LYNDA DOERN, social worker; b. Milw., July 6, 1943; d. Ronald Oliver and Marian Elizabeth (Doern) B. B.A., U. Wis., 1965, MSW, 1969; student U. Hawaii, 1962, Mich. State U., 1965. Peace Corps vol., Chile, 1965-67; social worker Luth. Social Svcs. of Wis. and Upper Mich., Milw., 1969-77, contract social worker, 1978-79; dist. supr. Children's Svc. Soc. Wis., Kenosha, 1977-78; social work supr. Sauk County Dept. Human Svcs., Baraboo, Wis., 1979-90; sales and relief mgr.-trainee, Wal-Mart, 1992-93, cashier, 1993—. Bd. dirs. Zoo Pride, Zool. Soc. Milw. County, 1975-77, Sauk County Mental Health Assn., 1979-84; mem. Harmony chpt. Sweet Adelines, West Allis, Wis., 1970-75, pres. chpt., 1971; pres. bd. dirs. Growing Place Day Care Center, Kenosha, 1977-78; mem. Baraboo (Wis.) Centennial Com., 1982; pres. bd. dirs. Laubach Literary Coun., Baraboo, 1986-88; mem. Sauk County Humane Soc., 1987—, sec., 1988-90. Mem. Nat. Assn. Social Workers, Acad. Cert. Social Workers, AAUW (br. sec. 1982-84), U. Wis. Alumni Assn. (life mem.), Am. Legion Aux., DAR, Nat. Soc. Magna Carta Dames, Eddy Family Assn. (life mem.), Nat. Soc. Ancient and Hon. Arty. Co. of Mass. (life mem.), Wis. Soc. Daus of 1812 (rec. sec. 1994—), Sauk County Hist. Soc., Internat. Crane Found. (patron), Daus. Colonial Wars, Daus. Am. Colonists, Zool. Soc. Milwaukee County (life), Am. Bus. Women's Assn., Friends of Baraboo Zoo, Vilas Park Zool. Soc., Order Eastern Star (grand rep. Miss. in Wis. 1988-90), Order White Shrine of Jerusalem, Ladies Aux. of Fraternal Order Eagles, Cameo Club, Alpha Xi Delta. Author: (with Clara Amelia Hess) Now-Won, A Collection of Feeling (poetry and prose), 1973. Home: 332 4th Ave Baraboo WI 53913-2029

BAYNE, DAVID COWAN, priest, legal scholar, law educator; b. Detroit, Jan. 11, 1918; s. David Cowan and Myrtle (Murray) B. AB, U. Detroit, 1939; LLB, Georgetown U., 1947, LLM, 1948; MA, Loyola U., Chgo., 1946, STL, 1953; SJD (grad. fellow), Yale, 1949; LLD (hon.), Creighton U., 1980. Bar: Fed. and D.C. 1948, Mich. 1960, Mo. 1963. Joined Soc. of Jesus, 1941; ordained priest Roman Catholic Ch., 1952; asst. prof. law U. Detroit, 1954-60; acting dean U. Detroit (Law Sch.), 1955-59, dean, 1959-60; research assoc. Nat. Jesuit Research Orgn., Inst. Social Order, St. Louis, 1960-63; vis. lectr. St. Louis U. Law Sch., 1960-63, prof. law, 1963-67; vis. prof. Mich. Law Sch., 1967, Inst. fur Auslandisches und Internationales Wirtschaftrecht, Frankfurt, 1967; prof. U. Iowa Coll. Law, Iowa City, 1967-88, prof. emeritus, 1988—; vis. prof. U. Koln, Germany, 1970, 74. Author: Conscience, Obligation and the Law, 1966, 2d edit., 1988; The Philosophy of Corporate Control, 1986; editor legal materials; contbr. articles to profl. jours. Research corp. law.

BAYNE, JAMES ELWOOD, oil company executive; b. Detroit, May 6, 1940; s. John David and Alice Angie (Davis) B.; m. Mary Lee Skinner. May 4, 1963; children: James E. Jr., Laura Lee Poe. BA, Yale U., 1962; MBA, Columbia U., 1967. Investment adminstr. Bankers Trust, N.Y.C., 1962-65; fin analyst Standard Oil, N.Y.C., 1967; sr. fin. analyst Esso Internat., N.Y.C., 1967-70; asst. treas. Esso S.A.P.A., Buenos Aires, 1970-71; treas. Intercol, Bogota, Colombia, 1971-74; asst. treas. Esso InterAm., Coral Gables, Fla., 1974-77; asst. gen. mgr. Esso Cen. Am., Coral Gables, Fla., 1977-80; mgr. Mexican Bus. Opportunity, Coral Gables, 1980-81; treas. Exxon Chem. Europe, Brussels, 1981-86; mgr., benefits fin. and investment Exxon, Dallas, 1986—; mem. CIEBA, Washington, 1986—; vice chmn. CIEBA, Washington, 1995-96, exec. com., 1994—, chmn. 1996-98; pension adv. com. N.Y. Stock Exch., 1995-99; bd. dirs. B.O.N.Y. Client Adv. Com.; mem. adv. bd. Wharton Trading Sys., 1993-96; mem. nat. commn. on retirement security CSIS, 1997-99; bd. dirs. S.W. Inst. Personal Fin. Savs. Steering com. Interforum; bd. dirs. Fin. Execs. Inst., 1996-98; pres. secretariat Dallas-Ft. Worth Cursillo Movement, 1992-96; co-chair Episcopal Renewal Ctr.; dir. Dallas-Ft. Worth Episcopal Renewal Ctr.; mem. bd. councillors U. Dallas, mem. bd. advisors; del. First White House Summit on Retirement Savs., 1998. Fellow George H. Gallup Internat. Inst.; mem. Pension 21 Club (N.Y.C.), Yale Club Dallas, Yale Club N.Y., Harbor Club (gov. Seal Harbor, Maine), Order St. John, Incarnation Found. (v.p.), Episcopal Found. Dallas (investment com., trustee Ch. Pension Fund). Episcopalian. Avocations: church work, walking, boating, reading, traveling. Home: 3204 Saint Johns Dr Dallas TX 75205-2919 Office: Exxon 5959 Las Colinas Blvd Irving TX 75039-2298

BAYNE, KATHRYN ANN LOUISE, veterinarian; b. Santa Monica, Calif., Feb. 4, 1959; d. Richard Harry and Loretta Mary Bayne; m. Mark Cofer Haines, May 19, 1990. BS cum laude, Calif. State Poly. U., 1979; MS, Wash. State U., 1982, PhD, 1986, DVM, 1987. Vet. behaviorist NIH, Bethesda, Md., 1987-94; assoc. dir Assn. for the Assessment & Accreditation of Lab. Animal Care, Rockville, Md., 1994—; Diplomate Am. Coll. Lab. Animal Medicine. Inventor in field; author publs. in field. Comdr. USPHS. Recipient Foster award, USPHS commendaton and achievement awards; named Alumnus of Yr. award Westlake Sch. Mem. AVMA, Animal Behavior Soc., Am. Soc. Lab. Animal Practitioners, Assn. Primate Vets. (past pres.), D.C. Vet. Med. Assn. (past pres.), Scientists Ctr. for Animal Welfare (past v.p. bd. dirs.). Avocations: gardening, birdwatching. Office: AAALAC International 11300 Rockville Pike Ste 1211 Rockville MD 20852-3040

BAYNES, THOMAS EDWARD, JR., judge, lawyer, educator; b. N.Y.C., Mar. 19, 1940; s. Thomas Edward and Ann Jane (Burke) B.; m. Maija Eva Kokko, Dec. 30, 1963; children: Cynthia Lynn, Barbara Ann. BBA, U. Ga., 1962; JD, Emory U., 1967, LLM, 1972; LLM, Yale U., 1973. Bar: Ga. 1968, U.S. Supreme Ct. 1971, Ct. of Mil. Appeals 1978, Fla. 1981. Dir. Legal Assistance to Inmates Program, Emory U., 1968-69; asst. dean, asst. prof. bus. law Ga. State U., 1969-72; acting regional dir. Nat. Ctr. for State Cts., Atlanta, 1973-74; prof. law and public adminstrn. Nova U. Law Ctr., Ft. Lauderdale, Fla., 1974-76, 77-81; jud. fellow U.S. Supreme Ct., 1976-77; speedy trial reporter U.S. Dist. Ct., So. Dist. Fla., 1977-81; ptnr. Peterson, Myers, Craig, Crews, Brandon & Mann, Lake Wales, Fla., 1981-87; U.S.

Bankruptcy Judge mid. dist. Fla., 1987—; State chmn., Ga., Nat. Council on Crime and Delinquency, 1971-72; legal counsel Reorgn. Study Commn. Ga., 1971-72. Author: (with W. Scott) Legal Aspects of Laboratory Medicine in Quality Assurance in Laboratory Management, 1978, Eminent Domain in Florida, 1979, Mortgage Law in Florida, 1982, (with others) Supreme Court Justices, Illustrated Biographies, 1993; supplement editor Fla. Real Estate Law and Procedure, 1976; contbg. editor Norton Bankruptcy Law and Practice, 1995. Bd. dirs. F. Lee Moffitt Cancer Ctr., Tampa, Fla., 1989-94, 97—. Comdr. JAGC, USNR, 1960-80, ret. Sterling fellow Yale U. Law Sch., 1972-73; Harry J. Loman Found. rsch. fellow, 1979. Mem. Ga. Bar Assn., Fla. Bar Assn., Am. Law Inst., Supreme Ct. Hist. Soc., Am. Arbitration Assn., Nat. Adv. Com. for Bankruptcy, Ferguson-White Inn (pres. 1992-93, master), Omicron Delta Kappa. Office: US Bankruptcy Ct 801 N Florida Ave Tampa FL 33602-3849

BAYNTON, DOUGLAS CAMERON, historian; b. Red Bank, N.J., Apr. 26, 1953; s. Robert August Baynton and Margaret Anna Post; m. Kirilka Stavreva, June 1, 1997. BS, We. Oreg. U., 1986; PhD, U. Iowa, 1993. Asst. prof. U. Iowa, Iowa City, 1993—. Author: Forbidden Signs: American Culture and the Campaign Against Sign Language, 1996. Irving K. Zola Emerging Scholar award Soc. Disability Studies, 1996; Postdoctoral fellow Smithsonian Instn., 1997-98. E-mail: douglas-baynton@uiowa.edu. Office: U Iowa Dept History 280 SH Iowa City IA 52240

BAYORGEON, JAMES THOMAS, judge; b. Kaukauna, Wis., May 7, 1935; s. Joseph F. and Lorraine (DeBrue) B.; m. Jeanne Marie Collins, Aug. 27, 1983. JD, Marquette U., 1958. Bar: U.S. Dist. Ct. (ea. dist.) Wis. 1958, U.S. Ct. Mil. Appeals, 1958, U.S. Ct. Appeals (7th cir.) 1961. Pvt. practice Appleton, Wis., 1962-83; judge Wis. Cir. Ct., Appleton, 1983—. With U.S. Army, 1958-61. Mem. ABA, Assn. Trial Lawyers Am., Outagamie County Bar Assn. Roman Catholic. Office: Outagamie County Br One Wis Cir Ct 410 S Walnut St Appleton WI 54911-5920

BAYS, JOHN THEOPHANIS, consulting engineer; b. Bklyn., July 17, 1947; s. Theophanis A. and Mildred Bays; BS, N.Y. Inst. Tech., 1972; BArch, CCNY, 1974; cert. in solar design, Ohio State U., 1975; m. Mindy Giardina, July 8, 1973; 1 dau., Nina. Cert. energy mgr., energy auditor, asbestos investigator, N.Y. Project mgr., head system designer Wormser Sci. Corp., Stamford, Conn., 1975-82, v.p. engring., 1982-85; pres. E.E. Linden Assocs., Cons. Engrs., Darien, Conn., 1985—. Recipient awards in solar design. Mem. ASHRAE. Home: 18 Marion Rd Westport CT 06880-2919 Office: 85 Old Kings Hwy N Darien CT 06820-4724

BAYS, MONA RAE, librarian; b. Mattoon, Ill., June 16, 1950; d. Alburn Marion and Doris Madelyn Reynolds Grafton; m. Michael Allan Bays, Mar. 20, 1999; children: Brent Allan, Clinton Andrew. BA in English, Ea. Ill. U., 1972; MA in Librarianship, U. Denver, 1973. Youth libr. Mattoon (Ill.) Pub. Libr., 1973-75, cataloger, 1975-76, libr., 1976-94, dir., 1994—. Author: A House Not Made With Hands, 1981. Elder First Christian Ch. of Mattoon, bd. chair 1999—. Named Best Boss in Ctrl. Ill. Decatur Herald and Rev., 1987, Young Careerist Bus. and Profl. Women's Assn., 1978. Mem. ALA, Am. Bus. Women's Assn. (Woman of Yr. Mattoon chpt. 1980, 95, Pegtown chpt. 1999), Women of the Moose, Ill. Libr. Assn. Avocations: golfing, traveling. E-mail: mbays@ltnet.ltls.org. Office: Mattoon Pub Libr 1600 Charleston Ave Mattoon IL 61938

BAYSAL, EDIP, executive; b. Istanbul, Turkey, Aug. 9, 1952; came to U.S., 1997; s. Nushet Zekai and Ayten (Eyinc) B.; m. Sema Semen Dalaman, Apr. 28, 1977; 1 child, Doga. PhD in Geophysics, U. Houston, 1982. Geophysicist Turkish Petroleum Corp., Ankara, 1977-79; rsch. asst. U. Houston, 1980-82; rsch. geophysicist Geophys. Devel. Corp., Houston, 1981-83; assoc. prof. Ankara U., Turkey, 1988-97; deputy exploration mgr. Turkish Petroleum Corp., 1983-97; v.p. rsch. & devel. Seismic Rsch. Corp., Houston, 1997-98; chief geophysicist Paradigm Geophys. Corp., Houston, 1998—. Mem. European Assn. Exploration Geophysicists, Soc. Exploration Geophysicists, Houston Geophys. Soc., Chamber Geophysical Engrs. Turkey. Office: Paradigm Geophys Corp 1200 Smith St Houston TX 77002-4313

BAYSAL, FATIH DOGAN, trading company executive; b. Diyarbakir, Turkey, Nov. 12, 1955; came to U.S., 1977; s. Selim and Servet (Oztekin) B.; m. Dilsat Baysal, Sept. 14, 1990; children: Mirel, Selim. BSCE, Bogazici U., Istanbul, Turkey, 1977; MSCE, La. State U., 1979. EIT, La. Rsch. asst. La. State U., Baton Rouge, 1977-79; regional mktg. mgr. Fugro Gulf, Inc., Houston, 1979-82; mktg. mgr. Syminex, Inc., Houston, 1982-83; pres. Seba Internat., Inc., Houston, 1982—; also bd. dirs. Co-author: (tech. book) Thermal and Loading Effects on Soil Parameters, 1979. Mem. Rep. presdl. task force, Washington, 1982—; permanent mem. Nat. Rep. Senatorial Com., Washington, 1984—. Mem. Am. Soc. Civil Engrs., Turkish Chamber of Civil Engrs., C. of C., Am. Turkish Assn. Republican. Avocations: skiing, tennis, swimming, reading, travel. Office: Seba Internat Inc 9801 Westheimer Rd Ste 203 Houston TX 77042-3953

BAYSINGER, STEPHEN MICHAEL, quality assurance professional; b. St. Louis, May 9, 1954; s. David Richard and Betty I. (Elledge) B.; children: Devin, Derrick, Corey, Jocelyn. BA in Polit. Sci., U. Denver, 1977; MS in Human Resource Mgmt., Troy State U., 1989. Commd. 2d lt. USAF, 1979, advanced through grades to maj., 1990; maintenance supr. 7th Bombardment Wing, Carswell AFB, Tex., 1979-82, 343d Fighter Wing, Eielson AFB, Alaska, 1982-85; logistics project mgr. Air Force Logistics Mgmt. Ctr., Gunter AFB, Ala., 1985-90; chief maintenance mgmt. 58 Figher Wing, Luke AFB, Ariz., 1990-91, maintenance supr., 1991, chief quality assurance, 1991-92; mgr. quality engring., project officer ISO 9001 K*Tec Electronics divsn., Houston, 1992-94; sr. quality audit engr. Lockheed Martin Manned Space Sys., New Orleans, 1994-96; sr. staff engr. Lockheed Martin Astronautics, Denver, 1996-97; process improvement specialist TeleTech, Denver, 1997-98; quality mgr. Moll Industries, Austin, Tex., 1998—. Author: The Complete Guide to the CQA; contbr. articles to profl. jours. Leader Boy Scouts Am., Luke AFB, 1991-92; bd. dirs. Ala. Am. Diabetes Assn., Montgomery, 1985-90. Lt. col. USAFR, 1995—. Mem. Am. Soc. for Quality Control (cert. quality auditor), Soc. Logistics Engrs. Achievements include development of the first-ever automated personnel and equipment performance trend identification and analysis program for USAF, of the automated information center, of the quality division. Office: Moll Industries 15407 Long Vista Dr Austin TX 78728

BAYT, ROBERT L., federal judge; b. 1940. AB, Butler U.; JD, Ind. U. Chief bankruptcy judge U.S. Dist. Ct. (so. dist.) Ind., Indpls., 1977—. Office: US Courthouse 46 E Ohio St Indianapolis IN 46204-1903

BAYUZICK, ROBERT J., materials scientist; b. Braddock, Pa., Sept. 6, 1937; s. John and Mary (Holub) B.; m. Jeannette A. Lyle, Apr. 22, 1961; children: Carrie Lynn Hargis, Kellie JoAnne. BS, U. Pitts., 1961; MS in Phys. Metallurgy, U. Denver, 1963; PhD in Material Sci., Vanderbilt U., 1969. Rsch. metallurgist Battelle Meml. Inst., Columbus, Ohio, 1964-65; instr. Vanderbilt U., Nashville, 1968-69, asst. prof. material sci., 1969-72, program dir. material sci., 1974-75, assoc. prof. material sci., 1972-77, dir. Ctr. for Space Processing of Engring. Materials, 1985-90, prof. material scis., 1977—, dir. material sci., 1993—; vis. rsch. prof. Cambridge (Eng.) U., 1977-78; vis. sr. sci. NASA, Washington, 1991-92; mem. metals and alloys discipline working group NASA, 1986-91, vice chmn. space processing tech. com., 1988-90, chmn. space sta. sci. and applications adv. com. 1989-91, mem. space sta. sci. and applications adv. com. 91-97, mem. space sta. adv. com. 1989-90, mem. Office Comml. Programs adv. com. 1989-90, mem. microgravity sci. and applications adv. com. 1989-91, mem. requirements integration group for space sta., shared lab. support equipment 1990-92, mem. requirements integration group for space sta., microgravity lab. support equipment 1990-92, mem. space sta. customer support team 1991-92, mem. exec. group life and microgravity scis. and applications adv. com. 1994-95; invited lectr. Beijing Rsch. Inst. of Materials and Tech., 1987, Luoyang (China) Inst. Tech., 1987, Northwest Polytechnic Inst., Xian, China, 1987; mem. Internat. Forum for Utilization of Space Sta., 1989-91; mem. com. on microgravity rsch. Space Studies Bd., NRC, 1995—, mem. com. on internat. progams, 1996-98; spkr. in field. Co-author: Solidification Processing of Eutectic Alloys, 1988, Space Commercialization: Platforms and Processing, Progress in Astronautics and Aeronautics 127, 1990; patentee in field; contbr. articles and papers to profl. jours. Recipient Pub. Svc. medal NASA, 1992. Mem. AIME Metall. Soc., Am. Inst. Aero. and Astro., Materials Rsch. Soc., Sigma Xi. Roman Catholic. Office: Vanderbilt U Rm 610 Olin Hall Nashville TN 37240

BAZANT, ZDENEK PAVEL, structural engineering educator, scientist, consultant; b. Prague, Czechoslovakia, Dec. 10, 1937; came to U.S., 1968, naturalized, 1976; s. Zdenek and Stepanka (Curikova) B.; m. Iva Marie Krasna, Sept. 27, 1967; children: Martin Zdenek, Eva Stephanie. Civil Engr., Tech. U., Prague, 1960; PhD in Mechanics, Czechoslovak Acad. Sci., 1963; postgrad. diploma in theoretical physics, Charles U., Prague, 1966; hon. doctorate, Czech Tech. U., Prague, 1991, Karlsruhe (Germany) U., 1998. Registered structural engr., Ill. Scientist, adj. prof. Bldg. Research Inst., Tech. U., Prague, 1963-67; docent habilitation Tech. U., Prague, Czechoslovakia, 1967; vis. research engr. Centre d'Étude et de Recherche du Bâtiment et des Travaux Publics, Paris, 1967, U. Toronto, 1967-68, U. Calif., Berkeley, 1969; assoc. prof. civil engring. Northwestern U., Evanston, Ill., 1969-73, prof., 1973-90, Walter P. Murphy prof., 1990—, coordinator structural engring. program, 1974-78, 92—; founding dir. Ctr. for Concrete and Geomaterials, 1981-86; cons. Argonne Nat. Lab., many other orgns. Author: Creep of Concrete in Structural Analysis, 1966, Stability of Structures: Elastic, Inelastic, Fracture and Damage Theories, 1991, Concrete at High Temperatures, 1996, Fracture and Size Effect, 1997; editor 13 books; editor in chief Jour. Engring. Mechanics, 1989-94; regional editor Internat. Jour. Fracture, 1991—; assoc. editor Applied Mechanics Rev., 1987—, Cement and Concrete Research Internat. Jour, 1970—, Materials and Structures, 1979— Solid Mechanics Archives, 1980-91, Materials and Structures, 1981—; mem. editl. bds. of 16 hours.; contbr. (with others) over 350 articles to profl. jours.; patentee in field. Recipient Best Engring. Book of Yr. award Soc. Am. Pubs., 1992, Outstanding New Citizen award Chgo. Citizenship Coun., 1976, IR100 award, 1982, A. von Humboldt award, 1990, Solin medal Czech Tech. U., Prague, 1998; grantee NSF, 1970—, ERDA, 1975-77, AOSR, 1975—, Los Alamos Sci. Lab., 1978-80, EPRI, 1980—, Office Naval Rsch., 1990—. Dept. Energy, 1984—; Ford Found. fellow, 1967-68, Guggenheim fellow, 1978-79, Kajima Found. fellow U. Tokyo, 1987, NATO fellow, Paris, 1988, JSPS fellow U. Tokyo, 1995-96. Fellow ASME (Worcester Reed Warner medal 1997), Am. Acad. Mechanics, ASCE (chmn. com. properties of materials 1976-78, 82-84, editor in chief Jour. Engring. Mechanics 1988-94, Walter L. Huber rsch. prize 1976, T.Y. Lin Prestressed Concrete award 1977, Newmark medal 1996, Croes medal 1997), Am. Concrete Inst. (chmn. fracture mechanics com. 1985-92), Internat. Assn. for Fracture Mechanics of Concrete Structures (pres. 1991-93), Internat. Union Testing and Rsch. Labs. Materials Structures, Internat. Union Rsch. Lab Materials Structures (chmn. com. on creep, gold medal 1975); mem. NAE, Internat. Assn. Structural Mechanics Reactor Tech. (coord. concrete structures divsn.), ASTM (mem. concrete com., skiing com.), Prestressed Concrete Inst., Am. Ceramic Soc., Internat. Assn. Soil Mech. Found. Engring., Internat. Assn. Bridge and Structural Engring., Soc. Exptl. Mechanics, Soc. Engring. Sci. (pres. 1993, Prager medal 1996), Am. Soc. Engring. Edn., Bldg. Rsch. Inst. Spain (hon., Torroja Gold medal 1990), Czech Soc. Civil Engring. (hon.), Czech Soc. Mechanics (award of merit 1993), Structural Engrs. Assn. Ill. (Meritorious Paper award 1992), Energy Acad. of Czech Republic (fgn. mem.). Home: 707 Roslyn Ter Evanston IL 60201-1721 Office: Northwestern Univ Dept Civil Engring Evanston IL 60208

BAZELIDES, DIANE, public relations executive. BS in Bus. Edn., U. Nebr. With dept. internal audit Enron Corp., Houston, 1976-80, with dept. pub. rels., 1980-83, comm. adminstr. dept. pub. rels., 1983-86, mgr. media rels., 1986-88, dir. media rels. dept. pub. rels., 1988-91, gen. mgr. dept. pub. rels., 1991-92, v.p. dept. pub. rels., 1992—. Bd. dirs. Alley Theater, Houston, Houston Ballet; mem. exec. com., pres. bd. dirs. Alzheimer's Assn., Houston. Mem. Pub. Rels. Soc. Am., Internat. Assn. Bus. Communicators. Office: Enron Corp 1400 Smith St Houston TX 77002-7369*

BAZELL, ROBERT JOSEPH, science correspondent; b. Pitts., Aug. 21, 1945; s. Irving and Beatrice (Robb) B.; m. Ilene Tanz, Sept. 11, 1966 (div.); children: Rebecca, Joshua; m. Margot Weinshel, July 31, 1979. BA, U. Calif., Berkeley, 1967; student, U. Sussex, Eng., 1968-69; postgrad., U. Calif., 1971. Writer Sci. Mag., Washington, 1971-72; reporter N.Y. Post, N.Y.C., 1972-76; network corr. NBC News, N.Y.C., 1976—. Contbr. articles to mags. Mem. Phi Beta Kappa. Office: NBC News 30 Rockefeller Plz Fl 3 New York NY 10112-0036*

BAZERMAN, STEVEN HOWARD, lawyer; b. N.Y.C., Dec. 12, 1940; s. Solomon and Miriam (Kirschenberg) B.; m. Christina Ann Gray, Aug. 28, 1981 (div. June 1988). BS in Math., BS in Engring., U. Mich., 1962; JD, Georgetown U., 1966. Bar: D.C. 1967, N.Y. 1968, U.S. Dist. Ct. (so. dist.) N.Y. 1970, U.S. Dist. Ct. (ea. dist.) N.Y. 1973, U.S. Claims Ct. 1976, U.S. Ct. Appeals (2d cir.) 1978, U.S. Cts. Customs and Patents Appeals 1981-82, U.S. Ct. Appeals (fed. cir.) 1982. Assoc. Arthur, Dry & Kalish, N.Y.C., 1967-80, Offner & Kuhn, N.Y.C., 1980-83; ptnr., head litigation dept. Kuhn, Muller & Bazerman, N.Y.C., 1983-87; ptnr. Moore, Berson, Lifflander, Eisenberg & Mewhinney, N.Y.C., 1987-88; of counsel Lerner, David, Littenberg, Krumholz & Mentlik, Westfield, N.J., 1988, Sutton, Basseches, Magidoff & Amaral, N.Y.C., 1988-90, Graham, Campaign & McCarthy P.C., N.Y.C., 1990-96, Bazerman & Drangel, P.C., N.Y.C., 1996—; governing counsel Community Law Offices Legal Aid Soc., N.Y.C., 1974-83, treas., 1979-82. Author: Guide to Treatment Regulation; co-author: Guide to Registering Trademarks; contbr. articles to profl. jours. Vol. counsel community law offices Legal Aid Soc., N.Y.C., 1974-82, treas., 1979-82. Mem. Assn. of Bar of City of N.Y., Am. Intellectual Property Law Assn., N.Y. Patent, Trademark & Copyright Law Assn. Jewish. Avocations: horses, classic automobiles. Office: Bazerman & Drangel PC 60 E 42nd St Rm 1158 New York NY 10165-1132

BAZLER, FRANK ELLIS, retired lawyer; b. Columbus, Ohio, Jan. 17, 1930; s. Frank Hayes and Minnie Maybrum (Rucker) B.; m. Virginia Ann Hutchison, Oct. 17, 1954. BSBA, Ohio State U., 1951, JD, 1953. Bar: Ohio 1953, U.S. Dist. Ct. (we. dist.) Ohio 1956, U.S. Ct. Mil. Appeals 1957, U.S. Supreme Ct. 1957, U.S. Ct. Appeals (6th cir.) 1964. Assoc. Robert S. Miller, Atty., Troy, Ohio, 1955-57; ptnr. Miller, Bazler & Schlemmer, Troy, 1957-71; asst. corp. counsel Hobart Mfg. Co., Troy, 1971-74; corp. atty., asst. sec. Hobart Corp., Troy, 1974-95; ret., 1995; of counsel Dungan & LeFevre, Troy, 1995—; v.p. Bazler Transfer & Storage, Inc., Columbus, Ohio, 1950-58; sec., bd. dirs. Golden Triangle Farms, Inc., Troy, 1972—. Pres. Troy United Fund, Inc., 1960, Troy Mus. Corp., 1990; chmn. Miami County chpt. ARC, 1955-59, Miami County (Ohio) Rep. Fin. Com., 1981-84; mem. Miami County Gen. Bd. Health, 1992—; commn. on cert. of Attys. as Specialists of Supreme Ct. of Ohio, 1994-99, chmn., 1994-96. Capt. JAG, USAFR, 1953-61. Named one of Outstanding Young Men in Troy and Ohio, Troy Jaycees, 1957, Ohio Jaycees, 1961; recipient Disting. Citizen award Troy C. of C., 1985, Citizenship award Ohio State U., 1993. Fellow Am. Bar Found. (Ohio chair 1995—), Ohio State Bar Found. (pres. 1992); mem. ABA (ho. of dels. 1984—), Ohio State Bar Assn. (pres. 1984-85, coun. of dels. 1979-88, Ohio Bar medal 1990), Miami County Bar Assn. (pres. 1966, Meritorious Svc. award 1985), Nat. Coun. Bar Pres. (exec. coun. 1988-91), Kiwanis (pres. 1964), Masons, Scottish Rite. Republican. Presbyterian. Avocations: photography, travel, golf. Home: 741 Gloucester Rd Troy OH 45373-1223 Office: Dungan & LeFevre 210 W Main St Troy OH 45373-3287

BAZZAZ, FAKHRI A., plant biology educator, administrator; b. Baghdad, Iraq, June 16, 1933; came to U.S., 1958; s. Abdul-Latif and Munifa Bazzaz; m. Maarib Bazzaz, Aug. 25, 1958; children: Sahar, Ammar. B.S., U. Baghdad, 1953; M.S., U. Ill., 1960, Ph.D., 1963; A.M. (hon.), Harvard U., 1984. Prof. U. Ill., Urbana, 1977-84, head dept. plant biology, acting dir. Sch. Life Scis., 1983-84; prof. Harvard U., Cambridge, Mass., 1984—; Mallinckrodt prof. biology Harvard U., Cambridge; fellow Clare Hall, Cambridge (Eng.) U., 1981—. Editor: Oecologia, 1983—. Guggenheim fellow. Fellow AAAS, Am. Acad. Arts and Scis.; mem. Ecol. Soc. Am., Brit. Ecol. Soc, Humboldt Forschungspreise, Germany (1997 award). Office: Harvard U Biol Labs 16 Divinity Ave Cambridge MA 02138-2020*

BEA, BARBARA ANN, legal secretary; b. Richmond, Va., Nov. 26, 1957; d. Arthur and Edith (Thompson) B.; 1 child, Michael T. Sec. IEEE, Washington, 1981-83, Greenhoot, Inc., Washington, 1983-85; legal sec. Friedlander, Misler, Friedlander, Sloan & Herz, Washington, 1985-88, Arnold & Porter, Washington, 1988-97, Dickstein, Shapiro, Morin & Olshinsky, Washington, 1997-99, Hale and Dorr, Washington, 1999—. Democrat. Mem. Seventh-Day Adventist Ch. Home: 2329 White Owl Way Suitland MD 20746-1063

BEA, ROBERT G., civil engineering educator. BS, U. Fla., 1959, MS, 1960. Sr. staff civl engr. Shell Oil Co., 1959-76; chief engr., v.p. Ocean Engring. Divsn., Woodward-Clyde Cons., 1976-81; v.p. PMB Sys. Engring., Inc., 1981-88; prof. dept. civil engring., naval arch. and offshore engring U. Calif., Berkeley, 1988—; cons. prof. engring Stanford U., 1985-89. Recipient J. Hillis Miller Engring. award. Mem. ASCE (Croes medal, 1959), Nat. Acad. Engring. Achievements include projects and research in coastal, offshore and ocean engineering; development of methods to define design criteria for fixed and mobile offshor structures; development of guidelines for the requalifications and rehabilitation of marine structures and ships; evaluation of forces due to waves, currents, earthquakes, ice and sea floor slides; development of technology for evaluation of the dynamic response characteristics of marine foundations and structures. Office: U Calif 215 Mclaughlin Hall Berkeley CA 94720-1712*

BEACH, ARTHUR O'NEAL, lawyer; b. Albuquerque, Feb. 8, 1945; s. William Pearce and Vivian Lucille (Kronig) B.; BBA, U. N.Mex., 1967, JD, 1970; m. Alex Clark Doyle, Sept. 12, 1970; 1 son, Eric Kronig. Bar: N.Mex. 1970. Assoc. Smith & Ransom, Albuquerque, 1970-74; assoc. Keleher & McLeod, Albuquerque, 1974-75, ptnr., 1976-78, shareholder Keleher & McLeod, P.A., Albuquerque, 1978—; teaching asst. U. N. Mex., 1970. Bd. editors Natural Resources Jour., 1968-70. Mem. ABA, State Bar N.Mex. (unauthorized practice of law com., adv. opinions com., med.-legal panel, legal-dental-osteo.-podiatry com., jud. selection com., specialization bd.), Albuquerque Bar Assn. (dir. 1978-82). Democrat. Mem. Christian Sci. Ch. Home: 2015 Dietz Pl NW Albuquerque NM 87107-3240 Office: Keleher & McLeod PA PO Drawer AA Albuquerque NM 87103

BEACH, BARBARA PURSE, lawyer; b. Washington, June 12, 1947; d. Clifford John and Lillian (Natarus) B. BA, U. Ky., 1968; MSW, U. Md., 1972; JD, Am. U., 1980. Bar: D.C. 1980, Va. 1980. Law clk. to presiding justice benefit rev. bd. U.S. Dept. Labor, Washington, 1980; asst. city atty. City of Alexandria, Va., 1981-85; atty. Ross, Marsh, Foster, Myers & Quiggle, Alexandria, 1985-90, Beach, Butt & Assocs., P.C., Alexandria, 1990-92; prin. Beach & Assocs., Alexandria, 1992—; town atty. Town of Herndon (Va.), 1992-94. Vice chmn. Va. Health Svcs. Cost Rev. Coun., 1989-92; mem. Va. Commn. on Women and Minorities, 1990-92; bd. divs. Am. Heart Assn., Alexandria, 1996—, divsn. pres., 1998-99. Mem. Va. Trial Lawyers Assn., Alexandria Bar Assn. (pres. 1987-88), Kiwanis (bd. dirs.). Office: Beach & Assocs 416 Prince St Alexandria VA 22314-3114

BEACH, BERT BEVERLY, clergyman; b. Gland, Vaud, Switzerland, June 15, 1928; s. Walter Raymond and Gladys (Corley) B.; m. Eliane Marguerite Palange, Apr. 8, 1954; children: Danielle, Michele. BA, Pacific Union Coll., 1948; postgrad., Stanford U., 1948-49, 51; PhD, U. Paris, 1958; ThD, Christian Theol. Acad., 1986. Prin. West Liberty Union Intermediate Sch., Gridley, Calif., 1949-50, Italian Jr. Coll., Florence, Italy, 1952-58; chmn. history dept. Columbia Union Coll., Takoma Pk., Md., 1958-60; dir. edn. No. Europe-West Africa Div. of SDA, St. Albans, Eng., 1960-75, gen. sec., 1973-80; sec. Conf. of Secs. Christian World Communions, Silver Springs, Md., 1970—; dir. pub. affairs Gen. Conf. of Seventh-day Adventists, Silver Spring, Md., 1980-95; gen. sec. Coun. on Inter-Ch. Rels., 1980—; sec. gen. Internat. Religious Liberty Assn., Silver Spring, Md., 1980-95; pres. Internat. Religious Liberty Assn., Silver Spring, 1996; v.p. Internat. Commn. for Prevention of Alcoholism and Drug Dependency, 1980—, pres., 1991, 97. Chmn. bd. John H. Weidner Found. Altruism, 1996—. Recipient Citation, Senate of State of Md., 1984; named Paul Harris fellow Rotary Internat., 1984, Order of Bishop Hodura, Polish Nat. Cath. Ch., 1986, Order of St. Magdalene, Polish Orthodox Ch., 1987, Honored Alumnus of Yr. Pacific Union Coll., 1997, Knight's Cross of Order of Merit of Polish Republic, 1998, Human Rights Leadership award Freedom Mag., 1998, Pres. medallion for Leadership Andrews Univ., 1999. Mem. Rotary Club of Silver Spring, Md., Cosmos Club, Nat. Press Club, Sons of Am. Revolution, Md. Assn. Founders and Patriots of Am. (gov. 1998—). Seventh-day Adventist. Avocation: prestidigitation. Home: 14508 Cutstone Way Silver Spring MD 20905-7430 Office: 12501 Old Columbia Pike Silver Spring MD 20904-6601

BEACH, BETH, elementary educator; b. Binghamton, N.Y., June 5, 1951; d. Martin Patrick and Mildred (Neary) Regan; 1 child, Martin Robert. BA in Elem. Edn., SUNY, Cortland, 1973; MS in Elem. Edn., Binghamton U., 1976. Cert. tchr., N.Y. Kindergarten tchr. Christ the King Sch., Endwell, N.Y., 1973-74, Blessed Sacrament Sch., Johnson City, N.Y., 1974-85; kindergarten tchr. Chenago Forks Schs., Binghamton, 1985-90, 2d grade tchr., 1990-96, 5th grade tchr., 1996-98, 4th grade tchr., 1998—; lectr. grad. edn. Binghamton U., 1988; mem. adv. bd. Hearts and Hands, Inc., Binghamton; leader workshops in field. Author: (with Muriel Rossie) Discipline and Self-Esteem, 1987. Tchr. safety town program Jr. League of Binghamton, 1982-90. Mem. N.Y. State United Tchrs., Binghamton Area Reading Coun., Binghamton Assn. for Edn. of Young Children (local bd. dirs., publs. com. 1984-86, historian 1986-88, nominating com. 1992). Avocations: sewing, reading. Home: 55 Lathrop Ave Binghamton NY 13905-4224 Office: Chenango Forks Cen Schs 1 Gordon Dr Binghamton NY 13901-5614

BEACH, CHRISTOPHER JOHN, American literary arts educator; b. Mpls., Nov. 12, 1959; s. Northrop and Myrtle Mary (Webb-Johnson) B.; m. Carrie Jaurès Noland, Aug. 18, 1958; children: Julian, Francesca. BA, Pomona Coll., 1981; AM, Harvard U., 1985, PhD, 1988. Asst. prof. Bates Coll., Lewiston, Maine, 1989-90, Columbia U., N.Y.C., 1990-92, Claremont (Calif.) Grad. Sch., 1992-93, U. Mont., Missoula, 1993-95, U. Calif., Irvine, 1995—. Author: ABC of Influence, 1992, Politics of Distinction, 1996, Artifice and Indeterminacy, 1998, Poetic Culture, 1999. Avocations: yoga, hiking, travel. Office: U Calif Irvine CA 92697

BEACH, DIANA LEE, psychotherapist, priest; b. Calgary, Alta., Can., Sept. 4, 1946; d. Hugh Hamilton and Lucille (Allen) B.; m. John Romig Johnson, Oct. 13, 1973 (div. June 1995). AB, Smith Coll., 1968; MDiv cum laude, Yale U., 1971; postgrad., Jung Inst., Zürich, Switzerland, 1973, 77; D in Ministry, N.Y. Theol. Sem., 1980. Ordained priest Diocese of N.Y., 1978, received into Diocese of Newark, 1997. Chaplain The Taft Sch., Watertown, Conn., 1971-72; nat. staff Episcopal Ch. Nat. Coun. Chrs., United Presbyn. Women, N.Y.C., 1972-75; dean pastoral studies N.Y. Theol. Seminary, 1975-83; priest in charge Grace Ch. Van Vorst, Jersey City, 1982-83; pvt. practice Jungian psychotherapy N.Y., N.J., 1983—; lectr. C.G. Jung Found., N.Y.C., 1975—; faculty profl. enrichment program Wainwright House, Rye, N.Y., 1982-90; core faculty Interweave Ctr. in Spirituality, 1991—; priest-in-charge St. Matthew's Ch., Jersey City, 1994-95; priest assoc. Christ Ch., Short Hills, N.J., 1996—. Author: Sex Role Sterotyping in Protestant Church School Curricula, 1972. Recipient Disting. Alumni award Berkeley Div. Sch. at Yale, 1982. Democrat. Episcopalian. Avocations: scuba diving, traveling. Home: 497 Jersey Ave Jersey City NJ 07302-3457 Office: 346 W 20th St New York NY 10011-3302

BEACH, DOUGLAS RYDER, lawyer, educator; b. Kittery, Maine, Sept. 20, 1948; s. Raymond Homer and Carolyn (Ryder) B.; m. Deborah C.M. Henry; children: Lindsay Alison, Garrett Wesley, Katherine Henry. BS, Central Conn. State U., 1970; JD cum laude, New Eng. Sch. Law, 1973; grad. with honors, U.S. Army Judge Sch., U. Va., 1976. Bar: Mass. 1973, Mo. 1977, U.S. Dist. Ct. (ea. and we. dists.) Mo. 1977, U.S. Ct. Mil. Appeals, 1973. Gen. ptnr. Paule & Beach, Inc., Clayton, Mo., 1977-81, Kaveney, Beach, Russell, Bond & Mittleman, Clayton, 1981-88, Beach, Burcke & Helfers, P.C., 1988—; instr. bus. law Washington U., St. Louis, 1980-89; city atty. Cit y Chesterfield, Mo. Contbr. chpt. to Medical Records, Property Distribution, Trial Tactics in Domestic Relations, 1984, Elder Bonhomme Presbyterian Ch., Chesterfield, Mo., 1984. Treas. Y's Men's Internat., St. Louis, 1977-80; mem. exec. bd. John Marshall Rep. Club, 1969-72. Lt. col. USMCR, 1973-91. Mem. ABA, Am. Acad. Matrimony Lawyers (pres. Mo. chpt., Best Atty. U.S. Am. 1990-91, 92-93, 94-95, 96-97, 98-99), St. Louis County Bar Assn. (named Outstanding Young Lawyer 1983, pres. 1984-85), Met. Bar St. Louis, Trial Lawyers Assn. St.

Louis. Home: 1535 Walpole Dr Chesterfield MO 63017-4614 Office: Beach Burcke & Helfers PC 222 S Central Ave Ste 900 Saint Louis MO 63105-3575

BEACH, EDWARD LATIMER, writer, retired naval officer; b. N.Y.C., Apr. 20, 1918; s. Edward Latimer and Alice (Fouché) B.; m. Ingrid Schenck, June 4, 1944; children: Inga, Edward A., Hugh S., Ingrid A. BSEE, U.S. Naval Acad., 1939; M.Internat. Affairs, George Washington U., 1963; ScD (hon.), Am. Internat. U., 1961; LLD (hon.), Bridgeport (Conn.) U., 1963. Commd. USN, 1939, advanced through grades to capt., 1956, ret., 1966; comdr. during 1st submerged circumnavigation of world USS Triton, 1960; prof. U.S. Naval War Coll., Newport, R.I., 1967-69; sec., staff dir. U.S. Sen. Rep. Policy Com., Washington, 1969-77; adminstrv. asst. to Senator Jeremiah Denton, 1980-81. Author: Submarine, 1952, Run Silent, Run Deep, 1955 (Nat. Book award 1956), Around the World Submerged, 1962, The Wreck of the Memphis, 1966, Dust on the Sea, 1972, Cold is the Sea, 1978, The United States Navy: 200 Years, 1986, Scapegoats!, 1995, Salt and Steel, 1999, others; co-author: Naval Terms Dictionary, 3rd edit., 1971, 4th edit., 1979, 5th edit., 1987-88, Keepers of the Sea, 1983; contbr. articles to profl. jours. Naval aide to U.S. Pres., 1953-57. Decorated Navy Cross, others; recipient Mahan award USN League, Theodore and Franklin D. Roosevelt award for history and lit., Am. Philos. Soc. Magellanic Premium award, Samuel Eliot Morison award USS Constn. Mus., Theodore Roosevelt Disting. Svc. medal Theodore Roosevelt Assn. Mem. Cosmos Club (Washington), Met. Club (N.Y.C.). Avocations: ship models, plumbing, electricity.

BEACH, FRANKLIN DARREL, minister; b. South Charleston, W.Va., June 24, 1938; s. Elwood James and Virgie (O'Dell) B.; m. Brenda Pauley, Oct. 4, 1968; children: Frank Jr., Deanna Dawn. Grad. high sch., Alum Creek, W.Va. Ordained min. Bapt. Ch., 1967. Welder, boilermaker Putnam Fabricators, Bandcroft, W.Va., 1972; welder South Charleston, W.Va., 1963-70; assoc. pastor, tchr. Dollie Hill Christian Acad. and God's Ch. Alum Creek, W.Va., 1973-79; min. King (N.C.) Christian Ctr., 1983—; TV min. CAT TV Channel 6, Winston-Salem, N.C., 1994—. Pres. Forsyth County Right to Life, Winston-Salem, 1993-95. With U.S. Army, 1956-61. Recipient award Concerned Citizens of Kanawha County, 1974. Avocations: private pilot, oil painting, auto mechanics. Home: 4673 Hyatt Dr Winston Salem NC 27101-2223

BEACH, GEO, journalist, poet; b. Boston, Feb. 14, 1957; s. George Richard Plagenz and Faith Hanna-Williams; m. Sydney Liane Webb, March 16, 1991; children: Miranda Rose, Isabel Gallan. Lit., Phillips Exeter Acad., N.H., 1975; Theatre, Yale U., 1979. Dir. commn. Yale U. Tutoring Agency, New Haven, 1979-82; public info. officer Dept. Pub. Safety, Homer, Alaska, 1983-87; columnist, editor Tempest Media Prodn., Arcata, Calif., 1988—; editor Marlowe & Co., N.Y., 1995—; anchor Peninsula Pub. Radio News, Kenai, AK, 1997—; judge Alaska State Coun. on Arts, Anchorage, 1998—; spokesman Alaska Childrens Trust, Anchorage, 1998. Featured essayist Monitor Radio News, Boston, 1993-97, (Pub. Radio Series) Tales of The Great North, 1995, Living on Earth, Boston, 1997—, The Savvy Traveler, L.A., 1997—. Trustee, Homer Fire Dept. Inc., 1983-87. Recipient Poetry prize Atlantic Monthly mag., 1975, Rescuer op-ed of Yr. award Homer Fire Dept., 1987, Mencken award Free Press Assn., 1994, Davidoff Journalist award, Wesleyan Writers Conf., 1996, Sigma Delta Chi award Radio Commentaries, 1997, Broadcast award AP, breaking news, 1997, live anchoring, 1998, World medal for best writing N.Y. Festivals Internat. Radio Awards, 1999; Murray fellowship Poynter Inst. Media Studies, 1998, guest author, Lila Wallace, Reader's Digest Fund Proj. Common Rhythms: Writing About Work, Wash., 1994. Mem. Nat. Soc. of Newspaper Columnists, Soc. of Profl. Journalists (sports reporting, 1995, radio commentaries 1997), Nat. Press Club, Alaska Press Club (columnist, sports analysis, radio essayist, live anchoring 1994-98). Home: Lookout Dr Homer AK 99603-9121 Office: Tempest Media Prodn PO Box 3600 Homer AK 99603-3600

BEACH, HARRY LEE, JR., mechanical engineer, aerospace engineer; b. Richmond, Va., Aug. 16, 1944; married, 1966; 3 children. BS, N.C. State U., 1966, MS, 1968, PhD in Mech. Engring., 1970. Rsch. engr. Langley Rsch. Ctr., NASA, Hampton, Va., 1970-75, head combustion sect., 1975-77, leader performance analysis group, 1977-80, asst., 1980-81, head hypersonic propulsion br., 1981-89, head nat. aerospace plane, 1989-92, dep. dir., 1992—; asst. prof. Joint Inst. Advanced Flight Sci., George Washington U., 1977—; adj. prof. Christopher Newport Coll., 1980—. Fellow AIAA (Air Breathing Propulsion award 1997). Achievements include research in supersonic combustion ramjet propulsion, combustion fundamentals, computational fluid dynamics, combustion diagnostics, inlet and combuster conceptual design and testing, inlet-combustor component integration. Home: 104 Blair Ct Williamsburg VA 23185-8912 Office: NASA Langley Rsch Ctr 11 Langley Blvd MS 102 Hampton VA 23681

BEACH, HAZEL ELIZABETH, nurse; b. Oakdale, Tenn., June 27, 1929; d. Michael Thomas and Susie Margaret (Babinchak) Semanick; m. Edward Junior Beach, Oct. 7, 1961; children: Monica Ann, Edward Michael. RN La., Tenn. Staff nurse Meml. Hosp., Chattanooga, 1952-61, head nurse, 1961-66; evening supr. Downtown Hosp., Chattanooga, 1977-83; staff nurse East Ridge Hosp., Chattanooga, 1983-91, charge nurse, 1991-95; ret., 1996—. Profl. artist. Vol. ARC, Washington, 1960—. Mem. ANA, Cath. Nurses Assn. Roman Catholic. Avocations: art, sewing, fishing, ceramics. Home: 8419 Oak Dr Chattanooga TN 37421-4342

BEACH, JOHN ARTHUR, lawyer; b. Syracuse, N.Y., Apr. 30, 1932; s. Arthur Myron and Norma Irene (Vergason) B.; m. Victoria Regina Gorcoff, 1954 (div. 1985); children: Carolyn, Ann, Ellen, George; m. Joyce Ann Gruka, 1985. AB summa cum laude, Syracuse U., 1954; JD, U. Mich., 1957. Bar: N.Y. 1958, Fla. 1983. Assoc. Bond, Schoeneck & King, various cities in N.Y. and Fla., 1957-65, ptnr., 1965—, chmn. exec. com., 1983-91; interim dean Coll. Law Syracuse U., 1973-74; interim pres., CEO Albany Med. Ctr., 1989-90. Sr. editor U. Mich. Law Rev., 1957; contbr. articles to profl. jours. Mem. ABA, N.Y. State Bar Assn., Albany County Bar Assn., Onondaga County Bar Assn., Fla. Bar Assn., Nat. Assn. Coll. and Univ. Attys. (pres. 1985-86), Phi Beta Kappa, Phi Kappa Phi. Home: 7 Birchwood Ct Albany NY 12211-2057 Office: Bond Schoeneck & King 111 Washington Ave Albany NY 12210 also: 1 Lincoln Ctr Syracuse NY 13202-1324

BEACH, LEE ROY, psychologist, educator, academic administrator; b. Gallup, N.Mex., Feb. 29, 1936; s. Dearl and Lucile Ruth (Krumtum) B.; m. Barbara Ann Heinrich, Nov. 13, 1971. B.A., Ind. U., 1957; M.A., U. Colo., 1959, Ph.D., 1961. Aviation psychologist U.S. Sch. Aviation Medicine, Pensacola, Fla., 1961-63; human factors officer Office of Naval Research, Washington, 1963-64; postdoctoral research U. Mich., Ann Arbor, 1964-66; faculty dept. psychology U. Wash., Seattle, 1966-89; faculty mgmt. & policy, psychology U. Ariz., Tucson, 1990—, McClelland chair mgmt. & policy, 1989—, vice dean Sch. Bus., 1998—. Contbr. articles to profl. jours. Recipient Feldman rsch. award, 1981, Disting. Tchr. award U. Wash., 1986, Prof. of Yr. award State of Wash., 1989, nat. teaching award Coun. for Advancement and Support Edn., 1989; fellow NIMH, 1964-66. Fellow Am. Psychol. Soc.; mem. Soc. for Orgnl. Behavior. Office: Univ Arizona Coll Bus & Pub Adminstrn Tucson AZ 85721

BEACH, MILO C., art museum director; b. Rochester, N.Y., July 12, 1939; m. Robin Cook. BA, Harvard U., 1962, PhD, 1969. With dept. Asiatic art Mus. Fine Arts, Boston, 1963-66, asst. curator dept. Islamic art, 1967; jr. fellow Am. Inst. Indian Art, India, 1967-68; asst. curator dept. Oriental art Fogg Art Mus. Harvard U., 1968-69; mem. faculty dept. art Williams Coll., Williamstown, Mass., 1969-84, chmn. dept. art, 1981-84; asst. dir. Freer Gallery of Art, Arthur M. Sackler Gallery, Washington, 1984-87, acting dir. Freer Gallery of Art, 1987-88, dir., 1988—; adj. prof. art history U. Mich.; vis. prof. art history U. Md.; adv. coun. dept. art and archaeology Princeton U.; chmn. com. sr. fellows Harvard U. Ctr. Studies in Landscape and Architecture. Author: The Imperial Image: Paintings for the Mughal Court, 1981, The Adventures of Rama, 1983, Early Mughal Painting, 1987, Mughal and Rajput painting, 1992, King of the World: A Mughal Manuscript from the Royal Library, Windsor Castle, 1997; co-author: (with Glenn D. Lowry) An Illustrated and Annotated Checklist of the Vever Collection, 1989, (with Andrew Topsfield) Indian Paintings and Drawings from the Collection of Howard Hodgkin, 1991, (with Abolala Soudavar) Art of the Persian Courts, 1992. Mem. vis. com. Boston Mus. Fine Arts; mem. dept. of art and archaeology adv. coun. Princeton (N.J.) U. Mem. Am. Fedn. Arts (exhbns. com.). Office: Sackler Gallery/Freer Gallery Art Smithsonian Instn 1050 Independence Ave SW Washington DC 20560*

BEACH, ROBERT MARK, biologist; b. Athens, Ga., Oct. 7, 1957; s. Robert Ervin and Frances (Myers) B.; m. Catherine Cesaro, Oct. 3, 1987; 2 children: Katelyn Marie, Joseph Mark. BS, Clemson U., 1979; PhD, U. Ga., 1985; MS in Bus., Johns Hopkins U., 1999. Rsch. asst. Clemson (S.C.) U., 1979-81, U. Ga., Athens, 1981-85, 1985-87; scientist Crop Genetics Internat., Columbia, Md., 1987-91, project mgr., 1991-92, dir. bioinsecticides, 1993-94; dir. field sales biosys, Columbia, Md., 19975-97; global project mgr. Abbott Labs., North Chgo., 1997—. Contbr. articles to profl. jours. Mem. Entomol. Soc. Am., Internat. Orgn. Biocontrol, Soc. Invertebrate Pathologists. Achievements include commercial development of biological insecticides. Home: 972 Tylerton Cir Grayslake IL 60030-1199 Office: Abbott Labs 6131 Oakwood Rd Long Grove IL 60047-9513

BEACH, ROGER C., oil company executive; b. Lincoln, Nebr., Dec. 5, 1936; s. Melvin C. and L. Mayme (Hoham) B.; m. Elaine M. Wilson, Oct. 1954 (div. 1972); children: Kristi, Mark, Anne; m. Karen Lynn Ogden, July 27, 1974. BS, Colo. Sch. Mines, 1961. Profl. petroleum refining engr., Calif. With Unocal Corp., L.A., 1961—; mgr. spl. projects Unocal Corp., Los Angeles, 1976-77, dir. planning, 1977-80, v.p. crude supply, 1980-86, pres. refining and mktg., 1986-92, corp. sr. v.p., 1987-1992, pres., 1992-94, CEO, 1994—, now chmn. and COO, 1994-98, CEO, 1998—. Chmn. bd. trustees Nat. 4-H Coun. Mem. Pres.'s Interchange Exec. Alumni Assn. Office: Unocal Corp 2141 Rosecrans Ave Ste 4000 El Segundo CA 90245-4746

BEACH, SANDRA MARIE YUDICHAK, secondary education educator; b. Niagara Falls, N.Y., Jan. 21, 1946; d. Thomas Stephen and Helen (Kosko) Yudichak; m. Fred Ellsworth Beach, Aug. 28, 1965 (div., May, 1994); 1 child, Gary Nathan. BA, SUNY, Buffalo, 1969; MA in Tchg., Niagara U., 1973. Cert. secondary English tchr., N.Y. Tchr. Grand Island (N.Y.) Middle Sch., 1969—; tutor, Lewiston, N.Y., 1969—; superintendent's advisory com., Lewiston-Porter H.S., N.Y., 1994-95, mem. decision making team; tchr. stakeholder Grand Island Middle Sch. Shared Decision Making, 1992-94. Named delegate to Spain, ASCD, 1995. Mem. ASCD, Power of Positive Students, N.Y. State United Tchrs. Avocations: writing, needle crafts. Home: PO Box 197 Lewiston NY 14092-0197 Office: Grand Island Sr High Sch Veronica E Connor Mid Sch 1100 Ransom Rd Grand Island NY 14072-1199

BEACH, STEPHEN HOLBROOK, lawyer; b. Highland Park, Mich., June 3, 1915; s. Stephen Holbrook and Katherine Jean (Campbell) B.; m. Mary Frances Mulvihill, July 6, 1951; children: Jennifer Katherine Beach Buda, Stephen Holbrook III. AB with honors in Polit. Sci, Kalamazoo Coll., 1936; LLB cum laude, U. Detroit, 1941; postgrad., Georgetown U., 1945, Columbia U., 1970. Bar: Mich. 1941, U.S. Dist. Ct. (ea. dist.) Mich., 1941, U.S. Supreme Ct. 1944, N.Y. 1947, U.S. Dist. Ct. (so. dist.) N.Y. 1947, U.S. Dist. Ct. (ea. dist.) N.Y. 1949, D.C. 1949, Conn. 1975. Assoc. Winthrop, Stimson, Putnam & Roberts, N.Y.C., 1946-48, Cann, Lamb & Kittelle, N.Y.C., 1948-56, Willkie, Farr, Gallagher, Walton and Fitzgibbon, N.Y.C., 1956-60; staff atty. IBM Corp., N.Y.C., 1960-61; of counsel supplies div. IBM Corp., N.Y.C. and Dayton, N.J., 1961-65; v.p., gen. counsel, sec. The Svc. Bur. Corp., N.Y.C., 1965-75; v.p., gen. counsel Data Svcs. Control Data Corp., Greenwich, Conn., 1976-78; gen. counsel Computer Co. Control Data Corp., Mpls., 1979-80, v.p., assoc., gen. counsel, 1980-82, sr. v.p. telecommunications policy, corp. sec., 1983-85; of counsel Rogers, Hoge & Hills, White Plains, N.Y., 1985-86; pvt. practice law Greenwich and Stamford, Conn., 1986—; bd. dirs., corp. sec. Dataware Techs., Inc. Editor-in-chief U. Detroit Law Jour., 1937-41. Capt. U.S. Army, 1943-46. Mem. ABA (sci. and tech. sect., banking and bus. law sect.), Conn. Bar Assn (intellectual property and computer law sects.), N.Y. State Bar Assn. (banking and bus. law sect.), D.C. Bar Assn., Assn. of Data Processing Svcs. Orgns. (v.p. govt. rels., bd. dirs. 1978-84), The Wee Burn Country Club, Delray Dunes Golf and Country Club. Republican. Episcopalian. Avocation: golf. Home: 52 Brushy Hill Rd Darien CT 06820-6007 Office: PO Box 1202 Darien CT 06820-1202

BEACH, WALTER EGGERT, retired publishing organization executive; b. North Adams, Mass., Aug. 24, 1934; s. W. Edwards and Liselotte Josephine Sophie (von Usedom) B. BA, Dickinson Coll., 1956; MA, George Washington U., 1961. Staff assoc., asst. dir. Am. Polit. Sci. Assn., Washington, 1965-80; sr. staff mem. Brookings Instn., Washington, 1980-90; dir. Heldref Publs. Helen Dwight Reid Ednl. Found., Washington, 1990-97. Treas. D.C. Dem. Party, 1981-84; mem. adv. bd. Hubert H. Humphrey Inst. Pub. Affairs, U. Minn., Mpls., 1990-99; trustee Dickinson Coll., 1984—, Mt. Vernon Coll., 1971-97, Helen Dwight Reid Ednl. Found., 1982—; pres. Internat. Eye Found., 1993-95; mem., bd. dirs. various polit. coms. With U.S. Army, 1956-58. Recipient Disting. Alumni award Dickinson Coll., 1991. Mem. Internat. Polit. Sci. Assn., Am. Polit. Sci. Assn. (Frank Goodnow award 1998), Ctr. Study Presidency, Hist. Soc. D.C., Midwest Polit. Sci. Assn., Nat. Capital Area Polit. Sci. Assn., Policy Studies Orgn., So. Polit. Sci. Assn., UN Assn. Nat. Capital Area, Western Polit. Sci. Assn., Cosmos Club, Pi Sigma Alpha. Democrat. Unitarian. Home: 5719 Chevy Chase Pky NW Washington DC 20015-2521 Office: Heldref Pubs 1319 18th St NW Washington DC 20036-1826

BEACHLEY, DEANNA EILEEN, history educator; b. Somerset, Pa., Aug. 22, 1963; d. Ronald D. and Linda E. (Brougher) B.; m. John M. Ziebell, Jan. 13, 1993. BA, Youngstown State U., 1985, MA, 1988; PhD in History, No. Ariz. U., 1997. Prof. history C.C. of So. Nev., North Las Vegas, 1992—. Active Nev. Women's History Project. Mem. Orgn. Am. Historians, Western Women's History Assn. Avocations: hiking, camping, kayaking. Office: CC of So Nev 3200 E Cheyenne Ave S2C North Las Vegas NV 89030-4228

BEACHLEY, DONALD E., federal judge. Apptd. part-time magistrate judge U.S. Dist. Ct. Md. Address: PO Box 1269 Hagerstown MD 21741-1269

BEACHLEY, NORMAN HENRY, mechanical engineer, educator; b. Washington, Jan. 13, 1933; s. Albert Henry and Anna Garnet (Eiring) B.; m. Marion Ruth Iglehart, July 18, 1959; children: Brenda Ruth, Rebecca Sue, Barbara Joan. B.M.E., Cornell U., 1956, Ph.D., 1966. Mem. tech. staff Hughes Aircraft Co., Culver City, Calif., 1956-57; mem. tech. staff Space Tech. Labs., Redondo Beach, Calif., 1959-63; mem. faculty U. Wis., Madison, 1966—, prof. mech. engring., 1978-94, prof. emeritus, 1994—; cons. numerous orgns., 1967—. Co-author: Introduction to Dynamic System Analysis, 1978. Served with USAF, 1957-59. Sci. and Engring. Research Council Gt. Britain fellow, 1981-82. Fellow Soc. Automotive Engrs.; mem. ASME, Sigma Xi. Research in field of energy storage powerplants for motor vehicles, 1970—. Home: 2332 Fitchburg Rd Verona WI 53593-9278 Office: U Wis 1513 University Ave Madison WI 53706-1539

BEACHUM, JAMES CURTIS, stockbroker; b. East Lansing, Mich., Apr. 26, 1960; s. James Curtis Beachum Sr. and Carmen Joan Brown. Bachelor's degree, U. Ind., 1981; postgrad., U. Mich., 1987-89. With Dean Witter-Morgan Stanley, N.Y.C., 1992-93, Merrill Lynch Pierce Fenner Smith, Farmington Hills, Mich., 1993; pres. Bloomfield Fin., Inc., Bloomfield Hills, Mich., 1993—; with Woodward Securities Inc., Birmingham, Mich., 1995. Contbr. articles to newspapers. Mem. Nat. Assn. Securities Dealers (lic. series 7, 63). Republican. Roman Catholic. Avocations: skiing, tennis, squash. Fax: (248) 644-5576. Home: 6730 Colby Ln Bloomfield Hills MI 48301 Office: 6730 Colby Ln PO Box 7884 Bloomfield Hills MI 48302

BEACHY, WILLIAM R., non-profit executive; b. Hutchinson, Kans., July 5, 1948; s. Vernon Mahlon and Nora M. (Miller) B. BA in Polit. Economy, Antioch Coll., Washington, 1973; M.Pub.Affairs, Ind. U., 1990. Rsch. asst. Washington Ctr. for Met. Studies, Washington, 1971-75; assoc. instr. Ind. U., Bloomington, 1975-76; adminstrv. asst. Congressman Dan Glickman, Washington, 1977-82; campaign mgr. Gov. John Carlin, Topeka, Kans., 1982; exec. dir. Kans. Dem. Party, Topeka, 1983-85, Kans. Nat. Priorities Project, Topeka, 1988-89, Topeka Ctr. for Peace and Justice, 1991—, Common Cause Kans., Topeka, 1997—. Editor Cooperation Times newsletter. Bd. sec. Concerned Citizens for Topeka, 1997—; rep. CDBG (Community Development Adv. Com.) Adv. Com., Topeka, 1995—. Recipient Martin Luther King Jr. Legacy award WIBW Radio and Kans. Sch. Dist. 501, 1996. Mem. Nat. Polit. Sci. Assn. Mennonite/Unitarian. Home: 122 SW Hampton St Topeka KS 66612-1415 Office: Common Cause Kansas 1248 SW Buchanan St Topeka KS 66604-1274

BEADLE, CHARLES WILSON, retired mechanical engineering educator; b. Beverly, Mass., Jan. 24, 1930; s. Thomas and Jean (Wilson) B.; m. Dorothy Elizabeth Struyk, May 5, 1956; children: Steven C., Sara E., Gordon S. BS, Tufts U., 1951; MSE, U. Mich., 1954; PhD, Cornell U., 1961. Registered mech. engr., Calif. Research engr. Gen. Motors Research Labs., Detroit, 1951-54, RCA Research Labs., Princeton, N.J., 1954-57; prof. mech. engring. U. Calif., Davis, 1961-91, ret., 1991. Contbr. articles to profl. jours. Fellow ASME. Home: 420 12th St Davis CA 95616-2023 Office: U Calif Davis Dept Mech Engring Davis CA 95616

BEADLE, JOHN GRANT, retired manufacturing company executive; b. Chgo., Dec. 16, 1932; s. John G. and Katharine (Brady) B.; m. Lee Oliver, Apr. 11, 1955; children: Katharine, John. B.A., Yale U., 1954. Salesman Pure Oil Co., Jacksonville and Tampa, Fla., 1957-59, Kordite Co., Tampa, New Orleans, 1959-61; with Union Spl. Corp., Chgo., 1961—; exec. v.p. Union Spl. Corp., 1972-75, pres., chief operating officer, 1975-76, pres., chief exec. officer, 1976-84, chmn., chief exec. officer, 1984-96; bd. dirs. Batts, Inc., Oliver Products Co., Learning Scis. Corp., Woodward Governor Co., Portec Corp., William Blair Mut. Funds; past pres., bd. dirs. Juvenile Protection Assn.; past chmn., bd. dirs. Midwest Indsl. Mgmt. Assn.; past chmn. Internat. Coun. Machinery and Allied Products Inst. Trustee, past pres. Castle Park Assn. Served with USAF, 1954-57. Mem. Northwestern U. Assocs., Chgo. Com., Am. Apparel Machinery Mfrs. Assn., Riomar Country Club, Riomar Bay Yacht Club. Republican. Episcopalian. Clubs: Skokie Country (Glencoe, Ill.), Commonwealth, Comml.

BEAGLE, BENJAMIN STUART, JR., columnist; b. Staunton, Va., Apr. 24, 1927; s. Benjamin Stuart Sr. and Mamie Virginia (Smith) B.; m. Mary Ann John, June 25, 1952; children: Ann Beheler, Benjamin III, Lucinda Casey. BA in English, Roanoke Coll., 1952. Reporter Radford (Va.) News Jour.; pub. rels. asst. Roanoke Coll., Salem, Va., 1952-53; reporter Staunton News Leader, 1953-54; sr. writer Roanoke (Va.) Times & World News, 1954-92, columnist, 1957—. Author: The World I Never Made, 1986, El Viejo Writes Again, 1990, J. Lindsay Almond, Virginia's Reluctant Rebel. With U.S. Army, 1945-46, ATO. Named Disting. Alumnus Roanoke Coll., 1992. Avocations: reading, writing, outdoor work, woodworking. Home: 5571 Highfields Rd Roanoke VA 24018-4109 Office: Roanoke Times & World News 201 Campbell Ave SW # 209 Roanoke VA 24011-1100

BEAGLE, JOHN GORDON, real estate broker; b. Spokane, Wash., Dec. 31, 1943; s. Gordon Avril and Sylvia Alberta (Dobbs) B.; m. Shihoko Ledo, Nov. 14, 1964; children: James, Steven, Kevin, Melanie. BS, Mont. State U., 1970; GRI, Realtors Inst., Helena, Mont. Cert. real estate broker. Instr. Kalispell (Mont.) High Sch., 1970-71; gen. mgr. Equity Coop. Assn., Harlem, Mont., 1971-76; owner, operator Howards Pizza, Livingston, Mont., 1976-79; broker, owner Beagle Properties, Sidney, Mont., 1979—. Appointed to Mont. Bd. Realty Regulation, 1995. With USN, 1963-67. Mem. Mont. Assn. Realtors (v.p. ea. dist. 1982-84, 90-94), Gateway Bd. Realtors (pres. 1987-88), Kiwanis, Masons (past master). Republican. Mem. Ch. of Christ. Avocations: computers, readings, fishing. Office: ERA Beagle Properties 120 2nd Ave SW Sidney MT 59270-4018

BEAGLE, PETER SOYER, writer; b. N.Y.C., Apr. 20, 1939; s. Simon and Rebecca (Soyer) B.; m. Enid Nordeen, May 8, 1964 (div. 1980); children: Vicki Lynn, Kalisa, Daniel Nordeen; m. Padma Hejmadi, Sept. 21, 1988. BA, U. Pitts., 1959; student, Stanford U., 1960-61. Author: (novels) A Fine and Private Place, 1960, The Last Unicorn, 1968, The Inkeeper's Song, 1993, I See By My Outfit, 1965, The California Feeling, 1969, (with Pat Derby) The Lady and Her Tiger, 1976, The Fantasy Worlds of Peter Beagle, 1978, The Garden of Earthly Delights, 1982, The Folk of the Air (novel), 1987; screenwriter: The Dove, 1974, The Greatest Thing That Almost Happened, 1977, The Lord of the Rings: Part One, 1978, The Last Unicorn, 1982, (opera libretto) The Midnight Angel, 1993, In the Presence of Elephants, 1995; co-editor: Peter S. Beagle's Immortal Unicorn, 1995, (novel) The Unicorn Sonata, 1996, (stories) Giant Bones, 1997, (stories) The Rhinoceros Who Quoted Nietzsche, 1997, Friends in the Night, 1999; free-lance writer for Ladies Home Jour., Saturday Evening Post, Holiday, others. Vice chmn. Santa Cruz chpt. ACLU, 1968-69. Address: 2135 Humboldt Ave Davis CA 95616-3084

BEAGLES, DOROTHY BOETTICHER, office administrator, homeopathic consultant; b. Garfield, N.J., Feb. 15, 1937; d. Rudolph Paul and Dorothy (Zibulsky) Boetticher; m. J. Keith Beagles, Apr. 23, 1960; children: Bradley Keith, J. Kevin. BS, Brigham Young U., 1961; D of Homeopathic Medicine, Brit. Inst. Homeopathy, London, 1995. Bd. cert. naturopathic doctor. Homeopathic cons. Dolosos, Las Vegas, 1986-91; office mgr. Tri-Chiropractic Kinesiology, Las Vegas, 1991—; instr. Environ. Stress Mgmt. Fellow Brit. Inst. Homeopathy; mem. Internat. Coll. Applied Kinesiology, Am. Naturopathic Med. Assn. Office: Tri Chiropractic Kinesiology 3750 S Jones Blvd Las Vegas NV 89103-2283

BEAGRIE, GEORGE SIMPSON, dentist, educator, dean emeritus; b. Peterhead, Scotland, Sept. 14, 1925; emigrated to Can., 1968, naturalized, 1973; s. George and Eliza Lawson (Simpson) B.; m. Marjorie McVie, Sept. 30, 1950; children: Jennifer, Lesley, Ailsa, Elspeth. LDS, Royal Coll. Surgeons, Edinburgh, Scotland, 1947; DDS, U. Edinburgh, 1966, DDS (hon.), 1987; DSc (hon.), McGill U., Can., 1985; D degree, U. Montreal, Can., 1991. Prof., chmn. dept. restorative dentistry U. Edinburgh Dental Sch., 1963-68; prof., chmn. dept. clin. scis. U. Toronto Dental Sch., 1968-78, dir. postgrad. div., 1974-78; dean faculty dentistry U. B.C., Vancouver, Can., 1978-88, dean emeritus, 1989—; sci. officer grants com. dental scis. Med. Rsch. Coun. Can., 1971-76, dir. dental tng. grants programme, 1971-78; mem. Nat. Dental Examining Bd. Can.; chmn. written exams com. Nat. Dental Examining Bd., Can., 1984-93; cons. in field. Contbr. over 100 articles to dental jours. Mem. United Ch. Can. Served to flight lt. RAF, 1948-50. Fellow Nuffield Found., 1957-58; grantee Med. Research Council U.K., 1962-64; grantee Med. Research Council Can., 1968; grantee Commonwealth Found., 1973. Fellow Royal Coll. Dentists Can. (pres. 1977-79), Am. Coll. Dentists, Internat. Coll. Dentists; fellow in dental surgery Royal Coll. Surgeons Edinburgh and Eng.; mem. ADA (hon.), Internat. Assn. Dental Research (pres. 1977-78), Fedn. Dentaire Internat. (chmn. commn. on dental edn. and practice 1981-87), Can. Dental Assn. (editor tape cassette program 1972-76), Omicron Kappa Upsilon. Office: Univ BC Faculty Dentistry, 345-2194 Health Scis Mall, Vancouver, BC Canada V6T 1W5

BEAHM, FRANKLIN D., lawyer; b. Independence, Kans., Jan. 18, 1953; s. Edgar Hiram and Dorothy S.; m. Tawny L. McIntyre, Jan. 7, 1994; children: F. David Beahm Jr., Patrick Stuart Beahm, Kristin Sanders, Stephen McWilliams. BBA, So. Methodist U., 1975; JD, Tulane U., 1977. Bar: La. 1977, Colo. 1993, U.S. Dist. Ct. (ea. dist.) La. 1977, U.S. Dist. Ct. (mid. dist.) La. 1980, U.S. Dist. Ct. (we. dist.) La. 1985, U.S. Ct. Appeals (5th cir.), U.S. Tax Ct. 1989, U.S. Supreme Ct. 1993. Assoc. Manard & Schenberger, New Orleans, 1977-80, Bourgeois, Bennett, Metairie, La., 1980; assoc. Hammett, Leake & Hammett, New Orleans, 1980-83, ptnr., 1983-85; ptnr. Thomas, Hayes & Beahm, New Orleans, 1985-95, Chehardy, Sherman, Ellis, Breslin, Murray, Metairie, 1995-97, Beahm & Green, New Orleans, 1997—. Mem. Am. Health Lawyers Assn., Am. Soc. Law and Medicine, La. Assn. Def. Counsel, La. Bar Assn. (Interprofl. com. 1997-98), La. Med. Soc. (Interprofl. com. 1997-98), La. Soc. Hosp. Attys. of the La. Hosp. Assn., Denver Bar Assn., Def. Rsch. Inst. (med. malpractice com., product liability com.), Beta Alpha Psi. Office: 145 Robert E Lee Blvd Ste 408 New Orleans LA 70124-2581

BEAHRS, OLIVER HOWARD, surgeon, educator; b. Eufaula, Ala., Sept. 19, 1914; s. Elmer Charles and Elsa Katherine (Smith) B.; 1 child, Gean Beahrs Landy; m. Helen Edith Taylor, July 27, 1947; children: John Randolf, David Howard, Nancy Ann Beahrs Oster. BA, U. Calif., Berkeley, 1937; MD, Northwestern U., 1942; MS in Surgery, Mayo Grad. Sch. Medicine, 1949; D of Mil. Medicine honoris causa, Uniformedc Svcs. U. Hlth. Sci., 1999. Diplomate Am. Bd. Surgery. Fellow surgery Mayo Grad. Sch. Medicine, Rochester, Minn., 1942, 46-49, prof. surgery, 1966-79, prof.

emeritus, 1979—; asst. surgeon Mayo Clinic, 1949-50, head sect. gen. surgery, 1950-79, vice-chmn. bd. govs., 1964-75; Bd. dirs. Rochester Meth. Hosp.; trustee Mayo Found.; mem. cancer control and rehab. adv. com. Nat. Cancer Inst., 1975-84; mem. Am. Joint Com. on Cancer, 1975-78, exec. dir., 1980-92. Editor: Surgical Consultations; editorial bd.: Surgery, Surg. Techniques Illustrated; contbr. over 400 articles to profl. jours. Hon. life, bd. dirs. Am. Cancer Soc., 1975—; trustee Rochester Meth. Hosp.; adv. bd. Uniform Svcs. Univ. Health Scis.; med. cons. Pres. and Mrs. Reagan. Capt. USNR, 1942-64, ret. Recipient Leadership and Humanitarian awards Am. Cancer Soc. Fellow Royal Coll. Surgery in Ireland (hon.), Royal Australasian Coll. Surgery (hon.); mem. AMA, ACS (mem. exec. com., bd. govs., chmn. cen. jud. com., long-range planning com., chmn. bd. govs., chmn. bd. regents, pres. 1988-89), Am. Group Practice Assn. (sec.-treas. 1974-75), Minn. Surg. Soc. (pres. 1960-61), Am. Thyroid Assn., James IV Assn. Surgeons, Am. Surg. Assn. (pres. 1979-80, chmn. com. on issues 1980-83), So. Surg. Assn., Cen. Surg. Assn., Western Surg. Assn., Soc. Head and Neck Surgeons (pres. 1966-67), Am. Assn. Endocrine Surgeons (pres. 1986-87), Am. Assn. Clin. Anatomists (pres. 1986-87), Soc. Surgery Alimentary Tract, Soc. Pelvic Surgeons (pres. 1983-84), Soc. Surg. Oncology, Am. Assn. Clin. Anatomists (pres.), Philippine Coll. Surgeons (hon.), Hellenic Coll. Surgery (hon.), Assn. Française de Chirurgie Française, Northwestern U. Alumni Assn. (Merit award), Sigma Xi, Phi Kappa Epsilon, Phi Beta Pi, Theta Delta Chi. Republican. Methodist. Home: 2253 Baihly Ln SW Rochester MN 55902-1023 Office: 200 1st St SW Rochester MN 55905-0001

BEAIRD, CHARLES T., publishing executive; b. Shreveport, La., July 17, 1922; s. James Benjamin and Mattie Connell (Fort) B.; m. Carolyn Williams, Feb. 6, 1943; children: Susan, Marjorie, John. B.A., Centenary Coll., 1966; Ph.D. in Philosophy, Columbia U., 1972. Vice pres., asst. gen. mgr. J.B. Beaird Corp., Shreveport, 1946-57; cons. in oil and investments Shreveport, 1957-59; pres. Beaird-Poulan Inc., Shreveport, 1959-73; chmn. bd. Beaird-Poulan div. Emerson Electric Co., 1973-76; pres., pub. Shreveport Jour., 1976—; dir. Fed. Res. Bank of Dallas, 1972-78, dep. chmn., 1973-78; dir. Winrock Enterprises, Inc., Little Rock; adj. prof. Centenary Coll., Shreveport, 1969-95, prof. emeritus, bd. dirs. Mem. Caddo Parish Police Jury, 1956-60; bd. dirs. Woodrow Wilson Nat. Fellowship Found., Princeton, N.J., 1975-78 bd. dirs. Community Found. of Shreveport-Bossier, 1975-85, chmn., 1979-80 Served to capt. USMCR, 1943-46. Mem. Shreveport Club, Shreveport Country, Demoiselle Club, Cambridge Club, So. Trace Country. Office: PO Box 31110 Shreveport LA 71130-1110

BEAIRD, JAMES RALPH, law educator, dean; b. 1925. BS, U. Ala., 1949, LLB, 1951; LLM, George Washington U., 1953. Bar: Ala. 1951, D.C. 1973. Atty. U.S. Dept. Labor, 1951-56, asst. solicitor, 1956-59; assoc. gen. counsel NLRB, 1959-60; assoc. solicitor U.S. Dept. Labor, 1960-65; vis. prof. U. Ga., 1965-66, prof. law, 1967-89, prof. emeritus, dean, 1976-87, dean emeritus; John Sparkman Vis. Disting. Prof., U. Ala., 1988—; mem. Sec. Labor's Adv. Council on Welfare and Pension Plans, 1968—. Mem. adv. com. for Ga. SBA, 1969—. Mem. Farrah Order Jurisprudence. Office: U Ga Sch Law Athens GA 30602

BEAK, PETER ANDREW, chemistry educator; b. Syracuse, N.Y., Jan. 12, 1936; s. Ralph E. and Belva (Edinger) B.; m. Sandra J. Burns, July 25, 1959; children: Bryan A., Stacia W. B.A., Harvard U., 1957; Ph.D., Iowa State U., 1961. From instr. to prof. chemistry U. Ill., Urbana, 1961—, Roger Adams prof. chemistry, 1997—, Jubille prof. liberal arts and sci., 1997—; cons. Abbott Labs., North Chgo., Ill., 1964—, Monsanto Co., St. Louis, 1969—; G.D. Searle Co., Ill., 1987—. Contbr. articles to profl. jours. A.P. Sloan Found. fellow, 1967-69; Guggenheim fellow, 1968-69. Fellow AAAS (chmn. chemistry sect. 1999); mem. Am. Chem. Soc. (editl. and adv. bds., sec. and divsn. officer, A.C. Cope scholar 1993, Mosher award 1994, Gilman award 1997). Home: 304 E Sherwin Ave Urbana IL 61802

BEAKE, JOHN, professional football team executive; m. Marcia Beake; children: Jerilyn, Chip, Christopher. Grad., Trenton (N.J.) State Coll.; M degree, Pa. State U. Asst. coach Pa. State U., 1961-62, Kansas City Chiefs, NFL, 1968-74, New Orleans Saints, NFL, 1976-77; offensive coordinator Colo. State U., 1974-76; dir. profl. personnel Denver Broncos, NFL, 1979-83, dir. football ops., 1983-84, asst. gen. mgr., 1984-85, gen. mgr., 1985—. Office: Denver Broncos 13655 Broncos Pky Englewood CO 80112-4150*

BEAL, GRAHAM WILLIAM JOHN, museum director; b. Stratford-on-Avon, Eng., Apr. 22, 1947; came to U.S., 1973; s. Cecil John Beal and Annie Gladys (Barton) Tunbridge; m. Nancy Jane Andrews, Apr. 21, 1973: children: Priscilla Jane, Julian William John. BA, Manchester U., Eng., 1969; MA, U. London, 1972. Acad. asst. to dir. Sheffield City (Eng.) Art Galleries, 1972-73; gallery dir. U. S.D., Vermillion, 1973-74, Washington U., St. Louis, 1974-77; chief curator Walker Art Ctr., Mpls., 1977-83; dir. Sainsbury Ctr. for Visual Arts, Norwich, Eng., 1983-84; chief curator San Francisco Mus. Modern Art, 1984-89; dir. Joslyn Art Mus., Omaha, 1989-96, Los Angeles County Mus. Art, 1996—; mem. Fed. Adv. Com. on Internat. Exhbns., 1991-94. Author: (book, exhbn. catalog) Jime Dine: Five Themes, 1984; co-author: (book, exhbn. catalog) A Quiet Revolution, 1987, David Nash: Voyages and Vessels, 1994, Joslyn Air Museum: Fifty Favorities, Joslyn Art Musuem: A Building History, 1998; contbg. to Apollo Mag., London, 1989-91. Trustee Djerassi Found., Woodside, Calif., 1987-89. Mem. Assn. Art Mus. Dirs. Avocations: history, cooking, music. Office: LA County Mus Art 5905 Wilshire Blvd Los Angeles CA 90036-4504

BEAL, JACK, artist; b. Richmond, Va., June 25, 1931; s. Walter Henry and Marion Watkins (Baker) B.; m. Sondra Freckelton. Student, Coll. of William and Mary, 1950-53, Art Inst. Chgo.; studies with Briggs Dyer, Isobel MacKinnon and Kathleen Blackshear, 1953-56; D of Fine Arts (hon.), Art Inst. Boston, 1992; LittD (hon.), Hollins Coll., 1994. vis. lectr. over 100 schs. and univs. Represented in permanent collections Whitney Mus. Am. Art, N.Y.C., Walker Art Ctr., Mpls., Art Inst. Chgo., San Francisco Mus. Fine Arts, Nat. Gallery Art, Washington, Met. Mus., N.Y.C., Del. Mus., Wilmington, Washington and Lee U., Lexington, Va., U.S. Dept. Interior, Washington; executed mural U.S. Labor Bldg., Washington; paintings exhibited Allan Frumkin Gallery, N.Y.C., 1965-93, Galerie Claude Bernard, Paris, Boston U., 1973-84, Va. Mus., 1973-74, Mus. Contemporary Art, Chgo., 1973-74, Madison (Wis.) Art Ctr., 1977-78, Art Inst. Chgo., 1977-78, Chrysler Mus., Norfolk, Va., 1980, Whitney Mus., Fairfield County, Conn., 1981, Munson-Williams-Proctor Inst., Utica, N.Y., 1982, Del. Art Mus., 1983. Mem. Youth Bd., Gouverneur, N.Y., 1970-73; bd. govs. Skowhegan (Maine) Sch., 1972-82; bd. visitors Sch. Visual Arts, Boston U; bd. trustees La Napoule Art Found., 1983-89; co-founder, advisor N.Y. Acad. Art. Recipient Neysa McMein Purchase award Whitney Mus., 1965, award Nat. Acad. & Inst. Arts and Letters, 1996; Nat. Endowment for Arts grantee, 1973; Hermitage Found. fellow, 1953-56; occupant Class of 1939 Endowed Chair Coll. William and Mary, 1992; subject of monograph by Eric Shanes, 1993. Office: care George Adams Gallery 41 W 57th St New York NY 10019-3409

BEAL, MERRILL DAVID, conservationist, museum director; b. Richfield, Utah, June 26, 1926; s. Merrill Dee and Bessy (Neill) B.; m. Jean Lorraine Wood, Feb. 24, 1947; children: John David, James Merrill. B.A., Idaho State Coll., 1950; M.S., Utah State U., 1952. Park ranger, naturalist Yellowstone Nat. Park, 1953-60; chief park naturalist Grand Canyon Nat. Park, 1960-69; asst. supt. Great Smoky Mountains Nat. Park, Gatlinburg, Tenn., 1969-72; assoc. regional dir. Midwest region Nat. Park Service, Omaha, 1972-75, regional dir., 1975-78; supt. Gt. Smoky Mountains Nat. Park, Gatlinburg, Tenn., 1978-83; asst. dir. Ariz.-Sonora Desert Mus., Tucson, 1983-91. Author: Grand Canyon, the Story Behind the Scenery, 1967. Mem. bd. Grand Canyon Sch., 1964-69. Served with USN, 1944-46. Recipient Meritorious Service award U.S. Dept. Interior, 1975. Mem. Wildlife Soc., Gt. Smoky Mountains Natural History Assn. (bd. dirs. 1993-95), S.W. Parks and Monument Assn., Ea. Nat. Park and Monument Assn. (bd. dirs. 1989-95), Sigma Xi.

BEAL, MYRON CLARENCE, osteopathic physician; b. N.Y.C., Dec. 4, 1920; s. Clarence Joseph and Birdice Elvira (Flint) B.; m. Esther Naomi DeLong, Sept 11, 1948; children: Rebecca Johnson, Myron Flint, Shelley Rees, Julie Wilson, Christina Beal Bailey. A.B., U. Rochester, 1942; D.O., Chgo. Coll. Osteo. Medicine, 1945; M.S. in Physiology, U. Chgo., 1949. Asst. dir. clinics Chgo. Coll. Osteo. Medicine, 1946-49; instr. London Coll. Osteopathy, 1949-51; pvt. practice osteo. medicine Rochester, N.Y., 1951-74; prof. biomechanics Coll. Osteo. Medicine, Mich. State U., East Lansing, 1974-81; prof. family medicine Coll. Osteo. Medicine, Mich. State U., 1981-89, prof. emeritus, 1989—, acting chmn. biomechanics, 1975-77; Mem. Nat. Bd. Examiners for Osteo. Physicians and Surgeons, 1960-84, cons., 1984-89; mem. N.Y. State Bd. Medicine, 1961-73. Trustee Chgo. Coll. Osteo. Medicine 1969-93, chmn. bd. dirs. 1985-91. Fellow Am. Acad. Osteopathy (editor 1987—); mem. Am. Osteop. Assn., N.Y. State Osteo. Soc., Mich. Assn. Osteo. Physicians and Surgeons, Chgo. Osteo. Health Systems (bd. dirs. 1986-90). Congregationalist. Office: 5873 Seneca Point Rd Naples NY 14512-9763

BEAL, ROBERT LAWRENCE, real estate executive; b. Boston, Sept. 10, 1941; s. Alexander Simpson and Leona M. (Rothstein) B. BS cum laude, Harvard U., 1963, MBA, 1965. Vice pres., ptnr. Beacon Cos., Boston, 1965-76; ptnr. The Beal Cos., Boston; pres. Beal and Co., Inc., Boston, 1976—; corporator, dir., mem. exec. com., lending com. Provident Instn. Savs., 1975-86; co-chmn. bd. dirs. Mass. Devel. Fin. Agy., 1976—; instr. real estate Northeastern U., 1969-75; mem. East Cambridge rezoning adv. com., 1989—; dir. Artery Bus. Com., 1989—, chmn., 1995—, treas., 1989-95. Bd. dirs. Boston Zool. Soc., 1972-86, pres., 1980, chmn., 1981-84, hon. chmn., 1985; mem. vis. com. Sch. Mus. Fine Arts, Boston, 1974-76, 88-89; overseer Boys Club Boston, 1975-93; mem. corp. Belmont Hill Sch.; trustee Beth Israel Deaconess Med. Ctr., 1981—, mem. bldg. and grounds com., 1976-82, 86-90; dir. Harvard Coll. Fund Coun., 1972-73, capital fund dr. Class '63, 1979-85, co-chmn. 25th reunion, co-chmn. 35th reunion, class gift; exec. bd. Boston chpt. Am. Jewish Com., 1987—, mem. bd. govs., 1989-92; bd. dirs. Boston Mcpl. Rsch. Bur., 1978—, treas., 1988-89, 92, vice chmn., 1990-93, chmn., 1994-96; bd. dirs. Met. Boston Housing Partnership, Inc., 1983-95; trustee The Partnership, Inc., 1981-89, New Eng. Aquarium, 1987—, bd. govs., 1993-98; mem. adv. task force John F. Kennedy Libr., 1982; bd. overseers Mus. Fine Arts, Boston, 1988—; mem. vis. com. Harvard Div. Sch., 1989—, adv. com. Taubman Ctr., John F. Kennedy Sch. Govt., Harvard U., 1989—. Mem. Nat. Realty Com. (dir., past sec., mem. exec. com. 1974—, v.p., vice chmn.), Mass. Assn. Realtors (dir. 1979-81), Greater Boston Real Estate Bd. (bd. dir. 1970-72, 76-90, pres. 1978-79), Am. Soc. Real Estate Counselors, Bldg. Owners-Mgrs. Assn. Boston (dir. 1970-72), Ripon Soc. (co-founder, nat. treas. 1968-73, nat. governing bd. 1979-85), Nat. Assn. Real Estate Appraiser (cert.), Mass. Taxpayers Found. (dir. 1980-86), Inst. Property Taxation (affliate), Internat. Assn. Assessing Officers (primary subscribing mem. 1982—), Beacon Hill Civic Assn. (bd. dir. 1975-79), Bostonian Soc. (life), Greater Boston C. of C. (bd. dirs.), The Vault (coord. com. 1978-97), Combined Jewish Philanthropies Greater Boston (vice chmn. 1992-93, exec. com.), Greater Boston C. of C. (bd. dirs. 1992—). Republican. Jewish. Home: 21 Brimmer St Boston MA 02108-1001 Office: Beal and Co Inc 177 Milk St Ste 2A Boston MA 02109-3410

BEALE, BETTY (MRS. GEORGE K. GRAEBER), columnist, writer; b. Washington; d. William Lewis and Edna (Sims) B.; m. George Kenneth Graeber, Feb. 15, 1969. A.B., Smith Coll. Columnist, Washington Post, 1937-40; reporter and columnist Washington Evening Star, 1945-81; weekly columnist North Am. Syndicate (formerly Field Newspaper Syndicate), 1953-89; ret., 1989; lectr. in field. Author: Power at Play: A Memoir of Parties, Politicians and The Presidents in My Bedroom, 1993; columnist Georgetown and Country, 1998—. Recipient Freedom Found. award, 1969, named Woman of Distinction, 1987. Address: 2926 Garfield St NW Washington DC 20008-3536

BEALE, CHRISTOPHER WILLIAM, banker; b. Sydney, New South Wales, Australia, Sept. 13, 1947; s. Jack Gordon Beale and Pamela June Anne (Wallis) Scott; m. Francesca May Macartney, May 6, 1972; children: Julian Macartney, Andrew Macartney. BA, U. Sydney, 1968, LLB, 1971; MBA, Harvard U., 1974. Bar: N.Y. 1975. Atty. Dibbs, Crowther & Osborne, Sydney, 1968-71, Price Waterhouse & Co., Sydney, 1972; assoc. The First Boston Corp., N.Y.C., 1974-77, v.p., 1978-83, mng. dir., 1984-88; chmn. Beale Lynch & Co., N.Y.C., 1988-93; mng. dir. Morgan Stanley & Co., Inc., N.Y.C., 1993-95; mng. dir., global head project fin. Citibank, N.A., N.Y.C., 1995—. Bd. dirs. Am. Australian Assn., N.Y.C., 1984—; mem. adv. bd. Inst. for Internat. Fin., Washington, 1997—. Home: 301 E 52nd St New York NY 10022-6319 Office: Citibank NA 399 Park Ave Fl Lc New York NY 10022-4699

BEALE, GEORGIA ROBISON, historian, educator; b. Chgo., Mar. 14, 1905; d. Henry Barton and Dora Belle (Sledd) Robison; m. Howard Kennedy Beale, Jan. 2, 1942; children: Howard Kennedy, Henry Barton Robison, Thomas Wight. AB, U. Chgo., 1926, AM, 1928; PhD, Columbia U., 1938; postgrad., Sorbonne and Coll. de France, 1930-34. Reader in history U. Chgo., 1927-29; lectr. Barnard Coll., 1937-38; instr. Bklyn. Coll., 1937-39; asst. prof. Hollins (Va.) Coll., 1939-41, Wellesley Coll., 1941-42, Castleton (Vt.) State Coll., 1968-70; vis. assoc. prof. U. Ky., Lexington, 1970-72; professorial lectr. George Washington U., 1983-84. Author: Revellière-lépeaux, Citizen Director, 1938, 72, Academies to Institut, 1973, Bosc and the Exequatur, 1978, The Botanophiles of Angers, 1996; contbg. author Historical Dictionary of the French Revolution, 1985; also articles. Mem. Madison (Wis.) Civic Music Assn. and Madison Symphony Orch. League, 1958—; hon. trustee Culver-Stockton Coll., 1974—. Univ. fellow Columbia U., 1929-30. Mem. AAUW (European fellow 1930-31), Am. Hist. Assn., So. Hist. Assn., Soc. French Hist. Studies, Western Soc. French History (hon. mem. exec. coun.), Am. Soc. 18th Century Studies, Brit. Soc. 18th Century Studies, Reid Hall Club (Paris), Brit. Univ. Women's Club (London), Phi Beta Kappa, Pi Lambda Theta, Phi Alpha Theta, Pi Kappa Delta. Office: The Ridge Orford NH 03777

BEALE, GUY OTIS, engineering educator, consultant; b. Cleve., June 16, 1944; s. Guy Otis and Hilda (Booth) B.; m. Susan Ann Weaver, Dec. 16, 1967; 1 child, Michael Scott. BSEE, Va. Poly. Inst., 1967; MS in Physics, Lynchburg Coll., 1974; PhDEE, U. Va., 1977. Engr. Babcock & Wilcox, Lynchburg, Va., 1971-81; asst. prof. Vanderbilt U., Nashville, 1981-86; assoc. prof. George Mason U., Fairfax, Va., 1986—; cons. David Taylor Rsch. Ctr., Carderock, Md., 1987—, Advanced Control Tech., Nashville, 1987-88, Vanderbilt U. Med. Ctr., Nashville, 1984-85, Syerdrup Tech., Tullahoma, Tenn., 1982-83. Co-author: Digital Simulation of Dynamic Systems, 1994; contbr. more than 50 articles to profl. jours. 1st lt. U.S. Army, 1968-70. Recipient Teaching Excellence award Tau Beta Pi, 1983. Mem. IEEE (sr. mem.), Sigma Xi, Eta Kappa Nu. Lutheran. Avocation: photography. Office: George Mason U Elec/Computer Engring Fairfax VA 22030

BEALE, MARK DOUGLAS, psychiatrist, educator; b. Richmond, Va., May 11, 1962. BA, U. Va., 1984; MD, Ea. Va. Med. Sch., 1989. Diplomate Am. Bd. Psychiatry and Neurology; lic. S.C. State Bd. Med. Examiners. Intern Med. U. S.C., Charleston, 1989-90, resident in psychiatry, 1989-93, fellow in electroconvulsive therapy, 1992-93, instr. dept. psychiatry and behavioral scis., 1993-94, asst. prof. dept. psychiatry and behavioral scis., 1994—; cons. electroconvulsive therapy, attending psychiatrist Inst. Psychiatry, Med. U. S.C., Charleston, 1993—, Ralph Johnson VA, Charleston, 1996—; cons. electroconvulsive therapy Charleston Meml. Hosp., 1993-96; lectr. in field. Author: (with others) Handbook of ECT, 1996, (book chpts.) Handbook of Child and Adolescent Psychiatry, 1996, Textbook of Consultation-Liaison Psychiatry, 1996; referee: (jours.) Convulsive Therapy, Psychosomatics, Neuropsychiatry/Neuropsychology & Behavioral Neurology; book reviewer: Clinical Gerontologist. Recipient Young Investigator award Nat. Alliance Rsch. on Schizophrenia and Depression, 1998. Mem. Am. Psychiat. Assn., Assn. Convulsive Therapy, S.C. Psychiat. Assn. Avocations: guitarist in The Psychodymanics band, saltwater fly fishing. Office: Med U of SC Dept Psychiatry/Behav Sci 171 Ashley Ave Dept Charleston SC 29425-0001

BEALKE, LINN HEMINGWAY, bank executive; b. St. Louis, Nov. 14, 1944; s. Charles Francis and Miriam Frances (Hemingway) B.; m. Jean Long Wells, Sept. 6, 1969; children: David Q.W., Emily R., Linn H. BA, U. Ark., 1966; MBA, Washington U., 1969. Fin. analyst Edison Brothers Stores, St. Louis, 1969-74; sr. v.p. Commerce Bank of St. Louis, 1975-78; v.p. fin. and adminstrn. Curlee Clothing Co., Lexington, Ky., 1978-80; vice chmn. County Bank of St. Louis, 1980-84, Southwest Bank of St. Louis, 1984—; bd. dirs. Zoltek Cos., Inc.; bd. dirs. Miss. Valley Bancshares, pres., 1984—. Treas. Forsyth Sch., St. Louis, 1980-87; pres. Edgewood Childrens Ctr., Webster Groves, Mo., 1986-88; dir. Mo. Colls. Fund, Jefferson City, Mo., 1990-93. Mem. Mo. Bankers Assn. (dir. 1988-90), Fin. Execs. Inst. (pres. St. Louis chpt. 1989-90, dir. 1991-94), Am. Bankers Assn. Leadership Conf. (del. 1990-92), Racquet Club (v.p. 1987-89), Bellerive Country Club, Boone Valley Golf Club. Office: SW Bank St Louis 2301 S Kingshighway Blvd Saint Louis MO 63110-3498

BEALL, BURTCH W., JR., architect; b. Columbus, Ohio, Sept. 27, 1925; s. Burtch W. and Etta (Beheler) B.; m. Susan Jane Hunter, June 6, 1949; children: Brent Hunter, Brook Waite. Student, John Carroll U., 1943; BArch, Ohio State U., 1949. Draftsman Brooks & Coddington, Architects, Columbus, 1949-51, William J. Monroe, Architects, Salt Lake City, 1951-53, Lorenzo Young, Architect, Salt Lake City, 1953-54; prin. Burtch W. Beall, Jr., Architect, Salt Lake City, 1954—; vis. lectr. Westminster Coll., 1955; adj. prof. U. Utah, 1955-85, 92-97; treas. Nat. Coun. Archtl. Registration Bds., 1982-84. Restoration architect Salt Lake City and County Bldg; contbr. projects to: A Pictorial History of Architecture in America, America Restored, This Before Architecture. Trustee Utah Found. for Arch., 1985, pres., 1987-91; mem. Utah State Bd. Fine Arts, 1987-95, chmn., 1991-93; chmn. Utah State Capitol Adv. Com., 1986-90, Western States Art Fedn., Bd. trustees, 1991-94; mem. exec. residence com. State of Utah, 1991-97; mem. Utah: A Guide to the State Found. With USN, 1943-45. Recipient several merit and honor awards; Found. fellow Utah Heritage Found., 1985. Fellow AIA; mem. Masons, Sigma Alpha Epsilon. Methodist. Home: 4644 Brookwood Cir Salt Lake City UT 84117-4908 Office: Burtch W Beall Jr Arch 2188 Highland Dr Salt Lake City UT 84106-2896

BEALL, CYNTHIA, anthropologist, educator; b. Urbana, Ill., Aug. 21, 1949; d. John Wood and J. Alene (Beachler) B. BA in Biology, U. Pa., 1970; MA in Anthropology, Pa. State U., 1972, PhD in Anthropology, 1976. Asst. prof. Case Western Res. U., Cleve., 1976-82, assoc. prof. of anthropology, 1982-87, prof. anthropology, 1987—. Co-editor Jour. of Cross-Cultural Gerontology, 1986-95; contbr. articles to profl. jours. Active Internat. Rsch. Exch. Program, 1990, 91. Rsch. grantee NSF, 1981, 83, 86, 87, 93, 94, 95, 97, Am. Fedn. for Aging. Rsch., 1983, 86, Nat. Geog. Soc., 1983, 86-87, 93, 95; Nat. Program for Advanced Study and Rsch. in China fellow NAS, 1986-87, 97. Mem. AAAS, U.S. Nat. Acad. Scis., Am. Anthrop. Assn., Am. Assn. Phys. Anthropology (exec. com. 1989-92), Human Biology Coun. (exec. com. 1989-92, pres. 1992-94), Soc. for Study Human Biology, Assn. for Anthropology and Gerontology. Achievements include field research in Peru, Bolivia, Nepal, Tibet, Mongolia and Ethiopia. Office: Case Western Res U Dept Anthropology 238 Mather Memorial Bldg Cleveland OH 44106-2699

BEALL, DENNIS RAY, artist, educator; b. Chickasha, Okla., Mar. 13, 1929; s. Roy A. and Lois O. (Phillips) B.; 1 son, Garm. Musician,, Okla. City U., 1950-52; B.A., San Francisco State U., 1953, M.A., 1958. Registrar Oakland (Calif.) Art Mus., 1958; curator Achenbach Found. for Graphic Arts, Calif. Palace of the Legion of Honor, San Francisco, 1958-1965; asst. prof. art San Francisco State U., 1965-69, assoc. prof., 1969-76, prof. art, 1976-92; prof. emeritus, 1992—. Numerous one-man shows of prints, 1957—, including: Award Exhbn. of San Francisco Art Commn., Calif. Coll. Arts and Crafts, 1978, San Francisco U. Art Gallery, 1978, Los Robles Galleries, Palo Alto, Calif.; numerous group shows 1960— including Mills Coll. Art Gallery, Oakland, Calif., Univ. Gallery of Calif. State U., Hayward, 1979, Marshall-Meyers Gallery, 1979, 80, Marin Civic Ctr. Art Galleries, San Rafael, Calif., 1980, San Francisco Mus. Modern Art, 1985; touring exhibit U. Mont., 1987-91; represented in numerous permanent collections including Libr. of Congress, Washington, Mus. Modern Art, N.Y.C., Nat. Libr. of Medicine, Washington, Cleve. Mus., Whitney Mus., Phila. Mus., U.S. embassy collections, Tokyo, London and other major cities, Victoria and Albert Mus., London, Achenbach Found. for graphic Arts, Calif. Palace of Legion of Honor, San Francisco, Oakland Art Mus., Phila. Free Libr., Roanoke (Va.) Art Ctr., Worcester (Mass.) Art Mus., Whitney Mus. Am. Art, Cleve. Mus., various colls. and univs. in U.S. Served with USN, 1947-50, PTO. Office: San Francisco State Univ Art Dept 1600 Holloway Ave San Francisco CA 94132-1722

BEALL, DONALD RAY, multi-industry high-technology company executive; b. Beaumont, Calif., Nov. 29, 1938; s. Ray C. and Margaret (Murray) B. BS, San Jose State Coll., 1960; MBA, U. Pitts., 1961; postgrad., UCLA; D of Engring. (hon.), GMI Engring. and Mgmt. Inst., 1994, Milw. Sch. Engring., 1994. With Ford Motor Co., 1961-68; fin. mgmt. positions Newport Beach, Calif., 1961-66; mgr. corp. fin. planning and contracts Phila., 1966-67; controller Palo Alto, Calif., 1967-68; exec. dir. corp. fin. planning N.Am. Rockwell, El Segundo, Calif., 1968-69, exec. v.p. electronics group, 1969-71; exec. v.p. Collins Radio Co., Dallas, 1971-74; pres. Collins Radio Group, Rockwell Internat. Corp., Dallas, 1974-76; corp. v.p., pres. Electronic Ops., Dallas, 1976-77; exec. v.p. Rockwell Internat. Corp., Dallas, 1977-79; pres., chief operating officer Rockwell Internat. Corp., Pitts., 1979-88; chmn. bd., chief exec. officer Rockwell Internat. Corp., Costa Mesa, Calif., 1988-98; chmn. Rockwell Internat. Corp., Seal Beach, 1997-98, chmn. of exec. com. of bd., 1998—; mem. bd. overseers and Grad. Sch. of Mgmt.; bd. visitors U. Calif., Irvine, 1988—; trustee Calif. Inst. Tech.; bd. dirs. Procter & Gamble Co., Amoco Corp., Times-Mirror Corp., L.A. World Affairs Coun.; mem. Bus. Higher Edn. Forum, Bus. Coun., Bus. Roundtable, SRI Adv. Coun., Coun. on Competitiveness. Recipient Exemplary Leadership in Mgmt. award John E. Anderson Sch. Mgmt., UCLA, 1991, Excellence in Tech. award Gartner Group, 1991, Spirit of Achievement award Jr. Achievement of So. Calif., 1993, Adm. Chester W. Nimitz award Navy League's Fleet, 1995, Inaugural Front and Ctr. award Calif. State U., Fullerton, 1996, Human Rels. award Am. Jewish Com., Orange County, 1996; named hon. chmn. Nat. Engrs. Week, 1994. Fellow AIAA, Soc. Mfg. Engrs.; mem. Navy League U.S., Young Pres.'s Orgn., Sigma Alpha Epsilon, Beta Gamma Sigma. Office: Rockwell Internat Corp 2201 Seal Beach Blvd Seal Beach CA 90740

BEALL, FRANK CARROLL, science director and educator; b. Balt., Oct. 3, 1933; s. Frederick Carroll Beall and Virginia Laura (Ogier) McNally; m. Mavis Lillian Holmes, Sept. 7, 1963; children: Amanda Jane Fee, Mark Walter Beall, Alyssa Joan Beall. BS, Pa. State U., 1964; MS, Syracuse U., 1966, PhD, 1968. Rsch. technologist U.S. Forest Products Lab., Madison, Wis., 1966-68; asst., then assoc. prof. Pa. State U., University Park, 1968-75; assoc. prof. U. Toronto, Can., 1975-77; scientist, mgr. Weyerhaeuser Co., Federal Way, Wash., 1977-88; Fred E. Dickinson chair in wood sci. and tech. U. Calif. Forest Products Lab., Richmond, 1997—, prof., dir., 1988—. Contbr. articles in wood and sci. tech.; patentee for wood forming method, method of measuring content of dielectric materials, vertical progressive lumber dryer, bond strength measurement of composite panel products, hybrid pultruded products and method for their manufacture, pultrusion method for condensation resin injection, others. Fellow Acoustic Emission Working Group (chmn. 1996-98), Internat. Acad. Wood Sci. (sec.-treas. 1996—); mem. ASTM (com. DO7 on wood, chmn. 1994-98), Internat. Union Forestry Rsch. Orgns. (chmn. non-destructive evaluation working group), Am. Soc. for Non-destructive Testing, Forest Products Soc. (v.p. 1999—), Soc. Wood Sci. and Tech. (pres. 1991-92). Office: U Calif Forest Products Lab 1301 S 46th St Richmond CA 94804-4600

BEALL, GEORGE, lawyer; b. Frostburg, Md., Aug. 17, 1937; s. James Glenn and Margaret (Schwarzenbach) B.; m. Nancy Roche, Dec. 30, 1964 (div. 1979); m. Carolyn Campbell, June 1, 1979; 1 child, Rebecca S. AB, Princeton U., 1959; LLB, U. Va., 1963. Bar: Md. 1963, U.S. Dist. Ct. Md. 1963, U.S. Dist. Ct. Del. 1988, U.S. Ct. Appeals (4th cir.) 1963, U.S. Ct. Appeals (3d cir.) 1988, U.S. Supreme Ct. 1968. Ptnr. Hogan & Hartson, Balt., 1988—. U.S. atty, Md., 1970-75. Office: Hogan & Hartson 111 S Calvert St Ste 1600 Baltimore MD 21202-6191

BEALL, JAMES ROBERT, toxicologist; b. Stillwater, Okla., June 29, 1940; s. James Arthur and Annabel (Hess) B.; m. Sandra L. Morseth, Aug. 31, 1985; children by previous marriage: Jimmie Karlene, Sidney Sharleen, Tracy Darlene. AAS, Amarillo Coll., 1960; BS, Okla. State U., 1963; MS, U. Okla., 1965, PhD, 1970. Cert. toxicology, 1980—. Sect. leader toxicology Schering Corp., Lafayette, N.J., 1969-77; biol. sci. adminstr. EPA, Washington, 1977-79; spl. asst. OSHA, Washington, 1979-80; sr. policy advisor, toxicologist U.S. Dept. Energy, Washington, 1980-97; dir. Cytomed. Lab., 1970-71, Am. Bd. Toxicology, Washington, 1981-85, Toxicology Lab. Accreditation Bd., Washington, 1983-87; cons. in field. Author: Uterine Lipid Biosynthesis During Reproductive Cycles, 1970; contbr. articles to profl. jours. Mem. Ambulance Squad, N.J., 1974-76. Recipient award of appreciation Consumer Product Safety Commn., 1981, plaque of appreciation Am. Bd. Toxicology, 1985, Md. Govt. award, 1992,. Mem. Soc. Toxicology, Teratology Soc., Assn. Govt. Toxicologists (pres. 1983-88, bd. dirs. 1983-88), N.Y. Acad. Scis., Sigma Xi. Avocations: backpacking, photography, writing. Office: 4804 Old Middletown Rd Jefferson MD 21755-8315

BEALL, KENNETH SUTTER, JR., lawyer; b. Evanston, Ill., Aug. 9, 1938; s. Kenneth Sutter and Helen Cantlon (Koenig) B.; m. Blair Hamilton Bissett, May 25, 1975; children: Kevina Anne, Hunter Bissett, Baret Bissett. BA, Washington and Lee U., 1961, LLB, 1963. Bar: Fla. 1964. With Gunster, Valdes-Fauli, Yoakley & Stewart, P.A., West Palm Beach, Fla., 1964—, ptnr., 1970—, pres., 1994—. Bd. dirs. The Whitehall Found., The Wells Family Found., The Fuller Found.; chmn. Palm Beach County Environ. Control Hearing Bd., 1970-1992; mem. law coun. Washington and Lee U., 1997—; trustee, sec. Caribbean/Latin Am. Action. Served with USMCR, 1963-68. Mem. ABA, Fla. Bar (Pres. Pro Bono Svc. award 1982), Palm Beach County Bar Assn., Fed. Bar Assn. (pres. Palm Beach County chpt. 1981), Bath and Tennis Club, Everglades Club, Sailfish Club (Palm Beach). Democrat. Roman Catholic. Office: 777 S Flagler Dr Ste 500 E West Palm Beach FL 33401-6161

BEALL, ROBERT JOSEPH, foundation executive; b. Washington, May 19, 1943; s. William Joseph and Louise Rachel (Tayman) B.; m. Mary Ellen O'Connor, June 24, 1967; children: Thomas Joseph, Robert Andrew. BS, Albright Coll., 1965; MA, SUNY, Buffalo, 1970, PhD, 1970. Asst. prof. dept. physiology Case-Western Reserve U., Cleve., 1971-74; asst. prof. Case-Western Reserve U. (Sch. Dentistry), 1972-74; grants asso. div. research grants NIH, 1974-75; program dir. metabolic diseases program Nat. Inst. Arthritis, Metabolism & Digestive Diseases, 1975-79; med. dir. Cystic Fibrosis Found., Rockville, Md., 1980-93; nat. dir. Cystic Fibrosis Found., Bethesda, Md., 1981-84; exec. v.p. Cystic Fibrosis Found., Bethesda, 1984-93, pres., CEO, 1994—. Recipient Merit award NIH, 1980. Mem. AAAS, N.Y. Acad. Scis., Am. Soc. Human Genetics, Sigma Xi. Presbyterian. Office: Cystic Fibrosis Found 6931 Arlington Rd Bethesda MD 20814-5231

BEALL, ROBERT MATTHEWS, II, retail chain executive; b. Fresno, Calif., Aug. 7, 1943; s. Egbert Ruffin and Lynda Topp (Matthews) B.; m. Aldona Louise Kupchella, June 15, 1943; children: Jennifer, Lydia, Alexis, Robert. BSBA, U. Fla., 1965; MBA with distinction, NYU, 1969. Asst. buyer Bloomingdale's, N.Y.C., 1969-70; mgr. to CEO/chmn. bd. Beall's, Inc., Bradenton, Fla., 1970—; bd. dirs. SunTrust Bank, Gulfcoast, Fla., Fla. Power & Light Corp., Blue Cross Blue Shield Fla. Divsn. chmn. United Way, Bradenton, 1991; bd. dirs. St. Stephens Sch., Bradenton, 1977-80, Tilton (N.H.) Sch., 1988-92, Fla. Coun. Econ. Edn., 1992—. Capt. U.S. Army, 1965-67. Mem. Nat. Retail Fedn. (bd. dirs. 1982—), Fla. C. of C. (chmn. 1994), Fla. Coun. 100 (bd. dirs., exec. com.), Pi Kappa Phi. Episcopalian. Office: Beall's Inc PO Box 25207 Bradenton FL 34206-5207

BEALS, JENNIFER, actress; b. Chgo., Dec. 19, 1963. Grad., Yale U. Actress: (films) My Bodyguard, 1980, Flashdance, 1983, The Bride, 1985, Split Decisions, 1988, Vampire's Kiss, 1989, Blood and Concrete, 1991, Day of Atonement, 1992, In the Soup, 1992, Dear Diary, 1994, Dead on Sight, 1994, Mrs. Parker and the Vicious Circle, 1994, Devil in a Blue Dress, 1995, Let it Be Me, 1995, Four Rooms, 1995, Arabian Knight, 1995, Wishful Thinking, 1996, The Search for One-eye Jimmy, 1996, The Prophecy II, 1998, Body and Soul, 1998, The Last Days of Disco, 1998, Fear of Flying, 1999; (TV movies) Terror Stalks the Class Reunion, 1992, Indecency, 1992, Night Owl, 1993, The Picture of Dorian Grey, The Twilight of the Golds, 1998, The Spree, 1998; (TV spl.) Cinderella, Faerietale Theatre, 1985; (TV series) 2000 Malibu Road, 1992, Nothing Sacred, 1997; TV guest appearance The Outer Limits, 1995. Office: 14755 Ventura Blvd # 710 Sherman Oaks CA 91403-3669*

BEALS, NANCY FARWELL, state legislator; b. El Paso, July 21, 1938; d. Fred Whitcomb and Katharine Doane (Pier) Farwell; m. Richard William Beals, June 30, 1962; children: Katharine, Robert, Susannah. BA in Polit. Sci., Bryn Mawr Coll., 1960; MA in Teaching, Harvard U., 1961. Group leader Exptl. Internat. Living, Putney, Vt.; jr. high sch. tchr. Winchester (Mass.) Pub. Schs., 1961-62; high sch. tchr. Hamden (Conn.) Pub. Schs., 1962-64; state rep. Conn. Gen. Assembly, Hartford, 1993—; Flemming fellow Ctr. for Policy Alternatives, 1995. Mem. various local and regional offices PTA, Chgo. and Hamden, 1970-83; local pres., state bd. dirs. LWV, Conn., 1979-92; mem., sec., chmn. Hamden Bd. Edn., 1983-92. Recipient Citizenship award for Conn. Philip Morris Corp., 1992, Hamden Notable award Friends of Hamden Libr., 1986, Children's Hero award Children's Trust Fund, 1995, Disting. Legislator award Conn. Assn. Bds. of Edn., 1998; named Legislator of Yr. Conn. Libr. Assn., 1994, Caucus of Conn. Dems., 1997. Democrat.

BEALS, PAUL ARCHER, religious studies educator; b. Russell, Iowa, Feb. 18, 1924; s. Archer Edwin and Myrtle Mae (Kelsey) B.; m. Vivian Brown, Sept. 29, 1945; children: Lois Ruth, Stephen Paul, Samuel Archer, Timothy Joel. AB, Wheaton (Ill.) Coll., 1945; diploma, Moody Bible Inst., Chgo., 1948; ThM with high honors, Dallas Theol. Seminary, 1952, ThD, 1964. Missionary in Cen. African Republic Bapt. Mid-Missions, Cleve., 1952-64; prof. of missiology Grand Rapids (Mich.) Bapt. Seminary, 1964-97, prof. emeritus missiology, 1998—, dir. continuing edn., 1977-90; theol. cons. Bapt. Mid-Missions, 1969—; conf. speaker. Author: A People for His Name, 1985, rev. edit., 1995; contbr. articles to profl. jours. Mem. Evang. Theol. Soc., Evang. Missiological Soc. (pres. 1990-93), Am. Soc. Missiology, Pi Gamma Mu. Home: 2111 Audley Dr NE Grand Rapids MI 49525-1517

BEALS, RALPH E., economist, educator; b. Lexington, Ky., Oct. 30, 1936; s. Wendell Everett and Gratia Marie (Burns) B.; m. Mildred Ann Hubbard, Sept. 3, 1960; children—Gerald E., Ellen H. BS, U. Ky., 1958; MA, Northwestern U., 1959; PhD, MIT, 1970; MA (hon.), Amherst Coll., 1971. Asst. prof. econs. Amherst (Mass.) Coll., 1962-63, assoc. prof., 1966-71, prof. econs., 1971—, Clarence Francis prof. econs., 1980—, acting dean of faculty, 1988-89, acting pres., 1991; asst. prof. econs. Northwestern U., 1963-66; cons. Harvard U. Inst. Internat. Devel., 1973-90, project assoc., Indonesia, 1973-75, 80-82; cons. Boston Inst. for Developing Econs., 1991; cons. U.S. Treasury Office of East Europe and Former Soviet Union, 1993-95; cons. in field. Author: Statistics for Economists: An Introduction, 1972, (with others) Tax and Investment Policies for Hard Minerals: Public and Multinational Enterprises in Indonesia, 1979; also articles. Chmn. bd. Hampshire Community Action Commn., 1969-73. Mem. Am. Econ. Assn. Home: 164 Columbia Dr Amherst MA 01002-3127 Office: Amherst Coll Dept Econs Amherst MA 01002

BEALS, VAUGHN LE ROY, JR., retired motorcycle manufacturing executive; b. Cambridge, Mass., Jan. 2, 1928; s. Vaughn Le Roy and Pearl Uela (Wilmarth) B.; m. Eleanore May Woods, July 15, 1951; children: Susan Lynn, Laurie Jean. BS, M.I.T., 1948, MS, 1954. Research engr. Cornell Aero. Lab., Buffalo, 1948-52, MIT Aero Elastic and Structures Research Lab., 1952-55; dir. research and tech. N.Am. Aviation, Inc., Columbus, Ohio, 1955-65; exec. v.p. Cummins Engine Co., Columbus, Ind., 1965-70, also dir.; chmn. bd., chief exec. officer Formac Internat., Inc., Seattle, 1970-75; dep. group exec. Motorcycle Products Group, AMF Inc., Milw., 1975-77; v.p. and group exec. Motorcycle Products Group, AMF Inc., Stamford, Conn., 1977-81; chief exec. officer Harley-Davidson, Inc., Milw., 1981-89, chmn., 1981-96, chmn. emeritus, 1996-98; bd. dirs. Lindsay Mfg. Mem. Desert Mountain Club, Desert Forest Golf Club, Forest Highlands Golf Club. Home: PO Box 3260 Carefree AZ 85377-3260 Office: Harley-Davidson Inc Box 653 3700 W Juneau Ave Milwaukee WI 53208-2865

BEAM, CLARENCE ARLEN, federal judge; b. Stapleton, Nebr., Jan. 14, 1930; s. Clarence Wilson and Cecile Mary (Harvey) B.; m. Betty Lou Fletcher, July 22, 1951; children—Randal, James, Thomas, Bradley, Gregory. BS, U. Nebr., 1951, JD, 1965. Feature writer Nebr. Farmer Mag., Lincoln, 1951; with sales dept. Steckley Seed Co., Mount Sterling, Ill., 1954-58, advt. mgr., 1958-63; from assoc. to ptnr. Chambers, Holland, Dudgeon & Knudsen, Berkheimer, Beam, et a, Lincoln, 1965-82; judge U.S. Dist. Ct. Nebr., Omaha, 1982-87, chief judge, 1986-87; cir. judge U.S. Ct. Appeals (8th cir.), 1987—; mem. com. on lawyer discipline Nebr. Supreme Ct., 1974-82; mem. Conf. Commrs. on Uniform State Laws, 1979—, chmn. Nebr. sect., 1980-82; mem. jud. conf. com. on ct. and jud. security, 1989-93, chmn., 1992-93. Contbr. articles to profl. jours. Mem. Nebr. Rep. Cen. Com., 1970-78. Capt. U.S. Army, 1951-53, Korea. Regents scholar U. Nebr., Lincoln, 1947, Roscoe Pound scholar U. Nebr., Lincoln, 1964. Mem. Nebr. State Bar Assn. Office: US Ct Appeals 8th Cir 435 Federal Bldg 100 Centennial Mall N Lincoln NE 68508-3859

BEAM, JAMES C. (JIM BEAM), editor, newspaper; b. Cameron, La., Oct. 7, 1933; s. Charles Cleveland and Carrie (Welch) B.; m. Jo Ann Drachenberg, Aug. 20, 1954; children: Jamie Lynn Meek, Bryan Carroll. BA, McNeese State, 1955; MA, La. State, 1962. Tchr. Calcasieu Sch. Bd., Lake Charles, La., 1958-62; reporter Lake Charles (La.) Am. Press, 1962-65, city editor, 1965-81, co-editor, 1981-92, editor, 1992-98, dir. polit. and pub. affairs, 1998—. Lt. U.S. Army, 1955-57. Recipient 1st place column La. Press Assn., 1979, Hal Boyle award La. Miss AP Assn., 1985-86, 1st place Personal Column, 1997. Mem. Soc. Profl. Journalists, Phi Kappa Phi. Democrat. Methodist. Home: 4824 Gentilly St Lake Charles LA 70607-6341 Office: Lake Charles Am Press PO Box 2893 4900 Highway 90 E Lake Charles LA 70615-4037

BEAM, RICHARD KENNETH, college administrator; b. Barberton, Ohio, Apr. 17, 1943; s. Archie Alexander and Mildred Irene (Bland) B.; m. Ruthanne Marlene Brown, Aug. 21, 1964; children: Richard Paul, Robert Kenneth, Derrick Douglas. BA, Ky. Christian Coll., 1965; MA, Morehead State U., 1975; EdD, U. Ky., 1981. Lic. minister, Ohio. Minister Salineville (Ohio) Ch. of Christ, 1965-69; tchr. So. Local H.S., Salineville, 1967-68; minister First Christian Ch., DuQuesne, Pa., 1969-73, Little Rock Christian Ch., Paris, Ky., 1973-76; v.p. Eastern Christian Coll., BelAir, Md., 1976-78; from asst. to assoc. prof. English Johnson Bible Coll., Knoxville, Tenn., 1978-84; prof. English and Lit. Johnson Bible Coll., Knoxville, 1984—, coord. for planning, 1984, dir. grad. and video edn., 1987-94, v.p. for acads., 1994—; cons. Tenn. Temple U., Chattanooga, 1996; commr. Accrediting Assn. Bible Colls., 1996—, chair accrediting commn., 1999: self study dir. Johnson Bible Coll., Knoxville, Commn. Colls. of So. Assn. Colls. & Schs. Accrediting Assn. Bible Colls., 1985, 87, 95, Accrediting Assn. Bible Colls., 1989, 95. Contbr. articles to religious and ednl. publs., 1983—. Elder Woodlawn Christian Ch., Knoxville, 1996—. Named Disting. Alumnus, Ky. Christian Coll., 1988. Mem. Tenn. Conf. Grad. Schs., Tenn. Assn. Instnl. Rsch. Republican. Avocations: fishing, racquetball, gardening. Home: 8003 Boling Ln Knoxville TN 37920-9728 Office: Johnson Bible Coll 7900 Johnson Dr Knoxville TN 37998-0001

BEAM, ROBERT THOMPSON, retired lawyer; b. What Cheer, Iowa, Oct. 27, 1919; s. Clyde O. and Mary Ethel (Thompson) B.; m. Eunice C. Beam. B.S., U. Ill., 1951, J.D., 1954; LL.M., NYU, 1956. Bar: Ill., N.Y. 1954. Assoc. firm Kramer, Marx, Greenlee & Backus, N.Y.C., 1954-57; ptnr. Sidley & Austin, Chgo., 1957-87, ret., 1987. Served to lt. col. USAAF, 1941-47, ETO; PTO. Mem. ABA, Ill. Bar Assn., Chgo. Bar Assn., Mid-Day Club, Univ. Club, Naples Sailing and Yacht Club, Masons. Republican. Episcopalian. Home: 4756 Crayton Ct Naples FL 34103-3012*

BEAM, WILLIAM WASHINGTON, III, data coordinator; b. L.A., Jan. 21, 1960; s. William Washington and Ada Frances (Towler) B. BS, UCLA, 1982; MA, U. Wash., 1985. Paralegal Arco, L.A., 1985-88, programmer, 1988-90, data coord., 1990-94, network adminstr., 1994-98; network analyst ARCO IT, L.A., 1998—. Mem. Am. Econ. Assn. Office: ARCO IT 333 S Hope St Ste 1342 Los Angeles CA 90071-2201

BEAMAN, MARGARINE GAYNELL, scrap metal broker; b. Feb. 26; d. Margaret Lena Geisweidt; m. Robert W. Beaman; children: Richard Beaman, Ronald Beaman, Lorene Barrera, Jessica Barrera. Student, U. Houston, U. Mich. V.p. Beaman Metal Co., Inc., Austin, 1972—; pres. Beaman Acctg. and Cons., Austin, 1975—. Chair Capital Area Workforce Devel. Bd., 1995-97; vol. RIF; mem. bd. Austin Crime Stoppers Edn., Austin C. of C., Homeless Com., Cmty. Action Network; vice chair Trans County Hist. Commn. Recipient Gov.'s Vol. of Yr. award, 1982, Mayor's Meritorious award, 1982, Svc. awards Sertoma Club, N.Y. Am. Coun. of Blind, Nat. Community Schs. award, Citizen Leadership award Freedom Found. at Valley Forge, 1986, Migel Medal award Am. Found. for Blind N.Y.C., 1992, Outstanding Contrbn. award Blinded Vets. Assn., 1995, Outstanding Svc. award Reading is Fundamental; inducted into Tex. Assn. Pvt. Colls. Hall of Fame, Austin Women's Hall of Fame; named Outstanding Blind Worker of Tex., 1982, Most Worthy Citizen of Austin, 1989, Austin's Most Worthy Citizen, 1989. Mem. Tex. Fedn. Bus. and Profl. Women's Clubs (Outstanding Dist. Businesswoman 1996), Exec. Women Internat. (past state pres., Outstanding Svc. award), Internat. Cert. Consumer Credit Execs., Nat. Assn. Fin. Aid Adminstrs., Austin C. of C., Austin Women's C. of C., Gen. Fedn. Women's Club, Pvt. Industry Coun., Am. Coun. of Blind, Zonta Internat., Rotary (pres. East Austin chpt. 1995-96). Home: 1406 Wilshire Blvd Austin TX 78722-1129 Office: 3409 E 5th St Austin TX 78702-4911

BEAMAN, WILLIAM C., federal judge; b. 1945. BA, Ariz. State U., 1967; JD, U. Wyo., 1971. Law clk. to Hon. Ewing T. Kerr U.S. Dist. Ct. Wyo., 1971-73; pvt. law practice Cheyenne, Wyo.; magistrate judge U.S. Dist. Ct. Wyo., Cheyenne, 1975—. Served with Air N.G., 1967-73. Office: 2120 Capitol Ave Cheyenne WY 82001-3633

BEAMER, LAURA, women's health and genetic health nurse; b. Chgo., Jan. 26, 1956; d. Frederick Richard and Bernice Elaine (Linklater) Curr; children: David, Amy, James, Daniel. ADN, Purdue U., 1983, BSN, 1988, MSN, 1990; postgrad., Rush U., 1996—. RN, Ind., Ill.; cert. high risk perinatal nurse, family nurse practitioner. Instr. prenatal Porter Meml. Hosp., Valparaiso, Ind., staff nurse; staff nurse, staff educator Northwestern Meml. Hosp., Chgo.; lectr. Ind. U., Gary. Mem. ANA, AWHONN, Internat. Soc. Nurses in Genetics, Ind. State Nurses Assn., Sigma Theta Tau. Home: 404 Orchid St SE Demotte IN 46310-8787 Office: Ind U Northwest 3400 Broadway Gary IN 46408-1101

BEAMER, YVONNE MARIE, psychotherapist, counselor; b. Cumberland, Md., Jan. 6, 1947; d. William Walter and Ruthella Louise (Smith) Barr; m. Charles Wesley Beamer, Jan. 5, 1974; children: Marie Lynn, Ann Christine. BA, W.Va. U., 1969. Cert. chem. dependency counselor, Ohio; nat. cert. chem. dependency counselor. Tchr. English and lang. arts Ft. Ashby (W. Va.) High Sch., 1969-70; field advisor, field dir. Shawnee G.S. Coun., Cumberland, Md., 1970-73; job counselor Md. Correctional Tng. Ctr., Hagerstown, Md., 1973-74; home tchr. Frederick (Md.) County Bd. of Edn., 1984-86; addictions counselor Frederick County Substance Abuse Program, 1986-88; intake admissions counselor Laurelwood Hosp., Willoughby, Ohio, 1988-92; intake/admissions counselor Glenbeigh Hosp., 1992; addictions counselor Cmty. Action Against Addiction, 1993—. Ch. organist All Souls Episc. Ch., Balt., 1976-82, St. James Episc. Ch., Mt. Airy, Md. 1982-88; mem. choir St. Andrew's Episcopal Ch., 1998—. Mem. Buckeye Squares, Phi Beta Kappa, Sigma Phi Omega. Avocations: dancing, piano, organ, singing, swimming, reading. Home: 3920 Spokane Ave Cleveland OH 44109-3834 Office: Cmty Action Against Addiction 5209 Euclid Ave Cleveland OH 44103-3703

BEAMISH, MARY KATHRYN, copy editor; b. Mpls., Oct. 26, 1958; d. George Edward and Ardis Edith (Zeigler) B. BA in Am. Studies, Augsburg Coll., 1981; MA in Journalism, U. Wis., 1991. Comms. coord. Ctr. for Global Edn. Augsburg Coll., Mpls., 1984-88; features editor, edn. reporter Holland (Mich.) Sentinel, 1992-96; copy editor LaCrosse (Wis.) Tribune, 1996—. Methodist. Avocations: travel, biking, cross-country skiing, films, concerts.

BEAMON, MARY ANN, retired nursing administrator; b. Mar. 20, 1931. Grad., Courter Sch. Practical Nursing, Bethesda Hosp. Sch. Nursing, Cin., 1975; student, U. Cin., 1979. RN, Ohio. Group leader, key punch operator U.S. Treasury Dept., Cin., 1953-59; dir. nursing Lincoln Crawford Home for Aged, 1975-78, nursing supr., 1982-83, day supr., 1985-86; charge practical nurse, charge nurse ob-gyn unit Bethesda Hosp., 1967-75, staff nurse med.-surg. unit, 1987-88; nursing dir. Empress Manor, Cin., 1988-90, Dr. Lucy O. Oxley Family Practice Ctr., Cin., 1990-92; dir. of nursing Grace Manor Nursing Home, Cin., 1992-95; ret., 1995; grief counselor Donald and Stewart Funeral Home, Cin. Ohio. Coord. parish nurse program St. Andrews Episcopal Ch., 1999. Mem. Ohio Nurse Assn. (RN evaluator Ohio nurse testing svc. 1993—). Episcopalian. Home: 3554 Idlewild Ave Cincinnati OH 45207-1012

BEAN, BENNETT, artist; b. Cin., Mar. 25, 1941; s. William Bennett and Abigail (Shepard) B.; m. Cathy Bao, Dec. 17, 1966; 1 child, William Bao. Student, Grinnell Coll., 1959-62; postgrad., U. Iowa, 1963, U. Wash., 1963; MFA, Claremont Grad. Sch., 1966. Asst. prof. art Wagner Coll., S.I., N.Y., 1966-79; trustee Am. Craft Enterprises, New Paltz, N.Y., 1982-85, Am. Craft Coun., N.Y.C., 1980-84; former chmn. bd. dirs. Peters Valley, Layton, N.J. One-man show Royal Marks Gallery, N.Y.C., 1969, Henri Gallery, Washington, 1969; one-person retrospective exhbn. lifetime work Ark. Arts Ctr. Decorative Arts Mus.; exhibited in numerous groups show, including Whitney Mus. Am. Art, 1968-69, Newark Mus., 1968, 80, 89, 91, Am. Craft Mus. II, 1982, 86, N.J. State Mus., 1984, Newport Art Mus., 1984, Hunter Mus., Chattanooga, 1990; represented in permanent collections Whitney Mus. Am. Art, The White House, Washington, Boston Mus. Fine Arts, Newark Mus., N.J. State Mus., St. Louis Mus. Art, Royal Ont. Mus., Ariz. State U., Grinnell Coll., Milw. Art Mus., Crocker Art Mus., Calif., Toledo Mus. Art, Cin. Art Mus., J.P. Speed Art Mus., Ky., others. Recipient editorial award Met. Home mag., 1990; rsch. grantee Wagner Coll., 1968, 70, 77, 78; fellow N.J. Coun. on Arts, 1978, 88, Nat. Endowment for Arts, 1980. Tibetan Buddhist. Studio: 357 County Road 661 Blairstown NJ 07825-4054

BEAN, BOURNE, lawyer; b. Louisville, Oct. 16, 1920; s. Richard M. and Rella (Bourne) B.; m. Byrd Chamness, Feb. 16, 1944; children: Courtney B. Obata, Christy B. Fox, Tracy B. Chivetta. AB, Princeton U., 1942; LLB, Harvard Coll., 1948. Bar: Mo. 1948. Of counsel Armstrong, Teasdale, Schlafly & Davis, St. Louis, 1948—; sec. M&W Packaging U.S. Inc., Cape Girardeau, Mo., 1989—, also bd. dirs.; sec. Swan Corp., St. Louis, 1972—. Lt. USN, 1942-45. Mem. ABA, Mo. Bar Assn. Republican. Epscopalian. Avocations: golf, tennis, traveling, fishing. Office: Armstrong Teasdale 1 Metropolitan Sq Ste 2600 Saint Louis MO 63102-2740*

BEAN, EDWIN TEMPLE, JR., lawyer; b. Washington, Feb. 17, 1926; s. Edwin Temple and Mary (a'Becket) B.; m. Susan Roberts, May 22, 1952; children: Douglas C., Philip O., Emelie R. Bean Ventling. BS, MIT, 1946; LLB, Georgetown U., 1950. Bar: D.C. 1950, N.Y. 1951, U.S. Dist. Ct. (we. dist.) N.Y. 1952, U.S. Ct. Appeals (2nd cir.) 1975, U.S. Supreme Ct. 1978, U.S. Ct. Appeals (fed. cir.) 1982. Examiner U.S. Patent Office, Washington, 1946-50; assoc. Bean, Brooks, Buckley & Bean, Buffalo, 1950-61; ptnr. Christel & Bean, Buffalo, 1961-78, Christel, Bean & Linihan, Buffalo, 1978-85; pres. Christel, Bean & Linihan, P.C., Buffalo, 1985-89; ptnr. Hodgson, Russ, Andrews, Woods & Goodyear, Buffalo, 1989—; lectr., asst. prof. Law Sch., SUNY, Buffalo, 1987—. Pres. Children's Aid, Buffalo, 1968-70; bd. dirs. Child and Family Svcs., Buffalo, 1982—; trustee Gow Sch., South Wales, N.Y., chmn., 1991-95. Mem. ABA, N.Y. State Bar Assn., Erie County Bar Assn., Am. Intellectual Property Law Assn., Licensing Execs. Soc., Buffalo Tennis and Squash Club (pres. 1974), Buffalo Yacht Club, Mid-Day Club (pres. 1972). Republican. Presbyterian. Office: Hodgson Russ Andrews Woods & Goodyear Ste 2000 One M&T Plz Buffalo NY 14203

BEAN, GLEN ATHERTON, entrepreneur; b. Mpls., Aug. 30, 1962; s. Douglas Atherton Bean and Eleanor Green (Caswell) Nolan; m. Mary Catherine Slingsby, June 16, 1990. BS, Ariz. State U., 1988. Promotion specialist John Deere & Co., Waterloo, Iowa, 1987; regional mgr. Elliott Meat Co., Duluth, Minn., 1989-90; gen. ptnr. No. Star Food Brokerage, Savage, Minn., 1990-92; pres. Rochester (Minn.) Bus. Group, Ltd., 1993-98, Hunter Holdings Ltd., Savage, 1998—; dir. McGab Agribusiness Scholar., Ariz. State Univ., 1989—. Media coord. U.S. Olympic Festival, Mpls. 1990; vol. Multiple Sclerosis Soc., 1989—; founder Ariz. State Univ. Agribus. Speakers Bur., 1987; bd. mem. alumni assn. Phoenix County Day Sch., Phoenix, 1983-89; guarantor Minn. Orch. Mem. Nat. Cattlemens Assn., Ariz. Cattle Growers Assn., Clan MacBean in N.Am., Universidad Iberoamericana (assoc.), Ducks Unlimited (publicity chmn. Phoenix 1986-88, dinner chmn. Burnsville 1990, 91, zone chmn. 1992—, state conv. chmn. 1998—), Trout Unlimited, T.C. Pub. TV, Mustang Club Am., Sigma Nu. Republican. Episcopal. Avocations: hunting, camping, conservation, internat. travel. Office: Hunter Holdings Ltd PO Box 276 Savage MN 55378-0276

BEAN, JACK VAUGHAN, author, publisher; b. Ft. Worth, June 30, 1957; s. Charles Jack Bean and Nan (Vaughan) Kennemer. BBA, BBA in Bus. and Mktg., Tex. Christian U., 1979; postgrad., Southwestern Paralegal Inst., 1988. Owner Ft. Worth (Tex.) Sound Studios, 1980-88; paralegal various law firms, Dallas and Ft. Worth, 1988-92; author, pub. Holographic Books, Ft. Worth, 1992—. Author: The Dream Diary, 1992, The ABC's of Meditation and More..., 1994, Remember The Future (The Prophecies of Nostradamus), 1998. Avocations: performing classic rock and rhythm and blues music, sailing, fishing, bicycling, target shooting. Office: Holographic Books PO Box 101862 Fort Worth TX 76185-1862

BEAN, MAURICE DARROW, retired diplomat; b. Gary, Ind., Sept. 9, 1928; s. Everett Thomas and Vera Mae (Curry) B.; m. Dolores J. Winston, Apr. 9, 1972; children: Linda D., Karen M., Laura L., James W., Jennifer J. BA in Govt., Howard U., 1950; MA in Social and Tech. Assistance, Haverford Coll., 1953; postgrad., cert., Sch. Advanced Internat. Studies, Johns Hopkins, 1959. With U.S. Bur. Census, 1950-51, AID, 1951-61; with Peace Corps, 1961-66; ops. officer for Peace Corps, Malaysia and Indonesia, 1961-62; regional program officer for Peace Corps, Far East, 1962-63; dep. regional dir. Peace Corps, 1963-64; dir. Peace Corps, Phillipines, 1964-66, Malaysia and Singapore affairs Bur. East. Asian and Pacific Affairs, Dept. State, 1966-70; mem. Sr. Seminar in Fgn. Policy, 1970-71; Am. consul Ibadan, Nigeria, 1971-73; dep. chief mission Am. Embassy, Monrovia, Liberia, 1973-76; sr. fgn. service insp., 1976-77; ambassador to Socialist Republic of Union of Burma, 1977-79; diplomat-in-residence Case Western Res. U., Cleve., 1979-80; State Dept. adv. to comdr. Air U., Maxwell AFB, Ala., 1980-86. Active Neighbors, Inc., Washington; bd. dirs. Watts Found. Cmty. Trust, L.A. Recipient Superior Honor award Dept. State, 1977, Outstanding Service award Gary Host and Hostess Club, 1979, Benjamin Hooks award NAACP, 1980, Meritorious Civilian Svc. award USAF, 1986, Meritorious Svc. award U.S. Dept. State, 1986; Named to Roosevelt High Sch. Hall of Fame, 1980; Christopher Reynolds Found. fellow, 1953; William E. Mosher Meml. scholar, 1961. Mem. Am. Fgn. Svc. Assn., Am. Sch. Assn., Manila, Urban League, Royal Bangkok Club, Sports Club (life), Omega Psi Phi. Home and Office: 285 E California Blvd Apt 308 Pasadena CA 91106-3645 *Opportunity does not knock. It must be sought, pursued, developed and, ultimately, utilized to the fullest.*

BEAN, VIRGINIA ANN, marketing executive; b. Grand Rapids, Mich., June 23, 1952; d. John Theunis and Muriel Naughton (Reeves) B.; m. Ronald Eugene Daley, Nov. 7, 1986; children: Jackson Phillip Wesley Daley, Bryan Augustin Daley, Geoffrey Eugene Daley. BA in Theater, Hiram Coll., 1974; MBA, NYU, 1987. Dir. fiscal ops. Cultural Coun. for Arts, N.Y.C., 1980-86; exec. dir. mktg. devel. Swiss Colony, Monroe, Wis., 1987—; pres. Ginny's, Monroe, 1995—. Creator: (catalog) Ginny's, 1992—. Bd. dirs. Rainbow Day Care, Monroe, 1989-92. Avocations: theater, sewing, parenting. Office: Ginny's 1112 7th Ave Monroe WI 53566-1364

BEANE, JUDITH MAE, psychologist; b. Durham, N.C., Mar. 28, 1944; d. Joseph William Sr. and Antoinette Gwathmey (Dew) B. BA, Campbell U., 1967; MRE, Golden Gate Bapt. Theol. Sem., Mill Valley, Calif., 1972; PhD, Profl. Sch. of Psychology, San Francisco, 1988. Lic. psychologist, Calif.; mental health therapist II, Northern Neck-Middle Peninsula Cmty. Svcs. Bd., 1995-97; cert. rehab. provider. Home missionary So. Bapt. Home Mission Bd., Atlanta, 1967-69; loan officer Coop Credit Union, Corte Madera, Calif., 1969-70; emergency svcs. specialist Community Action Marin, San Rafael, 1976-78; program coord. Marin Treatment Ctr., San Rafael, Calif., 1980-85; church sec. St. Paul's Episcopal Church, San Rafael, 1979-81; psychol. intern Raleigh Hills Hosp., Redwood City, Calif., 1984; psychol. asst. Lic. Psychologists, San Anselmo, Calif., 1985-92; bd. dirs. The Open Door Ministries, Inc., Sausalito, Calif., 1971—; psychologist Mill Valley, Calif., 1992-93; mng. dir. Ch. Resource Svcs. Inc., Lancaster, Va.,

1997—; deacon Kilmarnock Bapt. Ch., Lancaster, Va., 1996—; cons. Ross (Calif.) Hosp., 1991; guest spkr. Turn on Marin, San Rafael, Calif., 1985; mng. dir. Ch. Resources Svcs., Inc., Lancaster, Va. Mng. dir. Ch. Resource Svcs., 1997—. Recipient award Marin County People Speaking, 1985. Mem. APA (assoc.), Calif. State Psychol. Assn., Marin County Psychol. Assn., Am. Counseling Assn., Am. Assn. Christian Counselors. Baptist. Avocations: handcrafts, reading. Home: PO Box 172 Lancaster VA 22503-0172

BEANE, MARJORIE NOTERMAN, academic administrator; b. Adams, Minn., Oct. 3, 1946; d. Matthias Hubert and Anna Helen (Boegeman) Noterman. BA, Marillac Coll., St. Louis, 1969; MEd, U. Ariz., 1979; PhD, Loyola U., Chgo., 1988. Tchr. St. Alphonsus Sch., Prospect Heights, Ill., 1969-73; tchr., asst. prin. St. Raphael Sch., Chgo., 1973-75; prin. St. Theresa Sch., Palatine, Ill., 1975-84; pres. Mallinckrodt Coll. of the North Shore, Wilmette, Ill., 1986-90; assoc. v.p. for adminstn. Loyola U., Chgo., 1991—; trustee Mallinckrodt Coll. of the North Shore, 1980-90; cons. Jospehinum High Sch., Chgo., 1976, St. Viator High Sch., Arlington Heights, Ill., 1986. Mem. History of Women Religious, Fedn. Ind. Ill. Colls. and Univs. (exec. com. 1989), Wilmette C. of C., Sisters of Christian Charity (councilor 1980-88). Rotary. Roman Catholic. Avocations: sewing, bicycling, swimming, travel. Office: Loyola U 820 N Michigan Ave Chicago IL 60611*

BEAR, DONALD, law firm executive director; b. Pensacola, Fla., Apr. 6, 1945; s. Lewis and Peggy (Loeb) B.; m. Janis Getz, Apr. 3, 1981; children: Emily Louise, Daisy Rose. BBA, Tulane U., 1967, MBA, 1970. CPA. Ga. Mgr., acct. Touche Ross and Co., N.Y.C. and Atlanta, 1970-78; mgr. internal audit Transcon, Inc., El Segundo, Calif., 1981-83; dir. fin. and adminstrn. O'Melveny and Myers, L.A., 1983-85; exec. dir. Rosen, Wachtell and Gilbert, L.A., 1986-88, Hill, Betts and Nash, N.Y.C., 1988-91, Carpenter, Bennett and Morrissey, Newark, 1991-95, Richards, Spears, Kibbe & Orbe, N.Y.C., 1995—; bd. dirs. The Lewis Bear Co., Inc. Contbr. articles to profl. jours. Mem. Little Red Fathers Group, N.Y.C., 1991-92; treas., bd. trustees Little Red Sch. House/Elizabeth Irwin H.S., 1995—. Mem. AICPA, Assn. Legal Adminstrs. (bd. dirs. 1990-92, com. chmn. 198-92, spkr. 1988-92), Assn. Law Firm Execs. Avocations: wine collector, golf, reading, music, elementary education. Home: 69 5th Ave New York NY 10003-3005 Office: Richards Spears Kibbe & Orbe One Chase Manhattan Plz New York NY 10005

BEAR, GREGORY DALE, writer, illustrator; b. San Diego, Aug. 20, 1951; s. Dale Franklin and Wilma (Merriman) B.; m. Astrid May Anderson, June 18, 1983; children: Erik William, Alexandra. AB in English, San Diego State U., 1973. Tech. writer, host Reuben H. Fleet Space Theater, 1973; freelance writer, 1975—. Author: Hegira, 1979, Psychlone, 1979, Beyond Heaven's River, 1980, Strength of Stones, 1981, The Wind From a Burning Woman, 1983, The Infinity Concerto, 1984, Blood Music, 1985, Eon, 1985, The Serpent Mage, 1986, The Forge of God, 1987, Eternity, 1988, Tangents, 1989, Heads, 1990, Queen of Angels, 1990, Anvil of Stars, 1992, Moving Mars, 1993 (Nebula award 1994), Songs of Earth and Power, 1993, Legacy, 1995, Slant, 1997, Dinosaur Summer, 1998, Foundation and Chaos, 1998, Darwin's Radio, 1999; short stories: Blood Music (Hugo and Nebula awards), 1983, Hardfought (Nebula award), 1993, Tangents (Hugo and Nebula awards), 1987; editor: New Legends, 1995. Cons. Citizen's Adv. Council on Nat. Space Policy, Tarzana, Calif., 1983-84. Mem. Sci. Fiction Writers of Am. (editor Forum 1983-84, chmn. grievance com. 1985-86, v.p. 1987, pres. 1988-90). Avocations: book collecting; science; music; movies, history. Home: 506 Lakeview Rd Lynnwood WA 98037-2141

BEAR, LARRY ALAN, lawyer, educator; b. Melrose, Mass., Feb. 28, 1928; s. Joseph E. and Pearl Florence B.; m. Rita Maldonado, Mar. 29, 1975; children: Peter, Jonathan, Steven. BA, Duke U., 1949; JD, Harvard U., 1953; LLM, (James Kent fellow), Columbia U., 1966. Bar: Mass. 1953, P.R. 1963, N.Y. 1967. Trial lawyer Bear & Bear, Boston, 1953-60; cons. legal medicine P.R. Dept. Justice, 1960-65; prof. law sch. U. P.R., 1960-65; legal counsel, then commr. addiction svcs. City of N.Y., 1967-70; dir. Nat. Action Com. Drug Edn. U. Rochester, N.Y., 1970-77; pvt. practice N.Y.C., 1970-82; pub. affairs radio broadcaster Sta. WABC, N.Y.C., 1970-82; U.S. legal counsel Master Enterprises of P.R., 1982-90; pres. Found. for a Drug Free Pa., 1991-92; adj. prof. markets, ethics and law Stern Sch. Bus. NYU, 1986—; lectr. in legislation and ethics Wharton Sch., U. Pa., 1996—; vis. prof. legal medicine Rutgers U. Law Sch., 1969; vis. prof. legal, social and ethical context of bus. Athens Lab. for Bus. Adminstrn., Greece, 1996; mem. alcohol and drug com. Nat. Safety Coun., 1972-82; cons. in field of substance abuse prevention, edn. programming, 1980—; mem. Atty. Gen.'s Med./Legal Adv. Bd. on Drug Abuse, Pa., 1992. Author: Law, Medicine, Science and Justice, 1964, The Glass House Revolution: Inner City War for Interdependence, 1990, Free Markets, Finance, Ethics, and Law, 1994; contbr. articles to profl. jours. Mem. adv. com. on pub. issues Advt. Coun., 1972-95; mem.-at-large Nat. coun. Boy Scouts Am., 1972-85; chmn. Bd. Ethics, Twp. of Mahwah (N.J.), 1990-91; mem. alumni admissions adv. com. Duke U., 1987—. Mem. ABA, N.Y. State Bar Assn., Forensic Sci. Soc. Great Britain, Acad. Colombiana de Ciencias Medico-Forenses, Harvard Club (N.Y.C.). Home: 95 Tam Oshanter Dr Mahwah NJ 07430-1526 Office: Dept Fin Mgmt Edn Ctr 44 W 4th St Ste 9-190 New York NY 10012-1106

BEAR, ROBERT EMERSON, secondary education art educator; b. Artesia, Calif., Oct. 6, 1953; s. Samuel Ronald and Erlene Mable (Wobick) B.; m. Katherine Luella Culp, Aug. 14, 1976; children: Nathaniel Emerson, Benjamin Robert, Aaron Anthony. BS in Art Edn., Bemidji (Minn.) State U., 1978; MS in Art, Tex. A&I U., 1987; postgrad., Tex. A&M U., 1997—. Cert. K-12 art tchr., Minn.; cert. 7-12 spl. edn., K-12 art tchr., Tex.; cert. supr. Tex. Tchr. art Ind. Sch. Dist. 710, Virginia, Minn., 1978-79, Ind. Sch. Dist. 363, Northome, Minn., 1979-81; exhibit specialist John E. Conner Mus., Kingville, Tex., 1985-87; tchr. spl. edn., art Webb Consol. Ind. Sch. Dist., Bruni, Tex., 1987-89; tchr. spl. edn. Cotulla (Tex.) Ind. Sch. Dist., 1989-90; edn. svc. specialist USAR, Indpls., 1989; tchr., art specialist Bryan (Tex.) Acad. Visual and Performing Arts, 1990-96; tchr. art secondary sch. Somerville (Tex.) Ind. Sch. Dist., 1998—; art dir. print shop Trinity Ch., Lubbock, Tex., 1984; tchr. photography Eveleth (Minn.) Area Vocat. Tech. Sch., 1989; judge Odessy of the Mind, 1999; guest lectr. art dept. Tex. A&I U., Kingsville, 1987; condr. workshops in field; guest artist Bee Frame Shop, Alexandria, Minn., 1983, Ducks Unltd. and Landmark Gallery, Redwood Falls, Minn., 1984; tchr. spl. edn. Big Horn (Wyo.) Sheridan County Sch. Dist. #1, 1997-98. Exhibited in group shows at Nat. Audubon Soc., 1979, Wildlife Heritage Found., 1984, Nat. Wildlife Art Collectors Soc., 1985, Okla. Wildlife Festival, 1983, No. Minn. Wildlife Art Show, 1983, Thief River Falls Art Coun., 1983, Okla. Wildlife Art Festival, 1984, 85 (2 1st pl. awards 1984, Best of Show 1985), Nat. Wildlife Art Collectors Soc., 1985; one man shows include Bemidji State U., 1978, Ducks Unltd., 1984, Tex. A&I U., 1987; pres., founder "Cool"ality Kid Found., 1995; inventor curriculum and instructional unit appraisal and rating instrument, 1998, MIA PATCHArts Lesson Plan, std. rsch., summary sheet, collegiate rsch. summary sheet; author: Oh Ho Ho game, 1993, Bear Classroom Management Portfolio, 1995, Curriculum and Instructional Unit Appraisal and Rating Instrument, 1998. Asst. scoutmaster Boy Scouts Am., Indpls., 1989, Cotulla, 1990-91, Webelos leader, Bryan, 1990-91. With U.S. Army, 1972-74. Scholar Leigh Yawkey Woodson Art Mus., Wausau, Wis., 1986. Mem. Nat. Art Edn. Assn., Tex. Art Edn.Assn., Braxos Valley Art Educators Assn. (pres. 1991-93), Brazos Valley Art League, Kappa Delta Pi. Avocations: building houses, carpentry, ornithology. Home: 5008 N Oakland Ln Bryan TX 77808-6155

BEARAK, COREY B(ECKER), lawyer; b. Forest Hills, N.Y., Oct. 7, 1955; s. Stephen Irwin Bearak and Phyllis (Stone) Stark; m. Rachelle Pamela Confino, Mar. 24, 1985; children: Jonathan Marc, Marisa Jean. BA in Polit. Sci., Hofstra U., 1977, JD, 1981. Bar: N.Y. 1982. Asst. to sec. of state N.Y. State, Albany and N.Y.C., 1978; pvt. practice Queens, N.Y., 1982—; counsel, chief staff Councilman Sheldon S. Leffler, N.Y.C., 1982-99; legis. counsel to Bronx Borough Pres. Fernando Ferrer, N.Y.C., 1999—; mem. bd. edn., chair legal, budget and legis. coms. N.Y.C. Cmty. Sch. Dist. 26, 1989-93. Contbr. publs. to law digest. Mem. Cmty. Planning Bd. 13, Queens, N.Y.C., 1980-88; mem. nat. bd. N.Y. State Dem. Action; chmn., mem. Nat. Jewish Dem. Coun., 1994-97; Dem. Liberal candidate for State Assembly from 25th dist., 1988; alt. del. Dem. Nat. Conv., 1984—; bd. dirs. Queens Jewish Cmty. Coun., 1987-94, fin. sec., 1994, v.p., 1995—; del. N.E. Queens Jewish Cmty. Coun., 1986, legis. chmn., 1987-95, sec., 1989-91, pres., 1991-98, chair exec. com., 1998—; v.p. Ea. Queens Civic Coun., 1994-97; co-chmn. Cmty. Advocates for Pub. Edn., 1995; founder, v.p. Queens Civic Congress, 1997—; co-chair Fedn. Civic Councils the Borough Queens, 1995-97; pres. North Bellerose Civic Assn., 1991-97, v.p. 1997—; 1st v.p. Queens County Line Dem. Assn., Glen Oaks, N.Y., 1980-82, pres., 1982-84, 93—, exec. sec., 1985-93; trustee Hofstra Law Sch. Alumni Bd., 1994—, v.p., 1996—. Recipient Cert. of Merit Boy Scouts Am., 1983, Cmty. Svc. award Young Israel New Hyde Park, 1997, Outstanding Svc. to Cmty. N.E. Queens award Queens Jewish Coun., 1998. Mem. N.Y. State Bar Assn. (legis. policy com., environ. law sect.), Queens Bar Assn. (assoc. editor jour. 1983-86, real property com., legis. and law reform com.). Avocations: family, friends, softball, music, football. Home: 82-35 251st St Bellevue NY 11426-2527 Office: 250 Broadway Fl 22 New York NY 10007-2516

BEARCE, JEANA DALE, artist, educator; b. St. Louis; d. Clarence Russell and Maria Emily Dale; m. Lawrence F. Rakovan, June 7, 1969; children: Barbara Emily, Luke, Francesca. B.F.A., Washington U., St. Louis, 1951; M.A., N.Mex. Highlands U., 1954. Vis. artist, various lectureships India, Pakistan, 1961-62, 93; founder art dept. U. Maine, Portland, 1965, chmn. and dept. rep., 1965-70, asst. prof. art, 1967-70; assoc. prof. U. Maine, 1970-81, prof., 1982—; Reflections South India sabbatical, 1992-93. Exhibited one-woman shows, Portland Mus. Art, Maine, 1958, U. Maine, Orono, 1958, 65, 69, 77, 80, Madras Govt. Mus., India, 1962, Gallery 65, Paris, 1964, Bristol Mus. Art, R.I., 1965, Center Gallery, N.Y.C., 1974, Benbow Gallery, Newport, R.I., 1979, Ctr. for the Arts, Chocolate Ch., Bath, Maine, 1988, USM Gallery, 1991, Main Gallery U. So. Maine, 1991, others, group show, Boston Mus. Art, Library of Congress, Phila. Print Club, Springfield Mus., Mo., Birmingham Mus. Art, Ala., others; represented permanent collection, St. Louis Art Mus., U.S. Edn. Found. in India, New Delhi, U. Maine, Orono and Portland, Bklyn. Mus. Art, Cornell U. Mus. Art, Calif. Coll. Arts and Crafts, Sarasota Art Assn., Fla., Bowdoin Coll., Brunswick, Maine; executed murals, N.Mex. Highlands U., Bowdoin Longfellow-Hawthorn Library, Brunswick, sculpture reliefs, St. Bartholomew, Cape Elizabeth, Maine, St. Charles Ch. Brunswick; retrospective, Maine Ctr. for the Arts, 1988. Mem. artist's com. Maine Art Gallery, 1957-75, 80-87; mem. Maine com. Skowhegan Sch. Painting and Sculpture, 1972—. Recipient various awards; recipient Fannie Cook award People's Competition, 1958, 59; sabbaticals to India: Return to India-Creative Paintings and Printmaking, 1987, South India-Painting and Printmaking, 1993, The Maine to India Series USM Environ. Studies Ctr., 1996, Tibet The Maine Art Gallery, Wiscasset, 1999. Mem. Bowdoin Coll. Mus. Assocs. Home: 327 Maine St Brunswick ME 04011-3310 Office: U So Maine College Ave Gorham ME 04038-1004

BEARD, AMANDA, swimmer, Olympic athlete; b. Irvine, Calif., Oct. 29, 1981. Mem. Pan Pac Team, 1995; swimmer U.S. Olympic Team, Atlanta, 1996. Recipient 2 silver medals in 100 meter breaststroke and 200 meter breaststroke Olympic Games, Atlanta, 1996, gold medal in 4x100 medley relay Olympic Games, Atlanta, 1996; holder Am. record for 100 meter breastroke, 1996. Office: US Swimming Inc One Olympic Plz Colorado Springs CO 80918*

BEARD, ANN SOUTHARD, government official, travel company executive, art framing company executive; b. Denver, Jan. 13, 1948; d. William Harvey and Cora Alice Cornelia (Caldwell) Southard; m. Terrill Leon Beard, Dec. 20, 1970 (div. Oct. 1980); 1 son, Jeffery Leon; m. Rainer G. Froehlich, Feb. 12, 1988 (div. 1992). BA, Willamette U., 1970; postgrad U. Calif.-San Diego, 1981-82. Exec. asst. Kidder Peabody & Co., San Francisco, 1970-72; adminstrv. aide Arthur Anderson & Co., Portland, Oreg., 1972-73; owner, mgr. Beard's Frame Shoppes, Inc., Portland, 1973-80; dir. mktg. Multnomah County Fair, Portland, 1979; owner, CEO Ann Beard Spl. Events, San Diego, 1980-82; pres. Frame Affair, Inc., San Diego, 1982-86, Jack Oil Co., Inc., Greeley, 1982—; co-owner, v.p. Froehlich Internat. Travel, La Jolla, Calif., 1987-92; chief of protocol Mayor Susan Golding's Office, City of San Diego, 1993—; v.p. 146 Co., Inc., Greeley, pres., 1970-88; lectr., cons. SBA, San Diego, 1980-85. Mem. Civic Light Opera, Old Globe Theatre; bd. dirs. San Diego Master Chorale, 1981-92; mem. state bd. Miss Calif. Pageant/Miss Am., 1982-87; mem. citizens adv. bd. Drug Abuse Task Force/Crime Prevention Task Force, San Diego, 1983-87; campaign coord. Bill Mitchell for City Coun., 1985; candidate for Congress; staff aide to dep. mayor, 1987; mem. Lead San Diego Alumni, 1988, Scripps Hosp. Aux., 1992—, Internat. Visitors Coun., 1993—, San Diego County Commn. on the Status of Women, 1993-96; mem. Internat. Affairs Bd., San Diego, 1993—; bd. dirs. La Jolla Rep. Women Fedn., 1992—. Mem. Am. Mktg. Assn., World Affairs Coun., San Diego C. of C., Save Our Heritage Orgn., Charter 100 San Diego, San Diego 1988 Alumna Willamette U., 1909 Univ. Club (bd. dirs. 1992—, pres. 1996—), Univ. Club San Diego (mktg., devel. and social dir. 1987-88), Delta Gamma. Home and Office: 934 Santa Helena Park Ct Solana Beach CA 92075-1543

BEARD, CHARLES EDWARD, library director, consultant; b. New Orleans, July 21, 1940; s. Julius Brown and Lucy Glenn (Dannelly) B.; divorced. BA, U. Ala., 1962; MS in Libr. Sci., Fla. State U., 1964. Adminstrv. officer libr. U.S. Army Command and Staff Coll., Ft. Leavenworth, Kans., 1964-66; head reference dept. Gorgas Libr. U. Ala., Tuscaloosa, 1966-69; head acquisition dept. U. Ala., 1969-70; dir. libr. svc. Judson Coll., Marion, Ala., 1970-71; dir. librs., assoc. prof./coord. edn. libr. media dept. Ga. Coll., Milledgeville, Ga., 1971-78; dir. univ. librs. State U. of West Ga., Carrollton, 1978—. Editor: Solutions to Your Public Relations Problems, 1991, The Ga. Libr., 1975-79; assoc. editor: The Southeastern Libr., 1975-79; contbr. articles to profl. jours. Trustee Freedom to Read Found., Chgo., 1998—; co-chair White House Conf. on Librs. and Info. Svc. Task Force, 1991-92; pres. Positive Response, Inc., Carrollton, 1997, 98—; v.p. Carrollton County Hist. Soc., 1994-96. Capt. U.S. Army, 1964-66. Recipient Juanita Skelton Disting. Svc. award Ga. Assn. Instrnl. Technologists, 1995, Commendation medal U.S. Army, 1966. Mem. ALA (exec. bd. 1993-97), Southeastern Libr. Assn. (pres. 1986-88), Ga. Libr. Assn. (Nix-Jones Disting. Svc. award 1991, pres. 1981-83), Ga. State Bd. Certification of Librs., Ga. Ctr. for the Book (adv. bd.), Kiwanis (pres. 1975, Outstanding Pres. award 1996), Omicron Delta Kappa (faculty advisor 1990-96), Beta Phi Mu, Phi Alpha Theta. Episcopalian. Avocations: bridge, swimming, gardening, reading. Home: 105 Briarwood Dr Carrollton GA 30117-4104 Office: State U of West Ga Ingram Libr Carrollton GA 30118

BEARD, CHARLES JULIAN, lawyer; b. Detroit, Dec. 24, 1943; s. James F. and Ethel W. (Coveney) B.; m. Roslyn M. Watson, June 29, 1974 (div. 1988); m. Vivian C. Male, Aug. 11, 1990; 1 child, James Anthony. AB, Harvard U., 1966, JD, 1969. Bar: Mass. 1969, U.S. Dist Ct. Mass. 1976. Spl. asst. to adminstr. Boston Model City Adminstrn., 1969-70, asst. adminstr. for community svcs., 1970-74; assoc. Foley, Hoag & Eliot, Boston, 1974-78, ptnr., 1979—; bd. dirs. Blue Cross-Blue Shield Mass., Boston. Trustee WGBH Ednl. Found., Boston, 1990-99; chmn. bd. trustees Emerson Coll., 1998—, Boston, Phillips Acad., Andover, Mass. Avocations: golfing, sailing, cross-country skiing. Office: Foley Hoag & Eliot One Post Office Sq Boston MA 02109

BEARD, ELIZABETH LETITIA, physiologist, educator; b. New Orleans, Apr. 2, 1932; d. Howard Horace and Irene (Handley) B. BA in Biology, Tex. Christian U., 1952, BS in Med. Tech., 1953, MS in Med. Tech., 1955; postgrad., Smith Coll., 1953-54, Vanderbilt U., 1954-55; PhD in Animal Physiology, Tulane U., 1961. Instr. dept. biol. scis. Loyola U., New Orleans, 1955-58, asst. prof., 1958-62, assoc. prof., 1962-68, prof., 1969—, chmn. premed. com., 1978—; rsch. assoc. dept. physiology Sch. Medicine Tulane U., New Orleans, 1960-63; prof. biology med. reinforcement and enrichment program Sch. Medicine Tulane U., 1968-94; vis. prof. dept. physiology and biophysics Med. Sch. Harvard U., 1983-84; vis. scientist Am. Indian Rsch. Opportunities Programs at Mont. State U., 1994. Contbr. articles on rsch. in physiology to profl. publs. Mem. project rev. com. New Orleans Health Planning Coun., 1974-77, bd. dirs., 1975-78; soprano soloist Holy Name of Jesus Ch., 1978—, pres. sch. bd., 1976-79; mem. grad. rsch. com. La. chpt. Am. Heart Assn., 1970-72, 81-83, mem. undergrad. rsch. com., 1978-81, 89-93; mem. Met. Mus. Art, New Orleans Mus. Art; participant med. mission Christian Med. and Dental Soc., Tepic Navjarit, Mex., 1993, La Esperanza, Honduras, 1994, 95, Muisine, Ecuador, 1996, Tena, Ecuador, 1997, Med. Ministry Internat., San Jose de Los Matas, Domincan Rep., 1998. NIH grantee, 1962-64, 67-69, La. Heart Assn. grantee, 1966-67, Edward Schleider Found. grantee, 1974-77, New Orleans Cancer Assn. grantee, 1962-63; Libby rsch. fellow Sch. Medicine Tulane U., 1961. Mem. AAUP, AAAS, Am. Physiol. Soc., Soc. Exptl. Biology and Medicine, Sigma Xi. Home: 6127 Garfield St New Orleans LA 70118-6040 Office: 6363 St Charles Ave New Orleans LA 70118-6143

BEARD, EUGENE P., advertising agency executive; b. Pittsburgh, Pa.. G-grad., Duquesne U., 1959. Exec. v.p., chief fin. officer Interpublic Group of Cos. Inc., N.Y.C., vice chmn. fin. & opers., cfo. Office: Interpublic Group Cos Inc Ste C3-31 1271 Avenue Of The Americas Fl 44 New York NY 10020-1459*

BEARD, JOHN JACKSON, III, journalist; b. Fayetteville, N.C., Aug. 24, 1948; s. John Jackson Jr. and Lillian (McBryde) B. BFA, East Carolina U., Greenville, N.C., 1975. Announcer, reporter WTSB Radio, Lumberton, N.C., 1968-70, WSIB Radio, Beaufort, S.C., 1970-72; news anchor, reporter WITN-TV, Washington, 1972-76, WXII-TV, Winston-Salem, N.C., 1976-77, WIVB-TV, Buffalo, 1977-81, KNBC-TV, Burbank, Calif., 1981-93; news anchor KTTV-TV, Los Angeles, 1993—. With USN, 1969-72. Named Outstanding Alumnus East Carolina U., Greenville, N.C., 1986. Presbyterian. Avocations: basketball, boating, swimming. Office: Fox News 1999 S Bundy Dr Los Angeles CA 90025-5203*

BEARD, LEO ROY, civil engineer; b. West Baden, Ind., Apr. 6, 1917; s. Leonard Roy and Barbara Katherine (Frederick) B.; m. Marian Janet Wagar, Oct. 21, 1939 (dec.); children: Patricia Beard Huntzicker, Thomas Edward, James Robert; m. Marjorie Elizabeth Pierce Wood, Aug. 30, 1974. A.A., Pasadena City Coll., 1937; B.S., Calif. Inst. Tech., 1939. Engr. U.S. Army C.E., Los Angeles, 1939-49; engr. Office Chief of Engrs., Washington, 1949-52; chief of Reservoir Regulation, Sacramento, 1952-64; dir. Hydrologic Engring. Center, Davis, Calif., 1964-72; prof. civil engring. U. Tex., Austin, 1972-87, prof. emeritus, 1987—; dir. (Center for Research in Water Resources), 1972-80; cons. Espey, Huston & Assos., Austin, 1980—; v.p. Internat. Commn. of Water Resource Systems; mem. NRC Water Sci. and Tech. Bd. Editor-in-chief: Water International; Editor: Jour. of Hydrology. Served with USNR, 1945-46. Recipient Meritorious Civilian Service award U.S. Army C.E., 1972. Fellow AAAS,. Internat. Water Resources Assn. (exec. bd.), ASCE (water resources exec. com., Julian Hinds award 1981, hon. mem. 1987, Hunter Rouse award 1993); mem. Am. Water Resources Assn. (hon.), Am. Geophys. Union (pres. hydrology sect.), Nat. Soc. Profl. Engrs., Internat. Assn. Hydrol. Scis., World Meteorol. Orgn. (chmn. com. on hydrol. design data), U.S. Com. on Irrigation, Drainage and Flood Control, Univs. Council on Water Resources (exec. bd.), Nat. Acad. Engring. Home: 606 Laurel Valley Rd Austin TX 78746-3508 Office: PO Box 519 Austin TX 78767-0519 *As you spend most waking hours at your work, choose to love it. The key is to select an occupation that serves others.*

BEARD, LILLIAN B. MCLEAN, physician, consultant; b. N.Y.; d. John Wilson and Woodie (Durden) McLean; m. Delawrence Beard, Aug. 20, 1967. BS, Howard U., 1965, MD, 1970. MD, 1970. Pvt. practice pediatrics Lillian M. Beard, Washington, D.C., 1973—; assoc. prof. pediatrics George Washington U., 1983—; asst. prof. community medicine Howard U., 1983—; contbg. editor Good Housekeeping Mag., N.Y., 1989-95; health adv. WUSA-TV, Washington, 1992-95; communications cons. to industry including: Carnation Nutritional Products; mem. bd. dirs. Nat. Women's Econ. Alliance, 1993—; Children's Hosp., 1993—. Recipient Disting. Leadership award Nat. Assn. Equal Opportunity in Higher Edn., 1993, Disting. Svc. award Nat. Med. Assn., 1990, Hall of Fame in Medicine award, 1994, Healthy Babies Project "Making a Difference" award, 1995, Howard U. Alumni Achievement award, 1996. Fellow Am. Acad. Pediatrics; mem. Nat. Med. Assn., Am. Acad. Pediatrics (physician recognition awards 1993—). Home: 10517 Alloway Dr Potomac MD 20854-1662 Office: 5505 5th St NW Washington DC 20011-6513

BEARD, RICHARD BURNHAM, engineering educator emeritus, researcher; b. Boston, Dec. 17, 1922; s. Daniel and Anne (Curran) B.; m. Marilyn D. W. Beard, Sept. 18, 1948; children: Beverly, Amy, Adrienne. BSChemE, Northeastern U., 1947; SM in Elec. Engring., Harvard U., 1950; PhD in Elec. Engring., U. Pa., 1965. Chemist Weymouth Artificial Leather, South Braintree, Mass., 1947-48; rsch. engr. Honeywell, Phila., 1950-58; instr. Drexel U., Phila., 1958-60; rsch. assoc. U. Pa., Phila., 1960-65; assoc. prof. elec. engring. Drexel U., Phila., 1965-73, prof. elec. engring., 1973-93, prof. emeritus, 1993—; dir. biomed. engring. and sci. inst. Drexel U., Phila., 1974-76. Contbr. articles to profl. jours. and procs. including Jour. Applied Polymer Sci., Polymer Bull., Procs. Soc. Photo-Optical Instrument Engrs. Vol. 2309, Vol. 2678. Cpl. U.S. Army, 1943-46. Mem. IEEE (sr.), AAAS, Acoustical Soc. Am., Am. Chem. Soc. Achievements include patents in field. Avocation: gardening. Home: 880 Willow Way Atco NJ 08004-1339 Office: Dept Elec Engring Drexel U Philadelphia PA 19104

BEARD, RONALD STRATTON, lawyer; b. Flushing, N.Y., Feb. 13, 1939; s. Charles Henry and Ethel Mary (Stratton) B.; m. Karin Paridee, Jan. 24, 1991; children: D. Karen, Jonathan D., Dana K. BA, Denison U., 1961; LLB, Yale U., 1964. Bar: Calif. 1964, U.S. Ct. Appeals (9th cir.) 1980, U.S. Dist. Ct. (cen. dist.) Calif. 1964. Ptnr. Gibson, Dunn & Crutcher, L.A., 1964—, chmn., mng. ptnr., 1991—. Trustee Denison U., Granville, Ohio, 1975—, chmn., 1998—; mem. steering com. Calif. Minority Coun. Program, 1991—; bd. dirs. L.A. Area Boy Scouts, World Affairs Coun.; mem. pub. coun. Constl. Rights Found., 1994—. Mem. ABA, Calif. Bar Assn., L.A. Bar Assn., Calif. Club, City Club (pub. counsel), Coun. Fgn. Rels., Chancery Club, Yale Club, Bear Creek Golf Club. Avocations: sports, travel, golf. Home: 120 Privateer Mall Marina Del Rey CA 90292-6796 Office: Gibson Dunn & Crutcher 333 S Grand Ave Ste 4400 Los Angeles CA 90071-3197*

BEARD, TIMOTHY, career officer; b. Mansfield, Ohio, Apr. 12, 1944; m. Melissa Cary Martinez; children: Amanda, Emily, Sarah. Diploma, U.S. Naval Acad., 1966; MS in Aero. Engring., USAF Test Pilot Sch. Commd. ensign USN, 1966, advanced through grades to rear adm.; stationed on USS Forrestal VA-94; dept. head VA-176; with Bur. Naval Pers. Office Sec. Def.; dep. dir. programming OPNAV Staff; commdg. officer Attack Squadron 176, USS Midway Air Wing 5, USS San Diego, USS John F. Kennedy; asst. to dep. chief staff Marine Corps Aviation; comdr. Carrier Group 1 & Tng. Command U.S. Pacific Fleet, dep. comdr., chief staff, comdr., chief, 1998—. Decorated Dep. Superior Svc. Medal, Legion of Merit, Bronze Star, Meritorious Svc. Medal, 11 Strike/Flight Air Medals, others. Office: USN Nav Strike Air Warfare Ctr Bldg 465 Salon NE 89496-5000*

BEARDEN, DENISE G(ODWIN), humanities educator, secondary education educator; b. Birmingham, Ala., Dec. 29, 1964; d. David Houston and Judith Elizabeth (Jordan) Godwin; m. Winn Allen Bearden, Sept. 22, 1990; children: Jessica Brooks, William Allen. BA in English, Ga. Southwestern Coll., 1987, MEd, 1996. Cert. tchr., Ga. Educator Americus (Ga.) H.S., 1987-89, South Ga. Tech. Inst., Americus, 1989-90, Sumter County Comprehensive H.S., Americus, 1991—; part-time instr. writing Ga. Southwestern State U., 1996—. Co-editor: SAMPLES from the Southwest Georgia Writing Project, 1998. Rep. Sumter County United Way, 1992-94. Fellow S.W. Ga. Writing Project (cons. 1997, mem. adv. coun. 1993—); mem. Nat. Coun. Tchr. of English, Sigma Tau Delta. Avocations: reading, creative writing, singing, family scrapbooks. Home: PO Box 464 Americus GA 31709-0464

BEARDEN, FRED B(URNETTE), JR., marketing executive; b. McKinney, Tex., July 25, 1923; s. Fred Burnette and Gladys (Chaddick) B.; m. Elizabeth Emery Jackman, Dec. 6, 1947 (div. Nov. 21, 1994); children: Devon Elizabeth Bearden Stiles, Fred Burnette III. BBA, So. Meth. U., 1946. Cert. practitioner Neuro Linguistic Programming NLP Ctr. for Counseling and Tng. Bus. mgr. Tom Galligan Prodns., Dallas, 1943-47; mfrs. rep. F.B. Bearden Co., Dallas, 1948-53; regional mgr. Waste-King Corp., Dallas, 1955-61; pres. Fred Bearden Co., Dallas, 1961—; founder, chmn. Inst. for Human Achievement/Self Realization; cons., speaker in field. Patentee; contbr. articles to profl. publs. Mem. Mktg. Agts. Food Svc. Industry (dir., pres. 1976-81), Richardson Jaycees (co-founder, pres. 1951), Mensa. Avocations: photography, writing, hiking. Office: 15726 El Estado Dr Apt 146 Dallas TX 75248-4450

BEARDEN, JAMES HUDSON, university official; b. Marion, Ala., Sept. 25, 1933; s. Joseph N. and Lula (Worrell) B.; m. Pauline Larkins, Mar. 31, 1961; children: James Hudson, Jr., Pauline B. Simonowich. B.S., Centenary Coll. La., 1956; M.A., East Carolina U., 1959; Ph.D., U. Ala., 1966. Bus. mgr. Marion Inst., 1959; mem. faculty East Carolina U., Greenville, N.C., 1959—; prof. bus. adminstrn. East Carolina U., 1964—, dir. bur. bus. research, 1964, dean, 1968-83, dir. BB&T Ctr. for Leadership Devel., 1983—. Author articles in field. Former trustee Campbell U.; pres., trustee N.C. Council Econ. Edn. Served with AUS, 1956-58. Mem. Newcomen Soc. N.Am., Assn. Leadership Educators, Fedn. Bus. Honor Socs. (pres. 1991—), Rotary, Beta Gamma Sigma (pres. 1986-90), Sigma Beta Delta (pres. 1994—). Home: 106 Crown Point Rd Greenville NC 27858-5718 Office: BB&T Ctr for Leadership Devel East Carolina U 1100 General Classroom Bldg Greenville NC 27858-4353

BEARDEN, JEFF R., hospital official; b. Longview, Tex., Mar. 13, 1954; s. B.E. and Rusty (Aston) B.; m. Mary Elizabeth Fitzgerald, Jan. 10, 1976; children: Christi, Clayton. BA in History, Tex. A&M U., 1976; MS in Social Work, U. Tex., Arlington, 1979. Psychotherapist Edgemeade of Tex. Inc., Mineral Wells, 1979; caseworker Pampa (Tex.) Family Svc. Ctr., 1980; regional outreach coord. Wichita Falls (Tex.) State Hosp., 1987-88; asst. dir. outreach svcs. Vernon (Tex.) State Hosp., 1980-85, dir. outreach svcs., 1985-87, chief treatment team coordinator, 1988-89, unit dir., 1990, dir. maximum security unit, 1990-96, dir. forensic psychiat. programs, 1996—; cons. Outreach Home Health Inc., Seymour, Tex., 1988-90; instr. Vernon Regional Jr. Coll., 1993; owner, operator Tex. Back Then, Vernon, 1994—. Chmn. hotel/motel tax com. City of Vernon, 1996; bd. dirs., v.p. Red River Valley Museum, 1997. Mem. Tex. Forensic Mental Health Network (pres. 1993), Rotary (pres. 1990-91), Santa Rosa Palomino club (pres. 1989). Avocations: rodeo horseback riding, living-history-chuck-wagon. Office: Vernon State Hosp PO Box 2231 Vernon TX 76385-2231

BEARDEN, THOMAS HOWARD, news program producer, correspondent; b. Washington, Feb. 14, 1948; s. Norman C. and Emma Dorothy (Jensen) B.; m. Ruth Ann Harrison, July 12, 1977; children: Jennifer Kate, Emily Jane. BS in Journalism, U. Miss., 1969, MA in Radio and TV, 1971. Reporter, anchorman Sta. WJTV-TV, Jackson, Miss., 1971-72; reporter, anchorman, assignment editor Sta. WHBQ-TV, Memphis, 1972-78; reporter, anchorman Sta. KMGH-TV, Denver, 1978-85; producer, correspondent MacNeil-Lehrer News Hour, Denver, 1985—. Producer/reporter TV news series documentary The Quicksilver Connection, 1984 (Emmy award 1984). 1st lt. U.S. Army, 1971-72. Mem. Sigma Delta Chi. Club: Denver Press (news series award 1983). Avocations: computers, photography. Office: MacNeil-Lehrer News Hour 2400 Syracuse St Denver CO 80207-3652

BEARDMORE, DOROTHY, state education official; b. Chgo.; m. William Beardmore; 2 children. BA, Cornell U. Cert. due process spl. edn. hearing officer Mich. Dept. Edn. Mem. bd. edn. Rochester Cmty. Schs., 1967-75; mem. Bd. Edn. Oakland Schs., Oakland County Intermediate Sch. Dist., 1974-84; treas., v.p., sec. State Bd. Edn., Lansing, Mich., 1984—, pres., 1990-92, sec., 1994-96, pres., 1999—; mem. profl. devel. adv. coms. State Bd., Dept. Edn., Mich. Legis., Mich. Assn. Sch. Bds.; chair study Nat. Assn. State Bds. Edn., 1988, bd. dirs. representing 12 midwestern states, chair bylaws com.; apptd. by gov. Midwestern Higher Edn. Com.; at-large del. Southeast Mich. Coun. Govts.; chmn. Health Schs. Network. Mem. Rep. Women's Forum. Recipient Disting. Svc. award Mich. Assn. Career Edn., 1989, Svc. award Phi Delta Kappa, 1989, Can Doer award Sci. and Tech. Quest Honor Roll, 1991, Spirit of Independence award Oakland-Macomb Counties Ctr. for Ind. Living, 1991, Paul Harris fellow Rotary Internat., 1989, Edn. Leadership award Mich. Elem. and Mid. Sch. Prins. Assn., 1995; inducted into Mich. Edn. Hall of Fame, 1996. Mem. Delta Kappa Gamma (hon.). Office: Edn Bd PO Box 30008 Lansing MI 48909-7508*

BEARDMORE, HARVEY ERNEST, retired physician, educator; b. Windsor, Ont., Can., Feb. 4, 1921; s. Harold and Marjorie (Harvey) B.; m. Frances Seymour Barnes, Sept. 1, 1945 (dec. Aug. 1995); children: Richard, Anne Beardmore Psaila, Patricia Beardmore Muldoon, Ian, Carol Beardmore Lamb, Diane Beardmore Lobb. BSc, McGill U., Montreal, Can., 1946, MD, CM, 1948. Diplomate Am. Bd. Pediat. Surgery. Intern Montreal Gen. Hosp., 1948-49; resident Queen Mary Vets. Hosp., Montreal, 1949-51; teaching fellow Tufts U., Boston, 1951-52; chief resident Montreal Children's Hosp., 1952-54, staff, 1954-92; practice medicine specializing in pediatric surgery Montreal, 1954-92; assoc. prof. surgery McGill U., 1954-92. Served with Princess Patricias Canadian Light Inf., 1943-45, Italy, N.W. Europe. Fellow Am. Acad. Pediatrics (chmn. sect. surgery 1972), ACS, Royal Coll. Surgeons Can.; mem. Can. Assn. Paediatric Surgeons (founding pres. 1967-72), Am. Pediatric Surg. Assn. (pres 1974), World Fed. Assn. Pediatric Surgeons (1st pres. 1974-77), Chevalier de la Chaine des Rotisseurs. Club: Chevalier de la Chaine des Rotisseurs. Home: 4501 Sherbrooke St W Apt 5B, Montreal, PQ Canada H3Z 1E7

BEARDON, RICHARD, beverage company executive; m. Nicole Beardon; children: Mark, Christopher (twins). Grad. in Bus., U. Coventry, Eng.; Mgmt. studies, Quality Coll., Winterpark, Fla.; grad. in Mgmt., Cornell U. Exec. UK Motor Industry, Perkins Engines; purchasing exec. Ford Motor Co.; gen. mgr. ops. TJ Raleigh; global logistics mgr. ICL Computer Co.; specialist logistics and ops. H.J. Heinz; ops. head Cadbury Schweppes-Coca Cola, 1989-94; head of global tech. ops. Cadbury Schweppes Global Beverages Mgmt., 1994-96; mem. Cadbury Acquisiton Team, 1996-98; pres., CEO Am. Bottling Co., Darien, Ill., 1998—. Office: Am Bottling Co 7955 S Cass Ave Ste 201 Darien IL 60561

BEARDSLEY, G(EORGE) PETER, pediatric oncologist, biochemical pharmacologist; b. N.Y.C., Dec. 29, 1940; s. G. Austin Beardsley and Sylvia Lucy (Davis) Eden; m. Diana S., June 10, 1971; Christopher Eden Marchant. BS, MIT, 1967; PhD in Bioorganic Chemistry, Princeton U., 1971; MD, Duke U., 1974. Resident in pediatrics Yale U., New Haven, 1974-76; fellow pediatric hematology/oncology Harvard Med. Sch., Boston, 1976-79, instr. pediatrics, 1979-81, asst. prof. pediatrics, 1981-85; assoc. prof. pediatrics Yale U. Sch. Medicine, New Haven, 1985-92, assoc. prof. pharmacology, 1989-92, prof. pharmacology, prof. pediatrics, 1992—, chief pediatric hematology/oncology, 1986—, dir. pediatric oncology program Yale Comprehensive Cancer Ctr., 1986. Contbr. articles, book chpts. related to biochem. pharmacology, chemistry or drug design and devel.; holder 4 patents. V.p. The Tommy Fund, Inc., New Haven, 1986—. Recipient Whitaker Found. Rsch. award, 1979, Jr. Faculty Rsch. award, 1981, Faculty Rsch. award Am. Cancer Soc., 1989. Mem. Am. Chem. Soc., Am. Assn. Cancer Rsch., Soc. for Pediatric Rsch. Office: Yale U Sch Medicine 333 Cedar St PO Box 3333 New Haven CT 06510-0333*

BEARDSLEY, JOHN RAY, public relations firm executive; b. Mpls., Jan. 10, 1937; s. Ray Homer Beardsley and Dorothy Louise (Refsell) Ripley; m. Sharon Ruth Olson, Aug. 24, 1960; children—Elizabeth Ruth, Alison Leigh, Leslie Anne. B.A., Augustana Coll., 1961. News editor Sioux Falls (S.D.) Argus Leadr, 1961-64; city editor Worthington (Minn.) Daily Globe, 1964; Corr. AP, Fargo, N.D. and Mpls., 1965-68; comms. mgr. Pillsbury Co., Mpls., 1968-69; pub. rels. mgr. Dayton Hudson Corp., Mpls., 1969-70; successively account exec., v.p., sr. v.p. Padilla and Speer, Inc., Mpls., 1970-83, CEO, 1983-86; chmn., CEO Padilla Speer Beardsley Inc., 1987—, nat. dir. at large, 1991-92, treas., 1993, pres.-elect, 1994, pres., 1995. Mem. Pub. Rels. Soc. Am. (pres. Minn. chpt. 1981), Nat. Investor Rels. Inst. (v.p., dir. Minn. chpt. 1981-84). Clubs: Mpls. Athletic, Minn. Home: 3904 Williston Rd Minnetonka MN 55345-2054 Office: Padilla Speer Beardsley Inc 224 W Franklin Ave Minneapolis MN 55404-2394

BEARDSLEY, ROBERT EUGENE, microbiologist, educator; b. Walton, N.Y., June 11, 1923; s. Harrison R. and Margaret (Sliter) B.; m. Philomena E. Pecora, Aug. 28, 1948; children: Luisa M., Margaret R., Robert E. B.S., Manhattan Coll., 1950; A.M., Columbia U., 1951, Ph.D., 1960. Instr. Manhattan Coll., 1951-54, asst. prof., 1954-58, asso. prof., 1958-68, prof., 1968-77; dir. Manhattan Coll. (Lab. Plant Morphogenesis), 1962-69, head dept. biology, 1969-77; prof. Iona Coll., New Rochelle, N.Y., 1977-89, prof. emeritus, 1989—; dean Iona Coll. (Sch. Arts and Sci.), 1977-83; vis. investigator Inst. Pasteur, Paris, 1966-67; Co-chmn. Scientists Com. Radiation Info., 1960. Contbr. articles to profl. jours. Dist. comdr. U.S. Power Squadrons, 1993. Served with AUS, 1943-46. Guggenheim fellow, 1966. Mem. Am. Pub. Health Assn., Am. Soc. Microbiologists, AAAS, Sigma Xi, Epsilon Sigma Pi. Home: 242 Mountaindale Rd Yonkers NY 10710-3512 Office: Dept Biology Iona Coll New Rochelle NY 10801 *In retrospect, I find that I have lived with the illusion of being guided by a desire to make some contribution toward a better world for all members of the human family. However, like all other people, I have only done what my unique combination of heredity, environmental programming and ego have compelled me to do.*

BEARDSLEY, THEODORE S(TERLING), JR., professional society administrator; b. East St. Louis, Ill., Aug. 26, 1930; s. Theodore Sterling and Margaret (Kienzle) B.; m. Lenora J. Fierke, May 26, 1955; children: Theodore Sterling III, Mark A., Mary Elizabeth. BS, So. Ill. U., 1952; MA (Max Bryant fellow), Washington U., St. Louis, 1954; postgrad., U. Heidelberg, Germany, 1955-56; PhD, U. Pa., 1961; linguistic rsch., Inst. Caro y Cuervo, Bogota, Colombia, summer 1973. Asst. in English Lycee Wilson, Chaumont, France, 1952-53; mem. faculty Rider Coll., 1957-61, chmn. dept. modern lang., 1959-61; asst. prof. Spanish So. Ill. U., 1961-62, U. Wis., 1962-65; dir. Hispanic Soc. Am., N.Y.C., 1965-95, pres., 1995—; adj. prof. NYU, 1967-69, 80, Adelphi U., 1966, 68, Columbia U., 1969, Eckerd Coll., 1997—; Fulbright lectr., Ecuador, 1974; guest lectr. U. Complutense, Madrid, 1990, 94, U. Salamanca, 1994, U. Rábida, Spain, 1996; diss. dir. U. Oviedo, Spain, 1992; vis. prof. U. Wis., 1995; chmn. Museums Coun. N.Y.C., 1972-73; spl. cons. Hispanic bibliography Libr. Congress, fall 1973, N.J. State Dept. Edn., spring 1975, NEH, 1978—. Narrator Spanish lang. recorded tours, Nat. Gallery Art, Met. Mus., Mus. Natural Sci., Boston Sci. Mus., Smithsonian Instn.; continuing series on Caribbean popular music in U.S, WBGO-FM, 1979; Xavier Cugat, 1980, USA Latino, 1981, Enrique Madriguera, Spanish Nat. Radio, 1985; author: Hispano-Classical Translations, 1482-1699, 1970, Tomas Navarro Tomas, A Tentative Bibliography, 1908-1970, 1971; also articles; recordings include: Charla con Camilo José Cela, 1966, Visita a la Hispanic Society, 1969; editor: Enrique Madriguera, 1994; co-editor: Celestina: Early Text, 1997; narrator-author: 4 part series Hispanic Immigration to the United States (text pub. 1976), CBS-TV, 1972; librettist: Ponce de Leon, 1973; mem. adv. bd.: Hispanic Rev., Studia humanitatis, Boletín de ANLE, Hispanic Sem. of Medieval Studies, Revista Caribe. Served with AUS, 1954-56. Decorated Orden de Mérito Civil, Spain ; Fulbright grantee, 1952-53; Jusserand traveling fellow, 1962; research grantee Am. Council Learned Socs., 1964; travel grantee, 1974; recipient Premio Bibliofilia Barcelona, Spain, 1973. Mem. ASCAP, Hispanic Soc. Am., Renaissance Soc. Am. (exec. coun., acting dir. 1981-82), Acad. Norteamericana Lengua Española, Internat. Inst. (Madrid), Internat. Linguistic Assn. (exec. coun.), Hispanic Sem. Medieval Studies (bd. dirs.), Ponce De Leon Conquistadors, Sigma Delta Pi, Sigma Tau Gamma; corr. mem. Royal Spanish Acad., Real Acad. Bellas Artes San Carlos (Valencia), Acad. Guatemalteca de Lengua, Assn. Bibliofilos Barcelona, Fundacion Odón Betanzos (Rociana), Fundacion Santa Maria de la Rabida, Fundacion Universitaria Espanola (Madrid), Inst. Valencia Don Juan (bd. dirs. Madrid). Office: Hispanic Soc Am 613 W 155th St New York NY 10032-7501

BEARE, GENE KERWIN, electric company executive; b. Chester, Ill., July 14, 1915; s. Nicholas Eugene and Minnie Cole (St. Vrain) B.; m. Doris Margaret Alt, Dec. 11, 1943 (dec.); children: Gail Kathryn, Joanne St. Vrain; m. Patricia Pfau Cade, Sept. 12, 1964 (dec.); m. Lee May Hollo, July 29, 1997. B.S. in Mech. Engring, Washington U., 1937; M.B.A., Harvard, 1939. Registered profl. engr., Ill. With Automatic Electric Co., Chgo., 1939-58, successively asst. to v.p. and gen. mgr., asst. to pres., mgr. internat. affiliated cos., gen. comml. mgr., 1939-54, v.p. prodn., 1954-58, dir., 1956-61; pres., dir. Automatic Electric Internat., Inc., Chgo., 1958-61; chmn., dir. Automatic Electric (Can.), Ltd., Chgo., Automatic Electric Sales (Can.), Ltd., 1958-61; pres., dir. Sylvania Internat., 1959-60; pres. Gen. Telephone & Electronics Internat., Inc., 1960-61, dir., 1960-72; also dir. numerous subs. in Gen. Telephone & Electronics Internat., Inc., Colombia, Mex., Venezuela, Argentina, Switzerland, Panama, Brazil, Bel; dir. Am. Research and Devel. Corp., 1967-74, Canadair Ltd., 1972-75; pres. Sylvania Electric Products, Inc., 1961-69, dir., 1961-72; exec. v.p. mfg., dir. Gen. Telephone & Electronics Corp., 1969-72; exec. v.p., dir. Gen. Dynamics Corp., St. Louis, 1972-77; pres. Gen. Dynamics Comml. Products Co., 1972-77; chmn. Asbestos Corp. Ltd., 1974-77; dir. Arkwright-Boston Mut. Ins. Co., Westvaco Corp., Emerson Electric Co., St. Joe Minerals Corp., Am. Maize-Products Corp., Datapoint Corp., Nooney Realty Trust, Inc. Served to lt. USNR, 1942-45. Mem. Pan Am. Soc., Nat. Elec. Mfrs. Assn. (bd. govs. 1963-72, v.p. 1964, pres. 1965-66), Armed Forces Communications and Electronics Assn., Nat. Security Indsl. Assn. (trustee 1969-72). Clubs: Wee Burn (Darien, Conn.) (gov. 1963-68); Union League (N.Y.C.), Econ. (N.Y.C.); St. Louis (dir. 1979—); Old Warson (Ladue, Mo.) (dir. 1979—), Univ. (St. Louis), The Ocean Club of Fla., Ocean Ridge. Home: 801 S Skinker Blvd Saint Louis MO 63105-3228 Office: Pierre Laclede Center 7701 Forsyth Blvd Ste 1070 Saint Louis MO 63105-1875

BEARE-ROGERS, JOYCE LOUISE, former research executive; b. nr. Pickering, Ont., Can., Sept. 8, 1927; d. Frederick John and Sarah May (Michell) Beare; m. Charles Graham Rogers, Dec. 30, 1961; 1 child, Anne Catherine. BA, U. Toronto, Ont., 1951, MA, 1952; PhD, Carleton U., Ottawa, Ont., 1966; DSc (hon.), U. Man., Winnipeg, Can., 1985, U. Guelph, Ont., Can., 1993. Rsch. assoc. U. Toronto, 1952-54; instr. Vassar Coll., Poughkeepsie, N.Y., 1954-56; chemist Food, Drug Directorate (name now Health Protect Br.), Ottawa, 1956-65, rsch. scientist, 1965-75; rsch. mgr. Bur. Nutritional Scis., Ottawa, 1975-91; rsch. mgr. Bur. Nutritional Scis., Ottawa, 1975-91; adj. prof. U. Ottawa, 1980-92; cons. Food and Agrl. Orgn. UN, 1992-94; Hilditch lectr. U.K., 1994; trustee Nat. Inst. Nutrition (Can.), 1997—. Editor: Methods for Nutritional Assessment of Fats, 1985, Fat Requirement for Development and Health, 1988; contbr. articles on dietary fats to profl. jours. Decorated Order of Can.; recipient Queen's Jubilee medal Govt. of Can., 1977, Medaille Chevreul award Inst. Corps Gras, 1984, Crompton award McGill U., 1986, Normann medal German Assn. for Fat Rsch., 1987, Commemorative medal for 125th Anniversary of Fedn. of Can., 1992. Fellow Royal Soc. Can., Am. Inst. Nutrition; mem. Am. Oil Chemists Soc. (pres. 1985-86; Lifetime Achievement award Can. sect. 1995), Internat. Soc. Fat Rsch. (pres. 1991-92), Can. Soc. for Nutrition Scis. (pres. 1984-85, Bordon award 1971, McHenry award 1993), Can. Biochem. Soc. Avocations: hiking, canoeing, cross-country skiing, reading. Home: 41 Okanagan Dr, Nepean, ON Canada K2H 7E9

BEARG, ESTHER MARILYN, school counselor; b. N.Y.C., Apr. 8, 1927; d. Frank and Ida D. (Zakim) Becker; widowed; children: Fredrica, Barry, Martin. BA, Queens Coll., 1947, MS in Edn., 1961; EdD, Fairleigh Dickinson U., 1979. Cert. elem. tchr., sch. counselor, prin., sch. social work. Tchr. 4th grade Elmont (N.J.) Bd. of Edn., 1947-50; tchr. 5th grade Woodmere (N.J.)-Hewlett Bd. of Edn., 1961-63; tchr. 5th grade West Orange (N.J.) Bd. of Edn., 1963-71, sch. counselor, 1971—; cons. in edn. and career Caldwell-West Caldwell Adult Sch., 1984—; advisor Nat. Honor Soc., West Orange H.S., 1976-96; leader numerous summer workshops on new math, child and youth study, career devel.; workshop co-leader NEAT: A Guide for Coll. Admission Counselors, 1985—. Author: Career Planning: Focus on Your Career, 1990; contbr. articles to newsletters, newspapers, mags. Co-chair adult edn. Oheb Shalom, South Orange, N.J., 1990-93; pres. local chpt., sec. N.J. region Am. Jewish Congress, 1988—. Named Essex County Counselor of Yr., N.J. Profl. Counseling Assn., 1989. Mem. NEA, N.J. Edn. Assn., N.J. Assn. Coll. Admission Counselors (sec. 1990-92), Essex County Edn. Assn., West Orange Edn. Assn., Essex County Sch. Counselor Assn. (pres., v.p. programming 1981-84, chair nat. sch. counseling week 1984—). Jewish. Avocation: family. Office: West Orange H S 51 Conforti Ave West Orange NJ 07052-2829

BEARMAN, TONI CARBO See CARBO, TONI

BEARMON, LEE, lawyer. BBA, U. Minn., JD. Bar: Minn. 1956. Sr. v.p., gen. counsel, sec. Carlson Cos., Inc, Mpls. Office: Carlson Cos Inc PO Box 59159 Minneapolis MN 55459-8200

BEARN, ALEXANDER GORDON, physician scientist, former pharmaceutical company executive; b. Surrey, Eng., Mar. 29, 1923; came to U.S., 1951; s. Edward Gordon B.; m. Margaret Slocum, Dec. 20, 1952; children: Helen B. Pennoyer, Gordon Clarence Frederic. Ed., Epsom Coll.; MB, BS, Guy's Hosp., U. London, Eng., 1945, MD, 1951; MD (hon.), U. René Descartes, Paris, 1974, Cath. U., Korea, 1968. Postgrad. Med. Sch., London, 1948-51; mem. staff Rockefeller Inst., Rockefeller U., N.Y.C., 1951-64, 88—, asso. prof., 1957-64, prof., sr. physician, 1964-66, adj. prof., vis. physician, 1966—; prof. medicine Cornell U., 1966-89, prof. emeritus, 1989—, Stanton Griffis Distinguished med. prof., 1976-80, chmn. dept., 1966-77; physician-in-chief N.Y. Hosp., 1966-77; sr. v.p. for med. and sci. affairs Merck, Sharp & Dohme Internat., Rahway, N.J., 1979-88; Disting. vis. fellow, fellow commoner Christ's Coll., Cambridge, Eng., 1996-97, 97—; exec. officer Am. Philos. Soc., 1997—; mem. Commn. Human Resources, Nat. Acad. Scis., 1974-77; chmn. div. med. scis. Assembly Life Scis., 1978-79; bd. sci. counselors Nat. Inst. Arthritis, Metabolism and Digestive Diseases, 1976-80; mem. Space Sci. Bd., 1978-79; cons. genetics tng. com., div. gen. med. scis. USPHS, 1961-65, cons. genetics study sect., 1966-70, coun. Fogarty Ctr NIH, 1990—; pres. Royal Soc. Medicine Found., Inc., 1976-78; now dir.; mem. bd. sci. overseers Jackson Lab., Bar Harbor. Editor: Am. Jour. Medicine; co-editor: Progress in Medical Genetics, 1962-87; asso. editor: Cecil-Loeb Textbook of Medicine; Contbr. articles to profl. jours. Trustee Rockefeller U., Helen Hay Whitney Found., Macy Found., Howard Hughes Med. Inst. Served as med. officer RAF, 1947-49. Recipient Alfred Benzon prize, Denmark, 1979. Fellow AAAS, Royal Coll. Physicians (Edinburgh, Scotland), Royal Coll. Physicians (London, Eng.); mem. Inst. Medicine NAS, Am. Philos. Soc. (exec. officer), Assn. Am. Physicians, Am. Soc. Clin. Investigation, Am. Soc. Human Genetics (pres. 1971), Genetics Soc. Am., Am. Soc. Biol. Chemists, Soc. Exptl. Biology and Medicine, Harvey Soc. (pres. 1972-73, Harvey lectr. 1975), Harveian Soc. London (Coun. 1959), Assn. Physicians Great Britain and Ireland, Med. Rsch. Soc. Great Britain, Med. Soc. London, Knickabocker, Sigma Xi (pres. Rockefeller chpt. 1962-63), fgn. assoc. Norwegian Acad. Sci. and Letters, Century Assn., Knickerbocker Club, Union League of Phila., Crail Golf Club (Scotland), Misquamicut Club (Watch Hill, R.I.). Presbyterian. Home: 241 S 6th St Apt 2111 Philadelphia PA 19106-3735 Office: Am Philosophical Soc 104 S Fifth St Philadelphia PA 19106

BEARSCH, LEE PALMER, architect, city planner; b. Binghamton, N.Y., July 5, 1942; s. Frederick James and Mildred Jane (Palmer) B.; m. Christine Cromer, Dec. 31, 1972; children: Frederick Cromer, Benjamin Palmer, Peter Furlong. BArch, Clemson U., 1965; M in Planning, Leverhulme Sch. Archtl. Assn., London, 1970. Registered profl. arch., N.Y., Pa., Md., Mass., Wis. Project dir. Llewelyn-Davies Assocs., London, N.Y., Racine, Wis., 1970-75; pres. Bearsch Compeau Knudson, Archs. and Engrs., P.C., Binghamton, 1976—; mem. N.Y. State Edn. Dept. Bd. for Arch. Lic. Bd., 1997—. Mem. Broome County Planning Adv. Bd., Binghamton, 1978-90, sec., 1986-88; bd. dirs. Broome County Small Bus. Coun., 1979-84, vice chmn., 1981-83; vestryman Christ Episcopal Ch., 1981-84; bd. dirs. Family and Childrens Soc. Broome County Inc., 1982—, pres., 1985-86; bd. dirs. Binghamton Symphony Orch.; mem. adv. bd. Endicott Trust divsn. Mfrs. and Traders Bank; mem. Binghamton U. Coun.; mem. N.Y. State Bd. for Arch. State Licensing Bd., 1995—. Fellow AIA (area dir. 1978-79, v.p. 1979-81, chpt. pres. 1981-82, state conv. chmn. 1983, state pres. 1990, nat. bd. dirs. 1990-93, nat. conv. chmn. 1996); mem. Am. Inst. Cert. Planners, N.Y. State Assn. Archs. (bd. dirs. 1985—, exec. com. 1987—, pres. 1990, mem. bd. archtl. registration 1995—), Archtl. Assn. (Eng.), Broome County C. of C. (bd. dirs. 1986—, chmn. 1990-91), Leadership Broome (adv. bd. 1988-90), Binghamton City Club (bd. govs.), Binghamton Country Club, Live Wire Club. Office: Bearsch Compeau Knndson A&E PC 41 Chenango St Binghamton NY 13901-2901

BEART, ROBERT W., JR., surgeon, educator; b. Kansas City, Mo., Mar. 3, 1945; s. Robert Woodward and Helen Elizabeth (Wamsley) B.; m. Cynthia Anne, Jan. 23, 1971; children: Jennifer, Kristina, Amy. AB, Princeton U., 1967; MD, Harvard U., 1971. Diplomate Am. Bd. Surgery, Am. Bd. Colon and Rectal Surgery. Intern U. Colo., 1971-72, resident, 1972-76; prof. surgery Mayo Clinic, Scottsdale, Ariz., 1976-87, 1987-92; prof. surgery U. So. Calif., L.A., 1992—. Maj. USMC, 1972-83. Fellow Am. Soc. Colon and Rectal Surgery (pres. 1994); mem. Commn. on Cancer (chmn.). Office: U So Calif Dept Surgery 1450 San Pablo St # 5400 Los Angeles CA 90033-1042

BEARY, JOHN FRANCIS, III, physician, pharmaceutical executive; b. Melrose, Iowa, Dec. 14, 1946; s. John F. and Dorothy (McGrath) B.; m. Bianca E. Mason, May 6, 1972; children: John Daniel, Vanessa, Webster, Nina. BS summa cum laude, U. Notre Dame, 1969; MD, Harvard U., 1973; MBA, Georgetown U., 1988. Diplomate Am Bd. Internal Medicine, Am. Bd. Rheumatology and Geriatric Medicine, Am. Bd. Clin. Pharmacology. Rsch. fellow Cornell Med. Coll., N.Y.C., 1978-80; from asst. prof. to clin. prof. Georgetown U. Sch. Medicine, Washington, 1980—; prin. dept. asst. sec. health affairs Dept. Def., Washington, 1981-83; assoc. dean strategic planning Georgetown U. Sch. Medicine, Washington, 1984-87; sr. v.p. regulatory and sci. affairs Pharm. Rsch. and Mfg. Assn., Washington, 1988-97; med. dir. arthritis rsch. Procter and Gamble Pharms., Cin., 1997—; mem. steering com. Internat. Conf. on Harmonization of Pharm. Stds., 1990-97. Editor: Manual of Rheumatology, 1981, 3d edit., 1993; mem. editorial bd. Jour. Pharm. Medicine, 1990—, Drug Devel. Rsch., 1992—. Bd. dirs. Scleroderma Found., Washington, 1982-92. Served to capt. USNR, 1984—. Recipient disting. pub. service medal Dept. Def., 1983, Navy and Marine Corps Commendatin medal, 1997. Fellow ACP, Am. Coll. Rheumatology, Am. Coll. Clin. Pharmacology; mem. AMA, Am. Geriatrics Soc., Am. Soc. Clin. Pharmacology and Therapeutics, Osteoarthritis Rsch. Soc., Res. Officers Assn., Johns Hopkins Med. and Surg. Assn., Chevy Chase Club. Office: Procter & Gamble Pharms 11450 Grooms Rd Cincinnati OH 45242-1408

BEARY, SHIRLEY LORRAINE, retired music educator; b. New Albany, Kans., Feb. 4, 1928; d. Howard Warren and Bertha Adelia (Wilcox) Fogelsanger; children: Stephanie Beary Johnson, Susan Beary Maloney. BA, Andrews U., 1949; MusM, U. Redlands, 1967; D Mus. Arts, Southwestern Bapt. Theol. Sem., 1977. Tchr. music Nevada, Iowa, 1949-50; prof. music Southwestern Adventist Coll., Keene, Tex., 1959-84, lectr. Christian ethics, 1978-84; prof. music Oakwood Coll., Huntsville, Ala., 1984-94; ret., 1994; ch. organist Seventh-day Adventist Ch., Kalamazoo, 1951-59, Keene, 1959-80, organist, min. music, 1980-82. Mem. bd. advisors Am. Biog. Inst., Raleigh, N.C. Mem. Coll. Music Soc., Am. Hymn Soc., Internat. Adventist Music Assn. Democrat. Avocations: travel, flower gardening, stamps and records collecting, gospel singing. Home: 2615 Oak Valley Dr Yreka CA 96097-9744

BEASLEY, BARBARA STARIN, sales executive, marketing professional; b. Nashville, Dec. 31, 1955; d. Donald Francis and Martha Murry (Bridges) S.; m. Johnny Mark Beasley, Oct. 22, 1983; children: John Thomas, Cara Nicole. BFA, So. Meth. U., 1976. Cert. strategic mktg. mgmt., Harvard Bus. Sch. Producer Bill Stokes Assn., Dallas, 1976-80; Mary Kay Cosmetics, Inc., Dallas, 1980-93; sr. v.p. mktg., 1987-89, exec. v.p. sales div., 1990-93; sr. v.p. mktg. Nest Entertainment, Dallas, 1994—. Mem. Leadership Tex., 1986. Avocation: birdwatching.

BEASLEY, BRUCE MILLER, sculptor; b. L.A., May 20, 1939; s. Robert Seth and Bernice (Palmer) B.; m. Laurence Leaute, May 21, 1973; children: Julian Bernard, Celia Beranice. Student, Dartmouth Coll., 1957-59; BA, U. Calif., Berkeley, 1962. One-man shows include Everett Ellin Gallery, L.A., 1963, Kornblee Gallery, N.Y.C., 1964, Hansen Gallery, San Francisco, 1965, David Stuart Gallery, L.A., 1966, Andre Emmerich Gallery, N.Y.C., 1971, DeYoung Mus., San Francisco, 1972, Santa Barbara Mus. Art, 1973, San Diego Mus. Art, 1973, Fuller-Goldeen Gallery, San Francisco, 1981, Hooks-Epstein Gallery, Houston, 1990, 93, 95, Pepperdine U., L.A., 1990, So. Oreg. State U., 1991, Sonoma State U., Rhonert Park, Calif., 1991, Fresno Art Mus., 1992, Oakland Mus., 1992, Utermann Gallery, Dortmund, Germany, 1993, Scheffel Gallery, Bad Homberg, Germany, 1993, Galerie Rudolfinum, Prague, 1994, Kunsthalle Mannheim, Germany, 1994, Harcourts Gallery, San Francisco, 1994, Galerie Wirth, Zurich, Switzerland, 1995, Yorkshire Sculpture Park, Eng., 1995, City Ctr., Dortmund, Germany, 1996, Atrium Gallery, St. Louis, 1997, Purdue U., West Lafayette, Ind., 1997, Solomon-Dubnick Gallery, Sacramento, 1997, Gwenda Jay Gallery, Chgo., 1998; exhibited in group shows at San Francisco Mus. of Modern Art, 1961, Mus. of Modern Art, N.Y.C., 1961,62, Dallas Mus. Contemporary Art, 1962, Musee d'Art Moderne, Paris, 1963, U. Art Mus., Berkeley, 1964, Fine Arts

Museums, San Francisco, 1965, Guggenheim Mus., 1966, Krannert Art Mus., Ill., 1969, Jewish Mus., N.Y.C., 1970, Milw. Art Ctr., 1970, Expo '70, Osaka, Japan, Stanford Art Mus., 1972, Musee d'Art Moderne, Paris, 1973, Nat. Mus. Am. Art, 1980, Musee d'Art Contemporain Bordeaux, France, 1984, Kunsthalle Mannheim, 1984, Palace of Exhbns., Budapest, Hungary, 1987, Middleheim Sculpture Park, Belgium, 1987, Yorkshire Sculpture Park, Eng., 1984, 87, Hakone Open-Air Mus., Japan, 1993, 95, Landesgartenschau, Germany, 1994, Sculpture '97, Bad Homberg, Germany, Pier Walk '97, 98, Chgo., Galerie Wirth, Zurich, Switzerland, 1997, Darmstadt (Germany) Sculpture Biennale, 1998, Cairo Biennale, Egypt, 1998; represented in permanent collections Mus. Modern Art, N.Y.C., Guggenheim Mus., N.Y.C., Musee d'Art, Paris, Nat. Mus. Am. Art, Washington, Kunsthalle Mannheim, Germany, San Franciso Mus. Modern Art, L.A. County Mus. Art, Sheldon Mem. Art Gallery, Lincoln, Nebr., Hood Mus. Art, Spencer Mus. Art, Lawrence, Kans., Laguna Art Mus., Franklin D. Murphy Sculpture Garden, UCLA, Crocker Art Mus., Sacramento, Bellevue Art Mus., Fresno Art Mus., Xantus Janos Mus., Hungary, Fine Art Muss., San Francisco, Oakland Mus. Calif., Santa Barbara Mus. Art, San Jose (Calif.) Mus. Art, Dartmouth Coll., N.H., Grounds for Sculpture, Hamilton, N.J., Nora Eccles Harrison Mus., Utah State U., Logan; commissions include State of Calif., Oakland Mus., City San Francisco, Miami Internat. Airport, San Francisco Internat. Airport, Fed. Home Loan Bank, San Francisco, Stanford U., City Anchorage, City Salinas, Calif., Fresno Art Mus. Bd. dirs. Internat. Sculpture Ctr., Washington. Home: 322 Lewis St Oakland CA 94607-1236

BEASLEY, DAVID MULDROW, former governor; b. Lamar, S.C., Feb. 26, 1957; s. Richard Lee and Jacqueline Adele (Blackwell) B.; m. Mary Wood Payne. Student, Clemson U., 1976-78; BA, U. S.C., 1979, JD. Mem. Dist. 56 S.C. Ho. Reps., 1979-92, majority leader, 1987, mem. joint legis. com. on edn., vice chmn. joint legis. com. on children, 1987-88; atty., 1992-94; gov. State of S.C., 1995-98. Office: Inst of Polit 79 JFK St Cambridge MA 02138*

BEASLEY, JAMES EDWIN, lawyer; s. James Edwin and Margaret Ann (Patterson) B.; children: Pamela Jane, Kimberly Ann, James Edwin. BS, Temple U., 1953, JD, 1956. Bar: Pa. 1956. Law clk. U.S. Dist. Ct. (ea. dist.) Pa., Phila., 1954-56; prin., owner Beasley, Casey & Erbstein, Phila., 1966—; instr. law Temple U., 1976-80, adj. prof., 1994; permanent del. 3d Cir. Jud. Conf.; chmn. standard civil jury inst. Pa. Supreme Ct.; bd. dirs. NATA; bd. trustees Pop Warner Little Scholars. Author: Products Liability and the Unreasonably Dangerous Requirement; contbr. articles to profl. jours. With USN, 1943-45, USAR, 1951-57. Mem. ABA, ATLA, FBA, Am. Jucicature Soc., Pa. Bar Assn., Phila. Bar Assn., Am. Law Inst., Am. Bd. Trial Advocates, Phila. Trial Lawyers Assn. (pres. 1970-71, Justice Michael Musmanno award), Pa. Trial Lawyers Assn. (pres. 1969-70), Inner Cir. Advs., Am. Bd. Profl. Liability Attys., Temple U. Gen. Alumni Assn. (cert. of honor), Pa. Soc., Aircraft Owners and Pilots Assn. (cert. flight instr. single-multi engine airplane and instrument FAA), Six Diamonds Aerobatic Flight Team, Nat. Air Racing Group, Union League. Episcopalian. Fax: 215-592-8360. E-mail: lawyers tortlaw.com. Office: 1125 Walnut St Philadelphia PA 19107-4918

BEASLEY, JAMES W., JR., lawyer; b. Atlanta, July 13, 1943; s. James W. and Sara Capal (Tucker) B.; m. Elizabeth Barno Marshall-Beasley, Nov. 28, 1986. AB cum laude, Davidson Coll., 1965; LLB cum laude, Harvard U., 1968. Bar: N.Y. 1969, D.C. 1971, Fla. 1972, U.S. Supreme Ct. 1973. Assoc. Sullivan & Cromwell, N.Y.C., 1968, Wilmer, Cutler & Pickering, Washington, 1970-72; assoc., then ptnr. Paul & Thomson, Miami, Fla., 1972-78; mng. ptnr. Beasley, Olle & Downs, Miami, 1978-88; ptnr. Tew , Jordan, Schulte & Beasley, Miami, 1988-89, Cadwalader, Wickersham & Taft, Palm Beach, Fla., 1989-94, Tew & Beasley LLP, Palm Beach, 1994-97, Beasley, Leacock & Hauser, P.A., Palm Beach, 1997—. Author: Florida Corporations, 1985; contbr. articles to profl. jours. Mem. Urban Land Inst.; chmn. County Conv. Ctr. Adv. Bd., 1994-96. Capt. U.S. Army, 1968-70. Mem. ABA, ATLA, Fla. Bar Assn. (chmn. securities regulation com. bus. law sect. 1975-77), Acad. Fla. Trial Lawyers.

BEASLEY, JERRY LYNN, academic administrator; b. New Braunfels, Tex., July 18, 1944; s. Harold E. and Marguerite (Martin) B.; m. Jean Karen Dressler, Apr. 12, 1974; children: Heather Lauren, Sarah Elizabeth, Leah Ellen. AB, Harvard U., 1966, MEd, 1969; PhD, Stanford U., 1980. Admission officer Harvard Coll., Cambridge, 1966-69; dir. comprhensive planning W.Va Commn. Higher Edn., Charleston, 1969-70; asst. to chancellor W.Va. Bd. Regents, Charleston, 1970-71; v.p. Waynesburg (Pa.) Coll., 1974-82, W.Va. Wesleyan Coll., Buckhannon, 1982-85; pres. Concord Coll., Athens, W.Va., 1985—; cons. numerous fed., state and local govt. agys., schs., colls. and univs.; cons.. evaluator North Ctrl. Assn.; mem. planning and devel. com. Coll. Entrance Exam. Bd., 1986—. Author: Coal and Rural America, 1978. Active W.Va. Commn. Nat. and Cmty. Svc.; pres. W.Va. Campus Compact; dir. Mission W.Va.; mem. MErcer County Econ. Devel. Authority. NIMH fellow Stanford U., 1972. Mem. Am. Assn. State Colls. and Univs., W.Va. Assn. Colls. and Univs. Pres., Rotary (bd. dirs. Princeton Club). Methodist. Avocations: reading, writing, sports. Home: PO Box 902 Athens WV 24712-0902 Office: Concord Coll Office of the Pres Athens WV 24712*

BEASLEY, JIM SANDERS See LEE, JACK

BEASLEY, JOHN JULIUS, child and family development educator; b. Raleigh, N.C., July 9, 1947; s. Julius Helland and Ruth Christine (Richardson) B.; m. Mary Sandra Wortham, June 21, 1969; 1 child, Elizabeth. BA, E. Carolina U., 1969; MS, Va. Tech., 1972, PhD, 1978. Extension agent 4-H Va. Tech., Blacksburg, 1971-74, instr. extension, 1974-78, asst. prof. extension, 1978-81; chair Appalachian State U., Boone, N.C., 1981-86; assoc. prof. Appalachian State U., Boone, 1981-88; prof. Ga. So. U., Statesboro, 1988—, chair, 1988-96; cons. Head Start, Vienna, Va., 1995—; spkr. in field. Editor rsch. sect. Jour. Extension, 1979-81; reviewer Jour. of Family and Consumer Scis., 1994—; contbr. articles to profl. jours. Pres., University Optimist, Statesboro, 1991-92, adv. bd., 1996—; pres. Child Abuse Coun., Statesboro, 1995-97. Grantee Children's Trust Fund, 1991, Ga. Child Care Coun., 1992. Mem. Future Homemakers of Am./HERO (hon.), Am. Assn. Family Consumer Sci. (cert. family consumer scientist), Ga. Family Consumer Scis., Statesboro C. of C., Optimist Internat. (life), Phi Delta Kappa, Phi Kappa Phi, Phi Upsilon Omicron. Episcopalian. Home: 108 Turkey Trl Statesboro GA 30458-8957 Office: Ga So U PO Box 8021 Statesboro GA 30460-1000

BEASLEY, JOHN SNODGRASS, II, university administrator; b. Franklin, Tenn., Oct. 2, 1930; s. Thomas Earl and Elsie (Eggleston) B.; m. Mary D. Allison Tidman, Sept. 4, 1958; children: John III, Eleanor Christensen Beasley Nahley. BA, Vanderbilt U., 1952, JD, 1954. Bar: Tenn. 1954. Atty. Franklin, 1957-58; exec. sec. alumni assn. Vanderbilt U., 1958-61, asst. dean, asst. prof., 1962-64, assoc. dean, asst. prof., 1964-66, assoc. dean, assoc. prof., 1966-70, assoc. dean, prof., 1970-71, nat. alumni dir. centennial campaign, 1980-81, spl. asst. to chancellor, 1981-83, vice chancellor for alumni and devel., 1983—; sr. v.p. Commerce Union Bank, Nashville, 1971-74, exec. v.p., 1978-80, vice chmn. trust bd., 1978-80. Founding pres. Heritage Found. of Franklin and Williamson County, 1965-68; bd. dirs. Franklin Spl. Sch. Dist., 1974-76; trustee Battle Ground Acad., Franklin, 1970-74, Tenn. Bot. Gardens and Fine Arts Ctr. at Cheekwood, Nashville, 1969-75, pres. 1973-75; chmn. bd. Harpeth Hall Sch., Nashville, 1976-81; bd. dirs. Tenn. Performing Arts Ctr., 1986-92. Mem. Belle Meade County Club (bd. dirs. 1974-80, v.p. 1979-80), Univ. Club (N.Y.C., Nashville), Order of Coif, Phi Beta Kappa, Omicron Delta Kappa, Sigma Chi, Pi Delta Epsilon, Phi Delta Phi. Republican. Episcopalian. Avocation: piano. Fax: 615-343-8340. E-mail: beasley@uansv3.vanderbilt.edu. Home: 335 Fourth Ave South Franklin TN 37064 Office: Vanderbilt U 205 Kirkland Hall Nashville TN 37064

BEASLEY, LARRY, newspaper publishing executive; b. Alice, Tex., Jan. 7, 1945. Pub., pres., CEO Daily News, Woodland Hills, Calif., 1994—. Office: Daily News Mgmt 21221 Oxnard St Woodland Hills CA 91367-5081*

BEASLEY, MARY CATHERINE, home economics educator, administrator, researcher; b. Portersville, Ala., Nov. 29, 1922; d. Albert Otis and Beulah Green (Killian) Reed; m. Percy Wells Beasley, Dec. 15, 1956 (dec. Dec. 1958). BS in Home Econs., Bob Jones U., 1944; MS, Pa. State U., State College, 1954, EdD, 1968. Tchr. Geraldine and Collinsville (Ala.) High Sch., 1944-45; vocat. home econs. tchr. Glencoe (Ala.) High Sch., 1945-48, Washington County High Sch., Chatom, Ala., 1948-51; home econs. tchr. Homewood Jr. High Sch., Birmingham, Ala., 1958-60; asst. supr. and subject matter specialist Ala. Dept. Edn., Montgomery, 1951-57; asst. prof. Samford U., Birmingham, 1960-62; instr. U. Ala., Tuscaloosa, 1951, asst. prof. then assoc. prof., 1962-68, dir. continuing edn. in home econs., 1968-84, prof., 1984-88, prof. emeritus consumer sci. Coll. Human Environ. Sci., 1988—. Author: (with others) Human Ecological Studies, 1986. Pres. Joint Legis. Coun. of Ala., 1973-75; dir. On Your Own Program, 1970-80. Recipient Creative Programming award Nat. U. Extension Assn., 1979. Mem. Am. Home Econs. Assn. (chmn. rehab. com. 1973, 75, leader 1986), Southeastern Coun. on Family Rels. (pres. 1982-84, Disting. Svc. award 1988), Ala. Home Econs. Assn. (pres. 1961-63, leader 1985), Ala. Coun. on Family Rels. (pres. 1981-83, Disting. Svc. award 1987), Altrusa Club of Tuscaloosa (pres. 1988-89, exec. bd. Ft. Payne/DeKalb 1989-93, corr. sec. 1995-96), Collinsville Study Club (v.p. 1992-93, pres. 1996-98), Alpha Delta Kappa (treas. Tuscaloosa chpt. 1973-75), Phi Upsilon Omicron, Kappa Omicron Nu. Republican. Baptist. Home: 12860 US Highway 11 Collinsville AL 35961-4321

BEASLEY, MAURINE HOFFMAN, journalism educator, historian; b. Jan. 28, 1936; d. Mimmitt Heard and Maurine (Hieronymous) Hoffman; m. William C. McLaughlin, May 20, 1966 (div. 1969); m. Henry R. Beasley, Dec. 24, 1970; 1 child, Susan Sook. BA in History, U. Mo., 1958; MS in Journalism, Columbia U., 1963; PhD in Am. Civilization, George Washington U., 1974. Edn. editor Kansas City (Mo.) Star, 1959-62; staff writer Washington Post, 1963-67; from asst. prof journalism to prof. U. Md., College Park, 1975-87, prof., 1987—. Author: Eleanor Roosevelt and the Media: A Public Quest for Self-Fulfillment, 1987, (with others) Women in Media, 1977, The New Majority, 1988, Taking Their Place! Documentary History of Women and Journalism, 1993 (Acad. Books Choice 1994); editor: (with others) Voices of Change: Southern Pulitzer Winners, 1978, One Third of a Nation (hon. mention Washington Monthly Book award 1982), 1981, White House Press Conferences of Eleanor Roosevelt, 1983; adv. bd. Am. Journalism, 1983—, Jour. Mass Media Ethics, Mass Com. Rev.; corr. editor Journalism History, 1995—; contbr. articles to profl. jours. Violinist Montgomery County Symphony Orch., 1975—; pres. Little Falls Swimming Club, Inc. 1988-89. Gannett Tchg. Fellowships Program fellow, 1977, Pulitzer Travelling fellow Columbia U., 1963; Eleanor Roosevelt studies grantee Eleanor Roosevelt Inst., 1979-80, Arthur Schlesinger rsch. fellow and grantee Roosevelt Inst., 1998; named one of nation's outstanding tchrs. of writing and editing Modern Media Inst. and Am. Soc. Newspaper Editors, 1981, most outstanding woman U. Md. Coll. Park Pres. Commn. on Women's Affairs, 1993, Haiman award Speech Comm. Assn., 1995. Mem. Assn. Edn. in Journalism and Mass Comms. (exec. com 1990-91, 94-95, standing com. on profl. freedom and responsibility 1985, vice chair 1987-89, chair 1990-91, sec. history divsn. 1986-87, vice head 1987-88, head 1988-89, pres. elect 1992, pres. 1993-94, leader People-to-People delegation to China and Hong Kong 1994, Outstanding Contbn. to Journalism Edn. award 1994), Nat. Fedn. Press Women, Soc. Profl. Journalists (chair nat. hist. site com. 1986-87, bd. dirs. Washington chpt. 1988-90, pres. Washington chpt. 1990-91, dir. region 2, mem. nat. bd. 1991-92, award for disting. svc. 1994, First Amendment award 1998), Internat. Assn. Mass. Comms. Rsch., Am. Journalism Historians Assn. (pres.-elect 1988-89, pres. 1989-90, Kobre award lifetime achievement 1997, best paper award 1998), Am. News Women's Club (bd. govs. 1986-87), Women in Comms. (bd. dirs. Washington chpt. 1985-87), Orgn. Am. Historians, Am. Hist. Assn., Phi Beta Kappa, Omicron Delta Kappa. Democrat. Unitarian. Home: 4920 Flint Dr Bethesda MD 20816-1746 Office: U Md Coll Journalism College Park MD 20742

BEASLEY, ROBERT PALMER, epidemiologist, dean, educator; b. Glendale, Calif., Apr. 29, 1936. AB in Philosophy, Darmouth Coll., 1958; MD, Harvard U., 1962; MSc in Preventive Medicine, U. Wash., 1969. Diplomate Am. Bd. Preventive Medicine, Am. Bd. Internal Medicine. Intern King County Hosp., Seattle, 1962-63; resident CDC, USPHS, 1963-65, U. Wash., Seattle, 1965-67; resident preventive medicine U. Washington Hosp., Seattle, 1967-69; assoc. prof. dept. medicine, dept. epidemiology U. Wash., Seattle, 1969-72, assoc. prof. to rsch. prof., 1972-86; with U. Calif., San Francisco, 1986-87; dir. Am. U. Med. Ctr., Taipei, Taiwan, 1979—; dean Sch. Pub. Health, U. Tex. Health Sci. Ctr. at Houston, 1987—. Recipient King Faisal Internat. prize in medicine, 1985; co-recipient Mott medal GM Cancer Rsch. Found., 1987. Mem. Am. Epidemiological Soc., Am. Fedn. for Clin. Rsch., Am. Pub. Health Assn., Am. Soc. of Internal Medicine, Soc. for Epidemiological Rsch. Office: U Texas Health Sci Ctr Sch Pub Health PO Box 20186 Houston TX 77225

BEASLEY, TROY DANIEL, secondary education educator; b. Whitestone, Ga., Dec. 5, 1942; s. Amos Daniel and Imogene (Duckett) B.; m. Debbie L. Jones, Feb. 23, 1985; children: Flannery Meghan, Annalise Sarah, Ammelia Katherine. BA, Ga. State U., 1973, MA, 1981. Cert. tchr., Ga. Tchr. English, drama and theatre Murray County H.S., Chatsworth, Ga., 1973—; tchr. Rinehardt Coll., Waleska, Ga., 1975-96. Del. Gov. Ga. Conf. on Edn., Atlanta, 1993. Staff sgt. USAF, 1963-68. Recipient Star Tchr. award Ga. C. of C., 1976, 77, 82, 85, 86, 94. Mem. Nat. Assn. Educators, Nat. Coun. Tchrs. English, Ga. Assn. Educators, Ga. Coun. Tchrs. English, Murray Assn. Educators (pres. 1983-85). Democrat. Roman Catholic. Avocations: theatre, reading, swimming, movies. Home: 151 Sahara Ln Chatsworth GA 30705-2633 Office: Murray County HS 1001 Green Rd Chatsworth GA 30705-2011

BEASLEY, WILLIAM REX, judge; b. Tulsa, Aug. 29, 1934; s. O. Rex and W. S. B.; m. Donna Knight, Sept. 3, 1954; children: Bradley, Brenda, Barry. BS with honors, U. Tulsa, 1959, JD, 1967; grad., Nat. Jud. Coll., 1977. Bar: Okla. 1967. Asst. dist. atty. Tulsa County, 1968-71; chief prosecutor McAlester, Okla., 1971-73; assoc. dist. judge Tulsa, 1973—; chief juvenile judge Tulsa County Dist. Ct. Okla., Tulsa, 1981-88; chief criminal judge Tulsa County Dist. Ct., Tulsa, 1998; lectr. Okla. Hwy. Patrol Acad., Oklahoma City, 1971—; mem. exec. coun. Okla. Jud. Conf., 1989-92; bd. dirs. Ct. Apptd. Spl. Advs., 1985-88; leader Nat. Jud. Coll., 1978; co-chmn. Tulsa County Ct. Fund; mem. rules com. Criminal Ct. Appeals; mem. judicial legis. com., 1997. Mem. Tulsa Safety Coun.; chmn. State Foster Care Rev. Adv. Bd., 1983-88; mem. Okla. Commn. on Children and Youth; founder, bd. dirs. Ct. Appointed Spl. Advocate, Tulsa, 1985-86; mem. adminstrv. bd. local Meth. ch. Mem. ABA, Okla. Bar Assn., Okla. Jud. Conf. (v.p. 1978, 79, exec. coun. 1989, 90, 91, 92), Nat. Coun. Juvenile Judges, Lions (del. Okla. jud. conf. 1989-92, mem. legis. com. 1997-99), Kappa Sigma. Home: PO Box 3081 Tulsa OK 74101-3081 Office: 500 S Denver Ave Ste 706 Tulsa OK 74103-3838

BEATHARD, BOBBY, professional football team executive; b. Zanesville, Ohio, Jan. 24, 1937; m. Christine Beathard; children: Kurt, Jeff, Casey, James. Student, Calif. Poly. Inst. Scout Kansas City Chiefs, Am. Football League, 1963-68, Atlanta Falcons, NFL, 1968-72; dir. player personnel Miami Dolphins, NFL, 1972-78; gen. mgr. Washington Redskins, NFL, 1978-89, San Diego Chargers, NFL, 1990—. Office: San Diego Chargers Jack Murphy Field Qualcomm Stadium PO Box 609609 San Diego CA 92160-9609*

BEATIE, BRUCE ALAN, comparative and medieval studies educator; b. Oakland, Calif., Mar. 4, 1935; s. Charles Baldwin and Marion Berenice (Putnam) B.; m. Rita Virginia Nicklos, May 11, 1956 (dec. Nov. 1989); children: Robert Bruce, Edward Charles; m. Therese Marie Huzvar, Dec. 22, 1990. BA in Comparative Lit., U. Calif., Berkeley, 1959; MA in German, U. Colo., 1960; PhD in Comparative Lit., Harvard U., 1967. Asst. prof. German dept. U. Colo., Boulder, 1964-68; assoc. prof. comparative lit. dept. U. Rochester, N.Y., 1968-70; prof. modern langs. Cleve. State U., 1970—, chair modern langs., 1970-77, dir. honors program Coll. Arts and Scis., 1990-92, dir. classical and medieval studies program, 1992-96; bd. dirs. Peoples and Cultures, Cleve., 1980-83. Author books; contbr. articles to profl. jours. With USAF, 1954-57. Woodrow Wilson fellow U. Colo., 1959-60; NEH young scholar, Munich, 1970. Mem. MLA, Medieval Acad. Home: 324 Bonds Pky Berea OH 44017-1273 Office: Cleve State U Dept Modern Langs Cleveland OH 44115

BEATIE, RUSSEL HARRISON, JR., lawyer; b. Lawrence, Kans., Jan. 20, 1938; m. Julia Ferguson DuVall; children: Benjamin Wilson Parkhill, Amy Wilder. BA cum laude, Princeton U., 1959, LLB cum laude Columbia U., 1964. Bar: N.Y. 1964, U.S. Dist. Ct. (so. and ea. dists.) N.Y., U.S. Ct. Appeals (2d, 3d, 5th, 6th, 7th, 9th and 10th cirs.), U.S. Supreme Ct. Assoc. Dewey, Ballantine, Bushby, Palmer & Wood, N.Y.C., 1964-66, 68-72, Rogers & Wells, 1966-68; ptnr. Dewey Ballantine, 1972-83; pvt. practice, 1983-88; ptnr. Brown & Wood, N.Y.C., 1989-93, Beatie, King & Abate, N.Y.C., 1993-97, Beatie and Osborn, 1997—. 1st lt., arty. U.S. Army, 1959-61. Mem. Assn. of Bar of City of N.Y., Union Club. Republican. Author: Road to Manassas—The Growth of Union Command in the Eastern Theatre from the Fall of Fort Sumter to the First Battle of Bull Run, 1961. Office: 599 Lexington Ave New York NY 10022-6030

BEATON, REBECCA ANDREA, psychotherapist; b. West Covina, Calif., Dec. 3, 1964; d. Allen Ethan and Joan Delores (Graybill) Brogan; m. Robert Gifford Beaton II, Sept. 4, 1993. BA in Human Philosophy & Cultural Geog., U. Calif., Santa Barbara, 1986; MS in Cmty. Counseling, Ga. State U., 1995, specialist in edn., 1996, postgrad., 1997—. Health counselor Bragg Health Sci., Santa Barbara, Calif., 1986-87; counselor intern Anxiety Disorders Inst./Atlanta Ctr. for Eating Disorders, 1994-95; counselor intern employee assistance program Lockheed Aero. Sys. Co., Marietta, Ga., 1994-95; psychotherapist Anxiety Disorders Inst. Atlanta, 1995-98; pvt. practice Ctr. for Psychotherapy and Healing Arts, 1998—; grad. rsch. asst. Ednl. Rsch. Bur., Ga. State U., Atlanta, 1993-94, dept. counseling and psychol. svcs., 1993-96; therapy group leader Trauma Abuse and Resource Program, Atlanta, 1995-98; psychotherapist Atlanta Ctr. for Eating Disorders, Atlanta, 1995-98; growth group leader Ga. State U., Atlanta, 1995-98; trainer Wellness Inst., 1997—; process group leader for med. interns Ga. Bapt. Med. Ctr., 1998—; presenter in field. Contbr. articles to profl. jours. Vol. counselor Ga. Mental Health Inst., Atlanta, 1991-93; vol. rape crisic ctr. counselor, legal liaison Grady Meml. Hosp., Atlanta, 1992-98. Mem. APA (divsn. 17, divsn. 38, divsn. 30), ACA, Am. Ednl. Rsch. Assn., Assn. for Multi-cultural Counseling and Devel., Assn. for Transpersonal Psychology, Atlanta Assn. for Play Therapy, The Menninger Found. Avocations: wildlife photography, hiking, gardening, mountain bike riding, bird watching. Office: Ctr for Psychotherapy and Healing Arts 1014 Canton St Roswell GA 30075

BEATON, ROY HOWARD, retired nuclear industry executive; b. Boston, Sept. 1, 1916; s. John Howard and Mary Beaton (LaVoie) B.; m. Margaret Marchant, July 22, 1939 (dec. Oct. 4, 1978); m. Leora Lauer Schier, June 26, 1982; children: Constance Beaton Fegley, Roy Howard, Patricia Schier Briselden, Susan Schier Carter, Mary Schier Rieber. BS, Northeastern U., 1939, DSc (hon.), 1967; DEng, Yale U., 1942. Registered profl. engr., Wash., Wis., Fla., Calif. With E.I. DuPont, 1942-46, plant tech. supr. Manhattan (Nuclear Bomb) Project, 1943-44; chief chem. devel., chief engr., gen. mgr. constrn. enging. GE, Richland, Wash., 1946-56; gen. mgr. neutron devices dept. GE, Milw., 1957-63; gen. mgr. Apollo Systems, Daytona Beach, Fla., 1964-68; v.p., gen. mgr. electronics systems div. GE, Syracuse, N.Y., 1968-74; v.p., gen. mgr. energy systems and tech. div. GE, Fairfield, Conn., 1974-75; sr. v.p. Nuclear Energy Group, San Jose, Calif., 1975-81. Chmn. industry div. United Way Campaign, Santa Clara County, Calif., 1978-79. Fellow Am. Inst. Chemists, AAAS; mem. NSPE, Nat. Acad. Engring., Am. Ordnance Assn., Am. Nuclear Soc., Am. Inst. Chem. Engrs., IEEE, AIAA, Navy League U.S., Air Force Assn., Soc. Mil. Engrs., Santa Clara County Mfg. Group, Sigma Xi, Tau Beta Pi. Home: 12 Fawn Ln Sequim WA 98382-3887

BEATRICE, RUTH HADFIELD, hypnotherapist, retired educator, financial administrator; b. Phila., Feb. 6, 1931; d. Claude and Alice Elizabeth (Smith) Hadfield; m. Michael Joseph Beatrice, May 29, 1954. BS, West Chester State U., 1953; MS, Marywood Coll., 1978; postgrad., Temple U., Pa. State U., 1978-80; cert. clinl. hypnotherapist, Phila. Hypnosis Union Inst., 1980. Cert. hypno-anaesthesia therapist Nat. Bd. Hypnotherapy and Hypnotic Anaesthesiology, 1991. Educator Bristol Twp. (Pa.) Sch. Dist., 1953-54, Phila. Sch. Dist., 1954-55; recreation dir. Phila. Dept. Recreation, 1953-57; educator Worcester (Pa.) Sch. Dist., 1958-59, Springford (Pa.) Joint Sch. Dist., 1960-61, Souderton (Pa.) Sch. Dist., 1961-63, Ctrl. Bucks Sch. Dist., Doylestown, Pa., 1970-1993; ret., 1993; clin. hypnotherapist in pvt. practice Perkasie, Pa., 1980—; clin. hypnotherapist, pvt. practice Avalon, N.J., 1980—; bus. adminstr. Beatrice Adminstrs. Co-author books on tutoring for Ptnrs. at Learning Series, 1978, 1979, 1983. Bd. mem. Pierce Free Libr., Hilltown, Pa., 1970-75; union del. Office and Profl. Employees Internat. Union Internat. Conv., Vancouver, B.C., Can., 1995; treas. Newcomers Civic Assn., Perkasie, 1964-85; me. Avalon (N.J.) Civic Assn., avalon Sr. Assn. Mem. NEA (life), Nat. Assn. Profl. Therapists, Am. Legion Aux., Pa. State Edn. Assn. (life), Hypnotism Soc. of Pa. (v.p. Phila. br. 1993-95), Phila. Hypnosis Union Local 476 (v.p. 1993-95), Nat. Guild of Hypnotists, Nat. Bd. for Hypnotherapy and Hypnotic Anaesthesiology. Democrat. Presbyterian. Avocations: tennis, walking, biking, fishing, boating, cooking. Home and Office: 273 52nd St Avalon NJ 08202-1314 also: 1107 Rickert Rd Perkasie PA 18944-2614

BEATTIE, ANN, author; b. Washington, Sept. 8, 1947; d. James and Charlotte (Crosby) B.; m. Lincoln Perry. B.A., Am. U., 1969; M.A., U. Conn., 1970; L.H.D. (hon.), Am. U., 1983. Vis. asst. prof. U. Va., Charlottesville, 1976-77, vis. writer, 1980; Briggs Copeland lectr. English Harvard U., Cambridge, Mass., 1977. Author: Chilly Scenes of Winter, 1976, Distortions, 1976, Secrets and Suprises, 1979, Falling In Place, 1980, Jacklighting, 1981, The Burning House, 1982, Love Always, 1985, Where You'll Find Me, 1986, Alex Katz, 1987, Picturing Will, 1990, What Was Mine, 1991, My Life Starring Dara Falcon, 1997, Park City: New & Selected Stories, 1998. Recipient Disting. Alumnae award Am. U., 1980, award in lit. Am. Acad. and Inst. Arts and Letters, 1980; Guggenheim fellow, 1977. Mem. Am. Acad. and Inst. of Arts and Letters, 1992, PEN, Authors Guild. Office: care Janklow and Nesbit 598 Madison Ave New York NY 10022-1614*

BEATTIE, CHARLES ROBERT, III, lawyer; b. Red Wing, Minn., Aug. 25, 1948; s. Charles Robert Jr. and Dorothy Catherine (Shepherd) B.; m. Camilla Lawther Foot, Aug. 26, 1972; children: Virginia, Anne, Charles. BA with honors, U. Mich., 1970; JD, Yale U., 1973. Bar: Minn. 1973, U.S. Dist. Ct. Minn. 1973, U.S. Ct. Appeals (8th cir.) 1975. Assoc. Doherty, Rumble & Butler, St. Paul, 1973-78; ptnr. Doherty, Rumble & Butler, St. Paul and Mpls., 1978, chmn. dept. bus. law, 1987-89, 92-94, dir., 1989-92, 98—; lectr. on partnerships and banking, leasing, comml. law and electronic commerce, 1983-98; mem. Minn. Digital Signature Guidelines Task Force, 1997-98. Contbr. articles on ltd. partnerships and electronic commerce to profl. jours., 1983, 98. Mem. Citizens League, St. Paul and Mpls., 1979-93; officer Leadership St. Paul, 1981-86; bd. dirs. Civic Symphony Assn., 1976-80, St. John the Evangelist Episc. Ch., St. Paul, officer, 1981-93; pres., bd. dirs. Valley Chamber Chorale, 1996—; mem. Gillette Children's Specialty Healthcare Exec. Coun., 1995—. Mem. ABA (uniform comml. code com., com. on cyberspace law 1991—, article 2 task force 1993—, article 1 task force 1993—, co-chair working group on electronic writings and notices 1995-97, bus. law sect. adviser NCCUSL electronic contracting act drafting com. 1997—), Minn. Bar Assn. (corp. banking and bus. law sects.), Greater Mpls. C. of C. (bd. dirs. 1997—). Avocations: sailing, skiing, tennis.

BEATTIE, DIANA SCOTT, biochemistry educator; b. Cranston, R.I., Aug. 11, 1934; d. Kenneth Allen and Lillian Francis (Barton) Scott; m. Benjamin Howard Beattie, June 30, 1956 (div. 1975); children: Elizabeth, Sara, Rachel, Ruth; m. Robert Nathan Stuchell, Feb. 6, 1976 (div. 1991). B.A., Swarthmore Coll., 1956; M.S., U. Pitts., 1958, Ph.D., 1961. Research assoc. U. Pitts., 1961-67, VA Hosp., Pitts., 1967-68; faculty Mt. Sinai Sch. Medicine, N.Y.C., 1968-85; prof. biochemistry Mt. Sinai Sch. Medicine, 1976-85; prof., chmn. dept. biochemistry W.Va. U. Sch. Medicine, Morgantown, 1985—; mem. grad. faculty biomed. sci. CUNY, 1968-86, biochemistry, 1971-85, biology, 1974-85; mem. grad. faculty biochemistry W.Va. U. Sch. Medicine, Morgantown, 1985—; vis. prof. U. Louvain, Belgium, 1982, U. Nairobi, Kenya, 1993; mem. ad hoc biochemistry study sect. NIH, 1976-77, 79-81, mem. phys. biochemistry study sect., 1981-85, 1993-97; chmn. phys. biochemistry study sect., 1983-85, 1995-97; mem. metabolic biology panel NSF, 1986-89; mem. basic sci. merit rev. panel VA, 1989-92. Contbr. articles to profl. jours.; ed. bd. Archives of Biochemistry and Biophysics, 1975-78, 85—, Jour. Bioenergetics, 1975—.

Recipient award Met. N.Y. chpt. Assn. for Women in Sci., 1979; grantee NSF, 1970-92, 97—, NIH, 1966—; Fogarty internat. fellow, 1982, Fulbright fellow, 1993. Mem. Am. Soc. Biol. Chemists (membership com. 1987-89), Am. Soc. Cell Biology, Biophysics Soc., Assn. Med. Sch. Depts. Biochemistry (exec. com. 1989-92, pres.-elect 1995, pres. 1996), Am. Assn. Med. Schs. (mem. coun. acad. socs. 1989—, adminstrv. bd. 1994—, chair 1998), Nat. Bd. Med. Examiners (biochemistry test com. 1991-93, chair 1994-95, amatomy test com. 1998—), Nat. Caucus Basic Biomed. Chairs (vice chair 1991—). Home: 324 Dream Catcher Cir Morgantown WV 26508-9473 Office: W Va U Sch Medicine Dept Biochemistry Morgantown WV 26506

BEATTIE, DONALD A., energy scientist, consultant; b. N.Y.C., Oct. 30, 1929; s. James Francis and Evelyn Margaret (Hickey) B.; m. Ann Mary Kean, Mar. 27, 1973; children: Thomas James, Bruce Andrew. A.B., Columbia U., 1951; M.S., Colo. Sch. Mines, 1958. Regional geologist Mobil Oil Co., 1958-63; Apollo lunar expts. program mgr. NASA, 1963-72; dir. NASA energy systems div. NASA, Washington, 1978-82; v.p. Houston ops. BDM Corp., 1983-84; cons. on energy and space tech., 1984—; pres. Endosat Inc., 1991-96; dir. advanced energy research and tech. NSF, 1973-75; dep. asst. adminstr. ERDA, 1975-77; acting asst. sec. Dept. Energy, Washington, 1977-78; solar energy coordinator U.S./USSR Coop. in Sci. and Tech.; U.S. rep. Vienna Inst. for Comparative Econ. Studies Workshop on Energy. Author, editor: History and Overview of Solar Heat Technologies, 1997; contbr. numerous articles on lunar sci., energy to profl. jours. Active Boy Scouts Am., 1958-71. Served with AC USN, 1951-56. Recipient Exceptional Service medal NASA, 1971, Sr. Exec. Service and Outstanding Performance award, 1980; Superior Achievement award Dept. Energy, 1978. Fellow AAAS; mem. Geol. Soc. Am., Nat. Space Club. Home and Office: 808 Mill Pond Ct Jacksonville FL 32259-3027

BEATTIE, EDWARD JAMES, surgeon, educator; b. Phila., June 30, 1918; m. Nicole Mary; 1 son, Bruce Stewart. B.A., Princeton U., 1939; M.D., Harvard U., 1943. Diplomate Am. Bd. Surgery, Am. Bd. Thoracic Surgery (mem. bd. 1960-69, chmn. bd. 1967-69). Intern, surg. resident Peter Bent Brigham Hosp., Boston, 1942-46; Mosely traveling fellow (Harvard) to U. London, Eng., 1946-47; surg. fellow, Markle scholar George Washington U., 1947-52; chief thoracic surgery Presbyn. Hosp., 1952-54; chmn. dept. surgery Presbyn.-St. Luke's Hosp., 1954-65; cons. thoracic surgery Hines VA Hosp., Ill., 1953-65, Chgo. Tb San., 1954-65, Ill. Research and Edn. Hosp., 1956-65, Rockefeller U. Hosp., 1978-83; prof. surgery U. Ill., 1955-65; prof. surgery Cornell U., 1965-83, emeritus, 1983—; prof. surgery, prof. oncology U. Miami, Fla., 1983-85; prof. surgery Mt. Sinai Sch. Medicine, N.Y.C., 1988-94, Albert Einstein Coll. Medicine, 1994—; chief thoracic surgery Meml. Hosp., N.Y.C., 1965-75, chmn. dept. surgery, 1966-78, chief med. officer, 1966-83, gen. dir., chief oper. officer, 1975-83; chief thoracic surgery, dir. Kriser Lung Cancer Ctr., dir. clin. cancer programs Beth Israel Med. Ctr., N.Y.C., 1985-95, dir. emeritus Kriser Lung Cancer Ctr., 1995, med. dir. Cancer Ctr., 1994—. Mem. editl. bd. Jour. Thoracic and Cardiovascular Surgery, 1962-83, Pediat. Digest, 1962-85, Cancer Clin. Trials, 1977-85, Internat. Advances in Surg. Oncology, 1977. Fellow A.C.S.; mem. Am. Assn. Thoracic Surgery, Am. Surg. Assn., Soc. Vascular Surgery, AMA, Central, Western surg. assns., Internat. Soc. Surgery, Soc. Clin. Surgery, Am. Radium Soc., Soc. Thoracic Surgeons, Transplantation Soc., Am. Assn. Med. Colls., Pan Am. Med. Assn., Am. Cancer Soc., Am. Fedn. Clin. Research, Soc. Surg. Oncology.*

BEATTIE, GERALDINE ALICE (GERI BEATTIE), advocate; b. Harrisburg, Pa., Jan. 8, 1943; d. John Martin and Marian Pauline (Coulson) Ramsey; m. Robert Bruce Beattie, Nov. 22, 1969; children: Michelle Nichols, Bryan Scott, Todd Alan. Student, U. Pa., 1960-62, Germantown (Pa.) Med. Ctr., 1960-63. Staff nurse Germantown (Pa.) Med. Ctr., 1963; head nurse Shore Meml. Hosp., Somers Point, N.J., 1964; head nurse Children's Hosp., San Diego, 1965-73, nursing supr., 1977-81, founder, supr. child abuse evidentiary program, 1981-93, asst. dir., mgr. Ctr. Child Protection, 1993—; bd. suprs. Multi-Victim Protocol Task Force, San Diego, 1987-88, Victim Witness Protocol Task Force, San Diego, 1989—; mem. Strategic Plan Task Force, Dept. Social Svcs., San Diego, 1996-98; project dir. Calif. Child Sexual Abuse Prevention and Treatment Ctr., Calif. Med. Tng. Ctr.; internat. tng. and tech. assistance expert on multidiscipline investigation of child abuse and implemt mgmt. of child abuse programs. Author/editor: (protocol manual) Victim Witness Protocol, 1991, 98. Mem. Am. Humane Soc., Am. Profl. Soc. Abuse of Children, Calif. Profl. Soc. Abuse of Children, Calif. Sexual Assault Investigators Assn., Calif. Network Sexual Offending, San Diego Cmty. Child Abuse Coord. Coun. (chair sexual abuse rev. com. 1984-86, Outstanding Svc. to Cmty. award). Republican. Presbyterian. Avocations: crafts, cooking, camping, reading. Home: 2298 Windmill View Rd El Cajon CA 92020-1356 Office: Ctr Child Protection-Childrens Hosp 3020 Childrens Way San Diego CA 92123-4223

BEATTIE, JAMES LOUIS, professional sports team executive; b. Hampton, Va., July 4, 1954; m. Martha Johnson, Sept. 10, 1978; children: Sam, Nell, Sarah. BA, Dartmouth Coll., 1976; MBA, U. Wash., 1989. Pitcher N.Y. Yankees, 1978-79; pitcher Seattle Mariners, 1980-86, dir. player devel., 1989-95; v.p., gen. mgr. Montreal Expos, 1995—. Office: Montreal Expos, 4549 Pierre-de-Coubertin Av, Montreal, PQ Canada H1V 3N7*

BEATTIE, NORA MAUREEN, insurance company executive, actuary; b. Bklyn., July 10, 1925; d. Robert G. and Eileen (Geaney) B. B.A. summa cum laude, St. John's U., 1947, M.S., 1949, D.C.S. (hon.), 1983. Asst. actuary N.Y. Life Ins. Co., N.Y.C., 1960-63; asso. actuary N.Y. Life Ins. Co., 1963-67, actuary, 1967-71, 2d. v.p., 1971-74, v.p., actuary, 1974-88, ret., 1988. Fellow Am. Acad. Actuaries, Soc. Actuaries; mem. Bus. and Profl. Women's Club (treas. Wall St. Br. 1969-71, Woman of Yr., N.Y. br. 1968), N.Y. Guarantee Assn. (treas. 1981-86). Club: N.Y. Actuaries.

BEATTIE, TED ARTHUR, zoological gardens and aquarium administrator; b. Salem, Ohio, Jan. 13, 1945; s. Don Earl and Frances (Webster) B.; children: Lauralyn, Sean, Kimberly; m. Penelope Johnson, July 13, 1985. BA in Journalism, Ohio State U., 1971, MA in Pub. Rels., 1972. Advt./pub. rels. dir. Shaw-Barton Co., Coshocton, Ohio, 1972-78; mktg. dir. Cin. Zoo, 1978-81; assoc. dir. Brookfield Zoo, Chgo., 1981-87; exec. dir. Knoxville (Tenn.) Zool. Gardens, 1987-92; dir., CEO Ft. Worth Zool. Pk., 1992-94; pres., CEO John G. Shedd Aquarium, Chgo., 1994—; cons. Zoo Plan Assn., Wichita, Kans., 1981-88. Vice chmn. and chmn. United Way campaign, Coshocton, 1977-78; mem. Leadership Knoxville, 1988. With U.S. Army, 1967-69, Vietnam. Fellow Am. Assn. Zool. Pks. and Aquariums (bd. dirs. 1989-91, 94-2002); mem. Am. Zoo & Aquarium Assn. (v.p. 1998-99), Chgo. Econ. Club, Arts Club, Onwentsia Club, Sawgrass Country Club. Avocations: golf, boating. Home: 8 Court Of Conn River Vly Lincolnshire IL 60069-3209 Office: John G Shedd Aqarium 1200 S Lake Shore Dr Chicago IL 60605-2402

BEATTS, ANNE PATRICIA, writer, producer; b. Buffalo, Feb. 25, 1947; d. Patrick Murray Threipland and Sheila Elizabeth Jean (Sherriff Scott) B. BA with honors, McGill U., Montreal, Que., Can., 1966. Contbg. editor National Lampoon mag., N.Y.C., 1970-74; writer Saturday Night Live NBC, N.Y.C., 1975-80; creator, prodr. Square Pegs CBS, Los Angeles, 1982-83; co-exec. prodr. A Different World NBC, Los Angeles, 1987-88; exec. prodr. The Stephanie Miller Show, 1994-95. Co-editor: (humorous books) Titters, 1976, Saturday Night, 1977; co-author: (humorous books) Titters 101, 1984, The Mom Book, 1986; author book for Broadway mus. Leader of the Pack, 1985; humor columnist L.A. Times, 1997-98. Mem. AFTRA, Screen Actors Guild, Writers Guild Am. (award 1976), Dirs. Guild Am., Women in Film, Dramatists Guild, Acad. TV Arts and Scis. (2 Emmy awards, 5 Emmy award nominations 1975-80).

BEATTY, GROVER DOUGLAS, stockbroker; b. Little Rock, Feb. 16, 1952; m. Cheryl Christine Kiecksee, Dec. 1, 1979. BSBA, Lincoln U., Jefferson City, Mo., 1977, MS in Bus. and Fin., 1983. Lic. security dealer Nat. Assn. Securities Dealers. Auditor Mo. Div. Employment Security, Jefferson City, 1979-82; stockbroker Scherck Stein & Franc, Inc., Jefferson City, 1983-86; stockbroker Stifel Nicolaus & Co., Jefferson City, 1986—, mem. pres.'s coun., 1991—, mem. chmn.'s coun., 1997—; instr. Lincoln U., 1981-94; apptd. Stifel Nicolaus Brokers Adv. Com., 1996. Fin. chmn. 9th Dist. Ross Perot Campaign. Republican. Baptist. Office: Stifel Nicolaus & Co 222 Madison St Jefferson City MO 65101-3230

BEATTY, JOHN CABEEN, JR., judge; b. Washington, Apr. 13, 1919; s. John Cabeen and Jean (Morrison) B.; m. Clarissa Hager, Feb. 8, 1943 (dec. Apr. 4 1996); children: John Cabeen III, Clarissa Jean; m. Virginia R. Campbell, May 10, 1997. A.B., Princeton U., 1941; J.D., Columbia, 1948. Bar: Oreg. 1948. Practiced law Portland, 1948-70; ptnr. Dusenbery, Martin, Beatty, Bischoff & Templeton, 1956-70, of counsel, 1985-96; judge circuit ct., 1970-85, sr. judge, 1985—; mem. Oreg. Bd. Bar Examiners, 1953-54; chmn. legis. com. Oreg. Jud. Conf., 1976-82; mem. Oreg. CSC, 1962-64, Oreg. Law Enforcement Council, 1974-77; vice chmn. Oreg. Commn. Jud. Br., 1979-85; vice chmn., chmn. Oreg. Criminal Justice Council, 1985-90. Mem. legis. com. Nat. Sch. Bds. Assn., 1966-68, chmn. coun. large city sch. bds., 1967-68; counsel Dem. Party Oreg., 1956-58; co-chmn. Oreg. for Kennedy Com., 1968; bd. dirs. Portland Pub. Schs., 1964-70, chmn., 1967-69; chmn. policy adv. com. on hazardous waste Dept. Environ. Quality, 1985-86; mem. Mayor's Spl. Rev. Commn., 1986; chmn. various adv. coms. Dept. Environ. Quality, 1987-89; chmn. tech. adv. com. Willamette River Basin Water Quality Study, 1990-94; chmn. city club study Oreg. Initiative and Referendum, 1994-95; chmn. Oreg. Onitiative Com., 1996—. Capt. AUS, 1941-46, ETO. Decorated Bronze Star medal; recipient City Club of Portland award, 1967. Mem. ABA, Oreg. Bar Assn., Multnomah County Bar Assn., Oreg. Hist. Soc. (dir. 1973-92), City Club (past pres., bd. govs., Portland Yacht Club, Racquet Club. Home and Office: 3331 SW Mitchell St Portland OR 97201-1260

BEATTY, KENNETH ORION, JR., chemical engineer; b. East Lansdowne, Pa., Dec. 18, 1913; s. Kenneth Orion and Ada Pearl (Marshall) B.; m. Mary Catharine Carter, Aug. 8, 1936; children: Susan Jennifer, Prudence Carter, Lucy Margaret. BS, Lehigh U., 1935, MS, 1937; PhD, U. Mich., 1946. Registered profl. engr., N.C. Raybestos-Manhattan fellow Lehigh U., 1935-37; chem. engr. Dow Chem. Co., Midland, Mich., 1937-39; asst. prof. chem. engring. U. R.I., Kingston, 1939-44; rsch. assoc. U. Mich., 1944-46; assoc. prof. N.C. State U., Raleigh, 1946-48; prof. N.C. State U., 1948—, acting head dept. chem. engring., 1959-60, R.J. Reynolds Industries prof. chem. engring., 1961—, spl. cons. in forensic engring., 1982—; dir. Carolina Cons. Scientists and Engrs., 1979-87; vis. prof. chem. engring. Ohio State U., summer 1949; vis. engr. Pratt & Whitney Co., Middletown, Conn., summer 1957; resident cons. engr. Nat. Lead Co. of Ohio, Fernald, summer 1959; mem. Max Jakob Award Com., 1963-67, chmn., 1966; mem. Nat. Heat Transfer Conf. Coordinating Com., 1965-71, chmn., 1967; coordinating chmn. 9th Nat. Heat Transfer Conf., Seattle, 1967; U.S. founding del. Assembly for Internat. Heat Transfer Conf., 1967-72; mem. sci. council Internat. Center for Heat and Mass Transfer, Yugoslavia, 1971-90. Contbr. articles to profl. jours. Mem. N.C. Gov.'s Sci. Adv. Com. Rsch. grantee NASA, NSF, Wright Air Devel. Center, AEC, Am. Soc. Refrigerating Engrs.; Princeton U. fellow, 1967-68. Fellow AIChE; mem. Am. Chem. Soc., University Park Homeowners Assn. Fax: 919-515-3465. Home: 323 Shepherd St Raleigh NC 27607-4031 Office: NC State U Dept Chem Engring Raleigh NC 27695-7905

BEATTY, MICHAEL L., lawyer; b. 1947; s. Herbert Francis and Lola (Stuewe) B.; m. Kathleen Murphy; children: Erin, Piper. BA, U. Calif., 1969; JD, Harvard U., 1972. Bar: Tex. 1972. Assoc. mem. Vinson and Elkins, 1972-74; prof. U. Idaho, 1974-79; vis. prof. law U. Wyo., 1980-81; atty. Colo. Interstate Gas Co., 1981-84, gen. counsel, 1984-85; with The Coastal Corp., Houston, 1985-93, exec. v.p., gen. counsel, 1989-93; with Akin, Gump, Strauss, Hauer & Feld LLP, Houston, 1993-98; prin. Michael L. Beatty & Assocs., P.C., Denver, 1998—. Office: Michael L Beatty & Assocs PC 1401 17th St Ste 1600 Denver CO 80202-1239

BEATTY, NED, actor; b. Louisville, July 6, 1937; s. Charles William and Margaret (Lennis) B.; m. Dorothy Adams Lindsay, June 28, 1979; children: Douglas, Charlie and Lennis (twins), Wally, John, Blossom, Thomas, Dorothy. Student pub. schs., Ky. Actor: Barter Theatre, Abingdon, Va., 1957-66, Arena Stage, Washington, 1963-71, (films) include Deliverance, 1972, The Thief Who Came to Dinner, 1972, The Front Page, 1974, Nashville, 1975, W.W. and The Dixie Dancekings, 1975, Network, 1976, All the Presidents' Men, 1976, The Big Bus, 1976, Micky and Nicky, 1976, Silver Streak, 1976, Exorcist II: The Heretic, 1977, Superman, 1978, Gray Lady Down, 1978, The Great Georgia Bank Hoax, 1978, The Passage, 1979, Promises in the Dark, 1979, The Incredible Shrinking Woman, 1981, Superman II, 1981, The Toy, Hopscotch, Touched, 1983, Stroker Ace, 1983, Back to School, 1986, Restless Natives, 1986, The Big Easy, 1987, The Fourth Protocol, 1987, The Unholy, Switching Channels, 1988, Physical Evidence, 1989, A Cry In the Wilderness, 1990, Angel Square, 1990, Hear My Song, 1991, Prelude To A Kiss, 1992, Ed and his Dead Mother, 1993, Rudy, 1993, Radioland Murders, 1994, The Legend of O.B. Taggart, 1995, Just Cause, 1995, Cookie's Fortune, 1998, He Got Game, 1998, Spring Forward, 1999, Life, 1999; TV movies include: The Execution of Private Slovik, 1974, The FBI Story: The FBI Versus The Ku Klux Klan, 1975, The Deadly Tower, 1975, Hunter, 1976, Friendly Fire, 1979, The Last Days of Pompeii, 1984, Celebrity, 1984, Robert Kennedy and His Times, The Last Train Home, 1990, Lockerbie, 1990, Back to Hannibal, 1990, T. Bone and Weasel, 1992, The Affair, 1995; (miniseries) Trial, Larry McMurtry's Streets of Laredo, 1995, Gulliver's Travels, 1996; star: (TV series) Szysznyk, 1977, Homicide, 1993-95; numerous TV guest appearances including Kojak. Office: Miller & Co Mgmt 10850 Wilshire Blvd Ste 400 Los Angeles CA 90024*

BEATTY, PERRIN, broadcasting company executive; b. Toronto; married; two children. Student, Upper Can. Coll., Toronto, U. Western Ont. Elected mem. Parliament, 1972; cabinet min. Min. of State-Treasury Bd., 1979, Min. of Nat. Revenue, 1984; solicitor gen., 1985, min. of nat. def., 1986, min. of health, 1989, min. of comms., 1991, min. external affairs, 1993; pres., CEO Can. Broadcasting Corp., 1995—; hon. vis. prof. dept. polit. sci. U. Western Ont. Columnist Toronto Sun. Office: CBC, 250 Lanark Ave, Ottawa, ON Canada K1Y 1E4*

BEATTY, PRUDENCE CARTER, federal judge; b. Kingston, R.I., Nov. 19, 1942; d. Kenneth Orion and Mary Catharine (Carter) B.; 1 child, Andrea. B.A., U. Mich., 1964, J.D. cum laude, 1968. Bar: Mich. 1969, N.Y. 1971, U.S. Dist. Ct. for so. dist. N.Y. 1972, U.S. Dist. Ct. for eastern dist. N.Y. 1972, U.S. Ct. Appeals for 2d circuit 1972, U.S. Supreme Ct. 1979. Assoc. firm Breed Abbott & Morgan, N.Y.C., 1970-72, Weil Gotshal & Manges, N.Y.C., 1972-78, Krause, Hirsch & Gross, N.Y.C., 1978-79; ptnr. firm Stroock & Stroock & Lavan, N.Y.C., 1980-82; judge U.S. Bankruptcy Ct. (so. dist.) N.Y., N.Y.C., 1982—. Mem. ABA. Office: US Bankruptcy Ct US Custom House One Bowling Green 6th Fl New York NY 10004-1408

BEATTY, RICHARD SCRIVENER, lawyer; b. Washington, May 6, 1934; s. John Joseph and Helen Louise (Simpson) B.; m. Barbara Boyd, July 14, 1956; children—Charles, Alexandra, Nicholas. BA, Williams Coll., 1955; LLB, Georgetown U., 1962. Bar: D.C. 1962. Trial atty. Dept. Justice, Washington, 1962-66; assoc. chief counsel Office U.S. Comptroller of Currency, 1966-67; ptnr. firm Alston, Miller & Gaines, Washington, 1968-84; ptnr. Shaw, Pittman, Potts & Trowbridge, Washington, 1985-95, sr. counsel, 1996—. Chmn. devel. council Williams Coll.; sr. warden St. Patricks Episcopal Ch., 1980-85; trustee Mt. Vernon Coll., 1985-90; bd. dirs. The Episc. Ch. Found., 1991—; pres. Ho. of Mercy, 1999—; trustee The Key Sch., 1999—. With U.S. Army, 1956-59. Mem. Am. Law Inst., Am. Bar Assn., D.C. Bar Assn., Order St. John of Jerusalem, Met. Club (Washington, Chevy Chase (Md.) Club, Delta Psi. Home: 7001 Glenbrook Rd Bethesda MD 20814-1222 Office: Shaw Pittman Potts & Trowbridge 2300 N St NW Fl 5 Washington DC 20037-1172

BEATTY, ROBERT ALFRED (R. ALFRED), surgeon; b. Colchester, Vt., May 7, 1936; s. George Lewis and Leila Margaret (Ebright) B.; m. Frances Calomeni, Aug. 24, 1963; children: Bradford, Roxanna. BA, U. Oreg., 1959, BS, 1960, MD, 1961. Diplomate Am. Bd. Neurol. Surgery. Intern U. Ill. Rsch. and Edn. Hosp., Chgo., 1961-62; resident neurosurgery U. Ill., Chgo., 1962-66; practice neurosurgery Hinsdale, Ill., 1967—; mem. staff Hinsdale Hosp., 1967—, Cmty. Meml. Hosp., LaGrange, Ill., 1967—, U. Ill. Hosp., Chgo., 1967—, Good Samaritan Hosp., Downers Grove, Ill., Elmhurst (Ill.) Hosp.; clin. assoc. prof. neurosurgery U. Ill., 1967—; adviser Marion Joy Rehab. Center, Wheaton, Ill., 1969-7; mem. State Ill. Spinal Cord Injury Adv. Coun., 1995, vice-chmn. 1997. Contbr. articles to profl. jours. Mem. founder's coun. Field Mus. Capt. USMC, AUS, 1968. Rsch. fellow St. George's Med. Sch., London, 1966-67. Mem. AMA, A.C.S., SAR, Ill. Med. Soc., Dupage County Med. Soc., Am. Assn. Neurol. Surgeons, N.Am. Spine Soc., Congress Neurol. Surgeons, Soc. Brit. Neurol. Surgeons, Internat. Microsurg. Soc., English Speaking Union, John Evans Club (N.W. U.), Theodore Thomas Soc., Chgo. Symphony Orch. (governing mem.), Hinsdale Golf Club, Phi Beta Kappa, Phi Beta Pi, Phi Kappa Psi. Republican. Achievements include research on intracranial aneurysms, lumbar discs; inventor medical instruments; profl. sculptor (under name R. Alfred). Office: 333 Chestnut St Hinsdale IL 60521-3247

BEATTY, TINA MARIE, legal assistant; b. Charlotte, N.C., Dec. 21, 1955. BA, Winthrop Coll., 1976; MBA, U. N.C., Charlotte, 1984; cert., The Nat. Ctr. for Paralegal Tng., 1976; MLiberal Arts, Winthrop Coll., 1992. Legal asst. Whitesides and Robinson, Gastonia, N.C., 1979-80, Garland and Alala, P.A., Gastonia, 1980-81, Kennedy Covington Lobdell & Hickman, Charlotte, 1981-88; documentation policy supr. Corp. Banking Group, First Union Nat. Bank N.C., Charlotte, 1988-93; legal asst. Moore & Van Allen, PLLC, Charlotte, 1993—; asst. state dir. Am. Inst. for Paralegal Studies, Inc., Charlotte, 1990-91. Charlotte area alumni steering com. Winthrop Coll., 1984, alumni ann. fund class agt., 1991-92, 92-93. Alumni Grad. scholar Winthrop Coll., 1991-92. Avocations: travel, photography, pottery. Office: Moore & Van Allen PLLC NationsBank Corp Ctr 100 N Tryon St Fl 47 Charlotte NC 28202-4000

BEATTY, (HENRY) WARREN, actor, producer, director; b. Richmond, Va., Mar. 30, 1937; s. Ira O. and Kathlyn (MacLean) Beaty; m. Annette Bening; 1 child, Kathlyn. Student, Northwestern U., 1956, Stella Adler Theatre Sch., N.Y.C., 1957. Actor films Splendor in the Grass, 1961, The Roman Spring of Mrs. Stone, 1962, All Fall Down, 1962, Lilith, 1963, Mickey One, 1965, Promise Her Anything, 1965, Kaleidoscope, 1966, The Only Game in Town, 1969, McCabe and Mrs. Miller, 1971, Dollars, 1971, The Parallax View, 1974, The Fortune, 1975, Town and Country, 1999; appeared in Broadway play A Loss of Roses, 1960; actor, producer films include Bonnie and Clyde, 1967 (Acad. award nomination for best actor), Ishtar, 1987; producer, co-screenwriter, actor Shampoo, 1975 (Acad. award nomination for best screenplay), Love Affair, 1994; producer, co-dir., co-screenwriter, actor Heaven Can Wait, 1978 (Acad. award nominations for best actor, best dir. and best screenplay); producer, dir., co-screenwriter, actor Reds, 1981 (Acad. award for best dir.), Bulworth, 1998; producer, dir., actor Dick Tracy, 1990; co-producer, actor: Bugsy, 1991; Love Affair (also producer and writer), 1996; Town and Country, 1998; Bulworth (also producer and writer); 1998; actor (TV) A Salute to Dustin Hoffman, 1999; TB guest appearances include Studio One, 1948, What's My Line, 1950, Vibe, 1997. Mem. Dirs. Guild Am. Democrat. Office: CAA care Risa Gertner 9830 Wilshire Blvd Beverly Hills CA 90212-1804*

BEATTY, WILLIAM KAYE, medical bibliography educator; b. Toronto, Feb. 5, 1926; s. E.W. and Muriel (Swan) B.; m. Virginia L. Lewis, June 14, 1952; children: Margaret M., William B.K., Carol E. Student, Harvard Coll., 1946-49; BA, Columbia Coll., 1951; MS, Columbia U., 1952. Libr. intern Harvard U. Librs., Cambridge, Mass., 1949; circulation asst. Coll. Physicians of Phila., 1952-53, asst. libr., 1954-56; asst. prof. med. bibliography U. Mo., Columbia, 1956-57, assoc. prof., 1957-62; prof. Northwestern U., Chgo., 1962-94, prof. emeritus; mem. faculty Rockefeller Found. and China Med. Bd., Selective Info. System, Beijing, 1982; cons. in field. Co-author: The Medical Garden, 1971, paperback edit., 1973, Women in White: Their Role as Doctors through the Ages, 1972, Arabic transl., 1976, The Story of Medicine in America, 1973 (selected as one of outstanding sci.-tech. books Libr. Jour. 1974), The Precious Metals of Medicine, 1975, Epidemics, 1976, paperback edit., 1978 (selected as one of outstanding sci.-tech. books Libr. Jour. 1976); editor: Vital Notes on Medical Periodicals, 1955-76; contbr. articles, book revs. to profl. jours.; contbg. author numerous books; cons. Index Medicus, 1965-87; editorial cons. Stedman's Medical Dictionary, 25th, 26th edits., 1982-97. Mem. Human Rels. Commn. Evanston, Ill., 1972-79, Friends of the Parks, Evanston, 1965-70. With AUS, 1944-46, ETO. Fellow Med. Libr. Assn. (editor Jour. Notes 1959-90, chmn. med. schs. group 1960, bd. dirs. 1966-69, archivist 1979-86, Ida and George Eliot prize 1973, spl. award 1990); mem. AAUP, ALA (life), Am. Assn. for the History of Medicine (coun. 1965-68), Am. Osler Soc. (charter, bd. govs. 1976-79), Assn. Hosp. and Instl. Librs. (pres. 1965-66), Inst. Medicine Chgo. (bd. govs. 1986-91), Soc. Med. History of Chgo. (pres. 1982-84), Spl. Librs. Assn. (pres. Ill. chpt. 1969-70, chmn. biol. scis. div. 1963-64, chmn. hosp. div. 1960-61, bd. dirs. 1964-67, John Cotton Dana lectr. award 1968), Chgo. Literary Club (pres. 1979-80). Home: 1509 Forest Ave Evanston IL 60201-4611

BEATTY, WILLIAM LOUIS, federal judge; b. Mendota, Ill., Sept. 4, 1925; s. Raphael H. and Teresa A. (Collins) B.; m. Dorothy Jeanne Starnes, June 12, 1948; children: William S., Steven M., Thomas D., Mary C. Student, Washington U., St. Louis, 1945-47; LL.B., St. Louis U., 1950. Bar: Ill. 1950. Gen. practice law Granite City, 1950-68; circuit judge 3d Jud. Circuit Ill., 1968-79; U.S. dist. judge So. Dist. Ill., 1979—. Served with AUS, 1943-45. Mem. Madison County Bar Assn., Tri-City Bar Assn. Roman Catholic. Office: So Dist Ct 750 Missouri Ave Rm 377 East Saint Louis IL 62201-2954

BEATY, JAMES ARTHUR, JR., judge; b. 1949. BA cum laude, Western Carolina U., 1971; JD, UNC, 1974; postgrad., U. Nev., 1985-91. With Richard C. Erwin, Winston-Salem, N.C., 1974-77; atty. at law Erwin and Beaty, Winston-Salem, 1977-78, Beaty and Friende, Winston-Salem, 1980-81; pvt. practice Winston-Salem, 1978-79; judge N.C. Superior Ct., 1981-94; dist. judge U.S. Dist. Ct. (mid. dist.) N.C., 1994—. Mem. ABA, N.C. State Bar, N.C. Bar Assn., Forsyth County and 21st Judicial Dist. Bar, Winston-Salem Bar Assn., N.C. Acad. Trial Lawyers (outstanding trial ct. judge of the yr., 1990), N.C. Assn. Black Lawyers (sec. 1976, v.p. 1978), NAACP (life), Alpha Phi Alpha, Sigma Pi Phi, Rotary Club. Office: 251 N Main St Rm 248 Winston Salem NC 27101-3914

BEATY, SHANNON MICHELLE, financial consultant; b. Dotham, Ala., Feb. 8, 1968; d. Samuel Franklin Jr. and Sharon Elizabeth (Callahan) B. BS, Auburn U., 1992. Asst. client rel. mgr. Bank South, Atlanta, 1993-95; sr. retired svcs. rep. Northern Trust, Atlanta, 1995-96; various positions numerous cons. agys., 1996-98; office mgr. Stanford (Calif.) U. Med. Ctr., 1998—. Vol. Habitat for Humanity, Atlanta, 1994, Smithsonian Inst., Washington, 1996. Mem. NAFE, Fin. Mgmt. Assn., Auburn Alumni Assn. Home: 502 Lea Ave Daphne AL 26526 Office: Stanford U Med Ctr 300 Pasteur Dr MC 53 Stanford CA

BEAUBIEN, ANNE KATHLEEN, librarian; b. Detroit, Sept. 15, 1947; d. Richard Parker and Edith Mildred Beaubien. Student, Western Mich. U., 1965-67; BA, Mich. State U., 1969; AM in Libr. Sci., U. Mich., 1970. Reference libr., bibliographic instr. U. Mich. Libr., Ann Arbor, 1971-80, dir. MITS, 1980-85, head coop. access svcs., 1985—; head Business & Cooperative Access Svcs., 1995—. Author: (booklet) Psychology Bibliography, 1980; co-author: Learning the Library, 1982; contbr. articles to profl. jours., editor, conf. proc., 1987. Pres. Ann Arbor Ski Club, 1978-79; mem. vestry St. Clare's Episcopal Ch., Ann Arbor, 1986-89. Recipient Woman of Yr. award Ann Arbor Bus. and Profl. Women's Club, 1982, Disting. Alumnus award Sch. Info. and Libr. Studies, U. Mich., 1987. Mem. ALA, Assn. Coll. and Rsch. Librs. (pres. 1991-92). Avocations: skiing, bicycling, ballroom dancing. Office: U Mich Libr 106 Hatcher Grad Libr Ann Arbor MI 48109

BEAUBIEN, PHILIPPE DE GASPE, II, communications executive; b. Montreal, Que., Can., Jan. 12, 1928; m. Nan Bowles O'Connell, Jan. 29, 1956; children: Philippe III, Nanon, Francois. B.A., Montreal U., 1952; M.B.A., Harvard U., 1954; hon. degree in law, York U., 1979. Founding pres. Beaubien Distbrn., Montreal, 1960-63; mayor Expo '67, Montreal, 1963-67; pres. Telemedia Que. Ltd., Montreal, 1968-71; chmn., chief exec. officer Telemedia Inc., Montreal, 1971-97; chmn. Bus. Families Found., Montreal, 1994—; bd. dirs. Bombardier Inc., McDonald's Restaurants Can. Ltd. Bd. dirs. Harvard Bus. Sch. Vis. Com.; mem. York U. adv. bd.; hon. chmn. Participation. Decorated Order Of Can.; dir. Can. Centennial medal; decorated Govt. Czechoslovakia Gold medal; recipient B'nai Brith Award of Merit, CAB Gold Ribbon Award. Mem. Chief Exec. Orgn. (dir.). Clubs:

Mount Royal (Montreal); York (Toronto). Office: Telemedia Corp, Telemedia Comm Inc, 1 Place Ville-Marie Ste 3333, Montreal, PQ Canada H3B 3M2

BEAUCHAMP, JESSE LEE (JACK BEAUCHAMP), chemistry educator; b. Glendale, Calif., Nov. 1, 1942; m. Patricia Margaret Beauchamp; children: Melissa Ann, Thomas Alton, Amanda Jane, Ryan Howell. BS with honors in Chemistry, Calif. Inst. Tech., 1964; PhD in Chemistry, Harvard U., 1967. Arthur Amos Noyes instr. in Chemistry Calif. Inst Tech., Pasadena, 1967-69, asst. prof. chemistry, 1969-71, assoc. prof. chemistry, 1971-74, prof. chemistry, 1974—; panelist chem. rsch. evaluation Directorate of Chem. Scis. Air Force Office of Sci. Rsch., 1978-81, adv. panelist high energy density materials, 1988-92; exec. com. advanced light source users, LBL, 1984-87; exptl. evaluation com. TRIUMPH, U. B.C., 1985-88; grad. fellow selection panel, NSF, 1986-89; postdoctoral selection panel NATO, 1987-89; mem. com. critical techs.: role of Chemistry and Chem. Engring. Nat. Rsch. Coun., 1991-92; chmn. com. on comml. aviation security Nat. Materials Adv. Bd., Nat. Rsch. Coun., 1994-97; commr. White House commn. on aviation safety and security, 1996-97. Mem. editorial adv. bd. Chemical Physics Letters, 1981-87, Jour. Am. Chem. Soc., 1984-87, Jour Physical Chemistry, 1984-87, Organometallics, 1989-92, Interat. Jour. Chemical Kinetics, 1990—. Woodrow Wilson fellow Harvard U., 1964-65, NAS grad. fellow, 1965-67; fellow Alfred P. Sloan Found., 1967-70; tchr.-scholar Camille and Henry Dreyfus, 1971-76; meml. fellow John Simon Guggenheim, 1976-77. Fellow AAAS; mem. NAS (com. chem. scis., chem. kinetics subgroup 1980-83), Am. Chem. Soc. (award in pure chemistry 1978, exec. com. divsn. physical chem., 1980-82, Peter Debye award in phys. chemistry 1999), Am. Assn. Mas. Spectometry, Aircraft Owners and Pilots Assn., Soc. Fellows Harvard U. Office: Calif Inst Tech Dept of Chemistry Noyes Lab 127 # 72 Pasadena CA 91125

BEAUCHAMP, MILES PHILIP, newspaper editor-columnist, education consultant; b. L.A., Apr. 17, 1953; s. Henry and Kathrinjo (Shelton) B.; m. Michelle Colleen Ryan, July 1, 1989. BA, San Diego State U., 1993, MA, 1994. V.p. Beauchamp Co. Hotels, San Diego, 1972-84; editor, columnist Asian Jour. newspaper, San Diego, 1985—; educator Futures in Edn., San Diego, 1995—; instr. Nat. Univ., 1996—; cons. The Writing Ctr., San Diego, 1992-96, Main Street mag., San Diego, 1994-95. Co-author: The Exquisite Cadaver, 1993; author: A New Way of Looking, 1996; editor: Filipinos in America, 1992; columnist Still Amazed, 1985-96. Profl. devel. facilitator Grossmont Coll., San Diego, 1990—; tchr. writing St. Vincent De Paul Shelter, San Diego, 1992; tchr., facilitator Profls. in Schs., San Diego, 1990—. Recipient award of appreciation San Diego Journalism Edn. Assn., 1992, San Diego Pub. Libr., 1994, Georgi awards Writers Fedn. Am., 1993. Mem. Film and Video Artists Assn., Writers Haven, San Diego Press Club. Avocations: travel, boating, photography. Office: Futures in Edn 1450 Frazee Rd Ste 306 San Diego CA 92108-4340

BEAUCHAMP, ROY E., career officer; b. July 1, 1945. Commd. U.S. Army, advanced through grades to maj. gen., 1997; with U.S. Army Tank-Automotive and Armaments Command, Warren, Mich. Office: US Army Tank Automotive and Armaments Command Warren MI 48397-5000

BEAUDET, ROBERT ARTHUR, chemistry educator; b. Woonsocket, R.I., Aug. 18, 1935; s. Ralph Edgar and Blanche L. (Pelchat) B.; m. Julia Marie Hughes, Sept. 14, 1957; children: Susan, Donna, Debra, Stephanie, Michelle, David, Nicole. BS, Worchester Poly. Inst., 1957; MA, Harvard U., 1960, PhD, 1962. Asst. prof. chemistry U. So. Calif., Los Angeles, 1963-66, assoc. prof., 1966-72, prof., 1972—. Served to lt. U.S. Army, 1961-63. Fellow NSF, 1957-61, A.P. Sloan Found., 1966-67, Humboldt, Cologne, Germany, 1974-75. Mem. Am. Chem. Soc., Am. Phys. Soc. Roman Catholic. Home: 887 Vallombrosa Dr Pasadena CA 91107-5642

BEAUDETTE, MICHELE J., language educator; b. Oct. 19, 1969. BA, U. Memphis, 1991, MA, 1993. Lectr. Zapadoceska U., Plzen, Czech Republic, 1992, U. Sibiu, Romania, 1994-97; instr. U. Memphis, Tenn., 1997-98; pedagogical dir. Berlitz Lang. Ctr., Memphis, 1997—; adv. ARAPAMESU, Sibiu, Romania, 1996-97. E-mail: beaudette@juno.com. Home: 2121 Poplar 71 Memphis TN 38104 Office: 632 Lancelot Ln Collierville TN 38017-1618

BEAUDETTE, ROBERT LEE, transportation and logistics consultant; b. White City, Kans., May 28, 1943; s. Axle John and Beatrice A. (Beaudette) Olson; m. Beverly Ann Robell, May 14, 1971; children: Jason M., Sara Ann. A in Commerce, Henry Ford U., 1975; postgrad., U. Mich., 1986. Traffic mgr. Detroit Stoker Co., Monroe, Mich., 1981-83; chief exec. officer Timely Air Freight, Romulus, Mich., 1985, v.p. spl. projects, 1986-88; dir. logistics Wolverine Transp. Group, Wayne, Mich., 1988-89; ptnr. IBM bus. Chuck Schubert & Assocs. Inc., 1989; transp. agt., logistics cons. IBM, 1989—, mktg. dir., 1992-95; cons. Multiplex Systems, Wyandotte, Mich., 1985—. Served to sgt. U.S. Army, 1960-66. Mem. The Packaging Inst. (prof.), Am. Legion, FOP (sec.), Vietnam Vets. Am., Delta Nu Alpha (pres. chpt. 92 1991—). Republican. Roman Catholic. Lodges: Fraternal Order Police (pres. 1988), KC. Avocations: woodworking, golf, coaching soccer. E-mail: bbeaudette@provide.net. Home: 2050 22nd St Wyandotte MI 48192-3838 Office: RB Multiplex Svcs Inc 2050 22nd St #A Wyandotte MI 48192-3838

BEAUDIN, CHRISTY LOUISE, health care administrator, consultant; b. Riverside, Calif., Feb. 8, 1957; d. Cletus Robert Beaudin and Frieda Kuiper. BA, Calif. State U., San Bernardino, 1978; MSW, San Diego State U., 1981; PhD, UCLA, 1997. Lic. clin. social worker. Clin. social worker Mercy Hosp. and Med. Ctr., San Diego; dir. human svcs. Brotman Med. Ctr., Culver City, Calif., 1986-88; sr. program adminstr. Nat. Med. Mgmt. Svcs., Washington, 1988-90; cons. CL Beaudin & Assocs., Santa Monica, Calif., 1990-96; v.p. quality mgmt. Value Behavioral Health, Falls Church, Va., 1996-98; v.p. R&D Magellan Health Svcs., Columbia, Md., 1999—; com. chair Am. Managed Behavioral Healthcare Assn., Washington; mem. adv. com. George Washington U., Washington. Author: (book chpts.) Nonprofit Boards and Leadership, 1995, Research in Social Policy, 1996; contbr. articles to sci. jours. Recipient Innovation award Partnership for Behavioral Healthcare, Washington, 1997. Mem. APHA (Beverlee A. Meyers Meml. scholar 1995), Am. Coll. Healthcare Execs., Assn. for Health Svcs. Rsch., Assn. for Rsch. on Nonprofit Orgns. and Vol. Assns., Nat. Assn. for Healthcare Quality, Delta Omega. Avocations: music, sports, people. Fax: (703) 208-8560. Office: Magellan Health Svcs 6950 Columbia Gateway Dr Columbia MD 21046

BEAUDOIN, CAROL ANN, psychologist; b. Lowell, Mass., Mar. 30, 1949; d. Adrien P. and Rita J. (LeBlanc) B.; B.A. with honors, U. Fla., 1971; M.Ed. in Counseling, Boston U., 1973, Ed.D. in Counseling Psychology, 1979. Psychiat. aide U. Fla.-Shands Teaching Hosp., Gainesville, 1970-71; trainee VA Hosp., Gainesville, 1971-72; attendant Boston State Hosp., 1972, intern, 1973; intern Univ. Hosp., also Counseling Center, Northeastern U., Boston, 1973-74, Dorchester Mental Health Center, also Carney Hosp., 1974-75; staff psychologist Human Resource Inst., Boston, 1974-80, treatment team leader, 1975-80; pvt. practice psychology, Brookline, Mass., 1980—. Mem. Am. Psychol. Assn. Office: 1101 Beacon St Brookline MA 02446-5502

BEAUDOIN, FRANÇOIS, financial institution president, chief executive officer; b. Montreal, Jan. 12, 1951; s. Léon and Madeleine Beaudoin; m. Manon Laverdure, Aug. 1972; children: Marie-Caroline, Chantal. BBA, École des Hautes Études, 1972; MBA, Columbia U., 1973. Economist fin. planning sect. Hydro-Quebec, 1974; sr. analyst fin. planning Bank of Montreal, 1974-76, mem. pres. task force, 1976, mgr. planning and budgeting, 1976-78, comptroller Quebec divsn., 1978-80, dist. mgr. Montreal West Island, 1980-83, v.p. Ottawa dist., 1983-85, v.p. Western Quebec dist., 1985-90; exec. v.p., COO Bus. Devel. Bank of Can., Montreal, 1990-93, pres., CEO, 1993—. Former v.p. bd. dirs. St. Mary's Hosp. Ctr.; former bd. mem. St. Mary's Hosp. Found. Mem. Bd. Trade Met. Montreal, Young Pres.'s Orgn. (Quebec chpt.), Assn. des MBA du Québec, Club Saint-Denis, Royal Montreal Golf Club, Beta Gamma Sigma (mem. Alpha chpt. N.Y.). E-mail: info-bdc@x400.gc.ca. Office: Bus Devel Bank of Can, 400 5 Place Ville Marie, Montreal, PQ Canada H3B 5E7

BEAUDOIN, GÉRALD-A(RMAND), lawyer, educator, senator; b. Montreal, Que., Can., Apr. 15, 1929; s. Armand and Aldéa (St.-Arnaud) B.; m. Renée Desmarais, Sept. 11, 1954; children: Viviane, Louise, Denise, Françoise. BA summa cum laude, U. Montreal, 1950, LLL magna cum laude, 1953, MA in Law, 1954; postgrad. in comparative law (Carnegie scholar), U. Toronto, 1954-55; DESD cum laude, U. Ottawa, Ont., 1958; LLD, U. Louvain-la-Neuve, Belgium, 1989. Bar: Called to Que. bar 1954, created queen's counsel 1969. Practiced law with Paul Gérin-Lajoie, Montreal, 1955-56; adv. counsel Dept. Justice, Ottawa, 1956-65; sr. adv. counsel Dept. Justice, 1960-65; asst. parliamentary counsel Ho. of Commons of Can., Ottawa, 1965-69; civil law dean Faculty of Law, U. Ottawa, 1969-79, prof. constl. law, 1969-89, dir. Human Rights Ctr., 1986-88; mem. Senate of Can., 1988; mem. Goldenberg Com. on Constn., 1967, La Commn des Svcs. Juridiques du Quebec, 1972-73, Task Force on Can. Unity, 1977-79; vis. prof. U. Sorbonne, 1985; vis. prof. faculty of law U. Ottawa, 1989-94, prof. emeritus, 1994—; co-chmn. spl. joint com. of Senate and Ho. of Commons on process for amending Constn. of Can., 1991, on a renewed Can., 1991-92; mem. Senate Spl. Com. on Euthanasia and Assisted Suicide, 1994-95. Author: Essais sur la Constitution, 1979, Le Partage des Pouvoirs, 1980, 3d edit., 1983, La Constitution du Canada, 1990; (with others) Mecanismes pour une Nouvelle Constitution, 1981; co-editor: La Charte Canadienne des Droits et Libertés, 3d edit., 1996, Perspectives Canadiennes et Européennes des Droits de la Personne, 1986; editor: The Supreme Court of Can.-La Cour Suprême du Can., 1986, Charter Cases, 1986-87, Your Clients and the Charter, 1988, Vues Canadiennes et Européennes des Droits et Libertés, 1989, As the Charter Evolves, 1990, The Charter: Ten Years Later, 1992, Federalism for Tomorrow: Essential Reforms (with G. Robertson), 1998; contbr. numerous articles to Can. and fgn. law revs.; mem. Themis Law Rev., 1951-52. Mem. spl. com. to draft Can. Constn. in French, 1985-90. Recipient The Ramon John Hnatyshyn award, 1997. Mem. Royal Soc. Can., Acad. des Lettres du Quebec, Can. Bar Assn. (nat. chmn. sect. constl. and internat. law 1971-73, 86-87), Can. Inst. Pub. Affairs, Inst. Pub. Adminstrn. (Can.), Can. Law Deans (chmn. 1972-73), Can. Inst. Inter de Droit d'Expression Française (v.p. 1973—), Que. Law Deans (chmn. 1975-76), Internat. Assn. Comparative Law, Internat. Commn. Jurists (v.p. for Can. 1987-90, pres. for Can. 1990-92), Standing Senate Com. on Legal and Constl. Affairs (chmn. 1993-96), Order of Can. Roman Catholic. Club: Cercle Universitaire d'Ottawa. Home: 4 St-Thomas, Hull, PQ Canada J8Y 1L4 Office: Senate of Can Parliament Bldgs, Ctr Block Rm 474-F, Ottawa, ON Canada K1A 0A4

BEAUDOIN, LAURENT, industrial, recreational and transportation company executive; b. Laurier Station, Que., Can., May 13, 1938; s. P.A. and Yvonne (Rodrigue) B.; m. Claire Bombardier, Aug. 29, 1959; children—Nicole, Pierre, Elaine, Denise. B.A., Ste. Anne U., N.S., Can., 1957; M. Commerce, Sherbrooke U., 1960, D. Bus. Adminstrn. (hon.), 1971. Partner firm Beaudoin, Morin, Dufresne & Assos., Quebec, Que., 1961-63; comptroller Bombardier Ltd., Valcourt, Que., 1963-64; gen. mgr. Bombardier Ltd., Montreal, Que., 1964-66; pres. Bombardier, Inc., Montreal, Que., 1966-86, chmn., CEO, 1979—. Bd. govs. Faculté d'Adminstrn., U. Sherbrooke, Que. Decorated companion Order Can., Ordre National du Québec; comdr. de l'Ordre de Léopold II. Fellow Inst. Chartered Accts.; mem. C. of C. Que. (gov.). Office: Bombardier Inc, 800 Rene-Levesque Blvd W, Montreal, PQ Canada H3B 1Y8

BEAUDOIN, ROBERT LAWRENCE, small business owner; b. Newberry, Mich., Nov. 22, 1933; s. Leo Joseph and Edith Wilhelmina (Graunstadt) B.; m. Margaret Cecelia Linck, June 20, 1953; children: Eugene Robert, Kathleen Therese, Annette Marie, Suzanne Margaret. Student, Marquette U., 1952-53. With Fisher plant GM, 1953; dock hand State of Mich., St. Ignace, 1953; sch. bus driver Engadine (Mich.) Consol. Schs., 1957-96; owner, operator Beaudoin's Texaco, Beaudoin's Cafe, Naubinway, Mich., 1956-82, Beaudoin's Cafe and Marathon, Naubinway, 1982-83, Beaudoin's Cafe, Naubinway, 1956—; bd. dirs. Naubinway Mchts. Inc., 1985—. Mem. Naubinway July 4th Com., 1954—; past mem. Naubinway Port commn., Garfield Twp. Planning and Zoning Commn.; vol. fireman Garfield Twp. Fire Dept., Naubinway, 1980-94; mem. recreation com. Garfield Twp. Bd., Engadine, 1983; support fellow N.G. and Res., support mem. U.S. Army Recruiting Main Sta., Detroit; mem. USAF Ground Observer Corp. Recipient Cert. of Appreciation, U.S. Army Recruiting Main Sta., Detroit, 1971, Statement of Support, N.G. and Res., 1976. Mem. NRA (life, mem. Golden Eagles), Internat. Platform Assn., West Mackinac C. of C., Nat. Fedn. Ind. Bus. (adv. bd. 1971—, 20 Yr. award 1985), Hiawatha Sportsmans Club (bd. govs. Engadine 1965-67, 89-95, apptd. security officer 1996-98, teas. coun. 7472 1998—), Curtis C. of C., N.Am. Hunting Club (life), Engadine Trap Shooting Club, KC (grand knight 1979-83, coun. 7472 Naubiway membership and program dir. East Marquette diocese 1984-88, 96-98, dist. dep. 1988-92, supreme coun. dist. dep. 1988-92, state dir. coun. activities 1992-94, dep. grand knight coun. 7472 1995-96), Lions (3d v.p. Engadine club 1970-71). Roman Catholic. Avocations: hunting, fishing. Home: PO Box 143 Naubinway MI 49762-0143 Office: Beaudoins Cafe PO Box 143 US Hwy 2 Naubinway MI 49762

BEAUDRY, DIANE FAY PUTA, quality management executive; b. Manitowoc, Wis., Mar. 6, 1947; d. Ruben William and Gertrude Katherine (Novak) Puta. BSN, Alverno Coll., 1971; MS in Ednl. Adminstrn., U. Wis., Milw., 1979, PhD in Urban Edn., 1991. Staff nurse St. Mary's Hosp., Milw., 1971-72, St. Anthony's Hosp., Milw., 1972-74; nurse coord. Pvt. Initiative in PSRO, Wis., 1974-75; insvc. instr. Deaconess Hosp., Milw., 1975-77, insvc. coord., 1977-81; dir. nursing staff devel./quality assurance Good Samaritan Med. Ctr., Milw., 1981-84, dir. quality assurance, 1984-85, dir. utilization mgmt., 1985-88; mgr. quality mgmt. Sinai Samaritan Med. Ctr., Milw., 1988-89, dir. med. staff svcs. and quality mgmt., 1989-97; dir. quality mgmt. Sinai Samaritan Med. Ctr., St. Luke's Med. Ctr., Milw., 1997—. Author: (with others) Interdisciplinary QA: Issues in Collaboration, 1991; author poem. mem. Nat. Assn. for Healthcare Quality, Alverno Coll. Alumnae Assn., U. Wis. Alumni Assn., Delta Epsilon Sigma, Kappa Gamma Pi. Avocation: ballroom dancing. Home: 11047 N Riverland Ct # 36W Mequon WI 53092-4900 Office: Sinai Samaritan Med Ctr PO Box 342 Milwaukee WI 53201-0342 also: St Luke's Med Ctr PO Box 2901 2900 W Oklahoma Ave Milwaukee WI 53201-2901

BEAUDRY, GUY G., company executive, lawyer; b. Montreal, Que., Can., 1960; s. Germain J. Beaudry and Micheline Michelin; m. Marie Desjardine, Aug. 5, 1995; 1 child, William. DES, Coll. Notre-Dame, 1979, Coll. de St. Césaire, 1979; DEC in Bus. Adminstrn, Coll. Marie-Victorin, 1982; LLB, U. Montreal, 1983. Bar: Que. 1983. Assoc. Maritineau Walker, 1983-86; gen. counsel, corp. sec. Comterm Inc., 1986-88; corp. counsel, asst. sec. Le Group Vidéotron Ltd., 1988-89, v.p. corp. affairs, 1986-96, sr. v.p. corp. affairs, 1996—; chmn., pres., CEO Wavepath, Mountain View, Calif., 1998—; bd. dirs. Wireless Holdings Inc., Videotron Bay Area Inc., Galea Network Security Inc. Mem. Can. Cable TV Assn. (chmn. ann. conv. 1996, pres. 1998, pres. polit. task force 1994, mem. telecomm. policies com.), Bar of Province of Que., Can. Bar Assn. (mem. comml. law sect.), Commanderie de Bordeaux (chancellor), Le Cercle Universitaire d'Ottawa, Montreal Badminton and Squash Club. Avocations: flying, squash, hiking, sailing, cross-country skiing. Fax: (650) 237-9755. E-mail: gbeaudry@videotron.com. Office: Wavepath 500 Clyde Ave Mountain View CA 94043

BEAUFAIT, FREDERICK W(ILLIAM), civil engineering educator; b. Vicksburg, Miss., Nov. 28, 1936; s. Frank W. and Eleanor Chambliss (Haynes) B.; m. Lois Mary Erdman, Nov. 27, 1964; children: Paul Frederick, Nicole. BSc, Miss. State U., 1958; MSc, U. Ky., 1961; PhD, Va. Poly. Inst., 1965. Structural engr. U.S. Army C.E., Vicksburg, 1958-59; engr. L. E. Gregg & Assocs., Lexington, Ky., 1959-60; vis. lectr. civil engring. U. Liverpool, Eng., 1960-61; prof. civil engring. Vanderbilt U., Nashville, 1965-79; prof., chmn. dept. civil engring. W.Va. U., Morgantown, 1979-83, assoc. dean Coll. Engring., 1983-86; dean Coll. Engring. Wayne State U., Detroit, 1986-95; dir. NSF Greenfield Engring. Edn. Coalition, 1996-98; pres. N.Y.C. Tech. Coll. of the CUNY, 1999—; vis. prof. civil and structural engring. U. Wales, Cardiff, 1975-76; cons. in field; mem. Engring. Accreditation Commn. Accreditation Bd. for Engring. and Tech., 1988-93, Engring. Manpower Commn., 1988-92; bd. dirs. Ford (Motor) Design Inst., 1991-96. Co-author: Computer Methods of Structural Analysis, 1970; author: Basic Concepts in Structural Analysis, 1977; also over 40 articles to profl. jours. Vice chmn. stewardship com. 1st Presbyn. Ch., Morgantown, 1982, elder, 1983-85, mem. long-range planning com., 1985-86; deacon Southminster Presbyn. Ch., Nashville, 1968-69, elder, 1971-73, 78-79, clk. of session, 1971-73; bd. dirs. Presbyn. Campus Ministry, Nashville, 1972-78, treas., 1972-75, pres., 1976-78; mem. citizens adv. com. Met. Sch. System, Nashville, 1978-79. Named Outstanding Vol. of Yr. Mich. Ctr. for High Tech., 1991. Mem. ASCE, NSPE, Mich. Soc. Profl. Engrs. (bd. dirs. Detroit metro chpt. 1987-90, vice chmn. 1991, chmn.-elect 1992, chmn. 1993, pres. profls. in engring. edn. divsn. 1990-93, state bd. dirs., treas. 1995-97, v.p. 1997-98, Outstanding Engr. in Edn. 1994), Am. Soc. Engring. Edn. (chmn. civil engring. divsn. 1992-93, Centennial medallion 1993, George K. Wadlin award of Civil Engring. Divsn. 1994), Engring. Soc. Detroit (Coll. of Fellows 1994, gold award 1997), Order of Engrs. (bd. governance 1989-97), Chi Epsilon, Tau Alpha Pi, Tau Beta Pi. Home: 54 Pierrepont St Apt 3 Brooklyn NY 11201-2256 Office: NYC TEch Coll CUNY 300 Jay St Brooklyn NY 11201-2983

BEAUFORD, JUDITH ELAINE, mathematics educator; b. Sept. 3, 1945. MS, U. Tex., San Antonio, 1990; PhD, U. Tex., Austin, 1996. Faculty math. Schreiner Coll., Kerrville, Tex., 1990-96; asst. prof. math. U. Incarnate Word, San Antonio, Tex., 1996—. Office: 4301 Broadway San Antonio TX 78209

BEAULIEU, DENNIS E., videographer. Student, Middlesex Cmty. Tech. Coll., 1993—. Photographer dept. police City of E. Hampton, Conn., 1971-82; comm. facility tech. So. New England Tel., Middletown, Conn., 1984-98; owner, prodr., videographer Beaulieu Prodns., Middle Haddam, Conn., 1992—; editor, engr., videographer, photographer 1995 Spl. Olympic World Summer Games, New Haven, 1995; videographer Internat. Festival Arts and Ideas, 1996, Steven Spielberg's Survivors of the Shoah Visual History Found., L.A., 1996—; judge UNESCO award in Broadcast Humanities, 1996, 97, 98, Global Awards, 1998; cons., instr. in field. Cinematographer, editor Air War: Vietnam, 1968. Flightdeck Fire Fighting: USS Enterprise & USS Forestal Fires, 1968, Flightdeck Fire Fighting, 1968; studio design engr. Satellite TV Marketing Show, 1993-94; lighting dir., camera operator (TV show) Friday Night Folk, 1996; instr., prodr., editor (video) Fun Fantasy Footlights, 1996; dir., editor (video) Error Correction 2, 1996; prodr., dir., editor (video) A Day in the Life of a Middle School Student, 1997; videographer, assoc. prodr., supr. spl. effects (film) Blue Light, 1998; prodr., dir.: (video) A Tribute to Gretchen Ulion 1998 (Olympic Gold medal 1998). Mem. Internat. TV Assn. (life), Internat. Film and TV Festival (judge 1993-98). Office: Beaulieu Prodns PO Box 88 Middle Haddam CT 06456-0088

BEAUMIER, COLLEEN, member Canadian Parliament; b. Chatham, Ont., Nov. 8, 1946; m. Pierre Beaumier; children: Stephanie, Michael, John. BA in Psychology, U. Windsor, Ont. Mem. Can. Parliament for Brampton-West Mississauga, Ont., 1993—; mem. standing com. on fgn. affairs and internat. trade Can. Parliament, 1994—, vice chair, 1997—, chair human rights sub-com. of standing com. on fgn. affairs and internat. trade, mem. standing com. on procedure and ho. affairs, com. on citizenship and immigration, com. on govt. ops. Pas chair Greater Toronto (Ont.) Area Liberal Caucus sub-com. on limousine industry at Lester B. Pearson Airport; head Can. del. monitoring elections for Palestinian Nat. Authority, 1996; bd. dirs. Rapport Youth and Family Counseling, Gur AASRA Trust; coord. Operation Lifeline for Vietnamese Refugees, 1980. Office: Ho of Commons, Rm 223 W Block, Ottawa, ON Canada K1A 0A6*

BEAUMONT, MONA, artist; b. Paris; d. Jacques Hippolyte and Elsie M. (Didisheim) Marx. m. William G. Beaumont; children: Garrett, Kevin. Postgrad., Harvard U., Fogg Mus., Cambridge, Mass. One-woman shows include Galeria Proteo, Mexico City, Gumps Gallery, San Francisco, Palace of Legion of Honor, San Francisco, L'Armitiere Gallery, Rouen, France, Hoover Gallery, San Francisco, San Francisco Mus. Modern Art, Galeria Van der Voort, San Francisco, William Sawyer Gallery, San Francisco, Palo Alto (Calif.) Cultural Ctr., Galerie Alexandre Monnet, Brussels, Honolulu Acad. Arts; group shows include San Francisco Mus. Modern Art, San Francisco Art Inst., DeYoung Meml. Mus., San Francisco, Grey Found. Tour of Asia, Bell Telephone Invitational, Chgo., Richmond Art Ctr., L.A. County Mus. Art, Galerie Zodiaque, Geneva, Galerie Le Manoir, La Chaux de Fonds, Switzerland, William Sawyer Meml. Exhibit, San Francisco, 1st Internat. Flash Art Mus. Exhbn., Trevi, Italy, 1999, others; represented in permanent collections Oakland (Calif.) Mus. Art, City and County of San Francisco, Hoover Found., San Francisco, Grey Found., Washington, Bulart Found., San Francisco; also numerous pvt. collections. Mem. Soc. for Encouragement of Contemporary Art, Bay Area Graphic Art Coun., San Francisco Art Inst., San Francisco Mus. Modern Art, Capp Street Project, San Diego Mus. Contemporary Art, L.A. Mus. Contemporary Art. Recipient ann. painting award Jack London Square, 2 ann. awards San Francisco Women Artists, One-man Show award San Francisco Art Festival; purchase award Grey Found., San Francisco Women Artists (2), San Francisco Art Festival; included in Printworld Internat., Internat. Art Diary, Am. Artists, N.Y. Art Rev., Calif. Art Rev., Art in San Francisco Bay Area. Address: 1087 Upper Happy Valley Rd Lafayette CA 94549-2805

BEAUMONT, PAMELA JO, marketing professional; b. Valentine, Nebr., July 30, 1944; d. William Henry and Phyllis Faye (Zersen) (Mott) Bostrom; m. Fred H. Beaumont, Apr. 17, 1971 (div. May 1981). BS in Bus., U. Colo., 1966, MBA, 1968. Asst. product mgr. Ore-Ida Foods, Boise, Idaho, 1969-71, product mgr., 1971-73, sr. product mgr., 1973-75, gen. mgr. sales and mktg. services, 1975; v.p. consumer affairs Albertson's Inc., Boise, 1975-76, v.p. mktg., 1976-87; ptnr. Forrest/Beaumont & Andrus, Boise, 1987—; chair Garden City Urban Renewal Agy., 1995—. Home: 9304 N Pebble Falls Ln Boise ID 83703-1759 Office: 4948 Kootenai St Ste 201 Boise ID 83705-2082

BEAUMONT, RICHARD AUSTIN, management consultant; b. N.Y.C., Dec. 21, 1925; s. Martin Anthony and Katherine Anne (Salcite) B. AB, UCLA, 1950; MA, U. Hawaii, 1956; postgrad., Columbia U., 1958. Asst. dir. rsch. Hawaii Employers Coun., Honolulu, 1952-56; dir. adminstv. svcs. Am. Mgmt. Assn., N.Y.C., 1956-58; pres. Orgn. Resources Counselors, Inc., N.Y.C., 1959-70, chmn., CEO, 1971—; sr. v.p. Am. Hess Corp., N.Y.C., 1970-71; also bd. dirs. Amerada Hess Corp., N.Y.C.; dep. undersec. navy Dept. Navy, Washington, 1966-67; bd. dirs. Yokogawa ORC, Tokyo. Co-author: Executive Retirement and Effective Management, 1961, Management Automation and People, 1964; editor: People Progress and Employee Relations, 1976. Trustee emeritus Darden Grad. Sch. Bus., U. Va., Charlottesville. With USAAF, 1944-46. Fellow Nat. Acad. Human Resources; mem. Inst. Mgmt. Cons. (founding), Indsl. Rels. Rsch. Assn., Nat. Acad. Human Resources, Univ. Club (N.Y.C.), Chgo. Club, St. Francis Yacht Club (San Francisco).

BEAUMONT, RODERICK FRASER, education consultant; b. Gourock, Scotland, Dec. 3, 1955; came to U.S., 1984; s. Robert Charles and Cathrine (Kendall) B.; m. Mary Elizabeth Beaumon; children: Timothy Michael, Allyn Joseph, Kathryn Nicol. BS in Edn., U. Ctrl. Eng., Birmingham, 1977; MA in Comm. Arts, U. Birmingham, 1979; AAS in Aerospace Sci., Emery Sch. Aviation, 1985. Tchr. various schs., Eng., 1977-82; photojournalist UPI, Europe and Am., 1982-90; instr. U. N.D., Grand Forks, 1990-92; program cons. Paradigm Group, Prescott, Ariz., 1990—; tech. prep coord. Amite County, Liberty, Miss., 1992-94; sch.-to-work dir. Yavapai Coll., Prescott, 1994-96; editor-in-chief Sch.-To-Work News, Prescott, 1995—; cons., Kans., Miss., N.D., Ariz., Colo., 1990—. Editor, author: Fergusons Guide to School to Work, 1998; contbr. articles to profl. jours. Fellow Royal Geog. Soc., London, 1978, Inst. of Journalists, London, 1980. Democrat. Avocations: photography, computers. Office: 303 E Gurley St # 506 Prescott AZ 86301-3804

BEAUMONTE, PHYLLIS ILENE, secondary school educator; b. Seattle, Dec. 15; d. Albert Hendrix and Bessie Dorothy (Buford) Ratcliff; m. Pierre Marshall Beaumonte, Mar. 12, 1962 (div. Aug. 1974). BA, U. Wash., 1973, MPA, 1975; postgrad., N.W. Theol. Union, Seattle, 1990-92, Seattle U., 1995—. Cert. tchr. K-12, Wash. Adminstrv. intern Office of the City Coun., Seattle, 1974; guest lectr. Pacific Luth. U., Tacoma, Wash., 1975; tchr. The Hebrew Acad., Seattle, 1979; instr./tchr. Seattle Ctrl. C.C., 1988; tchr. Seattle Pub. Schs., 1980—; coord. h.s. Bus. Ptnrs. in Pub. Edn., Seattle, 1989-92; social studies chairperson Rainier Beach H.S., Seattle, 1992—; cons. RA Beau Enterprises, Seattle, 1987—; participant Ctr. for Rsch. and Devel. in Law-Related Edn., Wake Forest U., Winston-Salem, N.C., 1994; adv. com. Wash. State Commn. on Student Learning, Social Studies Acad. Learning Requirements, 1994—; part-time faculty South C.C., Seattle, 1998-

99. Author: (poetry) Satyagraha, 1992; author/editor: Roses and Thorns, 1994. Mem. King County Women's Polit. Caucus, Seattle, 1993—; mem. candidate evaluation com. Seattle Mcpl. League, 1972-74; Seattle edn. sch. rep. Seattle Tchrs. Union, 1983-85; v.p. Ch. Women United, State of Wash. and N. Idaho, 1976-78; alumni advisor Grad. Sch. Pub. Affairs, U. Wash., 1994—; v.p. Black Heritage Assn. of Wash. State, Inc. Recipient Internat. Poet of Merit award Internat. Soc. Poets, 1993; U. Wash. minority journalism scholar, 1972. Mem. Mus. of History and Industry, Nat. Coun. for History Edn. (Cert. of Appreciation 1993), Internat. Soc. Poets (life), Nat. Coun. for the Social Studies, Sigma Gamma Rho. Baptist. Avocations: singing, writing, reading, teaching. Home: Apt 402 9030 Seward Pk Ave S Seattle WA 98118

BEAUPAIN, ELAINE SHAPIRO, psychiatric social worker; b. Boston, Nov. 1, 1949; d. Abraham and Anna Marilyn (Gass) S.; m. Dean A. Beaupain, Feb. 14, 1987; 1 child, Andrew. BA, McGill U., Montreal, Que., 1971, MSW, 1974. Ind. clin. social worker, Mass.; cert. social worker, Maine; cert. social worker with ind. practice lic., Maine; lic. ind. clin. social worker, Mass. Psychiat. social worker Bangor (Maine) Mental Health Inst., 1974-75; outpatient therapist The Counseling Ctr., Bangor, 1975-76, The Counseling Ctr., Millinocket, Maine, 1979-86; asst. core group leader adolescent unit Jackson Brook Inst., Portland, Maine, 1986-87; area dir. Community Health and Counseling Svcs., 1981-86; pvt. practice social work, 1987—, psychotherapy with individuals, couples and families Millinocket and Bangor, 1987—. Mem. AAUW, Nat. Assn. Social Workers, Acad. Cert. Social Workers (diplomate 1992). Republican. Office: 122 Pine St Bangor ME 04401-5216

BEAUREGARD, LESLIE MICHELLE, budget analyst, legislative liaison; b. Atlanta, Feb. 5, 1970; d. David Robert and Marjorie Katherine (Minnix) B. BA, Va. Tech., 1992, MPA, 1996. Mgmt. intern City of Williamsburg, Va., 1996; fin. analyst City of Poquoson, Va., 1997; budget analyst City of Hampton, Va., 1997-99, sr. budget analyst, 1999—; rsch. asst. Ctr. PUb. Adminstrn. Policy, Blacksburg, 1995-96; intern, grant writer Town of Blacksburg, 1996; grant writer Newtown Improvement Civic Club, Inc., Hampton, 1997—; adj. tchr. Christopher Newport U., fall 1999. Loaned exec. United Way, Hampton, 1997; vol. United Way, coord. United Way Hampton, 1998. Named Vol. of Yr. United Way, 1997; recipient achievement award City of Hampton, 1997, 98. Mem. Internat. City Mgmt. Assn. (scholar 1997), Am. Soc. Pub. Adminstrn., Soc. for Women in Pub. Adminstrn., Assn. for Budgeting and Fin. Mgmt. Avocations: running, weight lifting, horseback riding, flute music, traveling. Office: City of Hampton Budget Office 22 Lincoln St Hampton VA 23669-3522

BEAUREGARD, LUC, public relations executive; b. Montreal, Que., Can., Aug. 4, 1941; s. Francois and Gertrude (Lévesque) B.; m. Michelle Beauregard; children: Valérie, Stéphanie, Francois, Philippe. BA, Coll. Stanislas, Montreal. Reporter, parliamentary corr. in Ottawa, city editor Montreal (Que.) Daily La Presse, Can., 1961-68; press sec. Que. Minister Edn., Quebec City, Que., 1968-69; founding ptnr. Beauregard, Landry, Nantel & Assocs. Pub. Rels. Cons., Montreal; pres., pub. Montreal-Matin Daily Newspaper, 1973-76; chmn., CEO Nat. Pub. Rels., Inc., Montreal, 1976—; chmn. Amarc, City of Montreal Corp. managing Man and His World (formerly Expo '67), 1982-86. Sec. info. commn. Que. Liberal Party, 1978-79, 80; chmn. Montreal BBB, 1983-84; bd. dirs. Nouvelle Compagnie Theatrale, 1984-94, St. Hubert food group, 1982—, Que. Heart Found., 1983-85; mem. exec. com. Montreal Mus. Contemporary Art, 1986-97; Found. Montreal Mus. Contemporary Art, chmn., 1987-90; chmn. Found. Montreal Island Sch. Coun., 1991-97; gov. Conseil du Patronat du Que., 1992—. Recipient Philip A. Novikoff award Can. Pub. Rels. Soc. Mem. N.Am. Pub. Rels. Coun. (chmn. 1985-86), Can. Pub. Rels. soc. (pres. 1984-85, chmn. Cons. Inst. 1982-83), Order of Can., Club des Quinze, Mt. Royal Club, St. Denis Club, Knowlton Golf Club. Avocations: golfing, tennis. Office: Nat Pub Rels, 770 Sherbrooke West Ste 1600, Montreal, PQ Canada H3A 1G1

BEAUSOLEIL, DORIS MAE, federal agency administrator, housing specialist; b. Chelmsford, Mass., Jan. 9, 1932; d. Joseph Honorious and Beatrice Pearl (Smith) B.;. Student, State Tchrs. Coll., Lowell, Mass., 1949-51; BA in Sociology and Psychology, Goddard Coll., Plainfield, Vt., 1954; MA in Human Rels., NYU, 1957; postgrad., CUNY, N.Y.C., 1988-97. With div. human rights N.Y. State, N.Y.C., 1960-69, housing dir., 1966-68; housing cons. Nat. Com. Against Discrimination in Housing, N.Y.C., 1969-70; housing cons. Edwin Gould Found., N.Y.C., 1970-71; human resources cons. interfaith housing strategy com., housing cons. Fedn. Prot. Welfare Agencies, Inc., N.Y.C., 1971-72; self-employed housing cons., 1972-74; equal opportunity compliance specialist N.Y./N.J. HUD, N.Y.C., 1975—, Fed. women's program coordinator, 1975-79; br. chief Title VI Sect. 109 Compliance div. fair housing and equal opportunity Region II, HUD, N.Y.C., 1979-84; founding mem. N.Y. State HUD Com.; adv. panel Housing Mag., 1979; cons., examiner N.Y. State Civil Svc. Commn., 1970-93. Mem. Nat. Assn. Human Rights Workers (Outstanding Svc. award 1974), Citizens Housing and Planning Coun., Nat. Assn. Housing and Devel. Ofcls., Goddard Coll. Alumni Assn. (sec. 1988-90), Rep. Bus. Women's Club (pres. 1985-88, bd. dirs. 1989-91). Republican. Unitarian. Home: 392 Central Park W New York NY 10025-5860 Office: 26 Federal Plz Rm 3543 New York NY 10025-5868

BEAVER, BONNIE VERYLE, veterinarian, educator; b. Mpls., Oct. 26, 1944; d. Crawford F. and Gladys I. Gustafson; m. Larry J. Beaver, Nov. 25, 1972 (dec. Nov. 1995). B.S., U. Minn., 1966, D.V.M., 1968; M.S., Tex. A&M U., 1972. Instr. vet. surgery and radiology U. Minn., 1968-69; instr. vet. anatomy Tex. A&M U., College Station, 1969-72, asst. prof., 1972-76, assoc. prof., 1976-82; prof. Tex A&M U., College Station, 1982-86; prof. vet. small animal medicine and surgery Tex A&M U., 1986—, chief medicine, 1990-99; mem. vet. medicine adv. com. HEW, 1972-74, nat. adv. food and drug com., HEW, 1975, com. on animal models and genetic stocks NAS, 1984-86, 87-89, panel on microlivestock NRC, 1986-87, task force on animal use study Inst. Lab. Animal Resources, 1986, adv. com. for Pew Nat. Vet. Edn. Program, Pew Charitable Trusts, 1987-92, 10th symposium on Vet. Med. Edn. Com., 1988-89. Mem. editl. bd. Applied Animal Ethology, 1981-82, 83-84, VM/SAC, 1982-85, Applied Animal Behavior Sci., 1982-84, 84-86, 86-88, 88—, Bull. on Vet. Clin. Ethology, 1994—, Jour. Am. Animal Hosp. Assn., 1995—; contbr. articles to profl. jours. Vice pres. Brazos Valley Regional Sci. and Engring. Fair, 1974—83, dir., 1983-85; bd. dirs. Brazos Valley unit Am. Cancer Soc., 1976-83, v.p., 1976-83. Named Citizen of Week, The Press, 1981, Outstanding Woman Veterinarian of 1982, Disting. Practitioner, Nat. Acads. Practice. Mem. AAAS, AVMA (Animal Welfare award 1996, exec. bd. 1997—), Tex. Vet. Med. Assn. (3d v.p. 1990, 2d v.p. 1991, 1st v.p. 1992, pres.-elect 1993, pres. 1994), Brazos Valley Vet. Med. Assn., Am. Animal Hosp. Assn., Am. Vet. Soc. Animal Behavior (pres. 1975-80), Am. Assn. Vet. Clinicians, Am. Assn. Equine Practitioners, Am. Vet. Neurology Assn., Animal Behavior Soc., Am. Coll. Vet. Behaviorists (chair organizing com. 1976-91, pres. 1991-96, exec. dir. 1996—, charter diplomat 1993—), Nat. Acad. Practice, Palomino Horse Breeders Am. (v.p. 1983-88, treas. 1984-85, pres.-elect 1988-89, pres. 1989-90), Tex. Palomino Exhibitors Assn., Alamo Palomino Exhibitors Assn., Houston Area Palomino Exhibitors, Am. Quarter Horse Assn., Am. Horse Coun., Phi Sigma, Sigma Epsilon Sigma, Phi Zeta (nat. pres. 1979-81), Phi Delta Gamma (pres. 1974-75). Office: Tex A&M Univ Coll Vet Medicine Vet Small Animal Medicine & Surgery College Station TX 77843-4474

BEAVER, FRANK EUGENE, communication educator, film critic and historian; b. Cleve., N.C., July 26, 1938; s. John Whitfield and Mary Louise (Shell) B.; m. Gail Frances Place, June 30, 1962; children: Julia Clare, John Francis, Johanna Louise. BA, U. N.C., 1960, MA, 1966; PhD, U. Mich., 1970. Instr. speech Memphis State U., 1965-66; instr. radio-TV-motion pictures U. N.C., Chapel Hill, 1966-68; asst. prof. speech comm. U. Mich., Ann Arbor, 1969-74, assoc. prof., 1974-79, assoc. prof. comm., 1979-84, prof., chmn. dept. comm., 1987-91, Arthur F. Thurnau prof., 1989-92, dir. grad. program in telecom. arts and film, 1991-96; gen. editor Twayne Pubs., N.Y., 1987—. Film critic radio Stas. WUOM, WVGR, WFUM, Ann Arbor, Grand Rapids, Mich., 1975—; author: Bosley Crowther, 1974, On Film, 1983, Dictionary of Film Terms, 1983, 94 (Mandarin-Chinese translation 1993), Oliver Stone: Wakeup Cinema, 1994; writer, dir. documentary film Under One Roof, 1967; editor (book series) Framing the Cinema. Bd. dirs. Mich. Theater Found., Ann Arbor, 1977-79, 86—; alumni adv. bd. Lambda Chi Alpha, Ann Arbor, 1989-94; advisor Ann Arbor Film Festival, 1975—. With M.I. Corps, U.S. Army, 1962-65, Vietnam. Recipient Playwriting award Carolina Playmakers, 1962, Major Hopwood writing awards for drama and essays U. Mich., 1969, Outstanding Teaching award Amoco Found., Ann Arbor, 1985; fellow NEH, 1975. Mem. Internat. Communication Assn., Speech Communication Assn., Assn. for Edn. in Journalism and Mass Communication, Assn. Schs. Journalism and Mass Communication, Univ. Press Club of Mich., Azazels Club, Racquet Club, Phi Kappa Phi, Kappa Tau Alpha. Democrat. Roman Catholic. Home: 1835 Vinewood Blvd Ann Arbor MI 48104-3609 Office: U Mich Dept Communication 2020 Frieze Ave Bldg Dept Ann Arbor MI 48104-4767

BEAVER, HOWARD OSCAR, JR., retired alloys manufacturing company executive; b. Lebanon, Pa., May 18, 1925; s. Howard Oscar and Lessie (Yocum) B.; m. Jean Lillian Shollenberger, June 14, 1945; children: Bonne Jean Beaver Riefenstahl, Thomas Arthur. Student, U.S. Naval Acad., 1944; BS in Metallurgy, Pa. State U., 1948; grad. exec. mgmt. program, U. Pitts., 1967; DSc (hon.), Albright Coll., 1982. Metallurgist Carpenter Tech. Corp., Reading, Pa., 1948-51, plant metallurgist, melting, 1951-57, mgr. mill metallurgy, 1957-60, asst. gen. supt., 1960-66, asst. v.p. steel mfg., 1966-68, v.p. prodn., 1968-69, group v.p. steel, 1969-71, dir., 1969-83, chmn. bd., 1981, chmn. bd., chief exec. officer, 1971-83, ret., now bd. dirs., ret. 1993; former mem. adv. panel Congl. Office Tech. Assessment, Washington. Contbr. articles to profl. jours.; patentee in field. Past pres. exec. bd. Boy Scouts Am. Hawk Mountain Coun., Reading, Pa.; past pres. adv. bd. Pa. State U., Berks Campus, Reading, gen. chmn. capital campaign; bldg. campaign com. Community Gen. Hosp., Reading; bd. trustees Chit Chat Found., Wernersville, Pa., Pa. State U.; active United Way of Berks County, Pennsylvanians for Effective Govt., Harrisburg, Keystone State Games. Recipient cert. of distinction Fin. World, 1979, Bronze award Fin. World, 1980, Silver award The Wall St. Transcript, 1980, Horatio Alger award, 1981, Humanitarian award B'nai Brith Internat., 1981, Billy Wallis Founders award Elec. Metal Makers Guild Inc., 1982, Disting. Alumnus award Pa. State U., 1991; named Disting. Pennsylvanian William Penn Com., Phila., 1981, Businessperson of Yr., Berks County C. of C., 1982, Wilbur B. Doran award United Way Berks County, 1985, Thun award Meridian Bank, 1990; named to Pa. Hall of Fame, Jr. Achievement Hall of Fame of Reading and Berks County, 1985. Fellow Am. Soc. Metals (Lehigh Valley chpt., Bradley Stoughton award 1967, David Ford McFarland award 1972, medal for advancement of rsch. 1980, Disting. Life Membership award 1988); mem. AIME (Benjamin F. Fairless award 1981), Am. Iron and Steel Inst. (hon. v.p.), Assn. Iron and Steel Engrs., Muhlenberg Lions Club, Berkshire County Club, Skytop (Pa.) Club. Republican. Lutheran. Home and Office: 1954 Meadow Ln Reading PA 19610-2710

BEAVER, WILLIAM HENRY, accounting educator; b. Peoria, Ill., Apr. 13, 1940; s. John W. and Ethel M. (Kostka) B.; m. Suzanne Marie Hutton, May 22, 1965; children: Marie, Sarah, David. BBA, U. Notre Dame, 1962, D (hon.), 1998; MBA, U. Chgo., 1965, PhD, 1965; D (hon.), Norwegian Sch. Econs., 1996. CPA, Ill. Asst. prof. U. Chgo., 1965-69; assoc. prof. acctg. Stanford U., 1969-72, prof., 1972—, Joan E. Horngren prof., 1977—; adv. com. on corp. disclosure SEC, 1976-77; cons. Fin. Acctg. Standards Bd., 1980-86. Author: Financial Reporting: An Accounting Revolution, 1981, 3d edit., 1998; edit. bd.: The Acctg. Rev., 1977-80, Jour. Acctg. Rsch., 1968—, Jour. Acctg. and Econs., 1978—, Fin. Analysts Jour., 1979-98; contbr. articles to profl. Jours. Recipient Lit. award Jour. Accountancy, 1978, Faculty Excellence award Calif. Soc. CPAs, 1978, Graham and Dodd award Fin. Analysts Fedn., 1979, Notable Contbn. to Acct. Lit. award, 1969, 79, 83, Outstanding Rsch. award Inst. Quantitative Rsch. in Fin., 1981, Nat. Acctg. award Alpha Kappa Psi Found., 1982, Wildman award Am. Acctg. Assn., 1985, Disting. Teaching award Stanford U., 1985, Seminal Contbn. to Acctg. Lit. award, 1989; named ot Acctg. Hall of Fame, 1996. Mem. AICPA, Am. Fin. Assn., Am. Acctg. Assn. (v.p. 1981-83, pres. elect 1986-87, pres. 1987-88, disting. internat. lectr. in acct. award 1979, outstanding educator award 1990), Fin. Acctg. Found. (trustee 1993-96), Fin. Svcs. Rsch. Initiative (co-dir. 1992-95). Home: 949 Wing Pl Palo Alto CA 94305-1028 Office: Stanford U Grad Sch Bus Stanford CA 94305

BEAVERS, ROY LACKEY, retired utility executive, essayist, activist; b. Joplin, Mo., Apr. 24, 1930; s. Roy L. Sr. and Margarette Nellie (Loughlin) B.; m. Valerie Evelyn Gurney; children: Leslie Anne, Brendan G. BS in Bus., U. Mo., 1952; MA in Polit. Sci., U. Md., 1970. Commd. ens. USN, 1952, advanced through grades to comdr., 1966, retired, 1972; agt., broker ins. agy., Lebanon, Mo., 1972-77; field rep. Nat. Rural Electric Coop. Assn., Washington, 1977-84; mgr. pub. info. and legis. liaison wholesale power coop. KAMO Power, Vinita, Okla., 1984-93; moderator internet discussion list EMF-L concerning electromagnetic field health hazards, 1995-99; advocate for regulation of electromagnetic radiation; assigned US Arms Control Disarmament Agy. (SALT I strategic arms negotiations), 1970-72. Contbr. polit. and mil. essays to newspapers and other publs. including An Absence of Accountability (U.S. policy failure in Vietnam), 1976. State hdqrs. dir. Va. Com. to Re-elect Nixon, Richmond, Va., 1972; mem. Bd. Mo. Cmty. Betterment Edn. Fund, 1990-93, Bd. Okla. Acad. for State Goals, 1990-93. Decorated Bronze, Silver, and Gold medals U.S. Naval Inst., Pres. Merit Svc. medal, Navy Commendation medal. Mem. U.S. Naval Inst., Internat. Platform Spkrs. Assn. Home: Lake Shore Estates 26555 Gene Dr Lebanon MO 65536-5776

BEAVERS, WILLIAM M., alderman; b. 1937; married; 3 children. Grad., Harold Washington Jr. Coll. Vice officer on narcotics, gambling, prostitution and gangs Chgo. Police Dept.; alderman Ward 7 Chgo. City Coun., 1983—; chmn. police and fire com., vice chmn. aviation com., mem. fin. and budget, govt. coms. Chgo. City Coun. City chmn. Cook County Dem. Com., 1994—. Office: 2552 E 79th St Chicago IL 60649-5124*

BEAVO, JOSEPH A., pharmacology professor. PhD in Physiology, Vanderbilt Col., 1970. Prof. Pharmacology U. Wash., 1977—. Mem. Nat. Acad. Scis. Office: U Washington Box 357280 Dept Pharmacology Seattle WA 98195-7280*

BEAZLEY, HAMILTON SCOTT, volunteer health organization executive; b. Houston, Dec. 21, 1943; s. Hamilton and Marjorie Virginia (Yates) B. BA, Yale U., 1966; MBA, So. Meth. U., 1977; PhD, George Washington U., 1998. Founder/exec. com. DyChem Internat. (U.K.) Ltd., Dallas, London, 1970-73; dir. corp. planning Hudon-Mueller Inc., Houston, 1973-75; fin. analyst Occidental Petroleum Corp., Houston, 1975-80; strategic planning cons. Houston, 1980-88; pres. Nat. Coun. on Alcoholism and Drug Dependence, N.Y.C., 1988-90, Soc. Ams. for Recovery, Washington, 1990-91. Co-creator TV series, BBC, Secrets Out, 1984-87; co-author: (with Bishop Payne) Let Down Your Nets, 1999. Bd. dirs. Total World Corp., Houston, 1985-97; adv. dir. Harvard Alcohol Project, Boston, 1989-90; liaison Nat. Inst. Alcohol Abuse and Alcoholism; bd. trustees Ednl. Advancement Found., 1996—; mem. adv. bd. divsn. on addictions Harvard Med. Sch., 1997—; mem. adv. bd. Discovery Learning Project, U. Tex., Austin, 1996—. Mem. Yale Club of N.Y.C. Republican. Episcopalian. Avocations: creative writing, sailing. Home: 2850 Spring Meadow Ct Indianapolis IN 46268-4228

BEBAN, GARY JOSEPH, real estate corporation officer; b. San Francisco, Aug. 5, 1946; s. Frank and Anna (Consani) B.; m. Kathleen Hanson, June 14, 1968; children: Paul, Mark. BA in History, UCLA, 1968. Real estate specialist, sales and mgr. positions CB Comml., Calif. and Ill., 1970-87; pres. CB Comml., L.A., Chgo., 1987-89; sr. exec., mng. dir. CB Richard Ellis, Chgo., 1984—. Mem. IDRC, 1986—, UCLA Assocs., 1980—; bd. trustee New Hampton Sch. Recipient Heisman Trophy award N.Y. Downtown Athletic Club, 1967; NCAA Scholar Athlete, 1968, Football Hall of Fame, 1988. Mem. Urban Land Inst., Nat. Realty Commn., UCLA Ctr. Fion. and Real Estate. Office: CB Richard Ellis 10 S Lasalle St Ste 2600 Chicago IL 60603

BEBER, ROBERT H., lawyer, financial services executive; b. N.Y.C., Aug. 17, 1933; s. Morris and Martha (Pollock) B.; m. Joan Parsons, June 14, 1957; children: Andrea, Judith, Deborah. A.B. in Econs, Duke U., 1955, J.D., 1957. Bar: N.Y., N.C. With Everett, Everett & Everett, N.C., 1957-58; atty. SBA, Washington, 1961-63; with RCA, 1963-81; sr. v.p., gen. counsel, sec. GAF Corp., N.Y.C., 1981-83, exec. v.p., dir., 1983-84, dir. subds.; sr. v.p., gen. counsel, sec. Phlcorp, Inc. (formerly Baldwin United Corp.), Phila., 1984-88; asst. gen. counsel litigation W.R. Grace & Co., N.Y.C., 1988-89, v.p., dir. litigation, 1989-91, sr. v.p., gen. counsel, 1991-93, exec. v.p., 1993-98, ret., 1999, cons., 1999—. Bd. vis. Sch. Law, Duke U., 1996—; chmn. bd. Health Care Plan N.J., 1975-78; v.p. South Jersey C. of C., 1974-77. Served with U.S. Army, 1958-61. Mem. ABA. Republican. Jewish. Home: 7228 Queenferry Cir Boca Raton FL 33496-5953 Office: WR Grace & Co 1 Town Center Rd Boca Raton FL 33486-1050

BEBKO-JONES, LINDA, state legislator. Student, Erie Bus. Acad., 1964-65. Legal sec. Silin, Eckert & Burke, Erie, Pa., 1964-66; office mgr., legal sec. Atty. Joseph Knowacki, Erie, 1975-83; adminstrv. asst. Hon. A. Buzz Andrezeski Pa. Senate, Erie, 1984-89; dir. Women Against Sexual Harassment, Erie, 1989-92; caseworker Community House for Women, Erie, 1990-92; caseworker Hon. Harris Wofford U.S. Senate, Erie, 1991-92; mem. Pa. Ho. Reps., Harrisburg, 1993—, sec. mil. and vets. affairs, mem. health and welfare com., state govt. com., aging and youth com., task force on violence as health concern, mem. firefighters caucus, freshman non-partisan caucus, Northwest caucus, substance abuse caucus, tax reform caucusm women's caucus; one on one reporter Presque Isle Mag., 1991-92; mem. adv. bd. Soldiers and Sailors Home; resident asst. Edmund Thomas Detention Hall; Erie County coord. Children's Lobby Kid Pix Program; apptd. to Pa. Commn. for Women; coord. Pa. Children's Legis. Conf./Coun. State Govts.; del. East Side Fedn. Mem. Dem. Exec. Com. Erie County, Dem. Women's Coun. Erie County; trainer in-svc. tng. program Mcpl. Police Officer's Edn. and Tng. Commn. Recipient Erie Woman of Yr. award, 1994. Mem. Am. Bus. Women's Assn., Slovsk Nat. Club (life). Home: 460 E 26th St Erie PA 16504-2802 Office: Pa Ho of Reps 112 South Office Bldg PO Box 202020 Harrisburg PA 17120-2020*

BEBOUT, ELI DANIEL, oil executive; b. Rawlings, Wyo., Oct. 14, 1946; s. Hugh and Dessie Bebout; m. Lorraine J. Tavares; children: Jordan, Jentry, Reagen, Taggert. BEE, U. Wyo., 1969. With U.S. Energy Co., Riverton, Wyo., 1972-75; field engr. Am. Bechtel Corp., Green River, Wyo., 1975-76; pres. NUPEC Resources, Inc., Riverton, 1976-83, Smith-Collins Pharm. Inc., Riverton, 1976-83; cons. Nucor Inc., Riverton, 1984-87; v.p. Nucor Drilling, Inc., Riverton, 1987—. Mem. Wyo. Ho. of Reps., mem. rules com. mgmt. coun., majority floor leader, spkr. Republican. Office: Nucor Inc PO Box 112 Riverton WY 82501-0112

BECATTI, LANCE NORMAN, finance company executive; b. Roseland, Ill., Feb. 11, 1959; s. Leroy J. Sr. and Shirley Ann Becatti. CFP, Fla. Dist. adminstr. Lanier Bus. Products, Inc., Sarasota and Ft. Myers, Fla., 1976-79; pres. Alpha I Inc. ADC, Ft. Myers, 1979-84; sr. fin. advisor Am. Express Fin. Advisors, Tampa, Fla., 1984—. Mem. adv. bd. Tampa's Downtown Spl. Svcs. Dist., 1993-96; campaign chmn. March of Dimes, Ft. Myers, 1978-79; mem. Tampa Planned Giving Coun. Mem. Internat. Assn. for Fin. Planning (practitioners divsn. 1992—), Tampa Bay Bus. Coun. Avocations: karate, raquetball, cycling. Home: 201 W Laurel St Apt 203 Tampa FL 33602-2935 Office: Am Express Fin Advisors 304 S Plant Ave Tampa FL 33606-2326

BECERRA, XAVIER, congressman, lawyer; b. Sacramento, Jan. 26, 1958; s. Manuel and Maria Teresa B.; m. Carolina Reyes, 1987. AB, Stanford U., 1980, JD, 1984. Atty., 1984—; dir. dist. office State Senator Art Torres, L.A.; dep. atty. gen. dept. justice, Calif., 1987-90; assemblyman, 59th dist. State of Calif., 1990-93; mem. 105th Congress from 30th Calif. dist., 1993—; mem. ways and means com.; chmn. Congl. Hispanic Caucus. Mem. Mexican-Am. Bar Assn., Calif. Bar Assn., Assn. Calif. State Attys. and Adminstrv. Law Judges. Democrat. Avocations: reading, carpentry, golf. Office: Ho of Reps 1119 Longworth Bldg Washington DC 20515-0530*

BECH, DOUGLAS YORK, lawyer, resort executive; b. Seattle, Aug. 18, 1945; s. Albert Richard and Vera Evelyn (Peterson) B.; m. Sheryl Annette Tucker, Aug. 9, 1968; children: Kristen Elizabeth, Allison York. BA, Baylor U., 1967; JD, U. Tex., 1970. Bar: Tex. 1970, N.Y. 1993. Ptnr. Andrews & Kurth, Houston, 1970-93, Akin, Gump, Strauss, Hauer & Feld, 1994-97; mng. dir. Raintree Capital Co., Houston, 1994—; chmn. Raintree Resorts Internat., Inc., Club Regina Resorts, Inc.; bd. dirs. Frontier Oil, efax.com, Pride Cos., Drexler Found. Sgt. USAR, 1968-74. Republican. Baptist. Avocations: running, snowskiing, travel, big game hunting, golf. Office: Raintree Resorts Internat 10000 Memorial Dr Ste 480 Houston TX 77024-3409

BECHAMPS, GERALD JOSEPH, surgeon; b. Flushing, N.Y., 1937. MD, Georgetown U., 1963. Diplomate Am. Bd. Surgery. Intern Meadowbrook Hosp., East Meadow, N.Y., 1963-64, resident in surgery, 1964-65; fellow surgery Mayo Clinic-Found., Rochester, 1965-69; clin. instr. U.Va. Sch. Medicine, 1971-99; pvt. practice Winchester Surg. Clinic, Ltd., 1971—; past pres. Fedn. State Med. Bds. of U.S.; surgeon Winchester Med. Ctr., Surgi-Ctr. of Winchester; mem. Va. State Bd. Medicine, 1980-92. Mem. ACS (past pres. Va. chpt.), So. Soc. Clin. Surgeons. Fax: 540-722-4515. Office: Winchester Surg Clinic Ltd PO Box 2698 Winchester VA 22604-1898

BECHER, ANDREW CLIFFORD, lawyer; b. Evanston, Ill., Jan. 24, 1946; s. Clifford C. and Ardeth M. (Johnson) B.; m. Deborah M. Bell, Jan. 18, 1969; children: Cory, Megan, Adam J. BS, Purdue U., 1968; JD, U. Ill., 1971. Bar: Ill. 1971, Minn. 1977, Tex. 1998. Assoc. McDermott, Will & Emery, Chgo., 1972-76; stockholder Briggs & Morgan, Mpls., 1976-87; sr. v.p. Dain Bosworth, Inc., Mpls., 1987-89; ptnr. Robins, Kaplan, Miller & Ciresi, Mpls., 1989-96; sr. v.p. Cal Dive Internat. Inc., Houston, 1996—; bd. dirs. Fantasy Flight Pub., Inc., Minn., Tri-Point Ptnrs., L.L.C., Houston, Energy Resource Technology, Inc., Houston, Hour Glass Golf, Inc., S.C.; lectr. in law Chgo. Kent Coll. Law-Ill. Inst. Tech., 1973-75; assoc. prof. Hamline U., St. paul, 1978-80. Chair local and state govt. com. St. Paul C. of C., 1978-80. Capt. U.S. Army, 1971-79, USAR. Mem. ABA, Minn. Bar Assn., Ill. Bar Assn., Tex. Bar Assn. Presbyterian. Avocations: family, travel, investments, golf, cars. Office: Cal Dive Internat Inc 400 N Sam Houston Pkwy E Houston TX 77060-3548

BECHER, WILLIAM DON, electrical engineering educator, engineering consultant; b. Bolivar, Ohio, Nov. 26, 1929; s. William and Eva Vernette (Richardson) B.; m. Helen Norma Hager, Aug. 31, 1950; children: Eric Alan, Patricia Lynn. BS in Radio Engring., Tri-State U., 1950; MSEE, U. Mich., 1961, PhD, 1968. Registered profl. engr., Mich., N.J. Project engr. Bogue Electric, Paterson, N.J., 1950-53; sr. devel. engr. Goodyear Aircraft Corp., Akron, Ohio, 1953-57; sr. systems engr. Beckman Instruments, Fullerton, Calif., 1957-58; engring. supr. Bendix Aerospace Systems, Ann Arbor, Mich., 1958-63; research engr. U. Mich., Ann Arbor, 1963-68; adj. prof. elec. engring., 1978-79, 81-94; prof. elec. engring. U. Mich., Dearborn, 1968-78; chmn., 1971-76; engring. dept. mgr. Environ. Research Inst. Mich., Ann Arbor, 1977-79, assoc. dir., 1981-87, tech. cons., 1988-90, engr. emeritus, 1990—; prof. elec. engring., dean Coll. Engring. N.J. Inst. Tech., Newark, 1979-81; pres. Mich. Computers & Instrumentation, Inc., Ann Arbor, 1983-87; prof., chmn. elec. engring. Calif. State U., Fresno, 1988. Author: Courses in Continuing Education for Electronics Engineers, 1975, 76, Logical Design Using Integrated Circuits, 1977. Served with U.S. Army, 1953-55. Gen. Electric Co. fellow, 1962-63. Mem. IEEE (life, sr.), Am. Soc. Engring. Edn., Order of Engrs., Sigma Xi, Alpha Sigma Lambda, Eta Kappa Nu, Phi Kappa Phi, Tau Beta Pi. Achievements include patents in field. Home and Office: 691 Spring Valley Rd Ann Arbor MI 48105-1060 Office: Environ Rsch Inst 3300 Plymouth Rd Ann Arbor MI 48105-2551

BECHERER, HANS WALTER, agricultural equipment manufacturing executive; b. Detroit, Apr. 19, 1935; s. Max and Mariele (Specht) B.; m. Michele Beigbeder, Nov. 28, 1959; children: Maxime (dec.), Vanessa. BA, Trinity Coll., Hartford, Conn., 1957; postgrad., Munich U., 1958; MBA, Harvard U., 1962. Exec. asst. office of chmn. Deere & Co., Moline, Ill., 1966-69; gen. mgr. John Deere Export, Mannheim, Germany, 1969-73; dir. export mktg. Deere & Co., Moline, 1973-77, v.p., 1977-83, sr. v.p., 1983-86, exec. v.p., 1986-87, pres., 1987-90, COO, 1987-89, CEO, 1989—, chmn., 1990—, also bd. dirs.; bd. dirs. Schering-Plough Corp., Allied Signal Inc., The Chase Manhattan Corp. and the Chase Manhattan Bank; mem. industry sector adv. com. U.S. Dept. Commerce, 1975-81; mem. Bus. Roundtable, 1989—; mem. adv. com. Chase Manhattan Bank Internat., 1990-98; trustee Com. for Econ. Devel., 1990—. Trustee St. Katherine's/St. Mark's Sch.,

Bettendorf, Iowa, 1983—. 1st lt. USAF, 1958-60. Mem. Coun. on Fgn. Rels., The Bus. Coun., Conf. Bd., Equipment Mfgs. Inst. (bd. dirs. 1987-90), Chgo. Club, Rock Island (Ill.) Arsenal Golf Club. Republican. Roman Catholic. Office: Deere & Co One John Deere Pl Moline IL 61265-8098

BECHERER, RICHARD JOHN, architecture educator; b. East St. Louis, Ill., Nov. 8, 1951; s. Adam Jacob and Agnes Evelyn (Baker) B.; m. Charlene Castellano, Aug. 13, 1982. Student Courtauld Inst., U. London, 1973; BA, BArch, Rice U., 1974; MA, Cornell U., 1977, PhD, 1981. Archtl. asst. Colin St. John Wilson and Ptnr., London, 1972-73; designer The Brooks Assn., Houston, 1973-74; grad. asst. Cornell U., Ithaca, N.Y., 1974-80, asst. prof. architecture, 1981; asst. prof. Auburn (Ala.) U., 1980-82, U. Va., Charlottesville, 1982-86; head grad. architecture program Carnegie Mellon U., Pitts., 1986-90, assoc. prof. architecture, 1987-96; assoc. prof. Cornell U., 1996; presenter seminars NEH, 1982, 88, 89, Am. Collegiate Schs. Architecture, 1988, 93, 97; lectr. Centre Canadien d'Architecture, Montreal, Carnegie Mus., Pitts., and various colls., univs. and nat. confs.; vis. assoc. prof. U. Pitts., 1997-99; assoc. prof. Am. U. Beirut, 1999—. Author: Science Plus Sentiment; César Daly's Formula for Modern Architecture, 1984, (mus. catalogue and display) Urban Theory and Transformation, 1976, (tourist guidebook) Canandaigua: A Walking Tour, 1977; contbr. articles to profl. jours.; prin. works include interiors Michael P. Keeley House, Belleville, Ill., 1978, Robert Becherer House, Stonybrook, 1990; selected exhibitor Venice Biennale, Prato della Valle, Padua, 1985; exhibitor Heart of the Park, Houston, 1992. Recipient Design Arts award Nat. Endowment for Arts, 1989-90, Graham Found. award, 1993; grad. fellow Cornell U., 1975-79, Eidlitz fellow, 1978, Soc. for Humanities and Mellon Found. fellow, 1984-85, NEH fellow, 1986, Paul Mellon vis. sr. fellow Ctr. for Advanced Study in Visual Arts, Nat. Gallery of Art; Travel to Collections grantee NEH, 1985. Mem. AAUP, Soc. Archtl. Historians (session chmn. ann. meeting 1989), Coll. Art Assn., Rice U. Alumni Assn. Democrat. Roman Catholic. Avocations: free-hand drawing, bicycling, ballroom dancing, French cinema. Home: 119 Race St Edgewood PA 15218-1337 Office: Cornell U Dept Architecture East Sibley Hall Ithaca NY 14853

BECHERER, RICHARD JOSEPH, science consulting firm executive, physicist; b. Boston, Mar. 19, 1941; s. Edward Charles and Grace Elizabeth (Dalton) B.; m. Kathleen Quinn, June 26, 1965 (div. Aug. 1984) children: Joan Elizabeth, Christine Diane, Carolyn Jean; m. Susan Jaeger, Sept. 30, 1989. BS in Physics, Boston Coll., 1962; MS in Physics, U. Ill., Champaign, 1964; NASA trainee, U. Rochester, 1969-71, PhD in Optics, 1972. Scientist Tech. Ops. Inc., Burlington, Mass., 1965-68, EIKONIX Corp., Bedford, Mass., 1968-71; sr. scientist, sect. mgr. Polaroid Research Labs, Cambridge, Mass., 1971-75; mem. tech. staff Lincoln Lab, MIT, Lexington, Mass., 1975-81; dir. optical sys. Sci. Applications Internat. Corp., Lexington, Mass., 1981-91; pres. Delta Sciences, Stow, Mass., 1991—; lectr. Northeastern U., Boston, 1966-83, U. Oulu, Finland, 1990, Nat. Tech. U., Ft. Collins, Colo., 1993—; cons. NAS Nat. Rsch. Coun., Washington, 1972-76; mem. Commn. Internat. l'Eclairage, Washington, 1973-76, USN Electro-Optics Working Group, 1977-80, NATO Rsch. Study Group, Munich, 1978-79; Strategic Def. Initiative Experimenters Working Group, 1986-91; instr. SPIE laser radar, sensor sys. courses Nat. Tech. U., 1983—; adj. prof. U. Conn., Storrs, 1992—; dep. dir. CONNECT-New Eng. Alliance Photonics Tech. Deployment, Storrs, 1994—; pres. coun. U. Ill., 1990—. Co-author: Optical Radiation Measurements, Vol. 1: Radiometry, 1979; editor: Adaptive Optics Systems and Technology, 1982, Laser Radar II, 1987, Laser Radar III, 1988, Laser Radar IV, 1989, Laser Radar V, 1990, Laser Radar VI, 1991, Laser Radar VII, 1992, Lidar for Remote Sensing, 1992, Lidar and Atmospheric Sensing, 1995; mem. editl. bd. Laser Focus, 1973-77; patentee optical filtering methods, optical heterodyne detection. Active Conservation Law Found., 1992—; com. mem. Rep. Nat. Com., Washington, 1994; campaign com. Mass. 5th Congl. Dist., Concord, 1994. Presidential scholar Boston Coll., 1962. Fellow Internat. Soc. Optical Engring.; mem. Optical Soc. Am. (chmn. edn. com.), Fides Soc., Pine Tree Soc., Sigma Xi, Sigma Pi Sigma. Roman Catholic. Avocations: history, politics, travel, tennis, skiing. Home: 6 October Ln Stow MA 01775-1037

BECHTEL, RILEY PEART, engineering company executive; s. Stephen Davison Bechtel, Jr. BA in Polit. Sci., Psychology, U. Calif., Davis, 1974; JD, MBA, Stanford U., 1979. Bar: Calif. 1979. With Bechtel Group, Inc., San Francisco, 1966-79, 81—, Thelen, Marrin, Johnson & Bridges, San Francisco, 1979-81; bd. dirs. Bechtel Corp. (formerly Bechtel Group Inc.), 1987—, pres., coo, 1989-1990, chmn. exec. com., ceo, 1990—, CEO, 1993—; mem. Bus. Coun., Bus. Roundtable policy com., Calif. Bus. Roundtable, J.P. Morgan Internat. Adv. Coun.; adv. coun. Stanford U. Grad. Sch. of Bus.; dean's adv. coun. Stanford Law Sch. Trustee Thacher Sch., Ojai, Calif. Mem. ABA. Office: Bechtel Corp PO Box 193965 San Francisco CA 94119-3965*

BECHTEL, STEPHEN DAVISON, JR., engineering company executive; b. Oakland, Calif., May 10, 1925; s. Stephen Davison and Laura (Peart) B.; m. Elizabeth Mead Hogan, June 5, 1946; 5 children. Student, U. Colo., 1943-44; BS, Purdue U., 1946, D. in Engring. (hon.), 1972; MBA, Stanford U., 1948; DSc (hon.), U. Colo., 1981. Registered profl. engr., N.Y., Mich., Alaska, Calif., Md., Hawaii, Ohio, D.C., Va., Ill. Engring. and mgmt. positions Bechtel Corp., San Francisco, 1941-60, pres., 1960-73, chmn. of cos. in Bechtel group, 1973-80; chmn. Bechtel Group, Inc., 1980-90, chmn. emeritus, 1990—; bd. dirs. Remington Arms, former chmn., mem. bus. coun., emeritus life councillor, past chmn. conf. bd.; chmn. emeritus Fremont Group, Inc., Sequoia Ventures, Inc., 1995—. Trustee, mem., past chmn. bldg. and grounds com. Calif. Inst. Tech.; mem. pres.'s coun. Purdue U.; adv. coun. Inst. Internat. Studies, bd. visitors, former charter mem., adv. coun. Stanford U. Grad. Sch. Bus. With USMC, 1943-46. Decorated officer French Legion of Honor; recipient Disting. Alumnus award Purdue U., 1964, U. Colo., 1978, Ernest C. Arbuckle Disting. Alumnus award Stanford Grad. Sch. Bus., 1974, Disting. Engring. Alumnus award 1979, Beta Theta PI Oxford Cup award 1997; named Man of Yr. Engring. News-Record, 1974, Outstanding Achievement in Constrn. award Moles, 1977, Chmn.'s award Am. Assn. Engring. Socs., 1982, Washington award Western Soc. Engrs., 1985, Nat. Medal Tech. from Pres. Bush, 1991, Golden Beaver award 1992, Herbert Hoover medal 1980. Fellow AAAS; mem. ASCE (hon., engring. mgmt. award 1979, pres. award 1985), Inst. Chem. Engrs. (U.K., hon.); mem. AIME, NSPE (hon. chmn. Nat. Engrs. Week 1990), Nat. Acad. Engring. (past chmn.), Calif. Acad. Scis. (hon. trustee), Am. Soc. French Legion Honor (bd. dirs., disting. achievement medal 1994), Royal Acad. Engring. (U.K., fgn. mem.), Pacific Union Club, Bohemian Club, San Francisco Golf Club, Claremont Country Club, Cypress Point Club, St. Francis Yacht Club, Bear River Club (Utah), Wild Goose Club (Calif.), Chi Epsilon, Tau Beta Pi. Office: Bechtel Group Inc PO Box 193965 San Francisco CA 94119-3965

BECHTEL, STEPHEN E., mechanical engineer, educator. BS in Engring. summa cum laude, U. Mich., 1979; PhD in Engring., U. Calif., Berkeley, 1983. Prof. dept. mech. engring. Ohio State U., Columbus, 1983—; reviewer design, mfg. and computer-integrated engring. divsn., fluid dynamics and hydraulics directorate NSF, 1985—; cons. Hoechst Celanese Corp., Los Alamos Nat. Lab., Battelle Meml. Inst., Corning, Inc. Referee Jour. Rheology, Jour. Applied Mechanics, Jour. Non-Newtonian Fluid Mechanics, others. James B. Angell scholar U. Mich., 1976-79. Mem. ASME (mem. fluid mechanics com. applied mechanics divsn. 1989—, rec. sec. gen. com. 1991-92, rec. sec. exec. com. 1992-93, Henry Hess award 1990), Am. Acad. Mechanics, Soc. Rheology, Tau Beta Pi. Achievements include research in modeling of industrial polymer processing and fiber manufacturing, viscoelastic fluid flows, free surface flows and instability mechanisms, material characterization, transducer characterization in non-destructive evaluation. E-mail: bechtel.3@osu.edu. Office: Ohio State Univ Applied Mechanics 155 W Woodruff Ave Columbus OH 43210-1117

BECHTLE, LOUIS CHARLES, federal judge; b. Phila., Dec. 14, 1927; s. Charles R. and Gladys (Kirchner) B.; m. Margaret Beck, Sept. 7, 1978; children: Barbara, Nancy, Amy; 1 stepchild, Samuel. B.S., Temple U., 1951, LL.B., 1954. Bar: Pa. 1954. Asst. U.S. atty. U.S. Dept. Justice, Phila., 1957-59, U.S. atty., 1969-72; pvt. practice law Jacoby & Maxmin, Phila., 1959-62; pvt. practice Wisler, Pearlstine, Talone, Gerber, Norristown, Pa., 1962-69; U.S. dist. judge U.S. Dist. Ct., Phila., 1972—; now sr. judge U.S. Dist. Ct. (Eastern Dist.), Phila.; adj. faculty Temple U. Law Sch., Phila., 1974-93, Villanova Law Sch., 1985-89; mem. Jud/ Panel on Multidist. Litigation, 1994—. Served with U.S. Army, 1946-47. Mem. Montgomery County Bar Assn., Fed. Bar Assn. Republican. Presbyterian. Office: US Dist Ct 17613 US Courthouse 601 Market St Philadelphia PA 19106-1713*

BECHTOL, LARRY OWEN, pastor; b. Gordon, Ohio, Oct. 14, 1937; s. Owen S. and Maudie B. B.; m. Betty J.; children: Julie, Lori, Stephen, Joan, Melissa, Sean, Tarla. BA, Asbury Coll., 1959; MDiv, United Theol. Sem., 1963. Ordained to ministry, United Ch. of Christ. Pastor Hollansburg (Ohio) UCC Ch., 1961-64, Frankford Congrl. Ch., Phila., 1964-66, Lansdale (Pa.) Schwenkfelder, 1966-68; pastor, counselor First E and R, Vermillion, Ohio, 1976-82; prof. Cin. Christian Coll., 1989—; instr. So. Ohio Coll., Ft. Mitchell, 1991—; pastor, counselor Matthew United Ch., Cin., 1969-76, 82—; chaplain Boy Scouts Am., Dayton, Ohio, 1960; youth leader Schwenkfelder Youth, 1968; chair Ch. Growth and Devel., Cleve., 1979-81. Bd. dirs. Winton Place Civic Assn., Cin., 1970-76. Mem. MLA, Am. Assn. Christian Counselors, Christian Educators Assn., Acad. Am. Poets. Avocations: writing, poems, reading, tennis.

BECICH, RAYMOND BRICE, healthcare consultant, mediator, trainer, educator; b. Chgo., Jan. 9, 1945; s. Nicholas Gabriel and Rose Christina (Spillar) B. BA, Ind. U., 1966; MS, Columbia U., 1968. Adminstrv. officer, then hosp. dir. Indian Health Svc., Harlem, Mont., 1968-72; hosp. dir. Indian Health Svc., Rapid City, S.D., 1972-78; hosp. adminstr. St. Elizabeth's Hosp., Washington, 1979-82, exec. officer, 1983-86; exec. officer NIH Clin. Ctr., Bethesda, Md., 1986-94; healthcare cons., mediator, trainer, educator, 1994—; adj. faculty Univ. Coll., U. Md., College Park, U. N.Mex., Albuquerque and Los Alamos, Coll. Santa Fe, Ctrl. Mich. U., Mt. Pleasant, 1995—. Bd. dirs. Ronald McDonald House, Washington, 1986-89; vol. Whitman-Walker Clinic, 1987-95. Fellow Am. Coll. Healthcare Execs. (life). Democrat.

BECK, ALBERT, manufacturing company executive; b. N.Y.C., Jan. 14, 1928; s. Albert Christian and Mabel Agnes (Dunn) B.; m. Jean Norma Russ, June 16, 1951; children—Nancy, Richard, Douglas. BS, Fairleigh Dickinson U., 1950; MS, Rutgers U., 1956. Product line mgr. Tung Sol Electric Inc. div. Wagner Electric, Bloomfield, N.J., 1951-66; dir. quality control IT&T, Brussels, Belgium, 1966-69; asst. dir. product ops. IT&T, N.Y.C., 1969-72, dir. N.Am. staff, 1972-73; v.p. ops. Grinnell Fire Protection Co., Providence, 1973-79, exec. v.p., 1979; exec. v.p. Grinnell Corp., 1986—. Mem. bd. edn. curriculum com. Wayne, N.J., 1964. Served with A.C., USN, 1945-47. Mem. Nat. Fire Sprinkler Assn. (bd. dirs. 1990), Sigma Xi. Republican. Avocations: golf, tennis, bridge, flying. Office: Grinnell Corp 3 Tyco Park Exeter NH 03833-2923

BECK, ANATOLE, mathematician, educator; b. Bronx, N.Y., Mar. 19, 1930; s. Morris and Minnie (Rosenblum) B.; m. Evelyn Torton, Apr. 10, 1954 (div.); children—Nina Rachel, Micah Daniel. B.A., Bklyn. Coll., 1951; M.S., Yale U., 1953, Ph.D., 1956. Instr. math. Williams Coll., Williamstown, Mass., 1955-56; Office Naval Rsch. rsch. assoc. Tulane U., New Orleans, 1956-57; traveling fellow Yale U., 1957-58; from asst. to assoc. prof. U. Wis., Madison, 1958-66, prof. math., 1966—; chmn. math. London Sch. Econ./U. London, England, 1973-75; vis. prof. Cornell U., 1960, Hebrew U., Jerusalem, 1964-65, U. Göttingen, Fed. Republic Germany, 1965, U. Warwick, 1968, Imperial Coll., U. London, 1969, U. Erlangen, Fed. Republic Germany, 1969, U. Md., 1971, Tech. U. Munich, Fed. Republic Germany, 1973, London Sch. Econs. and Univ. Coll., U. London, 1985, 91-92, 9 4, 95, 96, 97; v.p. Wis. Fedn. Tchrs., 1975-83; co-founder Wis. U. Union, 1984, pres., 1988-91. Author: Continuous Flows in the Plane, 1974, (with M.N. Bleicher and D.W. Crowe) Excursions into Mathematics, 1969, The Knowledge Business, 1997; contbr. articles to profl. jours. Recipient Disting. Alumnus award Bklyn. Coll., 1976. Mem. Am. Math. Soc. (council 1973-75), Math. Assn. Am., AAUP, Sigma Xi, Phi Beta Kappa, Pi Mu Epsilon. Democrat. Office: U Wis 480 Lincoln Dr 721 Van Vleck Hall Madison WI 53706-1329

BECK, ANDREW JAMES, lawyer; b. Washington, Feb. 19, 1948; s. Leonard Norman and Frances (Greif) B.; m. Gretchen Ann Schroeder, Feb. 14, 1971; children: Carter, Lowell, Justin. BA, Carleton Coll., 1969; JD, Stanford U., 1972; MBA, Long Island U., 1975. Bar; Va. 1972, N.Y. 1973, Pa., 1992. Assoc. Casey, Lane & Mittendorf, N.Y.C., 1972-80, ptnr., 1980-82; mng. ptnr. Haythe & Curley, N.Y.C., 1982—; gen. counsel Nat. Stroke Assn., 1992—. Bd. dirs. Allied Devices Corp., 1994—; trustee Bklyn. Heights Synagogue, 1980-81, Bklyn. Heights Montessori Sch., 1988-92, treas., 1990-92. Mem. ABA, Va. State Bar Assn., N.Y. Stat Bar Assn., Pa. Bar Assn., Assn. of Bar of City of N.Y., Nat. Stroke Assn. (gen. counsel 1992—). Avocations: squash, bridge. Home: 71 Willow St Apt 1 Brooklyn NY 11201-1657 Office: Haythe & Curley 237 Park Ave New York NY 10017-3140

BECK, ANDREW ROBERT, accountant; b. Churchville, Pa., Aug. 20, 1971; s. Francis Joseph and Dorothy Ann (VanWittkamp) B. BS in Bus. Adminstrn. cum laude, LaSalle U., 1993. CPA, Pa., N.J. Sr. acct. Zook, Dinon & Roman, P.A., Moorestown, N.J., 1993—. Mem. AICPA. Avocations: swimming, sports, reading.

BECK, ANGEL C., columnist, educator; b. Omaha, Aug. 18, 1951; d. James and Aleane (Fitz) Carter; m. Frank J. Beck, May 7, 1977 (div. May 12, 1988); children: Jaman, Angel Marie, Frank J. BGS, U. Nebr., 1975. Sports reporter Oakland (Calif.) Tribune, 1987-88; reporter Shoreline Times/Ft. Worth, 1988-89, Arlington (Tex.) Citizen Jour., 1989-90; talk show host WNET TV, N.Y.C., 1990-91; tchr. Stamford (Conn.) Pub. Schs., 1990—; syndicated columnist Tribune Media Svcs., Chgo., 1996-97, Zwita Prodns. Syndications, Stamford, Conn., 1997—; adv. 1 Have a Dream WCBS-TV, N.Y.C., 1995—. Author: History of Black Golfers, 1989, How To Play Bid Whist, 1995; contbr. articles to Black Enterprise jour. Mem. Nat. Assn. Black Journalists. Avocations: bid whist, jazz. Office: PO Box 112486 Stamford CT 06911-2486

BECK, BARBARA NELL, elementary school educator; b. Corpus Christi, Tex., Oct. 25, 1940; d. Marshall Joseph and Madie Ann (Spence) Robertson; m. Joel J. Beck, June 23, 1973. BA, Baylor U., 1964. Tchr. Killeen (Tex.) Ind. Sch. Dist., 1964—. Sunday sch. tchr., co-treas., ch. clk. First Bapt. Ch. of Nolanville. Mem. NEA, Tex. State Tchrs. Assn., Tex. Assn. for the Gifted and Talented, Killeen Edn. Assn. (treas., past pres., bd. dirs.), Clifton Park PTA (past treas.). Office: Clifton Park Elem Sch 2200 Trimmier Rd Killeen TX 76541-8599

BECK, CHRISTINE SAFFORD, photographer, publisher, volunteer; b. Phila., July 10, 1943; d. Elisha Jr. and Margaret (Tramdack) Safford; m. Leif Christian Beck, Nov. 21, 1964; children: C. Lars, Eric S., Anders. BA in German and French, Queens Coll., 1964; MA in German Lit., Bryn Mawr Coll., 1969; postgrad., N.Y. Inst. Photography. Co-founder, pres. Nat. Jr. Tennis League of Phila., 1969-79; pres., CEO Nat. Jr. Tennis League, N.Y.C., 1979-83; owner, photographer Christine S. Beck Photography, Villanova, Pa., 1990—; pub., owner Prism Light Press, Bryn Mawr, Pa., 1995—; pres. Phila. Tennis Patrons Assn., 1985-95, mem. adv. bd., 1995—; pres. Arthur Ashe Youth Tennis Ctr., Phila., 1985-95; chair adv. coun. Esperanza Health Ctr., Phila., 1994-97. Photographer (books): Beyond Me. Voices of the Natural World, 1993, Spirit of Summit County, Colorado, 1996; producer Broadway Comes to Queens benefit concert, Charlotte, N.C., 1999. Bd. dirs. Habitat for Humanity, Phila., 1988-90; coord. vols. Jimmy Carter Workcamp, North Phila., 1988; chair stewardship campaign Bryn Mawr Presbyn. Ch., 1992; trustee Queens Coll., Charlotte, N.C., 1995—, Gesu Sch., Phila., 1996—. Recipient Kennedy award Robert F. Kennedy Pro Celebrity Tennis Tournament, 1975, Jimmy Carter Hammer award Habitat for Humanity, 1988, Merit award for women Internat. Tennis Hall of Fame, 1988, Svc. Bowl, U.S. Tennis Assn., 1991, Take the Lead award Girl Scouts of Greater Phila., 1992. Mem. U.S. Tennis Assn. Middle States (treas. 1986-89, Mangan award 1990, Coren award 1973), N.Am. Nature Photographers Assn. (charter mem.), Rocky Mountain Book Pubs. Assn., Mountain and Plains Booksellers Assn., Summit County C. of C., Nikon Profl. Svcs. Avocations: golf, tennis, hiking. Office: Prism Light Press PO Box 766 Bryn Mawr PA 19010-0766

BECK, CRAFTON, music director; b. Memphis, Tenn., Dec. 18, 1956. PhD in conducting, Cincinnati Col. Conserv., 1987. Music dir. Boca Pops, Boca Raton, Fla., 1996—. Office: Boca Pops 100 NE 1st Ave Boca Raton FL 33432-3904*

BECK, CURT WERNER, chemist, educator; b. Halle/Saale, Germany, Sept. 10, 1927; came to U.S., 1950, naturalized, 1955; s. Curt Paul and Clara (Fischer) B.; m. Lily Yallourakis, Feb. 10, 1953; children—Curt Peter, Christopher Paul. Student. U. Munich, 1946-48; B.S., Tufts U., 1951; Ph.D., Mass. Inst. Tech., 1955. Instr. Franklin Tech. Inst., Boston, 1955-56; asst. prof. Roberts Coll., Istanbul, Turkey, 1956-57; lectr. Vassar Coll., Poughkeepsie, N.Y., 1957-59; asst. prof. Vassar Coll., 1959-62, asso. prof., 1962-66, prof. chemistry, 1966-93, Matthew Vassar Jr. prof., 1970-93, rsch. prof., 1993—. Co-editor Art and Archaeology Tech. Abstracts, 1966—; sect. editor Chem. Abstracts, 1967-95; editor: Archaeological Chemistry, 1974; mem. editl. bd. Jour. Field Archaeology, 1975-93, Jour. Archaeol. Sci., 1979-87. Mem. Zoning Bd. Appeals, La Grange, N.Y., 1965-91, chmn., 1974-91; mem. Dutchess County council Boy Scouts Am., 1965-67, Candidate supr., La Grange, 1967. Recipient Research award Mid-Hudson sect. Am. Chem. Soc., 1965. Fellow Royal Soc. Arts, Internat. Inst. for Conservation Historic and Artistic Works (London); mem. Am. Chem. Soc. (past sect. chmn.), Royal Soc. Chemistry (London), Gesellschaft Deutscher Chemiker, Archeol. Inst. Am., Internat. Union Prehistoric and Protohistoric Scis. (chmn. com. study of amber, mem. permanent coun., mem. exec. com.), Assn. for Field Archaeology, Sigma Xi. E-mail: beck@vassar.edu. Home: La Grange 149 Skidmore Rd Pleasant Valley NY 12569 Office: Vassar Coll Poughkeepsie NY 12604

BECK, DAVID EDWARD, surgeon; b. Geneva, Ill., May 1, 1953; s. George R. and Gloria M. (Zesch) B.; m. Sharon Mieir, Aug. 30, 1983; children: Allison, Lauren, John. BS, USAF Acad., 1975; MD, U. Miami, Fla., 1979; postgrad., USAF Aerospace Medicine Primary Course, Brooks AFB, Tex., 1978, Combat Casualty Care Course, Ft. Sam Houston, Tex., 1980, Hyperbaric Oxygen CourseB, Brooks AFB, 1982, ATLS Instr. Course, Ft. Sam Houston, 1986, Squadon Officers Sch., 1987-88, Mgmt. for Chief of Hosp. Svcs., Sheppard AFB, Tex., 1988, Sch. Pub. Health, Harvard U., 1990. Diplomate Am. Bd. Colon and Rectal Surgery. Lt. Col. USAF, 1975-93; resident in gen. surgery Wilford Hall USAF Med. Ctr., Lackland AFB, Tex., 1979-84, chief colorectal surgery, 1986-92; staff surgeon, chief colorectal surgery svc. Wilford Hall USAF Med. Ctr., Lackland AFB, 1986-92, asst. chmn. dept. gen. surgery, 1988, chmn. dept. gen. surgery, residency program dir., 1988-92; staff gen. surgeon Patrick AFB (Fla.) Hosp., 1984-85; fellow in colorectal surgery Cleve. Clinic Found., 1985-86; residency program dir. gen. surgery joint Mil. Med. Command, San Antonio, 1989-91; clin. assoc. prof. surgery U. Tex. Health Sci. Ctr., San Antonio, 1990-92, F. Edward Herbert Sch. Medicine, U. Health Scis., Bethesda, Md., 1992—; chief surgery 870 USAF Contingency Hosp., RAF Little Rissington, U.K., 1993; staff colorectal surgeon Ochsner Clinic, New Orleans, 1993—, chmn. dept. colon and rectal surgery, 1994—; cons. USAF Surgeon Gen., Washington, 1986-92. Author chpts. to books; co-editor (textbooks); (with David R. Welling) Patient Care in Colorectal Surgery, 1991, (with Steven D. Wexner) Fundamentals of Anorectal Surgery, 1992, 2nd edit., 1998, (with T.C. Hicks, F.E. Opelka, A.E., Timmcke) Complications of Colon and Rectal Surgery, 1996; editor: Handbook of Colorectal Surgery, 1997; mem. editl. bd. Current Surgery, 1990—; reviewer Diseases of the Colon and Rectum, 1990—, mem. editl. bd., 1992—, So. Me. Jour., 1988-92; mem. editl. bd. Perspectives in Colon and Rectal Surgery, 1997—; contbr. articles to profl. jours. Decorated Air Force Achievement medal with oak leaf cluster, Air Force Meritorious Svc. medal with oak leaf cluster. Fellow ACS; mem. AMA, Am. Soc. Colon and Rectal Surgeons (mem. socioecon./legis. com. 1991-94, pub. rels. com. 1993—, chmn. 1996—, Outstanding Young Investigator award, 1992), Assn. Mil. Surgeons U.S., La. State Med. Soc., Soc. Air Force Clin. Surgeons (treas. 1989-90, v.p. 1990-92, pres. 1992-93, Excalibur award 1992), Soc. Surgery of Alimentary Tract, So. Med. Assn. (mem. colon and rectal sect., sec. 1988-91, v.p. 1990-91, pres. 1991-92), Soc. Med. Cons. to Armed forces, St. Tamminy Parish Med. Soc., Tex. Soc. Colon and Rectal Surgeons (sec. 1991-93), Air force Assn., USAF Acad. Assn. Grads. Avocations: fishing, wood working, gardening. Home: 127 Deloaks Rd Madisonville LA 70447-9597 Office: Oschner Clin 1514 Jefferson Hwy New Orleans LA 70121-2429

BECK, DAVID PAUL, biochemist; b. Wilmington, Del., Aug. 3, 1944; s. David Franklin and Mary Jane (Lazar) B.; m. Jeanne Elaine Crawford, Nov. 19, 1966; children: Jennifer Jeanne, David Andrew. AB, Princeton U., 1966; PhD, Johns Hopkins U., 1971. Fellow Harvard U., Cambridge, Mass., 1971-74; staff scientist Md. Psychiat. Rsch. Ctr., Balt., 1974-77; health scientist, adminstr. NIH, Bethesda, Md., 1977-84; assoc. dir., sec. bd. dirs. Pub. Health Rsch. Inst., N.Y.C., 1984-91; pres. Coriell Inst. Med. Rsch., Camden, N.J., 1991—, sec. bd. trustees, 1991—; bd. dirs. CorCell, Inc., N.J. Tech. Coun. Contbr. articles to profl. jours. Active Baltimore County Bd. Recreation and Pks., 1977-84; bd. dirs. Hoff-Barthelson Music Sch., Scarsdale, N.Y., 1989-91, West Jersey Chamber Music Soc., Moorestown, N.J., 1992—. Mem. Assn. Ind. Rsch. Insts. (v.p. 1989-92, pres.-elect 1993-95, pres. 1995-97, exec. v.p. 1997-99), N.J. Assn. Biomed. Rsch. (bd. dirs. 1997—), N.J. Technology Coun. (bd. dirs. 1996—). Office: Coriell Inst Med Rsch 401 Haddon Ave Ste 102 Camden NJ 08103-1559

BECK, DENNIS L., magistrate judge; b. Belen, N.Mex., Dec. 7, 1947; m. Christine T. Beck, Mar. 2, 1968. BA, Coll. William & Mary, 1969, JD, 1972. Bar: Calif. 1972, U.S. Dist. Ct. (ea. dist.) Calif. 1978, U.S. Ct. Appeals (9th cir.) Calif. 1978. Asst. dist. atty. Fresno (Calif.) County, 1972-78, 79-83, 1987-90; assoc. Crossland Crossland Caswell & Bell, Fresno, 1978-79; judge Kings County Superior Ct., Hanford, Calif., 1983-85; assoc. Thomas, Snell, et al., Fresno, 1985-87; magistrate judge U.S. Dist. Ct. (ea. dist.) Calif., Fresno, 1990—. Office: US Dist Ct 1130 O St Rm 3489 Fresno CA 93721-2201

BECK, EARL RAY, historian, educator; b. Junction City, Ohio, Sept. 8, 1916; s. Ernest Ray and Mary Frances (Helser) B.; m. Marjorie Culbertson, Nov. 7, 1944 (dec. Feb. 1995); children: Ann, Mary Sue. A.B., Capital U., 1937; M.A., Ohio State U., 1939, Ph.D., 1942. Instr. Capital U., 1942-43, Ohio State U., 1946-49; asst. prof. Fla. State U., Tallahassee, 1949-52; assoc. prof. Fla. State U., 1952-60, prof. history, 1960-89, chmn. dept. history, 1967-72, chmn. grad. studies, 1982-87; prof. emeritus, 1989—; summer vis. prof. La. State U., 1955, Tulane U., 1959, Duke U., 1966. Author: Verdict on Schacht, 1956, The Death of the Prussian Republic, 1959, Contemporary Civilization I, 1959, On Teaching History in Colleges and Universities, 1966, Germany Rediscovers America, 1968, A Time of Triumph and of Sorrow: Spanish Politics During the Reign of Alfonso XII, 1874-1885, 1979, Under the Bombs: the German Home Front, 1942-1945, 1986, 89, European Homefronts, 1939-45, 1993, 98. Served with AUS, 1946-49. Mem. So. Hist. Assn. (chmn. European history sect. 1983-84), German Studies Assn. Presbyterian. Home: 2514 Killearney Way Tallahassee FL 32308-3163

BECK, EDWARD WILLIAM, lawyer; b. Atchison, Kans., Aug. 19, 1944; s. Russell Niles and Lucille Mae (Leighton) B.; m. Marshia Ablon, June 24, 1966; children: Michael Adam, David Gordon, Stephen Jared. BA cum laude, Yale U., 1967; JD cum laude, Harvard U., 1972. Bar: Calif. 1972. Assoc. firm Pillsbury, Madison & Sutro, San Francisco, 1972-77; gen. counsel Pacific Lumber Co., San Francisco, 1977-86; sec. Pacific Lumber Co., 1978-86, v.p., 1980-86, dir., 1985-86; v.p., gen. counsel, sec. Shaklee Corp., San Francisco, 1986-87, sr. v.p., gen. counsel, sec., 1987—; bd. dirs. Shaklee Corp., 1989—. Trustee, mem. exec. com. San Francisco Conservatory Music, 1988—, co-chmn. acad. affairs com., 1989-91, chmn. presdl. search com., 1991, chair trustees and offices com., 1993-96, exec. vice chair, 1994—, chair conservatory 2006 com., 1996—; mem. law com. United Way of Bay Area Campaign, 1991—, chmn., 1992. Mem. ABA, Calif. Bar Assn., San Francisco Bar Assn. (bd. dirs. 1991-94, nominating com. 1993), Bay Area Gen. Counsels Group (chmn. 1991), San Francisco C. of C. (leadership coun. 1987—, gen. coun., bd. dirs., exec. com. 1993-96), San Francisco Yale Alumni Assn. (schs. com.). Office: Shaklee Corp 444 Market St Ste 3600 San Francisco CA 94111-5378

BECK, ELAINE KUSHNER, elementary and secondary school educator; b. Phila., May 31, 1942; d. Joseph and Emma Kushner; m. Stuart Edwin Beck, June 20, 1964; children: Adam, Barry, Caroline. BS, Drexel U., 1963; Masters equivalent, Temple U., Pa. State U., West Chester U., 1984. Cert. tchr., Pa. Tchr. grades 4, 5, 6 Upper Darby (Pa.) Sch. Dist., 1963-64; tchr. high sch. Francis Hammond-Alexandria (Va.) Sch. Dist., 1964-65; tchr. adult edn. YMCA, Alexandria, 1966-67; tchr. mid. sch. Haverford Sch. Dist., Havertown, Pa., 1980—; bus. owner Lady Elaine Creations, Havertown, 1976-80. Contbg. editor: Passoverama, 1979-80; author (teaching program) The Equipment Scavenger Hunt, 1989. Mem. strategic plan com. Haverford Sch. Dist., Havertown, 1995-96; organizer sr. citizen dances, Havertown, 1992, 93, 94; pres., v.p., mem. adv. bds. sisterhood Temple Beth Hillel/Beth El, 1980-81. Recipient Dominick Recchiuti Humanitarian award, 1992; named one of Top 5 Home Econs. Tchrs. in U.S., Home Baking Assn., 1994; Ptnr. in Edn. grantee Sun Oil Co., 1989. Mem. NEA, Pa. Edn. Assn., Nat. Audubon Soc., Nature Conservancy, World Wildlife Fund, Sierra Club, Key and Triangle, Omicron Nu, Phi Sigma Sigma (honored Drexel U. chpt. 1998). Avocations: exotic bird training, wild bird watching, sailing, environmentalism, biking. Home: 624 Greythorne Rd Wynnewood PA 19096-2509 Office: Haverford Sch Dist 1701 Darby Rd Havertown PA 19083-3738

BECK, EVA-CAROL, musician; b. San Antonio, Oct. 9, 1938; d. Carl Addison, Jr. and Seldon (Sandlin) B.; m. Jay Kenneth Friedman, 1962 (div. 1974); children: Erika Ann, David Jay. MusB magna cum laude, U. Houston, 1960; postgrad., Yale U., 1960-61; MusM, Ind. U., 1964. Prin. viola Fla. Symphony, Orlando, 1961; viola sect. Lyric Opera, Chgo., 1964-66, 71—, acting asst. viola, 1982; viola sect. Grant Park Symphony, Chgo., 1970—, acting asst. prin. viola, 1981; asst. prin. Symphony II, Chgo., 1989—; del. Internat. Conf. Symphony Opera Musicians, 1984-97; mem. examining bd. Chgo. Fedn. Musicians, 1986-88; negotiator mems. com. Lyric Opera Orchestra, 1986-88, Grant Park Symphony, 1993. Mem. Mortarboard, Phi Kappa Phi. Democrat. Avocations: fitness, cooking. Home: 831 Hamlin Street Evanston IL 60201

BECK, GEORGE PRESTON, anesthesiologist, educator; b. Wichita Falls, Tex., Oct. 21, 1930; s. George P. and Amanda (Wilbanks) B.; m. Constance Carolyn Krog, Dec. 22, 1953; children: Carla Elizabeth, George P., Howard W. BS, Midwestern U., 1951; MD, U. Tex., 1955. Diplomate Am. Bd. Anesthesiology. Intern John Sealy Hosp., 1955-56; resident anesthesiology Parkland Meml. Hosp., Dallas, 1959-62, vis. staff, 1964—; practice medicine specializing in anesthesiology, Lubbock, Tex., 1964—; chief staff Meth. Hosp., Lubbock, 1967-68; asst. prof. anesthesiology Southwestern Med. Sch., Dallas, 1962-64, asst. clin. prof., 1964-71, prof. 1996—, assoc. clin. prof. anesthesiology U. Tex. Med. Br. at Galveston, 1971— assoc clin prof., 1980-95, clin prof. 1996—; pres. Gt. Plain Ballistics Corp., 1967—; clin. prof. Tex. Tech. U. Sch. Medicine, 1986—, pres. found. bd., 1972-73. Author: The Ideal Anesthesiologist, 1960, Mnemonics as an Aid to the Anesthesiologist, 1961, Anterior Approach to Sciatic Nerve Block, 1962; inventor Beck Airway Airflow Monitor. Pres. Luth. Ch. council, pres. congregation, 1965-66. With USAF, 1956-59. Fellow Am. Coll. Anesthesiologists; mem. Am. Soc. Anesthesiologists, Tex. Soc. Anesthesiologists (pres. 1974) Tex. Med. Soc., Lubbock County Med. Soc., Lubbock Surg. Soc. (pres. 1969); Named Asabel Smith disting. Alumnus award, 1994. Home: 4601 18th St Lubbock TX 79416-5713 Office: PO Box 16385 Lubbock TX 79490-6385

BECK, GEORGE WILLIAM, retired industrial engineer; b. Dayton, Ohio, Aug. 31, 1921; s. George A. and Florence I. (Hoskett) B.; m. Elizabeth A. Thatcher, Apr. 14, 1945 (died Nov. 8, 1992); children: Bruce, Christine, William. B.Indsl. Engring., Gen. Motors Inst., 1946. Registered profl. engr., Ohio. Sales rep. Inland Mfg. div. Gen. Motors Corp., Dayton, 1946-53; sr. project engr. Inland Mfg. div. Gen. Motors Corp., 1953-56, staff engr., 1956, asst. chief engr., 1956-62, chief engr., 1962-80, dir. engring., 1980-85; ret., 1985. Trustee Met. YMCA, 1964-71; chmn. bd. mgmt. Kettering YMCA, 1966-70; mem. Centerville City Sch. Dist. bd. edn., 1968-74, v.p., 1973-74. Served to lt. (j.g.) USNR, 1943-45. Mem. Soc. Automotive Engrs., Dayton C. of C., Aircraft Owners and Pilots Assn. (lic. pilot). Presbyterian. Clubs: MVMA, Sycamore Creek Country, Mission Valley Country. Inventor automotive products; holder of 10 patents in field. Home: 2120 Timucua Trl Nokomis FL 34275-5306

BECK, GORDON EUGENE, art history educator, consultant; b. Goshen, Ind., Mar. 23, 1929; s. Ralph Lea and Lydia Elizabeth (Greenlee) B.; m. Elizabeth Alice Arnholt, Mar. 22, 1951; children: Anne Elizabeth, Susan Elizabeth, Stephen Lea, John Lyons. BA, Bowling Green State U., 1951; MA, Western Res. U., 1952; PhD, U. Ill., 1964; postdoctoral student, Cini Found., Venice, Italy, 1979. Founder Studio 16, Washington, 1953-54; asst. instr. U. Ill., Urbana, 1954-56; instr. Bowling Green (Ohio) State U., 1956-57; instr., dir. univ. theatre U. Kans., Lawrence, 1957-65; asst. prof., dir. univ. theatre Cornell U., Ithaca, N.Y., 1965-71; prof. art history Evergreen State Coll., Olympia, Wash., 1971-94, prof. emeritus art history and archaeology, 1994—; cons. European travel, Euro-Files, Olympia; dir. U. Kans. Theatre, 1957-65, Cornell U. Cinema, 1965-70, Mus. and Monuments Program, Olympia, 1975—; vis. prof. cinema Am. U. Rome, 1973-74; del. Cannes Internat. Film Festival, 1996, 97, 98. Editor, Players Mag., 1961-67; contbr. articles to Theatre Ann., 1964-69, Ency. World Drama, 1969; producer feature film, Branches, 1970. Cpl. M.C., U.S. Army, 1952-54. Mem. Coll. Art Assn., Mediaeval Acad. Am., Am. Soc. Aesthetics, Am. Inst. Archaeology. Democrat. Home: 2406 18th Ave NW Olympia WA 98502-4119 Office: Evergreen State Coll 3602 Library Bldg Olympia WA 98505

BECK, IRENE CLARE, educational consultant, writer; b. N.Y.C., Dec. 18, 1944; d. James E. and Helen (Carroll) Clare; m. William J. Beck, Aug. 9, 1986; children: Daniel, James Chesire. BA, St. Mary's Coll., 1966; MA, Fairfield U., 1977; EdD, U. Rochester, 1982. Cert. tchr., N.Y. Tchr. Elem. Sch., N.Y.C., 1966-68, Montessori Acad. N.Y., Bklyn., 1968-73; faculty Housatonic Community Coll., Bridgeport, Conn., 1975-77, Nazareth Coll., Rochester, N.Y., 1977-83; faculty dir. Sheppard Pratt Nat. Ctr. Human Devel., Balt., 1983-91; exec. dir. William & Irene Beck Found., 1987—; cons. Headstart Programs, Rochester, 1980-83, Family Day Care Tng., Rochester, 1980-83; adj. faculty DePaul U. Women's Studies Program, 1999—; presenter workshops and seminars. Author: Expect Respect, Let Me Tell You (manuals), (No Hang Ups (telephone audiotape), 1987, In Tune With Teens (booklet), 1990; weekly news col. Parents and Teens, 1987-90; free-lance writer, 1986—; contbr. articles to profl. jours.; sr. editor What's Workikng for Girls in Illinois, 1996—. Mem. AAUW, Assn. Childhood Edn. Internat. Avocations: hiking, swimming, biking. Home: 424 W Armitage Ave Apt F Chicago IL 60614-4682

BECK, JERRY GUNTHER, development company executive, consultant; b. Danzig, Free City, (now) Poland, Apr. 10, 1926; came to U.S., 1939.; s. Fred and Margarete (Kamnitzer) B.; m. Ola Iwiansky, June 15, 1950 (dec. Aug. 1985); children: Annette, Sonia; m. Ruth H. Dorfman Schwartz, Aug. 15, 1986. B. Indsl. Engring., NYU, 1950; MS in Engring., Columbia U., 1951; JD, Wayne State U., 1958. Bar: Mich., 1958, U.S. Patent Office, 1960; registered profl. engr., Mich. Sr. engr. Ford Motor Co., Dearborn, Mich., 1951-90, patent atty., 1959-65, planning mgr., 1966-90; cons. Jerry G. Bech & Assocs., West Bloomfield, Mich., 1990—; gen. ptnr. EWS Golf Devel. Co., West Bloomfield, 1993—. Patentee in field. Pres. Condo Assn., West Bloomfield, 1988-91. With U.S. Army, 1945-46. Mem. ASME, Soc. Automotive Engrs. (auto. glazing com.). Home and Office: 5328 Fairway Ct West Bloomfield MI 48323-3420

BECK, JOHN CHRISTIAN, physician, educator; b. Audubon, Iowa, Jan. 4, 1924; s. Wilhelm and Marie (Brandt) B. MD, McGill U., 1947, MSc, 1951, DSc (hon.), 1994; PhD (hon.), Ben Gurion U. of the Negev. Diplomate Am. Bd. Internal Medicine (chmn., dir.). Intern Royal Victoria Hosp., Montreal, 1947-48; sr. asst. resident Royal Victoria Hosp., 1948-49; physician-in-chief, endocrinologist Royal Victoria Hosp., Montreal, 1964-74; chmn. dept. medicine, dir. Univ. Clinic McGill U., 1964-74; prof. medicine U. Calif., San Francisco, 1974-79; dir. Robert Wood Johnson Clin. Scholars Program, 1974-79; prof. geriat. medicine and gerontology UCLA, 1979—, dir. academic geriat. resource ctr., 1984-90; dir. long term car gerontology ctr. UCLA/U. So. Calif., 1980-85; dir. Calif. Geriatric Edn. Ctr., 1987-97, emeritus dir., 1993—; dir. multicampus program in geriat. medicine & gerontology UCLA, 1979-93; pres. Am. Bd. Med. Spltys.; vis. prof. numerous univs.; Simeone lectr. Brown U., 1977; John McCreary Meml. lectr. U. B.C., 1985; Bruce Hall Meml. lectr. Garvan Inst. Med. Rsch., U. N.S.W., Sydney, Australia, 1989—; Allen T. Bailey Meml. lectr. U. Sask., Can., 1989. Mem. editl. bd. Jour. Clin. Endocrinology and Metabolism, Current Topics in Exptl. Endocrinology, Psychiatry in Medicine, Health Policy and Edn., Jour. Am. Bd. Family Practice; cons. editor Roche Lab. Series on Geriatrics and Gerontology. Recipient Lifetime award Ben Gurion U. of Negev, Israel, 1985. Master ACP, fellow AAAS, Royal Coll. Physicians (Can., mem. coun., Duncan Graham award 1990), Royal Coll. Physicians (London), Royal Soc. Can., Inst. of Medicine, Internat. Soc. Endocrinology (sec.-gen.), Can. Soc. Clin. Investigation (pres.), Endocrine Soc. (v.p., chmn. postgrad. assembly), Am. Fedn. Clin. Rsch. (coun. East div.), Can. Med. Assn. (post-grad. edn. com.), Am. Diabetes Assn., Can. Diabetes Assn., McGill Osler Reporting Soc. (sec.), Montreal Physiol. Soc., Can. Physiol. Soc., Laurentian Hormone Conf. (bd. dirs.), Can. Assn. Profs. Medicine (Ronald V. Christie award 1987), Am. Clin. and Climatological Assn., Assn. Am. Med. Colls., Can. Med. Protective Assn., Internat. Soc. Neuroendocrinology, Soc. Exptl. Biology and Medicine (mem. editorial bd. jour.), Western Assn. Physicians, Am. Geriatrics Soc. (Milo F. Leavitt Meml. award 1988), Gerontol. Soc. Am. (mem. editorial bd. jour., Joseph T. Freeman award 1990), Am. Fedn. on Aging Rsch. (Irving S. Wright award 1991), Sigma Xi, Alpha Omega Alpha. Fax: 310-454-1944. E-mail: egebjcb@ucla.edu. Home: 1562 Casale Rd Pacific Palisades CA 90272-2714 Office: UCLA PO Box 951687 1562 Casale Rd Los Angeles CA 90095-1687

BECK, JOHN ROBERT, pathologist, information scientist; b. Cleve., Sept. 8, 1953; s. John Edward and Maralyn Janet (Smith) B.; m. Sharon Louise Dombkowski, Aug. 30, 1975; children: John Benjamin, Stefan Andrew, Meredith Louise. AB, Dartmouth Coll., 1974; MD, Johns Hopkins U., 1978. Diplomate Am. Bd. Pathology. Intern, then resident in pathology Dartmouth-Hitchcock Med. Ctr., Hanover, N.H., 1978-80, dir. bloodbank, 1984-89, dir. clin. pathology, 1987-89; fellow, clin. decision making New Eng. Med. Ctr., Boston, 1981; from asst. to assoc. prof. pathology Dartmouth Med. Sch., Hanover, 1982-89; prof., dir. biomed. info. communication ctr. Oreg. Health Scis. U., Portland, 1989-92; prof., v.p. info. tech. Baylor Coll. Medicine, Houston, 1992—; chmn. Health Outcome Techs., Inc., Portland, 1991-97; cons. Nat. Libr. Medicine, Bethesda, Md., 1988-92. Editor-in-chief Med. Decision Making, 1989-94. Recipient Rsch. Career Devel. award Nat. Libr. Medicine, 1986. Fellow Am. Coll. Med. Informatics, Am. Soc. Clin. Pathologists (coun. chmn. 1991-93), Coll. Am. Pathologists (com. vice-chair 1997—); mem. Soc. for Med. Decision Making (sec.-treas. 1985-87, v.p. 1987-88, pres. 1995-96), Acad. Clin. Lab. Physicians and Scientists (exec. councilor 1989-91, Young Investigator award 1981), Integrated Advanced Info. Mgmt. Sys. (chmn. 1994-96), AAMC Group on Info. Resources (exec. com. 1997—). Republican. Avocations: golf, bridge, trumpet. Office: Baylor Coll of Medicine Info Tech 1 Baylor Plz Houston TX 77030-3411

BECK, KAREN PORTSCHE, elementary education educator; b. Salt Lake City, June 30, 1950; d. Vernon Willis and Gretchen Ann (Roeser) Portsche; m. James Kenneth Vogler, Aug. 2, 1968 (div. May 1991); children: Philip Justin Vogler, Shaun Wade Vogler; m. Harvey William Beck, Mar. 18, 1995. BA, Boise (Idaho) State U., 1979, MA, 1994. Cert. tchr., Idaho. Tchr. Hillcrest Elem. Sch., Boise, 1979-84; tchr. Hawthorne Elem. Sch., Boise, 1984-98, computer coord., 1994-97; tchr. Riverside Elem. Sch., Boise, 1998—. Author: (tchrs. manual) Education Strategies FAS and FAE Students, 1994. Avocations: drawing, cross stitch, surfing the Internet, gardening.

BECK, LOIS GRANT, anthropologist, educator; b. Bogota, Colombia, Nov. 5, 1944; d. Martin Lawrence and Dorothy (Sweet) Grant; m. Henry Huang; 1 dau., Julia. BA, Portland State U., 1967; MA, U. Chgo., 1969, PhD, 1977. Asst. prof. Amherst (Mass.) Coll., 1973-76, Univ. Utah, Salt Lake City, 1976-80; from asst. to assoc. prof. Washington U., St. Louis, 1980-92, prof., 1992—. Author: Qashqa'i of Iran, 1986, Nomad, 1991; co-editor Women in the Muslim World, 1978. Grantee Social Scis. Rsch. Coun., 1990, NEH, 1990-92, 98, Am. Philos. Soc., 1998. Mem. Middle East Studies Assn. (bd. dirs. 1981-84), Soc. Iranian Studies (exec. sec. 1979-82, edit. bd. 1982-91, coun. mem. 1996-98). Office: Washington U Dept Anthropology 1 Brookings Dr Dept Saint Louis MO 63130-4899

BECK, LOUIS S., hotel executive. Pres., CEO Beck Summit Hotel Mgmt. Group, Boca Raton, Fla. Office: Beck Summit Hotel Mgmt Group 2300 Corporate Blvd NW Ste 232 Boca Raton FL 33431-7359*

BECK, LUKE FERRELL WILSON, insurance specialist; b. Granbury, Tex., Feb. 2, 1948; s. Don Elder and Georgia Ferrell (Wilson) B.; m. Susan Villars, Nov. 14, 1970 (div. Feb. 1974). BA in Psychology, U. Tex., 1970. CPCU. Claims rep. Employers Ins. Tex., Beaumont, 1975-86; home office supr. Employers Ins. Tex., Dallas, 1986-89; litigation specialist CNA Ins. Co., Dallas, 1989-93, litigation supv., 1993—. 1st lt. U.S. Army, 1971-75. Mem. Soc. of CPCU. Presbyterian. Avocations: cooking, history. Home: 2108 Barton Dr Arlington TX 76010-4750 Office: CNA Ins PO Box 219046 Dallas TX 75221-9046

BECK, MARILYN MOHR, columnist; b. Chgo., Dec. 17, 1928; d. Max and Rose (Lieberman) Mohr; m. Roger Beck, Jan. 8, 1949 (div. 1974); children: Mark Elliott, Andrea; m. Arthur Levine, Oct. 12, 1980. AA, U. So. Calif., 1950. Free-lance writer nat. mags. and newspapers Hollywood, Calif., 1959-63; Hollywood columnist Valley Times and Citizen News, Hollywood, 1963-65; West Coast editor Sterling Mags., Hollywood, 1963-74; free-lance entertainment writer L.A. Times, 1965-67; Hollywood columnist Bell-McClure Syndicate, 1967-72; chief Bell-McClure Syndicate (West Coast bur.), 1967-72; Hollywood columnist NANA Syndicate, 1967-72; syndicated Hollywood columnist N.Y. Times Spl. Features, 1972-78, N.Y. Times Spl. Features (United Feature Syndicate), 1978-80, United Press abroad, 1978-80, Internat. Editors News and Features, Chgo. Tribune/N.Y. Daily News Syndicate, 1980-97; Grapevine columnist TV Guide, 1989-92; creators syndicate, 1997—. Creator, host Marilyn Beck's Hollywood Outtakes spls. NBC, 1977, 78; host Marilyn Beck's Hollywood Hotline, Sta. KFI, L.A., 1975-77; Hollywood reporter Eyewitness News, Sta. KABC-TV, L.A., 1981, (TV program) PM Mag., 1983-88; on-air corr. E! TV, 1993—, CompuServe Entertainment Authority, 1994-96, eDrive Internet Authority, 1996-97, e!online Internet Hollywood Authority, 1997—; author: (non-fiction) Marilyn Beck's Hollywood, 1973, (novel) Only Make Believe, 1988; co-author: Unfinished Lives, What If...?, 1996. Recipient Citation of Merit L.A. City Coun., 1973, Press award Pub. Guild Am., 1974, Bronze Halo award So. Calif. Motion Picture Coun., 1982. Office: PO Box 11079 Beverly Hills CA 90213-4579 *Being the best isn't everything; it's the only thing. "Life is too short to be little" (Disraeli).*

BECK, MARTHA ANN, art curator, director. BA in English Lit., Vassar Coll., 1960; postgrad., NYU, 1963-67. Editor, writer, rschr. The Frick Collection, 1962-64; curatorial asst. drawings dept. The Mus. Modern Art, 1968-75; founder, dir. The Drawing Ctr., 1975-90, dir. emeritus, 1990—; founder, dir. The Ctr. for Internat. Exhbns., 1992—; served on numerous juries and panels including Nat. Endowment for the Arts, SUNY Thayer Family Fellowships, The Westchester Coun. on the Arts and the Jerome Found. Fellowships; lectr. in field. Recipient NYU scholarship, 1964-65. Home: 9 Gramercy Park S New York NY 10003-1742

BECK, MARY VIRGINIA, lawyer, public official; b. Ford City, Pa., Feb. 29, 1908; BA, U. Pitts., 1929, LLB, 1932, JD, 1968. Bar: Mich. 1944. Elected to Common Coun. City of Detroit, 1950-70; bd. suprs. County of Wayne, Mich., 1950-69; exec. dir. Ukrainian Info. Bur., Detroit; ret., 1995. Chmn. Policemen & Retirement Fund Commn., Detroit, 1958-62; chmn. Wayne County Port Commn., 1962-68; mem. Gov.s Commn. on Status of Women, 1962, Gov.'s Commn. on Econ. Devel., 1962, World Fedn. Ukrainian Women (hon.), Ukrainian Nat. League of Women Am. (hon.). Recipient Cert. of Merit Fashion Group of Detroit, 1955; Ruth Houston Whipple award Plymouth Bus. and Profl. Woman's Club, 1956; Sport Guild award Sprots Guild Detroit, 1956; award Detroit Dental Soc., 1957; citation Detroit Cancer Fighters, 1959; Ukrainian Community Service award Ukrainians of the Free World, 1960; Ukrainian of Yr. award Ukrainian Grad. Club of Detroit and Windsor, 1963; award Amvets of World War II, 1967; Woman of the Yr. award Soroptimist Club, 1968, inducted into Detroit's Bowling Hall of Fame, 1974, inducted into Mich.'s Women Hall of Fame, 1992, others. Mem. Mich. State Bar, Detroit Bar Assn., Women Lawyers Assn. Mich., Nat. Assn. Women Lawyers, Detroit Bus. Womans Club, Nat. Fedn. Profl. and Bus. Women, Internat. Platform Assn., World Fedn. Ukranian Women's Orgns. (hon.), Ukranian Nat. Women's League Am. (hon.).

BECK, MORRIS, allergist; b. Miami, Fla., Oct. 12, 1927; s. Max and Anna (Luks) B.; m. Hollis Schwartz, Aug. 6, 1960; children: Gayle Beck Finan, Anne Lin. BA, UCLA, 1949; MD, U. Zurich, Switzerland, 1957. Diplomate Am. Bd. Allergy and Immunology, Am. Bd. Pediatrics. Intern Queens Hosp. Ctr., 1958, resident in pediatrics, 1959-60; preceptor in allergy U. Miami (Fla.) Med. Sch., 1961-77; pvt. practice pediatrician Miami, 1961-77, pvt. practice allergist, 1978—; chief dept. allergy Miami Children's Hosp., 1986—, Miami VA Hosp., 1994—; clin. prof. pediatrics Nova U. Southeastern Med. Sch., 1998—; clin. asst. prof. U. Miami Med. Sch. With U.S. Army, 1950-52. Fellow Am. Coll. Allergy & Immunology, Am. Acad. Pediatrics, Am. Assn. Cert. Allergists; mem. Am. Acad. Allergy & Immunology, Am. Coll. Chest Physicians. Republican. Jewish. Avocations: photography, fishing, travel. Office: Ste C 340 7800 SW 87th Ave # C-340 Miami FL 33173-3570

BECK, PAUL ALLEN, political science educator; b. Logansport, Ind., Mar. 15, 1944; s. Frank Paul and Mary Elizabeth (Flanegin) B.; m. Maria Teresa Marcano, June 10, 1967; children: Daniel Lee, David Andrew. A.B., Ind. U., 1966; M.A., U. Mich., 1968, Ph.D., 1971. Asst. prof. U. Pitts., 1970-75, assoc. prof., 1976-79; prof. Fla. State U., Tallahassee, 1979-87, chmn. dept., 1981-87; prof. Ohio State U., Columbus, 1987—, chmn. dept., 1991—. Co-author: Political Socialization Across the Generations, 1975, Individual Energy Conservation Behaviors, 1980, Electoral Change in Advanced Industrial Democracies, 1984, Party Politics in America, 8th edit., 1997. Chmn. council Inter-Univ. Consortium for Polit. and Social Research, 1982-83, mem., 1980-83; mem. NSF polit. sci. panel, 1988-89. Mem. Am. Polit. Sci. Assn. (exec. coun. 1981-82, 93-94, book rev. editor 1976-79, program chair 1994), Midwest Polit. Sci. Assn. (exec. coun. 1987-90, mem. editl. bd. 1988-90, program chair 1991, v.p. 1996-98), So. Polit. Sci. Assn. (mem. editl. bd. 1982-87). Democrat. Home: 7003 Perry Dr Columbus OH 43085-2815 Office: Ohio State U Dept Polit Sci Columbus OH 43210-1373

BECK, PETER MICHAEL, economics researcher; b. June 23, 1967. BA, U. Calif., Berkeley, 1989; PhD, U. Calif., San Diego, 1999. Dir. rsch. and acad. affairs Korea Econ. Inst. Am., Washington, 1997—. E-mail: pmb@keia.com. Office: 1101 Vermont Ave NW Ste 401 Washington DC 20005

BECK, PHILIP S., lawyer; b. Chgo., Apr. 30, 1951. BA, U. Wis., 1973; JD, Boston U., 1976. Bar: Ill. 1977. Clerk U.S. Ct. Appeals D.C. cir., 1976-77; ptnr. Bartlit Beck Herman Palenchar & Scott, Chgo. Office: Bartlit Beck Herman et al 54 W Hubbard St Chicago IL 60610-4645*

BECK, ROBERT ALFRED, hotel administration educator; b. Boston, Nov. 1, 1920; s. Alfred and Laura Martha (Reissman) B.; m. Mary Kathryn Murray, Nov. 5, 1944; children: Susan Jane, Janice Barbara, Robin Marie. BS, Cornell U., 1942, MS in Edn., 1952, PhD, 1954. Food technologist, pers. mgr. Quincy Market Co., Boston, 1945-50; mem. faculty Sch. Hotel Adminstrn., Cornell U., 1954-84, prof., 1960-84, dean, 1961-81; dir. Internat. Inst. Hotel Mgmt., Cergy-Pontoise, France, 1981-84; prof., disting. scholar in residence Fla. Internat. U., 1984—; vis. lectr. USAF in PTO and ETO, U.S. Army in Europe, also numerous nat. and fgn. sems. and confs.; bd. dirs. Carrolls Devel. Corp., Consulan AG, Switzerland; mgmt. cons. U.S. Dept. Commerce, USAF, U.S. Army, USN, Govt. of Jamaica, Govt. of Barbados, Govt. of Bahama Is., Nat. Restaurant Assn., others. Contbr. articles to trade publs. Trustee, v.p. Ednl. Inst. of Am. Hotel and Motel Assn.; v.p. Nat. Inst. Foodservice Industry; trustee Caribbean Hotel Tng. Inst., Ithaca (N.Y.) Coll.; mem. bd. advisors Nova U., Ft. Lauderdale, Fla.; bd. dirs. Culinary Inst. Am., Internat. Hotel and Tourism Tng. Inst., Basel, Switzerland. 1st lt. F.A., AUS, 1942-45, ETO. Decorated Purple Heart. Mem. AAUP, Phi Kappa Phi, Phi Delta Kappa. Home: 1255 N Gulfstream Ave Apt 805 Sarasota FL 34236-8929

BECK, ROBERT BERYL, real estate executive; b. Dalton, Ga., Feb. 25, 1935; s. Carson W. and Gladys (Gray) B.; m. Martha Lucinda Cone, June 14, 1957; children: Perkie Cone Beck Cannon, Robert B. Jr., Carson W. Student, Vanderbilt U., 1953-57; LLB, JD, Nashville Sch. Law, 1964. Salesman Southeastern Inc., Nashville, 1957-64; purchasing agt. Nashville Bd. Edn., 1965-66; pres. Beck & Beck Realty, Nashville, 1967—; pres. Beck & Beck Ins. Co., Nashville, 1967-78, v.p., 1978—; pres. Tri-County Builders, Nashville, 1974—. Editor Grace Bapt. Monthly, 1985, real estate newsletter, 1986-87. Mem. Nashville Bd. Realtors, Profl. Ins. Assn. Democrat. Lodge: Masons. Avocations: fishing, hiking, cycling. Home: 3500 Brick Church Pike Nashville TN 37207-2002 Office: Beck & Beck 4205 Gallatin Rd Nashville TN 37216-2111

BECK, ROBERT EDWARD, computer scientist, educator; b. Denver, June 7, 1941; s. Arthur Walter and Caroline Adelheid (Petrie) B.; m. Barbara Ruth Pennell, Aug. 21, 1965; children: Philip Arthur, Christopher William, Jennifer Grove. BS in Math., Harvey Mudd Coll., Claremont, Calif., 1963; PhD in Math., U. Pa., 1969. Instr. Villanova (Pa.) U., 1966-69, asst. prof., 1969-74, assoc. prof., 1974-78, prof. computer sci., 1978—, dept. chair, 1992—; team chair Computing Sci. Accreditation Bd., 1986—. Author: Elementary Linear Programming, 2d edit., 1995; editor: Computers in Nonassociative Rings and Algebras, 1978. Fulbright Exchange fellow, 1981-82. Mem. AAUP, ACM (chair computer sci. conf. 1995, 96, chair preparing future faculty program 1998—), Am. Math. Soc., Sigma Xi. Office: Villanova U Dept Computing Sci Villanova PA 19085

BECK, ROBERT LEE, bookstore owner; b. Chgo., Apr. 9, 1921; s. Harvey Beck and Edith (Blitch) Eichelberg; m. Anna Nadine Wood, May 20, 1947; children: Linda Olson, Philip S. Grad. high sch., Chgo. Mgr. Faulkner's Ednl. Books, Chgo., 1945-55; owner Beck's Book Stores, Chgo., 1955—. Served with U.S. Coast Guard. Mem. Nat. Assn. Coll. Stores. Avocation: Cubs baseball fan. Office: Beck's Book Stores Inc 4520 N Broadway St Chicago IL 60640-5693

BECK, ROBERT N., nuclear medicine educator; b. San Angelo, Tex., Mar. 26, 1928; married, 1958. AB, U. Chgo., 1954, BS, 1955. Chief scientist Argonne Cancer Rsch. Hosp., 1957-67, assoc. prof., 1967-76; prof. radiological sci. U. Chgo., 1976; dir. Franklin McLean Inst., 1977-94, dir. Ctr. Imaging Sci., 1986-98; prof. emeritus U. Chgo., 1998—; cons. Internat. Atomic Energy Agency, 1966-68; mem. Internat. Com. on Radiation Units, 1968—, Nat. Coun. on Radiation, Protection & Measurements, 1970—. Recipient Aebersold award FDR, 1991. Mem. IEEE (Med. Imaging Sci. award 1996), Soc. Nuclear Med., Am. Assn. Physicists in Medicine, Soc. Magnetic Resonance. Achievements include research in development of a theory of the process by which images can be formed of the distribution of radioactive material in a patient in order to diagnose his disease. Office: U Chgo (MC 2026) Franklin McLean Meml Rsch Inst 5841 S Maryland Ave Chicago IL 60637-1463

BECK, ROBERT RAYMOND, priest; b. Waterloo, Iowa, Aug. 28, 1940; s. Paul Clayton and Mildred Anne (Klein) B. BA, Loras Coll., Dubuque, Iowa, 1962; ThM, Aquinas Inst. Theology, Dubuque, 1965; cert. of study, Ecole Biblique, Jerusalem, 1978; DMin, Cath. U., 1983. Assoc. pastor St. Columbkille Parish, Dubuque, 1966-71; with campus ministry U. No. Iowa, Cedar Falls, 1971-73; instr. of Scripture Aquinas Inst. Theology, 1973-81; prof. religious studies Loras Coll., 1981—, chair dept. religious studies, 1992—; co-founder, bd. dirs. Cath. Worker, Dubuque, 1976-94; co-founder, pastor Anawim Faith Community, Dubuque, 1981—; founder, dir. Ray Herman Peace Ctr., Dubuque, 1983-86. Author: Nonviolent Story: Narrative Conflict Resolution in the Gospel of Mark, 1996; composer: (rock opera) Mark, A Rock Gospel, 1975, 87, Our Father, 1968; columnist: Sunday's Word, 1982-87; editor: Loras Faculty Review, 1989—; contbr. articles to profl. jours. Mem. Soc. Bibl. Lit., Am. Acad. Religion, Cath. Theol. Soc. Am. Democrat. Home: 1450 Alta Vista St Dubuque IA 52001-4327

BECK, RODNEY ROY, baseball player; b. Burbank, Calif., Aug. 3, 1968. With Oakland (Calif.) Athletics, 1986-88; pitcher San Francisco Giants, 1988-98, Chgo. Cubs, 1998—; mem. Nat. League All-Star Team, 1993, 94. Office: Chgo Cubs 1060 W Addison St Chicago IL 60613-4305*

BECK, ROSEMARIE, artist, educator; b. N.Y.C., July 8, 1924; d. Samuel and Margit (Weisz) B.; m. Robert Phelps, Sept. 15, 1945 (dec.); 1 child, Roger Phelps. AB, Oberlin Coll., 1944; student, Inst. Fine Arts, 1944-45, Columbia U., 1945, Atelier Robert Motherwell, 1950. Instr. Vassar Coll., Poughkeepsie, N.Y., 1956-57, 60-61, 63-64, Middlebury (Vt.) Coll., 1958, 59, 62, Parsons Sch. Design, N.Y.C., 1965-69; instr. to prof. Queens Coll., N.Y.C., 1968-91, prof. emeritus, 1991—; lectr. Columbia U., N.Y.C., 1972, U. Pa., Phila., 1971, New Studio Sch., N.Y.C., 1991—; artist-in-residence Dartmouth Coll., N.H., 1992. One-person shows include Allen Art Mus., Oberlin, Ohio, 1944, Maverick Concert Hall, Woodstock, N.Y., 1948, Woodstock Artists Assn., 1948, Peridot Gallery, N.Y.C., 1953, 55, 56, 59, 60, 63, 65, 66, 68, 70, 72, Vassar Coll., 1957, 61, Wesleyan U., Middletown, Conn., 1960, SUNY, New Paltz, 1962, Kirkland Coll., Clinton, N.Y., 1971, Duke U. Mus., 1971, Zachary Waller Gallery, L.A., 1971, Washburn Gallery, 1972, Paul Klapper Libr., 1975, Poindexter Gallery, N.Y.C., 1975, 80, Mari Galleries, Westchester, N.Y., 1979, Middlebury Coll., 1980, Weatherspoon Gallery, Greensboro, N.C., 1980, Cornell U., 1980, Ingber Gallery, N.Y.C., 1980, 85, 89, N.Y. Studio Sch., 1992, N.Y. Mus. Annex, Bklyn., 1985, Am. U., Washington, 1990, Dartmouth Coll., 1992, Swarthmore Coll., 1996, Smith Coll., 1997, Queens Coll., 1999; group shows include Kootz Gallery, N.Y.C., 1951, Stable Gallery, 1954, 55, 56, Pa. Acad. Fine Arts, Phila., 1954, 66, Art Inst. Chgo., 1955, 57, 60, 62, Whitney Mus., N.Y.C., 1955, 57, 58, U. Wis., 1956, U. Mich., 1956, Martha Jackson Gallery, 1956, Woodstock Artists Assn., 1958, Tate Gallery, London, 1958, Butler Inst. Am. Art, Cin., 1962, Felix Landau Gallery, L.A., 1962, Wadsworth Atheneum, 1964, Kansas City Art Inst., 1964, Walters Art Gallery, Balt., 1965, Nat. Inst. Arts and Letters, 1968, 69, 73, 75, 78, 79, Bowery Gallery, 1970, Nat. Arts Club, 1970, Deutsch Gallery, N.Y.C., 1982, 83, Moorhead Gallery. Greensboro, N.C., 1982, Nat. Acad. Design, 1985, Joel Becker Gallery, Provincetown, Mass., 1987, 88, Am. U., Washington, 1990, Nat. Acad., 1991, 92, 93. Recipient Altman Figure prize NAD, 1986, 89; grantee Woodstock Found., 1951, Ingram Merrill, 1967, 78, Rockefeller Found., 1983, NEA, 1986-87. Office: 6 E 12th St New York NY 10003-4447

BECK, STEPHANIE G., lawyer; b. Endicott, N.Y., Jan. 10, 1964; d. Ray A. and Donna E. (Geesey) B. BA with honors, SUNY, Binghamton, 1986; JD, Syracuse U., 1989. Bar: N.Y. 1990, U.S. Dist. Ct. (no. dist.) N.Y. 1990. Atty. Young & Paniccia, Binghamton, 1990—. Advisor/vol. Drama Club for Mentally and Physically Impaired, Binghamton, 1992-96; mem. ch. coun. Our Saviour Luth. Ch., Endwell, N.Y., 1990-94, 96; asst. coach Boys and Girls Club, Endwell, 1986-91. Mem. N.Y. State Bar Assn., Broome County Bar Assn. Democrat. Lutheran. Avocations: softball, volleyball. Office: Young and Paniccia 22 Riverside Dr Binghamton NY 13905-4612

BECK, STUART EDWIN, lawyer; b. Phila., Aug. 12, 1940; s. Louis M. and Anna (Cooper) B.; m. Elaine Kushner, June 20, 1964; children: Adam, Barry, Caroline. BSME, Drexel U., 1964; JD, George Washington U., 1968. Bar: Va. 1968, U.S. Dist. Ct. D.C. 1969, Pa. 1970, U.S. Dist. Ct. (ea. dist.) Pa. 1971, U.S. Ct. Appeals (3d cir.) 1971, U.S. Supreme Ct. 1980, U.S. Ct. Appeals (4th cir.) 1989, U.S. Patent and Trademark Office. Assoc. Seidel, Gonda & Goldhammer, Phila., 1969-73; atty. pvt. practice, Phila., 1974-79, 91—; ptnr. Trachman, Jacobs & Beck, Phila., 1979-88, Weinstein, Trachtman, Beck & Kimmelman, Phila., 1988-91; adj. prof. patent law Rutgers U. Law Sch., Camden, N.J.; instr. patent, trademark and copyright law The Phila. Inst. Capt. Am. Cancer Soc., 1974, 75; bd. dirs. Jewish Family and Children Svc. Phila., 1973-89, legal, fin. and budget com., 1979—, spkrs. com., 1979—, bldg. and grounds com., 1980-82, trustee, 1989; bd. dirs., by-laws revision com., bldgs. and grounds com., edn. com. Temple Beth Hillel; bd. dirs. Phila. Vol. Lawyers for Arts, 1980-84, treas., 1980-82. Mem. ABA (patent trademark and copyright law sect., litigation sect., antitrust law sect.), Am. Intellectual Property Law Assn. (com. patent contracts other than govt. 1971-75), Pa. Bar Assn., Phila. Bar Assn. (com. profl. responsibility 1975-93, com. election procedures 1976-84, com. law and arts 1976-80), Phila. Patent Law Assn. (com. ethics 1977-83, com. pub. rels. 1974-77, com. profl. responsibility 1975-79). Avocations: sailing, travel.

BECK, TIMOTHY DANIEL, human resources specialist, consultant; b. Santa Monica, Calif., Mar. 21, 1953; s. James Daniel and Bettye June (Cisler) B.; m. Marcia Ann Smith, Jan. 16, 1977; children: Tracy Beth and Erica Brandy (twins), Jenna Michelle. AA, El Camino Community Coll., 1974; BA, Calif. State U., Northridge, 1979. Registered health underwriter, registered employee benefits cons. Candidate cert. employee benefit specialist, group claims supr. Prudential Ins. Co. Am., L.A., 1973-79; employee benefits cons. Olanie, Hurst & Hemrich, L.A., 1979-81; v.p. policyholder svc. dept. Health Maintenance Life Ins. Co., Fountain Valley, Calif., 1981; v.p. Robert E. French Ins. Svcs., Inc., Huntington Beach, Calif., 1981-85; v.p., mng. cons. employee benefits Warren, McVeigh & Griffin, Inc., Newport Beach, Calif., 1985-91; mng. cons. employee benefits A. Foster Higgins and Co., Inc., 1991-96; prin. Buck Cons., Inc., L.A., 1996—; mem. Kaiser Permanente Orange County Consumer Coun., 1987—; mem. pub. edn. com. Calif. Health Decision, 1988—; mem. bus. and health adv. panel Am. Health Pub.; speaker to confs. and profl. socs.; cons. Healthnet Adv. Coun., 1996—, Orange County Bus. Coun., Town Hall, 1996—; mem. Healthnet Cons. Adv. Coun., 1997—. Creator, contbg. editor Employee Benefits Mgmt. Letter, 1985-91; contbr. articles to profl. publs. Mem. Internat. Found. Employee Benefits, Nat. Assn. Health Underwriters, Calif. Assn. Health Underwriters, Employee Benefit Planning Assn. So. Calif. (bd. dirs. 1992-93), So. Calif. Assn. Benefit Plan Adminstrs., Orange County Assn. Health Underwriters (founder, 1st v.p. 1987-88), Orange County Bus. Coun., Orange County Employee Benefit Coun., Calif. State U. Northridge Alumni Assn. Avocations: fishing, hiking, backpacking, rock climbing.

BECK, WILLIAM HAROLD, JR., lawyer; b. Clarksdale, Miss., Aug. 18, 1928; s. William Harold and Mary (McGaha) B.; m. Nancy Cassity House, Jan. 30, 1954; children—Mary, Nancy, Katherine. BA, Vanderbilt U., 1950; JD, U. Miss., 1954. Bar: Miss. 1954, La. 1960. Atty., Clarksdale, Miss., 1954-57; asst. prof. Tulane U., 1957-59; ptnr. Foley & Judell, New Orleans, 1959-88; of counsel, 1988—. Served to capt., AUS, 1951-53. Mem. La. Bar Assn., Miss. Bar Assn., SAR, Soc. Colonial Wars, S.R., Mil. and Hospitaller Order of St. Lazarus of Jerusalem, Huguenot Soc., Mil. Order Fgn. Wars. Office: Foley & Judell 1 Canal Pl 365 Canal St Ste 2600 New Orleans LA 70130-1138

BECK, WILLIAM SAMSON, physician, educator, biochemist; b. Reading, Pa., Nov. 7, 1923; s. Myron Paul and Gertrude (Harris) B.; m. Helene Samuels, Oct. 24, 1947; children—Thomas Russell, Peter Dean; m. Hanne Troedsson, July 20, 1964; children—John Christopher, Paul Brooks. B.S. in Chemistry, U. Mich., 1943, M.D., 1946; A.M. (hon.), Harvard U., 1971. Diplomate Am. Bd. Internal Medicine. Instr., asst. prof. medicine UCLA, 1950-57; fellow in biochemistry NYU Coll. Medicine, 1955-57; mem. faculty dept. medicine Harvard U., Boston, 1957—; prof. Harvard U., 1979—, tutor in biochem. scis., 1957—; emeritus, 1996—; prof. div. health sci. and tech. Harvard-MIT, 1971—, chmn. admissions com., 1977-88; dir. clin. labs. Mass. Gen. Hosp., Boston, 1957-75, chief hematology unit, 1957-72, dir. hematology rsch. lab., physician, 1957-96; mem. adv. coun. Nat. Inst. Arthritis, Metabolism and Digestive Diseases, NIH, 1971-74; mem. hematology study sect. NIH, 1967-71; Austin S. Weisberger vis. prof. medicine, CWRU, 1996. Author: Modern Science and the Nature of Life, 1957, Life: An Introduction to Biology, 3d edit., 1991, (with K.F. Liem, G.G. Simpson), Human Design, 1971, Hematology, 5th edit., 1991 (CD-ROM) Hemavid, 1995; contbr. articles to profl. jours. Served with AUS, 1943-46. Fellow AAAS; mem. Am. Soc. Biochemistry and Molecular Biology, Am. Soc. Hematology (exec. com. 1979-84), Assn. Am. Physicians, Am. Soc. Clin. Investigation, Am. Assn. Cancer Rsch. Home: 85 Arlington St Winchester MA 01890-3734 Office: Mass Gen Hosp Boston MA 02114*

BECKEL, CHARLES LEROY, physics educator; b. Phila., Feb. 7, 1928; s. Samuel Mercer and Katherine (Linsky) B.; m. Josephine Ann Beck, June 27, 1958; children: Amanda S., Sarah Beckel Lentz, Timothy C., Andrea C. BS, U. Scranton, 1948; PhD, Johns Hopkins U., 1954. Asst. prof. physics Georgetown U., 1953-59, assoc. prof., 1959-64; rsch. staff mem. Inst. for Defense Analyses, Arlington, Va., 1964-66; assoc. prof. physics U. N.Mex., 1966-69, prof., 1969-94, prof. emeritus, 1995—, asst. dean, 1971-72, acting v.p. rsch., 1972-73; acting dir. Inst. Social R&D, 1972; vis. prof. theoretical chemistry Oxford U., 1973; vis. prof. chemistry and molecular scis. U. Sussex, U.K., 1987; Fulbright lectr. U. Peshawar, Pakistan, 1957-58, Cheng Kung U., Tainan, Taiwan, 1963-64; cons. Ballistics Rsch. Lab., Aberdeen Proving Ground, Md., 1955-57, Dikewood Corp., Albuquerque, 1967-72, 74-80, Albuquerque Urban Obs., 1969-71, Inst. Def. Analyses, 1962-64, 66-69, U.S. ACDA, 1981-84; phys. sci. officer U.S. Arms Control and Disarmament Agy., 1980-81; vis. prof. physics U. Scranton, 1995. Pres. Nat. Kidney Found. N.Mex. Inc., 1968-72, del. trustee, 1972-73, 76-80, exec. com., 1974-80, 83-86, v.p., 1982-83, bd. trustees, 1987-93; bd. dirs. Nat. Capitol Area Nat. Kidney Found., 1965-66, N.Mex. Combined Health Appeal, 1972-73; mem. edn. subcom. Navajo Sci. Com. 1975-82. Recipient Vol. award Nat. Kidney Found. of N.Mex., 1988, Frank J. O'Hara award for disting. achievement in sci. U. Scranton Nat. Alumni Soc., 1988, U.S. Dept. Energy award in solid state physics materials scis., 1988, Outstanding Teaching award Burlington Northern Found., 1989. Mem. Am. Phys. Soc., Bioelectromagnetics Soc., Nat. Eagle Scout Assn. Office: U NMex Dept Physics and Astronomy Albuquerque NM 87131

BECKEN, BRADFORD ALBERT, engineering executive; b. Providence, Oct. 5, 1924; s. Albert R. and Ruth M. (Stephenson) B.; m. Gaynelle M. Lane, Nov. 30, 1946; children: Bradford Albert, Brian A., Christian L., Anne Tracey. Student, U. R.I., 1942-43; B.S., U.S. Naval Acad., 1946; B.S. in Electronics, U.S. Naval Postgrad. Sch., 1952; M.S., UCLA, 1953, Ph.D., 1961. Commd. officer USN, advanced through grades to comdr.; cons. Airtronics-Spl. Warfare Lab., 1967; mgr. systems engring. lab. submarine signal div. Raytheon Co., Portsmouth, R.I., 1967-70, mgr. engring., 1970-82, dir. tech. Portsmouth Engring. Lab., 1982-94; cons., 1994—. Author: Advances in Hydroscience, 1964. Trustee Newport Hosp., 1977, chmn. bd., 1979-84; chmn. bd. dirs. Newport Health Care Corp., 1982-93; treas. Newport Hist. Soc., 1993-94, pres., 1994—. Recipient Asst. Chief Bur. Ships award, 1963, Am. Def. Preparedness Assn. Gold medal, 1995, Navy Undersea Warfare Ctr. Decibel award, 1997. Fellow Acoustical Soc. Am.; mem. Am. Def. Preparedness Assn., Naval War Coll. Found., U.S. Naval Inst., U.S. Naval Acad. Alumni Assn. Episcopalian. Home: 260 Fischer Cir Portsmouth RI 02871-5400

BECKENSTEIN, MYRON, journalist; b. Cleve., Mar. 11, 1938; s. Irwin and Rachel (Miller) B.; 1 child, Stacey Amanda. B.S., Northwestern U., 1959, M.S., 1960. Mem. staff Chgo. Daily News, 1959-78, Balt. Sun, 1978—. Served with AUS, 1961-64. Mem. Upper Patuxent Archeol. Group, Archeol. Soc. Md., Soc. Profl. Journalists. Home: 9256 Feathered Head Columbia MD 21045 Office: Balt Sun 501 N Calvert St Baltimore MD 21278-3604

BECKER, ALISON LEA, lawyer; b. Covington, Ky., Apr. 5, 1963; d. Richard L. and Rosalind M. (Schuppert) Ante; m. Patrick J. Becker, Apr. 4, 1992; 1 child, Christopher P. BA, No. Ky. U., 1984, JD, 1987. Bar: Ohio 1988, U.S. Dist. Ct. (so. dist.) Ohio 1988, U.S Ct. Appeals (6th cir.) 1988, U.S. Army Ct. Mil. Rev. 1990, U.S. Ct. Mil. Appeals 1992, U.S. Supreme Ct. 1992, Fla. 1998, U.S. Dist. Ct. (mid. dist.) Fla. 1998, U.S. Ct. Appeals (11th cir.) 1999. Sole practice Cin., 1988-89; trial def. atty. U.S. Army JAG Corps, Goeppingen, Germany, 1990-91; trial counsel, legal assistance atty. U.S. Army JAG Corps, Stuttgart, Germany, 1991-92; def. appellate counsel U.S. Army JAG Corps, Falls Church, Va., 1992-94; chief claims and adminstrv. law U.S. Army JAG Corps, Atlanta, 1994-97; sr. atty. Office Atty. Gen., Tampa, Fla., 1998—; coord. for appellate def. before U.S. Supreme Ct., U.S. Army, Falls Church, 1992-94. Office: Office Atty Gen 2002 N Lois Ave 7th Fl Tampa FL 33607

BECKER, BARBARA ANN STULAC (BOBBIE BECKER), small business owner; b. Chgo., Sept. 29, 1938; d. Josef Florian and Dagmar Adrienne Pakoneh Stulac; m. Raymond August Becker (div. 1980); children: Raymond August, Jr., Renay Dagmar. AA, Florissant Valley (Mo.) C.C., 1980; BA, U. Mo., St. Louis, 1981. Pvt. instrumental music instr. St. Louis, 1977-80, Dallas, 1981-83, Columbia, Mo., 1984—, Boonville, Fayette, Mo., 1987—; owner Bobbie Becker Music, Franklin, Mo., 1992—, piano tuner, instrument repair profl., 1992—. Mem. Mid-Mo. Music Tchrs. Assn., Mo. State Old Time Fiddlers Assn., Mo. Folkore Soc. Avocations: painting, travel, violin, guitar, piano. Office: Bobbie Becker Music 3764 State Route J Franklin MO 65250-9592

BECKER, BORIS, professional tennis player; b. Leimen, Federal Republic of Germany, Nov. 22, 1967; s. Karl-Hinez and Elvira Becker; m. Barbara Feltus, Dec. 1993; 1 child. Mem. Fed. Republic Germany championship team Davis Cup Tournament, Goteborg, Sweden, 1988. Winner numerous tennis tournaments, including West German Jr. Championship, 1983, Young Masters Tournament, Birmingham, Eng., 1985, Grand Prix Tournament, Queen's, 1985, Men's Singles Championship, Wimbledon, Eng., 1985, 86, 89, U.S. Open Singles Tournament, N.Y., 1989, Australian Open, 1991, 96, ATP World Championship, 1995;(with Michael Stich) Men's Doubles Gold Medal, Olympics, 1992. Office: USTA 70 W Red Oak Ln White Plains NY 10604-3602*

BECKER, BRANDON, lawyer; b. Berwyn, Ill., Mar. 19, 1954. BA summa cum laude, U. Minn., 1974; JD magna cum laude, U. San Diego, 1977; LLM, Columbia U., 1979. Bar: Calif. 1978, D.C. 1978. Atty. SEC, Washington, 1978-80, br. chief, 1980, legal asst., 1981-82, asst. dir., 1982-86, assoc. dir., 1986-91, dep. dir., 1991-93, dir. divsn. mkt. regulation, 1993-95, spl. advisor to the chmn. for internat. derivatives, 1995-96; ptnr. Wilmer, Cutler & Pickering, Washington, 1996—. Articles editor San Diego Law Rev. Avocation: chess. E-mail: bbecker@wilmer.com. Office: Wilmer Cutler & Pickering 2445 M St NW Ste 6W Washington DC 20037-1420

BECKER, BRUCE CARL, II, physician, educator; b. Chgo., Sept. 8, 1948; s. Carl Max and Lillian (Podzamsky) B; m. Irene Stepien-Thibault, 1991; one child, Joseph. BS in Aero. and Astron. Engring., U. Ill., 1970; MSME, Colo. State U., 1972; postgrad. Wright State U., 1973-74; MD, Chgo. Med. Sch., 1978; MS in Health Svcs. Adminstrn., Coll. St. Francis, Joliet, Ill., 1984; Diploma in Spanish, U. Chgo., 1988; Diploma in Polish, Coll. of Du Page, 1989. Diplomate Am. Bd. Med. Mgmt. Resident in surgery U. N.C.-Chapel Hill, 1978-79, in family practice St. Mary of Nazareth Hosp. Ctr., Chgo., 1979-81, chmn., program dir. dept. family practice, 1985-90; clin. instr. Chgo. Med. Sch., 1982, affiliate instr., 1982-83, asst. prof., 1983, vice chmn. dept. family medicine, 1983-91; asst. dir. med. edn. St. Mary of Nazareth Hosp. Ctr., Chgo., 1981-82, dir. family practice residency, 1983-90, chief Family Practice Ctr., 1983-85, chmn. dept. family practice, 1985-90, med. dir. Home Health Svc., 1985—, med. dir. HMO-Ill., 1985—, mem. fin. com. governing bd., 1987-91, planning and devel. com. governing bd., 1990—, v.p. med. affairs, 1989—; mem. adv. com. family practice residency Ill. Dept. Health, 1991—. Contbr. articles to profl. jours. Mem. editorial rev. bd. Postgrad. Medicine, 1987-89. Mem. Pub. Health Svc. Adv. Network Dept. Health & Human Svcs., 1990-91; bd. dirs. Inn Care of Am. Midwest Region, 1991—; mem. dinner com. Ill. chpt. Lupus Found. Am., 1991. Capt., USAF, 1970-75. Recipient Literary Key award St. Mary of Nazareth Hosp. Ctr., 1981, 85. Fellow Am. Acad. Family Physicians (rep. to accreditation rev. com. for physician assts. 1989-94, chmn. 1991-93), Am. Coll. Physician Execs., Am. Coll. Health Care Execs.; mem. AMA, Ill. Acad. Family Physicians (commn. on internal affairs 1986, commn. pub. and govt. policy 1987-89, chmn. 1989-90, bd. dirs. 1988-92, chmn. pub. rels. and info. com. 1988-92, state rep. family practice res. act com. 1990-92, vice speaker, 1991-92), Soc. Tchrs. of Family Medicine, Assn. Am. Med. Colls., Alliance Continuing Med. Edn., Am. Coll. Occupl. Medicine, Am. Acad. Med. Adminstrs., Chgo. Med. Soc. (councilor for Chgo. Med. Sch. 1986-91, alt. councilor for Chgo. Med. Sch. 1991-95, physicians stress ad hoc com. 1989-90, vice chmn. 1990-91, adv. com. on pub. health policy 1990—, presdl. adv. com. 1991—), Ill. State Med. Soc. (coun. on edn. and manpower 1986-96, chmn. com. on CME activities 1991-96, chmn. subcom. physican placement and practice issues 1986-90, third party payment and processes com. IAFP rep. 1990-92), Phi Delta Epsilon. Roman Catholic.

BECKER, BRUCE DOUGLAS, mechanical engineer; b. Tacoma, Mar. 19, 1959; s. Walter A. and Mary Jane (Barr) B.; m. Jamie M. Russell, Sept. 10, 1988; 1 child, Catherine Anne. BSME, Wash. State U., 1981. Registered profl. engr., Oreg. Design engr. Hyster Corp., Portland, Oreg., 1981-85; devel. engr. Precision Castparts Corp., Portland, 1985-95; design engr. Autostack Corp., Portland, 1995-96, Gunderson, Inc., Portland, Oreg., 1996—. Eagle scout Boy Scouts Am., Pullman, Wash., 1975; citizen amb. People to People Internat., People's Republic of China, 1985; mem. Milw. Lutheran Ch., 1996—. Mem. ASME (assoc.), NSPE. Avocations: sailing, skiing, photography, hiking, travel. Home: 18613 SE 24th Cir Vancouver WA 98683-1867 Office: Gunderson Inc 4350 NW Front Ave Portland OR 97210-1499

BECKER, CHARLES MCVEY, economics and finance educator; b. Cleve., Nov. 13, 1937; s. William Nevison and Helen (McVey) B.; m. Natalie Sage Slaughter, July 25, 1964; children: William Nevison II, James Pahl. BA cum laude, U. Ariz., 1960, MA, 1962, PhD, 1966. Chartered fin. analyst. Asst. prof. fin., econs. Nev. So. U., Las Vegas, 1965-67; asst. prof. Tex. Christian U., Ft. Worth, 1967-70, assoc. prof., 1970—; Asst. dir. Am. Free Enterprise Inst. Contbr. over 40 articles to profl. jours. Mem. Southwestern Econs. Assn. (pres. 1990-91), Southwestern Soc. Economists (pres. 1992-93), N.Am. Econs. and Fin. Assn. (adv. bd.), Assn. for Investment Mgmt. and Rsch., Am. Econ. Assn. (life), Alpha Kappa Psi, Beta Gamma Sigma, Phi Alpha Theta, Alpha Sigma Phi, Omicron Delta Epsilon, Order of Omega. Avocations: tennis, golf. Office: Tex Christian U Dept Economics TCU Campus Fort Worth TX 76129

BECKER, CHERI A(NN), marketing professional, business consultant; b. Ft. Wayne, Ind., Dec. 25, 1949; d. Van Watt Gardner and Margaret Joann Little Moore; m. Mark Davis Becker, Apr. 24, 1993. Cert. of Airline Op., Atlantic Sch., Kansas City, Mo., 1968; student, U. Ky., 1969; cert. completion, Ball State U., 1993; BS in Human Svcs. Mgmt., Ind. Inst. Tech., 1993. Owner Concept Advt. and Mktg., Kalamazoo, 1975-80; major accounts mgr., new product devel. mgr. Ft. Wayne Newspapers, 1980-85; dist. mgr. Modern Metals, Chgo., 1985-87; dir. product devel. Rho Lyn Engring., Detroit, 1985; exec. dir. Small Bus. Devel. Ctr., Ft. Wayne, 1987; pres. N.E. Ind. Bus. Assistance Corp., 1990-94; v.p. mktg. and sales Midland Inc., Ft. Wayne, 1994-95; dir. comms. Sterling Diagonostics Imaging, Inc., Greenville, S.C., 1997—; past mem. adv. bd. women's bus. program Ind. Small Bus. Devel. Corp., Ind. U.-Purdue U. Mktg. Club, 1987-88; mem. adv. bd. Young Entrepreneurs Success Program; co-chmn. Three Rivers Festival, 1993, v.p. adminstrn., 1994; instr. continuing edn. dept. Ind. U.-Purdue U., 1987-94, past mem. adv. coun. Sch. Fine Arts; past spkr. Entrepreneurs Day Conf., Ind. Inst. New Bus. Ventures, Indpls., Regional Conf., Women in Comms., Inc., 1995, 98; bd. dirs. Home For New Beginnings, Opportunity Greenville; advisor United Neighborhood Economic Devel. Corp. Past pres. bd. dirs. Speech Hearing & Learning Ctr., Connections, Leadership for Women, Greenville, S.C.; trustee S.C. Nature Conservancy; past event organizer Run Jane Run, 1983-84; fundraiser United Way, 1985, drive trainer, 1989; past chmn. mktg. com. Ft. Wayne Ballet, 1988, v.p., 1990-94; mem. Leadership Ft. Wayne, 1994, pres. Leadership Alumni Assn.; past mem. Ft. Wayne Adv. Com., 1988-94, mem. adv. com. mfg. tech. svcs. program, 1994; facilitator Ft. Wayne Workforce Conf., 1990; mem. task force Urban Land Inst., 1990; mem. Ft. Wayne Consensus Com., 1991; bd. dirs. Home for New Beginnings, Opportunity Greenville, 1999; active Franciscan Forum; advisor United Neighborhood Econ. Devel. Corp. Recipient Cert. of Recognition, Crossroads Children's Home, cert. Nat. Safety Coun., 1988, Cert. of Profl. Contbn., Delta Sigma Pi, Bus. award Urban League, 1992. Mem. Women's Bur., Small Bus. Inst. Dirs. Assn., Friends of the Urban League, Women's Bus. Owners Assn. (speaker 1988-90). Independent. Roman Catholic. Avocations: gardening, sailing, skiing, target shooting, painting. Home and Office: 121 Sanderling Dr Greenville SC 29607-5546

BECKER, DANIEL PAUL, medicinal chemist, researcher; b. Peru, Ind., June 12, 1960; s. Joseph Robert and Rosanna (Dorsam) B.; m. Michele Power, Aug. 18, 1984; children: Julia, Robert. BA in Chemistry, Kalamazoo Coll., 1982; PhD in Organic Chemistry, Ind. U., 1986. Rsch. assoc./assoc. instr. Ind. U., Bloomington, 1982-86; sr. rsch. scientist, group leader Searle/Monsanto, Skokie, Ill., 1987—, sustainable devel. facilitator, 1996—; adj. asst. prof. medicinal chemistry U. Ill., Chgo., 1993—; lectr. in field. Contbr. articles to profl. jours.; patentee (20) in field. Recipient DuPont Assoc. Instr. award for excellence in tchg. Ind. U., 1984. Mem. Am. Chem. Soc. (organic chemistry and medicinal chemistry divsns.). Roman Catholic. Avocation: baroque recorder. Office: Searle/Monsanto R&D 4901 Searle Pkwy Skokie IL 60077-2919

BECKER, DAVID, artist, educator; b. Milw., Aug. 16, 1937; s. Walter Gustav and Fern Bertha (Raddatz) B.; m. Catherine Claytor, Aug. 27, 1960 (div. 1981); children: Sarah Lynne, Amelia Elisabeth; m. Patricia Ann Fennell, Nov. 13, 1988; 1 child, Sloane Fennell. Student, Layton Sch. Art, 1956-58; BS, U. Wis., Milw., 1961; MFA, U. Ill., 1965. Asst. prof. Wayne State U., Detroit, 1965-71, assoc. prof., 1971-80, prof., 1980-85; assoc. prof. U. Wis., Madison, 1985-87, prof., 1987—; vis. prof. U. Wis., Madison, 1978-79; vis. artist Utah State U., Logan, 1981; art lectr. in field. Exhbns. include Mus. Fine Arts, Boston, 1965, 75, Butler Inst. Am. Art, Youngstown, Ohio, 1967, 68, 72, Lawrence Stevens Gallery, Detroit, 1968, Detroit Inst. Arts, 1971, 77, 86, 91, Richard Nash Gallery, Seattle, 1974, Franz Bader Gallery, Washington, 1974, 77, 80, Madison (Wis.) Art Ctr., 1975, 79, Libr. of Congress, Washington, 1975, Honolulu Acad. Arts, 1975, 83, ADI Gallery, San Francisco, 1975, London Arts Gallery, Detroit, 1976, Boston Ctr. Arts, 1976, 78, Museo de Arte Moderno, Cali, Colombia, 1976, 77, 81, Bawag Found., Vienna, Austria, 1976, Bklyn. Mus., 1976, 84, Met. Mus., Miami, Fla., 1977, 80, Habatat Galleries, Dearborn, Mich., 1977, Visual Arts Ctr. Alaska, Anchorage, 1978, 86, Cranbrook Acad. Art, Bloomfield Hills, Mich., 1980, Associated Am. Artists Gallery, Phila., 1980, Phila. Art Alliance/Phila. Print Club, 1980, Kalamazoo (Mich.) Inst. Arts, 1980, 86, Nat. Mus. Am. Art, Washington, 1982, DeCordova Mus., Lincoln, Mass., 1982, 86, USIA, 1983, Saginaw (Mich.) Mus. Art, 1984, Brockton (Mass.) Mus. Art, 1984, Mich. Gallery, Detroit, 1986, Neville-Sargent Gallery, Chgo., 1986, Intergrafic, East Berlin, 1984, 87, 9th Brit. Internat. Print Biennale, Bradford, 1986, Jane Haslem Gallery, Washington, 1987, 90, 92, 93, John Szoke Graphics, N.Y.C., 1988, Silvermine Gallery, Stamford, Conn., 1988, Elvehjem Mus. Art, Madison, 1989, Boston Printmaker's 42d and 43d Nat. Print Exhbn., 1993, Fitchburg (Mass.) Mus. Art, 1990, New Orleans Mus. Art, 1990, NAD, N.Y.C., 1986, 87, 90, 91, 92, 93, 94, The Hoyt Inst. Fine Arts, New Castle, Pa., 1992, Sodarco Gallery, Montreal, 1993, Davidson Galleries, Seattle, 1993, Galleria Mesa, Mesa, Ariz., 1993, Intergrafia, Katowice, Poland, 1994, Sapporo Internat. Print Biennale, Japan, 1993, Maastricht Internat. Print Biennale, The Netherlands, 1993; permanent collections include: Libr. of Congress, Washington, Art Inst. Chgo., Rose Art Mus., Waltham, Mass., Elvehjem Mus. Art, Madison, Wis., Butler Inst. Am. Art, Minot (N.D.) Art Assn., Silvermine Guild Arts, New Canaan, Conn., Honolulu Acad. Arts, N.Y. Pub. Libr., Detroit Inst. Art, Museo de Arte Moderno, Bklyn. Mus., Met. Mus., Miami, Nat. Mus. Am. Art, Washington, Portland (Oreg.) Art Mus., Art Ctr., South Bend, Ind., USIA, Prague, Czech Republic, and numerous colls. and univs. 1st lt. U.S. Army, 1961-63. Creative Artist grantee Mich. Coun. Arts, 1982; NEA Visual Arts fellow, 1993-94. Fellow The MacDowell Colony; mem. NAD (nat. academician). Subject of numerous articles and revs. Home: 2512 Lunde Ln Mount Horeb WI 53572-2440 Office: U Wis Art Dept 6241 Humanities Bldg Madison WI 53706

BECKER, DAVID MANDEL, law educator, author, consultant; b. Chgo., Dec. 31, 1935; m. Sandra Kaplan, June 30, 1957; children: Laura, Andrew, Scott. AB, Harvard Coll., 1957; JD, U. Chgo., 1960. Bar: Ill. 1960. Assoc. Becker and Savin, Chgo., 1960-62; instr. law U. Mich., Ann Arbor, 1962-63; asst. prof. law Washington U., St. Louis, 1963-66, assoc. prof., 1966-69, prof., 1969-93, Joseph H. Zumbalen prof. law, 1993. Author: (with David Gibberman) Legal Checklists, 1968, and ann. supplements; Legal Checklists-Specially Selected Forms, 1977, and ann. supplements; Perpetuities and Estate Planning: Potential Problems and Effective Solutions, 1993; contbr. numerous articles to profl. jours. Recipient Founders Day award Washington U. Alumni Assn., 1973, Tchr. of Yr. award Washington U., 1980, 89, Disting. Tchr. award Washington U. Sch. Law Alumni, 1988. Home: 843 Woodmoor Dr Saint Louis MO 63132-3518 Office: Washington U Sch Law Saint Louis MO 63130

BECKER, DON CRANDALL, retired newspaper executive; b. Sacramento, Dec. 31, 1933; s. Edwin Archibald B. and Georgiana (Holt) English; m. Maureen Ann Maguire, 1961; children: James Crandall, Brian Edward. A.B., San Jose State U., 1957. Reporter Santa Cruz (Calif.) Sentinel,

1957-58; reporter, editor UPI, San Francisco, 1958-59; corr., mgr. UPI, Singapore, 1960-62, Manila, 1962-67, San Juan, P.R., 1969-72, Miami, 1972-73; dep. commr. Nat. Profl. Soccer League, N.Y.C. and San Francisco, 1967-68; dir. corp. relations Knight-Ridder Newspapers, Miami, 1973-78; pub., chmn. Gary (Ind.) Post-Tribune, 1978-79; pres. Detroit Free Press, 1979-84; pub., pres. Jour. of Commerce, N.Y.C., 1985-97; ret., 1997; exec. sec. Fgn. Corrs. Assn. S.E. Asia, Singapore, 1961-62; pres. Manila Overseas Press Club, 1963-64. Bd. dirs. Kirov Internat. Opera, Medici Archives Project, Inc. Served to cpl. U.S. Army, 1954-56. Mem. Greater Detroit C. of C. (chmn. 1984), Palmilla Golf Club, Stanwich Country Club, Met. Club. Home: Greenwich Ct Riverside CT 06878

BECKER, DONALD EUGENE, animal science educator; b. Delavan, Ill., Feb. 2, 1923; s. George Edwin and Esther C. (Peters) B.; m. Elsie J. Hendrickson, Dec. 28, 1949; children: Esther A. Becker Gasser, Phyllis E. Becker Boerman, Donald Eugene, William E., Beth A. Becker Kasper. BS, U. Ill., 1945, MS, 1947; PhD, Cornell U., 1949. Cert. animal scientist. Asst. U. Ill., Urbana, 1945-47, prof. animal sci., 1950-84, head dept. animal sci., 1967-84; faculty, chmn. dept. animal sci. Ohio State U., 1984-87; asst. Cornell U., Ithaca, N.Y., 1947-49; assoc. prof. U. Tenn., Knoxville, 1949-50; ind. cons., 1987—; pres. Oxford Feeders Inc., 1989—; cons. Oak Ridge Lab., 1949-50. Contbr. numerous articles to profl. jours. Recipient Am. Feed Mfrs. award, 1957, Funk recognition award, 1972. Fellow AAAS, Am. Soc. Animal Sci. (editor Jour. 1967-70, pres. 1970-71, Morrison award 1977); mem. Am. Inst. Nutrition, Animal Nutrition Research Council (chmn. 1962-63), Council for Agrl. Sci. and Tech. (treas. 1972-73). Methodist. Home and Office: 2209 Combes St Urbana IL 61801-6811

BECKER, DONALD PAUL, surgeon, neurosurgeon; b. Cleve., 1935. MD, Case Western Res. U., 1961. Diplomate Am. Bd. Neurol. Surgery. Intern U. (Cleve.) Hosps., 1961-62, resident in surgery, 1962-63, resident in neurol. surgery, 1963-67; fellow in neurosurgery NIH, Bethesda, Md., 1966; prof. UCLA Med. Ctr., 1967-71; prof., chmn. divsn. neurol. surgery Med. Coll. Va., Richmond, 1971-85; chief neurosurgery UCLA Med. Ctr., 1985—; prof., chmn. divsn. neurol. surgery Med. Coll. Va., Richmond, 1971-85. Mem. ACS, AMA. Office: UCLA Med Ctr Divsn Neurosurgery PO Box 957039 Los Angeles CA 90095-7039

BECKER, DWIGHT LOWELL, physician; b. Mercer County, Ohio, July 21, 1918; s. George and Maude R. (Purdyzz) B.; m. Mary Lauer, Sept. 6, 1942; children—Lawrence, Judith, George Edward. B.A., Ohio State U., 1940, M.D., 1943. Intern Christ Hosp., Cin., 1943-44; gen. practice medicine Lima, Ohio, 1946-65; emergency room practice Lima, 1965-87; mem. staff Lima Meml. Hosp.; med. dir. Blue Cross of Lima, 1970-87; past student health dir. Ohio No. U.; med. dir. Auglaize County Health Dept., Wapakoneta, Ohio, 1994—; ret., 1999; past chmn. bd. Ohio Med. Indemnity, Inc., Worthington; field med. cons. Ohio Vocat. Rehab.; past bd. dir. Met. Bank, Lima. Mem. Allen County Bd. Health, 1952-55; v.p. bd. dirs. Allen County Coun. on Aging; med. advisor Lima and Allen County Vis. Nurses Assn.; bd. dirs. Sta WIMA, Lima. Served to capt. M.C. AUS, 1944-46. Mem. Am. Coll. Emergency Physicians, AMA, Ohio Med. Assn., Phi Beta Kappa. Republican. Clubs: Masons, Shawnee Country, Elks. Home and Office: 1 Galvin Ln Lima OH 45805-3870

BECKER, EDWARD ROY, federal judge; b. Phila., May 4, 1933; s. Herman A. and Jeannette (Levit) B.; m. Flora Lyman, Aug. 11, 1957; children: James Daniel (dec. 1969), Jonathan Robert, Susan Rose, Charles Lyman. BA, U. Pa., 1954; LLB, Yale U., 1957. Bar: Pa. 1957. Ptnr. Becker, Becker & Fryman, Phila., 1957-70; U.S. Dist. Judge, 1970-82; judge U.S. Ct. Appeals (3d cir.), 1982—, chief judge, 1998—; counsel Rep. City Com., Phila., 1965-70; mem. task force on implementation of new jud. article Joint State Govt. Commn., 1969; lectr. law U. Pa. Law Sch., 1978-83; mem. edn. adv. com. concerning Comprehensive Crime Control Act, Fed. Jud. Ctr., 1981-90, Fed. Jud. Ctr. Com. on Sentencing, Probation and Pretrial Svcs., 1985-90; bd. dirs. Fed. Jud. Ctr., 1991-95; mem. faculty sr. appellate judges seminar Inst. Jud. Adminstrn., N.Y.C., 1992-94. Bd. editors Manual for Complex Litigation, 1981-90; contbr. articles to profl. jours. Trustee Magna Carta Found., Phila.; vis. com. U. Chgo. Law Sch., 1988-91; chair Rhodes Scholarship Selection Com. Dist. II (Pa., N.Y., Vt., N.H.), 1996-98. Fellow Am. Bar Found.; mem. ABA (jud. rep. antitrust sect. 1983-86), Phila. Bar Assn., Am. Judicature Soc., Am. Law Inst. (adv. com. restatement conflict of laws 2d, mem. ALI-ABA com. 1992—, chmn. program subcom. 1996—), Jud. Conf. U.S. (com. on adminstrn. probation system 1979-87, chmn. com. on criminal law and probation adminstrn. 1987-90, com. on long range planning 1991-96, exec. com. 1999—), Phi Beta Kappa. Jewish. Home: 936 Herbert St Philadelphia PA 19124-2417 Office: US Ct Appeals 19613 US Courthouse 601 Market St Philadelphia PA 19106-1713

BECKER, EDWIN DEMUTH, chemist, laboratory director; b. Columbia, Pa., May 3, 1930; married, 1953; 2 children. B.S., U. Rochester, 1952; Ph.D. in Chemistry, U. Calif., 1955. Instr. U. Calif., 1955; phys. chemist NIH, Bethesda, Md., 1955—, chief sect. molecular biophysics, 1962-72, chief lab. chem. physics, 1972-80; acting dir. Fogarty Internat. Ctr. NIH, 1979-80, assoc. dir. for research services, 1980-88, chief sect. NMR, 1972-98, scientist emeritus, 1998—, mem. faculty Grad. Sch., 1963—; lectr. Georgetown U., 1958-97. NSF fellow U. Calif. Fellow AAAS; mem. Am. Chem. Soc. Research in nuclear magnetic resonance, hydrogen bonding, molecular structure, infrared spectroscopy. Office: NIH Bldg 5 Rm 124 Bethesda MD 20892-0520

BECKER, FRED RONALD, lawyer; b. Phila., Apr. 7, 1937; s. Samuel and Molly (Cletter) B.; m. Judith Ellen Ettlinger, June 5, 1961. B.A., U. Pa., 1958; J.D. magna cum laude, Harvard U., 1961. Bar: D.C. 1963. Law clk. U.S. Ct. Appeals (9th cir.), 1961-62; asst. Stanford U. Law Sch., 1962-63; atty. tax div. U.S. Dept. Justice, 1963-65; atty. Office Tax Legis. Counsel U.S. Treasury, 1965-69; ptnr. Ropes & Gray, Boston, MA, 1969. Office: Ropes & Gray 1 International Pl Boston MA 02110-2602*

BECKER, FREDERIC KENNETH, lawyer; b. N.Y.C., Dec. 22, 1935; s. Max and Mary (Brandman) B.; m. Barbara Helene Kiesler, Dec. 4, 1960; children: Richard, Martin, Mary. AB, Brown U., 1956; JD, Harvard U., 1959. Bar: N.J. 1960, U.S. Dist. Ct. N.J. 1960, N.Y., U.S. Ct. Appeals (3d cir.), U.S. Supreme Ct. Pres. Wilentz, Goldman & Spitzer, P.C., Woodbridge, N.J., 1960—; trustee Newark Beth Israel Med. Ctr., 1976-86, chmn. editl. bd. N.J. Lawyer, 1994—; bd. dirs. Prudential Ins. Co. Am. Trustee, v.p. Temple B'Nai Jeshurun, 1996—. Fulbright scholar, 1959-60. Fellow Am. Coll. Trial Lawyers, Am. Bar Found.; mem. ABA, Assn. Fed. Bar N.J. (pres. 1993-95), N.J. Bar Assn. Home: 71 Troy Dr Short Hills NJ 07078-1365 Office: Wilentz Goldman Spitzer PC 90 Woodbridge Ctr Dr Ste 900 Woodbridge NJ 07095-1142

BECKER, FREDERICK FENIMORE, cancer center administrator, pathologist; b. N.Y.C., July 23, 1931; s. Louis I. and Ruth (Shurr) B.; m. Mary Ellen Terry, Nov. 23, 1971; 1 child, Bronwyn Elizabeth. BA, Columbia U., 1952; MD, NYU, 1956. Intern Harvard svc. Harvard service Boston City Hosp., 1956-57; resident Bellevue Hosp., N.Y.C.; pathology trainee NYU Sch. Medicine, N.Y.C., 1957-60, prof., dir. pathology, 1962-75; chmn. dept. pathology U. Tex. Cancer Center, M.D. Anderson Hosp. and Tumor Inst., Houston, 1976-79; v.p. rsch. U. Tex. M.D. Anderson Cancer Ctr., 1979-98, spl. advisor to the pres., 1998—. Contbr. numerous articles to various publs. Served with USN, 1960-62. Mem. Am. Assn. Pathologists (pres. 1980-81), Am. Assn. Cancer Research, Am. Soc. Cell Biology, Tex. Med. Assn. Club: Athenaeum (London). Office: U Tex MD Anderson Cancer Ctr 1515 Holcombe Blvd Houston TX 77030-4009

BECKER, GAIL ROSELYN, museum director; b. Long Branch, N.J., Oct. 22, 1942; d. Joseph and Adele (Michelsohn) B. BA, Vassar Coll., 1964. Exhibit project officer U.S. Info. Agy., Washington, 1967-87, chief devel. and prodn. exhibits, 1987-91; exec. dir. Louisville Sci. Ctr. (formerly Mus. History and Sci.), 1991—; mem. Ky. Sci. and Tech. Coun., bd. dirs., 1993—. Bd. dirs. Louisville Advanced Tech. Coun., 1993—, Louisville Con. Fgn. Rels.; active Leadership Louisville. Recipient Presdl. Design awards Nat. Endowment for the Arts, Washington, 1984, 88, 92, Special Achievement award U.S. Info. Agy., Washington, 1988. Mem. Am. Assn. Mus. (bd. dirs. 1994-97), Assn. Sci.-Tech. Ctrs. (bd. dirs. 1992—), Vassar Coll. Alumnae Assn., Rotary. Office: Louisville Sci Ctr 727 W Main St Louisville KY 40202-2681

BECKER, GARY STANLEY, economist, educator; b. Pottsville, Pa., Dec. 2, 1930; s. Louis William and Anna (Siskind) B.; m. Doria Slote, Sept. 19, 1954 (dec.); children: Judith Sarah, Catherine Jean; m. Guity Nashat, Oct. 31, 1979; children: Michael Claffey, Cyrus Claffey. AB summa cum laude, Princeton U., 1951, PhD (hon.), 1991; AM, U. Chgo., 1953, PhD, 1955; PhD (hon.), Hebrew U., Jerusalem, 1985, Knox Coll., 1985, U. Ill., Chgo., 1988, SUNY, 1990, U. Palermo, Buenos Aires, 1993, Columbia U., 1993, Warsaw (Poland) Sch. Econs., 1995, U. Econs., Prague, Czech Republic, 1995, U. Miami, 1995, U. Rochester, 1995. Asst. prof. U. Chgo., 1954-57; from asst. prof. to assoc. prof. Columbia U., N.Y.C., 1957-60, prof. econs., 1960-68, Arthur Lehman prof. econs., 1968-70; prof. econs. U. Chgo., 1970-83, prof. econs. and sociology, 1983—, chmn. dept. econs., 1984-85; Ford Found. vis. prof. econs. U. Chgo., 1969-70; assoc. Econs. Rsch. Ctr. Nat. Opinion Rsch. Ctr., Chgo., 1980—; mem. domestic adv. bd. Hoover Instn., Stanford, Calif., 1973-91, sr. fellow, 1990—; mem. acad. adv. bd. Am. Enterprise Inst., 1987-92; rsch. policy advisor Ctr. for Econ. Analysis Human Behavior Nat. Bur. Econ. Rsch., 1972-78, mem. and sr. research assoc., 1957-79; assoc. mem. Inst. Fiscal and Monetary Policy, Ministry of Japan, 1988—. Author: The Economics of Discrimination, 1957, 2d edit., 1971, Human Capital, 1964, 3d edit., 1993, Japanese transl., 1975, Spanish trans., 1984, Chinese trans., 1987, Romanian trans., 1997, Human Capital and the Personal Distribution of Income: An Analytical Approach, 1967, Economic Theory, 1971, Japanese transl., 1976, (with Gilbert Ghez) The Allocation of Time and Goods Over the Life Cycle, 1975, The Economic Approach to Human Behavior, 1976, German trans., 1982, Polish transl., 1990, Chinese transl., 1993, Romanian trans., 1994, A Treatise on the Family, 1981, expanded edit., 1991, Spanish transl., 1987, Chinese transl., 1988, Accounting for Tastes, 1996, Czech trans., 1998, Italian trans., 1999, (with Guity Nashat Becker) The Economics of Life, 1996, Chinese trans., 1997, German trans., 1998, Japanese trans., 1998, (in German) Family, Society, and State, 1996, (in Italian) L'approccio Economico al Comportamento Umano, 1998; editor: Essays in Labor Economics in Honor of H. Gregg Lewis, 1976; co-editor: (with William M. Landes) Essays in the Economics of Crime and Punishment, 1974; columnist, Bus. Week, 1985—; contbr. articles to profl. jours. Recipient W.S. Woytinsky award U. Mich., 1964, Profl. Achievement award U. Chgo. Alumni Assn., 1968, Frank E. Seidman Disting. award in Polit. Economy, 1985, merit award NIH, 1986, John R. Commons award Omicron Delta Epsilon, 1987, Nobel prize in Econ. Scis., 1992, Lord Found. award, 1995, Irene Taueber award, 1997. Fellow Am. Statis. Assn., Econometric Soc., Am. Acad. Arts and Scis., Am. Econ. Assn. (Disting., v.p. 1974, pres. 1987, John Bates Clark medal 1967); mem. NAS, NAE (founding mem., v.p. 1965-67), Am. Philos. Soc., Internat. Union for Sci. Study Population, Mont Pelerin Soc. (exec. bd. dirs. 1985-94, v.p. 1989-90, pres. 1990-92), Western Econ. Assn. (pres. 1996-97), Pontifical Acad. Scis., Phi Beta Kappa. Office: U Chgo Dept Econs 1126 E 59th St Chicago IL 60637-1539

BECKER, GLENN ADAM, plastic surgeon; b. Bklyn., Mar. 13, 1958. BS with high honors, SUNY, Stony Brook, 1980; MD, SUNY, Downstate, 1984. Diplomate Nat. Bd. Med. Examiners, Am. Bd. Surgery, Am. Bd. Plastic Surgery; lic. N.Y., Calif. Tchg. asst. gen. biology, organic chemistry SUNY, Stony Brook, 1983, asst. clin. instr. surgery Sch. Medicine, 1989-90; clin. asst. instr. surgery Coll. Medicine Health Sci. Ctr. SUNY, Bklyn., 1991-93, asst. prof. (GST) in surgery Coll. Medicine Health Sci. Ctr., 1997, dir. hand surgery divsn. plastic surgery Health Sci. Ctr., 1998, resident in plastic surgery Health Sci. Ctr., 1990-91, chief plastic surgery resident Health Sci. Ctr., 1992-93; resident in surgery dept. surgery NYU Med. Ctr., 1984-86, hand surgery fellow dept. plastic and orthopedic surgery, 1986-90; surg. resident dept. surgery Nassau County Med. Ctr., East Meadow, N.Y., 1986-89, mem. pharmacy, therapeutics com., ICU com., 1989-90; pvt. practice N.Y.C., 1993—; tchg. asst. surgery Sch. Medicine NYU, 1984-86; asst. attending Bellevue Hosp., N.Y.C., 1990-91; Presenter, researcher in field. Contbr. numerous articles to profl. jours. Fellow ACS (assoc.); mem. AMA, Am. Soc. Plastic and Reconstructive Surgeons (mem. guidelines com. 1996-99, govt. rels. com. 1997—, physicians' current procedural terminology/relative values com.), Med. Soc. State N.Y., Assn. Academic Surgeons, Soc. Former Residents and Assocs. Plastic Surgery (v.p. 1997, pres. 1998). Office: 109 E 61st St New York NY 10021-8101

BECKER, HAROLD, film director, producer. Motion picture dir., prodr. Prodr., dir. films The Ragman's Daughter, 1972, Malice, 1993, City Hall, 1996; dir. The Onion Field, 1979, Taps, 1981, Vision Quest, 1985, Sea of Love, 1989, Bodily Harm, 1993, Mercury Rising, 1998, Solo, 1999, others. Office: c/o DGA 7920 Sunset Blvd Los Angeles CA 90046

BECKER, HERBERT LAWRENCE, writer, accountant; b. Hollywood, Fla., Aug. 12, 1956; s. Jack and Lorraine (Abrams) B.; m. Malka Gasner, Jan. 1, 1977 (div. Jan. 1990); children: Randi, Adam, Brian; m. Shelly Basser, Nov. 8, 1992; children: Gillah, Dovid, Nehemiah. BBA, Roosevelt U., Belgium, 1983, MBA, 1984; DBA, Columbia U., 1997. CPA, Belgium; cert. mgmt. acct., Soc. Pub. Accts. Dist. mgr. Coles Book Stores, U.S. and Can., 1976-83; pub. acct., U.S. and Can., 1983-87; sr. fin. mgr. Video One, Can., 1987-90; pres. Postal Plus Svcs., Can., 1990-93. Author: All the Secrets of Magic, 1994, Magic Secrets, 1996,, So That's How They Do It, 1996, Magic Secrets, 1997-98; (tv spls.) World's Greatest Magic Secrets . . . Revealed, More Magic Secrets, 1997, World's Greatest Magic Secrets, 1999. Democrat. Avocations: writing, magic, karate. Home: 2607 S Woodland Blvd Deland FL 32720-7001

BECKER, ISIDORE A., business executive; b. N.Y.C., May 10, 1926; s. Max and Eva (Chester) B.; m. Adele Sandler, Dec. 20, 1947; children: Steven Richard, Carol Ann. B.A., Bklyn. Coll., 1949. Partner Herbert D. Silver & Co., N.Y.C., 1956-63; fin. v.p., chmn. financial com. Rapid-Am. Corp., N.Y.C., 1966-72; vice chmn. bd. Rapid-Am. Corp., 1967-72, 76-82, dir., 1964-82, pres., 1972-76; chief financial officer, treas. McCrory Corp., N.Y.C., 1964-70; dir. McCrory Corp., 1964-82; vice chmn. bd., dir. Glen Alden Corp., N.Y.C., 1967-72; chmn. bd., dir. Schenley Industries, Inc., 1968-82; pres. Riviera Hotel, Inc., 1973-83; chmn. bd. Shaw-Ross Internat. Importers, Inc., 1983—, Southern Wine & Spirits, 1983—. Vice chmn. bd. Boys Town Jerusalem; founder Albert Einstein Coll. Medicine; asso. chmn., bd. govs. Anti Defamation League B'nai B'rith. Served with USMCR, 1944-46. Home: 10155 Collins Ave Bal Harbour FL 33154-1655 Office: 126 E 56th St New York NY 10022-3613

BECKER, IVAN, advertising executive; b. Newark, Nov. 5, 1948; s. Abraham and Rose B.; m. Nadeen Harriet Klein, Oct. 16, 1973; children: Amy Bree, Michael Pat. BS in Bus., Ohio State U., 1971; MA in Radio and TV, Northwestern U., 1972. Asst. media dir. Sullivan Stauffer Colwell & Bayles (now Lintas), N.Y.C., 1973-75; assoc. planning dir. Needham Harper & Steers, N.Y.C., 1975-76; sr. planner Ogilvy & Mather, N.Y.C., 1976; media dir. Keyes Martin & Co., Springfield, N.J., 1976-78; sr. v.p., assoc. media dir. BBDO Worldwide, N.Y.C., 1978—. Recipient Creative Media awards ADWEEK Mktg. and Media Edn., N.Y.C., 1987, 88. Democrat. Jewish. Avocations: tennis, golf, music. Office: BBDO NY 1285 Avenue Of The Americas New York NY 10019-6028*

BECKER, IVAN ENDRE, plastics company executive; b. Budapest, Hungary, June 14, 1929; came to U.S., 1946, naturalized, 1953; s. Dezsö and Kato (Irsai) B.; student NYU, 1953-54, New Sch. for Social Rsch., 1953-54; m. Nancy Helen Greenglass, Feb. 11, 1962; children—David Michael, Kenneth Andrew. With mktg. and prodn. depts., asst. prodn. mgr. Exxon Film div. Exxon Co., N.Y.C. and Pottsville, Pa., 1955-67, tech. services mgr., 1958-64; founder, pres. Edison Plastics Co. div. Blessings Corp., mems. Am. Stock Exchange, South Plainfield, N.J., 1967—, dir. 1976-78, mem. adv. com. to bd. dirs., 1978—; pres. Blessings Internat. Inc., Piscataway, N.J., 1980-88, pres., chief exec. officer, 1988-94, ret., 1994, dir., also bd. dirs.; pres., chief exec. officer Blessings Corp. Cpl. Signal Corps, U.S. Army, 1951-53. Mem. Soc. Plastics Industry, Soc. Plastics Engrs., Flexible Packaging Assn., Internat. Disposables Assn., TAPPI, Econ. Club, Chemists Club (N.Y.C.), Econ. Club N.Y. Home: 306 Shadybrook Ln Princeton NJ 08540-4156

BECKER, JAMES MURDOCH, surgeon, educator; b. Cleve., Jan. 7, 1949; s. Norman O. and Mildred Edith (Murdoch) B.; m. Christine Louise Lohmann, Dec. 30, 1972; children: Alexander, Selby, Catherine, Anne. BA in Biology, Yale U., 1971; MD, Case Western Res. U., 1975. Diplomate Nat. Bd. Med. Examiners, Am. Bd. Surgery; lic. surgeon, Minn., Utah, Mo., Mass. Intern in surgery U. Utah Hosps., Salt Lake City, 1975-76, resident in gen. surgery, 1976-79, chief resident in surgery, 1976-79; research fellow in surgery U. Utah Sch. Medicine, 1977-78, asst. prof. surgery, 1982-86; mem. surg. staff VA Hosp., Salt Lake City, 1982-86, chief green service, 1983-86, head nutritional support team, 1983-86; mem. cons. staff Intermountain Unit Shriners Hosps. for Crippled Children, Salt Lake City, 1984-86; assoc. prof. surgery, dir. gastrointestinal surgery Washington U. Sch. Medicine, 1986-89; assoc. prof surgery, chief divsn. gen. and gastroint. surg. Harvard Med. Sch./Brigham and Women's Hosp., Boston, 1989-94; James Utley prof. and chmn. surgeon-in-chief Boston U. Sch. Medicine/Boston Med. Ctr., 1994—. Contbr. articles to profl. jours., chpts. to books. NIH fellow, Mayo Clinic, 1980-82; grantee Johnson & Johnson Products, Inc., 1985, NIH, 1985—, Sandeoz Corp., 1985-87, Ethicon, Inc., 1985-86. Mem. ACS, AMA, Am. Gastroenterol. Assn., Am. Motility Soc., Am. Pancreatic Assn., Assn. Acad. Surgery, Am. Soc. Parenteral and Enteral Nutrition, Internat. Biliary Assn., Collegium Internat. Chirurgiae Digestivae (Grassi prize 8th World Congress 1984), Soc. for Surgery Alimentary Tract, Soc. Univ. Surgeons, Yale U. Alumni Assn., Am. coll. Surgeons, Am. Surg. Assn., We. Surg. Assn., Cen. Surg. Assn., New Eng. Surg. Assn., Am. Soc. Colorectal Surgeons, Soc. Internat. Chirugiae, Alpha Omega Alpha. Office: Boston Med Ctr 88 E Newton St Boston MA 02118-2308

BECKER, JAMES RICHARD, lawyer; b. San Juan, P.R., Sept. 25, 1954; s. John Joseph and Patricia (Doherty) B.; m. Mary E. McGurk; children: Colette Anne, Robert Charles II. BA in English, Va. Tech., 1977; JD, George Mason Law Sch., 1982. Bar: Va. 1982, U.S. Dist. Ct. (ea. and we. dists.) Va. 1982, U.S. Ct. Appeals (4th cir.) 1982. Atty. James R. Becker, Esquire, Middleburg and Chantilly, Va., 1982-93; assoc. atty. Nichols, Bergere & Zauzig, P.C., Woodbridge, Va., 1993-94, Joel Atlas Skirble and Assocs., Falls Church, Va., 1994-98; of counsel Anderson & Corrie, Fairfax, Va., 1998—. Editor Law Rev., 1980-82. Mem. Fairfax Bar Assn. Avocations: computers, software development. Home: 4515 Fillingame Dr Chantilly VA 20151-2820 Office: 12600 Fair Lakes Circle Ste 220 Fairfax VA 22033

BECKER, JEROME DAVID, writer; b. June 6, 1941. BA, U. Richmond, Va., 1965; MA, Pa. State U., State Coll., 1967; PhD, Am. U., Washington, 1974. Sports writer Hopewell (Va.) News, 1964-65; columnist, editl. writer Cin. Enquirer, 1974-84; editor, writer USA Today, Rosslyn, Va., 1984-86; assoc. dir. pub. affairs The White House, Washington, 1986-89; dep. dir. speechwriting Dept. Health and Human Svcs., Washington, 1989-91; speech writer to dir. Office Thrift Supervision, Washington, 1991-93; pub. affairs analyst, speechwriter Am. Petroleum Inst., Washington, 1993—. E-mail: becker@api.org. Office: 1220 L St NW Washington DC 20005

BECKER, JIM, gem historian, jeweler; b. Sault Sainte Marie, Mich., Apr. 28, 1953; s. Wade Moore and Mary Bonnie (Law) B. BA, U. Ctrl. Fla., 1977; grad., Gemological Inst., 1991. Assoc. Zales Jewelers, Jensen Beach, Fla., 1987-88, Mayor's Jewelers, Jensen Beach, 1988-91; pres., owner Gem Advice Co., Stuart, Fla., 1991—; owner Am. Jewelry Co., Vero Beach, Fla., 1994—; gem historian Christie's Auction House, Geneva, 1988—, Smithsonian Inst., 1994—; head American Jewelry Co., Vero Beach, Fla.; lectr. and conductor of workshops Sotheby's; gem and fraud cons. FBI, 1997—. Tracer of jewels to major owners, including Catherine the Great, Empress Eugenie, Czarina Alexandra, Maharanee of Baroda, Enid Annenberg Haupt, Queen Mary, Lady Cullinan, others; traced 423 carat Logan Sapphire to Imperial Russia; presented Cullinan Blue Diamond Necklace to Smithsonian Inst., 1994; assisted Smithsonian Inst. to obtain their first Black Pearls for the Gem and Mineral Hall; contbr. articles to profl. jours. Promoter Am. Heart Assn., Stuart, 1991—; mem., sponsor Vero Beach (Fla.) Ctr. for Arts, 1991. Credited in Lord Ian Balfour's latest edit. of Famous Diamonds. Mem. Jewelers of Am., C. of C. Chmn.'s Club Ctr. for Arts, Rotary Internat. Known internationally as the "Gem Sleuth", reputed to be the only living person in the jewelry industry with a career-related nickname. Avocations: collecting jewelry, films, writing, theater. Office: Gem Advice Co 3905 12th St Sebastian FL 32976-2829 also: Am Jewelry Co 2855 Ocean Dr Vero Beach FL 32963-2039

BECKER, JON ANDREW, arts and education consultant; b. Milw., Aug. 9, 1953; s. Raymond Matthias and Adeline (Yellen) B. BMus, Lawrence U., 1975; MS in Music Edn., U. Ill., 1987. Cert. K-12 music tchr. life Wis., N.J., K-12 music, Mich., supervision N.J. Tchr. Oconomowoc (Wis.) Public Schs., 1976-84; prof. Ripon (Wis.) Coll., 1987-88, Westminster Choir Coll., Princeton, N.J., 1988-91; arts edn. cons. Traverse City, Mich., 1991-99, Madison, Wis., 1999—; cons. Ednl. Testing Svc., Princeton, 1989-91, Bridgeton Symphony Orch., 1990-93, Wis. Edn. Assn. Coun., 1994—, others. Prodr. (CDs) Dancing Bear Music, 1998, NMC Music Department Presents!, 1998. Bd. dirs. Traverse Area Arts Coun., Traverse City, 1993-99, Mich. Assn. Cmty. Arts Agys., Southfield, Mich., 1995—; pres.-elect Grand Traverse County Planning Commn., 1995. U. Ill. fellow, 1984-86. Mem. ASCD, Internat. Soc. of Music Educators (lect. 1990, St. Petersburg, Russia), Am. Fedn. of Musicians, Internat. Trombone Assn., Soc. of Music Tchr. Educators. Democrat. Avocations: environmental advocacy, outdoor activities.

BECKER, JULIETTE, psychologist, marriage and family therapist; b. L.A., Sept. 22, 1938; d. Louis Joseph and Elissa Cecelia (Bevacqua) Cevola; m. Richard Charles Sprenger, Aug. 13, 1960 (div. Dec. 1984); children: Lisa Anne, Stephen Louis, Gina Marie, Paul Joseph, Gretchen Lynette; m. Vance Benjiman Becker, Nov. 7, 1986. BA in Psychology, Calif. State U., Fullerton, 1983; M in Marriage and Family Therapy, U.S. Internat. U., 1985; PhD in Clin. Psychology, William Lyon U., 1988. Therapist Villa Park (Calif.) Psychol. Svcs., 1985-88, psychologist, 1988—. Mem. APA, Am. Assn. Marriage, Family and Child Therapists, Calif. Assn. Marriage, Family and Child Therapists. Avocations: painting, opera, classical piano, interior design, writing. E-mail: jbecker586@aol.com. Fax: (714) 283-3701. Office: Villa Park Psychol Svcs 17871 Santiago Blvd Ste 206 Orange CA 92861-4131 also: Newport Coast Psychol Svcs 260 Newport Center Dr Ste 320 Newport Beach CA 92660-7525

BECKER, KARL MARTIN, lawyer; b. Glenridge, N.J., May 30, 1943; s. Alfred Martin and Helen K. (Gramse) B.; m. Barbara A. Benton, Feb. 19, 1966; children—Glenn M., Mark W. A.B., Yale U., 1965; J.D., U. Chgo., 1968. Bar: Ill. 1968, S.C. 1994. Assoc. Vedder Price Kaufman Kammholz, Chgo., 1968-75, ptnr., 1975-78; asst. gen. counsel Esmark, Inc., Chgo., 1978-83, assoc. gen. counsel, 1983-84; v.p., gen. counsel, sec. Swift Ind. Corp., Chgo., 1985-86, sr. v.p., gen. counsel, sec., 1986; sr. v.p., gen. counsel Beatrice Cos., Inc. and BCI Holdings Corp., Chgo., 1986-87, E-II Holdings, Inc., Beatrice Co., Chgo., 1987-88, Beatrice Co., Chgo., 1988-90; dir. Mathers Fund, Inc., Bannockburn, Ill., 1991-98. Mem. ABA, S.C. Bar Assn., Chgo. Bar Assn. Avocations: skiing; sailing. Home: 31 Hearthwood Dr Hilton Head Island SC 29928-2906

BECKER, LAWRENCE CARLYLE, philosopher, educator, author; b. Lincoln, Nebr., Apr. 26, 1939; s. Albert Carlyle and Harriette (Toren) B.; m. Charlotte Ann Burner, June 10, 1967. BA in History, Midland Coll., 1961; MA in Philosophy, U Chgo., 1963, PhD in Philosophy, 1965; LHD (hon.), Midland Luth. Coll., 1994. Instr. philosophy Hollins Coll., Roanoke, Va., 1965-67, asst. prof. philosophy, 1967-71, assoc. prof., 1971-78, prof., 1978-89, fellow of coll., 1989—, dir. summer inst. for ethics and pub. policy, 1990-92; prof. philosophy, William R. Kenan, Jr. prof. humanities Coll. William and Mary, Williamsburg, Va., 1989—, acting chair, 1992-93; mem. summer conf. in metaphysics Coun. for Philos. Studies, 1968, mem. summer conf. on moral problems in medicine, 1974; vis. fellow in philosophy Harvard U., Cambridge, Mass., 1975-76; invited lectr. in field. Author: On Justifying Moral Judgments, 1973, Property Rights: Philosophic Foundations, 1977, Reciprocity, 1986, A New Stoicism, 1998; editor: (with Kenneth Kipnis) Property: Cases, Concepts and Critiques, 1984 (with Charlotte B. Becker) A History of Western Ethics, 1992, Encyclopedia of Ethics (2 vols.), 1992; mem. editl. bd. Ethics, 1979-85, assoc. editor, 1985—, acting editor, 1994-95, book rev. editor, 1998—; contbr. over 70 articles and book revs. to profl. jours. Woodrow Wilson grad. fellow, 1961-62; Danforth grad. fellow, 1961-65, Woodrow Wilson dissertation fellow (hon.), 1964-65, fellow NEH, 1971-

72, 93-94, Oxford (Eng.) U., 1971-72, Harvard U., 1975-76, Am. Coun. Learned Socs., 1975-76, humanities fellow Rockefeller Found., 1982-83, Ctr. for Advanced Study in Behavioral Scis., 1983-84. Mem. Am. Philos. Assn. (com. on philosophy and law 1984-87, adv. com. to program com. ethics divsn. 1989-92, com. on status and future of profession 1993-96), Am. Soc. for Legal and Polit. Philosophy, Va. Philos. Assn. (sec. 1978-79, v.p. 1979-80, pres. 1980-81). Office: Coll William and Mary Dept Philosophy Williamsburg VA 23187

BECKER, MARVIN BURTON, historian; b. Phila., July 20, 1922; s. Benjamin and Florence (Wachs) B.; m. Beatrice Lapayowker, Jan. 16, 1944; children: Wendy, Dana. BS, U. Pa., 1946, MA, 1947, PhD, 1950. Asst. prof. history U. Ark., 1950-52, Baldwin-Wallace Coll., Berea, Ohio, 1952-56; asso. prof. Western Res. U., 1957-63; prof. U. Rochester, N.Y., 1964-73; prof. history U. Mich., Ann Arbor, 1973—; chmn. dept. U. Mich., 1977-79, Richard Hudson research prof., 1984-85; seminar presenter Spelman Villa of Johns Hopkins U., Florence, Italy, 1995. Author: Florence in Transition, 2 vols., 1967-68, Medieval Italy: Constraints and Creativity, 1981, transl. into Italian, 1986, Civility and Society in Western Europe, 1300-1600, 1988, The Emergence of Civil Society in the 18th Century: A Privileged Moment in the History of England, Scotland, and France, 1994, Indiana Law Jour., vol. 72, 1997; series gen. editor Studies in Medieval and Early Modern Civilization for U. Mich. Press. Served with AUS, 1944. Fulbright fellow, 1953-55; fellow Guggenheim Found., 1956-57; fellow Am. Council Learned Socs., 1963-64; fellow Inst. Advanced Study, Princeton, N.J., 1968-69; Harvard fellow I Tatti, 1963-64; sr. fellow Humanities Inst., Johns Hopkins U., 1966-67; hon. mem. Deputazione di Storia Patria per la Toscana, 1976. Mem. Medieval Acad., Renaissance Soc. Am., Am. Hist. Assn., Nat. Humanities Faculty, Soc. Scholars (Johns Hopkins U. 1992). Jewish. Home: 2335 Hill St Ann Arbor MI 48104-2651 Office: 4609 Haven Hall Ann Arbor MI 48109

BECKER, MARY LOUISE, political scientist; b. St. Louis; d. W. R. and Evelyn (Thompson) Becker; divorced; children: James, John. BS, Washington U., St. Louis, 1949, MA, 1951; PhD, Radcliffe Coll., 1957; postgrad., U. Karachi (Pakistan), 1953-54. Intelligence rsch. analyst Dept. State, Washington, 1957-59; internat. rels. officer AID, Washington, 1959-64, community rels. officer, 1964-66, sci. rsch. officer, 1966-71, UN rels. officer, 1971-91; pres. Internat. Devel. Enterprises, Washington, 1992—; adviser U.S. dels. 19th, 21st, 23d, 24th, 26th, 28th, 30th, 32d, 34th Governing Coun. sessions UN Devel. Program; adv. U.S. del. 3d prep. com. meeting World Conf. UN Decade for Women; adviser U.S. dels. UNICEF exec. bd. sessions, 1987-91; lectr. internat. rels. civic orgns., student groups, 1954—; mem. U.S. Com. for UN Fund for Women. Author: Muhammed Iqbal, 1965; contbg. editor: Concise Ency. of Middle East, 1973; contbr. articles to govt. publs. Mem. adv. bd. chmn. internat. student placement Washington Citizenship Seminar, Nat. YMCA-YWCA, Washington, 1961-71. Blewett fellow Washington U., 1951, Resident fellow Radcliffe Coll., 1952-56; Fulbright scholar U. Karachi, 1953-54. Mem. AAUW, Am. Polit. Sci. Assn., Soc. Internat. Devel., Assn. Asian Studies, Asia Soc., Middle East Inst., UN Assn. (bd. dirs. Nat. Capital area 1991—), South Asian Muslim Studies Assn. (v.p. 1992—), Mo. Soc. Washington (sec. 1959-60), Mortar Bd., Chimes, Internat. Club, Harvard Club (Washington), Alpha Lambda Delta, Beta Gamma Sigma, Eta Mu Phi, Pi Sigma Alpha. Presbyterian. Office: North Bldg Ste 700 601 Pennsylvania Ave NW Washington DC 20004-2601

BECKER, MICHAEL ALLEN, physician, educator; b. N.Y.C., Oct. 3, 1940; s. David S. and Sylvia M. (Salomon) B.; m. Mary E. Baim; children: David, Jonathan, Abigail, Arielle, Daniel. BA, U. Pa., Phila., 1961, MD, 1965. Diplomate Am. Bd. Internal Medicine, with subspecialty in rheumatology. Intern Barnes Hosp., Washington U., St. Louis, 1965-66, resident, 1969-70; asst. prof. U. Calif., San Diego, 1972-77, assoc. prof., 1977-80; prof. medicine Pritzker Sch. Medicine U. Chgo., 1980—; mem. biochemistry study sect. NIH, Bethesda, Md., 1991-95. Contbr. numerous rsch. articles ot profl. publs. Sr. asst. surgeon USPHS, 1966-69. Fellow John Simon Guggenheim Meml. Found.; mem. Am. Soc. Clin. Investigation, Assn. Am. Physicians, Am. Coll. Rheumatology. Office: U Chgo Med Ctr MC0930 Chicago IL 60637

BECKER, MICHAEL EDWARD, police and emergency medical services executive; b. Flint, Mich., Dec. 29, 1947; s. Rolland Nelson and Jeanine (Bellamey) B.; m. Roberta Caverly, Oct. 8, 1966 (div 1978); children: Richard Michael, Michelle Ilene; m. Kylene Becker, Oct. 11, 1980; children: Alisha May, Michael James, David Alan, Kristina Lynn, Shanna Kaye. AS in Health Scis., Mott C.C., Flint, Mich., 1979, AS in Criminal Justice, 1985; BA, Spring Arbor Coll., 1994; cert. completion, FBI Acad., Quantico, Va., 1995. Police officer Genesee Twp., Mich., 1971-74; police dep. Genesee County Sheriff, Flint, Mich., 1974-76, 77-79; police sergeant Genesee County Sheriff, Flint, 1979-87, corrections lt., 1987, police sergeant, 1987-90, police lt. assigned comdg. officer paramedic section, 1990—; police officer Montrose Twp. Police, 1976-77; treas. Regio 5 EMS Coun., Flint, 1981-82, bd. dirs., 1982-84; bd. dirs. Genesee County Med. Control, Flint, 1990—; mem. Genessee County local emergency planning com., Flint, 1990—. Advocate for EMS mileage, Com. to pass, Flint, Mich., 1996. Recipient Care a Medic award SWM Systems, Mich. State Senate, 1995. Mem. FBI Nat. Acad. Assocs. Avocations: Japanese karate, family activities, running, weight lifting. Office: Genessee County Sheriff Dpt 1002 S Saginaw St Flint MI 48502-1410

BECKER, MICHAEL KELLEHER, university administrator, consultant; b. L.A., June 27, 1941; s. George Joseph and Marion Julia (Kelleher) B.; m. Eugenia Margosian, June 11, 1963; children: Gwendolyn Becker O'Keefe, Sean Michael Becker, Katherine Becker. BA, Swarthmore Coll., 1963; MA, U. Calif., Berkeley, 1965; PhD, U. Calif., 1970. Contract negotiator Oakland Naval Supply Ctr., 1966-67; instr., asst., assoc. prof. Ctrl. Conn. State U., New Britain, 1967-77; dean pers. adminstrn. Ctrl. Conn. State U., 1978-89; dir. employee rels. So. Ill. U. Sys., Carbondale, 1989-92; asst. v.p. acad. affairs-faculty rels. U. Toledo, 1992-96; dir. human resources Western Washington U., Bellingham, 1996—. Mem. New Britain Sch. Bd., 1983-89 (pres. 1988-89). Woodrow Wilson fellow Woodrow Wilson Found., 1963. Mem. Acad. for Acad. Pers. Adminstrn., Coll. and Univ. Pers. Assn., Soc. for Human Resource Mgmt. Unitarian. E-mail: mikebecker@wwu.edu. Home: 3014 Windtree Ct Bellingham WA 98226-5937 Office: Western Wash Univ Human Resources Mail Stop 9021 Bellingham WA 98225

BECKER, MURRAY LEONARD, corporate financial consultant, consulting actuary; b. Phila., July 30, 1933; s. Simon and Bertha B. (Berlin) B.; m. Anita Goodman, Apr. 3, 1955; children: Mark, Lynn, Donna (dec.). BS in Econs., U. Pa., 1955. Actuary Mutual of N.Y., N.Y.C., 1955-70; v.p., cons. actuary Johnson & Higgins, N.Y.C., 1970-88; pres. Becker & Rooney, Inc., Teaneck, N.J., 1988-95; pres. Becker & Rooney divsn. Kwasha Lipton, Ft. Lee, N.J., 1995-97; v.p. J.P. Morgan Investment Mgmt., N.Y.C., 1997-98. Mem. actuarial adv. com. N.Y.C. Retirement System, 1990. Named Advisor of Yr., Pension World Mag., 1986; voted by his peers for the Investment Mgmt. Inst.'s 1996 most respected GIC/Stable Value profl. award. Fellow Soc. of Actuaries; mem. Am. Acad. Actuaries, Actuarial Soc. N.Y. (pres. 1982-83). Home: 631 James Ln River Vale NJ 07675

BECKER, NANCY ANNE, state supreme court justice; b. Las Vegas, May 23, 1955; d. Arthur William and Margaret Mary (McLoughlin) B. BA, U.S. Internat. U., 1976; JD, George Washington U., 1979. Bar: Nev. 1979, D.C. 1980, Md. 1982, U.S. Dist. Ct. Nev. 1987, U.S. Ct. Appeals (9th cir.) 1987. Legis. cons. D.C. Office on Aging, Washington, 1979-83; assoc. Goldstein & Ahalt, College Park, Md., 1980-82; pvt. practice Washington, 1982-83; dep. city atty., prosecutor criminal div. City of Las Vegas, 1983; judge Las Vegas Mcpl. Ct., 1987-89, Clark County Dist. Ct., Las Vegas, 1989—; cons. MADD, Las Vegas, 1983-87. Contbr. articles to profl. publs. Pres. Clark County Pro Bono Project, Las Vegas, 1984-88. Mem. So. Nev. Assn. Women Attys. (past officer), Am. Businesswomen's Assn. (treas. Las Vegas chpt. 1985-86), NCCJ, Las Vegas and Latin C. of C., Vietnam Vets Am., Soroptimist Internat. Office: Nevada Supreme Court Capital Complex 201 S Carson St Carson City NV 89701-4702

BECKER, NETTIE, preschool administrator; b. Bklyn., Aug. 29, 1930; d. Harry and Molly (Small) Shames; m. Paul Becker, Dec. 26, 1954; children: Lynn, Lesley. BS in Health and Phys. Edn., Bklyn. Coll., 1953; M in Profl. Studies, Adelphi U., 1988. Cert. tchr., N.Y. Phys. edn. and dance tchr. Wash. Irving H.S., N.Y.C., 1953-56, Abraham Lincoln H.S., Bklyn., 1956-59, Springfield Gardens H.S., Queens, N.Y., 1967-87; interactive movement specialist early intervention program Kennedy Child Study Ctr., N.Y.C., 1988-94; child devel. therapist for presch. children, N.Y.C. and Rockville Ctr., 1994—. Author: A Special Kind of Love: A Guide for Parents and Teachers of Children with Disabilities, 1994, A Comprehensive Guide for Caregivers in Day-Care Settings, 1999. Vol. Cmty. Dance Programs, Queens, 1967-87. Mem. AAHPERD, Acad. Dance Therapy (registered), Laban Movement Inst., United Fedn. Tchrs. (sec. Springfield Gardens chpt. 1986-87). Democrat. Avocations: dance, mountain climbing, theatre, travel. Home and Office: PO Box 504 Rockville Centre NY 11571-0504

BECKER, QUINN HENDERSON, orthopedic surgeon, army officer; b. Kirksville, Mo., June 11, 1930; s. Quinn Henry B. and Sarah Lucille (Henderson) Finley; m. Gladys Marie Roussell, Aug. 11, 1951; children: Quinn E., Terri K., Paul Eric. Grad., N.E. La. State Coll., 1952; MD, La. State U., 1956; student, Armed Forces Staff Coll., 1969-70, Command and Gen. Staff Coll., 1971, U.S. Army War Coll., 1974-75. Diplomate: Am. Bd. Orthopedic Surgery. Commd. 2d lt. U.S. Army, advanced through grades to lt. gen., 1985; intern Tripler Gen. Hosp., 1956-57; resident in orthopedic surgery Confederate Meml. Med. Ctr., Shreveport, La., 1958-61; orthopedic surgeon Ft. Gordon, Ga., 1962-63; chief orthopedic service Ft. Rucker, Ala., 1963-64; comdg. officer 5th Surg. Hosp. (Mobile Army), Heidelberg, W. Ger., 1964-65; surgeon 3d Inf. Div., Wurzburg, W. Ger., 1965-66; chief orthpedic surgery 33d Field Hosp., Wurzburg, 1965; asst. chief orthopedic service Walter Reed Gen. Hosp., 1966-69; chief profl. services 85th Evacuation Hosp., Vietnam, 1970; div. surgeon and bn. comdr. 15th Med. Bn. 1st Cavalry Div., Vietnam, 1970-71; chief orthopedic service and orthopedic residency tng. Tripler Army Med. Ctr., 1971-74; surgeon 18th Airborne Corps., Ft. Bragg, 1975-77; comdr. Med. Activity Womack Army Hosp., Ft. Bragg, 1976-77; dir. health care ops. Office Surgeon Gen., 1977-80; comdt. Acad. Health Scis., U.S. Army, Ft. Sam Houston, Tex., 1980-81; dep. surgeon gen. Washington, 1981-83; comdr. 7th Med. Command, Heidelberg, 1983-85; Surgeon Gen. Dept. Army, 1985-88, ret., 1988; asst. prof. orthopedic surgery Howard U., Washington, 1967-69; clin. assoc. prof. Sch. Medicine U. Hawaii, Honolulu, 1973-74; chief of staff VA Hosp., Asheville, N.C., 1989-92, ret. 1992. Contbr. papers to publs. and confs. in field. Decorated Legion of Merit, Meritorious Service medal, Bronze Star, Air medal, Disting. Service medal. Fellow Am. Acad. Orthopedic Surgeons (chmn. mil. affairs com. 1981-85), ACS, Am. Coll. Physician Execs. (disting.); mem. AMA (ho. of dels.), Am. Orthopaedic Assn., Masons (33d degree, Grand Cross 1993), Civitan (pres. Asheville club 1992, chmn. internat. rsch. com. 1996—). Home: PO Box 2388 Dillon CO 80435-2388

BECKER, RALPH LEONARD, psychologist; b. Cin., July 15, 1927; s. Morris and Sarah Ruth B.; m. Evelyn Zeifman, Aug. 15, 1976. BA in Sci., Ohio State U., 1958, BS in Edn., 1960, MA in Psychology, 1961, PhD in Psychology, 1979. Lic. psychologist, Ohio; cert. counselor, Ohio. Spl. tchr. Columbus (Ohio) City Schs., 1962-64; staff psychologist Ohio Dept. Mental Retardation/Devel. Disabilities, Columbus, 1964-68, research scientist, 1968-72, research assoc., 1972-82; research dir. Elbern Pubs., Columbus, 1982—. Author: Reading-Free Vocational Interest Inventory, 1981, rev. edit. 1988, Occupational Title List, 1984, rev. edit. 1992, Becker Work Adjustment Profile, 1989; contbr. articles to profl. jours. Grantee State of Ohio, 1966, 67, U.S. Office of Edn., 1968. Fellow Am. Assn. on Mental Retardation; mem. Coun. for Exceptional Children, Ohio Psychol. Assn., Ohio State Alumni Assn., Am. Psychol. Assn. Avocations: carpentry, elec. wiring, gardening, woodcraft. Office: Elbern Publs PO Box 09497 Columbus OH 43209-0497

BECKER, RAY EVERETT, management consultant; b. Grand Rapids, Mich., Jan. 14, 1937; s. Lawson Everett and Virginia Jane (Shellman) B.; m. Mary Rita Warren, Aug. 18, 1960 (div. 1972); children: Elizabeth Anne, Catherine Virginia; m. Arlyss Ellen Roeber, Aug. 12, 1974. AB in Engring., Dartmouth Coll., 1959, MS in Engring and Bus. Adminstrn., 1960; MS in Mgmt., MIT, 1974. Project adminstr. Astro Electronics div. RCA, Hightstown, N.J., 1961-65; bus. mgr.radar lab. Missile Systems div. Raytheon Corp., Bedford, Mass., 1965-68; mgr. mgmt. systems Missile Systems div. Raytheon Corp., Bedford, 1968-70, mgr. adminstrn. and data processing, 1970-73; program mgr. Missile Systems div. Raytheon Corp., Lowell, Mass., 1981-85; mgr. comml. svcs. Raytheon Svc. Co., Burlington, Mass., 1974-75; dir. mktg. Raytheon Svc. Co., Burlington, 1975-80; v.p., mgr. Mideast area Raytheon Overseas Ltd., Riyadh, Saudi Arabia, 1980-81; v.p., gen. mgr. Info. Svcs. div. Keane Inc., Boston, 1985-95; mgmt. cons. to info. svcs. cmty., 1995—. Avocations: skiing, reading. Home and Office: 785 Lamoine Beach Rd Lamoine ME 04605-4748

BECKER, REX LOUIS, architect; b. St. Louis, May 20, 1913; s. Louis Herman and Elsie (Schroeder) B.; m. Ada Sylva Schmidt, Nov. 20, 1937; children: Susan (Mrs. Robert L. Barley), Kathryn (Mrs. Russell Kisling), Rex Louis, Roger G. B.Arch., Washington U., St. Louis, 1934, M.Arch., 1935. With archtl. firm Johnson & Maack, St. Louis, 1935-42; ptnr. Froese, Maack & Becker, St. Louis, 1946-73; pres. Becker & Flowers, St. Louis, 1973-81; cons., mem. architects com. Luth. Ch.-Mo. Synod, 1980-96, chmn. 1986-87. Works include: Luth. Hosp., St. Louis, Civil Engring. Bldg., Math & Computer Bldg U. Mo. at Rolla, over 150 ch. projects. Pres. Council Luth. Chs. Greater St. Louis, 1960-61. Served with C.E. U.S. Army, 1942-45. Recipient Disting. Alumni award Washington U., 1995. Fellow AIA (pres. St. Louis 1956, regional dir. 1966-69, treas. 1969-71, Gold Medal award St. Louis chpt. 1998), Mo. Assn. Registered Architects (pres. 1955), Guild Religious Architecture, Scarab. Clubs: Mo. Athletic (St. Louis) (gov. 1973-76, treas. 1975-76), Engrs. (St. Louis). Home: 9 Wakefield Dr Saint Louis MO 63124-1463

BECKER, RICHARD CHARLES, retired college president; b. Chgo., Mar. 1, 1931; s. Charles Beno and Rose Mildred (Zak) B.; m. Magdalene Marie Kypry, June 19, 1954; children: Richard J., Daniel P., Douglas F., Steven G., Pamela J. *Richard J. (8/28/55), M.S. Virginia Polytech (1980), Lt. Commander, USN-retired (1997), Engineering Test Pilot, Sikorsky Aircraft Corporation, West Palm Beach, Fla.; Daniel P. (7/11/57), DVM University of Illinois, Boulder Terrace Animal Hospital, Naperville, IL.; Douglas F. (12/29/59), Ph.D. University of Iowa, Senior Project Director Measurement Research, Riverside Publishing/Houghton Mifflin Co. Itasca, IL.; Steven G. (6/12/62), M.S. University of California-Berkeley; Manager Technology/Business Strategy and Communications, American Express Corporate Services, Rolling Meadows, IL.; Pamela J. Becker-Radcliff (3/18/64), B.A. Illinois Benedictine College, President, Management Innovation Associates, Officer Evergreen Consulting, Tyrone, Georgia.* BS in Elec. Engring, Fournier Inst. Tech., 1953; MS in Elec. Engring, U. Ill., 1954, MS in Math., 1956, PhD in Elec. Engring, 1959; postgrad., Harvard Inst. Ednl. Mgmt., 1976. Engr. Ill. Bell Tel. Co., Chgo., 1952, Andrew Corp., Chgo., 1953; rsch. asst. U. Ill., Urbana, 1954-58, asst. prof., 1959; sr. staff engr. Amphenol Corp., Chgo., 1959-60; sr. rsch. scientist Amphenol Corp., 1961-64, dir. program mgmt., 1965-67; dir. Amphenol Corp. (Far Eastern ops.), 1968; group v.p., corporate dir. adminstrn. Bunker Ramo Corp., Oak Brook, Ill., 1968-73; chief exec. officer and chmn. bd. Fortune Internat. Enterprises, Inc., Oak Brook, 1973-76; pres. Benedictine Univ. (formerly Ill. Benedictine Coll.), Lisle, 1976-95, pres. emeritus, 1995—; Trustee, prof. Midwest Coll. Engring., Lombard, Ill., 1968-86; trustee Ill. Benectine Coll., Lisle, 1973-76; bd. dir. Amphenol Tyree Proprietary, Ltd., Australia, Amphetronix, Ltd., India, Oxbow Resources, Ltd., Can.; v.p. Bonita Sprgs. Incorporation Com., Inc., 1998-99. Contbr. articles and chpts. to profl. jours. and books. Gov. Brook Forest Community Assn., 1971-74; del. Oak Brook Caucus, 1970; trustee, pres. Arthur J. Schmitt Found., Ill. Benedictine Coll.; chmn. Coun. West Suburban Colls., Chgo. Met. Higher Edn. Coun., officer Fedn. Ind. Ill. Colls. and Univs.; chmn. Associated Colls. of Ill., West Suburban Regional Acad. Consortium. Named Disting. Eagle Scout, 1989, Regent Nat. Eagles Scout Assn.; Arthur J. Schmitt fellow U. Ill., 1953-56. Mem. Am. Phys. Soc., Nat. Assn. Ind. Colls. and Univs. (bd. dirs.), Albertus Magnus Guild, Rotary (Paul Harris fellow), Equestrian Order of the Holy Sepulchre of Jerusalem, Sigma Xi, Eta Kappa Nu, Tau Beta Pi.

BECKER, RICHARD STANLEY, music publisher; b. Hillside, N.J., Nov. 9, 1934; s. Nat Edward and Hattie Adele (Perkel) B. Student, U. Miami, Fla., 1953. Pres. Richie Becker's Music, Inc. Pub. Music pub.: Moody River (No. 1 song in nation), Pat Boone, 1961, Anna, Beatles, 1963 (million selling album), You Better Move On, Rolling Stones, 1966 (Gold Record award), December's Children album, Moody River, Frank Sinatra, 1969 (Gold Record award), Cycles album, You Better Move On, Dean Martin, 1974, Moody River, Readers Digest, 1975, mgr., Alex Bradford, star of Broadway show, Don't Bother Me, I Can't Cope, 1975; pub.: musical Your Arm's Too Short to Box with God, 1975; dir. first country music show in history, Madison Sq. Garden, 1964; Contbr.: Moody River to, Colliers Yearbook, 1961, Anna to, Ency. Brit., 1963. Recipient Broadcast Music award, 1961, Key to City Memphis, 1973, Ark. Traveler award, 1973; named Hon. Citizen Tenn., 1973, Hon. lt. col. aide-de-camp George C. Wallace, 1973; Alex Bradford Meml. Music scholar Spelman Coll., 1996. Mem. Friars Club, Broadcast Music, Inc. Established Richard S. Becker scholarship Juilliard Sch. Music, 1976. Office: PO Box 144 Deal NJ 07723-0144

BECKER, ROBERT A., advertising executive; b. Mar. 3, 1920; s. William and Eva (Kats) B.; m. Pearl Pehr, Aug. 22, 1948; son, David Jonathan; m. Nancy Gibbs, 1977. BS in Mktg., NYU, 1941; BS in Pharmacy, L.I. U., 1949; DCS (hon.), St. John's U., 1989. Copywriter Plough Inc., Memphis, 1941-42, Murray Breese Assocs., N.Y.C., 1944-48; copywriter, product mgr. Squibb, N.Y.C., 1949-52; profl. advt. mgr. Squibb, 1955-57; advt. dir. Nepera Pharm. Co., Yonkers, N.Y., 1953-54; v.p. Burdick & Becker Inc., N.Y.C., 1957-61; pres. Robert A. Becker, Inc., N.Y.C., 1961-88, chmn. bd. emeritus, 1988—; pres. Hosp. Publs., Inc., 1963-84. Bd. visitors Fordham U. Sch. Law, 1987—; trustee George London Found. for Singers, N.Y.C., 1993—, Guild Hall Mus., East Hampton, N.Y., 1995-97. Recipient Decoration of honor in Gold, Govt. Austria; officer's cross Order of Merit, Fed. Republic Germany, 1985; Distinction of Merit in Gold, City of Vienna; elected to Med. Advt. Hall of Fame, 1997. Mem. Lotos Club. Home: 875 Park Ave New York NY 10021-0341

BECKER, ROBERT ALLEN, data processing executive; b. Chgo., June 27, 1942; s. Sig Herman and Dorothy (Shaw) B.; m. Babs Lee Hefter, Dec. 24, 1964; children: David, Edie. BS in Indsl. Mgmt., Purdue U., 1964. Programmer analyst Standard Oil Co. (Amoco), Chgo., 1964-67; programmer analyst R.R. Donnelley & Sons, Chgo., 1967-68, project leader, 1968-71, supr. computer ops., 1971-72, supr. tech. svcs., 1972-79; mgr. data ctr. ops. Chic Merc. Exch., Chgo., 1979-82; dir. info. resources Richard D. Irwin, Homewood, Ill., 1982-87; dir. system svcs. Holy Cross Health System, South Bend, Ind., 1987-89; dir. info. systems and communications Elkhart (Ind.) Gen. Hosp., 1989-92; dir. info. systems Mt. Sinai Hosp. Med. Ctr., Chgo, 1992—, Schwab Rehab. Hosp., Chgo, 1993—; instr., Thornton Community Coll., South Holland, Ill., 1970-71, Prairie State Coll., Chicago Heights, Ill., 1982-87. Asst. cub master, Boy Scouts Am., Homewood, Ill., 1976; mgr. Homewood Little League. Mem. Guide Internat. (bd. dirs. 1971-80), Computer Ops. Mgmt. Assn., Data Processing Mgmt. Assn., (bd. dirs. 1984-88, pres. Calumet chpt. 1987-88, Individual Performance award 1988), Soc. Info Mgmt., Healthcare Info. and Mgmt. Sys. Soc. (sec.-treas. region III med. users software exchange, 1994-95, treas. med. users software exchg. internat., 1996—), Purdue Alumni Assn. (dir. Region 17, 1997—), Purdue Club (bd. dirs. 1987, treas. 1989—), Alpha Epsilon Pi. Home: 12996 Pierce Ct Crown Point IN 46307-9255 Office: Mt Sinai Hosp Med Ctr California 15th Chicago IL 60608

BECKER, ROBERT CLARENCE, retired clergyman; b. N.Y.C., June 19, 1927; s. Clarence Henry and Lillian (Butler) B.; m. Harriet Louise Egland, June 23, 1951; children: John, Ruth, Paul, Carol, Joel. Student, Providence Bible Inst., 1944-47, Gordon Coll. Theology and Missions, 1947-48; B.A., Upsala Coll., 1951. Ordained to ministry Baptist Ch., 1951; pastor First Bapt. Ch., Sedgwick, Maine, 1952-54, Ticonderoga, N.Y., 1954-58; pastor Garden View Bapt. Ch., Williamsport, Pa., 1958-67, First Bapt. Ch., Clayton, N.J., 1967-73; sr. minister First Bapt. Ch., Bloomfield, N.J., 1973-97; pres. Conservative Bapt. Assn. Am., 1979-82; chmn. Am. Council, Africa Evangelical Fellowship, 1981-86. Bd. dirs. Denver Conservative Bapt. Theol. Sem., 1972-84, Eastern Conservative Bapt. Sem., 1982-84, Northeastern Bible Coll., 1983-86, Conservative Bapt. Fgn. Mission Soc., 1988-94. Mem. Nat. Assn. Evangelicals, Conservative Bapt. Fgn. Mission Soc., Conservative Bapt. Home Mission Soc., Conservative Bapt. Assn. (eastern v.p. 1984). Home: PO Box 57 Sedgwick ME 04676-0057

BECKER, ROBERT JEROME, allergist, health care consultant; b. Milw., May 29, 1922; s. Jacob and Sarah (Saxe) B.; m. June Granof, June 25, 1950; children: Scott M., Jill Becker Wilson, Jon G. BS, U. Wis., Milw., 1943; MD, Med. Coll. Wis., 1949. Intern Michael Reese Hosp., Chgo., 1949-50; resident in internal medicine VA Hosp., Wood, Wis., 1950-53; resident in allergy Roosevelt Hosp., N.Y.C., 1955-56; pvt. practice specializing in allergy Joliet, Ill., 1956-82; founder, chmn. bd. dirs. HealthCare COMPARE, 1982-90, chmn. bd. dirs. emeritus, 1990—; cons. health care utilization co., 1982-90; founder, pres. Becker Cons. Corp., 1990—; founder, chmn. bd. dirs. Healthcare Comm. Mgmt. Corp., 1990-93; med. dir. Quad river Found. Med. Care, 1976-84; pres. Am. Assn. Profl. Stds. Rev. Orgns., 1980-82; exec. v.p. Joint Coll. Allergy and Immunology, 1978-86; mem. adv. coun. Nat. Inst. Environ. Health Scis., 1984-88; bd. dirs. Impac Corp., Am. Psych Sys.; vice chmn, bd. dirs. Madison Info. Technologies, Inc.; chmn. Utilization Rev. Accreditation Commn., 1991-94, bd. dirs., 1994-96. Author articles in field. Pres. bd. edn. Joliet Twp. H.S. Dist. 204, 1969-70, 75-76; mem. bus. adv. com. U. Ill. Sch. Bus., Chgo., 1987—. Recipient Clemens von Pirquet award Georgetown U. Internat. Interdisciplinary Ctr. Immunology, 1978; named Entrepreneur of Yr. Arthur Young/Venture Mag., 1988. Fellow ACP, Am. Acad. Allergy, Am. Coll. Allergists (pres. 1987), Am. Coll. Chest Physicians; mem. Ill. Soc. Internal Medicine (pres. 1984-86), Asthma and Allergy Assn. Am. (bd. dirs. 1987—), Asthma and Allergy Found. Am. (bd. dirs. 1990-94), Am. Managed Care and Rev. Assn. (bd. dirs. 1989-95), Am. Assn. Preferred Providers Assn. (bd. dirs. 1989—), Utilization Rev. Accreditation Commn. (chair 1991-94, bd. dirs. 1991-96), Am. Assn. Preferred Provider Orgns. (bd. dirs. 1988-93), Am. Psychiat. Sys. (bd. dirs. 1994—), Alpha Omega Alpha, Alpha Sigma Nu. Office: 1S 045 Spring Rd Oakbrook Terrace IL 60181 *Whatever success I have achieved has occurred with the following rules of my life: 1) Individual and public accountability for decisions made; 2) Kindness to all persons in my sphere of contact; 3) Hard work; 4) Humility, truth, and respect for human dignity have been uppermost elements in my interpersonal relations; and, 5) I have accepted my humanness when I fall short of these rules.*

BECKER, ROBERT JOSEPH, database consultant, computer science specialist, database software developer and educator; b. Grand Rapids, Mich., Apr. 22, 1946; s. Leon Joseph and Alfreda Mary (O'Rielly) B.; m. Kathleen Zbikowski, Jan. 16, 1970; children: Steven, Michael, Kimberly, John. BS in Computer Sci., Mich. State U., 1970. Computer sci. specialist Wolverine World Wide, Rockford, Mich., 1970-73; data base adminstr. Foremost Ins. Co., Grand Rapids, 1973-80, with data base, data communications, 1980-86, mgr. data base adminstrn., 1986-88, cons. of tech. directions, 1988—; keynote data base performance speaker U.S. and European Software AG Confs., 1973—; tchr. computer basics to elem. sch. students, 1988-93; actor cmty. theater, 1995—. Editor (data base products) Software Ag Connections, 1987-98, author performance courses, 1993—; contbr. articles to profl. jours. Community edn. instr., Wyoming, Mich., 1974-80; vol. examiner FCC, Grand Rapids, 1975-85; vol. religious edn. instr., 1980—. Mem. Software AG Internat. Users Group (cert., chmn. performance spl. interest group 1978—, tech. rep. 1983-85, data base products rep. 1987-94, chmn. data base future directions 1989—, comm. and client-server software rep. 1994-96, bd. dirs. 1996—, best presentation award 1978, 82, best speaker award 1979), Am. Radio Relay League, Nat. Train Collectors Assn. Republican. Roman Catholic. Avocations: amateur radio, commercial broadcasting, community and semi-professional theater. Home: 4560 Bremer St SW Grandville MI 49418-2238 Office: IBM/Foremost Ins Co PO Box 1233 Grand Rapids MI 49501-1233

BECKER, ROBERT OTTO, orthopedic surgery educator; b. River Edge, N.J., May 31, 1923; s. Otto and Elizabeth (Blank) B.; m. Lillian J. Moller, Sept. 6, 1946; children: Lisa, Michael, Adam. B.A., Gettysburg Coll., 1946; M.D., NYU, 1948. Am. Bd. Orthopedic Surgery Nat. Bd. Med. Examiners. Intern Bellevue Hosp., N.Y.C., 1948-49; resident Mary Hitchcock Meml. Hosp., Hanover, N.H., 1950-51, SUNY Downstate Med. Ctr., 1953-56; practice medicine specializing in orthopedic surgery, 1956—; prof. orthopedics SUNY Upstate Med. Ctr., Syracuse, 1966—; clin. prof. orthopedics La. State Coll. Medicine, Shreveport, 1980—; v.p. rsch. Becker

Biomagnetics, 1992—. Author: Electromagnetism and Life, 1982, The Body Electric, 1985, Cross Currents, 1990; editor: Mechanisms of Growth Control, 1981; patentee electric stimulation of growth, iontophoretic method for tissue healing and regeneration. Served to 1st lt. USMC, 1951-53. Faculty exchange scholar SUNY, 1979; recipient Middletown research award VA, 1960, disting. alumnus award NYU Coll. Medicine, 1966, Nicolas Andry award Assn. Bone and Joint Surgery, 1979. Mem. AAAS, N.Y. Acad. Scis., Bioelectronics Soc., Internat. Soc. for Bioelectricity. Republican. Home: Star Route Lowville NY 13367 Office: Becker Biomagnetics Star Route Lowville NY 13367 *Any success I have enjoyed in research has been due to the fact that it has been the most exciting and all-consuming endeavor I ever engaged in.*

BECKER, ROGER VERN, information science educator; b. Omaha, Apr. 12, 1947; s. LaVern Herman and Doris Bessie (Smith) B.; m. D'Lea Brauner; 1 child, Lindsey Vern. Student, U. Nebr., 1965-67, JD, 1970; LLM, U. Wash., 1971; Specialist in Libr./Info. Svcs., Ind. U., 1981. Dir. info. svcs. U. Va. Sch. Law, Charlottesville, 1971-73; dir. legal rsch. U. N.D. Sch. Law, Grand Forks, 1973-80; dir. tech. U. Ark. Sch. Law, Fayetteville, 1981-83; planner, systems strategist, dir. tech. U. Puget Sound, Tacoma, Wash., 1983-94; dir. info. tech. Sch. Law Seattle U., 1994-97; chief info. officer, endowed prof., dean libr. info. svc. Centenary Coll. La., 1996—; bus. and mktg. advisor P.S. The Last Word in Personal Style, Mercer Island, Wash., 1984—. Prodr. various videos; program designer various computer programs; author articles in field. Mem. Govs. Commn. on Libraries, N.D., 1974-76. Mem. Order of Coif, Beta Phi Mu. Avocations: Christian radio, pastoral writing. Office: Centenary College PO Box 4118 2911 Centenary Blvd Shreveport LA 71104-3396

BECKER, RONALD LEONARD, archivist; b. N.Y.C., Feb. 16, 1950; s. Bernard and Frieda (Miller) B.; m. Christine Lee Johnsen, Jan. 6, 1974; children: Nathan James, Bernard William. AB in History, Duke U., 1971; AM in History, Rutgers U., 1972, MLS, 1973. Cataloger, bibliographer N.J. Hist. Soc., Newark, 1973-74; curator manuscripts Rutgers U., New Brunswick, N.J., 1974—, head spl. collections, 1991—; grant reviewer NEH, 1977—, U.S. Dept. Edn., 1992-94; program evaluator N.J. Com. for Humanities, Trenton, 1983—; mem. N.J. State Hist. Records Adv. Bd., 1997—. Author: Checklist of New Jersey Periodicals, 1982; co-author: Union List of New Jersey Annual Publications, 1977, History of the Jewish Community in Newark, N.J., 1995; editor Mid-Atlantic Archivist, 1983-92. Mem., v.p. bd. trustees Metuchen (N.J.) Pub. Libr., 1977-82. Mem. Soc. Am. Archivists, Mid-Atlantic Regional Archives Conf. (pres. 1975-77), Fedn. Jewish Men's Clubs (v.p. 1986-88, trustee 1988-92). Democrat. Jewish. Fax: (732) 932-7012. E-mail: rbecker@rci.rutgers.edu. Home: 84 Highland Ave Metuchen NJ 08840-1913 Office: Spl Collections Univ Archives Rutgers U Libr 169 College Ave New Brunswick NJ 08901-1163

BECKER, SEYMOUR, hazardous materials and wastes specialist; b. Bronx, N.Y., Feb. 14, 1924; m. Ruth Schmitt, Aug. 30, 1958. MS, U. Wis., 1949; PhD, Pacific Western U., 1981. Nationally cert. hazardous materials mgr. and hazardous control mgr. Radiation control insp. Suffolk County Dept. Health Svcs., Hauppauge, N.Y., 1960-81; tech. cons., 1981-83; hazardous materials and wastes cons. Environ. Svcs., Portland, Maine, 1983-85, Mercy Hosp., Portland, 1985—; del. to China, People to People, Spokane, Wash., 1987, del. to Russia and Ukraine, 1992; advisor and cons. State of Maine Hosp. Assn., Augusta, 1988-90, Low Level Radioactive Wastes Authority, Augusta, 1989-93, Dept. Environ. Protection, Augusta, 1989-93. Contbr. articles to profl. jours. Cons. Emergency Mgmt. Agy., Windham, Maine, 1983—, Local Emergency Planning Com., Windham, 1989—, chair, Cumberland, Maine, 1996—; rep. State Emergency Response Commn., Maine, 1998—. Mem. APHA, Acad. Hazardous Materials Mgmt., Health Physics Soc., N.Y. Acad. Scis., Maine Pub. Health Assn. Achievements include development of N.Y. State radiation code; initiation of radiation control program in Suffolk County, N.Y. Home: 169 High St Apt 312 Portland ME 04101-2852 Office: Mercy Hosp 144 State St Portland ME 04101-3795

BECKER, STEPHEN A., physicist, designer; b. Evanston, Ill., Sept. 11, 1950; s. John N. and Irene A. (Wlodarski) B.; m. Wendee M. Brunish, May 30, 1980. BA, Northwestern U., 1972; MS, Case Western Res. U., 1974; PhD, U. Ill., 1979. Rsch. and teaching assoc. U. Ill., Champaign, 1979-80; postdoctoral fellow Calif. Inst. Tech., Pasadena, 1980-82; mem. staff Los Alamos (N.Mex.) Nat. Lab., 1983—. Contbr. articles to Astrophys. Jour. Mem. Los Alamos Cable TV Bd., 1991-97. Recipient Recognition of Excellence award U.S. Dept. Energy, 1989. Mem. Am. Astron. Soc., Internat. Astron. Union. Roman Catholic. Office: Los Alamos Nat Lab PO Box 1663 Mail Stop B220 Los Alamos NM 87545*

BECKER, STEPHEN BRADBURY, fraternal organization administrator; b. Toronto, Canada, Aug. 17, 1947; s. Jack and Anne (Havill) B.; m. Trudy Ann Gaar, Dec. 27, 1968; two children. BSc, U. Fla., 1969. Asst. mgr. distbn. Composers Authors & Publs. of Canada, Toronto, 1969-71; employee rels. adminstr. Canadian Imperial Bank Commerce, Toronto, 1971-80; dir. personnel & mgmt. tng. Mother's Restaurants, Inc., Burlington, Ont., Canada, 1980-83; dist. mgr. Radio Shack, Toronto, 1983-85; mgr. devel. & cmty. rels. Oakville (Ont.)-Trafalgar Meml. Hosp., 1985-88; v.p. Navion Fund Raising Cons., Toronto, 1988-92; dir. advancement Beta Theta Pi Found., Oxford, Ohio, 1992-94; v.p., prin. Navion Fund Raising Cons., 1995-97; assoc. adminstrv. sec. Beta Theta Pi Fraternity, Oxford, 1997—. Fellow Inst. Canadian Bankers; mem. Nat. Soc. Fund Raising Execs. (cert.), Fraternity Execs. Assn. Home: 10 University Ave Oxford OH 45056-1348

BECKER, SUSAN KAPLAN, management consultant, educator; b. Newark, Jan. 4, 1948; d. Charles and Janet Kaplan; m. William Paul Becker, 1969 (div. 1977). BA in English cum laude, with distinction, U. Pa., 1968, MA, 1969, PhD, 1973, MBA in Fin., 1979. Instr. English Bryn Mawr (Pa.) Coll., 1972-74; assoc. editor U. Pa., Phila., 1975, asst. dir., lectr. urban studies, 1975-77; fin. analyst Phila. Nat. Bank, 1979-82; asst. v.p. Chem. Bank, N.Y.C., 1982-84; v.p. Bankers Trust Co., N.Y.C., 1984-85; prin. Becker Cons. Svcs., N.Y.C., 1985—; adj. assoc. prof. mgmt. comm. Stern Sch. Bus. N.Y.U., 1990—; cons./evaluator Pa. Humanities Council, Phila., 1977-78; mem. editorial bd. Mgmt. Comm. Quar., 1993-97. Author: How to Develop Profitable Financial Products for the Institutional Marketplace, 1988; contbr. articles and revs. to profl. jours. Vol. N.Y. Cares, 1989-92, N.Y.C. affiliate Am. Heart Assn., 1995-97. U. Pa. fellow, 1968-72; E.I. DuPont de Nemours fellow, 1979, N.Y. Regents Coll. Teaching fellow, 1968-70. Mem. Am. Soc. Tng. & Devel., Internat. Comm. Assn. (reviewer tech. and comm. divsn. 1991), Fin. Women's Assn. N.Y. (profl. devel. com. 1995—), Women's Econ. Round Table, Profl. Assn. Investment Comm. Resources. Democrat. Avocations: painting and drawing, swimming. Office: 155 E 29th St New York NY 10016-8173

BECKER, THEODORE MICHAELSON, lawyer; b. Chgo., Feb. 18, 1949; s. Michael and Hazel Becker; m. Tamara B. Kaplan, June 11, 1983; children: Adam Michael, Alex Jordan, Ian David. AB summa cum laude, Washington U., St. Louis, 1970; MA in Sociology, Northwestern U., 1972, JD summa cum laude, 1974, PhD in Sociology, 1981. Bar: Ill. 1975, U.S. Dist. Ct. (no. and so. dist.) Ill. 1975, U.S. Ct. Appeals (7th and 10th cirs.) 1975, U.S. Ct. Appeals (9th cir.) 1976, U.S. Supreme Ct. 1978, U.S. Dist. Ct. (cen. dist.) Ill. 1979, U.S. Dist. Ct. (no. dist. trial bar) Ill. 1982, U.S. Ct. Appeals (Fed. cir.) 1983. Russell Sage fellow, instr. Yale U., New Haven, 1974-75; pvt. practice Chgo., 1975—. *Theodore Becker represents clients ranging from individuals and small companies to financial institutions and the largest multinational corporations. He has obtained a number of multi-million dollar recoveries for his clients and has successfully defended multi-million dollar actions against his clients. Mr. Becker achieved national recognition when he obtained a verdict of $52 million on behalf of a small Chicago ice cream supplier against the fast food giant McDonald's Corporation for breach of a "handshake agreement. The verdict was the largest in Cook County (Chicago) Court history. That case is presently included in the curricula of major law schools and colleges.* Contbr. articles to books and profl. jours. Mem. ABA, Ill. Bar Assn., Chgo. Bar Assn., Phi Beta Kappa, Order of Coif. Office: Becker Assocs 19 S La Salle St Ste 1500 Chicago IL 60603-1407

BECKER, THOMAS BAIN, lawyer; b. St. Charles, Mo., Sept. 3, 1944; s. John Bruere and Marie Louise (Denker) B.; m. Linda Ann Flynn, May 25, 1974; children: Thomas Bain Jr., Shannon Flynn. BSBA, Georgetown U., 1966; MBA, U. Mo., Columbia, 1968, JD, 1976. Bar: Mo. 1976. Acct. Kerber, Eck & Braeckel, St. Louis, 1966, Rothaus, Bartels & Earley, St. Louis, 1968; acctg. analyst U.S. Dept. Commerce, Washington, 1971-73; shareholder Stinson, Mag & Fizzell, Kansas City, 1976-98, Gilmore & Bell, P.C., Kansas City, 1998—. Bd. dirs., v.p., pres. Westport Citizens Action Coalition, Kansas City, 1987—; bd. dirs. Hist. Kansas City Found., 1981-89, Kansas City Union Sta., Inc., 1988-97; bd. commrs., vice chair Mo. Housing Devel. Commn., 1995-98; mem. task force Mayor's Odyssey 2000, Kansas City, 1993; bd. dirs., vice chmn. Citizens Assn. Kansas City, 1996—. Recipient Community Svc. award Westport Coop. Svcs., 1991. Mem. ABA, Nat. Assn. Bond Lawyers, Rockhill Tennis Club (bd. govs., treas. 1999—). Democrat. Roman Catholic. Avocations: sports, politics, reading, travel. Home: 816 Gleed Ter Kansas City MO 64109-2617 Office: Gilmore & Bell PC 2405 Grand Blvd Ste 1100 Kansas City MO 64108-2521

BECKER, WALTER HEINRICH, vocational educator, planner; b. St. Louis, Mar. 20, 1939; s. Anthon and Maria (Fleischman) B.; m. Ayse Nur Alpyoruk, Aug. 3, 1971; children: Volkan P., Kristal S. BS, S.E. Mo. State U., 1963; MS, U. Mo., Columbia, 1969; PhD, St. Louis U., 1978; MS, Fontbonne Coll., 1989. Cert. tchr. Secondary tchr. Sch. Dist. of Hancock Pl., Lemay, Mo., 1963-64, Mascoutah (Ill.) Sch. Dist., 1964-65, U.S. Dept. of Def., Japan, Turkey, Philippines, 1965-70; vocat. edn. supr. Mo. Divsn. of Mental Health, Farmington, Mo., 1971-79; program analyst Arabian Am. Oil Co., Dhahran, Saudi Arabia, 1979-80, planning and programs analyst, 1981-85; vocat. edn. supr. Mo. Dept. of Corrections, Jefferson City, 1990-93.

BECKER, WESLEY CLEMENCE, psychology educator emeritus; b. Rochester, N.Y., Mar. 17, 1928; s. William Henry and Alcey (Cole) B.; m. Barbara Ann Beckel, June 15, 1950 (div. Sept. 1968); children: Jill, Jeffrey, Linda, James; m. Janis Lynn Wetherell, Oct. 14, 1968 (div. May 1972); 1 dau., Karen; m. Julia Lee Molloy, July 20, 1972 (div. Apr. 1980); children: David, Brandin. A.B., Stanford, 1951, M.A., 1953, Ph.D., 1955. Instr. U. Ill., Urbana, 1955-56; asst. prof. U. Ill., 1956-60, assoc. prof., 1960-63, prof., 1963-70; prof. U. Oreg., Eugene, 1970-92; prof. emeritus U. Oreg., 1992—, assoc. dean Coll. Edn., 1978-89; cons. U.S. Office Edn., 1968-78; dir. Oreg. Research Inst., 1977-86. Author: Teaching: A Course in Applied Psychology, 1971, An Empirical Basis for Change in Education, 1971, Parents Are Teachers, 1971, Successful Parenthood, 1974, Teaching 1, Classroom Management, 1975, Teaching 2, Cognitive Learning and Instruction, 1975, Teaching 3, Evaluation of Instruction, 1976, Applied Psychology for Teachers: A Behavioral Cognitive Approach, 1986. Served with AUS, 1946-49. Fellow Am. Psychol. Soc., Phi Beta Kappa, Sigma Xi. Research in behavior modification, edn. of disadvantaged children, instructional psychology. Home: 65 Stardust Ln Sedona AZ 86336-3739

BECKER, WILLIAM WATTERS, lawyer; b. New Orleans, Apr. 1, 1943; s. Ralph Elihu and Ann Marie (Watters) B.; m. Joan A. Alper; children: Kirsten Anne, Gevry Danielle. BA, Dartmouth Coll., 1964, MBA, 1965; LLB, Harvard U., 1968. Bar: Mass. 1968, D.C. 1970, U.S. Supreme Ct. 1978, Md. 1978. Staff atty., Reginald Heber Smith fellow Community Legal Assistance Office, Cambridge, Mass., 1968-69; ptnr. Landfield, Becker & Green, Washington, 1969-89, Breed, Abbott & Morgan, 1989-92; prin. William W. Becker, Chtd., Washington, 1993—; gen. counsel, dir. Voice Found., N.Y.C., 1976—; assoc. gen. counsel John F. Kennedy Ctr. Performing Arts, Washington, 1977-93, gen. counsel, 1993—; gen. counsel Kennedy Ctr. Prodns., Inc., 1972—; dir. Greater Washington Bd. Trade, 1978-92, gen. counsel, 1981-85. Dir., treas. Washington Architectural Found., 1998—. Mem. Mass. Bar Assn., D.C. Bar Assn., Fed. Bar Assn.

BECKER-ROUKAS, HELANE RENÉE, securities analyst, financial executive; b. N.Y.C., May 7, 1957; d. Arnold and Ella Florence (Feldman) Becker; m. George Paul Roukas, Sept. 6, 1980; children: Samuel Matthew, Hannah Beth. BA, Montclair State U., 1979; MBA in Fin., NYU, 1984. Options coord. Donaldson Lufkin & Jenrette, N.Y.C., 1979-81; mktg. coord. E.F. Hutton & Co., N.Y.C., 1981-82; securities analyst Prudential-Bache Securities, N.Y.C., 1982-86; v.p., analyst Drexel Burnham Lambert, N.Y.C., 1986-87; mng. dir., analyst Lehman Bros., N.Y.C., 1987-94, Smith Barney, N.Y.C., 1995-98; sr. v.p., prin. Buckingham Rsch. Group, N.Y.C., 1998—; speaker various airline industry confs. and panels; instnl. investor. Columnist Corp. Travel Mag., 1990. Mem. Senate Commn. on Civil Tilt Rotor. Named to Investor All-Am. Rsch. Team, 1985-94. Mem. Soc. Airline Analysts (pres. 1996-98), Profl. Women in Bus., Wings Club, Short Hills Assn., NYU Alumni Assn. N.J. Avocations: skiing, tennis, swimming, golf. Office: Buckingham Rsch Group 630 3rd Ave Fl 6 New York NY 10017-6705

BECKERS, JACQUES MAURICE, astrophysicist; b. Arnhem, The Netherlands, Feb. 14, 1934; came to U.S., 1962; s. Wilhelmus B.H. and Maria H. (Hermans) B.; m. Gerda M. Van Vuurden, Mar. 24, 1959 (div. Aug. 1995); children: Christina M., Michael P. PhD, U. Utrecht, The Netherlands, 1959. Astrophysicist Sacramento Peak Obs., Sunspot, N.Mex., 1962-79; astrophysicist, dir. Multiple Mirror Telescope Obs., Tucson, 1979-84, Advanced Devel. program Nat. Optical Astronomy Observatories, Tucson, 1984-88; astrophysicist European So. Obs., Garching, Fed. Republic of Germany, 1988-93, VLT Program Scientist, 1991-93; dir. Nat. Solar Observatory, Tucson, Ariz., 1993-98. Mem. Norwegian Acad. Scis. (fgn.), Royal Netherlands Acad. Scis. (corr.). Office: Nat Solar Obs Sacramento Peak PO Box 62 Sunspot NM 88349

BECKETT, KURT A., legislative staff member. BA, U. Wash., 1994. Dep. campaign mgr. Rep. Norm Dicks, Tacoma, 1996, dist. dir., 1997—. Office: Office Rep Norm Dicks Ste 2244 1717 Pacific Ave Tacoma WA 98402-4411*

BECKETT, THEODORE CHARLES, lawyer; b. Boonville, Mo., May 6, 1929; s. Theodore Cooper and Gladys (Watson) B.; m. Daysie Margaret Cornwall, 1950; children: Elizabeth Gayle, Theodore Cornwall, Margaret Lynn, William Harrison, Anne Marie. BS, U. Mo., Columbia, 1950, JD, 1957. Bar: Mo. 1957. Since practiced in Kansas City; mem. firm Beckett Law Firm; instr. public pol. sci. U. Mo., Columbia, 1956-57; asst. atty. gen. State of Mo., 1961-64. Former mem. bd. dirs. Kansas City Civic Ballet; mem. City Plan Commn., Kansas City, 1976-80; mem. bd. curators U. Mo., 1995—, pres. 1998. 1st lt. U.S. Army, 1950-53. Mem. Am., Mo., Kansas City bar assns., Lawyers Assn. Kansas City, Newcomen Soc. N.Am., SAR, Order of Coif, Sigma Nu, Phi Alpha Delta. Presbyterian. Clubs: Kansas City (Kansas City, Mo.), Blue Hills Country (Kansas City, Mo.). Office: 1400 Commerce Trust Bldg 922 Walnut St Kansas City MO 64106-1809

BECKETT, VICTORIA LING, physician; m. Peter G.S. Beckett, 1954 (dec. 1974); 1 child, Paul T. (dec.); m. Joseph C. Sharp, 1996. BA, Mt. Holyoke Coll., 1945; MD, U. Mich., 1949; MA, St. Mary's U., 1995. Intern Mpls. Gen. Hosp., 1949-50; resident Northwestern Hosp., Mpls., 1950-51; fellow Mayo Grad. Sch., 1951-55; clin. instr. Wayne State U. Sch. Medicine, Detroit, 1956-67; staff cons. internal medicine oncology svc. Henry Ford Hosp., Detroit, 1957-60; rsch. physician Darling Meml. Ctr., Detroit, 1965-69; asst. prof. oncology Wayne State U. Sch. Medicine, 1968-69, rsch. assoc. rheumatology, 1970-72, postgrad. tutor, 1972-73, dir., 1973-76; cons. physician in rheumatology Federated Dublin Vol. Hosps., 1973-76; cons. rheumatology Mayo Clinic, 1976-90, emeritus staff, 1990—; asst. prof. medicine Mayo Med. Sch., 1976-90. Mem. Meth. Ch. choir. Fellow ACP; mem. Alumni Assn. Mayo Fedn., Am. Coll. Rheumatology (ret. mem.), Minn. State Med. Assn., Zumbro Valley Med. Soc., Rochester Health Care Ctr. (med. dir. 1985-90), Sigma Xi, Phi Beta Kappa. Avocations: teaching exercise class, taking piano lessons, creative writing, computers, psychology research. Office: Mayo Clinic 200 First St SW Rochester MN 55905

BECKHAM, EDGAR FREDERICK, educational consultant; b. Hartford, Conn., Aug. 5, 1933; s. Walter Henry and Willabelle (Hollinshed) B.; m. Ria Haertl, Aug. 16, 1958; 1 child, Frederick Hollinshed. BA, Wesleyan U., 1958; MA, Yale U., 1959, postgrad., 1959-61; DHL, Olivet Coll., 1997. Instr. German Wesleyan U., Middletown, Conn., 1961-66, dir. lang. lab., 1963-66, lang. lab. dir., lectr. German, 1967-69, assoc. provost, 1969-73, dean, 1973-90, dean emeritus, 1996—; program officer The Ford Found., N.Y.C., 1990-96; coord. Campus Diversity Initiative, 1996-98; sr. fellow Assn. Am. Colls. and Univs., 1998—; lectr. English U. Erlangen, Germany, 1966-67; cons. Nat. Endowment for Humanities; mem. Commn. on Instns. of Higher Edn., 1981-84; pres. Rockfall Corp., 1985-86; bd. dirs. Assn. Am. Colls., 1985-90. Chmn. Conn. Humanities Coun., 1979-80, Conn. Com. on Edn. Equity and Excellence, 1994-95, Conn. State Bd. Edn., 1993-95; mem. Dem. Town Com., Middletown, 1972-90; pres. bd. dirs. Conn. Housing Investment Fund, 1981-83; chmn. bd. dirs. Middlesex Hosp., 1983-85, dir. emeritus; trustee emeritus Vt. Acad.; chmn., bd. dirs. Conn. Pub. Broadcasting, 1990-92; chmn. bd. trustees Donna Wood Found. With AUS, 1954-57. Recipient Outstanding Contbn. to Higher Edn. award Nat. Assn. Student Pers. Adminstrs., 1997, Raymond E. Baldwin medal Wesleyan U. Alumni Assn., 1991, Outstanding Svc. award, 1998. Mem. MLA, Am. Assn. for Higher Edn., Am. Assn. Tchrs. German. Office: Assn Am Colls and Univs 1818 R St NW Washington DC 20009

BECKHAM, WALTER HULL, JR., lawyer, educator; b. Albany, Ga., Apr. 18, 1920; m. Ethel Koger, Mar. 13, 1943; children: Barbara, Walter III, James K. AB, Emory U., 1941; LLB cum laude, Harvard U., 1948. Bar: Fla. 1949, U.S. Supreme Ct. 1956, D.C. 1978. Assoc. prof. law U. Miami, Fla., 1948-49; ptnr. Nichols, Gaither, Beckham et al, 1950-67; of counsel Podhurst, Orseck, Josefsberg, Eaton, Meadow, Olin & Perwin P.A., Miami, 1967—; prof. law U. Miami, 1967-82, prof. emeritus, 1982—. Editor Harvard Law Rev. Pres. Greater Miami YMCA, 1963-68, Crippled Children's Soc. Dade County, 1968-69; mem. Dade County Mental Health Bd., 1971-73; chmn. bd. trustees YMCA Blue Ridge Assembly, 1977-79; trustee Nat. Jud. Coll., 1990-96, trustee, chmn., 1995-96, chmn. emeritus, 1996—. With USNR, 1941-46; capt. USNR, ret. Recipient The Perry Nichols award, Acad. Fla. Trial Lawyers, 1984. Mem. ABA (spl. com. on tort liability system 1979-84, spl. commn. on assn. governance 1983-84, chmn. tort and ins. practice sect. 1974-75, Ho. of Dels. 1979-85, 87-95, sec.-elect 1986-87, sec. 1987-90), Am. Bar Found., Am. Coll. Trial Lawyers, Am. Law Inst., Assn. Trial Lawyers Am. (chmn. aviation sect. 1966-68), Fla. Bar Assn. (past mem. bd. of govs. jr. bar sect.), Dade County Bar Assn. (pres. jr. bar sect. 1952-53, exec. com. 1953-54), Internat. Acad. Trial Lawyers (pres. 1973), Internat. Acad. Law and Sci., Law Sci. Inst., Maritime Law Assn. U.S., Nat. Inst. Trial Adv. (trustee 1976-86, chmn. 1983-85), Inner Circle of Advs., Med. Inst. for Attys. (dir. 1968-83), Nat. Bd. Trial Adv. (founding mem.), Phi Beta Kappa, Omicron Delta Kappa, Phi Alpha Delta, Chi Phi, Kiwanis. Home: 3612 SW 57th Ave Miami FL 33155-5031 Office: Podhurst Orseck Josefsberg Eaton Meadow Olin Perwin City Nat Bank Bldg 25 W Flagler St Ste 800 Miami FL 33130-1720

BECKHARD, HERBERT, architect; b. N.Y.C., Jan. 28, 1926; s. Julius and Erna (Sinn) B.; m. Eleanor Sabesin, Nov. 4, 1951; children: Susan, Karen, Thomas, Jane. BS with honors, Pa. State U., 1949; MFA, Princeton U., 1950. Draftsman, assoc., ptnr. Marcel Breuer & Assocs.— Archs., N.Y.C., 1951-83; ptnr. Beckhard, Richlan & Assocs., N.Y.C., 1983—; guest lectr. Syracuse U., N.Y. Inst. Tech., U. N.Mex., Ill. Inst. Tech., Pa. State U. Subject of book: Architecture without Rules—The Houses of M. Breuer and H. Beckhard (D. Masello), 1993; prin. works include IBM Bldg., Boca Raton, Fla., U. Mass. Campus Ctr., Amherst, Philip Morris mfg. facility, Charlotte, N.C., Internat. Fin. Ctr., Jersey City, Cornell U. Sch. Indsl. Labor Rels., Ithaca, N.Y., Pa. State U. new rsch. ctr., University Park, Franklin Twp. Tech. Ctr., N.J., Pineles Nursing Home, Hackensack, N.J., Drew Meth. Ch., Pt. Jervis, N.Y., Temple Emeth, Teaneck, N.J., Housing Police Precinct, N.Y.C., office bldg. complex, Englewood Cliffs, N.J., Somerset, N.J. Lt. (j.g.) USNR, 1944-46, PTO. Recipient Disting. Alumnus award Pa. State U., 1974, Alumni fellow, 1982; IBM fellow Aspen Design Conf., 1983. Fellow AIA (AIA nat. honor awards for St. Francis de Sales Ch., Muskegon, Mich., Koerfer House, Ascona, Switzerland, HUD and HEW hdqrs. bldgs., Washington, Archtl. Record Houses 11 times), NAD (awards). Avocations: photography; tennis. Avocations: photography, tennis (Ea. and nat. rankings). Home: Red Spring Ln Glen Cove NY 11542-1700 Office: Beckhard Richlan & Assocs 307 7th Ave New York NY 10001-6007

BECKHOLT, ALICE, clinical nurse specialist; b. N.Y.C., Aug. 7, 1941; d. Julius and Mary (Katz) Kalkow; m. Richard H. Polakoff, Aug. 12, 1962 (div. 1984); children: Katherine, Michael, Matthew; m. Kenneth Eugene Beckholt, Feb. 3, 1990. BA, Syracuse U., 1962; ADN, El Centro Coll., 1977; BSN, U. Tex., Arlington, 1980; MS, Tex. Woman's U., 1988. RN, Tex., Ohio. Staff nurse, outpatient mgr. Irving (Tex.) Cmty. Hosp., 1977-86; staff nurse Meth. Hosp., Dallas, 1986-89, U. Tex. S.W. Med. Ctr., Dallas, 1989-90; pediat. home care nurse various agys., Columbus, Ohio, 1990-94; advanced practice nurse, pub. speaking Columbus Health Dept., 1994—. Sec., 2nd v.p., 1st v.p., pres. Am. Cancer Soc., 1971-76, bd. dirs. Irving, Tex., 1971-90, BSE instr., nurse's com., 1990—, triple touch coord., 1991—, BSE faculty, 1986-90; vol., auction subchair Sta. KERA-TV, Dallas, 1972-84; CPR instr. Am. Heart Assn., 1984-98. Recipient Outstanding Svc. award Am. Cancer Soc. Columbus chpt., 1992-93; named Outstanding Vol., Am. Cancer Soc., Irving, Tex., 1973, 74, 76. Mem. Ohio Pub. Health Assn., Toastmasters Internat., Sigma Theta Tau. Avocations: gourmet cooking, classical music, travel. Home: 2605 Brookwood Rd Columbus OH 43209-2904 Office: Columbus Dept Health 181 Washington Blvd Columbus OH 43215-4022

BECKJORD, ERIC STEPHEN, nuclear engineer, energy researcher; b. Evanston, Ill., Feb. 17, 1929; s. Walter Clarence and Mary Amelia (Hitchcox) B.; m. Caroline Wendell Gardner, Feb. 28, 1953; children—Eric H., Amy W., Charles A., Sarah H. AB cum laude, Harvard U., 1951; MS in Elec. Engring., MIT, 1956; MBA, U. Chgo., 1984. Devel. engr. GE, San Jose, Calif., 1956-60; project engr. GE, Pleasanton, Calif., 1960-63; engring. mgr. Westinghouse Electric Corp., Pitts., 1963-70; project dir., mgr. strategic planning-nuclear Westinghouse Electric Corp., 1973-75; v.p. Westinghouse Nuclear Europe, Brussels, 1970-73; dep. dir. FEA, Washington, 1975; dir. div. reactor devel. and demonstration ERDA, Washington, 1976-77; dir. nuclear power devel. Dept. of Energy, Washington, 1977-78; coordinator internat. nuclear study Dept. of Energy, 1978-80; dep. dir. Argonne Nat. Lab., Ill., 1980-84; vis. prof. nuclear engring. MIT, Cambridge, 1984-86; dir. rsch. U.S. Nuclear Regulatory Commn., Washington, 1986-95, cons., 1995—; chmn. com. safety of nuclear installations NEA-DECD, Paris, 1995. Author: Boiling Water Reactor Design, 1962; contbr. articles to profl. jours. Mem. vis. com. for nuclear engring. dept. MIT, 1992-98; mem. bd. visitors dept. materials and nuclear engring. U. Md., 1995—; vestry St. Alban's Ch., Washington, 1989-93. Lt. (j.g.) USNR, 1951-54. Fellow Am. Nuclear Soc. (bd. dirs. 1995-98, vice chair nuclear installations safety divsn. 1999—); mem. IEEE (sr.), Sigma Xi (Presdl. Meritorious award 1992). Avocation: history.

BECKLAKE, MARGARET RIGSBY, physician, educator; b. London, May 27, 1922; d. James Thomas and Dorothy Mabel (Mills) B.; m. Maurice McGregor, Mar. 20, 1948; children: James, Margaret. MBBCh, U. Witwatersrand, 1944, MD, 1951, MD (hon.), 1974. Lectr. U. Witwatersrand, 1950-57; asst. prof. exptl. medicine McGill U., 1961-65, prof., 1967-96, prof. epidemiology and medicine, 1973-96, prof. emeritus, 1996—; career investigator Med. Rsch. Coun. Can., 1968-93. Contbr. articles to med. jours. Named hon. prof., U. Witwatersrand, 1984-85. Fellow Royal Coll. Physicians, Royal Soc. (Can.); mem. Am. Thoracic Soc. (Disting. Achievement award 1997), Can. Thoracic Soc., Am. Physiol. Soc. E-mail: becklake@meakins.lan.mcgill.ca. Home: 532 Pine Ave W, Montreal, PQ Canada H2W 1S6 Office: McGill Univ Dept Epidem, 1110 Pine Ave W, Montreal, PQ Canada H3A 1A3*

BECKLER, DAVID ZANDER, government official, science administrator; b. June 29, 1918; s. William J. and Thekla (Levy) B.; m. Harriet Levy, Aug. 1, 1943; children: Stephen, Paul, Rochelle. BSChemE, U. Rochester, N.Y., 1939; JD, George Wash. U., 1943. Bar: D.C. 1942. Patent atty. Pennie, Davis, Marvin & Edmonds, Washington, 1939-42; tech. aide fgn. liaison office Office Sci. R & D Exec. Office of Pres., Washington, 1942-45; patent atty. Eastman Kodak Co., Rochester, N.Y., 1946; dep. tech. historian Ops. Crossroads Joint Chiefs of Staff, Washington, 1946; chief tech. intelligence br. R & D Bd. Office of Sec. of Def., Washington, 1947-49; mem. internat. sci. policy survey group Dept. of State, Washington, 1949-50; exec. dir. com. atomic energy R & D Bd., Washington, 1950-52; asst. dir. office indsl. devel. AEC, Washington, 1952-53; exec. officer Pres. Sci. Adv. Com., Washington, 1953-73; asst. to pres. NASSA, Washington, 1973-76; dir. sci. tech. and industry OECD, Paris, 1976-83; assoc. dir. Carnegie Commn. on Sci. Tech. and Govt., Paris, 1988-94; spl. asst. to dir. Office of Def. Mobilzation, Washington, 1954-57; asst. to spl. asst. to pres. for sci. and tech. The White

House, Washington, 1957-62; asst. to dir. Office Sci. and Tech., Exec. Office of Pres., Washington, 1962-73; cons. sci. and tech. policies, 1983-88, 94—. Recipient cert. of appreciation War and Navy Depts., Washington, 1945. Fellow AAAS; mem. Coun. Fgn. Rels., Cosmos Club (Washington chpt.). Home: 8709 Duvall St Fairfax VA 22031-2711 Office: Carnegie Commn Sci Tech and Govt 8709 Duvall St Fairfax VA 22031-2711

BECKLEY, DAVID LENARD, academic administrator; b. Shannon, Miss., Mar. 21, 1946; s. George and Georgianna (Fields) B.; m. Gemma Douglas, June 1, 1968; children: Jacqueline, Lisa. BA, Rust Coll., 1967; MEd, U. Miss., 1975, PhD, 1986. Dir. advancement Rust Coll., Holly Springs, Miss., 1967-87; pres. Wiley Coll., Marshall, Tex., 1987-93, Rust Coll., Holly Spring, Miss., 1993—. Mem. NAACP (life). Named Outstanding Alumni, U. Miss., Oxford, 1989. Mem. Tex. Assn. Developing Colls. (chmn. 1991-93), Edn. Ins. Assn. (bd. dirs. 1988-93), United Negro Coll. Fund (bd. dirs. 1990—), Omega Psi Phi (Citizen of Yr. award 1986, Man of Yr. award 1984). Democrat. Methodist. Avocations: reading, traveling, collecting antiques. Office: Rust Coll 150 E Rust Ave Holly Springs MS 38635-2330

BECKLEY, DONALD K., fundraiser; b. Washington, Mar. 27, 1916; s. Frank Ross and Lila Strock (Kauffman) B.; m. Eugenie E. Smith, Nov. 14, 1942 (div. 1972); m. Flora Mack, June 26, 1980 (dec. 1999). A.B., Columbia U., 1936, M.S., 1937; Ph.D., U. Chgo., 1948. Dept. store work, 1936-39; instr. retailing Rochester (N.Y.) Inst. Tech., 1939-42; prof. retailing and dir. Prince Sch. Retailing, Simmons Coll., Boston, 1946-58; exec. dir. Boston Center for Adult Edn., 1958-62; dir. devel. ops. and donor relations NYU, 1962-68; cons. Frantzreb & Pray Assos., Inc., 1968-75; devel. coordinator Am. Mus. Natural History, N.Y.C., 1976; coordinator N.Y. State com. Nat. Health Agys. for Fed. Campaigns, N.Y.C., 1977-81. Author: (with Edwina B. Hogadone) Merchandising Techniques, 1942, (with W. B. Logan) The Retail Salesperson at Work, 1948, (with John W. Ernest) Modern Retailing, 1950, (with Wenzil K. Dolva) The Retailer, 1950. Served with USAAF, 1944-45; staff U.S. Armed Forces Inst., U. Chgo., 1942-43; tchr. naval flight prep. Sch. Monmouth (Ill.) Coll., 1943-44. Home: 511 Ives Dairy Rd Miami FL 33179-5486

BECKLEY, MICHAEL JOHN, hotel executive; b. Watford, Eng., Mar. 24, 1942; arrived in Can., 1981; s. Reginald and Louise (Hart) B.; m. Elke Beckley, Sept. 9, 1966 (div. 1978); children: Kim, Christopher, Sarah; m. Janet Dorothy Brandon, Mar. 29, 1979; children: Justin, Julian. Grad., Westminster Hotel Sch., London, 1961. Cert. hotel adminstr., 1988. Asst. mgr. pers., food and beverage Brit. Transport Hotels, Eng., France, Fed. Republic Germany, 1961-66; gen. mgr. Pink Beach Club, Bermuda, 1966-68, Discovery Bay Hotel, Barbados, 1968-72; Caribbean area dir. St. James Beach Hotels, Barbados, 1972-76; dir. ops. Commonwealth Hospitality Ltd., London, 1976-81, v.p. ops., Toronto, Ont., Can., 1981-87, pres., 1987-97; exec. v.p. UNI Host Corp., Mississauga, Ont., Can., 1997—. Trustee Ednl. Inst., East Lansing, Mich., 1988—; former chmn. Experience Can.-A Travel Partnership; chmn. ministry adv. com. Tourism Strategy for Province of Ont.; chmn. Ont. Tourism Coun. Fellow Hotel and Catering-Mgmt. Inst. (cert. hotel adminstr.), SKAL. Avocations: golf, tennis, skiing, cooking. Office: UNI Host Corp, 5090 Explorer Dr 6th Fl, Mississauga, ON Canada L4W 4T9

BECKLEY, MICHELE ANISE BENNETT, elementary education educator; b. Pontiac, Mich., May 18, 1954; d. Russell Gene Bennett and Roberta (Bray) Bennett-Hunter; m. Wayne E. Beckley, Dec. 24, 1980; children: Nicole Anise, Drew Douglas. BA in Edn., U. Mich., 1976. Cert. tchr. K-8 core curriculum, K-12 bilingual, Mich., elem. self-contained 1-8, elem. bilingual/Spanish, early childhood edn., Tex. Tchr. first grade El Paso (Tex.) Ind. Sch. Dist., 1976-83, tchr. pre-kindergarten/kindergarten, 1992—; tchr. pre-kindergarten/kindergarten First Presbyn. Christian Pre-Sch., 1989-92; mem. adv. coun. presch. program for children with disabilities, 1995-96; mem. Campus Improvement Team, El Paso, 1993-96; mentor for new tchrs. El Paso Ind. Sch. dist., 1994-97. Grantee Target, 1998. Mem. ASCD, Assn. for Childhood Edn. (mem. Hall of Excellence El Paso com. br. 1996, rep. El Paso br. at internat. conf. in Portland, Oreg., Hall of Excellence award), Nat. Assn. for Edn. of Young Children (1st v.p., co-chair fall conf. 1995 El Paso br., pres.-elect, mem. chair 1996, other offices). Avocations: fine arts fairs. Office: Cielo Vista Elem Sch El Paso TX 79925

BECKLEY, ROBERT MARK, architect, educator; b. Cleve., Dec. 24, 1934; s. Mark Ezra and Marie Elizabeth (Kuhl) B.; m. Jean Dorothy Love, Feb. 26, 1956 (div. May 1988); children: Jeffery, Thomas, James; m. Jytte Dinesen, Oct. 24, 1992. BArch, U. Cin., 1959; MArch, Harvard U., 1961. Registered Architect Mich., Ohio, Ill., Wisc. From asst. to assoc. prof. U. Mich., Ann Arbor, 1963-69; from assoc. prof. to prof. U. Wisc., Milw., 1969-86; dean, prof. U. Mich., Ann Arbor, 1987-97, prof., 1997—; prin. Beckley-Myers, Architects, Milw., 1980-91. Prin. designs include: Theater Facilities, 1980-81 (award 1983), Theater Dist., 1981-82 (award 1984), Bellevue Downtown Park, 1985 (1st place award 1985). Recipient Distinction award Milw. Art Mus., 1986. Fellow Am. Inst. Architects, Inst. Urban Design, Graham Found. Home: 1016 Scott Pl Ann Arbor MI 48105-2585 Office: U Mich Coll Arch 2000 Bonisteel Dr Ann Arbor MI 48109-2069

BECKMAN, ARNOLD ORVILLE, analytical instrument manufacturing company executive; b. Cullom, Ill., Apr. 10, 1900; s. George W. and Elizabeth E. (Jewkes) B.; m. Mabel S. Meinzer, June 10, 1925; children: Gloria Patricia, Arnold Stone. BS, U. Ill., 1922, MS, 1923; PhD, Calif. Inst. Tech., 1928; DSc (hon.), Chapman Coll., 1965, Whittier Coll., 1971, Clarkson U., 1989, Rockefeller U., 1992, Scripps Rsch. Inst., 1994; LLD (hon.), U. Calif., Riverside, 1966, Loyola U., L.A., 1969, U. Ill., 1982, Pepperdine U., 1977, Ill. Wesleyan U., 1991; DHL (hon.), Calif. State U., Fullerton, 1984, Ill. State U., 1990. Rsch. assoc. Bell Tel. Labs., N.Y.C., 1924-26; chem. faculty Calif. Inst. Tech., 1926-39; v.p. Nat. Tech. Lab., Pasadena, Calif., 1935-39; pres. Nat. Tech. Lab., 1939-40, Helipot Corp., 1944-58, Arnold O. Beckman, Inc., South Pasadena, Calif., 1946-58; founder, chmn. Beckman Instruments, Inc., Fullerton, Calif., 1940-65, chmn. emeritus, 1988—; vice chmn. SmithKline Beckman Corp., 1984-86; bd. dirs. Security Pacific Nat. Bank, 1956-72, adv. dir., 1972-75; bd. dirs. Continental Airlines, 1956-71, adv. dir., 1971-73; bd. dirs. So. Calif. Edison, 1957-72. Author articles in field; inventor; patentee in field. Mem. Pres.'s Air Quality Bd., 1970-74; chmn. System Devel. Found., 1970-88; chmn. bd. trustees emeritus Calif. Inst. Tech.; hon. trustee Calif. Mus. Found.; bd. overseers House Ear Inst., 1981—; trustee Scripps Clinic and Rsch. Found., 1971—; bd. dirs. Hoag Meml. Hosp.; co-founder, chmn. emeritus, bd. dirs. Beckman Laser Inst. and Med. Clinic, 1982—; mem. bd. overseers U. Calif., Irvine, 1982—; founder, chmn. emeritus, bd. dirs. Arnold and Mabel Beckman Found., 1977—. With USMC, 1918-19. Benjamin Franklin fellow Royal Soc. Arts; named to Nat. Inventors Hall of Fame, 1987; recipient Nat. Medal Tech., 1988, Presdl. Citizens medal, 1989, Nat. Medal of Sci., 1989, Order of Lincoln award State of Ill., 1991, Bower award for Bus. Leadership, 1992. Fellow Assn. Clin. Scientists; mem. NAM, AAAS, Am. Acad. Arts and Scis., L.A. C. of C. (bd. dir. 1954-58, pres. 1956), Calif. C. of C. (dir., pres. 1967-68), Nat. Acad. Engring. (Disting. Honoree, 1986, Founders Award, 1987), Am. Inst. Chemists (Gold medal 1987), Instrument Soc. Am. (pres. 1952), Am. Chem. Soc., Social Sci. Rsch. Coun., Am. Assn. Clin. Chemistry (hon.), Newcomen Soc., Auto Club So. Calif. (bd. dirs. 1965-73, hon. dir. 1973—), Sigma Xi, Delta Upsilon, Alpha Chi Sigma, Phi Lambda Upsilon. Clubs: Newport Harbor Yacht, Pacific. Office: Arnold & Mabel Beckman Found 100 Academy Irvine CA 92612-3002

BECKMAN, JAMES WALLACE BIM, economist, marketing executive; b. Mpls., May 2, 1936; s. Wallace Gerald and Mary Louise (Frissell) B. BA, Princeton U., 1958; PhD, U. Calif., 1973. Pvt. practice, Berkeley, Calif. 1962-67; cons. Calif. State Assembly, Sacramento, 1967-68; pvt. practice, Laguna Beach, Calif., 1969-77; cons. Calif. State Gov.'s Office, Sacramento 1977-80; pvt. practice real estate cons., L.A. 1980-83; v.p. mktg. Gold-Well Investments, Inc., L.A. 1982-83; pres. Beckman Analytics Internat., econ. cons. to bus. and govt., L.A. and Lake Arrowhead, Calif., 1983—, East European/Middle East Bus. and Govt., 1992—; adj. prof. Calif. State U. Sch. Bus., San Bernardino, 1989—, U. Redlands, 1992—; cons. E European, environmental issues. Contbr. articles to profl. jours. Ordained elder, commr. Maj. USMC 1958-67. NIMH fellow 1971-72. Fellow Soc. Applied Anthropology; mem. Am. Econs. Assn., Am. Statis. Assn., Am. Mktg. Assn. (officer), Nat. Assn. Bus. Economists (officer). Democrat. Presbyterian. Office: PO Box 1753 Lake Arrowhead CA 92352-1753

BECKMAN, L. DAVID, university chancellor; b. Denver, Aug. 21, 1926. BA, Wheaton Coll., 1947; MTh, Dallas Theol. Sem., 1952, ThD, 1956; MA, Columbia U., 1962; DD, Colo. Christian Coll., 1987. Instr. Dallas Bible Inst., 1952-55, London (Ont., Can.) Bible Inst. and Theol. Sem., 1955-61; chmn. Bible dept. The King's Coll., Briarcliff Manor, N.Y., 1961-63; pres. Rockmont Coll., Longmont/Denver, Colo., 1963-81; pres. emeritus Rockmont Coll., Lakewood, Colo., 1981-83, Lakewood, 1983-85; pres. Colo. Christian Coll./Colo. Christian U., Lakewood, 1985-91; pres. Colo. Christian U., Lakewood, 1991-93, chancellor, 1993-95, pres. emeritus, 1995—. Home: 6325 W Mansfield Ave Apt 221 Denver CO 80235-3015

BECKMANN, DAVID MILTON, minister, economist, social activist; b. Kearney, Nebr., Feb. 22, 1948; s. Milton W. and Leona (Lange) B.; m. Janet L. Williams, June 17, 1972; children: Andrew, John. BA, Yale Coll., 1969; MDiv, Christ Sem., St. Louis, 1974; MSc, London Sch. Econs., 1975; DHH (hon.), Capital U., Columbus, Ohio, 1993; DD (hon.), Berkely Sch. of Div. at Yale, 1996. Ordained pastor Evang. Luth. Ch. Am., 1974. Student pastor First Luth. Ch., Omaha, 1972-73; devel. officer Rangpur Dinajpur Rehab. Svc., Thakurgaon, Bangladesh, 1975-76; urban projects officer World Bank, Washington, 1976-81, speech writer for pres., 1982-85, adviser on nongovernmental orgns., 1985-91; pres. Bread for the World, Bread for World Inst., Washington, 1991—; chmn. Medford Group Anti-hunger Orgns., 1995-97; exec. com. Inter Action. Author: Where Faith and Economics Meet, 1981, Bread for the World: Who We Are and What We Stand For, 1996; co-author: (books) The Overseas List, 1979, 85, Friday Morning Reflections at the World Bank, 1991, Transforming the Politics of Hunger, 1993. Recipient Disting. Alumni award Luth. Sch. of Theology, Chgo., 1993. Achievements include leadership of Bread for the World which won passage of Africa' Seeds of Hope Act and helped win back food stamps for the most vulnerable legal immigrants in U.S. Office: Bread for the World 1100 Wayne Ave Ste 1000 Silver Spring MD 20910-5643

BECKMANN, JOHN, architect, designer, writer; b. Mt. Kisco, N.Y., Sept. 3, 1960; s. Norman Peter and Margret Rose (Gorog) B.; m. divorced; 1 child, Kyra. BFA in Environ. Design, Parsons Sch. of Design, 1982. Established Axis Mundi, 1987; design cons. Met. Mus. of Art, N.Y.C., 1991-92; adj. prof. architecture N.J. Inst. Tech., 1999. Designer: included in group exhibitions, The Am. Crafts Mus., N.Y., 1988, The Nat. Arts Club, N.Y., 1988, Via Salon, Paris, 1989, Museo Alchimia, Milan, Italy, 1990, Gallery 91, N.Y., 1991, Mcpl. Art. Soc., N.Y., 1993; individual projects: Randolph Duke boutique, N.Y.C., 1987-88, Collaboration w/Uvegi Assoc., Final Image, N.Y., 1992, Aerotik Furniture Collection, 1990, Barbara Kramer Showroom, 1991, chinaware for Swid-Powell, 1992, Magnum, N.Y.C., 1998; author: International Interiors: Showrooms, 1993; editor: the Virtual Dimension: Architecture, Representation and Crash Culture, 1998. Grantee Graham Found. for Advanced Visual Studies in the Fine Arts, 1996. E-mail: jbeckmann@axismundi.com. Office: Axis Mundi 72 Seaman Ave New York NY 10034

BECKMANN, JON MICHAEL, publisher; b. N.Y.C., Oct. 24, 1936; s. John L. and Grace (Hazelton) B.; m. Barbara Ann Efting, June 26, 1965. BA, U. Pa., 1958; MA, NYU, 1961. Sr. editor Prentice-Hall Inc., Englewood Cliffs, N.J., 1964-68; v.p., editor Barre Pubs., Mass., 1970-73; pub. Sierra Club Books, San Francisco, 1973-94; pres. Beckmann Assocs. and Millennium Press, Sonoma, Calif., 1994—. Contbr. articles, book revs., poetry to publs. Mem. Book Club of Calif. Office: Beckmann Assocs & Millennium Press 18185 7th St E Sonoma CA 95476-4797

BECKMANN, MICHELE LILLIAN, secretary; b. Bklyn., Feb. 15, 1957; d. Anton and Alice Naomi (Williams) Prudich; m. Robert Westcott Beckmann, Apr. 18, 1981; children: Andrew Isaac, Walter Ian (twins). BA, Ea. Wash. U., 1978. Cert. prof. sec. Lead sec. New Way Homes, Spokane, 1980-81; libr. asst. Spokane Pub. Librs., 1981-82; office asst. Spokane County Assessor's Office, 1982; data processing clk. Aztech-Comstock, Spokane, 1983-84; finishing opr. Hollister-Stier Labs., Spokane, 1984; pvt. sec. Danial Kallestad, CLU, ChFC, Spokane, 1985; office asst. Wash. State U., Pullman, 1986-87, sec. III, 1987-89, project sec., 1989-92; owner Bhunkey Bros. Ink, Colfax, 1992—. Mem. Pullman Fair Housing Commn., 1989—, vice chmn., 1989-90; mem. local coun. Camp Fire, Inc., 1989-90; precinct officer Whitman County Dems., Colfax, Wash., 1988-90; mem. Whitman County Safety and Health Network, 1996-98, chmn., 1996-97. Recipient WO-HE-LO Medallion Camp Fire Ind., 1975; cert. appreciation Pullman Fair Housing Commn., 1989, 91. Avocations: sewing, crochet, quilting, reading, homeschooling. Home and Office: 1702 N Riverside Ln Colfax WA 99111-9755

BECKNER, WALTON THOMAS (TOM), adult education educator, academic administrator; b. Hamilton, Ohio, Oct. 28, 1946; s. Walton Estil and Lella Mae (Williams) B.; m. Beverly Sue Rice, Oct. 2, 1965; 1 child, Monica Lyn. BA, Milligan Coll., 1974; MA, Kent State U., 1979; MS, Ga. State U., 1984; PhD, U. Tenn., 1994. Ordained to ministry. Chaplain Stone Mountain (Ga.) Correctional Facility, 1982-84; dir. personal prison ministry Atlanta, 1982-87; pres. Am. Chaplaincy Tng. Sch., Ft. Wayne, Ind., 1985—; assoc. prof. Milligan Coll., 1988-95, Taylor U., Ft. Wayne, 1995—; dir. Ctr. Justice & Urban Leadership, Ft. Wayne, 1998—; chmn. Allen Co. Jail Chaplaincy Adv. Bd., Ft. Wayne, 1997—; v.p. Restorative Justice Ministry Network Am., Ocala, Fla., 1998—. Author, prodr.: (video series) I was in Prison... Did You Visit Me?, 1987; co-author: At Risk Youth: Theory, Practice, and Reform, 1997; editor: Effective Jail & Prison Ministry, 1998. Univ. rep. Cmty. Svc. Coun., Ft. Wayne, 1998—. Recipient Citizen of the Yr. award Dept. Pub. Safety, 1983; Appalachian Mellon fellow Mellon Found., 1992, Faculty Program scholar, 1994. Mem. Am. Correctional Assn., Am. Protestant Correctional Chaplain Assn., Am. Correctional Chaplains Assn., Ind. Correctional Assn. Avocations: hiking, reading, scuba diving, traveling. Office: Taylor U 1025 W Rudisill Blvd Fort Wayne IN 46807-2197

BECKNER, WILLIAM, mathematician; b. Kirksville, Mo., Sept. 15, 1941; s. William Horace and Bessie Mae Beckner; m. Chandra Muller; children: Amalia Marise, Chiara Lisa. BS, U. Mo., 1963; PhD, Princeton (N.J.) U., 1975. L.E. Dickson Instr. U. Chgo., 1975-76; lectr. Princeton U., 1975; asst. prof. U. Chgo., 1976-83; assoc. prof. U. Tex., Austin, 1983-90, prof., 1992—; vis. prof. U. Chgo., 1990-91, UCLA, 1992. Contbr. articles to profl. jours. Salem prize French Math., 1975; Sloan fellowship Sloan Found., 1976-78. Mem. Am. Math. Soc., Transactions of the Am. Math. Soc., Tex. Inst. for Computational and Applied Math. E-mail: beckner@math.utexas.edu. Office: U Tex at Austin Dept of Math Austin TX 78712

BECKS, RONALD ARTHUR, film producer; b. N.Y.C., July 9, 1953; s. Wellington and Vivian (Newkirk) B. Student, York Coll., 1969-71; cert. for prodrs., Cintel Corp., 1974-75; cert., Ch. Religious Sc., 1975-77; D of Religious Communication (hon.), Temple Faith, 1974. Owner, pres., chmn. Ronald A. Becks Internat. Theatre Soc., N.Y.C., 1978-90; v.p. Miracle Prodns., N.Y.C., 1978-90; pres. Magic Circle Players, Australia and Hong Kong, Sodeko Films, Australia and Hong Kong; mktg. dir. V.R.B. Enterprises, Australia and Hong Kong, Multi-Media Svcs., Australia and Hong Kong; pres. Noduki Films, Australia and Hong Kong, 1990, Face Affair, Beverly Hills, Calif., 1991, Film Gods Prodns., Beverly Hills, 1991—; founder, pres. STN TV Network, 1994; prodr. Blues TV, Century Cable, 1996, Inside Press TV, 1997, MASC TV, 1997; artistic dir. Beverly Hills Cmty. Theatre, 1997; v.p. BBH Cosmetics Labs., Beverly Hills, 1994; mem. adv. coun. Internat. Biog. Ctr., Cambridge, Eng., 1995, Inside Press TV Show, Blues TV; pres. Sir Ronald Blues Band, 1996; artistic dir. Beverly Hills Cmty. Theatre Co., 1997; exec. dir. United Citizens Com. Am., 1997. Author: The 3rd Testament, 1990, Legend of Billy Blue, 1988, Black Diamond, 1989, Come and Get It, 1991, Say a Little Prayer, 1991, Stagecoach Mary, 1993, Gigi and the Bogey-Man, 1993; prodr.: You Bring Out the Best in Me, 1984 (top 40 song); inventor phone device; songwriter Perfume in My Coffee; prodn. coord. Asian Belle, 1995. Dep. chmn. UN Assn., 1979, dep. amb., 1979, chmn. Song Quest, 1979; entertainment coord. Keep Australia Beautiful, 1980; prodr. children's show Consulate of Peru, 1979; prodr. and host I Love New York, N.Y.C., 1978; mem. notary pub. commn., 1996. Recipient Internat. Order of Merit, Cambridge. Fellow Highlander Club (life); mem. Prodrs. and Dirs. Guild, Prodrs. Assn., PEN Internat., Am. Soc. Notaries, NAACP, Internat. Platform Assn., Rainbow Coalition, Writers Guild, Journalists Club, Hollywood Press Club, Noetic Scis. Avocations: sports, writing, martial arts, horses, farming. Home and Office: 264 S La Cienega Blvd Ste 364 Beverly Hills CA 90211

BECKUM, LEONARD CHARLES, academic administrator; b. Winnsboro, La., Nov. 10, 1937; s. Charlie and Julia (Boyd) B.; m. Eva Lee Handy, Apr. 16, 1956 (div. 1974); children: Shinita La Joy, Leonard Charles Jr.; m. Sandra Ann Melia, June 3, 1978; children: Alisha Revira, Nicole DeAnna, Tiffany Marie. BA, San Francisco State U., 1969; AA, San Francisco City Coll., 1973; PhD, Stanford U., 1973. Truck driver Motor Assessory, P&S Co., Pueblo, Colo., 1958-60; psychiatric technician Colo. State Hosp., Pueblo, 1960-63, U. Calif. Med. Ctr., San Francisco, 1963-64; security officer San Francisco Gen. Hosp., 1964-66; police officer San Francisco Police Dept., 1966-69, police insp., 1969-75; edn. researcher Far West Edn. Lab., San Francisco, 1974-85; dean Sch. Edn. CCNY, CUNY, 1985-90; univ. v.p., vice provost, prof. of Practice of Edn. Duke U., 1990-96, prof. pub. policy studies, 1996—; mem. Calif. Task Force for Integrated Edn., Sacramento, 1978-82, Task Force for Bilingual Edn., Sacramento, 1977-79; mem. State N.Y. Tchr. Certification Practices Bd., 1987-90, Task Force Tchr. Preparation for N.Y. State, 1987-88. Contbr. articles in field to profl. jours. Test developer San Francisco Civil Svc. Commn., 1972-80; mem. Advanced Cert. Peace Officers Standards and Tng., Sacramento, 1970-75; bd. dirs. NAACP Legal Def. Fund, San Francisco, 1982-85, San Francisco Edn. fund, 1984-85, Pacific Grad. Sch. Psychology, Palo Alto, Calif., 1984-88, River Vale (N.J.) Dist. Sch. Bd., 1986-90, Wachovia Bank, 1990—, Am. Assn. Univ. Adminstrs., 1993-95; trustee Stanford U., 1990-95; mem. bd. advisors U.S. Army Command Coll., 1995-97. Postdoctorate study in edn. adminstrn. Rockefeller Found., 1976-78. Mem. Am. Edn. Research Assn., Am. Assn. Colls. of Tchr. Edn. (bd. dirs. N.Y. state chpt. 1986-90, chmn. multicultural task force 1986-90, pres. N.Y. chpt., nat. bd. dirs. 1990), Nat. Alliance Black Sch. Adminstrs. (life), Stanford U. Edn. Assn. (pres. 1971-72), Stanford Alumni Assn. (life), Alpha Tau Boulé. Avocations: jogging, bowling, fishing, traveling. Office: Duke U 209 Terry Sanford Inst PO Box 90011 Durham NC 27708-0011

BECK-VON-PECCOZ, STEPHEN GEORGE WOLFGANG, artist; b. Munich, Oct. 18, 1933; came to U.S., 1937; s. Wolfgang Anton Willibald Maria and Martha Jeanette (Morse) Beck-von-P.; m. Dorothy Ann Freytag, June 16, 1956 (div. 1971); m. Michele Marie Perry, Jan. 8, 1972; children: Stephen Jr., David, Kenneth, Lisa. BEE, Cornell U., 1956; MA in Art, Calif. State U., San Diego, 1974. Electronic engr. Stromberg Carlson Co., San Diego, 1958-60; project mgr. Control Data Corp., San Diego, 1960-65, Digital Devel. Corp., San Diego, 1965-66; project engr. Stromberg Datagraphix, Inc., San Diego, 1966-69; project mgr. Digital Sci. Corp., San Diego, 1969-71; artist San Diego, 1974—; cons. elec. engring., San Diego, 1974-78. Served to 2d lt. USAF, 1956-58. Mem. Internat. Sculpture Ctr., Kappa Alpha Soc. Avocations: art, travel. Home and Studio: 636 Nardito Ln Solana Beach CA 92075-2306

BECKWITH, BARBARA JEAN, journalist; b. Chgo., Dec. 11, 1948; d. Charles Barnes (dec.) and Elizabeth Ann (Nolan) B. BA in Journalism, Marquette U., 1970. News editor Lake Geneva (Wis.) Regional News, 1972-74; asst. editor St. Anthony Messenger, Cin., 1974-82, mng. editor, 1982—; mem. U.S. Cath. Conf. Communications Com., 1990-92. Mem. Cath. Press Assn. (bd. dirs. 1986-96, v.p. 1988-90, pres. 1990-92, best interview 1982, best photo story 1985, St. Francis de Sales award for outstanding contbn. to Cath. journalism 1994, best poetry 1997), Women in Comms., Cin. Editors Assn., Fedn. Ch. Press Assns. of Internat. Cath. Union of the Press (3d v.p. 1989-92, pres. 1992—), Nat. Cath. Assn. for Broadcasters and Communicators (bd. dirs. 1989-96, 97-98), Cath. Journalism Scholarship Fund (bd. dirs. 1993—, v.p. 1995-96, pres. 1996—). Office: St Anthony Messenger 1615 Republic St Cincinnati OH 45210-1298

BECKWITH, DAVID E., lawyer; b. Madison, Wis., Mar. 5, 1928; m. Natalie Biart, Nov. 19, 1948; children: Steven V.W., John B., David T. BS, U. Wis., 1950, LLB, 1952. From assoc. to ptnr. Foley & Lardner, Milw., 1952-98; ret., 1998. Bd. editors Fed. Litigation Guide Reporter, 1985—. Mem. bd. regents U. Wis., Madison, 1977-84, pres., 1982-84; dir., chmn. U. Wis. Madison Found. With USN, 1945-46. Fellow Am. Bar Found., Am. Coll. Trial Lawyers; mem. Order of Coif, Phi Beta Kappa. Unitarian. Avocations: golf, skiing, fishing. Office: Foley & Lardner Firstar Ctr 777 E Wisconsin Ave Ste 3800 Milwaukee WI 53202-5367

BECKWITH, EDWARD JAY, lawyer; b. Paterson, N.J., July 18, 1949; s. David and Beverly Beckwith; m. Iris Kailo; children: Jessica, Jason, Jenna. BS, Pa. State U., 1971; JD, Georgetown U., 1974, ML in Taxation, 1983. Bar: D.C., U.S. Supreme Ct., U.S. Ct. Appeals (fed. cir.), U.S. Ct. Appeals (D.C. cir.), U.S. Dist. Ct. D.C., U.S. Tax Ct., U.S. Claims Ct. Staff asst. Coun. on Environ. Quality Exec. Office of Pres., Washington, 1973; assoc. Fried, Frank, Harris, Shriver & Kampelman, Washington, 1974-82, Baker & Hostetler, Washington, 1982-83; ptnr. Baker & Hostetler, 1984—; adj. prof. law Georgetown U. Law Ctr., Washington, 1984—; bd. advisors Jour. Taxation Trusts and Estates, 1989-92; mem. Greater Washington Bd. Trade. Contbr. articles to profl. publs. Mem. steering com. sect. on trusts and probate law D.C. Bar, 1985-87. Alumni fellow honoree Pa. State U., 1998. Fellow Am. Coll. Trust and Estate Counsel (state chair); mem. ABA, Am. Law Inst. (estate planning coun. Washington chpt.), Pa. State U. Alumni Assn., Omicron Delta Kappa. Office: Baker & Hostetler 1050 Connecticut Ave NW Washington DC 20036-5304

BECKWITH, F. W., food products executive. CEO Fareway Stores, Boone, Iowa, chmn. bd., 1998—. Office: Fareway Stores Inc PO Box 70 Boone IA 50036-0070*

BECKWITH, JOHN, musician, composer, educator; b. Victoria, B.C., Can., Mar. 9, 1927. BMus, U. Toronto, 1947, MMus, 1961; DMus (hon.), Mt. Allison U., Sackville, N.B., 1974, McGill U., Montreal, 1978, U. Guelph, Ont., 1995; LLD (hon.), Queen's U., Kingston, Ont., 1998. Pvt. piano studies Alberto Guerrero, Royal Conservatory of Music, Toronto, 1945-50; pvt. composition studies Nadia Boulanger, Paris, 1950-51; pub. relations dir. Royal Conservatory of Music, Toronto, 1948-50; staff writer for radio music continuity Can. Broadcasting Corp., Toronto, 1953-55; freelance radio programmer and writer, 1955-70; spl. lectr. U. Toronto, 1952-53, lectr., 1954-60, asst. prof. music, 1960-66, assoc. prof., 1966-70, dean, 1970-77, prof., 1977-90, 1st holder Jean A. Chalmers chair in Can. music, 1984-90. Debut: Toronto, 1950; over 100 compositions including 4 operas, works for orch., chorus, etc.; 30 works published including: 4 songs to poems by E.E. Cummings, 1950; Fall Scene and Fair Dance, 1956; Music for Dancing, 1959; Jonah, 1963; Sharon Fragments, 1966; Circle, with Tangents, 1967; Gas, 1969; Taking a Stand, 1972; Musical Chairs, 1973; 3 Motets on Swan's China, 1981; Sonatina in 2 Movements, 1982; Harp of David, 1985; recorded compositions include: Music for Dancing; The Trumpets of Summer; Sharon Fragments; Circle, with Tangents; Quartet; Keyboard Practice; 3 Motets on Swan's China; Upper Can. Hymn Preludes; Etudes, Arctic Dances, Harp of David; recordings: Music at Sharon, 1982; Musical Toronto, 1984; arranger, dir. of instrumental ensemble; editor: The Modern Composer and His World, 1961; Contemporary Canadian Composers, 1975; Canadian Composer series, 1975-90, Musical Canada, 1988; Canadian Consultant, The New Grove, London, 1980; author: Music Papers, 1997; contbr. articles to profl. jours. Recipient Can. Music Coun. ann. medal, 1972, Arts Found. of Greater Toronto ann. music award, 1994; named to Order of Can., 1987. Mem. Can. League of Composers (former sec.), Ency. of Music in Can. (bd. dirs. 1972-94), Can. Musical Heritage Soc. (editl. bd. 1981—). Office: 121 Howland Ave, Toronto, ON Canada M5R 3B4

BECKWITH, JONATHAN ROGER, geneticist; b. Cambridge, Mass., Dec. 25, 1935; s. Manuel and Mildred B.; m. Barbara Shutt, Dec. 26, 1960; children—Benjamin Hunter, Anthony Rhys. BA, Harvard U., 1957, PhD, 1961. Mem. faculty Harvard U. Med. Sch., 1965—, prof. genetics, 1969—, Am. Cancer Soc. prof., 1979—; mem. Sci. for The People, 1971—; mem. Nat. Acad. Scis., 1984—. Recipient Eli Lilly award, 1970, Genetics Soc. Am. medal, 1993. Fellow AAAS; mem. Am. Acad. Arts and Scis., European Molecular Biology Orgn. (assoc.), Am. Soc. Exptl. Biologists, Am. Soc. Microbiology, Genetics Soc. Am. Research and publs. in bacterial genetics and social implications of genetics. Home: 8A Appleton Rd Cambridge MA 02138-2226 Office: Harvard Univ Medical Sch Boston MA 02115

BECKWITH, KAREN DANETTE, artist, printer; b. Corry, Pa., Oct. 31, 1964; d. Duane Karl and Janet Mae Beckwith. BFA, Cleve. Inst. Art, 1987; cert. master printer, Tamarind Inst., Albuquerque, 1998. Prodn. coord., creative advisor Hamilton Arts Rubber Stamp Co., Cleve., 1989-94; asst. studio dr. Hamilton Press, Cleve., 1991-96; artist, master printer Cleve., 1998—. Editor: Aluminum Plate Lithography, 1999. Grantee Ohio Arts Coun., 1992. Avocations: cycling, reading, home improvement, meditation. E-mail: lithogds@yahoo.com. Office: 18913 Nottingham Rd Cleveland OH 44110

BECKWITH, LARRY EDWARD, mechanical engineer; b. Pierre, S.D., Oct. 21, 1943; s. Charles Edward and Junebelle Ann (Robley) B.; m. AnhTuyet Thi Pham, Mar. 3, 1970. BSME, S.D. Sch. Mines Tech., Rapid City, 1966. Mil. engring. officer USACE, 1967-69; from mech. engr. to ptnr. Dunham Assocs., Bloomington, Minn., 1966, 70—; bd. dirs. Beckwith Hardware, Inc., Presho, S.D., 1977-92. State chmn. S.D. Coll. Reps., 1965-66; life mem. Rep. Nat. Com., 1994—; bd. govs. Walden Assn., 1994-96, pres., 1996. Capt. U.S. Army, 1967-69, Vietnam. Recipient bronze star U.S. Army, 1968, w/oak leaf cluster, 1969. Mem. VFW (life), Am. Legion, Decathlon Club, Oxford Club. Avocations: chess, golf. Office: Dunham Assocs Inc 8200 Normandale Blvd Ste 500 Bloomington MN 55437-1075

BECKWITH, LEWIS DANIEL, lawyer; b. Indpls., Jan. 30, 1948; s. William Frederick and Helen Lorena (Smith) B.; m. Marcia Ellen Ride, June 27, 1970; children: Laura, Gregory. BA, Wabash Coll., 1970; JD, Vanderbilt U., 1973. Bar: Ind. 1973, U.S. Dist. Ct. (so. dist.) Ind. 1973. Assoc. Baker & Daniels, Indpls., 1973-80, ptnr., 1981—. Articles editor Vanderbilt Law Rev., 1972-73. Mem. ABA, Ind. Bar Assn., Indpls. Bar Assn., Ind. C. of C. (com. occupational safety and health law 1982—), Associated Gen. Contractors of Ind. (com. occupational safety and health 1988—, safety and health counsel), Indpls. Athletic Club, ORder of Coif, Eta Sigma Phi, Beta Theta Pi. Republican. Lutheran. Avocation: sports. Office: Baker & Daniels 300 N Meridian St Ste 2700 Indianapolis IN 46204-1782

BECKWITH, MARLIN, aeronautics program manager; b. Emmett, Idaho, Jan. 1, 1938; children: Randy, Brenda. BA in history, U. Idaho, 1991; postgrad. in Pub. Adminstr., Calif. State U. Various positions Dept. of Pub. Works, Calif., 1964-73; various positions Dept. of Transp., Calif., 1976-83, chief, divsn. of Info. Svcs., 1983-94; program mgr, aeros. program Caltrans, Calif., 1994—. 1st lt. U.S. Army, 1961-63. with Res. 1963-1970. Mem. Nat. Assn. of State Aviation Offices (regional v.p. region 6), SW Chpt. of AM. Assn. of Airport Execs.

BECKWITH, SANDRA SHANK, judge; b. Norfolk, Va., Dec. 4, 1943; d. Charles Langdale and Loraine (Sterneberg) Shank; m. James Beckwith, Mar. 31, 1965 (div. June 1978); m. Thomas R. Ammann, Mar. 3, 1979. BA, U. Cin., 1965, JD, 1968. Bar: Ohio 1969, Ind. 1976, Fla. 1979, U.S. Dist. Ct. (so. dist.) Ohio 1971, U.S. Dist. Ct. Ind. 1976, U.S. Supreme Ct. 1977. Sole practice Harrison, Ohio, 1969-77, 79-81; judge Hamilton County Mcpl. Ct., Cin., 1977-79, 81-86, commr., 1989-91; judge Ct. Common Pleas, Hamilton County Divsn. Domestic Rels., 1987-89; assoc. Graydon, Head and Ritchey, 1989-91; judge U.S. Dist. Ct. (so. dist.) Ohio, 1992—; mem. Ohio Chief Justice's Code of Profl. Responsibility Commn., 1984, Ohio Gov.'s Com. on Prison Crowding, 1984-90, State Fed. Com. on Death Penalty Habeas Corpus, 1995—; pres. 6th Cir. Dist. Judges Assn., 1998-99; chair So. Dist. Ohio Automation Com., 1997-98. Office: Potter Stewart US Courthouse Ste 810 Cincinnati OH 45202

BECKWITH, SIDNEY JOHNSON, director special programs, curriculum administrator; b. East Grand Rapids, Mich., Dec. 30, 1947; d. William Judson and Betty Dame (Bonisteel) Johnson; m. James Luther Beckwith, Aug. 17, 1974; children: Crystina Ann, Betty Bonisteel-Chaffee, William James. BS, Western Mich. U., 1969; MS in Guidance and Counseling, Boston State Coll., 1974, cert. advanced grad. studies, 1976; adminstrv. cert., Syracuse U., 1981. Cert. tchr. reading and English, N.Y.; cert. guidance counselor, Mass. Tchr. English and reading Boston Pub. Schs., 1970-76; coord. K-12 reading, lang. arts, and compensatory program Union Springs (N.Y.) Cen. Schs., 1976-91, chair com. spl. edn., 1984-98, dir. spl. programs and curriculum, 1990-98, cons. K-12 program cons.; dir. nat. difussion network IPIMS Reading Ctr. Union Springs Cen. Schs., 1984-90; co-dir. Wellsprings Leadership Summer Camp, 1993-98; co-founder, co-dir. Wellsprings Leadership Curriculum and Summer Camp. Mem. Cayuga County children's com. United Way, 1983-89; bd. dirs. YMCA-WEIU, 1978-81. Grantee NDN, N.Y. State ESEA. Mem. ASCD, Midlakes Reading Coun. (pres. 1978-79), Cayuga County Prins. Assn. (sec. 1986-87), Regional Com. for Reading, Spl. Edn., Gifted and Talented, Fingerlakes Reading Assn., Phi Delta Kappa.

BECOFSKY, ARTHUR LUKE, arts administrator, writer; b. N.Y.C., Sept. 17, 1950; s. Arthur and Frances (Oliva) B. BA in Polit. Sci., Duke U., 1972; MA in Polit. Sci., Columbia U., 1974. Adminstr. Cunningham Dance Found., N.Y.C., 1974-79, exec. dir., 1980-94; pres. Art Plus Mgmt. Svcs., 1994—; world booking agt. Merce Cunningham Dance Co., N.Y.C., 1976-94; cons. Found. for Ext. and Devel. of Am. Profl. Theatre, N.Y.C., 1985, Found. for Dance Promotion, 1995—, Ringside/Elizabeth Streb, 1995—, The Armitage Found., 1995, Cross Performance, Inc., 1995-98, Stephen Petronio Dance Co., 1995—, Gotham Dance, Inc., 1995, ODC/San Francisco, 1995—, Twyla Tharp, 1996, David Dorfman Dance, 1996—, Ballet Hispanico, 1996—, David Rousseve/Reality, 1996—, Susan Marshall Dance Co., 1996—, Rena Shagan Assocs., 1996—, Margaret Jenkins Dance Co., 1997—, Bill Young and Dancers, 1997—, Bridgehampton Chamber Music Assocs., 1997, Ananda Shankar Dance Co., Calcutta, 1997—, Nest/Tokyo, 1997—, Garth Fagan Dance, 1998—, Moving Education, 1998—, Richard Alston Dance Co., London, 1998—, Grupo Corpo/Brazil, 1998—, Rosy Co./Tokyo, 1998—, Siobhan Davies Dance Co., London, 1998—, Lines Contemporary Ballet, 1998—, Joe Goode Performance Group, 1999—, Pentacle Help Desk, 1999—, Art Plus Care to Dance, 1999—; mem. dance panel NEA, 1983-94. Guitarist with Rhys Chatham & The Din, 1981; composer: Secretarial Suite, 1980, Track, 1983, Get Real, Cassandra, 1985, Space Into Action, 1986; author: The Road Show Abroad, 1985, On Commissioning New Art, 1989, MMerce, 1991. Bd. dirs. Dancing for Life, 1987; U.S. Performing Arts subcom. CULCON for U.S.-Japan cultural exch., 1989-93. Mem. Dance/U.S.A. (bd. dirs. 1983-88, 91-98, treas. 1983-86, vice chair 1993-96), World Dance Alliance (bd. dirs. 1993-97), Am. Arts Alliance (bd. dirs. 1983-87). Democrat. Avocation: photography. E-mail: ckdance@aol.com. Home: 324 E 9th St Apt 8 New York NY 10003-7962 Office: Stuyvesant Station PO Box 759 New York NY 10009-0759

BECTON, HENRY PRENTISS, JR., broadcasting company executive; b. Englewood, N.J., Oct. 16, 1943; s. Henry Prentiss and Jean Sprague (Coggan) B.; m. Jean Campbell Redpath, Sept. 28, 1968; children: Sara Campbell, Wilson Prentiss, Elizabeth Campbell. BA magna cum laude, Yale U., 1965; JD cum laude, Harvard U., 1968. Tchr. Cambridge Sch., Weston, Mass., 1968-69; tel. producer WGBH Ednl. Found., Boston, 1970-73; program mgr. WGBH Ednl. Found., 1974-78, v.p., gen. mgr., 1978-84, pres., 1984—; bd. dirs. Becton, Dickinson & Co., Pub. Broadcasting Svc., A.H. Belo Co., Mass. Corp. for Ednl. Telecoms., Banff Internat. TV Festival; trustee Scudder Funds, Conn. Coll., 1992-97, Com. for Econ. Devel., 1992—, Ethics Resource Ctr., 1994-97. Bd. dirs. mass. Com. for Prevention of Child Abuse, 1979-81; trustee Boston Ballet, 1976-78, Met. Cultural Alliance, Boston, 1974-76, New Eng. Aquarium, 1981—, boston Mus. Sci., 1984—, Wang Ctr. for Performing Arts, 1985-93, Concord Acad., 1993—, v.p., 1994—; bd. overseers Boston Mus. Fine Arts, 1990-98. Mem. NATAS (bd. dirs. New Eng. chpt. 1980-84), Mass. Bar Assn., Kollegewidgwok Yacht Club (Blue Hill, Maine), Phi Beta Kappa. Office: Sta WGBH-TV & WGBH-FM 125 Western Ave Allston MA 02134-1008

BEDARD, DONNA LEE, environmental microbiologist; b. Adams, Mass., May 5, 1947; d. Leo H. and Gertrude; m. Michael Brennan Dick, July 9, 1977; children: Christopher Michael Dick, Jonathan Leo Dick. BS, Tufts U., 1969; PhD in Biology, U. Chgo., 1973. Postdoctoral fellow U. Rochester (N.Y.), 1974, Johns Hopkins U., Balt., 1975-78; prof. Bennington (Vt.) Coll., 1978-80; rsch. scientist N.Y. State Dept. Health, Albany, 1980-82; staff scientist GE Corp. R&D, Schenectady, N.Y., 1982-90, staff scientist, group leader, 1990—. Author: (with others) Microbial Reductive Dechlorination of Polychlorinated Biphenyls, 1995; editl. bd. Microbial Ecology, 1993-96; contbr. articles to profl. jours. Recipient Am. Chem. Soc. award for Creative Advances in Environ. Sci. and Tech., 1995, Dushman award, 1992. Mem. Am. Soc. Microbiology (chair div. environ. and gen. microbiology 1992-93, mem. editl. bd. Applied and Environ. Microbiology 1997—). Achievements include 5 patents for microbial degradation of PCBs; discovery of several novel mechanisms of PCB degradation; first demonstration of accelerated PCB dechlorination in situ. Office: GE Corp R&D Bldg K-1, Rm 3B12 PO Box 8 Schenectady NY 12301-0008

BEDARD, EMIL R., career officer; b. Argyle, Minn., Dec. 3, 1943; m. Linda Kathleen Deck; children: Jason, Jordan, Camille. Grad., Univ. N.D., 1967. 2nd lt., 1967; commander, staff occier Sch. Demo. Troops, Quantico, Va.; lt. col., asst. ops. officer MAF-G3; col. Marine Corps., Twentynine Palms, Calif.; asst. G-3 for ops. 7th Marine Expeditionary Brigade, 1991-93; asst. divsn. commander 1st Marine Divsn., Camp Pendleton, Calif., 1993; pres. Marine Corps. Univ., Quantico, 1994; major gen., 1997. Decorated Def. Superior Svc. medal, Legionof Merit with gold star, Bronze star with Combat V, Navy Commendation medal with Combat V, two gold stars, Def. Meritious Svc. medal, Meritorious Svc. medal, Navy and Army Achievement medals, Air Medal with numeral 16, Combat Action Ribbon with Gold star, Vietnam Cross of Gallantry with Silver Star. Office: 2 Marine Divsn Box C 20003 Camp Lejeune NC 28542*

BEDARD, PATRICK JOSEPH, editor, writer, consultant; b. Waterloo, Iowa, Aug. 20, 1941; s. Gerald Joseph and Pearl Leona (Brown) B. B.S. in Mech. Engring, Iowa State U., 1963; M.Automotive Engring., Chrysler Inst. Engring., 1965. Product engr. Chrysler Corp., Highland Park, Mich., 1963-67; tech. editor Car and Driver mag., N.Y.C., 1967-69; exec. editor Car and Driver mag., 1969-78, editor-at-large, 1978—; race driver, cons. in field; freelance writer mags. and TV films. Author: Expert Driving, 1987. Mem. Soc. Automotive Engrs., U.S. Ultralight Assn., Sports Car Club Am., Pi Tau Sigma. Roman Catholic. First driver to win profl. road race in N.Am. in Wankel-powered car, 1973; raced at Indpls. 500, 1983-84; 1st driver to go 200 miles per hour at Indpls. in Stockblock-powered car, 1984. Home: Rt 1 Box 779 Port Saint Joe FL 32456 Office: Car and Driver 2002 Hogback Rd Ann Arbor MI 48105-9795

BEDAU, HUGO ADAM, philosophy educator; b. Portland, Oreg., Sept. 23, 1926; s. Hugo Adam and Laura (Romeis) B.; m. Jan Lisbeth Peterson Mastin, 1952 (div. 1988); children—Lauren, Mark Adam, Paul Hugo, Guy Antony; m. Constance Elizabeth Putnam, 1990. Student, U. So. Calif., 1944-45; B.A. summa cum laude, U. Redlands, 1949; M.A., Boston U., 1951, Harvard, 1953; Ph.D., Harvard, 1961. Instr. Dartmouth, 1953-54; instr. Princeton, 1954-57, lectr., 1958-61; assoc. prof. Reed Coll., 1962-66; prof. philosophy Tufts U., 1966-72, Austin Fletcher prof. philosophy, 1972—, Romanell-Phi Beta Kappa prof. philosophy, 1994-95; vis. prof. law faculty U. Natal, South Africa, 1981, U. Westminster, London, 1994; vis. life fellow Clare Hall, Cambridge U., 1980; vis. fellow Wolfson Coll., Oxford, 1988; hon. rsch. fellow Bentham Project, U. London, 1997-99. Author: The Courts, The Constitution and Capital Punishment, 1977, Death is Different, 1987, Thinking and Writing About Philosophy, 1996; co-author: Victimless Crimes, 1974, Current Issues and Enduring Questions, 1987, 5th edit., 1999, In Spite of Innocence, 1992, Critical Thinking, Reading, and Writing, 3d edit., 1999; editor: Death Penalty in America, 1964, 4th edit., 1997, Civil Disobedience, 1969, Justice and Equality, 1971, Civil Disobedience in Focus, 1991; co-editor: Capital Punishment in the U.S., 1976; contbr. articles and essays on social, polit., and legal philosophy to books and profl. jours. Bd. dirs. Am. League to Abolish Capital Punishment, 1959-72, pres., 1969-72; bd. dirs. ACLU of Mass., 1984-87, 88-93, 95—, v.p., 1987; chmn. Nat. Coalition Against Death Penalty, 1990-93. Danforth fellow, 1957-58, Liberal Arts fellow in law and philosophy Harvard U. Law Sch., 1961-62. Mem. Am. Philos. Assn., AAUP, Am. Soc. Polit. and Legal Philosophy (v.p. 1981), Phi Beta Kappa. Office: Tufts U Dept Of Philosophy Medford MA 02155

BEDDALL, BARBARA GOULD, science historian, writer; b. Tarrytown, N.Y., Oct. 28, 1919; d. Gerald Blenkiron and Anna Rosetta (Curtiss) Gould; m. Edward A. Beddall, Oct. 29, 1949 (dec. Dec. 1992); 1 child, Thomas G. BA, Swarthmore Coll., 1941; BS in Libr. Sci., Columbia U., 1942; MS in Zoology, Yale U., 1962. Rsch. libr. Time Inc., N.Y.C., 1944-52. Author: Wallace and Bates in the Tropics, 1969; contbr. articles to profl. jours. Avocation: ornithology. Home: 297 Crosslands Dr Kennett Square PA 19348-2034

BEDDOW, RICHARD HAROLD, judge; b. Springfield, Mass., Jan. 3, 1932; s. Richard Harold and Elizabeth Christine (Geehern) B.; m. Trudy C. Howells, Jan. 14, 1967; children: Catherine Elizabeth, Elissa Christine. BS, U. Mass., 1953; LLB, Boston Coll, 1959. Bar: Mass. 1960. Atty. ICC, Washington, 1959-69, mem. rev. bd., 1969-73, adminstrv. law judge, 1973-81; adminstrv. law judge NLRB, Washington, 1981—. With USN, 1953-55. Roman Catholic. Avocation: landscape gardening. Home: 2406 Rockwood Rd Accokeek MD 20607-9584 Office: NLRB 1099 14th St NW Washington DC 20570

BEDEIAN, ARTHUR GEORGE, business educator; b. Davenport, Iowa, Dec. 22, 1946; s. Arthur and Varsenick (Donjoian) B.; m. Lynda L. Kennon, June 29, 1968; children: Katherine Nicole Kingsmill, Thomas Arthur. BBA, U. Iowa, 1967; MBA, Memphis U., 1968; DBA, Miss. State U., 1973. Instr. Mgmt. Miss. State U., Mississippi State, 1969-71; asst. prof. Ga. So. Coll., Statesboro, 1971-73; adj. asst. prof. Boston U., 1973-74; Edward L. Lowder prof. mgmt. Auburn (Ala.) U., 1974-85; Ralph and Kacoo G. Olinde Disting. prof. mgmt. La. State U., 1985-96; Boyd prof., 1996—; dir. Found. for Adminstrv. Rsch., 1982-93, pres., 1989-90; cons. in field. With USAR, 1968-73, pres. Acad. Mgmt., 1987-89. Fellow Acad. Mgmt. (dean 1997-99), Internat. Acad. Mgmt., So. Mgmt. Assn.; mem. APA, Inst. Decision Scis. (nat. coun. 1976-79), Southeastern Inst. Decision Scis. (pres. 1978-79), So. Mgmt. Assn. (pres. 1982-83), Am. Sociol. Assn., Beta Gamma Sigma, Delta Mu Delta, Phi Kappa Phi, Sigma Iota Epsilon. Armenian Apostolic. Author: Organizations: Theory and Design, 1991, Management Laureates, 1992, 93, 96, 98; Standarization of Selected Management Concepts, 1986, Management, 3d edit., 1993, Management in Extension, 3d edit., 1995; editor Jour. of Mgmt., 1977-79. Fax: 225-388-6140. E-mail: abede@lsu.edu. Home: 838 High Plains Ave Baton Rouge LA 70810-4349 Office: La State U Dept Mgmt Baton Rouge LA 70803-6312

BEDELIA, BONNIE, actress; b. N.Y.C., Mar. 25, 1948; d. Philip and Marian (Wagner) Culkin; m. Kenneth Luber, Apr. 15, 1969; children: Yuri, Jonah. Student, Hunter Coll., N.Y.C.; studied with Uta Hager, Herbert Berghof studios; studied with Lee Strasberg, Actors Studio. Stage appearances include The Glass Menagerie, 1970, The Sea Gull, 1970, As You Like It, 1970, Midsummer Night's Dream, 1970; Broadway appearances include Isle of Children, 1960, Enter Laughing, 1963, The Playroom, 1965, Happily Never After, 1966, My Sweet Charlie, 1967 (Theatre World award 1967); film appearances include Gypsy Moths, 1969, They Shoot Horses, Don't They?, 1969, Lovers and Other Strangers, 1970, Rosalie, 1972, Between Friends, 1973, The Big Fix, 1978, Heart Like a Wheel, 1983, Death of an Angel, 1986, The Boy Who Could Fly, 1986, Violets are Blue, 1986, The Stranger, 1987, Die Hard, 1988, Prince of Pennsylvania, 1988, Fat Man & Little Boy, 1989, Presumed Innocent, 1990, Die Hard II, 1990, Needful Things, 1993, Speechless, 1994, Judicial Consent, 1994, Homecoming, 1996, Any Mother's Son, 1997, Bad Manners, 1998; TV series Love of Life, 1961-67, The New Land, 1974, mini-series Salem's Lot, 1979, A Season in Purgatory, 1996; TV films Then Came Bronson, 1969, Sandcastles, 1972, Hawkins on Murder, 1973, A Message to My Daughter, 1973, A Time for Love, 1973, Heatwave, 1974, A Question of Love, 1978, Walking Through the Fire, 1979, Fighting Back, 1980, Million Dollar Infield, 1982, Memorial Day, 1983, The Lady from Yesterday, 1985, Alex, The Life of a Child, 1986, When the Time Comes, 1987, Somebody Has to Shoot the Picture, 1990, Switched At Birth, 1991, A Mother's Right: The Elizabeth Morgan Story, 1993, The Fire Next Time, 1993, Fallen Angels (The Quiet Room), 1993 (Emmy nomination, Guest Actress - Drama, 1994), Shadow of a Doubt, 1995, Legacy of Sin: The William Coit Story, 1995, Her Costly Affair, 1996, To Live Again, 1998. Recipient Golden Globe award, 1983. Office: care ICM c/o Michael Black 8942 Wilshire Blvd Beverly Hills CA 90211-1934*

BEDELL, ARCHIE WILLIAM, family physician, educator; b. Detroit, Sept. 22, 1938; s. Archie Arnold and Mary (Barson) B.; m. Linda Suzanne Boos, Apr. 15, 1952; children: Robert, Marty, Jim, Amy. BS, Detroit Inst. Tech., 1961; MS in Biology, U. Detroit, 1963; MS in Human Anatomy, Wayne State U., 1964, PhD, 1967, MD, 1970. Diplomate Am. Bd. Family Practice. Med. intern Bon Secours Hosp., Grosse Point, Mich., 1969-71, Holden fellow, 1969-71; dir. inpatient tng. Bon Secours Hosp., Grosse Pointe, Mich., 1971-73; founding dir. family practice residency Bon Secours Hosp., Grosse Pointe, 1974-88; founding chmn. dept. family practice Henry Ford Hosp., Detroit, 1988-91, founding dir. family practice residency program, 1988-91; pvt. family practice Grosse Pointe, Mich., 1991-95; chmn., family practice Macomb Hosp., Warren, Mich., 1994; dir. family practice residency Mercy Hosp., Toledo, 1995—, dir. med. edn., 1995; trustee Detroit Inst. Tech., 1974-78; merit project bd. mem. Family Health Found. Am. Acad. Family Physicians, Kansas City, Mo., 1982; chmn. bd. Mich. Health Coun., Lansing, 1996—. Provider Homeless, Toledo, 1995. Recipient Holden award Sisters of Bon Secour, Grosse Pointe, 1969, 71, Semmes award, 1970. Mem. Mich. Acad. Family Physicians (chmn. risk mgmt. 1980-90, bd. mem., v.p., pres.-elect 1994-95, pres. 1996-97, past pres. 1997-98), Wyndgate County Club (charter mem.), Ohio Acad. Family Physicians (dir. family practice residencies 1996-97), Mich. Health Coun. (chmn. bd. dirs. 1996-98). Methodist. Avocations: duck carving, golfing, hunting, fishing. Office: Mercy Family Practice Ctr 2127 Jefferson Ave Toledo OH 43624-1117

BEDELL, BARBARA LEE, journalist; b. Annapolis, Md., July 10, 1936; d. Royal Lee and Kathryn Rosalee (Alton) Sweeney; m. Raymond Lester Bedell, July 1, 1955 (div. 1979); children: Patricia Bedell Pulito, Barbara Ann Bedell Porrini, Raymond, Robert. *As a child who grew up during World War II, Barbara Bedell's patriotism is unwaivering. An avid reader who loves American history, she strives to share her knowledge with her family, especially the eight grandchildren. Her legacy is family first. She enjoys sharing an appreciation of heritage, patriotism, and service to community.* Dir. woman's programming, host daily talk show Sta. KLME, Laramie, Wyo., 1962-68, Sta. WKIP, Poughkeepsie, N.Y., 1968-70; asst. soc. editor, feature writer Poughkeepsie Jour., 1968-70; dir. communications and publs. Spackenkill Sch. Dist., Poughkeepsie, 1970-73; columnist, reporter Times Herald-Record Newspaper, Middletown, N.Y., 1973—; bd. dirs. Middletown Day Nursery, 1988—; mem. steering com. Dr. Martin Luther King. Jr. Cmty. Wide Celebration, 1992—; lectr. on various topics to civic, polit., religious, social orgns., 1961—. Mem. 75th Anniversary Com., Cheyenne, Wyo., 1965; mem. Rep. Precinct Com., 1961-68, Albany County Bd. Electors, 1966-68; mem. com. history and heritage collection Orange County Community Coll., Middletown, 1984; mem. 100th Anniversary Com., Middletown, 1983-88; bd. dirs. divsn. marshal 1988 Parade; apptd. del. Gov. Mario Cuomo's N.Y. State Conf. on Librs., 1981; campaign chair United Way, 1996; bd. dirs. Literacy Vols. of Am. *As a respected journalist, Barbara Bedell has been writing a popular column about community events and the people who make them work for more than 25 years.Through her work, she has won more than 400 community service awards and honors and has participated in many programs as a motivator and speaker.* Recipient 1st in N.Y. feature writing award Am. Cancer Soc., 1973; Disting. Svc. award NAACP, 1980, 96, Hadassah Myrtle Wreath award, 1979, Cmty. Svc. award Boy Scouts Am., 1990, Humanitarian award Human Rights Commn., 1997, Svc. awards from numerous svc. clubs and lodges, chs., assns.; named Mrs. Wyoming, Mrs. Am. Pageant, 1967; N.Y. State All-Am. Family, 1972, Orange County Agr. Soc. award. Mem. Nat. Fedn. Press Women (8 awards for feature writing 1967-70, top Wyo. state award for radio script writing 1966), Elks (Mother of Yr. award 1989), SAR (Woman of Year award 1991). Mem. Kiwanis, Lions. Republican. Home: PO Box 458 Walker Valley NY 12588-0458 Office: Times Herald-Record Box 2046 Middletown NY 10940-6302

BEDELL, GEORGE CHESTER, retired publisher, educator, priest; b. Jacksonville, Fla., May 13, 1928; s. Chester and Edmonia (Hair) B.; m. Elizabeth Reed Phillips, Jan. 22, 1983; children: George Chester III, Frank Moor, Nathan Gale. BA, U. of South, Sewanee, Tenn., 1950; MDiv, Va. Theol. Sem., Alexandria, 1953; MA, U. N.C., 1966; PhD, Duke U., 1969; DCL (hon.), U. of South, 1991. Ordained priest Episcopal Ch.; parish priest Episc. Ch., Lake City, Panama City and Tallahassee, Fla., 1953-64; asst. prof. religion Fla. State U., Tallahassee, 1967-73; assoc. prof. Fla. State U., 1973-74; dir. humanities and fine arts State U. System of Fla., 1971-72, dir. pers. and faculty rels., 1972-76, assoc. vice chancellor, 1976-77, exec. asst. to chancellor, dir. pub. affairs, 1977-79, vice chancellor, 1979-80, interim chancellor, 1980-81, exec. vice chancellor, 1981-86, vice chancellor for adminstrv. affairs, 1986-87; dir. U. Press of Fla., 1987-94; mng. editor AAR Studies in Religion, 1972-76; historiographer Episc. Diocese of Fla., 1968-76. Author: Kierkegaard and Faulkner: Modalities of Existence, 1972, Religion in America, 1975, 82. Mem. Tallahassee City Park Bd., 1972-76, Leon County Dem. Exec. Com., 1970-74; trustee Jessie Ball du Pont Fund, 1985-98, chmn., 1988-89, 93-95, 97-98; mem. jud. nominating commn. Fla. Supreme Ct., 1990-94; mem. fee arbitration com. Fla. Bar, 1994-98; trustee Newberry Libr., 1995—; bd. dirs. The Presiding Bishop's Fund for World Relief, 1996—. Arthur N. Morris fellow, 1964-67; Duke-Danforth fellow, 1965-67. Mem. MLA, Fla. Hist. Soc., Nat. Trust for Hist. Preservation, Rotary. Democrat. Episcopalian. Home: 2810 NW 38th Dr Gainesville FL 32605-2680

BEDELL, GEORGE NOBLE, physician, educator; b. Harrisburg, Pa., May 1, 1922; s. George Harold and Elsie Clair (Noble) B.; m. Betty Jane Goldzier, Nov. 4, 1950 (dec. Mar. 1970); children: David, Mark, Barbara, Bruce; m. Mirriel Shields Hummel, Oct. 17, 1970; step-children: Judy, Jeffrey, Eric, Deborah, Andrew. B.A., DePauw U., 1944; M.D., U. Cin., 1946. Intern U. Iowa, 1946-47, resident in pathology, 1947-48, resident in internal medicine, 1950-52, research fellow in internal medicine, specializing in cardiology, 1952-54; research fellow physiology Postgrad. Sch. Medicine, U., Pa., 1954-55; asst. prof. dept. medicine Coll. Medicine, U. Iowa, 1955-59, asso. prof. dept. medicine, 1959-68, prof., 1968—; dir. Pulmonary Disease div. Dept. Medicine, 1968-81; cons. VA Hosp., Iowa City, 1954—; mem. staff U. Hosps., Iowa City. Contbr. articles to profl. jours. Mem. Johnson County Democratic Central Com., 1956-69, treas., 1958-64. Served with AUS, 1948-50. NIH Spl. fellow, 1954-55; recipient Career Devel. award, 1960-70, Walter L. Bierring award Am. Lung Assn. Iowa, 1973. Mem. ACP, Am. Lung Assn. (dir. 1972-80), Am. Lung Assn. Iowa (dir. 1971-81), Am. Fedn. Clin. Research, Am. Thoracic Soc., Iowa Thoracic Soc. (v.p. 1960-61, pres. 1962-63), Iowa Tb and Health Assn. (dir. 1961-65, 67-71), AMA (vice chmn. sect. council on diseases of chest 1971-73, chmn. sec. council diseases of chest 1974-76, Am. Thoracic Soc. del. to AMA 1979-85), Iowa, Johnson County med. socs., Soc. Exptl. Biology and Medicine, Iowa Clin. Soc. Internal Medicine, Central Soc. Clin. Research, Am. Coll. Chest Physicians, Am. Physiol. Soc., Am. Soc. Clin. Investigation, A.C.P., Central Clin. Research Club. Democrat. Unitarian. Home: 327 Blackhawk St Iowa City IA 52246-3803 Office: University Hosps Iowa City IA 52242

BEDELL, JAY DEE, educator, writer; b. Monterey, Calif., Oct. 20, 1946; s. John Dewhirst and Lucille (Huffman) B. BA, U. Calif.-Davis, 1968. Tchr. Antioch Schs., Calif., 1969-84, v.p., dir. Credit Union, 1979-81; owner Bedell Enterprises, 1986—; pvt. cons., 1985—; supr. security Chevron U.S.A., 1988-90; mem. Adv. Coun. for Spl. Edn., Antioch, Calif., 1979-81; mem. State Dept. Conf. on Spl. Edn., 1978. Bd. dirs. Storyland Theater, Antioch, 1979; mem. staff devel. com. Supt. of Schs., Contra Costa County, Calif., 1979-81. Writer poetry (Golden Poet awards World of Poetry Press, 1985, 86, 87, 88, 89, 90, 91, 92); author: (poems) The Golden Eagle, 1984, Dreams, 1986, Lady Liberty, 1986, Sierra-Nevada, 1986, Grand Canyon, 1986, Mother Teresa, 1987, The Eyes of a Child, 1988, A Prayer for Ann Naputi, 1989, Monarch, 1989, Eternal Flame, 1989, Heartbreak, 1989, Blood and Roses, 1990, Crystal Tears, 1990, San Francisco Morning, 1990, Little Sheba, 1991, I Remember Ann, 1992, Battle of Isandhlwana, 1994, Beauty, 1996, King Cobra, 1996, (poems) Chariots in the Sky, 1997, Mountain Meadow, 1997, The Sea, 1999. Deacon Adventist Ch., Antioch, Calif.; active sch. bd. Hilltop Christian Sch., Antioch, Calif. With U.S. Army, 1971-73. Fellow Am. Biog. Inst. Rsch. Assn. (life); mem. Internat. Platform Assn., Libr. of Congress (assoc.), Smithsonian (assoc.), Knight Order of Templars Jerusalem, Delta Upsilon. Democrat. Home: 1020 Claudia Ct Apt 11 Antioch CA 94509-3449

BEDERSON, BENJAMIN, physicist, educator; b. N.Y.C., Nov. 15, 1921; s. Abraham Michael and Lena (Waxlowsky) B.; m. Betty Weintraub, Jan. 20,

1956; children: Joshua Benjamin, Geoffrey Adam, Aron Gregory, Benjamin Boris. B.S., CCNY, 1946; M.S., Columbia U., 1948; Ph.D., NYU, 1950. Spl. engring. detachment Los Alamos Sci. Lab., 1944-46; research scientist MIT, Cambridge, 1950-52; mem. faculty dept. physics NYU, 1952-92, prof., 1967-92, prof. emeritus, 1992—, chmn. dept., 1973-76, spl. advisor for sci. to dean Faculty Arts and Scis., 1983-86, dean Grad. Sch. Arts and Scis., 1986-89; chmn. Internat. Conf. Physics of Electronic and Atomic Collisions, 1983-85; chmn. vis. panel Ctr. for Absolute Phys. Quantities, Nat. Bur. Standards, 1980-83. Editor-in-chief emeritus Am. Phys. Soc., 1992-96; editor Phys. Rev. A, 1978-91; assoc. editor Atomic Data and Nuclear Data Jour., 1969-98; editor (with Herbert Walther) Advances in Atomic, Molecular, and Optical Physics, 1974—; contbr. articles to profl. jours.; patentee in field. Served with U.S. Army, 1942-46, PTO. Fellow AAAS, APS. E-mail: ben.bederson@nyu.edu. Home: 60 E 8th St Apt 24K New York NY 10003-6522 Office: NYU Physics Dept 4 Washington Pl New York NY 10003-6621

BEDERSON, JOSHUA BENJAMIN, neurosurgeon; b. Feb. 26, 1957. BA in Neurobiology, Cornell U., 1978; MD, U. Calif., San Francisco, 1983. Resident in neurosurgery U. Calif., San Francisco, 1983-90; fellow in cerebrovascular surgery Borrow Neurol. Inst., Phoenix, 1990; asst. prof. neurosurgery Montefiore Med. Ctr., N.Y.C., 1990-91; dir. cerebrovascular surgery Mt. Sinai Sch. Medicine, N.Y.C., 1992—. E-mail: jbederson@mssm.edu. Office: Mt Sinai Med Ctr Dept Neurosurgery New York NY 10029

BEDFORD, AMY ALDRICH, public relations executive, corporation secretary; b. Pendleton, Oreg., July 13, 1912; d. Edwin Burton and Elsie (Conklin) Aldrich; m. J.M. Bedford (wid.); 1 child, Jacqueline Bedford Brown. BS, Oreg. State U., 1933. Mgr. comml. dept. East Oregonian, Pendleton, 1950-75, mgr. pub. rels., 1975—; corp. sec. East Oregonian Pub. Co., Pendleton, 1950—. Bd. dirs. Oreg. Status of Women Com., 1972-75, Oreg. Law Enforcement Commn., 1975-82; mem. Arts Coun. Pendleton. Recipient Pendleton First Citizen award C. of C., 1962, Gov.'s award for the Arts, 1988, Woman of Achievement award Oreg. Commn. for Women, 1998. Mem. Women in Communications, Oreg. Press Women, AAUW (pres. 1956-58, grantee 1965), LWV, Pendleton River Parkway Found., World Affairs Coun. Oreg., Altrusa. Avocations: reading, travel, music, theatre. Home: PO Box 1456 Pendleton OR 97801-0360 Office: East Oregonian Pub Co PO Box 1089 Pendleton OR 97801-1089

BEDFORD, BRIAN, actor; b. Morley, Yorkshire, Eng., Feb. 16, 1935; s. Arthur and Ellen (O'Donnell) B. Student, Royal Acad. Dramatic Art, London. Actor: (plays) A View From the Bridge, 1958, Five Finger Exercise, 1959, The Tempest, 1959, Write Me A Murder, 1962, Lord Pengo, 1962, The Doctor's Dilemma, 1963, The Private Ear, 1963, The Knack, 1964, The Unknown Soldier and His Wife, 1967, 73, Astrakhan Coat, 1967, The Cocktail Party, 1968, The Seven Descents of Myrtle, 1968, Hamlet, 1969, Private Lives, 1969, Three Sisters, 1969, Blithe Spirit, 1970, The Tavern, 1970, School for Wives, 1971 (Tony award for Best Actor 1971), Jumpers, 1972, Butley, 1973, Measure for Measure, 1975, Twelfth Night, 1975, Equus, 1976, Richard III, 1977, The Guardsman, 1977, As You Like It, 1977, The Winter's Tale, 1978, Uncle Vanya, 1978, Death Trap, 1979, The Seagull, 1980, Much Ado About Nothing, 1980, Whose Life Is It Anyway?, 1980, The Misanthrope, 1981, Arms and the Man, 1982, Blithe Spirit, 1982, Tartuffe, 1983, Richard II, 1983, 86, A Midsummer Night's Dream, 1984, Waiting for Godot, 1984, The Real Thing, 1985, The Tempest, 1985, Private Lives, 1986, Opera Comique, 1987, No Time for Comedy, 1987, The Merchant of Venice, 1988, Educating Rita, 1988, The Relapse, 1989, The Merchant of Venice, 1989, The Lunatic, The Lover and The Poet, 1989, Macbeth, 1990, Julius Caesar, 1990, Timon of Athens, 1991, Much Ado About Nothing, 1991, School for Wives, 1991, Two Shakespearean Actors, 1991, 92 (Tony award nominee for Lead Actor in a Play 1992), Measure for Measure, 1992, Timon of Athens, 1993, 94 (Tony award nominee for Lead Actor in a Play 1994), Twelfth Night, 1994, The Molière Comedies, 1994, 95, (Tony award nominee for Lead Actor in a Play 1995), Amadeus, 1995, 96, The Little Foxes, 1996, London Assurance, 1997 (Tony award nominee for Lead Actor 1997), Equus, 1997, Much Ado About Nothing, 1998, A Midsummer Night's Dream, 1999, The School for Scandal, 1999; (films) Man of the Moment, 1955, Miracle in Soho, 1957, The Angry Silence, 1960, Number Six, 1961, The Pad and How to Use It, 1966, Grand Prix, 1966, Robin Hood, 1973, Nixon, 1995, others; also numerous TV appearances; dir.: (plays) Titus Andronicus, 1978, The Rivals, 1981, Coriolanus, 1981, Blithe Spirit, 1982, Phaedra, 1990, Othello, 1994, Waiting for Godot, 1996, 98, Equus, 1997, The Winter's Tale, 1998. Inducted into Theatre Hall of Fame, 1996. Address: Stratford Festival, P.O.Box 520, Stratford, ON Canada N5A 6V2 Office: PO Box 298 Hurley NY 12443-0298

BEDFORD, DANIEL ROSS, lawyer; b. Berwyn, Ill., Aug. 19, 1945; s. Fred Doyle and Nelda Elizabeth (Dittrich) B.; children: Ian, Kate. BS, Stanford U., 1967, JD, 1971, MBA, 1971. Bar: Calif. 1972. Assoc. Thelen & Martin, San Francisco, 1971-78, ptnr., 1979-86; ptnr. Orrick, Herrington & Sutcliffe, San Francisco, 1986—. Mem. ABA, Calif. Bar Assn., San Francisco Bar Assn., Am. Coll. of Investment Counsel. Democrat. Episcopalian. Home: 2 Townsend St Apt 1-1006 San Francisco CA 94107-2043 Office: 400 Sansome St San Francisco CA 94111-3304

BEDFORD, DANIELLE, public relations specialist; b. L.A., Oct. 20, 1970; d. Roderick and Beverly Bedford; 1 child, Simeon Bonnell. Student, Santa Monica Coll., 1991, West L.A. Coll., 1994. Switchboard operator Midway Hosp., L.A., 1989-97, hosp. transporter, 1996-97; pub. rels. specialist Levine Comms., L.A., 1998-99, Davina Douthard & Co., 1999—. Author: (poems) Season's, 1997. Democrat. Avocations: reading, writing poetry, making gift baskets.

BEDFORD, KEITH WILSON, civil engineer, atmospheric science educator; b. Schenectady, N.Y., May 5, 1945; s. Alexander Wilson and Elsie Maude (Flickinger) B.; m. Marilyn Kay Bettoney, Aug. 18, 1972; children: Nathaniel Keith, Hilary Alexis. BSME with honors, Union Coll., 1969, MSME, 1971; PhD, Cornell U., 1974. Rsch. asst. Union Coll., 1968-70; rsch. fellow EPA Cornell U., 1970-73, teaching asst. hydaulics/hydrology lab., 1973; asst. prof. civil engring. Ohio State U., 1973-78, assoc. prof., 1978-83, prof. civil engring. and atmospheric sciences, 1983—; chmn. dept. civil and environ. engring., 1994-96, chmn. dept. civil and environ. engring. and geodetic sci., 1996—; fellow Coop. Inst. Limnology and Ecosystem Rsch., NOAA Great Lakes Environ. Rsch. Lab./U. Mich., 1990—; rsch. cons. U.S. Fish and Wildlife Svc., 1977-78, Geotechnics, Inc., 1980-82, U.S. Army Corps. Engrs., 1982-83, 89-90, HRC corp., 1984-86, UN, 1985-87, Camp, Dresser and McKee, 1991—, others. Contbr. articles to profl. jours. Fed. Water Quality Adminstrn. Rsch. fellow Cornell U., 1970-71, EPA Rsch. fellow, 1971-73. Mem. ASCE (Outstanding Svc. award 1976, 77, Huber prize 1986, Karl Emil Hilgard prize 1989, Review Article of Yr. award hydraulics divsn. 1991), Am. Geophysical Union, Internat. Assn. Great Lakes Rsch. (bd. dirs.), Internat. Assn. Hydraulic Rsch., Sigma Xi, Tau Beta Pi, Chi Epsilon. Unitarian. Achievements include development of Great Lakes Forecasting System, Acoustic Resuspension Measurement System, HANDS high frequency non-destructive particle sizer, Dynamic Water Quality Planning Model; research includes measurements of erosion rates and scour, closure free turbulence models. Office: Ohio State U Dept Civil/Environ Engring 2070 Neil Ave Columbus OH 43210-1226

BEDFORD, NORTON MOORE, accounting educator; b. Mercer, Mo., Nov. 11, 1916; s. Cornelius David and Mary (Moore) B.; m. Helen Grace Horn, Mar. 19, 1943; children—Norton Mark, Martha Ann. B.B.A., Tulane U., 1940, M.B.A., 1947; Ph.D., Ohio State U., 1950. CPA 1947. Faculty Ohio State U., 1947-50, Washington U., St. Louis, 1950-53; prof. U. Ill., Urbana, 1954-90, prof. emeritus, 1987—, Arthur Young prof., 1974-87; prof. Harvard U., 1981-82, U. Calif., Santa Barbara, 1987-92, Claremont Coll., 1993-95, Calif. Inst. Tech., 1996—; mgmt. cons. Author: Income Determination Theory, 1965, Advanced Accounting, 1961, 2d edit., 1967, 3d edit., 1973, 4th edit., 1979, Introduction to Modern Accounting, 1968, Future of Accounting in a Changing Society, 1970, Extensions in Accounting Disclosures, 1973; Contbr. articles to profl. jours. Served with AUS, 1942-46. Named Sch. Bus. Outstanding Alumnus, Tulane U., 1963, Acct. of Yr., Beta Alpha Psi, 1976; inducted into Acctg. Hall of Fame, 1988; Weldon Powell prof., 1969; Fulbright scholar, 1972. Mem. AICPA (bd. dirs., Outstanding Educator 1988), Am. Acctg. Assn. (pres., named Outstanding Educator 1980), Nat. Assn. Accts. (v.p., bd. dirs.), Rotary. Home: 101 W Windsor Rd Urbana IL 61802-6663 Office: U Ill 302 Commerce W Urbana IL 61801 *Success requires admiration for excellence in all things, concern for the human condition, a willingness to sense and accept change, an interest in being respected by others, great sensitivity to criticism, and a desire to learn and generalize knowledge coupled with a belief in the role and effectiveness of education as a means for developing civilization.*

BEDFORD, ROBERT FORREST, anesthesiologist; b. Boston, Oct. 6, 1942; s. Nathaniel Forrest and Roberta Lelia (Skinner) B.; m. Faith Goodwin Andrews, Dec. 28, 1963; children: William, Eleanor, Sarah. AB in Biology, Princeton U., 1964; MD, Cornell U., 1968. Diplomate Am. Bd. Anesthesiology (assoc. examiner 1987-90). Intern Va. Mason Hosp., Seattle, 1968-69; resident/fellow anesthesiology U. Pa. Hosp., Phila., 1969-72; chief anesthesiology, operating svcs. U.S. Walson Army Hosp., Ft. Dix, N.J., 1972-74; asst. clin. prof. anesthesiology Columbia U. Coll. Physicians and Surgeons, N.Y.C., 1974-77; from asst. prof. to prof. anesthesiology U. Va. Sch. Med., Charlottesville, Va., 1977-86; chmn. dept. anesthesiology Meml. Sloan-Kettering Cancer Ctr., N.Y.C., 1986-90; clin. prof. anesthesiology U. Va. Sch. Med., Charlottesville, 1990-96; prof. anesthesiology U. South Fla., Tampa, 1996—; chief anesthesia svc. James Haley VA Med. Ctr., Tampa, 1996—; spl. govt. employee anesthetic and life support drug adv. com. FDA, Rockville, Md., 1991-94, acting dir. pilot drug divsn. 1994-95, divsn. anesthetics, 1995-96. Contbr. over 85 articles to profl. jours., 15 chpts. to books. Maj. USAR, 1972-74. Grantee Found. Anesthesia Edn./Rsch., 1981; recipient Univ. Bordeaux II medal, 1988, Physician Recognition award AMA, 1991—. Mem. Soc. Neurosurg. Anesthesia (sec., treas., v.p., pres.), Va. Soc. Anesthesiologists (sec., treas., v.p., pres.), Am. Soc. Anesthesiologists (chair neurosci. com. 1986-88, resident rsch. essay award, 1973). Presbyterian. Avocations: sailing, fishing, skiing. Home: 5311 Ambrose Ct Tampa FL 33647-1010 Office: James Haley VA Med Ctr Anesthesia Svc 1300 Bruce B Downes Blvd Tampa FL 33600

BEDINI, SILVIO A., historian, author; b. Ridgefield, Conn., Jan. 17, 1917; s. Vincent and Cesira (Stefanelli) B.; m. Gerda Hintz, Oct. 20, 1951; children: Leandra, Peter. Ed., Columbia U., 1935-42; LLD, U. Bridgeport, 1970. Curator divsn. mech. and civil engring. U.S. Nat. Mus., Smithsonian Instn., Washington, 1961-65; from asst. dir. to dep. dir. Mus. History and Tech., 1965-78, keeper rare books, 1978-87; historian emeritus Smithsonian Inst., 1987—. Author: Ridgefield in Review, 1958, The Scent of Time, 1963, Early American Scientific Instruments and Their Makers, 1964; (with F.R. Maddison) Mechanical Universe, 1966; (with W. Von Braun and F.L. Whipple) Moon, Man's Greatest Adventure, 1970, The Life of Benjamin Banneker, 1972, rev. and expanded edit., 1999; (with others) The Unknown Leonardo, 1974, Thinkers and Tinkers, Early American Men of Science, 1975, The Spotted Stones, 1978, Declaration of Independence Desk: Relic of Revolution, 1981, Thomas Jefferson and His Copying Machines, 1984, At the Sign of the Compass and the Quadrant, 1984, Clockwork Cosmos, 1985, Thomas Jefferson Statesman of Science, 1990, The Pulse of Time, 1990, The Trail of Time, 1993, Science and Instruments in Seventeenth Century Italy, 1994, The Pope's Elephant, 1997, The Mace and the Gavel: Symbols of Government in America, 1997, The Jefferson Stone, 1999, Patrons, Artisans and Instruments of Science, 1999. Fellow Washington Acad. Scis.; mem. Am. Philos. Soc., Am. Antiquarian Soc., Soc. Am. Historians, History Sci. Soc., Soc. for History Tech., Astrolabe Soc. Home: 4303 47th St NW Washington DC 20016-2449 Office: Smithsonian Instn Washington DC 20560

BEDKE, ERNEST ALFORD, retired air force officer; b. Oakley, Idaho, Oct. 16, 1934; s. Herschel McIntosh and Ethel Marie (Alford) B.; m. Marilyn Meils, June 8, 1955; children: Curtis, Michael. B.S. in Bus. Adminstrn., U. Idaho, 1955; grad., Air Command and Staff Coll., 1967, Air War Coll., 1973. Commd. 2d lt. U.S. Air Force, 1955, advanced through grades to maj. gen., 1977; instr. pilot Reese AFB, Tex., 1957-62; air ops. officer Chaumont Air Base, France, 1962; fighter pilot Phalsbourg Air Base, France, 1962-63, Holloman AFB, N.Mex., 1963-66, Da Nang Air Base, Vietnam, 1966; air liaison officer, forward air controller Cat Lai, Vietnam, 1967-68; ops. staff officer NATO, Ramstein Air Base, Fed. Republic Germany, 1968-71; chief Europe-NATO, plans & policy, Hdqrs. U.S. Air Force, Wash., 1971-72; dep. comdr. ops. Eglin AFB, Eglin, Fla., 1973-74; comdr. 56 Tactical Fighter Wing Macdill AFB, Fla., 1975-77; dep. comdr. tng., testing and range facilities Nellis AFB, Nev., 1977-79; insp. gen. Tactical Air Command Langley AFB, Va., 1979-80; dep. chief staff ops. and intelligence Hdqrs. Pacific Air Forces Hickam AFB, Hawaii, 1980-83; ret., 1983; mgmt. cons. Decorated AF Disting. Svc. medal, Legion of Merit (2), D.F.C. (2), Air medal (20), M.S.M., Air Force Commendation medal. Mem. Air Force Assn., Order of Daedalians. Home: 18509 Turtle Dr Lutz FL 33549-4461

BEDNAR, CHARLES SOKOL, political scientist, educator; b. N.Y.C., Nov. 3, 1930; s. Karel and Anna (Tomcala) B.; m. Beluse Alzbeta Pokorny, Aug. 31, 1959. A.B., Rutgers U., 1951, M.A., 1952; Ph.D., Columbia, 1960. Asso. prof. Lynchburg Coll., 1958-62; prof., chmn. dept. polit. sci., asso. dean of coll. Muhlenberg Coll., 1962—, Eve Elizabeth Muhlenberg Disting. Svc. prof., 1989—; adj. prof. grad. program in gen. edn., chmn. social sci. panel Temple U., 1963-86. Contbr. articles to profl. jours. Chmn. Lehigh Valley Citizens for Progress, 1972-75; pres. Allentown YMCA, 1979-80. Recipient award Lindback Found., 1965, Paul E. Empie Meml. award, 1983. Mem. Czechoslovak Acad. Arts and Scis. (v.p.), AAUP, Phi Beta Kappa, Delta Phi Alpha, Tau Kappa Alpha, Omicron Delta Kappa, Pi Sigma Alpha. Home: 1285 Sheridan Rd Coopersburg PA 18036-1816 Office: Muhlenberg Coll 2400 W Chew St Allentown PA 18104-5564

BEDNAR, MICHAEL JOHN, architecture educator; b. Cleve., Mar. 19, 1942; s. Peter and Mary (Rohal) B.; m. Mary Kathryn Gillman; children: Richard Earl, Matthew Scott, Rachel Catherine; m. Elizabeth Waddel Lawson. BArch, U. Mich., 1964; MArch, U. Pa., Phila., 1967. Registered architect, Pa., N.Y., Va. Jr. designer I.M. Pei & Ptnrs., N.Y.C., 1965-66; project architect Geddes, Brecher, Qualls, Cunningham, Phila., 1967-68; asst. prof. Rennselaer Polytech. Inst., Troy, N.Y., 1968-72; assoc. prof. U. Va., Charlottesville, 1972—, co-chmn. div. of architecture, 1976-81, assoc. dean for academics, 1992-95; prin. Michael Bednar, FAIA Architect, Charlottesville, 1973-90, Bednar Lawson Architects, 1990—. Author: Architecture for Handicapped, 1973, The New Atrium, 1986;, Interior Pedestrian Places, 1989; editor: Barrier-Free Environment, 1977. Mem., chair City Planning Commn., Charlottesville, 1982—; chmn. Urban Design Task Force, Charlottesville, 1985-88; mem. Bd. of Architectural Review, Charlottesville, 1983-86. Booth fellow U. Mich., 1972, NEA fellow, 1984, Graham Found. fellow, 1988; recipient Nat. Book award Am. Assn. of Publs., 1986, Nichols award Preservation Alliance Va., 1997, Cmty. Svc. award, 1997. Fellow Am. Inst. Architects (Disting. Achievemnt award 1997). Avocations: jazz music, tennis, travel, photography. Home: 1201 E Jefferson St Charlottesville VA 22902-5414 Office: U Va Sch of Architecture Charlottesville VA 22903

BEDNARZ, JAMES C., wildlife ecologist educator. BS in Wildlife and Fishery Biology, N.Mex. State U., 1976; MS in Animal Ecology, Iowa State U., 1979; PhD in Biology, U. N.Mex., 1986. Wildlife biologist U.S. Fish and Wildlife Svc., 1977-78; wildlife cons., 1979-80, 85-91; rsch. assoc. U. N.Mex., 1985-91; dir. higher edn. and rsch. Hawk Mountain Sanctuary Assn., 1987-90; prin. investigator Greenfalk Cons., 1990-91; asst. prof. wildlife ecology Ark. State U., State Univ., 1993-96, assoc. prof. wildlife ecology, 1997—; rsch. asst. part-time Iowa State U., 1977-78; invited mem. Eastside Forests Scientific Panel; bd. dirs., chair conservation com. Raptor Rsch.; referee Science, Ecology, Auk, Jour. Mammalogy, Wilson Bull., Raptor Rsch, NSF, and others. Contbr. articles to profl. jours. Recipient Rsch. award Hawk Mountain, Marcia Brady Tucker Travel award; Ding Darling scholar. Am. Ornithologists' Union, Animal Behavior Soc., Wildlife Soc., Cooper Ornithological Soc., Wilson Ornithological Soc., Raptor Rsch. Found., Acad. Nat. Scis. Phila. (assoc. in ornithology), Hawk Watch Internat. (rsch. adv. com.). Achievements include research in conservation biology, the influence on human disturbance on wildlife populations, the effects on habitat alterations on wildlife populations, social behavior of birds and mammals, evolution of mating systems, the influence of ecology on animal social systems, migratory strategies of birds, and the application of basic ecological and evolutionary principles to conservation and wildlife management. Office: Ark State U Dept Biological Scis PO Box 599 State University AR 72467-0599

BEDNASH, GERALDINE POLLY, association executive; b. San Antonio, May 6, 1943; d. David Anthony and Bernice (Brewer) Parrott; m. Thomas Francis Bednash, June 24, 1967; children: Thomas F. Jr., Joseph Andrew. B of Nursing, Tex. Women's U., 1965; M of Nursing, Cath. U. Am., 1977; PhD, U. Md., 1989. Cert. nurse practitioner. Nurse Binghamton (N.Y.) Gen. Hosp., 1967-69; instr. Broome County Community Coll., Binghamton, 1967-71; asst. prof. No. Va. Community Coll., Annandale, 1977-78, George Mason U., Fairfax, Va., 1978-86; dir. govt. rels. Am. Assn. Coll. Nursing, Washington, 1986-89, exec. dir., 1989—; co-chmn. Nat. Com. Nursing Implementation Project, Washington, 1990-91; cons. in field. Contbr. articles to profl. jours. Polit. action chmn. Va. Nurses Assn., 1979-83; nurse clinician So Others Might Eat, Washington, 1981-83. Capt. U.S. Army, 1963-67. Primary Care fellow Robert Wood Johnson Found., U. Md., 1981-82, Nat. Rsch. Svc. fellow, Washington, 1983-87. Fellow Am. Acad. Nursing; mem. ANA, Sigma Theta Tau. Roman Catholic. Avocations: skiing, horticulture. Office: Am Assn Coll Nursing 1 Dupont Cir NW Ste 530 Washington DC 20036-1135

BEDRICK, BERNICE, retired science educator, consultant; b. Jersey City, Sept. 29, 1916; d. Abraham Lewis and Esther (Cowan) Grodjesk; m. Emanuel Arthur Bedrick, Dec. 25, 1938 (dec. 1967); children: Allen Paul, Jane Bedrick Abels; m. Samuel Milberger, Sept. 23, 1984 (dec. 1984); stepchildren: Susan Milberger Rafael, Stanford. BS, U. Md., 1938; MA, NYU, 1952. Cert. tchr., N.J. Tchr. Linden (N.J.) Pub. Sch. System, 1950-69, supr. sci. curriculum, 1969-79, sch. prin., 1979-87; ret., 1987. Co-author: A Universe to Explore, 1969; developer program of safety and survival N.J. Dept. Edn., 1975. Founder, mem., bd. dirs., v.p. edn. Temple Mekor Chayim, Linden; pres. bd. trustees Linden Pub. Libr., 1989-90, v.p., 1991; pres. Friends of Linden Libr., 1987-92, 95-97; bd. trustees Temple Beth-El Mekor Chayim, Cranford, N.J., 1999-2000. Recipient Cmty. Vol. Svc. award B'Nai B'Rith, 1993, Outstanding Sr. Citizen of Yr., City of Linden, 1996. Mem. NEA (life), N.J. Edn. Assn. (life), Am. Fedn. Sch. Adminstrs. (chpt. pres. 1984-86), Linden Edn. Found. (bd. dirs.), N.Y. Acad. Scis., N.J. Prins. and Suprs. Assn., N.J. Sci. tchrs. Assn., Nat. Sci. Tchrs. Assn., Alumni Assn. U. Md. (life), N.J. PTA (life), Hadassah (life), Linden Ceramics Club (sec. 1991-92, 95-99), Nat. Coun. Jewish Women (life), Alpha Lambda Delta, Phi kappa Phi. Home: 2016 Orchard Ter Linden NJ 07036-3719

BEDRIJ, OREST, investment banker, scientist; b. Ukraine, May 24, 1933; arrived in U.S., 1949, naturalized, 1955; s. Eustachy and Olha (Banach) B.; m. Oksana Cymbalista, Nov. 10, 1956; children: Orest W., Roksasa Bedrij Arpa, Chrystyna Bedrij Stecyk. BSEE, Rochester Inst. Tech., 1956, MS in Humanities; PhD in Physics, Columbia Pacific U., 1986. Various mgmt. positions IBM Corp., Poughkeepsie, N.Y. and Los Angeles, 1956-68; IBM tech. dir. Space Flight Facility, Jet Propulsion Lab., Calif. Inst. Tech., 1962-63; founder, pres., dir. Securities Coun., Inc., 1965-83, Profit Tech., Inc., 1983-89, Griffin Capital Mgmt. Corp., N.Y.C., 1989-97; co-founder, dir. Advance Memory Sys. Inc. (merged with GE) as Intersil, Inc., Sunnyvale, Calif., 1968-71, Inst. for Math. Physics, 1972—, Internat. Jour. Nonlinear Math. Physics, Kiev, 1992, Griffin Securities, Inc., N.Y.C., 1997—; mem. exec. com., treas., dir. Ukrainian Studies Fund, Harvard U., 1959-72. Author: Yes, It's Love: Your Life Can Be a Miracle, 1974, One, 1977, 2d rev. edit., 1978, You, 1988; contbr. articles to profl. jours.; patentee in field. Trustee, treas. John E. Fetzer Found., 1987-89. With USAR, 1954-60. Recipient Outstanding Contribution award IBM, 1967. Mem. N.Y. Acad. Arts and Scis., Shevchenko Sci. Soc., The Ukrainian Engrs. Soc. of Am., Sci. and Med. Network, London, Am. Inst. Physics, The Libr. of Congress Assn., The World Trade Ctr. Club. Achievements include research in physics of the First Principle. Office: Griffin Securities Inc 140 Broadway Fl 29 New York NY 10005-1101

BEDROSIAN, EDWARD, electrical engineer; b. Chgo., May 22, 1922; s. Charles and Hazel (Najarian) B.; m. Evelyn Patricia Gardner, Apr. 16, 1971; children—William C., Barbara A., Charles E., Edward G., Victoria G. BS, Northwestern U., 1949, MS, 1950, PhD, 1953. Aero. engr. Convair, San Diego, 1942, Hughes Aircraft Co., Culver City, Calif., 1943-44; elec. engr. Motorola, Chgo., 1953-57; sr. scientist Rand Corp., Santa Monica, Calif., 1957-98; adj. prof. U. So. Calif., 1968-71. Contbr. articles to profl. jours. Served with USMC, 1944-46. Fellow IEEE, Inst. Advancement Engring.; mem. Sigma Xi, Eta Kappa Nu, Tau Beta Pi. Home: 3923 Sierks Way Malibu CA 90265-5214

BEDROSIAN, EDWARD ROBERT, investment management company executive; b. Chgo., June 30, 1932; s. Kesrow and Rebecca (Babian) B.; m. Diane Yvonne Morse, Aug. 25, 1956; children: Dawn Eve, Cynthia Sarah, Edward Robert. B.S.C.E., Ill. Inst. Tech., 1954; M.S.C.E., M.I.T., 1955; M.B.A., Harvard U., 1964. CFA; registered profl. engr., Mass. Treas. Ea. Shokcrate Corp., Bound Brook, N.J., 1964-65; v.p., treas. Polaroid Corp., Cambridge, Mass., 1965-87; chmn. Merganser Capital Mgmt. Corp., Cambridge, Mass., 1987—. Served with USNR, 1955-60. Mem. Assn. for Investment Mgmt. and Rsch. Conglist. Office: Merganser Capital Mgmt Corp 1 Cambridge Ctr Ste 402 Cambridge MA 02142-1605

BEDROSIAN, GREGORY RONALD, investment banker; b. Phila., Sept. 14, 1966; s. Samuel D. and Agnes Bedrosian. BS in Econs., U. Pa., 1988; MBA, Harvard U., 1992. Investment banker Salomon Bros., Inc., N.Y.C., 1988-90; investment banker Credit Suisse First Boston Ltd., London, Moscow, 1992-95; co-founder, mng. dir. Sputnik Funds (Renaissance Capital), Moscow, 1995—. Mem. Coun. on Fgn. Rels., Harvard Club of N.Y., Met. Club. Republican. Home: 35 Bryan Ave Malvern PA 19355-3007

BEDWORTH, DAVID ALBERT, health educator; b. Cortland, N.Y., Mar. 31, 1949; s. Albert Ernest and Agnes Sheldon (Franklin) B.; children: Jodi Michele, Michael David. BS, Butler U., 1971; MS, U. Ill., 1972, PhD, 1976. Instr. Russell Sage Coll., Troy, N.Y., 1973-75; asst. prof. SUNY, Brockport, 1976-78; program coord. Heart Health Edn. R.I., Pawtucket, 1978-79; prof. SUNY, Plattsburgh, 1979—; cmty. edn. cons. STOP Ctr. for Domestic Violence, Plattsburgh, 1982; drug edn. cons. Federal Correction Instn., Ray Brook, N.Y., 1982, Ticonderoga (N.Y.) Ctrl. Sch. Dist., 1985. Author: (with Albert E. Bedworth) Health Education: A Process for Human Effectivess, 1978, Health for Human Effectiveness, 1982, The Profession and Practice of Health Education, 1992; contbr. articles to profl. jours., chpts. to books. Task force on youthful alcohol abuse N.Y. State Dept. Mental Hygiene, 1977; profl. edn. com. Am. Lung Assn., 1980-84, exec. com., 1981-82. Mem. APHA, ASCD, N.Y. State Fedn. Profl. Health Educators (pres. 1977). Democrat. Avocations: antiques, travel. Office: SUNY Plattsburgh NY 12901

BEE, CLAIR FRANCIS JR., . b. Oct. 9, 1948. Student, N.Y. Mil. Acad., 1971-73, FBI Hazardous Device Sch., 1984, DEA Drug Narcotics Sch., John Jay Coll., N.Y.C. From cook supervisor to correction officer Woodbourne N.Y. State Dept. Correctional Facilities, 1975-81, from sr. weapons and chem. agts. instr. Ctrl. Office Tng., 1981-83, asst. to dir. CERT Ops. Ctrl. Office Tng., 1983-84, sr. investigator, 1981-87, correctional security tech. specialist, 1987-95, sr. correctional security tech. specialist, 1995-96, asst. commr. correctional facilities, 1996—. Served in U.S. Army, 1967-70, Vietnam. Office: NY State Dept Corrections Bldg 2 St Campus Albany NY 12226

BEE, ROBERT NORMAN, banker; b. Milw., Mar. 4, 1925; s. Clarence Olson and Norma Pern (Pitt) B.; m. Dolores Marie Cappelletti, Apr. 23, 1955; children: Diane, John, Leslie. Ph.B., Marquette U., 1949; B.S. in Fgn. Service, Georgetown U., 1950, M.A., 1955. With Dept. Treasury, various locations, 1950-65; fin. attache Stockholm, 1952-54, Ankara, Turkey, 1956-60; chief fin. affairs Am. embassy, Bonn, Germany, 1960-65; dep. dir. AID, Karachi, Pakistan, 1965-67; 1st. v.p. 1st Wis. Nat. Bank, 1967-71; sr. v.p. Wells Fargo Bank; also pres. Wells Fargo Internat. Investment Corp., San Francisco, 1971-78; mng. dir., chief exec. officer London Interstate Bank Ltd., Eng., 1978-87; mng. dir. TSB Pvt. Bank Internat. SA, London, 1987-90; chmn. U.S. Fin. adv. Svc., London, 1990-91, SAJ Investments Ltd., London, 1991-95; Sr. fellow Center Internat. Banking Studies, Charlottesville, Va. Chmn. World Affairs Coun. Milw., 1970-71; bd. dirs. Adam Smith Inst., London, chmn., 1985-87; chmn. Am. Soc. in London, 1986-87. With

AUS, 1943-46. Mem. Bankers Assn. for Fgn. Trade (pres. 1977-78). Home and Office: 1940 Vallejo St Apt 5 San Francisco CA 94123-4918

BEEBE, GRACE ANN, special education educator; b. Wyandotte, Mich., Feb. 16, 1945; d. Cecil Vern and Elizabeth Lucille (Tamblyn) B. BA, Ea. Mich. U., 1967; MEd, Wayne State U., 1970; postgrad., U. Mich., 1973-78. Cert. spl. edn. tchr., Mich. Tchr. POHI 1st grade Grand Rapids (Mich.) Pub. Schs., 1967-69; tchr. title VI Taylor (Mich.) Pub. Schs., 1970-73, tchr. Physically or Otherwise Health Impaired pre-kindergarten, 1973-79, tchr. POHI 1st-3rd grades, 1979-81, tchr. POHI pre-kindergarten, 1981-84, tchr., cons. POHI, 1984—. Area coord. Indian Trails Camp, Grand Rapids, 1979-97; Brownie troop leader Girl Scouts U.S., 1997—. Recipient Recognition award 4-H Wayne County Handicapped Riding, 1986, Indian Trails Camp, 1990; Ronald McDonald Children's Charities grantee, 1990; State of Mich. Spl. Edn. scholar, 1966-67, Vocat. Rehab. scholar, 1969-70. Mem. SCADS (alt. rep.), N.Am. Riding for the Handicapped Assn., Mich. Fedn. Tchrs., Physically Impaired Assn. Mich., Taylor Fedn. Tchrs. (ancillary v.p. 1990-92), Taylor Handicapped Assn., Allen Park Assn. for Handicapped, Trenton Hist. Soc. (exec. bd. 1988-97), Coun. for Exceptional Children, Phi Delta Kappa, Alpha Delta Kappa. Democrat. United Methodist. Avocations: horseback riding, gardening, walking. Home: 2225 Emeline St Trenton MI 48183-3653 Office: Taylor Spl Edn Dept 11010 Janet St Taylor MI 48180-4079

BEEBE, HANK, composer; b. Woodbury, N.J., July 16, 1926; s. Harold Henry and Miriam Priscilla (Davidson) B.; m. Nancy Neal Ault, Mar. 29, 1952; children: Selby Lane, Jane Heston Beebe Bertolini. BA, U. N.C., 1947, MusM, 1951; studied composition Vincent Persichetti, Phila. Conservatory of Music, 1953-54. Dir. music The Childrens Hour WCAU-TV Weekly Program, Phila., 1954-58; organist, choirmaster Ch. of St. Matthew and St. Timothy, N.Y.C., 1968-72, St. Alban's Episcopal Ch., Cape Elizabeth, Maine, 1981-88; cons. for musical presentations GM, Detroit, 1956-78, RCA, Indpls., 1962-78, McDonalds Corp., Oakbrook, Ill., 1973-77. Composer, writer (off-Broadway musical) Tuscaloosa, 1975-76 (Outer Critics Circle award 1976), (ch. anthem) Go Out With Joy, 1975, 12 musical plays, 300 choral works, hymns in Episcopal, Roman Cath., and Japanese United Ch. of Christ hymnals. Parent bd. mem. St. Matthew and St. Timothy Cmty. Ctr., N.Y.C., 1967-78; composer campaign song Re-election of John Lindsay as Mayor, N.Y.C., 1969; bd. mem. Embassy Players Cmty. Theater Orgn., Portland, Maine, 1983-97. Lt. (j.g.) USNR, 1944-55. Mem. Broadcast Music, Inc., Dramatist Guild, Phi Beta Kappa. Episcopalian. Avocation: family activities.

BEEBE, JOHN ELDRIDGE, financial service executive; b. Freeport, N.Y., Jan. 30, 1923; s. Henry W. and Edna (Eldridge) B.; m. Margaret Sands Hubbell, Sept. 7, 1946; children: John Eldridge, Martha. B.A. cum laude, Princeton U., 1947. Vice pres. Chase Manhattan Bank, 1947-65; sr. v.p. Paine, Webber, Jackson & Curtis, Inc., N.Y.C., 1965-80; v.p. corp. fin. F. Eberstadt & Co., Inc., N.Y.C., 1981-83; dir. corp. fin. Ingalls & Snyder, N.Y.C., 1983-85; chmn. Scott Macon Ltd., 1985-91, ret., 1991; bd. dirs. Balchem Corp. Served to 1st lt. U.S. Army, 1942-46. Mem. Univ. Club, Princeton Club, S.C. Yacht Club, Bear Creek Golf Club. Episcopalian.

BEEBE, LEO CLAIR, industrial equipment executive, former educator; b. Williamsburg, Mich., July 20, 1917; s. Fred Grant and Rena (Allton) B.; m. Jan Wyss, Mar. 11, 1966; children—Leo Peter, Anne Lorraine. BS in Edn., U. Mich., 1939; postgrad., Wayne U., 1942-43; MA, Glassboro State Coll., 1985. With Ford Motor Co. (various locations), 1945-72; gen. mgr. consumers products div. Philco-Ford, Phila.; also exec. v.p. Philco-Ford, until 1972; prof. mgmt. Glassboro State Coll., 1972-85, dean bus. sch., 1977-85; chmn. bd. John Hancock Health Plan of Pa., 1982-89; dir. K-Tron Internat., 1976—, chmn., chief exec. officer, 1985-92, chmn. bd., 1992—, CEO, 1995-97, chmn. emeritus, 1998—; mgr. winning Ford Motor racing team culminating in 1st U.S. 1-2-3 victory in 24 hour endurance race, LeMans, France, 1966; cons. Nat. Council Better Bus. Burs., 1972-74; cons. to sec. HEW, 1978-81. Author numerous manuals, articles speeches on refugee and hardcore disadvantaged employment. Vice chmn. Pres. Eisenhower's Com. for Hungarian Refugees; dir. program to resettle 36,000 refugees; dir. Cuban Refugee Center, Miami, 1960; chief exec. Pres. Johnson's Program for Hardcore Employment, 1968; mem. Pres. Johnson's Commn. for Exec. Exchange; chmn. Civic Com. on Sch. Needs, Dearborn, Mich., 1958; pres. Dearborn Boys' Club, 1955-60; chmn. numerous campaigns YMCA, United Fund; bd. dirs. Reading is Fundamental; trustee Va. Union U.; Trustee Misericordia Coll., 1983-92; chmn. bd. dirs. United Way Gloucester County, 1989-92. Served with USNR, 1942-45. Recipient Gold plate award for achievement Nat. Acad. Achievement, 1969. Mem. Nat. Alliance Businessmen (founding pres.), Indsl. Audio Visual Assn. (past pres.), C. of C. So. N.J. (past chmn. bd.), Rotary (past dist. gov.). Episcopalian. Home and Office: 108 Glenn Rd Ardmore PA 19003-2500

BEEBE, MARY LIVINGSTONE, curator; b. Portland, Oreg., Nov. 5, 1940; d. Robert and Alice Beebe. B.A., Bryn Mawr Coll., 1962; postgrad. Sorbonne, U. Paris, 1962-63. Curatorial asst. Fogg Art Mus., Harvard U., Cambridge, Mass., 1966-68; Apprentice Portland Art Mus., 1963-64, Boston Mus. Art, 1964-65; exec. dir. Portland Ctr. for Visual Arts, 1973-81; dir. Stuart Collection U. Calif.-San Diego, La Jolla, 1981—; cons. in field. Mem. art steering com. Portland Devel. Commn., 1977-80; bd. dirs. Henry Gallery, U. Wash., Seattle, 1977-80; project cons. Nat. Rsch. Ctr. for Arts, N.Y.C., 1978-79; bd. dirs. Western Assn. Art Museums, Art Mus. Assn. San Francisco, 1978-84; bd. dirs., trustee Art Matters Inc., 1985-96; trustee Russell Found., 1982-94; hon. mem. bd. dirs. Portland Ctr. for Visual Arts, 1984-91; mem. arts adv. bd. Centre City Devel. Corp., San Diego, 1982-94; arts adv. bd. Port of San Diego; panel mem., cons. Nat. Endowment Arts; juror numerous art shows and exhbns. Nat. Endowment Arts fellow, 1979. Recipient Allied Professions award AIA, 1992. Contbr. articles to profl. jours. Office: U Calif San Diego The Stuart Collection 9500 Gilman Dr La Jolla CA 92093-0010

BEEBE, MIKE, state senator, lawyer; b. Amagon, Ark., Dec. 28, 1946; s. Lester Kendall and Meadean Louise (Quattlebaum) B.; m. Ginger Croom, Mar. 2, 1979; 1 child, Kyle. B.A., Ark. State U., 1968; J.D., U. Ark., 1972. Bar: Ark. Ptnr. Lightle, Beebe, Raney, Bell & Simpson, Searcy, Ark., 1972—; mem. Ark. Senate, 1982—. Editor-in-chief U. Ark. Sch. Law. Trustee Ark. State U., Jonesboro, 1974-79, chmn. bd. trustees, 1977-79; chmn. Central Ark. Gen. Hosp., Searcy, 1985-93. Mem. Ark. Trial Lawyers Assn. (outstanding trial lawyer award 1982), Ark. Mcpl. League (dist. svc. award 1985), Searcy C. of C. Democrat. Episcopalian. Avocation: golf. Office: 211 W Arch Ave Searcy AR 72143-5301

BEEBE, SANDRA E., retired English language educator, artist, writer; b. March AFB, Calif., Nov. 10, 1934; d. Eugene H. and Margaret (Fox) B.; m. Donald C. Thompson. AB in English and Speech, UCLA, 1956; MA in Secondary Edn., Calif. State U., Long Beach, 1957. Tchr. English, Garden Grove (Calif.) High Sch., 1957-93, attendance supr., 1976-83, ret., 1993; tchr. watercolor courses, Asilomar, Calif., 1997; jury chmn. N.W.S., 1997. Contbr. articles to English Jour., chpts. to books; watercolor artist; exhbns. include AWS, NWS, Okla. Watercolor Soc., Watercolor West, Midwest Watercolor Soc., Butler Inst. Am. Art, Youngstown, Ohio, Kings Art Ctr., Audubon Artists N.Y.; cover artist Exploring Painting, 1990, title page Understanding Watercolor, American Artist, 1991. mem. faculty Asilomar, 1997; chmn. of jurors N.W.S. Open, 1997. Named one of the Top Ten Watercolorists The Artists Mag., 1994; recipient Best Watercolors award Rockport Press, 1995; chosen for Design Poster selection, 1995, 97. Mem. Am. Watercolor Soc. (dir. 1999—), Nat. Watercolor Soc., Midwest Watercolor Soc., Watercolor West, Allied Artists N.Y., Knickerbocker Artists N.Y., Audubon Artists N.Y., West Coast Watercolor Soc., Rocky Mountain Nat. Watermedia Honor Soc., Jr. League Long Beach, Kappa Kappa Gamma. Republican. Home: 7241 Marina Pacifica Dr S Long Beach CA 90803-3899 Studio: B-Q Gallery 3920 E 4th St Long Beach CA 90814-1656 also: 239 Mira Mar Ave Long Beach CA 90803-6153

BEEBE, STEPHEN A., agricultural products company executive; b. 1945. JD, U. Idaho. Bar: Idaho 1969. Legal asst. U.S Dist. Judge, 1969-70; staff atty. J.R. Simplot, Co., Boise, 1970—, pres., CEO, dir., 1994—. Office: JR Simplot Co PO Box 27 Boise ID 83707-0027*

BEEBE, SUSAN JANE, English language educator; b. Sacramento, Calif., Nov. 20, 1952; d. William Herbert and Janie Lou (Jennings) Dye; m. Steven A. Beebe, May 25, 1974; children: Mark, Matthew. BSE in Comm., Ctrl. Mo. State U., 1973; MA in English Lit., U. Miami, Coral Gables, Fla., 1979. Cert. secondary edn. tchr., Mo. Tchr. English, debate coach Moberly (Mo.) H.S., 1974-76; tchr. English Deerborne Sch., Coral Gables, 1977; lectr. Sch. Comm., U. Miami, 1980-86; coord. San Marcos (Tex.) Consol. Ind. Sch. Dist., 1989-93, mem. ednl. improvement coun., 1995—; lectr., assoc. dir. first-year English, dept. English, S.W. Tex. State U., San Marcos, 1988—. Co-author: (textbooks) Interpersonal Communication: Relating to Others, 1996, 2d edit., 1999. Public Speaking: An Audience-Centered Approach, 3d edit., 1997, (manual) Instructor's Manual for Communicating in Small Groups: Principles and Practices, 2d edit., 1986. Bd. dirs. Tex. Assn. Ptnrs. in Edn., 1992-93; founding coord. Volunteers in Pub. Schs., San Marcos, 1987—. Recipient Gov.'s Ednl. Excellence award, Tex., 1991, pvt. citizen award Tex. Classroom Tchrs. Assn., 1993. Mem. Conf. of Coll. Tchrs. of English, Tex. Coun. Tchrs. of English, Nat. Coun. Tchrs. of English. Democrat. Mem. Reorganized Ch. of Jesus Christ of Latter-Day Saints. Avocations: reading, music. Office: SW Tex State U Dept English San Marcos TX 78666

BEEBY, THOMAS H., architect. Architect C.F. Murphy, Chgo., 1965-71; ptnr. Ruppert Ainge Inc. (formerly Hammond, Beeby & Babka), Chgo., 1971—; mem. faculty dept. architecture Ill. Inst. Tech., Chgo., 1973-80; dir. Sch. Architecture U. Ill.-Chgo., Chgo., 1980-85; dean, prof. archtl. design Yale U. Sch. Architecture, 1985-91; adj. prof. Archtl., Yale U., 1992—; mem. adv. bd. dept. arch. Ill. Inst. Tech., 1993—, bd. dirs., 1997—. Designs exhibited: Art Inst. Chgo., Mus. Contemporary Art, Chgo., Cooper-Hewitt Mus., N.Y.C., Walker Art Ctr., Mpls., Venice Biennale; contbr. articles to profl. jours. Recipient Progressive Architecture citation, 1976, 87, 89, Louis Sullivan award, 1989. Fellow AIA (mem. nat. com. on design awards, nat. honor award 1984, 87, 89, 91, 93); mem. Soc. Archtl. Historians (bd. dirs. 1996—), U.S. State, Office Fgn. Bldg., Archtl. adv. bd., 1989-93, Graham Found. (bd. dirs. 1992—). Office: Rupert Ainge Inc 440 N Wells St Ste 630 Chicago IL 60610-4546*

BEECH, JOHNNY GALE, lawyer; b. Chickasha, Okla., Sept. 18, 1954; s. Lovell Gale and Lucille L. (Phillips) B.; m. Judy Carol Schroeder, Dec. 31, 1977. BS, Southwestern Okla. State U., 1977; JD, U. Ark., Little Rock, 1980; LLM in Energy-Environment, Tulane U., 1985. Bar: Okla. 1980, U.S. Dist. Ct. (we. dist.) Okla. 1982, U.S. Dist. Ct. (no. dist.) Tex. 1983, U.S. Dist. Ct. (no. dist.) Okla. 1986, U.S. Dist. Ct. (ea. dist.) Okla. 1997. Assoc. Meacham, Meacham and Meacham, Clinton, Okla., 1980-84, Ford & Brown, Enid, Okla., 1985-86, Wright & Sawyer, Enid, 1986-88, Phillips, McFall, McCaffrey, McVay, Sheets and Lovelace, Oklahoma City, 1988-90; ptnr., mng. dir. Lester & Bryant, Oklahoma City, 1990-96; mgr. Beech Edwards and Percival PLLC, 1996—; mcpl. judge Town of Arapaho, Okla., 1982-84; assoc. gen. counsel Proserv Basketball, 1996—. Bd. dirs. Jr. Achievement Garfield County, Enid, 1986-88; commr. Little League Baseball; bd. dirs., treas. Edmond All Sports, Inc., 1999; mem. Bus. Sch. adv. coun. Southwestern U. Mem. ABA (real property, probate and trusts sect.), ATLA, Okla. Bar Assn. (law sch. com. 1989-91, uniform laws com. 1994-96, chmn. desk manual com. young lawyers div., uniform laws com. 1994—), Okla. Assn. Def. Counsel, Garfield County Bar Assn. (treas. 1988-89), Am. Bus. Club, Southwestern Okla. State U. Alumni Assn. (pres. 1983-86, parliamentarian 1992, exec. counsel 1986—, pres. 1997—), Southwestern Sch. Bus. Alumni Assn. (v.p. 1980-92, pres. 1992-93), Jaycees, Am. Bus. Club, Phi Alpha Delta (sec. 1979). Democrat. Methodist. Avocations: reading, bike racing. Home: 702 N Cook St Cordell OK 73632-3002 Office: Beech Edwards & Percival PLLC PO Box 54367 Oklahoma City OK 73154-1367

BEECHER, DONNA D., human resources administrator. BA, Drew U., 1967; MBA, Syracuse U., 1968. Dep. dir. office of pers. HUD, Washington, 1978; dir. office of pers. policy and comms., dir. pers. ops. U.S. Dept. Health and Human Svcs., Washington, 1979-87; asst. dir. office sys. and innovation and simplification Office of Pers. Mgmt., Washington, 1987—, dep. assoc. dir. employment svcs., 1987—, dir. office contracting and adminstrn. svcs., 1987—. Office: Human Resources and Equal Employment Opportunity Office of Pers Mgmt 1900 E St NW Washington DC 20415

BEECHER, WILLIAM JOHN, zoologist, museum director; b. Chgo., May 23, 1914; s. Edward J. and Anna (Lawlor) B. PhB, BS, U. Chgo., 1947, MS, 1949, PhD, 1954. Zoology asst. Chgo. Natural History Mus., 1937-54; sr. naturalist Conservation Dept., Cook County Forest Preserve Dist., 1955-57; dir. Chgo. Acad. Scis., 1958-82, dir. emeritus, 1982—; Chmn. Chgo. Conservation Council, 1964—; pres. Beecher Research Co., mfg. Beecher Mirage spectacle binocular, 1983—, Beecher Research Found. Author: Nesting Birds and the Vegetation Substrate, 1942, Attracting Birds To Your Backyard, 1954; contbr. numerous articles to profl. jours. Mem. open lands project Welfare Coun. Met. Chgo.; mem. policy com. Chgo. com. Ill. Sesequicentennial; mem. Ill. Nature Preserves Commn., 1971—, Ill. Endangered Species Commn., 1973—; mem. biology com. Ill. Bd. Higher Edn., 1970—; environmental aspects com. Northeastern Ill. Planning Commn.; sec. Wetlands Research, 1985— bd. dirs. Chgo. coun. Girl Scouts U.S.A.; rsch. assoc. Bird div. Field Mus. Nat. History; mem. coun. div. Biol. Scis. and Pritzker Sch. Med. U. Chgo.; hon. life mem. Lincoln Park Zool. Soc., 1971—. With AUS, 1942-45, PTO. Recipient ann. sci. award Adult Edn. Soc. Greater Chgo., 1963, Ecology award Chgo. Outdoor Art League, 1970, Environ. Quality award U.S. EPA, 1975, 20 Yrs. Svc. award Open Lands Project, citation Univ. Club Chgo., 1975, Gaylor/Donnelley Nature of Ill. Found. award, 1993, others. Fellow AAAS, Royal Soc. Arts, Royal Geog. Soc., Am. Ornithol. Union; mem. Nature Conservancy (vice chmn. Ill. chpt., Green Leaf award 1969), Ecol. Soc. Am., Wilson Ornithol. Soc., Cooper Ornithol. Soc., Geog. Soc. Chgo. (v.p. 1971—), Am. Soc. Zoologists, Ill. Audubon Soc., Chgo. Audubon Soc. (dir.), Explorers Club, Sigma Xi (award for lifelong contbn. to sci. 1981). Clubs: Garden of America (mem. conservation com.), Kennicott, Bandar Log, Adventurers. Spl. research anatomy and classification birds of world, ecologist, conservationist; wildlife photographer; inventor spectacle binocular for bird study. Home: 1960 N Lincoln Park W Chicago IL 60614-5456 Office: Chgo Acad Scis 2001 N Clark St Chicago IL 60614-4712 *Man is the only species with an aesthetic appreciation of natural beauty, and his very ability to stand off from nature and look at it deludes him into the view that he is not really part of it, vulnerable if impoverished or polluted ecosystems die.*

BEECHER, WILLIAM MANUEL, government official; b. Framingham, Mass., May 27, 1933; s. Samuel and Gertrude (Kradelman) B.; m. Eileen Brick, June 8, 1958; children: Debbie, Diane, Lori, Nancy. BA, Harvard U., 1955; MS, Columbia U., 1956. Reporter St. Louis Globe-Democrat, 1956-59; corr. Fairchild Pubs., Washington, 1959-60, Wall Street Jour., Washington, 1960-66, N.Y. Times, Washington, 1966-73; asst. sec. def. U.S. Dept. Def., Washington, 1973-75; corr. Boston Globe, Washington, 1975-87; Washington bur. chief Mpls. Star Tribune, Washington, 1987-92; pub. affairs dir. U.S. Nuclear Regulatory Commn., Washington, 1993—; mem. U.S. Sr. Exec. Svc., 1993—. Author: Mayday Man, 1990; co-author: (newspaper study) U.S.-Soviet Relations, 1983 (Pulitzer prize 1983); bd. of editors Foreign Svc. Jour. 2d lt. U.S. Army, 1956. Recipient Disting. Pub. Svc. medal Def. Dept., 1975, Excellence awards Overseas Press Club, N.Y.C., 1975, 79, 86, Weintal award Georgetown U., Washington, 1983. Mem. Internat. Inst. for Strategic Studies, State Dept. Corrs. Assn. (pres. 1982), Overseas Writers Assn. (pres. 1978-79), Aviation/Space Writers Assn. (pres. 1970-71), Coun. Fgn. Rels., Gridiron Club, Army and Navy Club. Home: 7911 Robison Rd Bethesda MD 20817-6928 Office: US Nuclear Regulatory Commn 02-H1 1 White Flint N Washington DC 20555

BEEDLE, LYNN SIMPSON, civil engineering educator; b. Orland, Calif., Dec. 7, 1917; s. Granville L. and Carol (Simpson) B.; m. Ella Marie Grimes, Oct. 20, 1946; children: Lynn, Helen, Jonathan, David, Edward. BS, U. Calif., 1941; MS, Lehigh U., 1949, PhD, 1952. With Todd-Calif. Shipbldg. Corp., Richmond, Calif., 1941; instr. Postgrad. Sch., U.S. Naval Acad., 1941-42; officer-in-charge Underwater Explosions Research div. Norfolk Naval Shipyard, Va., 1942-47; dir. Lehigh U. Fritz Engring. Lab., Bethlehem, Pa., 1960-84; prof. civil engring. Lehigh U., 1958-77, Univ. Disting. prof., 1978—, prof. emeritus, 1988—, dir. High-Rise Inst., 1983-89; coord., chair Fazlur Rahman Khan, 1983—. Author: Plastic Design of Steel Frames, 1958, (with others) Structural Steel Design, 2d edit., 1974, Tall Buildings of the World, 1987; editor-in-chief: Planning and Design of Tall Buildings, 5 vols., 1978-81, Recent Developments in Tall Buildings, 1983, Advances in Tall Buildings, 1986, High-Rise Buildings-Recent Progress, 1986, Second Century of the Skyscraper, 1988, Tall Buildings: 2000 and Beyond, 1990, Cast-in-Place Concrete in Tall Building Design and Construction, 1992, Cladding, 1992, Building Design for Handicapped and Aged Persons, 1992, Fire Safety in Tall Buildings, 1992, Semi-Rigid Connections in Steel Frames, 1992, Cold-Formed Steel in Tall Buildings, 1993, Structural Systems for Tall Buildings, 1995, Architecture of Tall Buildings, 1995, Habitat and the High-Rise, 2 vols., 1995, Tall Building Structures--A World View, 1996, Structural, Design, Codes and Special Building Projects, 1997, (with others) 100 of the World's Tallest Buildings, 1998; contbr. (with others) articles to profl. jours. Served with USNR, 1941-47. Recipient Robinson award Lehigh U., 1952, Hillman award, 1973, Silver medal Am. Welding Soc., 1957, Regional Tech. Mfg. award Am. Iron and Steel Inst., 1958, Constrn. award Engring. News Record, 1965, 73, Engr. of Yr. award Lehigh Valley sect. NSPE, 1977, Internat. Contbns. award Japan Soc. Civil Engrs., 1994, John Fritz medal by various profl. engring. assns., 1994; named Acad. Specialist U. Jordan, 1987, Bangladesh U. Engring. and Tech., 1988. Fellow ASCE (hon., bd. dirs. 1974-77, bd. dirs. Lehigh Valley sect. 1979-82, past chmn. structural divsn. exec. com., past mem. rsch. com., E.E. Howard award 1963, Rsch. prize 1956, Shortridge Hardesty award 1993), Royal Soc. Arts; mem. AIA (liaison mem. regional & urban design com.), Structural Stability Rsch. Coun. (life, exec. com. 1947—, chmn. 1966-70, dir. 1970-93, dir. emeritus 1993—), Welding Rsch. Coun., Am. Inst. Steel Constrn. (T.R. Higgins Lectureship award 1973, Spl. Citation award 1991), Nat. Acad. Engring., Fritz Engring. Rsch. Soc. (hon. pres. 1995-96), Coun. Tall Bldgs. & Urban Habitat (chmn. 1970-76, dir. 1976—), Internat. Assn. Bridge & Structural Engring. (hon.). Presbyterian (elder 1957—). Home: 102 Cedar Rd Hellertown PA 18055-2303 Office: Lehigh U 11 E Packer Ave Bethlehem PA 18015-3101

BEEDLES, WILLIAM LEROY, finance educator, financial consultant; b. Independence, Kans., Apr. 9, 1948; s. Roy William Beedles and Opal Irene (Connor) Hunter; m. Margaret Ann Vanderlip, Dec. 21, 1974; children: Margaret Micaela, Patricia Opal, Cyrus Dean. BS, Kans. State U., 1970, MS, 1971; PhD, U. Tex., 1975. Asst. prof. Ind. U., Bloomington, 1975-78; vis. prof. Monash U., Melbourne, Victoria, Australia, 1984, U. NSW, Sydney, Australia, 1985; assoc. prof. to prof., dir. Masters program U. Kans., Lawrence, 1978—; vis. rsch. fellow Pub. Utilities Commn., Austin, Tex., 1981. Contbr. articles to profl. jours. Capt. U.S. Army, 1970-78. Mem. Am. Fin. Assn., Western Fin. Assn., So. Fin. Assn. (assoc. editor jour. 1979-84), Fin. Mgmt. Assn. Congregational. Avocation: raquetball. Office: U Kans Summerfield Hall Lawrence KS 66044-7585

BEEGLE, EARL DENNIS, family physician; b. Ashland, Ohio, July 24, 1944; s. Ray Benjamin and Alice Mae (Imhoff) B.; m. Isabel Sloan-Kerr Adamson, Sept. 3, 1964; children: Ryan Benjamin, Kevin Ian. BA, Manchester Coll., 1967; MS, Purdue U., 1970; MB BChir, MD, BAO, Queen's U., Belfast, No. Ireland, 1978. Diplomate Am. Bd. Family Practice. Life scis. tchr. Elkhart (Ind.) Schs., 1967-72; house officer Nat. Health Svc. of U.K., 1978-79; resident in family practice Riverside Hosp. Med. Coll. Ohio, Toledo, 1979-81, chief resident, 1981-82; pvt. practice Everett, Wash., 1982-93; med. dir. Providence Primary Care Network, Everett, 1993-96; v.p., med. dir. Medalia Healthcare, Seattle, 1997-98, exec. v.p. managed care, 1998-99; CEO Medalia Med. Group N.W. Wash., 1999—; credentials com. Providence Gen. Med. Ctr., 1996—, physician well-being com., 1997—; med. dir. Planned Parenthood, Everett, 1983-86; chmn. utilization Providence Hosp., Everett, 1987-90, chmn. quality assurance, 1991-92; chmn. dept. family practice Providence-Gen. Med. Ctr., Everett, 1993-94; dir. Sisters of Providence Health Plans, Seattle, 1993-98. Active Friends of the Somme, No. Ireland, 1991—. NSF fellow, 1967-70. Fellow Am. Acad. Family Practice; mem. Irish and Am. Pediatric Soc., Snohomish County Med. Soc., Associated Physicians of Snohomish County (bd. dirs.), Internat. Soc. Travel Medicine. Avocations: international travel, period furniture, antiquities. Office: Providence Claremont Clinic 5007 Claremont Way Everett WA 98203-3321

BEEGLE, PHILIP H., JR., plastic and reconstructive surgeon; b. Tucson, Apr. 16, 1949; s. Philip H. Sr. and Geraldine B. Beegle. BS, U. Ga., 1971; MD, Med. Coll. Ga., 1975. Asst. clin. instr. surgery Wright State U., Dayton, Ohio, 1982-84; pvt. practice Atlanta Plastic Surgery, 1984—; clin. asst. prof. dept. surgery divsn. plastic surgery Emory U., Atlanta. Maj. USAF, 1982-84. Fellow ACS; mem. AMA, Am. Assn. Plastic Surgeons, Am. Soc. Plastic and Reconstructive Surgeons, Southeastern Soc. Plastic and Reconstructive Surgeons, Ga. Soc. Plastic Surgery. Office: Atlanta Plastic Surgery Ste 500 975 Johnson Ferry Rd Atlanta GA 30342

BEEHAN, CATHY, government official, lawyer; b. St. John's, Newfoundland, Can.. Attended, Meml. U. of Newfoundland, 1974-75; MusB with honors cum laude, U. Ottawa, Can., 1979; LLB cum laude, U. Ottawa, 1982; cert. in French lang., Université de Savoie, France, 1985. Law clk. Osler, Hoskin & Harcourt, Toronto, Ont., Can., 1982-83; spl. asst. to Min. Justice and Atty. Gen. of Can., 1985-86; policy advisor to Min. Transport Govt. of Can., 1986-88, sr. policy advisor to Min. Internat. Trade, 1988-91, exec. asst. to Min. for Atlantic Can. Opportunities Agency, 1991-92; Can. sec., binational secretariat, Canadian sect. Can.-U.S. Free Trade Agreement, 1992-94; sec. NAFTA Secretariat, Ottawa, 1994—. Violinist Ottawa Symphony Orch., 1976-79, 86—. Mem. Can. Bar Assn., Law Soc. Upper Can. Avocations: skiing, tennis. Office: NAFTA Canadian Sect, 90 Sparks St # 705, Ottawa, ON Canada K1P 5B4

BEELER, BULAH RAY, medical/surgical nurse; b. San Saba, Apr. 8, 1929; d. Noah Bassett and Cora Estelle (Lawrence) Gillentine; m. Waddie O.J. Beeler, June 1, 1948; 1 child, Hubert Dale. Diploma, Lubbock Voct. Sch. Nursing, 1972. Lic. vocat. nurse, Tex.; cert. in CPR. Staff nurse Crosbyton (Tex.) Clinic Hosp., 1957—; dept. mgr. pharmacy, 1992—. Named Lic. Vocat. Nurse of Yr. Lubbock div., 1987. Home: 263 E 44th St San Bernardino CA 92404-1257

BEELER, DONALD DARYL, retail executive; b. Hettinger, N.D., Nov. 13, 1935; s. Earl Aaron and LaVera Grace (Krause) B.; m. Laurice Marianne Fish, May 23, 1954; children: Jillayne Marianne, Jacalyn Faye, Donald Earl. Grad. high sch., Lemmon, S.D. Owner, operator Lemmon (S.D.) Recreation, 1954-55; owner D&M Gifts, Lemmon, 1956-57; mgr. trainee to store mgr. Snyder Drug Stores, Inc., Hopkins, Minn., 1964-67, dist. mgr. to dir. of franchise ops., 1967-77, v.p. franchise ops. to v.p. gen. mgr., 1977-82, sr. v.p., gen. mgr., 1982, pres., 1982-86, chmn., pres., chief exec. officer, 1986-94, chmn., CEO, 1994—. Bd. dirs. Variety Club Children's Hosp., U. Minn., 1991—, "Braun's", 1992—; mem. U.S. Olympic Com., Minn., 1986—; vis. exec. United Fund, Mpls., 1988, sect. chmn., 1989; pres. Food, Drug and Liquor Coun., City of Hope, Mpls., 1984-87; exec. coun., 1987—. Served with U.S. Army, 1957-64. Recipient Spirit of Life award City of Hope, 1984. Mem. Nat. Assn. of Chain Drug Stores (bd. dirs. 1990—, exec. com. 1996-99), So. Drug Stores Assn., Minnetonka Country Club (bd. govs. 1988—, v.p. 1991, pres. 1992). Republican. Presbyterian. Avocations: golf, sports fan. Home: 4450 Manitou Rd Excelsior MN 55331-9447 Office: Snyders Drug Stores Inc 14525 Hwy 7 Minnetonka MN 55345

BEELER, THOMAS JOSEPH, lawyer, general management consultant; b. Marion, Ind., June 5, 1933; s. Thomas James and Margaret B. (Milford) B.; m. Jennifer Cunningham; children: Honor, Tessa; children from previous marriage: Kristin, Mark, Laura. BSBA cum laude, Notre Dame U., 1956, JD, 1957. Bar: Ind. 1957. Sole practice Anderson, 1958-61; asst. sec., counsel The Weatherhead Co., Cleve., 1961-68; asst. gen. counsel, corp. sec. Figgie Internat. Inc., Willoughby, Ohio, 1968-74; corp. atty., sec. Outboard Marine Corp., Waukegan, Ill., 1974-76, sr. v.p., gen. counsel, chief adminstrv. officer, 1976-92; gen. mgmt. cons., Libertyville, Ill., 1992—. Served to 1st lt. AUS, 1957-58. Mem. Am., Ind. bar assns., Am. Soc. Corp. Secs. Home and Office: 28390 N Oak Ln Libertyville IL 60048-9762

BEELER, VIRGIL L., lawyer; b. Inpls., June 6, 1931; s. Elmer L. and Margaret Gwendolyn (Turney) B.; m. Patricia McAtee Walker; children: Stephen L., Philip E. AB in Econs., Ind. U., 1953, JD, 1959. Bar: Ind. 1959, U.S. Dist. Ct. Ind., U.S. Ct. Appeals (7th cir.), U.S. Supreme Ct., U.S. Tax Ct. Assoc. Baker & Daniels, Indpls., 1959-65, ptnr., 1966-95, of counsel, 1995—. Contbr. to profl. jours. 1st lt. U.S. Army, 1954-56. Fellow Am. Coll. Trial Lawyers, Ind. Bar Found.; mem. Indpls. Bar Assn., Ind. State Bar Assn., 7th Cir. Bar Assn., Order of Coif, Phi Beta Kappa. Office: Baker & Daniels 300 N Meridian St Ste 2700 Indianapolis IN 46204-1782

BEEM, JACK DARREL, lawyer; b. Chgo., Nov. 17, 1931. AB, U. Chgo., 1952, JD, 1955. Bar: Ill. 1955. Assoc. firm Wilson & McIlvaine, Chgo., 1958-63; ptnr. firm Baker & McKenzie, Chgo., 1963—. Mem. vis. com. Ctr. for East Asian Studies U. Chgo. Mem. ABA, Chgo. Bar Assn., Japan-Am. Soc. Chgo. (pres. 1988-92), Am. Fgn. Law Assn. (chmn. Chgo. br.), Phi Beta Kappa. Home: 175 E Delaware Pl Apt 8104 Chicago IL 60611-7746 Office: Baker & McKenzie 1 Prudential Plz 130 E Randolph St Ste 3700 Chicago IL 60601-6342

BEEM, JOHN KELLY, mathematician, educator; b. Detroit, Jan. 24, 1942; s. William Richard and June Ellen (Kelly) B.; m. Eloise Masako Yamamoto, Mar. 24, 1964; 1 child, Thomas Kelly. A.B. in Math., U. So. Calif., 1963, M.A. in Math., 1965, Ph.D. in Math., 1968. Asst. prof. math. U. Mo., Columbia, 1968-71, assoc. prof., 1971-79, prof., 1979—. Author: (with P. Y. Woo) Doubly Timelike Surfaces, 1969, (with P. E. Ehrlich) Global Lorentzian Geometry, 1981, (with P.E. Ehrlich and K.L. Easley), 2d edit., 96; condr. research in differential geometry and gen. relativity. Recipient Kemper Tchg. award, 1996; NSF fellow, 1965, 68. Mem. Math. Assn. Am., Am. Math. Soc., Phi Beta Kappa. Home: 5204 E Tayside Cir Columbia MO 65203-5191

BEEMAN, BOB JOE, minister; b. Billings, Mont., Nov. 3, 1952; s. Marvin Joe and Bonnie Berteen (Boegler) B. CE, Mont. Inst. of the Bible, 1972. Ordained to ministry Sanctuary Internat., 1980. Dir. Acts Alive! Ministries, Billings, 1976-80, Bob Beeman Evangelistic Assn., Calif., 1980-85; pastor, founder Sanctuary Chs. Inc., Redondo Beach, Calif., 1985-94; exec. dir. Sanctuary Internat., Mt. Juliet, Tenn., 1994—. Office: Sanctuary International PO Box 1477 Mount Juliet TN 37121-1477

BEEMAN, JOSIAH HORTON, diplomat; b. San Francisco, Oct. 8, 1935; s. Josiah Horton and Helen Virginia (Hooper) B.; m. Susan Louise Sturman, Oct. 28, 1995; 1 child, Olivia Louise. BA, Calif. State U., 1957. Adminstrv. asst. Congressman Phillip Burton, Washington, 1964-66; mem. San Francisco Bd. Suprs., 1967-68; sec. internat. affairs Presbyn. Ch., N.Y.C., 1969-70; dir. Washington Office Presbyn. Ch., Washington, 1970-75; staff dir. Democratic Caucus U.S. Ho. of Reps., Washington, 1975; chief dep. dir. fin. State Calif., Washington, 1975-80; polit. and legis. dir. Am. Fedn. State, County and Mcpl. Employees, Washington, 1980-83; dir. Dem. Nat. Conv., San Francisco, 1983-84; pres. Beeman and Assocs., Washington, Sacramento, 1983-94; U.S. amb. to New Zealand and Samoa, 1994—. Chmn. gen. assembly coun. Presbyn. Ch. U.S.A., 1988-89. Democrat. Office: Psc 467 Box 1 APO AP 96531-0001

BEEMAN, MALINDA MARY, artist, program administrator; b. Pomona, Calif., Jan. 23, 1949; d. Earl Wilson and Mary (Alvey) B. BA, San Diego State U., 1971; MFA, San Francisco Art Inst., 1973. Area coord. printmaking U. Houston, 1985-92; program dir. Anderson Ranch Art Ctr., Snowmass Village, Colo., 1992—. Recipient Visual Artists award Nat. Endowment for Arts, 1988, 96, Covision Recognition award Colo. State Arts Coun., 1992. Office: Anderson Ranch Arts Ctr 5263 Owl Creek Rd Snowmass Village CO 81615

BEEMAN, RICHARD ROY, historian, educator; b. Seattle, May 16, 1942; m. Pamela Jane Butler, Dec. 26, 1964; children: Kristin Dowds, Joshua Douglas. AB in History, U. Calif., Berkeley, 1964; MA in History, Coll. of William and Mary, 1965; PhD in History, U. Chgo., 1968. Asst. prof. history U. Pa., 1968-73, assoc. prof., 1973-82, prof., 1982—, acting chmn. dept., 1986-87, chmn., 1987-91, assoc. dean, 1991-96; vis. prof. Am. studies U. Hull, Eng., 1976-77; dean coll. arts & scis. U. Pa., 1998—; William R. Kenan prof. history, chmn. Colby Coll., 1979-80; dir. Phila. Ctr. for Early Am. Studies, 1980-85. Author: The Old Dominion and the New Nation, 1788-1801, 1972, Patrick Henry: A Biography, 1974, The Evolution of the Southern Backcountry, 1984; editor: Beyond Confederation: The Origins of the American Constituion and National Identity, 1987; also articles and book revs. Dept. of History fellow Coll. William and Mary, 1964, Univ. fellow U. Chgo., 1966-67, Newberry Library jr. fellow, Chgo., 1967-68, U. Pa. summer research grants, 1969, 71, Am. Philos. Soc. research grants, 1971, 76, 89, Social Sci. Research Council post-doctoral fellowship, 1972-73, Nat. Book Award nominee, 1974, Fulbright sr. lectr., U.K., 1976-77, NEH basic research grant, 1983-84, summer seminar grant, 1986, sr. fellow, 1989—; fellow Inst. Advanced Study, 1989-90, Huntington Libr., 1997. Home: 301 Glenwood Ave Media PA 19063-4131

BEEMER, JOHN BARRY, lawyer; b. Scranton, Pa., Sept. 4, 1941; s. Ellis and Rose Mary (Costello) B.; m. Diane Montgomery Fletcher, July 18, 1964; children: David, Bruce. BS, U. Scranton, 1963; LL.B., George Washington U., 1966. Bar: Pa. 1966, U.S. Supreme Ct. 1980; cert. civil trial adv. Nat. Bd. Trial Advocacy. Law clk. U.S. Ct. Claims, 1966-67; clk. to judge U.S. Dist. Ct. (mid. dist.) Pa., 1967-68; assoc. Warren, Hill, Henkelman & McMenamin, Scranton, 1968-72; ptnr. Beemer, Brier, Rinaldi & Fendrick, 1972-77; pres. Beemer, Rinaldi, Fendrick & Mellody, P.C., Scranton, 1977-83; ptnr. Beemer & Beemer, Scranton, 1984—; lectr. in law U. Scranton, 1969-70. Chmn. com. constn. and by-laws revision Lackawanna (county Pa.) United Fund., 1971; nat. chmn. U. Scranton Alumni Fund Drive, 1972. Mem. ABA, Pa. Bar Assn., Lackawanna Bar Assn. (bd. dirs. 1988—), Assn. Trial Lawyers Am., Pa. Trial Lawyers Assn., Phi Delta Phi. Office: 114116 N Abington Rd Clarks Summit PA 18411

BEER, ALAN EARL, physician, medical educator; b. Milford, Ind., Apr. 14, 1937; s. Theo and Naoma Marguerite (Speheger) B.; m. Dorothy Gudeman, Aug. 17, 1958; children—Michael, Elizabeth, Margaret, Laura. B.S., Ind. U., 1959, M.D., 1962. Diplomate: Am. Bd. Ob-Gyn. Resident in Ob-Gyn Hosp. of U. Pa., Phila., 1965-68; USPHS/Ford Found. fellow Dept. Med. Genetics and Ob-Gyn, U. Pa., Phila., 1968-70; asst. prof. dept. Ob-Gyn, U. Tex. Southwestern Med. Sch., Dallas, 1971-73; assoc. prof. Ob-Gyn, U. Tex. Southwestern Med. Sch., 1973-76, prof., 1976-79; Bates prof., chmn. dept. Ob-Gyn, U. Mich., Ann Arbor, 1979-84; prof. Ob/Gyn, dir. Reproductive Immunology Labs., 1984-87; prof. microbiology, immunology, obstetrics and gynecology Chgo. Med. Sch., 1987—. Assoc. editor: Jour. Reproductive Immunology, 1979, editor-in-chief, 1979—; contbr. articles to profl. jours. Served with USPHS, 1963-65. Recipient Lalor Found. award, 1969; Carl F. Hartman award Am. Fertility Soc., 1970. Mem. Am. Coll. Obstetricians and Gynecologists, Am. Fertility Soc., Internat. Transplantation Soc., AMA, Soc. for Study of Reprodn., Soc. for Gynecol. Investigation, Am. Assn. Ob-Gyn., Am. Soc. Immunology of Reprodn. (pres. 1985). Office: Finch U Health Scis Chgo Med Sch 3333 Green Bay Rd North Chicago IL 60064-3037*

BEER, ALICE STEWART (MRS. JACK ENGEMAN), retired musician, educator; b. Redwood Falls, Minn., Sept. 29, 1912; d. Robert and Isabel (Montgomery) Stewart; m. Jack Engeman, Dec. 14, 1974; children by previous marriage: W. Robert, Jane K. Beer Mosher, Elizabeth S. Beer-Shilling. MusB, Northwestern U., 1934, MusM, 1952; postgrad., Johns Hopkins U., 1954, 60, Mexico City Coll., 1956, U. Md., 1957. Tchr. pub. schs., Lawton, Mich., 1934-39, Battle Creek, Mich., 1949-51; tchr. Balt. Pub. Schs., 1951-53, supr. music, 1953-77; tchr. summer sessions various colls. and univs., 1957-85; adj. faculty Peabody Inst., John's Hopkins U., Balt., 1981-85; cons. Alliance for Arts in Edn., Balt. County Pub. Schs., 1982-90, cons. curriculum, 1984-91; pres. Pickersgill Retirement Cmty. Apt. Residents Assn., 1996-97. Author: Teaching Suggestions, Birchard Music Series II and III, 1962, Teaching Music: What, How and Why, 1973, Teaching Music to the Exceptional Child: A Handbook for Mainstreaming, 1980, Teaching Music, 1982, Patriotic Color Sound Filmstrips/Videos, 1967-69; mem. editorial bd. Maryland Music Educator Jour., 1990—; contbr. articles to profl. jours. Mem. bd. lady mgrs. Balt. Street Clinic, 1986—; ordained elder Towson Presbyn. Ch., chmn. nominating comm. Prebyterian women. Recipient Director's Recognition award for commitment to music edn. and extraordinary contbn. to art of teaching, 1986; inductee Md. Music Educators Hall of Fame, 1989. Mem. AAUW (mem. Towson br.), Nat. Conf. Music Educators, Md. Music Educators Assn., Pres.'s Club Cir. U. Md., Officers and Faculty Club of U.S. Naval Acad., Pres.'s Club Circle, Phi Beta. Republican. Home: 615 Chestnut Ave Apt 1401 Baltimore MD 21204-3767

BEER, BARRETT LYNN, historian, educator; b. Goshen, Ind., July 4, 1936; s. Peter J. and Mabel M. Beer; m. Jill Parker, 1965. B.A., DePauw U., 1958; M.A., U. Cin., 1959; Ph.D., Northwestern U., 1965. Instr. history Kent State U., Ohio, 1962-65; assoc. prof. Kent State U., 1968-76, prof., 1976—; asst. prof. U. N.Mex., Albuquerque, 1965-68; asst. dean Coll. Arts and Scis. U. N.Mex., 1966-68; Fulbright prof. U. Tromso, Norway, 1983. Author: Northumberland: The Political Career of John Dudley, Earl of Warwick and Duke of Northumberland, 1973, Rebellion and Riot: Popular Disorder in England during the Reign of Edward VI, 1982, (with others) Recent Historians of Great Britain, 1990; editor: (with S.M. Jack) The Letters of William, Lord Paget of Beaudesert, 1547-1563, 1974, The Life and Raigne of King Edward the Sixth (John Hayward), 1993, Tudor England Observed: The World of John Stow, 1998. Am. Philos. Soc. grantee, 1966; Am. Council Learned Socs. grantee, 1973; fellow Newberry Libr., 1991, Folger Shakespeare Libr., 1997. Fellow Royal Hist. Soc.; mem. Conf. on Brit. Studies, Ohio Acad. History, Phi Beta Kappa. Episcopalian. Home: 445 Dansel St Kent OH 44240-2626 Office: Kent State U Dept History Kent OH 44242

BEER, CLARA LOUISE JOHNSON, retired electronics executive; b. Bisbee, Ariz., Jan. 14, 1918; d. Franklin Fayette and Marie (Sturm) Johnson; m. Philip James McElmurry, May 15, 1937 (div. July 1944); children—Leonard Franklin, Philip James Jr.; m. William Sigvard Beer, July 15, 1945 (dec. Aug. 31, 1977); 1 son, Douglas Lee; m. Kenneth Christy Huntwork, May 1, 1982. Student, Merritt Bus. Sch., Oakland, Calif., 1935, Bus. Instrn. Sch., Palo Alto, Calif., 1955. Sec., artist M.R. Fisher Studios, Oakland, 1936-40; piano, organ instr. Anna May Studios, Palo Alto, 1948-50; pvt. piano, organ instr. Palo Alto, 1949-56; sec. Stanford Electronics Labs., Stanford U., 1955-58; corporate sec. and exec. sec. to chmn. bd. Watkins-Johnson Co., Palo Alto, 1958-88; dir., sec. Watkins-Johnson Internat., 1968-88, Watkins-Johnson Ltd., 1971-88, Watkins-Johnson Assocs., 1977-88. Mem. Nat. Secs. Assn., Christian Bus. and Profl. Women's Coun. (sec. 1966-67, adviser 1968). Home: 24157 Hillview Rd Los Altos CA 94024-5222

BEER, DANIEL JACKSON, sales executive; b. Altoona, Pa., Apr. 15, 1948; s. Bernard Hale and Rhea Virginia (Tie) B. BA in History and Polit. Sci., SUNY, Albany, 1989. Enlisted USAF, 1967, human resource mgr., warehouse supr., warehouseman, 1967-88, ret., 1988; sr. store assoc. Army and Air Force Exch. Svc., Wright-Patterson AFB, Ohio, 1989—. Mem. Libr. Congress (assoc.), Regents Coll. Alumni Assn. Avocations: reading, American history, astronomy. Home: 35 S Broad St Apt A Fairborn OH 45324-4659

BEÉR, JÁNOS MIKLÓS, engineering educator; b. Budapest, Hungary, Feb. 27, 1923; s. Sandor and Gizella (Trismai) B.; m. Marta Gabriella Csato, Oct. 27, 1944. Dipl. Ing., Jozsef Nador U. Tech., Budapest, 1950; PhD, U. Sheffield, Eng., 1960, DSc, 1968; Dr honoris causa, U. Miskolc, Hungary, 1987, U. Tech. Scis., Budapest, Hungary, 1997. Research engr. Heat Research Inst., Budapest, 1949-56; head combustion div. Heat Research Inst., 1952-56; prin. lectr. combustion Budapest Tech. U., 1953-56; research engr. Babcock & Wilcox Ltd., Renfrew, Scotland, 1956-57; head research sta. Internat. Flame Research Found., Ijmuiden, Holland, 1960-63; prof. fuel sci. Pa. State U., 1963-65; Newton Drew prof., head dept. chem. engring. and fuel tech. U. Sheffield, 1965-76, dean engring., 1973-75; prof. chem. and fuel engring. MIT, 1976-93, prof. emeritus, 1993—; vis. fellow Australian Commonwealth, 1972; mem. joint com. Internat. Flame Research Found., 1972-89, supt. research, 1972-89; bd. dirs. Combustion Inst., Pitts., 1974-86; adv. council research and devel. fuel and power U.K. Dept. Energy, 1973-76; mem. Clean Air Council, Dept. Environ., U.K., 1974-76; mem. chem. tech. com. U.K. Sci. Research Council, 1972-75; mem. combustion sci. com. Italian Nat. Research Council, 1974—; chmn. clean coal utilization project NAS, 1987-88; mem. adv. coun. U.S. Sec. Energy Nat. Coal Coun., 1994—. Co-author: Combustion Aerodynamics, 1972; editor: Fuel and Energy Science Monograph Series, 1972; co-editor: Heat Transfer in Flames, 1972, Industrial Flames, 1972, Combustion Technology, 1974; author articles; patentee in field. Recipient BCURA Coal Sci. gold medal, 1986. Alfred Egerton gold medal Combustion Inst., 1986, Axel Axelson Johnson medal Swedish Acad. Engring. Scis., 1995, AIAA Energy Sys. award, 1998; named Hon. Supt. Rsch., Internat. Flame Rsch. Found., 1991. Fellow ASME (Moody award 1964, Percy Nicholls award 1988), Inst. Energy (sr., Melchett medal 1985), Royal Acad. Engring. U.K.; mem. Am. Inst. Chem. Engrs., Inst. Chem. Engring., Hungarian Acad. Scis. (hon.), Hungarian Nat. Acad. Engring. (hon.), Finnish Acad. Tech. (fgn.). Office: MIT 66-548 Dept Engring Cambridge MA 02139

BEER, JOSEPH ERNEST, telecommunications manager; b. Pasadena, Calif., June 5, 1959; s. Joseph Andrew and Pauline Sylvia (Micciche) B.; m. Amy Shun-Fong Wu, Oct. 13, 1984. BS in Internat. Bus., Calif. State U., L.A., 1982; MBA in Info. Tech. Mgmt., U. So. Calif., 1987. Asst. engr. ARCO-Electronics & Telecommunications, L.A., 1979-83, sr. coord., 1983-84, project engr., 1984-85, sr. project engr., 1985-87; mgr. Ernst & Young, L.A., 1987-91; dir. telecommunications and network svcs. South Coast Air Quality Mgmt. Dist., L.A., 1991-94; mgr. info. tech. svcs. Tosco Northwest Co., Seattle, 1994-96; dir. profl. svcs. Mosaix Inc., Seattle, 1996-98; sr. mgr. Ernst & Young, Seattle, 1999—. Recipient scholarship, Ebell Found., L.A., 1981, Bank Am. scholarship, Bank Am. Found., 1981. Mem. Soc. Telecommunications Consultants, Project Mgmt. Inst. Republican. Avocations: biking, hiking, antique car and telephone collecting and restoration. Home: 24012 SE 37th Pl Issaquah WA 98029-6320 Office: Ernst & Young Ste 3500 999 3d St Seattle WA 98101

BEER, PAMELA JILL PORR, writer, retired vocational school educator; b. Denver, Sept. 23, 1941; d. Wyeth Wittwer and Mary (DuReece) Porr; m. Calvin George Beer, Dec. 25, 1968. BS, Pittsburg State U., Kans., 1963, MBE, 1979. Bookkeeper Hubbard Auto Supply, Pittsburg, 1960-63; tchr. bus. edn. Sabetha High Sch., Kans., 1963-65; tchr. bus. edn. Nevada High Sch., Mo., 1965-71; head bus. dept. Nevada Vocat. Area Sch., 1971-93, ret. 1993; feeelance writer 1993—. mem. nat. adv. bd. Today's Sec., N.Y.C., 1982-83; instr. continuing edn. Mo. Southern State Coll., Joplin, 1987—, mem. articulation com., 1986-87. Contbr. articles to profl. jours; mem. editorial adv. bd. Roxburg Pub. Co., 1984—. Instr. 4-H, 1987. Named Nev. R-5 Tchr. of Yr. 1992, Mo. Southwest Dist. Bus. Edn. Tchr. of Yr., 1993, Mo. Bus. Edn. Assn. S.W. Dist. Tchr. of Yr. Mem. Nat. Bus. Edn. Assn., Am. Vocat. Assn., Nev. C. of C. (Area Educator of Yr. 1987), Delta Kappa Gamma, Delta Pi Epsilon, Alpha Gamma Delta. Methodist. Avocations: bowling, swimming, bridge, tennis, golfing. Home: 1827 F Kennedy Pittsburg KS 66762

BEER, PETER HILL, federal judge; b. New Orleans, Apr. 12, 1928; s. Mose Haas and Henret (Lowenburg) B.; children: Kimberly Beer Bailes, Kenneth, Dana Beer Long-Innes; m. Marjorie Barry, July 14, 1985. BBA, Tulane U., 1949, LLB, 1952; LLM, U. Va., 1986. Bar: La. 1952. Successively assoc., ptnr., sr. ptnr. Montgomery, Barnett, Brown & Read, New Orleans, 1955-74; judge La. Ct. Appeal, 1974-79, U.S. Dist. Ct. (ea. dist.) La., New Orleans, 1979—; vice chmn. La. Appellate Judges Conf.; apptd. by chief justice of U.S. to state-fed. com. Jud. Conf. U.S., 1985-89; apptd. by chief justice of U.S. to Nat. Jud. Coun. State and Fed. Cts., 1993—. Mem. bd. mgrs. Touro Infirmary, New Orleans, 1969-74; mem. exec. com. Bur. Govtl. Rsch., 1965-69; chmn. profl. divsn. United Fund New Orleans, 1966-69; mem. New Orleans City Coun., 1969-74, v.p., 1972-74. Capt. USAF, 1952-55. Decorated Bronze Star. Mem. ABA (mem. ho. dels.), Am. Judicature Soc., Fed. Bar Assn., La. Bar Assn., Fed. Judges Assn. U.S. (bd. dirs. 1985, 5th cir. rep. bd. govs.), Nat. Lawyers Club, So. Yacht Club, St. John Golf Club. Jewish. Home: 133 Bellaire Dr New Orleans LA 70124-1008 also: 204 3rd Ave Pass Christian MS 39571-3214 Office: US Dist Ct US Courthouse 500 Camp St New Orleans LA 70130-3313

BEER, REINHARD, atmospheric scientist; b. Berlin, Germany, Nov. 5, 1935; came to U.S., 1963, naturalized, 1979; s. Harry Joseph and Elisabet Maria (Meister) B.; m. Margaret Ann Taylor, Aug. 11, 1960. B.Sc. with Honors, U. Manchester, Eng., 1956, Ph.D., 1960. Rsch. asst. physics U. Manchester, 1956-60, sr. asst. astronomy, 1960-63; sr. scientist Jet Propulsion Lab., Pasadena, Calif., 1963-70; group supr. tropospheric sci. Jet Propulsion Lab., 1970—, sr. rsch. scientist, 1985—, mgr. atmospheric and oceanographic scis. sect., 1990-92, flight team leader, 1997—; vis. assoc. prof. astronomy U. Tex., Austin, 1974; vis. astronomer Kitt Peak Nat. Obs., 1979-81, Mauna Kea Obs., 1982-86; prin. investigator tropospheric emission spectrometer NASA Earth Observing System, 1989—, airborne emission spectrometer program NASA, 1992—; co-investigator NASA Atlas 1 mission, 1992, Atlas 2, 1993. Author: Remote Sensing by Fourier Transform Spectrometry, 1992; contbr. articles to profl. jours. Hon. Turner and Newall fellow, 1961; recipient medal for exceptional sci. achievement NASA, 1974; NASA group achievement award for Pioneer Venus, 1980, Spacelab 3 ATMOS experiment and sci., 1986. Mem. AAAS, Am. Geophys. Union, Optical Soc. Am., Internat. Astron. Union. Discoverer of extra-terrestrial deuterium (heavy hydrogen), 1972, of carbon monoxide in Jupiter, 1975. Office: 183-301 Jet Propulsion Lab Pasadena CA 91109

BEERBOWER, CYNTHIA GIBSON, lawyer; b. Dayton, Ohio, June 25, 1949; d. Charles Augustus and Sarah (Rittenhouse) Gibson; m. John Edwin Beerbower, Aug. 28, 1971; children: John Eliot, Sarah Rittenhouse. BA, Mt. Holyoke Coll., 1971; JD, Boston U., 1974; LLB, Cambridge U., Eng., 1976. Bar: N.Y. 1975. Assoc., Cadwalader, Wickersham & Taft, N.Y.C., 1975-76; assoc. Simpson, Thacher & Bartlett, N.Y.C., 1977-81, ptnr., 1981-93; internat. tax counsel U.S. Dept. Treasury, Washington, 1993-94, dep. asst. sec. tax policy, 1994-96; chmn., CEO Reeve Ct. Ins. Ltd., 1997—. Mem. ABA, Assn. Bar City N.Y., N.Y. State Bar Assn. (com. co-chmn. 1987-93). Presbyterian. Home: 720 Park Ave New York NY 10021-4954 Office: Richmond House PO Box HM 1067, 12 Par-La-Ville Rd, Hamilton HM EX, Bermuda

BEERBOWER, JOHN EDWIN, lawyer; b. Columbus, Ohio, Jan. 7, 1948; m. Cynthia Gibson, Aug. 28, 1971; children: John Eliot, Sarah Rittenhouse. BA, Amherst Coll., 1970; JD, Harvard U., 1973; student, Trinity Coll., Cambridge (Eng.) U. Bar: N.Y. 1975. Mem. Cravath, Swaine & Moore, N.Y.C. Bd. govs. Mannes Coll. Music, New Sch. Social Rsch.; trustee Madison Ave. Presbyn. Ch.; mem. Langdell com. Harvard U. Law Sch., Cambridge, Mass., 1994-96. Mem. ABA, N.Y. State Bar Assn., N.Y. Law Inst. (mem. nominating com.), Assn. of Bar of City of N.Y. (chmn. profl. and jud. ethics com. 1990-93), Soc. of Alumni Amherst Coll. (pres. 1994-95), Phi Beta Kappa. Office: Cravath Swaine & Moore Worldwide Plz 825 8th Ave Fl 38 New York NY 10019-7475

BEERING, STEVEN CLAUS, academic administrator, medical educator; b. Berlin, Germany, Aug. 20, 1932; came to U.S., 1948, naturalized, 1953; s. Steven and Alice (Friedrichs) B.; m. Catherine Jane Pickering, Dec. 27, 1956; children: Peter, David, John. BS summa cum laude, U. Pitts., 1954, MD, 1958; DSc (hon.), Ind. Cen. U., 1983, U. Evansville (Ind.), 1984; ScD (hon.), U. Pitts., 1998; DSc (hon.), Ramapo Coll., 1986, Anderson Coll., 1987; ScD (hon.), Ind. U., 1988; LLD (hon.), Hanover Coll., 1986. Intern Walter Reed Gen. Hosp., Washington, 1958-59; resident Wilford Hall Med. Center, San Antonio, Tex., 1959-62, chief internal medicine, edn. coordinator, 1967-69; prof. medicine Ind. U. Sch. Medicine, Indpls., 1969—, asst. dean, 1969-70, assoc. dean, dir. postgrad. edn., 1970-74, dir. statewide med. edn. system, 1970-83, dean, 1974-83; chief exec. officer Ind. U. Med. Center, Indpls., 1974-83; pres. Purdue U. and Purdue U. Research Found., West Lafayette, Ind., 1983—; prof. pharmacology and toxicology Purdue U.; bd. dirs. Arvin Industries, Eli Lilly Co., NIPSCO Industries, Am. United Life, Veridian Corp.; cons. Indpsl. VA Hosp., St. Vincent Hosp.; chmn. Ind. Commn. Med. Edn., 1973-83, Med. Edn. Bd. Ind., 1974-83, Liaison Com. on Med. Edn., 1976-81. Contbr. articles to sci. jours. Sec. Ind. Atty. Gen.'s Trust, 1974-83; regent Nat. Library Medicine, 1987-91; mem. Lafayette Community Council. Served to lt. col. M.C. USAF, 1957-69. Fellow ACP, Royal Soc. Medicine; mem. Am. Fedn. Clin. Rsch., Am. Diabetes Assn., Endocrine Soc., Assn. Am. Med. Colls. (chmn. 1982-83), Coun. Med. Deans (chmn. 1980-81), Assn. Am. Univs. (chair 1995-96), Nat. Acad. Sci. Inst. of Medicine, Ind. Acad., Indpls. Athletic Club, Columbia Club, Skyline Club, Woodstock Club, Meridian Hills Club, Phi Beta Kappa, Sigma Xi, Alpha Omega Alpha, Phi Rho Sigma (U.S. v.p. 1976-85). Presbyterian (elder). Home: 500 Mccormick Rd West Lafayette IN 47906-4911 Office: Purdue U Office of Pres Rm 200 Hovde Hall Purdue University IN 47907

BEERMAN, JOSEPH, health educator; b. N.Y.C., Aug. 31, 1937; s. Herbert and Frances B.; m. Andrea Ellenhorn, Aug. 15, 1987; 1 child, Eric Hunter. BA, Hunter Coll., 1959; MA, NYU, 1963; diploma Tchr.'s Coll., Columbia U., 1970. Cert. in health and phys. edn., N.Y. Tchg. asst., track coach NYU, 1959-61; tchr. health edn. Herman Ridder Jr. H.S., N.Y.C., 1961-65; prof. health and phys. edn. Manhattan C.C.-CUNY, N.Y.C., 1965-96, assoc. dean faculty, 1978-79, prof. emeritus, 1996—, adj. prof., 1996—; cons. Nat. Coun. Jr. Colls., NEA, Washington, 1965—; rep. Coun. Health Educators, CUNY, 1965—. Author: Chemical Dependency and the Minorities, 1993, Basic Tennis: Skills and Strategies, 1995. Guest speaker YMCA and sr. citizen orgns., N.Y.C., 1965—; presenter tennis clins. Ea. Tennis Patrons, N.Y.C., 1965-75; presenter seminars N.Y.C. Bd. Edn., 1961-70. Sgt. U.S. Army, 1959-61. Nat. Humanities Faculty grantee, 1978; recipient McGovern award U.S. Tennis Assn., 1987; inducted into Hunter Coll. Athletic Hall of Fame, 1993. Fellow Internat. Inst. Cmty. Svc., Friends of Penn Relay's; mem. Am. Alliance Phys. Edn., Health, Recreation and Dance (mem. various coms. 1960—), Democrat. Jewish. Avocations: philately, numismatics, antiques, tennis. Home: 16-70 Bell Blvd Apt 113 Bayside NY 11360 Office: CUNY 199 Chambers St New York NY 10007-1044

BEERMAN, MIRIAM, artist, educator; b. Providence; d. William and Rose (Nochemsohn) B.; m. Julian F. Jaffe (dec. 1973); 1 child, William Jaffe. BFA, R.I. Sch. Design, 1945; postgrad., Art Students League, N.Y.C., 1945-46, New Sch. for Social Rsch., NYU. Prof. painting and drawing Queensborough C.C., CUNY, 1972-95; instr. Jersey City State Coll., 1973-75; instr. Montclair (N.J.) Art Mus. Art Sch., 1974-90, resident, 1980-90; instr. Montclair State Coll., 1980-89; artist-in-residence MacDowell Colony, 1959, Ossibaw Island, Ga., 1974, Camargo Found., Cassis, France, 1980—, Va. Ctr. for Creative Arts, Sweet Briar, 1983, 84, 86, 89, 90, 91, 92, 93, 94, 97, 98, Leighton Artist's Colony, Banff Ctr., Alta., Can., 1986-87, Blue Mountain Ctr., N.Y., 1988, 93, 95, 97, Millay Colony for Arts, 1976, 91, Camargo Found., 1980. One-woman shows include Bklyn. Mus., 1971, Montclair Art Mus., 1974, 87-88, Graham Gallery, N.Y.C., 1972, 78, Mus. of St. John the Divine, N.Y.C., 1978, N.J. State Mus., Trenton, 1991, Klarfeld Perry Gallery, N.Y.C., 1993, Suffolk C.C., N.Y., 1993, Bergen Mus., Paramus, N.J., 1996, Jersey City Mus., 1997-98, also others; exhibited in group shows Inst. Contemporary Art, New Orleans, 1986, Newark Mus., 1985-86, Roanoke Mus. Fine Art, 1985, Bayly Mus., 1985, Corcoran Gallery of Art, Washington, 1994, Bergen Mus., Paramus, N.J., 1996, Montclair Mus., N.J., 1997, Ctr. for Book Arts, N.Y.C., 1996, 98, Women of the Book, 1997—, numerous others; represented in permanent collections Israel Mus., U. Oreg., Newark Mus., Whitney Mus., Am. Art, Bklyn. Mus., Montclair Art Mus., Arnot Art Mus., Morris Mus., Met. Mus. Art, Mus. of Art, RISD, Queens Mus., N.Y., Jersey City Mus., Jewish Mus., N.Y.C., others. Recipient numerous awards including Childe Hassam purchase award AAAL, 1977, prize 11th R.I. Arts Festival, 1969, Ives prize RISD, Disting. Artist award N.J. Coun. on Arts, 1987; N.Y. State Coun. on Arts grantee, 1971, Womens Rsch. and Devel. Fund, CUNY grantee 1986, N.J. Coun. on Arts grantee, 1978, 83, 87, Rutgers Ctr. for Innovative Printmaking grantee, 1987, 97, Joan Mitchell Found. grantee, 1994, Mid Atlantic NEA grantee, 1996, Dodge Found. grantee for residency, 1998; Fulbright fellow, Paris, 1953-55, 54-55; Forest fellow Millay Colony, 1992, others. Home and Studio: 6 Macopin Ave Montclair NJ 07043-2002

BEERMANN, ALLEN J., former state official; b. Sioux City, Iowa, Jan. 14, 1940. B.A., Midland Lutheran Coll., Fremont, Nebr., 1962; J.D., Creighton U., Omaha, 1965; LLD (hon.), Midland Luth. Coll., 1995. Bar: Nebr. 1965. Legal counsel, adminstrv. asst. to sec. state State of Nebr., 1965-67, dep. sec. state, 1967-71; sec. of state, 1971-95; mem. Fed. Election Commn. adv. panel. Bd. dirs. NebraskaLand Found.; exec. bd. Cornhusker coun. Boy Scouts Am. Lt. col. U.S. Army, ret. Recipient Disting. Svc. plaque Omaha Legal Aid Soc., 1964, Silver Beaver award Boy Scouts Am., 1979; named Outstanding Young Man Lincoln Jaycees, 1975, Outstanding Young Man Nebr. Jaycees, 1975. Mem. ABA, Nat. Assn. Secs. State (pres. 1976-77), Nebr. Bar Assn. (exec. dir. 1995—), Nebr. Press Assn., Am. Legion (fed. election commn. adv. panel, Cert. Appreciation). Lutheran. Office: Nebr Press Assn 845 S St Lincoln NE 68508-1226

BEERS, ANNE, protective services official. BA in Edn., Hamline U., 1975. Trooper trainee Minn. State Patrol, 1975-76, trooper East Metro dist. 2400, 1976-80, trooper 1, 1981-83, lt., 1984-88, capt., 1988-92, comdr. East Metro dist. 2400, 1993-95, maj., 1995-97, chief, 1997—. Named Woman of Yr. Women's Transp. Sem. of Minn., 1998. Mem. Minn. Chiefs of Police Assn., Internat. Assn. of Women Police, Internat. Assn. of Chiefs of Police, Law Enforcement Opportunities, Minn. Assn. of Women Police (Carolen Bailey Mentoring award 1992), Minn. Police and Peace Officers Assn. Office: Minn State Patrol 444 Cedar St Ste 130 Saint Paul MN 55101-5130

BEERS, ANNE COLE, real estate broker; b. Beverly, Mass.; d. Samuel Dodge Cole and Georgianna Wescott; m. Rowland A. Beers, Dec. 27, 1947 (div. 1979); children: Daniel C., Natalie Beers Davis, Janet Beers Heirtzler. Student, Beaver Coll., 1943-44; BS in Psychology magna cum laude, Tufts U., 1947. Sales agt., broker Ray Blanchard Real Estate, Richardson, Tex., 1965-71, Detrick Realtors, Tulsa, 1971-73; mgr. exceptional properties in Conn. Preview, Inc., N.Y.C., 1973-75; sales agt., broker Helen Benson Assocs. Realtors, Westport, 1975-82; sales mgr. Westport office William Ravies Real Estate, 1983-88; luxury homes mgr. William Ravies Real Estate, Westport, 1988, exec. v.p. exceptional properties, 1988—. Bd. dirs. New Neighbors, Westport, 1974; troop leader Boy Scouts Am., Girl Scouts U.S., 1957-59; trustee Unitarian Ch., Westport, 1975. With USN, 1944-46. Mem. AAUW, LWV, Women's Coun. Realtors, Westport-Weston Bd. Realtors, Fairfield Bd. Realtors, Westport Womens Club, Gourmet Club, Westport Hist. Soc., Richardson Symphony Assn. Republican. Congregationalist. Avocations: backgammon, theater, boating, sports. Office: William Raview Real Estate PO Box 961 Fairfield CT 06430-0961 also: 47 Riverside Ave Westport CT 06880-4215

BEERS, CHARLOTTE LENORE, advertising agency executive; b. Beaumont, Tex., July 26, 1935; d. Glen and Frances (Bolt) Rice; m. Donald C. Beers, 1971; 1 dau., Lisa. B.S. in Math. and Physics, Baylor U., Waco, Tex., 1958. Group product mgr. Uncle Ben's Inc., 1959-69; sr. v.p., dir. client services J. Walter Thompson, 1969-79; chief operating officer Tatham-Laird & Kudner, Chgo., from 1979, mng. ptnr., chmn. and chief exec officer; vice chmn. RSCG Group Roux Seguela, Cayzac & Goudard, France; chmn., CEO Ogilvy & Mather Worldwide, N.Y.C.; chmn., CEO Ogilvy Group Inc., N.Y.C., chmn. emeritus, 1997-99; chmn. J. Walter Thompson, N.Y.C., 1999—. Named Nat. Advt. Woman of Yr. Am. Advt. Fedn., 1975. Mem. Am. Assn. Advt. Agencies (chmn. from 1987), Women's Advt. Club Chgo., Chgo. Network. Republican. Episcopalian. Office: J Walter Thompson 466 Lexington Ave New York NY 10017*

BEERS, RAND, narcotics and law enforcement administrator; married; 2 children. BA in History, Dartmouth U., 1964; MA in History, U. Mich., 1971. With Fgn. Svc., Washington, 1971; dep. for strategy, ops. coord. regional affairs and security Dept. of State, Washington, dir. Office of Security Analysis, Office of Internat. Security Policy, dep. dir. Office of Policy Analysis, dep. polit. advisor to Supreme Allied Comdr., Europe, dep. asst. sec. regional affairs and export control Bur. Polit. Mil. Affairs, asst. sec. Internat. Narcotics and Law Enforcement Affairs, 1998—; dir. global issues NSC, Washington, spl. asst. to Pres., sr. dir. for intelligence programs. With USMC. Office: Dept of State Narcotics Law Enforcement 2201 C St NW Washington DC 20520-0001

BEESLEY, H(ORACE) BRENT, savings and loan executive; b. Salt Lake City, Jan. 30, 1946; s. Horace Pratt and Mary (Brazier) B.; m. Bonnie Jean Matheson, Dec. 20, 1980; children: Laura Jean, Sarah Janice, Mary Roslyn, Amy Elizabeth, David Brent, Katherine Ann, Daniel Pratt. BA, Brigham Young U., 1969; MBA, Harvard U., 1973, J.D., 1973. Bar: Utah 1973. Instr. U. Utah, Salt Lake City, 1973-81; ptnr. Ray, Quinney & Nebeker, Salt Lake City, 1977-81; dir. Fed. Savs. and Loan Ins. Corp., Washington, 1981-83; chmn., chief exec. officer Charter Savs. Corp., Jacksonville, Fla., 1983-86; pres., chief exec. officer Farm Credit Corp. Am., Denver, 1986-88; chmn., chief exec. officer Heritage Savs. Bank, St. George, Utah, 1988—. Bd. dirs. Fed. Home Loan Bank, Seattle, 1992-95, Savs. and Cmty. Bankers Am., 1992-96, Utah Heritage Found., 1978-81, Utah Arthritis Found., 1978-81. Mem. Utah State Bar Assn. Club: Alta (Salt Lake City). Home: 1492 Kristianna Cir Salt Lake City UT 84103-4221 Office: 95 E Tabernacle St Saint George UT 84770-2307

BEESON, JACK HAMILTON, composer, educator, writer; b. Muncie, Ind., July 15, 1921; children: Christopher Sigerist (dec.), Miranda. Student of music, U. Rochester, Columbia U.; studied with Béla Bartók. Tchr. Juilliard Sch. Music; former chmn. dept. music, assoc. dir. opera workshop Columbia U., N.Y.C.; MacDowell prof. emeritus Columbia U.; former sec. Alice M. Ditson Fund; former chmn. music publ. com. Columbia U. Press.; bd. dirs. Composers Recs., Inc., other mus. orgns. Composer: (operas) Jonah, Hello Out There, The Sweet Bye and Bye, Lizzie Borden (commd. by Ford Found.), My Heart's in the Highlands (commd. by NET), Captain Jinks of the Horse Marines (commd. by Nat. Endowment of Arts), Dr. Heidegger's Fountain of Youth (commd. Nat. Arts Club), Cyrano, Sorry, Wrong Number, Practice in the Art of Elocution, (for orch.) Hymns and Dances, Symphony in A, Transformations, Interludes and Arias from Cyrano (for baritone and orchestra), Two Concert Arias (for soprano and orchs.), (chamber music) Sonata for Viola and Piano, Interlude, Song, 4th and 5th Piano Sonatas, Two Diversions, Round and Round, Sonata Caronica, Old Hundredth for Organ, (vocal works) Six Lyrics, Five Songs, Eldorado, Piazza Piece, Big Crash Out West, Indiana Homecoming, Margret's Garden Aria, To a Sinister Potato, (cycles) From a Watchtower, Two by Betjeman, (countertenor and chamber ensemble) The Daring Young Man on the Flying Trapeze, numerous others, also works for voice and string quartet, and choral works including Knots, Magicke Pieces, Epitaphs. Recipient Rome prize, City of Rochester prize, Marc Blitstein Mus. Theatre award Nat. Inst. Arts and Letters, gold medal for music Nat. Arts Club, 1976, Gt. Tchrs. award Columbia U., 1979, Alumni Achievement award U. Rochester, 1985, award for Lifetime Achievement award Nat. Opera Assn., 1998; Guggenheim fellow; Fulbright fellow to Italy. Mem. ASCAP (bd. dirs. 1991-95), AAAL (treas., v.p. for music), Phi Beta Kappa. Home: 18 Seaforth Ln Huntington NY 11743-9714 Home: 404 Riverside Dr New York NY 10025-1861 Office: Columbia U Dept Music New York NY 10027

BEESON, PAUL BRUCE, physician; b. Livingston, Mont., Oct. 18, 1908; s. John Bradley and Martha Gerard (Ash) B.; m. Barbara Neal, July 10, 1942; children: John, Peter, Judith. Student, U. Wash., 1925-28; M.D., C.M., McGill U., 1933, D.Sc., 1971; D.Sc., Emory U., 1968, Albany Med. Coll., 1975, Yale U., 1975, Med. Coll. Ohio, 1979. Asst. Rockefeller Inst., 1937-39, Harvard Med. Sch., 1939-40; asst. prof. medicine Emory U. Med. Sch., 1942-46, prof., chmn. dept., 1946-52; Ensign prof. medicine, chmn. dept. internal medicine Yale Med. Sch., 1952-65; physician-in-chief univ. service Grace-New Haven Community Hosp., 1952-65; Nuffield prof. clin. medicine Oxford (Eng.) U., 1965-74; prof. medicine U. Wash., Seattle, 1974-81. Named Alumnus summa laude dignatus U. Wash., 1968, hon. knight comdr. Brit. Empire, 1973; recipient 50th Anniversary Gold medal Peter Bent Brigham Hosp., 1962; Bristol award Infectious Diseases Soc. Am., 1972; Kober medal Assn. Am. Physicians, 1973; Abraham Flexner award Assn. Am. Med. Colls., 1977; Willard Thompson award Am. Geriatrics Soc., 1984; Founders award So. Soc. Clin. Research, 1982; fellow Berkeley Coll.; fellow Yale; fellow Magdalen Coll. (hon.); fellow Green Coll. (hon.); fellow Oxford U.; Paul Buson Scholarship in Aging Rsch., 1995. Fellow Royal Coll. Physicians (London), Royal Soc. Medicine (hon.); mem. Nat Acad. Scis., Am. Acad. Arts and Scis., A.C.P. (master, John Phillips Meml. award 1976, Disting. Tchr. award 1990), Soc. Expel. Biology and Medicine, Am. Soc. Clin. Investigation, Assn. Am. Physicians (pres. 1967), Assn. Physicians Gt. Britain and Ireland. Episcopalian. Home: 21013 NE 122nd St Redmond WA 98053-5323

BEESON, VIRGINIA REED, naval officer, nurse; b. Franklin, N.J., Mar. 14, 1951; d. Colin Reed and Marion (Dailey) B. BSN magna cum laude, U. Vt., Burlington, 1973; MS in Nursing Adminstrn., Boston U., 1987. RN, Vt.; cert. in nursing adminstrn.; cert. ATLS. Commd. ensign USN, 19, advanced through grades to capt., 1994; staff and charge nurse various locations, 1973-85; charge nurse gen. surgery ward Nat. Naval Med. Ctr., Bethesda, Md., 1987-89; Nurse Corps assignment officer U.S. Navy Annex, Washington, 1989-91; head leadership tng. div. Naval Sch. Health Scis., Bethesda, 1991-95; dir. Nursing Svcs. Naval Hosp., Jacksonville, Fla., 1995-98; dep. dir. USN Nurse Corps, Washington, 1998; speaker in field. Decorated Naval Commendation medal (3), Navy Achievement medal, Meritorious Svc. medal (2). Mem. ANA, Va. Nurses Assn., Women Officers Profl. Assn., Am. Coll. Healthcare Exec., Am. Orgn. of Nurse Exec., Sigma Theta Tau. Avocations: travel, classical music, sailing. Home: #503N 2111 Jefferson Davis Hwy Arlington VA 22202 Office: Bur Medicine Surgery Code OONCB 2300 E St NW Washington DC 20372-0001

BEESTON, PAUL, professional baseball executive; b. Welland, Ont., Can.; m. Kaye Doherty, Aug. 29, 1969; children: Aimee, David. BA in Econs. and Polit. Sci., U. Western Ont., 1968. Chartered acct., Can. With Coopers and Lybrand, London, 1968-76, mgr., 1973-76; v.p. adminstrn. Toronto (Can.) Blue Jays, 1976-77, v.p. bus. ops., 1977-84, exec. v.p. bus., 1987-89, pres., COO, 1989-97, pres., CEO, 1997; pres., COO Major League Baseball, N.Y.C., 1997—; bd. dirs. Maj. League Baseball Promotion Corp., mem. com. examining Am. League expansion. Office: Major League Baseball 245 Park Ave New York NY 10167*

BEETHAM, STANLEY WILLIAMS, international management consultant; b. Montpelier, Idaho, Nov. 2, 1933; s. Harry Stanley and Mary (Williams) B.; m. Barbara Burnham, June 20, 1987; 1 child, Lara Mary. BA, Wesleyan U., 1956; MA, U. Amsterdam, The Netherlands, 1957; postgrad., Harvard U., 1958-59, U. Wash., 1959-60. Internat. market mgr. U.S. Rubber/Uniroyal, N.Y.C., 1960-63; corp. mktg. cons. GE, N.Y.C., 1963-65; assoc. dir. Benton & Bowles, Inc., N.Y.C., 1965-67; dir. corp. planning Esmark, Chgo., 1967-72, Consol. Packaging Co., Chgo., 1972-74; sr. cons. Booz Allen Hamilton/Hay Assocs., N.Y.C. and Phila., 1975-80; sr. v.p. U.S. Tobacco Co., Greenwich, Conn., 1981-87; pres. S.W. Beetham & Co., Seattle, 1987—. Contbr. articles in field. Candidate for U.S. Congress from 13th Ill. Dist., 1972, 74; chmn. roundtable Westchester (Conn.) Planning Forum; bd. dirs. AHA Internat., Rural Devel. Inst. Fulbright scholar, 1956, Marshall scholar, 1957; Woodrow Wilson fellow, 1958. Mem. N.Am. Soc. Corp. Planning, Nat. Assn. Bus. Economists, Coun. for Urban Econ. Devel., Internat. Soc. for Planing and Strategic Mgmt., Rainier Club, Phi Beta Kappa. Office: 1223 Spring St Apt 501 Seattle WA 98104-3572

BEETON, ALFRED MERLE, laboratory director, limnologist, educator; b. Denver, Aug. 15, 1927; s. Charles Frederick and Edna F. (Smith) B.; m. Mary Eileen Wilcox, July 20, 1945; children—Maureen Ann, Heather Ann, Celeste Nadine; m. Ruth Elizabeth Holland, June 4, 1966; children—Jonathan Eugene, Daniel Paul. BS, U. Mich., 1952, MS, 1954, PhD, 1958. Fishery biologist U.S. Bur. Comml. Fisheries, Ann Arbor, Mich., 1957-65; chief environ. research U.S. Bur. Comml. Fisheries, 1960-65; prof. zoology U. Wis.-Milw., 1965-76; asst. dir. U. Wis.-Milw. (Center for Gt. Lakes Studies), 1965-69, assoc. dir., 1969-73; assoc. dean U. Wis.-Milw. (Grad. Sch.), 1973-76; dir. Gt. Lakes and Marine Waters Center; prof. U. Mich., Ann Arbor, 1976-86; dir. Gt. Lakes Environ. Research Lab., Nat. Oceanic and Atmospheric Adminstrn. Dept. Commerce, Ann Arbor, 1986-96; acting chief scientist Nat Oceanic & Atmospheric Adminstrn. Dept. Commerce, Washington, 1996-97; lectr. biology Wayne State U., 1957-61; lectr. civil engring. U. Mich., 1961-65; mem. Mich. Toxic Substance Control Commn., 1987-89; U.S. chmn. Sci. Adv Bd. Internat. Joint Commn., 1986-91; mem. research adv. council Wis. Dept. Natural Resources; mem. water quality criteria com. Nat. Acad. Scis.; cons. U.S. Army C.E., 1967-73, Met. San. Dist. Chgo., 1968-76, EPA, 1973-83; adviser to Smithsonian Instn. on projects in, Ghana, Laos, Yugoslavia, 1972-82; to WHO/Pan Am. Health Orgn. in, Venezuela, 1978; mem. environ. studies bd. NRC, 1976-82, internat. environ. program com., 1977-82; adj. prof. Sch. Pub. Health U. Mich., 1993—; vis. prof. Oreg. State U., 1982; chmn. sci. adv. bd. NOAA, 1998—; mem. Ocean Rsch. Adv. Panel/Nat. Oceanographic Partnership Program. Contbr. chpts. to books; articles Ency. Brit. Mem. Internat. Assn. Theoretical and Applied Limnology, Am. Soc. Limnology and Oceanography (treas. 1962-81), Internat. Assn. Gt. Lakes Research, Mich. Acad. Sci., Arts and Letters. Home: 2761 Oakcleft St Ann Arbor MI 48103-2247

BEETS, FREEMAN HALEY, retired government official; b. Chickasha, Okla., Apr. 17, 1919; s. Daniel Walter and Ida Belle (Alverson) B.; m. Margaret Elizabeth Edwards, Dec. 25, 1941; 1 child, Susan Belle. B.A. in Journalism, U. Okla., 1946, M.A., 1948, Ed.D., 1954; LL.D., Drury Coll., Springfield, Mo., 1974. Instr. journalism Okla. Bapt. U., 1948, asst. prof. journalism and bus., 1950, dir. night sch., chmn. div. applied arts and sci., 1951-53; asst. exec. sec. edn. commn. So. Bapt. Conv., Nashville, 1953-55; dir. admissions, registrar Hardin-Simmons U., 1955-56; asst. to pres., prof. journalism U. Scis. and Arts Okla., 1956-58, pres., 1958-61; regional rep. div. coll. and univ. assistance U.S. Office of Edn., 1961-66; regional asst. commr. edn. U.S. Office of Edn., Kansas City, Mo., 1966-70; dir. div. ednl. sers. U.S. Office Edn., Kansas City, Mo., 1970-80; dep. regional rep. Office of Sec., U.S. Dept. Edn., Kansas City, Mo., 1980-84; ret., 1984. Served to 1st lt. AUS, 1941-45. Decorated Bronze Star, Purple Heart. Mem. Nat. Assn. Securities Dealers (arbitrator 1987—). Home: 107 Riviera Dr Chickasha OK 73018-7264

BEEVER, JAMES WILLIAM, III, biologist; b. Balt., Aug. 17, 1955; s. James William Jr. and Virginia Irene (Ruhlmann) B.; m. Lisa Britt Dodd, May 26, 1990. BS, Fla. State U., 1977, MS, 1979; postgrad., U. Calif., Davis, 1991. Environ. specialist Fla. Dept. of Environ. Regulation, Ft. Myers, 1984-88; resource mgmt. and rsch. coord. South West Fla. Aquatic Preserves, Bokeelia, Fla., 1988-90; biol. scientist III Fla. Game and Fresh Water Fish Commn., Punta Gorda, 1990-98, biol. scientist IV, 1998—; adj. faculty biology Edison C.C., Charlotte County; mem. tech. adv. bd. Sarasota Bay and Tampa Bay Nat. Estuary Program, Sarasota, 1989—, mem. policy com. and tech. adv. com. Charlotte Harbor Nat. Estuary Program; chair sci. com. on Mangrove Tech. Adv. Com. Fla. Dept. Environ. Protection, 1994-95; chair Fla. com. on rare and endangered plants and animals, 1994-96; expert witness in field, 1986—; coord. Conservation Plan for the Hillsborough River Greenway Area, 1995; founder Frog Listening Network, 1997. Author: Lemon Bay Aquatic Preserve Management Plan, 1988, The Cedar Point Study, 1992, Hydric Pine Flatwoods of Southwest Florida, 1994, (computer database) Resource Inventory of Species in S.W. Fla.; contbr. articles to profl. jours. Chair Grad. Student Assn., Davis, 1981-83. Regents fellowship U. Calif, 1983-84; recipient Grad. Rsch. award, 1982-83, Outstanding Profl. Achievements award Fla. DNR, 1989. Mem. Fla. Acad. Sci., Estuarine Rsch. Fedn., Soc. Wetland Scientists, Soc. for Conservation Biology, Ecol. Soc. Am., Phi Beta Kappa, Sigma Xi. Achievements include rsch. on mangrove tree crab and arboreal folivore, mangrove cutting, endangered species protection, red cockaded woodpeckers; hydric pine flatwoods, xeric oak scrub, regional wildlife habitat/wildlife corridor planning; designation Fla. ecosystems, hydrogeomorphic method for the Everglades. Office: Fla Game & Freshwater Fish 29200 Tuckers Grade Punta Gorda FL 33955-2207

BEEVER, LISA BRITT-DODD, transportation and environmental planner, researcher; b. Alton, Ill., Apr. 16, 1960; d. Ralph Everett and Martha Guinilda (Ebbersten) D.; m. James William Beever III, May 26, 1990. BS in Landscape Architecture, Tex. A&M, 1982, PhD, 1987; MLA, N.C. State U., 1983. Registered landscape architect; cert. planner. Landscape designer Dave Bost Group, Round Rock, Tex., 1983-84; teaching asst. Tex. A&M U., College Station, 1984-85; landscape planner Richardson-Verdoorn, Austin, Tex., 1985; planner Austin Parks and Recreation Dept., 1985-88; prin. planner divsn. planning Lee County, Ft. Myers, Fla., 1988-89; dir. environ. scis. Lee County, Ft. Myers, 1989-92; dir. Charlotte County-Punta Gorda (Fla.) Met. Planning Orgn., 1993—; adj. faculty Barry U., 1994—. Author several environ. regulations and transp. tech. reports, Lee County Wildlife Corridor Plan, Charlotte County Long Range Transp. Plan; contbr. articles to profl. jours. Mem., vol. landscape architect Calusa Land Trust, Pine Island, Fla., 1990—; vol. Children's Sci. Ctr., N. Ft. Myers, Fla., 1992, Profl. Placement Network, Ft. Myers, 1993. Recipient County Achievement award Nat. Assn. Counties, 1990, 91, 92, award of excellence Fla. Planning Assn., Nat. award for outstanding met. transp. planning Assn. Met. Planning Orgns., 1997, award of environ. excellence Fed. Hwy. Adminstrn., 1999. Mem. Am. Planning Assn., Fla. Native Plant Soc. (Landscape Design award), Inst. Transp. Engrs., Am. Inst. Cert. Planners, Fla. Acad. Scis. (chair urban and regional planning sect. 1991-94, pres. 1995-96). Democrat. Unitarian. Avocations: gardening, art, travel, dachshunds, hiking. Home: 306 Little Grove Ln Fort Myers FL 33917-3929 Office: Charlotte County-Punta Gorda Met Planning Orgn 28000 Airport Rd Ste A6 Punta Gorda FL 33982-2409

BEEVERS, HARRY, biologist; b. Shildon, Eng., Jan. 10, 1924; came to U.S., 1950, naturalized, 1958; s. Norman and Olive (Ayre) B.; m. Jean Sykes, Nov. 19, 1949; 1 child, Michael. BSc, U. Durham, Eng., 1945, PhD, 1947; DSc, U. Newcastle-on-Tyne, 1974, Purdue U., 1972, Nagoya U., 1986. Research fellow Oxford U., Eng., 1946-50; asst. to prof. Purdue U., West Lafayette, Ind., 1950-69; prof. biology U. Calif., Santa Cruz, 1969-90, prof. emeritus, 1990—; fellow Crown Coll. U. Calif., Santa Cruz, 1969—. Author: Respiratory Metabolism in Plants, 1961; contbr. articles to profl. jours. Recipient von Humboldt Sr. Scientist award, 1987. Mem. NAS, Am. Soc. Plant Physiologists (Stephen Hales award 1970, pres. 1960), Am. Soc. Biol. Chemists, Am. Acad. Arts and Scis., Accademia Nazionale dei Lincei, Deutsche Botanische Gesselschaft (hon.), Academia Europaea (fgn.), Bayerische Akademie der Wissenschaften (corr.). Home: 46 S Circle Dr Santa Cruz CA 95060-1816 Office: U Calif Santa Cruz Dept Biology Santa Cruz CA 95064

BEEZER, ROBERT RENAUT, federal judge; b. Seattle, July 21, 1928; s. Arnold Roswell and Josephine (May) B.; m. Hazlehurst Plant Smith, June 15, 1957; children: Robert Arnold, John Leighton, Mary Allison. Student, U. Wash., 1946-48, 51; BA, U. Va., 1951, LLB, 1956. Bar: Wash. 1956, U.S. Supreme Ct. 1968. Ptnr. Schweppe, Krug, Tausend & Beezer, P.S., Seattle, 1956-84; judge U.S. Ct. Appeals (9th cir.), Seattle, 1984-96, sr. judge, 1996—; alt. mem. Wash. Jud. Qualifications Commn., Olympia, 1981-84. 1st lt. USMCR, 1951-53. Fellow Am. Coll. Trust and Estate Counsel, Am. Bar Found.; mem. ABA, Seattle-King County Bar Assn. (pres. 1975-76), Wash. Bar Assn. (bd. govs. 1980-83). Clubs: Rainier, Tennis (Seattle). Office: US Ct Appeals 802 US Courthouse 1010 5th Ave Seattle WA 98104-1130

BEGALA, JOHN ADELBERT, human service administrator; b. Akron, Ohio, Nov. 29, 1950; s. Joseph William and Harriet (Kilb) B.; m. Carole Tate, Dec. 18, 1981; 1 child, Stephen T. BA, Kent State U., 1972, MA, 1975. Councilman-at-large City of Kent, 1973-76; mem. Ohio Ho. of Reps., Columbus, 1977-82; dep. dir. Ohio Dept. Mental Retardation/Developmental Disabilities, Columbus, 1983-85; v.p. Greater Cin. Hosp. Coun., 1986-90; assoc. v.p. U. Cin. Med. Ctr., 1991-94; sr. v.p. MetroHealth Sys., Cleve., 1994-97; exec. dir. Fedn. Cmty. Planning, Cleve., 1998—; adj. faculty U. Cin., 1986-94. Columnist Planning & Action, 1998—. Avocation: music. Office: Fedn Cmty Planning 614 W Superior Ave Ste 300 Cleveland OH 44113

BEGALA, KATHLEEN, consumer safety organization administrator. BS, U. Tex., 1981. Dir. info. and pub. affairs Consumer Product Safety Commn., 1994—. Office: Consumer Product Safety Commn 4330 East West Hwy Bethesda MD 20814

BEGAM, ROBERT GEORGE, lawyer; b. N.Y.C., Apr. 5, 1928; s. George and Hilda M. (Hirt) B.; m. Helen C. Clark, July 24, 1949; children—Richard, Lorinda, Michael. B.A., Yale U., 1949, LL.B., 1952. Bar: N.Y. bar 1952, Ariz. bar 1956, U.S. Dist. Ct. Ariz. 1957, U.S. Ct. Appeals (9th cir.) 1958, U.S Supreme Ct. 1973. Assoc. firm Cravath, Swaine & Moore, N.Y.C., 1952-54; spl. counsel State of Ariz., Colorado River Litigation in U.S. Supreme Ct., 1956-58; pres. Begam, Lewis Marks & Wolfe, P.A., Phoenix. Author: Fireball, 1987. Pres. Ariz. Repertory Theater, 1960-66, trustee Atla Roscoe Pound Found.; bd. dirs. Phoenix Theater Ctr., 1955-60, 87-92, Boys Clubs of Met. Phoenix; bd. govs. Welzmann Inst. Sci., Rehovot, Israel; pres. Am. Com. for Welzmann Inst. of Sci. Fellow Internat. Soc. Barristers; mem. Assn. Trial Lawyers Am. (pres. 1976-77, chmn. polit. action com. 1979-86), Western Trial Lawyers Assn. (pres. 1970), Am. Bd. Trial Advocates (bd. dirs.), State Bar Ariz. (cert. specialist in injury and wrongful death litigation). Clubs: Yale (N.Y.C.), Desert Highlands Country (Scottsdale, Ariz.), Pinetop Country (Pinetop, Ariz.), Wig and Pen (London). Avocations: writing, theater, golf. Office: Begam Lewis Marks & Wolfe 111 W Monroe St Ste 1400 Phoenix AZ 85003-1787

BEGANDO, JOSEPH SHERIDAN, retired university chancellor, educator; b. Roseland, Kans., Jan. 7, 1921; s. James and Bessie (Barcus) B.; m. Virginia DeVillo Suttee, Aug. 6, 1943; children: DeVillo Begando Janecek, Dana Ann Begando Rodziewicz, Darcy V. BS, Pittsburg (Kans.) State U., 1942; MS, U. Ill., 1947, PhD, 1951. Asst. in mktg. U. Ill., 1946-47, instr., 1948-51; instr. commerce Pittsburg State U., 1947-48, asst. prof. econs., summer 1951; asst. prof. mktg. U. Kans., 1951-53; asst. dean, asso. prof. pharmacy adminstrn. U. Ill., Chgo., 1953-58, asst. to pres., 1958-61, v.p. univ., 1961-66; chancellor U. Ill. Med Center, Chgo., 1966-83; chancellor emeritus U. Ill. Med Center, 1983—, prof. health resources mgmt. Sch. Pub. Health, 1982-95. Citizen fellow Inst. Medicine, Chgo., 1985. Served to lt. (s.g.) USCG, 1942-45. Recipient Meritorious Achievement award Pittsburg State U., 1959, Disting. Service award U. Ill. Alumni Assn., 1983. Mem. Assn. Acad. Health Centers (pres. 1976-77), Assn. Am. Med. Colls., Pi Omega Pi, Beta Gamma Sigma, Alpha Kappa Psi, Rho Chi, Delta Kappa Sigma, Phi Delta Chi. Club: Univ. (Chgo.). Home: 842 Washington St Elmhurst IL 60126-4841

BEGELL, WILLIAM, publisher; b. Wilno, Poland, May 18, 1928; came to U.S., 1947, naturalized, 1953; s. Ferdinand and Liza (Kowarski) Beigel; m. Esther Kessler, May 27, 1948; children: Frederick Paul (dec.), Alissa Maya. BChemE, CCNY, 1953; MChemE, Poly. Inst. Bklyn., 1958; postgrad., Columbia U., 1958-59; DSc, Acad. Sci. BSSR, Minsk, 1984. Engring. mgr. heat transfer research facility dept. chem. engring. Columbia U., 1953-59; co-founder, exec. v.p. Scripta Technica, Inc., Washington, 1959-74; founder, pres. Hemisphere Publishing Corp., Washington, 1974-91, Begell House, Inc., Pubs., N.Y.C., 1991—; pres., chief scientist Byelocorp Sci., Inc., 1991—; dir. Supco Internat. Engring. Corp., Milan, 1994—; lectr. pub. George Washington U., Washington, also N.Y. U.; cons. Heat Transfer Research Lab., Columbia U.; cons. in field. Editor 7 books; contbr. numerous articles on heat transfer to profl. jours. Mem. nat. adv. bd. ctr. for the Book, Libr. of Congress; chmn. exec. coun. Profl. and Scholarly Pubs.; bd. dirs. Am. Fedn. for the Blind. Recipient Benjamin Gomez award book pub. div. Anti-Defamation League, 1984. Mem. AAAS, Am. Inst. Chem. Engrs., Am. Soc. for Engring. Edn., ASME (communications bd. Fellow, 1996, Disting. Svc. award 1992), Assn. Am. Publishers (dir.), N.Y. Acad. Scis. (publs. bd.), Internat. Centre for Heat and Mass Transfer, Washington Book Publishers (founder), Am. Assn. Engring. Socs. Jewish. Patentee in field. Home: 46 E 91st St New York NY 10128-1350 Office: Begell House Inc Pubs 79 Madison Ave New York NY 10016-7802*

BEGELMAN, MITCHELL CRAIG, astrophysicist, educator. AB, AM, Harvard U., 1974; PhD, U. Cambridge, Eng., 1978. Asst. prof. dept. astrophys., planetary and atmospheric scis. U. Colo., Boulder, 1982-87, assoc. prof., 1987-91, prof., 1991—, assoc. chair, 1992-95, chmn., 1995-98, fellow Joint Inst. for Lab. Astrophysics, 1984—. Recipient Presdl. Young Investigator award, 1984, Sci. Writing award Am. Inst. Physics, 1996; Alfred P. Sloan Found. rsch. fellow, 1987-91; John Simon Guggenheim fellow, 1998-99. Fellow Royal Astron. Soc., Cambridge Phil. Soc.; mem. Am. Astron. Soc. (Helen B. Warner prize 1988). Office: U Colo Joint Inst Lab Astrophysics PO Box 440 Boulder CO 80309-0440

BEGERT, JEROME FRANCIS, writer; b. Lewiston, Maine, July 13, 1927; s. James Henry and Agnes Victorine Begert; m. Eleanor Mathilda Couri, Feb. 16, 1952; children: Kathleen Diane (dec.), Jerome Karl. BA in Philosophy, U. Maine, Orono, 1950. Civil servant U.S. Govt., Washington, 1950-74, cons., 1987-93. Author: Door Openings, 1997. With USN, 1945-46, PTO. Recipient WWII Victory medal USN, 1945-46, Am. Area medal, 1945-46, Civilian Svcs. medal U.S. Govt., Vietnam, 1969-71, cert. of exceptional svc., 1969-71. Avocation: philosophy. Home: 40 Whistler Landing Scarborough ME 04074

BEGERT, MATTHEW, engineering company official; b. Topeka, July 19, 1950; s. John Frederick and Betty Lykel (Prosser) B.; m. Pamela Helen Weidman, Nov. 12, 1982; 1 child, Eric Matthew. BS in Journalism and Mass Comm., U. Kans., 1972, BA in Anthropology, 1973; grad. with honors, Naval War Coll., 1994. Commd. officer USMC, 1973, advanced through grades to lt. col., 1991; exec. officer 1st Air and Naval Gunfire

Liaison Co., Oceanside, Calif., 1984-87; ops. action officer 3d Marine Aircraft Wing, El Toro, Calif., 1987-88; adminstr., exec. officer Marine Strike Fighter Squadron 121, El Toro, 1988-89; ops. officer Marine Aircraft Group 11, El Toro, 1989-91; exec. officer Marine Aviation Tng. Support Group, Oak Harbor, Wash., 1991-94; dep. dir. Precision Guided Weapons Countermeasures, White Sands Range, N.Mex., 1994-99; project leader The Aerospace Corp., El Segundo, Calif., 1999—; mem. integrated process team J.F. Begert and Sons, Lawrence, Kans., 1985—; cons. Abraxas Techs., Burbank, Calif., 1994-96; contbr. Nat. Security Studies Program, Calif. State U., San Bernardino, 1995-96; investigative reporter Wings Pub. Co., Houston, 1995-96. Screenwriter Beck Prodns., La Canada, Calif., 1994-96; dir., playwright White Sands Missile Range Cmty. Theatre, 1995-97. Decorated Navy Commendation medal with gold star Sec. of the Navy, 1987, Air medal with combat V, Sec. of the Navy, 1993, Meritorious Svc. medal Sec. of the Navy, 1994. Mem. Nat. Def. Indsl. Assn., Nat. Tactical Officers Assn., Airplane Owners and Pilots Assn., Mesilla Valley Track Club, Nat. Geog. Soc. Office: Nat Law Enforcement and Corrections Tech Ctr Western Region 2350 El Segundo Blvd El Segundo CA 90245-4691

BEGERT, WILLIAM J., lieutenant general United States Air Force. BS, U.S. Air Force Acad., 1968; grad., Squadron Officer Sch., Maxwell AFB, Ala., 1974; MPA, U. Colo., 1980; student, Air Command and Staff Coll., Maxwell AFB, Ala., 1981, Nat. War Coll., Ft. Lesley J. McNair, Washington, 1985; Mgmt. Program for Execs., U. Pitts., 1990; Program for Sr. Execs. in Nat. Security, John F. Kennedy Sch. Govt., Harvard, 1995. Pilot, aircraft comdr. 20th Mil. Airlift Squadron USAF, Dover AFB, Del., 1969-71; combat crew tng. USAF, Hurlburt Field, Fla., 1971; forward air controller, flight examiner pilot 20th tactical support squadron USAF, DA Nang Air Base, Vietnam, 1972-73; pilot, flight examiner 9th mil. airlift squadron 436th Airlift Wing, Dover AFB, Del., 1973-77; mil. instr. U.S. Air Force Acad., Colorado Springs, 1977-78, air officer commanding Cadet Squadron 20, 1978-80; comdr. and wing exec. officer 436th Mil. Airlift Wing, Dover AFB, Del., 1981-82; squadron comdr. 3d Mil. Airlift Squadron, Dover AFB, Del., 1983-84; from mobility forces programmer to chief mobility forces divsn., directorate of programs Hdqtrs. USAF, Washington, 1985-88; vice comdr. then comdr. 436th Mil. Airlift Wing USAF, Dover AFB, Del., 1988-90; comdr. 60th Mil. Airlift Wing USAF, Travis AFB, Calif.; chief of staff Hdqtrs. U.S. Transp. Command, Scott AFB, Ill., 1992-94; comdr. USAF Mobility Warfare Ctr., Air Mobility Command, McGuire AFB, N.J., 989-90; dir. ops. and logistics Hdqtrs. U.S. Transp. Command, Scott AFB, Ill., 1995-97; vice comdr. Hdqtrs. U.S. Forces in Europe, Ramstein Air Base, Germany. Decorated Defense Disting. Svc. medal, Defense Superior Svc. medal, Legion of Merit with oak leaf cluster, Disting. Flying Cross with oak leaf cluster, Meritorious Svc. medal with oak leaf cluster, Air medal with 11 oak leaf clusters. Office: USAFE/CV Unit 2050 Box 1 APO AE 09094-0501

BEGG, CYNTHIA I., health facility administrator; b. Legazpi, Albay, The Philippines, Oct. 28, 1957; d. Maximo and Leonila Imperial; m. Gerard J.A. Begg, Dec. 28, 1983; 1 child, Kristen. BSN, Aquinas U., Albay, The Philippines, 1980; M in health adminstrn., Chapman Univ., 1998. Staff nurse St. Joseph Hosp., Orange, Calif., 1985-90; supr. Magnolia Outpatient Surgery Ctr., Westminster, Calif., 1991-94, adminstr., 1995—. Office: Magnolia Outpatient Surgery Ctr 14571 Magnolia St Westminster CA 92683-5574

BEGGS, DONALD LEE, university chancellor; b. Harrisburg, Ill., Sept. 16, 1941; s. C. J. and Mary (Fitzgerald) B.; m. Shirley Malone, Mar. 19, 1963; children: Brent A., Pamela A. B.S. in Edn., So. Ill. U., 1963, M.S. in Edn., 1964; Ph.D., U. Iowa, 1966. Prof. So. Ill. U., Carbondale, 1966—, assoc. dean grad. sch., 1970-71, asst. dean edn., 1973-75, acting asst. v.p. acad. affairs, 1975-76, assoc. dean edn., 1975-81, dean Coll. Edn., 1981-96, chancellor, 1996-98; pres. Wichita (Kans.) State U., 1998—; cons. Quincy Pub. Schs., Ill., 1974-79, Chgo. Pub. Schs., 1977-80, Ill. State Bd. Edn., 1966—, Nat. Inst. Edn., Washington, 1983. Author: Measurement and Evaluation in the Schools, Evaluation and Decision Making in the Schools, 1971, Research Design in the Behavioral Sciences, 1969, Nat. Standardized Tests, 1980. Mgr. sports, Carbondale, 1979; active United Way Campaign, 1978, Carbondale Schs. PTA, 1972-83. Named Outstanding Tchr. in Edn. Coll. Edn., 1969; Ill. State Bd. Edn. grantee, 1979; Ill. Supt. Pub. Instrn. grantee, 1968; U.S. Office Edn. grantee, 1969. Mem. Am. Edn. Research Assn. (sec. div. D. 1976-79), Ill. Pub. Sch. Deans of Edn. (chmn. 1982-83), Research and Evaluation Adv. Council Ill. Office Edn. (chmn. 1982-83), Phi Delta Kappa (named one of 75 Young Leaders 1981). Office: Wichita State Univ Office of Pres 1845 Fairmount Wichita KS 67260-0001*

BEGGS, PATRICIA K., performing company executive. BA, Stephens Coll.; MBA, U. Cin. Mktg. dir. Provident Bank; with pub. rels. dept. Ctrl. Trust Co.; dir. mktg. Cin. Opera, 1984-91, asst. mng. dir., 1991-97, mng. dir., 1997—. Office: Cin Opera Assn Music Hall 1241 Elm St Cincinnati OH 45210-2231*

BEGHE, RENATO, federal judge; b. Chgo., Mar. 12, 1933; s. Bruno and Emmavve (Frymire) B.; m. Bina House, July 10, 1954; children: Eliza Ashley, Francesca Forbes, Adam House, Jason Deneen. B.A., U. Chgo., 1951, J.D., 1954. Bar: N.Y. 1955. Practiced in N.Y.C.; assoc. Carter, Ledyard & Milburn, 1954-65, ptnr., 1965-83; ptnr. Morgan, Lewis & Bockius, 1983-89; judge U.S. Tax Ct., Washington, 1991—; lectr. N.Y. U. Fed. Tax Inst., 1967, 78, U. Chgo. Fed. Tax Conf., 1974, 80, 86, also other profl. confs. Mng. editor U. Chgo. Law Rev., 1953-54; contbr. articles to profl. jours. Mem. ABA, Internat. Bar Assn., N.Y. State Bar Assn. (chmn. tax sect. 1977-78), Assn. of Bar of City of N.Y. (chmn. art law com. 1980-83), Am. Law Inst., Internat. Fiscal Assn., Am. Coll. Tax Counsel, America-Italy Soc. Inc. (bd. dirs. 1980-92), Phi Beta Kappa, Order of Coif, Phi Gamma Delta. Home: 633 E St SE Washington DC 20003-2716 Office: US Tax Ct 400 2nd St NW Washington DC 20217

BEGLARIAN, GRANT, foundation executive, composer, consultant; b. Tiflis, Republic of Georgia, Dec. 1, 1927; came to U.S., 1947, naturalized, 1954; s. Boghos and Arax (Boghosian) B.; m. Joyce Heeney, Sept. 2, 1950; children: Eve, Spencer. B.M., U. Mich., 1950, M.Mus., 1952, D.M.A.; univ. Regents creative arts fellow, 1958. Ford Found. composer in residence Cleveland Heights (Ohio) Schs., 1959-60; editor Prentice Hall Inc., 1960-61; pres. Music Book Assocs., N.Y.C.; also field rep. and project dir. Ford Found., 1961-68; dean, prof. music Sch. Performing Arts, U. So. Calif., 1969-82; pres. Nat. Found. for Advancement of Arts, 1982-91; lectr. and cons. in arts and edn.; adv. for arts in state and nation, pub. and pvt. sectors; mem. music coun. Yale U., 1974-76; mem. music adv. coun. Princeton U.; mem. panel Inst. Internat. Edn., NEA; founding prin. The Group, N.Y., 1991—; sr. adv. Am. Mus., Giverny, France, 1992-94, Fund for Arts and Culture Ctrl. and Ea. Europe, 1993—; Nat. Guild Cmty. Schs. for Arts, 1994-96; internat. coord. Advance Network and Svcs., 1996—. Compositions include String Quartet, 1947, Violin Sonata, 1949, Cello Sonata, 1952, Divertimento for Orchestra, 1957, Nurse's Song; for chorus and orch., 1960, Sinfonia for Orch., 1961, A Hymn for Our Times; for multiple bands, 1967, Fables . . . for Cellist and Actor, 1971, Diversions, 1973, Sinfonia for Strings, 1974, To Manitou!, 1976, Elegy for Cellist, 1979, Partita for Orch., 1986. Served with U.S. Army, 1952-54. Recipient Gershwin award Meml. Found., 1959, Grammy award, 1996; Ford Found. grantee, 1959, 62, 68. Mem. ASCAP (ann. award com. 1965-85), Am. String Tchrs. Assn. (Disting. Svc. award 1992), Internat. Coun. Fine Arts Dean (pres. 1980-82), Am. Music Ctr., Coll. Music Soc., Nat. Ad Hoc Forum of Film/Video Schs., Arts Edn. Consultancy in U.S., Gt. Britain, USSR, Eastern Europe, Israel, Mex., Japan, Iran, Century Assn. (N.Y.). Mem. Armenian Apostolic Ch. Office: 141 River Rd Scarborough NY 10510-2429 *As a composer and teacher I am convinced that artists inform, instruct, change, improve and affect society through their work. Art is a product of a person's craft, genius and dreams. It is essentially a private activity. The marvel of art is that this private vision has an enduring public impact.*

BEGLEY, DENNIS, radio station executive. Intern Sta. WPEN/WMGK, Bala Cynwyd, Pa., 1981, account exec., 1982-86, v.p., gen. mgr., 1996—; with CBS Radio Reps., 1986-89; nat. sales mgr., gen. mgr. Sta. WOGL, 1989-96; v.p., gen. mgr. Sta. WMMR-WXXM. Mem. Phila. Advt. Club (v.p.). Office: WPEN 1 Bala Plz Fl 3D Bala Cynwyd PA 19004-1403*

BEGLEY, ED, JR., actor; b. Hollywood, Calif., Sept. 16, 1949; s. Edward James and Allene Jeanne (Sanders) B.; m. Ingrid Margaret Taylor (div.); children: Amanda, Nicholas. Student, Los Angeles Valley Coll. Actor (theatre) Love Letters, The Cryptogram, (films) including Cat People, The In-Laws, Goin' South, Citizen's Band, Blue Collar, Stay Hungry, Private Lessons, Buddy Buddy, The One and Only, Airport 79, Showdown, Transylvania 6-5000, Protocol, The Accidental Tourist, Meet The Applegates, Scenes from The Class Struggle in Beverly Hills, She Devil, Dark Horse, Mastergate, Page Master, Even Cowgirls get the Blues, Cooperstown, Sensations, Renaissance Man, Greedy, Batman Forever, Santa With Muscles, Lay of the Land, Ms. Bear, Joey, I'm Losing You, Addams Family Reunion, others; (TV movies) A Shining Season, Elvis, Amateur Night at the Dixie, Dead of Night, Rascals & Robbers, Hot Rod, An American Love Affair, Spies, Lies and Naked Thighs, The Incredible Ida Early, Roman Holiday, Home, In the Best Interest of the Child, Not a Penny More, Not a Penny Less, 1990, A Change of Heart, Story Lady, Stand Off At Marion, Exclusive, World War II: When the Lions Roared, Jacks, The Late Shift, Alone, Not in This Town, Murder She Purred: A Mrs. Murphy Mystery; (TV series) Mary Hartman, Mary Hartman, Battlestar Galactica, Roll Out, Room 222, St. Elsewhere, Parenthood, Winnetka Road, Todays Environment, Meego, Maggie Day, Meego; also numerous TV commls., night club performances; dir. Enemies of Laughter, 1999; TV guest appearances include Quincy, The Love Boat, Touched by an Angel, 3rd Rock from the Sun, Star Trek: Voyager, Sabrina, The Teenage Witch, The Drew Carey Show, Ellen, The Simpsons, others. Chmn. Santa Monica Mountains Conservancy; commr. environ. affairs, L.A. Democrat. Roman Catholic. Avocations: carpentry; organic gardening, environmental concerns. *

BEGLEY, EVELYN MARIA, special education educator; b. N.Y.C., July 7, 1953; d. Peter Francis and Theresa Rose Begley. BA in English, L.I. Univ., 1977; MA in Spl. Edn. with Splty. in Deaf Edn., Columbia U., 1983. Cert. in transliteration, sign. lang. interpreter. Interpreter N.Y. Soc. for the Deaf, N.Y.C., 1975-83, 86-93; tchr. of the deaf St. Francis De Sales Sch., Bklyn., 1983-86, La Guardia C.C., Queens, N.Y., 1992—. Contbr. to book Insider's Baseball, 1983. Avocations: baseball, movies, arts and crafts, writing. Home and Office: 625 E 14th St New York NY 10009

BEGLEY, KATHLEEN A., communications trainer and writer; b. Phila., Mar. 28, 1948; d. Thomas and Kathleen (Harvey) B.; m. Joseph J. Strub, Sept. 11, 1993. BA in English Lit., Temple U., 1970; MA in Polit. Sci., Villanova U., 1974; postgrad., Wilmington Coll., 1998. Cert. Myers-Briggs Type Indicator Adminstr., Internat. Bd. Certified Trainers. Reporter Delaware County Daily Times, 1966-69, Camden (N.J.) Courier Post, 1970, Phila. Inquirer, 1971-76, Chgo. Daily News, 1977-78; prodr. Sta. WITF-TV, Hershey, Pa., 1979; pres. Bear Group Inc., Tampa, Fla., 1980-82; writer Seattle Times, 1983-87; prin. The Write Co., Wilmington, Del., Del./Pa., West Chester, Pa., 1987—; leader onsite programs DuPont, J.P. Morgan, Land Rover, Bell Atlantic, County of Maui, Hawaii, others; clients include The Castle Group, Dun & Bradstreet, and Skillpath; trainer of more than 20,000 people in N.Am., Europe, and Asia. Author: Deadline, 1977; also 6 multimedia tng. programs, including workbooks, instr. manuals, and videos. Mem. ASTD, Am. Mgmt. Assn. Avocations: walking, dogs, movies, self-help. Home: 1212 Fox Glove Ln West Chester PA 19380-5837 Office: Write Co Plus 1554 Paoli Pike Ste 301 West Chester PA 19380-6123

BEGLEY, LOUIS, lawyer, writer; b. Stryj, Poland, Oct. 6, 1933; came to U.S., 1948, naturalized, 1953; s. Edward David Begley and Frances Hauser; m. Sally Higginson, Feb. 11, 1956 (div. May 1970); children: Peter Higginson, Amey B. Larmore, Adam C.; m. Anne Muhlstein Dujarric le la Riviere, Mar. 30, 1974. AB summa cum laude, Harvard U., 1954, LLB magna cum laude, 1959. Bar: N.Y. 1961. Assoc. Debevoise & Plimpton, N.Y.C., 1959-67, ptnr., 1968—; sr. vis. lectr. Wharton Sch., U. Pa., Phila., 1985, 86; lectr. legal topics People's Republic China, 1983, 87, 88, 89. Author: Wartime Lies, 1991, The Man Who Was Late, 1993, As Max Saw It., 1994. With U.S. Army, 1954-56. Recipient Jeanette Schocken Preis, 1955, Irish Times-Aer Lingus Internat. Fiction Prize, 1991, Ernest Hemingway Found. award, 1992, Prix Medicis Etranger, 1992. Mem. Am. Arbitration Assn. (arbitrator), Assn. Bar of City of N.Y. (various voms. 1960—), PEN Am. Ctr. (pres. 1993-95), Coun. Fgn. Rels., Century Assn. Democrat. Office: Debevoise & Plimpton 875 3rd Ave Fl 23 New York NY 10022-6256

BEGLEY, SHARON LYNN, journalist; b. Englewood, N.J., June 14, 1956; d. John Joseph and Shirley (Wintner) B.; m. Edward Groth III, July 24, 1983; children: Sarah, Daniel. BA, Yale U., 1977. Sci. editor Newsweek, N.Y.C., 1982—. Office: Newsweek 251 W 57th St New York NY 10019-1802*

BEGLEY, THOMAS D., JR., lawyer; b. Phila., May 2, 1938; s. Thomas Devlin and Margaret (Moore) B.; m. Anne E. Glass, June 24, 1961 (dec. Feb. 1977); children: Thomas D. III, Sharon A., Mark L., Colleen I. Student, Georgetown U., 1959, Georgetown U., 1962. Pvt. practice Begley, Begley & Fendrick, P.C., Moorestown, N.J., 1962—; senator Georgetown U. Senate, Washington, 1962—. Author: How to Develop and Manage a Successful Trust & Estates/Elde-Law Practice, 1997; (with others) New Jersey Elder Law Practice, 1997. V.p. South N.J. Alzheimers Assn.; bd. dirs. Moorestown Bd. Edn. Found. Fellow Nat. Acad. Elder Law Attys. (bd. dirs.); mem. N.J. Bar Assn. (past chmn. elder law sect., past chmn. bd. consultors real property probate and trust law sect. 1989—). Republican. Roman Catholic. Avocations: swimming, boating, travel. Office: Begley Begley & Fendrick PC 509 S Lenola Rd Bldg 7 Moorestown NJ 08057-3310

BEGLINGER, SUSAN MARIE, marriage and family therapist, rehabilitation counselor; b. Huntington Park, Calif., Nov. 21, 1948; m. William Christian Beglinger, Jan. 29, 1969; children: Bryen, Erin. BS in Med. Microbiology, No. Ariz. U., 1976; MS in Counseling, U. Nev., Las Vegas, 1992. Lic. marriage and family therapist, Nev.; cert. rehab. counselor, family therapist, disability analyst, drug and alcohol abuse counselor, Nev. Rehab. cons. Lynn Maguire Phys. Therapy, Las Vegas, 1992-97, Green Valley Spine and Sports, Henderson, Nev., 1995-97; marriage and family therapist, program dir. Cmty. Counseling Ctr., Las Vegas, 1993-96; patient and family therapist Columbia Sunrise Health Strategies, Las Vegas, 1996—; co-chmn. Nev. Partnership for a Drug Free Am., Las Vegas, 1994-96; therapist U. Nev. Sch. Medicine, Las Vegas, 1998. Bd. dirs., v.p. Susan G. Komen Breast Cancer Found., 1998, pres., 1999—. Named Disting. Women of So. Nev., 1995, 97, 99. Fellow Am. Bd. Disability Analysts; mem. ACA, Am. Soc. Clin. Hypnosis, Am. Assn. Marriage and Family Therapists (clin. mem.), Am. Soc. Clin. Pathologists (assoc.). Office: 3131 La Canada Ste 108 Las Vegas NV 89109

BEHA, ANN MACY, architect; b. N.Y.C., June 26, 1950; m. Robert A. Radloff, June 21, 1975; children: Macy, Allison. BA, Wellesley Coll., 1972; MArch, MIT, 1975; Loeb fellow, Harvard U., 1987-88. Registered architect, Mass., N.Y., Conn., Maine, R.I., Fla., N.H., Oreg., Mich. Asst. to head archtl. dept. MIT, Cambridge, 1975-78; pres. Ann Beha Assocs., Inc., Boston, 1978—. Featured in and contbr. articles to profl. jours. Trustee Soc. for Preservation New Eng. Antiquities, Boston; mem. adv. bd. Hist. Mass. Inc., Boston. Recipient Lifetime Achievement award Victoria Soc. Am., 1994, Conservation award, 1979, Merit award Am. Wood Coun., 1989, 25th Anniversary Preservation award Mass. Hist. Commn., 1988, Gov.'s Preservation award citation, 1982, Gov.'s Design award Commonwealth Mass., 1986, Tucker award for Design Excellence Bldg. Stone Inst., 1985, 86, Preservation award Hist. Neighborhoods Found., 1985. Fellow AIA; mem. Assn. for Preservation Tech., Boston Soc. Architects, Alpha Ro Chi. Avocation: painting. Office: 33 Kingston St Boston MA 02111-2208

BEHARRELL, STEVEN RODERIC, lawyer; b. Harpenden, Hertfordshire, Eng., Dec. 22, 1944; s. Douglas Wells and Pamela (Pearman) B.; m. Julia Elizabeth Powell, June 10, 1967 (dec.); children: Victoria Jane, Rebecca Clare; m. Mary Rebecca Mortimer, Sept. 1, 1995; 1 child, Natasha R. Cours de civilisation, Brit. Inst., Paris, 1963, Coll. Law, London, 1968. Articled clk. Denton Hall Burgin & Warrens, London, 1966-68, ptnr., 1973-90; founder, sr. ptnr. Beharrell, Thompson & Co., London, 1990-93; ptnr. Coudert Bros., London, 1993—. Mem. Internat. Bar Assn. (mem. law soc.), Worshipful Co. Drapers (freeman). Avocations: shooting, fishing, sailing. Office: Coudert Bros. 60 Cannon St, London EC4N 6JP, England

BEHARRIELL, FREDERICK JOHN, German and comparative literature educator; b. Toronto, Ont., Can., June 5, 1918; came to U.S., 1946, naturalized, 1958; s. Frederick Roy and Anna Beatrice (Moffatt) B.; m. Barbara Jean McBroom, June 16, 1942; children—Ruth, Shirley. *Beharelles lived in northern France (Arras) as early as 1500 and are still found there. By 1581 Protestant Beharelles had fled to Canterbury, England; in 1628 others emigrated from Ghent and Leiden to Hull, Yorkshire. In the twentieth century two were knighted. Great-great-grandfather Isaac Beharrell emigrated to Canada from Hull in the 1840's with eight children.* B.A. with honors, U. Toronto, 1939, M.A., 1946; Ph.D., U. Wis., 1950. Lectr. U. Toronto, 1945-46; instr. Ind. U., Bloomington, 1948-53; asst. prof. German Ind. U., 1953-58, assoc. prof., 1958-64, prof., 1964-69; prof. German and comparative lit. SUNY, Albany, 1968—. Contbr. over 30 studies in books and profl. jours. Served with RCAF, 1942-45. Guggenheim fellow, 1965; Fulbright sr. research fellow, Austria, 1965; fellow Inst. Humanistic Studies, 1977—. Mem. MLA, AAUP, Am. Assn. Tchrs. German, Nat. Assn. Psychoanalytic Criticism, Internat. Arthur Schnitzler Research Assn., Am. Comparative Lit. Assn., Am. Assn. Advancement Humanities, Am. Com. Study of Austrian Lit., Am. Goethe Soc. Home: 1969 Village Rd Niskayuna NY 12309-5535

BEHBEHANI, ABBAS M., clinical virologist, educator; b. Iran, July 27, 1925; came to U.S., 1946, naturalized, 1964; s. Ahmad M. and Roguia B. (Tasougi) B.; married; children—Ray, Allen, Bita. B.A., Ind. U., 1949; M.S., U. Chgo., 1951; Ph.D., Southwestern Med. Sch., U. Tex., 1955. Asst. prof. Baylor U. Coll. Medicine, Houston, 1960-64; assoc. prof. pathology U. Kans. Sch. Medicine, Kansas City, 1967-72; prof. U. Kans. Sch. Medicine, 1972-90, prof. emeritus, 1990—. Author three books, more than 70 articles. Fellow Am. Acad. Microbiology; mem. AAAS, Am. Soc. Microbiology, Soc. Exptl. Biology and Medicine. Moslem. Current research on history of smallpox, history of yellow fever and Persian founders of Islamic medicine during middle ages. Home: 5415 Hazen Ave Kansas City KS 66106-3229 Office: U Kans Med Ctr Dept Pathology & Lab Med Kansas City KS 66160

BEHLAR, PATRICIA ANN, political science educator; b. New Orleans, Jan. 16, 1939; d. James Edward and Maude Albertine (Davis) B. BA, U. New Orleans, 1966; MA, La. State U., 1968, PhD, 1974. Instr. Northwestern State U. of La., Natchitoches, 1971-72; instr. Pan Am. U., Edinburg, Tex., 1974-76; asst. prof. Pan Am. U., Edinburg, 1976-77, U. Ark., Pine Bluff, 1977-84; asst. prof. Pittsburg (Kans.) State U., 1986-92, assoc. prof., 1992—; mem. U. Ark. Pine Bluff Winthrop Rockefeller lectures steering com., 1980-82; referee Ark. Polit. Sci. Jour., 1983-84; alt., edit. com. Univ. Press of Kans., 1991-93; mem., edit. com. Univ. Press of Kans., 1993-95; book rev. editor, The Midwest Quarterly, 1994—. Contbg. author ref. books. Audio reader for the blind, Pittsburg, 1992. Recipient La. State U. fellowship, 1970-71. Mem. Am. Polit. Sci. Assn., Sou. Polit. Sci. Assn., Kans. Polit. Sci. Assn., Southwestern Social Sci. Assn., Phi Kappa Phi. Democrat. Roman Catholic. Avocations: reading, walking, bird watching. Home: 508 Hobson Dr Pittsburg KS 66762-6315 Office: Pittsburg State U Dept Social Sci Pittsburg KS 66762

BEHLER, ROBERT F., military officer; m. Naomi Behler. BS in Aerospace Engring. magna cum laude, U. Okla., 1970, MS in Aerospace Engring. summa cum laude, 1972; MBA, Marymount U., 1991. Commd. 2nd lt. USAF, 1972, advanced through grades to brig. gen., 1996—; instr. C-9A aircraft comdr. 11th Aeromed. Airlift Squadron, Scott AFB, Ill., 1973-76; instr. Air Force test Pilot Sch., Edwards AFB, Calif., 1976-80; ops. officer Office of Advanced Manned Vehicle, Edwards AFB, Calif., 1980-81; SR-71 aircraft comdr., T-38 instr. pilot, ops. officer 1st Reconnaissance Squadron, Beale AFB, Calif., 1982-85; dep. comdr. ops. Detachment 4, 9 SRW RAF, Mildenhall, Eng., 1985-86; comdr. 31st Test and Evaluation Squadron, Edwards AFB, 1986-88; asst. for strategic sys. to dir. operational test/eval. Office of Sec. Def., 1988-90; Nat. Security fellow Harvard U., Cambridge, Mass., 1990-91; spl. asst. to dir. ops. 9th Ops. Group, Beale AFB, Calif., 1991, comdr., 1991-93; chief Senate Liaison Office Office of Sec. Air Force, Washington, 1993-95; comdr. 9th Reconnaissance Wing, Beale AFB, 1995-97; dir. C41 Sys., J-6 USSTRATCOM, Offutt AFB, Nebr., 1997—, dir. command control, comm. and computer sys., 97-. Decorated Legion of Merit, Air Medal with 2 oak leaf clusters, Air Force Commendation medal with one oak leaf cluster, others. Office: C41 Sys J-6 USSTRATCOM USN 901 Sac Blvd Ste 2b9 Offutt AFB NE 68113-6600*

BEHLING, CHARLES FREDERICK, psychology educator; b. St. George, S.C., Sept. 8, 1940; s. John Henry and Floy (Owings) B.; m. Jennifer Crocker; children: John Charles, Andrew Crocker. BA, U. S.C., 1962, MA, 1964; MA, Vanderbilt U., 1966, PhD, 1969. Asst. dean of students U. S.C., Columbia, 1962-63; asst. state news editor The State Newspaper, Columbia, 1963-64; asst. prof. psychology Lake Forest (Ill.) Coll., 1968-74; assoc. prof. Lake Forest Coll., 1974-88, chmn. dept., 1977-84; pvt. practice psychotherapy Lake Bluff, Ill., 1970-88, Buffalo, 1988-95; clin. assoc. prof. SUNY, Buffalo, 1988-95; dir. of undergraduate studies, 1989-95; adj. prof. U. Mich., Ann Arbor, 1995—; dir. intergroup rels., conflict and cmty., 1995—. Contbr. articles to profl. jours. Bd. dirs. Nat. Abortion Rights Action League, Planned Parenthood; mem. long-range planning com. Lake Bluff Bd. Edn. Named Outstanding Prof., Underground Guide to Colls., 1971, Birnbaum Guide, 1992, Outstanding Tchr., Lake Forest Coll., 1981, SUNY, Buffalo, 1991; NASA fellow. Mem. Am. Psychol. Assn., Soc. Psychol. Study of Social Issues, Assn. Humanistic Psychology, AAUP, Univ. S.C. Alumni Assn., Psi Chi, Sigma Delta Chi. Democrat. Home: 1325 Wynnstone Dr Ann Arbor MI 48105-2894 Office: U Mich Dept Psychology Ann Arbor MI 48109

BEHLMAR, CINDY LEE, business manager, consultant; b. Smyrna, Tenn., July 4, 1959; d. James Wallace and Barbara Ann (Behlmar) Gribble. BBA, Coll. William and Mary, 1981; MBA, Old Dominion U., 1995. Cert. mgmt. acct. Adminstrv. extern Hampton (Va.) Gen. Hosp., 1981-82; from mktg. rep. to supr. mktg. svcs. PruCare of Richmond, Va., 1983-85; exec. dir. PhysicianCare, Inc., Newport News, Va., 1986-89; provider rels. cons. Va. Health Network, Richmond, 1989-91; ind. cons. Tidewater Health Care, Virginia Beach, Va., 1991-92; COO Tidewater Phys. Therapy, Inc., Newport News, 1993-95; ind. cons. Yorktown, Va., 1996-97; contract mgr. Sentara Health Mgmt., Virginia Beach, 1998-99; state mgr. managed care Va. Oncology Assocs., 1999—; sec., bd. dirs. Greater Peninsula Area Med.-Bus. Coalition, Newport News, 1987-89; symposium faculty mem. Am. Hosp. Assn., Orlando, Fla., 1987, Washington, 1988. Mem. ch. coun. St. Mark Luth. Ch., Yorktown, Va., 1988-91. Fin. Exec. Inst. scholar, 1993. Mem. Inst. Mgmt. Accts., Toastmasters Internat. (club pres. 1997-98, area gov. 1998-99, Club Toastmaster of Yr. 1997-98, Dist. Spirit Success award 1998, Advanced Toastmaster gold award 1999), Phi Kappa Phi, Beta Gamma Sigma. Avocations: reading, music theory and piano, art and fashion. Home: 103 Jean Pl Yorktown VA 23693-3007 Office: Va Oncology Assocs Bldg 200 895 Middle Ground Blvd Newport News VA 23606

BEHLMER, RUDY H., JR., director, writer, film educator; b. San Francisco, Oct. 13, 1926; s. Rudy H. and Helen Mae (McDonough) B.; 1 child by previous marriage, Curt; m. Stacey Endres, Oct. 1992. Student, Pasadena Playhouse Coll., 1946-49, Los Angeles City Coll., 1949-50. Dir. Sta. KLAC-TV, Hollywood, Calif., 1952-56; network TV dir. ABC-TV, Hollywood, 1956-57; TV comml. producer-dir., exec. Grant Advt., Hollywood, 1957-60; exec. producer-dir. Sta. KCOP-TV, Hollywood, 1960-63; v.p., TV comml. producer-dir. Hollywood office Leo Burnett USA, 1963-84; lectr. film Art Ctr. Coll. of Design, Pasadena, Calif., 1967-92, Calif. State U., Northridge, 1984-92, UCLA, 1988. Author: Memo from David O. Selznick, 1972, (with Tony Thomas) Hollywood's Hollywood, 1975, America's Favorite Movies-Behind the Scenes, 1982, Inside Warner Bros., 1985, Behind the Scenes: The Making of..., 1990, Memo From Darryl F. Zanuck, 1993, W.S. Van Dyke's Journal-White Shadows in the South Seas, 1996; co-author: The Films of Errol Flynn, 1969; text on Warner Bros. Fifty Years of Film Music, 1973; editor: The Adventures of Robin Hood, 1979, The Sea Hawk, 1982 (Wis./Warner Bros. screenplay series), Warner Bros. 75 Years of Film Music, 1998; contbr. articles on film history, booklets for film music CDs; writer and narrator for laserdiscs, DVD's, and video documentaries. Served with AC, USNR, 1944-46. Mem. Dirs. Guild Am.

BEHM, FORREST EDWIN, glass manufacturing company executive; b. Lincoln, Nebr., July 31, 1919; s. Forrest E. and Lisle (Jacobson) B.; m. Ethel

E. Groth, Aug.11, 1943; children: Courtney Ann, Douglas, Brian, Gregory. B.S., U. Nebr., 1941, LL.D., 1965, LHD, 1991. Foreman to plant mgr. Corning (N.Y.) Glass Works and affiliates, 1946-55; div., sales and mfg. mgr. Corning Glass Works, 1955-61, v.p., 1961-65; pres., bd. dirs. Corning Internat. Corp., 1965-75; sr. v.p., mem. mgmt. com., bd. dirs. Corning Glass Works, 1975-82, sr. v.p. ops., 1982-83, dir. quality, 1983-87; pvt. practice, 1987—; bd. examiners Malcolm Baldridge Nat. Quality award, sr. examiner, 1989, 90, judge for N.Y. State Quality award, 1991, 92. Served to maj. AUS, 1942-46. Mem. Nebr. Football Hall of Fame; elected to Nat. Coll. Football Hall of Fame, 1988. Mem. Electronic Industries Assn. (bd. govs.), Beta Gamma Sigma. Republican. Presbyterian. Clubs: Corning Country. Home: 3 Briarcliff Dr Corning NY 14830-3328 Office: 80 E Market St Ste 303 Corning NY 14830-2722

BEHN, ROBERT DIETRICH, public policy educator, writer; b. Washington, Sept. 5, 1941; s. Victor Dietrich and Nona (Heffley) B.; m. Judith Howe, May 4, 1968; 1 son, Mark Dietrich. BS in Physics, Worcester Poly. Inst., 1963; SM, Harvard U., 1965, PhD in Decision and Control, 1969. Research dir. The Ripon Soc., Cambridge, Mass., 1968-69, exec. dir., 1970-72; asst. to gov. Commonwealth of Mass., Boston, 1969-70; lectr. Harvard Bus. Sch., 1972-73; assoc. prof. Terry Sanford Inst. Pub. Policy Duke U., Durham, N.C., 1973-88, prof., 1988—, dir. Inst. Policy Scis. and Pub. Affairs, 1982-85; dir. Gov.'s Ctr., 1984—; scholar-in-residence Ctr. for Excellence in Govt., Washington, 1985-86, adj. scholar, 1986-94; cons. RAND Corp., Santa Monica, 1966, Urban Acad., N.Y.C., 1978-79, Ford Found., N.Y.C., 1977; vis. prof. Kennedy Sch. Govt. Harvard U., 1993. Author: (with others) Quick Analysis for Busy Decision makers, 1982, Leadership Counts; editor: The Lessons of Victory, 1969; co-editor: Innovations in American Government, 1997; columnist Governing mag., 1993-98, The New Pub. Innovator, 1998—; editl. bd. State and Local Govt. Rev., 1993-96, Jour. Pub. Adminstrn. Rsch. and Theory, 1996—; bd. editors: Internat. Pub. Mgmt. J., Jour. Pub. Affairs Edn., 1998—; contbr. articles to mags. and profl. jours. Chmn. Gov.'s Task Force Intercity Transp., Boston, 1970-71; alt. del. Republican Nat. Conv., 1972; mem. Mass. Rep. State Com., 1973; nat. governing bd. Ripon Soc., 1966-79; mem. Mass. adv. com. U.S. Civil Rights Commn., 1971-73, Com. to Study Need for Inpatient Services for Children with Chronic Phys. Disabilities, Raleigh, N.C., 1978; campaign advisor Hatch for Gov. Com., Boston, 1977-78; bd. dirs. Pub. Svc. Curriculum Exchange, 1992—; mem. Ind. Study Commn. on Reorgn. of N.C. Dept. Human Resources, 1996-97. Fellow Nat. Acad. Pub. Adminstrn (program com. chair 1997); mem. Assn. Pub. Policy Analysis and Mgmt. (treas. 1983-89, v.p. 1987-88, rsch. conf. program com. chair 1983, 94), Am. Soc. Pub. Adminstrn., Pub. Policy and Mgmt. Program for Case/Course Devel. (chmn. quantitative methods panel 1982-83). Home: 105 Amber Ct Carrboro NC 27510-4110 Office: Duke U Terry Sanford Inst Pub Policy PO Box 90246 Durham NC 27708-0246

BEHNER, ELTON DALE, dentist; b. Oberlin, Ohio, Sept. 6, 1952; s. Wayne Edwin and Velma Jean (Sevison) B.; m. Brenda Kay Crabtree, Aug. 18, 1974 (div. July 1982); m. Annette Lynn Brunst, Oct. 27, 1984: children: Nicolas, Ryan, Tadd. Student, Andrews U., 1971-74; BS, Loma Linda U., 1976; DDS, Ind. U., 1984. Dipolmate Am. Bd. Dental Examiners. Staff technologist clin. lab. Loma Linda (Calif.) U. Hosp., 1976-77, rsch. technologist, 1977-79; sr. technologist Ind. U. Hosp., Indpls., 1982-84; asst. prof. sch. dentistry Ind. U., Indpls.; grad. residency Ind. U. Med. Ctr., Indpls., 1984; pres. E. Dale Behner DDS PC, Indpls., 1985—; coord., cons. dental svc. Am. Surgery Ctr., Indpls., 1987—; active mem. staff dental svc. Wishard Meml. Hosp., Indpls. Fellow Acad. Gen. Dentistry; mem. ADA, Ind. Dental Assn., Indpls. Dist. Dental Soc., Crown Coun. Avocations: flying, model bldg., restoring sport cars, skiing, boating. Office: E Dale Behner DDS PC 5987 E 71st St Ste 103 Indianapolis IN 46220-4049

BEHNEY, CLYDE JOSEPH, health services researcher; b. Williamstown, Pa., May 19, 1946; s. Clyde J. Behney and Gladys Yvonne (Host) Williams; m. Nancy L. Kenney, Sept. 12, 1981; children: Lindsay, Fletcher, Taylor. BS, Lehigh U., 1968; MBA, U. Md., 1972; postgrad., George Washington U., 1975-82. Staff asst. U.S. Dept. Health, Edn., & Welfare, Washington, 1972-74, mgmt. intern, 1974-77; analyst/project dir. Office Tech. Assessment U.S. Congress, Washington, 1977-81, health program mgr. Office Tech. Assessment, 1981-93, asst. dir. Office Tech. Assessment, 1993-96; dir. divsn. health care svcs. Inst. Medicine, NAS, 1996-97, dep. exec. officer, 1997—, interim exec. officer, 1998; exec. dir. The Sorcerer's Apprentice Network, Washington, 1981-85; mem. steering com. Nat. Health Policy Forum, 1998—; mem. quality awards adv. bd. Health Improvement Inst., 1998—. Co-author: Toward Rational Technology in Medicine, 1981; author/co-author chpts. in 9 books; editor: (newsletter) The Sorcerer's Apprentice, 1981-85; mem. editl. bd. Internat. Jour. Tech. Assessment in Health Care, 1985-98; contbr. articles to profl. jours. Treas. Glebe Elem. PTA, Arlington, Va., 1990-94, Swanson Mid. Sch. PTSA, Arlington, 1994-96; mem. tech. adv. bd. Milbank Meml. Fund. Sgt. U.S. Army, 1969-71. Home: 2515 N Vermont St Arlington VA 22207-4125

BEHNKE, CARL GILBERT, beverage franchise executive; b. Seattle, May 13, 1945; s. Robert Joseph and Sally (Skinner) B.; m. Reneé; children: Marisa Winifred, Merrill West. BA, Princeton, 1967; MBA, Harvard, 1973. Adminstrv. asst. ALPAC Corp., Seattle, 1973-75, v.p., 1978-84, pres., 1984-93, also bd. dirs.; sales mgr. Pepsi-Cola/7Up, Honolulu, 1974-76; chmn. bd. Skinner Corp.; pres. REB Enterprises, Seattle, 1993—; bd. dirs. Sage Terrace Inc., The Commerce Bank of Washington, Northwestern Trust, Internat. Yogurt Co. Bd. dirs. Pres.'s Club, U. Wash., 1980-84, Jr. Achievement Puget Sound, 1981—, chmn. bd., 1988; bd. dirs. United Way Washington, 1982-86; pres. Bellevue Boys and Girls Club, 1985-87; trustee U. Puget Sound, Patrons of N.W. Civic Cultural and Charitable Orgns., pres., 1990; chmn. bd. dirs. Eastside Performing Arts Ctr., 1987-90; chmn. bd. Seattle-King County Conv. and Visitors Bur., 1989; mem. exec. bd. Seattle Organizing Com./Goodwill Games, 1987; bd. dirs. Croquet Found. Am., Pacific N.W. Ballet. Named One of 100 Newsmakers of Tomorrow, Time Mag.-Seattle C. of C., 1978. Mem. Nat. Soft Drink Assn. (bd. dirs.), Wash. State Soft Drink Assn. (bd. dirs.), Pepsi-Cola Bottlers Assn. (bd. dirs. 1986), 7UP Bottlers Assn. (bd. dirs.), Young Pres's. Orgn., Cen. Park Tennis Club, Men's Univ. Club, Rainier Club, Columbia Tower Club, Puget Sound Croquet Club, Washington Athletic Club. Republican. Home: 10501 NE 47th Pl Kirkland WA 98033-7610 Office: REB Enterprises 520 Pike St Ste 2620 Seattle WA 98101-4082

BEHNKE, ROY HERBERT, physician, educator; b. Chgo., Feb. 24, 1921; s. Harry and Florence Alice (MacArthur) B.; m. Ruth Gretchen Zinszer, June 3, 1944; children: Roy, Michael, Donald, Elise. A.B., Hanover Coll., 1943; Ph.D. (hon.), 1972; M.D., Ind. U., 1946. Diplomate: Am. Bd. Internal Medicine. Intern Ind. U. Med. Center, 1946-47, resident, 1949-51, chief resident medicine, 1951-52; instr. medicine Ind. U. Sch. Medicine, Indpls., 1952-55, asst. prof. medicine, 1955-58, assoc. prof., 1958-61, prof., 1961-72; chief medicine VA Hosp., Indpls., 1957-72; prof. medicine U. South Fla. Coll. Medicine, Tampa, 1972—, chmn. dept. medicine, 1972-95, chmn. dept. head emeritus, 1995—; AMA rep. to residency rev. com. in internal medicine, 1970-75; mem. exec. and adv. com. Inter-Soc. Commn. Heart Disease Resources, 1968-72, chmn. pulmonary study sect., 1969-72; chmn. career devel. com. VA, 1980-83. Mem. Met. Sch. Bd. Washington Twp., 1968-72, pres., 1971; bd. dirs. Southside Community Health Center, 1968; trustee Tampa Gen. Hosp. Found., 1979-85; mem. research coordinating com. Am. Lung Assn., 1983-85, chmn., 1985-87, bd. dirs., 1983-87. Served with AUS, 1943-45, 47-49. Recipient Std. Oil Found. award Ind. U., 1971, Alumni Achievement award Hanover Coll., 1971; named Hon. Alumnus, USF Coll. Medicine, 1995; John and Mary Markle scholar, 1952, 57. Fellow and master ACP (gov. Fla. chpt. 1980-84, Laureate award 1991); fellow Am. Coll. chest Physicians; mem. AMA, Am. Fedn. Clin. Rsch., Ctrl. Soc. Clin. Rsch., So. Soc. Clin. Rsch., Alpha Omega Alpha. Home: 5111 Rolling Hill Ct Tampa FL 33617-1024 Office: Dept Internal Medicine 12901 N 30th St # 19 Tampa FL 33612-4742

BEHNKE, WALLACE BLANCHARD, JR., consultant, engineer, retired utility executive; b. Evanston, Ill., Feb. 5, 1926; s. Wallace Blanchard and Dorothea (Bull) B.; m. Joan F. Murphy, Sept. 24, 1949; children: Susan F., Ann B., Thomas W. BS, Northwestern U., 1945, BSEE, 1947. Registered profl. engr., Ill. With Commonwealth Edison Co., Chgo., 1947-89; dist. supt. Commonwealth Edison Co., Crystal Lake, Ill., 1956-58; div. engr. Commonwealth Edison Co., Joliet, Ill., 1958-60; area mgr. Commonwealth Edison Co., Mount Prospect, Ill., 1960-62; div. v.p. Commonwealth Edison Co., Chgo., 1962-66, asst. to pres., 1966-69, v.p., 1969-73, exec. v.p., 1973-80, vice chmn., 1980-89; bd. dirs. Duff & Phelps Utilities, Inc. Hon. dir. Northwestern Meml. Hosp.; mem. U.S. Nat. Com. Cigrè. Lt. USNR, 1943-46. Fellow IEEE (bd. dirs. 1990-91; mem. NAE, IEEE Power Engring. Soc. (pres. 1987-88), Am. Nuclear Soc., Western Soc. Engrs. (pres. 1987-88), Comml. Club Chgo., Kiawah Island Club, Exch. Club Kiawah-Seabrook, Phi Delta Theta. Home and Office: 323 Glen Eagle Ct Johns Island SC 29455-5728

BEHNKE, WILLIAM ALFRED, landscape architect, planner; b. Cleve., Jan. 7, 1924; s. Walter William and Constance Helen (Ireson) B.; m. Virginia E. Woolever, Sept. 18, 1948; children: Lee, Deborah, Mitchel, Mark. B.Landscape Architecture, Ohio State U., 1951. Designer Grier Riemer Assos., Cleve., 1951-55; prin. William A. Behnke, Cleve., 1955-57; asso. Charles L. Knight, Cleve., 1957-58; partner Behnke, Szynyog & Ness, Cleve., 1958-61, Behnke, Ness & Litten, Cleve., 1961-70; mng. partner William A. Behnke Assoc., Cleve., 1970-89, ret.; assoc. prof. Kent State U., 1973-74; pres. Ohio State Bd. Landscape Archtl. Examiners, 1973; vice-chmn. Ohio Bd. Unreclaimed Strip Mined Lands, 1973-74; bd. dirs. Landscape Architecture Found., 1981-85, pres., 1983; mem. adv. bd. Trust for Pub. Lands, 1988—. Mem. Ohio Arts Coun., 1983-84; pres. metro bd. Lake County YMCA, 1989-90. Served with USNR, 1943-46. Named Distinguished Alumnus Ohio State U., 1978; inductee Eastlake Sch. Dist. Hall of Fame, 1999. Fellow Am. Soc. Landscape Architects (v.p. 1977-79, pres. 1980-81). Home: 37334 Harlow Dr Willoughby OH 44094-5758 Office: William Behnke Assocs Inc 700 St Clair Ave W # 416 Cleveland OH 44113-1230 *I am gratified with the knowledge that my livelihood is achieved from a profession that has as its goal the betterment of mankind.*

BEHNKEN, WILLIAM JOSEPH, art educator, artist; b. N.Y.C., Mar. 29, 1943; s. William Henry and Margaret Mary (Hoolan) B. BA, CCNY, 1968, MA, 1995. Dir. art sch. Provincetown (Mass.) Art Assn. Mus., 1984-93; prof. art Bronx (N.Y.) C.C., 1973-83, CCNY, 1970—; instr. studio art Art Students League, N.Y.C., 1998—. Artist print edits. lithographs, aquatints, mezzotints; represented in permanent collections at N.Y. Pub. Libr. Print Divsn., Bklyn. Mus., Bowdoin Coll. Mus., Indpls. Mus. Fine Arts, Mus. Nat. Acad. Design, Jane Voorhees Zimmerli, Mus. Rutgers U., Mus. City N.Y. Recipient Louis Lozowick awards Audubon Artists Soc., N.Y.C., 1991, 92. Mem. Soc. Am. Graphic Artists (pres. 1998), Nat. Acad. Design (graphics prize 1992), Boston Printmakers, Phi Beta Kappa. Democrat. Home: 3415 Fort Independence St Bronx NY 10463-4507

BEHR, ALAN ANDREW, lawyer, writer; b. Paterson, N.J., Aug. 18, 1954; s. Ludwig Louis B. and Sary Behr Fox; m. Julie Lyn Hackett, Sept. 24, 1994. BA cum laude, U. Pa., 1976; JD, Columbia U., 1979, postgrad., 1980. Bar: N.Y., U.S. Ct. Appeals (2d cir.), U.S. Dist. Ct. (so. and ea. dists.) N.Y. With Mfrs. Hanover Leasing Corp., N.Y., 1984-85; assoc. Dreyer and Traub, N.Y., 1985-86, Newman, Tannenbaum, Helpern, Syracuse & Hirschtritt, N.Y., 1986-87; atty. intellectual property and corp. Met. Life Ins. Co., N.Y.C., 1987-95; v.p. legal affairs GT Interactive Software Corp., N.Y.C., 1995—; Spkr. in field. Contbr. numerous articles to profl. jours., newspapers, mags., and lit. revs. Trustee Film/Video Arts, Inc. Mem. Am. Intellectual Property Law Assn., Copyright Soc. U.S.A., Assn. of Bar of City of N.Y., N.Y. New Media Assn., Christian Den Fjerdes Laug, Penn Club. Republican. Avocations: opera/concerts, mus., lit., theatre, skiing. Home: 190 E 72nd St New York NY 10021-4370 Office: GT Interactive Software Corp 417 5th Ave New York NY 10016-2204

BEHR, MARION RAY, artist, author, business executive; b. Rochester, N.Y., Sept. 12, 1939; d. Justin Max and Sophie Gusta (Koffler) Rosenfeld. B.Art Edn., Syracuse U., 1961, M.F.A., 1962; m. Omri Marc Behr, June 24, 1962; children: Dawn Marcy Yael, Darrin Justin Mason, Dana Marisa Jana. *Father, Justin Rosenfeld, born 1901 in Schopfloch, Bavaria. Studied law and economics. 1926, employed by bankers Wilhelm Vogt & Co, full responsibility for stories, casting, advertising, licensing, production and distribution of films for German speaking and foreign countries, film producer, president Orbis Film, Berlin. 1936, very successfully produced film Mademoiselle Josette, Ma Femme. 1937, compelled by Nazi laws to cease operations completely. Fled to United States in 1938 with wife, Sophie Koffler Rosenfeld. Died in 1947 at 47. Mother-Sophie Koffler Rosenfeld Lustik-teacher and translator of five languages lived to be 92* Has contr. publications for stories, crafts, mag. covers and toy designs to nat. mags. including McCall's, Good Housekeeping, Lady's Circle, 1962-77; one-woman shows include Douglas Coll., 1983, Pargot Gallery, 1989, New Jersey Small Works Show, 1992, 12x12 Exhibition, 1992, Eldorado Gall., 1992, Beamsderfer Gall., 1992, Artsquad Gall., 1993, Hunterdon Art Gall., 1993, Hunterdon Mus. Art, 1998; exhibited in group shows at Contemporary Am. Artists, Scarsdale, N.Y., 1964, Am. Women Artists, Douglass Coll., 1977, Internat. Miniature Print Biennial John Szoke Gallery, 1989, 15th Ann. Print Exhbn., Kanagawa Prefectual Gallery, Yokohama, Japan, 1989, 14th Ann. Small Works Exhbn., 80 Washington Sq. East Gallery, N.Y.C., 1990, 3d Micrographics Triennale, Riga, Latvia, USSR, 1990, 17th Ann. Print Exhbn., Kanagawa, Japan, 1991, Juniper Gallery, Napa, Calif., 1991, Eldorado Gallery, Colorado Springs, Colo., 1992, B. Beamsderfer Gallery, Highland Park, N.J., 1992, Artsquad Gallery, Easton, Pa., 1993, 7th Nat. Print Exhbn., Hunterdon, Clinton, N.J., 1993, Traveling Show, Johnson & Johnson, 1994, NAWA Juried Show, Lever House, 1995, 18th Independante Print Exhibition, 1996, Male Formi Grafiki, 1996, Cork Gall., 1996, Cheltenham Ctr. for Arts, 1996, Krasdale Gall., 1998, Natl. Acad. Mus., 1998, Stark and Stark, 1998, New Arts Prog., 1999, Inst. Cult. Peruano Norteamericano, 1999, Nat. Assn. Women Artists Ann. Exhbn., N.Y.C., 1990, Nat. Acad. Mus., 1998, Krasdale Gallery, 1998, Audubon Artists, 1998, Zimmerli Art Mus., Rutgers U., New Brunswick, N.J.; permanent print collection Smithsonian Instn. Nat. Mus. Am. History, 1995, Jane Vorhees Zimmerli Art Mus., 1993, 96, Thai Royal Art Collection, Bangkok, Thailand, 1995; creator survey Women Working Home— the Invisible Workforce, 1978; pres. Women Working Home, Inc., Edison, N.J., 1980—; condr. workshops; author: (with others) Women Working Home: The Homebased Business Guide and Directory, 1981, 2d edit., 1983; contbr. articles to popular mags., 1988-89; contbr. articles to profl. art jours., 1991-98; illustrator: Jewish Holiday Book, 1977; inventor (with Omri Behr) acid free, environmentally safe graphic etching process; installed Electrotech processor and taught first non toxic intaglio etching class at Stanford University, 1999; extensive radio and TV appearances rep. Nat. Alliance Homebased Businesswomen, Co-author, Women Working Home: The Homebased Business Guide and Directory, 1981, 2d edit., 1983, contbr. numerous articles ot profl. jours.; Recipient, Woman of the Year in Bus. and Ind., NJ Women in Bus. Advocate of the Year Awd.; Mem. Kean for Gov. campaign, 1981; mem. White House Conf. on Free Enterprise Zones, 1982, Natl. Assn. of Women Artists, 1992, Soc. Amer. Graphic Artists, Southern Graphics Counc., 1992, Print COunc. of New Jersey, 1993; trustee Women's Bus. Ownership Ednl. Conf., Inc., N.J., 1985; apptd. to N.J. Devel. Authority for Small, Minority and Women's Bus. Commn., 1986; Presdl. del. White House Conf. on Small Bus., 1986. Recipient N.J. Women in Bus. Advocate of the Yr. award SBA, 1984, Merit award Am. Artist Profl. League, Woman of Yr. in Bus. and Industry award, 1985, Audubon Artists Merit award, 1995; Syracuse U. alumni grantee, 1957; Arts and Humanities grantee Charles E. Lindbergh Fund, 1993-94. Mem. Nat. Alliance Homebased Businesswomen (pres. 1980-82, legis. chair 1982-85; originator, founder), Women's Caucus for Art. Jewish. Office: 325 Pierson Ave Edison NJ 08837-3123

BEHREN, ROBERT ALAN, lawyer, accountant; b. N.Y.C., Dec. 29, 1929; s. Jeremiah E. and Sue (Windman) B.; m. Judith Sandra Morgan, Dec. 20, 1971. BBA, CUNY, 1951, MBA, 1956; JD, NYU, 1956, LLM, 1958. CPA, N.Y. Prof. CUNY, N.Y.C., 1957-72; pvt. practice N.Y.C., 1958—; pub., CEO, founder Inst. Continuing Profl. Devel., N.Y.C., 1967-87; CEO Behren Fin. Strategies, West Palm Beach, Fla., 1990—. Contbr. over 1000 articles to profl. mags., fin. pubs., newsletters. Pres. Musician's Emergency Fund, N.Y.C., 1991—. Maj. USAF, 1952-53. Recipient numerous awards, scholarships and grants. Mem. Flight Instructors Assn., U.S. Polo Assn., Mensa. Home: 2417 Golf Brook Dr West Palm Beach FL 33414-7067 Office: Behren Fin Strategies 270 Mason St Greenwich CT 06830

BEHREND, BETTY ANN, municipal official; b. Canton, Mo., Feb. 26, 1948; d. James Marvin and Frieda Leora (Ludwig) DeWitt; m. Jerry Lee Behrend, Aug. 18, 1973; children: Jeffrey Lee, James Robert. BA in biology, Culver-Stockton Coll., 1970; MS in biology, U. N.Mex., 1972. Lab. technician Village of Los Lunas, N.Mex., 1983-88; wastewater supt. Village of Los Lunas, 1988-92, utilities dir., 1992—; pres. N.Mex. Mcpl. Environ. Quality Assn., Santa Fe, 1997—; mem. Mid Rio Grande Tech. Adv. Com., Albuquerque, 1995—. Named Successful Woman of '90s Valencia News-Bulletin, 1993. Mem. N.Mex. Water/Wastewater Assn. (bd. dirs. 1984—, Outstanding Plant Ops. 1990, 91), Rocky Mountain Water Environment Fedn. (Analytical Merit award 1988), Solid Waste Assn. N.Am., Optimists (pres. Los Lunas club 1993). Republican. Methodist. Avocations: birdwatching and photography, gardening. Office: Village of Los Lunas 660 Main St NW PO Box 1209 Los Lunas NM 87031-1209

BEHREND, DONALD FRASER, educator, university administrator; b. Manchester, Conn., Aug. 30, 1931; s. Sherwood Martin and Margaret (Fraser) B.; m. Joan Belcher, Nov. 9, 1957; children: Andrew Fraser, Eric Hemingway, David William. BS with honors and distinction, U. Conn., 1958, MS, 1960; PhD in Forest Zoology, SUNY, Syracuse, 1966. Forest game mgmt. specialist Ohio Dept. Natural Resources, Athens, 1960; res. asst. Coll. Forestry, SUNY, Newcomb, 1960-63, res. assoc., 1963-67; dir. Adirondack ecol. ctr. Coll. Environ. Science and Forestry, SUNY, Newcomb, 1968-73; acting dean grad. studies Syracuse, 1973-74; asst. v.p. research programs, exec. dir. Inst. Environ. Program Affairs, 1974-79, v.p. acad. affairs, prof., 1979-85, prof. emeritus, 1987—; asst. prof. wildlife mgmt. U. Maine, Orono, 1967-68; provost, v.p. acad. affairs U. Alaska Statewide System, Fairbanks, 1985-87, exec. v.p., provost, 1988; chancellor U. Alaska, Anchorage, 1988-94, chancellor emeritus, 1994—; mem. patent policy bd. SUNY, 1983-85, chmn. Res. Found. com. acad. res. devel., 1984-85; chmn. 6-Yr. planning com. U. Alaska, 1985-86; bd. dirs. Commonwealth North, 1991-92, Alaska Internat. Ednl. Found., 1997; mem. selection com. Harry S. Truman Scholarship Found.; mem. Pres.'s Commn., NCAA, 1992-95; chmn. spl. com. on student athlete welfare access and equity, 1993-95; chmn. 20th Great Alaska Shootout, 1997. Contbr. numerous articles and papers to profl. jours. Mem. Newcomb Planning Bd., 1967-69; mem., pres. Bd. Edn. Newcomb Cent. Sch., 1967-73; chmn. governing bd. N.Y. Sea Grant Inst., 1984-85; trustee U. Ala. Found., 1990-94. Served with USN, 1950-54. Mem. Alaska Internat. Edn. Found. (bd. dirs. 1997—), Wildlife Soc., Soc. Am. Foresters, AAAS, Phi Kappa Phi (hon.), Sigma Xi, Gamma Sigma Delta, Sigma Lambda Alpha (hon.). Lodges: Rotary (bd. dirs. Fairbanks club 1985-86), Lions (bd. dirs. Newcomb club 1966-67). Avocations: reading, writing, photography, fishing, bagpiping. Home: 333 M St Apt #403 Anchorage AK 99501-1902

BEHREND, WILLIAM LOUIS, electrical engineer; b. Wisconsin Rapids, Wis., Jan. 11, 1923; s. Albert and Eva Mae (Barney) B.; m. Manet Louise Whitrock, July 7, 1945; children: Jane Louise, Ann Behrend Luther. B.S. in Elec. Engring., U. Wis., 1946, M.S., 1947. Research engr. David Sarnoff Research Ctr., RCA, 1947-64; advanced devel. engr. comml. systems div. RCA, Meadows Lands, Pa., 1964-66, preliminary design and systems analyst, 1966-84; ret., 1984, cons. engr., 1984-90. Contbr. articles on elec. engring. to profl. jours.; patentee in field. Served with USNR, 1944-46. Recipient RCA David Sarnoff Rsch Ctr. Outstanding Rsch. award, 1956, 59, 63, RCA Comml. Systems Div. Outstanding Contbns. to Product Tech. award, 1974. Fellow IEEE (Scott Helt award 1971); mem. N.Y. Acad. Scis., Sigma Xi. Address: 6436 Antietam Ln Madison WI 53705-2934

BEHRENDT, DAVID FROGNER, journalist; b. Stevens Point, Wis., May 25, 1935; s. Allen Charles and Vivian (Frogner) B.; m. Mary Ann Weber, Feb. 4, 1961; children: Lynne, Liza, Sarah. BS, U. Wis., 1957, MS, 1960. Reporter Decatur (Ill.) Review, 1957-58; reporter Milw. Jour., 1960-70, copy editor, 1970-71, editorial writer, 1971-84, editorial page editor, 1984-95; Crossroads sect. editor Milw. Jour. Sentinel, 1995-98. Home: 1928 Hillside Ct Delafield WI 53018-2302

BEHRENDT, JOHN CHARLES, research geophysicist; b. Stevens Point, Wis., May 18, 1932; s. Allen Charles and Vivian Eulaine (Frogner) B.; m. Donna Miriam Ebben, Oct. 6, 1961 (div.); children: Kurt A., Marc R. Student, Cen. State Coll., Stevens Point, 1950-52; BS in Physics, U. Wis., Madison, 1954, MS in Geology, 1956, PhD in Geophysics, 1961. Asst. seismologist Arctic Inst. N.Am., Ellsworth Sta., Antarctica, 1956-58; research assoc. U. Wis., Madison, 1958-64; research geophysicist U.S. Geol. Survey, Denver, 1964-72, Liberia, West Africa, 1968-70; research geophysicist, Antarctic coordinator, 1977-95; geophysicist emeritus U.S. Geol. Survey, 1995—; chief br. of Atlantic-Gulf of Mex. marine geology Woods Hole, Mass., 1974-77; fellow Inst. Arctic and Alpine Rsch U. Colo., Boulder, 1996—; frequent pub. spkr. on Antarctica and other rsch.; advisor U.S. Depts. State and Interior, Washington, 1977—; mem. U.S. del. to Antarctic Treaty Meetings, various countries, 1977-95, various working groups NAS-NRC; rsch. on Antarctic, earthquakes in ea. U.S., Rocky Mountain tectonics, Gt. Lakes geologic structure, Atlantic continental margin of N.Am. and West Africa. Author: Innocents on the Ice: A Memoir of Antarctic Exploration, 1957, 1998; contbr. over 200 articles to sci. jours. Recipient Antarctic Svc. medal U.S. Dept. Def., 1966, Meritorious Svc. award Dept. Interior, 1992. Fellow Geol. Soc. Am., Explorers Club; mem. Am. Geophys. Union, Soc. Exploration Geophysicists, AAAS. Avocations: photography, outdoor activities, music.

BEHRENS, BEREL LYN, physician, academic administrator; b. New South Wales, Australia, 1940. MB, BS, Sydney (Australia) U., 1964. Cert. pediatrics, allergy and immunology. Intern Royal Prince Alfred Hosp., Australia, 1964; resident Loma Linda (Calif.) U. Med. Ctr., 1966-68; with Henrietta Egleston Hosp. for Children, Atlanta, 1968-69, T.C. Thompson Children's Hosp., Chattanooga, 1969-70; instr. pediatrics Loma Linda U., 1970-72, with dept. pediatrics, 1972—, dean Sch. Medicine, 1986-91, pres., 1990—. Office: Loma Linda U Office of the Pres Loma Linda CA 92350

BEHRENS, DIANE R., nursing educator; b. East Orange, N.J., Dec. 9, 1941; d. Samuel N. and Sylvia Irene (Lucas) Rankin; m. Otto Karl Behrens, Jr., Dec. 22, 1962; children: Connie, Cheryl, Karl, Carrie. BSN, Columbia U., 1964; MA in Nursing, Ball State U., 1984; MSEd, Ind. U., 1991. Cert. oncology nurse, med. surg. nurse, clin. specialist in med.-surg. nursing, CPR instr. Paramed. examiner Prudential Ins. Co., Merrillville, Ind., 1979-81; instr. pharmacology Valparaiso (Ind.) U., 1983; staff nurse St. Joseph Hosp., Ft. Wayne, Ind., 1978-81, relief nurse, nutritional support team, 1981; instr., assoc. prof. Luth. Coll. Health Professions, Ft. Wayne, 1981-93; asst. prof. St. Francis Coll., Ft. Wayne, 1993—. Mem. ANA (cert.), Ind. State Nurses Assn., Oncology Nursing Soc. (Three Rivers chpt.), Ind. Mental Health Assn., Sigma Theta Tau, Kappa Delta Phi. Home: 1202 S 500 E Columbia City IN 46725-9049

BEHRENS, ELLEN ELIZABETH COX, writer, counselor, educator; b. Fremont, Ohio, July 25, 1957; d. William Luther and Dorothy Cox. BA in English, Denison U., 1979; MFA in Creative Writing, Bowling Green State U., 1990. Writer in residence Ohio Arts Coun., 1991-94; ednl. devel. counselor Sch. Social Work Delphi Chassis Sys. facility U. Mich., Sandusky, Ohio, 1994—; adj. faculty Firelands Coll., Terra Tech. Coll., 1988-94; cons. Bowling Green State U., 1991-94. Author: None But the Dead and Dying, 1996; asst. editor: Mid-American Review, 1988-90, fiction editor, 1990-94, advisory editor, 1994—; contbr. short stories to anthologies, Descant, Fiction, Echoes, Paragraph, other literary mags. Individual Artist fellow Ohio Arts Coun., 1992. Mem. Bowling Green State U. Creative Writing Alumni Assn. (bd. dirs. 1990—), Associated Writing Programs, Tchrs. and Writers Collaborative, Ohioana Lib. Assn. Home: PO Box 1643 Sandusky OH 44871-1643 Office: Delphi Automotive 2509 Hayes Ave Sandusky OH 44870-5359

BEHRENS, HILDEGARD, soprano; b. Oldenburg, Germany, 1937; m. Seth Scheidman. Student, Music Conservatory, Freiburg, Fed. Republic of Germany. Opera debut in Freiburg, 1971; resident mem. Deutsche Opera Am Rhein, Dusseldorf, Fed. Republic of Germany; debut Covent Garden, 1976, as Leonore in Fidelio, in Salzburg, 1977, as Salome; appeared in Tosca, N.Y. Met., 1985, as Brünnhilde in Siegfried, N.Y. Met., 1988, title role in Elektra, N.Y. Met., 1994; appeared in new Production of The Ring, Bayreuth, 1988; appeared with Frankfurt (Fed. Republic of Germany) Opera,

Teatro Nacional de San Carlo, Lisbon, Portugal, Vienna Staatsoper, Met. Opera, N.Y.C., Orchestre Nat. de Paris, 1990; soloist Chgo. Symphony Orch., 1984. Office: Herbert H Breslin Inc 119 W 57th St New York NY 10019-2303

BEHRENS, JAMES WILLIAM, physicist, administrator, author; b. Litchfield, Ill., Apr. 29, 1947; s. George William and Norma Clara Marie (Boeker) B.; m. Pamela Jane Breese, July 7, 1973 (div. Jan. 1980); 1 child, Jaime Rhea; m. Linda Sue Lawrence, July 5, 1984. BS in Engring. Physics, U. Ill., 1970; MS in Engring and Applied Sci., U. Calif., Davis, 1976, postgrad., 1976-78. Physicist Lawrence Livermore (Calif.) Nat. Lab., 1969-78, U.S. Dept. Commerce, Nat. Bur. Stas., Gaithersburg, Md., 1978-89; sci. tech. advisor Joint Chiefs of Staff, U.S. Dept. Def. Joint Staff, Washington, 1989-91; asst. exec. program mgr. Office Asst. Sec. Def. U.S. Dept. Def., Washington, 1991-92; sr. spl. projects mgr. U.S. Dept. Def., USN, Indian Head, Md., 1992-93; asst. dir. U.S. Dept. Def., Interagy. Tng. Ctr., Ft. Washington, Md., 1993-95; dep. dir. Interagy. Tng. Ctr. U.S. Dept. Def., Ft. Washington, Md., 1995-97; dir. U.S. Dept. Def. Ft. Washington Facility, 1997—; tech. cons., pres. I.Q. in Nuc. Electronics Sys. & Tech., Inc., Rockville, Md., 1983-89; guest scientist Commissariat à l'Energie Atomique (CEA), Bruyere-le-Chatel, France, 1984. Author: Symbols and Fragments, 1993, Record of the House of Braunschweig-Illinois-Hannover, 1995, The 1995 Behrens Chronicle: A Complete Work, 1996, The 1995 Boeker Chronicle: A Complete Work, 1996, The 1996 Behrens-Boeker Chronicles: A Combined Work, 1997; co-editor: Fifty Years with Nuclear Fission, 1989; contbr. tech. articles to profl. pubs. Mem. Nat. Geneal. Soc., Nat. Writers Assn., Internat. Platform Assn., Nat. Audubon Soc., Nat. Wildlife Fedn., Am. Nuc. Soc. (cert. Appreciation 1989). Independent. Lutheran. Achievements include investigation of fast neutron-induced fission cross section measurements of the actinide elements, improvement of accuracy of neutron-induced fission cross section values which are used in broad areas of applied nuclear physics. Home: 16712 Baederwood Ln Rockville MD 20855-2009 Office: Ft Washington Facility 10530 Riverview Rd Fort Washington MD 20744-5821

BEHRENS, MYLES MICHAEL, neuro-ophthalmologist; b. N.Y.C., Oct. 26, 1938; s. Alvin Behrens and Anne Beth (Sleppin) Figman; m. Roberta Alice Kinstler Jaeger, Aug. 23, 1964 (div. 1967); m. Susan Ruth Page, Nov. 20, 1970 (div. 1976); m. Marsha Carole Miller, June 7, 1981; 1 child, Adam James. BA, Yale U., 1958; MD, Columbia U., 1962, D in Med. Sci., 1970. Diplomate Nat. Bd. Med. Examiners, Am. Bd. Ophthalmology. Intern and resident in medicine Columbia-Presbyn. Hosp., N.Y.C., 1962-64; clin. assoc. NIH-NIAID, Bethesda, Md., 1964-66; resident in ophthalmology Columbia-Presbyn. Hosp., 1966-70; Heed fellow in neuro-ophthalmology U. Calif. Med. Ctr., San Francisco, 1970-71; attending in ophthalmology, chief neuro-ophthalmology clinic Columbia-Presbyn. Hosp., 1971—; prof. clin. ophthalmology Columbia U., 1987—. Contbr. over 90 articles to profl. jours.; mem. editl. bds. major ophthalmol. and neurol. jours. Mem. adv. bd. Heed Found. Lt. comdr., USPHS, 1964-66, Bethesda. Recipient Lucien Howe prize N.Y. State Med. Soc., 1989, Philip Knapp Meml. tchg. award Harkness Eye Inst., 1992, Heed Found. award, 1986. Fellow Am. Acad. Ophthalmology (sr. honor award 1990), N.Am. Neuro-Ophthalmology Soc., N.Y. Acad. Medicine (chmn. sect. ophthalmology 1996-97). Jewish. Office: Columbia-Presbyn Med Ctr 635 W 165th St New York NY 10032-3701

BEHRING, DANIEL WILLIAM, educational administrator; b. Sheboygan, Wis., Jan. 9, 1940; s. Melvin William and Frieda (Ostwald) B.; m. Nancy Jean Steeno, July 28, 1962; children: Deanna, Shelley, Tanya, Jonathan. BA, Ripon Coll., 1962; MA, Ohio U., 1964, PhD, 1969. Teaching fellow Ohio U., Athens, 1965-66, acting instr., 1966; asst. prof. So. Ill. U., Edwardsville, 1966-71; dean students, asst. prof. Monmouth Coll., Ill., 1971-76; assoc. prof., v.p. Alma Coll., Mich., 1976-86; v.p. acad. affairs, Adrian (Mich.) Coll., 1986-91, interim pres., 1988-89; v.p., dir. of schs. Cranbrook Edn. Community, 1991-95; pres., SQT syss., 1995—; cons. colls., high schs., mental health orgns., businesses and mfrs. Contbr. articles to profl. jours. Bd. dirs. Hoogerland Meml. Workshop, St. Louis, Mich., 1977-86, Lenawee Tomorrow Econ. Devel. Assn., 1989-91, Lenawee Symphony, 1986-91, Farm Credit Svcs., 1990-94; reviewer United Way, Alma, 1983, 84; bd. dirs. Prodn. Credit Assn., 1990-94. Capt. U.S. Army, 1966-68. Kellogg Found. grantee, 1976-80; U.S. Office Edn. grantee, 1977, 78, 79, Lilly grantee, 1988, Towsely Found. grantee, 1989, State of Michigan grantee, 1989, 91. Mem. Am. Psychol. Assn., Am. Assn. Higher Edn., Rotary (pres. 1983-84, bd. dirs. Adrian chpt.), Oakland County Bus. Roundtable, Sigma Xi, Sigma Chi (Grand Consul Merit award 1984). Avocations: numismatics, Studebaker automobiles, model trains, science, sailing. Home and Office: 3695 Lakeshore Dr Manistee MI 49660-9760

BEHRING, KENNETH E., professional sports team owner; b. Freeport, Ill., June 13, 1928; s. Elmer and Mae (Priewe) B.; m. Patricia Riffle, Oct. 16, 1949; children: Michael, Thomas, David, Jeffrey, Scott. Student, U. Wis., 1947. Owner Behring Motors, Monroe, Wis., 1953-56, Behring Corp., Ft. Lauderdale, Fla., 1956-72; owner Blackhawk Corp., Danville, Calif., 1972—, also chmn. bd. dirs.; owner Seattle Seahawks, NFL, 1988-97; Calif. land developer; mem. policy adv. bd. real estate and urban econs. U. Calif., Berkeley.; chmn. bd. dirs. Behring-Hofmann Ednl. Inst., Inc. U. Calif. Trustee U. Calif., Berkeley; regent St. Mary's Coll., Moraga, Calif., Holy Name Coll., Oakland, Calif.; hon. trustee Mt. Diablo Hosp. Found., Concord, Calif.; hon. chmn. Seattle Art Mus., Am. Cancer Soc., Muscular Dystrophy, Silverado Concours. Named Man of Yr. Boys Town Italy, Entrepreneur of Yr. INC mag. Mem. Am. Acad. Achievement (honoree 1989), Assn. Wash. Bus., Seattle Master Builders Assn., Blackhawk Club, Vintage Club, Seattle Yacht Club, Wash. Athletic Club. Office: Blackhawk Corp PO Box 807 Danville CA 94526-0807

BEHRLE, FRANKLIN CHARLES, retired pediatrician and educator; b. Ansonia, Conn., June 4, 1922; s. Frank Edward and Irene Elizabeth (Bannon) B.; m. Margaret Ann Begley, June 16, 1945; children: Barbara, Susan, Carol, Richard, Robert. A.B., Dartmouth Coll., 1944; M.D., Yale U., 1946. Diplomate Am. Bd. Pediatrics, Am. Bd. Neonatal and Perinatal Medicine. Intern Nat. Naval Med. Center, Bethesda, Md., 1946-47; resident U. Kans. Med. Center, Kansas City, 1949-51; from instr. to assoc. prof. pediatrics U. Kans. Sch. Medicine, 1951-61; prof. dept. pediatrics U. Medicine and Dentistry, N.J.-N.J. Med. Sch., Newark, 1961-64, chmn. dept. pediatrics, 1964-85; prof. emeritus U. Medicine and Dentistry-N.J. Med. Sch., Newark, 1992—; exec. dir. Statewide Perinatal Services and Research Ctr., Newark, 1985-90. Contbr. chpts. to books; Contbr. numerous articles to profl. jours. Served to lt. (j.g.) M.C. USN, 1946-49. Fellow Am. Acad. Pediatrics; mem. Soc. for Pediatric Research. Home: PO Box 437 Grantham NH 03753-0437

BEHRMAN, EDWARD JOSEPH, biochemistry educator; b. N.Y.C., Dec. 13, 1930; s. Morris Harry and Janet Cahn (Solomons) B.; m. Cynthia Fansler, Aug. 29, 1953; children—David Murray, Elizabeth Colden, Victoria Anne. B.S., Yale, 1952; Ph.D., U. Calif. at Berkeley, 1957. Research asso. biochemistry Cancer Research Inst., Boston, 1960-64; bd. tutors biochem. scis. Harvard, 1961-64; asst. prof. chemistry Brown U., Providence, 1964-65; mem. faculty Ohio State U., Columbus, 1965—; asso. prof. biochemistry Ohio State U., 1967-69, prof., 1969—. Contbr. articles profl. jours. USPHS fellow, 1955-56, 57-60; NSF grantee, 1966-73; NIH grantee, 1973-81. Mem. Am. Chem. Soc., Royal Soc. Chemistry, Phi Beta Kappa, Sigma Xi. Home: 6533 Hayden Run Rd Hilliard OH 43026-9642 Office: Ohio State U Dept Biochemistry Columbus OH 43210

BEHRMAN, HAROLD RICHARD, endocrinologist, physiologist, educator; b. Sask., Can., Nov. 26, 1939; s. Henry Fred and Minnie Alice (Waslenko) B.; m. Carol Hope O'Rourke, Aug. 8, 1981; children: Tracy Lee, Terri Lynne, Russell Norman, Kevin Michael, Kathleen Hope. B.S., U. Man. (Can.), 1962, M.A., 1965; Ph.D., N.C. State U., 1967; M.S. (hon.), Yale U., 1982. Research fellow Harvard U. Med. Sch., Boston, 1967-71, asst. prof., 1971-72; dir. reproductive biology Merck Inst., Rahway, N.J., 1972-75; assoc. prof. gynecology and pharmacology Yale U., New Haven, 1975-81, prof. ob-gyn. and pharmacology, 1981—; dir. reproductive biology sect., 1975—; cons. NIH, 1978-83, 91-95, USDA, 1985, NSF, 1985, Med. Rsch. Coun. Can., 1990-91. Recipient Research award Lalor Found., 1971-72; Fulbright-Hays Disting. prof., 1978; MRC Can. fellow, 1967-70; recipient Alta. Heritage Vis. Prof. award, 1983. Mem. AAAS, Am. Physiol. Soc., Endocrine Soc., Soc. Study of Reprodn., Soc. Endocrinology, Can. Physiol. Soc. Home: 790 Green Hill Rd Madison CT 06443-2404 Office: Yale U Dept Ob-Gyn 1303A Yale Sta New Haven CT 06520

BEHRMAN, RICHARD ELLIOT, pediatrician, neonatologist, university dean; b. Phila., Dec. 13, 1931; s. Robert and Vivian (Keegan) B.; m. Ann Nelson, Aug. 14, 1954; children: Amy Jane, Michael Jameson, Carolyn Ann, Hillary. A.B., Amherst Coll., 1953; J.D., Harvard U., 1956; M.D. (Univ. scholar), U. Rochester, 1960. Diplomate Am. Bd. Pediatrics (examiner). Intern Johns Hopkins Hosp., Balt., 1960-61; resident in pediatrics Johns Hopkins Hosp., 1963-65; asst. prof. pediatrics U. Oreg. Sch. Medicine, Portland, 1965-67; asso. prof. U. Oreg. Sch. Medicine, 1967-68; prof. U. Ill. Coll. Medicine, Chgo., 1968-71; prof., chmn. dept. pediatrics Columbia U. Coll. Physicians and Surgeons, N.Y.C., 1971-76; prof., chmn. dept. Case Western Res. U. Sch. Medicine, Cleve., 1976-81, dean Sch. Medicine, 1980-89, v.p. med. affairs, 1987-89; dir. dept. pediatrics Rainbow Babies and Children's Hosp., Cleve., 1976-81; sr. v.p. med. affairs Lucile Packard Found. for Children's Health, Palo Alto, Calif., 1999, chmn. bd., 1996-99; dir. Lucile S. Packard Children's Hosp./Stanford Health Svcs., Stanford, UCSF-Stanford Health Care. Author: Neonatology: Diseases of the Fetus and Infant, 1973, Neonatal-Perinatal Medicine, 1977; editor: Nelson's Textbook of Pediatrics, 1978, 83, 87, 92, 95, Essentials of Pediatrics, 1989, 93, 97, The Future of Children, 1990; mem. editl. bd., sect. editor fetal and neonatal medicine Jour. Pediats., 1970-85; assoc. editor, mem. editl. bd., cons. editor Pediat. Rsch. Jour., 1971-80. With USPHS, 1961-63. Served with USPHS, 1961-63. Whipple scholar, 1960-61; Wyeth pediatric fellow, 1963-65. Fellow Am. Acad. Pediatrics; mem. Soc. Pediatric Rsch. (v.p. 1976-77), Inst. Medicine of Nat. Acad. Scis., Am. Pediatric Soc., Perinatal Rsch. Soc. (coun. 1970-73), Soc. Gynecol. Investigation, Century Assn., Sigma Xi. Episcopalian. Home: 15 Crest Rd Belvedere Tiburon CA 94920-2433

BEHRMANN, JOAN GAIL, newspaper editor; b. N.Y.C.; d. Jerome and Jeannette (Silverman) Metzner; m. Larry Jinks, Oct. 2, 1960 (div. 1970); children: Laura Jinks Kastigar, Daniel Carlton; m. Nicolas Lee Behrmann, Dec. 21, 1972. BA, Queens Coll., 1956; MS, Columbia U., 1958. Reporter Charlotte (N.C.) Observer, 1958-60, Miami (Fla.) Herald, 1960-64, Miami News, 1965-66; asst. prof. Miami Dade C.C., 1968-72; assoc. prof. Boston U., 1975-78; Sunday editor The Saragotan, Saratoga Springs, N.Y., 1979-80; editor Gannett Westchester, Westchester County, N.Y., 1981-83; page one editor, entertainment editor USA Today, Rosslyn, Va., 1983-87; exec. editor The Desert Sun, Palm Springs, Calif., 1987-95; arts editor The Detroit News, Detroit, 1996—. Co-author: Questioning Media Ethics, 1978. Bd. dirs. Coll. of the Desert Found., Palm Desert, 1993-95, Jewish Family Svcs., Palm Springs, 1994-95, Palm Springs Opera Guild, 1989-91, Adult Well-Being Svcs., Detroit, Mich., 1997—; founder Every Women's Coun., Glens Falls, N.Y., 1978-80. Recipient Athena award Palm Springs C. of C., 1991. Mem. Assn. Press Mng. Editors Orgn. (bd. dirs. 1991-96, com. chair 1996-97), Am. Soc. Newspaper Editors. Avocations: travel, reading. Office: Detroit News 615 W Lafayette Blvd Detroit MI 48226-3197

BEHROUZ, ELIZABETH J., service director; b. New London, Conn., May 6, 1957; d. Dale and Jane (Senne) Daggett; m. Homayoun Behrouz, Jan. 1983; twins: Darmaan, Shaheen. BS in English, Mt. Scenario Coll., 1982. Exec. asst. to dean grad. studies Lincoln U., 1983-85, prison ednl. program coord., 1983-85; exec. asst. to sales tax divsn. mgr. Mo. Dept. Revenue, 1985-87; staff asst. Office of Senator Christopher S. Bond, 1989-91, dir. Office Constituent Svcs., 1992—.

BEHUNIAK, PETER, JR., educational administrator, consultant; b. Derby, Conn., Feb. 11, 1950; s. Peter and Stella (Spak) B.; m. Gail Ann Tomala, Mar. 8, 1986; 1 child, Alexander T. BS with high honors, U. Conn., 1971, MA, 1973, PhD, 1981; postgrad., U. Mass., 1975-77. Cert. tchr., Conn. Tchr. Glastonbury (Conn.) Pub. Schs., 1971-78; research asst. U. Conn. Bur. Ednl. Research, Storrs, 1979-80; pres. Edn. Resource Assocs., Glastonbury, 1980-83; edn. cons. Conn. Dept. Edn., Hartford, 1983-89, coord. student assessment, 1989-91, chief Bur. Evaluation and Student Assessment, 1991-92, dir. student assessment and testing, 1992—; lectr. U. Bridgeport, Conn., 1982-83, U. Conn., Storrs, 1980-85, Ea. Conn. State U., 1987-89; adj. faculty U. Hartford, dir. student assessment, 1988—. Contbr. articles to profl. jours. Mem. evaluation com. Cmty. Coun. of the Capitol Region, Hartford, 1984-87; bd. dirs. S.E. Conn. Livil Liberties Union, Windham, 1977-80; bd. overseers N.E. Regional Labs.; pres. Edn. Adminstrs. Union, Conn. State Dept. Edn.; chmn. tech. guidelines for performance assessment Coun. of Chief State Sch. Officers; Nat. Coun. Measurement in Edn. rep. to Joint Com. on Testing Practices. Mem. Am. Ednl. Research Assn. (presenter), Nat. Council on Measurement in Edn. (presenter), Am. Evaluation Assn. (presenter), N.E. Ednl. Research Assn. (presenter, program reviewer 1983), Phi Delta Kappa. Avocation: photography. Office: Conn State Dept Edn PO Box 2219 Hartford CT 06145-2219

BEIDEL, JOHN MICHAEL, headmaster, pastor; b. El Paso, Tex., June 11, 1941; s. Arthur Henry and Emajosephine (Curry) B.; m. Helen Beatrice Medlin, June 28, 1963; children: Mary, Sarah, Elizabeth, Rebecca. BA in Math., U. Tex., 1963, MA in Math., 1968. Cert. sec. sch. teacher. Tchg. asst. U. Tex., Austin, 1964-66; math. instr. Austin Ind. Sch. Dist., 1965-67, St. Mark's Sch., Dallas, 1967-77; head math. dept. Trinity Christian Acad., Addison, Tex., 1977-80, headmaster, 1980-93; ednl. cons. Richrdson, Tex., 1993—; pastor of discipleship Trinity Bible Ch., Richardson, Tex., 1993-96; sch. head Covenant Christian Acad., Colleyville, Tex., 1996-97; headmaster 1st Bapt. Acad., Dallas, 1997—; instr. in math. U. Tex., Dallas, 1985-89, reader, table leader AP calculus, 1991—. Contbr. chpt. to book Home Schooling, 1985. Co-chmn. Adam's Parent Tchr., 1999. Mem. ASCD, Tex. Assn. Non-Pub. Schs. (regional bd. dirs. 1985-87, v.p. 1987-89, pres. 1989-92), Nat. Coun. Tchrs. Math. Republican. Avocations: tennis, camping, reading, singing. Office: PO Box 868 Dallas TX 75221

BEIDEMAN, RONALD PAUL, chiropractic physician, college dean; b. Norristown, Pa., Mar. 22, 1926; s. Jonas Paul and Bertha May (Cane) B.; student Temple U., 1948; D. Chiropractic, Nat. Coll. Chiropractic, Chgo., 1952; postgrad. Wheaton Coll.; B.A., Lewis U., 1976; m. Lorraine Marian Barrett, Aug. 19, 1950 (dec.); children—Ronald Paul, J. Kirk; m. 2d, Peggy Ann Bartlett, May 31, 1980. Dir. dept. diagnosis Nat. Coll. Chiropractic, Chgo., 1952-66, sr. tenured prof., 1963—, registrar, 1966-78, dean admissions and records, 1973-88, ofcl. coll. historian, 1987—; dean of records 1988-94, coll. archivist, 1994—; exam. physician Chgo. Gen. Health Service, 1954-65; lectr. in field; pvt. practice chiropractic Chgo., 1954—; mem. nat. prof. standards rev. council, Health Care Financing Adminstrn., HHS, 1982; prof. Nat.-Lincoln Sch. Postgrad. Edn., 1964—; accrediting evaluator Council on Chiropractic Edn., 1978—, mem. task force panels on admissions Commn. on Accreditation, 1980, 84—; accrediting evaluator Western Assn. Schs. and Colls., 1985. Served with USAAF, 1944-46. Fellow Internat. Coll. Chiropractors (faculty); mem. Nat. Coll. Chiropractic (corp. sec. 1972-94), Nat. Bd. Chiropractic Examiners (chmn. test com. 1967-69), Ill., Chgo. Chiropractic Socs., Am. Chiropractic Assn. (vet. affairs com. 1979-81), Am. Legion (post comdr. 1957-58), Am., Ill. Assns. Collegiate Registrars and Admissions Officers, Ill. Assn. Student Financial Aid Adminstrs., Nat. Assn. Coll. Admissions Counselors, Pa. Assn. Drugless Physicians (hon. life), Nat. Coll. Chiropractic Alumni Assn. (Outstanding Alumnus of Yr. 1995), Sigma Phi Kappa (grand chancellor), Lambda Phi Delta. Author: In The Making of a Profession: The National College of Chiropractic 1906-1981, 1995; contbr. over 70 articles to profl. pubs. Office: 200 E Roosevelt Rd Lombard IL 60148-4539

BEIDLER, MARSHA WOLF, lawyer; b. Bridgeton, N.J., Feb. 29, 1948; d. Benjamin and Esther (Lourie) Wolf; m. John Nathan Beidler, Aug. 18, 1974; children: Dora E., Evan A. BA, Dickinson Coll., Carlisle, Pa., 1969; JD, Rutgers U., Camden, N.J., 1972; LLM in Taxation, NYU, 1979. Bar: Pa. 1972, Fla. 1973, N.J. 1975; Fla. bar bd. cert. tax lawyer. Estate and gift tax atty. IRS, Phila., 1972-74, Trenton, N.J., 1974-76; atty. McCarthy & Hicks, Princeton, N.J., 1976-81; ptnr. Pinto & Beidler, Princeton, 1981-83; prin. Smith, Lambert, Hicks & Miller, Princeton, 1983-88; ptnr. Drinker, Biddle & Reath, Princeton, 1988—; Sec. Mercer County Estate Planning Council, 1977-86; prof. paralegal studies Rider Coll., Trenton, 1982; lectr. estate planning various corps. and univs. Bd. dirs. Birth Alternatives, Princeton, 1980; bd. dirs. Mercer Council on Alcoholism, Trenton, 1985-86. Fellow Am. Coll. Trusts and Estate Counsel; mem. ABA (taxation sect., real property, probate and trust sect.), Fla. Bar Assn., N.J. Bar Assn. (taxation sect.). Office: Drinker Biddle & Reath 105 College Rd E PO Box 627 Princeton NJ 08542-0627

BEIDLER, PETER GRANT, English educator; b. Bethlehem, Pa., Mar. 13, 1940; s. Paul Henry and Margaret (Grant) B.; m. Anne E. Gilbert, June 15, 1963; children: Paul, Kurt, Gretchen, Nora. B.A., Earlham Coll., 1962; M.A., Lehigh U., 1965, Ph.D., 1968. Asst. prof. English Lehigh U., Bethlehem, Pa., 1968-72; assoc. prof. Lehigh U., Bethlehem, 1972-77, prof., 1977—, Lucy G. Moses Disting prof. English, 1978—, acting v.p. for student affairs, 1982-83; Robert Foster Cherry disting. tchg. prof. Baylor U., 1995-96. Author: Fig Tree John: An Indian in Fact and Fiction, 1977; co-author: (bibliography) The Indian in American Short Fiction, 1979; editor: John Gower's Literary Transformations, 1982, Ghosts, Demons and Henry James, 1989, Writing Matters, 1992, Henry James's The Turn of the Screw: Case Studies in Contemporary Criticism, 1995, Geoffrey Chaucer's The Wife of Bath: Case Studies in Contemporary Criticism, 1996, Masculinities in Chaucer, 1998, Chaucer's Wife of Bath: Prologue and Tale: An Annotated Bibliography, 1990-1995, 1998, A Reader's Guide to the Novels of Louise Erdich, 1999. Served with USAF, 1962-68. Named Nat. Prof. of Yr. Coun. for Advancement and Support of Edn., 1983; Fulbright lectr. Sichuan U., Chengdu, Peoples Republic of China, 1987-88; recipient Robert Foster Cherry Disting. Teaching chair Baylor U., 1995-96. Mem. MLA, New Chaucer Soc., Medieval Soc. Am., Phi Beta Kappa, Phi Beta Delta. Office: Lehigh U English Dept 35 Sayre Dr Bethlehem PA 18015-3116

BEIERLE, HERBERT LEONARD, dean; b. Milw., Apr. 2, 1927; s. Herbert Frank and Ella (Kammer) B.; m. Faith Flora Wangemann, June 23, 1950 (div. 1970); 1 child, Mark Herbert. DD, Coll. Divine Metaphysics, Indpls., 1948; PhB, Univ. Healing, Campo, Calif., 1975, PhD, 1985, M in Healing Scis., 1994. Ordained to ministry Ch. of God Unlimited 1975; lic. real estate broker. Editor STAR/Saturday Graphic, West Allis, Wis., 1950-52, Hartley Publs., Columbus, Ohio, 1952-54, Prairie Du Chien (Wis.) C-Press, 1954-56, Atwater (Calif.) Signal, 1956-58; editor, pub. Newark (Calif.) Sun, 1958-60; editor Newport Harbor Ensign, Corona del Mar, Calif., 1960-63, Neporter Mag., Newport Beach, Calif., 1963-65, Orange County Indsl. Pub., Santa Ana, Calif., 1965-67, El Toro (Calif.) Reporter, 1967-70, Sci. of Mind Mag., L.A., 1971-73; dean, chmn. bd. dirs. God Unlimited, Univ. Healing, Campo, 1975—; chmn. bd. dirs., dean Univ. Philosophy, Campo, 1985, Absolute Monastaery, Campo; min. various chs. and univ., Wis., Ill., INd., Nev., Minn., Del., N.Y., N.J., Conn., Calif., Montreal, Can., Munich, Lugano, Switzerland, Zurich, Switzerland, Prague, Chechoslovakia, Moscow, St. Petersburg, Russia, Cairo.lectr. Univ. Moscow, Univ. Leningrad; founding min. Jonathan Chapel, Mpls., Chapel by the Water, Duluth, Minn., Ch. of God Unlimited Internat.; min. Forest Glenn Congl., Chgo., Livingston (Calif.) Congl. Ch., Imperial Valley Ch. Religious Sci., El Centro, Calif., Andromeda, Chapel of Open Door, Lake Minnetonka, Minn.; presenter in field. Author: Art and Science of Wholeness, 1975, Song of the Spirit, 1976, Illumination, Handbook of Ascended Masters, 1977, How To Give a Healing Treatment, 1979, Ministers Manual, 1995, A Gift from Self to Self, 1981, Practice Reality, 1982, I Am Number One, 1983, Practitioners Manual, 1995, Relative, 1990, Law of Cause and Effect, 1991, Relative/Absolute, Absolute, My Inner Journey, 1996, Autobiography of God, 1979, Why Can I Say I Am God?, The Weathering, 1994, Three Hour Meditation, 1995, Inexhaustible Laughter of Heaven-Bliss, 1997, ; editor Merced County Farm & Ranch, 1956-58, Mercer News, West Allis Star, Rochester Clarion, Hilltop Record, West Side Leader, South Side News, Franklin County News, Newport Unity, Orange County Bus. Mag., Orange County Bus. Digest, Inside/Outside, Gist. Chmn. West Allis (Wis.) Civil Def. Orgn., 1951-52; pres. Merced (Calif.) County Crippled Children's Soc., 1958; cubmaster Cub Scouts, Newport Beach, 1961, sunday sch. supt. Wauwatosa (Wis.) Congl. Ch., Prairie du Chien Meth. Ch., choir dir., Milw. Unity Ch., dir. youth. With USN, 1945-48. Recipient Journalism award Calif. Newspaper Pub. Assn., 1956. Mem. Newspaper Pub. Assn. N.Y. (Photojournalism award 1951), Calif. Real Estate Assn., Newport Harbor Real Estate Assn., Kiwanis, Atwater Jr. C. of C. (past pres., Jaycee Leadership award 1957), Saddleback Exchange Club, Atwater Rotary. Avocations: flying, water skiing, climbing, photography, singing. Home & Office: God Unlimited Univ Healing 1101 Far Valley Rd Campo CA 91906-3213

BEIERWALTES, WILLIAM HENRY, physician, educator; b. Saginaw, Mich., Nov. 23, 1916; s. John Andrew and Fanny (Aris) B.; m. Mary Martha Nichols, Jan. 1, 1942; children: Andrew George, William Howard, Martha Louise. AB, U. Mich., 1938, MD, 1941. Diplomate: Am. Bd. Internal Medicine and Nuclear Medicine. Intern, then asst. resident medicine Cleve. City Hosp., 1941-43; mem. faculty U. Mich. Med. Center, 1944-87, prof. medicine, 1959-87, prof. emeritus, 1987—; dir. nuclear medicine, also dir. Thyroid Research Lab., 1952-86, cons., 1987-95; cons. nuclear medicine depts. St. John Hosp., Detroit, Wm. Beaumont Hosp., Royal Oak and Troy, Mich., 1987-95, The UpJohn Co. Rsch. div., 1952-65, The Abbott Labs. Rsch. div., 1960-67; sr. med. cons. MD (Med. Fedn.), Bagdad, Iraq, 1963; mem. exec. com. Inst. Sci. and Tech., 1963; lectr. Nat. Naval Med. Ctr., 1964-88, Ctr. for Environ. Health Mich. State Dept. Health, 1988-89; Peter Heimann lectr. 34th meeting Internat. Congress Surgery, Stockholm, Sweden, 1991; adv. panel on radionuclide labeled compounds for tumor diagnosis Internat. AEC, 1974-75; mem. Mich. State Radiation Bd., 1980-84; co-chmn. Nat. Coop., Thyroid Cancer Therapy Group, 1978-81. Author: Clinical Use of Radioisotopes, 1957, Manual of Nuclear Medicine Procedures, 1971, Love of Life Autobiog. Sketches, 1996; contbr. numerous articles to profl. jours.; assoc. editor Jour. Lab. and Clin. Medicine, 1954-60; editl. bd. Jour. Nuclear Medicine, 1964-69, assoc. editor, 1975-81; editl. bd. Jour. Clin. Endocrinology and Metabolism, 1963; adv. bd. Annals of Saudi Medicine, 1986-90; patentee for monoclonal antibodies to HCG, and radionuclide in vivo biochem. imaging of endocrine glands, 1951; first to treat a patient for cancer with radio labeled antibodies, 1951; co-inventor radiopharms, 1971; originator of radioimmunodetection of human cancer; first description of cytogenetic evolution of thyroid cancer; first description of fall of serum antithyroid antibodies during pregnancy with rise after delivery, other med. techniques. Guggenheim fellow, 1966-67; Commonwealth Fund fellow, 1967; recipient Hevesy Nuc. Medicine Pioneer award, 1982, Disting. Faculty award U. Mich., 1982, Johann-Geor-Zimmerman Trust for Cancer Rsch. Sci. prize for greatest contbn. to treatment of thyroid cancer, 1983, WWJ 950 Detroit Citizen of Week award, 1994; named Internat. Man of Yr. Internat. Biog. Ctr., Cambridge, Eng., 1992-93. Mem. AMA (Outstanding Scientific Achievement award 1994), ACP, Am. Fedn. Clin. Rsch. (pres. 1954-55), Soc. Nuclear Medicine (pres. 1965-66, Disting. Educator's award 1989, The Best Doctors in Am. award 1993-95), Ctrl. Clin. Rsch. Club (pres. 1958-59), Am. Thyroid Assn. (v.p. 1964-65, 66-67, Disting. Svc. award 1972), Ctrl. Soc. Clin. Rsch. (councillor 1964-67, 67-71), Galens Med. Soc., Assn. Am. Physicians, Mich. Med. Soc., Am. Endocrine Soc., Am. Soc. Clin. Oncology. Home: 917 Whittier Rd Grosse Pointe MI 48230-1873

BEIGHEY, LAWRENCE JEROME, packaging company executive; b. Akron, Ohio, June 24, 1938; s. Jac Laverne and Martha Rose (Vestal) B.; m. Carole Anne LaFlamme, Dec. 11, 1970; children: Basil, Susan, Thomas, Timothy, Elizabeth, Anne. BS in Indsl. Engring., Pa. State U., 1960. Registered profl. engr., Pa.; cert. data processor. Mgr. internat. div. Brockway (Pa.), Inc., 1968-76, mgr. energy div., 1976-78, project mgr., 1978-79, plant mgr., 1979-81, mgr. mfg. staff and services, 1981-83; exec. v.p. Brockway Standard, Atlanta, 1983-86, pres., 1986-89; v.p. Brockway, Inc., Jacksonville, Fla., 1986-89; pres. Transition Mgmt. Resources, Atlanta, 1989; v.p., gen. mgr. All-Pak, Inc., Decatur, Ga., 1990; pres. Plastite Corp., 1990-95; mfg. cons., 1995—. Bd. dirs. Boy Scouts Am., DuBois, Pa., 1978-80, YMCA, DuBois, 1981-83; mem. sch. bd. Brockway Area Sch. Dist., 1981-83; pres. Jaycees, DuBois, 1964. Mem. Steel Shipping Container Inst. (bd. dirs. 1986), Data Processing Mgmt. Assn. (bd. dirs. 1966-68), Dunwoody (Ga.) Country Club, Amelia Island (Fla.) Ocean Club. Avocations: golf, tennis.

BEIGHLE, DOUGLAS PAUL, electric power industry executive; b. Deer Lodge, Mont., June 18, 1932; s. Douglas Paul Beighle and Clarice Janice (Driver) Kiefer; m. Gwendolen Anne Dickson, Oct. 30, 1954 (dec. Jan. 1996); children: Cheryl, Randall, Katherine, Douglas J. B.S. in Bus. Adminstrn., U. Mont., 1954; J.D., U. Mont, 1958; LL.M., Harvard U., 1960. Bar: Mont. 1958, Wash. 1959, U.S. Supreme Ct. 1970. Assoc. Perkins & Coie, Seattle, 1960-67, ptnr., 1967-80; v.p. contracts Boeing Co., Seattle, 1980-81, v.p. contracts, gen. counsel, sec., 1981-86; sr. v.p. Boeing Co., 1986-

97; chief legal counsel Puget Sound Energy Co., Bellevue, Wash., 1970-80, also bd. dirs., 1981—; exec. dir. Wash. State, U.S. West Comm., Denver, 1990-95; bd. dirs. Peabody Holding Co., St. Louis, 1982-90, Washington Mut. Inc., Seattle, 1989—, KCTS-9 TV, 1995—, chair 1996—. Nat. bd. dirs. Jr. Achievement, Colorado Springs, 1981-95; bd. dirs. Greater Puget Sound Jr. Achievement, 1983—, Intiman Theatre, Seattle, 1991-93; trustee Mcpl. League Seattle, 1983-88, U. Mont. Found., Missoula, 1983-91, Mansfield Found., Missoula, 1990-95, Pacific Sci. Ctr., Seattle, 1992—, pres. 1996; trustee Corp. Coun. for the Arts, Seattle, 1994—, chair, 1995-96; active Voice Corp., 1998—. 1st lt. USAF, 1954-56. Harvard U. Law Sch. fellow, 1959. Mem. ABA, Mont. Bar Assn., Wash. State Bar Assn. (chmn. adminstrv. law sect. 1959-60), Seattle-King County Bar Assn., Nat. Assn. Mfrs. (bd. dirs., regional vice chmn. 1988-93), Greater Seattle C. of C. (chair 1994-95), Rainier Club Seattle, Seattle Yacht Club, Poulsbo Yacht Club. Republican. Presbyterian. Office: 1000 2nd Ave Ste 3700 Seattle WA 98104-1053

BEIHL, FREDERICK, lawyer; b. St. Joseph, Mo., Jan. 26, 1932; s. Ernst F. and Evelyn E. (Kline) B.; m. Lillis Prater, Mar. 3, 1962. AB, U. Mo., 1953, LLB, 1955. Bar: Mo. 1955, U.S. Supreme Ct. 1968. With Shook Hardy & Bacon, Kansas City, 1955—, ptnr., 1961—, shareholder, 1992—. Chmn. bd. dirs. UMKC Conservatory of Music, Kansas City, 1988-91, Visiting Nurses Assn., Kansas City, 1977-79; pres. Heart of Am. Family and Children Svcs., Kansas City, 1982-84, Friends of Art Nelson Mus., Kansas City, 1979-81. Avocations: tennis, skiing, art collecting. Office: Shook Hardy & Bacon 1200 Main St Ste 2100 Kansas City MO 64105-2118

BEIL, LARRY, sports announcer; b. Jan. 7, 1961. BA in Journalism, U. Hawaii, Manoa, 1982. Sports dir. KGMB-TV, Honolulu, 1982-89; weekend sports anchor, field reporter KTVU-TV, Oakland, Calif., 1989-95; anchor/reporter SportsCenter ESPN, 1995—. Office: c/o ESPN ESPN Plaza Bristol CT 06010*

BEILENSON, ANTHONY CHARLES, former congressman; b. New Rochelle, N.Y., Oct. 26, 1932; s. Peter and Edna (Rudolph) B.; m. Dolores Martin, June 20, 1959; children: Peter, Dayna, Adam. B.A., Harvard Coll., 1954; LL.B., Harvard U., 1957. Bar: Calif. 1957. Mem. Calif. Assembly from 59th Dist., 1963-66, Calif. Senate from 22d Dist., 1967-76, 95th-104th Congresses from 23rd (now 24th) Calif. Dist., 1977-96; ranking minority mem. subcom. on Rules & Orgn. of Ho. Democrat. Home: 8109 Kerry Ln Chevy Chase MD 20815-4811*

BEILENSON, PETER LOWELL, public health official; b. L.A., Feb. 6, 1960; s. Anthony Charles and Dolores (Martin) B.; children: Valerie, Alex, Jane. AB, Harvard U., 1981; MD, Emory U., 1987; MPH, Johns Hopkins U., 1990. Family practice intern U. Md., Balt., 1987-88; resident in preventive medicine Johns Hopkins U., Balt., 1989-91, chief resident, 1991-92; commr. Balt. City Health Dept., 1992—. Mem. AMA, APHA (Milton and Ruth Roemer award for creative pub. health 1996). Avocations: sports, coaching youth sports. Office: Balt City Health Dept 210 Guilford Ave Baltimore MD 21202-3621

BEILIN, KATARZYNA OLGA, educator; b. June 2, 1966. MA, U. Warsaw, Poland, 1990; PhD, U. Chgo., 1998. Lectr. U. Notre Dame, Ind., 1996-98; vis. asst. prof. Williams Coll., Mass., 1998—. E-mail: kbeilin@williams.edu. Home: 74 Spring St Apt 5 Williamstown MA 01267-2886

BEIM, DAVID ODELL, investment banker, educator; b. Mpls., June 2, 1940; s. Raymond Nelson and Moana (Odell) B.; m. Elizabeth Lucile Artz, Aug. 29, 1964; children—Amy Marie, Nicholas Frederick. B.A. with honors, Stanford U., 1963; MPhil (Rhodes scholar), Oxford (Eng.) U., 1965. With First Boston Corp., N.Y.C., 1966-75; v.p. First Boston Corp., 1971-75, head project finance, 1973-75; exec. v.p. Export-Import Bank U.S., Washington, 1975-77; head corp. fin. Bankers Trust Co., N.Y.C., 1978-87, sr. v.p., 1978-79, exec. v.p., 1979-86, mem. mgmt. com., 1986-87; mng. dir. Dillon Read & Co., 1987-89; prof. Bus. Sch. Columbia U., N.Y.C., 1990—. Chmn. Wave Hill, Inc.; chmn. Outward Bound, Inc. Mem. Council Fgn. Relations. Home: 4684 Dodgewood Rd Bronx NY 10471-3604 Office: Columbia U Uris Hall 410 New York NY 10027

BEIM, NORMAN, playwright, actor, director; b. Newark; s. Herman and Frieda (Thau) B.; m. Virginia Rapkin (div.). Student, Ohio State U., Hedgerow Theatre Sch., Phila., Inst. Contemporary Art, Washington. Appeared in Broadway play Inherit the Wind, 1956-58, off-Broadway play Coriolanus, 1953, Black Visions, 1973; nat. touring prodn. Tribute, 1980; plays include The Deserter, 1979, Success, 1983, Pygmalion and Galatea, 1984, Archie's Comeback, 1986, Jewel Thieves, 1990 (James Ellis Meml. award 1992), Death Amid the Rich and Famous, 1991, Cri de Coeur, 1991, Dreams (No Empty Theater New Play award 1993), Shakespeare Revisited (Maxim Mazumdar New Play award 1993); author: Six Award Winning Plays, Plays at Home and Abroad, My Family, The Jewish Immigrants, 1997, Hymie and the Angel, 1998. Served with F.A. U.S. Army. Mem. SAG, AFTRA, Dramatists Guild Am., Actors Equity Assn. Home: 425 W 57th St New York NY 10019-1764

BEIMERS, GEORGE JACOB, financial executive; b. Grand Rapids, Mich., Dec. 30, 1930; s. Jacob Beimers and Betty Marie (Ashby) Gerold; m. Susannah Shrack, June 5, 1952 (div. 1972); m. Gertrude Hii, Apr. 5, 1986; children: Linda Sue Barrie, Mark George, Pamela Ann. BS in Edn., Western Mich. U., 1952; MEd in Adminstrn., U. Ariz., 1960, MEd in Psychology, 1976; degree in internat. rels., Johns Hopkins U., Bologna, Italy, 1970. Instr. polit. sci. Tucson Pub. Schs., 1957-87; instr. psychology and sociology U. Ariz., Tucson, 1972-87; v.p. New Era Corp., Tucson, 1970-71; pres. Beimers Properties and Investment Co., Tucson, 1972—. Author: Luck, the Human Factor, 1983, Never Kiss a Chinese Dragon, 1992, Gift From the Gods, 1993, Out of the Mouth of a Chinese Dragon, 1996; editor: Blackboard mag., 1960. With U.S. Army, 1953-55. Recipient Golden Poet award World of Poetry, 1987, 91, award of merit, 1987, 90. Mem. U.S. Boat Owners Assn., Sierra Club, Met. Yacht Club. Republican. Avocations: sailing, photography, scuba diving, tennis, golf. Office: Beimers Properties & Investments PO Box 2667 Port Aransas TX 78373-2667 Home: 19 La Playa Port Aransas TX 78373

BEIN, WOLFGANG WALTER, computer science educator; b. Flensburg, Germany, Nov. 22, 1957; came to U.S., 1985; naturalized U.S. citizen.; s. Walter and Elli Bein. MS in Math., U. Osnabrueck, Germany, 1981, PhD, 1987. Rsch. asst. prof. Duke U., Durham, N.C., 1986-88; asst. prof. U. N.Mex., Albuquerque, 1988-92; ops. rsch. analyst Am. Airlines, Ft. Worth, 1992-94; sr. lectr. U. Tex., Dallas, 1994-98; asst. prof. computer sci. U. Nev., Las Vegas, 1998—. Contbr. articles to profl. jours. Deutscher Akademischer Austauschdienst scholar, 1983, 85. Mem. Assn. Computing Machinery (conf. chair 1994—), Sierra Club. Lutheran. E-mail: bein@cs.unlv.edu. Office: U Nev Dept Computer Sci 4505 Maryland Pkwy Las Vegas NV 89154-4019

BEINECKE, CANDACE KRUGMAN, lawyer; b. Paterson, N.J., Nov. 26, 1946; d. Martin and Sylvia (Altshuler) Krugman; m. Frederick W. Beinecke II, Oct. 2, 1976; children: Jacob Sperry, Benjamin Barrett. BA, NYU, 1967; JD, Rutgers U., 1970. Bar: N.Y. 1971. Assoc., then ptnr. Hughes, Hubbard & Reed, N.Y.C., 1970—; lectr., chmn. Practising Law Inst., N.Y.C. Bd. dirs. Merce Cunningham Found., N.Y.C., Jacob's Pillow Dance Festival, Lee, Mass., First Eagle Trust; mem. vis. com. Met. Mus. Art Watson Libr. Mem. ABA, Assn. Bar City of N.Y., River Club, Women's Forum. Office: Hughes Hubbard & Reed One Battery Park Plaza New York NY 10004-1466

BEINECKE, FREDERICK WILLIAM, investment company executive; b. Stamford, Conn., June 3, 1943; s. William S. and Elizabeth (Gillespie) B.; m. Candace Krugman, Oct. 2, 1976; children—Jacob Sperry, Benjamin Barrett. B.A., Yale U., 1966; J.D., U. Va., 1972; P.M.D., Harvard U., 1977. Bar: N.Y. 1973. Assoc. firm Hughes Hubbard & Reed, N.Y.C., 1972-73; gen. counsel South Street Seaport Mus., N.Y.C., 1973-75; with Sperry and Hutchinson Co., N.Y.C., 1975-82; pres. Gunlocke Co. subs., 1979-80, corp. v.p., 1977-80, pres., 1980-82, dir., 1977-82; pres. Antaeus Enterprises, Inc., 1982—, also bd. dirs.; bd. dirs. Catalina Mktg. Corp. Trustee Phillips Acad, Andover, Mass., 1981—, Wildlife Conservation Soc., 1984—, Outward Bound USA, 1987—; trustee Trudeau Inst., Saranac Lake, N.Y., 1971-98, chmn., 1984-91, 95-97, chmn. emeritus, 1998—; bd. dirs. N.Y.C. Ballet, 1978-88, 92—, Prospect Hill Found., 1962—, Samuel H. Kress Found., 1997—; bd. dirs. Sperry Fund, 1977—, pres., 1982—. Capt. USMC, 1966-69. Decorated Bronze Star. Mem. Assn. Bar City N.Y., River Club, Sky Club, Yale Club, Hollenbeck Club, Clove Valley Club, Knickerbocker Club. Office: Antaeus Enterprises 99 Park Ave New York NY 10016-1601

BEINECKE, WILLIAM SPERRY, corporate executive; b. N.Y.C., May 22, 1914; s. Frederick William and Carrie (Sperry) B.; m. Elizabeth Barrett Gillespie, May 24, 1941; children: Frederick W. II, John B., Sarah S., Frances G. B.A., Yale U., 1936, M.A. (hon.), 1971; LL.B., Columbia U., 1940; LL.D. (hon.), Southwestern U., 1967, Cath. U. Am., 1972, Yale U., 1986. Former asso. firm Chadbourne, Wallace, Parke & Whiteside; cofounder firm Casey, Beinecke & Chase; became gen. counsel The Sperry and Hutchinson Co., N.Y.C., 1952; v.p. The Sperry and Hutchinson Co., 1954-60, pres., 1960-67, chmn. bd., chief exec. officer, 1967-80; bd. dirs. Antaeus Enterprises, Inc. Pres., bd. dirs. The Prospect Hill Found.; chmn. emeritus Hudson River Found. for Sci. and Environtl. Rsch.; dir. The Sperry Fund; hon. trustee Am. Museum of Natural History, The Pingry Sch.; life trustee Ctrl. Park Conservancy. Served to comdr. USNR, World War II. Recipient Alumni medal Alumni Fedn. Columbia U., 1971. Mem. Coun. Fgn. Rels., Yale U. Club, Sky Club, Baltusrol Golf Club, Eastward Ho Country Club, Gulf Stream Golf Club, Ocean Club, Little Club. Home: 21 E 79th St New York NY 10021-0125 Office: Antaeus Enterprises Inc 99 Park Ave #2200 New York NY 10016-1601

BEINEKE, LOWELL WAYNE, mathematics educator; b. Decatur, Ind., Nov. 20, 1939; s. Elmer Henry and Lillie Agnes (Snell) B.; m. Judith Rowena Wooldridge, Dec. 23, 1967; children: Jennifer Elaine, Philip Lennox. BS, Purdue U., 1961; MA, U. Mich., 1962, PhD, 1965. Asst. prof. Purdue U., Ft. Wayne, Ind., 1965-68, assoc. prof., 1968-71, prof., 1971-86, Jack W. Schrey prof., 1986—; tutor Oxford (Eng.) U., 1974, The Open U., Milton Keynes, Eng., 1974, 75; vis. lectr. Poly. N. London, Eng., 1980-81; vis. scholar Wolfson Coll., Oxford U., 1993-94. Co-author, co-editor: Selected Topics in Graph Theory, 3 vols., 1978, 83, 88, Applications of Graph Theory, 1979, Graph Connections, 1997; mem. editl. bd., assoc. editor Jour. Graph Theory, 1977-80, 89-94; mem. editl. bd. Internat. Jour. Graph Theory, 1991-95, co-editor: congressus Numerantium, Vols., 1963-64, 1988; contbr. numerous articles to profl. jours. Corp. mem. Bd. for Homeland Ministries, United Ch. of Christ, N.Y., 1988-91, del. Gen. Synod, 1989, 91. Recipient Outstanding Tchr. award AMOCO Found., 1978, Friends of the Univ., 1992, Disting. Svc. award Ind. Sect., 1998, Outstanding Rsch. award, 1999; Fulbright Found. grantee London, 1980-81, rsch. grantee Office Naval Rsch., Washington, 1986-89; fellow Inst. Combinatorics and its Applications, 1990—. Mem. AAUP, Math. Assn. Am. (chairperson Ind. sect. 1987-88, bd. govs. 1990-93, Disting. Tchg. award Ind. Sect. 1997), Am. Math. Soc., London Math. Soc., Common Cause, Amnesty Internat., Summit Book Club, Internat. Affairs Forum, Sigma Xi (club pres. 1984-86, chpt. pres. 1997-98), Phi Kappa Phi (chpt. pres. 1993). Achievements include characterization of line graphs and thickness of complete graphs; enumeration of multidimensional trees. Avocations: British culture, reading, gardening, stamp collecting, jogging. E-mail: beineke@ipfw.edu. Home: 4529 Bradwood Ter Fort Wayne IN 46815-6028 Office: Ind U-Purdue U Dept of Math Scis 2101 E Coliseum Blvd Fort Wayne IN 46805-1445

BEINERT, HELMUT, biochemist; b. Lahr, Germany, Nov. 17, 1913; came to U.S., 1947; m. Elisabeth Meyhoefer, 1955; 4 children. Dr rer nat, U. Leipzig, 1943; DSc, U. Wis., Milw., 1987, U. Konstanz, Germany, 1994. Rsch. assoc. Kaiser Wilhelm Inst. Med. Rsch., Germany, 1943-45; biochemist Air Force Aeromed Ctr., Germany, 1946, USAF, Sch. Aviation Medicine, 1947-50; postdoctoral rschr. U. Wis., Inst. Enzyme Rsch., Madison, 1950, rsch. assoc., 1951-52, asst. prof. to prof. enzyme chemistry, 1952-84, chmn. section III, 1958-84, prof. biochemistry, 1967-84, emeritus prof. enzyme chemistry and biochemistry, 1984—; prof. biochemistry, dist. scholar residence Med. Coll. Wis., 1985-94; permanent guest prof. U. Konstanz, Germany, 1967. Recipient Rsch. Career award NIH, 1963, Sr. Scientist award Alexander von Humboldt Found., 1981, Keilin medal Biochem. Soc. London, 1993, Warburg medal German Soc. Biochem. and Molecular Biology, 1994. Fellow Am. Acad. Arts and Sci.; mem. NAS, Am. Chemical Soc., Am. Soc. Biol., Chemistry and Molecular Biology, Soc. Biol. Inorganic Chemistry. Office: Univ Wis Inst Enzyme Rsch 1710 University Ave Madison WI 53705-4098

BEIRNE, MARTIN DOUGLAS, lawyer; b. N.Y.C., Oct. 24, 1944; s. Martin Douglas and Catherine Anne (Rooney) B.; m. Kathleen Harrington; children: Martin, Shannon, Kelley. BS, Spring Hill Coll., 1966; JD with honors, St. Mary's U., 1969. Bar: Tex. 1969, U.S. Dist. Ct. (ea. dist.) Tex. 1972, U.S. Dist. Ct. (so. dist.) Tex. 1971, U.S. Dist. Ct. (no. dist.) Tex., U.S. Dist. Ct. (we. dist.) Tex., U.S. Ct. Appeals (5th and 11th cirs.) 1974, U.S. Dist. Ct. (ea. dist.) Calif., U.S. Supreme Ct. 1975. Ptnr. Fulbright & Jaworski, Houston, 1971-85; mng. ptnr. Beirne, Maynard & Parsons, Houston, 1985—. Editor-in-chief St. Mary's Law Rev. Bd. dirs. St. Thomas U., Houston Law Rev. Capt. U.S. Army, 1969-71. Fellow Tex. Bar Found.; mem. ABA, Tex. Bar Assn., Houston Bar Assn., Coronado Club, The Houstonian Club, Legatus-U. Houston Law Sch. Found. Roman Catholic. Office: Beirne Maynard & Parsons LLP Wells Fargo 1300 Post Oak Blvd Fl 24 Houston TX 77056-3028

BEIRNE-PATEY, MARIAN JOSEPHINE, secondary educator; b. Somers Point, N.J., Mar. 30, 1954; d. Owen Joseph and Helen (Smith) Beirne; m. Carl Edward Patey, Aug. 27, 1983. BA, Rutgers U., 1976; MFA, George Washington U., 1985, MEd, 1997. Cert. secondary tchr. Resident costume designer South Jersey Regional Theatre, Somers Point, N.J., 1976-81; costume designer George Washington U., Washington, 1989-91; secondary educator Chantilly (Va.) H.S., 1993—; adj. prof. Cath. U., Washington, 1985-87, George Mason U., Fairfax, Va., 1988. curriculum developer Chantilly H.S., Fairfax, 1996-98, staff devel. in-svc., 1994-98; gifted and talented liaison Fairfax County Pub. Sch., 1994-96. Mem. Prince William County Dem. Com., 1994—; v.p. Quail Hollow Homeowners Assn., Manassas, Va., 1997—. Douglass Coll. scholar, 1972-76, Women's Club Fedn. of N.J. scholar, 1972-76. Mem. AAUW, Douglas Coll. Alumni Assn., Nat. Coun. of Tchrs. of English, English Tchrs. Assn. of Northern Va. (Promise award, Outstanding Tchr. 1994), Contbg. Assn. in Support of GWU Theatre. Democrat. Avocations: reading, cross-stitching, sewing. E-mail: pateywomyn@aol.com. Home: 7563 Kimberton Ct Manassas VA 20111-1762

BEISNER, JOHN HERBERT, lawyer; b. Salina, Kans., Feb. 24, 1953; s. Herbert J. and Matilda (Cordel) B.; m. Diane G. Klinke, Apr. 26, 1980; 1 child, Laura Ann. BA, U. Kans., 1975; JD, U. Mich, 1978. Bar: Calif. 1978, D.C. 1980. Assoc. O'Melveny & Myers, Washington, 1978-85, ptnr., 1985—, mgmt. com., 1996—. Mem. State Colls. Coord. Com. Kans. Bd. Regents, 1974-75. Mem. ABA, Am. Law Inst., Fed. Comm. Bar Assn. Office: O'Melveny & Myers 555 13th St NW Ste 500W Washington DC 20004-1159

BEISSER, SALLY RAPP, educator; b. Ft. Dodge, Iowa, Nov. 11, 1949; d. Alvin LeRoy Rapp and Betty (Williams) Tuttle; m. Kim David Beisser, July 19, 1975; children: Andrea Lynn, Sarah Ann. BS, Iowa State U., 1971, MS, 1977, PhD, 1999. Cert. tchr., Iowa. Tchr. Maquoketa (Iowa) Community Schs., 1971-73; tchr., gifted and talented facilitator Ames (Iowa) Community Schs., 1974-90, West Des Moines (Iowa) Community Schs., 1992; supr. student tchrs. U. Iowa, Iowa City, 1991-92; instr. Coll. Edn. Iowa State U., Ames, 1992-99; prof. effective teaching Drake U., Des Moines, 1999—; ednl. cons. Crayola Kids mag., 1994; ind. edn. cons., cen. Iowa. Contbr. to profl. publs. Bd.dirs. Friends of the Libr., West Des Moines, 1992; mem. literacy com. Greater Des Moines Literacy Coalition. Mem. NEA, ASCD, AAUW, SITE, SHSI, Iowa State Edn. Assn., Nat. Assn. Gifted Children, Iowa Talented-Gifted Assn. (bd. dirs. 1994—, co-chair, conf. coord., speakers bur. 1988—), Nat. Assn. Soc. Studies, Am Ednl. Rsch. Assn., Assn. Tchrs. Educators, Phi Delta Kappa, Delta Kappa Gamma, Phi Kappa Phi. Avocations: classical music, creative writing, church activities. Home: 3126 Sycamore Rd Ames IA 50014-4510 Office: Drake U Sch Edn 3206 University Ave Des Moines IA 50311

BEISSINGER, MARGARET HIEBERT, educator; b. San Francisco, Jan. 20, 1954; d. Erwin Nick and Elfrieda Lillian (Franz) Hiebert; m. Mark Richard Beissinger, June 14, 1984; children: Jonathan David, Rebecca Helen. BA, Harvard Coll., 1976; PhD, Harvard U., 1984. Teaching asst. Harvard U., Cambridge, Mass., 1984-88; vis. asst. prof. U. Wis., Madison, 1989-93, lectr., 1993-99, asst. prof., 1999—. Author: The Art of the Lăutar: The Epic Tradition of Romania, 1991; editor: Epic Traditions in the contemporary World: The Poetics of Community, 1999. Grantee Fulbright Found., Romania, 1979-80, Internat. Rsch. & Exch. Bd., Romania, 1979-80, 85, 87, 89, 98; Am. Coun. Learned Socs. fellow, 1988-89. Mem. Am. Assn. Advancement Slavic Studies, Am. Assn. Tchrs. Slavic & East European Langs., Am. Folklore Soc., Modern Lang. Assn. Am., Soc. Romanian Studies (nat. bd. dirs. 1987-88, 94—), Gypsy Lore Soc. (bd. dirs. 1998—). Home: 1719 Madison St Madison WI 53711 Office: U Wis Dept Slavic Langs 1220 Linden Dr Madison WI 53706

BEISSINGER, MARK RICHARD, political scientist, educator; b. Phila., Nov. 28, 1954; s. Walter and Muriel Beissinger; m. Margaret Helen Hiebert, June 14, 1984; children: Jonathan, Rebecca. BA in Polit. Sci., Duke U., 1976; PhD in Govt., Harvard U., 1982. Asst. prof. govt. dept. Harvard U., Cambridge, Mass., 1982-87; asst. prof. polit. sci. dept. U. Wis., Madison, 1988-90, assoc. prof. polit. sci. dept., 1990-95, prof. polit. sci. dept., 1995—, founding dir. Ctr. for Russia, East Europe and Ctrl. Asia, 1992-98; v.p. Assn. for the Study of Nationalities, N.Y.C., 1994-98; chair univ. libr. com. U. Wis., Madison, 1996-97. Author: Scientific Management, Socialist Discipline, and Soviet Power, 1988; editor: The Nationalities Factor in Soviet Politics and Society, 1990; mem. editl. bd. Slavic Rev., 1992-96; mem. internat. adv. bd.: Encyclopedia of Nationalism, 1997—; contbr. chpts. to books and articles to profl. jours. Fulbright-Hays fellow, Moscow, 1990-91, fellow Woodrow Wilson Internat. Ctr. for Scholars, Washington, 1995-96; grantee NSF, Washington, 1993-96. Mem. Am. Polit. Sci. Assn., Am. Assn. for the Advancement Slavic Studies. Democrat. E-mail: mbeissin@facstaff.wisc.edu. Home: 1719 Madison St Madison WI 53711 Office: U Wis Madison Dept Polit Sci 110 North Hall Madison WI 53706

BEISTLINE, EARL HOOVER, mining consultant; b. Juneau, Alaska, Nov. 24, 1916; s. Ralph H. and Catherine (Krinach) B.; m. Dorothy Ann Hering, Aug. 24, 1946; children—Ralph Robert, William Calvin, Katherine Noreen, Lynda Marie. B. Mining Engring., U. Alaska, 1939, E.M., 1947, LL.D. (hon.), 1969. Mem. faculty U. Alaska, 1946-82, dean Sch. Mines, 1949-61, dean Coll. Earth Sci. and Mineral Industry, 1961-75, provost Coll. Earth Sci. and Mineral Industry, 1970-75, exec. officer no. region, 1970-73, dean Sch. Mineral Industry, 1975-82, dean emeritus, prof. mining engring. Sch. Mineral Industry, 1982—; mining cons. Served to maj. AUS, 1941-46. Fellow AAAS, Explorers Club; mem. NSPE, Am. Inst. Mining and Metall. Engrs., Mining and Metall. Soc. Am., Arctic Inst. N.Am., Am. Soc. Engring. Edn., N.W. Mining Assn., Alaska Mining Assn., Pioneers of Alaska. Home and Office: PO Box 80148 Fairbanks AK 99708-0148*

BEISWANGER, GARY LEE, lawyer; b. Billings, Mont., May 31, 1938. BA in Philosophy, History-Polit. Sci., U. Mont., 1960, LLB, 1963. Bar: Mont. 1963, U.S. Dist. Ct. Mont. 1963, U.S. Ct. Appeals (9th cir.) 1987. Pvt. practice, Billings, 1965—. Mem. ABA, ATLA, State Bar Mont., Mont. Trial Lawyers Assn., Yellowstone County Bar Assn. Office: Rocky Village Ctr I 1500 Poly Dr Billings MT 59102-1748

BEITER, THOMAS ALBERT, crystallographer, research scientist, consultant; b. Lancaster, Ohio, Jan. 21, 1947; s. Paul Clement and Marie Julia (Mullen) B. BS in Math., Ohio State U., 1970; MS in Physics, Miami U., Oxford, Ohio, 1984, PhD in Chemistry, 1992. Rsch. scientist, cons. in crystallography Mansfield, Ohio, 1992—. Mem. Am. Chem. Soc., Am. Crystallographic Assn., Am. Phys. Soc., Am. Math. Soc., Assn. for Symbolic Logic, Sigma Xi, Phi Beta Kappa. Achievements include development of new methods for solving mathematical problems in x-ray diffraction crystallography; structure determination from powder data; indexing of triclinic powder data; space group determination for atomic arrangements; analysis of disorder in crystalline samples; research in number theory (Fermat Conjecture). Avocation: flying. Office: PO Box 3532 Mansfield OH 44907-0532

BEITLER, STEPHEN SETH, private equity and venture capital executive; b. N.Y.C., Oct. 1, 1956; s. Stanley Samuel and Arline (Mandell) B.; m. Deborah Joy Gottlieb, Jan. 16, 1982; children: Grace Jacqueline, Elinore Meredith. BA, cert. of Asian Study, Am. U. Sch. Internat. Studies, Washington, 1977; postgrad., U. Chgo., 1977-78; MS, Def. Intelligence Coll., 1986. Legis. aide U.S. Ho. of Reps., Washington, 1975-77; commd. 2d lt. U.S. Army, 1977, advanced through grades to maj., 1989; intelligence briefing officer to Sec. Def. and Chmn. Joint Chiefs of Staff, Washington, 1984-86; asst. to asst. sec. of def. Office Sec. Def., Washington, 1987-88, asst. to undersec. of def., 1988-89; resigned U.S. Army, 1989; mgr. ops. devel. Helene Curtis, Inc., Chgo., 1989-90, corp. mgr. strategy and devel., 1990-92, dir. strategy and devel., 1993; nat. mgr. operational planning and info. Sears Merchandise Group, Hoffman Estates, Ill., 1993-95; sr. dir. fin. processes and systems Sears, Roebuck and Co., Hoffman Estates, Ill., 1995-97, asst. corp. contr., 1997-98; ptnr. Trident Capital, Chgo., 1998—; comdr. 305th psychol. ops. bn. USAR, Arlington Heights, Ill., 1992-96; comdr. 16th psychol. ops. bn. USAR, Ft. Sheridan, Ill., 1996-97; cons. MGA, Inc., Chgo., 1985—; founding chmn. Conf. Bd. Coun. Competitive Analysis. Contbg. author: The Military Intelligence Community, 1986; contbr. articles to profl. publs. Vol. Bus. Vols. for the Arts, Chgo., 1991-94. Lt. col. USAR, ret. 1998. Decorated Green Beret for valor and svc. Fellow Interuniv. Seminar on Armed Forces and Soc., Soc. Competitive Intelligence Profls. (bd. dirs. 1991-94); mem. Spl. Forces Club, Army and Navy Club. Home: 156 Lakewood Pl Highland Park IL 60035-5010 Office: Trident Capital 272 E Deerpath Ste 304 Lake Forest IL 60045

BEITZ, ALEXANDRA GRIGG, political activist; b. Cin., Oct. 15, 1960; d. Kenneth Andrew and Betty Ann (Carpenter) Grigg; m. Charles Arthur Beitz III, Oct. 17, 1987; 1 child, Madeleine Grigg Beitz. BA, Vassar Coll., 1982; MBA, Wake Forest U., 1985. Asst. buyer Bloomingdale's, N.Y.C., 1982-83; dept. mgr. Bloomingdale's, Stamford, Conn., 1983; intern Ciba-Geigy Corp., Greensboro, N.C., 1984; retail sales promotion mgr. Hanes Hosiery, N.Y.C., 1985-86; market rep. May Co., N.Y.C., 1986-87; freelance polit. cons. Winston-Salem, N.C., 1990-98. Vol. Planned Parenthood, Winston-Salem, N.C., 1988-98, Southeastern Ctr. for Contemporary Art, Winston-Salem, 1992-98, exec. bd. dirs. Friends, 1983, v.p.-pres. elect, 1994, pres., 1995, exec. bd. dirs., 1995-98; vol. Am. Cancer Soc., Winston-Salem, 1992-94; bd. dirs. Planned Parenthood of the Triad, Winston-Salem, 1995-98. Avocations: photography, gastronomy.

BEITZ, WILLIAM CHARLES, religious charity executive; b. Saginaw, Mich., Apr. 10, 1943; s. Wilbert Charles and Edna Martha (Brieske) E.; m. Lynette Diane Beitz, Feb. 14, 1985. MA, St. John Provincial Sem., Plymouth, Mich., 1982; MPA, Ctrl. Mich. U., 1984. Adminstr. Cath. Diocese of Saginaw, 1969-82; asst. exec. dir. Cath. Family Svc., Saginaw, 1982-87; exec. dir. Cath. Charities, Jacksonville, Fla., 1987—. Mem. Emergency Svcs. and Homeless Coalition, Jacksonville, 1987—; mem. study team Jacksonville Cmty. Coun., Inc., 1988—. Mem. ASAP (past treas., v.p., pres.), Soc. Human Resource Mgrs., Jacksonville Downtown C. of C. (treas. 1989—), Deercreek Country Club. Democrat. Roman Catholic. Avocations: camping, walking, sports fan. E-mail: bbeitz@medione.net. Office: Catholic Charities 134 E Church St Jacksonville FL 32202

BEIZER, LANCE KURT, lawyer; b. Hartford, Conn., Sept. 8, 1938; s. Lawrence Sidney and Victoria Merriam (Kaplan) B. BA in Sociology, Brandeis U., 1960; MA in English, San Jose State U., 1967; JD, U. San Diego, 1975. Bar: Calif. 1975. Selective svc. affairs coord. U. Calif., 1969-73, vet. affairs coord., 1973-75; vet. outreach coord. San Diego Community Coll. Dist., 1975-76; dep. dist. atty. Santa Clara County, Calif., 1976—. Bd. mgrs. Santa Clara Valley S.W. YMCA, Saratoga, Calif., 1988—, chair, 1991-93; bd. dirs. The Lumen Found., San Francisco, 1985—. Bd. dirs. Fedn. Cmty. Ministries, Calif., 1992—, chair, 1996—; bd. dirs. South Bay Homeless Teenagers Alliance, 1997—, chair, 1997—. Lt. USNR, 1961-65. Mem. Calif. Dist. Attys. Assn., Santa Clara County Bar Assn., Am. Profl. Soc. on Abuse of Children, Nat. Assn. Counsel for Children, Am. Weil Soc., Mensa, Commonwealth Club. Republican. Episcopalian. Home: 1197 Capri Dr

Campbell CA 95008-6002 Office: Santa Clara County Dist Atty 70 W Hedding St San Jose CA 95110-1768

BEIZER, ROBERT A., lawyer; b. Hartford, Conn., Dec. 13, 1939. AB, Harvard U., 1961; LLB, Yale U., 1964. Bar: Conn. 1964, D.C. 1965. Law clerk U.S. Ct. Appeals 2d cir., 1964-65; ptnr. Sidley & Austin, Washington, 1994; with Venable, Baetjer, Howard & Civiletti, 1994—; tutor law Yale U., 1964-65; lectr. comm. law U. Va. Law Sch., 1968-84; v.p. law & devel. Gray Comm. Sys., Inc., 1996—. Named Disting. Practitioner Residence Comms. Law Inst. Cath. U. Law Sch., 1994. Mem. Fed. Comm. Bar Assn. (exec. com. 1979-81, pres. 1992-93). Office: Venable, Baetjer, Howard & Civiletti 1201 New York Ave NW Washington DC 20005-3917

BEJA, MORRIS, English literature educator; b. N.Y.C., July 18, 1935; s. Joseph and Eleanor (Cohen) B.; children: Andrew Lloyd, Eleni Rachel; m. Ellen Carol Jones, 1990. BA, CCNY, 1957; MA, Columbia U., 1958; PhD, Cornell U., 1963. From instr. to prof. English, Ohio State U., Columbus, 1961—, chmn. dept., 1983-94; vis prof. U. Thessaloniki, Greece, 1965-66, Univ. Coll. Dublin, 1972-73. Author: Epiphany in the Modern Novel, 1971, Film and Literature, 1979, Joyce the Artist Manqué and Indeterminacy, 1989, James Joyce: A Literary Life, 1992; editor: Virginia Woolf's Mrs. Dalloway, 1996, Joyce in the Hibernian Metropolis, 1996, Perspectives on Orson Welles, 1995, Samuel Beckett's Humanistic Perspectives, 1983, James Joyce Newestlatter, 1977—, James Joyce's Dubliners and Portrait of the Artist, 1973, 5 other books. Pres. Internat. James Joyce Found., 1982-90, sec., 1990—; dir. Internat. James Joyce Symposia, 1982, 86, 92. With USAR, 1958-63. Guggenheim fellow, 1972-73; Fulbright lectr., 1965-66, 72-73. Mem. Virginia Woolf Soc. (trustee 1976-84), MLA, Am. Conf. Irish Studies. Jewish. Avocations: photography; travel; cycling. Home: 1135 Middleport Dr Columbus OH 43235-4060 Office: Ohio State U Dept of English 164 W 17th Ave Columbus OH 43210-1326

BEJAN, ADRIAN, mechanical engineering educator; b. Sept. 24, 1948; married; 3 children. SB in Mech. Engring., MIT, 1972, SM in Mech. Engring., 1972, PhD Mech. Engring., 1975; PhD (hon.), Poly. U. Bucharest, 1992, U. Galati, Romania, 1995, U. Constantza, Romania, 1997. Engr. Sci. Energy Systems, Inc., Watertown, Mass., 1972; rsch. asst. dept. mech. engring. MIT, 1971-74, lectr., rsch. assoc., dept. mech. engring., 1975-76; fellow Miller Inst. Basic Rsch. Sci., U. Calif., Berkeley, 1976-78; asst. prof., dept. mech. engring. U. Colo., Boulder, 1978-81; Croft prof. U. Colo. Coll. Engring., 1981-82; assoc. prof., dept. mech. engring. U. Colo., Boulder, 1981-84; prof., dept. mech. engring. and materials sci. Duke U., Durham, N.C., 1984-89, J.A. Jones prof., dept. mech. engring., 1989—. Author: Entropy Generation Through Heat and Fluid Flow, 1982, Convection Heat Transfer, 1984, 2d edit., 1995, Advanced Engineering Thermodynamics, 1988, Heat Transfer, 1993, Entropy Generation Minimization, 1996; co-author: Convection in Porous Media, 1992, Thermal Design and Optimization, 1996; hon. editorial bd.: International Journal of Heat and Mass Transfer, 1992, International Communications in Heat and Mass Transfer, 1992, Termotehnica, 1993; bd. editors: Internat. Journal for Engineering Analysis and Design; adv. editor: Heat Transfer Japanese Rsch., 1990, Internat. Jour. Heat and Fluid Flow, 1988, Numerical Heat Transfer, 1995, Jour. Non-Equilibrium Thermodynamics, 1996, Energy-The Internat. Jour., 1997, Revue Générale de Thermique, 1997; reviewer manuscripts for numerous jours.; contbr. over 260 articles to profl. jours. Recipient Ralph R. Teetor award Soc. Automotive Engrs., 1980, De Florez award MIT, 1969, Heat Transfer Meml. award, 1994, Worcester Reed Warner medal 1996; Faculty fellow U. Colo., 1984-85; F. Mosey Vis. scholar U. Western Australia. Fellow ASME (Gustus L. Larson award 1988, James Harry Potter Gold medal 1990); mem. Am. Acad. Mechanics, Tau Beta Pi, Pi Tau Sigma. Office: Duke U PO Box 90300 Dept Mech Engring Sc Durham NC 27708-0300*

BEJCZY, ANTAL KÁROLY, research scientist, research facility administrator; b. Ercsi, Hungary, Jan. 16, 1930; came to U.S., 1966; s. Jenö and Erzsébet (László) B.; m. Margit Tóth, Oct. 12, 1957. BSEE, Tech. U., Budapest, Hungary, 1956; PhD in Physics, Sci. U., Oslo, 1963. Univ. lectr. Sci. U., Oslo, 1963-66; rsch. scientist Norwegian Rsch. Coun., Oslo, 1963-66; sr. rsch. fellow Calif. Inst. Tech., Pasadena, 1966-69; mem. tech. staff Jet Propulsion Lab., Pasadena, 1969-79, tech. mgr., 1979—, sr. rsch. scientist, 1985—; bd. dirs. Zoltán Bay Applied Scis. Found., Budapest, Hungary, 1993—; affiliate prof. Washington U., St. Louis, 1983—. Contbr. articles on robotics and telerobotics to profl. jours.; assoc. editor Automatic Control Trans., 1982-85; patentee in field. Recipient Jean Vertut award Robotics Internat., 1987; NASA Exceptional Svc. medal, 1991. Fellow IEEE; mem. Robotics and Automation Soc. of IEEE (pres. 1986-87, adminstrv. com. 1991—). Avocations: tennis, gardening, music. Office: Jet Propulsion Lab MS 198-219 4800 Oak Grove Dr Pasadena CA 91109-8001

BEKAVAC, NANCY YAVOR, academic administrator, lawyer; b. Pitts., Aug. 28, 1947; d. Anthony Joseph and Elvira (Yavor) B. BA, Swarthmore Coll., 1969; JD, Yale U., 1973. Bar: Calif. 1974, U.S. Dist. Ct. (cen. dist.) 1974, (no. dist.) Calif. 1975, (so. dist.) Calif. 1976, U.S. Ct. Appeals (9th cir.) 1975, (8th cir.) 1981, U.S. Supreme Ct. 1979. Law clk. at large U.S. Ct. Appeals (D.C. cir.), Washington, 1973-74; assoc. Munger, Tolles & Rickershauser, L.A., 1974-79, ptnr., 1980-85; exec. dir. Thomas J. Watson Found., Providence, 1985-87, cons., 1987-88; counselor to pres. Dartmouth Coll., Hanover, N.H., 1988-90; pres. Scripps Coll., Claremont, Calif., 1990—; adj. prof. law UCLA Law Sch., 1982-83; mem. Calif. Higher Edn. Roundtable, 1996—; trustee Am. Coun. Edn., 1994-97. Bd. mgrs. Swarthmore Coll., 1984—; trustee Wenner-Gren Found. for Anthr. Rsch. 1987-94; bd. trustees Am. Coun. Edn., 1994-97; chair Assn. Ind. Colls. and Univs., 1996-97. Recipient Human Rights award L.A. County Commn. on Civil Rights, 1984; Woodrow Wilson fellow, Thomas J. Watson fellow, 1969. Mem. Assn. Ind. Calif. Colls. and Univs. (chair 1996), Sierra Club. Avocations: hiking, reading, traveling. Office: Scripps Coll Office of Pres 1030 N Columbia Ave Claremont CA 91711-3948

BEKEY, GEORGE ALBERT, computer scientist, educator, engineer; b. Bratislava, Slovakia, June 19, 1928; came to U.S., 1945, naturalized, 1956; s. Andrew and Elizabeth B.; m. Shirley White, June 10, 1951; children: Ronald Steven, Michelle Elaine. BS with honors, U. Calif., Berkeley, 1950; MS, UCLA, 1952, PhD, 1962. Research engr. UCLA, 1950-54; mgr. computer center Beckman Instruments, L.A. and Berkeley, 1955-58; mem. sr. staff, dir. computer center TRW Systems Group, Redondo Beach, Calif., 1958-62; mem. faculty U. So. Calif., L.A., 1962—, prof. elec. and biomed. engring. and computer sci., 1968-82, chmn. dept. elec. engring. systems, 1978-86, dir. Robotics Lab., 1983-98, chmn. computer sci. dept., 1984-89, dir. Ctr. for Mfg. and Automation Research, 1987-94, assoc. dean rsch. Sch. Engring., 1996—; chair computer sci. Gordon Marshall, 1990—; cons. to govt. agys. and indsl. orgns. Author: (with W.J. Karplus) Hybrid Computation, 1968, (with K. Goldberg) Robotics and Neural Networks, 1994; editor 6 books; mem. editorial bd. 3 profl. jours.; founding editor IEEE Trans. Robotics and Automation; editor Autonomous Robots; contbr. over 200 articles to profl. jours.; patentee in field. Served with U.S. Army, 1954-56. Recipient Disting. Faculty award, 1977, Sch. Engring. and Service award U. So. Calif., 1990. Fellow AAAS, IEEE, Am. Inst. Med. and Biol. Engring., Am. Assn. Artificial Intelligence; mem. IEEE Robotics and Automation Soc. (pres. 1996-97), NAE, Assn. for Computing Machinery, Soc. for Computer Simulation, Neural Network Soc., Biomed. Engring. Soc., World Affairs Coun., Sigma Xi, Tau Beta Pi, Eta Kappa Nu. Office: U So Calif Office of the Dean Los Angeles CA 90089-4500

BEKEY, SHIRLEY WHITE, psychotherapist; b. L.A.; d. Lawrence Francis and Alice (King) White; m. George Albert Bekey, June 10, 1951; children: Ronald S., Michelle E. BA in Psychology, Occidental Coll., L.A., 1949; MSW in Psychiat. Social Work, UCLA, 1954; PhD in Edn. Psychology, U. So. Calif., 1980. Lic. clin. social worker, Calif.; cert. in pupil pers., parent-child edn. Caseworker outpatient svcs. Calif. State Dept. Mental Health, Montebello; caseworker Lowman Sch. for Handicapped, L.A. Unified Sch. Dist., North Hollywood, Calif., 1971-72; psychotherapist Hofmann Psychiat. Clinic, Glendale (Calif.) Adventist Hosp., 1973-75; pvt. practice Encino, Calif., 1980—; sprk. in field.; TV expert on children's emotional problems. 1st hosp. vol. candystriper in U.S., Hollywood Hosp, L.A., 1942; mem. World Affairs Coun., L.A., 1960—. Fellow Soc. for Clin. Social Work; mem. NASW, APA, Am. Ednl. Rsch. Assn., Nat. Assn. Gifted Children, Assn. Transpersonal Psychology, Inst. Noetic Sci., Assn. Ednl. Therapists, So. Calif. Soc. for Clin. Hypnosis, Analytical Psychology Club L.A., Nat. Assn. Poetry Therapy, Calif. Assn. for Gifted. Avocations: clinical hypnosis, gifted and talented, learning disabilities. Office: 4924 Balboa Blvd # 199 Encino CA 91316-3402

BEKHECHI, MOHAMMED ABDELWAHAB, lawyer; b. Tlemlen, Algeria; s. Chaib Bekhechi and Cherifa Medroumi; m. Karima Triqui, Apr. 14, 1975; children: Nassima, Nael, Chaib Mohammed Riad. ML, Sorbonne Paris 1, 1973; PhD in Law, Sorbonne Paris 2, 1986. Prof. internat. law U. Oran, Algeria, 1974-84; vice-rector U. Oran, 1980-86; sr. counsel World Bank, Washington, 1994—; prof. internat. law U. Paris, 1984-88; mem. Constnl. Coun. Algeria, 1989-94. Author of three books on internat. law; editor 2 books on polit. scis.; contbr. articles to profl. jours. Lt. Algerian Air Force, 1976-78. Mem. Internat. Union for Conservation, Profl. Bankers Assn. Home: 7204 Taveshire Way Bethesda MD 20817 Office: World Bank 1818 H St NW Washington DC 20433

BEKKEDAHL, BRAD DOUGLAS, dentist; b. Williston, N.D., Nov. 23, 1957; s. Oliver Lawrence Jr. and Gudrun Joan (Sundby) B. BA, Jamestown (N.D.) Coll., 1979; BS, U. Minn., 1982, DDS, 1984. Gen. practice dentistry Williston, 1984—; chmn. dental staff Mercy Med. Ctr., 1991-93. Scoutmaster Boy Scouts Am., Williston, 1984-86; pastoral com. Gloria Dei Luth. Ch., Williston, 1986-88, coun. mem., 1993-96, congregation pres., 1995; pres. Am. Legion Drum and Bugle Corps, Williston, 1986; edn. officer Luth. Brotherhood br. 8334, 1989-93; mem. exec. com. Raymond Family Cmty. Ctr., 1988-96; city commr. Williston, 1996—; mem. Williston Pk. Bd., 1988-96, pres., 1988-92; dist. dir. USA Hockey, 1999—. Capt. Dental Corps, USAR. Recipient New Dentist of Yr. award N.Dakota Dental Assn., 1997. Mem. ADA, N.D. Dental Assn. (New Dentist of Yr. 1997), N.W. Dist. Dental Assn., Williston Dental Soc. (sec.-treas.), N.D. Amateur Hockey Assn. (v.p. 1990-93, cmty. rep., pres. 1986-90, pres. 1993—). Avocations: youth coaching, camping, woodworking, sports. Home: PO Box 2443 Williston ND 58802-2443 Office: PO Box 2443 2204 2d Ave W Williston ND 58801

BELAFONTE, HARRY, singer, concert artist, actor; b. N.Y.C., 1927; s. Harold George and Melvine (Love) B.; m. Julie Robinson, Mar. 8, 1957; children—Adrienne, Shari, David, Gina. Student pub. schs.; LHD (hon.), Park Coll., Mo., 1968; HHD (hon.), Park Coll.; Doctorate Liberal Arts (hon.), ArtsD (hon.), New Sch. Social Research; MusD (hon.), Morehouse Coll., 1987; DFA (hon.), SUNY, Purchase, 1987, Spelman Coll., 1990; DHL (hon.), CCNY, 1990, Columbia U., 1993; DSc (hon.), Tufts U., 1991, Brandeis U., 1991, Long Island U., 1991; DA (hon.), Bard Coll., 1993; DLitt, U. West Indies, Kingston, Jamaica, 1996; hon. degree, U. Mass., 1996; LLD(hon.), McMaster U., Hamilton, Ont., Can., 1996; D (hon.) in Civil Law, U. Newcastle, Britain, 1998; LHD (hon.), Bklyn. Coll., 1998. Pres. Belafonte Enterprises, Inc., N.Y.C. Singer, actor in Broadway shows John Murray Anderson's Almanac (Tony award 1953), Three for Tonight, 1955; motion pictures: Bright Road, 1952, Carmen Jones, 1954, Island in the Sun, 1957, The World, the Flesh and the Devil, 1958, Odds Against Tomoroow, 1959, The Angel Levine, 1969, Buck and the Preacher, 1971, Uptown Saturday Night, 1974, White Man's Burden, 1995, Kansas City, 1996; prodr. stage play To Be Young Gifted and Black, 1969; appeared in TV movies Grambling's White Tiger, 1981, Swing Vote, 1999; prodr. TV spls. A Time for Laughter, 1967, Harry and Lena, 1969; TV program Tonight with Belafonte, 1960 (Emmy award); appeared on German TV spl. I Sing What I See, 1980; concert performances in Cuba, Jamaica, Europe, 1980, Australia, N.Z., U.S., Europe, 1981, Can., 1982, U.S., Europe and with Can. symphony orchs., 1983, U.S., 1985, U.S., Can., Japan, Europe, 1986; prodr. Strolling Twenties-TV; co-prodr. Beat Street, 1984; appeared at Golden Nugget, Atlantic City and Las Vegas, 1985, 86; initiator, performer rec. We Are the World, 1985 (Grammy award 1985); performer concert tours, U.S., Can. and Europe including 60 city tour, 1988, concerts in U.S., Europe, Can., 1989, 90, 93, concerts in U.S., Japan and Can., 1991, concert tour U.S., 1992, concerts U.S., Can. and Europe, 1995, U.S., Can., Europe and Far East, 1996, 50-city European tour, 1998; 1st N.Y. appearance in 30 yrs. Avery Fisher Hall, Lincoln Ctr., 1993. Chmn. Martin Luther King., Jr. Holiday Commn., 1987; goodwill amb. UNICEF, 1987; bd. dirs. N.Y. State Martin Luther King, Jr. Inst. for Nonviolence, 1989—; N.Y. State Employees Brotherhood com. (Benjamin Potocker brotherhood award 1993). Recipient award of appreciation for initiation of and work for USA for Africa, Am. Music, 1986, Leader for Peace award Peace Corps, 1988, Danny Kaye award U.S. Com. for UNICEF, 1989, Africa's Future award, 1994, Whitney M. Young Jr. Svc. award Boy Scouts Am., 1989, Golden Acorn award Bronx Community Coll., 1989, Kennedy Ctr. honors, 1989, Mandela Courage award (inaugural presentation), 1990, Tribute to a Black Am. award Nat. Conf. Black Mayors, Inc., 1991, Bill of Rights award ACLU So. Calif., 1991, Internat. House Berkeley award, 1994, Food and Hunger Hotline award, 1994, Humanitarian award N.Y. Assn. New Americans, 1994, Brotherhood award 100 Black Men, 1994, Children's Champion award UNICEF Com. Greater Boston-joint award with Julie Belafonte, 1994, Nat. Medal of the Arts, 1994, Letelier-Moffitt Human Rights award, 1994, Best Supporting Actor (Kansas City), 1996, N.Y. Film Critics Cir., Jesse Owens Humanitarian award, 1996, Man of the Yr. award N.Y. chpt. Hadassah, 1996, Hadassah Internat. First Citizen of the World award, 1996, Medal of Distinction, Lenox Hill Hosp., N.Y.C., 1996, South African-Am. Orgn. Leadership award, 1996, Florinda Lasker Civil Liberties award, 1997, Living Landmark award N.Y. Landmarks Conservancy, 1997, Humanitarian of Yr. award WLIW/21, 1997, William Moses Kunstler Racial Justice award, 1997, N.Y. Arts & Bus. Coun. award, 1997, Chmn.'s award NAACP Image Awards, Ronald H. Brown award Nat. Child Labor Com.; inducted into Miami Children's Hosp. Internat. Pediat. Hall of Fame, 1996.

BELAG, ANDREA SUSAN, artist; b. N.Y.C., Nov. 21, 1951; d. Julius Belag and Harriet (Goldberg) Belag-Lange; m. James Cole Bowness, Apr. 20, 1980 (div. Aug. 1989). Student, N.Y. Studio Sch., 1971-74. Lectr. visual arts program Princeton (N.J.) U., 1995; instr. Sch. Visual Arts, 1995—, SUNY., Purchase, 1992, Md. Inst. Coll. of Art, Baltimore, 1993; curator Eight Painters, Jersey City Mus., 1980, 1981 Invitational, Selected Drawings, 1983, Ralph Hilton 1946-84, 1985, Mystery Show, 1985, The Mirror in Which Two Are Seen as One, 1989, Drawn Out, Kansas City (Mo.) Art Inst., 1987.; vis. artist N.Y. Studio Sch., 1983, Bard Coll., 1984, N.J. Coun. of Arts (fellowship juror), 1985, Kansas City Art Inst., 1987, N.Y. Feminist Art Inst., 1989, R.I. Sch. of Design, Providence, 1993, Hampshire Coll., 1999. One-woman shows include Jersey City Mus., 1979, N.J. State Mus., Trenton, 1984, John Davis Gallery, Akron, 1985, N.Y.C., 1987, 88, David Beitzel Gallery, N.Y.C., 1991, (monotypes), Richard Anderson Fine Arts, N.Y.C., 1992, 93, 94, Rutgers U., New Brunswick, N.J., 1995, Littlejohn Contemporary Art, N.Y.C., 1996, Bill Maynes Gallery, N.Y.C., 1998, Galerie Heinz Holtmann, Cologne, Germany, 1998; numerous group shows include John Davis Gallery, N.Y.C., 1986, Graham Modern, N.Y.C., 1991, Tibor de Nagy Gallery, N.Y.C., 1992, Galerie Bernhard Steinmetz, Bonn, Germany, 1992, 93, Newhouse Ctr. for Contemporary Art, Snug Harbor, N.Y., 1997, Michael Schneider Zeitgenossische Kunst, Bonn, 1997, Rhona Hoffman Gallery, Chgo., 1997; represented in mus. collections including Newark Mus., N.J. State Mus., Moriss Mus. of Arts and Scis.; work represented in numerous publs. Fellow N.J. Coun. for Arts, 1984, Nat. Endowment for Arts, 1987, Mariposa Found. fellow Corp. of YADDO, 1994; grantee Blue Mountain Ctr., 1993; Guggenheim fellow, 1999. Home: 7 Harrison St Apt 40 New York NY 10013-2832

BÉLAIR, RÉGINALD, Canadian government official; b. Hearst, Ont., Can., Apr. 16, 1949; m. Jo-Anne Béland; children: Annie, Julie. BA, Hearst Coll. Constituency exec. asst. to Keith Penner; mem. Parliament, Ottawa, Ont., 1988—, assoc. critic for forestry, 1990—, assoc. critic for sec. of state, 1990—, assoc. critic for official langs., 1990—; natural resources com. Parliament, Ottawa. Founding mem. PTA Jeanne-Mance Sch., Kapuskasing, Can.; mcpl. councillor Town of Kapuskasing, 1985-88. Mem. Can.-Europe Paliamentary Assn., Can.-Japan Inter-Parliamentary Group, Commonwealth Parliamentary Assn., Internat. Assn. French Speaking Parliamentarians, Can.-France Inter-Parliamentary Assn. (bd. dirs.), Knight of Columbus. Office: Ho of Commons, Rm 223 Confedn Bldg TJ Bay, Ottawa, ON Canada K1A 0A6*

BELAK, MICHAEL JAMES, information systems executive; b. Cleve., Nov. 26, 1961; s. John James and Violet Mae (Yamek) B.; children: Michael James II, Nathaniel Hinds. BS in Computer Engring., Ohio State U., 1985; MBA in Info. Systems Mgmt., George Washington U., 1990. Application programmer, office of registrar Ohio State U., Columbus, 1984-85; project leader database adminstrn. IBM, Gaithersburg, Md., 1985-88; cons. svcs. mgr. Gen. Electric, Rockville, Md., 1988-91; dir. fleet svcs. devel. PHH Corp., Hunt Valley, Md., 1991-94; dir. data quality mgmt. Nat. Assn. Securities Dealers, Rockville, Md., 1994-97; sr. dir. data mgmt. and tech. program mgmt. Marriott Internat., Bethesda, Md., 1998—. Contbr. articles to profl. jours. Mem. allocation panel United Way, 1993-94. Mem. Internat. DB2 Users Group (conf. com. 1990-92), Washington Case Users Group (sec. 1991), Assn. for Computing Machinery (profl. devel. com. 1989-91), Soc. Info. Mgmt. (East Coast working group on client server tech.; bd. dirs. D.C. chpt. 1997). Republican. Avocations: tennis, weight training, golf. Home: Kentlands 301 Ridgepoint Pl Gaithersburg MD 20878-5704 Office: Marriott Internat 10400 Fernwood Rd Bethesda MD 20817-1109

BELANGER, CHERRY CHURCHILL, elementary school educator; b. Berea, Ky., May 14, 1923; d. David Carroll and Anna Eleanor (Franzen) Churchill; m. Paul Adrien Belanger, Oct. 15, 1950 (dec. Feb. 1987); children: Peter Carroll, Karen Michelle Belanger-Magon. *Parents Carroll and Eleanor Churchill, who met each other as missionaries in India, founded the Churchill Weavers in Berea, Kentucky, in 1922. Churchill Weavers became the largest hand-weaving enterprise in the United States. Husband Paul Adrien Belanger, pianist, composer, musicologist, writer, director, was a television pioneer with CBS Television in New York City in the late 40's and early 50's. Son, Peter Carroll Belanger, an Eagle Scout, is president of Outbound Resources, a consulting firm for business to business telemarketing. His children are Christopher Patrick, Luke Philip and Lily Kathleen. Daughter Karen Belanger-Magon, is Director of Creative Affairs, Intermedia Films.* BA, Pomona Coll., Claremont, Calif., 1944; MA in Elem. Edn., Calif. State U., Northridge, 1983. Cert. tchr. early childhood edn. Actress Actor's Equity Assn., 1944-49; retail promotion asst. Bloomingdale's, N.Y.C., 1948-52; editor Living for Young Homemakers, N.Y.C., 1953-54, Bride-To-Be Mag., N.Y.C., 1955; off-camera editor NBC Home Show, N.Y.C., 1955-56; publicist home furnishing Alfred Auerbach, Bell & Stanton, N.Y.C., 1956-61; retail rep. Betsy Ross Martin Assocs., L.A., 1961-66; exec. sec. So. Calif. Assn. Bedding Mfrs., L.A., 1966-70; retail rep. Hercules Corp., L.A., 1971; tchr. early childhood edn. Carthay Nursery, Beverly Hills, Calif., 1971-78; tchr. early childhood edn. L.A. Unified Sch. Dist., 1976-79, tchr. kindergarten and 1st grade, 1979—. Den mother, treas., chmn., inst. rep. Boy Scouts Am., Beverly Hills, 1961-85; troop leader Brownies, Girl Scouts U.S., 1968-83. Recipient Silver Fawn award Boy Scouts Am., L.A., 1972, Elizabeth H. Brady Tchr. award So. Calif. Kindergarten Assn., 1997; honored Cherry Belanger Day in Beverly Hills, City Coun., 1976. Mem. DAR, AAUW, United Tchrs. of L.A. Avocations: drama, music, camping.

BELANGER, GERARD, economics educator; b. St. Hyacinthe, Que., Can., Oct. 23, 1940; s. Georges and Cecile (Girard) B.; 1 child, Marie-Jose. B.A., U. Montreal, 1960; B.So.Sc., Laval U., 1961, M.So.Sc., 1967; M.A., Princeton U., 1966. Asst. prof. econs. Laval U., 1967-71, assoc. prof., 1971-77, prof. econs., 1977—; research coordinator Howe Inst., Montreal, 1977-79; mem. fin. com. Council Univs., Que., 1971-73. Co-author: The Price of Health, 1974, Le Prix du Transport au Quebec, 1978; author: L'economique du secteur public, 1981, Croissance du secteur public et fédéralisme, 1988. Woodrow Wilson scholar, 1964-65; Walter N. Rothschild scholar, 1965-66. Fellow Royal Soc. Can. Office: Université Laval, Dept D'eco Pav Desève, Quebec, PQ Canada G1K 7P4

BELANGER, LUC, oncologist; b. Montreal, Que., Can., July 2, 1948. BA, Petit Seminaire Chicoutimi, 1967; MD, Laval U., 1971, PhD in Biochemistry, 1975. Fellow biochemistry and milecular biology Med. Rsch. Coun./Univ. Calif. San Diego, Salk Inst. and, Vanderbilt U., 1975-78; scholar molecular biology Med. Rsch. Coun. Can., 1978-83; dir. Cancer Rsch. Ctr. Laval U., Quebec City, 1983—; mem. cancer grants panel Med. Rsch. Coun., 1980-83, scholar panel, Nat. Cancer Inst., 1980-82; faculty medicine coun. Laval U., 1981-87, advisory com. cancer, Que Ministry Health, 1990-91.; mem. coun. Med. Rsch. Coun. Can., 1988—, Nat. Cancer Inst. Can., 1988—; pres., scholar bd. Fonds Recherche Sante Que, 1988-91, Meed Rsch. Coun. Bd. Eval Grants Programs Performances, 1990-93. Mem. Can. Soc. Cellular and Molecular Biology, Am. Soc. Cell Biology, Internat. Soc. Oncodevelop Biology and Medicine (bd. dirs. 1980-90). *

BELANGER, ROBERT EUGENE, lawyer; b. Pitts., June 10, 1958; s. Eugene Edward and Patricia Mickle (Pelikan) B.; m. Gale Elizabeth Lynam, May 21, 1988; children: Sean Robert, Katharine Anne. BA, John Carroll U., 1981; JD, Cleve.-Marshall Coll. of Law, 1986; cert. with honors, Naval Justice Sch., Newport, R.I., 1988. Bar: Ohio 1986, U.S. Ct. Mil. Appeals 1989, U.S. Dist. Ct. (no. dist.) Ohio 1990, U.S. Supreme Ct. 1992, Fla. 1993. Assoc. Svete McGee & Carrabine, L.P.A., Chardon, Ohio, 1990-94; supervising asst. state atty. 19th Jud. Cir., Stuart, Fla., 1994—. Bd. dirs. Geauga County Bd. Mental Health and Drug Addiction, Chardon, 1991-94; sustaining mem. Rep. Nat. Com., Washington, 1990—; chmn. Martin County (Fla.) Rep. Exec. Com. Capt. USMC, 1986-90. Mem. ABA, Fla. Bar Assn., SAR (compatriot Western Res. chpt. 1990—). Roman Catholic. Avocations: running, karate. Home: 3698 SW Thistlewood Ln Palm City FL 34990-7718 Office: Office of State Atty Constnl Bldg 4th Fl 120 E Ocean Blvd Stuart FL 34994-2206

BELANGER, WILLIAM JOSEPH, chemist, polymer applications consultant; b. Chgo., Mar. 20, 1925; m. Keltah Long, Feb. 1, 1947; children: William Joseph, Thomas, Kathryn, Michael, Jeanne, Judith, Elizabeth, John, Anne. B.S. in Chemistry, St. Louis U., 1948; Ph.D. in Organic Chemistry, Notre Dame U., 1951. Research chemist duPont Co., 1951-53; research chemist, then tech. service mgr. Devoe & Reynolds Co., 1953-60; tech. mgr. resin devel. Celanese Coatings & Specialties Co., Louisville, 1960-69; v.p. tech. and engring. Celanese Polymer Specialities Co., Jeffersontown, Ky., 1970-79; v.p. Specialties Group, Celanese Plastics & Specialties Co., 1979-82; Splty. polymer applications cons., 1982—; tchr. polymer chemistry U. Louisville, 1957; tchr. organic chemistry Ind. Univ. Southeast, 1986. Vice chmn. Jefferson County Housing Authority, 1975-78; trustee Audubon Hosp., 1979-82. Served with USNR, 1943-45. Mem. Am. Chem. Soc., Nat. Paint and Coatings Assn. Patentee in field. Home and Office: 1208 Creighton Hill Rd Louisville KY 40207-2244

BELASCO, SIMON, French language and linguistics educator; b. Phila., Dec. 21, 1918; s. Albert and Sara Gwendolyn (Wilson) B.; m. Elaine Pile (div. 1979); children: Laurence Jon, David Robert, Allyson Anne; m. Martha Catherine Freibert, 1981. BS in Edn., Romance Langs., Temple U., 1940; MA in French Linguistics, U. Pa., 1948, PhD in Romance Linguistics, 1953. Instr. French and Spanish Francis Mil. Acad., Laurel Springs, N.J., 1940-41, U. Pa., Phila., 1947-52, summers 1948-53; French interpreter, translator Mission Navale Française, 1942-44, Engring. div. Phila. Naval Base, 1942-44; instr. French and psychology Yokohama (Japan) Ctrl. AEP Sch., 1946-47; asst. prof. Romance langs. Pa. Mil. Acad., 1952-53; asst. prof. Romance linguistics Pa. State U., 1953-57, assoc. prof., 1957-62, prof., 1962-79; prof. emeritus Pa. State U., University Park, 1979—, dir. linguistics program, 1954-79; prof. French and linguistics U. S.C., Columbia, 1979-91, Disting. prof. French and classics emeritus, 1991—, acting chmn. dept. Fgn. Langs. and Lit., 1985, chmn. dept., 1988-91; assoc. in audiology U. Pa. Med. Sch., 1952-53; rsch. assoc. in psychoacoutics Jefferson Med. Coll., 1953-58; dir. linguistics programs summer lang. insts. for NDEA, Colgate U., 1959-61, Emory U., Besançon, France, 1962, Fla. State U., 1965, also Acad. Yr. Inst. Pa. State U., 1960-62; vis. prof. Linguistic Soc. Am. summer insts. U. Washington, 1963, Ind. U., 1964; chmn. listening and speaking com., N.E. Conf. Teaching of Fgn. Langs., 1963; mem. implementation com. major instl. grants NEH, 1981; chmn. various linguistic sects. Ky. Fgn. Lang. Conf., 1966-87; sect. chmn. ann. confs. Linguistic Symposium on Romance Linguistics, 1978, 82, 83; referee individual grants NEH, NSF. Co-author, editor: Manual of Applied Linguistics, 5 vols., 1960, Anthology of Applied Linguistics, 1960; co-author: (text, workbook tapes, records) College French in the New Key, 1965, Applied Linguistics and the Teaching of French, 1968; author: (with others) Son et Sens, 1972, 2d edit. and supplementary workbooks, tapes, 1977, Scènes et Séjours, 1972, 2d edit., 1977, Etudes de Linguistique Appliquée, 1973, Essays on the Teaching of Culture: A Festschrift to Honor H.L. Nostrand, 1974, Reading College French: A Bilingual Structural Approach, 1975, Studies in Lexicography as a Science and as an

Art, 1977, A Comprehension Approach: An Evolving Methodolgy in Foreign Language Instruction, 1981, others; editor: Critical Bibliography of Phonetics in American Speech, 1958-66, (series) Theoretical Studies in Second Language Acquisition, 1988—; editor Monographs in Theoretical Linguistics and Philosophy, 1992—; mem. editorial bd., adv. com. Am. Speech jour., 1965-67; editorial bd. Studies in Second Language Acquisition, 1979-91; contbr. numerous articles, revs. to profl. jours., conf. procs. Capt. AUS, 1944-47, PTO. Decorated chevalier dans l'Ordre des Palmes Académiques, 1991; named Tchr. of Yr. Pa. MLA, 1979; grantee Pa. State U. 1955-72, Am. Coun. Learned Socs., Eng., 1969, France, 1973; fellow Inst. Arts and Humanistic Studies Pa. State U., France, 1978, 79, U. S.C., France, 1980, 81, 83, 85, NDEA, 1960-62, Fulbright Rsch., France, 1984, others. Fellow Am. Coun. Learned Socs; mem. MLA (officer, sect. head numerous coms. 1955-80, chmn. Applied Linguistics Div. 1979-80), Linguistic Soc. Am., Linguistic Circle N.Y., Am. Assn. Tchrs. French, Am. Coun. Teaching of Fgn. Langs., Am. Libr. of Recorded Dialect Studies, Internat. Soc. Phonetic Scis. Office: U of SC Dept French and Classics Columbia SC 29208*

BELAU, JANE CAROL GULLICKSON, marketing, government affairs and public relations company executive; b. Fertile, Minn., Oct. 21, 1934; m. Paul G. Belau, June 22, 1957; children: Steven, Matthew, Nancy. Student, Concordia Coll., Moorhead, Minn., 1952-53; grad., RN, Fairview Hosp. Sch. Nursing, 1956; postgrad., U. Minn. Spl. events dir. Retail Mchts. Assn., 1966-71; cons. U.S. HEW, Washington, 1971-77; commr. Minn. State Corrections Authority, Mpls., 1974-75; cons. McKnight Found., Mpls., 1974-78; commr. Minn. State Cable Comm. Bd., 1975-78; v.p. state mktg. and govt. affairs Control Data Corp., Mpls., 1978-90; pres. Belau Cons. Group, 1990—; chair Nat. Adv. Coun. on Devel. Disabilities; mem. State Govt. Affairs Coun.; cons. in field. Illustrator: Fashiongrams; producer-host cable/pub. TV program Community Affairs; contbr. articles to profl. jours. Mem. bd. advisors U. Minn. Grad. Sch., 1985-91, U. Minn. Regent Candidate Selection Commn., Minn. Pvt. Coll. Coun.; bd dirs. Gov.'s Commn. on Dislocated Workers, vice chmn. Commn. on Computer Industry, Minn. State Commn. on Reform and Efficiency, 1992—, Minn. State Milestones Bd., 1990-92; chairperson nat. adv. coun. St. John's U.. Minn., 1986-92; bd. dirs. Minn. Meeting, 1986—, Minn. High Tech. Coun., 1986—, Minn. Alliance for Sci., 1986-90, Minn. Acad. Sci., 1985-89; founding pres. Rochester (Minn.) Area Econ. Devel.; chmn. Rochester Pub. Salary Commn., 1994-95, Nat. Adv. Coun. on Developmental Disabilites; pres. Rochester Charter Commn., Olmsted County Planning and Zoning, Airport Zoning Commn. Named Bus. and Profl. Woman of Yr., 1974; recipient Outstanding Leadership award Internat. Assn. Women Execs., 1981, Outstanding Svc. award Minn. Cmty. TV, 1995, Achievement award Minn. High Tech. Coun., 1996, Outstanding Svc. award Minn. High Tech. Assn., 1997. Mem. Am. Electronics Assn. (Minn. govtl. chmn.), Women's Econ. Roundtable Minn. (founder, bd. dirs.), U.S. C. of C. (nat. health care com.), Rochester Athletic Club, Rotary Internat. Avocations: art, music, reading, racquetball. Office: Belau Consulting Group 916 4th St SW Rochester MN 55902-2901

BELAVEK, DEBRA LOUISE, school psychologist; b. Detroit, Mar. 22, 1959; d. Richard Frank and Patricia Ann (Mitchell) Czerw; m. John Frank Belavek, June 29, 1985; children: Cameron, Trevor. BA, Mich. State U., 1982; MA, Gallaudet U., 1985, cert of advanced grad. studies, 1986. Nat. cert. sch. psychologist; cert. sch. psychologist, Mich. Tchr. Muskegon (Mich.) Pub. Schs., 1983-84; sch. psychologist Bloomfield Hills (Mich.) Sch. Dist., 1986—; ind. evaluator, expert on deafness, presenter workshops various sch. dists., Mich., 1986—. Mem. Nat. Assn. Sch. Psychologists. Avocations: reading, gardening, walking, swimming, crafts. Office: E Hills Mid 2800 Kensington Rd Bloomfield Hills MI 48304-1830

BELAY, BRENDA MAY, emergency room nurse; b. Flint, Mich., Oct. 23, 1948; d. Morris D. and Bernice M. (McInally) Ross; m. James P. Belay, Sept. 6, 1969; children: Wade P., Sha Lynn. Diploma, Deaconess Hosp. Sch. Nursing, Detroit, 1969; BSN, Wilmington Coll., 1998. RN, Mich., Md.; cert. ACLS, CEN, trauma nursing, emergency nursing, CPR, first aid instr. Team leader Deaconess Hosp.; head nurse, mgr. emergency dept. Union Hosp. Cecil County, Elkton, Md.; IV staff nurse Home Health Corp. Am., Newark, Del.

BELCASTRO, PATRICK FRANK, pharmaceutical scientist; b. Italy, June 3, 1920; came to U.S., 1927, naturalized, 1943; s. Samuel and Sarah (Mosca) B.; m. Hanna Vilhelmina Jensen, July 6, 1963; children—Helen Maria, Paul Anthony. B.S., Duquesne U., 1942; M.S. (Am. Found. Pharm. Edn. fellow), Purdue U., 1951, Ph.D. in Pharmacy and Pharm. Chemistry (Am. Found. for Pharm. Edn. fellow), 1953. Instr. pharmacy Duquesne U., 1946-49; asst. prof. pharmacy Ohio State U., 1953-54; prof. indsl. pharmacy Purdue U., 1954-90, prof. emeritus, 1990—. Author: Physical and Technical Pharmacy, 1963; contbg. editor: (with others) Internat. Phar. Abstracts, 1970—, Pharm. Tech, 1977—; contbr. to: (with others) Jour. Pharm. Scis. Served with U.S. Army, 1942-46. Mem. Am. Pharm. Assn., Am. Soc. Hosp. Pharmacists, AAUP, Rho Chi, Phi Lambda Upsilon. Roman Catholic. Home: 327 Meridian St West Lafayette IN 47906-2603 Office: Purdue U Sch Pharmacy and Pharm Scis West Lafayette IN 47907

BELCHER, DENNIS IRL, lawyer; b. Wheeling, W.Va., Aug. 24, 1951; s. Finley Duncan Belcher and Ellen Jane (Huffman) Good; m. Vickie Marie Early, Aug. 2, 1975; children: Sarah Anne, Matthew Irl, Benjamin Scott. BA, Coll. William and Mary, 1973; JD, U. Richmond, 1976. Bar: Va. 1976, U.S. Tax Ct. 1978. Assoc. McGuire, Woods, Battle & Boothe, Richmond, Va., 1976-83, ptnr., 1983—, mem. exec. com., 1996—; adj. prof. taxation Va. Commonwealth U., Richmond, 1985-88. Co-author: Business Tax Planning Forms for Businesses and Individuals, 1985. Chmn. Richmond chpt. Am. Heart Assn., 1984-85; mem. House of Delegates, 1998-99; mem., bd. trustees St. Christopher's Sch., 1993—. Fellow Am. Coll. Trust and Estate Counsel (bd. regents. 1999—); mem. ABA (real property and probate sect., sec. 1997-98, chmn. marital deduction com., vice chmn. lifetime transfers com., ho. of dels. 1998-99), Va. Bar Assn. (wills and trusts and taxations sects.), Bull and Bear Club, Country Club of Va. Presbyterian. Avocations: golf, farming. Office: McGuire Woods Battle & Boothe 1 James Ctr 901 East Cary St Richmond VA 23219

BELCHER, LA JEUNE, automotive parts company executive; b. Chgo., Nov. 16, 1960; d. Lewis Albert and Dorthy (Brandon) B. BA, Northwestern U., 1982; postgrad., Am. Inst. of Banking, 1983-84. Notary pub.; securities lic.; ins. lic., Ill. Securities processor Am. Nat. Bank, Chgo., 1983, divisional asst., 1983-84; mgmt. trainee Toyota Motor Distbrs., Carol Stream, Ill., 1984-85, dist. parts mgr., 1985-90, sr. customer rels. adminstr., 1990—; fin. rep. Waddell and Reed, 1992; rep. to Japan-U.S. Toyota Dealer Meeting, Tokyo, 1985; owner Crystal Clear Concepts. Author: (booklet) The Cutting Edge: 127 Tips to Improve Your Professional Image. Mem. alumni admissions coun. Northwestern U., Evanston, Ill.; bd. dirs. Boys and Girls Club; comty. docent Art Inst. Chgo. Mem. NAFE, NAACP, Northwestern Club Chgo., Toastmasters (edn. v.p. 1988, 94, 95, advt. v.p. 1989, pres. 1990-93), Delta Sigma Theta. Office: Toyota Motor Distbrs 2350 Sequoia Dr Aurora IL 60506-6211

BELCHER, LOUIS DAVID, marketing and operations executive, former mayor; b. Battle Creek, Mich., June 25, 1939; s. Louis George and Josephine (Johnson) B.; children: Debora Louise, Sheri Lynn, Stacy Elizabeth; m. Jane Elisabeth Dillon, May 8, 1987. Student, Kellogg Community Coll., 1959; B.S., Eastern Mich. U., 1962. With Gen. Motors Corp., Livonia, Mich., 1962; adminstr. U. Mich., Ann Arbor, 1962-63; with NCR, Lansing, Mich., 1963-69, Veda, Inc., Ann Arbor, 1969-72; owner, v.p., treas. First Ann Arbor Corp., 1972-83; owner, chief fin. officer Third Party Services, Inc. and Data Scan, Inc., Ann Arbor, Mich., 1983-84; pres., chief exec. officer Data Scan, Inc., Ann Arbor, 1984-86, Ann Arbor Rod & Gun Co., 1986-88; ptnr. Shipman, Corey, Belcher, Ann Arbor, 1984-86; sr. asst. to pres. and dir. tech. svcs. Environ. Rsch. Inst. Mich., Ann Arbor, 1988-93; owner, prin. L. D. Belcher and Assocs. Mgmt. Cons., Ann Arbor, 1993—; v.p. Cybernet Syss. Corp., Ann Arbor, 1996-97; bd. dirs. The Geosat Com., Inc., Washington; corp. dir. M.W. Microwave, Inc., Ann Arbor, Environment Tech. Corp., Ann Arbor, Innovative Rsch. & Svcs., Inc.; adv. bd. dirs. Mich. Consol. Gas Co.; mem. exec. com. Ann. Conf. Earth Observations and Decision Making - A National Partnership, Washington, 1988—, Ann. Internat. Symposium on Remote Sensing of Environment, 1990—, Thematic Conf. Geol. Remote Sensing, 1990, Ann. Thematic Conf. Coastal and Marine Environment, 1992—. Mem. City Coun., Ann Arbor, 1974-78, mayor pro tem, Ann Arbor, 1976-78, mayor, 1978-85; mem. adv. coun. region 5 SBA, Detroit, 1982-86; pres. bd. dirs. U. Mich. Theatre, 1983-85; bd. dirs. Marcel Marceau World Ctr. for Mime, Inc., Ann Arbor, 1986-89, Mich. Theatre Found., Ann Arbor, 1986-92; mem. nat. Rep. campaign team, 1980. Served to capt. Air N.G., 1956-70. Recipient Outstanding Alumni awards Kellogg C.C., Outstanding Alumni awards Ea. Mich. U. Coll. Bus., Silver Elephant award Rep. Party, Commendation Adminstr. Vets. Affairs, Commendation Ann Arbor Vets. Hosp.; Bügermedaille, City of Tübingen, Fed. Republic Germany; elected Mayor's Hall of Fame, 1995. Mem. Air Force Assn., U.S. Conf. Mayors (past pres.), Mich. Conf. Mayors (past pres.), Am. Soc. for Photogrammertry and Remote Sensing. Republican. Mem. Ch. of Christ. Home: 1352 Cobblestone Ct Ann Arbor MI 48108-9553 Office: LD Belcher & Assocs 1352 Cobblestone Ct Ann Arbor MI 48108-9553 *I have had incredible luck - I was born an American and given the opportunity and freedom to chase my dreams.*

BELCHER, MAX, social services administrator, college dean; b. East Lynn, W.Va., Mar. 16, 1942; s. George H. and Ella D. (Dickerson) B.; m. Linda L. Frey, Aug. 8, 1964; children: Kipling, Babbette, Andrew, Raleigh, Perry. BA, Berea (Ky.) Coll., 1969; ThM, Trinity Coll., 1972; ThD, Trinity Theol. Sem., 1973; MA, Liberty (Va.) U., 1994; DD, LLD (hon.), Internat. Free Prof. Episc. U., London, 1966; PhD, U. San Jose, 1996. From caseworker to dist. mgr. Mich. Dept. Social Svcs., Flint, 1964-97, dist. mgr., 1992-97; mem. faculty dept. psychology Baker Coll., Flint, 1987-98, dean for gen. edn., 1998—. Bd. dirs. Consortium on Child Abuse and Neglect, Flint, 1993-97. Recipient Cert. of Merit in Youth Employment, Genesee Intermediate Sch. Dist., 1979, Cert. of Appreciation, Health Care Access Project, 1990. Mem. Am. Counseling Assn., Ky. Counseling Assn., Am. Assn. Christian Counselors, Intercollegiate Studies Inst. (faculty advocate), Mich. County Social Svcs. Assn. (life). Home: 9421 McAfee Rd Montrose MI 48457-9123 Office: Baker Coll 1050 W Bristol Rd Flint MI 48507-5516

BELCO, KAREN MARIE, cardiology nurse; b. Cleve., Oct. 24, 1953; d. Arthur W. and Daniella E. (Lokar) Schultz, Nov. 24, 1979; m. Joseph E. Belco. BSN, St. John Coll., 1975. Staff nurse cardiac surgery Cleve. Clinic, 1976-79, 81, clin. instr. cardiac surgery, 1982-85, nurse clinician dept. cardiology, 1985-92, mgr. electrophysiology, 1989-92; sr. clin. electrophysiology specialist, mgr. Baylor Coll. Medicine, Houston, 1993-95, rsch. assoc., 1993-98; cardiac electrophysiology and device specialist Houston VA Med. Ctr., 1995-98; mgr. cardiac electrophysiology and device specialist Cardiology Assocs. of Lubbock, 1998—; lectr. in field. *Karen has over 14 years of experience in establishing and managing cardiac electrophysiology programs caring for heart patients with heart rhythm disorders. She has been a national leader among allied professionals in her field by presenting and publishing research, organizing and directing educational programs, and working on a credentialing process to assure appropriate education and competency of health care professionals caring for patients with implantable cardiac devices and heart rhythm disorders. She has contributed to health care policies by participating in policy conferences and task forces sponsored by North American Society of Pacing and Electrophysiology,American College of Cardiology, and American Heart Association.* Author book chpts.; contbr. to abstracts and manuscripts. Active The Woodlands Symphony Chorus. Mem. N.Am. Soc. Pacing and Electrophysiology (assoc., NASPEXAM writing com., trustee 1992-94, pubs. com. 1996—, credentialing com. 1997—, history com. 1998—, data base com. 1998—), Am. Coll. Cardiology, Coun. Associated Profls. (chair 1992-94), Am. Heart Assn., Houston Cardiology Soc., Coalition for Collaborative Cardiology Practice. Avocations: boating, golf.

BELDEN, DAVID LEIGH, professional association executive, engineering educator; b. Mpls., Jan. 9, 1935; m. Lois Marion Lind, June 14, 1956; children: Richard Alan, Grant David. B in Gen. Edn., U. Omaha, 1961; MS in Indsl. Engring., Stanford U., 1963, PhD, 1969; grad., Indsl. Coll. Armed Forces, 1973; DSc (hon.), Manhattan Coll., 1992. Registered profl. engr., Calif. rated navigator, aviator. Enlisted U.S. Air Force, 1954, commd. 2d lt., 1956, advanced through grades to col., 1973; served Thailand; asst. for procurement mgmt. to Sec. Air Force, Washington; ret., 1976; exec. dir. Inst. Indsl. Engrs., Norcross, Ga., 1976-87, ASME, N.Y.C., 1987—; adj. prof. Far East div. U. Md., 1970; asso. prof. George Washington U., 1974. Author articles in field. Bd. dirs. N.Y.C. Indsl. Tech. Assistance Corp. Decorated Legion of Merit, Meritorious Service medal, Commendation medal (3). Fellow ASME, Instn. of Engrs. of Ireland, Hong Kong Instn. of Engrs., Inst. Indsl. Engrs., Inst. Prodn. Engrs. (Eng., life); mem. Am. Assn. Engring. Socs. (bd. govs.), Coun. Engring. and Sci. Soc. Execs. (pres. 1984-85), Am. Soc. Engring. Edn., N.Y. Soc. Assn. Execs. (bd. dirs. 1996—), Am. Soc. Assn. Execs. (found. bd. 1992-94, bd. dirs. 1994-97), Australian Inst. Indsl. Engrs. (hon.), Japan Mgmt. Soc. (assoc.), Union League Club, Israeli Soc. Mech. Engrs. (hon.), Nat. Eagle Scout Assn., Alpha Pi Mu, Tau Beta Pi. Republican. Home: 6 Bates Farm Ln Darien CT 06820-3500 Office: ASME International Three Park Ave New York NY 10016-5990

BELDEN, URSULA, set designer; b. Weimar, Fed. Rep. Germany, Sept. 27, 1947; came to U.S., 1949; d. Ernest J. and Edith G. (Pütter) Mugdan; 1 child, Willow Allegra. MA, U. Mich., 1972; MFA in Design, Yale U., 1976. Prof., chair design dept. Sch. Theatre Ohio U., 1995. Designer Broadway, Off-Broadway, and internat. plays, including: The Mikado, 1977, The Eastern Opera Theatre, 1977, Patience, 1977, Where Memories are Magic and Dreams Invented, 1978, The Importance of Being Ernest, 1979, At Her Age, 1979, Galileo, 1979, Shortages, 1979, Dark Ages, 1980, A Dream Play, 1980 (Villager award for outstanding scene design 1981), Amadeus, 1980, 82, I Can't Keep Running in Place, 1981, Living Quarters, 1983, Weekend, 1983, Quilters, 1984, Pieces of Glass, 1987, A Murder of Crows, 1988 (Peggy Ezekiel award U.S. Inst. Theatre Tech. 1989), Spare Parts, 1989, Waitin' in the Wings, 1990, Trinity, 1991, Night of the Iguana, Cleve., 1993 (Peggy Ezekiel award U.S. Inst. Theatre Tech. 1993), Lay of the Land, 1994, Edith Stein, 1994, Awake and Sing, 1995, Conversations with My Father, 1993 (Peggy Ezekiel award 1995); (films) Pasta Paolo, 1997, You're Gonna Pass, 1999. Recipient Prague Quadrenial award, 1994, 99. Mem. United Scenic Artists (local 829). Office: 84 Prospect Ave Flushing NY 11363-1370

BELDOCK, DONALD TRAVIS, financial executive; b. N.Y.C., May 29, 1934; s. George and Rosa (Tribus) B.; m. Lucy Geringer, Apr. 23, 1971; children: John Anthony, Gwen Ann, James Geringer Christopher. B.A., Yale U., 1955. Mdse. and fin. exec. R. H. Macy & Co., N.Y.C., 1955-60; mng. ptnr., fin. cons. D. T. Beldock & Co., N.Y.C., 1961-66; pres., chief exec. officer, chmn. fin. com. BASIX Corp. (formerly Basic Resources Corp.), N.Y.C., 1966-69, chmn. bd., pres., chief exec. officer, 1970-88; chmn., dir. White Shield Greece Oil Corp., N.Y.C., 1969—; chmn., chief exec. officer Fundamental Properties, Inc., N.Y.C., 1989—, also bd. dirs.; chmn., pres., chief exec. officer Primavera Labs, 1989—; also bd. dirs. CRA Inc, Phoenix, 1982-89; chmn., CEO Packard Press Corp., Phila., 1987-88, bd. dirs., 1977-88; founding ptnr. Transp. Infrastructure Adv. Group; mng. dir. Hellenic Oil Co., 1989—. Patentee in field. Chmn. bd. trustees Strang Clinic-Preventive Medicine Inst., 1968-89, chmn. emeritus, 1989—, chmn. investment com., 1996—; mem. bd. advisors Chem. Bank, 1983-88; bd. dirs. Renewable enregy Inst., 1981-86; trustee Am. Symphony Orch., 1979-96; chmn. bd. dirs. Teamwork Found., 1980-89, trustee, 1989—; mem. com. Nat. UN Day, 1978-87; mem. N.Y. Gov.'s Commn. on Voluntary Enterprise, 1985-88; chmn. N.Y. Gov.'s Commn. Subcom. on Foster Care, 1986-88, Foster Care Ind. Living, 1986-89; bd. advisers free fellowship program U. Hawaii, 1982-86; mem. pvt. sector adv. panel on infrastructure financing of budget com. U.S. Senate, 1984-88; mem. devel. bd. Yale U., 1983-93, mem. exe. com., 1984-88. Honoree testimonial dinner United Jewish Appeal, 1960. Mem. Am. Mgmt. Assn., Fgn. Policy Assn., Assn. Yale U. Alumni (nat. class rep. 1983-86, bd. govs. 1986-89), Alumni Assn. N.Y. (hon., bd. dirs.), Yale Club, Westchester Country Club, Lotos Club. Office: Fundamental Properties Inc 99 Biltmore Ave Rye NY 10580-1837

BELDOCK, MYRON, lawyer; b. N.Y.C., Mar. 27, 1929; s. George J. and Irene (Goldstein) B.; m. Elizabeth G. Pease, June 28, 1953 (div. 1969); children: David, Jennifer, Hannah, Benjamin, Adam Schmalholz; m. Karen L. Dippold, June 19, 1986. BA, Hamilton Coll., 1950; LLB, Harvard U., 1958. Bar: N.Y. 1958, U.S. Dist. Ct. (ea. and so. dists.) N.Y. 1960, U.S. Ct. Appeals (2d cir.) 1960, U.S. Supreme Ct. 1973, U.S. Dist. Ct. (no. dist.) N.Y. 1983, U.S. Ct. Appeals (3d cir.) 1985, U.S. Ct. Appeals (5th cir.) 1992. Asst. U.S. Atty. U.S. Atty's Office, Eastern Dist., N.Y., 1958-60; assoc. Geist, Netter & Marx, N.Y.C., 1960-62; sole practice N.Y.C., 1962-64; ptnr. Beldock Levine & Hoffman LLP, N.Y.C., 1964—. Bd. dirs., v.p. Brotherhood-In-Action, N.Y.C., 1972—; bd. dirs. Brookdale Revolving Fund., N.Y.C., 1973-76. Served with U.S. Army, 1951-54. Mem. Assn. of Bar of City of N.Y. (spl. com. penology 1974-80), N.Y. County Lawyers Assn., Bklyn. Bar Assn., Kings County Criminal Bar Assn., N.Y. County Criminal Bar Assn., N.Y. State Assn. Criminal Def. Lawyers, Nat. Assn. Criminal Def. Lawyers, Nat. Lawyers Guild.

BELDON, SANFORD T., publisher; b. Scranton, Pa., Nov. 9, 1932; s. Benjamin and Evelyn (Jacobson) B.; m. Jeanne Sherman, June 25, 1967 (dec. Nov. 1992); m. Patricia Wood, Feb. 4, 1995; children: Mary, Kenneth, Emily. BBA, CCNY, 1955; postgrad., NYU Grad. Sch. Bus., 1956-57. Publicist Prentice-Hall, Inc., N.Y.C., 1956-59; publicity dir. Fawcett Publs., Inc., N.Y.C., 1959-62; asst. dir. public relations Crowell-Collier-Macmillan, N.Y.C., 1963-65; dir. advt. and public relations, edn. group Litton Industries, White Plains, N.Y., 1966-68; dir. promotion Baker & Taylor divsn. W.R. Grace Co., 1968-71; dir. mktg. book div. Rodale Press, Inc., Emmaus, Pa., 1971-74; dir. advt. Organic Gardening mag., Emmaus, 1974-78, v.p., 1974-82, pub., 1978-86, group v.p., 1982-91, sr. v.p., 1991-98; pub. New Shelter mag., 1984-86, Pub. Prevention Mag., 1986-91, sr. v.p., 1991—; bd. dirs. Second Harvest Food Bank of Lehigh Valley, 1996—. Pres. ecology adv. com. Allentown (Pa.) City Coun., 1972-75; bd. dirs. Lehigh Valley Child Care, Allentown, 1974-82, pres. bd., 1976-80; bd. dirs. Lehigh Valley Conservancy, Allentown, 1976-77, Planned Parenthood Lehigh County, Pa., 1977-78; mem. bd. assocs. Cedar Crest Coll., 1985—; trustee, mem. corp. com., chmn. mktg. coms. Allentown Art Mus., 1992—, pres. bd. trustees, 1997—; mem. Pa. Housing Adv. Commn., 1997—. Mem. Players Club (N.Y.C.). Democrat. Jewish. Office: 33 E Minor St Emmaus PA 18098-0001

BELETZ, ELAINE ETHEL, nurse, educator; b. N.Y.C., Jan. 5, 1944; d. Harry and Rose (Friedman) B. RN, Mt. Sinai Hosp., N.Y.C., 1968; BSN, Fairleigh Dickinson U., 1970; MA, NYU, 1974; MEd, Columbia U., 1978, EdD, 1979. Staff nurse ICU Mt. Sinai Hosp., 1968-70, asst. head nurse, 1970, adminstrv. supervisory relief nurse, 1973-74, 77-78; clin. instr. Roosevelt Hosp. Sch. Nursing, N.Y.C., 1970-73; nurse gerontologist St. Luke's Hosp. Ctr., N.Y.C., 1974; asst. dir. nursing Bklyn. Hosp., N.Y.C., 1975-77; asst. prof. nursing Hunter Coll. CUNY, 1978-81; v.p. nursing Mt. Sinai Hosp. Med. Ctr., Chgo., 1982-83; assoc. prof. nursing Villanova (Pa.) U., 1983—; lectr.; cons. nursing adminstrn., labor rels. in health care; mem. task force on block grants Ill. Dept. Health. Contbr. articles to profl. jours.; internat. cons. and lectr. Bd. dirs. Hadassah Nurses Coun., Phila., 1993-94; pres.-elect, 1994-96, pres. 1996-98; Midatlantic Reg. v.p. nat. bd. Zionist Orgn. Am., 1998—, del. 91st nat. conv., 1998, nominating com., 1998; mem. religious affairs and fgn. rels. com. Am. Jewish Com., 1997—. Recipient Disting. Achievement award Columbia U. Nursing Edn. Alumni Assn., 1989. Fellow Am. Acad. Nursing; mem. Am. Nurses Assn. (bd. dirs. 1982-87, mem. polit. action com. 1982-86), N.Y. State Nurses Assn. (treas. 1977-78, pres.-elect 1978-79, pres. 1979-81, bd. trustees, cert. of appreciation 1981, hon. recognition award 1987), Pa. Nurses Assn. (nominating com. 1985-86, chair polit. action com. 1990-92), N.Y. Counties Registered Nurses Assn. (nominating com. 1973, dir. 1975-78, Amanda Silvers award 1981), Shershower Benevolent Assn., Nursing Edn. Alumni Assn. (Leadership award 1989), Sigma Theta Tau, Phi Kappa Phi, Phi Beta Delta (a founder 1998). Jewish. Office: Villanova U Grad Program Nursing Health Care Adminstrn Coll Nursing Villanova PA 19085

BELEW, ADRIAN, guitarist, singer, songwriter, producer. Lead singer, co-guitarist King Crimson; v-drummer Projekct Two; former pop band The Bears. Performed on record and on tour with numerous entertainers and bands including Frank Zappa, David Bowie, Talking Heads, Laurie Anderson, David Byrne, Herbie Hancock, Paul Simon, Nine Inch Nails, Crash Test Dummies, others; albums: (with King Crimson) Discipline, 1981, Beat, 1982, Three of a Perfect Pair, 1984, The Compact King Crimson, 1987, Vrooom, 1994, Thrak, 1995, Thrakattak, 1996, (solo) Lone Rhino, 1982, Twang Bar King, 1983, Desire Caught by the Tail, 1986, Mr. Music Head, 1989, Young Lions, 1990, Desire of the Rhino King, 1991, Inner Revolution, 1992, Here, 1993, The Acoustic Adrian Belew, 1994, The Guitar as Orchestra, 1995, Op Zop Too Wah, 1996, Belewprints, 1998, Project Two/Space Groove, 1998, Salad Days, 1999, (with The Bears) The Bears, 1987, Rise and Shine, 1988; writer: Fantasy (by Mariah Carey); appeared in films Baby Snakes, Home of the Brave, Return Engagement; prodr. Caifanes/BMG, Santa Sabina/BMG, Jars of Clay/Essential-Silvertone, Sara Hickman/Shanachie, Rick Altizer/KMG, Irresponsibles/ABP. Office: Umbrella PO Box 8385 Cincinnati OH 45208-0385

BELEW, JOHN SEYMOUR, academic administrator, chemist; b. Waco, Tex., Nov. 3, 1920; s. George H. and Mary (Seymour) B.; m. Ruth Edna McAfee, June 3, 1944; children—James Seymour, Janet Elizabeth. BS, Baylor U., 1941; MS, Wichita State U., 1947; PhD, U. Wis., 1951; LLD, Hong Kong Bapt. U., 1995. Instr. U.S. Army Air Corps Tech. Tng. Command, 1941-43; rsch. assoc. Brown U., Providence, 1951-53; acting. asst. prof. U. Va., 1953-56; asst. prof., then assoc. prof. and prof. chemistry Baylor U., Waco, Tex., 1956-91, prof. emeritus, 1991—, assoc. dean Coll. Arts and Scis., 1973-74, dean Coll. Arts and Scis., 1974-79, chief acad. officer, 1979-91, Jo Murphy chair in internat. edn., 1990-96, provost emeritus, 1991—; vis. fellow Manchester Coll., Oxford U., summer 1995. Bd. dirs. Waco Heart Assn., Goals for Waco, Clean Community Systems, Waco Performing Arts Co., Strecker Mus. Assocs.; trustee Midway Ind. Sch. Dist., Waco, 1962-73; bd. dirs. Tex. High Speed Rail Authority, 1992—. With USAAF, 1943-46. Wilton Park fellow, 1976; recipient Disting. Alumnus award Baylor U., 1993. Mem. Am. Chem. Soc. (chmn. sect. 1965), Royal Soc. Chemistry, Am.-Thai Edn. Found. (bd. dirs.), Am.-Philippines Edn. Found. (bd. dirs.), Turner Soc. London, Sigma Xi. Office: Provost Emeritus Baylor Univ Waco TX 76798-7121

BELFIGLIO, VALENTINE JOHN, political science educator, pharmacist; b. Troy, N.Y., May 28, 1934; s. Edmond Liberato and Mildred Elizabeth (Sherwood) B.; BS, Union U., 1956; MA, U. Okla., Norman, 1967, PhD, 1970; 1 child, by previous marriage, Valentine Edmond. Grad. asst., instr. U. Okla., 1967-70; prof. polit. sci. Tex. Woman's U., Denton, 1970—. Reviewer textbooks in internat. politics Holbrook Press, Boston, 1973-75. Served with USAF, 1959-67. Tex. Woman's U. Instl. Research grantee, 1973-74, 76-77; postdoctoral fellow Republic of South Africa, 1976; NEH grantee, 1978; decorated knight Order of Merit, Republic of Italy; recipient Guido Dorso prize U. Naples, 1985, C.K. Chamberlain award East Tex. Hist. Assn., 1990. Mem. Internat. Studies Assn. (sec.-treas. region 1974-76), Am. Polit. Sci. Assn., Am. Italian Hist. Assn., AAUP, MENSA, Kappa Psi. Republican. Roman Catholic. Avocations: chess, dancing, gourmet cookery. Author: The United States and World Peace, 1971; American Foreign Policy, 1979; The Italian Experience in Texas, 1983; The Best of Italian Cooking, 1985, Alliances, 1986, Go For Orbit, 1987, Pride of the Southwest, 1991, Italian Experience in Texas: A Closer Look, 1994, Honor, Pride, Duty: A History of the State Guard, 1995. Contbr. numerous articles on internat. relations, Asian politics to profl. jours. Home: 704 Camilla Ln Garland TX 75040-4622 Office: Tex Woman's U PO Box 425889 Denton TX 76204-5889

BELFORT, GEORGES, chemical engineering educator, consultant; b. Johannesburg, Transvaal, Republic of South Africa, May 8, 1940; came to U.S., 1964; s. Nathan Leveen and Sophie (Konviser) Belfort; m. Marlene Bertha Stern, Dec. 28, 1967; children: David, Gabriel, Jonathan. BScChemE, U. Capetown, 1963; MS in Engring., U. Calif., Irvine, 1969, PhD in Engring., 1972. Rsch. engr. Astropower Labs., McDonnel Douglas Corp., Newport Beach, Calif., 1964-70; acting instr. U. Calif., Irvine, 1971-72; sr. lectr. Hebrew U., Jerusalem, 1973-77; vis. assoc. prof. Northwestern U., Evanston, Ill., 1977-78; assoc. prof. Rensselaer Poly. Inst., Troy, N.Y., 1978-82, prof., 1982—; cons. Biogen Inc., Millipore Corp., PTI Technologies Inc., Baxter Corp., Danish Separations Sys. A/S, Baxter Corp.; chair Gordon Rsch. Conf. on Membranes, Materials and Processes, 1997. Mem. editorial bd. Jour. Membrane Sci., Desalination, Bioseparation (U.K.), Separation Sci. and Tech., internat. editor North, Central and South Amer. of Jour. Chem. Engring. Japan, editor, author: (with others) Synthetic Membrane Processes: Fundamentals, 1984; co-editor, author: (with others)

Fundamentals of Adsorption, 1984, Advanced Biochemical Engineering, 1987; contbr. over 100 articles to profl. jours. Fellow Japanese Soc. for Promotion Sci., 1981, 96; rsch. grantee U.S. Dept. Energy, 1994—, USN, 1990-94, NSF, 1995—. Mem. AIChE, Am. Chem. Soc. (Award in Separations Science and Technology 1995), N.Am. Membrane Soc. (pres. 1995, bd. of dirs. 1993—), European Membrane Soc. E-mail: belfog@tpi.edu. Office: Rensselaer Poly Inst Chem Engring Dept Troy NY 12180-3590

BELFORTE, DAVID ARTHUR, company president; b. Framingham, Mass., Oct. 25, 1932; s. Arthur David and Jean Louise (Purcell) B.; m. Virginia Elizabeth Crowley, Aug. 2, 1958; 1 child, Steven, David. BS, Northeastern U., 1963, MS, 1970. Staff scientist Raytheon Co., Waltham, Mass., 1957-65; v.p. Thomson Gen. Corp., Lynn, Mass., 1965-70; dir. mktg. Am. Optical Corp., Southbridge, Mass., 1970-73; mgr. Ferranti Elec. Inc., Sturbridge, 1973-76; dir. mktg. Avco Everett Metal Working Lasers, Somerville, Mass., 1976-81; pres. Belforte Assocs., Sturbridge, 1982—. Editor: Industrial Laser Handbook, 1986-92; editor Indsl. Laser Rev., 1986-98, Indsl. Laser Solutions, 1999—. Recipient Arthur L. Schawlow award Laser Institute of America, 1995. Fellow Laser Inst. Am. (Pres.'s award 1988, Arthur L. Schawlow Award, 1995); mem. Am. Welding Soc., Soc. Mfg. Engrs., Ukranian Acad. Engring. Scis. Office: Belforte Assocs PO Box 245 Sturbridge MA 01566-0245

BELFOUR, ED, professional hockey player; b. Carman, Man., Can., Apr. 21, 1965. Student, U. N.D. Goalie Chgo. Blackhawks, Dallas Stars; mem. NCAA All-Am. West second team, 1986-87, tournament team, 1986-87, WCHA All-Star first team 1986-87; player NHL All-Star game, 1992-93. Recipient Vezina trophy, 1990-91, 92-93, Calder Meml. trophy, 90-91, William M. Jennings trophy, 90-91, 92-93, Trico Goaltender award, 1990-91; co-recipient Garry F. Longman Meml. trophy, 1987-88; named Rookie of the Year, 1990-91, Sporting News All-Star 2nd team, 1992-93, NCAA All-Am. Second Team, 1986-87, NHL All-Rookie Team, 1990-91, NHL All-Star First Team, 1990-91, 92-93. Office: Dallas Stars 211 Cowboys Pkwy Irving TX 75063-5931*

BELGARD, STEPHEN L., airport administrator. Mgr. Ogdensburg Internat. Airport. Office: Ogdensburg Internat Airport 5840 State Hwy 812 Ogdensburg NY 13669*

BEL GEDDES, JOAN, writer; b. L.A.; d. Norman and Helen (Sneider) Bel G.; m. Barry Ulanov, Dec. 16, 1939 (div. 1968); children: Anne, Nicholas, Katherine. *Father Norman Bel Geddes (1893-1955) was a theatrical designer, director and producer. He was also the world's first industrial designer, producing many household products as well as streamlined trains, cars and aircrafts, including the first planes to cross the Atlantic. For the 1964 World's Fair, he designed the popular Futurama, a model of America's towns, cities and rural areas with multi-lane highways traversing them. Prior to this, only two-lane highways existed but, inspired by the exhibit, President Eisenhower launched today's nationwide Interstate Highway System. Her son Nicholas Ulanov, born on Norman's 63rd birthday, founded the Ulanov Partnership, which advises non-profit organizations in five countries.* B.A., Barnard Coll. Columbia U., 1937. Researcher and theatrical asst. to Norman Bel Geddes, Inc., N.Y.C., 1937-41; publicity dir. Compton Advt., Inc., N.Y.C., 1942; new program mgr. Compton Advt., Inc., 1943-47; pub. info. officer UNICEF, N.Y.C., 1970-76, chief editorial and publs. services, 1976-79, cons. devel. edn., Universal Children's Day (over 100 countries), 1979-85, editor Almanac World's Children, 1985-90; editor Pate Inst. Bull., 1988-94; tchr. drama Birch Wathen Sch., N.Y.C., 1950; mem. faculty Inst. Man and Sci., Rensellaerville, N.Y., 1969. Interviewer-hostess: weekly radio program Religion and the Arts, NBC, 1968; author: Small World: A History of Baby Care from the Stone Age to the Spock Age, 1964, How to Parent Alone: A Guide for Single Parents, 1974, To Barbara With Love--Prayers and Reflections by a Believer for a Skeptic (Catholic Press Assn. award 1974), Are You Listening, God?, 1994, Childhood and Children, a Compendium of Customs, Superstitious, Theories, Profiles, and Facts, 1997, Children Praying, Why and How to Pray with Your Children, 1999, (with others) Art, Obscenity and Your Children, 1969, American Catholics and Vietnam, 1970, The Future of the Family, 1971, Holiness and Mental Health, 1972, The Children's Rights Movement, 1977, And You, Who Do You Say I Am?, 1981; translator: (with Barry Ulanov) Last Essays of Georges Bernanos, 1955; editor: Magic Motorways (Norman B. Geddes), 1940, Earth: Our Crowded Spaceship (Isaac Asimov), 1974; editor in chief: My Baby mag, 1954-56, Congratulations mag, 1954-56. Rep. to UN Balkan-Ji-Bar Internat. Orgn. for Child and Youth Welfare of the World. Mem. Authors League Am., Assn. Former Internat. Civil Servants, The Coffee House, World Future Soc., Teilard de Chardin Assn., Mcpl. Arts Soc. N.Y., Internat. Inst. Rural Reconstrn. (mem. internat. coun.), Thomas More Soc. (pres. 1966), Barnard Coll. Alumnae Assn. (class v.p. 1972-76, 92—, pres. 1976-82), N.Y. City Mission Soc., Guilford Friends of Music, Pate Inst. Human Survival (bd. dirs. 1989-95), The Charles A. and Anne Morrow Lindbergh Fund, Citizens Against Govt. Waste. Roman Catholic. Home and Office: 60 E 8th St New York NY 10003-6514 *The longer I live the more I relish life. People praise and envy youth but, to my great surprise, I find that growing older is even better than being young. Pleasures taken for granted before become valued, enlarged, prolonged. Like a baby chortling joyfully at seeing things for the first time, I marvel at seeing things for the hundredth or last time. I don't think of life as a right one can in any way earn or deserve but as an inexplicably, unbelievably amazing gift to enjoy and to use and to learn from —so each day is, to me, wondrous, surprising, full of unimagined possibilites.*

BELGIORNO, JOHN, career consultant, educator; b. Rochester, N.Y., Sept. 26, 1948; s. Angelo and Julia Mary (Brancatisano) B.; m. Lynn Ann Keegan, Nov. 13, 1971; 1 child, Kristen. B in Profl. Scis., SUNY Empire State, Rochester, 1993, Assoc. degree, 1993. Ops. officer, supr. Chase Lincoln First Bank, N.A., Rochester, N.Y., 1968-90; instr. Am. Inst. Banking, Rochester, 1986—; mng. cons. Drake Beam Morin, Inc., Rochester, 1991—. Bd. dirs. Cancer Action, Inc., Rochester, 1985-92, asst. treas., 1989-92; nat. trainer United Ostomy, Inc., Irvine, Calif., 1986-92, N.Y. state rep., 1986-90, nat. pres., 1990-92; chmn. ho. of dels. The 7th World Congress, Internat. Ostomy Assn., Rio de Janeiro, 1991. Mem. Soc. Human Resource Mgrs. (pres. Genesee Valley Chpt., 1998—). Avocations: public speaking, music. Home: 72 Judy Ann Dr Rochester NY 14616-1940

BELICH, JOHN PATRICK, SR., journalist; b. Peekskill, N.Y., Dec. 6, 1938; s. John Andrew and Iris Patricia (Brown) B.; m. Louise Daniel, June 4, 1971; children: Mary Louise, John P., Andrew J. Student, N.Y. Inst. Photography, St. Petersburg Jr. Coll. Staff news photographer UPI, 1963-69; So. div. photo mgr. Atlanta, 1969-72; photo editor, dir. photography St. Petersburg Times and Evening Independent, 1972-87, mgr. newsroom projects, 1987-94, asst. to pres., 1994—. V.p., bd. dirs. N.W. Fla. Little Mag. League Assn.; mem. photography adv. com. St. Petersburg Vocat. Tech. Inst.; guardian ad litem 6th Jud. Ctr., Fla.; Skywarn vol. Amateur Radio Emergency Svc. Corp., Nat. Weather Svc.; bd. advisors Coll. Comm., Fla. State U. Recipient Pres.'s medal Nat. Press Photographers Assn., 1978, citation of excellence, 1979. Mem. Nat. Press Photographers Assn. (bd. dirs., chmn. info. com. 1978), Atlanta Press Photographers Assn. (past treas., v.p.), Fla. News Photographers Assn., Nat. Press Photographers Found., Am. Meteorol. Soc., Nat. Weather Assn., Am. Radio Relay League, Amateur Radio Satellite Corp., NRA, Wyo. Antelope Club, St. Petersurg Police Pistol Club, Skyway Trap and Skeet Club, Clearwater Amateur Radio Soc., Soc. Newspaper Design, Bass Anglers Sportsman Soc., Sigma Delta Chi. Office: 490 1st Ave S Saint Petersburg FL 33701-4204

BELIN, GASPARD D'ANDELOT, retired lawyer; b. Scranton, Pa., May 30, 1918; s. Gaspard d'Andelot and Margery (Jenks) B.; m. Harriet Lowell Bundy, Oct. 11, 1941; children: Harriet Lowell Belin Winkelman, Constance Belin Gibb, Richard, Margaretta Belin, Alletta Belin Farmer. B.A., Yale U., 1939, LL.B., 1946. Bar: Mass. 1947. With firm Choate, Hall & Stewart, Boston, 1947-62, ptnr., 1955-62, 65-90; gen. counsel Dept. Treasury, 1962-65. Past pres. Yale U. Coun., Cambridge Civic Assn.; trustee Mus. Sci.; v.p. Boston Athenaeum; dir. Mus. Trustee Assn.; past trustee Brigham & Women's Hosp.; past city councillor Cambridge. Capt. AUS, 1942-45, ETO. Fellow Am. Acad. Arts and Scis.; mem. ABA, Boston Bar Assn., Am. Law Inst. Episcopalian. Home: 4 Willard St Cambridge MA 02138-4837 Office: Choate Hall & Stewart 53 State St Exchange Pl Boston MA 02109

BELIN, JACOB CHAPMAN, paper company executive; b. DeFuniak Springs, Fla., Oct. 28, 1914; s. William Jacob and Addie (Leonard) B.; m. Myrle Fillingim, Nov. 28, 1940; children: Jacob Chapman, Stephen Andrew. Student, George Washington U., 1935-38. Dir. sales St. St. Joe Paper Co., Fla., 1949-56; v.p. St. Joe Paper Co., 1956-68, pres., dir., 1968—, chmn. bd., chief exec. officer, 1982-91; dir. St. Joseph Land & Devel. Co. Bd. dirs. Nemours Found., Alfred I. duPont Found.; trustee Estate of Alfred I. DuPont. Mem. Elks, Rotary, Kappa Alpha. Baptist. Office: St Joe Paper Co 1650 Prudential Dr Ste 400 Jacksonville FL 32207-8176

BELINGER, HARRY ROBERT, business executive, retired; b. Phila., Sept. 16, 1927; s. Harry and Florence (McGovern) B.; m. Jean Marie O'Neill, Nov. 30, 1957; 1 child, Lizanne. BS, Temple U., 1957. Reporter UPI, Phila., 1957-62; reporter Phila. Daily News, 1962-63, asst. city editor, 1963-66, city editor, 1966-68, 70-71; city editor Phila. Inquirer, 1968-70; city rep., dir. commerce City of Phila., 1972-76; v.p. pub. affairs ARAMARK Inc., Phila., 1976-95; ret., 1995; bd. dirs. Fitzgerald Mercy Hosp. Former ex-officio mem. City Planning Commn.; former v.p. Phila. Indsl. Devel. Corp.; past dir., mem. exec. com. Phila. Port Corp.; former mem. sch. bd. Archdiocese of Phila.; past bd. dirs., mem. exec. com. Conv. and Tourist Bur., Phila.; past bd. dirs. Phila. Civic Ctr. With inf., AUS, 1950-52. Mem. Phila. Press Assn. (bd. dirs. 1964-66). Home: 830 Strawberry Ln Wynnewood PA 19096-1644

BÉLISLE, PAUL C., Canadian government official; b. St. Joachim, Ont., Can., Nov. 14, 1950; m. Danielle Parent. B in Social Sci. (hon.), U. Ottawa, Ont., 1974, cert. in pub. adminstrn., 1975, LLL, 1980. Bar: Que. Clk. Coms. and Pvt. Legis. Directorate, 1979-84, asst. dir., 1984-94; sec. gen. Can.-France Interparliamentary Assn., 1989-91; clk. of the Senate, clk. of the Parliaments Senate of Canada, Ottawa, Ont., 1994—. Mem. editl. bd. Can. Parliamentary Rev. Mem. Assn. Clks.-at-the-Table Can., Commonwealth Parliamentary Assn. (exec. sec. treas.), Assn. of Secs. Gen. of Parliaments. Fax: 613-992-7959. Office: Senate of Can Parlmt Bldgsa, Rm 185-S Centre Block, Ottawa, ON Canada K1A 0A4

BELITT, BEN, poet, educator; b. N.Y.C., May 2, 1911; s. Joseph and Ida (Lewitt) B. B.A., U. Va., 1932, M.A., 1934, postgrad., 1934-36. Asst. lit. editor Nation, 1936-37; prof. English Bennington (Vt.) Coll., 1938—; mem. faculty dance summer schs. Bennington Coll., Mills Coll., 1939, Conn. Coll., 1948-49. Author: (poems) The Five-Fold Mesh, 1938, Wilderness Stair, 1955, The Enemy Joy; New and Selected Poems, 1964, Nowhere But Light, Poems, 1964-1969, The Double Witness, 1970-75, Possessions: New and Selected Poems (1938-1985), 1986, This Scribe My Hand: The Complete Poems of Ben Belitt, 1998, Graffiti, 1990; (prose) School of the Soldier, 1949; (essays) Adam's Dream: A Preface to Translation, 1978, The Forged Feature: Toward A Poetics of Uncertainty, 1994; editor and translator: Four Poems by Rimbaud: The Problem of Translation, 1947, Poet in New York (Federico García Lorca), 1955, Selected Poems of Pablo Neruda, 1961, Juan de Mairena and Poems from the Apocryphal Songbooks (Antonio Machado), 1963, The Selected Poems of Rafael Alberti, 1965, Pablo Neruda: A New Decade: Poems, 1958-67, 1969, Poems from Canto General, 1969, To Painting (Rafael Alberti), 1972, Splendor and Death of Joaquín Murieta (Pablo Neruda), 1972, New Poems: 1968-70 (Pablo Neruda), 1972, Five Decades: Poems 1925-70, 1974, Skystones 1981, Late and Posthumous Poems (1968-1974) (Pablo Neruda), 1988; contbr. to: The Selected Poems of Federico García Lorca, 1955, Cántico, Selections (Jorge Guillén), 1965, Selected Poems (Eugenio Montale), 1965, Jorge Luis Borges: Selected Poems, 1923-67), 1972. Served with AUS, 1942-44. Recipient Shelley Meml. award in poetry 1936, Oscar Blumenthal award in poetry 1956, Chgo. Civic, Arts award 1957, Brandeis Creative Arts award in poetry 1962, Nat. Inst. Arts and Letters award in poetry 1965, Williams/Derwood award for poetry, 1986; Guggenheim fellow, 1947; Nat. Endowment for the Arts grantee, 1967-68; Ben Belitt lectureship endowment Bennington Coll., 1977; Russell Loines award for poetry Am. Acad. and Inst. Arts and Letters, 1981; Rockefeller Found. grantee, Bellagio, Italy, 1984. Fellow Vt. Acad. Arts and Scis.; mem. P.E.N., Authors Guild, Phi Beta Kappa. Address: PO Box 88 North Bennington VT 05257-0088

BELITZ, PAUL EDWARD, lawyer; b. Omaha, July 11, 1951; s. Edward Paul and Jo Anna Beverly (Brown) B.; m. Joanne Deborah Nilson, June 9, 1973; children: Nicholas P., Christopher T. BS with high distinction, U. Nebr., 1973; JD magna cum laude, Creighton U., 1976. Bar: Nebr. 1976, Colo. 1982. Assoc., then ptnr. Kutak Rock, Omaha, 1976-81; ptnr. Kutak Rock, Denver, 1982—. Bd. dirs. Fleischer Found., Scottsdale, Ariz., 1986—, Fleischer Mus., Scottsdale, 1989—. Mem. ABA, Nebr. Bar Assn., Denver Bar Assn. Avocations: reading, skiing, golf. Office: Kutak Rock 717 17th St Ste 2900 Denver CO 80202-3329

BELJAN, JOHN RICHARD, university administrator, medical educator; b. Detroit, May 26, 1930; s. Joseph and Margaret Anne (Brozovich) B.; m. Bernadette Marie Marenda, Feb. 2, 1952; children: Ann Marie, John Richard, Paul Eric. B.S., U. Mich., 1951, M.D., 1954. Diplomate: Am. Bd. Surgery. Intern U. Mich., Ann Arbor, 1954-55, resident in gen. surgery, 1955-59; dir. med. services Stuart div. Atlas Chem. Industries, Pasadena, Calif., 1965-66; from asst. prof. to assoc. prof. surgery U. Calif. Med. Sch., Davis, 1966-74, from asst. prof. to assoc. prof. engring., 1968-74, from asst. dean to assoc. dean, 1971-74; prof. surgery, prof. biol. engring. Wright State U., Dayton, Ohio, 1974-83, dean Sch. Medicine, 1974-81, vice provost, 1974-78, v.p. health affairs, 1978-81, provost, sr. v.p., 1981-83; prof. arts and scis., assoc. v.p. med. affairs Cen. State U., Wilberforce, Ohio, 1976-83; provost, v.p. acad. affairs, dean Sch. Medicine Hahnemann U., Phila., 1983-85, prof. surgery and biomed. engring., 1983-86, spl. adviser to pres., 1985-86; v.p. acad. affairs Calif. State U., Long Beach, 1986-89, prof. anat., physiology and biomed. engring., 1986-91, provost, 1989-91; pres. Northrop U., L.A., 1989-93, pres. emeritus, 1993—; trustee Cox Heart Inst., 1975-77, Drew Health Ctr., 1977-78, Wright State U. Found., 1975-83, CSULB Found., 1986-89, 49er Athletic Found., 1986-89; trustee, regional v.p. Engring. and Sci. Inst. Hall of Fame, 1983—; bd. dirs. Miami Valley Health Sys. Agy., 1975-82, UCI Ctr. for Health Edn., 1987-90, Long Beach Rsch. Found., 1989-94; cons. in field. Author articles, revs., chpts. in books. Served with M.C. USAF, 1955-65. Decorated Commendation medal; Braun fellow, 1949; grantee USPHS, NASA, 1968—. Fellow A.C.S.; mem. Los Angeles County Med. Assn., Mich. Alumni Club (Dayton, Outstanding Alumnus award 1976), Oakwood Fur Club, Fin and Feather Club, Phi Beta Delta, Phi Beta Kappa, Alpha Omega Alpha, Phi Eta Sigma, Phi Kappa Phi, Alpha Kappa Kappa. Home and Office: 6490 E Saddle Dr Long Beach CA 90815-4740

BELK, F. NORMAN, librarian; b. Greenville, S.C., June 8, 1947; s. Francis Norman and Louellen Vinny (Davis) B. BA, Furman U., 1969; MLS, U. S.C., 1975. Reference librarian Greenville County Libr., 1970-77, br. libr. mgr., 1977-84, outreach librarian, 1984-85, audiovisual sect. mgr., 1985-86, acquisitions-automation librarian, 1986-89, coord. cmty. rels., 1989-98, coord. main libr. svc., 1998—. Rschr., contbr.: Tales from the Dark Corner: Documenting the Oral Tradition, 2 vols., 1995; contbr. articles to profl. jours. Mem. ALA (mem. intellectual freedom com. 1997—), Pub. libr. Assn. (mem. audiovisuals com. 1995—), S.C. Libr. Assn. (chair awards com. 1988-91, chair intellectual freedom com. 1991-93, Outstanding Librarian award 1994), Met. Arts Assn., Palmetto Soc. of United Way, Greenville East Rotary (program chair 1996-97, bd. dirs. 1995—), Furman Club (founder), S.C. Libr. Assn. (v.p., pres.-elect 1999). Home: 107 Richbourg Rd Greenville SC 29615-1354 Office: Greenville County Libr 300 College St Greenville SC 29601-2015

BELK, IRWIN, retail executive; b. Charlotte, N.C., Apr. 4, 1922; s. William Henry and Mary Leonora (Irwin) B.; m. Carol Grotnes, Sept. 11, 1948; children: William Irwin, Irene Belk Miltimore, Marilyn Belk Wallis, Carl Grotnes. BS in Commerce, U. N.C., 1946; LLD (hon.), Mo. Valley Coll., 1977; HHD (hon.), Erskine Coll., 1979; LLD (hon.), Elon Coll., 1990. Dir. Belk Fin. Co.; officer and dir. Belk Group Stores, Charlotte; chmn., dir. PMC, Inc., Raleigh, N.C.; chmn. bd. Monroe Hardware Co.; dir. First Union Nat. Bank of N.C., Charlotte, Lumbermen's Mut. Casualty, Co., Chgo., Stonecutter Mills, Spindale, N.C.; Past pres. men's council N.C. Synod, Presbyn. Ch.; mem. exec. com. Hist. Found. Presbyn and Reformed Chs. (Montreat), N.C. Past pres. N.C. div. Am. Cancer Soc.; trustee N.C. Symphony Soc.; chmn. U.S. Olympic Com. for N.C.; past mem. City of Charlotte Urban Redevel. Com.; mem. N.C. Ho. of Reps., 1959-60, 61-62, N.C. Senate, 1963-66, N.C. Legis. Coun., 1963-64, Legis. Rsch. Commn., 1965-66, Democratic nat. committeeman for, N.C., 1969-72; del. Dem. Nat. Convs., 1956, 60, 64, 68, 72; bd. dirs. Med. Found. N.C., N.C. State Bus. Found. N.C., Chapel Hill, Ednl. Found., Found. of U. N.C., Charlotte, Sch. of Design, N.C. State U.; bd. dirs., mem. exec. com. N.C. Assn. for Blind; bd. dirs., past pres. N.C. chpt. Nat. Soc. Prevention Blindness; ho. dels. Am. Cancer Soc.; bd. dirs. Charlotte Opera Assn.; bd. govs. U. N.C., Presbyn. Coll., Clinton, S.C.; bd. advisors Belk Found.; former bd. assocs. Meredith Coll., Raleigh; bd. counselors Erskine Coll., Due West, S.C.; bd. advisers Western Carolina U., Cullowhee, N.C.; former bd. advisers Campbell Coll., Buies Creek, N.C.; dir. N.C. Citizens for Bus. and Industry, Raleigh, N.C., 1990-94. Served with USAAF, World War II. Recipient Outstanding Young Man award Charlotte, 1954-57. Mem. Charlotte Mchts. Assn., Charlotte C. of C. (exec. com., dir.), N.C. Presbyn. Hist. Soc. (past pres.), Charlotte Country Club, Myers Park Country Club, Charlotte City Club, Sky Club, Masons, Shriners, Lions (past pres., past dist. gov.), Kappa Alpha, Delta Sigma Pi. Democrat. Presbyterian (elder, past deacon). Clubs: Masons (Charlotte, dist. gov.), Shriners (Charlotte, dist. gov.), Lions (Charlotte, dist. gov.) (past pres.); Charlotte City (Charlotte), Charlotte Country (Charlotte), Charlotte Execs. (Charlotte) (past pres.), Charlotte Carrousel (Charlotte) (past pres.), Myers Park Country (Charlotte); Sky (N.Y.C.). Home: 9200 Winged Bourne Rd Charlotte NC 28210-5948 Office: Belk Group Stores 6100 Fairview Rd Ste 640 Charlotte NC 28210-4258

BELK, JOHN M., retail company executive; b. Charlotte, N.C., 1920. Student, Davidson Coll., 1943. Chmn. Belk Stores Svcs. Inc., now CEO; chmn. Belk Bros. Co.; bd. dirs. Bros. Investment Co., Chaparral Steel Co., Coca Cola Bottlin Co. Consolidated, Lowe's Cos., Inc. Mem. Nat. Retail Fedn. (bd. dirs.). Office: Belk Stores Svcs Inc 2801 W Tyvola Rd Charlotte NC 28217 4525*

BELKIN, BORIS DAVID, violinist; b. Sverdpovsk, USSR, Jan. 26, 1948; s. David Boris and Anna Alexandre Belkin; children: Julian, Alexander, Maïa. Student, Central Music Sch., Moscow, 1969, Moscow Conservatory, 1969-74; studied with, Yankelevitch and Andrievsky. Violinist; appeared with orchs. throughout world, including, N.Y. Philharm., Israel Philharm., Chgo. Symphony Orch., Los Angeles Philharm., Cleve. Symphony Orch., Boston Symphony Orch., Berlin Philharm., Royal Philharm., Phila. Symphony Orch., Paris National, Vienna Symphony, London Philharm., Pitts. Symphony Orch.; also rec. artist, Decca. Recipient 1st prize Nat. Violin Competition USSR, 1973. Office: care ICM Artists Ltd 40 W 57th St New York NY 10019-4001*

BELKNAP, JODI PARRY, graphic designer, writer, business owner; b. New Canaan, Conn., June 4, 1939; d. Corliss Lloyd and Joan (Pike) Parry; m. William Belknap III, Feb. 20, 1970 (div. Nov. 1982). AB in English and Writing, Barnard Coll., 1962; MA in Drama and Theater, U. Hawaii at Manoa, Honolulu, 1988. Life elem. tchr. credential, Calif. Tchr. grade 6 Ruth Fyfe Sch., Las Vegas, Nev., 1963-64; tchr. grades. 2,3 Schilling Sch., Hayward, Calif., 1964-69; master tchr. U. Calif., Hayward, 1967-69; editor Island Heritage Ltd., Honolulu, 1970-73; Pacific bur. chief OAG Publs. (Dun and Bradstreet), Honolulu, 1972-82; freelance writer, columnist various mags. and publs., 1976-88; owner Belknap Pub. and Design, Honolulu, 1987—. Author: (books) Majesty, The Exceptional Trees of Hawaii, 1982, Kaanapalī, 1981, Halekulani, 1982, (children's book) Felisa and the Magic Tikling Bird, 1973; book designer: How the B-52 Cockroach Learned to Fly, 1995, Hula Is Life, 1998; prin. design projects for Sheraton Hotels in Hawaii, 1988—, others; Hawaiian corr. Sr. Travel Tips, 1997. Recipient Gold award Hospitality Mktg. Assn. Internat., 1995, award Hawaii chpt. Pub. Rels. Soc. Am., 1993, 94, Ilima award of excellence Internat. Assn. Bus. Communicators, 1989, 90. Mem. Am. Inst. Graphic Arts, Soc. Children's Book Writers, Small Bus. Hawaii. Avocations: swimming, hiking, family trips. Address: Belknap Pub PO Box 22387 Honolulu HI 96823-2387

BELKNAP, MARIA ANN, writer; b. Portland, Oreg., Mar. 28, 1958; d. Russell Lee B. Student, U. Calif. Santa Barbara, 1976-78; BS in Resource Mgmt., U. Oreg., 1980. Buyer Splendiferous Inc., L.A., 1982-83; co-proprietor Am. Croissant, L.A., 1983-90; writer L.A., 1989—. Author: The Horseman's Spanish-English Dictionary, 1991, The Horseman's German-English Dictionary, 1994, The Horseman's English-Spanish Dictionary, 2d edit., 1996, The Equine Dictionary, 1997. Democrat. Avocations: horseback riding, skiing, tennis, sky diving, scuba diving. Home and Office: PO Box 15452 Beverly Hills CA 90209-1452

BELKNAP, MICHAEL H. P., real estate developer; b. South Bend, Ind., Oct. 27, 1940; s. Paul E. and Mary Elizabeth (Gibb) B.; m. Dorothy Callaway, Aug. 12, 1967 (div. Dec. 1989); children: Michael, Jenny Warner, Matthew Gibb; m. Martha Burke-Hennessy, May 25, 1996; children: Helene Lesterlin, Roland Lesterlin. BA, Harvard U., 1963, JD, 1967; LLB, Cambridge (Eng.) U., 1965. Bar: N.Y. 1969; assoc. Sullivan & Cromwell, N.Y.C., 1967-70; dir. Coun. on Environment, Office of Mayor City of N.Y., 1970-72; v.p., gen. counsel Corp. Property Investors, N.Y.C., 1972-75; v.p. Levitt & Sons Inc., Greenwich, Conn., 1975-78; pres. Belknap Co. Ltd., Canaan, N.Y., 1978—; adj. prof. Western New Eng. Coll. Sch. Law. Fellow English Speaking Union, 1963-64. Mem. Berkshire Natural Resources Coun. (trustee), Harvard Club. Democrat. Episcopalian. Home: PO Box 94 Canaan NY 12029-0094 Office: Warner Crossing Rd Canaan NY 12029

BELKNAP, NORTON, petroleum company consultant; b. Topeka, June 17, 1925; s. Paul Edward and Twila Norton Belknap; m. Mary Lonam, June 7, 1950; children: Paula Belknap Reynolds, David Barrett, Randall Page. B.S., MIT, 1950, M.S., 1951. Various tech. and supervisory positions Exxon, 1951-60; v.p., dir. Esso Japan, 1961-65; chmn., mng. dir. Esso Australia, 1966-69; v.p., exec. v.p., dir. Esso Europe, 1969-73; v.p. corporate planning Exxon Corp., N.Y.C., 1973-79; sr. v.p. Exxon Internat., N.Y.C., 1979-82; trustee Carnegie Hall, N.Y.C., 1974—, mng. dir., 1983-88; petroleum cons., 1982—; bd. dirs. So. Pacific Petroleum USA. Pres. bd. dirs. Paul Taylor Dance Co.; bd. dirs., chmn. exec. com. US/China C. oF C., 1998—. Decorated Air medal with oak leaf cluster. Mem. Tau Beta Pi. Clubs: Union, Century Assn., Metropolitan Opera (N.Y.C.). Home: 563 Park Ave New York NY 10021-7314

BELKNAP, ROBERT LAMONT, Russian and comparative literature educator; b. N.Y.C., Dec. 23, 1929; s. Chauncey and Dorothy (Lamont) B.; m. Josephine E. Hornor, Aug. 20, 1955 (separated 1992); children: Lydia Duff, Ellen Belknap, Abigail Krueger; m. Cynthia H. Whittaker, Aug. 24, 1997. AB, Princeton U., 1951; postgrad., U. Paris, 1951-52; MA, Columbia U., 1954; cert., Russian Inst., 1957, PhD, 1960; postgrad., Leningrad U., 1963-64. Instr. Russian, Columbia U., 1957-60, asst. prof., 1960-63, chmn. freshman humanities, 1963, 67-68, 88-91, assoc. prof., 1963-68, assoc. dean student affairs, 1968-69, prof., 1968—, acting dean of Coll., 1976-77; dir. Russian Inst., 1977-80; vis. assoc. prof. Russian Ind. U., 1966, 67; adj. prof. Russian Yale U., 1967; vis. foreign scholar, Hokkaido U., 1999—. Author: The Structure of the Brothers Karamazov, 1967, reprint, 1989, Russian translation, 1997, The Genesis of The Brothers Karamazov, 1990; co-author: General Education and the Reintegration of the University, 1977; editor, Russianness, 1990. Pres. bd. trustees Brearley Sch., N.Y.C., 1981-87; trustee Whiting Found., 1985—; served with U.S. Army, 1953-55. Fellow Kennan Inst., 1987-88, Guggenheim, 1994-95. Home: 501 E 79th St New York NY 10021-0735 Office: Columbia U Slavic Dept New York NY 10027 *Students rarely learn anything they are told. They often learn the things they say themselves. Good teaching wrestles them into saying sensible, verifiable, interesting, and sometimes important things.*

BELL, ALAN, lawyer, environmental health activist; b. N.Y.C., Aug. 13, 1954; s. Julius and Vivian B.; 1 child, Ashlee. BBA magna cum laude, U. Miami, 1976, JD, 1979. Bar: Fla. 1979, U.S. Dist. Ct. (so. dist.) Fla. 1980. Asst. state atty., prosecutor Broward County, Ft. Lauderdale, Fla., 1980-86; corp. counsel and atty. The Travelers Insur. Co., Ft. Lauderdale, Fla., 1986-89; lawyer pvt. practice, 1989-91; chmn., founder Environ. Health Found., Tucson, Ariz., 1992—. Chief justice Student Supreme Ct., U. Miami, 1976. Mem. Omicron Delta Kappa (hon., pres.), Delta Sigma Pi, Phi Kappa Phi. Home: 4161 N Camino Del Celason Tucson AZ 85718

BELL, ALEXIS T., chemical engineer; b. N.Y.C., Oct. 16, 1942. BS, MIT, 1964, ScD, 1967. From asst. prof. to prof. U. Calif., Berkeley, 1967-76, prof.

chem. engring., 1976-99, asst. dean Coll. Chemistry, 1979-81, dean Coll. Chemistry, 1994-99, chmn. Dept. Chem. Engring., 1981-91; Cons. Tracer Labs., Calif., 1967-69, Internat. Plasma Corp., 1969—, Tegal Corp. & Lockheed Space & Missile Co.; sr. scientist Lawrence Berkeley Nat. Lab. Contbr. articles to profl. jours. Recipient Curtis W. McGraw Rsch. award Am. Soc. Engring. Edn., 1981, Paul E. Emmett award Catalysis Soc., 1985; Donald L. Katz lectr. U. Mich., 1984, B. F. Dodge lectr. Yale U., 1988, Langmuir lectr. Am. Chem. Soc., 1992. Fellow AAAS; mem. NAE, Am. Chem. Soc. (A. Glenn award 1978), AIChE (R.H. Wilhelm award 1992), Electrochem. Soc., Sigma Xi. Fax: (510) 642-4778. Office: U California Dept Chem Engineering 107 Gilman Hall Berkeley CA 94720-1462*

BELL, BAILLIS F., airport terminal executive. Budget analyst City of Wichita, Kans., 1970-75; dir. Wichita Airport Authority, Kans., 1975—. Office: Witchita Airport Authority 2173 Air Cargo Rd Wichita KS 67209-1958*

BELL, BRIAN MAYES, lawyer; b. Columbus, Tex., Aug. 21, 1940; s. Robert Harvey and Edith Virginia (Kimball) B.; m. Karen Ann Roof, May 25, 1962 (div. 1973); m. Charlotte Jean Starks, Dec. 28, 1973 (div. 1980); m. Sue Ann Curry, July 25, 1980; children: Robin L., Susan L., Michael K., Miles A. Franz, Alex F. Franz. BS, So. Meth. U., 1962; JD, U. Denver, 1968. Bar: Colo. 1969, U.S. Dist. Ct. Colo. 1969, U.S. Ct. Appeals (10th cir.) 1969. Assoc. Rovira, DeMuth & Eiberger, Denver, 1968-72; atty., asst. sec. Mountain Bell Tele. Co., Denver, 1972-83; sr. corp. counsel, asst. sec. U.S. West, Inc., Englewood, Colo., 1983-93; adj. prof. U. Colo., Denver, 1974-83; legal cons. 1993—. Mem. ABA, Am. Soc. Corp. Secs. (bd. dirs. 1990-93, pres. Colo. chpt. 1988-89), Am. Corp. Counsel Assn. (bd. dirs. Colo. chpt. 1989-95), Met. Club, Valley Country Club. Republican. Presbyterian. Home: 3233 Country Club Pkwy Castle Rock CO 80104-8300

BELL, BURWELL BAXTER, III, major general United States Army. BS in Bus. Adminstrn., U. Tenn.; MS in Systems Mgmt., U. So. Calif.; grad. armor officer advanced course, U.S. Army Armor Sch, Fort Knox, Ky., 1976; student, Army Command, Gen. Staff Colls, Fort Leavenworth, Kans., 1980-81, Nat. War Coll., Fort McNair, N.J., 1987-88. Commd. 2d lt. U.S. Army, 1969, advanced through grades to major gen., 1998; from platoon leader to exec. officer Troop M, 14th Cavalry U.S. Army Europe and Seventh Army, Germany, comdr. L troop, 3d Reconnissance Squadron, 14th Cavalry, 1971-72; comdr. D troop 5th Cavalry Squadron 1st Indivual Tng. Brig. U.S. Army Armor Sch., Fort Knox, Ky., 1974-75; chief individual tng. dept. U.S. Army Armor Ctr., Fort Knox, Ky., 1975-76; staff officer modernization coord. office Office Chief of Staff, Army, Washington, 1981-83; cmmdr. 2d squadron, 9th cavalry, 24th infantry divsn. U.S. Army, Fort Stewart, Ga., 1984-87; exec. officer to cmdr.-in-chief U.S. Ctrl. Command Operation Desert Shield/Desert Storm, Saudi Arabia, 1990-91; chief of staff 3d infantry divsn. U.S. Army Europe and Seventh Army, Germany, 1993-94, chief of staff V Corps, 1996-97, dep. chief of staff for ops., 1997-98, chief of staff, 1998—. Decorated Legion of Merit with 2 Oak Leaf Clusters, Bronze Star medal, Army Commendation medal with 2 Oak Leaf Clusters, Defense Superior Svc. medal, Meritorious Svc. medal with 2 Oak Leaf Clusters. Office: Chief of Staff US Army & 7th Army Europe APO AE 09014

BELL, CAROLYN SHAW, economist, educator; b. Framingham, Mass., June 21, 1920; d. Clarence Edward and Grace (Wellington) Shaw; m. Nelson S. Bell, Aug. 26, 1953; 1 dau. by previous marriage, Tova Maria. AB magna cum laude, Mt. Holyoke Coll., 1941; PhD, London Sch. Econs., 1949; LHD (hon.), Babson Coll., 1983, Denison U., 1988, North Adams State Coll., 1991. Economist OPA, 1941-45; rsch. economist London Sch. Econs., 1946-47, Social Sci. Rsch. Coun., Harvard, 1950-53; mem. faculty Wellesley Coll., 1950-89, prof. econs., 1962-89, chmn. dept., 1962-65, 79-82, Katharine Coman prof. econs., 1970-89, Katharine Coman prof. econs. emeritus, 1989—; cons. Lexington, Mass., 1989—; pub. mem. Fed. Adv. Coun. on Unemployment Inc., 1974-77, chmn., 1975-77; bd. econ. advisors Pub. Interest Econ. Ctr.; bd. overseers Amos Tuck Grad. Sch. Bus. Adminstrn., Dartmouth, 1973-79; mem. econs. policy coun. UN Assn., 1976-85, trustee, 1981-90; trustee Joint Coun. Econ. Edn., 1975-83, Tchrs. Ins. and Annuity Assn., 1977-85, Symmes Life Care, Inc., 1994—, NEADS, Inc., 1994—; mem. NRC Com. for Behavioral & Social Scis., 1977-83; bd. adv. Internat. Labour Rev. Author: Consumer Choice in the U.S. Economy, 1967, The Economics of the Ghetto, 1970; co-author: (with W.W. Cochrane) Economics of Consumption, 1956; co-author: Coping in A Troubled Society, 1974; contbr. articles to profl. jours.; radio and TV commentator; mem. bd. editors Challenge Mag. Mem. Hearing Dog Adv. Coun., 1990-93. Recipient Disting. Achievement award The Boston Club, 1996, WERT award for Tchg. Excellence, 1997, Acad. of Women Acheivers, YWCA, 1997. Mem. AAUP (pres. Wellesley chpt. 1965-66). AAUW (Shirley Farr fellow 1961-62), ACLU, Assn. for Advancement Socio-Econs., Manhattan Inst. (adv. bd.), Am. Econs. Assn. (chmn. com. on status women in econs. profession 1972-74, exec. com. mem. 1975-77), Assn. Evolutionary Econs. (bd. dirs. 1973-75), Ea. Econs. Assn. (exec. bd. 12983-85), Phi Beta Kappa (pres. Eta Mass chpt. 1978-80), Delta Soc. (svc. dog. adv. bd. 1994-95). E-mail: cbell@wellesley.edu. Home and Office: 1010 Waltham St Apt 8F Lexington MA 02421-8061

BELL, CHARLES A., hotel development and management executive; b. New Brighton, Pa., Aug. 30, 1925; s. Charles and Elizabeth (Pollock) B.; m. Claire Naughton, Oct. 1, 1949; children: Charles A. (dec.), Jane Bell Cammarata. BS, Cornell U.; student, U. Grenoble, France. Purchasing agt., cost contr. Hilton Internat./Caribe Hilton Hotel, P.R., 1949-51; chief steward Hotel Plaza Hilton, N.Y.C., 1952; restaurant mgr. Hotel Roosevelt-Hilton, N.Y.C., 1955; food and beverage mgr. Hotel New Yorker-Hilton, N.Y.C., 1956; asst. dir. food and beverage Hilton Hotels Corp., N.Y.C., 1960; v.p. food and beverage Hilton Hotels Internat., N.Y.C., 1965, sr. v.p. adminstrn., 1970, exec. v.p., COO, 1976-85; pres. inernat. hotel mgmt. and devel. Charles A. Bell, Ltd., N.Y.C., 1986—; Contbr. articles to profl. jours. Bd. dirs. Washington Sq. Assn., 1982-92; mem. Washington Sq. Coalition, 1986—. With USAF, 1943-46. Mem. Quaker Hill Country Club, Marco Polo Club, World Trade Club, Confrerie des Chevaliers du Tastevin (comdr.), Angler's Club N.Y., Alpha Sigma Phi, Phi Kappa Phi. Republican. Home: 29 Washington Sq W New York NY 10011-9180 Office: Charles Anderson Bell Ltd 29 Washington Sq W New York NY 10011-9180

BELL, CHARLES D., lawyer; b. McKeesport, Pa., Jan. 23, 1923; s. Charles R. and Bertha Beatrice (Davis) B.; m. Mary Porter Wilkin, Mar. 17, 1945 (dec. 1971); children—Betty Bell Williams, Peggy Jean Hrach, Charles William, Julie Bell Caldwell; m. Marjorie Wicks, Mar. 26, 1977. BS in Chemistry, Bethany Coll., 1944; JD, U. Mich., 1949. Bar: W.Va., 1951. Assoc. Schroeder, Merriam, Hofgren & Brady, Chgo., 1950-51, Bell, McMullen, Wellsburg, W.Va., 1951—; asst. pros. atty. Brooke County, Wellsburg, 1960-68, 72-76, 81-90; bd. dirs., sec. Banner Fibreboard Co., Wellsburg. Past bd. dirs. W.Va. Rehab. Found., North Ctrl. region Boy Scouts Am.; mem. W.Va. Ind. Coll. Found., chmn., 1992-95; bd. trustees Bethany Coll., 1976-97, chmn., 1977-97. Served with AUS, 1944-46. Mem. ABA, Brooke County Bar Assn., W.Va. State Bar Assn., Wheeling Country Club, Masons, Elks. Republican. Home: 1222 Pleasant Ave Wellsburg WV 26070-1345 Office: Bell McMullen 67 Town Sq Wellsburg WV 26070

BELL, CHARLES EUGENE, JR., industrial engineer; b. N.Y.C., Dec. 13, 1932; s. Charles Edward and Constance Elizabeth (Verbelia) B.; B. Engring., Johns Hopkins U., 1954, M.S. in Engring., 1959; m. Doris R. Clifton, Jan. 14, 1967; 1 son, Scott Charles Bell. Indsl. engr. Signode Corp., Balt., 1957-61, asst. to plant mgr., 1961-63, plant engr., 1963-64, div. indsl. engr., Glenview, Ill., 1964-69, asst. to div. mgr., 1969-76, engring. mgr., 1976-93; cons., 1993—; host committeeman Internat. Indsl. Engring. Conf., Chgo., 1984, 92. Served with U.S. Army, 1955-57. Registered profl. engr., Calif. Mem. Am. Inst. Indsl. Engrs. (pres. 1981), Indsl. Mgmt. Club Central Md. (pres. 1964), Nat. Soc. Profl. Engrs., Ill. Soc. Profl. Engrs., Soc. Plastics Engrs. Republican. Roman Catholic. Home: 1021 W Old Mill Rd Lake Forest IL 60045-3749

BELL, CHARLES ROBERT, JR., judge; b. Wichita, Kans., July 14, 1930; m. Janice Little; children: Barbara, Charles Robert III, Nancy, Bradley L., James S. AB, Princeton U., 1952; JD, Harvard U., 1955. Bar: Mass. 1955, Kans. 1959. Pvt. practice Boston, 1955-56; with Garvey Family Enterprises, 1958-60; ptnr. Morris, Laing, Evans & Brock, Wichita, 1960-74, Brick & Bell, Wichita, 1974-80; pres. C. Robert Bell, P.A., Wichita, 1980-88; judge Kans. State Dist. Ct., Wichita, 1988—; founding dir. Prepaid Legal Svcs. Kans., Inc. Mem. Am. Arbitration Assn. (mem. panel arbitrators). Home: 8018 Woodspring Way # 310 Wichita KS 67226 Office: 525 N Main St Wichita KS 67203

BELL, CHESTER GORDON, computer engineering company executive; b. Kirksville, Mo., Aug. 19, 1934; s. Roy Chester and Lola Dolph (Gordon) B.; m. Gwendolyn Kay Druyor, Jan. 3, 1959; children: Brigham Roy, Laura Louise. BSEE, MIT, 1956, MSEE, 1957; DEng (hon.), Worcester Poly. Inst., 1993. Engr. Speech Communication Lab., MIT, Cambridge, 1959-60; mgr. computer design Digital Equipment Corp., Maynard, Mass., 1960-66, v.p. engring., 1972-83; prof. computer sci. Carnegie-Mellon U., 1966-72; vice chmn. Encore Computer Corp., Marlboro, Mass., 1983-86; asst. dir. NSF, Washington, 1986-87; v.p. R & D Stardent Computer, Sunnyvale, Calif., 1987-89; cons. The Bell-Mason Group, 1989—; bd. dirs. Cynapps Design, Cradle Tech., Packetcom.; bd. dirs., trustee Computer Mus., 1982—; sr. researcher Microsoft Corp., 1995—. Author: (with Newell) Computer Structures, 1971, (with Grason, Newell) Designing Computers and Digital Systems, 1972, (with Mudge, McNamara) Computer Engineering, 1978, (with Siewiorek, Newell) Computer Structures, 1982, (with McNamara) High Tech Ventures, 1991. Recipient 6th Mellon Inst. award, 1972, Nat. Medal Tech., U.S. Dept. Commerce Tech. Adminstrn., 1991, award for greatest econ. contbn. to region Am. Electronics Assn., 1993, MCI Smithsonian award for Innovation, 1995. Fellow IEEE (McDowell award 1975, Eckert-Mauchly award 1982, von Neumann medal 1992), AAAS, Am. Acad. Arts and Scis., Assn. for Computing Machinery; mem. NAE, Eta Kappa Nu. Home and Office: 450 Old Oak Ct Los Altos CA 94022-2682

BELL, CHRIS, city councilman; m. Alison Ayres; 1 child, Atlee. JD, U. Tex. City councilman-at-large City of Houston, 1997—, mem. Charter Rev. Com., mem. Fiscal Affairs Com., mem. Competitive Svcs. Com.; former reporter Sta. KTRH Radio; atty. Bell & Henry, LLP. Episcopalian. Office: City of Houston PO Box 1562 Houston TX 77251-1562*

BELL, CLARENCE DESHONG, state senator, lawyer; b. Upland, Pa., Feb. 4, 1914; s. Samuel Robert and Belle (Hanna) B.; m. Mary James, Nov. 24, 1939; children: Clarence, Mary D. AB, Swarthmore Coll., 1935; JD, Harvard U., 1938; grad., U.S. Army Command and Gen. Staff Coll., 1942; advanced course, U.S. Army Field Arty. Sch., 1945. Bar: Pa. 1939. Pvt. practice law Delaware County, Pa., 1939—; mem. Pa. Ho. of Reps., 1954-60; mem. Pa. Senate, 1960—, chmn. joint legis. budget and fin. commn., chmn. consumer protection and profl. licensure com., vice-chmn. appropriations com. With U.S. Army, 1935-74; to brig. gen. Army N.G., 1964-74; to maj. gen. Pa. N.G., 1974—. Decorated Legion of Merit; named Labor's Man of Yr. Delaware County chpt. AFL-CIO; recipient awards and citations from Pa. Gold State Mothers, Jewish War Vets., VFW, Res. Officers Assn., Mil. Govt. Assn., B'nai B'rith, KC, Polish-Am. Citizens Club, SSS, N.G. Assn. Pa., Am. Legion, various others, Pa. Dist. Svc. medal (2). Mem. ABA, UAW (hon.), UA (hon.), Pa. Bar Assn., Fraternal Order Police (hon.), Teamsters (hon.), Transport Workers Union (hon.), Mil. Govt. Assn. (past nat. pres.), Res. Officers Assn (past state pres.), Mil. Order World Wars, N.G. Assn., Exch. Club (past state pres.), Masons (33d degree), also hon. mem. several other unions. Republican.

BELL, CLARK WAYNE, business editor, educator; b. Casper, Wyo., Feb. 7, 1951; s. Homer James and Jeanette (Hoban) B.; m. Victoria Anne Boucher, Jan. 2, 1971 (divorced); 1 child, Heidi Elizabeth; m. Suzanne Cerny, Mar. 6, 1989; 1 child, Natalie Taylor. BS, Drake U., 1973; MA, Loyola U., Chgo., 1978. Copy editor Chgo. Daily News, 1973-74, reporter, 1974-79; bus. columnist Chgo. Sun-Times, Chgo., 1979-84; exec. bus. editor Dallas Times Herald, 1984-86; editor, assoc. pub. Modern Healthcare Mag., Chgo., 1986—; lectr. Northwestern U., Evanston, Ill., 1980-83; cons. editor Sales & Mktg. Mgmt. mag., N.Y.C., 1982-84. Bd. dirs. Youth Comm., Chgo., 1981-84, Next Theatre Co., Evanston, 1982-84, Heartland Alliance, 1994—, Chgo. Health Outreach, 1995—. Sloan fellow Princeton U., 1975-76. Mem. United Ch. Christ. Office: Modern Healthcare Crain Comm 740 N Rush St Chicago IL 60611-2546

BELL, C(LYDE) R(OBERTS) (BOB BELL), foundation administrator; b. Balt., Apr. 12, 1931; s. William and Rachel (Roberts) B.; m. Carol Ann Murphy, June 14, 1980 (dec. Aug. 1997); children: Diane, Nancy, Mary Lynn, Catherine, Robert, Brian, Douglas, Jeffrey, Lawrenec, Laura; m. Jean Creighton Chapman, Feb. 13, 1999. BS with distinction, U.S. Naval Acad., 1953. Registered profl. nuclear engr. Commd. ensign USN, 1953, advanced through grades to vice adm., 1987, ret., 1988; pres. Greater Omaha C. of C., 1989—; bd. dirs. Guarantee Life Ins. Co., Omaha, Ctr. for Human Nutrition, Omaha, WELCOM, Omaha. Trustee Boy Scouts Am., Omaha, 1990—; bd. dirs. NCCJ, Omaha, 1991—. Mem. Omaha Country Club, Omaha Club (Man of Yr. 1991), Omaha Plaza Club, Omaha Press Club. Avocations: golf, reading, the arts, family. Office: Greater Omaha C of C 1301 Harney St Omaha NE 68102-1832

BELL, DAVID ARTHUR, advertising agency executive; b. Mpls., May 29, 1943; s. Arthur E. and Frances (Tripp) B.; m. Gail G. Galvani; children: Jenny L., Jennifer L., Jeffrey D., Ashley Tripp, Andrew Joseph. BA in Polit. Sci., Macalester Coll., 1965. Account exec. Leo Burnett, Chgo., 1965-67; pres. Knox Reeves, Mpls., 1967-74; pres. Atlantic div. Bozell & Jacobs, 1974-85; pres. Bozell, Jacobs, Kenyon & Eckhardt, 1986-92; chmn., CEO Bozell Worldwide Inc., 1992—, True North Comm., Inc.; bd. dirs. Bus. Publs. Audit; chmn. Am. Advt. Fedn. Nat. com. coord. United Way Am., Minn., 1975—; trustee Macalester Coll., 1986-88, 98—, Pitts. Theol. Sem., New Sch. Social Rsch., 1995—; bd. dirs. True North, 1998—; chmn. Advt. Ednl. Found., vice chmn. Ad Coun. Recipient charter centennial medallion Macalester Coll., 1974; named disting. alumnus Macalester Coll., 1978; recipient Minn. Airman of Yr. award, 1967. Mem. Am. Advt. Fedn. (chmn. nat. bd. dirs. 1988-91), Am. Assn. Advt. Agys. (chmn. 1996-97. Republican. Presbyterian. Home: 1 W 72nd St Apt 45 New York NY 10023-3418 Office: True North Comm Inc 101 E Erie St Chicago IL 60611 also: Bozell Worldwide Inc 40 W 23d St New York NY 10010

BELL, DAVID SHEFFIELD, physician; b. Beverly, Mass., Aug. 5, 1945; s. Charles Cox and Helen Bell; m. Karen Maziarz; children: Nadira, David, Omar. AB, Harvard U., 1967; MD, Boston U., 1971. Pvt. practice Lyndonville, N.Y., 1978-90, 95-97; asst. prof. Harvard U., Cambridge, Mass., 1990-95. Mem. Am. Acad. Pediat., Am. Assn. Chronic Fatique Syndrome (bd. dirs. 1994-97), Chronic Fatique Syndrome Assn. (bd. dirs. 1987-97, sci. advisor 1990-97). Author: Three Children, 1973, The Disease of a Thousand Names, 1988, Doctors Guide to Chronic Fatigue Syndrome, 1993. Office: 77 S Main St Lyndonville NY 14098-9771

BELL, DELORIS WILEY, physician; b. Solomon, Kans., Sept. 30, 1942; d. Harry A. and Mildren H. (Watt) Wiley; children—Leslie and John. B.A., Kans. Wesleyan U., 1964; M.D., U. Kans., 1968. Diplomate Am. Bd. Ophthalmology. Intern St. Luke's Hosp., Kansas City, Mo., 1968-69; resident U. Kans. Med. Ctr., Kansas City, 1969-72; practice medicine specializing in ophthalmology, Overland Park, Kans., 1973—. Mem. AMA, Kans. Med. Soc. (pres. sect. ophthalmology 1985-86, spkr of house 1994-97), Am. Acad. Ophthalmology (councillor 1988-93, chmn. state govtl. affairs 1993-97), Kans. Soc. Ophthalmology (pres. 1985-86), Kansas City Soc. Ophthalmology and Otolaryngology (sec. 1984-86, pres.-elect 1988, pres. 1989). Avocations: photography, travel. Office: 7000 W 121st St Ste 100 Shawnee Mission KS 66209-2010

BELL, DENISE LOUISE, newspaper reporter, photographer, librarian; b. Washington, Nov. 27, 1967; d. Richard Keith Bell and Kay Lorraine (Sutherland) Reynolds. Student, Inst. Adventiste du Saleve, Collonges, France, 1988; BA in French, Loma Linda U., 1990. Yearbook editor Loma Linda U., La Sierra, Calif., 1989-90; desk technician Loma Linda U., Loma Linda, Calif., 1990-92; staff writer Inland Empire Cmty. Newspapers, Colton, Calif., 1990-91; city editor Inland Empire Cmty. Newspapers, San Bernardino, Calif., 1991-94; asst. circ. supr. Del Webb Meml. Libr. Loma Linda (Calif.) U., 1994—; reporter City Newspaper Group, Colton, Calif., 1995—. Asst. leader Girl Scouts U.S.A., Walla Walla, Wash., 1986; co-leader Girl Scouts Switzerland, Geneva, 1987, Girl Scouts U.S., Loma Linda, 1988-93. Mem. Toastmasters. Avocations: photography, writing, archery. Home: 9 Crooks St Loma Linda CA 92354-1935

BELL, DEREK, baseball player; b. Tampa, Fla., Dec. 11, 1968. With Toronto Blue Jays, 1991-92, San Diego Padres, 1993-95; outfielder Houston Astros, 1995—. Named Nat. League Player of the Week, 1995, 97. Office: Houston Astros PO Box 288 Houston TX 77001-0288

BELL, DERRICK ALBERT, law educator, author, lecturer; b. Pitts., Nov. 6, 1930; s. Derrick Albert and Ada Elizabeth (Childress) B.; m. Jewel Allison Hairston, June 26, 1960 (dec. Aug. 1990); m. Janet Dewart, June 28, 1992; children: Derrick Albert III, Douglass Dubois, Carter Robeson. AB, Duquesne U., 1952; LLB, U. Pitts., 1957; hon. degree in law, Toogaloo Coll., 1983, Northeastern U., 1985, Mercy Coll., 1988, Allegheny Coll., 1989, Howard U., 1995, Bates Coll., 1997. Bar: D.C. 1957, Pa. 1959, N.Y. State 1966, Calif. 1969. Atty. civil rights div. Dept. Justice, Washington, 1957-59; 1st asst. counsel NAACP Legal Def. Edn. Fund, N.Y.C., 1960-66; dep. dir. Office Civil Rights, HEW, Washington, 1966-68; exec. dir. Western Ctr. on Law and Poverty, 1968-69; lectr. law Harvard U., Cambridge, Mass., 1969-71; prof. law Harvard U., Cambridge, 1971-80, 86-92; dean U. Oreg. Law Sch., 1981-85;, 1991-93; vis. prof. NYU Sch. Law, 1991—, scholar-in-residence, 1993-94. Author: Race, Racism and American Law, 1973, 3d edit., 1992, Shades of Brown: New Perspectives on School Desegregation, 1980, And We Are Not Saved: The Elusive Quest for Racial Justice, 1987, Faces at the Bottom of the Well: The Permanence of American Racism, 1992, Confronting Authority: Reflections of an Ardent Protester, 1994. Mem. gospel choirs Psalms of Survival in an Alien Land Called Home, 1996, Constitutional Conflicts, 1997. 1st lt. USAF, 1952-54. Grantee Ford Found., 1972, 75, 91, 93, 94-96, NEH, 1980-81. Home: 444 Central Park W Apt 14B New York NY 10025-4358 Office: NYU Sch Law 40 Washington Sq S New York NY 10012-1005

BELL, DONALD LLOYD, retired engineer; b. Toledo, Ohio, May 17, 1925; s. Albert Lloyd and Sarah Amelia (Burrell) B.; m. Alice J. Ingwersen, Oct. 25, 1947 (dec. Apr. 1995); children: David J., Barbara A., Richard L.; m. Gerladine Ferguson, May 2, 1998. BME, Marquette U., Milw., 1945; MSE, U. Mich., Ann Arbor, 1965. Reg. profl. engr. Jr. engr. Electric Auto Lite Co., Toledo, Ohio, 1946-50; sr. engr. Electric Auto Lite Co., Toledo, 1950-57; sr. project engr. AC Spark Plug Divsn. GMC, Flint, Mich., 1957-82, devel. engr., 1982-85; ret., 1985. Scout master Troop 238 Boy Scouts of Am., Grand Blanc, Mich., 1972, 73; dist. camping chmn. Arrowhead Dist. Tall Pine Coun. Boy Scouts of Am., 1973-75. Mem. Soc. Automotive Engrs. Avocations: genealogy, golf. Home: 662 Perry Creek Dr Grand Blanc MI 48439-1474

BELL, ERNEST LORNE, III, lawyer; b. Boston, June 12, 1926; s. Ernest L. and Ellamay (Currier) B.; m. Margaret Van Nostrand Depue, Apr. 14, 1951 (dec. Oct. 1988); children: David E., Robin E., Roseanne Margaret; m. Sally Leavitt Cheney, Nov. 25, 1989. B.A. cum laude, Harvard Coll., 1949; J.D., U. Mich., 1952. Bar: N.H. 1952, U.S. Supreme Ct. 1962. Pvt. practice Keene, N.H., 1952; ptnr. firm Bell & Falk, P.A., 1972—. Author: An Initial View of Ultra as an American Weapon in World War II. Mem. exec. bd. Daniel Webster coun. Boy Scouts Am., 1970-79, 93—; chmn. bd. advisers Colony House Mus., 1984-91; trustee, treas. Keene Pub. Libr.; del. N.H. Constl. Convs., 1964, 74; mem. World War II Studies Assn.; mem. N.H. Aero. Commn., 1980-86. Recipient Silver Beaver award. Fellow Am. Bar Found. (N.H. chair 1993—); mem. ABA, N.H. Bar Assn (pres. 1978-79), N.H. Bar Found. (sec., bd. dirs. 1985-90, chmn. 1991-93), Cheshire County Bar Assn., Lawyer Pilots Bar Assn. (founding dir. 1962-68), Def. Rsch. Inst. (v.p. 1969-73, sec. 1973-76), Am. Kennel Club (del. 1979-81), Standard Schnauzer Club Am., Keene Country Club, Harvard Club (Boston). Episcopalian. Home: 35 Felt Rd Keene NH 03431-2103 Office: 8 Middle St Keene NH 03431-3305

BELL, FRANCES LOUISE, medical technologist; b. Milton, Pa., Apr. 28, 1926; d. George Earl and Kathryn Robbins (Fairchild) Reichard; m. Edwin Lewis Bell II, Dec. 27, 1950; children: Ernest Michael, Stephen Thomas, Eric Leslie. *Edwin Lewis Bell II, BS, MS, PhD, an emeritus professor of biology at Albright College, continues to research and publish about amphibians and reptiles. Ernest, BS Rensselaer Polytechnic Institute 1974, MS 1975, is an electrical engineer. His wife Christine Luddy, BS Simmons College 1974, MS 1977, is a medical librarian. Stephen, BS Franklin and Marshall College 1976, MD Jefferson Medical College 1980, is a cardiologist. His wife Wendy Stabolepszy, BS in business management Franklin and Marshall College 1979, is currently a homemaker and volunteer. Eric, BS Bucknell University 1977, MS Cornell University 1980, PhD 1985, is a research chemist. His wife Linda Kaszczuk, BS University of Connecticut 1981, MBA University of Rochester 1991, is a research scientist. Mrs. Bell has eight grandchildren.* BS in Biology cum laude, Bucknell U., 1948; MT, Geisinger Meml. Hosp., 1949. Registered med. technologist. Med. technologist Burlington County Hosp., Mt. Holly, N.J., 1949-50, Robert Packer Hosp., Sayre, Pa., 1950, Carle Hosp./Clinic, Urbana, Ill., 1951-52, St. Joseph Hosp., Reading, Pa., 1972-83. Vol. Crime Watch, City Hall, Reading, 1985-90, Am. Heart Assn., Reading, 1956—, March of Dimes, Reading, 1956-72, Am. Cancer Soc., Reading, 1956-71, Multiple Sclerosis, Reading, 1956-72, Reading Musical Found., 1985-90, Hist. Soc. Berks County; corr. sec. women's aux., 1986-90; fin. sec. aux. Albright Coll., 1988-95; hospitality co-chmn. women's com. Reading Symphony Orch., 1985-90, editor yearbook women's com., 1992-96; editor yearbook Reading Symphony Orch. League, 1996—; chmn. hospitality Reading-Berks Pub. Librs., 1988-91; mem. Friends Reading Mus., Berks County Conservancy. Mem. AAUW (assoc. editor bull. 1961-63, cultural interests rep. 1967-68), Woman's Club of Reading (treas. 1986-88, fin. sec. 1991—), United Meth. Women, World Affairs Coun. Berks County, Libr. Soc. Albright Coll., Phi Beta Kappa. Republican. Methodist. Avocations: music appreciation, photography, postcard art prints. Home: 1454 Oak Ln Reading PA 19604-1865 *Life and grace are cherished gifts to each one of us from our creator. We are spiritual beings, so our nature is to be loving, kind, understanding, forgiving and compassionate in all our relations with others.*

BELL, FRANK JOSEPH, III, architect; b. Paterson, N.J., Sept. 30, 1955; s. Frank Joseph and Evelyn Dorothy (Nemeth) B.; m. Greta Eichlin, Sept. 13, 1987; children: Marjorie Blair, Caroline Frances. Student, U. Miami, Coral Gables, Fla., 1976-78; BArch, N.J. Inst. Tech., 1981. Registered architect, N.J., N.Y., Pa.; cert. profl. planner, N.J. Staff architect Houghton-Quarty-Warr, Architects, 1981-86; prin. Frank Joseph Bell, Architect, Branchville, N.J., 1986—; apptd. county architect County of Hunterdon, 1990—; bd. dirs. constrn. housing Hunterdon County Housing Corp. Secretary, chmn. bd. dirs. Highlands Workshop/Easter Seal Soc., Franklin, N.J., 1981—; chmn. bldg. and grounds com. St. Joseph's Ch., Newton, 1984—; mem. Franklin Twp. Sch. Bd. Mem. AIA, N.J. Soc. Architects, Bldg. Ofcls. Code Adminstrn. Avocations: photography, water skiing, fly fishing. Office: PO Box 314 Pittstown NJ 08867-0314

BELL, FRANK OURAY, JR., lawyer; b. San Francisco, Aug. 13, 1940; s. Frank Ouray, Sr. and Clara Belle (McClure) B.; m. Sherrie A. Levie, Mar. 29, 1981; children: Aimee, David; children from previous marriage: Carin, Laurie. AB, San Francisco State U., 1963; JD, U. Calif., San Francisco, 1966. Bar: Calif. 1966, Calif. Supreme Ct. 1966, U.S. Dist. Ct. (no. dist.) Calif. 1967, U.S. Ct. Appeals (9th cir.) 1967, U.S. Supreme Ct. 1973. Dep. atty. gen. Calif. State's Atty.'s Office, Sacramento, 1966-68; ptnr. Goorjian & Bell, San Francisco, 1968-70; chief asst. Fed. Pub. Defender's Office, San Francisco, 1970-82; dir. Calif. State Pub. Defender's Office, 1984-87; pvt. practice law San Francisco, 1982-84; sr. litigation assoc. Olimpia, Whelan & Lively, San Jose, 1987-89; sole practice San Mateo, 1989—. Mem. San Mateo County Bar Assn., Calif. Pub. Defenders Assn. (bd. dirs. 1986-87). Democrat. Jewish. Office: 177 Bovet Rd Ste 600 San Mateo CA 94402-3122

BELL, GARY M., college dean; b. Feb. 10, 1945. MA, Brigham Young U., 1968; PhD, UCLA, 1974. Prof. history Sam Houston State Coll., Huntsville, Tex., 1978-93; dean Tex. Tech. U., Lubbock, Tex., 1993—. E-mail: gbell@ttu.edu.

BELL, GENE, newspaper publishing executive. Pres. and ceo San Diego Union-Tribune, San Diego, 1992—. Office: San Diego Union-Tribune 350 Camino De La Reina San Diego CA 92108-3003*

BELL, GEORGE EDWIN, retired physician, insurance company executive; b. Canton, Ohio, Dec. 6, 1923; s. George Edwin and Florence Lea (Clark) B.; m. Evelyn Maxine Adams, Apr. 20, 1946; children: Richard, John, Jeffrey, David. Student, Wooster Coll., 1941-42, Yale U., 1943; M.D., Ohio State U., 1947; postgrad., U. Pa., 1954-55. Am. Bd. Life Ins. Medicine. Intern Del. Hosp., Wilmington, 1947-48, resident in medicine, 1948-49; resident in pathology Aultman Hosp., Canton, Ohio, 1949-50; resident in medicine Ohio State U. Hosp., Columbus, 1955-56, asst. clin. prof. medicine, 1970-89; ltd. practice medicine Central Ohio Med. Group, Columbus, 1971-89; dir. med. service Columbus State Hosp., 1958-66, dir. research lab., 1966-69, med. dir., 1968-89; v.p. Nationwide Ins. Co., Columbus, 1980-89; chmn. dept. medicine Grant Hosp., Columbus, 1975-77; cons. City of Columbus, 1989. Contbr. articles to profl. jours.; programmer computer programs for use in lab. office, 1967—; co-compiler first Chinese-English dictionary with an alphanumeric index; contbr. abstracts to med. jours. Advisor Columbus Pub. Health Nursing Dept., 1967-79; vol. physician Ecco Family Practice Clinic, 1970-74; bd. dirs. Columbus Council on Alcoholism, 1973-77, League Against Child Abuse, 1979-83, Recreation Unltd., 1985—; ad hoc data processing com. chmn. Columbus Acad. Medicine, 1980-81. Served as med. officer USAF, 1951-53. Fed., state, pvt. research grantee, 1958-59; recipient Vol. Services cert. Ohio Dept. Mental Health, 1981, Service plaques J.C. Penney Co., 1981, Service plaques Columbus Health and Life Claim Assn., 1983. Fellow ACP, Am. Life Ins. Med. Dirs. Assn.; mem. AMA, Am. Council Life Ins. (chmn. human resources com.), Acad. Medicine Columbus and Franklin County (history and archives com. 1982—), Midwestern Med. Dirs. Assn. (pres. 1985-86), Pres.'s Club, Kappa Mu Epsilon. Home: 66 W Campus View Blvd Columbus OH 43235-1436

BELL, GEORGE IRVING, biophysics researcher; b. Evanston, Ill., Aug. 4, 1926; s. George Irving and Hazel (Seerley) B.; m. Virginia Lotz, Jan. 13, 1956; children—Carolyn Bell Prince, George Irving Jr. B.S. in Physics, Harvard U., 1947; Ph.D. in Theoretical Physics, Cornell U., 1951. Staff mem. Los Alamos Nat. Lab, 1951-70, assoc., alt. or acting div. leader, 1970-80, leader theoretical biology and biophysics group, 1974-90, theoretical div. leader, 1980-89; acting dir. Ctr. for Human Genome Studies, 1988-89, project mgr., functional genomics, 1998—; Gordon McKay lectr. Harvard U., Cambridge, Mass., 1962-63; mem. Basel Inst. Immunology, Switzerland, 1979-80; scholar in human biology Eleanor Roosevelt Inst. Cancer Rsch., Denver, 1977-90; bd. sci. counselors Nat. Cancer Inst., Bethesda, 1985-89, chmn. supercomputer mgmt. oversight group, 1989—; mem. human genome steering com. U.S. Dept. Energy, 1988-89; mem. Joint Informatics Task Force for Human Genome, 1990-92, Nat. Adv. Rsch. Resources Coun., NIH, 1992-94; sci. bd. Santa Fe Inst., 1988—; mem. various mountaineering expeditions, 1948-60. Author (with S. Glasstone) Nuclear Reactor Theory, 1970; editor: Theoretical Immunology, 1978, Computers and DNA, 1989; contbr. articles to profl. publs. RCA Corp. fellow, 1945-47, AEC fellow, 1948-50. Fellow AAAS, Am. Phys. Soc., Am. Nuclear Soc. (cert. merit 1966); mem. Biophys. Soc., Am. Alpine Club (David A. Sowles medal 1981), Himalayan Club (India). Achievements include rsch. in nuclear reactor theory such as methods for treating effective cross sections in dense lattices, anisotropic scattering, fluctuations in neutron populations; and in theoretical biology such as theoretical models of immune system, binding of antigens to cells and cell-cell adhesion, evolution of repetitive DNA sequences, functional genomics. Office: K 710 PO Box 1663 Los Alamos NM 87545

BELL, GRIFFIN B., lawyer, former attorney general; b. Americus, Ga., Oct. 31, 1918; s. A.C. and Thelma (Pilcher) B.; m. Mary Foy Powell, Feb. 20, 1943; 1 son, Griffin B. Student, Ga. Southwestern Coll.; LL.B. cum laude, Mercer U., 1948, LL.D., 1967. Bar: Ga. bar 1947. Practice in Savannah and Rome, 1947-53; partner firm King and Spalding, Atlanta, 1953-59; mng. partner King and Spalding, 1959-61; U.S. judge 5th Circuit, 1961-76; sr. partner firm King and Spalding, Atlanta, 1976, 79—; atty. gen. U.S., 1977-79; served chief of staff Gov. Vandiver of Ga., 1959-61; chmn. Atlanta Commn. on Crime and Delinquency, 1965-66; Mem. vis. com. Law Sch., Vanderbilt U.; trustee Mercer U.; bd. dirs. Fed. Jud. Center, 1974-76; chmn. Madrid Conf. on Security and Cooperation in Europe, 1980; co-chmn. Nat. Task Force on Violent Crime, 1981. Co-chmn. Pres. Bush's Com. on Fed. Ethics, 1989. Served to maj. AUS, 1941-46. Mem. ABA (chmn. divsn. jud. adminstrn. 1975-76), Am. Coll. Trial Lawyers (past pres.), Am. Law Inst., Order of Coif. Baptist. Office: King & Spalding 191 Peachtree St NE Atlanta GA 30303-1740

BELL, HANEY HARDY, III, lawyer; b. Staunton, Va., Aug. 20, 1944; s. Haney Hardy Jr. and Maud (Deekens) B.; m. Alice Tester, Feb. 17, 1968; 1 son, Landon D. BA, U. Va., 1966; JD cum laude, U. Wis., 1973. Bar: Va. 1974. Group ins. rep. Prudential Ins. Co. Am., Milw., 1969-70; assoc. Woods, Rogers & Hazelgrove, Roanoke, Va., 1973-78; assoc. counsel R.J. Reynolds Industries, Inc., Winston-Salem, N.C., 1978-79; sec., gen. counsel RJR Foods, Inc., 1979-80; sr. internat. counsel R.J. Reynolds Tobacco Internat., Inc., 1980-87; assoc. gen. counsel Fieldcrest Cannon Inc., Eden, N.C., 1987-95, Lorillard Tobacco Co., Greensboro, N.C., 1996—. Lt. AUS, 1967-69. Mem. ABA, Va. State Bar, Order of Coif, Twin City Club, Bermuda Run Country Club. Office: 714 Green Valley Rd Greensboro NC 27408-7018

BELL, HARRIETTE ELIZABETH, stock agency administrator; b. Washington, Dec. 29, 1958; d. Richard Lewis Jr. and Mable Harriette (Diggs) B. Student, U. D.C., 1980; cert. in pvt. investigation, No. Va. Security Acad., 1987; paralegal cert., Barclay Career Sch., 1989. Freelance investigator D.C. Superior Ct., Washington, 1980-84; customer svc. rep. Nat. Bank Washington, 1984-89; pvt. investigator Associated Investigators Inc., Washington, 1989-92; adminstrv. asst. NIH, Rockville, Md., 1992—; mem. adv. bd. EEO, Rockville, 1994—. Author (poetry) Seasons to Come, 1994, Journey of the Mind, 1995, Treasured Poems of America, 1995, Beyond the Stars, 1995, Voices, 1995. Active Blacks in Govt., 1992—. Nominated Poet of Yr. Internat. Libr. Poetry, 1995. Mem. Songwriter's Assn. Democrat. Avocations: writing, swimming, reading, badminton, skating. Home: 3400 Dean Dr Apt 201 Hyattsville MD 20782-1201

BELL, HARRY EDWARD, quality consulting company executive; b. Jamaica, N.Y., Aug. 28, 1947; s. Harry Edward and Margaret Florence (Ketcham) B.; m. Rosann Branciforte, Sept. 2, 1967; children: Michael Harry, Brian Scott. BS in Chemistry, CCNY, 1970, MA in Organic Chemistry, 1975. Sr. chemist NL Industries, Inc., West Caldwell, N.J., 1970-73; sales svc. chemist Alcan Ingot & Powders, Union, N.J., 1973-74; tech. mgr. pigments Alcan Ingot & Powders, 1974-75, tech. mgr. div., 1975-84; corp. spc coordinator Alcan Aluminum Corp., Cleve., 1984-85; mgr. productivity Alcan Rolled Products Co., Cleve., 1985-90; pres., CEO Quality Resources Internat., Hudson, Ohio, 1987—; bd. dirs., cons. Branch Cons., E. Brunswick, N.J., 1978-82. Contbr. articles to profl. jours.; patentee in field. Pratt Inst. Tech. art scholar, 1961; NSF geophysics scholar, 1963. Mem. ACS, ASTM (chmn. D1 subcom. metallic pigments 1979-83), Assn. for Quality and Participation, Am. Soc. for Quality Control, Aluminum Assn. (chmn. pigments and powders tech. com. 1979-83). Avocations: golf, swimming, travel, oil painting. Fax: (330) 963-4153. E-mail: qri@quality-qri.com. Office: Quality Resources Internat PO Box 426 Hudson OH 44236-0426

BELL, HENRY MARSH, JR., banking executive; b. Tyler, Tex., Jan. 23, 1928; s. Henry Marsh and Elizabeth (Loftin) B.; m. Dorothy Nell Allen, Dec. 8, 1951; children: Henry Marsh III, John Allen. Student, The Citadel, 1944-46; BS in Indsl. Adminstrn., Yale U., 1948; LHD (hon.), Tex. Coll., 1992. Various operational positions 1st City Tex.-Tyler (formerly known as 1st City Nat. Bank Tyler), 1948-50, asst. v.p., 1950-52, asst. v.p., dir., 1952-55, v.p., trust officer, 1955-62, sr. v.p., 1962-64, exec. v.p., 1964-67, pres., 1967-70, chmn. bd. dirs., pres., 1970-81, chmn. bd. dirs., chief exec. officer, 1981-87, chief exec. officer, 1987-88, sr. chmn. bd., 1988-93; cons., 1988—; bd. dirs., cons. Tyler Bank & Trust Co., N.A., 1993—; bd. dirs. Indsl. Devel. Corp. Tex., Smith County Indsl. Corp.; chmn. bd. dirs. Tyler Health Facilities Corp. Trustee Tchr. Retirement Sys. Tex., Tex. Chest Found.; pres., bd. dirs. East Tex. Mental Health, Inc.; mem. exec. com., chmn. bd. dirs. East Tex. Hosp. Found., Inc., Tyler Indsl. Found.; treas., chmn. bd. dirs. Better Bus. Bur. Cen. East Tex.; bd. dirs. Tex. Rose Festival Assn., United Way Greater Tyler, Tyler Health Ctr., East Tex. Cancer Ctr., Tex. Coll., Tyler Salvation Army; mem. devel. bd. U. Tex.; vestry, sr. warden Episc. Ch. Named one of Men of Achievement in Tex., 1974; recipient W.C. Windsor award, 1961, T.B. Butler award, 1971. Mem. Philos. Soc. Tex., Tyler Petroleum Club, Willow Brook Country Club, Masons. Office: Ste # 816 100 E Ferguson St Tyler TX 75702-7253*

BELL, HUBERT THOMAS, government official; b. Mobile, Ala., July 9, 1941; m. Satwant Bell; children: Naydja, Nileah, Anthony, Andrew. BS in Math., Ala. State U., 1965. Agt.-in charge Honolulu field office Secret Svc., 1984-86, agt.-in-charge Vice Presdl. Protective Divsn., 1987-89, dep. asst. dir. Office Investigations, 1989, asst. dir. Office Protective Ops., 1989-92, asst. dir. Office Inspection, 1992-94, exec. dir. work force planning and diversity mgmt., 1994-96; inspector gen. Nuclear Regulatory Commn., Washington, 1996—. Office: US Nuclear Regulatory Commn Office Inspector Gen Mail Stop T5-D28 Washington DC 20555*

BELL, JACK ATKINS, percussionist, educator; b. Knoxville, Tenn., Oct. 16, 1944; s. Jack Atkins Sr. and Sara (Allen) B.; m. Patricia Duran, June 4, 1967 (div. June 1980); 1 child, Jack Aquiles; m. April Darlene Salyer, June 18, 1983. BMusic Edn., Oberlin Coll., 1966, M Music, 1967; pvt. study, Cloyd Duff, Cleve. Orch. Band dir., choir dir. Columbia H.S., 1967-68; from instr. to assoc. prof. Ga. State U., Atlanta, 1968—, coord. percussion div.; prin. percussionist Atlanta Symphony; presenter in field. Recs. with Atlanta Symphony Orch. include Peter and the Wolf, The Carnival of the Animals, Daphnis and Chloe, Stabat mater, Karelia Suite, Finlandia, William Tell, The Canyon, Te Deum Laudamus, numerous others. Mem. Nat. Assn. Rudimental Drummers, Past Pres. of Ohio Student Music Educators Assn., Nat. Percussive Arts Soc. (past pres. Ga. chpt.), Pi Kappa Lambda, Pi Mu Alpha (past pres.). Avocations: seamanship, power boating, water sports. Home: Atlanta Symphony Orchestra 6791 Gaines Ferry Rd Flowery Branch GA 30542 Office: Ga State U Sch Music University Plz Atlanta GA 30303

BELL, JAMES BACON, business executive; b. Monroe County, Tenn., Aug. 3, 1952; s. James Orbia and Elizabeth (Bacon) B.; m. Camille Marie Carter, June 17, 1978. AA in Agrl. Econs., Hiwassee Coll., 1972; BS in Biology and Plant and Soil Sci., Tenn. Technol. U., 1975; MS in Environ. Health and Safety, Western States U., 1995. Registered environ. mgr.; Cert. hazardous material mgr., environ. auditor. Prin. Jim Bell Landscaping Svc., Lenoir City, Tenn., 1974-79; asst. county agt. U. Tenn. Coop. Extension Svc., Celina, 1976-79; owner, mgr. Midwestern Pecan Co., Inc., Nevada, Mo., 1979—, Bell-Bacon Farms, Inc., Nevada, 1979—; co-owner Possum Pete's Recreational Vehicle Park, Nevada, 1990—; pres., co-owner Cape Canaveral Marine Svcs., 1991—; v.p. Used Oil Recyclers & Transports of Fla., 1992—; mem. small bus. adv. coun. U.S. Rep. Ike Skelton, Mo., 1986; vice-chmn. Vernon County Agri-Extension Coun., Nevada, 1988-89. Chmn. Dandelion Days, Nevada Spring Festival, 1986; mem. solid waste adv. com. City of Nevada, 1987; bd. dirs. Quality Products Sheltered Workshop, Nevada, 1989-91; mem. environ. svcs. steering com. Brevard County Sch. Dist., 1996—; mem. restoration adv. bd. Patrick AFB, 1997—. Recipient Outstanding Agribus. award State of Mo., 1988. Mem. Hazardous Waste Mgmt. Assn. (bd. govs. 1996—), Nat. Assn. Environ. Profls., Nat. Contract Mgmt. Assn., Nat. Environ. Tng. Assn., United Assn. Used Oil Svcs., World Safety Orgn., Fla. Assn. Environ. Profls., Nevada-Vernon County C. of C. (chmn. tourism div. 1987, bd. dirs. 1986-89, pres. 1988), Sons Spanish-Am. War Vets, Sons Union Vets., Mil. Order Stars and Bars, Sons of Confederate Vets. Presbyterian. Avocations: quail hunting, reading, cooking, travel. Home: 427 Brightwaters Dr Cocoa Beach FL 32931-3837 Office: Cape Canaveral Marine Svcs 350 Imperial Blvd Cape Canaveral FL 32920-4211

BELL, JAMES FREDERICK, retired lawyer; b. New Orleans, Aug. 5, 1922; s. George Bryan and Sarah Barr (Perry) B.; m. Jill Cooper Arden, Apr. 14, 1951; children: Bradley Cushing, Sara Perry, Ashley Arden. A.B. cum laude, Princeton U., 1943; LL.B., Harvard U., 1948. Bar: D.C. 1949. Assoc. Pogue & Neal, Washington, 1948-53, ptnr., 1953-88, cons., 1988-89; ret., 1988; gen. counsel Conf. State Bank Suprs., 1951-87. Chmn. com. on canons and other bus. Episcopal Diocese of Washington, 1960-78; pres. Episc. Ctr. for Children, Washington, 1966-67. Lt. USNR, 1943-46. Mem. ABA, D.C. Bar Assn. Home: 2103 R St NW Washington DC 20008-1933 *The fragmentation of human thought into an increasing number of disciplines has proliferated standards of judgment as to the rightness or wrongness of human conduct to a point where consensus as to viable guidelines becomes impossible.*

BELL, JAMES THOMAS, town official; b. N.Y.C., Oct. 17, 1949; s. Jane Bell Davis; m. Leslie Toombs, June 25, 1977; children: Guy K., Colin J., Kate E. BA in English Edn. cum laude, Boston Coll., 1971; MPA, L.I. U., 1985. Cert. tchr., N.Y., Conn., Mass. With pers. office Nassau County Dept. Recreation and Parks, N.Y., 1971-72; with pub. info. office Town of Oyster Bay, N.Y., 1972-76, dir. cmty. rels., 1977-80, founding mem., vice chmn. Indsl. Devel. Agy., 1980-82, exec. asst. to town supr., 1980-82, dep. supr., 1982-87, comptr., 1988-97, chmn. town geog. info. sys. commn., 1995-97; dep. town supr. Town of Oyster Bay, 1998—; instr. L.I. U., 1998—. Mem. Nassau County Rep. Com.; exec. committeeman Sea Cliff (N.Y.) Rep. Com.; N.Y. rep. committeeman 15th A.D.; del. 10th Jud. Dist. Rep. Conv.; trustee Inc. Village Sea Cliff, 1978-80. Recipient Fin. Reporting Achievment award Govt. Fin. Officers Am. and Can., 1996. Mem. Am. Soc. for Pub. Adminstrn., Sea Cliff Civic Assn., Friends Sea Cliff Mus., Kiwanis, Met. Boston Coll. Club, Club N.Y., Alumni chpt. L.I. U., Pi Alpha Alpha. Home: 9 Leonard Pl Sea Cliff NY 11579-2011 Office: Town of Oyster Bay Audrey Ave Oyster Bay NY 11771

BELL, JAY STUART, baseball player; b. Eglin AFB, Fla., Dec. 11, 1965. With Cleve. Indians, 1986-88; shortstop Pitts. Pirates, 1989-96, Kansas City (Mo.) Royals, 1997, Ariz. Diamondbacks, 1997—; mem. Nat. League All-Star Team, 1993. Named Nat. League leader short stop putouts, 1990, 91, short stop assists, 1991, 92; Nat. League Gold Glove, 1993. Office: Ariz Diamondbacks Bank One Ballpark 401 E Jefferson St Phoenix AZ 85004-2438*

BELL, JOHN, state agency executive; b. Brookhawen, Miss.. M, Wayne State U., 1967, U. San Francisco, 1987. Exec. dir. Pub. Svcs. Divsn., Mobile, Ala., 1994—; mgr. Nat. Registry Environ. Mgrs., 1997. Patentee odor emissions. Office: Pub Svcs Divsn Govt Plaza 205 Government St Mobile AL 36644-0002*

BELL, JOHN ALTON, lawyer, judge; b. Greer, S.C., Dec. 1, 1958; s. Dallas Frank Sr. and Una Merle (Gay) B.; m. Vida Ivy, June 30, 1984; children: Luke, Meredith. BA, Carson-Newman Coll., 1980; JD, Memphis State U., 1982. Bar: Tenn. 1983, U.S. Dist. Ct. (we. dist.) Tenn. 1983, U.S. Army Ct. Mil. Rev. 1984, U.S. Ct. Mil. Appeals 1987, U.S. Dist. Ct. (ea. dist.) Tenn. 1988. Assoc. Litigation Support, Inc., Memphis, 1983; officer ops. and tng. U.S. Army, Ft. Knox, Ky., 1983-84; legal assistance atty. U.S. Army, Ft. Knox, 1984-86, defense counsel, 1986-87; assoc. King & King, Greeneville, Tenn., 1987-89; ptnr. King, King & Bell, Greeneville and Newport, Tenn., 1989-90, Bell & Bell P.C., Newport, 1990-98; judge Cooke County Sessions and Juvenile Ct., Newport, 1998—; instr. bus. law Sullivan Jr. Coll., Ft. Knox, 1986-87; adj. prof. bus. law Walter State C.C., 1989-90, 97—. Columnist It's The Law, Newport Plain Talk, 1984-85, 89-98. Bd. dirs. Extended Sch. Program, Greeneville, 1988; co-vice chmn. Rep. Com. Cocke County, Tenn., 1989-95. Named Ky. Col., Gov. Ky., 1986. Mem. ABA, Fed. Bar Assn., Tenn. Bar Assn., Assn. Trial Lawyers Am., Judge Advocate Gen.'s Assn. Republican. Baptist. Avocations: sports, church activities. Office: Cooke County Sessions Ct 111 Court Ave Newport TN 37821

BELL, JOHN PERRY, minister, religious organization administrator; b. Columbia, La., Feb. 8, 1948; s. John Dixon and Laverne (Beck) B.; m. Gwendolyn Jean McKay, Dec. 18, 1971; children: Felicia, Peter, Rachel. BA, N.E. La. U., 1970, MA, 1971; ThM, Southern Meth. U., 1973; DMin, Garrett Evang. Sem., 1989. Ordained to ministry United Meth. Ch., 1974. Min. youth United Meth. Ch., Athens, Tex., 1972; pastor United Meth. Ch., Argyle, Wis., 1973-76, Sheboygan Falls, Wis., 1976-84, Waupaca, Wis., 1984-91; assoc. conf. min. United Ch. of Christ, 1991-97; exec. dir. United Meth. Found., 1998—; bd. dirs. Bell Press, Waupaca, 1990—; sec. Coun. on Fin. Adminstrn., Sun Prairie, Wis., 1984-92; del. World Meth. Conf., Honolulu, 1981, Nairobi, 1986, New World Mission, Bangalore, India, 1989, UNCED, Rio de Janeiro, 1992, UN Conf. on Population, Cairo, Egypt, 1994. Pres. Am. Cancer Soc., Waupaca, 1988-90, Mental Health Assn., Waupaca, 1988-91. Recipient Superior award Am. Cancer Soc., 1989-90. Mem. World Future Soc., Kiwanis (local pres. 1983). Democrat. Home: 2212 Stockton Dr Springfield IL 62703-5268 Office: 400 Chatham Rd Ste 26 Springfield IL 62704 *Life is both internal and external. We have to place equal emphasis on both. Our internal life needs as much care as any other part of life. How we think and feel will determine what we do and say. Faith, then, is the foundation for life.*

BELL, JOHN TEDFORD, civil engineer; b. Live Oak, Fla., May 18, 1960; s. Wilbur Seale and Mary Bond (Benson) B.; m. Kathryn Elizabeth Gill, July 21, 1993. BSCE, U. Fla., 1983; postgrad., U. S.C., Ga. Tech. Registered profl. engr., Fla., Ga., S.C., Tenn., Ala. Design engr. Campbell Wallace Cons. Engrs., Knoxville, Tenn., 1983-85, Jordan, Jones & Goulding, Inc., Charleston, S.C., 1985-89; pres., owner Gen. Inspection Svcs. Inc., Charleston, 1987; project mgr. Jordan, Jones & Goulding, Inc., Atlanta, 1989-90; regional mgr. Jordan, Jones & Goulding, Inc., Knoxville, 1991-95, Tallahassee, 1995-96; pres., owner The Coloney Co., Tallahassee, 1996—. Contbr. articles to profl. jours. Asst. scoutmaster Boy Scouts Am., Charleston, S.C., 1986-89; bd. dirs. So. Shakespeare Festival, Tallahassee, 1996—. Mem. ASCE, NSPE, Am. Water Works Assn., Governor's Club. Methodist. Achievements include successfull opening of engineering design office. Avocations: hunting, fishing, model railroading, skiing. Office: The Coloney Co 1014 N Adams St Tallahassee FL 32303-6133

BELL, JONATHAN ROBERT, lawyer; b. Bklyn., Oct. 2, 1947; s. Saul A. and Hope R. (Rosenblat) B.; children: Gabriel J., Nicholas R.; m. Catherine Janow, May 5, 1989. BA, Yale U., 1969; JD, Harvard U., 1973. Bar: Mass. 1974, U.S. Tax Ct. 1977, N.Y. 1978, U.S. Dist. Ct. (so. dist.) N.Y. 1980. Assoc. Nutter, McClennen & Fish, Boston, 1973-77; assoc. Debevoise & Plimpton, N.Y.C., 1977-83, ptnr., 1984-93; ptnr. Paul, Weiss, Rifkind, Wharton & Garrison, N.Y.C., 1993—. Bd. dirs. United Way, N.Y.C., 1984-95, Studio in A School, 1988—, v.p., 1991-98, N.Y.C. Ballet, 1995—. Fellow Am. Coll. Trust and Estate Counsel; mem. N.Y. State Bar Assn. (trusts and estates law sect.), Assn. Bar City of N.Y. (chair trusts, estates and surrogate's cts. com. 1995-98). Home: 35 Bethune St New York NY 10014-7201 Office: Paul Weiss Rifkind Wharton & Garrison Rm 202 1285 Avenue Of The Americas Fl 21 New York NY 10019-6028

BELL, KEVIN J., zoological park administrator; b. N.Y., Aug. 14, 1952; s. Joseph L. and Muriel E. (Beck) B.; m. Catharine Kleiman, Sept. 8, 1991. BS in Biology, Syracuse U., 1974; MS Zoology, SUNY, Brockport, 1976. Rsch. asst. Nat. Audubon Soc., Ea. Egg Rock, Maine, 1975; curator of birds Lincoln Park Zoological Gardens, Chgo., 1975-92, dir., 1993—; pres., CEO Lincoln Park Zool. Soc., Chgo., 1995—; leader Zoo Soc. Tours to Africa, India, Nepal and Thailand. Contbr. articles to jours. in field. Office: Lincoln Pk Zool Gardens 2001 N Clark St Chicago IL 60614-4712 also: PO Box 14903 Chicago IL 60614*

BELL, LARRY STUART, artist; b. Chgo., Dec. 6, 1939; s. Hyman David and Rebecca Ann (Kriegmont) B.; three children. Student, Chouinard Art Inst., L.A., 1957-59. One man exhbns. include Stedelijk Mus., Amsterdam, 1967, Pasadena (Calif.) Art Mus., 1972, Oakland (Calif.) Mus., 1973, Ft. Worth Art Mus., 1975, Santa Barbara (Calif.) Mus. Art, 1976, Washington U., St. Louis, 1976, Art Mus. So. Tex., Corpus Christi, 1976, Erica Williams, Anne Johnson Gallery, Seattle, 1978, Hayden Gallery, MIT, Cambridge, Mass., 1977, Hudson River Mus., Yonkers, N.Y., 1981, Newport Harbor Art Mus., 1982, Marian Goodman Gallery, N.Y.C., 1982, Ruth S. Schaffner Gallery, Santa Barbara, Calif., Arco Ctr. Visual Arts, L.A., 1983, Unicorn Gallery, Aspen, Colo., 1983, Butler Inst. Am. Art, Youngstown, Ohio, 1984, Leigh Yawkey Woodson Art Mus., Wausau, Wis., 1984, Colorado Springs, Colo. Fine Arts Ctr., 1987, Cleve. Ctr. for Contemporary Art, Ohio, 1987, Mus. Contemporary Art, L.A., 1987, Am. Acad. and Inst. Arts and Letters, N.Y.C., 1987, Boise (Idaho) Gallery Art, 1987, Gilbert Brownstone Gallery, Paris, 1987, Braunstein/Quay Gallery, San Francisco, 1987, 89, Fine Arts Gallery, N.Mex. State Fairgrounds, 1987, Laguna Art Mus., Laguna Beach, Calif., 1987, High Mus. Art, Atlanta, 1988, Sena Galleries West, Santa Fe, 1989, Kiyo Higashi Gallery, L.A., 1989, 90, 94, Musee D'Art Contemporain, Lyon, France, 1989, Contemporary Art Ctr., Kansas City, Mo., 1989, San Antonio Art Inst., 1990, New Gallery, Houston, 1990, Braunstein/Quay Gallery, San Francisco, 1990, Galerie Rolf Ricke, Koln, Fed. Republic Germany, 1990, Galerie Montenay, Paris, 1990, 95, The Works Gallery, L.A., 1990, Galerie Kammer, Hamburg, Germany, 1990, Tony Shafrazi Gallery, N.Y.C., 1991, Tucson Mus. Art, 1991, New Gallery, Houston, 1991, Janus Gallery, Santa Fe, 1992, Kiyo Higashi Gallery, L.A., 1992, 93, New Gallery, Houston, 1992, Tampa Mus. Art, 1992, Kiyo Higashi Gallery, L.A., 1993, 94, New Directions Gallery, Taos, N.M., 1993, Dartmouth St. Gallery, Albuquerque, 1994, Braunstein/Quay Gallery, San Francisco, 1994, Leedy/Voulkos Gallery, Kansas City, 1994, Kiyo Higashi Gallery, L.A., 1994, U. Wyo. Art Mus., Laramie, 1995, Denver Art Mus., 1995, Indigo Gallery, Boca Raton, Fla., 1995, Harwood Mus. U. N. Mex., Taos, 1995, Galerie Montenay, Paris, 1995, Joy Tash Gallery, Scottsdale, Ariz., 1996, Kiyo Higashi Gallery, L.A., 1996, Boulder Mus. Contemporary Art, 1996, Braunstein/Quay Gallery, San Francisco, 1996, Art et Industrie Gallery, N.Y.C., 1996, The Albuquerque Mus., 1997, The Reykjavik Mcpl. Art Mus., Iceland, 1997, Bergen (Norway) Kunstmus., 1998, Seljord (Norway) Art Assn., 1998, Wood Street Galleries, Pittsburgh, PA, 1999; group exhbns. include Mus. Modern Art, N.Y.C., 1965, 79, Jewish Mus., N.Y.C., 1966, Whitney Mus. Am. Art, 1966, Guggenheim Mus., N.Y.C., 1967, Tate Gallery, London, 1970, Hayward Gallery, London, 1971, Detroit Inst. Arts, 1973, Nat. Collections Fine Arts, 1975, San Francisco Mus. Modern Art, 1976, Museo de Arte Contemporaneo de Caracas, Venezuela, 1978, Aspen Ctr. for Visual Arts, 1980, Fruit Market Gallery, Edinburgh, Scotland, 1980, Albuquerque Mus., 1980, Art Inst. Chgo., 1982, Santa Barbara Art Mus., 1984, The Rufino Tamayo Mus., Mexico City, 1985, Colorado Springs Fine Art Ctr., 1986, Mus. Comtemporary Art, 1986, AAAL, 1986, Ariz. State U., Tempe, 1987, Phoenix Art Mus., 1987, Braunstein/Quay Gallery, 1987, The Works Gallery, Long Beach, 1987, Davis/McClain Gallery, Houston, 1987, Basel (Switzerland) Art Fair, 1989, Galerie Joan Prats, Barcelona, Spain, 1989, Musee d'Art Contemporain, Lyon, 1989, Harcus Gallery, Boston, 1989, Colorado Springs Gallery Contemporary Art, 1990, Mus. Contemporary Art, L.A., 1990, Musee de Grenoble, France, 1990, L.A. County Mus. Art, 1991, U. So. Calif. Fisher Gallery, L.A., 1991, Espace Lyonnais d'Art Contemporain, France, 1991, Galerie Montenay, Paris, 1991, Galerie Rolf Ricke, Köln, Germany, 1991, Arolsen, Germany, 1992, Leedy/Voulkos Gallery, Kansas City, Mo., 1993, Musee du Palais du Luxembourg, Paris, 1993, Denver Art Mus., 1993, New Gallery, Houston, 1993, Whitney Mus. Am. Art, N.Y.C., 1993, Conn., 1994, Parrish Art Mus., Southampton, N.Y., 1994, Kiyo Higashi Gallery, L.A., 1994, Madison (Wis.) Art Ctr., 1994, Whitney Mus. Am. Art, 1995, Galerie Ncht St. Stephen, Vienna, 1995, Galerie Rolf Ricke, Cologne, 1996, Colorado Springs Fine Art Ctr., 1996, Mus. N.Mex., Santa Fe, 1996, Orange County Mus. Art, Newport Beach, Calif., 1997, Harwood Mus. U. N.Mex., Taos, 1997, Louisiana Mus. Modern Art, Humlebaek, Denmark, 1997, Milw. Art Mus., 1997, Whitney Mus. Am. Art, N.Y., 1997, San Jose (Calif.) Mus. Art, 1997, Grounds for Sculpture, Mercerville, N.J., 1998-99, Frederick R. Weisman Mus. Art, Pepperdine U. Malibu, Calif., 1998, Calif. Ctr. Arts, Escondido, Calif., 1999; represented in permanent collections including Nat. Collection Fine Arts, Musee de Art Contemporaine, Lyon, France, Mus. of Fine Arts, Santa Fe, N.Mex., Whitney Mus. Am. Art, N.Y.C., 1994, Laguna Gloria Mus., Austen, 1994, H & W Bechtler Gallery, Charlotte, 1994, Calif. Crafts Mus., San Francisco, 1994, Parrish Art Mus., Southampton, 1994, Tate Gallery, London, Gallery New South Wales, Australia, Albright-Knox Gallery, Buffalo, Art Inst. Chgo., Denver Art Mus., Dallas Mus. Fine Arts, Guggenheim Mus., Houston, L.A. County Mus., Victoria and Albert Mus., London, San Antonio Mus. Art, The Menil Collection, Houston, Mpls. Inst. Arts, Mus. Ludwig, Koln, Albuquerque Mus., Mpls. Inst. Arts, others; instr. sculpture, U. South Fla., Tampa, U. Calif., Berkeley, Irvine, 1970-73, So. Calif. Inst. of Architecture, 1988, Taos (N.Mex.) Inst. of Art, 1989-94. Copley Found. grantee, 1962; Guggenheim Found. fellow, 1970; Nat. Endowment Arts grantee, 1975; recipient Gov.'s award for excellence in visual arts, N.Mex., 1990. Office: PO Box 4101 Taos NM 87571-9998

BELL, LAWRENCE A., city official; b. Balt., Nov. 14, 1961. BA, U. Md., 1983. City councilman Balt., 1987-95; pres. City Coun., Balt., 1995—; chmn. exec. appointments com. and pub. safety com., vice-chmn. land use com., mem. edn., judiciary and planning com.; chmn., founder Network Inc. Named one of 30 Leader of Future, Ebony Mag., 1988; one of 40 Influential

People Under 40, Balt. Bus. Jour., 1993, Balt.'s Best City Councilman, Balt. Mag., 1994. Office: Balt City Hall 100 Holliday St Ste 400 Baltimore MD 21202-3417

BELL, LEE PHILLIP, television personality, television producer; b. Chgo.; d. James A. and Helen (Novak) P.; m. William Joseph Bell, Oct. 23, 1954; children: William J., Bradley, Lauralee. B.S. in Microbiology, Northwestern U., 1950. With CBS-TV, Chgo., 1952-86; pres. Bell-Phillip TV Prodns., 1985—; bd. dirs. William Wrigley, Jr. Co., Chgo. Bank Commerce, Phillips Flowers Inc. TV and radio shows include Lee Phillip Show, Chgo., from 1952, Lady and Tiger Show WBBM Radio, from 1962, WBBM TV from 1964; hostess Noon Break, numerous TV Spls. including Forgotten Children, The Rape of Paulette (nat. Emmy award, duPont Columbia award); Children and Divorce (Chgo. Emmmy award) co-creator: (with William Bell) The Young and the Restless CBS-TV daytime drama, 1973 (Emmy award); co-creator, exec. producer The Bold and the Beautiful, 1987—. Bd. dirs. United Cerebral Palsy, Chgo. Unlimited, Northwestern U. Hosp., Chgo. Heart Assn., Nat. Com. Prevention of Child Abuse, Mental Health Assn., Children's Home and Aid Soc., Salvation Army (L.A. bd. dirs.), Family Focus; mem. Chgo. Maternity Ctr.; life mem. Northwestern U. Bd. Trustees. Recipient 16 Chgo. Emmys; Top Favorite Female award TV Guide mag., 1956, Outstanding Woman of Radio and TV award McCall's mag., 1957-58, 65, bd. govs. award Chgo. chpt. Nat. Acad. TV Arts and Scis., 1977, William Booth award for community svc. Salvation Army, 1990; named Person of Yr. Broadcast Advt. Club, Chgo., 1980. Mem. Am. Women Radio and TV (Golden Mike award 1968, Broadcaster of Yr. 1993), Acad. TV Arts and Scis. (bd. dirs.), Chgo. chpt. Acad. TV Arts and Scis., Women's Athletic Club of Chgo., Comml. Club, Delta Delta Delta. Office: CBS c/o Bold and Beautiful 7800 Beverly Blvd Los Angeles CA 90036-2188*

BELL, LEO S., retired physician; b. Newark, N.J., Nov. 7, 1913; s. Alexander M. and Marie (Saxon) B.; m. Edith Lewis, July 3, 1938; children; Jewyl Linn, David Alden. AB, Syracuse U., 1934, MD, 1938. Diplomate Am. Bd. Pediatrics. Intern N.Y.C. Hosp., 1938, Bklyn. Hosp., 1939-40; resident Sea View Hosp., N.Y.C., 1940-41, N.Y.C. Hosp., 1941-42; pediatrician pvt. practice, San Mateo, Calif., 1946-84; staff mem. Mills Meml. Hosp., San Mateo, Peninsula Hosp. & Med. Ctr., Burlingame, Children's Hosp., San Francisco; assoc. clin. prof. pediatrics U. Calif. Med. Sch., San Francisco; prof. clin. emeritus Stanford Med. Sch., Palo Alto; mem. curriculum & ednl. affairs com. U. San Francisco Med. Sch., adminstrv. coun. Columnist San Mateo Times; contbr. articles to profl. jours. Bd. dirs. Mills Hosp. Found., San Mateo, U. Calif. San Francisco Hosp., San Mateo County Heart Assn., Hillsborough Schs. Found. (Calif.), 1980-83. Capt. USAAF, 1942-46. Recipient bronze and silver medals Am. Heart Assn. Fellow Am. Acad. Pediatrics, Am. Pub. Health Assn.; mem. AMA (alt. del. to ho. of dels), U. Calif. San Francisco Clin. Faculty Assn. (pres.), Calif. Fedn. Pediatric Socs. (pres.), Am. Fedn. Pediatric Socs. (pres.), Calif. Med. Assn., Am. Pyub. Health Assn., Air Force Assn., Calif. Med. Assn. (ho. of dels.), San Mateo County Med. Assn. (vice chmn. quality assurance com. San Mateo county health plan), Internat. Scuff Bottle Soc., Hong Kong Snuff Bottle Soc., San Francisco Gem & Mineral Soc., World Affairs Coun. San Francisco, U. San Francisco Med. Sch. Clin. Faculty Assn. (coun., pres.), Peninsula Golf & Country Club, Commonwealth Club. Home: 220 Roblar Ave Burlingame CA 94010-6846 Office: PO Box 1877 San Mateo CA 94401-0946

BELL, LORI JO, crisis counselor, psychiatric nurse; b. Pitts., Dec. 16, 1960; d. John Spencer and Nancy Carol (Schleicher) B. ADN, C.C. Allegheny Co., Pitts., 1987; BS in Devel. Psychology, U. Pitts., 1984; MSEd in Cmty. Counseling, Duquesne U., 1996. Nat. cert. counselor, cert. in adult psychiat./mental health nursing, crisis intervention specialist, cert. critical incident stress debriefing, instr. for non-violent crisis prevention, cert. pre/post HIV counseling. Primary counselor Mon Yough Mental Health/Mental Retardation, McKeesport, Pa., 1984; residential advisor Chartiers Mental Health/Mental Retardation, Bridgeville, Pa., 1985-87; counselor, 1985-87; psychiat. nurse in acute/admissions bldg. Eastern State Hosp., Williamsburg, Va., 1987; psychiat. nurse St. Francis Med. Ctr., Pitts., 1987-90, Mercy Psychiat. Inst., Pitts., 1990-92; coord. emergency outpatient psychiat. svcs. Meadville (Pa.) Med. Ctr., 1997-99; cmty. HIV/AIDS educator; microbiology tutor Duquesne U., 1994. Contbr. articles to profl. jours. Mem. ANA, Am. Mental Health Counselor's Assn., Am. Assn. Suicidology, Pa. Counseling Assn., Pa. Mental Health Counselor's Assn., Crisis Intervention Assn. Pa., Internat. Critical Incident Stress Found., Internat. Assn. Addiction and Offender Counselors, Chi Sigma Iota Nat. Counseling Honor Soc. Home: 337 Shadowlawn Ave Pittsburgh PA 15216-1239

BELL, M. JOY MILLER, financial planner, real estate broker; b. Enid, Okla., Dec. 29, 1934; d. H. Lee and M.E. Madge (Hatfield) Miller; m. Richard L.D. Berlemann, July 21, 1957 (div. Nov. 1974); children: Richard Louis, Randolph Lee; m. Donald R. Bell, Aug. 17, 1996; children: Jeri Lynn, Johnna Kay, Nolan Ray, Charles, Mary. BSBA, N.Mex. State U., 1956. CFP; grad. Realtors Inst.; fellow Life Underwriting Tng. Coun. Tchr. of bus. and mathematics Alamogordo (N.Mex.), Las Cruces (N. Mex.) and Omaha Pub. Schs., 1956-63; tchr., dir. Evelyn Wood Reading Dynamics Southern N.Mex. Inst., 1967-68; registered rep. Westamerica Fin. Corp., Denver, 1968-76; gen. agt. Security Benefit Life, Topeka, 1969—, Delta Life & Annuity, Des Moines, 1969—; registered rep. AGF Sponsors, Inc., Denver, 1976—; pres., broker Fin. Design Corp. R.E. (name changed to Bell, Inc. 1997), Las Cruces, 1977—; Mrs. U.S. Savings Bonds ofcl. goodwill amb. U.S. Treasury, U.S. Savs. Bond Divsn., Washington, 1968-70. Contbr. articles to profl. jours. Vice pres. Dona Ana County Fedn. Rep. Women. Recipient Top Sales Person award Investment Trust and Assurance, 1976-77. Mem. Nat. Assn. Realtors, Nat. Assn. Life Underwriters, Nat. Assn. Ret. Fed. Employees (program chmn. local chpt.), Internat. Assn. Registered Fin. Planners, S.W. N.Mex. Assn. Life Underwriters (treas. 1990-91, pres.-elect 1991-92, pres. 1992-93), Las Cruces City Alumnae Panhellenic, Altrusa, Order Ea. Star, Delta Zeta. Methodist. Home: 4633 Lamar Rd Las Cruces NM 88005-3558 Office: Bell Inc PO Box 577 Las Cruces NM 88004-0577

BELL, MARCIA MALONE, marriage and family therapist, researcher; b. Cin., Sept. 26, 1956; d. Wayne P. and Elizabeth (Malone) B.; divorced; children: Natalie Claie Postel, Ryan Joseph Postel, John Christian Postel; m. Thomas E. Bickel, Dec. 22, 1985. BS in Family Studies, U. Ky., 1994, MS in Family Studies, 1997, grad. cert. in women's studies, 1998. Accredited in marriage and family therapy edn., Ky. Nat. sales adminstr. Sta. WSVN-TV, NBC, Miami, Fla., 1980-82; customer svc. mgr. Champion Cable, Inc., Hialeah, Fla., 1988-89; exec. mktg. and advt. asst., asst. to dir. sales and mktg. Ben Franklin Properties/Mystic Poine on Bay, Miami, 1989-91; adminstrv. med. asst. Women's Care Ctr., Lexington, Ky., 1991-92; undergrad tchg. asst. dept. family studies U. Ky., Lexington, 1994, grad. tchg. asst., 1995-97, project coord., 1995-97, staff therapist Family Ctr., 1996-97, rsch. asst., 1997; marriage and family therapist, Lexington, 1997—; exec. prodr., prodn. dir. Piecing It Together: Essential Skills for Single Parent Families, 1997-98, dir. edn., 1999—; paper presenter in field; guest lectr. Georgetown (Ky.) Coll., 1998, Ea. Ky. U., Richmond, 1998. Vol. Multiple Sclerosis Soc., 1978, Ky. Spl. Olympics, 1979, Barry Gibb Love and Hope Tennis Festival, Diabetes Inst. Miami, 1991, Am. Cancer Soc., 1991-94; fundraiser Ronald McDonald House, U. Miami, 1981, Hospice of Windsor, Eng., 1985-86, Children's Miracle Network, 1992, Lexington Children's Theater, 1992-94; founder, pres. Miss Miami Scholarship Found., 1980-84; treas. Thames Valley Am. Women's Club, Windsor, 1984-85, pres., 1985-86; dir., publicity coord. Windsor Monarch's Brit. Am. Football Team, 1984-88; mem. youth free time task force Lesington-Fayette Urban County Govt., 1992; advisor Ultimate Children's Christmas Party, 1993; v.p., founding mem. Miss Ky. Scholarship Orgn., 1991-94; banquet chmn. Southland Steelers Youth Football Assn., 1993-94; publicity coord. co-chmn. Oktoberfest, Mary Queen of Holy Rosary Ch., Lexington, 1993-94, facilitator divorced and separated recovery group; mem. auction com. Living Arts and Sci. Ctr., 1995; mem. recognition com. Nat. Assn. Women Bus. Owners, 1995; co-chmn. fundraising for scholarhips to children of victims Oklahama City bldg. disaster Lexington Cath. AAU, 1995; active Family Resource Ctr., Harrison Elem. Sch., Lexington. Named gen. of Adair County, hon. citizen Columbia, Ky., Ky. Col., Disting. Citizen Lexington, Ky. Amb. of Good Will; recipient key to city of Maysville, Ky. and Flint, Mich., cert. of recognition Diabetes Inst. Miami, U. Miami Sch. Medicine Ctr. for Juvenile Diabetes, award of merit U. Miami Student Activities Homecoming Orgn., lt. gov.'s outstanding citizen award State of Ky.; former Miss Ky.; Miss Am. scholar, 1978, Ky. Found., 1993, 95, 96, James V. Brown scholar U. Ky. Coll. Human Environ. Scis., 1995-96, Alda Henning scholar, 1996-97, Lisa Barclay scholar, 1997. Mem. AAUW, Am. Assn. for Marriage and Family Therapy, Nat. Coun. on Family Rels., Nat. Assn. for Edn. Young Children, Am. Assn. Christian Counselors, Regional Human Svcs. Orgn., Ky. Assn. for Marriage and Family Therapy, Ky. Assn. for Play Therapy, U. Ky. Coll. Human Environ. Scis. Alumni Assn., U. Ky. Alumni Assn., 191st Airborne Divsn. Air Assault Team (hon., cert. of recognition), Phi Upsilon Omicron. Home: 2336 Harrodsburg Rd Lexington KY 40503-1706

BELL, MARTIN ALLEN, investment company executive; b. N.Y.C., Apr. 29, 1951; s. Bernard B. and Helene (Spiro) B.; m. Carol J. del Aguila, June 13, 1998; children: Daniel Warren, Frances Annelies. BA, U. Mich., 1974; JD, NYU, 1977. Bar: N.Y. 1978. Ptnr. Finley, Kumble, Wagner, Heine, Underberg, Manley & Casey, N.Y.C., 1977-85; pres. Svc. Resources Corp., N.Y.C., 1985-90; gen. counsel D.H. Blair Investment Banking Corp., N.Y.C., 1991—, vice chmn., 1995—; bd. dirs. Venus Exploration Corp., Rand Pub. Corp. Democratic. Jewish. Home: 1035 5th Ave New York NY 10028-0135 Office: D H Blair Investment Banking Corp 44 Wall St New York NY 10005-2401

BELL, MARVIN HARTLEY, poet, English language educator; b. N.Y.C., Aug. 3, 1937; s. Saul and Belle (Spector) B.; m. Mary Mammosser, 1958 (div.); m. Dorothy Murphy; children: Nathan Saul, Jason Aaron. BA, Alfred U., 1958, LHD (hon.), 1986; MA, U. Chgo., 1961; MFA, U. Iowa, 1963. Mem. faculty, Writers' Workshop U. Iowa, Iowa City, 1965—, Flannery O'Connor prof. of letters, 1986—; vis. lectr. Goddard Coll., 1970; disting. vis. prof. U. Hawaii, 1981; vis. prof. U. Wash., 1982; Lila Wallace-Reader's Digest Writing fellow U. Redlands, 1991-92, 92-93; Woodrow Wilson vis. fellow St. Mary's Coll. of Calif., 1994-95, Nebr. Wesleyan U., 1996-97, Pacific U., 1996-97; judge Lamont Award-Acad. Am. Poets, 1989-91, Pushcart Prizes, 1991, 97, Western Book Awards-Western States Arts Fedn., 1991, Nat. Poetry Series, NEA, N.C. Arts Coun., Coordinating Coun. Lit. Mags., Discovery Contest-Poetry Ctr. of 92nd St Y, N.Y.C., Poetry Soc. Am., Hopwood Awards, Tulsa Arts Coun., Anhinga Poetry Prize-Fla. State U. Press, numerous others. Author: (poems) Things We Dreamt We Died For, 1966, A Probable Volume of Dreams, 1969 (Lamont award Acad. Am. Poets 1969), The Escape into You, 1971, 94, Residue of Song, 1974, Stars Which See, Stars Which Do Not See, 1977 (Nat. Book award finalist 1977), 92, These Green-Going-To-Yellow, 1981, Drawn by Stones, by Earth, by Things That Have Been in the Fire, 1984, New and Selected Poems, 1987, Iris of Creation, 1990, The Book of the Dead Man, 1994, Ardor: The Book of the Dead Man, vol. 2, 1997, Wednesday: Selected Poems, 1998, Poetry for a Midsummer's Night, 1998; (essays) Old Snow Just Melting: Essays and Interviews, 1983; (anthology) A Marvin Bell Reader, 1994; co-author: Segues: A Correspondence in Poetry, 1983, Annie-Over, 1988, editor, pub. Statements, 1959-64; poetry editor The Iowa Rev., 1969-71, guest poetry editor, 1980; poetry editor The Pushcart Prize, vol. XXI, 1996-97, editor-at-large vol. series, 1994-96, series editor, poetry, 1997—; columnist The Am. Poetry Rev., 1975-78, 90-92; contbr. and commd. poetry to numerous mags. and anthologies. Fellow Guggenheim Found., 1977, NEA, 1978, 84; Sr. Fulbright scholar to Yugoslavia, 1983, Sr. Fulbright scholar to Australia, 1986; recipient Bess Hokin award Poetry, 1969, Emily Clark Balch prize Va. Quar. Rev., 1970, Am. Poetry Rev. prize, 1982, Lit. award Am. Acad. Arts and Letters, 1994. Home: 1416 E College St Iowa City IA 52245-4409 also: PO Box 1759 Port Townsend WA 98368-0180 Office: U Iowa Writer's Workshop Dey House Iowa City IA 52242

BELL, MARY E. BENITEAU, accountant; b. San Antonio, Dec. 20, 1937; d. Thomas Alfred and Mary Elizabeth (McMurrain) Beniteau; BBA, Baylor U., 1959; MBA, U. Tex., 1960; m. William Woodward Bell, May 31, 1969; children: Susan Elizabeth, Carol Ann. tchg. asst. U. Tex., Austin, 1959-60; prin. Deloitte & Touche CPA, Dallas, 1960-69; county auditor Brown County, Tex., 1972-78; pvt. practice acctg., Brownwood, Tex., 1969-95; ptnr. Bell & Isbell, LLP, CPA, 1996—; acct. Brownwood Regional Med. Ctr. Aux., 1969—. Mem. bus. and audit com. Bapt. Gen. Conv. Tex., 1985-90, 97—, vice chmn., 1987-88, chmn., 1988-89; bd. dirs., sec. Brownwood Civic Improvement Found., Inc., 1991—, pres., 1993-95, treas., 1995—. Recipient W.R. White Meritorious Svc. award Baylor U., 1996; named Outstanding 4-H Leader, Dist. 8, Tex., 1992, Outstanding Woman Over 35, Brownwood Jaycees, 1986, Outstanding Com. Chmn., Dallas chpt. CPA, 1968-69; CPA, Tex. Mem. Brownwood C. of C. (dir. 1979-82, sec.-treas. 1981-82), Tex. Soc. CPA (dir. 1979-82, chair rels. with AICPA com. 1988-89, trustee found. 1981-89, sec.-treas. 1982-84, pres. 1984-86, Kenneth W. Hurst fellow 1990, peer rev. com. 1993-96, CPA helping Schs. Com., 1994-95), AICPA, DAR (Mary Garland chpt., vice-regent 1994-98, regent 1998—), Abilene Chpt. CPA (dir. 1984-85, 87-88, CPA of Yr. 1984-85), Brownwood Com. CPA (pres. 1987-88), Pi Beta Phi, Baylor U. Alumni Assn. (dir. 1979-82). Baptist. Clubs: Brownwood Woman's (pres. 1980-81), Rotary Ann of Brownwood (pres. 1983-84. Home: PO Box 1564 Brownwood TX 76804-1564 Office: 109 N Fisk Ave Brownwood TX 76801-8207

BELL, MELODIE ELIZABETH, artist, massage therapist; b. Long Beach, Calif., Apr. 21, 1958; d. Robert I. and Bettymay (Shelley) Bell; m. Timothy Monroe Roach, Feb. 4, 1993; children: Chelsea Ann Bell, Rory Michael Bell. Student, Calif. State U., Long Beach, 1976-78, Humboldt State U., 1978-79; BA in Art (Photography), Calif. State U., Fullerton, 1984. Cert. massage therapist, L.A. Coll. Massage and Phys. Therapy, 1978. Owner Mel's Place, Cypress, Calif., 1982-91; mgr. George Galanoudes Apts., Garden Grove, Calif., 1991-93; massage therapist Office of Stephen Waldman, MD, Fullerton, Calif., 1992-97, drug study site coord., 1996-98; freelance portrait artist, photographer, 1984—; buyer Pegasus Rsch. Corp., Santa Ana, Calif., 1998—. Solo exhbns. include Calif. State U., Fullerton, 1979, 84, Rossmoor Pub. Libr., Seal Beach, Calif., 1992, Six Flags Magic Mountain, Saugus, Calif., 1983-85; commd. portraits and paintings in pvt. collections. Leader Webelos Boy Scouts Am., Garden Grove, 1994-95; vol. Thanksgiving for the Homeless, Santa Ana, Calif., 1996, Fryberger Elem. Sch., Westminster, Calif., 1995-96, Choc Walk, 1995, AIDS Dance-a-Thon, 1997. Mem. Humboldt State Alumni Assn. Democrat. Jewish. Avocations: camping, fine furniture repair and restoration, ceramics, fine art. Home: 8642 Gloria Ave Apt C Garden Grove CA 92844-1939

BELL, MICHAEL G., trade association administrator; b. Atlantic City, May 1, 1954; s. Daniel and Bertha (Zaleski) B.; m. Monica Piaskowski, June 9, 1979 (div. 1997); children: Melissa S., Maria D. B Liberal Studies in Econs. Bus. Adminstrn., Hillsdale Coll., 1976; Grad., N.Y. Inst. Photography, 1991. Account exec. Mgmt. Recruiters, Southfield, Mich., 1978-80; mgr. profl. interests Soc. Mfg. Engrs., Dearborn, Mich., 1980-91; dir. ednl. svcs. Fedn. of Socs. for Coatings Tech., Blue Bell, Pa., 1991—. Guest columnist Indsl. Finishing Mag., 1985-86, Coatings Mag., 1995; contbg. writer Assn. Educator, 1995. Mem. indsl. adv. bd. Ea. Mich. U., Ypsilanti, 1984-87; mem. Greater Detroit Econ. Devel. Task Force, 1988; mem. Rep. Presdl. Task Force, Washington, 1984-89. Recipient Outstanding Photograph award Mich. Renaissance Festival, Holly, 1988-89. Mem. Am. Soc. Assn. Execs. (edn. tech. subcom. 1994-95), Am. Mgmt. Assn., Intersoc. Polymer Edn. Coun. (treas. 1997—, bd. dirs. 1997—), Hillsdale Coll. Alumni Assn. (pres. Detroit area 1989-91), Ancient Order of Hibernians. Roman Catholic. Avocation: photography. Home: 150 Montgomery Dr Harleysville PA 19438-2131 Office: Fedn Socs for Coatings Tech 492 Norristown Rd Blue Bell PA 19422-2355

BELL, MILDRED BAILEY, lawyer, educator; b. Sanford, Fla., June 28, 1928; d. William F. and Frances E. (Williford) Bailey; m. j. Thomas Bell, Jr., Sept. 18, 1948 (div.); children: Tom, Elizabeth, Ansley. AB, U. Ga., 1950, JD cum laude, 1969; LLM in Taxation, N.Y. U., 1977. Bar: Ga. 1969. Law clk. U.S. Dist. Ct. No. Dist. Ga., 1969-70; prof. law Mercer U., Macon, Ga., 1970-94; prof. emeritus Mercer U., 1994—; mem. Ga. Com. Constl. Revision, 1978-79; bd. dirs. Arrowhead Travel, Inc. Bd. editors Ga. State Bar Jour., 1974-76; contbr. articles to profl. jours., chpts. in books. Mem. ABA, Ga. Bar Assn., Phi Beta Kappa, Phi Kappa Phi,. Republican. Episcopalian. Home: 615 Laurel Lake Dr Apt A-233 Columbus NC 28722-7420

BELL, NANCY LEE HOYT, real estate investor, middle school educator, volunteer; b. L.A., Oct. 25, 1929; d. James and Mabel Ruth (Lockard) Hoyt; m. Ralph Rogers Bell, July 3, 1953; children: Linda Lee, John Curtis, James Hoyt, Martha Chambers, Ralph Rogers II, Nancy Lee II. Student, Whittier Coll., 1948, San Jose State Coll., 1949; BA in Edn., U. Calif., Santa Barbara, 1950; postgrad., San Francisco State Coll., 1952, UCLA, 1953; MS in Edn., U. So. Calif., 1955. Tchr. John Adams Jr. H.S., Santa Monica, Calif., 1950-54; real estate investor. Pres. Santa Clarita Cmty. Concerts, Saugus, Calif., 1968-69; vol. worker USO, YWCA, 1944-45, Cancer Crusade, Calif. and Wash., 1960-90. Mem. AAUW (charter life; pres.), Big Bear Valley Hist. Soc. (life; sec.), DAR (charter life; treas.), Gen. Soc. Mayflower Descs. (life; bd. dirs.), Alpha Delta Pi. Republican. Methodist. Avocations: world travel, collecting antiques, genealogy researcher, activities with children and grandchildren, music. Home: 615 Main St Ste B Edmonds WA 98020-3029

BELL, NORMAN HOWARD, physician, endocrinologist, educator; b. Gainesville, Ga., Feb. 11, 1931; s. Kenneth Rush and Henrietta Maria (Howard Rankin) B.; m. Claude Handy, June 27, 1959 (dec. 1967); children: Douglas Howard, Julianne Rankin; m. Mary Virginia Baughman, Aug. 24, 1968 (div. July 1972); m. Ledlie Laird Dinsmore, Dec. 16, 1972; 1 child, Bayard Gardiner. A.B., Emory U., 1951; M.D., Duke U., 1955. Intern Duke U. Med. Ctr., Durham, N.C., 1955-56, resident, 1956-57; clin. assoc. Nat. Inst. Allergy and Infectious Diseases, NIH, Bethesda, Md., 1957-59; mem. staff clin. endocrinology br. Nat. Heart, Lung and Blood Inst., NIH, Bethesda, 1959-63, assoc. in medicine, 1963-65; asst. prof. medicine Northwestern U. Sch. Medicine, Chgo., 1965-68; assoc. prof. Ind. U. Med Sch., Indpls., 1968-71; prof. Ind. U. Med Sch., 1971-79; prof. medicine and pharmacology Med. U. S.C., Charleston, 1979—, disting. univ. prof., 1998—; mem. gen. medicine B study sect. NIH, Bethesda, 1982-86, chmn., 1985-86; trustee Nat. Osteoporosis Found., Washington, 1984-88, chmn. sci. adv. bd., 1985-88; mem. spl. grants rev. com. Nat. Inst. Arthritis, Musculo-Skeletal and Skin Diseases, NIH, 1990-95, chmn., 1993-94. Edit. bd. Calcified Tissue Internat., 1978-83, 94—; Jour. Clin. Endocrinology and Metabolism, 1982-87, Jour. Bone and Mineral Rsch., 1989-93, Italian Jour. Mineral and Electrolyte Metabolism, 1990—, Revs. in Endocrinology and Metabolism, 1999—. Served with USPHS, 1957-63. Recipient Career Devel. award USPHS, 1965-68, VA med. investigator award, 1979, 81-87, Thomas A. Roe Found. award S.C. Med. Assn., 1982; William S. Middleton VA award, 1983; Frederic C. Bartter award Am. Soc. Bone and Mineral Rsch., 1992, Career Recognition award Vitamin D Workshop, 1997. Mem. Am. Soc. Clin. Investigation, Am. Soc. Bone and Mineral Research (sec.-treas. 1978-85, pres. 1986-87, Shirley Hohl Svc. award 1998), Am. Soc. Pharmacology and Exptl. Therapeutics, Assn. Am. Physicians, Assn. Osteobiology (councillor 1997—), Endocrine Soc., Alpha Omega Alpha. Democrat. Episcopalian. Home: 1 Johnson Rd Charleston SC 29407-7514 Office: VA Med Ctr 109 Bee St Charleston SC 29401-5703

BELL, P. JACKSON, computer executive; b. Portsmouth, Va., Dec. 31, 1941; s. John Henry and Lois Belle (Hendrix) B.; m. Virginia Phillips Inman, Apr. 11, 1981; children by previous marriage: Scarlett Lee Talamantes, Christopher J. Bell, John R. Bradley, Lynda I. Kleene. B.S.B.A., Northwestern U., 1963; M.A., U. S.C., 1964. Mgmt. cons. McKinsey & Co., Washington, 1967-73; dir. corp. planning Washington Post Co., 1973-77; asst. to pres. Allegheny Airlines, Washington, 1977-78; v.p.-long range planning USAir Inc, Washington, 1978-83, sr. v.p.-fin., 1983-86, exec. v.p.-fin., 1986-89; v.p.-fin., chief fin. officer USAir Group, 1984-89; exec. v.p., chief fin. officer Burlington Northern Inc., Ft. Worth, 1989-91; sr. v.p. planning Am. Airlines Inc., Ft. Worth, 1991-92, sr. v.p. strategic programs, 1992-93; exec. v.p., CFO Conner Peripherals Inc., San Jose, Calif., 1993-96; exec. v.p., CFO, chief adminstrv. officer Adobe Systems, Inc., San Jose, 1996-98. Served to capt. USMC, 1964-67, Vietnam.

BELL, PHILIP WILKES, accounting and economics educator; b. N.Y.C., Oct. 24, 1924; s. Samuel Dennis and Miriam Ball (Wilkes) B.; m. Katherine Elizabeth Hubbard, June 16, 1945 (div. May 1980); children: Susan, Geoffrey, Mary Ellen, James; m. Virginia Wood Crozier, June 14, 1980; stepchildren: Thomas, Steven, Peter. BA, Princeton U., 1947; MA, U. Calif., Berkeley, 1949; PhD, Princeton U., 1954. Instr. Princeton (N.J.) U., 1948-51; rsch. assoc. Inst. for Advanced Study, Princeton, 1951-52; asst. prof. Haverford (Pa.) Coll., 1952-56, assoc. prof., then prof., 1960-68; assoc. prof. U. Calif., Berkeley, 1957-60; prof. Merrill Coll., U. Calif., Santa Cruz, 1968-79, provost, 1968-72; William A. Kirkland prof. Rice U., Houston, 1979-89; prof. acctg. and econs. Boston U., 1989-92; assoc. dir. Rockefellor Found., 1963-68; dir. Edn. Abroad Program U. Calif., Kenya, 1972-74; vis. prof. Univ. Sains Malaysia, Penang, 1976-77, Norges Handelshoyskole, Bergen, Norway, spring 1982, U. Pa., Phila, fall 1982. Author: Sterling Area in the Postwar World, 1956, Toward Greater Logic and Utility in Accounting: The Collected Writings of Philip W. Bell, 1997; co-author: Theory and Measurement of Business Income, 1961, Accounting for Economic Events, 1979, Financial Accounting: Principles and Issues, 1992; also monographs; contbr. numerous articles to profl. jours. 2d lt. USAF, 1943-45. Rsch. fellow Social Sci. Rsch. Coun., London, 1956-57, Ford Found. fellow, Berkeley, 1959. Mem. Am. Acctg. Assn., Brit. Acctg. Assn., European Acctg. Assn., Royal Econ. Soc. (U.K.), Acctg. Assn. Australia and New Zealand. Mem. Soc. of Friends. Home: 3300 Darby Rd C # 503 Haverford PA 19041-1064

BELL, PHILLIP MICHAEL, curator; b. Toronto, Ont., Can., Dec. 31, 1942; s. William Harvey and Alice W. (Stone) B.; m. Natalie Marie Luckyj, Aug. 15, 1977. BA with honors, U. Toronto, 1966, MA, 1967. Curator Pub. Archives of Can., Ottawa, Ont., 1969-73; dir. Anges Etherington Art Gallery, Kingston, Ont., 1973-78; visual arts officer Ont. Arts Council, Toronto, 1978-79; asst. dir. pub. programs Nat. Gallery Can., Ottawa, Ont., 1979-81; acting dir. Nat. Gallery Can., Ottawa, 1981; dir. McMichael Canadian Collection, Kleinburg, Ont., 1981-86; assoc. curator Agnes Etherington Art Centre Queen's U., Kingston, Ont., 1986-92; dir. Carleton U. Art Gallery, Ottawa, Ont., 1992—. Author: Painters in a New Land, 1973 (Gov. Gen.'s award for Non-Fiction), Braves and Buffalo: Plains Indian Life in 1837, 1973, William Goodridge Roberts, Drawings, 1976, William Sawyer: Portrait Painter, 1978, Empowering the Word: Sorel Cohen, Will Gorlitz Al McWilliams, Carroll Moppett, 1993, Kanata, Robert Houle's Histories, 1993, Transitions, Hugh Mackenzie, 1994, Being Seen: Alex Colville: The Serigraphs, 1994, The Other Alberta Sculpture, Isla Burns: Catherine Burgess: Peter von Tiesenbausen, 1996, The Voluptuous Gardener, 1996, The Whole Hogg: Drawings by Barry Callagham, 1997, Romancing the Stone: The Lithographs of Frederick Hagan, 1998. Chmn. Inuit Art Quar.; trustee Nat. Museums of Can., 1987-90, Nat. Gallery Gallery Can., 1990-91, The State Hermitage Found. Can., Inc., 1998—. Mem. Can. Hist. Assn. (appraisal bd.), Can. Mus. Assn. (bd. dirs. 1983-86), Ont. Assn. Art (galleries bd. 1974-78), Univ. and Coll. Art Galleries of Can. (pres.). Office: Carleton U, Art Gallery, Ottawa, ON Canada K1S 5B6

BELL, PRISCILLA J., academic administrator. BA, Tex. Tech. U., 1971; MS, Calif. State U., L.A., 1976; PhD, U. Tex., 1986. Dir. student programs, activities Tacoma (Wash.) C.C., 1978-81, dean student svcs., 1978-95, assoc. dean student devel., 1981-86; pres. Fulton-Montgomery C.C., Johnstown, N.Y., 1995—. E-mail: pbell@ps.fmcc.suny.edu. Office: 2805 State Hwy 67 Johnstown NY 12095

BELL, RALPH ROGERS, retired superintendent schools, genealogist; b. Nanaimo, B.C., Can., Jan. 31, 1922; came to U.S., 1948; s. John and Madrid Rogers (Stone) B.; m. Nancy Lee Hoyt, July 3, 1953; children: Linda Lee, John Curtis, James Hoyt, Martha Chambers, Ralph Rogers Jr., Nancy Lee. BSA, U. B.C., Vancouver, 1944, BEd, 1947; MS, Oreg. State U., 1949; EdD, U. So. Calif., 1959. Cert. in edn. adminstrn., Calif. Tchr. Ladysmith (B.C.) Jr.-Sr. H.S., 1945-47; tchg. asst. U. So. Calif., L.A., 1949-50, part-time lectr., 1967-68; tchr. sci., sci. coord. Crozier Mid. Sch., Inglewood, Calif., 1950-51; dist. supt. Sulphur Springs Union Sch. Dist., Saugus, Calif., 1951-69, Bear Valley Unified Sch. Dist., Big Bear Lake, Calif., 1969-78; ret., 1978; off-campus dir. San Bernardino Valley C.C., Big Bear Lake, 1969-78; nat. spkr. Nat. Coun. on Year-Round Edn., 1972-78. Author: A Rogers Family Ancestry, 715 A.D. to 2000 A.D., of Dr. Ralph Rogers Bell, 1999. Pres. Soledad Twp. Coordinating Coun., Newhall, Calif., 1955-56. Recipient commendation for cmty. svc. Los Angeles County Bd. Suprs., 1956, resolution of recognition San Bernardino County Bd. Suprs., 1978; postdoctoral scholar UCLA, 1967-68. Mem. Seattle Geneal. Soc., Sno-Isle Geneal. Soc., Calif. PTA (life). Republican. Methodist. Avocations: world travel, photography, classical music, gardening, genealogy research on his forefather King Edward I and family barons who signed the Magna Charta in 1215. Home: Bell's Soundview 615 Main St Ste B Edmonds WA 98020-3029

BELL, RAYMOND MARTIN, retired physics educator; b. Weatherly, Pa., Mar. 21, 1907; s. Frank T. and Marion E. (Seibert) B.; m. Lillian Mae Kelly, Mar. 28, 1942; children: Carol A., Martha J., Edward F. AB, Dickinson Coll., 1928; AM, Syracuse U., 1930; PhD, Pa. State U., 1937; ScD (hon.), Washington and Jefferson Coll., 1976. Prof. physics Washington (Pa.) and Jefferson Coll., 1937-75; ret., 1975. Author numerous books on physics, astronomy, history, and genealogy, including Ancestry of Richard Nixon, 1972, Ancestry of Samuel Clemens (grandfather of Mark Twain), 1984; contbr. numerous articles to profl. jours. Fellow Am. Soc. Genealogists, Geneal. Soc. Pa.; mem. AAUP, Phi Beta Kappa, Sigma Xi. Republican. Methodist. Avocations: radio, television, genealogy. Home: 1506 1st Ave Apt 3 Coralville IA 52241-1199

BELL, RICHARD EUGENE, grain and food company executive; b. Clinton, Ill., Jan. 7, 1934; s. Lloyd Richard and Ina (Oglesby) B.; m. Maria Christina Mendoza, Oct. 22, 1960; children—David Lloyd, Stephen Richard. B.S. with honors, U. Ill., 1957, M.S., 1958. Internat. economist Dept. Agr., Washington, 1959-60; dir. grain div. Dept. Agr., 1969-72; agrl. attache Am. embassies in Ottawa, Can., Brussels, and Dublin, Ireland, 1961-68; asst. sec. agr. internat. affairs and commodity programs, 1973-77; pres. Riceland Foods Inc., Stuttgart, Ark., 1977—; now also chief exec. officer Riceland Foods Inc.; bd. dirs. First Comml. Corp., GTE S.W. Inc., Fed. Res. Bank St. Louis; pres., dir. Commodity Credit Corp., also Fed. Crop Ins. Corp., 1975-77; exec. sec. Pres.'s Agrl. Policy Com., 1976-77; rep. Internat. Wheat Coun., London, 1970-77; adviser World Food Conf., Rome, 1974; trustee Ark. State U., 1997—. Recipient Disting. Service award Dept. Agr., 1975. Mem. Alpha Gamma Rho, Alpha Zeta. Republican. Mem. Christian Ch. (Disciples of Christ). Office: Riceland Foods Inc PO Box 927 2120 S Park Ave Stuttgart AR 72160-6822

BELL, RICHARD G., lawyer; b. Billings, Mont., Sept. 16, 1947; s. George A.W. and Mary Helen (Sharp) B.; m. Linda Carol Riggs, June 21, 1969; children: Stephen, Geoffrey. AB, Stanford U., 1969; JD, U. Calif., San Francisco, 1972. Bar: Calif.; U.S. Supreme Ct., 1990; U.S. Ct. Appeals Calif. (9th cir.) 1973; U.S. Dist. Ct. Calif. (no. dist., 1972, cen. dist., 1976). Assoc. Finch, Sauers, Player & King, Palo Alto, Calif., 1972-76; ptnr. Finch, Sauers, Player & Bell, Palo Alto, 1976-83; gen. counsel Watkins-Johnson Co., Palo Alto, 1983-90; v.p., gen. counsel Watkins-Johnson Co., 1990-97; ptnr. Corp. Advisory Law Group, Los Altos, Calif., 1998—. Bd. dirs. Family Svc. Assn., Palo Alto, 1981-87; trustee Mountain View Los Altos Union H.S. Dist., 1990-98; pres. bd. Los Altos Conservatory Theater, 1991-95. Mem. ABA, Calif. Bar Assn., Santa Clara County Bar Assn., Palo Alto Area Bar Assn. Republican. Episcopalian. Office: Corp Adv Law Group 40 Main St Los Altos CA 94022-2902

BELL, ROBERT DANIEL, religious studies educator; b. Fresno, Calif., July 11, 1942; s. Oran Robert and Arshaloos (Bedrosian) B.; m. Kathryn L. Kruse, July 29, 1967; children: Jonathan Adam, David Benjamin. BA, Bob Jones U., 1964, MA, 1966, PhD, 1970. Prof. Bible and ancient langs. Bob Jones U., Greenville, S.C., 1968—, chmn. divns. grad. sch. of religion and seminary, 1979—. Asst. editor (jour.) Bibl. Viewpoint, 1979—; contbr. articles to profl. jours. Republican. Ind. Bapt. Avocations: computers, baseball, stamp collecting. Home: 102 Buena Vista Ave Greenville SC 29607-1203 Office: Bob Jones U Greenville SC 29614

BELL, ROBERT EUGENE, anthropologist educator; b. Marion, Ohio, June 16, 1914; s. Harry Thew and Clara (Stouffer) B.; m. Emily Virginia Merz, Aug. 31, 1938; children—Patricia (Mrs. Paul Lindsey), David Eugene. Student, Ohio State U., 1936-38; B.A. with honors, U. N.M., 1940; M.A., U. Chgo., 1943, Ph.D., 1947. Asst. prof. anthropology U. Okla., 1947-51, assoc. prof., 1951-55, prof., 1955-69; prof. George L. Cross Research prof., 1969-80, emeritus, 1980—; chmn. dept., 1947-55, 61-64; head curator Stovall Mus., 1947-85; dir. Mississippi Valley Dendochronology Lab. U. Chgo., 1942-43, 46-47, Oklahoma River Basin Salvage Lab., 1962-78. Author: Oklahoma Archaeology: an Annotated Bibliography, 1969, 2d edit., 1978, The Harlan Site, CK-6, A Prehistoric Mound Center in Cherokee County, Eastern Oklahoma. Archaeol. investigations at site of El Inga, Ecuador; Editor: Am. Antiquity, 1966-70, Bull. Okla. Anthrop. Soc, 1963-66, Prehistory of Oklahoma, 1984. Served with M.C. AUS, 1943-46. Recipient Clarence H. Webb award Outstanding Contbns. to Caddoan Archeology, 1985, Presentation in Recognition of Outstanding Contbn. to Ecuadorian Archeology, Govt. of Ecuador, 1986; subject of Festschrift Okla. Anthrop. Soc., Okla. Archeol. Survey, 1983, Shirk Meml. award for Hist. Preservation, 1987; named to Okla. Hist. Soc.'s Hall of Fame, 1994, Plains Anthropol. Soc. Disting. Svc. award 1994; Fulbright fellow, New Zealand, 1955-56. Mem. Am. Anthrop. Assn., Am. Assn. Phys. Anthropology, AAAS, Okla. Hist. Soc., Am. Ethnol. Soc., Soc. for Am. Archaeology (50th Anniversary award 1985), Mo., Ark., Tex., Kans. archaeol. socs., Inst. Gt. Plains, Southeastern Archaeol. Conf., Polynesian Soc., Soc. for Hist. Archaeology, Soc. for Conservation Archaeology, Explorers Club, Phi Beta Kappa (hon.), Sigma Xi. Home: 1120 Berry Cir Norman OK 73072-6307

BELL, ROBERT FRED, German language educator. BA in German, U. Ill., 1959, MA in German, 1962, PhD, 1969. Fulbright teaching asst. German high schs., Munich, 1959-60; grad. instr. U. Ill., 1964-65; instr. Purdue U., 1965-68; instr. U. Ky., 1968-69, asst. prof., 1969-72; asst. prof. U. Ala, Tuscaloosa, 1972-76, assoc. prof., 1976-82, prof., 1982—, chair dept. German and Russian, 1976-78, acting chair dept. German and Russian, 1994-95, summer acting chair dept. Modern Langs. and Classics, 1998; mem. exec. com. Ky. Fgn. Lang. Conf., U. Ky., 1970-72, chair German 3 sect., 1986; co-organizer symposium German exile lit. U. Ala., 1975; chair sect. German war novels South Atlantic Modern Lang. Convention, Atlanta, 1979. Co-editor: Protest-Form-Tradition: Essays on German Exile Literature, 1979, Exile: The Writer's Experience, 1982; consulting editor Critique: Studies in Modern Fiction, 1983—; mem. editorial adv. bd. Classical and Modern Lit.: A Quar., 1981—; contbr. over 50 articles, revs. and papers to profl. jours., confs.; translator poems. Grantee U. Ala. Rsch. Grants Com., 1973. Mem. MLA (organizer spl. sect. ann. meeting 1982, 83, del. assembly 1989-93, South Atlantic affiliate, sec. German II sect. 1969-70, chmn. German II sect. 1970-71, sect. nominating com. 1971-74, chmn. nominating com. 1973-74, exec. com. 1974-77, sec. German III sect. 1980-81, chmn. 1981-82, sect. nominating com. 1982-85, chmn. sect. nominating com. 1984-85, presider German gen. session 1984, 86, 95, 97, SAMLA studies award com. 1985-88, chmn. ad hoc com. on constitution and by-laws, 1996, exec. dir. 1989-94, editor South Atlantic Rev. 1989-94), Am. Assn. Tchrs. German (sec. SAMLA region 1979-80, pres. 1980-81), Soc. for Exile Studies, German Studies Assn. (moderator session 71 16th ann. conf. 1992), Ala. Assn. Fgn. Lang. Tchrs. (v.p. 1979-80, pres. 1980-81), Phi Beta Kappa (3 term exec. com. U. Ala. chpt. 1982-85, 90-92, 98—, v.p. 1983-84, pres. 1984-85), Delta Phi Alpha (faculty sponsor U. Ala. chpt. 1975, 76, 79—), Phi Kappa Phi. Home: 708 Greystone St Northport AL 35473-2648 Office: U Ala Dept Modern Langs and Classics PO Box 870246 Tuscaloosa AL 35487-0246

BELL, ROBERT G., federal agency official; b. Birmingham, Ala., Aug. 26, 1947; m. Rosemary Jackson; children: Nathan, Stefan. BS with honors, U.S. Air Force Acad., 1969; MA in Internat. Security Studies, Tufts U., 1970. Defense analyst Congl. Rsch. Svc. Libr. Cong., 1975-78, 80; staff dir. milit. com. Atlantic Assembly, Brussels, 1979; prin. staff aide for defense policy, arms control issues to Chmn. Charles H. Percy, Com. Fgn. Rels., U.S. Senate, Washington, 1981-84; prin. staff asst. for arms control issue to Chmn. Sam Nunn, Com. Armed Svcs., U.S. Senate, 1984-93; sr. dir. def. policy and arms control Nat. Security Coun., Washington, 1993—; spl. asst. to Pres. for nat. security affairs, 1993—. Served to Capt. USAF, 1975. Office: National Security Council 1600 Pennsylvania Ave NW Washington DC 20500-0005

BELL, ROBERT HOLMES, federal judge; b. Lansing, Mich., Apr. 19, 1944; s. Preston C. and Eileen (Holmes) B.; m. Helen Mortensen, June 28, 1968; children: Robert Holmes Jr., Ruth Eileen, Jonathan Neil. BA, Wheaton Coll., 1966; JD, Wayne State U., 1969. Bar: Mich. 1970, U.S. Dist. Ct. (we. dist.) Mich. 1970. Asst. prosecutor Ingham County Prosecutor's Office, Lansing, Mich., 1969-72; state dist. judge Mich. State Cts., 1973-78; state cir. judge Mich. State Cts., Mason, 1979-87; judge U.S. Dist. Ct. Mich., Grand Rapids, Mich., 1987—. Office: US Dist Ct 411 Fed Bldg 110 Michigan St NW Grand Rapids MI 49503-2363*

BELL, ROBERT M., state chief judge court of appeals; b. Rocky Mount, N.C., July 6, 1943. AB with honors, Morgan State Coll., 1966; JD, Harvard U., 1969. Bar: Md. 1969. Judge Md. Dist. Ct. Dist. 1, Balt., 1975-79; former judge Cir. Ct. Md. 8th Jud. Cir.; assoc. judge Md. Ct. Spl. Appeals, 1980-91; assoc. judge Md. Ct. Appeals, Balt., 1991-96, chief judge, 1996—. Mem. ABA, Nat. Bar Assn., Md. State Bar Assn., Inc., Bar Assn. Balt. City, Monumental City Bar Assn. Office: Court of Appeals 634 Courthouse East 111 N Calvert St Baltimore MD 21202-1904 Office: Court of Appeals 361 Rowe Blvd Annapolis MD 21401-1672*

BELL, ROBERT MATTHEW, pharmaceutical company consultant; b. London, Dec. 3, 1932; came to U.S., 1972; s. George Frederick and Patricia (Brusso) B.; m. Jeanette Edna Head, Sept. 19, 1955; children: Adrian R., Colette M. MB,ChB, Birmingham U., Eng., 1968; postgrad., Godfrey Huggins Sch. Medicine, Salisbury, Rhodesia. Diplomate Am. Bd. Family Practice; cert. pharm. chemist Pharm. Soc. Great Britain. Relief mgr. Boots Chemists, Eng., 1955-57; owner Bell's Pharmacy, Rhodesia, 1958-61; joint owner Strachan's Pharmacy, Rhodesia, 1962-69; asst. lectr. Godfrey Huggins Sch. Medicine, Rhodesia, 1970-72; clin. project dir. Sterling Winthrop Rsch. Inst., Renesselaer, 1973-75; chief clin. pharmacology ICI Americas, Wilmington, Del., 1975-78; pres., owner RAMA Med. Clinic, Charlotte, N.C., 1980-86; from assoc. dir. to sr. dir. healthcare info. svcs. Searle, Inc., Skokie, Ill., 1986-96; prin. Bell and Assocs., Libertyville, Ill., 1996—; mem. drug rev. com. Drugs Control Coun. of Rhodesia, Salisbury, 1971-72; mem. adv. bd. Upjohn Healthcare Servers, Charlotte, N.C., 1983-84; chmn. adv. bd. Med. Office Asst. Program Piedmont Comty. Coll., Charlotte, N.C., 1983-84; mem. exec. bd. Am. Acad. Pharm. Physicians, Cary, N.C., 1995-96. Co-author: (book) The Practical Management of Renal Failure, 1969; co-editor: (book) The Endorphins, Marcel Dekker, N.Y., 1982. Grantee Malvern Trust, Rhodesia, 1963; named Metrolina Vol. of Yr., Am. Lung Assn., N.C., 1985; recipient Outstanding Svc. award Drug Info. Assn., Ambler, Pa., 1997. Mem. AMA, Am. Acad. Pharm. Physicians (v.p. AMA rels.), Am.-Zimbabwe Med. Assn. (chmn. 1996-98). Avocations: postal history, reading, exercising. Office: Bell & Assocs PO Box 672 Libertyville IL 60048-0672

BELL, ROBERT MORRALL, lawyer; b. Graniteville, S.C., Feb. 15, 1936; s. Jonathan F. and Ruby Lee (Carpenter) B.; m. Cecelia Richardson Coker, June 11, 1965 (dec.). AB, U. S.C., 1958, LLB, 1965. Bar: S.C. 1965, U.S. Dist. Ct. S.C. 1965, U.S. Ct. Appeals (4th cir.) 1970. With Watkins, Vandiver, Kirven & Long, Anderson, S.C., 1965-67; sr. law clk. to chief judge U.S. Dist. Ct. S.C., Greenville, 1967-69; mem. Abram, Bowen & Townes, Greenville, 1969-71, Bell, Surasky & Anderson, P.A., Langley, S.C., 1971-76, sr. ptnr., 1976—; county atty. Aiken County (S.C.), 1982—. Mem. S.C. Hwy. Commn., 1982-86; state exec. committeeman S.C. Dem. Com., 1980-86; mem. S.C. Bd. Chiropractic Examiners, 1978-80; mem. Svc. Coun. of Aiken County, 1976-82, Aiken County Planning Commn., 1976-80, Chmn. Aiken County Transportation Com., 1993-96; bd. dirs. Aiken County Crippled Children's Soc., 1976-82, Gregg-Graniteville Found., 1984—, chmn., 1998—; del. gen. & jurisdictional confs. United Meth. Ch., 1988-92. With USAR, 1959-60. Mem. ABA, ATLA, Aiken County Bar Assn., S.C. Bar Assn., S.C. Trial Lawyers Assn., Masons, Shriners, Kappa Sigma Kappa, Tau Kappa Alpha, Phi Delta Phi, Chi Psi. Democrat. Methodist. Office: PO Box 1890 2625 Jefferson Davis Hwy Langley SC 29834

BELL, RONALD MACK, university foundation administrator; b. Atlanta, Mar. 4, 1937; m. Deborah Jean Slaton, Dec. 28, 1989. BS in Indsl. Mgmt., Ga. Inst. Tech., 1959; MBA, U. Mich., 1965; attended, Cornell U., 1980. Commd. USN, 1959, advanced through grades to capt., 1979, ret., 1985; assoc. dir. rsch. contracts Ga. Inst. Tech., Atlanta, 1985-88; v.p., gen. mgr. Ga. Tech. Rsch. Corp., Atlanta, 1988-97; dir. S.C. Rsch. Inst., Columbia, 1997—; bd. dirs., past pres., now dir. emeritus Nat. Supply Corps. Assn.; cons. Wesvaco/Post, Buckley, Coastal Cons., Inc., UCRF Support Assocs., others, 1985—; expert witness ELSCO, U. Tenn., others, 1987-90; nat. chmn. Univ. Connected Rsch. Found., 1990-91. Past chmn., dir. emeritus Naval Supply Corps. Sch. Mus. Com., Athens, mem., 1983—; mem. Exec. Roundtable, Atlanta, 1985-97; resource staff Gov.'s Com. Tech. & Devel., Atlanta, 1992-97; bd. dirs. Ga. Tech. Sch. Mgmt., 1995-98. Decorated Legion of Merit (2), Meritorious Svc. medal (2). Mem. Soc. Rsch. Adminstrs. (nat. coms., chair regional com. 1985—), Licensing Execs. Soc., Nat. Coun. Univ. Rsch. Adminstrs. (chair regional com., nat. panelist 1985—), Coun. Rsch. and Tech. (dir. workshop, tax com. 1986-92), Ga. Tech. Nat. Alumni Assn. (various coms.), Nat. Conf. on the Advancement of Rsch., Assn. Univ. Tech. Mgrs., Theta Chi (past chpt. pres.), Phi Kappa Phi, Beta Gamma Sigma. Avocations: golf, woodworking. Home: 113 Thompson Cv Saint Simons Island GA 31522-3768 Office: S Carolina Rsch Inst 901 Sumter St Ste 517 Columbia SC 29208-3961

BELL, SAMUEL H., federal judge; b. Rochester, N.Y., Dec. 31, 1925; s. Samuel H. and Marie C. (Williams) B.; m. Joyce Elaine Shaw, 1948 (dec.); children: Henry W., Steven D.; m. Jennie Lee McCall, 1983. BA, Coll. Wooster, 1947; JD, U. Akron, 1952. Pvt. practice Cuyahoga Falls, Ohio, 1956-68; asst. pros. atty. Summit County, Ohio, 1956-58; judge Cuyahoga Falls Mcpl. Ct., Ohio, 1968-73, Ct. of Common Pleas, Akron, Ohio, 1973-77, Ohio Ct. Appeals, 9th Jud. Dist., Akron, 1977-82, U.S. Dist. Ct. (no. dist.) Ohio, Akron, 1982—; adj. prof. Coll. Wooster; adj. prof., adv. bd. U. Akron Sch. Law, past trustee Dean's club; bd. dirs. Jos. R. Miller Found. Co-author: Federal Practice Guide 6th Cir., 1996. Recipient Disting. Alumni award U. Akron, 1988, St. Thomas More award, 1987. Fellow Akron Bar Found. (trustee 1989-94, pres. 1993-94); mem. Fed. Bar Assn., Ohio Bar Assn., Akron Bar Assn., Fed. Judges Assn. (bd. dirs.), Akron U. Sch. Law Alumni Assn. (Disting. Alumni award 1983), Charles F. Scanlon Akron Inn Ct. (pres. 1990-92), Ohio Hist. Soc., Supreme Ct. Hist. Soc., Akron City Club, Masons, Phi Alpha Delta. Republican. Presbyterian. Office: US Dist Ct 526 Fed Bldg & US Courthouse 2 S Main St Akron OH 44308-1813

BELL, SCOTT LEE, pastor; b. Madison, Wis., Mar. 5, 1954; s. LeRoy Joseph and Joyce (Johnson) B.; m. Kathleen D. Wade, July 21, 1979; children: Major, Cody, Gabriel. Diploma, Inst. of Christian Studies, 1980; BA, Rollins Coll., 1985. Youth min. Good Shephard Episcopal, Maitland, Fla., 1977-83; dir. pastoral care Orlando (Fla.) Christian Ctr., 1984-88; pastor Restoration Christian Ctr., Bedford and Seymour, Ind., 1988—. Host: (radio show) Battle Belongs to the Lord, 1989-94; host local show Trinity Broadcasting Network, 1997—. Mem. Orgn. Bd. for Habitat for Humanity, Bedford, 1991; candidate for city councilman Dem. Party, Bedford, 1991; grad. Leadership Lawrence County, Bedford, 1991; mem. sch. bd. North Lawrence Cmty. Schs., 1996—. Mem. Bedford-North Lawrence Ministerial Assn. (v.p., pres. elect 1990—, pres. 1991—).

BELL, SHARON KAYE, small business owner; b. Lincoln, Nebr., Sept. 14, 1943; d. Edwin B. and Evelyn F. (Young) Czachurski; m. James P. Kittrell (div. Sept. 1974); children: Nathan James, Nona Kaye; m. Joseph S. Bell, June 5, 1976; stepchildren: Eugene, Patricia, Bobbie, Linda. Continuing edn./active tax preparer/interviewer assoc., H&R Block, Laguna Hills, 1987—. Various positions mgmt., bookkeeping, 1961-71; bookkeeper Internat. Harvester, Chesapeake, Va., 1971-73, Cheat'AH Engring., Santa Ana, Calif., 1973-74, Fre Del Engring., Santa Ana, Calif., 1974-75; bookkeeper/mgr. Tek Sheet Metal Co., Santa Ana, Calif., 1975-79; owner, bookkeeper Bell's Bookkeeping, Huntington Beach, Calif., 1979-86, Fountain Valley, Calif., 1986—, Laguna Hills, Calif., 1986—; tax preparer H.R. Block, 1989—. Mem. Inst. Mgmt. Accts. (bd. dirs. 1985-86, sec. 1986-87, v.p. 1987-90, dir. manuscripts 1990-91), Nat. Notary Assn., NAFE, Wives of Submarine Vets. World War II (v.p. L.A. chpt. 1986-87, treas. 1990-92), Nat. Soc. Pub. Accts., Internat. Platform Assn. Republican. Avocations: gardening, dancing, grandchildren and great grandchildren. Office: Bells Bookkeeping PO Box 2713 Laguna Hills CA 92654-2713

BELL, SHEILA SUE, primary school educator; b. Breckenridge, Mich., May 24, 1957; d. Clayton Glenn and Carol Jean Peters; m. Randy Alan Bell, Aug. 14, 1982; children: Laurel Rhea, Trevor Clayton Robert. BEd, Ctrl. Mich. U., 1979, early childhood endorsement, 1987; M in Curriculum and Tchg., Mich. State U., 1995. Child devel. instr. N.W. Mich. Coll., Traverse City, Mich., 1988-90; tchr. Headstart Program, Traverse City, 1988-92; kindergarten tchr. Benzie County (Mich.) Ctrl. Schs., 1992—; presenter in field. Contbg. author: Teaching and Change, NEA, Washington, 1996. Named Outstanding Educator, Benzie County Ctrl. Edn. Assn., 1999. Mem. Assn. for Curriculum Devel., Grand Traverse Assn. for the Edn. Young Children (bd. mem., mem.-at-large 1997-99). Avocations: gardening herbs and flowers, hiking, reading. E-mail: bell@msue.msu.edu. Home: 316 10th St Frankfort MI 49635-9697

BELL, STEPHEN ROBERT, lawyer; b. Menominee, Mich., July 10, 1942; s. John Martin and Catherine Irene (Goodman) B.; m. Linden Tucker, May 22, 1976. AB, Georgetown U., 1964; JD, U. Wis., 1967. Bar: D.C., Minn., U.S. Ct. Appeals (4th and 5th cirs.), U.S. Supreme Ct. Assoc. Dorsey & Whitney, Mpls., 1967-68; ptnr. Wilkinson, Cragun & Barker, Washington, 1971-82, Squire, Sanders & Dempsey, Washington, 1982-96, Willkie, Farr & Gallagher, Washington, 1996—. Contbr. article to profl. jours. Lt. USNR, 1968-71. Mem. ABA, D.C. Bar Assn., Fed. Communications Bar Assn., Computer Law Assn. (bd. dirs. 1987-93), Order of Coif. Office: Wilkie Farr & Gallagher Three Lafayette Ctr 1155 21st St NW Fl 6 Washington DC 20036-3384

BELL, STEPHEN SCOTT (STEVE BELL), journalist, educator; b. Oskaloosa, Iowa, Dec. 9, 1935; s. Howard Arthur and Florance (Scott) B.; m. Joyce Dillavou, June 16, 1957; children: Allison Kay, Hilary Ann. B.A., Central Coll., Pella, Iowa, 1959, Ph.D. (hon.), 1959); M.S. in Journalism, Northwestern U., 1963. Announcer Radio Sta. KBOE, Oakaloosa, 1955-59; reporter WOI-TV, Ames, Iowa, 1959-60; news writer WGN Radio-TV, Chgo., 1960-61; reporter, anchorman WOW-TV, Omaha, 1962-65; anchorman Radio Sta. WNEW, N.Y.C., 1965-66; corr. ABC News, 1967-86; assignments include corr. ABC News, Vietnam, 1970-71; polit. corr. ABC News, 1968, 72, chief Asia corr., 1972-73; White House corr. ABC News, Washington, 1974-75; news anchorman World News This Morning and Good Morning Am., 1975-86; news anchor KYW-TV, Phila., 1987-91, USA Network Updates, 1989-92; prof. telecomm. Ball State U., Muncie, Ind., 1992—. Recipient Emmy nominations, 1965, 73, Overseas Press Club award, 1969, Headliner award, 1975. Mem. AFTRA, Council Fgn. Relations. Presbyterian (elder). Office: Ball State U Dept Telecommunications Muncie IN 47306 *As a journalist, the older I get, the less inclined I am to "play God."*

BELL, STEVEN DENNIS, lawyer; b. Akron, Ohio, Feb. 11, 1953; s. Sam H. and Joyce E. (Shaw) B.; m. E. Jane White (div. Feb. 1995); children: Colleen, Patrick. BA, U. Notre Dame, 1975; JD, U. Akron, 1978. Bar: Ohio 1979, D.C. 1989, U.S. Dist. Ct. (no. dist.) Ohio 1980, U.S. Ct. Appeals (6th cir.) 1980, U.S. Ct. Appeals (D.C. cir.) 1987, U.S. Supreme Ct. 1989, U.S. Dist. Ct. (so. dist.) Ohio 1990, U.S. Dist. Ct. (ea. dist.) Mich. 1996. Pvt. practice Akron, 1979-81; chief trial atty. City of Akron, 1981-84; asst. U.S. atty. no. dist. Ohio U.S. Atty.'s Office, Cleve., 1984-88, chief civil divsn., 1986-88, chief appellate litigation, 1987; ptnr. Janik & Bell, Cleve., 1988-91, Ulmer & Berne LLP, Cleve., 1991—. Mem. ABA, Ohio State Bar Assn., Nat. Health Lawyers Assn. Office: Bond Ct Bldg 1300 E 9th St Lbby 9 Cleveland OH 44114-1503

BELL, STEVEN H., financial company executive; b. Cedar Rapids, Iowa, Nov. 5, 1947; s. Hugh Burl and Dorothy Lorraine (Weidersberg) B.; m. Diana Carol Haubert, June 1, 1971 (div. Dec. 1986); m. Robin Leigh Marisco, July 1, 1989; children: Joshua Jacob, Jorden Lyn, Lindsey Rebecca. BS, Colo. State U., 1969; MS, U. Ariz., 1971. Sr. v.p., mgr. Hanifen Irghoff, Inc., Denver; 1st v.p. E.F. Hutton & Co., Denver; dir. Prudential Securities, Denver; sr. v.p. Kemper Securities, Denver; mng. dir. Dain Rauscher, Inc., Denver; sr. v.p. mgr. fixed income div. Hanifen, Imhoff Inc. Pres. Jefferson Edn. Found., Lakewood, Colo.; baseball coach Jefferson County, Arvada, Colo. Mem. Colo. Wrestling Ofcksl. Assn. (bd. dirs. 1976-83). Republican. Avocations: water skiing, snowboarding, guitar, fitness training. Home: 15463 W 73rd Ave Arvada CO 80007-7860 Office: Hanifen Imhoff Inc 1125 17th St Ste 1600 Denver CO 80202

BELL, STOUGHTON, computer scientist, mathematician, educator; b. Waltham, Mass., Dec. 20, 1923; s. Conrad and Florence Emily (Ross) B.; m. Mary Carroll O'Connell, Feb. 26, 1949 (div. 1960); children: Karen, Mark; m. Laura Joan Bainbridge, May 24, 1963 (div. 1979); children: Nathaniel Stoughton, Joshua Bainbridge. Student, Harvard U., 1946-49; A.B., U. Calif., Berkeley, 1950, M.A., 1953, Ph.D., 1955. Mem. staff Sandia Corp., Albuquerque, 1955-66; div. supr. Sandia Corp., 1964-66; vis. lectr. U. N.Mex., 1957-66, dir. computing center, 1966-79, assoc. prof. math., 1966-71, prof. math. and computer sci., 1971-92; prof. emeritus, 1992—; vis. lectr. N.Mex. Acad. Scis., 1965—; nat. lectr. Assn. for Computing Machinery, 1972-74. Co-author: Linear Analysis and Generalized Functions, 1965, Introductory Calculus, 1966, Modern University Calculus, 1966, Mathelatical Analysis for Modeling, 1999. Served with AUS, 1943-44. Mem. Assn. for Computing Machinery, Am. Math. Soc., Math. Assn. Am., Soc. Indsl. and Applied Math., Am. Statis. Assn., Ops. Research Soc. Am. Office: U NMex Computer Sci Dept Albuquerque NM 87131-1386

BELL, SUSAN JANE, nurse; b. Columbus, Ohio, July 24, 1946; d. Donald Richard Bell and Martha Jane (McDowell) Nichols; m. Robert Earlin Ward, Oct. 24, 1964 (div. 1984); children: Duane Allen Ward, Melissa Jane Ward, Bryan Thomas Ward. Degree in nursing, Columbus Sch. Practical Nursing, 1986; ADRN, Columbus State C.C., 1989; student, Franklin U., 1993—. RN, Ohio; cert. CPR; notary pub., Ohio. Nurse's asst. Riverside Meth. Hosp., Columbus, 1970-80, Norworth Convalescent Ctr., Columbus, 1980-86; lic. practical nurse, charge nurse Heartland Thurber Care Ctr., Columbus, 1986-89; staff nurse Am. Nursing Care, Columbus, 1989—; medicare home visitation, staffing and pvt. duty nurse Telemed, Columbus, 1989—; asst. head nurse Northland Terr., Columbus, 1989; supr. Elmington Manor, Columbus, 1989; staff nurse cardiac step down unit Grant Hosp., Columbus, 1989-92; nurse med. ICU, CCU and pediatric ICU, 1992-93; charge nurse critical/skilled unit First Cmty. Village Health Care Ctr., Columbus, 1992-95; pres. Bell Mktg. Distbrs., pvt. duty ALS ventilator patients Med. Pers. Poole. Mem. NAFE, ASPCA, World Wildlife Found., Nature Conservancy, Ohio Hist. Found. (archives/libr. divsn.), Nat. Audubon Soc., Environ. Def. Fund, Nat. Wildlife Fedn., Humane Soc. U.S., Columbus Met. Mus. Art, Rotary. Avocations: body building, power lifting, swimming, music, crocheting.

BELL, THEODORE AUGUSTUS, advertising executive; b. Tampa, Fla., July 3, 1946; s. Theodore A. and Mary Trice (Howell) B.; m. Evelyn Byrd Lorentzen, Mar. 31, 1978; 1 child, Evelyn Byrd. BA in English, Randolph-Macon Coll., 1969; DFA (hon.), Kendall Coll., 1990. Copywriter Wilson, Haight, Welsh Advt., Hartford, Conn., 1970-71, Tinker, Dodge & Delano, N.Y.C., 1971-72; v.p., creative dir. Doyle Dane Bernbach, N.Y.C., 1972-82; pres., chief creative officer Leo Burnett USA, Chgo., 1982-93; vice-chmn., worldwide creative dir. Young & Rubican, N.Y.C., 1993—; creative cons. Heart of Am. America's Cup Challenge, Chgo., 1985-86. Bd. dirs. Lincoln Park Zoo, 1988—, Prentice Women's Maternity Ctr. Northwestern Meml. Hosp., Chgo., 1981—. Recipient Gold Lion award Cannes (France) Internat. Festival du Film Publicitaire, 1988. Mem. Racquet Club (Chgo. and N.Y.C.), Field Club (Greenwich, Conn.). Republican. Episcopalian. Avocations: sailing, golf, screenwriting, gamebird hunting. Office: Young & Rubican Advt 285 Madison Ave New York NY 10017-6486*

BELL, THOMAS DEVEREAUX, JR., advertising company executive; b. Niagara Falls, Nov. 2, 1949; s. Thomas Devereaux and Lenore (Chisholm) B.; m. Margaret McDaniel, Jan. 17, 1975 (div.); 1 child, Thomas Devereaux III; m. Jennifer Holtzman, Dec. 27, 1987; children: Kevin Holtzman Bell, Hannah Holtzman Bell. Student, U. Tenn., 1967-70, George Washington U., 1973, NYU, 1984-88. Exec. dir. Presdl. Inaugural Ball Com., Washington, 1972; dep. div. dir. Com. to Reelect the Pres., Washington, 1971-72; adminstrv. asst. U.S. Senator William Brock, Washington, 1973-75; pres., CEO Bell and McDaniel, Washington, 1975-76, Holder, Kennedy, Dye & Bell, Nashville, 1976-79, Creative Com. Corp., Washington, 1979-82, Hudson Inst., Indpls., 1982-87; exec. v.p. Ball Corp., Muncie, Ind., 1987-89; vice chmn., COO Burson-Marsteller, 1989-94; vice chmn. Gulfstream Aerospace Corp., Savannah, Ga., 1994-95; pres., CEO Burson-Marsteller, N.Y.C., 1995-98; also bd. dirs. Gulfstream Aerospace Corp., Savannah, Ga.; chmn., CEO Young & Rubicam Advt., N.Y.C., 1998—; bd. dirs. Lincoln Nat. Corp., Ft. Wayne, Ind., Young & Rubicam, Inc., N.Y.C., Hudson Inst., Indpls., Lincoln Life & Annuity Co. N.Y. Mem. Transition Team for Pres. Ronald Reagan, Washington, 1981; ptnr. N.Y.C. Partnership. Mem. U.S. C. of C. (bd. dirs. Washington chpt.), Skyline Club, Univ. Club (Indpls.), Econ. Club (N.Y.), Burning Tree Club (Bethesda, Md.), Arthur Page Soc., Union

League Club (N.Y.C.), Georgetown Club (Washington), Field Club (Greenwich, Conn.), Blind Brook Club (Harrison, N.Y.), Gold Club of Purchase (N.Y.). Republican. Office: Young & Rubicam Advt 285 Madison Ave New York NY 10017

BELL, THOMAS EUGENE, psychologist, educational administrator; b. Okmulgee, Okla., Feb. 20, 1945; s. Wilmer Ordell and Betty Jean (Good) Bell; m. Ramona Kay Ashlock, Aug. 26, 1965; 1 child, Stacie Lane. BA, Cen. State U., Edmond, Okla., 1972, MEd, 1975; postgrad., Okla. State U., 1986-88. Lic. profl. counselor, Okla. Psychometrist Guthrie (Okla.) Pub. Schs., 1975-79, sch. psychologist, 1979-89, dir. counseling, 1989-94; pvt. practice Edmond, 1994—. Developer Teen Buddies, 1990. With USAF, 1965-67. Recipient Parent Edn. award Okla. Juvenile Justice, Oklahoma City, 1991. Mem. Mensa Internat. (proctor 1979-86), Okla. Psychol. Assn. (rep. 1986-87), Okla. Sch. Psychology Assn. (area rep. 1987-88), Nat. Assn. Sch. Psychologists, Youth Suicide Prevention Assn. (v.p. 1991—). Democrat. Mem. Ch. of Christ. Avocations: scuba diving, swimming, golf, travel. Home: 1101 Apollo Cir Edmond OK 73003-6013 Office: Meridian Med Tower Bldg 400 Ste A Ste 304 Oklahoma City OK 73120

BELL, TONY CLIFFTON, radio show host, producer; b. Collinsville, Okla., Apr. 26, 1963; s. Robert Norris and Delores Ann (Cannon) B.; m. Joleta Faye Miller, Jan. 4, 1985; children: S. Luke, Hannah Mae, Joshua Robert. BS in Music, So. Nazarene U., 1986. Radio show host Saturday Morning Raptunes Sta. KOKF Radio, Oklahoma City, 1990—. Recipient Gabriel award Unda-U.S.A., 1991, Angel award Excellence in Media, 1995. Avocations: family, fitness, crafts, reading. Office: Sta KOKF Radio 7704 N Council Rd Oklahoma City OK 73132-4147

BELL, WALLACE EDWARD, minister; b. Jackson, Tenn., Feb. 23, 1950; s. William and Marvelyne Eugenia (Wallace) B.; m. Johnnie Mae Mitchell, Sept. 12, 1974; children: Jonathan Edward, Candace Michelle. Student, Lambuth Coll., 1970; BS, Union U., 1972; postgrad., Calif. State U., L.A., 1973-74, Midwestern Sem., 1990-91. Lic. to ministry Ch. of Christ (Holiness) U.S.A., 1973; ordained, 1979. Assoc. pastor Good News Ch., Pasadena, Calif., 1973-78; assoc. pastor Christ Temple Ch., Jackson, Tenn., 1978-79, pastor, 1979-87; pastor Greater Peace Ch., Aurora, Colo., 1987-88, Christ Temple Ch., Kansas City, Kans., 1988-95, 1st Ch. Christ (Holiness) USA, Kansas City, Mo., 1998—; trustee C. M. & I. Coll. Nat. Bd., Jackson, 1980-92; sec. Northcentral Diocese, St. Louis, 1982-90; dir. comms. Nat. S.S. Congress CoCHUSA, Jackson, 1989-96; career agt. Am. Nat. Life Ins., 1995-97; agt. Woodmen Accident & Life, 1997; personal ins. cons. Sitel, 1997-98; dist. chmn. midwest dist. Ch. of Christ (Holiness) USA, Kansas City, Mo., 1997—, dist. pres. 1997—; ins. licensing trainer, 1998—; lic. trainer Sitel Corp., 1998—. Bd. dirs. Aspell Manor, Jackson, 1985-87. Recipient E.M. Wills award Tenn.-Ky. Dist., 1986. Mem. Jaycees (chaplain 1984-85). Home: 907 N 89th St Kansas City KS 66112-1659 Office: 1st Ch Christ (Holiness) USA 2425 Van Brunt Ave Kansas City MO 64128

BELL, WALLY, umpire; b. Ravenna, Ohio, Jan. 10, 1965; m. Vickie Lynn, Jan. 3, 1997. Umpire N.Y.-Pa. League, South Atlantic League, Carolina League, So. League, Dominican Republic League, Triple Alliance, Internat. League, Nat. League, 1993—. Avocations: golf, fishing. Office: Nat League 350 Park Ave New York NY 10022 Office: Umpires Union 1735 Market St Philadelphia PA 19103

BELL, WALTER CLAYTON, drag car racer, small business owner; b. Endicott, N.Y., Feb. 2, 1942; s. Harold Van Fleet and Edith May (Dempsey) B.; m. Sara V. Perugino, Jan 4, 1965 (div. Oct. 1982); 1 child, Victoria Edith; m. Beverly Jeanne Quick, Nov. 26, 1982. Student, Pottsdam Conservatory, 1964. Auto sales mgr. Bill Graham Chevrolet, Gault Chevrolet, Owego, Endicott, N.Y., 1964-67; sales mgr. Prudential Ins. Co., Binghamton, N.Y., 1967-77; ins. agt. Wally Bell & Assocs., Endicott, N.Y., 1977-80; dir. sales Sentry Ins. Co., Stevens Point, Wis., 1980-84; sales rep Sentry Ins. Co., Charlotte, N.C., 1984-87; racer Wally Bell Motorsports, Charlotte, N.C., 1987—, pres., 1988—; cons. Denver Racing, Mooresville, N.C., 1986-89; past officer Life Underwriters Ins. Assn. Contbr. to Book on History Drag Racing, 1971. Named Most Popular Driver, Argus Publ. Co., Calif., 1990, 91.; Nat. record holder in 2 classes of racing, 1965, 69. Mem. KC (4th degree 1989). Democrat. Roman Catholic. Avocations: golf, boating, music. Home: PO Box 237 Harrisburg NC 28075-0237

BELL, WENDELL, sociologist, educator, futurist; b. Chgo., Sept. 27, 1924; s. Wendell and Blanche (Leiferman) B.; m. Lora-Lee Edwards, June 15, 1947; children: Karen Ann, Sharon Lee, David Howard. BA with highest honors, Calif. State U., Fresno, 1948; MA, UCLA, 1951, PhD, 1952; MA (hon.), Yale U., 1963. Asst. prof. sociology, acting dir. survey rsch. facility Stanford U., 1952-54; assoc. prof. sociology Northwestern U., 1954-57; from assoc. prof. to prof. sociology, dir. West Indies study program UCLA, 1957-63; prof. sociology Yale U., New Haven, 1963-95, chmn. dept., 1965-69, dir. comparative sociology tng. program, 1969-77, dir. undergrad. studies, 1976-83, dir. grad. studies, 1984-89, 94; prof. emeritus, 1995—; mem. exec. com. div. behavioral scis. NRC, 1968-69; tng. grant dir. NIMH, 1969-77; vis. fellow Inst. Advanced Studies, The Australian Nat. U., 1985. Author: (with E. Shevky) Social Area Analysis, 1955; (with R.J. Hill and C.R. Wright) Public Leadership, 1961; (with I. Oxaal) Decisions of Nationhood, 1964, Jamaican Leaders, 1964, Foundations of Futures Studies, Vol. I. History, Purposes, and Knowledge, Vol II Values, Objectivity, and the Good Society, 1997; editor, contbr.: The Democratic Revolution in the West Indies, 1967; (with James A. Mau) The Sociology of the Future, 1971; (with Walter Freeman) Ethnicity and Nation-Building, 1974; editor Internat. Studies in Polit. and Social Change, 1966-76; assoc. editor Am. Sociol. Rev., 1958-61; mem. editl. adv. bd. Sage Profl. Papers in Internat. Studies, 1972-84, Sage Rsch. Papers in Social Sci., Series Social Orgn. of Cmty., U. Iowa, 1974-84, Futurics, 1976—, Cultural Futures Rsch., 1976-87, Technological Forecasting and Social Change, 1995-96; editl. cons. Sociometry, 1959-61; mem. editl. bd. Internat. Studies Quar., 1970-80, Plantation Soc. in the Americas, 1978-90, Political Behavior, 1978-80, Jour. Conflict Resolution, 1980-97, Futures Rsch. Quar., 1992—, The Jour. of Contingencies and Crisis, 1992—; cons. editor D.C. Heath and Co., 1971-84. Gov.'s appointee Commn. on Conn.'s Future, 1987-89; mem. adv. coun. Inst. for Global Ethics, 1990—. Aviator USNR, 1943-46, CBI. Recipient Disting. Alumnus award Calif. State U., Fresno, 1988; Rsch. Tng. predoctoral fellow Social Sci. Rsch. Council, 1951-52; Faculty fellow, 1956-59; rsch. grantee, 1978; Carnegie Corp. N.Y. grantee, 1960-63; fellow Center Advanced Study Behavioral Scis., 1963-64; NSF grantee, 1969-70. Mem. AAUP, Internat. Sociol. Assn., Am. Sociol. Assn., Eastern Sociol. Assn., Pacific Sociol. Assn. (v.p. 1960-61), Sociol. Rsch. Assn., Internat. Studies Assn. (v.p. 1970-71), Caribbean Studies Assn. (v.p. 1978, pres 1979, Meritorious Service award 1985, mem. coun. 1988-89), World Future Soc., World Futures Studies Fedn. E-mail: wendell.bell@yale.edu. Home: 364 Sperry Rd Bethany CT 06524-3542 Office: Yale U Dept Sociology PO Box 208265 New Haven CT 06520-8265

BELL, WILLIAM HENRY, JR., banker; b. Schenectady, Oct. 15, 1918; s. William Henry and Elizabeth (Lambert) B.; m. Alice Creedon, Sept. 13, 1947 (dec. 1988); children: Susan, Martha, Patricia, Barbara, Alexandra, Madeline; m. Barbara Page, June 24, 1989. B.A., Princeton U., 1939. With J.P. Morgan & Co., N.Y.C., 1939-49, First Nat. Bank, Jersey City, 1950-52, Heritage Bank, Cherry Hill, N.J., 1953-83; pres., dir., chief exec. officer, chmn., Heritage Bancorp., 1971-82, vice chmn., 1982-83; vice chmn., dir. Duralith Corp., Millville, N.J., 1980-85; bd. dirs. Midlantic Bank South, 1985-89; chmn. Coriell Inst. Med. Rsch., Camden, 1970-85; bd. mgrs. Cooper Med. Ctr., Camden, 1976-78. Pres. Camden (N.J.) Housing Improvement Projects, 1967-74; mem. N.J. Gov.'s Commn. To Evaluate Capital Needs, 1968; treas. class of 1939, Princeton U., 1969-89, v.p., 1989; mem. Gov.'s Task Force for Improving N.J.'s Econ. and Regulatory Climate, 1982; mem. planning and evaluation com. Landings Assn., Savannah, 1990-92; bd. dirs. Hospice Savannah, 1990-94. Lt. comdr. USNR, 1941-46, PTO. Mem. Assn. Bank Holding Cos. (legis. com. 1976-82), Fed. Res. Assn. (nominating adv. com. 1966-69), N.J. Bankers Assn. (exec. com. 1964, 81-85, chmn. task force on interstate banking 1982-85), Pine Valley Golf Club (Clementon, N.J.), The Landings Club (Savannah, Ga.), Oglethorpe Club (Savannah), St. Andrews Soc. (Savannah), Phi Beta Kappa. Republican. Episcopalian. Home: PO Box 503 Highlands NC 28741-0503

BELL, WILLIAM JOSEPH, cable television company executive; b. Jersey City, Dec. 10, 1939; s. William Joseph and Mary Jane (Egan) B.; m. Ellen Jules McInerney; children: Michael, Sally, Thomas, Timothy, Jennifer. BA in Econs., St. Peter's Coll., 1961. With Dun & Bradstreet, Union Carbide, Riegel Paper Corp., 1962-71; asst. treas. Gen. Instrument Corp., 1971-79; exec. v.p., then pres. Cablevision Systems Corp., Woodbury, N.Y., from 1979, vice chmn., 1979—, also dir.; bd. dirs. Continental Bank, Garden City, N.Y. Office: Cablevision Systems Corp 1 Media Crossways Woodbury NY 11797-2013*

BELL, WILLIAM WOODWARD, lawyer; b. May 15, 1938; s. Charles Smith and Janie Mae (Woodward) B.; m. Mary Elizabeth Beniteau, May 31, 1969; children: Susan Elizabeth, Carol Ann. BBA, Baylor U., 1960, JD, 1965. Bar: U.S. Dist. Ct. (we. dist.) Tex. 1967, U.S. Supreme Ct. 1971. Ptnr. Sleeper, Boynton, Burleson, Williams & Johnson, Waco, Tex., 1965-68, Holloway, Slagle & Bell, Brownwood, 1968-71, Johnson, Slagle & Bell, Brownwood, 1971-74; pvt. practice Brownwood, 1974-80; atty. City of Brownwood, 1980-99; ptnr. Bell and Ellis, Brownwood, 1980-89, Bell, Franklin & Morelock and Investment Co., Brownwood, 1962-86. Capt. USMC, 1960-63. Named Vol., 1991, Developer of Yr., Tex. Indsl. Devel. Coun. Fellow Tex. Bar Found.; mem. Tex. Bar Assn. (chmn. dist. 15B grievance com. 1986-87), Brown County Bar Assn., Am. Judicature Soc., Phi Alpha Delta. Baptist. Home: PO Box 1564 Brownwood TX 76804-1564 Office: PO Box 1726 Brownwood TX 76804-1726

BELLA, JONATHAN NORIEGA, internist; b. Cotabato City, The Philippines, Apr. 12, 1965; came to U.S., 1991; s. Primitivo Jr. and Patrocinio (Noriega) B. BA in Humanities, U. of The Philippines, 1985; MD, U. of the East, The Philippines, 1989. Cert. in internal medicine. Intern Atlantic City Med. Ctr., N.J., 1991-92; resident Montefiore Med. Ctr., N.Y.C., 1992-94; fellow in cardiology N.Y. Hosp.-Cornell Med. Ctr., 1994-97, fellow in echocardiography, 1997-98; dir. echocardiology Louis Stokes Cleve. VA Med. Ctr., 1998—; asst. prof. medicine Sch. Medicine Case Western Res. U., 1998—. Mem. Am. Coll. Cardiology, Am. Heart Assn., Am. Soc. Echocardiography. Roman Catholic. Office: Louis Stokes Cleveland VA Med Ctr 10201 East Blvd Cleveland OH 44106

BELLACK, ALAN SCOTT, clinical psychologist; b. N.Y.C., Nov. 27, 1944; s. Jack and Yetta B.; m. Barbara Bartlett, Nov. 16, 1969; children: Jonathan, Adam. B.S., CCNY, 1965; M.S., St. John's U., 1967; Ph.D., Pa. State U., 1970. Diplomate Am. Bd. Profl. Psychology. Asst. prof. psychology Pa. State U., 1970; mem. faculty U. Pitts., 1971-82, prof. psychology and psychiatry, 1980-82; prof. psychiatry Med. Coll. Pa., Phila., 1982-95, U. Md., 1995—; vice chmn., dir. clin. psychology Med. Coll. Pa., Phila.; chmn., dir. clin. psychology; prof. psychiatry U. Md. Sch. Medicine; cons. in field. Author: Behavioral Assessment: A Practical Handbook, 1976, 2nd edit., 1981, 3rd edit., 1988, Behavior Modification: An Introduction, 1977, Introduction to Clinical Psychology, 1980, The Clinical Psychology Handbook, 1983, 2nd edit., 1991, others; editor: Clin. Psychology Rev., 1981—, Behavior Modification, 1977—; contbr. articles to profl. jours. USPHS fellow, 1968-70. Mem. Am. Psychol. Assn., Assn. Advancement Behavior Therapy. Office: Univ of Maryland at Balt Dept Psychiatry 737 W Lombard St 5th Fl Baltimore MD 21201*

BELLACOSA, JOSEPH W., state supreme court justice; b. Bklyn., Sept. 1, 1937; s. Frank and Antoinette Bellacosa; m. Mary Bellacosa; children: Michael, Peter, Barbara. BA in English, St. John's U., 1959, LLB, 1961. Bar: N.Y. 1961. With N.Y. Life Ins. Co., 1961-63; law asst., law sec. to Hon. Marcus G. Christ N.Y. Cts. Appellate Divsn., 1963-70; assoc. prof. law St. John's U., 1970-75, asst. dean academics and admissions, 1970-73; prof. law, dir. govt. law ctr. Union U., 1970-75, 83-85; chief clk., counsel N.Y. Ct. Appeals, 1975-83; judge N.Y. Ct. Claims, 1985-87; chief adminstrv. judge N.Y. State Cts., 1985-87; assoc. judge N.Y. Ct. Appeals, Albany, 1987—; vis. prof. St. John's U., 1979-83; chmn. N.Y. State Sentencing Guidelines Com., 1983-85; mem. Chief Judge's Media Adv. Com. on TV and Cts. Author: Criminal Procedure Law of the State of New York, 1974-85; assoc. editor St. John's Law Rev. Mem. Albany chpt. Fund for Modern Cts. Bd. and Strategic Planning Com. City of Albany; communicant, law scripture reader, lay eucharistic min. St. Madeleine Sophie, Guilderland, N.Y. Mem. Am. Law Inst., Assn. of Bar of City of N.Y. (arbitration com. 1965-69, ethics com. 1969-73), N.Y. State Bar Assn. (criminal justice sect., Outstanding Contbn. to Criminal Justice Edn. criminal justice sect. 1981). Office: NY Ct of Appeals Court of Appeals Hall 20 Eagle St Albany NY 12207-1009*

BELLAH, C. RICHARD, lawyer; b. San Antonio, Jan. 11, 1955; s. Max and Charlotte (Arant) B.; m. Erin P. Jones, Oct. 1987. BS in Gen. Bus. Adminstrn., Ariz. State U., 1977; JD, U. Ariz., 1980. Bar: U.S. Dist. Ct. Ariz. 1980, U.S. Ct. Appeals (9th cir.) 1981, U.S. Tax Ct. 1985, U.S. Supreme Ct. 1985. Law clk. to presiding justice Ariz. Supreme Ct., Phoenix, 1980-81; assoc. Crotts & Laird, Phoenix, 1981-82; ptnr. Charles, Smith & Bellah, Glendale, Ariz., 1982-86; pvt. practice Glendale, 1986-88; ptnr. Bellah & Harrian, Glendale, 1988—; councilman City of Glendale, 1984-92, vice mayor, 1991-92; justice of peace pro tem Maricopa County Justice Ct., Glendale, 1985-90. Committeeman precinct Maricopa County Reps.; bd. dirs. Glendale Youth Ctr., Faith House Women's Shelter, Fiesta Bowl, Phoenix Christian H.S., 1993—; mem. fin. com. and policy com. N.W. Cmty. Christian Sch.; deacon Bapt. Ch. Recipient Outstanding Service award Am. Legion, 1979, Cert. of Appreciation Ariz. State Legis., 1979, Maricopa Services Commn., 1985, Phoenix of Realtors, 1985, Soroptimist Internat., 1985, City of Glendale, 1985, Glendale Sr. Ctr., 1986. Mem. ATLA, ABA (Silver Key award 1979), Ariz. Bar Assn., Ariz. Trial Lawyers Assn., Phi Alpha Delta (chpt. justice, vice justice alumni assn.), Sigma Phi Epsilon (Hall of Honor). Avocation: jogging. Home: 6301 W Aster Dr Glendale AZ 85304-1638 Office: Bellah and Harrian 5622 W Glendale Ave Glendale AZ 85301-2525

BELLAH, ROBERT NEELLY, sociologist, educator; b. Altus, Okla., Feb. 23, 1927; s. Luther Hutton and Lillian Lucille (Neelly); m. Melanie Hyman, Aug. 17, 1949; children: Jennifer, Harriet. BA, Harvard U., 1950, PhD, 1955. Rsch. assoc. Inst. Islamic Studies, McGill U., Montreal, Can., 1955-57; with Harvard U., Cambridge, Mass., 1957-67, prof., 1966-67; mem. faculty dept. sociology U. Calif., Berkeley, 1967-97, Elliott prof. emeritus, 1997—. Author: Tokugawa Religion, 1957, Beyond Belief, 1970, The Broken Covenant, 1975 (Sorokin award Am. Sociol. Assn. 1976), (with Charles Y. Glock) The New Religious Consciousness, 1976, (with Phillip E. Hammond) Varieties of Civil Religion, 1980, (with others) Habits of the Heart, 1985, (with others) The Good Society, 1991. With U.S. Army, 1945-46. Fulbright fellow, 1960-61; recipient Harbison award Danforth Found., 1971. Mem. Am. Acad. Arts and Scis., Am. Sociol. Assn., Am. Acad. Religion, Am. Philos. Soc. Episcopalian. Office: U Calif Dept Sociology Berkeley CA 94720-1980

BELLALTA, ESMÉE CROMIE, landscape architect, retired educator; b. London, Oct. 6, 1927; came to U.S., 1976; d. Bernard Patrick and Irene Maud (Belcher) Cromie; m. Jaime Juan José; children: Esmée, Alexandra, Barbara, Antoniou, Angela, Josephine, Maria, Jaime, Diego, Felipe. BA, Harvard U., 1951, M in Landscape Architecture, 1952. Registered cert. landscape architect, Ind. Assoc. prof. Sch. Architecture U. Notre Dame, Notre Dame, Ind., 1976-95, assoc. prof. emerita, 1995; coord., faculty Justice Edn. Program St. Mary's Coll., Notre Dame, 1981-97; vis. prof. Pontifica Univ. Cath. Chile, 1997, Harvard U. Grad. Sch. Design, 1993-94, Ball State U. Coll. Architecture & Planning, Landscape Dept., 1978-93; prof. landscape architecture U. Chile, 1974-76; prof. environ. design Coll. Architecture Cath. U. Chile, Santiago, 1973-76; tchr. Centro Nat. Familia, Chile, 1968-75, counselor, 1967-75; tchr. Calvert Sch., 1968-70; tchr. art Santiago Coll., 1955-75; co-dir. Inst. R&D Holistic Design Divsn. Ecology, Evanston, Ill., 1972—; cons. in field; rschr. in field. Contbr. articles to profl. jours. Mem Diocesan Liturgical Art & Environment Com., Ft. Wayne, South Bend, Ind., 1985-91; mem. cons. com. disabled U. Notre Dame, 1985-91; counselor Cath. Marriage Adv. Coun., Gt. Britain, 1964-67; apptd. Diocesan Liturgical Commn., 1989. Lily grantee St. Mary's Coll., 1989, 90; Environic Found. Internat. grantee, 1985, Kellogg Seed Money grantee Helen Kellogg Inst. Internat. Studies, 1984. Mem. Am. Soc. Landscape Archs. (elected mem.-at-large Ind. chpt. 1985-88, Merit award 1981, spl. award 1980), Royal Horticulture Soc., Amnesty Internat. Roman Catholic. Home: 1132 N Saint Joseph St South Bend IN 46617-1254

BELLAMY, CAROL, international organization executive; b. Plainfield, N.J., 1942. BA with honors, Gettysburg Coll., 1963; JD, NYU, 1968. Asst. commr. Dept. Mental Health and Mental Health Retardation Svc., N.Y.C.; with Peace Corps., Guatemala, Ctrl. Am.; assoc. Cravath, Swaine & Moore, N.Y.C.; mem. N.Y. State Senate; prin. Morgan Stanley & Co., N.Y.C.; mng. dir. Bear Stearns, N.Y.C.; dir. Peace Corps., Washington, 1993-95; exec. dir. UNICEF, 1995—. Office: UNICEF Office of Exec Director 3 United Nations Plz New York NY 10017-4486*

BELLAMY, JAMES CARL, insurance company executive; b. Detroit, Oct. 15, 1926; s. Robert Maxwell Belllamy and Mamie (Moery) B.; m. Marie Alice Brakebill, Jan. 20, 1951; children: James Carl, Janet Marie. B.S., U. Tenn., 1950. C.L.U. Agt., asst. mgr. Nat. Life & Accident Ins. Co., Chattanooga, Louisville, 1950-58; dist. mgr. Nat. Life & Accident Ins. Co., Little Rock, Nashville, 1958-73; 2d v.p. Nat. Life & Accident Ins. Co., Nashville, 1973-78, v.p., 1978-82; sr. v.p., dir. Am. Gen. Life & Accident Ins. Co., Nashville, 1982-87; sr. v.p. mktg. Southlife Holding Co., Nashville, 1987-91, ret., 1991; exec. v.p. mktg. Pub. Savs. Life Ins. Co., Charleston, S.C.; vice chmn. Security Trust Life Ins. Co., Macon, Ga., bd. dirs.; pres. Southlife Gen. Agys., Nashville; bd. dirs. Pub. Savs. Life Ins. Co., Charleston. Solicitor United Way, Nashville, 1968-74; solicitor Boy Scouts Am., 1968-74. Served with USNR, 1944-46, PTO. Mem. Nat. Assn. Life Underwriters, Nashville Assn. Life Underwriters (pres. 1970-71), Nashville Gen. Agts. and Mgrs. Assn. (pres. 1967), Ins. Mktg. Research Assn. (exec. com.), Hillwood Country Club (bd. dirs.), Univ. Club, Kiwanis, Sigma Chi. Republican. Baptist.

BELLAMY, JENNIFER RACHELLE, artist; b. Clio, S.C., Aug. 9, 1944; d. Leland and Myrtle Lee (Wise) Wiggins; m. Marvin James Bellamy, May 19, 1963; 1 child, Audrey Katherine Rollins. BA in Art & Performance magna cum laude, U. Tex., 1989, postgrad., 1992-93, 95—. Dist. sec. Corning Glass Works, Richardson, Tex., 1977-80; adminstrv. asst. The Chase Manhatten Bank, Dallas, 1981-85; owner The Bellamy Studio, Richardson, Tex., 1990-93, 95—. Recipient tchg. assistantships U. Tex., Dallas, 1993. Mem. AAUW, Coll. Art Assn., Richardson Civic Art Soc., Phi Theta Kappa. Lutheran. Avocations: writer, child care advocate, gardener, cooking, walking. Office: The Bellamy Studio 404 Summit Dr Richardson TX 75081-5118

BELLAMY, JOE DAVID, English language educator, writer; b. Cin., Dec. 29, 1941; s. Orin Ross and Beulah Pearl (Zutavern) B.; m. Connie Sue Arendsee, Sept. 16, 1964; children: Lael Elizabeth, Samuel Ross Carlos. Student, Duke U., 1959-61; B.A., Antioch Coll., 1964; M.F.A., U. Iowa, 1969. Editor The Antiochian, 1965-67; instr. English Pa. State Coll., Mansfield, 1969-70, asst. prof., 1970-72; asst. prof. English St. Lawrence U., Canton, N.Y., 1972-74, assoc. prof., 1974-80, prof. English, 1980-91; dir. lit. program Nat. Endowment for Arts, Washington, 1991—; disting. vis. writer George Mason U., Fairfax, Va., 1987-88; pub., editor Fiction Internat. mag. and press, 1972-83; dir. Fiction Internat./St. Lawrence U. Writer's Conf. at Saranac lake, 1974-80; dir. St. Lawrence Award for Fiction, 1973-84; cons. editor U. Ill. Press, Champaign, 1974—; program cons. NEH, 1976—; book reviewer Sat. Rev., 1975-78, N.Y. Times, 1975—, Washington Post, 1975—; judge Drue Heinz Lit. prize, 1989-90; contbg. editor The Pushcart prize, 1990—. Editor: Apocalypse: Dominant Contemporary Forms, 1972, Superfiction, or the American Story Transformed, 1975, Moral Fiction, 1980, New Writers for the Eighties, 1981, Love Stories/Love Poems, 1982, American Poetry Observed, 1984; author: The New Fiction, 1974, Olympic Gold Medalist, 1978, The Frozen Sea, 1988, Suzi Sinzinnati, 1989. Recipient Fels award for editing Coordinating Council Lit. Mags., 1976, fiction prize Kans. Quar./Kans. Art Commn., 1982, Editors' Book award, 1988; grantee NEH, 1974, Nat. Endowment for Arts, 1985; CAPS fellow in fiction, 1984. Mem. Nat. Book Critics Circle, Coordinating Coun. Lit Mags. (pres., chmn. bd. dirs. 1979-81), Associated Writing Programs (bd. dirs. 1989-91, pres., chmn. bd. dirs. 1990-91). Home: 1145 Lawson Cove Cir Virginia Beach VA 23455-6824 Office: Nat Endowment for Arts Office Dir Lit Program Washington DC 20506

BELLAMY, JOHN CARY, civil engineer, meteorologist; b. Cheyenne, Wyo., Apr. 18, 1915; s. Benjamin Charles and Alice Elizabeth (Cary) B.; m. Josephine Marie Johnston, Sept. 21, 1940; children: John Cary, Agnes Louise, Charles Fulton, William Delaney, Mary Elizabeth. BCE, U. Wyo., 1936; PhM, U. Wis., 1938; PhD in Meteorology, Chgo. U., 1947. Registered profl. engr., Wyo. Ptnr. Bellamy & Sons Engrs., Lamont, Wyo., 1938-42; asst. prof. U. Chgo., 1942-47; assoc. dir. Cook Rsch. Labs., Chgo., 1947-60; dir. NRRI U. Wyo., Laramie, 1960-73; prof. civil engring. U. Wyo., 1973-81; prin. Bellamy & Sons Engrs., Laramie, 1981—; dir. Inst. Tropical Meteorology, U. P.R., 1943-44; spl. cons. U.S. Army Air Corps, Washington, 1944-45; mem. Western Interstate Nuclear Bd., Denver, 1964-75. Contbr. articles to profl. jours.; contbr. to books; patentee in field. Recipient Losey award, Inst. Aero. Sci., 1944, Medal of Freedom, Pres. U.S.A., 1946, Thurlow award Inst. Navigation, 1946. Fellow Am. Meteorol. Soc. (dir. 1948-52), Inst. Navigation (pres. 1962); mem. Wyo. Engring. Soc., Am. Geophys. Union, Nat. Soc. Profl. Engrs. (chpt. pres. 1976), Lions (chpt. pres. 1981, 84). Avocations: golf, bowling, computer programming. Home and Office: 2308 Holliday Dr Laramie WY 82070-4847

BELLAMY, JOHN STARK, II, librarian; b. Cleve.; s. Peter and Jean (Dessel) B.; m. Laura A. Serafin, Aug. 9, 1996; children: Sarah, Catherine. BA, Goddard Coll., Plainfield, Vt., 1971; M.History, U. Va., 1977; MLS, Case Western Res. U., 1978. Pub. svcs. libr. Cuyahoga County Pub. Libr., Beachwood, Ohio, 1982-89; subject specialist libr. Cuyahoga County Pub. Libr., Fairview Park, Ohio, 1989—. Author: Angels on the Heights, 1991, They Died Crawling, 1995, The Maniac in the Bushes, 1997, The Corpse in the Cellar, 1999. Roman Catholic. Office: Cuyahoga County Pub Library 21255 Lorain Rd Fairview Park OH 44126-2120

BELLAMY, WALTER JONES, retired basketball player. Student, Ind. U., 1957-60. With Chgo. Packers, 1961-62, Chgo. Zephyrs (formerly Chgo. Packers), 1962-63, Balt. Bullets, 1963-66, N.Y. Knicks, 1965-68, Atlanta Hawks, 1970-72, New Orleans Jazz, 1974-75; mem. U.S. Olympic Basketball Team, 1960. Pres. Atlanta Police Athletic League; trustee Gate City Day Nursery Assn.; bd. dirs. S.W. Youth Bus. Orgn.; founder, 1st pres. Men of Tomorrow, Inc., Md.; membership chmn. Campbelltown/Cascade YMCA Men internat. Club. Named Rookie of Yr., 1962, Basketball Hall of Fame, 1993; winner Gold medal U.S. Olympics, 1960; named to U.S. Olympic Hall of Fame, N.C. Sports Hall of Fame, 100% Wrong Club Atlanta Hall of Fame, Ind. U. Sports Hall of Fame, NBA Hall of Fame. Mem. Ind. U. Alumni Club, Alpha Phi Alpha, Alpha Phi Omega. Achievements include mem. gold-medal-winning U.S. Olympic Team, 1960, holds single-season record for most games played-88, 1969. Address: PO Box 42751 Atlanta GA 30311-0751

BELLANCA, JOSEPH PAUL, engineering construction executive; b. Rochester, N.Y., Nov. 25, 1936; s. Sam and Anna (Cani) B.; m. Joy Eleanor Gaston, Dec. 5, 1964 (dec.); children: Joseph Jr., Victoria Ann Gordon, Lizabeth Ann Wilbur, Lorraine Thacker. BS in Civil Engring., Purdue U., 1958. Registered profl. engr., D.C. and 10 states. Assoc./project mgr. TAMS Consultants, Dallas/Ft. Worth, 1968-73; assoc./resident mgr. TAMS Consultants, Washington, 1973-77; pres. Bellanca Engring. Consultants, Atlanta, others, 1977-85; dir. Schal Assocs., Chgo., 1985-86; v.p. Greiner, Inc., Orlando (Fla.), Denver, 1986-88, Bechtel Internat. Inc., Vienna, Va., 1988-92, Turner Constrn. Co., Atlanta, 1992-98; exec. v.p. Bovis Constrn. Co., Atlanta, 1998—; lobbyist Airport Consultants Coun. Author/editor: (jour.) Airports--Challenges of the Future, 1973, (design compendium) World Travel Center--Detroit Met. Airport (won design competition for $1 billion new air terminal complex. Named Young Engr. Yr. Mid-Cities chpt. Tex. Soc. Profl. Engrs., 1971. Mem. ASCE (sec. 1973, vice chmn. 1979, exec. com., air transport divsn.), NSPE (pres. Mid-Cities chpt. Tex. Soc. Profl. Engrs. 1972-73). Achievements include managing and coordinating airfield design for future 2 million pound aircraft at Dallas/Ft. Worth airport; executive role in 11 major airport development programs (Dallas/Ft. Worth, Atlanta, Chicago, Denver, 2-Jordan, 4-Saudi Arabia, New Seoul) and Detroit Downtown People Mover. Avocations: travel, reading, sports, history/govt. Home: 9295 Heatherton Walk Duluth GA 30097-2492 Office:

Bovis Constrn Corp 7000 Central Pkwy NE Ste 1400 Atlanta GA 30328-4596

BELLANGER, BARBARA DORIS HOYSAK, biomedical research technologist; b. Syracuse, N.Y., Oct. 24, 1936; d. Edward George and Bernardine Elizabeth (Blaney) Hoysak; m. Ronald Patrick Bellanger, July 1, 1961; children: Laura Jeanne, Andrea Lynne, Janis Anne. BS, Syracuse U., 1958. Cert. lab. animal technician. Tech. asst. Bur. of Labs., Syracuse, 1958; rsch. scientist Bristol Labs., Syracuse, 1958-63; rsch. assoc. Syracuse Cancer Rsch. Inst., 1973—. Pres. CNS Northstars Band Parents, Inc., Cicero-North Syracuse, N.Y., 1986-87. Mem. Am. Assn. Lab. Animal Sci. (cert. and registered lab. animal technician, sec. Upstate N.Y. br. 1990—, Technician of Yr. award 1992, Harlan Teklad award 1998), N.Y. Acad. Scis., Alpha Gamma Delta (pres. Alpha alumnae chpt. 1959-60, treas. 1989—). Home: 410 David Dr North Syracuse NY 13212-1929 Office: Syracuse Cancer Rsch Inst Presdl Plz 600 E Genesee St Syracuse NY 13202-3111

BELLANGER, SERGE RENÉ, banker; b. Vimoutiers, France, Apr. 30, 1933; s. René Albert and Raymonde Maria (Renard) B. MBA, Paris Bus. Sch., 1957. With Citibank, 1966-73, mem. Paris br., 1966-69; world corp. rels. officer for Europe Citibank, N.Y.C., 1969-73, asst. v.p., 1969-71, v.p., 1972-73; sr. v.p., gen. mgr. Compagnie Financière de CIC et de l'Union Européenne, N.Y.C., 1973-79, exec. v.p., gen. mgr., 1979—; U.S. gen. rep. CIC Group, N.Y.C., 1973—; prof. banking French Banking Inst., 1961-64; mem. adv. com. French House, Columbia U., 1976—, chmn., 1996—; mem. adv. com. Ctr. for Study of French Civilization and Culture, NYU, 1988—; mem. adv. bd. French Inst. Culture and Tech. U. Pa., 1992—, chmn. adv. bd., 1992-95; dir. Am. Ctr. in Paris, 1985-93; mem. U.S. Com. Fgn. Trade Advisors for France, 1979—, v.p. U.S. com., 1992-93, exec. v.p., 1985-93, mem. bd. dirs. nat. com., 1986—, mem. Paris exec. com., 1994-95; chmn. internat. banking course New Sch. Social Rsch., N.Y.C., 1981-83. With French Air Force, 1958-60. Decorated Algeria Commemorative medal, Officer Legion of Honor, Comdr. Nat. Order of Merit. Mem. French-Am. C. of C. (councillor 1973-74, exec. com. 1974-80, v.p. 1980-82, exec. v.p. 1982-83, nat. pres. 1983—, pres. N.Y. chpt. 1983—), European-Am. C. of C. (pres., CEO 1990-96, hon. chmn. 1996—), N.Y. C. of C. (mem. internat. bus. initiative 1994-95), N.Y.C. Partnership and C. of C. (ptnr. 1992—), Assn. French C. of C. and Industry Abroad (v.p. 1991-96, first v.p. 1996—), French Overseas Assn., Inst. Fgn. Bankers (trustee 1975-77, v.p. 1977-79, chmn. legis. and regulatory com. 1977-79, chmn. 1979-80), Lyonnaise de Banque (bd. dirs. 1986-89), Assn. for Promotion of French Sci., Industry and Tech. (pres. 1986-91), Banque de l'Union Européenne, bd. dirs. 1989-90), Food and Wines from France (SOPEXA) (bd. dirs. 1983—), N.Y. Futures Exchange (dir. 1980-87, chmn. fgn. exchange steering com. 1981-82), N.Y. Cotton Exchange (bd. dirs. fin. instrument exchange divsn. 1985-95), Bank Adminstrn. Inst. (mem. editl. bd. World of Banking Mag., 1981-87, columnist Banker's Mag. 1986-96), Univ. Club, River Club, Automobile Club de France. Home: 860 U N Plz Apt 2324C New York NY 10017-1810 Office: 520 Madison Ave New York NY 10022-4213

BELLAS, ALBERT CONSTANTINE, investment banker, advisor; b. Steubenville, Ohio, Sept. 15, 1942; s. Constantine Michael and Kiki (Michalopoulos) B.; m. Kay Mazzo, Dec. 21, 1978; children: Andrew James, Kathryn Kiki. BA, Yale U., 1964; JD, U. Chgo., 1967; MBA, Columbia U., 1968. Summer intern The White House, 1963; assoc. Dillon, Read & Co., Inc., N.Y.C., 1968-72; v.p. Goldman Sachs & Co., N.Y.C., 1973-76; gen. ptnr. Loeb Rhoades & Co., N.Y.C., 1976-78; sr. exec. v.p., mem. mgmt. com. Shearson Lehman Bros., N.Y.C., 1979-90; sr. exec. v.p., mem. bd. dirs. Lehman Bros., Inc., 1990-91; mng. dir., mem. mgmt. com. Offitbank, N.Y.C., 1992—; allied mem. N.Y. Stock Exch., 1976-92. Bd. dirs. Lincoln Ctr. for Performing Arts, N.Y.C., 1987—, mem. audit com., 1989—, investment com., 1990-93; bd. dirs. Guild Hall, East Hampton, N.Y., 1989—, mem. exec. com., treas., 1994-96; bd. dirs. 1128 Park Ave. Corp., 1988-94, Sch. Am. Ballet, N.Y.C., 1975-85, vice chmn., 1986-87, chmn., 1987—; mem. bd. regents Mercersburg Acad., Pa., 1992—, mem. investment com., 1992—, mem. exec. com., 1993—, chmn. fin. com., 1994—; chmn. investment com., The Century Assn., 1995—; mem. day sch. com. Brick Ch., N.Y.C., 1985-88. McKinsey scholar, 1968. Mem. ABA, Ohio Bar Assn., Maidstone Club, Yale Club, Century Assn., India House, Univ. Club. Avocation: tennis. Home: 1130 Park Ave New York NY 10128-1255 Office: 520 Madison Ave Fl 27 New York NY 10022-4213

BELLATTI, LAWRENCE LEE, lawyer; b. Oklahoma City, Apr. 19, 1944; s. Lawrence Fitzhugh and Esther Lee (Swank) B.; m. Barbara Gail Wolfinger, June 25, 1977; children: Julie M., Jenny E., Jill N. BS, Okla. State U., 1966; JD, Okla. U., 1969. Bar: Okla. 1969, Tex. 1974, U.S. Dist. Ct. (so. dist.) Tex. 1975, U.S. Ct. Mil. Appeals 1978, U.S. Dist. Ct. (ea. dist.) Tex. 1979, U.S. Ct. Appeals (5th cir.) 1979, U.S. Ct. Appeals (11th cir.) 1981, U.S. Ct. Appeals (10th cir.) 1982, U.S. Dist. Ct. (we. dist.) Tex. 1983, U.S. Dist. Ct. (we. dist.) Okla. 1983, U.S. Dist. Ct. (no. dist.) Tex., 1984, U.S. Dist. Ct. (no. dist.) Okla., 1992, U.S. Dist. Ct. (ea. dist.) Okla. 1994. Assoc. Andrews, Kurth, Campbell & Jones, Houston, 1974-80; ptnr. Andrews & Kurth, Houston, 1980—; bd. dirs. Interface-Samaritan Counseling Ctrs., Inc., Houston. Mem. Harris County Flood Control Dist. Task Force, Houston, 1984. Lt. comdr. JAGC, USNR, 1969-74. Mem. Tex. Bar Assn., Okla. Bar Assn., Houston Bar Assn., Order of Coif, Phi Kappa Phi, Sigma Chi, Phi Delta Phi. Republican. Baptist. Office: Andrews & Kurth 600 Travis St Ste 4200 Houston TX 77002-2910

BELL-BROWN, BRENDA YVETTE, arts administrator; b. Memphis, Apr. 2, 1959; d. Benny Frank Bell and Mary Barbara (Horton) Saunders; m. John Alexander Bronw, Jr., Dec. 21, 1984; children: Naima Taaj Ajmal, Malik Babatunde. BA in Theatre Arts, Brown U., 1982; MA in Mus. Studies, Hampton U., 1986. Edn. specialist Smithsonian Instn., Washington, 1986-87; program, devel. officer African Am. Mus. Assn., Washington, 1987-88; asst. to the dir. Euphrat Gallery, Cupertino, Calif., 1990-91; curator of edn. Triton Mus. of Art, Santa Clara, Calif., 1991-92; mgr. traveling exhibits program Minn. Hist. Soc., St. Paul, 1993-96; project coord. for diversity planning Minn. Minority Edn. Partnership, Mpls., 1996; mgmt. analyst State Coun. on Black, St. Paul, 1997-98; adv. com. Ordway Music Theatre, St. Paul, 1996—, chair steering com. Children, Family and Cmty. Invitational, St. Paul, 1994-97; bd. dirs. Met. Regional Arts Coun., St. Paul, 1996-97; free-lance artist Non-Union Talent Svc., Edina, Minn., 1995—; master of ceremonies SASE: The Write Place, St. Paul, 1994—. Commr. Gov.'s Commn. on the King Holiday, Minn., 1994—. Recipient Douglas Turner Ward/Alice Childress Scriptwriting award Gwendolyn Brooks Writers Ctr., Chgo., 1997; Many Voices fellow Playwrights' Ctr., Mpls., 1997; emerging artist-in-lit. Twin Cities Juneteenth Celebration Com., Mpls., 1995-97. Mem. OES, Daus. of Isis. Avocations: storytelling, dollmaking, poetry writing. Home: 296 Thomas Ave Saint Paul MN 55103-1737

BELLE, ALBERT JOJUAN, professional baseball player; b. Shreveport, La., Aug. 25, 1966. Student, La. State U. With Cleve. Indians, 1987-1996, Chgo. White Sox, 1997-99, Balt. Orioles, 1999—. Player Am. League All-Star Game, 1993-96; ranked 1st in Am. League for runs batted in, 1993; named to Am. League Silver Slugger Team, 1993-95, Sporting News Am. League All-Star Team, 1993-94; named Player of Yr. Sporting News, 1995. Leader Maj. League home runs, 1995; mem. Am. League champions, 1995. Office: Balt Orioles Oriole Park at Camden Yards 333 W Camden St Baltimore MD 21201*

BELLE-ISLE, DAVID RICHARD, organization and management consultant; b. Springfield, Mass., Mar. 26, 1950; s. Richard Alfred and Eda (Carra) Belle-Isle; divorced; children: Justin, Melissa, Michelle, Megan. AA, Kendall Coll., 1969; BS magna cum laude, Springfield Coll., 1971, MEd, 1972; PhD, U. North Colo., 1975; postgrad., MIT, 1979-80. Asst. dean Western New Eng. Coll., Springfield, 1972-73, U. No. Colo., Greeley, 1973-75, W.Va. Inst. Tech., Montgomery, 1975-76; sr. cons. Digital Equipment Corp., Maynard, Mass., 1976-80; dir. corp. planning Martin Marietta Corp., Bethesda, Md., 1980-84; exec. dir. Sara Lee Corp., Chgo., 1984-86; sr. v.p. Electrolux Corp., Stamford, Conn., 1986-87; pres. David Belle-Isle Corp., Fairfield, Conn., 1987-88; chief human resources officer Epic Health Care Group, Dallas, 1988-94; pres. Tex. chpt. Nat. Esop Assn., 1992-94, Insight Consulting, Inc., 1994—; prof. Suffolk U., Boston, 1976-78, Clark U., Worcester, Mass., 1977-79, U. Mich., Ann Arbor, 1985-87; bd. dirs. Mgmt. Techs., Houston. Mem. Grace Commn., U.S. Presdl. Pvt. Sector Study on Cost Control, Washington, 1983-84. Mem. Psi Chi Nat. Honor Soc. Republican. Avocations: reading, skiing, aerobic training. E-mail: belleuis-leuinsight@msw.com. Home and Office: Belle-Isle Insight Cons Inc 2100 Parker Lawe Austin TX 78741

BELLEMARE, DAVID JOHN, architectural designer; b. Waterbury, Conn., Dec. 25, 1960; s. John Arthur and Lucille (Cianciolo) B. Student, Boston Archtl. Ctr., 1984-89. Drafter Monacelli Assocs., Inc., Cambridge, Mass., 1984-85; designer, drafter The Architects Group, Boston, 1986-89; fed. regulations coord. John Errichetti Assocs., Waterbury, Conn., 1989—. Served with USMC, 1980-84. Mem. Boston Soc. Architects. Avocations: running, football, movies, cars, dancing. Home: 90 Frost Rd Waterbury CT 06705-2103 Office: John Errichetti Assocs 34 Prospect St Waterbury CT 06702-1310

BELLEMARE, EUGENE, member of parliament. MBA, U. Ottawa. Mem. of parliament House of Commons, Ottawa, Can., 1988—. Office: House of Commons, Consideration Bldg/Rm 650, Ottawa, ON Canada K1A0A6*

BELLENGER, GEORGE COLLIER, JR., physics educator; b. Gadsden, Ala., Oct. 15, 1926; s. George Collier Sr. and Corrie Anna (Sitz) B.; m. Anna Conwell Hubbard, July 4, 1959; children: Baily, George III, James Thomas. B in Indsl. Engring., Ga. Inst. of Tech., 1952. Constrn./indsl. engring. E.I. DuPont Co., Augusta, Ga., 1952-54, Richmond, Va., 1955-58; ops. rsch. E.I. DuPont Co., Wilmington, Del., 1958-63; group supr.-engring. E.I. DuPont Co., Chattanooga, 1963-65; sr. supr. systems E.I. DuPont Co., Wilmington, 1965-67; chief supr. E.I. DuPont Co., Deep Water, N.J., 1967-70; systems mgr. E.I. DuPont Co., Wilmington, 1970-78, mgr. project devel., 1978-87; math/physics educator Wilmington Coll., New Castle, Del., 1987-91; chair gen. studies divsn. Wilmington Coll., New Castle, 1991—, chair faculty senate, 1998—. PTA pres. Mt. Pleasant Sch. Dist., Wilmington, 1972-76; commr. North Brandywine Youth Baseball, Wilmington, 1974-77; head coach Mt. Pleasant Youth Football, Wilmington, 1977-79. Lt. U.S. Army, 1944-47. Mem. Rotary Internat. (pres. 1983-84, Paul Harris fellow 1987), Nat. Norwich/Norfolk Terrier Assn. (pres. 1993-96), Army and Navy Club, Phi Delta Theta. Achievements include rsch. on a micro/macro production and inventory system based on a stochastic deterministic, partial differential set of equations, a manufacturing capacity expansion plan based on combining a unique LP model and computer simulation methods. Home: PO Box 449 Unionville PA 19375-0449 Office: Wilmington Coll 320 Dupont New Castle DE 19720

BELLER, DANIEL J., lawyer; b. N.Y.C., Aug. 4, 1946. BA, Harvard U., 1968; JD, Yale U., 1972. Bar: N.Y. 1973, U.S. Dist. Ct. (so. and ea. dists.) N.Y. 1978, D.C. 1984, U.S. Supreme Ct. 1987. Law clk. to Hon. Irving R. Kaufman U.S. Ct. Appeals (2nd cir.) N.Y., 1972-73; asst. U.S. atty. U.S. Dist. Ct. (so. dist.) N.Y., 1974-78, chief major crimes unit, 1977-79; ptnr. Paul, Weiss, Rifkind, Wharton & Garrison, N.Y.C. Fellow Am. Coll. of Trial Lawyers; mem. Fed. Bar Coun., Assn. Bar City N.Y., D.C. Bar, N.Y. Criminal Def. Lawyers Assn., Anti-Defamation League (co-chair lawyer's divsn.). Office: Paul Weiss Rifkind Wharton & Garrison Ste 2-c 1285 Avenue Of The Americas Fl 21 New York NY 10019-6065

BELLER, GARY A., lawyer, insurance company executive; b. N.Y.C., Oct. 16, 1938; s. Charles W. and Jeanne A. B.; m. Carole P. Wrubel, Nov. 22, 1967; 1 child, Jessie Melissa. BA, Cornell U., 1960; LLB, NYU, 1963, LLM, 1971. Bar: N.Y. 1963. Various positions gen. counsel's office Am. Express Co., N.Y.C., 1968-82, exec. v.p. and gen. counsel, 1983-94; exec. v.p., chief legal officer Met. Life Ins. Co., N.Y.C., 1995—. Bd. dirs. Lenox Hill Neighborhood Assn.; bd. dirs., chmn. Citizens' Crime Commn. N.Y. Mem. ABA, Assn. Bar City N.Y. Office: Met Life Ins Co 1 Madison Ave Ste 10A New York NY 10010-3642*

BELLER, GEORGE ALLAN, medical educator; b. N.Y.C., 1940. MD, U. Va., 1966. Diplomate Am. Bd. Internal Medicine. Intern U. Wis. Hosp., Madison, 1966-67, resident, 1967-68; resident in medicine Boston Med. Svc., 1968-69; fellow in cardiology Thorndike Meml. Lab. Harvard Med. Unit/Boston City Hosp., 1969-70; mem. staff cardiac unit Mass. Gen. Hosp., Boston, 1973-77; instr. medicine Harvard U., Boston, 1974-75, asst. prof., 1975; prof. medicine U. Va., Charlottesville, 1977—, head div. cardiology, 1977—, vice-chmn. dept. of medicine, 1997—. Maj. M.C., U.S. Army, 1970-73. Mem. Am. Soc. Clin. Investigation, Am. Fedn. Clin. Rsch., Assn. Am. Physicians, Am. Coll. Cardiology (chmn. bd. govs. 1994-95, pres.-elect 1998—), Assn. Profs. Cardiology (pres. 1995). Office: U Va Med Ctr Box 158 Dept of Cardiology Charlottesville VA 22908-0158

BELLER, GERALD STEPHEN, professional magician, former insurance company executive; b. Phila., Aug. 6, 1935; s. Nathan and Adelaide B. (Goldfarb) B.; m. Nancy R. Nelson, June 8, 1968; children: Fay A., Mark S., Royce W., Merrilee A., Marie A., Frank A. CLU, Am. Coll., Bryn Mawr, Pa., 1972. Spl. agt. Prudential Ins. Co., San Bernardino, Calif., 1959-62, div. mgr., 1962-66; agy. supr. Aetna Life & Casualty, L.A., 1966-69, gen. agt., 1969-77; rsch. analyst Investigative Svcs. Bur. San Bernadino County Sheriff's Dept., 1991-95; capt. specialized svcs. bur. San Bernardino County (Calif.) Sheriff's Dept.; profl. magician, 1982—; mem. Magician Magic Castle, Hollywood, Calif. mem. sheriff's coun. San Bernardino County Sheriff's Dept., Apple Valley sheriff's adv. bd. Served with USAF, 1953-57. Recipient Man of Year award, 1961; Manpower Builders award, 1966-69; Agy. Builders award, 1970-72; Pres.'s Trophy award, 1973-74. Mem. Am. Soc. CLUs, Golden Key Soc., Internat. Exec. Svc. Corps. (vol.), Acad. Magical Arts, Internat. Brotherhood of Magicians (Outstanding Magic Lectr. of Yr. 1989-90, Aldini Meml. award 1990), Soc. Am. Magicians. Home: 20625 Tonawanda Rd Apple Valley CA 92307-5736

BELLER, HERBERT N., lawyer; b. Ill., 1943. BSBA, Northwestern U., 1964, JD cum laude, 1967. Bar: Ill. 1967, D.C. 1969; CPA, Ill. Law clk. to Hon. Theodore Tannenwald, Jr. U.S. Tax Ct., 1967-68; ptnr. Sutherland, Asbill & Brennan, Washington; adj. prof. law Georgetown U., Washington, 1972-81. Editor-in-chief: The Tax Lawyer, 1993-96. Mem. ABA (mem. sect. taxation, vice chair 1993-96, mem. coun. 1989-92, liaison to Am. Law Inst. fed. income tax project on integration of individual and corp. income taxes 1990—, chmn. govt. submissions com. 1988-89, chmn. closely held corps. com. 1981-83), Am. Coll. Tax Counsel, D.C. Bar Assn., Ill. State Bar Assn. Office: Sutherland Asbill & Brennan LLP 1275 Pennsylvania Ave NW Washington DC 20004

BELLER, LUANNE EVELYN, accountant; b. Ft. Dodge, Iowa, Feb. 5, 1950; d. Gerald L. and Evelyn E. (Liston) Heyl; m. Stephen M. Beller, June 28, 1970; children: Clancy Dee, Corby Lu. BA, Oreg. State U., 1977; MBA, Rochester Inst. Tech., 1981. CPA, Ill. Plant acct. DuBois Plastic Products, Avon, N.Y., 1977-79; coll. acct. SUNY, Geneseo, 1979-81; gen. acctg. supr. M&M/Mars, Inc., Cleveland, Tenn., 1981-83, Hackettstown, N.J., 1983-84; sales rep. M&M/Mars, Inc., Jacksonville, Ill., 1984-86, terr. sales supr., 1986-88; gen. acctg. coord. Kal Kan Foods, Inc., Columbus, Ohio, 1988-90, fin. info. coord., 1990-92, gen. acctg. supr., 1992-97; site svc. and fin. supr. Kal Kan Foods, Inc., Columbus, 1997—. Vol. Girl Scouts U.S.A., Jacksonville, 1985-88, Bexley, Ohio, 1988—; mem. edn. com., chmn, 1998—, mem. sound control com. Bexley United Meth. Ch., 1989—, Sunday Sch. tchr., 1996—, LOGOS vol., 1996—. Mem. Inst. Mgmt. Accts., Phi Kappa Phi, Beta Gamma Sigma, Beta Alpha Psi. Democrat. Avocations: children, pets, reading.

BELLER, MARTIN LEONARD, retired orthopaedic surgeon; b. N.Y.C., Apr. 30, 1924; s. Abraham Jacob and Ida (Fishkin) B.; m. Wilma Gertrude Kjelgaard, June 29, 1947; children: Alan Lewis, Beatrice Ann Beller Foreman Heck, Peter James. AB with honors, Columbia U., 1944, MD, 1946. Diplomate Am. Bd. Orthopaedic Surgery. Intern Mt. Sinai Hosp., N.Y.C., 1946-47; resident in orthopaedic surgery Hosp. Joint Diseases, N.Y.C., 1949-52; pvt. practice Phila., 1952-87; asst. prof. orthopaedic surgery U. Pa. Sch. Medicine, Phila., 1967-72; assoc. prof. U. Pa. Sch. Medicine, 1972-80, clin. prof., 1980-87; attending orthopaedic surgeon Hosp. U. Pa., 1963-87; assoc. attending orthopaedic surgeon Albert Einstein Med. Center, Phila., 1960-70; chmn. dept. orthopaedic surgery Albert Einstein Med. Center (Daroff divsn.), 1970-79. Author: (with I. Stein and R. O. Stein) Living Bone in Health and Disease, 1955, (with I. Stein) Clinical Densitometry of Bone, 1970. Vestryman Episcopal Ch., 1966-87, 90-93, 96-99; trustee St. Paul's Episcopal Ch., Wellsboro, Pa., 1999—. Capt. M.C., AUS, 1947-49. Am. Orthopaedic Assn. exchange fellow Gt. Britain, 1963. Fellow ACS, Am. Acad. Orthopaedic Surgeons (bd. councilors 1978-81, Pa. rep. commn. on trauma 1984-87), Internat. Soc. Orthopaedic Surgery and Traumatology; mem. Am. Orthopaedic Assn., Pa. Orthopaedic Soc. (pres. 1975-77), Orthopaedic Rsch. Soc., Am. Coll. Rheumatology, N.Y. Acad. Sci., Phi Beta Kappa, Alpha Omega Alpha, Phi Delta Epsilon (nat. pres. 1975-76, chmn. bd. trustees 1984-85, assoc. exec. sec. 1991-95, exec. com. 1995—). Republican. Home: RR 1 Box 256-B Gaines PA 16921-9768

BELLER, MELANIE, federal agency administrator; b. Feb. 23, 1959. BA, U. Kans., 1981, MPA. Legis. intern U.S. Rep. Dan Glockman, Washington, 1982-83; sr. legis. asst. U.S. Sen. Harry Reid, Washington, 1986-89; legis. dir. U.S. Rep. Richard Lehman, Washington, 1989-91; staff dir. House Interior Com. Gen. Oversight & Calif. Desert Lands, Washington, 1991-93, House Natural Resources (formerly Interior), Washington, 1993; deputy dir. Congrl. Legis. Affairs, Office of Sec. Dept. Interior, Washington, 1993-94, asst. to sec. & dir., 1994—. Office: Dept of Interior 1849 C St NW Washington DC 20240-0002

BELLER, MICHAEL, epidemiologist; b. L.A., Dec. 25, 1950; s. George and Anne B. BA, U. Calif., 1973; MD, McGill U., 1982; MPH, U. Calif., Berkeley, 1986. Epidemic intelligence svc. officer U.S. Ctrs. Disease Control & Prevention, Atlanta, 1987-89; county health officer Washington County, Hillsboro, Oreg., 1989-90; epidemiologist State of Alaska, Anchorage, 1991—. Contbr. articles to profl. jours. With USPHS, 1987-89. Office: Sect Epidemiology POB 240249 Anchorage AK 99524

BELLER, STEPHEN MARK, university administrator; b. Chgo., Aug. 14, 1948; s. I.E. and De Vera (Jameson) B.; m. Luanne Evelyn Heyl, June 28, 1970; children: Clancy Dee, Corby Lu. BS, U. Ill., 1970; MS, Western Ill. U., 1972; PhD, Oregon State U., 1977. Asst. head ed. Awards of Rotary Found., Evanston, Ill., 1972-73; asst. dean of students SUNY, Geneseo, N.Y., 1977-81; dean of student svcs. Tenn. Wesleyan Coll., Athens, 1981-83, MacMurray Coll., Jacksonville, Ill., 1984-88, Capital U., Columbus, Ohio, 1988—. Mem. Nat. Assn. Student Pers. Adminstrs., Am. Coll. Personnel Assn., Assn. of Student Jud. Affairs, Ohio Coll. Pers. Assn., Phi Kappa Phi, Phi Delta Kappa. Methodist. Avocations: railroading, photography. Home: 2474 Seneca Park Pl Bexley OH 43209-1750 Office: Capital U 2199 E Main St Columbus OH 43209-2394

BELLES, CHRISTINE FUGIEL, office administration educator; b. Hamtramck, Mich., Sept. 6, 1945; d. Ted and Theresa (Ellman) Fugiel; m. Duane Allen Belles, Aug. 10, 1973; children: Douglas, Michael. BA, Mich. State U., 1967, MA, 1970. Clk. Warren Schs. Credit Union, Centerline, Mich., 1963; sec. to dean of students Mich. State U., East Lansing, 1964-67, Consumers Power Co., East Detroit, 1964-65; key punch oper. Fisher Body div. GMC, Warren, Mich., 1966, sec., 1967, 69; legal sec. Rollins, Genser and White, Detroit, 1974; tchr. Lakeview High Sch., St. Clair Shores, Mich., 1967-73; prof. bus. info. sys. Macomb Community Coll., Warren, 1973—, cert. profl. sec., 1974—, prof. bus. info. syss.; exam. proctor Profl. Secs. Internat., 1983-89. Recipient Excellence in Teaching award, 1993. Mem. Nat. Bus. Edn. Assn., Delta Pi Epsilon, Pi Omega Pi. Avocations: piano, knitting, reading. Office: Macomb Community Coll 14500 E 12 Mile Rd Warren MI 48093-3870

BELLES, DONALD ARNOLD, pastoral therapist, mental health counselor; b. Sayre, Pa., Mar. 7, 1948; s. William and Alice (Arnold) B.; m. Linda Scheel, July 9, 1981. BA, St. Martin's U., 1973; MDiv, Fuller Theol. Sem., 1977; PhD, Calif. Grad. Sch. Theology, 1981; MBA, City U. Bellevue, 1994; postgrad., Seattle Pacific U., 1997—. Lic. amateur radio operator; ordained to ministry Worldwide Congl. Fellowship, 1989; cert. c.c. tchr., Calif., mental health counselor, Wash., profl. stage hypnotist. Chaplain Vols. of Am., L.A., 1976-78; therapist Greater life Found., Seattle, 1979-81; industrial engr. commercial airplane divsn. Boeing, 1979-80, program planner aerospace divsn., 1980-86, sr., lead program planner electronics divsn., 1986-89, systems analyst, contract tech. mgr., 1989-92, analyst software engring. practices, mgr. total quality improvement project, 1992-95, lead, mgr. computing infrastructure archtl. design team, 1995—, mgr. computing infrastructure design, 1996-97; therapist, dir. clinic Creative Therapies, Seattle, 1982-83; clin. dir. Applied Hypnosis, Tacoma, 1984-87; dir. Active Therapy Assoc., Tacoma, 1988-89; dean of students Coll. Therapeutic Hypnosis, Puyallup, Wash., 1989-93; cons. theological issues, abduction rsch., psychic phenomena, paranormal events; adult edn. instr. Tacoma C.C., 1987-88, Pierce Coll., 1990-92; mem. U.S. Acad. Team to CIS, U. St. Petersburg, Russia, 1994; presenter, lectr. in field; instr. Olympia Diocese Sch. of Theology, 1995; adv. bd. mem. Software Support Profls. Orgn.; cons. Wash. State Offices Supr. of Pub. Instrn. Contbr. articles to profl. jours., prodr. hypnosis, mental health videos in field. Exec. dir. Nat. Assn. to Prevent and Eliminate Child Abuse, Tacoma, 1987-89. Maj. U.S. Army, 1969-75, USAR, 1975-92. Fellow Am. Assn. Profl. Hypnotherapists; mem. Nat. Assn. Clergy Hypnotherapists (bd. dirs. 1987-88, editor jour. 1987), Internat. Med. Dental Hypnotherapy Assn., Wash. State Head Injury Found. Avocations: backpacking, swimming, reading, amateur radio.

BELLES, MARTIN RUSSEL, manufacturing engineer; b. Ft. Wayne, Ind., Sept. 4, 1952; s. Russel Elwin and Irene (Crossley) B. Student, U. Calif., Berkeley; BS in Computer Sci., Armstrong Atlantic State U., Savannah, Ga., 1999. Aircraft assembler Rockwell Internat., Bethany, Okla., 1974-83; process planner Gulfstream Aerospace, Bethany, 1984-85; mfg. engr. Gulfstream Aerospace, Savannah, 1985—. Contbg. author: Stupid Windows Tricks, 1992. Mem. Ga. Hist. Soc., Historic Savannah Found., Telfair Acad. of Arts and Scis. Mem. IEEE, Assn. Computing Machinery, Epsilon Data Pi, Upsilon Pi Epsilon. Avocation: computer programming. Office: Gulfstream Aerospace 500 Gulfstream Rd Savannah GA 31407-9643

BELLEVILLE, PHILIP FREDERICK, lawyer; b. Flint, Mich., Apr. 24, 1934; s. Frederick Charles and Sarah (Adelaine) B.; m. Geraldean Bickford, Sept. 2, 1953; children—Stacy L., Philip Frederick II, Jeffrey A. BA in Econs. with high distinction and honors, U. Mich., 1956, J.D., 1960. Bar: Calif. 1961. Assoc. Latham & Watkins, LA., 1960-68; ptnr. Latham & Watkins, L.A. and Newport Beach, Calif., 1968-98; ptnr., chmn. litigation dept. Latham & Watkins, L.A. and Newport Beach, 1973-80; ptnr. Latham & Watkins, L.A., Newport Beach, San Diego, Washington, 1980—, Chgo., 1983—, N.Y.C., 1985—, London and San Francisco, 1990—, Moscow, 1992—, Hong Kong, 1995—, Tokyo, 1995—, Singapore, 1997—, Silicon Valley, 1997—. Asst. editor Mich. Law Rev., Ann Arbor, 1959-60. Past mem. So. Calif. steering com. NAACP Legal Def. Fund, Inc., L.A.; mem. cmty. adv. bd. San Pedro Peninsula Hosp., Calif., 1980-88. James B. Angell scholar U. Mich., 1955-56. Mem. ABA (antitrust and trade regulation and bus. law sects.), L.A. County Bar Assn. (bus. trial lawyers sect.), Assn. Bus. Trial Lawyers, Order of Coif, Portuguese Bend (Calif.) Club, Palos Verdes (Calif.) Golf Club, Caballeros, Phi Beta Kappa, Phi Kappa Phi, Alpha Kappa Psi. Republican. Avocations: antique and classic autos, public service, sports, art, antiques. Office: Latham & Watkins 633 W 5th St Ste 4000 Los Angeles CA 90071-2005

BELLIN, HARVEY FORREST, television producer, director; b. New Haven, Apr. 25, 1944; s. Milton and Ida M. (Slutsky) B. BA, Yale U., 1966, MFA in directing, 1969. Pres. The Media Group of Conn., Inc., Weston, 1974—, Instructional Media Inst., Inc., Weston, 1989—; project dir. 5 U.S. dept. edn. nationally disseminated drug and alcohol abuse prevention tng. videos. Co-producer, dir. (documentary): Ancient Moderns: Greek Island Art 3,000-2,000 B.C. (PBS TV series) The Shakespear Hour hosted by Walter Matthau, 1985-86; co-producer, dir. (TV docu-drama) Blake (Gold medal 1984); overseas producer Big Blue Marble (Emmy 1975, 76); writer, dir. (documentaries) Bali Mask of Rangda, Sacred Trances of Java and Bali, 1972-74; co-producer, dir. (indsl.) Worlds of Pepsico (Silver medal 1985); co-producer Pepsi-Soviet Partnership Video, 1990, Disney's World of English. *. Dir. Weston Bicentennial Video Program (Emmy 1987); treas. Weston Dem. Town Com., 1986—, acting chmn., 1992, vice chmn., 1993-97, chmn., 1998—; super-coord. Conn. Clinton/Gore campaign, 1992; campaign coord. Lieberman U.S. Senate, 1994. Recipient Emmy award for outstanding dir.

NATAS, 1989. Avocations: visual arts, kung fu, politics. Office: Media Group of Conn Inc 7 Maple St Weston CT 06883-1026

BELLIN, HOWARD THEODORE, plastic surgeon; b. N.Y.C., Apr. 8, 1936; s. Maurice and Etta (Rosenbloom) B.; m. Christina Paolozzi, Oct. 27, 1964 (dec. Apr. 27, 1988); children: Marco, Andy. BA, Amherst Coll., 1957; MD, N.Y. Med. Coll., 1962. Diplomate Am. Bd. Plastic Surgery. Intern U. Calif. Hosp., San Francisco, 1962-63; resident Met. Hosp., N.Y.C., 1963-66; resident in plastic surgery Columbia Presbyn. Med. Ctr., N.Y.C., 1968-70; instr. in surgery Columbia Coll. Physicians and Surgeons, N.Y.C., 1968-70; asst. clin. prof. surgery N.Y. Med. Coll., N.Y.C., 1970-84, asst. clin. prof. dermatology, 1975-83; chief plastic surbery Cabrini Med. Ctr., N.Y.C., 1973-80; pres. Cosmedica Plastic Surgery Ctr., N.Y.C., 1980—; pres. Cortec, Inc., N.Y.C., 1983—, Life Signs, Inc., N.Y.C., 1989—, Motor Vehicle Protection Systems, Inc., N.Y.C., 1993—, also chmn. bd.; bd. dirs. Novamed, Inc.; mem. sci. adv. com. Inst. for Ecosystem Studies, 1998—. Author: Dr. Bellin's Beautiful You Book, 1981; patentee on cardiac monitoring system, 1991, portable EKG monitoring device, 1985, system for subliminal signals, 1992, systems for cancellation...artifacts, 1992, auto theft prevention system, 1995, patient monitor sheets, 1995, automobile security device, 1998. Capt. USAF, 1966-68. Fellow N.Y. Acad. Medicine; mem. AAAS, Am. Soc. Plastic and Reconstrv. Surgeons, Explorers Club (nominating com. 1985). Avocations: auto racing, helicopter flying, archaeology, computer programming. Office: Cosmedica 105 E 73rd St New York NY 10021-3502

BELLINGER, EDGAR THOMSON, lawyer; b. N.Y.C., Sept. 23, 1929; s. John and Margaret (Thomson) B.; children from previous marriage: Edgar Jr., Robert, Margaret; m. Ann Clark, Feb. 25, 1989. BA, Haverford Coll., 1951; JD with honors, George Washington U., 1955. Bar: D.C. 1955, Md. 1955. Law clk. to chief judge U.S. Dist. Ct. D.C., 1955-57; asst. U.S. atty. for Washington, 1957-59; ptnr. Pope, Ballard & Loos, Washington, 1959-81, Zuckert, Scoutt and Rasenberger, Washington, 1981-94; ptnr. Bellinger & Assocs., Washington and Md., 1995—; chmn. unauthorized practice com. D.C. Ct. Appeals, 1972-78; mem. D.C. jud. conf., 1972-90; bd. mgrs. Chevy Chase Village, 1983-86. Mem. ABA, D.C. Bar Assn. (D.C. Ct. Appeals orgn. com. 1972), Md. Bar Assn., Talbot County Bar Assn., Am. Arbitration Assn. (panel of arbitrators), Nat. Assn. Securities Dealers (panel of arbitrators), Met. Club, Chevy Chase Club (bd. govs. 1972-77, pres. 1976-77), Barristers. Home: 27497 West Point Rd Easton MD 21601-8439 Office: 888 17th St NW Washington DC 20006-3939 also: PO Box 739 Easton MD 21601-0739

BELLINGER, MARK F., urology educator; b. Syracuse, N.Y., Apr. 20, 1948; s. Richard F. and Nancy K. Bellinger; m. Catherine Irene Mahardy, June 14, 1969; children: Deborah, Michael, Todd, Karen. BS, Lemoyne Coll., 1970; MD, SUNY, Syracuse, 1974. Surg. intern Med. Coll. Va., Richmond, 1974-75, resident in surgery, 1975-76, resident in urology, 1976-79; fellow in pediatric urology Children's Hosp., Phila., 1979-80; asst. prof. Pa. State U. M.S. Hershey Med. Ctr., 1980-85; prof. dept. pediatric urology U. Pitts., 1985—. Fellow Am. Acad. Pediat.; mem. Am. Urol. Assn. Northeastern Sect. Am. Urol. Assn. (sec. 1997—). Avocation: rowing. E-mail: markbell @pitt.edu. Office: U Pitts Dept Pediatric Urology 125 Desoto St Pittsburgh PA 15213-2583

BELLINGER, PATRICIA MCHUGH, oncology and adult nurse practitioner; b. Scotland, Mar. 20, 1940; d. Patrick and Margaret Kathleen (Docherty) McHugh; m. David L. Bellinger, July 27, 1962; children: Tania K., David M. Diploma, Knightswood Hosp. Sch. Nursing, Glasgow, 1960; student, U. St. Thomas, Houston, 1985; BSN, U. Tex., Houston, 1987, MSN, 1994. RN, Tex.; oncology cert. nurse; cert. clin. nurse specialist, advanced nurse practitioner. Staff oncology nurse, med.-surg. Princess Margaret Hosp., Toronto, 1962-64, pediatric nurse, 1964-66; staff nurse Kelsey-Seybold Clinic, Houston, 1966-78, Houston Allergy Clinic, 1980-85; staff nurse med. and cardiac intermediate care units Hermann Hosp., Houston, 1987-90, rsch. clinician radiotherapy, 1992; rsch. clinician radiotherapy M.D. Anderson Cancer Ctr., 1992-95; Adult Nurse Practitioner, clinic mgr. Tex. Med. Ctr. Baylor Coll. of Med., Houston, Tex., 1996—. Mem. AACCN, AAUW, ANA, Tex. Nurses Assn., U. Tex. at Houston Alumni Assn., Sigma Theta Tau. E-mail: mpb@bcm.tmc.edu. Home: 11303 Bexley Dr Houston TX 77099-1650

BELLIOTTI, RAYMOND ANGELO, philosopher, educator, lawyer; b. Dansville, NY, June 17, 1948; s. Angelo Richard and Louise Mary (Leonardo) B.; m. Marcia Helen Dalby, May 31, 1986; children: Angelo, Vittoria. BA, Union Coll., 1970; MA, U. Miami, 1976, PhD, 1977; JD, Harvard U., 1982. Bar: N.Y. 1983. Asst. prof. Va. Commonwealth U., Richmond, Va., 1978-79; lawyer Barrett Smith Schapiro Simon & Armstrong, N.Y.C., 1982-84; prof. SUNY, Fredonia, 1984—. Author: Justifying Law, 1992, Good Sex, 1993, Seeking Identity, 1995, Stalking Nietzsche, 1998. Chmn. Chautauqua Italian Am. Orgn., Fredonia, 1986—. Mem. Nat. Italian Am. Found., Nat. Italian Am. Hist. Soc., Am. Soc. Legal Philosophers, Am. Philos. Assn., Chautauqua Italian Am. Soc. (cultural chair 1986). Democrat. Roman Catholic. Avocations: running, softball, basketball. Home: 104 Central Ave Fredonia NY 14063-1308 Office: SUNY Fredonia Dept Philos Fenton 2109 Fredonia NY 14063

BELLIS, ARTHUR ALBERT, financial executive, government official; b. Worcester, Mass., June 16, 1928; s. Frank Clayton and Ruth Porter (Gordon) B.; m. Barbara Swift, Feb. 22, 1952 (div. 1969); children: Bradford, Susan; m. E. Deborah Shea, May 28, 1972 (div. 1997); children: Cynthia, Michael. BSBA, Boston U., 1952. Asst. credit mgr. Procter & Gamble, N.Y.C., 1955-56; asst. supr. capital budget Western Union, N.Y.C., 1956-58; corp. budget analyst CBS, N.Y.C., 1958-64; account exec. Edwards & Hanley, N.Y.C., 1964-66, Spencer Trask, Worcester, 1966-70; sr. securities compliance examiner SEC, Boston, 1970-90; retired, 1990; treas., CFO, chief compliance officer Burlington Securities Corp., Chatham, Mass., 1993-97. Advisor Explorer program Mohegan council Boy Scouts Am., 1966-70; mem. Worcester Rep. Com., 1952-53, Rep. Presdl. Task Force, 1984-85; mem. fin. com. Town of Yarmouth, 1982-86; v.p. Sheriff's Cmty. Patrol, 1997. Recipient Superior Performance award SEC, 1976, 1986; Medal of Merit, Pres. of U.S., 1985. Mem. Internat. Platform Assn., Masons (treas. Howard lodge 1988-91, trustee 1992-97). Roman Catholic. Avocations: flying, hiking, camping. Address: Lot #32 9701 E Highway 25 Belleview FL 34420-7436

BELLISARIO, DOMENIC ANTHONY, lawyer; b. Pitts., May 14, 1953; s. Domenic and Mary (Murgia) B.; m. Barbara Marie Johns, May 25, 1990. BA, U. Pitts., 1975, JD, 1978. Bar: Pa. 1978; U.S. Dist. Ct. (we. dist.) Pa., 1978; U.S. Ct. Appeals (3d cir.) 1985. Trial atty. Nat. Labor Rels. Bd., Pitts., 1978-83; human resource counsel Western Res. Care Sys., Youngstown, Ohio, 1986-89; ptnr. Bellisario & Pontier, Pitts., 1984-90; pvt. practice Pitts., 1991—. Author: Preventing and Defending Sexual Harassment Claims in Pennsylvania, 1996, Basic Wage and Hour Law in Pennsylvania, 1997. Mem. coun. Nat. Italian Am. Found., Washington, 1991. Mem. ABA, Pa. Bar Assn., Allegheny County Bar Assn., Pa. Trial Lawyers Assn., Italian Cultural Heritage Soc. West Pa. Avocations: travel, skiing. Office: 1000 Law & Finance Bldg Pittsburgh PA 15219

BELLISARIO, DONALD P., TV writer, director, producer; b. Cokeburg, Pa., Aug. 8, 1935; s. Albert and Dana (Lapcevic) B.; m. Vivienne Lee, Nov. 27, 1998; 7 children. TV dir., writer, prodr. series Black Sheep Squadron (also known as Baa Baa Black Sheep), 1977-78; writer, exec. prodr. series Quincy, M.E., 1978; dir., supervising prodr. co-author series Battlestar Galactica, 1978-79; creator (with Glen A. Larson), dir., writer, exec. prodr. series Magnum, P.I., 1980-88 (Emmy award nomination outstanding drama series 1981, 82, Edgar Allen Poe award Mystery Writers Am. best tv series episode China Doll 1981); exec. prodr. (with Stephen J. Cannell), writer series Stone, 1980; creator, exec. prodr., writer Tales of the Gold Monkey, 1982-83; creator, dir., exec. prodr., writer series Quantum Leap, 1989-93 (Emmy award nominations outstanding drama series 1989, 90, Writers Guild Am. award nomination best tv episode 1991), Tequila and Bonetti (also known as Tequila and Boner), 1992; TV pilots: Magnum, P.I., 1980, Tales of the Gold Monkey, 1982, Airwolf, 1983, Quantum Leap, 1989, Tequila and Bonetti, 1992; TV movies: creator, dir., exec. prodr. Three on a Match, 1987; screenwriter, dir., exec. prodr. (film) Last Rites, 1988; TV series writer Kojak, 1973, Airwolf, 1984; creator, exec. producer, writer TV series JAG, dir. pilot JAG, 1995. Roman Catholic. Office: care Norman Kurland Broder Kurland Webb Uffner 9242 Beverly Blvd Ste 200 Beverly Hills CA 90210-3731 Address: Belisarius Prodns 5555 Melrose Bow Bldg #204 Los Angeles CA 90038

BELLIVEAU, GERARD JOSEPH, JR., librarian; b. Waltham, Mass., May 27, 1940; s. Gerard Joseph and Mary Teresa (Reilly) B. BA in English Lit., Boston Coll., 1963; MA in Philosophy, Boston U., 1972; MLS in Libr. Svc., Rutgers U., 1973. Lectr. U. Rouen (France), 1965-66; philosophy bibliographer Boston Pub. Libr., Boston, 1967-68; asst. libr. Racquet & Tennis Club: Libr. of Sport, N.Y.C., 1971-78, head libr., 1979—; libr. gen. rsch. div. N.Y. Pub. Libr., N.Y.C., 1973-79, libr. in charge gen. rsch. div., 1980-81, asst. chief pub. catalog sect. gen. rsch. div., 1981-88, asst. chief libr. gen. rsch. div., 1988-95; mem. coop. acquisitions program com. METRO Ref. and Rsch. Libr. Agy., N.Y.C., 1984-88, chair coop. acquisitions program com., 1985-86, mem. resources devel. com., 1986-89. Bd. dirs. Peabody-Mason Music Found., Boston, 1972-87. Mem. Williams Club. Democrat. Avocations: architecture, travel, French medieval history. Office: Racquet & Tennis Club Libr 370 Park Ave New York NY 10022-5968

BELLM, JOAN, civic worker; b. Alton, Ill., June 20, 1934; d. Harvey Jacob and Alma Lorene (Roberts) Goldsby; m. Earl David Bellm, Oct. 1, 1955; children: David, Lori, Michael. Bd. dirs. Drug Watch Internat., 1991-98, lifetime hon. dir., 1998—. Editor Best of IDEA newsletter, 1991-96, Drug Watch World News, 1996-98. Organist, dir. jr. choir St. Mary's Cath. Ch., 1958-78; mem. adv. bd. Carlinville (Ill.) Area Hosp., 1981-86; trustee Blackburn Coll., Carlinville, 1983-86; bd. dirs. Cath. Children's Home, Diocese of Springfield, Ill., 1986—; founder, bd. dirs., state networker Ill. Drug Edn. Alliance, 1982-86, pres., 1987-89; bd. dirs., nat. networker Nat. Fedn. Parents for Drug-Free Youth, Washington, 1984-86; mem. Ill. Gov.'s Adv. Coun. on Alcoholism and Substance Abuse, 1989-93; founder Drug Watch Internat., 1991, Internat. Drug Strategy Inst., 1993, invited participant Internat. Private Sector Conf. on Drugs, Seville, 1993, advisor U.N. Internat. Drug Ctrl. Program, 1994 ; numerous others. Recipient letter of endorsement Pres. of U.S., 1981, citation of recognition Ill. Dept., Am. Legion, 1981, Meritorious Svc. award, 1982, award Ill. Drug Edn. Alliance award, 1984, Southwestern Ill. Law Enforcement Commn., 1984, Carlinville Sch. Bd., 1985, Outstanding Svc. award Nat. Fedn. Parents, 1986, award Ill. Alcohol and Drug Dependence Assn., 1986, Optimist Internat., 1987, Ill. Drug Edn. Alliance, 1988, Outstanding Citizen award Blackburn U., 1989, Citizen of Yr. award, Carlinville, 1990. Home: PO Box 227 Carlinville IL 62626-0227

BELLMAN, MICHAEL STANLEY, forester, freelance writer; b. Wadena, Minn., Apr. 8, 1947; s. Stanley and Margaret (Hoffman) B.; m. Virginia Ann Arnold, June 21, 1969; children: William Michael, Matthew James. BS, U. Mont., 1969. Forester Bur. Land Mgmt., Salem, Oreg., 1969-74, Boise Cascade Corp., Monmouth, Oreg., 1974-79, Avison Lumber Co., Molalla, Oreg., 1979-98, Quality Veneer & Lumber, Lyons, Oreg., 1998—; editl. advisor Oreg. Fish and Wildlife Jour., 1988—. Columnist Molalla Pioneer, 1992-98, Itemizer Observer, 1994-98. Mem. Oreg. Writers Colony, Salem Writers and Pubs. (treas. 1995-96). Republican. Roman Catholic. Avocations: writing short stories, hunting, reading. Home: 5840 Basil St NE Salem OR 97301-3323

BELLMORE, LAWRENCE ROBERT, JR., financial planner; b. Flint, Mich., May 1, 1947; s. Lawrence R. and Vaneta O. (Wortz) B.; m. Patricia Antonopolos, Dec. 27, 1969; (div. 1973); 1 son, Lawrence Robert III; m. Susan Marie Thompson, Aug. 1979; children: Samuel Ryan, Stuart Logan; 1 stepchild, Stacy Marie Thompson. B.S. in Mech. Engring., Gen. Motors Inst., 1970; MBA, U. Pitts., 1987; postgrad., Widener U., 1996—. Cert. fin. planner. Engr. in tng. Gen. Motors Inst., Flint, Mich., 1969-70; dist. service and parts mgr. Detroit zone Buick Motor Div., Flint, Mich., 1970-72; mgr. fleet maintenance N.Am. Van Lines, Ft. Wayne, Ind., 1972-74, Eazor Express, Pitts., 1974-75; asst. br. mgr. Pullman Trailmobile, Inc., Jersey City, Pa., 1974-75; br. mgr. Pullman Trailmobile, Inc., Jersey City, N.J., 1976-77, Balt., 1977-79; pres. Lyco Truck Sales & Svc., Inc. and Lyco Leasing, Inc., Montoursville, Pa., 1979-81, L.R. Bellmore & Assocs., Montoursville, Pa., 1981—; registered rep. Waddell & Reed, Inc., 1981-84, FSC Securities Corp., 1984-87; nat. sales mgr. R. Dummont & Co., GMBH W.Ger. in U.S., 1982-84; mktg. dir. DKM Bldg. Enterprises, 1989-90, v.p. sales, 1990-92, v.p. adminstrn., corp. planning, 1993—; branch mgr. Am. Home Loans Mortgage Bankers, 1997—; founder LRBA Advisory Inc., Bus. Brokers, Mortgage Brokers & Investment Mgmt., 1987—; mng. exec. Integrated Resources Equity Corp., Montoursville, 1987-89; mktg. dir. Muncy Homes Inc.; mng. exec. Royal Alliance Assocs., 1989-99. Bd. dirs. Black Hawk Home Owners Assn., 1972-74. Mem. Internat. Assn. Cert. Fin. Planners, Full Gospel Bus. Men's Fellowship, Internat. Republican. Home: PO Box 157 604 S Main St Muncy PA 17756-1732 Office: L R Bellmore & Assocs 330 Pine St Williamsport PA 17701-6261

BELLO, JUDITH HIPPLER, lawyer; b. Alexandria, Va., May 31, 1949. BA in History summa cum laude, U. N.C., 1971; JD, Yale U., 1975. Bar: D.C. 1975. Office legal adviser Dept. State, Washington, 1977-82; dep. to dep. asst. Sec. Commerce for Import Adminstrn., Washington, 1982-84, from dep. gen. counsel to gen. counsel, U.S. trade rep. and chmn. Sect. 301 Com., 1985-89; ptnr. Sidley & Austin, Washington, 1989-96; exec. v.p. policy and strategic affairs Pharm. Rsch. and Mfrs. of Am., Washington, 1996—; lectr. internat. trade seminar Yale U., 1984-85, 85-86; mem. Pres. Commn. on Fed. Ethics Law Reform, 1989; mem. adv. bd. Corp. Counsel's Internat. Adviser, 1985—; adj. prof. Georgetown U. Law Ctr., 1989-90; mem. adv. com. Export-Import Bank, 1990-92. Author: (with Alan F. Holmer) The Antidumping and Countervail Duty Laws: Key Legal and Policy Issues, 1987, Guide to U.S.-Can. Free-Trade Agreement, 1990; editor: North American Free Trade Agreement, 1994; contbr. numerous articles to profl. jours. Mem. adv. coun. on pub. policy and edn. Brookings Inst.; mem. adv. bd. Maxwell Sch. Citizenship and Pub. Affairs Syracuse (N.Y.) U., 1993-98, G.W.J. Internat. Law and Econs., 1984-97, Georgetown J.L. & Poly Internat. Bus., 1993-97, also corporate counsel. Recipient Overall Excellence award D.C. Bar Com., 1985, Meritorious Pub. Svc. award USCG, 1978. Mem. ABA (internat. sect. co-chmn. trade com. 1986-90, couns. 1987-90), D.C. Bar (internat. sect., chmn. steering com. 1987-88; co-chmn. trade com. 1983-86), Am. Soc. Internat. Law (editl. adv. bd. 1982-89, coun. 1994-96), Washington Internat. Trade Assn., Coun. on Fgn. Rels., Phi Beta Kappa. Home: 1710 Chesterbrook Vale Ct Mc Lean VA 22101-3244 Office: PhRMA 1100 15th St NW Ste 900 Washington DC 20005-1763

BELLO, MARIA, actress; b. Norristown, Pa., Apr. 18, 1967. BS in Polit. Sci., Villanova U. Appeared in off-Broadway plays, including The Killer Inside Me, Small Town Gals with Big Problems, Urban Planning, After the Fact, Young Frankenstein; appeared in TV series, including ER, 1997—, The Commish, Misery Loves Company, Simon, Nowhere Man, Due South, Mr. and Mrs. Smith. Co-founder Dream Yard Drama Project for Kids, Harlem, N.Y.C. Office: Warner Bros TV Prodns c/o ER 4000 Warner Blvd Burbank CA 91522

BELLO, SHERE CAPPARELLA, foreign language educator; b. Norristown, Pa., Sept. 4, 1956; d. Anthony and Patsy (Robbins) Capparella. BA in Spanish and French, Rosemont (Pa.) Coll., 1978; BA in Mktg., Ursinus Coll., 1991; student, Institut Internat. D'Enseignement de la Langue Française, France, 1992, Escuela de Idiomas, Spain, 1992; MEd in Multicultural Edn., Eastern Coll., 1993; postgrad., 1994-97; ballet student, Novak and Kovalska; Spanish flamenco/castanet student, José Greco; dance student, Harrisburg Dance Conservatory; postgrad., 1994—. Cert. in French/Spanish. Salesperson Spectrum Communications Corp., Norristown, 1977-79, sales and mktg. mgr., 1986-87; asst. sales and adminstrv. asst. Tettex Instruments, Inc., Fairview Village, Pa., 1979-83; owner, instr. Shere's World of Dance and Fine Arts, Jeffersonville, Pa., 1982-88; multilingual adminstrv. asst. Syntex Dental Products, Inc., Valley Forge, 1984-86; v.p. Captrium Devel. Corp., Exton, Pa., 1987-89; cons. Mary Kay Cosmetics, 1988-96; sales mgr. Spectrum Communications, 1989-92; tchr. Spanish and French Middletown (Pa.) Area Sch. Dist., 1992-94; adj. prof. Spanish Messiah Coll., Grantham, Pa., 1996—; market rsch. analyst Capital Health Sys., Harrisburg, Pa., 1995; Spanish and French tchr. Elizabethtown (Pa.) Area Sch. Dist., 1996-97; Spanish, French, and German tchr. The Milton Hershey Sch., 1997-98; fgn. lang. rep. United Concordia Cos., Inc.; v.p. La Bella Modeling Agy., Collegeville, Pa., 1979-82; choreographer and dance instr. La Bella Sch. Performance, Collegeville, 1979-82. Judge state and nat. pageants Miss Am. Scholarship, Jr. Miss. Nat. Teen and Pre-Teen, All-Am. Talent, Ofcl. Little Miss Am., Little Miss Diamond, Talent Olympics, Talent Unltd., 1979—; producer, choreographer Miss Montgomery County Pageant, Plymouth Meeting, Pa., 1985; co-producer, choreographer Miss Del. Valley Pageant, Horsham, Pa., 1983-84; confraternity Christian Doctrine kindergarten tchr. Visitation Parish, 1987-88. Recipient award Internat. Leaders in Achievement, 1989, Community Leaders of Am., 1989. Mem. ASTD, Am. Coun. Tchrs. Fgn. Langs., Am. Assn. Tchrs. French, Pa. State MLA, Pa. State Edn. Assn., Christian Children's Fund, Am. Assn. Tchrs. Spanish, Kappa Delta Pi. Roman Catholic. Avocations: health and fitness, travel, ballroom and Latin dance, fashion, historical home restoration. Home: 4700 Cumberland St Harrisburg PA 17111-2725

BELLOCK, PATRICIA RIGNEY, state legislator; b. Chgo., Oct. 14, 1946; d. John Dungan and Dorothy (Comiskey) Rigney; m. Charles Joseph Bellock, Nov. 8, 1969; children: Colleen, Dorothy. BA, St. Norbert Coll., 1968. With customer rels. 3M Corp., Chgo., 1968-69; tchr. jr. h.s. Milw. and Fairbanks, Alaska, 1970-72; v.p. sports corps. Dor-Mor-Pat Corp., River Forest, Ill., 1976-84; mem. DuPage County Bd. from Dist. 3, Wheaton, Ill., 1992-98, Ill. Ho. of Reps., Springfield, 1999—; asst. treas. DuPage County Forest Preserve Dist. Mem. sch. bd. St. Isaac Jogues Sch., Hinsdale, Ill., 1989-91; bd. dirs. Hinsdale Cmty. House, 1987-89, U. Ill. Gerontology Rsch., 1988-91, Hinsdale Youth Ctr., 1987-90, DuPage County Bd. Health, Wheaton, 1990—, Care and Counseling Ctr., Downers Grove, 1977—, pres., 1986-89. Recipient award Ill. Health Dept., 1992, Woman of Yr. award Serenity House, Addison, Ill. Roman Catholic. Home: 138 E 6th St Hinsdale IL 60521-4650 Office: 6301 S Cass Ave Westmont IL 60559-3276

BELLOW, ALEXANDRA, mathematician, educator; b. Bucharest, Romania, Aug. 30, 1935; d. Dumitru and Florica Bagdasar; m. Cassius Ionescu Tulcea, Apr. 1956 (div. 1969); m. Saul G. Bellow, Oct. 1974 (div. 1986); m. Alberto P. Calderon, Sept., 1989. M.S. in Math, U. Bucharest, 1957; Ph.D. in Math., Yale U., 1959. Research assoc. Yale U., New Haven, Conn., 1959-61; research assoc. U. Pa., Phila., 1961-62, asst. prof., 1962-64; assoc. prof. U. Ill., 1964-67; prof. Northwestern U., Evanston, Ill., 1967-96, prof. emeritus, 1996—; Emmy Noether lectr., 1991. Author: (with C. Ionescu Tulcea) Topics in the Theory of Lifting, 1969; assoc. editor: Annals of Probability, 1979-83, Advances in Math., 1979—. Recipient Sr. Disting. Scientist award Alexander von Humboldt Found., 1987; Fairchild Disting. scholar Calif. Inst. Tech., 1980; NSF grantee. Mem. Sigma Xi. Office: Northwestern U Dept of Math 2033 Sheridan Rd Evanston IL 60208-2730

BELLOW, DONALD GRANT, mechanical engineering educator; b. Winnipeg, Man., Can., Aug. 5, 1931; s. Walter William and Lillian Christine (Hnappdal) B.; m. Jean Marion Daye, May 18, 1956; children: Jonathan Mark, Denise Gisele. BASc in Applied Sci., U. B.C., 1956; MS, U. Alta, 1960; PhD, U. Alta., 1963. Registered profl. engr., Alta., Can. Project engr. Can. Industries Ltd., Kingston, Ont., 1956-57, Gen. Motors Diesel Ltd., London, Ont., Can., 1957-58; lectr., asst. prof., assoc. prof., prof. U. Alta., Edmonton, Can., 1958—, chmn. dept., 1975-84, assoc. v.p. facilities, 1989-94, spl. asst. to v.p. fin. and adminstrn., 1994-96; ret. U. Alta., Edmonton, 1996. Recipient L.C. Charlesworth award Assn. Profl. Engrs., Geologists and Geophysicists of Alta., 1982; Cert. of Recognition, Alta. Soc. Engring. Technologists, 1986. Fellow Can. Acad. Engring., Can. Soc. Mech. Engrs.; mem. ASME, Soc. for Exptl. Mechanics, Assn. Profl. Engrs., Geologists and Geophysicists of Alta. (2d v.p. 1983-84, 1st v.p. 1984-85, pres. 1985-86, hon. life mem. 1987-93). Conservative. Anglican.

BELLOW, SAUL C., writer; b. Lachine, Que., Can., June 10, 1915; s. Abraham and Liza (Gordin) B.; m. Anita Goshkin, 1937 (div.); 1 child, Gregory; m. Alexandra Tschacbasov, 1956 (div); 1 child, Adam; m. Susan Glassman, 1961 (div.); 1 child, Daniel; m. Alexandra Ionesco Tuleca, 1974 (div.); m. Janis Freedman, Sept., 1989. Student, U. Chgo., 1933-35; BS, Northwestern U., 1937, LittD, 1962; LittD, Bard Coll., 1962, NYU, 1970, Harvard U., 1972, Yale U., 1972, McGill U., 1973, Brandeis U., 1974, Hebrew Union Coll.-Jewish Inst. Religion, 1976, Trinity Coll., Dublin, Ireland, 1976. Instr. Pestalozzi-Froebel Tchrs. Coll., Chgo., 1938-42; mem. editl. dept. "Great Books" project Ency. Brit., Inc., Chgo., 1943-46; mem. English dept. U. Minn., Mpls., 1946, asst. prof., 1948-49, assoc. prof. English, 1954-59; vis. lectr. NYU, 1950-52; creative writing fellow Princeton (N.J.) U., 1952-53; faculty mem. Bard Coll., Annandale-on-Hudson, N.Y., 1953-54; vis. prof. English U. P.R., Rio Piedras, 1961; celebrity in residence U. Chgo., 1962, Grunier Disting. Svcs. prof., 1962—, mem. com. on social thought, 1962—, chmn. com. on social thought, 1970-76; Tanner lectr. Oxford U., Romanes lectr., 1990. Author: (novels) Dangling Man, 1944, The Victim, 1947, The Adventures of Augie March, 1953 (Nat. Book award 1954), Seize the Day, 1956, Henderson the Rain King, 1959, Herzog, 1964 (Prix Internat. de Litterature 1965, Nat. Book award 1964, Soc. Midland Authors Fiction award 1976), Mr. Sammler's Planet, 1970 (Nat. Book award 1970), Humboldt's Gift, 1975 (Pulitzer prize for fiction 1976), The Dean's December, 1982, More Die of Heartbreak, 1986, A Theft, 1989, The Bellarosa Connection, 1989, The Actual, 1997, (short stories) Mosby's Memoirs, and Other Stories, 1968, Him with His Foot in His Mouth, and Other Stories, 1984, Something to Remember Me By: Three Tales, 1991, Occasional Pieces, 1993; (plays) The Wrecker, 1954, The Last Analysis, 1964, Under the Weather, 1966, (nonfiction) To Jerusalem and Back: A Personal Account, 1976, It All Adds Up: From the Dim Past to the Uncertain Future, 1994; contbr. fiction to Esquire and lit. quars.; criticisms appear in New Leader, others; short story to Atlantic's 125th Anniversary Edit., 1982. Decorated Croix de Chevalier, France, 1968, Comdr. Legion of Honour, France, 1983, Comdr. Order of Arts and Letters, France, 1985; Guggenheim fellow, 1948, Neil Gunn Internat. fellow, 1977; Nat. Inst. Arts and Letters grantee, 1952, Ford Found. grantee, 1959-61; recipient O. Henry prize for The Gonzaga Manuscripts, 1956, for A Silver Dish, 1980, Friends of Lit. Fiction award, 1960, James L. Dow award, 1964, Jewish Heritage award B'nai B'rith, 1968, Formentor prize, 1970, Nobel prize for lit., 1976, Gold medal Am. Acad. Arts and Letters, 1977, Brandeis U. Creative Arts award, 1978, Medal of Honor for lit. Nat. Arts Club, 1978, Malaparte Lit. award, 1984, Premio Scanno Lit. award Italy, 1988, Nat. Medal of Arts, 1988, Lifetime Achievement award Nat. Book Award, 1990, Lifetime Cultural Achievement award YIVO Inst. for Jewish Rsch., 1996. Mem. Am. Acad. Arts and Scis. (Emerson-Thoreau medal 1977). *

BELLOWS, A. ROBERT, ophthalmologist; b. Manchester, N.H., May 14, 1937; s. Arnold Leo and Eleanora Bellows; m. Jean Blunt Farley, May 30, 1964; children: Matthew, Kristen, Nathaniel. BA, Brown U., 1959; MD, Boston U., 1963. Diplomate Am. Bd. Ophthalmology. Intern Univ. Hosp., Boston, 1963-64; asst. resident in internal medicine VA Hosp., Boston, 1964-65; opthal. resident Yale New Haven (Conn.) Hosp., 1967-70, cheif resident, 1970; W.M. Grant MD Glaucoma Fellowship Mass. Eye and Ear Infirmary, Boston, 1971-72; partner Ophthalmic Consultants of Boston, Inc., 1974—; instructor in ophthal. surgery, Yale U., 1969-70, asst. clin. prof. ophthal., Harvard U., 1972—, Tufts U., 1992—. Capt. USAF, 1965-67, Libya. Mem. ACS, Mass. Med. Soc., Ophthal. Assn. in Rsch. to Prevent Blindness, Mass. Soc. Eye Physicians and Surgeons, Am. Acad. Ophthal. (Honor award 1984, Sr. Honor a ward 1996), Assn. for Rsch. in Vision and Ophthal., New England Ophthal. Soc., Am. Eye Study Club. Home: 167 Marlborough St Boston MA 02116-1822 Office: Ophthalmic Cons of Boston 50 Staniford St Ste 600 Boston MA 02114-2587

BELLOWS, HOWARD ARTHUR, JR., marketing research executive; b. N.Y.C., Mar. 10, 1938; s. Howard Arthur and Rita Jennie (Maffitt) B.; m. Mary Josephine Boyd, Sept. 7, 1968; children—Maffitt Vodrey, Alexander Scott, Hillary Newland, Jennifer Pacheteau. B.A., Princeton U., 1960; M.B.A., Harvard U., 1964. Dir. mktg. Olga Co., Van Nuys, Calif., 1964-66; chmn. bd., co-chief exec. officer Triangle Corp., Stamford, Conn., 1967-71; chmn. bd., pres., chief exec. officer Triangle Corp., 1971-95; pres. Audits & Surveys Worldwide, Inc., N.Y.C., 1995—, also bd. dirs.; bd. dirs. Audits and Surveys Worldwide, Inc., Tools Ins. co. Ltd.,. Trustee Western Res. Acad., Hudson, Ohio, dir., Boys and Girls Club of Greenwich and Arch St. Teen Ctr., Served to lt. (j.g.) USNR, 1960-62. Mem. Links Club, Blind Brook Club, Racquet and Tennis Club, Round Hill Club, Eagle Springs Golf Club. Office: Audits & Surveys Worldwide 650 Avenue Of The Americas Fl 6 New York NY 10011-2098

BELLOWS, MICHAEL DONALD, foreign service officer; b. Spirit Lake, Iowa, Mar. 7, 1952; s. Donald Morris and Dolores Elizabeth (Thiesen) B.; m. Toni Leder, July 27, 1974; 1 child, Melissa Elizabeth. BA in History, Morningside Coll., Sioux City, Iowa, 1974; diploma, Nat. Def. U., 1990. Vice consul U.S. Embassy, Manila, 1975-77, U.S. Consulate Gen., Frankfurt, Germany, 1978-80; dep. prin. officer U.S. Consulate Gen., Halifax, Can., 1980-82; consul U.S. Embassy, Suva, Fiji, 1982-84, polit. officer, 1985-87; polit. and econ. officer U.S. Dept. State, Washington, 1987-89; consul gen. U.S. Consulate Gen., Auckland, New Zealand, 1990-93; dean Auckland Consular Corps, 1992-93; dir. Office Pub. and Diplomatic Liaison Dept. State, Washington, 1994-96; spl. asst. Bur. of Consular Affairs Dept. State, Washington, 1996—; min.-counselor U.S. Embassy, Ottawa, Can., 1997—; vis. fellow Inst. Nat. Strategic Studies, Nat. Def. U., 1993-94. Editor: Asia in the 21st Century: Evolving Strategic Priorities, 1994. Mem. Am. Fgn. Svc. Assn., Am. Defenders of Bataan & Corregidor, Am. Club of New Zealand. Avocations: reading, music, basketball. Office: US Dept State Fgn Svc Lounge Washington DC 20520

BELLOWS, RANDALL TRUEBLOOD, ophthalmologist, educator; b. Chgo., June 1, 1946; s. John D. and Mary Frances (Trueblood) B. B.S., Northwestern U., 1968, M.D., 1971. Intern Los Angeles County-U. So. Calif., 1972; resident U. Fla., Gainesville, 1972-75; practice medicine specializing in eye surgery and diseases Chgo., 1975—; assoc. dir. Am. Soc. Contemporary Medicine, Surgery and Ophthalmology, 1975—; chmn., head dept. surgery Henrotin Hosp., 1981-83. Editor: Glaucoma Jour, Annals of Ophthalmology, Jour. Ocular Therapy and Surgery, Comprehensive Therapy; contbr. chpts. to textbooks, articles to profl. jours. Recipient cert. of competence in ophthalmic practice. Mem. AMA (recognition awards 1981-98), Am. Soc. Contemporary Ophthalmology, Am. Soc. Contemporary Medicine and Surgery, AAAS, Am. Acad. Ophthalmology, Am. Intraocular Implant Soc., Chgo. Med. Soc., Ill. Med. Soc., Chgo. Inst. Medicine, Chgo. Ophthmol. Soc., Pan-Am. Assn. Ophthalmology, Internat. Glaucoma Congress, Internat. Assn. Ocular Surgeons. Office: 4711 Golf Rd Ste 408 Skokie IL 60076-1242

BELLOWS, THOMAS JOHN, political scientist, educator; b. Chgo., Aug. 15, 1935; s. Charles Everett and Dorothy (Morrison) B.; m. Marilyn Denise Corbell; children: Scott Anthony, Justin Thomas, Trevor Cullen, Ethan Forrest; children by previous marriage: Roderick Alan, Adrienne Marie, Jeannine Louise, Derek John, Marshall Everett. Student, Am. U., 1956, UCLA, 1956-57; BA, Augustana Coll., 1957; MA, U. Fla., 1958, Yale U., 1960; PhD, Yale U., 1968. Asst. prof. polit. sci. West Ga. Coll., Carrollton, 1962-64, 66; from asst. prof. to prof. polit. sci. U. Ark., Fayetteville, 1967-81; chmn. dept. U. Ark., 1971-78; dir. divsn. social policy scis. U. Tex., San Antonio, 1981-88, prof. polit. sci., 1981—, interim dir. office internat. programs, 1996—; Vis. lectr. depts. history, polit. sci. Nanyang U., Singapore, 1965; vis. prof. Nat. Chengchi U., Taiwan, 1979. Author: The People's Action Party of Singapore: Emergence of a Dominant Party System, 1970, (with S. Erikson and H. Winter) Political Science: Introductory Essays and Readings, 1971, Taiwan's Foreign Policy in the 1970's, 1976, (with H. Winter) People and Politics: An Introduction to Political Science, 1985, Bridging Tradition and Modernization: The Singapore Bureaucracy, 1989, (with H. Winter) Conflict and Compromise, 1992; author, editor The Republic of China: The First Eighty Years, 1993; (with F. Almaraz) Texas Politics, 1996; editor Am. Jour. Chinese Studies, 1999—. Mem. Southwest Conf. Asian Studies (pres. 1995), Am. Assn. for Chinese Studies (pres. 1998—), Assn. Asian Studies, Phi Beta Kappa, Phi Alpha Theta, Phi Kappa Phi. Methodist. Office: U Tex Internat Programs San Antonio TX 78249

BELLSON, LOUIS PAUL, drummer; b. Rock Falls, Ill., July 6, 1924; s. Louis and Carmen (Bartolucci) B.; m. Pearl Bailey, Nov. 19, 1952; children: Tony, Dee Dee. Student, Augustana Coll., Rock Island, Ill., 1942. With Ted Fio Rito, 1942, Benny Goodman, 1943, 46, Tommy Dorsey, 1947-50, Duke Ellington, 1951-54, Jazz at Philharm., 1954; concert artist, 1955—; mem. Big Band Now. Albums include Louis Bellson at the Flamingo, Big Band at the Summit, Louis Bellson's Septet Recorded Live at the 1976 Concord Jazz Festival, Louis Bellson and His Jazz Orch., 1989, Peaceful Thunder, 1992, Big Band Explosion, 1994, Louie Bellson and His Big Band Live from New York, 1994, Cool, Cdool blue, 1995, Live at the Concord Summer Festival, 1995, Their Time was the Greatest, 1996; composer: Skin Deep, Halk Talks, Ting-a-Ling, Drumology, ballet The Marriage Vows (Las Vegas Jazz Festival), Symphony in Jazz Americana, Composition for Piano and Orch., London Ste. Served with AUS, 1943-46. Mem. Musicians Union. Office: Concord Jazz PO Box 845 Concord CA 94522-0845 Office: Thomas Cassidy Inc 11761 E Speedway Blvd Tucson AZ 85748-2017*

BELL-TOLLIVER, LAVERNE, social worker; b. Little Rock, Feb. 28, 1949; d. Louis Anthony and Ruby Jewell (Fleming) Bell; 1 child, Stephen Anthony Bell; m. Johnny Marvin Tolliver, Dec. 20, 1970 (div. Apr. 1975); 1 child, Amani Malaika. BA in Sociology and Spanish, Drury Coll., 1971; MSW, U. Ark., 1973; MA in Biblical Counseling with honors, Dallas Theol. Sem., 1996. Lic. master social work, Tex. Clin. social worker Ctrl. Counties Mental Health Mental Retardation, Temple, Tex., 1973-75; worker, supr., trainer Tex. Dept. Human Svcs., Dallas, 1975-91; owner, dir. Empowerment Svcs., Dallas, 1991—; satellite dir. Child Guidance Clinic of Dallas, 1991-96; clin. dir. Our Brother's Keeper-NDUGU, Inc., Dallas, 1997-99; owner, dir. Empowerment Svcs., Dallas, 1991—; adj. faculty Dallas County C.C., Mesquite, Tex., 1987-91; contract therapist Family Place, Dallas, 1991-94, Family Place, 1998—; contract facilitator Tex. Dept. Protective and Regulatory Svcs., Arlington, Tex., 1991—; tech. expert Health and Scis. TV Network, 1999. Author, pub. My Very Own Parent's Training Manual, 1994, also trainers guide, 1994; contbr. Thomas Nelson Women's Study Bible, 1995. Youth dir. Cmty. Bapt. Ch., Dallas, 1979-87, Bexar St. Bapt. Ch., Dallas, 1987—; choir mem. St. Luke Cmty. United Meth. Ch., Dallas, 1991—; adj. mem. Oak Cliff Child Guidance Bd., Dallas, 1993-96; mem. ednl. task force Dallas Pub. Schs., 1995 -96; mem. health fair task force Dallas Urban League, 1995—; chair Dallas Mental Health Assn. Adolescent Symposia, 1998-99. Named Master Trainer, Tex. Dept. Human Svcs., Austin, 1983; recipient award of excellence Assn. for Retarded Citizens, Dallas, 1990, scholastic recognition N.Am. Profs. of Christian Edn., 1995. Mem. Am. Assn. Marriage and Family Therapists (clin. mem.), Nat. Assn. Black Social Workers, Assn. Play Therapists (registered play therapist), Tex. Assn. Play Therapists, Oak Cliff C. of C. (edn. adv. bd. 1993—). Democrat. Avocations: reading, singing, exercising. Home: 5729 Arlington Park Dr Dallas TX 75235-6203 Office: Empowerment Svcs 2018 S Marsalis Dallas TX 75216

BELLUOMINI, FRANK STEPHEN, accountant; b. Healdsburg, Calif., May 19, 1934; s. Francesco and Rose (Giorgi) B.; m. Alta Anita Gifford, Sept. 16, 1967; 1 child, Wendy Ann. AA, Santa Rosa Jr. Coll., 1954; BA with honors, San Jose State U., 1956. CPA, Calif. Staff acct. Hood, Gire & Co., CPA's, San Jose, Calif., 1955-60, ptnr., 1960-66; ptnr. Touche Ross & Co., CPA's, San Jose, 1967-89, ptnr.-in-charge San Jose office, 1971-85, sr. ptnr. San Jose office, 1985-89; ptnr. Deloitte & Touche, San Jose, 1989-95. Bd. dirs. Santa Clara Valley chpt. ARC, 1993-99, chmn. bd. dirs. 1995-97; mem. adv. bd. Salvation Army, San Jose, 1979-85, San Jose Children's Coun., 1982-89; mem. citizens adv. coun. Via Rehabilitation Svcs., Inc., 1989-94, bd. dirs., 1995—, sec./treas., 1996-98, vice chair, 1998—; trustee Santa Clara County (Calif.) United Way, 1979-95, v.p. planning and allocations, 1981-83, vice chmn., 1985-87, chmn. 1987-89; bd. dirs. San Jose Mus. Art, 1984-86; mem. Presentation High Sch. Devel. Bd., 1989-92; mem. dean's adv. coun. San Jose State U. Bus. Sch., 1990-95, mem. adv. bd. The Acad. of Fin., 1992-94. Named Disting. Alumnus, San Jose State U. Sch. Bus., 1978. Mem. Santa Clara County Estate Planning Council (pres. 1979-80), Calif. Soc. CPA's (pres. chpt. 1968-69, state v.p. 1976-77), Am. Inst. CPA's (chmn. state and local govt. com. 1976-79), San Jose State Alumni Assn. (treas. 1960-61, dir. 1961-62, exec. com. 1961-62), San Jose State Acctg. Round Table (bd. dirs., treas. 1982-87, 92-97, pres. 1994-95), Beta Alpha Psi (San Jose State U. Outstanding Alumnus award 1986). Clubs: San Jose Rotary (dir. 1979-81, trustee and treas. San Jose Rotary Endowment 1976-83).

BELLUOMINI, RONALD JOSEPH, secondary education educator, poet; b. Chgo., July 19, 1946; m. Marilyn Lucille Naselli, Sept. 27, 1969; children: Thomas, Marc. BS in Edn., Chgo. State U., 1968, MA in Geography, 1971. Cert. 6-12 Tchr., ILL. Tchr. St. Basil Sch., Chgo., 1968-71, Northbrook (Ill.) Dist. II 28, 1971—. Author: The Thirteenth Labor, 1985 (Robert and Hazel Ferguson Meml. award for poetry Friends of Lit. Chgo. 1986); contbr. to lit. revs. Mem. Poetry Soc. Am. Home: 1721 Juliet Ln Libertyville IL 60048

BELLUS, RONALD JOSEPH, marketing and communications executive; b. Travis AFB, Calif., Feb. 25, 1951; s. Vincent Joseph and Katherine Veronica (Giudice) B.; m. Beth Ann Johnson, June 26, 1976 (div.); children: Veronica Lee, Joseph Vincent, Kenneth James; m. Gina Jean Prom, Aug. 9, 1990; children: Anthony Taylor, Andrew Tyler. BA in Communications, Brigham Young U., 1977. Lic. FCC radio telephone operator, 1979. Sports dir. Sta. KGUY-AM, Palm Desert, Calif., 1979; news, sports dir. Sta. KBLQ-AM/FM, Logan, Utah, 1979-80; gen. sales mgr. Sta. KSTM-FM/KVVA-AM, Phoenix, 1980-84, Sta. KLFF-AM/KMZK-FM, Phoenix, 1984-85; media cons. Mediacorp Planning & Buying, Phoenix, 1985-86; press sec. Gov. of Ariz., Phoenix, 1986-87; asst. dir. Ariz. Office of Tourism, Phoenix, 1987-88; media cons. Bellus Media, Phoenix, 1988-93; pres. Taska Ltd. (formerly Bellus Media), Phoenix, 1993—; ptnr. Desertwest Media Group, Inc., Phoenix, 1988-96; v.p. Nat. Restaurant Group, Inc., Phoenix, 1990-91; media cons. Mecham for Gov. com., Glendale, Ariz., 1986; host cable TV show Arizona-Now and Then, Cox Cable, 1990—; v.p. Infosystems, Tempe, 1991-94, Green Valley Health Group, Phoenix, 1992-98; co-founder Cinema Concepts Found., Scottsdale, 1994—; co-founder, CEO Bronze Memories Ltd., Phoenix, 1994—; co-founder, pres. Taurus, Inc., 1998—; assoc. dir. Southwest Ctr. for Ethics, Scottsdale C. C., 1998—. Author: Mecham: Silence Cannot Be Misquoted, 1988, Ariz. Tourism Travel Planner, 1988. Comm. mem. Phoenix Boys Choir, 1988; precinct committeeman Rep. State Com., Phoenix, 1987-89, del., 1988; candidate for state senate, Phoenix, 1988; bd. dirs. Cinema Concepts Found., 1994—; mem. Gilbert Anti-Gang Task Force, 1994—, Gilbert Action Inter-Faith Network, 1994—; chmn. adv. bd. Original Kids TV, Inc. Named one of Outstanding Young Men Am., 1987. Mem. Phoenix Press Box Assn. (treas. 1984-85, exec. dir. 1985-86). Ch. of Latter Day Saints. Avocations: golf, travel, reading. Office: 15812 N 32d St Ste 9 Phoenix AZ 85032-3857

BELLUSCHI, ANTHONY C., architect; b. Portland, Oreg., Aug. 2, 1941; s. Pietro and Helen (Hemila) B.; m. Helen Risom, June 25, 1966 (div. 1975); children: Pietro Antonio, Catharine Camilla; m. Martha Mull Page, July 17, 1992. BArch, RISD, 1966. Lic. arch. 28 states including N.Y., Mass., R.I., Calif., N.J., Oreg., Ill., Fla., Ga. Draftsman Ernest Kump Assocs., San Francisco, 1964; designer Zimmer-Gunsel-Frasca, Portland, 1965; assoc. Jung/Brannen Assocs., Boston, 1968-73; prin., treas. Belluschi/Daskalakis Inc., Boston, 1973-77; sr. v.p. Charles Kober Assocs., L.A., 1977-84; mng. ptnr. Kober/Belluschi Assocs., Chgo., 1984-87; pres. Anthony Belluschi Assocs. Inc., 1984-87; founder Anthony Belluschi Archs., Ltd., Chgo., 1988; archtl. cons. U.S. Peace Corps, El Salvador, 1966-68; trustee RISD, 1986—, vice chmn., 1995—. Bd. adv. Inland Arch. Mag., 1992-95. Bd. dirs. Friends of the Park, Chgo., 1993—. Recipient First prize sculpture contest RKO & Redevel. Agy., Boston, 1973, award of merit Mass. Commn. Housing, 1975, Alumni of Yr. award RISD, 1982-83. Mem. AIA (award of excellence 1997), Urban Land Inst. (award of excellence 1997), Internat. Coun. Shopping Ctrs. (design awards for Erieview Galleria, Clevel., Bridgewater Commons, N.J., 1989, Sportsgirl Office/Retail Hirise Bldg., Melbourne, Australia, 1991, Park Meadows Retail Resort, Denver, Univ. Retail Ctr., Tampa, Fla., 1996, The Falls, Miami, 1996, Northwood Cafe, Appleton, Wis., 1999), RISD Alumni Assn. (founder Chgo. chpt.). Avocations: photography, collecting stamps and coins, automobiles, skiing. Home: The Coach House 119 W Chestnut St Chicago IL 60610-3254 Office: Anthony Belluschi Architects Ltd 55 W Monroe St Ste 200 Chicago IL 60603-5001

BELLUZZO, RICHARD E., computer company executive. BS in Acctg., Golden Gate State U. Acctg. positions disk memory divsn. Hewlett-Packard Co., exec. and mgmt. positions printer and peripherals ops., exec. v.p., gen. mgr. computer orgn.; chmn., CEO Silicon Graphics, Inc., 1998—; bd. dirs. Proxima Corp. Office: 2011 N Shoreline Blvd Mountain View CA 94043

BELL-VILLADA, GENE H., literature educator, writer; b. Port-au-Prince, Haiti, Dec. 5, 1941; came to U.S. 1959; s. Gene H. Bell and Carmen (Villada) Romero; m. Audrey M. Dobek, Aug. 9, 1975. BA, U. Ariz., 1963; diploma, U. Paris, 1966; MA, U. Calif., Berkeley, 1967; PhD, Harvard U., 1974. Instr. SUNY, Binghamton, 1971-73; lectr. Yale U., New Haven, 1973-74; from asst. to prof. dept. romance langs. Williams Coll., Williamstown, Mass., 1975—, chair dept., 1993-95; instr. Middlebury (Vt.) Coll., summer 1971-72; reader, grader Advance Placement Readings, Ednl. Testing Svc., 1978-85; vis. prof. Wellesley (Mass.) Coll., 1984-85, 89-90; resident dir. Acad. Yr. in Spain program Hamilton Coll., Madrid, 1986-87, 95-96; freelance edit. cons., 1987—. Author: Borges and His Fiction, 1981, Garcia Marquez, 1990 (Best Book award New England L.Am. Studies 1991), The Carlos Chadwick Mystery, 1990, Art for Art's Sake and Literary Life, 1996 (finalist Nat. Book Critics Cir. award 1997), The Pianist Who Liked Ayn Rand: A Novella & 13 Stories, 1998; contbr. articles to profl. jours. and gen. interest mags. Nat. Endowment for Humanities fellow, 1979; Am. Philos. Soc. grantee, 1982. Mem. MLA, Latin Am. Studies Assn., Am. Assn. Tchrs. Spanish and Portuguese. Avocations: music, travel, films. Office: Williams Coll Dept Romance Langs Williamstown MA 01267

BELL WILSON, CARLOTTA A., state official, consultant; b. Detroit, Dec. 7, 1944; d. Albert Powell (dec.) and Elfrieda (Bertram) Bell; divorced; children: Lizette C. Wilson, SaMia M. Wilson, Shira M. Ingram. AA, Wayne County C.C., Detroit, 1975; BS, Wayne State U., 1979; MEd, Bowling Green State U., 1983. Dental asst. Fred Colvard, DDS, Detroit, 1968-73; edn. coord. Merrill Palmer Inst., Detroit, 1979-81; head start evaluator Cmty. Devel. Inst., Wayne County, 1981; grad. asst. Bowling Green (Ohio) State U., 1981-83; child care worker Meth. Children's Village, Detroit, 1984-85; tchr. New Calvary Head Start, Detroit, 1985; child welfare specialist Mich. Dept. Social Svcs., Detroit, 1985-93; resource program analyst teen parent program Mich. Family Independence Agy., Lansing, 1993—; conf. presenter U. Mich., Ann Arbor, 1995, Mich. Assn. Cmty. and Adult Edn., Bellaire, 1995, Baker Coll., Flint, Mich., 1996. Mem. Toastmasters. Roman Catholic. Avocations: gardening, pottery, cultural activities, travel. Office: Michigan Family Independence Agy 235 S Grand Ave Ste 510 Lansing MI 48933-1805

BELMAN, A. BARRY, pediatric urologist; b. Columbus, Ga., Oct. 16, 1938; s. David Joseph and Ruth (Radin) B.; m. Paula Yonover, June 14, 1964; children: Peter, Lisa, Trina, Jessica. BA with distinction, U. Ariz., 1960; MD, Northwestern U., 1964, MS, 1969. Diplomate Am. Bd. Urology (exam. com. 1980-84, guest oral examiner). Intern Passavant Meml. Hosp., Chgo., 1964-65; resident dept. urology Northwestern U. Med. Sch., 1965-70, from instr. to assoc. prof. urology, 1969-76; attending pediatric urologist Children's Meml. Hosp., Chgo., 1970-76; assoc. prof. urology and pediatrics George Washington U. Sch. Medicine, Washington, 1976-78, prof. urology and pediatrics, 1978—; chmn. dept. pediatric urology Children's Nat. Med. Ctr., Washington, 1976-96, chmn. emeritus, 1996—; cons. Nat. Naval Hosp., Walter Reed Army Hosp., NIH. Co-author: Genitourinary Problems in Pediatrics, 1981; assoc. editor: Clinical Pediatric Urology, 1976, co-editor, 2d edit., 1985, 3rd edit., 1992; mem. editorial bd. Current Problems in Urology, 1989-93, Jour. Urology, 1991—. Mem. AMA (rep. urology residency rev. com. 1995—), ACS, Am. Urol. Assn. (ped. cons., mem. residency edn. and fellowship com. Mid-Atlantic sect.), Am. Acad. Pediat. (sec. urology sect. 1984-87, chmn.-elect 1987-88, chmn. 1988-89), Soc. Pediat. Urology (mem. exec. com. 1990-96, pres. 1995-96), Cosmos Club. Office: Childrens Nat Med Ctr 111 Michigan Ave NW Washington DC 20010-2916*

BELMAN, MURRAY JOEL, lawyer; b. Omaha, June 11, 1935; s. Hymen Belman and Margarette (Margolin) Yudelson; m. Laura Haines, Aug. 20, 1966; children—John Chase, Owen Wolcott. AB, Cornell U., 1957; JD cum laude, Harvard U., 1960. Bar: D.C. 1960. Dep. legal adviser, asst. legal adviser Dept. State, Washington, 1961-69; gen. counsel IOS Devel. Co., Geneva, 1969-70; sole practice Washington, 1972-77; ptnr. Pepper, Hamilton & Scheetz, Washington, 1977-84, Thompson Coburn (formerly Thompson & Mitchell), Washington, 1984—; professorial lectr. law George Washington U., Washington, 1972-74; adj. prof. Georgetown U. Sch. Law, Washington, 1975-76. Trustee St. John's Child Devel. Ctr., Washington, 1984-92, v.p., 1987-90, pres. 1990-92. Mem. ABA, D.C. Bar Found. (adv. bd. 1991—), Am. Soc. Internat. Law, Internat. Law Inst. Democrat. Jewish. Office: Thompson Coburn 700 14th St NW Ste 900 Washington DC 20005-2024

BELMARES, HECTOR, chemist; b. Monclova, Coahuila, Mex., Feb. 21, 1938; s. Armando and Guadalupe (Sarabia) B.; B.Sc., Instituto Tecnológico de Monterrey (Mex.), 1960; Ph.D. (Todd fellow 1961-63), Cornell U., 1963; postdoctoral student Calif. Inst. Tech., 1965; m. Eleanor Johanna Wold, Aug. 28, 1965; children: Michelle Anne, Michael Paul, Elizabeth Myrna, Mary Eleanor. Sr. research chemist Rohm and Haas Co., Phila., 1965-71; gen. mgr. tech. and quality control Fibras Químicas, S.A., Monterrey, Mex., 1972-75; sr. research chemist Centro de Investigación en Química Aplicada, Saltillo Coahuila, Mex., 1976-83, Sola Optical USA Inc., 1984—; mem. adv. panel Modern Plastics Mgmt., 1986-87; cons. on polymers for industry; cons. UN Indsl. Devel. Orgn. Community rep. Against Indsl. Air Pollution, Moorestown, N.J., 1968-70. Mem. Am. Chem. Soc., N.Y. Acad. Scis., AAAS, Sigma Xi. Mem. Christian Evangelical Ch. Patentee in field. Contbr. articles to profl. jours. Home: 1100 Shadyslope Dr Santa Rosa CA 95404-2743

BELMONT, LARRY MILLER, retired public health executive; b. Reno, Apr. 13, 1936; s. Miller Lawrence and Madeline (Echante) B.; m. Laureen Metzger, Aug. 14, 1966; children: Miller Lawrence, Rebecca Madeline, Amie Echante, Bradley August. BA in Psychology, U. Nev., 1962; MPH, U. Mich., 1968; cert. in environ. mgmt., U. So. Calif., 1978; MPA, U. Idaho, 1979. Rep. on loan to city health depts. USPHS, Los Angeles and Long Beach, 1962-63; advisor pub. health on loan to Alaska dept. health & welfare USPHS, Anchorage, 1963-64, Juneau and Anchorage, 1964-67; dep. dir. Wash./Alaska Regional Med. Program, Spokane, Wash., 1968-71; dir., sec.-treas. bd. of health Panhandle Health Dist., Coeur d'Alene, Idaho, 1971-98; ret., 1998; past adj. faculty Whitworth Coll., Spokane; presenter in field. Chmn. nominating com. Kootenai Econ. Devel. Council, Idaho, 1985, bd. dirs. 1981-86; mem. adv. com. Kootenai County Council Alcoholism, 1979-80; regional coordinator Gov.'s Com. Vol. Services, Idaho, 1979-80; chmn. Montessori Adv. Bd., Idaho, 1975-79; chmn. personnel com. North Idaho Hospice, 1985-88, bd. dirs. 1985-88; bd. dirs. North Idaho Spl. Services Agy., 1972-76; bd. dirs., vice-chmn. Pub. Employees Credit Union, 1990-95; bd. dirs. United Way of Kootenai County, Inc., 1990-91; mem. nat. steering com. APEX/PH, 1987-91; others; treas. Friends of Head Start Bd. USPHS trainee U. Mich., 1967-68, EPA trainee U. So. Calif., 1978. Mem. APHA, Nat. Assn. Home Health Agys. (chmn. legis. com. 1979-82, bd. dirs. 1978-81), Nat. Assn. County Health Ofcls. (bd. dirs. 1986-88, registry com. 1990), Idaho Pub. Health Assn. (bd. dirs. 1998—, treas. 1973-77), Idaho Conf. Dist. Health Dirs. (bd. dirs. 1998, vice-chmn. and chmn. 1993-95), Idaho Forest Owners Assn. (tree farmer), Kootenai County Environ. Alliance, Idaho Conservation League, Area Agy. on Aging (legis. com., adv. coun.), Idaho Rural Health Coalition, The Nature Conservancy, Ducks Unltd., Dem. Club (natural resources com.), Senior Coalition. Democrat. Avocations: hunting, fishing, wood carving, music, camping.

BELMONT, MADRA ALVIS, lawyer; b. Bluefield, W.Va., Apr. 22, 1970; d. Danny Ray and Dianna Sue (Shumate) Alvis; m. Philip James Belmont Jr., Apr. 25, 1995. BA, Duke U., 1991, JD, 1994. Bar: U.S. Dist. Ct. Md. 1995, Md. 1995, D.C. 1997. Atty. Muldoon, Murphy & Faucette, Washington, 1994-96; assoc. counsel M.G.A., Inc., Dothan, Ala., 1996-98; corp. counsel Am. Club Sys. Inc., Columbus, Ga., 1998—.

BELMONTE, STEVEN JOSEPH, hotel chain executive; b. Oak Park, Ill., Aug. 25, 1952; s. Silvio J. and Vilma (Giannini) B.; m. Dwyonia Conrad; children: Gino Anthony, Kellie Rose, Michael Steven. BA in Hotel Mgmt., Wright Coll., Chgo., 1974; student Holiday Inn U., Memphis, 1974; BM in Innkeeping, Harper Coll., Rolling Meadows, Ill., 1981; D Applied Pub. Svc. (hon.), Hocking Coll., 1993. Gen. mgr., regional dir. Holiday Inns, Chgo., 1972-84; pres. CEO Equity Hotel Corp, Rolling Meadows, Ill., 1984-91; pres, CEO Ramada Franchise Sys., Inc., 1991—; chmn. Ramada Inns Nat. Assn.; founding sponsor Childreach; speaker Ill. Budget for Tourism, 1978-81. Bd. advisors Wright Jr. Coll.; mem. Joint Civic Com. Italian Ams.; hon. chmn. Childreach Plan Internat. 1996; bd. dirs. Chgo. chpg. Inner City Games, 1998—; active fund raiser for various charities and retirement homes. Recipient citation Italo-Am. War Vets. U.S., 1980, Humanitas award PLAN Internat. Charities, 1994. Mem. Am. Soc. Travel Agts., Am. Hotel & Motel Assn. (bd. trustees ednl. inst.), Am. Hotel Fedn., Hotel Sales Mgmt. Assn., Soc. Mng. Execs., Chgo. Innkeepers Assn. (v.p. 1979-81), Am. Hotel Found. (exec. com. 1997—, chmn. devel. com. 1997—) Office: Ramada Franchise Sys Inc 1 Sylvan Way Parsippany NJ 07054-3707

BELNAP, DAVID F., journalist; b. Ogden, Utah, July 27, 1922; s. Hyrum Adolphus and Lois Ellen B.; m. Barbara Virginia Carlberg, Jan. 17, 1947. Student, Weber Coll., Ogden, 1940. Asst. city editor Seattle Star, 1945-47; bur. chief UP Assns., Helena, Mont., 1947-50, Honolulu, 1950-52; regional exec. Pacific N.W., 1952-55, dir. Latin Am. services, 1955-67; Latin Am. corr. L.A. Times, 1967-80, asst. fgn. news editor, 1980-93. Recipient Overseas Press Club Am. award for best article on Latin Am., 1970, Maria Moors Cabot prize, 1973. Mem. Overseas Press Club Am., Greater Los Angeles Press Club, Audiophile Soc. Clubs: Am. of Buenos Aires; Phoenix of Lima (Peru). Home: 1134 W Huntington Dr Arcadia CA 91007-6308 Office: Times Mirror Sq Los Angeles CA 90053

BELNAP, NUEL DINSMORE, JR., philosophy educator; b. Evanston, Ill., May 1, 1930; s. Nuel Dinsmore and Elizabeth (Dafter) B.; m. Joan Gohde, Oct. 23, 1953; children: Nuel Dinsmore, Christopher William, Mary Jo, Tyler Kristan; m. Gillian Hirth, Apr. 7, 1982; m. Birgit Herbeck, Dec. 31, 1997. B.A., U. Ill., 1952; M.A., Yale U., 1957, Ph.D., 1960. Instr. philosophy Yale U., New Haven, 1958-60, asst. prof., 1960-63; assoc. prof. philosophy U. Pitts., 1963-66, prof., 1966—, prof. sociology, 1967—, prof. dept. history and philosophy of sci., 1971—, prof. in intelligent systems program, 1988-93; vis. prof. U. Calif.-Irvine, winter 1973; vis. Oscar R. Ewing prof. Ind. U., Bloomington, fall, 1977, 78, 79, Alan Ross Anderson lectr., 1983-84, Alan Ross Anderson Disting. prof. philosophy, 1984—; vis. fellow Australian Nat. U., 1976; cons. Office Naval Research, 1960-63, System Devel. Corp., 1961-67, U. Pitts. Knowledge Availability Ctr., 1963-66, Westinghouse Research Lab., 1981; vis. Leibniz prof. Leipzig U., summer 1996. Author: (with Thomas B. Steel) The Logic of Questions and Answers, 1976, (with Alan Ross Anderson) Entailment: The Logic of Relevance and Necessity, vol. I, 1975, (with Alan Ross Anderson and J. Michael Dunn), Vol. II, 1992, (with Anil Gupta) The Revision Theory of Truth, 1993; mem. editorial bd. Am. Philos. Quar., 1966-78, Jour. Philos. Logic, 1970—, v.p., 1976-82—, chmn. bd. govs., 1982-88; mem. editorial bd. Notre Dame Jour. of Formal Logic, 1970, Philosophy of Sci., 1975—, Studia Logica, 1976—, Philos. Research Archives, 1976—; author: computer programs Tester, 1974, Bindex, 1974. Mem. U. Ill. Found., Urbana, 1973—. Served to 1st lt. USAF, 1952-54. Sterling Jr. fellow, 1955-56; Fulbright fellow, 1957-58; Morse Research fellow, 1962-63; Guggenheim fellow, 1975-76; Ctr. for Advanced Study in Behavioral Scis. fellow, 1982-83. Fellow AAAS; mem. Am. Philos. Assn., Assn. for Symbolic Logic (exec. com. 1970-73, com. on revs. policy 1974-76, oversight com. 1988-89), Soc. for Exact Philosophy (v.p. 1971-74, pres. 1974-76, treas. 1979-80), Mind Assn. (U.S. treas. 1974-94).

BELNICK, MARK ALAN, lawyer; b. Elizabeth, N.J., Oct. 30, 1946; s. Ben B. and Rhoda Helen (Dubrowsky) B.; m. Randy Lee Birer, Mar. 23, 1974; children: Kelly Ann, Cory Frances, Jason Todd. BA cum laude, Cornell U., 1968; JD, Columbia U., 1971. Bar: N.Y. 1972, U.S. Tax Ct., 1972, U.S. Ct. Appeals (2d cir.) 1972, U.S. Dist. Ct. (so. dist.) N.Y. 1973, U.S. Supreme Ct. 1975, U.S. Dist. Ct. (ea. dist.) N.Y. 1978, U.S. Ct. Appeals (9th cir.) 1980, D.C. 1981, U.S. Ct. Appeals (4th cir.) 1982. Assoc. Marshall, Bratter, Greene et al, N.Y.C., 1971-72; assoc. Paul, Weiss, Rifkind, Wharton & Garrison, N.Y.C., 1972-79, ptnr., 1979-98; exec. v.p., chief corp. counsel Tyco Internat. Ltd., N.Y.C., 1998—; adj. prof. law Benjamin N. Cardozo Sch. Law, N.Y.C., 1982-86; mem. panel mediators and fact finders N.Y. State Pub. Employment Rels. Bd., Albany, 1972-79; deputy chief counsel U.S. Senate select com. on secret mil. assistance to Iran and Nicaraguan opposition, 1987-88; chief counsel select com. on structure and governance Nat. Assn. Security Dealers, 1994-96; bd. visitors Columbia Law Sch., 1996—; dir. Cornell U. prelaw program, 1999—. Mem. com. on alumni trustee nominations Cornell U., 1993-97, mem. coun., 1992-96, 98—, mem. adv. coun. Coll. Arts and Scis., 1993—, dir. prelaw program, 1999—; mem. adminstrv. bd. Cornell Coun., 1999—; bd. trustees Ethical Culture Fieldston Schs., 1999—. Harlan Fiske Stone scholar, 1971. Fellow Am. Coll. Trial Lawyers (downstate N.Y. com., fed. civil procedure com.); mem. ABA, N.Y.

State Bar Assn., Assn. Bar City N.Y., Univ. Club N.Y.C. Office: Tyco Internat Ltd 712 Fifth Ave 48th Fl New York NY 10019

BELOBRAIDICH, SHARON LYNN GOUL, elementary education educator; b. Detroit, Oct. 21, 1940; d. William A. and Lillian Mae (Atkinson) Goul; m. Frank Glen Belobraidich, Mar. 24, 1962 (dec. May 1987); children: Caryn Lyn, Ellyn Elizabeth Christensen. BA, Mich. State U., 1962; MA, Ea. Mich. U., 1968. Tchr. Waverly Schs., Lansing, Mich., 1962-63, Plymouth (Mich.) - Canton Schs., 1963—; bldg. rep. Plymouth Canton Edn. Assn., 1963-97, sec., 1974-90, v.p., 1990—; del. to rep. assembly NEA, Mich. Edn. Assn., 1990—. Experienced Tchr. fellow U.S. Govt., 1967-68. Mem. AAUW (play dir. 1977, 83, 90; treas. 1997—), Mich. Diabetes Assn. (bd. dirs. 1971-87), Beacon Hollow Condo Assn. (pres. 1994—), Alpha Delta Kappa (sec. 1968-70, pres. 1972-74, 76-78). Avocations: literature, drama, travel. Home: 12498 Pinecrest Dr Plymouth MI 48170-3061

BELOFF, ZOE, artist, educator. Student, Edingburgh (Scotland) U.; MFA in Film, Columbia U. Tchr. digital media Pratt Inst., City Coll. N.Y. Prodr. (CD-ROM) Beyond (First prize QuickTime VR Competition), Where There There There Where, (film) Life Underwater, Lost. Found. Contemporary Arts grantee, 1997.

BELOK, LENNART C., neurologist; b. N.Y.C., July 1, 1949; s. John Belok and Anne Schubert. BA, NYU, 1969; MD, N.Y. Med. Coll., 1973. Diplomate Am. Bd. Neurology. Office: 401 E 20th St New York NY 10010

BELONGIE, MICHAEL EUGENE, English language educator, poet; b. Escanaba, Mich., Nov. 1, 1946; s. Cyril and Anne (Strazzinski) B.; m. Jane Comerford, Apr. 15, 1974; children: Shaun, Ryan. BS, U. Wis., Oshkosh, 1970. Instr. English, curriculum and staff devel. facilitator Randolph (Wis.) Sch. Dist., 1970—; mem. adv. bd. Scholastic, Inc., N.Y.C., 1979-86; instr. interactive TV, broadcaster South Cen. Instrnl. Network Group, 1995—; drama critic Beaver Dam Daily Citizen, 1978—. Sgt. USAR, 1970-76. Recipient Congl. Tchg. award Congressman Scott Klug, 1991, 95. Mem. ASCD, Wis. Fellowship of Poets (life, pres. 1992-95), So. Edn. Inservice Orgn. (pres. 1995-96), Phi Delta Kappa. Avocations: supporting the arts, exercise. Home: 1421 Hiawatha Dr Beaver Dam WI 53916-1041 Office: Randolph Sch Dist 110 Meadowood Dr Randolph WI 53956-1318

BELONICK, CYNTHIA ANN, psychiatric-mental health nurse; b. New Britain, Conn., Mar. 21, 1957; d. Steven and Anne (Kochanowski) B. Diploma, St. Francis Hosp. Sch. Nursing, Hartford, Conn., 1982; BA cum laude, U. Conn., 1979; MSN, Yale U., 1992. Cert. clin. specialist in adult psychiat. and mental health, advanced practice RN. Nurse educator The Inst. of Living, Hartford, Conn., 1993—; co-rschr. forgiveness & cognitions; lectr. in field. Contbr. Psychiat. Nursing Diagnoses: A Comprehensive Manual of Manual Health Care. Mem. Conn. Nurses Assn., Conn. Soc. Nurse Psychotherapists, Sigma Theta Tau, Delta Mu.

BELOVARSKI, BORISLAV V., scriptwriter, writer; b. Sofia, Bulgaria, May 9, 1961; s. Vassil B. and Tania Dakova (Dilova) B.; m. Radositina Luleva Kozarova Belovarski, Dec. 8, 1982 (widow dec. 30, 1985); children: Emanuela, Bojana; m. Viktoria Dimitrova Archimedova Belovarski, Aug. 20, 1990; children: Ioan, David, Joshua. PhD in Bible Lit., Am. Coll. Metaphys. Theology, Golden Valley, Minn., 1999—. Artist, asst. producer Nat. Radio TV Ctr., Sofia, Bulgaria, 1980-87; INDIE producer Inri Films, Sofia, Bulgaria, 1992-95, Johannesburg, South Africa, 1995-97; writer, scriptwriter pvt. practice, Albuquerque, 1997-. Author: The Most Dead Artizans of Happiness, 1980, Air Mail, 1983, Timeship, 1997-99. Avocations: videography, digital art, webdesign, composing. E-mail address: belovarski@aol.com. Home: 6367 Sandpiper Tr NE Rio Rancho NM 87124

BELOW, CLIFTON C., state legislator; b. Memphis, Aug. 26, 1956; s. Ralph Wilson and Caroline B.; m. Kathryn A. Petuck, 1989. BA, Dartmouth Coll., 1980; MSCED, N.H. Coll., 1985. Mem. N.H. Ho. of Reps., 1992—, mem. sci., tech. and energy com.; mem. N.H. Senate; v.p. mgmt. svcs. Ardent Realty Svcs., Ltd., 1992—. Mem. Lebanon (N.H.) Planning Bd., 1996—; dir. Lebanon Opera House Improvement Corp., 1991—, Friends of No. Rail-Trail, 1996—. Mem. Lebanon Garden Club (treas. 1986—). Address: 25 Perley Ave Lebanon NH 03766-1816*

BELSHAW, GEORGE PHELPS MELLICK, bishop; b. Plainfield, N.J., July 14, 1928; s. Harold and Edith (Mellick) B.; m. Elizabeth Wheeler, June 12, 1954; children: Richard, Elizabeth, George. B.A., U. of South, 1951, DD (hon.), 1994; S.T.B., Gen. Theol. Sem., N.Y.C., 1954, S.T.M., 1959, D.D. (hon.), 1975. Ordained to ministry, Episcopal Ch., consecrated bishop. Vicar St. Matthew's Ch., Waimanalo, Hawaii, 1954-57; fellow, tutor Gen. Theol. Sem., N.Y.C., 1957-59; rector Christ Ch., Dover, Del., 1959-65, St. George's Ch., Rumson, N.J., 1965-75; suffragan bishop Diocese of N.J., Trenton, 1975-83, bishop of N.J., 1983-94; vis. lectr. Gen. Theol. Sem., 1969, 70; governing bd. Episc. Urban Caucus, 1982—, pres., 1986-89; mem. Commn. Peace of Episc. Ch., 1979-85, Econ. Justice Implementation Com., Episc. Ch., 1988-95. Editor: Lent with Evelyn Underhill, 1964, Lent with William Temple, 1966; contbr. articles to theol. jours. Trustee Gen. Theol. Sem., 1975—, chmn. 1992—, acting dean, pres., 1997-98; trustee Westminster Choir Coll., 1976-82. Mem. Am. Teilhard de Chardin Assn. (bd. dirs. 1976—), N.J. Coalition Religious Leaders (pres. 1986), Bd. Anglican Theol. Rev. (1993—). Home: 15 Boudinot St Princeton NJ 08540-3007

BELSKY, MARTIN HENRY, law educator, lawyer; b. Phila., May 29, 1944; s. Abraham and Fannie (Turnoff) B.; m. Kathleen Waits, Mar. 9, 1985; children: Allen Frederick, Marcia Elizabeth. BA cum laude, Temple U., 1965; JD cum laude, Columbia U., 1968; cert. of study Hague (Netherlands) Acad. Internat. Law, 1968; diploma in criminology Cambridge (Eng.) U., 1969. Bar: Pa. 1969, Fla. 1983, N.Y., 1987, U.S. dist. ct. (ea. dist.) Pa. 1969, U.S. Ct. Appeals (3d cir.) 1970, U.S. Supreme Ct. 1973. Chief asst. dist. atty. Phila. Dist. Atty.'s Office, 1969-74; assoc. Blank, Rome, Klaus & Comisky, Phila., 1975; chief counsel U.S. Ho. of Reps., Washington, 1975-78; asst. adminstr. NOAA, Washington, 1979-82; dir. Ctr. for Govtl. Responsibility, assoc. prof. law U. Fla. Holand Law Ctr., 1982-86; dean Albany Law Sch., 1986-91, dean emeritus, prof. law, 1991-95; dean U. Tulsa Coll. of Law, 1995—; chair Select Commn. on Disabilities, N.Y., Spl. Commn. on Fire Svcs.; bd. advs. Ctr. Oceans Law and Policy; mem. corrections task force Pa. Gov.'s Justice Commn., 1971-75; adv. task force on cts. Nat. Adv. Commn. on Criminal Justice Standards and Goals, 1972-74; mem. com. on proposed standard jury instrns. Pa. Supreme Ct., 1974-81; lectr. in law Temple U., 1971-75; mem. faculty Pa. Coll. Judiciary, 1975-77; adj. prof. law Georgetown U., 1977-81. Chmn. Phila. council Anti-Defamation League, 1975, N.Y. region, mem. D.C. bd., 1977-78, chair N.Y. region, mem. nat. leadership Coun.; exec. v.p. Urban League Northeastern N.Y.; bd. dirs. Coun. on Aging & Disability. Stone scholar and Internat. fellow Columbia U. Law Sch. Mem. N.Y. State Bar Assn., Albany County Bar Assn., Phila. Bar Assn. (chmn. young lawyers sect. 1974-75), Pa. Bar Assn. (exec. com. young lawyers sect. 1973-75), ABA (del. young lawyers sect. exec. bd. 1973-75), Fla. Bar Assn., Fed. Bar Assn., Am. Judicature Soc., Nat. Dist. Attys. Assn., Am. Soc. Internat. Law, Am. Arbitration Assn. (referee N.Y. State Commn. on Jud. Discipline), Temple U. Liberal Arts Alumni Assn. (v.p. 1971-75), Am. Law Inst., Fund for Modern Cts. (bd. dirs.), Hudson-Mohawk Assn. Colls. and Univs. (v.p.), Sword Soc. Jewish. Club: B'nai B'rith (v.p. lodge 1973-75), Cardoto Soc., United Jewish Fedn. Northeastern N.Y. (v.p., pres. elect). Author: (with Steven H. Goldblatt) Analysis and Commentary to the Pennsylvania Crimes Codes, 1973; Handbook for Trial Judges, 1976, Oceans and Capital Law and Policy, 1994; contbr. articles to legal publs.; editor in chief Jour. Transnat. Law, Columbia Law Sch., 1968; mem. bd. advisors Territorial Sea Jour. Office: U Tulsa Coll Law 3120 E 4th Pl Tulsa OK 74104-2418

BELSOM, JOHN ANTON (JACK), writer, researcher; b. Roaring Spring, Pa., June 21, 1933; s. John and Mary Ottilia (Schiele) B. BA, Tulane U., 1955; MA, La. State U., 1972. Personnel technician Dept. Civil Svc., New Orleans, 1957-70, personnel divsn. chief, 1970-76, dir. personnel, 1976-88. Author: (monograph) Opera In New Orleans, 1993, Celebrating 200 Years of Opera in New Orleans, 1998; contbr. articles to publs. Pres. Lower Quarter Crime Watch Assn., New Orleans, 1981-82; pres. Cath. Bookstore Found., New Orleans, 1984-85, recording sec., 1995—; recording sec. Vieux Carré Property Owners Assn., New Orleans, 1989-91. With U.S. Army, 1955-57. Mem. Internat. Personnel Mgmt. Assn. (chpt. treas. 1977—). Democrat. Roman Catholic. Avocations: genealogy, opera, traveling, music, writing. Home: 721 Barracks St New Orleans LA 70116-2516

BELSON, JAMES ANTHONY, judge; b. Milw., Sept. 23, 1931; s. Walter W. and Margaret (Taugher) B.; m. Rosemary P. Greenslade, Jan. 11, 1958; children: Anthony James, Marie Taylor, Elizabeth Ann, Stephen Griffin. AB cum laude, Georgetown U., 1953, JD, 1956, LLM, 1962. Bar: D.C. 1956, Md. 1962. Law clk. U.S. Ct. Appeals (D.C. cir.), 1956-57; assoc. Hogan & Hartson, Washington, 1960-67, ptnr., 1967-68; trial judge D.C. Superior Ct., 1968-81, presiding judge civil divsn., 1978-81; assoc. judge D.C. Ct. Appeals, Washington, 1981-91, sr. judge, 1991—; faculty mem. Nat. Jud. Coll., 1973-80; bd. dirs. Coun. for Ct. Excellence, 1982—, Cath. Legal Immigration Network, Inc., 1994-98; bencher Am. Inn of Ct. VI, 1983-90. Bd. editors Georgetown Law Jour., 1955-56. Bd. dirs. Project SHARE D.C., Inc., 1992—, chmn., 1997—. With JAGC, U.S. Army, 1957-60. Mem. ABA, Bar Assn. of D.C. (bd. dirs. 1966-67, chmn. jr. bar 1965-66), Am. Judicature Soc. (bd. dirs. 1980-85), Am. Bar Found., John Carroll Soc. (bd. govs. 1978-85, 1st v.p. 1989-91), Sovereign Mil. Order of Malta Fed. Assn. (pres. 1991-94, bd. dirs. 1988-95, 97—, chmn. task force on Cuba 1994—). Home: 12 W Severn Ridge Rd Annapolis MD 21401-5844 Office: DC Ct Appeals 500 Indiana Ave NW Rm 5510 Washington DC 20001-2131

BELT, DAVID LEVIN, lawyer; b. Wheeling, W.Va., Jan. 13, 1944; s. David Homer and Mae Jean (Duffy) B.; m. Carolyn Emery Copeland Belt, July 22, 1967; children: David Clifford, Amy Elizabeth. BA, Yale U., 1965, LLB, 1970. Bar: Conn. 1970. Assoc. Jacobs, Grudberg, Belt & Dow, P.C., New Haven, Conn., 1970-74, mem., 1974—. Co-author: The Connecticut Unfair Trade Practices Act, 1994; contbr. articles to profl. jours. 1 lt. USAR, 1965-67, Vietnam. Fellow Conn. Bar Found.; mem. Conn. Bar Assn. (exec. com. antitrust and trade regulation sect. 1978—), Conn. Trial Lawyers Assn., Yale Club N.Y.C. Office: Jacobs Grudberg Belt & Dow PC 350 Orange St New Haven CT 06511-6415

BELT, EDWARD SCUDDER, sedimentologist, educator; b. N.Y.C., Aug. 4, 1933; s. Charles Banks and Emma Willard (Keyes) B.; m. Emily Hillen Macsherry, Feb. 4, 1961; children: Emily H., Anne Banks, Agnes Keyes, Catherine Kilty. BA, Williams Coll., 1955; AM, Harvard U., 1957; PhD, Yale U., 1963. Asst. prof. Villanova (Pa.) U., 1962-66; asst. prof. geology Amherst (Mass.) Coll., 1966-70, assoc. prof., 1970-78, prof., 1978—, chmn. dept. geology, 1971-76, 92-93, dir. Pratt Mus. Natural History, 1987—; hon. prof. U. St. Andrews, Fife, Scotland, 1972-73; vis. prof. Colo. State U., Ft. Collins, 1979-80; cons. in uranium exploration, 1958, cons. in surface water, 1969, cons. in coal, 1975-79, cons. in oil, 1983; cons. in sedimentology Nat. Sci. & Engring. Rsch. Coun. Can., 1994; geologist, coal br. U.S. Geol. Survey, Denver, 1980-84, Reston, Va., 1986—; geologist N.D. Geol. Survey, Grand Forks, 1983, Earth Scis. and Resources Inst., Columbia, S.C., 1983; dir. Keck Found. project, eastern Mont., 1987-89, 92-93, Yellowstone-Bighorn Res. Assoc., 1986—. Contbr. chpts. to books, articles to profl. jours. Served with U.S. Army, 1957-62. Grantee Geol. Soc. Am., 1960-61, NSF, 1961, 64-67, 85-87, 89-91, Sigma Xi, 1967-68, Am. Philos. Soc., 1972-73, Nat. Geog. Soc., 1972-73, Que., 1970-79, Keck Found., 1987-89, 92-93, Amherst Coll., 1997—. Fellow Geol. Soc. Am., Geol. Soc. London; mem. Am. Assn. Petroleum Geologists, Geol. Assn. Can., Am. Inst. Profl. Geologists, Internat. Assn. Sedimentologists, Soc. for Sedimentary Geology, Nat. Assn. Geology Tchrs. Republican. Roman Catholic. Home: 116 Alpine Dr Amherst MA 01002-1617 Office: Amherst Coll 123 Pratt Mus Natural Hist Amherst MA 01002-5000

BELTH, JOSEPH MORTON, retired business educator; b. Syracuse, N.Y., Oct. 22, 1929; s. Irving and Helen Rose (Bright) B.; m. Marjorie Helen Lavine, June 12, 1955; children: Ann Irene, Michael Irving, Jeffrey Edward. A.A.S., Cayuga Community Coll., 1958; B.S. summa cum laude, Syracuse U., 1958; Ph.D., U. Pa., 1961. C.L.U., C.P.C.U. Asst. purchasing agt. Onondaga Supply Co., Syracuse, N.Y., 1947-53; agt. Continental Am. Life Ins. Co., Syracuse, 1953-58; asst. dir. continuing edn. Am. Soc. Chartered Life Underwriters, Bryn Mawr, Pa., 1961-62; asst. prof. Ind. U., Bloomington, 1962-65, assoc. prof., 1965-68, prof., 1968-93, prof. emeritus, 1993—. Author: Participating Life Insurance Sold by Stock Companies, 1965, The Retail Price Structure in American Life Insurance, 1966; Life Insurance: a Consumer's Handbook, 1973, 2d edit., 1985, The A.L. Williams Replacement Empire, 1987, 2d edit., 1989; editor newsletter The Ins. Forum, 1974— (George Polk award 1990). Mem. Am. Risk and Ins. Assn. (pres. 1973-74, Elizur Wright award, 1966, Jour. Risk and Ins. awards 1962,64,65, 67,71,79), AAUP, Beta Gamma Sigma, Phi Kappa Phi. Democrat. Jewish. Home: 5125 N Starnes Rd Bloomington IN 47404-9358

BELTON, DEBORAH CAROLYN KNOX, state information systems administrator; b. Manchester, Tenn., Mar. 31, 1962; d. Eugene Clarke and Myrtle Carolyn (Bell) Knox; m. Joseph Burton Belton, May 23, 1992. BBA in Acctg., Middle Tenn. State U., 1984. CPA, Tenn.; cert. govt. fin. mgr. Sr. fin. planner Lincoln Fin. Group, Brentwood, Tenn., 1986; staff acct. Charles Tharp & Assocs., Nashville, 1987; staff acct. dept. treasury State of Tenn., Nashville, 1984-85, supr. pension payroll dept. treasury, 1987, compliance analyst, policy planner, 1988, dir. program acctg. dept. fin. and adminstrn., 1988-93; from data adminstr. to mgr. application devel. and support Dept. of Fin. and Adminstrn., Nashville, 1993-99, asst. dir. info. sys. mgmt., 1999—. Mem. Assn. Govt. Accts., Nat. Assn. CPAs (John Lewis award 1984). Avocations: snow and water skiing, raising and training horses and dogs.

BELTON, JOHN, English educator; b. June 18, 1945. BA, Columbia U., 1967; PhD, Harvard U., 1975. Prof. Rutgers U., New Brunswick, N.J., 1988—. E-mail: belton@fas-english.rutgers.edu.

BELTON, JOHN THOMAS, lawyer; b. Yonkers, N.Y., Feb. 24, 1947; s. Harry James and Anne Marie (Kupko) B.; m. Linda Susanne Cheugh, jan. 6, 1973; 1 child, Joseph Timothy. BA, Ohio State U., 1972, postgrad. in bus. adminstrn., 1972-73; JD, Ohio No. U., 1976. Bar: Ohio 1977, U.S. Ct. of Claims. Sole practice Columbus, Ohio, 1976-83; ptnr. Belton & Marlin, and predecessor firm Belton, Goldwin & Cheugh, Columbus, 1983—; arbitrator Franklin County Ct. Common Pleas, 1983—; dir. Weeks-Finneran Inc. Rep. precinct chmn., 1983; v.p. Far Northwest Coalition, 1984. Mem. ch. coun. St. Peter's Parish, 1984—, Pub. Bd. Zoning Appeals, 1991—; pres. Dublin Youth Athletics, 1985—. With USAF, 1968-71. Mem. ABA, ATLA, Columbus Bar Assn. (com. chmn. 1976—), U.S. Dist. Ct. Fed. Bar, U.S. Supreme Ct. Bar, Ohio Bar Assn. (bd. govs. 1993—), Dublin Jr. C. of C., The Pres., Ohio State Alumni, Republican Glee, Columbus Shamrock, K.C., Order of Barristers, Omicron Delta Kappa, Phi Alpha Delta (justice 1975). Roman Catholic. Avocations: reading, chess, golfing, racquetball, recreational activities. Home: 8649 Dunsinane Dr Dublin OH 43017-8757 Office: Belton Wherry & Marlin 2066 Henderson Rd Columbus OH 43220-2452

BELTON, ROBERT, law educator; b. 1935. BA, U. Conn., 1961; JD, Boston U., 1965. Bar: N.Y. 1966, N.C. 1970, Tenn. 1980. Asst. counsel legal def. fund NAACP, N.Y.C., 1966-70; ptnr. Chambers, Stein, Ferguson & Lanning, Charlotte, N.C., 1970-75; lectr., dir. fair employment clinic Vanderbilt U., Nashville, 1975-77, assoc. prof., 1977-82, prof., 1982—; vis. prof. Harvard U. Law Sch., Cambridge, Mass., 1986-87, U. No. Car., 1990-91, Charles Hamilton Houston Disting. vis. prof. N.C. Ctrl. Law Sch., 1997. Author: Remedies in Employment Discrimination Law, 1992; co-author Casebook on Employment Discrimination Law, 1999; contbr. articles to profl. jours. Mem. ABA, Nat. Bar Assn., Am. Assn. Law Schs. (exec. com. 1991-94), Am. Law Inst., Nat. Employment Lawyers' Assn. (exec. bd. 1996—). Office: Vanderbilt U Sch Law 21st Ave S Nashville TN 37240

BELTRAMO, MICHAEL NORMAN, management consultant; b. L.A., Feb. 9, 1942; s. Blase and Violette (Murphy) B.; m. Susan Annette Lawton, Dec. 24, 1969 (div. 1980); m. Jane Sinden Spiegel, Apr. 21, 1984; children: Helen Weedon, Anna Sinden, Emily Murphy. AB, UCLA, 1964; MPA, U. So. Calif., 1967; PhD, Rand Grad. Inst., Santa Monica, Calif., 1983. Cert. cost estimator/analyst. Mem. tech. staff The RAND Corp., Santa Monica, 1969-75; dep. mgr. Sci. Applications Internat. Corp., L.A., 1975-80; pres. Beltramo and Assocs., L.A., 1980—. Author: LA County Economic Adjustment Strategy for Defense Reduction; contbr. articles to profl. publs. Named Ky. Col. Commonwealth of Ky., 1973. Mem. Soc. Cost Estimating and Analysis (cert., bd. dirs. 1987-88). Republican. Methodist. Avocations: fly fishing, surfing. Home and Office: 13039 Sky Valley Rd Los Angeles CA 90049-1037

BELTRAN, EUSEBIUS JOSEPH, archbishop; b. Ashley, Pa., Aug. 31, 1934; s. Joseph C. and Helen Rita (Kozlowski) B. Ed., St. Charles Sem., Overbrook, Pa. Ordained priest Roman Cath. Ch., 1960. Consecrated bishop, 1978; pastor chs. in Atlanta and Decatur, Ga., 1960; notary, then vice officialis Atlanta Diocesan Tribunal, 1960-62; vice chancellor Archdiocese Atlanta, 1962; officialis Archdiocesan Tribunal, 1963-74; pastor chs. in Atlanta and Rome, Ga., 1963-66; vicar gen. Archdiocese of Atlanta, 1971-78; pastor St. Anthony's Ch., Atlanta, 1972-78; bishop of Tulsa, 1978-92; archbishop of Oklahoma City Archdiocese of Oklahoma, 1992—; mem. com. liturgy Nat. Conf. Cath. Bishops; also com. for Am. Coll., Louvain, Belgium; bd. regents Conception Sem.; bd. dirs. St. Gregory's Coll., Shawnee, Okla. Mem. Equestrian Order Holy Sepulchre, NCCJ. Club: K.C. Home: 2151 N Vancouver Ave Tulsa OK 74127-2218 Office: Archdiocese of Oklahoma City PO Box 32180 Oklahoma City OK 73123-0380*

BELTZ, CHARLES ROBERT, engineering executive; b. Pitts., Feb. 23, 1913; s. Charles Fred and Ester (Johnston) B.; m. Amy Margaret Ferguson, Oct. 23, 1935; children: Charles R., A.M. Bonnie Beltz Hatch, Homer F., William T., Carol E. Beltz Marks, M. Joy Beltz O'Keefe. Student, Greenbrier Mil. Sch., 1930-33; MSE, Cornell U., 1934; MS in Aero. Engring., U. Pitts., 1937. Engr. Crane Co., 1937-39; design engr. Stout Skycraft Corp., 1939-43; project engr. Cycle-Weld Labs., 1943-44; project engr., mgr. Fairchild E&A Corp., Roosevelt Field, 1944-46; corp. engr. Chrysler Corp., 1946-47; pres. Charles R. Beltz & Co., Detroit, 1947-85, Beltz Engring., 1950—, Beltemp, Inc., 1969-81. Author: Ice Skating, Skating Weather or Not, ABC's Air-conditioning, Rotatable Aircraft; designer in field. Mem. Nat. Aero. Assn. (past pres.), Air Conditioning Inst. (past pres.), Inst. Aero. Scis. (vice chmn.), ASHRAE (contbg. author), Engring. Soc. Detroit, Air Force Assn., Grosse Pointe Hist. Soc., English Speaking Union, Air Force Found., Yankee Air Force, Toledo Zool. Soc., Am. Philatelic Soc., Aero Club (bd. dirs.), Econ. Club, Curling Club (Detroit), Grosse Pointe Yacht Club, Lost Lake Woods Club. Address: 500 Lakeland St Grosse Pointe MI 48230-1655

BELTZ, WILLIAM ALBERT, publisher; b. Meriden, Conn., Aug. 24, 1929; s. Albert Henry and Marie Adelade (Heusel) B.; m. Beverly Sawyer, May 31, 1958; children—John, Jane, Kurt, Adam. A.B., Tufts U., 1951. With Bur. Nat. Affairs, Inc., Washington, 1956—; assoc. editor, then exec. editor Nat. Affairs, Inc., 1965-79; pres., editor in chief Bur. Nat. Affairs, Inc., 1979-96, chief exec. officer, 1980-96; chmn. Nat. Affairs, Inc., 1991—; bd. dirs. McArdle Printing Co., Silver Spring, Md. Trustee The Washington Opera Co., 1989-91, The Shakespeare Theater at Folger, 1991—; Washington trustee Fed. City Coun., 1992—. Mem. The White House Corrs. Assn., Info. Industry Assn. (dir.), Wash. Theater Awards Soc. (dir. 1986—, pres. 1988—), Econ. Club Washington. Democrat. Episcopalian. Club: Nat. Press (Washington). Office: Bur Nat Affairs Inc 1231 25th St NW Washington DC 20037-1197

BELTZNER, GAIL ANN, music educator; b. Palmerton, Pa., July 20, 1950; d. Conon Nelson and Lorraine Ann (Carey) Beltzner. BS in Music Edn. summa cum laude, West Chester State U., 1972; postgrad., Kean State Coll., 1972, Temple U., 1972, Westminster Choir Coll., 1972, Lehigh U., 1972. Tchr. music Drexel Hill Jr. High Sch., 1972-73; music specialist Allentown (Pa.) Sch. Dist., 1973—; tchr. Corps Sch. and Cmty. Devel. Lab., 1978-80, Corps Cmty. Resource Festival, 1979-81, Corps Cultural Fair, 1980, 81; Integrate music and scienceinto the curriculum to reiforce what has been learned from the scientists in the Growing With Science presentations with concepts such as the National Standards for Music dev. by MENC, Kodaly, Orff Schulwerk, Dalcroze Eurhythmics, Howard Garner's Multiple Intelligences, Heidi Hayes Jacobs Integrating the Curriculum, Dr. Sue snyder Intergrating Music into the Curriculum, Pam Robbins Brain Research. Mem. Mus. Fine Arts, Boston, aux. Allentown Art Mus., aux. Allentown Hosp.; mem. woman's com. Allentown Symphony, The Lyric Soc. of the Allentown Orch.; mem. Allentown 2d and 9th Civilian Police Acads.; bd. dirs. Allentown Area Ecumenical Food Bank; mem. Growing with Sci. partnership—Air Products and Chems., Inc. and Allentown Sch. Dist., Good Shepherd Home Aux. Decorated Dame Comdr., Ordre Souverain et Militaire de la Milice du St. Sepulcre; recipient Cert. of Appreciation, Lehigh Valley Sertoma Club; Excellence in the Classroom grantee Rider-Pool Found., 1988, 91-92. Mem. AAUW, NAFE, ASCD, Am. String Tchrs. Assn., Am. Viola Soc., Internat. Reading Assn., Internat. Platform Assn., Allentown Edn. Assn., Music Educators Nat. Conf., Pa. Music Educators Assn., Am. Orff-Schulwerk Assn., Phila. Area Orff-Schulwerk Assn., Soc. Gen. Music, Am. Assn. Music Therapy, Internat. Soc. Music Edn., Internat. Tech. Edn. Assn., Assn. for Tech. in Music Instrn., Choristers Guild, Lenni Lenape Hist. Soc., Lehigh Valley Arts Coun., Allentown Symphony Assn., Midi Users Group, Pa.-Del. String Tchrs. Assn., Nat. Sch. Orch. Assn., Lehigh County Hist. Soc., Confedn. Chivalry, Maison Internat. des Intellectuels Akademie, Order White Cross Internat. (apptd. dist. comdr. for Pa./ U.S.A. dist., nobless of humanity), Airedale Terrier Club of Greater Phila., Kappa Delta Pi, Phi Delta Kappa, Alpha Lambda. Republican. Lutheran. Home: PO Box 4427 Allentown PA 18105-4427

BELUSHI, JAMES A., actor; b. Chgo., June 15, 1954; s. Adam and Agnes Belushi; divorced; 1 child, Robert. Student, Coll. DuPage; grad., So. Ill. U. Mem., musician James Belushi & The Sacred Hearts, Blues Brothers Band; mem. Second City comedy troupe, 1977-78, 80. Actor: (stage prodns.) Under Milkwood, Born Yesterday, Dumbwaiter, Sexual Perversity in Chicago, Apollo Theatre, Chgo., 1979, Baal in the Twenty-first Century, Goodman Theatre, Chgo., 1980, Pirates of Penzance, Minscoff Theatre, N.Y., 1982, True West, Cherry Lane Theatre, N.Y., 1983, Moon Over Miami, Williamstown Theater, 1987, Conversations with my Father, Royale Theatre, 1993, Bobby Gould in Hell, 1997, (TV series) Who's Watching the Kids, NBC, 1978, Working Stiffs, CBS, 1979, Saturday Night Live, NBC, 1983-85, (writer, prodr., dir.) Birthday Boy, 1986, Cinemax, others, (TV films) Best Legs in Eighth Grade, 1986, HBO, Wild Palms, ABC, 1993, Royce, 1994, Sahara, 1995, Totay Security, 1997, (feature films) Thief, 1981, Trading Places, 1983, The Man with One Red Shoe, 1985, Salvador, 1986, About Last Night..., 1986, Real Men, 1987, Principle, 1987, Red Heat, 1988, K-9, 1988, Homer and Eddie, 1988, To Forget Palermo, 1989, Taking Care of Business, 1990, Mr. Destiny, 1991, Traces of Red, 1992, Only the Lonely, 1991, Curlie Sue, 1991, Once Upon a Crime, 1992, Separate Lives, 1995, Destiny Turns ofn the Radio, 1995, Streets of Gold, 1996, Jingle All The Way, 1996, Jumpin Jack Flash, 1986, Total Security, 1997, Justice, 1997, Gang Related, 1997, Living in Peril, 1997; (features) Race the Sun, 1996, Retroactive, 1997, Criminal Intent, 1997, Peril of Walter Wood, 1996 (cameo appearences) Harry Crumb, Little Shop of Horrors, Monsters of Menace, 1989, Wedding Band, 1989, The Last Action Hero, Diary of a Hit Man, 1992; (voice overs) The Pebble and the Penguinm 1995, Bad Baby, Mighty Duck's, Duckman, Ahh, Monsters, Animaniacs, Superman. Pinky and the Brain, 3 Little Pigs, Dog's Best Friend, 1997, Babes In Toyland, 1997, Hey Arnold!, 1997, Blues Brothers, 1997; co-screenwriter Number One With a Bullet; writer SNL, 1983-85. Mem. Actors Equity Assn., Screen Actors Guild, AFTRA, Writers Guild Am., Acad. Motion Picture Arts and Scis., Acad. TV Arts and Scis. Office: care ICM 8942 Wilshire Blvd Beverly Hills CA 90211-1934*

BELYTSCHKO, TED BOHDAN, civil, mechanical engineering educator; b. Proskurov, Ukraine, Jan. 13, 1943; came to U.S., 1950; s. Stephan and Maria (Harpinak) B.; m. Gail Eisenhart, Aug. 1967; children: Peter, Nicole, Justine. BS in Engring. Sci., Ill. Inst. Tech., 1965, PhD in Mechanics, 1968; PhD (hon.), U. Liege, 1997. Asst. prof. structural mechanics U. Ill., Chgo., 1968-73, assoc. prof., 1973-76, prof., 1976-77; Walter P. Murphy prof. civil and mech. engring. Northwestern U., Evanston, Ill., 1977—, chair mech. engring., 1998—. Assoc. editor Computer Methods in Applied Mech. and Engring., 1977-83, Jour. Applied Mechanics, 1979-85; editor Nuclear Engring. and Design, 1980-88, Engring. with Computers, 1984-88, Internat. Jour. Numerical Methods in Engring., 1988—. NDEA fellow, 1965-68; recipient Thomas Jaeger prize Internat. Assn. Structural Mechanics in Reactor Tech., 1983, Japanese Soc. Mech. Engrs. Computational Mechanics award, 1993,

Gold medal Internat. Conf. on Computational Engring. and Scis., 1996, Computational Mechanics award Internat. Assn. for Computational Mechanics, 1998. Fellow ASME (chmn. applied mechanics div. 1991, Pi Tau Sigma Gold medal 1975, Theodore von Karman medal 1999), Am. Acad. Mechanics; mem. ASCE (chmn. engring. mechanics div. 1982, Walter Huber rsch. prize 1977, structural dynamics and materials award 1990), Assn. for Computing Machnery (pres. 1992-94, Computational Structural Mechanics award 1997), NAE (elected 1992). Office: Northwestern Univ Mech Engring Dept 2145 Sheridan Rd Evanston IL 60208-0834

BELZ, MARK, lawyer; b. Marshalltown, Iowa, July 19, 1943; s. Max Victor and Jean (Franzenburg) B.; m. Linda Cole, July 24, 1965; children: Aaron Sanderson, Jane Evangelyn. BA, Covenant Coll., Lookout Mountain, Ga., 1965; JD, U. Iowa, Iowa City, 1970; MDiv, Covenant Theol. Sem., St. Louis, 1981. Bar: Iowa 1970, Mo. 1976. Ptnr. Rosenberger, Peterson, Conway & Belz, Muscatine, Iowa, 1970-72, Keyes & Crawford, Cedar Rapids, Iowa, 1972-78, Belz & Belz, St. Louis, 1983-87; prin. Belz & Beckemeier, P.C., St. Louis, 1987-94, Belz & Jones, P.C., Clayton, Mo., 1995—. Author: Suffer the Little Children, 1989. Bd. dirs. Westminster Acad., 1977-85, Covenant Coll., 1972-81, Cono Christian Sch., 1993—; moderator Presbyn. Ch. Am., Atlanta, 1991-92, mem. standing jud. com., 1989—. Named Alumnus of Yr., Covenant Coll., 1989. Republican. Office: Belz & Jones PC 7777 Bonhomme Ave Ste 1710 Clayton MO 63105-1911

BELZ, RICHARD A., federal judge; b. 1935. BA, Marist Coll.; JD, U. Fla. Magistrate judge U.S. Dist. Ct. (no. dist.) Fla., Gainesville, 1994—. Office: 401 SE First Ave Gainesville FL 32607-0268

BELZBERG, SAMUEL, investment professional; b. Calgary, Alta., Can., June 26, 1928; s. Abraham and Hinda (Fishman) B.; m. Frances Cooper; children: Cheryl Rae, Marc David, Wendy Jay, Lisa. B.Comm., U. Alta., Edmonton, 1948. Chmn. Balfour Holdings, Inc., 1992-97; pres. 1st City Fin. Corp. Ltd., Vancouver, B.C., Can., 1970-83, 86-91, chmn., 1983-91; pres. Gibralt Capital Corp., Vancouver, 1995—, Bel-Fran US Inc., 1997—; bd. dirs. C.E. Franklin Ltd., D. Grant MacDonald Capital Corp., Westminster Capital, Inc., N.Am. Energy Systems Corp., Metromedia Asia Corp., Emultek Ltd., Bar Equipment of Am. Home: 3711 Alexandra St, Vancouver, BC Canada V6J 4C3 Office: 1177 W Hastings St Ste 2000, Vancouver, BC Canada V6E 2K3

BELZER, ELLEN J., negotiations and communications consultant; b. Kansas City, Mo., May 22, 1951; d. Meyer Simmon and Fay (Weinstein) B. Student, U. Okla., 1969-70, U. Ibero-Americana, Mexico City, 1971; BA, Northwestern U., 1973; MPA, U. Mo., Kansas City, 1976. Rsch. asst. dept. polit. sci. Northwestern U., Evanston, Ill., 1970-73; adminstrv. asst. Ctrs. for Regional Progress Midwest Rsch. Inst., Kansas City, 1974; various positions to dir. socioecons. div. Am. Acad. Family Physicians, Kansas City, 1974-86; pres. Belzer Seminars and Cons., Kansas City, 1986—; instr. communication Avila Coll., Kansas City, 1987-92, dept. continuing edn. U. Kans., Lawrence, 1989-92; speaker on negotiation strategies, conflict resolution techniques, communication skills, 1986—; mediator for hosps., physician groups, state health depts., community health ctrs., others. Contbr. articles to profl. publs., also monographs. Campaign vol. for local candidate, Kansas City, 1970, 82, 99. Democrat. Home: 21 W Bannister Rd Kansas City MO 64114-4009 Office: 7140 Wornall Rd Ste 203 Kansas City MO 64114-1300

BELZER, RICHARD, comedian, TV show host, actor; b. Bridgeport, Conn., Aug. 4, 1944; s. Charles and Francis B.; m. Gail Susan Ross (div.); m. Dalia Danoch (div.); m. Harlee McBride. Student, Dean Jr. Coll. Appeared in (films) Fame, Author! Author!, The Groove Tube, Night Shift, Scarface, The Puppet Masters; stand-up comedian N.Y.C. and Los Angeles clubs; host (cable TV show) Hot Properties; performer (TV show) Thicke of the Night, The Late Show David Letterman, Tonight Show with Johnny Carson; TV (series) Homicide, 1993—, Lois & Clark/Superman; author: (book) How To Be a Standup Comic. Office: care Panacea Entertainment 2705 Glendower Ave Los Angeles CA 90027-1116

BEMENT, ARDEN LEE, JR., engineering educator; b. Pitts., May 22, 1932; s. Arden Lee and Edith Ardelia (Bigelow) B.; m. Mary Ann Baroch, Aug. 24, 1952 (dec.); children: Kristine, Kenneth, Vincent, Cynthia, Mark, David, Paul, Mary. Deg. of Engr. in Metallurgy, Colo. Sch. Mines, 1954; MSMetE, U. Idaho, 1959; PhD, U. Mich., 1963; Hon. Doctorate degree, Cleve. State U., 1989. Rsch. metallurgist Hanford Labs., GE, Richland, Wash., 1954-65; sr. rsch. mgr. Pacific N.W. Lab., Battelle Meml. Inst., Richland, 1965-70; prof. nuclear materials MIT, 1970-76; dir. Def. Advanced Rsch. Projects Agy. Office Materials Sci., DARPA, DOD, Washington, 1976-79, dep. undersec. rsch. and advanced tech., 1979-80; v.p. tech. resources TRW, Lyndhurst, Ohio, 1980-89, v.p. sci. and tech., 1990-92; Basil S. Turner disting. prof. engring. Purdue U., West Lafayette, Ind., 1992-98, head sch. nuclear engring., 1998—; tech. assistance expert to Mexico UNIAEA, 1974-76; cons. NRC, Taiwan, 1975; mem. Nat. Sci. Bd., 1988-94; mem. sci. adv. com. Electric Power Rsch. Inst., 1987—, Advanced Tech. Inc., 1993—; bd. dirs. Keithley Instrument Co., Lord Corp. Author publs. in field; editor: Biomaterials: Structural and Biomedical Bases for Hard Tissue and Soft Tissue Substitutes, 1971; co-editor: Dislocation Dynamics, 1968, Creep of Zirconium Alloys in Nuclear Reactors, 1983; mem. editl. bd. Jour. Nuclear Materials, 1970-77, Materials Tech., 1987-99; contbr. articles to profl. jours. Chmn. bd. health Mental Health/Mental Retardation, Benton-Franklin Counties, Wash., 1968-70; mem. Richland, Wash. city coun., 1968-70; pres. Arts Coun., Richland, Pasco and Kennewick, Wash., 1968-70; bd. dirs. Cleve. Opera Bd., treas., 1982-86, v.p., 1986-91, nat./internat. bd. mem., 1992—; bd. dirs. LaFayette Symphony, 1998—; bd. overseers Fermi Nat. Accelerator Lab., 1999—. Lt. col. USAR, 1954-79. Recipient Outstanding Achievement award Colo. Sch. Mines, 1984, Melville F. Coolbaugh award, 1991, Disting. Engr. award UCLA, 1987, Honor Roll award U. Idaho Alumni Assn., 1991, Engring. Alumnus of Yr. award U. Mich. Alumni Assn. (Cleve. br.), 1992, Merit award U. Mich. Alumni Assn., 1993, Nat. Mats. Adv. award Fedn. of Mats. Socs., 1997. Fellow Am. Nuclear Soc., Am. Soc. Metals (Disting. Life mem. 1998), Am. Inst. Chemists; mem. Nat. Acad. Engrs., ASTM, AIME, Metals Soc. of AIME (Leadership award 1988), Sigma Xi, Tau Beta Pi, Sigma Gamma Epsilon. Republican. Roman Catholic. Home: 4709 Doe Path Ct Lafayette IN 47905-8542

BEMENT, JILL LEIGH, occupational therapist; b. Amarillo, Tex., Feb. 21, 1973; d. Lee and Nelda (Vanderburg) Callaway; m. Matthew Thomas Bement, Dec. 30, 1995. Occupational therapy, Tex. Tech. Univ., 1995. Registered therapist, Tex. Dir. of occupational therapy Sherwood Health Care, Inc., Bryan, Tex., 1996—. Mem. Tex. Occupational Therapy Assn., Am. Occupational Therapy Assn. Republican. Baptist. Avocations: needlework, flower arranging, tennis, golf, aerobics. Office: Sherwood Health Care Inc 1401 Memorial Dr Bryan TX 77802-5218

BEMILLER, C. RICHARD, II, consultant; b. Hanover, Pa., Aug. 21, 1955; s. Carl Richard and Patricia Naomi (Houck) B.; m. Debra E. Smith, May 23, 1992. BA in Govt., Franklin and Marshall Coll., 1977; MBA in Fin. Mgmt., St. Joseph's U., 1990. Mfr.'s rep. Josten's Inc., Mpls., 1981-85; v.p. mktg. L.F. Manze, Inc., East Aurora, N.Y., 1985-86; grad. bus. program St. Joseph's U., Phila., 1987-90; edn. sales mgr. Gen. Computer Corp., Tamaqua, Pa., 1991-92; pres. Consumers Group Telephone, Orwigsburg, Pa., 1992-94; exec. dir. Schuylkill Symphony Orch., Pottsville, Pa., 1994—; mng. ptnr. Global Control, Orwigsburg, 1990—. Mem. bd. dirs. Ashland Regional Med. Ctr. Found., 1996-97, Schuykill County Coun. for Arts, 1995-96. Mem. Mfr.'s Assn. Mideastern Pa., Schuylkill Leadership Assn. (pres. 1995—), Schuykill C. of C., Schuylkill Symphony Orch. (bd. dirs. 1995—). Avocations: tennis, classical music, reading. Home: 1002 Village Rd Orwigsburg PA 17961-9692 Office: Global Control 1002 Village Rd Orwigsburg PA 17961-9692

BEMILLER, JAMES NOBLE, biochemist, educator; b. Evansville, Ind., Apr. 7, 1933; s. LaMar N. and Mabel (Gruber) BeM.; m. Paraskevi Mavridis, Aug. 6, 1960; children: Byron N., Philip J. BS, Purdue U., 1954, MS, 1956, PhD, 1959. Asst. prof. biochemistry Purdue U., 1959-61; asst. prof. biochemistry dept. chemistry and biochemistry So. Ill. U., Carbondale, 1961-65; assoc. prof. So. Ill. U., 1965-68, prof., 1968-85, chmn. dept. chemistry and biochemistry, 1966-67; prof. biochemistry So. Ill. U. Sch. Medicine, 1971-85; asst. dean curriculum Sch. Medicine So. Ill. U., 1977-79, dean Coll. Sci., 1976-77, chmn. dept. med. biochemistry, 1980-83; prof. dept. food sci. Purdue U., West Lafayette, Ind., 1986—; dir. Whistler Ctr. for Carbohydrate Rsch. Purdue U., 1986—; Pres. U.S. adv. com. Internat. Carbohydrate Symposia, 1982—. Editor: Industrial Gums, 1959, 73, 93, Methods in Carbohydrate Chemistry, 1-10, 1962—, Starch: Chemistry and Technology, 1965, 67, 84; mem. adv. bd. Carbohydrate Research, 1971-95, Jour. Carbohydrate Chemistry, 1984—, Food Hydrocolloids, 1985-89, Carbohydrate Polymers, 1988—; assoc. editor: Cereal Chemistry, 1975-78, 94-97. Mem. exec. bd. Egyptian coun. Boy Scouts Am., 1982-85, pres., 1985, Sagamore coun., 1989-92; bd. dirs. Luth. Sch. Theology, Chgo., 1967-73, sec., 1971-73; bd. dirs. ACS group ins. trust, 1974-76; bd. dirs. Christ Sem., 1976-79, mem. devel. com., 1979-86; exec. bd. Ill. Synod Luth. Ch. Am., 1978-85. Mem. AAAS, AAUP, TAPPI, Am. Chem. Soc. (councilor 1967-95), Am. Soc. Biochem. Molecular Biol., Am. Assn. Cereal Chemists, Internat. Carbohydrate Orgn. (U.S. rep. 1978—, pres. 1986-88, 1998—), Am. Inst. Chemists (dir. 1982-84, sec. 1985, pres. 1988-89), Ins. Food Technologists, Ill. Acad. Scis., Sigma Xi, Phi Tau Sigma, Alpha Chi Sigma, Alpha Tau Omega. Home: 2829 Bentbrook Ln West Lafayette IN 47906-5275 Office: Purdue U Whistler Ctr Carbohydrate Rsch 1160 Food Sci Bldg West Lafayette IN 47907-1160

BEMIS, MARY FERGUSON, magazine editor; b. N.Y.C., Dec. 28, 1961; d. Edmund Augustus and Anne Adoian (Nalbandian) B. BFA in Writing, Johnson State Coll., 1983. Co-editor, co-pub. Ave. Literary Rev. Ave. Publs. Inc., Burlington, Vt., 1983-85; editor Unique Hair and Beauty Mag., 1994; editor Lady's Circle Mag. Lopez Publs., N.Y.C., 1987-94, editor, 1989-94; freelance editor, writer Mus. Sci., Boston, 1991-93; freelance editor Woman's Day Spl. Interest Publs., 1995-97. Co-editor: The Green Mountain Rev., 1982-83, Nature Through Her Eyes; Art and Literature by Women, 1994, Journey Into the Wilderness, 1994; sr. editor Am. Spa mag., Am. Salon mag., 1996—; editor-in-chief Am. Spa mag., 1998—. Mem. Women in Comm., Inc. Democrat. Mem. Unitarian Ch. Home and Office: 36 E 20th St Fl 5 New York NY 10003-1315

BEN, MANUEL, chemist; b. Syracuse, N.Y., July 30, 1916; s. David and Sarah (Slater) B.; m. Evelyn Ben, July 14, 1940 (dec. Mar. 1988); children: Allan Wayne Ben, Francine Adele Savin. BS, U. Mich., 1939, postgrad., 1939-40. Cert. electroplater finisher. Sr. rsch. chemist AC Spark Plug divsn. GM Corp., Flint, Mich., 1940-53; supr. electrochemistry dept. GM Rsch. Labs., Warren, Mich., 1953-67; sr. chem. engr./supr. GM Mfg., Warren, 1967-72; sr. design engr./plating specialist Chevrolet divsn. GM Corp., Warren, 1972-74; staff devel. engr. GM Mfg. Staff, Warren, 1974-81; cons. in field. Contbr. articles to profl. jours.; patentee in field. Vol. counselor Svc. Corps of Ret. Execs., Detroit, 1983— (Platinum award 1998). Fellow Am. Electroplaters and Finishers Soc. (Saginaw Valley br. pres. 1954, Detroit br. pres., Charles Henry Proctor Meml. award 1964); mem. Electrochemistry Soc. (Detroit chmn., emeritus mem.), Inst. Metal Finishing (England chpt., emeritus). Avocations: music, travel, counseling, volunteering. Home: 5734 Templar Xing West Bloomfield MI 48322-1367

BENACERRAF, BARUJ, pathologist, educator; b. Caracas, Venezuela, Oct. 29, 1920; came to U.S., 1939, naturalized, 1943; s. Abraham and Henriette (Lasry) B.; m. Annette Dreyfus, Mar. 24, 1943; 1 child, Beryl. B es L, Lycee Janson, 1940; BS, Columbia U., 1942; MD, Med. Sch. Va., 1945; MA, Harvard U., 1970; MD (hon.), U. Geneva, 1980; DSc (hon.), NYU, 1981, Va. Commonwealth U., 1981, Yeshiva U., 1982, U. Aix-Marseille, 1982, Columbia U., 1985, Adelphi U., 1988, Weizmann Inst., 1989, Harvard U., 1992, U. Bordeaux, 1993, U. Vienna, 1995. Intern Queens Gen. Hosp., N.Y.C., 1945-46; rsch. fellow dept. microbiology Med. Sch. Columbia U., 1948-50; charge de recherches Centre Nat. de Recherche Scientique Hosp. Broussais, Paris, 1950-56; asst. prof. pathology Sch. Medicine NYU, 1956-58, assoc. prof. Sch. Medicine, 1958-60, prof. Sch. Medicine, 1960-68; chief immunology Nat. Inst. Allergy and Infectious Diseases NIH, Bethesda, Md., 1968-70; Fabyan prof. comparative pathology, chmn. dept. Med. Sch. Harvard U., 1970-91; ret. Med. Sch., Harvard U., Cambridge, Mass., 1991; pres., CEO Dana-Farber Cancer Inst., 1980-91, Dana-Farber Inc., 1990-95; mem. immunology study sect. NIH; pres. Fedn. Am. Socs. Exptl. Biology, 1974-75; chmn. sci. adv. com. Centre d'Immunologie de Marseille. Bd. govs. Weizmann Inst. Medicine; mem. sci. adv. com. Children's Hosp. Boston; mem. award com. GM Cancer Rsch. Found., also chmn. selection com. Sloan prize, 1980. Capt. M.C. AUS, 1946-48. Recipient T. Duckett Jones Meml. award Helen Hay Whitney Found., 1976, Rabbi Shai Shacknai lectr. and prize Hebrew U. Jerusalem, 1974, Waterford award, 1980, Nobel prize, 1980, Corr. Emerite de l'Institut de la Sante et de la Recherche Scientifique, Nat. Medal of Sci. NSF, 1990. Fellow Am. Acad. Arts and Scis.; mem. NAS, Nat. Inst. Medicine, Am. Assn. Immunologists (pres. 1973-74), Brit. Assn. Immunology, French Soc. Biol. Chemistry, Internat. Union Immunology Socs. (pres. 1980-83). Home: 111 Perkins St Jamaica Plain MA 02130-4313 Office: Dana-Farber Cancer Inst 44 Binney St Boston MA 02115-5347

BENACH, SHARON ANN, physician assistant; b. New Orleans, Aug. 28, 1944; d. Wilbur G. and Freda Helen (Klaas) Cherry; m. Richard Benach, Dec. 6, 1969 (div. Oct. 1976); children: Craig (dec.), Rachel. Degree, St. Louis U., 1978. Physician asst. VA Hosp., St. Louis, 1982-84, Maricopa County Health Svcs., Phoenix, 1984—. Served with USPHS, 1978-82. Recipient Outstanding Performance award HHS. Mem. Maricopa Faculty Assn. (div. internal medicine), Mensa. Jewish. Avocation: pre-Columbian archaeology. Home: 5515 N 7th St Apt 5-600 Phoenix AZ 85014-2531

BENAK, JAMES DONALD, lawyer; b. Omaha, Jan. 22, 1954; s. James R. and Norma Lea (Roberts) B.; Patricia Ann Duffy, Mar. 1995; 1 child, James Duffy. BA, U. Nebr., 1977; JD, Creighton U., 1980. Bar: Nebr. 1980, U.S. Dist. Ct. Nebr. 1980, U.S. Ct. Appeals (7th cir.) 1988, U.S. Ct. Appeals (6th cir.) 1989, Ill. 1990, U.S. Dist. Ct. (no. and ctrl. dists.) Ill. 1991. Assoc. Kennedy, Holland, DeLacy & Svoboda, Omaha, 1980-84; asst. gen. atty. Union Pacific R.R. Co., Omaha, 1984-87, gen. atty., 1987-90; ptnr. Jenner & Block, Chgo., 1990—. Bd. dirs. Combined Health Agys. Drive/Nebr., 1985-90, Automated Monitoring and Control Internat., Inc., 1987-90, Coll. World Series, 1989-90. Mem. ABA (litigation sect.), Nebr. Bar Assn., Chgo. Bar Assn. (pub. utility and ins. law com.). Republican. Roman Catholic. Home: 225 Ravine Rd Hinsdale IL 60521-3713 Office: Jenner & Block One IBM Plz Chicago IL 60611

BENAKIS, GEORGE JAMES, lawyer; b. N.Y.C., June 24, 1971; s. James G. and Voula (Aneson) B. BA, Brooklyn Coll., 1992; JD, Fordham U., 1995. Bar: N.Y. Legal asst. Wachtell, Lipton, Rosen & Katz, N.Y.C., 1992-94; intern N.Y. State Atty. Gen., N.Y.C., 1994; case mgr. Paine Webber, Inc., Weehawken, N.J., 1995-96; contract atty. Cleary, Gottleib, N.Y.C., 1996-97; assoc. Ateshoglou, Kavourias & Chrysanthem, P.C., N.Y.C., 1997-98, Capitol Lease Funding L.P., N.Y.C., 1998—. Mem. ABA, N.Y. State Bar Assn., Assn. Bar City of New York, New York County Lawyer's Assn., Ea. Orthodox Lawyers Assn., N.Y. State Hellenic-Am. Rep. Assn. (mem. pub. rels. sect. 1997), Pan-Imbrian Benevolent Assn. (pres. 1995-98). Greek Orthodox. Avocations: fishing, basketball. Office: Capital Lease Funding LP 111 Maiden Ln 36th Flr New York NY 10005

BEN-AKIVA, MOSHE EMANUEL, civil engineering educator; b. Tel Aviv, June 11, 1944; came to U.S., 1968; s. Eliezer and Rivka (Reiner) B.A.; children: Ori, Lea, Danna, Elana, Erez. BSCE, Technion-Israel Inst. Tech., Haifa, 1968; MSCE, MIT, 1971, PhD in Transp. Systems, 1973; docteur honoris causa, U. Lumiere Lyon, France, 1992. Registered profl. engr., Israel. Edmund K. Turner prof. civil engring. MIT, Cambridge, Mass., 1973-96; vis. prof. Technion-Israel Inst. Tech., Haifa, 1978-79, 81-82, Tel Aviv, 1981-82; vis. scholar NTT Rsch. Labs., 1988; cons. Am. Airlines, 1987, Atty. Gen. Mass., Boston, 1985-88, Hague (The Netherlands) Cons. Group, 1985—, Cambridge Systematics, Inc., 1972—. Assoc. editor: Intelligent Transportation Systems Jour. and Transp. Sci.; mem. editl. bd. Jour. Retailing and Consumer Svcs., Jour. Transp. and Statistics. Lady Davis fellow Technion-Israel Inst. Tech., 1978. Mem. Transp. Rsch. Bd., Transp. Rsch. Forum, Regional Sci. Assn., Ops. Rsch. Soc. Am. (award 1973), World Conf. on Transp. Rsch. Soc. Office: MIT 77 Massachusetts Ave Rm 1-181 Cambridge MA 02139-4307

BENAMATI, DENNIS CHARLES, law librarian, editor, consultant; b. Orlando, Fla., Oct. 30, 1948; s. Thomas Guy and Ann (Clements) B.; m. Evelina Estella Lemelin, Aug. 19, 1983; children: Suzette, Alicia, Marcus. BA, St. Francis Coll., Loretto, Pa., 1970; MA, Fordham U., 1974; MLS, So. Conn. State U., 1975. Law libr. Conn. State Libr., Stamford, 1976-78; reference libr. U. Bridgeport (Conn.) Sch. Law, 1979; asst. law libr. for tech. svcs. U. Maine Sch. Law, Portland, 1979-83; asst. law libr. Aetna Life & Casualty Co., Hartford, Conn., 1983-84; head cataloging U. Conn. Sch. Law, Hartford, 1984-88; dir. The Dewey Grad. Libr. SUNY, Albany, 1988-93; adj. faculty Sch. Criminal Justice SUNY, Albany, 1993-95; vis. elec. info. svcs. libr., instr. advanced legal rsch. U. S.C. Sch. Law, 1995-97; asst. libr. dir. Marist Coll., 1997—; ptnr. Lemelin & Benamati; cons., Kinderhook, N.Y., 1985—; cons. to various law firms, Lawyers Coop. Pub. Co., European Inst. for Crime Prevention and Control. Co-author: Publication Opportunities for Law Librarians, 1995, Criminal Justice Information: How to Find It, How to Use It, 1998; rapporteur World Criminal Justice Libr. Network Conf., 1997; contbr. articles to profl. jours. Mem. Am. Assn. Law Librs., Law Librs. New England (bd. dirs. 1985-87). Roman Catholic. Home: 26 Hawthorne Dr Valatie NY 12184-5004 Office: PO Box 692 Kinderhook NY 12106-0692

BENARDE, ANITA E., artist; b. Oct. 11, 1927. Student, Bklyn. Coll., St. Martins Sch., London. Solo exhbns. include Art Bank, Norristown, Pa., Turkish Consulate Gallery, N.Y.C., 1986, AT&T Corp. Edn. Ctr., Princeton, N.J., 1989, Johnson & Johnson World Headquarters, New Brunswick, N.J., 1993; group exhbns. include Hunterdon Art Ctr., Clinton, N.J., 1988-91, Newark Mus., 1988, Milberg Gallery, Princeton Univ., 1988, Rider U., Lawrenceville, N.J., 1990, Soviet Art Exch., Moscow, 1990, The Scanticon, Princeton, 1990-94, The Bianco Gallery, Doylestown, Pa., 1996, The Lobby Gallery, N.Y.C., 1996, Gratella Gallery, Princeton, 1998, Bristol-Myers-Squibb, 1999, Home Box Office, N.Y.C., 1999; represented numerous pvt. and corp. collections including Art Bank, Emmee Gallery, Best Portfolio, Williams Collection, Schulte Gallery. Home: 6 Thorngate Ct Princeton NJ 08540

BENARIO, HERBERT WILLIAM, classics educator; b. N.Y.C., July 21, 1929; s. Frederick and Ilse (Kessler) B.; m. Janice M. Martin, Dec. 23, 1957; children: Frederick M., John H. B.A., CCNY, 1948; M.A., Columbia U., 1949; Ph.D., Johns Hopkins U., 1951. Instr. Greek and Latin Columbia U., 1953-58; asst. prof. Greek and Latin Sweet Briar Coll., 1958-60; mem. faculty Emory U., 1960—, prof. classics, 1967-87; chmn. dept., 1968-73, 76-78, prof. emeritus, 1987; dir. Vergilian Soc. Summer Sch. in, Italy, 1963, 67, 73, 81, asst. dir., 1957, 59; dir. Roman Britain tour, 1977, 86, Roman Germany tour, 1981, 88, Rome and North Italy, 1982; vis. prof. Intercollegiate Center Classical Studies, Rome, spring 1967, co-prof. in charge, 1984-85; vis. prof. U. Colo., summer 1969; Fulbright Sr. prof. U. Passau, Fed. Republic Germany, 1990; co-exec. sec. Vergilian Soc., 1992-93; mem. Latin achievement test com. Coll. Entrance Exam. Bd., 1963-66; dir. Roman Germany tour Mediterranean Soc., 1998. Author: Tacitus, Agricola, Germany, Dialogue on Orators, 1967, rev. edition, 1991, An Introduction to Tacitus, 1975, A Commentary on the Vita Hadriani in the Historia Augusta, 1980, Tacitus Annals 11 and 12, 1983, The Classical Association of the Middle West and South, 1989, Caesaris Augusti Res Gestae et Fragmenta, 1990, Thusnelda. A German Princess in Ancient Rome, 1993, Tacitus Germany, 1999; co-editor: Basil Lanneau Gildersleeve, An American Classicist, 1986. Served with AUS, 1951-53. Fulbright grantee, 1956; research grantee Am. Philos Soc.; Am. Council Learned Socs. fellow, 1978. Mem. Am. Philol. Assn., Classical Assn. Middle West and South (pres. 1971-72, pres. So. sect. 1968-70), Classical Soc. of Am. Acad. in Rome (pres. 1965), Vergilian Soc. Am. (trustee 1960-65, 69-73, pres. 1980-82), Am. Classical League, Phi Beta Kappa (pres. Emory U. chpt. 1968- 69). Home: 430 Chelsea Cir NE Atlanta GA 30307-1269 Office: Emory U Classics Dept Atlanta GA 30322

BEN-ASHER, DANIEL LAWRENCE, legislative researcher, writer; b. Newark, Apr. 15, 1946; s. Jerry and Florence (Tasoff) B.; m. Michele Lauren Cohn, July 16, 1978; children: Sarah, Joshua. AB, Rutgers Coll., 1968; MA, U. Minn., 1970. Plant pers. adminstr. Tanatex Chem. Co. div. Sybron Corp., Lyndhurst, N.J., 1970-71; rsch. asst. Office Legis. Svcs. N.J. State Legislature, Trenton, 1971-76, rsch. assoc., 1976-87, sr. rsch. assoc., 1987-98, sr. rsch. analyst, 1999—; staff N.J. Assembly Labor Com., 1974-81, Assembly Commerce and Industry Com., 1981-82, Alcoholic Beverage Control Study Commn., 1986-88, Assembly Drug and Alcohol Abuse Policy Com., 1990-91, Assembly Housing Com., 1995; mem. N.J. Tobacco Age-of-Sale Enforcement Task Force, 1994-96; mem. politics and govt. judges panel The Best in America spl. edit. U.S. News and World Report, 1990. Mem. Ewing Twp. (N.J.) Rent Control Bd., 1976-77; fin. coord. Lawrence Twp. (N.J.) Hist. Preservation Adv. Com., 1985-92; twp. chmn. A Guide to Lawrenceville's Historic Landmarks, 1991-93; chmn. Mason Gross Presdl. Meml., Rutgers-New Brunswick, 1992-94; mem. nat. alumni adv. com. on admissions Rutgers U., 1992-94; Rutgers Alumni Admissions Rep., 1994—. Recipient Loyal Son award for extraordinary svc. to alma mater Rutgers Alumni Assn., 1995. Home: 11 Bennington Dr Lawrenceville NJ 08648-1536 Office: NJ Office Legis Svcs PO Box 68 Trenton NJ 08625-0068

BEN-ASHER, M. DAVID, physician; b. Newark, June 18, 1931; s. Samuel Irving and Dora Ruth (Kagan)B.; m. Bryna S. Zeller, Nov. 22, 1956. BA, Syracuse U., 1952; MD, U. Buffalo Sch. Med., 1956. Intern E.J. Meyer Mem. Hosp., Buffalo, N.Y., 1956-57; resident Jersey City Med. Ctr., 1957-58; asst. chief med. service U.S. Army Hosp., Ft. McPherson, Ga., 1958-60; resident Madigan Gen. Hosp., Tacoma, Wash., 1960-62; chief gen. med. service Walson Army Hosp., Ft. Dix, N.Y., 1962-64; attending staff St. Mary's Hosp., Tucson, Ariz., 1964—; pvt. practice Tucson, 1964—. Bd. dirs. Tucson Symphony, 1971-73; mem. Ariz. State Bd. Med. Examiners, 1978-88, joint bd. for regulation of physicians' assts., 1990-97; bd. trustees United Synagogue Am., 1981-87, nat. adv. bd., 1987-91. Fellow ACP; mem. Pima County Med. Soc. (bd. dirs. 1971-77, pres. 1976), Ariz. Med. Assn., AMA. Democrat. Avocations:health club, music, computers. Home: 3401 N Tanuri Dr Tucson AZ 85750-6735 Office: So Ariz Med Specialists 4711 N 1st Ave Tucson AZ 85718-5610

BENATAR, LEO, packaging company executive; b. Atlanta, Feb. 21, 1930; s. Morris H. and Mary (Levy) B.; m. Louise Cure, Sept. 2, 1956; children: Morris L., Ann Marie, Ruth Eileen. B. Indsl. Engring., Ga. Inst. Tech., 1951; postgrad., Rochester Inst. Tech., 1956, Harvard Bus. Sch., 1970. Formerly pres. Mead Packaging Co., Atlanta; chmn. Engraph, Inc., Atlanta; bd. dirs. Sonoco Products Co., Johns Manville Corp., Interstate Bakeries Corp., Mohawk Industries, Inc., Aaron Rents, Inc.; past mem. internat. adv. coun. Trust Co. Ga., Trust Co. Bank; past mem. adv. bd. Arkwright-Boston Ins.; past chmn. Fed. Res. Bank Atlanta. Past bd. dirs. Rsch. Atlanta, Jr. Achievement, ARC, Nat. Minority Purchasing Coun., Keep Am. Beautiful, Peachtree Corners; past bd. visitors Emory U.; bd. dirs. Atlanta Partnership Bus. and Edn., Ga. Coun. on Econ. Edn.; steering com. Nat. Found. Ileitis and Colitis; past indsl. mgmt. adv. coun., nat. adv. bd. Ga. Inst. Tech.; mem. adv. coun. Coll. Bus. Adminstrn., Ga. State U.; mem. alumni adv. bd. Sch. Indsl. and Systems Engring. Ga. Tech.; bd. trustees Ga. Tech. Found.; past chmn. Pvt. Industry Coun.; past mem. DeKalb Reorgn. Com., Ga. Bd. Industry and Trade. With USN, 1951-53. Recipient Arcdiocesan medal of St. Paul Greek Orthodoc Archdiocese of North and South Am.; Lion of Judah award, Cmty. Achievement award ORT. Mem. Bus. Coun. Ga., Nat. Alliance Bus. (past chmn. Met. Atlanta, bd. dirs.), Japan-Am. Soc. Ga., Commerce Club, Standard Club, Buckhead Club. Home and Office: 121 Burdette Rd NW Atlanta GA 30327-4803

BENATAR, SOLOMON ROBERT, internist; b. Selukwe, Zimbabwe, Feb. 6, 1942; s. Haim Solomon and Suzette Sultana (Albagli) B.; m. Evelyn Mary Goldberg, Oct. 26, 1943; children: David, Michael, Brian. B Medicine, B Surgery, U. Capetown, Republic of South Africa, 1965. Fellow faculty anaesthetists Coll. of Medicine of South Africa, 1971; intern Groote Schuur Hosp., Capetown, 1966; pvt. practice Port Elizabeth, Republic of South Africa, 1967-68; resident anesthesiology Groote Schuur Hosp., U. Capetown, 1969-70; resident internal medicine Grooote Schuur Hosp., U. Capetown, 1971; rsch. fellow Northwick Park and Brompton Hosps., London, 1972; rsch. fellow, hon. resident Brompton Hosp. and Cardiothoracic Inst., London, 1973; cons. physician Groote Schuur Hosp. and U. Capetown, 1974—, prof., chmn. dept. medicine, 1980—; physician-in-chief dept. medicine Groote Schuur Hosp., Capetown, 1980—; dir. Bioethics Ctr. U.

Capetown, 1992—; hon. registrar Coll. Medicine South Africa, 1978-80, elected councillor, 1980—, chmn. faculty medicine, 1980-91, v.p. 1986-95; internat. vis. scholar Hastings Ctr., N.Y.C., 1986; internat. advisor Jour. Respiratory Medicine and Theoretical Medicine and Bioethics; fellow Program in Ethics and the Professions, Harvard U., 1994-95; vis. prof. Harvard U. Med. Sch., 1994-95, U. Coll. London Med. Sch., 1997—; co-dir. Centre For Med. Ethics, 1997—. Mem. editorial bd. South African Med. Jour., 1983-92. Trustee South Africa Med. Students Trust, 1980-90; mem. coun. U. Capetown, 1990-96; chmn. selection com. Imperial Chem. Industries Rsch. Scholarship, 1992-95, Sandoz Rsch. Scholarship, Johannesburg, 1989-95; commr. U. Witswatersrand Enquiry on Baragwanath Hosp., 1988. Recipient African Oxygen Gold medal Coll. Medicine South Africa, 1971, Hamilton Maynard Meml. medal South African Med. Jour., 1977; rsch. fellow Imperial Chem. Industries, 1971. Fellow ACP (hon.), Royal Coll. Physicians, Coll. Medicine South Africa, Royal Soc. South Africa; mem. NAS, Am. Acad. Arts and Scis. (fgn. hon.), Acad. Sci. South Africa (founder), Inst. Medicine. Jewish. Avocations: philosophy, medical ethics, health economics, international health, music. Home: 41 Willow Rd Newlands, Capetown 7700, South Africa Office: U Capetown, Capetown 7925, South Africa

BENAVIDES, FORTUNATO PEDRO (PETE BENAVIDES), federal judge; b. 1947. BBA, U. Houston, 1968, JD, 1972. Atty. Rankin, Kern & Martinez, McAllen, Tex., 1972-74, Cisneros, Beery & Benavides, McAllen, 1974, Cisneros, Brown & Benavides, McAllen, 1975, Cisneros & Benavides, McAllen, 1976; pvt. practice McAllen, 1977; judge Hidalgo County Ct.-at-Law # 2, Edinburg, Tex., 1977-79; prin. Law Offices of Fortunato P. Benavides, McAllen, 1980-81; judge 92nd Dist. Ct. of Hidalgo County, Tex., 1981-84, 13th Ct. Appeals, Corpus Christi, Tex., 1984-91, Tex. Ct. Criminal Appeals, Austin, 1991-92; atty. Atlas & Hall, McAllen, 1993-94; judge U.S. Ct. Appeals (5th cir.), Austin, 1994—; commr. Tex. Juvenile Probation Commn., 1983-89; vis. judge to cts. in Tex., 1993. Active Mex.-Am. Dems. of Tex., 1990-92, Mustangs of Corpus Christi, 1990-91, hon. mem., 1992, St. Michael Episc. Ch., Austin, 1992—. Mem. ABA, State Bar Tex., Hidalgo County Bar Assn. Office: US Ct Appeals 5th cir Homer Thornberry Judicial Bldg 903 San Jacinto Blvd Rm 450 Austin TX 78701-2450*

BENAVIDES, MARY KATHLEEN, anesthesiologist, nutritional consultant; b. Alhambra, Calif., Sept. 10, 1958; d. Duane Joseph B. and Janet Leona Johnson; m. John Gerard Migliori, May 27, 1946. BS, U. Calif., 1980, MD, 1985. Diplomate Am. Bd. Anesthesiology, Nat. Bd. Med. Examiners. Intern Wadsworth-VA Hosp., L.A., Calif., 1985-86; resident Loma Linda (Calif.) Med. Ctr., 1986-89; attending physician L.A. Children's Hosp., 1989-90; anesthesiologist Inland Valley Regional Med. Ctr., Wildomar, Calif., 1990-91, Mission Bay Hosp., San Diego, 1991-96, Treasure Valley Hosp., Boise, 1996—; nutritional cons. BodyWise Internat., San Diego, 1994—, Boise, 1996—. Mem. Am. Soc. Anesthesiologists, Soc. Ambulatory Care Anesthesiology, Idaho Soc. Anesthesiology. Avocations: hiking, skiing, reading, being a caring, nurturing mother. Home: PO Box 418 Boise ID 83701-0418

BENBOW, CAMILLA PERSSON, psychology educator, researcher; b. Lund, Sweden, Dec. 3, 1956; came to U.S., 1965, naturalized, 1985; m. David Lubinski; children: Wystan R., Bronwen G., Trefor A., Evan M., Lovisa D., G. Byron, Lena C. BA in Psychology with honors, Johns Hopkins U., 1977, MA in Psychology, 1978, MS in Edn. of the Gifted, 1980, EdD with distinction in Edn. of Gifted, 1981. Dir. Office of Precollegiate Programs for Talented & Gifted Iowa State U., 1987-98; dir. Office of Precollegiate Programs for Talented & Gifted Johns Hopkins U., Balt., 1977-79, asst. dir. Study of Mathematically Precocious Youth, 1979-81, assoc. dir., 1981-85, co-dir., 1985-86, dir., 1986—; assoc. rsch. scientist dept. psychology Johns Hopkins U., 1981-86, asst. prof. sociology, part-time, 1983-86; assoc. prof. psychology Iowa State U., Ames, 1985-90, prof. psychology, 1990-95, chair dept. psychology, 1992-98, disting. prof., 1995-98, interim dean coll. edn., 1996-98; dean Peabody Coll. of Edn. and Human Devel., Vanderbilt U., Nashville, 1998—. Sr. editor: Academic Precocity: Aspects of Its Development, 1983, Intellectual Talent: Psychometric and Social Issues, 1996; contbr. articles to profl. jours. Recipient John curtis gowan prize Nat. assn. Gifted children, 1980, 81; Rsch. award Am. Ednl. Rsch. Assn., 1982; Spencer fellow, alt., 1984, 85, 86, Rsch. paper award Mensa, 1985, 86, 89, 94, 95; Early Scholar award Nat. Assn. Gifted Children, 1985, Disting. Scholar award 1992, George A. Miller award, APA, 1999. Mem. Johns Hopkins Soc. Scholars, Phi Beta Kappa, Sigma Xi. Office: Vanderbilt Univ Deans Office Peabody Coll Edn/Human Deve Nashville TN 37203

BENBOW, CHARLES CLARENCE, retired writer, critic; b. Moore Haven, Fla., Feb. 23, 1929; s. Clarence Oliver and Rosalie Florence (King) B.; m. Lois Chandler, Oct. 10, 1954; children—Margot Britton, Claudia King. B. Applied Arts, U. Fla., 1951; M.S. in Art Edn., Fla. State U., 1961, postgrad., 1965-66. Art dir. sta. WJXT-TV, Jacksonville, Fla., 1955-58; tchr. art Duval County (Fla.) Pub. Schs., 1958-62; instr. humanities U. Fla., 1962-65; writer-critic St. Petersburg (Fla.) Times, 1966-86. Co-author Fla. state guide for art in secondary schs.; Contbr. articles to profl. jours. Mem. City St. Petersburg Arts Commn. Served with USN, 1951-55. Named Best Architecture Critic in Fla. Fla. Assn. Am. Inst. Architects, 1978, 80. Mem. Fla. Art Edn. Assn. (v.p., treas. 1958-63, Disting. Service award 1989). Democrat. Presbyn. Home: 135 20th Ave S Saint Petersburg FL 33705-2759

BENBOW, RICHARD ADDISON, psychological counselor; b. Las Vegas, Dec. 27, 1949; s. Jules Coleman and Bonnie Ray B. BBA, U. Nev. 1972, MS in Counseling, 1974; AAS in Bus. Mgmt. and Real Estate, Clark County Community Coll., 1980; PhD in Clin. Psychology, U. Humanistic Studies, 1986. Cert. tchr., Nev.; cert. clin. mental health counselor, secondary sch. counselor, Nev., substance abuse counselor, Nev., substance abuse program adminstr., Nev.; nat. cert. counselor. Jud. svcs. officer Mcpl. Ct. City of Las Vegas, 1983-88, pretrial program coord., 1988—; inmate classification technician Detention and Correctional Svcs., 1982-83; stress mgmt. cons. Mem. Biofeedback Soc. Am., Assn. Humanistic Psychology, Nat. Assn. Psychotherapists, Am. Counseling Assn., Am. Mental Health Counselors Assn., Am. Acad. Crisis Interveners, Jr. C. of C., U.S. Jaycees (presdl. award of honor 1978-79), Delta Sigma Phi. Democrat. Christian Scientist. Office: Mcpl Ct Intake Svcs City of Las Vegas 400 Stewart Ave Las Vegas NV 89101-2927

BENC, TAMARA SUSAN, reading and language arts educator; b. Johnstown, Pa., June 16, 1966; d. Mim George Evanisko III; m. Gregory Benc. BS, U. Pitts., 1988. Tchg. cert. elem. edn. Reading and lang. arts tchr. Garwood (N.J.) Sch. Dist., 1989—; workshop presenter Star-Ledger, Newark, 1994-98. Vol. preliminary pageants Miss N.J. Pageant, Union, Essex, and Somerset, 1992—; team capt. Walk Am., March of Dimes, No. N.J., 1994—. NJEA Frederick L. Hipp grantee, 1998-99. Mem. Nat. Coun. Tchrs. English, Suburban Reading Coun. Republican. Eastern Orthodox.

BENCH, JOHNNY LEE, retired professional baseball player; b. Oklahoma City, Dec. 7, 1947; s. Ted Bench. Grad. high sch. Catcher Cin. Reds, Nat. League, 1967-83; spl. cons. to gen. mgr. Cin. Reds, 1997-98; speaker Keppler Assocs. Inc., Arlington, Va., 1998—; broadcaster; propr. bowling alley, Cin.; spokesman, bd. dirs. Interactive Mktg. Tech., Inc., Tarzana, Calif., 1999—. Profl. nightclub singer, from 1970; host TV interview show MVP-Johnny Bench, until 1976; baseball instructional show The Baseball Bunch, 1981, 82, 83; toured Vietnam with Bob Hope Christmas Show, 1970, 71; author: Catch You Later. Named Minor League Player of Yr., Sporting News, 1967, Nat. League Rookie of Yr., Sporting News, 1968, Nat. League Rookie of Yr., Baseball Writers Assn. Am., 1968, Nat. League Most Valuable Player, 1970, 72, Major League Player of Yr., Sporting News, 1970, Nat. League Player of Yr., Sporting News, 1970, Most Valuable Player, 1976 World Series; player Nat. League All-Star Fielding Team, 1968-77, 79-80, Nat. League All-Star Team, Sporting News, 1968-70, 72, 73-77; inducted into Baseball Hall of Fame, 1989; recipient Gold Glove award 10 times. Catcher over 100 games a yr. for 13 consecutive seasons. Address: Interactive Mktg Tech Inc 5120 Whitsett Ave Valley Village CA 91607*

BENCHLEY, PETER BRADFORD, author; b. N.Y.C., May 8, 1940; s. Nathaniel Goddard and Marjorie Louise (Bradford) B.; m. Winifred B. Wesson, Sept. 19, 1964; children: Tracy, Clayton, Christopher. BA cum laude, Harvard U., 1961. Gen. assignment reporter Washington Post, 1963; assoc. editor Newsweek mag., N.Y.C., 1963-67; staff asst. to Pres. White House, Washington, 1967-69; freelance writer, 1969—. Author: Time and a Ticket, 1964, (novels) Jaws, 1974, The Deep, 1976, The Island, 1978, The Girl of the Sea of Cortez, 1982, Q Clearance, 1986, Rummies, 1989, Beast, 1991, White Shark, 1994; author screenplays (with others) Jaws (Br. Acad. Award nomination), 1975, The Deep, 1977, The Island, 1979; co-author: Ocean Planet, 1995; writer, narrator, host episodes The Am. Sportsman TV show, 1974-83, Galapagos TV spl., 1987; host, narrator Expedition Earth TV series, 1990-93; co-creator Dolphin Cove TV series, 1989; exec. producer Beast minseries, 1996; host, narrator Ocean Reports pub. radio series, 1997—; contbr. articles to newspapers and mags. including Nat. Geographic, The N.Y. Times. Served with USMCR, 1962-63. Clubs: Coffee House. Office: care ICM 40 W 57th St New York NY 10019-4001

BENCHOFF, DENNIS L., career officer; b. Dec. 23, 1939. Commd. U.S. Army, advanced through grades to lt. gen., 1996. Office: 5001 Eisenhower Ave Alexandria VA 22333

BENCHOFF, JAMES MARTIN, manufacturing company executive; b. Hagerstown, Md., May 18, 1927; s. J. Thompson and Marie (Hickey) B.; m. Brigitte R. Puhringer, July 1, 1978 (div.); children by previous marriage—Helen Marie, James Martin II. Student, U. Pa., 1944-45. With Grove Mfg. Co. div. Hanson Industries, Shady Grove, Pa., 1954—, v.p., 1962-66, 1st v.p., 1966, 1st v.p., asst. gen. mgr., 1966-68, exec. v.p., gen. mgr., 1968-69, pres., chief exec. officer, 1969-80, chmn., chief exec. officer, 1980-88, chmn. emeritus, 1988—; pres. Monta Vista Inc., Waynesboro, Pa., 1959—; pres., chmn. Ben Mar Holdings Ltd., Waynesboro, 1970—. Clubs: Waynesboro Country; Fountain Head Country (Hagerstown, Md); Met. (N.Y.C.). Office: PO Box 308 Waynesboro PA 17268-0308

BENCINI, SARA HALTIWANGER, concert pianist; b. Winston Salem, N.C., Sept. 2, 1926; d. Robert Sydney and Janie Love (Couch) Haltiwanger; m. Robert Emery Bencini, June 26, 1954; children: Robert Emery, III, Constance Bencini Waller, John McGregor. Mus. B., Salem Coll., 1947; postgrad. grad. Juilliard Sch. Music, 1948-50; M.A., Smith Coll., 1951; D In Mus. Arts, U. N.C., Greensboro, 1989. Head piano dept. Mary Burnham Sch. for Girls, Northampton, Mass., 1949-51; pianist, composer dance and drama dept. Smith Coll., 1951-52; head music dept. Walnut Hill Sch. for Girls, Natick, Mass., 1952-54; pvt. piano tchr., High Point, N.C., 1954-66; concert pianist appearing in Am. and Europe, 1948—; duo-piano performances with PBS-TV, Columbia, S.C., 1967, Winston Salem Symphony, N.C., 1964-68, Ea. Mus. Festival, Greensboro, N.C., 1969. Democrat. Presbyterian.

BENCKE, RONALD LEE, financial executive; b. Maynard, Iowa, Feb. 9, 1940; s. Floyd B. and Emilie W. (Reinhardt) B.; m. Mary Kay Scott, Dec. 19, 1961; children: Stephen, Patrick, Desiree, Matthew, Joshuah. BA, Wartburg Coll., 1962; PMD, Harvard U., 1981. Fin. analyst Gen. Electric, Danville, Ill., 1962-65; controller Ansul Co., Marinette, Wis., 1965-66; systems mgr. Chamberlain Corp., Elmhurst, Ill., 1966-69; cons. Westinghouse Electric, Pitts., 1969-74; v.p., controller Westinghouse Credit Corp., Pitts., 1974-83, v.p., CFO, 1983-88, also bd. dirs.; pres. Westinghouse Evaluation Svcs. Group, Pitts., 1988-92; CFO QED Communications, Pitts., 1992-94; v.p., CFO Lasertechnics, Inc., Albuquerque, 1994-96; chmn. The Murdoch Group, 1997—. Scoutmaster Boy Scouts Am., Chgo., 1967; chmn. United Way, 1985; elder Presbyn. Ch. Mem. Fin. Execs. Inst., Harvard U. Bus. Sch. Assn. (pres.), Nat. Rev. Appraisers, Mortgage Underwriters Assn. Republican. Club: Harvard-Yale-Princeton (Pitts.). E-mail: ronald@bencke.com. Office: Murdoch Group Inc The Overlook Placitas NM 87043-8903

BEN-DAK, JOSEPH DAVID, political scientist, educator, consultant. BA, Hebrew U., Jerusalem, 1966; MA, U. Mich., 1969, PhD, 1976; diploma, Grad. Sch. Internat. Tng., Brattleboro, Vt., 1976; PhD (hon.), Mongolian Tech. U., 1994. Assoc. rsch. sociologist program dir. Ctr. for Rsch. on Conflict Resolution, U. Mich., 1967-70; asst. prof. orgn., sociology and policy scis. Am. U. and Cath. U. Am., 1971-74; coord., prof. internat. mgmt. studies, peace studies Grad. Sch. for Internat. Tng., 1971-77; prof. mgmt. and policy scis. U. Haifa, Israel, 1977-84, acad. head Sch. for Internat. Programs, 1982-84; prof. mgmt. and internat. econs. Kyunghee U., Seoul, 1983-86; rsch. prof. mgmt. and policy scis. Poly. U., N.Y., 1993—; chmn. World Ecotourism Group, 1979—; corp. advisor, bd. dirs. numerous bus. entrepreneurships, 1987-92; chmn. bd. Telesense Holdings and Internat., Nahariya, 1986-92; advisor Govt. Tanzania, Papua New Guinea, Colombia, Brazil and others, 1979-86; leader task force on reorganizing internat. strategy Ministry of Internat. Trade, Govt. of Japan, Korean Advanced Inst. for Sci. and Tech., 1985-88; sr. rsch. sociologist The World Bank, 1988-91; pres. Found. for Arab Israeli Reconciliation, Washington, 1974-77, 84-91; chmn. bd., CEO Practical Concepts Inc. Internat., 1977-87; acad. dir. Israeli Air Force Sch. for Sr. Officers, Israeli Air Force Tech. Acad., 1977-84; cons. UN, 1989-91; sr. UN ofcl. Mgmt. Capacity Bldg. in Less Developed Countries and Tech. Sci. Policy, 1992—; vis. prof. U. Lund, Sweden, 1975-76; guest prof. mgmt. and policy studies U. São Paulo, Brazil, 1995-96, Nat. Rsch. Coun. prof. in comms., 1996-97; acting dir. Inst. for Creative Studies, Washington, 1970-72; sr. cons. Caribbean Applied Tech. Ctr. Ltd., Jamaica, 1990-92; UN rep. World Assn. Indsl., Tech. and Rsch. Insts., Aarhus, Denmark, 1993—; prin. advisor sci., tech. and pvt. sector UN Devel. Program, N.Y.C., 1991-96; chief global tech. group, UN, N.Y.C., 1996—; chmn. Internat. Indsl. Devel. Found., 1997—; pres. Internat. Indsl. Devel. Found. N.Y. and Va., 1996—; chmn. Internat. Regenesis Found. for UN, N.Y.C., 1996—; chmn. Internat. Rebound Tech. Found., N.Y., Nairobi, 1997—. Assoc. editor Jour. Conflict Resolution, 1970-80; assoc. editor Korea Bus. Weekly, 1983-88; bd. editors The Monthly YAM, 1987—; contbg. editor Globes, Monitin, and Monies, 1989—. Recipient award Internat. Gundaker Found., 1966, award Nat. Pub. Health Inst., 1967-70, Lisle fellowship, Denmark, 1968, grant Advanced Rsch. Projects Agy. and NSF, 1968, Rsch. award and Travel grant Scandinavian Coun. on Conflict and Peace Rsch., 1969-70, UNESCO fellowship, 1969, grant Lilly Endowment, 1977-78, Golden Record award Nashville C. of C., 1982, Premier Decoration of Merit, East New Britain Provincial Govt., Papua New Guinea, 1986, spl. travel and insight gathering grantee Govt. Lithuania, 1990, grantee Brit. Commonwealth and OECD, 1992, St. Louis Econ. Conversion Project award, 1993—. Fellow AAAS; mem. Internat. Soc. Soil Mechanics and Found. Engrng. (bd. dirs. 1992—), Simulation Coun. (sr.), The Math. Assn. Am., Fgn. Policy Assn. Avocations: chess, scuba diving, sharpshooting, poetry. Home: PO Box 38 Mount Vernon NY 10552-0038

BEN DANIEL, DAVID JACOB, entrepreneurship educator, consultant; b. Phila., Nov. 10, 1931; s. Daniel and Rosella (Soffian) Berkowitz; m. Judith Milgram, June 3, 1957 (div. Nov. 1975); children: Matthew, Elisabeth; m. Claire S. Berman, Nov. 19, 1991. BA with honors, U. Pa., 1952, MS in Physics, 1953; PhD in Engring., MIT, 1960. Physicist GE, Schenectady, N.Y., 1961-67, mgr. advanced programs R & D Ctr., 1967-70, mgr. tech. ventures ops., 1970-76; area mgr. advanced energy Exxon Corp., Florham Park, N.J., 1976-79; group v.p. Exxon Enterprises Co., Florham Park, 1979-81; sr. v.p. Am. R & D, Boston, 1981-83; exec. v.p. Genesis Venture Capital, Boston, 1983-84; Berens prof. entrepreneurship Johnson Grad. Sch. Mgmt., Cornell U., Ithaca, N.Y., 1984—; cons. Venture Capital Partnerships, 1984-89; vis. prof. Keio U., Japan, 1997-98. Co-editor Handbook of International Mergers and Acquisitions, 1991, Internat. M&A, Jt. Ventures and Beyond, 1997; contbr. articles to profl. jours. Chmn. Human Rights Commn., Schenectady, 1970-73; trustee Union Am. Hebrew Congregations, N.Y.C., 1972-80. Lt. USN, 1953-56. Recipient Disting. Svc. award Jaycees of Am., 1968; vis. fellow Harvard Bus. Sch., 1970. Mem. Harvard Club (Boston), Cornell Club (N.Y.C.), Sigma Xi. Republican. Jewish. Avocation: mathematical foundations. Home: 111 Kelvin Pl Ithaca NY 14850-2319 Office: Johnson Grad Sch Mgmt Cornell U Ithaca NY 14853

BENDER, BETTY BARBEE, food service professional; b. Lexington, Ky., Apr. 29, 1932; d. Richard Carroll and Sarah Elizabeth (Rodes) Barbee; m. David H. Bender, Dec. 14, 1957; children: Bruce, Carroll. BA in Home Econs., Mont. State U., 1954; MS in Food Service Mgmt., Miami U., Oxford, Ohio, 1980. Adminstrv. dietitan Mass. Gen. Hosp., Boston, 1955-56; asst. chief dietitian Meth. Hosp., Indpls., 1957-61; chief dietitan Community Hosp., Indpls., 1961-63; supervising dietitian Chgo. Area ARA, 1963-67; asst. food service supr. Dayton (Ohio) Bd. Edn., 1969, mgr. food service, 1969—; cons. Nat. Frozen Food Assn., Washington, 1983, Crescent Metal Products Co., Cleve., 1985. Contbr. articles to profl. jours. Recipient 26th Ann. Foodsvc. Facilities Design award Instrs. Mag. for Commissary Design, 1972, Silver and Gold Plate awards Internat. Foodsvc. Mfrs. Assn., 1985, Pres.'s award Ohio Sch. Food Svc. Assn., 1987, FAME Golden Star award, 1992; recognized for outstanding contbns. to child nutrition program Ohio Ho. of Reps., 1972, 84. Mem. Am. Sch. Food Svc. Assn. (nat. pres. 1983, chmn. 1978-80, maj. city sect.), Ohio Sch. Food Svc. (pres. 1977), Dayton Sch. Adminstr. Assn., Dayton Sch. Mgmt. Assn. (pres. 1993-94), Am. Dietetic Assn. (cert., chair dietary practice group 1990-91, award for Excellence in Mgmt. Practice 1992, Food Svc. Dir. Yr. 1994), Ohio Dietetic Assn., Dayton Dietetic Assn., Soc. Nutrition Edn. (panel 1983). Democrat. Avocations: bridge, golf, swimming. Home: 1953 E Hickman Rd Nicholasville KY 40356

BENDER, BETTY WION, librarian; b. Mt. Ayer, Iowa, Feb. 26, 1925; d. John F. and Sadie A. (Guess) Wion; m. Robert F. Bender, Aug. 24, 1946. B.S., N.Tex. State U., Denton, 1946; M.A., U. Denver, 1957. Asst. cataloger N. Tex. State U. Library, 1946-49; from cataloger to head acquisitions So. Meth. U., Dallas, 1949-56; reference asst. Ind. State Library, Indpls., 1951-52; librarian Ark. State Coll., 1958-59, Eastern Wash. Hist. Soc., Spokane, 1960-67; reference librarian, then head circulation dept. Spokane (Wash.) Public Library, 1968-73, library dir., 1973-88; vis. instr. U. Denver, summers 1957-60, 63, fall 1959; instr. Whitworth Coll., Spokane, 1962-64; mem. Gov. Wash. Regional Conf. Libraries, 1968, Wash. Statewide Library Devel. Council, 1970-71. Bd. dirs. N.W. Regional Found., 1973-75, Inland Empire Goodwill Industries, 1975-77, Wash. State Library Commn., 1979-87, Future Spokane, 1983-88, vice chmn., 1986-87, pres., 1987-88. Recipient YWCA Outstanding Achievement award in Govt., 1985. Mem. ALA (mem. library adminstrn. and mgmt. assn. com. on orgn. 1982-83, chmn. nominating com. 1983-85, v.p./pres.-elect. 1985-86, pres. 1986-87), Pacific N.W. Library Assn. (chmn. circulation div. 1972-75, conv. chmn. 1977), Wash. Library Assn. (v.p./pres.-elect 1975-77, pres. 1977-78), AAUW (pres. Spokane br. 1969-71, rec. sec. Wash. br. 1971-73, fellowship named in honor 1972), Spokane and Inland Empire Librarians (dir. 1967-68), Am. Soc. Pub. Adminstrn. Republican. Lutheran. Club: Zonta (pres. Spokane chpt. 1976-77, dist. conf. treas. 1972). Home: 221 E Rockwood Blvd Apt 504 Spokane WA 99202-1274

BENDER, BRUCE F., book publishing executive; b. Toledo, Ohio, Oct. 4, 1949; s. Richard S. and Joan B. Bender; B.A., Muskingum Coll., 1971; M.B.A., Rutgers U., 1972; m. Margaret Norris, Sept. 4, 1971; children—Courtney, Meghan. Supr., Coopers & Lybrand, C.P.A.s, N.Y.C., 1972-76; pres. Lyle Stuart, Inc., Secaucus, N.J., 1989—, also bd. dirs.; pres. Carol Pub. Group, 1989—. Pres. Brightwood Assn.; bd. dirs. Westfield Symphony. Mem. Am. Inst. C.P.A.s, Assn. Am. Pubs., Pub. Fin. Round Table, N.J. Inst. C.P.A.s. Club: Echo Lake (Plainfield). Office: 120 Enterprise Ave S Secaucus NJ 07094-1902 also: Carol Pub Group 600 Madison Ave New York NY 10022-1615

BENDER, BYRON WILBUR, linguistics educator; b. Roaring Spring, Pa., Aug. 14, 1929; s. Ezra Clay and Gertrude Magdalene (Kauffman) B.; m. Lois Marie Graber, Aug. 25, 1950; children: Susan Alice, Sarah Marie, Catherine Anne, Judith Lee, John Richard. BA, Goshen Coll., 1949; MA, Ind. U., 1950, PhD, 1963. Edn. specialist Trust Terr. of Pacific Islands, Majuro, Marshall Island, 1953-59, Saipan, Marianas Island, 1962-64; asst. prof. Goshen (Ind.) Coll., 1960-62; assoc. prof. linguistics U. Hawaii at Manoa, Honolulu, 1964-69, prof., 1969—, chmn. dept., 1969-95; bd. dirs. U. Hawaii Profl. Assembly, Honolulu, 1978-88, 92-98, pres., 1982-88. Author: Spoken Marshallese, 1969, Linguistic Factors in Maori Education, 1971, (with others) Marshallese-English Dictionary, 1976; editor Oceanic Linguistics Spl. Publs., 1965—, Studies in Micronesian Linguistics, 1984, Oceanic Linguistics, 1991—; mng. editor Oceanic Linguistics, 1965-90. Trustee Hawaii Pub. Employees Health Fund Bd., 1987-95. Recipient Merit awards U. Hawaii 1971, 76, 86. Mem. NEA (standing com. higher edn. 1985-89), Linguistic Soc. Am. (dir. Linguistic Inst. summer 1977, program com. 1987-89, parliamentarian), Polynesian Soc. Mem. Soc. of Friends. Home: 7268 Kauhako St Honolulu HI 96825-2221 Office: U Hawaii Dept Linguistics 1890 E West Rd Honolulu HI 96822-2318

BENDER, CARL MARTIN, physics educator, consultant; b. Bklyn., Jan. 18, 1943; s. Alfred and Rose (Suberman) B.; m. Jessica Dee Waldbaum, June 18, 1966; children—Michael Anthony, Daniel Eric. AB summa cum laude with distinction, Cornell U., 1964; AM, Harvard U., 1965, PhD, 1969. Mem. Inst. for Advanced Study, Princeton, N.J., 1969-70; asst. prof. math. MIT, Cambridge, 1970-73, assoc. prof., 1973-77; prof. physics Washington U., St. Louis, 1977—; research assoc. Imperial Coll., London, 1974; cons. Los Alamos Nat. Lab., 1979—; vis. prof. Imperial Coll., London, 1986-87, 95-96, Technion Israel Inst. of Technology, Haifa, Israel, 1995. Author: Advanced Mathematical Methods for Scientists and Engineers, 1978; editor: Am. Inst. Physic series on math. and computational physics; mem. edtl. bds. Jour Math. Physics, 1980-83, Advances in Applied Math., 1980-85; contbr. more than 150 articles to sci. jours. Telluride scholar, 1960-63, NSF fellow, 1964-69, Woodrow Wilson fellow, 1964-65, Sloan Found. fellow, 1973-77, Fulbright fellowship to U.K., 1995-96, Lady Davis fellowship to Israel, 1995; recipient Burlington No. Found. Faculty Achievement award 1985. Fellow Am. Phys. Soc.; mem. Phi Beta Kappa, Phi Kappa Phi. Home: 509 Warren Ave Saint Louis MO 63130-4155 Office: Washington U Dept Physics Saint Louis MO 63130

BENDER, CHARLES CHRISTIAN, retail home center executive; b. Bklyn., July 4, 1936; s. Charles C. and Virginia R. (Rahlfs) B.; m. Jean Ann Couper; children: Lori Ann Grenier, Hallie Couper. BA, Hillsdale Coll., 1959; MBA, U. Mich., 1960. Buyer Dayton Hudson, Detroit, 1962-69; v.p., gen. mdse. mgr. Wickes Lumber, Saginaw, Mich., 1969-81; gen. mgr. Wickes B.V., Utrecht, Netherlands, 1981-84; pres., CEO, investor Busy Beaver Bldg. Ctrs., Pitts., 1984—, also chmn. bd. dirs. Bd. dirs., vice chmn. St. Margaret's Meml. Hosp. Found. Served with U.S. Army, 1960-61. Mem. Home Ctr. Industry Pres. Coun. (adv. bd. 1986—), Home Ctr. Inst. (bd. dirs. 1998), Rotary. Republican. Presbyterian. Clubs: Pitts. Field. (bd. dirs. 1996). Avocations: golf, sailing. Home: 310 Buckingham Rd Pittsburgh PA 15215-1527 Office: Busy Beaver Bldg Ctrs Inc 3130 William Pitt Way Pittsburgh PA 15238-1360

BENDER, CHARLES WILLIAM, lawyer; b. Cape Girardeau, Mo., Oct. 2, 1935; s. Walter William and Fern Evelyn (Stroud) B.; m. Carolyn Percy Gavagan, June 20, 1961 (div. 1983); children: Theodore Marten, Christopher Percy; m. Betty Lou Port, May 5, 1983; stepchildren: Courtney Elizabeth, Cameron Ann. AB magna cum laude, Harvard U., 1960, LLB magna cum laude, 1963. Bar: Calif. 1965, U.S. Dist. Ct. (cen. dist.) Calif. 1965, U.S. Ct. Appeals (9th cir.) 1969, U.S. Supreme Ct. 1979, D.C. 1984. Assoc. O'Melveny & Myers, Los Angeles, 1965-71, ptnr., 1972-84, mng. ptnr., 1984-92; chmn., 1993—. Editor Harvard U. Law Rev., 1961-62, articles editor, 1962-63. Advisor campaign Alan Cranston for Senator, Calif., 1968, 74, 80; mgr. campaign Jess Unruh for Gov., Calif., 1970; trustee Los Angeles Legal Aid Found., 1971, Lawyers' Com. for Civil Rights Under Law, Washington, 1985—. Served with U.S. Army, 1956-57. Sheldon Traveling fellow Harvard U., 1963-64. Mem. ABA, Calif. Bar Assn., Los Angeles Bar Assn. Democrat. Home: 2831 The Strand Hermosa Beach CA 90254-2400 Office: O'Melveny & Myers 400 S Hope St Los Angeles CA 90071-2899*

BENDER, DAVID RAY, library association executive; b. Canton, Ohio, June 12, 1942; s. John Ray and Mary Elizabeth (Witmer) B.; children: Robert Ray, Scott David, Lori Jo Ryan. BS, Kent State U., 1964; MS in LS, Case Western Res. U., 1969; PhD, Ohio State U., 1977. Librarian South High Sch., Willoughby, Ohio, 1964-68; cons. sch. library services Ohio Dept. Edn., Columbus, 1969-70; grad. research assoc. Ohio State U., Columbus, 1970-72; br. chief sch. library media services Md. Dept. Edn., Balt., 1972-79; exec. dir. Spl. Librs. Assn., Washington, 1979—; lectr. Rutgers U., New Brunswick, N.J.; vis. prof. Towson State U., Balt.; cons., project dir. various stated depts. edn. and colls. and univs., profl. assns. also internat., state and local orgns.; mem. adv. com. on naval history, USN, 1991-95. Author: Learning Resources and the Instructional Program in Community College, 1980, Library Media Programs and the Special Learner, 1981; co-author (with others): Nat. Information Policies: Strategies for the Future, 1991; contbr. numerous articles to profl. jours. Mem. adv. coun. Kent (Ohio) State U. Sch. of Libr. and Info. Sci., 1991—, Washington Nat. Cathedral Fund

Com., 1998—. Recipient award for outstanding svc. Md. Ednl. Media Orgn., 1980, H.W. Wilson Co. award, 1989. Mem. Spl. Librs. Assn. (President's award 1986), Nat. Libr. and Info. Assns. (chmn. 1990-91), Internat. Fedn. Libr. Assns. and Instns. (chmn. round table for Mgmt. of Libr. Assn. 1993—), Am. Soc. Assn. Execs. Found. (chmn. 1988), Beta Phi Mu, Kappa Sigma. Republican. Episcopalian. Home: Unit 34 2126 Connecticut Ave NW Washington DC 20008-1729 Office: Spl Librs Assn 1700 18th St NW Washington DC 20009-2506

BENDER, DEAN, public relations executive. Ptnr. Bender/Helper Impact (formerly Bender, Goldman & Helper), L.A. Office: Bender/Helper Impact 11500 W Olympic Blvd Ste 655 Los Angeles CA 90064-1597*

BENDER, EDWARD ERIK, geology educator, researcher; b. Bronxville, N.Y., Dec. 9, 1962; s. Edward Joseph and Mae Virgina (Camera) B.; m. Linda Dee Young, June 8, 1964; 1 child, Alexandra Dominique. BS in Geology, Rider U., 1985; MS, Vanderbilt U., 1990; PhD, U. So. Calif., 1994. Instr. Calif. State U., Fullerton, 1991-92; asoc. prof. Orange Coast Coll., Costa Mesa, Calif., 1994—; adj. prof. Chaffey Coll., Alta Loma, Calif., 1991—, Mt. San Antonio Coll., Walnut, Calif., 1992-93, Pasadena (Calif.) City Coll., 1992-94; adv. com-edn. So. Calif. Earthquake Ctr., L.A., 1995—; spkr. Earthquake Awareness Orange Coast Coll., 1996, Costa Mesa Mineral Soc., 1995. Contbr. articles to profl. jours. Mem. Seismological Soc. Am., Geol. Soc. Am. (Penrose grant 1986), Am. Geophys. Union, Mineralog. Soc. Am. Achievements include examination of growth of North American continent, mechanisms and timing; discovery that many terranes of California have not travelled as previously believed. Office: Orange Coast Coll 2701 Fairview Rd Costa Mesa CA 92626-5563

BENDER, HAROLD, beverage company consultant; b. Boston, Oct. 2, 1910; s. Samuel and Clara Rebecca (Wernon) B.; m. Lilyan Alpert, Mar. 24, 1935; children: M. Barbara, Laurence Howard. BSBA, Boston U., 1931. Sales exec. Ideal Wine and Spirits Co., Inc., Boston, 1933-68; treas. John Gilbert Jr. Co., Boston, 1968-87, cons., 1987—. Grantee Lilyan Bender Endowment Fund, Boston, 1990. Mem. Assn. for Devel. Bordeaux Wines (Champagnon de Bordeaux 1955), Wine and Spirits Club (life, Boston U., Brandeis U., award of merit 1965), Masons (50 Yr. mel 1989). Republican. Avocation: researching major hist. events. Home: 250 Hammond Pond Pkwy Apt 16115 Chestnut Hill MA 02467-1533

BENDER, HARVEY A., biology educator; b. Cleve., June 5, 1933; m. Eileen Adelle Teper, June 16, 1956; children: Leslie Carol, Samuel David, Philip Michael. AB in Chemistry, Case Western Res. U., 1954, student, 1954-55; MS, Northwestern U., 1957, PhD, 1959. Diplomate Am. Bd. Medical Genetics (founding). Post-doctoral fellow USPHS U. Calif., Berkeley, 1959-60; asst. prof. biology U. Notre Dame, Ind., 1960-64, assoc. prof., 1964-69, prof., 1969—; adj. prof. law U. Notre Dame, 1974—; dir. No. Ind. Regional Genetics Ctr., Meml. Hosp. South Bend (Ind.), 1979—, Gt. Lakes Regional Genetics Group, 1991—; NSF In-Svc. Inst. prof., fall term 1962-63; vis. prof. human genetics, rsch. assoc. Yale U., 1973-74; vis. prof. zoology So. Ill. U., Carbondale, summer 1978; adj. prof. medical genetics Ind. U., 1979—; vis. prof. natural scis. Washington Coll., Chestertown, Md., 1984; cons. Ednl. Rsch. Coun. Am., 1967-69, Pres.'s Com. on Mental Retardation, 1973, N.J. Inst. Tech., 1975-76, Ind. State Bd. of Health, 1991—, mem. sickle cell commn., 1987—, chronic disease commn., 1989—; genetics cons. Ind. State Bd. Health, 1991—. Editorial reviewer various profl. jours. Bd. dirs. Internat. Rels. Coun., 1961-69, v.p., 1962-64, pres., 1964-65; bd. dirs. Coun. for Retarded of St. Joseph County, 1964-76, 1st v.p., 1967-76; chmn. human rights com. No. Ind. State Hosp., 1980—. Predoctoral fellow USPHS, 1957-59, Cross-disciplinary fellow Yale U., 1973-74; grantee NIH, 1961-67, DOE, 1961—, United Health Svc., 1963-73, NSF, 1978-81, HEW, HHS, others. Fellow AAAS; mem. AAUP, Am. Assn. Mental Deficiency, Am. Inst. Biol. Scientists, Am. Soc. Human Genetics, Genetics Soc. Am., Ind. Acad. Sci., Radiation Rsch. Soc., Soc. Devel. Biology, Soc. for Values in Higher Edn., Sigma Xi (regional lectr. 1977—, mem. nat. com. on sci. and society 1978-89, chmn. 1981-89, mem. nat. com. awards, 1981-86, chmn. 1981-83, dir.-at-large 1980-86, bd. dirs. nat. exec. com. 1983-84, long range planning com. 1986—). Office: U Notre Dame Dept Biol Scis Notre Dame IN 46556

BENDER, HARVEY W., JR., cardiac and thoracic surgeon; b. Corpus Christi, Tex., 1933. MD, Baylor U., 1959. Diplomate Am. Bd. Surgery. Intern. Johns Hopkins Hosp., 1959-60, res., 1960-61, 1963-67; surgeon John Hopkins Hosp., 1967-71; asst. prof. surgery John Hopkins U., Sch. Medicine, 1967-70; assoc. prof. surgery John Hopkins U. Sch. Medicine, 1970-71; sr. asst. surgeon US PHS, 1961-63; prof. cardiac & thoracic surgery, chmn. Vanderbilt U. (Sch. Medicine), 1971—; cons. Va. Hosp., Balt., 1968-71; consulting surgeon Good Samaritan Hosp., Balt., 1968-71, prof. emeritus cardiac thoracic surgery, 1997—; formerly chmn. Am. Bd. Thoracic Surgery. Mem. Am. Assn. for Thoracic Surg., Am. Coll. of Surgeons (bd. regents), Am. Surgical Assn. Office: Vanderbilt U Hosp 2986 Vanderbilt Clinic 1301 22nd Ave S Nashville TN 37232-5734*

BENDER, HOWARD JEFFREY, software engineering educator; b. Phila., Dec. 18, 1946; s. Irving Monroe and Ethel (Hellman) B.; m. Randi Laine Anderson, May 22, 1971; children: Rebecca Jennifer, Heidi Julia (dec.). BS, Pa. State U., 1969; MS, Polytech. Inst. N.Y., 1980; PhD, U. Md., 1992. Sr. programmmer, analyst ITEL Corp., White Plains, N.Y., 1977-80; computer scientist CSTA, Greenbelt, Md., 1980-82; systems engr. Lockheed Corp., Greenbelt, Md., 1982-85, CTA, Inc., Rockville, Md., 1985-93; instr. U. Md., College Park, 1981-85, adj. asst. prof., 1986-94, assoc. dir., 1994-98, cons., 1994—; pres. Edn. Process Improvement Ctr., Hyattsville, Md., 1995—. Author tech. articles; programmer (software) Personal Computing to Aid the Handicapped, 1981. Welcome wagon host University Park Civic Assn., 1989—. Mem. ASCD, Assn. for the Advancement of Computing in Edn., Computer Profls. Social Responsibility. Avocations: tennis, bridge, banjo. Home: 4200 Sheridan St Hyattsville MD 20782-2137

BENDER, HY, writer; b. Bronx, N.Y., May 14, 1958. BA, NYU, 1981. Author: Excel Quick Reference, 1990, PC Tools Deluxe: The Complete Reference, 1990, PC Tools: The Complete Reference, 2nd Edition, 1991, Essential Software for Writers, 1994, Getting Started with Windows 95, 1995, (with M. Young) Dummies 101: The Internet for Windows 95, 1996, (with M. Young) Dummies 101: Netscape Navigator, 1996, (with M. Young, J. Levine and C. Baroudi) The Internet for Dummies, Starter Kit Edition, 1997, Dummies 101: Netscape Communicator 4, 1997, Dummies 101: The Internet for Windows 98, 1998, The Sandman Companion, 1999; contbr. nat. mags., including PC Week, PC Mag., Am. Film, Advt. Age, Spy, Mad Mag., PC World, Folio: The Mag. for Mag. Mgmt., Bottom Line/Personal, and Yahoo! Internet Life.

BENDER, JANET PINES, artist; b. Chgo., June 14, 1934; d. Nathan and Hana (Leff) Pines; m. Irwin Robert Bender, Feb. 25, 1956. BS, U. Wis., 1955; MA, Northwestern U., 1956; postgrad., U. Ill./Loyola U., Chgo., 1955-56, Tyler Sch. Fine Arts, Phila., 1957. One-woman shows include One Ill. Ctr., Chgo., 1979, 87, Olive Hyde Gallery, Fremont, Calif., 1980, 81, N.A.M.E. Gallery, Chgo., 1982, W.A.R.M. Gallery, Mpls., 1984, A.R.C. Gallery, Chgo., 1985, 87, 89, 94, 96, 98, 99, R.H. Love Galleries, Chgo., 1989, 92, Soho 20 Gallery, N.Y.C., 1990, Galerie Thea Fischer-Reinhardt, Berlin, Germany, 1990, 98, catalog, exhib. travels to Munich & Antwerp, R.H. Love Contemporary Gallery, Chgo., 1992, 97; exhibited in group shows at Mus. Sci. and Industry, Cho., 1995, 96, 98, Artimesia Gallery, Chgo., 1996, Gallery 750, Sacramento, 1996, Women's Nat. Art Gallery, Washington, 1995, Rockford (Ill.) Art Mus., 1994, U. Wis. Art Gallery, Madison, Amos Enos Gallery, N.Y.C., 1993, Tonali Gallery, Mexico City, 1992, Renaissance Soc., Chgo., 1986, Ill. State Mus., 1983, 72nd Newport (R.I.) Nat. Exhbn., 1983, Chauttaqua Nat. Exhbn., 1981, Zolla Leiberman Gallery, Chgo., 1980, Holter Mus., Helena, Mont., 1997, Swan Gallery, Sydney (Australia) Coll. Art Gallery, 1998, Atelierhof Kunsthandwerkev, Bremen, Germany, 1999, ; represented in permanent collections at Mus. Sci. and Industry, Chgo., Young & Rubicam, Chgo., Brown-Forman Corp., Louisville, Nugent Wenckus Corp., Chgo., Louis Zahn Drug Co., Melrose Park, Ill, Fuller Comml. Brokerage Co., Chgo., Dynamark Inc., Chgo., Aabott Distbn., Miami, Art Beasley Inc., San Diego, Siegel, Denberg, Vanasco, Shivkovsky, Moses and Shoenstadt, Chgo., Altschuler, Melvoin & Glassner, Chgo., Shafer, Meltzer & Lewis Assocs., Wilmette, Ill., Schiff, Hardin & Waite, Chgo, art res. Bardcliff Art Colony, 1998. Bd. dirs. Art Residents Chgo. Gallery, Chgo., 1984—; juror Ill. Assn. Fine Arts Awards, 1993. Recipient Ill. Arts Coun. Project Completion grants, 1979, 81-82, Visual Arts Fellowship grant Ill. Arts Coun., 1983; fellow Northwestern U., 1955-56. Mem. NAFE, Women's Caucus for Art, Nat. Woman's Mus., Mus. Contemporary Art, Art Inst. Chgo., Chgo. Artist Coalition, Ill. Arts Alliance, Met. Mus. Art (N.Y.), Coll. Art Assn., Peace Mus., Ill. State Gallery, Com. fr Artist Rights (organizing com. 1988), Siam House, Pi Lambda. Avocations: reading, tennis, swimming, travel, theater. Studio: 2001 N Elston Ave Chicago IL 60614-3901 *"Art is a metaphor for life", the trick is to keep our priorities straight...success in the visual arts depends on one's personal definitions and goals. Hard work, good luck, strong focus, and good slides; the challenge is not to take rejection personally, nor to let a temporary "success" stifle the creative impulse and the nerve to fail.*

BENDER, JOHN CHARLES, lawyer; b. N.Y.C., May 17, 1940; s. John H. and Cecilia B.; m. Helen Hadjiyannakis; 1 child, Marianna Celene. BSME, Northea. U., 1964; JD, NYU, 1968, LLM, 1971. Bar: N.Y. 1968, U.S. Dist. Ct. (so. dist.) N.Y. 1972, U.S. Supreme Ct. 1997. Atty. Marshall, Bratter, Greene, Allison and Tucker, 1968-69; asst. dir, NYU Ctr. for Internat. Studies, N.Y.C., 1969-71; atty. Poletti Freidin Prashker Feldman & Gartner, N.Y.C., 1971-75; spl. counsel Moreland Act Commn. on Nursing Homes and Residential Facilities, N.Y.C., 1975-76; gen. counsel N.Y. State Fin. Control Bd., N.Y.C., 1976-80; v.p., gen. counsel News Am. Pub. Inc., N.Y.C., 1980-85; group v.p., gen. counsel Simon & Schuster Inc., N.Y.C., 1985-90; sr. v.p., dir., gen. counsel Maxwell Macmillan Group, 1991-95; dir. Black Book Mktg. Group, Inc., 1994-96. Chmn., trustee Trust for Cultural Resources of City of N.Y., 1981—; chmn., trustee Mary McDowell Ctr. for Learning, 1993—. Mem. ABA, Assn. of Bar of City of N.Y. (mem. com. on com. law 1981-85, mem. spl. com. on edn. and the law 1982-85). Home: 27 W 67th St New York NY 10023-6258 Office: 150 E 58th St New York NY 10155-0002

BENDER, JOHN HENRY, JR. (JACK BENDER), editor, cartoonist; b. Waterloo, Iowa, Mar. 28, 1931; s. John Henry and Wilma (Lowe) B.; divorced; children: Thereza, John Henry IV, Anthony; m. Carole R. Humphrey, 1995. BA, U. Iowa, 1953; MA, U. Mo., 1962; postgrad., Art. Inst. Chgo., 1956, Washington U., St. Louis., 1957. Art dir., asst. editor Commerce Pub. Co., St. Louis, 1953-54, 56-58; editor Florissant Reporter, 1958-61; edit. cartoonist Waterloo Courier, 1962-84, assoc. editor, 1975-83; art. dir., editor Alpha VII Corp., Tulsa, 1984-87; head dept. prodn. art Platt Coll., Tulsa, 1987-92; cartoonist Don Martin Studio, Miami, Fla., 1989-92; cartoonist Alley Oop comic strip United Media Syndicate, N.Y.C., 1991—; sports cartoonist Basketball Weekly, Baseball Digest Mag., U. Iowa, others. Author: Pocket Guide to Judging Springboard Diving, (with Dick Smith) Inside Diving, (with Ed Gagnier) Inside Gymnastics. With USAF, 1954-56, col. USAFR, ret. Recipient Best Editl. award Mo. Press Assn., 1960, Grenville Clark Editl. Page award, 1968, Freedoms Found. award, 1969, 71, 75, Ignatz award Orlandocon, 1992, Air Force Commendation medal, 1981; named to Hall of Fame East H.S., Waterloo, Iowa, 1972, Names on Main, Cedar Falls, Iowa, 1997. Mem. Assn. Am. Editl. Cartoonists, Nat. Cartoonists Soc., Comic Art Profl. Soc., Sigma Chi. Home: RR 1 Box 540 Terlton OK 74081-9740 Office: 3289 S Cincinnati Ave #499 Tulsa OK 74105-1947

BENDER, LARRY WAYNE, vocational educator; b. Indpls., May 23, 1942; s. Wayne Crawford and Margaret Dell (Ramer) B.; m. Barbara Agnes Kroll, Aug. 26, 1967; children: Anissa Gayle, Timothy Alan. BS in Indsl. Edn., Purdue U., 1967, MS in Indsl. Edn., 1972. Tchr. South Newton Sch. Corp., Kentland, Ind., 1967-81; tchr. tech. edn. Franklin (Ind.) Community Schs., 1981—. Recipient IPALCO Golden Apple award 1997, Newmast award 1997; Eli Lilly Found. grantee. Mem. Internat. Tech. Edn. Assn. (Outstanding Program of Yr. award 1987), Tech. Educators of Ind. (Meritorious Tchr. award 1987). Episcopalian. Avocations: photography, computers, bowling, golf, woodworking. Home: 4215 North Graham Rd Whiteland IN 46184-9326 Office: Custer Baker Middle Sch 101 W State Road 44 Franklin IN 46131-8936

BENDER, PAUL E., title insurance executive; b. Decatur, Ill., June 5, 1951; s. Kenneth D. and Martha Bender Heinzelmann; m. Anne Scartabello, Dec. 31, 1976 (div. Aug. 1978); 1 child, Anthony. BA, Millikin U., 1973; JD, Hamline U., 1976; MBA, U. Phoenix, San Francisco, 1997. Assoc. Halloran & Alfueby, Mpls., 1977-78; pvt. practice Arthur, Ill., 1978-79; atty. Chgo. Title, Peoria, Ill., 1979-82; ptnr. Cordis & Bender, Princeville, Ill., 1982-84; office counsel Chgo. Title, Champaign, Ill., 1984-88, mgr., 1988-96; mgr. McLean Title, Bloomington, Ill., 1996—, Decatur (Ill.) Title, 1997—; lectr. Ill. Bankers Assn. Mem. Rep. Nat. Com. Masons, Shriner. Avocations: chess, college basketball. Home: 303 N Cottage Ave Normal IL 61761-4264

BENDER, PAUL S., management consultant. Degree, MIT, Poly. Sch., Paris, Swiss Inst. Tech. Pres. Bender Cons., Inc. a SynQuest Co.; also bd. dirs.; lectr. MIT, Stanford U., Columbus U., Northwestern U., USAF Inst. Tech., Japan Inst. Sys. Rsch., Chinese Mech. Enging. Soc., TsingHua U., Beiming, Singapore Inst. Sys. Sci., U. NSW, other schs., cos., profl. and tech. orgns. Mem. Inst. Mgmt. Cons. (cert., founding mem.), Am. Assn. Artificial Intelligence, Assn. Computing Machinery, Am. Mktg. Assn., Japan Mktg. Assn., Nat. Purchasing Mgmt. Assn., Assn. for Mfg. Excellence, Coun. Logistics Mgmt., Inst. Mgmt. Scis. Office: Bender Mgmt 3500 Parkway Ln Ste 555 Norcross GA 30092

BENDER, PEGGY WALLACE, fundraising consultant; b. Athens, Ohio, Apr. 29, 1957; d. Allen Riley and Carol Jean (Jago) Wallace; children: Meghan Elizabeth, Erin Michelle. AS, Ohio U., 1986, BA, 1988. Cert. Fund Raising Exec., 1988. Asst. to dean Ohio U. Col. Bus. Admin., Athens, 1981-86; asst. dir. planned giving U. Cin. Fed., 1986-88; dir. planned/major gifts Western Md. Col., Westminster, 1988-89; dir. planned giving Am. Red Cross, Cleve., 1991-93; pres. Strategies for Planned Giving, Cleve., 1993—; bd. dirs. Nat. Com. Planned Giving, Indpls. Mem. Kindergarten Curriculum Com. Family Life Ctr., Berea, Ohio, 1996-97; bd. dirs. Nat. Com. Planned Giving, 1998—. Named Outstanding Fund Raising Exec., 1997. Mem. Northern Ohio Planned Giving Council (pres., 1993-96), Nat. Soc. Fund Raising Execs. (v.p., 1992), Ohio Council Fund Raising Execs., Ohio Assn. Healthcare Philanthropy. Avocations: reading, travel, boating. Office: Strategies Planned Giving 15300 Pearl Rd Cleveland OH 44136-5091

BENDER, RANDI LAINE, occupational therapist; b. Omaha, July 17, 1947; children: Rebecca Jennifer, Heidi Julia (dec. Mar. 1991). BS, U. Ill., 1970; MS, Calif. Coll. for Health Scis., 1996. Registered occupational therapist. Occupl. therapist Westchester County Med. Ctr., Valhalla, N.Y., 1970-76, UCP Therapeutic Nursery, Washington, 1987-89, Edward Mazique Parent Child Ctr., Washington, 1989, Great Oak Ctr., Silver Spring, Md., 1989-93, Montgomery Primary Achievement Ctr., Silver Spring, 1993—, Pediat. Svcs. Am., Inc., Washington, 1996—. Mem. Coun. for Exceptional Children, Am. Occupational Therapy Assn., DAR, Riverdale Presbyn. Ch. Avocations: writing poetry, painting portraits, jigsaw puzzles. Home: 4200 Sheridan St Hyattsville MD 20782-2137

BENDER, RICHARD, university dean, architect, educator; b. N.Y.C., Jan. 19, 1930; s. Edward and Betty (Okun) B.; m. Sue Rosenfeld, Aug. 9, 1956; children: Michael, David. BCE, CCNY, 1951; MArch, Harvard U., 1956. Architect Walter Gropius, 1951-53, William Lescaze, 1958-60; with Town Planning Assocs., N.Y.C., 1960-66; ptnr. Town Planning Assocs., 1961-66, prin., 1966—; pvt. practice Berkeley, 1966—; bd. dirs. Bridge Housing Corp., San Francisco; lectr. Columbia U., N.Y.C., 1957-60; asst. prof. Cooper Union, 1961; prof. architecture U. Calif., Berkeley, 1969—, chmn. dept., 1974-76; vis. prof. urban design and constrn., endowed vis. chair U. Tokyo, 1989—; dir. bldg. rsch. bd. Nat. Acad. Sci., 1974-80, mem. adv. bd. on the built environment; adv. panels HUD, Nat. Endowment Arts; mem. design rev. bd. City of San Francisco, U. Calif., J.P. Getty Trust; cons. univ campus planning U. Calif., Berkeley, 1972—, U. Calif., San Diego, 1987-90, U. Calif., Davis, 1989-93, U. Calif., Santa Cruz, 1992-96, master plan Benesse Inst. of Arts, Naoshima Island, Japan, 1993—, master plan for MediaPolis, Taipei, Taiwan, 1997—, master plan for New Town Cergy-Pontoise, France, 1993—. Author: A Crack in the Rearview Mirror, 1973. Bd. dirs. Bridge Housing, San Francisco, 1980—; trustee Mills Coll., 1993—. With U.S. Army, 1954-55. Home: 804 Santa Barbara Rd Berkeley CA 94707-2018 Office: U Calif Coll Environ Design Berkeley CA 94720

BENDER, ROBERT JOHN, ceramic engineer; b. Oil City, Pa., Nov. 28, 1956; s. Robert G. and Virginia (Russell) B.; m. Lee Dennis, May 26, 1987; children: Matthew, Christopher. BS in Ceramic Sci. and Enging., Pa. State U., 1979. Engr. Johns-Manville, Denver, 1979-84; rsch. engr. Manville, Denver, 1985-90; sect. mgr., market mgr. Schuller Internat., Waterville, Ohio, 1990—; sales dir. Evanite Fiber Corp., Corvallis, Oreg. Mem. Ceramic Enging. Soc. (pres. Rocky Mountain sect. 1985-90), Tech. Assn. Pulp and Paper Industry (session developer 1994, divsn. editor newsletter 1998, 99). Home: 294 Hunter Ridge Dr Saline MI 48176-9296

BENDER, ROSS THOMAS, minister; b. Tavistock, Ont., Can., June 25, 1929; came to U.S., 1960, naturalized, 1966; s. Christian and Katie (Bender) B.; m. Ruth Eileen Steinmann, Dec. 22, 1950 (dec. Dec. 1997); children: Ross Lynn, Elizabeth, Michael, Deborah, Anne. BA, Goshen Coll., 1954, BD, 1956; MA, Yale U., 1961, PhD, 1962. Ordained to ministry Mennonite Ch., 1958. Prin. Rockway Mennonite sch., Kitchener, Ont., 1956-60; prof. Christian edn. Associated Mennonite Bibl. Sem., Ind., 1962-96; dean Assoc. Mennonite Bibl. Sems., Elkhart, Ind., 1964-79; dean emeritus Assoc. Mennonite Bibl. Sems., Elkhart, 1996; dir. Inst. Mennonite Studies, 1990-97; pres. Mennonite World Conf., 1984-90. Author: The People of God, 1969, Christians in Families, 1982, Education for Peoplehood, 1997; co-editor: Baptism, Peace and the State in the Reformed and Mennonite Traditions, 1991. Rockefeller fellow, 1960-61; Am. Assn. Theol. Schs. fellow, 1961-62; NIMH postdoctoral fellow U. Pa., 1970-71.

BENDER, SHEILA SUE, essayist, poet, author; b. Richmond, Va., Mar. 6, 1948; d. Bertrand J. Lillian and Arline Chernin; m. Kurt C. Vandersluis, Nov., 24, 198 6; children: Emily Ruth, Seth Michael; m. Arthur J. Bender, Aug., 21, 1969 (div. May, 1980). BA in English, U. Wis., 1970; MAT, Keane Coll., 1972; MA in Creative Writing, U. Wash., 1981. Tchr. Matawan N.J. Sch. Dist., 1970-72; day care dir./program coord. Temple Day Care, Seattle, 1972-75; instr. Shoreline Comm. Coll., Seattle, 1982-95; vis. writer Seattle U., 1996-97, U. Ariz. and Pima C. C., Tucson, 1995-99; Instr. Pima Writer's Conf., Tucson, 1997, S.W. Writer's Conf., 1999; critic Seattle Times, 1996-98. Author: (books) Love From the Coastal Route, 1991, Writing Personal Essays, 1995, Sustenance, 1999, Writing Personal Poetry, 1999; co-author: Writing in a New Convertible with the Top Down, 1997; editor: The Writer's Journal, 1997. Recipient fellowship Residency Centrum Found., Port Townsend, Wash., 1994. Mem. Nat. Book Critics, Internat. Women's Writing Guild. Jewish.

BENDER, THOMAS, history and humanities educator, writer; b. Redwood City, Calif., Apr. 18, 1944; s. Joseph Charles and Catherine Frances (McGuire) B.; m. Sally Hill, June 8, 1966 (div. 1983); 1 child, David William; m. Gwendolyn Wright, Jan. 14, 1984; 1 child, Sophia Wright. B.A., U. Santa Clara, 1966; M.A., U. Calif.-Davis, 1967, Ph.D., 1971. Asst. prof. history and urban studies U. Wis., Green Bay, 1971-74; asst. prof. history NYU, N.Y.C., 1974-76, assoc. prof. history, 1976-77, prof. history, 1977—, Samuel Rudin prof. humanities, 1977-82, Univ. prof. humanities, 1982—, dean for the humanities, 1995-98; mem. research planning com. N.Y.C. Social Sci. Research Council, 1985-88; dir. Internat. Ctr. Advanced Studies NYU, 1997—. Author: Toward an Urban Vision, 1975 (Frederick Jackson Turner prize 1975), Community and Social Change in America, 1978, (with Edwin Rozwenc) The Making of American Society, 1978, New York Intellect, 1987, Intellect and Public Life, 1993; editor: Democracy in America, 1981, Intellectual History Group Newsletter, 1978-85, The University and the City, 1988, The Anti-Slavery Debate: Capitalism and Abolitionism as a Problem in Historical Interpretation, 1992; co-editor: (with Carl Schorske) Budapest and New York: Studies in Metropolitan Transformation 1870-1930, 1994, (with Carl Schorske) The Tranformation of American Academic Culture, 1998; cons. editor New Studies in American Intellectual and Cultural History, 1981-94; mem. editorial bd. Readers Encyclopedia of American History, 1988-91, Am. Hist. Rev., 1991-94; assoc. editor American National Biography, 1990-97. Bd. dirs. Mcpl. Art Soc. N.Y., N.Y.C., 1983-84, N.Y. Coun. for the Humanities, 1989-96, chair, 1992-95; mem. gov. coun. Rockefeller Archives Ctr., Pocantico Hills, N.Y., 1987-92; trustee Grace Sch., N.Y.C., 1987-94. N.Y. Inst. Humanities fellow, 1977-88; Guggenheim fellow, 1980-81; Rockefeller Found. fellow, 1984-85; Getty scholar Getty Ctr. for Study of Art and Humanities , 1992-93. Fellow Am. Acad. Arts and Scis.; mem. Am. Hist. Assn., Orgn. Am. Historians, Soc. Am. Historians, Writers Guild, PEN. Democrat. Home: 54 Washington Mews New York NY 10003-6608 Office: NYU Dept History 53 Washington Sq S New York NY 10012-1098

BENDER, VICTOR M., educational administrator; b. Pitts., Apr. 18, 1946; m. Patricia Ann Pike, Jan. 27, 1968; children:Trisha Ann Bender-Labbe, John Scott Bender, Michael Ray Bender. BS, Northeast La. U., 1969; MEd, Southeastern La. U., 1973. Football coach Northeast La. U., Monroe, 1974, Miss. State U., Starkville, 1974-76; exec. asst. Tangipahoa Parish Sheriff's Office, Amite, La., 1976-78; supr. Davill Petroleum, Natalbany, La., 1978; pogram dir. City of Hammond (La.) Recreation Dept., Hammond, La., 1978; acct., bookkeeper Triangle Timber, Hammond, 1978-79; tchr., coach Kentwood (La.) H.S., 1979-80; prin. Ponchatoula (La.) Jr. H.S., 1990—; emergency mgmt. coord. Tangipahoa Parish Pike Jury, Amite, 1982. Capt. U.S. Army Inf., 1969-71. Recipient award for contbrn. to amateur athletics Nat. Football Found. and Coll. Hall of Fame, 1996. Mem. Nat. Assn. Secondary Prins., La. Assn. Prins., La. Assn. Sch. Execs., Am. Legion (vice-comdr. 1989), K.C. (patriotic chair 1980—, Knight of Yr. 1980), Phi Delta Kappa (pres. 1995-97). Avocations: camping, hiking, golf, fishing. Home: 47191 Bender Rd Hammond LA 70401-6829

BENDICKSON, MARCUS J., company executive. Pres. Dynetics, Inc., Ala. Address: Dynetics Inc 1000 Explorer Blvd NW Huntsville AL 35806-2806*

BENDIG, WILLIAM CHARLES, editor, artist, publisher; b. Corry, Pa., Dec. 1, 1927; s. William Charles and Hazel Grace Mae (Dailey) B. BA with honors, Trinity Coll., 1953; postgrad., U. London, 1955-56. Founding editor Erie (Pa.) Tribune, 1944-48; mgr. Nat. Symphonic Choir, Erie, 1946-49; program mgr. Erie Philharmonic Orch., 1947-49; instr. Cheshire (Conn.) Acad., 1953-54, Brunswick Sch., Greenwich, Conn., 1954-55; editor in chief, pub. theARTgallery Mag., Ivoryton, Conn., 1957-84; prin., pub. Hollycroft Pubs., Ivoryton, 1987—; editor in chief Botswana Rev., Ivoryton and Gaborone, 1988-90; curator, archivist theARTgallery Archive, 1990—; pres. Hollycroft Found., 1992—; cons. Kuwait Info. Office, Washington, 1993-96; cons. Submarine Force Libr. & Nautilus Mus., Groton, Conn., 1994—; dep. dir. U.S.-Africa Arts Found., Gaborone, 1988-93, life trustee; trustee Contemporary Sculptors Guild, 1994-95; dep. dir. Sculptors Guild, N.Y.C., 1997—; juror nat. art exhbns.; lectr. univs. and mus. Designer, fabricator Pentecost rose window All Sts.' Episcopal Ch., Ivoryton, 1988; contbr. works in various art exhbns. V.p. Essex Art Assn., 1960-62; founding v.p. Ivoryton Village Assn.; mem. Essex Landmark Commn., 1981-82; trustee Ivoryton Pub. Libr., Ivoryton Playhouse Found. (founding); dir. art seminar program. Episcopal Conf. Ctr., Ivoryton, 1982-92. Mem. Mediaeval Acad. Am., Africa Studies Assn., Friends of Trinity Libr., Naval Submarine League, Trinity Coll. Alumni Assn. (pres. New London chpt. 1963-67), Grad. Club, New Haven Club. Episcopalian (vestryman 1970-92). Home and Office: Hollycroft Found Main St Ivoryton CT 06442

BENDINER, ROBERT, writer, editor; b. Pitts., Dec. 15, 1909; s. William and Lillian (Schwartz) B.; m. Kathryn Rosenberg, Dec. 24, 1934; children: David, William, Margaret. Student, CCNY, 1928-33; LHD (hon.), L.I. U., 1994. Mng. editor The Nation, N.Y.C., 1937-44, assoc. editor, 1946-50, freelance writer, 1951-68, 78—; lectr., program chmn. Wellesley Summer Inst. Social Progress, 1946-53; mem. Faculty Salzburg Sem. in Am. Studies, 1956; vis. lectr. pub. affairs Wesleyan U. (Conn.), 1983. Contbg. editor The Reporter, N.Y.C., 1956-60; U.S. corr. New Statesman, London, 1959-61; mem. editorial bd. N.Y. Times, 1969-77; author: The Riddle of the State Department, 1942, White House Fever, 1960, Obstacle Course on Capitol Hill, 1964, Just Around the Corner, 1967, The Politics of Schools, 1969, The Fall of the Wild, The Rise of the Zoo, 1981; TV documentary NBC White Paper, The Man in the Middle, The State Legislator, 1961. Served with AUS, 1944-45. Guggenheim fellow, 1962-63; grantee Carnegie Fund;

recipient Benjamin Franklin Mag. award U. Ill., 1955, NEA award, 1960. Mem. Nat. Press Club. Club: Coffee House (N.Y.C.). Home and Office: Southampton Estates 238 Street Rd Apt A202 Southampton PA 18966-3128

BENDITT, THEODORE MATTHEW, humanities educator; b. Phila., Oct. 23, 1940; m. Anne Rosamond Shaw, Feb. 3, 1968; 1 child, David Shaw. AB, U. Pa., 1962, LLB, 1965, MA, 1967; PhD, U. Pitts., 1971. Instr. Duke U., Durham, N.C., 1970-71, asst. prof., 1971-75; asst. prof. U. So. Calif., Los Angeles, 1975-78; assoc. prof. U. Ala., Birmingham, 1978-83, prof., 1983—, dean, Sch. Arts and Humanities, 1984-98. Author: Law as Rule and Principle, 1978, Rights, 1982; contbr. articles to profl. jours. Recipient Younger Humanist Fellowship, NEH, 1974-75. Mem. Am. Philos. Assn., Am. Soc. for Polit. and Legal Philosophy, Amintaphil. Office: Univ of Ala at Birmingham Dept Philosophy Birmingham AL 35294-1260

BENDIX, HELEN IRENE, lawyer; b. N.Y.C., July 24, 1952; d. Gerhard Max and Eva Gabriela (Sternberger) B.; m. John A. Kronstadt, Nov. 29, 1974; children: Jessica Claire Kronstadt, Erik Bendix Kronstadt, Nicola Eva Kronstadt. BA, Cornell U., 1973; JD, Yale U., 1976. Bar: Calif. 1976, D.C. 1978, U.S. Dist. Ct. D.C. 1980, U.S. Dist. Ct. (ctrl. dist.) Calif. 1986, U.S. Ct. Appeals (D.C. cir.) 1981, U.S. Ct. Appeals (9th cir.) 19887, U.S. Dist. Ct. (so. dist.) Calif. 1990. Law clk. to Hon. Shirley M. Hufstedler U.S. Ct. Appeals (9th cir.), L.A., 1976-77; assoc. Wilmer Cultler & Pickering, Washington, 1977-79; asst. prof. law UCLA, 1979-80; from assoc. to ptnr. Leva Hawes Symington Martin & Oppenheimer, Washington, 1980-85; of counsel Gibson Dunn & Crutcher, L.A., 1986-89; ptnr. Heller Ehrman White & McAuliffe, L.A., 1989-96; sr. v.p., gen. counsel KCET Cmty. TV of So. Calif., 1996—; judge Mcpl. Ct. L.A. Jud. Dist., 1997—; vis. prof. law UCLA, 1985-86. Co-author: Moore's Federal Practice, Vols. X and XI, 1976, Vols. XII and XIII, 1979; contbr. articles to profl. jours. Violinist Palisades Symphony, Pacific Palisades, Calif., 1989-97. Mem. D.C. Bar Assn., Calif. State Bar Assn. (chairperson internat. law sect. 1990-91), Calif. Judges Assn., Mcpl. Ct. Judges Assn., L.A. County Bar Assn. (chair dispute resolution svcs.), Nat. Charity League (chmn. 11th grade class), Chancery Club, Phi Beta Kappa. Office: 1945 S Hill St Los Angeles CA 90007-1413

BENDIXEN, HENRIK HOLT, physician, educator, dean; b. Fredriksberg, Denmark, Dec. 2, 1923; came to U.S., 1954, naturalized, 1960; s. Carl Julius and Borghild (Holt) B.; m. Karen Skakke, Dec. 20, 1947 (dec. 1984); children: Nils, Birgitte; m. Lilo M. Laver, May 29, 1985. Cand. Phil., U. Copenhagen, 1943, CM, CChir, 1951, MD (hon.), 1987; MD (hon.), Jagiellonian U., Krakow, Poland, 1985. Diplomate Am. Bd. Anesthesiologists. Intern Copenhagen County Hosp., 1951-52; resident in surgery and anesthesia Denmark and Sweden, 1952-54; resident in anesthesia Mass. Gen. Hosp., Boston, 1954-57, anesthetist, 1957-69; asst. clin. prof. Harvard U., Boston, 1957-69; prof. anesthesia, chief dept. U. Calif., San Diego, 1969-73; med. dir. Univ. Hosp., San Diego, 1971-72; prof. anesthesiology Columbia U., N.Y.C., 1973—, chmn. dept. anesthesiology, 1973-85, acting provost Coll. Physicians and Surgeons, 1980-81, alumni prof., 1984, v.p. health scis., dean faculty medicine, 1984-89, E.M. Papper prof. anesthesiology, 1985-86; sr. assoc. v.p. health scis., sr. assoc. dean medicine, 1989—. Author: Respiratory Care, 1965; contbr. numerous articles to profl. jours. Mem. bd. visitors sch. medicine U. Pitts., 1985; trustee Mary Imogene Bassett Hosp., Cooperstown, N.Y., 1986—. Fellow AAAS, Faculty of Anesthetists, Royal Coll. Surgeons Eng.; mem. Minn. Surg. Soc. (hon.), Inst. Medicine, Am. Soc. Anesthesiologists, Am. Urological Assn., Belgian Soc. Anesthesiologists (hon.), Scandinavian Soc. Anesthesiologists (hon.). Clubs: Harvard (Boston); Univ., Century (N.Y.C.). Home: Daisy Ln Irvington NY 10533-2015 Office: Columbia U Coll Physicians & Surgeons 630 W 168th St New York NY 10032-3795*

BEN-DOR, GISÈLE, conductor, musician; b. Montevideo, Uruguay; came to U.S., 1982; m. Eli Ben-Dor; children: Roy, Gabriel. Student, Acad. of Music, Tel Aviv; artist diploma, Rubin Acad. Music, Tel Aviv; M, Yale Sch. of Music, 1982. Music dir. Annapolis Symphony, Md., Pro Arte Chamber Orch. of Boston; condr. Norwalk (Conn.) Youth Symphony; conducting fellow L.A. Philharm. Inst., 1984, Tanglewood Music Ctr., 1985; resident condr. Houston Symphony, 1991; music dir. Santa Barbara Symphony, Calif., 1994—; resident condr. Houston Symphony; condr. variety conducting activities including prestigious summer festivals, competitions, 1983-87, Hungarian Nat. Symphony, Budapest Philharm., others; guest condr. orchs. in Uruguay, Ea. Europe, Israel and U.S. including Barvarian Radio Orch., Boston POPS, New World Symphony, Women's Philharm, San Francisco, Minn. Orch. in Summerfest Festival, 1986, N.Y. Philharm., 1993, 95, Orquestra del Teatro Nacional, Brazil, Ulster Orch., Israel Philharm., 1991, Carnegie Hall, 1991, others; past music dir. Houston Youth Symphony; past acting orch. dir. Shepherd Sch. Music Rice U.; music dir. Boston ProArte Chamber Orch., Annapolis Symphony. Condr. Israel Philharm. Orch. (play) The Rite of Spring; recs. with London Symphony, Israel Chamber Orch., (CD) London Symphony Orch., Sofia Soloists, Boston ProArte Chamber Orch.; numerous TV appearances. Am.-Israel Cultural Found scholar, Frances Wickes scholar; Leonard Bernstein fellow; recipient Bartók prize Hungarian TV Internat. Condrs. Competition, 1986. E-mail: delrosdra@aol.com. Office: Santa Barbara Symphony Orch Arlington Theatre 1900 State St Ste G Santa Barbara CA 93101-8424 Office: Del Rosenfield Assoc 714 Ladd Rd Bronx NY 10471-1204*

BENEDEK, ARMAND, landscape architect; b. N.Y.C., Feb. 25, 1931; s. Manfred and Lia (Shakno) B.; m. Phyllis Roby, Nov. 15, 1957; children: Lia, Amanda. BS in Landscape Architecture, U. Ga., 1955. Registered landscape arch., N.Y., Conn., Mass., Pa., Md., Va., W.Va. Sr. landscape arch. Bye & Herrman Landscape Archs., Rye, N.Y., 1957-61; pvt. practice White Plains and Bedford, N.Y., 1961-89; sr. ptnr. Armand Benedek & Ptnrs., Bedford, N.Y., 1989—; vis. critic N.Y. Inst. Tech.; guest lectr. numerous archtl. and landscape archtl. schs. Prin. works include Holocaust Meml., Westchester County, N.Y., Chem Bank Gardens at Sterling Forest, N.Y. (Comml. Landscape award Am. Assn. Nurserymen). With USAF, 1955-57. Recipient Honor award L.I. Assn. Commerce and Industry, Presdl. award Am. Assn. Nurserymen, 1973, Bldg. of Yr. award Bldg. Owners and Mgrs. Assn., 1990, 92, Honors cert. N.Y. State Assn. Architects/AIA, 1975, HUD award for design excellence, 1976. Fellow Am. Soc. Landscape Archs. Office: Armand Benedek & Ptrns Ltd Hunting Ridge Mall 4448H Old Post Rd Bedford NY 10506*

BENEDEK, GEORGE BERNARD, physicist, educator; b. N.Y.C., Dec. 1, 1928. BS, Rensselaer Poly. Inst., 1949; MA, Harvard U., 1952, PhD in Physics, 1953. Mem. staff joint Harvard-Lincoln Lab. MIT Project, 1953-55; rsch. fellow, lectr. in solid state physics Harvard U., 1955-57, asst. prof. applied physics, 1958-61; assoc. prof. MIT, Cambridge, 1961-65, prof. physics, 1965—, now Alfred H. Caspary prof. physics and biol. physics, dept. chmn., 1979—; mem. physics adv. com. NSF, 1983-86. Recipiant Proctor medal award ARVO, 1997, Sci. pour l'art award Louis Vuitton Co., 1995; Guggenheim fellow, 1960; profl. fellow Atomic Energy Rsch. Establishment, Harwell, Eng., 1967. Fellow Am. Phys. Soc. (Irving Langmuir prize in chem. physics 1995), Am. Acad. Arts and Scis.; mem. NAS (inst. medicine 1983), Am. Inst. Physics (bd. govs. 1971-74). Office: MIT Dept Physics Rm 13-2005 77 Massachusetts Ave Cambridge MA 02139

BENEDETTO, ANTHONY DOMINICK See BENNETT, TONY

BENEDETTO, M. WILLIAM, investment banker; b. N.Y.C., May 20, 1941; s. Francis Michael and Betty Rita (Yula) B.; m. Lois Mary Leonard, Apr. 20, 1968; children—Michael, William. A.B. in Philosophy, Georgetown U., 1962. Chmn., co-founder Benedetto, Gartland & Co., Inc., N.Y.C., 1988—; bd. dirs. Donna Karan Internat., N.Y.C.; chmn. bd. Georgetown U. Sch. Medicine, Washington, 1999—. Fin. advisor City of Chgo., 1974; trustee, pres. St. David's Sch., N.Y.C., 1982-94. Capt. USAF, 1962-67, Vietnam. Mem. Securities Ind. Assn. (chmn. corp. fin. com. 1983-87), Fin. Execs. Inst. (bd. dirs. 1978-80). Office: Benedetto Gartland & Co Inc 1330 Avenue Of The Americas New York NY 10019-5400

BENEDICK, JAMES MICHAEL, psychotherapist; b. Winston Salem, N.C., Dec. 16, 1942; s. Michael Anthony and Isla May (McSperrin) B.; m. Janice Yantzer-Benedick, Sept. 15, 1978; children: Jesse Mathew, Jason Kirk. BA, Coll. William and Mary, 1975; MSW, Norfolk State Coll., 1977; postgrad., U. Sarasota, 1993—. Bd. cert. diplomate in clin. social work, in clin. sexology; lic. clin. social worker, Fla. Staff social worker Peninsula Group Home, Hampton, Va., 1977-78; sch. social works supr. Mandan (N.D) Pub. Sch., 1978; clin. social worker S.E. Human Svc. Ctr., Fargo, N.D., 1978-84, Coastal Recovery Ctrs., Sarasota, Fla., 1989-90; mgr. community svcs. div. Red River Human Svcs. Found., Fargo, 1984-89; psychotherapist Lifestyle Profl. Ctr., Sarasota, 1990-92; pvt. practice Sarasota, 1992—; psychotherapist Neurobehavioral Medicine Ctr., Sarasota, 1997. With U.S. Army, 1960-63. Fellow Am. Acad. Clin. Sexologists; mem. NASW, Acad. Cert. Social Workers, Register Clin. Social Workers, Fla. Soc. Clin. Social Work. Avocations: physical fitness, jogging, reading, study. Home: 4028 72nd Ave E Sarasota FL 34243-5153 Office: 1620 Main St Ste 8 Sarasota FL 34236-5824

BENEDICK, RICHARD ELLIOT, diplomat; b. N.Y.C., May 10, 1935; s. Lester and Jean (Shamski) B.; m. Hildegard K.G. Schulz, June 1, 1957 (div.); children: Andreas Peter Anselm, Julianna Valeska.; m. Helen Ruth Freeman, Sept. 10, 1983 (div.); m. Irene E. Federwisch, 1997. AB summa cum laude, Columbia U., 1955; MA, Yale U., 1956; postgrad., Oxford U., 1956; DBA, Harvard U., 1962. Program economist AID U.S. Dept. State, Washington, 1958, Tehran, Iran, 1959-61, Karachi, Pakistan, 1962-64; economist OECD, Paris, 1964-66; 1st sec. Am. Embassy, Bonn, Germany, 1966-71; dir. Office Devel. Fin., Washington, 1971-75; counselor for econ. and comml. affairs Am. Embassy, Athens, Greece, 1975-77; mem. sr. seminar Dept. State, Washington, 1977-78; coord. population affairs with rank amb. U.S. Dept. State, Washington, 1979-84, dep. asst. sec. for environ., health and natural resources, 1984-87; sr. fellow World Wildlife Fund, 1987-98; dep. dir. Battelle Pacific N.W. Nat. Lab., 1998—; spl. advisor to sec. gen. UN Conf. on Environ. and Devel., 1990-92, Internat. Conf. on Population and Devel., 1993-94, pres. com. for Nat. Inst. for Environ., 1994—; vis. prof. Academie Internationale de l'Environnement, Geneva, 1992-96; lectr. in field; head U.S. del. to numerous confs.; chief U.S. negotiator Montreal Protocol on protection of ozone layer, 1985-87; bd. dirs. Population Resource Ctr., 1984—, Pacific Inst., 1990—, Transparency Internat., 1994—, Environ. and Energy Study Inst., 1994—; mem. internat. adv. bd. Battelle, 1994—, Environ. Tech. Ctr., Berlin, 1996; v.p. OECD Environ. Com., 1984-87; v.p. Transboundary Air Pollution Conv., Econ. Commn. for Europe, 1985-87; vis. fellow Nat. Ctr. Atmospheric Rsch., 1988, 89, Ostwestwirtschafts Akademie, Berlin, 1991-96, Wissenschaftszentrum Berlin, 1995—. Author: Industrial Finance in Iran, 1964, The High Dam and the Transformation of the Nile, 1979, Ozone Diplomacy, 1991, 2d edit., 1998; contbr. articles to profl. jours. Recipient Presdl. Meritorious Svc. award, 1984, 90, Superior Honor medal Dept. State, 1985, 87, John Jacob Rogers award, 1993, Presdl. Disting. Svc. award, 1988, ann. award Climate Inst., 1988, UN Global Ozone award, 1997; Evans fellow Oxford U., 1956, Population Ref. Bur. hon. fellow, 1986. Fellow World Acad. of Art and Sci. (elected 1991); mem. Toenissteiner Kreis (Germany), Phi Beta Kappa. Home: 4111 27th St N Arlington VA 22207-5211 Office: Battelle Washington Ops 901 D St SW Washington DC 20024-2169

BENEDICT, BURTON, retired museum director, anthropology educator; b. Balt., May 20, 1923; s. Burton Eli Oppenheim and Helen Blanche (Deiches) B.; m. Marion MacColl Steuber, Sept. 23, 1950; children: Helen, Barbara MacVean. AB cum laude, Harvard U., 1949; PhD, U. London, 1954. Sr. rsch. fellow Inst. Islamic Studies, McGill U., Montreal, Que., Can., 1954-55; sociol. rsch. officer Colonial Office, London and Mauritius, 1955-58; sr. lectr. social anthropology London Sch. Econs., 1958-68; prof. anthropology U. Calif., Berkeley, 1968-91, prof. emeritus, 1991—, chmn. dept., 1970-71, dean social scis., 1971-74, dir. Hearst Mus. Anthropology, 1989-94; dir. emeritus Hearst Mus. Anthropology, 1994—; dir. U. Calif. Study Ctr. for U.K. and Ireland, London, 1986-88. Author: Indians in a Plural Society, 1961; author and editor: Problems of Smaller Territories, 1967, (with M. Benedict) Men, Women & Money in Seychelles, 1982, The Anthropology of World's Fairs, 1983; contbr. numerous articles to profl. jours. Sgt. USAF, 1942-46. Recipient Western Heritage award Nat. Cowboy Hall of Fame, 1984; rsch. fellow Colonial Office, 1955-58, 60, U. Calif., Berkeley, 1974-75; grantee NEH, 1981-83. Fellow Royal Anthrop. Inst. (mem. coun. 1962-65, 67-68, 86-89), Am. Anthrop. Assn.; mem. Assn. Social Anthropologists of Brit. Commonwealth, Athenaeum Club (London). Avocations: museums, zoos, bird watching, postcards, world's fairs. Office: U Calif Berkeley Dept Anthropology Berkeley CA 94720

BENEDICT, CAROL ANN, educator; b. Kalamazoo, Mich., Dec. 26, 1955; d. James Stephen and Muriel Gertrude Benedict; m. Paul Ashin, Feb. 19, 1990; 1 child, Mark Stephen. BA, U. Calif., Santa Cruz, 1980; MA, Stanford U., 1985, PhD, 1992. Asst. prof. Williams Coll., Williamstown, Mass., 1991-95; asst. prof. Georgetown U., Washington, 1995-98, assoc. prof., 1999—. Author: Bubonic Plague in 19th Century China, 1996. Mem. Am. Hist. Assn., Assn. for Asian Studies/China Inner Asia Coun. Office: Georgetown U Dept of History Washington DC 20057

BENEDICT, DOROTHY JONES, genealogist, researcher; b. Bronxville, N.Y., Mar. 23, 1916; d. Harry Edwin and Katherine Jones; m. Mark Charles Benedict; children: Ann Benedict Johnson, Sharon Benedict Bash, Gail Benedict Bain, Faye. BA, Goucher Coll., 1938. Statistician E.W. Axe Co., N.Y.C., 1938; with Nat. Labor Rels. Bd., N.Y.C., 1938-39. Leader Girl Scouts of Am., Glastonbury, Conn., 1957-64; creator convalescent homes Sunday mini-svc. Asbury Ch., Glastonbury, 1960-70. Mem. Nat. Soc. Magna Carta Dames, Arts Soc. Orlando Mus., DAR, Delta Delta Delta, Phi Beta Kappa. Methodist. Avocations: golf, walking, art. Home: 100 S Interlachen Ave Winter Park FL 32789-4438

BENEDICT, GREGORY BRUCE, business administration/finance professional, legal consultant; b. San Antonio, Tex., June 16, 1955; s. Bruce Oren and Joan (Baker) B.; m. Rita Marie Willefsky, Nov. 25, 1978; children: Elizabeth Culhane, Zoe Katherine, Erin Fisher. BS in Fin., U. Colo., 1977; JD, U. N.Mex., 1984; MBA, 1984. Bar: N.Mex. 1984, U.S. Dist. Ct. N.Mex. 1987. Atty. Erwin & Davidson, P.C., Raton, N.Mex., 1984-87; pvt. practice Albuquerque, 1987; v.p. Fisher Automatic Svc., Inc., Bryan, Ohio, 1988-96, pres., 1997, 1997—; lectr. N.Mex. Bar Assn., Santa Fe, 1987. bd. dirs. Black Swamp Coun. Boy Scouts Am., Findlay, Ohio, 1989—. Recipient Pro Bono award N.M. Lawyer Referral for Elderly, 1986, Am. Jurisprudence award Am. Jurisprudence, 1983. Mem. ABA, N.M. Bar Assn., Williams County Bar Assn. (pres. 1995-96), Nat. Automatic Merchandising Assn., Ohio Automatic Merchandising Assn., Bryan Rotary Club (treas. 1992—), First Presbyn. Ch. (elder 1996—). Avocations: skiing, fishing, Am. history, computers. E-mail: fasico@bright.net. Home: PO Box 852 Bryan OH 43506-0852 Office: Fisher Automatic Svc Inc PO Box 447 Bryan OH 43506-0447

BENEDICT, JAMES NELSON, lawyer; b. Norwich, N.Y., Oct. 6, 1949; s. Nelson H. and Helen (Wilson) B.; m. Janet E. Fagal, May 8, 1982. B.A. magna cum laude, St. Lawrence U., 1971; J.D., Albany Law Sch. of Union U., 1974. Bar: N.Y. 1975, U.S. Dist. Ct. (no., ea. and so. dists.) N.Y. 1975, U.S. Ct. Appeals (2d cir.) 1975, U.S. Ct. Appeals (8th cir.) 1977, U.S. Ct. Appeals (10th cir.) 1978, U.S. Ct. Appeals (11th cir.) 1982, U.S. Supreme Ct. 1978. Assoc. Rogers & Wells, N.Y.C., 1974-82, ptnr., 1982—. Mem. bd. contbg. editors and advisors The Corp. Law Rev., 1976-86. Contbr. articles to profl. jours. Bd. dirs. Reece Sch., N.Y.C., 1984-89, Stanley Isaacs Neighborhood Ctr., N.Y.C., 1984-89; trustee St. Lawrence U., Canton, N.Y., 1985-91. Mem. ABA (chmn. securities litigation subcom. on 1940 Act matters 1984-86, 96—), Fed. Bar Council, N.Y. State Bar Assn., Assn. Bar City N.Y. (mem. com. on securities regulation, fed. legislation com., fed. cts. com.) Am. Soc. Writers on Legal Subjects, Sky Club (N.Y.C.), Scarsdale Golf Club, Phi Beta Kappa. Home: 26 Kensington Rd Scarsdale NY 10583-2217 Office: Rogers & Wells 200 Park Ave Fl 8E New York NY 10166-0800

BENEDICT, JEFFERY WEST, planner, estimator; b. Harrison, Ark., July 7, 1957; s. Danny Lee B. and Marilyn Edith (West) Julian; m. Kathleen A. LeMons, June 29, 1991. BSBA cum laude, Christopher Newport U., 1997; postgrad, Coll. William and Mary Grad. Sch. Bus., 1998—. Engring. logistics tech. Inst. Modern Procedures, Inc., Chesapeake, Va., 1986-88; planner, estimator Assoc. Naval Archs., Inc., Portsmouth, Va., 1988—; pres., bd. dirs. Tidewater Maritime Tng. Inst., Norfolk, Va., 1991—. Bd. dirs. Poquoson Is. Players, Inc. (former pres.), Poquoson, Va., 1994-96. Served with USN, 1978-86. Mem. South Tidewater Assn. Ship Repairers, Inc. (mem. contracts com. 1990—), Alpha Chi Nat. Honor Soc. Coll. William and Mary Grad. Sch. Bus. Avocation: golf. Home: 61 Queens Ct Newport News VA 23606-2034

BENEDICT, JOHN ANTHONY, II, army officer; b. Morgantown, W.Va., July 24, 1970; s. John Anthony Benedict and Diana Lynn (Pennington) Jones. BA, Va. Tech. U., 1992. Commd. 2d lt. U.S. Army, 1992; advanced through ranks to capt., 1996; platoon leader, ops. officer 257th Signal Co., Camp Humphreys, Korea, 1993-94; platoon leader, co. exec. officer 82d Signal Battalion, Ft. Bragg, N.C., 1995-96; dep. sec. gen. staff 82d Airborne Divsn., Ft. Bragg, 1995-96; squadron signal officer 17th Cavalry, Ft. Bragg, 1996-97; brigade signal officer 69th Air Def., Giebelstadt, Germany, 1997-99; co. comdr. 17th Signal Bat., Kitzingen, Germany, 1999—. Mem. Assn. U.S. Army, Armed Forces Comm.-Elect Assn., 82d Airborne Divsn. Assn., Am. Legion, Signal Corps Regimental Assn. Republican. Roman Catholic. Avocations: volleyball, football, reading, hiking, golf. Home: 954 Cmr 408 APO AE 09182-9998 Address: Box 954 APO AE 09182-9998

BENEDICT, LAWRENCE NEAL, foreign service officer; b. Independence, Mo., Dec. 17, 1942; s. Albert Michael and Audentia Elizabeth (Thomas) B.; m. Gloria Kay Bruning, July 2, 1966. BA, Calif. State U., Long Beach, 1974. V.p. A.M. Benedict & Assocs., Long Beach, Calif., 1966-72; vice consul Am. Embassy, Dahka, Bangladesh, 1974-77; comml. officer Am. Consulate Gen., Rio de Janeiro, 1977-79; desk officer for Bangladesh U.S. Dept. of State, Washington, 1979-80, desk officer for Turkey, 1980-82, dep. dir. devel. fin., 1986-89; fin./devel. officer Am. Embassy, Ankara, Turkey, 1982-86; counselor econ. affairs Am. Embassy, Islamabad, Pakistan, 1989-92; dep. chief of mission Am. Embassy, Khartoum, Sudan, 1992-95; amb. Am. Embassy, Praia, Cape Verde, 1996—. Staff sgt. USANG, 1963-69. Mem. Am. Fgn. Svc. Assn. Avocations: tennis, reading, collecting books and wine. Home and Office: Am Embassy PRAIA Dept of State Washington DC 20520

BENEDICT, MANSON, chemical engineer, educator; b. Lake Linden, Mich., Oct. 9, 1907; s. C. Harry and Lena I. (Manson) B.; m. Marjorie Oliver Allen, July 6, 1935 (dec. 1995); children: Mary Hannah (Mrs. Myran C. Sauer, Jr.), Marjorie Alice (Mrs. Martin Cohn). B in Chemistry, Cornell U., 1928; MS, MIT, 1932, PhD, 1935. NRC fellow chemistry, 1935-36; rsch. assoc. geophysics Harvard, 1936-37; rsch. chemist M.W. Kellogg Co., 1938-43; in charge process design gaseous diffusion plant for uranium-235 Kellex Corp., 1943-46; dir. process development Hydrocarbon Rsch., Inc., 1946-51; tech. asst. to gen. mgr. AEC, 1951-52; prof. nuclear engring. MIT, 1951-69, Institute prof., 1969-73, prof. emeritus, 1973—, head dept. nuclear engring., 1958-71; dir. Burns & Roe, Inc., 1979-85; sci. advisor Nat. Rsch. Corp., 1951-58, dir., 1962-67; mem. gen. adv. com. AEC, 1958-68, chmn., 1962-64; dir. Atomic Indsl. Forum, 1966-72; mem. energy R & D adv. coun. FEA, 1973-75. Co-editor: Engineering Developments in the Gaseous Diffusion Process, 1949; co-author: Nuclear Chemical Engineering, 1981. Recipient Indsl. and Engring. Chemistry award Am. Chem. Soc., 1962; Perkin medal Soc. Chem. Industry, Robert E. Wilson award in nuclear chem. engring., Fermi award AEC, 1972, John Fritz medal Engring. Founder Socs., 1974, Nat. Medal Sci., 1975, Henry D. Smyth Nuclear Statesman award Atomic Indsl. Forum, 1979, Washington award Western Soc. Engrs., 1982. Fellow AIChE (William H. Walker award 1947, Founders award 1965), Am. Nuclear Soc. (pres. 1962-63, Arthur H. Compton award), Am. Acad. Arts and Scis., Am. Philos. Soc.; mem. NAS, Nat. Acad. Engring. (Founders award 1976), Weston Golf Club (Mass.), Country Club Naples (Fla.), Sigma Xi. Home: 108 Moorings Park Dr Apt B206 Naples FL 34105-2155

BENEDICT, MARY-ANNE, educator; b. Cambridge, Mass., Apr. 14, 1944; d. Preston E. and Mary Rose (Murphy) Woodward; m. Charles A. Benedict, Sept. 20, 1969; children: Annmarie, Helene, Laura. BS in Nursing, Boston Coll. Sch. Nursing, 1967; MSN, Salem State Coll., 1995. Cert. orthopedic nurse. Instr. Sch. Nursing New Eng. Bapt. Hosp., Boston, 1969-79, edn. specialist, 1979-96; coord. edn. and tng. Emerson Hosp., Concord, Mass., 1997—. Lt. (j.g.) USN, 1966-69. Mem. Nat. Assn. Orthopedic Nurses, Sigma Theta Tau (Alpha Chi chpt.). Home: 84 Rockland Pl Newton MA 02464-1234

BENEDIKT, MICHAEL, poet, educator, author, editor, free-lance consultant; b. N.Y.C., May 26, 1935; s. John and Helen (Davis) B. BA in English and Journalism, NYU, 1956; MA in Comparative Lit, Columbia U., 1961. Assoc. editor Horizon Press, N.Y.C., 1959-61; N.Y. corr. Art Internat., 1965-67; editorial assoc. Art News mag., N.Y.C., 1962-72; assoc. prof. Bennington Coll., 1968-69, Sarah Lawrence Coll., 1969-73, Hampshire Coll., 1973-75; Sexton prof. poetry Boston U., 1975, vis. prof. English and creative writing, 1977-79; vis. prof. Vassar Coll., 1976-77; judge Nat. Book award in translation, 1974; guest lectr. various colls. and univs.; judge Coordinating Council of Lit. Mags., 1970, 73, Lamont Poetry awards Acad. Am. Poets, 1970-72; mem. CAPS-N.Y. State Council on Arts panel in mixed media, 1976, Mass. Arts and Humanities Found. panel in poetry, 1977. Contbg. editor: Am. Poetry Rev., 1973—; editor (poetry) The Paris Rev, 1974-78; author: (poetry) The Body, 1968, Sky, 1970, Mole Notes, 1971, Night Cries, 1976, The Badminton at Great Badminton, or Gustave Mahler and the Chattanooga Choo-Choo, 1980, Subject: Benedikt: A Profile, 1978, Subject: Library of Congress Videotape, 1986; editor: (Am. drama anthology) Theatre Experiment, 1968; co-editor: (internat. drama anthologies) Modern Spanish Theatre, 1968, Post-War German Theatre, 1967, Modern French Theatre: The Avant-Garde, Dada and Surrealism, 1964; editor: (poetry anthologies) The Poetry of Surrealism, 1975, The Prose Poem: An International Anthology, 1976; guest poetry and fiction editor: Chelsea, 1968; guest poetry editor: Modern Poetry Studies, 1971; contbr. articles on lit. and arts to Minimal Art, 1968, Jean-Luc Godard, 1968, The Grand Eccentrics, 1972, New Artists Video, 1978, numerous other critical anthologies, also scholarly, lit., arts and popular mags.; author (song lyrics) for feature films: Out of It, 1966, Jenny, 1968, others.; has performed his poetry at more than 100 colls. and univs., and on radio; poetry represented at numerous websites. Recipient Hokin award for best poems in single year Poetry Mag., 1969; Guggenheim fellow in poetry, 1968-69; Nat. Endowment for Arts prize for single poem, 1970; Fels award for excellence in mag. editing, 1975; CAPS poetry grantee, 1975; Nat. Endowment for Arts fellow in poetry, 1979-80; Poet Laureate of the Net, About.com, 1999. Mem. MLA, PEN, Poetry Soc. Am., Am. Assn. for Advancement of the Humanities, Am. Studies Assn., others. Home: 315 W 98th St New York NY 10025 *As one desires to do one's best in important things, one appreciates acknowledgements of one's achievements, such as this. Therefore, one comes to require the company of those who desire to do their best in important things; and comes to desire the company of those who have accomplished much, and who also have done that much well. In short, I believe that it behooves us, by acts of will, to seek out all the best in ourselves, and all the best that is in art, life, and society as a whole.*

BENEKE, PATRICIA JANE, federal agency administrator; b. Ames, Iowa; married; 2 children. BA, Iowa State U., 1976; JD, Harvard U., 1979. Bar: Iowa 1979, D.C. 1980. Atty. advisor office of gen. counsel USDA, 1979-80; trial atty. land and natural resources divsn. U.S. Dept. Justice, Washington, 1981-83; litigation assoc. McDermott Will & Emery, 1983-85; minority counsel Com. on Energy and Natural Resources, Washington, 1985-86, sr. counsel, 1987-93; assoc. solicitor for energy and resources U.S. Dept. Interior, Washington, 1993-95, dep. asst. sec. for water and sci., 1995, asst. sec. for water and sci., 1995—. Office: Water & Sci Dept Interior 1849 C St NW Washington DC 20240-0001

BENEN, ELAINE CAROL, educational administrator; b. N.Y.C., Mar. 22, 1938; d. Sidney and Lee (Chesneau) Lowenstern; m. Arthur Swartz; children: Troy, Robert, Julie, Sandy, Paula. BA, George Mason Coll., Fairfax, Va., 1970, MEd, 1973; EdD, U. Pacific, Stockton, Calif., 1983. Cert. elem. tchr. and prin., K-12 reading tchr., Va. Elem. tchr. Alexandria (Va.) Pub. Schs., 1974-84; tchr. spl. projects, reading specialist Fairfax County Pub. Schs., Fairfax, Va., 1984-92, elem. asst. prin., 1992—; reader funding bilingual proposals U.S. Dept. Edn.; conf. presenter NSTA, Nat. Core Knowledge Found. Contbr. articles to profl. publs. Impact II grantee, McDonald's grantee, minority achievement grantee; Fulbright scholar, 1997. Mem. ASCD, NAESP, Nat. Coun. for Social Studies, Va. Edn. Assn., Fairfax Edn. Assn., Phi Delta Kappa, Delta Kappa Gamma. Home: 20853 Waterbeach Pl Sterling VA 20165-7410 Office: Forestville Elem Sch 1085 Utterback Store Rd Great Falls VA 22066

BENENSON, CLAIRE BERGER, investment and financial planning educator; b. N.Y.C.; d. Nathan H. and Alice E. (Zeisler) B.; m. Lawrence A. Benenson; children: Harold, Gary. BA, Wellesley Coll.; postgrad. N.Y. Inst. Fin., New Sch. Social Rsch., 1965-69. Security analyst Merrill Lynch, N.Y.C., 1940-43; rsch. assoc. Conn. Coll., 1943-45; lectr. NYU Mgmt. Inst., N.Y.C., 1960-68; lectr. New Sch. for Social Rsch., N.Y.C., 1963-86, dir. ann. conf. Wall St. and Economy, 1967-87, dir. ann. conf. Futures and Options, 1979-86, chmn. dept. investment and fin. planning, 1974-86; cons. fin. confs., N.Y.C., 1987—; mem. adv. bd. The First Women's Bank, N.Y.C., 1984-86; bd. dirs. Drexel Burnham Fund, DBL Cash Fund, DBL Tax Free Cash Fund, Drexel Series Trust, N.Y.C., 1970-89, Burnham Fund, Zweig Cash Fund, Zweig Tax Free Fund, Zweig Series Trust, N.Y.C., 1989—; trustee Simms Global Fund, 1987-89, Euclid Mkt. Neutral Fund, 1998—; pres. Money Marketeers, NYU, N.Y.C., 1979-80. Contbg. editor Exec. Jeweler, 1981-83; creator, moderator NBC-TV series, Wall St. for Everyone, 1967-68. Mem. bd. overseers Parsons Sch. of Design, N.Y.C., 1974-93; br. librs. and annual fund com. and coun. conservaters N.Y. Pub. Libr., 1990—, chair N.Y. Pub. Libr. SIBL com., 1994—; mem. bd. dirs. 92nd St. YM and YWHA, N.Y.C., 1993—; mem. bus. leadership coun. Wellesley Coll., 1991—, bd. dirs. Ctrs. for Women, 1998—; bd. dirs. 92d St YMCA & YWCA, N.Y.C., mem. lecture com. Named Disting. Alumna Wellesley Coll., 1968, Durant Scholar, Wellesley Coll.; Alt. fellow in econs. Columbia U., 1938-39. Mem. Fin. Women's Assn. (bd. dirs., chair dirs. resource adv. com., co-chair program com. 1988-89), Nat. Assn. Bus. Econs., Women's Econ. Roundtable, Econ. Club N.Y., N.Y. Assn. Bus. Economists, Money Marketeers NYU, Durant Soc. Wellesley Coll., Women's Bond Club, Harmonie Club (co-chair forum com.), Cosmopolitan Club (investment and fin. com.), Phi Beta Kappa. Jewish.

BENENSON, DAVID MAURICE, engineering educator; b. Bklyn., Jan. 22, 1927; s. Louis and Bella (Hirschcowitz) B.; m. Lydia Kathleen Chapman, June 11, 1957; children—Kathleen Ann, Patricia Janice. SB, MIT, 1950; MS, Calif. Inst. Tech., 1953, PhD, 1957. Project engr. So. Calif. Coop. Wind Tunnel, Pasadena, Calif., 1950-53; research engr. Westinghouse Rsch. Labs., Pitts., 1957-63; prof. SUNY, Buffalo, 1963—, chmn. dept. elec. and computer engring., 1983-89; instr. Carnegie Inst. Tech., Pitts., 1958-63; cons. Bell Aerospace Co., 1969-70, Westinghouse Electric Co., 1963-68; treas. Gaseous Electronics Conf., 1971-73. Served with USNR, 1945-46. NSF grantee, 1964—; Air Force Sci. Research grantee, 1970—; Aero. Research Labs. grantee, 1964-67; Guggenheim fellow in jet propulsion Calif. Inst. Tech., 1953-55. Fellow AIAA (assoc.; chmn. Niagara Frontier sect. 1966-67), IEEE (sr., assoc. editor Trans. Plasma Sci. 1976-89, mem. switchgear com. 1971—), Am. Phys. Soc. (mem. exec. com. gaseous electronics conf. 1970—, sec. 1978), Current Zero Club, Sigma Xi. Rsch. on analysis and devel. diagnostic techniques for study of steady-state and time varying plasmas; non-invasive diagnostics of time varying mech. systems. Home: 53 Andover Ln Buffalo NY 14221-3308 Office: SUNY Sch Engring/Applied Sci Buffalo NY 14260

BENENSON, EDWARD HARTLEY, realty company executive; b. N.Y.C., Mar. 27, 1914; s. Robert C. and Nettie B.; m. Gladys Steinberg, Apr. 5, 1962; 1 dau., Lisa; children by previous marriage: Thomas Hartley, James Stuart, Amy Roberta. B.A., Duke, 1934. Chmn. Benenson & Co., Benenson Funding Corp., Benenson Investment Corp., Greenwich Devel. Corp., Sedgefield Realty N.C., Thomas James Corp., Arbee Properties of Fla. Author: The Benenson National Restaurant Guide, 1985-94, The Benenson Guide (Manhattan), 1991, 93, 95, 97, 98. Host Hiroshima Maidens, 1955-56; chmn. Urban-Patron Redevel. Commn., Stamford, Conn., 1957-58; mem. N.Y.C. Mayor's Youth Adv. Group, 1956-58; chmn. Friends Duke U. Mus. Art; bd. dirs. Duke Med. Ctr.; trustee emeritus Duke U.; bd. overseers Albert Einstein Coll. Medicine; trustee, mem. governing bd. Am. Ballet Theatre; mem. Rep. Nat. Com.; pres. YM-YWHA, 1958-63, now bd. dirs.; donor Benenson Arts awards Duke U.; univ. rep. com. Corp. Support for Pvt. Univs.; mem. President's Citizens Com.; donor Benenson Scholar award for Duke U. Lt. 77th inf. div. AUS, 1939-43. Decorated officer Ordre de Merite, Legion of Merit (France), knight Order St. John of Malta; recipient gold medal Renaissance Francaise, bronze medal City of Paris; Donor-Benenson scholar. Mem. Confrerie des Chevaliers du Tastevin (Grand Camerlingue d'Amerique), Culinary Inst. Am. (co-founder and trustee), Les Amis d'Escoffier Soc., Grand Jury Assn., Commerce and Industry Assn. N.Y., Nat. Bd. Realtors, Internat. Real Estate Fedn. (charter), Order of Lafayette, Fedn. War Vets. (France), Chaine des Rotisseurs (former chmn., Chaine Man of Yr. award 1991), Conseil d'Honneur, Am. Soc. Italian Legions Merit (Cavaliere d'Italia), Les Chevaliers de la Croix de Lorraine, Commanderie de Bordeaux, Res. Officers Assn., Conseil de la Croix du Combattant de l'Europe, Les Vingt-Six Soc. (founder), Presidents Club, Paris Am. Club, Wine and Food Soc., Century Country Club, Noyac Country Club, Palm Beach Country Club, Southampton Golf Club, Princeton Club, Army-Navy Club. Office: 445 Park Ave New York NY 10022-2606

BENENSON, JAMES, JR., manufacturer; b. Moultrie, Ga., Mar. 9, 1936; s. James and Mary (Camp) B.; m. Sharen Statler, Aug. 28, 1966; children: James, Clement. BS, MIT, 1958; postgrad., Yale U., 1960. With F. Eberstadt & Co., N.Y.C., 1960-65, Walker, Hart & Co., N.Y.C., 1965-68, James Benenson & Co., Inc., N.Y.C., 1968—; chmn. bd. Vesper Corp., Newtown Square, Pa., 1978—, Arrowhead Holdings Corp., Cleve., 1983—. Served with U.S. Army Chem. Corps, 1959. Woodrow Wilson scholar, 1959-60; Andover Teaching fellow, 1958-59. Mem. Horticultural Soc. N.Y., N.Y. Bot. Garden (dir.), Soc. of Cincinnati, Century Assn., Racquet Club (Phila.), Buck's Harbor Yacht Club (Brooksville, Maine), N.Y. Yacht Club. Episcopalian. Office: care Vesper Corp 3400 W Chester Pike Newtown Square PA 19073-4638

BENENSON, MARK KEITH, lawyer; b. N.Y.C., Oct. 13, 1929; s. Aaron and Luba (Stein) B.; m. Letizia Pitigliani, Dec. 29, 1959; children: Alexander, Daniela. B.S.S., CCNY, 1951; J.D., Columbia U., 1956. Bar: N.Y. 1956. Atty. Dept. Labor, Washington, 1957-58; practiced in N.Y.C., 1958—; Bd. dirs. Amnesty Internat. U.S.A., 1966-80, sec., 1966-67, chmn., 1968-71, vice chmn., 1972-73, gen. counsel, 1972-80; pres. Vanguard Found., Inc., 1962—. Contbr. articles to profl. jours., mags. and newspapers. Exec. sec. Nat. Found. for Firearms Edn., 1983-91, Pres. 1991—. With U.S. Army, 1951-53. Recipient John Amber Gun Digest Writing award, 1998. Home: 585 W End Ave New York NY 10024-1715 Office: 185 Madison Ave Fl 6 New York NY 10016-4325

BENENSON, WALTER, nuclear physics educator; b. N.Y.C., Apr. 27, 1936; s. Charles and Sylvia (Ogush) B.; m. Antje Semsrott, Dec. 4, 1969; children: Arleigh Ann, Tanya. B.S., Yale U., 1957; MS, U. Wis., 1959, PhD, 1962. Rsch. assoc. U. Strasbourg, 1962-63; asst. prof. nuclear physics Mich. State U., East Lansing, 1963-68; assoc. prof. Mich. State U., 1968-72, prof., 1972-97; u. disting. prof. Nat. Superconducting Cyclotron Lab., 1997—, assoc. dir., 1980-82, 90-95; vis. fellow Australian Nat. U., 1968; vis. prof. U. Grenoble, 1970; vis. lectr. Inst. for Nuclear Sci., Moscow, 1975; cons. Lawrence Berkeley Lab., 1979; participation profl. confs.; mem. nuclear sci. adv. com. U.S. Govt., 1993—. Assoc. editor: Phys. Rev. C; contbr. articles to profl. jours., mags. and newspapers. Bd. dirs. Happendance Dance Co., 1994-96. Nat. Acad. Scis. fellow, 1974; A.V. Humboldt Sr. Scientist award Fed. Republic of Germany Govt., 1988, Eminent Scientist award Riken, Japan, 1997. Fellow Am. Phys. Soc. (chmn. 6th Internat. Conf. on Atomic Masses 1979, mem. exec. com. divsn. nuclear physics); mem. Lansing Sailing Club (commodore 1987), Univ. Club, Golden Key Hon. Soc. (hon.). Home: 6111 Skyline Dr East Lansing MI 48823-1604

BENERIA, LOURDES, economist, educator; b. Boi, Lleida, Spain, Oct. 8, 1939; came to U.S., 1964; d. Agusti Beneria and Josepa Farre; children: Jordi, Marc. Licenciatura, U. Barcelona, Spain, 1961; MPhil, Columbia U., 1974, PhD in Econs., 1975. Coord. program on rural women ILO, Geneva, 1977-79; asst. prof. Rutgers U., New Brunswick, N.J., 1975-81, assoc. prof., 1981-86; prof. city and regional planning and women's studies Cornell U., Ithaca, N.Y., 1987-92, 99—, dir. program on gender & global change, 1987-92; dir. Latin Am. studies program, 1993-97, prof., 1997—. Office: Cornell Univ CRP W Sibley Hall Ithaca NY 14853-7601

BENERITO, RUTH ROGAN (MRS. FRANK H. BENERITO), chemist; b. New Orleans, Jan. 12, 1916; d. John Edward and Bernadette (Elizardi) Rogan; m. Frank Henshaw Benerito, Aug. 22, 1950. BS, H. Sophie Newcomb Coll., 1935; postgrad., Bryn Mawr Coll., 1935-36; MS, Tulane U., 1938, DSc (hon.), 1981; PhD, U. Chgo., 1948. Instr. chemistry Randolph-Macon Woman's Coll., Lynchburg, Va., 1940-43, Newcomb Coll., New Orleans, 1943-47; asst. prof. chemistry Tulane U., New Orleans, 1947-53, mem. grad. faculty, 1960-86, adj. prof. dept. biochemistry Med. Sch., 1960-86, prof. emeritus, 1986; phys. chemist fat emulsion program So. Regional Lab., USDA, New Orleans, 1953-58, supervisory phys. chemist, head phys. chem. investigations natural polymers lab., 1958-86; cons. phys. chemistry of cellulose, adj. prof. chemistry U. New Orleans, 1986-96. Contbr. articles to profl. publs. Recipient Disting. Svc. USDA award, 1970, New Orleans Fed. Exec. Assn., 1967, Fed. Woman's award U.S. CSC, 1968; named one of 75 Most Important Women in U.S., Ladies Home Jour., 1971. Fellow Am. Inst. Chemists (Honor Scroll L.A. chpt. 1977); mem. AAAS, Am. Chem. Soc. (So. Chemist award 1968, Garvan medal 1970, S.W. Regional award 1972), Am. Oil Chem. Soc., Am. Assn. Textile Chemists and Colorists, Sci. Rsch. Soc. Am., Sigma Xi, Sigma Delta Epsilon, Delta Kappa Gamma (hon.), Iota Sigma Pi (hon.). Home: 4733 Marigny St New Orleans LA 70122-5020 Office: USDA PO Box 19687 New Orleans LA 70179-0687 *Happiness comes only by contributing to the development and happiness of others; it abounds with selflessness and can be found without travelling to far off places.*

BENES, ANDREW CHARLES, professional baseball player; b. Evansville, Ind., Aug. 20, 1967. Student, U. Evansville. With San Diego Padres, 1988-95, Seattle Mariners, 1995, St. Louis Cardinals, 1996-98, Ariz. Diamondbacks, 1998—; mem. U.S. Olympic Baseball Team, 1988, Nat. League All-Star Team, 1993. Named Sporting News Rookie Pitcher of Yr., 1989. Office: care Ariz Diamondbacks Bank One Ballpark 401 E Jefferson Phoenix AZ 85004

BENEŠ, NORMAN STANLEY, meteorologist; b. Detroit, July 1, 1921; s. Stanley and Cecelia (Sereneck) B.; m. Elinor Simson, May 5, 1945 (div. Feb. 1972); children: Gregory, Heather, Michelle, Francine; m. Celia Sereneck, Mar. 3, 1972. BS, U. Wash., 1949; postgrad., U. Calif., Davis, 1963, U. Mich., 1966. Chief meteorologist Hawthorne Sch. of Aero., Moultrie, Ga., 1951-55; meteorologist U.S. Weather Bur., Phoenix, 1955-57, 59-60; meteorologist in charge NSF, Hallett, Antarctica, 1958; sta. sci. leader NSF, Byrd, Antarctica, 1960-61; meteorologist Nat. Weather Service, Sacramento, Calif., 1962-84; mem. Exec. Com. Range Benes Peak, Antarctica. Contbr. articles to profl. jours. Pres. local chpt. PTA, 1965. With USN, 1943-46, PTO. Mem. AAAS, Am. Meteorol. Soc., Am. Geophys. Union, Nat. Weather Assn., Masons. Avocation: model trains. Home: 3311 Holiday Ln Placerville CA 95667-9076

BENES, SOLOMON, biomedical scientist, physician; b. Iasi, Romania, Mar. 28, 1925; came to U.S., 1978; s. Moritz and Cecilia (Abramovici) B.; m. Liudmila Topor, Mar. 27, 1954. MD, Sch. of Medicine, Bucharest, Romania, 1952. Intern microbiology lab. Mil. Hosp., Bucharest, 1949-50, fellow microbiology lab., 1950-51, dir. clin. lab. outpatient dept., 1951-52; dir. rsch. lab. Ctr. for Radiobiology Rsch., Bucharest, 1953-57, 59-66; chief physician microbiology lab. Mil. Hosp., Bucharest, 1967-73; chief physician clin. lab. Ctr. of Haematology, Bucharest, 1973-76; assoc. in medicine Havard Med. Sch., Boston, 1978-81; asst. rsch. scientist, asst. prof. SUNY Health Sci. Ctr., Bklyn., 1982-95; sr. rsch. scientist, asst. prof. SUNY Rsch. Found., Bklyn., 1995-98; ret., 1998. Author: (with others) Seminars in Infectious Diseases, 1983; contbr. articles to Sexually Transmitted Diseases, Antimicrobial Agts. and Chemotherapy, Jour. Clin. Microbiology, Proceedings of the 6th Internat. Symposium on Human Chlamydial Infections. Col., Romanian Army Med. Svc., 1946-73. Achievements include discovery that the Trachoma biovar of Chlamydia trachomatis is able to achieve intercellular propagation in cell culture and that, in a proper cell setting, this bacterium spreads from cell to cell in cell culture, contrary to what was generally believed. Home: 2421 Shellpot Dr Wilmington DE 19803

BENESCH, WILLIAM MILTON, molecular physicist, atmospheric researcher, educator; b. Balt., Apr. 22, 1922; s. Jerome William and Blanche (Koshland) B.; m. Joan Sagner, June 1, 1946; children—Amy Joan, Sarah Elizabeth, Jane Margaret. B.A., Lehigh U., 1942; M.S., Johns Hopkins U., 1950, Ph.D., 1952. Asst. prof. U. Pitts., 1953-60; asst. prof. molecular physics U. Md., College Park, 1962-63, assoc. prof., 1964-66, prof., 1967—, prof. emeritus, 1992—, dir. Inst. Molecular Physics, 1973-76; cons. Argonne Nat. Lab., Ill., 1978-80. Contbr. numerous articles to profl. jours. Served as sgt. USAR, 1944-66. Fellow Commn. for Relief of Belgium, Liege, 1952-53, Weizmann Inst., Rehovoth, Israel, 1960-62, Johns Hopkins U., Balt., 1977—. Fellow Am. Phys. Soc., Optical Soc. Am. (assoc. editor jour. 1978-84), Washington Acad. Sci. (bd. mgrs. 1988-89, v.p. adminstrv. affairs 1989-90), Philosophical Soc. Washington; mem. Am. Geophys. Union, Soc. Applied Spectroscopy, Cosmos Club (Washington), Johns Hopkins U. Club (Balt.). Avocation: bird watching, duplicate bridge, Bronze Life master. Home: 4444 Linnean Ave NW Washington DC 20008-2317 Office: U Md Inst Phys Sci Ipst Bldg College Park MD 20742

BENET, CAROL ANN, journalist, career counselor, teacher; b. Albany, N.Y., Mar. 21, 1939; d. Morton Harold and Ethel Leona (Maitland) Levin; m. Leslie Z. Benet, Sept. 8, 1960; children: Reed Michael, Gillian Vivia. AB, U. Mich., 1961, MA, 1964; PhD, U. Calif., Berkeley, 1987. Freelancejournalist, arts critic Ark newspaper, Belvedere, Calif., 1975—; book seminar tchr. U. Calif. Extension, Berkeley, San Francisco, 1991-98; book group leader several different univs., Marin County, San Francisco, 1987—; PhD career advisor/counselor U. Calif., Berkeley, 1993-97; journalist, arts critic Bay City News Svc., San Francisco, 1993-97; adj. prof. Antioch Coll., Yellow Springs, Ohio, 1995-96, lectr. grad. humanities program, Dominican Coll, San Rafael, Calif., 1996-97. Author: The German Reception of Sam Shephard, 1990. Docent Asian Art Mus., San Francisco, 1987, De Young Mus., San Francisco, 1984. Jewish. Avocations: swimming, travel, gardening, hiking/walking, reading. Home: 53 Beach Rd Belvedere CA 94920

BENET, LESLIE ZACHARY, pharmacokineticist; b. Cin., May 17, 1937; s. Jonas John and Esther Racie (Hirschfeld) B.; m. Carol Ann Levin, Sept. 8, 1960; children: Reed Michael, Gillian Vivia. AB in English, U. Mich., 1959, BS in Pharmacy, 1960, MS in Pharm. Chemistry, 1962; PhD in Pharm. Chemistry, U. Calif., San Francisco, 1965; PharmD (hon.), Uppsala U., Sweden, 1987; PhD (hon.), Leiden U., The Netherlands, 1995; DSc (hon.), U. Ill., Chgo., 1997, Phila. Coll. Pharm. & Sci., 1997, L.I. U., 1999. Asst. prof. pharmacy Wash. State U., Pullman, 1965-69; asst. prof. pharmacy and pharm. chemistry U. Calif., San Francisco, 1969-71, assoc. prof., 1971-76, prof., 1976—, vice chmn. dept. pharmacy, 1973-78, chmn. dept. pharmacy, 1978-96, dir. drug studies unit, 1977—, dir. drug kinetics and dynamics ctr., 1979—, chmn. dept. biopharm. scis., 1996-98; mem. pharmacology study sect. NIH, Washington, 1977-81, chmn., 1979-81, mem. pharmacol. scis. rev. com., 1984-88, chmn., 1986-88; mem. generic drugs adv. com. FDA, Washington, 1990-94, mem. Sci. Bd., 1992—; mem. sci. adv. bd. SmithKline Beecham Pharms., 1989-92, Pharmetrix, 1989-92, Alteon, Inc., 1993—, TheraTech, Inc., 1993-96, Roche Biosci., 1998—; chmn. bd. AvMax, Inc., 1994—; bd. dirs. Oxon Medica, Inc., InforMedix, Inc., Josman Labs., Inc. Editor Jour. Pharmacokinetics and Biopharmaceutics, 1976-98; assoc. editor Pharmacology and Therapeutics, 1995—; editl. bd. Pharmacology, 1979-98, Pharmacy Internat., 1979-82, Pharmaceutical Rsch., 1983-95, ISI Atlas of Sci.: Pharmacology, 1988-89, Pharmaceutical News, 1994—, The Effect of Disease States on Drug Pharmacokinetics, 1976, Pharmacokinetic Basis for Drug Treatment, 1984, Pharmacokinetics: A Modern View, 1984, ISI Atlas of Sci.: Pharmacology, 1988-89, Integration of Pharmacokinetics, Pharmacodynamics and Toxicokinetics in Rational Drug Development, 1992, Clinical Applications of Mifepristone (RU486) and Other Antiprogestins, 1993; contbr. more than 380 articles to profl. jours. Appt. to Forum on Drug Devel. and Regulation, 1988. Fellow Acad. Pharm. Scis. (pres. 1985-86, chmn. basic pharmaceutics sect. 1976-77, mem.-at-large exec. com. 1979-83, Rsch. Achievement award 1982), AAAS (mem.-at-large exec. com. pharm. scis. sect. 1978-81, 91-95, chair 1996-97), Am. Assn. Pharm. Scientists (pres. 1986, treas. 1987, bd. dirs. 1988-93, Disting. Pharm. Scientist award 1989, Disting. Svc. award 1996); mem. Inst. Medicine NAS (forum on drug devel. and regulation 1988-94, chmn. com. on antiprogestins, 1993, membership com. 1994-97, chmn. other health professions sect. 1995-97, chmn. com. pharmacokinetics & drug interactions in elderly 1996-97, mem. Round Table R & D Drugs, Biologics & Med. Devices 1997—), AAUP, Am. Found. for Pharm. Edn. (bd. dirs. 1987—, Disting. Svc. "Profile" award 1993), Am. Coll. Clin. Pharmacology (Disting. Svc. award 1988), ISSX (councillor 1992-96, treas. 1998—), Am. Pharm. Assn., Am. Soc. Clin. Pharmacology and Therapeutics (Rawls-Palmer award and lectureship 1995), Am. Soc. for Pharmacology and Exptl. Therapeutics, Generic Pharm. Industry Assn. (mem. blue ribbon com. on generic medicines 1990), Internat. Pharm. Fedn. (bd. pharm. scis. 1988, chair 1996—), Drug Info. Assn., Am. Coll. Clin. Pharmacy (therapeutic frontiers lectr. 1995), Am. Assn. Colls. Pharmacy (Volwiler Rsch. Achievement award 1991, pres. 1993-94, bd. dirs. 1992-95), Sigma Xi, Rho Chi (Ann. Lecture award 1990), Phi Lambda Sigma. Home: 53 Beach Rd Belvedere CA 94920-2364 Office: U Calif San Francisco Dept Biopharm Scis San Francisco CA 94143

BENEWITZ, MAURICE CHARLES, labor arbitrator, educator; b. Hartford, Conn., Nov. 16, 1923; d. Doris L. Benewitz; m. Lesley Frank Alan Benewitz. AB in Econs., Harvard U., 1947; PhD in Econs., U. Minn., 1954. From asst. prof. to prof., dept. chair Baruch Coll., N.Y.C., 1955-75; arbitrator Manhasset, N.Y., 1958—; dir. Nat. Ctr. for the Study of Collective Bargaining in Higher Edn., N.Y.C., 1970-73. Author: Higher Education Arbitration, 1988. Mem. Am. Arbitration Assn. (panel mem.), Fed. Mediation and Conciliation Svc. (panel mem.), N.Y. State Pub. Employee Rels. Bd. (panel mem.), N.Y.C. Office Collective Bargaining (panel mem.), N.J. State Med. Bd., Nat. Acad. Arbitrators, Phi Beta Kappa. Home and Office: 261 Thompson Shore Rd Manhasset NY 11030-2240

BENEZET, LOUIS TOMLINSON, retired psychology educator, former college president; b. La Crosse, Wis., June 29, 1915; s. Louis Paul and Genevieve (Tomlinson) B.; m. Mildred Twohy, 1940 (dec. 1977); children: Joel (dec.), Laura, Julia , Barbara, Martha; m. Virginia Iglehart Clifford, 1988. A.B., Dartmouth, 1936, LL.D., 1966; A.M., Reed Coll., 1939; Ph.D., Columbia, 1942; LL.D., Mt. Union Coll., U. Pitts., U. Denver, Knox Coll., Loyola U., Chgo., Colo. Coll., U. Colo., U. Calif.; L.H.D., Westminister (Utah) Coll., Hebrew Union Coll. Instr. The Hill Sch., 1936-38; assoc. in psychology Reed Coll., 1938-40; assoc. prof. psychology, asst. dir. admissions Knox Coll., 1942-43; asst. dean Univ. Coll., Syracuse U., 1946-47, asst. to chancellor, 1947-48; pres. Allegheny Coll., 1948-55, Colo. Coll., 1955-63; pres. emeritus, 1995—; pres. Claremont Grad. U., 1963-70, SUNY, Albany, 1970-75; rsch. prof. human devel. SUNY, Stony Brook, 1975-85, cons. on coll. adminstrn., 1987-90; pres. Pa. Assn. Colls. and Univs., 1951-52; chmn. Ind. Coll. Funds of Am., 1961-62; chmn. Rhodes scholar selection com., Colo., Calif., N.Y., 1958-74; mem. instl. rels. com. NSF, 1967-70, chmn., 1969-70; mem. Calif. Gov.'s Commn. on Tax Reform, 1969, N.Y. Gov.'s Task Force on Financing Higher Edn., 1972-73. Author: General Education in the Progressive College, 1943, Private Higher Education and Public Funding, 1976, Style and Substance: Leadership in the College Presidency, 1981, People Versus Pyramids, 1999; contbr. articles to profl. jours. Trustee Aspen Inst., 1956-68, moderator Exec. Seminar, 1958-79. Served with USNR, 1943-46, PTO. Named Disting. Alumnus Columbia Tchrs. Coll., 1984. Mem. Western Coll. Assn. (pres. 1969-70), Assn. Am. Colls. (chmn. commn. on acad. freedom and tenure 1955-58), Am. Coun. on Edn. (exec. com. 1955-58, bd. dirs. 1961-64, chmn. 1965-66), Phi Beta Kappa. Home: 5101 Shelter Bay Ave Mill Valley CA 94941-6019

BENFER, DAVID WILLIAM, hospital administrator; b. Toledo, Ohio, May 28, 1946; s. Wilson L. and Marjorie (Baringer) B.; m. Mary Sturner, Sept. 5, 1970; children: Emily, Matthew, Andrew. BA, Wittenberg U., 1968; MBA in Hosp. Adminstrn., Xavier U., 1970. Asst. adminstrn. Med. Coll., Ohio Hosp., Toledo, 1971-76, exec. dir., CEO, 1976-81; exec. dir., CEO Bon Secours Hosp., Grosse Pointe, Mich., 1982-84, Henry Ford Hosp., Detroit, 1985-92; pres., CEO St. Joseph Med. Ctr., Joliet, Ill., 1992-99, St. Raphael Healthcare System, New Haven, Conn., 1999—. Co-author: Issues in Health Care Management, 1982; contbg. author: Sisters of Bon Secours Centennial, 1982. Trustee, chmn. Family Svcs., Detroit and Wayne County, 1992-92; chmn. AIDS Consortium Southeastern Mich., Toledo, 1988-92l v.p. Med. Value Plan, Inc., 1986-91; chmn. S.E. Mich. Hosp. Coun.; bd. dirs. U. St. Francis, Joliet, 1993—; vice chmn. New Ctr. Area Coun., 1991-92; chair-elect Mich. Tastefest, 1996; bd. dirs., chmn. Ctr. Econ. Devel., Will County C. of C., Ill. Recipient Commendation 114th Ohio Gen Assembly, 1981. Fellow Am. Coll. Health Care Execs. (coun. regents 1989-92, bd. govs. 1992—, Robert S. Hudgens award 1982, chair 1998—); mem. Am. Hosp. Assn., White Eagle Golf Club (Naperville, Ill.), Joliet Country Club, Detroit Country Club. Roman Catholic. Avocations: jogging, golf. Office: St Raphael Healthcare System 659 George St New Haven CT 06511

BENFIELD, ANN KOLB, lawyer; b. Reading, Pa., May 1, 1946; d. Curtis Kepler and Stella (Kolb) B. BA, George Washington U., 1969, MA, 1974; JD, U. Ky., 1983. Ky. 1983, U.S. Ct. Appeals (6th cir.) 1985, U.S. Supreme Ct. 1987. Probation officer Superior Ct. of D.C., Washington, 1973-78; jud. law clk. to chief judge U.S. Dist. Ct. (we. dist.) Ky., Louisville, 1983-86, jud. atty. to fed. sr. judge, 1989-95; trial atty. Ogden & Robertson, Louisville, 1986-89; adj. prof. U. Louisville Sch. Law, 1993. Mem. exec. com., bd. dirs. Ky. chpt. ACLU, 1988-89, 91—, nat. bd. dirs., 1992-94, sec., 1995-96, treas., 1998; Reproductive Freedom Adv. Com., 1994—; mem. steering com. Fellowship Reconciliation, Louisville, 1997—; mem. governing coun. U. Louisville Women's Ctr., 1998; rape crisis advocate Ctr. for Women & Families, 1997—, domestic violence advocate, 1998; bd. dirs., gen. counsel Depressed Self-Help Svcs., Inc., 1998. Fellow Ky. Bar Found. (charter, bd. dirs.); mem. Ky. Bar Assn., Louisville Bar Assn., Louisville Women's Law Assn., Order of Coif, Phi Beta Kappa. Home: 1113 Holly Springs Dr Louisville KY 40242-7762 Office: 2d Fl 1326 S 3d St Louisville KY 40208-2306

BENFIELD, JAMES HAINES, treasurer; b. Mineola, N.Y., June 8, 1953; s. Clifford John and Eunice (Patrick) B.; m. Lois Mary Scordamaglia, Aug. 26, 1978; children: Kathryn, Anne. BA, Union Coll., 1975; MBA, NYU, 1982. Asst. v.p. Mfrs, Hanover Trust Co., N.Y., 1975-80; v.p., treas. Transammonia, Inc., N.Y., 1980—. chmn. The Heritage Park Rowing Found., Norwalk, Conn., 1993-94. Mem. Norwalk River Rowing Club (pres. 1990), Sprite Island Yacht Club. Episcopalian. Avocations: rowing, sailing. Office: Transammonia Inc 350 Park Ave Rm 400 New York NY 10022-6022

BENFIELD, JOHN RICHARD, surgeon; b. Vienna, Austria, June 24, 1931; came to U.S., 1938, naturalized, 1945; s. Richard and Charlotte Lola Benfield; m. Joyce A. Cohler, Dec. 22, 1963; children: Richard L., Robert E., Nancy J. A.B., Columbia U., 1952; M.D., U. Chgo., 1955. Diplomate Am. Bd. Surgery, Am. Bd. Thoracic Surgery (bd. dirs. 1982-88). Intern Columbia-Presbyterian Hosp., N.Y.C., 1955-56; E.H. Andrews fellow in thoracic surgery U. Chgo., 1956-57; chief resident and instr. in surgery U. Chgo. Clinics, 1962-64, resident in surgery, 1956-57, 59-63; asst. prof. surgery U. Wis., 1964-67; asst. prof. UCLA, 1967-69, assoc. prof., 1969-73, prof., 1973-77, clin. prof., 1978-88; prof. surgery, chief cardiothoracic surgery, vice chmn. surgery U. Calif. Davis Med. Ctr., Sacramento, 1988-95, prof. surgery, chief thoracic surgery, 1995-98, prof. emeritus, 1998—; attending surgeon V.A. Martinez Med. Ctr., 1988-98; courtesy staff Kaiser Permanente Med. Ctr., Sacramento, 1988-98; James Utley prof. surgery, chmn. dept. surgery Boston U., 1977; chmn. surgery City of Hope Nat. Med. Ctr., Duarte, Calif., 1978-87; bd. dirs. Am. Bd. Thoracic Surgery, 1982-88; cons. U.S. Naval Med. Ctr., San Diego, 1968-88; mem. sr. staff VA Wadsworth Med. Ctr., L.A., 1978-88. Editor Current Problems in Cancer, 1975-86; mem. editorial bd. Annals of Thoracic Surgery, 1979—, Annals of Surg. Oncology, 1994—; assoc. editor Annals of Thoracic Surgery, 1987—; contbr. articles to prof. jours., chpts. to books. Sec., trustee Univ. Synagogue, Los Angeles. Served as capt. M.C. U.S. Army, 1957-59, Korea. Grantee Life Ins. Med. Rsch., 1962-64, Am. Heart Assn., 1968-71; USPHS, 1971-92. Mem. ACS (bd. govs. 1982-88, 92-98), Am. Surg. Assn., Am. Assn. Thoracic Surgery, Am. Assn. Cancer Rsch., Am. Med. Writers Assn., Internat. Assn. Study Lung Cancer, Internat. Soc. Surgery, Calif. Med. Soc., Ctrl. Surg. Assn., L.A. Acad. Medicine, The Royal Soc. Medicine (Gt. Britain), The Transplantation Soc., Soc. Thoracic Surgeons (v.p. 1994-95, pres. 1995-96), Soc. Univ. Surgeons, Pacific Coast Surg. Assn. (v.p. 1995-96), Soc. Surg. Oncology, Am. Coll. Chest Physicians (pres. Calif. chpt. 1996-97), Western Thoracic Surgeons Assn. (pres. 1989-90), Internat. Surg. Soc., Thoracic Surgery Dirs. Assn. (pres. 1995-97). Office: U Calif Davis Med Ctr 4301 X St Sacramento CA 95817-2214

BENFIELD, MARION WILSON, JR., law educator; b. Belwood, N.C., July 26, 1932; s. Marion Wilson and Gazzie Cleo (Martin) B.; m. Dalida Quijada, Feb. 21, 1964; children: Marion, Steve, Robin, Rosalina, Christopher, Jeanette, Antonio, Maria. AA, Gardner-Webb Coll., Boiling Springs, N.C., 1951; AB in English, U. N.C., 1953; LLB, Wake Forest U., 1959; LLM, U. Mich., 1965. Bar: N.C. 1959. Asst. dir. Inst. Govt. U. N.C., 1959-61; individual practice law Hickory, N.C., 1961-63; asst. prof. law U. Ga., 1963-65; assoc. prof. Case Western Reserve U., 1965-66; assoc. prof. U. Ill., 1966-68, prof., 1968-88, Albert E. Jenner, Jr. prof. law, 1988-90, assoc. dean, 1980-85; disting. chair law Wake Forest U., 1990-97, adj. prof., 1997-98; vis. prof. U. Tex., 1998—; vis., prof. U. Houston, 1976-77, Duke U., 1979, NYU, 1984, Peking U., 1985, Shenzhen U., China, 1986, Loyola U., L.A., 1995, U. Tex., 1998—; mem. Nat. Conf. of Commrs. on Uniform State Laws, 1973—. Reporter, draftsman: The Uniform Land Transactions Act and Uniform Simplification of Land Transfers Act, 1970-77, Revised Uniform Commercial Code, Article 2A, 1995—; author: Social Justice through Law-New Approaches in the Law of Contracts, 1970, (with W.H. Hawkland) Cases and Materials on Sales, 1979, 3d edit., 1992, (with Peter Alces) Commercial Paper and Alternative Payment Systems, 1987, (with Peter Ales) Payment Systems, 1993; mem. editl. bd.: Uniform Commercial Code, 1974—, Uniform Land Transactions Act and Uniform Simplification of Land Transactions Act, 1982-93. Served with U.S. Army, 1954-56. Mem. Am. Law Inst., ABA. Home: 10 Overlook Cir New Braunfels TX 78132-4728

BENFORADO, DAVID M., environmental engineer; b. N.Y.C., Nov. 17, 1925; s. Mark Joseph and Mathilde (Abraham) B.; m. Ruthann Martin, May 5, 1950; children: Mark Andrew, Marcia Ann, David Dean. B.S. in Chem. Engrng., Columbia, 1948; student, CCNY, 1942-44. Registered profl. engr., N.Y. Engr., Skelly Oil Co., Eldorado, Kans., 1948-53; applied research engr. Walter Kidde Nuclear Labs., Garden City, N.Y., 1953-56; heat transfer specialist Trane Co., La Crosse, Wis., 1956-61; mgr. application engrng. Penn Brass & Copper, Erie, Pa., 1961-65; product mgr. air pollution control equipment Air Preheater Co., Wellsville, N.Y., 1965-69; sr. environ. engrng. specialist 3M, St. Paul, 1969-94; cons. control odorous indsl. emissions; mem. com. odors from stationary and mobile sources NRC, 1978; gen. conf. chair nat. meeting Air Pollution Control Assns., 1986; cons. for subcom. on pollution prevention EPA Sci. Adv. Bd. Environ. Engrng. Com., 1991. Mem. City of Woodbury (Minn.) Solid Waste Adv. Commn., 1987-95; apptd. pub. mem. Minn. Emergency Response Commn., 1991; active Boy Scouts Am., 1937—; mem. Am. Inst. Pollution Prevention, 1990-96; pres. BMD Environ. Vols. Fellow Air and Waste Mgmt. Assn. (dir. 1968—, pres. 1972-73, hon. mem. 1981—, chmn. gen. conf. ann. nat. meeting 1986); mem. Am. Inst. Chem. Engrs., Am. Acad. Environ. Engrs. (diplomate, trustee 1981-84, pres. 1990), Woodbury Lions Club (sec. 1970, bd. dirs. 1971—, pres. 1978). Home: 7100 Glenross Rd Woodbury MN 55125-1624

BENFORD, ANNE MICHELE, pediatric nurse practitioner, clinical nurse specialist; b. N.Y.C., Apr. 17, 1965; d. William Kenneth and Panthie (Hopper) S.; m. Maurice R. Benford. BSN, SUNY, Buffalo, 1989; MSN, Emory U., 1995. RN, Tex., Ga.; cert. pediatric nurse practitioner. Staff nurse orthopedics Buffalo Gen. Hosp., 1989; charge nurse gen. surgery Millard Fillmore Hosp., Buffalo, 1990; staff nurse newborn nursery, postpartum unit USAF Wilford Hall Med. Ctr., Lackland AFB, Tex., 1990-94; childbirth educator Wilford Hall, 1993-94. 1st lt. USAF, 1990-94. Mem. Nat. Assn. Pediat. Nurse Assocs. & Practitioners, Am. Heart Assn., Internat. Nursing Honor Soc., Sigma Theta Tau (Alpha Epsilon chpt.). Baptist. Avocations: performing African, modern and jazz dance, aerobics, reading, music.

BENFORD, HARRY BELL, naval architect; b. Schenectady, Aug. 7, 1917; s. Frank Albert and Georgia (Rattray) B.; m. Edith Elizabeth Smallman, Apr. 26, 1941; children—Howard Lee, Frank Alfred, Robert James. B.S.E. in Naval Architecture and Marine Engrng, U. Mich., 1940. With Newport News Shipbldg. Co., Va., 1940-48; mem. faculty U. Mich., Ann Arbor, 1948-59, 60-83; prof. naval architecture U. Mich., 1959-83, prof. emeritus, 1983—, chmn. dept. naval architecture and marine engring., 1967-72; exec. dir. maritime rsch. adv. com. NRC, 1959-60. Author 4 books, 150 tech. papers. Fellow Soc. Naval Architects and Marine Engrs. (hon. mem., pres.'s award 1957, Linnard prize 1962, Taylor medal 1976), Royal Instn. Naval Architects; mem. Tau Beta Pi, Phi Kappa Phi. Home: 6 Westbury Ct Ann Arbor MI 48105-1411 Office: U Mich Dept Naval Architecture Ann Arbor MI 48109-2145

BENGHIAT, RUSSELL, advertising agency executive; b. N.Y.C., July 10, 1948; s. Isaac and Pearl (Feld) B.; m. Nancy Joseph, Nov. 8, 1987; children: Joshua Laurence, Gabriel William. BA in English Lit., Swarthmore Coll., 1970; MS in Advt., U. Ill., 1972. Copywriter Kight, Cowman, Abram, Columbus, Ohio, 1972-73; assoc. creative dir. Johnson & Dean, Grand Rapids, Mich., 1973-76; mktg. analyst FTC, Cleve., 1976-81; v.p. Nicholes & Benghiat Advt., Cleve., 1981-83; pres. Benghiat Mktg. and Comm., Inc., Cleve., 1983—. Pres. bd. dirs. Cleve. Dancers, 1983; del. Dem. Nat. Convention, San Francisco, 1984. Recipient Nat. Addy award Am. Advt. Fedn., 1974. Mem. Greater Cleve. Growth Assn. (com. chmn., COSE Vol. of Month 1989). Office: 3628 Walnut Hills Ave Ste 200 Cleveland OH 44122-4484

BENGLIS, LYNDA, artist, sculptor; b. Lake Charles, La., Oct. 25, 1941; d. Michael A. and Leah Margaret (Blackwelder) B. B.F.A., Sophie Newcomb Coll., 1964. Asst. prof. sculpture U. Rochester, 1970-72; vis. artist Yale-Norfolk, summer 1972; prof. Hunter Coll., 1972-73; vis. artist Calif. Inst. Arts, 1974, 76, Kent State U., 1977, Skowhegan Sch. Painting Sculpture, 1979, 99; vis. prof. Princeton, 1975; asst. prof. Hunter Coll., 1980, prof., 1981; prof. U. Ariz., Tucson, 1981, Sch. Visual Arts fine arts workshop, 1985-90; Avery prof. Bard Coll., 1987; master artist Atlanta Ctr. Arts, New Symerna, Fla., 1989; prof. Quinnipiac Coll., 1998, 99. One-woman shows include U. R.I., 1969, Paula Cooper Gallery, N.Y.C., 1970-71, 74-78, 80, 82, 84, 87, 90, 94, Hayden Gallery, Cambridge, Mass., 1971, Kans. State U., 1971, Fuller-Gross Gallery, 1972-74, 77, 79, 82, 86, 88-89, Portland Center Visual Arts, 1972, The Clocktower, N.Y.C., 1972, The Tex. Gallery, Houston, 1974-75, 77, 79-81, 84, 89, Margo Leavin Gallery, Los Angeles, 1977, 80, 83, 85, 87, 89, 91, Dart Gallery, Chgo., 1979, 81-83, 85, Richard Gray Gallery, Chgo., 1990, 93, Tilden Foley, New Orleans, 1989, Real Art Ways, New Haven, 1979, Ga. State U., Atlanta, 1979, Galerie Albert Baronian, Belgium, 1979, 81, Galerie Six Friedrich, Munich, 1998, Charim Klocker Gallery, Vienna, 1998, Kappatos Gallery, Athens, 1998, Cheim & Read Gallery, N.Y., 1998, Galerie Simmoniece Sterne, New Orleans, 1999; one-person retrospective shows include U. South Fla., Tampa, 1980, Lowe Art Mus., Miami, 1980, Atlanta Ctr. Arts, New Symerna, Fla., 1989, David Heath Gallery, Atlanta, 1980, 85, 92, Chatham Coll., Pitts., 1980, Susanne Hilberry Gallery, Birmingham, Mich., 1980, 83, 85, U. Ariz., 1981, Tilden-Foley Gallery, New Orleans, 1984, 86, 89, Landfall East, N.Y.C., 1987, Cumberland Art Gallery, Nashville, 1988, High Mus. Art, Atlanta, 1991; exhibited in group shows Bellas Artes, Sante Fe, 1991, Illeme Biennale de Sculpture, Monte Carlo, Monaco, 1991, Am. Acad. and Inst. Arts and Letters 43d annual exhbn., 1991, 94, CU Art Galleries, U. Colo. at Boulder, A. B. Galeries, Paris, 1992, Morris Mus., Morristown, N.J., 1993, Okla. Mus. Fine Art, 1993, Fine Arts Mus. of South, Mobile, Ala.,1993, Rhone Hoffman Gallery, 1992, Julian Pretto, N.Y.C., 1992, Brooke Alexander Editions, N.Y.C., 1993, Penine Hart Gallery, N.Y.C., 1993, Hunter Coll. Art Gallery, N.Y.C., 1993, Auckland (N.Z.) City Art Ctr., 1993, Bykert Gallery, N.Y.C., 1969, Detroit Inst. Arts, 1969, Milw. Art Ctr., 1971, Walker Art Ctr., Mpls., 1971, 81, Balt. Mus. Art, 1975, Mus. Contemporary Art, Chgo., 1977, 80, Stedelijk Mus., Amsterdam, 1978, Mus. Modern Art, N.Y.C., 1979, 86-87, Palazzo Reale, Milan Italy, 1979, Guggenheim Mus., N.Y.C., 1979, 87, Contemporary Arts Mus., Houston, 1980, San Diego Mus. Art, 1980, Whitney Mus., N.Y.C., 1981; Between the Geometry and the Gesture, N.Am. Sculpture 1965-75 by minister of culture Valesquez Palace, Madrid, 1986, Wadsworth Atheneum, Hartford, 1987, Albright Knox Art Gallery, Buffalo, 1987, The New Sculpture, 1965-67: Between Geometry and the Gesture, Whitney Mus., 1990, others; numerous other one and two-person and group exhbns. nationally and internat.; represented in permanent collections Mus. Modern Art, N.Y.C., Guggenheim Mus., Whitney Mus., Walker Art Ctr.; Olympic Com. artist, 1983, High Mus. Art, Atlanta, Balt. Mus. Art, Canberra , Nat. Gallery Australia, Mus. Fine Arts, Houston, New Orleans Mus. Art, Phila. Mus. Art, Burroughs-Wellcome Corp., Research Triangle Park, N.C., Hokkaido Mus. Modern Art, Sapporo, Japan, "American Sculptors", N.Y., L.A., Kamakura Gallery, Tokyo, Suzanne Hillberry Gallery Group Show, 1990, Nat. Mus. Am. Art, Washington; works are subject of hundreds of mag. and jour. articles and books; juror, participant nat. competitive exhbn. co-sponsored by South Bend Regional Mus. art, Ind. Women's Caucus for Art, 1992. Recipient Australian Art Coun. award 1976, Distinction award Nat. Coun. Art Adminstr., 1989; Yale-Norfolk scholar, 1963, Max Beckman scholar, 1965; Guggenheim fellow, 1975, Avery fellow, Bard Coll., 1987; Artpark grantee, 1976, Nat. Endowment for Arts grantee, 1979, 90. Address: Cheim & Read Gallery 521 W 23rd St New York NY 10011

BENGSTON, BILLY AL, artist; b. Dodge City, Kans., June 7, 1934. Exec. dir. Westfall Art, Venice, Calif., 1996-98. One-man show Galerie Neuendorf, Frankfurt, Germany, 1993; exhibited in group shows at Art Inst. Chgo., 1963, 72, Sao Paolo, Brazil, 1965, Whitney Mus. Am. Art, 1N.Y.C., 1967-69, Biennial Exbhn., 1979, retrospective L.A. County Mus. Art, 1968, 88, Stedelijk van Abbemuseum, Eindhoven, The Netherlands, 1969, retrospective Contemporary Arts Mus., Houston, 1988, Oakland (Calif.) Mus., 1988, The Contemporary Mus., Honolulu, 1988; represented in permanent collections Mus. Modern Art, N.Y.C., Art Inst. Chgo., L.A. County Mus. Art, Whitney Mus. Am. Art, Ft. Worth Art Ctr. Mus., Guggenheim Mus., Beauborg, Paris, N.Y.C., Nat. Gallery, Washington; founder Artist Studio, Venice, Calif., 1960; established Pelican Club Prodns., Ltd., 1982; commd. Calif. State Office Bldg., L.A., 1990; contbr. articles to art jours. Nat. Found. Arts grantee, 1967, Ford Found. grantee Tamarind Lithography Workshop, 1968, 87; Guggenheim fellow, 1975. Home and Studio: 805 Hampton Dr Venice CA 90291-3020

BENGTSON, ROGER DEAN, physicist; b. Wausa, Nebr., Apr. 29, 1941; s. Fridolph M. and Edith E. (Pearson) B.; m. Billie A. Spies, June 15, 1963; children—Nissa C., Hans E. B.S., U. Nebr., 1962; M.S., Va. Poly. Inst. and State U., 1964; Ph.D., U. Md., 1968. Aerospace engr. NASA-Langley Research Ctr., Hampton, Va., 1962-67; research assoc. U. Tex., Austin, 1968-70, asst. prof. physics, 1970-75, assoc. prof., 1975-81, prof., 1981—, chmn. dept., 1984-88. Mem. Am. Phys. Soc., AAAS, Sigma Xi. Home: 411 Honeycomb Rdg Austin TX 78746-5324 Office: U Tex Dept Physics Rm 5208 Austin TX 78712

BEN-HAIM, ZIGI, artist; b. Baghdad, Iraq, Nov. 28, 1945; came to U.S., 1970; s. Jacob and Violet (Halawe) B.-H.; m. Tsipi Inberg, July 28, 1980; 1 child, Yori Lee. Diploma, Avni Inst. Fine Arts, Tel Aviv, 1970, Calif. Coll. Arts and Crafts, 1971; MFA, San Francisco State U., 1974. guest artist fellow Artists Union, Russia, 1992. Prin. works include sculptures Bklyn. Mus., Buscaglia-Castellani U. Mus., Ghent (Belgium) Mus., Israel Mus., Jerusalem, Malmo Mus., N.Y.C., Jewish Mus., N.Y.C., Tel Aviv Mus., U. Md., College Park, Westminster Bank, N.Y.C., Chelouche Gallery, Tel Aviv, Herbert Johnson Mus., Cornell U., Ithaca, N.Y., Jewish Mus., N.Y.C., Baumgartner Gallery, Washington, Art Gallery Hamilton, Ont., Can., Munro Gallerie, Hamburg, Germany, Cleve. Mus. Art, Jersey City Mus., Touchstone Gallery, N.Y.C., Las Vegas Art Mus. N.Y. State Coun. on Arts grantee, 1983, NEA grantee, 1984, Pollock Krasner Found. grantee, 1990, 96; recipient Achievement award Israel Ministry Culture, 1971. Home: 94 Mercer St New York NY 10012-4425

BENHAM, JAMES H., state official; b. Twin Falls, Idaho, July 14, 1944; s. James Henry and Matilda (Riggs) B.; m. Ann Elizabeth McIntosh, Mar. 27, 1965; 2 children. BA in Polit. Sci., Idaho State U., 1990, MPA, 1992. From police officer to chief of police Pocatello (Idaho) Police Dept., 1988-94; U.S. marshal dept. justice U.S. Dist. Idaho, Boise, 1994—. Contbr. articles to profl. jours. Bd. dirs. Nat. Criminal Justice Assn., 1992-93. Mem. Idaho Peace Officers Assn. (pres. 1986), Idaho Chief of Police Assn. (pres. 1990-91), Pocatello Police Relief Assn., Lions, Phi Kappa Phi. Methodist. Avocations: golf, fishing, exercizing, hunting, gardening. Office: US Marshal for Dist Idaho 550 W Fort St # 010 Boise ID 83724-0101*

BENHAM, LELIA, small business owner, social/political activist; b. Cartersville, Ga., July 15, 1945; d. Emory and Nellie Pearl (Carson) Benham; m. Larry L. Mabins, Jan. 15, 1966 (div. 1970); children: Gary K., Margo L., Berrie E. Student, North Cen. Tech. Coll., Mansfield, Ohio, 1981-83, 91—, Mansfield Bus. Coll., 1964-66, 84-85. Bookkeeper/sec. M-R-M Cmty. Action Program, 1970-72; with The Tappan Co., 1972-81; sec./bookkeeper daycare ctr. Mansfield Opportunities Industrialization Ctr., 1983-84; office svcs. contractor FSC Ednl., Inc., Mansfield, 1988-89; sales asst. Hill's Dept. Store, Mansfield, 1988-90; pres./dir. Benham & Co., Mansfield, 1988—; ind. sales distbr. Shaklee Products, 1985-86; home health habilitation aide, waiver/supportive living provider Ohio Dept. Mental Retardation and Developmentally Disabled, 1992—, Richland Newhope Ctr., Mansfield, 1992—; nurse asst. Mansfield Meml. Geriatric Ctr., 1994; nat. and internat. cons. in field. Editor Richland NOW News, 1985-87, 91-92. Cand. Mansfield Sch. Bd. and City Coun., 1987, 89, 91; founding mem. adv. bd., bd. dirs. Litter Prevention and Recycling/KAB (Mid-Ohio Clean Scene), 1982-96; v.p., founding treas. Sister Cities Assn., Mansfield, 1986-94; active various charitable orgns.; bd. dirs. Ohio Women Inc.; mem. alumni bd. Canton Regional Transit Authority, 1989-96, Cleve. Sch. Bd., 1989-93, Ohio Dept. Adminstrv. Svcs. Minority Bus. Enterprise, 1989-96, others; adv. bd. mem. Keep Yourself Alive, 1992, 93. Recipient 10 billboard advt. awards Cleve. Regional Transit Authority Community Minority Taskforce, 1991, Keeper of the Flame Proclamation award Ohio Sec. of State, 1990, award AFrican Am. Women Agenda of Ohio,. 1991, others. Mem. NOW (Richland County founder, pres. 1985-96, Scholarship award 1987, task force chair state bd. racial and ethnic diversity 1993—), NAACP (Ohio rep. to state orgns. 1989—, Pres.'s award 1982, Cmty. award 1988). Democrat. Ch. of God in Christ. Avocations: reading, sewing, travel. Home and Office: Benham & Co 140 Wood St Apt 309 Mansfield OH 44903-2263

BENHAM, LINDA SUE, civil engineer; b. Toledo, Oct. 31, 1954; m. William H. Benham; children: William H. IV, Katherine L. BS in Civil Engrng., U. Toledo, 1977. Structural engr. Itil and Assocs., Toledo, 1977-78; environ. unit mgr., assoc. Finkbeiner, Pettis and Strout, Inc., Toledo, 1978—; pres. A Mind's Eye Photography, Sylvania, 1997—. Trustee Huntington Community Ctr., Sylvania, Ohio, 1990-92; mem. coun. St. Joseph Sch., 1999—. Recipient Spirit of Am. Woman in Bus. award, 1990. Mem. Tech. Soc. Toledo, Kiwanis (past pres.). Republican. Avocations: private pilot, writer, canoeing, camping, pianist. Office: Finkbeiner Pettis and Strout Inc 4405 Talmadge Rd Toledo OH 43623-3591

BENHAM, PRISCILLA CARLA, religion educator, college president; b. Berkeley, Calif., Jan. 30, 1950; d. Carl Thomas and Bebe (Harrison) Patten; m. Donald W. Benham, Mar. 30, 1986; 1 child, Charmaine P. Benham. BS summa cum laude, Patten Coll., 1969; BA in Psychology, Coll. Holy Names, 1971; MA in New Testament with honors, Wheaton Coll., 1972; PhD in New Testament, Drew U., 1976. Prof. New Testament Patten Coll., Oakland, Calif., 1975—, pres., 1983—; coor. music Christian Cathedral, Oakland, 1989—; co-founder Christian Cathedral Chorale, Oakland, 1975—; tree planting participant David Ben Gurion Forest, Israel, 1975. Co-author: Before the Times, 1989, The World of the Early Church, 1991; mem. editorial bd. Pentecostal Theology; contbr. articles to profl. jours. Violinist Redwood Symphony. Mem. AAUP, Am. Assn. Higher Edn., Am. Assn. Pres. Ind. Colls. and Univs. (bd. dirs.), Am. Coun. Edn., Assn. Ind. Calif. Colls. and Univs., Soc. Bibl. Lit., Am. Acad. Religion, Bar-Ilan Assn. of the Greater Bay Area, Western Coll. Assn. Pres. Small Ind. Colls., Regional Assn. East Bay Colls. and Univs. (mem. at-large exec. com.), Oakland C. of C., Nat. Assn. Intercollegiate Athletics, Rotary of Oakland, Phi Delta Kappa. Office: Patten Coll 2433 Coolidge Ave Oakland CA 94601-2630

BENHAM, ROBERT, state supreme court justice; m. Nell (Dodson) B.; children: Corey Brevard, Austin Tyler. BS in Polit. Sci. with honors, Tuskegee U.; JD, U. Ga.; LLM, U. Va. Judge Ga. Ct. Appeals, Ga., 1984-89; justice Supreme Ct., State of Ga., Atlanta, 1989—, presiding justice, chief justice; mem. adv. bd. 1st So. Bank. Chmn. Gov.'s Commn. on Drug Awareness and Prevention, State of Ga.; mem. Ga. Hist. Soc.; trustee Fa. Legal Hist. Found.; bd. dirs. Cartersville (Ga.) Devel. Authority, Cartersville-Bartow C. of C.; deacon, former Sunday Sch. supt. The Greater Mt. Olive Bapt. Ch.; notably one of first black individuals elected to a statewide position in the history of Ga. Mem Atlanta Bar Assn. (bd. dirs, jud. sect.), Ga. Bar Found., Lawyers Club Atlanta, Masons, Shriners, Elks. Office: Ga Supreme Ct 244 Washington St SW Rm 572 Atlanta GA 30334-9007

BENHAMOU, ERIC A., computer company executive. MSEE, Stanford U.; diplome d'Ingenieur, Ecole Nationale Superieure d'Arts et Metiers, Paris. Project mgr., software mgr., design engr. Zilog, Inc.; v.p. Bridge Comm., 1981; chmn., chief exec. officer 3Com Corp., Santa Plz., Calif., 1990—; bd. dirs. Smart Valley Inc., Cypress Semiconductor, Legato, Santa Clara U. Sch. Bus.; chair Am. Electronics Assn. Nat. Info. Infrastructure Task Force. Recipient Pres. Environ. and Conservation Challenge award, 1992. Office: 3COM Corp 5400 Bayfront Plz Santa Clara CA 95052-3600

BENI, GERARDO, electrical and computer engineering educator, robotics scientist; b. Florence, Italy, Feb. 21, 1946; came to U.S., 1970; s. Edoardo and Tina (Bazzanti) B.; m. Susan Hackwood, May 24, 1986; children: Catherine Elizabeth, Juliet Beatrice. Laurea in Physics, U. Firenze, Florence, Italy, 1970; PhD in Physics, UCLA, 1974. Research scientist AT&T Bell Labs., Murray Hill, N.J., 1974-77; research scientist AT&T Bell Labs., Holmdel, N.J., 1977-82, disting. mem. tech. staff, 1982-84; prof. elec. and computer engrng. U. Calif., Santa Barbara, 1984-91, dir. Ctr. for Robotic Systems in Microelectronics, 1985-91; prof. elec. engring., dir. distbn. robotic system lab. U. Calif., Riverside, 1991—, chmn. elec. engring. dept., 1997-98. Founder, editor: Jours. Robotic Systems, 1983 (Jour. of Yr. award 1984); editor: Recent Advances in Robotics, 1985, Vacuum Mechatronics, 1990; contbr. more than 130 articles to tech. jours.; 16 patents in field. Fellow Am. Physics Soc. Office: U Calif-Riverside Coll Engring Riverside CA 92521 *Produce in freedom; give in freedom; and in freedom enjoy.*

BENICA, SHERRY LYNN, pediatric critical care nurse; b. Phila.; d. Harry W. and Katherine P. (Coulter) Waples; m. Arthur G. Benica, Mar. 26, 1983. Diploma, Chestnut Hill Hosp., Phila., 1974; BS in Biology, Chestnut Hill Coll., Phila., 1976; BSN, U. Pa., 1981, MSN, 1987; postgrad., Am. Sch. Prof. Psychology. Staff nurse, head nurse, ednl. nurse specialist Children's Hosp. of Phila., 1976-91; head nurse pediatric and neonatal critical care Robert Wood Johnson U. Hosp., New Brunswick, N.J., 1989-92; adminstrv. dir. Children's Nat. Med. Ctr., Washington, 1992—; lectr. in field. Contbr. articles to profl. jours. AACN, Soc. Critical Care Medicine, Am. Orgn. Nurse Execs., Sigma Theta Tau. Office: 111 Michigan Ave NW Washington DC 20010-2916

BENIGNI, ROBERTO, actor, writer, director, producer; b. Misericordia, Arezzo, Italy, Oct. 27, 1952. Appeared in films, including Berlinguer ti voglio bene, 1977, I, Giorni cantati, 1979, Chiedo asilo, 1979, Womanlight, 1979, Luna, 1979, In the Pope's Eye, 1981, Il Minestrone, 1981, Tu mi turbi, 1983, F.F.S.S., 1983, Nothing Left To Do But Cry, 1984, Coffee and Cigarettes, 1986, Down by Law, 1986, The Little Devil, 1988, Voice of the Moon, 1989, Johnny Toothpick, 1991, Night on Earth, 1991, Son of the Pink Panther, 1993, The Monster, 1994, Life Is Beautiful, 1997 (Oscar Best Fgn. Film 1998, Oscar Best Actor 1998), Asterix and Obelix vs. Caesar, 1999; writer (films) Berlinguer ti voglio bene, 1977, Chiedo asilo, 1979; writer, dir. (films) Tu mi turbi, 1983, Nothing Left To Do But Cry, 1984, The Little Devil, 1988, Johnny Toothpick, 1991, Life Is Beautiful, 1997; writer, dir., prodr. (film) The Monster, 1994. Recipient Nastro d'Argento, David di Donatello, 1989; named hon. citizen of Cesena; Toronto Intl Film Festival, People's Choice Award, Life is Beautiful, 1998; Vancouver Intl Film Festival, Most Popular Film, Life is Beautiful, 1998; National Board of Review, NBR Award, Special Achievement in Filmmaking, Life is Beautiful, 1998; Montreal World Film Festival, People's Choice Award, Life is Beautiful, 1998; Los Angeles Intl Film Festival, Audience Award, Best Feature Film, Life is Beautiful 1998; European Film Awards, Best Actor, Life is Beautiful, 1998; Ft Lauderdale Intl Film Festival, Critic's Choice Award, Best Director, Best Actor, Life is Beautiful, 1998; Screen Actors Guild, SAG Award, Best Actor, Life is Beautiful, 1999; David di Donatello Awards, David (Italian Oscar), Best Actor, Best Director, Best Screenplay, Life is Beautiful, 1998; Cannes Film Festival, Grand Jury Prize, Life is Beautiful, 1998; Chicago Film Critics Assoc Awards, Best Foreign Language Film, Life is Beautiful, 1999; Cesar Awards, Best Foreign Film, Life is Beautiful, 1999; British Academy Awards, BAFTA Film Award, Best Actor, Life is Beautiful, 1999; American Comedy Awards, Best Comedic Actor, Life is Beautiful, 1999; American Academy Awards, Oscar for Best Actor, Life is Beautiful, 1999. Office: via S Anselmo 29, I-00153 Rome Italy*

BENIGNO, THOMAS DANIEL, lawyer; b. Queens, N.Y., July 29, 1954; s. John Baptiste and Ernesta Mary (Yannaco) B.; m. Maria Angelica Vasquez, Jan. 26, 1980; children: Diana Maria, Laura Michelle, John Frederick. BA with honors, Hofstra U., 1976; JD, Benjamin Cardozo Law Sch., 1979. Bar: N.Y. 1981, U.S. Dist. Ct. (so. and ea. dists.) N.Y. 1985. Atty. Legal Aid Soc., Bronx, N.Y., 1979-84; ptnr. Benigno, Cassisi & Casissi, Floral Park, N.Y., 1984-87; mng. ptnr., gen. counsel Benigno/Gurrieri Real Estate Mgmt. and Devel., Bklyn., 1984-95; pres. Gurben Properties, Inc., Floral Park, 1987-88, Movies for Kids Inc., Valley Stream, N.Y., 1989-90; gen. counsel Our Gang Assocs. Inc. (doing bus. as Thin White Line), Cedarhurst, N.Y., 1988-90. Mem. N.Y. Bar Assn., Rotary Internat. Office: 269 Hempstead Ave Ste 2 Malverne NY 11565-1224

BENING, ANNETTE, actress; b. Topeka, May 29, 1958; m. Steven White (div.); m. Warren Beatty, 1992; children: Kathlyn Bening Beatty, Benjamin Beatty, Isabel Ashley Ira Beatty. Student, Mesa Coll.; theatre degree, San Francisco State U.; studied at, Am. Conservatory Theatre. Films include The Great Outdoors, 1988, Valmont, 1989, The Grifters, 1990 (Acad. award nomination best supporting actress 1990), Postcards from the Edge, 1990, Guilty by Suspicion, 1991, Regarding Henry, 1991, Bugsy, 1991, Love Affair, 1994, Richard III, 1995, The American President, 1995, Mars Attacks!, 1996, Blue Vision, 1998, Against All Enemies, 1998, The Siege, 1998, American Beauty, 1999, In Dreams, 1999; stage appearances Coastal Disturbances, 1986, (Tony award nomination 1986, Clarence Derwin award 1987, Theatre World award 1987), Spoils of War, 1988; TV movies Manhunt for Claude Dallas, 1986, Hostage, 1988. Blue Vision, 1998; Against All Enemies, 1998. Avocations: scuba diving. Office: CAA c/o Kevin Huvane 9830 Wilshire Blvd Beverly Hills CA 90212-1804*

BENIRSCHKE, STEPHEN KURT, orthopedic surgeon; b. Boston, Aug. 16, 1953; s. Kurt and Marion Elizabeth (Waldhausen) B.; m. Elizabeth Williamson Abu-Haydar, Aug. 25, 1984; children: Leila Maria, Kurt Karim, Kristina Suraya. BA in Biology, U. Calif., San Diego, 1975; MD, Case Western Res. U., 1979. Diplomate Am. Bd. Orthopaedic Surgery. Intern surgery Case Western Res. U., Cleve., 1979-81, resident in orthopaedics, 1984; A.O. fellow Chur, Switzerland, 1984; acting instr. U. Wash., Seattle, 1985-86, asst. prof. dept. orthopaedics, 1987-91, assoc. prof., 1992—; assoc. chief orthopaedics Harborview Med. Ctr., U. Wash., Seattle, 1987—. Rsch. grantee A.O. Found., 1988. Democrat. Roman Catholic. Avocations: tennis, skiing, automobile restoration, computers. Office: Harborview Med Ctr 325 9th Ave Seattle WA 98104-2420*

BENITIZ, MANNY, manufacturing company executive; b. June 21, 1959. Pres. Am. Fastners Corp., Miami, 1981—. Office: 7323 Northwest 66th St Miami FL 33166

BENJAMIN, ADELAIDE WISDOM, community volunteer and activist; b. New Orleans, Aug. 23, 1932; d. William Bell and Mary (Freeman) Wisdom; m. Edward Bernard Benjamin Jr., May 11, 1957; children: Edward Wisdom, Mary Dabney, Ann Leith, Stuart Minor. Student, Hollins Coll., 1950-52; BA in English, Newcomb Coll., 1954; JD, Tulane U., 1956; student, Loyola U., New Orleans, 1980-81; grad. extension program Sewanee Theol. Sch., U. South, 1982. Assoc. Wisdom, Stone, Pigman and Benjamin, New Orleans, 1956-58; tchr. ext. courses Sewanee Theol. Sem., 1984-88; spkr., panelist on sch. issues various local and nat. groups. Mem. Tulane Law Rev., 1954-56. Pres. bd. New Orleans Symphony, 1984-89; mem. exec. bd. La. Philharm. Orch., 1992—; trustee, Mary Freeman Wisdom Charitable Found., sec., 1987-92, pres., 1990-94, treas., 1994—; pres. E&A Charitable Found., New Orleans, 1983—; bd. dirs. Nat. Symphony Orch., Washington, 1992-98, RosaMary Charitable Found., New Orleans, 1978—, Loyola U., New Orleans, 1989—, mem. exec. com., 1996—, bd. dirs. Nat. D-Day Museum, New Orleans, 1998—, La. Mus. Found. Bd., New Orleans, 1989—, mem. exec. com., 1991—, Children's Hosp., New Orleans, 1976-79, S.E. La. coun. Girl Scouts U.S., New Orleans, 1989-97, Louise S. McGehee Sch., New Orleans, 1990-97, v.p., 1991-97, hon. mem. bd. dirs., 1998—, Newcomb Children's Ctr., New Orleans, 1991-94, New Orleans Mus. Art Fellows Forum, 1991—; mem. adv. bd. dept. psychiatry La. State U. Med. Ctr.,

1992—; active Trinity Episc. Ch., New Orleans, sec. parish coun., 1973-75, sec. vestry, 1975-79, leader Trinity Quartet, 1979-84; local YWCA, 1967-75, 76-79, sec. bd. dirs., 1967-68, 1st v.p., 1968-69; trustee Metairie Park Country Day Sch., 1971-79, sec., 1976-79, pres. PTA, 1975-76; mem. Loving Cup selection com. New Orleans Times Picayune, 1985; mem. adv. bd. Pub. Radio Sta. WWNO, 1980—; bd. dirs Parenting Ctr., 1981—mem. adv. bd Tulane Summer Lyric Theatre, Tulane U., 1972—, pres. adv. bd., 1977-79. Recipient Weiss Brotherhood award Nat. Conf. Christians and Jews, 1986, Outstanding Philanthropist, Nat. Soc. Fundraising Execs., 1986, Volunteer Activist Award, St. Elizabeth Guild, 1986, Jr. League Sustainer award, 1987, Disting. Alumna award McGehee Sch., 1987, George Washington Honor Medal for Individual Achievement, Freedom Found. at Valley Forge, 1988, Living and Giving award Juvenile Diabetes Found. 1991, Outstanding Citizen New Orleans award La. Colonials, 1994, Jacques Yenni award Outstanding Community Svc. Sch. Bus. Adminstrn. Loyola Univ., 1994, Integritas Vita award for outstanding cmty. svc. Loyola U., 1994, Classical Arts Patron award Tribut to the Classical Arts, 1998; named Goodwill Ambassador for Louisiana Gov.'s Commn. Internat. Trade, Industry and Tourism, 1987, Sweet Art, Contemporary Arts Ctr., 1988, Significant Role Model, Young Leadership Coun., 1988, Woman of Distinction S.E. La. Girl Scout Coun., 1992. Mem. ABA, LWV, La. Bar Assn., New Orleans Bar Assn., Jr. League New Orleans (exec. com. 1971-72, bd. dirs. 1967-72), Ind. Women's Orgn., Com. 21, Am. Symphony Orch. League, Quarante Club (2d v.p. 1978-79), Sybarites Club, Debutante Club, Le Debut des Jeunes Filles Club, New Orleans Town Gardners (pres. 1979-80), Thomas Wolfe Soc. (life mem.). Home: 1837 Palmer Ave New Orleans LA 70118-6215

BENJAMIN, BARBARA BLOCH, writer, editor; b. N.Y.C., May 26, 1925; d. Emil William and Dorothy (Lowengrund) B.; m. Joseph B. Sanders, Aug. 3, 1944 (div. 1961); children: Elizabeth Sanders, Ellen Janice Benjamin; m. Theodore S. Benjamin, Sept. 20, 1964 (dec.). Student, NYU, 1943-45, New Sch. Social Rsch., 1966. Office mgr. Writers War Bd., N.Y.C., 1943-45, Westchester Dem. Com., White Plains, N.Y., 1955-56; mgr. Westchester Symphony Orch., 1957-62; mng. editor Cooking Ency., Rutledge Books, N.Y.C., 1970-71; pres. Internat. Cookbook Services, White Plains, 1978—; columnist House Beautiful, 1984-87; cookbook editor Benjamin Co., 1990—; cons. in field; tchr. cooking classes White Plains, 1975-80; lectr. in field. Author: Anyone Can Quilt, 1975; Meat Board Meat Book, 1977; If It Doesn't Pan Out, 1981; Garnishing Made Easy, 1983, Microwave Party Cooking, 1988, A Little Jewish Cookbook, 1989, A Little New England Cookbook, 1990, A Little Southern Cookbook, 1990, A Little New York Cookbook, 1990; editor/author: All Beef Cookbook, 1973; In Glass Naturally, 1974; Fresh Ideas with Mushrooms, 1977; Holly Farms Complete Chicken Cookbook, 1984; Gulden's Cookbook, 1985, A Centennial Celebration of Recipes from Solo, 1988, Salute to the Great American Chefs, 1988, TCBY and More, 1989, GoldStar Micro-Convection Cookbook, 1991, Healthy Cooking with Amway Queen Cookware, 1993, McCormick/Schilling's New Spice Cookbook, 1994, Simply the Best Chicken, 1997, Fabulous Things To Do With Chocolate, 1998, The Pasta Pack, 1998; Am. adapter The Cuisine of Olympe, 1983, Baking Easy and Elegant, 1984, series of 3 English cookbook mags., 1984-87, Best of Cold Foods, 1985, Cakes and Pastries, 1985, series of 12 Creative Cuisine books, 1985, The Art of Cooking, 1986, The Art of Baking, 1987, Perfect Pasta, 1992, Rocky Food, 1994; editor contbr. various books; contbr. articles to profl. jours. Nat. bd. dirs. Emcampment for Citizenship, N.Y.C., 1966-72; bd. dirs. YWCA Central Westchester, 1965-71, Westchester Ethical Humanist Soc., 1968—; exec. com., pres. Internat. Student Exchange of White Plains, 1955-70; bd. dirs. Westchester Chamber Music Soc., 1986—; co-chmn. Concerned Citizens for Open Space, 1997—. Jewish. Fax: 914-997-7214. Home and Office: Internat Cookbook Svcs 21 Dupont Ave White Plains NY 10605-3537

BENJAMIN, BEZALEEL SOLOMON, architecture and architectural engineering educator; b. Anand, India, Feb. 21, 1938; came to U.S., 1971; s. Solomon and Penninah (Ellis) B.; m. Nora Jacob David, Feb. 25, 1962; children—Ashley Bezaleel, Jennifer Elana. B.E. in Civil Engring., Bombay U., India, 1957; D.I.C., Imperial Coll., London, 1958; M.S. in Engring., London U., 1959, Ph.D., 1965. Design engr. M.N. Dastur & Co., Bombay, 1961-63; postdoctoral fellow U. Surrey, Eng., 1965-66; prin. lectr. Hatfield Poly., Eng., 1966-71; asst. prof. archtl. engring. U. Kans., Lawrence, 1971-72; assoc. prof. U. Kans., 1972-76, prof., 1976—; vis. Fulbright prof. Technion, Haifa, Israel, 1987-88. Author: The Analysis of Braced Domes, 1963, Structural Design with Plastics, 1969, Structures for Architects, 1975, Building Construction for Architects and Engineers, 1978, Structural Evolution: An Illustrated History, 1990, Statics, Strenths and Structures for Architects, 1992; (novels) Rampaging Lovers, 1988, A Nazi Among Jews, 1990, Bene Israel Tales, 1991, The Jewish Amendment, 1992, David Rahabi, 1993. Democrat. Jewish. Avocation: writing. Office: U Kans Sch Architecture Lawrence KS 66045

BENJAMIN, DAVID NICHOLAS, architect, researcher; b. Cleve., Mar. 18, 1957; arrived in Norway, 1984; s. Stanley Solomon and Jeanne Ruth Benjamin. BA, Washington U., St. Louis, 1979, MArch, 1982; PhD, Norwegian Inst. Tech., 1993. Architect trainee Stewart Farnet Architect, New Orleans, 1982, Planned Expansion Group, White Plains, N.Y., 1983; architect Richard Fleischman Architects, Cleve., 1984, Per Knudsen Arkitekt, Trondheim, Norway, 1984-85, Trond Thommesen Arkitekt, Trondheim, Norway, 1985-88; rschr. The Norwegian Inst. of Tech., Trondheim, 1988-93; prin. environ. design Ptnrs., Inc., 1998—; pvt. cons. in architecture and cultural heritage mgmt., 1994—; cons. Lejre Hist. Archaeol. Rsch. Ctr., UN Spl. Commns. of Experts on War Crimes Geneva, 1993-94. Bd. dirs. Naturfolkenes Verden, Copenhagen, 1986—; with Program for Housing the Homeless in Broward County, Fla., 1993. Mem. Norske Arkitekters Landsforbund. Avocation: music. Office: Naturfolkenes Verden, Dronningensgade 14, 1420 Copenhagen K, Denmark

BENJAMIN, DONNA MILLER, university official, elementary education educator; b. May 1, 1942. BA, Wesleyan U., Middletown, Conn., 1970; MBA, U. New Haven, 1982. Various positions U. Conn., 1972-86; dir., counselor, site supr. Upward Bound, U. Conn., Storrs, 1986-91, dir. student support svcs., 1991-94; dir. ednl. talent search U. Conn., New Haven, 1994—. Office: Jackie Robinson Mid Sch 150 Fournier St New Haven CT 06511

BENJAMIN, EDWARD BERNARD, JR., lawyer; b. New Orleans, Feb. 11, 1923; s. Edward Bernard and Blanche (Sternberger) B.; m. Adelaide Wisdom, May 11, 1957; children: Edward Wisdom, Mary Dabney, Ann Leith, Stuart Minor. BS, Yale U., 1944; JD, Tulane U., 1952. Bar: La. 1952. Practiced in New Orleans, since 1952; ptnr. Jones, Walker, Waechter, Poitevent, Carrere & Denegre, New Orleans; pres. Am. Coll. Probate Counsel, 1986-87, Internat. Acad. Estate and Trust Law, 1976-78; vice chmn. bd. trustees Southwestern Legal Found., 1980-88, bd. dirs., 1988-90; chmn. bd. Starmount Co., Greensboro, N.C., 1968-88, chmn. emeritus, 1988—. Editor-in-chief Tulane U. Law Rev., 1951-52; mem. editorial bd. Community Property Jour., 1974-89. Trustee Hollins Coll., 1966-87; chancellor Episcopal Diocese of La., 1984—. Trinity Episcopal Ch., New Orleans, 1974-92; mem. adv. bd. CCH Estate & Fin. Planning Svc., 1982-88; chmn. Salavation Army City Commd. Adv. Bd., 1965-68; pres. New Orleans Jr. C. of C., 1953. 1st lt., F.A. pilot, U.S. Army, 1943-46. Mem. Am. Coll. Tax Counsel, Am. Law Inst., ABA (sec. taxation sect. 1967-68, coun. 1976-79, coun. real property, probate and trust law sect. 1978-81), La. Bar Assn. (chmn. taxation sect. 1959-60), La. Law Inst., La. Bar Found. (trustee 1998-99), New Orleans Country Club, Southern Yacht Club, New Orleans Lawn Tennis Clu. Home: 1837 Palmer Ave New Orleans LA 70118-6215 Office: Jones Walker Waechter Poitevent Carrere & Denegre 201 St Charles Ave 51st Fl New Orleans LA 70175-5100

BENJAMIN, GEORGES CURTIS, emergency physician, consultant; b. Chgo., Sept. 28, 1952; s. George and Tessie Cozie (Edwards) B.; m. Yvette Josphanie Janisse; children: Stephanie, Kali. BS, Ill. Inst. Tech., 1973; MD, U. Ill., 1978. Diplomate Am. Bd. Internal Medicine, Am. Bd. Med. Examiners. Intern and resident internal medicine Brooke Army Medical Ctr., San Antonio, Tex., 1978-81; dept. emergency medicine Madigan Army Medical Ctr., Tacoma, Wash., 1981-83; chief emergency medicine Walter Reed Army Med. Ctr., Washington, 1983-87; chair. dept. com. health & ambulatory care Dist. Columbia Gen. Hosp., Washington, 1987-90; commr. pub. health Dist. Columbia, 1990-91; health policy cons., 1992-95; emergency physician Holy Cross Com. Hosp., Silver Spring, Md., 1991-95; dep. sec. Pub. Health State of Md., Balt., 1995-99; sec. Dept. Health and Mental Hygiene, Balt., 1999—; emergency physician Patuxent Naval Air Station, Patuxent River, Md., 1989, Nisqually Clinic, Yelm, Wash., 1981-82, Allenmore Com. Hosp., Tacoma, 1981-82; house internist Greater Southeast Com. Hosp., Washington, 1985-87; clinical instr. emergency medicine, Georgetown U., 1988-95; adj. prof. Health Care Scis., 1993, asst. prof. medicine Uniformed Svcs. U. Health Scis., Bethesda, Md., 1984-87. Editorial bd. Jour. Nat. Medical Assn., 1986-93; reviewer Am. Coll. Physician Execs., 1989—, Am. Jour. Emergency Medicine, 1986-94, Military Medicine, 1983-87; contbr. articles to profl. jours. Bd. dirs. Hosp. Sock Children, Boarder Baby Project, Inc. Whiteman Walker Clinic Inc.; adv. bd. D.C. Commn. Pub. Health Disability and Injury Prevention Program, 1993, Montgomery County HIV/AIDS Citizens, 1992-93; bd. trustees Am. Cancer Soc.; bd. govs. Medico Chirurgical Soc. D.C.; mem. D.C. Emergency Med. Svcs. Com., 1990-91, D.C. State Health Coord. Coun., 1990-91; gov. commn. Welfare Policy State of Md., 1993. With M.C. U.S. Army, 1978-87, USAR, 1974-78. Recipient Cert. Recognition, 1993, Coun. Govs. Svc. award, 1991, Disting. Pub. Svc. award, 1991, Cert. Appreciation Best Friends of D.C., 1991, Cert. Appreciation D.C. Pub. Schs., 1991, Svc. award Medico Chirurgical Soc., 1990, Recognition award D.C.G.H. Medical/Dental staff, 1990; decorated Army Commendation medal, 1983, Commanders award, 1981, Eisenhower Proclamation medal, 1970. Fellow ACP, Am. Coll. Emergency Physicians (Nat. Key Contact 1987-90, 92-95, gov. affairs com. 1993, D.C. chpt. v.p. 1988-90, D.C. chpt. pres. 1989-90, liaison rep. emergency nurses assn. 1992-95, nat. health policy com. Dallas 1992-93); mem. APHA, Nat. Med. Assn. (mil. and aerospace medicine sect. sec. 1983, nat. co-chmn. 1985, 86, nat. chmn. 1987, emergency medicine nat. chmn. 1990-93), Medico Chirurgical Soc. (violence task force chmn. 1992-94), Am. Coll. Physicians Execs.

BENJAMIN, JANICE YUKON, foundation development executive; b. Kansas City, Mo., Aug. 12, 1951; d. Stanley and Frances (Weneck) Yukon; m. Bert Lyon Benjamin, June 14, 1975; children: Brett David, Blair Yukon. AS, Bradford Coll., 1971; BA, Newcomb Coll., 1973; MA, U. Mo., 1978. Tchr. secondary, dept. chmn. Shawnee Mission (Kans.) Sch. Dist., 1973-80; career counselor Career Mgmt. Ctr., Kansas City, 1980-82, pres., owner, 1982-97; v.p., chief devel. officer Menorah Med. Ctr. Found., 1997—; ptnr. Career Mgmt. Press, Kansas City, 1983—, The MBL Human Resources Cons. Group, 1989-91. Contbr. articles to profl. jours.; co-author career planning book. Bd. dirs. Cmty. Jr. League, Kansas City, 1988-89, v.p., 1989-90, pres.-elect, 1990-91, pres., 1991-92; bd. dirs. Menorah Med. Ctr., Overland Park, Kans., 1995-97, gen. chair grand hosp. opening, 1996; bd. dirs. Menorah Med. Ctr. Aux., 1984-97, auditor, 1990-92, v.p., 1994-96; bd. dirs. Health Partnership Clinic of Johnson County, 1997—; bd. dirs. Women's Found. Greater Kansas City, 1991-96, chmn. bd. devel., 1993-95; bd. dirs. Kansas City Friends of Alvin Ailey, 1992-94, co-chmn. planning com.; bd. dirs. Ctrl. Exch., Kansas City, 1988-90, co-chair capital campaign, 1999; mem. adv. bd. women's coun. U. Mo. Kansas City, 1988-89; initiator, sponsor Kansas City Youth Vol. Svc. awards United Way, 1989-90, adv. com. Heart of Am. United Way, 1994-97; mem. Promise Project steering com. Kansas City Consensus, 1994-96; co-chmn. Youth Declaration; mem. adv. com. Vol. Connection, 1998; bd. dirs. The New Reform Temple, 1999. Recipient Miss T.E.E.N. Encouraging Excellence award, 1990; named One of 25 Up and Comers award Jr. Achievement of Mid. Am., 1994. Mem. Assn. Healthcare Philanthropy, Mid-Am. Planned Giving Coun. Republican. Jewish. Office: Menorah Med Ctr Found 5721 W 119th St Overland Park KS 66209-3722

BENJAMIN, JEFF, lawyer, pharmaceutical executive; b. Bklyn., Dec. 28, 1945; s. Haskell and Lillian (Sikofski) B.; m. Betty Gae Meckler, Mar. 21, 1971; children: Lily Meckler, Ross Meckler. B.A., Cornell U., 1967; J.D. cum laude, NYU, 1971. Bar: N.Y. 1971, U.S. Dist. Cts. (so. and ea. dists.) N.Y. 1972. Assoc., Kronish, Lieb, Shainswit, Weiner & Hellman, N.Y.C., 1971-74; atty. Ciba-Geigy Corp., Ardsley, Tarrytown, N.Y., 1974—, counsel for regulatory affairs, 1976—, div. counsel, 1978—, asst. gen. counsel, 1985—; dir. legal dept. and assoc. gen. counsel, 1986-89, v.p., assoc. gen. counsel, 1989-96, v.p. gen. counsel, 1996-97; v.p. assoc. gen. counsel, compliance with law officer Novartis Corp., Summit, N.J., 1997—. Contbr. law articles to profl. jours.; lectr. in the field. Mem. Citizens Adv. Com., Town of Ramapo, N.Y. Served with USAR, 1969-74. Eagle Scout. Mem. ABA, Order of Coif, Cornell U. Alumni Assn. (admissions amb.). Home: 13 Park Ave New City NY 10956-1107 Office: Novartis Corp 564 Morris Ave Summit NJ 07901-1315

BENJAMIN, KARL STANLEY, art educator; b. Chgo., Dec. 29, 1925; s. Eustace Lincoln and Marie (Klamsteiner) B.; m. Beverly Jean Paschke, Jan. 29, 1949; children: Beth Marie, Kris Ellen, Bruce Lincoln. Student, Northwestern U., 1943, 46; BA, U. Redlands, 1949; MA, Claremont Grad. Sch., 1960. With dept. arts Pomona Coll., Claremont, Calif., 1979-97, Loren Barton Babcock Miller prof., artist-in residence, 1978-94, prof. emeritus, 1997—; prof. art Claremont Grad. Sch. Traveling exhbns. include New Talent, Am. Fedn. Arts, 1959, 4 Abstract Classicists, Los Angeles and San Francisco museums, 1959-61, West Coast Hard Edge, Inst. Contemporary Arts, London, Eng., 1960, Purist Painting, Am. Fedn. Arts, 1960-61, Geometric Abstractions in Am, Whitney Mus., 1962, Paintings of the Pacific, U.S., Japan and Australia, 1961-63, Artists Environment, West Coast, Amon Carter Mus., Houston, 1962-63, Denver annual, 1965, Survey of Contemporary Art, Speed Mus., Louisville, 1965, The Colorists, San Francisco Mus., 1965, Art Across Am, Mead Corp., 1965-67, The Responsive Eye, Mus. Modern Art, 1965-66, 30th Biennial Exhbn. Am. Painting, Corcoran Gallery, 1967, 35th Biennial Exhbn. Am. Painting, 1977, Painting and Sculpture in California: The Modern Era, San Francisco Mus. Modern Art, 1976-77, Smithsonian Nat. Collection Fine Arts, Washington, 1976-77, Los Angeles Hard Edge: The Fifties and Seventies, Los Angeles County Mus. Art, 1977, Corcoran Gallery, Washington, Cheney Cowles Mus., Spokane, 1980, Calif. State U., Bakersfield, 1982, Henry Gallery, U. Wash., 1982, U. Calif., Santa Barbara, 1984, L.A. Mcpl. Art Galleries, Barnsdall Park, 1986, Turning the Tide: Early Los Angeles Modernists, Santa Barbara Mus. Art, Oakland Mus., others, 1989-91, L.A. County Mus. Art, 1996; rep. permanent collections, Whitney Mus., L.A. County Mus. Art, San Francisco Mus. Art, Santa Barbara (Calif.) Mus. Art, Pasadena (Calif.) Art Mus., Long Beach (Calif.) Mus. Art, La Jolla (Calif.) Mus. Art, Fine Arts Gallery San Diego, U. Redlands, Mus. Modern Art, Israel, Pomona Coll., Scripps Coll., Univ. Mus., Berkeley, Calif., Wadsworth Atheneum, Nat. Collection Fine Arts, Seattle Mus. Modern Art, Newport Harbor Mus., U. N.Mex. Mus. Art, Wash. State U., L.A. Mus. Contemporary Art; retrospective exhbn. covering yrs. 1955-87 Calif State U. at Northridge, 1989, retrospective exhbn. 1979-94, Pomona Coll., 1994, 450 year survey Calif. art Orange County Mus. Art, Newport Beach, 1998-99. Served with USNR, 1943-46. Visual Arts grantee NEA, 1983, 89. Office: Pomona Coll Dept Arts 333 N College Way Dept Arts Claremont CA 91711-4429 also: Claremont Grad Sch Art Dept 251 E 10th St Claremont CA 91711-3913

BENJAMIN, LAWRENCE, food service executive. Pres., CEO Specialty Foods Corp., Deerfield, Ill. Office: Specialty Foods Corp 520 Lake Cook Rd Ste 550 Deerfield IL 60015-4927

BENJAMIN, LAWRENCE, retired research chemist; b. Tonypandy, Wales, Mar. 17, 1932; came to the U.S., 1960; s. Thomas and Ada (Whiston) B.; m. Shirley Gladys Brown, Aug. 7, 1954; children: Stephen, Christa, Karla, Gareth. BSc in Chemistry, U. London, 1953, PhD in Chemistry, 1957. Rsch. fellow Imperial Coll., London, 1956-58, NRC, Ottawa, Can., 1958-60; chemist, mgr. Procter & Gamble Co., Cin., 1960-89, group leader, 1963-66, sect. head, 1966-89; ret., 1989. Contbr. articles to profl. jours.; patentee in field. Home: 2200 Victory Pkwy Cincinnati OH 45206-2837

BENJAMIN, LENI BERNICE, elementary education educator; b. Durham, N.C., Aug. 15, 1945; d. Irving Jack and Svea Elisabeth (Wohlers) Kruger; m. Stuart Dychtwald, Sept. 21, 1968 (div. May 1985); children: Dana Kyle, Scott Eric, Rachel Ann; m. Wellington Leon Benjamin, Nov. 30, 1985. BA, Newark (N.J.) State Coll., 1967; MA, NYU, 1969; postgrad., Drake U., 1980-81, Kean Coll., 1984-85. Cert. reading tchr., N.J., Iowa; cert. elem. tchr., N.J., Iowa, Mass.; cert. prin./supr., N.J. Tchr. Elizabeth (N.J.) Bd. Edn., 1967-69, 84-85, Diocese of Green Bay, Wis., 1977-79, Diocese of Des Moines, 1979-81; acting dept. mgr., sales assoc. Lord & Taylor, Northbrook, Ill., 1981-82; tchr. Diocese of Metuchen-St. Helena's, Edison, N.J., 1982-83; instr. Edison Job Corps Ctr., 1983-84; tchr. Plainfield (N.J.) Bd. Edn., 1985-87, Pleasantville (N.J.) Bd. Edn., 1987—; team leader mid. level, tchr. 8th grade; coord. PRISM math. project Pleasantville (N.J.) Bd. Edn., career awareness specialist elem. sch., 1995—; chairperson Reading Curriculum Com., Green Bay, 1978-79; mem. English Curriculum Com., Des Moines, 1979-81, Family Life Edn. Curriculum Com., Plainfield, 1985-86, Dist. Test Com., Pleasantville, 1987—. Treas. Boy Scouts Am., Green Bay, 1977. Recipient Elizabeth Edn. Assn. scholarship, 1963. Mem. NEA, N.J. Edn. Assn., Nat. Reading Assn., Nat. Coun. Tchrs. Math., N.J. Tchrs. Math., Nat. Reading Assn., Assn. Supervision and Curriculum Devel., Kean Coll. Alumni Assn., NYU Alumni Assn. Democrat. Jewish. Avocations: reading, needlework. Home: 39 Masters Cir Marlton NJ 08053-3745

BENJAMIN, LORNA SMITH, psychologist; b. Rochester, N.Y., Jan. 7, 1934; d. Lloyd Albert and Esther Smith; children: Laureen, Linda. AB, Oberlin Coll., 1955; PhD, U. Wis., 1960. NIMH fellow dept. psychiatry U. Wis., 1958-62, clin. psychology intern, 1960-64, asst. prof., 1966-71, assoc. prof., 1971-77, prof. psychiatry, 1977-88; prof. psychology U. Utah, 1988—; research asso. Wis. Psychol. Inst., Madison, 1962-66. Contbr. articles to profl. jours. Mem. Am. Psychol. Assn., Soc. Psychotherapy Research, Phi Beta Kappa. Office: Univ Utah Dept Psychology 390 S 1530 E Dept Salt Lake City UT 84112-8936 *I attribute my success to a high energy level, and to some teachers and friends who supported me in times and places women were unwelcome.*

BENJAMIN, MARTIN, anthropologist; b. Flushing, N.Y., July 6, 1968; s. Albert Herbert and Ellen Nichol (Sparer) Bindman. BA in Anthropology, Columbia U., 1990; MPhil, Yale U., 1993, PhD, 1999. Gen. editor Kamusi Project, New Haven, Conn., 1995—; anthropologist Yale U., Malangali, Tanzania, 1995-97, Dublin, Ireland, 1997-98; vis. scholar Cornell U., Ithaca, N.Y., 1994. Gen. editor, Kamusi Project, Print, Electronic and Internet Dictionaries and Resources, 1995—; co-author: Lonely Planet Swahili Phrasebook, 1998. Recipient Hochschild fellowship Yale Ctr. for Internat. and Area Studies, Tanzania, 1995, Mellon Pre-dissertation fellowships, E. Africa, 1992, 93; Fulbright-Hays GPA Lang. grantee U.S. Govt., Tanzania, 1993; grantee for Kamusi Project, 1995-2000; Mellon writing fellow, 1996-97. Mem. Am. Anthropol. Assn., African Studies Assn. Home: RR 1 Box 532 North Bennington VT 05257-9748 Office: Yale Dept of Anthropology 51 Hillhouse Ave New Haven CT 06520-8277

BENJAMIN, MILTON KEMP, computer scientist, engineer, physicist; b. N.Y.C., June 4, 1942; s. Howard and Beatrice (Kempner) B.; m. Patricia Reva Loewy, June 19, 1965; children: Michael, Steven. BA, Bklyn. Coll., 1963; DSc, Columbia U., 1969. Profl. engr. N.Y. Prof. engring. sci. CUNY, Staten Island, 1969-74; engr., mgr. Ebasco Svs., N.Y.C., 1974-81; cons. Energy Svcs., N.Y.C., 1981-86; lead engr. Singer Corp., Wayne, N.J., 1986-89; lead mem. engring. staff Gen. Elec. (now Lockheed-Martin), Moorestown, N.J., 1989—. Technology chair N.J. Reform Party, Cherry Hill, 1997. Mem. N.Y. Acad. Scis. Home: 12 Webster Ave Cherry Hill NJ 08002-3729 Office: Lockheed Martin Borton Landing Rd Moorestown NJ 08057

BENJAMIN, ROBERT SPIERS, foreign correspondent, writer, publicist; b. Bklyn., Aug. 17, 1917; s. Harry Asher and Alice (Spiers) B.; m. Dorothy Calhoun, Apr. 25, 1945 (dec. 1961); children: Robert C. and Gordon R. (twins), Geraldine Benjamin Ameriks, Alan; m. Sarah Graves, Nov. 7, 1970 (div.); 1 dau., Diana Lee; m. Patricia Chamberlin, Aug. 16, 1986. Student Sch. Journalism, Rutgers U., 1940. Staff writer Panama Star & Herald, 1940; asst. editor Dodd, Mead & Co., 1941; chief publs., office coordinator Inter-Am. Affairs Dept. State, Washington, 1942-43; chief Time-Life Bur., Santiago, Chile, 1946-47, Buenos Aires, Argentina, 1947-48, Mexico City, 1949-51; corr., dir. Latin Am. ops. Vision Mag., 1951-56; stringer N.Y. Times, Mexico, 1951-56; founder, chief exec. officer Robert S. Benjamin & Assocs., Mexico City, 1957—. Author: Call To Adventure, 1934, (several fgn. edits.), The Vacation Guide, 1940, The Inside Story, 1940, Europa Para Todos, 1973; editor: Eye Witness, 1940, I'm An American, 1941; assoc. editor: New World Guide to the Latin American Republics, 1943; contbr. numerous articles to various publs.; lectr. on Inter-Am. affairs. Served with CIC, U.S. Army, 1943-46. Recipient Honor award Ohio U. Coll. Communications, 1971. Mem. Overseas Press Club (founder, hon. life mem.), Pub. Rels. Soc. Am. (v.p. internat. com. 1971-74, dir. 1975-76), Time-Life Alumni Assn., Interam. Fedn. Pub. Rels. Assns. (v.p. 1973-75), Univ. Club Mex. (pres. 1977-78). Address: 2502 W Sunset Dr Tampa FL 33629-5339 *Almost all my career has been spent in Latin American communication activities. As early as public school days I had my goal set on writing about the countries 'south of the border'. I hope that I have been able to contribute to better understanding between peoples of the U.S. and the Latin American Republics.*

BENJAMIN, RUTH, writer; b. Tacoma, Mar. 5, 1934; d. Samuel David Turteltaub and Rebecca Shallit; m. Arthur Isaac Rosenblatt, Aug. 5, 1956; children: Paul, Judy. BA, Sarah Lawrence Coll., 1956. Circulation dept. staff The Am. Inst. Physics, N.Y.C., 1953-54; prodn. asst. Esquire, Inc., N.Y.C., 1955-56; asst. editor Hillman Periodicals, N.Y.C., 1957-58; devel. dept. staff Poets & Writers, Inc., N.Y.C., 1983-84; adminstrv. asst. RKK&G Mus. & Cultural Facilities Cons., 1995—. Author: Naked at Forty, 1984, Movie Song Catalog, 1993. Mem. The Authors Guild, Inc., The Players. Avocations: reading, theater, cabaret. Home: 1158 Fifth Ave New York NY 10029

BENJAMIN, SARAGAIL KATZMAN, writer, performer, composer; b. Omaha, July 13, 1953; d. Daniel and Ruth (Goldberg) Katzman; children: Joshua, Aaron. BA, Sarah Lawrence Coll., 1975. Creative residencies N.Y.C., 1988—; performer Joyful Noise, N.Y.C., 1990—. Author: My Dog Ate It, 1994; composer, lyricist The Furnished Room, 1990, A Joyful Noise, 1990, The Alexandria, 1986, The Dybbuk, 1992. Office: Holiday House Inc 425 Madison Ave Fl 12 New York NY 10017-1140

BENJAMIN, SHEILA PAULETTA, secondary education educator; b. Sept. 28, 1948. AA, Montreat-Anderson Coll., 1966; BA in History, Belhaven Coll., 1968; MEd in History, U. Tampa, 1979. Cert. gifted, social studies and bible tchr. Tchr. Hillsboro County, Fla., 1970-98, Bloomingdale H.S., Valrico, Fla., 1998—; clinician tchr. Suncoast Area Tchr. Tng. Honors Program; supervising tchr. Fla. Beginning Tchr. Program; dir. workshops in field. Aviation educator USAF-CAP; vol. Nat. Pks. Svc. 99s-Internat. Women's Pilot Assn. Recipient Photography awards Fla. Strawberry Festival and Hillsborough County Fair; Latin Am. Studies grantee NEH, 1983, African Studies, 1985; Fulbright-Hays scholar in Egypt, 1986, Honduras, 1993. Mem. ASCD, DAR, Nat. Space Soc., Nat. Coun. Social Studies, World Aerospace Edn. Orgn. (U.S. del., Amman, Jordan), Internat. World Aerospace Edn. Assn., Women in Aviation, Gulf Coast Archeol. Soc., Fla. Alliance for Geography, Fla. Aerospace Edn. Assn. (founding pres.), Fla. Anthrop. Soc. (bd. dirs., Appreciation award, Preservation award), Men of Menendez (Historic Fla. Militia Inc.), Mid. East Educators Network, Hillsborough Classroom Tchr. Assn. (NEA), Hillsborough County/Fla. Social Studies Coun., Challenger Ctr. Found. (founding sponsor), Fulbright Alumni Asns., Sun-N-Fun EAA, Phi Delta Kappa. Avocations: flying and soaring, scuba diving and snorkeling, archaeology. Home: 605 Fieldstone Dr Brandon FL 33511-7936 Office: Bloomingdale High Sch 1700 Bloomingdale Ave Valrico FL 33594-6220

BENJAMIN, STEPHEN ALFRED, veterinary medicine educator, environmental pathologist, researcher; b. N.Y.C., Mar. 27, 1939; s. Frank Benjamin and Dorothy (Zweighaft) Fabricant; m. Barbara Larson, July 25, 1982; children: Jeffrey, Karen, Susan, Douglas. AB, Brandeis U., 1960; DVM, Cornell U., 1964, PhD, 1968. Diplomate Am. Coll. Vet. Pathologists. Fellow pathology Johns Hopkins U., Balt., 1966-67; asst. prof. comparative medicine M.S. Hershey (Pa.) Med. Ctr. of Pa. State U.; exptl. pathologist Inhalation Toxicology Research Inst., Albuquerque, 1970-77; prof. pathology, environ. health and radiol. health scis. Colo. State U., Ft. Collins, 1977—, dir. collaborative radiol. health lab., 1977-91, assoc. dean grad. sch., 1986-94, co-dir. ctr. for environ. toxicology and tech., 1991—. Contbr. sci. articles to profl. mags. Mem. Am. Vet. Med. Assn., U.S. and Can. Acad. Pathology, Radiation Rsch. Soc., Nat. Coun. for Radiation Protection (liver task group), Soc. Toxicologic Pathology. Office: Colo State U Dept Pathology Ctr Environ Toxic Fort Collins CO 80523

BENJAMIN, THOMAS EDWARD, music educator, composer, conductor; b. Bennington, Vt., Feb. 17, 1940; s. Paul Alfred and Frances (Stern) B.; m. Elizabeth Klein, Aug. 25, 1963 (div. 1986); children: Matthew, Sarah; m. Carol Jean Russell, May 28, 1994. BA, Bard Coll., 1961; MA, Harvard U., 1963; PhD, Eastman Sch. Music, 1968. Prof. U. Houston, 1968-87; tchr. Nat. Music Camp, Interlochen, Mich., 1969-71, 77-83; prof. music theory Peabody Conservatory, Balt., 1987—. Author: The Craft of Modal Counterpoint, 1978, Counterpoint in the Style of Bach, 1986; co-author: Techniques and Materials of Tonal Music, 4th edit., 1992, Music for Analysis, 4th edit., 1996; mem. editl. bd. Jour. Music Theory Pedagogy, 1989-96; 40 published compositions. Resident fellow MacDowell Colony, 1982, 83, 96; composer grantee Meet-the-Composer, 1980, 86, 88; Composer award NEA, 1978; resident fellow Yaddo, 1978, 80, 84. Mem. ASCAP (Std. Music award 1975-97), Am. Soc. Univ. Composers, Nat. Coun. Coll. Music Soc. Avocations: gardening, sailing. Home: 4093 Fragile Sail Way Ellicott City MD 21042-5018 Office: Peabody Conservatory Mt Vernon Pl Baltimore MD 21202

BENJAMIN, WILLIAM CHASE, lawyer; b. Glen Cove, N.Y., Dec. 2, 1947; s. Park and Beatrix B.; m. Karen Horton, Dec. 21, 1974; children: Sarah, Lisa, Alexandra. AB, Princeton U., 1969; postgrad., Grad. Inst. Internat. Affairs, Geneva, 1969-70; JD, Harvard U., 1973. Bar: N.Y. 1974, U.S. Tax Ct. 1978, Mass. 1983. Assoc. Cleary, Gottlieb, Steen & Hamilton, Brussels, 1975-78, N.Y.C., 1978-82; assoc. Hale and Dorr, Boston, 1982-84, jr. ptnr., 1984-86, sr. ptnr., 1986—. Fulbright scholar, 1969-70. Mem. ABA, Internat. Bar Assn., Mass. Bar Assn., Boston Bar Assn., Internat. Fiscal Assn. Avocations: skiing, tennis, swimming, sailing. Office: Hale and Dorr LLP 60 State St Ste 25 Boston MA 02109-1816

BENJAMIN-KRUGE, SIONA, artist, educator; b. Bombay, Dec. 11, 1960; came to U.S., 1986; d. Judah and Sophie (Joseph) Benjamin; m. Michael Anthony Kruge, Aug. 14, 1993; 1 child, Rachel-Sophia. Diploma in Fine Arts, J.J. Sch. Arts, Bombay, 1981, Diploma in Metals, 1983; MFA, So. Ill. U., 1989, U. Ill., 1993. adj. instr. So. Ill. U., Carbondale, 1995—; roster artist Ill. Arts Coun., Chgo., 1996—; profl. muralist, painter, 1984—; vis. artist Unity Point Sch., Eastern Ill. U., Cobden Elem. Sch., MaComb H.S. 1996, others; art instr. Shawnee C.C., Ullin, Ill., 1989. Artist (series of paintings) Resurrection, 1989-92, Body and Soul, 1992-98, Finding Home, 1996—, Man-Woman, 1984-86; contbr. articles to profl. jours.; exhibited in one-woman shows at Beacon St Gallery, Chgo., 1994, 95, Maison des Dimes, Gondreville/Nancy, France, 1994, New Harmony Gallery of Contemporary Art, Ind., 1992, Waltuch Art Gallery, Tenefly, N.J., 1990, Tarble Arts Ctr., 1998, Lorimier Gallery, 1998, Jewish Cmty. Ctr., Fairfax, Va., 1998; exhibited in group shows at Palais Thurm und taxis, Bregenz, Austria, 1991, Galerie Ovadia, Nancy, 1994, Stage Art at the I-Space, Chgo., 1994, Gallery at Work: East West, Chgo., 1995, Walsh Gallery, Chgo., 1995, 96, 97, Wood St. Gallery, Chgo., 1996, Bockrath Gallery, Cleve., 1997, Gallery at 678, N.Y.C., 1997, others; scene designer Ill. Repertory Theater, Urbana, 1993, Little Theater on the Sq., Sullivan, Ill., 1993, Ill. Opera Theater, Urbana, 1993, St. Louis Black Repertory Co., 1992-93; asst. scene designer Ill. Repertory Theater, 1992, 93, others. Recipient Ill. Arts Coun. Arts-in-Edn. Svc. Recognition award, 1998, Women Studies and Profl. Advancement Juried Competition award So. Ill. U., 1998-99; grantee Ill. Arts Coun., 1994, 1999—, Mo. Art. Coun., 1999—. Mem. The Enamelist Soc. Jewish. Home and Studio: 913 S Glenview Dr Carbondale IL 62901-2541

BENKARD, JAMES W. B., lawyer; b. N.Y.C., Apr. 10, 1937; s. Franklin Bartlett and Laura Derby (Dupee) B.; m. Margaret Walker Spofford, Dec. 12, 1964; children: Andrew Minturn, James Robinson, Margaret Mercer. AB, Harvard U., 1959; LLB, Columbia U., 1963. Bar: N.Y. 1963. Assoc. Davis Polk & Wardwell, N.Y.C., 1963-73, ptnr., 1973—. Trustee Vassar Coll., Poughkeepsie, N.Y., Tchrs. Coll., N.Y.C., Environ. Def. Fund, N.Y.C., St. Mark's Sch., Southborough, Mass, Columbia Law Sch. Alumni Assn., Scenic Am. Mem. Knickerbocker Club, River Club (N.Y.C.), Fishers Island Country Club. Home: 1192 Park Ave Apt 11A New York NY 10128-1314 Office: Davis Polk & Wardwell 450 Lexington Ave New York NY 10017-3911

BENKE, PAUL ARTHUR, college president; b. Michigan City, Ind., May 27, 1921; s. Paul Rol and Virginia (Peterson) B.; m. Beverly Anne Benke, Mar. 14, 1982; children: Janet, Eric. Student, Ind. U., 1941-42; A.B., Ind. State U., Terre Haute, 1948; M.A., U. Chgo., 1951, M.B.A., 1954. Gen. mgr. war prodn. div. Cline Electric Mfg. Co., Chgo., 1951-55; gen. mgr. Paasche Airbrush Co., Chgo., 1955-58; asst. to pres. H.K. Porter Co., 1956-57; gen. mgr. div. Coldform, 1957-58, Coldform (Thermoid div.), 1958-63; pres. (Colt's Firearms Div.), Hartford, Conn., 1963-73; v.p. Colt Industries Inc., 1969-73; group exec., marine products group, v.p. AMF Inc., White Plains, N.Y., 1973-81; pres. Jamestown (N.Y.) Community Coll., 1981-91; bd. dirs. Bush Industries, Inc.; mem. Marine Midland Regional Adv. Bd. Pres., CEO Roger Tory Peterson Inst. Natural History, 1982-96. 1st lt. Ordnance Corps U.S. Army, 1942-45, CBI. Pres., exec. dir. Roger Tory Peterson Inst. Natural History, 1982-96. Served to 1st lt. Ordnance Corps. U.S. Army, 1942-45, CBI. Mem. Blue Key, Beta Gamma Sigma, Alpha Phi Gamma, Pi Gamma Mu. Office: Roger Tory Peterson Inst 311 Curtis St Jamestown NY 14701-9620

BENKEN, ERIC W., career officer; b. Cin., Aug. 20, 1951; m. Johnne Ceravolo; children: Erica, Brian, Kyle. Student, Tactical Air Command Noncommissioned Officer Leadership Sch., Bergstrom AFB, 1977, Tactical Air Command Noncommissioned Officer Acad., Tyndall AFB, 1986, USAF Sr. Noncommissioned Officer Acad., Gunter AFB, 1989; AAS, C.C. of the Air Force, 1994. Adminstrv. specialist USAF, 1970, advanced through grades to chief master sgt., adviser to the sec. and chief of staff, 1996—, chief of staff. Decorated with Legion of Merit, Legion of Merit, Republic of Vietnam Gallantry Cross with Palm, Republic of Vietnam Campaign Medal, others. Office: HQ USAF/CCC 1670 Air Force Pentagon Washington DC 20330-1670*

BENKERT, MARY RUSSELL, pediatrics nurse, researcher; b. Boston, Aug. 27, 1961; d. Charles Edward and Ann Russell (Schork) Doherty. BS in Nursing, St. Anselm Coll., Manchester, N.H., 1983; MS in Nursing, U. Colo., Denver, 1993. Cert. pediatric nurse. Clin. nurse III, preceptor pediatric med. unit Children's Hosp. Nat. Med. Ctr., Washington, 1983-87; staff nurse pediat. ICU The Children's Hosp., Boston, 1987-88; flex team nurse The Children's Hosp., Denver, 1992-96; sr. staff nurse pediatric clin. rsch. ctr. U. Colo. Health Scis. Ctr., Denver, 1988-90; asst. nursing dir. The Children's Hosp., Denver, 1990-91, clin. nurse IV, 1991-92; neurology nurse health care program for children spl. needs Colo. Dept. Health, Denver, 1995; nurse care coord. Denver Health Children & Families Program, 1996—. Mem. Soc. Pediatric Nurses (co-chair program com. 1995-96). Home: 5655 South Routt St Littleton CO 80127

BENKOVIC, STEPHEN JAMES, chemist; b. Orange, N.J., Apr. 20, 1938; s. Stephen and Mary (Zamadics) B.; m. Patricia Doran, June 10, 1961. A.B. in English Lit., Lehigh U., 1960, B.S. in Chemistry, 1960; Ph.D. in Organic Chemistry (NIH fellow 1961-63. Teeple fellow 1960-61), Cornell U., 1963. Research asso. U. Calif., Santa Barbara, 1964-65; asst. prof. chemistry Pa. State U., University Park, 1965-67; assoc. prof. Pa. State U., 1967-70, prof., 1970—, Evan Pugh prof., 1977, univ. chair in biol. scis., 1984, Univ. prof., Eberly chair in chemistry, 1986—. Contbr. articles to profl. jours. Alfred P. Sloan Found. fellow, 1968-70; Guggenheim fellow, 1976; recipient NIH career devel. award., 1969-74, Pfizer award in enzyme chemistry Pa. State U., 1977, Gowland Hopkins award, 1986, Arthur Cope Scholar award, 1988, NIH Merit award, 1988, Alfred R. Bader award Am. Chem. Soc., 1995. Mem. Fedn. Am. Biologists., Am. Acad. Arts and Scis., Nat. Acad. Scis., Chem. Soc., Am. Chem. Soc., Inst. Medicine, Sigma Xi, Phi Beta Kappa. Home: 771 Teaberry Ln State College PA 16803-3183 Office: Pa State U 414 Wartik Laboratory University Park PA 16802-6300*

BENMOSCHE, ROBERT H., insurance company executive. BA in Math., Alfred U., 1966. With Chase Manhattan Bank; with Paine Webber, 1982, sr. v.p. mktg., 1984-86, CFO retail bus., 1986-87, dir. securities ops., 1987, exec. v.p.; exec. v.p. individual bus. dept. Met. Life Ins. Co., pres., COO, 1997—, also bd. dirs. Bd. dirs. N.Y. Philharm. Lt. U.S. Army Signal Corps, 1966-68. Mem. Life INs. Mktg. and Rsch. Assn. (bd. trustees). Office: Met Life 1 Madison Ave New York NY 10010-3603*

BENN, DENNA M., veterinarian; b. Toronto, Ont., Canada, Dec. 27, 1950; d. Denzil John and Maizie Mabel (Lane) Drake; children: Tricia, Wesley, Emilee. BSc, U. Guelph, 1973, DVM, 1976, Diploma in Medicine, 1977, MSc, 1983. Intern clin. studies U. Guelph, Ont., Canada, 1976-77; teaching master Seneca Coll., King City, Ont., Canada, 1977-81, 83; rsch. assoc. clin. studies U. Guelph, 1979-81, staff vet. animal care svcs., 1980-87, acting dir. animal care svcs., 1984, 87, dir. animal care svcs., 1988—; adj. prof. pathology Ont. Vet. Coll., 1989—; mem., chair vet. programs adv. com. Seneca Coll. Applied Arts & Tech., 1983—; mem. animal welfare com. Ont. Vet. Med. Assn., Milton, 1990-95; cons. Atomic Energy Bd. Can., Ottawa, Ont., 1993-96. Recipient Merck award, 1976, Frederick A. McGrand award Can. Fedn. Human Socs., 1993, Humane award Can. Vet. Med. Assn., 1993, Charles River award, 1995; Ayerst fellow, 1978; Patricia McKeown Meml. scholar, 1979. Mem. Am. Soc. Lab. Animal Practitioners, Am. Assn. Lab. Animal Sci., Can. Assn. lab. Animal Medicine, Can. Assn. Lab. Animal Sci. (bd. dirs. 1983-84, 94—, pres. 1998—), Can. Vet. Med. Assn., Scientist Ctr. Animal Welfare, Ctr. Study Animal Welfare (mem. steering com. 1989—). Avocations: hobby farm, coin collecting, animals. Office: Animal Care Svcs, U Guelph, Guelph, ON Canada N1G 2W1

BENN, DOUGLAS FRANK, information technology and computer science executive; b. Detroit, May 8, 1936; s. Frank E. and Madeline (Pond) B.; m. Shirley M. Flanery, July 16, 1955; children—Christopher, Susan, Kathy. BS in Math., Mich. State U., 1960, MA, 1962; cert. data processing (NSF scholar), Milw. Inst. Tech., 1965; postgrad., U. Wis., 1965-66; Ed.Adminstrn., Washington U., 1972; MS in Computer Sci., So. Meth. U., 1982, D of Engring. in Computer Sci., 1990. Tchr. math. and sci. Lansing (Mich.) Public Schs., 1960-64; chmn. computer sci. dept. Kenosha (Wis.) Area Tech. Inst., 1964-67, mgr. data processing, 1965-67; sr. project leader Abbott Labs., North Chicago, Ill., 1967-68, sr. IT cons., 1968-69; dir. data processing div. St. Louis Public Schs., 1969-74; dir. info. systems div. mental health State of Ill., Springfield, 1974-78; dir. data processing div. Med. Computer Systems, Inc., Dallas, 1978; dir. bus. adminstrn. Dallas County Mental Health Center, 1979-80; prof. computer sci. So. Meth. U., Dallas, 1979-82, 89-96; sr. dir. corp. research and devel. Blue Cross & Blue Shield of Tex., Dallas, 1980-83; v.p. mgmt. info. services Western States Adminstrs., Fresno, Calif., 1984-88; chmn., pres. D.F. Benn & Assocs. Inc., 1989—; chief info. officer Tex. Natural Resource Conservation Commn., 1996-98; prof. Info. Tech. U. Tex., Dallas, 1990-92; exec. dir. for tech. Corpus Christi Ind. Sch. Dist.; lectr. and adv. coun. Great Cities Pub. Sch. Sys., 1969-74; cons. Ill. Med. Soc., 1976-78, Wis. Bd. Vocat. Tech. and Adult Edn., 1964-67; co-dir. mgmt. adv. group Ill. Dept. Mental Health, 1974-78; mem. adv. group Tex. Gov.'s Task on Mental Health, 1980; adj. prof. computer info. sys. Wash. U., 1972-74; expert witness/software appraisal svcs. U.S. Tax Ct., 1995, Info. Tech. State of Tex., 1997—, Strategic Planning Coun., 1997, Geog. Info. Sys. Coun., 1997—, Nat. Gov.'s Assn./EPA Joint Task Force Electronic Commerce, 1997—. Contbr. articles on info. techs., engring. mgmt., and software valuation to profl. jours. Arbitrator computer and bus. contract cases, 1976—. Mem. Data Processing Mgmt. Assn., Assn. for Sys. Mgmt. (Disting. Svc. award 1980, Merit award 1976, Achievement award 1978, chpt. pres. 1976-77, dist. dir. 1976-78), Am. Arbitration Assn., Data Processing Mgmt. Assn. (bd. dirs. 1987-89), Am. Soc. Engring. Mgmt. Presbyterian. E-mail: DougBenn@AOL.COM. Home and Office: 14721 Whitecap Blvd Corpus Christi TX 78418-7712

BENN, JULIE EVE AREND, writer, communications specialist; b. Highland Park, Ill., Mar. 11, 1971; d. Robert Lee Arend and Andrea Diann (Pries) Kuipers; m. John Tyler Benn, Oct. 21, 1995. Assoc. in Psychology, Mira Costa Coll., 1994; B Journalism, San Diego State U., 1996. Editl. intern San Diego Mag., 1993; reporter The Beach News, Encinitas, Calif., 1993-96; intern KGTV Channel 10, San Diego, 1994, KOCT Oceanside (Calif.) Cmty. TV, 1996; comms. specialist Try J Advt., Carlsbad, Calif., 1996—; newsrm. asst. Rep. Convention programming CBS News, San Diego, 1996; media advisor Married Students Club, San Diego State U., 1995-96. Commentator Morning Edition program Nat. Pub. Radio, 1996; guest commentator KPBS Radio, San Diego, 1997. Recipient Bear award for automotive newspaper advt. in Calif., 1996, Critiquers Choice award for poetry 14th Ann. Writers Conf., San Diego State U., 1998, Effective Advt. in Radio award, 1998, Achievement in Radio award, 1999, Summit Creative award, 1999.

BENN, RAYMOND CHRISTOPHER, materials engineer; b. London, Oct. 20, 1946; came to U.S., 1977; s. Frank Abraham and Eileen Mabel (Ashford) B.; m. Pamela Scott Woodhouse, Apr. 8, 1979; children: Briana Crawford, Britanny Ashford. Chem. engring. candidate, London U., 1965-66; BSc with 1st class honors in Metallurgy, U. Surrey, Eng., 1970; MBA, U. New Haven, 1995. Chartered engr., U.K. Devel. metallurgist Delta Materials Rsch., 1970-74; rsch. metallurgist Inco Alloys Ltd., Hereford, Eng., 1974-77; sect. mgr. Inco Alloy Products Co. Rsch. Ctr., Suffern, N.Y., 1977-82, prin. metallurgist, 1982-84; group leader, sr. metallurgist Inco Alloys Internat., Inc., Huntington, W.Va., 1984-89; staff engr. Allied Signal Engines (Textron-Lycoming), Stratford, Conn., 1989-95; chief technologist Wyman-Gordon Co., Groton, Conn., 1995—; tech. presenter in field. Contbr. more than 50 articles to profl. publs.; co-author 2 books in field. Recipient Innovative P/M award European Powder Metallurgy Assn., 1992. Fellow ASM (chmn. specialty materials divsn. 1988-92, chmn. W.Va. chpt. 1986-87, chmn. Hudson Valley chpt. 1983-84, chmn. heat resistant materials group 1983-88, Chpt. chmn. award 1984, 87, nominating com. 1985), Inst. Materials; mem. TMS-AIME, Sigma Xi. Congregational. Achievements include research in developing alloys (including mechanical alloying techniques) and materials technology for high temperature/performance applications in aerospace and industry; over 20 patents in field. Avocations: boating, archery, calligraphy, rowing. Office: Wyman-Gordon Co 839 Poquonnock Rd Groton CT 06340-0999

BENNACK, FRANK ANTHONY, JR., publishing company executive; b. San Antonio, Feb. 12, 1933; s. Frank Anthony and Lula W. (Connally) B.; m. Luella M. Smith, Sept. 1, 1951; children: Shelley, Laura, Diane, Cynthia, Julie. Student, U. Md., 1954-56, St. Mary's U., 1956-58. Advt. account exec. San Antonio Light, 1950-53, 56-58, adv. mgr., 1961-65, asst. pub., 1965-67, pub., 1967-74; gen. mgr. newspapers Hearst Corp., N.Y.C., 1974-76, exec. v.p., chief oper. officer, 1975-78, pres., chief exec. officer, 1978—; chmn. Mus. of Television and Radio, N.Y.C., 1991—; dir. Mfrs. Hanover Trust Co., N.Y.C., Am. Home Products Corp. Chmn. bd. San Antonio Symphony, 1973-74; Trustee Our Lady of Lake Coll.; hon. trustee Witte Meml. Mus.; bd. govs. N.Y. Hosp., N.Y.C. Served with AUS, 1954-56. Mem. Tex. Daily Newspaper Assn. (pres. 1973—), Am. Newspaper Pubs. Assn. (dir.), Greater San Antonio C. of C. (pres. 1971—). Club: Rotarian (pres. 1974-75). *

BENNER, CHARLES HENRY, retired music educator; b. Fort Recovery, Ohio, Feb. 4, 1912; s. Henry Farraday and Ida Matilda (Denney) B.; m. Mary Arbutus Kautz; children: Charles Jonathan, Susan Elizabeth, Daniel Farraday. BS in Edn., Wittenberg U., 1935; MEd, U. Cinn., 1947; PhD, Ohio State U., 1963. Tchr. music, gen. subjects Pub. Schs., Butler County, Ohio, 1934-42; prin. Lemon-Monroe Sch., Ohio, 1946-48; tchr. music, math. Wyoming, Ohio, 1948-58; mem. faculty Sch. Music Ohio State U., Columbus, 1958-68; mem. faculty Coll. Conservatory Music U. Cinn., 1968-79, ret., 1979, prof. emeritus, 1979—; pres. N. Ctrl. Divsn. Music Educators Nat. Conf., 1965-67; U.S. del. internat. symposium October-Art-Children, Moscow, 1977; cons. to Australia coun. and Australia Soc. Music Edn., Canberra, 1980; vis. prof. music edn. Cath. U., Washington, 1981-82; mem. faculty Brigham Young U., Provo, Utah, summer 1974. Author: From Research to the Classroom: Teaching Performing Groups, 1972; co-author: Music in General Education, 1965. Reader Radio Reading Svc., Cinn., 1990—. With USCG, Maryland, 1942-43, Deck Ofcr., Lt. jg., PTO, 1944-46. Recipient Disting. Svc. award Ohio Music Edn., 1971, Ohio Music Edn. Dist. Svc. Awd., 1971, Canticum Novum award Wittenberg U., Springfield, Ohio, 1973, U. Cincinnati Coll., Conservatory of Music, Dist. Svc. Awd., 1979. Mem. Ohio Music Assn. (pres. 1958-60, disting. svc. award 1971), Internat. Soc. Music Edn. (bd. dirs. 1974-76), Music Educators Nat. Conf. (life, pres. 1974-76). Home: 5610 Windridge Dr Cincinnati OH 45243-2987

BENNER, RICHARD BYRON, philosophy educator; b. Somers Point, N.J., Dec. 6, 1936; s. Theodore Roosevelt and Carolyn Mildred (Wilkinson) B.; m. Ethel Barbara Blair, June 7, 1958 (div. Oct. 1996); children: Richard Byron Jr., Kathryn Lynn, Cheryl Susan; m. Linda Jean Foster, Dec. 24, 1996; 1 stepchild, Genevieve Lynn Fox. BA, Villanova U., 1969; MS, Fla. State U., 1972; postgrad., U. Pa., 1972—. Clin. lab. chief Shore Meml. Hosp., Somers Point, N.J., 1961-62; med. rschr. Bryn Mawr (Pa.) Hosp., 1962-71; office mgr. O.C. Plumbers, Inc., Ocean City, N.J., 1972-79; plumbing contractor Doctor's Plumbing and Heating, Ocean City, 1979-85; hist. preservationist R.B. Benner and Son, Ocean City, 1985-93; animal care specialist Wildlife Aid, Inc., English Creek, N.J., 1993-95; instr. philosophy Atlantic C.C., Mays Landing, N.J., 1995—; spkr. in field; adj. assoc. prof. philosophy Ocean County Coll., Toms River, N.J., 1998—. Contbr. articles, photographs to profl. publs. Founder, pres. Ocean City Hist. Preservation Soc., 1986-90. With U.S. Army, 1958-61; vol. U.S. Dept. Interior, N.J. Divsn. Fish and Game. Recipient 1st place photo award Egg Harbor Twp., 1995, 96, cert. of recognition Exch. Club, 1991. Mem. Am. Philos. Assn., Audubon Soc., Nature Conservancy, Nat. Wildlife Fedn., World Wildlife Fund, Sierra Club. Avocations: outdoor and wildlife photography, conservation. Home: 6037 Main St Mays Landing NJ 08330

BENNER, RICHARD EDWARD, JR., management and marketing consultant, investor; b. Jersey City, Dec. 7, 1932; s. Richard E. and Dorothy (Linstead) B.; m. Virginia Hart; children: Linda, Richard III, Christopher. BS, Lehigh U., 1954; postgrad., NYU, 1959-63. Sales exec. IBM Corp, Norwalk, Conn., 1955-58; with Avon Products, Inc., N.Y.C., 1959-78, group v.p. mktg. and internat., 1972-78; exec. v.p. The Fuller Brush Co., Kansas City, Mo., 1979-86; mktg. cons. Kansas City, 1987—; bd. dirs. Game Hill, Inc., Weston, Mo., exec. com., chmn. Exec. Svc. Corp., 1993—, LINC, Local Investment commn., 21st Century Initiative; bd. dirs. Ctr. for Mgmt. Assistance, 1996—; mentor Helzberg Entrepreneurial Mentoring Program, 1998—. Bd. dirs., pres. Northland Homes Partnership for the Homeless, 1988-94; active Eccumedia, 1987—; maj. corp. com. chmn. United Way, N.Y.C., 1976; Rep. committeeman, Bergan County, 1973; mem. SCORE, 1990—, vice chmn., 1991-92; vice chair cmty. rels. SCORE, 1990—. Mem. Direct Selling Assn. Edn. Found. (bd. dirs. 1982-84). Lutheran. Club: Beaverkill Trout (Livingston Manor, N.Y.) (bd. dirs. 1975-78); Old Pike Country (bd. dirs. 1987-90). Lodge: Rotary (bd. dirs., Polio Plus area coord., pres.). Avocations: fly fishing, investing, gardening. Home and Office: 4404 NW Normandy Ln Kansas City MO 64116-1553

BENNER, RICHARD WALTER, oil company executive, geologist, engineer; b. Dayton, Ohio, June 2, 1922; s. Frederick and Edna Marie B.; m. Parnel Gillilan, Mar. 19, 1949 (dec. Apr. 1970); m. Donna Tschappat, Nov. 24, 1978 (dec. Sept. 1995). BS in Geology, U. Mich., 1947, MS in Geology, 1948. Registered profl. engr., Colo. Photo geologist Texaco, Inc., Lewistown, Mont., 1947-48; field geologist Texaco, Inc., Lewistown, 1948-59; dist. geologist Texaco, Inc., Denver, 1959-66, spl. projects geologist, 1966-77; v.p. Kissinger Petroleum Corp., Englewood, Colo., 1977-81, Kissinger Drilling & Exploration, Englewood, 1981-86; pres. Kissinger Exploration, Inc., Denver, 1981-86; cons. Corpus Christi, Tex., 1987—. Author, co-author: Ann. Field Book Publs., Rocky Mountain Geol. Soc. and Montana Geol. Soc., 1949-77; co-author Geological Atlas of Rocky Mountain Region, Wind River Basin, Wyo., 1970, U.S. Geol. Bull., Reserves of Oil and Gas in Rocky Mountain Region, 1977. With U.S. Coast Guard, 1943-44, lt. U.S. Navy, 1944-46, ETO, PTO. Mem. Am. Assn. Petroleum Geologists, Sigma Gamma Upsilon. Home and Office: 5206 Wooldridge Rd Corpus Christi TX 78413

BENNET, DOUGLAS JOSEPH, JR., university president; b. Orange, N.J., June 23, 1938; s. Douglas Joseph and Phoebe (Benedict) B.; m. Susanne Klejman, June 27, 1959 (div. 1995); children: Michael, James, Holly; m. Midge Bowen Ramsey, July 27, 1996. B.A., Wesleyan U., Middletown, Conn., 1959; M.A., U. Calif., Berkeley, 1960; Ph.D., Harvard, 1968. Asst. to econ. adv. AID, New Delhi, India, 1963-64; spl. asst. to Am. ambassador to India, 1964-66; asst. to Vice Pres. Hubert H. Humphrey, 1967-69; adminstrv. asst. to U.S. Senator Thomas Eagleton, 1969-73, to U.S. Senator Abraham Ribicoff, 1973-74; staff dir. com. budget U.S. Senate, 1974-77; asst. sec. state congressional relations, 1977-79; adminstr. AID, Washington, 1979-81; pres. Roosevelt Ctr. for Am. Policy Studies, 1981-83; pres., CEO Nat. Pub. Radio, Washington, 1983-93; asst. sec. state Internat. Orgnl. Affairs Dept. State, Washington, 1993-95; pres. Wesleyan U., Middletown, Conn., 1995—. Bd. dirs. Salzburg Seminar. Mem. Coun. Fgn. Rels., Cosmos Club. Democrat. Home: 269 High St Middletown CT 06457-3208 Office: Office of Pres Wesleyan U 229 High St Middletown CT 06459-3208

BENNETT, ALAN JEROME, electronics executive, physicist; b. Phila., June 13, 1941; s. Leon Martin and Reba (Perry) B.; m. Frances Kitey, June 16, 1963; children: Sarah, Rachel, Daniel. BA, U. Pa, 1962; MS, U. Chgo., 1963, PhD, 1965. Physicist R & D ctr. GE, Schenectady, N.Y., 1966-74, br. mgr. R & D ctr., 1975-79; dir. electronics lab. Gould Inc., Rolling Meadows, Ill., 1979-84; v.p. R & D Varian Assocs., Palo Alto, Calif., 1984-91; dir. program devel. Lawrence Livermore Nat. Lab., Livermore, Calif., 1992-96, dir. indsl. partnerships and commercialization, 1997—, mgr. program devel. Contbr. articles to profl. jours. Fellow NSF, 1963-65, 66. Mem. IEEE (sr.), Phi Beta Kappa, Sigma Xi. Avocations: linguistics, amateur radio. Home: 233 Tennyson Ave Palo Alto CA 94301-3737 Office: Lawrence Livermore Nat Lab PO Box 808 Livermore CA 94551-0808

BENNETT, ALEXANDER ELLIOT, lawyer; b. Houston, Aug. 9, 1940; s. William Ernest and Verna Evelyn (Donelan) B.; m. Marilyn A. Bennett, June 6, 1960 (div. 1981); children: Andrew, Laura, Peter; m. Brooksley Born, Oct. 9, 1982; children: Nicholas Landau, Ariel Landau. BA, U. Mich., 1961, JD, 1963. Bar: D.C. 1964. Assoc. Covington & Burling, Washington, 1964-66; assoc. Arnold & Porter, Washington, 1966-70, ptnr., 1971—. Editor U. Mich. Law Rev., 1963. Mem. ABA, D.C. Bar Assn., Order of Coif. Democrat. Avocations: sailing, tennis. Home: 2319 Tracy Pl NW Washington DC 20008-1640 Office: Arnold & Porter Thurman Arnold Bldg 555 12th St NW Washington DC 20004-1206

BENNETT, ANNA DELL, minister, religion educator, retired elementary school educator; b. Cobb Hill, Ky., Jan. 11, 1935; d. James Edison Shoemaker and Chrystal (Abney) Shoemaker-Hurst; m. Stanley Bennett, Oct. 7, 1950 (dec. Jan. 1987); children: Eddie Wayne, James Lloyd, Kathryn Melissa. BS, U. Dayton, 1966; MS in Elem. Classroom Teaching, Wright State U., 1974, M in Gifted Teaching, 1980; Assoc. Bibl., Centerville Bible Coll., 1985, degree in theology, 1987. Lic. minister, Ohio; ordained minister Open Bible Standard Chs., 1992. Tchr. West Carrollton (Ohio) Bd. Edn., 1966-86; dir. Christian edn., Way of the Cross Ch., Dayton, Ohio, 1989-96; retired, 1996; founder, adminstr. Noah's Ark Pre-Sch., 1994; adj. prof. Mt. St. Joseph Coll., Cin., 1981-85. Recipient plaque Mt. St. Joseph Coll., Cin., 1985. Republican. Home: 1916 Hickory Ridge Dr Beavercreek OH 45432-4036

BENNETT, ANNE MARIE, nursing administrator; b. Savannah, Ga., July 29, 1968; d. Rex and Sherry Louise (Edenfield) Duggar; m. Joseph Cleveland Bennett, Jr., Dec. 18, 1992. BSc with honors, Armstrong Atlantic State U., 1992; MSc, U. Mobile, 1996. Cert. critical care nurse, registered nurse, Ga., Miss., La., Ala. Charge nurse Bulloch Meml. Hosp., Statesboro, Ga., 1992-94; critical care clinical specialist Springhill Meml. Hosp., Mobile, Ala., 1994-98; dir. critical care Thomas Hosp., Fairhope, Ala., 1998-99; dir. Thomas Hosp., Fairhope, 1999—; adj. faculty U. Mobile, Ala., 1995-96; cons. in field. Reviewer Jour. Nursing Staff Devel., 1998. Big Sister Big Brothers/Big Sisters, Savannah, 1989-91; medical missionary, Nicaragua, 1995; team captain Am. Cancer Soc., Mobile, 1997, Healthcare Olympics, Mobile, 1997; bd. dirs. Ala. Southern Cmty. Coll. Nursing Bd., Monroeville, 1996-97. Recipient Lamplighter award Ala. League for Nursing, Mobile, 1997, Nurse Educator of Yr. award Nurse's Soc., Mobile County, 1997. Mem. Am. Assn. Critical Care Nurses (sec. Mobile Bay Area chpt. 1993—, Circle of Excellence award 1997), Am. Nurses Assn., Emergency Nurses Assn., Mensa, Sigma Theta Tau (Virginia Henderson fellow 1997). Home: 35 Lake Shore Dr Daphne AL 36526-7439

BENNETT, ARLIE JOYCE, clinical social worker emeritus; b. Central Lake, Mich., Nov. 22, 1921; d. Charles Herbert and Bernice Evelyn (Miller) B. Student, Alma (Mich.) Coll., 1946-48; BA, U. Mich., 1950, MSW, 1955. Bd. cert. diplomate emerita Am. Bd. Examiners in Clin. Social Work. Social worker Ypsilanti (Mich.) State Hosp., 1950-54; staff social worker Kalamazoo Child Guidance Clinic, 1955-67, chief social worker, 1967-71; clin. social worker State Tech. Inst. Rehab. Ctr., Plainwell, Mich., 1971-90; pvt. practice, Kalamazoo, 1991-92; field instr. Mich. State U., 1959-76, Western Mich. U. Sch. Social Work, Kalamazoo, 1971-90, U. Mich., 1967-71. Author: Pie Is in the Eye of the Beholder, 1980, War and Memory, 1991; editor newsletter Late Show Connection, 1993—; also articles. Vol. record reviewer Cath. Family Svcs. Agys., Kalamazoo; bd. dirs. Youth Opportunities Unltd., Kalamazoo, 1968—. Tech. sgt. WAC, AUS, 1944-46, ETO. Mem. NASW (past chmn. and officer), AAUW (legis. chmn. Kalamazoo br. 1985-89, 93-95, pres. 1991-93), Mensa (local coord. 1990—), Loners Am. (pres. Mich. chpt. 1990-92, 97-98), U. Mich. Alumnae Club (past pres. and officer), Phi Kapa Phi. Avocations: poetry, writing, camping, seat weaving, upholstery. Home: 1110 W Maple St Kalamazoo MI 49008-1846

BENNETT, BETTY T., English language educator, university dean, writer; children: Peter, Matthew. BA, Bklyn. Coll., 1962; MA, NYU, 1963, PhD, 1970. Adj. asst. prof. dept. English and comparative lit. SUNY, Stony Brook, 1970-75, asst. chmn. comparative lit., 1971-72, asst. to dean Grad. Sch., 1970-79, adj. assoc. prof., 1975-79; assoc. prof. English and humanities Pratt Inst., Bklyn., 1979-81, prof., 1981-85, dean Sch. Liberal Arts and Scis., 1979-85; dean Coll. Arts and Scis. Am. U., Washington, 1985-97, disting. prof. lit., 1997—; fellowship reader Danforth Found., 1978-79; edn. liaison officer N.Y. State, 1977-80; co-dir. NEH Inst., 1989-90. Author: British War Poetry in the Age of Romanticism: 1793-1815, 1976, The Letters of Mary Wollstonecraft Shelley, Vol. I, 1980, Vol. II, 1983, Vol. III, 1988, Mary Wollstonecraft Shelley: An Introduction, 1998; editor: (with Donald H. Reiman and Michael Jaye) The Evidence of the Imagination, 1978; (with Charles Robinson) The Mary Shelley Reader, 1990, Proserpine and Midas and Relation of the Cenci, 1992, Mary Diana Dods: A Gentleman and a Scholar, 1991, paperback edit., 1994; editor The Selected Letters of Mary Wollstonecraft Shelley, 1995, editor: (with Stuart Curran) Shelley: Poet & Legislator of the World, 1996, Mary Wollstonecraft Shelley: An Introduction, 1998; consulting editor and author gen. introdn. The Novels and Selected Works of Mary Wollstonecraft Shelley, 1996; book rev. editor Keats-Shelley Jour., 1976-94. Keats-Shelley Assn. Am. Disting. scholar, 1992; NEH fellow, 1974-75, Henry E. Huntington Libr. fellow, 1976, Am. Coun. Learned Socs. fellow, 1977-78; Am. Philos. Soc. grant, 1980-81, NEH grant, 1984-87. Mem. MLA, Byron Assn., Keats-Shelley Assn. Am. (bd. dirs.), Soc. for Textual Scholarship (exec. com. 1993—), Bklyn. Coll. Alumni Assn., NYU Alumni Assn., Phi Beta Kappa (founding pres. Zeta chpt. of D.C.). Office: Am U Dept Lit Coll Arts and Scis 4400 Massachusetts Ave NW Washington DC 20016-8001

BENNETT, BILL, publishing company executive. Pres. Folio Corp., Provo, Utah. Office: Folio Corp 5072 N 300 W Provo UT 84604-5652*

BENNETT, BRIAN RICHARD, investment broker; b. Sweet Home, Oreg., May 21, 1950; s. Clinton J. and Hilda (Ditchfield) B.; children: Brian Richard Jr., Drew Edward. BA, Drake U., Des Moines, 1971. Account exec. E.F. Hutton & Co., Colorado Springs, Colo., 1976-78, Dean Witter Reynolds, Colorado Springs, 1978-79; account exec. Boettcher & Co., Colorado Springs, 1979-82, spl. ptnr., 1982-87; sr. v.p. sales Boettcher & Co., Inc., Colorado Springs, 1987-91; v.p. D.E. Frey & Co., Inc., Colorado Springs, 1991; pres. Bennett & Rawlings Fin. Group LLC, dba D.E. Frey & Co., Inc., Colorado Springs, 1994—. Pres. bd. Consumer Credit Counseling Svc. Pikes Peak region, Colorado Springs, 1987-97; bd. dirs. Consumer Credit Counseling Svc. of Greater Dallas, 1998—, Better Bus. Bur. of Pikes Peak region, 1998—; mem. investment oversight com. Regis Univ.; trustee El Paso Club, 1999. Mem. East Colorado Springs Rotary (pres. 1990-91), Rotary Internat. (Paul Harris fellow 1989). Republican. Episcopalian. Home: 17 Sequoyah Rd Colorado Springs CO 80906-4300 Office: D E Frey & Co Inc 111 S Tejon St Ste 100 Colorado Springs CO 80903-2247

BENNETT, BROOKE, Olympic athlete; b. May 6, 1980. Grad. high sch., Plant City, Fla., 1998. Swimmer; winner gold and silver medals Pan-Am Games, 1995; winner gold medal Pan Pacific Games, 1995, 97; gold medalist 800m freestyle Olympic Summer Games, 1996; sponsor Brandon Blue Wave. Avocation: horse-back riding. Office: c/o USA Swimming 1 Olympic Plz Colorado Springs CO 80918*

BENNETT, BRUCE MICHAEL, mathematician, educator, musician; b. N.Y.C., Mar. 25, 1941; s. Edwin P. and Frances (Neuschatz) B.; m. Bonnie Charley, Aug. 2, 1962 (div.); children: Raphael Sebastian, Kamala Sati; m. Rhonda Kyrias, Sept. 26, 1991. Student, Harvard U., 1958-61; BA, L.I. U., 1964; PhD, Columbia U., 1968. Asst. prof. in math. Harvard U., Cambridge, Mass., 1968-71, Stanford U., Palo Alto, Calif., 1971-74; assoc. prof. U. Calif., Irvine, 1974-88, prof., 1988—. Co-author: Observer Mechanics, 1989; saxophonist/composer: (CD) Little Owl, 1995; contbr. articles to profl. publs. Bd. dirs. Trabuco Canyon (Calif.) Water Dist., 1979-85. Office: U Calif Dept Math Irvine CA 92717

BENNETT, BRUCE W., construction company executive, civil engineer; b. St. Joseph, Mo., Dec. 24, 1930; s. Bruce W. and Laura Louella (Clark) B.; m. Barbara Gail Haase, July 26, 1957; children: Stacy Suzanne, Bruce W. B.S. in Civil Engring., U. So. Calif., 1954. Project mgr. George A. Fuller & Co., Chgo., 1956-61; contract mgr. Huber, Hunt & Nichols, Indpls., 1961-70, v.p., 1970-82, exec. v.p., 1982-84, pres., 1984-95, ret., 1995; pres. Hunt Corp., 1988-95, bd. dirs. Served to capt. USAF, 1954-57. Mem. Archimedes Circle, David Wilson Assocs., Newcomen Soc. Republican. Clubs: Indpls. Athletic, Skyline (Indpls.). Avocations: tennis; golf. Home: 437 Seville Ave Newport Beach CA 92661-0656

BENNETT, C. LEONARD, consulting engineer; b. Lowell, Mass., Oct. 5, 1939; s. C. Leonard and Ruth E. (Glow) B.; m. Patricia Ann Derival, Aug. 22, 1966; children: Craig, Dawn Marie. B.S. in Elec. Engring., Lowell Tech. Inst., Mass., 1961; M.S., N.C. State U., Raleigh, 1964; Ph.D., Purdue U., 1968. Registered profl. engr., Mass. Research engr. Purdue U., 1968; mem. tech. staff Sperry Research Ctr., Sudbury, Mass., 1968-73; mgr. systems applications Sperry Research Ctr., Sudbury, 1973-83; cons. engr. Raytheon, Marlboro, Mass., 1983—; lectr. in field. Contbr. chpts. to books, articles to profl. jours.; patentee field. Chmn. Groton Fin. Com., Mass., 1970-76; treas. Groton Ctr. for the Arts, 1976-78; coach Groton Jr. Hockey, 1979-86, Groton Little League Baseball, 1981-84; mem. com. local troop Boy Scouts Am., 1983—; bd. dirs. Groton Dunstable Soccer Club, 1981-92, Nashoba Valley Youth Soccer League, 1986—; soccer referee U.S. Youth Soccer Assn., 1987—. Fellow IEEE (assoc. editor Trans. on Antennas and Propagation 1983-96); mem. Internat. Union of Radio Scis., Eta Kappa Nu, Tau Beta Pi, Phi Kappa Phi, Sigma Pi Sigma. Home: 304 Reedy Meadow Rd Groton MA 01450-1408 Office: Raytheon 1001 Boston Post Rd E Marlborough MA 01752-3789

BENNETT, CARL, retired discount department store executive; b. Greenwich, Conn., Jan. 27, 1920; s. Mayer and Rebecca (Lipsky) B.; m. Dorothy Becker, June 24, 1951; children: Marc Mitchell, Robin Cheryl Bennett Kanarek, Bruce Kenneth. Student, NYU, 1937-38. Wholesale liquor salesman Conn., 1940-51; founder, ret. chmn. bd., chief exec. officer Caldor, Inc., Norwalk, Conn., 1951-84; ptnr. DorCal Assocs., Norwalk, Conn., 1984—. Chmn. Bi-Cultural Day Sch., Stamford, Conn., 1965-67, treas., 1967-68; bd. dirs. Stamford Hosp., nat. bd. dirs. NCCJ; mem. Am. com., internat. bd. govs. Weizmann Inst. Served with AUS, 1942-45. Recipient Amudin award outstanding work Hebrew day schs., 1965, disting. service award Prime Minister Israel, 1973; named Retailer of Yr., 1982; named to Retailers Hall of Fame, 1983. Mem. World Bus. Council (charter), Nat. Retail Mchts. Assn. (bd. dirs.). Clubs: Sailfish Point Country (Stuart, Fla.); Quaker Ridge Country (Scarsdale, N.Y.). Home: Windrose Way Greenwich CT 06830 Office: DorCal Assocs 607 Main Ave Norwalk CT 06851-1058

BENNETT, CARL ROOSEVELT, secondary education teacher; b. Dover, Okla., Aug. 29, 1932; s. Carl A. Bennett and Harriet (Gracey) Bennett-Riley; m. Barbara Pope, Aug. 22, 1964; children: Bradley Carlton, Bianca Cherie. BS, Langston (Okla.) U., 1954; MEd, Howard U., 1970; EdD, U. Md., 1988. Cert. secondary tchr. Farm mgr. Dover, 1954-55; counselor Dept. Welfare, Washington, 1960-62; tchr. English D.C. Pub. Sch. Sys., 1962—; bd. dirs. policy bd. Teacher Ctr., Washington, 1978-86. V.p. Pennyton Civic Assn., Clinton, Md., 1973-80; bd. dirs., v.p., pres. parental adv. bd. Town & Country Day Sch. and New Port Prep. Sch., Kensington, Md., 1974-84. With USAF, 1955-59. Mem. Washington Tchr.'s Union (rep. 1979-94), Alpha Phi Alpha. Democrat. Methodist. Avocations: photography, gardening, writing. Home: 9402 Pella Pl Clinton MD 20735-3530 Office: DC Pub Schs Duke Ellington Sch Arts 3500 R St NW Washington DC 20007-2326

BENNETT, CAROL(INE) ELISE, reporter, actress; b. New Orleans, Dec. 27, 1938; d. Gerald Clifford Graham and Edna Doris (Toennies) Kerr; m. Ralph Decker Bennett Jr., Feb. 27, 1966; children: Ralph Decker III, Katherine Elise. BA, U. B.C., Vancouver, Can., 1960; BLS, McGill U., Montreal, Que., Can., 1962. Libr. various locations, 1962-76; reporter TV/radio Washington-Ala. News Report, Washington, 1981—. Appeared on stage Girl in My Soup, 1978; in film Prime Risk, 1984; host weekly TV program Modern Maturity, 1986-88. Vol. reader Rec. for Blind, Washington, 1985—. Mem. SAG, AFTRA, AAUW, Soc. Profl. Journalists. Avocation: tennis. Home: 115 Southwood Ave Silver Spring MD 20901-1918

BENNETT, CAROLYN L., journalist, writer; b. Augusta, Ga., Feb. 11, 1943; d. Thomas Judson and Laura Lou (Pickett) B. BS in Music Edn., Knoxville Coll., 1964; MMus in Music Edn., DePauw U., 1969; PhD in Curriculum Tchr. Edn., Mich. State U., 1976; MA in Journalism and Pub. Affairs, Am. U., Washington, 1996. Peace corps tchr. Annie Walsh Secondary Sch., Freetown, Sierra Leone, 1964-66; tchr. French and English Boggs Acad. Secondary Sch., Keysville, Ga., 1966-67; tchr., counselor St. Cyril Sch., Detroit, 1969-71; grad. asst., instr. Mich. State U., East Lansing, 1973-76; asst. prof., asst. curriculum reviewer Paine Coll., Augusta, Ga., 1976-77; asst. prof., acad. affairs adminstr. Fayetteville State U., N.C., 1977-79; founding pub., editor Network of N.C. Women, Fayetteville, 1979-81; copyright examiner Libr. of Congress, Washington, 1982-96; journalism lectr. Howard U., Washington, 1997-98; asst. prof. journalism and mass comm. U. Maine, Orono, 1998—. Author: You Can Struggle Without Hating, 1990, Come Home America, 1991, America's Human Connection, 1992, 94; author, compiler: (manuscript) Writings of Mary McLeod Bethune, 1983; columnist: Chgo. Defender, City News, About Time mag.; contbr. articles to profl. jours. Mem. Nat. Writers Guild, Women's Inst. for Freedom of the Press (assoc.), Internat. Women's Writing Guild, Assn. for Edn. in Journalism and Mass Comm., Nat. Assn. Black Journalists, Am. Journalism Historians Assn., Peace and Justice Ctr. Ea. Maine, Maine Writers and Publ. Alliance, Phi Kappa Phi. Avocations: informal discussion, bicycling, tennis, public affairs reading, radio and TV. Home: 15 Grove St Orono ME 04473-1520 Office: Univ Maine Dept Journalism & Comm 5724 Dunn Hall Orono ME 04469-5724

BENNETT, CATHERINE JUNE, data processing manager, educator, consultant; b. Augusta, Ga., June 19, 1950; d. Robert Stogner and Catherine Sue (Jordan) Robinson; m. Danny Marvin Bennett, Sept. 5, 1971; children: Timothy Jordan, Robert Daniel. BS in Stats., U. Ga., 1971, MA in Bus., 1973. Programmer William M. Shenkel & Assocs., Athens, Ga., 1971-73; sys. analyst U. Ga., Athens, 1973-76; product cons. ISA/SUNGUARD, Atlanta, 1976-78, mgr. product support, 1980-85, hotline mgr., sr. fin. specialist, 1986-88, mem. edn. staff Investment Client Support, 1988-90, mgr. investment reporting, 1991-93, mgr. devel., 1993-95; dir. Fin. Reporting Solutions, 1998-99; project mgr. CGI, Atlanta, 1999—. Den leader pack 419 Cub Scouts, 1989-90, treas., 1990-95; head ofcl. Duluth Thunderbolts, 1994; mem. Gwinnett Swim League (sec. 1995—). Avocations: bridge, swimming, travel. Office: CGI 3080 Northwoods Cir Ste 200 Norcross GA 30071

BENNETT, CHARLES EDWARD, former congressman, educator; b. Canton, N.Y., Dec. 2, 1910; s. Walter James and Roberta Augusta (Broadhurst) B.; m. Jean Bennett; children: Bruce, James, Lucinda. JD, U. Fla., 1934; HHD (hon.), U. Tampa, 1950; LLD (hon.), Jacksonville U., 1972, Edward Waters Coll., 1988, U. North Fla., 1990; DSc (hon.), Maine Maritime Acad., 1989; LLD (hon.), St. Lawrence U., 1992, U. Fla., 1994. Bar: Fla. 1934. Practiced Jacksonville; mem. Fla. Ho. of Reps., 1941-42; mem. 81st-102d Congresses, 3d Fla. Dist., chair ethics com., mem. armed svcs. com., chmn. seapower subcom.; prof. Jacksonville (Fla.) U., 1992—. Author: Laudonniere and Fort Caroline, 1964, Settlement of Florida, 1968, Southernmost Battlefields of the Revolution, 1970, Three Voyages, 1974, Florida's French Revolution, 1981, Twelve on the River St. Johns, 1989; co-author: Congress and Conscience, 1970, A Quest for Glory, 1991. Capt. AUS, 1942-47; overseas in New Guinea andthe Philippines, including guerrilla fighting in Luzon. Decorated Silver Star, Bronze Star, Philippine Legion of Honor and Gold Cross, 1968, French Legion of Honor, 1976; recipient Disting. Service award Pres.'s Com. on Employment of Handicapped, 1969. Mem. DAV, Am. Legion, VFW, Fla. Bar Assn., Jacksonville Bar Assn., Jacksonville Jr. C. of C. (pres. 1939), U. Fla. Alumni Assn. (pres.). Democrat. Mem. Disciples of Christ Ch. Clubs: Masons, Lions, Rotary. Office: Jacksonville U Dept History Jacksonville FL 32211

BENNETT, CHARLES FRANKLIN, JR., biogeographer, educator; b. Oakland, Calif., Apr. 10, 1926; s. Charles Franklin and Charlotte Louise (Normand) B.; m. Carole Ann Messenger, Nov. 30, 1947; 1 child, Ashley Lynn. PhD, UCLA, 1959. Instr. UCLA, 1959-60, asst. prof., 1960-65, assoc. prof., 1965-69, prof. biogeography, 1969—; prof. emeritus, 1993—; cons. in field. Author: Human Influence on Zoogeography of Panama, 1968, Man and Earth's Ecosystems, 1976, Conservation of Natural Resources, 1983; contbr. articles to profl. jours. Guggenheim fellow, 1970-71. Fellow AAAS, Royal Geog. Soc.; mem. Ecol. Soc. Am., Brit. Ecol. Soc., Assn. Tropical Biology, Soc. for Conservation Biology, Fauna and Flora Preservation Soc., Am. Inst. Biol. Scis. Avocation: collecting natural history books. Home: 317 S Anita Ave Los Angeles CA 90049-3805 Office: UCLA Dept Geography 405 Hilgard Ave Los Angeles CA 90095-9000

BENNETT, CHARLES H., director programs. Fellow IBM T.J. Watson Rsch. Ctr., Yorktown Heights, 1995—. Mem. Nat. Acad. of Scis. Office: IBM TJ Watson Rsch Ctr PO Box 218 Yorktown Heights NY 10598-0218*

BENNETT, CHARLES LEON, vocational and graphic arts educator; b. Salem, Oreg., Feb. 5, 1951; s. Theodore John and Cora Larena (Rowland) B.; m. Cynthia Alice Hostman, June 12, 1976 (div.); m. Lynn Marie Toland, Aug. 12, 1977 (div.); children: Mizzy Marie, Charles David; m. Christina M. Crawford, Dec. 19, 1987 (div.). AS in Vocat. Tchr. Edn., Clackamas C.C., 1977; AS in Gen. Studies, Linn Benton C.C., 1979; BS in Gen. Studies, Ea. Oreg. State Coll., 1994. Tchr. printing Tongue Point Job Corps, Astoria, Oreg., 1979-80; tchr., dept. chmn. Portland (Oreg.) pub. schs., 1980—; owner, mgr. printing and pub. co., Portland, 1981-87. With AUS, 1970-72. Mem. NRA, Oreg. Vocat. Trade-Tech. Assn. (dept. chmn., pres. graphic arts div., Indsl. Educator of Year 1981-82), Oreg. Vocat. Assn. (Vocat. Tchr. of Yr. 1982-83), Graphic Arts Tech. Found., In-Plant Printing Mgmt. Assn., Internat. Graphic Arts Edn. Assn. (v.p. N.W. region VI), Oreg. Assn. Manpower Spl. Needs Personnel, Oreg. Indsl. Arts Assn., Internat. Platform Assn. Nat. Assn. Quick Printers, Am. Vocat. Assn., Pacific Printing & Imaging Assn., Inplant Printing Mgmt. Assn., Portland Club Lithographers and Printing House Craftsmen. Republican. Home: 20295 S Unger Rd Beavercreek OR 97004-8884 Office: 546 NE 12th Ave Portland OR 97232-2719

BENNETT, CORNELIUS, professional football player; b. Birmingham, Ala., Aug. 25, 1965; m. Tracey Bennett. Student, U. Ala. With Buffalo Bills, 1987-96, Atlanta Falcons, 1996-98; linebacker Indianapolis Colts, 1999—. Named to Pro Bowl team, 1988, 90-93, Sporting News All-Pro team, 1988, Sporting News Coll. All-Am. team, 1984-86; recipient Lombardi award, 1986. Office: Indianapolis Colts Atlanta Falcons Complex 7001 W 56th St Indianapolis IN 46254*

BENNETT, DONALD DALTON, grocery stores executive; b. Jefferson City, Mo., June 16, 1936; s. Dalton and Lola (Hudson) B.; m. Donna Waggaman, Oct. 18, 1958; children: David, Donna Kay, Dennis, Deanna. BA, Butler U., 1959; MA, Mich. State U., 1961. Owner, mgr. Kroger, Jefferson City, 1951-58, Model Markets, San Antonio, 1958-62, Colonial Stores, Cin., 1962-68; v.p. procurement and distbn. P. A. & S. Small, York, Pa., 1968-74; v.p. distbn. Carr Gottstein, Anchorage, 1974-79; div. pres., exec. v.p., bd. dirs. Wetterau, Inc., St. Louis, 1979-90; pres., chief exec. officer Richfood, Inc./Richfood Holdings, Inc., Richmond, Va., 1990—, chmn., chief exec. officer, 1995-98; bd. dirs. Richfood, Inc./Richfood Holdings, Inc., Richmond, 1998—. Mem. Nat. Am. Wholesale Grocers Assn. (bd. dirs.), Nat. Grocers Assn. (bd. dirs.), Food Mktg. Inst. (bd. dirs.), Internat. Grocers Alliance. Office: Richfood Inc/Richfood Holdings Inc 4860 Cox Rd Ste 300 Glen Allen VA 23060-9250*

BENNETT, DOUGLAS CARLETON, academic administrator; b. Rochester, N.Y., June 25, 1946; s. Frank Clinton Jr. and Roberta Lincoln (Evans) B.; m. Dulany Young Ogden, June 20, 1981 (div. 1993); 1 child, Thomas Baldrige; m. Ellen Trout, 1997. BA magna cum laude, Haverford Coll., 1968; M of Philosophy, Yale U., 1971, PhD, 1976. Asst. prof. dept. polit. sci. Temple U., Phila., 1976-80, assoc. prof., 1980-88, prof., assoc. dean Coll. Arts and Scis., 1988-89; provost Reed Coll., Portland, Oreg., 1989-93; exec. dir. Portland Area Libr. Sys., 1993-94; v.p. Am. Coun. Learned Socs., N.Y.C., 1994-97; pres. Earlham Coll., Richmond, Ind., 1997—. Author: Transnational Corporations v.s. the State, 1985; contbr. numerous articles and book revs. to polit. sci. jours. Mem. nat. community rels. com. Am. Friends Svc. Commn., Phila., 1982-86, mem. Latin Am. panel internat. div., 1985-89, clk. Latin Am. panel, 1988-89; bd. trustees Germantown Friends Sch., 1985-89, Friends Sem., N.Y.C., 1996-97; trustee Germantown monthly meeting Soc. of Friends Ch., 1984-89. Recipient Alumni award Haverford Coll., 1988; fellow Woodrow Wilson Internat. Ctr. for Scholars, 1980-81; fellowship grantee Am. Coun. Learned Socs./Social Sci. Rsch. Coun., 1976-77, Carnegie Endowment for Internat. Peace, 1976-77. Mem. Ctr. for Rsch. Librs. (bd. dirs. 1997—). Democrat. Avocations: reading, films. Office: Earlham Coll 801 National Rd W Richmond IN 47374-4021

BENNETT, DOUGLAS PHILIP, real estate executive, lawyer; b. White Plains, N.Y., Feb. 24, 1942; s. Philip Chauncy and Anne Blythe Bennett; m. Sandra Seton Benedikt, May 18, 1968; children: Heather Seton, Douglas Stratton, Robyn Kirsten, Rebecca Blythe, Alexandra Benedikt, Jon Christian; m. Susan Hurley, Sept. 13, 1990. BS, U.S. Mil. Acad., 1964; MBA magna cum laude, Am. U., 1971; JD, George Washington U., 1975. Bar: D.C. 1977, U.S. Ct. Appeals D.C. 1977. Commd. 2d lt. U.S. Army, 1964, advanced through grades to maj., resigned, 1970; congl. asst. U.S. Congress, Washington, 1971-72; exec. Firestone Corp., Washington, 1972-73; asst. to sec. U.S. Dept. Treasury, Washington, 1974-75; asst. to pres. The White House, Washington, 1975-77; pvt. practice law Washington, 1977-88; pres. Hudson River Ptnrs., Washington, 1989—. Bd. visitors U.S. Mil. Acad., West Point, N.Y., 1977-80, trustee, 1980-90; acting gen. counsel U.S. Dept. Edn., Washington, 1981; mem. various presdl. bds., Washington. Mem. Mil. Order of Carabao, Congl. Country Club, Met. Club Washington, Day Club. Republican. Roman Catholic. Avocations: golf, skiing, reading, travel. E-mail: hrptrs@aol.com. Office: Hudson River Ptnrs Ste 415 700 New Hampshire Ave NW Washington DC 20551

BENNETT, EDITH LILLIAN, lay church worker, radio personality; b. Livermore, Ky., June 21, 1931; d. Dorsey Slade and Isa Carey (Taylor) B. AS, Owensboro (Ky.) Bus. Coll., 1950; student, Mid Continent Bible Coll., Owensboro, Ky., 1991-96. Various positions including sec., office mgr., writer-dir. Sta. WOMI, Owensboro, 1950—; fin. sec. Third Bapt. Ch., Owensboro, 1981—; pres. West Central Kentucky Fam. Research Assn. Radio personality 4-VOC, Haiti, WOMI & WVJS Radio weekly; author, compiler, editor numerous publs. on Livermore history, genealogy and slavery. Sunday sch. tchr. Third Bapt. Ch.; 2d v.p. Hunt Family Found., Ky., 1958—; instr. AARP 55-Alive Dirving, started video section (with DAR) in new Livermore Lib. Named to Honorable Order of Ky. Colonels, 1969, Someone Spl., Owensboro, 1984, honored for 47 years in radio with keys to cities, Livermore and Owensboro, 1997. Mem. Owensboro Choral Soc. (co-chmn., presenter MESSIAH benefits 1940—), DAR (local officer 1960—, state officer 1989—). Home: 725 Scherm Rd Apt 5C Owensboro KY 42301-6067 Office: Third Bapt Ch PO Box 808 527 Allen St Owensboro KY 42302 also: WOMI/WVJS Radio PO Box 1330 Owensboro KY 42302-1330

BENNETT, EDWARD HENRY, reinsurance executive; b. Glens Falls, N.Y., July 22, 1917; s. Harry and Elizabeth Chandler (Clark) B.; m. Louise Faris, Aug. 3, 1946; children: Faris Elizabeth Ramseur, Anne Louise Petronis. AB, Princeton U., 1940. With Guy Carpenter & Co., Inc., N.Y.C., 1940-51; asst. v.p. Guy Carpenter & Co., Inc., 1951-54, v.p., dir., 1954-76, vice chmn., chief adminstrv. officer, 1976-82; dir. Mitsui Marine & Fire Ins. Co. of Am., N.Y.C., 1987—; bd. dirs. Bartlett Carry Club, Inc., Tupper Lake, N.Y., 1988—. Maj. USAAF, 1942-46, lt. col. USAFR. Decorated Legion of Merit. Mem. SAR, Res. Officers Assn., Princeton Club of N.Y., Nassau Club of Princeton, The Down Town Assn. N.Y. Republican. Episcopalian. Address: 6 Heerdt Farm Rd Pound Ridge NY 10576-1616

BENNETT, EDWARD VIRDELL, JR., surgeon; b. Nashville, July 17, 1947; s. Edward Virdell and Florence Elaine (Nelson) B. *Parents were graduates of Fisk University. Father was a general surgeon in Dayton, Ohio for over 20 years after clinical and research fellowships at Peter Bent Brigham Hospital, Boston. Three daughters all graduated from Spelman College. Elizabeth is a medical student in Nashville. Christina, lives in Atlanta. Melanie is also a medical student* BA in Biology, Fisk U., 1969; MD cum laude, Ohio State U., 1973. Fellow in surgery Johns Hopkins U., Balt., 1973-75; intern, then resident Johns Hopkins Hosp., Balt., 1973-75; resident in surgery and cardiothoracic surgery Albany Med. Ctr. Hosp., N.Y., 1975-80, instr. in surgery, 1976-80; asst. prof. surgery Health Ctr., U. Tex.-San Antonio, 1980-83; practice medicine specializing in cardiothoracic surgery, Sayre, Pa., 1983-91; chief cardiac surgery Guthrie Clin. Ltd., Sayre, 1990-91; mem. staff Robert Packer Hosp., Sayre, 1983-91; mem. Guthrie Clinic, Ltd., Sayre, 1983-91; cardiac surgeon Albany Cardiothoracic Surgeons, P.C., 1991—; mem. staff Albany Med. Ctr. Hosp., 1991—, St. Peters Hosp., Albany, 1991—; clin. asst. prof. surgery Albany Med. Coll., 1991—; chief cardiac surgery St. Peter's Hosp., Albany, 1997—. Mem. N.Y. State Cardiac Adv. Com., 1995—. *Extensive experience in clinical practice and research. Selected to Top Doctors in the Northeast, 1997 and Top Doctors in America, 1998. As chief of cardiac surgery at St. Peters Hospital was leader of development and reorganization of program that has earned many recognitions. The cardiac surgery program received five star rating by Health Care Report Cards, 1998; named Top 100 Cardiac Hospitals and Top 100 hospitals for Benchmarks of Success. The only program in New York State to be selected and ranked in top 10 nationally for bypass and valve surgery results* Contbr. articles to med. jours. Producer med. motion picture. Fellow Am. Coll. Chest Physicians, Am. Coll. Cardiology, ACS; mem. Soc. Thoracic Surgeons, Internat. Soc. for Heart Transplantation, Sigma Xi, Alpha Omega Alpha, Omega Psi Phi. Republican. Episcopalian. Avocations: sailing; scuba diving; skiing. Fellow ACS, Am. Coll. Chest Physicians, Am. Coll. Cardiology; mem. Soc. Thoracic Surgeons, Internat. Soc. for Heart Transplantation, Am. Heart Assn. (bd. dirs. NE Pa. chpt.), Sigma Xi, Alpha Omega Alpha, Omega Psi Phi. Office: Albany Cardiothoracic Surgeons 319 S Manning Blvd Ste 301 Albany NY 12208-1790

BENNETT, EILEEN PATRICIA, copy editor, reporter; b. Garfield, N.J., July 12, 1954; d. Jerry Ralph and Marie Ann (Mangano) Tedesco; m. Charles Corson Bennett, Sr., May 26, 1979; stepchildren: Charles Jr., Wendy; adopted daughter, Unity. AA, Cumberland County Coll., 1974; BA, Glassboro State Coll., 1976. Reporter Today's Sunbeam, Salem, N.J., 1975; reporter Bridgeton (N.J.) Evening News, 1976-81, city editor, 1981-86, mng. editor, 1986-90, editor, 1990-93; editor Millville (N.J.) News, 1991-93; reporter, stringer Phila. Bull., 1979, Phila. Inquirer, 1979; copy editor, staff writer Press of Atlantic City, 1993-95, 96; asst. editor The Current Newspapers, Pleasantville, 1995-96; staff writer Press of Atlantic City, 1996—. Recipient Voice of Am. award VFW, Bridgeton, Best Column award Am. Pub. Co., 1992. Mem. Soc. Profl. Journalists, Nat. Hist. PreservationTrust, Mauricetown Hist. Soc. Roman Catholic. Home: 2 D St Mauricetown NJ 08329 Office: Press Atlantic City Devins Ln Pleasantville NJ 08232

BENNETT, FRED GILBERT, lawyer; b. May 28, 1946. HBA magna cum laude, U. Utah, 1970; JD, U. Calif., 1973. Bar: Calif. 1974. Ptnr. Gibson, Dunn & Crutcher, L.A., 1980-98; sr. ptnr. Quinn Emanuel Urquhart Oliver & Hedges, 1998—; mem. nat. com. on arbitration U.S. Coun. for Internat. Bus., 1984—, chmn. subcom., 1989—; comml. and constrn. arbitrator Internat. C. of C./Am. Arbitration Assn. Large Complex Case Panel; chmn. continuing edn. com. Am. Aarbitration Assn. Large Complex Case Panel. Mng. editor UCLA Law Rev., 1972-73. Mem. ABA, Internat. Bar

Assn., L.A. County Bar Assn., Phi Beta Kappa. Office: Quinn Emanuel Urquhart Oliver & Hedges 865 S Figueroa St Los Angeles CA 90017-2543

BENNETT, GENEVIEVE, artist; b. Chgo., Feb. 11, 1927; d. Joseph and Mary Sieczka; m. William A. Bennett, Jan. 31, 1953; children: William George, J. Daniel, Gordon Dean. BA, Calif. State U., Fullerton, 1974; MA, Calif. State U., Long Beach, 1978. Artist Anaheim, Calif.; part-time tchr. art Ebell Club Anaheim, 1985-97, art tchr. Whittier and Anaheim, Calif.; lectr. on N.Am. temple mound builders. One-woman shows include Calif. Poly. U., Ponoma, 1995, Orange County Fair, Calif., 1995, Anaheim Mus., 1997. Mem. Nat. League Am. Pen Women (state v.p. 1997-98, Orange County br. pres. 1997-98, recipient Women of Achievement award, 1998), Calif. State U. Art Alliance, So. Calif. Women's Caucus for Art, Orange County Fine Arts, Phi Delta Gamma (Phi chpt.). Avocations: archaeology, piano, music, travel, art meetings. Home: 2026 W Judith Ln Anaheim CA 92804-6511

BENNETT, GEORGE FREDERICK, investment manager; b. Quincy, Mass., Aug. 16, 1911; s. Wallace Cherrington and Lois E. (Williams) B.; m. Helen F. Brigham, Oct. 25, 1935; children—Peter C., George Frederick, Robert B. A.B. cum laude, Harvard, 1933. With First Boston Corp., Boston, 1934-37, Newton, Abbe & Co., Boston, 1937-43; with State Street Research & Mgmt. Co., Boston, 1943—; partner State Street Research & Mgmt. Co., 1946—; chmn. State St. Exchange Fund, Boston; pres. State St. Investment Corp., Boston, Fed. St. Fund, Inc., Boston; dir. Campbell Taggert, Inc., Dallas, Middle South Utilities, Inc., N.Y.C., N.E. Electric System, Hewlett Packard Co., Palo Alto, Calif., Fla. Power & Light Co., Miami, Ford Motor Co., Detroit, John Hancock Mut. Life Ins. Co., Boston, Hanna Mining Co., Cleve. Treas. Harvard U., Harvard-Yenching Inst.; trustee Wheaton (Ill.) Coll., Rockefeller U., Gordon Conwell Theol. Sem., Com. Econ. Devel., Washington. Mem. Pi Eta. Clubs: Harvard (Boston and N.Y.C.); Union (Boston); Links (N.Y.C.). Home: 712 Main St Hingham MA 02043-3327 Office: State Street Rsch & Mgmt Co One Financial Ctr Boston MA 02111

BENNETT, GEORGE H., JR., lawyer, healthcare company executive. BS, U. Miami, 1975; JD, Ohio State U., 1978. Bar: Ohio 1978. Assoc. Mortiz McClure Hughes & Kerscher, 1978-80, Baker & Hostetler, 1980-83; gen. counsel Cardinal Distbn. Inc., 1984-86, v.p., 1986-91, v.p., chief adminstrv. officer, 1991-94; exec. v.p., gen. counsel Cardinal Health Inc., Dublin, Ohio, 1994—. Office: Cardinal Health Inc 5555 Glendon Ct Dublin OH 43016-3249*

BENNETT, GEORGE NELSON, biochemistry educator; b. St. Edward, Nebr., Oct. 26, 1946; s. Glenn Nelson and Esther Adelaide (McBride) B.; m. Lolin T. Wang, Dec. 11, 1983; children: Alan N., Neal K. BS, U. Nebr., 1968; PhD, Purdue U., 1974. Postdoctoral fellow Stanford U., Palo Alto, Calif., 1975-78; asst. prof. Rice U., Houston, 1978-84, assoc. prof., 1984-92, prof., 1992—. Grantee NIH, NSF, USDA, Dept. of Energy, Army Rsch. OFfice, R.A. Welch Found. Mem. Am. Chem. Soc., Am. Soc. for Microbiology, Fedn. Soc. Exptl. Biology. Office: Rice Univ Biochemistry & Cell Biology 6100 Main St Houston TX 77005-1892

BENNETT, GERARD PAUL, computer scientist; b. Windsor, Ont., Can., Oct. 31, 1937; came to U.S., 1955; s. Onias and Yvonne (Barnier) B.; m. Patricia Flach, Aug. 30, 1969; 1 child, Douglas Paul. BA in Bus. Mgmt./BA in Computer Info., U. North Tex., 1974. Computer systems programmer The Banks of N.Y., N.Y.C., 1961-67, LTV Electrosystems, Greenville, Tex., 1967-70; software devel. mgr. Cybertek Data Systems, Dallas, 1970-75, Data Gen. Corp., Dallas, 1975-76; computer systems engr. Datapoint Corp., San Antonio, 1976-85; computer rsch. analyst USAA, San Antonio, 1985—. Bd. dirs. Boerne (Tex.) Fine Arts Found., 1985-90; exec. dir. Lordel Inst., Fair Oaks, Tex., 1989-99; sci. fair judge Boerne Ind. Sch. Dist., 1986—; tech. cons. Boerne Pub. Libr., 1989-98. Mem. NRA, The Planetary Soc., Nat. Space Soc., Kiwanis of Boerne (v.p., pres. 1978-87, Pres.'s award 1984). Republican. Episcopalian. Avocations: astronomy, archaeology, native American history. Home: 146 Steel Valley Dr Boerne TX 78006-7018 Office: USAA Applied Rsch Group 9800 Fredericksburg Rd San Antonio TX 78288

BENNETT, GROVER BRYCE, engineering consultant; b. Shelley, Idaho, Apr. 9, 1921; s. Grover T. and Guila (Young) B.; m. Barbara A. Beedle, July 30, 1944; children—William G., Rebecca I., Alan B. B.S. in Civil Engring, U. Idaho, 1943; M.S. (Research fellow), U. Wash., 1949. Constrn. engr. Pan Am. Airways, Seattle, 1943-44; instr. civil engring. Seattle U, 1946-48; asst. prof. U. Idaho, 1949-51; materials engr. Idaho Dept. Hwys., 1951-53, asst. state hwy. engr., 1955-56, state hwy. engr., 1956-64; asphalt mgr. Shell Oil Co., Sacramento, 1953-55; with Internat. Engring. Co., Inc., 1964-83; v.p., gen. mgr. Internat. Engring. Co., Inc., San Francisco, 1967-71; exec. v.p. Internat. Engring. Co., Inc., 1971-83, also dir.; mem. engring. adv. bd. U. Idaho, 1968-74; adv. com. Project Mgmt. Inst., 1976-82. Served with USNR, 1944-46. Fellow ASCE. Home: 29 Medina Way Rancho Mirage CA 92270-4715

BENNETT, HAROLD CLARK, clergyman, religious organization administrator; b. Asheville, N.C., July 30, 1924; s. Charles C. and Emily H. (Clark) B.; m. Phyllis Jean Metz, Aug. 17, 1947; children: Jeffrey Clark, John Scott, Cynthia Ann Bennett Howard. Student, Asheville Biltmore Jr. Coll., 1946, Mars Hill Coll., 1946-47; B.A., Wake Forest U., 1949; postgrad., Duke U. Div. Sch., 1949-51; M.Div., So. Bapt. Theol. Sem., 1953; LL.D. (hon.), Stetson U., 1968; D.D. (hon.), Campbell U., 1982, Wake Forest U., 1985; STD (hon.), Southwest Bapt. U., 1991. Clk. FBI, Washington, 1942-43; ordained to ministry Baptist Ch., 1948; pastor Glen Royal Bapt. Ch., Wake Forest, N.C., 1948-51; chaplain Ky. State Reformatory, LaGrange, 1951-53, Ky. Woman's Prison, 1951-53; pastor Westport (Ky.) Bapt. Ch., 1952; asst. pastor First Bapt. Ch., Shreveport, La., 1953-55; pastor Beech St. Bapt. Ch., Texarkana, Ark., 1955-60; supt. new work Sunday Sch. Dept., Sunday Sch. bd. So. Bapt. Conv., Nashville, Tenn., 1960-62; interim pastor Little West Fork Bapt. Ch., Hopkinsville, Ky., 1960, Two Rivers Bapt. Ch., Nashville, 1962; sec. met. missions home mission bd. So. Bapt. Conv., Atlanta, Ga., 1962-65; dir. missions div. Bapt. Gen. Conv. Tex., Dallas, 1965-67; exec. sec., treas. Fla. Bapt. Conv., Jacksonville, 1967-79; pres., treas. exec. com. So. Bapt. Conv., Nashville, 1979-92, pres. emeritus, 1992—; vice chmn. Religion in Am. Life, 1979-91; mem. bd. incorporators Covenant Life Ins. Co., Phila., 1990-93; chmn. U.S. Ch. Leaders, 1987-89, active, 1979-83; mem. Bapt. Joint Com. on Pub. Affairs, Washington, 1979-91, Internat. Adv. Com. for World Evangelization, 1986-89; vis. prof. So. Bapt. Theol. Sem., Louisville, 1993-94; pres. N.Am Bapt. Fellowship, 1994-96, mem., 1979-97. Compiler: God's Awesome Challenge, 1980; Contbr. numerous articles to religious publs.; author: Reflections of Faith, 1983—. Mem. adv. coun. Fla. State Alcoholism, 1973-78; trustee Fla. Meml. Coll., Miami, 1967-74, Am. Bible Soc., N.Y.C., 1980—; mem. Nashville Literacy Task Force; deacon First Bapt. Ch., Nashville, 1991-94, 98—. With A.C. USN, 1942-45. Named Ky. Col.; recipient Good Shepherd award Boy Scouts Am., 1986. Mem. Assn. Bapt. State Exec. Secs. (pres. 1978-79), Assn. Bapt. State Conv. Ch. Bond Plans (pres. 1978-79), Fla. Bapt. State Bd. Missions (exec. dir., treas., sec. 1967-79), Bapt. World Alliance (mem. gen. coun. 1979—, v.p. 1990-95), Am. Bible Sioc. (trustee 1980—, corp. sec. 1995-96, vice-chmn. 1996—), Nashville C. of C. (mem. law and justice com. 1984-93), dir. First Am. Nat. Bank, TN, 1987-94, mem. Souper Bowl of Caring, Columbia, SC, 1997 (chmn. 1997—). Home: 202 Long Valley Rd Brentwood TN 37027-4945 *In my life, with the variety of conflicts and demands thrust my way, I have discovered that a personal relationship with Jesus Christ is the only way to maintain an inner peace. It is a joy to be a Christian and to have the privilege of serving as an ambassador for Him. I long for others to come to have a similar peace with God.*

BENNETT, HARRY LOUIS, college educator; b. Ansonia, Conn., Dec. 22, 1923; s. Louis and Florence (Swole) B.; m. Claire Davis, July 2, 1949; 1 dau., Lisa Brierley. BA, Yale U., 1944, MA, 1948, PhD, 1954. Welfare investigator Conn., 1950-51; mem. faculty Quinnipiac Coll., Hamden, Conn., 1951—; prof. history, dean coll. Quinnipiac Coll., 1956-67, v.p. acad. affairs, 1967-69, 72-90, prof., chmn. history, 1969-72, provost, 1972-90, acting pres., 1978-79, provost emeritus, 1990, emeritus prof. history, 1992—; sec.-treas. Conn. Conf. Community and Jr. Colls., 1955-62, v.p., 1962-64, pres., 1964-65; chmn. standing com. accreditation Conn. Council Higher Edn., 1964-65, vice chmn., 1985-86; chmn. Conn. Adv. Com. on Accreditation, 1986-88. 1st lt., inf. AUS, 1944-46, MTO. Mem. Am. Hist. Assn., Am. Cath. hist. Assn., New Eng. Hist. Assn., Orgn. Am. Historians, Assn. Study Conn. History, Am. Mil. Inst., U.S. Naval Inst., Conn. Hist. Soc., New Haven Colony Hist. Soc. Roman Catholic. Home: 21 Knollwood Rd North Haven CT 06473-4328

BENNETT, HERD LEON, lawyer; b. Portsmouth, Ohio, Oct. 17, 1934. BA, Duke U., 1956; JD, Cornell U., 1959. Bar: Ohio 1959. Ptnr. Bennett & Bennett, Eaton, Ohio, 1959—; asst. atty. gen. of Ohio, 1962-63; spl. counsel to atty. gen. of Ohio, 1963-70; trustee Ohio State Bar Found., 1984-92, chair planning and rsch. com., 1986-92, awards com., 1988-90, pres. 1991-92; trustee Preble County Law Libr. Assn., 1970-72; trustee Ohio Legal Continuing Edn. Inst., 1990-91, 93-99, treas., 1993-94, vice chmn., 1994-95, chmn., 1995-96; trustee Eaton Found., 1978—, v.p., 1980—; trustee Nat. Hummel Found. and Mus., 1982—; bd. dirs. Ohio Bar Title Ins. Co., 1991-98, Northedge Shopping Ctr., Inc., Miller's Super Markets, Inc. Trustee Eaton Cmty. Improvement Corp., 1981-94 (v.p. 1987-94), trustee Preble County Area Cmty. Improvement Corp., 1994— (pres. 1994—); mem. Eaton Area C. of C., 1959—; mem., moderator, Sunday Sch. tchr. Concord United Ch. of Christ, Eaton H.S. Alumni Assn. (pres. 1983-84, permanent advisor); exec. officer Duke U. Offie Devel., 1956-90, admissions interview chmn. for S.W. Ohio, 1994-97. Mem. ABA (real property, probate and trust law sect.), Nat. Assn. Criminal Def. Lawyers, Am. Judicature Soc., Ohio State Bar Assn. (mem. bd. govs. 1997—, mem. legal ethics and profl. conduct com. 1981—, coun. dels. 1981—), Preble County Bar Assn. (v.p. 1972-74, pres. 1974-76). Office: Bennett & Bennett 200 W Main St Eaton OH 45320-1748

BENNETT, JACK FRANKLIN, oil company executive; b. Macon, Ga., Jan. 17, 1924; s. Andrew Jackson and Mary Eloise (Franklin) B.; m. Shirley Elizabeth Goodwin, Sept. 17, 1949; children: Jackson Goodwin, Philip Davies, Hugh Franklin, Elizabeth Fraser. BA, Yale U., 1944; MA, Harvard U., 1949, PhD, 1951. Negotiator Joint U.S.-U.K. Export Import Agy., Berlin, Germany, 1946-47; teaching fellow finance Harvard, 1949-51; spl. asst. to adminstr. Tech. Assistance Program, U.S. Dept. State, Washington, 1951-52; economist U.S. Mut. Security Agy., Washington, 1952-53; sr. economist Presdl. Commn. on Fgn. Econ. Policy, 1954; sr. fgn. exch. analyst Exxon Corp., N.Y.C., 1955-58; dep. European fin. rep. Exxon Corp., London, 1958-60; treas. Esso. Petroleum Co., Ltd., London, 1960-61; asst. treas. Exxon Corp., N.Y.C., 1961-65; mgr. gen. econs. dept. Exxon Corp., 1965-66, mgr. coordination and planning dept., 1966-67; gen. mgr. supply dept. Exxon Co., U.S.A., Houston, 1967-69; v.p., dir. Exxon Internat., N.Y.C., 1969-71; sr. v.p. Exxon Corp., N.Y.C., 1975-89, also bd. dirs., ret., 1989; dep. undersec. for monetary affairs U.S. Dept. Treasury, Washington, 1971-74, undersec. for monetary affairs, 1974-75. Contbr. articles to profl. jours. Trustee Com. Econ. Devel. With USNR, 1943-46. Mem. University Club (N.Y.C.), Stanwich Club (Greenwich, Conn.), York (Maine) Club, Blind Brook Club, John's Island Club (Fla.), Wentmouth-by-the-Sea Club. Republican. Office: 141 Taconic Rd Greenwich CT 06831-3113

BENNETT, JACQUELINE BEEKMAN, school psychologist; b. Santa Paula, Calif., Sept. 4, 1946; d. Jack Edward and Margaret Blanche (MacPherson) Beekman.; m. Thomas LeRoy Bennett Jr., Aug. 5, 1972; children: Shannon, Brian, Laurie. BA, U. Calif., Davis, 1968; MS, Colo. State U., 1975, PhD, 1984. Histologist Sch. Veterinary Medicine, Davis, 1969-71; sch. psychologist Poudre Sch. Dist. R-1, Ft. Collins, Colo., 1983-95, Brain Injury Recovery Program, Ft. Collins, 1995—. Mem. augment panel Colo. State Grievance Bd., 1988-94; nominating chmn. United Presbyn. Women, Timnath, Colo., 1982, pres., 1986; mem. Women and the Ch. com. Boulder Presbytery, Colo., 1985-86; elder Timnath Presbyn. Ch., 1985—. Mem. Colo. Soc. Sch. Psychologists (cert.), Nat. Assn. Sch. Psychologists (cert.), NEA, Am. Psychol. Assn., Ft. Collins Parents of Twins (pres. 1977-78), Sigma Xi, Phi Kappa Phi. Democrat. Club: Squaredusters (Ft. Collins) (v.p. 1977-78). Avocations: camping, gardening, swimming, cooking. Home: 213 Camino Real Fort Collins CO 80524-8907 Office: Brain Injury Recovery Program 1049 Robertson St Fort Collins CO 80524-3926

BENNETT, JAMES CHESTER, computer consultant, real estate developer; b. Chico, Calif., May 14, 1932; s. George Clerk and Georgia Mae (James) B.; m. Grace M. Schutrum, Feb. 14, 1955 (div. 1967); children: Ronald, Becky Ann, Todd Bryant. BA in Bus., Calif. State U., Long Beach, 1965. Sgt. USAF, 1947-62; customer engr. IBM, L.A., 1962-70; mgr. computer systems Continental Airlines, L.A., 1970-82; instr. ITT Tech. Inst., Buena Park, Calif., 1982-84; dir. Ramasat Comm., LTD, Bangkok, Thailand, 1984-89; instr. ITT Tech. Inst., San Diego, 1989-90; pres. The Systems Group, Inc., Ramona, Calif., 1990—. Avocations: computer graphics, amateur radio. Home: PO Box 2032 1446 Cedar St Ramona CA 92065-1326

BENNETT, JAMES EDWARD, retired plastic surgeon, educator; b. Burlington, Wis., May 19, 1925; s. John Francis and Florence (Mauer) B.; m. Ellen MacPherson, June 18, 1956; children: David, Martha, Thomas, Jonathan. Student, Notre Dame U., 1943-44, Mass. Inst. Tech., 1944-45; M.D., Northwestern U., 1950. Diplomate Am. Bd. Plastic Surgery (dir. 1978-84, chmn. 1983-84, chmn. residency rev. com. 1978-79), Am. Bd. Surgery. Intern Milw. County Hosp., 1949-50; resident in surgery U. Mich. Hosp., 1953-58; gen. practice medicine Burlington, 1950-51; exchange fellow in plastic surgery Wales, 1956-57; resident in plastic surgery U. Tex. Sch. Medicine, Galveston, 1958-61; asst. prof. surgery, dir. plastic surgery Ohio State U. Sch. Medicine, 1961-64; prof. surgery, dir. plastic surgery Ind. U. Med. Center, 1964-91, Willis D. Gatch prof. surgery, 1981-91, Willis D. Gatch prof. emeritus, 1991—. Fellow ACS (2d v.p. 1991-92); mem. Plastic Surgery Rsch. Coun. (chmn. 1970), Frederick A. Coller Surg. Soc. (councillor 1981-83), Am. Soc. Plastic and Reconstructive Surgeons, Am. Assn. Surgery Trauma, Am. Assn. Plastic Surgeons (sec. 1978-81, v.p. 1981-82, pres. 1983-84), Am. Surg. Assn., Ind. Trotting and Pacing Horse Assn. (chmn. 1993-94), Phi Rho Sigma. Home: PO Box 243A Monrovia IN 46157-0243

BENNETT, JAMES MARVIN, consulting company executive; b. St. Louis, June 28, 1939; s. Marvin L. and Florence Anntonette (Rumph) B.; m. Barbara Virginia Rostron, July 2, 1965; children: J. Austin, Bradley Alexander. BS, Washington U., St. Louis, 1963, PhD in Botany, 1968. Prof. biology NYU, 1968-70; Ford Found. lectr. New Sch. Social Rsch., 1968-70; dir. environ. affairs Joseph Schlitz Brewing Co., Milw., 1970-75, dir. environ. and indsl. affairs, 1975-78, dir. govt. rels., 1978-82; exec. v.p., gen. mgr. Consultancy Intenrat., N.Y.C., 1984-86; pres., CEO Bennett & Assocs. (name now Bennett Environ. Mgmt., Inc.), N.Y.C., 1982—; assoc. prof. environ. engring., N.Y.I.T., 1994—; cons. A.T. Kearney, Inc., N.Y., 1986—, Castlton Environ. Contractors, 1998—. NSF fellow, 1965-68. Mem. AAAS, N.Y. Acad. Scis. Office: Bennett Environ Mgmt Inc PO Box 8505 FDR Station New York NY 10022

BENNETT, JAMES PATRICK, healthcare executive; b. Huntsville, Ala., Oct. 20, 1957; s. Raymond Arthur and Shirley Marie (Breach) B.; m. Marcella Joanne Lakebrink, Sept. 28, 1979; children: Stephanie Erin, James Patrick Jr. BS, U. North Ala., 1979. CPA, Ala. With Ernst & Whinney, Birmingham, Ala., 1979-87, supr., 1983-86, sr. mgr., 1986-87; v.p. fin. Russ Pharms., Inc., Birmingham, 1987-89, v.p. ops., bd. dirs., 1989-91; group v.p. inpatient rehab. ops. HealthSouth Rehab. Corp., Birmingham, 1991-92, pres. inpatient ops., bd. dirs., 1992-95; pres. HealthSouth Rehab. Hosp., 1992-95; pres., COO Healthsouth Corp., Birmingham, 1995—; dir. Managed Care USA, Inc., Charlotte, N.C., 1996—, Physician Solutions, Inc., Dallas, 1997—, Biomed. Disposal, Inc., Atlanta, 1998—; bd. dirs. FAHS, 1998—, Arthritis Found. Ala. chpt., Am. Canfer Soc., Ala. chpt., 1996—. Treas. Shelby Com. of 100, Birmingham, 1987-89; chmn. U. North Ala. Ann. Fund Drive, 1995; chmn. rehab. com. Fedn. Am. Hosps., 1995-96; hon. chmn. Birmingham Multiple Sclerosis Soc., 1996; bd. dirs. Birmingham chpt. Am. Cancer Soc., 1996, Am. Sports Medicine Inst., 1995—. Nominee Leadership Birmingham, 1994, 95; recipient Cmty. Leadership award Multiple Sclerosis Soc., 1994; named outstanding alumnus, U. North Ala., 1997, Vol. of Yr., Ala. chpt. Am. Heart Assn., 1998. Mem. AICPA, Ala. Soc. CPAs, Am. Mgmt. Assn., Healthcare Fin. Mgmt. Assn. (regional v.p. 1987-88, Outstanding Mem. 1987), Nat. Assn. Accts., Secession Golf Club, Greystone Golf Club, Shoal Creek Golf Club, Elks. Roman Catholic. Avocations: golf, hiking, football. Home: 3732 Shady Cove Dr Birmingham AL 35243-2448 Office: Healthsouth Corp 1 Health S Pkwy Birmingham AL 35243

BENNETT, JAMES RONALD, secretary of state; b. Red Oak, Iowa, Jan. 3, 1940; s. George T. and Florence B. (Olson) B.; m. Luan Atkins, June 11, 1989; children: Donald B., Tara L.; 1 stepchild, Megan L. Scott. BS, Jacksonville State U., 1961; MA, U. Ala., 1979. Mem. Ala. Ho. of Reps., 1978-83; senator State of Ala., 1983-93, sec. of state, 1993—. Bd. trustees Jacksonville State U.; dir. Tammehill Ironworks Hist. State Park, 1990-93. Mem. Nat. Assn. Secs. of State (so. regional v.p.). Home: 1600 Shades Park Cove Birmingham AL 35209-5400 Office: PO Box 5616 Montgomery AL 36103-5616*

BENNETT, JAMES THOMAS, economics educator; b. Memphis, Oct. 19, 1942; m. Sara Ellen Dorman, Sept. 2, 1967. B.S. in Ops. Research magna cum laude, Case Inst. Tech., 1964, M.S. in Mgmt. Sci., 1966; Ph.D. in Econs., Case Western Res. U., 1970; student Grad. Sch. Bus., Columbia U., 1964-65. Teaching fellow Case Inst. Tech., 1968-69; instr. bus. Cleve. State U., 1967-68; asst. prof. econs. George Washington U., Washington, 1970-75; assoc. prof. econs. George Mason U., Fairfax, Va., 1975-77; Eminent Scholar and William P. Snavely prof. polit. economy and pub. policy George Mason U., 1975—; dir. John M. Olin Inst. for Employment Practice and Policy. Co-author: The Political Economy of Federal Government Growth: 1958-1978, 1980; Better Government at Half the Price, 1981; Deregulating Labor Relations, 1981; Underground Government: The Off-Budget Public Sector, 1983; Destroying Democracy: How Government Funds Partisan Politics, 1985, Unfair Competition: The Profits of Nonprofits, 1989, Patterns of Corporate Philanthrophy: Ideas, Advocacy and the Corporation, 1989, Health Research Charities: Image and Reality, 1990, Health Research Charities II: The Politics of Fear, 1991, Official Lies: How Washington Misleads Us, 1992, Unhealthy Charities: Hazardous to Your Health and Wealth, 1994, Cancer Scam: The Diversion of Federal Cancer Funds to Politics, 1998, The Food and Drink Police: America's Nanies, Busybodies, and Petty Tyrants, 1999; contbr. chpts. to books, articles to profl. jours.; editor Jour. Labor Rsch. Ford Found. scholar, 1960-64; Continental Grain Corp. fellow; McKinsey scholar; Case Inst. fellow, 1965-67; Fed. Res. Bank Cleve. fellow, 1969-70. Mem. Am. Econ. Assn., So. Econ. Assn., Pub. Choice Soc., Western Econ. Assn., Am. Statis. Assn., Phila. Soc., Mont Pelerin Soc., Phi Beta Kappa, Sigma Xi, Tau Beta Pi. Office: George Mason U Dept Econs Fairfax VA 22030

BENNETT, JANET HUFF, legislative staff member; b. Portland, Oreg., Oct. 6, 1932; d. Stephen Loren and Melba Sperry (Stout) Huff; m. Gerald Randolph Petrey, Oct. 11, 1950 (div. 1968); m. Michael Jesse Bennett, Dec. 30, 1968; children: Mark Randall, Karee Meg Petrey Cannon, Creighton Loren; also stepchildren. Student, U. Wash. With ZCMI Dept. Store, Salt Lake City, 1975-77; office mgr. Promised Valley Theatre, Salt Lake City, 1977-79; asst. state dir. U.S. Sen. Orrin Hatch, Utah, Salt Lake City, 1979-92; dep. state dir. Senator Robert Bennett, 1993—. Chair Utah Women's Conf., Salt Lake City, 1985-92, Conf. for Srs., 1989-92; mem. task force Prevention Ritual Abuse, 1991-93, 3d Dist. Judicial Nominating Commn., 1992-94; mem. Gov.'s Commn. on Women and Families, 1993—, chair, 1996-97; co-chair legis. issues Women's Legis. Coun., 1989-97, co-chair revenue-tax. com., 1998—; chair bd. dirs. Children's Mus. of Utah, Salt Lake City, 1989-90; bd. dirs. Utah Symphony, 1991-97, Utah Coun. for Crime Prevention, 1989—, Coalition for Utah Families, 1995—; pres. Utah Symphony Guild, 1992-93; hon. mem., bd. dirs. Utah Chamber Artists, 1995—; chair Gov.'s Conf. on Marriage, 1997-98. Mem. Nat. Assn. for Commns. for Women (bd. dirs. 1995—), Profl. Rep. Women, Utah Fedn. Rep. Women. Mem. LDS Ch. Avocation: painting. Office: Office of Senator R Bennett 4225 Bennett Federal Bldg Salt Lake City UT 84138

BENNETT, JANET SANDHOFF, physical education educator; b. Goodrich, Mich., Apr. 19, 1951; d. William John and Lucille Marie (Bates) Sandhoff; m. Gerald Alan Bennett; children: Richard Jay Permuy, Julie Lauren Huber, Kaycee Lynn Huber. AA, Manatee Jr. Coll., Bradenton, Fla., 1971; BA in Phys. Edn., U. South Fla., 1973, MA in Adaptive Phys. Edn., 1986; EdD, Nova Southeastern U., 1999. Dir. presch., tchr. Bayshore Reform Ch., Bradenton, 1983-86; tchr. gifted Bradenton Christian Sch., 1985-86; tchr. phys. edn. Harlee Mid. Sch., Bradenton, 1986-87; perceptual motor specialist Snitz Products, Bradenton, 1875-89; owner, dir., tchr. Jungle Gym, Mt. Pleasant, S.C., 1987-90; instr. Parent Workshops, Charleston, S.C., 1987—; owner, tchr. Jumpnastics, Charleston, 1987—, also bd. dirs., 1990—; instr. Trident Tech. Coll., Charleston, 1999—. Author: (book and tape) 5 and 10 You Can Do It Again, 1986; producer movement edn. movie, 1974. Mem. Nat. Phys. Edn. Assn., Nat. Assn. Parents and Tchrs. Children Under Six. Republican. Avocation: golf. Home: 2047 Hallahan Ct Mount Pleasant SC 29464-6250

BENNETT, JAY BRETT, medical device company executive; b. Durham, N.C., Dec. 13, 1961; s. James Leonard Jr. and Yoalder Kathleen (Brunson) B.; m. Trisha Helen Folds, Feb. 3, 1990; children: Lydia Helen, William Chisholm. BA in Econs., Wake Forest U., 1984; M Health Adminstrn., Duke U., 1986. Sr. cons. Ernst and Whinney (now Ernst and Young), Charlotte, N.C., 1986-89; assoc. dir. strategic planning SSI Med. Svcs., Inc., Charleston, S.C., 1989-92, dir. strategic planning, 1992-94; dir. planning and bus. devel. Hill-Rom, Inc., Charleston, S.C., 1994-96, bus. unit dir., 1996-99, v.p., 1999—; adj. prof. bus. and econs. Coll. Charleston, 1995—. Mem. alumni coun. Fuqua Sch. Bus., Duke U.; mem. Leadership Charleston '99. Mem. Am. Coll. Healthcare Execs., Nat. Trust for Historic Preservation, Am. Hosp. Assn., Nat. Subacute Care Assn. (industry adv. bd.), Soc. for Healthcare Planning and Mktg., Nat. Soc. SAR, Ducks Unltd., Quail Unltd., Trout Unltd. Avocations: outdoors, history of American South, photography.

BENNETT, JAY D., lawyer; b. Albany, Ga., June 3, 1952; s. J. Donald and Clara Louise (Jordan) B.; m. Susan Parker, June 9, 1974; children: Summer, Lillian, Sky. BA with honors, U. N.C., 1974; JD cum laude, Harvard U., 1977. Bar: U.S. Dist. Ct. (no. and mid. dist.) Ga., U.S. Ct. Appeals (4th, 5th, and 11th cirs.), U.S. Supreme Ct. Assoc. Alston & Bird, Atlanta, 1977-83, ptnr., 1983—. Morehead scholar Morehead Found. 1970-74. Mem. State Bar Ga., Atlanta Bar Assn., Lawyers Club Atlanta, Trial Attys. Am., Phi Beta Kappa. Avocations: flying, skydiving, motorcycling, fishing. Office: Alston & Bird LLP One Atlantic Ctr 1201 W Peachtree St NW Ste 4200 Atlanta GA 30309-3424*

BENNETT, JEAN LOUISE MCPHERSON, physicist, research scientist; b. Kensington, Md., May 9, 1930; d. Archibald Turner and Margaret Fitch (Willcox) McPherson; m. Harold Earl Bennett, Aug. 17, 1952 (div. Nov. 1984). BA summa cum laude, Mt. Holyoke Coll., 1951, DSc (hon.), 1992; MS, Pa. State U., 1953, PhD in Physics, 1955. Physicist Wright Air Devel. Ctr., Dayton, Ohio, 1955-56; physicist Naval Ordnance Test Sta. (now Naval Air Warfare Ctr. Weapons Div.), China Lake, Calif., 1956-85, sr. research scientist, 1987-93, 95; vis. prof. U. Ala., Huntsville, 1986-87, Mt. Holyoke Coll., South Hadley, Mass., 1994-95; ret., 1996—; mem. NRC Evaluation Panel Nat. Bur. Stds., Ctr. for Radiation Rsch., 1979-85, Nat. Inst. Stds. and Tech. Mfg. Engring. Lab., 1988-94, U.S. Nat. Com. for Internat. Commn. for Optics, 1984-85, 88-95; vis. scientist Inst. Optical Rsch., Royal Inst. Tech., Stockholm, Mar.-Sept., 1988, 98, 99. Author: (with Lars Mattsson) Introduction to Surface Roughness and Scattering, 1989, revised 1999; author: Surface Finish and Its Measurement, 1992; contbr. sci. articles to profl. jours.; patentee in field. Recipient Tech. Achievement award Soc. Photo-Optical Instrumentation Engrs., 1983, L.T.E. Thompson award Naval Weapons Ctr., 1988, Women in Sci. and Engring. Lifetime Achievement award, 1993; named sr. fellow Naval Weapons Ctr., 1989, Disting. Fellow, 1994. Fellow Optical Soc. Am. (v.p. 1984, pres.-elect 1985, pres. 1986, past pres. 1987, chmn. book publ. com. 1991-94, David Richardson medal 1990); mem. Am. Inst. Physics (subcom. on books 1990-94), Phi Beta Kappa, Sigma Xi, Sigma Delta Epsilon, Iota Sigma Pi, Pi Mu Epsilon, Sigma Pi Sigma. First woman to receive PhD in Physics at Pa. State U., 1955; first woman pres. Optical Soc. of Am.; avocations: backpacking, kayaking, photography. Home: 1275 Sage Ct Ridgecrest CA 93555-2622 Office: Code 4T41A0D Michelson Lab Naval Air Warfare Ctr China Lake Nwc CA 93555

BENNETT, JESSIE F., lawyer; b. Bridgeport, Conn.; d. Cornelius T. and Jessie F. (Sutcliffe) B.; m. Ronald J. Canuel, Nov. 3, 1990. BS in Fin. with honors, Fairfield U., 1980; JD magna cum laude, U. Bridgeport, 1986. Bar: Conn., 1986; U.S. Dist. Ct. Conn., 1987, U.S. Dist. Ct. (so. and ea. dists.)

N.Y. 1989, U.S. Ct. Appeals (2d cir.) 1989, D.C. Ct. of Appeals, 1989, U.S. Supreme Ct., 1989. Jud. clk. to Judge Ellen Bree Burns U.S. Dist. Ct., New Haven, 1986; atty. Cohen & Wolf, Danbury, Conn., 1987-88, Davidson & Naylor, Norwalk, Conn., 1988-92; law clk. jud. dept. State of Conn., Waterbury, 1992-96; asst. state's atty. State of Conn. Divsn. Criminal Justice, 1996—. Mem. ABA, ATLA, Conn. Bar Assn., Nat. Dist. Attys. Assn., Conn. Trial Lawyers Assn., D.C. Bar Assn., Phi Delta Phi, Phi Alpha Delta (Am. Jurisprudence award in Remedies and Family Law, Kristin Ann Carveth Meml. Scholastic award, Code Enforcement Ofcl. of Yr. 1999, Pres. award 1999, Cert. Appreciation award 1999). Roman Catholic. Avocations: exercise, music, cooking, travel. Office: States Attys Office 80 Washington St Hartford CT 06106-4405

BENNETT, JOE CLAUDE, pharmaceutical executive; b. Birmingham, Ala., Dec. 12, 1933; s. Claude and Clara Lucille (Clark) B.; m. Nancy Miller, June 17, 1958; children: Katherine Diane, Miller, Clark Barton. A.B., Samford U., 1954; M.D., Harvard U., 1958; DSc (hon.), U. Ala., 1992. Diplomate Am. Bd. Internal Medicine (governing bd. 1987—, cert. exam. com. for 1989, ind. com. R & D, 1988—), Am. Bd. Rheumatology, Nat. Bd. Med. Examiners. Intern Univ. Ala. Hosp., Birmingham, 1958-59, resident, 1959-60; rsch. assoc. molecular biology NIH, Bethesda, Md., 1962-64; sr. rsch. fellow div. biology Calif. Inst. Tech., Pasadena, Calif., 1964-65; asst. prof. dept. medicine, assoc. prof. dept. microbiology, asst. dir. div. clin. immunology and rheumatology U. Ala. Med. Sch., Birmingham, 1965-70; dir. div. clin. immunology and rheumatology U. Ala. Med. Sch., 1970-83, prof., chmn. dept. microbiology, 1970-82, prof., chmn. dept. medicine, 1982-92, Spencer Prof. Med. Sci., 1992—, dir. multipurpose arthritis center, 1977-84, disting. faculty lectr., 1979; pres. U. Ala., Birmingham, 1993-96; pres., COO BioCryst Pharms., Birmingham, 1996—; physician in chief U. Ala. Hosp.; vis. prof. U. Mo.-Columbia Sch. Medicine, 1987, U. Leiden, The Netherlands, 1988, Baylor U. Coll. Medicine, Houston, 1989, others; invited lectr. various univs., confs. including IX Pan-Am. Congress Rheumatology, Buenos Aires, 1986, U. Mo.-Columbia Sch. Medicine, 1987, Cornell Med. Sch., 1986, U. Colo., 1986; mem. sci. adv. bd. Merck Sharp & Dohme Rsch. Labs., 1987-89, Gorgas Meml. Inst. Tropical and Preventive Medicine, 1985—, others; mem. bd. health sci. policies, NIH, NAS, 1988—. Editor: Vistas in Connective Tissue Diseases, 1968; co-editor: Rheumatology and Immunology, 2d edit., 1986, Cecil Textbook of Medicine, 1988—, Cecil Essentials of Medicine; editor-in-chief Am. Jour. Medicine, 1986-97, Arthritis and Rheumatism, 1975-80; mem. editorial bd. Protein and Peptide Revs., 1980—, Current Opinion in Rheumatology, 1988—, Arthritis and Rheumatism, 1969-75; contbr. numerous articles, papers, book revs., abstracts to profl. publs. Recipient Ala. Acad. Honor award, 1987, Seale Harris award So. Med. Assn., 1987; John and Mary R. Markle Found. scholar in acad. medicine, 1965-70; recipient Rsch. Career Devel. award NIH, 1965-75; fellow Arthritis and Rheumatism Found., Harvard Med. Sch., Mass. Gen. Hosp., 1960-62. Fellow AAAS (sec. N. Med. scis. nominating com. 1989—); mem. Am. Bd. Internal Medicine (exec. com. 1992), Federated Coun. of Internatl Medicine, Assn. of Am. Med. Colls. (adv. panel on biomed. rsch. 1991-92), Inst. Medicine NAS, ACP (master 1990), Am. Assn. Immunologists, Am. Fedn. Clin. Rsch., Am. Coll. Rheumatology (pres. 1981-82, bd. dirs. planning group 1986-87), Am. Soc. Biol. Chemists, Am. Soc. Clin. Investigation, Am. Soc. Microbiology, more. Home: 3520 River Bend Rd Birmingham AL 35243-4832 Office: BioCryst Pharms 2190 Parkway Lake Dr Birmingham AL 35244-1803*

BENNETT, JOEL HERBERT, construction company executive; b. Chgo., Nov. 7, 1936; children: Evan Alan, Julie Andrea. BSChemE, U. So. Calif., L.A., 1958, MSChemE, 1962; MBA in Ops. Rsch., UCLA, 1960. Chem. process engr. C. F. Braun & Co., Alhambra, Calif., 1960-65, with bus. devel., 1965-73; v.p. Arthur G. McKee & Co., Cleve., 1973-78, Parsons Engring. Sci., Inc., Pasadena, Calif., 1978-81; sr. v.p. Santa Fe Braun Inc., Alhambra, 1981-89; exec. v.p. The Parsons Corp., Pasadena, 1989-92, 96—; pres. Parsons Environ. Svcs. Inc., Pasadena, 1992-96, Harland Bartholomew & Assocs., 1992-95; exec. v.p. The Parsons Corp., 1995-96; sr. v.p. Parsons Brinckerhoff, Inc., N.Y.C., 1996—, also mem. bd. dirs.; chmn., pres. PB Power Inc., N.Y.C., 1998—; bd. dirs. Inst. Redesign Lng.; mem. environ. mgmt. adv. bd. U.S. Dept. Energy, 1994—. Author: (with others) Project Management, 1989. Dir. Calif. State U. L.A. Found.; mem. bd. advisors The Asian Am. Architects/Engrs. Assn. Mem. Am. Inst. Chem. Engrs., Jonathan Club (L.A.). Avocations: skiing, jogging, tennis, music. Home: 30 W 61st St # 9D New York NY 10023 Office: Parsons Brinckerhoff Inc One Penn Plz New York NY 10119

BENNETT, JOHN JOSEPH, professional services company executive; b. Camden, N.J., Sept. 4, 1923; s. John Henry and Margaret Katherine (Bloxsum) B.; m. Dolores Florence Griffiths, June 17, 1943; children: Jill, T. Robert, T. Richard. Student, Centenary Coll., 1951-55; MBA, Mich. State U., 1961; D in Bus. Adminstrn., George Washington U., 1974. Commd. 2d lt. USAAF, 1943; advanced through grades to col. USAF, officer various operational and mgmt. jobs,, 1942-60; asst. comptroller Hdqrs. AFSC, Washington, 1961-66; asst. to Asst. Sec. Air Force and dep. chief staff, Personnel Hdqrs. USAF, Washington, 1967-69; ret. USAF, 1969; exec. dir. Mauchley Edn. Inst., Washington, 1969-70; pres. Sycom, Inc., Washington, 1969-70; mgr. aerospace def. practice Peat, Marwick, Mitchell & Co., Washington, 1970-74; prin. dep. asst. U.S. Sec. of Def., Washington, 1975-76, Asst. Sec. of Navy, Washington, 1976-77; dir., exec. office pres. Fed. Acquisition Inst., Washington, 1977-79; chief exec. officer ANADAC, Inc., Washington, 1979-88, chmn. bd., 1988-92, chmn. emeritus, 1992—; lectr. George Washington U., 1979-89; chmn. bd. dirs. TBG Reliance Corp., 1997—. Author: The Next Generation Management Systems for Systems Management, 1967, Department of Defense Systems Acquisition Management, 1974, Program Management Principles and Practices, 1994; author: (with others) Systems Concepts for Human Resources Management, 1968. Decorated Legion of Merit, D.F.C., Air medal with 4 oak leaf clusters; recipient Disting. Civilian Svc. award, 1976, Disting. Pub. Svc. award, 1977. Mem. Acad. Mgmt., Am. Soc. Naval Engrs., Am. Mgmt. Assn. Methodist. Home: 316 100th St Stone Harbor NJ 08247-1332 Office: ANADAC 2200 Claridon Blvd Ste 900 Arlington VA 22201

BENNETT, JOHN MORRISON, medical oncologist; b. Boston, Apr. 24, 1933; s. Theodore and Gladys B.; m. Carol F. Rosenblum, Dec. 22, 1957; children: Robert, Elizabeth, Douglas. AB cum laude, Harvard U., 1955; MD cum laude, Boston U., 1959. Intern Mass. Meml. Hosp., Boston, 1959-60; resident Beth Israel Hosp., Boston, 1960-62; instr. medicine Harvard Med. Sch., 1965-66; head morphology and histochem. sect. clin. pathology dept. NIH, 1966-68; asst. prof. medicine Sch. Medicine Tufts U., 1968-69; dir. outpatient labs. Boston City Hosp., 1968-69; dir. hematology and med. oncology Highland Hosp., Rochester, N.Y., 1969-74; prof. oncology in medicine, pathology and lab. medicine U. Rochester Sch. Medicine, 1976-98; prof. medicine emeritus, 1999—; assoc. dir. clin. affairs U. Rochester Cancer Ctr., 1978-94; head med. oncology unit Strong Meml. Hosp., Rochester, 1974-95. Editor: Leukemia Research, 1993; contbr. more than 400 articles to profl. jours. Chmn. Myelodysplastic Syndromes Founds., 1996—. With USPHS, 1966-68. Mem. ACP, AMA, Am. Soc. Clin. Oncology, Am. Soc. Hematology, Internat. Soc. Hematology, European Soc. Oncology. Home: 335 Avalon Dr Rochester NY 14618-2731 Office: 601 Elmwood Ave Rochester NY 14642-0001 *The major principle that has guided my academic career has been to treat patients with compassion but also in a setting of clinical trials research. Participation of patients in innovative studies and randomized trials offers the best opportunity for quality care and improved results in the field of oncology. My research has focused on classifcation of leukemias and establishing clinical correlations.*

BENNETT, KATHI, women's basketball coach; b. Clintonville, Wis., Jan. 23, 1963. Student, U. Wis., Stevens Point; BS in Exercise Sci., U. Wis., Green Bay, 1986. Asst. coach Carroll Coll., 1987-88; head coach women's basketball Teiyko Marycrest, 1987-88, U. Wis., Oshkosh, 1989-96, U. Evansville, Ind., 1996—. Office: U Evansville 1800 Lincoln Ave Evansville IN 47722-1506

BENNETT, KEITH GEORGE, nurse; b. Springfield, Clarendon, Jamaica, Aug. 31, 1929; came to the U.S., 1968; s. Aubrey Samuel and Ethel Ann Bennett; m. Marjorie Joyce Smith, Apr. 21, 1956; children: Evon Claude, Keith George Jr., Keitha Lois, Judith Marjorie. BS in Cmty. Mental Health, N.Y. Inst. Tech., 1981; MPH, Loma Linda U., 1984; BSN, Coll. Mt. St. Vincent, 1991. RN, N.Y. Pub. health inspector, water quality control inspector Ministry of Health, Jamaica, 1952-68; mental health therapy asst. N.Y. State Psychiat. Inst., N.Y.C., 1976-86; nurse Bronx Lebanon Hosp. Ctr., N.Y., 1975-96; dir. Melaleuca Ind. Mktg. Exec., Bronx, 1996—. Fellow Royal Soc. Health. Democrat. Adventist. Home: 3331 Pearsall Ave Bronx NY 10469-2921 Office: 3331 Pearsall Ave Bronx NY 10469-2921

BENNETT, KENNETH ALAN, retired biological anthropologist; b. Butler, Okla., Oct. 3, 1935; s. Kenneth Francis and Lillian Imogene (McDaniel) B.; m. Helen Lucille Maze, Sept. 6, 1959; children: Letitia Arlene, Cheri Lynn. AS, Odessa Coll., 1956; BA, U. Tex., 1961; MA, U. Ariz., 1966, PhD, 1967. Asst. prof. anthropology U. Oreg., 1967-70; assoc. prof. U. Wis., Madison, 1970-75, prof., 1975-97, ret., 1997. Author: The Indians of Point of Pines, Arizona, 1973, Fundamentals of Biological Anthropology, 1979, Skeletal Remains from Mesa Verde National Park, 1975, A Field Guide for Human Skeletal Identification, 1987, 2nd edit., 1993; editor Yearbook of Phys. Anthropology, 1976-81; contbr. editor Social Biology, 1981-87; mem. editl. com. Ann. Revs. in Anthropology, 1987-91; contbr. articles to profl. jours. Mem. Wis. Burial Sites Preservation Bd., 1988. With U.S. Army, 1956-58. NIH fellow, 1964-67. Mem. Am. Assn. Phys. Anthropologists, Am. Soc. Naturalists, Human Biology Council, Soc. for Study Evolution, Am. Acad. Forensic Scis., Soc. for Study Human Biology, Soc. Systematic Zoology, Am. Assn. Physical Anthropologists (exec. com. 1976-81), Sigma Xi. Home: 5718 Hammersley Rd Madison WI 53711-3450

BENNETT, LAWRENCE ALLEN, psychologist, criminal justice researcher; b. Selma, Calif., Jan. 4, 1923; s. Allen Walter and Eva Eleanor (Hall) B.; m. Beth J. Thompson, Aug. 14, 1948; 1 son, Glenn Livingston; 1 child, Yvonne Irene Solis. B.A., Fresno State Coll., 1949; M.A., Claremont Grad. Sch., 1954, Ph.D., 1968. Supervising psychologist Calif. med. facility Calif. Dept. Corrections, Vacaville, 1955-60, departmental supr. clin. psychology, Sacramento, 1960-67, chief of research, Sacramento, 1967-76; dir. Center for Study of Crime, Delinquency and Corrections, So. Ill. U., Carbondale, 1976-79; dir. Office of Program Evaluation, 1979-84; dir. Crime Prevention and Enforcement Div. Nat. Inst. of Justice, Washington, 1985-86; dir. Adjudication and Corrections Div., 1987-88; criminal justice cons., Sacramento, 1988—; practice clin. psychology, Sacramento, 1988—; mem. part-time faculty U. Calif., Davis, U. Calif., Berkeley, 1959-76, Calif. State U., Sacramento, 1988—; mem. bd. Calif. Crime Technol. Research Found., 1970-75; mem. Calif. State Interdepartmental Coordinating Council, 1967-76, chmn., 1970; bd. dirs. Am. Justice Inst., Sacramento, 1970-79, 88—, v.p., 1989-90, pres., 1991—; mem. juvenile adv. bd. State of Ill., 1977-79; commr. Calif. Blue Ribbon Commn. on Inmate Population Mgmt., 1988-90. Served with U.S. Army, 1942-45, 49-50. Decorated Bronze Star with oak leaf cluster. Mem. Acad. of Criminal Justice Scis., Am. Psychol. Assn., Am. Soc. Criminology, Am. Correctional Assn. (mem. rsch. coun. 1992—), Evaluation Research Soc., Assn. for Correctional Rsch. and Info. Mgmt. (pres. 1989-90). Unitarian. Author: (with Thomas S. Rosenbaum and Wayne R. McCollough) Counseling in Correctional Environments, 1978; contbr. articles in field to profl. jours. Home: 1129 Rivara Cir Sacramento CA 95864-3720 Office: Am Justice Inst 1129 Rivara Cir Sacramento CA 95864-3720

BENNETT, LAWRENCE HERMAN, physicist; b. Bklyn., Oct. 17, 1930; s. Harold and Irene (Kamel) B.; m. Devora Mae Spintman, Mar. 22, 1953; children: Claire Ann Bennett Freeland, Charles Leonard, Craig David. BA cum laude, Bklyn. Coll., 1951; MS, U. Md., 1955; PhD, Rutgers U., 1958. Physicist Naval Ordnance Lab., White Oak, Md., 1950-58, Nat. Bur. Stds., Gaithersburg, Md., 1958-96; adj. prof. physics U. Md., College Park, 1959-94, rsch. prof. Inst. for Magnetics Rsch. The George Washington U., Washington, 1995—. Author: (with G.C. Carter and D.H. Kahan) Metallic Shifts in NMR, 1977; editor: Thoery of Alloy Phase Formation, 1980, Computer Modeling of Alloy Phase Diagrams, 1986, High Temperature Superconductors: Magnetic Interactions, 1989, Magnetic Multilayers, 1994; contbr. articles to profl. jours. Recipient Gold medal Dept. Commerce, 1971. Fellow Am. Phys. Soc. (chair magnetism group 1999—), Am. Soc. for Metals (Burgess Meml. award 1964); mem. IEEE Metall. Soc., Materials Rsch. Soc., Phi Beta Kappa, Sigma Xi (pres. bur. of stds. 1987). Home: 6524 E Halbert Rd Bethesda MD 20817-5414 Office: George Washington U Inst Magnetic Rsch Ashburn VA 20147

BENNETT, LERONE, JR., magazine editor, author; b. Clarksdale, Miss., Oct. 17, 1928; s. Lerone and Alma (Reed) B.; m. Gloria Sylvester, July 21, 1956; children: Alma Joy, Constance, Courtney, Lerone III. BA, Morehouse Coll., 1949, LittD (hon.), 1966; HHD (hon.), Wilberforce U., 1977; DLitt (hon.), Marquette U., 1979, Voorhees Coll., 1981, Morgan State U., 1981; LHD (hon.), U. Ill., 1980, Lincoln Coll., 1980, Dillard U., 1980; LittD (hon.), Howard U., 1982; LHD (hon.), Boston U., 1987; DLitt (hon.), Tuskegee U., 1989. Reporter Atlanta Daily World, 1949-51, city editor, 1952-53; assoc. editor Ebony mag., Chgo., 1953-58; sr. editor Ebony mag., 1958-87, exec. editor, 1987—; vis. prof. history Northwestern U., 1968-69. Author: Before the Mayflower: A History of Black America, 1619-1964, 1962, rev., 1964, 82, The Negro Mood, 1964, What Manner of Man, A Biography of Martin Luther King, Jr, 1964, Confrontation: Black and White, 1965, Black Power U.S.A, 1968, Pioneers in Protest, 1968, The Challenge of Blackness, 1972, The Shaping of Black America, 1975, Wade in the Water, 1979; Contbr. to: New Negro Poets: USA, 1964, American Negro Short Stories, 1966. Trustee Morehouse Coll., Columbia Coll.; mem. Pres.'s Com. Arts and Humanities. Recipient Patron Saints award Soc. Midland Authors, 1965; Book of Year award Capital Press Club, 1963; AAAL Acad.-Inst. lit. award, 1978. Mem. Phi Beta Kappa, Kappa Alpha Psi., Sigma Delta Chi. Office: Ebony Mag 820 S Michigan Ave Chicago IL 60605-2103*

BENNETT, LOIS, real estate broker; b. N.Y.C., Dec. 23, 1933; d. Richard and Fern (Steinberg) B.; m. Barry Silverstein, June 8, 1958 (div. May 1978); children: Mark Shale, Susan Beth, Thomas Benjamin; m. Milt Felsen, Aug. 1998. BA, Smith Coll., 1955. Cert. residential specialist, broker/salesman, Fla. Counselor Women's Health Ctr., Sarasota, Fla., 1977-78; investment counselor, stockbroker Pvt. Bourse Inc., Sarasota, 1978-79; realtor-assoc. Harrison Properties, Inc., Sarasota, 1984-86; broker/salesman Mt. Vernon Realty Co., Inc., Sarasota, 1986-91; broker-salesman Re/Max Properties, Sarasota, 1991-96. Bd. dirs. Planned Parenthood S.W. Fla., Sarasota, 1978-84, fundraising chmn., 1982-84; bd. dirs. Family Counseling Ctr., Sarasota, 1978-81, 90, Sarasota County Arts Coun.; mem. exec. com., bd. dirs. Fla. West Coast Symphony, Sarasota, 1982-88, nominating chair 1995, 96, sec.; chmn. spl. events 1st ann. Sarasota French Film Festival, 1989, co-chmn. spl. events, 1990; bd. dirs. Asolo Performing Arts Ctr., Sarasota, 1990-95; bd. dirs. Sarasota French Film Festival, 1989-96; mem. film commn. Com. of 100, 1989-92; chmn. Sarasota County Arts Day, 1994, 95; exec. com., sec., pres. Smith Cub of Sarasota. Mem. Women's Coun. Realtors, Realtors Inst. (grad.), Re/Max 100% Club (Michael Saunders Circle of Excellence). Avocations: gardening, reading, collecting art, travel. Office: Michael Saunders & Co 61 S Blvd Of Presidents Sarasota FL 34236-1423

BENNETT, LORI JAYNE, elementary school educator; b. Sioux City, Iowa, Jan. 19, 1957; d. George S. and Bertha M. (Gunderson) Kaspar; m. David M. Bennett, June 2, 1981; 1 child, Anna Kathleen. BA in Edn., Nat. Coll. Edn., 1978; MA in Edn., Tex. Woman's U., 1991; postgrad., U. North Tex., 1995—. Cert. tchr., Tex. 7th grade tchr. East Main Schs., Des Plaines, Ill., 1978-79; 6th-8th grade tchr. Grand Prairie (Tex.) Schs., 1979-81, Rocksprings (Tex.) Schs., 1982-84; coord. cmty. edn. Ctrl. Tex. Coll., Killeen, 1984-87; K-5, 8th grade tchr. White Settlement Schs., Ft. Worth, 1987-94; 4th-6th grade tchr. Hurst-Euless-Bedford (Tex.) Schs., 1994—; cons. in field. Author: Plug In The sun, 1991, Think Plus Science, 1992, Aviation Explorations, 1994. Recipient Letter of the Month award Ft. Worth Star Telegram, 1988, 91. Mem. ASCD, Nat. Assn. for Gifted Children, Assn. Tex. Profl. Educators, Tex. Assn. for Gifted and Talented. Lutheran. Office: Harrison Lane Elem Sch 1000 Harrison Ln Hurst TX 76053-5002

BENNETT, MARGARET AIROLA, lawyer; b. San Francisco, July 20, 1950; d. Virgil Raymond and Caroline (Maccoun) Airola; m. Eugene Le Brun Bennett, Mar. 1, 1980; children: Scott, Brad, Elizabeth. AB cum laude, U. Calif., Berkeley, 1972; JD, U. San Francisco and Loyola U., 1976. Bar: Ill.1976, U.S. Dist. Ct. (no. dist.) Ill. 1977, U.S. Ct. Appeals (7th cir.) 1983. Intern Cook County State's Atty.'s Office, Chgo., 1975-76; assoc. Dunlap, Thompson & Boyd, Ltd., Libertyville, Ill., 1977-79; ptnr. Bennett & Bennett, Ltd., Oak Brook, Ill., 1980-96; pvt. practice The Law Offices of Margaret A. Bennett, Oak Brook, 1996—; atty. rep. McDonald's Corp., Oak Brook, 1982—, County of DuPage, Wheaton, Ill., 1990-95. Counsel fo DuPage Ill. Fair and Exposition Authority, County of DuPage, 1991-95, co-chmn. next generation com.; mem. devel. coun. Good Samaritan Hosp., 1988-92. Mem. DuPage County Bar Assn. (chmn. real estate law com. 1994-95, Cert. of Appreciation 1989, Bd. Dirs. award 1998, chmn. profl. responsibility com. 1996-97, chmn. family law com. 1997-98), Ill. State Bar Assn. (assembly mem., Cert. of Appreciation 1990), Womens Bar Assn. DuPage County, Evang. Health Found. (bd. sponsors 1988-92). Republican. Episcopalian. Avocations: golf, reading, skiing, travel. Home: 11 Lochinvar Ln Oak Brook IL 60523-1612 Office: 720 Enterprise Dr Oak Brook IL 60523-1908

BENNETT, MARGUERITE M., college administrator, mathematics educator; b. Mar. 17, 1945. MEd, U. Ill., 1971, PhD, 1976. Dir. instnl. rsch., math. prof. Mt. Vernon Nazarene Coll., 1976—; pres. Mt. Vernon City Schs. Bd. Edn., 1988-99; v.p. Knox County Career Ctr. Bd. Edn., 1992-99. Mem. Mt. Vernon-Knox County C. of C. E-mail: mbennett@mvnc.edu. Office: 800 Martinsburg Rd Mount Vernon OH 43050

BENNETT, MARK WARREN, lawyer, educator; b. Milw., June 4, 1950. BA in Polit. Sci., Gustavus Adolphus Coll., 1972; JD, Drake U., 1975. Bar: Iowa 1975, U.S. Dist. Ct. (so. dist.) Iowa 1975, U.S. Dist. Ct. (no. dist.) Iowa 1978, U.S. Ct. Appeals (7th cir.) 1981, U.S. Supreme Ct. 1978. Ptnr. Babich, Bennett and Nickerson, Des Moines, 1975—; judge U.S. Dist. Ct., Sioux City; vis. prof. polit. sci. and sociology U. S.D., Vermillion, 1975-76; asst. prof. law enforcement adminstrn. Western Ill. U., Macomb, 1976-77; adj. prof. law Drake U., Des Moines, 1981—; lectr. law U. Iowa, summers 1984-85; guest lectr. on civil rights, employment discrimination and constl. litigation, 1981—. Del. Dem. Nat. Conv., 1972; trustee Legal Aid Soc. Polk County, 1978-83, pres. 1980-81; bd. dirs. ACLU, 1987—. Named Civil Libertarian of Yr. Iowa Civil Liberties Union, 1986. Fellow Iowa Acad. Trial Lawyers; mem. Iowa Bar Assn. (com. legal aid 1985—, study com. women and minorities involvement in bar assn. and jud. system Iowa 1987—, com. labor law 1988-89), Polk County Bar Assn. (pro bono com. 1985—), Iowa Assn. Trial Lawyers (co-chmn. amicus curiae com. 1986—, co-chmn. constl. law com. 1987—). Avocations: making brass mobiles, gardening, golf. Office: US Dist Ct Federal Bldg 320 6th St Ste 311 Sioux City IA 51101-1262*

BENNETT, MARSHALL GOODLOE, JR., state official, lawyer; b. Lexington, Miss., Dec. 25, 1943; s. Marshall G. and Tavia (Childress) B.; m. Shirley Shelton, July 15, 1963; children—Steven, Elizabeth, Russell. B.A., U. Miss., 1965, J.D., 1967. Bar: Miss. 1967, U.S. Supreme Ct. 1971. Exec. dir. Miss. Crime Commn., Jackson, 1967-68; asst. atty. gen. State of Miss., Jackson, 1970-72, 74-79; asst. dist. atty. 7th Dist., State of Miss., Jackson, 1972-74; adminstrv. asst. to gov. State of Miss., Jackson, 1980-81; chmn., commr. Miss. Workmen's Compensation Commn., Jackson, 1981-87, elected state treas., 1987—; ptnr. Peters, Royals, Bennett, & Jackson, 1972-74. Chmn. Miss. Spl. Task Force on Econ. Devel.; chmn. bd. trustees Pub. Employees Ret. System; Pres. Nat. Soc. Prevent Blindness, Jackson, 1984-85, So. Workers Compensation Adminstrs., Atlanta, 1984; treas., bd. dirs. State YMCA, Jackson, 1980; bd. dirs. Community Trust Found. Miss., Jackson, 1985. Served to capt. U.S. Army, 1968-70. Mem. Miss. State Bar Assn., So. Treas.'s Assn. (chmn. 1990), Nat. Assn. State Auditors, Comptrs., Treas. (exec. com. 1989-90, v.p.), Jackson Young Lawyers Assn. (sec. 1972), N.J. Assn. State Treas. (pres.). Democrat. United Methodist. Home: PO Box 421 Jackson MS 39205-0421 Office: Treasury Dept PO Box 138 Jackson MS 39205-0138*

BENNETT, MARY See THOMPSON, DIDI CASTLE

BENNETT, MICHAEL VANDER LAAN, neuroscience educator; b. Madison, Wis., Jan. 7, 1931; s. Martin Toscan and Cornelia (Vanderlaan) B.; m. Ruth Berman, July 19, 1963 (div. 1993); children: Nicholas Toscan, Elena Paula; m. R. Suzanne Zukin Nov. 19, 1997. BS, Yale U., 1952; DPhil, Oxford U., Eng., 1957. Research worker Coll. of Physicians and Surgeons Columbia U., N.Y.C., 1957-58, rsch. assoc., 1958-59, asst. prof. neurology, 1959-61, assoc. prof. neurology, 1961-66; co-dir. neurobiology Marine Biol. Lab., Woods Hole, Mass., 1970-74; prof. anatomy Albert Einstein Coll. Medicine, Bronx, N.Y., 1967-74, prof. neurosci., 1974-96, chmn. neurosci., 1982-96, Sylvia and Robert S. Olnick Prof. of Neurosci., 1986—; Editor rev. jours.; contbr. articles to profl. jours. Hon. Pepsi Cola scholar, 1948, Rhodes scholar, 1952; Grass Fellow, 1958. Fellow AAAS; mem. NAS, Am. Physiol. Soc., Am. Soc. Cell Biology, Biophys. Soc., Soc. Neurosci., N.Y. Road Runners Club, Phi Beta Kappa. Avocations: running, skiing, scuba. Office: Albert Einstein Coll of Medicine Dept Of Neurosci Bronx NY 10461

BENNETT, MICHAEL WAYNE, social services administrator, consultant; b. Palatka, Fla., May 17, 1951; s. Hubert Clyde and Betty Lou (Hodges) B.; m. Janice Marie Moller, Dec. 28, 1975; children: Christi Renee, Leah Michelle, Chelsea Elizabeth. AA in Liberal Arts, Fla. C.C., Jacksonville, 1972; BA in Sociology, U. North Fla., 1974; MBA in Health Care Adminstrn., Century U., 1997. Cert. addictions profl. Cert. Bd. for Addictions Profls. Fla.; internat. cert. alcohol and drug counselor Internat. Cert. Reciprocity and Consorium-Alcohol and Other Drug Abuse, Inc.; cert. criminal justice master counselor Nat. Assn. Forensic Counselors. Social worker Fellowship Luth. Ch., Jacksonville, 1972-74; counselor City of Jacksonville, 1974-76; dir. methadone svcs. River Region Human Svcs., Inc., Jacksonville, 1976-84, dir. non-residential svcs., 1984-86, dir. residential svcs., 1986-91, dir. planning, 1991-93, assoc. exec. dir., 1993—; substance abuse prevention specialist Edward Waters Coll., Jacksonville, 1988-90; nat. accreditation surveyor Rehab. Accreditation Commn., Tucson, 1993—; cons. Johnson, Bassin & Shaw, 1999; cons. and trainer in field. Participant Coalition for a Drug and Crime Free Jacksonville, 1993-95; chair healthcare com. Emergency Svcs. and Homeless Coalition Jacksonville, 1996-99; asst. pastor Vineyard Christian Fellowship, Jacksonville, Fla., 1998; bd. dirs. Nat. Treatment Accountability for Safer Cmties., 1999. Mem. Fla. Alcohol and Drug Abuse Assn. Avocations: computers, photography, music. Home: 2408 Summer Tree Rd E Jacksonville FL 32246-2448 Office: River Region Human Svcs Inc 660 Park St Jacksonville FL 32204-2933

BENNETT, MICHELE MARGULIS, women's health nurse; b. Oakland, Calif., Mar. 16, 1962; d. Frank and Rosalyn Barbara (Danneman) Margulis; m. Dennis Kerry Bennett, Jan. 1, 1991 (div. Jan. 12, 1995); 1 child, Caitlyn Anne. BA, U. Fla., 1984; BSN, Fla. Internat. U., 1990. Cert. childbirth educator. Staff nurse maternity Lyster Army Cmty. Hosp., Ft. Rucker, Ala., 1991-94; clin. staff nurse maternity Darnall Army Cmty. Hosp., Ft. Hood, Tex., 1994-96; clinical staff nurse WOMACK Med. Ctr., Ft. Bragg, N.C., 1996-1998; Head Nurse OB/Gyn Clinic, 1998-99, 121st Gen. Hosp., Korea, 1999—; mem. jr. officer coun. Ft. Hood, 1994-96; creative memories cons. CPT. U.S. Army, 1984—. Mem. AWHONN. Republican. Jewish. Avocations: quilting.

BENNETT, NOËL, artist, author; b. San Jose, Dec. 23, 1939; d. Charles Faris and Merton (Meyer) Kirkish; m. John N. Bennett, II; children: John N. III, Brockington LeLand; m. Jim Wakeman. BA cum laude with honors in humanities, Stanford U., 1961, MA in Edn. and Fine Art, 1962; postgrad., U. N.Mex., 1984-86. Art faculty Coll. Notre Dame, Belmont, Calif., 1963-67, U. N.Mex., Albuquerque, 1971-75; founder Navajo Weaving Restoration Ctr., 1978; faculty Internat. Coll., L.A., 1979-84; rschr. A Place in the Wild, N.Mex., 1984—; founder, dir. Shared Horizons, 1981—; condr. multimedia presentations, workshops on Navajo weaving and Native Am. concepts to numerous mus., univs. and guilds; coord. seminars on S.W. textiles, culture, fiber and dye identification, storage and conservation, 1980, 82. Author: Working With the Wool -- How to Weave a Navajo Rug (with Tiana Bighorse), 1971, Genuine Navajo Rug -- Are You Sure?, 1973, 2d edit. 1980, The Weaver's Pathway -- A Clarification of the "Spirit Trail" in Navajo Weaving, 1974, Designing with the Wool -- Advanced Navajo Weaving Techniques, 1979, Shared Horizons/Navajo Textiles (with Susan McGreevy and Mark Winters), 1981, Patterns of Power -- Art, Life, Self (cassette), 1982, Halo of the Sun -- Stories Told and Retold, 1987, Navajo Weaving Way -- The Path From Fleece to Rug (with Tiana Bighorse), 1997; editor: Bighorse The Warrior, 1990; contbr. articles to profl. jours.; art exhbns. include Univ. Art Ctr., Stanford U., Coll. Notre Dame, Mus. No. Ariz., Flagstaff, Convergence, San Francisco, St. John's Episc. Cathedral, Albuquerque, Denver Mus. Natural History, U. N.Mex., Statements 86, Albuquerque, Art Ctr. Los Alamos, N.Mex., 1996, Woman Made Gallery, Chgo., 1996; works in permanent collections of Sheehan, Sheehan and Stelzner, P.A., Albuquerque, Corrales (N.Mex.) Pub. Libr., San Jose State Coll., Grant St. Apts., San Francisco, Viking Apts., Eugene, Oreg., Simmons Inst. Human rels., Redwood City, Calif., Padre House, Carmel, Calif. and numerous private collections. Recipient Comm. Arts award, 1982, Mortimer C. Levintritt award for most outstanding work in dept. of art and arch., Stanford U., 1961; grantee Weatherhead Found., 1975, Tenn. Humanities Found., 1982, L.J. and Mary C. Skaggs Found., 1986, 89, Richard C. and Susan B. Ernst Found., 1989, NEA, 1990. Home: 976 Vallecitos Rd Jemez Springs NM 87025-9380

BENNETT, OLGA SALOWICH, civic worker, graphic arts researcher, consultant; b. Detroit, June 30, 1925; d. Nicholas Stefanovich and Maria Elarionovna (Mikuliak) Salowich; m. Robert William Bennett, Dec. 20, 1947; 1 child, Susan Roberta. Student, U. Mich., 1943-45, Parsons Sch. Design, 1948, U. Md., Nagoya, Japan, 1959; BA, NYU, 1975. Graphic artist Silver & Co., N.Y.C., 1948-50; editor, pub. Bull., organizer radio series LWV, Pitts., 1950-55; instr. Nanzan U., Nagoya, 1959; aide, cons. to U.S. hon. consul, Safi, Casablanca, Morocco, 1962-65; chmn. internat. affairs LWV, Montclair, N.J., 1966-73; conf. coord. UN Assn., Madison, N.J., 1974; weekly broadcaster LWV, San Juan, P.R., 1979-81; lectr. color theory Cunard, Ltd., London, Miami, Fla., 1985-88; bd. dirs., docent Ctr. Fine Arts, Miami, 1990-92; docent Bass Mus. Art, Miami Beach, Fla., 1990-92, Vizcaya Mus. Art, Miami, 1983—; cons. on corp. overseas placement. Author artist brochures, ednl. pamphlets; translator Russian-Am. Conf., Miami, 1990. Mem. panel theater award com. New Theater, Miami, 1991; mem. Nat. Mus. of Women in the Arts. Mem. AAUW, LWV, UN Assn., NYU Alumni Assn., New Sch. Alumni Assn., Fgn. Policy Assn., Great Decisions Program. Democrat. Russian Orthodox. Home: Kings Creek S Apt A1-402 7727 SW 86th St Miami FL 33143-7283

BENNETT, PAMELA YVONNE, diabetes resource nurse, pediatrics nurse; b. Mt. Carmel, Ill., Aug. 9, 1959; d. Donald Burris and Joan Carey; m. Timothy Bennett, Apr. 9, 1980. ADN with honors, Pima Coll., 1989; BSN with honors, U. Phoenix, 1996; MS with honors, Ariz. State U., 1999. Cert. pediatric ALS. Clin. nurse Tucson Med. Ctr., 1988—; mem. quality mgmt. com., leader pediatric quality improvement team, night owl conf. com., nurse practice com. Recipient Student Nurse of Yr. award Ariz. State Nurses Assn. Mem. Student Nurses Assn. (sec. 1987-88, v.p. 1988-89), United Way (team leader 1989-98), Sigma Theta Tau. Home: 7820 S Glasgow St Tucson AZ 85747-9248

BENNETT, PAUL EDMOND, engineering educator; b. Somerville, Mass., June 27, 1924; s. William Francis and Ellen Elizabeth (Cotter) B.; m. Carolyn Stevens Gove, June 16, 1956; children: Cynthia, David P., Steven W. BSEE, U. Mass., 1950; MSEE, Pa. State U., 1974. Registered profl. engr., Pa. Electronic engr. USN Underwater Sound Lab., New London, Conn., 1950-51, Woods Hole (Mass.) Oceanographic Inst., 1951-55; sr. engr., staff engr., sect. mgr. HRB-Singer, State College, Pa., 1956-67; rsch. assoc. Ordnance Rsch. Lab., State College, 1967-72; rsch. asst. Ionosphere Rsch. Lab., University Park, Pa., 1972-74; staff engr. Locus, State College, 1974-76; prof. engrng. tech. U. So. Ind., Evansville, 1976-92, prof. emeritus, 1992—, adj. prof., 1992-95; mem. Ind. Vocat. Tech. Coll. Joint Adv. Com., 1987-92. Author: Advanced Electrical Circuit Analysis, 1991; contbr. articles to profl. jours. Coord. vols. Peregrine Hacking Project Ind. Dept. Natural Resources, 1994; steering com. Friends Ayrshire, 1997-99; Hoosier Audubon Coun. delegate, 1997-99, Ind. IBA tech. com., 1999—; mem. citizen adv. com. Evansville Urban Transp., 1999. Mem. IEEE (faculty sponsor U. So. Ind. student br. 1978-85, 91, mem. regional student affairs com. 1978-85, chair sect. ednl. activities com. 1978-79, sect. chair 1979-80, chair sect. membership com. and nominations com. 1980-81, exec. bd. 1978-84, bd. govs. 1980-84), Am. Soc. for Engrng. Edn. (reviewer Jour. Engrng. Tech. 1986-97, sect. moderator internat. divsn. ann. conf. 1987, vice chair programs-elect internat. divsn. 1989-90, program internat. divsn. 1990-91, chair 1991-93, past chair 1993-95), Friends of Ayrshire, Tau Beta Pi, Tau Alpha Pi (chpt. sponsor 1980-92). Avocations: birdwatching, sailboat racing. Home: 7321 Washington Ave Evansville IN 47715-4440

BENNETT, PAUL WILLIAM, lawyer; b. Tyler, Tex., Aug. 19, 1967; s. Paul Amon and Altha Jeanette (Rouse) B.; m. Janet Elizabeth Risley, July 25, 1992. BA, Austin Coll., Sherman, Tex., 1989; JD, Tex. Tech U., 1993. Bar: Tex. 1993, U.S. Dist. Ct. (no. dist.) Tex. 1995. Legis. asst. Tex. Ho. of Reps., Austin, 1989; law clk. Office of Staff Judge Advocate USAF, Lubbock, Tex., 1992-93; law cl. Office of Tex. Atty. Gen., Lubbock, 1993; atty. Corley & Corley, L.L.P., Dallas, 1993-95, Law Offices of Ira Thomas King, Dallas, 1995—. Mem. governing coun. Austin Coll., 1986-87. Mem. ABA, Def. Rsch. Inst., Dallas Bar Assn. (history and meml. com.). Republican. Baptist. Home: 120 Spyglass Dr Coppell TX 75019-3162 Office: Law Offices of Ira Thomas King 4311 Oak Lawn Ave Ste 200 Dallas TX 75219-2311

BENNETT, PEGGY ELIZABETH, librarian, library director, educator; b. Columbus, Ga., Aug. 22, 1935; d. William Osborne and Ola Lee (McMahan) B. BA in Chemistry, So. Coll., 1956; cert. med. technologist, Glendale Sch. Med. Tech., Glendale, 1957; MS in Libr. Sci., Fla. State U., 1971. Med. technologist Glendale (Calif.) Hosp., 1957-59, Columbus (Ga.) Med. Ctr., 1960-61; sec. Seventh-Day Adventists Ch. Orgns., various, 1961-67; med. technologists Warm Springs (Ga.) Found., 1967-69, Thrash Labs., Columbus, Ga., 1969-70; libr. So. Coll. Seventh-Day Adventist, Collegedale, Tenn., 1971—; dir. librs. So. Coll. of Seventh-Day Adventist, Collegedale, 1986—; presenter in field, 1979-87; developer Processing Ctr. for Southeastern Adventist Sch. Librs., 1981; cons. Adventist Network of Gen. Ednl. Librs., Collegedale, 1981—, Girl's Preparatory Sch., Chattanooga, 1984-85; mem. Sirs Mandarain Adv. Bd. Author: Library Pathfinder for MIT, 1972; contbr. articles to profl. jours. Mem. ALA, Assn. of Seventh-Day Adventists Librs. (v.p. 1981-82, pres. 1982-83), Southeastern Libr. Assn., Chattanooga Area Libr. Assn., Solinet Lambda Users' Group (exec. com. 1984, steering com.), Beta Phi Mu. Seventh Day Adventist. Avocations: tennis, aerobic walking, crafts. Home: 4640 Pierson Dr Collegedale TN 37315 Office: So Adventist U Industrial Dr Collegedale TN 37315

BENNETT, PETER BRIAN, researcher, hyperbaric medicine; b. Portsmouth, Hampshire, Eng., June 12, 1931; s. Charles Risby and Doris Isobel (Peckham) B.; m. Margaret Camellia Rose, July 7, 1956; children: Caroline Susan, Christopher Charles. BSc, U. London, 1951; PhD, U. Southampton, 1964, DSc, 1984. Asst. head surg. sect. Royal Navy Physiol. Lab., Alverstoke, Eng., 1953-56, head inert gas narcosis sect., 1953-66; dep. dir., prin. sci. officer, head pressure physiology sect. Royal Naval Physiol. Lab., Alverstoke, 1968-72; head pressure physiology group Can. Def. and Civil Inst. for Environ. Rsch., Toronto, Ont., 1966-68; prof. biomed. engrng. Duke U., Durham, N.C., 1972-75, assoc. prof. physiology, 1975—, prof. anesthesiology, 1972—, dir. rsch. dept. anesthesiology Med. Ctr., 1973-84, dir. Nat. Divers Alert Network, 1980—; dep. dir. F.G. Hall Lab. Environ. Rsch., 1973-74; co-dir. F.G. Hall Lab. Environ. Research, 1974-77, dir., 1977-88; sr. dir. Hyperbaric Ctr., 1988—; cons. in field. Author: The Aetiology of Compressed Air Intoxication and Inert Gas Narcosis, 1966; author, editor: The Physiology and Medicine of Diving and Compressed Air Work, 1969, Russian edit., 1987, 4th edit., 1993; contbr. over 200 articles to profl. jours. With RAF, 1951-53. Recipient Letter of Commendation, Pres. Ronald Reagan, 1981, Sci. award Underwater Soc. Am., 1980, Leonard Greenstone Safety award Nat. Assn. Underwater Instrs., 1985, 1st Prince Tomohito of Mikasa Japan prize, 1990, Craig Hoffman Meml. award, 1992, Dan Seap Mentor award, 1998. Mem. Undersea Med. Soc. (pres. 1975-76, mem. exec. com. 1972-75, editor jour. 1976-79, 1st Oceaneering Internat. award 1975, Albert R. Behnke award 1983), Am. Physiol. Soc., European Undersea Biomed. Soc., Russian Acad. Sci. (fgn. mem.), Aerospace Med. Soc., Marine Tech. Soc., Croatian Undersea and Hyperbaric Med. Soc. (hon.), Nat. Acad. Scuba Educators (Meritorious Svc. award 1997), Internat. Divers Alert Network. Avocations: gardening, swimming, boating. Home: 213 Lancaster Dr Chapel Hill NC 27514-3430 Office: Duke U Med Ctr FG Hall Lab PO Box 3823 Durham NC 27702-3823

BENNETT, PETER DUNNE, retired marketing educator; b. Mt. Pleasant, Tex., Feb. 19, 1933; s. Alvin Lowell and Jessie Lorene (Wintz) B.; m. Mary Lou Sanders, Aug. 23, 1953; children—Bonnie Kathleen, Blythe Allison. BBA, U. Tex., Austin, 1955, MBA, 1961, PhD, 1965. Mktg. rep. IBM Corp., Lubbock, Tex., 1957-60; lectr. U. Tex., Austin, 1961-63; vis. researcher U. Chile, Santiago, 1963-64; prof., chmn. dept. mktg., assoc. dean, bus. Pa. State U., University Park, 1964-97; gen. contractor State College, Pa., 1997—; bd. dirs. Walshire Asurance; cons. and lectr. in field. Author: Consumer Behavior, 1973, Marketing, 1988, Dictionary of Marketing Terms, 1989, 2d edit. 1995; editor numerous books in field; contbr. chpts. to books. Served to capt. USAF, 1955-57. Named Disting. Visitor, U. Tex., 1979. Mem. Assn. Consumer Research, Am. Mktg. Assn. (v.p. mgmt. 1983-85, editor 1982-84). Democrat. Presbyterian. Avocations: Golf, sailing, water skiing, house building, wood working.

BENNETT, REBECCA EATON, artist; b. Decatur, Ala., Sept. 27, 1957; d. Herbert Jess and Eleanor Alice Eaton; divorced; 1 child, Rachel Katherine. AS, Calhoun Coll., 1991; BA in Art and Bus. Adminstrn., Athens State Coll., 1993. Owner Ye Ole Abode Studio, Decatur, 1993—. Republican. Baptist. Avocations: ballet, theatre, symphonies, museums. Office: Ye Ole Abode Studio PO Box 843 Decatur AL 35602-0843

BENNETT, RICHARD CARL, social worker; b. Eau Claire, Wis., July 25, 1933; s. Ira Anthony and Marion Rhoda (Johnson) B.; BA, Hamline U., St. Paul, 1955; MS, George Williams Coll., 1957; MS (Lou Hougttellian fellow, Am. Lutheran Ch. fellow), U. Chgo., 1962; postgrad. Loyola U., Chgo., Roosevelt U., Chgo., Forest Inst., Chgo., 1988; grad. Ind. Family Mediation Tng., 1992; PhD Clayton Sch, Birmingham, Ala., 1996; cert. EEG Biofeedback BCIA, 1996; Diplomate Am. Bd. of Examiners in Clin. Social Work. m. Patricia Ann Work, Oct. 27, 1972; children: Matthew, Elizabeth, Kimberly, Timothy. Caseworker, Rock County Welfare Dept., Janesville, Wis., 1957-61; area dir. Luth. Family Service Oreg., Eugene, 1962-67; exec. dir. Family Service Travelers Aid, Fort Worth, 1967-70; mgr. agy. ops. Tarrant County United Way, Fort Worth, 1970-73; mile coord. Hands Accross Am., 1986, coord. Porter County Share Food, 1986-87; exec. dir. Luth. Family Service N.W. Ind., Merrillville, 1973-80; exec. v.p. Listening Inc., 1979—; mem. clin. staff Ctr. Children and Families, Kouts, Ind., 1998; exec. dir. Inst. for Family Life Porter County, 1982-93; CEO Environtech, 1988-94; cons. Ind. sentencing; lectr. Calumet Coll., Hammond, Ind., 1988-94, Purdue U., Westville, 1991-94, adult edu. instr, Indiana U., coord. of telecourses Calumet Coll., 1989-97; instr. Davenport Coll., 1998—; cons. Support Group Adult Attention Deficit Disorder, 1992, 98. Apptd. by gov. Ind. Social Work and Marriage and Family Therapist and Mental Health Counselor Licensing Bd., 1991, chmn., 1998; host TV show Life's Dimensions, 1985-90; cons. internat. bd. Parents without Ptnrs.; cons. numerous social agys.; founding bd. mem. Dunes Shakespeare Repitory Theater. With USAR, 1958-62. Mem. Nat. Assn. Social Workers (dir. Ind. chpt.), Acad. Cert. Social Workers (diplomate in clin. social work), Assn. Marriage and Family Therapists, Nat. Orgn. Forensic Social Workers, Ind. Pub. Defender Coun., Assn. Family and Conciliatory Cts. Author: Second Opinion: A Holistic Approach to Treating Adults with ADD, 1994, Reversing Attention Deficit Disorder in Adult, 1996; author divorce mgmt. materials and newspaper column, Author: QSort 10 an interactive diagnostic/treatment instrument for ADD Adults and other DSMIV diagnosis, 1996; profl. manuals; pub. Step Families and Beyond, 1979—; editor: The Business of Social Work, 1983-84, ADD-Up Bi-monthly Newsletter dor ADD-Adults, The "Violence Chronicles", 1998—. Home and Office: 8716 Pine Ave Gary IN 46403-1441

BENNETT, RICHARD THOMAS, retired manufacturing executive; b. Trenton, N.J., Jan. 7, 1930; s. George and Gladys (Burgess) B.; m. Bertha B. Wilson, Jan 24, 1958; children: Sandra, Richard, Terri, David. BS in Chemistry, Yale U., 1952; MS in Organic Chemistry, Rutgers U., 1954, PhD in Organic Chemistry, 1956. Rsch. chemist E.I. duPont de Nemours & Co., Wilmington, Del., 1956-58, Phila., 1958-59; tech. rep. E.I. duPont de Nemours & Co., Wilmington, 1959-62; tech. dir. Am. Bag and Paper Corp., Phila., 1962-64; research assoc. Allied Chem. Corp., Morristown, N.J., 1964-66, tech. supr., 1966-67, product mgr., 1967-70, bus. mgr., 1970-73, asst. to pres., 1973-74, mem. of task force, 1975-76; gen. mgr. Allied Chem. Corp., Toledo, 1974-79; pres. Plaskon Products, Inc., Toledo, 1979-84, PLK Corp., Toledo, 1984-86, Congoleum Corp., Kearny, N.J., 1986-88; plastic cons. Hillside Capital, N.Y.C., 1988-91; bd. dirs. Ohio Chem. Council, 1978-86, pres. 1981. Vestryman St. Michael's Episc. Ch., Toledo, 1979-81; sr. warden St. Michael's Ch., Toledo, 1980-81; bd. dirs. United Way, Toledo, 1981-86, vice chmn. spl. gifts, 1978-86, chmn., 1983; vice chmn. Toledo Council Boy Scouts Am., 1981-83; chmn. Blue Guardian Corp. of Blue Cross, 1984-86; trustee Blue Cross of Northwest Ohio, 1981-86, Med. Coll. Ohio at Toledo Found., 1983-86; past vice chmn. and bd. dirs. Toledo Area C. of C. Mem. Ohio Mfrs. Assn. (vice chmn. 1983-86), Am. Mgmt. Assn., Pres.'s Assn.

BENNETT, ROBERT F., senator; b. Salt Lake City, Utah, 1933; s. Wallace F. Bennett; m. Joyce McKay; 6 children. BS, U. of Utah, 1957. Various staff positions U.S Ho. of Reps., U.S. Senate, Washington; CEO Franklin Quest, Salt Lake City, 1984-90; U.S. senator from Utah, 1993—; chmn. legis. br. appropriations subcom. Senate GOP, chmn. fin. instns. subcom.; chmn. spl. com. Yr. 2000 Tech. Problem; mem. banking, housing, urban affairs com., appropriations com., environ. and pub. works com., joint economic com., small bus. com.; chmn. task force Senate reorganization; lobbyist various orgns., Washington; head Dept. Transp.'s Congl. Liaison. Author: Gaining Control. Chmn. Education Strategic Planning Commn. Utah State Bd. Edn. (mem. Edn. Strategic Planning Com.). Recipient Light of Learning award for Outstanding Contbns. to Utah edn., 1989; named Entrepreneur of Yr. for Rocky Mtn. region INC. magazine, 1989. Republican. Office: US Senate Office Of Senate Mems Washington DC 20510

BENNETT, ROBERT FREDERICK, lawyer, former governor; b. Kansas City, Mo., May 23, 1927; s. Otto F. and Dorothy Bess (Dodds) B.; m. Olivia Fisher, July 16, 1971; children: Robert Frederick, Virginia Lee, Cathleen Kay, Patricia Ann. AB, U. Kans., 1950, LLB, 1952, JD, 1970. Bar: Kans. 1952, Mo. 1952, U.S. Supreme Ct. 1967. Practiced in Johnson County, Kans., 1952—; assoc. Bennett, Lytle, Wetzler, Martin & Pishny, 1952-74, 79-97; gov. State of Kans., 1975-79; assoc. Lathrop & Gage LC, 1998—; mem. city coun. City of Prairie Village, Kans., 1955-57, mayor, 1957-65; pres. Kans. League Municipalities, 1959; mem. Kans. Senate, 1965-75, pres., 1973-75; chmn. com. on urban and rural devel. Nat. Gov.'s Conf., 1976, mem. exec. com., 1976-79; vice chmn. Rep. Gov.'s Conf., 1976-77, chmn., 1977-78. Chmn. nat. com. on child abuse and neglect Edn. Commn. of States, 1975-78; mem. bd. govs. U. Kans. Law Sch.; co-chmn. Kans. Citizens Justice Initiative Commn., 1987—. Recipient Disting. Alumni award U. Kans., 1979, Disting. Svc. citation, 1984, Fred Ellsworth Medallion award, 1990. Fellow Am. Bar Found. (life); mem. ABA, Mo. Bar Assn., Kans. Bar Assn. (past sec.-treas. exec coun.), Johnson County Bar Assn., VFW, Am. Legion, Rotary, Masons, Shriners. Office: 9401 Indian Creek Pkwy Ste 1050 Overland Park KS 66210-2019 *A meaningful life is the daily dedication of time and energy to the service of others. I hope mine has been no exception to this rule.*

BENNETT, ROBERT LEROY, computer software development company executive; b. Salt Lake City, May 16, 1937; s. Edward L. and Helen (Hofheins) B.; m. Linda Lou Anderson, Aug. 25, 1961; children: Keri Lynn, Troy, Nicole, Jessica, Candice, Chelsea. *Daughter Keri Lynn, MD and board certified psychiatrist and child psychiatrist, is clinical director of pediatric psychiatry at Utah State Hospital. Keri Lynn and her husband Kurt Herrmann, have five children. Son Troy, BA 1988 BYU, teacher and coaches high school history and volleyball, respectively, in Skokie, IL. Troy and his wife Elizabeth have three children. Daughter Nicole, BA 1991, MA 1994 BYU, teacher in the English Department at Brigham Young University. Nicole and her husband Brian Wistisen, have three children.* BA, Brigham Young U., 1962; JD, UCLA, 1965. Bar: Calif. 1966, U.S. Supreme Ct. 1969. Atty., advisor CIA, Washington, 1965-70; exec. v.p., chief operating officer Mead Data Central, Inc. (now Lexis-Nexis), Washington and N.Y.C., 1970-81; assoc. Heidrick and Struggles, Inc., N.Y.C., 1982-83; pres., chief exec. officer Mirror Systems, Inc., Cambridge, Mass., 1983-92; prin. Bennett, Fisher, Giuliano and Gottsman: The Electronic Publishing Group, N.Y.C., 1993—; bd. dirs. Raytech Corp., Trumbull, Conn., ADVOCAST, Provo, Utah. Mem. ABA. Mormon.

BENNETT, ROBERT MENZIES, retired gas pipeline company executive; b. Louisville, Oct. 24, 1926; s. Donald Menzies and Irene Marie (Schubring) B.; m. Elizabeth Lois Sherman, June 11, 1949; children: James, Elizabeth, Emily, Robert Jr. BEE, U. Louisville, 1950. Registered profl. engr., W.Va. Engr. Louisville Gas and Electric, 1950-55; engr. Columbia Gas div. United Fuel Gas Co., Charleston, W.Va., 1955-61, supervisory engr., 1961-71; mgr. Columbia Gas W.Va., Charleston, 1971-73; dir. planning Columbia Gas Transmission Corp., Charleston, 1973-80, v.p. gas procurement, 1980-85, sr. v.p. mktg., 1985-87, pres., 1987-88, vice chmn., 1988-90, also bd. dirs.; co-owner Enerco Oil and Gas Corp., Charleston, 1990—. Served with U.S. Army, 1945-46, PTO. Mem. IEEE (chmn. W.Va. sect. 1972). Republican. Episcopalian. Club: Kanawha Country. Lodge: Rotary. Avocations: golf, hiking. Home: 5120 Kanawha Ave SE Charleston WV 25304-2114 Office: Enerco Oil and Gas Corp PO Box 4296 Charleston WV 25364-4296

BENNETT, ROBERT ROYCE, engineering and management consultant; b. Spokane, Wash., May 7, 1926; s. Fred Alonzo and Rebecca Jane (Sommerville) B.; m. Margaret Stewart Keyes, Aug. 20, 1950; children—Susan Bennett Olson Nelson, Philip K., Laurie B. Mapes. B.S., Calif. Inst. Tech., 1945, M.S., 1947, Ph.D., 1949. Registered profl. engr., Oreg.; lic. surveyor, Oreg. Mem. tech. staff Hughes Aircraft, Culver City, Calif., 1949-54; v.p. TRW Systems, Redondo Beach, Calif., 1954-65; engrng. mgmt. cons., Eugene, Oreg., 1965—. Contbr. articles to profl. jours. Patentee in field. Served to lt. (j.g.) USNR, 1944-54. Fellow IEEE. Republican. Presbyterian. Home and Office: 85334 S Willamette St Eugene OR 97405-9568

BENNETT, ROBERT THOMAS, lawyer, accountant; b. Columbus, Ohio, Feb. 8, 1939; s. Francis Edmund and Mary Catherine (Weiland) B.; B.S., Ohio State U., 1960; J.D., Cleve. Marshall Law Sch., 1967; m. Ruth Ann Dooley, May 30, 1959; children—Robert Thomas, Rose Marie. Admitted to Ohio bar, 1967; C.P.A., Ernst and Ernst, Cleve., 1960-63; with tax assessing dept. Cuyahoga County (Ohio) Auditor's Office, Cleve., 1963-70; mem. firm Bartunek, Bennett, Garofoli and Hill, Cleve., 1975-79; mem. firm Bennett & Klonowski, Cleve., 1979-83; mem. firm Bennett & Harbarger, Cleve., 1983-88. Exec. vice chmn. Cuyahoga County Rep. Orgn., 1974-88; state chmn. Ohio Rep. Orgn., 1988—; mem. Rep. Nat. Com., 1988—; bd. dirs. Univ. Hosp. of Cleve. and S.W. Gen. Health Ctr. Republican. Roman Catholic. Mem. Citizens League Club, Capitol Hill Club (Washington). Contbr. articles to profl. publs. Home: 4800 Valley Pky Cleveland OH 44126-2847 Office: Ohio Rep Party 211 S 5th St Columbus OH 43215-5203*

BENNETT, ROBERT WILLIAM, law educator; b. Chgo., Mar. 30, 1941; s. Lewis and Henrietta (Schneider) B.; m. Harriet Trop, Aug. 19, 1979. B.A., Harvard U., 1962, LL.B., 1965. Bar: Ill. bar 1966. Legal asst. FCC commr. Nicholas Johnson, 1966-67; atty. Chgo. Legal Aid Bur., 1967-68; asso. firm Mayer, Brown & Platt, Chgo., 1968-69; faculty Northwestern U. Sch. Law, Chgo., 1969—; prof. law Northwestern U. Sch. Law, 1974—, dean, 1985-95. Author: (with LaFrance, Schroeder and Boyd) Hornbook on Law of the Poor, 1973. Knox Meml. fellow London Sch. Econs., 1965-66. Fellow Am. Bar Fedn. (bd. dirs., treas.); mem. Chgo. Council Lawyers (pres. 1971-72), Am. Law Inst., ABA. Home: 2130 N Racine Ave Chicago IL 60614-4002 Office: Northwestern U Sch Law 357 E Chicago Ave Chicago IL 60611-3059*

BENNETT, RONALD THOMAS, photojournalist; b. Portland, Oreg., Nov. 6, 1944; s. E.E. Al and Donna Mae (Thomas) B.; children: R. Thomas, Gardinas. Student, Portland State U., 1964-67; student in photojournalism, U. Wash., 1965; student pre-law and bus. mgmt, Multnomah Coll., Portland, 1963-64. Lab. technician, photographer Sta. KATU-TV, Portland, 1963-65; staff photographer Oreg. Jour., Portland, 1965-68, UPI Newspictures, L.A., 1968-70; staff photojournalist UPI at White House, 1970-88; sr. photo editor The San Diego Union, 1988-89; owner, CEO Capital TV, La Jolla, Calif., 1989-97; graphic artist, illustrator, 1997—; internat. launch svcs. mission integrator, 1998—; instr. photojournalism Portland State U., 1967; mem. standing com. U.S. Senate Press Photographers Gallery, 1980-89, sec.-treas.; CEO, Ronald T. Bennett Photography Frameable Original Photos & Note Cards, 1995—. Photographer: Assassination, 1968; one-man show Lake Oswego, Oreg., 1979; group exhbns. Libr. of Congress, 1971-89; exhibited in juried art shows in Calif. and Ariz., show photography, Offtrack Gall. Mem. coun. Town of La Jolla, Calif., active Associated Volume Buyers, chmn. Brown Goods. Recipient 1st prize World Press Photo Assn., 1969, Calif. Press Photographers, 1968, 69, Gold Seal competition, 1968, 69; nominated for Pulitzer prize, 1968, 76, 77, 78, first prize, Internatl. Exhibition of Photography, 1996-97. Mem. White House News Photographers (bd. dirs. photo exhbn. com, 1974-78, 1st prize 1976, 77, 78, 80, 84, 86, 87), Nat. Headliner Club (1st prize 1969, 78), Nat. Press Photographers Assn. (1st prize 1972), San Diego Art Guild and Colo. Art Assn., Calif. Press Photographers Assn., Rotary (staff photographer La Jolla chpt., Achievement award Am. Project 1992, 93), German Shepherd Dog Club. Baptist. e-mail: RonPhoto@worldnet.att.net. Home: 12907 La Tortola San Diego CA 92129-3057

BENNETT, SAUL, public relations agency executive; b. N.Y.C., Oct. 21, 1936; s. Philip and Ruth (Weinstein) Ostrove; m. Joan Marian Abrahams, Aug. 15, 1965; children: Sara (dec.), Charles, Elizabeth. BS in Journalism, Ohio U., Athens, 1957. Engaged in public relations, 1963—; account supr., then v.p. Rowland Co. (public relations), N.Y.C., 1965-74; v.p., then sr. v.p. Robert Marston and Assocs., N.Y.C., 1974-78; exec. v.p. Robert Marston and Assocs., 1978-86, partner, 1979—, sr. exec. v.p., 1986—; pres. Robert Marston Mktg. Communications Inc., 1988-96; ind. cons., 1997—. Author: New Fields and Other Stones, Jesus Matinees and Other Poems, 1998. With USAR, 1958-59, 61-62.

BENNETT, SCOTT BOYCE, librarian; b. Kansas City, Kans., July 22, 1939; s. Preston Theodore Bennett and Viola Louise (Scott) Mayberry; m. Carol Jean Glass, June 20, 1960; children: Beth Louise, Theodore David, Myron Richard, Kristellen Anne. AB magna cum laude, Oberlin Coll., 1960; MA in English, Ind. U., 1966, PhD in English, 1967; MS in Libr. Sci., U. Ill., 1976. Woodrow Wilson teaching intern St. Paul's Coll., Lawrenceville, Va., 1964-65; asst. prof. English U. Ill., Urbana-Champaign, 1967-74, from instr. to asst. prof. to assoc. prof. libr. adminstrn., 1974-81; asst. libr. collection mgmt. Northwestern U., Evanston, Ill., 1981-89; dir. Milton S. Eisenhower Libr. Johns Hopkins U., Balt., 1989-94; univ. libr. Yale U., New Haven, 1994—. Contbr. articles to profl. jours. Adv. panel library and archival preservation Ill. State Libr., adv. bd. Ill. State Archives; rev. panelist NEH; chair project Rsch. Librs. Group; prin. state-wide preservation planning Md. Woodrow Wilson Nat. fellow 1960-61, Ind. U. Dissertation Yr. fellow, Haskell fellow, 1966-67, U. Ill. Faculty fellow, 1969, Hon. Vis. Rsch. fellow Victorian Studies Ctr. U. Leicester, Eng., 1979, Am. Coun. Learned Socs. fellow, 1978-79. mem. AAUP (pres., sec. Urbana-Champaign chpt. 1975-78, various other offices), Rsch. Soc. Victorian Periodicals (exec. bd. 1971-73, pres. 1977-82). Office: Yale U Univ Libr PO Box 208240 New Haven CT 06511-8240*

BENNETT, SCOTT LAWRENCE, lawyer; b. N.Y.C., July 8, 1949; s. Allen J. and Rhoda (Maltz) B. A.B. with high distinction, U. Mich., 1971; J.D.,

Cornell U., 1974. Bar: N.Y. 1975, U.S. Dist. Ct. (so. dist.) N.Y. 1976, U.S. Ct. Appeals (2d cir.) 1976, U.S. Supreme Ct. 1977. Assoc. Donovan, Leisure, Newton & Irvine, N.Y.C., 1974-79; sr. v.p., assoc. gen. counsel, sec. The McGraw-Hill Cos., Inc., N.Y.C., 1979—. Mem. Assn. Am. Pubs. (lawyers com.), Assn. of Bar of City of N.Y. (corp. law com.), ABA, N.Y. State Bar Assn., Phi Beta Kappa. Home: 101 W 12th St Apt 10J New York NY 10011-8120 Office: The McGraw Hill Co Inc Ste 383 1221 Avenue Of The Americas New York NY 10020-1095

BENNETT, SHARON KAY, music educator; b. West Jefferson, Ohio. BMus, Eastman Sch. Music, 1960, MMus, 1962. Asst. prof. U. Iowa, Iowa City, 1980-84; from asst. prof. to assoc. prof. Capital U., Columbus, Ohio, 1992—; adj. lectr. Otterbein Coll., Westerville, Ohio, 1986-87, Capital U., 1985-92; resident coloratura Nurnberg (Germany) Opera, 1970-73, Hamburg (Germany) State Opera, 1973-76; resident guest artist Scottish Opera, Glasgow, 1976-77; presenter symposium. Author: 40 Vocalises, 1993, Class Voice Simplified, 1994. Recipient 1st place Iowa Symphony competition, 1981; named to Women of Achievement, YWCA, 1986; Rockefeller Found. grantee, N.Y.C., 1966-68; Old Gold fellow U. Iowa, Iowa City, N.Y. and Paris; Capital U. faculty devel. grantee, 1995. Mem. Nat. Assn. Tchrs. of Singing, Internat. Assn. Women Composers, Vocal Arts Resource Network, Coll. Music Soc., Sigma Alpha Iota (sec. 1985-87). Avocations: gardening, painting.

BENNETT, SHOSHANA STEIN, post partum counselor, consultant, lecturer; b. N.Y.C., Sept. 5, 1954; . Herman David and Charmion Kerr (Goldfarb) S.; m. Henry Joseph Bennett, May 24, 1981; children: Elana Michelle, Aaron Daniel. BA, Grinnell Coll., 1975; MA, San Francisco State U., 1977; PhD in Clin. Psychology, Calif. Coast U., Santa Ana, 1998. Cert tchr. learning handicapped, multiple subjects, Calif.; cert. c.c. tchr., Calif.; cert. in clin. hypnotherapy. Founder, coord. Postpartum Assistance for Mothers, Castro Valley, Calif., 1987—; instr. in handling postpartum depression Hayward (Calif.) Adult Sch., 1988-90; group leader Acalanes Adult Sch., Walnut Creek, Calif., 1988-90; guest spkr., cons. Western Regional Postpartum Support Internat. Seminar, Oakland (Calif.) Children's Hosp., 1990, ASPO Lamaze Conf., Walnut Creek, Calif., 1990, Nat. Assn. Postpartum Care Svcs. Conf., Oakland, 1992, Ob.Gyn. Conf., Kaiser Oakland Med. Ctr., 1992, 95, Calif. Healthy Mothers, Healthy Babies Conf., Oakland, 1993, Calif. Diabetes and Pregnancy Program, Warrack Hosp., Santa Rosa, Calif., 1994, San Joaquin County Comprehensive Perinatal Svc. Program, Stockton, Calif., 1995, Family Practitioner Grand Rounds, San Joaquin Gen. Hosp., Stockton, 1995, Dept. Psychiatry Kaiser Permanente Med. Group, Redwood City, Calif., 1995, Walnut Creek, Calif., 1998, Kaiser Lactation Assocs. Conf., Hayward Med. Ctr., 1996, others. Speaker on People are Talking TV program, 1987, KLOK radio From Birth and Beyond, 1992; author hosp. manuals on postpartum depression. Mem. Sch. Site Coun., Castro Valley, Calif., 1995—. Mem. Am. Counseling Assn., Postpartum Health Alliance (v.p.), Postpartum Support Internat. (bd. dirs.), Depression After Delivery. Office: Postpartum Assistance for Mothers PO Box 20513 Castro Valley CA 94546-8513

BENNETT, SONJA QUINN, administrative assistant; b. Dallas, Sept. 27, 1942; d. Cabe Terrell and Iva Pearle (McAuley) Quinn; m. Thomas Rae Bennett, May 27, 1961 (div. Dec. 1980); children: Richard James, Gary Don, Regina Anne. Student, U. Ark., 1983—. Tchr. Springdale (Ark.) Schs., 1975-80; adminstrv. asst. U. Ark., Fayetteville, 1980—; mem. staff senate U. Ark., 1998—. Mem. exec. bd. West Ark Area coun. Boy Scouts Am., Ft. Smith, 1972-90; EYC youth min. St. Thomas Episcopal Ch., Springdale, 1975-89; house mother internat. students Spring Internat., 1993—. Recipient Silver Beaver award Boy Scouts Am., 1976. Mem. Nat. Thespian Soc., Order Eastern Star. Republican. Home: 2060 N Juneway Ter Fayetteville AR 72703-2737

BENNETT, STEVEN ALAN, lawyer; b. Rock Island, Ill., Jan. 15, 1953; s. Ralph O. and Anne E. B.; m. Jeanne Aring; children: Preston, Spencer, Hunter, Whitney. BA in Art History, U. Notre Dame, 1975; JD, U. Kans., 1982. Bar: Tex. 1983, Ohio 1995, U.S. Dist. Ct. (no. dist.) Tex. 1983, U.S. Ct. Appeals (5th cir.) 1983, U.S. Supreme Ct. 1995. Atty. Freytag, Marshall, et al, Dallas, 1982-84, Baker, Mills & Glast, Dallas, 1984-87; ptnr. Shank, Irwin, Conant et al, Dallas, 1987-89; gen. counsel Bank One, Tex., N.A., Dallas, 1989-94; sr. v.p., gen. counsel, sec. Banc One Corp., Columbus, Ohio, 1994-99; exec. v.p., chief legal officer, sec. Cardinal Health, Inc., Dublin, Ohio, 1999—. City councilman, mayor pro tem Mesquite, Tex., 1984-86; trustee Meadowview Sch., Mesquite, 1985-92; chair fin. com. St. Brendan Ch., Hilliard, Ohio, 1998—; treas. Kress for Congress Com., Dallas, 1988-91; pres., bd. dirs. Dallas Dem. Forum, 1993-94; bd. dirs. Ohio Hunger Task Force, Columbus, 1995—; trustee Woodrow Wilson Internat. Ctr. for Scholars, Washington, 1996—, vice-chmn., 1999—. Fellow, Ohio State Bar Found.; mem. ABA (banking law com.), Tex. Assn. Bank Counsel, Dallas Bar Assn., Ohio State Bar Assn., Columbus Bar Assn., St. Thomas More Soc. (Dallas bd. dirs. 1990-94), Am. Corp. Counsel Assn. (bd. dirs. 1996—, chair policy com. 1997—), The Bankers Roundtable (lawyers' coun. 1994-98), Phi Beta Kappa. Avocation: landscape photography. Office: Cardinal Health Inc 7000 Cardinal Pl Dublin OH 43017

BENNETT, THOMAS B., federal judge; b. 1949. BS, W.Va. U., 1970, MA, 1973, JD, 1976. Bar: W. Va., 1976, Tex., 1979. Instr. econs. W.Va. U., 1971-76; law clk. hon. John R. Brown U.S. Ct. Appeals 5th Cir., 1976-77; assoc. Bowles, Rice, McDavid, Graff & Love, 1977-79; ptnr. Bowles, Rice, McDavid, Geoff, Slove, 1980-95; judge US Bankruptcy Ct. for Northern Dist. of Alabama, Birmingham, 1995—. Fax: 205-714-3882. Office: 1800 5th Ave North Rm 128 Birmingham AL 35203

BENNETT, THOMAS LEROY, JR., clinical neuropsychology educator; b. Norwalk, Conn., Sept. 25, 1942; s. Thomas LeRoy and Gertrude Upson (Richardson) B.; m. Jacqueline Beekman, Aug. 5, 1972; children: Dean, Shannon, Brian, Laurie. B.A., U. N. Mex., 1964, M.S., 1966, Ph.D., 1968. Diplomate Am. Bd. Profl. Neuropsychology (examiner, treas. 1993-96, pres.-elect 1995-97, pres. 1997-99), Am. Bd. Forensic Examiners, Am. Bd. Profl. Disability Cons., Am. Bd. Profl. Psychology. Asst. prof. Calif. State U., Sacramento, 1968-70; assoc. prof., then prof. psychology and physiology Colo. State U., Ft. Collins, 1970-98, coord. exptl. psychology sect., 1978-81, 92-95; pvt. practice neuropsychology Ft. Collins, 1981—; mem. allied health staff Poudre Valley Hosp., Ft. Collins; clin. dir. Brain Injury Recovery Program, Ft. Collins. Author: Brain and Behavior, 1977, The Sensory World, 1978, The Psychology of Learning and Memory, 1979, Exploring the Sensory World, 1979, Introduction to Physiological Psychology, 1982, The Neuropsychology of Epilepsy, 1992, Brainwave-R: Cognitive Strategies for Brain Injury Rehabilitation, 1997, Mild Traumatic Brain Injury, 1999, Psychology Video Teaching Modules: The Brain, 2d edit., 1997, Psychology Video Teaching Modules: The Mind, 1999; also articles and book chpts.; assoc. editor Rehab. Psychology, Archives of Clinical Neuropsychology; mem. editl. bd. Cognitive Rehab., Archives Clin. Neuropsychology, Jour. Head Injury, Bull. of Nat. Acad. Neuropsychology, Neuropsychology Rev., others. Elder Timnath Presbyterian Ch. Fellow APA, Nat. Acad. Neuropsychology (editl. bd. Bull., bd. dirs. 1993-95, conv. chmn. 1993, 94), Am. Psychol. Soc., Am. Coll. Profl. Neuropsychology (pres. 1997-99); mem. Am. Coll. Forensic Examiners, Psychonomic Soc., Rocky Mountain Psychol. Assn., Soc. for Cognitive Rehab., Nat. Head Injury Found. (provider's coun.), Colo. Head Injury Found. (provder's coun.), Internat. Neuropsychol. Soc., Colo. Neuropsychol. Soc., Sigma Xi (named Colo. State U. Honored Scientist 1996). Home: 213 Camino Real Fort Collins CO 80524-8907 Office: Colo State U Dept Psychology Fort Collins CO 80523 *Always look for something good in everyone you meet.*

BENNETT, TONY (ANTHONY DOMINICK BENEDETTO), entertainer; b. Astoria, N.Y., Aug. 3, 1926; s. John and Anna (Suraci) Benedetto; m. Patricia Beech, Feb. 12, 1952 (div. 1971); children: D'Andrea, Daegal; m. Sandra Grant, Dec. 29, 1971 (div. 1984); children: Joanna, Antonia. Ed., Am. Theatre Wing, N.Y.C.; MusD, U. Berkeley. Classic pop vocalist, entertainer; frequent appearances on TV, in concert; recs. for Columbia Records including The Art of Excellence, 1986, Bennett/Berlin, 1988, Astoria: Portrait of the Artist, 1990, Perfectly Frank, 1992 (Grammy award best traditional vocal performance), Steppin' Out, 1993 (Grammy award, Best Traditional Pop Vocal), The Essence of Tony Bennett, 1993, MTV Unplugged, 1994 (Grammy award Album of the Year, Best Traditional Pop Vocal), Here's to the Ladies, 1995, The Playground, 1998, Tony Bennett on Holiday, 1997, Tribute to Billie Holiday; owner, rec. artist for Improv Records; paintings exhibited Butler Inst. of Am. Art, Youngstown, Ohio, 1994; appeared in (films) The Scout, 1994, (TV movies) Men, Movies & Carol, 1994, Men, Movies & Carol, 1994, The Scout, 1994, Sinatra: 80 Years My Way, 1995; (TV shows) The Simpsons, 1989, Muppets Tonight, 1996, (TV spl.) tony Bennett on Holiday: A Tribute to Billy Holiday, 1997, (TV guest appearance) Suddenly Susan, 1997; author: The Good Life: The Autobiography of Tony Bennett. Served with inf. AUS, World War II. Recipient Gold records for recs. Because of You, I Left My Heart in San Francisco, Best Male Vocalist award Cash Box mag., 1951, Grammy award for best solo vocal and record of year, 1962, Grammy award for best traditional pop vocal performer, 1998. Address: 130 W 57th St Apt 9D New York NY 10019-3311*

BENNETT, VERNA GREEN, employee relations executive; b. Memphis, Oct. 4, 1942; d. Agee and Philistine Louvenia (Jackson) Green; m. John Paul Bennett, Sept. 24, 1966 (div. Dec. 3, 1978). BS in Bus. Edn., Knoxville Coll., 1965. Tchr. Stevens Lee High Sch., Asheville, N.C., 1965-66; adminstr. external affairs Youth in Action, Bklyn., 1966-67; adminstr. cmty. rels., pub. rels. Pepsi Cola Co., N.Y.C., 1967-70; staff asst., coll. rels. coord., hdqrs. recruiter Mobil Corp., N.Y.C., 1970-80; western region recruiter Mobil Corp., L.A., 1980-87; EEO rels. mgr. Mobil Corp., Fairfax, Va., 1987-96; head ednl. non-profit orgn. CCDM Inc., Dallas, 1996—; mem. corp. adv. bd. Nat. Assn. Minority Engr. Adminstrs., Fla., 1980-96, Am. Indian Sci. and Engring., Boulder, 1990-96, NAACP ACTSO, Balt., 1989-96; motivational spkr., lectr. on recruitment. Pres. New Dominion chpt. Nat. Coalition of 100 Black Women, 1992-96, mem. nat. membership com., 1998-99, chmn. chpt. devel. com., nat. bd. dirs., 1993-99, also v.p. membership Dallas chpt., 1998-99; chmn. bd. Coun. on Career Devel. for Minorities, Dallas, 1986-96, exec. dir. elect, 1997—; mem. No. Va. Urban League, Alexandria, 1990-96; mem. adv. bd. I Am That I Am Acad., Dallas, 1999. Recipient Presdl. Achievement and Nat. Amigo of Yr. awards SER-Jobs for Progress, Dallas, 1988, 89, 90, 94, Donald H. McGannon award Nat. Urban League, N.Y.C., 1992, youth award Delta Sigma Theta, 1992. Mem. NAACP (life), Bus. and Profl. Women (corp. adv. resource devel. 1992-96). Avocations: antiques, gardening, reading, walking, music. Home: 8017 N Macarthur Blvd Apt 1063 Irving TX 75063-7634 Office: CCDM Inc Ste # 722 E 1341 W Mockingbird Ln Dallas TX 75247-4939

BENNETT, WILLIAM, oboist. Grad. with honors, Yale U.; student, Julliard Sch. Music. Assoc. prin. San Francisco Symphony Orch., 1979, prin. oboe, Edo de Waart chair, 1987—; mem. faculty San Francisco Conservatory of Music. Performer Marlboro Music Festival, 1979, 81; debut Carnegie Hall, 1980; co-soloist in Bach's Double Concerto in D minor San Francisco Symphony 1983 tour, soloist Haydn's Sinfonia concertante in B-flat, Mozart's C major Oboe Concerto, world premier Alvaro Cordero-Saldivia's Ciro Notturno for oboe and orch. on symphony's New and Unusual Music Series, 1986 and reconstructed version Mozart's Sinfonia concertante for flute, oboe, bassoon and horn, 1987; frequent recital soloist San Francisco Bay area; co-founder Caselli Ensemble; founding mem. Chamber Music Sundaes; mem. chamber orch. PARLANTE, performer West Coast premier Barber's Canzonetta for oboe and strings. Fellow Tanglewood Berkshire Music Ctr., 1977, 78; 1st prize winner Artists Internat. Competition, 1979. Office: San Francisco Symphony Orch Savies Symphony Hall 201 Van Ness Ave Ste 107 San Francisco CA 94102-4585*

BENNETT, WILLIAM LEO, JR., management consultant; b. Bklyn., Nov. 7, 1921; s. William L. and Anna Christine (Lawless) B.; m. Mary Louise Short, Aug. 18, 1948 (div. 1971); children: Mary Christine Bennett Cooke, Elizabeth Nancy Bennett Payne (dec.), Susan Laura Bennett Smith, William Leo III; m. Mary-Louise Aspinwall, Nov. 23, 1972; children: Lucy Knapp Richardson, Molly Knapp Gloss, John F. Knapp, Jr. BS in Naval Sci., U.S. Navl Acad., 1943; postgrad., Test Pilot Sch., 1950, Armed Forces Staff Coll., 1954. Commd. ensign USN, 1943, advanced through grades to capt., ret., 1972; project mgr. ENSCO, Inc., Springfield, Va., 1972-76; dir. quality div. Nat. R.R. Passenger Corp., Washington, 1976-81; v.p. ops. Intertek Svcs. Corp., Fairfax, Va., 1981-88; pvt. practice cons. Falls Church, Va., 1988-94. Mem. Fairfax County Rep. Com., 1981-84. Decorated Legion of Merit. Mem. Early and Pioneer Naval Aviators Assn., Am. Soc. Quality Control, Am. Helicopter Soc., The Retired Officers Assn., U.S. Naval Acad. Alumni Assn., U.S. Naval Acad. Athletic Assn., USS Yorktown Assn. (v.p., bd. dirs.), Army-Navy Country Club. Episcopalian. Avocation: golf. Home: 46910 Grissom St Sterling VA 20165-3576

BENNETT, WILLIAM MICHAEL, physician; b. Chgo., May 6, 1938; s. Harry H. and Helen A. (Kaplan) B.; m. Sandra S. Silen, June 12, 1977; four children. Student, U. Mich., 1956-59; B.S., Northwestern U., 1960, M.D., 1963. Diplomate Am. Bd. Internal Medicine, Am. Bd. Nephrology, Am. Bd. Clin. Pharmacology. Intern U. Oreg., 1963-64; resident Northwestern U., 1964-66; practice medicine specializing in internal medicine Portland, Oreg. and; Boston; mem. staff Mass. Gen. Hosp., 1969-70; asst. prof. medicine U. Oreg. Health Scis. Center, 1970-74, asso. prof., 1974-78, prof. medicine and pharmacology, 1978—. Author: Pharmacology and Management of Hypertension, 1994, Manual of Nephrology, 1990, Drug Therapy in Renal Failure, 1994; contbr. articles to med. jours. Served with USAF, 1967-69. Fellow ACP; mem. Am. Soc. Nephrology (pres. 1998-99), Transplantation Soc., Internat. Soc. Nephrology, Am. Soc. Pharmacology and Exptl. Therapeutics. Office: Oreg Health Sci U Portland OR 97201

BENNETT, WILLIAM RALPH, JR., physicist, educator; b. Jersey City, Jan. 30, 1930; s. William Ralph and Viola (Schreiber) B.; m. Frances Commins, Dec. 11, 1952; children: Jean, William Robert, Nancy. AB, Princeton U., 1951; MA, PhD, Columbia U., 1957; MA (hon.), Yale U., 1965; D.Sc. (hon.), U. New Haven, 1975. Rsch. asst. physics Columbia Radiation Lab., 1952-54; mem. Pupin Cyclotron Group, 1954-57; mem. faculty Yale U., New Haven, 1957-59, 62—, prof. physics and applied sci., 1965-72, Charles Baldwin Sawyer prof. engring. and applied sci., prof. physics, 1972-98, prof. emeritus, 1998—, fellow Berkeley Coll., 1963-81, master Silliman Coll., 1981-87, life fellow Silliman Coll., 1981—; tech. staff Bell Telephone Labs., Murray Hill, N.J., 1959-62; Cons. Tech. Rsch. Group, Melville, N.Y., 1962-67, Inst. Def. Analysis, Washington, 1963-70; vis. scientist Am. Inst. Physics Vis. Scientist Program, 1963-64; vis. prof. Brandels Summer Inst. Theoretical Physics, 1969; cons. mem. bd. dirs. Laser Scis. Corp., Bethel, Conn., 1968-71; mem. adv. panels atomic physics and astrophysics Nat. Bur. Standards, 1964-69; cons. CBS Labs., Stamford, Conn., 1967-68, AVCO Corp., 1978-81, Reeves Sci. Co., New Haven, 1989-91, Oak Ridge Assn. Univs., Washington, 1991-92, MCG Internat., New Haven, 1992-93; mem. lab. adv. bd. for rsch. Naval Rsch. Adv. Com., 1968-78; visitor Soviet Union, 1967, 69, 79; researcher gas lasers and atomic physics, gravitational physics, applications of computers to med. diagnostics. Author: Introduction to Computer Applications, 1976, Scientific and Engineering Problem Solving With the Computer, 1976, The Physics of Gas Lasers, 1977, Atomic Gas Laser Transition Data: A Critical Evaluation, 1979, Health and Low Frequency Electromagnetic Fields, 1994; editorial adv. bd. Jour. Quantum Electronics, 1965-69; guest editor Applied Optics, 1965. Recipient Western Electric Fund award for outstanding tchg. Am. Assn. Engring. Educators, 1977, Outstanding Patent award R & D Coun. N.J., 1977, Eli Whitney Patent award Conn. Patent Lawyers Assn., 1994; fellow Alfred P. Sloan Found., 1967, Guggenheim Found., 1967, John Fenders fellow, 1987. Fellow IEEE (life, Morris Liebmann award 1965), Am. Phys. Soc., Optical Soc. Am.; mem. Sigma Xi. Office: Yale U 102 Dunham Lab 10 Hillhouse Ave New Haven CT 06511-6814

BENNETT-MACCUBBIN, JUSTEN MICHAEL, journalist, producer; b. St. Louis, June 12, 1973. BA in Journalism, George Washington U., 1998. Adminstrv. asst. Whitman-Walter, Washington, 1994-96; reporter The Washington Intowner, 1997-98; polit. unit intern CNN's Inside Politics, Washington, 1998; prodn. asst. C-SPAN, Washington, 1998—. Mem. nat. steering com. 1993 March on Washington for Lesbian, Gay and Bisexual Equal Rights and Liberation, 1991-93; mem. zoning com. Adv. Neighborhood Commn., Washington, 1997. Mem. Soc. Profl. Journalists. Avocations: movies, science-fiction, plants. Home: 1215 N St NW Apt 4 Washington DC 20005 Office: C-SPAN 444 N Capitol Washington DC 20001

BENNIE, BOB, investment company executive; b. Canton, Ill., Sept. 28, 1960; s. Robert Ray and Janet Ann B.; m. Vicki Marie Monaghan Schuarz, Oct. 14, 1983 (div. Aug. 1987); 1 child, Jake; m. Angelia Lynn Clark, Nov. 25, 1989; childre; Jessie, Sadie. BS in Agrl., U. Nebr., 1983; MBA, Kans. State U., 1993. Sales rep. Monsanto Agrl. Co., Manhattan, Kans., 1984-94; investment rep. Edward Jones Investments, Lincoln, Nebr., 1994-97; CEO Bob Bennie Retirement Planning, Inc., Lincoln, Nebr., 1997—; mem. adv. bd. St. Elizabeth Hosp. Found., Lincoln, 1998—; bd. dirs. People's City Mission, Lincoln. Tchr. Sunday sch. Capital City Christian Ch., Lincoln, 1996—. Mem. Lincoln Independent Bus. Assn., Rotary. Republican. Avocations: fishing, waterfowl hunting, camping. Home: 1331 N 37th St Lincoln NE 68503 Office: Bob Bennie Retirement Planning Inc 5701 S 34th St Ste 101 Lincoln NE 68516

BENNING, JOSEPH RAYMOND, principal; b. Streator, Ill., May 23, 1956; s. Joseph Charles and Shirley Ann (Smith) B.; m. Katherine Marie Turner, Apr. 24, 1976; children: Jennifer Nichole, Joseph Donald. BA, Augustana Coll, 1978; MS in Edn., No. Ill. U., 1988. Cert. state supr., teaching, Ill. Tchr., coach Fulton (Ill.) High Sch., 1978-79; recreation dir. Fulton Recreation Corp., 1979; tchr., coach Streator (Ill.) High Sch., 1979-80, Woodland High Sch., Streator, 1980-83; program dir. Ill. State Bd. Edn., Ottawa, 1983-85; prin. St. Mary Grade Sch., Streator, 1985-89; assoc. supt. schs. Cath. Diocese Peoria, Ill., 1989-91, supt. schs., 1991-94; prin. St. Bede Acad., Peru, Ill., 1994—. Pres. Streator Youth Football League, 1984-90; adv. bd. Streator High Sch., 1985-89; prins. adv. bd. Cath. Diocese Peoria, 1987-89. Recipient CJ McDonald award Streator Youth Football League, 1989. Mem. Nat. Cath. Edn. Assn., Nat. Assn. Secondary Sch. Prin., Nat. Assn. Elem. Sch. Prin., Assn. Supervision and Curriculum Devel., Cath. Conf. Ill., KC. Roman Catholic. Avocations: sports, music. Office: Saint Bede Acad Rt 6 W Peru IL 61354*

BENNINGER, EDWARD C., JR., petroleum and natural gas company executive; b. 1942. BBA, Tex. Tech U., 1965. Mgmt. trainee West Tex. Utilities, 1965-66; sr. auditor Haskins & Sells, 1969-75; asst. v.p. internat. audit Lo Vaca Gathering Co., 1975-77, v.p. treasury svcs., 1977-79; treas. Valero Energy Corp., San Antonio, 1979-83, v.p. corp. financing, 1983-85, v.p., treas., 1985-86, sr. v.p., treas., 1986-92, bd. dirs., 1990—, exec. v.p., CFO, 1992—; exec. v.p. Valero Energy Co., 1992—; pres. Valero Natural Gas, L.P. Cos., 1992—, exec. v.p., COO, bd. dirs., 1992—, exec. v.p. fin. and adminstrn., 1995-96; pres., CFO Valero Energy Corp., San Antonio, Tex., 1996—. Served to lt. (j.g.) USN, 1966-69. Office: Valero Energy Corp 7990 I H IOW San Antonio TX 78230-4715*

BENNINGFIELD, CAROL ANN, lawyer; b. San Antonio, Dec. 8, 1952; d. Gordon Lane Benningfield and Ann Benningfield McCraw. BA in Polit. Sci., S.W. Tex. State U., 1975; JD, U. Tex., 1979. Bar: Tex. 1979, U.S. Dist. Ct. (so. dist.) Tex. 1996. Staff atty. Tex. Dept. Labor and Stds., Austin, 1979; staff counsel Tex. Chem. Coun., Austin, 1979-80; assoc. Wiley, Garwood, San Antonio, 1981-83; account exec. Dean-Witter Reynolds, San Antonio, 1983-89; pvt. practice Rockport, Tex., 1990—. Mem. gala com. San Antonio Stock Show and Rodeo, 1981-83; mem. Target 90 Goals for San Antonio, 1984-85; deacon First Presbyn. Ch., Rockport, 1992-95, mem. choir, 1990-96; mem. Rockport Art Assn., 1990—; trustee Aransas County Ind. Sch. Dist., Rockport, 1993-96, sec., 1993-96. Fellow Tex. Bar Found. Tex.; mem. San Antonio Young Lawyers (membership chmn. 1982), Rockport Fulton C. of C. (dir. 1992-94, awards com. chmn., v.p. 1993), Rotary. Office: 2602 Highway 35 N Rockport TX 78382-5707

BENNINGFIELD, TROY LEE, language arts educator; b. Lebanon, Ky., Sept. 3, 1969; s. Leroy and Betty Lou (Adams) B. BA, U. Ky., 1992. Cert. tchr. Ky. Facilitator, scorer Advanced Systems in Measurement and Evaluation, Inc., Louisville, 1992-93; program presenter The Sci. Ctr., Louisville, 1992-93; English, journalism tchr. Newport (Ky.) Ind. Schs., 1993-97, Washington County Schs., Springfield, Ky., 1997—. Mem. Nat. coun. of Tchrs. of English, U. Ky. Alumni Assn., Ky. H.S. Journalism Assn. (steering com. 1997). Democrat. Baptist. Home: 1425 Bradfordsville Rd Lebanon KY 40033-9718

BENNINGTON, LESLIE ORVILLE, JR., insurance agent; b. Sedalia, Mo., Dec. 29, 1946; s. Leslie Orville Sr. and Eunice May Marguerite (Cole) B.; m. Susan Frances Grotha, June 1, 1968; children: Leslie O. III, Jeremy Lawrence. BSME, U. Mo., Rolla, 1968; postgrad., U. Tenn. Space Inst., 1969; ChFC, Am. Coll., 1988. CLU; chartered fin. cons.; registered profl. engr., Wash., Wyo. Design engr. Arnold Research Orgn., Tullahoma, Tenn., 1968-70; engr. Pacific Power & Light, Glenrock, Wyo., 1973-75; agt., asst. gen. agt. Am. Nat. Ins. Co., Casper, Wyo., 1975-85; gen. agt. Ins. Sales, Glenrock, 1985—; pres. Cen.Wyo. Estate Planning Coun., Casper, 1985-86. Mem. Glenrock Vol. Fire Dept., 1973—, asst. chief, 1982, pres., 1993-97; pres., v.p. Converse County Recreation Bd., Douglas, Wyo., 1980-90; judge dist. h.s. speech contests, Glenrock; bd. dirs. Converse County Sch. Dist. 2, 1976; bd. dirs. Glenrock Cmty. Recreation Dist., 1990-97, pres., 1992-94; guide Helluva Hunt for physically disabled hunters, 1986—, bd. dirs., 1991—; bd. dirs. Nat. Bow Hunt, Glenrock, 1994—; baseball coach Little League and Babe Ruth, 1983-93. Mem. Nat. Assn. Life Underwriters (Nat. Quality award, Health Ins. Quality award, Nat. Sales Achievement award), Cen. Wyo. Life Underwriters (pres. 1978-80), Wyo. Life Underwriters Assn. (chmn. membership com. 1985-87, nat. com. 1982-87, v.p. 1986-87, bd. dirs. 1980-90, Ins. Agt. of Yr., 1980, pres. 1988-89), West Cen. Wyo. CLUs (pres. 1986-88), Million Dollar Round Table, Nat. Pony Express Assn. (pres. Ea. Wyo. div. 1985—, v.p. Wyo. div. 1989-97, pres. 1997—), KC (grand knight, faithful navigator). Republican. Roman Catholic. Avocations: cattle, livestock. Home: 6 Shannon Dr Glenrock WY 82637 Office: PO Box 2049 1260 East US Hwy 20-26-87 Glenrock WY 82637-2049

BENNINGTON, RONALD KENT, lawyer; b. Circleville, Ohio, July 16, 1936; s. Ralph P. and Delorice (Dudley) B.; m. Barbara Schumm, June 19, 1959; children: Scott C., Amy E. BA magna cum laude, Kenyon Coll., 1958; JD summa cum laude, Ohio State U., 1961. Assoc. Black, McCuskey, Souers & Arbaugh, Canton, Ohio, 1961-65, ptnr., 1965—; sec. Hoover Worldwide Corp., 1969-86; bd. dirs. United Hard Chrome, Inc. Bd. trustees Plain Twp., Canton, 1972-78, Malone Coll., Canton, 1982—, chmn. 1984-86, Timken Mercy Med. Ctr., Canton; adv. com. Kenyon Coll., Gambier, Ohio; mem. Leadership Canton; bd. dirs. ARC, Canton; fundraising United Way Fund Drive; trust com. Hoover Found.; ambassador Ohio Found. Ind. Colls.; steering com. Pro Football Hall of Fame, 1985—; Big Ten football ofcl., 1984—; trustee The Hoover Found., Canton, Greater Canton C. of C.; bd. assocs. Union Coll., Alliance, Ohio. Fellow Am. Bar Found., Ohio State Bar Found.; mem. ABA, Ohio Bar Assn., Stark County Bar Assn., Greater Canton C. of C. (bd. trustees), Ea. Ohio Football Ofcls. Assn. (pres. 1986—), Stark County Law Libr. Assn. (pres.). Republican. Presbyterian. Home: 3528 Darlington Rd NW Canton OH 44708-1714 Office: Black McCuskey Souers & Arbaugh 1000 United Bank Plz Canton OH 44702

BENNINK, JACK RICHARD, microbiologist, researcher; b. Corry, Pa., Feb. 18, 1953; s. Ivan Guy and Mary Lou (Hurlbert) B.; m. Cindi Sue Merkle, May 29, 1976; children: Nathanael Scott, Tara Susanne. BA, Asbury Coll., 1975; PhD, U. Pa., 1978. Staff mem. Basel (Switzerland) Inst. for Immunology, 1980-82; asst. prof., assoc. prof. Wister Inst., Phila., 1982-87; sr. investigator NIH, Bethesda, Md., 1987—. Contbr. articles to profl. jours. Recipient Pub. Health Svc. award, 1990, 94, 95. Mem. Am. Soc. Virology. Office: NIH Bldg 4 Rm 213 Bethesda MD 20892-0440*

BENNION, JOSEPH WOOD, potter; b. Salt Lake City, Sept. 4, 1952; s. Owen Cannon and Lenore (Wood) B.; m. Lee Patrica Udall, June 29, 1976; children: Louisa Bonelli, Zina Lenore, Adah Lee. Student, Tuscarora (Nev.) Pottery Sch., 1980; BFA in ceramics, Brigham Young U., 1982, MFA, 1986. Potter Horseshoe Mountain Pottery, Spring City, Utah, 1976—; lectr., workshop leader in field. City coun. mem. Spring City Coun., 1980-84. Fellow Nat. Endowment Arts, 1991; subject of documentary A Potter's Meal, 1992. Mem. Nat. Coun. Edn. in Ceramic Arts. Mormon. Avocations: river running, backpacking. Home and Office: PO Box 186 Spring City UT 84662-0186*

BENNION, SCOTT DESMOND, physician; b. Casper, Wyo., July 26, 1948; s. Desmond and Wanda Bennion; m. Mary Marie Blanton; children: Scott, Beau, Brandon. BS summa cum laude, U. Wyo., 1970, MS, 1972;

MD, U. Utah, 1975. Diplomate Nat. Bd. Med. Examiners, Am. Bd. Internal Medicine, Am. Bd. Dermatology, Am. Bd. Dermatologic Immunology/Diagnostic and Lab. Immunology. Intern U. Rutgers Med. Sch., 1975-76, resident in internal medicine, 1976-78, chief resident dept. medicine, 1978; commd. 2d lt. U.S. Army, 1976, advanced through grades to col., 1991; resident in dermatology Fitzsimons Army Med. Sch., Denver, 1981-84, chief dept. clin. investigations, 1994-96, chmn. lab. animal use and care com., 1994-96; asst. chief dermatology svc. 98th Gen. Hosp., Nuremburg, Germany, 1986, chief dept. health clinics, 1987-88; chief immunodermatology sect. dermatology svc. Fitzsimons Army MC, Aurora, Colo., 1989—; command surgeon ARTASK, Kuwait, 1992; command surgeon joint task force Kuwait and Army Ctrl. Command-Forward, 1992; dermatology cons. to the Army Surgeon Gen., 1996-99; chief Troop Med. Clin. Fitzsimmons Army Garrison, 1996—; asst. clin. prof. dept. dermatology U. Colo. Health Sci. Ctr., 1992—. Contbr. chpts. to books: Military Dermatology, 1994, Secrets of Dermatology, 1996, Dubois Lupus, 1997, also articles to profl. publs. Pres. Nuremburg Elem. Sch. PTSA; asst. cubmaster, cubmaster, chmn. Volksmarch com. Boy Scouts Am., 1986; pres. Foxrdige Improvement Assn., 1992—, pres., 1994—. Named to Order of Mil. Med. Merit, 1987; named Cubmaster of Yr. Bavaria dist. Boy Scouts Am., 1987. Fellow ACP, Am. Acad. Dermatology (mem. govt. medicine task force 1996—; Colo. Dermatology Soc. rep. to adv. bd. 1997—), Assn. Mil. Surgeons, Assn. Mil. Dermatologists (Residents award 1984, sec.-treas. 1990-96, guest editor jour. 1991, pres. 1998-99), Soc. for Investigative Dermatology, Phi Kappa Phi. Avocations: skiing, diving. Home: 7944 S Olive Dt Englewood CO 80112 Office: Fitzsimons Army Garrison Health Clinic NSAG-Fitzsimons Aurora CO 80045

BENNIS, WARREN GAMELIEL, business administration educator, author, consultant; b. N.Y.C., Mar. 8, 1925; s. Philip and Rachel (Landau) B.; m. Clurie Williams, Mar. 30, 1962 (div. 1983); children: Katharine, John Leslie, Will Martin; m. Mary Jane O'Donnell, Mar. 8, 1988 (div. 1991); m. Grace Gabe, Nov. 29, 1992. AB, Antioch Coll., 1951; hon. cert. econs., London Sch. Econs., 1952; PhD, MIT, 1955; LLD, Xavier U., Cin., 1972, George Washington U., 1977; LHD (hon.), Hebrew Union Coll., 1974, Kans. State U., 1979; DSc (hon.), U. Louisville, 1977, Pacific Grad. Sch. Psychology, 1987, Gov.'s State U., 1991; LHD (hon.), Doan Coll., 1993. Diplomate Am. Bd. Profl. Psychology. Asst. prof. psychology MIT, Cambridge, 1953-56, prof., 1959-67; asst. prof. psychology and bus. Boston U., 1956-59; prof. Sloan Sch. Mgmt., 1959-67; provost SUNY-Buffalo, 1967-68, v.p. acad. devel., 1968-71; pres. U. Cin., 1971-77; U.S. prof. corps. and soc. Centre d'Etudes Industrielles, Geneva, Switzerland, 1978-79; exec.-in-residence Pepperdine U., 1978-79; George Miller Disting. prof.-in-residence U. Ill., Champaign-Urbana, 1978; Disting. prof. Bus. Adminstrn. Sch. Bus., U. So. Calif., L.A., 1980-88; univ. prof. U. So. Calif., L.A., 1988—; vis. lectr. Harvard U., 1958-59, Indian Mgmt. Inst., Calcutta; vis. prof. U. Lausanne (Switzerland), 1961-62, INSEAD, France, 1983; bd. dirs. The Foothill Group. Author: Planning of Change, 4th edit., 1985, Interpersonal Dynamics, 1963, 3d and 4th edits., 1975, Personal and Organizational Change, 1965, Changing Organizations, 1966, repub. in paperback as Beyond Bureaucracy, 1974, The Temporary Society, 1968, Organization Development, 1969, American Bureaucracy, 1970, Management of Change and Conflict, 1972, The Leaning Ivory Tower, 1973, The Unconscious Conspiracy: Why Leaders Can't Lead, 1976, Essays in Interpersonal Dynamics, 1979; (with B. Nanus): Leaders, 1985, On Becoming a Leader, 1989, (with I. Mitroff) The Unreality Industry, 1989, Why Leaders Can't Lead, 1989, Leaders on Leadership, 1992, An Invented Life: Reflections on Leadership and Change, 1993, Beyond Bureaucracy, 1993, (with J. Goldsmith) Learning to Lead, 1994, (with M. Mische) Reinventing the 21st Century, 1994, Beyond Leadership, 1994, Herding Cats: Bennis on Leadership, 1996, Organizing Genius, 1997, The Temporary Society, 1998, Co-Leaders, 1999, Old Dogs, New Tricks, 1999; co-headers, 1999, cons. editor Calif. Mgmt. Rev., Mgmt. Series Jossey-Bass Pubs. Mem. Pres.' White House Task Force on Sci. Policy, 1960-70; mem. FAA study task force U.S. Dept. Transp., 1975; mem. adv. com. N.Y. State Joint Legis. Com. Higher Edn., 1970-71; mem. Ohio Gov.'s Bus. and Employment Coun., 1972-74; mem. panel on alt. approaches to grad. edn. Coun. Grad. Schs. and Grad. Record-Exam Bd., 1971-73; chmn. Nat. Adv. Commn. on Higher Edn. for Police Officers, 1976-78; adv. bd. NIH, 1978-84; trustee Colo. Rocky Mountains Sch., 1978-82; bd. dirs. Am. Leadership Forum, 1984-89; mem. vis. com. for Humanities MIT, 1975-81; trustee Antioch Coll., Salk Inst. Capt. AUS, World War II. Decorated Bronze Star, Purple Heart; recipient Dow Jones award, 1987, McKinsey Fedn. award, 1967, 68. Mem. Am. Acad. Arts and Scis. (co-chmn. policy coun. 1969-71), Am. Mgmt. Assn. (dir. 1974-77), U.S. C. of C. (adv. group scholars). Office: U So Calif Sch Bus University Park Los Angeles CA 90089-1421

BENNISON, ALLAN PARNELL, geological consultant; b. Stockton, Calif., Mar. 8, 1918; s. Ellis Norman Lambly and Cora Mae (Parnell) B.; m. DeLeo Smith, Sept. 4, 1941; children: Victor, Christina, Mary. BA, U. Calif., Berkeley, 1940. Cert. petroleum geologist, cert. profl. geologist. Geology fellow Antioch Coll., Yellow Springs, Ohio, 1940-42; photogrammetrist U.S. Geol. Survey, Arlington, Va., 1942-45; stratigrapher, asst. chief geologist Companias Unidas de Petroleos, Cartagena, Colombia, 1945-49; staff stratigrapher Sinclair Oil & Gas Co., Tulsa, 1949-69; geol. cons. Tulsa, 1969—; cons. in field. Editor: Tulsa's Physical Environment, 1973; compiler maps; contbr. articles to profl. jours. Fellow AAAS, Geol. Soc. Am., Explorers Club; mem. Am. Assn. Petroleum Geologists (hon., trustee assoc., Disting. Svc. award 1986), Soc. Econ. Paleontologists and Mineralogists (Disting. Svc. award 1990), Tulsa Geol. Soc. (pres. 1965), Tulsa Astronomy Club (v.p. 1965), Explorers Club, Sigma Xi. Republican. Episcopalian. Avocations: photography, astronomy, reading, travel. Home and Office: 1410 Terrace Dr Tulsa OK 74104-4626 also: 11200 Butler Rd Grass Valley CA 95945

BENNON, SAUL, electrical engineer, transformer consultant; b. Phila., Aug. 9, 1914; s. Harry and Rose (Lipschutz) B.; m. Monica M. Delnick, Sept. 6, 1945; children: Lois, Nora, Betty, Alice, Robert, William. BSEE, U. Pa., 1936, MSEE, 1937. Registered profl. engr., Pa. With Westinghouse Electric Co., Sharon, Pa., 1937-79, design engr. power transformer div., 1937-43, project engr. underwater ordnance div., 1943-49, section mgr. distbn. transformer div., 1949-51, section mgr. large power transformer div., 1951-62, section mgr. power transformer devel., 1962-66, engring. mgr. large power transformers, Muncie, Ind., 1966-79; transformer cons. Muncie, 1979—. Contbr. articles to profl. jours.; holder 10 U.S. patents. Fellow IEEE (chmn. transformers com. 1977-78); mem. Phi Beta Kappa, Sigma Xi. Avocation: amateur radio. Office: 2701 W Twickingham Dr Muncie IN 47304-1050

BENO-CLARK, CANDICE LYNN, chemical company executive; b. New Brunswick, N.J., Mar. 25, 1951; d. Andrew Jule and Claire May (Blanchard) Beno; m. John W. Clark, Sr., Dec. 8, 1990. BA magna cum laude, U. Conn., 1973, MS in Biochemistry, 1974, postgrad., 1974-75. Grad. asst. U. Conn., 1973-75; lab. technician Linde div. Union Carbide Corp., Keasbey, N.J., 1976-78, sr. lab. technician Linde div., 1978-79; regional tech. supr. Linde div. Union Carbide Corp., South Plainfield, N.J., 1979; asst. staff engr. Linde div. Union Carbide Corp., Springfield, N.J., 1979-82, staff engr. Linde div., 1982-84; tech. bus. cons. Linde div. Union Carbide Corp., Danbury, Conn., 1984-85; staff engr. Linde div. Union Carbide Corp., Somerset, N.J., 1985-87; mgr. Linde div. Union Carbide Corp., Springfield, 1987-89; mgr. Linde div. Union Carbide Indsl. Gases, Inc., Danbury, Conn., 1989-96, internat. mgr., 1991-96; dir. internat. mgr. Praxair, Inc., Danbury, 1996; dir. N.Y. Blood Ctr., N.Y.C., 1997-98, spl. asst. to pres., 1998-99, chief learning officer, 1999—; supr. Landmark Edn., Edison, N.J., 1984-87; guest seminar leader, 1985-96, course mgr., 1984-86. Mem. Am. Soc. Quality Control, Compressed Gas Assn. (chmn. 1984-91, vice chmn. 1982-88, Svc. award 1991), Semicondr. Equipment and Material Inst. (co-chmn. 1987-91, editor jour. 1982-88, Outstanding Svc. award 1884-89, Leadership award 1988, Mortar Board, Phi Beta Kappa, Phi Kappa Phi. Democrat. Avocations: reading, swimming, jogging, nutrition, holistic health. Home: 405 Newark Ave Point Pleasant Beach NJ 08742-4143

BENOIT, JEAN-PIERRE ROBERT, pneumologist, consultant; b. Cotonou, Dahomey, May 19, 1930; s. Samuel Pierre and Renée (Meffre) B.; m. Isabelle Rappard, Apr. 10, 1969; children: Laurence, Arnaud. MD in Pneumo-phtisiology, Paris U., 1964, PhD in Econs., 1968. Intern in medicine Paris Hosp.; resident in pneumology-indsl. medicine Corbeil (France) Hosp.; sr. cons., dept. head Pneumology Hosp. Fontenoy, Chartres, France, 1970—; v.p. Ligue contre le Cancer, Chartres, 1990—. Contbr. articles to profl. jours. Officer French Med. Svc., 1957-59. Mem. Am. Thoracic Soc., Soc. Pneumology de Langue Francaise, N.Y. Acad. Scis., Nat. Geog. Soc., European Respiratory Soc., Imagery Thoracic Soc. Avocations: viola, bridge, music composition, archeology. Office: Hôpital Fontenoy Ctr, Hospitalier, Chartres 28018, France

BENOIT, RICHARD ARMAND, retired police chief, lawyer; b. New Bedford, Mass., Jan. 29, 1942; s. Oliver Maurice and Delina Marie (Barie) B.; m. Elizabeth Joan Nobrega, Nov. 17, 1962; children: Karen Marie Carvalho, Richard Michael. AS, Bristol Community Coll., Fall River, Mass., 1972; BS, Salve Regina U., 1975, MS, 1979; JD, So. New Eng. Sch. Law, New Bedford, 1989. Bar: Mass. 1990. Police officer New Bedford Police Dept., 1967-71, sgt., 1971-75, lt., 1975-82, capt., 1982-86, chief of police, 1986—; pvt. practice law New Bedford, 1990—; dir., instr. New Bedford Police Acad., 1975-85. Mem. Mayor's Task Force on Drug Free Community, New Bedford, Neighborhood Crime Watch, New Bedford, YMCA, New Bedford. With U.S. Army, 1959-62. Mem. ABA, Mass. Bar Assn., Boston Bar Assn., Mass. Chiefs of Police Assn., Internat. Assn. Chiefs of Police. Avocations: swimming, golf, reading. Home: 209 Maywood St New Bedford MA 02745-5108 also: 154 N Main St Fall River MA 02720-2107

BENOLIEL, JOEL, lawyer; b. Seattle, June 11, 1945; s. Joseph H. and Rachel (Maimon) B.; m. Maureen Alhadeff, Mar. 1971; 1 child, Joseph D. BA in Polit. Sci., U. Wash., 1967, JD, 1971. Bar: Wash., U.S. Dist. Ct. (we. dist.) Wash., U.S. Ct. Appeals (9th cir.), U.S. Mil. Ct. Appeals. Assoc. atty. MacDonald, Horgue & Bayless, Seattle, 1971-73, ptnr., 1973-78; v.p., gen. counsel Jack A. Benaroya Co., Seattle, 1978-84; ptnr. Trammell Crow Co., Seattle, 1985-87, Spieker Ptnrs., Bellevue, Wash., 1987-92; sr. v.p. law and real estate, gen. counsel Price Costco, Inc., Issaquah, Wash., 1992—. Bd. dirs. Overlake Sch., Redmond, Wash., 1995—, Congretation Ezra Bessaroth, Seattle, 1992-95. With U.S. Army, 1968-74. Avocations: tennis, boating, skiing, reading fiction. Office: Price Costco Inc 999 Lake Dr Issaquah WA 98027-5367*

BENOWITZ, ROY, composer, orchestrator, copyist, organist, pianist; b. Bklyn., Oct. 10, 1924; s. David and Bertha Miriam Benowitz; divorced; 1 child, Nathan. Piano accompanist for Zelda Benowitz (sister) (A.K.A. Zelda Bennett), N.J., 1938-40; orch. pianist Catskill Mtns., N.Y., 1945-50, throughout U.S., 1950-54; orchestrator Atlanta Pops Concert Orch., 1954-55; keyboardist throughout continental U.S., 1959—; organist for beauty pageant, San Bernardino, Calif., 1973-80. Composer music for TV series The Russ Lewis Show, 1959, (stage book show) Cafe Frisco, 1966, At the Stroke of Midnight, 1983, All Right God, 1985-86, An American Tradition, 1985-88, Trilby, 1985-89; composer score to Speak in Time, 1990 (on behalf of the problems faced by people who stutter); (prodn. number) On With the Show, 1965, Love Has Me Going in Circles, 1980, It's Over Now, 1986; adapted drama A Inner Panic to musical A Panic Within, 1995 (also pro-stuttering); appeared in movies: A Cold Wind in August, 1961, Seven Thieves, 1960. Mem. ASCAP, Am. Fedn. Musicians, Songwriters Guild of Am., Dramatists Guild, Nat. Ctr. for Stuttering, Nat. Stuttering Project, Creative Arts Temple. Jewish. Avocations: golf, chess, Am. history, swimming, self improvement.

BENSCH, KLAUS GEORGE, pathology educator; b. Miedar, Germany, Sept. 1, 1928; married; 3 children. M.D., U. Erlangen, Germany, 1953. Diplomate: Am. Bd. Pathology. Intern U. Hosps. of Erlangen, 1953-54; resident in anat. pathology U. Tex. and; M.D. Anderson Hosp., Houston, 1954-56, Yale, 1956-57; instr. pathology Yale Med. Sch., 1958-61, asst. prof., 1961-64, assoc. prof., 1964-68; prof. pathology Stanford Med. Sch., 1968—, acting chmn. dept. pathology, 1984-85, chmn. dept. pathology, 1985-99. Office: Stanford U Med Sch Dept Pathology 300 Pasteur Dr Palo Alto CA 94304-2203

BENSCHIP, GARY JOHN, manufacturing company executive; b. Chgo., Aug. 27, 1947; s. Melville John and Eleanor (Melin) B.; m. Susan Diane Mattson, Sept. 19, 1970; 1 child, Jaclyn. BS in Fin., U. Ill., Chgo., 1969; MBA, DePaul U., 1971. Budget analyst R.R. Donnelly & Sons, Chgo., 1969-73; rep. DuPont Walston, Chgo., 1973-74; mgr. fin. ops. Sun Electric Corp., Crystal Lake, Ill., 1974-78; dir. fin. analysis Cenco, Inc., Oak Brook, Ill., 1979-83; treas. Amerace Corp., Hackettstown, N.J., 1983-91, Curtiss-Wright, Lyndhurst, N.J., 1991—. Mem. Beta Gamma Sigma, Delta Mu Delta. Avocations: running, golf, coaching athletic youth teams. Office: Curtiss-Wright Corp 1200 Wall St W Lyndhurst NJ 07071-3677

BENSE, CHARLES JAMES, English educator; b. Sacramento, June 17, 1948; s. Charles Augustus and Joan Marie Bense; m. Susan Jane Pengray, 1966 (div. 1970); 1 child, Heidi Susan; m. Caroline Collins, Dec. 2, 1988. BA in English, Calif. State U., Sacramento, 1970, MA in English, 1973; MA in English, U. Calif., Davis, 1984, PhD in English, 1989. Cert. secondary tchr., Mont. Tchr. reading Hellgate H.S., Missoula, Mont., 1975-78; lectr. European div. U. Md., Heidelberg, Germany, 1978-81; tchg. asst. English U. Calif., Davis, 1982-85, assoc. English, 1985-89, lectr. English, 1989-90; asst. prof. Moorhead (Minn.) State U., 1990-95, assoc. prof., 1995—; interim chair dept. English Moorhead State U., 1997. Assoc. editor Jour. Mind and Behavior: An Interdisciplinary Jour., 1980-93, assessing editor, 1993—; panel reviewer Am. lit. younger scholars program NEH, 1993; contbr. articles to profl. jours. Faculty Rsch. grantee Moorhead State U., 1995. Mem. MLA (mem. Am. lit. sect.), Minn. State Univs. Inter Faculty Orgn. Office: Dept English Moorhead State U Moorhead MN 56563

BENSEL, CAROLYN KIRKBRIDE, psychologist; b. Orange, N.J., Sept. 21, 1941; d. William Everitt and Margaret Mary (McGlynn) B.; A.B. with honors in Psychology, Chestnut Hill Coll., 1963; M.S., U. Mass., 1964, Ph.D. (Univ. fellow), 1967. Teaching asst. U. Mass., Amherst, 1963-64, research asst., 1964-66; human factors psychologist Grumman Aerospace Corp., Bethpage, N.Y., 1967-71; chief human factors group U.S. Army Natick (Mass.) Research, Devel. and Engring. Ctr., 1971—. Lic. psychologist, Mass. Fellow Human Factors Soc., APA; mem. Ergonomics Soc., Soc. Engring. Psychologists, Internat. Ergonomics Assn., AAAS, Sigma Xi. Editor: Proc. 23d Ann. Meeting of Human Factors Soc., 1979. Office: Sci & Advanced Tech Directorate Army Natick Research Devel Engring Ctr Kansas St Natick MA 01760

BENSELER, DAVID PRICE, foreign language educator; b. Balt., Jan. 10, 1940; s. Ernest Parr and Ellen Hood Escar (Turnbaugh) B.; m. Suzanne Shelton, May 25, 1985; children: James Declan, Derek Justin. BA, West Wash. U., 1964; MA, U. Oreg., 1966, PhD, 1971. Prof. german, dept. chair Ohio State U., 1977-85; chair dept. modern langs. and lits. Case Western Reserve U., 1991-98, Louis D. Beaumont U. Prof. Humanities, 1991-98, Emile B. de Sauzé prof. modern lang. and lit., 1998—; disting. vis. prof. fgn. langs. U.S. Mil. Acad., West Point, N.Y., 1987-88, N.Mex. State U., Las Cruces, 1989; dir. German Studies program Case Western Reserve U.; mem. numerous coms. Case Western Res. U., U.S. Military Acad., U.S. Naval Acad., U. Akron, Ohio State U., Wash. State U., Ind. U., Emory U., U. Md., U. Cin., U. Wis., Pa. State U., U. Va., U. Mich., various others; lectr., panel mem., workshop condr., cons. in field. Compiler, editor: (with Suzanne S. Moore) Comprehensive Index to the Modern Language Journal, 1916-1980; editor 50 books, bibliographies, jours.; contbr. chpts. to books and articles to profl. jours. With USN, 1958-60. Recipient Bundesverdienstkreuz I. Klasse, Pres. Fed. Republic Germany, 1985, Army Commendation medal for disting. civilian svc. U.S. Mil. Acad., 1988; Lilly Found. Faculty Renewal fellow, Stanford U., 1975, Fullbright Graduate fellow, 1967-68, NDEA fellow, U. Oreg., 1964-67; various other grants, fellowships, scholarships. Mem. MLA, TESOL, Am. Assn. Applied Linguistics, Am. Assn. Tchrs. of German, Am. Assn. Univ. Profs., Am. Goethe Soc., Am. Soc. for 18th Century Studies, German Studies Assn., Lessing Soc., Soc. German-Am. Studies, Ohio Fgn. Lang. Assn., Phi Sigma Iota, Sigma Kappa Phi, Delta Phi Alpha. E-mail: dpb5@po.cwru.edu. Office: Case Western Res U Dept Modern Langs and Lits Cleveland OH 44106-7118

BEN SHAUL, YOCHANAN MENASHSHEH See **MISHLER, JOHN MILTON**

BENSINGER, DAVID AUGUST, dentist, university dean; b. St. Louis, May 14, 1926; s. William and Esther (Lissner) B.; m. Myra Blass, Dec. 24, 1944 (div. June 1972); children: Judith Ann (Mrs. William Thomas Haynes), Scott David; m. Susan Cohn Hartman, May 31, 1975. B.A., Washington U., St. Louis, 1944; D.D.S., St. Louis U., 1948; postgrad. health systems mgmt. Harvard U. Sch. Bus. Adminstrn., 1977. Mem. faculty, adminstrn. Sch. Dentistry Washington U., St. Louis, 1949—, assoc. prof. dept. periodontics, 1956-76, prof., 1976-90, assoc. dean, 1970-76, acting dean, 1976-83, exec. assoc. dean, 1983-87; dean Washington U. Sch. Dental Medicine, 1987-90, dean, prof. emeritus, 1990; practice dentistry, specializing in periodontics St. Louis, 1949-90; mem. staff Barnes, Jewish hosps., both St. Louis; mem. deans com. VA Hosp.; mem. nat. adv. com. Dental Edn. Rev. Com., NIH, 1969-72; cons. Scott AFB, St. Louis, 1956-62; mem. adv. coun. SBA, 1975. Editor: Jour. Greater St. Louis Dental Soc. 1963-70; asso. editor: Jour. Mo. Dental Assn, 1966-73. Mem. exec. bd. Ladue (Mo.) Sch. Sys., 1964-67; chmn. bd. counselors U. Calif. Med. Ctr., San Francisco, 1995-98; chmn. regional cabinet Wash. U., San Francisco, 1996—; elected trustee Coll. of Notre Dame, Belmont, Calif., 1998—. Lt. M.C., U.S. Army, 1948-49, capt. med. dept. USAF, 1955-56. Fellow Am. Coll. Dentists, Internat. Coll. Dentists; mem. ADA (ho. of dels.), Mo. Dental Assn. (pres. 1973-74, jud. coun.), Greater St. Louis Dental Soc. (bd. dirs. 1963-70, Svc. award 1971), Am. Acad. Peridontology, Internat. Assn. Dental Rsch., Midwest Soc. Peridontology (pres. 1972-73), Pierre Fouchard Acad., Royal Soc. Medicine (Eng.), Inst. Internat. Edn. (vice chmn. bd. dirs., chmn. exec. com. 1996-98), Washington U. Alumni Assn. (Alumnus of Yr. 1968), Univ. Club (St. Louis), Harvard Club (Boston and N.Y.C.), Omicron Kappa Upsilon. Home: 2100 Pacific Ave San Francisco CA 94115-1585

BENSINGER, PETER BENJAMIN, consulting firm executive; b. Chgo., Mar. 24, 1936; s. Benjamin Edward and Linda Elkus (Galston) B.; m. Judith S. Bensinger; children: Peter Benjamin, Jennifer Anne, Elizabeth Brooke, Virginia Brette. Grad., Phillips Exeter Acad., 1954; BA, Yale, 1958; hon. degree, San Marcos U., Peru, 1978; LLD (hon.), Dan Kook U., Seoul, Republic of Korea, 1980. Various mktg. positions Brunswick Corp., Chgo., 1958-65; new products mgr. Brunswick Corp., 1966-68; gen. sales mgr. Brunswick Internat., Europe, 1965-66, spl. products mgr., 1966-68; chmn. Ill. Youth Commn., 1969-70; dir. Ill. Dept. Corrections, Chgo., 1970-73; exec. dir. Chgo. Crime Commn., 1973; adminstr. Drug Enforcement Adminstrn., Washington, 1976-81; pres. Bensinger, DuPont & Assocs., Chicago, 1982—; chmn. Ill. Criminal Justice Info. Authority, 1991—; cons. various orgns.; del. White House Conf. on Corrections, 1971, Drug Abuse, 1988, U.S. Del. to Interpol, 1978. Pres. Lincoln Park Zool. Soc., Chgo., 1962-63; governing life mem., also mem. men's council Chgo. Art Inst.; mem. Ill. Alcoholism Adv. Council; Ill. Law Enforcement Commn., Ill. Council on Diagnosis and Evaluation Criminal Defendants, Ill. Narcotics Adv. Council; adv. com. Center for Studies in Criminal Justice, So. Ill. U., Center for Studies in Criminal Justice, U. Chgo.; vice chmn. ad hoc adv. com. U.S. Dept. Justice Nat. Inst. Corrections; mem. exec. com. Am. Bar Assn. Nat. Commn. Corrections; chmn. Ill. Task Force on Corrections, 1969; mem. bd. Fed. Prison Industries, Inc., 1973-85; bd. dirs. Jewish Fedn. Met. Chgo., Council Community Services Met. Chgo., Ill. Commn. on Children, Children's Meml. Hosp., Chgo., 1988—; bd. dirs., mem. exec. council Anti-Defamation League; regional bd. dirs. NCCJ; trustee Phillips Exeter Acad.; chmn. nat. law enforcement explorers conf. Boy Scouts Am., 1981, U.S. del. to, Interpol, 1978. Recipient Young Leadership award Jewish Fedn.-Welfare Bds. Met. Chgo., 1969, award for excellence John Howard Assn., 1972, Disting. Svc. award Govt. of Peru, 1978, U.S. Dept. of Justice award, EEO award, 1979, Disting. Svc. medal USCG, 1981, John Phillips award Phillips Exeter Acad., 1990, Lincoln medal Lincoln Acad., 1998. Mem. Am. Correctional Assn. (bd. dirs.), Assn. State Correctional Adminstrs. (sec. 1971-72, pres. 1972-73), Internat. Assn. Chiefs of Police (mem. exec. com.), Nat. Sheriffs Assn. (life), Chgo. City Club (bd. dirs.), Arts Club, Comml. Club Chgo., Yale Club (N.Y.C.), Shoreacres Club (Lake Bluff), Casino Club (Chgo.). Office: 20 N Wacker Dr Chicago IL 60606-2806

BENSMAIA, REDA, French studies educator, researcher; b. Kouba, Algeria, Oct. 15, 1944; came to U.S., 1979; s. Kaddour and Saleha (Benouniche) B.; m. Joelle Proust, Feb. 2, 1947 (div. June 1989); children: Sliman, Djamel; m. Maurizia Natali, Oct. 22, 1995. Licence es-lettres, Facultes des lettres, Aix-En-provence, France, 1969, MPhil, 1971; BA, Ecole Pratique, Paris, France, 1977, PhD, 1981. Asst. prof. Institut d' Etudes Politiques, Algiers, Algeria, 1973-74, U. Algiers, Algeria, 1974-76; prof. philosophy Lycée Français, San Francisco, 1979-81; assoc. prof. U. Minn., Mpls., 1981-85; dir. Paris Ctr. for Critical Studies, 1985-88; assoc. prof. U. Minn., Mpls., 1988-89; prof. U. Va., Charlottsville, Va., 1989-91, Brown U., Providence, 1991—; dir. Paris Ct. for Critical Studies, Paris, France, 1985-88. Author: The Barthes Effect, 1987, The Year of Passages, 1995, Alger ou la maladie de la mémoire, 1997; editor: On Gilles Deleuze, 1989; contbr. articles to profl. jours. Recipient award Am. Inst. for Maghrebi Studies, 1995; NEH grantee, 1983; EDP grantee U. Minn., Mpls., 1989. Mem. MLA, Continuum (adv. bd.), Lendemains (adv. bd.), Sites (adv. bd.), Coun. for Internat. Ednl. Exch. (steering com., adv. bd. curriculum). Avocations: writing poetry and fiction, music, hiking. Office: Brown U Dept French Studies PO Box 1961 Providence RI 02912-1961

BENSON, AARON LEE, art educator; b. Athens, Tenn., Jan. 31, 1958; s. Wayne Lee and Mary Nell (Gentry) B.; m. Elizabeth Jane Brown, Dec. 17, 1994; children: Aaron Tennessee, Mary Elizabeth, Zachriah Chyanne, Sarah Blessing. BFA, U. Tenn., 1985, BS in Art Edn., 1987, MFA, 1990. Asst. prof. art Shorter Coll., Rome, Ga., 1991-96, Union U., Jackson, Tenn., 1996—. One-man shows include Arts Ctr., Rome, Ga., 1995, Rome Area Coun. for the Arts, 1996, Asbury (Ky.) Coll., 1996, Tenn. Arts. Commn., 1997, Adam Gallery, Wheaton, Ill., 1997, West Tenn. Regional Art Ctr., Humbolt, 1998, U. Nebr. (Omaha); exhibited in group shows in Carbondale, Ill., 1988, Knoxville, Tenn., 1989, Phoenix, 1990, Sacred Arts, Wheaton, Ill., 1990, Portland (Ore.) Mus. Art, 1994, Nexus Gallery, Atlanta, 1996, Jackson, Tenn., 1997; permanent sculptures include Trump Corp., Knoxville, 1990, Ala. Inst. for the Deaf and Blind, Talladega, 1995, Corp. Olympic Devel., Atlanta, 1995, Rome Coun. for the Arts, 1996; contbr. articles to profl. jours. With USN, 1988-90. Grantee So. Artist Fedn., 1996, Patterson Barclay, Churches Holmes Found. Home: 79 Countrywood Dr Jackson TN 38305-3523 Office: Union Univ 1050 UU Dr Jackson TN 38305

BENSON, ANDREW ALM, biochemistry educator; b. Modesto, Calif., Sept. 24, 1917; s. Carl Bennett and Emma Carolina (Alm) B.; m. Ruth Carkeek, May 22, 1942 (div. 1969); children: Claudia Benson Matthews, Linnea; m. Dorothy Dorgan Neri, July 31, 1971. BS, U. Calif., Berkeley, 1939; PhD, Calif. Inst. Tech., 1942; Phil D h.c., U. Oslo., 1965; Docteur h.c., U. Paris, 1986. Instr. chemistry dept. U. Calif., Berkeley, 1942-43, asst. dir. Bio-organic group Radiation Lab., 1946-54; rsch. assoc. dept. chemistry Stanford U., 1944-45; assoc. prof. agrl. biol. chemistry Pa. State U., 1955-60, prof., 1960-61; prof.-in-residence biophys./physiol. chemistry UCLA, 1961-62; prof. Scripps Instn. Oceanography, U. Calif., San Diego, 1962-88, prof. emeritus, 1988—; Fulbright vis. prof. Agrl. Coll. Norway, 1951-52. Contbr. articles on biochem. rsch. on photosynthesis, lipids, coral metabolism, arsenic metabolism, methanol application in agr. to profl. jours. Trustee Found. for Ocean Rsch., San Diego, 1970-88; mem. adv. council The Costeau Soc., 1976—; mem. internat. adv. bd. Marine Biotech. Inst. Co. Ltd., Tokyo, 1990-98. Recipient Sugar Rsch. Found. award, 1950, Ernest Orlando Lawrence Meml. award, 1962, Rsch. award Supelco/Am. Oil Chemists Soc., 1987; Sr. Queen's fellow Australia, 1979; Eminent Scientist of RIKEN, Japan, 1995; named Hon. Citizen Alert Bay, B.C., Can., 1988. Fellow AAAS; mem. Am. Acad. Arts and Sci., NAS, Royal Norwegian Soc. Sci. and Letters, Am. Oil Chemists Soc., Am. Chem. Soc. (emeritus), Am. Soc. Plant Physiologists (Stephen Hales prize 1972), Am. Soc. Biochemistry and Molecular Biology, Inst. Marine Biology, Far East Br., Acad. Sci. Russia (hon.). Home: 6044 Folsom Dr La Jolla CA 92037-6711 Office: Scripps Instn Oceanography La Jolla CA 92093-0202

BENSON, BARBARA ELLEN, state agency administrator; b. Rockford, Ill., June 5, 1943; d. Olander Anton and Eleanor Margaret (Lydon) B. BA, Beloit Coll., 1965; MA, Ind. U., 1969, PhD, 1976. Editor Eleutherian Mills-Hagley Found., Wilmington, Del., 1973-80; dir. libr. Hist. Soc. Del., Wilmington, 1980-90, exec. dir., 1990—. Author: Logs and Lumber, 1989, (with Michael Biggs) Wilmington: the City and Beyond, 1990; contbr. articles to jours., chpts. to books. Vice chairperson Del. Humanities Forum, 1987-92, chairperson, 1992-94; bd. dirs. Sister Cities, Wilmington, 1985-89, ofcl.

visitor to Kalmar, Sweden, 1985; bd. dirs. State Records Commn. Del., 1987—; mem. rev. bd. Del. Hist. Preservation, 1990-96; bd. dirs. Hist. Red Clay Valley, 1994-96, Wilmington Rotary; mem. adv. com. Del Hist. Records, 1987—. Mem. Nat. Soc. of Fund Raising Execs., Am. Assn. of Mus., Am. Assn. State and Local History (state awards chmn. 1987-94, state membership com. 1996—), Mid Atlantic Regional Archivists (bd. dirs. 1983-87). Office: Hist Soc Delaware 505 N Market St Wilmington DE 19801-3004*

BENSON, BERNICE LAVINA, elementary education educator; b. Wolford, N.D., Sept. 30; d. Therman George and Annie Catherine (Hittle) Ritzman; m. Benjamin Melvin Benson, June 11, 1941 (dec.); 1 child, Beverly Ann. Student, Jamestown Coll.; BS in Edn., No. State Coll., 1964, MA equivalent. Cert. elem. tchr., S.D.; commd. Stephen's min., 1995. Tchr. 1st-6th grade Southam (N.D.) Sch. System, 1935-41; tchr. 1st grade Pierre (S.D.) Sch. System, 1953-84; tchr. Title I Fed. Devel. Reading Program, Pierre, 1984-87; tchr.-tutor Title IV Fed. Tutorials for Native Americans, Pierre; supr. student tchrs. No. State Coll., Pierre. Past officer, past mem. various state coms. Delta Kappa Gamma; charter mem. Capital U., Pierre; sponsor Discovery Ctr., Pierre; mem. YMCA, Pierre; spl. events worker VFW Aux., Pierre; mem. Fine ARts Coun., Pierre; actress Never Too Late, Pierre Players Drama Assn.; mem. planning com. for new bldg., mem. meml. com. Luth. Meml. Ch. Mem. NEA (state exec. uni-serve com.), Pierre Edn. Assn., S.D. Edn. Assn., Pierre Tchrs. Assn. (pres.), Internat. Reading Assn., Assn. for Childhood Edn., AAUW, DAR (past offices), PEO (past pres., all offices), Annie D. Tallent Club. Avocations: bridge, reading, traveling, gardening. Home: 324 Mary Ln Pierre SD 57501-2213

BENSON, D(AVID) MICHAEL, plant pathologist; b. Dayton, Ohio, Aug. 28, 1945; s. Phillip Wayne and Edna Mae (Yowler) B.; m. Patricia D. Miller, Jan. 28, 1967; children: Julie Ann, Jeremy M., Jamie M. BS, Earlham Coll., Richmond, Ind., 1967; MS, Colo. State U., 1968, PhD, 1973. Postdoctoral fellow U. Calif., Berkeley, 1973-74; prof. plant pathology N.C. State U., Raleigh, 1974—. Editor: Phytopathology, 1988-90, Crop Prot., 1993-96, Can J. Microbiology, 1993-96; contbr. articles to profl. jours. Fellow Am. Phytopathol. Soc.; mem. Sigma Xi (v.p. 1987, Young Rschr. award 1980), Gamma Sigma Delta (treas. 1991-93, pres. 1994-95). Office: N C State Univ Dept Plant Pathology Box 7616 Raleigh NC 27695

BENSON, DEE VANCE, federal judge; b. Salt Lake City, Aug. 25, 1948; s. Gilbert and Beryl Butler (Despain) B.; children: Angela, Natalie, Lucas, Katherine. BA, Brigham Young U., 1973, JD, 1976. Bar: Utah 1976, U.S. Dist. Ct. Utah 1976, U.S. Ct. Appeals (10th cir.) 1976, U.S. Supreme Ct. 1984, U.S. Ct. Appeals (5th cir.) 1988. Ptnr. Snow, Christensen & Martineau, Salt Lake City, 1976-84; legal counsel Senate Judiciary Com., Washington, 1984-86; chief of staff Senator Orrin Hatch's Office, Washington, 1986-88; legal counsel U.S. Senate Select Com., Washington, 1987; assoc. dep. atty. gen. U.S. Dept. Justice, Washington, 1988; U.S. atty. dist. Utah U.S. Dept. Justice, Salt Lake City, 1989-91; judge U.S. Dist. Ct., Salt Lake, 1991—; legal counsel Iran-Contra Congl. Investigating Com., Washington, 1987. Contbg. author univ. law rev. Mem. ABA, Utah State Bar (com. on cts. and judges), Salt Lake County Bar Assn., Phi Alpha Delta. Mem. LDS Ch. Avocations: soccer, skiing, mountain biking, basketball, running. Office: US Dist Ct 350 S Main St Ste 251 Salt Lake City UT 84101-2153*

BENSON, DONALD ERICK, holding company executive; b. Mpls., June 1, 1930; s. Fritz and Annie (Nordstrom) B.; children: Linda K., Nancy A., Stephen D.; m. Roberta Mann, 1992. BBA in Acctg., U. Minn., 1955. CPA, Minn. From staff to partnership Arthur Andersen & Co., Mpls., 1955-68; pres. MEI Corp., Mpls., 1968-86, MEI Diversified Inc., Mpls., 1986-94; exec. v.p. Marquette Bancshares, Inc., Mpls., 1992—; also bd. dirs.; bd. dirs. Mesaba Holdings, Inc., Minn. Twins Baseball Club, Mut. Fund Corp. Investors, Mass. Mut. Participation Investors, Delta Beverage Group, Inc., Nat. Merc. Bancorp.; chmn. Health Systems Minn.; dir. Swedish Coun. Am. and its Royal Round Table. Past chmn. Bethel Coll. Found., St. Paul, Meth. Hosp., Mpls.; past pres. Boys and Girls Clubs Mpls. Served with U.S. Army, 1951-53. Mem. AICPA, Minn. CPA Soc., Mpls. Club, Interlachen Country Club. Office: Marquette Bancshares Inc 3900 Dain Bosworth Plz Minneapolis MN 55480-1000

BENSON, EDWIN WELBURN, JR., trade association executive; b. Nashville, Tenn., Feb. 18, 1945; s. Edwin Welburn and Mildred B.; m. Jamie Suzanne Parks, Aug. 14, 1982; 1 child, Edwin III. BA, Vanderbilt U., 1967. V.p. The Benson Co., Nashville, 1970-78; assoc. exec. dir. Country Music Assn., Nashville, 1979-91, exec. dir., 1992—. Bd. dirs. Leonard Bernstein Ctr. for Learning Through Arts; bd. govs. Nashville C. of C. With U.S. Army, 1967-70. Mem. Leadership Music Alumni, Leadership Nashville Alumni, The Recording Acad., Acad. TV Arts and Scis., Am. Soc. Assn. Execs. Avocations: golf, travel, music. Office: Country Music Assn 1 Music Cir S Nashville TN 37203-4312

BENSON, ELIZABETH POLK, Pre-Columbian art specialist; b. Washington, May 13, 1924; d. Theodore Booton and Rebecca Dean (Albin) B. BA, Wellesley Coll., 1945; MA, Cath. U. Am., 1956. Mus. aide, curator Nat. Gallery of Art, Washington, 1946-60; curator Pre-Columbian Collection Dumbarton Oaks, Washington, 1962-79, dir. Ctr. for Pre-Columbian Studies, 1971-79; rsch. assoc. Inst. Andean Studies, Berkeley, Calif., 1980—; lectr. Cath. U. Am., Washington, 1968-69; adj. prof. Columbia U., N.Y.C., 1973; sr. lectr. U. Tex., Austin, 1985; Andrew S. Keck disting. vis. prof. Am. U., Washington, 1987; cons. Montreal Mus. Fine Arts, 1980-84, 90-92; adv. ed. L.Am. Indian Lits. Jour., Pitts., 1989—; mem. adv. com. Found. for Advancement of Mesoamerican Studies, Crystal River, Fla., 1994—; co-curator traveling exhbn. Birds and Beasts of Ancient L.Am., 1995-98. Author: The Maya World, 1967, 72, 77, The Mochica, 1972, Birds and Beasts of Ancient Latin America, 1997; co-author: Museums of the Andes, 1981, Atlas of Ancient America, 1986; co-editor: Olmec Art of Ancient Mexico, 1996. Mem. Soc. Woman Geographers (co-chair mus. com. 1994—), The Lit. Soc., Latin Am. Indian Lits. Assn. (v.p. 1989—). Home and Office: 8314 Old Seven Locks Rd Bethesda MD 20817-2005

BENSON, FRANCES GOLDSMITH, editor-in-chief; b. Orange, N.J., Oct. 27, 1945. BA, Wells Coll., 1967. Dir. ILR Press Cornell U., Ithaca, N.Y., 1982-95; editor-in-chief Cornell U. Press, Ithaca, N.Y., 1995—. Mem. Indsl. Rels. Rsch. Assn. Office: Cornell U Press Ithaca NY 14850

BENSON, FRANCIS M., production engineer, radio producer; b. Bklyn., Oct. 7, 1958; s. Francis Gerald Benson and Grace Angela (Superty) Brothers; children: Megan Kristine, Lindsey Nicole; m. Lucena Arcila, Feb. 14, 1998. Student, Palmdale High Sch., Calif. Cert. Airframe & Powerplant Mechanic, Calif. Structure mechanic B Lockheed Aircraft Co., Palmdale, Calif., 1979-80, final assembly mechanic, 1980-83, structure mechanic B, 1985-86, mfg. supr., 1986-87; structure mechanic B Rockwell Internat., Palmdale, Calif., 1983-85, hydraulic checkout mechanic, 1985; structure mechanic A Northrop B-2 Division, Palmdale, Calif., 1987-88, mfg. supr., 1988, mfg. planner, 1988-89, mfg. engr., 1989-92; program coord., prodr. Disney/ABC, 1992-94, prodn. coord./prodr., 1994-97; computer and audio-visual technician Palos Verdes Peninsula Unified Sch. Dist., Palos Verdes Estates, Calif., 1998—; union steward Internat. Assn. Machinists & Aerospace, Palmdale Calif. Democrat. Roman Catholic. Avocations: snow skiing, running, triathlon, golf, camping. Home: 3520 Maricopa St Unit 19 Torrance CA 90503-4994 Office: 3801 Via La Selva Palos Verdes Estates CA 90274

BENSON, IRENE M., nurse; b. Chgo.. BSN, Loyola U., 1980; MS, Saint Xavier U., 1993. RN, Ill. Staff nurse hematology and operating rm. Michael Reese Hosp. and Med. Ctr., Chgo., 1980-86; staff nurse trauma ICU Loyola U., Maywood, Ill., 1986-87; staff nurse telemetry U. Ill., Chgo., 1987-88; staff nurse, tour supr. emergency rm. Cook County Hosp., Chgo., 1988-91, clin. nurse specialist med. nursing, 1993—; staff nurse emergency rm. St. Francis Hosp., Blue Island, Ill., 1991-94; staff emergency rm. U. Ill. Chgo., 1992—; clin. instr. Triton Coll., River Grove, Ill., 1998—; trauma nurse instr. USAF, 1990—. Maj. USAF Res., 1982—. Mem. Emergency Nurses Assn., Acad. of Med.-Surg. Nurses, Ill. Nurses Assn., Internat. Assn. of Forensic Nurses, Res. Officers Assn. (life), Sigma Theta Tau Internat. Roman Catholic. Avocations: reading, sky diving, traveling. Office: Cook County Hosp 1835 W Harrison St Chicago IL 60612-3785

BENSON, JAMES DEWAYNE, university administrator; b. Fairbury, Nebr., June 23, 1925; s. Earl Mark and Cleone Matilda (Wycoff) B.; m. Maran Schueller, May 29, 1948; children—David, Barbara, Mary, Stephen. B.Sc., Creighton U., 1949; M.A., U. Iowa, 1952, Ph.D., 1958. Asst. prof. mktg. Iowa State U., 1952-54, 55-57; asso. prof. So. Ill. U., 1957-62, U. Iowa, 1962-70; dean Coll. Bus. Administrn., No. Ariz. U., 1970-73; dir. corp. mktg. Motorola Inc., Chgo., 1973-75; dean Coll. Bus., No. Ill. U., 1975-84, v.p. bus. affairs, 1984-86; prof. U. Wis., La Crosse, 1986-90; vol. exec. Internat. Exec. Svc. Corp., Slavjansk, Ukraine, 1994-95; vol. Internat. Exec. Svc. Corp., Bhatislava, Slovakia, 1996—; bd. dirs. BeeLine Motor Freight Inc., Benson Color Tech., Rockford Spring Inc.; cons. Jefferson Davis and Assocs., Corn Belt Coop., Northwestern Bell Telephone Co., Motorola, Inc. Contbr. articles to profl. jours. Pres. No. Ariz. Social Welfare, 1971-73. Served to 2nd lt., AC AUS, 1943-45. Mem. Am. Mktg. Assn., Midwest Econs. Assn., Midwest Bus. Assn., Am. Assembly Collegiate Schs. Bus. (pres. Mid-continent East region), Western and Mid-Western Deans Colls. of Bus., DeKalb (Ill.) C. of C., Omicron Delta Epsilon, Beta Gamma Sigma, Phi Eta Sigma. Club:, (). Home: 1051 Calico Ridge Dr Henderson NV 89015-3008

BENSON, JAMES M., investment company executive. BA in Econs., U. Ill., 1968; MBA, U. So. Calif., 1972. CLU. With Pacific Mut. Life Inst. Co., 1968-84; ptnr. Mgmt. Compensation Group, 1984-93; former pres., COO Equitable Life Assurance Soc. U.S., N.Y.C., former bd. dirs.; pres., CEO New Eng. Fin., Boston, 1997-98, chmn., CEO, 1998—. Bd. dirs. Achilles Track Club, The Am. Coll., Christopher Reeve Found., Alliance Francaise, Hosp. for Spl. Surgery, African Wildlife Found.; founder, chmn. World T.E.A.M. Sports. Office: New Eng Fin 501 Boylston St Boston MA 02116*

BENSON, JOANNE E., former lieutenant governor; b. Jan. 4, 1943; m. Robert Benson; 2 children. BS, St. Cloud State U. Mem. Minn. Senate, St. Paul, 1991-94; lt. gov. State of Minn., St. Paul, 1994-98. *

BENSON, JOHN ALEXANDER, JR., physician, educator; b. Manchester, Conn., July 23, 1921; s. John A. and Rachel (Patterson) B.; m. Irene Zucker, Sept. 29, 1947; children: Peter M., John Alexander III, Susan Leigh, Jeremy P. BA, Wesleyan U., 1943; MD, Harvard Med. Sch., 1946. Diplomate Am. Bd. Internal Medicine (mem. 1969-91, sec.-treas. 1972-75, pres. 1975-91, pres. emeritus 1991—), Subsplty. Bd. Gastroenterology (mem. 1961-66, chmn. 1965-66). Intern Univ. Hosps., Cleve., 1946-47; resident Peter Bent Brigham Hosp., Boston, 1949-51; fellow Mass. Gen. Hosp., Boston, 1951-53; rsch. asst. Mayo Clinic, Rochester, Minn., 1953-54; instr. medicine Harvard U., 1956-59; head divsn. gastroenterology U. Oreg. Med. Sch., Portland, 1959-75, prof. medicine, 1965-93; prof. emeritus Oreg. Health Sci. U., Portland, 1993—; interim dean Sch. Medicine Oreg. Health Sci. U., 1991-93, dean emeritus, 1993—; cons. VA Hosps., Madigan Gen. Army Hosp., John A. Hartford Found. Editorial bd.: Am. Jour. Digestive Diseases, 1966-73; Contbr. articles to profl. jours. Mem. Oreg. Med. Ednl. Found., 1967-73, dir., 1967-73, pres., 1969-72; bd. dirs. N.W. Ctr. for Physician-Patient Comm., 1994—, Am. Acad. on Physician and Patient, 1994-99; bd. dirs. Found. for Med. Excellence, 1996—, pres., 1998—; trustee Oreg. Health Scis. Found., 1999—. With USNR, 1947-49. Mem. AAS, AMA, ACP (master), Am. Gastroenterol. Assn. (sec. 1970-73, v.p. 1975-76, pres.-elect. 1976-77, pres. 1977-78), Am. Clin. and Climatol. Assn. (v.p. 1997), Am. Soc. Internal Medicine, Western Assn. Physicians, North Pacific Soc. Internal Medicine, Am. Fedn. Clin. Rsch., Federated Coun. for Internal Medicine, Am. Assn. Study Liver Disease, Western Soc. Clin. Investigation, Soc. Health and Human Values, Assn. Health Svcs. Rsch., Inst. Medicine NAS (sr.), Phi Beta Kappa, Sigma Xi, Alpha Omega Alpha. Office: Oreg Health Scis U Sch Medicine L102 Portland OR 97201

BENSON, JOHN T., state agency administrator; married; three children. BA in Elem. Edn., Luther Coll., 1960; MS in Sch. Adminstrn., U. Minn., Winona, 1963, postgrad.; postgrad., U. Minn., Madison. Elem. tchr. Harmony (Minn.) Pub. Schs., 1960-62; prin. Burlington (Wis.) Elem. and Jr. H.S., 1962-65; dist. adminstr. Barneveld (Wis.) pub. Schs., 1965-68; owner, operator farm equipment dealership, Barneveld, 1968-71; prin. Evansville (Wis.) Mid. Sch., 1971-72; dist. adminstr. Marshall (Wis.) Pub. Schs., 1971-82, 89-93; asst. state supt. Divsn. Instrnl. Svcs. Wis. Dept. Pub. Instrn., 1981-89, state supt. of pub. instrn., 1993—. Bd. regents U. Wis.; mem. State Bd. of Vocat., Tech. and Adult Edn.; bd. dirs. Jr. Achievement of Wis., Inc., Very Spl. Arts of Wis., Higher Edn. Aids Bd., numerous others. Mem. Coun. of Chief State Sch. Officers, Am. Assn. Sch. Dist. Adminstrs., Edn. Commn. of the States, Nat. Coun. for Accreditation of Tchr. Edn., FFA Alumni Assn., Lions, Phi Delta Kappa. Lutheran. Office: Office of State Supt Wis Dept Pub Instrn PO Box 7841 Madison WI 53707-7841

BENSON, JOHNNY, professional race car driver; b. Grand Rapids, Mich., June 27, 1963; s. John and Judy Benson; m. Debbie Benson; children: Katelyn and Mikayla. 1989 Berlin Raceway Champion, competed Amer. Speed Assoc. Series, 1990-93 with 9 wins, 48 top-10 finishes ; winner 1995 NASCAR Busch Series Grand Nat. Divsn. championship, 1995, NASCAR Winston Cup Series, 1996—, ranked 11th in 1997 with 8 top-10 finishes. Named Rookie of Yr. 1990, Rookie of Yr. 1994, Busch Grand National. Office: care NASCAR Bahari Racing 208 Rolling Hill Rd Mooresville NC 28117-6845 Office: care NASCAR PO Box 2875 Daytona Beach FL 32120-2875*

BENSON, JOSEPH FRED, journalist, legal historian; b. St. Louis, Dec. 14, 1953; s. Max and Addie Marie (Klein) B.; m. Lynn Walker, July 31, 1993 (div. 1995). AA, St. Louis C.C., 1974; AB cum laude, St. Louis U., 1976, AM, 1977, JD, 1985. Legal historian, archivist Cir. Ct. St. Louis County, Clayton, Mo., 1978-85; columnist St. Louis Daily Record and St. Louis Countian, 1987—, spl. corres., 1989—, editl. writer, 1990—, cons. in constl. law, 1995—; editl. writer St. Peters Courier, 1998—; asst. law libr. St. Louis County Ct. House Law Libr., 1979-85; adj. instr. Am. history Harris-Stowe State Tchrs. Coll., St. Louis, 1987; rsch. cons. law firm David C. Godfrey, Clayton, 1981—, Zwibelman, Edelman & Walter, Clayton, 1989-95, Law Firm of Scott E. Walter, P.C., 1997—; friend of the ct. 21st cir. Cir. Ct. St. Louis County, Mo., 1993-94; instr. Am. history Van Buren (Mo.) R-1 Pub. Schs., 1994-95; instr. Am. history and Am. govt. East Carter County R-II Pub. Schs., Ellsinore, Mo., 1995, U. City (Mo.) H.S., 1995-96; cons. in field. Author newspaper column Law In History, 1987—; contbr. Wentzville Union (Mo.) Legal Newspaper, 1995—; contbr. articles on internat. law to profl. jours. including Mo. Lawyers Weekly. Judge St. Louis County Bd. Elections, Clayton, 1978-84, supr., 82-84; incorporator Hist. Soc. St. Louis County, 1978, exec. dir., asst. sec., 1979-87, comm. Bicentential U.S. Constn., 1983-91; sexton, prayer leader Shaare Zedek Synagogue, University City, Mo., 1998—. Sam. A. Kessler Meml. scholar, 1981, Project '87: Bicentennial scholar, 1985-91; faculty fellow St. Louis U., 1983, 84. Mem. Supreme Ct. Hist. Soc., B'nai B'rith, Rotary, Phi Alpha Theta, Phi Theta Kappa. Democrat. Jewish. Avocations: cooking, tennis, gardening. Home: 7812 Delmar Blvd University City MO 63130-3711

BENSON, KENNETH J., federal judge, educator; b. 1946. JD, Duquesne U., 1979. Bar: Pa. 1979. Law clk. to Hon. Henry X. O'Brien, Pa. Supreme Ct., Harrisburg, 1979-80; assoc. Zimmer & Dice, Pitts., 1981-82; asst. dist. atty. Allegheny County, Pitts., 1982-87; dep. atty. gen. Commonwealth of Pa., Pitts., 1987-90; magistrate judge for western Pa., U.S. Magistrate Ct., Pitts., 1990—; adj. prof. Duquesne U. Law Sch., Pitts., 1986—. With USN, 1967-71. Office: US Magistrate Ct 733 US PO and Courthouse 700 Grant St Pittsburgh PA 15219-1906

BENSON, KENNETH VICTOR, manufacturing company executive, lawyer; b. New Lisbon, Wis., Aug. 2, 1929; s. Carl W. and Ottilia (Olson) B.; m. Alice May Drewry, June 23, 1951; children: Jennifer, Elizabeth, Kenneth, Jonathan, Nathan. BBA, U. Wis., 1951, JD, 1957. Bar: Wis. 1957. Sales trainee, sales corr. Marathon Corp., Menasha, Wis., 1953-54; practice law with Benson & Day, Marshfield, Wis., 1957-58; sr. v.p., dir., exec. com. Kohler Co., Wis., 1959-81; pres., mem. exec. com., dir. Vollrath Co., Sheboygan, Wis., 1982-89; ptnr. Benson, Zufelt & Donohue, Sheboygan, 1990-92; bd. dirs., mem. exec. com. EnzoPac, Sheboygan, Wis. Bd. dirs. Sheboygan United Fund, 1969-75, Wis. 4-H Found., Inc., 1988-92, Sheboygan YMCA, 1971-79, sec., 1975-76, v.p., 1977-79; pres. Sheboygan Comty. Players and Civic Orch., 1967-69, bd. dirs., 1963-76; bd. dirs. Sheboygan Retirement Home, 1976-85, v.p., 1979-80, pres., 1980-81; trustee Lakeland Coll., 1978-92. With AUS, 1951-53. Mem. Home: 125 White Ash Dr Pine Knoll Shores NC 28512

BENSON, LUCY PETERS WILSON, political and diplomatic consultant; b. N.Y.C., Aug. 25, 1927; d. Willard Oliver and Helen (Peters) Wilson; m. Bruce Buzzell Benson, Mar. 30, 1950 (dec. Mar. 1990). B.A., Smith Coll., 1949, M.A., 1955; L.H.D. (hon.), Wheaton Coll., Norton, Mass., 1965; LLD (hon.), U. Mass., 1969; L.H.D. (hon.), Bucknell U., 1972; LLD (hon.), U. Md., 1972; L.H.D. (hon.), Carleton Coll., 1973; LLD (hon.), Amherst Coll., 1974, Clark U., 1975; H.H.D., Springfield Coll., 1981; L.H.D. (hon.), Bates Coll., 1982. Mem. jr. exec. tng. program Bloomingdale's, N.Y.C., 1949-50; asst. dir. pub. rels. Smith Coll., 1950-53; rsch. asst. dept. Am. studies Amherst Coll., 1956-57; pres. Amherst LWV, Mass., 1957-61; pres. Mass. LWV, 1961-65, nat. pres., 1968-74; mem. Gov.'s cabinet and sec. human svcs. Commonwealth of Mass., 1975; mem. spl. commn. on adminstrv. rev. U.S. Ho. of Reps., Washington, 1976-77; under sec. State Security Assistance, Sci. and Tech. U.S. Dept. State, Washington, 1977-80; cons. U.S. Dept. State and SRI Internat., Washington, 1980-81; pres. Benson and Assocs., Amherst and Washington, 1981—; vice chmn. Citizen Network for Fgn. Affairs; trustee N.E. Utilities, 1971-74, 76-77; bd. dirs. Continental Group, Inc., Dreyfus Fund, Dreyfus Liquid Assets, Dreyfus Asset Allocation Fund, Dreyfus 401K Fund, Dreyfus Third Century Fund, Inc., Comms. Satellite Corp., Gen. Reins. Corp., Dreyfus Worldwide Dollar Money Market Fund, Inc., Logistics Mgmt. Inst. Mem. steering com. Urban Coalition, 1968, exec. com., 1970-75, 80-84, co-chmn., 1973-75; mem. Gov. Mass. Spl. Com. Rev. Sunday Closing Laws, 1961; mem. spl. commn. Mass. Legislature to Study Budgetary Powers of Trustees U. Mass., 1961-62; mem. Gov. Mass. Com. Rev. Salaries State Employees, 1963, Mass. Adv. Bd. Higher Ednl. Policy, 1962-65, Mass. Bd. Edn. Adv. Com. Racial Imbalance and Edn., 1964-65, Mass. adv. com. U.S. Commn. Civil Rights, 1964-73; vice chmn. Mass. Adv. Council Edn., 1965-68; mem. Mass. Com. Children and Youth Com. to Study Report by U.S. Children's Bur., Mass. Youth Svc. Div., 1967; mem. pub. adv. com. U.S. Trade Policy, 1968; mem. vis. com. John F. Kennedy Sch. Govt.; mem. Trilateral Commn., Coun. Fgn. Rels. Mem. town meeting, Amherst, 1957-74, finance com., 1960-66; trustee Edn. Devel. Center, Newton, Mass., 1967-72, Nat. Urban League, 1974-77, Smith Coll., 1975-80, Brookings Instn., 1974-77, Alfred P. Sloan Found., 1975-77, 81—, Bur. Social Sci. Rsch., Inc., 1985-87; bd. dirs. Catalyst, 1972-90, Internat. Exec. Svc. Corps, Atlantic Coun. of U.S., 1988—, vice chmn., 1993—; former bd. govs. Am. Nat. Red Cross, Common Cause, Women's Action Alliance; bd. govs. Internat. Ctr. on Election Law and Adminstrn., 1985-87; trustee Lafayette Coll., 1985—, vice chmn., 1990—. Recipient Achievement award Bur. Govt. Research, U. Mass., 1963; Distinguished Service award Boston Coll., 1965; Smith Coll. medal, 1969; Distinguished Civil Leadership award Tufts U., 1965; Distinguished Service award Northfield Mount Hermon Sch., 1976; Radcliffe fellow Radcliffe Inst., 1965-66, 66-67. Mem. NAACP, ACLU, Nat. Acad. Pub. Adminstrn., UN Assn., Urban League, Assn. Am. Indian Affairs, East African Wildlife Soc., Jersey Wildlife Preservation Trust Channel Islands, Internat. Inst. Strategic Studies. Home and Office: 46 Sunset Ave Amherst MA 01002-2018

BENSON, ROBBY, actor, director, writer, producer; b. Dallas, Jan. 21, 1956; s. Jerry Ann (Benson) Segal; m. Karla DeVito; children: Lyric, Zephyr. Student, Am. Acad. Dramatic Arts. film instructor, U. So. Carolina. Actor: (Broadway debut) Zelda, 1969, The Rothschilds, 1970, The Pirates of Penzance, 1981-82; (TV series) Search For Tomorrow, 1971-73, Tough Cookies, 1986, Road To Avonlea, 1992, Prince Valiant, 1993, Exo-Squad, 1993; (TV movies) The Virginia Hill Story, 1974, Remember When (also known as Four Stars in the Window, 1974, All the Kind Strangers, 1974, Death Be Not Proud, 1975, Our Town, 1978, The Death of Richie, 1977, Two of a Kind, 1982, California Girls, 1985, Invasion of PRivacy, 1992, Homewrecker, 1992,Lincoln, 1992, Precious Victims, 1993, Belle's Magical World, 1997, Beauty & The Beast: The Enchanted Christmas, 1997; (films) Jory, 1972, Jeremy, 1973, Lucky Lady, 1975, Ode to Billy Joe, 1976, One on One, 1977, The End, 1978, Ice Castles, 1978, Walk Proud (also known as Gang), 1979, Die Laughing, 1980, Tribute, 1980, National Lampoon Goes to the Movies, 1981, The Chosen, 1982, Running Brave, 1983, Harry and Son, 1984, City Limits, 1985, Rent-A-Cop, 1988, White Hot (dir., also known as Crack in the Mirror and Do It Up), 1989, Modern Love, 1990 (writer, producer, dir., composer songs), Beauty & The Beast, 1991, Invasion of Privacy, 1992, The Webbers, 1993, Deadly Exposure, 1993, Exosquad, 1993, Homewrecker, 1993; (TV series) Sabrina, the Teenage Witch, 1996, (TV) Precious Victims, 1993; Voice of the Beast in Beauty and the Beast, 1991, (voice) Lincoln, 1997, Belle's Magical World, 1997; dir. 3 TV episodes of Evening Shade; writer: (with Jerry Segal) One on One, 1977, (with Don Peake, also composer) Walk Proud, 1979, (with Jerry Segal and Scott Parker, also composer with J. Segal) Die Laughing, 1980; song composer: The Breakfast Club, 1985, White Hot, 1989; numerous TV guest appearances; dir. (TV series) Jesse, 1998, Brother's Keeper, 1998, Reunited, numerous others. also Address: PO Box 1305 Woodland Hills CA 91365-1305 Address: Krost Chapin Management 9465 Wilshire Blvd Ste 430 Beverly Hills CA 90212-2613*

BENSON, ROBERT ELLIOTT, investment banker, consultant; b. Bklyn., June 13, 1916; s. Philip Adolphus and Louise A. (Melville) B.; m. Elena Vittoria, June 13, 1942; children: Elena V. Benson Ganzenmuller, Christine L. Benson Pell, Robert Elliott, William M., David Philip. S.B., Mass. Inst. Tech., 1937; postgrad., Bklyn. Poly. Inst., 1938-39; M.B.A., Harvard, 1941; grad., Program for Execs., Carnegie Inst. Tech., 1957. Student engr. Consol. Edison Co. N.Y., Inc., N.Y.C., 1937-39; security analyst City Bank Farmers Trust Co., N.Y.C., 1940; asst. engr. L.I. Lighting Co., Mineola, N.Y., 1941-42; security analyst Equitable Life Assurance Soc. U.S., 1946, 2d v.p., 1956-60, v.p., 1960-66; exec. asst. to pres. Internat. Tel. & Tel. Corp., N.Y.C., 1966; v.p. Internat. Tel. & Tel. Corp., 1967-76; sr. cons. White, Weld & Co. Inc., N.Y.C., 1976-78; v.p. Merrill Lynch, Pierce, Fenner & Smith Inc., 1978-85; sr. v.p., chief fin. officer Finacopro N.V., Curaćao, Netherland Antilles and N.Y.C., 1985-86; cons. Drexel Burnham Lambert Inc., 1986-90; cons. corp. fin. Locust Valley, N.Y., 1990—; trustee, dir. Dime Savs. Bank of N.Y., 1963-88. Pres., trustee YWCA Retirement Fund, 1956-90; trustee, v.p. McAuley Water St. Mission; trustee, mayor, police commr. Village of Matinecock; vestryman, chmn. fin. com. St. John's of Lattingtown. Maj. AUS, 1942-46. Decorated Legion of Merit. Mem. Beaver Dam Winer Sports Club (Locust Valley), The Creek Club. Republican. Episcopalian. Home and Office: Duck Pond Rd Locust Valley NY 11560

BENSON, ROBERT EUGENE, lawyer; b. Red Oak, Iowa, Apr. 7, 1940; s. Paul J. and Frances (Sever) B.; m. Ann Marie Lucke, July 20, 1968; children: Steven J., Robert J., Katherine A. BA, U. Iowa, 1962; LLB, U. Pa., 1965. Bar: Colo. 1965. Assoc. Holland & Hart, Denver, 1965-71, ptnr., 1971—; adj. faculty U. Denver Coll. Law, 1992. Author: The Power of Arbitrators and Courts to Order Discovery in Arbitration, 1996, Application of the Pro Rata Liability, Comparative Negligence and Contribution Statues, 1994; co-author: How to Prepare For, Take and Use a Deposition, 5th edit., 1994; editor: Colorado Constitution Law, 1999; contbr. articles to profl. jours. Capt. USAF, 1965-73. Mem. ABA, Colo. Bar Assn., Denver Bar Assn. Avocations: golf, skiing. Home: 5454 Preserve Pky N Littleton CO 80121-2185 Office: Holland & Hart 555 17th St Ste 3200 Denver CO 80202-3950

BENSON, SALLY JEAN, development manager; b. Gary, Ind., Apr. 2, 1958; d. Dale Robert and Dorothy Jean (Weber) B. BA, Purdue U., Hammond, Ind., 1980, MA, 1992. Cert. fund raising exec. Reporter, anchor WJOB Radio, Hammond, Ind., 1981-83; press sec. City of Hammond, 1983-84; dir. devel., pub. rels. Girl Scouts, Highland, 1984-87; asst. dir. fund raising Jackson Pk. Hosp., Chgo., 1987-88; devel. mgr. ACS, Chgo., 1992—. Recipient Thanks badge Calumet Coun. Girl Scouts U.S., Highland, 1991. Mem. Nat. Soc. Fund Raising Execs. (cert. fund-raising exec., bd. dirs. 1995—), Chgo. Symphony Orch. Assocs. (v.p. vol. activities 1996-97). Avocations: music, amateur violinist, tennis, theatre, horses. Office: Am Coll Surgeons 633 N Saint Clair St Chicago IL 60611-3234

BENSON, SANDRA JEAN, media specialist; b. Winona, Minn., Apr. 13, 1949; d. Artha B.O. and Virginia H. (McNamer) Thompson. BS, U. Wis., River Falls, 1975, MAT in Elem. Edn., 1982. Libr. Cen. High Sch., Paddock Lake, Wis., 1974-76; media specialist Hudson (Wis.) Pub. Schs., 1976—; instr. U. Wis., River Falls, 1991—; cons. tech. several ednl. and bus. orgns., River Falls, 1990—. Mem. ALA, Wis. Ednl. Media Assn., Soc. Sch.

Librs. Internat., Assn. for Ednl. Communications and Tech. (div. sch. media specialist), St. Croix Valley Reading Coun. (sec.), Wis. Assn. Mid. Level Edn. Avocations: antiques, computers. Office: Hudson Mid Sch 1300 Carmichael Rd Hudson WI 54016-7711

BENSON, SARA ELIZABETH, real estate broker, real estate appraiser; b. Columbia, S.C., Nov. 29, 1960; d. Herbert Lankford Benson and Anna Marian (Stanley) Tucker; m. Donald Joseph DeBat, Aug. 20, 1994; children: D. Edward, Herbert L. Benson IV. Student, U. S.C., 1977, Am. Conservatory Music, Chgo., 1978-81. Lic. real estate broker, Ill., S.C.; designated cert. real estate brokerage mgr.; approved ind. fee appraiser; cert. real estate appraiser, Ill. Pres., owner Benson Stanley Realty, Chgo., 1990—; owner Sara Benson Cons., Inc., Chgo., 1992—; fee appraiser FHA, HUD, Chgo., 1986—; speaker, author in field. Bd. dirs. Chgo. Child Care Soc. Mem. NAFE, Nat. Assn. Realtors, Assn. Fed. Appraisers, Real Estate Buyer's Agt. Coun., Ill. Assn. Realtors, Chgo. Assn. Realtors (chair profl. standards com.), North Shore Bd. Realtors, Real Estate Brokerage Mgrs. Coun., MLS No. Ill., Nat. Assn. Ind. Fee Appraisers, Bus. Execs. Assn. Chgo., Chgo. Child Care Soc. (bd. dirs. 1997—). Avocations: piano, literature, interior design. Office: Benson Stanley Realty 980 N Michigan Ave Ste 1400 Chicago IL 60611-7500

BENSON, SHARON JOAN, mathematics educator; b. Glendale, Calif., Aug. 23, 1964; d. Paul John and Arleen Camille (Green) B. BS in Math., Calif. Poly. State U., 1987; MST in Math., U. N.H., 1992; postgrad., N.Mex. State U., 1998—. Cert. single subject clear math., Calif. Tchr. math. Victor Valley Union High Sch. Dist., Victorville, Calif., 1988-98; grad. asst. dept. curriculum and instrn. N.Mex. State U.; part-time instr. Victor Valley C.C., Victorville, 1993-98. Mem. Nat. Coun. Tchrs. Math., Calif. Math. Coun., Oreg. Coun. Tchrs. of Math., Assn. Women in Math. Republican. Roman Catholic. Avocations: cross-stitch, reading, collecting carousel horses and cherished teddies.

BENSON, SHARON STOVALL, primary school educator; b. Clovis, N.Mex., Apr. 18, 1946; d. Travis and Anna Gene (Crump) Stovall; m. Merle John Benson, Aug. 21, 1966; children: Brenda Kay, Linda Carol. BS, U. N.Mex., 1968, MA, 1980. Cert. tchr., N.Mex. Kindergarten aide Albuquerque Pub. Schs., 1976-78; tchr. LaMesa Little Sch., Albuquerque, 1987-88, Congl. Presch., Albuquerque, 1991—; parent rep. South Atlantic Regional Resource Ctr., Plantation, Fla., 1986-87; sec. bd. Albuquerque Spl. Presch., 1975. Trained evaluator Assn. Retarded Citizens, Albuquerque, 1988—. Mem. Parents Reaching Out, Assn. Retarded Citizens, N.Mex. Assn. Edn. Young Children, Pi Lambda Theta. Methodist. Avocations: bell choir, programs for handicapped. Home: 7409 Carriveau Ave NE Albuquerque NM 87110-1490

BENSON, SIDNEY WILLIAM, chemistry researcher; b. N.Y.C., Sept. 26, 1918; m. Anna Bruni, 1986; 2 children. A.B., Columbia Coll., 1938; A.M., Harvard U., 1941, Ph.D., 1941; Docteur Honoris Causa, U. Nancy, France, 1989. Rsch. asst. Gen. Electric Co., 1940; rsch. fellow Harvard U., 1941-42; instr. chemistry CCNY, 1942-43; group leader Manhattan Project Kellex Corp., 1943; asst. prof. U. So. Calif., 1943-48, assoc. prof., 1948-51, prof. chemistry, 1951-64, 76-89, distng. prof., 1986—, Disting. prof. emeritus, 1989—, dir. chem. physics program, 1962-63; dir. dept. kinetics and thermochemistry Stanford Rsch. Inst., 1963-76; sci. dir. Hydrocarbon Rsch. Inst. U. So. Calif., 1977-90, sci. dir. emeritus, 1991—; rsch. assoc. dept. chemistry and chem. engring. Calif. Inst. Tech., 1957-58; vis. prof. UCLA, 1959, U. Ill., 1959; hon. Glidden lectr. Purdue U., 1961; vis. prof. chemistry Stanford U., 1966-70, 71, 73; mem. adv. panel phys. chemistry Nat. Bur. Standards, 1969-72, chmn., 1970-71; hon. vis. prof. U. Utah, 1971; vis. prof. U. Paris VII and XI, 1971-72, U. St. Andrews, Scotland, 1973, U. Lausanne, Switzerland, 1979; Frank Gucker lectr. U. Ind., 1984—; Brotherton prof. in phys. chemistry U. Leeds, 1984; cons. G.N. Lewis; lectr. U. Calif., Berkeley, 1989. Author: Foundations of Chemical Kinetics, 1960, rev. edit. 1982, Thermochemical Kinetics, 1968, 2d edit., 1976, Critical Survey of the Data of the Kinetics of Gas Phase Unimolecular Reactions, Reactions, 1970, Chemical Calculations, 3d edit., 1971, Atoms, Molecules and Chemical Reactions, 1972; founder, editor-in-chief Internat. Jour. Chem. Kinetics, 1967-83; mem. editl. adv. bd. Combustion Sci. and Tech., 1973-94, Oxidation Comms., 1978—, Revs. of chem. Intermediates, 1979-87, Hydrocarbon Letters, 1980-81, Jour. Phys. Chemistry, 1981-85; sci. adv. coun. Annales Medicales de Nancy, 1993—. Recipient Polanyi medal Royal Soc. Eng., 1986; faculty rsch. award U. So. Calif., 1984, Presdl. medal, 1986, Peter Kapitsa Gold Medal award Russian Acad. Natural Sci., 1997; Guggenheim fellow, 1950-51, Fulbright fellow, France, 1950-51, fellow NSF, 1957-58, 71-72. Fellow AAAS, Am. Phys. Soc.; mem. NAS, Am. Chem. Soc. (Tolman medal 1977, Hydrocarbon Chem. award 1977, Langmuir award 1986, Orange County award 1986), Faraday Soc., Indian Acad. Sci., Phi Beta Kappa, Sigma Xi, Pi Mu Epsilon, Phi Lambda Upsilon, Phi Kappa Phi. Home: 1110 N Bundy Dr Los Angeles CA 90049-1513 Office: U So Calif University Pk MC-1661 Los Angeles CA 90089

BENSON, STEPHEN EDWARD, writer; b. June 14, 1949. BA, Yale U., 1971; MFA, U. Calif., Irvine, 1973; PhD, Wright Inst., 1995. Author: As Is, 1978, Blindspots, 1979, Blue Book, 1990, Reverse Order, 1991, Roaring Spring, 1998.

BENSON, STEVEN CLARK, management and engineering executive; b. Chillicothe, Ohio, Sept. 27, 1954; s. Myron Clark and Velma Lucille (Dye) B.; m. Mary Ellen Hill, Mar. 9, 1979; children: Michael Lee, Kelly Dawn. BSCE, Ohio U., 1976. Registered profl. engr., Ohio, Ky., Pa., Va., W.Va., Fla. Project engr. McNally Pittsburg, Inc., Wellston, Ohio, 1976-87; pres. SBA Cons., Inc., Jackson, Ohio, 1985—; pres. SBA Assocs., Inc., Jackson, 1989—, also bd. dirs.; city engr., asst. svc., safety dir. City of Jackson, Ohio. Mem. NRA (life), NSPE, Ohio Soc. Profl. Engrs., Ohio Design Profls. and Code Analysts, Ohio Gun Collectors Assn., Bldg. Ofcls. and Code Adminstrs., Aircraft Owners and Pilots Assn., Cousteau Soc. Avocations: flying, scuba diving, camping, travel, hunting. Home: 54399 Benson Rd Ray OH 45672-8947 Office: SBA Inc PO Box 962 Jackson OH 45640-0962

BENSON, STEVEN DONALD, sheet metal research and marketing executive, sheet metal mechanic, programmer, author; b. Longview, Wash., Oct. 11, 1953; s. Steven Hughes Benson and Donna Ruth (Johnson) McKinney; m. Patricia Joyce Krauss, Feb. 14, 1982; children: Steven William, Patricia Ann. AA in Drafting, South Salem Indsl. Arts Coll., 1973; AA in Robotics, AMADA Sch., Buena Park, Calif., 1997. Precision sheet metal mechanic Ariz. Precision Sheet Metal, Phoenix, 1980-86, Neilson Mfg. Inc., Salem, Oreg., 1986—; owner, operator Time Honored Gifts, Salem, 1988—; pres. Advanced Sheet Metal Applications, Salem, 1986—; instr. Oreg. Advanced Tech. Consortium, Wilsonville, 1990—; sheet metal instr. Clackamas C.C., Oregon City, Oreg., 1997—; editor, pub. Precision Sheet Metal Chronicle, electronic mag., 1998—. Author: (textbooks) Introduction to Precision Press Brake, 1991, Intermediate Press Brake, 1992, Advanced Precision Press Brake, 1994, Press Brake Technology, 1997, (software) Advanced Sheet Metal Applications (ASMA 4.0), 1982, 90, 92, 95, 97. Sec., treas. Bike PAC of Oreg., Salem, 1988—, lobbyist, 1992; mem. A Brotherhood Against Totalitarian Enactments (ABATE), Oreg., Inc. Mem. Fabricators and Mfrs. Assn. (mem. adv. com. precision sheet metal adv. 1997—, mem. coun.), Soc. Mfg. Engrs., Internat. Sheet Metal Workers (local #16). Avocations: family activities, children, politics, Indian moto-cycles, British sports cars. Fax: 206-727-8729. E-mail: steve@asmachronicle.com. Home: 395 23d St NE Salem OR 97301-4440 Office: Advanced Sheet Metal Applications 398 Rose St NE Salem OR 97301-4468

BENSON, THOMAS WALTER, rhetoric educator, writer; b. Abington, Pa., Jan. 25, 1937; s. Walter Adelbert and Beatrice (Newton) B.; m. Margaret Sandelin, Sept. 3, 1960; children: Margaret, Sarah Beverly. AB, Hamilton Coll., 1958; MA, Cornell U., 1961, PhD, 1966. From asst. to assoc. prof. SUNY, Buffalo, 1963-71; assoc. prof. Pa. State U., University Park, 1971-75, prof., 1975—, Sparks prof. rhetoric, 1990—; vis. asst. prof. U. Calif., Berkeley, 1969-70; Shorenstein fellow Harvard U., 1999. Co-author: (books) Reality Fictions, 1989, Documentary Dilemmas, 1991; editor: (books) American Rhetoric, 1989, Rhetoric and Political Culture, 1997, (jours.) Comm. Quar., 1976-78, Quar. Jour. of Speech, 1987-89, CRTNET, 1985-97. Shorenstein fellow Harvard U., 1999. Mem. Internat. Soc. for History of Rhetoric, Nat. Comm. Assn. (Kibler award 1983, Presdl. citation 1997, Disting. Scholar 1997, Disting. Rhetorical Scholar 1997), Ea. Comm. Assn. (Distng. Rsch. fellow), Soc. for Cinema Studies, Univ. Film and Video Assn. Home: 327 Mcbath St State College PA 16801-2744 Office: Pa State U 227 Sparks Bldg University Park PA 16802-5201

BENSON, TOM, professional football executive; b. New Orleans, LA, 1927; s. Tom Sr. and Carmen B. Benson; m. Grace Trudeau; children: Rene, Tootsie, Donn, Susan, Rick, Mirian. Student, Loyola U., New Orleans, HHD (hon.); DSc and Bus. (hon.), Cleary Coll. Bookkeeper Cathey Chevrolet Co., New Orleans, LA, 1948; mgr. Chevrolet Dealership, San Antonio, TX, 1956-62; founder Tom Benson Chevrolet Co. name changed to Benson Automobile World, San Antonio, TX, 1962; owner, gen. ptnr. New Orleans Saints, NFL, New Orleans, LA, 1985—. Mem. pres.' council Loyola U., New Orleans. Recipient Brotherhood award NCCJ, Order St. Louis medallion Archdiocese of New Orleans. Avocations: ranching, horse racing. Office: care New Orleans Saints 5800 Airline Hwy Metairie LA 70003-3876*

BENSON, TRAVIS THEO "DOC", minister, association administrator; b. Carnegie, Okla., Oct. 8, 1929; . Joe Travis and Edith Lee (Taggart) B.; m. Hattie MarEllen McCartney, Aug. 4, 1960; children: Brooks LeRoy, Bryant Leslie, Tammy Lynn Benson Argento. BA, Okla. City U., 1957; BD, So. Meth. U., 1960; grad., Tex. Sch. Addiction Problems, Austin, 1968, Rutgers Sch. Alcohol Problems, 1971. Ordained minister Meth. Ch., Okla., 1957. Minister Fittstown, Pontotoc (Okla.) Chs., 1957-60, Lakeside United Meth. Ch., Okla. City, 1960-62, Marietta (Okla.) United Meth. Ch., 1962-66, Waurika (Okla.) United Meth. Ch., 1966-71, Mangum (Okla.) United Meth. Ch., 1971-75, Shawnee (Okla.) Wesley United Ch., 1975-77, Douglas Blvd. United Meth. Ch., Okla. City, Okla., 1977-81; minister, dir. Skyline Urban Ministry, Okla. City, Okla., 1981-87, The Education & Employment Ministry, Okla. City, 1987—; mem. Bd. Hosps. and Homes, Okla., 1960-64; bd. dirs. North Conway (N.H.) Inst., 1966-72. Mem. Alcohol and Drug Problems Assn. N. Am., 1966-80, State Commn. on Alcoholism, Okla., 1967-73, liason to state legislators, chair of alcohol and drug concerns com. Bd. Ch. and Soc., Okla., 1968-76; chair prison ministries com. Bd. of Global Ministries, Okla., 1968-75,. Named 719th Point of Light, Pres. George Bush, 1992, Homecoming Family of Yr., Oklahoma City Univ., 1997; recipient Harry Chapin awar, World Hunger Found., 1994, Elwin D. Hatfield award, Dean A. McGee awards, 1997, Disting. Alumnus award Perkins Sch. Theology, 1998; Recognition of achievment certs. from Okla. Congressman J.C. Watts, and Senator Don Nickles, Okla. city Mayor, Ron Norick and others; Sept. 19, 1995 proclaimed Doc. Benson Day by then Gov. Frank Keating, Okla. Mem. Nat. Soc. Fund-Raising Execs., Okla. City Downtown Rotary Club. Democrat. United Methodist. Avocations: quail hunting, antique automobiles. E-mail: teem98@swbell.net. Office: Edn & Employment Ministry 14 NE 13th St Oklahoma City OK 73104-1426

BENSON, WARREN FRANK, composer, educator; b. Detroit, Jan. 26, 1924; s. Fred William and Ella Alma (Hermenau) B.; m. Patricia Louise Vander Velde, Nov. 19, 1949; children: Erika, Dirk, Kirsten, Sonja. MusB in Theory, U. Mich., 1949, MusM in Theory, 1951. Timpanist Detroit Symphony Orch., 1946, Ford Sunday Evening Hour Orch., 1946, Brevard Music Ctr. Orch., 1949, 53, 54; Fulbright tchr. music Anatolia Coll., Salonica, Greece, 1950-52; dir. orch. and band Mars Hill Coll., 1952-53; prof. music, composer in residence Ithaca Coll., 1953-67; prof. composition Eastman Sch. of Music U. Rochester, N.Y., 1967-93; Kilbourn prof. composition Eastman Sch. of Music U. Rochester, 1980-93, prof. emeritus, 1994—; Disting. vis. prof. Meadows Sch. Arts, So. Meth. U., Dallas, 1986-88; guest condr., lectr. at festivals and ednl. ctrs., U.S., Can., Mex., S.Am., Europe; bd. advisors The Chestnut Brass Co., The Harvey Phillips found.; mem. MacDowell Colony, 1955, 63. Author: Creative Projects in Musicianship, 1967, ...And My Daddy Will Play the Drums, 1999; compositions include Concertino for Alto Saxophone, 1954, Trio for Percussion, 1956, Psalm XXIV for womens voices and string orch., 1957, Symphony for Drums and Wind Orch., 1962, The Leaves are Falling for wind ensemble, 1963, The Solitary Dancer for wind ensemble, 1966, Helix for tuba and wind ensemble, 1966, Bailando, ballet for orch., 1965, The Mask of Night for wind ensemble, 1968, Shadow Wood, song cycle for soprano and orch. or wind ensemble, 1968, String Quartet, 1969, Concerto for Horn and Orch, 1971, The Dream Net for alto saxophone and string quartet, 1972, Five Lyrics of Louise Bogan for mezzo-soprano and flute, 1977, Largo Tah for bass trombone and marimba, 1978, Songs For the End of the World, for mezzo-soprano, horn and chamber ensemble, 1980, The Man With The Blue Guitar, for orch., 1980, Beyond Winter: Sweet Aftershowers for string orch., 1981, Moon Rain and Memory Jane for soprano and two cellos, 1981, Hills, Woods, Brook: Three Love Songs for soprano and chamber ensemble, 1982, Symphony II-Lost Songs, 1982, The Putcha Putcha Variations for solo singer, 1983, A Score of Praises for a cappella chorus, 1983, Concertino for Flute, Strings and Percussion, 1983, Wings for wind ensemble, 1984, Other Rivers for wind ensemble, 1984, The Hearth Within for a cappella chorus, 1985, String Quartet II-Hawk Music, 1986, Fair Game chamber ensemble, 1986, The Stevens Gambit for solo cello, 1986, Steps for brass quintet, 1987, Dawn's Early Light for band, 1987, The Red Lion for vibraphone and piano, 1988, Still for solo clarinet, 1989, Still, A Love Song for solo cello, 1990, Meditation on I Am For Peace for band, 1990, Concerto for clarinet and winds, 1991, Danzon-Memory for band, 1991, Trio Tertulio for clarinet, violin and cello, 1991, Adagietto for wind ensemble, 1992, Dux Variations for Symphonic Winds, 1992, Shadow Wood, 1992, Divertissement I, 1993, 14 Duos for trumpet and guitar, 1994, Aurora Moring for organ, 1994, Harwen's Ground Bass for wind ensemble, 1995, String Quartet III-Cat's Cradle, 1995, A Gift from Cordoba for wind ensemble, 1996, Tango Largo, 1997, The Drums of Summer for winds and voices, 1997, Daughter of the Stars for wind ensemble, 1998; recs. include Gasparo CD, Centaur CD, Nonesuch CD, CRI, Golden Crest, Orion, Coronet, USAF and USMC bands CD, Nanset (Norway) CD, Kosei, Japan CD, Albany CD, Crystal CD; commns. include Nat. Endowment for Arts, N.Y. State Coun. on Arts, Ohio Music Educators Assn., Charlotte Symphony Orch., Internat. Horn Soc., Baldwin-Wallace Conservatory, Am. Wind Symphony Orch., Rochester Philharm. Orch., Mich. State U., U. Conn., The Cantata Singers, U. Mich., USAF Band, Chestnut Brass Company, Cricklade Music Festival (Eng.), Kronos Quartet, U.S. Marine Band, Emory U., Uster Festival of Switzerland, So. Meth. U. Recipient Diploma de Honor Argentina, 1970, Lillian Fairchild Meml. prize in arts U. Rochester, 1971, Citation of Excellence Nat. Band Assn., 1976; Warren Benson Disting. tchr. award established at Ithaca Coll., 1965; Ford Found. grantee, 1963, 65; Guggenheim fellow, 1981-82. Mem. ASCAP (Serious Music awards 1960—), Am. Bandmasters Assn., Pi Kappa Lambda, Phi Mu Alpha (nat. hon. mem. Orpheus award), Kappa Kappa Psi. Home: 10 Reitz Pky Pittsford NY 14534-2206 *My goal is to write music worthy of the best in the art which speaks to the best in people of my time.*

BENSON, WILLIAM EDWARD (BARNES), geologist; b. West Haven, Conn., May 15, 1919; s. John Edward and Lucia Purdy (Barnes) B.; m. Mary Freda Hill, July 11, 1944; children—Sharon (Mrs. J.G. Rachel), Lynn (Mrs. J.D. Walker), William Edward. B.A., Yale, 1940, M.S., 1942, Ph.D., 1952. Geologist Conn. Geol. and Natural History Survey, 1940-42; geologist U.S. Geol. Survey, 1942-54, br. chief, 1953-54; exec. sec. div. earth sci. Nat. Acad. Scis./NRC, 1954-55; chief geologist Manidon Mining Inc., N.D., 1955-56; program dir., sect. head NSF, 1956-75, chief scientist earth sci. div., 1975-79; sci. advisory to Office of Pres., Washington, 1976-77; pvt. cons., 1980—; vis. prof. U. Hawaii, 1980; sr. staff assoc. NAS, 1980—. Contbr., editor profl. jours. Served with USNR, 1944-45. Yale fellow, 1940-42. Fellow Geol. Soc. Am., Am. Geophys. Union, AAAS (sec. sect. E 1969-73, chmn. sect. E 1974-75); mem. Geol. Soc. Washington (v.p. 1958), Pick and Hammer Soc. (chmn. 1970-73), Phi Beta Kappa, Sigma Xi. Home: 7531 Parish Ln Falls Church VA 22042-3521*

BENSOUSSAN, ABRAHAM, rabbi; b. Agadire, Morocco, July 21, 1948; came to U.S., 1961; s. Elias Eliyahou and Esther Bensoussan; m. Linda E. Rabinsky, Aug. 23, 1973; children: Haim, Yudit. B. Religious Edn., Kaminetz Yeshiva, 1970; MA, Y. Detroit, 1974; EdS, Wayne State U., 1976. Ordained rabbi, 1972. Dir. Jafo Sch., Yafo, Israel, 1971-72; tchr. religious studies Akiva Day Sch., Detroit, 1973-76; guidance counselor Akiva Day Sch., Southfield, Mich., 1974-76; prof. advanced studies Medrasha Coll., Southfield, 1976—; rabbi Rinat Israel Congregation, Cleve., 1976—; exec. dir. Yabi, Multi Program Torah Inst., Cleve., 1976—; tchr. of Jewish law Rinat Israel, Cleve., 1989—; spiritual leader Rose Nursing Home, Cleve., 1976-80; youth, religious dir. Nat. Conference of Synagogue Youth, University Heights, Ohio, 1976—; mem. orthodox rabbinical coun., trustee Merkaz Harabonim, Cleve., 1978—; ednl. adviser Betsefer Mizrachi, 1980-85, 80-91; rabbinical adviser Coll. Jewish Studies, 1980-83; speaker in field. Contbr. articles to profl. publs. Mem. campaign cabinet United Way, Cleve., 1989, Cleve. Jewish Community Fedn., 1990-91; rabbinical cons. University Heights City Hall, 1989-91. Mem. Orthodox Rabbinical Coun. (sec. 1978-91), Jewish Educators Coun. (pres. 1987-88). *In order for an individual to acquire a closeness to G-d, he must be sincere with his fellow man. In order for one to be sincere with fellow man, one must be honest with himself. This would eventually bring the individual close to G-D.*

BENSTON, GEORGE JAMES, accountant, economist; b. N.Y.C., Mar. 18, 1932; s. William and Rose L. B.; m. Alice N. Schwartz, July 28, 1951; children: Kimberly Wayne, Randall Craig. BA, Queens Coll., 1952; MBA, NYU, 1953; PhD, U. Chgo., 1963. CPA, N.C. Acct. CPA firms, 1952-53; acctg. and tax specialist 1st Nat. Bank of Atlanta, 1956-57; asst. prof. acctg. Ga. State U., 1957-58, U. Chgo., 1962-66; assoc. prof. acctg. and fin. U. Rochester, 1961-69, prof. fin., acctg. and econs., 1969-87; Harlan prof. fin., acctg. and econs. Emory U., Atlanta, 1987—, assoc. dean faculty rsch. and ctr. devel., 1990-92, area coord. fin., 1988-90, 92-96, area coord. acctg., 1993; vis. prof. U. Calif., Berkeley, Grad. Sch. Bus. Studies, London, London Sch. Econs., Hebrew U., Jerusalem; hon. vis. prof. City U. London, Oxford U.; trustee Coll. Retirement Equities Fund; Disting. Internat. Lectr. Am. Acctg. Assn., 1980. Author: Corporate Accounting Disclosure in the UK and the USA, 1976, Contemporary Cost Accounting and Control, 1970, 77, Analysis of Causes of SLA Failures, 1985, The Separation of Commercial and Investment Banking: The Glass-Steagall Act Revisited and Reconsidered, 1990; co-editor: Jour. Fin. Svcs. Rsch.; assoc. editor, mem. editorial bd. Jour. Money and Credit Banking, Jour. Acctg. Pub. Policy; others; contbr. articles to profl. jours. Ford Found., U.S. Steel and Woodrow Wilson fellow, 1958-59; Olin Disting. fellow Oxford U. Mem. Shadow Fin. Regulation Com., Am. Acctg. Assn., Am. Fin. Assn., Am. Econ. Assn., Fin. Mgmt. Assn., Phi Beta Kappa, Beta Gamma Sigma. Home: 3572 Knollwood Dr NW Atlanta GA 30305-1022

BENT, ALAN EDWARD, political science educator, administrator; b. Shanghai, China, June 22, 1939; s. Walter J. and Tamara (Rocklin) B.; m. Dawn Bickler, Aug. 13, 1977; 1 son by previous marriage, Ronald Geoffrey. B.S., San. Francisco State U., 1963; M.A., U. So. Calif., 1968, Claremont Grad. Sch., 1970; Ph.D., Claremont Grad. Sch., 1971; M.B.A., Xavier U., 1985. Instr. polit. sci. Chapman Coll., Orange, Calif., 1969-70; research assoc. Mcpl. Systems Research, Claremont Grad. Sch., 1970-71; asst. prof. polit. sci., assoc. dir. Inst. Govtl. Studies and Research Memphis State U., 1971-74; assoc. prof., chmn. dept. pub. adminstrn. Calif. State U., Dominguez Hills, 1974-77; prof. polit. sci. U. Cin., 1977-81, 82-92, head dept. polit. sci., 1977-81; dean Coll. Arts and Scis. U. No. Colo., Greeley, 1981-82, prof. polit. sci., 1981-82; prof. pub. adminstr. Troy State U., Europe, 1989-92; cons. police agys., govtl. and pvt. instns. Author: Escape from Anarchy: A Strategy for Urban Survival, 1972; The Politics of Law Enforcement: Conflict and Power in Urban Communities, 1974, 2d edit., 1976; co-author: Police, Criminal Justice and the Community, 1976, Collective Bargaining in the Public Sector: Labor-Management Relations and Public Policy, 1978; co-editor, contbr. Urban Administration: Management, Politics and Change, 1976, 2d edit. 1977; contbr. articles to profl. jours.; bd. editors: Rev. Pub. Personnel Adminstrn., 1980-89, Spectrum, A Jour. of Comparative Politics and Devel., New Delhi, 1984-92. Served to capt. USAF, 1964-69. NASPAA fellow, 1981-82. Mem. AAUP. Home: 1006 Oro St Laguna Beach CA 92651-3534

BENT, GEOFFREY STEVEN, artist, librarian; b. Chgo., June 28, 1950; s. William Harvey and Merle Elaine (Benson) B.; m. Jeanette Sue Alexander, June, 21, 1992. BA, Northeastern Ill. U., 1972; MA, Loyola U., Chgo., 1989. Libr. Sonnenschein, Nath & Rosenthal, Chgo., 1977—. One-man shows include Beverly Art Ctr., Chgo., 1982, Sonnenschein, Nath & Rosenthal, Chgo., 1987, Mars Gallery, Chgo., 1988, Space Gallery, Chgo., 1990, Nash Gallery, 1997, U. Tenn., 1998, U. Wis., 1999; exhibited in group shows at Limelight, Chgo., 1988, ARC Gallery, Chgo., 1990, Edge of the Looking Glass Gallery, Chgo., 1990, Wustum Mus., Racine, Wis., 1991, N.W. Art Coun. Gallery, Chgo., 1991, Chgo. Cultural Ctr., 1992, Indpls. Art Ctr., 1993 (1st pl.), Plan B Gallery, Memphis, 1994, M. Ward Gallery, Chgo., 1994, Clara Van Storch Gallery, Dexter, Mich., 1994, Three Rivers Arts Festival, Pitts., 1994-96, Agora Gallery, N.Y.C., 1995, Mus. Art, Springfield, Mass., 1995, Resurgam Gallery, Balt., 1995, Alternative Mus., N.Y.C., 1995-96, Pa. Mus., Allentown, 1996, Mcpl. Gallery, Raleigh, N.C., 1996, U. Oreg., Eugene, 1996, Salmagundi Club, N.Y.C., 1996, La. Mus. Art, Alexandria, 1996, Orange County Ctr. Contemporary Art, Calif., 1997, Hyde Park Art Ctr., 1997; contbr. articles to profl. jours. Mem. Chgo. Artists Coalition, Hyde Park Art Ctr. Home: 587 Wilshire Ave Glen Ellyn IL 60137-4975 Office: Sonnenschein Nath & Rosenthal 8000 Sears Tower Chicago IL 60606

BENT, ROBERT DEMO, physicist, educator; b. Cambridge, Mass., Dec. 22, 1928; s. Henry Edward and Florence (Demo) B.; m. Mary Alice Keating, June 9, 1956; children—Lisa Clare, Jason Robert, Alan Demo. Student, U. Mo., 1945-46; B.A., Oberlin Coll., 1950; M.A., Rice U., 1952, Ph.D., 1954. Research assoc. Rice U., Houston, 1954-55, Columbia U., 1955-58; vis. research assoc. Brookhaven Nat. Lab., Upton, N.Y., summer 1955; asst. prof. physics Ind. U., Bloomington, 1958-62; assoc. prof. Ind. U., 1962-66, prof., 1966-95, prof. emeritus, 1995—. Contbr. articles on nuclear physics to profl. jours. Guggenheim fellow Oxford, Harwell, 1962-63. Fellow Am. Phys. Soc. Home: 1315 S Longwood Dr Bloomington IN 47401-6073

BENTAS, LILY H., retail executive. CEO Cumberland Farms, Canton, Mass., chmn., pres. Office: Cumberland Farms Inc 777 Dedham St Canton MA 02021-1484*

BENTEL, FREDERICK RICHARD, architect, educator; b. N.Y.C., Jan. 2, 1928; s. Carl August and Mary (Muller) B.; m. Maria L. R. Azzarone, Aug. 16, 1952; children: Paul Louis, Peter Andreas, Maria Elisabeth. BArch., Pratt Inst., 1949; grad. fellow, Mass. Inst. Tech., MArch., 1950; DArch., Technische Hochschule, Graz, Austria, 1953. Registered architect, N.Y., N.J., Va., Vt., Conn., profl. planner, N.J. Architect, partner Bentel & Bentel (AIA), Locust Valley, N.Y., 1957—; pres. Correlated Designs Inc., Locust Valley, 1961—; ptnr. Old Path Realty, Cobblestone Enterprises; prof. Sch. Architecture, Pratt Inst., 1955-70; prof. Sch. Architecture, N.Y. Inst. Tech., 1969—. Author publs. in field. Founding mem. com. Locust Valley Bus. Dist. Planning; adv. bd. Oyster Planning and Hist. Preservation Commn., 1970-73; mem. Oyster Bay Hist. Preservation Commn., 1975-91; alt. APD panel N.Y. State Coun. on Arts, 1985-86, St. Joseph's Coll. Libr. Arch., L.I., chpt. AIA, 1990, St. Stephen's Ch., Warwick, N.Y., L.I. chpt. AIA, 1991, Pavilion, Old Westbury, N.Y. Fulbright scholar, 1952-53; recipient awards in field including 1st pl. commn. Islip Bay Shore downtown redevel. competition, 1976, Suffolk County Ct. Complex, 1985. Fellow AIA (task force for archtl. graphic stas., St. Joseph's Coll. Libr. Arch. L.I. chpt. 1990, St. Stephen's Ch., Warwick, N.Y., L.I. chpt. 1991, Pavilion, Old Westbury, N.Y., Gramercy Tavern, N.Y.C., L.I. chpt. 1996); mem. N.Y. Soc. Architects (numerous awards), Am. Italy Soc., MIT Alumni Assn. (ednl. coun.),. Home: 23 Frost Creek Dr Locust Valley NY 11560-1029 Office: Bentel & Bentel Architect & Planner 22 Buckram Rd Locust Valley NY 11560-1928

BENTEL, MARIA-LUISE RAMONA AZZARONE (MRS. FREDERICK R. BENTEL), architect, educator; b. N.Y.C., June 15, 1928; d. Louis and Maria-Teresa (Massaro) Azzarone; m. Frederick R. Bentel, Aug. 16, 1952; children: Paul Louis, Peter Andreas, Maria Elisabeth. BArch, MIT, 1951; Fulbright scholar, Scuola d'Architettura, Venice, Italy, 1952-53. Registered profl. architect, Conn., N.Y., N.J., Va., Vt. registered profl. planner, N.J. Partner Bentel & Bentel (Architects), Locust Valley, N.Y., 1955—; pres. Tesstoria Realty Corp., N.Y.C., 1961—; v.p., sec.-treas. Correlated Designs, Inc., Locust Valley, 1961—; partner Cobblestone Enterprises, 1967; founding mem. Locust Valley Bus. Dist. Planning Commn., 1968—; regional vice chair MIT Ednl. Coun.; adv. mem. MIT Coun. for the Arts; assoc. prof. architecture Sch. Architecture and Fine Arts N.Y. Inst. Tech.; mem. APD panel N.Y. State Coun. for Arts, 1985-89. Archtl. works include C.W. Post Coll.

L.I. U (N.Y. State Assn. Architects award 1975, Gold Archi award L.I. Assn. Architects 1974), Hempstead Bank, Nassau Centre Office Bldg., North Shore Unitarian Sch., Plandome, N.Y., Shelter Rock Library, Searingtown, N.Y., St. Anthony's Ch., Nanuet, N.Y., Kinloch Farm, Va., Steinberg Learning Center-Woodmere (N.Y.) Acad., St. Francis de Sales Ch., Bennington, Vt., Neitlich residence, Oyster Bay Cove, N.Y., Amityville (N.Y.) Pub. Library, Jericho (N.Y.) Pub. Library, John B. Gambling residence, Lattingtown, N.Y., Glen Cove (N.Y.) Boys' Club at Lincoln House, Salten Hall, N.Y. Inst. Tech., N.Y. Coll. Osteo. Med. at N.Y. Inst. Tech., Old Westbury, Commack (N.Y.) Pub. Library, St. Mary Star of the Sea Ch., Far Rockaway, Oberlin Residence, St. Hyacinth's Ch.; Museums at Stony Brook, St. Joseph's Coll. Libr., N.Y. Inst. Tech. Libr., 1989, Simpson residence, St. Stephen's Ch., Warwick, N.Y., 1991, Pavilion Old Westbury (N.Y.); contbr. religious architecture chpt. to Time Saver Standards (De Chiara and Callender), 1973. Mem. comml. panel Am. Arbitration Assn.; bd. dirs. L.I. Soc. AIA; chmn. adv. panel on govt. bldg. projects GSA, 1976; chmn. Inst. Internat. Edn.; mem. nat. adv.-selection com. Fulbright-Hays awards, 1976-78, 80, 82; chair Locust Valley Libr. Adv. Bd., 1973-80. Named Woman Architect of Year Nassau-Suffolk County, 1976. Fellow AIA (corp. mem., chmn. design com., dir. L.I. chpt.); mem. N.Y. State Assn. Architects (chmn. design awards com.), Nat. Council Archtl. Registration Bds., MIT Alumnae Assn., MIT Alumni L.I. Home: 23 Frost Creek Dr Locust Valley NY 11560-1029 Office: 22 Buckram Rd Locust Valley NY 11560-1928

BENTIVEGNA, PETER IGNATIUS, architectural company executive; b. N.Y.C., Dec. 2, 1941; s. Peter and Catherine Bentivegna; m. Louise Catherine Foulkrod, Aug. 20, 1989. BArch, Pratt Inst., 1963. Registered architect, D.C., Ky., Mass., N.C., N.J., N.Y., Pa., Tex., W.Va. Mng. ptnr. Bentivegna, Lindsay Maron Merlino Architects, Bala Cynwyd, 1983—; pres. BLM Group, Bala Cynwyd, 1983—. Contbr. articles to profl. jours. Lt. U.S. Army, 1964-66. Mem. AIA (com. on architecture for health), Pa. Soc. Architects, Constrn. Specifications Inst., Nat. Fire Protection Assn. Office: BLM Group 161 Rockhill Rd Bala Cynwyd PA 19004-2048*

BENTLEY, ANTHONY MILES, lawyer; b. N.Y.C., July 16, 1945; s. Herbert A. and Dorothy Dene (Hyman) B. BA, U. Pa., 1967; JD, Fordham U., 1971. Bar: N.Y. 1971, U.S. Ct. Appeals (2d cir.) 1971, Pa. 1973, U.S. Dist. Ct. (so. and ea. dists.) N.Y. 1973, U.S. Tax Ct. 1976, U.S. Supreme Ct. 1976, U.S. Ct. Appeals (fed. cir.), 1995, U.S. Claims Ct. 1996, U.S. Dist. Ct. Ariz. 1996, U.S. Ct. Internat. Trade 1996. Assoc. Hughes Hubbard & Reed, N.Y.C., 1970, Cahill Gordan & Reindel, N.Y.C., 1971-75, Goldstein Shames Hyde, N.Y.C., 1975-76; sole practice N.Y.C., 1977—; spl. master N.Y. County Supreme Ct., 1977—, N.Y. County Civil Ct., 1994—; arbitrator N.Y.C. Ct. N.Y. Coun. Editor Fordham Law Rev., 1970-71; founding editor Fordham Urban Law Jour., 1971. Trustee Am. Judges Found. With U.S. Army, 1963-65. Recipient Disting. Svc. award FTC, 1976, 79. Mem. ABA, Assn. of Bar of City of N.Y., Assn. Trial Lawyers Am., Pa. Bar Assn., Phila. Bar Assn., Mensa, Intertel, Am. Judges Assn. (N.Y. del.), N.Y. County Lawyers Assn., N.Y. Civil and Criminal Cts. Bar Assn. Jewish. Address: 116 W 72nd St New York NY 10023-3315

BENTLEY, CHARLES RAYMOND, geophysics educator; b. Rochester, N.Y., Dec. 23, 1929; s. Raymond and Janet Cornelia (Everest) B.; m. Marybelle Goode, July 3, 1964; children: Molly Clare, Raymond Alexander. BS, Yale U., 1950; PhD, Columbia U., 1959. Rsch. geophysicist Columbia U., 1952-56; Antarctic traverse leader and seismologist Arctic Inst. N.Am., 1956-59; project assoc. U. Wis., 1959-61, asst. prof., 1961-63, assoc. prof., 1963-68, prof. geophysics, 1968-98, A.P. Crary prof. geophysics, 1987-98, prof. emeritus, 1998—. Recipient Bellingshausen-Lazarev medal for Antarctic rsch. Acad. Scis. USSR, 1971; NSF sr. postdoctoral fellow, 1968-69; NAS-USSR Acad. Sci. exch. fellow, 1977, 90. Fellow AAAS, Am. Geophys. Union, Arctic Inst. N.Am., Am. Polar Soc. (hon., bd. dirs.); mem. AAUP, Soc. Exploration Geophysicists, Internat. Glaciological Soc. (Seligman Crystal award 1990), Am. Quaternary Assn., Oceanography Soc., Am. Geol. Inst., Geol. Soc. Am., Phi Beta Kappa, Sigma Xi. Achievements include research on Antarctic glaciology and geophysics, satellite studies of geomagnetic anomalies, magnetotelluric exploration of Earth structure, satellite radar and laser altimetry. Home: 5618 Lake Mendota Dr Madison WI 53705-1036 Office: U Wis Geophys & Polar Rsch Ctr Weeks Hall 1215 Dayton St Madison WI 53706

BENTLEY, CLARENCE EDWARD, savings and loan executive; b. Ranger, Tex., Oct. 9, 1921; s. Clarence Edward and Rosa Estelle (Bryant) B.; m. Gloria Gill, Oct. 9, 1943; children: Jon, Kitty, Perry (dec.). Student, McMurry U., Abilene, Tex., 1939-42. Pres. Abilene Savs. Assn., 1944-77, Southwestern Group Fin. Co., Houston, 1976-77; pres. United Savs. Assn. Tex., Houston, 1977-80; chmn. bd. United Savs. Assn. Tex., 1980-85; dir., chmn. bd. Sandia Fed. Savs. & Loan, Albuquerque, 1986-89; dir. Kaneb Pipeline Partners, 1990—; chmn. bd. dirs. United Fin. Mortgage Co., Dallas, United Fin. Group, Inc., Houston, 1980-86; bd. dirs. Kaneb Services Inc., Investors Mortgage Ins. Co., Boston. Contbr. articles to profl. publns. Pres. Abilene Indsl. Found., 1970, United Fund Abilene, 1962; mem. bd. Tex. State Hosps., 1962-64; mem. Tex. Fin. Commn., 1964-76, chmn., 1971. Served with USAAF, 1942-43. Recipient Outstanding Citizen award City of Abilene, 1964, Disting. Alumnus award McMurry U., 1971. Mem. Nat. Savs. and Loan League (pres. 1970-71), Tex. Savs. and Loan League (pres. 1970-71), Assn. Thrift Holding Cos. (chmn. bd. 1985-87), Abilene C. of C. (pres. 1964). Episcopalian. Club: Abilene Country (pres. 1951). Home: 52 Rue Maison St Abilene TX 79605-4710

BENTLEY, FRED DOUGLAS, SR., lawyer; b. Marietta, Ga., Oct. 15, 1926; s. Oscar Andrew and Ima Irene (Prather) B.; children from previous marriage: Fred Douglas, Robert Randall; m. Jane Morrill McNeel, Nov. 7, 1997. BA, Presbyn. Coll., 1949; JD, Emory U., 1948. Bar: Ga. 1948. Sr. mem. Bentley & Dew, Marietta, 1948-51; ptnr. Bentley, Awtrey & Bartlett, Marietta, 1951-56, Edwards, Bentley, Awtrey & Parker, Marietta, 1956-75, Bentley & Schindelar, Marietta, 1975-80, Bentley, Bentley & Bentley, Marietta, 1975-80, 1980—; pres. Beneficial Investment Co., Newmarket, Inc., Happy Valley, Inc., Bentley & Sons, Inc.; founder, chmn. bd. Charter Bank and Trust Co.; founder, trustee emeritus Kennesaw Coll. Mem. Ga. Ho. Reps., 1951-57, Ga. Senate, 1958; past pres. Cobb County (Ga.) C. of C.; founder, hon. curator Bentley Rare Book Galleries-Brenau U., Kennesaw State U.; mem., past chmn. Ga. Coun. Arts, 1976-89; mem. Gov.'s Fine Arts Com., 1990-92, Cummer Mus. of Art (hon. life); attache Ghana Olympic Com.; founder Cobb Emergency Svcs., bd. advisors Emory U-Woodruff. Served with USN. Recipient Blue Key Cmty. Svc. award, Founder's award, 1992, Clarisse Baquell award for outstanding svc., Spl. Svc. award Kennesaw State Coll., Robert Cleveland award for lifetime achievement in law; named Citizen of Yr., C. of C., 1951, Leader of Tomorrow, Time mag., 1953, Vol. Citizen of Yr., Atlanta Jour./Constn., 1981, Kennesaw Historical Soc. Man of Yr., 1996, Brenau Univ. Man of Yr., 1996; fellow J. Pierpont Morgan Libr.; Oct. 15 Fred Bentley Day City & Coun. Mem. ABA, Ga. Bar Assn., Ga. Mus. Art (bd. advisors, hon. life mem.), Nat. PTA (hon. life), Cobb Landmarks Soc. (founder), Kennesaw Mountain Jaycees (founder), Rotary (hon. life), Georgian Club (bd. dirs.), The Grolier Club (hon.), Fellows of Marietta Cobb Mus. of Art (founder, chmn.), Ga. Mus. (life, bd. advisors). Republican. Methodist. Home: 1441 Beaumont Dr Kennesaw GA 30152-3201 Office: 241 Washington Ave NE Marietta GA 30060-1958

BENTLEY, JAMES DANIEL, hospital association executive; b. Jamestown, N.Y., Feb. 17, 1945; s. John Alexander and Pauline Ruby (Norberg) B.; m. Lorraine Kay Anderson, June 17, 1967; children: Kimberly, Andrew. BA, Mich. State U., 1967; PhD, U. Mich., 1971. Asst. dir. teaching hosps. Assn. Am. Med. Colls., Washington, 1976-80, assoc. dir.teaching hosps., 1980-86, v.p. for clin. svcs., 1987-91; sr. v.p. policy Am. Hosp. Assn., Washington, 1991-97, sr. v.p. strategic policy planning, 1997—; tech. advisor Health Care Financing Adminstrn., Washington, 1984-87. Mem. editorial bd. Health Adminstrn. Press, Ann Arbor, Mich., 1988-91. Pres. Ch. Coun. St. Luke Luth., Silver Spring, Md., 1986-88; exec. com. Holy Cross Hosp., Silver Spring, Md., 1990-96. Lt. USN, 1971-76. Recipient traineeship USPHS, 1967-71. Office: Am Hosp Assn Liberty Pl 325 7th St NW Washington DC 20004-2818

BENTLEY, JAMES LUTHER, journalist; b. Panama City, Fla., Jan. 24, 1937; s. Thomas Pierce and Sara Pope (Woodruff) B.; m. Patricia Ann Daniel, July 30, 1965. Student Ga. Inst. Tech, Ga. State U., 1958-61, N.C. State U., 1962. Reporter Atlanta Constitution, 1958-64, asst. city editor, 1964-66, night city editor, 1966-71, city editor, 1971-79; corr. Reuters Ltd., 1967-79; dir. info. TVA, 1979; mng. editor Cox News Svc., Washington, 1979—. Served with U.S. Army, 1961-63. Mem. Soc. Profl. Journalists, Rotary. Lutheran. Home: 317 Old Plantation Rd Jekyll Island GA 31527-0857 Office: Ste 10000 2000 Pennsylvania Ave NW Washington DC 20006-1812*

BENTLEY, JAMES ROBERT, association curator, historian, genealogist; b. Louisville, Feb. 14, 1942; s. Francis Getty and Katharine Elizabeth (Wescott) B; BA, Centre Coll. Ky., 1964; MA, Coll. William and Mary, 1971. Research asst. Colonial Williamsburg (Va.), 1966-68; asst. to curator Filson Club, Louisville, 1964-65, curator, 1968-83, sec., 1972-84, acting dir., 1983-84, dir., 1984-92; dir. G.R. Clark Press, Louisville, 1974—; mem. adv. com. to photograph archives U. Louisville, 1971-72; mem. Hist. Zoning Task Force Louisville and Jefferson County, 1971-73; mem. hist. protection and preservation com. Bd. Aldermen Louisville, 1972-73; mem. Mayor's Com. Public Amenities, 1991—; mem. Jefferson County Comm. Ky. Bicentennial Comn., 1991-92; commr. Hist. Landmarks and Preservation Dists. Commn., Louisville, 1973-79. Mem. SAR (registrar 1970-93, library com.), Ky. Soc. Mayflower Descs. (historian, librarian 1970-78, gov. 1978-84, dep. gov. gen. 1981-87 , 5 generation project com. 1979-80), Ky. Soc. Colonial Wars (councillor 1971-76, registrar 1976—), Jeffersontown Hist. Soc. (dir. 1972-73, v.p. 1974-76, pres. 1976-78), Soc. Am. Archivists, Manuscript Soc., Nat. Trust Hist. Preservation, Hist. Homes Found. Louisville, Vt. Hist. Soc. (life), New Eng. Hist. Geneal. Soc., English Speaking Union, Nat. Geneal. Soc. (life), Vt. Geneal. Soc., Ind. Hist. Soc., Vt. Old Cemetery Assn., Louisville Hist. League, Alden Kindred Am., Soc. Stukely Westcott Descs., Edmund Rice 1638 Assn., Soc. Descs. Robert Bartlett of Plymouth Colony, Harleian Soc., Order Ky. Cols., Sigma Chi. Episcopalian. Clubs: Pendennis (Louisville), Filson (life). Editor, pub. Ky. Genealogist, 1979-86. Home: 1048 Cherokee Rd Louisville KY 40204-1231

BENTLEY, KENNETH CHESSAR, oral and maxillofacial surgeon, educator; b. Montreal, Que., Can., Sept. 22, 1935; s. Albert Edwin and Lilian Beatrice (Hoare) B.; m. Jean Wadsworth, Aug. 19, 1961; children: Douglas, Margaret. DDS, McGill U., 1958, MD, CM, 1962. Intern, then resident Montreal Gen. Hosp. and Bellevue Hosp., N.Y., 1962-66; from asst. prof. to assoc. prof. McGill U., 1966-67, prof. dentistry, 1975-98, prof. emeritus, 1998; dean McGill U. Sch. Dentistry, 1977-87; jr. asst. dental surgeon Montreal Gen. Hosp., 1966, assoc. dental surgeon, assoc. dir. dentistry, 1968, dental surgeon-in-chief, 1970—; cons. oral and maxillofacial surgery Montreal Children's Hosp., Royal Victoria Hosp., St. Mary's Hosp.; bd. dirs. Thistle Coun. Montreal, Griffith-McConnell Residence. Co-author: Advanced Oral Radiographic Interpretation, 1979. Fellow Am. Coll. Dentists, Internat. Coll. Dentists, Royal Coll. Dentists Can., Pierre Fauchard Acad., Academie Dentaire Du Quebec; mem. Assn. Oral and Maxillofacial Surgeons Que., Bellevue Soc. Oral Surgeons, Can. Dental Assn. (chmn. council hosp. services 1971-75, council edn. 1982-85), Can. Assn. Oral and Maxillofacial Surgeons (sec.-treas. 1970-71), Internat. Assn. Study Pain, Internat. Assn. Oral Surgeons, Montreal Dental Club (sec. 1968, pres.1992), Nat. Dental Examining Bd. Can., Order Dentists Que., St. Andrew's Soc. Montreal (1st v.p.). Avocations: music, pipe organ, Scottish country dancing. Office: B3-149, 1650 Cedar Ave, Montreal, PQ Canada H3G 1A4

BENTLEY, MARGARET ANN, librarian; b. Tawas City, Mich., June 13, 1956; d. Rupert A. and Joy A. (Bills) B. AB in English, Gordon Coll., 1978; MA in Libr. Sci., U. Mich., 1979. Cert. libr., Mich. Adult svcs. libr., asst. dir. Shiawassee Dist. Libr. (formerly Owosso Pub. Libr.), Owosso, Mich., 1979—. Author: 75 Years of Service, 1989. Mem. AAUW (treas. 1984-99), Mich. Libr. Assn., Beta Phi Mu, Lambda Iota Tau, Phi Alpha Chi. Avocations: reading, crafts, camping. Office: Shiawassee Dist Libr 502 W Main St Owosso MI 48867-2607

BENTLEY, ORVILLE GEORGE, retired agricultural educator, dean emeritus; b. Midland, S.D., Mar. 6, 1918; s. Thomas O. and Ida Marie (Sandal) B.; m. Enolia J. Anderson, Sept. 19, 1942; children: Peter T., Craig E. B.S., S.D. State Coll., 1942; M.S. in Biochemistry, U. Wis., 1947, Ph.D., 1950, hon. degree, 1984; hon. degree, S.D. State U., 1974. Asst. prof. animal sci. Ohio Agrl. Expt. Sta.; also mem. dept. animal sci. and dept. agrl. biochemistry Ohio State U., 1950-58; dean Coll. of Agr. and Biol. Scis., S.D. State U., 1958-65, Coll. Agr., U. Ill. at Urbana, 1965-82; asst. sec. agr. for sci. and edn. USDA, Washington, 1982-89; dean emeritus, coll. agr. U. Ill., Urbana, 1986—; mem. comm. animal nutrition NRC-Nat. Acad. Scis., 1958-67; mem. Coun. U.S. Univs. for Rural Devel. in India, 1967-74; mem. ad hoc adv. com. Ill. Inst. for Environ. Quality, 1971; mem. tech. adv. com. on food and agr. U.S. Dept. Agr., Vietn Nam, 1966; mem. panel NAS to meet mems. Indonesian Acad. Scis., 1968; co-chmn. Agrl. Rsch. Policy Adv. Com., 1973-77; mem. Bd. for Internat. Food and Agrl. Devel., 1976-80; co-chmn. U.S. Dept. Agr. Joint Coun. for Food and Agrl. Scis., 1982-89; mem. NAS Govt.-Univ. Industry Rsch. Roundtable, 1985-89; mem. com. of earth sci., com. on life scis., biotech. sci. coordinating com. Fed. Coordinating Coun., Soc., Engring., and Tech.; head U.S. del. U.S./Indo Subcommn. on Agr., 1986-88, Ohio Coun. Rsch. and Econ. devel., 1989-90, U.S.-Japan high level adv. panel Sci. and tech. agreement, 1989-92; co-chair USDA Joint Venezuela-U.S. Agrl. Commn., 1990-95. Mem. editorial bd. Jour. Animal Sci., 1956-59; contbr. articles to profl. jours. Bd. trustees Am. U. Beirut, Midwest Univs., 1973-92, Consortium for Internat. Activities, 1966-76; chmn. bd. dirs. Farm Found., 1971-78. Served to maj., chem warfare svc. AUS, 1942-45. Named Young Man of Year Wooster Jr. C. of C., 1953; recipient Distinguished Alumnus award S.D. State U., 1967, U. Ill., 1985. Fellow Am. Soc. Animal Sci. (pres. midwestern sect. 1963, Am. feed mfrs. award 1958); mem. Am. Inst. Nutrition, Am. Soc. Animal Sci., Am. Dairy Sci. Assn., Internat. Union of Nutritional Scis., Farm House (hon.), AAAS (committeeman-at-large 1971-82), Sigma Xi, Phi Kappa Phi. Club: Rotary. Home and Office: 2030 Bentbrook Dr Champaign IL 61822-9221

BENTLEY, PETER, lawyer; b. Jersey City, Sept. 1, 1915; s. Peter and Emma (Patterson) B.; m. Signe Von Krusenstierna, Apr. 15, 1944 (dec. Mar. 1984); 1 child, Frederique Bentley Boire; m. Jane Morfoot Chapman, Apr. 19, 1986. B.A., Princeton U., 1938; JD, Yale U., 1941. Bar: N.Y. 1942, U.S. Ct. Appeals (2d cir.) 1943, U.S. Dist. Ct. (so. dist.) N.Y. 1944, Conn. 1952, U.S. Dist. Ct. Conn. 1954. Assoc. Simpson, Thacher & Bartlett, N.Y.C., 1941-52, Maguire, Cole, Bentley & Babson (and predecessors), Stamford, Conn., 1952-81; mem. Bentley, Mosher, Babson & Lambert, P.C. and predecessors, Stamford, 1981-90; of counsel Bentley, Mosher, Babson, & Lambert P.C., Greenwich, Conn., 1990—. Rep. Greenwich Town Meeting, 1966-68; bd. dirs., pres. The Carl J. Herzog Found. Inc., 1978—; bd. dirs. Ferris Found. Am. Inc., 1983-90; bd. dirs. The Royal Soc. of Medicine Found., Inc., 1991-96; mem Rockefeller U. Coun., 1994—. Mem. ABA, Conn. Bar Assn., Stamford Bar Assn. (pres. 1971-72, bd. dirs.), Am. Skin Assn. (bd. dirs., chmn. 1988-96). Republican. Mem. Soc. of Friends. Home: Crawford 232 7 Riverwoods Dr Exeter NH 03833-4374 Office: Bentley Mosher Babson & Lambert PC 321 Railroad Ave Greenwich CT 06830-0788

BENTLEY, PETER JOHN GERALD, forest industry company executive; b. Vienna, Austria, Mar. 17, 1930; s. Leopold Lionel Garrick and Antoinette Ruth B.; m. Sheila Farrington McGiverin, May 23, 1953; children: Michael Peter, Barbara Ruth, Susan Patricia, Joan Katherine, Lisa Marie. Ed., U. B.C. Sch. Forestry, Banff Sch. Advanced Mgmt.; LLD (hon.), U. B.C. Chmn., dir. Canfor Corp., Vancouver, B.C., Can., Can. Forest Products Ltd., Vancouver; co-chmn., dir. Howe Sound Pulp & Paper Ltd.; co-chmn. Canwel Distbn. Ltd.; ret., 1995; bd. dirs. Bank Montreal, Shell Can. Ltd., B.C. Chem. Ltd.; gov. Olympic Trust Can.; mem. internat. adv. coun. Chase Manhattan Corp. on N.Y.C. Bd. dirs. Jr. Achievement of Can.; past chmn., trustee Vancouver Hosp. and Health Sci. Ctr.; vice chmn. Bus. Coun. on Nat. Issues, Ottawa, past chmn. Bus. Coun. B.C.; bd. dirs. Can. Inst. for Advanced Rsch.; mem. adv. coun. to faculty commerce and bus. adminstrn., mem. forestry adv. com. U. B.C., bd. govs. Banff Ctr. for Continuing Edn. hon.; dir. Can. Profls. Golfers Assn. Decorated officer Order of Can. Mem. B.C. Forestry Assn. (hon. life, past pres., hon. dir.). Clubs: Capilano Golf and Country, Marine Drive Golf, Vancouver, Vancouver Lawn Tennis and Badminton; Thunderbird Country (Rancho Mirage); Morningside (Rancho Mirage, Calif.); Royal and Ancient Golf (St. Andrews, Scotland). Office: Canfor Corp, POB 49420 Bentall Postal, Vancouver, BC Canada V7X 1B5

BENTLEY, RICHARD NORCROSS, regional planner, writer, educator; b. Chgo., Mar. 17, 1937; s. Richard and Phoebe Wrenn (Norcross) B.; m. Carolyn Stiglic, Sept. 10, 1977; children: Nicholas Northrup, Julia Wrenn. BA, Yale U., 1959; MFA, Norwich U., 1992; writers workshop, U. Iowa, 1995. Chief project mgr. Kate Maremont Found., 1965-70, Rose Assocs., N.Y.C., 1973-75, Adv. Svcs. for Better Housing, N.Y.C., 1975-78, Mass. Dept. Community Affairs, Boston, 1978-83; chief planner Mayor's Office Housing, Boston, 1983-86; planning dir. Boston Housing Authority, 1986-87; sr. planning mgr. Pioneer Valley Planning Commn., West Springfield, Mass., 1987-88; instr. Internat. City Mgmt. Assn., Washington, 1982—; instr. creative writing U. Mass., 1992—, Cambridge Coll., 1994—, Mass. Coll. Liberal Arts, 1995—, Holyoke C.C., 1997—; instr. MFA program Vt. Coll., 1997. Editor Peregrine Mag., 1991-93. Bd. govs. Groton (Mass.) Sch., 1990-95; gov.'s appointee Mass. Mortgage Rev. Bd., 1984—. Served with U.S. Army, 1960-62. Recipient Internat. Fiction award Paris Writers' Workshop, 1994. Mem. Nat. Assn. Housing and Redevelopment Officals, Am. Planning Assn., Assn. Personal Historians (founding), Amherst Yacht Club, Soc. Mayflower Descendants. Clubs: Yale (Boston), Harvard (Boston). Home: 24 N Prospect St Amherst MA 01002-2014

BENTLEY, SHEILA CARVER, communication consultant, education educator; b. Provo, Utah, Jan. 3, 1949; d. John James Sr. and Dorothy Lee (Eskew) Carver; m. Joseph Charles English, Feb. 2, 1968 (div. June 1979); children: Christine Elizabeth English, Joseph Scott English; m. Gary Michael Bentley, June 4, 1983. BA, U. Utah, 1970; MA, Ariz. State U., 1977, PhD, 1988. Cert. tchr. grades kindergarten through 12 and cmty. coll., Ariz. Tchr. Bryant Jr. H.S., Salt Lake City, 1970-71, Scottsdale (Ariz.) Unified Schs., 1972-83; faculty assoc. Ariz. State U., Tempe, 1977-81; mem. adj. faculty U. Memphis, 1986—; comm. cons. Bentley Cons., Collierville, Tenn., 1983—; cons. Honeywell Inc., Phoenix, 1983-90, Internat. Paper Co., Memphis, 1987—, U.S. Army, Ft. Campbell, Ky., 1993—, Vanderbilt U., Nashville, 1994—, numerous other orgns. Contbr. (chpt.) Perspectives on Listening, 1993; contbr. articles to numerous profl. jours. Bd. dirs. Leadership Collierville, 1997—, pres. elect, 1998; pres. Woods Homeowners Assn., Collierville, 1991. Mem. ASTD (Memphis chpt. pres. 1999, v.p. nat. issues Memphis chpt. 1995-96, chpt. bd. dirs. 1993-94), Internat. Listening Assn. (pres. 1994-95, 1st v.p. 1993-94, 2nd v.p. 1990-91, Pres.'s award 1991, 94), Collierville pres. elect, 1998. Republican. Avocations: snow skiing, scuba diving, gourmet cooking, watercolors, travel. Office: Bentley Cons 1035 W Tree Dr Collierville TN 38017-1305

BENTLEY, THOMAS ROY, educator, writer, consultant; b. Belfast, No. Ireland, June 5, 1931; s. Thomas and Anne (Hill) B.; m. Joan M. Williams, Dec. 24, 1955; children: Kimberley, Shannon, Carolyn. B.A., U. Toronto, 1960, M.A., 1966; Ed.B., Ont. Coll., 1961; Ph.D., Meml. U., Nfld., Can., 1970. Assoc. dean edn. U. B.C., Vancouver, Can., 1973-77, head lang. edn., 1978-79, dean (acting) edn., 1979-81, adv. internat. affairs, 1981-83, prof. edn., 1983-96; cons. to major cos. on communication and transp. issues; co-founder Internat. Lifewriting Network. Author 4 books on English communications; editor 12 books on Can. lit.; contbr. articles to profl. jours. Broadcaster many programs on radio and TV. Mem. Nat. Assn. Tchrs. English (chmn. internat. assembly 1981), Nat. Conf. for Research English, Can. Council Tchrs. English (editor, bd. dirs. 1975-78), Vancouver Club, Faculty Club. Office: 5529 University Blvd, Vancouver, BC Canada V6T 1K5

BENTLEY, WILLIAM ARTHUR, electro-optical consultant, engineer; b. Jan. 21, 1931; s. Garth Ashley and Helen (Dieterle) B.; m. Erika Bernadette Seuthe, Nov. 17, 1956; children: David Garth, Barbara Bentley Smith. BS inPhysics, Northwestern U., 1952; MS in Systems Engring., Calif. State U., Fullerton, 1972. Engr. N. Am. Aircraft, Downey, Calif., 1956-69; chief engr. Fairchild Optical, El Segundo, Calif., 1969-72; sr. staff engr. Advanced Controls, Irvine, Calif., 1975-80; prin. Instrument Design Cons., Santa Ana, Calif., 1978—; mgr. mfg. research and devel. Xerox Electro-Optical, Pomona, Calif., 1980-83; cons. Kasper Industries, Sunnyvale, Calif., 1977-78, Lincoln Laser Co., Phoenix, 1983—, Coopervision, Irvine, 1984-88, Baxter, 1988-90, Indsl. Dynamics Co., 1990—, Polyscan Corp., Tucson, 1992-96, Pacific Optical, 1995—. Patentee in field including 1st automatic optical PWB inspector. Mem. Soc. Photo-optical Instrumentation Engrs., Optical Soc. Am., Mensa. Democrat. Home: 170 The Masters Cir Costa Mesa CA 92627-4640 Office: Instrument Design Cons PO Box 2203 Santa Ana CA 92707-0203

BENTLEY-SCHECK, GRACE MARY, artist; b. Troy, N.Y., Apr. 20, 1937; d. John Franklin and Gladys Serena B.; m. George Frederick Scheck, July 22, 1967. BFA, SUNY, Alfred, 1959, MFA, 1960. Tchr. art Riverhead (N.Y.) Jr. High Sch., 1963-67, North Colonie Ctrl. Schs., Latham, N.Y., 1967-72; artist, printmaker Oswego, N.Y., 1972-83, Narragansett, R.I., 1983—. Chair art scholar Wickford (R.I.) Art Assn., 1986—; graphic designer, fundraiser South County Cmty. Action, Wakefield, R.I., 1996, 97, 98. Mem. Soc. Am. Graphic Artists (Paul Cadmus award 1997), Printmakers Network So. New England, Boston Printmakers, 19 on Paper (treas. 1994—). Avocations: cooking, literature, canoeing, walking dog. Home and office: 63 Sassafras Trl Narragansett RI 02882-2503

BENTLY, DONALD EMERY, electrical engineer; b. Cleve., Oct. 18, 1924; s. Oliver E. Bently and Mary Evelyn (Conway) B.; m. Susan Lorraine Pumphrey, Sept. 1961 (div. Sept. 1982); 1 child, Christopher Paul. BSEE with distinction, U. Iowa, 1949, MSEE, 1950; DS (hon.), U. Nev., 1987. Registered profl. engr., Calif., Nev. Pres. Bently Nev. Corp., Minden, 1961-85, chief exec. officer, 1985—; chief exec. officer Bently Rotor Dynamics and Research Corp., Minden, 1985—; also chmn. bd. dirs. Bently Nev. Corp., Minden; chief exec. officer Gibson Tool Co., Carson City, Nev., 1978—; bd. dirs. Sierra Pacific Resources, 1982-83. Contbr. articles to profl. jours.; developer electronic instruments for the observation of rotating machinery, and the algorithm for rotor fluid-induced instability; inventor in field. Trustee Inst. World Politics. With USN, 1943-46, PTO. Named Inventor of Yr., State of Nev. Innovation and Tech. Coun., 1983; recipient first Decade award Vibration Inst., Myklestad award; inducted to Jr. Achievement of Northern Nev. Bus. Leaders' Hall of Fame. Mem. ASME (industry adv. bd.), Am. Petroleum Inst., St. Petersburg (Russian Fedn.) Acad. Engring., Sigma Xi, Eta Kappa Nu, Tau Beta Pi, Sigma Alpha Epsilon. Episcopalian. Avocations: skiing, hiking, biking. Office: Bently Nev Corp 1711 Orbit Way Minden NV 89423-4114

BENTO, ANTONIO MIGUEL R., banking consultant; b. Sept. 19, 1972. BA, U. Nova de Lisboa, Lisbon, Portugal, 1996; postgrad., U. Md. Rsch. asst. U. Md., College Park, 1996-98; cons. World Bank, Washington, 1998—. Rotary Internat. scholar, 1997-98. Email: abento@worldbank.org. Office: Apt T-1 6020 Westchester Park Dr College Park MD 20740

BENTON, ALLEN HAYDON, biology educator; b. Ira, N.Y., Sept. 4, 1921; s. Haydon Willey and Pearl Amelia (Diddy) B.; m. Marjorie Lois Hall, Aug. 16, 1947; children: Thomas Hall, Christopher Allen, Holly Anne. B.S., Cornell U., 1948, M.S., 1949, Ph.D, 1952. Jr. wildlife biologist U.S. Fish and Wildlife Service, 1949; asst. prof. biology SUNY-Albany, 1949-57, assoc. prof., 1957-62; prof. biology SUNY-Fredonia, 1962-73, disting. teaching prof., 1973-84, faculty exchange scholar, 1975-84, prof. emeritus, 1984—; vis. prof. Stephen F. Austin Coll., 1957, Concord Coll., Athens, W.Va., 1969-70, U. Minn. Biol. Sta., 1970; cons. Nuclear Fuel Services Inc., Fla. Arthropod Collection, Roger Tory Peterson Inst. for the Study of Natural History. Author: (with W.E. Werner Jr.) Field Biology and Ecology, 3rd edit., 1974, Atlas of Fleas of the Eastern United States, 1980, Manual for Field Biology and Ecology, 6th edit., 1983, Wild Worlds, 1988, Light and Natural, 1992; columnist Dunkirk (N.Y.) Evening Observer, Albany (N.Y.) Knickerbocker News, Jamestown (N.Y.) Post Jour.; freelance writer on nature and sci.; contbr. articles to profl. jours. Served with cav. U.S. Army, 1942-46. Decorated Bronze Star; grantee Research Found. SUNY, 1963, 83; NSF grantee, 1972; E.N. Huyck Found. grantee, 1976-78. Mem. Am. Ornithologists Union, Am. Soc. Mammalogists, Wilson Ornithol. Soc., Fedn. N.Y. State Bird Clubs (pres.), PTA (life), Sigma Xi, Phi Kappa Phi. Home: 292 Water St Fredonia NY 14063-2025

BENTON, AUBURN EDGAR, lawyer; b. Colorado Springs, Colo., July 12, 1926; s. Auburn Edgar and Ella Dot (Heyer) B.; m. Stephanie Marie Jakimowitz, June 8, 1951; children—Margrit Laura, Mary Ellen. BA, Colo.

Coll., 1950; LLB, Yale U., 1953. Bar: Colo. 1953, U.S. Dist. Ct. Colo. 1953, U.S. Ct. Appeals (10th cir.) 1954. Assoc. Holme Roberts & Owen, Denver, 1953-57, ptnr., 1957-91, of counsel, 1992—. Mem. Bd. Edn. Denver Pub. Schs., 1961-69; mem. Colo. Commn. Higher Edn., Denver, 1975-85; mem. Colo. Bd. Ethics, Denver, 1975-98; mem. Nat. Common Cause Bd., Washington, 1975-85; dir. soc. sci. found. U. Denver. Mem. Colo. Bar Assn., Denver Bar Assn., Cactus Club (Denver), Phi Beta Kappa. Democrat. Home: 901 Race St Denver CO 80206-3735 Office: Holme Roberts & Owen 1700 Lincoln St Ste 4100 Denver CO 80203-4541

BENTON, BILL BROWNING, human services consultant; b. L.A., Sept. 13, 1943; s. Bill B. and Mary I. (Linman) B.; m. Lynn Shaub, July 13, 1968; children: Melissa, Michael. BA, George Washington U., 1965; M Govt. Adminstrn., U. Pa., 1966; D Pub. Adminstrn., U. So. Calif., 1983. Dir. Planning-Programming-Budgeting Systems N.J. Dept. Community Affairs, Trenton, N.J., 1968-70; asst. sec. Md. Dept. Human Resources, Balt., 1970-75; sr. rsch. assoc. Urban Inst., Washington, 1975-77; dep. dir. U.S. Office Human Devel. Svc., Washington, 1977-78; dep. sec. Md. Dept. Human Resources, Balt., 1978-80; vis. dir. New Zealand Dept. Social Welfare, Wellington, 1980-81; exec. v.p. Urban Systems Rsch. and Engring., Washington, 1981-85; pres. human svc. MAXIMUS, Falls Church, Va., 1985-94; v.p. Benton & Assocs., Ellicott City, Md., 1994—; mem. coun. Internat. Conf. Social Welfare, 1985-88. Author: Social Services, 1978. Health svc. officer USPHS, 1966-68, with Res. 1968—. Mem. ASPA (com. chairperson 1980-81), Am. Pub. Welfare Assn. (mem. nat. coun. 1975-80). Home: 12237 Carroll Mill Rd Ellicott City MD 21042-1311 Office: Benton & Assocs 12237 Carroll Mill Rd Ellicott City MD 21042

BENTON, DONALD STEWART, publishing company executive, lawyer; b. Marlboro, N.Y., Jan. 2, 1924; s. Fred Stanton and Agnes (Townsend) B. Student, U. Leeds, Eng., 1945; BA, Columbia U., 1947, JD, 1949; LLM, NYU, 1953. Bar: N.Y. 1953. Practiced in N.Y.C., 1953-56; atty. N.Y. State Banking Dept., 1954-55; v.p. Found. Press, Inc., Bklyn., 1957-60; exec. asst. to exec. v.p. N.Y. Stock Exchange, 1960-61; dir. reference book dept. and spl. projects editor Appleton Century Crofts, N.Y.C., 1962-71; sr. editor Matthew Bender & Co., Inc., N.Y.C., 1974-77; sr. legal editor Warren, Gorham & Lamont, Inc., N.Y.C., 1977-89. Author: Thorndike Encyclopedia of Banking and Financial Tables, 3rd edit., 1999 yearbook, Federal Banking Laws, 3rd edit., 1987, Real Estate Tax Digest, 1984, Criminal Law Digest, 3rd edit., 1983, Modern Real Estate and Mortgage Checklists, 1979. Mem. Cresskill (N.J.) Zoning Bd. Adjustment, 1969-71, 82-83, 86—. Cresskill Planning Bd., 1971-74; councilman City of Cresskill, 1972-74. With AUS, 1943-46, 50-52. Decorated Bronze Star. Mem. Phi Delta Phi. Mem. Reformed Ch. in Am. Home: 117 Heatherhill Rd Cresskill NJ 07626-1020 Office: AS Pratt & Sons Warren Gorham & Lamont 395 Hudson St New York NY 10014-3669

BENTON, FLETCHER, sculptor; b. Jackson, Ohio, 1931. BFA, Miami U., Oxford, Ohio, 1956, DFA (hon.), 1993; DFA (hon.), Rio Grande U., 1994. Mem. faculty Calif. Coll. Arts and Crafts, 1959, San Francisco Art Inst., 1964-67; prof. art Calif. State U., San Jose, 1967-81; prof. Calif. State U., 1981-86. One-man shows include, San Francisco Mus. Modern Art, 1965, Albright-Knox Mus., Buffalo, 1970, Galeria Bonino, N.Y.C., 1969, Galerie Francoise Mayer, Brussels, San Francisco Mus. Modern Art, 1970, London Arts Gallery, Detroit, 1970, Galeria Bonino, Buenos Aires, Estudio Actual, Caracas, Venezuela, 1970, Landry-Bonino Gallery, N.Y.C., 1972, Phoenix Mus. Art, 1973, Galeria Bonino, Rio de Janiero, 1973, Calif. State U.-Berkeley, 1973, Neuberger Mus., N.Y., 1974, Hirshhorn Mus., 1974, Phila. Art Alliance, 1974, Elvehejem Mus. Art, Wis., 1976, San Francisco Modern Mus. Art, 1976, Huntsville Mus. Modern Art, Ala., 1977, Alrich Mus. Contemporary Art, Conn., John Berggruen Gallery, San Francisco, 1978, 84, 89, 96, Am. Acad. and Inst. Arts and Letters, N.Y.C., 1979, Chgo. Arts Club, 1979, Milw. Art Ctr., 1980, Suermondt-Ludwig Mus., Asschen, Fed. Republic Germany, Klingspor Mus., Offenbach, Fed. Republic Germany, 1981, 96, Kunsthandling Brigitte Haasner, Wiesbaden, Fed. Republic Germany, 1987, 92, 96, Sung Dem Fine Arts, Seoul, Korea, 1991, Dorothy Goldeen Gallery, Santa Monica, Calif., 1988, 93, Gallerie Simone Sterne, New Orleans, 1990, 93, Riva Yares Gallery, Scottsdale, 1991, Miami U., Oxford, 1993, Gallery Camino Real, Boca Raton, Fla.; group shows include San Francisco Art Inst., 1964, San Francisco Modern Mus. Art, 1964, Calif. Pal. of Legion of Honor, 1964, Whitney Mus. Am. Art, N.Y.C., 1966, 68, Los Angeles County Mus., 1967, Phila. Art Mus., 1967, Walker Art Ctr., Mpls., 1968, Art Inst. Chgo., 1968, Internat. Mus. Fine Arts, Osaka, Japan, 1970, Hayward Gallery, London, 1970, Stanford (Calif.) Mus., 1971, Am. Acad. and Inst. Arts and Letters, N.Y.C., 1981, Amerika Haus, Frankfurt, 1981, Whitney Mus. Am. Art, N.Y.C., 1981, Oakland Mus., 1982, John Berggruen Gallery, 1983, Olympic Arts Festival, Los Angeles, France, Fed. Republic Germany, Eng., Norway, 1984, John Berggruen Gallery, 1985, 89, 92, Chapman Coll. (Calif.), 1985, The Adrich Mus. Contemporary Art, Conn., 1985, Centro de Arte Moderna, Lisbon, Portugal, 1986, Kleinewefers, Krefeld, Fed. Repbulic Germany, 1987, Kundsthandlung Brigitte Haasner, Wiesbaden, Fed. Republic Germany, 1987, 88, Dorothy Goldeen Gallery, Santa Monica, Calif., 1988, Andre Emmerich Gallery, 1991, 92, Rio Grande (Ohio) U., 1994, Miami Art Mus., Oxford, Ohio, 1996, others; major collections Euroclear Hdqs. Brussels, Belgium, 1993, Modernesstadt Cologne, 1993, Gothaer, Cologne, Top Gallant, 1994, Pauling, N.Y., 1994; subject of book, Fletcher Benton by Paul Karlstrom and Edward Lucie-Smith, 1990. Served with USN, 1949-50. Recipient Disting. Svc. award to arts Am. Acad. and Inst. Arts and Letters, 1979, Career award Ohioana Libr. Assn., 1994; Pres.'s Scholar award San Jose State U., 1980. *

BENTON, JACK MITCHELL, management consultant; b. Bakersfield, Calif., July 15, 1941; s. James Edwin and Alice Kathryn (Hawthorne) B.; m. Suzanne Wilken, June 14, 1964; children: Mitchell Brian, Andrea Katherine. BS in Acctg., Calif. State U., Chico, 1964. CPA, Calif., N.Y. Acct. Arthur Young & Co., Los Angeles, 1964-68; chief fin. officer Newport Nat. Bank, Newport Beach, Calif., 1968-70; mng. dir. human resources Chase Manhattan Bank & Chase Manhattan Capital Markets Corp., N.Y.C., 1970-87; sr. v.p., mgr. human resources Bank Tokyo, Ltd.-N.Y. Agy. Bank Tokyo Trust Co., N.Y.C., 1987-93; mng. dir. Alec Peters Assoc., N.Y.C., 1993-95, Cromwell Ptnrs., Inc., N.Y.C., 1995-96, Ward Howell Internat., N.Y.C., 1996-98; v.p. human resources Mitsubishi Materials, N.Y.C., 1998—. Served with USCG, 1960-61, USCGR, 1961-68. Mem. AICPA, Soc. Human Resource Mgmt., Calif. Soc. CPAs, N.Y. State Soc CPAs, Soc. CPAs, Shek-O Country Club, Hong Kong. Home: PO Box 2026 Hoboken NJ 07030-1308 Office: Mitsubishi Materials USA Corp 399 Park Ave 38th Fl New York NY 10022-4619

BENTON, KAY MYERS, sales executive; b. Balt.; d. Brenton Ellsworth and Kevera (Hauf) Myers; m. Gregory W. Lewis, June 29, 1962 (div. Sept. 1986); children: Stacy Kay French, Gregory Lawrence; m. Robert David Benton, Nov. 19, 1988. BA, U. Md. Profl. model Washington, 1971-76; sr. mgr. Unisys, McLean, Va., 1976-86; dir. bus. devel. Planning Rsch. Corp., McLean, 1986-87, Baxter Travenol, Reston, Va., 1987-88; real estate assoc. Prudential, Potomac, Md.; dir. bus. devel. ISN Corp., 1989-91, TRW, 1991-95; global strategic sales mgr. Sun Microsys., McLean, Va., 1995—; cons. Andersen Cons., Washington, 1988-89. Contbr. articles to profl. pubs. Mem. AIAA, Am. Assn. Airport Execs., Airports Cons. Coun., Air Traffic Control Assn., Industry Adv. Coun., Washington Transp. Seminar, Md. Realtors Assn., Montgomery County Bd. Realtors, Washington Club, The City Club, Army-Navy Country Club, Congl. Country Club, Kappa Delta. Republican. Methodist. Avocations: golf, tennis, travel. Home: 9712 Kendale Rd Potomac MD 20854-4523

BENTON, MARJORIE CRAIG, federal agency administrator. LHD, Nat. Coll. Edn., 1981, Lincoln Coll., 1982, Columbia Coll., 1983, Northwestern U., 1983; LLD (hon.), John Marshall Law Sch., 1984; D of Pub. Svc. (hon.), St. Xavier Coll., Chgo., 1987; PhD (hon.), Mundelein Coll., 1988. Pub. del. U.S. Mission to UN, 1977, del. spl. session on disarmament, 1978; mem. commn. UN Assn., 1978-79; spl. adv. UN Disarmament Commn., 1979; U.S. rep. UNICEF, 1980-83; mem. Commn. on White House Fellowships, Washington, 1993, chmn. bd. dirs., 1994; vice chair Pub. Media, Inc., Chgo.; bd. dirs. Royal Packaging Industries, Van Leer, The Netherlands; co-chair Am. for Strategic Arms Limitation Talks, 1977-79; U.S. Commr. Internat. Yr. of Child; mem. adv. com. Agy. Internat. Devel. Private Voluntary Orgns., 1981-82; co-chair Symphony for Survival, Chgo., 1982. Co-founder The Peace Mus., Chgo., Chgo. Found. for Women, Women's Issues Network, Chgo.; hon. chair Save the Children Fedn., N.Y.; pres. Chapin Hall Ctr. for Children U. Chgo.; chair bd. dirs. Coun. on Founds., Washington; mem. com. on univ. resources Harvard U., Cambridge, Mass., Internat. Humn Rights Law Inst. DePaul Coll. of Law, Chgo., Inst. Social & Econ. Policy in the Middle East, Harvard U., Middle East Policy Coun., Washington; mem. Bernard Van Leer Foundation, The Netherlands, The Van Leer Group Foundation, The Netherlands; trustee Benton Foundation, Washington, DC; del. Dem. Nat. Conv., 1972, 76, 82, 88, 92; commn. del. selection Dem. Nat. Com., 1973, 88; del. Dem. Mid-Term Conv., 1974, 78, 83; mem. procedures com. Dem. Nat. Conv., 1978; mem. Ill. Dem. Platform com., 1975; Ill. co-chair Inaugural Com., 1977; mem. rules com. Dem. Nat. Conv., 1980, 87; mem. affirmative action com. Ill. Dems., 1984; del.-at-large Dem. Nat. Conv., 1984. Recipient Oustanding Pub. Svc. award UNICEF, 1978, Alumni Svc. award Nat. Coll. Edn., 1979, Woman of Achievement award, Cleve. City Women's Club, 1980, Adlai Stevenson award, 1981, Outstanding Achievement in Cmty. Leadership award YMCA, 1982, Better Govt. Assn. award, 1983, Lincoln award Ill. Citizenx for Handgun Control, Louis Lerner Disting. Svc. award Ill. Pub. Action Coun., Leadership award Chgo. Chpt. Nat. Assn. Fundraising Execs., Woman of Achievement award, Girl Scouts of Am., Chgo., Jane Addams Internat. Women's Leadership award, 1991, Full Circle award, 1993; Midwest Women's Ctr. 10th Anniversary Honoree, 1986. Mem. Chgo. Pediat. Soc. (hon.), Am. Orthopsychiatric Assn., Arts Club Chgo., Econ. Club Chgo., River Club N.Y. Office: Commn White House Fellows Office of Chmn 712 Jackson Pl NW Washington DC 20006-4901*

BENTON, NICHOLAS, theater producer; b. Boston, Oct. 18, 1926; s. Jay Rogers and Frances (Hill) B.; m. Kate Lenthal Bigelow, June 5, 1954; children: Frances Hill, Kate, Emily Weld, Louisa Barclay. *Nicholas Benton's daughter Kate married James Francis Doughan, the son of Leo Doughan and Nancy Berry, in Wareham, Massachusetts on August 27, 1988. They have two sons, Charles Benton Dougham born in Los Angeles, California on April 22, 1991, and Henry Leo Bigelow Doughan, born in Los Angeles, California on December 1, 1993. His daughter Emily Weld Benton married John Francis Morgan, son of James Paul Morgan and Joan Margaret Fitzgerald, in Wareham, Massachusetts on August 29, 1998.* Grad., Phillips Exeter Acad., 1945; AB, Harvard U., 1951. Promotion writer Life mag., N.Y.C., 1951-55, Fortune mag., N.Y.C., 1955-56; staff writer Time Mag., N.Y.C., 1956-57; advt. promotion mgr. Archtl. Forum, N.Y.C., 1957-64; gen. promotion mgr. Time-Life Books, Alexandria, Va., 1965-68, dir. pub. rels., 1968-83, v.p., 1977-83; lectr. pub. procedures course Radcliffe Coll., 1976-82; producing dir. Am. Kaleidoscope Theatre, 1983-85; mem. Nat. Book Awards Com., 1971; co-chmn. Nat. Book Awards Week Com., 1975-79; vice-chmn. Am. Book Awards, 1981-82. Author: A Benton Heritage, 1964; co-producer musical Phoenix '55, 1955, Salad Days, 1958, The Golden Age, 1984, the Perfect Party, 1986, Love Letters, 1989, The Heart's a Wonder, 1990; author, dir. (play) Not So Long Ago, 1995. Pres. East 69th St. Assn., 1963-64; 1st v.p. Soc. Meml. Sloan-Kettering Cancer Ctr., 1963-64, asst. treas., 1964-66, treas., 1967-68; exec. com. Friends of the Theatre Collection, Mus. of City of N.Y., 1983-86; pres. Land Owners Assn. Indian Neck, Wareham, Mass., 1993-95; chmn. Harvard Crimson Impact tutoring program, NY H.S., 1991—. With AUS, 1945-46. Mem. Pubs. Publicity Assn. (pres. 1970-71), New Eng. Historic Geneal. Soc. (trustee 1979-95, corr. sec. 1982-88, v.p. 1988-93), N.Y. Geneal. and Biog. Soc., Assn. Am. Pubs. (freedom to pub. com. 1979-82), Time-Life Alumni Soc. (bd. dirs. 1994—), Soc. of Colonial Wars, Harvard Club (bd. mgrs. N.Y.C. chpt. 1971-73), Bourne Cove Yacht Club (commodore Wareham, Mass. chpt. 1988-91), N.Y. City Opera (bd. dirs. 1995-99, guild pres. 1995-99, editor Tempo newsletter 1993—). Home and Office: 129 E 82nd St New York NY 10028-0836 also (summer): Indian Neck Wareham MA 02571

BENTON, NICHOLAS FREDERICK, publisher; b. Ross, Calif., Feb. 9, 1944; s. Frederick C. H. and Jeanne Emma (Brun) B.; m. Donna Carley, Apr. 15, 1979 (div. Oct. 1984); m. Janine Schollnick, Oct. 20, 1985. AA, Santa Barbara City Coll., Calif., 1963; BA, Westmont Coll., 1965; MDiv cum laude, Pacific Sch. Religion, Berkeley, Calif., 1969. Reporter Santa Barbara News Press, 1961-66; dir. Christian edn. Plymouth Ch., Oakland, Calif., 1966-69; chief corr. Berkeley Barb, 1970-72; dir. advt. display Syufy Enterprises, San Francisco, 1973-76; regional dir. Fusion Energy Found., Washington, 1976-87; chief Washington corr. Century News Svc., Falls Church, Va., 1987—; chmn., chief exec. officer Century News Svc., Falls Church, 1987—; pub., editor Falls Church News Press, 1991—, chmn., chief exec. officer, 1991—. Pres. Falls Church Baseball, Inc., 1991—; clk. Emmaus Ch., 1989-92; bd. dirs. Arlington (Va.) Symphony, 1992-93. Mem. Greater Falls Church C. of C. (bd. dirs. 1991—, pres. 1993-94, Pillar of Cmty. award 1993), LWV of Falls Church, Optimists Club of Falls Church, White Ho. Corrs. Assn., Nat. Press Club (Washington). Mem. United Ch. Christ. Office: Falls Church News Press 929 W Broad St Ste 200 Falls Church VA 22046-3121

BENTON, ROBERT, film director, screenwriter; b. Waxahachie, Tex., Sept. 29, 1932. BA, U. Tex. Screenwriter: (with David Newman) There Was A Crooked Man, 1962, Bonnie and Clyde, 1967, What's Up Doc?, 1972, (with Mario Puzo and Tom Mankiewicz) Superman, 1978; dir., writer: Bad Company, 1972, The Late Show, 1976, Kramer vs. Kramer, 1979 (Best Dir. Acad. award 1979, Best Screenplay Acad. award 1979), Still of the Night, 1982, Places in the Heart, 1984 (Best Screenplay Acad. award 1984), Nadine, 1987, Nobody's Fool, 1994; dir.: Billy Bathgate, 1991; co-exec. prodr.: The House on Carroll Street, 1988. Mem. Dirs. Guild Am. *

BENTON, ROBERT DEAN, educational organization executive; b. Guthrie Center, Iowa, July 22, 1929; s. John H. and Luella M. (Rawlings) B.; m. Rachel Swanson, July 29, 1951; children: Camille, John, Scott. B.A., U. No. Iowa, 1951, M.A., 1956; Ed.D., U. No. Colo., 1961. Tchr. Ruthven, Ia., 1953-56, Mason City, Iowa, 1956-58; dir. pub. info., coordinator secondary edn. Rapid City, S.D., 1958-61; asst. supt. in charge of instrn., 1961-66; supt. schs. Council Bluffs, Iowa, 1966-72; dir. dept. edn. State of Iowa, 1972-87; dean Coll. Edn. and Human Services, U. Wis., Oshkosh, 1987-94; exec. sec. Tchr. Edn. Coun. State Colls. and Univs., Oshkosh, 1994—; part-time journalism tchr. summer sessions U. No. Colo., 1959-61; mem. Iowa Adv. Council for Vocat. Edn., 1970-72. Hon. chmn., mem. founding com. Friends of Music Community Concert Series, 1967; Bd. dirs. Chanticleer Community Theater, 1968-72, Christian Home, 1968-72. Served with USMC, 1951-53. Named Boss of the Year Jaycees, Council Bluffs, 1970; Outstanding Young Man of the Year Jr. C. of C., Rapid City, 1965. Mem. NEA, Am. Assn. for Colls. Tchr. Edn., Phi Delta Kappa, Theta Alpha Phi. Methodist.

BENTON, W. DUANE, chief justice; b. Springfield, Mo., Sept. 8, 1950; s. William Max and Patricia F. (Nicholson) B.; m. Sandra Snyder, Nov. 15, 1980; children: Megan Blair, William Grant. BA in Polit. Sci. summa cum laude, Northwestern U., 1972; JD, Yale U., 1975; MBA in Accounting, Memphis State U., 1979; student Inst. Jud. Adminstrn., NYU, 1992; LLD (hon.), Ctrl. Mo. State U., 1994; LLM, U. Va., 1995; LLD (hon.), Westminster Coll., 1999. Bar: Mo. 1975; CPA, Mo. Ensign USN, 1972; advanced through grades to capt., 1993; judge advocate USN, Memphis, 1975-79; chief of staff for Congressman Wendell Bailey, Washington, 1980-82; pvt. practice Jefferson City, Mo., 1983-89; dir. revenue Mo. Dept. of Revenue, Jefferson City, 1989-91; judge Mo. Supreme Ct., Jefferson City, 1991—, chief justice, 1997—; adj. prof. Westminster Coll., U. Mo.-Columbia Sch. Law. Contbr. articles to profl. jours.; mng. editor Yale Law Jour., 1974-75. Chmn. Multistate Tax Commn. Washington, 1990-91; chmn. Mo. State Employees Retirement System, Jefferson City, 1989-93; regent Ctrl. Mo. State U., 1987-89; dir. Coun. for Drug Free Youth, Jefferson City, 1989—; mem. Mo. Mil. Adv. Com., 1989-91; mem. Mo. Commn. Intergovernmental Coop., Jefferson City, 1989-91; trustee, deacon 1st Bapt. Ch., Jefferson City. Danforth fellow JFK Sch. Govt. Harvard U., 1990. Mem. ABA (tax com. 1975—), Mo. Bar Assn. (tax com. 1975—), AICPA (tax com. 1983—), Mo. Soc. CPA's (tax com. 1983—), Navy League, Mil. Order of World Wars, Vietnam Vets of Am., VFW, Am. Legion, Phi Beta Kappa, Beta Gamma Sigma, Rotary (sgt. at arms 1990—). Baptist. Lt. USN, 1975-80. Capt. JAGC USNR. Office: Supreme Court PO Box 150 Jefferson City MO 65102-0150

BENTON, WILLIAM PETTIGREW, advertising agency executive; b. Laurinburg, N.C., Nov. 4, 1923; s. William P. and Carlie (Austin) B.; m. Blanche Marilyn Lampke, June 26, 1948; children: Barbara, Mary Anne, Judy, Nancy. Student, U. N.C., 1946. With Ford Motor Co., Dearborn, Mich., 1947-84, v.p. mktg., 1971-73, v.p. parent co., gen. mgr. Lincoln-Mercury div., 1973-75, v.p. parent co., gen. mgr. Ford div., 1975-77, v.p. parent co., v.p. mktg. worldwide, 1981; v.p. sales Ford of Europe, 1977-81; dep. chmn. Brit. Car Group, Eng., 1984-86; chmn. Brit. Car Group Inc. U.S., 1984-86, Group Lotus Inc., 1985-86, Sandgate Corp., 1985-86; vice chmn. Wells, Rich, Greene/BDDP, Dearborn, 1986-96; exec. dir. Ogilvy & Mather, Dearborn, 1997—; dir. automotive div. United Fund Campaign, Detroit, 1971. Gen. chmn. Meadowbrook Theatre and Music Festival, Oakland U., Rochester, Mich., 1972; bd. dirs. emeritus Sch. Bus. Adminstrn. Sponsors, Inc., Coll. William and Mary, 1976-86; bd. dirs. Marian H.S. Dads Club, 1973-76; mem. exec. com. Internat. Fedn. Multiple Sclerosis Worldwide, pres., 1985-93, pres. emeritus, 1994; bd. dirs. Beaumont Found., Ind. for Life, 1989-95. With USAAF, 1943-45. Decorated Bronze Star, Croix de Guerre (France). Mem. Advt. Coun. (bd. dirs. 1983-85), Detroit C. of C. (bd. dirs. 1983-84), Econ. Club Detroit, Bloomfield Hills Country Club, Lost Tree Club, Everglade Club, Palm Beach Yacht Club, Harry's Bar (London). Home: 355 Martell Dr Bloomfield Hills MI 48304-3451

BENTROVATO, DONALD A., genito-urinary surgeon; b. Sept. 17, 1947. BS, Union Coll., 1969; MD, St. Louis U., 1973. Diplomate Am. Bd. Urology. Attending physician Ellis Hosp., Schenectady, N.Y., 1978—, Albany Meml. Hosp., 1978—, Samaritan Hosp., Troy, N.Y., 1978—. Fellow ACS, Am. Soc. Reproductive Medicine. Office: 903 Bedford Rd Schenectady NY 12309

BENTSEN, KENNETH E., JR., congressman; b. Houston, June 3, 1959; m. Tamra Bentsen; children: Louise, Meredith. BA, U. St. Thomas, Houston, 1982; M in Pub. Adminstrn., Am. U., 1985. Mem. staff Congressman Ronald D. Coleman, 1983-87; assoc. staff U.S. House Appropriations Com., 1985-87; chair Harris County Dem. Party, 1990-93; investment banker Houston, 1987-94; mem. 104th Congress from 25th Tex. dist., 1995—. Presbyterian. Office: US House Reps 326 Cannon House Ofc Bldg Washington DC 20515-4325*

BENTSEN, KENNETH EDWARD, architect; b. Mission, Tex., Nov. 21, 1926; s. Lloyd Millard and Edna Ruth (Colbath) B.; m. Mary Dorsey Bates, Dec. 3, 1953; children: Molly Bates, Elizabeth Jean, Kenneth Edward Jr., William Lloyd. B.S., U. Houston, 1951, B.A., 1952. Pvt. practice architecture, prin. Kenneth Bentsen Assocs., Houston, 1958-91. Projects include Baylor Coll. Medicine, Jones and Anderson Med. Research Tower, M.D. Anderson-R. Lee Clark Clinic Bldg., West Tower, Clin. Care Ctr., Tex. Children's Hosp., Houston, Tex. Med. Ctr., Agnes Arnold Hall, Philip Hoffman Hall, U. Houston, M.D. Anderson Library, U. Houston, Pan Am. U., Grad. Sch. Bus., U. Tex, M.D. Anderson Environ. Rsch. Ctr., U. Tex, Learning Ctr., Allied Health Sci. & Nursing, U. Tex. Med. Br., Galveston, Compact, Houston Sports Arena, State Law Ctr., Austin, Tex., Harris County Adminstrn. Bldg., Houston, Tex. Commerce Bldg. Complex, McAllen, Tex. Bd. dirs. Tex. Children's Hosp., Cultural Trust Coun. Tex.; past bd. dirs. Tex. Commn. on the Arts, Mayor's Com. Bd. Appeals, Mus. Fine Arts, Blaffer Gallery; past mem. adv. coun. U. Tex. Sch. Architecture Pres.'s Adv. Com. Recipient numerous design awards. Mem. AIA, Tex. Soc. Architects, Houston C. of C. Office: Kenneth Bentsen FAIA 12 E Greenway Plz Ste 1100 Houston TX 77046-1201

BENTSEN, LLOYD, former government official, former senator; b. Mission, TX, Feb. 11, 1921; s. Lloyd M. and Edna Ruth (Colbath) B.; m. Beryl Ann Longino, Nov. 27, 1943; children: Lloyd M. III, Lan, Tina. J.D., U. Tex., 1942. Bar: Tex. 1942. Practice law McAllen, Tex., 1945-48; judge Hidalgo County, Tex., (hdqs. Edinburg), 1946-48; mem. 80th-83d congresses from 15th Tex. Dist.; pres. Lincoln Consol., Houston, 1955-70; U.S. Senator from Tex., 1971-93, chmn. senate fin. com.; mem. senate commerce, sci., transp. and joint com. on taxation and congl. joint econ. com.; sec. Dept. Treasury, Washington, 1993-94; ptnr. Verner, Lipfert, Bernhard, McPherson and Hand; Democratic nominee for Vice Pres. U.S., 1988. Served to maj. USAAF, 1942-45. Decorated D.F.C., Air Medal with 3 oak leaf clusters.

BENTY, CAMERON TODD, magazine editor; b. Highland Park, Mich., Dec. 4, 1956; s. John Louis and Florence May (Bailey) B.; m. Suzanne Margo Acosta, Apr. 11, 1987; children: Jenna Marie, Jordan Cameron. BA in Journalism, U. Pacific, 1978. Assoc. editor Hot Rod Mag., L.A., 1978-81; editor Argus Pub., L.A., 1981-87, Car Craft Mag., L.A., 1987-90; editor, dir. devel. Custom Pub., L.A., 1990-91; editor SPORT, L.A., 1991-98, Petersen's Golfing, L.A., 1995-97; editl. dir. Real Edge mag., L.A., 1998—; mem. nominating com. ESPN Espy Awards, 1992-98; mem. Victor Awards com., 1991—. Author 12 books of sports facts. Avocations: writing, sports. Office: Petersen Publishing 6420 Wilshire Blvd Los Angeles CA 90048-5502

BENTZ, DALE MONROE, librarian; b. York County, Pa., Jan. 3, 1919; s. Solomon Earl and Mary Rebecca (Wonders) B.; m. Mary Gail Menius, June 13, 1942; children: Dale Flynn, Thomas Earl, Mary Carolyn. A.B., Gettysburg Coll., 1939; B.S.L.S., U. N.C. Chapel Hill, 1940; M.S., U. Ill., 1951. With Periodicals dept. U. N.C. Library, Chapel Hill, 1940-41, Serials Dept., Duke U. Library, Durham, N.C., 1941-42; asst. librarian E. Carolina Tchrs. Coll., Greenville, N.C., 1946-48; head processing dept. U. Tenn. Library, Knoxville, 1948-53; assoc. dir. libraries U. Iowa, Iowa City, 1953-70, univ. librarian, 1970-86, univ. librarian emeritus, 1986—. Editor U. Tenn. Library Lectures, 1952; contbr. articles to profl. jours. Pres. Iowa City Bd. Edn., 1962-63. Mem. Iowa Library Assn. (pres., 1959-60), ALA (pres. resources and tech. services div. 1975-76), AAUP, Assn. Coll. and Research Libraries, Beta Phi Mu (pres. 1966-67). Lutheran. Clubs: Triangle (pres. 1958-59), Univ. Athletic (sec. 1979-80). Home: 701 Oaknoll Dr # 430 Iowa City IA 52246-5168 Office: U Iowa Libraries Iowa City IA 52242

BENTZ, MICHAEL LLOYD, plastic and reconstructive surgeon; b. Pitts., May 9, 1958; s. Joe Denton and Ida Mae (Troxell) B.; m. Kim Marie Livingstone, Nov. 19, 1988. BA, Ind. U., 1980; MD, Temple U., 1984. Diplomate Am. Bd. Surgery, Am. Bd. Plastic Surgery, Nat. Bd. Med. Examiners. Resident in gen. surgery Temple U. Hosp., Phila., 1984-89; rsch. fellow U. Pitts., 1989-90, resident in plastic and reconstructive surgery, 1990-92; asst. prof. surgery and pediat. U. Pitts., Pa., 1992-99; assoc. prof. surgery and pediat. U. Pitts., 1999—; instr. advanced trauma life support U. Pitts., 1989—. Contbr. articles to profl. jours. Rsch. grantee Am. Soc. for Surgery of Hand, 1990-91, Plastic Surgery Ednl. Found., 1991-92, 92-93; recipient 1st prize rsch. Ohio Valley soc. Plastic and Reconstructive Surgeons, 1990, Ivy Soc., 1991, Clin. Tour award Coller Soc., 1989, Humaneness in Medicine award Philadelphia County Med. Soc., 1989. Fellow ACS, Am. Acad. Pediatrics; mem. Am. Cleft Palate-Craniofacial Assn., Am. Soc. Plastic and Reconstructive Surgeons, Plastic Surgery Rsch. Coun. Republican. Presbyterian. Home: 2440 Dogwood Dr Wexford PA 15090-7705 Office: Childrens Hosp of Pitts DeSoto 4A447 3705 5th Ave Pittsburgh PA 15213-2524

BENTZ, WARREN WORTHINGTON, federal bankruptcy judge; b. Fairfield, Nebr., Jan. 8, 1926; s. Ivan Vincent and Marie Elizabeth (Weyenberg) B.; m. Maria Bentz, Sept. 9, 1951; children: Virginia Bentz Chestek, Linda Bentz Welles, James W. BSCE-Structures, U. Mich., 1946; postgrad., George Washington U., 1947, U. Toledo, 1950-51; LLB, Harvard U., 1954. Bar: Ohio 1954, Pa. 1955. Engr. Sun Oil Co., Toledo, 1948-51; assoc. I.J. Silin, Esq., Erie, Pa., 1954-58; pvt. practice, Erie, 1958-85; judge Bankruptcy Ct., we. dist. Pa., Erie, 1985—; lectr. in field. Past. v.p. Erie Philharm.; past bd. dirs. Erie Preservation Project. Lt. (j.g.) USNR, 1943-46. Mem. ABA, Pa. Bar Assn., Erie County Bar Assn. (pres. 1978), Am. Judicature Soc , Pa. Soc. Profl. Engrs., Erie Yacht Club, Kiwanis (past pres. Erie), Sigma Chi. Democrat. Methodist. Avocations: boating, fishing, handball. Office: US Bankruptcy Ct 717 State St Ste 700 Erie PA 16501-1355

BENVENISTE, JACOB, retired physicist; b. Portland, Oreg., Dec. 21, 1921; s. Nissim Aslan and Boule (Capeluto) B.; m. Lucie Almeleh, Apr. 23, 1944; children: Richard Nissim, David Mark, Daniel Stephen. BA, Reed Coll., 1943; PhD, U. Calif., Berkeley, 1952. Physicist Lawrence Livermore (Calif.) Nat. Lab., 1950-63; dir. nuclear effects subdiv. Aerospace Corp., San Bernardino, Calif., 1963-68; v.p., dir. research Physics Internat. Corp., San Leandro, Calif., 1968-72; sr. staff scientist Aerospace Corp., El Segundo, Calif., 1972-82; chief scientist Northrop Research and Tech. Ctr., Palos Verdes, Calif., 1982-88; mem. adv. rsch. panel Def. Nuclear Agy., Washington, 1965-68; chmn. adv. tech. panel USAF, El Segundo, 1973-77. Patentee in field; contbr. articles to profl. jours. Chmn. Livermore Joint Union High Sch. Dist., 1955-63. Served with USNR, 1944-45. KERR Scholar, Reed Coll., 1941. Mem. AAAS, Am. Phys. Soc., Phi Beta Kappa, Sigma Xi. Jewish. Avocations: auto mechanics, needlepoint. Home: 4458 170th Ave SE Bellevue WA 98006-6500

BEN-VENISTE, RICHARD, lawyer; b. N.Y.C., Jan. 3, 1943; s. Isaac and Sylvia (Schultz) B.-V. AB, Muhlenberg Coll., 1964, LLD (hon.), 1975; JD, Columbia U., 1967; LLM, Northwestern U., 1968. Bar: N.Y. 1968, U.S. Dist. Ct. (so. dist.) N.Y. 1968, U.S. Ct. Appeals (2nd cir.) 1969, U.S. Supreme Ct. 1974, D.C. 1975, U.S. Ct. Appeals (1st cir.) 1976, U.S. Ct. Appeals (3rd cir.) 1980, U.S. Ct. Appeals (D.C. cir.) 1982, U.S. Ct. Appeals (4th cir.) 1983, U.S. Dist. Ct. (no. dist.) Calif. 1983, U.S. Dist. Ct. D.C. 1983. Asst. U.S. atty. U.S. Attys. Office (so. dist.) N.Y., 1968-73; asst. spl. prosecutor Watergate Spl. Prosecution Task Force, 1973-75; spl. counsel Senate Subcom. on Govtl. Ops., Washington, 1976-77; ptnr. Melrod, Redman & Gartlan, 1975-81, Ben-Veniste & Shernoff, 1981-90, Weil, Gotshal & Manges, Washington, 1991—; chief minority counsel Senate Whitewater Com., 1995-96; co-founder Trial Lawyers for Pub. Justice, 1982. Co-author: Stonewall, The Real Story of the Watergate Prosecution, 1977. Recipient Outstanding Pub. Svc. award Seymour Assn., 1976.

BENVENUTTI, PETER J., lawyer; b. Gulfport, Miss., June 24, 1949; s. Peter J. and Elizabeth Cullen (Beyer) B.; m. Lise A. Pearlman, May 31, 1974; children: Anna B., Jamie E., Amalia R. AB, Harvard U., 1971; JD, U. Calif., Berkeley, 1974. Bar: Calif. 1974, U.S. Dist. Ct. (no. dist.) Calif. 1974, U.S. Dist. Ct. (ea. dist.) Calif. 1977, U.S. Dist. Ct. (ctrl. and so. dists.) Calif. 1989, U.S. Dist. Ct. Ariz. 1990, U.S. Ct. Appeals (9th cir.) 1984. Assoc. Dinkelspiel & Dinkelspiel, San Francisco, 1974-80, ptnr., 1981-88; ptnr. Heller, Ehrman, White & McAuliffe, San Francisco, 1988—; mng. ptnr. San Francisco Office, 1995-97. Bd. dirs. ARC, 1981-83. Mem. ABA, Bar Assn. San Francisco (pres. Calif. bankruptcy forum 1993-94, lawyer rep. 9th Cir. Jud. Conf. 1994—). Democrat. Home: 1147 Clarendon Cres Oakland CA 94610-1807 Office: Heller Ehrman White & McAuliffe 333 Bush St San Francisco CA 94104-2806*

BEN-YAACOV, GIDEON, computer system designer; b. Bney Brack, Israel, July 26, 1941; came to U.S., 1979; s. Abraham and Henda (Natel) B-Y.; m. Miriam R. Schultz, May 11, 1967; children: David, Saul. BSEE, Technion Israel Inst. Tech., Haifa, 1966. R&D engr. Israeli Ministry of Def., Haifa, 1967-69; sci. asst. U. of the Witwatersrand, Johannesburg, Republic of South Africa, 1969-71; head office engr. ESCOM, Johannesburg, 1971-79; staff engr. Gibbs & Hill, Omaha, 1979-82; head process computer engring. HDR, Omaha, 1982-83; cons. engr. Power Utility Process Computer Engring., Omaha, 1983-92; sr. engr. advanced transp. techs. MFS Network Techs., Omaha, 1992-96, MFS Transp. Sys., Mt. Laurel, N.J., 1996—. Contbr. tech. articles to Process Computer Systems Engring.; author tech. papers. Mem. IEEE (sr.), Instrument Soc. Am. (sr., Philip P. Sprague Application award for devel. advanced operator interface, 1980). Achievements include research on human-factors in power and transportation industries; development of operator interface terminals for power plant computer systems, sound verification and validation procedures to enhance software QA process; technical and administrative leadership for the design of more than 30 advanced computer systems for the process industries; introduction of application of distributed controls for electrostatic precipitators. Home: 1870 Mayfair Dr Omaha NE 68144-1050

BENZ, DONALD RAY, nuclear safety engineer, researcher; b. Carbondale, Ill., Feb. 16, 1950; s. Raymond and Estella (Ebersohl) B.; m. Betty Jo Ring, Dec. 30, 1972; children: Kathy Lynn, Jeffrey Alan. BSEE, So. Ill. U., 1972; MA in Bus. Adminstrn., Sangamon State U., (now U. Ill.), 1982. Registered profl. engr., Ill. Design engr. Moldovan & Assocs. Cons. Engrs., Salem, Ill., 1973-75; elec. estimator McWilliams Electric Co., Vandalia, Ill., 1975-77, Volle Electric, Springfield, Ill., 1977-78; evaluation engr. Ill. Capitol Devel. Bd., Springfield, 1978-82; sect. head engring. div. Ill. Dept. Nuclear Safety, Springfield, 1982-96, sr. project engr., 1996—; program dir. Nat. Clean Air com. Conf. Radiation Control, 1984-85; presenter in field, 1990. Mem. bldg. com. Faith Evang. Luth. Ch., Jacksonville, Ill., 1988-90; mem. precinct com. Prentice-Sinclair (Ill.) Rep. Com.; vol. during 1993 floods ARC, bd. dirs. Morgan-Cass Counties chpt., 1995—. Mem. Am. Nuclear Soc. (chmn. Ctrl. Midwest sect. 1986-87, cert. of governance 1987, 93-96), Ill. Soc. Profl. Engrs. (pres. 1986-87, President's award Capital chpt. 1987), Health Physics Soc. (charter, by-laws com. Prairieland chpt. 1989-90), Am. Contract Bridge League (sect. master 1989). Achievements include the design, development and installation of the Ill. Dept. of Nuclear Safety's continuous radiation monitoring system consisting of isotopic stackmonitors, environmental detection network and liquid effluent monitors for nuclear power plants, the establishment of programs and goals for the development of a research and testing center for radiation monitoring systems. Home: RR 1 Box 90A Ashland IL 62612-9621

BENZ, EDWARD JOHN, retired clinical pathologist; b. Pitts., June 11, 1923; s. Henry John and Gertrude Nora (Heffernan) B.; m. Verna Marie Cuddyre, June 20, 1945; children: Edward John, Thomas James, Gregory Paul, Mary Louise. BS, U. Pitts., 1943, MD, 1946; MS, U. Minn., 1952. Intern, St. Joseph's Hosp., Pitts., 1946-47; resident, fellow Mayo Found., Mayo Clinic, 1949-53; pathologist, dir. labs. St. Luke's Hosp., Bethlehem, Pa., 1953-84, v.p. med. affairs, 1984-89; med. dir. utilization rev. Sacred Heart Hosp., Allentown, Pa., 1990-98; adj. prof. microbiology Lehigh U., Bethlehem, 1956-64; pres. Lab. Clin. Pathology, Bethlehem, 1956-88, ret., 1988; cons. Palmerton (Pa.) Hosp., Allentown (Pa.) State Hosp.; past dir. Miller Meml. Blood Bank, Bethlehem Mem. adv. com. Pa. Sec. Health on Clin. Labs., 1973-89; mem. health sci. adv. com. Lehigh U., 1973-89. Trustee St. Luke's Hosp., 1968-71; pres. Pa. Assn. Clin. Pathologists, 1966-67. Served as capt. M.C., AUS, 1947-49. Fellow Coll. Am. Pathologists (past chmn. anat. path. commn., past del. from Pa.), Am. Soc. Clin. Pathologists; mem. Internat. Acad. Pathology, Am. Assn. Pathologists and Bacteriologists, Am. Assn. Blood Banks, Am. Coll. Physician Execs., Sigma Xi, Alpha Omega Alpha. Club: Saucon Valley Country (Bethlehem). Contbr. articles to profl. publs. Home and Office: 1564 Saucon Valley Rd Bethlehem PA 18015-5260

BENZ, EDWARD JOHN, JR., physician, educator; b. Pitts., May 22, 1946; s. Edward John and Verna Marie (Cuddyre) B.; m. Margaret A. Vettese; children: Timothy Edward, Jennifer Kirsten. AB in Biology cum laude, Princeton U., 1968; MD magna cum laude, Harvard U., 1973. Diplomate Am. Bd. Internal Medicine, Am. Bd. Hematology. Resident Peter Bent Brigham Hosp., Boston, 1973-75; fellow pediatric hematology Children's Hosp. Med. Ctr., Boston, 1974-75; fellow adult hematology Yale U. Sch. of Medicine, New Haven, Conn., 1978-79; asst. prof. internal medicine Yale U. Sch. of Medicine, New Haven, 1979-82, assoc. prof. internal medicine, human genetics, 1982-87, prof. internal medicine, human genetics, 1987-92, chief sect. hematology, 1987-92, chmn. dean's curriculum task force, 1987-88, assoc. chmn. dept. internal medicine, 1988-92; Jack D. Myers prof., chmn. dept. medicine U. Pitts. Sch. Medicine, 1993-95; Sir William Osler prof., dir. dept. medicine Johns Hopkins U. Sch. Medicine., Balt., 1995—; physician-in-chief Johns Hopkins Hosp., Balt., 1995—; prof. molecular biology and genetics Johns Hopkins U. Sch. of Medicine, 1995—; research assoc. molecular hematology Nat. Heart, Lung, Blood Inst., Bethesda, Md., 1975-78; chmn. curriculum com. Yale Sch. of Medicine, New Haven, Conn., 1985-88; lectr. Am. Assn. Blood Banks, 1986, William B. Castle, 1995, Baldini lectr. Harvard Med. Sch., 1996; prof. pro-tem, hon. vis. chief of svc. Brigham & Women's Hosp., 1997; surgeon USPHS, 1975-78, Bethesda; adj. prof. biol. scis. Carnegie Mellon U., 1993-95; Harvard Hiatt vis. prof. Harvard Med. Sch., 1998. Author: Molecular Genetics Methods, 1987; co-editor: Hematology, Principles and Practice, 1990, 3d edit., 1999; assoc. editor Blood, 1988-94; contbr. more than 150 articles to profl. jours. Recipient Career Devel. award nat. Inst. Health, 1982, Edward Paradiso Research award Cooley's Anemia Found., N.Y.C., 1985, Basil O'Connor award March of Dimes, 1980. Fellow ACP, Molecular Med. Soc.; mem. Am. Soc. Clin. Investigation (nat. coun. 1987-91, pres. 1991-92), Assn. Am. Physicians, NIH (study sect. 1984—, chmn. 1993-95), Am. Fedn. Clin. Rsch., Am. Soc. Hematology (exec. coun. 1994, v.p. 1998, pres.-elect 1999), Am. Clin. and Climatological Soc., Am. Bd. Internal Medicine (hematology com.), Am. Soc. Human Genetics, Assn. Profs. Medicine, Inst. Medicine (elected), Interurban Clin. Club, Princeton Elm Club, Johns Hopkins Club, Phi Beta Kappa, Sigma Xi, Alpha Omega Alpha. Office: Johns Hopkins Sch Medicine 1830 E Monument St Dept Medicine Baltimore MD 21287-0003

BENZ, GEORGE ALBERT, economic consultant, retired educator; b. St. Louis, Feb. 21, 1926; s. George and Genevieve Beatrice (Klueg) B.; m. Dorris Jean Tabor, Apr. 14, 1951; 1 dau., Lynda Kaye. BBA, North Tex. State U., 1953, MS, 1955; PhD, U. Okla., 1969. Mgmt. trainee Montgomery Ward, 1953-54; tchr. social studies, coach Bryson (Tex.) High Sch., 1954-55; tchr. mathematics, coach Grapevine (Tex.) High Sch., 1955-56; instr. social studies N.W. Mo. State Coll., Maryville, 1956-57; grad. asst. U. Okla., Norman, 1957-59; asst. prof. econs. and sociology Central State Coll., Edmond, Okla., 1959-66; asso. prof. econs. St. Mary's U., San Antonio, 1966-79; prof. econs. St. Mary's U., 1979-93; dir. Univ. Research Center, 1979-93, chmn. dept. urban studies; retired, 1993; cons. in field; econ. advisor Greater San Antonio C. of C.; bus. advisor, various small bus. loan orgns.; research dir. Scientific Profit Analysis for Restaurants, 1979—; dir. Urban Adv. Group, 1980—; econ. expert witness in loss of income and anti-trust cases, 1973—; mem. Tex. State adv. com. U.S. Civil Rights Com., 1969-77. Contbr. articles to profl. jours. Campaign treas. various local and nat. candidates. Served with U.S. Army, 1943-49. Decorated Bronze Star, Purple Heart.; named Tchr. of Yr. St. Mary's U.; recipient KBAT Tex. Star award Sta. KBAT, Outstanding Centennial Alumnus U. North Tex., 1990. Mem. Am. Econs. Assn., Southwestern Social Sci. Assn., So. Econ. Assn., Assn. for Evolutionary Econs., AAUP, San Antonio Bus. and Econ. Soc. Democrat. Unitarian. Home: 206 E Sunshine Dr San Antonio TX 78228-3119

BENZEL, ILONA FRAN, artist; b. Bklyn., Mar. 20, 1952; d. George Borofsky and Miriam (Schenkman) Carroll; m. Bruce D. Benzel, May 10, 1985; children: Aaron Denutte, Amy Denutte. BA in Comml. Art, Notre Dame Coll., Manchester, N.H., 1985. Paste-up artist, acting prodn. mgr. The N.H. Times, Concord, 1985-86; printshop artist Curry Copy/Sir Speedy, Manchester, 1986-89; paste-up/computer artist Concord Monitor, 1989-94; artist N.H. Tech. Inst., Concord, 1994-97. Avocations: writing, oil painting.

BENZER, SEYMOUR, neuroscience educator; b. N.Y.C., Oct. 15, 1921; s. Mayer and Eva (Naidorf) B.; m. Dorothy Vlosky, Jan. 10, 1942 (dec. 1978); children: Barbara Ann Benzer Freidin, Martha Jane Benzer Goldberg; m. Carol A. Miller, May 11, 1980; 1 child, Alexander Robin. B.A., Bklyn. Coll., 1942; M.S., Purdue U., 1943, Ph.D., 1947, D.Sc. (hon.), 1968; D.Sc., Columbia U., 1974, Yale U., 1977, Brandeis U., 1978, CUNY, 1978, U. Paris, 1983, Rockefeller U., N.Y.C., 1993. Mem. faculty Purdue U., 1945-67, prof. biophysics, 1958-61, Stuart distinguished prof. biology, 1961-67; prof. biology Calif. Inst. Tech., 1967-75, Boswell prof. neurosci., 1975—; biophysicist Oak Ridge Nat. Lab., 1948-49; vis. asso. Calif. Inst. Tech., Pasadena, 1965-67. Contbr. articles to profl. jours. Rsch. fellow Calif. Inst. Tech., 1949-51; Fulbright rsch. fellow Pasteur Inst., Paris, 1951-52; sr. NSF postdoctoral fellow Cambridge, Eng., 1957-58; recipient Award of Honor Bklyn. Coll., 1956, Sigma Xi rsch. award Purdue U., 1957, Ricketts award U. Chgo., 1961, Gold medal N.Y. City Coll. Chemistry Alumni Assn., 1962, Gairdner award of merit, 1964, McCoy award Purdue U., 1965, Lasker award, 1971, T. Duckett Jones award, 1975, Prix Leopold Mayer French Acad. Scis., 1975, Louisa Gross Horwitz award, 1976, Harvey award Israel, 1977, Warren Triennial prize Mass. Gen. Hosp., 1977, Dickson award, 1978, Rosenstiel award, 1986, T.H. Morgan medal Genetics Soc. Am., 1986, Karl Spencer Lashley award, 1988, Gerard award Soc. Neurosci., 1989, Helmerich award, 1990, Wolf Found. Prize (in medicine), Israel, 1991, Bristol-Myers Squibb Neurosci. award, 1992, Crafoord prize Royal Swedish Acad. Scis., 1993, Mendel award Brit. Genetical Soc., 1994, Alberto Feltrinelli prize Accademia dei Lincei, Italy, 1994. Fellow Indian Acad. Scis. (hon.); mem. Nat. Acad. Scis., Am. Acad. Arts and Scis., Am. Philos. Soc. (Lashley award 1988), Harvey Soc., N.Y. Acad. Scis., AAAS, Royal Soc. London (fgn. mem.), Royal Acad. of Scis. of Spain (fgn. mem.). Home: 2075 Robin Rd San Marino CA 91108-2831

BENZING, CYNTHIA DELL, economics educator; b. Upper Darby, Pa., Oct. 23, 1951; d. Martin Paul and Alyce (Chapman) Dell; m. William Thomas Benzing, Oct. 21, 1972; children: William, Daniel, Edward, James. BS in Psychology, Pa. State U., 1972; MBA, Drexel U., 1977, PhD in Bus., 1987. Asst. controller Parade Publs., Inc., Phila., 1972-76; teaching asst. Drexel U., Phila., 1976-77; acctg. instr. St. Joseph's U., Phila., 1977-80; teaching fellow Drexel U., Phila., 1983-87; prof. West Chester (Pa.) U., 1987—, chair, 1996—. Editor-in-chief Pa. Econ. Rev., 1991-94; contbr. articles to profl. jours. Instr. Thresholds Vols. in Prison, Delaware County, Pa., 1989; foster parent Children and Youth Svcs., Delaware County, 1986-88, 90-98. Mem. Pa. Econ. Assn. (bd. dirs. 1989-91, treas. 1991-93, v.p. 1994-95, pres. elect 1996, pres. 1997), So. Econ. Assn., Ea. Econ. Assn., Atlantic Econ. Assn., Fin. Mgmt. Assn. Avocations: camping, reading. Home: 331 Caswallen Dr West Chester PA 19380-4119 Office: West Chester U Dept Econs and Fin West Chester PA 19383

BENZIO, DONNA MARIE, cardiopulmonary rehabilitation nurse, educator; b. Connellsville, Pa., June 5, 1955; d. John Robert and Ewaldina Marie (Kosisko) Bartholomai; m. Benjamin Arthur Benzio, Nov. 18, 1978; children: Benjamin, Ashley, Zachary. Diploma in nursing, Mercy Hosp., Pitts., 1978; student, Pa. State U., Fayette. RN, Pa.; BLS, Am. Heart Assn.; cert. outpatient cardiac rehab. nursing Nursing Cons., Inc. Med. staff nurse Uniontown Hosp., 1976-77, staff nurse ICU, 1977-80, cardiac rehab. nurse, 1980-87, dir. cardiac diagnostics, 1987-91, cardiopulmonary rehab. nurse, 1991—; health asst. instr. North Fayette Vo-Tech., 1996—; leader cardiac club Uniontown Hosp.; bd. dirs. Am. Heart Assn., Uniontown. Recipient Appreciation award Am. Heart Assn., 1990-92, Walk-A-Thon cert., 1992. Mem. Am. Assn. Cardiovascular and Pulmonary Rehab. Roman Catholic. Avocations: swimming, walking, gardening, public speaking, biking. Home: 568 Narrows Rd Connellsville PA 15425-9201

BENZLE, CURTIS MUNHALL, artist, art educator; b. Lakewood, Ohio, Apr. 20, 1949; s. Arthur George and Martha (Munhall) B; m. Suzan Scianamblo, Feb. 6, 1972 (div. 1995); children: Elliott, Kyle, Marisa; m. Sally Jo Havas, Aug. 28, 1996 (div. 1999). Student, Hillsdale Coll., 1967-69; BFA, Ohio State U., 1972; postgrad., Rochester Inst. Tech., 1973, MA, No. Ill. U., 1978. Owner, mgr. Oz Crafts, Hilton Head, S.C., 1973-76, Benzle Porcelain Co., Columbus, Ohio, 1980-93, Benzle Applied Arts, Hilliard, Ohio, 1988—; owner Creative Spirit Workshop; exec. dir. Ohio Designer Craftsmen, 1996-99; instr. U. S.C., Beaufort, 1978-79, Columbus (Ga.) Coll. Art and Design, 1982—; pres. Japan-USA Exch. Exhbn., 1988-92; bd. overseers Am. Craft Assn., 1991-96, chmn., 1994-95; bd. trustees Am. Crafts Coun., 1992-96. One-man show U. S.C., 1979, Indpls. Mus. Art, 1984, Lawrence Gallery, Portland, Oreg., 1986, Running Ridge Gallery, Santa Fe, 1986, Akasaka/Green Gallery, Tokyo, 1987, 90, Zanesville Art Ctr., 1988, Swidler Gallery, 1990, Tsukushi Gallery, Kitakyushu, Japan, 1991, del Mano Gallery, 1998, also others; exhibited in numerous group shows, 1971—, including Smithsonian Instn., 1980, 83, Suntory Art Mus., Tokyo, 1984, Cermaic Nat. Everson Mus., Syracuse, 1988, Internat. Competition of Ceramics, Mino, Japan, 1989; represented in numerous permanent collections, including Smithsonian Instn., Everson Mus. Art, Los Angeles County Mus. Art, Cleve. Mus. Art., White House Collection Contemporary Craft. Mem. Ohio Citizens Com. for Arts, 1986—. Nat. Endowment for Arts fellow, 1980, Ohio Arts Coun. fellow, 198l, 83, 84, 86, 88, Greater Columbus Arts Coun. fellow, 1987. Mem. Am. Crafts Coun. (bd. overseers 1991-96, trustee 1992-96), Nat. Coun. on Edn. in Ceramic Art, Ohio Designer Craftsmen (bd. dirs. 1984—, pres. 1985-87). Avocation: gardening.

BENZO-BONACCI, ROSEMARY ANNE, health facility administrator; b. Utica, N.Y., Apr. 28, 1955; d. Rocco Anthony and Grace Lillian (Maggi) B.; m. Michael V. Bonacci. AAS, Mohawk Valley C.C., 1988; BS, New Sch. for Social Rsch., 1992, postgrad., 1994—. With Mohawk Valley C.C., Utica, 1977-89, alumni asst., 1989-93; dir. cmty. rels. Charles T. Sitrin Health Care Ctr., New Hartford, N.Y., 1993—; program dir. Youth Mentorship Activities Program in Health Care Svcs. Dept. Health N.Y. Pres. Vol. Horizons, 1993—, Coalition for Tobacco Control, 1994; bd. dirs., mem. task force pub. edn. sector Utica Coalition for a Smoke-Free Cmty., 1989-93, chair ann. coalition meeting, 1990-91; chair search com. for tech. asst. Mohawk Valley C.C., 1990. Mem. Mohawk Valley C.C. Alumni Assn. (bd. dirs. 1991-93). Democrat. Roman Catholic. Avocations: writing short stories, reading, collecting figurines, weight training. Home: 16 Symphony Pl Whitesboro NY 13492-2227 Office: Charles T Sitrin Health Care Ctr Box 2050 Tilden Ave New Hartford NY 13413

BENZON, HONORIO TABAL, anesthesiologist; b. Ilocos Sur, The Philippines, Sept. 12, 1946; came to U.S., 1972,; s. Alejo Gonzales and Concepcion Tacto (Tabal) B.; m. Julieta Palpal-latoc, May 30, 1970; children: Barbara Hazel, Hubert Anthony. BS, Far Eastern U., Manila, Philippines, 1966, MD, 1971. Diplomate Am. Bd. Anesthesiology, Am. Bd. Pain Mgmt. Intern Overlook Hosp., Summit, N.J., 1972-73; resident in anesthesia U. Cin. Med. Ctr., 1973-75, Northwestern U. affil. hosps., 1975-76; pvt. practice anesthesiology Chgo., 1976—; asst. prof. dept. anesthesia Northwestern U. Med. Sch., 1980-85, assoc. prof., 1985-94, prof. dept. anesthesiology, 1994—, chief sect. pain medicine, 1990—, program dir. pain mgmt. fellowship program; assoc. staff Northwestern U. Meml. Hosp., 1976-82, attending staff, 1982—; attending staff VA Lakeside Hosp., 1976—, Brigham and Women's Hosp., 1985-86; instr. dept. anesthesia Harvard Med. Sch., 1985-86; cons. staff Rehab. Inst. Chgo. Editor: Regional Anesthesia and Pain Medicine; assoc. editor: Pain Digest; chief editor: (book) Essentials of Pain Medicine and Regional Anesthesia; contbr. numerous articles to profl. jours. Fellow Am. Coll. Anesthesiologists; mem. AMA, Am. Soc. Anesthesiologists, Internat. Anesthesia Rsch. Soc., Am. Soc. Regional Anesthesia, Am. Pain Soc. Roman Catholic. Home: 161 E Chicago Ave #48F Chicago IL 60611-6681 Office: Northwestern U Med Sch Dept Anes 303 E Superior St Rm 360 Chicago IL 60611-4804

BEN-ZVI, JEFFREY STUART, gastroenterologist, internist; b. Bklyn., Aug. 19, 1957; s. Seymour and Doris (Salzman) B.-Z.; m. Julie Genuth, May 11, 1982; children: Chana, Adina, Ilana, Aviva, Samuel, Sara. BSc, CUNY, Bklyn., 1979; MD, Columbia U., 1983. Diplomate Am. Bd. Internal Medicine, Am. Bd. Gastroenterology, Am. Bd. Geriatrics. Intern St. Luke's-Roosevelt Hosp., N.Y.C., 1983-84, resident in internal medicine, 1984-86, fellow in gastroenterology, 1986-88; asst. prof. clin. med. Columbia U., N.Y.C., 1988—; attending physician Columbia-Presbyn. Med. Ctr., Lenox Hill Hosp., Beth Israel Med. Ctr., N.Y.C. Contbr. articles to profl. jours. Med. dir./advisor Hatzolah Vol. Ambulance Corp., N.Y.C., 1985—; bd. dir. Coun. Jewish Organ. of Flatbush, Ave. N. Jewish Cmty. Ctr. Fellow ACP, Am. Coll. Gastroenterology; mem. AMA, Am. Gastroent. Assn., Am. Soc. Gastrointestinal Endoscopy, Am. Soc. Internal Medicine, Royal Soc. Medicine (U.K.), Am. Radio Relay League (life), Agudath Israel Am. (life), Am. Geriatric Soc., Am. Soc. for Parenteral and Enteral Nutrition, N.Y. Acad. Sci. Avocations: philately, photography, amateur radio (KC2ND), personal computers, aquaria. Home: 2414 Avenue R Brooklyn NY 11229-2430 Office: 911 Park Ave New York NY 10021-0337 also: 315 W 57th St New York NY 10019-3158 also: 2907 Kings Hwy Brooklyn NY 11229-1805

BEPKO, GERALD LEWIS, university administrator, law educator, lecturer, consultant, lawyer; b. Chgo., Apr. 21, 1940; s. Lewis V. and Geraldine S. (Bernath) B.; m. Jean B. Cougnenc, Feb. 24, 1968; children: Gerald Lewis Jr., Arminda B. B.S., No. Ill. U., 1962; J.D., Ill. Inst. Tech.-Chgo. Kent Coll. Law, 1965; LL.M., Yale U., 1972. Bar: Ill. 1965, U.S. Supreme Ct. 1968, Ind. 1973. Assoc. Ehrlich, Bundesen, Friedman & Ross, Chgo., 1965; spl. agt. FBI, 1965-69; asst. prof. law Ill. Inst. Tech.-Chgo. Kent Coll. Law, 1969-71; prof. Ind. U.-Indpls., 1972-86, assoc. dean acad. affairs, 1979-81, dean, 1981-86, v.p. Ind. U., 1986—; vis. prof. Ind. U.-Bloomington, summers 1976, 77, 78, 80, U. Ill., 1976-77, Ohio State U., 1978-79; cons. and reporter Fed. Jud. Ctr.; bd. dirs., First Ind. Bank/Corp., 1988—, Ind. Energy Inc. & Ind. Gas Co., Inc., 1989-97, USA Group and USA Funds, 1996—, Indpls. Life Ins. Co., 1997—; mem. Conf. Commrs. on Uniform State Laws, 1982, Permanent Editl. Bd. for the Uniform Comml. Code, 1993—; vice chair Ind. Lobby Registration Commn., 1992-96, chair, 1996—. Indpls. Chgo. Title and Trust Co. Found. scholar, 1962-65; Ford Urban law fellow, 1971-72. Fellow Am. Bar Found., Ind. State Bar, Indpls. Bar Found.; mem. ABA, Ind. State Bar Assn., Indpls. Bar Assn. Methodist. Club: Country of Indpls. Lodge: Rotary. Author: (with Boshkoff) Sum and Substance of Secured Transactions, 1981; contbr. articles on comml. law to profl. jours. Office: Ind U 355 Lansing St Indianapolis IN 46202-2815

BEQULIEU, EUGENE W., federal judge; b. 1929. BA, St. Joseph's U., 1950; LLD, Suffolk U., 1958. Judge Maine Dist. Ct.; justice Maine Superior Ct.; magistrate judge U.S. Dist. Ct. Maine, Bangor, 1992—. Fax: (207) 945-0362. Office: US Dist Ct Maine 202 Harlow St Rm 300 Bangor ME 04401

BERACHA, BARRY HARRIS, food company executive; b. Bronx, N.Y., Feb. 28, 1942; s. Nissim Macy and Celia Grace (Sides) B.; m. Barbara Marie Capobianco, Dec. 23, 1967; children: Brian, Bradley, Bonnie. BChE, Pratt Inst., 1963; MBA, U. Pa., 1965. Ops. researcher Celanese Corp., 1965-67; tech. economist Sun Oil Co., 1964-65; with Anheuser-Busch Cos., Inc., 1967-96, v.p. corp. planning, 1974-76, v.p., group exec., 1976-96; chmn., CEO Earthgrains Co., Clayton, Mo., 1996—. Office: Earthgrains Co 8400 Maryland Ave Clayton MO 63105-3647

BERALL, FRANK STEWART, lawyer; b. N.Y.C., Feb. 10, 1929; s. Louis J. and Jeannette F.; m. Christiana Johnson, July 5, 1958 (dec. July 1972); children: Erik Dustin, Elissa Alexandra; m. Jenefer M. Carey, Sept. 1, 1980. BS, Yale U., 1950, JD, 1955; LLM in Tax, NYU, 1959. Bar: N.Y. 1955, Conn. 1960; accredited estate planner. Assoc. firm Mudge, Stern, Baldwin & Todd, N.Y.C., 1955-57, Townley, Updike, Carter & Rodgers, N.Y.C., 1957-60; atty. Conn. Gen. Life Ins. Co., Bloomfield, Conn., 1960-65; atty. trust dept. Hartford Nat. Bank & Trust Co., Conn., 1965-67; assoc. Cooney & Scully, Hartford, Conn., 1968-70; ptnr. Copp & Berall and predecessors, Hartford, 1970—; v.p., sec., gen. counsel, bd. dirs. John M. Blewer, Inc., Essex, Conn., 1969-86; asst. in instrn. Yale U. Law Sch., 1954-55; lectr. U. Conn. Sch. Ins., 1964-72, Law Sch., 1972-73; instr. estate planning Am. Coll. Life Ins., 1968-69; adj. asst. prof. grad. tax program U. Hartford, 1973-74; counsel Conn. Gov.'s Strike Force for Full Employment, 1971-72, Conn. Gov.'s Commn. on Tax Reform, 1972-73, State Tax Commr.'s Commn., 1972-75, Com. on Tax Law Clarification, 1984-88; lectr. in field. Co-author: A Practitioners Guide to the Tax Reform Act of 1969, 1970, Estate Planning and the Close Corporation, 1970, Planning Large Estates, 1970, Revocable Inter Vivos Trusts, 1985, The Migrant Client: Tax, Commnity Property, and Other Considerations, 1994; sr. editor Conn. Bar Jour., 1969—; mem. editl. bd. Estate Planning mag., 1973—, Practical Tax Lawyer, 1988—, Jour. Taxation of Trusts and Estates, 1988-92. Bd. dirs. Bloomfield Interfaith Homes, 1967-71; mem. adv. council U. Hartford Tax Inst., 1970-82; co-chmn. adv. council Hartford Tax Inst., 1986-94; co-chmn. Notre Dame Estate Planning Inst., 1977—; trustee Culver Ednl. Found., 1997—. 1st lt., F.A. U.S. Army, 1951-52. Fellow Am. Coll. Trust and Estate Counsel (chmn. Conn. chpt. 1975-81, editl. bd. 1975-87, chmn. estate and gift tax com. 1976-81, chmn. accessions tax com. 1984-88, regent 1977-83), Am. Coll. Tax Counsel; mem. ABA (chmn. com. estate planning and ins. 1979-85, chmn. task force on retroactivity and constitutionality of tax law changes 1985-89, vice chmn. comm. estate planning and drafting 1992-96, co-chmn. com. non-tax issues in drafting wills and recovable trusts and co-chmn. tax litig. and controversy of real property probate and trust sect. 1995—, chmn. mem. com. 1977-79, chmn. com. on income of estates and trusts 1983-85, chmn. com. econ. tax practice 1987-89, chmn. CLE com. tax sect., co-founder, convener estate planning seminar group 1972-78), Conn. Bar Assn. (exec. com., estates and probate sect. 1973—, chmn. 1984-86, chmn. tax sect. 1969-72, exec. com. 1969—, vice chmn. com. on specialization 1974-77), Hartford County Bar Assn. (chmn. com. liaison with IRS 1972-74, com. charter and by-laws 1975), Am. Law Inst. (tax adv. group 1980-89), Internat. Acad. Estate and Trust Law (exec. coun. 1978-82, spkr. numerous seminars), Tax Club of Hartford (pres. 1975-76), Culver Summer Schs. Alumni Assn. (v.p. 1975-85, pres. 1997—, bd. dirs. 1985-91, 93—), Culver Club (pres. 1996—), Yale Club of Hartford (dir. 1998—, pres. 1999—). Home: 9 Penwood Rd Bloomfield CT 06002-1520 Office: Copp & Berall 55 Farmington Ave Ste 703 Hartford CT 06105-3790 *As a tax lawyer, I view my job as helping to keep the system going by seeing to it that my clients pay the government all it is legally entitled to receive in taxes, but no more, and doing pro bono work for the improvement of the entire federal and state tax law system.*

BERAN, GEORGE WESLEY, veterinary microbiology educator; b. Riceville, Iowa, May 22, 1928; s. John and Elizabeth (Buresh) B.; m. Janice Ann Van Zomeren, Dec. 21, 1954; children: Bruce, Anne, George. DVM, Iowa State U., 1954; PhD, Kans. U., 1959; LHD, Silliman U., Philippines,

1973. Diplomate Am. Coll. Vet. Preventive Medicine, Am. Coll. Epidemiology. Epidemic intelligence officer USPHS, 1954-56; asst. prof. biology Silliman U., Dumaguete City, Philippines, 1960-63, chmn. dept. agr., 1962-71, assoc. prof. microbiology, 1963-67, prof. microbiology, 1967-73; prof. vet. microbiology and preventive medicine Iowa State U., Ames, 1973-93, Disting. prof. microbiology, immunology, preventive medicine, 1993—; cons. WHO, Belize, Ecuador, Mex., India, Laos, Malaysia, Philippines, Jamaica, Surinam, Barbados; rsch. del. USSR/Iowa State U. exch. program, Moscow, 1989-90, Latvia, 1993; rsch. cons., Taiwan, 1983, 96, 98, Hungary, 1988, 90, U. Yucatan, 1989-90, 97, 98, Ukraine, 1996, Japan, 1998; vis. lectr. Nat. Inst. Vet. Bioproducts and Pharms., Beijing, Faculty Vet. Medicine, Huazhong Agrl. U. Wuhan, Peoples Republic of China, 1988; cons. Pan Am. Health Orgn., 1979, 85, 93, 95, 96, 98, 99; cons., mem. WHO Expert Panel on Zoonoses, 1980—; Fulbright prof. Ahmadu Bello U., Zaria, Nigeria, 1980; mem. subcom. on drug use in animals NRC, 1993-98, mem. nat. adv. com. on microbiol. criteria for foods, 1997—; adv. com. Wellcome Trust, 1998-99. Editor, co-editor books on zoonoses; contbr. articles to profl. jours., chpts. to books. Active Ames Humane League, Ptnrs. of the Americas, UN Assn., Ames chpt.; advisor Ames Eagles 4-H Club. Recipient James H. Steele award World Vet. Epidemiology Soc., 1979, Nat. Meritorious Svc. award Livestock Conservation Inst., 1989, Gold Head Cane award Am. Vet. Epidemiology Soc., 1993. Mem. AVMA (mem. coun. pub. health and regulatory vet. medicine, Internat. Svc. award 1996), Am. Coll. Vet. Preventive Medicine (pres.), Conf. Pub. Health Veterinarians (pres.), Am. Assn. Food Hygiene Veterinarians (Outstanding Tchr. award 1978), Assn. Tchrs. Vet. Pub. Health and Preventive Medicine, Iowa Vet. Med. Assn. (chair pub. health com.), Iowa Pork Producers Assn. (pseudorables com.), U.S. Animal Health Assn. (com. on pseudorables, pub. health, food safety, feed safety, chair com. on feral swine), Cardinal Key, Sigma Xi, Phi Beta Delta, Phi Kappa Phi (pres.), Gamma Sigma Delta (Svc. to Agr. Merit award 1995), Phi Zeta, Alpha Zeta, Phi Eta Sigma. Home: 304 24th St Ames IA 50010-4834 Office: Coll Vet Medicine Iowa State U Rm 2134 Ames IA 50011

BERANEK, CARLA TIPTON, music educator; b. Aberdeen, Md., Nov. 8, 1964; d. B.G. Carl William and Shirley Ann (Sanders) Tipton; m. John Fred Beranek, Mar. 23, 1996. B in Music Edn., James Madison U., 1986; MusM, U. Tex., 1988. Provisional cert. middle grade prin., Ky., tchg. instrumental music K-12, Ky., tchg. vocal music K-12, Ky., tchg. all-level music, Tex., tchg. elem. self-contained 1-8, Tex., cert. temporary mid-mgmt. adminstr., Tex. Tchr. gen. music, choir Temple (Tex.) Ind. Sch. Dist., 1989-92, Ft. Worth Ind. Sch. Dist., 1992-96; tchr. band, orch., keyboard Fayette County Pub. Schs., Lexington, Ky., 1996; itinerant staff asst. Sch. for the Creative & Performing Arts, 1998—; presenter in field. Del. leader student exchange Ft. Worth Sister Cities Internat., 1994. Mem. ASCD, Ky. Music Educators Assn., Music Educators Nat. Conf., Ky. Edn. Assn., Fayette County Edn. Assn., U. Tex. Ex-Student Assn. (life), Kappa Kappa Psi (chpt. sec. 1985-86, s.w. dist. pres. 1987-88), Phi Delta Kappa. Democrat. Methodist. Home: 905 Medley Dr Richmond KY 40475-6807

BERANEK, LEO LEROY, acoustical consultant; b. Solon, Iowa, Sept. 15, 1914; s. Edward Fred and Beatrice (Stahle) B.; m. Phyllis Knight, Sept. 6, 1941 (dec. Nov. 1982); children: James Knight, Thomas Haynes; m. Gabriella Sohn, Aug. 10, 1985. A.B., Cornell Coll., 1936, D.Sc. (hon.), 1946; M.S., Harvard U., 1937, D.Sc., 1940; D.Eng. (hon.), Worcester Poly. Inst., 1971; D.Comml. Sci. (hon.), Suffolk U., 1979; LL.D. (hon.), Emerson College, 1982; Dr. Pub. Service (hon.), Northeastern U., 1984. Instr. physics Harvard U., 1940-41, asst. prof., 1941-43; dir. Electro-Acoustics and Systems Rsch. Labs., 1941-46; assoc. prof. communications engring. MIT, 1947-58, lectr., 1958-81; tech. dir. Acoustics Lab., 1947-53; pres., dir., chief exec. officer Bolt Beranek & Newman, Cambridge, Mass., 1953-69, chief scientist, 1969-71, dir., 1953-84; pres., chief exec. officer, dir. Boston Broadcasters, Inc., 1963-79, chmn. bd., 1980-83; pres. Am. Acad. Arts and Scis., Cambridge, 1989-94, chair develop. com., 1995—; part-owner WCVB-TV, Boston, 1972-82; chmn. bd. Mueller-BBM GmbH, Munich, 1962-86; bd. dirs. Tech. Integration Inc., Bedford, Mass., 1987—. Author: Principles of Sound Control in Airplanes, 1944, Acoustic Measurements, 1949, 2d edit., 1986, Music, Acoustics and Architecture, 1962, Noise Reduction, 1960, Noise and Vibration Control, 1971, 2d edit., 1988, Noise and Vibration Control Engineering, 1992, Concert and Opera Halls: How They Sound, 1996; contbr. articles on acoustics, audio and TV comm. sys. to tech. publs. Charter mem. bd. overseers Boston Symphony Orch., 1968-80, chmn., 1977-80, trustee, 1977-87, chmn. bd. trustees, 1983-86, hon. chmn., 1987, life trustee 1994—; mem. bd. overseers Harvard U., 1984-90; mem. coun. for arts MIT, 1972—; mem. Mass. Commn. on Jud. Conduct, 1986-88, others in past. Guggenheim fellow, 1946-47; recipient Presdl. certificate of merit, 1948; Cornell Coll. Alumni Citation, 1953; 1st Silver medal le Groupement des Acousticiens de Langue Francaise Paris, 1966; Abe Lincoln TV award So. Bapt. Conv., 1976; named Sta. WCRB Person of the Yr., 1987. Fellow NAE (bd. dir, marine bd., com. pub. engring. policy, aeros. and space engring. bd.), AAAS, IEEE (chmn. profl. group audio 1950-51), Am. Phys. Soc., Am. Acad. Arts and Scis., Audio Engring. Soc. (pres. 1967-68, Gold medal 1971, gov. 1966-71), Acoustical Soc. Am. (mem. coun. 1944-47, v.p. 1949-50, pres. 1954-55, Bienniel award 1944, Sabine award 1961, Gold medal 1975, Hon. mem. 1994); mem. Inst. Noise Control Engring. (charter pres. 1971-73, dir. 1973-75, 1st Disting. Noise Control Engr. 1997), Mass. Broadcasters Assn. (bd. dirs. 1973-80, pres. 1978-79, Disting. Svc. award 1980), Cambridge Soc. Early Music (pres. 1963-71, dir. 1961-79), Acad. Disting. Bostonians, Greater Boston C. of C. (dir. 1973-79, v.p. 1976-79, Disting. Cmty. Svc. award 1980, 83), St. Botolph Club, Phi Beta Kappa, Sigma Xi, Eta Kappa Nu. Episcopalian. Home and Office: 975 Memorial Dr Ste 804 Cambridge MA 02138-5755

BERARD, ANDRÉ, bank executive; b. Bedford, Que., Can., Aug. 13, 1940. Fellow's diploma, Can. Bankers' Assn.; grad. spl. mgmt. program, Harvard U., 1985; PhD (Hon.), U. Ottawa, 1991. With Nat. Bank of Can., Montreal, 1958—, asst. br. mgr., br. mgr., 1963-72, successively asst. mgr., supt., mgr. internat., asst. gen. mgr. internat. div., 1972-77, v.p., 1977-80, sr. v.p., gen. mgr. internat., 1980-81, sr. v.p. and gen. mgr. credit, 1981-82, exec. v.p. nat. accounts, 1982-84, sr. exec. v.p. banking, 1984-86, pres., chief oper. officer, 1986-89, pres., chief exec. officer, 1989-90, chmn. bd., chief exec. officer, 1990—; also bd. dirs. Nat. Bank of Can.; chmn. bd. dirs. Nat. Bank Export Fin. Co., Inc., NBC Export Devel. Corp., Inc.; bd. dirs. Natcan Fin. (Asia) Ltd., Noranda, Inc., MacDonald Stewart Found.; bd. dirs., mem. audit com. Groupe Vidéotron Ltée, Télé-Métropole Inc. Mem. policy com., mem. internat. trade adv. com. Bus. Coun. on Nat. Issues; mem. coun. of govs. Assn. U. Montreal; mem. adv. com. to Prime Minister of Bus./Govt. Exec. Exch. Program. Mem. Can. Bankers Assn. (chmn. exec. coun. 1986-89), Can./France Bus. Rels. Club. Office: Nat Bank Can Pub Rels Dept, 600 de La Gauchetiere St W Fl 8, Montreal, PQ Canada H3B 4L2

BERARDELLI, CATHERINE MARIE, women's health nurse, nurse educator; b. Portland, Oreg., Aug. 22, 1949; d. Francis Lawrence and Jean Carolyn (Petersen) Ison; m. Victor Francis Berardelli Jr., May 28, 1988. BSN, U. Oreg., 1972; MSN, U. So. Maine, Portland, 1985; PhD, Adelphi U., 1994, FNP, 1995. RN; cert. family nurse practitioner. Night staff nurse Dornbecker Childrens Hosp., Portland, Oreg., 1972-73; night charge nurse Maine Med. Ctr., Portland, 1973-78; evening supr. St. Andrews Hosp., Boothbay Harbor, Maine, 1978-82, DON, 1982-85; instr. nursing Cen. Maine Med. Ctr. Sch. Nursing, Lewiston, 1985-88, U. So. Maine Sch. Nursing, Portland, 1986-90; clin. nurse specialist Long Island Jewish Med. Ctr., New Hyde Park, N.Y., 1990-92; clin. learning lab. coord. Adelphi U., Garden City, N.Y., 1991-94; dir. nursing programs U. New Eng., Westbrook Coll. Campus, 1995—; adj. assoc. prof. Simmons Coll., 1995—; expert witness Kelly Remmel & Zimmerman, Portland, 1989-92; test item writer Nat. League Nursing, N.Y.C., 1991; vis. prof. Sch. Nursing Adelphi U., 1993-95. Co-author patient edn. brochure. Mem. Maine People's Alliance, Portland, 1985-90; mem. New Eng. Women's Studies Assn., 1987; bd. dirs. Kaler Vaill Home for Older Women, 1996, Park Danforth, 1997, Vis. Nurse Svc. So. Maine, 1997. U. So. Maine rsch. grantee, 1989. Mem. ANA, Assn. Women's Health Obstetrics and Neonatal Nurses, Nat. League Nursing, Maine Nursing Honor Soc. (charter), Maine Nurse Practitioners Assn., Sigma Theta Tau. Home: 149 Pine Point Rd Scarborough ME 04074-8855

BERARDI, RONALD STEPHEN, pathologist, educator; b. Rochester, Pa., Jan. 12, 1943; s. Desiderio John and Florence (Salvaggio) B.; m. Diane Lenore Wytaske, June 17, 1967; children: Lenore Christine, James Ronald, Anne-Marie. BS in Chemstry, U. Pitts., 1963; MD, Loyola U., Chgo., 1967. Diplomate Am. Bd. Pathology. Intern Presbyn.-St. Lukes Hosp., Chgo., 1967-68, resident in pathology, 1968-69; resident in pathology Malcolm Grow USAF Med. Ctr., Washington, 1969-71, New Eng. Deaconess Hosp., Boston, 1971-72, U. Pitts. Health Ctr. Hosp., 1972-73; Sarah Mellon Scaife fellow in immunopathology U. Pitts., 1973-74; assoc. pathologist Latrobe (Pa.) Area Hosp., 1974-80, chief pathologist, dir. labs., 1980—; co-dir. labs. Henry Clay Frick Community Hosp. Latrobe Area Hosp., Mt. Pleasant, Pa., 1974-80; assoc. instr. U. Ill., Chgo., 1967-69; teaching fellow U. Pitts., 1972-74, teaching faculty, 1974-76; instr. Thomas Jefferson Coll. Medicine, Phila., 1977—; med. dir. Sch. Med. Tech. Ind. U. Pa., 1980—; lab. insp. Coll. Am. Pathology, Chgo., 1980—; chmn. infection control com., tissue transfusion com., cancer registry, cost containment com. Latrobe Area Hosp., 1980—. Reviewer jour. Cancer, 1994; editl. bd. Physicians News Digest 1994—; contbr. articles to profl. jours. Mem. Nat. Adv. Bd. Am. Security Council, Boston, 1985; mem. Rep. Presdl. Task Force, Washington, 1985-88; mem. Rep. Nat. Com., Washington, 1985. Senatorial scholar, 1961-63; mem. Rep. Senatorial Inner Circle, U.S. Senatorial Bus. Adv. Bd., 1988, state advisor to U.S. Congl. Adv. Bd.; U.S. Congressional Adv. Bd. (state advisor). Fellow Am. Soc. Clin. Pathologists, Coll. Am. Pathologists, U.S.-Can. Acad. Pathology Inc., Internat. Biographical Assn.; mem. Am. Assn. Blood Banks, AMA (Physicians Recognition award 1985), Am. Chem. Soc., N.Y. Acad. Scis., Internat. Platform Assn., Am. Biographical Inst. (disting. leadership award), Am. Inst. Chemists, Am. Med. Writers Assn., Westmoreland County Med. Soc. (editor bulletin), Pitts. Cancer Inst. (affiliate), Latrobe Country Club, Univ. Club, U.S. Senatorial Club, Phi Eta Sigma, Alpha Epsilon Delta. Roman Catholic. Avocations: astronomy, golf, horseback riding, hunting, fishing. Home: 811 Spring St Latrobe PA 15650-2025 Office: Latrobe Area Hosp 2D Avenue E Latrobe PA 15650-3225

BERCAW, JOHN EDWARD, chemistry educator, consultant; b. Cin., Dec. 3, 1944; s. James Witherow and Mary Josephine (Heywood) B.; m. Teresa Diane Ingram, July 10, 1965; children—David Lawrence, Karin Elizabeth. B.S. in Chemistry, N.C. State U., 1967; Ph.D. in Chemistry, U. Mich., 1971. Postdoctoral U. Chgo., 1971-72; A.A. Noyes fellow Calif. Inst. Tech., Pasadena, 1972-74, asst. prof. chemistry, 1974-77, assoc. prof. chemistry, 1977-79, prof. chemistry, 1979-93, Centennial prof. chemistry, 1993—, Shell Disting. prof., 1985-90; cons. Exxon Corp., Annandale, N.J., 1979—. Fellow Am. Acad. Arts and Scis.; mem. NAS, AAAS, Am. Chem. Soc. (chmn. divsn. inorganic chemistry 1988-89, organometallic subdivsn. chair 1980, chmn. Gordon Rsch. Conf. on Organometallic Chemistry 1991, award in pure chemistry 1980, award in organometallic chemistry 1990, award for disting. svc. in inorganic chemistry 1997, George A. Olah award for hydrocarbon or petroleum chemistry 1999). Home: 1455 Afton St Pasadena CA 91103-2702 Office: Calif Inst Tech 1201 E California Blvd Pasadena CA 91125-0001

BERCEL, NICHOLAS ANTHONY, neurologist, neurophysiologist; b. Budapest, Hungary, Aug. 20, 1911; came to U.S., 1940; s. Desiré and Julia (Kapos) B.; m. Eva Mindszenti, Mar. 25, 1982; children: Diana, Anthony, Christopher, Patrick, Yvette. MD, U. Rome, 1936., 1940; Resident U. Rome, 1936-38, U. Paris, 1938-40; intern Swedish Hosp., Mpls., 1958—; assoc. prof. in physiology U. So. Calif., L.A., 1948-67; mem. staff St. John Hosp., Santa Monica, 1954-84; mem. staff dept. neurodiagnosis Queen of Angels Hosp., L.A., 1960-80; neuro-psychiat. cons. Social Security Adminstrn., West Los Angeles, 1958—. Author: Textbook on Etiology of Schizophrenia, Psychopathology, 1959; contbr. numerous articles to profl. publs., including Diseases of the Nervous System, Jour. of Neuropsychiatry, Jour. AMA, Calif. Medicine, Am. Jour. Med. Scis., others. Republican. Achievements include research on experimental epilepsy for testing the comparative activity of anticonvulsants; schizophrenic serum influence on spider beahvior; schizophrenic model psychoses induced with LSD-25.

BERCHEM, ROBERT LEE, SR., lawyer; b. Milford, Conn., Aug. 17, 1941; s. Robert W. and Barbara (Maher) B.; m. Lee Contrucci, Feb. 19, 1966; children: Kerry, Robert L. Jr., Jonathan. AB, Fairfield U., 1962; LLB, Villanova U., 1965; LLM, U. Mich., 1967. Bar: Conn. 1965. Law clk. U.S. Dist. Ct., Conn., 1965-66; prin. Berchem, Moses & Devlin, P.C., Milford, 1967—. Trustee Fairfield (Conn.) U.; chmn. Milford Hist. Dist. Commn., 1976—. Mem. ABA, Conn. Bar Assn., New Haven County Bar Assn., Milford Bar Assn. Democrat. Roman Catholic. Avocations: golf, skiing. Home: 125 W River St Milford CT 06460-3420 Office: Berchem Moses & Devlin PC 75 Broad St Milford CT 06460-3331

BERCOVICI, MARTIN WILLIAM, lawyer; b. Omaha, Nov. 7, 1942; s. Jacob and Ethelyn (Kramer) B.; m. Ellen Pokress, Aug. 7, 1971; children: Jason M., Lauren P., Nicole J. BS, U. Mo., 1964; JD, NYU, 1967. Bar: D.C. 1968, Calif. 1969, U.S. Ct. Appeals (D.C. cir. 1969), U.S. Supreme Ct. 1973, U.S. Ct. Appeals (5th cir.) 1980, U.S. Ct. Appeals (fed. cir.) 1985, U.S. Ct. Appeals (7th cir.) 1987, U.S. Ct. Appeals (6th cir.) 1990. Teaching fellow George Washington U. Law Sch., Washington, 1967-68; law clk. to Hon. Joseph C. Waddy U.S. Dist Ct. D.C., 1968; asst. prof. San Diego State Coll., 1968-69; assoc. Keller & Heckman, Washington, 1969-73, ptnr., 1973—; v.p. legal Waterway Comms. System, Inc., Jeffersonville, Ind., 1986-93; mem. U.S. Del. to World Adminstrv. Radio Conf. for the Mobile Svcs.; vice-chmn. Fed. Adv. Comm. for the World Adminstrv. Radio Conf. for the Mobile Svcs., Washington, 1985-87, Fed. Comms. Commn., Geneva, 1987; exec. dir. Alliance for Rail Competition, Washington. Mem. ABA. Office: Keller & Heckman 1001 G St NW Ste 500W Washington DC 20001-4545

BERCOVITCH, SACVAN, English language professional, educator; b. Montreal, Que., Can., Oct. 4, 1933; s. Alexander and Brytha (Avrutick) B.; children: Eytan, Alexander. B.A., Sir George William Coll., 1961; M.A., Claremont (Calif.) Grad. Sch., 1963, Ph.D., 1965; LittD (hon.), Concordia U., 1993. Asst. prof. English and Am. lit. Brandeis U., 1966-68; asso. prof. U. Calif., San Diego, 1968-70; prof. English and Am. Lit. Columbia U., 1970-83; prof. English and Am. lit. Harvard U., 1983—; lectr., Kyoto, Tokyo, Shanghai, Beijing, Amsterdam, Frankfurt, Konstanz, Lisbon, Jerusalem, Tel Aviv, Salzburg, Coimbra, Montreal, Rome, Budapest, Paris, Venice, Bologna, Toronto, Oxford, Berlin, Yale U., Princeton U., U. Pa., U. Calif., Berkeley, L.A., San Diego, Irvine, Cornell U., Dartmouth Coll., Concordia Coll., Claremont Grad. Sch.; advisor, cons. in field. Author: Typology and Early American Literature, 1972, The American Puritan Imagination, 1974, The Puritan Origins of the American Self, 1975, The American Jeremiad, 1978, Reconstructing American Literary History, 1986, Ideology and Classic American Literature, 1986, The Office of the Scarlet Letter, 1991, The Rites of Assent: Transformations in the Symbolic Construction of America, 1992; gen. editor: Cambridge History of American Literature. Am. Philos. Soc. fellow, 1968-69, Guggenheim fellow, 1969-70, Am. Coun. Learned Socs. fellow, 1971-72, Nat. Humanities Inst. fellow, 1975-76, Ctr. for Advanced Study in Behavioral Scis. fellow, 1978-79, NEH fellow, 1978-79, 86-87, Woodrow Wilson Ctr. fellow, 1990-91, Time-Life fellow Huntington Libr., 1994—, Cabot fellow for achievement in humanities; recipient James Russell Lowell prize for scholarship, award for excellency in teaching. Fellow Am. Acad. Arts and Scis.; mem. MLA (mem. exec. com. Am. sect. 1976-78), English Inst., Am. Studies Assn. (pres. 1982-84).

BERCU, BARRY B., pediatric endocrinologist; b. Montreal, Aug. 10, 1944; m. Sandra Minkin, 2 children. BS, U. Md., 1965, MD, 1969. Diplomate Nat. Bd. Med. Examiners, Am. Bd. Pediatrics, Am. Bd. Pediatric Endocrinology; lic. physician, Mass., Md., Fla. Med. intern V and VI Med. Svc. Boston City Hosp., 1969-70; asst. and sr. resident pediatrics Mass. Gen. Hosp., Boston, 1970-72; clin. and rsch. fellow pediatric endocrinology & metabolism Harvard Med. Sch., Boston, 1974-77; clin. and rsch. fellow endocrinology dept. internal medicine Tufts U. Med. Sch., New Eng. Med. Ctr., Boston, 1974-77; clin. assoc. Nat. Inst. Child Health and Human Devel., NIH, Bethesda, Md., 1977-79, head pediatric endocrine unit neonatal & pediatric med. br., 1979-82, head pediatric endocrine unit, pregnancy rsch. br., 1982-84; assoc. prof. pediatrics Uniformed Svcs. U., Bethesda Naval Ctr., 1980-84; assoc. rsch. prof. child health and devel. George Washington U. Sch. Medicine and Health Scis., Washington, 1983-84; prof. pediatrics, prof. pharmacology and therapeutics U. South Fla. Coll. Medicine, Tampa, 1984—, pres. faculty coun., 1990-97; grant reviewer various orgns.; chmn., Univ. IRB Com.; mem. Dir.'s Conf. on Uses and Abuses of Growth Hormone in Children, Nat. Inst. Child Health and Human Devel., NIH, 1983—; mem. med. adv. bd. Parent Coun. for Growth Normality, 1985—; mem. pediatric clin. oncology group Community Clin. Oncology Program, 1989—; mem. staff All Children's Hosp., St. Petersburg, 1984—, Shriners Hosp., Tampa, 1985—, Tampa Gen. Hosp., 1986—, others; chmn. Internat. Symposium on Growth Hormone, Tampa, 1985, Perinatal Thyroidology, Longboat Key, Fla., 1990, Growth Hormone, Tarpon Springs, Fla., 1992, Internat. Symposium on Growth Hormone Releasing Secretagogues, 1994, Second Internat. Symposium on Growth Hormone Secretagogues, 1997, Therapeutic Outcome of Endocrine Disorders: Efficacy, Innovation and Quality of Life, 1997, Internat. Symposium on Endocrine and Molecular Interventions in Aging, 1998, Forum on Drug and Hormone Interventions in Aging, 1998, Endocrinology of Aging, 1999. Mem. editorial bd. Jour. Clin. Endocrinology and Metabolism, 1986-89, Jour. Anti-Aging Medicine, 1998—; editorial manuscript reviewer Acta Endocrinologica, Am. Jour. Nutrition, Biol. Psychiatry, Biology of Reprodn., Clin. Endocrinology, Clin. Pediatrics, Endocrine Jour., Endocrine Revs., Endocrinology, European Jour. Pediatrics, Hormone and Metabolic Rsch., Jour. AMA, Jour. Clin. Endocrinology and Metabolism, Jour. Clin. Investigation, Metabolism, others; contbr. articles to profl. jours.; patentee in field. Bd. dirs. Birth Defects Found., Fla. Bay Area chpt., 1991—, chmn. med. adv. com., 1991; mem. expert divsn. vaccine injury compensation and mem. bd. dirs. USF Divsn. Sponsored Rsch., 1994-95. Grantee BioNebr., Eli Lilly and Co., Genentech Corp., Daniel Pharm. Corp., Serono Labs., Am. Cancer Soc. Fla., ICN Pharms., Merck & Co., Novonordisk, Pharmacia Peptides, Inc., Pharmacia & Upjohn, Wyeth-Ayerst, Alkermes. Mem. AMA, Am. Acad. Pediatrics (endocrinology sect.), Am. Assn. Clin. Endocrinologists, Am. Fedn. Clin. Rsch., Am. Pediatric Soc., Am. Pituitary Assn., Endocrine Soc., Fla. Endocrine Soc., Fla. Med. Assn., Hillsborough County Med. Assn., Hillsborough County Pediatric Soc., Lawson Wilkins Soc. Pediatric Endocrinology, Soc. Pediatric Rsch., So. Soc. Pediatric Rsch., Tampa Bay Area Soc. Neurosci. Office: All Childrens Hosp USF Coll Medicine 801 6th St S Saint Petersburg FL 33701-4899

BERCZI, ANDREW STEPHEN, academic administrator, educator; b. Budapest, Hungary, Aug. 15, 1934; s. Stephen Andrew and Iren Maria (Bartha) B.; m. Susan Bartok, Aug. 30, 1958; children—Thomas Edgar, Peter Alexander. E.E., U. Tech. Scis., Budapest, 1956; B.Sc., Sir George Williams U., 1961, B.A., 1963; M.B.A., McGill U., 1965, Ph.D., 1972. Engr. Bell Telephone Co., Montreal, 1956-59, mem. hdqrs. staff acctg., 1959-62, supr. computer systems, 1962-65; prof. quantitative methods, chmn. dept. quantitative methods Sir George Williams U., 1965-71; dean Faculty of Commerce and Adminstrn. Concordia U., Montreal, 1971-77; dean Faculty of Grad. Studies Wilfrid Laurier U., Waterloo, Ont., Can., 1978-87, v.p. fin. and adminstrn., 1987-98, prof. mgmt. scis., 1998-99; prof. ops. and decisions scis. Wilfrid Laurier U., Waterloo, Ont., 1999—; cons. govtl. agys., pvt. industry; lectr. U. Calif. at Berkeley, U. Va., U. Chgo. Author: Exercises in Management Science, 1968, Problems in Managerial Operations Research, Vol. I and II, 1969, The Stock Exchange - A Total System Approach, 1970; contbr. over 80 articles and papers to profl. jours. and assns. McConnell fellow, 1965-66; Canada Council fellow, 1966-67; Quebec Province scholar, 1967-68. Fellow AAAS.; mem. IEEE, Operations Research Soc. Am., Canadian Operations Research Soc., Inst. Mgmt. Scis., Assn. Systems Mgmt., Fin. Execs. Inst., Acad. of Mgmt., Am. Statis. Assn. Home: 76 McCarron Crescent, Waterloo, ON Canada N2L 5N1 Office: 75 University Ave W, Waterloo, ON Canada N2L 3C5*

BERDAHL, ROBERT MAX, academic administrator, historian, educator; b. Sioux Falls, S.D., Mar. 15, 1937; s. Melvin Oliver and Mildred Alberta (Maynard) B.; m. Margaret Lucille Ogle, Aug. 30, 1958; children—Daphne Jean, Jennifer Lynne, Barbara Elizabeth. B.A., Augustana Coll., 1959; M.A., U. Ill., 1961; Ph.D., U. Minn., 1965. Asst. prof. history U. Mass., Boston, 1965-67; asst. prof. history U. Oreg., Eugene, 1967-72; assoc. prof. U. Oreg., 1972-81, prof., 1981-86; dean U. Oreg. (Coll. Arts and Scis.), 1981-86; prof. U. Ill., 1986-93, vice chancellor academic affairs, 1986-93; pres. U. Tex., Austin, 1993-97; chancellor U. Calif., Berkeley, 1997—; research asso. Inst. for Advanced Study, Princeton, 1972-73. Author: The Politics of Prussian Nobility, 1988; (with others) Klassen und Kultur, 1982; contbr. articles to profl. jours. Fulbright fellow, 1975-76; Nat. Endowment Humanities fellow, 1976-77. Office: U Calif at Berkeley 200 California Hall Berkeley CA 94720-7464

BERDICK, LEONARD STANLEY, insurance broker; b. New Rochelle, N.Y., Aug. 13, 1938; s. Julius and Fay (Jaffe) B.; m. Arlene Jean Kaufman, Oct. 31, 1968. B.A., Colgate U., 1960; M.A., Columbia U., 1963; student, U. N.C. Law Sch., 1960-61. Mem. Nat. Assn. Life Underwriters, Acad. Polit. Sci., Colgate U., Columbia U., U. N.C. alumni assns. Jewish. Club: Colgate Univ. Home: 80 Richmond Hill Rd Staten Island NY 10314-7581 Office: 5 E 41st St # 129 New York NY 10017-6205

BERDON, ROBERT IRWIN, state supreme court justice; b. New Haven, Dec. 24, 1929; s. Louis J. and Jean (Cohen) B.; m. Nancy Tarr, Aug. 30, 1964 (dec. Mar. 1992); 1 child, Peter A. BS, U. Conn., 1951, JD, 1957; LLM in Jud. Process, U. Va., 1988. With Bank of Manhattan, 1953-54; pvt. practice New Haven, 1957-73; treas. State of Conn., 1971-73; judge Superior Ct., State of Conn., New Haven, 1973-91; justice Supreme Ct., State of Conn., 1991—; adj. prof. law U. Bridgeport Sch. Law, 1986-91; lectr. in law U. Conn. Sch. of Law, 1993; assoc. fellow Saybrook Coll., Yale U., 1986—; lectr. Am. Bd. Trial Advs., 1986; mem. Conn. Bd. Pardons, 1991-92. Contbr. articles to profl. jours. Recipient Judiciary award Conn. Trial Lawyers Assn., 1976, Disting. Alumni award U. Conn., 1977, Outstanding State Trial Judge in U.S. award Assn. Trial Lawyers in Am., 1982, Pub. Svc. award U. Conn. Sch. Law Alumni Assn., 1989, Judiciary award Conn. Bar Assn., 1991. Home: 245 Pleasant Point Rd Branford CT 06405-5609 Office: Conn Supreme Court Drawer Z Sta A 231 Capitol Ave Hartford CT 06106-1548

BEREK, PETER, English educator; b. Bklyn., June 20, 1940; s. Leo and Ida (Kantrowitz) B.; m. Ellen H. Stark, June 10, 1962; children—Rachel, Martha, Elizabeth. B.A., Amherst Coll., 1961; M.A., Harvard U., 1963, Ph.D., 1967. Instr. English, Hamilton Coll., Clinton, N.Y., 1965-67; asst. prof. English, Williams Coll., Williamstown, Mass., 1967-72, assoc. prof., 1972-77, prof., 1977-90, dept. chmn., 1980-86, Morris prof. rhetoric, 1984-90, dean of coll., 1975-78, spl. asst. to pres., 1987-90; prof. English Mt. Holyoke Coll., South Hadley, Mass., 1990—, dean faculty, provost, 1990-98, interim pres., fall 1995; cons. NEH, Washington, 1973-76, 86-87, 89. Contbr. articles to profl. jours. Woodrow Wilson Found. fellow, 1961-62; NEH fellow, 1971-72, 82-83. Mem. MLA, Shakespeare Assn. Am., AAUP. Jewish. Home: 87 Woodlot Rd Amherst MA 01002-3452 Office: Mt Holyoke Coll Dept English South Hadley MA 01075

BERENATO, AGNUS MCGLADE, women's basketball coach; b. Dec. 9, 1956; m. Jack Berenato; children: Theresa Marie, Andrew, Joey, Clare, Christina. Student, U. N.C., 1976-77; BA in Sociology and Theology, Mt. St. Mary's Coll., Emmitsburg, Md., 1980, DHL (hon.), 1995. Profl. basketball player Entente Senonaise, Sens, France, 1975-76; head coach Rider Coll., 1981-85; asst. coach Ga. Tech U., 1986-88, head coach women's basketball, 1988—. Recipient Disting. Alumni award Mt. St. Mary's Coll., 1984; Sports Ethics fellow Inst. Internat. Sports, 1996. Mem. Atlanta Tipoff Club (nat. adv. bd.), Atlanta Women's Network Inc., Women's Basketball Coaches Assn., Ga. Women's Intersport Network, Atlanta Women in Sports, Naismith Hall of Fame. Office: Ga Tech Athletic Assn 150 Bobby Dodd Way NW Atlanta GA 30313-2551

BERENATO, ANTHONY FRANCIS, financial executive; b. Phila., Dec. 3, 1922; s. Frank A. and Eleanor A. (Siderio) B.; m. Dena Marie Marchione, Sept. 5, 1946; children—Anthony F., Mark Anthony. B.S. in Econs., Villanova U., 1949; postgrad., Am. U., Biarritz, France, 1945-46; student-philosophy and art appreciation, Barnes Found., 1966-68. C.P.A., Pa. Ptnr. Steinberg, Spiegel & Berenato, Springfield, Pa., 1956-91; pres. Roger Fin. Corp., Phila., 1961-63, Sure Loan Corp., Phila., 1961-65, Cobbs Fla. Cupboard Inc., Bala Cynwyd, Pa., 1965-67, Phila. Arena Corp., 1961-65; chmn. Crescent Iron Works, Phila., 1974-85; chmn., chief exec. officer Custom Art Metals Inc., Barrington, N.J., 1967-89; co-founder, mng. dir. OSA Environ. Svcs., Southampton, N.J., 1996; founder, chmn. Crescent Cab Co., Phila.; pres., CEO Custom Art Metals P.R. Inc., 1987-90. Trustee Anthony F. and Dena Marie Berenato Charitable Trust. Served with U.S.

Army, 1942-46, ETO, active Res. 1946-49. Fellow Am. Inst. Mgmt., Navy League of U.S. (life mem.), Pa. Soc., AICPA, Pa. Inst. CPAs, U.S. Naval Inst. (life), Am. Sec. Coun., Bala Golf Club (treas. 1974-76), Rio Mar Country Club (P.R.), Greate Bay Country Club, Rolling Green Golf Club, Hamilton Club. Republican. Roman Catholic. Home: 411 Scholar Ln Springfield PA 19064-0178

BERENBAUM, MAY ROBERTA, entomology educator; b. Trenton, N.J., July 22, 1953. BS, Yale U., 1975; PhD, Cornell U., 1980. Asst. prof. entomology U. Ill., Urbana-Champaign, 1980-85, assoc. prof. entomology, 1985-90, prof. entomology, 1990-95, head dept., 1992—, Swanlund prof. entomology, 1996—. Assoc. editor Am. Midland Naturalist, 1982-85; mem. editl. bd. Jour. Chem. Ecology, Chemoecology, Proceedings of the Nat. Acad. Scis. USA. Recipient Presdl. Young Investigator award NSF, 1984, Founder's award Entomol. Soc. Am., 1994; U. Ill. scholar, 1985-88. Mem. AAAS, NAS, Am. Philos. Soc., Am. Assn. Arts and Scis., Entomol. Soc. Am., Ecol. Soc. Am., Phytochem Soc. Am., Internat. Soc. Chem. Ecology, Sigma Xi. Achievements include research in chemical aspects of insect-plant interaction, evolutionary ecology of insects, phototoxicity of plant products, host-plant resistance. Office: U Ill Dept Entomology 320 Morrill Hall 505 S Goodwin Ave Urbana IL 61801-3707

BERENBAUM, MICHAEL GARY, foundation adminstrator, theology educator; b. Newark, July 3, 1945; s. Saul Berenbaum and Rhea Kass; m. Linda Bayer, Aug. 25, 1968 (div. July 1992); children: Ilana, Lev, Joshua; m. Melissa Patack, June 25, 1995. Student, Jewish Theol. Sem., 1963-67, Hebrew U., 1965-66; AB in Philosophy, Queens Coll., 1967; postgrad., Boston U., 1967-69; PhD in Religion and Culture, Fla. State U., 1975; DD (honoris causa), Narazeth Coll., Rochester, N.Y., 1995. Instr. dept. philosophy and religion Colby-Sawyer Coll., 1969-71; adj. asst. prof. religion, Jewish chaplain Wesleyan U., 1973-80; assoc. professorial lectr. dept. religion George Washington U., 1981-83; opinion page editor Washington Jewish Week, 1983-86, acting editor, 1985; sr. scholar Religious Action Ctr., 1986-88; Hymen Goldman prof. theology Georgetown U., 1983-97; rsch. fellow U.S. Holocaust Meml. Mus., 1987-88, project dir., 1988-93, dir. U.S. Holocaust Rsch. Inst., 1993-97; pres., CEO Survivors of Shoah Visual History Found., 1997—; prof. theology U. Judaism, 1998—; adj. prof. Judaic studies Am. U., 1987; assoc. dir.-Zachor: Holocaust Resource Ctr., 1978; dep. dir. Pres. Commn. on Holocaust, 1979-80; vis. prof. Hebrew Studies U. Md., 1983; assoc. Gannett Ctr. Media Studies Columbia U. Author: The Vision of the Void: Theological Reflections on the Works of Elie Wiesel, 1979, paper, 1987, reprinted as Elie Weisel: God, The Holocaust and the Children of Israel, 1994, The World Must Know: The History of the Holocaust as Told in the U.S. Holocaust Museum, After Tragedy and Triumph, 1990; editor: From Holocaust to New Life, 1985, Witness to the Holocaust, 1997, The Holocaust and History: The Known, The Unknown, The Disputed and The Reexamined, 1998; co-editor: Holocaust: Religious and Philosophical Implications, 1989, Anatomy of the Auschwitz Death Camp, 1996, What Kind of God?, 1997, The Holocaust and History, 1998; mem. editl. bd. Tikkun, Jour. Holocaust and Genocide Studies; contbg. editor Sh'ma; editor Together, 1986-89, The Holocaust and History, 1998. Recipient Simon Rockower Meml. award in Jewish journalism for Disting. Editl. Writing by Am. Jewish Press Assn., 1986, Disting. Coverage of Arts, 1987, Silver Angel award Religion and the Media, 1981, Outstanding Informational Emmy award for One Survivor Remembers, 1995, Cable Ace award for One Survivor Remembers, 1996; Ezra Styles fellow Yale U., 1979, Danforth Found. Underwood fellow, 1976-77, George Wise Tel Aviv U., 1974, Charles E. Merrill fellow Fla. State U., 1972-73. Fellow Soc. Values in Higher Edn. Democrat. Home: 2101 Hillsboro Ave Los Angeles CA 90034-1120 Office: Suvivors of the Shoah Visual History Found PO Box 3168 Los Angeles CA 90078-3168

BERENBEIM, RONALD EVERETT, business writer, educator; b. Denver, May 5, 1944; s. Samuel Leonard and Joan Madelon (Goodney) B.; m. Jane Susan Rosen, Mar. 25, 1979; children: Jessica Lucy, Sarah Katherine. AB cum laude, Cornell U., 1971; BA, Oxford (Eng.) U., 1968, MA, 1971; JD, Harvard U., 1971. Bar: Wash. 1973, Mass. 1974. Atty. Nat. Labor Rels. Bd., Seattle, 1971-73; bus. rep. Motion Picture and TV Union, N.Y.C., 1975-77; rsch. assoc. The Conf. Bd., Inc., N.Y.C., 1977-80, sr. rsch. assoc., 1980-97; dir. Working Group of Bus. Ethics Prins., N.Y.C., 1997—; prin. rschr. The Conf. Bd., Inc., N.Y.C., 1998—; prof. NYU, N.Y.C., 1990, Stern Sch. Bus. Adminstrn., 1995; dir. Working Group on Global Bus. Ethics Principles, N.Y.C., 1997—. Contbr. articles to profl. jours., chpts. to books. Keasbey Meml. scholar Balliol Coll., Oxford U., 1966. Mem. Nat. Assn. Corp. Dirs. (blue ribbon commn. on profl. bd. 1996). Home: 172 E 95th St New York NY 10128-2511 Office: The Conf Bd 845 3rd Ave New York NY 10022-6601

BERENBERG, WILLIAM, physician, educator; b. Haverhill, Mass., Oct. 29, 1915; s. Louis and Eva (Shapiro) B.; m. Blanche Berger, June 17, 1939 (dec.); children: Jeffrey, Richard (dec.), Barbara. AB, Harvard U., 1936; MD, Boston U., 1940. Diplomate Am. Bd. Pediatric Medicine. Intern Children's Hosp., Boston, 1941, resident, 1942-44, chief resident, 1945; instr. med. sch. Harvard U., Boston, 1945-50, assoc. prof., 1950-60, prof. pediatrics, 1960-80; prof. pediatrics Harvard-MIT Health Scis. & Tech., Cambridge, Mass., 1980-90; prof. emeritus Harvard-MIT Health Scis. & Tech., Cambridge, 1990—. Contbr. over 65 articles to profl. jours. V.p. med. affairs United Cerebral Palsy, N.Y.C., 1972, chmn. rsch. coun., 1972; life trustee Roxbury Latin Sch., West Roxbury, Mass., 1975. Recipient Presdl. Gold medal Govt. of Ecuador, Guayaquil, 1977, Weinstein award United Cerebral Palsy, 1978. Mem. Am. Acad. Cerebral Palsy (pres. 1968, Presdl. award 1987), Am. Acad. Pediatrics (state chmn. 1960), Am. Pediatric Soc., Soc. Pediatric Rsch., New Eng. Pediatric Soc. (pres. 1962), Rehab. Engring. Soc. N.Am. (E&J award 1984). Jewish. Avocations: swimming, boating. Office: Children's Hosp 300 Longwood Ave Boston MA 02115-5737

BERENDES, HEINZ WERNER, medical epidemiologist, pediatrician; b. Dortmund, Germany, May 1, 1925; came to U.S., 1953; s. Johannes and Swanette (Kayma) B.; children: Christoph Mathias, Andrea Maria, David Michael. MD, U. Goettingen, Germany, 1949; Dr. Medicine, U. Munich, 1952; MHS, Johns Hopkins U., 1972. Diplomate: Am. Bd. Epidemiology. Intern Abbott Hosp., Mpls., 1954; intern U. Minn. Hosp., 1954-55, resident, 1955-56; instr. dep. pediatrics U. Minn., Mpls., 1954-59, asst. prof., 1959-60; asst. dir. collaborative research Nat. Inst. Neurology Disorders and Stroke, NIH, Bethesda, Md., 1960; chief perinatal research br. Nat. Inst. Neurology Disorders and Stroke, NIH, Bethesda, 1960-73; chief contraceptive eval. br. Nat. Inst. Child Health and Human Devel. Bethesda, 1974-79; dir. epidemiology and biometry research program Nat. Inst. Child and Human Devel., Bethesda, 1979—; dir. prevention rsch. Nat. Inst. Child and Human Devel., 1990-91, assoc. dir. prevention rsch., 1987, dir. divsn. epidemiology, statistics and prevention rsch., 1991—, sr. investigator, 1999—; clin. prof. dept. pediatrics Howard U., Washington, 1961—; sr. assoc. dept. epidemiology Johns Hopkins U., Balt., 1982—; rsch. prof. pediatrics George Washington U., Washington, 1994—; mem. WHO Sci. Adv. Group, Geneva, 1979; cons. fertility and maternal health drug adv. com. FDA, Rockville, Md., 1979-86. Editor: (monograph) Pharmacology of Steroid Contraceptive Drugs, 1977; mem. editl. bd. Am. Jour. Pub. Health, 1993—, assoc. editor, 1996—. Pres. Watergate Assn., Bethany Beach Del., 1976-79. Recipient NIH Dirs. award NIH, 1979, Superior Svc. award U.S. Pub. Health Svc., 1991. Fellow Am. Coll. Epidemiology; mem. Soc. Epidemiol. Research. Home: 7020 Barkwater Ct Bethesda MD 20817-4402 Office: NICHD Divsn Epidem Stats Prevent 6100 Executive Blvd Bethesda MD 20892

BERENDI, ERLINDA BAYAUA, physician surgeon; b. Santiago, Isabela, The Philippines, Oct. 31, 1947; came to U.S., 1972; d. Jeremias Carreon and Amanda (Florentin) Bayaua; m. S. Alexander Berendi, Jan. 2, 1981. BS, U. Santo Tomas, Manila, 1966, MD, 1971. Med. dir. Great Pacific Life Ins. Co., Manila, 1971-72; intern, resident Michael Reese Hosp., Chgo., 1973-77; pres., physician, surgeon Consultative Exams., Inc., Chgo., 1980—; med. dir. Intracorp. Med. Rev. Svcs., Arlington Heights, Ill., 1987-89; pres. Finnegan's Choice, Inc., Chgo., 1985—; med. cons. Dept. Health and Human Svcs., Chgo., 1977-83, State of Ill., Dept. Rehab. Svcs., Chgo., 1981—; acting chmn. med. quality rev. com. Bur. of Program Integrity, Ill. Dept. Pub. Aid, Chgo., 1977—; physician cons. Comprehensive Health Svcs, Inc., Chgo., 1978-79; chief med. cons. U.S. R.R. Retirement Bd., 1981-95. Mem. AMA, Am. Acad. Family Physicians, Nat. Assn. Disability Examiners, N.Y. Acad. Scis. Avocations: running, weightlifting, piano. Home: 6666 N Tower Circle Dr Lincolnwood IL 60646-3221 Office: Consultative Exams Inc 55 E Washington St Ste 2101 Chicago IL 60602-2219

BERENDT, JOHN LAWRENCE, writer, editor; b. Syracuse, N.Y., Dec. 5, 1939; s. Ralph Sidney and Carol (Deschere) B. A.B., Harvard U., 1961. Assoc. editor Esquire Mag., N.Y.C., 1961-69; sr. staff editor Holiday Mag., N.Y.C., 1969; assoc. producer David Frost Show, N.Y.C., 1969-71; writer Dick Cavett Show, N.Y.C., 1973-75; editor N.Y. Mag., N.Y.C., 1977-79; columnist Esquire Mag., N.Y.C., 1982-94. Author: Midnight in the Garden of Good and Evil, 1994 (Pulitzer prize finalist for general non-fiction 1995); contbr. articles to profl. jours. Mem. PEN, Century Assn. Home and Office: 20 W 76th St New York NY 10023-1556

BERENDT, ROBERT TRYON, lawyer; b. Chgo., Mar. 8, 1939; s. Alex E. and Ethel L. (Tryon) B.; m. Sara Probert, June 15, 1963; children: David, Elizabeth, Katherine. BA, Monmouth Coll., 1961; JD with distinction, U. Iowa, 1965. Bar: Iowa 1965, Ill. 1968, U.S. Dist. Ct. (no. dist.) Ill. 1968, U.S. Ct. Appeals (7th cir.) 1968, Mo. 1979, U.S. Dist. Ct. (ea. dist.) Mo. 1979. Assoc. Schiff Hardin & Waite, Chgo., 1968-73, ptnr., 1973-78; litigation counsel Monsanto Co., St. Louis, 1978-83, asst. gen. counsel, 1983-85, assoc. gen. counsel, 1986-96; of counsel Thompson Coburn, St. Louis, 1996—; Disting. Neutral, Ctr. for Pub. Resources; editl. adv. bd. Alternatives, Inside Litigation, Product Safety and Liability Reporter-Bur. Nat. Affairs. Contbr. articles to profl. jours. Lt. USNR, 1965-68. Mem. ABA (litigation sect., coun. mem. 1993-96), Mo. Bar Assn., Ill. Bar Assn., Iowa Bar Assn., Bar Assn. Met. St. Louis, Product Liability Adv. Coun. (bd. dirs., exec. com., Inst. for the Judiciary, pres.-trustee Found. 1992-98). Avocations: golf, tennis, reading. Office: Thompson Coburn 1 Mercantile Ctr Saint Louis MO 63101-1643

BERENDZEN, RICHARD, astronomer, educator, author; b. Walters, Okla., Sept. 6, 1938; s. Earl Emmanuel and Florine Adora (Harrison) B.; m. Gail Anita Edgar, Nov. 26, 1964; children: Deborah Carol, Natasha Karina. BS, MIT, 1961; MA, Harvard U., 1967, PhD, 1969; LLD (hon.), W.Va. Wesleyan U., 1979, Kean Coll. of N.J., 1984, Seton Hall U., 1985, U. Charleston, 1986; LHD (hon.), Bridgewater Coll., 1983; DS (hon.), U. Columbo, Sri Lanka, 1985; LLD (hon.), U. Balt., 1990. Staff scientist Geophysics Corp. Am., 1959-64, Ling-Temco-Vought, 1961-62; lectr. Harvard U., 1964, 66; mem. staff Project Physics, 1965; mem. faculty Boston U., 1965-73, assoc. prof. astronomy, 1971-73, acting dept. chmn., 1971-72; prof. physics, dean Coll. Arts and Scis., Am. U., Washington, 1974-76; univ. provost Am. U., Washington, 1976-79, pres., 1980-90, prof., 1990—; commentator on edn. and astronomy Stas. WUSA-TV/WTOP, Washington, 1984-90; cons. NASA, 1991, 98; cons. space sci. bd. NAS, 1973-74, mem. panel astron. survey com., 1971-73; cons. acad. affairs Am. Coun. on Edn., 1973-74; cons. to pub. cos.; holder numerous lectureships; Am. specialist in Asia Am. Council Edn. and Dept. State; adv. Am. Inst. Physics, Library of Congress, Internat. Communication Agy., UNESCO, Smithsonian Instn., NSF; univ. evaluator Commn. Higher Edn. Middle States Assn. Colls. and Secondary Schs.; chmn. priorities and planning com. Assn. Am. Colls., 1978-80, chmn. pres.'s adv. com., 1977-79; program evaluator U.S. Armed Forces Inst.; mem. rev. panel human resources NRC; lectr. USIA; host spls. on astronomy and higher edn. NBC-TV, 1976-77; organizer Space 2000 Symposium, 1998; frequent guest radio and TV shows; researcher on cosmology, history of astronomy, sci. and soc., Am. and internat. edn. Author: Education in and History of Modern Astronomy, 1972, Life Beyond Earth and the Mind of Man, 1973, Man Discovers the Galaxies, 1976, Is My Armor Straight? A Year in the Life of a University President, 1986, Come Here: A Man Overcomes the Tragic Aftermath of Childhood Sexual Abuse, 1993; founding editor Jour. Coll. Sci. Teaching; contbr. numerous articles and revs. to profl. jours. Bd. dirs. Bus. Coun. for Internat. Understanding, 1980-84, Assn. Am. Colls., 1981-83, European Inst., Group Hospitalization Med. Svc. Inc., Nat. Network for Youth, Inc., 1994-97; chmn. Com. on Fng. Students and Instl. Policy, 1981-82; chmn. Employment/Edn. Bur. Greater Washington Bd. Trade, 1989; co-chmn. AIDS project Meyer Found., 1988-90; mem. D.C. Com. on Pub. Schs., 1988—; chmn. D.C. Commn. on Budget and Fin. Priorities, 1989-90, 94; mem. NASA Exploration Adv. Task Force, 1988-91; chmn. bd. dirs. Orphan Found. Am., 1996-97. Named one of Top Young Educators Change: Mag. of Learning, 1978; recipient Mortar Bd. Faculty award, 1977, Freedoms Found. Valley Forge award, 1982, Glenn T. Seaborg award Internat. Platform Assn., 1997; fellow Com. Scientists Investigating Claims of the Paranormal, 1977-78. Fellow AAAS; mem. Internat. Astron. Union, Internat. Assn. Univ. Pres., Am. Astron. Soc., Am. Assn. U. Adminstrs., Am. Assn. for Higher Edn., Internat. Assn. Univs., N.Y. Acad. Scis., Am. Assn. Physics Tchrs., Astron. Soc. Pacific, History of Sci. Soc., Nat. Sci. Tchrs. Assn., Am. Assn. Higher Edn., Am. Conf. Acad. Deans, Washington Inst. Fgn. Affairs, Cosmos Club, Sigma Xi, Kappa Mu Epsilon, Phi Eta Sigma, Phi Kappa Phi. Home: 1300 Crystal Dr Arlington VA 22202-3234 Office: Am U Dept Physics Washington DC 20016-8058

BERENFELD, MARK M., chemist; b. Moscow, Aug. 14, 1940; s. Moisey I. Berenfeld and Fanya I. Prosmushkina; m. Genya Berenfeld, Oct. 9, 1971; children: Benjamin, Sonya. BS, Engring. Inst., Moscow, 1965; MS, Lomonossov U., Moscow, 1970; PhD, Karpoff Sci. Inst. Physics, Moscow, 1974. Sr. scientist Pigment and Varnishes Co., Moscow, 1971-77, Dyestuff Co., Moscow, 1977-89; R&D chemist Fabricolor, Inc., Paterson, N.J., 1991-95; sr. sci. chemist Jos. H. Lowenstein, Inc., Bklyn., 1996—. Mem. Am. Chem. Soc. Home: 33 Sanderson Ave West Caldwell NJ 07006-7974

BERENGER, TOM (THOMAS MICHAEL MOORE), actor; b. Chgo., May 31, 1950. Actor stage prodns. The Rose Tattoo, Streetcar Named Desire, End as a Man, Electra; motion pictures include Beyond the Door, 1975, The Sentinel, 1977, Looking for Mr. Goodbar, 1977, In Praise of Older Women, 1979, Butch and Sundance: The Early Days, 1979, The Dogs of War, 1981, The Big Chill, 1983, Eddie and the Cruisers, 1983, Firstborn, 1984, Fear City, 1984, Rustler's Rhapsody, 1985, Platoon, 1987 (Oscar nomination), Someone to Watch Over Me, 1987, Betrayed, 1988, Love at Large, 1990, At Play in the Fields of the Lord, 1991, Sniper, 1993, Sliver, 1993, Gettysburg, 1993, Major League 2, 1994, Chasers, 1994, Last of the Dogmen, 1995, The Substitute, 1996, An Occasional Hell, 1996, The Gingerbread Man, 1997; TV movies include Johnny We Hardly Knew Ye, 1977, Flesh and Blood, 1979, Body Language, 1995, Avenging Angel, 1995; TV series include One Life to Live. Office: care CAA 9830 Wilshire Blvd Beverly Hills CA 90212-1804

BERENS, BETTY KATHRYN MCADAM, community program administrator; b. Wheeling, W.Va., Dec. 17, 1927; d. Will and Elizabeth Margaret (Wickham) McAdam; m. Alan Robert Berens, June 18, 1949; children: Robert Seton, Kathryn Elizabeth. Student, Radcliffe Coll., 1945-47; BA cum laude, Case Western Res. U., 1949; postgrad., Kent State U., 1967. Vol. various cities, Ohio, 1963-88; founder Western Res. Human Svcs., Akron, Ohio, 1975-84; cons. Hudson (Ohio) Local Schs., Addison County, Vt., 1968-88, coord. cmty./sch. vol. program (VIP); pres. aux. bd. Porter Med. Ctr., Middlebury, Vt., 1990-92; vol. Hawthornden State Hosp., Cleve., 1963-65; vol. probation officer Mcpl. Ct., Cuyahoga Falls, Ohio, 1973-74; comm. chmn. Elderly Svcs. Inc., Middlebury, 1990-95; cmty. sch. vol. cons. Ohio Dept. Edn., Columbus, 1984-88; bd. dirs. Addison County Home Health Care Agy., Champlain Valley Agy. on Aging. Bd. dirs. Porter Med. Ctr., 1990-92; bd. dirs. Internat. Inst., Akron, 1983-88, pres., 1986-87; mem. Summit County Bd. Edn., Akron, 1977-88, pres., 1981, 86; chmn. Hudson Cares, 1974-76; comm. chmn. Addison County United Way. Recipient Cmty. Svc. award Hudson Jaycees, 1984, Commendation for Outstanding Svc. in Edn., Pres. Ronald Reagan, 1988. Mem. Phi Delta Kappa (Leader in Edn. 1977, 88). Avocations: volunteering, family, knitting, cross-country skiing, canoeing. Home: 5931 Snake Mountain Rd Weybridge VT 05753-9749

BERENS, E. ANN, writer, mental health and youth advocate; b. Worthing, Eng., Sept. 28, 1930; came to U.S., 1962; d. Samuel Lister and Edith Emily (Harragin) James; m. Robin Hugh Berens, Sept. 22, 1956; children: Carolyn, Keith. Student, Bedford (Eng.) Tng. Coll., 1949-52. Tchr.'s cert. Nat. Froebel Found. Kindergarten and primary tchr. Copythorne Sch. and Ringwood Sch., Hampshire, Eng., 1952-55; childcare worker Protestant Children's Homes, Toronto, Ont., Can., 1956-59; v.p. Berens Assocs. Inc., Emeryville, Calif., 1966-92; presenter 5th World Congress Logotherapy, 1985, 8th,, 1991. Contbr. articles to profl. publs. Vol., chmn. mini course program Claremont Jr. H.S., Oakland, Calif., 1972; vol. for mentally ill Creative Living Ctr., Berkeley, Calif., 1975-97, chmn. adv. bd., 1996-97; group facilitator search for meaning Life Plan Ctr., San Francisco, 1996—; sec. bd. dirs. The Orgn. for Youth Svcs. Toys, Lafayette, Calif., 1994-97, editor newsletter, 1995-97; sec., bd. dirs. KLOUT for Kids. Mem. Inst. Logotherapy (bd. dirs. 1985-89). Mem. United Ch. of Christ. Home: 56 Camino Del Diablo Orinda CA 94563-2037

BERENS, MARK HARRY, lawyer; b. St. Paul, Aug. 4, 1928; s. Harry C. and Gertrude M. (Scherkenbach) B.; m. Barbara Jean Steichen, Nov. 20, 1954; children: Paul J., Joseph F. (dec.), John M., Stephen M., Thomas M., Michael M., Lisa M., James M., Daniel M. BS in Commerce, Acctg. magna cum laude, U. Notre Dame, 1950, JD magna cum laude, 1951; postgrad., U. Chgo., 1951-53. Bar: Ill. 1951, D.C. 1955, U.S. Supreme Ct. 1971; CPA, Ill. James Nelson Raymond grad. rsch. fellow U. Chgo. Law Sch., 1951-53; assoc. Mayer, Brown & Platt, and predecessors, Chgo., 1956-61; ptnr. Mayer, Brown & Platt, and predecessors, 1961-96; chmn., CEO Attys.' Liability Assurance Soc., Inc., Chgo., 1987-95; ptnr. Altheimer & Gray, Chgo., 1996—; chmn. bd. dirs. Attys.' Liability Assurance Soc. (Bermuda) Ltd., 1979-95; bd. dirs. Lancer Fin. Group, Accts. Liability Assurance Co.; nat. chmn. Nat. Assn. Law Rev. Editors, 1950-51. Editor-in-chief Notre Dame Law Rev., 1950-51; contbr. articles to profl. jours. 1st lt. JAGC U.S. Army, 1953-56. Mem. ABA, D.C. Bar Assn., Chgo. Bar Assn., Internat. Bar Assn., Am. Law Inst., The Comml. Bar Assn. (London), Am. Assn. Atty.-CPAs, Union League Club, Law Club, Legal Club, Met. Club, Sunset Ridge Country Club (Northbrook). Republican. Roman Catholic. Home: 1660 North Ln Northbrook IL 60062-4708 Office: Altheimer & Gray 10 S Wacker Dr Fl 35 Chicago IL 60606-7482

BERENS, WILLIAM JOSEPH, lawyer; b. New Ulm, Minn., Dec. 12, 1952; s. Robert J. and Lorraine M. (O'Brien) B.; m. Janet Christiansen, June 13, 1975; children: Margaret, Elizabeth, Catherine. BA, Coll. St. Thomas, 1975; JD, U. Minn., 1978. Bar: Minn. 1978. Assoc. Dorsey & Whitney, LLP, Mpls., 1978-83, ptnr., 1984—; adj. prof. William Mitchell Coll. of Law, St. Paul, 1981-84. Fellow Am. Coll. Trust and Estate Counsel. Home: 1601 Beechwood Ave Saint Paul MN 55116-2409 Office: Dorsey & Whitney LLP 220 S 6th St Ste 2200 Minneapolis MN 55402-1498

BERENSON, PAUL STEWART, advertising executive; b. Boston, Aug. 28, 1944; s. Joseph and Estelle Ada (Isenberg) B.; m. Tilly Lemler, Nov. 19, 1966 (div. 1984). AAS in Nuclear Engring., Wentworth Inst., 1964; Diploma in Bus. Adminstrn., Northeastern U., 1968. Editor Sylvania Electric Systems, Waltham, Mass., 1965-67; editor, writer Honeywell EDP, Newton, Mass., 1967-69; ptnr., writer Waldon Assocs., Newton, 1969-71; ptnr. Insight Advt., Boston, 1971-73; chair, CEO Berenson and Isham, Inc., Boston, 1973—; chmn. New Market Ventures, Boston, 1995, Data Applications Inc., Boston, 1995; instr. direct mktg. mgmt. Bentley Coll., 1989—; advt. cons. Silver Edits., Larkspur, Calif., 1985-86; cons. various mktg. groups, 1973—. Author: Venture Capital and Management, 1971; writer, editor computer course, 1987. Dir. Mass. Found. for Children, 1993-94. With Army N.G., 1964-70. Recipient awards Advt. Club Greater Boston, Art Dirs. Club, Good Samaritans, Bus./Profl. Advt. Assn., Addy award. Mem. Am. Mktg. Assn., New Eng. Direct Mktg. Assn. (pres. 1995-96), Art Dirs. Club, Advt. Club (trustee), Direct Mktg. Club, Gt. Dane of N.E. Club (pres. 1979-82). Avocations: fishing, boating, collecting stamps and coins. Office: Berenson Isham & Ptnrs Inc 31 Milk St Boston MA 02109-5104

BERENSON, ROBERT LEONARD, advertising agency executive; b. Chgo., Nov. 14, 1939; s. James Morton and Harriet Ruth (Fisher) B.; m. Terry Reiner, Nov. 14, 1993; 1 child, Cindy Elizabeth. BA, Syracuse U., 1961; MS in Journalism, Northwestern U., 1962. Mgmt. trainee Grey Advt., Inc., N.Y.C., 1964-67; v.p., account supr. Grey Advt., Inc., 1967-70, v.p., mgmt. supr., 1970-71, sr. v.p., mgmt. rep., 1971-77, exec. v.p., 1977-82, exec. v.p. adminstrn. and account mgmt., 1982-92; pres. Grey Advt., Inc., N.Y.C., 1993—; guest lectr. mktg. U. Conn., Syracuse U., Northwestern U., St. John's U., 1974-88; bd. dirs. Burgundy Wine Co. Bd. dirs. Better Bus. Bur.; chmn., bd. dirs. Fed. Law Enforcement Found. 1st lt. U.S. Army, 1962-64. Jewish. Home: 777 Third Ave New York NY 10017 Office: Grey Advt Inc 777 3rd Ave New York NY 10017-1401*

BERENSON, STEPHEN, actor, educator; b. N.Y.C., Mar. 29, 1953; s. Jerome and Veronica Shirley (Grumbach) B. BFA, Drake U., 1975; cert. of completion, Hartman Theatre Conservatory, 1977. Acting instr. AMAS Reperatory Theatre, N.Y.C., 1977-85; master acting tchr. Ednl. Testing Svc., Miami, 1985; mem. acting co., theatre assoc. Bread Loaf Sch. of English, Middlebury, Vt., 1984—; mem. Trinity Repertory Co., Providence, R.I., 1989—; co-dir. Trinity Repertory Conservatory, Providence, 1990—; vis. artist Profl. Children's Sch., N.Y.C., 1983-85; mem. acting faculty Roundabout Theatre Conservatory, N.Y.C., 1984-85; adj. faculty R.I. Coll., Providence, 1996—; mgr. subscriptions/groups N.Y.C. Ctr., 1982-84; supr. Vivian Beaumont Theatre-Lincoln Ctr., N.Y.C., 1981-82. Bd. dirs. Perishable Theatre, Providence, 1985-88. Grantee Nat. Endowments for Arts, Nelal Tchg. grant. Mem. AFTRA, Actor's Equity Assn. (dep. coun. on conversion contracts 1981), Screen Actors Guild. Democrat. Jewish. Office: Trinity Reperatory Co 201 Washington St Providence RI 02903-3297

BERENSON, WILLIAM KEITH, lawyer; b. Nashville, Nov. 23, 1954; s. Leon and Lorraine Florence (Keiles) B; m. Mara Lynn Rubinton; 1 child, Marissa Laurel. BA with honors, U. Tex., 1976; JD, So. Meth. U., 1979. Bar: Tex. 1979, U.S. Dist. Ct. (no. dist.) Tex., U.S. Ct. Appeals (5th and 11th cirs.), U.S. Supreme Ct.; cert. personal injury trial law, Tex. Bd. Legal Specialization. mem. Supreme Ct. Jury Task Force. Author: Evaluating Settlement Offers, 1990, Texas Automobile Injury Guide, 1993, Trying the Automobile Injury Case in Texas: Plaintiff's Perspective, 1995, Automobile Injury Cases in Texas, 1996, Quantification of Personal Injury Claims, 1997; mem. editl. bd. Ins. Settlement and Litigation Reporter; mem. editl. adv. bd. Ins. Issues Annotated. Chmn. Longhorn Coun. Boy Scouts Am., Ft. Worth; bd. dirs. So. Meth. U. Alumni Assn., AIDS Interfaith Network; dir. Regional Coun. of Parents and Alumni, So. Meth. U.; vol. atty. North Tex. Humane Soc. Fellow Tarrant County Bar Found.; mem. ABA, ATLA (sustaining mem. pub. interest group com.), State Bar Tex., Tex. Bar Assn., Tarrant County Bar Assn. (jud. evaluation com., fee arbitration com.), Tarrant County Lawyrs Assn. (bd. dirs. 1994-99), Tex. Trial Lawyers Assn., Coll. State Bar Tex., Nat. Coll. Advocacy, Roscoe Pound Found., Phi Alpha Delta. Avocations: golf, snow skiing. Office: 900 River Plaza Tower 1701 River Run Fort Worth TX 76107-6579

BERENT, IRWIN MARK, writer, software executive; b. Norfolk, Va., Feb. 10, 1958; s. Nathan and Selma Faye (Caplan) B. BA in History, Old Dominion U., 1980; MA in Am. History, East Carolina U., 1982. Dir. Monitor Rsch. and Recovery Found., Norfolk, 1980-82; exec. dir. The Speakers' Agy., Norfolk, 1988—; v.p. StoryCraft Corp., Norfolk, 1994—; speaker in field. Author: Fundamentalism, 1988, The Crew of the USS Monitor: A Biographical Dictionary, 1981, The Right Words, 1992, Drug Legalization: For and Against, 1992, Getting Your Words Worth, 1993, Jewish Genealogy, 1984, The Monuments and Statues of the Capitol Square of North Carolina, 1985, Weird Words, 1995, More Weird Words, 1995, History of Tidewater Jewry: 1900-1950, 1986, The Quotable Conservative, 1996, ABC of Cat Trivia, 1996, The Dictionary of Highly Unusual Words, 1997; developer Story Craft Fiction Writers Software. Avocations: philosophy, literature, ham radio, tennis. Home: 930 Rockbridge Ave Ste 134 Norfolk VA 23508 Office: StoryCraft Corp 930 Rockbridge Ave Ste 134 Norfolk VA 23508

BERENT, STANLEY, psychologist, educator, researcher, consultant; b. Norfolk, Va., Mar. 10, 1941; s. David and Esther (Laibstain) B.; m. Joy McKeever; children: Melissa Virginia, Alison Reneé, Rachel Irene. BS, Old Dominion U., 1966; MS, Va. Commonwealth U., 1967; PhD, Rutgers U., 1972. Diplomate Am. Bd. Profl. Psychology. Prof. U. Va., Charlottesville, 1972-79, U. Mich., Ann Arbor, 1979—; chief of psychology, VA Med. Ctr., Ann Arbor, 1979-85; vis. prof. U. London, 1988-89, China Rehab. Rsch. Ctr., Beijing, 1998—; pres., CEO, bd. dirs. NeuroBehavioral Resources, Inc., 1998—. Author 4 books, 18 book chpts.; contbr. more than 200 articles to profl. jours. Bd. dirs. Arbor Hills Assn., 1986-88. Served with USMC, 1959-63. Fellow Am. Psychol. Assn.; mem. Assn. Advancement Sci.,

Neurosci. Soc., Am. Epilepsy Soc., Am. Acad. Neurology. E-mail: sberent@umich.edu. Office: U Mich Hosps Box 0840 Med Inn Bldg Suite 480 Ann Arbor MI 48109-0840

BERENTSEN, KURTIS GEORGE, music educator, choral conductor; b. North Hollywood, Calif., Apr. 22, 1953; s. George O. and Eleanor J. (Johnson) B.; m. Jeanette M. Sacco, Aug., 1975 (div. 1977); m. Floy I. Griffiths, March 17, 1984; 1 child, Kendra Irene. MusB, Utah State U., 1975; MA in Music, U. Calif., Santa Barbara, 1986; cert. colloguy, Concordia Coll., 1996. Cert. cmty. coll. tchr., Calif., pub. tchr., Calif.; commd. minister Luth. Ch., Mo. Synod, 1996. Dir. music Hope Luth. Ch., Daly City, Calif., 1975-81; gen. mgr. Ostara Press, Inc., Daly City, Calif., 1975-78; condr. U. Calif., Santa Barbara, 1981-86; dir., condr. Santa Barbara oratorio Chorale, 1983-85; dir. music 1st Presbyn. Ch., Santa Barbara, 1983-84, Goleta (Calif.) Presbyn. Ch., 1984-85; minister music Trinity Luth. Ch., Ventura, 1985-92, Christ Luth. Ch. & Sch., Little Rock, Ark., 1992-98; dir. choral music Concordia U., Portland, Oreg., 1998—; instr. Ventura Coll., 1987-88; music dir., condr. Gold Coast Community Chorus, Ventura, 1988-92; choir dir. Temple Beth Torah Jewish Community, Ventura, 1982-87; adj. prof. Pepperdine U., Malibu, Calif., 1988; chorus master Ventura Symphony Orch., 1987; owner Music and Ch. Discount Suppliers, 1989-92. Condr. oratorios Christus Am Oelberg, 1983, Elijah, 1984, Hymn of Praise, 1988, cantata Seven Last Words, 1979, 84, Paukenmesse, 1989, Mozart's Requiem, 1990, Requiem-Fauré, 1991, Judas Maccabaeus-Handel, 1992; soloist 15 major oratorio and opera roles, 1971-92, Nat. Anthem, L.A. Dodgers, 1989; dir. (with John Rutter) Gold Coast Community Chorus, Carnegie Hall, N.Y.C., 1991, Tribute to America, Lincoln Ctr. Concert, N.Y.C., 1991. Min. music, tchr. Christ Luth. Ch. and Sch., Little Rock, 1992—. First place winner baritone vocalist Idaho Fedn. Music Clubs, 1971, recital winner Utah Fedn. Music Clubs, 1974. Mem. Choral Condrs. Guild, Assn. Luth. Ch. Musicians, Am. Guild of English Handbell Ringers, Sigma Nu (sec., song leader 1973-75). Home and Office: 2811 NE Holman St Portland OR 97211-6067

BERENZWEIG, JACK CHARLES, lawyer; b. Bklyn., Sept. 29, 1942; s. Sidney A. and Anne R. (Dubowe) B.; m. Susan J. Berenzweig, Aug. 8, 1968; children: Mindy, Andrew. B.E.E., Cornell U., 1964; J.D., Am. U., 1968. Bar: Va. 1968, Ill. 1969. Examiner U.S. Pat. Off., Washington, 1964-66; pat. adviser U.S. Naval Air Systems Command, Washington, 1966-68; ptnr. Brinks, Hofer, Gilson & Lione and predecessor firm, Chgo., 1968—. Editorial staff Am. U. Law Rev., 1966-68; contbr. articles to profl. jours. Mem. ABA, Chgo. Bar Assn., Ill. State Bar Assn., Bar Assn. 7th Fed. Cir., Va. State Bar, Internat. Trademark Assn. (bd. dirs. 1983-85), Brand Names Edn. Found. (bd. dirs. 1993-98), Meadow Club (Rolling Meadows, Ill.), Miramar Club (Naples, Fla., Delta Theta Phi. Home: 4119 Terramere Ave Arlington Heights IL 60004-1359 Office: Brinks Hofer Gilson & Lione Ltd Ste 3600 455 N Cityfront Plaza Dr Chicago IL 60611-5599

BERES, MICHAEL JOHN, plant engineer; b. Gary, Ind., June 26, 1950; s. Edward Kenneth and Joan Marie (Petrovich) B.; m. Susan Eileen Heminger, Oct. 26, 1973; children: Amanda Eileen, Matthew James. AAS, Purdue U., 1972, BS, 1973. Registered profl. engr., Ill. Estimator, field engr. J.M. Foster, Inc., Gary, 1973-74; civil engr. Brown & Root, Inc., Oakbrook, Ill., 1974-76; field piping engr. Dedelow, Inc., Gary, 1977; plant facilities engr. Reynolds Metals Co., McCook, Ill., 1977-88; constrn. mgr. midwest region Waste Mgmt. of N.Am., Inc., Westchester, Ill., 1988-91; project supt. Exec. Constrn., Inc., Downers Grove, Ill., 1992—; pres. Beres Engring., Downers Grove, 1993—; v.p. White-Whitfield & Assocs., Downers Grove, 1993—; plant engr. Heinemann's Bakeries, Inc., 1994—. Team leader Dupage County Pub. Action to Deliver Shelter, Downers Grove, Ill., 1983-92. Recipient Cert. of Recognition Gov. James R. Thompson. Roman Catholic. Club: Waste Mgmt., Inc. Midwest Region Golf League (pres. 1989-90), Reynolds Golf League (McCook, pres. 1981-87). Avocations: golf, basketball, tennis. Home and Office: 4210 Highland Ave Downers Grove IL 60515-2133

BERESFORD, BRUCE, film director; b. Sydney, New South Wales, Australia, Aug. 16, 1940; s. Leslie and Lona (Warr) B.; m. Rhoisin Patricia Harrison, 1965; children: Benjamin, Cordelia, Adam; m. Virginia Patricia Mary Duigan, 1985; 1 child, Trilby. BA, Sydney U., 1961. Films officer Brit. Film Inst., London, 1965-70; film advisor Arts Council of Great Britain, London, 1967-70. Dir. films Dons Party, 1976 (Best Dir. award Australian Film Inst.), The Getting of Wisdom, 1977, Money Movers, 1978, The Club, 1980, Tender Mercies, 1981, Puberty Blues, 1982, King David, 1984, Her Alibi, 1989, Driving Miss Daisy, 1989, Mr. Johnson, 1990, The Black Robe, 1991, Rich in Love, 1992, A Good Man in Africa, 1994, Silent Fall, 1994; dir., writer: Breaker Morant, 1980, Fringe Dwellers, 1985, Crimes of the Heart, 1986, (segment) Aria, 1988; producer, dir.: The Adventures of Barry McKenzie, 1972, Barry McKenzie Holds His Own, 1974. Mem. Dirs. Guild U.S.A. Avocations: opera, skiing, Australian football, tennis. *

BERESFORD, DOUGLAS LINCOLN, lawyer; b. Washington, June 1, 1956; s. Spencer Moxon and Ann (Lincoln) B.; m. Lori Anne Mainous, Sept. 22, 1990; children: Alexander Gould, Erik Mainous. AB cum laude, Harvard U., 1978; JD, Georgetown U., 1982. Bar: D.C. 1982, U.S. Ct. Appeals (D.C. cir.) 1984, U.S. Supreme Ct. 1986. Assoc. Morgan, Lewis & Bockius, Washington, 1982-83; assoc. Newman & Holtzinger, P.C., Washington, 1983-89, ptnr., 1989-94; ptnr. Long, Aldridge & Norman, Washington, 1994—. Office: Long Aldridge & Norman 701 Pennsylvania Ave NW Ste 600 Washington DC 20004-2692

BERESFORD, WILMA, elementary and gifted education educator; b. Kensett, Ark., Nov. 3, 1931; d. Newton A. and Anna Lucille Murray (Bedair) Graham; m. Robert B. Beresford, Aug. 5, 1949; children: Anna C. Walker, Angela D. Thomas, Robert L. BS, Lamar State Coll., 1963; MEd, McNeese State U., 1971; postgrad., Lamar U. Cert. tchr., Tex. Tchr. Groves (Tex.) Pub. Schs.; spl. assignment tchr. Port Neches Ind. Sch. Dist., Groves, 1963—; Chpt. I tchr., tchr. ESL and computer literacy Port Neches Groves Ind. Sch. Dist.; cons., presenter workshops in field. Mem. ASCD, Tex. Tchrs. Assn., Tex. Gifted and Talented Assn. (cert.), Tex. Computer Edn. Ass., Future Problem Solvers Tex. (cert. evaluator), Tex. States Tchr. Assn., Am. Bus. Women's Assn., Tex. Classroom Tchrs. Assn., Phi Delta Kappa.

BERETTA, GIORDANO BRUNO, computer scientist, researcher; b. Brugg, Aargau, Switzerland, Apr. 14, 1951; came to U.S., 1984; PhD, ETH, Zurich, Switzerland, 1984. Mem. rsch. staff Xerox Palo Alto (Calif.) Rsch. Ctr., 1984-90; charter mem., sr. scientist Canon Info. Systems, Palo Alto, 1990-93; mem. tech. staff Hewlett-Packard Labs., 1994—; chmn. various confs. Contbr. articles to profl. jours.; patentee digital color reprodn. and colorimetry. Mem. The Internat. Soc. for Optical Engring., Inter-Soc. Color Coun., Soc. for Imaging Sci. and Tech. (svc. award 1998), Swiss Math. Soc., Alumni Orgn. of Swiss Fed. Inst. of Tech. Zurich. Office: Hewlett-Packard Labs 1501 Page Mill Rd Palo Alto CA 94304-1100

BEREUTER, DOUGLAS KENT, congressman; b. York, Nebr., Oct. 6, 1939; s. Rupert Wesley and Evelyn Gladys (Tonn) B.; m. Louise Meyer, June 1, 1962; children: Eric David, Kirk Daniel. BA, U. Nebr., 1961; M in City Planning, Harvard U., 1966, MPA, 1973. Urban planner HUD, San Francisco, 1965-66; dir. div. state and urban affairs Nebr. Dept. Econ. Devel., 1967-68, state planning dir., 1968-70; coord. fed.-state relations Nebr. State Govt., 1967-70, urban planning cons., 1971-78; assoc. prof. U. Nebr., Kans. State U., 1971-78; mem. Nebr. Legislature, 1974-78, 96th-105th Congresses from 1st Nebr. Dist., 1979—; mem. com. on banking and fin. svcs., vice chmn. internat. rels. com., chmn. Asia-Pacific subcom.; mem. Nebr. State Crime Commn., 1969-71; chmn. standing com. on urban devel. Nat. Conf. State Legislatures, 1977-78; mem. Nat. Agrl. Export Commn., 1985-86. Served as officer U.S. Army, 1963-65. Mem. Am. Planning Assn., Phi Beta Kappa, Sigma Xi. Republican. Lutheran. Office: Ho of Reps 2184 Rayburn Ofc Bldg Washington DC 20515-2701

BEREZIN, SERGEI, professional hockey player; b. Voskresenska, Russia, Nov. 5, 1971. Mem. Toronto Maple Leafs, Ont., Can., 1994—. Named to All-Star Team, 1996; mem. Russian Hockey Team, 1994 Olympics; winner Silver medal 1991 World Jr. Champaionships. Office: Toronto Maple Leafs, 60 Carlton St, Toronto, ON Canada M5B 1L1*

BEREZIN, TANYA, acting coach, actress; b. Phila., Mar. 25, 1941; d. Maurice and Bettye (Shifrin) Berezin; m. Robert Leeming Thirkield, June 29, 1969 (div. June 1977); children: Lila Joy, Jonathon Schuyler; m. Mark Beers Wilson, Oct. 18, 1987. Student, Boston U., 1959-63. Co-founder Circle Repertory Co., N.Y.C., 1969, artistic dir., 1986-94; resident acting coach All My Children, ABC, N.Y.C., 1994-98; resident acting coach Another World, NBC, N.Y.C., 1997-98; resident acting coach As the World Turns, CBS, N.Y.C., 1998—. Appeared in (TV shows) St. Elsewhere, 1984, Law and Order, 1992, 93, 94, (play) Angels Fall, 1983, Moundbuilders, 1975 (Obie award), Sympathetic Magic, 1997, (film) Awakenings, 1993; producer Prelude to a Kiss, Destiny of Me, Three Hotels. Avocation: gardening.

BEREZINSKY, VENIAMIN SERGEEVICH, physicist; b. Volgograd, Russia, Apr. 17, 1934; arrived in Italy, 1990; s. Sergei Borisovich and Sofia Yakovlevna (Akselrod) B.; m. Julia Yakovlevna Dubinskaya, Jan. 29, 1962. Physicist, Moscow State U., Moscow, Russia, 1960; PhD, P.N. Lebedev Physical Inst., Moscow, 1967, D in sci. prof., 1979. Jr. scientist, sr. scientist P.N. Lebedev Physical Inst., Moscow, 1961-71; sr. scientist Inst. for Nuclear Rsch., Moscow, 1971-76, leading scientist, 1976-91; dir. of rsch. Lab. Nazionali del Gran Sasso, Assergi, Italy, 1991—; mem. editorial bd. Soviet Astronomy Letters, Moscow, 1985-97; Italian coord. European Network TAN, 1993-97. Author: Neutrino, 1965, Astrophysics of Cosmic Rays, 1990; contbr. numerous articles to profl. jours.; editor: Astroparticle Physics, 1992—. Recipient The Humboldt award Alexander Von Humboldt, 1991. Home: Via Dei Farnese 2A Apt 12B, 67100 L'Aquila Italy Office: Lab Nazionali del Gran Sasso, 67010 Assergi Italy

BERG, ALAN, lawyer, government official; b. Scranton, Pa., June 5, 1947; s. Donald and Lucile (DeLugo) B.; m. Rita A. Samin, June 15, 1975; children: Thomas M., Matthew P., Andrew J. BA, Hartwick Coll., Oneonta, N.Y., 1969; JD, St. John's U., 1972; LLM in Labor Law, NYU, 1975. Bar: N.Y. 1973, U.S. Dist. Ct. (dists. N.Y.) 1973, U.S. Ct. Appeals 1973, U.S. Supreme Ct. 1976. Atty., N.Y. State Labor Relations Bd., 1972-79, adminstrv. law judge, 1979-80, chief judge, 1980-84, gen. counsel, 1984-91; gen. counsel N.Y. State Employment Rels. Bd., 1991—; judge N.Y. Law Sch. Wagner Moot Ct.; advisor NYU Law Sch. student adv. program. Trustee, Freeport Meml. Library (N.Y.), 1976-81; coach Freeport High Sch. summer basketball team, 1973—(12 league championships), N.Y. all-star team N.Y.-Phila. basketball festival, 1985-86, 88-97; arbitrator Better Bus. Bur. Recipient George Emma Meml. Sportsmanship award, 1986, Outstanding Citizen award Freeport Boosters Club, 1987. Mem. N.Y. State Bar Assn., Indsl. Relations Research Assn., St. John's Law Sch. Alumni Assn. Home: 108 Delaware Ave Freeport NY 11520-1313 Office: NY State Employment Rels Bd 1 Penn Plz New York NY 10119-0002

BERG, ALFRED OREN, epidemiology and famiy practice medicine educator; b. Wichita, Kans., July 3, 1949. BA, Tabor Coll., 1970; MD, Washington U., 1974; MPH, U. Wash., 1979. Prof., assoc. chmn. U. Wash., 1979—. Assoc. editor Jour. Am. Bd. Family Practice, 1991—. Mem. Am. Acad. Family Physicians, NAS, Soc. Tchrs. Family Medicine, Inst. Medicine.

BERG, A(NDREW) SCOTT, author, biographer. Author: Lindbergh, 1999, Goldwyn: A Biography, Max Perkins: Editor of Genius. Guggenheim fellow, 1996.

BERG, BARBARA KIRSNER, health education specialist; b. Cin., Dec. 6, 1954; d. Robert and Mildred Dorothy (Warshofsky) Kirsner; m. Howard Keith Berg, Apr. 8, 1984; children: Arielle, Allison, Stacy. BA, Brandeis U., 1976; MEd, U. Cin., 1977. Cert. health edn. specialist Nat. Commn. for Health Edn. Credentialing, Inc., Mass. Health educator S.W. Ohio Lung Assn., Cin., 1977-79; coord. adminstrv. edn. N.E. Regional Med. Edn. Ctr., Northport, N.Y., 1979-81; patient health edn. coord. VA Med. Ctr., Buffalo, 1981-87; clin. asst. prof. SUNY, Buffalo, 1982-87; dir. cmty. health edn. N.W. Hosp. Ctr., Balt., 1987-89; coord. law and health care program U. Md. Sch. Law, Balt., 1989-90; med. mgmt. cons. Dr. Howard K. Berg, Owings Mills, Md., 1990—; cons. health edn. Edward Bartlett, Assoc., Rockville, Md., 1987-88; mem. adult edn. com. Chizuk Amuno Congregation, Balt., 1993—, mem. bd. dirs., 1996-98, chair cultural arts com., 1996-98. Bd. dirs., mem. Am. Lung Assn. Western N.Y., Buffalo, 1983-86, Pumpkin Theater, Balt., 1990-91; chair domestic concerns com. Balt. Jewish Coun., 1994-96, chair govt. rels. com., 1996-98, sec., bd. dirs., 1996-98, 2d v.p. 1998—; sec. women's dept. Associated Jewish Charities, Balt., 1994-97; mem. sch. bd. nominating conv. Baltimore County, 1995—; co-pres. Pikesville Mid. Sch. PTA, 1998—. Mem. APHA, Soc. for Pub. Health Edn., Am. Jewish Com., Phi Delta Kappa. Jewish. Avocations: reading, travel, advocacy. Home and Office: 12116 Heneson Garth Owings Mills MD 21117-1629

BERG, DANIEL, science and technology educator; b. N.Y.C., June 1, 1929; s. Jack and Hattie (Tannenbaum) B.; m. Frances Helena Ely, Aug. 18, 1956; children: Brian, Laura, Meredith. BS, CCNY, 1950; MS, Yale U., 1951, PhD, 1953; grad. execs. program, Carnegie-Mellon U., 1972. With Westinghouse Electric Corp., Pitts., 1953-77; research div. mgr., then tech. dir. Westinghouse Electric Corp., 1976-77; prof. sci. and tech. Carnegie-Mellon U., 1977-83, dean Mellon Coll. Sci., 1977-81, univ. provost, 1981-83; v.p. acad. affairs, provost, Inst. prof. sci. and tech. Rensselaer Poly. Inst., Troy, N.Y., 1983-85, pres., 1985-87, Inst. prof., 1987—; bd. dirs. Duquesne Light, Hy-Tech. Machine Co., Inc.; chmn. bd. Crystek Inc.; mem. Pa. Sci. and Engring. Found., 1975-76; mem. vis. coun. sci. and engring. CCNY, 1980-84; mem. vis. coun. Sch. Computer Sci., Carnegie-Mellon U., 1992—; mem. Yale U. Coun., 1981-85; assoc. fellow Jonathan Edwards Coll., 1982—; cons. to industry and govt. Author, editor, patentee in field. Fellow IEEE, AAAS, Am. Inst. Chemists, N.Y. Acad. Scis.; mem. Nat. Acad. Engring. (coun. 1985-88), Am. Chem. Soc., Am. Phys. Soc., Cosmos Club of Washington, River Club of Pitts., Century Club N.Y.C., Phi Beta Kappa, Sigma Xi, Alpha Chi Sigma, Tau Beta Pi. Home: 12 The Crossways Troy NY 12180-7263 Office: Rensselaer Poly Inst 5015 CII Troy NY 12180-3522

BERG, DAVID, author, artist; b. Bklyn., June 12, 1920; s. Morris Isaac and Bessie (Freidman) B.; m. Vivian Lipman, Mar. 3, 1949; children—Mitchel Ian, Nancy Anne Iva. Student, Cooper Union, Pratt Inst., U. Wis., New Sch., Iona Coll., Rochelle, N.Y., Coll. New Rochelle; Th.D. (hon.), Reconstructionist Rabbinical Coll., 1973. Artist-writer Will Eisner Prodns., N.Y.C., 1940-41; assoc. editor Timely Comics, 1945—; artist-writer Fawcett Publs., N.Y.C., 1941—, Warner Books, also Signet Books, 1956—, Mad mag.; also contbr. regular feature Lighter Side of; creative cons. NBC-TV, 1979—; guest tchr. Westchester (N.Y.) Schs., lectr. colls. and univs., 1968—; Army war corr., Iwo Jima. Author, artist: My Friend God, 1972, sects. reprinted in Eng. Celtic Press, rev. edit., 1994, Roger Kaputnik and God, 1974, also series of 14 mad books, 1964—; illustrator: (children's book) The Story Hour, 1994, vol. 2, 1995. Field commr., scoutmaster local Boy Scouts Am., 1950-75; bd. dirs. local Girl Scouts, 1962-66; coach Little League, 1962; recreation commr. New Rochelle, 1967; judge state contest Miss Am. Beauty Contest, Internat. Cultural Exch. Program, 1965. Served with USAAF, 1942-45. Recipient B'nai B'rith Youth Svcs. award, 1978, Tzivos Hashem award Chabad House, 1987; named to Chair of Great Cartoonists UCLA student body, 1975; David Berg Day named by Westchester County, N.Y., May 7, 1978 (nominated second annual comedy awards). Mem. Authors League, Writers Guild West, Nat. Cartoonists Soc. Democrat. Jewish. Club: B'nai B'rith (pres. Marina Del Ray, Calif. chpt., 1984-85, 85-87). Home: 14021 Marquesas Way Apt 307C Marina Dl Rey CA 90292-6047 Office: Mad Mag 1700 Broadway New York NY 10019-5905 *To succeed while having a ball: Make your hobby your livelihood.*

BERG, DAVID HOWARD, lawyer; b. Springfield, Ohio, Mar. 4, 1942; s. Nathan Stewart Berg and Mildred (Besser) Berg-Filion; children: Geoffrey Alan, Gabriel Adam, Caitlin Hannah; m. Kathryn Page, July 10, 1994. Student, Tulane U., 1963; BA in English, U. Houston, 1964, JD, 1967. Bar: Tex. 1967, U.S. Dist. Ct. Tex. 1967, N.Y. 1989, U.S. Dist. Ct. (so. dist.) N.Y. 1990, U.S. Ct. Appeals (2d, 4th, 5th, 8th and 11th cirs.) 1990, U.S. Supreme Ct. 1990. Law clk. NLRB, Washington, 1967-68; ptnr. David Berg & Assocs., Houston, 1968-77, Berg & Androphy, 1977-98, Berg Androphy & Wilson, 1998—; mem. fed. ct. lawyers adv. com. U.S. Dist. Ct. (so. dist.) Tex.; mem. U. Houston Law Found., 1996—; spl. counsel commn. on lawyer discipline, Tex. State Bar, 1996—. Contbr. articles and essays to mags. Issues staff Jimmy Carter Campaign, Atlanta, 1976; adviser Jimmy Carter Transition Govt., Washington, 1976; adviser Mayor Kathy Whitmire campaigns, 1980-91; patron Friends of Menil Collection, 1990-91; adviser campaign Mayor Bob Lanier, 1991; chmn. City of Houston's "Imagine Houston"; bd. dirs. "Camp for All"; bd. dirs. U. Houston Law Found., 1996. Recipient 1st pl. for best feature article in a scholarly jour. Nat. Assn. Publ., 1991. Fellow Internat. Acad. Trial Lawyers, Houston Bar Found.; mem. ATLA, Tex. Bar Assn. (chmn. grievance com. 1984-85), Tex. Bar Found., N.Y. State Bar Assn., Tex. Trial Lawyers Assn., Houston Trial Lawyers Assn., U. Houston Law Alumni Assn. (bd. dirs. 1992-95), Am. Bd. Trial Advocates (assoc.). Democrat. Jewish. Avocations: writing, running, fishing. Home: 16 Sunset Blvd Houston TX 77005-1838 Office: Berg Androphy & Wilson 3704 Travis St Houston TX 77002-9550

BERG, DEBORAH JEAN, construction management owner; b. Calif., Aug. 28, 1952; m. Tom Berg, Oct. 12, 1974; children: Tom, Lindsé, Alicia. BA, UCLA, 1974; MPPA in Pub. Works, Calif. State U., Long Beach, 1998. Cert. tchr., Calif. Founder, prin. Berg and Assocs., Inc., San Pedro, Calif., 1980-94, CEO, 1994—; cons. Alameda Corridor Transp. Project; bd. dirs. Women's Transp. Seminar, L.A.; bd. dirs. bus. adv. coun. Met. Transp. Agy., L.A. Recipient grant Dance for Life/Rim Ed Found., 1995. Mem. Women Constrn. Owners and Execs. (bd. dirs.), Nat. Assn. Women and Bus. Owners, Phi Kappa Delta. Office: Berg and Assocs Inc 302 W 5th St Ste 203B San Pedro CA 90731

BERG, GORDON HERCHER, banker; b. New Haven, May 14, 1937; s. John Edward and Dazma Charlotte (Hercher) B.; m. Ruth I. Gardner, Aug. 26, 1961; (div. Feb. 1985); children: Elizabeth, Deborah, Mary, Beatrice, Gordon; m. Patricia Pridham, Apr. 27, 1985. AA, Mitchell Coll.; BA, Ohio Wesleyan U., 1959; MBA, NYU, 1963; grad., Stonier Grad. Sch. Banking, 1967; MTS, Harvard U., 1988. Asst. sec. Irving Trust Co., N.Y.C., 1959-64; v.p. New England Merchants Bank, Boston, 1964-68; ptnr. The Sprague Co., Boston, 1968-70; pres., chief exec. officer Berg & Co. Inc., BMFC, Inc., Boston, 1970-84; pres. Berg & Co., Inc., Boston, 1984—; med. ethicist. Contbr. articles to prfl. jours. Past pres., trustee emeritus Derby Acad., Hingham, Mass., 1972. Mem. Mortgage Bankers Assn. Am. (cert. mortgage banker award, 1983), Masons. Republican. Avocations: theology, precision cabinet making, offshore sailing, celestial navigation, mountain glacier climbing. Office: Berg & Co Inc 200 High St Fl 6 Boston MA 02110-3036

BERG, HOWARD C., biology educator; b. Iowa City, Iowa, Mar. 16, 1934; s. Clarence P. and Esther M. (Carlson) B.; m. Mary E. Guyer, Dec. 19, 1964; children—Henry G., Alexander H., Elena C. BS in Chemistry, Calif. Inst. Tech., Pasadena, 1956; AM in Physics, Harvard U., 1960, PhD in Chem. Physics, 1964. Jr. fellow Harvard Soc. Fellows, Cambridge, Mass., 1963-66; asst. prof. dept. biology Harvard U., Cambridge, 1966-69, assoc. prof. dept. biochemistry and molecular biology, 1969-70, prof. dept. molecular and cellular biology, 1986—; prof. physics, 1997—; assoc. prof. to prof. dept. molecular, cellular and developmental biology U. Colo., Boulder, 1970-79; prof. div. biology Calif. Inst. Tech., Pasadena, 1979-86; mem. Rowland Inst. Sci., Cambridge, 1986—. Author: Random Walks in Biology, 1983, revised edit., 1993; contbr. articles to profl. jours. Fulbright fellow, 1956-57; NSF Sci. Faculty Devel. awardee, 1978-79; recipient Biol. Physics prize, Am. Phys. Soc., 1984. Mem. AAAS, Am. Phys. Soc., Biophys. Soc., Am. Soc. Microbiology, Am. Soc. Biochemistry and Molecular Biology, N.Y. Acad. Sci., Nat. Acad. Sci., Am. Acad. Arts and Sci., Am. Acad. Microbiology. Office: Harvard U Biology Labs 16 Divinity Ave Cambridge MA 02138-2020 also: Rowland Inst Sci 100 Edwin H Land Blvd Cambridge MA 02142

BERG, JEFFREY SPENCER, talent agency executive; b. L.A., May 26, 1947. B.A. in English with honors, U. Calif., Berkeley, 1969. Vice pres., head lit. div. Creative Mgmt. Assocs., Los Angeles, 1969-75; v.p. motion picture dept. Internat. Creative Mgmt., Los Angeles, 1975-80; pres. Internat. Creative Mgmt., 1980-85, chmn., chief exec. officer, 1985—; dir. Josephson Internat., Inc., Marshall McLuhan Ctr. of Global Communication. Trustee U. Berkeley Found.; bd. govs. Music Ctr. L.A. County; pres. letters and sci. exec. bd. U. Calif. Berkeley; co-chmn. Calif. Info. Tech. Coun.; bd. vis. Anderson Grad. Sch. of Mgmt., UCLA. Mem. U. Calif. Berkeley Alumni Assn. Offices: Internat Creative Mgmt 8942 Wilshire Blvd Beverly Hills CA 90211-1934*

BERG, JOHN RICHARD, chemist, former federal government executive; b. Chippewa Falls, Wis., Apr. 24, 1932; s. John and Florence Agnes (Heagle) B.; m. Virginia Marie Binet, June 16, 1956; children: John E., Thomas A., James E., Joseph M. BS in Chemistry, Coll. St. Thomas, 1954; PhD in Physical Chemistry, Iowa State U., 1961. Sr. chemist then tech mgr. 3M Co., St. Paul, 1961-82; fed. govt. mgr. 3M Co., Washington, 1982-86; prin. dep. asst. sec. Dept. of Energy, Washington, 1986-88, asst. sec., 1988-89; pvt. cons., 1990—; cons. in field, 1992—; bd. dirs. Columbia Rsch. Corp. Patentee in field. Former mem. Cmty. Svcs. Program, Roseville (Minn.) Sch. Dist.; past leader, commr. Boy Scouts Am.; candidate for U.S. Congress from 4th dist. Minn.; mem. ad hoc task force Arlington County Mandatory Recycling, 1993-95, Arlington County Four Mile Run Watershed Joint Planning Commn., 1994—, Arlington C. of C., 1994—, Arlington County Environment and Energy Conservation Commsn., 1997—. Named Scouter of Yr., Boy Scouts Am., St. Paul, 1969. Mem. Am. Inst. Chemists, Am. Chem. Soc., AAAS, Phi Lambda Upsilon, Sigma Xi. Avocations: fishing, gardening, model railroading, travel. Home: 3202 N Tacoma St Arlington VA 22213-1340

BERG, LEONARD, neurologist, educator, researcher; b. St. Louis, July 17, 1927; s. Jacob and Sara (Kessler) B.; m. Gerry Saltzman, Mar. 25, 1948; children: Kathleen, John, Nancy. A.B. cum laude, Washington U., St. Louis, 1945, M.D. cum laude, 1949. Diplomate: Am. Bd. Psychiatry and Neurology (dir. 1978-85, pres. 1985). Intern Barnes Hosp., St. Louis, 1949-50; resident Barnes Hosp., 1950-51, Neurol. Inst., N.Y.C., 1951-53; clin. assoc. Nat. Inst. Neurol. Diseases and Blindness, NIH, 1953-55; mem. faculty Washington U. Med. Sch., 1955—, prof. clin. neurology, 1972-89, prof. neurology, 1989—; attending neurologist Barnes Hosp., Jewish Hosp., St. Louis; dir. Alzheimer's Disease Rsch. Ctr., Washington U., 1985-97; expert U.S. FDA, 1992-96; mem. U.S. Congress Adv. Panel on Alzheimer's Disease, 1993-96. Co-author: Atlas of Muscle Pathology in Neuromuscular Diseases, 1956. Bd. dirs. Temple Israel, St. Louis, 1972-74, Jewish Center for Aged, 1981—. With USPHS, 1953-55. Mem. AMA, Am. Acad. Neurology, Am. Neurol. Assn. (1st v.p. 1988-89), Soc. for Neurosci., Alzheimer's Assn. (Chgo.) (bd. dirs. 1989-95, 96-98, chair med. and sci. adv. bd. 1991-95), Phi Beta Kappa, Sigma Xi, Alpha Omega Alpha. Home: 816 S Hanley Rd Apt 7D Saint Louis MO 63105-2678 Office: Washington U Alzheimer's Disease Rsch Ctr Ste 130 4488 Forest Park Ave Saint Louis MO 63108-2293

BERG, LILLIAN DOUGLAS, chemistry educator; b. Birmingham, Ala., July 9, 1925; d. Gilbert Franklin and Mary Rachel (Griffin) Douglas; m. Joseph Wilbur Berg, June 26, 1950; children: Anne Berg Jenkins, Joseph Wilbur III, Frederick Douglas. BS in Chemistry, Birmingham So. Coll., 1946; MS in Chemistry, Emory U., 1948. Instr. chemistry Armstrong Jr. Coll., Savannah, Ga., 1948-50; rsch. asst. chemistry Pa. State U., University Park, 1950-54; instr. chemistry U. Utah, Salt Lake City, 1955-56; prof. chemistry No. Va. C.C., Annandale, 1974-96, 98—, adj. prof., 1998—. Mem. Am. Chem. Soc., Am. Women in Sci., Am. Guild Organists, Mortar Bd. Soc., Iota Sigma Pi, Sigma Delta Epsilon, Phi Beta Kappa. Avocation: music. Home: 3319 Dauphine Dr Falls Church VA 22042-3724

BERG, LLOYD, chemical engineering educator; b. Paterson, N.J., Aug. 8, 1914; s. Olav and Anita (Schneider) B.; m. Edna Barrowclough, Jan. 1, 1938; children: Sally, Charles, John, Ann. BSChemE, Lehigh U., 1936; PhD, Purdue U., 1942. Registered profl. engr., Mont., Pa. Tech. svc. engr. Sherwin-Williams Co., Newark, 1936-39; rsch. engr. Gulf R & D Co., Pitts., 1942-46; assoc. prof. chem. engring. U. Kans., Lawrence, 1946; prof., head dept. chem. engring. Mont. State U., Bozeman, 1946-79, prof., 1979—; v.p. Brix-Berg Co., Bozeman, 1995—; cons. Hoechst Celanese, EXXON, Ga. Gulf, ADM, Glitsch; pres. Brix-Berg Co. Contbr. articles in extractive distillation to profl. jours.; holder over 300 patents in field of azeotropic and extractive distillation. With U.S. Army, 1936-42. Fellow AIChE; mem. Am. Soc. Engring. Edn., Am. Chem. Soc. Home: 1314 S 3rd Ave Bozeman MT 59715-5506 Office: Mont State U Dept Chem Engring Bozeman MT 59717

BERG, LOUIS LESLIE, investment executive; b. Vienna, Austria, Dec. 27, 1919; s. Gustav and Hedwig (Kohn) B.; came to U.S., 1938, naturalized, 1943; student U. Vienna, 1937-38, Coll. City N.Y., 1941-43; m. Minnette Whitman, Aug. 28, 1959; children: Sharon, Randee, Michel. Pres., Gt. Empire Corp., N.Y.C., 1946—, Bendalou Real Estate Corp., N.Y.C., 1950-60, Netherlands Securities Co., Inc., N.Y.C., 1959-62, Imported Automotive Parts, Ltd., L.I. City, N.Y.; chmn., bd. dirs. IAP Inc., Avenel, N.J., IAP West Inc., Los Angeles; bd. dirs., exec. com. Auto Internat. Assn.; advisor U.S. Congl. Adv. Bd. dir. Internat. Aviation Corp., Cosmos Industries, Kane-Miller Corp., Knickerbocker Toy Co., Inc., Vernitron Corp., Jet Aero Corp., Fidelity Am. Finance Corp., S.W. Fla. Enterprises, Sulray Inc., U.S. Airlines, Commuter Airlines, Aviation Equipment. Mem. Am. Mgmt. Assn. Club: Wings. Office: IAP Inc 26 Engelhard Ave Avenel NJ 07001-2217 also: IAP West Inc 2939 Bandini Blvd Los Angeles CA 90023-4508

BERG, SISTER MARIE MAJELLA, university chancellor; b. Bklyn., July 7, 1916; d. Peter Gustav and Mary Josephine (McAuliff) B. BA, Marymount Coll., 1938; MA, Fordham U., 1948; DHL (hon.), Georgetown U., 1970, Marymount Manhattan Coll., 1983. Registrar Marymount Sch., N.Y.C., 1943-48; prof. classics, registrar Marymount Coll., N.Y.C., 1949-57; registrar Marymount Coll. of Va., Arlington, 1957-58, Marymount Coll., Tarrytown, N.Y., 1958-60; pres. Marymount U., Arlington, Va., 1960-93, chancellor, 1993—; pres. Consortium for Continuing Higher Edn. in Va., 1987-88; mem. com. Consortium of Univs. in Washington Met. Area, 1987-93, chmn., 1992-93. Contbr. five biographies to One Hundred Great Thinkers, 1965; editor Otherwords column of N.Va. Sun newspaper, Arlington. Bd. dirs. Internat. Hospice, 1984-96, Ballston Partnership, 1992—, Hope, SOAR, 10th Dist. Congl. Award Coun., No. Va.; vice chmn. bd. Va. Found. Ind. Colls., 1992-93; cmty. advisor Jr. League No. Va., 1992—; mem. Friends of TACT, 1994—. Recipient commendation Va. Gen. Assembly, Richmond, 1990, 93, Elizabeth Ann Seton award, 1991, Arlington Notable Women award Arlington Commn. on Status of Women, 1992, Voice and Vision award Arlington Cmty. TV Channel 33, 1993, Pro Ecclesia et Pontifice medal Holy See, 1993; elected to Va. Women's Hall of Fame, 1992; named Washingtonian of Yr., Washingtonian mag., 1990; named to Washington Bus. Hall of Fame, Washingtonian mag. 1998, Jr. Achievement, 1998. Roman Catholic. Avocations: sewing, crocheting, reading. Home and Office: Marymount U Office of Chancellor 2807 N Glebe Rd Arlington VA 22207-4224

BERG, OLENA, investment company executive, former federal official; b. Dec. 31, 1949; d. Clarence Millard and Anna Elizabeth (Schlegel) Nave; 1 child. BA in English summa cum laude, Calif. State U., 1974; MBA, Harvard U., 1984. Budget and estimates analyst State of Calif. Depts. Fin. and Benefits Payments, 1975-77; asst. to sec. State of Calif. Bus. and Transp. Agy., 1977-78; chief dep. dir. State of Calif. Dept. Housing and Community Devel., 1978-82; project mgr. McNeil Consumer Products, 1983; pres., COO Gerson Bakar and Assocs., 1984-88; exec. v.p. Lowe Assocs., 1988-91; chief dep. state treas. State of Calif., 1991-93; asst. sec. pension and welfare benefits adminstrn. Dept. of Labor, Washington, 1993-98; sr. adv. Fin. Engines Inc., Palo Alto, Calif., 1998—. Baker scholar Harvard U. Mem. Century Club. Office: Fin Engines Inc 1804 Embarcadero Rd # 100 Palo Alto CA 94303-3318*

BERG, PAUL, biochemist, educator; b. N.Y.C., June 30, 1926; s. Harry and Sarah (Brodsky) B.; m. Mildred Levy, Sept. 13, 1947; 1 son, John. BS, Pa. State U., 1948; PhD (NIH fellow 1950-52), Western Res. U., 1952; DSc (hon.), U. Rochester, 1978, Yale U., 1978, Wash. U., St. Louis, 1986, Oreg. State U., 1989, Pa. State U., 1995. Postdoctoral fellow Copenhagen (Denmark) U., 1952-53; postdoctoral fellow sch. medicine Washington U., St. Louis, 1953-54; Am. Cancer Soc. scholar cancer research dept. microbiology sch. medicine Washington U., 1954-57, from asst. to assoc. prof. microbiology sch. medicine, 1955-59; prof. biochemistry sch. medicine Stanford U., 1959—, Sam, Lulu and Jack Willson prof. biochemistry sch. medicine, 1970-94; Robert W. Cahill prof. cancer rsch., 1994—; chmn. dept. sch. medicine Stanford U., 1969-74; dir. Stanford U. Beckman Ctr. for Molecular and Genetic Medicine, 1985—, Affymetrix, 1993—, Nat. Found. Biomed. Rsch., 1994—; non-resident fellow Salk Inst., 1973-83; adv. bd. NIH, NSF, MIT; vis. com. dept. biochemistry and molecular biology Harvard U.; bd. sci. advisors Jane Coffin Childs Found. Med. Rsch., 1970-80; chmn. sci. adv. com. Whitehead Inst., 1984-90; bd. sci. adv. DNAX Rsch. Inst., 1981—; internat. adv. bd. Basel Inst. Immunology; chmn. nat. adv. com. Human Genome Project, 1990-92. Contbr. profl. jours.; Editor: Biochem. and Biophys. Research Communications, 1959-68; editorial bd.: Molecular Biology, 1966-69. Trustee Rockefeller U., 1990-92. Served to lt. (j.g.) USNR, 1943-46. Recipient Eli Lilly prize biochemistry, 1959; V.D. Mattia award Roche Inst. Molecular Biology, 1972; Henry J. Kaiser award for excellence in teaching, 1969, 72; Disting. Alumnus award Pa. State U., 1972; Sarasota Med. awards for achievement and excellence, 1979; Gairdner Found. annual award, 1980; Lasker Found. award, 1980; Nobel award in chemistry, 1980; N.Y. Acad. Sci. award, 1980; Sci. Freedom and Responsibility award AAAS, 1982; Nat. Medal of Sci., 1983; named Calif. Scientist of Yr. Calif. Museum Sci. and Industry, 1963; numerous disting. lectureships including Harvey lectr., 1972, Lynen lectr., 1977, Priestly lectrs. Pa. State U., 1978, Dreyfus Disting. lectrs. Northwestern U., 1979, Lawrence Livermore Dir.'s Disting. lectr., 1983, Linus Pauling lectr., 1993. Fellow AAAS; mem. NAS, Inst. Medicine, Am. Acad. Arts and Scis., Am. Soc. Biol. Chemists (pres. 1974-75), Am. Soc. Cell Biology (chmn. pub. policy com. 1994—), Am. Soc. Microbiology, Am. Philos. Soc., Internat. Soc. Molecular Biology, Japan Biochem. Soc. (elected fgn. mem. 1978), French Acad. Sci. (elected fgn. mem. 1981), Royal Soc. (elected fgn. mem. 1992). Office: Stanford Sch Medicine Beckman Ctr B-062 Stanford CA 94305-5425

BERG, PETER, actor; b. N.Y.C., N.Y., Mar. 11, 1964; married. Film appearances include Demonstrator, 1971, Miracle Mile, 1988, Heart of Dixie, 1989, Never on Tuesday, 1989, Shocker, 1989, Genuine Risk, 1991, Late for Dinner, 1991, Aspen Extreme, 1993, Fire in the Sky, 1993, Across the Moon, 1994, The Last Seduction, 1994, Girl 6, 1996, Coveat White Hype, 1996, Cop Land, 1997, others; appeared as Dr. William Kronk in Chgo. Hope TV series, 1994—, Chicago Hope, 1994. *

BERG, ROBERT LEWIS, physician, educator; b. Spokane, Wash., Sept. 10, 1918; s. Evan and Rachel Myfanwy (Lewis) B.; m. Florence Mitcham Foster, June 18, 1943 (dec. 1985); children—Erik Christian, Astri Maren. B.S., Harvard, 1940, M.D., 1943. Successively intern, resident, chief med. resident Mass. Gen. Hosp., Boston, 1944-46, 50; asst. to dir. rsch. and edn. Mass. Gen. Hosp., 1951-54, asst., then assoc. physician, 1951-58; Moseley traveling fellow Royal Caroline Inst., Stockholm, 1948-49; from instr. to asst. prof. medicine Harvard Med. Sch., 1951-58, Albert D. Kaiser prof., also chmn. dept. preventive, family and rehab. medicine, 1958-89; assoc. dean planning Univ. Rochester, 1982-89, assoc. prof. medicine, 1958-69, prof. medicine, 1969-89, prof. emeritus, 1989—; sr. assoc. physician Strong Meml. Hosp., 1958-69, physician, 1969-89; acting adminstr., 1960-61; mem. NIH Epidemiology and Biometry Tng. Com., 1962-66, 67-71, chmn., 1969-70; mem. U.S. Com. Vital and Health Statistics, 1965-69, chmn., 1967-69. Author: (with M. Roy Brooks, Jr. and Miomir Savicevic) Health Care in Yugoslavia and the United States, 1976; editor: Health Status Indexes, 1973, (with Joseph S. Cassells) The Second Fifty Years: Promoting Health and Preventing Disability, 1990. Trustee Eastman Dental Center, 1971-97, chmn., 1975-79. Mem. Am. Pub. Health Assn., Assn. Tchrs. Preventive Medicine (treas. 1963-69, v.p. 1969-70, pres. 1970-72), Internat. Epidemiological Assn. Home: 45 Songbird Ln Rochester NY 14620-3174 Office: Box 644 601 Elmwood Ave Rochester NY 14642-0001

BERG, ROBERT RAYMOND, geologist, educator; b. St. Paul, May 28, 1924; s. Raymond F. and Jennie (Swanson) B.; m. Josephine Finck, Dec. 22, 1946; children: James R., (dec.), Charles R., William R. B.A., U. Minn., 1948, Ph.D., 1951. Geologist, Calif. Co., Denver, 1951-56; cons. Berg and Wasson, Denver, 1957-66; prof. geology, head dept. Tex. A&M U., 1967—, Michel T. Halbouty prof. geology, 1982—; dir. univ. research Tex. A & M U., 1972—; cons. petroleum geology, 1959—. Contbr. papers in field. Served with AUS, 1943-46. Recipient Disting. Achievement award U. Minn., 1992. Fellow Geol. Soc. Am.; mem. Am. Assn. Petroleum Geologists (disting. lectr. 1972, hon. mem. 1985, Sidney Powers Meml. award 1993), Am. Inst. Profl. Geologists (pres. 1971, hon. mem. 1988), Nat. Acad. Engring. Home: 414 East Brookside Bryan TX 77801 Office: Texas A&M Univ Geology Dept College Station TX 77843

BERG, STANTON ONEAL, firearms and ballistics consultant; b. Barron, Wis., June 14, 1928; s. Thomas C. and Ellen Florence (Nedland) Silbaugh; m. June K. Rolstad, Aug. 16, 1952; children: David M., Daniel L., Susan E., Julie L. Student, U. Wis., 1949-50; LLB, LaSalle Ext. U., 1951; postgrad., U. Minn., 1960-69. Claim rep. State Farm Ins. Co., Mpls., Hibbing and Duluth, Minn., 1952-57, claim supt., 1966-70; regional mgr.. State Farm Fire and Casualty Co., St. Paul, Minn., 1970-84; firearms cons. Mpls., 1961—; bd. dirs. Am. Bd. Forensic Firearm and Tool Mark Examiners, 1980—; instr. home firearms safety, Mpls., 1975—; cons. to Sporting Arms and Ammunition Mfrs. Inst., 1974-84; internat. lectr. on forensic ballistics Adv. Bd. Milton Helpern Internat. Ctr. for Forensic Scis., 1975—; mem. bd. cons. Inst. Applied Sci., Chgo., 1974—; cons. for re-exam. of ballistics evidence in Robert Kennedy assassination/Sirhan case Superior Ct. L.A., 1975; ct. expert witness in most state cts., Mil. Gen. Ct. Martial and U.S. Dist. Cts., Supreme Ct. of Ont., Can.; mem. Nat. Forensic Ctr., 1979—, internat. study group in forensic scis., 1985—; chmn. internat. symposiums on forensic ballistics, Edinburgh, Scotland, 1972, Zurich, 1975, Bergen, Norway, 1981, Dusseldorf, Germany, 1993. Contbg. editor Am. Rifleman mag., 1973-84; mem. editl. bd. Internat. Microform Jour. Legal Medicine and Forensic Scis., 1979—, Am. Jour. Forensic Medicine and Pathology, 1979-91; contbr. articles on firearms and forensic ballistics to profl. publs. With CIC, RA, 1948-52. Fellow Am. Acad. Forensic Sci., Am. Coll. Forensic Examiners (life, bd. cert. forensic examiner and diplomate); mem. ASTM (criminalistics subcom. 1989—, non powder guns subcom. 1990—, paintball guns and sys. subcom. 1994—), NRA, Assn. Firearms and Tool Mark Examiners (exec. coun. 1970-71, charter mem., life mem., editl. com. AFTE jour., 1989-92, Disting. Mem. and Key Man award 1972, exam. and standards com. 1975-76, spl. honors award 1976, nat. peer group on cert. of firearms examiners 1978—), Forensic Sci. Soc., Internat. Assn. forensic Scis., Internat. Assn. for Identification (mem. firearms subcom. of sci. and practice com. 1961-74, 86-99, chmn. firearm subcom. 1964-66, 69-70, 91-95, lab. rsch. and techniques subcom. 1980-81, life and disting. mem., life charter mem. Minn. divsn.), Internat. Wound Ballistics Assn. (full mem.), Western. Conf. Criminal and Civil Problems (sci. adv. com.), Am. Legion (life), Army Counter-Intelligence Corp. Vets. Assn. (life), Browning Arms Collectors Assn. (life 1988—), Am. Ordnance Assn. (life), Minn. Weapons Collectors, Internat. Cartridge Collectors Assns. (life), Internat. Reference Orgn. Forensic Medicine and Scis., Internat. Assn. Bloodstain Pattern Analysts. Address: 6025 Gardena Ln NE Minneapolis MN 55432-5840

BERG, STEPHEN WARREN, government official; b. Washington, Jan. 21, 1948; s. Isidore and Dorothy (Faust) B.; BA, Tulane U., 1970; MS, Shippensburg U., 1976; children: Ashley Michelle, Marcus Alan. Program analyst Dept. Army, New Cumberland, Pa., Ft. Monmouth, N.J., Chambersburg, Pa., 1972-75; program mgr. Army Office Environ. Program, Washington, 1975-76; chief, directorate support br. Army Corps of Engrs., Washington, 1976-78; chief coordination and support br. Pub. Bldgs. Svc., Washington, 1978-79, chief mgmt. control and analysis br., 1979-82, sr. planner policy and planning office, 1982-86; operational dir. Office Assoc. Adminstr. for Ops., GSA, Washington, 1986—; exec. officer Coop. Adminstrv. Support Program, 1987—, Pres.'s Coun. on Mgmt. Improvement, 1987-92; realty specialist Office of Bus., Industry & Govt. Affairs, 1990—; spl. asst. to dir. mgmt. & adminstrn. divsn. Info. Resource Mgmt. Svc., Washington, 1992-95; dir. human resources and mgmt. svcs. ctr. Info. Tech. Svc., Washington, 1995-96; dir. investment analysis staff Office of the Chief Info. Officer, 1996-98, dir. Ctr. for Info. Tech. Acquisition Office of the CIO, dir. GSAITA Svcs. Ctr. Federal Tech. Svc., Mem. Nat. Contract Mgrs. Assn. Home: 10626 Tuppence Ct Rockville MD 20850-3930 Office: 18th and F Sts NW Washington DC 20405

BERG, THOMAS, manufacturing executive; b. Sparta, Wis., Dec. 28, 1914; m. Evelyn Sweet, Nov. 13, 1937; children: Barbara Caryl, James Richard. B.S.E.E., U. Wis., 1937. Engr. Gen. Electric Co., Schenectady, 1937-48; instr. Rensselaer Poly. Inst., Troy, N.Y., 1943-44; pres., owner, welding specialist, application engr. Arcway Equipment Co., Phila., 1948-58; pres. Airco Welding Products div. Air Reduction Co., N.Y.C., 1958-68; pres., chief exec. officer, dir. Friedrich Refrigerators Inc., San Antonio, 1968-75; chmn. Friedrich Refrigerators Inc., 1975-86; chmn. bd., CEO Character Edn. Inst., San Antonio; v.p., dir. Crutcher Resources Corp., Houston; v.p. Wylain Inc.; dir. Universal Bookbindery Inc.; v.p., dir. Ellison Industries Inc.; pres. Ray Ellison Devels. Inc.; bd. dirs., chmn. S.W. Research Inst.; founder Skills Tng. Center, San Antonio, 1971; dir. First Nat. Bank, San Antonio, Jim Berg Publs., Inc.; dir., chmn. exec. com., pres. J.E.T. Properties, Inc., San Antonio. Author: Aim for a Job in Welding, 1967. chmn. adv. council Sch. Bus., 1976-77, San Antonio; chmn. bd. City Pub. Service Bd., San Antonio; bd. dirs. Prevent Blindness of San Antonio.; pres., bd. dirs. Nat. Myasthenia Gravis Found., N.Y.C., bd. dirs., San Antonio; founding dir. Tex. Research & Tech. Found., San Antonio; chmn. bd., dir., chief exec. officer Am. Inst. for Character Edn., San Antonio; dir., exec. com. German Heritage Park, Inc., San Antonio; mem. Am. 2000 Initiative. Named hon. citizen City of San Antonio, 1978. Mem. AIEE, Am. Welding Soc. (life, founder ann. Airco award 1965), San Antonio C. of C. (bd. dirs. 1972—, chmn. econ. devel. coun. 1973—), Trinity U. Assocs., San Antonio Country Club, City Club, Argyle Club, Giraud Club, Plaza Club, Majectic Club, Rotary (bd. dirs.). Presbyterian. Featured on front cover of Iron Age Mag., June 1967. Developer universal jeep welder and energizer systems, 1942-44. Office: PO Box 6583 San Antonio TX 78209-0583

BERG, THOMAS CHARLES, law educator; b. Chgo., Aug. 18, 1960; s. Roy Charles and Anne (Ingebretson) B.; m. Maureen Kane, Nov. 23, 1961; children: Brendan, Aidan. BS, Northwestern U., 1982; JD, U. Chgo., 1987; MA, Oxford U., 1993, U. Chgo., 1992. Bar: Ill. 1989. Law clk. U.S. Ct. Appeals (5th cir.), Baton Rouge, La., 1987-88; atty. Mayer, Brown & Platt, Chgo., 1988-92; law prof. Samford U. Cumberland Law Sch., Birmingham, Ala., 1992—; adv. bd. DePaul U. Ctr. Church-State Studies, Chgo., 1994—; mem. adv. bd. Nat. Coun. Chs., 1998—. Author: The State and Religion in a Nutshell, 1998; editor: The Structures of American Churches, 1998. Vol. Clinton/Gore campaign, Birmingham, 1992. Named religious liberty defender of yr. Christian Legal Soc., 1996; Rhodes scholar, 1982-84. Mem. ABA, Assn. Am. Law Schs., Supreme Ct. Hist. Soc. Episcopalian. Office: Samford U Cumberland Law Sch 800 Lakeshore Dr Birmingham AL 35229-0001

BERG, THOMAS KENNETH, lawyer; b. Willmar, Minn., Feb. 10, 1940; s. Kenneth Q. and Esther V. (Westlund) B.; m. Margit Kathryn Larson, July 31, 1965; children: Erik, Jeffrey. BA, U. Minn., 1962, LLB, 1965. Bar: Minn. 1965, U.S. Dist. Ct. Minn. 1968, U.S. Ct. Appeals (8th cir.) 1974, U.S. Supreme Ct. 1980. Atty. Dept. Navy, Washington, 1965-67; assoc. Carlsen, Greiner & Law, Mpls., 1967-79; state rep. Minn. Ho. of Reps., St. Paul, 1970-78; U.S. atty. Dept. of Justice, Mpls., 1979-81; ptnr. Popham, Haik, Schnobrich & Kaufman, Mpls., 1981-97, Hinshaw & Culbertson, Mpls., 1997—. Chair Gov.'s Re-election Com., St. Paul, 1984-86, Gov.'s Commn. for Drug Abuse, Mpls., 1989; U.S. Senate candidate for endorsement Dem. Farmer Labor Party, Mpls., 1994; chmn. bd. dirs. St. Paul Rehab. Ctr., 1995-97. Recipient Outstanding Narcotics Prosecution award U.S. Drug Enforcement Adminstrn., 1981. Mem. Am. Health Lawyers Assn. Office: HInshaw & Culbertson 3200 Piper Jaffray Tower 222 S 9th St Minneapolis MN 55402-3389

BERG, WARREN STANLEY, retired banker; b. Lynn, Mass., Jan. 17, 1922; s. Carl W. and Gladys (Colburn) B.; m. Marjorie E. Coleman, Mar. 25, 1944; children—Peter C., Carolyn (Mrs. John Spengler), Dana S. BS, Harvard U., 1943; grad. exec. devel. program, Cornell U., 1944. Dir. pub. relations and sales promotion Arthur D. Little, Inc., Cambridge, Mass., 1951-65; with Shawmut Bank of Boston (N.A.), 1965-87, sr. v.p., 1969-87. Author: History of Harvard Baseball, 1964, History of Massachusetts Institute of Technology Athletics, 1950. Trustee, pres. Museum of Sci.; chmn. bd. dirs. Freedom House, Freedom Trail; pres. Freedom Trail Found.; chmn. Freedom Trail Commn.; exec. com. Wang Ctr. for Performing Arts. Served to capt. USMCR, 1943-46. Named to Harvard U. Athletic Hall of Fame (baseball). Mem. Pub. Relations Soc. Am. (presdl. citiation for meritorious service 1962), Assoc. Grantmakers of Mass. (v.p.). Clubs: Harvard (Boston), Harvard Varsity (Boston); Winchester Country. Home: 635 Witchtrot Rd Sanbornville NH 03872-4224

BERG, WILLIAM JAMES, French language educator, writer, translator; b. Dunkirk, N.Y., Oct. 26, 1942; s. Francis John and Adalyn Huldah (Goodwin) B.; m. Verity Anne Fry, July 2, 1966 (div. 1985); children—Jennifer Anne, Jessica Lyn; m. Laurey Kramer Martin, Feb. 1, 1986; stepchildren: Stirling Brooke Martin, Hunter Kirk Martin. Cert. pratique, Sorbonne, Paris, 1962-63; B.A., Hamilton Coll., 1964; M.A., Princeton U., 1966, Ph.D., 1969. NDEA inst. asst. Hamilton Coll., Clinton, N.Y., 1964; teaching asst. Princeton (N.J.) U., 1966; instr. French U. Wis., 1967-68, asst. prof., 1968-73, assoc. prof., 1973-79, prof., 1979—, assoc. chmn. French dept., 1974-75, 78-79, 79-80, 90-92, chmn. dept. French and Italian, 1982-85; dir. Acad. Yr. Abroad, Paris and N.Y.C., 1973-74; outside examiner Swarthmore Coll., 1978, No. Ill. U., 1985, 86; outside program evaluator U. Mich., 1979; tenure reviewer Swarthmore Coll., 1982, Tulane U., 1985, Marquette U., 1992; invited lectr. Rice U., 1985, U. Tenn., 1993; full prof. reviewer Georgetown U., 1984, Swarthmore Coll., 1992, U. Mich., 1994, Northwestern U., 1996, U. Colo., 1997; editl. bd. Summa Publs., Birmingham, Ala., 1983—; reviewer panel for travel and collections NEH, 1989. Author: (with P. Schofer and D. Rice) Poèmes, Pièces, Prose, 1973, (with G. Moskos and M. Grimaud) Saint/Oedipus. Psychocritical Approaches to Flaubert's Art, 1982, (with L. Martin) Images, 1989, The Visual Novel, 1992, (with L. Martin) Emile Zola Revisited, 1992, Gustave Flaubert, 1997; author study guides on Twain's Huckleberry Finn, 1986, Tom Sawyer, 1987, (with L. Martin) Flaubert's Madame Bovary, 1989, Zola's Germinal, 1989, Maupassant's Short Stories, 1992; translator: (with P. Scott) Graphics and Graphic Information-Processing, 1981; Semiology of Graphics (design award Midwest Books Competition 1983), 1983-84; mem. editl. bd. Substance, 1971-79; contbr. articles to profl. jours. Travel grantee Am. Philos. Soc., 1969, rsch. grantee U. Wis., 1969, 75, 81-82, 86, 87; Vilas assoc., 1991-93, honors fellow, 1994—; Halverson-Bascom professorship, 1995—; recipient U. Wis. Chancellor's award for excellence in tchg., 1995. Mem. Midwest MLA (French nominating com. 1975-78), Com. on Instnl. Cooperation (Romance lang. chairs 1982-85), MLA, Am. Coun. Tchrs. of Fgn. Langs., Phi Beta Kappa. Avocations: tennis, guitar. Home: 5201 Pepin Pl Madison WI 53705-4724 Office: U Wis Dept French and Italian Madison WI 53706

BERGA, SARAH LEE, women's health physician, educator; b. San Benito, Tex., May 22, 1954; d. John Orrin and Nancy Estelle (Michael) B.; m. Frederick S. Sherman, Sept. 26, 1981 (div. 1994); children: Alexis Estelle, Nathaniel Abbott; m. Lockwood Hoehl, Oct. 28, 1995. BA, U. Va., 1976, MD, 1980. Diplomate Am. Bd. Ob-Gyn., Am. Bd. Reproductive Endocrinology. From asst. to assoc. prof. U. Pitts., 1988—; dir. reproductive endocrinology fellowship U. Pitts. Sch. of Medicine, 1995—; med. dir. menopause ctr. Magee-Womens Hosp.; assoc. med. dir. Gen. Clin. Rsch. Ctr.; bd. dirs. U. Pitts. Physicians. Mem. Soc. Gynecologic Investigation (coun. mem. 1999—). Home: 5432 Northumberland St Pittsburgh PA 15217-1129 Office: U Pitts Magee Womens Hosp 300 Halket St Pittsburgh PA 15213-3108

BERGAMO, RON, marketing executive; b. Palm Springs, Calif., Nov. 26, 1943; s. Ralph and Dorothy (Johnson) B.; m. Jane E. Reed; children: Brad, Doug, Steve. BS, U. Ariz., 1965; MBA, Northwestern U., 1972. With Leo Burnett, 1966-68, NBC Network, 1968-69, AVCO TV Sales, 1969-72, Eller Outdoor, 1972-74, Sta. KMBC-TV Sales, 1974-77, LSM Sta. WFAA-TV, 1977-80; gen. mgr. Sta. KFDM-TV, Beaumont, Tex., 1980-82, Sta. KWCH-TV, Wichita, Kans., 1983-88; pres., gen. mgr. KSAZ-TV, Phoenix, 1988-95; exec. v.p., gen. mgr. KWBA TV58, Tucson, Ariz., 1997—. Bd. dirs. Greater Phoenix Leadership, Phoenix Art Mus., Boys/Girls Club, Fiesta Bowl. With U.S. Army NG, 1965-71. Bd. dirs. Phoenix Charities, Phoenix Meml. Hosp. Recipient Gen. Mgr. of Yr. award Am. Women in Radio and TV, 1990, Phoenix award Pub. Rels. Soc. Am., 1992; named Wichita Ad Person of Yr., 1985, Person of Yr. Phoenix Ad Club, 1993. Mem. Ariz. Broadcasters Assn. (pres. 1993), Ariz. C. of C. (bd. dirs.), Sigma Chi. Republican. Methodist. Avocations: reading, travel, Porsches. Home: 5901 E Stella Ln Paradise Vly AZ 85253-4276 Office: KWBA-TV58 3481 E Michigan St Tucson AZ 85714-2025

BERGAN, EDMUND PAUL, JR., lawyer; b. N.Y.C., May 6, 1950; s. Edmund Paul and Alice (Gordon) P. B.; m. Patricia Ann Gallagher, Jan. 31, 1987; children: Annabel (dec.), Caroline. BA, Holy Cross Coll., 1971; JD, Fordham U., 1975. Bar: N.Y. 1976. Staff atty. SEC, Washington, D.C., 1975-77; v.p., assoc. gen. counsel Securities Industry Assn., N.Y.C., 1977-81; v.p., asst. gen. counsel Alliance Capital Mgmt. LP, N.Y.C., 1981-88; v.p. gen. counsel Alliance Fund Distbrs., N.Y.C., 1988-94; v.p., gen. counsel Alliance Fund Svc. Subs., N.Y.C., 1988-94; sr. v.p., gen. counsel Alliance Fund Distbrs. and Alliance Fund Svcs., N.Y.C., 1994—. Mem. ABA (mem. fed. securities com. 1982—), Investment Co. Inst. (SEC rules com. 1986—, closed-end fund com. 1989—, chmn. 1992-97, various subcoms.). Republican. Roman Catholic. Avocations: historical studies, athletics. Office: Alliance Capital Mgmt LP 1345 Ave of Americas New York NY 10105-3198

BERGAN, JOHN JEROME, vascular surgeon; b. Tampico, Mex., Apr. 4, 1927; s. Ernest and Arva Elizabeth (Yeagley) B.; m. Elisabeth Molnar; children: Elizabeth Anne, Margaret Alice, John Widener. B.S., Purdue U., 1950; M.D., Ind. U., 1954. Intern Ind. U. Med. Center, 1954-55; resident in surgery Northwestern U. Med. Sch., Chgo., 1955-59; mem. faculty Northwestern U. Med. Sch., 1959-88, Magerstadt prof., 1967-88, chief div. vascular surgery, 1970-88, prof. emeritus, 1988—; mem. staff Northwestern Meml. Hosp., VA Lakeside Hosp., 1959-89; clin. prof. surgery U. Calif., San Diego, 1989—; attending staff Scripps Meml. Hosp., La Jolla, Calif., 1988—; clin. prof. surgery USUHS, Bethesda, Md., 1989—; prof. surgery Loma Linda U. Med. Sch., 1994—; hon. prof. surgery U. Belgrade. Editor: (with James Yao) Venous Problems, 1978, Gangrene and Severe Ischemia of the Lower Extremities, 1978, Surgery of the Aorta, 1979, Surgical Techniques in Vascular Surgery, 1980, Aneurysms, 1981, Cerebrovascular Insufficiency, 1982, Management of Circulatory Disorders, 1983, Surgery of the Veins, 1984, Reoperative Arterial Surgery, 1985, Emergency Vascular Surgery, 1986, Arterial Surgery: New Developments, 1987, Aortic Surgery, 1988, Techniques in Arterial Surgery, 1989,Venous Disorders, 1990, (with R. Kistner) Atlas of Venous Surgery, 1992, (with P. S. van Bemmelen) Quantitative Measurement of Venous Incompetence, 1992, (with V. Guzzetta) Sailing and Yachting First Aid, 1992, (with M. Goldman) Varicose Veins and Telangiectasias: Diagnosis and Management, 1993, Malattie delle Vene, 1993, Atlante di Chirurgia delle Vene, 1993, Ambulatory Treatment of Venous Disease, 1995; Yearbook of Vascular Surgery, 1986, 87, 88, 89, 90, 91, 92, (with P. Gloviszcki) Atlas of Sub Fascial Endoscopic Perforator Vein Surgery, 1997; editor: Arterial Surgery, 1984; founding editor Postgraduate Vascular Surgery, Internat. Vascular Surgery; founder, editor Venous Digest; mem. editl. bd. Surgery, Jour. Vascular Surgery, Annals Vascular Surgery, Brit. Jour. Surgery, Phlebology, Vascular Surgery, Jour. Endovasc. Surgery, Dermatol. Surgery; founder, editor Internat. Venous Digest by Fax; editor emeritus Vascular Forum; contbr. numerous articles to profl. jours. Served with USN, 1946-48. Recipient Rovsing medal Danish Surg. Soc. Fellow ACS (dir. internat. transplantation registry 1971-75), Royal Coll. Surgeons (hon.); mem. Am. Surg. Assn., Ctrl. Surg. Assn. (recorder 1976—), Internat. Cardiovasc. Soc. (v.p. 1973), Soc. Vascular Surgery (pres. 1985), Internat. Assn. Vascular Surgeons (pres. 1986), Soc. Univ. Surgeons (hon. lectr. 1979), Soc. Clin. Vascular Surgery (hon.), Assn. Surgeons (hon.), Vascular Soc. Great Britain and Ireland (hon.), Midwestern Vascular Surg. Soc. (founding mem., pres. 1978-79), Gulf Coast Vascular Soc. (pres. 1988), Chgo. Surg. Soc. (v.p. 1972, pres. 1987), New England Vascular Soc. (hon., lectr. 1988), Soc. Clin. Vascular Surgery (hon., lectr. 1988) South Assn. Vascular Surgery (hon., lectr. 1988), Vascular Surgery Sect. Royal Australasian Soc., Am. Venous Forum (founding mem. 1988, pres. 1989), So. Calif. Vascular Soc. (pres. 1996), Vascular Surg. Soc. South Africa (hon. lectr. 1991), Swedish Surg. Soc., Russian Vascular Soc. (hon. lectr. 1992), Soc. Phlebologicas Scandanavicas (hon. lectr. 1992). Home: 7744 Ludington Pl La Jolla CA 92037-3806 Office: 9850 Genesee Ave Ste 800 La Jolla CA 92037-1219

BERGAN, WILLIAM LUKE, lawyer; b. Auburn, N.Y., Sept. 3, 1939; s. Luke Joseph and Mary Beatrice (Twyne) B.; m. Marilyn Terese Meister, Aug. 8, 1964 (dec. May 1990); children: William Luke, Elizabeth M., Ann G.; m. Frances Maureen West, Jan. 2, 1993. BA summa cum laude, Niagara U., Niagara Falls, N.Y., 1961; JD magna cum laude, Syracuse U., 1964.

Bar: N.Y. 1964, U.S. Dist. Ct. (we. dist.) N.Y. 1977, U.S. Dist. Ct. (no. dist.) N.Y. 1968, U.S. Ct. Appeals (2d cir.) 1970. Sr. ptnr. Bond, Schoeneck & King, Syracuse, 1966—. Trustee, past pres. parish coun. St. John the Evangelist Ch., Syracuse, 1993—. Capt. U.S. Army, 1964-66. Fellow Am. Bar Found., Coll. Labor and Employment Lawyers; mem. ABA, N.Y. State Bar Assn. (chmn. labor and employment law sect. 1981-82, exec. com. 1976—), Onondaga County Bar Assn., Nat. Assn. Coll. and Univ. Attys., Am. Arbitration Assn. (bd. dirs. 1984—), Greater Syracuse C. of C. (bd. dirs. 1992-96), Niagara U. Alumni Assn., Century Club Syracuse. Democrat. Roman Catholic. Avocation: tennis.

BERGÉ, CAROL, author; b. N.Y.C., 1928; d. Albert and Molly Peppis; m. Jack Bergé, June 1955; 1 child, Peter. Asst. to pres. Pendray Public Relations, N.Y.C., 1955; disting. prof. lit. Thomas Jefferson Coll., Allendale, Mich., 1975-76; instr. adult degree program Goddard Coll. at Asilomar, 1976; tchr. fiction and poetry U. Calif. Extension Program, Berkeley, 1976-77; assoc. prof. U. So. Miss., Hattiesburg, 1977-78; vis. prof. Honors Ctr. and English dept. U. N.Mex., 1978-79, 87; vis. lectr. Wright State U., 1979, SUNY, Albany, 1980-81; tchr. Poets and Writers, Poets in the Schs. (N.Y. State Council on Arts), 1970-72, Poets in the Schs. (Conn. Commn. Arts); propr. Blue Gate Gallery of Art and Antiques, 1988-99. Author: (fiction) The Unfolding, 1969, A Couple Called Moebius, 1972, Acts of Love: An American Novel, 1973 (N.Y. State Coun. on Arts CAPS award 1974), Timepieces, 1977, The Doppler Effect, 1979, Fierce Metronome, 1981, Secrets, Gossip & Slander, 1984, Zebras, or, Contour Lines, 1991; (poetry) The Vulnerable Island, 1964, Lumina, 1965, Poems Made of Skin, 1968, The Chambers, 1969, Circles, as in the Eye, 1969, An American Romance, 1969, From a Soft Angle: Poems About Women, 1972, The Unexpected, 1976, Rituals and Gargoyles, 1976, A Song, A Chant, 1978, Alba Genesis, 1979, Alba Nemesis, 1979, (reportage) The Vancouver Report, 1965; editor Ctr. Mag., 1970-84, pub., 1991—; editor Miss. Rev., 1977-78, Subterraneans, 1975-76, Paper Branches, 1987, LIGHT YEARS: The N.Y.C. Coffeehouse Poets of the 1960's, 1999; contbg. editor Woodstock Rev., 1977-81, Shearsman mag., 1980-82, S.W. Profile, 1981; editor, pub. CENTER Press, 1991-93; pub.: Medicine Journeys (Carl Ginsburg), Coastal Lives (Miriam Sagan), 1991; co-pub.: Zebras (Carol Berge). Nat. Endowment Arts fellow, 1979-80. Mem. Authors' League, Poets and Writers, MacDowell Fellows Assn., Nat. Press Women. Home: 2070 Calle Contento Santa Fe NM 87505-5406

BERGE, SCOTT JERRY, accountant; b. Ft. Francis, Ont., Can., Feb. 16, 1972; (parents Am. citizens); s. Jerry Leroy and Mary Dawn (Severinson) B. B Acctg. with honors, U. N.D., 1994. CPA, N.D. Sr. staff acct. Drees, Riskey & Vallager, Ltd., Grand Forks, 1994—. Mem. N.D. Soc. CPA's (pub. rels. com. 1997—, v.p. Grand Forks chpt. 1997—), Greater Grand Forks Jaycees (bd. dirs. 1998—). Avocations: golf, tennis, hunting, automobile racing. Home: 2702 Cherry St Grand Forks ND 58201-7454 Office: Drees Riskey & Vallager Ltd 1405 Library Cir Grand Forks ND 58201-6317

BERGEL, MENY, physician, researcher; b. Rosario, Santa Fe, Argentina, Mar. 26, 1925; s. Simon and Alegria Bergel. MD, U. Litoral, Rosario, 1947. Postdoctoral fellow, rsch. fellow U. Rochester, N.Y., 1952-53; dir. rsch. Sommer Leprosarium, Buenos Aires, 1958-63, Inst. Leprology, Rosario, 1963-85; prof. biology J.F.K. U., Buenos Aires, 1976—; prof. postgrad. studies Argentine Med. Assn., Buenos Aires, 1983—; med. dir. Leprosy Rsch. Inst., Buenos Aires, 1985—; guest investigator Rockefeller Inst., N.Y.C., 1959; cons. dermatologist Ferroviario Hosp. Rosario, 1956—, Pub. Health Svc.-Dermatology, Buenos Aires, 1960—; cons. researcher Centro Leprologico S. Araujo, Curitiba, Brazil, 1975—. Author: Elements of Leprosy, 1963, Leprosy as a Metabolic Disease, 1989, Leprosy: Etiology, Pathology, Treatment, 1990, Metabolic Theory of Leprosy, 1992. Recipient Rosendhal award of Weizman Inst., Mitsuda award Inst. of Leprology; Fulbright scholar, 1959; grantee Pub. Health Svc., U.S., 1961, WHO, Switzerland, 1972, Muscular Dystrophy Assn. Am., 1973; nominated for Gandhi Internat. award, 1993. Mem. Argentine Soc. Pharmacology (hon. pres. 1971), Nat. Acad. Scis. (Hansen award), Argentine Med. Assn. (Sommer award 1958), Soc. of Dermatology (hon., Peru), Soc. of Dermatology (hon., Greece), Soc. of Leprology (hon., Korea), Soc. of Leprology (hon., Philippines), Italian Soc. Pharmacology (hon.), Denmark Soc. of Biology (hon.), Order of Malta (comdr. 1973), Rotary (Order of Garay 1987), Lancisian Acad. (hon.). Jewish. Avocations: painting, sculpture. Office: Inst of Leprology, Paraguay 1365, 1057 Buenos Aires Argentina

BERGELSON, JEFFREY MICHAEL, pediatrician , educator; b. Phila., 1950. MD, U. Penn., 1981. Diplomate Am. Bd. Pediatrics. Resident in pediatrics U. Calif., San Francisco, 1981-84; fellow in infectious diseases Children's Hosp., Boston, 1985-88; instr. Harvard Med. Sch., Boston, 1988-94; asst. prof. Dana-Farber Cancer Inst., Boston, 1994-97; pediatrician Children's Hosp., Phila., 1997—; asst. prof. pediats. U. Pa., Phila., 1997—; asst. prof. pediatrics Harvard Med. Sch., 1994—. Recipient Established Investigator award Am. Heart Assn., 1995. Office: Childrens Hosp Philadelphia Abramson 1202 E 34th St & Civic Ctr Philadelphia PA 19104

BERGEN, CANDICE, actress, writer, photojournalist; b. Beverly Hills, Calif., May 9, 1946; d. Edgar and Frances (Westerman) B.; m. Louis Malle, Sept. 27, 1980 (dec. 1995); 1 dau., Chloe. Ed., U. Pa. Model during coll. Films include The Group, The Sand Pebbles, The Day the Fish Came Out, Live for Life, The Magus, Soldier Blue, Getting Straight, The Hunting Party, Carnal Knowledge, T.R. Baskin, The Adventurers, 11 Harrowhouse, Bite the Bullet, The Wind and the Lion, The Domino Principle, The End of the World in Our Usual Bed in a Night Full of Rain, Oliver's Story, Starting Over, Rich and Famous, Gandhi, 1982, Stick, 1985; TV series: Murphy Brown, 1988-98 (Emmy award, Leading Actress in a Comedy Series, 1988-89, 89-90, 91-92, 93-94, 94-95); TV films Arthur the King, 1985, Murder by Reason of Insanity, 1985, Mayflower Madam, 1987, Tim, 1996; TV miniseries Hollywood Wives, 1985, Trying Times, Moving Day; author Knockwood; photojournalist credits include articles for Life, Playboy; dramatist: (play) The Freezer (included in Best Short Plays of 1968). Recipient Emmy awards for lead actress in a comedy series, 1989, 90, 92, 94, 95.

BERGEN, CHRISTOPHER BROOKE, opera company administrator, translator, editor; b. L.A., Jan. 11, 1949; s. Edward Grinnell Bergen and Alvina Ellen (Temple) Stevens; m. Mary Novella Tilman, Apr. 11, 1998. BA, UCLA, 1971; MA, Yale U., 1977. Conf. officer IAEA, Vienna, Austria, 1973-75, data analyst, 1979-81; import mgr. COBEC Trading Corp., N.Y.C., 1978-79; assoc. Geissler Engring. Co., Oakland, Calif., 1982-83; dir. Yale Cons. Assocs., San Francisco, 1983-84; editor INPUT, Mountain View, Calif., 1984; adminstr. surtitles San Francisco Opera, 1985-98. Editor profl. jours.; translator operatic texts for projection during performances at San Francisco Opera, Met. Opera, Lyric Opera of Chgo., Washington Opera, many other opera cos., symphonies and conservatories in U.S., abroad. Mem. Amnesty Internat., Sierra Club. Democrat. Avocations: literature, rowing. Home: 1115 Prospect Ave # 306 Brooklyn NY 11218

BERGEN, JOHN DONALD, communications, public affairs executive; b. Bronx, N.Y., Sept. 16, 1942; s. John D. and Alice Jean (Almand) B.; m. Linda L. Rosewall, Nov. 21, 1964; children: John M., Michael L. BS in Engring., U.S. Mil. Acad., 1964; MA in English, Ind. U., 1971. Commd. 2d lt. U.S. Army, 1964, advanced through grades to lt. col., 1968; battalion advisor Vietnam, 1968-69; comdr. U.S. Army, Republic of Korea, 1974-76; prof. U.S. Mil. Acad., West Point, N.Y., 1971-74; strategic planner Dept. Def., Washington, 1976-81; dir. speechwriting and issue mgmt. Office of Sec. Def., Washington, 1981-84; v.p., corp. affairs RCA, N.Y.C., 1984-86; mgr. corp. affairs Gen. Electric Corp., Fairfield, Conn., 1986; sr. v.p., chief adminstrv. officer Hill & Knowlton, Inc., N.Y.C., 1987, exec. v.p., gen. mgr. ea. region, 1988-90, also bd. dirs.; pres., COO, Hill and Knowlton USA, N.Y.C., 1990-91; pres., CEO, GCI Group, N.Y.C., 1991-96; sr. v.p. corp. rels. Westinghouse/CBS, N.Y.C., 1996-98; pres. Coun. of PR Firms, 1998—. Author: Military Communications: A Test for Technology, 1987; contbr. articles to profl. and tech. jours. Chmn. Inst. of Pub. Rels. Named Outstanding Young Am., Jaycees, 1973. Mem. West Point Soc., Am. Mgmt. Assn. (mktg. coun.), Pub. Rels. Soc. Am., Pub. Rels. Seminar. Roman Catholic. Avocations: tennis, soccer, sports officiating. Home: 1789 Wrightstown Rd Newtown PA 18940-2603 Office: CPRF Ste 5029 11 Penn Plaza New York NY 10001

BERGEN, KENNETH WILLIAM, lawyer; b. Harlingen, N.J., Sept. 13, 1911; s. Edward Burgess and Adelia (Mertz) B.; m. Emily Fetter; children: Bruce, Carol Franklin, Nancy Flint, Roger. AB, Rutgers U., 1934; LLB, Harvard U., 1937; DHL (hon.), Colby Coll., 1983. Bar: N.Y. 1938, Mass. 1943. Atty. Tax Ct. U.S., 1942-43; ptnr. Bingham Dana LLP, Boston, 1954-83; assoc. White & Case, N.Y.C., 1937-42; of counsel Bingham Dana LLP, Boston, 1983—; pres.; pres. Mass. Continuing Legal Edn.-New England Law Inst., Inc., 1974-77, trustee, 1969-78, pres. 1976-77; co-chmn. Conf. Reps. of ABA and trust div. Am. Bankers Assn., 1974-78; mem. adv. com. U.S. Ho. of Reps. Ways and Means Com. on Adminstrn. Fed. Tax Laws, 1956, income taxation estates and trusts, 1958; bd. dirs., co-founder, exec. dir. Tax Inst. New England, 1948—, pres., 1994—; mem. adv. com. Tax Lawyer, 1975—; mem. planning com., co-founder Colby Coll. Estate Planning and Tax Inst., 1953—; mem. Mass. Bd. Registration C.P.A.'s, 1956-60; dir., lectr. grad. tax program Northeastern U. Sch. Law, 1946-52; adv. com., lectr. Boston U. Law Sch. Grad. Tax Program; mem. adv. group Commr. of IRS, 1987. Moderator Town of Lincoln, Mass., 1966-78, 94-95; mem. Lincoln-Sudbury Regional H.S. Com., 1956-62, Lincoln Rep. Town Com., 1950-87, chmn., 1954-62; chmn. Rural Land Found. of Lincoln, 1966-92. Mem. ABA (tax sect., past sec., mem. coun.), Am. Coll. Trust and Estate Counsel (past regent), Am. Coll. Tax Counsel, Am. Law Inst., Am. Bar Found., Boston Bar Assn. (past mem. coun., chmn. sect. profl. responsibility, chmn. com. on legislation, co-chmn. peer support com.), Internat. Acad. Estate and Trust Law (exec. coun.), Mass. Soc. CPAs (hon.). Office: 150 Federal St Boston MA 02110-1713

BERGEN, POLLY, actress; b. Bluegrass, Tenn.; d. William and Lucy (Lawhorn) Burgin; m. Freddie Fields, Feb. 13, 1956 (div. 1976); children: Kathy, Pamela, Peter. Pres. Polly Bergen Cosmetics, Polly Bergen Jewelry, Polly Bergen Shoes. Author: Fashion and Charm, 1960, Polly's Principles, 1974, I'd Love To, But What'll I Wear, 1977; author, producer for TV: Leave of Absence, 1994; Broadway plays include Champagne Complex, John Murray Andersons' Almanac, First Impression, Plaza Suite, Love Letters; films include Cape Fear, Move Over Darling, Kisses for My President, At War with the Army, The Stooge, That's My Boy, The Caretakers, A Guide for the Married Man, Making Mr. Right, Cry-Baby, 1990, Dr. Jekyll and Ms. Hyde, When We Were Colored, 1994; performed in one woman shows in Las Vegas, Nev., and Reno; albums: Bergen Sings Morgan, The Party's Over, All Alone By the Telephone, Polly and Her Pop, The Four Seasons of Love, Annie Get Your Gun and Do Re Mi, My Heart Sings, Act One Sing Too; numerous TV appearances including star of The Polly Bergen Show, NBC-TV; other TV appearances include The Helen Morgan Story, 1957 (Emmy award as best actress), To Tell the Truth, The Lightning Field, The Surrogate, For Hope; miniseries include The Winds of War (Emmy nomination), 79 Park Ave, War and Remembrance, 1988 (Emmy nomination); writer, prodr. NBC movie Leave of Absence, 1994. Bd. dirs. Martha Graham Dance Ctr., The Singer Co., Soc. Singers, Calif. Abortion and Reproductive Rights Action League, Show Coalition; hon. canister campaign chairperson Cancer Care, Inc., Nat. Cancer Found.; founder Nat. Bus. Coun. for ERA; mem. Planned Parenthood Fedn., Am. Bd. Advs.; mem. nat. adv. com. NARAL, Hollywood Women's Polit. Com. Recipient Fame award Top Ten in TV, 1957-58, Troupers award Sterling Publs., 1957, Editors and Critics award Radio and TV Daily, 1958, Outstanding Working Woman award Downtown St. Louis, Inc., Golden Plate award Am. Acad. Achievement, 1969, Outstanding Mother's award Nat. Mothers' Day Com., 1984, Best Achievement in New Jewelry Design award, 1986, Cancer Care award, 1989, Woman of Achievement award LWV, 1990, Extraordinary Achievement award Nat. Women's Law Ctr., 1991, Freedom of Choice award Calif. Abortion and Reproductive Rights Action League, 1992; Polly Bergen Cardio-Pulmonary Rsch. Lab., Children's Rsch. Inst. and Hosp., Denver dedicated, 1970. Mem. AFTRA, AGVA, SAG, Actors Equity. Office: 101 W 55th St New York NY 10019-5343

BERGEN, STANLEY SILVERS, JR., retired university president, physician; b. Princeton, N.J., May 2, 1929; s. Stanley Silvers and Leah (Johnson) B.; m. Suzanne E. Miller, Nov. 16, 1965; children: Steven Richard, Victoria Elizabeth, Stuart Vaughn; children by previous marriage: Stanley Silvers III, Amy Dorle. AB, Princeton U., 1951; MD, Columbia U., 1955; hon. degrees, Bloomfield Coll., 1972, Stevens Inst., 1985; LLD (hon.), Princeton U., 1995. Resident St. Luke's Hosp., N.Y.C., 1955-58; chief resident, Francis Zabriskie fellow St. Luke's Hosp., 1958-59, asst. chief dept. medicine, 1959-60, asst. attending physician, 1962-64; med. dir. Convalescent and Research Unit, Greenwich, Conn., 1962-64; chief medicine Cumberland Hosp., Bklyn., 1964-68; asst. dir. dept. medicine Bklyn.-Cumberland Med. Center, 1964-68, chief community medicine, 1968-70; sr. v.p. N.Y.C. Health & Hosps. Corp., 1970-71; instr. medicine Columbia, 1959-64; asso. prof. medicine Downstate Med. Sch., Bklyn., 1964-71; pres. U. Medicine and Dentistry N.J., Newark, 1971-98, founding pres. emeritus, 1998—; prof. medicine N.J. Med. Sch., Robert Wood Johnson Med. Sch., Sch. Osteo. Medicine; prof. cmty. dentistry N.J. Dental Sch.; attending med. staff Univ. Hosp., Newark, 1971—, VA Hosp., East Orange, 197298—, Robert Wood Johnson U. Hosp., 1981-98; trustee Univ. HealthCare Corp., 1993—; chair bd. trustees Univ. Health Plans N.J., 1994—; trustee University Heights Sci. Park, 1995—, chmn. bd., 1996—. Author articles in field. Mem. Mayor's Commn. Health and Hosps., N.Y.C., 1969-70; mem. N.J. Comprehensive Health Planning Coun., 1971-91; chmn. N.J. Commn. to Study Structure and Function N.J. Dept. Health, 1973, N.J. Abortion Commn., 1975, Adv. Coun. Grad. Edn. N.J., 1978-98; adv. com. mcpl. health svc. program R.W. Johnson, also, Nat. Conf. Mayors, 1980-85; mem. Bd. Comprehensive Health, Newark, 1976-81, treas., 1972-80; bd. dirs. Cancer Inst. N.J., 1974-78; bd. dirs. Ednl. Commn. Fgn. Med. Grads., 1982-91, sec., vice chmn., 1985-86, chmn., 1986-91; bd. dirs., mem. exec. com. Hastings Ctr. on Biomed. Ethics, 1976—, chmn. devel. com., 1980-95, mem. governance com., 1995—, chmn. elect, 1997, chmn., 1998—; bd. dirs., mem. exec. com. Art Center No. N.J., 1978-82; chmn. N.J. Blood Banks Task Force, 1980-90; trustee Robert Wood Johnson U. Hosp., 1985-98, exec. com. 1987-98; trustee Hackensack Med. Ctr., 1990—, exec. com., 1992—; bd. joint mgrs. Cancer Inst. N.J., 1991-98, trustee 1998—; trustee Bergen Pines County Hosp., 1994-98, exec. com. 1994-98, trustee Univ. Healthcare Corp. of N.J., 1993-97, Gilda's Club No. N.J., 1997, treas., mem. exec. com., 1998—, Kessler Med. Rehab. Rsch. Edn. Corp., 1998—, Matheny Sch. and Hosp., 1998—, Internat. Ctr. Pub. Health Inc., 1999—; treas. Pres.'s Coun. N.J. Commn. Higher Edn., 1996-98; chmn. bd. trustees U. Health Plan N.J., 1997—; chair bd. mgrs. N.J. Ctr. Biomaterials, 1997—. First recipient Woodrow Wilson medal for pub. svc. leadership Gov. of N.J., 1987, Univ. medal UMDNJ, 1995. Fellow ACP, Assn. Am. Med. Colls., Am. Fedn. Clin. Rsch., Endocrine Soc., Clin. Soc. N.Y., Diabetes Assn. (v.p. 1969-70, chmn. clin. soc. 1968-69), N.Y. Acad. Scis., Am. Inst. Nutrition; mem. AMA (ho. dels. sect. on med. schs. 1978-98), Assn. Acad. Health Ctrs., Am. Diabetes Assn. (bd. dirs. N.J. affiliate), Am. Soc. Clin. Nutrition, Am. Coll. Healthcare Execs. (hon. fellow), Essex County Med. Soc., Med. Soc. N.J., Am. Hosp. Assn. (trustee 1992-94, chmn. com. grad. med. edn. 1974-76, mem. coun. profl. svcs. 1973-76, mem. governing coun. sect. met. hosps. 1984-87, com. med. edn. 1984-91, ad hoc com. on AIDS 1987-91, chmn. tech. com. biomed. ethics 1986-91, alt. del. Ho. Dels., 1991, mem. AHA regional policy bd., 1988-94, mem. internat. med. scholars program 1987-92, mem. com. to study single pathway to nat. med. licensure 1987-90, mem. com. to study clin. med. skills assessment 1988-92, trustee 1991-94, trustee regional plan commn. 1995-98), Greater Newark C. of C. (dir. 1978-84), Nat. Assn. Pub. Hosps. (trustee 1982-88), State N.J. Health Coord. Coun., Univ. Health System N.J. (trustee, exec. com. 1987-98), Univ. Hosp. Consortium (trustee 1988-92, exec. com. 1990-92). Home: 164 Glenwood Rd Englewood NJ 07631-1951 Office: U Medicine & Dentistry NJ 100 Bergen St Newark NJ 07103-2407 *My career has taken many significant turns, most of which have improved my ability to lead efforts toward better and more accessible health services. I have been fortunate in the opportunity to lead a variety of activities and to express creativity through institutions and individuals. My successes are due to the extent to which this nation still rewards those willing to work hard and learn from experience, as well as to the many intelligent, compassionate mentors with whose guidance I have been blessed.*

BERGEN, VIRGINIA LOUISE, principal, language arts educator; b. St. Louis, Apr. 5, 1945; d. Roland Daniel Paton and Gladys (Crawford) Gibson; m. Robert Elwood Bergen, July 11, 1964; children: Robert Brandon, Jennifer Lynn. BA, So. Ill. U., 1971, MS, 1973, EdS, 1975; Ednl. Adminstrn. Cert., U. Oreg., 1981. Cert. K-12 Ed. Ad., K-9 tchr., K-12 spl. edn., speech corr., reading specialist, Colo., Oreg., Ill, Mo., N.Mex. Speech therapist Dist. #175, Belleville, Ill., 1971-73; K-12 clin. tchr. Collinsville (Ill.) Unit #10, 1973-74, jr. high sch. LD tchr., 1974-78; edn. resource cons. Douglas Edn. Svc. Dist., Roseburg, Oreg., 1978-80; child devel. specialist Roseburg Dist. #4, 1980-82; asst. prin. Mesa County Valley Dist. #51, Grand Junction, Colo., 1982-85, prin., 1985—; vis. lectr. So. Ill. U., 1976-78; instr. Met. State Coll., Denver, 1989-91; lectr. Mesa State Coll., Grand Junction, 1991-92; in-svc. provider Mesa County Valley Sch. Dist. #51, 1982—, mem. standards and assessment steering com.; founding mem. governance bd. Basil T. Knight Staff Devel. Ctr., Dist. #51, Grand Junction, 1986-89. Mem. Colo. Assn. Sch. Execs., Phi Delta Kappa. Avocations: reading, alpine skiing, travel, Nordic skiing. Office: Fruitvale Elem Sch 585 30 Rd Grand Junction CO 81504-5602

BERGER, ANDREW L., investment banker, lawyer; b. N.Y.C., Dec. 10, 1946; s. Harry and Jennie (Kronenberg) B.; m. Brook Jaye Horowitz, June 16, 1968; children—Adam Linley, Douglas Bradley. BS, Lehigh U., 1968; JD, Columbia U., 1971. Bar: N.Y. 1972. Assoc. Cravath, Swaine & Moore, N.Y.C., 1971-78; ptnr. Rivkin, Sherman & Levy, N.Y.C., 1979-81; mem. exec. com., adminstrv. mng. dir. L.F. Rothschild & Co. Inc., N.Y.C., 1981-88, pres., 1987-88; mem. exec. com. L.F. Rothschild Holdings Inc., 1986-88; chmn. bd., trustee L.F. Rothschild Managed Trust, 1986-88; chmn. bd. L.F. Rothschild Fund Mgmt. Inc., 1986-88, also bd. dirs., 1986-88; chmn. bd., trustee Hampton Utilities Trust, 1988; mng. dir. Wertheim Schroder & Co. Inc., N.Y.C., 1988-94, Lehman Bros., London, 1994-98; mem. exec. mgmt. Union Bancaire Privee, Geneva, 1998—; bd. dirs. Nordfinanz Bank, Zurich, Switzerland; mem. bd. govs. Nat. Assn. Securities Dealers, 1990-93. Mem. ABA, N.Y. Bar Assn., Grolier Club. Office: Union Bancaire Privee, 96-98 rue du Rhone, 1204 Geneva Switzerland

BERGER, ANITA HAZEL, psychotherapist, adult educator, organizational consultant; b. N.Y.C., Mar. 27, 1930; d. Harry William and Sadye (Lauzar) Fink; m. Ramon Francis Berger, May 6, 1951, (dec.); children: Elizabeth Harrie, Gideon Samuel. BA cum laude, Bklyn. Coll., 1951; MSW, U. Pa., 1953; postgrad., Columbia U., NYU. Cert. social worker, N.Y.; lic. ind. clin. social worker R.I., Mass. Psychotherapist Jewish Community Svcs. L.I., N.Y.C., 1953-57; psychotherapist, field work instr. Jewish Family Svc., N.Y.C., 1957-60; supr. lower Manhattan social svc. dept., dir. student unit N.Y.C. Housing Authority, 1972-74; asst. prof. SUNY Grad. Sch. Social Work, Buffalo, 1974-75; psychotherapist Ch. Mission of Hope Family Svc., Erie County Mental Health Svcs., Buffalo, 1975-77; pvt. practice Providence, 1978—; instr. Brown Learning Community Brown U., 1988-92, 98—; cons. orgnl. and leadership devel., career performance Quest for Excellence, Providence, 1992-94, staff assoc., 1992-94; cons. Non-Profit Resources, 1996-98; orgnl. cons., 1995—; cons. orgnl. devel. Bus. Vol. for the Arts, Greater Providence C. of C. Coord. Community Ctr. Art Show, N.Y.C., 1964; rep. community planning bd. 2 Congressman Koch's, N.Y.C., 1968-71; mem. adv. com. to bd. dirs. Mental Health Clinic, Buffalo, 1976-77; bd. dirs., chmn. tng. and edn. com., trainer Vols. in Action, Providence, 1979-85; mem. R.I. adv. com. U.S. Commn. on Civil Rights, 1981-85; rep. R.I. Coalition Against Bigotry, 1982-85; mem. allocations and budget com. United Way Southeastern New Eng., Providence, 1981-84; mem. R.I. Gov.'s Adv. Commn. on Women, 1982-85; vol. Greater Providence C. of C., Cmty. Svcs. Coun., R.I., Options for Working Parents, 1997—. Recipient Woman of Yr. award Providence Bus. and Profl. Women's Orgn., 1984. Fellow N.Y. State Soc. Clin. Social Work Psychotherapists; mem. Nat. Assn. Social Workers, R.I. Group Psychotherapy Assn. (pres. 1988-89), Alpha Kappa Delta. Jewish.

BERGER, BARBARA PAULL, social worker, marriage and family therapist; b. St. Louis, June 18, 1955; d. Ted and Florence Ann (Vines) Paull; m. Allan Berger, Dec. 27, 1980; children: Melissa Dawn, Tammi Alyse, Jessica Lauren. BS, U. Tex., 1977; MSSW, U. Wis., 1978. Diplomate Am. Bd. Clin. Social Work; lic. social worker, Tex., Ky.; cert. marriage and family therapist. Clin. social worker Child and Family Svcs., Buffalo, 1980-81, United Cerebral Palsy Assn., St. Louis, 1982-83; clin. social worker/coord. Jewish Family Life Edn. Jewish Family Svc., Dallas, 1984-85, 88-90; instr. Miss. Delta C. C., Greenville, 1991; child and adolescent therapist United Behavioral Systems, Louisville, 1993-94; therapist Inpsych, Louisville, 1994-98, Beacon Behavioral Health Group, Louisville, 1998—. Mem. NASW, Acad. Cert. Social Workers, Am. Assn. Marriage and Family Therapy, Phi Kappa Phi, Pi Lambda Theta, Omicron Nu. Home: 2719 Avenue Of The Woods Louisville KY 40241-6281

BERGER, BERNARD BEN, environmental and civil engineer, former educator and public health officer; b. N.Y.C., Aug. 21, 1912; s. Louis and Pauline (Margil) B.; m. Neoma Miller, 1939; children—Paul S., David R., Susan Beth Berger Atkins. B.S., MIT, 1935; M.S., Harvard U., 1948; Sc.D. (hon.), U. Mass., 1979. Registered profl. engr., Mass. Field engr. Met. Boston Housing Assn. Inc., 1935-39; sanitary engr. Kent County Dept. Health, Mich., 1939-41; commd. officer USPHS, 1941-66; liaison officer U.S. Biol. Labs., U.S. Army Chem. Corps., Fort Detrick, 1950-54; dir. water supply and water pollution control research activities Robert A. Taft Sanitary Engring. Ctr., Cin., 1954-63; ret., 1966; dir. water resources research ctr., prof. civil engring. U. Mass., Amherst, 1966-78, prof. emeritus, 1978—; water resources specialist Office Sci. and Tech., Washington, 1968-69; cons. EPA, Dept. Interior, NSF, Nat. Research Council, Israel, Water Research Commn., South Africa. Author: (report) Engineering Evaluation of the Virus Hazard in Water, 1970 (Rudolph Hering award ASCE 1971); editor: Control of Organic Substances in Water and Wastewater, 1983. Mem. Mass. Pub. Health Council, 1966-73; chmn. sci. adv. com. New Eng. River Basins Commn., 1975-78; mem. water com. Town of Amherst, 1970-78. Fellow Inst. Water and Environ. Mgmt. (U.K.) (hon.), ASCE; mem. Am. Water Works Assn., Am. Water Resources Assn., Boston Soc. Civil Engrs., Assn. Environ. Engring. Profs. (emeritus), Nat. Acad. Engring., Internat. Assn. Water Pollution Research (hon.), Water Environment Fedn. (hon.). Home: 230 Santa Maria St Apt 434E Venice FL 34285-1848

BERGER, BILLIE DAVID, corrosion engineer; b. Yale, Okla., May 30, 1919; s. Edward James Berger and Ada Lucy Botts Berger Roam; m. Twylla I. Briggs, Oct. 11, 1942; children: Nancy Berger Rano, Kay Berger Fritchman, Boise David. AA, Okla. State U., 1951; B.Indsl. Arts, Oklahoma City U., 1960. Cert. corrosion engr., Tex. Elec. contr. Okla., 1945-49; engr. Cities Svc. Gas Co., Oklahoma City, 1951-55, supt. comms. dept., 1956-66; elec. engr. Point Four Program, Ethiopia, 1955-56; supt. comms. Am. Ind. Oil Co., Kuwait, 1966-70; dept. head Occidental of Libya, Inc., Tripoli, 1970-74; instr., acting dept. head Okla. State U., Stillwater, 1974-79; cons., corrosion engr. Berger Cons. Svcs., 1979-94; engr. Municipality of Yale, 1994—. Author: Refinery Operations, 1979, Gas Handling and Field Processing, 1980, Basic Processing Knowledge, 1979, Modern Petroleum, 3d edit., 1992. With USN, 1940-45. Recipient Cert. of Spl. Congl. Recognition, Bill K. Brewster, Mem. of Congress, Washington, 1991, Award for Outstanding Achievement in Writing "Lest We Forget", VFW, Post 1118, Cushing, Okla., 1991, Gov.'s Commendation, State of Okla., 1991. Mem. VFW (jr. vice comdr. 1994-95), Am. Legion, Pearl Harbor Survivors Assn. (Medal), Yale C. of C., Jim Thorpe Meml. Found. (co-chmn. 1987-93). Democrat. Christian Ch. Avocations: acting, movie making, ranching, fishing, flying. Home: RR 2 Box 39 Yale OK 74085-9403

BERGER, CHARLES LEE, lawyer; b. Evansville, Ind. Oct. 14, 1947; s. Sydney L. and Sadelle (Kaplan) B.; m. Leslie Lilly, Apr. 20, 1973; children—Sarah, Rebecca, Leah. B.A., U. Evansville, 1969; J.D. cum laude, Ind. U., 1972. Bar: Ind. 1972, U.S. Dist. Ct. (so. dist.) Ind. 1972, U.S. Ct. Appeals (7th cir.) 1972, U.S. Ct. Appeals D.C. 1975, U.S. Supreme Ct. 1977, U.S. Dist. Ct. (we. dist.) Ky. 1981, U.S. Ct. Appeals (6th cir.) 1984. Ptnr., Berger & Berger, Evansville, 1972—; mem. study com. Ind. Supreme Ct. Rules of Evidence, 1993—; mem. Ind. Jud. Qualifications Disciplinary Commn., 1998—. Bd. dirs. Leadership Evansville, 1977. Fellow Ind. Bar Found.; mem. Ind. Bar Assn. (chmn. trial lawyers sect. 1982-83), Am. Bd. Trial Advocates, Ind. Trial Lawyers Assn. (bd. dirs. 1973-77, 77-84, v.p. 1984—). Jewish. Home: 7408 E Sycamore St Evansville IN 47715-3762 Office: Berger & Berger 313 Main St Evansville IN 47708-1485

BERGER, CHARLES MARTIN, food company executive; b. Wilkes-Barre, Pa., May 2, 1936; s. Edward and Sadie (Zwass) B.; m. Jane Elrod Purdy, June 5, 1960; children: Cary John Aaron, Elizabeth Anne, Valerie Ann. A.B., Princeton U., 1958; M.B.A., Harvard U., 1960. Mktg. mgmt.

Procter and Gamble Co., Cin., 1960-64; with H.J. Heinz Co., 1964—; gen. mgr. mktg. U.S.A. div. H.J. Heinz Co., Pitts., 1964-69, dir. corp. planning world hdqrs., 1969-70; mktg. dir. Heinz-London, 1970-72; mng. dir. Plasmon SpA, Milan, Italy, 1972-78; pres., CEO, chmn. Weight Watchers Internat. Inc., Jericho, N.Y., 1978—; chmn., CEO Heinz India Pvt. Ltd., Bombay, 1994—; dir. Stern's Miracle Gro, Inc., Sports & Fitness Corp. of Am.; lectr. Carnegie-Mellon Grad. Sch. Indsl. Adminstrn., 1968-69. Chmn. bd. dirs. Am. Sch. Milan, 1975-78; dir. Buckley Country Day Sch., Manhasset, N.Y., 1983-89. Mem. World Pres' Assn. (bd. dirs.), Met. Pres. Assn. (bd. dirs.). Republican. Jewish. Clubs: Princeton (N.Y.), Village Club of Sands Point (N.Y.). Office: Scotts Co 14111 Scottslawn Rd Marysville OH 43041

BERGER, DAVID, lawyer; b. Archbald, Pa., Sept. 6, 1912; s. Jonas and Anna (Raker) B.; children—Jonathan, Daniel. AB cum laude, U. Pa., 1932, LLB cum laude, 1936. Bar: Pa. 1938, D.C., N.Y. Asst. to prof. U. Pa. Law Sch., Phila., 1936-38, spl. asst. to dean; law clk. Pa. Supreme Ct., Phila., 1939-40; spl. asst. to dir. enemy alien identification program U.S. Dept. Justice, Washington, 1941-42; law clk. U.S. Ct. Appeals, 1946; pvt. practice Phila., Washington and N.Y.C.; city solicitor Phila., 1956-63; founder, chmn. Berger & Montague, P.C., Phila.; former counsel Sch. Dist. Phila.; former chmn. adv. com. Pa. Superior Ct.; mem. drafting com. fed. rules evidence U.S. Supreme Ct.; lectr. on legal subjects. Author numerous articles on law. Nat. commr. Anti-Defamation League; assoc. trustee U. Pa., mem. bd. overseers Law Sch.; Presdl. appointee U.S. Holocaust Meml. Coun.; dir. Internat. Tennis Hall of Fame; trustee Game Conservancy USA; bd. dirs. ARC, Palm Beach, Fla.; founder, mem. Friends of Art and Preservation in Embassies. Decorated Silver Star and Presdl. Unit Citation; Fellow Duke of Edinburgh's Award World Fellowship; David Berger chair of law for the improvement of the adminstrn. of justice established at U. Pa. Law Sch.; enshrined in U. Pa. Tennis Hall of Fame, 1997. Fellow Am. Coll. Trial Lawyers, Internat. Acad. Trial Lawyers, Internat. Soc. Barristers; mem. ABA (vice-chair tort and ins. practice sect. com. on comml. torts 1988-89), Phila. Bar Assn. (pres., bd. govs., chancellor), Phila. Bar Found. (past pres.), The Athenaeum Phila., Penn Club (N.Y.C., founder), Order of Coif, The Queens Club (London), Royal Ascot Racing Club (Ascot, Eng.). Home: Elephant Walk 109 Jungle Rd Palm Beach FL 33480-4809 Office: Berger & Montague PC 1622 Locust St Philadelphia PA 19103-6305

BERGER, DAVID, history educator; b. Bklyn., June 24, 1943; s. Isaiah and Shirley (Kravitz) B.; m. Pearl Rabinowitz, June 14, 1965; children: Miriam, Yitzhak, Gedalyah. BA, Yeshiva Coll., 1964; MA, Columbia U., 1965, PhD, 1970. Ordained rabbi, 1967. Instr. Yeshiva Coll., N.Y.C., 1968-70; asst. to assoc. prof. Bklyn. Coll., 1970-80; prof. Bklyn. Coll. and the Grad. Sch., CUNY, 1980—. Author: The Jewish-Christian Debate in the High Middle Ages (John Nicholas Brown prize 1983); co-author: Judaism's Encounter with other Cultures: Rejection or Integration?, 1997, Jews and "Jewish Christianity", 1978; editor: History and Hate: The Dimensions of Anti-Semitism, 1986. Bd. trustees Beth Din of Am., N.Y.C., 1995—. Recipient Bernard Revel Meml. award Yeshiva Coll. Alumni Assn., 1990. Fellow Am. Acad. for Jewish Rsch.; mem. Am. Hist. Assn., Medieval Acad. Am., Assn. for Jewish Studies (pres. 1997—), Internat. Assn. of Socs. for the Study of Jewish History (chair Am. sect. 1991—), Nat. Found. for Jewish Culture (vice-chair acad. adv. bd. 1996—), Am. Acad. for Jewish Rsch. (exec. com. 1992—). Office: Dept History Brooklyn Coll Brooklyn NY 11210

BERGER, DIANNE GWYNNE, educator; b. N.Y.C., Mar. 10, 1950; d. Harold and Mary Bell (Mott) Gwynne; m. Robert Milton Berger, Aug. 25, 1974; children: Matthew Robert Gwynne, Daniel Alan Gwynne. BS, Cornell U., 1971; MS, Drexel U., 1974; PhD, U. Pa., 1992. Cert. home econs. tchr., sexuality educator, family and consumer sci. educator and family life educator, Pa.; cert. supervision, curriculum and instrn. Tchr. family and consumer scis., sexuality edn. Wallingford-Swarthmore Sch. Dist., 1972—; cons., Swarthmore, 1986—, Swarthmore Presbyn. Ch., 1995, Elwyn Insts., Media, Pa., 1989-91, Phila. Task Force on Sex Edn., 1991-93. Cons. Trinity Coop. Day Nursery, Swarthmore, 1980-93, Renaissance Edn. Assn., Valley Forge, Pa., 1987-94, A Better Chance, Inc., Swarthmore, 1990-91. Grantee Impact, Inc., 1990. Mem. NEA, Am. Assn. Family and Consumer Scis., Soc. for Sci. Study of Sex (sec. ea. region, 1995-97), Nat. Coun. on Famly Rels., Am. Assn. Sex Educators, Counselors and Therapists (chmn. Delaware Valley sect. 1996-98). Home: 304 Dickinson Ave Swarthmore PA 19081-2001

BERGER, FRANK MILAN, biomedical researcher, scientist, former pharmaceutical company executive; b. Pilsen, Czech Republic, June 25, 1913; came to U.S., 1947, naturalized, 1953; s. Otto and Martha (Weigner) B.; m. Bozena Jahodova, Mar. 15, 1939 (dec. Nov. 1972); children: Franklin Milan, Thomas Jan; m. A. Christine Spade, May 21, 1975. M.D., U. Prague, Czechoslovakia, 1937, SUNY, 1948; D.Sc. (hon.), Phila. Coll. Sci. and Pharmacy, 1966. Research fellow physiology U. Prague, 1934-36, research asst. bacteriology, 1936-38; bacteriologist Czechoslovak State Inst. Health, 1938-39; sr. resident Monsall Hosp. Infectious Diseases, Manchester, Eng., 1941-43; chief pharmacologist Brit. Drug Houses, London, 1945-47; asst. prof. pediatrics U. Rochester, 1947-49; dir. research Carter-Wallace Inc., 1949-55, v.p., 1955-58; pres. Wallace Labs. div. Carter-Wallace Inc., Cranbury, N.J., 1958-73; mem. adv. council dept. biology Princeton U., 1961-74, lectr., prof., 1969-74; mem. sci. adv. com. Waksman Inst. Microbiology, Rutgers U., 1960-67; cons. Surgeon Gen., Walter Reed Army Med. Center, Washington, 1974-80; pres. Mario Negri Inst. Found. for Biomed. Research, Inc., 1973—; prof. psychiatry U. Louisville Med. Sch., 1974-90; hon. prof. microbiology Waksman Inst. Microbiology, Rutgers U., 1982. Fellow N.Y. Acad. Scis., Am. Coll. Neuropsychopharmacology, AAAS; mem. AMA, AAUP, Am. Pharm. Soc., Brit. Pharm. Soc., Can. Pharm. Soc., Am. Bacteriol. Soc., Soc. Exptl. Biology and Medicine, Am. Chem. Soc., Biometric Soc., Cosmos Club (Washington), Princeton Club (N.Y.C.), N.Y. Athletic Club, Sigma Xi. Discovered tranquilizer meprobamate, muscle-relaxant mephenesin, pain reliever carisoprodol, antiepileptic felbamate; also method purification penicillin. Office: 200 E 72nd St New York NY 10021-4537 *Concentrate on the important, rather than the urgent; try not to do what everybody else is doing; and remember that within limits of reason and decency, it is better to do what you like rather than what is expected of you.*

BERGER, FRANK STANLEY, management executive; b. N.Y.C., 1940; s. Ernest A. and Anna Berger; m. Judith Berger; children: Evan, Stacey. BA, Queens Coll., 1958; MBA, NYU, 1960; postgrad., N.Y. Law Sch., 1961, IBM Edn. Center, 1960. Supr. dept. mktg. and fin. analysis Lever Bros., 1959-61; v.p. fin. and adminstrn. Pacific Enterprises, 1961-62; mem. corp. mktg. staff Joseph E. Seagram & Sons, Inc., 1962-63; mktg. asst. to mgr. cen. div. Calvert Distillers, 1964, asst. mgr. Fla. region, 1965, mgr. N.J. region, 1966-67, asst. mgr. ea. div., 1967-68, mgr. so. div., 1969-70; v.p., gen. sales mgr. Frankfort Distillers, 1970-71, exec. v.p. mktg. and fin., 1972-73; pres. Gen. Wine & Spirits Co., N.Y.C., 1973-76, Seagram Distillers Co., 1976-77; pres., chief exec. officer House of Seagram, 1978-79; dir. Joseph E. Seagram & Sons, Inc., 1974-79; chmn. bd. Quadrillon Investments Inc., 1980-86, Viceroy Imports, Inc., 1981-86; chmn. Hazel Bishop Cosmetics Inc., N.J., 1981-87; dir. Majestic PLC, 1988-89; chmn. bd. dirs., pres. ICI, Inc., 1990-95; chmn., pres. Naturally Scientific Inc., 1996—. Trustee N.Y. Hall of Sci.; chmn. N.Y. Lunch-o-Ree Boy Scouts Am., United Jewish Appeal, Gaucho Basketball Assn., Cystic Fibrosis Soc.; exec. com. wine and spirits div. Anti-Defamation League, Pro-Am. tennis sponsor Cerebral Palsy; bd. dirs. Bronfman Found. With AUS, 1958. Mem. AIM, Nat. Assn. Chain Drug Stores, Am. Mgmt. Assn., Am. Mktg. Assn, N.Y. C. of C., Young Pres.' Orgn., Quality and Productivity Mgmt. Assn., Conf. Bd. (CEO program). Clubs: Advt. of N.Y, N.Y. Sales Execs.

BERGER, FREDERICK JEROME, electrical engineer, educator; b. Szatmar, Hungary, Nov. 26, 1916; came to U.S. 1929; s. Joseph and Goldie (Weiss) B. BS, CCNY, 1959, BEE, 1961; MEE, NYU, 1964; LLD, Frank Ross Stuart U., 1981; DSc, Capitol Coll., Laurel, Md., 1986. Tool and die maker Brewster Aero. Co., 1935-39, chief tool, gauge and plant engr., 1939-45; process engr. Arma Co., 1946-51; entrepreneur Elec. Electronic Communication Systems and Machine Shop Equipments, 1952-61; prof., dep. chmn., chmn. and engring. sci. coord. CUNY, 1962-82; evaluator Accrediting Bd. Engring., 1962-81; cons. NSF, 1969-80. Editor Jour. of Tau Alpha Pi, 1975-95. With U.S. Army, WWII. Recipient Letter of Recognition for Outstanding Contbn. to Edn. Pres. Ronald Regan, 1987, Pres. William Clinton, 1993. Fellow Am. Soc. Engring. Edn. (Frederick J. Berger ann. scholarship award 1990—, James H. McGraw award in Engring. Tech. Edn. 1992, Centennial cert. and medallion 1993); mem. IEEE (life, Engring. Svc. award 1964-81), Am. Nuclear Engring. Soc., Instrument Soc. Am. (life), Masons, Tau Alpha Pi (founding exec. dir. 1973—), Tau Beta Pi. *

BERGER, GEORGE, lawyer; b. N.Y.C., Jan. 21, 1936. BA summa cum laude, NYU, 1957, JD, 1960. Bar: N.Y. 1960, U.S. Dist. Ct. (so. dist.) N.Y. 1961, U.S. Ct. Appeals (2nd cir.) 1963, U.S. Supreme Ct. 1961, U.S. Ct. Appeals (5th cir.) 1974, U.S. Dist. Ct. (ea. dist.) N.Y. 1975, U.S. Dist. Ct. (we. dist.) 1980, U.S. Ct. Appeals (D.C. cir.) 1977, U.S. Ct. Appeals (10th cir.) 1985. Assoc. Phillips, Nizer, Benjamin, Krim & Ballon, N.Y.C., 1960-67, ptnr., 1967—; disting. neutral, N.Y. panel, Ctr. for Pub. Resources, 1992-93. Editor: Hazardous Waste and Toxic Torts: Law and Strategy, 1987-92. Mem. ABA, Assn. of Bar of City of N.Y. (general civil litigation, ins. and intellectual property). Office: Phillips Nizer Benjamin Krim & Ballon LLP 666 5th Ave New York NY 10103-0001

BERGER, HAROLD, lawyer, engineer; b. Archbald, Pa., June 10, 1925; s. Jonas and Anna (Raker) B.; m. Renee Margareten, Aug. 26, 1951; children: Jill Ellen, Jonathan David. BS in Elec. Engring, U. Pa., 1948, JD, 1951. Bar: Pa. 1951. Practiced in Phila.; judge Ct. of Common Pleas, Phila. County, 1971-72; chmn., moderator Internat. Aerospace Meetings Princeton U., 1965-66; chmn. Western Hemisphere Internat. Law Conf., San Jose, Costa Rica, 1967; chmn. internat. Confs. on Aerospace and Internat. Law, Coll. William and Mary; permanent mem. Jud. Conf. 3d Circuit Ct. of Appeals; mem. County Bd. Law Examiners, Phila. County, 1961-71; chmn. World Conf. Internat. Law and Aerospace, Caracas, Venezuela, Internat. Conf. on Environ. and Internat. Law, U. Pa., 1974, Internat. Confs. on Global Interdependence, Princeton U., 1975, 79; mem. Pa. State Conf. Trial Judges, 1972-80, Nat. Conf. State Trial Judges, 1972—; chmn. Pa. Com. for Independent Judiciary, 1973—; adv. coun. Biddle Law Libr., U. Pa., 1991—; mem. bd. overseers Sch. Engring. & Applied Scis., U. Pa., 1998—. Mem. editorial advisory bd.: Jour. of Space Law, U. Miss. Sch. of Law, 1973—; contbr. articles to profl. jours. Mem. We the People 200 Com. for Constn. Bicentennial, 1991—. Served with Signal Corps, AUS, 1944-46. Recipient Alumnus of Year award Thomas McKean Law Club, U. Pa. Law Sch., 1965, Gen. Electric Co. Space award, 1966, Nat. Disting. Achievement award Tau Epsilon Rho, 1972, Spl. Pa. Jud. Conf. award, 1981. Mem. Inter-Am. Bar Assn. (past chmn. aerospace law com.), Fed. Bar Assn. (past nat. chmn. com. on aerospace law, pres. Phila. chpt. 1983-84, mem. nat. exec. coun., past nat. chmn. fed. jud. com., Presdl. award 1970, Nat. Disting. Svc. award 1978, nat. com. 1987 bi-centennial of U.S. Constn., chmn. class action and complex litigation com. 3d cir. 1990—, nat. chmn., alternate dispute resolution com. 1992-95, pres. eastern dist. Pa. chpt. 1996—), ABA (Spl. Presdl. Program medal 1975, past chmn. aerospace law com., mem. state and fed. ct. com., nat. conf. of state trial judges), Phila. Bar Assn. (past chmn. jud. liaison com. 1975, chmn. internat. law com. 1977), Assn. U.S. Mems. Internat. Inst. Space Law Internat. Astronautical Fedn. (former bd. dirs.), Internat. Acad. Astronautics Paris. Office: 1622 Locust St Philadelphia PA 19103-6305

BERGER, HAROLD RICHARD, physician; b. Elizabeth, N.J., Oct. 31, 1914; s. Abraham and Frances (Herfield) B.; m. Minna Constance Wolfson, Aug. 22, 1943; children: Brian, Andrew, Alan, James. AB, Cornell U., Ithaca, N.Y.; MD, NYU Sch. Medicine. Diplomate Am. Bd. Pediatrics. Intern Elizabeth (N.J.) Gen. Hosp., 1940-41; maj. U.S. Med. Corp., 1941-46; resident in pediatrics Jersey City (N.J.) Med. Ctr., 1951-53; pvt. practice, 1946—; mem. child health program Elizabeth Bd. of Health, Hillside Bd. of Health; sch. physician Elizabeth Bd. Edn. Recipient award Am. Bd. Pediatrics, 1954. Mem. AMA, N.J. Med. Soc., Union County Med. Soc. Avocations: golf, reading, traveling. Home: 987 Harding Rd Elizabeth NJ 07208-1047 Office: 250 Elizabeth Ave Elizabeth NJ 07206-1649

BERGER, HARVEY ROBERT, psychologist; b. Quincy, Mass., Nov. 3, 1927; s. Joel Joseph and Helen Esther (Stone) B.; m. Thelma Lee Cohen, July 11, 1954. BA, Tufts U., 1949, MA, 1950; PhD, U. Mo., 1953. Diplomate Am. Bd. Examiners Profl. Psychology, Am. Bd. Psychol. Specialties, Am. Bd. Forensic Examiners, Prescribing Psychologists Register, cert. fellow; cert. fellow Am. Coll. Forensic Exam.; cert. prescribing psychologist. Psychologist Marblehead (Mass.) Pub. Schs., 1953-79; dir. psychol. svcs. federally assisted programs Salem (Mass.) Pub. Schs., 1967-76; cons. Revere (Mass.) Pub. Schs., 1979-90; nat. svc. officer Jewish War Vets. U.S.A., 1984—; assoc. prof. Salem State Coll., 1963; clin. dir. North Shore Psychol. Counseling and Testing Ctr., 1963-75; pres. Paul Revere Savs. & Loan Assn., 1971-76, William Dawes Realty Corp.; with U.S. Dept. Commerce, 1983-84. Mem. Nat. Commn. on Safety Edn., 1952-54; capt., Mass. comdt. U.S. Naval Cadet Program, 1966-86; col. Gov.'s staff Ky. N.G.; pres. Area Bd. on Mental Health and Retardation, 1975-78; vice chmn. Greater Lynn (Mass.) Coun. for Children, Mass. Office for Children, 1977-78; mem. governance bd. Greater Lynn Cmty. Mental Health Ctr., 1977-90; auditor Rep. City Com., Lynn, 1970-75; pres. Mass. Am. Legion Coll., 1964-66; pres. NEA Mut. Fund; chmn. bd. NEA Income Fund; trustee Ida C. Romanow Fund, Jewish Cmty. Rels. Coun. of Greater Boston; pres. Congregation Chevra Tehillim; diplomat World Jewish Congress; mem. Jewish Inst. for Nat. Security affairs, Friends of the Israel Def. Forces, Friends of Israel Disabled War Vets. With U.S. Army, 1945-47. Sch. Alcohol Studies fellow Yale U., 1957, John F. Kennedy Libr. fellow. Fellow APA; mem NASP (life), NEA (life, Disting. Svc. award), VFW (life), DAV (life, past comdr.), Am. Assn. Mental Retardation, Am. Orthopsychiat. Assn., Royal Soc. Health, Am. in Torah (life, patron, benefactor), Soc. for Personality and Social Psychology, Internat. Assn. for the Scientific Study of Intellectual Disabilities, Nat. Assn. Sch. Counselors, Mass. Schoolmasters Club (life). Am. Psychology-Law Soc., Soc. for Advancement Social Psychology, Soc. for Psychol. Study Social Issues, Am. Security Coun. Found. (congl. adv. bd.), USN Meml. Found. (mem. nat. adv. coun.), Soc. Behaviorists, Religious Zionists Am. (life), Jewish Inst. Nat. Security Affairs, Mass. Bar Assn., Am. Legion (life, past comdr.), Def. of Washington Garrison, Army and Navy Union USA, Mil. Order Purple Heart (life, comdr. Dept. Mass.), Navy League (life), U.S. Naval Inst. (life, Silver Citation award), Orders and Medals Soc. Am., Nat. Soc. Profs. (life), Am. Assn. Higher Edn. (life), Jewish War Vets (life, nat. svc. officer 1984—, Disting. Svc. award), Soc. Supporters of the Ho. of Sages, Tufts Jumbo Club, Charles Tufts Soc., Nat. Eagle Scout Assn., Masons (32 degree), Shriners (fire brigade chaplain), Legion of Honor, Supreme Grand Royal Arch Chpt. State Israel, Order Ea. Star (worthy patron, grand sentinal), Order of Amaranth (auditor), Phi Beta Kappa, Phi Delta Kappa. Home: 31 Tudor St Lynn MA 01902-4617 Office: John F Kennedy Federal Bldg Boston MA 02203

BERGER, IVAN BENNETT, magazine editor, writer; b. July 9, 1939; s. Leynard and Celia (Berlin) B.; m. Roberta Thumin, Sept. 13, 1985 (dec. Oct. 27, 1995). Editor electronics and camera divsn. Popular Mechanics mag., N.Y.C., 1972-77; sr. editor Popular Electronics mag., N.Y.C., 1977-79; tech. editor Audio mag., N.Y.C., 1982—. Author: The New Sound of Stereo, 1985. Mem. Am. Soc. Journalists and Authors. Avocations: poetry, cooking, photography. Home: 459 La Grande Ave Fanwood NJ 07023-1732 Office: Audio Mag 1633 Broadway Ste 4200 New York NY 10019-6741

BERGER, JACK CHANDLER, retired physician, surgeon, psychiatrist, educator; b. Kansas City, Mo., Dec. 12, 1923; s. John Joseph and Elsa (Dietrich) B.; m. Virginia Butts, Mar. 14, 1953. BS, U. Chgo., 1944, MD, 1946. Intern Presbyn. St. Luke's Hosp., Chgo., 1946-47, resident gen. surgery, 1949-50; resident gen. surgery U.S. Naval Hosp., Long Beach, Calif., 1947-48; resident plastic surgery U.S. Naval Hosp., St. Albans, N.Y., 1951-53; resident plastic and dental surgery Cook County Hosp., Chgo., 1954-56; preceptoship plastic surgery Wayne B. Slaughter, MD, DDS, Chgo., 1956-57; pvt. practice plastic surgery Chgo., 1958-64; chief plastic surgery Hines (Ill.) VA Hosp., 1960-68, resident psychiatry, 1968-70; resdient psychiatry Rush-Presbyn.-St. Luke's Med. Ctr., Chgo., 1971-72; pvt. practice psychiatry Chgo., 1971-90; ret., 1991; instr. anatomy U. Ill., 1946-47, 49-50; clin. instr. psychiatry Rush-Presbyn. St. Luke's Med. Ctr., Chgo., 1965-66, clin. asst. prof. psychiatry, 1969-70; clin. instr. plastic surgery Stritch Sch. Medicine, Loyola U., Chgo., 1956-64; clin. asst. prof. psychiatry Rush Med. Sch., Chgo., 1970-91; cons. Ill. Visually Handicapped Inst., 1971-81. Contbr. articles to profl. jours. Lt. USMC, 1950-51, Korea. Fellow Internat. Coll. Surgery (plastic surgery sect.); mem. AMA, Am. Soc. Plastic and Reconstructive Surgery (life), Harry Benjamin Internat. Gender Dysphoria Assn. (founding, bd dirs.), Ill. Med. Soc., Ill. Psychiatric Soc., Chgo. Soc. Plastic Surgery (founding), Chgo. Med. Soc. Avocations: music, art, travel. Home: 1338 Sutton Pl Chicago IL 60610

BERGER, JAMES (HANK), business broker; b. Lakewood, Ohio, July 27, 1951; s. James Henry and Joan Marie (Wertz) B.; m. Rochelle Anne Kiehl, Apr. 29, 1977; children: Justin Henry, Max Albert. Degree, Cooper Sch. Art, 1972. Owner H.M.S. Titanic Art Studio, Cleve., 1971-73; mgr. various rock groups Cleve., 1972-73; exec. producer TV show Music Your'e My Mother, 1975-76; owner Club Roundtable, Cleve., 1976, Deja Vu, Cleve., 1977-78, Club Traxx, Hanks Cafe, Cleve., 1976-88, Club Metropolis, 1988-90; Club U41A; owner Berger Bus. Brokerage, Rocky River, Ohio, 1990—; owned and marketed sections of original Hollywood (Calif.) Sign, 1980-82; owner The Probe-Disco, Hollywood, 1983-85; cons. in field. Author screen play When The Music's Over, 1980. Coach Rocky River Little League, 1990-95, Rocky River Recreation, 1994-95. With USN, 1969-71, Vietnam. Recipient High Pope of Pub. Rels., The Ch. of Sub Genius, 1983; named 78 Most Ineresting People Cleve., Cleve. mag., 1978; Club Probe voted # 1 disco So. Calif. D.J. Assn., 1984; featured in People mag., 1979, 80. Republican. Roman Catholic. Avocations: interior designing, literature, gardening. Home and Office: 24446 Lake Rd Bay Village OH 44140-2959

BERGER, JASON, artist, printmaker; b. Malden, Mass., Jan. 22, 1924; s. Simon and Frances Alice (Savel) B.; m. Estela Simoes Couto, Sept. 1, 1978; 1 son by previous marriage: Adam Joseph. Student, Boston Mus. Fine Arts Sch., 1942-43, 46-49, U. Ala., 1943-44, Ossip Zadkine Sch Sculpture, Paris, 1950-52. Vis. prof. SUNY-Buffalo, 1969-70; instr., then prof. painting Art Inst., Boston, 1973-88. Group shows, Art Inst. of Chgo., 1952, 54, Carnegie Inst. Mus., 1954, 55, Mus. Modern Art, 1954, 56, Boston City Hall, 1972, Boston State House, 1975, DeCordova Mus., 1986, others; represented: permanent collections Mus. Modern Art, Chase Manhattan Bank, Smith Coll. Mus. Art, Guggenheim Mus. Art, Brandeis U., others; works featured in (by Lois Katz) The Paintings of Jason Berger, 1998. Served with U.S. Army, 1943-46, ETO. Recipient Grand prize Boston Arts Festival, 1955; recipient 1st prize Boston Arts Festival, 1961; Boston Mus. Fine Arts Sch. traveling fellow. Jewish. Home: Rua Cândido de Figueiredo 89-7-G, 1500 Lisbon Portugal

BERGER, JAY VARI, executive recruiter; b. San Francisco, Aug. 31, 1944; s. Jack Vari and Ruth (Wasserman) B.; m. Margareta Ahlberg, June 14, 1969; children: Karin Britta Margareta, John Vari Sten. BS, U. So. Calif., 1966, MS, 1967, PhD, 1971. Assoc. dean admissions U. So. Calif., L.A., 1969-76, dir. admissions, 1976-82, asst. v.p. devel., 1982-86; prin. ptnr. Morris & Berger, Pasadena, Calif., 1986—. Author: (juvenile) Willie the Worm, 1986; columnist Venture Connections, 1988. Bd. dirs. The Sycamores, Pasadena, 1985-94, chair, 1992-94; bd. dirs. Foothill Friends of Music, 1989-92; bd. dirs. Covenant House Calif., 1992-99, pres., trustee Chandler Sch., Pasadena, 1993-89, chmn. bd., 1987-89; trustee Flintridge Preparatory Sch., 1992-98, chmn. bd. dirs. 1996-98; bd. councilors U. So. Calif. Coll. Letters, Arts & Scis. Mem. Calif. Exec. Recruiters Assn., Calif. Assn. Ind. Schs. (bd. trustees 1988-91), Annandale Golf Club, Rotary (bd. dirs. Pasadena chpt. 1988-92). Avocations: golf, traveling, fishing, reading, writing. Home: 1550 Arroyo View Dr Pasadena CA 91103-1903 Office: Morris & Berger Cons Exec Search 201 S Lake Ave Ste 700 Pasadena CA 91101-3019

BERGER, JEROME MORRIS, communications executive; b. Cleve., Dec. 7, 1951; s. Jack and Beatrice Berger; m. Francine Ellis, Oct. 9, 1977. BA, Boston U., 1973; MS in Journalism, Columbia U., 1976. Editor, reporter Marlboro (Mass.) Enterprise, 1977-82; reporter UP Internat., Boston, 1982-87, statehouse bur. chief, 1987-90; asst. prof. Sch Journalism Northeastern U., Boston, 1990-96; comms. dir. com. on ways and means Mass. Senate, Boston, 1996-98; comms. dir. Mass. Cultural Coun., Boston, 1998—; developer, cons. Nat. Polit. Awareness Test, Project Vote Smart, Boston, 1993-96. Media columnist The Middlesex News, 1996; editor-in-chief: Insuring American Health for the Year 2000, 1992; contbr. articles to profl. publs. Mem. adv. network State Fiscal Analysis Initiative, Boston, 1993-94; media cons. Graduated Income Tax Campaign, Boston, 1994. Mem. Soc. Profl. Journalists. Avocations: reading, walking. E-mail: jfberger@world.std.com. Office: Mass Cultural Coun 120 Boylston St Boston MA 02116

BERGER, JERRY ALLEN, museum director; b. Buffalo, Wyo., Oct. 8, 1943. BA in Psychology, U. Wyo., 1965, BA in Art, 1971, MA in Art History, 1972. Curator collections U. Wyo. Art Mus., Laramie, 1972-88, asst. dir., 1980-83, 87-88, acting dir., 1984-86; dir. Springfield (Mo.) Art Mus., 1988—. Office: Springfield Art Mus 1111 E Brookside Dr Springfield MO 65807-1899

BERGER, JOHN TORREY, JR., lawyer; b. St. Louis, Apr. 14, 1938; s. John Torrey Sr. and Maud Alice (Beattie) B.; m. Helen Lee Thompson, Aug. 26, 1961; children: John Torrey III, Helen E. JD, Washington U., 1963. Bar: Mo. 1963. Assoc. Lewis, Rice & Fingersh, L.C., St. Louis, 1963-70; mem. Lewis & Rice, St. Louis, 1971—, chmn. real estate sect.; bd. dirs. Carr Lane Mfg. Co., St. Louis, Presbyn. Children's Svc., Farmington, Mo., Logos sch., St. Louis; adv. bd. dirs. St. Louis Screw & Bolt Co. Deacon, elder, trustee Presbyn. Ch., St. Louis, 1970-75, 75—. Mem. ABA (corp. sect., real estate sect.), Mo. Bar Assn. (real estate sect., banking and securities com.), Bar Assn. Met. St. Louis, Internat. Conf. Shopping Ctrs., SAR, Phi Delta Phi. Avocations: fishing, birding, photography. Home: 1257 Takara Ct Saint Louis MO 63131-1013 Office: Lewis Rice & Fingersh 500 N Broadway Ste 2000 Saint Louis MO 63102-2147

BERGER, JONATHAN M., legislative staff member. Student, Hebrew U., Jerusalem, 1991-92; B in Middle East History, Occidental Coll., 1993. Press asst. House Fgn. Affairs Com., 1994, Leslie Byrne for Congress, 1994; account assoc. The November Group, 1994; rsch. asst. Washington Inst. for Near East Policy, 1995; legis. asst. Office Congressman Ackerman, 1995-97, sr. legis. asst., 1997-98; legis. dir. Office Congressman Gary L. Ackerman, 1998—. Co-founder Jewish Cultural Assn., Occidental Coll. Mem. Sigma Alpha Epsilon, Phi Alpha Theta. Home: Apt 204 3601 Wisconsin Ave Washington DC 20016

BERGER, JOSEPH, author, educator, counselor; b. Bklyn.; s. Harry and Rose (Diner) B.; m. Margaret Smith, July 9, 1966; children—Adam, Rachel, Gideon. A.B. magna cum laude, Bklyn. Coll., 1949; M.A., Harvard U., 1952, Ph.D. in Sociology, 1958. Lic. counselor. Instr. sociology Dartmouth, 1954-56, asst. prof., 1956-59; asst. prof. Stanford, 1959-62, assoc. prof., 1962-68, prof. sociology, 1968-95; prof. emeritus, 1995—; dir. Lab. for Social Research, 1968-70, 71-74, chmn. dept. sociology, 1977-83, 85-89; sr. fellow by courtesy Hoover Instn., 1984-86, 91—, sr. rsch. fellow, 1986-91. Author: (with others) Types of Formalization in Small Groups Research, 1962, Expectation-States Theory: A Theoretical Research Program, 1974, Status Characteristics and Social Interaction: An Expectation-States Approach, 1977, Status, Power and Legitimacy, 1998; editor: (with others) Sociological Theories in Progress, Vol. I, 1966, Vol. II, 1972, Vol. III (New Formulations), 1989, Status, Rewards, and Influence: How Expectations Organize Interaction, 1985, Theoretical Research Programs: Studies in the Growth of Theory, 1993, Status, Power and Legitimacy: Strategies and Theories, 1998; contbr. articles and papers to profl. jours., books. Served to 1st lt. AUS, 1943-46, ETO. Decorated Bronze Star medal, Army Commendation medal; recipient Cooley-Mead award Social Psychology sect. of Am. Sociol. Assn., 1991; NIMH spl. postdoctoral fellow, 1964, 70-71. Mem. Am. Sociol. Assn., Pacific Sociol. Assn., Am. Assn. for Marriage and Family Therapy, Propylea. Home: 955 Mears Ct Stanford CA 94305-1041

BERGER, LELAND ROGER, lawyer; b. N.Y.C., Feb. 3, 1956; s. Albert and Audrey Sybil (Ellenbogen) B.; m. Lisa M. Burk, Feb. 15, 1987 (div. Dec. 1998) ; 1 child, Robert Samson. Student, Am. U., 1977; BA, Dickinson Coll., 1978; JD, Lewis & Clark Coll., 1982. Bar: Oreg. 1983, U.S. Dist. Ct. Oreg. 1983, U.S. Ct. Appeals (9th cir.) 1990. Pvt. practice Portland, Oreg., 1983-84; assoc. Rieke, Geil & Savage, P.C., Portland, 1984-94; pvt. practice Portland, 1995—; mem. legal com. NORML. Mem. Oreg. Bar Assn. (ad hoc com. to study multi-state bar exam. 1983-84, uniform criminal jury instrn. com. 1989-90, sec. 1990-91, criminal law sect., appellate law sect.),

Multnomah County Bar Assn. (corrections com. 1987), Oreg. Young Attys. Assn. (bd. dirs. 1983-84), Nat. Lawyers Guild (co-chair criminal justice com. Portland chpt. 1983-84), Oreg. Criminal Def. Lawyers Assn. (rep. to Oreg. Health Divsn. adv. com. on med. marijuana 1999), Nat. Criminal Def. Lawyers Assn. Democrat. Jewish. Home: 3427 NE 11th Ave Portland OR 97212-2240 Office: 950 Lloyd Ctr Ste 3 Portland OR 97232-1262

BERGER, LEV ISAAC, physicist, educator; b. Rostov, USSR, June 23, 1929; came to U.S., 1978; s. Isaac Mark and Sara (Poltevsker) B.; m. Ninelle Rossine, July 2, 1956; 1 child, Yuri. MS in Physics, State U., Moscow, 1955; PhD in Physics, State U., Minsk, USSR, 1959; PhD in Tech. Scis., U. Steel and Alloys, Moscow, 1968. Lectr. physics U. Nonferrous Metals, Moscow, 1956-60; docent Physics U. Metallurgy, Moscow, 1960-62; prof. Poly. Inst., Moscow, 1962-77; sr. scientist New Eng. Research Ctr., Sudbury, Mass., 1979-81; lectr. physics San Diego State U., 1981-89, U. San Diego, 1989—; pres. Calif. Inst. Electronics & Materials Sci., Hemet, 1981—; dir. divsn. Inst. Spl. Purity Substances, Moscow, 1962-71, Introscopy Research Inst., Moscow, 1971-77. Author: Ternary Diamond-like Semiconductors, 1969, Semiconductor Materials, 1997; contbr. articles to profl. jours.; patentee in field. San Diego State U. grantee, 1983. Mem. ASTM (com. electronics, thermal measurements), Soc. for Advancement of Material and Process Engrng. (exec. bd.), Am. Phys. Soc., Am. Assn. Crystal Growth, Materials Rsch. Soc., Nat. Assn. Scholars. Home: 2115 Flame Tree Way Hemet CA 92545-7803 Office: Calif Inst Electronics & Materials Sci PO Box 832 Hemet CA 92546-0832

BERGER, LINDA FAY, writer; b. Ft. Worth, Mar. 12, 1943; d. Walter Bob and Bertha Fay (Christensen) B. AA, Tarrant County Jr. Coll., Ft. Worth, 1976; BBA, U. Tex., Arlington, 1981; MBA, North Tex. U., 1987. Cert. profl. sec. Profl. Sec. Assn. Internat. With Tex. Refinery Corp., Ft. Worth, 1961-91, file clk., telex operator, departmental sec., exec. sec., asst. pers. dir., pers. dir. Co-author: A Joyful Journey, 1995. Mem. Profl. Secs. Internat. (sec. 1969-79), Tex. Assn. Bus. (sec. 1990), Order Ea. Star (Riverside chpt. 834). Republican. Mem. Unity Ch. Avocations: travelling, yoga, reading, cooking.

BERGER, MARLEDA CARTER, student health nurse practitioner; b. Pa., Feb. 27, 1939; d. Clairmont Parks and Margaret (Riviello) Carter; m. Jonathan Berger, June 24, 1965; children: Keith, Margo. Diploma, Kings County Hosp. Ctr., 1959; student, Brigham Young U., 1979; BA, Ea. Conn. State U., 1984; MS, U. Conn., 1987. APRN, Conn.; cert. adult nurse practitioner ANA. Nurse cons. State of Conn. Dept. Mental Retardation; nurse practitioner/cons. Town of West Hartford (Conn.); nurse practitioner student health svcs. U. Conn., Storrs. Mem. ANA, CNA, Am. Acad. Nurse Practitioners, Conn. Nurse Practitioner Group.

BERGER, MELVIN, allergist, immunologist; b. Phila., Mar. 7, 1950. MD, Case Western Res. U., 1976, PhD in Biochemistry, 1976. Internship, resident pediatrics Children's Hosp. Med. Ctr., Boston, 1976-78; fellow allergy & immunology Nat. Inst. Allergy & Infectious Diseases, Bethesda, Md., 1978-81; pediatrician Rainbow Babies and Children's Hosp., Cleve., 1984—; prof. peds. & pathology Case Western Res. U. Lt. col. USPHS, 1978-81, U.S. Army Res., 1981-97. Fellow Am. Acad. Pediatrics. Office: Rainbow Babies Hosp Div Pediatrics/Immunology Cleveland OH 44106*

BERGER, MELVIN GERALD, lawyer; b. Bklyn., June 13, 1943; s. Louis and Lillian (Shapiro) B.; m. Ellen Terry Chelmow, Jan. 24, 1965 (dec. 1991); children—Michael R., Andrew R., Lee M.; m. Joyce Goldstein, Nov. 26, 1992. B.S., CCNY, 1965; M.S., NYU, 1967; J.D., George Washington U., 1971, LL.M., 1975. Bar: Md. 1972, U.S. Ct. Claims 1973, U.S. Ct. Customs and Patent Appeals 1972, D.C. 1986, U.S. Ct. Appeals (fed. cir.) 1989, (4th cir.) 1992, Fla. 1994. Patent examiner U.S. Patent Office, Washington, 1967-69; patent advisor Dept. of Navy, Naval Ordnance Lab., White Oak, Silver Spring, Md., 1969-72, patent atty., 1972-73; law clk. U.S. Ct. Claims, Washington, 1973-74; trial atty. Antitrust div. Dept. of Justice, Washington, 1974-79; trial atty. Office of Gen. Counsel, Fed. Energy Regulatory Commn., Washington, 1979-84; atty. Brand, Beeny, Berger & Whitler (formerly Brand & Leckie), 1984-86, ptnr. 1987-93; of counsel 1993—. Cub Scout leader, 1977-79, 81-82; com. mem. Boy Scouts Am., 1979-86. Recipient Superior Performance award Dept. of Navy, 1973; Spl. Achievement award Dept. of Justice, 1976; Superior Job Performance award Fed. Energy Regulatory Commn., 1980, 82. Mem. ABA, Phi Beta Kappa, Order of Coif. Club: B'nai B'rith. Home: 941 Paddington Ter Lake Mary FL 32746-5316 Office: 1730 K St NW Washington DC 20006-3868

BERGER, MIRIAM ROSKIN, creative arts therapy director, educator, therapist; b. N.Y.C., Dec. 9, 1934; d. Israel and Florence (Frankel) Roskin; m. Meir Berger, July 16, 1967 (div. June 1981); children: Jonathan Israel. Student, Barnard Coll., 1952-53; BA, Bard Coll., 1956; postgrad., CCNY, 1956-58; Dr. Arts, NYU, 1998. Alumni dir. Bard Coll., Annandale-on-Hudson, N.Y., 1958-59; dance therapist Manhattan Psychiatric Ctr., N.Y.C., 1959-60; performer, educator Jean Erdman Theater of Dance, N.Y.C., 1959-62; dir. adult program Hebrew Arts Sch., N.Y.C., 1981; faculty Dance Notation Bur., N.Y.C., 1974-75, 77; asst. prof. dance therapy program NYU, 1975—, acting dir. dance therapy program, 1991, dir. dance edn. program, 1993—; dir. creative arts therapies Bronx Psychiatric Ctr., N.Y.C., 1970-90; leader internat. workshops on dance/movement therapy, Gt. Britain, France, Sweden, Brazil, Italy, Yugoslavia, Germany, Holland, Russia, Czech Republic, Poland; mem. editl. bd. The Arts in Psychotherapy; keynote spkr. Internat. Congress on Dance Therapy, Berlin, 1994. Prodr. off-Broadway The Coach with the Six Insides, 1962-63; author, prodr. Non-Verbal Group Process, 1978; co-editor Am. Jour. Dance Therapy, 1991-94; led dance therapy session Senate hearing on Aging, 1992; contbr. articles to profl. jours. Bd. dirs. Theater Open Eye, 1978-82, v.p. bd. trustees, 1982-89, pres., 1989-94; bd. Dance Libr. Israel, 1996; bd. dirs. Internat. Cmty. Dance Libr. of Israel. Recipient NYU scholarship, 1981, Best Paper award Med Art World congress on Arts and Medicine, 1992. Mem. Am. Dance Therapy Assn. (founder, bd. dirs. 1967-76, v.p. 1974-76, 92, credential com. 1976, 82, keynote speaker at nat. conf. 1991, pres. 1994—), Acad. Registered Dance Therapists, Dance Libr. Israel (bd. dirs.). Home: 2 Horizon Rd Fort Lee NJ 07024-6525 Office: NYU 35 W 4th St New York NY 10012-1172

BERGER, NEWELL JAMES, JR., security professional; b. Pitts., Oct. 26, 1926; s. Newell James and Marjorie Ikler (Herndon) B.; m. Darlene Ingram, Sept. 6, 1950 (dec. Nov. 1990). BS, Mich. State U., 1958; grad., U.S. Army Command and Gen. Staff Coll., 1963, U.S. Army War Coll., 1972; MA, Webster U., 1993. Enlisted man U.S. Army, 1944, advanced through grades to staff sgt., 1948, commd. 2d lt., 1948, advanced through grades to col., 1970; chief corrections hdqrs. U.S. Army, Washington, 1970-72, dir. security Office Surgeon Gen., 1972-73; dir. security Health Svcs. Command U.S. Army, Ft. Sam Houston, Tex., 1973-78; ret. U.S. Army, 1978; security cons. Phoenix and San Diego, 1979-84; chief plant security Teledyne Ryan Aero. Co., San Diego, 1985-86; dep. dir. security Marconi Intergrated Systems, Inc., San Diego, 1986—. Decorated Legion of Merit with two oak leaf clusters. Mem. (life) Internat. Assn. Chiefs Police, Am. Soc. for Indsl. Security (cert. protection profl.). Republican. Episcopalian. Avocations: music, history. Home: 11872 Caminito Corriente San Diego CA 92128-4550 Office: Marconi Integrated Sys Inc PO Box 1198 Poway CA 92074-1198

BERGER, PATRICIA WILSON, retired librarian; b. Washington, May 1, 1926; d. Thomas Decatur Wood and Nina Hughes; m. George Hamilton Combs Berger, May 20, 1970. BA, George Washington U., 1965; MSLS, Cath. U. Am., 1974. Asst. libr., ops. rsch. office Johns Hopkins U., Chevy Chase, Md., 1949-51; asst. ops. rsch. analyst Johns Hopkins U., 1951-54; head libr. CEIR, Washington, 1954-55; chief, tech. info. and libr. svcs. Human Rels. Area Files Yale U., Washington, 1955-57; tech. info. officer, chief libr. Inst. for Def. Analyses, Washington, Arlington, Va., 1957-67; dir. tech. info. and security programs Lambda Corp., Arlington, 1967-71; chief libr. U.S. Commn. on Govt. Procurement, Washington, 1971-72; head gen. ref. br., later dep. chief libr. U.S. Patent and Trademark Office, Arlington, 1972-76; chief libr. divsn. U.S. Nat. Bur. Stds., Gaithersburg, Md., 1976-78; dir. info. resources and svcs. U.S. EPA, Washington, 1978-79; chief libr. and info. svcs. U.S. Nat. Bur. Stds., Washington, 1979-83; chief info. resources and svcs. U.S. Nat. Bur. Stds., 1983-91, dir. Office Info. Svcs., 1990-92; ret., 1992; cons. libr., info. and security matters, 1965-95; del. 1st White House Conf. on Librs. and Info. Svc., 1979; bd. dirs. Universal Serial and Book Exch., 1983-84; chmn. Nat. Info. Std. Orgn., Am. Nat. Std. Inst., 1981-83, elected Nat. Info. Std. Orgn. fellow, 1989. Mem. editl. bd. Sci. and Tech. Librs., 1979-92; contbr. articles to profl. jours. Apptd. by Govs. of Va. to Libr. of Va. Bd., 1986-90, 90-95, vice chair, 1992-93, chair, 1993-94; bd. dirs. Va. Commn. for Reenactment of Battle First Bull Run, 1960-61; bd. dirs. Freedom to Read Found., 1988-90, 92-94; apptd. U.S. Postmaster Gen's. Commn. Lit., 1990-92. Recipient Internat. Women's Yr. award Dept. Commerce, 1976, Bronze medal, 1980, Silver medal, 1984, Outstanding Adminstrv. Mgr. award, 1985, H.W. Wilson Pub. Co. award, 1980, Disting. Svc. award U. Richmond Librs., 1989, Cert. of Recognition, Gov. State of Va., 1989, Resolution of Esteem, Va. State Libr. Bd., 1988, award Coun. Libr. and Media Technicians, 1989; named Outstanding Alumnus in Libr. and Info. Sci., Cath. U. Am., 1988; Cert. of appreciation Martin Luther King Jr. Fed. Holiday Commission, 1996. Mem AAAS (elected assn. fellow 1992), Spl. Librs. Assn. (exec. bd. Washington chpt. 1970-71, pres. Washington chpt. 1977, elected assn. fellow 1987), ALA (coun. 1984-88, exec. bd. 1986-90, v.p./pres.-elect 1988-89, pres. 1989-90, immediate past pres. 1990-91), Va. Libr. Assn., D.C. Libr. Assn., Fed. Librs. Roundtable (pres. 1982-83, Achievement award 1985), Cosmos Club, Chi Omega, Beta Phi Mu. Episcopalian. Home: 105 Queen St Alexandria VA 22314-2610

BERGER, PAUL ERIC, artist, photographer; b. The Dalles, Oreg., Jan. 20, 1948; s. Charles Glen and Virginia (Nunez) B. B.A., UCLA, 1970; M.F.A., SUNY-Buffalo, 1973. Vis. lectr. U. Ill., 1974-78; prof. art U. Wash.-Seattle, 1978—. Exhibited one-man shows, photographs, Art Inst. Chgo., 1975, Light Gallery, N.Y.C., 1977, Seattle Art Mus., 1980, Light Gallery, N.Y.C., 1982, Univ. Art Mus., Santa Barbara, Calif., 1984, Cliff Michel Gallery, 1989, Seattle Art Mus., 1990, Fuel Gallery, 1993, Galerie Lichtblick GFFK, Cologne, Germany, 1996, SOHO Photo, N.Y.C., 1999. NEA Photographer's fellow, 1979, NEA Visual Artist's fellow, 1986; recipient Artist's Commn., Wash. State Arts Commn., 1990. Mem. Soc. Photographic Edn. Office: U Wash Sch Art PO Box 353440 Seattle WA 98195-3440

BERGER, PAUL S., lawyer; b. Blakely, Pa., Aug. 25, 1932; s. Louis and Lena (Eisenberg) B.; m. Debra Joyce Herman, Oct. 12, 1958; children: Meryl, Jessica, Louis. BS in Acctg. magna cum laude, U. Scranton, 1954; JD cum laude, NYU, 1957. Bar: N.Y. Sr. ptnr. Arnold & Porter, Washington; atty. subcom. legis. oversight U.S. Ho. of Reps.; cons. to Pres.'s Reorgn. Plan Task Force; mem. tax counsel Nat. Coord. Com. Multi-Employer Plans; mem. counsel Employee Benefit Rsch. Inst.; mem. Spl. Tax Counsel AFL-CIO; mem. Spl. Counsel Ministry Fin., Israel; trustee Law Ctr. Found. NYU. Contbr. articles to profl. jours. Chmn. emeritus bd. govs. Charles E. Smith Jewish Day Sch.; vice chmn. and mem. exec. com. Operation Independence; nat. vice-chmn. and trustee United Jewish Appeal; bd. govs. and mem. exec. com. Jewish Agy. for Israel; past chmn., pres. and mem. exec. coms. United Jewish Appeal Greater Washington. Mem. ABA, D.C. Bar Assn. Office: Arnold & Porter 555 12th St NW Washington DC 20004-1206

BERGER, PEARL, library director; b. N.Y.C., Nov. 30, 1943; d. Baruch Mayer and Tova (Brandwein) Rabinowitz; m. David Berger, June 14, 1965; children: Miriam Esther, Yitzhak, Gedalyah Aaron. B in Religious Edn., Yeshiva U.; BA, Bklyn. Coll., 1965; MLS, Columbia U., 1974. Diploma tchr. Hebrew. Tchr. Hebrew & Jewish studies Yeshiva of Crown Heights, Bklyn., 1963-65; asst. libr. YIVO Inst. Jewish Rsch., N.Y.C., 1976-80; head tech. svcs. Librs. Yeshiva U., N.Y.C., 1980-81, head libr. Pollack Libr., 1981-83, head libr. main ctr. librs., 1983-85, dean librs., 1985—; v.p. Coun. Archives and Rsch. Librs. in Jewish Studies, 1984-86, pres. 1986-89. Assoc. editor: Jour. Judaica Librarianship, 1983—; first v.p. Met. Reference and Rsch. Libr. Orgn., 1996—; contbr. articles to profl. jours.; compiler catalog Guide to Yiddish Classics on Microfiche, 1980. Recipient Benjamin Gottesman Libr. Chair Yeshiva U. Mem. Am. Libr. Assn., Metro. Ref. Rsch. Libr. Agency (trustee 1991—, sec. 1993—, 1st v.p. 1996—), Assn. Jewish Librs. (rsch., spl. librs. divsn., v.p. 1982-84, pres. 1984-86, voting rep. Nat. Info. Stds. Orgn. 1995—), Beta Phi Mu. Office: Yeshiva U Dean of Libraries 500 W 185th St New York NY 10033-3299

BERGER, P(HILIP) JEFFREY, animal science educator, quantitative geneticist; b. Newark, June 28, 1943; s. Philip Graham and Jean Bar (Weller) B.; m. Frances Ann Williams, June 25, 1965; children—Sarah Katherine, Philip Calvin. B.S., Delaware Valley Coll., 1965; M.S., Ohio State U., 1967, Ph.D., 1970. Research and teaching asst. Ohio State U., Columbus, 1965-70; mem. faculty Iowa State U., Ames, 1972—, prof. animal sci., 1982—; cons. computer applications, animal prodn. div. FAO, Rome, 1979; vis. coop. scientist Bet Dagan, Israel, 1980; participant 1st Animal prodn. Conf., San Jose, Costa Rica, 1981; developer mixed model animal prediction programs, 1972—; participant tech. transfer project to develop genetic evaluation program for dairy cattle in tunisia, 1988, Sabbatical Wageningen Agrl. U., The Netherlands, 1994. Contbr. articles to profl. jours. Mem. Am. Dairy Sci. Assn., Am. Soc. Animal Sci., Sigma Xi, Delta Tau Alpha. Republican. Methodist. Home: 2518 Kellogg Ave Ames IA 50010-4863 Office: Ia State U Dept Animal Sci 239 Kildee Hall Ames IA 50011

BERGER, RAOUL, retired law educator, violinist; b. Russia, Jan. 4, 1901; came to U.S.,, naturalized, 1910; s. Jesse and Anna (Kahn) B.; m. Helen Beck, Aug. 1930 (dec. Sept. 1958); m. Patricia Wolcott, 1967. Student, Franz Kneisel Inst. Mus. Art, N.Y.C., 1919-21; Carl Flesch pupil violin, Berlin; AB, U. Cin., 1932, LLD (hon.), 1975; JD, Northwestern U., 1935, LLD (hon.), 1989; LLM, Harvard U., 1938; LLD (hon.), U. Mich., 1978. Soloist Cleve. Orch., 1927; 1st violinist Cin. String Quartet; practiced law Chgo., 1935-37; with SEC, 1938-40; spl. asst. to atty. gen. U.S., 1940-42; assoc. gen. counsel, then gen. counsel Alien Property Custodian, 1942-46; pvt. practice Washington, 1946-62; vis. prof. U. Calif.-Berkeley Law Sch., 1962-65; Charles Warren sr. fellow Am. legal history Harvard U. Law Sch., Cambridge, Mass., 1971-76, ret. Author: Congress vs. the Supreme Court, 1969, Impeachment: The Constitutional Problems, 1973, Executive Privilege: A Constitutional Myth, 1974, Government by Judiciary: The Transformation of the Fourteenth Amendment, 1977, Death Penalties: The Supreme Court's Obstacle Course, 1982, Federalism: The Founder's Design, 1987, The Fourteenth Amendment and the Bill of Rights, 1989; contbr. articles to legal jours. Mem. ABA (past chmn. sect. adminstrv. law 1961-62, Gavel award 1978), Order of Coif. Address: 140 Jennie Dugan Rd Concord MA 01742-4823

BERGER, RICHARD STANTON, dermatologist; b. Flint, Mich., July 30, 1940; s. Frederick S. and Millicent (Petschau) B.; m. Brenda Gorne (div.); children: Adam, Lauren; m. Janice Marie Berger, Feb. 10, 1978. MD, U. Mich., 1965. Intern Walter Reed Gen. Hosp., Washington, 1965-66; resident U. Mich., Ann Arbor, 1968-71; asst. prof. medicine and dermatology U. Mo., Columbia, 1971-73; assoc. dir. clin. rsch. Johnson & Johnson, New Brunswick, N.J., 1973-78; clin. asst. prof. medicine and dermatology Rutgers Med. Sch., New Brunswick, N.J., 1973-77; assoc. prof. medicine and dermatology U. Medicine and Dentistry of N.J., New Brunswick, 1977-87, clin. prof., 1987—, chief dermatology, 1979-95; chief dermatology Robert Wood Johnson Univ. Hosp., New Brunswick, 1979-95; pvt. practice Kendall Park, N.J., 1983—; cons. for several cos. and hosps., including Rutgers Cmty. Health Plan, New Brunswick, 1976-89, Personal Products Rsch. Divsn., Milltown, N.J., 1978-95, Chicopee Mfg. Co., Rsch. Divsn., Milltown, 1978-94, VA Hosp., Lyons, N.J., 1978—, Greenbrook Regional Ctr., Green Brook, N.J., 1980—; med. dir. Hilltop Rsch., East Brunswick, N.J., 1979—. Contbr. more than 100 articles to profl. jours. Capt. Med. Corps, U.S. Army, 1966-68. Fellow Am. Acad. Dermatology (Silver award for Tchg. Value 1985); mem. Middlesex County Med. Soc., Soc. for Investigative Dermatology, Inc., Assn. of Profs. of Dermatology, Inc., N.J. Dermatol. Soc., Skin Pharmacology Soc. Avocation: swimming. Office: 3270 State Route 27 Kendall Park NJ 08824-1458

BERGER, ROBERT BERTRAM, lawyer; b. N.Y.C., Sept. 1, 1924; s. Edward William and Sophie (Berkowitz) B.; m. Phyllis Ann Korona, June 14, 1947; children: Barry Robert, Mark Alan, Karen Elizabeth Berger Adametz, James Michael; m. 2d, Arlene Kidder Wills, Dec. 27, 1980; 1 stepchild, Kimberly Kidder Wills Campbell. BS, Georgetown U., 1948; JD, U. Conn., 1952. Bar: Conn. 1952, U.S. Dist. Ct. Conn. 1953, U.S. Tax Ct. 1967, U.S. Ct. Appeals (2d cir.) 1968. Sole practice, 1952-56; ptnr. Berger & Alaimo, Enfield, Conn., 1956-82, Berger, Alaimo, Santy & McGuire, 1982-91, Berger, Santy & McGuire, 1991-94, Berger & Santy, 1994—; judge Probate Dist. of Enfield, 1989-94; dir. Enfield Vis. Nuses Assn., 1993-96; bd. dirs., mem. exec. com. Conn. Attys. Title Ins. Co., Rocky Hill. Chmn. Enfield Dem. Town Com., 1979-87, Conn. Psychiat. Security Review Bd., 1985—; pres. United Way of N. Cen. Conn., 1981-84; trustee St. Bernard's Roman Cath. Ch., 1977-90, 99—; trustee, exec. bd. mem. Johnson Meml. Hosp. and Johnson Meml. Corp., Stafford, Conn.; bd. dirs. United Way of Capitol Area, 1981-85, United Way N. Cen. Conn., 1977—. With USMCR, 1942-45. Decorated Purple Heart; recipient Disting. Svc. award Enfield Jr. C. of C., 1955, Clayton Frost award U.S. Jr. C. of C., 1959-60. Mem. ABA, Conn. Bar Assn., Hartford County Bar Assn., Enfield Lawyers Assn. (pres. 1973-74), Am. Judicature Soc. Club: Enfield Rotary (pres. 1970-71, Paul Harris fellow 1984). Contbr. monthly polit. column Enfield Press, 1980-84. Office: PO Box 1163 Enfield CT 06083-1163

BERGER, ROBERT LEWIS, retired biophysicist, researcher; b. Omaha, Sept. 2, 1925. BS, Colo. State U., Ft. Collins, 1950; MS, Pa. State U., 1953, PhD, 1956. Instr. Park Coll., Parkville, Mo., 1950-51; postdoctoral fellow Cambridge U., Eng., 1956-57; asst. prof. Utah State U., Logan, 1957-60, assoc. prof., 1960-62; sr. investigator Nat. Heart Inst., Bethesda, Md., 1962-77; chief biophysics sect. Nat. Heart, Lung and Blood Inst., NIH, Bethesda, Md., 1977-96; sr. sci. advisor Blood Rsch. Detachment Walter Reed Army Inst. Rsch., Washington, 1994-96; ret.; pvt. cons. Bethesda, 1996—; emeritus sr. investigator Walter Reed Army Inst. Rsch., 1998—; on-loan sci. exec. EEG, Inc., Las Vegas, Nev., 1959-60; vis. scientist dept. chemistry U. Calif., San Diego, 1969-71; organizer med. and biol. sect. 4th Internat. Conf. on Temperature, Washington, 1971; invention devel. coord. Nat. Heart Lung Blood Inst., 1990—. Author over 100 sci. articles and book chpts. on fast reaction methods, calorimetry, mixing, computer and protein chem. reactions; mem. editorial bd. J. Biochem. and Biophys. Methods, 1982—; inventor Berger Ball Mixer. Pres., chief exec. officer, fund raiser Karma House Inc., Rockville, Md., 1974-77; bd. dirs., fund raiser Protestant Student House, Utah State U., Logan, 1958-62; advisor Bd. Christian Edn., United Presbyn. Ch, 1960-68. Lt. (j.g.) USCG, 1943-45, PTO. Recipient Comdrs. award for Pub. Svc. Legion of Merit Equin, 1994-96, Disting. Svc. award Elerely Coll. of Sci. and PSH Alumni Soc., 1998. Fellow Am. Phys. Soc., AAAS; mem. Biophys. Soc. (chmn. discussions com. 1976-92), Soc. for Gen. Physiology, Am. Soc. Molecular Biology and Biochemistry. Democrat. Episcopalian. Email: rlberger@aol.com. Home: 4503 Avamere St Bethesda MD 20814-3930 Office: Blood Rsch Detachment Walter Reed Army Inst Rsch Rockville MD 20307

BERGER, ROBERT MARTIN, urologist; b. N.Y.C., Aug. 28, 1950; s. Samuel and Pearl Anna Berger; m. Amy Gail Dwork, June 16, 1974; children: Randy, Daniel, Seth. BA, SUNY, Binghamton, 1972; MD, SUNY Upstate Med. Ctr., Syracuse, 1976; postgrad., Children's Meml. Hosp., Chgo., 1982. Diplomate Am. Bd. Urology. Intern in gen. surgery George Washington U. Hosp., Washington, 1976-77, resident in gen. surgery, 1977-78, resident in urology, 1978-81; pediat. urology fellow Children's Meml. Hosp., Chgo., 1981-82; clin. instr. in urology Northwestern U., Chgo., 1981-82; clin. instr. in urology George Washington U., Washington, 1982-84, asst. clin. prof., 1984—; pvt. practice pediatric urology Fairfax, Va., 1982-98; mem. staff West End Med. Ctr., Washington, 1998—; clin. asst. prof. dept. surgery (urology) Georgetown U. Med. Ctr., 1998—; owner, cons. Med. Products Internat., Ltd., Bethesda, Md., 1995—, Berger Internat., Ltd., Great Falls, Va., 1996—; mem. exec. com. Fairfax Hosp., Falls Church, Va., 1987-90, mem. credentials com., 1987, chmn. med. records com., 1988-90; mem. credentials com. Reston (Va.) Hosp., 1987. Contbr. numerous articles to profl. publs., chpt. to book; rschr. in field FDA, 1989. Named one of Top Washington Drs., Washingtonian Mag., 1991, 93, 95, 99, one of Top Urologists in Washington, Washington Checkbook, 1993, one of Outstanding Physician Specialists, Washington Consumer Checkbook, 1998. Fellow ACS; mem. Am. Urol. Assn., No. Va. Pediatric Soc., Washington Urol. Soc. Avocations: collecting marine fish, beekeeping, swimming, tennis. Office: West End Med Ctr 2100 W Pennsylvania Ave NW Washington DC 20037-3202

BERGER, ROBERT MICHAEL, lawyer; b. Chgo., Jan. 29, 1942; s. David B. and Sophia (Mizock) B.; m. Joan B. Israel, Aug. 16, 1964; children: Aliza, Benjamin, David. AB, U. Mich., 1963; JD, U. Chgo., 1966. Bar: Ill. 1966, U.S. Supreme Ct. 1975. Law clk. to cir, judge Henry J. Friendly U.S. Ct. Appeals, 2d Circuit, N.Y.C., 1966-67; atty. Chgo. Legal Aid Bur. Law Reform Unit, 1967-68; mem. firm Mayer, Brown & Platt, Chgo., 1968-72; partner Mayer, Brown & Platt, 1972—; adjunct prof. Northwestern U. Law Sch., 1997—; lectr. Northwestern U. Law Sch., 1973; adj. prof. grad. program in real estate law John Marshall Law Sch., 1995-97; summer inst. faculty mem. Nat. Inst. Law-Focused Edn., Chgo., 1969-74; mem. hearing bd. Ill. Supreme Ct. Atty. Disciplinary Sys., 1973-79; mem. Ill. Sec. State Adv. Com. on Revised Uniform Ltd. Partnership Act, 1984-88, mem. spl. tax adv. commn. to Ill. Dept. Ins., 1972; bd. dirs., legal counsel Consumer Fedn. Ill., 1967-71; mem. regional consumer adv. coun. coun. FTC, 1969; bd. dirs., chmn. program com. Legal Assistance Found., Chgo., 1975-78; mem. Highland Park (Ill.) Zoning Bd. Appeals, 1984-86; chmn. blue ribbon com. Cook County Recorder, 1989-92; mem. real estate adv. bd. Dai-Ichi Kangyo Bank, Chgo., 1988-93; lectr. continuing legal edn. seminars. Comment editor: U. Chgo. Law Rev, 1965-66; author: Law and the Consumer, 1969, 74; author 500 page chpt. Lending, Finance and Banking, Construction Law, 1986, and ann. supplements; reporter Revised Uniform Ltd. Partnership Act, 1984-88; contb r. articles to law jours. Sec. Chgo. area Anti-Defamation League. Mem. ABA (chmn. subcom. on rev. uniform ltd. partnership act 1981-85, chmn. com. on partnerships and unincorporated bus. orgns. 1985-88), Am. Law Inst. (mems. consultative group), Am. Coll. Real Estate Lawyers (bd. govs. 1995-98, vice chmn. program com.), Chgo. Bar Assn. (bd. mgrs. 1970-72, chmn. com. on real estate fin. 1984-86, chmn. real property law com. 1987-88), Chgo. Coun. Lawyers (founder, bd. govs. 1969-71), Am.-Israel C. of C. (v.p.), Order of Coif, Phi Beta Kappa, Phi Kappa Phi. Office: Mayer Brown & Platt 190 S La Salle St Ste 3300 Chicago IL 60603-3410

BERGER, ROBERT STEVEN, dermatologist; b. Freeport, N.Y., July 14, 1954; s. Robert Henry and Barbara Ann (Neary) B.; m. Cathleen Ellen Shields, Aug. 14, 1976; children: Caitlin Shields, Meghan Aileen, Kerry Elizabeth. BS in Biology summa cum laude, Boston Coll., 1976; MD, N.Y. Med. Coll., 1980. Diplomate Am. Bd. Dermatology, Am. Bd. Med. Examiners; lic. physician Ala., Maine, Md., N.H. Intern Washington Hosp. Ctr., 1980-81; commd. med. officer USAF, 1981, advance through grades to maj., 1990, flight surgeon, 1981-85, resident in dermatology, 1985-88, stationed at Pease AFB, 1988-90; pvt. practice Waldorf, Md., 1990—; clin. prof. dept. dermatology Johns Hopkins U. Hosp., Balt.; staff Physicians Meml. Hosp., La Plata, Md.; courtesy staff Southern Md. Hosp. Ctr., Clinton, Md. Contbr. articles to profl. jours. Recipient Cert. Merit Soc. Investigative Dermatology, 1987, Silver medal Am. Acad. Dermatology, 1987, Achievement medal USAF, 1989. Mem. Phi Beta Kappa. Office: 11355 Pembrooke Sq Ste 108A Waldorf MD 20603-4805

BERGER, SAMUEL R., federal official; b. Sharon, Conn., Oct. 28, 1945. AB, Cornell U., 1967; JD cum laude, Harvard U., 1971. Bar: D.C. 1971. Legis. asst. Senator Harold E. Hughes, Iowa, 1971-72; spl. asst. Mayor John V. Lindsay, N.Y.C., 1972; dep. dir. policy planning staff Dept. of State, 1977-80; ptnr. Hogan & Hartson, Washington; asst. dir. nat. security Presdl. Transition Team, 1992; dep. asst. to the Pres. for nat. security affairs The White House, Washington, 1993-95, asst. to pres. for nat. security issues, 1995—. Author: Dollar Harvest, 1971, (with others) Manual of Foreign Investment in the United States, 1984. Mem. ABA. Office: National Security Council 1600 Pennsylvania Ave NW Washington DC 20500-0005*

BERGER, SANFORD JASON, lawyer, securities dealer, real estate broker; b. Cleve., June 29, 1926; s. Sam and Ida (Solomon) B.; m. Bertine Mae Benjamin, Aug. 6, 1950 (div. Dec. 1977); children: Bradley Alan, Bonnie Jean. B.A., Case Western Res. U., 1950, J.D., 1952. Bar: Ohio 1952, U.S. Supreme Ct. 1979, U.S. Ct. Appeals, 1981. Field examiner Ohio Dept. Taxation, Cleve., 1952; pvt. practice law, Cleve., 1952—; real estate cons., Cleve., 1960—; investment cons., Cleve., 1970—. Contbr. author: Family Evaluation in Child Custody Litigation, 1982, Child Custody Litigation, 1986, The Parental Alienation Syndrome and the Differentiation Between Fabricated and Genuine Child Sex Abuse, 1987, Family Evaluation in Child

Custody Mediation, Arbitration and Litigation, 1989; Copyright 10 songs, 1977. Candidate police judge, East Cleve., 1955, Bd. Edn., Beachwood, Ohio, 1963, mayor, Beachwood, 1967, judge ct. common pleas, Cuyahoga County, Ohio, 1984, 1986, Ct. Appeals, 1988, 90, 92, 94. Successful lawyer in U.S. Supreme Ct. Case of Cleveland Bd. of Edn. vs. Loudermill, 1985. With USMC, 1944-45, PTO. Recipient Cert. Appreciation Phi Alpha Delta, 1969, U.S. Supreme Ct. Chief Justice Warren E. Burger Healer Award, 1987, Outstanding Ohio Citizen award Ohio Gen. Assembly, 1987. Republican. Jewish. Lodge: B'nai B'rith (editor 1968-70). Avocations: poet, lyricist, legal writer, drag racer, scuba diving. Home: 1032 Som Center Rd Cleveland OH 44143-3527 Office: Sanford J Berger 1836 Euclid Ave # 305 Cleveland OH 44115-2234

BERGER, SEYMOUR MAURICE, social psychologist; b. Bklyn., Jan. 7, 1928; s. Leo and Bessie Ida (Okun) Berger; m. Sara Marilyn Nappen, Sept. 7, 1952; children: Evelyn Joyce, Nancy Faith. B.S., Okla. A&M Coll., 1949; M.A., Columbia U., 1950; Ph.D., Cornell U., 1959. Instr. Trinity Coll., Hartford, Conn., 1958-59; from instr. to assoc. prof. Ind. U., Bloomington, 1959-69; prof. social psychology U. Mass., Amherst, 1969-95, prof. emeritus, 1995—, acting dean social and behavioral scis., 1991-92, dean social behavioral scis., 1992-95. Contbr. articles on social psychology to profl. jours.; mem. editorial bd. Jour. Personality and Social Psychology. Served with USNR, 1945-46; served with USAF, 1951-55. Fulbright sr. research scholar, 1975-76,83; spl. fellow NIH, 1965-66. Democrat. Jewish. Home: 459 Flat Hills Rd Amherst MA 01002-1219

BERGER, SIDNEY L., theater educator, director; b. N.Y.C., Jan. 25, 1936; s. Sam B. and Pauline Schrank; m. Sandra Hopkins, Mar. 2, 1963; children: Jennifer, Erik. BA, Bklyn. Coll., 1957; MA, U. Kans., 1960, PhD, 1964. Asst. instr. U. Kans., 1958-63; asst. prof. Mich. State U., East Lansing, 1964-66, assoc. prof., 1966-69; prof., dir. Sch. Theater U. Houston, 1969-96, John & Rebecca Moores Disting. prof., 1996—; bd. dirs. Nat. Shakespeare Globe Ctr. Bd., Tex. Opera Theatre of Houston Grand Opera, Shakespeare Globe Ctr. Internat.; mem. theatre panel Cultural Arts Coun. Houston, 1978-82, 88; mem. adv. coun. Miller Theatre; cons. Arts and Sci. program NASA, 1974, Young Audiences, 1989-90, Woodlands Theatre Project, George Mitchell Interests, H.S. for Visual and Performing Arts, Houston; bd. trustees Nat. Theatre Conf.; chair Southwest Globe Ctr. Bd.; mem. adv. bd. Alley Theatre, 1988, assoc. artist, 1989—; regional chmn. Am. Coll. Theatre Festival, 1968, judge, 1970-73, 91-94. Author: plays including (book and lyrics) The Mudlark, 1970, (adapted book) The Fall and Rise of Bertolt Brecht, 1977, (book and lyrics) The Little Matchgirl, 1982, Bird Boy, 1985, (book and lyrics) The Last Temptation of Christ, 1984, Snow White, 1984, (book and lyrics, musical) America!, 1985, Rapunzel, 1990, (libretto with Robert Nelson, musical) American Anthem, 1991, opera librettoes include The Demon Lover, 1987, (with Robert Nelson) Tickets, Please, 1985, films include (documentary) Upstream U.S.A., 1985, House of the Jaguar, 1988, Reina de la Selva (Houston Internat. Film Festival award, 1989); author: (oratorio) Where is the Sun?, 1988; co-author, co-prodr.: (documentary film) The Search for Shakespeare, 1985-86; author, dir.: Was It a Dream?, 1991, End of the Line, 1992; sr. staff editor: Speech and Dram Svc. Ctr. Bulletin, 1959-64; editor: (with Jeane Luere) The Playwright Versus The Director, 1994, (with Jeane Luere) The Theatre Team, 1997; contbr. articles to profl. jours.; dir.: plays including Hamlet, West Side Story, Marat/Sade, Macbeth, Shadow Box, Home Coming, Richard III, Equus, King Lear, The Tempest, Sight Unseen, A Delicate Balance, Romeo and Juliet, Jacques Brel, Diary of Anne Frank, Taming of the Shrew, numerous others, films include (with Ben Vereen) Houston Proud, 1986, Crimestoppers, 1986-88, The Pear Tree, Alamo Dream; narrator documentary films including Honor Squadrons, Tiger Cruise, Norway, Texas Rangers; dir., adapter, prodr: films Duets for Cannibals (Red Ribbon Am. Film Festival 1992), Old Secrets (Silver award Corp. Pub. Broadcasting 1993, Outstanding New Work Nat. Video Festival Am. Film Inst.). Mem. screening com. Internat. Exch. of Persons, Washington, Cmty. Leaders of Am.; bd. dirs. Mus. and Arts mus., 1993; founding mem. Houston Coalition of the Arts; apptd. to State of Mich. Coun. on the Arts, 1968-69. Recipient Commendation State of Tex. for Crimestoppers program, 1981, Outstanding Contribution by a Performing Artist Mayor, 1986, Resolution of Commendation mayor and City Coun., 1991, award for contribution for arts Musicfest, 1992. Mem. Am. Theatre Assn. (chmn. overseas touring com. U.S.O. 1978-85, nat. U.S.O. shows com. 1978-83), Houston C. of C. (cultural com. 1970-73), Shakespeare Assn. Am. (pres., founder), Am. Ednl. Theater Assn. (regional chmn. Ohio, western Pa. 1968), Coll. Fellows Am. Theatre. Home: 4711 Imogene St Houston TX 77096-1713 Office: U Houston Sch of Theatre Houston TX 77204

BERGER, STANLEY ALLAN, mechanical engineering educator; b. Bklyn., Aug. 9, 1934; s. Jack and Esther (Bernstein) B.; m. Anna Ofman, Jan. 30, 1966 (div. Aug. 1984); children: Shoshana, Maya. BS, Bklyn. Coll., 1955; PhD, Brown U., 1959. Rsch. assoc. Princeton U., N.J., 1959-60; from lectr. to prof. U. Calif., Berkeley, 1961—; cons. IBM, The Rand Corp., Lockheed Missiles and Space Co., Sci. Applications, Inc., Aluminum Co. Am. Author: Laminar Wakes, 1971; editor: Introduction to Bioengineering, 1996; contbr. articles to profl. jours. Fellow AAAS, ASME, AIAA, Am. Phys. Soc. Home: 899 Arlington Ave Berkeley CA 94707-1926 Office: U Calif Dept Mech Engring Berkeley CA 94720

BERGER, STEPHEN, financial services company executive; b. N.Y.C., July 11, 1939; s. Saul and Paula (Rosenzweig) B.; m. Cynthia C. Wainwright, Sept. 24, 1977. BA, Brandeis U., 1959. Edito Crowell-Collier Publs., N.Y.C., 1961-62; exec. asst. to Rep. Jonathan Bingham N.Y.C., 1964-68; pres. PCM Corp., N.Y.C., 1969-73; exec. dir. N.Y. Study Commn. on N.Y.C., 1972-73; dir. Studies Commn. on Critical Choices for Americans, N.Y.C., 1973-74; commr. N.Y. Dept. Social Svcs., Albany, 1975-76; dir. N.Y. Office Planning Svcs., Albany, 1975; exec. dir. N.Y. Emergency Fin. Control Bd., N.Y.C., 1976; mem. N.Y. Bd. Social Welfare, 1977; dir. corp. devel. Oppenheimer & Co., Inc., N.Y.C., 1981-82; investment banker Odyssey Ptnrs., N.Y.C., 1983-85; chmn. U.S. Ry. Assn., Washington, 1980-87; prof. pub. adminstrn. N.Y.U., 1977-85; bd. dirs., chmn. fin. com. N.Y. Met. Transp. Authority, 1979-85; exec. dir. Port Authority, N.Y., N.J., 1985-90, Intergovtl. Policy Adv. Com. (office U.S. trade rep.), 1988-90; chmn., chief exec. officer Fin. Guaranty Ins. Co., N.Y.C., 1990-92; exec. v.p. GE Capital Corp., 1992-93; ptnr. Odyssey Ptnrs., L.P., N.Y.C., 1993—; chmn. Odyssey Investment Ptnrs., LLC., 1997—. Bd. trustees Brandeis U., 1994—. With U.S. Army, 1962-63. Democrat. Jewish.

BERGER, STEVEN R., lawyer; b. Miami, Aug. 23, 1945; s. Jerome J. and Jeanne B. B.; m. Francine Blake, Aug. 20, 1966; children: Amy, Charlie. BS, U. Ala., 1967; JD, 1969. Bar: Fla. 1969, Nev. 1991, U.S. Dist. Ct. (no. dist.) Fla. 1969, U.S. Dist. Ct. (so. dist.) Fla. 1971, U.S. Dist. Ct. (mid. dist.) Fla. 1989, U.S. Dist. Ct. Nev. 1991, U.S. Ct. Appeals (5th cir.) 1971, U.S. Ct. Appeals (11th cir.) 1981, U.S. Ct. Appeals (2nd and 9th cirs.) 1991, U.S. Supreme Ct. 1972, U.S. Ct. Claims 1977. Assoc. W. Dexter Douglass, Tallahassee, Fla., 1969-71, William R. Dawes, Miami, 1971; ptnr. Carey, Dwyer, Cole Selwood & Bernard, Miami, 1971-81; sole practice Steven R. Berger, P.A., 1981-89; ptnr. Wolpe, Leibowitz, Berger & Brotman, 1989-94, Berger & Chafetz, 1994—; mem. faculty Nat. Appellate Advocacy Inst., Washington, 1980; vice chmn. bench and bar adv. com. Ct. Appeals. 4th Dist., 1986-92. Chmn. City Miramar Planning Bd., 1975-76. Mem. ABA (vice chmn. app. practice com. litigation sect. 1981-83, chmn. 5th cir. sub-com. appellate practice com. 1978-81), Am. Judicature Soc., Am. Arbitration Assn., Tallahassee Bar Assn., Kendall-South Miami Bar Assn., Dade County Def. Bar Assn., Fla. Def. Lawyers Assn. (vice chmn. appellate rules com. 1989), Def. Rsch. Inst., Rep. Nat. Lawyers Assn., Internat. Assn. Def. Counsel, N.Y. State Bar Assn., State Bar Nev., N.Y. State Trial Lawyers Assn. Office: Berger & Chafetz PO Box 1627 Miami FL 33256

BERGER, SUE ANNE, secondary education educator, chemist; b. Wichita, Kans., Oct. 8, 1941; d. Oscar Henry and Josephine Mildred (Stucky) B. BE, Kans. State Tchrs. Coll., 1963; MS in Chemistry, U. Miss., 1968; MS in Mineral Econs., Colo. Sch. Mines, 1982. Cert. chemistry and math. tchr., Colo. Tchr. Davy Crockett Jr. High Sch., Amarillo, Tex., 1963-67, Bear Creek Sr. High Sch., Denver, 1968-94; dept. chmn. Bear Creek Sr. High Sch., 1980-85; adj. prof., Physics, (Golden) Colo. Schl. of Mines, 1994—. Author: (with others) Element of the Week, 1986, CHEM-PACS, 1989. Named Disting. Tchr., White House Commn. on Presdl. Scholars, 1987, 88; recipient Exemplary H.S. Sci. Tchg. award CIBA-Geigy, 1992, A Plus for Breaking the Mold award Mobile Sci. Show, 1993, Disting. Svc. to Sci. Edn. award Colo. Assn. Sci. Tchrs., 1994. Mem. Am. Chem. Soc. (named Tchr. of Yr. Colo. chpt. 1988), Nat. Sci. Tchrs. Assn., Colo. Assn. Sci. Tchrs., Colo. Chem. Tchr. Assn., Phi Delta Kappa. Democrat. Mennonite. Avocations: cross country skiing, golf, bridge. Home: 6372 S Annapurna Dr Evergreen CO 80439-5334

BERGER, THOMAS JAN, financial company executive; b. N.Y.C., June 3, 1952; s. Frank Milan and Bozena (Jahodova) B.; m. Diane May Levine, Feb. 3, 1979. BA cum laude, Harvard U., 1973, MBA, 1977. Acct. officer Citbank N.A., N.Y.C., 1973-75; v.p. Merrill Lynch Capital Markets, N.Y.C., 1977-83; advisor Saudi Arabian Monetary Agy., Riyadh, 1983-86; dep. asst. sec. for internat. monetary affairs U.S. Dept. Treasury, Washington, 1986-89; dir. Lombard Odier Internat. Portfolio Mgmt. Ltd., London, 1989-93, Mercury Asset Mgmt. plc, London, 1993-97, Invesco Asset Mgmt. Ltd., London, 1997—. Chmn. Reps. Abroad, U.K. Mem. Harvard Club (N.Y.C.), Cosmos Club (Washington), Carlton Club (London). Republican. Avocations: tennis, squash, antiques. Office: Invesco Asset Mgmt Ltd, 11 Devonshire Sq, London Ec2m 4YR, England

BERGER, THOMAS LOUIS, author; b. Cin., July 20, 1924; s. Thomas Charles and Mildred (Bubbe) B.; m. Jeanne Redpath, June 12, 1950. BA with honors, U. Cin., 1948; postgrad., Columbia U., 1950-51; LittD (hon.), L.I.U., 1986. Librarian Rand Sch. Social Sci., N.Y.C., 1948-51; staff mem. N.Y. Times Index, 1951-52; assoc. editor Popular Sci. Monthly, 1952-53; disting. vis. prof. Southampton Coll., 1975-76; vis. lectr. Yale U., 1981, 82; Regent's lectr. U. Calif., Davis, 1982. Author: Crazy in Berlin, 1958, Reinhart in Love, 1962, Little Big Man, 1964, Killing Time, 1967, Vital Parts, 1970, Regiment of Women, 1973, Sneaky People, 1975, Who Is Teddy Villanova?, 1977, Arthur Rex, 1978, Neighbors, 1980, Reinhart's Women, 1981, The Feud, 1983 (Pulitzer Prize nomination 1984), Nowhere, 1985, Being Invisible, 1987, The Houseguest, 1988, Changing the Past, 1989, Orrie's Story, 1990, Meeting Evil, 1992, Robert Crews, 1994, Suspects, 1996, The Return of Little Big Man, 1999, (play) Other People, 1970. Served with AUS, 1943-46, ETO. Recipient Rosenthal award Nat. Inst. Arts and Letters, 1965; Western Heritage award, 1965; Ohioana Book award, 1982; Dial fellow, 1962. Office: Don Congdon Assocs 156 5th Ave New York NY 10010-7002 *In my work I try to compete with that reality to which I must submit in life.*

BERGER, TOBY, electrical engineer; b. Sept. 4, 1940; s. Henry and Doris L. (Goldstein) B.; m. Florence Cohen, Aug. 27, 1961; children: Elizabeth, Lawrence. BS, Yale U., 1962; MS, Harvard U., 1964, PhD, 1966. Assoc. scientist Raytheon Co., Wayland, Mass., 1962-66, sr. scientist, 1966-68, cons., 1968-75; asst. prof. elec. engring. Cornell U., Ithaca, N.Y., 1968-72, prof., 1977-88, J. Preston Levis prof. engring., 1988-98, Irwin and Joan Jacobs prof. engring., 1998—, acting dir. dept. elec. engring., 1998—; cons. IBM, Owego, N.Y., 1975-94, Bell Labs., Murray Hill, N.J., 1987—, TCSI, Berkeley, Calif., 1986—; vis. prof. ENST, Paris, 1986, Princeton U., 1989-90, Northeastern U., 1990, U. Va., 1997. author: Rate-Distortion Theory, 1971, Digital Compression for Multimedia, 1998; contbr. articles to tech. jours. Fellow Guggenheim Found., 1975-76, Japan Soc. for Promotion of Sci., 1980-81, Peoples Republic of China Ednl. Ministry, 1981, Fulbright travel fellow, 1987. Fellow IEEE (pres. info. theory group 1979, editor-in-chief Transactions on Info. Theory 1987-89); mem. AAAS, Am. Soc. Engring. Tech. (Frederick E. Terman award 1982), Sigma Xi, Tau Beta Pi. Home: 422 Highland Rd Ithaca NY 14850-2216 Office: Sch Elec Engring Cornell U Ithaca NY 14853

BERGER, WILLIAM MERRIAM BART, investment management company executive; b. Denver, Nov. 3, 1925. *Wife, Bernadette Johnson Berger, is co-founder of The Berger Art Collection at the Denver Art Museum. In 1995, she became a member of the Huntington Library's Art Collectors Council. Bernadette has been a member of the Director's Roundtable of the J. Pierpont Morgan Library since 1996. In 1997,she was elected to the Executive Committee of the Friends of American Art at Yale and the Chairman's Council at the Metropolitan Museum of Art. Bernadettethen became a member of the Education Committee at the Denver Art Museum in 1998.* Grad., Hotchkiss Sch., Lakeville, Conn., 1943; BA, Yale U., 1948. V.p., investment mgr. Colo. Nat. Bank Denver, 1948-59; dir., chmn. bd. dirs. Centennial Mgmt. and Rsch. Corp., Denver, 1959-67; pres., dir. Centennial Fund, Inc. (merger Gyphon Fund), Denver, 1959, 2d Centennial Fund, Inc. (merger Gryphon Fund), Denver, 1959, Gryphon Fund, Inc. (now Founders Growth Fund), Denver, 1961-69; v.p., dir. Meridian Fund, Inc. (now Founders Income Fund), Denver, 1962-69; v.p., portfolio mgr. and dir. Fin. Programs, Denver, 1964-65; v.p. Fin. Indsl. Fund and Fin. Indsl. Income Fund, Denver, 1964-65; with Berger, Kent Adv. Corp., N.Y.C., 1969-73; gen. ptnr. Berger, Kent & Co., N.Y.C., 1966-70; v.p., dir. Founders Mutual Depositor Corp., Denver, 1967-69; prin. investment officer Fleming Berger Assocs. (formerly Fleming, Berger-Kent & Co.), Denver, 1969-73, gen. ptnr., 1970-73, pres., dir., 1973-75; chmn. bd., pres., prin. investment officer Fleming Berger Fund, Inc. (merger 100 Fund, Inc.), Denver, 1973; pres., dir. Berger Land Co., Estabrook, Colo., 1957—, 101 Fund, Inc., Denver, 1974-94, 100 Fund, Inc., Denver, 1974-94; pres., dir. Berger Assocs., Inc., Denver, 1975-94, chmn. bd., 1994—; shareholder, dir. The Berger 100 Fund, The Berger Growth and Income Fund, The Berger Small Co. Growth Fund; pres. Denver chpt. Am. Inst. Banking, 1951-52; mem. adv. fund. Denver Rsch. Inst., U.Denver, 1970-73. Trustee Mile High United Trust Fund, Denver, 1960—; chmn. Urban League Colo., 1964-68; art collector, co-found of The Berger Collection at the Denver Art Mus., 1995; found. of the WMBBerger Found., 1994; mem. investment com. Denver Art Mus. Found. and mem. investment com. Denver Found, 1997. With Am. Field Svc. with Brit. 8th Army, 1944-45; mem. adv. com. Mt. Vernon Ladies Assn.; mem. art collectors council, Huntington Libr., 1994; Overseer's comm., Huntington Library, 1994; mem. roundtable Pierpont Morgan Libr.; mem. pres.'s coun. Met. Mus., N.Y.C., 1998. Mem. Colo. Bankers Assn. (bond portfolio com. 1957-59), Denver Soc. Security Analysts (founding), Prouts Neck Assn., Prouts Neck Yacht Club, Prouts Neck Country Club, Univ. Club, Cactus Club, Yale Club N.Y.C., Mile High Club, The Leash (N.Y.C.). Office: Berger Assocs PO Box 6587 Denver CO 80206-0587 also: 2450 E Alameda Ave Unit 12 Denver CO 80209-3346*

BERGER, WOLFGANG H., oceanographer, marine geologist; b. Erlangen, Bavaria, Fed. Republic of Germany, Oct. 5, 1937; came to U.S., 1961; s. Helmut and Emilie Berger; m. Karen J. Thomas, June 9, 1966; children: Karl, Katrina. MS in Geology, U. Colo., 1963; PhD in Oceanography, U. Calif., San Diego, 1968. Wissensch. asst. Universität Kiel, Fed. Republic of Germany, 1969-71; rsch. asst. Scripps Inst. Oceanography U. Calif., La Jolla, 1963-68, asst. researcher, 1968-69, asst. prof., 1971-74, assoc. prof., 1974-80, prof. oceanography, 1980—; interim dir. Scripps Inst. Oceanography Scripps Inst. Oceanography U. Calif., 1996-97; dir. Calif. Space Inst. U. Calif., San Diego, 1998—; vis. prof. geology Universität Kiel, 1977, 80; guest researcher Universität Bremen, Fed. Republic of Germany, 1986—. Editor: Abrupt Climatic Change, 1987, Ocean Productivity, 1989. Mem. geology adv. bd. U. Colo., Boulder, 1989-92. Recipient Bigelow medal Woods Hole (Mass.) Oceanographic Inst., 1979, Huntsman medal Bedford Oceanographic Inst., Can., 1984, Humboldt award German Sci. Found., Bonn, Fed. Republic of Germany, 1986, Albert I medal, Paris, 1991, Balzan prize, 1993, Steinmann medal Geol. Vereingung, 1998; Lady Davis fellow Hebrew U., 1986. Fellow AAAS, Am. Geophysical Union (Ewing medal 1988), Geol. Soc. Am.; mem. European Geophysical Soc. Avocation: water color. Office: U Calif San Diego Scripps Inst Oceanography SI0-UCSD-0215 La Jolla CA 92093

BERGERON, CLIFTON GEORGE, ceramic engineer, educator; b. Los Angeles, Jan. 5, 1925; s. Lewis G. and Rose C. (Dengel) B.; m. Laura H. Kaario, June 9, 1950; children—Ann Leija, Louis Kaario. B.S., U. Ill., 1950, M.S., 1959, Ph.D., 1961. Sr. ceramic engr. A. O. Smith Corp., Milw., 1950-55; staff engr. Whirlpool Corp., St. Joseph, Mich., 1955-57; research asso. U. Ill., Champaign-Urbana, 1957-61; asst. prof. U. Ill., 1961-63, asso. prof., 1963-67, prof., 1967-78, head dept. ceramic engring., 1978-86, prof. emeritus, 1988—; cons. A. O. Smith Corp., Whirlpool Corp., Ingraham Richardson, U.S. Steel Corp., Pfaudler Corp., Ferro Corp. Editor, Ann. Conf. on Glass Problems. Served in U.S. Army, 1943-46, ETO. NSF grantee, 1961-82. Fellow Am. Ceramic Soc.; mem. AAAS, Nat. Inst. Ceramic Engrs., AAUP, KERAMOS, Am. Soc. Engring. Edn., Sigma Xi. Research in crystallization kinetics in glass; high temperature reactions. Home: 208 W Michigan Ave Urbana IL 61801-4944 Office: 105 S Goodwin Ave Urbana IL 61801-2901

BERGERON, EARLEEN FOURNET, actress; b. New Orleans, Aug. 7, 1938; d. Earl Joseph Fournet and Lucia (Cuccia) Wadsworth; m. James Ronald Bergeron Sr., June 17, 1961; children: Blanche Theresa, Michele Yvette, James Ronald Jr. B of Social Sci. in Theatre and Speech, Loyola U., 1960. bd. dirs. Port Players, Shreveport, La.; assoc. mem. The Co. Repertory Theatre, Inc., Project-Shakespeare in the Schs. Actor: (play) The Secret Affairs of Mildred Wilde, 1977, The Boyfriend, 1977, The Shadow Box, 1979, California Suite, 1980, Hay fever, 1985, Brighton Beach, 1986, Beyond Therapy, 1987, Steel Magnolias, 1988, 89, Nunsense, 1990, Broadway Bound, 1991, The Women, 1993, Nunsense II, 1995, Stomping Grounds, 1995, 96, Angels in America, Part I: Millenium Approaches, Part II: Perestroika, 1997, Spareribs, 1998, (TV series) Rescue 911, 1991, (film) Man in the Moon, 1990, (comml.) Goodwill, 1988, Schumpert Medical Center, 1991, Cunningham and McDonald, Plastic Surgeons, 1991, JB Cable Ads, 1995, Pierre Bossier Mall, 1996. Mem. Shreveport Opera Guild, 1972-97; area leader fund drive Am. Cancer Soc., Shreveport, 1985-89; active Shreveport Med. Aux., 1968-97, exec. bd. 1976-78. Named one of Outstanding Team Capts., United Way Fund, 1969. Mem. Shreveport Little Theatre Guild (bd. dirs. 1985-86), Shreveport Little Theatre, Majorie Lyons Playhouse, Strand Theatre. Roman Catholic.

BERGERON, NORMAND R., retired state legislator; b. Nashua, N.H., May 15, 1927; m. Carmen E. Bergeron; 3 children. Grad. h.s., Nashua. Selectman Ward 7, Nashua, 1953-54, Ward 3, 1992-95; mem. N.H. Ho. of Reps., Concord, 1994-97; mem. transp. com. N.H. Ho. Reps.; mem. Nashua Wholesale Grocers Inc., 1969-78, dir. Mem. Nat. Assn. Life Underwriters (v.p. 1964, pres. 1965), Young Businessmen's Club (v.p. 1964, pres. 1965). Address: 8 Overhill Ave Nashua NH 03060-1664

BERGERON, ROBERT FRANCIS, JR. (TERRY BERGERON), software engineer; b. Gloucester, Mass., Jan. 23, 1942; s. Robert Francis and Jean Ann (Francis) B.; children: Robert, Karin, Kristin; m. Marion Louise Pisarchuk, July 14, 1979; children: Steven, Tanya. ScB summa cum laude, Brown U., 1964; PhD math., MIT, 1968. Rsch. assoc. Bolt Beranek & Newman, Cambridge, Mass., 1968; instr. math MIT, Cambridge, 1969; mem. tech. staff Bell Lab., Whippany, N.J., 1969-72, supr., 1972-84; tech. mgr. AT&T Bell Lab., Warren, N.J., 1984-95; cons., sr. mgr. Cotelligent, Liberty Corner, N.J., 1996—. Patentee in field; contbr. articles to profl. jours. Home: 27 Kevin Dr Flanders NJ 07836-9762 Office: Cotelligent 150 Allen Rd Liberty Corner NJ 07938

BERGERON, RONALD JAY, computer programmer, analyst; b. North Tonawanda, N.Y., Aug. 23, 1955; s. Roland Adelard and Lois Jane (Burgin) B. AS in Gen. Biology, Monroe Cmty. Coll., Rochester, N.Y., 1982; AS in Nutritional Sci., U. Mass., Northampton, 1986; BS in Biomed. Computing, Rochester Inst. Tech., 1988. Dept. mgr. Burroughs Corp., Rochester, 1973-81; drywall contractor Major Drywall, Fairport, N.Y., 1981-87; jr. program specialist VA Hosp., Northampton, 1987-88; sr. programmer, analyst Shared Med. Systems, Malvern, Pa., 1988-92; programming specialist U. Rochester Med. Ctr., 1992-94; programmer, analyst Apex Mgmt., Rochester, 1994-97, Rsch. Inst. Am., Rochester, 1997—. Camp counselor United Cancer Coun., Rochester, 1981-93; apheresis donor, ARC, Rochester, 1973—. Mem. Knights of Columbus. Democrat. Roman Catholic. Avocations: tennis, construction projects, civic activities, racquetball. Office: Rsch Inst Am Group 175 Corporate Woods Ste 225 Rochester NY 14623-1461

BERGERON, SHEILA DIANE, retired science educator, educational consultant; b. Decatur, Ill., Aug. 17, 1940; d. Lewis F. and Elizabeth A. (Hoff) Brown; m. Richard A. Bergeron, Sept. 25, 1965; 1 child, Cynthia Diane. BS in Spl. Edn., Ill. State U., 1962; MA in Counseling, U. Colo., 1980. Tchr. Villa Park (Ill.) Dist. # 45, 1962-68, Jefferson County Schs. R-1, Golden, Colo., 1968-98; ret., 1998; cons. in field; adj. instr. U. No. Colo., Greeley, 1980-86, Met. State U., 1986-88, U. Colo., Denver, 1986-88, Colo. Christian U., 1998; staff devel. cons. Denver Pub. Schs., Summit County Schs., Dillon, Colo., Dallas Pub. Schs., Lake City Schs., Colo., 1982-93; team mem. North Ctrl. Accreditation Assn., 1978, 90. Steering com. mem., pres. Leadership Golden, 1986-98; emergency communicator ARC, Denver, 1990-98; vol. Pub. TV, KRMA-TV, Denver, 1991-98, Golden Civic Found., 1986-94. Named A-Plus Tchr. Rocky Mountain News and KCNC-TV, 1992; recipient Presdl. Excellence in Sci. Teaching award, 1995. Mem. ASCD, NSTA (Nat. Sci. Tchrs. Assn.), Nat. Staff Devel. Coun. Avocation: amateur radio operator. Home: 606 Alaska St Golden CO 80403-1308

BERGERON, TRACEY ANNE, mental health nurse, educator; b. Concord, N.H., Mar. 17, 1952; d. Ernest George and Yvette Sylvia (Hunneyman) Caldwell; m. Scott Martin Bergeron, Aug. 5, 1980. BA in Elem. Edn., Plymouth (N.H.) State Coll., 1974; diploma, Concord Hosp. Sch. Nursing, 1981; M in Edn. and Human Svcs., New Eng. Coll., Henniker, N.H., 1988; BSN, Graceland Coll., 1996. Lic. elem. tchr.; RN, N.H.; cert. psychiat.-mental health nurse; cert. med. asst., 1998. Sch. nurse Barrington (N.H.) Sch., 1984-89; charge nurse Wentworth Douglass Hosp., Dover, N.H., 1981-90, Seaborne Hosp., Dover, 1984-86; nurse reviewer W.B. Saunders Pub. Co., Phila., 1992—; nurse trainer, cons. Divsn. Devel. Svcs., Dover, 1995—; maternal/child nurse Portsmouth Pre Natal Clinic, 1989-95, Portsmouth Regional Hosp., 1989-95; psychiat. nurse Portsmouth Pavillion, 1987—; clin. instr. McIntosh Coll., Dover, N.H., 1990—. Contbr. articles to profl. jours.; co-author nursing newsletter The Grape Vine; nurse reviewer RN Mag. Mem. Devel. Disabilities Nurses Assn., Kappa Delta Phi. Avocations: study of foreign languages, dancing, reading, reiki, tai chi. Home: 732 Route 153 Middleton NH 03887-6102 Office: McIntosh Coll 23 Cataract Ave Dover NH 03820-3908

BERGERON, WILTON LEE, physician; b. Scott, La., Feb. 13, 1933; s. Lee and Ida (Duhon) B.; m. Juanita Marie Landry, Aug. 3, 1957; children: David, Marcel, René, Jeanne. BS, U. South La., 1956; MD, La. State U., 1958. Diplomate Am. Bd. Allergy and Immunology. Intern Confederate Meml. Med. Ctr. (now La. State U. Med. Sch.), Shreveport, 1958-59; resident Lafayette (La.) Charity Hosp., 1959-60; fellow in allergy Tulane U. Med. Sch., New Orleans, 1968-70; pvt. practice Lafayette and Scott, La., 1960—, allergist, 1970—. Pres. Secular Franciscan Order, 1990-93. Mem. La. Allergy Soc. (former pres.). Republican. Roman Catholic. Avocations: fishing, computers. Home and Office: PO Box 98 # 90 Scott LA 70583-0098

BERGERSON, DAVID RAYMOND, lawyer; b. Mpls., Nov. 23, 1939; s. Raymond Kenneth and Katherine Cecille (Langworthy) B.; m. Nancy Anne Heeter, Dec. 22, 1962; children—W. Thomas C., Kirsten Finch, David Raymond. BA, Yale U., 1961; JD, U. Minn., 1964. Bar: Minn. 1964. Assoc. Fredrikson Law Firm, Mpls., 1964-67; atty. Honeywell Inc., Mpls., 1967-74, asst. gen. counsel, 1974-82, v.p., asst. gen. counsel, 1983-84, v.p., gen. counsel, 1984-92; pvt. practice law Mpls., 1992-94; v.p., sec. Telcom Sys. Svcs., Inc., Plymouth, Minn., 1994-96, dir., cons., 1996-97; v.p. bd. dirs. Hogan Bergerson, Inc., Plymouth, Minn., 1997—. Bd. dirs. Pillsbury Neighborhood Svcs., Inc., Mpls., 1983-92. Republican. Club: Minneapolis. Avocations: tennis; bird-hunting. Home and Office: 2303 Huntington Point Rd E Wayzata MN 55391-9740 Office: Hogan Bergerson Inc 4040 IDS Ctr Minneapolis MN 55402

BERGES, JUNERIA PARR, middle school principal; b. Aug. 2, 1947. B in Music Edn., U. So. Miss., 1969; MEd, Tex. Women's U., 1988; EdD, E. Tex. State U., 1993. Choral dir. Grapevine (Tex.) H.S., 1983-88; asst. prin. Grapevine Colleyville Ind. Sch. Dist., 1988-92; prin. Grapevine Middle Sch., 1992-98, Coppel (Tex.) Middle Sch. North, 1998—. E-mail: jberges@coppell.ednet10.net. Home: 121 S Timberline Colleyville TX 76034-3502

BERGESEN, ROBERT NELSON, transportation company executive; b. Phila., Nov. 1, 1937; s. Bernhard E. and Carol Pearl (Nelson) B.; m. Jean Nicol, Apr. 23, 1966; children: Susan, Jean, Jeffrey. BA, Cornell U., 1959, MBA, 1961. Sys. analyst Price Waterhouse and Co., N.Y.C., 1961-63, Warner-Lambert, Morris Plains, N.J., 1963-66; fin. analyst Leaseco, N.Y.C., 1969-70; asst. controller C.T.I., N.Y.C., 1970-71; controller Flexi-Van Corp., N.Y.C., 1971-75; from controller to gen. mgr. Vt. Transit Co., Inc.,

Burlington, 1977—. Mem. New Eng. Bus. Assn. (bd. dirs. 1993—). Lutheran. Home: 24 Morningside St Middlebury VT 05753-1015 Office: Vt Transit Co Inc 106 Main St Burlington VT 05401-8420

BERGESON, JAMES, advertising executive. Pres., COO, CEO Colle and McVoy Inc., Mpls. Office: Colle & McVoy Inc Ste 2400 8500 Mormandale Lake Blvd Minneapolis MN 55437*

BERGESON, TERRY, state system administrator. BA in English, M in Counseling and Guidance, PhD in Edn. Tchr., j.h. sch. guidance counselor Mass., Alaska, Wash.; exec. dir. Ctrl. Kitsap Sch. Dist., 1989-92, Wash. State Commn. on Learning, 1993-95; state supt. pub. instrn. Olympia, Wash., 1997—. Fax: 360-753-6712. Office: PO Box 47200 Olympia WA 98504-7200

BERGETHON, KAARE ROALD, retired college president; b. Tromso, Norway, June 8, 1918; came to U.S., 1926, naturalized, 1930; s. Maximilian and Petra Ruud (Olsen) B.; m. Katherine Lind, Apr. 4, 1942; children: Bruce L., Peter R. A.B., DePauw U., 1938; M.A., Cornell U., Ithaca, N.Y., 1940, Ph.D., 1945; Litt.D., Brown U., 1959, Franklin and Marshall Coll., 1959; New England Coll.,, 1998; LL.D., Rutgers U., 1959, Muhlenberg Coll., 1959, Lehigh U., 1959, Waynesburg Coll., 1960, DePauw U., 1961, Gannon Coll., 1978, Lafayette Coll., 1978, Temple U., 1978, Allegheny Coll., 1979, Bloomfield Coll., 1980. With Walter Kidde Constructors Inc., N.Y.C., 1938-39, 41-44; instr. German Syracuse (N.Y.) U., 1945-46; instr. German Brown U., 1946-47, asst. prof. German, asst. to chmn. div. modern langs., 1947-52, assoc. dean, 1952-55, assoc. prof. German, 1953-58, dean, 1955-58, prof. German, 1958; pres. Lafayette Coll., Easton, Pa., 1958-78; pres. emeritus Lafayette Coll., 1978—; interim chief exec. and cons. Bloomfield (N.J.) Coll., 1979-80, interim pres., cons., 1986-87; vice chmn. Econ. Devel. Council of N.Y.C., Inc. and; exec. dir. Nat. Alliance of Bus. of N.Y.C., 1980-81; interim pres. New Eng. Coll., Henniker, N.H., 1981-82; pres. New Eng. Coll., Henniker, 1982-85; ednl. cons. Easton, 1985-95; interim pres., cons. Wells Coll., Aurora, N.Y., 1987-88. Author: Grammar for Reading German, 1950, alt. edit., 1963, rev. edit., 1979, also articles in profl. publs. Past pres. Presbyn. Coll. Union; past pres. Middle States Assn. Colls. and Secondary Schs.; trustee Charlotte W. Newcombe Found., Princeton, N.J. Mem. Northampton Country Club (Easton), Phi Beta Kappa, Phi Eta Sigma, Phi Kappa Phi, Beta Theta Pi, Sigma Delta Chi, Alpha Phi Omega. Unitarian. Home: 1312 Kirkland Village Cir Bethlehem PA 18017-4759

BERGEY, JOHN M., retired technology executive; b. Harleysville, Pa., Feb. 6, 1934; s. Norman L. and Verna A. Bergey; m. Joan Pumphrey; children: Kurt, Krista. B in Engring., Pa. State U., 1956, MBA, 1972. Registered profl. engr., Pa. Program mgr. Ordnance Prodn. Divsn., HMW, Lancaster, Pa., 1959-68; dir. R & D Hamilton Watch Co., Lancaster, Pa., 1968-71; pres. Pulsar Time Computer, Inc., Lancaster, Pa., 1971-77, Novatec, Inc., Lancaster, Pa., 1977-83; dir. bus. devel. Ferranti Techs., Lancaster, Pa., 1983-92; ret., 1992. Patentee in field of solid state digital watches. Pres. Lancaster County unit Am. Cancer Soc.; bd. mem. St. Joseph Hosp., Lancaster. 1st lt., USAF, 1952-56. Mem. Am. Mgmt. Assn., Air Force Assn., Lancaster C. of C., Lancaster Country Club, Conestoga Country Club, Tau Kappa Epsilon, Tau Beta Pi, Sigma Tau, Pi Eta Sigma. Avocations: tennis, golf.

BERGGREN, DICK, editor; b. Westerly, R.I., May 27, 1942; s. Richard and Lorraine Berggren; m. Kathy Berggren, July 19, 1964. BS, So. Conn. State, 1964; MS, Tufts U., 1967, PhD, 1970. Editor Gen. Media, Ipswich, Mass., 1977—; TV personality Stas. TNN, WTBS, CBS. Recipient Deery award Race Promoters Am., 1986, Frank Blunk award Ea. Motorsport Press Assn., 1979, McLemore award, Unocal Corp., 1983, Don Martin award, 1998. Mem. Am. Automobile Racing Writers and Broadcasters Assn., Ea. Motorsport Press Assn., Nat. Motorsports Press Assn. Office: General Media 65 Parker St Ste 2 Newburyport MA 01950-4600

BERGGREN, GERARD T., plant pathologist; b. New Orleans, Dec. 8, 1946; married; two children. BS, Southeastern La. U., 1969; MS, La. State U., 1971, PhD in Plant Pathology, 1974. Rsch. plant pathologist Ansul Co., 1974-75; mgr. product devel. Kalo Lab, Marion Labs, 1975-76; mgr. field rsch., 1976-77; prof. plant pathology La. State U., Baton Rouge; resident dir. St. Gabriel Rsch. St., La. Mem. Am. Phytopath Soc. Office: St Grabriel Rsch Sta Central Stations PO Box 34 Saint Gabriel LA 70776-0034*

BERGGREN, WILLIAM ALFRED, geologist, research micropaleontologist, educator; b. N.Y.C., Jan. 15, 1931; s. Wilhelm Fritjof and Lilly Maria (Skog) B.; m. Lois Albee, June 19, 1954 (div. July 1981); children—Erik, Anna Lisa, Anders, Sara Maria; m. Marie Pierre Aubry, June 19, 1982. BS, Dickinson Coll., 1952; MSc, U. Houston, 1957; PhD, U. Stockholm, 1960, DSc, 1962. Research micropaleontologist Oasis Oil Co., Tripoli, Libya, 1962-65; asst. scientist Woods Hole Oceanographic Inst., Mass., 1965-68; assoc. scientist Woods Hole Oceanographic Inst., 1968-71, sr. scientist, 1971-98, sr. scientist emeritus, 1998—; adj. prof. Brown U., Providence, 1968-93. Editor: (with others) Catastrophes and Earth History, 1984, Late Eocene-Early Oligocene Climatic and Biotic Change, 1992, Geochronology, Time-Scales and Global Stratigraphic Correlation, 1995; contbr. articles to sci. jours. Recipient Cushman Found. award for foramini feral rsch., 1995. Fellow Geol. Soc. Am., Geol. Soc. London (hon.); mem. NAS (Mary Clark Thompson medal 1982), Am. Assn. Petroleum Geologists, Soc. Econ. Paleontologists and Mineralogists (hon.), Paleontol. Soc. Am. (co-editor jour. 1980-84), Am. Geophys. Union, Geol. Soc. Switzerland. Avocation: skiing. Office: Woods Hole Oceanographic Inst Water St Woods Hole MA 02543

BERGGRUEN, JOHN HENRY, art gallery executive; b. San Francisco, June 18, 1943; s. Heinz and Lillian Z. B. Pres., owner John Berggruen Gallery, San Francisco. Office: John Berggruen Gallery 228 Grant Ave San Francisco CA 94108-4612*

BERGHAHN, KLAUS LEO, German and Jewish studies educator; b. Duesseldorf, Germany, Aug. 5, 1937; arrived in U.S., 1967; s. Wilhelm and Anna (Bong) B.; m. Doris E. Beyer, Aug. 10, 1966; 1 child, Marcus J. Student, U. Cologne, Germany, 1957-59; staatsexamen, U. Muenster, Germany, 1963, Dr phil, 1967. Tutor, asst. U. Muenster, 1963-67; asst. prof. German studies U. Wis., Madison, 1967-71, assoc. prof., 1971-73, prof., 1973—, chmn. German dept., 1994-97, mem. senate, 1974-78, 85-87, dir. ctr. German European studies, 1998—, Weinstein-Bascom prof. German and Jewish studies, 1999—; vis. prof. Free U. Berlin, 1978, U. Bielefeld, Germany, 1980-81, U. Giessen, Germany, 1983, 92, U. Mich., Ann Arbor, 1984, U. Calif., Davis, 1989, Hebrew U., Jerusalem, 1993; mem. adv. bd. German Am. Art Found., Chgo., 1995—; mem. German sect. Fulbright Commn., 1995-98; mem. adv. bd. German dept. Harvard U., 1994-95, 96-97; organizer spl. sessions, confs. and symposia, 1983—. Author: Formen der Dialogführung in Schillers klassischen Dramen, 1970, Friedrich Schiller: Vom Pathetischen und Erhabenen, 1970, Friedrich Schiller: Kallias oder über die Schönheit, 1971, Briefwechsel zwischen Schiller und Körner, 1973, Schillers Gedichte, 1980, G.E. Lessing: Hamburgische Dramaturgie, 1981, Schiller—Ansichten eines Idealisten, 1986, (with John Crean) Kritische Gespräche—Zehn Kapitel über Amerika, 1972, (with Beate Pinkerneil) Am Beispiel Wilhelm Meister, 2 vols., 1980; editor: (with Reinhold Grimm) Schiller—Zur Theorie und Praxis der Dramen, 1972, Wesen und Formen des Komischen im Drama, 1975, Utopian Vision—Technological Innovation—Poetic Imagination, 1990, (with Hans Ulrich Seeber) Literarische Utopien von Morus bis zur Gegenwart, 1983, 2d edit., 1985, (with Holub and Scherpe) Responsibility and Committment. Ethische Postulate der Kulturvermittlung. Festschift für Jost Hermand, 1996; editor: Schiller—Zur Geschichtlichkeit seines Werkes, 1976, The German-Jewish Dialogue-Reconsidered, 1996; mem. editl. bd. Monatshefte, 1970—, Mich. Germanic Studies, 1985—, Goethe Yearbook, 1988—; contbr. articles and revs. to profl. jours., chpts. to books. Vol. for local and state polit. campaigns. Fellow VW-Found., Germany, 1965-67, Am. Philos. Soc., 1969, 73, Inst. for Rsch. in Humanities, U. Wis., 1972, 89-94, Ctr. for Interdisciplinary Rsch., Bielefeld, 1980-81, German Acad. Exch. Svc., 1990, 99, also others; 14 summer rsch. grants U. Wis. Grad. Sch. Mem. MLA (19th and early 20th century German lit. divsn. exec. com. 1974-78, chmn. 1977, mem. 18th and early 19th century German lit. divsn. 1983-88, chmn. 1987, mem. adv. bd. MLA Profession 1997-99), Am. Assn. Tchrs. German (program and selection com. 1990), Internat. Union Germanists (program com. 1995), Lessing Soc., Schiller Soc. (medal 1984), Goethe Soc. Avocations: reading, writing, music, theater, chess. Home: 2908 Oxford Rd Madison WI 53705-2220 Office: U Wis Dept German 860 Van Hise Hall 1220 Linden Dr Madison WI 53706-1525

BERGHAHN, VOLKER ROLF, history educator; b. Berlin, Feb. 15, 1938; came to U.S., 1988; s. Alfred and Gisela (Henke) B.; m. Marion Ilse Koop, Dec. 29, 1969; children: Sascha, Vivian, Melvin. MA, U. N.C. Chapel Hill, 1961; PhD, U. London, 1964; Habil., U. Mannheim, 1966-69. Sr. scholar St. Anthony's Coll., Oxford, Eng., 1964-66; rsch. fellow U. Mannheim, 1966-69; lectr. U. East Anglia, Norwich, 1969-71; reader U. E. Anglia, Norwich, 1971-75; prof. U. Warwick, Coventry, 1975-88, Brown U., Providence, 1988-97, Columbia U., N.Y.C., 1998—. Author: Der Stahlhelm, 1966, Der Tirpitz Plan, 1970, Germany and the Approach of War, 1973, Modern Germany, 1982, The Americanization of West German Industry, 1945-1973, 1986, Otto A. Friedrich, 1902-1975, 1992, Imperial Germany, 1871-1914, 1995. Various grants and fellowships. Fellow Royal Hist. Soc.; mem. German History Soc. (pres. 1986-88), Am. Hist. Assn., German Studies Assn. Avocations: tennis, walking. Office: Columbia U Dept History New York NY 10027

BERGHOLZ, DAVID, foundation administrator; b. Chgo., Jan. 2, 1938; s. Arthur C. and Sarah (Tarler) B.; 1 child from previous marriage, Jonathan; m. Eleanor Jean Mallet, Sept. 17, 1970; children: Louis Daniel, Max Arthur. Student, U. Chgo., 1955-57; AB in Anthropology, U. Pitts., 1962. Asst. dir. com. on human resources Office of Mayor, City of Pitts., 1966-67; asst. to exec. dir. Allegheny Council to Improve Our Neighborhoods-Housing, Inc., Pitts., 1967-72; asst. to pres. Mallet & Co., Inc., Carnegie, Pa., 1972-73; assoc. planning Comprehensive Health Planning Assn. of Western Pa., Pitts., 1973-75; assoc. dir. cancer ctr. planning project Allegheny Gen. Hosp., Pitts., 1976-77; asst. exec. dir. Allegheny Conf. on Community Devel., Pitts., 1977-88; pres. Pub. Edn. Fund, Pitts., 1983-88; exec. dir. George Gund Found., Cleve., 1989—; adj. assoc. prof. cmty. devel. Carnegie Mellon U., Pitts., 1985-88; mem. adv. com. Health Policy Inst.; mem. steering com. Robert Wood Johnson Affordable Health Care Project. Recipient Recognition award Boys and Girls Club of Western Pa., 1984, Pitts. Bd. Edn. award, 1986. Mem. Coun. on Founds., Coun. on Basic Edn., Ind. Sector, Phi Delta Kappa (Lay Leader award 1985). Office: George Gund Found 1845 Guildhall Bldg 45 W Prospect Ave Cleveland OH 44115-1039*

BERGHOLZ, RICHARD CADY, political writer; b. Corvallis, Oreg., Apr. 13, 1917; s. William Orville and Mabel (Cady) B.; m. Elizabeth True Jamison, Feb. 22, 1941; children: Barbara Bergholz Stacy, Richard J., Elizabeth S.J. BA, U. Wash., 1938. Reporter Ventura (Calif.) Star-Free Press, 1938-41, AP, 1941-44; war corr. New Guinea, Philippines, China, Manchuria, 1944-46; reporter Glendale (Calif.) News-Press, 1946-47; polit. editor San Diego Evening Tribune, 1947-54, L.A. Mirror, 1954-62; polit. writer L.A. Times, 1962-83. Bd. dirs. Calif. First Amendment Coalition. Mem. Soc. Profl. Journalists, Pi Kappa Alpha. Home: 929 Crestview Dr Pasadena CA 91107-1950

BERGIA, ROGER MERLE, educational administrator; b. Peoria, Ill., Nov. 26, 1937; s. Merle Frederick and Doris Ann (Markham) B.; BA, Eureka Coll., 1960; MA, Bradley U., 1967, postgrad., 1968—; m. Valerie Jean Lane, Oct. 16, 1960; children: Lori, Amy, Beth. Tchr., coach Jr. H.S., Peoria Heights Sch., 1960-65; prin., Kelly Ave. Grade Sch., Peoria Heights, Ill, 1965-74; supt. Peoria Heights Schs., 1974—. Adminstrv. agent Ill. State Bd. of Early Childhood Edn. Early Childhood Exemplary Program. Named Sch. Adminstr. of Yr., Ill. Bd. Edn., 1981-82, recipient Exemplary Practices award, 1992. Mem. Phi Delta Kappa, Lambda Chi Alpha. Republican. Presbyterian. Home: 6723 N Gem Ct Peoria IL 61614-2901 Office: 1316 E Kelly Ave Peoria Heights IL 61614

BERGIN, ALLEN ERIC, clinical psychologist, educator; b. Spokane, Wash., Aug. 4, 1934; s. Bernard F. and Vivian Selma (Kullberg) B.; m. Marian Shafer, June 4, 1955; children: David, Sue, Cyndy, Kathy, Eric, Ben, Patrick, Daniel, Michael. BS, Brigham Young U., 1956, MS, 1957; PhD, Stanford U., 1960. Diplomate Am. Bd. Profl. Psychology. Postdoctoral fellow U. Wis., Madison, 1960-61; prof. psychology and edn. Tchrs. Coll., Columbia U., N.Y.C., 1961-72; prof. psychology Brigham Young U., Provo, Utah, 1972-99, dir. Values Inst., 1976-78, dir. clin. psychology, 1989-93; sr. rsch. fellow Nat. Inst. Health Care Rsch., 1992—; prof. emeritus Brigham Young U., 1999—; assessment officer Peace Corps, Washington, 1961-66; cons. NIMH, Rockville, Md., 1969-75, 90. Co-author: Changing Frontiers in Psychotherapy, 1972, A Spiritual Strategy for Counseling and Psychotherapy, 1997; co-editor: Handbook of Psychotherapy, 1971, 4th edit., 1994 (citation classic 1979), Handbook of Pyschotherapy and Religious Diversity, 1999. Bishop LDS Ch., Emerson, N.J., 1970-72, Provo, 1981-84, stake pres., 1992-95; mem. steering com. Utah Gov.'s Conf. on Families, Salt Lake City, 1979-80. Recipient Biggs-Pine award Am. Assn. Counseling and Devel., 1986, Maeser rsch. award Brigham Young U. Alumni Assn., 1986, exemplary paper award Templeton Found., 1996. Fellow APA (Disting. Contbn. to Knowledge award 1989, William James award div. 36, 1990); mem. Soc. for Psychotherapy Integration, Soc. for Sci. Study Religion, Soc. for Psychotherapy Rsch. (pres. 1974-75, Disting. Career award 1998), Am. Psychiat. Assn. (Pfister award 1998), Assn. Mormon Counselors (pres. 1979-80). Republican. Avocations: world travel, writing.

BERGIN, COLLEEN JOAN, medical educator; b. Foxton, New Zealand, May 13, 1953; came to U.S., 1981; d. Joseph Bernard and Mary Catherine (Butel) B.; m. Niall C.T. Wilton, May 22, 1992; children: Tessa, Sophie. MBChB, Auckland Med. Sch., 1979. Resident U. B.C., Vancouver, Can., 1981-87; faculty Stanford (Calif.) U., 1989-92; prof. U. Calif., San Diego, 1992—; cons. radiologist Auckland Hosp., 1998—. Contbr. articles to profl. jours. NIH Rsch. grantee, 1992—; Thoracic Radiology fellow Duke U., 1988. Mem. Am. Roentgen Ray Soc., Radiol. Soc. N.Am., Soc. Thoracic Radiology, Soc. Magnetic Resonance. Democrat. Roman Catholic. Avocations: golf, flying, photography, diving.

BERGLEITNER, GEORGE CHARLES, JR., investment banker; b. Bklyn., July 16, 1935; s. George Charles and Marie (Preitz) B.; m. Betty Van Buren, Oct. 29, 1966; children: George Charles III, Michael John, Stephen William. BBA, St. Francis Coll., Bklyn., 1959; MBA, CCNY, 1961; PhD in Bus. Adminstrn. (hon.), Colo. State Christian Coll. Dir. instl. sales A.T. Brod & Co., N.Y.C., 1965-66; dir. instl. sales Weis, Voisin & Cannon, Inc., N.Y.C., 1966-67, C.B. Richard, Ellis & Co., N.Y.C., 1967-68; pres. Stamford (N.Y.) Fin. Co., also bd. dirs.; pres. M.J. Manchester & Co., Fashion & Time, Inc., B.J.B. Graphics, Inc., First Coinvestors, Inc., Smart Fit Foundations, Inc., Jay Co., Computer Holdings Corp., Ltd., Delhi Mfg. Corp., Delhi Industries, Delhi Mfg., Inc., Delhi Internat., Inc., Luxemborg; bd. dirs. Alpha Capital Corp., Am. Energy Mgmt. Corp., Stamford Fin., Electronic Tax Ctrs., Inc., L.I.U.G., L.I. Venture Capital Group, L.I. Venture Group, High Tech Semiconductor Svcs., Del. County Indsl. Devel.; sponsor N.Y. Venture Group; bd. dirs. Indsl. Devel. Agy., Delaware County, N.Y. Chmn. Franciscan Fathers Devel. Program, 1967-71; mem. Pres's Coun., Franciscan Spirit award; 1959—; pres. South Kortright Ctrl. Sch.; chmn. No. Catskills Econ. Devel. Coun., Econ. Devel. Coun. Stamford, Econ. Devel. Coun. Delaware County; regent St. Francis Coll.; bd. dirs. Econ. Devel. Coun., Printing Trade Sch., Cmty. Hosp., Stamford, N.Y., Stamford Econ. Devel. Coun., Del. County Indsl. Devel. Agy., Cath. Charities Am., v.p., 1999; bd. dirs., sec. Indsl. Devel. Authority Delaware County; co-chair Project Strive, Albany, N.Y.; mem. fin. com. Sacred Heart Roman Cath. Ch.; pres. Otsego Del. Bd. Realtors; v.p. bd. dirs. Cath. Charities, 1999. With U.S. Army, 1952-55. Paul Harris fellow Rotary Internat.; Internat. Rotary Benefactor; recipient St. Francis Coll. Alumni Fund award, 1965, Del. County Youth award, 1991, John F. Kennedy Meml. award, 1972, Internat. award for Svc. to Investment Commn., 1982, Youth Bur. award, 1991, St. Francis Prep Sch. Alumni Achievement award, 1993; named Stamford Citizen of Yr., 1992, Realtor of Yr., 1992, Col. Harper Grange Citizen of Yr., 1993. Mem. N.Y. State Realtors Assn. (bd. dirs., chmn. polit. action, polit. action dir. 1999), Conn. Venture Capital Assn., Venture Assn. N.J. (bd. dirs.), Assn. Investment Bankers, Otsego-Delaware Bd. Realtors (P.A.F. chmn., bd. dirs., pres.-elect, pres. 1994, 99), Stamford C. of C. (pres. 1991-92), Am. Legion, Am. Inst. Mgmt., Cath. War Vets, Honor Legion N.Y.C. Police Dept., CCNY Alumni Assn., Elks, Loyal Order Moose, Univ. Club (Albany). Republican. Home: Red Rock Rd Stamford NY 12167 Office: Stamford Fin Bldg Off Bd Dirs Stamford NY 12167 *With all affluence, accomplishment, and success goes the responsibility of assistance; economic, social, and physical to the less fortunate of the world.*

BERGLES, ARTHUR EDWARD, mechanical engineering educator; b. N.Y.C., Aug. 9, 1935; s. Edward H. and Victoria (Winkelmann) B.; m. Priscilla Lou Maule, June 19, 1960; children: Eric, Dwight. SB, SM, MIT, 1958, PhD, 1962; DEng (hon.), U. Porto, Portugal, 1998, Rand Afrikaans U., 1999. Registered profl. engr., Mass. Research staff Nat. Magnet Lab., Cambridge, Mass., 1962-69; asst. prof. to assoc. prof. mech. engring. MIT, Cambridge, 1963-69, assoc. dir. heat transfer lab., 1966-69; prof. mech. engring. Ga. Inst. Tech., Atlanta, 1970-72; prof., chmn. dept. mech. engring. Iowa State U., Ames, 1972-83, prof., dir. heat transfer lab., 1983-86; Clark and Crossan prof. engring., dir. heat transfer lab. Rensselaer Poly. Inst., Troy, N.Y., 1986-97, dean of engring., 1989-92; Clark and Crossan prof. emeritus, 1997—; Martin Inst. prof. engring. U. Md., College Park, 1999—; U.S. rep. Internat. Heat Transfer Conf., 1978-82; chmn. U.S. group heat transfer U.S./USSR Agreement, Washington, 1979-82; cons. to industry, mem. numerous adv. groups. Co-author: Two-Phase Flow and Heat Transfer in the Power and Process Industries, 1981; co-editor: Two-Phase Heat Exchangers, 1988, Heat Transfer Enhancement of Heat Exchangers, 1999, others; editor: Heat Transfer in Electronic and Microelectronic Equipment, 1990; mem. editl. adv. bd. 17 jours.; contbr. numerous articles to tech. jours. Scoutmaster Boy Scout Am., Ames, 1976-84; bd. dirs. Ames Soc. for Arts, 1975-79. Fulbright fellow Technische Hochschule, Munich, Fed. Republic Germany, 1958-59; recipient U.S. Sr. Scientist award Alexander von Humboldt Found., U. Hanover, Fed. Republic Germany, 1979-80, Tech. U., Munich, 1996-97, Faculty Achievement award in research Iowa State U., 1986; named Anson Marston Disting. prof. engring., Iowa State U., 1981. Fellow AIAA (assoc.), ASHRAE (Edn. and Rsch. award N.E. chpt. 1993, Disting. Svc. award 1996), AAAS, NAE, ASME (hon. mem. 1996, v.p. 1981-85, chmn. heat transfer divsn. 1982-83, bd. govs. 1985-89, pres. 1990-91, Heat Transfer Meml. award 1979, Dedicated Svc. award 1984, Max Jakob Meml. award AIChE and ASME 1995), Internat. Ctr. Heat and Mass Transfer (exec. com. 1984—, chmn. exec. com. 1996-98, fellowship award 1988, Luikov medal 1998), Am. Soc. Engring. Edn. (Lamme award 1987, Centennial cert. and medal 1993); mem. AIChE (Donald Q. Kern award 1990), Soc. Automotive Engrs. (Ralph R. Teetor award 1987), Union Mech. and Elec. Engrs. and Technicians Yugoslavia (hon.), Polish Soc. Theoretical and Applied Mechanics (fgn.), Rotary (Paul Harris fellow), Theta Chi. Republican. Lutheran. Office: Rensselaer Poly Inst Mech Engring Aeronautical Engr Mech Troy NY 12180-3590 *My personal philosophy is to do as many things as I can, always striving for excellence and professionalism.*

BERGLUND, CARL NEIL, electronics company executive; b. Thunder Bay, Ont., Can., July 21, 1938; came to U.S., 1978; s. Anton Robert and Mary (Sideen) B.; m. Evelyn Jean McEvilla, Apr. 1, 1961; children: Cheryl Lynn, Gregory Neil, Carl Anton. B.S. with honors, Queen's U., Kingston, Ont., 1960; M.S. in Elec. Engring., MIT, 1961; Ph.D. in Elec. Engring., Stanford U., 1964. Mem. tech staff Bell Labs., Murray Hill, N.J., 1964-66; supr. semicond. devices Bell Labs., 1966-72; mgr. electronic materials Bell No. Research, Ottawa, 1972-73; v.p. tech. Microsystems Internat., Ottawa, 1973-74; dir. silicon technology Bell No. Research, Ottawa, 1974-78; dir. tech. devel. Intel Corp., Aloha, Oreg., 1978-83; pres., chief exec. officer ATEQ Corp., Beaverton, Oreg., 1983-87; pres. Northwest Tech. Group, Tigard, Oreg., 1987—; prof. elec. engring. and applied physics Oreg. Grad. Inst., Beaverton, 1994—. Contbr. articles to profl. jours.; patentee (in field). Fellow IEEE; mem. Electron Devices Soc. Home: 15361 S Clackamas River Dr Oregon City OR 97045-9489 Office: Northwest Tech Group 7340 SW Hunziker Rd Ste 103 Tigard OR 97223-2303*

BERGLUND, ROBIN G., child psychiatrist, former corporate executive; b. Milw., Oct. 12, 1945; s. Gunnar E. and V. June (Huebsch) B.; children: Victoria S., Christopher F. BS in Biochemistry magna cum laude, Mich. State, 1967; MBA, Harvard, 1971; MD, Med. U. S.C., 1995. Engr. Eastman Kodak Co., Rochester, N.Y., 1967-69; v.p. The First Nat. Bank of Chgo., 1971-75, Wells Fargo Bank, N.A., L.A., 1975-77; exec. v.p. Ponderosa Homes, Newport Beach, Calif., 1977-84; chmn., CEO Glenfed Devel. Corp., Encino, Calif., 1984-88; pres. Lowe Enterprises Northwest, Seattle, 1988-89, Met. Homes Inc., Portland, Oreg., 1989-90; pediatrician UCLA-Cedars Sinai Med. Ctr., L.A., 1995-96; psychiatrist UCLA Neuropsychiatric Inst. and Hosp., 1996-98, child psychiatrist, 1998—. Bd. dirs. United Svc. Orgn., Hollywood, Calif., 1975-80, Am. Youth Soccer Orgn., Newport Beach, Calif., 1980-84, Waring Libr. Soc., Charleston, 1992-95; scoutmaster Boy Scouts of Am., San Marino, Calif., 1984-89; vol. Children's Hosp., Seattle, 1990-91. Nat. Merit and Nat. Honor Soc. scholar, Mich. State U., 1964-67. Mem. Am. Psychiatric Assn., Am. Acad. Child & Adolescent Psychiatry, Young Pres.'s Orgn., Blue Key, Phi Kappa Phi, Phi Eta Sigma, Delta Phi Epsilon, Omicron Delta Kappa. Avocations: travel, sailing.

BERGMAN, ALAN, lyricist, writer; b. Bklyn., Sept. 11, 1925; s. Samuel and Ruth (Margulies) B.; m. Marilyn Keith, Feb. 9, 1958; 1 child, Julie Rachel. Grad., Ethical Culture Sch.; BA, U. N.C.; MA, UCLA; Doctorate (hon.), Berklee Coll. Music, 1995. TV dir. CBS, Phila., 1949-53; ind. lyricist, collaborator with Marilyn Bergman, 1956—. Compositions include numerous pop, TV theme, theatrical and film score songs including (TV themes) Bracken's World, 1969-70, The Sandy Duncan Show, 1972, Maude, 1972-78, Good Times, 1974-79, The Nancy Walker Show, 1976, The Dumplings, 1976, Alice, 1976-82, In the Heat of the Night, 1988-94, Brooklyn Bridge, 1991-93, The Powers That Be, 1993; (TV film lyrics) The Hands of Time (from Brian's Song), 1971, Queen of the Stardust Ballroom, 1975 (Emmy award best dramatic underscore 1975), (score only) Sybil, 1976 (Emmy award best dramatic underscore 1976), Too Many Springs (from Hollow Image), 1979; (theatrical scores) Something More, 1964, Ballroom, 1978 (Grammy award nominee for best cast show album 1979), The Lady and the Clarinet, 1980; (feature film songs) The Marriage-Go-Round, 1960 (from The Marriage-Go-Round), Any Wednesday, 1966 (from Any Wednesday), Make Me Rainbows, 1967 (from Fitzwilly), (score) In the Heat of the Night, 1967, The Windmills of Your Mind, 1968 (from The Thomas Crown Affair; Acad. award for best song 1968, Golden Globe award for best original song 1969), His Eyes, Her Eyes, 1968 (from The Thomas Crown Affair), You Must Believe in Spring, 1968 (from Young Girls at Rochefort), Maybe Tomorrow, 1969 (from John and Mary), Tomorrow Is My Friend, 1969 (from Gaily, Gaily), There's Enough to Go Around, 1969 (from Gaily, Gaily), A Smile, A Mem'ry and an Extra Shirt, 1969 (from A Man Called Gannon), Sugar in the Rain, 1969 (from Stiletto), What Are You Doing the Rest of Your Life?, 1969 (from The Happy Ending; Acad. award nominee for best song 1969), I Was Born in Love With You, 1970 (from Wuthering Heights), Sweet Gingerbread Man, 1970 (from The Magic Garden of Stanley Sweetheart), Nobody Knows, 1970 (from The Magic Garden of Stanley Sweetheart), Move, 1970 (from Move), Pieces of Dreams (AKA Little Boy Lost), 1970 (from Pieces of Dreams; Acad. award nominee for best song 1970), The Costume Ball, 1971 (from Doctors' Wives), All His Children, 1971 (from Sometimes a Great Notion; Acad. award nominee for best song 1971), Rain Falls Anywhere It Wants To, 1971 (from The African Elephant), The Summer Knows, 1971 (from Summer of '42; Grammy award nominee for song of the year 1972), A Face in the Crowd, 1971 (from Le Mans), Marmalade, Molasses and Honey, 1972 (from The Life and Times of Judge Roy Bean; Acad. award nominee for best song 1972), Love's the Only Game in Town, 1972 (from Pete and Tillie), Molly and Lawless John, 1972, The Way We Were, 1973 (from The Way We Were; Grammy award for song of the year 1973, Acad. award for best song 1973, Golden Globe award for best original song 1974, Grammy award for best original score 1974), Breezy's Song, 1973 (from Breezy), In Every Corner of the World, 1973 (from Forty Carats), Summer Wishes, Winter Dreams, 1973 (from Summer Wishes, Winter Dreams), Easy Baby, 1974 (from 99 and 44/100%), There'll Be Time, 1975 (from Ode to Billy Joe), Evening Sun, Morning Moon, 1975 (from The Yakuza), I Believe in Love, 1976 (from A Star is Born; Grammy award nominee for best original score 1977), I'm Harry, I'm Walter, 1976 (from Harry and Walter Go to New York), Hello and Goodbye, 1976 (from Noon to Three), Bobby Deerfield, 1977 (from Bobby Deerfield), The Last Time I Felt Like This, 1978 (from Same Time Next Year; Acad. award nominee for best song 1978), The One and Only, 1978 (from The One and Only), There's Something Funny Goin' On, 1979 (from ...And Justice For All), I'll Never Say Goodbye, 1979 (from The Promise; Acad. award nominee for best song 1979), Where Do You Catch the Bus for Tomorrow, 1980 (from A Change of Seasons), Ask Me No Questions, 1981 (from Back Roads), How Do You Keep the Music Playing?, 1982 (from Best Friends; Acad. award nominee best song 1982), Think About Love, 1982 (from Best Friends), Comin' Home to You, 1982 (from Author! Author!), Tootsie, 1982 (from Tootsie), It Might Be You, 1982 (from Tootsie; Acad. award nominee for best song 1982, Grammy award nominee for best original score 1983), If We Were in Love, 1982 (from Yes, Giorgio; Acad. award nominee for best song 1982), Never Say Never Again, 1983 (from Never Say Never Again), Papa, Can You Hear Me?, 1983 (from Yentl; Acad. award nominee best song 1983), The Way He Makes Me Feel, 1983 (from Yentl; Acad. award nominee for best song 1983), Will Someone Ever Look at Me That Way?, 1983 (from Yentl; Acad. award for best original score 1983, Grammy award nominee for best original score 1984), Little Boys, 1983 (from The Man Who Loved Women), Something New in My Life, 1984 (from Mickey and Maude), The Music of Goodbye, 1985 (from Out of Africa), I Know the Feeling, 1989 (from The January Man), The Girl Who Used to Be Me, 1989 (from Shirley Valentine; Acad. award nominee for best song 1989, Golden Globe nominee for best original song 1990, Grammy award nomination 1990), Welcome Home, 1989 (from Welcome Home), Most of All You, 1989 (from Major League), Dreamland, 1991 (from For the Boys), Places That Belong to You, 1991 (from The Prince of Tides), It's All There, 1991 (from Switch), Moonlight, 1995 (from Sabrina; Acad. award nominee for best original song 1996), Bogus, 1996; (pop songs) You Don't Bring Me Flowers (Grammy award nominee for song of the year 1978), In the Heat of the Night, The Summer Knows, Nice 'N' Easy (Grammy award nominee for song of the year 1960), Someone in the Dark, L.A. Is My Lady, After the Rain, I Was Born in Love With You, That Face, Look Around, I Love to Dance Like They Used to Dance, What Matters Most, One Day, A Child Is Born, Sleep Warm, Sentimental Baby, Live It Up, If I Close My Eyes, Yellow Bird, Like a Lover, Where Do You Start?, On My Way to You, Ordinary Miracles (Ace award and Emmy award for best original song); (albums) Never Be Afraid for Bing Crosby, The Ballad of the Blues for Jo Stafford; writer: Barbra Streisand: The Concert, 1995 (Ace nominee for writing of a spl., Emmy award for Best Music & Lyrics). Served with AUS, 1943-45. Named to Songwriters Hall of Fame, 1980; grantee Am. Film Inst., 1976; recipient Singers Salute to Songwriter award Clooney Foundation, 1986, Aggie award Songwriter's Guild, 1987. Mem. ASCAP, Motion Picture Acad. Arts and Scis. (gov.). Office: Gorfaine-Schwartz 13245 Riverside Dr Ste 450 Sherman Oaks CA 91423-2172*

BERGMAN, ANDREW, motion picture director; b. Queens, N.Y., 1945. Grad. magna cum laude, Harpur Coll.; PhD in History, U. Wis., 1970. Publicist United Artists. Author: We're in the Money, The Big Kiss-Off of 1944, Hollywood and Levine, Sleepless Nights; writer (Broadway comedy) Social Security, (films) Blazing Saddles, The In Laws, Fletch, Soapdish; writer, dir. So Fine, The Freshman, Honeymoon in Vegas, It Could Happen to You, Striptease. Office: CAA 9830 Wilshire Blvd Beverly Hills CA 90212-1804*

BERGMAN, ANNE NEWBERRY, civic activist; b. Weatherford, Tex., Mar. 12, 1925; d. William Douglas and Mary (Hunter) Newberry; m. Robert David Bergman, Aug. 17, 1947; children: Elizabeth Anne Bozzell, John David, William Robert. BA, Trinity U., San Antonio, 1945; postgrad., UCLA, 1946-47. Councilperson City of Weatherford, 1986-91, mayor pro tem, 1990-91; pres. Weatherford Libr. Found., 1987-97; mem. heritage gallery com. Weatherford Pub. Libr. (Mary Martin collection), 1993-98; bd. dirs. Manna Store House, Inc. Founder Hist. Home Tour, Weatherford, 1972; co-chair Spring Festival Bd., 1976, Weatherford Planning and Zoning Commn., 1980-85; fundraising chair Weatherford Libr. Found., 1985-86; chair Tex. State Rev. Com. Cmty. Devel. Block Grants, 1987-91; pres. Tex. Fedn. Rep. Women, 1975-77; regional coord. George Bush for Pres. campaign, 1980, 88; co-chair Congl. Dist. 12 Bush-Quayle campaign, 1992, Tex. Women Support Pres., 1983-84; del. Nat. Rep. Conv., 1988; mem. Episcopal Churchwomen's Cabinet, Diocese of Ft. Worth; del. Episcopal Ch. Women Triennial, Episcopal Ch. U.S.A., 1997, pres., 1999—; bd. dirs. Weatherford Libr. Found., 1989—, pres., 1989-96. Named Outstanding Rep. Woman, Tex. Fedn. Rep. Women, 1981. Mem. Parker County Rep. Women, DAR (Weatherford chpt.), Weatherford C. of C. (Outstanding Citizen of the Yr. 1988), Friends of Weatherford Pub. Libr. (life, charter pres. 1959-61, pres. 1973-74). Avocations: sailing, bridge. Home: 609 W Josephine St Weatherford TX 76086-4055

BERGMAN, BRUCE E., municipal official; m.; 2 children. BA, Simpson Coll., 1970; JD, U. Houston, 1972. Clk. to Hon. M.E. Rawlings Iowa Supreme Ct., 1973-74; assoc. Williams, Hart, Lavorato & Kirtley, West Des Moines, Iowa, 1974-78; ptnr. Williams, Hart, Lavorato & Kirtley, 1978-79, Davis, Baker & Bergman, Des Moines, 1984-85, Isaacson, Clarke & Bergman, P.C., Des Moines, 1985-89; asst. city atty. City of Des Moines Legal Dept., 1989-90, solicitor, 1990-91, chief solicitor, 1991-96, corp. counsel, 1996—. Mem. ABA, Iowa State Bar Assn., Polk County Bar Assn., Def. Rsch. Inst., Iowa Mcpl. Attys. Assn. (bd. dirs. 1996—). Home: 4508 49th St Des Moines IA 50310-2970 Office: Office of the Corp Counsel City of Des Moines City Hall 400 E 1st St Des Moines IA 50307

BERGMAN, BRUCE JEFFREY, lawyer; b. N.Y.C., May 15, 1944; s. Lawrence A. and Myrna (Coe) B.; m. Linda A. Cantor, May 30, 1971; children: Jennifer Dana, Jason Cole. BS, Cornell U., 1966; JD, Fordham U., 1969. Bar: N.Y. 1970, D.C. 1987, U.S. Dist. Ct. (so. dist.) N.Y. 1971, U.S. Supreme Ct. 1973, U.S. Dist. Ct. (ea. dist.) N.Y. 1973, U.S. Ct. Appeals (2d cir.) 1973. Assoc. law firm Jarvis, Pilz, Buckley & Treacy, N.Y.C., 1970-76; ptnr. law firm Pedowitz & Bergman, Garden City, N.Y., 1976-80; dep. county atty. Nassau County, Mineola, N.Y., 1980-84; counsel Jonas Libert & Weinstein, Garden City, 1981-84; ptnr. Roach & Bergman, 1984-90, Certilman Balin Adler & Hyman, East Meadow, N.Y., 1991—; adj. assoc. prof. NYU Real Estate Inst., N.Y.C., 1981—; faculty mem. Mortgage Bankers Assn. Am. Sch. of Mortgage Banking, 1994—; special lectr. Hofstra Law Sch., 1998—. Author: Bergman on New York Mortgage Foreclosures, vols. 1-3, 1990; rev. edit. 1999; contbr. numerous articles to legal jours.; contbg. editor: Mortgages and Mortgage Foreclosure in New York, 1982. Councilman City of Long Beach, N.Y., 1980-88. Mem. ABA, N.Y. State Bar Assn., Nassau County Bar Assn. (dir., chmn. real property law com.), Am. Coll. Real Estate Lawyers, Scribes, Am. Soc. Writers on Legal Subjects, Cornell Club (past pres.). Republican. Home: 12 Hawthorne Ln Lawrence NY 11559-2521 Office: Certilman Balin Adler & Hyman 90 Merrick Ave East Meadow NY 11554-1500

BERGMAN, CHARLES CABE, foundation executive; b. May 1, 1933; s. Sidney Meyer and Esther Rachel (Cabe) B. AB, Harvard U., 1954. Account asst. Ketchum, MacLeod & Grove, Inc., Pitts., 1955-57; assoc. dir. devel. and alumni affairs Browne & Nichols Sch., Cambridge, Mass., 1957-59; assoc. v.p. Lavin Co., Inc., Boston and N.Y.C., 1959-61; v.p. People to People Health Fedn., Washington, 1962-63, Inter-Am. Found. for the Arts, N.Y.C., 1963-65; exec. v.p., treas., trustee Acad. Religion and Mental Health, N.Y.C., 1965-72; exec. v.p., COO, dir. Insts. Religion and Health, 1972-78; sr. assoc. Jeffcoat Schoen & Morrell, 1981-82; exec. v.p., COO Pollock-Krasner Found., Inc., N.Y.C., 1985-99, chmn. bd., COO, 1999—; cons. UN Ctr. on Transnat. Corps., 1979-80; dir. George Nelson & Co., N.Y.C. Cons. Adminstrv. Psychiatry Program, Yale Med. Sch., New Haven, 1971, NIMH, Argentina, 1969, Ctr. for Studies Child and Family Mental Health, NIMH, Washington, 1971; spl. adviser Pres.'s Com. on Mental Retardation, Washington, 1971, White House Conf. on Children and Youth, Washington, 1970, Maurice Falk Med. Fund, 1971; vis. lectr. U. Colo.; Presdl. felow Aspen Inst. Humanistic Studies. Chmn. internat. coun. Am. Field Svc. Internat. Intercultural Programs; bd. mgrs. Silver Hill Found.; bd. dirs. City Harvest, Circle Repertory, The Alliance for Young Writers, Inc., N.Y., Very Specials Arts, Washington, Delfina Studios Trust, London, The Millay Colony for Arts; former cons. Marie Walsh Sharpe Found.; mem. bd. advisors Fund for Arts and Culture in Cen. and East Europe; bd. artistic advisors Creative Artists Network; former panelist N.Y. State Coun. on Arts Visual Arts Program; mem. N.Y. State Coun. on Arts, 1999—. Home: 24 E 82nd St # 4C New York NY 10028-0344 Office: 863 Park Ave New York NY 10021-0342

BERGMAN, EDWARD JONATHAN, lawyer, educator; b. Jersey City, Aug. 10, 1942; s. Abe and Ethel (Leitner) B.; m. Jennifer Shapiro, Feb. 1, 1969 (div.); children: Peter Jeremy, Jennifer Amy. BA, U. Pa., 1963; JD, Columbia U., 1966. Bar: N.J. 1974, U.S. Dist. Ct. N.J. 1974, U.S. Supreme Ct. 1989; cert. comml. mediator N.J. Assn. of Profl. Mediators. Ptnr. Bergman & Barrett, Princeton, N.J., 1975—; pub. defender Princeton Borough, 1986—, Princeton Twp., 1988—; fed. mediator U.S. Dist. Ct., N.J., 1992—; mediator N.J. Superior Ct., 1995—; lectr. Woodrow Wilson Sch., Princeton U., 1990-92; affiliated faculty U. Pa. Wharton Sch. of Bus. Dept. of Legal Studies, Phila., 1995—; vis. lectr. U. Calif. at Berkeley, St. Petersburg U. Joint Mgmt. Program, Russia, 1995—; official dispute resolver NHLA/AAHA; affiliate Bickerman Dispute Resolution Group, Washington, 1998—. Author: (with J. Bickerman) Court-Annexed Mediation: Perspectives on Selected State & Federal Programs, 1998. Trustee Princeton Ballet, 1942-92, Arts Coun. Princeton, 1998—. Mem. ABA (sec. on dispute resolution, mediation com., chmn. subcom. on ct.- annexed mediation), N.J. Bar Assn., Mercer County Bar Assn., Princeton Bar Assn. (pres. 1986-87), Nat. Inst. for Dispute Resolution, Soc. Profl. in Dispute Resolution, Penn Basketball Club (exec. bd. 1995—), Penn Club N.Y. Avocations: wine food, travel, sports, art and architecture. Home: 95 Wilson Rd Princeton NJ 08540-2601 Office: Bergman & Barrett PO Box 1273 Princeton NJ 08542-1273

BERGMAN, GEORGE MARK, mathematician, educator; b. Bklyn., July 22, 1943; s. Lester V. and Sylvia G. (Bernstein) B.; m. Mary Frances Anderson, Dec. 26, 1981; stepsons: Jeff E. Watson, Michael L. Anderson; children: Clifford I. and Rebecca N. Anderson-Bergman (twins). BA, U. Calif., Berkeley, 1963; PhD, Harvard U., 1968. Asst. prof. Dept. Math. U. Calif., Berkeley, 1967-72, assoc. prof., 1972-78, prof., 1978—. Contbr. articles to profl. jours. Mem. AAUP, Am. Math. Soc. Democrat. Avocations: linguistics, folk-dancing. Office: U Calif Dept Math Berkeley CA 94720-3840

BERGMAN, HERMAS JOHN (JACK BERGMAN), retired college administrator; b. Akiak, Alaska, May 3, 1926; s. Ruebin Eric and Esther (Schierman) B.; m. Jeanne Louise Culton, 1946 (div. 1961); children—Stephen, Kathleen, Marsha; m. Evelyn Alice Templeman, Apr. 6, 1963; children—Kristin, Robert. BA, Walla Walla Coll., 1948; MA, U. Puget Sound, 1963; PhD, Wash. State U., 1967. Tchr., Wash. Pub. Schools, Wenatchee and Tacoma, 1948-58, 61-64; bus. mgr. Totem Plywood, Inc., Tacoma, 1958-61; prof. history Western Oreg. U., Monmouth, 1966-79, dean Liberal Arts and Scis., 1980-85; pres. Walla Walla Coll., College Place, Wash., 1985-90; ret., 1990. Author: The Religious Fringe; contbr. articles to history journs. Mem. exec. com. Oreg. Conf. Seventh-day Adventists, 1981-85; chmn. bd. commrs. Polk County Parks and Recreation Commn., Dallas, Oreg., 1977-80; nat. adv. coun. Am. United for Separation of Ch. and State, 1992—; v.p. Wash. State Religious Liberty Assn. of Pacific N.W., 1991—; bd. trustees Walla Walla Gen. Hosp., 1985—; chmn. bd. Internat. Children's Care Inc., Vancouver, Wash., 1981-89; bd. dirs. Portland Adventist Med. Ctr., 1972-78, 85-90, Ind. Colls. of Wash., Seattle, 1985-90, United Way of Walla Walla, 1988-91, Wash. Friends of Higher Edn., Seattle, 1985-90. Seventh Day Adventist. Avocations: photography, geology, stamps, lapidary.

BERGMAN, JERRY RAE, science educator; b. Detroit, May 30, 1946; s. Ernest R. and Irene (Buck) B.; m. Marie Fox, June 20, 1970; children: Aeron, Mishalea; m. Dianne Haldiman, Dec. 28, 1985. BS, Wayne State U., 1969, MEd, 1971, PhD, 1976; MA, Bowling Green State U., 1986; PhD, Columbia Pacific U., 1992; MSBS, Med. Coll. of Ohio, 1999. Prof. Bowling Green State U., Bowling Green, Ohio, 1973-80, U. Toledo, Toledo, Ohio, 1981-86, Northwest Coll., Archbold, Ohio, 1987—; dir. Soc. for Study of Male Psychology and Physiology, Montpelier, Ohio, 1974—; rsch. assoc., adj. instr. Med. Coll. of Ohio, Toledo. Author 20 books and monographs; contbr. 500 articles (trans. into 12 langs.) to profl. jours. Fellow Am. Sci. Affiliation; mem. AAAS, Am. Chem. Soc. Office: Northwest State Cmty Coll 22-600 State Rt 34 Archbold OH 43502

BERGMAN, MARILYN KEITH, lyricist, writer; b. Bklyn., Nov. 10, 1929; d. Albert A. and Edith (Arkin) Katz; m. Alan Bergman, Feb. 9, 1958; 1 child, Julie Rachel. BA, NYU; DMus (hon.), Berklee Coll. Music, 1995. Lyricist, collaborator (with Alan Bergman) numerous pop, TV themes, theatrical and film score songs including (TV themes) Bracken's World, 1969-70, The Sandy Duncan Show, 1972, Maude, 1972-78, Good Times, 1974-79, The Nancy Walker Show, 1976, The Dumplings, 1976, Alice, 1976-82, In the Heat of the Night, 1988-94, Brooklyn Bridge, 1991-93, The Powers That Be, 1993; (TV film lyrics) The Hands of Time (from Brian's Song), 1971, Queen of the Stardust Ballroom, 1975 (Emmy award nominee for best dramatic underscore and best musical material 1975), (score only) Sybil, 1976 (Emmy award for best dramatic underscore 1976), Too Many Springs (from Hollow Image, 1979; (theatrical scores) Something More, 1964, Ballroom, 1978 (Grammy award nominee for best cast show album 1979), The Lady and the Clarinet, 1980; (feature film songs) The Marriage Go-Round, 1960 (from The Marriage Go-Round), Any Wednesday, 1966 (from Any Wednesday), Make Me Rainbows, 1967 (from Fitzwilly), (score) In the Heat of the Night, 1967, The Windmills of Your Mind, 1968 (from The Thomas Crown Affair, Acad. award for best song 1968, Golden Globe award best original song 1969), His Eyes, Her Eyes, 1968 (from The Thomas Crown Affair), You Must Believe in Spring, 1968 (from Young Girls at Rochefort), Maybe Tomorrow, 1969 (from John and Mary), Tomorrow Is My Friend, 1969 (from Gaily, Gaily), There's Enough to Go Around, 1969 (from Gaily, Gaily), A Smile, A Mem'ry and an Extra Shirt, 1969 (from A Man Called Gannon), Sugar in the Rain, 1969 (from Stiletto), What Are You Doing the Rest of You Life?, 1969 (from The Happy Ending; Acad. award nominee for best song 1969), I Was Born in Love With You, 1970 (from Wuthering Heights), Sweet Gingerbread Man, 1970 (from The Magic Garden of Stanley Sweetheart), Nobody Knows, 1970 (from The Magic Garden of Stanley Sweetheart), Move, 1970 (from Move), Pieces of Dreams, 1970 (from Pieces of Dreams; Academy award nominee for best song 1970), Little Boy Lost, 1970 (from Pieces of Dreams) The Costume Ball, 1971 (from Doctors' Wives), All His Children, 1971 (from Sometimes a Great Notion; Acad. award nominee for best song 1971), Rain Falls Anywhere It Wants To, 1971 (from the African Elephant), The Summer Knows, 1971 (from Summer of '42 (Grammy award nominee for song of the year 1972); A Face in the Crowd, 1971 (from Le Mans), Marmalade, Molasses and Honey, 1972 (from The Life and Times of Judge Roy Bean; Acad. award nominee for best song 1972), Love's the Only Game in Town, 1972 (from Pete and Tillie), Molly and Lawless John, 1972, The Way We Were, 1973 (from The Way We Were; Grammy award for song of the year 1973, Acad. award for best song 1973, Golden Globe award for best original song 1974, Grammy award for best original score 1974), Breezy's Song, 1973, (from Breezy), In Every Corner of the World, 1973 (from Forty Carats), Summer Wishes, Winter Dreams, 1973 (from Summer Wishes, Winter Dreams), Easy Baby, 1974 (from 99 and 44/100%), There'll Be Time, 1975 (from Ode to Billy Joe), Evening Sun, Morning Moon, 1975 (from The Yakuza), I Believe in Love, 1976 (from A Star is Born; Grammy award nomination best original score 1977), I'm Harry, I'm Walter, 1976 (from Harry and Walter Go to New York), Hello and Goodbye, 1976 (from Noon to Three), Bobby Deerfield, 1977 (from Bobby Deerfield), The Last Time I Felt Like This, 1978 (from Same Time Next Year; Acad. award nominee for best song 1978), The One and Only, 1978 (from The One and Only), There's Something Funny Goin' On, 1979 (from ...And Justice For All), I'll Never Say Goodbye, 1979 (from The Promise; Acad. award nominee for best song 1979), Where Do You Catch the Bus for Tomorrow, 1980 (from A Change of Seasons), Ask Me No Questions, 1981 (from Back Roads), How Do You Keep the Music Playing?, 1982 (from Best Friends; Acad. award nominee for best song 1982), Think About Love, 1982 (from Best Friends), Comin' Home to You, 1982 (from Author! Author!), Tootsie, 1982 (from Tootsie), It Might Be You, 1982 (from Tootsie; Acad. award nominee for best song, 1982, Grammy award nominee for best original score 1983), If We Were in Love, 1982 (from Yes, Giorgio; Acad. award nominee for best song 1982), Never Say Never Again, 1983 (from Never Say Never again), Papa, Can You Hear Me?, 1983 (from Yentl; Academy award nomination best song 1983), The Way He Makes Me Feel, 1983 (from Yentl; Acad. award nominee for best song 1983), Will Someone Ever Look at Me That Way?, 1983 (from Yentl; Acad. award best original score and Grammy award nomination for best original score 1984), Little Boys, 1983 (from The Man Who Loved Women), Something New in My Life, 1984 (from Mickey and Maude), The Music of Goodbye, 1985 (from Out of Africa), I Know the Feeling, 1989 (from The January Man), The Girl Who Used to Be Me, 1989 (from Shirley Valentine; Acad. award nominee for best song 1989, Golden Globe nominee for best original song 1990, Grammy award nominee 1990), Welcome Home, 1989 (from Welcome Home), Most of All You, 1989 (from Major League), Dreamland, 1991 (from For the Boys), Places That Belong to You, 1991 (from The Prince of Tides), It's All There, 1991 (from Switch), Moonlight, 1995 (from Sabrina; Acad. award nominee for best original song 1996), Bogus, 1996; (pop songs) You Don't Bring Me Flowers (Grammy award nominee for song of the year 1978), In the Heat of the Night, The Summer Knows, Nice 'N' Easy (Grammy award nominee for song of the year 1960), Someone in the Dark, L.A. Is My Lady, After the Rain, I Was Born in Love With You, That Face, Look Around, I Love to Dance Like They Used to Dance, What Matters Most, One Day, A Child Is Born, Sleep Warm, Sentimental Baby, Live It Up, If I Close My Eyes, Yellow Bird, Like a Lover, Where Do You Start?, On My Way to You, Ordinary Miracles (Cable Ace award and Emmy award for best original song); (albums) Never Be Afraid for Bing Crosby, The Ballad of the Blues for Jo Stafford, Barbra Streisand: The Concert (Ace nominee for writing of a spl.). Named to songwriters hall of Fame, 1980; grantee Am. Film Inst., 1976; recipient singers salute to songwriter award Clooney Found., 1986, Aggie award Songwriter's Guild, 1987. Mem. ASCAP (pres., chmn. bd. dirs. 1994—). Office: Gorfaine-Schwartz 13245 Riverside Dr Ste 450 Sherman Oaks CA 91423-2172 also: ASCAP One Lincoln Plz New York NY 10023*

BERGMAN, MARK, non-commissioned officer; b. Bklyn., Sept. 24, 1962; s. Edward and Myrtle L. B.; m. Trish L. Saffelle, Aug. 23, 1994; children: Elizabeth G. Pope, Marcus A., Jeffrey M., Ryan C., Kyle A. AD, Ctrl. Tech. Coll., 1987; B of Criminal Justice (cum laude), Fayetteville State U., 1990; MA, Webster U., 1994. Enlisted private U.S. Army, 1980, advanced through grades to master sgt., 1998—. Sponsor Funshine Olympics, Heidelberg, Germany, 1995; venue security mgr. World Spl. Olympics, 1999. Mem. Am. Soc. Indsl. Security (treas. 1992-93), Am. Soc. Law Enforcement Trainers, Am. Soc. Pub. Adminstrs., Assn. Cert. Fraud Examiners, Assn. Quatermasters (St. Martin's award 1999). Avocations: coin collecting, reading, bicycling, computer games. Home: 816 Makay Ct Hope Mills NC Office: US Army (Airborne) 46th Corps Support Group Fort Bragg NC 28307

BERGMAN, NANCY PALM, real estate investment company executive; b. McKeesport, Pa., Dec. 3, 1938; d. Walter Vaughn and Nellie (Sullivan) Leech; m. Donald Bergman; 1 child, Tiffany Palm Taylor. Student, Mt. San Antonio Coll., 1970, UCLA, 1989-93. Corporate sec. U.S. Filter Corp., Newport Beach, Calif., 1965—; pres. Jaguar Research Corp., Los Angeles and Atlanta, 1971—; owner Environ. Designs, Los Angeles, 1976—; pres. Prosher Corp., Los Angeles., 1978-83; now pres., dir. Futura Investments, L.A.; CEO Rescor, Inc. Author: Resident Managers Handbook. Home: 8 Fincher Way Rancho Mirage CA 92270-3036 also: 2257 Century Hl Los Angeles CA 90067-3506 Office: PO Box 67566 Los Angeles CA 90067-0566

BERGMAN, ROBERT GEORGE, chemist, educator; b. Chgo., May 23, 1942; s. Joseph J. and Stella (Horowitz) B.; m. Wendy L. Street, June 17, 1965; children: David R., Michael S. BA cum laude in chemistry, Carleton Coll., 1963; PhD (NIH fellow), U. Wis., 1966; PhD (hon.), Carleton Coll., 1995. NATO fellow in chemistry Columbia U., N.Y.C., 1966-67; Arthur Amos Noyes instr. chemistry Calif. Inst. Tech., Pasadena, 1967-69; asst. prof. chemistry Calif. Inst. Tech., 1969-71, assoc. prof. chemistry, 1971-73, prof., 1973-77; prof. chemistry U. Calif. at Berkeley, 1977—; asst. dean Coll. Chemistry U. Calif., Berkeley, 1987-91, 96, Miller Rsch. prof., 1982-83, 93; Sherman Fairchild Disting. scholar Calif. Inst. Tech., 1984; mem. panel NIH bioinorganic and metallobiochemistry study sect. NIH, 1977-80; cons. E.I. DuPont de Nemours, 1982-85, Chevron Rsch. Co., 1983-89, Union Carbide Corp., 1977-81, 90—; disting. vis. prof. U. N.C., Chapel Hill, 1999. Mem. editorial bd. Chem. Revs., Jour. Am. Chem. Soc., Organometallics, Tetrahedron Publs.; contbr. articles to profl. jours. Recipient Tchr. Scholar award Camille and Henry Dreyfus Found., 1970-75, Excellence in Tchg. award Calif. Inst. Tech., 1978, merit award NIH, 1991, E.O. Lawrence award for chemistry Dept. Energy, 1993; Alfred P. Sloan Found. fellow, 1970-72, Guggenheim fellow, 1999. Fellow Calif. Acad. Sci.; mem. AAAS, Nat. Acad. Scis., Am. Chem. Soc. (Organometallic Chemistry award 1986, Edward Fahs Smith award Pa. sect. 1990, Ira Remsen award Balt. sect. 1990, Arthur C. Cope award, 1996, Arthur C. Cope scholar 1987), Phi Beta Kappa, Sigma Xi, Phi Lambda Upsilon. Home: 501 Coventry Rd Kensington CA 94707-1316 Office: U Calif Dept Chemistry Berkeley CA 94720

BERGMAN, ROBERT PAUL, museum administrator, art historian, educator, lecturer; b. Bayonne, N.J., May 17, 1945; s. Abe and Ethel (Leitner) B.; m. Marcelle Posnak, June 30, 1971, 1 child, Maggie. BA, Rutgers U., 1966; MFA, Princeton U., 1969, PhD, 1972; DHL (hon.), U. Balt., 1993; Rutgers U., 1997; DFA (hon.), Md. Inst. Coll. of Art, 1993, Baldwin-Wallace Coll., 1995. Asst prof. history of art U. Rochester, N.Y., 1971-72; asst. prof. history of art Princeton U., N.J., 1972-76; assoc. prof. Harvard U., Cambridge, 1976-81; dir. Walters Art Gallery, Balt., 1981-93, Cleve. Mus. Art, 1993—; vis. instr. Lincoln U., fall 1968; adj. prof. Johns Hopkins U., Balt., 1981-93, Case Western Res. U., 1993—. Author: The Salerno Ivories, 1980, Santa Maria De Olearia in Maiori, 1995; cons. editor: Art Bull.; contbr. articles and revs. in art field. Vol. various mayoral and gubernatorial coms., Balt., Cleve.; fundraiser for various causes. Guggenheim fellow; Dumbarton Oaks fellow; Fulbright fellow; Henry Rutgers scholar. Fellow Am. Acad. in Rome; mem. AAUP, Am. Assn. Mus. (past chmn. bd. dirs.), Assn. Art Mus. Dirs. (trustee, pres.), Coll. Art Assn., Internat. Ctr. of Medeval Art (bd. dirs.), Soc. Archtl. Historians, Medieval Acad. Am., Am. Arts Alliance (bd. dirs., treas., chmn.), Phi Beta Kappa. Office: The Cleve Mus of Art 11150 East Blvd Cleveland OH 44106-1711

BERGMAN, ROGER CHARLES, ethics educator; b. Manhattan, Kans., Nov. 3, 1948; s. Frank V. and June (Zirkle) B.; m. Wendy Mae Wright, June 21, 1977; children: Emily, Elizabeth, Charles. BA, Kans. State U., 1970; MA, U. Ariz., 1977; M Theol. Studies, Weston Sch. Theology, Cambridge, Mass., 1991. Edn. coord. Los Niños, Santa Barbara, Calif., 1981-84; dir. New Covenant Ctr., Omaha, 1987-91; instr. ethics Creighton U., Omaha, 1989—, dir. justice and peace studies program, 1993—; columnist Signs of the Times, The Cath. Voice, 1990-97. Contbr. articles, essays and poems to various jours. Co-chair Social Ministry Commn., Archdiocese of Omaha, 1996—; mem. leadership team Sacred Heart Parish, Omaha Together One Cmty., 1993-97. Recipient Tchg. for Tomorrow award Omicron Delta Kappa and Alpha Sigma Nu, 1995, 97. Mem. Assn. for Moral Edn. Roman Catholic. Avocations: basketball, canoeing, hiking. Office: Creighton U Adminstrn 425 Omaha NE 68178

BERGMAN, YAACOV, performing company executive; m. Joan Behrens. Degree in conducting and composition, Rubin Acad., Hebrew U., Jerusalem; studied with Richard Westenburg, Mannes Coll. Music; studied with Charles Bruck, Leonard Bernstein. Music dir. Colorado Springs (Colo.) Symphony; music dir. Walla Walla (Wash.) Symphony; founder, music dir., condr. Heritage Orch. N.Y.; condr. Osaka (Japan) Opera Co., 1996. Office: Colorado Springs Symphony PO Box 1692 Colorado Springs CO 80901-1692

BERGMANN, BARBARA ROSE, economics educator; b. N.Y.C., July 20, 1927; d. Martin and Nellie (Wallenstein) Berman; m. Fred H. Bergmann, July 16, 1965; children: Sarah Nellie, David Martin. B., Cornell U., 1948; MA, Harvard U., 1955, PhD, 1959. Economist U.S. Bur. Labor Stats., N.Y.C., 1949-53; sr. staff ecomomist, cons. Council Econ. Advisors, Washington, 1961-62; sr. staff Brookings Inst., Washington, 1963-65; sr. econ. advisor AID, Washington, 1966-67; assoc. prof. U. Md., College Park, 1965-71, prof. econs., 1971-88; disting. prof. econs. Am. U., Washington, 1988-97, prof. emeritus, 1997—. Author: (with Chinitz and Hoover) Projection of a Metropolis, 1961; (with George W. Wilson) Impact of Highway Investment on Development, 1966; (with David E. Kaun) Structural Unemployment in the U.S., 1967; (with Robert Bennett) A Microsimulated Transactions Model of the United States Economy, 1985, The Economic Emergence of Women, 1986, Saving Our Children from Poverty: What the United States Can Learn from France, 1996, In Defense of Affirmative Action, 1996, Is Social Security Broke? A Cartoon Guide to the Issues, 1999; mem. editl. bd. Am. Econ. Rev., 1970-73, Challenge, 1978—, Signs, 1978-85; columnist econ. affairs N.Y. Times, 1981-82. Mem. Economists for McGovern, 1977; mem. panel econ. advisors Congl. Budget Office, Washington, 1977-87; mem. price adv. com. U.S. council on Wage and Price Stability, 1979-80. Mem. AAUP (coun. 1980-83, pres. 1990-92), Am. Econ. Assn. (v.p. 1976, adv. com. to U.S. Census Bur. 1977-82), Ea. Econ. Assn. (pres. 1974), Internat. Assn. for

Feminist Econs. (pres. 1999), Soc. for Advancement of Socio-Econs. (pres. 1995-96). Democrat. Home: 5430 41st Pl NW Washington DC 20015-2911

BERGMANN, CARL ADOLF, chemical engineer, researcher; b. Concordia, Mo., Mar. 27, 1932; s. Theodore H. and Clara A. (Brandenberg) B.; m. Elizabeth C. Moran, Apr. 16, 1960; children: Beverly E. Bergmann Hammer, William C. BS in Chem. Engring., U. Mo., 1954; MBA, U. Pitts., 1968. Sr. engr. Bettis Atomic Power Lab., Pitts., 1963-74; prin. engr. Westinghouse Electric Co., Pitts., 1975-96; cons. CDI, Pitts., 1996—; mem. com. Electric Power Rsch. Inst., Palo Alto, Calif., 1986-96; mem. indsl. adv. com. Brookhaven Nat. Lab. Alara Ctr., L.I., N.Y., 1987-96. Contbr. articles to profl. jours.; co-inventor process to inhibit corrosion in a nuclear reactor, 1992. Chmn. traffic bd. Mt. Lebanon (Pa.) Twp., 1978-79. Capt. USAF, 1955-58. Mem. Am. Nuclear Soc. Democrat. Unitarian-Universalist. Avocations: gardening, stamp collecting, walking. Home: 638 Briarwood Ave Pittsburgh PA 15228-2552

BERGMANN, CYNTHIA, pediatrics nurse, lawyer; b. Buffalo, Apr. 10, 1956; d. John L. and Helen C. (Pasierbowicz) Hiczewski; m. Dennis Bergman, July 28, 1990; children: Nicole, Todd, Lindsey. ASN, Rio Hando Coll., 1978; student, SUNY, Buffalo, 1987—; BSN, U. Buffalo, 1984, postgrad.; JD, SUNY, Buffalo, 1994. Bar: N.Y. 1995. Charge RN, staff nurse Children's Hosp. of Buffalo, 1978-85; RN instr. ARC, Buffalo; victim advocate Dist. Atty.'s Office State of N.Y., Buffalo, 1987-89; nurse instr. Erie Bus. Coll., 1992-95; nurse atty. Agate & Rosche, Snyder, N.Y., 1995-99; supr. workers' compensation CIGNA, Amherst, N.Y., 1999—. Mem. Western Coalition for Crime Victims, Erie County Bar Assn., Assn. of Nurse Attys. Home: 52 Candy Ln Orchard Park NY 14127-4605

BERGMANN, DENNIS WILLIAM, health facility administrator; b. Buffalo, Mar. 16, 1955; s. William John and Virginia (Chomiszewska) B.; m. Cynthia Hiczewski, July 28, 1990; children: Nicole, Todd, Lindsey. AAS in Occupational Therapy, Erie Community Coll., 1975; BS in Social Work, Edinboro U., 1984; MSW, U. Pitts., 1987. Cert. occupational therapy asst.; cert. in gerontology; lic. social worker, Pa. Cert. occupational therapy asst. Pavillion Skilled Nursing Facility, 1975-76; evening counselor Peoples Inc.'s, 1978-79; rehab. specialist S.E. Corp. V. Mental Health Day Treatment, 1979-81; personal care attendant Office of Disabled Students of Edinboro U. Pa., 1981-85; program mgr. Great Lakes Rehab. Hosp., 1987, dir. of neurology rehab. svcs., 1988-90; adminstr. Pegasus Integrated Living Ctr., 1990-92; program mgr. resource ctr. Gateways Mental Health Day Treatment Program, 1992—; mental health adminstr. Rsch. Ctr. M.H. Clinic Svcs., 1998—. Contbr. articles to profl. jours. Bd. dirs. Multiple Sclerosis Soc. Erie. Mem. NASW, Nat. Rehab. Assn. (pres.-elect Mid-Atlantic region 1990, pres. 1991), Pa. Rehab. Assn. (bd. dirs. 1986-92), Am. Occupational Therapy Assn., N.W. Pa. Ind. Living Task Force; mem. Chautaugua Co. M.H. Sch. Supts. Com., 1998—: mem.Chautaugua Co. M.H. Focus Group, 1998. Avocations: collecting demographic, social and economic statistical data, painting, drawing. Home: 52 Candy Ln Orchard Park NY 14127-4605 Office: The Resource Ctr. 186 Lakeshore Dr. West Dunkirk NY 14048

BERGMANN, DONALD GERALD, pharmaceutical company executive; b. Aug. 13, 1949; s. Edgar Frank and Dorothy Bertha Bergmann; m. Kathy Jeanne Dumont, Sept. 4, 1976; children: Karen Ann, Kim Jeanne. BS, Mich. State U., 1972; PhD, Ohio State U., 1978. Researcher UCLA, 1978-81; project leader Burroughes-Wellcome Co., Kansas City, Kans., 1981-83; scientist Genentech, Inc., South San Francisco, Calif., 1983, ops. mgr., 1983-87; sr. project mgr. Genentech, Inc., South San Francisco, 1987-88; dir. biopharmaceutical mfg. SmithKline Beecham Pharms., Phila., 1988-91, group dir. biopharm. tech. ops., 1991-95, gen. mgr. biopharms., 1995—. Contbr. articles to profl. jours. and publs. Fellow Nat. Cancer Inst., 1978-80; grantee Nat. Cancer Inst., Am. Cancer Soc. Mem. Internat. Soc. Pharm. Engring. (lectr.), Pharm. Rsch. and Mfrs. Assn. (lectr., com. chair, steering com.). Avocations: skiing, wine collecting.

BERGMANN, LINDA J., marketing professional; b. Milw., Jan. 3, 1955; d. Gordon Walter and Ann Leona (Mueller) Bertschy; m. Myron George Bergmann, June 30, 1984. BS, U. Wis., Milw., 1977. Translator Allis-Chalmers Power Systems, Milw., 1978-82; payroll coord. Utility Power Corp., Milw., 1982-84; mktg. adminstr. Utility Power/Siemens Power Corp., Bradenton, Fla., 1984-92; mgr., mktg. comms. Siemens Power Corp., Milw., 1992—. Contbr. articles to profl. jours. Mem. Dem. Leadership Coun., Washington, 1991—, Manatee County Dem. Exec. Com., Bradenton, 1990-92; treas. Waukesha County Dem. Party, 1997—; vice chair 4th Congl. Dist. Wis. Dem. Party. Mem. Am. Mktg. Assn., Ecology Assn. New Berlin (sec. 1994-95, pres. 1996-98), Phi Beta Kappa. Lutheran. Avocation: piano. Home: 16275 W Crescent Dr New Berlin WI 53151-6598 Office: Siemens Power Corp 1040 S 70th St Milwaukee WI 53214-3164

BERGMANN, MEREDITH GANG, sculptor; b. Passaic, N.J., Jan. 8, 1955; d. Lloyd and Ruth Gang; m. Michael Bergmann, May 11, 1986; 1 child, Daniel. Student, Wesleyan U., 1972-74, Parsons Sch. of Design, N.Y.C., 1975; BFA, Cooper Union Sch. of Art, N.Y.C., 1977. Selected one-woman shows include: West Side YMCA, N.Y.C., 1992-93, Asser Levy Ctr., N.Y.C., 1991-92, McGolrick Park, Bklyn., 1989, 10 on 8, N.Y.C., 1982, Ctr. for the Arts/Wesleyan U., Middletown, Conn., 1979; pub. sculpture commns. include: Ala. Inst. for Deaf and Blind, Talledega, 1997, Bronx Coun. on the Arts, N.Y., 1995, Town of Montclair/Barnet Sister Cities, Montclair, N.J. and Barnet, Eng., 1993; corp./instnl. collections include: N.Y. Pub. Libr., 1997, Abington Friends Sch., Jenkintown, Pa., Benco Dental Supply, Wilkes-Barre, Pa., Goldring Internat., Woodbury, N.Y.; prodn. designer Milk and Money, RKO Pictures, 1995, Practice to Deceive, 1990; scene and costume designer for theatre and film, 1979-97; contbr. essays to profl. jours. Recipient fellowships for sculpture N.Y. Found. for Arts, N.Y.C., 1997, N.J. State Coun. on the Arts, Trenton, N.J., 1983; recipient Eliot Lash award for sculpture Cooper Union, 1977. Mem. Internat. Sculpture Ctr., Nat. Sculpture Soc. Website: http://www.michaelandmeredith.com.

BERGON, FRANK, English language educator, writer; b. Ely, Nev., Feb. 24, 1943; s. Frank Albert and Lina Rose (Mendive) B.; m. Holly St. John Neil, July 28, 1979. BA in English summa cum laude, Boston Coll., 1965; postgrad., Stanford U., 1965-66; PhD in English, Harvard U., 1973. Fellow in teaching Harvard U., Cambridge, Mass., 1968-70, 71; dir. Am. Culture Program Vassar Coll., Poughkeepsie, N.Y., 1982-85, prof. English, 1972—; part time lectr. Newton Coll., 1971-72; vis. assoc. prof. U. Wash., 1980-81. Author: Stephen Crane's Artistry, 1975, Shoshone Mike, 1987, The Temptations of St. Ed & Brother S, 1993, Wild Game, 1995; editor: The Western Writings of Stephen Crane, 1979, The Wilderness Reader, 1980, A Sharp Lookout: Selected Nature Essays of John Burroughs, 1987, The Journals of Lewis and Clark, 1989; co-editor: Looking Far West: The Search for the American West in History, Myth and Literature, 1978. Fellow NEH, 1985-86, Am. Coun. of Learned Socs., 1979-80, Woodrow Wilson Found., 1966-67, Wallace Stegner Found., 1965-66; named to Nev. Writers Hall of Fame, 1998. Mem. MLA, Am. Studies Assn., Western Lit. Assn., Assn. Study of Lit. and the Environment, John Burroughs Assn. (bd. dirs.). Avocations: jogging, hiking. Home: 136 Chapel Hill Rd Highland NY 12528-2103 Office: Vassar Coll Raymond Ave Poughkeepsie NY 12601

BERGONIA, RAYMOND DAVID, venture capitalist; b. Spring Valley, Ill., May 21, 1951; s. Raymond A. and Elva M. (Bernadini) B.; m. Linda Goble, Dec. 31, 1988; children: Alexandra, Andrew, Caroline, Margot. BBA, U. Notre Dame, 1973; JD, Harvard U., 1976. Bar: Ill. 1976, U.S. Dist. Ct. (no. dist.) Ill. 1976, U.S. Tax Ct. 1977; C.P.A., Ill. Assoc. Winston & Strawn, Chgo., 1976-79; legal counsel, v.p. adminstrn. Heizer Corp., Chgo., 1979-86; v.p. corp. fin. Chgo. Corp., 1986-89; exec. v.p., prin. N.Am. Bus. Devel. Co. L.L.C., Chgo., 1989—; bd. dirs. numerous pvt. cos. Recipient Elijah Watts Sells award Am. Inst. C.P.A.s, 1973. Mem. ABA, Chgo. Bar Assn. Home: 605 Essex Rd Kenilworth IL 60043-1129 Office: NAM Bus Devel Co LLC 135 S La Salle St Chicago IL 60603-4105

BERGONZI, AL, company executive. Dir. rsch. HBO & Co., Atlanta, 1981-98, pres., COO, 1998—. Office: HBO and Co 301 Perimeter Ctr N Atlanta GA 30346-2402*

BERGOUST, ERIC, olympic athlete; b. Missoula, Mont., Aug. 27, 1969. Olympic athlete, aerials, 1988—. Winner 1998 Goldl medal in aerials competition, Nagano Olympics, World Cup, 1992; Silver medalist 1997 World Championships; 8 time World Cup aerial event champion; 2 time U.S. Nat. champion. Office: c/o US Ski and Snowboard Assn PO Box 100 Park City UT 84060-0100*

BERGQUIST, ED PETER, JR., music educator emeritus; b. Sacramento, Aug. 5, 1930; s. Ed Peter and Margaret (Rogers) B.; m. Dorothy Catherine Clark, June 16, 1956; children: Carolyn, Emily (dec.). Student, Eastman Sch. Music, Rochester, N.Y., 1948-51; BS, Mannes Coll. Music, N.Y.C., 1958; MA, Columbia U., 1960, PhD, 1964. Asst. prof. Sch. Music, U. Oreg., Eugene, 1964-69, assoc. prof., 1969-73, prof., 1973-95, prof. emeritus, 1995—. Editor: Orlando di Lasso, The Complete Motets, 21 vols., 1995—, Orlando di Lasso, Samtliche Werke neue Reihe, vol. 22-25, 1992-93; contbr. articles to profl. jours. Sr. warden, jr. warden, vestryman St. Mary's Episcopal Ch., Eugene. With USAF, 1951-55. Recipient Ersted award for disting. teaching U. Oreg., 1973; Fulbright sr. rsch. awardee, 1985; Nat. Endowment for Humanities grantee, 1994-98; rsch. and travel awardee DAAD, ACLS. Mem. AAUP, Am. Musicol. Soc., Internat. Musicol. Soc., Soc. for Music Theory, Music Libr. Assn., Coll. Music Soc. Democrat. Home: 3195 Portland St Eugene OR 97405-5140 Office: Sch Music 1225 U Oreg Eugene OR 97403-1225

BERGQUIST, GENE ALFRED, farmer, rancher, county commissioner; b. Paynesville, Minn., Aug. 5, 1927; s. Albin and Viola (Heinrich) B.; m. Ann Dorothy Corwin, Aug. 2, 1958; children: Wayne A., Viola M. Grad. high sch., Rhame, N.D. Self-employed farmer-rancher Rhame, 1948—; Slope County commr. Amidon, N.D., 1982—; bd. dirs. Rhame, N.D. Cenex, 1970-82; bd. dirs. Harper Twp. Rhame; com. mem. Slope County Agrl. Stabilization and Conservation Svc.-USDA Commn., Amidon, 1968-84. Bd. dirs. Rhame Rural Fire Dept., 1976—, Bowman-Slope Social Svc. Bd., Bowman, N.D., 1991—, Deep Creek Twp., 1958-64, Richland Center Twp. Bd., 1952-57; elder Lyle Presbyn. Ch.; youth leader 4-H Slope County, 1950-57. Mem. N.D. Assn. Counties. Presbyterian. Avocations: reading, painting, fishing, riding, gardening. Office: Courthouse Amidon ND 58620

BERGQUIST, JAMES MANNING, history educator; b. Council Bluffs, Iowa, Feb. 1, 1934; s. Reuben Neil and Irene Mary (Norton) B.; m. Joan Marie Solon, May 17, 1969; children: John Norton, Charles James. BA, U. Notre Dame, 1955; MA in History, Northwestern U., 1956, PhD in History, 1966. Instr. history Coe Coll., Cedar Rapids, Iowa, 1961-63; instr. history Villanova (Pa.) U., 1963-66, asst. prof., 1966-69, assoc. prof., 1969-86, prof., 1986—. Contbr. articles on Am. social history and immigration to profl. jours., chpts. to books. Trustee Balch Inst. for Ethnic Studies, Phila., 1988-92, 94—; mem. Pa. Task Force on Diversity in Higher Edn., 1991-94. Fellow NEH, summers 1967, 77, 80. Mem. AAUP (pres. Pa. divsn. 1988-90, mem. nat. coun. 1995—), Am. Hist. Assn., Orgn. Am. Historians, Am. Studies Assn., Immigration and Ethnic History Soc. (bd. dirs. 1995—), Am. Assn. for State and Local History, Ethnic Studies Assn. Phila. (pres. 1980-82). Democrat. Roman Catholic. Avocations: swimming, travel. Home: 217 Devon Blvd Devon PA 19333-1616 Office: Villanova U History Dept Villanova PA 19085

BERGQUIST, SANDRA LEE, medical and legal consultant, nurse; b. Carlton, Minn., Oct. 13, 1944; d. Arthur Vincent and Avis Lorene Portz; m. David Edward Bergquist, June 11, 1966; children: Rion Eric, Taun Erin. BSN, Barry U., 1966; MA in Mgmt., Central Mich. U., 1975; student U. So. Calif., 1980-82. RN, advanced registered nurse practitioner; cert. physician asst. Commd. 2nd lt. USAF, 1968, advanced through grades to lt. col., 1985; staff and charge nurse USAF, 1968-76, primary care nurse practitioner, McConnell AFB, Kans., 1976-79, officer in charge Wheeler Med. Facility, Wheeler AFB, Hawaii, 1979-83, supr. ambulatory care services, Elgin AFB, Fla., 1983-84; med.-legal cons., Pensacola, Fla., 1985—; risk mgr., quality assurance coordinator HCA-Twin Cities Hosp., Niceville, 1986-88. Bd. dirs. Elder Svcs. of Okaloosa County, Fla., 1984—; mem. adv. bd. Advanced Home Health, 1990—; chairperson Niceville/Valparaiso Task Force on Child Abuse Prevention, Fla., 1985-88; chmn. home and family life com. Twin Cities Women's Club, Niceville, 1985-88; chmn. advancement com. Gulf Coast coun. Boy Scouts Am., 1985-87; instr. advanced and basic cardiac life support Hawaii Heart Assn. and Tripler Army Med. Ctr., 1981-83. Decorated Commendation medal with 1 oak leaf cluster, USAF Meritorious Svc. medal, Air Force Commendation medal. Mem. AACN, Am. Assn. Physician Assts., Assn. Mil. Surgeons U.S., Soc. Ret. Air Force Nurses, Soc. Air Force Physician Assts., Twin Cities Women's Club. Lutheran. Avocations: computer programming, reading, handicrafts.

BERGREEN, BERNARD D., investment company executive. Pres. Gilman Investment Co. Inc., N.Y.C. Office: Gilman Investment Co Inc 111 W 50th St Fl 2 New York NY 10020-1202*

BERGREEN, MORRIS HARVEY, lawyer, business executive, private investor; b. Passaic, N.J., Sept. 28, 1917; s. Harold and Jennie (Dolgen) B.; m. Adele G. Bergreen, Sept. 1, 1947; children: Laurence, John. Student, NYU, 1935-38; LLB, Fordham U., 1941; postgrad., NYU. Bar: N.Y. 1942. Sr. ptnr. Bergreen & Bergreen, N.Y.C., 1953-86, 95—; ret. of counsel Milbank, Tweed, Hadley & McCloy, N.Y.C., 1986-95; sr. ptnr. Bergreen & Bergreen, N.Y.C., 1995—; pres. Croydon Co., Inc., Westminster Broadcasting Corp., Claridge Broadcasting Corp.; gen. mgr. Grosvenor Investment Co., Skirball Investment Co. Pres. The Skirball Found.; bd. dirs., founding mem. bd. trustees Skirball Mus. and Cultural Ctr.; mem. adv. bd. Skirball Inst. on Am. Values; trustee, bd. dirs. Audrey Skirball Kenis Theatre, Inc.; trustee, mem. acad. affairs com., adv. bd. Bronfman Ctr. for Jewish Student Life/NYU; trustee, mem. joint com. Med. Ctr. initiatives NYU Med. Ctr., mem. coordinating com.; bd. govs. Oxford Ctr. for Hebrew and Jewish Studies Oxford U.; trustee, mem. investment com. NCCJ, Inc.; bd. dirs., v.p. Grand St. Settlement; trustee Jewish Home and Hosp. for Aged; bd. dirs. Sarah R. Neuman Nursing Home, others. 1st lt. USAAF, 1942-46. Recipient Albert Gallatin medal for outstanding contbn. to society NYU, 1995. Mem. ABA, N.Y. State Bar Assn., Assn. Bar of City of N.Y., Fordham Law Rev. Assn., Harmonie Club (N.Y.C.), Sunningdale Country Club (Scarsdale, N.Y.), Club at Morningside (Rancho Mirage, Calif.), Tamarisk Country Club (Rancho Mirage, Calif.), Hillcrest Country Club (L.A.), N.Y. Athletic Club. Home: 24 Highland Farm Rd Greenwich CT 06831-2606 also: 980 5th Ave New York NY 10021-0126 Office: Bergreen & Bergreen 767 5th Ave Fl 43 New York NY 10153-0023

BERGREN, HELEN DUFFEY, retired nurse; b. Tacoma, Aug. 7, 1928; d. Joseph Clifford and Nancy Margaret (Johnson) Duffey; m. Bill G. Hollingsworth, Oct. 29, 1955 (dec. Sept. 1962), 1 child, Clint L.; m. Alfred C. Bergren, May 23, 1963. AA, Wenatchee (Wash.) Valley Coll., 1955. Supr. Ctrl. Wash. Deaconess Hosp., Wenatchee, 1955-56, Cascade Sanitarium, Leavenworth, Wash., 1957-60; 3-11 supr. Ctrl. Wash. Deconess Hosp., Wenatchee, 1961-66; pub. health nurse Chelan-Douglas Helath Dist., Wenatchee, 1966-75; staff nurse Cascade Gen. Hosp., Leavenworth, Wash., 1977-83, asst. dir. nursing, 1983-88, dir. nursing, 1988-90, ret., 1990; nurse Leavenworth Sch. Dist., 1966-72. Elizabeth Sterling Soule scholar, 1952; Pub. Health Dept. grantee, 1973-75. Mem. Ctrl. Wash. Deaconess Alumni Assn., Back Country Horsemen of Wash. and Am., Leavenworth Winter Sports Club, Chumstick Grange #819, Phi Theta Kappa. Avocations: horse-back riding, skiing, swimming, fishing, hunting. Home: 7675 Icicle Rd Leavenworth WA 98826-9318

BERGREN, SCOTT C., career officer; b. Mineola, N.Y.. BA in Econ., Clemson U., 1970; student navigator tng., Mather AFB, Calif., 1970-71; student, Squadron Officer Sch., 1974; M in Polit. Sci., Auburn U., 1981; student, Air Command and Staff Coll., 1981, Air War Coll., 1990, Harvard U., 1996. Commd. 2d lt. USAF, 1970, advanced through grades to maj. gen., 1999, various F-4 Phantom assignments, 1971-76; air staff ops. officer programs and resources Air Staff Tng. program, Hdqs. USAF, Pentagon, Washington, 1976-77, asst. exec. officer to dep. chief staff programs/resources, 1976-77; instr., navigator and exchange officer 237th Operational Conversion Unit, RAFB Honington, Eng., 1977-80; dir. ops. force analysis div. then spl. asst. comdr. Hdqs. Tactical Air Command, Langley AFB, Va., 1981-85; comdr. 325th Tactical Tng. Wing's Aircraft Generation Squadron, Tyndall AFB, Fla., 1985-87, asst. dep. comdr. maintenance, 1985-87; dep. comdr. maintenance 33rd Tactical Fighter Wing, Eglin AFB, Fla., 1987-89; Air Univ. chair for chief staff of Air Force Maxwell AFB, Ala., 1990-91; various comdr. positions Nellis AFB, Nev., 1991-93; stationed at U.S. Ctrl. Command, MacDill AFB, Fla., 1994-96; vice comdr. San Antonio Air Logistics Ctr., Kelly AFB, Tex., 1996-97; comdr. 82d Tng. Wing, Sheppard AFB, 1997-99; dir. maintenance, dep. chief staff installations & logistics HQ/USAF, 1999—. Decorated Silver Star, D.F.C. with silver oak leaf cluster, Purple Heart, Air medal with three silver oak leaf clusters and bronze oak leaf cluster, Small Arms Expert Marksmanship Ribbon, Rep. Vietnam Gallantry Cross with Palm, Rep. Vietnam Campaign medal. Office: HQUSAF/ILM 1030 Air Force Pentagon Washington DC 20330-1030

BERGRUN, NORMAN RILEY, aerospace executive; b. Green Camp, Ohio, Aug. 4, 1921; s. Theodore and Naomi Ruth (Stemm) B.; m. Claire Michaelson, May 23, 1943; children: Clark, Jay, Joan. BSME, Cornell U., 1943; LLB, LaSalle U. Ext., 1955; DSc, World U., 1983. Registered profl. mech. engr. Thermodynamicist Douglas Aircraft Co., El Segundo, Calif., 1943-44; rsch. scientist NACA Ames Rsch. Lab., Mt. View, Calif., 1944-56; mgr. analysis Lockheed Missile & Space Co., Sunnyvale, Calif., 1956-67, staff scientist, 1967-69; dir. mgmt. systems Nielsen Engring. and Rsch., Mt. View, 1969-71; CEO, scientist Bergrun Rsch. and Engring., Los Altos, Calif., 1971—; guest on radio and TV programs in the U.S., Can., Australia and Europe; spkr. L'Academie Europeene, 1987; Expo West lectr., 1996, CompuServe Conf. lectr.; instr. NASA Space Day, 1998; lectr. Independence H.S., San Jose, 1999. Author: Ringmakers of Saturn, 1986, Tomorrow's Technology Today, 1972, A Warming Trend for Icing Research, 1995, Air Travel Safety Forum Attracts Public Media Interest, 1997, The International Space Station: A Momentous Cultural, Scientific and Societal Undertaking, 1998; photographer including the Sir Francis Drake Collection, 1990; contbr. more than 90 articles and reports of profl. jours. Incorporator Aurora Singers Found., Palo Alto, Calif., 1989; co-founder NSPE Edn. Found., Sacramento, Calif., advisor to bd., 1985-92; mem. Steinman Coun., 1988—, steering com. mem. Congressmen Visits Day, 1997, 98, 99; mem. Cornell U. Concert Musician Carnegie Hall, 1989. Named Man of Yr., Am. Biog. Assn.; recipient Archimedes award, 1988, Cert. of Appreciation, Eglin AFB, 1961. Fellow AIAA (assoc., sr. judge 7th and 8th grade essay contest 1992, 93, 94, 95, 97, 98, 99, chair nat. pub.-policy comm. subcom. 1992—, regional dep. dir.-at-large 1995—, spl. svc. citation 1994, 98, advisor Airline Safety Initiative 1997, moderator Internat. Space St. Forum 1998); mem. NSPE (life), Profl. Engrs. Soc. (Calif. pres. 1988-89, Integrity award 1989, Outstanding Exec. Performance award 1986, Disting. Contbns. award 1985-86, 86-87, 98). Achievements include discoveries of existence of large, mobile cylindrical objects, identified at Saturn, Miranda, Iapetus, Mars, Neptune, Earth's moon, the Sun, and deep space; patents for Cyclic Electric Thermal Ice-Prevention System for Airplanes. Office: Bergrun Rsch and Engring 26865 Saint Francis Rd Los Altos CA 94022-1910

BERGSCHNEIDER, JOHN, city engineer; b. Atwater, Calif., Aug. 2, 1954; s. Francis Fabin and Sara Nell (Morris) B.; m. Frances Torres; children: Frank P., Sara M., John H. BS in Civil Engring., Auburn U., 1978. Registered profl. engr. Ala., Fla., Ga.; profl. surveyor Ala. Engr. Peace Corps, Khorant, Thailand, 1979-81; asst. county engr. Franklin County, Russelville, Ala., 1984-85; civil engr. Fulton County, Atlanta, Ga., 1985-86; asst. dir. engring. Columbus (Ga.) Consolidated Govt., 1986-90; city engr. Phenix City, Ala., 1990-93; city pub. works dir. Destin, Fla., 1993-94; city engr. Ft. Walton (Fla.) Beach, 1994—. Mem. Profl. Engrs. Assn. (pres. Emerald chpt 1996), Lions Club (tail twister, v.p.). Avocations: swimming, fishing, biking. Home: 332 Gardner Dr NE Fort Walton Beach FL 32548-5140

BERGSMA, DERKE PETER, minister, religious studies educator; b. Racine, Wis., Aug. 29, 1927; s. John Sietze and Johanna Jacoba (Vlaardingerbroek) B.; m. Doris Elaine Bielema, Oct. 28, 1950; children: Deborah, Derk, Diann, Danette. AB, Calvin Coll., 1951; BD, Calvin Sem., 1954; MA, Northwestern U., 1962; DTh, Free-U.-Amsterdam, 1964; D Religion, Chgo. Theol. Sem., 1968. Ordained to ministry Christian Reformed Ch. in Am., 1954. Instr. Calvin Coll., Grand Rapids, Mich., 1950-52; pastor Christian Reformed Ch., Grand Rapids, 1954-62; prof. Trinity Christian Coll., Palos Heights, Ill., 1968-81, Westminster Theol. Sem., Escondido, Calif., 1981—; co-founder Christian Counseling Ctr., Palos Heights, 1974-76; trustee Bd. Publs., Christian Reformed Ch., Grand Rapids, 1970-76. Author: Voices, 1976, Predestination: Islam and Calvinism, 1984, Redemption: The Triumph of God's Great Plan, 1988; contbr. articles to profl. jours. Trustee Calvin Theol. Sem., 1989-92. Capt. USN. (Ret.). Chgo. Ch. Fedn. grantee, 1977. Mem. Evang. Theol. Soc., DAV, Lions. Home: 8975 Lawrence Welk Dr Spc 424 Escondido CA 92026-6423 Office: Westminster Theol Sem 1725 Bear Valley Pky Escondido CA 92027-4128

BERGSMARK, EDWIN MARTIN, mortgage bank executive; b. July 14, 1941; married; 2 children. BBA, U. Cin., 1964; postgrad. in mgmt., U. Colo.; JD, U. Toledo, 1972; postgrad. in banking, U. Wis. Bar: Ohio 1972, U.S. Dist. Ct. Ohio, U.S. Tax Ct., Ct. Customs and Patent Appeals, U.S. Supreme Ct. 1975. Indsl. rels. pers. dir. Textileather div. Gen. Tire and Rubber, 1967-70; exec. v.p., gen. counsel TrustCorp, Inc., Toledo, 1970-89; chmn., CEO Cavista Corp.; chmn. Vista Capital Group Inc., Cavalear Corp., Cavalear Realty Co., Cavalear Ins.; bd. dirs. Unimast Corp., Vista Devel. Inc., Gen. Aluminum and Chem. Corp., N.Am. Travel Corp. Past chmn. Sta. WGTE-TV (PBS); past pres., trustee Toledo Zool. Soc.; trustee Lourdes Coll.; chmn., trustee Toledo Mud Hens Baseball Club; pres. bd. trustees Lucas County Recreation Ctr.; past pres. Kidney Found. Northwestern Ohio, Toledo Neighborhood Housing Svcs.; vice chmn., treas., commr. Ohio Turnpike Commn. Served to capt. U.S. Army, Vietnam. Named Toledo's Outstanding Young Man of Yr., 1972. Mem. ABA, Toledo Bar Assn., Fed. Bar Assn. (trustee), Legal Inst. of Gt. Lakes, Am. Econ. Coun., Burning Tree Golf Club, Inverness Country Club. Office: Vista Capital Group Inc 6444 Monroe St Ste C Sylvania OH 43560-1430

BERGSON, ABRAM, economist, educator; b. Balt., Apr. 21, 1914; s. Issac Burk and Sophia (Rabinovich) B.; m. Rita S. Macht, Nov. 5, 1939; children: Judith, Emily, Lucy. A.B., Johns Hopkins U., 1933; Ph.D., Harvard U., 1940; LL.D., U. Windsor, 1979; D.H.L., Brandeis U., 1985. Instr. econs. Harvard U., 1937-38, 39-40; asst. prof. econs. U. Tex., 1940-42; economist various agys. Fed. Govt., 1942-46; mem. U.S. delgation Moscow Reparations Conf., summer, 1945; assoc. prof. econs. Columbia U., 1946-50, prof., 1950-56; prof. econs. Harvard U., 1956-71, George F. Baker prof. econs., 1971-84, prof. emeritus, 1984—; dir. The Russian Research Center, Harvard U., 1964-68, 77-80; cons. Rand Corp., 1948-88. Author: Structure of Soviet Wages, 1944, Economics of Soviet Planning, 1964, Essays in Normative Economics, 1966, Planning and Productivity under Soviet Socialism, 1968, Productivity and the Social System, 1978, Welfare, Planning, and Employment, 1982, Planning and Performance in Socialist Economies, 1989; contr. to books, articles to profl. econ. jours.; co-editor: Economic Trends in the Soviet Union, 1963, The Soviet Economy: Toward the Year 2000, 1983. Mem. social sci. advisory bd. ACDA, 1966-73, chmn., 1972-73. Fellow Econometric Soc., Am. Acad. Arts and Scis., Am. Econ. Assn. (disting. fellow); mem. Nat. Acad. Scis., Am. Philos. Soc., Social Sci. Research Council (dir.-at-large 1963-69). Jewish. Home: 334 Marsh St Belmont MA 02478-1734

BERGSON, HENRY PAUL, professional association administrator; b. Boston, Dec. 22, 1942; s. Harry Jr. and Elizabeth (Paul) B.; m. Jacqueline Hope Wilson, June 11, 1966; children: Susan Elizabeth, Abigail Anne. BS, U. N.H., 1966. Various mgmt. positions Fed. Signal, Blue Island, Ill., 1970-78; dir. mktg. Tork, Mt. Vernon, N.Y., 1978-83; v.p. ops. G.C.S. Svc., Chappaqua, N.Y., 1983-85; exec. v.p. Nat. Elec. Mfrs. Reps. Assn., Armonk, N.Y., 1985-93, pres., 1994—, also bd. dirs.; bd. dirs. Elec. Industry Joint Bus. Productivity Coun.; fire commr. Katonah Fire Dist., 1992—; vice chmn. bd. fire commrs., Katonah, 1996—. Contbr. articles to profl. jours. Elder 1st Presbyn. Ch. of Katonah, N.Y., 1991-94; chief Katonah Vol. Fire Dept., 1980-84, v.p., 1984-87, pres., 1987-90, bd. dirs., 1990—, chmn. bd. dirs., 1995—; mem. Bedford Transp. Com., 1984-86; cmty. adv. bd. Taconic and Bedford Hills Correctional Facilities, N.Y. State Dept. Corrections. Capt. U.S. Army, 1967-70. Decorated Bronze Star for Valor with two oak leaf clusters, Air medal with three oak leaf clusters, Purple Heart, Army Commendation medal for Valor, Vietnam Medal of Honor. Mem. Nat. Elec. Mfrs. Assn. (assoc.), Nat. Assn. Elec. Distribrs. Republican. Avocations:

collecting firematic antiques. Home: PO Box 182 Katonah NY 10536-0182 Office: NEMRA 200 Business Park Dr Ste 301 Armonk NY 10504-1727

BERGSTEIN, DANIEL GERARD, lawyer; b. Nice, France, May 1, 1943; came to U.S., 1952; s. Max and Suzanne (Fenigstein) B.; children: Jordan, Elizabeth C. BA, CUNY, 1965; JD, Bklyn. Law Sch., 1968. Bar: N.Y. 1968, Fla. 1974. From assoc. to ptnr. Greenbaum, Wolff & Ernst, N.Y.C., 1982; ptnr. Reavis & McGrath, N.Y.C., 1982-85, Finley, Kumble, Wagner, Heine, Underberg, Manley, Myerson & Casey, N.Y.C., 1985-87, Paul, Hastings, Janofsky & Walker, N.Y.C., 1988—. Mem. ABA, French-Am. C. of C. in U.S. Office: Paul Hastings Janofsky & Walker LLP 399 Park Ave Fl 31 New York NY 10022-4697

BERGSTEIN, HARRY BENJAMIN, psychology educator; b. Sag Harbor, N.Y., Dec. 30, 1916; s. Joseph and Sarah (Baer) B.; children from previous marriage: Mary, Paul, David; m. Florence R. Markert, Jan. 2, 1989. A.B., SUNY, 1939, M.A., 1947; Ed.D., NYU, 1960. Tchr., counselor various schs., L.I., N.Y., 1945-60; guidance dir. Huntington (L.I.) Pub. Schs., 1960-67; vis. prof. CUNY, 1967-68; mem. faculty SUNY, Oneonta, 1968-90, prof. ednl. psychology, 1968-90; chmn. dept. ednl. psychology SUNY-Oneonta, 1978-82; cons. sch. psychologist to area pub. schs., 1970-82. Served with AUS, 1941-45. NYU teaching fellow, 1959-60. Mem. Am. Psychol. Assn., Am. Counseling Assn. (life), NEA (life), Phi Delta Kappa (life). Home: 34 College Ter Oneonta NY 13820-1204

BERGSTEIN, JACK MARSHALL, surgeon; b. Duluth, Minn., Apr. 21, 1955; s. Sherman and Muriel (Gilder) B.; m. Mary Beth Bergstein, May 21, 1982; children: Lauren, Julian. BA in Journalism, U. Minn., 1978, MD, 1982. Diplomate Am. Bd. Surgery with added qualifications in surg. critical care; diplomate Am. Bd. Forensic Examiners, Am. Bd. Forensic Medicine. Resident surgery U. Minn., Charlotte Med. Ctr., 1982-85, 85-87; surg. critical care fellow Lincoln Med. and Mental Health Ctr., Bronx, N.Y., 1987-88; sr. attending surgeon Froedert Hosp., Milw., 1988-97; dir. trauma and surg. critical care St. Francis Med. Ctr., Peoria, 1997-99; assoc. prof. surgery U. Ill. Coll. Medicine, Peoria, 1997-99; dir. surg. critical care, assoc. dir. trauma Jon Michael Moore Trauma Ctr. W.Va. U. Hosp., Morgantown, 1999—; prof. surgery W.Va. Sch. Medicine, Morgantown, 1999—; active staff St. Francis Hosp., Peoria, 1997—. Dir. at large Peace Studies Ctr., Milw., 1995-97; adv. bd. Peoria Safe Cmtys. Fellow ACS (chmn. Wis. com. on trauma 1995-97); mem. Am. Trauma Soc. (pres. Wis. 1992-97), Am. Assn. Surgery of Trauma, Ea. Assn. for the Surgery of Trauma (dir.-at-large 1999—, chmn. violence prevention task force, 1999—, vice chair violence prevention task force, 1994-99), Western Trauma Assn., Assn. Tchrs. Preventive Medicine, Assn. Acad.Surgery, Midwest Surg. Assn., Nat. Network Violence Prevention Practitioners. Avocations: bonsai, watercolor painting. Home: 264 Lakeside Dr Morgantown WV 26508 Office: WVa Sch Medicine Robert C Byrd Health Scis PO Box 9238 Rm 7700 HSCS Morgantown WV 26506-9238

BERGSTEIN, JERRY MICHAEL, pediatric nephrology; b. Cleve., June 26, 1939; s. Sol R. and Hilda (Nittscoff) B.; m. Renee M. Hillman, July 7, 1963; children: Stephanie, Michael, Jeffrey. BA, UCLA, 1961; MD, U. Minn., 1965. Diplomate Nat. Bd. Med. Examiners, Am. Bd. Pediat., Am. Bd. Pediat. Nephrology; lic. physician, Ind. Intern in pediat. U. Minn., Mpls., 1965-66, jr. pediat. resident, 1966-67, chief pediat. resident, 1969-70, postdoctoral fellow in pediat. nephrology, 1970-73; asst. prof., head pediat. nephrology UCLA, 1973-77; assoc. prof. Ind. U. Sch. Medicine, Indpls., 1977-82, head pediat. nephrology, 1977—, prof., 1982—; mem. adv. bd. Nat. Kidney Found. Ind., 1980—; mem. adv. coun. Am. Heart Assn., 1988—. Mem. editl. bd. Child Nephrology and Urology, 1980-90, Pediat. Nephrology, 1995—; contbr. chpts. to books. Lt. comdr. USN, 1967-69. Recipient Fellowship USPHS, Washington, 1970; grantee Thrasher Fund, 1980, Amgen, 1990. Mem. Am. Soc. Nephrology, Am. Soc. Pediat. Nephrology, Am. Soc. Investigative Pathology, Soc. Exptl. Biology and Medicine. Achievements include research on the role of the fibrinolytic inhibitor plasminogen activator inhibitor-1 in the pathogenesis and outcome of the hemolytic-uremic syndrome; development of anti-tubular basement membrane antibody disease; development of radiation nephritis in bone marrow transplant patients. Avocations: fishing, gardening, reading, racquetball. Office: James Whitcomb Riley Hosp for Children 702 Barnhill Dr Indianapolis IN 46202-5128

BERGSTEIN, STANLEY FRANCIS, horse racing executive; b. Pottsville, Pa., June 19, 1924; s. Milton Isidore and Esther Miriam (Rosenzweig) B.; m. June Carol Hanna, June 4, 1950; children: Alfred M., Lisa R. BS, Northwestern U., 1947. Writer James S. Kearns Assoc., Chgo., 1947-50, CBS TV, Chgo., 1956-57; racing sec. Sportsman's Pk., Chgo., 1957-60; exec. dir. Harness Racing Inst., Chgo., 1961-68; exec. v.p. Harness Tracks Am., Tucson, Ariz., 1961—; pres. Am. Horse Publs., Lexington, Ky., 1969-70; trustee Hall of Fame of Trotter, Goshen, N.Y., 1980—. Editor Hoof Beats Mag., Columbus, Ohio, 1968-75; columnist Harness Horse Mag., Harrisburg, Pa., 1979-90, Times: in Harness Mag., 1990—, Daily Racing Form, 1995—. Named Horseman of Yr. Horseman and Fair World Mag., Lexington, 1971; recipient Proximity award U.S. Harness Writers, Goshen, 1978, Writers Hall of Fame award, 1986, Hall of Fame of Trotter award Trotting Horse Mus., Goshen, 1987, Internat. award Racing Commrs., 1990, Amtote Internat. award, 1992. Mem. U.S. Trotting Assn. (v.p. publicity 1968-75). Avocation: antiquarian book and print collecting.

BERGSTEN, C. FRED, economist; b. Bklyn., Apr. 23, 1941; s. Carl Alfred and Lois Halkaline (Kirk) B.; m. Virginia Lee Wood, June 16, 1962; 1 son, Mark. AB, Ctrl. Meth. Coll., Fayette, Mo., 1961, LHD, 1995; MA, Fletcher Sch. Law and Diplomacy, Medford, Mass., 1962, MA in Law and Diplomacy, 1963, PhD, 1969. Internat. economist Dept. State, 1963-67; vis. fellow Council Fgn. Relations, 1967-68; asst. for internat. econ. affairs NSC, 1969-71; sr. fellow Brookings Instn., 1972-76; asst. sec. treasury internat. affairs, 1977-81; sr. assoc. Carnegie Endowment Internat. Peace, 1981; dir. Inst. Internat. Econs., 1981—; bd. dirs. Consumers Union, 1976-77, Consumers for World Trade, 1982-90, Atlantic Ins., 1973-77, Ovrseas Devel. Coun., 1974-77, Ctrl. Meth. Coll., 1982-88, Ctr. Law and Social Policy, 1973-77, Worldwatch Inst., 1975-77, Fletcher Sch. Law and Diplomacy, 1992—; dir. Overseas Pvt. Investment Corp., 1977-81, U.S.-Israel Binat. Rsch. and Devel. Found., 1977-81; U.S. coord. U.S.-Saudi Arabia Joint Econ. Commn., 1977-81; mem. def. mgmt. bd. Task Force on Fgn. Ownership and Control, 1989-90, competitiveness policy coun., 1991-97, chmn., 1991-97; mem. panel on pub.-pvt. cooperation in civilian tech. NAS, 1990-91; mem. exec. com. Trilateral Commn., 1991—, Bretton Wood Com., 1989—, Carnegie Endowment, Nat. Commn. Am. and the New World Order, 1992, Commn. Govt. Renewal, 1992; chmn. APEC Eminent Persons Group, 1993-95; vice chmn. adv. com. on fgn. econ. policy Dept. State, 1996—. Author: The Future of the International Economic Order: An Agenda for Research, 1973, Toward a New World Trade Policy, 1975, World Politics and International Economics, 1975, Toward a New International Economic Order: Selected Papers of C. Fred Bergsten, 1972-74, 1975, The Dilemmas of the Dollar: The Economics and Politics of United State International Monetary Policy, 1976, American Multinationals and American Interests, 1978, Managing International Economic Interdependence:Selected Papers of C. Fred Bergsten, 1975-76, 1977, The International Economic Policy of the United States: Selected Papers of C. Fred Bergsten, 1977-79, 1980,The World Economy in the 1980s: Selected Papers of C. Fred Bergsten, 1981, The United State in the World Economy: Selected Papers of C. Fred Bergsten, 1981-82,1983, Bank Lending to Developing Countries: The Policy Alternatives, 1985, The United States-Japan Economic Problem, 1985, Global Economic Imbalances, 1985, Auction Quotas and United States Trade Policy, 1987, America in the World Economy: A Strategy for the 1990's, 1988, International Adjustment and Financing, 1991, Pacific Dynamism and the International Economic System, 1993, Reconcilable Differences? United States-Japan Economic Conflict, 1993, Global Econ. Leadship and the Group of Seven 1996, Whither APEC?, 1997; mem. editl. bd. Fgn. Affairs, 1972-77, Internat. Orgn., 1973-77, Jour. Internat. Econs., 1977-80, Foreign Policy, 1987—. Recipient Meritorious Honor award Dept. State, 1965, Disting. Alumnus award Central Meth. Coll., 1975, Exceptional Service award Treasury Dept., 1980, French Legion of Honor, 1987. Fellow Chinese Acad. Social Scis. (hon.); mem. Am. Econ. Assn., Coun. Fgn. Rels. Home: 4106 Sleepy Hollow Rd Annandale VA 22003-2042 Office: Inst Internat Econs 11 Dupont Cir NW Washington DC 20036-1207

BERGSTROM, ALBION ANDREW, army officer, federal official; b. Salem, Mass., Sept. 2, 1947; s. Eric Jhalmar and Helen Lawrence (Andrew) B.; m. Angela Jane Feyerabend, May 11, 1997. BA, Colo. State U., 1969; MA, Ctrl. Mich. U., 1978; grad. Command and Gen. Staff Coll., U.S. Army, 1982. Commd. 2d lt. U.S. Army, 1969, advanced through grades to col., 1991; platoon leader, aide de camp U.S. Army, Vietnam, 1970-71; co. comdr. U.S. Army, Ft. Hood, Tex., 1974-75; br. exec. officer U.S. Army, Erlangen, Fed. Republic of Germany, 1980-81; assignment officer Arbor Br. U.S. Army, 1983-85, bn. comdr. 1-35 Armor, 1986-88; cols. assignment officer Pers. Command U.S. Army, Alexandria, Va., 1988-89; chief, officer divsn. DCS pers., The Pentagon U.S. Army, Washington, 1990-92; dep. comdr. U.S.Army Phys. Disability Agy., Washington, 1992-96; prof. jt. mil. ops., chief regional contingency planning and war fighting divsn. Naval War Coll., Newport, R.I., 1996—; program chmn. Abrams Ch.,Armor Assn., 1982-85; del. N.H. Rep. convs., 1966, 68. Decorated Legion of Merit, Bronze Star, Purple Heart, Bronze medal, Order of St. George, Forrestal award Naval War Coll.; Nat. Security fellow John F. Kennedy Sch. Govt., Harvard U., 1988-90. Mem. VFW, ArmorAssn., Am. Legion, Assn. U.S. Army, 1st Cavalry Divsn. Assn., U.S. Naval Inst., Naval War Coll. Found., U.S. Army War Coll. Alumni Assn., Nat. Sojourners, Colo. State U. Alumni Assn., Ctrl. Mich. U. Alumni Assn., B. U. Alumni Assn., Masons, Shriners, Mil. Order of Purple Heart, Order Ky. Cols., Phi Sigma Delta, Zeta Beta Tau. Congregationalist. Avocations: photography, cross-country skiing. Home: Quarters A Riggs Rd Newport RI 02840-1020

BERGSTRÖM, ANNA, foreign language educator; b. Sweden, Mar. 25, 1961; came to the U.S., 1976; d. Jan I. and Barbro I. (Feldt) B. BA, U. Wis., 1983, MA, 1986; PhD, Pa. State U., 1995. Tchr. French Glenbrook North H.S., Northbrook, Ill., 1986-88; vis. lectr. French Ind. U., Bloomington, 1993-95; asst. prof. French U. Del., Newark, 1995—, 1995-99; dept. chair Stockholm Inst. Edn., 1999—. Mem. NAFE, Am. Assn. Tchrs. French, Am. Assn. Applied Linguistics, European Second Lang. Acquisition, Del. Coun. on the Tchr. Fgn. Langs. Avocations: music, dance, horseback riding. Office: U Del, Stockholm Inst Edn, Box 34103, 10026 Stockholm Sweden

BERGSTROM, DEDRIC WALDEMAR, retired paper company executive; b. Neenah, Wis., Aug. 21, 1919; s. D. Waldemar and Agnes (Forsythe) B.; m. Jane Katherine Gibson, June 14, 1941; children—Dedric Waldemar IV, John F., Richard A., Jennifer M., William L. Grad., Northwestern Mil. and Naval Acad., Lake Geneva, Wis., 1936; student, Lawrence Coll., Appleton, Wis., 1936-38, U. Minn., 1939. With Bergstrom Paper, Neenah, Wis., 1936-84; successively gen. mill, office work, purchasing agt. Bergstrom Paper, 1945-50, treas., 1950-56, dir., 1950—, dir. purchases, 1950-71, dir. prodn. planning and scheduling, 1957-71, v.p., sec., 1956-62, exec. v.p., 1962-75, pres., chief operating officer, 1975-79; pres. Bergstrom divsn. P.H. Glatfelter Co., 1979-84; bd. dirs. Twin City Savs. and Loan Assn., 1951-90. Vice pres. Bergstrom Found., 1962-80, pres., 1980—; bd. regents Campion High Sch., 1968-72. Served to maj. AUS, 1942-45. Mem. Wis. Paper & Pulp Mfrs. Traffic Assn. (dir. 1967-72). Roman Catholic. Club: Bergstrom Paper Management. Home: 835 River Ln Neenah WI 54956-2931

BERGSTROM, MARIANNE ELISABETH, program coordinator, special education educator; b. Sodertalje, Sweden, Aug. 18, 1941; came to U.S., 1967; d. Uno G. Bergstrom and Agnes (L.B.) Gustafsson. BA, Linkopings Tchrs. Coll., Sodertalje, 1964, Pacific Luth. U., 1973; MA, Pacific Luth. U., 1979; EdD, Seattle U., 1988; profl. mediation cert., U. Wash. Cert. tchr., prin., program adminstr., Wash.; cert. in profl. meditation skills tng. Tchr. spl. edn. Jarna and Botkyrka Sch. Dists., Sweden, 1964-67; tchr. spl. edn. Bellevue (Wash.) Sch. Dist., 1969-80, head tchr., 1980-91, program coord., 1991—; ednl. advisor Swedish Sch., Bellevue, 1991-92, pres. bd. dirs., 1993-94. Recipient Outstanding Guardian Ad Litem for abused and neglected children King County Superior Ct., Seattle, 1967-91, Outstanding Tchrs. in Exceptional Edn. award Acad. Therapy Publs., 1975. Mem. ASCD, Coun. for Exceptional Children. Lutheran. Avocations: hiking, skiing, dancing, tennis, traveling. Office: Bellevue Sch Dist Bellevue WA 98009-9010

BERGSTROM, STIG MAGNUS, geology educator; b. Skovde, Sweden, June 12, 1935; s. Axel Magnus and Karin Margareta (Engberg) B.; m. Disa Birgitta Kullgren. Fil. lic., Lund U., Sweden, 1961, hon. doctorate, 1987. Amanuensis Lund U., 1958-62, asst. lectr., 1962-68; asst. prof. geology Ohio State U., Columbus, 1968-70, assoc. prof., 1970-72, prof., 1972—; dir. Orton Geol. Mus., 1968—. Contbr. numerous articles to profl. jours. Served with Swedish Army, 1955-56. Recipient numerous grants, 1958—, Assar Hadding prize 1995, Raymond C. Moore medal, 1999; Fulbright scholar, 1960; Am.-Scandinavian Found. fellow, 1964. Fellow Geol. Soc. Am., Ohio Acad. Sci.; mem. Royal Physiographic Soc. Office: Ohio State U Orton Geol Mus 155 S Oval Mall Columbus OH 43210-1308

BERICK, JAMES HERSCHEL, lawyer; b. Cleve., Mar. 30, 1933; s. Morris and Rebecca Alice (Gerdy) B.; m. Laura Ruth Greenfield, June 19, 1955; children: Michael, Daniel, Robert, Joshua. AB, Columbia U., 1955; JD, Case Western Res. U., 1958. Assoc. Burke, Haber & Berick, Cleve., 1958-60, ptnr., 1960-86, mng. ptnr., 1968-83; chmn. Berick, Pearlman & Mills Co. L.P.A., 1986—; bd. dirs. MBNA Corp., MBNA Am. Bank, N.A., MBNA Internat. Bank Ltd., The Town and Country Trust, The Town and Country Funding Corp.; lectr. law Case Western Res. U., 1969-78; sec. Cleve. Browns Football Co. LLC.; bd. visitors Case Western Res. U. Sch. Law, 1998—. Founding trustee Rock and Roll Hall of Fame and Mus.; mem. Shaker Heights (Ohio) Bd. Edn., 1980-83; bd. visitors Columbia Coll., 1981-87, 90-96; bd. dirs. Univ. Circle Inc., 1994—; mem. univ. coun. Case We. Res. U., 1994—, chmn., 1996—. Mem. Columbia Coll. Alumni Assn. (dir. 1976-85), Ct. of Nisi Prius, Soc. of Benchers, Cleve. 50 Club, Order of Coif, Hermit Club, Skating Club, Union Club (Cleve.). Home: 1701 E 12th St Apt 23GW Cleveland OH 44114-3237 Office: Berick Pearlman & Mills Co 1350 Eaton Ctr Cleveland OH 44114

BERING, EVA, healthcare executiver; b. Lebanon, Pa.; d. Harry R. and Minnie (Capretti) Greenawalt; children: Christine, Corey. Diploma, St. Joseph Hosp. Sch. Nursing, Lancaster, Pa., 1967; BSN, Lebanon Valley Coll., 1982; MS in Administrn., Cen. Mich. U., 1987; MSN, Widener U., 1992. RN, Pa., cert. nursing administr. Head nurse ICU/CCU St. Joseph Hosp., Lancaster, 1976-82; dir. nursing Good Samaritan Hosp., Lebanon, 1982-85, v.p., 1985-91; v.p. nursing Westmoreland Hosp., Greensburg, Pa., 1992-93; v.p. patient svcs. Susquehanna Health Svcs., 1993-96, v.p. ops., 1996—. Mem. Am. Coll. Healthcare Execs. (assoc.), Am. Orgn. Nurse Execs., Pa. Orgn. Nurse Execs. (pres. 1994), South Ctrl. Nurse Execs. (bd. dirs., pres. 1990), Pa. Nurses Assn. (chair practice com. 1993-95).

BERINGER, STUART MARSHALL, investment banker; b. N.Y.C., Jan. 27, 1923; s. Albert Frederick and Elizabeth Morris (Marshall) B.; m. Alice Joan Taylor, June 25, 1949; children: Stuart Stratton, Peter Marshall. BS, Harvard U., 1943; MBA, Columbia U., 1949. Pres. P.W. Brooks & Co. Inc., N.Y.C., 1947-66; sr. v.p. Blair & Co. Inc., N.Y.C., 1966-70, W.E. Hutton & Co., N.Y.C., 1970-74; v.p. Reynolds Securities Inc., N.Y.C., 1974-78; pres. Essex Chem. Corp., Clifton, N.J., 1978-80; sr. v.p. corp. fin. Thomson McKinnon Securities Inc., N.Y.C., 1980-89; chmn. TM Capital Corp., N.Y.C., 1989—; chmn. Servo-Tek Products Co., Inc., 1982—. With USN, 1944-46. Mem. Am. Yacht Club, Apawamis Club, Coral Beach & Tennis Club, The Club at Windermere. Office: TM Capital Corp One Battery Park Plz New York NY 10004

BERINGER, WILLIAM ERNST, mediator, arbitrator, lawyer; b. Madison, Wis., Oct. 24, 1928; s. William and Martha M. Beringer; m. Marilyn J. Walter, Aug. 4, 1984; children: Amy, Julia, Barry, Thomas, Maureen. BA summa cum laude, Lawrence Coll., 1950; JD with distinction, U. Mich., 1953. Bar: Mich. 1953, Wis. 1953, Ill. 1955, assoc. Ga., 1978. Assoc. Vedder, Price, Kaufman & Kammholz, Chgo., 1953-56; atty. law dept. Swift & Co., Chgo., 1956-71; dir. gen. law dept. Allis-Chalmers Corp., Milw., 1971-77; v.p., gen. counsel, sec. Siemens Energy & Automation, Inc., Alpharetta, 1978-94; assoc. gen. counsel Siemens Corp., 1987-94; bd. dirs. corp. banking and bus. law sect. Wis. Bar, 1976-78; mem. antitrust and corp. policy com. U.S. C. of C., 1974-80; mem. panels Am. Arbitration Assn., Resolution Resources Corp., NASD; mem. Soc. Profls. in Dispute Resolution, Ga. Coun. for Dispute Resolution. Editorial bd. Mich. Law Rev, 1952-53. Bd. dirs. Hinsdale (Ill.) Community Concert Assn., 1969-71, Dupage County (Ill.) Girl Scouts U.S., 1969-71, Clarendon Hills (Ill.) Community Chest, 1968-70; vice chmn. Clarendon Hills Human Relations Commn., 1968-70; mem. Chgo. study team Nat. Commn. on Causes and Prevention Violence, 1968; chmn. MAPI Law Coun. II, 1992-94. Mem. ABA, Am. Corp. Counsel Assn. (bd. dirs. Ga. chpt. 1985-88), Atlanta Bar Assn., Order of Coif, Cherokee Town and Country Club, Rotary. Republican. Congregationalist.

BERINSTEIN, WILLIAM PAUL, business executive; b. Elmira, N.Y., Dec. 25, 1935; s. Benjamin M. and Ann (Newhouse) B.; m. Phyllis Altman, Aug. 22, 1964; children: Benjamin M., Dorothy C. BA, U. Mich., 1957. Pres. Polk Properties, Inc., Syracuse, N.Y., 1960-89; ptnr. HLB Assocs. Investments, Syracuse, 1973—, ANB Assocs. Investments, Syracuse, 1964—; pres. Cortland Cinema Corp., Syracuse, 1967—, Cornell Theatres, Inc., Syracuse, 1973—; owner Euclid Enterprises, Syracuse, 1973—; pres. Bendor Mgmt. Ltd., 1992—; pres. 715 Realty Corp., 1990—. Trustee Temple Soc. of Concord, Syracuse, 1968-74, 90-92, treas, 1992-96, pres., 1997—. Named to Hall of Fame, Syracuse Men's Bowling Assn., 1990. Mem. Onondaga County Bowling Coun. (sec. 1985—), N.Y. State Bowling Props. Assn. (bd. dirs. 1958-65), Bowling Props. Assn. Am. (bd. dirs. 1958-64). Jewish. Avocations: genealogy, travel. Home: 4820 Candy Ln Manlius NY 13104-1604 Office: 1067 W Genesee St Syracuse NY 13204-2244

BERIO, BLANCA, editor; b. San Juan, P.R., Aug. 26, 1950; d. Gaspar and Blanca (Morales) B.; m. Martin Martino, Nov. 11, 1972; children: Blanca Iris, Martin, Bibiana. BA, U. P.R., 1968, MA, 1985, EdD, 1997. Prof. Guadalajara (Mex.) Autonomus U., 1973-76; tchr. Spanish Colegio de La Salle, Bayamón, P.R., 1980-88; prof. edn. U. Sacred Heart, Santurce, P.R., 1984-91; ednl. editor Editorial Norma, Cataño, 1991-92; chief editor Editorial Rio Ingenio, 1987-98; dir. grad. program U. Cen. Bayamon, P.R., 1998—; cons. Learn Aid, Rio Piedras, P.R., 1990-98. Author: De 13 a 19, 1969, El Paso, 1971, Tapatea, 1987, 2nd edit., 1994, Bibliografia de Literatura Puertorriqueña Para Niños, 1994; editor bull. Algo Nuevo, 1990, (software) Nos Comunicamos: K-3; contbr. articles to profl. jours. Recipient Excelsa Benjamina Assn. Autores Puertorriqueños San Juan, 1971. Mem. Internat. Reading Assn., Assn. Grads. U. P.R., Alpha Delta Kappa. Roman Catholic. Avocations: reading, stamp collecting, swimming, writing. Home: Rio Hondo 2 Ah14 Calle Rio Ingenio Bayamon PR 00961-3234 Office: Rio Ingenio Bayamon PR 00961

BERK, ALAN S., law firm executive; b. N.Y.C., May 11, 1934; s. Phil and Mae (Buchberg) B.; m. Barbara Binder, Dec. 18, 1960; children—Charles M., Peter M., Nancy M. BS in Econs., U. Pa., 1955; MS in Bus., Columbia U., 1956. CPA, 1960. Staff acct. Arthur Young & Co., N.Y.C., 1956-62; mgr., prin. Arthur Young & Co., 1962-67; sr. v.p. Avco Corp., Greenwich, Conn., 1967-75; dir. Arthur Young & Co., 1975—, ptnr., 1976—, chief fin. officer, 1979-89; nat. dir. fin., treas. Ernst & Young, 1989-92; exec. dir. Kelley, Drye & Warren, N.Y.C., 1993-94. Mem. nat. adv. group Nat. Tech. Inst. for the Deaf, Rochester, N.Y.; chmn. bd. dirs. Jewish Home for the Elderly of Fairfield County, Inc., 1997—; 1st v.p., treas. Bruce Mus., Greenwich, Conn., 1996—; trustee, treas. Fund for Peace, Washington; mem. golf bd. Town of Greenwich, Conn.. With U.S. Army, 1957. Mem. AICPA, N.Y. State Soc. CPAs, Fin. Execs. Inst., Landmark Club, Stockbridge (Mass.) Golf Club, Stockbridge Sportmen's Club, Lake Dr. Homeowner's Assn. Home: 14 Cornelia Dr Greenwich CT 06830-3906

BERK, HARLAN JOSEPH, numismatist, writer, antiquarian; b. Joliet, Ill., June 7, 1942; s. Sammy and Ruth (Press) B.; m. Ellen Landman, Sept. 20, 1966 (div. 1978); children: Aaron R., Shanna L.; m. Pamela Margaret Blade, June 22, 1982; 1 child, Sammy. Student, U. Ill., 1960-64. Vice pres. New Star Jewelers, Joliet, 1964-85; pres. Harlan J. Berk Ltd., Joliet, 1964, Chgo.; bd. dirs. OLICON Imaging Systems, Inc., Louisville; lectr., treas. N.Y. Internat. Numis. Conv.; Am. rep. Numismatica Ars Classica, Zurich. Author: Roman Gold Coins, 1985, Eastern Roman Successors, 1987, Roman Gold Coins of the Medieval World 383-1453 A.D. (Robert Friedberg award 1987), Eastern Roman Successors of the Sestertius; columnist World Coin News, 1989—, What's Old (Best Fgn. Column Numismatic Literary Guild, 1989, 90, 91, 92). Mem. exec. com. World Heritage Mus., Champaign, Ill., 1988—. Mem. Internat. Assn. Profl. Numismatists (pub. rels. for Am., chmn. 2000 internat. congress Chgo.), Profl. Numismatist Guild (edn. chmn., bd. dirs.), Am. Numismatists Assn. (dealer liaison com.). Democrat. Jewish. Avocations: art collecting, scuba diving, running, skiing, fishing. Office: 31 N Clark St Chicago IL 60602-2806

BERK, JACK EDWARD, physician, educator; b. Phila.; s. Samuel and Esther (Pill) B.; m. Adeline Elizabeth Alberts, June 26, 1937; children: Philip Howard (dec.), Richard Hanna. BA, U. Pa., 1932, MSc in Medicine, 1939, DSc in Medicine, 1943; MD, Jefferson Med. Coll., 1936; postgrad., Grad. Sch. Medicine, U. Pa., 1937-38. Diplomate Am. Bd. Internal Medicine, Am. Bd. Gastroenterology. Intern Walter Reed Gen. Hosp., Washington, 1936-37; resident in medicine No. divsn. Albert Einstein Med. Ctr., Phila., 1938-39; fellow gastroenterology Grad. Hosp., U. Pa., 1939-40; Ross V. Patterson fellow physiology Jefferson Med. Coll., Phila., 1940-41; instr. gastroenterology U. Pa., 1941-46; asst. prof. medicine Sch. Medicine, Temple U., 1946-54; asst. dir. Fels Research Inst., 1946-54; assoc. prof. clin. medicine Coll. Medicine, Wayne State U., 1954-62, prof. clin. medicine, 1962-63; prof. medicine Coll. Medicine, U. Calif., Irvine, 1963-79, Disting. prof. medicine, 1979—, chmn. dept. medicine, 1963-73, head div. gastroenterology, 1963-79, asst. dean, 1979-90; cons. VA Hosp., Long Beach, Calif., 1963-97, Cedars-Sinai Med. Ctr., 1963—, Meml. Hosp., Long Beach, 1964-97. Contbg. author: Bockus Gastroenterology, 1st and 2nd edits.; assoc. editor: Bockus Gastroenterology 3d edit., 1974, editor-in-chief 4th edit., 1985, cons. editor 5th edit., 1994; editor: Developments in Digestive Diseases, Vol. 1, 1977, Vol. 2, 1979, Vol. 3, 1980; co-editor: Gastrointestinal Symptoms: Clinical Interpretation, 1991; mem. editl. bd. 13 med. jours., 1959—; delivered 14 named lectureships; contbr. 196 articles to med. jours., 108 chpts. to more than 60 books. U.S. Dept. State rep. to S.Am. countries Cultural Exchange Program, 1961. Served to maj. M.C. AUS, 1941-46. Recipient Disting. Service award Mich. Med. Soc., 1959, Faculty Community Service award U. Calif.-Irvine Alumni Assn., 1971, also Faculty Univ. Service award, 1976, Disting. Achievement award Jefferson Med. Coll. Alumni Assn., 1977, Maimonides award Maimonides Soc., 1984, Centennial award N.E. High Sch., Phila., 1990, Disting. Univ. Svc. Aldrich award U. Calif., Irvine, 1993, Bockus medal World Orgn. Gastroenterology, 1994; named Disting. Physician Nat. Found. for Ileitis and Colitis, 1980; J. Edward Berk Lectr. established U. Calif. Irvine Gastroenterology Alumni Assn., Aug., 1991, J. Edward Berk Lectr. established U. Calif. Irvine Vol. Clin. Faculty, 1991, J. Edward Berk Alumni Med. Edn. Ctr. dedicated, May 30, 1996. Master ACP (gov. So. Calif. region II 1976-80, Laureate award So. Calif. region 1990), Am. Coll. Gastroenterology (pres. 1975-76, Rorer award 1970, 74, 78, 79, Disting. Sci. Achievement award 1982, Clin. Achievement award 1988, Samuel Weiss award 1995); mem. Am. Gastroent. Assn. (Disting. Educator award 1992), Am. Soc. Gastrointestinal Endoscopy (pres. 1958-59, Rudolf Schindler award 1966), Am. Fedn. Clin. Research (past chmn. Eastern sect.), Bockus Internat. Soc. Gastroenerology (pres. 1967-71), AMA (chmn. sect. gastroenterology 1965-66), Detroit Gastroent. Soc. (pres. 1960-61), So. Calif. Soc. Gastroenterology (pres. 1967-68), L.A. Acad. Medicine (gov. 1981-84), So. Calif. Soc. Gastrointestinal Endoscopy (hon.), Orange County Acad. Medicine, Orange County Gastroenterology Soc. (founding pres.), Interam. Gastroent. Assn. (life, hon. pres. 1981—), Sigma Xi, Alpha Omega Alpha; Acad. Med. Ecuador, Peruvian and Cuban Soc. Gastroenterology (hon.), Gastroenterology Socs. Colombia (corr.), Gastrointestinal Endoscopy Soc. Colombia (corr.), Ecuador, Venezuela and Brazilian Soc. of Gastroenterology and Nutrition, Fgn. Med. Soc. Home: 894 Ronda Sevilla # C Laguna Woods CA 92653-4748 Office: Univ Calif Irvine Med Ctr Dept of Medicine 101 The City Dr S Orange CA 92868-3201

BERK, JEREMIAH E., federal judge; b. 1941. BS, Wilkes Coll., 1963; JD, Union U., Albany, N.Y., 1966. Bar: N.Y. Ptnr. McCabe & Mack, Poughkeepsie, N.Y., 1968-80; bankruptcy judge for so. dist. N.Y., U.S. Bankruptcy Ct., Poughkeepsie, 1980%; founder, dir. Mid-Hudson Legal Svcs., Inc. Author coursebooks and manuals in field, including Consumer Bankruptcy—An Update to the General Practitioner, 1989; contbr. articles to law jours. Active Vassar Bros. Hosp. Assn., Dutchess County Soc. for Prevention Cruelty to Animals, Inc. Mem. ABA, Nat. Conf. Bankruptcy

Judges, N.Y. State Bar Assn., Dutchess County Bar Assn. Office: PO Box 1000 176 Church St Poughkeepsie NY 12601-4104

BERK, LEE ELIOT, college president. Pres. Berklee Coll. Mus., Boston, 1979—. Office: Berklee Coll Music Office of the President 1140 Boylston St Boston MA 02215-3631*

BERK, PAUL DAVID, physician, scientist, educator; b. Bklyn., Apr. 3, 1938; s. Charles and Helen (Goell) B.; m. Aviva Ancona, July 4, 1965 (div. Aug. 1990); children: Claire, Philip, Edward; m. Nicole Polak, 1991. B.A., Swarthmore Coll., 1959; cert., U. St. Andrews, Scotland, 1960; M.D., Columbia U., 1964. Diplomate Am. Bd. Internal Medicine, Am. Bd. Hematology. Intern Columbia-Presbyn. Med. Ctr., N.Y.C., 1964-65, resident, 1965-66, fellow in hematology, 1969-70; clin. assoc. metabolism br. Nat. Cancer Inst., Bethesda, Md., 1966-69; sr. investigator Nat. Cancer Inst., Bethesda, 1970-73; clin. asst. prof. medicine Georgetown U., Washington, 1971-75, clin. assoc. prof., 1975-77; chief sect. on diseases of the liver Nat. Inst. Arthritis, Metabolism and Digestive Diseases, NIH, Bethesda, 1973-77; prof. medicine Mt. Sinai Sch. Medicine, N.Y.C., 1977—, Albert and Vera List prof. medicine, 1980-89, prof. biochemistry, 1987-99, Henry and Lillian Stratton prof. molecular medicine, 1989—, chief divsn. hematology, 1977-89, acting chief, 1989-90, chief divsn. liver disease, 1989—; adj. prof. Rockefeller U., 1987-89; cons. in liver disease NIH, 1977-80, mem. adv. coun. Nat. Inst. Diabetes and Digestive and Kidney Diseases, 1990-94. Editor: (with others) Chemistry and Physiology of the Bile Pigments, 1977, Frontiers in Liver Disease, 1981, Myelofibrosis and the Biology of Connective Tissue, 1984, Hans Popper: A Tribute, 1992, Hepatic Transport and Bile Secretion, 1993, Polythemia Vera, 1994; editor-in-chief Seminars in Liver Disease, 1981-90, 96—, Hepatology, 1991-96; mem. editorial bd. Artificial Organs, 1979-92, Liver, 1980-93; contbr. articles to profl. jours. Served as sr. surgeon USPHS, 1966-69, 75-77. Recipient Merck award Columbia U., 1964; Fulbright scholar, 1959. Fellow ACP, Am. Coll. Gastroenterology; mem. Am. Soc. Clin. Investigation, Assn. Am. Physicians, Am. Assn. Study of Liver Disease (councillor 1985-93, v.p. 1988, pres. 1989), Internat. Assn. Study of Liver (councillor 1988-91), Am. Soc. for Hematology, Am. Clin. and Climatological Assn., Nat. Polychemia Vera Study Group (vice chmn. 1978-95), Soc. Exptl. Biol. Medicine (councillor 1993-96), N.Y. Soc. Study of Blood (pres. 1982-83), Sigma Xi, Phi Beta Kappa, Alpha Omega Alpha. Office: Mt Sinai Sch Medicine Box 1633 1 Gustave L Levy Pl New York NY 10029-6500

BERK, PHILIP WOOLF, journalist; b. Cape Town, South Africa, Feb. 13, 1933; came to U.S., 1952; s. Benjamin and Rebecca (Brenner) B.; m. Ruth Greenberg, June 20, 1954; children: Benjamin, Alexander, Ann, Melanie. BA, UCLA, 1955; gen. secondary life teaching credential, Calif. State U., Northridge, 1963; MA, Calif. State U., 1965. With The Argus Group, Johannesburg, South Africa, 1974-83; pres. Hollywood Fgn. Press Assn., 1989-92; internat. freelancer. Mem. Hollywood Fgn. Press Assn. (pres. 1990-92), Phi Eta Sigma. Home: 6829 Mclennan Ave Van Nuys CA 91406-4530 Office: The Argus Group, PO Box 1014, Johannesburg South Africa 2000*

BERKA, MARIANNE GUTHRIE, health and physical education educator; b. Queens, N.Y., Dec. 25, 1944; d. Frank Joseph and Mary (DePaul) Guthrie; m. Jerry George Berka, June 1, 1968; children: Katie, Keri. BS, Ithaca Coll., 1966, MS, 1968; EdD, NYU, 1990. High sch. tchr. Northport High Sch., 1966-67; full prof. health, phys. edn. and recreation Nassau Community Coll., Garden City, N.Y., 1968—; assoc. adj. prof., Hofstra U., Hempstead, N.Y., 1998—. Mem. AAHPERD, AAHPER, Assn. Women Phys. Educators N.Y. State (chpt. chmn. 1973-74, chpt. treas. 1980-84), N.Y. State Assn. Health, Phys. Edn. and Recreation (J.B. Nash scholarship com. 1983—), Am. Assn. Sex Educators, Counselors and Therapists (cert. sex educator), Am. Coll. Sports Medicine (cert. health/fitness instr.). Roman Catholic. Home: 90 Bay Way Ave Brightwaters NY 11718-2012 Office: P226 HPER Nassau Community Coll Garden City NY 11530

BERKE, AMY TURNER, health science association administrator; b. Cleve., Oct. 27, 1942; d. Elliott L. and Evelyn (Silverman) Glicksberg; m. Donald Alan Turner, Dec. 16, 1962 (div. 1979); children: Matthew, Kelli; m. Joseph Jerold Berke, June 21, 1981; children: Richard, Rachel, Jason. Student, Ohio State U., 1960-63; BS, Wayne State U., 1965, MA, 1966. Tchr. Waterford (Mich.) Sch. System, 1965-67; v.p. Apt. Referral Service, Oak Park, Mich., 1970-73; instr. Detroit Coll. Bus., Dearborn, Mich., 1975-79; exec. dir. Detroit Neurosurgical Found., 1979—. Past bd. dirs. Internat. Mus. Surg. Sci., Friends of Belle Isle; bd. dirs. Goodwill Industries Found., Alliance for Safer Greater Detroit; mem. Citizens Adv. Wayne County Youth; commr., vice chair Detroit Recreation Adv. Commn.; commr. Youth Sports and Recreation Commn. Mem. Coun. Mich. Founds., Project Pride Detroit C. of C., Wayne State U. Alumni Club, Ohio State U. Alumni Club, Coun. of Mich. Founds., Detroit Area Grantmakers. Avocations: reading, hiking, aerobics, traveling. Office: Detroit Neurosurg Found 8900 E Jefferson Ste 1117 Detroit MI 48214-2961

BERKE, IRVING, obstetrician-gynecologist, military officer; b. Bklyn., June 21, 1924; s. Abraham and Adela (Soffer) Berkowitz; m. Ruth E. Miller, Dec. 28, 1947 (dec. Feb. 1996); children: David, Laura, Nancy. Student, U. Wis., 1943; MD, Case Western Res. U., 1949. Cert. in obstetrics and gynecology; recert. Commd. 1st lt. U.S. Army, 1949, advanced through grades to col., 1972; ret., 1984; med. officer U.S. Army M.C., 1949-56; pvt. practice Youngstown, Ohio, 1956-63; med. officer USAR, Youngstown and L.A., 1956-84; pvt. practice Long Beach, Calif., 1963-83; physician Long Beach Dept. Health and Human Svcs., 1992—; med. advisor Calif. Blue Shield, L.A., 1967-73, Med. Bd. Calif., L.A., 1985-93; expert witness in ob-gyn., L.A., 1985—; asst. clin. prof. ob-gyn. Sch. Medicine, U. Calif., Irvine, 1977-83. Fellow ACOG, Internat. Coll. Surgeons; mem. Am. Acad. Anti Aging Medicine. Avocations: tennis, jogging, alternative medicine. Home and Office: 6430 E Mantova St Long Beach CA 90815-4658

BERKE, SARAH BALLARD, geriatrics nurse, mental health nurse; b. Bethesda, Md., Feb. 21, 1951; d. Edward B. and Pauline C. (Lowery) Ballard; divorced; children: Nathan M., Adam B. Diploma in nursing, Forsyth Hosp., 1974. RN, N.Mex., Tex. Acting unit dir. N.Mex. State Hosp., Las Vegas, 1976-78; head nurse adult unit U. N.Mex. Mental Health Ctr., Albuquerque, 1986-87; day charge nurse Americare Rio Rancho, N.Mex., 1987-89, St. Joseph West Mesa Hosp., Albuquerque, 1989-90; traveling nurse Rio Rancho, 1990-92; dir. clin. svcs. Kimberly Quality Care, Midland, Tex., 1992-93; DON Glenwood Psychiat. Hosp., Midland, 1993-95, Terrace West Nursing Ctr., Midland, 1995-98, Meadowbrook Terr. of Davie, Advance, N.C., 1998-99, In Home Care, Winston-Salem, N.C., 1999—.

BERKEBILE, CHARLES ALAN, geology educator, hydrogeology researcher; b. Queens, N.Y., Mar. 4, 1938; s. Charles Dean and Bernice (Manlove) B.; m. Jeanne Marie Kleypas, Oct. 21, 1994; children: Patricia Berlowe, Gregory Martin. BS, Allegheny Coll., 1960; MA, Boston U., 1961, PhD, 1964. Mem. rsch. staff MIT, Cambridge, 1963-64; asst. prof. Southampton (N.Y.) Coll. L.I. U., 1964-67, assoc. prof., dept. chair Southampton (N.Y.) Coll., 1969-75, prof., assoc. dir. Southampton (N.Y.) Coll., 1975-81; rsch. mineralogist Corning (N.Y.) Glass Works, 1967-69; prof., dept. chair Corpus Christi (Tex.) State U., 1981-91; prof., dir. Tex. A&M U., Corpus Christi, 1991-94, prof., asst. dean, 1994-98; vis. assoc. chemist Brookhaven Nat. Lab., Upton, N.Y., 1966-67; vis. sr. rsch. geologist Princeton (N.J.) U., 1979-80. Contbr. articles to profl. jours. Mem. Regional Stormwater Master Plan Adv. Com., Corpus Christi, 1989-90, Mayor's Adv. Com. on Water Issues, Corpus Christi, 1991-92; treas., bd. dirs. Rockport (Tex.) Country Club Estates Homeowners Assn., 1991-94. Fellow Geol. Soc. Am.; mem. Assn. Ground Water Scientists and Engrs., Nat. Ground Water Assn., Nat. Assn. Geology Tchrs., Tex. Ground Water Assn. (bd. dirs. 1990—, v.p. ground water sci. 1994, pres. 1995-96), Corpus Christi Geol. Soc. Avocations: golf, music. Home: 314 Champions Dr Rockport TX 78382-6906 Office: Tex A&M U 6300 Ocean Dr Corpus Christi TX 78412-5503

BERKELEY, BETTY LIFE, gerontology educator; b. St. Louis, May 25, 1924; d. James Alfred and Anna Laura (Voltmer) Life; m. Marvin Harold Berkeley, Feb. 7, 1947; children: Kathryn Elizabeth, Barbara Ellen, Brian Harrison, Janet Lynn. AB, Harris Tchrs. Coll., 1947; MA in Ednl. Adminstrn., Washington U., St. Louis, 1951; PhD, U. North Tex., 1980. Tchr. St. Louis pub. schs., 1946-48, Clayton pub. schs., Mo., 1948-49, Lamplighter Pvt. Sch., Dallas, 1964-67; program devel. specialist Richland Coll., Dallas, 1980-84, instr., 1981—; adj. prof. U. North Tex., Denton, 1981—, cons. Sch. Cmty. Svcs. Ctr. for Studies on Aging, 1981—; pres. Retirement Planning Svcs., Dallas, 1984—. Contbr. articles to profl. jours. Named Outstanding Alumna Coll. of Edn. U. of North Tex., 1992. Mem. Dallas Commn. on Status of Women, 1975-79; bd. dirs. Dallas Municipal Library, 1979-83, Sr. Citizen Greater Dallas, 1986-92; bd. dirs. Council on Adult Ministry Lovers Lane United Meth. Ch., 1982, trustee, 1997—; charter mem. bd. dirs., life mem. Friends of U. North Tex. Libr.; mem. Pres.'s Coun. U. North Tex., mem. vol. mgmt. edn. task force, 1978-82. Mem. AAUW (pres. 1973-75; Outstanding Woman of Tex. 1981). Club: Women's Council of Dallas County (v.p. 1977-79). Avocations: travel, cooking, gardening, needlework. Home and Office: 13958 Hughes Ln Dallas TX 75240-3510

BERKELEY, EDMUND, JR., retired archivist, educator; b. Charlottesville, Va., Apr. 1, 1937; s. Edmund and Dorothy A. Berkeley; m. Elizabeth Makaritis, June 9, 1963; children: Maria Randolph, Edmund III. BA, U. South, 1958; MA in Am. History, U. Va., 1961. Prep. sch. tchr., 1961-63; asst. archivist Archives divsn. Va. State Libr., 1963-65; sr. asst., curator Manuscripts divsn. U. Va., Charlottesville, 1965-69; univ. archivist Manuscripts divsn. U. Va., 1976-87, curator manuscripts, 1970-87, records adminstr., 1976-99; dir. spl. collections dept., 1987-93, sr. curator, 1994, univ. archivist, sr. assoc. dir., 1995-99; assoc. prof. Coll. Arts and Scis., 1976-99, ret., 1999; cons. U. Ga. Library, George C. Marshall Library, SUNY-Stony Brook. Nat. Hist. Publs. Editor: Autographs and Manuscripts: A Collector's Manual, 1978; author, editor articles to profl. jours. Commn. grantee Dept. Edn. Fellow Soc. Am. Archivists (coun. 1977-81); mem. Soc. Am. Architects, Mid-Atlantic Regional Archives Conf., Assn. Documentary Editing, Mid-west Archives Conf., Soc., Ga. Archivists, Va. Hist. Soc. Episcopalian. Home: 2403 Bennington Rd Charlottesville VA 22901-2205

BERKELEY, ELIZABETH, actress; b. Detroit, July 28, 1972. Appeared in films Molly & Gina, 1993, Armitage III (voice), 1994, White Wolves II: Legend of the Wild, 1995, Showgirls, 1995, The First Wives Club, 1996, the Real Blonde, 1997, The Tax Man, 1998, Random Encounter, 1998, Last Call, 1998, Last Call, 1998, Cross Country, 1998, (tv series) Saved By The Bell. Office: United Talent Agy 9560 Wilshire Blvd Fl 5 Beverly Hills CA 90212-2400*

BERKELEY, FRANCIS LEWIS, JR., retired archivist; b. Albemarle County, Va., Apr. 9, 1911; s. Francis Lewis and Ethel (Crissey) B.; B.S., U. Va., 1934, M.A., 1940; m. Helen Wayland Sutherland, June 12, 1937. Tchr. Va. pub. schs., 1934-38; curator manuscripts U. Va. Library, Charlottesville, 1938-41, curator and univ. archivist, 1946-63, asso. librarian, 1957-63, sec. of Rector and Visitors, 1953-58, exec. asst. to pres., 1963-74, archivist emeritus, prof. emeritus, 1974—; council Inst. Early Am. History and Culture. Fulbright research fellow U. Edinburgh, 1952-53; Guggenheim fellow U. London, 1961-62; sec. of navy adv. com. on naval history, 1958-74. Trustee Thomas Jefferson Meml. Found.; mem. adv. com. Papers of Thomas Jefferson, Papers of James Madison, Papers of George Washington; mem. Va. Com. on Colonial Records, 1955-71, Va. Commn. on Hist. Records, 1976—. Served with USNR, 1942-46; capt. ret. Fellow Soc. Am. Archivists; mem. Am. Antiquarian Soc., Mass., Va., (v.p. 1970-78, trustee 1979—), other hist. socs., Colonial Soc. Mass., Walpole Soc., Raven Soc., Phi Beta Kappa, Omicron Delta Kappa. Democrat. Episcopalian. Clubs: Colonnade (Charlottesville); Century (N.Y.). Editor and compiler: Dunmore's Proclamation of Emancipation, 1941; Annual Reports on Historical Collections, University of Virginia Library, 1945-50, with cumulative indexes, 1945, 50; Jefferson Papers of the University of Virginia, 1950; Papers of John Randolph of Roanoke, 1950; John Rolfe's True Relation. 1951; Introduction to Thomas Jefferson's Farm Book, 1953. Editorial bd. Va. Quar. Rev., 1961-74. Contbr. to Dictionary of Biography, Ency. Brit., Collier's Nat. Am. Cyclopedia; other reference works. Home: 2610 Barracks Rd Apt H226 Charlottesville VA 22901-2121

BERKELEY, MARVIN H., management educator, former university dean; b. St. Louis, Oct. 22, 1922; m. Betty L. Berkeley, Feb. 7, 1947; children: Kathryn Morton, Barbara Dietz, Janet Pittman, Brian Berkeley. BA, Harris Tchrs. Coll., 1944; AB, Washington U., St. Louis, 1947, PhD, 1952. Research psychologist Personnel Research Lab., San Antonio, 1951-54; dir. research White-Rodgers Co., St. Louis, 1954-57; personnel dir. to corp. personnel dir. Tex. Instruments, Dallas, 1957-73; dean Coll. Bus. U. North Tex., Denton, 1973-83; prof. U. North Tex., 1983—; bd. dirs. Irving Nat. Bancshare, United Micronesian Devel. Assn.; v.p. bd. Tex. Instruments Found., 1969-73; adv. bd. Nat. Inst. for Work and Learning, 1973-79, Fed. Exec. Inst., 1968; mem. Commn. on Career Advancement in Fed. Svc., 1967-68. pres. bd. edn. Dallas Ind. Sch. Dist., 1967-73; chmn. S.W. Regional Panel White House Fellows, 1968-70; bd. dirs. Dallas Symphony Orch., 1968-72; mem. Tex. Urban Devel. Commn., 1970-72; chmn. adminstrv. bd. Lover's Lane United Methodist Ch., 1963-65; bd. dirs., past pres. Mental Health Assn. Dallas County, Dallas Council on Alcoholism; mem. exec. com. Big City Bds. of Edn. 1969-73; co-founder, chmn. Tex. Council of Maj. Sch. Dists., 1968-71. Served to lt. (j.G.) USNR, 1943-46. Mem. Tex. Coun. Collegiate Edn. for Bus. (past pres. 1980), Southwestern Bus. Adminstrn. Assn. (past pres. 1981), Chief Exec. Round Table (bd. dirs. 1983-93), Sigma Xi, Beta Alpha Psi, Beta Gamma Sigma. Home: 13958 Hughes Ln Dallas TX 75240-3510

BERKELEY, SEAMUS OSBORNE, artist, consultant; b. Mar. 26, 1955. BA, Salem State Coll. Freelance artist Estes Park, Colo., cons. E-mail: seamus@sbart.com. Home and Studio: 1795 Moon Trailway Estes Park CO 80517

BERKELHAMER, JAY ELLIS, pediatrician; b. Tuscaloosa, Ala., Apr. 8, 1942; s. Louis H. and Belle F. B.; m. Jacqueline Beth Colman, June 12, 1966; children: Beth Carolyn, Sara Kay, Adam Colman. BS, U. Mich., 1963, MD, 1967. Resident U. Chgo., 1967-70, asst. prof., 1972-78, assoc. prof., 1978-84, prof., 1984-93, assoc. chair, dir. residency program, 1986-93, assoc. dean ambulatory care, 1983-88; chair pediatrics Henry Ford Health Sys., Detroit, 1993—; prof. pediatrics Case Western Res. U., Cleve., 1994—; clin. prof. pediatrics and communicable diseases U. Mich., Ann Arbor, 1994—. Lt. comdr. USPHS, 1970-72. Robert Wood Johnson Health Policy fellow NAS, Washington, 1978-79. Mem. Am. Acad. Pediatrics (pres. Ill. chpt. 1992), Chgo. Pediatric Soc. (pres. 1987, Archibald L. Hoyne award 1993), Ambulatory Pediatric Assn. (pres. 1986). Office: Henry Ford Health Sys 2799 W Grand Blvd Detroit MI 48202-2608

BERKELMAN, KARL, physics educator; b. Lewiston, Maine, June 7, 1933; s. Robert George and Yvonne (Langlois) B.; m. Mary Bowen Hobbie, Oct. 10, 1959; children: Thomas, James, Peter. BS, U. Rochester, N.Y., 1955; PhD, Cornell U., 1959. From asst. prof. to prof. physics Cornell U., Ithaca, N.Y., 1961—, dir. lab. nuclear studies, 1985—; sci. assoc. DESY, Hamburg, Fed. Republic of Germany, 1974-75, CERN, Geneva, 1967-68, 81-82, 91-92. Office: Cornell U Newman Lab Nuclear Studies Ithaca NY 14853

BERKENKAMP, FRED JULIUS, management consultant; b. Alma, Wis., Oct. 19, 1925; s. Julius Henry and Elisabeth Helen Berkenkamp; m. Ruth Ethelyn Taylor; children: Linda Birch, Vicki Fitzgerald, Thomas, JoAnne. B.S. in Electron Engring, U. Wyo., 1948; postgrad., U. Syracuse, N.Y., 1951. Quality control mgmt. Gen. Electric Co., Syracuse, 1948-55; corporate cons. mfg. mgmt. Gen. Electric Co., N.Y.C., 1955-65; mgr. planning jet engines Gen. Electric Co., Cin., 1966-68; mgr. nuclear fuels mfg. Gen. Electric Co., Wilmington, N.C., 1969; corp. exec. v.p., pres. Appliance Group, Roper Corp., Kankakee, Ill., 1970-80; pres., chief exec. officer, dir. Allied Structural Steel Co. subs. MSL Industries/Alleghany Corp., Chicago Heights, Ill., 1980-83; pres. Berkenkamp & Co. Inc., mgmt. cons., 1984—; pres., CEO FMH, Inc., Newport Beach, Calif., 1988-91. Trustee Community Coll., 1974-80. Served with USNR, 1944-46. Mem. Assn. Home Appliance Mfrs. (chmn. bd. dirs.), Gas Appliance Mfrs. Assn. (dir.), Sigma Chi. Home: 19815 N Alta Loma Dr Sun City West AZ 85375-5570

BERKENSTADT, JAMES ALLAN, lawyer; b. Chgo., June 26, 1956; s. Edward Jules and Lois Marion (Solomon) B.; m. Holly Lynn Cremer, Aug. 3, 1985; children: Rebecca, Bradley. BA, Northwestern U., 1978; JD, So. Ill. U., 1981. Bar: Ill., Wis. Litigation atty. Pollina & Phelan, Chgo., 1982-85; atty. for security dept. Chgo. Cubs Nat. League Ball Club, Chgo., 1982-84; litigation atty. Axley & Brynelson, Madison, Wis., 1986-87; v.p., corporate counsel The Wisconsin Cheeseman, Inc., Madison, 1987—. Author: Black Market Beatles: The Story Behind The Lost Recordings, 1995, Nevermind: Nirvana, 1998; prodr. The Beatle Tapes CD, 1994, 96, 97, The Best of the Big Bands CD, 1998; contbr. articles to Musician mag. Bd. dirs. Cremer Charitable Found., Madison, 1989—. Mem. NARAS. Avocations: racquetball, golf, music archivist, writer. Office: The Wisconsin Cheeseman Inc 301 Broadway Dr Sun Prairie WI 53590-1799

BERKEY, DENNIS D., mathematics educator; b. Wooster, Ohio, May 27, 1947; s. William Bruce and Mary Louise (Schrock) B.; m. Catherine Grooms, Aug. 24, 1974; children: Cristin, Aaron, Jessica. BA, Muskingum Coll., New Concord, Ohio, 1969; MA, Miami U., Oxford, Ohio, 1971; PhD, U. Cin., 1974. Lectr. U. Cin., 1972-73; instr. Miami U., Oxford, Ohio, 1973-74; asst. prof. math. Boston U., 1974-79, assoc. prof. math., 1979-93, prof. Math., 1993—, dean grad. sch., 1987—, dean arts and scis., 1987—, provost, 1987-91, 96—. Author: Calculus, 1983, 3d ecit., 1992, Applied Calculus, 1986, 3d edit., 1994, Calculus for Management, 1986, 3d edit., 1994. Recipient Metcalf Award for Excellence in Teaching, Boston U., 1978. Mem. Am. Math. Soc., Math. Assn. Am., Soc. for Indsl. and Applied Math. Home: 30 Nobscot Rd Weston MA 02493-1147 Office: Boston U Coll Arts and Scis Rm CLA 106 Boston MA 02215

BERKEY, DOUGLAS BRYAN, dental educator, researcher, gerontologist, clinician; b. L.A., Apr. 24, 1949; s. Harvey Garfield and Sytha Jean (Roberts) B.; m. Gail Jo Harmon, Aug. 4, 1972; children: Bryan, Lori, Kristen, Tyler. DMD, U. Louisville, 1977; MPH in Dental Pub. Health, U. Minn., 1981, MS in Oral Health Svcs. for Older Adults, 1983. Dir. postdoctoral geriat. fellowship programs VA Med. Ctr., Denver, 1985-87, Rocky Mountain coord. geriat. dental programs, 1985-87; dental dir. HHS geriat. tng. grant U. Colo. Health Scis. Ctr., Denver, 1988-95, assoc. dir. for dental area health edn. ctr., 1990-93, 96—, assoc. dir. for dental geriat. edn. ctr., 1991—; dir. advanced edn. in gen. dentistry programs U. Colo. Sch. Dentistry, Denver, 1991-93, chair dept. applied dentistry, 1992—. Mem. internat. editl. bd. (manuscripts) Gerodontology, 1997; author of monographs and manuscripts. Various leadership positions Boy Scout Am., Minn., Idaho and Colo., 1977—; cons. Ariz. Dept. Health Svcs., 1986—; reviewer, referee Am. Fund for Dental Health, Ill., 1990-95; mem. external adv. bd. Cmty. Oriented Dental Edn. (CODE), N.J., 1995-96. USPHS scholar, Mpls., 1980-81; Pew Nat. Dental Leadership fellow Pew Charitable Trusts, Phila., 1991-92, finalist for W.J. Fulbright Scholar, 1995. Mem. ADA (spkrs. bur. 1990-93, del. JCAHO, 1995—, 98, Prof. of Yr. Rocky Mtn. Study Club 1998), Internat. Assn. for Dental Rsch. (pres. geriat. oral rsch. group 1990), Gerontol. Soc. Am., Am. Soc. for Geriat. Dentistry (bd. dirs. 1985-91), Am. Assn. Dental Schs. (del. coun. faculties 1996—), Am. Assn. Pub. Health Dentistry, Internat. Dental Fedn. (chair-elect gerondontology sect. 1997-98), Phi Kappa Phi. Mem. LDS Ch. Avocations: bicycling, running, water sports. Office: U Colo Sch Dentistry 4200 E 9th Ave # C-284 Denver CO 80220-3706

BERKHOFER, ROBERT FREDERICK, JR., retired history educator; b. Teaneck, N.J., Nov. 20, 1931; s. Robert Frederick and Elsa Berkhofer; m. Genevieve Patricia Zito, June 9, 1962; 1 child, Robert Frederick III. BA, SUNY, Albany, 1953; MA, Cornell U., 1955, PhD, 1960. Instr. Ohio State U., Columbus, 1959-60; instr., asst. prof. U. Minn., Mpls., 1960-69; prof. U. Wis., Madison, 1969-73, U. Mich., Ann Arbor, 1973-91; grad. rsch. prof. U. Fla., Gainesville, 1984-85; prof. history U. Calif., Santa Cruz, 1991-97; ret., 1997. Author: Salvation and the Savage, 1965, A Behavioral Approach to Historical Analysis, 1969, The White Man's Indian, 1978, Beyond the Great Story, 1995. Recipient fellowships Social Sci. Rsch. Coun., 1957-59, Nat. Endowment for Humanities, 1973-74, John Simon Guggenheim Found., 1978-79, Stanford Humanities Ctr., 1987-88. Mem. Am. Studies Assn. (pres. 1980-82), Orgn. Am. Historians (exec. bd. 1981-84), Am. Hist. Assn.

BERKHOLTZ, NICHOLAS EVALD, engineering manager, consultant; b. Majori, Riga Beach, Latvia, Apr. 19, 1928; came to U.S., 1952; s. Gordian and Irmgard Rosalie (Hirv) B.; m. Elga Olita Martinsons, July 4, 1957; children: Karin Rana, Ingrid Maija. BS in Gen. Engring., Iowa State U., 1956; MS in Indsl. Mgmt., U. Minn., 1963, postgrad., 1963-67. Profl. engr., Minn., Calif. Adminstrv. svcs. officer UN-IRO, Augsburg, Bavaria, 1949-51; interpreter CIC U.S. Army, ETO, 1951-52; engr. Mpls.-Honeywell Regulator Co., Mpls., 1956-75; cons. engr. Stetter Assocs., Inc., Menlo Park, Calif., 1975-77; project engr. Honeywell Inc., New Brighton, Minn., 1977-79; translation mgr. Honeywell Inc., Edina, Minn., 1979-81; supr. Proving Ground Honeywell Inc., Elk River, Minn., 1981-84; program mgr. Honeywell Inc., Mpls., 1984-87; engring. supr. Alliant Techsystems Inc., Elk River, 1987-90, mgr., 1990-92. Author: (monographs) Standards for Management Control, 1963, Evolution of the Shaped Charge, 1985; originator recognition program 7 Wonders of Engring. in Minn., 1963. Pres. Christ Latvian Ch., Mpls., 1976-82, 97-99, Mean Old Men's Club, Mpls., 1973; found. The Baltic Caucus, Mpls., 1989. Fellow ASME (life, bd. dirs. Minn. sect. 1984-92, mem. bd. profl. practice and ethics 1992-97, mem. gen. awards com. 1988-94, 97—, mem. nat. nominating com. 1993-96, hons. awards com. 1997—, Quarter Century award 1986, Dedicated Svc. award 1997); mem. AIAA, Minn. Soc. Profl. Engrs. (life), U.S. Naval Inst. (life, Silver Mem. 1995), Assn. Latvian Engrs. (Can.), Friends of Immigration History Rsch. Ctr. (dir. 1989-91), Assn. for Advancement Baltic Studies (life), Am. Latvian Assn. (life, gold mem. 1989), Latvian Press Soc., Am. Def. Preparedness Assn./Nat. Def. Indsl. Assn. (life), Minn. Fedn. Engring. Socs. (sec.-treas. 1995—), Tau Beta Pi (life). Lutheran.

BERKLEY, EMILY CAROLAN, lawyer; b. Richmond, Va., Mar. 2, 1950; d. Charles Garvice and Edna Gray (Berkley) Broom; m. Richard E. Bird, Sept. 6, 1969 (div. Mar. 1988); children: Jessica A. Bird, Martel J. Bird. Student, Coll. of William and Mary, 1968-70; BS in Psychology cum laude, Tufts U., 1972; JD magna cum laude, Temple U., 1977. Ptnr. Ballard Spahr Andrews & Ingersoll LLP, Phila., 1977—; seminar panelist Pa. Bar Inst., 1992, 98, Practicing Law Inst., 1993, 94, 95, 96, 97, 98, 99. Mem. long range planning com. Performing Arts for Tredyffrin-Easttown Sch. Dist., Berwyn, Pa., 1989, chair subcom. on creativity, futures com., 1990; active United Way, 1989-91; bd. dirs. Devon-Strafford Little League, 1992-95. Fellow Am. Bar Found.; mem. ABA (mem. com. on legal opinions, mem. Uniform Comml. Code com., chair task force on exportation of Uniform Comml. Code 1995-97, vice chair internat. comml. law subcom. 1997—, bus. law sect. liaison to U.S. Sec. of State's adv. Com. on Pvt. Internat. Law 1998—, mem. comml. fin. svcs. com., vice chmn. interest and usury subcom. 1989-93, panelist satellite seminar fundamentals of asset based financing 1990, instr. Ctrl. and Ea. European law initiative 1993, internat. law sect.), Am. Coll. Comml. Fin. Lawyers (mem. bd. regents 1993—, pres.-elect 1999), Am. Law Inst., Pa. Bar Assn. (mem. steering com., legal opinions drafting group, mem. real estate opinion project, chair Article 9 com. bus. law sect.), Phila. Bar Assn., N.Y. TriBar Opinion Com. Office: Ballard Spahr Andrews et al 1735 Market St Ste 5100 Philadelphia PA 19103-7599

BERKLEY, EUGENE BERTRAM (BERT BERKLEY), envelope company executive; b. Kansas City, Mo., May 8, 1923; s. Eugene Bertram (Bert) Berkowitz and Caroline Newman (Newburger) B.; m. Joan Meinrath, Sept. 1, 1948; children: Janet Lynn Berkley Dubrava, William (Bill) Spencer, Jane Ellen Berkley Levitt. BA, Duke U., 1948; MBA, Harvard U., 1950. Pres., CEO Tension Envelope Corp., Kansas City, Mo., 1962-88, chmn. bd., 1967—. Bd. dirs. The Reference Press, TravelFest, The Inst. for Ednl. Leadership, Inc., Washington. Trustee, chmn. U. Kansas City, 1983-85 , vice chmn., 1981-83, North Campus Devel. Com., policy bd., charter mem. Univ. Assocs.; chmn. bd. dirs. Minority Supplier Coun., 1986-88, Ewing Marion Kauffman Found., Ctr. for Entrepreneurial Leadership, 1991; chmn. Ctr. for Bus. Innovation, 1987-89; bd. dirs. Nat. Youth Info. Network, 1997—; mem. adv. bd. Nat. Coun. Econ. Edn., 1993-95, human resources com. Heart of Am. United Way, 1983, chmn. Comprehensive Needs and Svc. Survey Com., 1971; pres. Civic Coun. of Greater Kansas City, 1967-68, charter mem., bd. dirs. 1982-83; pres. C. of C. of Greater Kansas City, 1968-69; bd. dirs. Menorah Med. Ctr. Bd., 1980-94; mem. Kitchen Cabinet, Kansas City, Mo. Sch. Dist, 1990-92; chmn. adv. com., bd. dirs. Ctr. for Workplace Preparation, U.S. C. of C., 1989—; trustee Midwest Rsch. Inst., exec. com., 1969-72; bd. dirs. Kansas City Area Health Planning Coun., Inc., 1982-83, Nat. Minority Supplier Devel. Coun. 1989—, Mid-Am. Coalition on Health Care;

chmn. bd. dirs. Human Svcs. Testing and Retng. Coun., 1983-90; active Bus. Roundtable Dept. Social Svcs. State of Mo., 1989—; adv. bd. U. Kans. Natural History Mus., 1994—, Nat. Parks and Conservation Assn., 1986—; bd. dirs. Can. Cellulose Co., Vancouver, BC, 1973-80, founder, LINC, 1992; chmn. local investment commn. LINC Mo. Dept. Social Svcs., 1992-95, exec. comm., 1992—, Eddie Jacobson Meml. Found.; mem. exec. com. Ctr. for Mgmt. Assistance, 1980-83; mem. Mayor's Prayer Breakfast Com., 1964-84; mem. exec. com., met. chmn. Nat. Alliance of Businessmen of Met. Kansas City, 1973; bd. govs. Am. Royal Assn., 1971-90; chmn. bd. dirs. Johnson Country Library, 1979-80; bd. dirs. Kansas City Minority Bus. Capital Corp., 1989—; mem. exec. coun. Am. Jewish Com., 1979-89, bd. dirs. Kansas City chpt., chmn., 1958-61; vice chmn. Jewish Fedn. and Coun. of Greater Kansas City, 1964, gen. chmn. campaign, 1961. 1st lt. AUS, 1943-46; 1950-52, PTO. Decorated Bronze Star; recipient Brotherhood award NCCJ, 1968, numerous other awards, including Mr. Kansas City award C. of C. of Greater Kansas City, 1972; Disting. Svc. award Johnson County Friends of the Library (Johnson County, Kans.), 1982; bd. dirs. NCCJ, 1956-74, chmn. citation dinner, 1972, sec., adv. com. to bd. dirs., 1981-89. Mem. Envelope Mfrs. Assn. (exec. com. 1960-63, 67-70, 76-79, vice chmn. exec. com. 1981-83, v.p. 1981-83, pres. 1983-85), Flexographic Tech. Assn. (bd. dir. 1993—). Clubs: Oakwood Country, Homestead Country. Patentee in field. Avocation: flyfishing, rafting, camping, white water rafting, backpacking. Office: Tension Envelope Corp 819 E 19th St Kansas City MO 64108-1781*

BERKLEY, GARY LEE, newspaper publisher; b. Omaha, Jan. 14, 1943; s. Dale Kenneth and Mildred Fern (Little) B.; m. M. Allison Brown, Dec. 28, 1960; children: Todd, Susan Berkley Markle, Jennifer. BA, U. Nebr., Omaha, 1968. Omaha br. mgr. computer sales and svc. Mohawk Data Scis., 1968-70; Chgo. br. mgr. Data Action Corp., 1970-72; v.p. mktg. Suburban Newspaper and Directory Group Sun Newspapers, Mpls., 1972-77; v.p. mktg. Belleville (Ill.) News-Democrat, 1978-87, pres., pub., 1987—. Bd. dirs. St. Louis Regional Commerce and Growth Assn., United Way of Greater St. Louis, Leadership Coun. Southwestern Ill.; mem. exec. com. Belleville Econ. Progress; bd. trustees McKendree Coll.; mem. adv. bd. Okaw Valley coun. Boy Scouts Am.; mem. adv. bd. Big Bros./Big Sisters; bd. dirs. So. Ill. U.-Edwardsville Found., Southwestern Ill. Devel. Authority; mem. Belle-Scott Com. Recipient award of merit St. Louis Urban League, 1991, Disting. Citizen award Mil. Airlift Command USAF, Human Dignity award YWCA, 1993, Disting. Svc. awrd So. Ill. U., 1995, Outstanding Svc. award Belleville Area Coll., 1995. Mem. Nat. Newspaper Assn., Ill. Press Assn., Inland Press Assn., St. Clair Country Club, Rotary. Avocations: family, photography, fiction, politics, golf. Office: Belleville News-Democrat 120 S Illinois St Belleville IL 62222-2130*

BERKLEY, JAMES DONALD, clergyman; b. Yakima, Wash., May 19, 1950; s. Donald William and Erma Ercile (Van Meter) B.; m. Deborah Milam, Aug. 18, 1974; children: Peter James, Mary Milam. BS, U. Wash., 1972; MDiv, Fuller Theol. Seminary, 1975, D Ministry, 1980. Intern First Presbyn. Ch., Yakima, Wash., 1971-73, Bel Air Presbyn. Ch., L.A., 1973-75; asst. pastor Community Presbyn Ch., Ventura, Calif., 1975-78; sr. pastor Dixon (Calif.) Community Ch., 1978-85; sr. assoc. editor Leadership jour. Christianity Today Inc., Carol Stream, Ill., 1985-90, editor Your Church, 1990-94; sr. assoc. pastor First Presbyn. Ch., Bellevue, Wash., 1994—. Author: Making the Most of Mistakes, 1987, Called into Crisis, 1988; gen. editor: Preaching to Convince, 1986, Leadership Handbooks of Practical Theology, Vol. I, 1992, Vols. II and III, 1994. Recipient 1st place award interview Evangelical Press Assn., 1991, 92. Republican. Avocations: bagpipes, hiking, tennis, golf, music. Home: 304 128th Ave NE Bellevue WA 98005-3242 Office: First Presbyn Ch 1717 Bellevue Way NE Bellevue WA 98004-2853

BERKLEY, PETER LEE, lawyer; b. Newark, Mar. 10, 1939; s. Irving S. and Goldie A. (Karp) B.; m. Nancy R. Margolis, Aug. 2, 1964; children: James, Alison, John. BA, Williams Coll., 1960; JD, Harvard U., 1963. Bar: N.J. 1963, U.S. Dist. Ct. N.J. 1963. Assoc. Riker, Danzig, Scherer & Brown, Newark, 1963-68; ptnr. Riker, Danzig, Scherer & Hyland, Newark and Morristown, N.J., 1969-83; mng. ptnr. Riker, Danzig, Scherer, Hyland & Perretti, Morristown, 1984-95, ptnr., 1996-99, of counsel, 1999—. Trustee Livingston (N.J.) Symphony Orch., 1975-89. Mem. ABA, N.J. State Bar Assn., Am. Coll. Real Estate Lawyers, Harvard Law Sch. Alumni Assn. N.J. (pres. 1980-81), Williams Coll. Alumni Assn. Ctrl. N.J. (pres. 1986-89), Phi Beta Kappa. E-mail: pberkley@riker.com. Home: 16 Fordham Rd Livingston NJ 07039-5507 Office: Riker Danzig Scherer Hyland & Perretti Hdqrs Plz 1 Speedwell Ave Morristown NJ 07962-1981

BERKLEY, SHELLEY, congresswoman; b. N.Y.C., Jan. 20, 1951. BA, U. NEv., 1972; JD, U. San Diego, 1976. Mem. 106th Congress from 1st Nev. dist., 1999—. mem. ho. com. on transp. and infrastructure, ho. com. on vet. affairs, Dem. Caucus (Freshman vp). Office: 1505 Longworth House Office Bldg Washington DC 20515 also: 2340 Paseo Del Prado Ste D 106 Las Vegas NV 89102*

BERKLEY, STEPHEN MARK, computer peripherals manufacturing company executive; b. N.J., 1944; s. Irving S. and Goldie A. Berkley; children: David, Michael; children: David, Michael. Student, London Sch. Econs., 1964-65; BA in Econs., Colgate U., 1966; MBA, Harvard U., 1968. Mgmt. cons. Boston Cons. Group, 1968, 71-73; mgr. strategic planning Potlatch Corp., 1973-77; v.p. bus. devel. Qume Corp. subs. ITT, Hayward, Calif., 1977-80; v.p., gen. mgr. memory products divs. Qume Corp. subs. ITT, Hayward, 1980-81; v.p. mktg. Quantum Corp., Milpitas, Calif., 1981-83; chmn., CEO Quantum Corp., Milpitas, 1987-92, chmn., 1992-93, 95-98; pres. Plus Devel. Corp. (Quantum subs.), 1983-87, chmn., CEO, 1987-92; pres. The Rosewood Found., 1991—; bd. dirs. Quantum Corp., Edify Corp., Coactive Computing Corp.; instr. bus. and econs. E. Carolina U., 1969-71. Served to lt. USNR, 1968-71. Mem. Corp. Planners Assn. (dir.), Harvard Bus. Sch. Club No. Calif., Los Altos Golf and Country Club, Phi Beta Kappa. Avocations: golf, modern art, travel. Office: Quantum Corp 500 McCarthy Blvd Milpitas CA 95035-7909

BERKLEY, WILLIAM ROBERT, insurance holding company executive; b. Oct. 31, 1945; m. Marjorie Adnepos, June 19, 1971; children: Lisa A., W. Robert Jr., Lauren E. BS, NYU, 1966; MBA, Harvard U., 1968. Founder, chmn., chief exec. officer W. R. Berkley Corp., 1967—; chmn. Pioneer Cos. Inc., The Greenwich Bank & Trust Co., Westport Nat. Bank; bd. dirs. Strategic Distbn., Inc., Middlesex Bank & Trust Co. Mem. bd. overseers Stern Sch. Bus., NYU; trustee NYU, Georgetown U.; vice chmn. U. Conn. Office: W R Berkley Corp PO Box 2518 165 Mason St Greenwich CT 06830-6608 also: Pioneer Cos Inc 700 Louisiana St Houston TX 77002-2700

BERKMAN, CLAIRE FLEET, psychologist; b. New Orleans, Dec. 5, 1942; d. Joel and Margaret Grace (Fishler) Fleet; m. Arnold Stephen Berkman, Apr. 27, 1975; children: Janna Samantha, Micah Seth Siegel. BA, Boston U., 1964; EdM, Harvard U., 1966; EdD, Boston U., 1970. Asst. prof. Counseling Ctr., Mich. State U., East Lansing, 1971-75, assoc. prof., 1975-78, assoc. prof. dept. psychiatry, 1975-82, clin. assoc. prof., 1986-87; pvt. clin. practice, 1975—; cons. Cath. Family Social Service, Lansing, 1979-83; mem. adv. bd. Cir. Ct. Family Counseling Program, 1982-88. V.p. Kehillat Israel Synagogue, 1975-76, pres. 1992-94; bd. dirs. Jewish Welfare Fedn., Lansing, 1974-75, 84-87; mem. children's task force State Bar Mich., 1993-95. NDEA fellow, 1968-70. Mem. Am. Psychol. Assn., Mich. Psychol. Assn., Mich. Soc. Forensic Psychologists, Nat. Soc. of Arts and Letters. Office: 4084 Okemos Rd Okemos MI 48864-3258

BERKMAN, DAVE, mass communications educator; b. Bklyn., May 6, 1934; s. Henry and Edna (Berkowitz) B.; m. Gloria Scnap, June 1953 (div. May 1963); 1 child, Linda; m. Jo Castellucci, Dec. 1989 (div. Nov. 1989); children: Elena, Neil; m. Margarita Dugek, Dec. 1998. BA cum laude, L.I. U., 1955; MS, Syracuse U., 1956; EdD, NYU, 1963. Prodr., dir. Sta. WHIZ-TV, Zanesville, Ohio, 1956-57, Sta. WTVS, Wayne State U., Detroit, 1957-59; dir. pub. rels. and edn. Dist. 65 AFL-CIO, N.Y.C., 1963-64; asst. prof. comm. Nassau C.C., SUNY, Garden City, 1964-65, Kingsborough C.C., CUNY, Bklyn., 1965-67; sr. media sys. specialist pub. divsn. Xerox Corp., N.Y.C. and Stamford, Conn., 1967-70; assoc. prof. mass comm. Am. U., Washington, 1970-71; program mgr. ESSA-TV, U.S. Office Edn., HEW, Washington, 1971-79; asst. dean telecom. Newhouse Sch., Syracuse (N.Y.) U., 1979-83; prof. mass comm. U. Wis., Milw., 1983—; v.p., chmn. bd. dirs. Alternative Publs., Inc., Milw., 1994-98; mem. minority affairs task force Corp. for Pub. Broadcasting, 1977-79. Media columnist Shepherd Express, Milw., 1989—; host call-in/interview program Media Talk, Wis. Pub. Radio Network, 1993—; mem. editl. bd. TV Quar., NATAS, 1983-98; contbr. over 125 articles to various publs. Active ACLU, 1957—, mem. Conn. state bd., 1968-70, mem. Wis. state bd., 1988-89. Sole non-minority recipient Minority Pub. Broadcasting Achievements award Nat. Assn. Ednl. Broadcasters, 1979. Mem. Broadcast Edn. Assn., Soc. Profl. Journalists (bd. dirs. Milw. chpt. 1984-85). Home: 3065 S Crosswinds Dr Cudahy WI 53110 Office: Univ Wis Dept Mass Comm PO Box 413 Milwaukee WI 53201-0413

BERKMAN, JAMES L., bicycle builder, publisher; b. Cleve., Jan. 12, 1952; m. Renee Eileen Lee, Oct. 15, 1994. BA in Philosophy, Youngstown State U., 1974; MA in Philosophy, Kent State U., 1975. Cert. bicycle mechanic, United Bicycle Inst. Instr. philosophy Lewis-Clark State Coll., Lewiston, Idaho, 1976-79; bicycle builder Ashland, Oreg., 1989—; owner Jim Berkman's Bikx, Ashland, 1989—; owner, pub. Runaway Publs., Ashland, 1977—. Author, editor poetry. Mem. Am. Philos. Assn., Christian Motorcyclists Assn. Republican. Office: Runaway Publs PO Box 1172 Ashland OR 97520-0040

BERKMAN, LILLIAN, foundation executive, corporation executive, art collector; b. N.Y.C.. B.A. summa cum laude, NYU, 1942, M.A. summa cum laude, 1943, H.H.D. (hon.), 1976; DFA (hon.), Marquette U., 1996. Dir. pub. relations J.I. Case Co., 1957-60; pres. Gen. Alarm Corp., N.Y.C., 1965—; corp. dir., head advt. and pub. relations Am. Tractor Corp., 1948-56; dir. Allied Stores Corp., 1974-86, Mich. Nat. Corp., 1977-86, Mich. Nat. Bank, Detroit, 1977-87, Mich. Nat. Investment Corp., 1978-87, MNC-Western Leasing, 1980-87; pres. Rojtman Found., Inc., 1967—; cultural advisor Coca Cola Co., 1978—; bd. dirs. Sterling Nat. Bank N.Y., Sterling Nat. Corp., Sterling Bancorp.; v.p., asst. to chmn. for corp. planning and devel. Associated Comm. Corp., 1988-94, vice chmn., 1990-94; v.p., asst. to chmn. long range planning Associated Group, Inc., 1995—. Fellow in perpetuity Met. Mus. Art, N.Y.C., 1964—; donor Rojtman Medieval Sculpture Gallery, 1964, trustee medieval art com., 1974—; mem. exec. council Inst. Fine Arts, N.Y. U., 1972—; trustee Am. Wing, 1976—, Poly. Inst. N.Y., 1977—; nat. adv. coun. St. Petersburg (Fla.) Mus. Fine Arts, 1990—; fellow Pierpont Morgan Library, 1969—, Frick Mus., N.Y., 1980—, Nat. Council San Francisco Museums, 1985—; bd. dirs. United Cerebral Palsy Research and Ednl. Found., Inc., 1973—, Inner City Scholarship Fund, 1980—; vice chmn., dir. Salvation Army, 1986—; mem. Met. Opera Nat. Council, 1973—; overseer U. Pa. Mus., 1982—; dir. Latin Am. Arts Council, 1988—; chmn. Theban expdn. to Valley of the Kings, Egypt, 1977—; cultural advisor to Costa Rica, 1978—; chmn., bd. dirs. Associated American Artists, Inc., 1983—; mem. dean's adv. bd., vis. com. overseers Harvard Law Sch., 1997. Recipient Highest Honor award Nat. Indsl. Advertisers Assn., 1956, Pere Marquette award Marquette U., 1966, Philippine Golden Heart Presdl. award for cultural interchange, 1976, Kairos award Marquette U., 1992, Friends of Inner-City Scholarship Fund award, 1996. Mem. Nat. Assn. Corp. Dirs., Economic Club of N.Y., Lotos Club, Univ. Club of N.Y. (mem. coun.), Harmonee Club of N.Y., Harvard Club of N.Y., Phi Beta Kappa Assocs. (bd. dirs., v.p. Middle Atlantic dist. awards com.). Home: 22 E 64th St New York NY 10021-7212

BERKMAN, MICHAEL G., lawyer, chemical consultant; b. Poland, Apr. 4, 1917; came to U.S., 1921; s. Harry and Bertha (Jay) B.; m. Marjorie Edelstein, Nov. 28, 1941; children—Laurel, William. BS, U. Chgo., 1937, PhD, 1941; JD, DePaul U., 1958; LLM in Intellectual Property, John Marshall Law Sch., 1962; spl. courses, Harvard U., 1943, MIT, 1943. Bar: U.S. Patent Office 1960. Research chemist Argonne Nat. Lab., 1946-51; assoc. dir., chief chemist Colburn Labs., Chgo., 1951-59; instr. chemistry Roosevelt U., Chgo., 1946-49; patent lawyer Mann, Brown & McWilliams, Chgo., 1959-63; ptnr. Kegan, Kegan & Berkman, Chgo., 1963-84, Trexler, Bushnell, Giangiorgi & Blackstone, Chgo., 1984-91; pvt. practice law Glenview, Ill., 1991—; chem. cons.; expert witness in patent law. Contbr. articles to profl. jours. Served to 1st lt. Signal Corps, U.S. Army, 1942-46. Mem. Am. Chem. Soc., ABA, Patent Law Assn., Chgo., Sigma Xi. Home and Office: 939 Glenview Rd Glenview IL 60025-3172

BERKMAN, RICHARD LYLE, lawyer; b. Pitts., Sept. 4, 1946; s. Allen H. and Selma (Wiener) B.; m. Toni Seidl, June 7, 1998; children: Benjamin, Lisa, Daniel. AB magna cum laude, Harvard U., 1968, JD cum laude, 1973. Bar: Pa. 1973, U.S. Dist. Ct. (ea. dist.) Pa. 1973, U.S. Ct. Appeals (3d cir.) 1975, U.S. Dist. Ct. (mid. dist.) Pa. 1979, U.S. Supreme Ct. 1986. Asst. to dir. Office Emergency Preparedness Exec. Office of U.S. President, Washington, 1970; law clk. to Hon. Edward R. Becker U.S. Dist Ct., Phila., 1973-74; ptnr. Dechert Price & Rhoads, Phila., 1974—. Co-author: Damming the West, 1971, Pennsylvania Evidence, 1974; contbr. articles to profl. jours. Bd. govs. Am. Jewish Com.; officer, bd. dirs. Congregation Rodeph Shalom; active Salzberg Seminar on AIDS. Lt. (j.g.) USN, 1968-70. Mem. ABA, Phila. Bar Assn., Am. Law Inst. Avocations: reading, charities, sports. Office: Dechert Price & Rhoads 4000 Bell Atlantic Tower 1717 Arch St Philadelphia PA 19103-2793

BERKMAN, RONALD M., dean, educator; b. Elizabeth, N.J., Apr. 17, 1947; s. Sidney and Hannah B.; m. Star Sandow, March 21, 1980 (div. Dec. 1984); m. Tricia Carol Maddox, Nov. 27, 1985; children: Cameron, Mikhaila. BA, William Patterson Coll., 1972; MA, Princeton U., 1974, PhD, 1976. Instr. pub. affairs Princeton (N.J.) U., 1976-78; prof. polit. sci. Bklyn. Coll., 1978-86; dean urban affairs CUNY Chancellors Office, N.Y.C., 1986-88, dean academic affairs, 1988-91; dean sch. pub. affairs Baruch Coll., N.Y.C., 1992—. Author: Opening the Gates, 1977, People, Power, Politics, 1978, Politics in the Mean Age, 1985, The Urban Summit, 1992. Dir. Regional Plan Assn., N.Y.C., 1992, Mayor's Urban Summit, N.Y.C., 1992; chair Metro Dade Strategic Planning, Miami, Fla., 1998. Recipient Svc. award U. Puerto Rico, Rio Pieoras, 1988; Guggenheim fellow Guggenheim Found., Bklyn., 1982. Fellow Alpha Phi Sigma; mem. Nat. Assn. Schs. Pub. Affairs, Assn. Policy and Mgmt., Urban Affairs Assn. Home: 13240 SW 82 Ave Miami FL 33156 Office: Florida Internat Univ Miami FL 33199

BERKMAN, SAMUEL ABBA, internist; b. Dayton, Ohio, Dec. 21, 1945; s. Sydney and Edna (Cohen) B.; m. Michele Ehrlich; children: Lauren, Jacqueline. BA, Syracuse U., 1967; MD, Tufts U., 1971. Cert. in internal medicine, hematology, med. oncology. Intern Cedars-Sinai Med. Ctr., L.A., 1971-72; resident Cedars-Sinai Med. Ctr., 1972-74; fellow U.C.L.A., 1974-76; fellow med. oncology NIH, Bethesda, Md., 1976-78; pvt. practice, 1978—. Contbr. articles to profl. jours. including Hosp. Practice, Blood Reviews, Annals of Internal Med. Avocation: foreign languages. Home: 3515 Alginet Dr Encino CA 91436 Office: 9400 Brighton Way Beverly Hills CA 90210

BERKMAN, WILLIAM ROGER, lawyer, army reserve officer; b. Chisholm, Minn., Mar. 29, 1928; s. Carl and Millie (Mikkelson) B.; m. Betty Ann Klamt, Dec. 17, 1950. AB, U. Calif., Berkeley, 1950, JD, 1957. Bar: Calif. 1957, D.C. Ct. Appeals 1957, D.C. 1957. Law clk. to judge U.S. Ct. Appeals 9th cir., 1957-58; assoc. Morrison & Foerster, San Francisco, 1958-67; mem. firm Morrison & Foerster, 1967-79; comdg. gen. 351st Civil Affairs Command, Mountain View, Calif., 1975-79; chief USAR, Washington, 1979-86; mil. exec., Res. Forces Policy Bd. Dept. of Def., Washington, 1986-92. Mng. editor: Calif. Law Rev, 1956-57. Pres. Sausalito (Calif.) Bd. Libr. Trustees, 1976-78; pres. Civil Affairs Assn., 1979-80, 93—; bd. dirs. Army Distaff Found., 1988-92; dir. Sausalito-Marin City Sanitary Dist. Maj. Gen. USAR, 1979—. Decorated Disting. Svc. medal with oak leaf cluster, Def. Disting. Svc. medal U.S. Army, Def. Superior Svc. medal U.S. Army, Navy, Coast Guard, Legion of Merit medal, Meritorious Svc. medal, Army Commendation medal, S. Order of Calif. award, U.S. Spl. Ops. command medal. Mem. ABA (chmn. standing com. on lawyers in armed svcs. 1988-91), State Bar Calif., Assn. U.S. Army, Res. Officers Assn., Civil Affairs Assn. (chief civil affairs corps., pres. civil affairs assn. 1992-99), World Trade Club, Sausalito Yacht Club, Army and Navy Club, Lions (dir. Sausalito Marin City sanitary dist.). Home: 33 Atwood Ave Sausalito CA 94965-2245

BERKNER, KLAUS HANS, laboratory administrator, physicist; b. Dessau, Anhalt, Germany, Mar. 2, 1938; came to U.S., 1948; s. Hans Otto and Sigrid Erika (Kuke) B. SB, MIT, 1960; PhD, U. Calif., Berkeley, 1964. NSF grad. fellowship U. Calif., Berkeley, 1960-61; NSF postdoctoral fellowship Culham, Eng., 1965-66; physicist Lawrence Berkeley (Calif.) Lab., 1964-79, sr. physicist, 1979—, deputy div. dir. accelerator and fusion research, 1982-84, acting div. dir., 1984-85, div. dir., 1985-91, assoc. lab. dir. for ops., 1991-94; dep. dir. ops., 1994—; mem. Basic Energy Scis. Adv. Com., 1991-96, co-chair, 1993-96; mem. Fusion Energy Adv. Com., 1991-93. Contbr. over 100 articles on atomic physics, accelerators and fusion research to profl. jours. Fellow Am. Phys. Soc. Office: Lawrence Berkeley Nat Lab Dep Dir Ops 1 Cyclotron Rd Berkeley CA 94720

BERKÓ, FERENC, photographer; b. Nagyvárad, Hungary, Jan. 28, 1916; came to U.S., 1947; s. René and Maria Theresa (Teleki) B.; m. Mirte Hahn-Beretta, Nov. 5, 1937; children: Nora, Gina. Student, U. London Extension, 1934-35. Freelance documentary photographer and filmmaker London, 1935-38; film cameraman Bhavnani Prodns., Bombay, India, 1938-39; free lance photographer and filmmaker Bombay, 1940-44; documentary film dir., staff capt. Brit. Directorate of Kinematography, Bombay, 1944-47; instr. film and photography Inst. Design, Chgo., 1947-48; photographer and filmmaker Container Corp. Am., Chgo., 1949-51; photographer Berko Photography, Aspen, Colo., 1951—; assoc. photographer Aspen Inst. Humanistic Studies, 1949—; photographer Aspen Skiing Corp., 1949-85, Mus. Assn. Aspen, 1949-82; selected portrait photographer cabinet ministers' photographs Carter Adminstrn., 1980; invited guest photography symposium Nat. Mus. Photography, Film and TV, Bradford, Eng., photographs of Guadeloupe, Martinique, Switzerland, Fed. Republic Germany, other countries. Contbr. books, mags., publs., 1938—; solo and group exhbns. 1937—, including Fotographie Forum, Frankfurt, Germany, 1991, Galleria Diaframma, Milan, 1993, Budapest, Hungary, 1994, Graphis, N.Y., 1995, 97, Midtown Gallery Internat. Ctr. Photography, 1996, Musée de l'Elysée, Lausanne, Switzerland, 1996, 97; represented in permanent collections Mus. Modern Art, Met. Mus. Art, San Francisco Mus. Art, Gernsheim Collection, Austin, Tex., Bibliotheque Nat., Paris, Ctr. Creative Photography, Tucson, Kunsthaus Zurich, Switzerland, Internat. Ctr. for Photography, N.Y.C., Hallmark Collection, Gruber Collection, Mus. Ludwig, Cologne, Fed. Republic Ger.; exhbns. in London, N.Y.C., U. Tex., Tucson, Phoenix, Scottsdale, Cin., Ft. Worth, Aspen, Ohio, Foto-Forum, Frankfurt, Fed. Republic Ger. retrospective exhbns in Arles, N.Y.C., Albert Schweitzer Found.; featured in Ferenc Berkow-60 Years of Photography-The Discovering Eye; work featured in United Airlines in-flight mag. Mem. Dr. Albert Schweitzer Found. (hon. com. mem.). Home: 223 E Hallam PO Box 360 Aspen CO 81612-0360

BERKOFF, CHARLES EDWARD, pharmaceutical executive; b. London, Sept. 29, 1932; came to U.S., 1963; naturalized, 1976; s. Maurice and Dora (Landy) B.; children: Timothy, David, Kevin; m. Heide-Gisela Triesch, 1997. BS in Chemistry (1st class honors), U. London, 1956, DIC, 1958; PhD, Imperial Coll., U. London, 1959. Chartered chemist. Dir. SmithKline Beecham Group, Phila., 1964-83; exec. v.p. ImuTech, Inc., Huntingdon Valley, Pa., 1983-84; pres., CEO Antigenics, Inc., Horsham, Pa., 1984-89; pres., chief exec. officer Creative Licensing Internat., Inc., Sarasota, Fla., 1987—, CEBRAL, 1987—; research fellow Johns Hopkins U., Balt., 1959-60; sr. research fellow Southampton U., Eng., 1960-61; mem. Adv. Council Smithsonian Sci. Info. Exchange, Washington, 1976-82. Contbr. articles to profl. jours.; patentee numerous U.S. and fgn. patents. Monsanto Research fellow Imperial Coll. Sci. and Tech., 1956-59; Fulbright scholar, 1959-60; recipient Statue of Victory World Culture prize Centro Studi e Ricerche Delle Nazioni, 1985. Fellow Am. Chem. Soc., Royal Soc. Chemistry; mem. Am. Arbitration Assn., Entomol. Soc., Am. Inst. Chem. Engrs., Licensing Execs. Soc. Republican. Unitarian. Club: Engrs. Club of Phila. Avocations: writing scientific humor, competitive tennis and swimming, classical guitar, bridge. E-mail: CEBRAL@ad.com. Office: CEBRAL PO Box 3376 Sarasota FL 34230-3376

BERKOFF, DAVID, Olympic athlete, swimmer. Olympic swimmer Barcelona, Spain, 1992. Recipient 100m Backstroke Bronze medal Olympics, Barcelona, 1992. Office: care US Swimming Inc One Olympic Plz Colorado Springs CO 80909*

BERKOFF, MARK ANDREW, lawyer; b. Boston, Aug. 8, 1961; s. Marshall Richard and Bebe R. B.; m. Susan Lynn Ochalek; children: Alexander, Rachel. BA with honors, U. Wis., 1983; JD, U. Chgo., 1986. Bar: Ill. 1987, U.S. Dist. Ct. (no. dist. Ill.) 1987, U.S. Ct. Appeals (7th cir.) 1990. Ptnr. Rudnick & Wolfe, Chgo., 1986—. Vol. Am. Cancer Soc., Chgo., 1993-96, Make-A-Wish Found. No. Ill., 1998—. Mem. ABA, Chgo. Bar Assn. Avocations: sports, collecting Currier & Ives prints, numismatics, family. Office: Rudnick & Wolfe 203 N LaSalle St Chicago IL 60601-1293

BERKOFF, MARSHALL RICHARD, lawyer; b. Milw., Apr. 10, 1937; s. Louis S. and Edith E. (Cohen) B.; m. Bebe R. Brandwein, June 19, 1960; children: Mark Andrew, Jonathan Hale, Adam Todd. BA, U. Wis., 1959; LLB, Harvard U., 1962. Bar: Wis. 1962, U.S. Dist. Ct. (we. and ea. dists.) Wis. 1962. Ptnr. Michael, Best & Friedrich, Milw., 1962—. Co-author: Employment Law Challenges of 1987, 1987, Labor Relations: The New Rules of the Game, 1984, The Legal Issues of Managing Difficult Employees, 1987; author/editor Currier and Ives "The New Best 50", 1991. Chmn. Charles Allis and Villa Terrace Art Mus., Milw., 1983-96; chmn. Milw. County War Meml. Corp., 1988-94, bd. dirs., 1983-96, vice chmn. 1996—; chmn. bd. dirs. St. Michael Hosp., Milw., 1988-89; bd. dirs. Covenant Health Care, 1993-95. Mem. ABA (labor and employment sect., hosp. and health care law sect.), Wis. Bar Assn., (chmn. labor law sect. 1977-78), Milw. Bar Assn., Am. Hist. Print Collector Soc. (pres. 1987-90). Avocations: collecting, speaking, writing, restoring and cataloguing antique Am. lithographs, fishing. Office: Michael Best & Friedrich 100 E Wisconsin Ave Ste 3300 Milwaukee WI 53202-4108

BERKOFSKY, MARTIN, concert pianist; b. Washington, Apr. 9, 1943; s. Benjamin and Ray B. BMus, Peabody Conservatory of Music, Balt., 1965, MMus, 1967. Co-founder, co-dir. L.I. Chamber Ensemble, N.Y.C., 1970-73; Fulbright fellow Vienna Acad. of Music, 1966-67; performer Marlboro (Vt.) Festival, 1968-69; Fulbright Prof. Titograd (Podgorica) Music Acad., Yugoslavia; head, advanced piano dept. State Conservatory of Music, Izmir, Turkey, 1987-89; touring artist/pianist U.S. State Dept., 1978-90; artistic dir. Cristofori Ensemble, Casanova, Va., 1994—; pres., founder Cristofori Found., Casanova, 1995—; bd. dirs. Internat. Peace Garden Found., Washington, 1994-97, Nicolae Bretan Music Found., McLean, Va., 1990-97. Pianist: (recs.) Works of Max Bruch with London Symphony, 1973, Works of Alan Hovhaness with L.I. Chamber Ensemble, 1971-72, Works of Bruch, Mendelsson, Lizst, Chopin, St. Saens with Berlin Symphony, 1975, Works of Alan Hovhaness with Seattle Symphony, 1997; solo albums with Cristofori Found. recs. Pianist for fundraising concerts worldwide, 1982—. Winner N.Y. Nat. Music League Young Artists Competition, 1965; recipient Fulbright scholarship, Vienna, 1966; named to "Five Who Made a Difference", Fauquier Citizen, Warrenton, Va., 1995. Mem. Cristofori Found. (founder, pres. 1995—). Avocation: amateur radio.

BERKON, MARTIN, artist; b. Bklyn., Jan. 30, 1932; s. Samuel F. and Sara (Hodes) B.; m. Eileen Phyllis Eichel, July 10, 1960. Student, Pratt Inst., 1952; BA, Bklyn. Coll., 1954; MA, NYU, 1959. Mem. adj. faculty Fairleigh Dickinson U., 1966, Nassau C.C., 1966-67; lectr. City Coll., CUNY, 1968-69; guest lectr. Middlebury Coll., 1977, Nassau C.C., 1982, St. Thomas Aquinas Coll., 1995; interviewed L.I. Art Scene TV, 1986. One-man shows include Smolin Gallery, N.Y.C., 1962, 20th Century West Gallery, N.Y.C., 1967, Soho Ctr. for Visual Artists, N.Y.C., 1974, Genesis Galleries, N.Y.C., 1978, Adelphi U., Garden City, N.Y., 1983, Blue Hill Cultural Ctr., Pearl River, N.Y., 1995; exhibited in group shows at Bklyn. Mus., 1958, Silvermine (Conn.) Guild Artists, 1963, Ohio U. Gallery, 1964, Ball State U., 1965, Wesleyan Coll. at Ga., 1965, Butler Inst. Am. Art, 1965, 67, 69, Aldrich Mus. Contemporary Art, Ridgefield, Conn., 1974, 75, 82, New Britain (Conn.) Mus., 1974, Am. Fedn. Arts traveling show, 1975-77, Meadowbrook Art Gallery Oakland U., Rochester, Mich. and Flint (Mich.) Inst. Art, 1974-76, Firehouse Gallery, Garden City, 1982, Barbara Walter Gallery, N.Y.C., 1982, Spaceport USA, Kennedy Space Ctr., 1985, 87, NASA collection traveling exhbn. Visions of Flight, 1988-91, Ctr. for Arts The Abstract Image, Vero Beach, Fla., 1996, Blue Hill Cultural Ctr., Pearl River, N.Y., 1997-98; represented in permanent collections Aldrich Mus. Contemporary Art, Texaco Inc., White Plains, N.Y., Pepsico Inc., Somers, N.Y.; commd. NASA, 1984, 87, NASA Gallery of Art, Kennedy Space Ctr.,

Ctr. for Arts, Vero Beach, Fla. Home: 503 Devries Ct Piermont NY 10968-1068

BERKOWITZ, ALAN STEVEN, educator, poet; b. N.Y.C., Mar. 20, 1954; s. Marvin and Gloria B.; m. Ellen Luisa Rapp, June 21, 1992. BA, U. Pa., 1976; PhD in English, CUNY, 1997. Adj. instr. John Jay Coll., N.Y.C., 1992-93, Touro Coll., N.Y.C., 1993—, Bronx C.C., N.Y., 1994, New Rockelle Coll., N.Y.C., 1994; adj. asst. prof. Yeshiva U., N.Y.C., 1997—, Hofstra U., Hempstead, N.Y., 1998, NYU, N.Y.C., 1998—; adj. instr. Touro Coll., N.Y.C., 1993—, Bronx (N.Y.) C.C., 1994, New Rochelle Coll., N.Y.C., 1994; adj. asst. prof. Yeshiva U., N.Y.C., 1997—, Hofstra U., N.Y., 1998, NYU, N.Y.C., 1998—, Fashion Inst. Tech., SUNY, 1999. Author: Colors of the Wind, 1999. Mem. MLA. Democrat; Jewish. Avocations: music, art, poetry, travel. Home: 334 East 5th St #10 New York NY 10009

BERKOWITZ, BERNARD JOSEPH, lawyer; b. Newark, Jan. 23, 1945; s. Sigmund and Gertrude (Zimmer) B.; m. Barbara Jean Haddock, Nov. 25, 1970; children: Brian, Gail, Mark. BA, Rutgers U., 1967; JD, Suffolk U., 1970. Assoc. Lewis B. Rothbart, Whippany, N.J., 1971-73, Yanowsky & Rosen, Boonton, N.J., 1973-76, Pressler & Pressler, Pine Brook, N.J., 1976-77; pvt. practice, Parsippany, N.J., 1977-98; ptnr. Berkowitz & Decker, Parsippany, 1982-87, Berkowitz & Raiken, Montville, N.J., 1998—; mcpl. ct. judge Rockaway Boro, 1988-96, Netcong Boro, 1991-96, Parsippany-Troy Hills Twp., 1983-87; atty. Parsippany Planning Bd., 1982-83; trustee Legal Svcs. of Morris County; active N.J. Supreme Ct. Com. on Mcpl. Cts. Mem. Suffolk U. Law Rev., 1969-70. Mem. Parsippany-Troy Hills Twp. Bd. Adjustment, 1978-82, Parsippany-Troy Hills Twp. Bd. Edn., 1988; bd. dirs. March of Dimes, 1979; v.p. Parsippany-Troy Hills Twp. Little League, 1987-90; pres. Parsippany Day Care Ctr. Mem. N.J. State Bar Assn., Morris County Bar Assn., Parsippany Area C. of C. (v.p. 1989-95). Republican. Jewish. Avocations: golf, bowling. E-mail: bjberk@aol.com. Fax: 973-227-4691. Home: 19 Ashwood Pl Parsippany NJ 07054-2261

BERKOWITZ, BERNARD SOLOMON, lawyer; b. Trenton, N.J., June 13, 1930; s. Samuel and Sarah R. (Jansil) B.; m. Edith A. Collins, June 11, 1960 (dec. Nov. 1975); children: Laura, Amy, Philip; m. Rita Sobel, Dec. 6, 1976; children: Alexa, Robert, Richard. BA, Cornell U., 1952, LLB with distinction, 1956; LLM, NYU, 1959. Bar: N.Y. 1956, N.J. 1957. With Hannoch Weisman, P.C., Roseland, N.J., 1956-60, ptnr., 1961—, pres., 1979—; lectr., panelist tax and corp. matters; prin. organizer, sec., dir. N.J Life Ins. Co., Newark, 1964—; organizer State St. Life Ins. Co., Boston. Bd. dirs., trustee, past pres. Community Found. N.J.; past pres. United Way Essex and West Hudson, The Whole Theatre Found. N.J.; bd. dirs. Orange Orphans Soc., Mountainside Hosp., Montclair, N.J., Bloomfield (N.J.) Coll.; trustee, bd. dirs. Nat. Soc. Prevent Blindness, N.J. 2d lt. AUS, 1952-54. Decorated Bronze Star. Mem. ABA, N.Y. County Bar Assn., N.J. Bar Assn., Essex County Bar Assn., Montclair Golf Club, Order of Coif. Republican. Unitarian. Avocations: golf, opera, art, skiing. Home: Llewellyn Park West Orange NJ 07052 Office: Hannoch Weisman 4 Becker Farm Rd Ste 11 Roseland NJ 07068-1734

BERKOWITZ, LAWRENCE M., lawyer; b. Leavenworth, Kans., Nov. 29, 1941; s. Barney and Sarah (Kramer) B.; m. Ursula Lustenberger, Sept. 2, 1969; children: Lizbeth Berkowitz, Leslie Berkowitz. BA Polit. Sci., U. Mich., 1963, JD, 1966. Bar: Mo. 1966. Law clerk U.S. Dist. Ct., Kansas City, Mo., 1966-68; assoc., ptnr. Stinson, Mag & Fizzell, P.C., Kansas City, Mo., 1968-97; ptnr. Berkowitz, Feldmiller, Stanton, et al, Kansas City, Mo., 1997—; mng. ptnr. Stinson, Mag & Fizzell, Kansas City, 1991-92. Bd. dirs. Nelson Gallery Bus. Coun., Kansas City, 1989—, Downtown coun., Kansas City, 1992-93; trustee Kansas City Art Inst., 1994—. Fellow Am. Coll. Trial Lawyers, Am. Bar Found.; mem. ABA, Am. Judicature Soc., Kansas City Met. Bar Assn., Lawyers Assn. Kansas City, Mo. Bar Assn., Am. Coll. Trial Lawyers (state bd. 1989—). Avocations: tennis, hiking, skiing, history, reading. Office: Berkowitz Feldmiller Stanton et al Ste 550419251 Two Brush Creek Blvd Kansas City MO 64112

BERKOWITZ, ROBERT, psychiatrist; b. Cleve., Feb. 17, 1941; s. Abraham Joseph and Minnie B.; m. Arlene Pearl Schultz, Oct. 28, 1973; children: Adam, Jessica. BA, U. Mo., 1963, MD, 1967. Diplomate Am. Bd. Psychiatry and Neurology, Am. Bd. Child Psychiatry, Am. Bd. Forensic Psychiatry. Sr. asst. surgeon USPHS, S.I., N.Y., 1967-70; resident in psychiatry Kings County Hosp., Bklyn., 1970-73; resident in child psychiatry S.I. Mental Health Soc., 1973-75; pvt. practice Toms River, N.J., 1975—. Mem. Am. Psychiat. Assn., Am. Acad. Psychology and Law, Am. Acad. Child and Adolescent Psychiatry, N.J. Psychiat. Assn. (Monmouth chpt.), N.J. Coun. Child and Adolescent Psychiatry. Avocation: playing recorder.

BERKOWITZ, STEVE, publishing company executive. Staff acct. J Herbert & Co, N.Y.C., 1980-81, Paramount Pictures, N.Y.C., 1981-83; fin. analyst Macmillan Pub., N.Y.C., 1983-85, bus. mgr., 1985-88, v.p. fin., 1988-91; v.p. pub. MIS Press, N.Y.C., 1991-94; pres. IDG Books Worldwide, Foster City, Calif., 1994—. *

BERKSON, JACOB BENJAMIN, lawyer, author, conservationist; b. Washington County, Md., Dec. 6, 1925; s. Meyer and Ida Evelyn (Berman) B.; m. Ann Goldstein, June 25, 1955 (div.); children: Daniel Jeremy, Susan Kay, James Meyer. BA, U. Va., 1947, LLB, 1949, JD, 1970; grad., Fed. Exec. Inst., Charlottesville, Va., 1972. Bar: Md. 1949, Va. 1949, U.S. Supreme Ct. 1965, Calif. 1975. Sole practice Hagerstown, Md., 1949-52, 54-64; ptnr. McCauley, Cooey, Berkson & Wright, Hagerstown, 1964-70; dep. gen. counsel U.S. GSA, Washington, 1970-76; pvt. practice law Hagerstown, 1976—; instr. Law Hagerstown Bus. Coll., 1986; trial magistrate, Hagerstown and Washington County, Md., 1951-52; mem. Legis. Coun. Md., 1955-58; del. Md. Legislature, 1955-58; trial magistrate, Hagerstown, 1958-59. Recipient commendation for svc. to U.S. Naval Acad. and pub. interest Chief of Naval Personnel, 1956. Lt. USNR, 1944-46, 52-54. Author: Shingahi Saburo and Short Stories, 1978, Comin' Home, 1993, A Canary's Tale, 1996; case editor, co-founder Va. Law Weekly, 1948; contbr. articles to profl. jours., address to Congrl. Record. Scoutmaster local coun. Boy Scouts Am.; organizer, dir. County Youth Conservation Corps; active Big Bros.; bd. dirs. Doub's Woods County Park, Devil's Backbone County Park; assisted in establishment of C&O Canal Nat. Histo. Park, 1954-70; camp sponsor YMCA; adv. Model Youth Legis.; pres. PTA; chmn. Washington County Park Commn., 1961-66; bd. dirs. Rachel Carson Coun., Inc., Chevy Chase, Md., 1996—. Mem. ABA, Calif. Bar Assn., Va. Bar Assn., Md. Assn. County Civil Attys. (pres., award for svc. as pres. 1966), Washington County Bar Assn. (pres.), Am. Legion, Hagerstown Club, Lions (pres.), Speakers Soc., Elks, Torch Club (Hagerstown). Republican. Jewish. Home and Office: 1419 Potomac Ave Hagerstown MD 21742-3315

BERKUS, JAMES, talent agent. Pres. United Talent Agy., Beverly Hills, Calif. Office: United Talent Agy 9560 Wilshire Blvd 5th Flr Beverly Hills CA 90212*

BERL, JOSEPH M., lawyer; b. Bklyn., Oct. 1, 1942. AB, Columbia U., 1964; JD with honors, George Washington U., 1967. Bar: N.Y. 1968, D.C. 1972, U.S. Supreme Ct. 1972. Law clk. to Hon. Frank H. Myers D.C. Ct. Appeals, 1967-68; trial atty. Div. Trading and Markets, SEC, Washington, 1968-70, br. chief, 1970-71; ptnr. Fortas & Koven, Washington, 1971-83, Stroock and Stroock and Lavan, Washington, 1984-86, Baker & Hostetler, Washington, 1986-98, Powell, Goldstein, Frazer & Murphy LLP, Washington, 1998—. Mem. ABA (mem. corp., banking and bus. law sect.), D.C. Bar. Office: Powell Goldstein Frazer & Murphy LLP 6th Flr 1001 Pennsylvania Ave NW Fl 6 Washington DC 20004-2505

BERLACK, EVAN RADEN, lawyer; b. N.Y.C., Apr. 1, 1934; s. Harris and Edith Ann (Raden) B.; m. Kay Baumler, July 15, 1963 (dec. July 1986); children: Andrew E., Kenneth H.; m. Phyllis Bonanno, Oct. 14, 1989. AB magna cum laude, Harvard U., 1956, LLB, 1962. Bar: N.Y. 1963, D.C. 1969. Fgn. service officer U.S. Dept. State, Washington and Paris, 1963-66; atty., adviser Office Legal Adviser U.S. Dept. State, Washington, 1966-68; assoc. Arent, Fox, Kintner, Plotkin & Kahn, Washington, 1968-73, ptnr., 1974—. Co-editor: Coping with U.S. Export Controls, 1985-86, 88-98. 1st lt. USAF, 1956-59. Mem. ABA, Am. Soc. Internat. Law, Harvard Club (N.Y.C., Washington). Clubs: Harvard (N.Y.C. and Washington). Avocations: swimming, baseball, classical music, history. Home: 67 Observatory Cir NW Washington DC 20008-3611 Office: Arent Fox Kintner Plotkin & Kahn 1050 Connecticut Ave NW Ste 500 Washington DC 20036-5339

BERLAGE, GAI INGHAM, sociologist, educator; b. Washington, Feb. 9, 1943; d. Paul Bowen and Grace (Artz) Ingham; m. Jan Coxe Berlage, Aug. 7, 1965; children: Jan Ingham, Cari Coxe. BA, Smith Coll., 1965; MA, So. Meth. U., 1968; PhD, NYU, 1979. Tchr. math. Piner Jr. High Sch., Sherman, Tex., 1968-69; asst. prof. sociology Iona Coll., New Rochelle, N.Y., 1971-83, assoc. prof., 1983-88, chmn. dept., 1981-90, 96—, prof., 1988—; coord. urban studies program, 1984-90, gerontology program, 1984-90, NCAA faculty athletic rep., 1996—. Author: Experience with Sociology: Social Issues in American Society, 1983, Understanding Social Issues: Sociological Fact Finding, 1987, 2d edit., 1990, 3d edit., 1993, Women in Baseball: The Forgotten History, 1994, Understanding Social Issues: Critical Thinking and Analysis, 1993, 5th edit., 1999; mem. editl. bd. Jour. Sport and Social Issues, 1990-94; contbr. articles to profl. jours. Commr. Wilton Commn. on Aging and Social Svcs., 1980-88, chmn., 1982-88; co-chmn. Wilton Task Force on Youth Coun., 1988; chmn. Wilton Task Force Com. for Outreach Program, 1981-82, Wilton Task Force on Day Care, 1983-88; mem. Wilton Task Force for Pub. Health Nursing Assn., 1981-82, Wilton Sport Coun., 1985-88; bd. dirs. Wilton Meals on Wheels, 1983-88; fellow N.Am. Faculty Network of Northeastern Univs. Ctr. for Study of Sport in Soc. Recipient Best Profl. Paper award Third Annual Cooperstown Symposium on Baseball and the Am. Cultre; named to Iona Coll. Women of Achievement, 1993. Mem. Am. Sociol. Assn., N.Am. Soc. Sociology of Sport (treas. 1992-93), Wilton Assn. for Gifted Edn. (pres. 1980-81), N.Am. Soc. for Sports History, Soc. for Am. Baseball Rsch., Women's Sport Found. (resources coun.). Office: Iona Coll Dept Sociology New Rochelle NY 10801

BERLAGE, JAN INGHAM, lawyer; b. Lewiston, N.Y., Nov. 17, 1969; s. Jan Coxe and Gai Elizabeth (Ingham) B. BA, Wesleyan U., Middletown, Conn., 1992; postgrad., Oxford U., 1992; JD, U. Va., 1995. Law clk. to hon. E. Stephen Derby U.S. Bankruptcy Ct. Dist. Md., Balt., 1995-96; assoc. Day, Berry & Howard, Hartford, Conn., 1996—. Exec. editor Jour. of Law and Politics, Charlottesville, 1994-95, editl. bd., 1993-94; author: (short story) Aguilar Expression, 1990. Deacon Avon Congl. Ch., 1997—; active Rep. Town Com., Avon, 1998—. Mem. Federalist Soc. (pres. U. Va. chpt. 1994-95, co-chmn. Hartford chpt. 1997—), Conn. Young Lawyers Assn. (co-chmn. comml. law and bankruptcy sect. 1997—), N.Y. Bar Assn. (mem. comml. law and fed. litigation sects., intellectual property subcom. 1998—), Jefferson Literary and Debating Soc., N.Am. Securities Adminstrn. Assn. (task force mem. 1994), Oxford U. Legal Soc., United Oxford/Cambridge U. Club, Phi Delta Phi, Psi Upsilon, Phi Beta Kappa. Office: Day Berry & Howard LLP City Place I Hartford CT 06103-3499

BERLAND, ABEL EDWARD, lawyer, realtor; b. Cin., Aug. 27, 1915; s. Samuel and Anne (Brod) B.; m. Meredith E. Tausig, Aug. 31, 1940; children: Michael Gardner, Richard Bruce, James Robert. JD, DePaul U., 1938, LHD, 1975. Bar: Ill. 1938. Vice chmn. Rubloff, Inc., Chgo.; real estate cons. Contbr. articles on real estate to profl. scholarly and trade jours. Life trustee, mem. acad. affairs com. DePaul U.; chmn. Civic Fedn. Chgo., 1989-90; bd. dirs. Crime Commn. Chgo.; mem. adv. bd. Salvation Army; mem. Newberry Libr. pres.'s coun. Fellow Brandeis U., 1958—; recipient Nat. Community Service award Jewish Theol. Sem. Am. Mem. Am. Chgo. Bar Assns., Nat. Assn. Realtors, Realtors Nat. Mktg. Inst. (C.C.I.M.), Am. Soc. Real Estate Counselors (pres. 1970), Pvt. Libraries Assn., Manuscript Soc., Am. Arbitration Assn. (nat. panel arbitrators), Shakespeare Soc. Am., Lex Legio, Assn. Internat. de Bibliophile, The Realty Club of Chgo. (pres. 1988), Gamma Mu, Pi Kappa Delta, Lambda Alpha, Omega Tau Rau. Clubs: Book of California; Caxton, Mid-Day, Economic, Brandeis University (founder 1949, pres. 1954), Standard (Chgo.); Grolier (N.Y.C.); Roxburghe of San Francisco; Philobiblon (Phila.). Home: 251 Sylvan Rd Glencoe IL 60022-1225 Office: 10 S La Salle St Ste 2600 Chicago IL 60603

BERLAND, DAVID I., psychiatrist, educator; b. St. Louis, Aug. 1, 1947; s. Harry I. and Mildred (Cornblath) B.; m. Elaine Prostak, May 22, 1977; children: Katharine J., Rachel P. BA, U. Pa., 1969; MD, U. Mo., 1973. Diplomate Am. Bd. Psychiatry and Neurology. Resident psychiatry Menninger Found., Topeka, Kans., 1973-78; staff child and adolescent psychiatrist Menninger Found., Topeka, 1978-83; dir. div. child and adolescent psychiatry St. Louis U. Med. Sch., 1983-93; with dept. adolescent psychiatry St. Luke's Hosp., Chesterfield, Mo., 1993-97; pvt. practice St. Louis, 1997—. Contbr. articles to profl. jours. Fellow Am. Acad. of Child and Adolescent Psychiatry; mem. AMA (rotating seat relative value update com. 1996-99), Soc. of Profs. of Child and Adolescent Psychiatry,. Jewish. Office: Ste 130 605 Old Ballas Rd Saint Louis MO 63141

BERLAND, JAMES FRED, software company executive; b. Chgo., July 12, 1943; s. Samuel Jesse and Lillian (Singer) B. Student, Reed Coll., 1961-64, UCLA, 1964-66; student exec. mgmt. program, Harvard U., 1980. Photographer with Elson-Alexandre, 1970-73; freelance journalist, 1970-74; pub. affairs dir. Sta. KPFK-FM-Pacifica, L.A., 1974-77; news dir., 1977-78; gen. mgr., v.p. Sta. KPFK-FM, Pacifica Found. Radio, 1978-84; pres., CEO News Wave Internat., Inc., L.A., 1984-85; CEO, Berland Techs., Inc., L.A., 1985—; mem. Calif. State Task Force on Telecom. Policy; active Californians for Pub. Broadcasting, chmn., 1980-81, pres., 1981-83. Mem. Assn. Calif. Pub. Radio Stas. (pres. 1980-82). Democrat. Office: 11242 Playa Ct Unit B Culver City CA 90230-6127*

BERLAND, KAREN INA, psychologist; b. N.Y.C., Nov. 14, 1947; d. Max and Lillian (Graf) B. BA in Psychology, SUNY, Buffalo, 1969; MEd in Ednl. Psychology, U. Ill., 1971; D. Psychology, U. Denver, 1984. Cert. sch. psychologist, clin. psychologist. Sch. psychologist City Sch. Dist. Rochester (N.Y.), 1971-73, Denver Pub. Sch., 1973—; psychology intern Vets. Hosp., West Haven, Conn., 1983-84; psychologist Aurora (Colo.) Community Mental Health Ctr., 1985-92; expert witness Denver County Ct. Mem. APA, Colo. Soc. Sch. Psychologists (pres. 1986-87, leadership award 1987), Colo. Psychol. Assn. (PAC chair, treas.), Colo. Women's Psychologists (western regional dir. and Colo. rep. 1976-83), Assn. Advancement of Behavior Therapy, Mensa. Democrat. Jewish. Avocations: tennis, skiing, reading. Home: 360 S Monroe St Ste 400 Denver CO 80209-3709

BERLAND, SANFORD NEIL, lawyer; b. N.Y.C., Aug. 12, 1950; s. Stephen Isaiah and Alice Lydia (Greenfield) B.; m. Susan A. Winston, Nov. 4, 1989; children: Laurence, Noah, Stephanie, Alexander, Schuyler, Grant. BA magna cum laude, SUNY, Buffalo, 1972, JD magna cum laude, 1977. Bar: N.Y. 1978, U.S. Ct. Appeals (2d, 10th and 11th cirs.), U.S. Dist. Ct. (ea., so. and no. dists.) N.Y., U.S. Supreme Ct. Law clk. to Hon. E.R. Neaher U.S. Dist. Ct. (ea. dist.) N.Y., 1977-79; assoc. Dewey, Ballantine, Bushby, Palmer & Wood, N.Y.C., 1979-83; assoc., ptnr. Law Offices of Russel H. Beatie, Jr., N.Y.C., 1983-88; counsel Kellner, Chehebar & Deveney, N.Y.C., 1988-90; corp. counsel-litigation Pfizer Inc., N.Y.C., 1990-93, sr. corp. counsel, 1993-99, dir. corp. risk mgmt., asst. sec., 1999—; teaching fellow Washington U., St. Louis, 1973-74; guest lectr. Pace U. Law Sch., 1989. Editor-in-chief Buffalo Law rev., 1976-77; contbr. articles to profl. jours. Mem. Huntington (N.Y.) Town Dem. Com., 1996—. Mem. ABA, N.Y. Bar Assn., Assn. Bar City N.Y., Phi Beta Kappa. Avocations: tennis, cycling. Home: 16 Wildwood Dr Dix Hills NY 11746-6041 Office: Pfizer Inc 235 E 42nd St New York NY 10017-5703

BERLE, MILTON (MILTON BERLINGER), actor; b. N.Y.C., July 12, 1908; m. Joyce Mathews; 2 children; m. Ruth Cosgrove, Dec. 9, 1953; children: Vicki, Billy; m. Lorna Adams, Nov. 26, 1991. HHD (hon.), McKendree Coll., Lebanon, Ill., 1984. Began profl. work as child actor in silent motion pictures for Biograph; later on stage in vaudeville; appearances on N.Y. legitimate stage include roles in Earl Carroll Vanities, Saluta, Life Begins at 8:40, Ziegfeld Follies, See My Lawyer, I'll Take the High Road, Seventeen, The Goodbye People, Last of the Red Hot Lovers, Norman, Is That You?; motion pictures include New Faces of 1937, Tall, Dark and Handsome, 1941, Sun Valley Serenade, 1941, Over My Dead Body, 1943, Always Leave Them Laughing, 1949, Let's Make Love, 1960, It's a Mad, Mad, Mad, Mad World, 1962, The Loved One, 1965, The Oscar, 1966, Who's Minding the Mint?, 1967, Where Angels Go, Trouble Follows, 1968, Can Hieronymus Merkin Ever Forget Mercy Humppe and Find True Happiness?, 1969, Lepke, 1974, The Muppet Movie, 1979, Broadway Danny Rose, 1984, Driving Me Crazy, 1991, Storybook, 1995; (TV movie Side by Side, 1988; conducted radio program; TV actor Texaco Star Theatre, 1948-54, Berle-Buick Show, TV series Kraft Music Hall, 1958-59, Jackpot Bowling, 1960-61, Doyle Against the House (Emmy nominee), Dick Powell Show, 1961, Chrysler TV Spl., 1962, The Milton Berle Show, 1966, The Legend of Valentino, 1975; appeared in TV series The Best of Everybody, 1975; cabaret appearances in Las Vegas, Nev., Miami Beach, Fla.; lyricist: Sam, You Made the Pants Too Long, I'm So Happy I Could Cry, Leave the Dishes in the Sink, Ma; author: Out Of My Trunk, 1945, Earthquake, 1959, Milton Berle: An Autobiography, 1974, B.S. I Love You, 1987, More of the Best of Milton Berle's Private Joke File, 1993; contbr. to Variety Mag. Recipient Golden award AGVA, 1977, Emmy award, 1979. Mem. ASCAP, Am. Guild Authors and Composers, Grand Street Boys, Friar's (re-elected hon. abbot emeritus 1968, pres. 1978— L.A.). *

BERLE, PETER ADOLF AUGUSTUS, lawyer, media director; b. N.Y.C., Dec. 8, 1937; s. Adolf Augustus and Beatrice (Bishop) B.; m. Lila Sloane Wilde, May 30, 1960; children: Adolf Augustus, Mary Alice, Beatrice Lila, Robert Thomas. BA (Knox fellow), Harvard U., 1958, LLB, 1964; LLD (hon.), Hobart Smith Coll., 1977, L.I. U., 1993, So. Vt. Coll., 1996; LLB (hon.), North Adams Tchrs. Coll., 1988. Bar: N.Y. 1964, U.S. Dist. Ct. (so. and ea. dists.) N.Y. 1966, U.S. Ct. Appeals (2d cir.) 1966, U.S. Supreme Ct. 1973. Assoc. Paul, Weiss, Rifkind, Wharton & Garrison, N.Y.C., 1964-71; ptnr. Berle, Butzel & Kass, N.Y.C., 1971-76; N.Y. state commr. environ. conservation, 1976-79; ptnr. Berle, Kass & Case, 1979-85; pres., CEO (pub. Audubon mag.) Nat. Audubon Soc., 1985-95; dir., host The Environment Show Nat. Pub. Radio, 1995—; trustee Twentieth Century Fund, Inc., 1971—, chmn., 1982-87; tchg. fellow econs. Harvard Coll., Cambridge, Mass., 1963-64; assoc. adj. prof. Sch. Urban Affairs Hunter Coll., 1974, 84; vis. prof. environ. sci. and forestry SUNY, 1980. Author: Does the Citizen Stand a Chance, 1974. Mem. N.Y. State Assembly, 1968-74; chmn. N.Y. Gov.'s Transition Task Force on Environment, 1974-75; commr. N.Y. State Moreland Act Commn. on Nursing Homes, 1975-77; bd. dirs. Clean Sites, Inc., 1986-93; chmn. Commn. on the Adirondacks in the 21st Century, 1989-90; mem. EPA adv. group on biotech., 1989-92, EPA adv. grout air quality; mem. nat. com. environ., 1991-92, nat. commn. superfund, 1992-94; mem. joint pub. adv. com. N.Am. Commn. on Environ. Coop., 1994—, commn. internat. environ. law World Conservation Union. 1st lt. USAF, 1959-61. Decorated Commendation medal; named Outstanding Legislator Eagleton Inst. Politics, 1971. Mem. ABA, N.Y. State Bar Assn., Assn. of Bar of City of N.Y. (environ. law com., profl. responsibility com., energy policy com., internat. human rights com., internat. environ. law com.). Episcopalian.

BERLEANT, ARNOLD, philosopher; b. Buffalo, Mar. 4, 1932; s. Bernard and Elizabeth (Barkun) B.; m. Riva Schiller, Aug. 1, 1958; children: Daniel, Andrea, Anne Nicole. Student, SUNY, Fredonia, 1949-51; MusB, Eastman Sch. Music; BM, U. Rochester, 1953, MA, 1955; PhD, SUNY, Buffalo, 1962. Teaching fellow SUNY, Buffalo, 1958-60; instr. SUNY, 1960-61, lectr., 1961-62; asst. prof. philosophy C.W. Post Campus, L.I.U., 1962-65; asso. prof. C.W. Post Center, L.I.U., 1965-70, prof., 1970-92, prof. emeritus, 1992—; Bingham prof. humanities U. Louisville, 1994; vis. assoc. prof. San Diego State Coll., 1966; mem. social sci. faculty Sarah Lawrence Coll., 1966-68. Author: The Aesthetic Field, 1970, Art and Engagement, 1991, The Aesthetics of Environment, 1992, Living in the Landscape: Toward an Aesthetics of Environment, 1997; contbr. articles to profl. jours. Served with U.S. Army, 1954-56. Am. Council Learned Socs. grantee, 1972, 76. Mem. AAUP, Internat. Assn. Aesthetics (sec.-gen. 1987-95, pres. 1995-98), Am. Soc. Aesthetics (sec.-treas. 1978-88), Internat. Inst. Applied Aesthetics (Lahti, Finland). Home: PO Box 52 Castine ME 04421-0052

BERLEKAMP, ELWYN RALPH, mathematic educator, electronics company executive,; b. Dover, Ohio, Sept. 6, 1940; s. Waldo and Loretta Berlekamp; m. Jennifer Joan Wilson, Aug. 21, 1966; children: Persis, Bronwen, David. BSEE, MIT, 1962, MSEE, 1962, PhD in Elec. Engring., 1964. Asst. prof. U. Calif., Berkeley, 1964-66; mem. tech. staff Bell Labs., Murray Hill, N.J., 1966-71; prof. math. U. Calif., Berkeley, 1971—, assoc. chmn. of elec. engring. and computer sci. dept., 1975-77; pres. Cyclotomics, Berkeley, 1981-89, Axcom, Berkeley, 1989-90; bd. dirs. Cylink, AK Peters, Ltd.; chmn. bd. Math. Sci. Rsch. Ins., Berkeley, 1994-98. Author: Key Papers in Coding Theory, 1974, Algebraic Coding Theory, 1984; co-author: Winning Ways, vols. 1 and 2, 1982, Mathematical Go, 1994; author or co-author more than 80 published articles and papers; holder 12 patents in field. Named Outstanding Young Elec. Engr., Eta Kappa Nu, 1971. Fellow IEEE (best rsch. paper award 1967, centennial medal 1984, Koji Kobayashi award 1990, Hamming award 1991), Info. Theory Soc. of IEEE (pres. 1973, Shannon award 1993); mem. NAE, AAAS, NAS, Am. Math. Soc. (bd. govs. 1980-82). Avocations: bridge, juggling. Home: 120 Hazel Ln Piedmont CA 94611-4033 Office: U Calif Dept Math Berkeley CA 94720

BERLEW, FRANK KINGSTON, lawyer; b. Bangor, Maine, Apr. 9, 1930; s. Herman David and Lillian (Kingston) B.; m. Jeanne Cadigan, Aug. 16, 1952; children: Derek K., Sarah. AB, Conn. Wesleyan U., 1951; JD, Harvard U., 1954. Bar: Mass. 1954, U.S. Dist. Ct. Mass. 1954, Maine 1980. Law clk. Hon. Bailey Aldrich U.S. Dist. Ct. Mass., Boston, 1956-57; assoc. Ropes & Gray, Boston, 1957-61; regional legal counsel U.S. AID, Washington, 1961-62; dir. U.S. Peace Corps, Lahore, Pakistan, 1962-64; assoc. dir. U.S. Peace Corps, Washington, 1964-66; legal dir., exec. v.p. ITT Africa and Mid. East, London, 1966-70; asst. group dir. consumer svcs. ITT, N.Y.C., 1970-72; pres. Canteen Internat., London, 1972-76, Berlew Bus. Devel. Internat., Boston, 1977-83; ptnr. Goldstein & Manello, Boston, 1984-88; ptnr. Palmer & Dodge, Boston, 1988-98, internat. legal cons., 1999—. Contbr. articles to profl. jours. Trustee Conn. Wesleyan U., Middletown, 1978-81; pres. World Law Group, 1987-90; chmn. bd. trustee Meth. Ch. York and Ogunquit, Maine, 1986-88. With U.S. Army, 1954-56. Mem. French-Am. C. of C. New Eng. (dir., pres. 1987-90), Japan Soc. Boston (dir. 1992-94). Avocations: guitar, singing, sports, wine. Home and Office: 130 Cider Hill Rd York ME 03909-5205 Office: Palmer & Dodge One Beacon St Boston MA 02108

BERLEY, DAVID RICHARD, lawyer; b. Bklyn., Apr. 9, 1942; s. Alexander and Ruth (Ginsburg) B.; m. Sharon Lee Freeman, Aug. 10, 1964 (div. 1975); children: Steven N., Barbara Robin; m. Katalin Fink, Feb. 14, 1992. BS, Boston U., 1963; JD, Boston Coll., 1966. Bar: Mass. 1966, U.S. Dist. Ct. Mass. 1966, U.S. Ct. Claims 1970, Fla. 1977, U.S. Dist. Ct. (so. dist.) Fla. 1977, U.S. Tax Ct., U.S. Ct. Appeals (11th cir.). Pvt. practice, 1966-77; gen. counsel Econocar Internat. Inc., Miami, Fla., 1976-77; v.p., gen. counsel Emergency Med. Services Assn., Inc., Miami, 1977-79, pvt. practice, 1979-85; ptnr. Berley & Littman, PA, Miami, 1985-94; pvt. practice Miami, 1994—. Active Greater Miami Heart Assn., Jewish Fedn. Greater Miami, Bus. Vols. for Arts; past chmn. City of Miami Waterfront adv. bd., Coconut Grove Playhouse Soc. of Stars; mem. citizens' adv. bd. Sta.-WLRN Pub. Radio. Mem. ABA, ATLA, Mass. Bar Assn., Fla. Bar Assn., Fla. Internat. Bankers Assn., Boston Coll. Law Sch. Alumni Assn., Greater Miami C. of C., Coconut Grove C. of C., Coconut Grove Playhouse Soc. Stars. Office: 848 Brickell Ave Ste 200 Miami FL 33131-2915

BERLEY, MARC S., foundation administrator, English educator; b. N.Y.C., Apr. 14, 1963; s. David I. and Madaleine B.; m. Vered Rachel Sussman, June 22, 1997. BA in English, Columbia Coll., 1985; MA in English, Columbia U., 1988, PhD in English and Comp Lit., 1993. Prof. English Lawrence U., Appleton, Wis., 1993-94, Rutgers U., Newark, 1995, Columbia U., N.Y.C., 1996-98; pres. Found. Acad. Stds., N.Y.C., 1996—. Author, editor: The Diversity Hoax, 1999; book reviewer; contbr. articles to profl. jours. Pres. fellow Colubmia U., 1990-93; Salvatori fellow Salvatori Found., 1999. Mem. MLA, Nat. Assn. Scholars, Assn. Lit. Scholars and Critics. E-mail: fast@gofast.org. Office: FAST 545 Madison Ave New York NY 10022

BERLIN, ALAN DANIEL, lawyer, international energy and legal consultant; b. Bklyn., Oct. 20, 1939; s. Joseph Jacob and Rose (Smith) B.; m. Renee Wellinger, Dec. 22, 1962; children—Nicole Suzanne, Allison Leigh. BBA, CCNY, 1960; LLB, NYU, 1963, LLM, 1968. Bar: N.Y. 1963. Assoc. Aranow, Brodsky, Bohlinger, Einhorn & Dann, N.Y.C., 1965-68; asst. counsel Gen. Electric Co., N.Y.C., 1968-70; tax counsel Norton Simon Inc., N.Y.C., 1970-77; asst. prof. Pace U. Grad. Sch. Bus., 1977-85; pres. Belco Petroleum Corp., N.Y.C., 1977-88, The Crown Group, White Plains,

N.Y., 1988-95; ptnr. Aitken Irvin Lewin Berlin Vrooman & Cohn L.L.P., 1995—; spl. cons. to UN Dept. Tech. Cooperation for Devel., 1989—, UN Ctr. for Transnat. Corps., 1990—; hon. assoc. Ctr. for Petroleum and Mineral Law & Policy, U. Dundee, Scotland, 1993—; bd. dirs. Chapparal Resources, Inc., Belco Oil & Gas Corp. Author monographs on fed. income tax. With U.S. Army, 1963-65. Mem. ABA, Internat. Bar Assn., N.Y. State Bar Assn., Assn. of Bar of City of N.Y., Inter-Am. Bar Assn., Assn. Internat. Petroleum Negotiators. Lodge: Masons. Office: Aitken Irwin Lewin Berlin Vrooman & Cohn LLP 2 Gannett Dr White Plains NY 10604-3403

BERLIN, CHESTON MILTON, JR., pediatrician, educator; b. Pitts., Mar. 28, 1936; s. Cheston Milton and Gladys Irene (Vance) B.; m. Anne Risher, July 9, 1960; children: Jean Vance, Douglas Cheston, Alexander Lindsay, Gordon Johnston. BA, Haverford (Pa.) Coll., 1958; MD, Harvard U., 1962. Intern Boston Children's Hosp., 1962-63, resident in pediatrics, 1965-67; asst. prof. pediatrics U. Ala. Sch. Medicine, Birmingham, 1967-68, George Washington U. Sch. Medicine, Washington, 1968-71; assoc. prof. pediatrics Pa. State U. Coll. Medicine, Hershey, 1971-75, prof. pediatrics and pharmacology, 1975-86, univ. prof. pediatrics, prof. pharmacology, 1986—; pediatric panel mem. U.S. Pharmacopeia, Rockville, Md., 1970-75, 80—. Contbr. articles to profl. jours. Sr. asst. surgeon USPHS, 1963-65. Markle Found. scholar, 1969, 74; recipient Cheston M. Berlin Alumni Svc. award Pa. State U. Coll. Medicine, 1987. Mem. Am. Acad. Pediatrics, Am. Soc. Experimental Pharmacology and Therapeutics, Am. Soc. Clin. Pharmacology and Therapeutics, Am. Pediatric Soc., Am. Inst. Nutrition, Phi Beta Kappa, Alpha Omega Alpha, Alpha Epsilon Delta. Episcopalian. Office: MS Hershey Med Ctr Dept Pediatrics PO Box 850 Hershey PA 17033-0850

BERLIN, DORIS ADA, psychiatrist; b. Newark, May 23, 1919; d. Samuel and Fanny (Lippman) B.; m. Saul R. Kelson; children: Joel, Tamar. BS in Pharmacy, Columbia U., 1940; MD, Med. Coll. Va., 1948; MPH in Community Mental Health, U. Mich., 1966. Cert. Am. Bd. Psychiatry and Neurology; lic. psychiatrist N.Y., Va., Ohio, Mich., Tex., Calif. Intern Beth Israel Hosp., N.Y.C., 1948-49; resident in psychiatry Bellevue Hosp., N.Y.C., 1949-52; pvt. practice N.Y.C., 1952-57, Toledo, 1957-66, Fishkill and Poughkeepsie, N.Y., 1984—; clin. asst. in psychiatry NYU Coll. Medicine, 1952-57; asst. in psychiatry U. Hosp., N.Y., 1952-53; clin. asst. vis. neuropsychiatrist Bellevue Hosp., N.Y., 1954-57; lectr. mental health Sch. Pub. Health U. Mich., 1966-68; dir. profl. edn. Toledo State Hosp., 1969-70; clin. assoc. prof. N.Y. Sch. Psychiatry, 1970-81; dir. residency program Hudson River Psychiat. Ctr., Poughkeepsie, 1970-83, others. Mem. citizen's adv. bd. Lucas County (Ohio) Welfare Dept., 1963-67, chair, 1965-66; bd. dirs. Jewish Family Svc., Toledo, 1969-70; mem. policy coun., rehab. com. Toledo Area Program on Drug Abuse, 1970; bd. dirs. Dutchess County Assn. for Sr. Citizens, 1993-96. Grantee NEH, 1979. Fellow Am. Psychiat. Assn. (chair editl. bd. Hosp. and Cmty. Psychiatric Jour., 1979-80, task force on cmty. mental health ctrs., 1983-88, com. on advertisers and exhibitors 1989-92, vice-chair lifers caucus, 1990-91, chair lifers orgn. 1992), Am. Coll. Psychiatrists (Laughlin fellowship com. 1976-79); mem. Am. Acad. Psychoanalysis (com. on psychoanalysis and cmty. mental health 1967-68), Dutchess County Med. Soc. (psychiatrists' rep. to coun. 1985-95, treas. 1987). Home and Office: 66 Mitchell Ave Poughkeepsie NY 12603-3423

BERLIN, FRED SAUL, psychiatrist, educator; b. Pitts., July 27, 1941; s. Sidney Danial and Pauline (Ritt) B.; m. Mary Ann Pazics, Oct. 3, 1969; children: Debra, Alison, Samantha, Ryan. BS, U. Pitts., 1964; MA, Fordham U., 1966; PhD, Dalhousie U., Halifax, N.S., Can., 1970, MD, 1974. Intern McGill U. Sch. Medicine, Jewish Gen. Hosp., Childrens Hosp., Montreal, Can., 1974-75; psychiat. resident Johns Hopkins Hosp., Balt., 1975-76; Johns Hopkins exch. resident Maudsley Hosp., London, 1977; chief resident dept. psychiatry and behavioral sci. Johns Hopkins Hosp., Balt., 1977-78; assoc. prof. dept. psychiatry and behavioral sci. Johns Hopkins U. Sch. Medicine; dir. Sexual Disorders Clinic Johns Hopkins Hosp.; attending physician Johns Hopkins Hosp., mem. house staff coun., 1976-77, mem. adv. com. house staff coun., 1977-78, mem. utilization rev. com., 1977-78, gender identity com., 1980-81; mem. Johns Hopkins U. Med. Sch. Coun., 1982-84; mem. bd. student advisors Johns Hopkins U. Sch. Medicine, 1980—; bd. dir. Nat. Inst. for Study Prevention and Treatment Sexual Trauma. Contbr. numerous articles to profl. publs. Recipient cert. appreciation Balt. County Police, 1989, 93. Fellow Am. Psychiat. Assn.; mem. AMA, Am. Acad. Psychiatry and Law (pres. Chesapeake Bay chpt.), Md. Psychiat. Assn. (legis. com. 1989—). Avocations: amateur radio, ponds and gardens. Office: John Hopkins Hosp 600 N Wolfe St Baltimore MD 21287-0005

BERLIN, HOWARD RICHARD, investment advisory company executive; b. White Plains, N.Y., Dec. 30, 1935; s. Simon and Frances (Held) B.; m. Joy Monte Shortino, June 10, 1961; children: Howard R. Jr., Asa Ward, Carter Franklin. BS in Econs., U. Pa., 1957; postgrad., NYU, 1962-63. Security analyst Merrill Lynch, N.Y.C., 1961-69, v.p. capital markets, 1969-86; portfolio mgr. Neuberger & Berman, N.Y.C., 1986-90, prin. ptnr., mem. exec. com., 1990—. Cmdr. USN, 1957-59. Mem. Fin. Analyst Fedn., N.Y. Soc. Security Analysts, Naval Res. Assn., Ret. Officers Assn., Williams Club (N.Y.C.), 101 Park Ave Club (N.Y.C.), U. Pa. Club (N.Y.C.). Avocations: land development, small business development. Office: Neuberger & Berman LLC 605 3rd Ave New York NY 10158*

BERLIN, JORDAN STUART, investment company executive; b. N.Y.C., May 26, 1952; s. Irving and Blossom (Lieberman) B.; m. Meredith Risé Brown, Aug. 13, 1988; children: Gregory, Lauren, Connor. BS, Cornell U., 1974. Acct. exec. UMIC, N.Y.C., 1975-78; sr. v.p. Lehman Bros., N.Y.C., 1978-81, A.G. Becker & Co., N.Y.C., 1981; gen. ptnr. Oppenheimer & Co. Inc., N.Y.C., 1981-97; mng. dir. CIBC Oppenheimer Corp., N.Y.C., 1998—. Mem. N.Y. Athletic Club. Office: CIBC Oppenheimer Corp 280 Park Ave West Bldg, 20th Fl New York NY 10017

BERLIN, KENNETH DARRELL, chemistry educator, consultant, researcher; b. Quincy, Ill., June 12, 1933; s. Kenneth Marion Fischer and Mary Esther (Beckley) B.; m. Grace Frances Smith, Apr. 3, 1937; children: Grace Esther, James Darrell. BA cum laude, North Cen. Coll., Naperville, Ill., 1955; PhD, U. Ill., 1958. Postdoctoral fellow U. Fla., Gainesville, 1958-60; asst. prof. chemistry Okla. State U., Stillwater, 1960-63, assoc. prof., 1963-66, prof., 1966-71, Regents prof., 1971—; spl. cons. Nat. Cancer Inst., Bethesda, Md., 1969—; cons. E.I. DuPont Co., Wilmington, Del., 1969-70, Am. Heart Assn., Oklahoma City, 1983-86, Ariz. Disease Control Commn., 1989—. Co-author: Organic Chemistry, 1972, Phosphorous Stereochem, 1977; contbr. research to Jour. Organic Chemistry, 1960—; contbr. over 270 papers to peer-reviewed jours. Recipient Regents Disting. Tchg. award, 1998, Sigma Xi rsch. award Okla. State U., Stillwater, 1969, Okla. Chemist of Yr. award, 1977. Fellow Okla. Acad. Sci. (scientist of yr. 1976, Burlington No. Faculty Achievement award 1988, Regent's Disting. Tchg. award 1998, Eminent Faculty award 1998); mem. Am. Chem. Soc. (sr.), Internat. Soc. Hetercyclic Chemists, Alpha Chi Sigma. Assembly of God. Office: Okla State Univ Dept Chemistry PS I Stillwater OK 74078

BERLIN, STEVEN RITT, business educator; b. Pitts., July 1, 1944; s. Sidney D. and Pauline (Ritt) B.; student Carnegie Mellon U., 1964-67; BBA, Duquesne U., 1967; MBA, U. Wis., 1969; m. Vera Y. Leffman, June 9, 1968; children—Leslie, Jessica, Loren. CPA. Prof., U. Houston, 1970-72; various fin. positions Cities Svc. Co., Tulsa, 1973-83; v.p. fin. Citgo Petroleum, Tulsa, 1983-85, gen. mgr., 1985-86, chief fin. officer, 1986-97; prof., assoc. dean U. Tulsa, 1997—; speaker various industry, profl. seminars; mem. Acctg. Edn. change Commn. Mem. bd. visitors U. Wis.; sec., treas. Green T Club of Tulsa, Am. Assembly of Collegiate Schs. of Bus. Mem. AICPA, Am. Acctg. Assn., Okla. Soc. CPAs, Stanford U. Alumni Assn., Beta Gamma Sigma. Jewish. Avocations: jogging, reading. Home: 230 E 19th St Tulsa OK 74119-5212 Office: U Tulsa Sch Bus 600 S College Ave Tulsa OK 74104-3126

BERLINCOURT, MARJORIE ALKINS, government official, retired; b. Toronto, Ont., Can., June 2, 1928; came to U.S., 1950, naturalized, 1956; d. Herbert John and Ellen Florence (Barker) Alkins; m. Ted Gibbs Berlincourt, Feb. 28, 1953; 1 child, Ellen Berlincourt Yale. BA, U. Toronto, 1950; MA, Yale U., 1951, PhD, 1954. Editl. dir. tech. publs. Rocketdyne, 1956-59; lectr. classics U. So. Calif., 1959-61; assoc. prof. classical history Calif. Luth. Coll., 1961-67, Calif. State U., Northridge, 1967-71; prof. Met. State Coll., Denver, 1971-72; program dir. div. fellowships for summer sems., fellowships NEH, Washington, 1972-78, dir. divsn. fellowships, seminars, 1991-94; ret., 1995; vis. lectr. Georgetown U., 1972. Author: De Surprise en Surprise, 1953, Entrez Petits Amis, 1954, Victory as a Coin Type, 1973; contbr. articles to profl. jours. Sterling fellow Yale U., 1950-53; recipient Calif. Faculty Rsch. award, 1970. Mem. Am. Assn. Ancient Historians. Episcopalian.

BERLIND, BRUCE PETER, poet, educator; b. Bklyn., July 17, 1926; s. Peter Sydney and Mae (Miller) B.; m. Doris Lidz, 1947 (div. 1950); m. Mary Elizabeth Dirlam, 1954 (div. 1983); children: Lise, Anne, John, Paul, Alexandra; m. Jo Anne Pagano, 1985. Student, Mercersburg Acad., 1941-43; AB, Princeton U., 1947; MA, Johns Hopkins U., 1950, PhD, 1958. Instr. English Colgate U., Hamilton, N.Y., 1954-58; asst. prof. Colgate U., 1958-63, assoc. prof., 1963-66, prof., 1966-80, Charles A. Dana prof. English, 1980-88, prof. emeritus, 1988—, chmn. dept. English, 1967-72, 80-83; poet in residence U. Rochester, 1966; USIS lectr., Germany, 1963, with Hungarian P.E.N. Translation Program, Budapest, 1977, 79, 86, 88, 91. Author: (poems) Ways of Happening, 1959, Companion Pieces, 1971; translator: (poems) Selected Poems of Agnes Nemes Nagy, 1980, Birds and Other Relations: Selected Poetry of Dezso Tandori, 1987, When You Became She by Imre Oravecz, 1994, The Journey of Barbarus by Ottó Orbán, 1997; assoc. editor: (poems) The Hopkins Rev., 1949-53; contbr. poems, essays, revs. to mags. 1st lt. AUS, 1945-46, 50-52. Recipient Meml. medal Hungarian PEN, 1986; Fulbright grantee, Hungary, 1983-84. Mem. PEN Am. Ctr., Poetry Soc. Am., Am. Lit. Translators Assn., AAUP (mem. council, past pres. N.Y. State Conf.). Home: PO Box 237 Hamilton NY 13346-0237

BERLIND, ROBERT ELLIOT, artist; b. N.Y.C., Aug. 20, 1938; s. Peter Sidney Berlind and Mae (Miller) Bach; m. Dorothy Welch, June 1963 (div. 1974); 1 child, Alexey Fuller; m. Nancy Lee Hubbard, June 17, 1978 (div. 1993); 1 child, Gabriel Peter; m. Mary Lucier, June 7, 1997. BA, Columbia U., 1960; BFA, Yale U., 1962, MFA, 1963. Assoc. prof. art N.S. Coll. of Art and Design, Halifax, Can., 1974-76; prof. SUNY, Purchase, 1979—. One man exhbns.: Alexander Milliken Gallery, N.Y.C., 1981, 82, Tomasulo Gallery, Union Coll., 1983, Ruth Siegel Gallery, N.Y.C., 1984, 86, 88, 90, Gallery One, Toronto, Can., 1985, Warren Wilson Coll., Swanano, N.C., 1986, St. Peter's Ch., N.Y.C., 1988, Delaware Valley Arts Alliance, Narrowsburg, N.Y., 1992, Tibor de Nagy Gallery, N.Y.C., 1994, 96, 98, Hampshire Coll. Main Gallery, Amherst, Mass., 1995, Reynolds Gallery, Richmond, Va., 1996, Wright State U., Dayton, Ohio, 1997, Newberger Mus. Art, Purchase, N.Y., 1998; group shows: N.Y. Studio Sch., 1986, The Bronx Mus. of the Arts, 1987, Sherry French Gallery, N.Y.C., 1987, One Penn Pla., N.Y.C., 1988, Fay Gold Gallery, 1988, Art Mus. Fla. Internat. U., 1989, Meml. Art Gallery U. Rochester, 1989, Found. Mona Bismarck, Paris, 1991, Am. Acad. and Inst. Arts and Letters, 1992, Neuberger Mus., Purchase, N.Y., 1994, Maier Art Mus., Lynchburg, Va., others. Recipient award in painting Am. Acad. Inst. Arts and Letters, 1992, Pollock-Krasner award, 1997; NEA fellow in painting, 1993. Mem. Coll. Art Assn., Internat. Assn. Art Critics. Home: 215 W 20th St Apt 4W New York NY 10011-3552

BERLIND, ROGER STUART, stage and film producer; b. N.Y.C., June 27, 1930; s. Peter Sydney and Mae (Miller) B.; m. Helen Polk Clark, July 7, 1962 (dec.); 1child, William Polk; m. Brook Wheeler, May 19, 1979. AB, Princeton U., 1952. Account exec. Eastman Dillon, Union Securities & Co., N.Y.C., 1956-60; gen. ptnr. Carter, Berlind & Weill, N.Y.C., 1960-65; chmn. exec. com. Cogan, Berlind, Weill & Levitt, Inc., N.Y.C., 1965-69; chief exec. officer Shearson Lehman Bros., N.Y.C., 1969-73, vice chmn. bd., 1974-75; bd. drs. Lehman Bros. Prodr.: (films) Aaron Loves Angela, 1975, Beyond Therapy, 1987; (plays) Rex, 1976, Music Is, 1976, Diversions and Delights, 1977, The Merchant, 1977, The 1940's Radio Hour, 1979, Passione, The Lady from Dubuque, Amadeus, 1980, Sophisticated Ladies, Lydie Breeze, 1981, Nine, 1982, All's Well that Ends Well, 1983, The Real Thing, The Rink, 1984, Joe Egg, After the Fall, 1985, Precious Sons, Big Deal, Long Day's Journey into Night, 1986, Ain't Misbehavin', 1988, Jerome Robbins' Broadway, 1989, City of Angels, 1989, Artist Descending A Staircase, 1989, Lettice and Lovage, 1990, Death and The Maiden, 1992, Guys and Dolls, 1992, Passion, 1994, Indiscretions, 1995, Hamlet, 1995, Getting Away with Murder, 1996, A Funny Thing Happened on the Way to the Forum, 1996, Skylight, 1996, Steel Pier, 1997, The Life, 1997, A View from the Bridge, 1998, The Judas Kiss, 1998, The Blue Room, 1998, Closer, Amy's View, 1999. Hon. trustee Am. Acad. Dramatic Arts. With CIC, U.S. Army, 1952-54. Mem. League Am. Theatres and Producers (gov.), Princeton Club (N.Y.C.), Univ. Club, River Club, Century Assn.

BERLINE, JAMES H., advertising executive, public relations agency executive; b. Youngstown, Ohio, Aug. 6, 1946; s. James Howard and Eloise Blanche (Smith) B.; children: Erin Michele, Jess Brandon, Quincy Blaine. B.A. in Econs., U. Mich., 1968; M.S. in Advt., U. Ill., 1971. Vice pres. Campbell-Ewald Co., Detroit, 1971-76; sr. v.p. Batten Barton Durstine & Osborn Inc., Troy, Mich., 1976-78; exec. v.p. Batten Barton Durstine & Osborn Inc., Southfield, Mich., 1984-85; pres. Yaffe Berline Inc., Southfield, 1980-82; pres., chief exec. officer The Berline Group, Birmingham, Mich., 1982—; bd. dirs. Leadership Detroit Alumni. Program chmn. United Found., Detroit, 1984; trustee Detroit Sci. Ctr., 1985—; adv. bd. Jr. League; trustee Juvenile Diabetes Found., 1994; chmn. comms. com. Leadership Detroit, 1993; trustee Young Pres. Orgn., office commn. chair, 1994; bd. dirs. Make-A-Wish Found.; founder Winning Futures. Mem. Young Presidents Orgn. (officer, com. chmn. Ea. Mich. chpt., trustee), Adcraft Club (bd. dirs. 1980-99, pres. 1988), Greater Detroit Alliance Bus. (bd. dirs. 1984-86), Detroit C. of C. (mktg. com. 1987-88), U. Mich. Club Detroit (past bd. govs.), U. Mich. Grad. M Club (Ann Arbor, bd. dirs. 1986). Avocation: squash. Office: The Berline Group 6001 N Adams Rd Bloomfield Hills MI 48304-1566

BERLINER, ALLEN IRWIN, dermatologist; b. N.Y.C., Apr. 18, 1947; s. Joseph Benjamin and Ruth (Kaplan) B.; m. Edwina. BA, Queens Coll., 1967; MD, SUNY, Buffalo, 1971. Diplomate Am. Bd. Dermatology. Intern Nassau County Med. Ctr., East Meadow, N.Y., 1971-72; resident in dermatology Boston U. Med. Ctr., 1974-76, chief resident, 1976-77; practice medicine specializing in dermatology Norwood, Mass., 1977—; asst. clin. prof. Tufts U., 1980-90, assoc. clin. prof., 1990—; chief dermatology sect. Norwood Hosp., 1986—; assoc. staff Boston U. Hosp., Tufts-New Eng. Med. Ctr.; bd. dirs. Mass. Acad. Dermatology. Served as surgeon USPHS, 1972-74. Mem. Am. Acad. Dermatology, New Eng. Dermatol. Soc., Mass. Acad. Dermatology (pres. 1994-95). Office: 95 Chapel St Norwood MA 02062-3161

BERLINER, BARBARA, librarian, consultant; b. Bklyn., July 14, 1947; d. Robert and Mildred M. (Sklar) Morris; 1 child, Stefanie Lauren. BA in Anthropology, NYU, 1969; MLS, Columbia U., 1970. Libr. N.Y. Pub. Libr., N.Y.C., 1970-81, sr. libr., telephone reference, 1981-86, supervising libr., telephone reference, 1986-92, head libr., Mid-Manhattan sci. and bus., 1992-93; coord. NYPL Express, N.Y.C., 1993—; cons. John Wright, N.Y.C., 1991; bibliographer Collier's Encyclopedia. Author: The Book of Answers, 1990. Mem. ALA, Spl. Librs. Assn., N.Y. Libr. Assn., Planetary Soc. Avocations: sports, astronomy. Home: 64 Meadowview Ct Leonia NJ 07605-2044 Office: NYPL Express 188 Madison Ave New York NY 10016-4314

BERLINER, DAVID C., foundation administrator; b. N.Y.C., Jan. 16, 1943; s. Martin M. and Miriam Weil B.; m. Donna G. Israel Berliner, Dec. 27, 1973; children: Lauren Samara, Debra Ellen, Robert Andrew. BA, NYU, 1964; student, Columbia U., 1971. Writer, corr. Newark Evening News, 1965-72; freelance writer, spl. corr. Washington Post N.Y. Times, N.Y.C., 1972-78; dir. office pub. info. Consumers Union, Yonkers, 1978-98; sr. dir. media and pub. rels. March of Dimes Birth Defects Found., White Plains, N.Y., 1999—. Co-author: Understanding Your Man, 1977. Commr. Greenburge Environ. Protection Commn., Westchester County, N.Y., 1979-90. Washington Journalism Ctr. fellow, 1968; Ford fellow in advanced internat. reporting Columbia U., 1971. Mem. Soc. Profl. Journalists, Pub. Rels. Soc. Am. (pres. Westchester-Fairfield, Conn. chpt. 1999), N.Y. Press Club. Avocation: creative writing. Home: 185 Woodlands Ave White Plains NY 10607

BERLINER, HERMAN ALBERT, university provost and dean, economics educator; b. N.Y.C., Apr. 6, 1944; s. Walter and Johanna (Aschenbrand) B. BA, CCNY, 1965; PhD, CUNY, 1970. Assoc. prof. econs. Hofstra U., Hempstead, N.Y., 1970-85, assoc. dean advisement, 1975-76, assoc. provost, 1976-83, dean Sch. Bus., 1980-82, 83-90, prof. econs., 1985—, provost, dean faculties, 1989—; Lawrence Herbert disting. prof., 1996—; mem. initial accreditation com. Am. Assembly of Collegiate Schs. of Bus., St. Louis, 1987-90; mem. N.Y. State Doctoral Coun., 1994—, The Coll. Bd. Regional Assembly, 1994-97. Assoc. editor Am. Economist, 1975-80, 83—. Home: 93 Plymouth Dr N Glen Head NY 11545-1126 Office: Hofstra U Office of Provost Hempstead NY 11550

BERLINER, JOSEPH SCHOLOM, economics educator; b. N.Y.C., Sept. 4, 1921; s. Michael and Yetta (Eisenberg) B.; m. Ann Korenbaum, Nov. 7, 1943; children: Paul, Carl, Nancy. B.A., Harvard U., 1947, Ph.D., 1953. Mem. faculty Syracuse (N.Y.) U., 1956-63; prof. econs. Brandeis U., Waltham, Mass., 1963-85; prof. emeritus Brandeis U., 1985—. Author: Factory and Manager in the USSR, 1957, Economy, Society and Welfare, 1972, The Innovation Decision in Soviet Industry, 1976, Soviet Industry From Stalin to Gorbachev, 1988, The Economics of the Good Society, 1999. Fellow Social Sci. Research Council; fellow Guggenheim Found., Kennan Inst.; grantee NSF, Nat. Council Soviet and East European Research. Mem. Assn. Comparative Econ. Studies (pres. 1975-76), Am. Assn. Advancement Slavic Studies (pres. 1963-64), Am. Econ. Assn. Democrat. Jewish. Home: 9 Chandler St Lexington MA 02420-3601 Office: Davis Ctr Russian Studies 1737 Cambridge St Cambridge MA 02138-3016

BERLINER, ROBERT WILLIAM, physician, medical educator, b. N.Y.C., Mar. 10, 1915; s. William Marcus and Anna (Weiner) B.; m. Leah Silver, Dec. 21, 1941; children: Robert William, Alice Hadler, Henry J., Nancy. BS, Yale U., 1936; MD, Columbia U., 1939; DSc (hon.), Med. Coll. Wis., 1973, Yale U., 1973. Intern Presbyn. Hosp., N.Y.C., 1939-41; resident Goldwater Meml. Hosp., N.Y.C., 1942-43, rsch. fellow, 1943-44, research asst., 1944-47; asst. in medicine NYU Coll. Medicine, 1943-44, instr. medicine, 1944-47; asst. prof. medicine Columbia U., 1947-50; rsch. assoc. dept. hosps., City of N.Y., 1947-50; chief Lab. Kidney and Electrolyte Metabolism, Nat. Heart Inst., NIH, Bethesda, Md., 1950-62, dir. intramural rsch., 1954-68; dir. labs. and clinics NIH, Bethesda, 1968-69, dep. dir. for sci., 1969-73; dean, prof. physiology and medicine Yale U., New Haven, 1973-84, dean emeritus, 1985—, prof. emeritus physiology and medicine, 1985—; dir. Pew Scholars Program in Biomed. Scis., New Haven, 1984-91; lectr. George Washington U. Sch. Medicine, 1951-73, Georgetown U. Schs. Medicine and Dentistry, 1964-73; mem. exec. com. assembly of life scis. NRC, 1973-78, chmn. div. med. scis., 1976-78. Contbr. articles to tech. jours. Served with USPHS, 1952-54. Recipient Disting. Service award HEW, 1962; Homer W. Smith Award in Renal Physiology, 1965, Alumni Award for Disting. Achievement, Coll. Physicians and Surgeons, Columbia U., 1966, Bicentennial Medal, 1967; Disting. Achievement award Modern Medicine, 1969; Research Achievement award Am. Heart Assn., 1970; Service award Assn. Chmn. Depts. Physiology, 1981; David M. Hume Meml. award Nat. Kidney Found., 1983; Mem. AAAS (bd. dirs., v.p. 1972), Am. Physiology Soc. (pres. 1967, Ray G. Daggs award 1982, Am. Soc. Clin. Investigation (pres. 1959), Am. Soc. Nephrology (pres. 1968), Internat. Soc. Nephrology (A.N. Richards award 1987), Assn. Am. Physicians (George M. Kober medal 1984), Inst. Medicine, Nat. Acad. Scis., (com. sci. and pub. policy 1978-81, council of acad. 1978-81), Soc. Exptl. Biology and Medicine (pres. 1978-81). Avocations: birdwatching, music. Home: 36 Edgehill Ter Hamden CT 06517-4016 Office: Yale Univ Sch Medicine 333 Cedar St New Haven CT 06510-3289

BERLING, JOHN GEORGE, academic dean; b. Melrose, Minn., June 26, 1934; m. Patricia Ann Ehlen, Feb. 23, 1957. BS in Bus. Edn., St. Cloud State U., 1957; MLS, Wayne State U., 1967; PhD in Ednl. Adminstrn., U. Nebr., 1975. Tchr. Holdingford Pub. Schs., Minn., 1957-62; tchr., libr. Staples H.S., Minn., 1962-68; dir. resource ctr. Apollo H.S., St. Cloud, Minn., 1969-75; reference libr. St. Cloud State U., 1968-69, dean learning resources ctr., dir. ctr. fo info. media, 1975—; cons. Control Data Corp., St. Paul, 1975, Cambridge Pub. Schs., Minn., 1976, Kearney State U., Nebr., 1977, St. Mary's U., San Antonio, 1979, U. Wis., Plattesville, 1989. Bd. dirs. Ctrl. Minn. Ednl. R&D Coun., 1985—; chmn. bd. Live Interactive Televised Edn. Supporting Programs and Networks; mem. Minn. Libr. Planning Task Force; mem. exec. com. Project for Automated Libr. Sys.; founding mem. Ctrl. Minn. Distance Learning Network; chair Minn. Ednl. Telecomms. Coun. Experienced Tchr. fellow Wayne State U., 1966-67; NDEA scholar, 1965. Mem. ALA, NEA, Minn. Edn. Assn., Minn. Ednl. Media Orgn., Assn. for Ednl. Comm. and Tech. Assn. (chair accreditation com. 1987-90), Assn. for Coll. and Rsch. Libr. Home: 3650 Plum Creek Dr Saint Cloud MN 56301-9521

BERLINGER, NORMAN THOMAS, physician, author; b. Detroit, Sept. 16, 1944; s. Stanley Edmund and Bernice (Glinka) B.; m. Patricia Ann Cybert, June 17, 1968; 1 child, Michael. BS, U. Mich., 1966, MD, 1970; PhD, U. Minn., 1978. Diplomate Am. Bd. Otolaryngology. Intern Henry Ford Hosp., Detroit, 1970-71; resident U. Minn. Hosps., 1971-73, 77-79; assoc. scientist Sloan-Kettering Inst. for Cancer Rsch., N.Y.C., 1973-77; instr. U. Minn. Med. Sch., Mpls., 1977-79; asst. prof. Uniformed Svcs. U. Health Scis., Bethesda, Md., 1979-81; surgeon, clin. br. NIH, Bethesda, 1979-81; assoc. prof. U. Minn. Med. Sch., 1981-88; surgeon Oakdale ENT, P.A., Mpls., 1988—; cons. FMC, Phila., 1986-88; advisor for marine mammals Minn. Zoo, Apple Valley, 1986-88. Contbr. numerous articles to textbooks, articles to profl. jours. and lay periodicals. Comdr. USNR, 1979-81. Grantee NIH, 1973-81, Am. Otological Soc., 1986-88; Nat. Cancer Inst. rsch. fellow, 1974-77. Fellow Am. Acad. Otolaryngology (Meritorious Svc. award 1987); mem. Assn. for Rsch. in Otolaryngology, Phi Rho Sigma. Avocations: piano, tennis, philately. Office: 2855 Campus Dr Ste 630 Plymouth MN 55441-2665

BERLINGER, WARREN, actor; b. Bklyn., Aug. 31, 1937; s. Elias and Frieda (Shapkin) B.; m. Betty Lou Keim, Feb. 18, 1960. Student, Profl. Children's Sch., 1952-55, Columbia, 1958. Broadway appearances include Annie Get Your Gun, 1946, Happy Time, 1950, Take a Giant Step, 1951, Anniversary Waltz, 1955, Roomful of Roses, 1957, Blue Denim, 1958 (Theatre World award 1959), Come Blow Your Horn, 1960, Bernardine, 1953; London appearance in How to Succeed in Business Without Really Trying, 1963-64; film appearances include The Long Goodbye, Spinout, The World According to Garp, My African Adventure, Outlaw Force, Hero, 1992, Crime and Punishment, 1994, Feminine Touch, 1994; TV appearances on Secret Storm, 1955-57, The Funny Side, 1971-72, Touch of Grace, 1973, My African Adventure, 1986, Take Two, 1987, Agatha Christie's Death on Safari, (TV series) Shades of L.A., 1991, Picket Fences, 1993; films include That Thing You Do!, Dear God, T.O. Friends, November Conspiracy; plays include Lend Me a Tenor. Named hon. mayor of Chatsworth Calif., 1968, hon. sheriff, 1975; recipient Theatre World award, 1958.

BERLINSKI, EDWARD GERARD, writing educator, writer; b. Spokane, Wash., Apr. 18, 1961; s. Edward Joseph and Dorothy Florence (Chojnowski) B. BA in History, Cath. U., Washington, 1984; MFA in Creative Writing, Am. U., Washington, 1990; PhD in Rhetoric and Composition, Cath. U., 1997. Writer/editor Naval Surface Warfare Ctr., Silver Spring, Md., 1984-90; writing instr. Cath. U., 1990-96; adj. prof. humanities Strayer U., Takoma Park, Md., 1993-97; lectr. profl. writing program U. Md., College Park, 1996—. Avocation: writing poetry. E-mail: eb127@umail.umd.edu. Home: PO Box 11038 Takoma Park MD 20913 Office: Univ Md Profl Writing Program 3119 Susquehanna Hall College Park MD 20742

BERLOFF, ANDREA, performing arts company official; b. Silver Springs, Md., Dec. 25, 1973; d. Howard Albert and Myra Lynn (Chudakoff) B. BA, Cornell U., 1995. Luncheon coord. New Dramatists, N.Y.C., 1995-96; assoc. prodr. festival Lincoln Ctr., N.Y.C., 1996-97; dir. devel. En Garde Arts, N.Y.C., 1996—. Author: (screenplay) Waiting, 1997. Mem. Cornell U. Alumni Assn.

BERLOW, ROBERT ALAN, lawyer; b. Detroit, Feb. 11, 1947; s. Henry and Shirley (Solovich) B.; m. Elizabeth Ann Goldin, Sept. 20, 1972; children: Stuart, Lisa. BA, U. Mich., 1968; JD, Wayne State U., 1971. Bar: Mich. 1971, U.S. Supreme Ct. 1978. Asst. to dean, instr. law sch. Wayne State U.,

Detroit, 1971-72; mem. Radner, Radner, Shefman, Bayer and Berlow, P.C., Southfield, Mich., 1972-78; gen. counsel Perry Drug Stores, Inc., Pontiac, Mich., 1978-80, gen. counsel, sec., 1980-82, v.p., gen. counsel, sec., 1982-88, sr. v.p., gen. counsel, sec., 1988-93, sr. v.p., chief adminstrn. officer, gen. counsel, sec., 1993-94, exec. v.p., gen. counsel, sec., 1994-95; sr. mem. Dykema Gossett, PLLC, 1995—. Pres. Agy. for Jewish Edn., Metro Detroit, 1993-95, v.p., 1987-93; bd. dirs. Jewish Cmty. Ctr. Met. Detroit, 1989—, v.p., 1992-93, treas., 1996-97, sec., 1997—. Mem. ABA, Bar of Supreme Ct. of U.S., Mich. Bar Assn. (chair comml. leasing and mgmt. of real estate com. of real property sect. 1993-98, mem. real property sect. coun. 1995—, frequent spkr. continuing legal edn. programs), Internat. Coun. Shopping Ctrs. (roundtable leader nat. law conf. 1986, 88-90, 93-98). Avocations: sports, photography. Office: Dykema Gossett PLLC 1577 N Woodward Ave Bloomfield Hills MI 48304-2837

BERLOWE, PHYLLIS HARRIETTE, public relations counselor; b. N.Y.C.; d. Louis and Rose (Jachez) Berlowe. Student, Hunter Coll., 1950-52. Account exec. Ted Sills & Co., N.Y.C., 1959-63, Harshe-Rotman & Druck, N.Y.C., 1963-65; exec. v.p. Edward Gottlieb & Assocs, N.Y.C., 1965-78; v.p. Hill & Knowlton, Inc., N.Y.C., 1972-79; v.p., group supr. Doremus & Co., N.Y.C., 1980-83, Marketshare divsn. Doremus & Co., N.Y.C., 1983-86; pres. The Berlowe Group, N.Y.C., 1986—. Named to founding roster Nat. Honor Roll of Women in Pub. Rels., No. Ill. U., 1993. Fellow Pub. Rels. Soc. Am. (citations 1976-78, 80-83, Silver Anvil 1977); mem. Counselors Acad. (chmn. 1981), Women Execs. in Pub. Rels. (pres. 1982), N.Y. Pub. Rels. Soc. (pres. 1990-91, citations 1993-95, John W. Hill award 1992). Office: The Berlowe Group 201 W 77th St New York NY 10024-6606

BERLOWITZ, LESLIE, cultural organization administrator. BA in English with honors, NYU, 165; MA in English, Columbia U., 1967. Mem. dept. English NYU, N.Y.C., 1967-96, asst. dean U. Coll. Arts and Scis., Washington Square Coll. Arts and Scis., 1969-73, dir. acad. program devel., 1973-81, asst. v.p. acad. affairs, 1981-84, assoc. v.p. acad. affairs, 1984-88, dep. v.p. acad. affairs, 1988-91, v.p. instnl. advancement, 1991-96; exec. officer Am. Acad. Arts and Scis., Cambridge, Mass., 1996—; founder, dir. The Humanities Coun., 1977-96, Faculty Resource Network, 1985-96; nat. dir. AmeriCorps, Project SafetyNet, 1995-96. Editor: (with Denis Donoghue and Louis Menand) America in Theory, 1988, Greenwich Village: Culture and Counterculture, 1990. Bd. dirs. Mass. Inst. Psychoanalysis; panelist Boston Jewish Film Festival; exec. bd. Corp. Yaddo; active Fund for Artists' Colonies, Inc., Coun. Internat. Edn. Exch., Urban Rsch. Ctr., Am. Jewish Congress, Fedn. Jewish Philanthropies, Joseph S. Gruss Found.; panelist NEH. Recipient Pacesetter award Tougaloo Coll., 1993. Fellow N.Y. Inst. Humanities; mem. MLA, Century Assn. (N.Y.). Fax: (617) 576-5055. Home: 1010 Memorial Dr Apt 8E Cambridge MA 02138-4854 Office: Am Acad Arts and Scis Norton's Woods 136 Irving St Cambridge MA 02138-1929*

BERLOWITZ TARRANT, LAURENCE, biotechnologist, university administrator; b. N.Y.C., Oct. 20, 1934; s. Israel and Beatrice (Rothenberg) B.; m. Sandra Kaplan, Jan. 13, 1954; children: Dion, Aviva; m. Susan Navarre, 1988. A.B., U. Calif., Berkeley, 1954, Ph.D., 1965; M.A., UCLA, 1958. Mem. tech. staff Thompson-Ramo-Wooldridge Corp., Los Angeles, 1958-60; human factors scientist Western Devel. Lab., Philco Corp., Palo Alto, Calif., 1960-61; instr. biol. sci. Chabot Coll., 1961-64; research fellow med. research council, epigenetics research group U. Edinburgh, Scotland, 1965-66; asst. prof. biology SUNY, Buffalo, 1966-70; assoc. prof. SUNY, 1970-75, co-chmn. dept., 1968-69; program dir. genetic biology NSF, Washington, 1975-76, spl. asst. biol. directorate, 1976-77; prof. biology, asst. v.p. acad. affairs NYU, N.Y.C., 1977-81; prof. biochemistry Clark U., Worcester, Mass., 1981-84, provost, v.p. acad. affairs, 1981-83; pres. Internat. Tech. Mgmt. Assocs., Ltd., Harvard, Mass., 1983—. Patentee cartilage healing, algal plastics, biopolymers. NIH spl. fellow U. Nijmegen, Netherlands, 1972-73; recipient John Belling prize U. Calif., 1970. Mem. AAAS, Soc. Developmental Biology, Am. Chem. Soc.

BERLYN, SHELDON, art educator; b. Worcester, Mass., Sept. 6, 1929; m. Diane C. Satterfield. Diploma, Worcester Art Mus. Sch., 1951; student, Yale-Norfolk Summer Sch. Art, 1949-50, Art Acad. Cin., 1954-55, SUNY Buffalo, 1959-62. Instr. drawing Worcester (Mass.) Art Mus. Sch., 1957-58; assoc. prof. painting (emeritus) SUNY Buffalo, 1962-99; ret., 1999—. With U.S. Army, 1951-53, Korea. Home: 813 Richmond Ave Buffalo NY 14222-1166 Office: SUNY 202-CFA Art Dept Buffalo NY 14260-6010

BERMACK, ELAINE, speech educator; b. Jersey City, N.J., Oct. 8, 1930; d. Morris and Irene (Hendel) Dalberg; m. Eugene Bermack, Mar. 18, 1951; children: Alison, Kiri, Marla. BA, NYU, 1951, PhD, 1988; MA, Columbia U., 1969. Lic. speech and lang. pathology, lic. tchr. of the deaf, N.Y. Tchr. of speech improvement N.Y.C. Bd. of Edn., 1951-57; asst. prof. speech Queensborough C.C., CUNY, Bayside, N.Y., 1971—, St. John's U., Queens, N.Y., 1989-94; instr. of comm. Nassau C.C., Garden City, 1973-80; chmn., CEO Presentations Plus, Manhasset Hills, N.Y., 1996—. Mem. Am. Speech and Hearing Assn. (cert. speech lang. pathology), L.I. Speech and Hearing Assn.

BERMAN, AARON, art appraiser, director, consultant; b. N.Y.C., Nov. 21, 1922; s. Harry and Minnie (Stillman) B.; m. Miriam Mosevitzky, July 4, 1955; children: David, Raphael, Michael. BA, Bklyn. Coll., 1943; BS, Notre Dame U., 1944; MA, Columbia U., 1947. Art dir. Spencer Enterprises, N.Y.C., 1948-72; art lectr. New Sch., N.Y.C., 1977-78; art dir. Aaron Berman Gallery, N.Y.C., 1976—; art cons. UJA-N.Y., 1970—, Nat. Council Art Jewish Life, 1983—; art appraiser Chai Art Inst., Bklyn., 1978—. Author: Grace Knowlton, 1981, Women's Art—Miles Apart, 1982, Michael Gleizer, 1993. Trustee Nat. Coun. Art, Am. Jewish Congress, 1984-87; assoc. Guggenheim, MOMA, Whitney, Jewish, Bklyn. museums. Ltd. USNR, 1944-47. Decorated Bronze Star. Mem. Appraisers Assn. Am., Knights of Pythias.

BERMAN, ALAN, physicist; b. Bklyn., Nov. 2, 1925; s. Hyman and Sarah (Levy) B.; m. Charlotte Bernstein, Apr. 28, 1962; children: Julia, Jessica, S. Jonathan, Margaret, James. A.B., Columbia U., 1947, Ph.D., 1952. Research scientist Hudson Labs., Columbia, N.Y.C., 1952-57; assoc. dir. Hudson Labs., Columbia, 1957-63, dir., 1963-67; dir. research Naval Research Lab., Washington, 1967-82; dean Sch. Marine and Atmospheric Scis. U. Miami, 1982-87; sr. rsch. fellow Ctr. Naval Analyses, 1987—; mem. Naval Research Adv. Com., 1982—; mem. panels of naval studies bd. Nat. Acad. Sci., 1982—, mem. ocean studies bd., 1985—; cons. Ctr. Naval Analyses, 1982—; gov. JOI Inc. Served with AUS, 1944-46. Recipient Superior Civilian Svc. award Dept. Navy, 1969, Disting. Civilian Svc. award Dept. Def., 1973, Robert Dexter Conrad award, 1982; named Disting. Sr. Exec., 1980. Fellow Am. Phys. Soc., Acoutical Soc. Am.; mem. Sigma Xi. Home: 5300 Holmes Run Pkwy Alexandria VA 22304-2834 Office: 4401 Ford Ave Alexandria VA 22302-1432

BERMAN, ARIANE R., artist; b. Danzig, Mar. 27, 1937; m. Mario La Rossa, 1965. B.F.A., Hunter Coll., N.Y.C., 1959; M.F.A., Yale, 1962; AAUW and Found. des Etats-Unis fellow, U. Paris, 1962-63. juror nat. screening com. Fulbright grants, 1976-77, chmn. screening com., 1977-78. One man shows at Center Gallery, Conn., 1963, Harry Salpeter Gallery, N.Y.C., 1966, Brentano's Art Gallery, N.Y.C., 1973, Graphic Art Gallery, Tel Aviv, 1973, Galleria San Sebastianello, Rome, 1973, Eileen Kuhlik Gallery, N.Y.C., 1971, 73, Pub. Mus., Oshkosh, Wis., 1974, Wustum Mus. Fine Arts, Racine, Wis., 1974, Fontana Gallery, Pa., 1963, 71, 74, Galleria d'Arte Helioart, Rome, 1974, Munson Gallery, Conn., 1975, Ward-Nasse Gallery, N.Y.C., 1975, 77, 80, Phila. Art Alliance, 1980, Silvermine Guild Artists, Conn., 1976, Kornblee Gallery, N.Y.C., 1982, Babson Coll., Mass., 1983, Northwood Inst., Mich., 1983, Westenhook Gallery, Mass., 1984, Phoenix Gallery, N.Y.C., 1985, 87, Concordia Coll., Bronxville, N.Y., 1989, Gallery 84 Inc., N.Y.C., 1992, L'Artisanat, Mass., 1992, others; exhibited in group shows at Galerie Atrium Artis, Geneva, Switzerland, 1975, F 15 Gallery, Norway, 1974, Galeries Raymond Duncan, Paris, 1964, Asso. Am. Artists, N.Y.C., 1971, Circle Galleries Ltd., N.Y.C., 1974, Margo Feiden Galleries, N.Y.C., 1972, Gallery 500, Pa., 1973, Van Straaten Gallery, Chgo., 1974, Genesis Gallery, N.Y.C., 1978, Marymount Coll., N.Y.C., 1983, NYU, 1982, Fairleigh Dickenson U., 1982, Allentown Art Mus., Pa., 1982, numerous others; represented in permanent collections at Am. Petroleum Inst., Israel Ministry of Tourism, USIA, McGregor-Doniger, Inc., Shipley Sch., Bryn Mawr, Pa., Readers Digest, N.J. Bd. Edn., Athena Gallery, New Haven, Charles E. Ellis Coll., Newton Square, Pa., Hearst Corp., Met. Mus. Art, Phila. Mus. Art, Phila. Art Alliance, Ms. mag., Seventeen, Redbook, Feminist Press, Duke U., Newspaper Advt. Bur., Purdue U., Phila. Child Guidance Ctr., others. Recipient Yale Painting prize, 1960, Purchase award Purdue U., 1964, Stella Drabkin Meml. award, ACPS Purchase prize, 1973, Catherine Lorillard Wolfe Arts Club Gold medal, 1973, Hon. mention Hudson River Mus., 1974, Artists Equity award, 1985. Mem. Am. Color Print Soc., Nat. Assn. Women Artists, Yonkers Art Assn., Women's Caucus for Art, Met. Painters and Sculptors, Pen and Brush, League of Present Day Artists, Sheffield Art League, Silvermine Guild of Artists, Soc. Women Artists (past corr. sec.), Hunter Coll. Alumni Assn. (Hall of Fame 1974). Home: 161 W 54th St New York NY 10019-5322 Office: care Gallery 84 50 W 57th St New York NY 10019-3914 *I use art as a means of communicating to people. My work is representational and tries to depict life in all its humor, sorrow, satiric aspects, and dream-like qualities of humanity as I see it. I particularly use color for emphasis in everything I do—paintings, graphics, plastics, and sculpture.*

BERMAN, ARTHUR LEONARD, state senator; b. Chgo., May 4, 1935; s. Morris and Jean (Glast) B.; m. Barbara Dombeck; children: Adam, Marcy Padorr. B.S. in Commerce and Law, U. Ill., 1956; J.D., Northwestern U., 1958. Bar: Ill., 1958. Pvt. practice, Chgo.; ptnr. White, White & Berman, Chartered, 1958-74, Maragos, Richter, Berman, Russell & White, Chartered, 1974-81, Chatz, Berman, Maragos, Haber & Fagel, 1981-82, Berman, Fagel, Haber, Maragos & Abrams, 1982-86, Karlin & Fleisher, 1986—; spl. atty. Bur. Liquidations, Ill. Dept. Ins., 1962-67; spl. asst. atty. gen. Ill., 1967-68; mem. Ill. Ho. of Reps., 1969-76, Ill. Senate, 1977—. Pres., 50th Ward Young Dems., 1956-60; v.p. Cook County Young Dems., 1956-60, 50th Ward Regular Dem. Orgn., 1955—; active 48th Ward Regular Dem. Orgn., 1985—, 49th Ward Regular Dem. Orgn., 1967—; exec. bd. Dem. Party, Evanston, Ill., 1973—; bd. govs. State of Israel Bonds. Mem. ABA, Ill. Bar Assn., Chgo. Bar Assn. (bd. mgrs. 1976-77), Decalogue Soc. Lawyers (bd. mgrs. 1988—), Nat. Assn. Jewish Legislators (pres. 1987-89), Am. Trial Lawyers Assn., Northwestern U. Alumni Assn., U. Ill. Alumni Assn., Phi Epsilon Pi, Tau Epsilon Rho. Office: 7344 N Western Ave Chicago IL 60645-1814

BERMAN, BARBARA, educational consultant; b. N.Y.C., Oct. 15, 1938; d. Nathan and Regina (Pasternak) Kopp; children: Adrienne, David. BS, Bklyn. Coll., 1959, MS, 196l; adminstrv./supervision cert., Coll. S.I., 197l; EdD, Rutgers U., 198l. Tchr. N.Y.C. Pub. Schs., 1959-70; project coord., dir. fed. projects Rutgers U., New Brunswick, N.J., 1976-80; math. cons. B & F Ednl. Cons., Inc., S.I., N.Y., 1978—; dir. fed. math. project Ednl. Support Systems, Inc., S.I., 1981-94; dir. Foresight Sch., S.I., 1985—, Great Beginnings Infant and Toddler Ctr., 1989—. Co-author of many books and articles on teaching mathematics for elem. and jr. h.s. tchrs. Mem. Nat. Coun. Tchrs. Math., Nat. Staff Devel. Coun., N.Y. Acad. Scis., Nat. Coun. Suprs. Math. Avocations: reading, travel, theatre. Home: 240 E 47th St Apt 13D New York NY 10017-2134 Office: B & F Ednl Cons 446 Travis Ave Staten Island NY 10314-6149

BERMAN, BRUCE, entertainment company executive, television producer; b. N.Y.C., Apr. 25, 1952. Grad., Calif. Inst. Arts Film Sch.; grad. magna cum laude in history, UCLA, 1975; JD, Georgetown U., 1978. Bar: Calif. 1978. Asst. to Jack Valenti Warner Bros., Burbank, Calif.; asst. to Peter Guber Casablanca Filmworks, 1979; asst. to Sean Daniel and Joel Silver Universal Pictures, 1979, v.p. prodn., 1982; v.p. prodn. Warner Bros., 1984, sr. v.p. prodn., 1988, pres. theatrical prodn., 1991-96, CEO Village Roadshow Pictures, 1998; pres. Worldwide Prodn., 1991-96; founder Plan B Entertainment, 1996—. Office: Village Roadshow Pictures care Warner Bros Studios 4000 Warner Blvd Burbank CA 91522*

BERMAN, BRUCE JUDSON, lawyer; b. Roslyn, N.Y., Oct. 9, 1946; s. Howard M. Berman and Soosha T. (Draizen) Marks; children: Daniel H., Ann N., Andrew J., Josie A.; m. Susan Leigh Readinger, Dec. 29, 1991. BA, Williams Coll., 1968; MBA, Columbia U., 1972; JD, Boston U., 1972. Bar: Fla. 1973, U.S. Dist. Ct. (so. dist.) Fla. 1980, U.S. Dist. Ct. (mid. dist.) Fla. 1990, U.S. Ct. Appeals (5th cir.) 1980, U.S. Ct. Appeals (11th cir.) 1981, U.S. Supreme Ct. 1976. Assoc. Guggenheimer & Untermyer, N.Y.C., 1973-79; from assoc. to ptnr. Myers, Kenin, Levinson, Frank & Richards, Miami, Fla., 1979-85; ptnr. Weil, Gotshal & Manges LLP, Miami, 1985—; mem. spl. ad hoc trial com. to Dade County (Fla.) Cir. Ct., 1988—; apptd. Supreme Ct. court reporter cert. planning com., 1995. Author: Florida Civil Procedure, 1998, 99. Mem. New World Symphony Cmty. Bd., Miami Beach, Fla., 1991—. Mem. Fla. Bar (civil procedure rules com. 1984—, chmn. 1988-90, jud. adminstrn. rules com. 1988—, chmn. 1993-94), Dade County Bar. Office: Weil Gotshal & Manges LLP 701 Brickell Ave Ste 2100 Miami FL 33131-2825

BERMAN, CAROL, commissioner; b. Bklyn., Sept. 21, 1923; d. Hyman and Sarah (Levy) B.; m. Seymour Jerome Berman, May 19, 1944; children: Elizabeth, Charles. BA, U. Mich., 1943. Trustee Bd. Edn., Lawrence, N.Y., 1973-77; senator State of N.Y., Albany, 1978-84; spl. rep. State Divsn. for Housing, Hempstead, N.Y., 1985-86; commr. N.Y. State Commn. on Lobbying, Albany, 1988-92, N.Y. State Commn. of Elections, Albany, 1992—. N.Y. co-chair Nat. Jewish Dem. Coun., 1988—, Met. Airport Noise Mitigation Rev. Commn., 1992—; del. Dem. Nat. Conv., N.Y., 1992; vice-chair Nassau Dem. County Com., Mineola, N.Y., 1970-72. Mem. Phi Beta Kappa, Phi Kappa Phi. Jewish. Avocations: grandchildren, golf. Home: 42 Lord Ave Lawrence NY 11559-1324 Office: NY State Bd Elections Empire State Plz Swan St Bldg Core 1 Albany NY 12223

BERMAN, CHRIS, sports anchor; b. May 10, 1955. BA in History, Brown U., 1977. Disc jockey WERI, Westerly, R.I., 1977-78; broadcaster WNVR Radio, Waterbury, Conn., 1978-79; weekend sports anchor WVIT-TV, Hartford, Conn., 1979; NFL studio host, anchor SportsCenter, baseball commentator ESPN, 1979—; host NFL PrimeTime, NFL GameDay, Sunday night NFL telecasts, NFL draft coverage, commentator major league baseball games, host Baseball Tonight, SportsCenter ESPN. Named nat. sportscaster of yr. Nat. Sportscasters and Sportwriters Assn., 1989, 90, 93, 94; named among top stars of the '90's TV Guide, 1990; winner sports Emmys for NFL GameDay, 1989, 92, 95, CableACE awards, 1989, 92, 93, 94; voted best cable sportscaster Cable Guide, 1987, 88, 90. Office: ESPN ESPN Plaza Bristol CT 06010*

BERMAN, DANIEL K(ATZEL), educational consultant, university official; b. Detroit, Nov. 17, 1954; s. Louis Arthur and Irene (Katzel) B. BS, Northwestern U., 1976, MS, 1977; AM, Harvard U., 1983; MA, U. Calif., Berkeley, 1984, PhD, 1991; cert. study, U. Paris, 1973, Peking (China) Normal U., 1981, Nat. Taiwan U., 1982. Subscription mgr. The N.Y. Times, 1983-84; editorial and rsch. asst. Inst. for Contemporary Studies, San Francisco, 1984-85; lang. cons. Berlitz Translation Svcs., San Francisco, 1986-89; v.p. Golden Gate Investment, San Francisco, 1985-87; lectr. St. Mary's Coll., Moraga, Calif., 1987; instr. U. Calif., Berkeley, 1984-90; chief exec. officer Pacific Fin. Svcs., San Francisco, 1987-92; editor Credit Report Newsletter for Consumer Edn., San Francisco, 1989-92; sales and mktg. cons. The Deerwood Corp./MRI, San Ramon, Calif., 1989-91; lectr. dept. mass comm. Calif. State U., Hayward, 1993-94; lectr. dept. elec. engring. San Jose State U., 1997-98; founder/dir. Acad. Cons. Internat., San Francisco, 1993—; assoc. provost Summit U. La., New Orleans, 1995—; founder CyberTip4theDay.com, San Francisco, 1998—. Author: The Hottest Summer in Peking, 1982, The Credit Power Handbook for American Consumers, 1988, 89, Words Like Colored Glass: The Role of the Press in Taiwan's Democratization Process, 1992; co-author: Proverb Wit & Wisdom, 1997; editor, translator: The Butterfly's Revenge and Other Chinese Mystery Stories, found. CyberTip4theDay.com, 1998—. Edn. scholar Rep. of China Ministry of Edn., 1979-82; rsch. grantee Pacific Cultural Found., 1981; fgn. lang. and area studies fellow in Chinese U. Calif., 1983-84. Fellow John F. Kennedy Libr. Found.; mem. The Harvard Club of San Francisco, Soc. of Profl. Journalists, Acad. of Polit. Sci., Nat. Ctr. for Fin. Edn. (profl. sponsor), Kappa Tau Alpha (grantee). Jewish. Avocations: computers, foreign languages, piano, t'ai-chi-ch'uan, tennis. Office: Acad Cons Internat PO Box 4489 Foster City CA 94404-0489

BERMAN, DANIEL LEWIS, lawyer; b. Washington, Dec. 14, 1934; s. Herbert A. and Ruth N. (Abramson) B.; children: Priscilla Decker, Jane, Katherine Ann, Sara Mark, Heather, Melinda. B.A., Williams Coll., 1956; LL.B., Columbia U., 1959. Bar: N.Y. 1960, Utah 1962. Asso. firm Chadbourne, Parke, Whiteside & Wolff, N.Y.C., 1959-60; asst. prof. law U. Utah, 1960-62; pvt. practice Salt Lake City, 1962-81; sr. ptnr. Berman, Gaufin, Tomsic & Savage, Salt Lake City, 1981—; vis. prof. U. Utah, 1970, 74, 77; Mem. Utah Coordinating Council Higher Edn., 1965-68. Mem. Salt Lake County Merit Coun., 1974-80; trustee Salt Lake Art Ctr., 1978-80; Dem. candidate for U.S. Senate from Utah, 1980. Mem. Am. Law Inst., Salt Lake Area C. of C. (bd. govs. 1976-79), Utah Transit Authority (bd. dirs. 1992-97). Democrat. Jewish. Office: Berman Gaufin Tomsic & Savage 50 S Main St Ste 1250 Salt Lake City UT 84144-2073

BERMAN, DAVID, lawyer, poet; b. N.Y.C., Sept. 11, 1934; s. Joseph and Sophie (Hersh) B. BA with honors, U. Fla., 1955; postgrad. Johns Hopkins U., 1955-56; JD, Harvard U., 1963. Bar: Mass. 1963. Teaching fellow Harvard Coll., 1962-63, 66-67; law clk. to justice Mass. Supreme Ct., 1963-64; asst. atty. gen. Commonwealth of Mass., 1964-67; assoc. Zamparelli & White, 1967, ptnr., 1968-74; pvt. practice, 1974-82, 1990—; ptnr. Berman & Moren, Medford, Mass., 1982-89. Author: Future Imperfect, 1982, Slippage, 1996, Early Mandamus in Massachusetts, Massachusetts Legal History, 1998. Trustee Cantata Singers, 1981—. Mem. ABA, Mass. Bar Assn., Mass. Bar Found., Middlesex Bar Assn. (Most Outstanding Trial Lawyer Appelate award, 1998), Harvard Club (Boston), Signet Soc., Confrerie de la Chaine des Rotisseurs, Ordre Mondial, Masons. Republican. Unitarian. Home: 33 Birch Hill Rd Belmont MA 02478-1729 Office: 100 George P Hassett Dr Medford MA 02155-3264

BERMAN, ELEANORE, artist; b. N.Y.C., Sept. 2, 1928; d. Isidor and Elsie (Goldstein) Berman; children: Deborah Nicholas, Jan Nicholas, Anthony Nicholas, David Lazarof. BA, UCLA, 1950. One-woman shows include Kirk De Gooyer Gallery, L.A., 1982, Kouros Gallery, N.Y.C., 1982, L.A. City Hall, 1984, Stuhr (Nebr.) Mus., 1984, U. Wyo. Art Gallery, 1984, U. Minn., Duluth, 1984, Gallery X, Brussels, 1985, New Eng. Ctr. for Contemporary Art, Mass., 1985, Mcpl. Gallery, Kampen, The Netherlands, 1986, Mcpl. Gallery, Amstelveen, The Netherlands, 1986, Rose Cafe, Venice, Calif., 1988, Lisa Kurts Gallery, Memphis, 1989, Boritzer/Gray Gallery, Santa Monica, Calif., 1991, L.A. Art Core, 1996; exhibited in group shows: LAART, N.Y.C., 1986, U. Hawaii, Hilo, 1986, L.A. County Mus. Art, 1981, Boston Ctr. for the Arts, 1981, Wesleyan Coll., Conn., 1980, Newport (R.I.) Harbor Mus., 1977, Nat. Acad. Western Art Traveling Exhbn., 1988, L.A.-U.K. Print Connection, 1989, Bonnie Fridholm Gallery, Asheville, N.C., 1989, San Bernardino County Mus., Calif., 1994, Wichita Falls (Tex.) Mus., 1995; represented in permanent collections: L.A. County Mus. Art, Bklyn. Mus., Milw. Art Ctr., Grunwald Graphic Art Ctr., UCLA, others. Mem. Nat. Assn. of Women Artists, So. Calif. Women's Caucus for the Arts, L.A. Printmaking Assn., Nat. Watercolor Soc., Artists Equity Assn.

BERMAN, ELLEN SUE, energy and telecommunications executive, theatre producer. Student, U. N.C., Greensboro, 1960-62, U. N.C., Chapel Hill, summer 1961, U. Calif., Berkeley, summer 1962; BA in Russian, Barnard Coll., 1964. Legis. asst. Senator Joseph Tydings, 1965-66; rsch. assoc. Washington Poverty Program United Planning Orgn., 1966-70; pres. Consumer Energy Coun. Am. Rsch. Found., Washington, 1973—; mem. Office Tech. Assessment Residential Energy Conservation Adv. Com., 1976-77, Magnetic Fusion Adv. Com., 1986-87, Aspen Inst. Energy Policy Forum; mem. coun. for the Arts MIT, 1995—; mem. Com. on Energy and Econ. Devel. NAACP; mem. German Marshall Fund Adv. Com. on Energy Efficiency in Swedish Bldgs. Co-author: A Decade of Despair, A Compendium of Utility-Sponsored Appliance Rebate Programs, Transportation, Energy and Environment: Balancing Goals and Identifying Policies, 1995, Restructuring the Electric Utility Industry: A Consumer Perspective, 1998; author: Equity and Energy: Rising Energy Prices and the Living Standards of Lower Income Americans, 1983, Oil, Gas or ..? A Guide to Saving Heating Dollars, The Consumer and Energy Impacts of Oil Exports, Operating Costs of Refrigerators/Freezers and Room Air Conditioners, If You Want to Lower Your Heating Bill, It's Time to Raise the Roof, A Comparative Analysis of Utility and Non-Utility Based Energy Services Companies, A State by State Compendium of Energy Efficiency Programs Using Oil Overchange Funds; (reports) The Consumer and Energy Impacts of Oil Exports, 1984, A Comprehensive Analysis of a Crude Oil Import Fee: Dismantling a Trojan Horse, 1982, A Comparison of Crude Oil Decontrol and Natural Gas Deregulation: An Analysis of the Impract of Immediate Decontrol of Crude Oil and Related Products on End Use Consumers, Natural Gas Deregulation: A Case of Trickle Up Economics, 1982; pub. The Quad Report, 1993—. Bd. dirs. Barnard in Washington, 1994—; bd. trustees Wider Opportunities for Women; bd. mgrs. Adas Israel Congregation, 1996—; chmn. bldgs. and gounds com. Woodley Park Towers condominium. Named Woman of the Eighties, Ladies Home Jour., 1979; grantee German Marshall Fund. Mem. Barnard Coll. Washington Alumnae Assn. (bd. dirs.), Cosmos Club. Home: 2737 Devonshire Pl NW Washington DC 20008-3479 Office: Consumer Energy Coun Am Rsch Found 2000 L St NW Ste 802 Washington DC 20036-4913

BERMAN, GEOFFREY LOUIS, turnaround management company executive; b. L.A., July 15, 1953; s. Geoffrey M. and Patricia A. (Meyer) B.; m. Autumn Joy Patton, Mar. 26, 1983; children: Arielle Louise, Michelle Elise. BA/BS in Bus. Adminstrn., U. of the Pacific, 1975; JD, Southwestern U., 1985. Loan officer Union Bank, L.A., 1975-80; adminstrv. asst. Credit Mgrs. Assn., L.A., 1980-82; asst. v.p. Mitsui Mfrs. Bank, L.A., 1982-86; asst. sec., mgr. adjustment bur. Credit Mgrs. Assn., Burbank, Calif., 1986-97; v.p. Devel. Specialists, Inc., L.A., 1997—; dir. Comml. Fin. Conf. Calif., L.A., 1978-80; co-chair insolvency laws com. Am. Bankruptcy Inst., Alexandria, Va., 1994—; mem. panel of mediators Ctrl. Dist. Bankruptcy Ct., L.A., 1996—. Co-author: (manual) ABI Creditor's Com. Manual, 1995; contbg. editor Am. Bankruptcy Inst. Jour., 1996—, Fed. G. Receiver, 1999—; contbr. articles to profl. jours. Task force mem. City of Buena Park (Calif.) Investment Policy Rev. Com., 1995. Recipient Recognition award Fed. Bar Assn., L.A., 1986. Mem. L.A. Bankruptcy Forum, Bay Area Bankruptcy Forum, Orange County Bankruptcy Forum. Office: Devel Specialists Inc 333 S Grand Ave Ste 2010 Los Angeles CA 90071-1524

BERMAN, GIZEL, sculptor; b. Sobrance, Slovakia, Aug. 26, 1919; came to U.S., 1946; d. Armin and Margit (Kaufman) Herskovits; m. Nicholas Berman, Dec. 23, 1941; 1 child, Margaret. Student, Uzhorod Bus. Coll., Czechoslovakia, 1935-37, Nagay Design Sch., Budapest, Hungary, 1938, Inst. Michot, Brussels, 1939. Lectr. in schs. and orgns. Survivors of the Holocaust, Seattle, 1980-90. Exhibited bronze sculptures at galleries in Seattle, Portland, Oreg. and Vancouver, B.C., Can., 1950—. Mem. Survivors of the Holocaust, Seattle, 1950—; with Herzl-Ner Tamid Conservative Congregation. Recipient Holocaust Meml. award Jewish Fedn. Greater Seattle, 1981; participant Album Internat., Geneva, 1979. Mem. Hadassah (life). Democrat. Avocations: horseback riding, skiing, tennis, hiking. Home: 6004 SE 32nd St Mercer Island WA 98040-2440

BERMAN, HARRY J., educator, college administrator; b. Phila., July 1, 1947; m. Deborah M. Berman, Dec. 29, 1968; children: Leah W., Dara V. BA, U. Chgo., 1969; PhD, Washington U., St. Louis, 1974. Asst. prof. Pa. State U., Uniontown, 1974-77; asst. prof. to prof. U. Ill., Springfield, 1977—; assoc. vice chancellor U. Ill. (formerly Sangamon State U.), Springfield, 1994—. Pres. Sr. Svcs. of Cen. Ill., 1995-96, Temple Israel, 1991-93; bd. dirs. City Day Sch. Recipient Disting. U. Svc. award Sangamon State U. Fellow Germtol. Soc. Am.

BERMAN, HERBERT E., councilman; b. Bklyn., Oct. 8, 1933; s. Sam and Sarah Berman; m. Frances Springer, 1960; children: Shari, Russell. BA, L.I. U.; LLD cum laude, NYU, 1959, JD, 1968. City councilman Dist. 46 N.Y.C. Coun., 1975—, chair fin. com.; chmn. edn. com. N.Y.C. Coun., 1983-89, chmn. fin. com., mem. govt. ops. and transp. coms.; adj. assoc. prof. Pace U. Spl. counsel Georgetown Civic Assn.; bd. dirs. Muscular Dystrophy Soc. Recipient Merit award Jewish War Vets. Mem. Bklyn. and Kings County Criminal Bar Assns., Futurama Civic Assn. (past pres.), Georgetown Civic Assn., Thomas Jefferson Club, Jewish War Vet., Internat. League for Repatriation Soviet Jewry (dir.). Office: 250 Broadway Fl 23 New York NY 10007-2516*

BERMAN, HOWARD ALLEN, rabbi; b. Paterson, N.J., June 21, 1949; s. Bernard and Elaine (Geller) B. BA, U. Cin., 1972; BA in Hebrew Letters, Hebrew Union Coll., 1973, MA in Hebrew Letters, 1974. Ordained rabbi, 1974. Asst. rabbi Temple Emanu-El, N.Y.C., 1974-79; assoc. rabbi Temple Beth Israel, Hartford, Conn., 1979-81; sr. rabbi Chgo. Sinai Congregation, 1982—; vis. prof. Luth. Sch. Theology, Chgo., 1988-96. Contbr. to World Book Ency. Year Book, 1984-93. V.p. Hyde Park Interfaith Coun., Chgo., 1988-91; mem. Chgo. Nuclear Free Zone City Commn., 1987-93; mem. adv. coun. Ctr. for Ethics and Corp. Policy, 1987-90; mem. met. task force Parliament of World Religions; mem. steering com. Interfaith Response to AIDS; mem., bd. dirs. Planned Parenthood of Chgo. Mem. Central Conf. Am. Rabbis, Greater Boston Bus. Coun., Religious Coalition for Human Rights, Pilgrim Soc., Boston Atheneum, Bostonian Soc. Avocations: collecting rare books, Pilgrim memorabilia, memorabilia of Diana, Princess of Wales. Office: Sinai Temple 15 W Delaware Chicago IL 60610

BERMAN, HOWARD LAWRENCE, congressman; b. L.A., Apr. 15, 1941; s. Joseph M. and Eleanor (Schapiro) B.; m. Janis Berman, 1979; children: Brinley Ann, Lindsey Rose. BA, UCLA, 1962, LLB, 1965. Bar: Calif. 1966. Vol. VISTA, Balt., San Francisco, 1966-67; assoc. Levy, Van Bourg & Hackler, L.A., 1967-72; mem. Calif. State Assembly from 43d dist., 1972-82 (majority leader); with 98th-105th Congresses from 26th Calif. dist.; freshman rep. steering and policy com., 1983, ranking mem. com. standards of ofcl. conduct, mem. jud. com., internat. law, immigration and refugees, intellectual property and jud. adminstrn., mem. internat. rels. com. Asia and Pacific. Pres. Calif. Fedn. Young Democrats, 1967-69 (budget com.); mem. adv. bd. Jewish Fund for Justice. Office: US Ho of Reps Rm 2330 Rayburn House Office Bldg Washington DC 20515

BERMAN, JEROME, museum director, curator. Exec. dir., curator Calif. Mus. Ancient Art, Beverly Hills, 1983—. Office: Calif Mus Ancient Art PO Box 10515 Beverly Hills CA 90213-3515*

BERMAN, JOSHUA MORDECAI, lawyer, manufacturing company executive; b. Rochester, N.Y., Aug. 4, 1938; s. Jeremiah Joseph and Rose (Rappaport) B.; m. Ruth Freed, Mar. 17, 1996; children: Marc Ethan, Eve. BBA summa cum laude, CCNY, 1958; JD cum laude, Harvard U., 1961. Bar: Mass. 1961, N.Y. 1984. With Goodwin, Procter & Hoar, Boston, 1961-80, ptnr., 1969-80; pres. Berman Engel P.C., 1980-85; counsel Kramer, Levin, Naftalis & Frankel, 1985—; adviser Fidelity Investments, 1971—, Brierley Investments Ltd., Wellington, New Zealand, 1988—; chmn. bd., CEO Tyco Internat. Ltd., 1970-73, bd. dirs., v.p. Founder, pres. Boston Children's Sch., 1965-66.

BERMAN, KEITH, solicitor, lawyer; b. Liverpool, Eng., Dec. 23, 1942; came to U.S., 1980; s. Joseph and Gerty Berman; children; Chloé Jo, Jade Kara, Kate Alexis. LLB with honors, U. Liverpool, 1963. Cert. solicitor Supreme Ct. Eng. and Wales, 1966; bar: N.Y. 1980, U.S. Dist. Ct. (so. and ea. dists.) N.Y. 1982, U.S. Ct. Internat. Trade 1992, U.S. Ct. Appeals (fed. cir.) 1992. Founding ptnr. Bermans English Solicitors, Liverpool, Manchester, 1967—, London, N.Y.C., 1980—. Trustee Fifth Ave Synagogue, N.Y.C., 1986—. Mem. ABA, Law Soc. Eng. and Wales, Liverpool Law Soc., Comml. Law League Am., Internat. Bar Assn. Jewish. Office: Bermans 9th Fl 805 Third Ave New York NY 10022-7503

BERMAN, LAURA, journalist; b. Detroit, Dec. 8, 1953; d. Seymour Donald and Rose (Mendelson) B. AB, U. Mich., 1975. Writer, reporter Detroit Free Press, 1976-86; columnist The Detroit News, 1986-93; freelance writer, 1994—; sr. writer The Detroit News, 1995-98; columnist Detroit News, 1998—. Mem. Am. Soc. Journalists and Authors, Inc. Office: The Detroit News 615 W Lafayette Blvd Detroit MI 48226-3197

BERMAN, LEWIS PAUL, financial executive; b. Cape Town, South Africa, Jan. 28, 1937; came to U.S., 1959, naturalized, 1969; s. Joshua Z. and Gertrude Berman; m. Karen Scott Dunlap, Oct. 18, 1969; children: Joshua Evans, Caroline Isabel. BCom, U. Cape Town, 1956, M. Com., 1958; MBA with high distinction, Harvard U., 1961. Vice-pres. Mgmt. Analysis Ctr., Cambridge, Mass., 1964-66; with Irwin Mgmt. Co. Inc., Columbus, Ind., 1966-68; asst. to chmn. Cummins Engine Co., Inc., Columbus, 1968-70; pres. Cummins Internat. Fin. Corp., Columbus, 1970-76; dir. fin. svcs. Cummins Engine Co., Inc., Columbus, 1976-80, treas., 1980-87; sr. v.p. Reams Asset Mgmt. Co., Columbus, 1987-99, ret.; chmn. Am. Fletcher Bank Suisse S.A., Geneva, Switzerland, 1970-82. Contbr. to textbooks. Trustee Columbus (Ind.) Regional Hosp., 1982-93; bd. dirs. Bartholomew County Hosp. Found., 1977-81; co-chmn. Uncommon Cause, Columbus, 1984-85; pres. Columbus Disting. Visitors, 1967. Baker scholar Harvard Bus. Sch., 1961. Home: 9675 W Marshall Dr Columbus IN 47201-9102

BERMAN, LISA, advertising executive. Media dir., sr. v.p. Hill, Holliday, Connors, Cosmopulos, Inc., Advertising, Boston, 1988—. Office: Hill Holliday Connors Cosmopulos Inc Advertising John Hancock Tower 200 Clarendon St Boston MA 02116-5021

BERMAN, LORI BETH, legislative staff member; b. N.Y.C., June 27, 1958; d. George Gilbert and Sara Ann (Abrams) B.; m. Jeffrey Ganeles, Nov. 26, 1983; children: Caryn Elissa, Steven Aaron. BA magna cum laude, Tufts U., 1980; JD, George Washington U., 1983. Assoc. Margolies, Edelstein & Scherlis, Phila., 1983-84, White and Williams, Phila., 1984-87, Brownstein Zeidman & Schomer, Washington, 1987-89; v.p. legal & compliance Pointe Savs. Bank, Boca Raton, Fla., 1990-95; dist. rep. Congressman Robert Wexler, Boca Raton, 1997—. Mem., Jour. Internat. Law and Econs. Mem. exec. coun. United Jewish Appeal Fedn., Washington, 1987-89, Boca Raton, 1990—, Leadership Boca, 1992. Mem. ABA, D.C. Bar Assn., Fla. Bar Assn., Boca Raton C. of C. Democrat. Jewish.

BERMAN, MALCOLM FRANK, health facility administrator; b. Boston, Oct. 30, 1941; s. Marcus Wolfe and Evelyn Bernice (Sachs) B.; m. Natalie Sue Peikin, June 27, 1965; children: Lisa, Wendy, Bradley. BA, U. Pa., 1963; MS, U. Pitts., 1966. Adminstrv. asst. St. Francis Med. Ctr., Pitts., 1965-66; adminstr. Meml. Hosp., Monongahela, Pa., 1966-67; asst. to exec. dir. St. Francis Med. Ctr., Pitts., 1967-82; adminstr. St. Francis Cmty. Mental Health Ctr., Pitts., 1972-85; assoc. dir. planning St. Francis Med. Ctr., Pitts., 1982-83, dir. planning, 1983-85, v.p. planning, 1985-90; v.p. planning St. Francis Health System, Pitts., 1990—; adj. asst. prof., preceptor U. Pitts. Grad. Sch. Pub. Health, 1980—; health care cons., 1983—; movie liaison St. Francis Med. Ctr. Contbr. articles to profl. jours. Bd. dirs., officer Rodef Shalom Congregation, Pitts., 1969-76, Group Against Smog and Pollution, Pitts., 1972-75, Pitts. Mineral and Lapidary Soc., 1973-77, B'Nai Israel Synagogue, Pitts., 1989-93, Jewish Residential Svcs., Pitts., 1989-90. 1st lt. USAR, 1963-69. Recipient citation Allegheny County Mental Health/Mental Retardation Bd., Pitts., 1982. Fellow Am. Coll. Health Care Execs. (cert.); mem. Assn. Mental Health Adminstrs. (cert. mental health adminstr.), Am. Hosp. Assn. (life), Hosp. Assn. Pa. Republican. Jewish. Avocations: rock, mineral collecting, home improvement. Home: 3 Knollwood Dr Pittsburgh PA 15215-1636 Office: St Francis Health System 4401 Penn Ave Pittsburgh PA 15224-1380

BERMAN, MARCELO SAMUEL, mathematics and physics educator, cosmology researcher; b. Buenos Aires, Apr. 10, 1945; s. Bernardo and Rosa (Soifer) B.; m. Geni Lima, June 21, 1986; children: Albert, Paula. EE, ITA, San José Campos, Brazil, 1967, MSc in Physics, 1981; DSc in Physics, Univ. Fed. Rio De Janeiro, 1988. Ptnr. Plasti-Tact Ltd., Curitiba, Brazil, 1974-79; ptnr., fin. dir. Constr. Gustavo Berman, Curitiba, 1979-88; prof. math. dept. exact scis. Fundaçao Educacional da Regiao de Joinville, Brazil, 1986-90; postdoctoral assoc. dept. astronomy U. Fla., Gainesville, 1989-90; asst adj. prof. dept. physics and astronomy U. Ala., Tuscaloosa, 1991; mng. ptnr. Editora Albert Einstein Ltda, Curitiba, Brazil, 1986—, Berman e Berman Ltd., 1993-94; vis. rschr. divsn. astrophysics INPE, São José dos Campos, Brazil, 1995; from vis. prof. to prof. dept. physics Tech. Inst. Aeronautics, 1995-97. Co-author: Tensor Calculus and General Relativity, 1987, Relativistic Cosmology, 1988; editor: The Illustrated A Brief History of Time, Brazilian version, 1997; contbr. over 50 articles to profl. jours. and 56 sci. articles in newspapers. Ministry Aeros. scholar, 1963-67, Pro-Nuclear Brazil scholar, 1980-81, CNPQ scholar, 1989-91, FAPESP scholar, 1995. Mem. AAAS, IEEE (sr.), Internat. Astron. Union, Am. Phys. Soc., Am. Astron. Soc., N.Y. Acad. Scis., Gen. Relativity and Gravitation Soc. Jewish. Achievements include presentation of models with constant deceleration parameter in cosmology, which cover and accept inflationary scenario. Home: Rua Itatiba 140 JD Apollo, 12243200 Sao Jose dos Campos SP, Brazil Office: ITA, Dept Physics, 12228-900 São José dos Campos SP, Brazil

BERMAN, MARLENE OSCAR, neuropsychologist, educator; b. Phila., Nov. 21, 1939; d. Paul Oscar and Evelyn (Hess) Oscar; m. Michael Brack Berman, June 23, 1963 (div. Feb. 1980); 1 son, Jesse Michael. BA, U.Pa., 1961; MA, Bryn Mawr Coll., 1964; PhD, U. Conn., 1968; postgrad., Harvard U., 1968-70. Research assoc. Boston VA Med. Ctr., 1970-72, clin. investigator, 1973-76, research psychologist, 1976—; assoc. prof. neurology Boston U. Sch. Medicine, 1975-82, prof. neurology and psychiatry, 1982—, dir Neuropsychology Lab. dept. psychiatry, 1981—; mem. Com. for Protection Human Participants in Rsch., 1979-82, chmn., 1983-85; affiliate prof. psychology Clark U., Worcester, Mass., 1975—; mem. biomed. rsch. initial rev. group Nat. Inst. Alcohol Abuse and Alcoholism, 1987-91, chmn. 1990-91; mem. initial rev. group Nat. Inst. Drug Abuse, 1996-97. Contbr. articles to profl. jours. Coordinator Newton Community Schs. (Mass.), 1978-80. Recipient rsch. scientist awards Nat. Inst. Neurol. and Communicative Disorders and Stroke, 1976-81, Nat. Inst. Alcohol Abuse and Alcoholism, 1981—, Method to Extend Rsch. in Time award, 1996—, clin. investigator award VA, 1973-76; grantee USPHS and HHS, 1964—; Fulbright sr. scholar, Australia, 1991. Fellow Mass. Psychol. Assn., Am. Psychol. Assn. (sec.-treas. 1981-83); mem. Acad. Aphasia, Soc. Neurosci., Internat. Neuropsychol. Soc., Psychonomic Soc., Huntington's Disease Soc. Am., New Eng. Psychol. Assn., Mass. Neuropsychol. Soc., N.Y. Acad. Scis., Eastern Psychol. Assn., Fulbright Found. Democrat. Jewish. Office: Boston U Lab Neuropsych Dept Psychiatry M-9 715 Albany St Dept M-9 Roxbury MA 02118-2526 *The four most significant helpers in my career have been hard work, luck, mentors, and a sense of humor.*

BERMAN, MARSHALL FOX, lawyer; b. Portsmouth, Va., Aug. 27, 1939; s. Israel and Etta (Fox) B.; m. Barbara Pressner, Aug. 29, 1965 (dec. Feb. 1993); m. Karen Orloff Kaplan, Nov. 18, 1996; children: Richard Joseph, Deborah Lynn. BA, U. Va., 1961, postgrad. in rhetoric, 1961-62; JD, Am. U., 1967; LLM in Labor Law with highest honors, George Washington U., 1970. Bar: Va. 1967, D.C. 1971, U.S. Supreme Ct. 1971. Tchr. reading pub. schs., Washington, 1965-66; staff D.C. Minimum Wage and Indsl. Safety Bd., 1966-67; atty. NLRB, Washington, 1968-71; assoc. Gall, Lane & Powell, Washington, 1971-75; ptnr. Dow, Lohnes & Albertson, Washington, 1975-91, Epstein, Becker and Green, Washington, 1992-98; sole practitioner Washington, 1998—. Co-author: Aviation Drug Testing Handbook, 1989, Aviation Drug Testing Operating Manual, 1990. Mem. ABA, Fed. Bar Assn., D.C. Bar Assn., Va. Bar Assn. Home: 7732 Canal Ct Mc Lean VA 22102 Office: 1101 30th St NW Ste 500 Washington DC 20007-3708

BERMAN, MILTON, history educator; b. N.Y.C., Apr. 18, 1924; s. Morris and Ida (Epstein) B.; m. Barbara Ann Roesch, Aug. 18, 1968. B.A., Hofstra Coll., 1953; A.M., Harvard U., 1954, Ph.D., 1959. Instr. history Harvard U., 1959-61, vis. assoc. prof., summer 1963; fellow Charles Warren Ctr., 1968-69; asst. prof. history U. Rochester, N.Y., 1961-63; assoc. prof. U. Rochester, 1963-70, prof., 1970-89, prof. emeritus, 1989—, assoc. chmn. dept., 1966-68. Author: John Fiske: The Evolution of a Popularizer, 1961. Served with U.S. Army, 1949-50. Mem. Am. Hist. Assn., Orgn. Am. Historians. Democrat. Jewish. Home: 16 Ranch Village Ln Rochester NY 14624-2857 Office: Univ Rochester Dept History Rochester NY 14627

BERMAN, MURIEL MALLIN, optometrist, humanities lecturer; b. Pitts.; d. Samuel and Dora (Coopersman) Mallin; m. Philip I. Berman, Oct. 23, 1942; children: Nancy, Nina, Steven. Student, U. Pitts., 1943, Carnegie Tech. U., 1944-45; BS, Pa. State Coll. Optometry, 1948; postgrad., U. Pitts., 1950, Muhlenberg Coll., 1954, Cedar Crest Coll., 1953; DFA (hon.), Cedar Crest Coll., 1972; hon. degree, Hebrew U., Israel, 1982; DHL (hon.), Ursinus Coll., 1987, Lehigh U., 1991. Lic. Pa., N.J. Practice optometry Pitts.; sec.-treas., dir. Philip and Muriel Berman Found.; underwriting mem. Lloyd's of London, 1974—; lectr. on travels, art, UN activities, women's status and affairs. Producer: weekly TV show College Speak-Out, 1967—; producer, moderator: TV show Guest Spot. Active in UNICEF, 1959—, ofcl. non-govtl. orgns., 1964, 74; U.S. State Dept. del. UN Internat. Women's Yr. Conf., Mexico City, 1975; mem. State Dept. Arts and Humanities Com. Nat. Commn. on Observance of Women's Yr., 1975; adv. com. U.S. Ctr. for Internat. Womens Yr., Washington; founder, donor Carnegie-Berman Coll. Art Slide Library Exchange; mem. Aspen (Colo.) Inst. Humanistic Studies, 1965, Tokyo, 1966; chmn. exhibits Great Valley council Girl Scouts U.S.A., 1966; adminstrv. head, chmn. various events Allentown Bicentennial, 1962; vice-chmn. Women for Pa. Bicentennial, 1976; co-chmn. Lehigh County Bicentennial Bell-Trek, 1976; patron Art in Embassies Program, Washington, 1965—; chmn. Lehigh Valley Ednl. TV, 1966—; program chmn. Fgn. Policy Assn. Lehigh County, 1965-67; treas. ann. ball Allentown Symphony, 1955—; mem. art adv. com. Dieruff High Sch., Allentown, 1966—; co-chmn. art. com. Episcopal Diocese Centennial Celebration, 1971; mem. Pa. Council on Status of Women, 1968-73; reappointed Pa. Gov.'s Commn. on Women, 1984; chmn. numerous art shows; mem. Art Collectors Club Am., Am. Fedn. Art, Friends of Whitney Mus., Mus. Modern Art, Mus. Primitive Art, Jewish Mus., Kemmerer Mus., Bethlehem, Pa., Univ. Mus., Phila., Archives of Am. Art, Met. Opera Guild, others; ofcl. del. Dem. Nat. Conv., 1972, 76, mem. Democratic Platform Com., 1972; mem. Pa. Humanities Coun., 1979—; bd. dirs. Heart Assn. Pa., Allentown Art Mus. Aux., Phila. Chamber Symphony, Baum Art Sch., Lehigh County Cultural Ctr., Heart Assn. Pa., Baum Art Sch., Young Audiences, Israel Mus., Hadassah Womens Orgn.; bd. govs. Pa. State System of Higher Edn., 1986—; trustee Kutztown State Coll., 1960-66, vice-chmn. bd., 1965; trustee, sec. bd. Lehigh Community Coll.; mem. nat. bd. UN-U.S.A., 1977—; trustee Pa. Council on Arts, Pa. Ballet, Smithsonian Art Council, Bonds for Israel, Hadassah (nat. bd. with portfolio), Am. Friends Hebrew U., 1984; bd. regents Internat. Ctr. for Univ. Teaching of Jewish Civilization, Israel, 1982—; fine arts chmn. Women's Club; mem. com. on Prints, Drawings, & Photography Pa. Mus. Art, 1984; hon. chmn. Bucks County Coillectors Art Show; hon. bd. dirs., trustee Phila. Mus. Art, 1997—. Named Woman of Valor State of Israel, 1965; recipient Centenial Yr. hon. citation Wilson Coll., 1969; Henrietta Szold award Allentown chpt. Hadassah; Outstanding Woman award Allentown YWCA, 1973; George Washington Honor medal Freedoms Found. at Valley Forge, 1985; Hazlett award Outstanding Service to Arts Pa.; Outstanding Citizen award Boy Scouts Am., 1982, Myrtle Wreath award Pa. Region Hadassah, Mt. Scopus award State of Israel Bonds, 1984, Woman of Yr. award Am. Friends Hebrew U., Phila., 1984, others; hon. fellow Hebrew U., 1975; Centennial citation Wilson Coll., 1969. Mem. LWV, NOW, Am. Fedn. of Art., Pa. Hist. Soc. (life), Jewish Publ. Soc. Am. (former pres., chmn. bd. 1984), Disting. Daus. Pa., Art Collector's Club Am., Wellesley Club. Jewish. Avocation: American and English sculpture art. Address: 1150 S Cedar Crest Blvd Ste 203 Allentown PA 18103-7900

BERMAN, MYLES LEE, lawyer; b. Chgo., July 11, 1954; s. Jordan and Eunice (Berg) B.; m. Mitra Moghimi, Dec. 19, 1981; children: Elizabeth, Calvin, Justin. BA, U. Ill., 1976; JD, Chgo.- Kent Coll. of Law, 1979. Bar: Ill. 1980, Calif. 1987, U.S. Dist. Ct. (no. dist.) Ill. 1980, U.S. Dist. Ct. (cen. dist.) Calif. 1988, U.S. Supreme Ct. 1992. Asst. state's atty. Cook County State's Atty.'s Office, Chgo., 1980-82; pvt. practice Offices of Myles L. Berman, Chgo., 1982-91; pvt. practice, L.A., 1988—; founder Nat. Drunk Driving Def. Task Force; traffic ct. judge pro tem Beverly Hills Mcpl. Ct., 1990—; traffic ct. judge pro tem adminstr. Culver Mcpl. Ct., 1991—; probation monitor State Bar Calif., 1992—. Editor: Century City Lawyer, 1992—. Mem. ABA, Santa Monica Bar Assn., Los Angeles County Bar Assn., Calif. Attys. for Criminal Justice, Nat. Assn. Criminal Def. Lawyers, Beverly Hills Bar Assn., Century City Bar Assn. (chmn. criminal law sect. 1989—, bd. govs. 1991—, Outstanding Svc. award 1990, 92, 93, 94, Spl. Recognition 1994, treas. 1994, sec. 1995, v.p. 1996, pres.-elect 1997, pres. 1998), Criminal Cts. Bar Assn. (evaluation profl. stds. and state bar com. 1996-97), Orange County Bar Assn., South Orange County Bar Assn., Cyberspace Bar Assn. Avocations: family, sports. Office: 9255 Sunset Blvd Ste 720 Los Angeles CA 90069-3304 also: 2659 Townsgate Rd Ste 101-24 Westlake Village CA 91361

BERMAN, NEIL SHELDON, chemical engineering educator; b. Milw., Sept. 21, 1933; s. Henry and Ella B.; m. Sarah Ayres, June 3, 1962; children—Jenny, Daniel. B.S., U. Wis., 1955; M.S., M.A., U. Tex., Austin, 1961, Ph.D., 1962. Engr. Standard Oil Co. Calif., Los Angeles, 1955-62; research engr. E.I. DuPont Co., Wilmington, Del., 1962-64; from asst. prof. to prof. chem. engring. Ariz. State U., 1964—, Grad. Coll. Disting. Rsch. prof., 1984-85; cons. air pollution, fluid dynamics; mem. Phoenix Air Quality Maintenance Area Task Force, 1976-77. Contbr. articles on fluid dynamics of polymer solutions, air pollution, thermodynamics and chem. engring. edn. to profl. jours. Served to capt. M.S.C. USAR, 1956-58. Recipient numerous grants for research in fluid dynamics and air pollution. Fellow Am. Inst. Chem. Engrs. (chmn. Ariz. sect. 1978-79), AAAS, Ariz.-Nev. Acad. Sci. (corr. sec. 1981-88, pres.-elect 1988-89, pres. 1989-90); mem. ASME, Am. Chem. Soc., Am. Phys. Soc., Ariz. Council Engring. and Sci. Assns. (chmn. 1980-81), Soc. Rheology, Am. Soc. Engring. Edn., Am. Acad. Mechanics, Nat. Assn. State Acads. Sci. (mem.-at-large bd. dirs.), Sigma Xi, Tau Beta Pi, Phi Kappa Phi. Home: 418 E Geneva Dr Tempe AZ 85282-3731 Office: Ariz State U Dept Chem Engring Tempe AZ 85287-6006

BERMAN, PHILIP AVERILL, journalist, consultant; b. N.Y.C., May 30, 1932; s. David and Eleanor (Davidson) B. BA in History, Stanford U., 1955. Journalist Chronicle Pub. Co., San Francisco, 1955-62; sr. editor Triangle Publs., Inc., N.Y.C., 1963-64, Fairchild Publs., Inc., N.Y.C., 1965-91; editorial cons. N.Y.C., 1991—. Mem. Internat. Platform Assn., Soc. Profl. Journalists, Nat. Writers Union, N.Y. Bus. Writers, Stanford Alumni Assn., Radio and TV News Dirs. Assn., N.Y. Press Club, The Deadline Club. Democrat. Jewish. Avocations: reading, travel, music. Home and Office: 177 E 75th St Apt 9D New York NY 10021-3232

BERMAN, PHILLIP LEE, religious institute administrator, author; m. Anne Kathleen Gordon. BA, U. Calif., 1979; MTS, Harvard U., 1982. Pres. Ctr. for Study Contemporary Belief, 1983-95; speaker in field. Author: The Courage of Conviction, 1986, The Courage to Grow Old, 1989, The Search for Meaning, 1990, The Ageless Spirit, 1993, The Journey Home, 1996, (with Jane Goodall) Reason for Hope, 1999; co-exec. prodr. (PBS documentary) Reason for Hope, 1999. Recipient Hobie Cat World Championships award, 1979, Lillich Davidson Book of Yr. award, 1989; nominated Pulitzer Prize. Mem. Am. Acad. Religion, Authors Guild. Home: 149 Fairview Rd Penn Valley PA 19072

BERMAN, RICHARD ANGEL, health and educational administrator; b. Cin., Jan. 23, 1945; s. Isidore Alexander and Cecilia (Angel) B.; m. Jean Berman; 1 child, Joshua. BBA with distinction, U. Mich., 1966, MBA with distinction, 1968, MHA, 1968. Spl. asst., asst. sec. health, dir. health policy Econ. Stblzn. Program, HEW, Washington, 1972-74; sr. program cons. Robert Wood Johnson Found., Princeton, N.J., 1974-77; asst. dean, assoc. hosp. dir. N.Y. Hosp.-Cornell Med. Ctr., N.Y.C., 1974-77; dir. N.Y. State Office Health Sys. Mgmt., Albany, 1977-80; commr. N.Y. State Divsn. Housing and Cmty. Renewal, 1981-83; exec. v.p. NYU Med. Ctr., N.Y.C., 1983-86; prof. health care mgmt. NYU Sch. Medicine, 1983-86; candidate for U.S. Congress 1986; spl. cons. McKinsey and Co., N.Y.C., 1987-90; v.p. Korn/Ferry Internat., N.Y.C., 1990-91; pres. N.Am. Howe-Lewis Internat., N.Y.C., 1991-92, pres., CEO, 1992-94; pres. Manhattanville Coll., Purchase, N.Y., 1995—; cons. in field; bd. dirs. Lillian Vernon, HCIA, 1st Med. Group, Stamford, Helath Ins. Plan Greater N.Y., HIP Plan of Fla., Westchester Edn. Coalition, Inc., White Plains, N.Y. Contbr. articles to profl. jours. Chmn. N.Y. State Bldg. Code Coun., 1981-83; mem. N.Y. State Housing Fin. Agy., 1981-83, N.Y. Statewide Health Coord. Coun.; mem. adv. bd. Ctr. Hosp. Fin. and Mgmt.; bd. dirs. N.Y.C. Pub. Devel. Corp., 1985-90; mem. Prospective Payment Assessment Commn., 1989-95; mem. exec. com. N.Y. March of Dimes Bd., 1980-95; mem. Mayor's Mgmt. Adv. Task Force, 1991-93; mem. nat. adv. coun. Nat. Inst. for Nursing Rsch., NIH, 1991-94; trustee SUNY, 1993-95; bd. dirs. Inst. for Student Achievement, Manhasset, N.Y., 1998—, Today's Students Tomorrow's Tchrs., Yorktown Heights, N.Y., 1998—. Recipient Horace M. Kallen Disting. Cmty. Svc. award Am. Jewish Congress, 1981, Brotherhood award NCCJ, 1985, Disting. Achievement award B'nai B'rith, 1997. Fellow Am. Coll. Health Care Execs., N.Y. Acad. Medicine (assoc.); mem. APHA, Am. Hosp. Assn., Pub. Health Assn. N.Y., Nat. Acad. Sci. Inst. Medicine. Home: 2900 Peachtree St Purchase NY 10577 Office: Manhattanville Coll 2900 Purchase St Purchase NY 10577-2103

BERMAN, RICHARD BRUCE, lawyer; b. Freeport, N.Y., Sept. 26, 1951; s. Nathan and Helen Dorothy (Raiden) B.; m. Laurie Michael, Nov. 2, 1985. BA in Speech Communication, Am. U., 1973; JD, U. Miami, 1976. Bar: Fla. 1976, U.S. Dist. Ct. (so. dist.) Fla. 1976, D.C. 1978. Atty. Travelers Ins. Co., Ft. Lauderdale, Fla., 1977-84; assoc. Frank & Flaster P.A., Sunrise, Fla., 1984-88, DeCasare & Salerno, Ft. Lauderdale, Fla., 1988-89; pvt. practice, 1989—; bd. dirs. Frosch Health Care Cons., Inc., Landerhill; mem. worker's compensation rules com. Fla. Bar, 1991-94; mem. Fla. Workers Advs., 1991—, bd. dirs., 1997—. Mem. panel health care Dem. Legis. Task Force, Ft. Lauderdale, 1985-87; mem. adv. bd. Reflex Sympathetic Dystrophy Syndrome Assn. Fla., 1992—; mem. B'nai Brith. Mem. ABA, ATLA, D.C. Bar, Fla. Bar Assn., Broward County Trial Lawyers Assn., B'nai Brith. Avocations: writing and performing music, theatre.

BERMAN, RICHARD KEITH, television producer, film producer; b. N.Y.C., Dec. 25, 1945. BA in Speech, U. Wis., Madison, 1967. Prodr., writer (story): Star Trek: Generations, 1994, Star Trek: First Contact, 1996, Star Trek: IMAX, 1998, Star Trek: Insurrection, 1998; prodr., writer (story), (TV): Star Trek: Deep Space Nine-Emissary/Emissary, 1993, Star Trek: Voyager-Caretaker, 1995; supervising prodr.: Star Trek: The Next Generation-Encounter at Farpoint, 1987, -All Good Things, 1994, (series) Star Trek: The Next Generation, 1987; creator (TV series) Star Trek: Deep Space Nine/DS9, 1993; co-creator (TV series) Star Trek: Voyager, 1995; creative cons. Star Trek: The Experience, 1998. Office: c/o Paramount Television Grp (divsn Paramount Pictures) 5555 Melrose Ave Hollywood CA 90038-3197*

BERMAN, RICHARD MILES, judge; b. N.Y.C., Sept. 11, 1943; s. Samuel and Sophie Berman; m. Emily Krasna, May 29, 1979 (div. Nov. 1983). BS, Cornell U., 1964; JD, NYU, 1967; Diploma Comparative Law, U. Stockholm, 1968, Diploma Internat. Law, 1970; MSW, Fordham U., 1996. Bar: N.Y. 1971. Assoc. Davis, Polk & Wardwell, N.Y.C., 1970-74; exec. asst. Sen. Jacob K. Javits, N.Y.C., 1974-78; gen. counsel, exec. v.p., dir. Warner Cable Comm. Inc., N.Y.C., 1978-86; gen. counsel, sec. MTV Networks, Inc., N.Y.C., 1983-86; ptnr. LeBoeuf, Lamb, Greene & MacRae, N.Y.C., 1986-95; mng. ptnr. L.A., 1989-91; judge Family Ct. of the State of N.Y., 1995-98, U.S. Dist. Ct. (so. dist.) N.Y., 1998—; exec. dir. N.Y. State Alliance to Save Energy Inc., N.Y.C., 1977-78; mem. fellowships and grants com. Am.-Scandinavian Found, N.Y.C., 1977-78; bd. dirs. Citizens Com. for N.Y.C. Inc., 1977-95; mem. N.Y.C. child abuse task force, 1995; N.Y. state permanent jud. commn. on Justice for Children, 1996—. Thord-Gray fellow Am.-Scandinavian Found., 1967-68; Donald Frank Sussman Meml. scholar Cornell U., Judge Valente, Clarence Palitz and Jacob Levy Found. scholar NYU Sch. Law, 1964-67. Mem. U.S. Jr. Davis Cup Squad (met. N.Y.C.), Assn. of Bar of City of N.Y. Avocations: tennis, horseback riding, house restoration. Office: US Dist Ct 40 Centre St New York NY 10007

BERMAN, ROBERT S., marketing consultant; b. N.Y.C., Apr. 13, 1932; s. Sydney and Beatrice (Lipman) B.; m. Eleanor Rae Greenwald, June 16, 1956 (div. 1973); children: Thomas, Eric, Terry; m. Sherry Rona Frawley, May 29, 1975 (div. 1994); m. Sharon Louise Erbe, Oct. 5, 1996. BA, Cornell U., 1953, MA, 1954; advanced mgmt. certificate, Harvard U., 1964. Vice pres. Marschalk, Inc., N.Y.C., 1962-64; exec. v.p. DeGarmo, Inc., N.Y.C., 1964-70, 1970-80; exec. v.p., gen. mgr. D'Arcy MacManus & Masius, N.Y.C., 1980-83; chmn. exec. com. Margeotes Fertitta & Weiss, 1984-88; ptnr. Ber/Cam Ptnrs., 1987-89; pres. Berman Mktg. Network, Naples, 1983—; instr. dept. communications Parsons Sch., 1968-70, Pratt Inst., 1974-76; columnist Madison Ave. Mag., N.Y.C., 1968-72. Dir. Collier County Spl. Olympics Internat. Served to 1st lt. U.S. Army, 1954-56. Named Advt. Accountman of the Yr. N.Y. Advt. Council, 1969. Mem. Unity of Naples (bd. dirs.), The Conservancy, Civil War Roundtable N.Y., Komos Aiden Theatrical Assn., Quill and Dagger Club, Cornell Club, The Vineyards Golf Club, Naples Bath and Tennis Club. Home: 1031 Oriole Cir Naples FL 34105-7425

BERMAN, RONALD CHARLES, lawyer, accountant; b. Chgo., July 7, 1949; s. Joseph and Helen Berman; m. Kristine K. Topp, May 1, 1993;

children: Daniel J. Lohr, Joseph James. BBS with highest honors, U. Ill., 1971, JD with honors, 1974. Bar: Ill. 1974, Wis. 1976; CPA, Wis. Mem. tax staff Grant Thornton, Chgo., 1974-76; tax supr. Grant Thornton, Madison, Wis., 1976-78, tax mgr., 1978-81, ptnr. tax dept., 1991-94; assoc. Neider & Boucher, Madison, 1995-96, shareholder, 1997—. Mem. editl. adv. bd. Physician's Tax Advisor Newsletter, 1986-89, Physician's Tax and Investment Advisor, 1989-93. Scoutmaster Boy Scouts Am., Middleton, Wis., 1978—, fin. chmn. Mohawk Dist. Four Lakes coun., Madison, 1981-85, chmn. endowment fund, 1984-92, v.p. fin., 1992-94, exec. bd., 1982—, treas., 1994-96, nat. rep., 1996—; bd. dirs. Scouts on Stamps Soc. Internat., 1986-96, v.p., 1996-98; bd. dirs. Madison Pension Coun., 1986-98, pres., 1988-89. Recipient Silver Beaver award Boy Scouts Am., 1981. Mem. ABA (employee benefits com. taxation sect.), AICPA, Wis. Soc. CPAs (chmn. fed. tax com. 1990-92), State Bar Wis., Ill. Bar Assn., Madison Estate Coun. (bd. dirs. 1991-97), Wis. Planned Giving Coun., Nat. Com. Planned Giving, Web Network Benefits Profls., Optimists, Order of Coif, Alpha Pi Omega, Phi Kappa Phi, Phi Alpha Delta. Avocations: photogrphy, philately, camping. Home: 3906 Rolling Hill Dr Middleton WI 53562-1224

BERMAN, RUTH SHARON, chiropractor; b. Plainfield, N.J., May 24, 1964; d. Morris H. and Paula (Mahler) B.; m. Michael J. Arra, Sept. 4, 1988. BS in Liberal Arts, SUNY; D of Chiropractic cum laude, Life Chiropractic Coll., Marietta, Ga., 1987. Diplomate Nat. Bd. Chiropractic Examiners; cert. Am. Chiropractic Bd. Sports Physicians, electric therapeutic modalities, Ga. Bd. Chiropractic Examiners; certificate in rating of permanent impairment for disability evaluation, Fla. Workers Compensation; lic. chiropractor Fla., Ga. Exam. dr. Berman Chiropractic Ctr., North Miami Beach, Fla., 1987; clinic dir. Alameda Plz. Clinic, Decatur, Ga., 1988-89; pvt. practice Arra Berman Chiropractic, Boynton Beach, Fla., 1990—; relief dr. various chiropractors, Ga., 1989—, Fla., 1990—; staff chiropractor Cory Everson's Fitness and Aerobics, 1995. Mem. Fla. Chiropractic Assn., Parker Chiropractic Resource Found., Palm Beach County Chiropractic Soc., Life Chiropractic Alumni Assn., Toastmasters Internat. (v.p. membership Boca Raton chpt. 1998—). Avocations: travel, music, painting. Office: Arra Berman Chiropractic 342 N Congress Ave Boynton Beach FL 33426-3465

BERMAN, SANFORD SOLOMON, motion picture sound designer, composer, arranger, artist; b. Long Branch, N.J., Nov. 14, 1951; s. Jerome Sidney and Marion (Solomon) B. BFA, Phila. Coll. Art, 1974. Freelance sound designer, record prodr./arranger, musician/composer. Sound designer, supr. (features) Double Jeopardy, Analyze This, Brokedown Palace, Neil Simon's Odd Couple 2, Hard Rain, Hush, Multiplicity, Jade, Virtuosity, Wings of Courage, Bad Girls, Tombstone, Striking Distance Aladdin (Golden Reel winner, FX Editl., Oscar nomination), Love Field, Unlawful Entry, J.F.K. (FX Editl., Brit. Acad. award, Golden Reel nominee), Hot Shots!, Back to the Future (The Ride), Revenge (Golden Reel nominee), Immediate Family, Oliver & Company (Golden Reel winner), The Princess Bride (Golden Reel nominee), The Seventh Sign (Golden Reel nominee), da, Big Bad John, Going Under Cover, Mac & Me, Weeds, Jaws III, Cloak & Dagger, The Stone Boy, Wolfen, Strange Invaders, That Championship Season, The Sword & The Sorcerer, History of the World Part I, Miss Lonelyhearts, Ten to Midnight, The House on Sorority Row, Evilspeak, Q, Summerspell, Suburbia, Roar, Sweet Sixteen, The Fatal Game, Radioactive Dreams, The Glory of Khan, (short subjects) A Hard Rain, Ballet Robotique (Oscar nomination), The Wizard of Change, The Quest, A Trip to Tomorrow, Bird & The Robot, The Water Engine, Lean Machine, Wind Tunnel, Environmental Effects, New Magic, The Collector, Niagara, Lets Go!, Tour of the Universe, Runaway Train, Zargon, Deep Water Rescue, Rollercoaster, Monte Carlo Race, Alpine Highway, Toyota, Chevrolet, Jet Helicopter, Call from Space; keyboardist for James Brown "Static", 1996; creator comic effects Eat It (Grammy nomination), Like a Surgeon (Grammy nomination), New Duck (Grammy nomination); prodr., arranger, keyboardist Secret Smiles; composer (feature film scores) Screamers, Cataclysm, (commls.) Toyota, 1986, Celica, 1986; appeared with Bruce Springsteen, Steel, Hall & Oates, Chuck Berry, Dwayne Eddy, Jr. Walker & The All-Stars, James Brown, others. Mem. ACLU, So. Calif., 1985—, People for the Am. Way, So. Calif., 1985—, Am. Jewish Congress, 1982—. Recipient Brit. Acad. award Brit. Acad. of Film and TV Arts, Gt. Britain, 1992. Mem. Motion Picture Sound Editors (pres. 1992—, Golden Reel award 1988, 92), Acad. of Motion Picture Arts and Scis., Nat. Acad. Recording Arts and Scis., Am. Soc. Music Arrangers and Composers, Motion Picture Editors Guild. Democrat. Avocations: drawing, antique and classic automobiles, books.

BERMAN, SAUL JAY, strategic consultant; b. Phila., Jan. 1, 1946; s. Sherwood and Leona (Habelson) B.; m. S. Jann Gillen, June 6, 1980; 1 child, Ashley Scott. BS in Econs., U. Pa., 1967; MBA, Columbia U., 1969, PhD, 1973. Asst. prof. U. So. Calif., L.A., 1972-77; divisional v.p. Broadway Dept. Stores, L.A., 1977-82; case leader Boston Consulting Group, L.A., 1982-86; mng. ptnr. Price Waterhouse Strategic Change Group, 1986-98; global and Ams. leader corp. and ops. strategy PricewaterhouseCoopers, 1998—; active Strategic Leadership Forum, 1986—. Bd. dirs. Love is Feeding Everyone, L.A., 1988-89; mem. L.A. County Beach Commn., 1978-80, Planning Forum, L.A., 1987—, Town Hall, L.A., 1987-94. Mem. U. Pa. Alumni Club (bd. dirs. 1986-88, So. Calif. assoc. alumni trustee 1990—), Columbia Bus. Sch. Club of So. Calif. (bd. dirs. 1992-95). Avocations: tennis, running. Office: PricewaterhouseCoopers 1880 Century Park E Ste 1200 Los Angeles CA 90067-1600

BERMAN, SIEGRID VISCONTI, interior designer; b. Bremen, Germany, May 22, 1944; came to U.S., 1951, naturalized, 1956; d. Walter L. and Annegrete M. (Wolf) Knapp; self-educated. Designer, Shepard Martin Assocs., N.Y.C., 1968-76; facilities mgr. Unifert, USA, N.Y.C., 1976-78; owner Siegrid Visconti Berman Interiors, N.Y.C., 1978—; dir. interiors DAT Cons., N.Y.C., 1980-83; dir. design Ralph Mancini Assocs., N.Y.C., 1983-85; sr. designer Karco-Davis, 1985-91; sr. mng. dir. Meli Borrelli Assocs., Architects and Designers, 1991-95, John Frances Borrelli, Architect, P.C., 1996—. Composer songs; illustrator book. Bd. dirs. Temple Spiritual Rsch. and Learning, 1981-82; reader Lighthouse for Blind. Colo. State Coll. scholar, 1962. Mem. AFTRA, SAG. Address: 13 E 37th St New York NY 10016

BERMAN, STEVEN RICHARD, software engineer; b. N.Y.C., Dec. 30, 1947; s. Harold and Norma (Bystock) B.; m. Susan Segall, Aug. 3, 1969; 1 child, Russell T. BS in Meteorology, CCNY, 1968; postgrad., U. Chgo., 1968-69; MS in Tech. Mgmt., Pepperdine U., 1993. Programmer, analyst Logicon, Inc., San Pedro, Calif., 1970-73, 75-78, Hughes Aircraft Co., Culver City, Calif., 1973-75; sr. analyst Argosystems, Inc., Sunnyvale, Calif., 1978-80; mgr. software support Ultrasystems, Inc., Irvine, Calif., 1981-86; sr. rsch. engr. Northrop Grumman Inc., Hawthorne, Calif., 1986-98; sr. software engr. TRW Inc., L.A., 1998—. Author (computer programs) Recording Input-Output, 1983, Batch Jobs from Fortran, 1988, Marking Files No Backup, 1988. NDEA Title IV fellow, Chgo., 1968. Mem. Am. Contract Bridge League, Mensa. Avocations: bridge, travel. Home: 17336 Flame Tree Cir Fountain Valley CA 92708

BERMAN, TRESSA LYNN, anthropologist, writer; b. Phila., Dec. 31, 1960; Eugene Adam Berman and Judith Ann Bateman. BA cum laude, San Francisco State U., 1982; MA, U. Colo., 1987; PhD, UCLA, 1994. Asst. curator and acting collections mgr. Calif. Acad. Scis., San Francisco, 1982-85; asst. curator U. Colo. Mus., Boulder, 1985-86; tchg. assoc. U. Calif., Davis, 1990, rsch. assoc., 1990; ethnologist Nat. Mus. Natural History Smithsonian, Washington, 1992-94; vis. scholar Macquarie U., Sydney, Australia, 1998; asst. prof. Ariz. State U., Phoenix, 1995—; advisor Three Affiliated Tribes Mus., Fort Berthold, N.D., 1991-92; mem. adv. bd. Cañon Jour. of Am. Studies, Phoenix, 1997-99; mem. editl. adv. bd. Collegiate Press, San Diego, Calif., 1999—; exec. dir. Border Zone Arts, San Francisco, 1999—. Contbr. (books) Encyclopedia of North America, 1996, It Takes More Than Class, 1997; also to jours. Cultural Survival Quarterly, 1988, Art Papers, 1998. Lectr. to pub., Nat. Mus. Natural History, Smithsonian, Washington, 1993, Queensland Coll. Art, Brisbane Australia, 1998; panel reviewer Ariz. State Commn. on Ats, Phoenix, 1995; project evaluator Boys and Girls Club Am., Phoenix, 1997. Grantee: Jacobs Rsch. Fund, Whatcom Mus., Bellingham, Wash., 1991-92, Phillips Grant, Am. Philos. Soc., Phila., 1992, rsch. grant Macquarrie U., Sydney, Australia, 1998; named Inst. of Am. Cultures fellow, UCLA, 1991=92. Mem. Soc. for Applied Anthropology (pres. anthropology and intellectual propertyrights group 1997—), Native Am. Art Studies Assn. (mem. exec. com., scholarship fund com.), Am. Anthrop. Assn., Internat. Assn. for Study of Common Property. Avocations: poetry, modern dance. Office: Ariz State U West 4701 Thunderbird Rd Phoenix AZ 85069

BERMAN, WILLIAM H., publishing company executive; b. Stamford, Conn., 1936. Grad., U. of Pa., 1959. Exec. v.p. Houghton Mifflin Co., Boston, Md.; retired Houghton Mifflin Co., Boston, 1993.

BERMAN-HAMMER, SUSAN, public relations executive; b. Buffalo, Sept. 12, 1950; d. Leonard and Judith H. (Goldenberg) Berman; m. Tony Hammer, Aug. 17, 1975; 1 child, Erik Jason. BA, Northwestern U., 1972, MS, 1975. Pub. info. asst. Sta. WBBM-TV, Chgo., 1972; news asst. exec. trailer Dem. Nat. Conv. ABC-TV News, Miami, Fla., 1972; writer Chgo. Conv. and Visitors Bur., 1973-75; Washington corr. Sta. WYEN, Des Plaines, Ill., 1975; sr. v.p. Herbert H. Rozoff Assocs., Inc., Chgo., 1976-82; pres., owner Susan L. Berman Assocs., Inc., Deerfield, Ill., 1982—; v.p. corp. communications Sheldon Good & Co., Chgo., 1988-89; chairperson Chgo. Communications/10, a consortium in field, 1982-83. Asst. regional dir. Nat. Movement for Student Vote, Chgo., 1972; bd. dirs. Chgo. Women in Broadcasting, 1972-76, Younger Set Jewish Fedn., Dallas, 1985-87; vice chair, spokesperson North Shore Sch. Dist. 112 Edn. Found.; mem. North Shore Sch. Dist. 112 Caucus, 1995; mem. exec. bd., chair Safe Home, liaison to North Shore Sch. Dist. 112, 1995-96, Edgewood Mid. Sch. PTA, 1995-97; also Dist. 112 crisis intervention team advisor, 1997-98; founder, chair steering com. Safe Home Program, serving 7500 students, North Shore Sch. Dists. 112 & 109, 1994—; Sherwood Sch. PTO liaison to North Shore Sch. Dist. 112 & CIC Legis. Com., Highland Park, Ill., 1994—; mem. young women's exec. bd., v.p. cmty. devel., co-chair Trendsetter luncheon, co-chair Insights com., nominating com. Shalom Chgo. com., mem. campaign cabinet Jewish United Fund Chgo., 1991-96; bd. dirs. nat. women's com. North Shore chpt. Brandeis U., 1991-93; exec. bd., v.p. programming, reenrollment and membership, nominating com. Tamarisk chpt. ORT, Deerfield, Ill., 1990-95; chair comm. com. North Shore Congregation Israel, Glencoe, Ill., 1993-94; spokesperson and co-leader Parents Against Proposed Annexation of Deerfield subdivsns. from North Shore Sch. Dist. 112 into Deerfield Sch. Dist. 109, 1993-94. Recipient Recognition award City Coun. of Highland Park, Ill. Mem. North Shore Congregation Israel, Northwestern U. Alumni Club, Alpha Lambda Delta, Multiplex. Avocations: aerobics, tennis, golf, synchronized swimming. E-mail: sbhsba@aol.com. Office: 9 Tamarisk Ln Deerfield IL 60015-5075

BERMANN, SANDRA LEKAS, English language educator; b. Chgo., Mar. 30, 1947; d. Clarence and Theria Belle (Pollard) Lekas; m. George Alan Bermann, Dec. 28, 1969; children: Sloan Douglas, Suzanne Evelyne, Grant Alexander. AB, Smith Coll., 1969; MA, Columbia U., 1971, PhD, 1976. Asst. prof. Princeton (N.J.) U., 1976-83, assoc. prof., 1983-94, prof., 1994—, chmn. comparative lit. dept., 1998—; dir. undergrad. studies dept. comparative literature Princeton U., 1978-82, 83-84, master of Stevenson Hall, 1984-92, dir. grad. studies dept. comparative literature, 1993-95. Author: The Sonnet Over Time, 1988; translator, introducer: Manzoni's On the Historical Novel, 1984; contbr. articles to profl. jours. Fellow Fulbright Commn., Italy, 1969-70, Mrs. Giles Whiting Found., Columbia U. and Paris, 1974-75. Mem. MLA, Internat. Comparative Literature Assn., Am. Comparative Literature Assn. (chair undergrad. com. 197-90, adv. bd. 1989-92, chair constitution 1991-93). Avocations: dance, music. Office: Princeton Univ Dept Comparative Literature 325 E Pyne Princeton NJ 08544

BERMARD, THEODORE G., marketing executive; b. Cleve., Jan. 2, 1962; s. Lewis A. Jr. and Geraldine S. Bernard; m. Lauren F. Bernard, Aug. 22, 1992; children: Rachel, Jessica. BA in Econs., Washington U., St. Louis, 1983; M Mgmt., Northwestern U., 1991. Rsch. assoc. Fed. Res. Bank, Cleve., 1985-88; jr. economist Coun. Econ. Advisors, Exec. Office Pres., Washington, 1988-89; sr. mgr. new product devel. Am. Express Travel Related Svcs. Co., N.Y.C., 1991-95; dir. portfolio mgmt. GE Capital Consumer Fin. Svcs., Cin., 1995-98; sr. v.p. Interactive Telesvcs. Corp., Columbus, Ohio, 1998—. Contbr. articles to profl. jours. Trustee, v.p. Hillel Found., U. Cin., 1995—; chmn. United Jewish Appeal, 1996-98; trustee Hillell Internat., 1998—. Mem. Omicron Delta Epsilon.

BERMAS, STEPHEN, lawyer; b. N.Y.C., Apr. 27, 1925. BS, Cornell U., 1949, JD, 1950; LLM, NYU, 1957. Bar: N.Y. 1950. Assoc. Wagner, Quillinan, Wagner & Tennant, N.Y.C., 1950-51; law sec. to chief justice U.S. Dist. Ct. (so. dist.) N.Y., N.Y.C., 1951-55; assoc. Gordon, Brady, Caffrey & Keller, N.Y.C., 1955-59; ptnr. Medine & Bermas, N.Y.C., 1959-63, Feltman & Bermas, N.Y.C., 1964-66; sr. atty. Columbia Gas System Corp., N.Y.C., 1966-69; asst. gen. counsel Continental Group Inc., N.Y.C., 1970-77, assoc. gen. counsel, 1978-82; v.p., gen. counsel Continental Can Co. Inc., Norwalk, Conn., 1982-86, exec. v.p., gen. counsel, 1987-91; v.p., gen. counsel Continental Plastic Containers, Inc., Norwalk, 1991—; instr. law Queen's Coll, N.Y.C., 1964-68; adminstrv. law judge Office Profl. Med. Conduct N.Y. State Dept. Health, N.Y.C., 1993—. Mem. ABA. Office: Continental Plastic Containers Inc 1 Aerial Way Syosset NY 11791

BERMINGHAM, JOHN SCOTT, associate dean; b. Jackson, Wyo., Nov. 1, 1951; s. George Carpenter and Harriet (McVaugh) B. BA in English, U. N.C., 1974; MA in Edn. Psychology, Northwestern U., Evanston, Ill., 1977, MA in Counseling Psychology, 1979. Cert. clin. mental health counselor. Tchr. Tabor Acad., Marion, Mass., 1974-76, Lake Forest (Ill.) Country Day Sch., 1977-78; counselor, coord. crisis Lake County Youth Svc. Bur., Lake Villa, Ill., 1978-79; clin. dir., co-founder Greenhouse Youth Svcs., Inc., Mundelein, Ill., 1979-86; assoc. dean Lake Forest Grad. Sch. Mgmt., 1987-96; chmn. NewCo Internat., Inc., 1996—; instr. Northwestern U., Evanston, summer 1977; exec. v.p., sec.-treas., bd. dirs. Chpt. Ho., Ltd., Lake Forest, 1981-85; mng. dir. Mgmt. Resource Cons., Lake Bluff, Ill., 1986—. Bd. dirs. Cen. Lake County United Way, Libertyville, Ill., 1985, Condell Meml. Hosp. Found., Libertyville, 1989—; chmn. bd. Lake County Youth Svc. Network, Waukegan, Ill., 1983-85, CROYA-Lake Forest Youth Commn., 1985—. Recipient Cert. of Recognition, Kiwanis Libertyville, 1985, Cert. of Honor, Village Bd. Libertyville, 1986, City Coun. Lake Forest, 1989. Mem. APA (assoc.), AACD, Ill. Psychol. Assn., Nat. Acad. Cert. Clin. Mental Health Counselors. Republican. Episcopalian. Avocations: racquet sports, dancing, piano, art collecting, wood working. Home: 36 Sunset Pl Lake Bluff IL 60044-2738 Office: 1000 Oak Spring Ln Libertyville IL 60048

BERMINGHAM, JOSEPH DANIEL, lawyer; b. Lackawanna, N.Y., July 26, 1938; s. Joseph Daniel and Marian Rita (Mahon) B.; m. Ann Barbara Goslin, Aug. 20, 1966; children: Christopher, David, Sarah, Elizabeth. BA, Canisius Coll., 1959; JD, Boston Coll., 1962. Bar: N.Y. 1962, U.S. Dist. Ct. (we. dist.) N.Y. 1964, U.S. Ct. Appeals (2d cir.) 1970, U.S. Supreme Ct. 1977. Assoc. Vincent E. Doyle, Esquire, Buffalo, 1964-67; ptnr. Doyle, Diebold & Bermingham and successor firms, Buffalo, 1967-88, Bermingham, Cook & Mahoney, P.C., Buffalo, 1988-93, Bermingham & Cook, P.C., 1993-98; prin. law clk. Erie County Surrogate Ct., Buffalo, 1998—. Co-author: Course Handbook, New York State Director of Criminal Justice Service, 1980. Pres. Amherst (N.Y.) Soccer Assn., 1984; bd. dirs. Neighborhood Legal Svcs., Inc., Buffalo, 1984-86. 1st lt. U.S. Army, 1962-64. Mem. Erie County Bar Assn. (v.p. and pres. 1986-88, bd. dirs. 1981-84, Lawyer of Yr. 1993), Western N.Y. Trial Lawyers Assn. (v.p. and pres. 1984-85), N.Y. State Bar Assn. (ho. of dels. 1986-90, 8th jud. dist. v.p. 1991-97). Office: Erie County Surrogate's Ct 92 Franklin St Buffalo NY 14202-3902

BERMUDEZ, EUGENIA M. See DIGNAC, GENY

BERN, HOWARD ALAN, science educator, research biologist; b. Montreal, Que., Can., Jan. 30, 1920; m. Estelle Bruck, 1946; children: Alan, Lauren. BA, UCLA, 1941, MA, 1942, PhD in Zoology, 1948; D (hon.), U. Rouen, France, 1996; LLD (hon.), U. Hokkaido, Japan, 1994; DPhil (hon.), Yokohama City U., 1997. Nat. Rsch. Coun. predoctoral fellow in biology UCLA, 1946-48; instr. in zoology U. Calif., Berkeley, 1948-50, asst. prof., 1950-56, assoc. prof., 1956-60, prof., 1960-89, prof. integrative biology, 1989-90, prof. emeritus, 1990—; rsch. endocrinologist Cancer Rsch. Lab., U. Calif., Berkeley, 1960—; chair group in endocrinology U. Calif., Berkeley, 1962-90, faculty rsch. lectr., 1988; rsch. prof. Miller Inst. for Basic Rsch. in Sci., 1961; vis. prof. pharmacology U. Bristol, 1965-66, U. Kerala, India, 1967, Ocean Rsch. Inst., U. Tokyo, 1971, 86, U. P.R., 1973, 74, U. Tel Aviv, 1975, Nat. Mus. Natural History, Paris, 1981, Toho U., Funabashi, Japan, 1982-84, 86-89, U. Hawaii, 1986, 91-93, Hokkaido U., 1992, 94, U. Fla., 1991, 92; James vis. prof. St. Francis Xavier U., Antigonish, N.S., 1986; Walker-Ames prof. U. Wash., 1977; disting. visitor U. Alta., Edmonton, Can., 1981; John W. Cowper Disting. vis. lectr. SUNY-Buffalo, 1984; Watkins vis. prof. Wichita (Kans.) State U., 1984; vis. scholar Meiji U., Tokyo, 1986; internat. guest prof. Yokohama City U., Japan, 1988, 95; lectr., spkr. in field; mem. adv. com. on instl. rsch. grants Am. Cancer Soc., 1967-70; mem. adv. com. Nat. Cancer Inst., 1975-79; mem. NIH adv. com. in Endocrinology and Metabolism, 1978-79; mem. GM Cancer Rsch. Found., Sloan Medal Selection Com., 1984-85, Japan Internat. Prize in Biology Selection Com., 1987, 92, 96. Mem. editl. bd. Endocrinology, 1962-74, Gen. and Comparative Endocrinology, Jour. Exptl. Zoology, 1965-69, 86-89, Internat. Rev. Cytology, Neuroendocrinology, 1974-80, Cancer Rsch., 1975-78, Jour. Comparative Physiology B, 1977-84, Am. Zoologist, 1978-83, Acta Zoologica, 1982-96, Zool. Sci., Tokyo, Animal Biol., Italy; contbr. articles to profl. publs. Assoc. Nat. Mus. Natural History, Paris, 1980; mem. adv. com. Contra Costa Cancer Rsch. Fund, 1984—, Stazione Zoologica Anton Dohrn de Napoli, 1987-92. Recipient Disting. Tchg. award U. Calif., Berkeley, 1972, The Berkeley Citation, 1990, Disting. Svc. award Soc. Adv. Chicanos and Native Americans in Sci., 1990; Guggenheim fellow, 1951-52, NSF fellow U. Hawaii, 1958-59, fellow Ctr. for Advanced Study in Behavioral Scis., Stanford, 1960, NSF fellow Stazione Zoologica, Naples, 1965-66, Japan Soc. Promotion of Sci. Rsch. fellow U. Toyama, Japan, 1993. Fellow NAS, AAAS, Am. Acad. Arts and Scis., Indian Nat. Sci. Acad. (fgn.), Società Nazionale di Scienze Lettere e Arti Napoli (fgn.), Calif. Acad. Sci., Accademia Nazionale dei Lincei (fgn.); mem. Soc. Integrative Comparative Biology (hon., pres. 1967), Am. Assn. Cancer Rsch., Am. Physiol. Soc., Endocrine Soc., Internat. Soc. Neuroendocrinology (coun. 1977-80), Exptl. Biology and Medicine (coun. 1980-83), Am. Soc. Molec. Marine Biol. Biotech., Western Soc. Naturalists, Japan Soc. Zootech. Sci. (hon.), Japan Soc. Comparative Endocrinology (hon.), Cosmos Club. E-Mail: bern@socrates.berkeley.edu. Home: 1010 Shattuck Ave Berkeley CA 94707-2626 Office: U Calif Dept Integrative Biology Berkeley CA 94720-3140

BERN, LYNDA KAPLAN, women's health and pediatric nurse; b. N.Y.C., Apr. 17, 1960; d. Melvin and Marilyn Kaplan; m. Jay Bern, June 1986. BSN, SUNY, Binghamton, 1981. RN, N.Y., Md., D.C., Va., N.J. Clin. nurse Gt. Neck (N.Y.) Pediatrics, 1981-82, North Shore Ob-Gyn, Bayside, N.Y., 1982-84; clin. ladder level three nurse North Shore U. Hosp., Manhasset, N.Y., 1981-88; breast feeding cons., instr. childbirth preparation Shady Grove Adventist Hosp., Rockville, Md., 1989-90, 91-92; relief nurse Md. Profl. Staffing Svc., Bethesda, Md., 1989-92; staff nurse St. Peter's Med. Ctr., New Brunswick, N.J., 1993—; instr. maternal-child series St. Peter's Med. Ctr., 1994-96, cert. preceptor, 1997—; nurse cons. Sons of Israel, Manalapan, N.J., 1998—; mgr. nursing hon. com. SUNY, mem. hosp. stds. of care com., nursing preceptor Adelphi Sr. Nursing Students, Vol. March of Dimes/Health Screening Fair. Nursing scholar Good Citizenship League.

BERN, MURRAY MORRIS, hematologist, oncologist; b. Montgomery, Ala., Feb. 26, 1944; s. Hymie and Ruth Edith (Schaeffer) B.; m. Nancy Frazee, Nov. 23, 1967; 1 child, Alan. BA, Vanderbilt U., 1966; MD, Tulane U., 1970. Diplomate Am. Bd. Internal Medicine, Am. Bd. Hematology, Am. Bd. Oncology. Intern, then resident New Eng. Deaconess Hosp., Boston, 1970-72; resident in medicine Boston City Hosp., 1972-73; fellow in hematology & oncology New Eng. Deaconess Hosp.; Am. Cancer Soc. fellow Ctr. for Blood Rsch., Boston, 1973-75; sect. chief hematology New Eng. Deaconess Hosp., Boston, 1975-86; co-founder Cancer Ctr. of Boston, 1986; lab. dir. bone marrow transplantation Cancer Ctr. Boston, Boston and Plymouth, Mass., 1986—; dir. Cancer Ctr. of Boston and its stem cell support care, 1990-97; asst. prof. medicine Harvard U., 1987-94, asst. clin. prof. medicine, 1978-87. Author, editor: Urinary Track Bleeding, 1985, Hematologic Disorders in Maternal and Fetal Medicine, 1990. Mem. bd. med. advisors Am. Cancer Soc., Mass., 1976-80, fellow, 1973-75; bd. dirs. N.E. region ARC, 1994—. Recipient Tullis award for rsch. Fellow ACP (jr. faculty fellow 1973-77); mem. Am. Soc. Hematology (clin. practice com. 1996—), Am. Soc. Clin. Oncology. Avocations: camping, fishing. Office: Cancer Ctr Boston 125 Parker Hill Ave Boston MA 02120-2847

BERN, PAULA RUTH, columnist; b. Pitts., July 27, 1934; children: Bruce, Caryn, Marshall, Samuel, Rona. BA, Pa. State U., 1956; MA, U. Pitts., 1978. Editor-in-chief Jaffe Pub. Co., L.A., 1958-63; on-air producer Sta. WQED-TV, Pitts, 1963-65; dir. univ. rels. and devel. Robert Morris Coll., Pitts. and Coraopolis, 1965-69, Poin Park Coll., Pitts, 1969-72; pres. Bern Asocs., Inc., 1972—; CEO The Exec. TV Workshop, Pitts., 1987—; tchr. sr. exec. seminars grad. sch. Urban and Pub. Affairs, Carnegie Mellon U., 1985-90; trustee Ptts. Ballet Theatre, Inc., 1973-95. Contb. editor New Women mag., 1988—; syndicated columnist Scripps Howard NewsSvc., Washington, 1988—; Author: Point Park College: A Histor, 1980; How to Work for awoman Boss (Even if You'd Rather Not)., 1987, Keep your Feet Off the Desk, 1999. Bd. dirs. council for Internat. Visitors, 1975-91; Exec. Women's Council, 1980—; adv. council Internat. Poetry forum, 1979—, Pa. Comn. for Women; bd. dirs. Assn. Commns. Women, bd. dirs. Conflict Resolution Ctr. Internat., Inc., 1998—. Recipient Am. Coun. on Edn. awad, 1982;. Mem. Women i Comm., Pub. Relations Soc. Am., Delta Sigma Rho, Phi Beta Kappa. Office: Scripps Howard News Svc 1090 Vermont Ave NW Ste 1000 Washington DC 20005-4906

BERN, RONALD LAWRENCE, consulting company executive; b. Anderson, S.C., Aug. 23, 1936; s. Samuel Harris and Minnie (Siegel) B.; m. Elaine Kay Lefkowitz, Dec. 25, 1960; children: Brett Alan, Melissa Lynn. BA in Journalism, U. S.C., 1958, MA in Journalism, 1961. Writer William Barton Marsh Co., N.Y.C., 1958-59; editor, writer Univac div. Sperry Rand, N.Y.C., 1959-60; editor, mgr. Bell Tel. Labs., N.Y.C., 1961-63; pres. Ronald Bern Co., N.Y.C., 1964-85; corp. sr. v.p. The LVI Group, Inc., N.Y.C., 1985-90; cons. AT&T Co., N.Y., N.J., 1966-85, The LVI Group, Lehr Constrn.; bd. dirs. Talon Corp., The Bern Cos., Inc., Healing Images Inc. Author: An American in the Making, 1960, The Successful Salesman, 1972, The Legacy, 1975; Gone Fishin': The 100 Best Spots in New Jersey, 1998; contbr. articles to profl. pubs. Bd. dirs. North Brunswick Little League, N.J., 1975-79; mem. North Brunswick Planning Commn., 1984. With U.S. Army, 1958-59, 61-62. Fellow S.C. Press Assn., 1960. Mem. South Caroliniana Soc. Democrat. Jewish. Avocations: reading, travel. Home: 37 Hidden Lake Dr New Brunswick NJ 08902-1213

BERNABEI, RAYMOND, management consultant; b. New Castle, Pa., Nov. 26, 1925; s. Leo and Maria Bernabei; m. Rosella E. Taucher, May 4, 1946; children: Raymond L., Alan J., Rosemary, Leo J., Lori J. BS in Math. and Geography, Indiana U. of Pa., 1947; MEd in Ednl. Adminstrn., U. Pitts., 1950; cert. in guidance and counseling, Duquesne U., 1960; DEd, Western Res. U., 1966. Math. tchr. Clymer (Pa.) H.S., 1947-50, Tarentum (Pa.) H.S., 1950-54; dir. guidance and testing Tarentum Sch. Dist., 1954-61; asst. jr.-sr. H.S. prin. Hampton Twp. (Pa.), 1961-63; grad. asst. Western Res. U., Cleve., 1963-64; dir. secondary edn. Mentor Pub. Schs., Ohio, 1964-65, asst. supt., 1965, supt., 1965-67; asst. exec. dir. Bucks County (Pa.) Schs., 1967-80; mgmt. cons. I.E. Banreb Assocs., Longwood, Fla.; vis. tchr. John Carroll U., Cleve., 1965, Bowling Green (Ohio) U., 1966, N.S. Summer Sch./Dalhousie U., Halifax, Can., 1967, Wis. State U., Eau Claire, 1968, U. Ala., University, 1969, 71, U. Nev., Las Vegas, 1970, 72, 93, Cleve. State U., 1970, Laurence U., Sarasota, Fla., 1971, 72, 73; adj. prof. U. Ala., 1974, 75, 76, Lehigh U., Bethlehem, Pa., 1978, 80, 81, 82, Rollins Coll., Winter Park, Fla., 1983—; presenter in field. Recipient Disting. Prof. award Nat. Acad. Sch. Execs., 1973, Recognition award Nat. Soccer Coaches Athletic Assn., 1983, Bill Jeffrey award, 1985, Honor award Nat. Soccer Coaches Athletic Assn., 1991, Honor award Nat. Intercollegiate Soccer Ofcls. Assn., 1975, Disting. Svc. award Pa. State Athletic Dirs. Assn., 1987; named to Western Pa. Hall of Fame, 1977, Nat. Soccer Hall of Fame, 1978, Allegheny-Kiski Valley Hall of Fame, 1979, Nat. Assn. Intercollegiate Athletics Hall of Fame, 1994, Nellie DelCamp Excellence in Tchg. award Rollins Coll., 1995. Home and Office: 541 Woodview Dr Longwood FL 32779-2614

BERNACCHI, RICHARD LLOYD, lawyer; b. Los Angeles, Dec. 15, 1938; s. Bernard and Anne (Belluomini) B. B.S. with honors in Commerce (Nat. Merit Found. scholar), U. Santa Clara, 1961; LL.B. with highest honors (Legion Lex scholar, Jerry Geisler Meml. scholar), U. So. Calif., 1964. Bar: Calif. 1964. Assoc. Irell and Manella, Los Angeles, 1964-70, ptnr., 1970—;

lectr. Am. Law Inst., 1972-73; lectr. data processing contracts and law U. So. Calif., Los Angeles, 1972, 78, 81; co-chmn. Regional Transp. Com., 1970-72; mem. adv. bd. U. So. Calif. Computer Law Inst., 1979—, Ariz. Law and Tech. Inst., 1982-86; U. Santa Clara Computer and High Tech. Law Jour., 1982-90. Author: (with Gerald H. Larsen) Data Processing Contracts and the Law, 1974, (with Frank and Statland) Bernacchi on Computer Laaw, 1986; editor-in-chief U. So. Calif. Law Rev., 1962-64; mem. adv. bd. Computer Negotiations Report, 1983—, Computer and Tech. Law Jour., 1984-93, Computer Law Strategist, 1984-94. Served to capt. AUS, 1964-66, PTO. Mem. ABA (mem. adv. com. on edn. 1973-74, chmn. subcom. taxation computer sys. of sect. sci. and tech. 1976-78), L.A. Bar Assn., Computer Law Assn. (bd. dirs. 1973-86, chmn. preconf. symposium on law and computers 1974-75, West Coast v.p. 1976-79, sr. v.p. 1979-81, pres. 1981-83, adv. bd. 1986—), Internat. Bar Assn. (co-chmn. sect. on bus. law mem. com. on internat. computer and tech. law 1995-98, steering com. 1998—), Am. Fedn. Info. Processing Socs. (mem. spl. com. electronic funds transfer sys. 1974-78), Order of Coif, Scabbard and Blade, Beta Gamma Sigma, Alpha Sigma Nu. Office: Irell & Manella 1800 Avenue Of The Stars Los Angeles CA 90067-4276

BERNARD, ALEXANDER, airport police official; b. L.A., Apr. 23, 1952; s. Louis and Hannah (Bergman) B.; m. Diana LoRee Winstead, Dec. 17, 1976; children: Michael Alexander, Andrew Alexander. AA magna cum laude, L.A. Valley Coll., 1976; BS summa cum laude, Calif. State U., L.A., 1989. Parking meter collector L.A. City Clk.'s Office, 1973-79; police officer L.A. Airport, 1979-95; sgt. police svcs. divsn. L.A. Airport, Ontario, Calif., 1995—. Contbr. articles to profl. jours. Active Boy Scouts Am. Mem. NRA (life), Internat. Police Assn. (life), Indsl. Rels. Rsch. Assn., Calif. Peace Officers Assn., Peace Officers Rsch. Assn. Calif. (chpt. pres. 1982-84, 85-87, state bd. dirs. 1984-85, 88—, ethnic rels. com. 1993-94, exec. com. 1994—, sec. 1999—), L.A. Airport Peace Officers Assn. (pres. 1981-89, 94-95, bd. dirs. 1992-94), Airport Supervisory Police Officers' Assn. L.A. (bd. dirs. 1996, v.p. 1997-98, pres. 1999—), Fraternal Order of Police, Calif. Rifle and Pistol Assn. (life), Golden Key (life), Phi Kappa Phi (life). Democrat. Mem. Assemblies of God Ch. Avocations: travel, record collecting. Office: Police Svcs Divsn Ontario Internat Airport 1070 S Vineyard Ave Ontario CA 91761-8007

BERNARD, DAVID GEORGE, retired management consultant; b. Cambridge, Mass., Oct. 30, 1921; s. Frederick and Fayetta (Smith) B.; m. Edith Barnes, Dec. 10, 1960; 1 child, Andrew; children by prior marriage: Jeffrey, Frederick, Joan, Peter. B.S., Harvard U., 1943, M.B.A., 1947. Gen. sales mgr. Am. Can. Co., N.Y.C., 1958-61; sr. v.p. Medusa Corp., Cleve., 1961-63; v.p. Internat. Paper, N.Y.C., 1968-78, Nat. Can Corp., Chgo., 1978-81; exec. v.p. Fischbach Corp., N.Y.C., 1981-83; pres. Delta Marine Supply Corp., N.Y.C., 1983-84; bd. dirs. Trojan Techs. Inc. Bd. dirs. Jobs for Youth. Served to lt. USN, 1943-46, PTO. Mem. Newcomen Soc., Bay Head Yacht Club (N.J.). Democrat. Episcopalian. Home: 254 E 68th St Apt 27E New York NY 10021-6017*

BERNARD, DAVID KANE, minister, writer, editor; b. Baton Rouge, Nov. 20, 1956; s. Elton David and Loretta (Artigue) B.; m. Connie Jo Sharpe, June 6, 1981; children: Jonathan David, Daniel Kent, Lindsey Renee. BA magna cum laude, Rice U., 1978; JD with honors, U. Tex., 1981. Ordained to ministry United Pentecostal Ch. Internat., 1981—; bar: Tex. 1981. Dean of students Jackson (Miss.) Coll. Ministries, 1981-82, asst. v.p., 1982-86; assoc. editor United Pentecostal Ch. Internat., Hazelwood, Mo., 1986—; pastor New Life United Pentecostal Ch., Austin, 1992—. Author: In Search of Holiness, 1981, The Oneness of God, 1983, 19 others, also author booklets. Presbyter Tex. Dist. Bd.-United Pentecostal Ch. Internat., 1995—. Named Writer of the Yr., World Aflame Press, Hazelwood, 1987. Mem. State Bar Tex., Order of the Coif, Phi Beta Kappa. Avocations: reading, travel, racquetball, swimming. Home: 4405 Andalusia Dr Austin TX 78759-4906 Office: New Life Ch 4001 Adelphi Ln Austin TX 78727-5319

BERNARD, EDDIE NOLAN, oceanographer; b. Houston, Nov. 23, 1946; s. Edward Nolan and Geraldine Marie (Dempsey) B.; m. Shirley Ann Fielder, May 30, 1970; 1 child, Elizabeth Ann. BS, Lamar U., 1969; MS, Tex. A&M U., 1970, PhD, 1976. Geophysicist Pan Am. Petroleum Co., 1969; rsch. asst. oceanographic rsch. Tex. A&M U., College Station, Tex., 1969-70; rschr. NOAA, 1970-73; dep. dir. pacific marine environ. lab. NOAA, Seattle, 1980-82; rschr. Joint Tsunami Rsch. Effort, 1973-77; dir. Nat. Tsunami Warning Ctr., 1977-80; dir. Pacific Marine Environ. Lab., Seattle, 1982—, chmn. Nat. Tsunami Hazard Mitigation Program, 1997—; dir. NOAA hydrothermal vents program, fisheries oceanography program; exec. com. Coop. Inst. for Marine Resource Studies Oreg. State U.; adminstrv. bd. Joint Inst. Marine and Atmospheric Rsch. U. Hawaii; mem. Panel on Wind and Seismic Effects U.S.-Japan Coop. Program in Nat. Resources, 1981—; mem. Washington Sea Grant Steering Com., 1987—; mem. sci. coun. Joint Inst. for Marine Observations, Scripps Instn. of Oceanography, 1992—, bd. dirs. Pacific Northwest Reg. Marine Rsch. Program, 1992—; exec. com. Cooperative Inst. for Arctic Rsch. U. Alaska. Editor: Tsunami Hazard: A Practical Guide for Tsunami Hazard Reduction, 1991; contbr. articles to profl. jours. Recipient Best of New Generation award Esquire Mag., 1984, Meritorious Presdl. Rank award Pres. Clinton, 1993. Mem. Internat. Union of Geodesy and Geophysics (chmn. Tsunami commn. 1987-95), Am. Geophys. Union. Office: Pacific Marine Environ Lab 7600 Sand Point Way NE Bldg 3 Seattle WA 98115-6349

BERNARD, H. RUSSELL, anthropology educator, scientific editor; b. N.Y.C., June 12, 1940; s. Herman Fink and Lillian (Rosenfeld) B.; m. Carole May Phillips, Jan. 28, 1962; children: Elyssa Lynn, Sharyn Kymm. BA, CUNY, 1961; MA, PhD, U. Ill., 1968. From asst. prof. to assoc. prof. Wash. State U., Pullman, 1966-72; rsch. assoc. Scripps Inst. Oceanography, La Jolla, Calif., 1972; from assoc. prof. to prof. W.Va. U., Morgantown, 1972-79; prof. anthropology U. Fla., Gainesville, 1979—; prof. Nat. Mus. Ethnology, Osaka, Japan, 1991, U. Cologne, 1994-95. Editor: (with B.P. Pelto) Technology and Social Change, 1972, 2d edit., 1987, Research Methods in Cultural Anthropology, 1988, 2d edit., 1994, Handbook of Methods in Cultural Anthropology, 1998; (with J. Salinas) The Otomi, 1978, Native Ethnography, 1989; (with W. Penn Handweker) Data Analysis with MYSTAT, 1994; collaborator (film) Aegean Sponge Divers, 1969 (Chris Plaque award 1975); contbr. articles to profl. jours. Recipient Alexander von Humboldt Rsch. award, 1994-95; Fulbright Rsch. scholar, 1969-70; grantee NSF, 1967—, NEH, 1976-85, Am. Philol. Soc., 1972. Mem. Soc. for Applied Anthropology (editor Human Orgn. 1976-81), Am. Anthrop. Assn. (editor-in-chief Am. Anthropologist 1981-89). Office: U Fla Dept Anthropology 1350 Turlington Hall Gainesville FL 32611

BERNARD, JOHN MARLEY, lawyer, educator; b. Phila., Feb. 6, 1941; s. Edward and Opal (Marley) B.; children: John Marley Jr., Kendall M., Katherine M., James M.; m. Esther L. von Laue, May 31, 1986. BA, Swarthmore Coll., 1963; LLB, Harvard U., 1967. Bar: Pa. 1967. Assoc. Montgomery McCracken Walker & Rhoads, Phila., 1967-73, ptnr., 1973-86; ptnr. Ballard Spahr Andrews & Ingersoll, LLP, Phila., 1986—; lectr. Temple U. Law Sch., Phila., 1975-95; instr. Phila. Acad. for Employee Benefits Tng., 1996-99; guest instr. U.S. Dept. Labor, Washington, 1984-96; instr. U. Pa. Wharton Sch., Phila., 1989-90; bd. dirs. PENJERDEL Employee Benefits Assn., Phila. Contbg. author: Handbook of Employee Benefits, 1989. Mem. ABA, Pa. Bar Assn. Office: Ballard Spahr Andrews & Ingersoll LLP 1735 Market St Fl 51 Philadelphia PA 19103-7501

BERNARD, LOUIS JOSEPH, surgeon, educator; b. Laplace, La., Aug. 19, 1925; s. Edward and Jeanne (Vinet) B.; m. Lois Jeannette McDonald, Feb. 1, 1976; children: Marie Antonia, Phyllis Elaine. BA magna cum laude, Dillard U., New Orleans, 1946; MD, Meharry Med. Coll., 1950. Diplomate: Am. Bd. Surgery. Instr. surgery Sch. Medicine, Meharry Med. Coll., Nashville, 1958-59, prof., 1973-90, chmn. dept. surgery, 1973-87, dean, 1987-90, v.p. for health svcs., 1988-90; practice medicine specializing in surgery, 1959-69; mem. clin. faculty U. Okla., 1959-69, assoc. prof., vice chmn. dept. surgery, 1969-73, chmn. dept. surgery, 1973-87, disting. prof. emeritus, 1990—; dir. Drew-Meharry Morehouse Consortium Cancer Ctr., 1990-96. Contbr. articles in field to profl. jours. Mem. Okla. State Bd. Corrections, 1968-69. With M.C. U.S. Army, 1951-53. USPHS research fellow NCI, U. Rochester, 1953-54. Fellow ACS, Southeastern Surg. Congress; mem. Soc. Surg. Oncology, Internat. Surg. Soc., Am. Assn. Cancer Edn., Alpha Omega Alpha. Democrat. Roman Catholic. Home: 156 Queens Ln Nashville TN 37218-1826

BERNARD, LOWELL FRANCIS, academic administrator, educator, consultant; b. Long Beach, Calif., Dec. 14, 1931; s. Francis Montgomery and Irma Viola (Phillips) B.; m. Diana Gypson, June 15, 1957; children: Deborah Diana Bernard North, Steven Lowell, Jocelyn Dawn Bernard Jablonski. BA in Microbiology, UCLA, 1955, MS in Pub. Health and Pre Medicine, 1959. Registered sanitarian, Calif. Instr. pub. health edn. UCLA, 1955-59; asst. dir. Heart and Tb Assn., Poughkeepsie, N.Y., 1959-60; instr. Dutchess Community Coll., Poughkeepsie, 1960-66; dir. edn. Cleve. Health Edn. Mus., 1966-69, exec. dir., 1969-88; adj. asst. prof. Med. Sch. Case Western Res. U., Cleve., 1969-83, adj. asst. prof. pediatrics, 1985-89, dir. Cleve. Health Edn. Project, 1989-97, adj. asst. clin. prof. family medicine, 1990-99, rsch. cons., 1997-98; adminstr. Case Western Res. U. Urban Area Health Edn. Ctr., 1991-97; internat. cons. to mus., 1969—; speaker, media appearances in field. Author profl. publs. Bd. dirs. Cleve. chpt. Epilepsy Found. Am., 1972-76; trustee Doan's Ctr. Inc., Retinal Vascular Found., 1984-89. Recipient Outstanding Service to City award City of Cleve., 1972; fellow in pub. health Case Western Res. U. Med. Sch., 1985-97. Mem. WHO (cons. Internat. Union of Health Edn.), Am. Alliance for Health, Phys. Edn., Recreation and Dance, Am. Assn. Health and Med. Mus. (v.p. 1971-73, pres. 1973-75), Assn. Sci. and Tech. Ctrs. (bd. dirs. 1976-83, sec.-treas. 1978-83, program chmn. 1979), Am. Assn. Mus. (program chmn. nat. meeting 1979, mus. assessment program evaluator 1982-89, mem. mus. accreditation team 1983-89), Aesculapian Soc., Am. Pub. Health Assn., Cleve. Acad. Medicine (hon.), Am. Soc. Sex Educators, Therapists and Counselors (cert. sex educator), Mid-West Mus. Conf., Ohio Mus. Assn., Greater Cleve. Growth Assn. Republican. Presbyterian. Avocations: sports; travel. Home: 72 Governor's Dr Kiawah Island SC 29455-3134

BERNARD, MICHAEL MARK, lawyer, city planning consultant; b. N.Y.C., Sept. 5, 1926; s. H.L. and Henryetta (Siegel) B.; m. Laura Jane Pincus, Aug. 28, 1958; 1 dau., Daphne Michelle. AB, U. Chgo., 1949; JD, Northwestern U., 1953; MCity Planning, Harvard U., 1959. Bar: Ill. 1952, U.S. Dist. Ct. (no. dist.) Ill. 1953, N.Y. 1955, U.S. Ct. Appeals (1st cir.) 1956. Pvt. practice law Chgo. and N.Y.C., 1953-55; rsch. asst. Law Sch. Harvard U., 1955-56; city planning cons., atty.-adviser Puerto Rico, 1956-58; rsch. atty. Model Laws Project Am. Bar Found., 1959-60; city planner, legal adviser Chgo. Dept. City Planning, 1960-64; cons. planning and land regulation, 1964—; cons. Chgo. Area Transp. Study, 1965; mem. exec. faculty Boston Archtl. Ctr., 1967—; adv. to Gov.'s Exec. Office on reorgn. Commonwealth Mass., 1968-72; cons. A.I.A. Rsch. Corp., 1974; cons. Mass. Atty. Gen., 1981—; mem. com. urban devel. and housing World Peace Through Law Ctr., 1965—; mem. com. transp. law transp. research bd. NRC-NAS, 1966—; cons. White House Policy Adv. Com. to D.C., 1966; del. World Congress Housing and Planning, Paris, France, 1962, Tokyo, Japan, 1966; fellow Ctr. Advanced Visual Studies, M.I.T.; prin. investigator Northwestern U. Transp. Ctr.; lectr. in field; vis. prof. urban and regional planning U. Iowa, 1969-70; vis. lectr. Harvard U., MIT, U. Mich.; mem. faculty Am. Law Inst., 1978—. Author: Constitutions, Taxation and Land Policy, 2 vols., 1979-80, Airspace in Urban Development, 1963; co-editor: Policy Studies Jour.; editor, pub.: Reflections on Space; revision project mgr.: Constitutional Uniformity & Equality in State Taxation, 2 vols., 1984, Transformation of Property Rights in the "Space Age", 1993; spl. editor: Urban Law Ann. Washington U. Sch. Law; columnist: Jour. Real Estate Devel.; bd. editors: Real Estate Fin.; contbr. articles to profl. jours. Patron Hull House Assn., Chgo., 1965; v.p., trustee Cambridge Community Art Ctr., 1971-73; mem. standing com. Unitarian Ch.; mem. founding site com. Mus. Contemporary Art, Chgo. With USN, 1944-46. Recipient cert. of commendation for teaching Boston Archtl. Ctr., 1984; grantee NRC-NAS, 1964-66. Fellow Lincoln Inst. Land Policy; mem. ABA (land use, planning and zoning com., chmn. T.D.R. subcom. 1984-89, air and space com.), Internat. Fedn. Housing and Planning, Am. Arbitration Assn. (cert., bldg. and constrn. arbitrator),Am. Soc. Pub. Adminstrn., Policy Studies Orgn., Am. Planning Assn. (chmn. legis. com. Met. Chgo. sect. 1963-65, Mass. state reporter planning and law div. 1990—), Boston Soc. Architects (affiliate), Nat. Space Soc. (bd. dirs., space law com. Boston chpt.), Am. Underground Space Assn., Internat. Ctr. for Land Policy Studies, Urban Affairs Assn. (jour. rev. editor), Am. Crafts Coun., Mass. Assn. Craftsmen (v.p. 1975-78), Boston Visual Artists Union (hon., sec.-gen. 1971-72), New England Poetry Club (life), U. Chgo. Club Boston (bd. dirs.), Boston Athenaeum (life, dir. Poetry program). Home: 25 Stanton Ave Newton MA 02466-3005 *It seems to me that man's random, specialized intervention in the universe will prove to be the most constant cause for concern in the future. The problem might be seen not so much as how to keep the earth whole, but as how man may keep whole himself: this remains the role and strength of creative, intuitive endeavor, the source of everything I find of true value. Hopefully, ours will not become the "Age of the Idiot Savant".*

BERNARD, RICHARD LAWSON, geneticist, retired; b. Detroit, Aug. 12, 1926; s. Clarence Rolla and Ilda Gentry (Lawson) B.; m. Ruth V. Thorne, June 14, 1952 (div. 1975); children: Betty Ruth Marnell, Richard Thorne, Alice Jean Woodley, Daniel Lawson. Student, U. Mich., 1943-45, Okla. State U., 1947-48; B.S., Ohio State U., 1949, M.S., 1950; Ph.D., N.C. State U., 1960. Research geneticist USDA, Urbana, Ill., 1954-88; prof. plant genetics U. Ill., Champaign, 1966-92, prof. emeritus, 1992—. Served with USAF, 1945-47. Democrat. Baptist.

BERNARD, RICHARD MONTGOMERY, retired physician; b. Long Beach, Calif., Feb. 21, 1925; s. Francis M. and Irma V. (Phillips) B.; m. Virginia Marie Thompson, Sept. 19, 1946 (div. Mar. 1971); children: Richard Jr., David, Mary, Danielle; m. Nancy Johnston, Nov. 18, 1971; stepchildren: Vivienne Kouba, N. Catherine Thompson. BS in Chemistry, U. Calif. Berkeley, 1945; MD, U. Chgo., 1950. Charter Diplomate Am. Bd. Family Practice. Assoc. physician Dr. G. Alan Fisher, Gresham, Oreg., 1953-54; pvt. practice Westslope, Portland, Oreg., 1954-60, Beaverton, Oreg., 1960-86; assoc. with Dr. D. Graham, Beaverton, 1986-90; family practitioner St. Vincent Tanesbourne Med. Plz., Beaverton, 1990-91; locum tenens Oreg., 1991-92; family practitioner Providence Health Sys., Wilsonville, Oreg., 1992-98; clin. prof. medicine, family practice dept., Oreg. Health Sci. U., Portland, 1994—. Commr. Wilsonville Long Range Planning Commn. Capt. USNR, WWII, 1942-46, Korea, 1950-53, ret., 1985. Recipient Meritorious Achievement award Oreg. Health Science U., 1988. Mem. Wilsonville Rotary. Republican. Avocations: fishing, golf, travel, photography, toy and model making. Home: 31530 SW Village Green Ct Wilsonville OR 97070-8426

BERNARD, RICHARD PHILLIP, lawyer; b. Chgo., May 29, 1950; s. Martin Joseph Jr. and Ruth (Hadka) B.; m. Svetlana Shoutova; children: Rachel, Benjamin, Alex. BA, Mich. State U., 1972; JD, NYU, 1976; M of Pub. Affairs, Princeton U., 1976; grad. Advanced Mgmt. Program, Harvard U., 1998. Bar: N.Y. 1977. Assoc. Milbank, Tweed, Hadley & McCloy, N.Y.C., 1976-84, ptnr., 1985-94; exec. v.p., gen. counsel New York Stock Exchange, N.Y.C., 1996—; exec. dir., resource sec. Russian Securities Commn., Moscow, 1995. Participating atty. Legal Aid Soc. Community Law Offices, N.Y.C., 1977-80. Mem. ABA (banking and bus. sects., com. on fed. regulation of securities). Democrat. Avocations: Russia, carpentry. Office: New York Stock Exchange 11 Wall St New York NY 10005-1905

BERNARD, ROBERT WILLIAM, plastic surgeon; b. N.Y.C., Aug. 18, 1942. Student, U. Mich., 1959-60; BA with honors in zoology, U. Vt., 1963, MD cum laude, 1967. Diplomate Am. Bd. Surgery, Am. Bd. Plastic Surgery. Intern U. Pa. Hosp., Phila., 1967-68; resident in gen. surgery NYU Hosp., 1968-72, resident in plastic surgery, 1972-74; chief plastic surgery No. Westchester Hosp., Mt. Kisco, N.Y., 1982-87, 96—, White Plains (N.Y.) Hosp., 1979-86, United Hosp., Port Chester, N.Y., 1986-94. Author, editor: Aesthetic Restoration of the Aging Face, 1997; editor Aesthetic Surg. Jour., 1993-98; contbr. articles to profl. jours. Fellow ACS; mem. AMA (Physicians Recognition award 1983, 84, 86, 88, 90, 92, 95, 98), Am. Soc. Plastic and Reconstructive Surgery, Am. Soc. for Aesthetic Plastic Surgery (nominating com. 1993-94, 95-96, practice rels. com. 1992—, strategic planning com. 1992-93, 96, chair sci. program surg. subcom. 1991-92, vice chair local arrangements com. 1989-90, parliamentarian 1997, historian 1998, sec. 1999, exec. com. 1999), Assn. for Hand Surgery, N.Y. State Med. Soc. (pres. plastic surgery sect. 1983-84), N.Y. Regional Soc. Plastic and Reconstructive Surgery (chair sci. program com 1984-85, pres. 1986-87, exec. com. 1987-88), N.Y. Soc. for Surgery of the Hand, Westchester County Med. Soc., Am. Cancer Soc. Office: 10 Chester Ave White Plains NY 10601 also: 91 Smith Ave Mt Kisco NY 10549

BERNARD, THELMA RENE, property management professional; b. Phila.; d. Michael John and Louise Thelma (Hoffman) Campione; m. Gene Bernard (div.). Sec. Penn. Mut. Life Ins. Co., Phila., Suffolk Franklin Savs. Bank, Boston, Holmes and Narver, Inc., Las Vegas; constrn. site office mgr. Miles R. Nay, Inc., Las Vegas; adminstrv. asst to pres. N.W.S. Constrn. Corp., Inc., Las Vegas, 1982-86, corp. sec., 1982-86; gen. mgr., corp. sec. property mgmt. com. D.A.P., Inc., Las Vegas, 1991-97, pres. property mgmt. com., 1991—. Author: Blue Marsh, 1972, Winds of Wakefield, 1972, Moonshadow Mansion, 1973, 2d edit., 1976, Spanish transl., 1974, German transl., 1977; author, concept creator, prodr. (CD) Knight Flights, 1999; contbr. articles to Doll Reader, Internat. Doll World, other mags.; past editor Cactus Courier; editor, pub. The Hoyer Enthusiastic Ladies Mail Assn., 1980-90, 96—; Friendly Tymes, 1991—, Lady Charleen, 1995—; writer song lyrics. Mem. Keats-Shelley Assn. Am. Inc., Broadcast Music Inc., Nat. League Am. Pen Women (v.p. Red Rock Canyon br. 1986-88), Original Paper Doll Artists Guild, Heritage Rose Soc., Bookmark Collector Club, Byron Soc. Am. Office: PO Box 14002 Las Vegas NV 89114-4002

BERNARD, WALTER, art director; b. Jersey City, July 2, 1937. Designer Ingenue Mag., N.Y.C., until 1962, Am. Heritage, N.Y.C., 1962-64; asst. art dir. Esquire Mag., N.Y.C., 1964-68; art dir. N.Y. Mag., N.Y.C., 1968-77, Time Mag., N.Y.C., 1977-80; ptnr., prin. Walter Bernard & Milton Glaser, N.Y.C., 1983—; tchr. Cooper Union, NYU; lectr. in field. Designer, cons. for numerous publs. including Washington Post, La Vanguardia (Barcelona), O Globo (Rio de Janeiro), L.A. Times, Boston Globe, Dallas Times Herald, East Hampton Star, L'Espresso (Italy), Time, Fortune, U.S. News & World Report, Adweek, Ms., Money, The Nation, L'Express (Paris), Barron's; designer movie titles (with Milton Glaser) Sleepless in Seattle, 1993, You've Got Mail, 1998; co-creator (visual 20th-century ency.) Our Times. Recipient numerous Gold and Silver medals. Mem. Soc. Publ. Designers (pres. 1993-94). Office: WBMG 207 E 32nd St New York NY 10016-6305

BERNARDI, MARIO, conductor; b. Kirland Lake, Ont., Can., Aug. 20, 1930; s. Leone and Rina (Onisto) B.; m. Mona Kelly, May 12, 1962; 1 d., Julia. Ed., Coll. Piox, Treviso, Italy, Benedetto Marcello Conservatory, Venice, Italy, Mozarteum, Salzburg, Austria, Royal Conservatory, Toronto. Began career as pianist Italy; music dir. Sadler's Wells Opera Co., 1967-69; music dir., condr. Nat. Arts Centre, Ottawa, Ont., 1969-82; music dir. Calgary Philharm. Orch., 1984-93; prin. condr. CBC Vancouver Orch., 1982—; guest condr. with San Francisco Opera, Royal Opera House at Covent Garden, Vancouver Opera, Canadian Opera Co., Met. Opera, Chgo. Symphony, Washington Opera, Houston Symphony Orch.; prin. condr. with CBC, Vancouver Orch. Decorated companion Order of Can. Club: Savage. Office: Columbia Artists Mgmt ATT Judie Janowski 165 W 57th St New York NY 10019-2201*

BERNARDINI, CHARLES, alderman. BS, U. Ill.; LLM, John Marshall Law Sch. Legis. asst. to Spkr. Ill. Ho. of Reps., 1972-73; sr. counsel Am. Hosp. Supply Corp., 1974-81; alternate del. Dem. Nat. Conv., 1980; spl. prosecutor for election fraud Cook County, Ill., 1981-83; commr., 1986-92; mem. Gov.'s Election Reform Commn., 1985; del. Dems. Abroad Dem. Conv., 1992; alderman City of Chgo., 1993-99; ptnr. Dykewia Gossett Law Firm, Chgo., 1999—; instr. internat. law Loyoa U. Chgo., Rome campus, 1981; counsel Allstate Ins. Co., 1983-91. Mem. Chgo.-Milan Sister City Com., 1988—. Mem. Am. C. of C. in Italy (mng. dir.). E-mail: crb43@aol.com. Office: Dykewia Gossett Law Firm 55 E Monroe St Ste 3050 Chicago IL 60603-5709*

BERNARDO, ALDO SISTO, foreign language educator, retired; b. Molise, Italy, May 17, 1920; came to U.S., 1924; s. Ernesto Bernardo and Adele De Orchis; m. Claudia Louise Marcantonio, Oct. 25, 1942 (wid. May 1976); children: Donald, Joanne, Adele; m. Reta Anne Mohney, Nov. 6, 1976. BA, Brown U., 1942, MA, 1946; PhD, Harvard U., 1950. From instr. to Disting. Prof. SUNY, Binghamton, 1949-87, chair Humanities Div., 1959-67, emeritus, 1987—; vis. prof. Johns Hopkins U., Balt., 1970, Folger Shakespeare Libr., Washington, 1974; pres. Verrazzano Coll., Saratoga Springs, N.Y., 1973-75. Author: (book) Petrarch, Scipio and The Africa, 1962, Petrarch, Laura and The Triumphs, 1974; translator: Petrarch, Familiares, 3 vols., 1975-84; editor: The Classics in the Middle Ages, 1990, Petrarch, Letters of Old Age, 2 vols., 1992, (with Reta Bernardo) A Concordance to Petrarch's Familiares, 2 vols., 1994. Chair Concerned Citizens for Rational Alternatives, Johnson City, N.Y., 1989-94; chair State Task Force for Excellence in Ednl. Methods, 1994—. Recipient Fulbright Rsch. grant U.S. Govt., Vatican Libr., Rome, 1955-56, Order of Merit, Italian Govt., 1966, Guggenheim fellowship Guggenheim Fund., Florence, Italy, 1964-65. Mem. MLA (life), Am. Assn. Tchrs. of Italian (Disting. Svc. award 1988), Am. Civic Assn. (pres. 1992-95), N.Y. Assn. of Scholars (v.p. 1990—, acting pres. 1995). Home: 25 3rd St Johnson City NY 13790-1816

BERNARDO, SUSAN MARIE, English educator; b. Fall River, Mass., 1958; d. Edward and Idalina Bernardo; m. Mark Wagner, 1990. BA in History summa cum laude, Gordon Coll., 1980; MA in History, Harvard U., 1981; MA in English Lit., Bryn Mawr Coll., 1983, PhD in English Lit., 1988. Vis. asst. prof. English Franklin & Marshall Coll., Lancaster, Pa., 1988-89, Susquehanna U., Selinsgrove, Pa., 1989-91; asst. prof. English Wagner Coll., S.I., N.Y., 1991-95; assoc. prof. English Wagner Coll., S.I., 1995—; presenter in field. Contbr. articles to profl. jours. Mem. AAUW, MLA, N.E. MLA. E-mail: sbernard@wagner.edu. Office: Wagner Coll Dept Langs & Lit One Campus Rd Staten Island NY 10301

BERNATH, MARY THERESE, special education educator; b. Trenton, N.J., Mar. 15, 1960; d. Joseph Michael and Nellie E. Bernath. BS in Edn., Trenton State Coll., 1983; MEd, U. Ctrl. Fla., 1989. Tchr. homebound/profoundly mentally handicapped Osceola County Sch. Bd., Kissimmee, Fla., 1983-84; tchr. educable mentally handicapped St. Cloud (Fla.) Mid. Sch., 1983-85, tchr. behavior disordered, 1985-86; tchr. educable mentally handicapped Highlands Elem. Sch., Kissimmee, 1986-87; tchr. trainable mentally handicapped Michigan Ave. Elem. Sch., St. Cloud, 1987-88, Ventura Elem. Sch., Kissimmee, 1989-90; tchr. profoundly, educable, trainable mentally handicapped Sidney Lanier Ctr., Gainesville, Fla., 1990—. Vol. Osceola County Spl. Olympics, Kissimmee, 1983-89, chmn. publicity com., 1984-87. Mem. Coun. for Exceptional Children, Kappa Delta Pi. Republican. Roman Catholic. Avocations: reading, gardening, crafts, swimming.

BERNAU, SIMON JOHN, mathematics educator; b. Wanganui, New Zealand, June 12, 1937; came to U.S., 1969; s. Earnest Lovell and Ella Mary (Mason) B.; m. Lynley Joyce Turner, Aug. 11, 1959; children: Nicola Ann, Sally Jane. B.Sc., U. Canterbury, Christchurch, New Zealand, 1958, M.Sc., 1959; B.A., Cambridge (Eng.) U., 1961, Ph.D., 1964. Lectr. U. Canterbury, 1964-65, sr. lectr., 1965-66; prof. math. U. Otago, Dunedin, New Zealand, 1966-69; assoc. prof. U. Tex., Austin, 1969-76, prof., 1976-85; prof., head math. dept. Southwest Mo. State U., Springfield, 1986-88; prof., chmn. dept. math. scis. U. Tex., El Paso, 1988-95; dean Coll. Sci. Calif. State Poly., Pomona, 1995—. Researcher numerous publs. in field, 1964—; referee profl. jours., 1965—. Gulbenkian jr. research fellow Churchill Coll., Cambridge U., 1963-64. Mem. Am. Math. Soc. (reviewer 1965—), Math. Assn. Am., London Math. Soc. Home: 1415 Ashland Ave Claremont CA 91711-3308 Office: Calif State Poly U Coll of Sci 3801 W Temple Ave Pomona CA 91768-2557

BERNBACH, JOHN LINCOLN, corporate strategies consultant; b. 1944; s. William Bernbach. Grad. polit. sci., Georgetown U. Trainee account mgmt., then v.p. account services Gilbert Advt., 1966-72; with DDB Needham Worldwide, Inc. (formerly Doyle Dane Bernbach), Paris, 1972-79, London, 1979-84; pres., chief exec. officer internat. div. DDB Needham Worldwide, Inc. (formerly Doyle Dane Bernbach), N.Y.C., 1984-86, pres., 1986-93, vice chmn., 1993-94; chmn., CEO The Bernbach Group, Inc., N.Y.C., 1994—. Office: The Bernbach Group Inc 800 3rd Ave Fl 13 New York NY 10022-7604

BERNBECK, VOLKERT JOACHIM, retired plastic surgeon; b. Apr. 15, 1928. MD, Munich U., 1953. Intern in plastic surgery and gen. surgery Newark; resident in plastic surgery Cottage Hosp.; assoc. prof. U. Calif., 1963—; pvt. practice Newport Beach and Laguna, Calif.; ret. Newport Beach and Laguna, 1991. Author: Research in Infant Cleft Lip and Cleft Palate. Mem. Am. Soc. Aesthetic Plastic Surgery (chmn. ethics com.), Am. Soc. for Plastic and Reconstructive Surgeons, Internat. Soc. Clin. Plastic Surgeons, Calif. Soc. Plastic Surgeons, Am. Aesthetic Soc., Internat. Soc. Aesthetic Plastic Surgeons.

BERNDT, ELLEN GERMAN, company executive; b. N.Y.C., 1953. BS, Denison U., 1975; JD, Capital U., 1984. Legal asst. Borden Inc., Columbus, Ohio, 1978-84, corp. atty., 1984-90, asst. sec., corp. atty., 1990-96, corp. sec., asst. gen. counsel, 1996—. Mem. Am. Corp. Counsel Assn., Ctrl. Ohio Corp. Counsel Assn. (pres. 1997). Office: Borden Inc 180 E Broad St Columbus OH 43215-3799

BERNDT, ERNST RUDOLF, economist, educator; b. Crespo, Entre Rios, Argentina, Apr. 13, 1946; came to U.S., 1949; s. Markus William and Charlotte Marie (Zimmerman) B.; m. Martha Ann Mirly, June 10, 1967 (div. 1982); children: Jeffery, Nathan; m. Joan Margaret Curran, May 15, 1994. BA with honors, Valparaiso U., 1968; MS., U. Wis., 1971, PhD, 1972; PhD (hon.), Uppsala U., 1991. Staff economist Exec. Office of the Pres. U.S. Govt., Washington, 1971-72; asst. prof. U. (Vancouver) B.C., Can., 1973-78, assoc. prof., 1978-80; prof. applied econs. MIT, Cambridge, Mass., 1980—; rsch. assoc. Nat. Bur. Econ. Rsch., Cambridge, 1980—; acad. affiliate Analysis Group, Inc., Belmont, Mass., 1985—. Contbr. profl. articles. Most cited economist under age 40 in 1985. Mem. Am. Econ. Assn., Econometric Soc., Conf. Rsch. in Income and Wealth. Independent. Lutheran. Office: MIT Sloan Sch of Mgmt 50 Memorial Dr # E52 452 Cambridge MA 02142-1347

BERNDT, JANE ANN, writer, researcher, educator; b. Portsmouth, Ohio, May 24, 1954; d. John William Berndt and Anna L. Rickey. BS in Edn., Ohio U., 1977, MEd, 1986; EdD, W.Va. U., 1993, George Washington U., 1993. Curriculum specialist, rschr., tchr. Washington D.C. Pub. Schs.; instr. W.Va. U., Ohio U., George Washington U.; adj. faculty Marshall U., Huntington, W.Va.; cons. in natural resources scis. Curriculum writer: A Science Based History Curiculum Walking Through Time; book reviewer Presdl. Studies Quar. Ind. candidate for 6th dist. U.S. Ho. of Reps., 1996; vol. D.C. Cathedral Literacy Program, Ky. Horse Park. Grantee W.Va. U., 1986-89, Mem. Bd. Govs. Who's Who in Edn., who's Who Emerging Leaders in Am.; Am. Biographical Assn. (life bd. govs.), Phi Kappa Phi, Sigma Alpha Epsilon, Phi Delta Kappa. Avocations: poetry, drawing.

BERNDT, MARTIN R., career officer. Grad., West Chester U., 1969; student, Amphibious Warfare Sch., 1980, USMC Command and Staff Coll., 1984, U.S. Army War Coll., 1987. Commd. 2d lt. USMC, 1969, advanced through grades to maj. gen., 1998; weapons platoon commdr. 9th Marines, Okinawa, Japan, 1969; rifle platoon comdr., co. exec. officer 7th, 1st Marines, Vietnam; instr., platoon comdr. Officer Candidate Sch., 1971, The Basic Sch.; officer selection officer N.Y.; ops. officer 3d Reconnaissance Bn.; various assignments Marine Aircraft Group 26, 1980-84, 2d Marine Divsn., 1987-90, Stuttgart, Germany, 1990-94; polit.-mil. planner Office Joint Chiefs Staff, 1984-86; exec. officer Marine Forces Panama, 1988-89; comdr. MEU (SOC), 1994-95; dep. comdr. USMC Forces, Atlantic, 1995; dir Joint Tng, J-7 U.S. Atlantic Commd. Office: Joint Training J-7 USACOM 116 Lake View Pkwy Suffolk VA 23435-2663

BERNE, BRUCE J., chemistry educator. B.S., Bklyn. Coll., 1961; Ph.D. (NASA fellow, NSF fellow), U. Chgo., 1964. NATO postdoctoral fellow U. Brussels, 1964-65; asst. prof. chemistry Columbia U., N.Y.C., 1966-69, assoc. prof., 1969-72, prof., 1972—; Miller Inst. prof. U. Calif., Berkeley, 1993-94; vis. prof. U. Tel Aviv, 1972-73, Sackler Disting. lectr., 1985; vis. scientist IBM Thomas J. Watson Rsch. Labs., Yorktown, N.Y., 1990-92; Reilly lectr. U. Notre Dame, 1998; Davidson lectr. U. Kans., 1998. Mem. editl. bd. Jour. Statistical Physics, 1976-79, Advances in Chemical Physics, 1984—, Jour. Phys. Chemistry, 1985-88, Jour. Chem. Physics, 1985-88. Recipient Alexander von Humboldt Found. award 1998, award in theoretical chemistry Am. Chem. Soc., 1995; Alfred P. Sloan Found. fellow, 1968-71, John Simon Guggenheim Found. fellow, 1972-73. Fellow AAAS, Am. Phys. Soc., Am. Acad. Arts and Scis.; mem. NAS. Office: Dept Chemistry Columbia U MC 3103 3000 Broadway New York NY 10027-6941

BERNE, ROBERT MATTHEW, physiologist, educator; b. Yonkers, N.Y., Apr. 22, 1918; s. Nelson and Julia (Stahl) B.; m. Beth Goldberg, Aug. 18, 1944; children: Julie, Amy, Gordon, Michael. AB, U. N.C., 1939; MD, Harvard U., 1943; DSc, Med. Coll. Ohio, 1973. Intern Mt. Sinai Hosp., N.Y.C., 1943-44; resident Mt. Sinai Hosp., 1946-48; rsch. fellow Western Res. U. Sch. Medicine, Cleve., 1948-49; instr. physiology Western Res. U. Sch. Medicine, 1949-50, sr. instr., 1950-52, asst. prof., 1952-55, assoc. prof., 1955-61, prof., 1961-66; prof., chmn. dept. physiology U. Va. Sch. Medicine, Charlottesville, 1966-88, Alumni prof. physiology, 1988-95; mem. sci. adv. bd. Alfred I. duPont Inst., 1988-94; prof. emeritus U. Va. Sch. Medicine, Charlottesville, 1995—; mem. evaluation com. on post doctoral fellowships in life scis. Nat. Acad. Scis., 1963-65; mem. physiology tng. com. NIH, 1964-65, mem. heart and vascular disease panel, nat. research and devel. demonstration rev. com., 1973-74; mem. tng. com. Nat. Heart Inst., 1966-70; mem. cardio-pulmonary tng. program VA, 1968-71; mem. physiology test Com. Nat. Bd. Med. Examiners, 1969-70, mem. study com., 1983-84; mem. panel on heart and blood vessel diseases, task force Nat. Heart, Lung, and Blood Inst., 1972, mem. heart and lung program project com., 1975-79, mem. hypertension task force, 1976-79; adminstrv. bd., council acad. socs. Assn. Am. Med. Colls., 1975, chmn. council acad. socs., exec. com., 1977-78, disting. service mem., 1982—; Nathanson Meml. lectr. U. So. Calif., 1973; mem. selection com. award for hypertension CIBA Found, 1975-77; Coordinating com. N.Y. State Doctoral Programs rev., 1982-89, bd. sci. counsel Nat. Heart Lung and Blood Inst., 1986-89; mem. Council Internat. Union Physiol. Scis., 1986-97. Author: (with M.N. Levy) Cardiovascular Physiology, 1967, 7th edit., 1997, Physiology, 4th edit., 1998, Principles of Physiology, 1990, 2d edit., 1996, Case Studies in Physiology, 1994; editor: Circulation Rsch., 1970-75; sect. editor Am. Jour. Physiology, Jour. Applied Physiology, 1964-65; editl. bd. Circulation Rsch., 1961-70, 75—, Jour. Molecular and Cellular Cardiology, 1969-71, Proc. Soc. Exptl. Biology and Medicine FASEB Jour., 1962-64, Ann. Rev. Physiology, 1976-81, assoc. editor, 1980-82, editor, 1982-88. Trustee Cleve. Area Heart Soc., 1962-65, pres. sci. council, 1964-65; steering com. Circulation Group Physiol. Soc., 1969-71. Served with M.C. AUS, 1944-46. Recipient Carl J. Wiggers award, 1975, Va. Lifetime Sci. Achievement award 1988, Daggs award, 1990, Inventor or Yr. award U. Va. Alumni Assn., 1992. Fellow Am. Coll. Cardiology (hon.); mem. AAAS, NAS, Am. Acad. Arts and Scis., Am. Physiol. Soc. (mem. coun. 1970-72, mem. fin. com. 1966-70, 75-78, pres. 1972-73, publs. com. 1976-80, Perkins Meml. Award com. 1977-80), Am. Soc. for Clin. Investigation (award com. Lita Annenberg Hazen awards 1984-86, mem. nat. adv. com. Pew Scholars program 1984-89), Am. Heart Assn. (com. on med. edn. 1963-66, vice chmn. on coun. basic sci., mem. med. adv. bd. coun. high blood pressure rsch. 1976-78, 79-80, 83, chmn. publs. com. 1981-85, award of merit 1978, rsch. achievement award 1979, Gold Heart award 1985, Jacobi Medallion award 1987), Am. Physiol. Soc. (hon. membership com. 1987-89), Raven Soc. of U. Va., Cardiac Muscle Club, Assn. Chmn. Depts. Physiology (pres. 1970-71, teaching award 176), Microcirculatory Soc. (mem. coun. 1971-72, liaison com. 1973-75, chmn. Landis award com. 1977-78), Inst. of Medicine (membership com. 1984-85), Phi Beta Kappa, Sigma Xi (v.p. 1984-85, pres. 1985-86), Alpha Omega Alpha. Home: 1851 Wayside Pl Charlottesville VA 22903-1630 Office: U Va Sch Med Dept Molecular Physiology Biol Physics Health Scis Ctr PO Box 10011 Charlottesville VA 22906-0011

BERNE, STANLEY, author; b. Staten Island, N.Y., June 8, 1923; s. William and Irene (Daniels) B.; m. Arlene Zekowski, May 17, 1952. BS, Rutgers U., 1951; MA, N.Y.U., 1952; postgrad. fellow, La. State U., 1954-59. Cert. tchr. of mentally retarded, N.Y. Tchg. fellow La. State U., Baton Rouge, La., 1954-59; assoc. prof. English Ea. N. Mex. U., Portales, 1960-80, rsch. assoc. prof. in English, 1980—; chmn. of the bd. Am.-Canadian Publishers, Inc., Santa Fe, N. Mex., 1980-97; bd. dirs. New Arts Found., Inc., Santa Fe, N. Mex., 1990—; guest lectr. U. Ams., 1965, U. S.D., 1968, Styrian Hauptshulen Paedagogische Akademie, Graz, Austria, 1969; founder, developer first dept. for tchg. mentally retarded, Dallas Pub. Schs., 1952-53. Author: A First Book of the Neo-Narrative, 1954, Cardinals and Saints, 1958, The Dialogues, 1962, The Multiple Modern Gods and Other Stories, 1964, The Unconscious Victorious and Other Stories, 1969, The New Rubaiyat of Stanley Berne, 1973, Future Language, 1976, The Great American Empire, 1981, Every Person's Little Book of P-L-U-T-O-N-I-U-M, 1992, Alphabet Soup, 1998, To Hell with Optimism!!, 1996, Gravity Drag, 1998; (inclusion in anthologies) Trace, 1965, First Person Intense, 1978, Breakthrough Fictioneers, 1979, American Writing Today, 1992, Dictionary of the Avant-Gardes, 1993, New World Writing (11), 1957, The Living Underground, 1996; prodr. and co-host (with Arlene Zekowski) 9 Part TV Series for PBS, Future Writing Today. With USAF, 1942-46, PTO. Decorated Medal of Philippine Liberation; recipient Rsch. awards Ea. N. Mex. U., 4 awards; recipient St.-John Perse award for internat. prose, 1998. Mem. PEN, Com. of Small Mags., Editors, Poets, New Eng. Small Press Assn., Rio Grande Writers Assn., Santa Fe Writers Coop. Avocations: painting, design, collage. Home: PO Box 4595 Santa Fe NM 87502-4595 Address: Rising Tide Press N Mex PO Box 6136 Santa Fe NM 87502-6136

BERNEIS, KENNETH STANLEY, physician, educator; b. Bloomington, Ind., Dec. 25, 1951; s. hans Ludwig and Regina (Fischhoff) B.; m. Karen Lou Sachs, Nov. 23, 1975; children: Erica, Erin, Ellen, Elaina, Elyse. BS, U. Mich., 1973, MD, 1977. Diplomate Am. Bd. Family practice; cert. geriats. Intern, resident Bronson Hosp. and Borgess Med. Ctr., 1977-80; pvt. practice Ostego, Mich., 1980—; owner Ostego Family Physicians, 1981—; clin. instr. Mich. State U., 1980—; preceptor Southwestern Mich. Area Health Edn. Ctr., 1980—; chief of staff Pipp Cmty. Hosp., 1985-86, vice-chief of staff, 1985-86, chief of staff, 1986—, chief ob-gyn., 1985—, chief pharmacy and therapeutics, 1984—; chief quality assurance Mirnet Rsch. Network, 1981—; med. dir. Bronson Healthcare Group Nursing Homes; geriatrics quality officer, Borgess-Pipp. Mem. AMA, NRA, Am. Geriatrics Soc. (cert.), Am. Acad. Family Physicians. Home: 131 N Sunset St Plainwell MI 49080-1296 Office: 900 Dix St Otsego MI 49078-1563 also: 1576 Main St Martin MI 49070

BERNER, ANDREW JAY, library director, writer; b. Bronx, N.Y., Apr. 5, 1952; s. Bernard and Phyllis (Stern) B. BA in History cum laude, Herbert H. Lehman Coll., 1974, MA in History, 1979; MS in Libr. and Info. Sci., Pratt Inst., 1982. Tchr. N.Y.C. Bd. Edn., 1979-82; asst. libr. The Univ. Club Libr., N.Y.C., 1982-84, assoc. libr., 1984-86, acting dir., 1986-87, dir., 1987-93, dir., curator of collections, 1993—; co-founder, dir. OPL Resources, Ltd., 1984—. Author: Time Management in the Small Library, 1987, (with Guy St. Clair) The Best of OPL, 1990, The Best of OPL II, 1997, Time Management in Libraries and Information Services, 1999; author, editor The Illuminator, 1990—, The Univ. Club Libr. Quar., 1984-90; editor (newsletter) The One-Person Libr., 1984-98; contbr. articles to profl. jours. Mem. ALA, Spl. Librs. Assn. (chair, chair-elect mus., arts and humanities divsn. 1990-92; pres.-elect, pres. N.Y. chpt. 1994-96, bylaws chair, pub. rels. chair, dir. awards), N.Y. Met. Ref. and Rsch. Librs. Agy. (legis. com.), Century Assn., Grolier Club. Office: The Univ Club Libr 1 W 54th St New York NY 10019-5404

BERNER, FREDERIC GEORGE, JR., lawyer; b. Washington, May 7, 1943; s. Frederic George and Florence Grace (Carlton) B.; m. Lorraine Ann Ouellette, Sept. 28, 1968; children: Frederic George, III, Christina Lorraine, Jennifer Jane. BA, Middlebury Coll., 1965; MBA, Am. U., 1970; JD, George Washington U., 1973. Bar: D.C. 1973, U.S. Dist. Ct. (D.C. Dist.) 1973, U.S. Ct. Appeals (D.C. cir.) 1974, U.S. Ct. Appeals (4th cir.) 1977, U.S. Supreme Ct. 1980, U.S. Ct. Appeals (11th cir.) 1984, U.S. Ct. Appeals (10th cir.) 1994. Econ. intellignece officer CIA, Washington, 1965-67, 70; assoc. Sidley & Austin, Washington, 1973-80, ptnr., 1980—. Contbr. articles to legal publs.; bd. editl. advisors Pub. Utilites Fortnightly. Gen. counsel, bd. dirs. Washington chpt. Nat. Hemophilia Found., 1976-80. Served to 1st lt. U.S. Army, 1967-70. Mem. Fed. Energy Bar Assn. (com. chmn. 1983-89, bd. dirs.), D.C. Bar, ABA, Order of Coif. Republican. Presbyterian. Home: 7605 Glenbrook Rd Bethesda MD 20814-1319 Office: Sidley & Austin 1722 I St NW Fl 7 Washington DC 20006-3795*

BERNER, KEITH, foundation administrator executive; b. Cleve., Dec. 23, 1959; s. Jerome and Shirley (Kaplan) B. BA in Speech, Northwestern U., 1982; MA in Internat. Rels., Johns Hopkins U., 1989. Bus. mgr. MoMing Dance & Arts Ctr., Chgo., 1983-85; assoc. dir. Physicians for Social Responsilbiity, Chgo., 1986-87; rsch. analyst Congl. Rsch. Svc., Libr. Congress, Washington, 1991-94; pub. info. officer Internat. Rsch. Exchanges Bd., 1994-95; asst. dir. programs Assn. Profl. Schs. Internat. Affairs, Washington, 1995-96; exec. dir. Potomac Area Coun. Hostelling Internat.-Am. Youth Hostels, Washington, 1996—; freelance editor, Swedish lang. tchr., Swedish and German translator, 1986-96. Fellow Olmsted Found., 1987-89, Fulbright, 1989-90. Home: 2315 40th St NW Apt 4 Washington DC 20007-1748 Office: Potomac Area Coun Hostelling Internat 1108 K St NW Fl 2D Washington DC 20005-4010

BERNER, LEO DE WITTE, JR., retired oceanographer; b. Pasadena, Calif., Feb. 11, 1922; s. Leo De Witte and Maude Alena (Wright) B.; m. Arvetta Jo Hankins, June 28, 1947; children: Jo Anne Berner Thomas, Ernestine Elizabeth Berner Ice. B.A., Pomona Coll., 1943; M.S., UCLA-Scripps Instn. Oceanography, 1952, Ph.D., 1957. Fishery biologist U.S. Fish and Wildlife Service, La Jolla, Calif., 1957-58; asst. research biologist Scripps Instn. Oceanography, La Jolla, 1958-60; acting curator marine invertebrates Scripps Instn. Oceanography, 1960-61; vis. asst. prof. U. Oreg., Oreg. Inst. Marine Sci., 1961; asso. program dir. NSF, Washington, 1961-65; adminstrv. scientist Tex. A&M U., College Station, 1965-66; asso. prof. Tex. A&M U., 1966-72; asst. dean Tex. A&M U. (Grad. Coll.), 1967-71, assoc. dean, 1971-84, dean, 1984-87, prof. oceanography, 1972-87, prof. emeritus, dean emeritus, 1987—. Served with USNR, 1943-47. Fellow AAAS; mem. Am. Soc. Limnology and Oceanography, Oceanographic Soc., Assn. Tex. Grad. Schs. (1st v.p. 1981-82, pres. 1982-83), Sigma Xi. Home: 1108 Neal Pickett Dr College Station TX 77840-2611 Office: Tex A&M U Oceanography College Station TX 77843

BERNER, MARY, publisher. Publisher, v.p. Glamour Mag. Office: Conde Nast Publications 350 Madison Ave New York NY 10017-3704*

BERNER, ROBERT ARBUCKLE, geochemist, educator; b. Erie, Pa., Nov. 25, 1935; s. Paul Nau and Priscilla (Arbuckle) B.; m. Elizabeth Marshall Kay, Aug. 29, 1959; children: John Marshall, Susan Elizabeth, James Clark. BS, U. Mich., 1957, MS, 1958; PhD, Harvard U., 1962; D honoris causa, U. Aix-Marseille, France, 1991. Sverdrup fellow Scripps Inst. Oceanography, LaJolla, Calif., 1962-63; asst. to assoc. prof. geochemistry U. Chgo., 1963-65; assoc. prof. geochemistry Yale U., New Haven, 1965-71, prof., 1971-87, Alan M. Bateman prof., 1987—; chmn. Gordon Rsch. Conf. on Chem. Oceanography, 1986; chmn. sect. geochem. of the earth surface Internat. Assn. of Geochemistry and Cosmochemistry; mem. fellowship com. NSF, 1985; disting. vis. scientist SUNY, Stony Brook, 1985, Nat. Ctr. for Atmospheric Rsch., 1987, Univ. Ctr., Ga., 1990, U. N.C., 1993, U. Hawaii, 1994, Mich. State U., 1995, U. Wash., 1996; Watkins vis. prof. Wichita State U., 1997; Edison lectr. U. Notre Dame, 1993; Steinbach fellow Woods Hole Oceanographic Inst., 1996; vis. com. Harvard U., Woods Hole Oceanographic Inst., SUNY, Stony Brook, Rosenstiel Sch. Marine and Atmospheric Scis. U. Miami; NATO lectr. France, 1981, 84. Author: Principles of Chemical Sedimentology, 1971, Early Diagenesis, 1980 (Sci. Citation classic Inst. for Sci. Info.); co-author: The Global Water Cycle, 1987, Global Environment, 1996; editor Am. Jour. Sci., 1980-90, assoc. editor, 1990—, sports editor, 1992—; contbr. articles to profl. jours. Mem. earth sci. adv. com. NSF, 1990-93, com. on oceanic carbon cycle Nat. Rsch. Coun., 1992-94, ocean studies bd., 1994. Recipient Huntsman medal in Oceanography, Can., 1993, V.M. Goldschmidt medal, 1995, Murchison medal Geol. Soc. London, 1996, Arthur L.Day medal, 1996; Alfred P. Sloan fellow, 1968-72, Guggenheim fellow, 1972. Fellow Am. Acad. Arts and Scis., Geol. Soc. Am. (chmn. hon. fellows com. 1986-87), Mineral. Soc. Am. (life, award 1971); mem. NAS (chmn. geochem. cycles panel 1988-90), Geochem. Soc. (councillor 1976-79, v.p. 1982, pres. 1983), Conn. Acad. Sci. and Engring., Chevaliers du Tastevin, Phi Beta Kappa, Sigma Xi, Beta Theta Pi. Home: 15 Hickory Hill Rd North Haven CT 06473-2916 Office: Yale U Dept Geology And Geoph New Haven CT 06511*

BERNER, ROBERT FRANK, managerial statistics educator, administrator; b. Cleve., Nov. 30, 1917; s. Frank Otto and Marie (Gideon) B.; m. Ruth Harriet Levis, Nov. 6, 1943; children: Robert Frank, Mary Elizabeth, John David, Jean Harriet (dec.). BS, U. Buffalo, 1939, MBA, 1948; PhD, U. Chgo., 1961. Tchr. Palmyra (N.Y.) H.S., 1939-41; instr. stats. U. Buffalo, 1946-48, acting chmn. dept., 1948-49; asst. dean U. Buffalo (Evening Coll.), 1949-52, asst. prof. stats., 1952-63; assoc. prof. dept. mgmt. sci. SUNY, Buffalo, 1963-65, prof. mgmt. sci. and ops. analysis, 1965-81, prof. emeritus, 1981—; pres. emeritus Ctr. of SUNY, Buffalo, 1983-85; chmn. MBA program com., 1976-81; adj. prof. internat. exec. program, 1986—, acting dean divsn. continuing edn., 1952-55, dean, 1955-76; Fulbright prof. Robert Coll., Istanbul, Turkey, 1968-69, U. Nairobi, Kenya, 1975-76. Chmn. adult edn. com. Cmty. Welfare Coun. Buffalo and Erie County, 1962-64; bd. dirs. Creative Edn. Found., 1969-89, emeritus trustee, 1990; bd. dirs. Ch. Mission Help Western N.Y., 1990-96, sec., 1992, treas., 1993-96. Capt. F.A., 10th Mountain divsn. AUS, 1941-45. Decorated Bronze Star, Silver Star. Mem. AAUP, Assn. Univ. Evening Colls. (past pres.), Nat. Univ. Extension Assn., Am. Coun. Edn., Assn. Continuing Higher Edn., Am. Assn. Univ. Adminstrs., Am. Soc. Tng. Dirs. (chpt. sec. 1952-56), Theta Chi, Beta Gamma Sigma, Alpha Sigma Lambda (past nat. pres.). Episcopalian (warden Calvary Ch. 1973-74, 76-77, 86-88, treas. 1996—, mem. commn. ministry Diocese Western N.Y. 1971, 95—, chmn. commn. on continuing edn. 1974-76, diocesan coun. 1988-91, diocese planning and vision com. 1989-92). Club: Equality (pres. 1986-87). Home: 33 Monarch Dr Buffalo NY 14226-1518 Office: SUNY 316 Jacobs Management Ctr Buffalo NY 14260-0113

BERNER, ROBERT LEE, JR., lawyer; b. Chgo., Dec. 9, 1931; s. Robert Lee and Mary Louise (Kenney) B.; m. Sheila Marie Reynolds, Jan. 12,. 1957; children: Mary, Louise, Robert, Sheila, John. A.B., U. Notre Dame, 1953; LL.B., Harvard U., 1956. Bar: Ill. 1956, N.Y. 1989. With Petit, Olin, Overmyer & Fazio, Chgo., 1956-63, Baker & McKenzie, Chgo., 1963—; ptnr., 1964—; mem. vis. com. Northwestern U. Law Sch., 1981-85; mem. legal adv. com. N.Y. Stock Exch., 1995-98. Mem. adv. bd. Catholic Charities, Chgo., 1971—; mem. vis. com. U. Chgo. Div. Sch., 1972—; mem. legal aid com. United Charities, Chgo., 1971—, bd. dirs., 1982—, chmn., 1983-85; bd. dirs. Link Unltd., Chgo., 1975—, pres., 1991-93; mem. adv. bd. Loyola U., 1972—. Mem. ABA (chmn. bus. law sect. 1987-88), Ill. State Bar Assn., Chgo. Bar Assn., Legal Club Chgo. (pres. 1974-75), Law Club Chgo. (pres. 1991-92). Home: 932 Euclid Ave Winnetka IL 60093-1418 Office: Baker & McKenzie One Prudential Plz 130 E Randolph St Ste 3700 Chicago IL 60601-6342

BERNER HARRIS, CYNTHIA KAY, librarian; b. Concordia, Kans, Aug. 31, 1958; d. William Clifford and Donna Darlene (Brown) B.; m. Dwight Harris, May 1, 1999. AA, Cottey Coll., 1978; BA, U. Kans., 1980; MALS, U. Denver, 1981. System cons. Panhandle Libr. Network, Scottsbluff, Nebr., 1981-82; dir. Winfield (Kans.) Pub. Libr., 1982-84; from Westlink br. mgr. to coord. ext. svcs. Wichita (Kans.) Pub. Libr., 1984-95, coord. adminstrv. svcs., 1995—. Editor Propeller mag., 1995-96 (Jr. League Wichita); editor (newsletter) LWV, Wichita Met., 1993. Pres. Philanthropic Ednl. Orgn. (chpt. IM), Wichita, 1989-90; active Jr. League Wichita; project chair STARBASE, 1997-98, dir. cmty. rels., 1998-99. Mem. ALA, Pub. Libr. Assn. (dir. pub. libr. systems sect. 1995-98, dir. pub. libr. sys. com. 1998—), Mountain Plains Libr. Assn. (chair profl. devel. grants com. 1983-84, 86-87, chair pub. libr. sect. 1988-89, chair intellectual freedom com. 1988-90, sec. 1996-97), Kans. Libr. Assn. (chair pub. libr. sect. 1988-89, mem. legis. com. 1997—). Methodist. Home: 6418 Oneil St Wichita KS 67212-6327 Office: Wichita Pub Libr 223 Main St Wichita KS 67202

BERNERS-LEE, TIM, World Wide Web executive. Dir. World Wide Web Consortium MIT, Cambridge, Mass. Recipient Koji Kobayashi Computers and Comm. award Inst. Elec. and Electronics Engrs., 1997. Office: World Wide Web Consortium MIT/545 Technology Square Cambridge MA 02139

BERNFELD, PETER HARRY WILLIAM, biochemist; b. Leipzig, Germany, June 1, 1912; s. Isidor and Elsa (Gutfreund) B.; M.S., U. Leipzig, 1935; Ph.D., U. Geneva (Switzerland), 1937; m. Helen Cecily Kroch, Nov. 21, 1940; children: Michele Marion, Mark Raymond. Came to U.S., 1949, naturalized, 1955. Research fellow U. Geneva, 1937-39, chief chemist dept. chemistry, 1939-49, privat docent enzymology, faculty sci., 1947-49; asst. prof. Sch. Medicine Tufts U., 1949-51, assoc. prof., dept. biochemistry and nutrition 1951-57, biochemist, cancer research unit, 1949-57; sr. v.p., dir. research Bio-Research Inst. and Bio-Research Cons., Cambridge, Mass., 1957-88, ret., 1988. Recipient Werner medal Swiss Chem. Soc., 1948. Mem. Am. Soc. Biol. Chem. and Molecular Biology, Soc. Exptl. Biology and Medicine, Am. Chem. Soc., Am. Inst. Chemists, Am. Assn. Cancer Research, AAAS, N.Y. Acad. Sci., Am. Coll. Toxicology, Sigma Xi. Editor, contbg. author Biogenesis of Natural Compounds, 1963, 2d edit., 1967. Contbr. articles to profl. jours. Home: 247 Farm Ln Westwood MA 02090-1111

BERNFIELD, LYNNE, psychotherapist; b. N.Y.C., Mar. 16, 1943; d. Meyer and Lilian Claire (Pastel) B.; m. Arthur Dawson Richards, June 16, 1982. BA, Hofstra U., 1964; MA, Asuza Pacific U., 1981. Lic. marriage, family, and child therapist, Calif., Fla. Founder, dir. Writers & Artists Inst., L.A., 1984—; ptnr. Next Step Unltd., 1997—. Author: When You Can You Will, 1993. Mem. ASCAP, Calif. Assn. Marriage and Family Therapists, Am. Assn. Marriage and Family Therapists. Office: PO Box 35156 Sarasota FL 34242-5156

BERNFIELD, MERTON RONALD, pediatrician, scientist, educator; b. Chgo., Apr. 9, 1938; s. Harry B. and Adeline A. (Fischer) B.; m. Audrey A. Rivkin, Aug. 30, 1959; children: Susan, James, Mark. BS, U. Ill., 1957, MS, 1961; MD, U. Ill., Chgo., 1961. Intern U. Ill. Research Hosps., Chgo., 1961-62; asst. resident in pediatrics N.Y. Hosp.-Cornell U. Med. Center, N.Y.C., 1962-63; research assoc. NIH, Bethesda, Md., 1963-65; research investigator Nat. Inst. Child Health and Human Devel., U. Calif., San Diego, 1965-66; chief resident in pediatrics Stanford U. Med. Center, 1967; asst. prof. pediatrics Stanford U., 1967-70, assoc. prof., 1970-75, prof., 1975-89, Josephine Knotts Knowles prof. human biology, 1977-89, dir. med. scientist MD-PhD tng. program, 1974-77, chmn. program in human biology, 1977-80, dir. fellowship program in membrane pathobiology, 1975-85, dir. fellowship program in developmental and neonatal biology, 1982-89; dir. cystic fibrosis rsch. devel. program Stanford (Calif.) U., 1987-89; Clement A. Smith prof. pediatrics, prof. cell biology Harvard U Med. Sch., 1989—; chief div. newborn medicine Children's Hosp., Boston; chmn. newborn medicine Brigham and Women's Hosp., Boston, Beth Israel Hosp., Boston, 1990—; mem. rsch. com. Cystic Fibrosis Found., 1972-76; mem. developmental biology panel NSF, 1976-77; mem. physiol. chemistry research com. Am. Heart Assn., 1979-83; mem. craniofacial anomalies evaluation panel Nat. Inst. Dental Research, 1980-81; mem. health adv. com. Calif. Medfly Eradication Project, 1981-82; mem. sci. adv. bd. Collagen Corp., 1981-90; chmn. Neonatal Biology Group, 1984-91; chmn. Ciba Symposium, Basement Membranes and Cell Movement, 1984; chmn. Gordon Rsch. Conf. on Basement Membranes, 1986; cons. in field. Contbr. articles to profl. jours.; mem. editorial bd. Archives Biochemistry and Biophysics, 1972-79, Cell Differentiation and Devel., 1980-90, Jour. Craniofacial Genetics and Devel. Biology, 1980-83, Jour. Biol. Chemistry, 1987-93, Am. Jour. Respiratory Cell and Molecular Biology, 1988—, Molecular Biology of the Cell, 1989—; assoc. editor Developmental Biology, 1981-95; exec. editor MATRIX, 1989—; sect. editor Current Opinion in Cell Biology, 1988-92. Mem. working group Organ Systems Program Nat. Cancer Inst., 1986-89, selection com. Pediatric Scientist Tng. Program, Assn. Med. Sch. Pediatric Dept. Chairmen, 1987-91, Mid. Grades Life Sci. Adv. Bd. Carnegie Corp., N.Y., 1988—, Maternal and Child Health Rsch. Com. Nat. Inst. Child Health and Human Devel., 1988-92; mem. working group on Early Life and Adolescent Health Policy, Harvard U., 1989—; mem. sci. adv. bd. Neose Techs., 1992—, Peregrine Pharms., 1993-97, Exilexsis Pharms., 1994-97, Genzyme Corp., 1994—. With USPHS, 1963-66. Guggenheim fellow, 1972-73; Josiah Macy scholar, 1980-81; recipient Merit award Nat. Inst. Child Health and Human Devel., 1988. Mem. Am. Pediatrics Soc. (Centennial Symposium lectr. 1988), Am. Acad. Pediatrics, Am. Soc. for Biochemistry and Molecular Biology, Am. Soc. Cell Biology (chmn. pub. policy com., treas.), Am. Assn. Physicians, Inst. Medicine of U.S. Nat. Acad. Scis., Internat. Soc. for Devel. Biology, Perinatal Research Soc., Soc. Devel. Biology (pres. 1991), Soc.

Pediatric Research, Teratology Soc., Western Soc. Pediatric Research (Ross award 1973). Home: 25 Brimmer St Boston MA 02108-1040 Office: Harvard Med Sch Joint Program In Neonatal Boston MA 02115

BERNHARD, ALEXANDER ALFRED, lawyer; b. New Orleans, Sept. 20, 1936; s. John Helanus and Dora (Solosko) B.; m. Martha Ruggles, Nov. 21, 1959 (div.); children: John, Jason, Frederic; m. Joyce Harrington, Dec. 30, 1976 (div.); m. Myra Mayman, Nov. 2, 1986. BS, MIT, 1957; LLB, Harvard U., 1964. Bar: Calif. 1964, Oreg. 1965, Mass. 1966, N.H. 1991. Law clk. to judge U.S. Ct. Appeals (9th cir.), 1964-65; assoc. Johnson, Johnson & Harrang, Eugene, Oreg., 1965-66, Bingham, Dana & Gould, Boston, 1966-71; assoc. Hale and Dorr, Boston, 1971-73, jr. ptnr., 1973-75, sr. ptnr., 1975—. Trustee, bd. dirs. Mass. Eye and Ear Infirmary, chmn., 1992-96, chmn. emeritus, 1996—. Lt. submarines USNR, 1957-61. Mem. ABA, Boston Bar Assn., Union Boat Club, Longwood Cricket Club. Democrat. Office: Hale and Dorr 60 State St Ste 25 Boston MA 02109-1803

BERNHARD, BERL, lawyer; b. N.Y.C., Sept. 7, 1929; s. Morris and Celia B.; children—Peter Berl, Robin Churchill, Andrew Morris. B.A. in Govt. magna cum laude (Rufus Choate scholar), Dartmouth Coll., 1951, A.M., 1974; J.D., Yale U., 1954; LL.D., Central Ohio State Coll., 1963. Bars: D.C., 1954, U.S. Supreme Ct., 1957. Assoc. Davis, Polk, Wardwell, Sunderland & Kiendl, N.Y.C., summer 1953; law clk. to U.S. dist. judge, 1954-56; assoc Turney & Turney, 1956-59; staff dir. U.S. Commn. on Civil Rights, 1961-63; ptnr. Verner, Liipfert, Bernhard, McPherson and Hand and predecessor firms, 1959, 63—, Hughes, Hubbard & Reed, Washington, 1972-75; chmn. Verner Liipfert Bernhard McPherson & Hand; bd. dirs. UNC Inc.; gen. counsel, dir. Evening Star Newspaper Co., Washington, 1974-78, WJLA, Inc., Washington, 1976-80; staff dir. U.S. Commn. on Civil Rights, 1961-63, cons. under sec. polit. affairs Sec. State, 1963-65; adj. prof. law Georgetown U. Law Ctr., 1963-65; spl. counsel, dir. The White Ho. Conf. "To Fulfill These Rights," 1966; counsel Lawyers Com. for Civil Rights Under Law. Contbr. articles to profl. jours. Gen. counsel Dem. Senatorial Campaign Com., 1965-71; spl. counsel Dem. Nat. Com., 1965-71; staff dir. Senator Edmund S. Muskie, 1971, nat. campaign mgr., 1972; mem. D.C. Bd. Higher Edn., chmn. fin. com.; trustee Dartmouth Coll., 1974-84, Joe Davies Found., 1968-87; sr. advisor to Sec. of State, 1980-81; chmn., CEO Washington Federals, U.S. Football League; bd. dirs. Harriman Polit. Action Com., 1980-89; mem. bd. visitors Nelson A. Rockefeller Ctr. for Social Scis., 1983-90; mem. bd. overseers The Amos Tuck Sch. Bus. Adminstrn., Dartmouth Coll., 1985-90; bd. dirs. Aspen Inst., 1988—, chmn., 1991-96; trustee Fed. City Coun., 1988-92; bd. trustees Mushie Found., 1997. Recipient Arthur S. Flemming award D.C. Jr. C. of C., 1960, Ten Outstanding Young Men award U.S. Jr. C. of C., 1962. Mem. Am. Bar Assn., Bar Assn. D.C., Assn. Interstate Practitioners, Nat. Panel Arbitrators, Am. Arbitration Assn., Casque and Gauntlet, Phi Beta Kappa, Sigma Nu, Phi Delta Phi. Clubs: Metropolitan (Washington); Yale (N.Y.C.). Home: 1693 Epping Farms Rd Annapolis MD 21401-6673 Office: Verner Lipfert Bernhard McPherson & Hand 901 15th St NW Ste 700 Washington DC 20005-2327

BERNHARD, HERBERT ASHLEY, lawyer; b. Jersey City, Sept. 24, 1927; s. Richard C. and Amalie (Lobl) B.; m. Nancy Ellen Hirschaut, Aug. 8, 1954; children: Linda, Alison, Jordan, Melissa. Student, Mexico City Coll., 1948; BEE, N.J. Inst. Tech., 1949; MA in Math., Columbia U., 1950; JD cum laude, U. Mich., 1957. Bar: Calif. 1958, U.S. Dist. Ct. (cen. dist.) Calif. 1958, U.S. Dist. Ct. (no., ea. and so. dists.) Calif. 1963, U.S. Ct. Claims 1966, U.S. Dist. Ct. (ea. dist.) Wis. 1982, U.S. Dist. Ct. (ea. and we. dists.) Ark. 1982, U.S. Dist. Ct. Nebr. 1982, U.S. Ct. Internat. Trade 1979, U.S. Tax Ct. 1969, U.S. Ct. Appeals (2d, 3d, 4th, 5th, 7th, 8th, 9th, 10th, 11th and D.C. cirs.) 1969, U.S. Supreme Ct. 1965. Research engr. Curtis-Wright Co., Caldwell, N.J., 1950-52, Boeing Aircraft Co., Cape Canaveral, Fla., 1952-55; assoc. O'Melveny & Myers, Los Angeles, 1957-62; ptnr. Greenberg, Bernhard, et al, Los Angeles, 1962-85, Jeffer, Mangels, Butler & Marmaro, Los Angeles, 1985—; instr. math. U. Fla., Cape Canaveral, 1952-55; instr. elec. engrng. U. Mich., Ann Arbor, 1955-57; referee L.A. Superior Ct., 1985—, arbitrator, 1988—, judge pro tem, 1988—; judge pro tem L.A. Mcpl. Ct., 1985—, Beverly Hills Mcpl. Ct., 1989—, Malibu Mcpl. Ct., 1994—. Contbr. articles to profl. jours. Chmn. adv. com. Skirball Mus., 1976-98; bd. overseers Hebrew Union Coll., 1976-98. With USAF, 1946-47. Recipient Disting. Minn. Achievement award N.J. Inst. Tech., 1998. Mem. Jewish Publ. Soc. (trustee 1986-96). Home: 1105 Tower Rd Beverly Hills CA 90210-2130 Office: Jeffer Mangels Butler & Marmaro 2121 Avenue Of The Stars Fl 10 Los Angeles CA 90067-5010

BERNHARD, JEFFREY DAVID, dermatologist, editor, educator; b. Buffalo, Oct. 31, 1951. AB, Harvard Coll., 1973; MD, Harvard Med. Sch., 1978. Diplomate Am. Bd. Dermatology. Chief resident dermatology Harvard Med. Sch., Boston, 1982; fellow photomedicine Mass. Gen. Hosp., 1983; mem. faculty Med. Sch. U. Mass., Worcester, 1983—, dir. dermatology, assoc. prof. Sch. Medicine, 1986—, assoc. dean for admissions Med. Sch., 1989-95, prof. Med. Sch., 1992—. Author: Itch: Mechanisms and Management of Pruritus, 1994; asst. editor Jour. Am. Acad. Dermatology, 1993-98, editor, 1998—; mem. editl. bd. Jour. European Acad. Dermatology and Venereology, Yearbook of Cancer, 1981-88, Yearbook of Dermatology, 1988-97, Internat. Jour. Dermatology, Jour. Geriat. Dermatology, 1993-97. Knox fellow St. John's Coll., U. Cambridge, 1973-74. Mem. Am. Acad. Dermatology, Soc. for Investigative Dermatology, European Acad. Dermatology and Venereology, Am. Dermatol. Assn., Royal Soc. Medicine, Sir James Saunders Soc., Aesculapian Club Boston, Assn. Profs. Dermatology, New Eng. Dermatol. Soc. (pres. 1990-91), Quinsigamond Dermatol. Soc., Phi Beta Kappa, Sigma Xi. Office: U Mass Meml Med Ctr 55 Lake Ave N Worcester MA 01655-0002

BERNHARD, ROBERT JAMES, mechanical engineer, educator; b. Algona, Iowa, July 28, 1952; s. David Louis and Darlene Justine (Kohlhaas) B.; m. Deborah S. Kell; children: Jay David, Jacqueline Elizabeth, Jonathan Christian, Justin Brian. BS in Mech. Engrng., Iowa State U., 1973, PhD, 1982; MS, U. Md., 1976. Engr. Westinghouse Electric, Inc., Balt., 1973-77; asst. prof. Iowa State U., Ames, 1977-82; asst. prof. dept. mech. engrng. Purdue U., West Lafayette, Ind., 1982-87, assoc. prof., 1987-91, prof., 1991—; dir. Ray W. Herrick Labs Purdue U., 1994—, Inst. for Safe, Quiet, and Durable Hwys, 1998—; cons. to GM, Electricite de France, Automated Analysis; prin. investigator many firms; lectr. CETIM, U. Wis., U. Mich. Assoc. editor: Noise Control Engrng. Jour., 1984-85, 90—. Fellow ASME (co-editor procs. 1989), Acoustical Soc. Am.; mem. AIAA, Soc. Automotive Engrs., Inst. Noise Control Engrs. (bd. dirs. 1988-97, pres. 1994), Am. Soc. Engrng. Educators. Office: Purdue U 1077 Ray W Herrick Labs Purdue University IN 47907

BERNHARD, SANDRA, actress, comedienne, singer; b. Flint, Mich., June 6, 1955; d. Jerome and Jeanette B. Stand-up comedienne nightclubs, Beverly Hills, Calif., 1974-78; films include Cheech and Chong's Nice Dreams, 1981, The King of Comedy, 1983 (Nat. Soc. Film Critics award), Sesame Street Presents: Follow That Bird, 1985, Track 29, 1988, Without You I'm Nothing, 1990, Hudson Hawk, 1991, Truth or Dare, 1991, Inside Monkey Zetterland, 1993, Dallas Doll, 1994, Unzipped, 1995, Catwalk, 1995, Plump Fiction, 1996, Somewhere in the City, 1997, Lover Girl, 1997, The Apocalypse, 1997, An Alan Smithee Film: Burn Hollywood Burn, 1997, I Woke Up Early the Day I Died, 1998, Exposé, 1998, Wrongfully Accused, 1998; also appears in Heavy Petting, 1988, Perfect, 1985, The Whoopee Boys, 1986, Casual Sex?, 1988; stage appearances (solo) Without You I'm Nothing, 1988, Giving Till It Hurts, 1992; TV appearances (host) Living in America, 1990; regular guest The Richard Pryor Show, Late Night with David Letterman; TV series Instant Comedy with the Groundlings, The Hitchhiker, The Full Wax, Tales from the Crypt, Roseanne, Space Ghost Coast to Coast, The Larry Sanders Show, Clueless, Chicago Hope, Highlander, Superman (voice), Ally McBeal, Hercules; (TV movies) Freaky Friday, 1995, The Late Shift, 1996; albums (co-author 8 songs) I'm Your Woman, 1985, Without You I'm Nothing, 1989; books include Confessions of a Pretty Lady, 1988, Love Love and Love, 1993. Office: Noe-Man Mgmt Scott Noe 26500 W Agoura Rd Ste 575 Calabasas CA 91302-1952 Home: care Susan DuBow 9171 Wilshire Blvd Ph Beverly Hills CA 90210-5532*

BERNHARDT, HERBERT NELSON, law educator, labor arbitrator; s. Michael Maurice and Rose (Miller) B.; children: Beth Margo, Suzanne Piper (twins). BS, Cornell U., 1956; LLB, Yale U., 1961; LLM, NYU, 1971. Bar: N.Y. 1962, U.S. Supreme Ct. 1965. Instr., rsch. assoc. Rutgers U., 1961-62; asst. prof. law U. S.C., 1962-64; atty. NLRB, 1964-67; assoc. prof. Dickinson Sch. Law, 1967-68; assoc. prof. law Northeastern U., Boston, 1968-69; prof. law U. Balt., 1971-98, prof. emeritus, 1998—; labor arbitrator Am. Arbitration Assn., Fed. Mediation and Conciliation Service; hearing examiner EEOC; cons. to City of Balt. Affirmative Action in Employment. Mem. editl. bd. Employee Rights and Employment Policy Jour.; contbr. articles to legal jours. NDEA fellow, 1969-71. Mem. ABA, Indsl. Rels. Rsch. Assn. (v.p. Balt. chpt.), Soc. Profls. in Dispute Resolution, Internat. Soc. Labor Law and Social Legislation, Assn. Am. Law Schs. (nat. sec. labor law sect. 1971-72, nat. sec. employment discrimination sect. 1995-96, nat. chair-elect 1996-97, nat. chair 1997-98), Common Cause, Balt. Folk Music Soc., Balt. Bicycle Club. Democrat. Jewish. Home and Office: 3415 Clarks Ln Apt C2 Baltimore MD 21215-2546

BERNHARDT, JEAN LOUISE, special education educator; b. Manitowoc, Wis., Jan. 22, 1961; d. Donald James and Lelah Alvira (Wimme) Cauley; m. Dennis William Bernhardt, July 21, 1984; children: Jeffrey William, Kevin Michael. BS in Edn., U. Wis., Whitewater, 1983. Cert. tchr., early childhood, exceptional ednl. needs. Tchr. pre-sch. and exceptional ednl. needs Owen (Wis.) -Withee Pub. Schs., 1983-84; tchr., exceptional ednl. needs CESA # 7, Chilton, Wis., 1984—. Mem. Coun. Exceptional Children, Phi Kappa Phi, Phi Eta Sigma. Roman Catholic.

BERNHARDT, JOHN BOWMAN, banker; b. Norton, Va., Aug. 7, 1929; s. Claude Bowman and Mabel (Dixon) B.; m. Ada Nuckels, Aug. 29, 1952; children: Jared B., J. Carter. B.A., U. Va., 1954, LL.B., 1957; postgrad., Rutgers U., 1967. Exec. v.p. Va. Nat. Bank, Norfolk, 1969-79; pres. Va. Nat. Bank, 1980-83; exec. v.p. Va. Nat. Bankshares, 1972-79, pres., 1980-83; vice chmn. bd. Sovran Fin. Corp. and Sovran Bank N.A., 1984-88; pres., chief exec. officer Sovran Services, 1986-88; mng. dir. Bernhardt/Gibson Fin., Newport News, Va.; bd. dirs. Dominion Resources Inc., Resource Bank. Fin. dir. First Source; bd. dirs. United Way, pres., 1976; bd. dirs. Forward Hampton Rds.; mem. Va. Fuel Converson Authority. Mem. Va. Bankers Assn. (pres. 1979), Va. C. of C. Presbyterian. Clubs: St. Croix (V.I.) Country, Caram Bola Golf (St. Croix), Cedar Point (Suffolk, Va.). Home: 8020 Quail Hollow Suffolk VA 23433-1010 Office: 90 Old York Rd Williamsburg VA 23185-5826

BERNHARDT-KABISCH, ERNEST KARL-HEINZ, English and comparative literature educator; b. Chemnitz, Germany, Nov. 15, 1934; came to U.S., 1955; s. Karl-Heinz and Brunhild Anna Bertha (Kabisch) Bernhardt; m. Eva Carolyn Dessau, Sept. 1, 1956; 1 child, Ethan Karl. BA, U. Calif., Berkeley, 1957, MA, 1959, PhD, 1962. Instr. Ind. U., Bloomington, 1962-64, asst. prof., 1964-68, assoc. prof., 1968-80, prof., 1980-99, prof. emeritus, 1999—; dir. Living Learning Ctr., Ind. U., Bloomington, 1977-90, resident dir. Overseas Study Program, Hamburg, Germany, 1990-91, 94-95. Author: Robert Southey, 1977, Begegnungen mit Erda, 1991; co-editor: Yearbook of Comparative and General Literature, 1977-90; contbr. articles to profl. jours. Mem. AAUP, Am. Comparative Lit. Assn., Modern Lang. Assn., Oesterreichischer Alpenverein, N.Am. Soc. for Study of Romanticism. Democrat. Avocations: mountain climbing, skiing, gardening, music, poetry. Home: 616 S Jordan Ave Bloomington IN 47401-5122 Office: Dept English Ind Univ Bloomington IN 47405

BERNHEIMER, MARTIN, music critic; b. Munich, Germany, Sept. 28, 1936; came to U.S., 1940, naturalized, 1946; s. Paul Ernst and Louise (Nassauer) B.; m. Lucinda Pearson, Sept. 30, 1961 (div. Feb. 1989); children: Mark Richard, Nora Nicoll, Marina and Erika (twins); m. Linda Winer, Sept. 27, 1992. MusB with honors, Brown U., 1958; student, Munich Conservatory, 1958-59; MA in Musicology, NYU, 1961. Free-lance music critic, 1958—; contbg. critic N.Y. Herald Tribune, 1959-62; mem. music faculty NYU, 1959-62; contbg. editor Mus. Courier, 1961-64; temporary music critic N.Y. Post, 1961-65; N.Y. corr. for Brit. Publ. Opera, 1962-65, L.A. corr., 1965—; corr. West Coast Brit. Opera Mag., 1965—; asst. to music editor Saturday Rev., 1962-65; mng. editor Philharmonic Hall Program, N.Y.C., 1962-65; music editor, chief critic L.A. Times, 1965-96; mem. faculty U. So. Calif., 1966-71, music faculty UCLA, 1969-75, Calif. Inst. Arts, 1975-82, Calif. State U., Northridge, 1978-81, Rockefeller Program for Tng. of Music Critics; mem. Pulitzer Prize Music Jury, 1984, 86, 90; L.A. corr. for Swiss publ. Opernwelt, 1984—. Contbg. author New Groves Dictionary; contbr. liner notes for recordings; appearances on radio and TV, Met. Opera Broadcasts; contbr. articles to Vanity Fair, Music Quar., The Critic, Opera News, Mus. Am., Fin. Times, London, Sidewalk N.Y. (internet), others; contributing feature writer Fin. Times, N.Y. Newsday, Met. Opera Broadcast. Recipient Deems Taylor award ASCAP, 1974, 78, Headliners award, 1979, Pulitzer Prize for disting. criticism, 1981, Lifetime Achievement award Svc. to Music, Calif. Assn. Profl. Music Tchrs., 1990. Mem. Nat. Opera Inst. (ind. selection com. 1980), Pi Kappa Lambda (hon.).

BERNICK, CAROL LAVIN, corporate executive; m. Howard Bernick; three children. BA, Tulane U., 1974. Mem. mktg. staff Alberto-Culver Co., Melrose Park, Ill., 1974-79, dir. new products, 1979-81, dir. new bus. devel. group, 1981-84, v.p., 1984-88; co-dir., 1984; group v.p. Alberto-Culver Co., Melrose Park, Ill., 1988-90, exec. v.p. worldwide mktg., 1990-92, exec. v.p., 1994—; pres. Alberto-Culver USA, Melrose Park, Ill., 1994—; vice chmn., pres. N.Am. Alberto-Culver Co., Melrose Park. Founder Friends of Prentice; bd. dirs. Northwestern Meml. Hosp. Corp.; active women's bd. Ptnrs. Home Care, Boy's and Girls Clubs of Chgo.; regent Lincoln Acad. Ill.; mem. adv. bd. Kellog Sch., Northwestern U. Recipient Leadership in Bus. award YWCA Met. Chgo., 1992. Mem. Young Pres. Orgn., Econ. Club Chgo., Exec. Club Chgo. Office: Alberto-Culver Co 2525 Armitage Ave Melrose Park IL 60160-1163

BERNICK, HOWARD BARRY, manufacturing company executive; b. Midland, Ont., Can., Apr. 10, 1952; came to U.S., 1974, naturalized, 1976; s. Henry and Esther (Starkman) B.; m. Carol Lavin, May 30, 1976; children: Craig, Peter, Elizabeth. B.A., U. Toronto, Ont., 1973. Investment banker Wood Gundy Ltd., Toronto, 1973-74, First Boston Corp., Chgo., 1974-77; dir. of profit planning Alberto Culver Co., Melrose Park, Ill., 1977-79, v.p. corp. devel., 1979-81, group v.p., chief fin. officer, 1981-85, exec. v.p., 1985-88, pres., COO, 1988-94, also bd. dirs.; pres., CEO, 1994—; bd. dirs. AAR Corp. Mem. Cosmetic, Toiletry & Fragrance Assn., Econ. Club Chgo. Office: Alberto-Culver Co 2525 Armitage Ave Melrose Park IL 60160-1163*

BERNIER, GEORGE MATTHEW, JR., physician, medical educator, medical school dean; b. Portland, Maine, June 29, 1934; s. George Matthew and Lillian Theresa (Wallace) B.; m. Mary Jane Marron, June 29, 1963; children: George Matthew, III, Elizabeth Wallace. A.B., Boston Coll., 1956; M.D., Harvard U., 1960. Intern Univ. Hosps., Cleve., 1960-61; resident Univ. Hosps., 1961-62, 65-66, U. Fla. Hosps., Gainesville, 1964-65; fellow in biochemistry U. Fla., 1962-64; instr. Case Western Res. U., Cleve., 1966-67, asst. prof. medicine, 1967-72, assoc. prof., 1972-75, prof., 1975-78; dir. div. med. oncology Univ. Hosps., Cleve., 1974-78; prof., chmn. dept. medicine Dartmouth Med. Sch., Hanover, N.H., 1978-86, Joseph M. Huber prof. medicine, 1982-86; dean, prof. medicine U. Pitts. Sch. Medicine, U. Pitts., 1987-95; dean medicine, v.p. acad. affairs U. Tex. Med. Br., Galveston, 1995—. Contbr. articles to profl. jours. Trustee Jackson Labs., Bar Harbor, Maine, 1973—. Served to lt. col. M.C. U.S. Army, 1967-70. Leukemia Soc. Am. scholar, 1970-75. Fellow A.C.P.; mem. Am. Soc. Hematology, Am. Soc. Clin. Oncology, Am. Soc. Clin. Investigation, Am. Assn. Immunologists, Assn. Am. Physicians, Am. Clin. and Climatological Assn. Office: U Tex Med Br 301 University Blvd Galveston TX 77555-0133

BERNIER, GILLES, member of parliament; b. Grand Falls, New Bruns., Can., Aug. 6, 1955; m. Rosita Bernier; children: Cory, Michel, Monica. Owner G. Bernier Painting, Grand Falls, 1981-89; acting pres. Wal-Cor Enterprises, Ltd., 1989-93; owner Tilley Convenience Store, Tilley, NB, Can., 1993—; elected to House of Commons, Tobique-Mactaquac, 1997—; apptd. Progressive Conservative critic for Pub. Works and Govt. Svcs., Can. Active several cmty. orgns. including St. Mary's Ch. Coun., Victoria Snowmobile Club, Royal Can. Legion. Mem. Tobique-Mactaquac Progressive Conservative Assn. (founding pres.), Victoria-Tobique Progressive Conservative Assn. (dir.), KC, Rotary, Atlantic Can. Entrepreneurial Inst. for Sml. Bus. Office: 466 W Block, 279 Confederation Bldg, Ottawa, ON Canada K1A OA6*

BERNIERI, FRANK JOHN, social psychology educator; b. Bklyn., May 2, 1961; s. Gene J. and Rose (Autunnale) B.; divorced; 1 child, Jennifer. BA, U. Rochester, 1983; PhD, Harvard U., 1988. Asst. prof. social psychology Oreg. State U., Corvallis, 1988-93, assoc. prof., 1993-94; assoc. prof. U. Toledo, Ohio, 1994—. Author: (with others) Coordinated Movement in Human Interaction, 1991; mem. editorial bd. Jour. Nonverbal Behavior, 1990—; contbr. articles to profl. jours. Fellow Harvard U., 1987; grantee NIH, 1988, Oreg. State U. Coll. Liberal Arts, 1990; NSF Young Investigator awardee, 1992. Mem. AAAS, APA, Am. Psychol. Soc., Soc. for Personality and Social Psychology, Soc. for Exptl. Social Psychology. Democrat. Office: U Toledo Dept Psychology Toledo OH 43606

BERNIKOW, LEONARD, federal judge; b. 1934. BA, CUNY, 1956; LLB, NYU, 1959. Bar: N.Y. With criminal br. Legal Aid Soc., N.Y.C., 1965-68; with N.Y.C. Counsel's Office, 1968-71, chief gen. litigation divsn., 1971-75; magistrate judge for so. dist. N.Y., U.S. Magistrate Ct., 1975—. With U.S. Army, 1959-60, 61-62. Office: US Magistrate Ct US Courthouse 500 Pearl St New York NY 10007-1316

BERNIKOW, LOUISE, writer; b. Sept. 19, 1940. BA, Barnard Coll., 1961; MPhil, Columbia U., 1973. lectr. Author: The American Women's Almanac, 1997; contbr. articles to mags. Home and Office: 318 W 105th St New York NY 10025-3463

BERNING, LARRY D., lawyer; b. Kendallville, Ind., Oct. 21, 1940; s. Melvin and Dolores (Sorge) B.; m. Phyllis Low Cameron, Oct. 24, 1987; children—Emily Lyn, Scott Michael. A.B., Ind. U., 1963, J.D., 1968. Bar: Ill. 1968, Ind. 1968. Assoc. Sidley & Austin, Chgo., 1968-74, ptnr., 1974—. Trustee Old People's Home of Chgo.; pres. William H. Miner Found. Served with U.S. Army, 1963-65. Mem. ABA, Ill. Bar Assn., Chgo. Bar Assn., Ind. Bar Assn., Am. Coll. Trust and Estate Counsel, Chgo. Estate Planning Council. Clubs: Mid-Day, Law, Legal. (Chgo.), Skokie C.C. Office: Sidley & Austin 1 First Natl Plz Chicago IL 60603-2003

BERNING, ROBERT WILLIAM, librarian; b. Carroll, Iowa, Dec. 2, 1949; s. Norbert John and Marjorie Lavine (Miller) B. BSE, N.W. Mo. State U., 1972; MLS, Emporia State U., 1974. Cert. pub. libr., Iowa. Sch. libr. Mount Ayr (Iowa) Cmty. Schs., 1974-76, Wall Lake (Iowa) Cmty. Schs., 1977-79, West Point (Nebr.) Pub. Schs., 1979-81; dir. Dubuque County Libr., Farley, Iowa, 1981-82; sch. libr. HLV Cmty. Schs., Victor, Iowa, 1982-84; dir. Carlisle (Iowa) Pub. Libr., 1985—; mem. adv. bd. State Libr. Iowa, Des Moines, 1987, 89; mem. adv. com. Ctrl. Iowa Regional Libr., Clive, 1992-94, 98—. Libr. rep. Lanning Bequest com. City of Carlisle, 1995-97, Mng. Info. for Rural Am. (MIRA), 1998; mem. com., task force Iowans Can't Wait (Enrich Iowa), State Libr. Iowa, Des Moines, 1995-96. Mem. ALA, KC, Iowa Libr. Assn. (govtl. affairs com. 1988-91), Iowa Small Libr. Assn. (sec. 1985-87), Carlisle Lion's Club, Carlisle C. of C. (libr. rep. 1990—), Mayor's Select Com. on Property Taxes, Des Moines, 1998-99. Roman Catholic. Avocations: collecting antiques, travel, gardening. Office: Carlisle Pub Libr 135 School St PO Box S Carlisle IA 50047

BERNISH, PAUL, public relations executive, consultant. Dir. pub. rels. The Kroger Co., Cin., 1980—. Office: The Kroger Co 1014 Vine St Cincinnati OH 45202-1100*

BERNS, KENNETH IRA, physician; b. Cleve., June 14, 1938; s. Charles and Delnet (Cohn) B.; m. Laura Louise Lawless, June 26, 1964; children: Jonathan Charles, Deborah Louise. Student, Harvard U., 1956-59; A.B., Johns Hopkins U., 1960, Ph.D., 1964, M.D., 1966. Intern Johns Hopkins Hosp., 1966-67; asst. prof. microbiology Johns Hopkins U. Sch. Medicine, 1970-74, asst. prof. pediatrics, 1970-76, asso. prof. microbiology, 1974-76; dir. Johns Hopkins U. Sch. Medicine (Year I program), 1973-76; prof., chmn. dept. immunology and med. microbiology, prof. pediatrics U. Fla. Coll. Medicine, Gainesville, 1976-84; R.A. Rees Pritchett prof., chmn. dept. microbiology Cornell U. Med. Coll., 1984-97; dean U. Fla. Coll. Medicine, 1997—, interim v.p. health affairs, 1998—; Howard Hughes med. investigator, 1970-75; mem. microbiology test com. Nat. Bd. Med. Examiners, 1979-82, chmn., 1983-86, mem. exec. bd., 1986-95; mem. Recombinant DNA adv. com. NIH, 1980-83, chmn., 1982-83; mem. genetic biology panel NSF, 1981-84; Fogarty sr. internat. fellow virology dept. Weizmann Inst. Sci., Rehovot, Israel, 1982-83; ad hoc mem. Bd. Sci. Counselors, Nat. Inst. Allergy and Infectious Diseases, 1981-82, perm. mem., 1992-96; del. U.S.-Japan Coop. Program on Recombinant DNA, 1981; mem. Internat. Com. Taxonomy of Viruses, 1981—; mem. virology study sect. NIH, 1985-89; mem. virology and microbiology adv. com. Am. Cancer Soc., 1985-89, liaison com. on med. edn., 1989-92; mem. composite com. U.S. Med. Licensing Exam., 1995-98; nat. adv. coun. Nat. Ctr. Rsch. Resources, 1999—. Served with USPHS, 1967-70. Recipient faculty research award Am. Cancer Soc., 1975-76; grantee NIH, 1970-76, 80—; grantee NSF, 1973-75, 77-80; grantee Am. Cancer Soc., 1970-72; Shell Oil fellow, 1963-64. Mem. AAAS, NAS, Am. Acad. Microbiology, Am. Soc. Biol. Chemists, Am. Soc. Microbiology (bd. pub. and sci. affairs, pres. 1996-97), Assn. Med. Sch. Microbiology Chairmen (counselor 1980-83, chmn. com. pub. policy 1979, pres. 1985), Am. Soc. Virology (pres. 1988-89), Soc. Gen. Microbiology, Soc. Pediatric Rsch., Internat. Union Microbiol. Socs. (v.p. 1990-94), Inst. Medicine, Phi Beta Kappa, Sigma Xi. Office: Univ Fla Office of Dean Miller Health Ctr PO Box 10014 Gainesville FL 32610-0014

BERNSEN, CORBIN, actor; b. North Hollywood, Calif., Sept. 7, 1954; s. Jeanne Cooper; m. Amanda Pays. BA in Theater Arts, UCLA, MFA in Playwriting. Teaching asst. UCLA. Appeared in (films) King Kong, 1976, S.O.B., 1981, Hello, Again, 1987, Bert Rigby, You're A Fool, 1989, Major League, 1989, Disorganized Crime, 1989, Shattered, 1992, Frozen Assets, 1993, Major League 2, 1994, Tales From the Hood, 1995, Menno's Mind, 1996, Kounterfeit, 1996, Bloodhounds, 1996, The Great White Hype, 1996, Circuit Breaker, 1997, An American Affair, The Misadventures of Margaret, 1998, Drop Dead, 1998, Beings, 1998, Major League: Back to the Minors, 1998, The Misadventures of Margaret, 1998, Young Hearts Unlimited, 1998, Two of Hearts, 1999; (TV Series) Ryan's Hope, L.A. Law, A Whole New Ballgame, The Cape; (TV Movie) Breaking Point, Danielle Steel's 'Full Circle', 1996, The Cape, 1996, The Dentist, 1996, Tidal Wave: No Escape, 1997, Loyal Opposition: Terror in the White House, 1998, Nightworld: Riddler's Moon, 1998, Recipe for Revenge, 1998, Two of Hearts, 1999; TV guest appearances include Star Trek: The Next Generation, 1987, Dear John, 1988, Anything But Love, 1989, Seinfeld, 1990, The Larry Sanders Show, 1992, The Nanny, 1993, Touched by an Angel, 1994. Office: ICM 8942 Wilshire Blvd Beverly Hills CA 90211*

BERNSEN, HAROLD JOHN, marketing executive, political affairs consultant, retired naval officer; b. Boston, Nov. 25, 1936; s. Harold Arthur and Solveig Bachrud (Birkrem) B.; m. Doris Ann Champion, Mar. 5, 1960. BA, Dartmouth Coll., 1958. Commd. ensign USN, 1958, advanced through grades to rear adm., 1988, comdg. officer USS LaSalle, 1980-82; comdg. officer USS Lexington USN, Pensacola, Fla., 1983-84; dir. plans and policy, staff comdr. in chief U.S. Cen. Command USN, Tampa, Fla., 1985-86; comdr. Mideast Force USN, 1986-88; dir. plans and policy staff comdr. in chief Atlantic Fleet USN, Norfolk, 1988-91; dep., chief of staff, comdr. in chief Atlantic Fleet, 1991, ret., 1991; v.p. internat. devel. World Building Systems Ltd., 1995—; spkr. on Mid. East issues. Chmn. bd., pres. 21st Century Coatings, Inc.; bd. dirs. Am. Bahraini Friendship Soc., Nat. Coun. on U.S.-Arab Rels.; v.p. trustees Physicians for Peace; bd. dirs. Nat. U.S. Arab C. of C. Decorated Disting. Svc. Medal, Def. Superior Svc. Medal, Legion of Merit, Royal Norwegian Order of Merit (Norway); Order 1st Class (Bahrain). Mem. U.S. Naval Inst., Assn. Naval Aviation, Naval Order U.S., N.Y. Yacht Club. Avocations: sailing, golf, cooking, gardening. E-mail: hal.fpu@juno.com. Office: 301 N Fairfax St Ste 100A Alexandria VA 22314

BERNSON, HAL, city councilman; b. L.A., Nov. 19, 1930; m. Robyn Goewert; children: Nicole, Sarah. Student, L.A. City Coll. City councilman 12th Dist., L.A., 1979—, chair planning and land use mgmt. com., bd. referred powers, mem. transp. com.; businessman; columnist San Fernando Valley Chronicle newspaper, 1978-79. Coord. City of L.A. Earthquake Preparedness; chair ad hoc com. Northridge Earthquake Recovery; ad hoc com. devel. reform; mem. local agy. formation com. L.A. City Coun.; mem. State Calif. Seismic Safety Commn., Pub. Safety Com., League of Calif.

Cities, City Planning Dept. Task Force, L.A., 1991; dir. alt. Met. Transp. Authority, L.A. County; bd. dirs. So. Calif. Regional Rail Authority; chmn. standing com. on implementation SCAG; mem. Regional Coun.; co-founder (with Mayor Richard Riordan) Develop Reform Com., 1995; mem. Entertainment Industry Devel. Bd., 1996; mem. Chatsworth Coord. Coun.; mem. Chatsworth Friends of Libr.; mem. Temple Ramat Zion Men's Club; mem. adv. bd. Am. Jewish Com., L.A.; mem. CSUN Pres.'s Club; founder North Valley YMCA Booster Club. Recipient Linz award San Fernando Bar Assn., 1982-83, Man of Yr. award Temple Ramat Zion, 1982-83, Newsmaker of Yr. award Valley Press Club, 1984, Gov.;s award for earthquake preparedness, Spl. award for seismic edn. Fed. Emergency Mgmt. Agy., Benefactor of Youth award North Valley YMCA, Golden Helmet award SAFE MOVES, Man of Yr. award Assn. Commuter Transit, 1995, Hon. Mem. award Structural Engrs., 1996. Mem. So. Calif. Assn. Govts. (chair valley area transp. study 1991), San Fernando Valley Industry Assn., Kiwanis, Jaycees (hon., life). Office: City Hall 200 N Main St Rm 319 Los Angeles CA 90012-4801*

BERNSON, MARCELLA SHELLEY, psychiatrist; b. N.Y.C., Aug. 24, 1952; d. Maxwell Isaac and Priscilla Edith (Zuckerman) Bernson. BA in Biology summa cum laude, Hofstra U., 1973; MD, Albert Einstein Coll. Medicine, 1976. Diplomate Am. Bd. Psychiatry and Neurology. Resident in psychiatry Bronx (N.Y.) Mcpl. Hosp. Ctr., 1976-79; assoc. dir. med. student edn. in psychiatry U. Medicine and Dentistry of N.J.-N.J. Med. Sch., Newark, 1979-81; pvt. practice psychiatry Westfield, N.J., 1981-86; cons. psychiatrist Healthwise EAP, Elizabeth, N.J., 1985-86; med. chief adult ambulatory svcs. dept. psychiatry Elizabeth Gen. Med. Ctr., 1986-87, asst. dir. dept. psychiatry, 1987-88; dir. tng. psychiat. svc. VA Med. Ctr., E. Orange, N.J., 1988-89; med. dir. partial care Occupl. Ctr. Union County, Roselle, N.J., 1989-92; cons. psychiatrist Union County Ednl. Svcs. Commn., Westfield, 1992-95; med. dir. Richard Hall CMHC, Bridgewater, N.J., 1995-99; with devel. disabilities ctr. Morristown (N.J.) Meml. Hosp., 1999—; instr. U. Medicine and Dentistry of N.J.-N.J. Med. Sch., Newark, 1979-81, asst. prof. clin. psychiatry, 1988-89; staff psychiatrist Elizabeth Gen. Med. Ctr., 1985-88, 92-95; profl. adv. com. Somerset County Mental Health Bd. Mem. Am. Psychiat. Assn., N.J. Psychiat. Assn. (tri-county chpt., Union County rep. 1989-90), Assn. Women Psychiatrists. Avocations: Am. art pottery, short fiction. Office: DDC Morristown Meml Hosp Box 60 100 Madison Ave Morristown NJ 07962

BERNSTEIN, AARON, magazine editor. BA, U. Calif., Santa Cruz. Corr UPI, London; reporter Forbes; mem. editl. staff Bus. Week mag. McGraw-Hill Cos., N.Y.C., 1983-85, labor editor, 1985—. Office: Bus Week McGraw-Hill Cos 1200 G St Washington DC 20005*

BERNSTEIN, AL, sports commentator; b. Sept. 15, 1950. Boxing analyst ESPN, 1980—; reporter all major championship fights SportsCenter ESPN; boxing analyst NBC Summer Olympics coverage, 1992. Author: Boxing for Beginners, 1978; contbr. KO Mag., The Ring mag.; contbg. editor Boxing Illustrated, 1978-80; editor Lerner Publs., Chgo., 1971-80; appeared in (film) Streets of Gold, 1986, Rocky V, (HBO mini-series) Glory Days; stage singer Las Vegas; singer (album) Al Bernstein—My Very Own Songs, 1987. Named commentator of yr. Boxing Illustrated, 1994, outstanding boxing commentator of yr. World Boxing Assn., 1989, broadcaster of yr. Rocky Marciano Found., 1993; named among Top 100 in Sports, Sport Mag., 1990; recipient Sam Taub award Boxing Writers Assn. Am., 1988, award for best news story Chgo. Newspaper Guild, 1975. Office: ESPN ESPN Plaza Bristol CT 06010*

BERNSTEIN, ALAN ARTHUR, oil company executive; b. Bklyn., Feb. 20, 1944; s. Lawrence and Ida (Slutsky) B.; m. Eleanor Gale Thorner, June 26, 1965; children: Andrew, Adam, Aaron, Aric. B.S. in Chem. Engring., CUNY, 1965; M.S. in Chem. Engring., U. Pa., 1966; M.B.A., Fairleigh Dickinson U., 1971. Engr. Exxon, Florham Park, N.J., 1966-69; planning engr. Amerada Hess Corp., N.Y.C., 1969-72, mgr. refinery econs., 1972-80, v.p., 1980-87, sr. v.p., 1987—. Mem. Am. Inst. Chem. Engrs. Jewish. Office: Amerada Hess Corp 1185 Ave Of The Americas New York NY 10036-2601

BERNSTEIN, BERNARD, lawyer, corporate executive; b. Bklyn., Feb. 9, 1929; s. Irving and Esther (Schriro) B.; m. Carmel Roth, June 24, 1973. AB, Syracuse U., 1950; JD, Harvard U., 1953. Bar: N.Y. 1955. With Philipp Bros., Inc. subs. Salomon Inc. (formerly Minerals and Chems. Philipp, Englehard Minerals & Chems. Corp., Phibro-Salomon, Inc.), N.Y.C., 1965—; now pres., gen. counsel, sec. Philipp Bros., Inc. subs. Salomon Inc. (formerly Phibro-Salomon, Inc.), N.Y.C., also bd. dirs. Chmn. Speculum Musicae. With AUS, 1953-55. Mem. ABA, Am. Arbitration ASsn. (bd. dirs.). Home: 25 E 86th St New York NY 10028-0553 Office: Philipp Bros Inc 7 World Trade Ctr Fl 29 New York NY 10048-1102*

BERNSTEIN, BONNIE, reporter; b. Howell, N.J., Aug. 16, 1970. BS in Broadcast Journalism, U. Md. Sports and news dir. Sta. WXJN Radio, Lewes, Del., 1992-93; weekend news anchor Sta. WMDT-TV, Salisbury, Md., 1993; weekend sports anchor Sta. KRNV-TV and Sta. KRNV Radio, Reno, Nev., 1993-95; Chgo.-based corr. SportsCenter ESPN, 1995—; acad. All-Am. gymnast U. Md. Office: c/o ESPN ESPN Pla Bristol CT 06010*

BERNSTEIN, DANIEL LEWIS, lawyer; b. Durham, N.C., Aug. 19, 1937; s. Edward Morris and Edith (Lewis) B.; m. Ann Lust; children: Kenneth, Margaret. AB, Amherst Coll., 1959; LLB, Harvard U., 1962. Bar: N.Y. 1962, D.C. 1976. Assoc. Law Offices of A.L. Bienstock, N.Y.C., 1962-66; assoc. Hale Russell & Gray, N.Y.C., 1966-69, ptnr., 1970-84; ptnr. Reid & Priest, N.Y.C., 1984-91, mng. ptnr., 1990-91; ptnr. Mannheimer Swartling, Stockholm, Sweden, N.Y.C., 1991-93, Law Office of Daniel L. Bernstein, N.Y.C., 1994—; sr. v.p., gen. counsel Lantis Eyewear Corp., N.Y.C., 1996—; trustee Georges Lurcy Charitable and Ednl. Trust, N.Y.C., 1982—. Dir. The Arts and Scis. Found. U. N.C., Chapel Hill, 1994—, The Colleen Giblin Endowment Fund for Child Neurology Rsch., Oradell, N.J., 1994—. Mem. ABA, Bar Assn. of City of N.Y., Internat. Bar Assn. Office: 90 Park Ave Rm 1500 New York NY 10016-1301

BERNSTEIN, DONALD CHESTER, brokerage company executive, lawyer; b. St. Louis, July 29, 1942; s. Michael Charles and Laura (Schmidt) B.; m. Estelle Marla Cohen, Jan. 17, 1946; children: Kimberleigh, Chad, Aaron. BSBA, Washington U., 1964, JD, 1967; LLM, U. London, 1968. Bar: Mo. 1967. V.p., counsel A.G. Edwards & Sons, Inc., St. Louis, 1969—. Mem. Mo. Bar Assn., Bar Assn. Met. St. Louis. Republican. Jewish. Home: 22 Twin Springs Ln Saint Louis MO 63124-1138 Office: A G Edwards & Sons Inc One N Jefferson Ave Saint Louis MO 63103

BERNSTEIN, EDWIN S., judge; b. Long Beach, N.Y., Aug. 15, 1930; s. Harry and Lena (Strizver) B.; children: Debora, Andrea, David. BA, U. Pa., 1952; LLB, Columbia U., 1955. Bar: N.Y. 1955, U.S. Ct. Appeals (2d cir.) 1962, U.S. Dist. Ct. (ea. and so. dists.) N.Y. 1962, U.S. Tax Ct. 1962, U.S. Supreme Ct. 1964, Md. 1981, D.C. 1982. Mem. bd. contract appeals Dept. Army, Heidelberg, Fed. Republic Germany, 1968-72; regional counsel U.S. Navy, Quincy, Mass., 1972-73; adminstrv. law judge U.S. Dept. Labor, Washington, 1973-79, Fed. Mine Safety and Health Rev. Commn., Washington, 1979-81, U.S. Postal Svc., Washington, 1981-87, USDA, Washington, 1987—; liaison rep. Administrv. Conf. of U.S., Washington, 1983-84; guest lectr. SUNY-Albany, 1978, U. Md., 1982, George Washington U., 1984. Author: U.S. Army Procurement Handbook, 1971; Establishing Federal Administrative Law Judges as an Independent Corps, 1984, also articles. Bd. dirs. Washington Hebrew Congregation, 1985-88. Recipient Meritorious Civilian Svc. award Dept. Army, 1972. Mem. ABA, Fed. Bar Assn., D.C. Bar Assn., Fed. Adminstr. Law Judges Conf. (pres. 1983-84), Papermill Assn. (pres. 1980-81). Lodge: Masons. Avocations: golf; bridge; sailing; wines; opera. Home: 5702 Balsam Grove Ct Rockville MD 20852-5551 Office: USDA 1049 South Bldg Independence Ave and 14th St SW Washington DC 20250

BERNSTEIN, ELLIOT LOUIS, television executive; b. N.Y.C., May 14, 1934; s. George Rubin and Renee (Horlick) B.; m. Marcy Adrienne Rosen, June 3, 1979; children: Joan, Daniel, Julie, Lisa. B.A., Bklyn. Coll., 1958. Writer, reporter, editor, TV producer UPI, N.Y.C., 1958-63; with ABC News, N.Y.C., 1963-66; bur. chief ABC News, Saigon, 1966-67, Chgo., 1967-69; dir. news KGO TV, San Francisco, 1969-71; asst. news dir. ABC TV, N.Y.C., 1971; weekend news producer ABC TV, 1972, spl. events producer, 1972-78; news producer CBS, N.Y.C., 1978; adj. faculty Grad. Sch. Journalism, Columbia U. Producer: Sunday Morning, 1978-79, Morning News, 1979-80; exec. producer: Morning with Charles Kuralt, 1980-81; producer: Sixty Minutes, 1981-85, West 57th, 1985—; sr. producer: On the Road with Charles Kuralt, 1983—, The American Parade, 1984—, Try To Remember, 1988—, Sunday Morning, 1988—. Served with AUS, 1958. Recipient Silver Gavel, 1976, Janus award Am. Mortgage Bankers Assn., 1976, Emmy award, 1984, EDI award Nat. Easter Seals Soc., 1994, Peabody award, 1998. Mem. Writers Guild Am. East. Office: CBS News Sunday Morning 524 W 57th St New York NY 10019-2924

BERNSTEIN, ELLIOT ROY, chemistry educator; b. N.Y.C., Apr. 14, 1941; s. Leonard H. Bernstein and Geraldine (Roman) Goldberg; m. Barbara Wyman, Dec. 19, 1965; children—Jephta, Rebecca. A.B., Princeton U., 1963; Ph.D., Calif. Inst. Tech., 1967. Postdoctoral fellow U. Chgo., 1967-69; asst. prof. Princeton U., N.J., 1969-75; assoc. prof. Colo. State U., Ft. Collins, 1975-80, prof. chemistry, 1980—; cons. Los Alamos Nat. Lab., 1975-83, Philip Morris, 1984-91, Du Pont Corp., 1985-92. Contbr. articles to profl. jours. NSF fellow, 1961-62; Woodrow Wilson fellow, 1963-64, JSPS fellow, 1996, Third Cycle in Chemistry lectr., Switzerland, 1998. Fellow Am. Phys. Soc.; mem. AAAS, Am. Chem. Soc., Sigma Xi. Office: Colo State U Dept Chemistry Condensed Matter Scis Lab Fort Collins CO 80523

BERNSTEIN, ERIC MARTIN, lawyer; b. Passaic, N.J., May 5, 1957; s. Abbot Alan and Jean Hausman (Schwartz) B. BA, Drew U., 1979; JD, U. Okla., 1982; MS in Indsl. and Labor Rels., Cornell U., 1985. Bar: N.J. 1982, U.S. Dist. Ct. N.J. 1982, D.C. 1985, U.S. Ct. Appeals (3d cir.) 1985, U.S. Supreme Ct. 1986. Assoc. Mandelbaum Salsburg Gold & Lazaris, East Orange, N.J., 1982-83; pvt. practice Clifton, N.J., 1983-84; sr. assoc. Gerald L. Dorf, P.A., Rahway, N.J., 1984-87; of counsel Vaida & Vaida, P.C., Flemington, N.J., 1987-88; pvt. practice Bridgewater, Clifton and Three Bridges, N.J., 1988-92; ptnr. Weiner Lesniak, Parsippany, N.J., 1992-97, Mauro Savo Camerino & Grant, Somerville, N.J., 1998—; lectr. Bur. Govt. Rsch., Rutgers U., New Brunswick, N.J., 1983—; mem. adj. faculty Raritan Valley C.C., Somerville, N.J., 1988-90; city atty. City of Passaic, N.J., 1990-92; mcpl. atty. Washington Twp.-Warren County, 1991—, Hardwick Twp.-Warren County, 1992—, West Windsor-Mercer County, 1993-97, North Plainfield-Somerset County, 1997—, Bethlehem Twp.-Hunterdon County, 1998—, Stillwater Twp.-Sussex County, 1998—, Paramus Borough-Bergen County, 1999—, Franklin Township-Hunterdon County, 1999—, Union City-Hudson County, 1999—; bd. atty. Englewood Bd. Edn.-Bergen County, 1996-99, Lincoln Park Bd. Edn.-Morris County, 1997—. Asst. editor, coauthor: Governing New Jersey Municipalities, 1984, co-editor, author, 6th edit., 1995; asst. editor N.J. Mcpl. Attys. Mag., 1984-92; editor N.J. State Bar Assn. Local Govt. Law Newsletter, 1995—. Vol. atty. Lawyers for the Arts, N.J., 1986—. Mem. ABA, Fed. Bar Assn., N.J. Bar Assn. (1st vice chair local govt. law sect. 1995—), D.C. Bar Assn., Passaic County Bar Assn., Somerset County Bar Assn. Republican. Jewish. Avocations: tennis, golf, stamp collecting, classical and jazz music. Home: 10 Timberline Dr Bridgewater NJ 08807-1204 Office: PO Box 1277 77 N Bridge St Somerville NJ 08876-1918

BERNSTEIN, FLORENCE HENDERSON See HENDERSON, FLORENCE

BERNSTEIN, GEORGE L., lawyer, accountant; b. Phila., Feb. 22, 1932; s. Leon B. and Elizabeth (Seidman) B.; m. Phyllis Wagner, June 27, 1954; children: Harris, Lisa. BS in Econs., U. Pa., 1953, JD cum laude, 1956. Bar: Pa. 1957; CPA, Pa. Accountant Laventhol & Horwath, Phila., 1950-90, exec. ptnr., chief exec. officer, 1980-90; chief oper. officer Dilworth, Paxon, Attys., Phila., 1991-94; CFO, CAO HFA, Inc., Exec. Search Cons., Phila., 1994—. Nat. chmn. profl. divsn. State of Israel Bonds, 1988-90; co-chmn. bd. trustees Am. Jewish Congress, Phila., 1988-90; bd. dirs. Mann Music Ctr., Phila.; trustee Einstein Health Care Network, Phila. Recipient Humanitarian award State of Israel Bonds, 1989. Mem. AICPA (coun. 1976-79, 81-87, strategic planning com. 1986-90, v.p. 1986-87, bd. dirs. 1981-84, com. small and medium sized firms 1978-80, MAS exec. com. 1971-75), Pa. Inst. CPAs (pres. 1976-77, com.m on past pres., chmn. MAS com., long-range objectives com., budget and fin. com.), Locust Club (pres. 1990-92, exec. com., bd. dirs.). Democrat. Avocations: golf, walking, music, theatre.

BERNSTEIN, GERALD WILLIAM, management consultant, researcher; b. Boston, Nov. 25, 1947; s. Alan Irwin and Anne (Fine) B.; m. Kathleen Ann Chaikin, Jan. 12, 1985. BS in Aero. Engring., Rensselaer Poly. Inst., 1969; MS in Engring., Stanford U., 1978. Transp. engr., dept. transp. State of N.Y., Albany, 1969-70; transp. planner Kennebec Regional Planning Com., Winslow, Me., 1974-77; dir. transp. dept. SRI Internat., Menlo Park, Calif., 1979-95; v.p. BACK Mgmt. Svcs., San Francisco, 1995-98; mng. dir. Stanford Transp. Group, San Francisco, 1998—; session chmn. aviation workshop NSF, 1985, 91; profl. conf. chmn.; bd. dirs. GlobTran Corp., 1993-98. Contbr. articles to profl. jours. Chmn. transp. com. Glenn Park Neighborhood Assn., San Francisco, 1982-85; dir. Balboa Terrace Neighborhood Assn., San Francisco, 1986-88; trustee Congregation Beth Israel-Judea, 1991-93. With U.S. Army, 1970-72. Recipient Cert. Appreciation City of Waterville, Maine, 1977. Mem. Am. Inst. Aeronautics and Astronautics (sr. mem.), Transp. Research Bd. of Nat. Research Council. Democrat. Jewish. Club: Toastmasters (Menlo Park, pres. 1986). Avocations: flying, skiing. Office: Stanford Transp Group 236 W Portal Ave Ste 359 San Francisco CA 94127-1423

BERNSTEIN, H. BRUCE, lawyer; b. Omaha, Dec. 9, 1943; s. David and Muriel (Krasne) B.; m. Janice Ostroff, Aug. 27, 1967; children: Daniel J., Jill M. AB, Cornell U., 1965; JD, Harvard U., 1968. Bar: Ill. 1968. Ptnr. Sidley & Austin, Chgo., 1974—. Bd. dirs. Jewish Family and Community Svc. Agy. Mem. ABA, Ill. Bar Assn., Chgo. Bar Assn., Am. Coll. Comml. Fin. Lawyers, Am. Coll. Bankruptcy, Nat. Bankruptcy Conf., Standard Club, Mid-Day Club, Northmoor Country Club, Harvard Club. Avocation: golf. Home: 1740 W Summit Ct Deerfield IL 60015-1817 Office: Sidley & Austin 1 First Natl Plz Ste 4500 Chicago IL 60603-2003

BERNSTEIN, I(RVING) MELVIN, university official and dean, materials scientist; b. N.Y.C., N.Y., Oct. 14, 1938; s. Emanuel and Helen (Wolitzer) B.; m. Katherine Sarah Russo, June 7, 1964; 1 child, Elana. B.S., Columbia U., 1960, M.S., 1962, Ph.D., 1965. Postdoctoral assoc. Central Electricity Generating Bd., Berkeley, Eng., 1966-67; scientist U.S. Steel Research Lab., Monroeville, Pa., 1967-72; from asst. prof. to prof. Carnegie-Mellon U., Pitts., 1972-87, assoc. dean engring., 1978-82, prof., head dept. metall. engring and materials sci., 1982-87; provost, acad. vice pres. Ill. Inst. Tech., Chgo., 1987-90, chancellor, 1990-91; v.p. arts, scis. & tech., dean of faculty Tufts U., Medford, Mass., 1991—; chief cons. MCL, Monroeville, 1972-82; liaison scientist Office Naval Research, London, 1977-78; mem. Nat. Materials adv. bd., 1990-96. Co-editor: Handbook of Stainless Steel, 1977, Hydrogen Effects in Metals, 1973, 76, 1981; assoc. editor Metall. Trans., 1977-82. Mem. Pitts. Dem. Com., 1971-75; bd. govs. Ben Gurion U., Israel, 1993—. Jewish.

BERNSTEIN, JANE, writer; b. Bklyn., June 10, 1949; d. David and Ruth (Levinson) B.; m. Paul Glynn; children: Charlotte, Rachel. BA, NYU, 1971; MFA, Columbia U., 1977. Asst. prof. creative writing Carnegie Mellon U., Pitts. Author: Departures, 1979, Seven Minutes in Heaven, 1986, (nonfiction) Loving Rachel, 1988, various short stories, screenplays, mag. articles. Fellow N.J. Council on the Arts, 1981, 86, Nat. Endowment for the Arts, 1983. Mem. Authors Guild, Writers Guild Am. East, Nat. Writers Union, PEN.

BERNSTEIN, JAY, pathologist, researcher, educator; b. N.Y.C., May 14, 1927; s. Michael Kenneth and Frances (Kaufman) B.; m. Carol Irene Kritchman, Aug. 11, 1957; children: John Abel, Michael Kenneth. BA, Columbia U., 1948; MD, SUNY, Bklyn., 1952. Diplomate Am. Bd. Pathology. Asst. pathologist Children's Hosp. Mich., Detroit, 1956-58, assoc. pathologist, 1959, attending pathologist, 1960-62, cons., 1975—; attending pathologist Bronx Mcpl. Hosp. Ctr., N.Y.C., 1962-68; asst. prof. pathology Albert Einstein Coll. Medicine, Bronx, N.Y., 1962-64, assoc. prof. pathology, 1964-68; dir. dept. anatomic pathology William Beaumont Hosp., Royal Oak, Mich., 1969-90, dir. Rsch. Inst., 1983-98, assoc. med. dir., 1990-98, hon. consulting staff, 1999—; chmn. sci. adv. bd. Nat. Kidney Found. Mich., 1986-88, nat. sci. adv. bd. mem., 1976-82; sci. advisor Nat. Inst. Child Health, USPHS, 1976-81; mem. profl. adv. bd. Nat. Tuberous Sclerosis Assn., 1990-93; clin. prof. pathology Wayne State U., Detroit, 1977—; clin. prof. health sci. Oakland U., Rochester, Mich., 1980-90; vis. prof. pathology Albert Einstein Coll. Medicine, Bronx, 1974—; mem. com. on renal disease WHO; cons. pathologist Internat. Study of Kidney Diseases in Children, Lupus Study Group. Co-editor: Perspectives in Pediatric Pathology; past contbg. editor Jour. Pediatrics; past mem. editl. bd. Pediatric Nephrology; mem. editl. bd. Jour. Urologic Pathology; contbr. articles to profl. jours. With USN, 1945-46. Recipient Henry L. Barnett award Am. Acad. Pediats., 1997. Mem. AAAS, Am. Soc. Investigative Pathology, Internat. Acad. Pathology (U.S.-Can. divsn.), Am. Soc. Clin. Pathologists, Soc. Pediatric Pathology (co-founder, past pres., Farber lectr. 1982, Spl. Disting. Colleague award 1987, 97), Am. Pediatric Soc., Am. Soc. Nephrology, Renal Pathology Soc. (past pres., Renal Pathology Founder award 1997), Am. Soc. Pediatric Nephrology (founder's award 1999). Office: William Beaumont Rsch Inst 3601 W 13 Mile Rd Royal Oak MI 48073-6712

BERNSTEIN, JOAN Z., government official; m. Lionel Bernstein; 3 children. BA in Econs., U. Wis.; JD, Yale U. Pvt. practice Washington; gen. counsel EPA, Washington, Dept. Health and Human Svcs., Washington; asst. to dir., dep. dir. and acting dir. Bur. Consumer Protection, FTC, Washington, 1970-76, dir., 1995—; chmn. Commn. on Wartime Relocation and Internment of Civilians. Mem. Yale U. Law Sch. Alumni Assn. (past pres.). Office: Federal Trade Commn 6th and Pennsylvania Ave NW Washington DC 20580*

BERNSTEIN, JONINE LISA, biometry researcher, epidemiologist, educator; b. San Francisco, Aug. 4, 1958; d. Cal and Roz (Kasden) B.; m. Randy M. Mastro; 1 child, Arianna Clara. AB, Brown U., 1981; MS in Applied Biometry, U. So. Calif., 1983; PhD in Epidemiology, Yale U., 1992. Indsl. hygienist divsn. occupational health and radiation control R.I. Dept. Health, Providence, 1978; project dir. Policy Rsch. Inc., Balt., 1980; biostatis. cons. dept. biometry, project coord. dept. ophthalmology U. So. Calif., L.A., 1981-83, biostatistician, project coord. divsn. occupational medicine, 1983; rsch. asst. environ. scis. lab. Mt. Sinai Sch. Medicine, N.Y.C., 1978-79, 80, biostatistician dept. biomath. scis., 1983-86, instr. biostats. and epidemiology, 1983-87, rsch. assoc., 1986-87, biostatis. cons. dept. cardiology, 1987-92; rsch. asst. prof. lab. epidemiology and biostats. Kaplan Ctr. and Inst. Environ. Med./NYU Med. Ctr., N.Y.C., 1992-94; asst. prof. dept. cmty. medicine Mt. Sinai Sch. Medicine, 1994—; student project coord. Brown U., Providence, 1979-80, student instr. occupational safety and health, 1980; project coord. L.A. Com. on Occupational Safety and Health, 1981-83; rsch. assoc. Sch. Epidemiology and Pub. Health, Yale U., New Haven, 1991-92; teaching asst. dept. biometry U. So. Calif., 1982; presenter profl. confs. Co-contbr. articles to sci. jours. Vol. coord. R.I. Com. on Occupational Safety and Health, Providence, 1977-81. Nat. Rsch. Svc. tng. grantee Yale U., 1987-89, 89-91, rsch. grantee dept. med. affairs Conn. divsn. Am. Cancer Soc., 1991. Mem. AAAS, Am. Assn. Cancer Rschrs., Am. Soc. Preventive Oncology (Best Poster award 1994), Soc. Epidemiologic Rsch. (Abraham M. Lilienfeld Student Prize Competition award 1992), N.Y. Acad. Scis. Democratic. Jewish. Home: 8 E 96th St # 16C New York NY 10128-0706 Office: Mt Sinai Sch Medicine Dept Cmty & Preventive Med PO Box 1043 New York NY 10029-0310

BERNSTEIN, JOSEPH, lawyer; b. New Orleans, Feb. 12, 1930; s. Eugene Julian and Lola (Schlemoff) B.; m. Phyllis Maxine Askanase, Sept. 4, 1955; children: Jill, Barbara, Elizabeth R, Jonathan Joseph. BS, U. Ala., 1952, LLB, Tulane U., 1957. Bar: La., 1957. Clk. to Justice E. Howard McCaleb of La. Supreme Ct., 1957; assoc. Jones, Walker, Waechter, Poitevent, Carrere & Denegre, 1957-60, ptnr., 1960-65; pvt. practice New Orleans, 1965—; former gen. counsel Alliance for Affordable Energy. Past pres. New Orleans Jewish Community Ctr., Met. New Orleans chpt. March of Dimes. Trustee New Orleans Symphony Soc.; past mem. adv. council New Orleans Mus. Art; past nat. exec. com. Am. Jewish Com. 2d lt. AUS, 1952-54. Mem. ABA, La. Bar Assn., New Orleans Bar Assn., Phi Delta Phi, Zeta Beta Tau. Republican. Jewish. Home: 708 Explanade Ave Bay Saint Louis MS 39520

BERNSTEIN, JOSEPH, orthopedic surgeon, philosopher; b. N.Y.C., Dec. 18, 1962. AB magna cum laude, Columbia Coll., 1984; MD, Cornell Med. Coll., 1990; MS, Harvard U., 1990. Diplomate Nat. Bd. Med. Examiners. Orthopedic surgeon U. Pa., Phila., 1990—, asst. prof. orthopedic surgery, 1996—; sr. fellow Leonard Davis Inst. of Health Econs., 1993—; team physician U. Pa., 1996—; mem. Ivy League Team Physicians Group, 1996—. Recipient Founder's award Ea. Orthopedic Assn., 1993. Mem. AMA, Am. Acad. Orthopedic Surgery, Medicine & Philosophy Soc. (Scheiss prize 1996), Pa. Med. Soc., Phila. Med. Soc., Phila. Soc. Sports Medicine, Phi Beta Kappa, Alpha Omega Alpha. Jewish. Office: U Pa 3400 Spruce St Philadelphia PA 19104-4204

BERNSTEIN, LESTER, editorial consultant; b. N.Y.C., July 18, 1920; s. Isidore and Rebecca (Axelrod) B.; m. Jacqueline Lipscomb, Feb. 6, 1946; children: Lynn, Nina, Paul, Daniel. A.B., Columbia U., 1940. Reporter N.Y. Times, 1940-48; writer, fgn. corr., editor Time mag., 1948-58; dir. info. NBC, 1958-60, v.p. corp. affairs, 1960-62; nat. affairs editor Newsweek, 1963-65, exec. editor, 1965-69, mng. editor, 1969-72, editor, 1979-82; editorial cons., 1982-85; v.p. corporate communications RCA Corp., 1973-79. Cons. N.Y. Internat. Festival of the Arts, 1987-92. Club: Century Assn. Home: 44 Buxton St Long Beach NY 11561-5009

BERNSTEIN, LIONEL M., gastroenterologist, educator; b. Chgo., Sept. 10, 1923; married, 1952; 3 children. BS, U. Ill., 1944, MD, 1945, MS, 1951, PhD in Physiology, 1954. Diplomate Am. Bd. Internal Medicine. Rsch. assoc. med. and clin. sci. U. Ill., 1952-53, instr. med. and physiology, 1953-54; chief metabolism rsch. divsn. Med. Nutrition Lab. Fitzsimmons Army Hosp., Denver, 1954-55; physician sr. grade VA Hosp., Sepulveda, Calif., 1955-56; chief gastroent. sect. VA Hosp., Hines, Ill., 1956-57, assoc. chief of staff, 1957-62; chief med. svcs. VA West Side Hosp., Chgo., 1962-67; dir. rsch. svc. VA Ctr. Office, 1967-70; assoc. dir. extramural programs Nat. Inst. Arthritis and Metabolism Disorders, 1970-73; dir. office program ops. HEW, 1973-74; spl. asst. Office Asst. Sec. Health, 1975-77; asst. dep. dir. rsch. and edn. Lister Hill Nat. Ctr. Biomed. Nat. Libr. Medicine, 1977-78, dir., 1978-83; prof. health professions edn. Coll. Medicine, acting head U. Ill., 1985-88, 88-90, prof. med. edn. Coll. Medicine, 1988—; vet. adminstrn. mem. Gen. Med. Study Sect., NIH, 1962-67; clin. prof. medicine George Washington U., 1982—; pres. Knowledge Sys., Inc., 1983—. Fellow AAAS, ACP; mem. Inst. Med.-NAS, AMA, Am. Gastroent. Assn., Am. Fedn. Clin. Rsch., Am. Med. Informatics Assn., Am. Coll. Med. Informatics. Office: 1802 Kalorama Sq NW Washington DC 20008-4022*

BERNSTEIN, MARK R., retired lawyer; b. York, Pa., Apr. 7, 1930; s. Phillip G. Bernstein and Evelyn (Greenfield) Spielman; m. E. Louise Bernstein, May 10, 1955; children: Phillip, Cary, Adam, Andrew, Jonathan, Evan. BA, U. Pa., 1952; JD, Yale U., 1957. Bar: N.C., U.S. Dist. Ct. (we. dist.) N.C., U.S. Ct. Appeals, U.S. Custom Ct. Atty. Kennedy, Covington, Lobdell, & Hickman, Charlotte, N.C., 1957-60, Haynes, Graham, Bernstein & Baucom, Charlotte, N.C., 1960-67; atty. Parker, Poe, Adams & Bernstein, Charlotte, N.C., 1968-98, chmn., 1963-68; bd. dirs. Family Dollar Stores, Inc., Nat. Welders Supply Co., Inc. Bd. dirs., vice-chmn. The Found. of the Carolinas, Inc., Charlotte Symphony Orchestra, The Wildacres Found.; past pres. Charlotte Symphony Assn.; past chmn. mayor's com. for a Performing Arts Ctr., 1983-85, com. mem. Performing Arts Ctr. Task Force, 1987; chmn. N.C. Econ. Devel. Bd.; past pres. Temple Beth El, Charlotte Jewish Cmty. Ctr., Charlotte Civitan Club, Am. Symphony Orch. League, Golden Circle Theatre, Found. of Shalom Park; past mem. exec. com. Yale Law Sch.; past mem. bd. N.C. Blumenthal Performing Arts Ctr. Recipient Disting. Svc. award Jaycees, 1961, State of Israel Humanitarian award, 1981, Charlotte Fedn. of Jewish Charities A Man of the Ages award, 1985, Silver Medallion award NCCJ, 1995, Israel Humanitarian award, The Vanguard award for personal svcs. Arts and Sci. Coun., 1998. Mem. Mecklenburg County Bar Assn. (past pres.), Charlotte City Club, The Tower Club (bd. dirs.), Olde Providence Racquet Club (past pres.). Democrat. Home: 5300 Hardison Rd Charlotte NC 28226-6426

BERNSTEIN, MARTIN, musicologist, bassist; b. N.Y.C., Dec. 14, 1904; s. Joseph and Ida (Colodny) B.; m. Juliet Danziger, Apr. 26, 1930 (dec. June 1948); children: Ellen, James; m. Virginia Leila Lubkin, Aug. 26, 1949; children: Roger, John. BS, N.Y.U., 1925, MusB, 1927. Bassist N.Y. Philharm. Orch., N.Y.C., 1926-28; from instr. to prof. emeritus NYU, N.Y.C., 1926-72, prof. emeritus, 1972—, head dept., 1955-70; condr. Purcell Operas, 1933-41, Bach Cantatas, 1936-43, 1951-72; lectr. in field 1950-72; music faculty Harvard U., 1965. Author: Score Reading, 1936,98; co-author: Introduction to Music, 1937, 4th edit., 1941. 1st lt. Mil. Intelligence, 1943-45, ETO. Recipient Great Teacher award, N.Y.U. Alumni Assn., 1971. Mem. Am. Bach Soc. (hon.), Am. Beethoven Assn. (bd. dirs.), Am. Musicological Soc., Am. Topical Assn., Music Libr. Assn. Avocations: photography, philately. Home: One Blackstone Pl Bronx NY 10471

BERNSTEIN, MERTON CLAY, lawyer, educator, arbitrator; b. N.Y.C., Mar. 26, 1923; s. Benjamin and Ruth (Frederica (Kleeblatt)) B.; m. Joan Barbara Brodshaug, Dec. 17, 1955; children: Johanna Karin, Inga Saterlie, Matthew Curtis, Rachel Libby. B.A., Oberlin Coll., 1943; LL.B., Columbia U., 1948. Bar: N.Y. 1948, U.S. Supreme Ct. 1952. Assoc. Schlesinger & Schlesinger, 1948; atty. NLRB, 1949-50, 50-51, Office of Solicitor, U.S. Dept. Labor, 1950; counsel Nat. Enforcement Commn., 1951, U.S. Senate Subcom. on Labor, 1952; legis. asst. to U.S. Sen. Wayne L. Morse, 1953-56; counsel U.S. Senate Com. on R.R. Retirement, 1957-58; spl. counsel U.S. Senate Subcom. on Labor, 1958; assoc. prof. law U. Nebr., 1958-59; lectr., sr. fellow Yale U. Law Sch., 1960-65; prof. law Ohio State U., 1965-75; Walter D. Coles prof. law Washington U., St. Louis, 1975-96, Walter D. Coles prof. emeritus, 1997—; mem. adv. com. to Sec. of Treas. on Coordination of Social Security and pvt. pension plans, 1967-68; prin. cons. Nat. Commn. on Social Security Reform, 1982-83; vis. prof. Columbia U. Law Sch., 1967-68, Leiden U., 1975-76; mem. adv. com. rsch. U.S. Social Security Adminstrn., 1967-68, chmn., 1969-70; cons. Adminstrv. Conf. of the U.S., 1989, Dept. Labor, 1966-67, Russell Sage Found., 1967-68, NSF, 1970-71, Ctr. for the Study of Contemporary Problems, 1968-71. Author: The Future of Private Pensions, 1964, Private Dispute Settlement, 1969, (with Joan B. Bernstein) Social Security: The System That Works, 1988; contbr. articles to profl. jours. Mem. Bethany (Conn.) Planning and Zoning Commn., 1962-65, Ohio Retirement Study Commn., 1967-68; co-chmn. transition team for St. Louis Mayor Freeman Bosley Jr., 1993; bd. dirs. St. Louis Theatre Project, 1981-84; pres. bd. Met. Sch. Columbus, Ohio, 1974-75; del. White House Conf. Aging, 1995. With AUS, 1943-45. Fulbright fellow, 1975-76, Elizar Wright award, 1965. Mem. ABA (sec. sect. labor rels. law 1968-69), Internat. Assn. for Labor Law and Social Security (bd. dirs. U.S. chpt. 1973-83, 88-91), Fulbright Alumni Assn. (bd. dirs. 1976-78), Indsl. Rels. Rsch. Assn., Nat. Acad. Arbitrators, Am. Arbitration Assn. (mem. adv. com. St. Louis region 1987—), Nat. Acad. Social Ins. (founding mem., bd. dirs. 1986-91). Democrat. Jewish. E-mail: bernstem@wulaw.wustl.edu. Office: Washington U Sch Law Campus Box 1120 Saint Louis MO 63130

BERNSTEIN, MICHAEL ALAN, history educator, department chairman; b. 1954. BA in Econs. magna cum laude, Yale U., 1976, MA in Econs., 1978, MPhil in Econs., 1980, PhD in Econs., 1982. Instr. for the preliminary examinations in econs. Faculty Econs. and Politics, U. Cambridge, Eng., 1976-77; staff economist Office of Integrative Analysis Energy Info. Adminstrn., U.S. Dept. Energy, Washington, 1978; lectr. in econs. Mills Coll., Oakland, Calif., 1979; acting instr. econs. Yale U., 1980, asst. prof. history and associated faculty mem. dept. econs., 1982-87; asst. prof. history U. Calif., San Diego, 1987-88, assoc. prof. history, 1988-91, assoc. prof. history, associated faculty mem. dept. econs., 1991—, chair dept. history, 1992—; chair undergrad. program com. and departmental rep. dept. history Princeton U., 1983-84, 85-86, mem. priorities com. on the budget, 1985-87; co-chair Columbia U. Seminar in Econ. History, 1985-86; dir. grad. studies in U.S. history dept. history U. Calif., San Diego, 1988-89, mem. chancellor's com. on the status of women, 1989-91, mem. rep. assembly of the acad. senate, 1990-92, chair undergrad. curriculum and advising com. dept. history, 1990-92, vice-chair dept. history, 1990-92, prin. investigator Calif. History-Social Sci. Project, 1994—, mem. adv. com. Office of Sexual Harassment Prevention and Policy, 1994—; mem. steering com. U. Calif. Intercampus Group in Econ. History, 1988—. Author: The Great Depression: Delayed Recovery and Economic Change in America, 1929-39, 1987, Japanese edit., 1991; co-editor (with D. Adler) Understanding American Economic Decline, 1994; mem. editl. bd. Jour. Econ. History, 1989-94; contbr. articles to profl. jours. Fulbright scholar Christ's Coll., Cambridge, Eng., 1976-77, Univ. Grad. fellow and Falk Found. fellow in econs. Yale U., 1977-81, ACLS fellow for studies in modern soc. and values, 1985, ACLS Postdoctoral fellow for sr. scholars, 1990, Andrew E. Mellon fellow Nat. Humanities Ctr., Research Triangle Park, N.C., 1990; Hoover scholar Herbert Hoover Presdl. Libr. Assn., West Branch, Iowa, 1991; recipient Grant-in-Aid, Econ. History Assn., 1982. Mem. Am. Econs. Assn., Am. Hist. Assn. (mem. com. on the Albert J. Beveridge Award and the John H. Dunning Prize 1991-93, chair 1993), Econ. History Assn. (com. on rsch. in econ. history 1994—), Orgn. Am. Historians (mem. Ellis Hawley Prize Organizing Com. 1994—), Am. Coun. Learned Socs. (mem. acad. adv. com. of the Am. studies program 1990—). Home: 4608 Delaware St San Diego CA 92116-1006 Office: U Calif San Diego Dept History 0104 9500 Gilman Dr La Jolla CA 92093-0104*

BERNSTEIN, MITCHELL HARRIS, lawyer; b. N.Y.C., Sept. 19, 1949; s. Melvin and Gladys (Weissman) B.; m. Barbara Veitch, Oct. 8, 1978; children: Jonathan, Matthew, Emily. AB, U. Pa., 1970; JD, Yale U., 1973. Bar: N.Y. 1974, U.S. Ct. Appeals (2d cir.) 1974, U.S. Dist. Ct. (so. and ea. dists.) N.Y. 1974, U.S. Ct. Appeals (5th and D.C. cirs.) 1980, U.S. Supreme Ct. 1980, D.C. 1981, U.S. Ct. Appeals (4th cir.) 1981, U.S. Dist. Ct. D.C. 1982, U.S. Ct. Appeals (3d cir.) 1985. Assoc. Breed, Abbott & Morgan, N.Y.C., 1974-77; sr. atty. U.S. EPA, Washington, 1977-81; assoc. Skadden, Arps, Slate, Meagher & Flom, Washington, 1981-83, ptnr., 1983-93; mem. Van Ness Feldman, Washington, 1994—. Bd. advisors Chem. Waste Litigation Reporter, Washington, 1985—. Mem. ABA, D.C. Bar. Assn. Office: Van Ness Feldman Ste 7 1050 Thomas Jefferson St NW Washington DC 20007-3837

BERNSTEIN, PAUL, retired academic dean; b. Phila., Jan. 19, 1927; s. Abraham and Jennie (Geek) B.; m. Irma Shuster, Apr. 10, 1949; children: Jay Ira, Lisa Beth. BS, Temple U., 1949, MEd, 1950; PhD, U. Pa., 1955. Tchr. social scis. Phila. pub. schs., 1949-55; prof. European history, chmn. social scis. dept. Lock Haven (Pa.) State Coll., 1955-64, Plattsburg (N.Y.) State U. Coll., 1964-66; dean Coll. Gen. Studies, Rochester Inst. Tech., 1966-76, dean grad. studies, 1976-92, ret., 1993; tchr. Elderhostel, Bradenton, Fla., 1998-99. Author: (with R. Green) History of Civilization, 2d edit., 1962, Career Education and the Quality of Working Life, 1980, American Work Values, 1997; mng. editor Lock Haven Bull., 1959-64; author articles on Swedish labor mgmt. issues capitalism and consumerism; manuscript reviewer Polity Press, 1998. Co-chmn. Citizens for Humphrey, Monroe County, N.Y., 1968. Served with AUS, 1944-47. Grantee Am. Philos. Soc., 1959; Grantee Swedish Bicentennial Com., 1980. Mem. Ind. Rel. Research Assn., Assn. Gen. and Liberal Studies (exec. bd., pres. 1978-79). Republican. Jewish. Club: Elks. Home: 1 Linden Cove Pittsford NY 14534-4614 Office: Rochester Inst Tech Rochester NY 14623

BERNSTEIN, PETER WALTER, publisher; b. N.Y.C., Oct. 27, 1951; s. Robert Louis and Helen (Walter) B.; m. Amy Brooks Daunis, Jan. 14, 1978; children: Elisabeth, Alexander, Nicholas. BA, Brown U., 1973; MA, Cambridge U., Eng., 1976. Reporter Pretoria (South Africa) News, 1973-74, N.Y. Daily News, N.Y.C., 1976-77; assoc. editor Fortune Mag., N.Y.C., 1977-82; bd. editors, Washington editor Fortune Mag., 1982-85; exec. editor U.S. News and World report, Washington, 1985-96; pub. Times Books, Random House, Inc., N.Y.C., 1996-99. Editor: Ernst & Young Tax Guide, 1985—; co-author: (with Amy Bernstein) Quotations from Speaker Newt, 1995; co-editor: (with Christopher Ma) The Practical Guide to Practically Everything, 1995, 3d edit., 1997. Trustee WETA, Washington, 1986-92, Tougaloo Coll., Jackson, Miss., 1988-94, Brown U., 1998—. Mem. Coun. on Fgn. Rels., Brown U. Alumni Assn. (pres. 1997-9).

BERNSTEIN, PHYLISS LOUISE, psychologist; b. Balt., Nov. 27, 1940; d. Samuel Wilfred and Helen Dorothy (Gerson) Wilke; m. Robert Bernstein, June 7, 1964; children: Steve, Susan, David. BA in Psychology summa cum laude, Avila Coll., 1980, MS in Psychology summa cum laude, 1981; PhD in Counseling Psychology with high honors, U. Mo., Kansas City, 1986. Lic. psychologist, Mo. Psychotherapist Community Counseling Ctr., Kansas City, Mo., 1983-85; assoc. psychologist Counseling and Human Devel. Svcs., Kansas City, Mo., 1985-86; ptnr., psychologist Profl. Psychol. Inst., Kansas City, Mo., 1996—; staff priviliges Bapt. Med. Ctr., Menorah Med. Ctr.; dir. Jewish Vocat. Svcs., Kansas City, 1988-91, U. Mo. Edn. Dept., Kansas City, 1991—, Jewish Family and Children Svcs., 1992—. Contbr. articles to profl. jours. Life mem. Nat. Coun. Jewish Women. Kansas City; bd. dirs. Avila Coll. Mem. APA, Nat. Register Health Svc. Providers in Psychology, Greater Kansas City Psychol. Assn., Phi Kappa Phi, Pi Lambda Theta, Psi Chi. Avocations: scuba diving, bungy jumping, snow skiing, horseback riding. Office: Counseling Psychologists 4901 Main St Ste 400 Kansas City MO 64112-2635

BERNSTEIN, RICHARD ALLEN, company executive; b. N.Y.C., June 28, 1946; s. Sidney and Ethel Helen (Shankman) B.; m. Amelia Fishman, Nov. 21, 1944; children: Bradley Ross, Jennifer Anne. BA in Econs., NYU, 1968. V.p. Pease & Ellman Inc., N.Y.C., 1968-70; pres. P&E Properties Inc., N.Y.C., 1970—; chmn. Western Pub. Co. Inc., N.Y.C., 1984-96; chmn., pres., CEO Western Pub. Group Inc., N.Y.C., 1984-96; chmn. Gen. Med. Corp., Richmond, Va., 1987-93, Harris Wholesale Co., Cleve., 1988-92; chmn., pres., CEO Rabco Health Svcs., Inc., N.Y.C., 1991-93; chmn. Millbrook Distbn. Svcs., Inc., Leicester, Mass., 1997—; chmn., CEO, Rabco Luxury Holdings LLC, 1997—, Breguet LLC, 1997—, B. Manischewitz Co., 1998—; chmn., pres., CEO Penn Corp., 1986-96; mem. adv. bd. Chase Manhattan Bank, 1985—; chmn., CEO, R.A.B. Holdings, Inc., 1996—, Millbrook Distbn. Svcs., Inc., 1997—, Breguet LLC, N.Y.C., 1997—, Rabco Luxury Holdings LLC, N.Y.C., 1997—. Trustee Police Athletic League, N.Y.C., 1982—, NYU, 1988—; bd. dirs. Big Apple Circus, Inc., 1992—, Hosp. for Joint Diseases, N.Y.C., N.Y. State Employee Retirement Sys., N.Y.C.; mem. N.Y. State Legis. Commn. on Expenditure Rev.; chmn. N.Y. State Commn. on Regulation of Lobbying, Albany, 1982-86; bd. overseers Stern Sch. Bus., NYU; candidate for compt. City of N.Y., 1981. With U.S. Army, 1969. Fellow Yeshiva U., N.Y.C., 1986. Mem. Econ. Club N.Y. Republican. Jewish.

BERNSTEIN, ROBERT, advertising executive; m. Phyliss Bernstein; children: Steven, David, Susan. Grad., U. Okla., 1960. With Potts Woodbury Advt., 1962-64; founder Bernstein-Rein, Kansas City, Mo., 1964—, pres, CEO; bd. dirs., chmn. Mark Twain Bank Kansas City. Active Youth Vol. Corps, Epilepsy Found., Heart Am. Shakespeare Festival, Met. Luth. Ministry, STOP Violence Coalition, Children's Pl., Children's Mercy Hosp., Genesis Sch., Ronald McDonald Houses, Variety Club Kansas City; pres. Starlight Theatre Assn.; bd. dirs. Kansas City Art Inst. Recipient Spirit of Kansas City award, 1991, Hy Vile Cmty. Svc. award, 1995, Advt. Profl. of Yr. award Am. Advt. Fedn., 1995, Manking award Cystic Fibrosis award, 1995. Mem. Am. Assn. Advt. Agys., Nat. Assn. Broadcasters. Office: Bernstein-Rein Advt Inc 4600 Madison Ave Ste 1500 Kansas City MO 64112-3012*

BERNSTEIN, ROBERT, retired physician, state official, former army officer; b. N.Y.C., Feb. 20, 1920; s. Morris and Rose (Gordich) B. BA, Vanderbilt U., 1942; MD, U. Louisville, 1946. Diplomate Nat. Bd. Med. Examiners, Am. Bd. Internal Medicine. Commd. 2d lt. U.S. Army, 1942, advanced through grades to maj. gen., 1973; intern Grasslands Hosp., Valhalla, N.Y., 1946-47; resident Walter Reed Army Med. Ctr., Washington, 1952-55, dep. comdr., 1972-73, comdg. gen., 1973-78; surgeon U.S. Mil. Assistance Command, Vietnam, 1970-72; ret., 1978; commr. for spl. health svcs. Tex. Dept. Health, Austin, 1978-80; commr. of health Tex. Dept. Health, 1980-91; adj. prof. U. Tex. Health Sci. Ctr., 1982—. Contbr. articles to mil. and med. jours. Decorated D.S.M. with oak leaf cluster, Legion of Merit with two oak leaf clusters, Bronze Star with oak leaf cluster, Purple Heart. Fellow ACP; mem. Soc. Med. Consultants to Armed Forces, Internat. Soc. Internal Medicine, Phi Delta Epsilon, Phi Kappa Phi, Alpha Epsilon Pi, Alpha Omega Alpha. Home: 3805 Greystone Dr Austin TX 78731-1505

BERNSTEIN, ROBERT LOUIS, publishing company executive; b. N.Y.C., Jan. 5, 1923; s. Alfred and Sylvia (Bloch) B.; m. Helen Walter, Nov. 23, 1950; children: Peter Walter, Tom Alfred, William Samuel. Grad., Lincoln Sch., N.Y.C., 1940; BS, Harvard U., 1944; LLD, New Sch. for Social Rsch., 1991; LLD (hon.), Swarthmore Coll., 1997. Gen. sales mgr. Simon & Schuster, Inc., N.Y.C., 1946-57; sales mgr. Random House, Inc., N.Y.C., 1957-62, 1st v.p., 1962-66, pres., 1966-67, chief exec. officer, 1967-89, chmn., 1975, chmn., pres., CEO, 1975-89; pub.-at-large John Wiley & Sons, N.Y.C., 1991-98; Bd. dirs. Am. Book Pubs. Bd. dirs. Dr. Seuss Found., Aaron Diamond Found.; chmn. Human Rights Watch, 1975—, founding chmn., 1990; mem. Human Rights Watch/Africa, Human Rights Watch/Ams., Human Rights Watch/Asia, Human Rights Watch/Middle East; founding chmn. Human Rights Watch/Helsinki, 1992; adv. com. Carter-Meril Human Rights Found.; mem. adv. bd. Robert F. Kennedy Found. Human Rights Award. With USAAF, 1943-46. Recipient Florina Lasker award N.Y. Civil Liberties Union, 1976, Human Rights award Lawyers Com. for Human Rights, 1987, Spirit of Liberty award People for the Am. Way, 1989, Merit medal Lotus Club, 1989, Barnard medal of distinction Barnard Coll., 1990, Liberty award Brandeis U., 1994. Mem. Assn. Am. Pubs. (chmn. 1972-73, chmn. com. Soviet-Am. pub. rels. 1973, com. on internat. freedom to pub. 1973-76, The Curtis G. Benjamin award for Creative pub. 1996), Coun. on Fgn. Rels., Asia Soc. Clubs: Century Assn. (N.Y.C.), University (N.Y.C.); Century Country (White Plains, N.Y.). Office: 10 E 53rd St Fl 20 New York NY 10022-5244*

BERNSTEIN, SANFORD IRWIN, biology educator; b. Bklyn., June 10, 1953; s. Harold and Adele Dorothy (Kutner) B.; m. Laurel Spear, July 10, 1983. BS, SUNY, Stony Brook, 1974; PhD, Wesleyan U., 1979. Research fellow U. Va., Charlottesville, 1979-82; asst. prof. biology San Diego State U., 1983-85, assoc. prof., 1985-88, prof. 1988—; assoc. dir. Molecular Biology Inst., 1987-92, dir. 1992-95; co-dir. DNA cert. program, 1983—, chair biology dept., 1995—. Established investigatorship Am. Heart Assn., 1989-94; Mem. grant rev. panels NIH, Am. Heart Assn. Assoc. editor Developmental Biology, 1991-95; contbr. articles to profl. jours. Muscular Dystrophy Assn. fellow, 1979-82, grantee, 1984—; grantee NIH, 1983—, NSF, 1997—. Mem. Genetics Soc. Am., AAAS, Am. Soc. Cell Biology, Am. Soc. Biochemistry and Molecular Biology, Am. Soc. Microbiol., Soc. Devel. Biology, Sigma Xi. Achievements include research in developmental regulation of muscle gene expression in Drosophila, muscle protein isoform function, alternative RNA splicing. Office: San Diego State U Biology Dept and Molec Bio Inst San Diego CA 92182-4614

BERNSTEIN, SOL, cardiologist, educator; b. West New York, N.J., Feb. 3, 1927; s. Morris Irving and Rose (Leibowitz) B.; m. Suzi Maris Sommer, Sept. 15, 1963; 1 son, Paul. AB in Bacteriology, U. Southern Calif., 1952, MD, 1956. Diplomate Am. Bd. Internal Medicine. Intern Los Angeles County Hosp., 1956-57, resident, 1957-60; practice medicine specializing in cardiology L.A., 1960—; staff physician dept. medicine Los Angeles County Hosp. U. So. Calif. Med. Center, L.A., 1960—, chief cardiology clinics, 1964, asst. dir. dept. medicine, 1965-72; chief profl. services Gen. Hosp., 1972-74; med. dir. Los Angeles County-U So. Calif. Med. Center, L.A., 1974-94; med. dir. central region Los Angeles County, 1974-78; dir. Dept. Health Services, Los Angeles County, 1978; assoc. dean Sch. Medicine, U. So. Calif., L.A., 1986-94, assoc. prof., 1968—; med. dir. Health Rsch. Assn., L.A., 1995—; cons. Crippled Childrens Svc. Calif., 1965—. Contbr. articles on cardiac surgery, cardiology, diabetes and health care planning to med. jours. Served with AUS, 1946-47, 52-53. Fellow A.C.P., Am. Coll. Cardiology; mem. Am. Acad. Phys. Execs., Am. Fedn. Clin. Research, N.Y. Acad. Sci., Los Angeles, Am. heart assns., Los Angeles Soc. Internal Medicine, Los Angeles Acad. Medicine, Sigma Xi, Phi Beta Phi, Phi Eta Sigma, Alpha Omega Alpha. Home: 4966 Ambrose Ave Los Angeles CA 90027-1756 Office: 1640 Marengo St Los Angeles CA 90033-1036

BERNSTEIN, STAN, federal judge; b. 1941. BA, Brandeis U., 1962; MA, U. Chgo., 1964; PhD, Harvard U., 1970; JD, Rutgers U., 1974. Bar: Mich., Ohio, Calif., Mass. Mem. faculty U. Calif., Davis, 1967-70, Rutgers U., 1970-73; lawyer Honigman, Miller, Schwartz & Cohn, Detroit, 1974-82; bankruptcy judge for ea. dist. Mich. Detroit, 1982-84; with Gender, Raskoff, Shapiro & Quittner, L.A., 1984-85, Dickinson, Wright, Detroit, 1985-89, Brown & Bain, Phoenix, 1989-90, Foley, Hoag & Eliot, Boston, 1991-96; bankruptcy judge for ea. dist. N.Y. Westbury, 1996—. Mem. ABA, Am. Bankruptcy Inst., Nat. Conf. Bankruptcy Judges. Office: US Bankruptcy Ct 1635 Privado Rd Westbury NY 11590-5298

BERNSTEIN, STANLEY JOSEPH, manufacturing executive; s. David William and Irene Mildred (Eisenman) B.; children: Michael A., Geoffrey T. BA, Brown U., 1965; JD, U. Pa., 1968. Bar: Mass. 1968. Mgr. Am. Biltrite Inc., Chelsea, Mass., 1968-71; div. gen. mgr. Am. Biltrite Inc., Cambridge, Mass., 1971-78, v.p. corp. devel., 1978-82; exec. v.p. The Biltrite Corp., Waltham, Mass., 1983-85, chmn., chief exec. officer, 1986—; also bd. dirs. The Biltrite Corp., Waltham; bd. dirs. K-Swiss Inc., Chatsworth, Calif., Shenzhen Biltrite-SPEC Soling Co., Ltd., Shenzhen, China, Atlanta, Sr. Tour Players Devel., Inc., Boston. Life trustee Roxbury Latin Sch., West Roxbury, Mass.; trustee Brown U., Combined Jewish Philanthropies Boston. Office: The Biltrite Corp PO Box 9045 51 Sawyer Rd Waltham MA 02454-9045

BERNSTEIN, STUART M., federal judge; b. 1950. BA cum laude, CUNY, 1972; JD cum laude, Foreham U., 1975. Bar: N.Y. Asst. U.S. atty. for so. dist. N.Y., U.S. Dept. Justice, N.Y.C., 1978-82; bankruptcy judge for so. dist. N.Y., U.S. Bankruptcy Ct., N.Y.C., 1993—; adj. assoc. prof. law Fordham U. Law Sch., 1984-86; lectr. Am. Law Inst.-ABA. Contbr. articles to law jours. With N.Y. Army Res. N.G., 1970-76. Mem. ABA, Fed. Bar Coun., Nat. Conf. Bankruptcy Judges, N.Y. State Bar Assn. (lectr.), Assn. Bar City N.Y. Office: US Bankruptcy Ct One Bowling Green Rm 627 New York NY 10004-1408

BERNSTEIN, THERESA, artist; b. Phila.; d. Isidore and Anne (Ferber) B.; m. William Meyerowitz, 1919. Student, Pa. Acad., Phila. Sch. Design, Art Students League; PhD (hon.), Moore Coll. Art, 1991. Dir. Salons of Am. Ind. Artists, 1924-30; life mem. Grand Central Art Galleries, N.Y. Author: William Meyerowitz, The Artist Speaks, 1986, The Poetic Canvas, 1988, The Journal, 1991, The Israeli Journal, 1994; contbr. articles to mags., newspapers.; one-woman shows Butler Inst. Am. Art, 1973, Smith Gerard Gallery, Stamford, Conn., 1976, Summit Gallery, N.Y.C., 1979, Smithsonian Inst., Fitchburg Art Mus., Doll & Richards, Inc., Boston Publick House, Sturbridge, Mass., U. Maine, Orono, Columbus Mus., Mus. Women of Art, Washington, 1989, Mus. City of N.Y., 1990, 91; represented in permanent collections U.S. Nat. Mus., Washington, Library of Congress, Phillips Meml. Art Gallery, Chgo. Art Inst., Met. Mus. Art, N.Y. Pub. Library, Bklyn. Mus., others; also pvt. collections; represented Art U.S.A. by painting Jazz Players; exhbns. include: Carnegie Inst., NAD, Cooper Union Mus., Butler Inst. Am. Art, Boston Pub. Library, N.Y. Hist. Soc. Phila. Mus. Art, Yose Gallery, Boston, N.Y. Hist. Soc., 1983-84, Paterson Pub. Library, 1984, Grand Central Galleries, N.Y.C., 1985-86, Cape Ann Hist. Assn., Gloucester, Mass., 1986; represented in permanent collection New England Ladies, Cape Ann Hist. Assn., N.Y. Hist. Soc., N.Y. Pub. Library; dir. summer art show, Gloucester, Mass., Weston U.; chmn. Meml. Exhibit Cape Ann Festival, 1958—. Recipient Phillips prize for Progressive Painting, 1946; Green traveling fellow; John Sartain scholar; Phila. Bd. Edn. scholar; Robert Dain prize, 1964; hon. mention Soc. Am. Graphic Artists, 1954, Knickerbocker Artists, 1956, Ogunquit Art Center; Carl Matson portrait award Rockport Art Assn., 1967; figure prize for Friends, 1981; New Eng. Artists award, N. Shore Arts Assn; John A. Johnson award, 1972; Johnson Meml. prize, 1975; Clark Meml. prize, 1977; Cantorella prize Nat. Assn. Women Artists, Nat. Acad., N.Y., 1968; Watson Meml. prize 1979; World Culture prize Italian Acad. Art, 1984; North Shore (Mass.) Artist of Yr. award, 1984; Medal of Honor, Rockport Art Assn., 1986; Oscar of Art, Italian Acad. Art, 1986; Mary Mintz Koffler award Audobon Artists Annual, 1988; Medal for Artistic Achievement, Rockport Art Assn., 1986. Mem. Nat. Assn. Women Artists (jury of awards 1948-50, jury oil painting 1959, Margaret Cooper prize for oil portrait Sarah 1951, Jane Peterson prize 1955, nominating com. 1963-64, Klein Figurative award 1977), Boston Printmakers Assn., Cape Ann Soc. Artists, Nat. Assn. Women Painters and Sculptors (jury of award 1920-29), N.Y. Soc. Woman Artists (chmn. 1935-36, dir. 1959—, hon. dir. 1969—), North Shore Arts Assn. (hon.), Cape Ann Soc. Artists, Conn. Acad. Artists Am. (oil jury 1957-58), Allied Artists Am. (Horgan award 1975), Italian Acad. Fine Arts (hon. mem., Gold medal 1980). Subject of book The Sketch Book 1910-1950, 1992. Studio: Sragow Gallery 73 Spring St New York NY 10012-5800

BERNSTEIN, WILLIAM, film company executive; b. N.Y.C., Aug. 30, 1933; s. Philip and Sadie (Lazar) B.; m. Evelyn Pauline Schnur, Aug. 3, 1958; children: Marian Suzanne, Steven Laurence. BA, NYU, 1954; LLB, Yale U., 1959. Atty. United Artists Corp., N.Y.C., 1959-67, v.p. bus. affairs, 1967-72, sr. v.p. bus. affairs, 1972-78; exec. v.p. Orion Pictures Corp., N.Y.C., 1978-91, pres., chief exec. officer, dir., 1991-92; exec v.p. Paramount Pictures Corp., L.A., 1992—. Mem. ABA, Acad. Motion Picture Arts and Scis. Home: 282 Bentley Cir Los Angeles CA 90049-2414 Office: Paramount Pictures Corp 5555 Melrose Ave Los Angeles CA 90038-3197

BERNSTEIN, WILLIAM JOSEPH, glass artist, educator; b. Newark, Dec. 3, 1945; s. Jacob and Rosalind (Merliss) B.; m. Katherine Schachter, July 21, 1968; children: Joshua, Alex. BFA, Phila. U. of Arts, 1968. Artist in residence Penland (N.C.) Sch. of Crafts, 1968-70; instr. Summervail Workshop, Vail, Colo., U. So. Calif., L.A., Pilchuck Glass Ctr., Stanwood, Wash., Naples (N.Y.) Mill Sch.; tchr. Bezalel Acad., Jerusalem, Israel, 1997—. One-man show Hodges Taylor Galley, Charlotte N.C., 1997; exhibited in group shows at Somerhill Gallery, Chapel Hill, N.C., Grohe Glass Gallery, Boston, Marx Gallery, Chgo., Am. Craft Mus., N.Y.C., John Michael Kohler Arts Ctr., Sheboygan, Wis., Spaso House, Moscow, U.S.S.R., The Denver Art Mus., Laguna Art Mus., Laguna Beach, Calif., Milwaukee Art Mus., J.B. Speed Art Mus., Louisville, Ky., Va. Mus. Fine Arts, Richmond, Ark. Arts Ctr. Decorative Arts Mus., Little Rock, Galerie Angela Hollings, Hameln, Germany, J&L Lobmeyr, Vienna, Austria, Galerie Rob van den Doel, The Hague, The Netherlands, Isetan Galleries, Japan; represented in permanent collections the Corning (N.Y.) Mus. of Glass, the Mint Mus. Art, Charlotte, N.C., Nat. Collection Fine Art, Washington, Greenville (S.C.) County Mus. Art, Austrialian Coun. for the Arts, Sidney, Morse Gallery Art, Winter Park, Fla., Ft. Lauderdale (Fla.) Mus. Arts, R.J. Reynolds Collection, Winston-Salem, N.C., Craft and Folk Mus., L.A., Glasmus., Frauenau, Germany, Ark. Art Ctr., Little Rock, Glasmus., Ebeltoft, Denmark, J&L Lobmeyr, Vienna, Austria, Asheville (N.C.) Mus. Art, Yamaha Corp., Japan, Chrysler Mus. Norfolk, Va., Newark (N.J.) Mus., Charles A. Wustan Mus. Arts, Racine, Wis. Louis Comfort Tiffany Found. grantee, 1975, NEA Master Craftsman Apprenticeship, 1976; NEA fellow, 1974, N.C. Arts Coun. fellow, 1983, masterworks fellow Creative Glass Ctr. Am., 1990. Office: 469 Hannah Branch Rd Burnsville NC 28714-7569

BERNSTEIN, WILLIAM ROBERT, banker; b. Newark, Apr. 14, 1947; s. Leonard H. and Gwen (Burstein) B.; m. Roberta Ann Sipkin, June 25, 1972; children: Carrie, Elizabeth, Michael. BS, Rensselaer Poly. Inst., 1969, BArch, 1970; M of Urban Planning, U. Wash., 1972. Project planner Jersey City Redevel. Agy., 1972-74; v.p. Matthews & Wright Inc., N.Y.C., 1974-79, Thompson Mckinnon Securities, N.Y.C., 1979-81; mng. dir. Drexel Burnham Lambert, N.Y.C., 1981-89; sr. v.p. The Tokai Bank, Ltd., N.Y.C., 1990-99; mng. dir. Mesco Ltd., Ridgefield, Conn., 1999—; pres. Nat. Leased Housing Assn., Washington, 1987-88, chmn., 1988-89, chmn. emeritus, 1989—. Home: 29 Wampus Lake Dr Armonk NY 10504-1122 Office: Mesco Ltd 470 Main St Ridgefield CT 06877

BERNSTINE, DANIEL O'NEAL, law educator, university president; b. Berkeley, Calif., Sept. 7, 1947; s. Annias and Emma (Jones) B.; m. Nancy Jean Tyler, July 27, 1971 (div. Mar. 1986); children: Quincy Tyler, Justin Tyler. BA, U. Calif., Berkeley, 1969; JD, Northwestern U., Chgo., 1972; LLM, U. Wis., 1975. Bar: D.C. 1970, Wis. 1979. Prof. law Howard U. Law Sch., Washington, 1975-78, gen. counsel, interim dean, 1987-90; prof. law U. Wis. Law Sch., Madison, 1978-97, dean, 1990-97; pres. Portland (Ore.) State Univ., 1997—. Author: Wisconsin and Federal Civil Procedure, 1986. Bd. dirs. Madison Cmty. Found., 1990-94, Portland Urban League, Legacy Health Sys.; mem. Portland Multnomah Progress Bd., 1998—, Kellogg Commn. on the Future of State and Land-Grant Univs., 1997—. Mem. Am. Law Inst. Office: Portland State Univ PO Box 751 Portland OR 97207-0751

BERNT, BENNO ANTHONY, financial executive, entrepreneur and investor; b. Bielitz, Austria, Mar. 14, 1931; came to U.S., 1953, naturalized, 1961;

s. Victor and Grete (Meissner) B.; m. Constance Smigel, June 22, 1957; children: Karin, Eric, Steve. BS in Engrng. cum laude, Fed. Inst. Tech., Vienna, Austria, 1952; DCS in Bus. and Econs. cum laude, U. Econs. & Bus. Adminstrn., Vienna, 1953; MBA, Carnegie Mellon U., 1954. Fin. and mfg. exec. Chrysler Corp., 1954-59; mfg. and bus. planning exec., subs. gen. mgr. Whirlpool Corp., 1959-68; pres. Cissell Mfg. Co., Louisville, 1968-70; gen. mgr. Simonds Abrasive Co., Phila., 1970-73; v.p. fin. ESB Ray-O-Vac Corp., Phila., 1973-76, exec. v.p., dir., 1977-78; pres., CEO RAYOVAC, Madison, Wis., 1979-82; sr. v.p. fin. and planning, CFO Nat. Intergroup Inc., Pitts., 1983-87; chmn. The Griffin Group, Pitts., 1988—, Univ. Ptnrs., Inc., 1997—; interim CEO Carnegie Tech. Edn., Inc.; bd. dirs. Claritech Corp., QED Comm., Pitts. Tissue Eng. Initiative; dir. tech. transfer Carnegie Mellon U., 1992-97. Bd. dirs. Pitts. Symphony; adv. bd. of sch. of computer sci. and dept. music Carnegie Mellon U., 1993—. Mem. Duquesne Club, Fox Chapel Golf Club, Pitts. Golf Club. also: Univ Partners Inc 308 Schenley Rd Pittsburgh PA 15217-1173 *I believe the measure of one's true success lies in how well we are using our own potential, and how well we are serving others.*

BERNTHAL, DAVID G., federal judge; b. 1950. BA, U. Ill., 1972, JD, 1976. Sole practitioner, 1976-86; assoc. cir. judge Fifth Jud. Cir., Vermilion County, Ill., 1987-95; magistrate judge Ill. Ctrl., Urbana, 1995—. Mem. Fed. Magistrate Judges Assn. Office: US Courthouse Rm 114 201 S Vine St Urbana IL 61802-3369

BERNTHAL, FREDERICK MICHAEL, association executive; b. Sheridan, Wyo., Jan. 10, 1943; s. Erwin and Erna Bernthal; m. Heather A. Lancaster; 1 child, Justin. B.S., Valparaiso U., 1964; Ph.D., U. Calif.-Berkeley, 1969. Research staff Yale U., New Haven, 1969-70; prof. Mich. State U., East Lansing, 1970-80; legis. asst. Senator Howard Baker, Washington, 1978-80, chief legis. asst., 1980-83; mem. U.S. Nuclear Regulatory Commn., Washington, 1983-88; asst. sec. oceans, environment, and sci. Dept. of State, Washington, 1988-90; dep. dir. NSF, Washington, 1990-94; pres. Univs. Rsch. Assn., Washington, 1994—; bd. dirs. Pa. Power and Light Co., Challenger Ctr. Space Sci. Edn., Cecil and Ida Green Ctr. Sci. and Pub. Policy. Contbr. 45 articles to sci. jours. NATO Sr. Scientist fellow U. Copenhagen, 1977; Congl. Sci. fellow Am. Phys. Soc., 1978-79. Fellow Am. Phys Soc.; mem. AAAS, Am. Chem. Soc., Cosmos Club of Washington. Republican. Lutheran. Office: Univs Rsch Assn 1111 19th St NW Ste 400 Washington DC 20036-3627

BERNTHAL, HAROLD GEORGE, health care company executive; b. Frankenmuth, Mich., June 11, 1928; s. Wilfred Michael and Olga Bertha (Stern) B.; m. Margaret Hrebek, Jan. 25, 1958; children: Barbara Anne, Karen Elizabeth, James Willard. B.S. in Chemistry, Mich. State U., 1950. Pres. Am. Hosp. Supply Corp., Evanston, Ill., 1974-85; chmn. Cobern Inc., Lake Forest, Ill., 1986—; bd. dirs. Nat. Standard Corp., Nalco Chem. Co., Butler Mfg. Co. Trustee Northwestern Meml. Hosp., Chgo., Valparaiso (Ind.) U., Wheat Ridge Found; governing mem. Chgo. Symphony Orch. Served with AUS, 1950-52. Recipient Lumen Christi medal Valparaiso U., 1988. Mem. Health Industries Assn. (past pres.), Health Industry Mfr.'s Assn. (past mem. exec. com.), Pharm. Mfrs. Assn. (past chmn. med. device com.). Clubs: Chgo. Comml.; Knollwood; Old Elm. Office: 225 E Deerpath Rd Lake Forest IL 60045-1952

BERO, R.D., manufacturing executive; b. Uniontown, Pa., 1941. BS in Mech. Egring., Ohio State U., 1967, MS in Syss. Engring., 1969. CEO Menasha; v.p. mfg. and engrng. U.S. Industries; opers. dir. Amsted Industries; v.p. plastics group Menasha Corp., Neenah, Wis., 1979, v.p. material handling group, 1991, pres., 1992—, also bd. dirs., 1992—, CEO, 1993—; bd. dirs. First Nat. Bank, Fox Valley, United health Group. Officer Jr. Achievement; pres., chmn. Future Neenah Devel. Corp.; campaign chmn., officer United Way; bd. advs. engring. dept. Ohio State U.; pres., dir. Fox Valley United Way. Mem. Fox Cities C. of C. (bd. dirs.). Office: Menasha Corporation 1645 Bergstrom Rd Neenah WI 54956-9766 Office: PO Box 367 Neenah WI 54957-0367*

BEROLZHEIMER, KARL, lawyer; b. Chgo., Mar. 31, 1932; s. Leon J. and Rae Gloss (Lowenthal) B.; m. Diane Glick, July 10, 1954; children: Alan, Eric, Paul, Lisa. BA, U. Ill., 1953; JD, Harvard U., 1958. Bar: Ill. 1958, U.S. Ct. Appeals (7th cir.) 1964, U.S. Ct. Appeals (9th cir.) 1969, U.S. Supreme Ct. 1976. Assoc. Ross & Hardies, Chgo., 1958-66, ptnr., 1966-76, of counsel, 1993—; v.p. legal Centel Corp., Chgo., 1976-77, v.p., gen. counsel, 1977-82, sr. v.p., gen. counsel, 1982-88, sr. v.p., gen. counsel, sec., 1988-93; v.p., gen. counsel, sec., 1988-93; mem. nat. adv. bd. Ctr. for Informatics Law, John Marshall Law Sch., Chgo., 1988-93; mem. Corp. Counsel Ctr., Northwestern U. Law Sch., 1987-93, mem. emeritus, 1993—; mem. adv. bd. Litigation Risk Mgmt. Inst., 1989-95; bd. dirs. Milton Industries, Chgo., Devon Bank, Chgo.; cons. Mt. Pulaski Tel. and Elec. Co., Lincoln, Ill., 1981-86; sec., gen. counsel Consol. Water Co., Chgo., 1968-72; mem. human rels. task force Chgo. Cmty. Trust, 1988-90. Bd. dirs. The Nat. Conf. Commn. and Justice, Chgo., presiding co-chmn., 1987-90, mem. nat. exec. bd. dirs., 1988-98, chair investment com., 1991-94, nat. co-chair, 1992-95, pres., 1993-94, chair, 1995-98; mem. exec. bd. Internat. Coun. Christians and Jews, 1996—, v.p., 1998—; bd. dirs. Evanston (Ill.) Mental Health, 1975-82, chair, 1978-80; dir. Evanston Comty. Found., 1996—, vice chair, chair grants com., 1996-98, chair, 1999—; bd. dirs. Beth Emet Found., 1997; trustee Northlight Theatre, Evanston, 1992—, vice-chair, 1993—; mem. coun. The Communitarian Network, 1993-96; trustee Beth Emet Synagogue, Evanston, 1985-87, 89, sec., 1985-89; chair Capital Campaign Plan com., 1994-97; mem. discrimination priority com. United Way, 1990-97, vice-chair, 1993; mem. assembly Parliament of the World's Religions, 1993; mem. Ill. atty. gen.'s ad hoc com. for creation of justice commn., 1994; mem. adv. com. Ill. Justice Commn., 1995-96; mem. adv. bd. Nat. Underground R.R. Freedom Ctr., 1997—. 1st lt. U.S. Army, 1953-55. Fellow Am. Bar Found.; mem. ABA (chair telecom. com. bus. law sect. 1982-86, dispute resolution com. 1986-90, office com. 1991-95, mem. Coalition for Justice 1993-97, bd. editors Bus. Law Today 1995-97, co-chair conflicts of interest com. 1997—), Chgo. Bar Assn. (mem. devel. of law com. 1963-67, chair 1971-73), Chgo. Coun. Lawyers. Democrat. Home: 414 Ashland Ave Evanston IL 60202-3208 Office: Ross & Hardies 150 N Michigan Ave Ste 2500 Chicago IL 60601-7567

BERRA, P. BRUCE, computer educator; b. Smiths Creek, Mich., Apr. 14, 1935; s. Mike John and Dorothy (Nelson) B.; 1 son, Marshall R. B.S., U. Mich., 1958, M.S., 1962; Ph.D., Purdue U., 1968. Sr. engr. Hughes Aircraft Corp., Culver City, Calif., 1958-60; engr., tech. advisor Bendix Corp., Ann Arbor, Mich., 1960-63; instr. U. Mich.-Dearborn, 1964-65; asst. prof. info. engring. Boston U., 1965-66; assoc. prof. Syracuse U. (N.Y.), 1968-74, 74—, prof., chmn. indsl. engrng. and ops. research, 1978-82, prof. elec. and computer engring., 1982-96; dir. N.Y. State Ctr. for Advanced Tech./Software Engring., 1991-96; dir. Info. Tech. Rsch. Inst., disting. prof. info. tech. Wright State U., Dayton, 1997—; cons. IBM Corp., Bell No. Rsch., IITRI, PAR Tech., SCEEE, Singer Link, TRW, KAMAN, Opticomp. Gen. chmn., organizer Workshop on Database Machines, 1980-89. USAF Office of Sci. Research univ. resident research fellow, 1982-83. Fellow IEEE; mem. IEEE Computer Soc. (editor-in-chief CS Press 1981-83, vice chmn. publs. bd. 1984-85, governing bd. 1985-86, 89-91, disting. visitors program 1986-88, 89-91, gen. chmn. internat. conf. on data engring. 1986). Office: Wright State Univ Computer Sci and Engring 351 Russ Dayton OH 45435

BERRA, ROBERT LOUIS, human resources consultant; b. St. Louis, June 24, 1924; s. Angelo John and Clara Catherine B.; m. Vivian Lorene Miles, Nov. 11, 1944; children—Kathleen Patricia Berra Schrage, Patricia Susan Berra Babcock. B.S. in Econs, St. Louis U., 1947; M.B.A., Harvard U., 1947. Faculty mem. St. Louis U., 1947-51; with Monsanto Co., 1951-70, 74-89, v.p. personnel, 1974-80; sr. v.p. adminstrn. St. Louis, 1980-89; v.p. pers. and pub. rels. Foremost-McKesson, Inc., San Francisco, 1970-74; adj. faculty Washington U., U. Ill., Urbana-Champaign. Bd. trustees St. John's Mercy Med. Center, St. Louis; trustee Maryville Coll. Recipient Alumni Merit award St. Louis, U., 1977, Tchr. Yr. award Washington U. Olin Sch. Business, 1994. Fellow Nat. Acad. Human Resources; mem. Soc. Human Resource Mgmt., Indsl. Rels. Assn. St. Louis (past pres.), Bellerive Country Club, Isla Del Sol Country Club, Vinoy Renaissance Country Club. Roman Catholic.

BERRA, YOGI (LAWRENCE PETER BERRA), professional baseball coach; b. St. Louis, May 25, 1925; s. Peter and Pauline (Longsoni) B.; m. Carmen Short, Jan. 26, 1949; children—Lawrence A., Timothy Thomas, Dale Anthony. PhD (hon.), Montclair State U., 1996. Profl. baseball player with N.Y. Yankees, 1946-63, mgr., 1964, coach, 1975-84, mgr., 1984-85; coach N.Y. Mets, 1965-72, mgr., 1972-75; coach Houston Astros, 1986-89; former v.p. Yoo-Hoo Chocolate Beverage Co. Author (with Tom Horton): It Ain't Over ..., 1989. Served with USNR, 1943-46. Recipient Am. League Most Valuable Player award, 1951, 54, 55; elected to Baseball Hall of Fame, 1972; established Am. League record for most home runs by a catcher, lifetime: 313. Clubs: Lion, Elk, Moose. Mem. Am. League All-Star Team, 1949-62, World Series Championship team, 1947, 49-53, 56, 58, 61-62; inducted into Baseball Hall of Fame, 1972. Office: Yogi Berra Mus Montclair State U 8 Quarry Rd Little Falls NJ 07424*

BERRESFORD, SUSAN VAIL, philanthropic foundation executive; b. N.Y.C., Jan. 8, 1943; d. Richard Case and Katherine Vail (Marsters) Berresford Hurd; m. David F. Stein (div.); 1 son, Jeremy Vail Stein. Student, Vassar Coll., 1961-63; B.A. cum laude in Am. History, Radcliffe Coll., 1965. Vol. UN Vol. Services, N.Y.C., summer 1962; sec. to Theodore H. White, summer 1964; program officer Neighborhood Youth Corps, N.Y.C., 1965-67; program specialist Manpower Career Devel. Agy., N.Y.C., 1967; human resources adminstrn. specialist Manpower Career Devel. Agy., 1968; freelance cons., writer Europe and U.S., 1968-70; program officer nat. affairs div. Ford Found., N.Y.C., 1970-80; program officer in charge Ford Found., 1980-81, v.p., 1981-95, exec. v.p., COO, 1995-96, pres., 1996—.

BERREY, ROBERT FORREST, lawyer; b. Oak Park, Ill., Dec. 7, 1939; s. Rhodes Clay and Regina (Kasprovich) B.; m. Rebecca L. Newell, Apr. 10, 1993; children from previous marriage: Adam Forrist, Ellen Catherine, Kevin Joseph. AB, Harvard U., 1962; JD, U. Chgo., 1968. Bar: Ill. 1969, Ohio 1986. Atty. Torshen, Fortes & Eiger, Chgo., 1970-75; atty. Jewel Cos., Inc., Chgo., 1975-76, sec., 1976-80, v.p., sec., gen. counsel, 1980-85; v.p., gen. counsel Tomkins (formerly Philips) Industries, Inc., 1986-91; ptnr. Chernesky, Heyman & Kress, Dayton, Ohio, 1991-98; formerly of counsel Bieser, Greer & Landis LLP, Dayton, Ohio; pvt. practice Chapel Hill, N.C. With AUS, 1962-65. Mem. ABA, Ohio State Bar Assn., Dayton Bar Assn., NCR Country Club, Governors Club. *

BERREY, ROBERT WILSON, III, retired judge, lawyer; b. Dec. 6, 1929; s. Robert Wilson and Elizabeth (Hudson) B.; m. Katharine Rollins Wilcoxson, Sept. 5, 1950; children: Robert Wilson IV, Mary Jane, John Lind. AB, William Jewell Coll., 1950; MA, U. S.D., 1952; LLB, Kansas City U., 1955; LLM, U. Mo., Kansas City, 1972; grad. Trial Judges Coll., U. Nev., 1972; postgrad., Ariz. State U., U. Nev. Bar: Mo. 1955, Kans. 1955. Assoc. Shugert and Thomson, 1955-56, Clark, Krings & Bredehoft, 1957-61, Terry and Welton, 1961-62; judge 4th Dist. Magistrate Ct., Jackson County, Mo., 1962-79; assoc. cir. judge 16th Cir. Ct., Jackson County, 1979-81, cir. judge, 1981-83, mem. mgmt.-exec. com., 1979-83; judge Mo. Ct. Appeals (we. dist.), Kansas City, 1983-97, chief judge, 1994, chmn. rules com., 1990-91, mem., 1993-95, conf. sec., 1992-93, mem. security com., 1992-94; ret., 1997; mem. Supreme Ct. Com. to Draft Rules and Procedures for Mo.'s Small Claims Ct., 1976-86. Vol. legal cons. Psychiat. Receiving Ctr. Del. Atlantic Coun. Young Polit. Leaders, Oxford, Eng., 1965; Kansas City rep. to Pres.'s Nat. Conf. on Crime Control; del.-at-large White House Conf. on Aging, 1972; former pack chmn. Cub Scouts Am.; counselor, com. mem. Boy Scouts Am., sponsor Eagle Scouts; vice chmn. water fowl com. Mo. Conservation Fedn., 1968-69, chmn. water fowl com., 1971-73; v.p. Cook PTA, 1967-68; mem. cts. and judiciary com. Mo. Bar, 1969-73; mem. Midwest region adv. com. Nat. Pks. Svcs., 1973-78, chmn., 1973-78; mem. Mo. State Judicial Planning Commn., 1977; chmn. Senatorial Redistricting Com., Mo., 1991; bd. dirs., founder Kansas City Open Space Found., 1976; regional dir. Young Rep. Nat. Fedn., 1957-59, gen. counsel, 1959-61, nat. vice-chmn.; chmn. Mo. Young Rep. Fedn., 1960, nat. committeeman, 1959-60, 61-64; Mo. alt.-at-large Rep. Nat. Conv., 1960, asst. gen. counsel, 1964, del. state and dist. convs., 1960, 64, 68; bd. dirs. Naturalization Coun., Kansas City, pres., 1973—, Native Sons of Kansas City, 1987—, chmn. long-range planning com., 1992, 1st v.p., 1994, pres., 1995; trustee Kansas City Mus., 1972-73, Hyman Brand Hebrew Acad., 1983—, Woods Meml. Christian Ch., 1988—, chmn., deacon, 1988-91, elder, 1991-94, 96—, chmn. trustees, 1992—, chmn. property, 1991-97, vice chmn. bd. dirs., 1998-99, chmn. bd. dirs., 1998-99, chmn. strategic and bldg. planning com., 1995, chmn. ofcl. bd., 1998-99; mem. status coun. LEAA, 1993-96; hon. life dir. Rockhurst Coll. Mem. Mo. Bar (Disting. Svc. award 1973, agr. law com., com. coun. 1980-81), Kansas City Bar Assn., Urban League (past exec. com. dir.), SAR (registrar 1998-99), Kansas City Mus. Natural Sci. Soc. (charter), Tex. Longhorn Breeders Assn. (life), Am. Royal (bd. govs.), Am. Forestry Assn. (life), Mo. Longhorn Breeders Assn. (life), Mo. Farm Bur., Clay County Lodge (life, Mo. Marshall 1993, jr. warden 1994, sr. warden 1995, worshipful master 1995-97), Nat. Soc. SAR (law commendation medal 1995, 98), Shrine, Ararat Temple (hon. life, provost), DeMolay Legion Honor (life), Waldo Optimist Club (v.p. 1967-68), Ducks Unltd. (life, nat. trustee 1986-89, state trustee/nat. del. 1992, 94, nat. spl. projects com. 1990-95, trustee emeritus 1993, life sponsor U.S., Can., Mex., state coun. 1985—, Sportsman of Yr. 1985, Conservation Svc. award 1992, Absentee Conservation Farmer Lubbock County Soil and Water Conservation Dist. 1994), The Explorers Club, Kansas City Club, Hartwell Hunt Club (dir. 1994-97), U. Club Kansas City, J Club, William Jewell Coll., Alpha Phi Omega, Delta Theta Phi (life, Toast 1990), Pi Gamma Mu, Tau Kappa Epsilon (Hall of Fame 1986). Home: 31694 W 132d St Excelsior Springs MO 64024-9402 also: RR 2 Battle Lake MN 56515-9802

BERRIDGE, GEORGE BRADFORD, retired lawyer; b. Detroit, June 9, 1928; s. William Lloyd and Marjorie (George) B.; m. Mary Lee Robinson, July 6, 1957; children: George Bradford, Elizabeth A., Mary L., Robert L. AB, U. Mich., 1950, MBA, 1953, JD, 1954. Bar: N.Y. 1954. Assoc. Chadbourne & Parke, N.Y.C., 1954-61; gen. atty., v.p. law Am. Airlines, Inc., N.Y.C., 1961-71; sr. v.p., gen. counsel Americana Hotels, Inc., N.Y.C., 1971-74, Nat. Westminster Bank U.S.A., N.Y.C., 1975-89, Nat. Westminster Bancorp, N.Y.C., 1989-93; ret., 1993. Contbr. articles to U. Mich. Law Rev. Served to lt. (j.g.) USN, 1951-53. Recipient Howard P. Coblentz prize U. Mich. Law Sch., 1954. Episcopalian. Home: 2 Circle Ave Larchmont NY 10538-4219

BERRIDGE, MARY, photographer. BA in Arts and Ideas-Lit. & Photography, U. Mich., 1986; MFA in Photography, Yale U., 1991. adj. instr. Concordia Coll., Bronxville, N.y., 1992, Fairleigh Dickinson U., Rutherford, N.J., 1992-94, Nassau C.C., Garden City, N.Y., 1994-96, Sch. Visual Arts, N.y.C., 1997; artist-in-residence, adj. instr. Coll. New Rochelle, N.Y., 1993; lectr. Princeton (N.J.) U., 1998-99. Selected exhbns. include The Ctr. for Photography, Woodstock, N.Y., 1991, Mus. Modern Art, N.Y.C., 1991, Berkshire Mus., Pittsfield, Mass., 1992, OPSIS Found., N.Y.C., 1992, Coll. New Rochelle, 1993, Midtown Y Photography Gallery, N.Y.C., 1993, Ind. Arts Gallery, Jamaica, N.Y., 1994, U. Rochester, N.Y., 1995, Blue Sky Gallery, Portland, Oreg., 1996, San Marino Mus. Photography, 1997, Robert Mann Gallery, N.Y.C., 1997, Soc. for Contemporary Photography, Kansas City, 1997-98, Mus. Fine Arts, Houston, 1997, M.H. de Young Meml. Mus., San Francisco, 1997, Cathedral of St. John the Divine, N.Y.C., 1997, Portland (Maine) Mus. Art, 1998, San Francisco Camerawork, 1998, U. Mich., Ann Arbor, 1999, Ctr. for Documentary Studies Duke U., Durham, N.C., 1999; publs. include Pleasures and Terrors of Domestic Comfort, 1991, The Human Condition/Photography 1995, 1996, Double Take, 1996-97, A Positive Life: Portraits of Women Living with HIV, 1997. Recipient The Ernst Haas award Maine Photographic Workshops, 1996, The Dorothea Lange-Paul Taylor prize Ctr. for Documentary Studies, Duke U., 1996, Fellowship award Soc. for Contemporary Photography, Kansas City, Mo., 1997, The Romeo Martinez Internat. award Ministry Culture of the Republic of San Marino, 1997; Artist's fellow N.Y. Found. for the Art, 1996, John Simon Guggenheim Meml. fellow, 1997. E-mail: berridge@princeton.edu. *

BERRIDGE, PAUL THOMAS, minister; b. Marion, Ohio, July 1, 1937; s. John Howard and Bertha Jane (Dulaney) B.; m. Marguerite Lucille Sheeks, Mar. 16, 1957 (dec. Mar. 1996); children: Pamela Rae, Janice Elaine, Valerie Kaye. AA, Ministerial Inst., 1968; postgrad., Wesleyan Ch., Indpls., 1972—. Ordained to ministry Wesleyan Ch., 1967. Pastor Pilgrim Holiness Ch., Lima, Ohio, 1967-69; sr. pastor Wesleyan Ch., Sandusky, Ohio, 1969-70, Springfield, Ohio, 1970—; v.p. Western Ohio Youth, Leesburg, 1962-68; dir., mem. coun. Wesleyan Ch., Vandalia, Ohio, 1972-92; sec. Bd. Ministerial Standing, Westerville, Ohio, 1974-93; dir. Holy Land/Greece Tour, 1971. Fellow Clark Ministerial Assn. Republican. Home: 411 N Shaffer St Springfield OH 45504-2429 *An investment with unlimited potential to achieve established goals, to be an inspiration to those persons facing devastating circumstances, and with Divine enablement I shall be a "Beacon Light" to offer hope in a troubled world.*

BERRIER, J. ALAN, transportation executive, entrepreneur; b. Lexington, N.C., Jan. 14, 1951; s. John Pitts and Etta Kaye (Hiatt) B. Student, Brevard (N.C.) Coll., 1969-70, High Point (N.C.) U., 1970-72. Shipping coord. Furnitureland South, Inc., Jamestown, N.C., 1992-96; over-the-road mgr. Royal Transp., Inc., Jamestown, 1996-98, MGM Transport Corp., Jamestown, 1998—. Mem. Nat. Audubon Soc., Soc. Hist. Preservation, Libr. Congr., Smithsonian Inst. Avocations: photography, travel. Home and Office: 106 Thomas St Apt F High Point NC 27263-2194

BERRIGAN, HELEN GINGER, federal judge; b. 1948. BA, U. Wis., 1969; MA, Am. U., 1971; JD, La. State U., 1977. Staff rschr. Senator Harold E. Hughes, 1971-72; legis. aide Senator Joseph E. Biden, 1972-73; asst. to mayor City of Fayette, Miss., 1973-74; law clk. La. Dept. Corrections, 1975-77; staff atty. Gov. Pardon, Parole and Rehab. Commn., 1977-78; prin. Gravel Brady & Berrigan, New Orleans, 1978-94, Berrigan, Litchfield, Schonekas, Mann & Clement, New Orleans, 1984-94; judge U.S. Dist. Ct. (ea. dist.) La., New Orleans, 1994—; active La. Sentencing Commn., 1987. Active Com. of 21, 1989, pres., 1990-92, ACLU of La., 1989-94, Forum for Equality, 1990-94, Amistad Rsch. Ctr. Tulane U., 1990-95. Mem. La. State Bar Assn. (mem. fed. 5th cir. 1986—), La. Assn. Criminal Def. Lawyers, New Orleans Assn. Women Attys. Office: US Dist Ct 500 Camp St C-556 New Orleans LA 70130-3313*

BERRINGTON, CRAIG ANTHONY, lawyer; b. Chgo., Aug. 9, 1943; s. Leo and Geraldine (Dale) Berrington; m. Susan Dale Olsen, Sept. 3, 1967; children: Jennifer, Emily, Lacy. BA, Am. U., 1965; JD, Northwestern U., 1968. Bar: D.C. 1969, U.S. Supreme Ct. 1989. Atty. U.S. Dept. Labor, Washington, 1968-75, assoc. solicitor, 1975-77, exec. asst. to under sec., 1977-79, dep. asst. sec. Employment Standards Adminstrn., 1979-86; sr. v.p., gen. counsel Am. Ins. Assn., Washington, 1986—. Mem. ABA, U.S. Supreme Ct. Bar, D.C. Bar. Home: 5920 Granby Rd Rockville MD 20855-1419 Office: Am Ins Assn 1130 Connecticut Ave NW Washington DC 20036-3904

BERRIS, BRIAN A., investment company executive. Gen. ptnr. Brown Bros. Harriman & Co., N.Y.C. Office: Brown Bros Harriman & Co 59 Wall St New York NY 10005-2808*

BERRY, ANN ROPER, diplomat; b. Cleve., Nov. 9, 1934; d. Frank Carson and Doris (Decker) Roper; m. Maxwell K. Berry, Feb. 11, 1959; children: Walter F., Helen D. BA, Ohio Wesleyan U., 1956; MEd, U. Md., 1964. Asst. budget and fiscal officer Am. Embassy, Baghdad, Iraq, 1958-59; various tchg. positions Turkey, Zambia and U.S., 1961-75; internat. economist Dept. of State, Washington, 1975-77, asst. chief textiles divsn., 1977-80; econ. officer Am. Embassy, Athens, Greece, 1980-82; dep. chief textile negotiator U.S. Trade Rep., Washington, 1982-84; mem. NATO Def. Coll., Rome, 1984; counselor for econ. affairs Am. Embassy, Paris, 1985-89; min. econ. affairs Am. Embassy, London, 1989-93; dep. chief of mission USOECD, Paris, 1993-96; econ. min. counselor U.S. Embassy, Pretoria, South Africa, 1996—. Recipient Superior Honor awards Dept. of State, 1980, 89. Mem. Phi Beta Kappa. Home: 331 Anderson St, Brooklyn Pretoria South Africa Office: US Embassy Pretoria, 877 Pretorius St, Arcadia 0083, South Africa Office: US Embassy Pretoria Dept State Washington DC 20521

BERRY, BEVERLY A., real estate investment executive; b. Wayne County, Ohio, Aug. 3, 1939; d. Arleigh Lester and Mabel Bell (Weltmer) Cooper; m. David P. Berry, June 9, 1957; children: Wesley, Tamala, Stephanie. Student, Akron U., 1976-78. Cert. real estate broker, residential specialist, Ohio. Sec., asst. underwriter Westfield Ins. Cos., Westfield Center, Ohio, 1957-69; office mgr., sec. of bd. Johnson Mfg. Co., West Salem, Ohio, 1972-76; prin. acct. Johnson Mfg. Co., West Salem, 1974-76; real estate agt. Gerspacher Realty, Lodi, Ohio, 1976-79, Rickel Realty, Lodi, 1979-82; pres., owner Bev Berry Ins. Agy., Inc., Lodi, 1982-90, Bev Berry Realty, Inc., Auction Co., Lodi, 1982—; mem. of Bus. Option Adv. Com. at Wayne Gen. and Tech. Coll., U. Akron, 1989-90. Mem. Ind. Ins. Agt.'s Assn., Women's Coun. Realtors, Realtors Polit. Action Com. (life), Medina County Bd. Realtors (sec. 1986-87, bd. dirs. 1982-86, sec., trustee 1991, Broker of Yr. 1986, Sales Achievement award 1981, Realtor of Yr. 1991), Wayne County Bd. Realtors, Ashland County Bd. Realtors, Lodi C. of C., Ashland C. of C., Medina C. of C., Ruritan. Lutheran. Avocations: reading, golfing, boating, gardening. Office: PO Box 131 Lodi OH 44254-0131

BERRY, BRIAN JOE LOBLEY, geographer, political economist, urban planner; b. Sedgley, Stafford, Eng., Feb. 16, 1934; came to U.S., 1955, naturalized, 1965; s. Joe and Gwendoline Alice (Lobley) B.; m. Janet Elizabeth Shapley, Sept. 6, 1958; children: Duncan Jeffrey, Carol Anne (dec.), Diane Leigh. BSc with honors, Univ. Coll., London, 1955; MA, U. Wash., 1956, PhD, 1958; AM (hon.), Harvard U., 1976. Instr. geography, civil engrng. U. Wash., Seattle, 1957-58; asst. prof. geography U. Chgo., 1958-62, assoc. prof., 1962-65, prof., 1965-72, Irving B. Harris prof. urban geography, 1972-76, dir. Ctr. Urban Studies, chmn. dept. geography, 1974-76; Frank Backus Williams prof. urban and regional planning Harvard U., 1976-81, chmn. Ph.D. Program in Urban Planning, dir. Lab. for Computer Graphics and Spatial Analysis, fellow Inst. Internat. Devel., 1976-81, prof. sociology, 1978-81; dean H. John Heinz III Sch. of Pub. Mgmt. Carnegie-Mellon U., 1981-86, Univ. prof. urban studies and pub. policy, 1981-86; founders prof. U. Tex., Dallas, 1986-91, prof. polit. econ., 1986—; Lloyd Viel Berkner Regental prof., 1991—; chmn. Bruton Ctr. for Devel. Studies U. Tex., Dallas, 1988-95. Author numerous books; contbr. articles to profl. jours. Fellow Univ. Coll., U. London, 1983; recipient Victoria medal Royal Geog. Soc., 1988, Rockefeller prize Dartmouth U., 1992. Fellow AAAS, Am. Acad. Arts and Scis., Urban Land Inst., Brit. Acad. (corr.), Weimer Inst. Real Estate and Land Econs., Royal Geog. Soc., So. Regional Sci. Assn.; mem. NAS (coun. 1999—), Assn. Am. Geographers (hon. award 1968, pres. 1978-79, Anderson medal 1987), Am. Inst. Cert. Planners, Regional Sci. Assn., Inst. Brit. Geographers, Sigma Xi. Office: U Tex-Dallas Sch Social Sci Richardson TX 75083-0688

BERRY, CAROL ANN, insurance executive; b. Walla Walla, Wash., Sept. 8, 1950; d. Alan R. and Elizabeth A. (Davenport) B.; m. Mark Brooks, June 27, 1998. BA, Wash. State U., 1972. Asst. mgr. L.A. reg. claims CIGNA, Santa Monica, Calif., 1981-83; reg. adminstr. Equicor, Sherman Oaks, Calif., 1983-89; dir. sys. for managed care Blue Cross of Calif., Woodland Hills, Calif., 1989-90; dir. field account svcs. Managed Health Network, L.A., 1990-93; pres. VertiHealth Adminstrs., Chatsworth, Calif., 1993—; lectr. in field. Mem. Pres.'s Commn. on Status of Women. Mem. NAFE, Assn. Info. Mgrs. Healthcare Industry, Health Fin. Mgmt. Assn., Health Care Adminstrs. Assn., Wash. State U. Alumni Assn. Home: 6155 Lockhurst Dr Woodland Hills CA 91367-1203

BERRY, CECILIA ANNE, nephrology nurse practitioner; b. Brighton, Sussex, Eng., Nov. 14, 1945; came to U.S., 1969; d. Dominic and Vera Denise (Lewry) Marini; children: Anne Da-Silva, Tuan Samahon, Yasmin Samahon, Rohan Samahon; m. Robert H. Berry, July 28, 1990. Diploma, Brighton and Hove Sch. Nursing, 1967; BSN, U. Rochester, N.Y., 1989, MS, 1995. RN, N.Y.; cert. nephrology nurse. Surg. staff nurse U. Rochester Med. Ctr., 1969-72, float staff nurse, pvt. duty nurse, 1972-77; staff nurse in dialysis Monroe Comty. Hosp., Rochester, 1977-82; from staff nurse dialysis level II to level IV, leader U. Rochester (N.Y.) Med. Ctr., 1982-91; dialysis clinician Park Ridge Health Care Sys., Rochester, 1991-96; adminstr. CEO Lake Plains Dialysis Ctr. Medina (N.Y.) Meml. Hosp., 1996—; dialysis nurse educator St. Mary's Hosp., Rochester, 1994. Contbr. articles to profl. jours. Pres. Young Women's Orgn.-Brockport Ward. Mem. Am. Nephrology Nurses Assn. (pres. Gt. Lakes chpt. 1991-93), Nat. Kidney Found. (coun. for nephrology nurses and technicians), Brockport Ward Young Women's Orgn. (pres.). Mormon. Home: 102 Hollybrook Rd

Brockport NY 14420-2504 Office: Medina Meml Hosp 11020 W Center Street Ext Medina NY 14103-9557

BERRY, CHARLES HORACE, economist, educator; b. Ottawa, Ont., Can., Jan. 6, 1930; came to U.S. 1956, naturalized 1965; s. F. William and Lucinda B. (Pratt) B.; m. Gisella Erdody, May 15, 1965; children: William, Rachel, Katherine. BS, McGill U., 1951; MS, U. Conn., 1953; PhD, U. Chgo., 1956. Asst. prof. econs. Yale U., New Haven, Conn., 1957-63, dir. undergrad. studies, 1959-62; mem. sr. staff Brookings Instn., Washington, 1963-66; assoc. prof. Princeton U., N.J., 1966-71, prof., 1971-95, prof. emeritus, 1995—; master John D. Rockefeller III Coll., 1986-91; dir. Sloan Found. fellowships in econ. journalism, 1975-80, dir. grad. program Woodrow Wilson Sch., 1975-78, assoc. dean, 1975-78, 80-85; trustee Princeton Med. Ctr., 1981-85. Author: Voluntary Medical Insurance and Prepayment, 1965, Corporate Growth and Diversification, 1975. Mem. Regional Planning Bd., Princeton, 1975, Princeton Hosp. Liaison Com., 1975-79. Mem. Nat. Bur. Econ. Rsch. (dir. 1969-89), Cons. in Industry Econs. (dir.), Gatineau Fish and Game Club. Home: 47 Maclean Cir Princeton NJ 08540-5620 Office: 213 Woodrow Wilson Sch Princeton U Princeton NJ 08544

BERRY, CHARLES MILES, cardiac surgeon; b. N.Y.C., Mar. 21, 1948; s. Charles Miles and Ruth Marie Berry; m. Cynthia Fair, Jan. 23, 1982; children: Margaret Florence, Nicholas Tennant. MD, U. Okla., 1977. Intern U. Ala., 1977-78, resident gen. surgery, 1978-82; resident cardiothoracic U. Utah, 1982-84; staff surgeon St. Francis Hosp., Tulsa, 1984—; assoc. clin. prof. surgery U. Okla., Tulsa, 1986—; cardiac surgeon Cardiac Surgery of Tulsa. Mem. Alpha Omega Alpha. Republican. Unitarian. Avocations: rollerblading, endurance motorcycling, children. E-mail: docursus@aol.com. Home: 28918 Ono Blvd Orange Beach AL 36561 Office: Cardiac Surgery of Tulsa 6151 S Yale Ave Tulsa OK 74136

BERRY, CHARLES RICHARD, lawyer; b. Louisville, Apr. 19, 1948; s. Charles Russell and Lillie Juanita (Crady) B.; m. Joan Phyllis Rosenberg, Aug. 29, 1970; children: Kevin Charles, Ryan Andrew. BA, Northwestern U., 1970, JD, 1973. Bar: Ariz. 1973, U.S. Dist. Ct. Ariz. 1973, U.S. Ct. Appeals (9th cir.) 1983. Assoc. Snell & Wilmer, Phoenix, 1973-77; ptnr. Tilker, Burke & Berry, Scottsdale, Ariz., 1978-80, Norton, Berry, French & Perkins, P.C. and predecessor firm Norton, Burke, Berry & French, P.C., Phoenix, 1980-86; dir. Fennemore Craig, Phoenix, 1986-90; ptnr. Titus, Brueckner & Berry, Scottsdale, 1991—. Mem. Ariz. Bar Assn. (chmn. securities regulation sect. 1996-97), Paradise Valley Rotary Club (pres. 1995-96). Mem. Unitarian Ch. E-mail address: tbandb@uswest.net. Fax: 480-483-3215. Home: 6148 E Mountain View Rd Scottsdale AZ 85253-1807 Office: Titus Brueckner & Berry 7373 N Scottsdale Rd Ste B252 Scottsdale AZ 85253-3513

BERRY, DAVID J., financial services company executive; b. Columbus, Ohio, Apr. 14, 1944; s. Maurice Glenn Berry and Janice (Eshelman) Read; m. Janet Lynn Tewksbury, Mar. 24, 1977; children: Jeffrey James, Jennifer Jean, Jon Andrew, Amy Jo. Student, Miami U., Oxford, Ohio, 1963-64, Ohio State U., 1965-66. Registered prin. SEC. Ind. fin. svc. salesman, 1966-74; gen. agt. Sun Life Assurance Co. Can., Columbus, 1975-85; pres. Strategic Info. Svcs., Columbus, 1986-87; v.p. IDS Life Ins. Co., Mpls., 1990—; assoc. mgr. IDS Fin. Svcs. Inc., Columbus, 1988, region dir., 1989; v.p. IDS Life Ins. Co., Mpls., 1991—; chmn. Agy. Mgmt. Tng. Coun., Columbus, 1982-83. Bell ringer Salvation Army, Columbus, 1975-85; vol. instr. Learning Disabled Children, Columbus, 1980-83; pres. PTA, Worthington, Ohio, 1983. Fellow Life Underwriting Tng. Coun., Columbus, 1981. Mem. Nat. Assn. Securities Dealers, Gen. Agts. and Mgrs. Assn. (pres. 1979-82), Mpls. Life Underwriters Assn. Avocations: travel, various sport participation, writing poetry. Office: IDS Life Ins Co Ids Tower # 10 Minneapolis MN 55402-2100

BERRY, DAVID VAL, newspaper editor; b. Hoisington, Kans., May 20, 1948; s. Lester Maxwell and Neva Ethel Grace (Bridenstine) B.; m. Martha Katheryn York, Dec. 24, 1972; children: Christina, Karen. BS in journalism, Kans. State U., 1970. News editor Manhattan (Kans.) Mercury, 1970; combat corr. U.S. Army, Vietnam, 1971-72; copy editor Tulsa (Okla.) Tribune, 1972-77; mng. editor Brazosport Facts, Lake Jackson, Tex., 1977-82; v.p., exec. editor Dallas-Ft. Worth Suburban Newspapers, Arlington, Tex., 1982-90; editor Messenger-Inquirer, Owensboro, Ky., 1991-93; mng. editor Tyler (Tex.) Morning Telegraph, 1994—; pres., owner Tex. Ink Editorial Svcs., Arlington, 1990-91. Grad. Leadership Arlington, 1984-85, Leadership Owensboro, 1992-93. Decorated Bronze Star medal U.S. Army, 1972; recipient Best Small Daily Newspaper award Dallas Press Club, 1982. Mem. AP Mng. Editors. Avocations: photography, writing, historical research, history. Office: Tyler Morning Telegraph 410 W Erwin St Tyler TX 75702-7133

BERRY, DAWN BRADLEY, writer, lawyer; b. Peoria, Ill., Mar. 11, 1957; d. Raymond Coke and Clarette (Williams) Bradley; m. William Lars Berry, July 12, 1980. BS, Ill. State U., 1979, MS, 1982; JD, U. Ill., 1988. Bar: N.Mex. 1988, U.S. Dist. Ct. N.Mex. 1988, U.S. Ct. Appeals (10th cir.) 1993. Assoc. Modrall, Sperling, Roehl, Harris and Sisk, Albuquerque, 1988-90; pvt. practice Tijeras and Albuquerque, 1990—; assoc. Hinkle Law Offices, Albuquerque, 1995-96. Author: Equal Compensation for Women, 1994, The Domestic Violence Sourcebook, 1995, The Divorce Sourcebook, 1995, The Fifty Most Influential Women in American Law, 1996, The Divorce Recovery Source Book, 1998, The Estate Planning Sourcebook, 1999. Pres., bd. dirs. Talking Talons Youth Leadership, Tijeras, 1993-98, v.p., 1998—. Recipient Outstanding Young Alumni award Ill. State U., 1996; Rickert scholar for pub. svc. U. Ill., 1988. Mem. NAFE, ACLU, N.Mex. Women's Bar Assn., S.W. Writer's Workshop, Parrot Heads of N.Mex., Communication Artists of N.Mex., F. Scott Fitzgerald Soc. Avocations: travel, dance, falconry, gardening, Renaissance fairs. Home and Office: 222 Raven Rd Tijeras NM 87059-8016

BERRY, DEAN LESTER, lawyer; b. Chgo., Jan. 20, 1935; s. Ruben W. and Leonore C. (Nelson) B.; m. Donna J. Zack, Nov. 16, 1962; children: Megan, Thomas. BA with distinction, DePauw U., 1955; JD with distinction, U. Mich., 1960. Bar: Ohio 1961, U.S. Dist. Ct. (no. dist.) Ohio 1962. Assoc. Squire, Sanders & Dempsey L.L.P., Cleve., 1960-70, ptnr., 1970—; lectr. various programs, Order of Coif. Author: Local Government in Michigan, 1960; contbr. articles to profl. jours.; participant in Quiz Kids radio program, 1945-47. Mem. council City of Rocky River, Ohio, 1967-71; mem. cen. com. Cuyahoga County Rep. Orgn., Ohio, 1963-75, mem. exec. com., 1969—. Served to 1st lt. USAF, 1955-57. Mem. ABA, Ohio Bar Assn., Greater Cleve. Bar Assn. (com. chmn. 1978) Soc. Profl. Journalists, Sigma Delta Chi. Methodist. Avocations: traveling, crossword puzzles. Home: 2638 Fairmount Blvd Cleveland OH 44106-3648 Office: Squire Sanders & Dempsey LLP 4900 Key Tower 127 Public Sq Cleveland OH 44114-1216

BERRY, DONALD LEE, accountant; b. Ft. Dodge, Iowa, Nov. 8, 1940; s. John Donald and Margaret Ann (Lichter) B.; m. Barbara B. Beyer, Aug. 11, 1962; children: Patrick Curtis, Dawn Marie. AA, Edison Community Coll., 1965; BS in Acctg., Fla. Atlantic U., 1967. CPA, Fla. Sr. acct. Haskins & Sells, CPAs, Ft. Lauderdale, Fla., 1967-71; corp. controller King Motor Ctr., Ft. Lauderdale, 1971-73, Krehling Industries, Naples, Fla., 1973-74; stockholder Wentzel, Berry, et. al., Naples, 1974-89; mng. prin. Wentzel, Berry & Alvarez PA, Naples, 1989—. active Mornings Park, Inc., Mother of God, House of Prayer. Recipient Outstanding Citizen award Naples Daily News, 1990. Mem. AICPA, Fla. Inst. CPAs (exec. com. 1989-91, bd. govs. 1984, pres. S.W. Fla. chpt. 1978-79, pres. PAC 1993-94, Pub. Svc. award 1993), Naples Area C. of C. (former pres., bd. govs.), Fellowship of Christian Athletes (former pres.), Fla. Inst. CPAs Ednl. Found., Inc. (v.p., past pres.), KC (past pres.), Pelican Bay Bus. Assn. (past pres.), Leadership S.W. Fla., Naples H.S. Quarterback Club (former pres.), Pelican Bay Rotary (former pres.). Republican. Roman Catholic. Avocations: golf, fishing, bird watching. Office: Wentzel Berry & Alvarez 801 Laurel Oak Dr Ste 303 Naples FL 34108-2767

BERRY, ELIOT WARD, writer, appraiser; b. N.Y.C., May 21, 1949; s. Charles Rynn and Nancy (Ward) B.; m. Gloria Signorelli, May 21, 1988; 1 child, Christopher. BA in History, U. Pa., 1971; MA in Creative Writing, Boston U., 1973; PhD in English, U. London, 1979. Profl. squash player, coach, Munich, Monte Carlo, Boston, 1974-77; tchr. Am. Sch. Paris, 1975; jr. Fulbright prof. Am. lit. U Kassel, Germany, 1979-80; appraiser, N.Y.C., 1985—. Author: (novel) Four Quarters Make A Season, 1973, (lit. criticism) The Fiction and Plays of John Hawkes: A Poetry of Force and Darkness, 1980, Tough Draw, 1992 (best narrative book on tennis NEC and Tennis Week 1992), Topspin, 1996 (best narravive book on tennis NEC and Tennis Week 1996); contbr. articles to newspaper and mags. Mem. Am. Soc. Appraisers. Avocations: tennis, squash, music. Office: 9 E 40th St New York NY 10016

BERRY, EVALENA HOLLOWELL, retired secondary educator, writer; b. Akron, Ohio, Feb. 5, 1921; d. James Emmett and Theresa (King) H.; m. Albert Allen Pool Jr., Nov. 2, 1942 (dec. Nov. 1949); 1 child, Albert Allen III (dec. 1979); m. Homer L. Berry, June 6, 1954 (dec. Dec. 1955). BA, Ark. Coll., 1942; MSE, U. Ark., 1954. Tchr. Pulaski County Pub. Schs., Little Rock, 1943-52, Capital City Bus. Coll., Little Rock, 1952-54, USAF Inst., Little Rock AFB, 1954-55, Little Rock Pub. Schs., 1952-61; asst. exec. sec. Ark. Edn. Assn., Little Rock, 1961-81. Editor: Jour. Ark. Edn., 1961-68; author: Time and the River, 1982, Sugar Loaf Springs, 1984. Coord. learning program Shepherds Ctr. of Little Rock, 1981-92; older adult enabler Synod of the Sun Presbyn. Ch., 1989-96. Recipient Disting. Alumni award Ark. Coll., Batesville, 1988. Mem. NEA (life), Ark. Edn. Assn. (life). Avocations: reading, history, writing, teaching. Home: 11300 Bainbridge Dr Little Rock AR 72212-1704

BERRY, GLENN, educator, artist; b. Glendale, Calif., Feb. 27, 1929; s. B. Franklin and Heloise (Sloan) B.; BA magna cum laude, Pomona Coll., 1951; BFA (Honnold fellow), MFA, Sch. Art Inst. Chgo., 1956. Faculty, Humboldt State U., Arcata, Calif., 1956-81, prof. art, 1969-81, emeritus, 1981—. Exhibited one-man shows Ingomar Gallery, Eureka, Calif., 1968, Ankrum Gallery, L.A., 1970, Esther Bear Gallery, Santa Barbara, Calif., 1971, Coll. Redwoods, Eureka, Calif., 1989; exhibited in group shows Palace of Legion of Honor, San Francisco, Pasadena (Calif.) Art Mus., Rockford (Ill.) Coll., Richmond (Calif.) Art Mus., Henry Gallery U. Wash., Seattle; represented in permanent collections at Storm King Art Center, Mountainville, N.Y., Kaiser Aluminum & Chem. Corp., Oakland, Calif., Palm Springs (Calif.) Desert Mus., Hirshhorn Mus., Washington, others; mural Griffith Hall, Humboldt State U., 1978. Mem. Phi Beta Kappa. Home: PO Box 2241 Mckinleyville CA 95519-2241

BERRY, GUY CURTIS, polymer science educator, researcher; b. Greene County, Ill., May 11, 1935; s. Charles Curtis and Wilma Francis (Wickes) B.; m. Marilyn Jane Montooth, Jan. 26, 1957; children: Susan Jane, Sandra Jean, Scott Curtis. B.S.Ch.E., U. Mich., 1957, M.S. in Polymer Sci., 1958, Ph.D., 1960. Fellow Mellon Inst., Pitts., 1960-65, sr. fellow, 1965—; assoc. prof. chemistry Carnegie-Mellon U., Pitts., 1966-73, prof., 1973—, acting dean, 1981-82, acting head dept. chemistry, 1983-84, head dept. chemistry, 1990-95; vis. prof. U. Tokyo, 1973, Colo. State U., Ft. Collins, 1979, U. Kyoto, Japan, 1983. Editor Jour. Polymer Sci., 1988-93; mem. editl. bd. Jour. Rheology, 1990—, Chemtracts-Macromolecular Chemistry, 1990-94; contbr. over 200 articles to sci. jours. Recipient Bingham medal Soc. of Rheology, 1990. Fellow Am. Phys. Soc.; mem. AAAS, Am. Chem. Soc. (Pitts. Chemistry prize 1994), Soc. Rheology. Office: Carnegie Mellon U Dept Chem 4400 5th Ave Pittsburgh PA 15213-2617

BERRY, HALLE, actress; b. Cleve., Aug. 14, 1968; d. Jerome and Judith (Hawkins) B.; m. David Christopher Justice, Jan. 1, 1993 (div.). Appeared in films Jungle Fever, 1991, The Last Boy Scout, 1991, Strictly Business, 1991, Boomerang, 1992 (Image award nominee 1992), Father Hood, 1993, The Program, 1993, The Flintstones, 1994, Losing Isaiah, 1995, The Rich Man's Wife, 1996, Executive Decision, 1996, Race The Sun, 1996, Girl 6, 1996, B*A*P*S, 1997, , Bulworth, 1998, Victims of Fashion, 1999, Ringside, 1999; TV mini-series Queen, 1992, Solomon & Sheba, 1995, The Wedding, 1998, Dorothy Dandridge, 1999; TV series include Living Dolls, 1989, Knots Landing, 1992; also appeared in episodes of Amen, A Different World, They Came From Outer Space, Frasier (voice). Named Miss Teen All-Am., 1985, Miss U.S.A., 1987. Office: William Morris Agy c/o Bill Butler 1325 Avenue Of The Americas New York NY 10019-6026*

BERRY, JAMES FREDERICK, lawyer, biology educator; b. Washington, Dec. 22, 1947; s. James Frederick and Joyce (Drummond) B.; m. Lynn M. Latzel, Aug. 2, 1997; children: Jennifer, Andrea L. BS, Fla. State U., 1970, MS, 1973; PhD, U. Utah, 1978; JD, Chgo.-Kent Law Sch., 1990. Bar: Fla. 1990, Ill. 1991, U.S. Dist. Ct. (mid. dist.) Fla. 1991, U.S. Dist. Ct. (no. dist.) Ill. 1991, U.S. Ct. Appeals (11th cir.) 1991. Teaching asst. Fla. State U., Tallahassee, 1969-73; chemist Fla. Dept. Agr., Tallahassee, 1973-74; teaching fellow U. Utah, Salt Lake City, 1974-78; rsch. assoc. Carnegie Mus., Pitts., 1983—; prof. biology Elmhurst (Ill.) Coll., 1978—; assoc. Burke, Bosselman & Weaver, Chgo., 1990-93; cons. ENCAP, Inc., DeKalb, Ill., 1983-84; rsch. asst. IIT Chgo.-Kent Law Sch., 1989-90; instr. law Am. Planning Assn., Chgo., 1992-94; adj. prof. Stuart Sch. Bus., Ill. Inst. Tech., 1995—. Contbr. articles to profl. jours. Bd. trustees Chgo. String Ensemble, 1989-94. Rsch. grantee U.S. Fish and Wildlife Svc., Washington, 1983-85, Elmhurst Coll., 1979-86. Mem. ABA, Ill. State Bar Assn., Sigma Xi, Phi Kappa Phi. Roman Catholic. Avocations: environmental protection activities, classical music. Office: Elmhurst Coll 190 Prospect Ave Elmhurst IL 60126-3271

BERRY, JANET CLAIRE, librarian; b. Jonesboro, Ark., Dec. 1, 1948; d. Troy Berry and Olivia Rosetta (Irwin) Thompson; m. Julius Jerome Mitcham, Mar. 27, 1970 (div. 1981); m. Gary Neville Hays, Nov. 10, 1987 (div. 1989). BSE, U. Cen. Ark., 1970; MLS, Vanderbilt/Peabody U., 1981. Libr./tchr. Greenbrier (Ark.) High Sch., 1970-72; employment counselor Dixie Employment Agy., Little Rock, 1973-76; sr. libr. asst. U. Ark. for Med. Sci., Little Rock, 1976-85; coord. cataloging svc. Ark. State Libr., Little Rock, 1985—; Instr. U. Ark., Little Rock, 1986-88. Editor La Docere for Am. Bus. Women's Assn. newsletter (regional top 5 award 1991, 92). Mem. West Baseline Neighborhood Assn., sec., 1997—; mem. Leion Hut Neighborhood Assn., sec., 1997—, Southwest Little Rock United for Progress, 1998—, v.p., 1999. Mem. ALA, Ark. Libr. Assn. (pres. 1983-84), Ark. Region Sports Car Club of Am. (editor 1988—), Am. Bus. Women's Assn. (La Petite Roche chpt., editor 1990-92, 1992 Woman of Yr.). Methodist. Avocations: road rallies, working sports car races. Office: Ark State Libr One Capitol Mall Little Rock AR 72201

BERRY, JAY ROBERT, JR., English educator; b. Cleve., Oct. 12, 1957; s. Jay Robert and Nettie Marie (Stanish) B.; m. Regenia Dee Bailey, Nov. 25, 1989. PhB, Miami U., 1979; MA, U. Iowa, 1983. Instr. U. Iowa, Iowa City, 1980-87, 88-93; instr. Iowa State U., Ames, 1994-97, adj. asst. prof., 1997—; vis. instr. Carleton Coll., Northfield, Minn., 1987-88, Mt. Mercy Coll., Cedar Rapids, Iowa, 1991-93. Mem. MLA, Am. Studies Assn., Coll. Lang. Assn. E-mail: jberry@iastate.edu. Office: Iowa State U Dept English 206 Ross Hall Ames IA 50011

BERRY, JEFFREY ALAN, film director; b. Albany, N.Y., Mar. 5, 1958; s. Gary and Judith Deborah (Epstein) B. BA in Motion Picture Prodn., UCLA, 1980. Rsch. asst. British Broadcasting Corp., London, 1980; copywriter Kaleidoscope Films, L.A., 1981-84; owner, producer Jeff Berry Prodns., L.A., 1985—; entertainment editor UCLA Daily Bruin, 1977-80; freelance feature writer L.A. Weekly, 1982; book reviewer in field. Dir. (film) including P.I.S.T., 1984, You're Not Alone, 1985, Secret of Easter Island, 1990, (video) Jock Jokes, 1988. Recipient Best Critical Article, 2nd Pl. award Calif. Intercollegiate Press Assn., 1979, Golden Eagle award CINE, 1985, 91, Blue Ribbon award Am. Film & Video Festival, 1987, Gold award Houston Internat. Film Festival, 1987, Key Art award Hollywood Reporter, 1990, 91, N.Y. Expo Jury award, 1991. Mem. Phi Eta Sigma Honor Soc. Home and Office: Jeff Berry Prodns 7760 Paseo Del Rey Apt 309 Playa Del Rey CA 90293-8340

BERRY, JOHN CHARLES, clinical psychologist, educational administrator; b. Modesto, Calif., Nov. 29, 1938; s. John Wesley and Dorothy Evelyn (Harris) B.; A.B., Stanford, 1960; postgrad. Trinity Coll., Dublin, Ireland, 1960-61; Ph.D., Columbia, 1967; m. Arlene Ellen Sossin, Oct. 7, 1978; children—Elise, John Jordan, Kaitlyn. Research assoc. Judge Baker Guidance Center, Boston, 1965-66; psychology asso. Napa State Hosp., Imola, Calif., 1966-67, staff psychologist, 1967-75, program asst., 1975-76; program dir. Met. State Hosp., Norwalk, Calif., 1976-77; asst. supt. Empire Union Sch. Dist., Modesto, Calif., 1977-93, dep. supt., 1993—. Mem. Am. Psychol. Assn., Assn. Calif. Sch. Adminstrs., Sigma Xi. Contbg. author: Life History Research in Psychopathology, 1970. Home: 920 Eastridge Dr Modesto CA 95355-4672 Office: Empire Union Sch Dist 116 N Mcclure Rd Modesto CA 95357-1329

BERRY, JOHN COLTRIN, insurance executive; b. Chgo., Nov. 23, 1937; s. Fred and Dorthy (Hubbard) B.; m. Hazel Janette Garrett, June 4, 1961; children: Cheryl, Pat, Andy. BS in Mgmt., No. Ill. U., 1968. Dir. for svcs. U.S. Army, Savanna (Ill.) Army Depot, 1963-73; dir. Office Mgmt. Scis. HHS, Health Care Financing Adminstrn., Dallas, 1973-76; dir. Bur. Program Operation HHS, Health Care Financing Adminstrn., Washington, 1976-87; sr. v.p. Trigon Blue Cross Blue Shield, Roanoke, 1987—; speaker various health care issues. Mem. Savanna (Ill.) City Coun., 1968-72; bd. dirs. United Way of Roanoke Valley, 1987-98, Comprehensive Health Investment Project, Roanoke, 1988-93, Total Action Against Poverty, Roanoke, 1989-93, Roanoke chpt. Am. Heart Assn., 1991-93; bd. dirs. Art Mus. of Western Va., 1995-97, Downtown Roanoke, Inc., 1995—, Lewis-Gale Found., 1995-97. Recipient Prodn. Mgmt. award Northern Ill. U., 1968, Meritorious Exec. award presented by Pres. of U.S., Wash., 1985. Mem. Am. Assn. Indsl. Engrs. (bd.dirs.), Roanoke Regional C. of C. (bd. dirs. 1992-93). Republican. Methodist. Avocations: golf, bridge, auto racing. Home: 5192 Fox Ridge Rd SW Roanoke VA 24014-4919 Office: Trigon Blue Cross Blue Shield 602 S Jefferson St Roanoke VA 24011-2406

BERRY, JOHN NICHOLS, III, publishing executive, editor; b. Montclair, N.J., June 12, 1933; s. John Nichols and Marian Petrea (Chase) B.; m. Louise Parker, June 5, 1982; children: Elizabeth Ann, John Nichols IV, Thomas Parker. A.B. in History, Boston U., 1958; M.S. in L.S, Simmons Coll., Boston, 1960. Youth-reference librarian Reading (Mass.) Pub. Library, 1959-60; reference librarian Simmons Coll., 1960-62, asst. dir. library, 1962-64; lectr. Sch. Library Sci., 1961-64; asst. editor Library Jour., R. R. Bowker Co. (div. Xerox), N.Y.C., 1964-66; editor book editorial dept. R. R. Bowker Co. (div. Xerox), 1966-68, editor-in-chief Library Jour., 1969-89; v.p., editor-in-chief Libr. Jour. Cahners Pub. Co., N.Y.C., 1989—; journalist in residence Sch. of Libr. and Info. Sci. La. State U., 1989; vis. prof. Sch. Info. and Libr. Sci., Pratt Inst., Bklyn., 1994—; lectr. Sch. Libr. and Info. Sci., U. Pitts., 1972-73, Sch. Libr. and Info. Studies, U. Wash., Seattle, 1982; William Gillard lectr. dept. libr. and info. sci. St. John's U., 1986; Rudi Weiss lectr. N.Y. Libr. Assn., 1988. Contbg. author: Library Issues The Sixties, 1970; editor: Directory of Library Consultants, 1969, Bay State Libr., 1962-64 (ALA-H.W. Wilson Libr. periodical award 1962); contbr. articles to profl. jours. Served with AUS, 1955-57. Recipient First Annual Alumni Achievement award Sch. Library Sci. Simmons Coll., 1970, Joseph W. Lippincott award Am. Lib. Assn., 1992, Spl. Svc. award Assn. Lib. and Info. Sci. Edn., 1993. Mem. ALA, Am. Soc. for Info. Sci., Spl. Libr. Assn. (chmn. div. pub. 1969), Archons of Colophon, Beta Phi Mu. Democrat. Home: 41 Chester St Stamford CT 06905-3945 Office: Bowker Mags/Cahners Pub 249 W 17th St New York NY 10011-5300

BERRY, JONI INGRAM, hospice pharmacist, educator; b. Charlotte, N.C., June 6, 1953; d. James Clifford and Patricia Ann (Ebener) Ingram; div.; children: Erin Blair, Rachel Anne, James Rosser. BS in Pharmacy, U. N.C., 1976, MS in Pharmacy, 1979, postgrad., 1999. Lic. pharmacist, N.C. Resident in pharmacy Sch. Pharmacy, U. N.C., Chapel Hill, 1977-79, adj. asst. prof., 1985—; pharmacist Durham County Gen. Hosp., Durham, N.C., 1977-79; coord. clin. pharm. Wake Med. Ctr., Raleigh, N.C., 1979-80; co-dir. pharmacy edn. Wake Area Health Edn. Ctr., Raleigh, 1980-85; pharmacist cons. Hospice of Wake County, Raleigh, 1980—; co-owner Integrated Pharm. Care Systems, Inc., 1995—. Mem. editorial adv. bd. Hospice Jour., 1985-91, 94—, Jour. Pharm. Care in Pain and Symptom Mgmt., 1992—; reviewer Am. Jour. Hospice Care, 1996-98; editor pharmacy sect. notes NHO Coun. Hospice Profls.; contbr. articles to profl. jours. Troop leader Girl Scouts U.S.A., Raleigh, 1987—, trainer, 1989-91, mgr. svc. unit, 1990-94; Sunday sch. tchr. St. Phillips Luth. Ch., Raleigh, 1990-92, 94-95, asst. min., 1995—, choir mem. 1998—. Recipient Silver Pinecone award Girl Scouts U.S., 1991, Golden Rule award J.C. Penney Co., 1991. Mem. Nat. Coun. Hospice Profls. (pharmacy sect. leader 1998—), Am. Pharm. Assn. (hospice pharmacist steering com. 1990—), Acad. of Pharmacy Practice and Mgmt. (mem.-at-large 1996—, chair-elect specialized sect. 1998—), Am. Soc. Hosp. Pharmacists, Nat. Hospice Orgn., Am. Pain Soc., N.C. Pharm. Assn. (Don Blanton award 1985, mem. continuing edn. com. 1986-87, com. chair 1981-84), N.C. Soc. Hosp. Pharmacists (bd. dirs. 1984-86, program com. 1988-91), Wake County Pharm. Assn. (sec. 1982-85), Rho Chi. Democrat. Avocations: gardening, weight lifting, aerobics. Office: Hospice Wake County 1300 Saint Mary's St Raleigh NC 27605

BERRY, JOYCE CHARLOTTE, university press editor; b. Chgo., Feb. 12, 1937; d. George Carlisle and Myrtle Dorothy (Olsen) B. B.S., U. Colo.; cert., Institute de Touraine and U. Grenoble, France, 1960-61; diploma in French studies, The Sorbonne, Paris, 1962; postgrad., Columbia U., 1964-65. Cartographic map editor Corps Engrs., San Francisco, 1958-60; asst. editor Field Enterprises, Chgo., 1962-63; assoc. editor Grolier, Inc., N.Y.C., 1963-65; sr. editor Oxford U. Press, N.Y.C., 1965—. Vol. Lexington Democratic Club, 1964; copywriter Citizens for Clean Air, 1965-66; editor INFORM, N.Y.C., 1979-80; mem. adoption group Amnesty Internat. U.S.A., 1978—. Mem. Gamma Theta Upsilon. Office: Oxford Univ Press 198 Madison Ave New York NY 10016-4308*

BERRY, KATHRYN ALLEN, editor in chief science publication; b. Binghamton, N.Y., July 9, 1958; d. William Earl Berry and Barbara (Ellis) Dickay; m. Mark Robert Bertram, Aug. 17, 1996. BA, Wittenberg U., 1980; M in Pub. Adminstrn., Ind. U., 1983. Assoc. instr. Ind. U., Bloomington, 1980-81; ranger, spokesperson U.S. Park Svc. Denali (Alaska) Nat. Park and Preserve, 1981-84 summers; sci. and investigative reporter Fairbanks (Alaska) Daily News Miner, 1984-88; publs. editor, br. mgr. Alaska Natural History Assn., Denali Park, 1988-89; free lance writer and editor Alaska Bus. Monthly, Anchorage Daily News, Alask Geographic, Fairbanks, Alaska, 1989-91; sci. editor-in-chief Geophys. Inst. U. Alaska, Fairbanks, 1991—. Co-author, editor: (book) Black Tides: The Alaska Oil Spill, 1989; editor: (books) A Backcountry Companion, 1989, The Geology of Denali National Park, 1989; editor Geophys. Inst. Quarterly Newsletter, 1991— (1st pl. writing and editing Alaska Press Women, 1995, Nat. Press Women, 1995, Bronze award Coun. for Advancement and Support of Edn., 1994). Officer United Way, Fairbanks, Alaska, 1994—; bd. dirs. Presbn. Hospitality House, Fairbanks, 1995—. Recipient Alaska Legislature citation for publ. excellence, 1994, 95, 96, First Place Nat. award for editing and producing "Global Change and Polar Regions" Jour. of Govt. Info., 1995. Mem. Alaska Press Women, Nat. Press Women, Soc. Profl. Journalists. Democrat. Lutheran. Avocations: lead singer jazz and folk bands, dog musher, outdoor enthusiast. Office: Geophys Inst U Alaska 903 Koyukuk Dr Fairbanks AK 99775-7320

BERRY, KIM LAUREN, artist; b. Hollywood, Calif., June 5, 1962; d. Gary and Judith Debra (Epstein) B.; m. Stanley Mark Carroll, Dec. 2, 1990. Studied with Jon Serl, Lake Elsinore, Calif., 1983-90; cert. in biomed. art, Calif. State U., Long Beach, 1985, BFA in Illustration, 1985; MFA in Painting, Claremont (Calif.) Grad. Sch., 1990. Instr. visual art Bixby Sch., Long Beach, Calif., 1993-94; cons. visual art, artist Fullerton (Calif.) Sch. Dist., 1990-91. Art dir.: (film) The Secret of Easter Island, 1991 (Cine Golden Eagle award 1991); one-man show West Gallery, Claremont Grad. Sch., 1990; represented in group shows Double Rocking G Gallery, L.A., 1983, Coll. Bd., Princeton, N.J., 1984, Gallery C Calif. State U., Long Beach, 1985, DA Gallery, Pomona, Calif., 1988, West and East Galleries Claremont Grad., 1989, Helen Lindhurst Gallery, U. So. Calif., L.A., 1990, Am. Film Inst. Warner Theatre,L.A., 1991, Out of Darkness Gallery, Long Beach, 1991, 92, IPSO FACTO Gallery, Fullerton, Calif., 1992, Found. Art Resources, L.A., 1993, The Caged Chameleon Gallery, Santa Ana, Calif., 1993, A.R.C. Gallery William Rainey Harper Coll., Palatine, Ill., 1993, Nat. Congress Art Design, Salt Lake City, 1995, Aids Resource Ctr., Milwaukee, 1995, Fairfield (Calif.) Cultural Ctr., 1995, Huntington Beach (Calif.) Cultural Ctr., 1996, Orange County Ctr. Contemporary Art, Santa Ana, 1997, Gallery by the Sea, San Pedro Art Assn., 1997; contbr. to profl. jours. Active benefit exhibit Art for AIDS, AIDS Resource Ctr. of Wis., Milw., 1995, Animal Assistance League Benefit Exhibit, Ipso Facto Gallery, Fullerton, 1992, Homeless Benefit Exhibit, The Caged Chameleon Gallery, Santa Ana, Calif., 1993; vol. Brit. Petroleum Bird Rescue, Long Beach, 1990,

Hemopet Greyhound Rescue, Irvine, Calif.; bd. dirs., co-dir., curator spl. projects Gallery by the Sea, San Pedro, 1998-99; panelist Orange County Ctr. for Contemporary Art Roundtable Forum, 1998. Calif. State Grad. fellow in Humanities, 1990; Claremont Grad. Sch. Travel and Rsch. grantee, 1989. Home and Studio: 5891 Pinon Dr Huntington Beach CA 92649-4927

BERRY, LAURIE ANN, critical care nurse; b. Duluth, Minn., Dec. 13, 1954; d. Robert Reginald and Claire Olivia (Hood) Johnson. RN, St. Luke's Hosp., Duluth, Minn., 1976. Gen. staff nurse med./neurosurgery Mercy San Juan Hosp., Citrus Hts., Calif., 1979-80; gen. staff nurse MSICU St. Luke's Hosp., Duluth, 1980-84; gen. staff nurse SICU St. Francis Hosp., Tulsa, 1984-85; gen. staff nurse bone marrow transplant Fairview U. Hosp., Mpls., 1985-98; staff nurse, med., surg., ICU Abbott Northwestern Hosp., Mpls., 1998—. Mem. Minn. Nurses Assn.

BERRY, LEORA MARY, school nurse; b. Peoria, Ill.; d. William Henry and Harrietta Estella (Booker) Wilson; div. ADN, Ill. Ctrl. Coll., 1971; BSN, Wright State U., 1984; MS, Ohio State U., 1990. Cert. sch. nurse, Ohio. Staff nurse U. Ill. Hosp., Chgo., 1971-72; burn unit head nurse Childrens Med. Ctr., Dayton, Ohio, 1973-80, recovery rm. nurse, 1980-86; grad. tchg. asst. Ohio State U., Columbus, 1987-88; staff nurse VA Med. Ctr., Dayton, 1988-89; clin. instr. Dayton Sch. Practical Nursing, 1990-91; sch. nurse Dayton Pub. Schs., 1991—; mem. adv. bd. Horizons in Nursing, Wright State U., 1989-90. Vol. health screening Delta Sigma Theta, Health Fair, 1985. Mem. Ohio Nurses Assn. (polit. action com. 1988-90, dist. 10 pres. 1992-94, dist. 10 bd. dirs. 1988-94, Nurse of Yr. 1994), Dayton Black Nurses Assn., Sigma Theta Tau. Methodist. Avocations: horseback riding, traveling, camping.

BERRY, LOREN CURTIS, lawyer, consultant; b. N.Y.C., Apr. 30, 1912; s. Gordon Lockwood and Katharine Wolcott (Dwight) B.; m. Florence Hoyt Bateson, May 10, 1941; children: Rosina B. Dixon, Roger Wolcott, Lucinda B. AB, Yale U., 1934; LLB, Columbia U., 1938. Bar: Miss. 1937, N.Y. 1939. Assoc. Rogers & Wells and predecessor firms, N.Y.C., 1939-41, 45-53, ptnr., 1953-83, cons. on estates & trusts, 1983-90, sr. counsel, 1990—; dir. Church & Dwight Co., Inc., 1961-84. Councilman Town of Huntington, N.Y., 1953-57; v.p. Assn. Towns State of N.Y., Albany, 1957-60; del. from 2d senatorial dist. to N.Y. State Constl. Conv., 1967; clerk of vestry St. John's Ch., Cold Spring Harbor, N.Y., 1982-88; mem. Suffolk County N.Y. Rep. Com., 1952-85. With USNR, 1941-45, lt. commdr. 1944-45, WWII Navy Scouting Squadron Assn. (cons. 1994—). Mem. N.Y. State Bar Assn., Suffolk County Bar Assn., Huntington C. of C. (dir. 1958-63), Elks, Union Club N.Y., Tahawus Club. (sec. 1975-95). Home: PO Box 23664/Fairfield Sta Hilton Head Island SC 29925-3664 Office: Rogers & Wells Trust Dept 200 Park Ave New York NY 10166

BERRY, LYNN MARINA, healthcare administrator; b. Chgo., June 15, 1955; d. Frank William and Ruth Wyatt (Sieber) Latzel; m. James F. Berry, Aug. 2, 1997. AA, Coll. DuPage, 1986; BA, Elmhurst Coll., 1988. Bd. commrs. specialist Jt. Commn. on Accreditation of Healthcare Orgns., 1999—. Mem. ACLU, U.S. Holocaust Meml. Mus. (founding mem.), Chgo. Geneal. Soc., Jewish Geneal. Soc., Mensa, Psi Chi, Phi Theta Kappa. Avocations: reading, films, dining out, geneal. rsch., baking. Office: Joint Commn on Accreditation Healthcare Orgns 1 Renaissance Blvd Oakbrook Terrace IL 60181

BERRY, MARION, congressman; b. Aug. 27, 1942; m. Caroyn Berry; 2 children. BS, U. Ark., 1965. Ptnr., gen. mgr. family farm Gillett, Ark.; commr. Ark. Soil and Water Conservation Commn., 1986-94, chmn., 1992; spl. asst. to Pres. Agrl. Trade and Food Assistance, 1993; mem. 105th Congress from 1st Ark. dist., 1997—; mem. agr. com., transp. and infrastructure com. Avocations: hunting, fishing. Office: 1113 Longworth HOB Washington DC 20515*

BERRY, MARY FRANCES, federal agency administrator, history and law educator; b. Nashville, Feb. 17, 1938; d. George Ford and Frances Southall (Wiggins) B. B.A., Howard U., 1961, M.A., 1962; Ph.D., U. Mich., 1966, J.D., 1970; hon. degree, Cen. Mich. U., Howard U., U. Akron, 1977, Benedict Coll., U. Md., Grambling State U., 1979, Bethune-Cookman Coll., Clark Coll., Del. State Coll., 1980, Oberlin Coll., Langston U., 1983, Marian Coll., Haverfod Coll., 1984, Colby Coll., CUNY, 1986, DePaul U., 1987. Bar: D.C. 1972. Asst. prof. history Central Mich. U., Mt. Pleasant, 1966-68; asst. prof. Eastern Mich. U., Ypsilanti, 1968-69; assoc. prof. Eastern Mich. U., 1969-70, U. Md., College Park, 1969-76; acting dir. Afro-Am. studies, 1970-72, dir., 1972-74, acting chmn. div. behavioral and social scis., 1973-74, provost div. behavioral and social scis., 1973-76; prof. history, prof. law U Colo. at Boulder, 1976-80, chancellor, 1976-77; prof. history and law Howard U., Washington, 1980—; Geraldine R. Segal prof. Am. Social Thought U. Pa., 1987—; asst. sec. for edn. HEW, Washington, 1977-80; mem., now chmn U.S. Commn. on Civil Rights, 1980—, now chmn.; adj. assoc. prof. U. Mich., 1970-71; mem. com. visitors U. Mich. Law Sch., 1976-80; mem. nat. adv. panel on minority concerns Coll. Bd., 1980-84; mem. adv. bd. Feminist Press, 1980—; mem. research adv. com. Joint Ctr. for Polit. Studies, 1981—; mem. editorial adv. com. Marcus Garvey Papers, 1981—; mem. adv. bd. Inst. for Higher Edn. Law and Governance, U. Houston, 1983—; Geraldine R. Segal prof. of am. social thought U. Pa., 1987—. Author: Black Resistance/White Law, 1971, Military Necessity and Civil Rights Policy, 1977, Stability, Security and Continuity, Mr. Justice Burton and Decision-Making in the Supreme Court, 1945-58, 1978, (with John Blassingame) Long Memory: The Black Experience in America, 1982; Why ERA Failed, 1986; asso. editor Jour. Negro History, 1974-78; contbr. articles, revs. to profl. jours. Bd. dirs. ARC, Washington, 1980—; trustee Tuskegee U., 1980—; mem. adv. bd. Project '87, 1978—; mem. council UN U., 1986—. Recipient Athena (disting. alumni) award U. Mich., 1977, Roy Wilkins Civil Rights award NAACP, 1983, Image award, 1983, Allard Lowenstein award, 1984, President's award Congl. Black Caucus Found., 1985, Woman of Yr. award Nat. Capital Area YWCA, 1985, Hubert H. Humphrey Civil Rights award Leadership Conf. on Civil Rights, 1986, Rosa Parks award SCLC, Black Achievement award Ebony Mag., Woman of Yr. award Ms. Mag., 1986. Mem. ABA, Nat. Bar Assn., D.C. Bar Assn., Nat. Acad. Public Adminstrn., Orgn. Am. Historians (exec. bd. 1974-77), Assn. Study of Afro-Am. Life and History (exec. bd. 1973-76), Am. Hist. Assn. (v.p. for profession 1980-83), Am. Soc. Legal History, Coalition 100 Black Women (hon.), Delta Sigma Theta (hon.). Office: Commn on Civil Rights Office of Chmn 624 9th St NW Washington DC 20425-0002*

BERRY, MICHAEL A., physician, consultant; b. San Francisco, June 2, 1946; s. Charles Alden and Addella (Nance) B.; m. Mary Frances Cauthen, Mar. 5, 1977; children: Jennifer Alice, Michael David, Matthew Alden. BS, Tex. Christian U., 1968; MD, U. Tex., Dallas, 1971; MS, Ohio State U., 1977. Diplomate Am. Bd. Preventive Medicine (bd. dirs., trustee 1990-98, vice chmn. aerospace medicine), Am. Bd. Med. Specialties (rep. 1995-98, database com. 1998—). Intern in gen. surgery Wilford Hall USAF Med. Ctr., San Antonio, 1971-72; flight surgeon USAF, Madrid, Spain, 1972-75, chief physician, 1974-75; comdr. 401st Air Transport Hosp., 1974; flight surgeon USAF, Lakenheath, Eng., 1975-76; resident in aerospace medicine Ohio State U., Columbus, 1976-78, Johnson Space Ctr., Houston, 1976-78; chief flight medicine clinic NASA Johnson Space Ctr., 1978-81; ptnr. Preventive & Aerospace Medicine Cons., P.A., Houston, 1982—; adj. asst. prof. aerospace medicine U. Tex. Sch. Pub. Health, Houston, 1979—; vis. lectr. space medicine USAF Sch. Aerospace Medicine, Brooks AFB, Tex., 1979—. Author book chpts.; contbr. articles to profl. jours. V.p. Am. Heart Assn., 1979-80, pres., 1981-82, Mission Glen Elem. PTA, 1986; mem. fin. com. Mission Bend United Meth. Ch., 1984-88, mem. adminstrv. bd., 1985-89, chmn., 1987, 88. Maj. USAF, 1970-76. Decorated D.S.M. Fellow Am. Coll. Preventive Medicine (chair sci. program 1981); mem. AMA (Physicians Recognition award 1982, 97), Aerospace Med. Assn. (pres. 1991-92, first v.p./pres.-elect 1989-91, v.p. 1988-89, chair sci. program 1985, mem. edn. and tng. com., mem. awards com., mem. coun. 1984-97, , rep. to AMA, Julian E. Ward Meml. award 1979), Civil Aviation Med. Assn., Soc. USAF Flight Surgeons, Soc. NASA Flight Surgeons (v.p. 1988, pres. 1990), Wilderness Med. Soc. (founding mem.), Internat. Acad. Aviation and Space Medicine (dir. 1996), Tex. Med. Assn., Harris County Med. Soc. Avocations: snow skiing, scuba diving, fishing, cooking. Office: Preventive & Aerospace Med Cons PA 10777 Westheimer Rd Ste 935 Houston TX 77042-3460

BERRY, MICHAEL JOHN, author, medical and dental management consultant; b. Waynesville, Mo., Dec. 30, 1957; s. John Patrick and Gloria Mae (Flynn) B.; m. Mary Ellen Larson, Oct. 31, 1981; children: Justin Michael, Amy Leah, Jessica Ann, Allison Marie. Student, U. Md., 1982-83, Ind. U., 1979-80, Purdue U., 1976-79. Med. and dental mgmt. cons./liaison Monticello, Ind.; adv. cons. Health Care Info. Network, Monticello; ind. subcontr./writer Am. Med. News (AMA), Chgo., 1992—; condr. seminars and table clinics in field. Author: Collections Made Easy, 1992, 2d edit., 1999, Reality Check (fiction), 1995; contbr. numerous articles to profl. jours.; book reviewer Chgo. Medicine, 1992, Health Care Fin. Mgmt., 1994. Ch. adv. bd. on fin. Yeoman (Ind) United Meth. Ch., 1988-91. Fax: 219-583-3015. E-mail: mjbconsult@email.com. Home and Office: 742 Canary Ln Monticello IN 47960-2111

BERRY, MORRELL JOHN, cultural organization administrator. BA summa cum laude, U. Md., 1980; MPA, Syracuse U., 1981. Asst. to chief Office of cable TV, Montgomery County, 1982-84; staff dir. Md. State Fin. Com., Annapolis, 1984-85; legis. asst. Rep. Steny H. Hoyer, 1985-86; assoc. staff House Appropriations Com., Washington, 1986-94; dep. asst. Sec. of Treasury, acting asst. sec. Dept. Treasury, Washington, 1994-95; dir. Office Govt. Rels., sr. policy advisor to under sec. Smithsonian Inst., Washington, 1995-97; asst. sec. for policy, mgmt. budget U.S. Dept. Interior, Washington, 1997—. Herbert H. Lehman fellow, 1981. Office: U.S. Deptartment of the Interior Office Sec for Policy Mgmt/Budget 1849 C St NW Washington DC 20240-0001*

BERRY, NANCY MICHAELS, philanthropy consultant; b. Kansas City, Mo., Sept. 3, 1928; d. William Wilson and Allene (Hart) Michaels; children: C. Nelson, Michaels C., Christopher N. (dec.), David S. Student, Wellesley Coll., 1945-48; B.A., Okla. U., 1971, M.A., 1978. Exec. dir. Oklahoma City Community Found., 1974-78; v.p. World Neighbors, Oklahoma City, 1978-80; v.p. Project Orbis N.Y.C., 1980-83; v.p. Nat. Exec. Svc. Corps, N.Y.C., 1983-95. Mem. Jr. League. Democrat. Episcopalian. Home: 71 E 77th St New York NY 10021-1834

BERRY, PETER DUPRE, real estate executive; b. Augusta, Ga., July 25, 1943; s. James A. and Carrie A. (Dupre) B.; children: Daniel D., David E., Katherine M. AB, Wofford Coll., Spartanburg, S.C., 1965; MBA, U. S.C., 1966. Treas. Landmarks Group, Inc., Atlanta, 1968-72; ptnr. Berry & Freyer Land Co., Atlanta, 1972-75; project developer Cochran Properties, Atlanta, 1975-77; pres. Berry Bros. Enterprises, Inc., Union, S.C., 1977—; bd. dirs. S.C. Nat. Bank, Union, S.C.; adv. bd. Wachovia Bank; permanent mem. adv. com. S.C. State Devel. Bd., 1986—, downtown revitalization bd., 1984-92; mem., permanent adv. bd. S.C. State Devel. Bd., 1980-90; gov.'s health care adv. com., 1994; pvt. industry coun., 1993—. 1st lt. U.S. Army, 1966-68. Named to Outstanding Young Men Am., 1970. Mem. Carolina Lumber Dealers Assn. (bd. dirs. 1979-84), Young Carolinians Assn., Union C. of C. (bd. dirs. 1980-82), Equal Compensation Commn. S.C. United Meth. Ch., Downtown Merchants Assn., Union Country Club (pres.), Debordieu Beach Club (Georgetown, S.C.). Methodist. Avocations: ham radio, tennis, golf, jogging. Office: Paradise Home Ctrs 600 Buffalo Rd Union SC 29379

BERRY, PHILLIP REID, beverage distribution executive; b. Owensboro, Ky., Apr. 4, 1950; s. Patrick Henry and Dorothy Lee (Best) B.; children: Patricia Brooke, Phillip Benjamin. BA in Psychology, Western Ky. U., 1972. Dir. Otis Bowen Ctr. for Human Svcs., Warsaw, Ind., 1982-84; exec. dir. Fourth Freedom Forum, Goshen, Ind., 1984-88; pres. NBI, Goshen, Ind., 1988-95. Chmn. strategic planning com. Jaycees Internat., Coral Gables, Fla., 1989-91 (world pres., 1987). With USAR, 1972-78. Recipient Don Cavalli Meml. award U.S. Jaycees, Tulsa, 1984-85; Rep. of China Order of Merit #30. Mem. Jr. Chamber Internat., Lambda Chi Alpha. Avocations: golf, travel, cartooning. Office: Bryant Distbg. Co Inc 7849 National Tpke Louisville KY 40214-4901

BERRY, RICHARD DOUGLAS, architectural educator, urban planner and designer; b. Denver, Oct. 28, 1926; s. Howard Thomas and Susie Ann (Ross) B. B.A. in Humanities, U. Denver, 1951; B.Arch., U. Calif-Berkeley, 1957. Assoc., project dir. Victor Gruen Assocs., Architects and Planners, Los Angeles and N.Y.C., 1957-63; mem. faculty urban planning and architecture depts. U. So. Calif., Los Angeles, 1963-75, prof. architecture, 1976-87, prof. emeritus, 1988—; planning, programming and design cons. on new community devel. Irvine Co., Newport Beach, Calif., 1964-65, GE, 1967-68, HUD, 1973-74; cons. GE Found., 1967-68; ednl. cons. U. N.C., 1971-73; vis. prof. urban design U. Wash., Seattle, 1969; lighting designer, scenic artist University City Theatre, Denver, 1947-48. Served with arty. U.S. Army, 1951-53, Korea. Recipient urban design award for Downtown Cin. Renewal Plan, Progressive Architecture, 1963, rsch. achievement award for solar zoning and design Nat. Endowment for Arts, 1984; various rsch. and ednl. grants from pub. and pvt. orgns. Mem. AAAS, AAUP, Am. Inst. Cert. Planners, Am. Planning Assn., Nat. Trust for Hist. Preservation. Office: U So Calif Sch Architecture Los Angeles CA 90089

BERRY, RICHARD LEWIS, author, magazine editor, lecturer, programmer; b. Greenwich, Conn., Nov. 6, 1946; s. John William and Dorothy May (Buck) B.; m. Eleanor von Auw, June 7, 1968. BA, U. Va., 1968; MSc, York U., Can., 1972. Research asst. MacMaster U., Hamilton, Ont., Can., 1973-74; project engr. Intraspace Internat., Toronto, Ont., Can., 1974-75; tech. editor Astronomy mag., Milw., 1976-78, editor, 1978-82, editor in chief, 1982-91; editor Telescope Making Mag., Milw., 1978-92; editorial dir. Earth mag., 1990-91, cons., 1992; freelance writer, programmer, lectr., 1991—; editor Cookbook Camera Newsletter, 1994—; cons. editor Willmann-Bell, Richmond, Va., 1983—. Author: Build Your Own Telescope, 1985, Discover the Stars, 1987, (with others) The Star Book, 1984, Introduction to Astronomical Image Processing, 1991, AIP Image Processing Software, 1991, BatchPIX Image Processing Software, 1992, Choosing and Using a CCD Camera, 1992, The CCD Camera Cookbook, 1994, The Dobsonian Telescope: A Practical Manual for Building Large Aperture Telescopes, 1997; contbg. author: Robotic Observatories, 1989, ST6PIX Image Processing Software, 1992, CB245 Image Processing Software, 1994, Multi245 Image Compositing Software, 1995, QColor Color Synthesis Software, 1997; editor: Telescope Optics, Design and Evaluation, 1988. Mem. adv. bd. Global Network of Automatic Telescopes. Recipient Clifford-Holmes award Astronomy for Am., 1981, Dorothea Klumpke-Roberts award Astron. Soc. Pacific, 1990, Omega Centauri award Tex. Star Party, Clyde W. Tombaugh award for tech. innovation in astronomy Riverside Telescope Makers Conf., 1995, G. Bruce Blair award for Achievement in Amateur Astronomy by the Western Amateur Astronomers, 1998; Asteroid 3684 Berry named in his honor by Internat. Astron. Union, 1990. Mem. Internat. Amateur Profl. Photoelec. Photometry, Internat. Dark Sky Assn., Am. Astron. Soc. Avocation: photography.

BERRY, RICHARD STEPHEN, chemist; b. Denver, Apr. 9, 1931; s. Morris and Ethel (Alpert) B.; m. Carla Lamport Friedman, Sept. 4, 1955; children: Andrea, Denise, Eric. AB, Harvard U., 1952, AM, 1954, PhD, 1956. Instr. chemistry Harvard U., 1956-57, U. Mich., 1957-60; asst. prof. Yale U., 1960-64; assoc. prof. U. Chgo., 1964-67, prof., 1967—, James Franck Disting. Svc. prof., 1989—; Arthur D. Little prof. MIT, 1968; Phillips lectr. Haverford Coll., 1968; Lôwdin lectr. Uppsala U, 1989; cons. Avco-Everett Research Labs., 1964-83, Argonne Nat. Lab., 1976—, Oak Ridge Nat. Labs., 1978-81, Los Alamos Sci. Lab., 1975—, mem. adv. com. theory; vis. prof. U. Copenhagen, 1967, 79; mem. adv. panel for chemistry NSF, 1971-73; mem. rev. com. radiol. and environ. research div. Argonne Nat. Lab., 1970-76; mem. evaluation panel measures for air quality Nat. Bur. Standards; mem. numerical data adv. bd. NRC, 1978-86, chmn., 1981-86, mem. com. strengthening linkages between math. and scis., 1997—; mem. steering com. panel on environ. monitoring, mem. com. on atomic and molecular sci., 1984-89, com. on chem. scis. NAS-NRC, 1977-79; mem. adv. panel on health of sci. and tech. enterprise, mem. adv. panel on nat. labs. Office Tech. Assessment; mem. adv. bd. Environ. Health Resource Center, Inst. for Theoretical Physics, Santa Barbara, 1989-91; mem. vis. com. div. applied physics Harvard U., 1977-81; Hinshelwood lectr. Oxford (Eng.) U., 1980, Newton-Abraham prof., 1986-87; mem. adv. panel dept. chemistry Princeton U., 1978-81; prof. associé U. Paris-Sud, 1979-80; Newton Abraham prof. Oxford U., 1986-87; Phi Beta Kappa lectr. 1989-90; Welch Symposium lectr., 1995; pres. Telluride Summer Rsch. Ctr., 1989-93; chair com. transnat. exchange sci. data Nat. Rsch. Coun., 1994-97; Frederick Kaufman lectr. U. Pitts., 1996; Sackler lectr. Tel Aviv (Israel) U., 1999, F.C. Bartell lectr. U. Mich., 1999. Author: Understanding Energy, 1988; co-author: TOSCA, The Total Social Cost of Fossil and Nuclear Power, 1979, Physical Chemistry, 1980, Thermodynamic Optimization of Finite Time Processes, 1999; assoc. editor: Jour. Chem. Physics, 1971-74, Accounts Chem. Rsch., 1975-90, Revs. Modern Physics, 1983-95, Phys. Rev. A, 1986-92, Phys. Rev. E, 1992-94; bd. dirs. Bull. Atomic Scientists, 1974-83; adv. editor: Resources and Energy, 1978-92; contbr. articles to profl. jours. Recipient Heyrovsky medal Czech Acad. Sci., 1997; Alfred P. Sloan fellow, 1962-66; Guggenheim fellow, 1972-73; MacArthur prize fellow, 1983; Alexander von Humboldt Stiftung prize fellow, 1993. Fellow AAAS (chmn. chemistry sect. 1993-94), Am. Phys. Soc. (coun. 1993-95, publs. oversight com. 1996—, chmn. few-body sys. topical group 1994-95), Am. Acad. Arts and Scis. (v.p. 1987-90, 95-98), Japan Soc. for Promotion of Sci.; mem. NAS (home sec. 1999—), Am. Chem. Soc., Royal Danish Acad. Arts and Letters (fgn.), Sigma Xi (nat. lectr. 1976-77).

BERRY, RITA KAY, medical technologist; b. Borger, Tex., July 2, 1958; d. Thomas Vickers, Floy (Martin) Livingston; m. James William Berry, Feb. 20, 1982; children: Matthew Tyler, Rachael Breanne. AAS, Amarillo Coll., 1978; BS, West Tex. State U., 1980. Cert. med. technologist, blood bank technologist, specialist in blood banking. Phlebotomist Coffee Meml. Blood Ctr., Amarillo, 1977-78; med. lab. tech. Northwest Tex. Hosp., Amarillo, 1978-80, med. technologist, 1980-82; med. technologist St. Anthony's Hosp., Amarillo, 1982-84, program dir. Sch. of Med. Technology, 1984-88; med. technologist VAMC, Amarillo, 1988-90, High Plains Bapt. Hosp., Amarillo, 1990—; mem. bone marrow transplant team, High Plains Bapt. Hosp., Amarillo, 1996; inspector lab. accreditation program Coll. of Am. Pathologists, Northfield, Ill., 1991—. Designer greeting card/Rubber Stamper's World Mag., 1995 (2nd place award 1995); painting exhibit: Tri-State Fair (1st and 3d place), 1998; author poetry. Coach Odyssey of the Mind Amarillo Ind. Sch. Dist., 1995-97; coach cheerleading Kids Inc., Amarillo, 1993. Mem. Am. Assn. Blood Banks (lead assessor accreditation program 1998), Am. Soc. Clin. Pathologists, Internat. Soc. Poets (chmn. student poetry contest com., v.p., publicity chmn. 1997-98, pres. 1998, newsletter editor, yearbook editor Hi-Plains chpt., Web master poetry Web site), Poetry Soc. Tex. (pres. Hi-Plains Chapt., 1998), Inspirational Writers-Alive, Acad. Am. Poets, Amarillo Fine Arts Assn., Lone Star Pastel Soc., Tri-State Artists Assn., West Tex. Watercolor Soc. Republican. Baptist. Avocations: poetry, painting, rubber art stamping, music, reading. Home: 2914 Trigg St Amarillo TX 79103-7125

BERRY, ROBERT BASS, construction executive; b. Tulsa, Jan. 29, 1948; s. Guy Leonard and Barbara (Bass) B.; m. Catherine Cowles, Jan. 16, 1971; children: Matthew Knipe, Eli Benjamin. BA in Fin., Okla. U., 1970. Ops. mgr. D.C. Bass & Sons Constrn., Inc., Enid, Okla., 1971-73, chief exec. officer, exec. v.p., 1973-75, pres., 1975—; chief exec. officer, pres. Mosher Devel. Co., Enid, 1975—; pres. Bobsfarm, Inc., Enid, 1975—. Mem. Okla. Acad. State Goals, Oklahoma City, 1985—, Gov.'s Internat. Trade Team, 1986-88; trustee Okla. chpt. The Nature Conservancy; mem. Leadership Okla., Oklahoma City, 1991, Habitat for Humanity, Enid, 1984; chmn. State Alcohol Beverage Law Enforcement Commn., Oklahoma City, 1984-88, State Tort and Liability Task Force, 1986-87; bd. dirs. Enid Wellness Ctr., 1985-87, Enid Joint Indsl. Found., 1984—. Capt. C.E. U.S. Army, 1971. Named Exec. of Yr., Profl. Secs. Internat., 1981; recipient Pres.'s Coun. award Phillips U., 1984, Developer's award Heritage League Enid, 1985. Mem. Okla. State C. of C. (bd. dirs. 1986—, chmn. 1989), Enid C. of C. (bd. dirs. 1975-78, 81-84, Vol. of Yr.), Associated Gen. Contractors (legis. team 1985-87), Young Pres.' Orgn. Republican. Presbyterian. Avocations: running, skiing, hunting, scuba, climbing. Office: DC Bass & Sons Constrn Co 205 E Maine Ave Enid OK 73702-1069

BERRY, ROBERT JOHN, architect; b. Concord, Mass., Nov. 10, 1947. A in Archtl. Engring., Wentworth Inst. Tech., 1967; BArch, U. Ariz., 1971. Registered architect, Mass. Asst. prof. Wentworth Inst. Tech., Boston, 1974-81, 90-94; prin. Robert J. Berry, Architect, Boxborough, Mass., 1974—. Mem. Am. Soc. Archtl. Perspectivists (exhibitor 1986). Avocations: photography, golf, oil painting. Home and Office: 171 Summer Rd Boxboro MA 01719

BERRY, ROBERT VAUGHAN, retired electrical manufacturing company executive; b. Newark, Mar. 24, 1933; s. Harold Silver and Elizabeth Lippincott (Vaughan) B.; m. Victoria Shaw, Mar. 8, 1958; children—Patricia E., Michael V. B.A., Dartmouth Coll., 1954. With Thomas & Betts Corp., Memphis, 1957-95, dir., 1972-85, v.p. fin., 1975-83, sr. v.p., 1983-95; ret., 1995; pres. Thomas & Betts Internat., Inc., 1975; bd. dirs. Ames Rubber Corp., Hamburg, N.J. Trustee Carrier Found. Psychiat. Hosp., Belle Mead, N.J., 1984-92. 1st lt. Airborne Corps U.S. Army, 1954-57. Mem. Baltusrol Golf Club (Springfield, N.J.), Harbor Ridge Golf Club (Stuart, Fla.), Summerlea Golf and Country Club (Montreal, Que., Can.), Mid Ocean Club (Bermuda), Royal and Ancient Golf Club of St. Andrews (Scotland). Republican. *Have a little fun each day - if you wait until the end you might miss it.*

BERRY, ROBERT WORTH, lawyer, educator, retired army officer; b. Ryderwood, Wash., Mar. 2, 1926; s. John Franklin and Anita Louise (Worth) B. B.A. in Polit. Sci., Wash. State U., 1950; J.D., Harvard U., 1955; M.A., John Jay Coll. Criminal Justice, 1981. Bar: D.C. 1956, U.S. Dist. Ct. (D.C.) 1956, U.S. Ct. of Appeals (D.C. cir.) 1957, U.S. Ct. Mil. Appeals 1957, Pa. 1961, U.S. Dist. Ct. (ea. dist.) Pa. 1961, U.S. Dist. Ct. (ctrl. dist.) Calif. 1967, U.S. Supreme Ct. 1961, Calif. 1967, U.S. Ct. Claims 1975, Colo. 1997, U.S. Dist. Ct. Colo. 1997, U.S. Ct. Appeals (10th cir.) 1997. Research assoc. Harvard U., 1955-56; atty. Office Gen. Counsel U.S. Dept. Def., Washington, 1956-60; staff counsel Philco Ford Co., Phila., 1960-63; dir. Washington office Litton Industries, 1967-71; gen. counsel U.S. Dept. Army, Washington, 1971-74, civilian aide to sec. army, 1975-77; col. U.S. Army, 1978-87; prof., head dept. law U.S. Mil. Acad., West Point, N.Y., 1978-86; ret. as brig. gen. U.S. Army, 1987; mil. asst. to asst. sec. of army, Manpower and Res. Affairs Dept. of Army, 1986-87; asst. gen. counsel pub. affairs Litton Industries, Beverly Hills, Calif., 1963-67; chair Coun. of Def. Space Industries Assns., 1968; resident ptnr. Quarles and Brady, Washington, 1971-74; dir., corp. sec., treas., gen. counsel G.A. Wright, Inc., Denver, 1987-92, dir., 1987—; pvt. practice law Fort Bragg, Calif., 1993-96; spl. counsel Messner & Reeves LLC, Denver, 1997—; foreman Mendocino County Grand Jury, 1995-96. Served with U.S. Army, 1944-46, 51-53, Korea. Decorated Bronze Star, Legion of Merit, Disting. Service Medal; recipient Disting. Civilian Service medal U.S. Dept. Army, 1973, 74, Outstanding Civilian Service medal, 1977. Mem. FBA, Bar Assn. D.C., Calif. Bar Assn., Pa. Bar Assn., Colo. State Bar Assn., Army-Navy Club, Army-Navy Country Club, Phi Beta Kappa, Phi Kappa Phi, Sigma Delta Chi, Lambda Chi Alpha. Protestant.

BERRY, ROBERTA MILDRED, civic worker; b. Feb. 27, 1926; d. Judson Stewart and Anna Doretha (Neddermyer) Lawrence; m. Moses Berry, June 29, 1948; children: Scott, Mark. MusB, Cornell Coll., 1948. Choir dir. Presbyn., Meth. chs., Cedar Rapids, Iowa, 1949-71; tchr. assoc. Cedar Rapids Comty. Schs., 1963-73; dir. Pioneer Village, Cedar Rapids, 1982-83, Linn Comty. Food Bank, Cedar Rapids, 1983—; pres. Chs. United, Cedar Rapids, 1984-85, v.p. Iowa state bd., 1994-97; orginator Grade Sch. Picture Lady Program, Cedar Rapids, 1968-69; pres. Seminole Valley Farm, Cedar Rapids, 1980-81; pres. Ch. Women United, Cedar Rapids, 1985-86, also bd. dirs., editor newsletter for Iowa State. Bd. dirs. YWCA, Cedar Rapids, 1970-72, Cedar Rapids Symphony Guild, 1983-88, Iowa Rails to Trails, Cedar Rapids, 1983-88; pers. Methwick Manor Aux., Cedar Rapids, 1985; sec. Coun. on Aging, Cedar Rapids, 1984-85; rep. Civic Newcomers, 1986-93; pres. Cedar Rapids Area Peace Network Guide, Guide Brucemore Hist. Home, 1982—. Mem. UN Assn. (Iowa state bd. 1993—, Linn County pers. 1996-99), Beethoven Club (pres. 1964-65), Coll. Club (pres. 1965-66), PEO (pres. 1982-83), Demolay Mothers Aux. (pres. 1974-75), Postal Workers Aux. (pres. 1974-75). Avocations: oil painting, needlework, tennis, biking. Home: 1118 Maplewood Dr NE Cedar Rapids IA 52402-4710

BERRY, RUSSELL W., historic site administrator. Supt. Wright Bros. Nat. Meml., Manteo, N.C., V.I. Nat. Park. Office: Wright Bros Nat Meml RR 1 Box 675 Manteo NC 27954-9708*

BERRY, STEPHEN JOSEPH, reporter; b. Ft. Jackson, S.C., May 2, 1948; s. Charles Berry and Marjorie (Sheehan) B.; m. Cheryl C. Berry, Nov. 24, 1973; 1 child, Stephen Richard. BA in Polit. Sci., U. Montevallo, 1970; MA, U. N.C. at Greensboro, 1984. Mem. city staff Dothan (Ala.) Eagle, 1970-71; reporter Greensboro (N.C.) News & Record, 1972-81, copy editor, 1981-84, reporter, 1984-89; reporter The Orlando (Fla.) Sentinel, 1989-96, L.A. Times, 1996—. Recipient 3d pl. Spot News award N.C. Press Assn., 1978, Benjamin Fine award, 1985, N.C. Sch. Bell award, 1986, 2d pl. Spot News award N.C. Press Assn., 1987, 3d pl. Lead Reporter award Fla. Soc. Newspaper Editors, 1992, Pulitzer Prize for investigative reporting, 1993, 1st place Soc. Profl. Journalism's Excellence award in sports reporting, 1994. Mem. Phi Alpha Theta. Home: 4945 Reforma Rd Woodland Hills CA 91364-2934 Office: LA Times Times Mirror Sq Los Angeles CA 90053*

BERRY, WILLIAM BENJAMIN NEWELL, geologist, educator, former museum administrator; b. Boston, Sept. 1, 1931; s. John King and Margaret Elizabeth (Newell) B.; m. Suzanne Foster Spaulding, June 10, 1961; 1 child, Bradford Brown. A.B., Harvard U., 1953, A.M., 1955; Ph.D., Yale U., 1957. Asst. prof. geology U. Houston, 1957-58; asst. prof. to prof. paleontology U. Calif., Berkeley, 1958—; prof. geology, 1991—; curator Mus. of Paleontology U. Calif., Berkeley, 1960-75, 87—, dir., 1975-87, chmn. dept. paleontology, 1975-87; marine scientist Lawrence Berkeley Lab., 1989—; cons. U.S. Geol. Survey., Environ. Edn. to Ministry for Environ., Catalonia, Spain. Author: Growth of a Prehistoric Time Scale, 1968, revised edit., 1987, Principles of Stratigraphic Analysis, 1991; assoc. editor Paleoceanography; contbr. numerous articles on stratigraphic, paleontol. and environ. subjects to profl. jours.; editor publs. in geol. scis. Guggenheim Found. fellow, 1966-67. Fellow Calif. Acad. Scis.; mem. Paleontol. Soc., Geol. Soc. Norway, Internat. Platform Assn., Explorers Club, Commonwealth Club Calif. Home: 1366 Summit Rd Berkeley CA 94708-2139 Office: U Calif Dept Geology and Geophysics McCone Hall Berkeley CA 94720

BERRY, WILLIAM LEE, business administration educator; b. Indpls., Dec. 24, 1935; s. George Lee and Anna Marie (Hansert) B.; m. Jane Frances Wilkinson, Sept. 23, 1980; children—Ann Kathleen, Lee Michael, Lynn Colleen, Michael Plenov. BS, Purdue U., 1957; MS, Va. Poly. Inst., 1964; DBA, Harvard U., 1969. Mfg. trainee GE, various locations, 1957-60; supr. mfg. GE, Salem, Va., 1960-64; from asst. prof. to assoc. prof. indsl. mgmt. Purdue U., West Lafayette, Ind., 1968-76; prof. prodn. mgmt. Ind. U., Bloomington, 1976-82; C. Maxwell Stanley prof. prodn. mgmt. U. Iowa, Iowa City, 1982-88; sr. assoc. dean Coll. Bus. Adminstrn. U. Iowa, 1983-87, dir. Mfg. and Productivity Ctr., 1986-87; Belk prof. bus. adminstrn., chmn. ops. mgmt. area U. N.C., 1988-92; prof. bus. adminstrn. Ohio State U., 1992—, Richard Ross chair in mgmt., dir. Ctr. Excellence in Mgmt., 1995—; cons. in field. Co-author: Operations and Logistics Management, 1972, Production Planning, Scheduling and Inventory Control: Concepts, Techniques and Systems, 1974, Master Production Scheduling: Principles and Practice, 1979, Manufacturing Planning and Control Systems, 1984, 2d edit., 1988, 3rd edit., 1992, 4th edit., 1997, ITEC: Manufacturing Planning and Control/Manufacturing Strategy Simulation, 1992, Production and Inventory Control Integrated, 1992; contbr. articles to profl. jours. 1st Enterprise fellow Kenan Inst., 1988-90. Fellow Decision Scis. Inst. (v.p. 1983-84, sec. 1985-86, pres.-elect 1987, pres. 1988); mem. Inst. Indsl. Engrs. (v.p. 1979-81, dir., Disting. Service award 1979), Ops. Mgmt. Assn. (v.p. 1981-85, pres.-elect 1985-86, pres. 1986-87, dir., Disting. Leadership award 1987), Am. Prodn. and Inventory Control Soc., Inst. Mgmt. Sci., Ops. Research Soc. Office: Fisher Coll of Bus Ohio State U Columbus OH 43210

BERRY, WILLIAM MARTIN, financial consultant; b. Chgo., June 21, 1920; s. William John and Mary Frances (Martin) B.; m. Julia McIntire Vail, Dec. 19, 1972; children: William E., Mary P., Peter D. BS, St. Mary's Univ., 1941; MA, DePaul U., 1949. Divsn. contr. Hughes Aircraft Co., Culver City, Calif., 1950-55; div. contr. TRW, Redondo Beach, Calif., 1955-58; mgr. mgmt. cons. dept. Peat, Marwick, Mitchell and Co., L.A., 1958-61; v.p. Litton Industries Inc., Beverly Hills, Calif., 1961-74; chmn., CEO NN Corp., Milw., 1974-80; chmn. Northwestern Nat. Ins. Group, 1981-84; bd. dirs. PK Tool & Die Mfg. Co., Chgo. Bd. dirs. Columbia Hosp., Milw., 1976—, Milw. Assn. Commerce, 1976-81, Milw. Symphony Orch., 1974-81, United Performing Arts Fund., Milw., 1977-81. With U.S. Army, 1941-46. Mem. Fin. Execs. Inst., Milw. Club, Milw. Country Club, Univ. Club. Avocations: woodworking, languages. Home and Office: 13800 N Birchwood Ln Mequon WI 53097-1702

BERRY, WILLIAM WELLS, lawyer; b. Nashville, Sept. 10, 1917; s. Allen Douglas and Agnes Wilkie (Vance) B.; m. Mary John Atwell, May 31, 1941 (dec.); children: William W., Edith Allen Berry Collier; m. Virginia N. Buntin, Jan. 4, 1986. B.A., Vanderbilt U., 1938, LL.B., 1940. Bar: Tenn. 1940. Pvt. practice law Nashville, 1940-42, 46—; ptnr. Bass, Berry & Sims, 1965—. Mem. Tenn. Inheritance Tax Study Com., 1977, 82; mem. adv. com. dental divsn. Tenn. Dept. Pub. Health, 1953-57; pres. Bill Wilkerson Hearing and Speech Ctr., 1959-67; bd. dirs. Noel Meml. Found., 1954-68; trustee Tenn. Fed. Tax Inst., 1973-79, pres., 1976-77; trustee Monroe Harding Home, 1971-93, Washington Found., 1978—, Nashville Found., 1965-82, Nelson Found., 1997—. Capt. AUS, 1942-46. Decorated Air medal with oak leaf cluster. Fellow Am. Coll. Estate and Trust Counsel (chmn. Tenn. chpt. 1975-81, bd. regents 1979-85), Internat. Acad. Trial Lawyers, Am. Bar Found., Tenn. Bar Found., Nashville Bar Found.; mem. ABA, Tenn. Bar Assn., Nashville Bar Assn. (bd. dirs. 1969-72, v.p. 1971-72), Am. Judicature Soc., Nashville Srs. Golf Assn. (pres. 1978-80), Nat. Soc. SAR, English Speaking Union (bd. dirs., past pres. Nashville chpt. 1991-93), 200 Club (bd. dirs., past comdr.), Belle Meade Country Club, Highlands Country Club. Democrat. Presbyterian (deacon, elder). Home: 5110 Boxcroft Pl Nashville TN 37205-3702 also: 312 Pipers Ct Highlands NC 28741-6634 Office: Bass Berry & Sims 2700 First American Ctr Nashville TN 37238

BERRY, WILLIAM WILLIS, retired utility executive; b. Norfolk, Va., May 18, 1932; s. Joel Halbert and Julia Lee (Godwin) B.; m. Elizabeth Mangum, Aug. 23, 1958; children: Preston Blackburn, John Willis, William Godwin. BSEE, Va. Mil. Inst., 1954; MS in Commerce, U. Richmond, 1964. Registered profl. engr., Va. Engr. Gen. Electric Co., 1954-55; with Va. Power, Richmond, 1957-92, v.p. div. ops., then sr. v.p. comml. ops., 1976-78, exec. v.p., 1978-80, pres., chief oper. officer, 1980-83, pres. chief exec. officer, 1983-85, chmn., chief exec. officer, 1985-86; chmn., chief exec. officer Dominion Resources Inc., 1986-90; chmn. Dominion Resources Inc., Richmond, 1990-92; bd. dirs. Ethyl Corp., Richmond, Universal Corp., Richmond. Chair ISO New England, Holyoke, Mass. Mem. Commonwealth Club, Country Club of Va., Norfolk Yacht and Country Club. Republican. Office: Three James Ctr 1051 E Cary St Ste 1201 Richmond VA 23219-4029

BERRYHILL, GEORGIA GENE, graphic designer, educator; b. Williamsport, Ind., Aug. 27, 1947; d. Detro Horace and Bliss Bernice (Bilbrey) Sells; m. Robert Earl Berryhill, Aug. 10, 1966; children: Deven Earl, Joel Eugene. BA in Biomed. Illustration, Calif. State U., Long Beach, 1979; MA in Graphic Design, Calif. State U., L.A., 1986; PhD, Walden U., Mpls., 1993. Graphic designer, art dir. Illustrated Sci., Seal Beach, Calif., 1976-86; bio-med. illustrator UCLA Med. Ctr., Torrance, Calif., 1979-80; design instr., curriculum developer Glendale (Calif.) C.C. Ext., 1984-88; creative dir. Berryhill Prodns., Laguna Beach, Calif., 1986—; art/design/photo instr. Biola U., La Mirada, Calif., 1987-89; art/design instr. Art Inst. of So. Calif., Laguna Beach, 1991-93; instr. computer graphics, digital arts U. Calif. Ext., Irvine, 1992—; cons. Martin Luther King Hosp., L.A., 1980, U. So. Calif., L.A., 1980, UCLA Med. Ctr., 1980-86, Beckman Found., 1996; program adminstr. Beckman Found., 1997; hon. prof. arts Yunnan Arts Inst., Kunming, China, 1999. Author: The Social Impact of Graphic Symbolism, 1993, Designing Website Images: A Practical Guide, 1999; contbr. articles to profl. jours.; spkr. in field; juried exhbns. include Festival of Arts/Pageant of the Masters, Laguna Beach, Calif., 1998, 99, Internat. Festival Arts, Kunming, 1999. Mem. Internat. Soc. Electronic Arts, Am. Inst. of Graphic Arts, Soc. of Environ. Graphic Design, Assn. for Advancement of Policy Rsch. Devel. in the 3d World, Coll. Art Assn., Kappa Pi, Crosshatch. Republican. Avocations: musician, songwriter. Office: U Calif PO Box 6050 Irvine CA 92616-6050

BERRYMAN, DONALD CARROLL, cattle rancher; b. Cedarvale, N.Mex., Aug. 28, 1934; s. Benjamin Carroll and Jodie Lou (Harrel) B.; m. Sharron Lou Luster, May 31, 1968; children: Penny Jo, Robert Todd. Student, Portales U., 1952-54. Reg. bull producer. Co-owner, operator Berryman Ranch, Cebolla, N.Mex., 1954-56, owner, operator, 1960—. Mem. Range Improvement Task Force, N.Mex. State U., 1988—; bd. dirs. Sunwest Bank, Espanola, N.Mex. Bd. dirs. Soil Conservation Agy., Chama, N.Mex., 1969-88. With U.S. Army, 1957-59. Recipient Excellence in Grazing award Soc. Range Mgmt., 1978. Republican. Avocations: woodworking, music, piano restoration. Office: Berryman Angus Ranch PO Box 188 Cebolla NM 87518-0188

BERRYMAN, RICHARD BYRON, lawyer; b. Indpls., Aug. 16, 1932; s. Herbert Byron and Ruth Katherine (Mayerhoefer) B.; m. Virginia Marie Asti, June 9, 1957; children: Steven, Susan, Kenneth. BA, Carleton Coll., 1954; JD, U. Chgo., 1957. Bar: D.C. 1957. Atty. bur. of aeronautics U.S. Dept. Navy, Washington, 1957-59, atty. office gen. counsel, 1959-62; assoc. Cox, Langford & Brown, Washington, 1962-65, ptnr., 1965-68; ptnr. Fried, Frank, Harris, Shriver & Jacobson, Washington, 1968-90; pvt. practice Washington, 1990—. Mem. vis. com. Law Sch. U. Chgo., 1978-82; trustee Carleton Coll., Northfield, Minn., 1982-86; dir. Pericles Inst., Washington, 1996—. Mem. ABA. Office: 1225 I St NW Ste 500 Washington DC 20005-3914

BERRYMAN, ROBERT GLEN, accounting educator, consultant; b. Freeport, Ill., Nov. 22, 1928; s. Loyd Vernon and Gladys Leone (Hicks) B.; m. Ruth Madelyn Bjorngjeld, Aug. 25, 1955; children: Peter, David, Kathryn. BSBA, Northwestern U., 1950, MBA, 1951; PhD, U. Ill., 1958. CPA, Ill. Staff auditor Deloitte & Touche, Chgo., 1951-54; mgr. Deloitte & Touche, Mpls., 1969-70; instr. U. Ill., Champaign, 1954-58; asst. prof. acctg. U. Minn., Mpls., 1958-61, assoc. prof., 1961-65, prof., 1965-95, dir. grad. studies in acctg., 1980-83, chmn. dept. acctg., 1963-65, 70-73, 1990-95; exec. dir. fin. Cedar Riverside Assocs., Mpls., 1974-75; cons. in field. Mem. editl. bd. Issues in Acctg. Edn., 1995-98; contbr. articles to profl. publs. Recipient Horace T. Morse-Amoco All Univ. Tchg. award U. Minn., 1976, Outstanding Tchr. award Carlson Sch. Mgmt., U. Minn., Green Eyeshade award Minn. Acctg. Assn., Tchg. award U. Minn. Alumni Assn., Mpls., 1978, Leon Radde Outstanding Educator award Inst. Internal Auditors, 1988. Mem. AICPAs (chmn. acctg. theory subcom. 1979-83, mem. continuing profl. edn. exec. com. 1979-82, bd. examiners 1980-83, Disting. Achievement in Acctg. Edn. award 1999), Inst. Internal Auditors (bd. regents 1979-83, bd. govs. Twin City chpt. 1981-91, cert. internal auditor), Minn. Soc. CPAs (bd. dirs. 1965-69, 78-83, first recipient and honoree R. Glen Berryman award 1976), Minn. Acctg. Aid Soc. (pres. and bd. dirs.), Am. Acctg. Assn. (Outstanding Acctg. Educator 1994, Auditing Educator 1992), Nat. Assn. Accts. Home: 1462 Brenner Ave Saint Paul MN 55113-1671 Office: Univ MN Carlson Sch of Mgmt 3-107 321 19th Ave S Minneapolis MN 55455

BERS, ABRAHAM, electrical engineering and physics educator; b. Cernauti, Bukovina, Romania, May 28, 1930; came to U.S., 1949; s. Isaias and Berta (Lechter) B.; m. Anita Alden Burrage, June 17, 1966; children: Rachel, Joshua. BS, U. Calif. with highest honors, Berkeley, 1953; SM, MIT, 1955, ScD, 1959. Rsch. asst. Rsch. Lab. Electronics MIT, Cambridge, Mass., 1953-58, instr. dept. elec. engring. and computer sci., 1958-59, asst. prof., 1959-63, assoc. prof., 1963-71, prof., 1971—; dir. rsch. Ecole Polytechnique, Paris, 1979-80; vis. prof. U. Paris-Orsay, 1981-92; vis. scientist CEA-Euratom, Cadarache, France, 1995, Limeil-Valenton, France, 1995. Co-author: Waves in Anisotropic Plasmas, 1963, Physique des Plasmas, Vols. 1-2, 1994; contbr. chpts. to books, articles to profl. jours. Faculty Exch. fellow Ford Found., Tech. U. Berlin, 1966, fellow J.S. Guggenheim Meml. Found., U. Paris, 1968-69. Fellow Am. Phys. Soc. (chmn. div. plasma physics 1991-92); mem. AAAS, Univ. Fusion Assn. (pres. 1988-89), St. Botolph Club Boston. Avocations: tennis, skiing.

BERS, DONALD MARTIN, physiology educator; b. N.Y.C., Dec. 13, 1953; s. Harold Theodore and Penny (Wall) B.; m. Kathryn Eileen Hammond, July 17, 1976; children: Brian Alexander, Rebecca Ann. BA, U. Colo., 1974; PhD, UCLA, 1978. Postdoctoral research fellow UCLA, 1978-79, asst. research physiologist, 1980-82, adj. asst. prof., 1981-87; postdoctoral research fellow Edinburgh (Scotland) U., 1979-80; asst. prof. U. Calif., Riverside, 1982-86, assoc. prof., 1986-89, prof., 1989-92, divisional dean, dir. biomed. scis. program, 1991-92; prof., chmn. dept. physiology Loyola U., Chgo., 1992—. Author: Excitation-Contraction Coupling and Cardiac Contractile Force, 1991; assoc. editor News in Physiol. Sci.; mem. editl. bd. Am. Jour. Physiology, Circulation Rsch., Jour. Pharm. and Exptl. Therapeutics, Jour. Molecular Cell Cardiology; contbr. articles to profl. jours. Bd. dirs. Am. Heart Assn., Riverside, 1985-92, pres., 1989-91. Fellow Am. Heart Assn., L.A., 1978-80, Brit.-Am., Am. Heart Assn., 1980-81; recipient New Investigator Rsch. award NIH, 1982-85, Rsch. Career Devel. award NIH, 1985-90. Mem. AAAS, Am. Physiol. Soc., Biophys. Soc. (mem. coun., mem. exec. bd.), Internat. Soc. Heart Rsch., Soc. Gen. Physiology.

BERSANO, BOB, newspaper editor. Formerly house and garden editor Dallas Morning News, now life styles editor, 1996—. Office: The Dallas Morning News 508 Young St Dallas TX 75202-4828*

BERSCHE, JAMES H., secondary education educator; b. Fairmount, W.Va., Jan. 24, 1933; s. G. Joseph and Jessie N. (Darling) B.; m. Mary J. Walton, Aug. 13, 1955 (dec. 1994); m. Linda F. Lombardo-Adelman, Dec. 16, 1995. BA, Wheaton Coll., 1955; MA, Eastern Mich. U., 1962; cert. edn. specialist, Bowling Green State U., 1977. Tchr. Crary Jr. H.S., Pontiac, Mich., 1955-62; treas. Bersche Constrn. Co., Pontiac, 1962-64; purchasing dir. Brass Craft Mfr., Detroit, 1964-70; tchr. Norwalk (Ohio) H.S., 1970—. Mem. NEA, Track Ofcls. Local Assn. Home: 48 Mariners Cv Vermilion OH 44089-2895

BERSH, PHILIP JOSEPH, psychologist, educator; b. Phila., Sept. 9, 1921; s. Michael and Sophie (Faggen) B.; m. Jacqueline Edith Fratkin, June 8, 1952; children: Lauren Helene, Marilyn Ellen. AB, Temple U., 1944; AM, Columbia U., 1947, PhD, 1949. Lectr. Columbia U., 1948-54, research assoc., 1951-54; lectr. U. Wis., 1951; chief intelligence and electronic warfare br. Rome Air Devel. Ctr., N.Y., 1954-62; lectr. Utica Coll., Syracuse U., N.Y., 1958-60, Hamilton Coll., 1961-62; chief combat systems div. U.S. Army Behavioral Sci. Research Lab., Washington, 1962-67, assoc. dir. human performance experimentation, 1966-67; lectr. George Washington U., 1966-67; prof. psychology Temple U., Phila., 1967—; vis. prof. dept. psychology Inst. Psychiatry U. London, 1979; cons. U.S. Army Research Inst. for Behavioral and Social Scis. Cons. editor: JSAS; Catalog Selected Documents in Psychology, 1976-79; mem. editorial bd. Jour. Exptl. Analysis of Behavior, 1980-83, 85-87; contbr. articles on psychology to profl. jours. Served with AUS, 1942-46, ETO. NRC postdoctoral fellow, 1950. Fellow Am. Psychol. Assn., AAAS, Am. Psychol. Soc.; mem. Assn. Behavior Analysis, Psychonomic Soc., Ctr. for Behavioral Studies, Ea. Psychol. Assn., Sigma Xi. Home: The Fairmont # 413 41 Conshohocken State Rd Bala Cynwyd PA 19004

BERSHAD, JACK R., lawyer; b. Phila., May 20, 1930; s. William and Anna (Goodman) B.; m. Helen Abby Jay, Apr. 7, 1957; children—Thomas, Daniel, Robert. BS, Temple U., 1951; JD, Harvard U., 1954; LHD, Moore Coll. Art. Bar: D.C. 1954, Pa. 1955, U.S. Supreme Ct. 1985. Mem. firm Blank, Rome, Comisky & McCauley, LLP, Phila., 1958—, chmn., 1991—; bd. dirs. Commerce Bancorp, Inc., Commerce Bank, N.A., Commerce Bank/Pa., N.A. Trustee Phila. Prisons, 1964-67; co-chair Juvenile Justice Project; mem. Phila. Fair Housing Commn., 1967; chmn. bd. mgrs. and trustees Moore Coll. Art, Phila., 1981-88; bd. trustees Phila. Mus. Art, 1989—; bd. dirs. Wilma Theatre, Phila., 1987-98, Greater Phila. Urban Affairs Coalition, 1989—, Opera Co. Phila., 1989—, v.p., 1990—; trustee Jewish Fedn. Greater Phila.; chmn., bd. dirs. Phila. chpt. Ben-Gurion U. of the Negev, 1997—. With U.S. Army, 1954-56. Mem. ABA, Pa. Bar Assn., D.C. Bar Assn., Phila. Bar Assn. (exec. com. sect. on corp. banking and bus. law 1972-75, 78, chmn. sect. on corp., banking and bus. law 1977, mem. conf. group to cooperate with Pa. Bankers Assn. 1975-80), Sons of Copper Beeches. Office: Blank Rome Comisky & McCauley 1 Logan Sq Fl 3 Philadelphia PA 19103-6998

BERSHAD, NEIL JEREMY, electrical engineering educator; b. Bklyn., Oct. 20, 1937; s. Milton Frank and Lila (Kaplan) B.; m. Susan Goldman; children: Brian, Melissa. BEE, Rensselaer Poly. Inst., 1958, PhD EE, 1962; MSEE, U. So. Calif., 1960. Mem. tech. staff Hughes Aircraft Co., Culver City, Calif., 1958-62, staff engr., 1964-69; prof. elec. engring. U. Calif., Irvine, 1966-94, prof. emeritus, 1994—. Contbr. more than 85 articles on communication theory, signal processing and adaptive filtering to profl. jours. 1st lt. USAF, 1962-65. Fellow IEEE (assoc. editor communications jour., acoustics, speech and signal processing jour.). Office: U Calif Dept Elec/Computer Engring Irvine CA 92717

BERSIN, RICHARD LEWIS, physicist, plasma process technologist; b. N.Y.C., July 4, 1929; s. Maxwell Hilary and Virginia (Greenfield) B.; m. Lillian Freda Braudy, Mar. 21, 1954 (div.); children: Joshua Morris, Adam Samuel; m. Ruth Ann Hargrave, July 25, 1976; children: Jacob David Antonio, Rebekah Bersin Contreras. BS in Physics, MIT, 1950; MS in Maths. and Physics, Northeastern U., Boston, 1962. Physicist Tracerlab, Inc., Boston, 1950-58; divsn. mgr. Lab. for Electronics Corp., Waltham, Mass., 1968-69; pres., founder Internat. Plasma Corp., Berkeley, Calif., 1969-74; exec. v.p. Dionex Gas Plasma Sys., Hayward, Calif., 1974-79; dir. of dry processing Perkin Elmer Corp., Wilton, Conn., 1979-83, dir. tech. mktg., 1983-84; pres., cons. Emergent Techs. Corp., New Haven, Conn., 1985—; engring. specialist Ulvac Japan, Ltd., Chigasaki, Japan, 1989-92; sr. tech. staff mem. Ulvac Techs., Inc., Methuen, Mass., 1992—. Patentee in field. Mem. IEEE, Am. Vacuum Soc., Electrochem. Soc., Semi Internat., Am. Chem. Soc., Computer Soc., ASM Internat. Democrat. Episcopalian.

BERSIN, RUTH HARGRAVE, priest, social services administrator; b. LaPorte, Ind., Sept. 16, 1939; d. Jacob Harold and Rowena Adeline (Hullett) Hargrave; m. Richard Lewis Bersin; children: Jacob David Antonio, Rebekah Bersin Contreras. BS in Edn., Ind. U., 1962; MA in Religion, Colgate Rochester Div. Sch., 1965; MDiv, Yale Div. Sch., 1982; D of Ministry, Grad. Theol. Found., 1993. Ordained priest, 1984. Dir. ednl. devel. ctr. Commodore, Japan, 1972-75; dir. spl. projects, refugees svcs. coord. Episcopal Social Svcs., Bridgeport, Conn., 1982-89; priest St. Peters, Cheshire, Conn., 1983-85, St. Lukes, Bridgeport, Conn., 1985-89; exec. dir. Tokyo English Lifeline, 1989-92; asst. dir. Interfaith Conf. Met. Washington, 1992-93; asst. priest Good Shepherd Episcopal Ch., Burke, Va., 1994; priest St. Monica's Capitol Hill, Washington, 1995-96; assoc. priest Grace Episcopal Ch., Lawrence, Mass., 1996-99; dir. Devel. Trauma Ctr., Brookline, Mass., 1996-99; pastoral psychotherapy fellow Greater Lowell Pastoral Counseling Ctr., 1997—; exec. dir. Refugee Immigration Ministries, 1998—; mem. Ecumenical commn. Diocese of Conn., 1984-89, Diocese of Washington, 1995, Diocese of Mass., 1996—; Episc. Congregation, U.S. Naval Base, Yokosuka, Japan, 1989-92; chaplain Washington Nat. Cathedral, 1995-96; chair task force on violence against women Diocese of Washington, 1995-96. Leader NOVA Trauma Team, Oklahoma City, 1995, Refugee Adv. Coun., State of Conn., 1984-89, Refugee Welfare Com. Nat. Ch. World Svc., 1986; bd. dirs. Women's Crisis Ctr., Norwalk, Conn., 1980-83; mem. Nat. Coalition Against Sexual Assault; mem. Mass. Immigrant and Refugee Advocacy Coalition, Boston Theol. Inst. Working Group on Restorative Justice, Women's Crisis Com. Diocese of Mass., Task Force on Domestic Violence, Lowell, Mass. Mem. Am. Assn. Pastoral Counseling, Internat. Assn. Trauma Counselors, Internat. Soc. Traumatic Stress Studies, Nat. Soc. Fund Raising Execs. (cert. fund raising exec.), Assembly of Episcopal Hosps. and Chaplains. Democrat. Avocations: music, swimming, reading, gourmet cooking.

BERSIN, SUSAN JOYCE-HEATHER (REIGNBEAUX JOYCE-HEATHER BERSIN), critical care nurse, police officer; b. Lakewood, Ohio, July 11, 1945; d. Richard George Sr. and Ireene Rose (Brenner) Bersin; m. Robert Joseph Okragley, Dec. 23, 1972 (div. Apr. 1993); 1 child, MaryRose Reignbeaux. BS in Zoology, Kent State U., 1975, BSN, 1976, BS in Chemistry, 1976; MS in Med.-Surg Nursing, Case Western Res. U., 1979. RN, Ohio; cert. critical care nurse. Driver Waite Transport, Akron, Ohio, 1967-68, Cleve. Transit System, 1968-70; CEO, chief technician Corvair Repair & Mobile Svc., Berea, Ohio, 1970—; critical care nurse Deaconess Hosp., Cleve., 1976-79, St. Luke's Hosp., Cleve., 1979-81, St. John Hosp., Cleve., 1981—; police officer Cleve. Police Dept., 1971—. Served with USN, 1963-67, Viet Nam. Mem. Sigma Theta Tau (charter mem. Delta Xi chpt.). Roman Catholic. Avocations: reading, ice figure skating, aeronautics and sky-diving. Home: 412 Waverly St Berea OH 44017-2145

BERSOFF, DONALD NEIL, lawyer, psychologist; b. N.Y.C., Mar. 1, 1939; s. Irving and Mina (Cohen) B.; children by previous marriage: David, Judith; m. Deborah Leavy, Oct. 16, 1988; 1 child, Benjamin. BS, NYU, 1958, MA, 1960, PhD, 1965; student, U. Va. Law Sch., 1973-74; JD, Yale U., 1976. Bar: Md. 1976, D.C. 1984, Pa. 1990. Asst. prof. Ohio State U.; assoc. prof. U. Ga., U. Md. Sch. Law; ptnr. Ennis, Friedman & Bersoff, Washington, 1982-88, Jenner & Block, Washington, 1988-89; coord. joint JD and PhD program in law and psychology U. Md. Sch. Law and Johns Hopkins U. Dept. Psychology, 1976-82; dir. law and psychology program Med. Coll. Pa.-Hahnemann U., Phila., 1990—, Villanova (Pa.) U. Law Sch., 1990—. Author: Learning to Teach: A Decision-Making System, 1976, Ethical Conflicts in Psychology, 1995, 2d edit., 1999, Law and Mental Health-Pennsylvania, 1999. With USAF, 1965-68. N.Y. State Regents coll. teaching fellow. Mem. ABA, APA (mem. coun. of reps. 1991-94, bd. dirs. 1994-97, chair policy and planning bd. 1999, coun. of reps. 1999—), Am. Psychology-Law Soc. (pres. 1980-81). Home: 780 College Ave Haverford PA 19041-1205 Office: Villanova Law Sch Villanova PA 19085

BERSON, ELIOT LAWRENCE, ophthalmologist, medical educator; b. Boston, 1937. MD, Harvard U., 1962. Intern Calif. Hosp., San Francisco, 1962-63; resident in ophthalmology Barnes and McMillan Hosps., St. Louis, 1963-66; clin. assoc. ophthalmologist Nat. Inst. Neurol. Diseases and Blindness, Bethesda, Md., 1966-68; asst. Mass. Eye and Ear Infirmary, Boston, 1968-73, asst. surgeon, 1974-78, dir. Berman-Gund Lab. for Study of Retinal Degenerations, Harvard Med. Sch., 1974—, assoc. surgeon in ophthalmology, 1979-84, surgeon in ophthalmology, 1984—; instr. Harvard U. Sch. Medicine, Boston, 1968-70, asst. prof., 1971-76, assoc. prof. ophthalmology, 1976-82, Chatlos prof. ophthalmology, 1982—. Surgeon USPHS, 1966-68. Mem. AMA, Assn. for Rsch. in Vision and Ophthalmology, Am. Acad. Ophthalmology, Am. Ophthal. Soc. Office: Berman-Gund Lab Mass Eye and Ear Infirmary 243 Charles St Boston MA 02114-3002

BERSON, JEROME ABRAHAM, chemistry educator; b. Sanford, Fla., May 10, 1924; s. Joseph and Rebecca (Bernicker) B.; m. Bella Zevitovsky, June 30, 1946; children: Ruth, David, Jonathan. B.S. cum laude, CCNY, 1944; M.A., Columbia U., 1947; Ph.D., 1949. NRC postdoctoral fellow Harvard U., 1949-50; asst. chemist Hoffmann-LaRoche, Inc., Nutley, N.J., 1944; asst. prof. U. So. Calif., 1950-53, asso. prof., 1953-58, prof., 1958-63; prof. U. Wis., 1963-69; prof. Yale U., 1969-79, Irénée du Pont prof., 1979-92, Sterling prof., 1992-94; Sterling prof. emeritus, 1994—; dir. div. phys. sci. and engring. Yale U., 1983-90; vis. prof. U. Calif., U. Cologne, U. Western Ont., U. Karlsruhe, U. Lausanne; Fairchild Disting. scholar Calif. Inst. Tech.; cons. Riker Labs., Goodyear Tire & Rubber Co., am. Cyanamid Co., IBM, Cord Labs., SMC Corp., B.F. Goodrich Corp., Lubrizol Corp.; mem. medicinal chemistry study sect. NIH, 1969-73; mem. adv. panel chemistry NSF, 1964-70. Mem. editorial adv. bd.: Jour. Organic Chemistry, 1961-65, Accounts of Chemical Rsch., 1971-77, 94-96, Nouveau Journal de Chimie, 1977-85, Chem. Revs., 1980-83, Jour. Am. Chem. Soc., 1988-93; contbr. articles to profl. jours. Served with AUS, 1944-46, CBI. Recipient Alexander von Humboldt award, 1980, Townsend Harris medal Alumni Assn. CCNY, 1984, Merit award NIH, 1989; John Simon Guggenheim fellow, 1980. Fellow Am. Acad. Arts and Scis.; mem. NAS, Am. Chem. Soc. (Calif. sect. award 1963, James Flack Norris award 1978, Nichols medal 1985, Roger Adams award 1987, Arthur C. Cope scholar 1992, Oesper award 1998, chmn. div. organic chemistry 1971), Chem. Soc. London, Phi Beta Kappa, Sigma Xi, Phi Lambda Upsilon. Home: 45 Bayberry Rd Hamden CT 06517-3401 Office: Yale U Dept Chemistry PO Box 208107 New Haven CT 06520-8107

BERSOUX, HENRI ROBERT, marketing executive; b. Liege, Belgium, Oct. 20, 1959; came to U.S., 1975; s. Roger Victor and Julia May (Jones) B.; m. Susan Adele Fowler, Nov. 10, 1990; children: Sarah, Natalie, Allison, Paul, Nicholas. BA, Samford U., 1980. Trainee European Econ. Communities, Brussels, Belgium, 1981; from jr. assoc. to acct. assoc. David Apter & Assocs., Washington, 1982-84; mng. ptnr. B2 Comm., Inc., Rockville,

Md., 1985-88; comm. assoc. Am. Coun. Life Insur., Washington, 1989-91, sr. comm. assoc., 1992-93; pub. rels. mgr. Ernst & Young, N.Y.C., 1993-94, asst. dir. nat. sales and mktg., 1994-95, assoc. dir. nat. mktg., 1995-96; assoc. dir. nat. corp. mktg., dir. innovative methods, internet site mgr. Ernst & Young, Cleve., 1996-97, dir. nat. mktg., 1997-98, dir. client connectivity, 1998—; lectr. in advtg., pub. rels., mktg. Geo. Washington U., 1985. Mgmt. cons. pro bono Internat. Student House, Washington, 1988-89. Republican. Roman Catholic. Avocations: riflery, chess, philately. Home: 8663 Treetop Trail Broadview Heights OH 44147-2567 Office: Ernst & Young 1200 Skylight Office Tower 1660 W 2nd St Cleveland OH 44113-1454

BERST, CHARLES ASHTON, English educator; b. Seattle, Sept. 30, 1932; s. Charles Ashton and Esther Anna (Weage) B.; m. Roelina Gerda den Ouden, June 8, 1962; children: Nelina, Caroline. BA, U. Wash., 1955, PhD, 1965. Asst. prof. U. Alta., Edmonton, Can., 1965-67; asst. prof. UCLA, 1967-73, assoc. prof., 1973-81, prof., 1981-94, prof. emeritus, 1994—; chair Coll. Letters & Sci. Faculty UCLA, 1977-81, vice chair and chair faculty senate, 1987-89. Author: Bernard Shaw and the Art of Drama, 1973, Pygmalion: Shaw's Spin on Myth and Cinderella, 1995; editor: Shaw and Religion, 1981. Office: UCLA Dept English PO Box 951530 Los Angeles CA 90095-1530

BERSTEIN, IRVING AARON, biotechnology and medical technology executive; b. Providence, Oct. 11, 1926; s. Robert Louis and Laura (Sperber) B.; m. Suzanne D'Amico, Apr. 16, 1972; children: Jonathan, Robert Laurance. ScB, Brown U., 1947; PhD, Cornell U., 1951. Assoc. tech. dir., sr. scientist Tracer Lab Inc., 1951-57; pres., tech. dir. Controls for Radiation, Inc., Cambridge, Mass., 1957-69, Controls for Radiation Inc. (acquired by Teledyne Inc.), Cambridge, Mass., 1969; v.p. Isotopes Inc. (subs. Teledyne Inc.), Cambridge, Mass., 1969-70; dir. med. div., v.p. AGA Corp., Secaucus, N.J., 1970-71; asst. dir. rsch. program devel. div. health sci. and tech. Harvard U.-MIT, 1972-86; founder and chmn. bd. Hygeia Scis. Inc., 1980-87; pres., CEO Hygeia Scis., Inc. (merged Hygeia Scis. Inc. into Tambrands, Inc.), 1985-87; sr. sci. advisor Hygeia Scis., Inc., 1988-90; chmn. bd. Endogen, Inc., Boston, 1990-95; bd. of advisors Rogers Foam Co., 1992—; pres. Berstein Tech. Corp., 1980—; cons. for Med. and Biotech., Corp. Devel. Francis Wayland scholar; Cornell U. fellow. Mem. Chief Execs. Orgn., Forty-Niners (pres. N.E. chpt. 1984, 96), Harvard Club Boston, Cornell Club Boston, Sigma Xi. Fax: (781) 862-3533. Home and Office: 42 Buckman Dr Lexington MA 02421-6040

BERSTICKER, ALBERT CHARLES, chemical company executive; b. Toledo, Mar. 22, 1934; s. Albert Charles and Lillian (Schorling) B.; m. Frances Ploeger, Sept. 15, 1956; children: Steven, Susan, Karen, Cristina. M.S. in Geo-Chemistry, Miami U., Oxford, Ohio, 1958. Chemist Interlake Iron Corp., Toledo, 1956; engr. Mobile Producing Corp., Billings, Mont., 1957-58; with Ferro Corp., Cleve., 1958—; asst. to group v.p. internat. Ferro Corp., 1973-74, group v.p. internat., 1974-76, exec. v.p. ops., chief oper. officer, 1976-86, pres., chief oper. officer, 1988-91, pres., CEO, also bd. dirs., 1991—, chmn., CEO, 1996—; bd. dirs. Cleve. Tomorrow, Greater Cleve. Growth Assn., Oglebay Norton Co., Brush Wellman, Inc., Key Corp., U. Hosps. Health Sys. Inc., Univ. Hosps./Case Western Res. U. Joint Coordinating Com. Editor: Symposium on Salt, 1963. Trustee Cleve. Roundtable. Mem. Chem. Mfg. Assn., Leadership Cleve. Episcopalian. Office: Ferro Corp 1000 Lakeside Ave E Cleveland OH 44114-1147

BERT, CAROL LOIS, educational assistant; b. Bakersfield, Calif., Oct. 15, 1938; d. Edwin Vernon and Shirley Helen (Craig) Phelps; m. John Davison Bert, Sept. 26, 1964; children: Mary Ellen, John Edwin, Craig Eric, Douglas Ethan. BS in Nursing, U. Colo., 1960. Med. surg. nurse U.S. Army, Washington, 1960-62, Ascom City, Korea, 1962-63, San Antonio, 1963, Albuquerque, 1964-65; ednl. asst. Jefferson County Schs., Arvada, Colo., 1979—. Sec. Parent, Tchr., Student Assn. Arvada West High Sch., 1987-88. Club: Colo. Quilting Coun. (1st v.p. 1988, 89, inducted into Hall of Fame, 1992). Avocations: reading, quilting, camping, fishing, tennis. Home: 5844 Oak St Arvada CO 80004-4739 Office: Allendale Elem Sch 5900 Oak St Arvada CO 80004-4741

BERT, CHARLES WESLEY, mechanical and aerospace engineer, educator; b. Chambersburg, Pa., Nov. 11, 1929; s. Charles Wesley and Gladys Adelle (Raff) B.; m. Charlotte Elizabeth Davis (June 29, 1957); children: Charles Wesley IV, David Raff. BSME, Pa. State U., 1951, MS, 1956; PhD in Engring. Mechanics, Ohio State U., 1961. Registered profl. engr., Pa., Okla. Jr. design engr. Am. Flexible Coupling Co., State Coll., Pa., 1951-52; aero. design engr. Fairchild Aircraft div. Fairchild Engine and Airplane Corp., Hagerstown, Md., 1954-56; prin. M.E. Battelle Inst., Columbus, Ohio, 1956-61; sr. research engr., 1961-62, program dir., solid and structural mechanics research, 1962-63, cons., 1964-65; assoc. prof. U. Okla., 1963-66, prof., 1966—; dir. Sch. Aerospace and Mech. Engring., 1972-77, 90-95, Benjamin H. Perkinson Chair prof. engring., 1978—; instr. engring. mechanics Ohio State U., Columbus, 1959-61; vis. scholar U. Calif., San Diego, 1996; cons. in field; chmn. Midwestern Mechanics Conf., 1973-75; Honor lectr. Mid-Am. State Univs. Assn., 1983-84; seminar lectr. Midwest Mechanics, 1983-84; Plenary lectr. Internal Conf. on Composite Structures, Paisley, Scotland, 1987. Mem. edit. bd. Composite Structures Jour., 1982—, Jour. Sound & Vibration, 1988—, Advanced Composite Materials, 1991—, Composites Engring., 1991-95, Mechanics of Composite Materials and Structures, 1993—, Applied Mechanics Revs., 1993—, Composites, 1996-98, Jour. of Sandwich Structures and Materials, 1997—; assoc. editor: Exptl. Mechanics, 1982-87, Applied Mechanics Revs., 1984-87; contbr. chpts. to books and articles to profl. jours. 1st lt. USAF, 1952-54. Sr. Rsch. scholar U. Calif., San Diego, 1996; recipient Disting. Alumnus award Ohio State U. Coll. engring., 1985. Fellow AAAS, AIAA (nat. tech. com. structures 1969-72, chmn. Cen. Okla. sect. 1966-67), ASME (Cen. Okla. sect. exec. com. 1973-78, 90-95, sec. 1990-91, region X mech. engring. dept. heads com. 1972-77, 90-95, chmn. 1975-77), Am. Acad. Mechs. (bd. dirs. 1978-82), Soc. Exptl. Mechanics (monograph com. 1978-82, chmn. 1980-82, sec. Mid-Ohio chpt. 1958-59, chmn. 1959-60, adv. bd. 1960-63), Soc. Engring. Sci. (bd. dirs. 1982-88); mem. NSPE, Am. Soc. Composites (bd. dirs. 1996-98), Okla. Acad. Sci., Okla. Soc. Profl. Engrs., Scabbard and Blade, Pa. State Alumni Assn. (Outstanding Engring. Alumnus award 1992), Sigma Xi, Sigma Tau, Pi Tau Sigma, Sigma Gamma Tau (Disting. Engr. award), Tau Beta Pi (Disting. Engr. award). Achievements include co-development of world's smallest pressure transducer capable of measuring both steady and fluctuating pressures; first general solution of cylindrically orthotropic plates of radially varying thickness under arbitrary body forces; origination of several minimum-weight optimal designs for multicell cylindrical pressure vessels, experimental techniques and associated data reduction equations for determining residual stresses in both flat-sheet and thick-walled cylindrical specimens of composite materials; first successful application of Kennedy-Pancu system identification method to shell structures, noninteger polynomial version of Rayleigh's method to heat conduction; first application of differential quadrature method to static structural problems, structural vibration problems and non-linear structural problems; first application of noninteger polynomial method to finite element analysis; first dynamic stability analysis of unicycles and monocycles; origination of concept of stress gages for composite materials; research on sandwich structures with bimodular facings, prediction of ply steer behavior of automobile tires, nonlinear flutter of laminated composite panels; many others. Home: 2516 Butler Dr Norman OK 73069-5059 Office: U Okla Sch Aerospace and Mech Engring 865 Asp Ave Norman OK 73019-1052 *Set high yet realistic goals, put forth the extra effort to achieve them, and practice the Golden Rule.*

BERT, CLARA VIRGINIA, home economics educator, administrator; b. Quincy, Fla., Jan. 29, 1929; d. Harold C. and Ella J. (McDaniel) B. BS, Fla. State U., 1950, MS, 1963, PhD, 1967. Cert. tchr., Fla.; cert. home economist; cert. pub. mgr. Tchr. Union County High Sch., Lake Butler, Fla., 1950-53, Havana High Sch., Fla., 1953-65; cons. rsch. and devel. Fla. Dept. Edn., Tallahassee, 1967-75, sect. dir. rsch. and devel., 1975-85, program dir. home econs. edn., 1985-92, program specialist resource devel., 1992-96, program specialist, spl. projects, 1996—; cons. Nat. Ctr. Rsch. in Vocat. Edn., Ohio State U., 1978; field reader U.S. Dept. Edn., 1974-75. Author, editor booklets. Mem. devel. bd., adv. bd. Fla. State U. Coll. Human Scis. Family Inst., 1994—. U.S. Office Edn. grantee, 1976, 77, 78; recipient Dean's award Coll. Human Scis., Fla. State U., 1995; named Disting Alumna Coll. Human Scis., Fla. State U., 1994. Mem. Am. Home Econs. Assn. (state treas. 1969-71), Am. Vocat. Assn., Fla. Vocat. Assn., Fla. Vocat. Home Econs., Fla. Home Econs., Am. Vocat. Edn. Rsch. Assn. (nat. treas. 1970-71), Nat. Coun. Family Rels., Am. Ednl. Rsch. Assn., Fla. State U. Alumni Assn. (bd. dirs. home econs. sect.), Havana Golf and Country Club, Fla. State U. Ctr. Club, Kappa Delta Pi, Kappa Omicron Nu (chpt. pres. 1965-66), Delta Kappa Gamma (pres. 1974-76), Sigma Kappa (pres. corp. bd. 1985-91), Phi Delta Kappa. Office: Fla Dept Edn FEC Tallahassee FL 32399

BERTAIN, G(EORGE) JOSEPH, JR., lawyer; b. Scotia, Humboldt County, Calif., Mar. 9, 1929; s. George Joseph and Ellen Veronica (Canty) B.; m. Bernardine Joy Galli, May 11, 1957; 1 child, Joseph F. AB, St. Mary's Coll. Calif., 1951; JD, Cath. U. Am., 1955. Bar: Calif. 1957. Assoc. Hon. Joseph L. Alioto, San Francisco, 1955-57, 59-65; asst. U.S. Atty. No. Dist. Calif., 1957-59; pvt. practice of law San Francisco, 1966—; panel mem. Theodore Granik's Am. Forum of The Air, Washington, 1955. Editor-in-Chief, Law Rev. Cath. U. Am. (vol. 5), 1954-55. Mem. bd. regents St. Mary's Coll. Calif., 1980—; chmn. San Francisco Lawyers Com. for Ronald Reagan, 1966-78, San Francisco lawyers com. for elections of Gov./U.S. Pres. Ronald Reagan, 1966, 70, 80, 84; spl. confidential advisor to Gov. Reagan on jud. selection, San Francisco, 1967-74; chmn. San Francisco Lawyers for Better Govt., 1978—; confidential advisor to Senator Hayakawa on judicial selection, 1981-82, to Gov. Deukmejian, 1983-90, to Gov. Wilson, 1991-92; bd. dirs. St. Anne's Home, Little Sisters of the Poor, San Francisco. Recipient De La Salle medal St. Mary's Coll. Calif., 1951, Signum Fidei award, 1976. Mem. ABA, Calif. Bar Assn., Fed. Bar Assn. (del. to 9th cir. jud. conf. 1967-76), St. Thomas More Soc. San Francisco, U.S. Supreme Ct. Hist. Soc., Assn. Former U.S. Attys and Asst. U.S. Attys. No. Calif. (past pres.), Commonwealth Club, Wester Assn., Knights of Malta, KC. Republican. Roman Catholic. Address: 2314 Ninth Ave San Francisco CA 94116

BERTANI, LILLIAN ELIZABETH T., biologist, researcher, educator; b. July 9, 1931. BS, U. Mich., 1953; PhD, Calif. Inst. Tech., 1957. Swedish Med. Rsch. Coun. fellow Karolinska Inst., Stockholm, 1966-75, asst. prof., 1975-85; vis. assoc. in biology Calif. Inst. Tech., Pasadena, 1981-85, 95—, lectr. biology, 1993—. E-mail: lebert@cco.caltech.edu. Home: 975 Dale St Pasadena CA 91106

BERTE, NEAL RICHARD, college president; b. May 7, 1940; s. Edward H. and Wenonah Maureen (Stevens) B.; m. Anne; children: Becky, Julie, Mark, Scott. BS in Polit. Sci, U. Cin., 1962, MS (Ford Found. scholar), 1963, EdD, 1966; Rockefeller Found. fellow, Union Theol. Sem., N.Y.C., 1962-63; postgrad., Garrett Theol. Sem., Evanston, Ill., 1966-67, Harvard U., 1966; LHD (hon.), U. Cin., 1993. Asst. dir. Coll. Entrance Exam. Bd., Evanston, 1966-68; exec. asst. to pres., asst. prof. Ottawa (Kans.) U., 1968-70; dean New Coll.; assoc. prof. U. Ala., 1970-74; v.p. ednl. devel., dean New Coll., 1974-76; pres. Birmingham (Ala.)-So. Coll., 1976—; project dir. NSF grants, 1972; chmn. session Internat. Council on Edn. for Teaching World Assembly, Nairobi, Kenya, 1973; mem. faculty Danforth Found. sponsored C.C. Inst., Stephens Coll., 1973; mem. steering com. Carnegie Found. funded project Coop. Assessment of Experiential Learning, 1974-77; mem. Commn. on Ednl. Credit, Am. Council Edn., 1975-81, Danforth Found. exec. com. for Danforth Fellows Program, 1974-75; mem. nat. adv. council for career edn. HEW, Office Edn., 1976-79; sec.-treas. So. U. Conf., 1977-80, v.p., 1984-85, pres., 1985-86; vis. scholar Inst. for Ednl. Mgmt., Harvard Grad. Sch Edn., 1990-91; co-chmn. Region 2020, Ala., 1997—. Contbr. articles to edn. jours. Mem. adminstrv. bd. Canterbury United Meth. Ch., Birmingham, 1977—, univ. senate United Meth. Ch., 1986-88; chmn. Univ. United Fund campaign, 1973; bd. dirs., mem. exec. com. United Fund, Tuscaloosa, Ala., 1974-75, chmn. edn. div., 1975; chmn. sect. for pvt. ednl. insts. Jefferson-Shelby-Walker Counties United Appeal, 1977; chmn. pub. employees div. United Way campaign, 1978; v.p. Coun. for Advancement Pvt. Colls. in Ala., 1977-82, pres., 1982-83; chmn. com. to select Man of Year in Birmingham, 1977; chmn. selection com. Rhodes Scholarships for Ala., 1976-81; bd. dirs. Jefferson-Shelby Counties Lung Assn., 1978-79, Ala. Partners for Progress with Guatemala Program, 1977—, Carraway Meth. Hosp., 1977-80, Brookwood Hosp., 1982-90, Neighborhood Housing Svc., Birmingham, 1977-78, Birmingham Symphony Assn., 1976-80, 82-87, Community Affairs Com., 1976-87, Operation New Birmingham, 1976-89; bd. govs. Relay House Club, Birmingham, 1983-87, Circle S Industries, Selma, Ala., 1983—, Parisian, Inc., Birmingham, 1983-88; bd. dirs. NCCJ, 1978—, Birmingham Summerfest, 1979—, March of Dimes, 1979-86, Am. Heart Assn., 1980-84, So. Rsch. Inst., 1982—, Leadership Birmingham, 1981—, Leadership Ala., 1990—; bd. dirs., chmn. long range planning com., chmn. program for Scout Exp. Jefferson County council Boy Scouts Am., 1977—; mem. exec. com. Men's Com., Birmingham Symphony Assn., 1977-84; bd. dirs. Jefferson Fed. Savs. and Loan Assn., Birmingham, 1978-91, Birmingham Festival Arts, 1982-89, bd. advisors, 1989, trustee, 1990, pres., 1981—; chmn. Birmingham Area United Way, 1983; trustee Advent Episc. Day Sch., 1977-87, Gorgas Scholarship Found., 1976-88, New Coll.-Sarasota, U. South Fla., 1977-79; founding mem., bd. dirs. Progressive Alliance, 1986—; bd. dirs. Met. Devel. Bd., 1987-88, Greater Birmingham Conv. and Visitors Bur., 1988; mem. commn. pub. rels. Nat. Assn. Ind. Colls and Univs., 1992-94, bd. dirs., 1994. Recipient Outstanding Citizens award Lawson State C.C. Coll., 1977, Outstanding Citizen award in Birmingham Erskine Ramsay Award Com., 1978, Brotherhood award NCCJ, 1984, Outstanding Service award Black Student Union, 1986, Outstanding Cmty. Svc. award Motar Bd., 1986, James M. Tingle award, 1986, Disting. Svc. award, Sigma Alpha Epsilon, 1991, Medal of Honor, DAR, 1995; elected to Ala. Acad. Honor, 1979; named one of 10 Outstanding Cmty. Leaders Birmingham Post-Herald, 1984, one of Top 10 Current Leaders in Birmingham, The Birmingham News, 1990, one of 10 leaders Bus. First jour., 1990, Birmingham Citizen of Yr. award for outstanding civic and cmty. svc., 1986, Outstanding Ala. Civic Leader Nat. Soc. Fund-Raising Execs., 1991, Disting. Citizen City Coun. of Birmingham, 1992, one of top ten mems. of 1997 Class of Movers and Shakers, Birmingham Bus. Jour.; named to Sigma Alpha Epsilon Leadership Sch. Hall of Fame, 1994. Mem. Am. Assn. Univ. Adminstrs. (pres. Alpha chpt. 1978-79), Greater Birmingham Area C. of C. (bd. dirs., exec. com. 1978-80, v.p. for govtl. rels., policy com. 1986, pres. 1988, chmn. exec. com. 1989), Am. Assn. Colls. (pres.'s adv. coun. 1977-78), Am. Assn. for Higher Edn. (chmn. Southeastern Regional Coun. 1973, chmn. panel on three-year degree programs 1973, program chmn. 1974, adv. bd. NEXUS Project 1974-75), Assn. for Innovation in Higher Edn. (adv. bd. 1973), Kiwanis Internat. (Disting. Pres. award 1992-93, George F. Hixon fellow 1995), Phi Beta Kappa (pres. 1975), Phi Delta Kappa. Club: The Redstone Club, The Jefferson Club, Downtown Birmingham Kiwanis (chmn. Ministers Day 1977, chmn. Youth-of-the-Year selection com. 1978, pres. 1992-93). Office: Birmingham So Coll Box 549002 Birmingham AL 35254-0001

BERTELE, WILLIAM, environmental engineer; b. Phila., Aug. 7, 1935; s. William J. and Viola H. (DeFant) B.; children: William Bradford, Theodore, Amanda. BS in Commerce and Engring., Drexel U., 1963. Registered profl. engr., N.J., Pa.; diplomate Am. Acad. Environ. Engrs. Field engr. Sam P. Wallace Co., Santurce, P.R., 1960-65; ptnr. Engineered Products Co., Santurce, 1965-68; sr. application engr. Am. Air Filter, Louisville, 1969-78; v.p. engring. Recon Systems Inc., Raritan, N.J., 1978-92; pvt. practice Bertele Environ., New Hope, Pa., 1991—. Active Del. Valley Coll. Mentor Program, 1994-97; dep. comdr. CAP, 1990-95, comdr., 1991. Recipient Commendation award CAP, 1984. Mem. Am. Conf. Govtl. Indsl. Hygienists, Air and Waste Mgmt. Assn., Ctrl. Bucks C. of C., Sigma Rho (hon.). Avocations: music, children, hiking, dancing, motorcycle touring. Fax: 215-862-1942. E-mail: wbertele@aol.com. Home and Office: 163 N Sugan Rd New Hope PA 18938-1035

BERTELSEN, THOMAS ELWOOD, JR., investment banker; b. Chgo., Feb. 13, 1940; s. Thomas Elwood and Virginia Marie (McKenna) B.; m. Sandra Lee Morgan, May 9, 1970; children: Derek, Page. AB, U. Kans., 1962; LLB, Stanford U., 1965; MBA, Columbia U., 1966; MA, Grad. Theol. Union, Berkeley, Calif., 1993. With Dean Witter Reynolds Inc., 1966-83; mgr. corp. fin. dept. Dean Witter Reynolds Inc., San Francisco, 1974-83, sr. v.p., 1975-80, mng. dir. investment banking, 1980-83, also dir.; exec. v.p. Sutro & Co. Inc., 1983-86, vice chmn., 1986-88; cons. Sutro Investment Ptnrs., 1990—; CFO Dominican Sisters of San Rafael, 1993—. Chmn. bd. trustees Grad. Theol. Union, 1990—; mem. bd. dirs. Hanna Boys Ctr., 1994—. Roman Catholic. Office: Dominican Sisters of San Rafael 1520 Grand Ave San Rafael CA 94901-2236*

BERTELSMAN, WILLIAM ODIS, federal judge; b. Cincinnati, Ohio, Jan. 31, 1936; s. Odis William and Dorothy (Gegan) B.; m. Margaret Ann Martin, June 13, 1959; children: Kathy, Terri, Nancy. B.A., Xavier U., 1958; J.D., U. Cin., 1961. Bar: Ky. 1961, Ohio 1962. Law clk. firm Taft, Stettinius & Hollister, Cin., 1960-61; mem. firm Bertelsman & Bertelsman, Newport, Ky., 1962-79; judge U.S. Dist. Ct. (ea. dist.) Ky., Covington, 1979—, chief judge, 1991-98; instr. Coll. Law U. Cin., 1965-72; city atty., prosecutor Highland Heights, Ky., 1962-69; adj. prof. Chase Coll. of Law, 1989—. Contbr. articles to profl. jours. Served to capt. AUS, 1963-64. Mem. ABA, Ky. Bar Assn. (bd. govs. 1978-79), U.S. Jud. Conf. (standing com. on practices and procedure 1989-95, liaison mem. adv. com. on civil rules 1989-95), No. Ky. C. of C. (pres. 1974, bd. dirs. 1969-77). Republican. Roman Catholic. Club: Optimist.

BERTENSHAW, BOBBI CHERRELLE, producer; b. Bklyn., Oct. 22, 1961; d. Eli and Marcia Janet (Forman) Slachofsky; m. William H. Bertenshaw III, Dec. 16, 1984. Diploma, Nat. Broadcast Sch., Phila., 1982, Health Maintenance Inst., Flushing, N.Y., 1985. Radio, TV prodr. Coun. of Chs., N.Y.C., 1981-84; prodr. Radio and TV Roundup Prodns., N.Y.C., 1982—; prodr., dir. WOR Radio, N.Y.C., 1982—; dir. comm. Delfon Rec. Soc., 1987—; CEO Radio & TV Roundup Prodns., 1991—; programming cons. N.J. Network Pub. TV, 1992—; comm. dir. Delfon Rec. Soc., 1987—; prodr.-dir. Sta. WOR Radio N.Y., 1983—; co-prodr. People Working for People, Sta. WWOR-TV N.Y. and Cable-TV Network of N.J., 1988—; judge N.J. Fresh, 1991. Judge N.J. Fresh, 1988—, Miss Jr. Miss N.J., 1997—. Recipient Cape TV award Cable TV Network N.J., 1987, N.J. State Fair awards, 1990-99. Mem. Women in Comm., Internat. Platform Assn., Am. Symphony Orch. League, N.J. Coun. of Chs. (dept. comm. 1983—, sec.), Feathered Fanciers Soc. (sec. 1992—), Nat. Lima Bean Assn. (co-chmn. 1988—, named Miss Lima Bean 1986-87). Home: 653 Sun Haven Dr Clayton NJ 08312-1955 Office: Delfon Rec Soc PO Box 1700 Livingston NJ 07039-7300

BERTENSHAW, WILLIAM HOWARD, III, radio and television producer; b. N.Y.C., Nov. 28, 1930; s. William Howard Jr. and Grace Annette (Miller) B.; m. Betty J. Underriner, July 7, 1956 (dec. Nov. 1975); children: Jane Ann, Judith Ann, Jo Ann; m. Bobbi C. Slachofsky, Dec. 16, 1984. BA in Communications, Ohio Wesleyan U., 1950. Asst. mktg. editor Bus. Week mag., N.Y.C., 1953-55; radio-TV dir. Hardy Burt Assocs., N.Y.C., 1955-57; radio-TV producer Empire Broadcasting Corp., N.Y.C., 1957-60, Nat. Episcopal Ch., N.Y.C., 1960-70; producer MBS, N.Y.C., 1970-75; dir. communications Council of Chs. City of N.Y., 1975-84; exec. producer, chief exec. officer Radio & TV Roundup Prodns., N.Y.C., 1984—; producer TKR Cable TV, N.Y.C., 1987—; guest lectr. So. Meth. U., Dallas, 1972, Seton Hall U., South Orange, N.J., 1974, Pace U., N.Y.C., 1980, Syracuse (N.Y.) U., 1982; vice chmn. dept. communications N.J. Coun. Chs., 1986—; host People Working for People, Sta. WOR-TV, N.Y.C., 1988; programmer Cable TV Network of N.J., 1985; producer The Jersey Cape TV series, 1990—. Host Inner-Dimension Community Concerns, Union Eyes and Perspective on the News Sta. WOR Radio, WOR Special Report, N.Y., 1970—. Pres. Rep. Club, West Cape May, N.J., 1986-87; vice chmn. communications N.J. Coun. Chs., 1986-89; committeman Cape May County N.J. Rep. Orgn., 1987-90, Essex Coun. N.J. Rep. Orgn., 1980-85. Sgt. U.S. Army, 1951-53. Recipient Gabriel award Washington Conf., 1966-67, Radio Programming award Ohio State U., 1969, Columbus Film Festival award Ohio Coun. Chs., 1970, Radio-TV award N.J. Coun. Chs., 1983, Olive award, 1984, Cape award Cable TV Network N.J., 1987, Angel award Excellence in Media, Hollywood, Calif., 1999. Mem. AFTRA, Nat. Lima Bean Assn. (founder), Alpha Sigma Rho, South Jersey Bird Club. Episcopalian. Club: Suburban Sports Car (N.J.) (v.p., co-founder 1956-61). Home: 653 Sun Haven Dr Clayton NJ 08312-1955

BERTENTHAL, BENNETT IRA, foundation administrator; b. N.Y.C., Mar. 22, 1949; married; 2 children. BA in Psychology, Brandeis U., 1971; MA in Devel. Psychology, U. Denver, 1976, PhD, 1978. Postdoctoral fellow Brain Rsch. Inst. and dept. pediats. UCLA Sch. Medicine, 1978-79; asst. prof. dept. psychology U. Va., 1979-85, assoc. prof., 1985, prof., 1991—, dir. devel. tng. program, 1989-96; asst. dir. NSF, Arlington, Va., 1997—; mem. human devel. and aging study sect, Nat. Inst. Child Health and Human Devel., 1987, 91-96, chair, 1994-96; extramural reviewer NSF, Nat. Inst. Neurol. Diseases & Communicative Disorders, NIMH; cons. NINCDS; mem. performance and safety monitoring com. NINCDS, 1981-88; program com. Internat. Conf. Infant Studies, 1984, 88, 96, Southeastern Conf. Human Devel., 1988; mem. MacArthur Network on Transition From Infancy to Childhood, 1987-92; mem. MacArthur Network Task Force-Devel. of Computer Workstas. for Psychol. Rsch., 1988-92. Assoc. editor Devel. Psychology, 1988-90, mem. editl. bd., 1988-90; mem. editl. bd. Jour. Exptl. Child Psychology, 1985-88, Child Devel., 1980-83; reviewer Psychophysiology, infant Behavior and Devel., Perception and Psychophysics, Devel. Psychology, Child Devel., SRCD Monographs, Internat. Jour. Behavioural Devel., Jour. Exptl. Psychology, Human Perception and Performance. Recipient Boyd R. McCandless Young Scientist award, 1985, rsch. career devel. awarrd NIH, 1985-90, Cattell Sabbatical award, 1990, MHTP postdoctoral fellowship, 1978-79; grantee U. Va. Rsch. Policy Coun., 1979-80, 87-90, 89—, NIMH, 1979-80, 85-90, 91—, NINCDS, 1980-81, NIH, 1982-84, 85-88, 89—, John D. and Catherine T. MacArthur Found., 1984-85, 89—, Va. Ctr. Innovative Tech., 1985-86, NATO, 1989—, United Cerebral Palsey Rsch. and Edn. Found., 1989-90, McDonnell-Pew Program Cognitive Neuroscis., 1991-93. Fellow APA (program com. 1987, 88, nominations com. divsn. 7 1988, mem.-at-large divsn. 7 exec. com. 1995-98, mem. com. on sci. awards, 1991-94, chair, 1994), Am. Psychol. Soc.; mem. AAAS, Soc. Rsch. in Child Devel. (co-chair program com. 1995-97), Assn. Rsch. in Vision and Ophthalmology, Internat. Soc. Infant Studies, Internat. Soc. Study Behavioural Devel., Internat. Soc. Study of Posture and Gait, Psychonomic Soc. Office: NSF 4201 Wilson Blvd Rm 905 Arlington VA 22230-0001

BERTHIAUME, WAYNE HENRY, electrical engineer; b. Worcester, Mass., Aug. 3, 1955; s. Henry Louis and Lorraine Anne (Beland) B.; m. Mary Louise Metivier, Aug. 21, 1976. ASEE cum laude, Worcester Jr. Coll., 1982; BEE cum laude, Cen. New Eng. Coll., Worcester, 1987. Profl. Ski Instr. Assn. Level II cert. Draftsman Henry L. Berthiaume Design Svcs., Northboro, Mass., 1969-71; TV repair technician Color Visual Tech., Northboro, 1971-72; technician Data Gen. Corp., Southboro, Mass., 1972-76, lead technician, 1974-76, final acceptance technician, 1976-77, lead technician, 1977, engr., 1977-83, sr. engr., 1983—. Marshal Boston Five Classic Golf Tournament, Danvers, Mass., Digital Sr. Golf Classic, Sudbury, Mass. Mem. NRA (life). Roman Catholic. Avocations: golf, skiing, windsurfing, woodworking. Home: 129 Wheeler Rd Princeton MA 01541-1917 Office: Data Gen Corp 4400 Computer Dr Westborough MA 01580-0001

BERTHOLD, JOHN WILLIAM, III, physicist; b. York, Pa., May 24, 1945; s. John William and M. Pauline (Decker) B.; m. Jacqueline Reed, Oct. 5, 1974; children: John William, Margaret H. BA, Gettysburg (Pa.) Coll., 1967; MS, U. Ariz., 1974, PhD, 1976. Sr. tech. aide Bell Telephone Labs., Inc., Murray Hill, N.J., 1967-69; rsch. asst., assoc. Optical Sci. Ctr. U. Ariz., Tucson, 1969-76; physicist U.S. Dept. Def., Ft. Meade, Md., 1976-79; sr. rsch. physicist Babcock & Wilcox Co./McDermott Technology, Inc., Alliance, Ohio, 1979-83; group supr. Babcock & Wilcox Co., Alliance, Ohio, 1983-84, sect. mgr., 1984-85, tech. advisor, 1985-90, scientist, 1990-94; sr. consulting engr., 1994—; cons. Iota Engring., Inc., Tucson, 1973-76; lectr. in field; sr. acad. coun. Ohio Acad. Sci., 1993—. Contbr. articles to profl. jours., chpts. to books; patentee in field. Owens-Ill. fellow, 1972-73; NASA Tech. Brief awardee, 1977. Fellow Internat. Soc. Optical Engring.; mem. Optical Soc. Am., Instrument Soc. Am. (sr.), IEEE (affiliate), Salem Golf Club. Achievements include 29 patents in field. Office: McDermott Tech Inc 1562 Beeson St NE Alliance OH 44601-2165

BERTHOT, JAKE, artist; b. Niagara Falls, N.Y., Mar. 30, 1939. Ed., New Sch. Social Rsch., 1960-61, Pratt Inst., 1960-62. Mem. faculty Cooper Union, 1960-62, Yale U., New Haven, 1982-90, Sch. Visual Arts, N.Y.C., 1992—; artist in residence Dartmouth U., fall 1995. One-man shows include Portland Ctr. Visual Arts, Oreg., 1973, Galerie de Gestlo, Hamburg, Fed. Republic Germany, 1973, 77, O.K Harris Gallery, N.Y.C., 1970, 72, 75, David McKee Gallery, N.Y.C., 1976, 78, 82, 83, 86, 88, 89, 91, 95, 96, U. Calif. Berkeley, 1984, Nina Nielsen Gallery, Boston, 1979, 84, 92, 95, 96,

Nat. Gallery, Washington, 1989, Nigel Greenwood Gallery, London, 1979, 91, Galleri Olsson, Stockholm, 1987, 90, 96, Cork Gallery Lincoln Ctr., N.Y.C., 1991, Jaffe-Friede and Strauss Gallery, Hanover, N.H., 1995, The Phillips Collection, Washington, 1996; group shows include Whitney Mus. Art, N.Y.C., 1969, 72, 74, 78, Art Inst. Chgo., 1971, Mus. Modern Art, N.Y.C., 1977, 81, 83, 84, 85, Meadows Art Gallery, Dallas, 1985, numerous others; represented in permanent collections Australian Nat. Gallery, Balt. Mus. Art, U. Calif. Berkeley Mus., Dallas Mus. Fine Arts, Fogg Art Mus. at Harvard U., Guggenheim Mus., Mus. Modern Art, Whitney Mus. Art., others. Guggenheim fellow, 1981; recipient Acad. Inst. award Am. Acad. Arts & Letters, 1994; named academician Nat. Acad. Design; grantee The Elizabeth Found., 1995-96. Address: David McKee 745 5th Ave New York NY 10151-0099*

BERTHOUEX, PAUL MAC, civil and environmental engineer, educator; b. Oelwein, Iowa, Aug. 15, 1940; s. George Albert and LaVadia Fay (McBride) B.; m. Susan Jean Powell, Sept. 8, 1962; 1 child, Stephanie Fay. BSCE, U. Iowa, 1963, MSCE, 1964; PhD, U. Wis., 1969. Registered profl. engr., Iowa. Instr. U. Iowa, Iowa City, 1964-65; asst. prof. civil engring. U. Conn., Storrs, 1965-67; chief rsch. engr. GKW Cons., Mannheim, Fed. Republic of Germany, 1969-71; prof. civil engring. U. Wis., Madison, 1971—. Author: Strategy of Pollution Control, 1978, Statistics for Environmental Engineers, 1994; contbr. over 100 articles to profl. jours. Recipient Radebaugh Prize, CSWPCA, 1989, 91. Mem. ASCE (Rudolf Herring medal 1974, 92), Water Environment Fedn. (Eddy medal 1971), Internat. Assn. Water Pollution Rsch. and Control, Assn. Environ. Engring. Profs. Office: U Wis 1415 Johnson Dr Madison WI 53706-1607

BERTHRONG, MERRILL GRAY, retired library director; b. Cambridge, Mass., July 18, 1919; s. Louis Paul and Helen (Gray) B.; m. Geraldine Brock; children—Peter Gray, Paul Merritt, Stephen Clark. B.A., Tufts U., 1941; M.A., Fletcher Sch. of Law and Diplomacy, Medford, Mass., 1946-47; Ph.D., U. Pa., 1958. Tchr. history U. Conn., New London, 1947-50, Drexel Inst., Phila., 1950-53, Rutgers U., Camden, N.J., 1950-55; library adminstr. U. Pa., Phila., 1956-64; dir. libraries Wake Forest U., Winston-Salem, N.C., 1964-89; ret., 1989. Served to capt. USAF, 1941-45; ETO. Fulbright grantee, Paris, 1955-56. Mem. Forsyth County Library Assn. (bd. dirs. 1984-86), ALA, Am. History Assn., AAUP, Southeastern Library Assn. Home: 2032 Faculty Dr Winston Salem NC 27106-5242 also: PO Box 132 Prospect Harbor ME 04669

BERTI, MARGARET ANN, early childhood education educator; b. Jersey City, Oct. 1, 1961; d. John Albert and Jane Matilda (McNair) Condon; m. Douglas Anthony Berti, Aug. 4, 1990; children: Matthew Douglas, Allison Nicole. BA, William Paterson Coll., Wayne, N.J., 1983, MEd, 1985. Tchr. 1st grade Paterson (N.J.) Pub. Schs., 1984-85; tchr pre-kindergarten and ESL Dallas Ind. Sch. Dist., 1985-92; tchr. kindergarten Pearland (Tex.) Ind. Sch. Dist., 1992-95; pre-sch. tchr. Early Childhood Program St. Paul's Cath. Ch., Nassau Bay, Tex., 1997—. Named Tchr. of Yr., George W. Truett Elem. Sch., 1988, Rustic Oak Elem. Sch., Pearland, 1994; named to Outstanding Young Women of Am., 1991; Title VII grantee Tex. Woman's U., 1987. Mem. Nat. Assn. Edn. Young Children, Classroom Tchrs. Dallas (bldg. rep. 1991), Dallas-Internat. Reading Assn. (corr. sec. 1992), Pearland Edn. Assn. (bldg. rep. 1993-95), Delta Kappa Gamma (Delta Rho chpt.). Roman Catholic. Avocations: reading, power walking, cycling, cooking. Home: 1526 Saxony Ln Houston TX 77058-3442

BERTI, PHYLLIS MAE, health information management specialist; b. Blue Island, Ill., Jan. 27, 1941; d. Louis J. and Helen Beatrice (Smola) Hankus; m. Jerome Leon Berti, May 27, 1967; children: James Louis, Jeffrey Jerome, Joseph Gregory, Cynthia Ann. AS in Health Info. Mgmt., Stark Tech. Coll., Canton, Ohio, 1992. Claims processor Mass. Mut. Ins. Co., Hazel Crest, Ill., 1981-84; physician billing rep. Ingalls Meml. Hosp., Harvey, Ill., 1984-87; coder, abstractor Timken Mercy Med. Ctr., Canton, 1987-89, Wooster (Ohio) Cmty. Hosp., 1989-92; coord. clin. records Quest Recovery Svcs., Canton, 1992-93; health info. mgmt. specialist So. Health Care Ctr., Southaven, Miss., 1994-99, Bapt. Progressive Care Ctr., Southaven, 1999—. Mem. Am. Health Info. Mgmt. Assn. (long term care sect., accredited records technician), Miss. Health Info. Mgmt. Assn., Memphis Health Info. Mgmt. Assn. Avocations: crafts, gardening, fishing, swimming, boating. Home: 4178 Star Landing Rd E Nesbit MS 38651-9202

BERTIN, JOHN JOSEPH, aeronautical engineer, educator, researcher; b. Milw., Oct. 13, 1938; s. Andrea and Yolanda G. (Pasquali) B.; m. Ruth Easterbrook; children: Thomas Alexander, Randolph Scott, Elizabeth Anne, Michael Robert. BA, Rice Inst., Houston, 1960; MS, Rice U., 1962, PhD, 1966. Aerospace technologist NASA Johnson Space Ctr., Houston, 1962-66; prof. U. Tex., Austin, 1966-89; program mgr. for space initiative MTS, Sandia Nat. Labs., Albuquerque, 1989-94; vis. prof. USAF Acad., Colorado Springs, Colo., 1988-89, prof. aero. engring., 1994—; cons. McGinnis, Lochridge & Kilgore, Austin, 1978-83, Sandia Nat. Labs., Albuquerque, 1980-89, BPD Difesa e Spazio, Rome, 1980-82, NASA, 1994-96, Sci. Applications Internat. Corp., 1996; detailed to Office of Space, U.S. Dept. Energy Hdqs., 1991-92; dir. Ctr. Excellence for Hypersonic Tng. and Rsch., 1985-89; mem. sci. adv. bd. USAF, 1989-93, mem. adv. group Flight Dynamics Labs., 1989-93; tech. chmn. Space 2000 Conf., 1998—. Author: Engineering Fluid Mechanics, 1987, Hypersonic Aerothermodynamics, 1994; co-author: Aerodynamics for Engineers, 1997; editor: Hypersonics, 1989, Advances in Hypersonics, 1992. Pres. Western Hills Little League, Austin, 1975; mem. arts subcom. NASA, 1987-91; mem. Aerospace Engring. Bd. Panel NRC, 1996-97, USAF hypersonics program rev. com., 1997-98. Recipient Gen. Dynamics tchg. award U. Tex. Coll. Engring., 1978, Tex. Exec. tchg. award Ex-Students Assn. U. Tex., 1982, faculty award Tau Beta Pi, 1986, award for meritorious civilian svc. Dept. Air Force, 1993, Gen. Daley award USAFA, 1996, Exemplary Civilian Svc. Award medal, 1996, F.J. Seiler Rsch. award, USAFA, 1997. Fellow AIAA (dir. region IV 1983-86, Disting. Lectr., Thermophysics award 1997, publs. bd. 1998—).

BERTINELLI, VALERIE, actress; b. Wilmington, Del., Apr. 23, 1960; m. Eddie Van Halen, Apr. 11, 1981; 1 child, Wolfgang. Student, Tami Lynn Acad. Artists, Calif. Owner Bertinelli, Inc. Actress: (TV movies) Young Love, First Love, 1979, The Promise of Love, 1980, The Princess and the Cabbie, 1981, I Was a Mail Order Bride, 1982, The Seduction of Gina, 1984, Shattered Vows, 1984, Silent Witness, 1985, Rockabye, 1986, Aladdin and His Magic Lamp, Murder of Innocence, 1993, The Haunting of Helen Walker, 1995, Two Mothers for Zachery, 1996, A Case for Life, 1996; (TV spls.) The Secret of Charles Dickens, The Magic of David Copperfield; (TV series) One Day at a Time, 1975-84, Sydney, 1990, Cafe Americain, 1993-94; (TV miniseries) Night Sins, 1997. Office: William Morris Agy care Marc Schwartz 151 S El Camino Dr Beverly Hills CA 90212-2775*

BERTINI, CATHERINE ANN, United Nations official; b. Syracuse, N.Y., Mar. 30, 1950; d. Fulvio and Ann (Vino) B.; m. Thomas Haskell, 1988. Degree, SUNY; DSc (hon.), McGill U., Montreal, Can., 1997; DHL (hon.), SUNY, Cortland, 1999. Youth dir. N.Y. Rep. State Com., 1971-74; with Rep. Nat. Com., 1975-76; mgr. pub. policy Container Corp. Am., 1977-87; dir. Office Family Assistance, U.S. Dept. Health and Human Svcs., 1987-89; acting asst. sec. U.S. Dept. Health and Human Svcs., 1989; asst. sec. U.S. Dept. Agrl., 1989-92; exec. dir. UN World Food Programme, Rome, 1992—; UN panel mem. sec. gen.'s High Level Personalities on African Devel., UN, 1992-95. Commr. Ill. State Scholarship Comm., 1979-84; mem. Ill. Human Rights Comm., 1985-87. Recipient Leadership in Human Svcs. award Am. Pub. Welfare Assn., 1990, Pub. Svc. award Am. Acad. Pediatrics, 1991, Leadership award Nat. Assn. WIC Dirs., 1992, Quality of Life award Auburn U., 1994, Disting. Alumni award Nelson A. Rockefeller Coll. Pub. Affairs and Policy, 1997. Fellow Harvard U., 1986. Office: UN World Food Program, Cesare Giulio Viola 68/70, 00148 Rome Italy

BERTINO, FRED, advertising executive. V.p., creative group head Della Femina McNamee WCRS; pres., co-creative dir. Anderson Veduccio Bertino Advt.; with Hill Holliday, Boston, 1990—, now pres., chief creative officer; mem. staff Art inst. New Eng. Recipient award N.Y. Advt. Club, N.Y. Art Dir.'s Club, One Show, Hatch Awards, Andy Awards, New Eng. Best of Broadcasting, Commn. Arts mag., Conn. Art Dir.'s Club, Grand Effie award for Creative Effectiveness, Arhena Newspapers, Stephen Kelly Awards, Grand Clio award. Office: Hill Holiday Coners Cosmopoulos Inc John Hancock Tower 200 Clarendon St Boston MA 02116

BERTINO, JOSEPH ROCCO, physician, educator; b. Port Chester, N.Y., Aug. 16, 1930; s. Joseph and Madaleine (Posillipo) B.; m. Mary Patricia Hagemeyer, Sept. 29, 1956; children—Frederick, Amy Marie, Thomas Allen, Paul Phillip. Student, Cornell U., 1947-50; M.D., Downstate Med. Center N.Y., 1954. USPHS Research fellow U. Wash. Sch. Medicine, Seattle, 1958-61; mem. faculty Yale U. Sch. Medicine, 1961-87, assoc. prof. pharmacology and medicine, 1964-67, prof., 1967-87, Am. Cancer Soc. prof., 1975—; head program molecular pharmacology and therapeutics Sloan Kettering Ctr., 1987—; prof. medicine and pharmacology Cornell U. Sch. Medicine, N.Y.C., 1987—; cons. USPHS, 1966—; N.Y. State scholar for medicine, 1950-54. Contbr. articles to profl. jours. Recipient Honor medal Am. Cancer Soc., 1992. Mem. Am. Soc. for Clin. Investigation, Am. Soc. Hematology, Biol. Chemists, Pharmacology and Therapeutics. Home: 117 Sunset Hill Rd Branford CT 06405-6419 Office: Meml Sloan Kettering Cancer Ctr 1275 York Ave New York NY 10021-6007

BERTLES, JOHN FRANCIS, physician, educator; b. Spokane, Wash., June 8, 1925; s. John Francis and Henrita Swart (Brown) B.; m. Jeannette Winans, 1948 (div. 1978); children: Mark Dwight, Jacquelyn Eve, John Francis.; m. Lila De Paganne, 1981. BS, Yale U., 1945; MD, Harvard U., 1952. Diplomate Am. Bd. Internal Medicine. Intern Presbyterian Hosp., N.Y.C., 1952-53; asst. resident in medicine Presbyterian Hosp., 1953-55; research fellow in hematology U. Rochester and Strong Meml. Hosp., 1955-56; research fellow in immunohematology Harvard U. Med. Sch. and Mass. Gen. Hosp., Boston, 1956-58; research fellow in hematology Harvard U. Med. Sch. and Mass. Gen. Hosp., 1958-59; instr. in medicine Harvard U. Med. Sch. at Mass. Gen. Hosp., 1959-61; dir. hematology-oncology div. St. Luke's Hosp. Center, N.Y.C., 1962-95; asst. attending physician St. Luke's Hosp. Center, 1962-64, assoc. attending physician, 1964-71, attending physician, 1971-95; dir. transfusion services St. Luke's Roosevelt Hosp. Ctr., 1981-95; sr. research asso. dept. biol. scis. Columbia U., 1970-71, asst. clin. prof. medicine, 1962-67, assoc. clin. prof., 1967-71, assoc. prof., 1971-74, prof., 1974-95, prof. emeritus of medicine, 1995—; attending physician Montefiore Med. Ctr., N.Y.C., 1995-97; clin. prof. medicine Albert Einstein Coll. Medicine, N.Y.C., 1995-97; vis. prof. medicine Nuffield dept. clin. medicine Radcliffe Infirmary, U. Oxford, Eng., 1977-78; cons. to various govt. agys., including hematology study sect. NIH, 1972-76, 82-84, blood rsch. rev. group, 1978-82; mem. dirs. coun. N.Y. Heart Assn., 1974-90; mem. basic rsch. adv. com. Nat. Found. March of Dimes, 1977-80. Contbr. articles to profl. publs. Ensign USNR, 1945-46. Fellow ACP; mem. Am. Soc. Clin. Investigation, Am. Physiol. Soc., Am. Soc. Hematology, Am. Fedn. Clin. Rsch., Am. Chem. Soc., Alpha Omega Alpha. Office: 67 Jared Dr White Plains NY 10605-3413

BERTMAN, SKIP, baseball coach; m. Sandy Bertman; children: Jan, Jodi, Lisa, Lori. BA in Health and Phys. Edn., U. Miami, 1961, M in Health and Phys. Edn., 1964. Asst. baseball coach U. Miami, 1976-83; head baseball coach La. State U., Baton Rouge, 1984—; led USA Baseball Team, 1995-96; asst. coach Olympic Baseball Team; asst. coach Interncontinental Baseball team, 1987, U.S. Olympic Baseball team, 1988; mgr. NCAA champion La. State U. Tigers, 1991, 93, 96, 97; head coach USA Baseball, 1995, 96. Author: Skip: The Man and The System, Coaching Youth Baseball. Named Nat. Coach of Yr., Baseball Am. and The Sporting News, 1986, Collegiate Baseball newspaper and Am. Baseball Coaches Assn., 1991, 93; named to U. Miami Sports Hall of Fame, 1994. *

BERTOLDO, JOSEPH RAMON, lawyer; b. Safford, Ariz., Nov. 24, 1950; s. Joe M. Bertoldo and Virginia (Burrell) Simmons. BS, U. Ariz., 1973, JD, 1976. Bar: Ariz. 1977, U.S. Dist. Ct. Ariz. 1977, U.S. Ct. Appeals (9th cir.) 1980, U.S. Supreme Ct. 1980. Asst. city atty. City of Flagstaff (Ariz.), 1977-81, city atty., 1981—. Bd. dirs. IMPACT, victim-witness advocacy group, Flagstaff, 1986; active Flagstaff unit Am. Cancer Soc. Mem. Ariz. Bar Assn., Coconino County Bar Assn. (v.p. 1989, pres. 1990), Ariz. City Attys. Assn. (pres. 1995-96), Internat. Mcpl. Lawyers Assn. (Ariz. state chair 1991-94, regional v.p. 1994—), Phi Delta Phi. Democrat. Roman Catholic. Avocations: fishing, bicycling, alpine skiing. Home: 1345 N Fox Hill Rd Flagstaff AZ 86004-7881 Office: City of Flagstaff 211 W Aspen Ave Flagstaff AZ 86001-5399

BERTOLET, RODNEY JAY, philosophy educator; b. Allentown, Pa., Mar. 22, 1949; s. Frank and Helen (Johnson) B. BA, Franklin & Marshall Coll., 1971; PhD, U. Wis., 1977. Asst. prof. philosophy Purdue U., West Lafayette, Ind., 1977-82; assoc. prof. philosophy Purdue U., West Lafayette, 1982-90, prof. philosophy, 1990—, dept. head, 1991—. Author: What Is Said, 1990. Mem. Am. Philos. Assn., Ind. Philos. Assn. (pres. 1983-84). Office: Dept Philosophy LAEB/Purdue Univ West Lafayette IN 47907

BERTOLLI, EUGENE EMIL, sculptor, goldsmith, designer, consultant; b. Boston, Feb. 19, 1923; s. Adolph and Julia (Manetti) B.; m. Jean Helen Tamburine, Apr. 21, 1956; children—Eugene Robert, Lisa Marie. A.B. (hons.) cum laude, Boston Coll., 1943; postgrad., Washington and Lee U., 1944. Dir. ednl. reconditioning Madigan Convalescent Hosp., Tacoma, 1945-47; sr. v.p. design Napier Co., Meriden, Conn., 1947-85; sculptor, goldsmith Bertolli Studio, Meriden, Conn., 1947—, also cons. design and jewelry techniques, 1947—; dir. City Savs. Bank, Meriden, Napier Co.; sculpture awards juror Am. Artists Profl. League, N.Y.C., 1993, Hudson Valley Art Assn., Inc., N.Y.C., 1984, 94. Works include bronze portrait The Outdoorsman (Am. Artists Profl. League award 1983). Mem. and officer Meriden Bd. Edn., 1958-63; pres. Meriden Pub. Libr. Bd., 1964-86; trustee Meriden-Wallingford Hosp. Recipient internat. outstanding jewelry design award Swarowski Internat., 1968, 69, John Manship Meml. award Rockport Art Assn., 1985, Franz Denghauser Meml. award for sculpture, 1988, award for sculpture Acad. Artists Assn., 1992, 94, Paul Manship Meml. award for excellence in sculpture North Shore Arts Assn., 1992, 93, portrait sculpture award Am. Artists Profl. League, 1994, L.J. Meiselman meml. award for Artistic Excellence of Sculpture for Portrait Bust, Am. Artists Profl. League, 1996 Grand Nat. Exhbn.; inducted into Meriden Hall of Fame for achievement in field of art, 1995. Mem. Acad. Artists Assn. (gold medal for sculpture 1982-84, 88-92), North Shore Arts Assn. (juror of awards and membership admission 1993, spl. portrait sculpture award 1980, Katharine Taylor Weems sculpture award 1989), Am. Artists Profl. League (juror of awards 1993), Hudson Valley Art Assn. (juror of awards 1994), Mfg. Jewelers and Silversmiths, Internat. Platform Assn., Meriden Art Assn. (pres. 1957-58), Guild Boston Artists, Salmagundi Club. Roman Catholic. Home and Studio: 73 Reynolds Dr Meriden CT 06450-2532 also: PO Box 1391 Madison CT 06443-1391

BERTOLONE, SALVATORE J., pediatric medicine educator; b. Bronx, N.Y., July 31, 1944. BS in Biology, Fordham U., 1966; MD, U. Louisville, 1970. Med. lic., Ky.; cert. Am. Bd. Pediatrics, Supspecialty Bd. Pediatric Hematology/Oncology. Pediatric intern U. Louisville (Ky.) Sch. Medicine, 1970-71, pediatric resident, 1971-72; fellow dept. pediatrics U. Colo., Denver, 1972-74; asst. clin. prof., dept. pediatrics, dept. neurosurgery U. Colo., Sch. Medicine, Denver, 1974-76; asst. prof. pediatrics, dept. pediatrics U. Louisville (Ky.) Sch. Medicine, 1976-82; assoc. in oncology U. Louisville (Ky.), James Graham Brown Cancer Ctr., 1977; assoc. prof. pediatrics, dept. pediatrics U. Louisville (Ky.) Sch. Medicine, 1982-92, prof. pediatrics, dept. pediatrics, 1992—, dir. pediatric Hematology, Oncology, 1998—; cons. Crippled Children's Svcs., State of Ky., 1976—, State of Ind., 1976, Hemophilia Clinic, Kosair Children's Hosp., Louisville, 1979—, Dept. Pediatrics Ireland Army Hosp., Fort Knox, Ky., 1979—, Jefferson County Dept. Health, Lead Poisoning Program, Louisville, 1983—; founder, bd. dirs. Pediatric Hospice of Louisville, 1979—, med. dir., 1979-84; active various coms. U. Louisville Sch. Medicine and Kosair Children's Hosp., many others; asst. chief pediatric clininc Fitzsimons Army Med. Ctr., Denver, 1974-76, chief pediatric hematology/oncology, 1974-76; active med. staff Kosair Children's Hosp., Louisville, 1976—, Humana Hosp., Audubon, Louisville, 1979—, U. Gen. Hosp., Louisville, 1979—, Humana Hosp., U., Louisville, 1986—, Meth. Evang. Hosp., Louisville, 1987-93; mem. med. staff Home of Innocents, Louisville, 1980-83; mem. courtesy staff Humana Hosp. Suburban, Louisville, 1981—, Jewish Hosp., Louisville, 1982—. Mem. editl. bd. Jour. Cancer Edn., 1986—; contbr. chpts. in books and numerous articles to profl. jours. Mem. adv. com. on childhood cancer Am. Cancer Soc., Louisville, 1979-80; mem. med. adv. com. ARC, Louisville, 1979—; bd. dirs. Help Our Parents Endure, Parent Support Group, Louisville, 1980-85; med., bd. dirs. Ronald McDonald House, Louisville, 1980—, chmn. planning com., 1980-82; co-chmn. Affiliate Instn. Com., Children's Cancer Group, 1984—; many others. Maj. U.S. Army, 1972-76. Recipient WLKY Bell award, 1991, Nat. Jefferson award, Washington, 1992; grantee Nat. Cancer Inst., 1977-82, Crusade for Children, 1978, 80, 82, 86, 90, 91, 92, Ky. Adv. Bd. on Hemophilia, State of Ky., 1981, 82, 83-85, 86-90, 91, Am. Cancer Soc., 1982, Louisville and Jefferson County Bd. of Health, 1983-90, 91, Children's Cancer Group, 1984-87, 87, 88, 89, 90, 91, 92, 93, Cabinet for Human Resources, 1988, 89, 90, Alpha Therapeutic Corp., 1991, others. Fellow Am. Acad. Pediatrics; mem. Am. Soc. Clin. Oncology, Am. Soc. Pediatric Hematology/Oncology, Am. Assn. Cancer Eductors, So. Soc. for Pediatric Rsch., Ky. Chpt. Am. Acad. Pediatrics, Ky. Med. Assn., Jefferson County Med. Soc., Louisville Pediatric Soc., Alpha Omega Alpha. Office: Dept Pediats Hemtology/Oncology 601 S Floyd St Ste 500 Louisville KY 40202-1837*

BERTOLUCCI, BERNARDO, film director; b. Parma, Italy, Mar. 16, 1941; s. Attilio and Ninetta B.; m. Clare Peploe, 1978. Attended, Rome (Italy) U. Dir. films The Grim Reaper, 1962, Before the Revolution, 1964 (Young Critics award Cannes Film Festival), La Via del Petrolio, 1965, His Partner, 1968, The Conformist, 1970 (Nat. Film Critics Best Dir. award), The Spider's Strategem, 1970, Last Tango in Paris, 1972, 1900, 1976, Luna, 1979, Tragedy of a Ridiculous Man, 1981, The Last Emperor (Golden Globe award for Best Dramatic Picture, 1986, Best Dir., Best Screenplay, Best Original Score, Best Editor, Best Cinematography, Best Sound, Best Prodn. Design, Art Dir., Best Costume Design, Acad. award for Best Picture of Yr., Best Dir., Best Screenplay Adaptation, Best Film honor Brit. Acad. Film and TV Arts), The Sheltering Sky, 1990, Little Buddha, 1994, Stealing Beauty, 1996; author: poems In Search of Mystery, 1962 (Viareggio prize, Italy). Office: care Recorded Picture Co, 24 Hanway St, London W1P 9DD, England also: care Jeff Berg ICM 8942 Wilshire Blvd Beverly Hills CA 90211-1934*

BERTON, PIERRE, journalist, author; b. Whitehorse, Yukon, Can., July 12, 1920; s. Francis George and Laura (Thompson) B.; m. Janet Walker, 1946; children: Penny, Pamela, Patricia, Peter, Paul, PeggyAnne, Perri, Eric. BA, U. B.C., 1941, DLitt (hon.), 1985; LLD (hon.), U. P.E.I., 1973, Dalhousie U., 1978, U. Brock, 1981, York U., 1974, U. Windsor, 1981, U. Athabasca, 1982, U. Victoria, 1983, McMaster U., 1983, U. Alaska, 1984, Royal Mil. Inst., 1985, Waterloo U., 1988. City editor Vancouver (B.C.) News Herald, 1941-42; feature writer Vancouver Sun, 1946-47; successive positions to mng. editor Maclean's Mag., Toronto, Ont., 1947-58; host The Pierre Berton Show, 1963-73; contbg. editor Maclean's Mag., 1963; asso. editor, daily columnist Toronto Daily Star, 1958-62; columnist Toronto Star, 1991-94; TV panelist Front Page Challenge, CBC, 1957-95; chancellor Yukon Coll., 1988-93. Author: 46 books including The Royal Family, 1953, Stampede for Gold, 1955, The Mysterious North, 1956, Klondike Fever, 1958, Just Add Water and Stir, 1959, Adventures of a Columnist, 1960, The New City, 1961, The Secret World of Og, 1961, Fast, Fast, Fast Relief, 1962, Big Sell, 1963, Comfortable Pew, 1965, The Cool, Crazy, Committed World of The Sixties, 1966, Smug Minority, 1968, The National Dream, 1970, The Last Spike, 1971, The Impossible Railway, 1972, Drifting Home, 1973, Hollywood's Canada, 1974, My Country, 1976, The Dionne Years, 1977, The Wild Frontier, 1978, The Invasion of Canada, 1812-1813, 1980, Flames across the Border, 1981, Why We Act Like Canadians, 1982, Klondike Quest, 1983, The Promised Land, 1984, Masquerade, 1985, Vimy, 1986, Starting Out, 1987, The Arctic Grail, 1988 (Periodical Marketers Can. Book of Yr. award), The Great Depression 1929-39, 1990 (Periodical Marketers Can. Authors award), Niagara, 1992, A Picture Book of Niagara Falls, 1993, Winter, 1994, My Times: Living with History 1947-1995, 1995, Farewell To The Twentieth Century, 1996, The Great Lakes, 1996, 1967-The Last Good Year, 1997, Seacoasts 1998, A Literary Resurrection, 1948-94, 1998, Worth Repeating, Pierre Berton's Canada, 1999, Welcome to the 21st Century, 1999; screenwriter; narrator City of Gold; contbr. to numerous mags.and newspapers. Past chmn. Heritage Can. Found. Capt. Can. Army, 1942-45. Decorated Companion Order Can.; recipient Gov. Gen.'s award for creative non-fiction, 1956, 58, 72; Stephen Leacock medal for humor, 1959; J.V. McAree award for columnist of year, 1959; Nat. Newspaper awards for feature writing and staff corresponding, 1960; Grand Prix film awards.; Beefeater Club prize for lit., 1982; Can. Booksellers award, 1982, Companion Order Can., 1986, Gabriele Leger Nat. Heritage award, 1989, Coles Book award, 1989, Great Trekker award U. B.C., 1990, Graeme Gibson award, 1992, Author's Leadership award Periodical Marketers Can., 1992, Pierre Berton award, 1994, Responsibilty in Journalism award Com. for Investigation of Paranormal, 1996, Biomed. Sci. Ambs. award, 1997; named to Can. Newspaper Hall of Fame, 1982, Order of Mariposa, 1990. Mem. Authors League Am., Heritage Can., Assn. Can. Radio and TV Artists (award for integrity in broadcasting 1972, award for pub. affairs 1977), Writers Union Can. Office: 21 Sackville St, Toronto, ON Canada M5A 3E1

BERTONAZZI, LOUIS PETER, federal agency administrator; b. Milford, Mass., Oct. 9, 1933; s. Peter John and Concetta (Rossi) B.; BA, Tufts U., 1955; MA, Suffolk U., 1960; D Pub. Adminstrn. (hon.), Mass. Maritime Acad.; m. Barbara Szymanski, June 7, 1957; 3 children. Guidance dir. Medway (Mass.) High Sch., 1961-65; 1st dep. commr. Mass. Dept. Youth Services, 1966-69; mem. Mass. Ho. of Reps., 1969-78, Mass. State Senate, 1979-96, Senate majority leader, 1996-97; asst. sec. Exec. Office Health and Human Svcs., Boston, 1996—; asst. adj. prof. Boston U. Sch. Medicine. Mem. adv. bd. Office of Children, Internat. Yr. of Child, 1979; mem. nat. consumer rep. W.K. Kellogg Found., 1978—; mem. Mass. Citizens Com. on Tort Law Reform, 1980-81; mem. com. on human resources Eastern Regional Conf. Council State Govts., 1981—; mem. adv. com. Mass. Cancer Registry; chmn. subcom. Joint Legis./Exec. Commn. on Hosp. Reimbursement Systems; mem. Gov.'s/MBA Com. on Alcoholic Client; mem. bd. overseers Tufts U. Sch. Dental Medicine. Served with U.S. Army, 1956-58. Mem. Nat. Conf. State Legislatures (fiscal affairs and oversight com.). Recipient Disting. Alumnus award Tufts U. Democrat. Roman Catholic. Office: Mass Exec Office Health & Human Svcs 1 Ashburton Pl Boston MA 02108-1518

BERTONE, ANDREW E., biological scientist, environmental scientist; b. Jersey City, N.J., Aug. 24, 1927; s. Anthony Dominic and Dellora B.; m. Paulin A. LiCalsi, Jan. 2, 1954; children: Pamela, Cynthia, Andrew, Mary Alice, Lisa. BS, Fairleigh Dickinson U., 1956. Reg. Med. Technologist; lic. radiol. tech. Med. tech. Clin. Lab., Newark, 1947-48; supr. lab. & x-ray Doctor's Hosp., Union City, N.J., 1948-50; med. tech. VA, Newark, 1950-53; supr. lab. & x-ray Mobil Oil, N.Y.C., 1953-76; prod. safety specialist Mobil Oil, Princeton, N.J., 1976-84; instr. med. tech. Easter Sch., N.Y.C., 1957-63; pvt. cons. health & safety industry N.Y., N.J., 1984—; chmn. N.J. Low Level Radioactive Waste Adv. Com., Trenton, N.J., 1988-90. Councilman borough Rutherford, N.J., 1970-92, mayor, 1992—. Mem. Unico Nat. Dist. VII (past dist. gov.), Rutherford Unico (past pres., Man of Yr. award 1993), Office Emergency Mgmt. (coord.), Rutherford Red Cross (bd. dirs., chmn.), Am. Heart Assn. (pres. 1993), Tribod Sewer Authority (chmn. 1992—), Am. Indsl. Hygiene Assn. Home: 159 W Newell Ave Rutherford NJ 07070-2239

BERTONE, THOMAS LEE, management consultant; b. Pittsburg, Kans., Nov. 15, 1938; s. Anthony and Gaye Kittle Bertone; m. Ellen Reville Kniffin, Sept. 6, 1969; children: Elizabeth Reville, Katherine Logan. AB, Harvard U., 1960; MA, Stanford U., 1963; D Pub. Adminstrn., George Washington U., 1971. Budget examiner on def. U.S. Bur. Budget, Washington, 1964-67; cons., assoc. Booz Allen & Hamilton, Washington, 1967-69, 78-80; dir. budget rev. Office Fiscal Affairs, N.J. Legislature, Trenton, 1973-75; exec. dir. Office Fiscal Affairs N.J. Ho. of Reps., Trenton, 1975-78; regional dir. state and local govt. cons. Coopers & Lybrand, Phila., 1980-82; dir. internat. cons. Grant Thornton, Chgo., 1986-90; pres. Thomas L. Bertone & Assocs., Pennington, N.J., 1982-86, 90—; World Bank decentralization adviser to permanent sec. Sri Lanka Ministry Local Govt., 1985-89; ADB advisor to budget dir. Budget Office, Federated States Micronesia, 1993-95; IMF budget advisor to min. fin. Palestine Authority, Gaza and West Bank, 1995; U.S. AID intergovtl. fiscal rels. advisor to prime min. and min. fin. Fedn. Bosnia Herzegovina, 1997. Sr. advisor on state fin. and mgmt. to gov. candidate State of W.Va., Charleston, 1970-72; pro bono cons. N.J. Office Mgmt. and Budget, Trenton, 1999. 2d lt. U.S. Army, 1964,

Korea. Mem. ASPA, Inst. Mgmt. Cons. (cert.), Assn. Govt. Accts. (cert. govt. fin. mgr.). Democrat. Avocations: scuba diving, skiing, horseback riding, shooting and gun collecting, dogs. E-mail: tomúbertoneúab60@post.harvard.edu. Home and Office: 153 E Delaware Ave Pennington NJ 08534

BERTONI, HENRY LOUIS, electrical engineering educator; b. Chgo., Nov. 15, 1938; s. Henry and Frances (Brisky) B.; m. Kathy Gutmuller, 1964 (div. 1978); children: Elliot, Rachel; m. Helene Ebenstein, 1990. BS, Northwestern U., 1960; MS, Poly. U., Bklyn., 1962, PhD, 1967. Prof. Poly. U., Bklyn., 1967—, head electric engring. dept., 1990-95; vice provost grad. studies Polytech. U., Bklyn., 1995-96; guest rsch. fellow Univ. Coll., London, 1982-83; summer rsch. fellow USAF Rome Air Ctr., Hanscom AFB, Mass., 1983; cons. Loral Electronics, Yonkers, N.Y., 1985-88, Panametrics, Waltham, Mass., 1987-91, Bio-Imaging Rsch., Lincolnshire, Ill., 1990-92, Pactel Cellular, Walnut Creek, Calif., 1991-95, Air Touch, Walnut Creek, Calif., 1997—. Co-editor 5 books; contbr. over 110 tech. articles to profl. jours., procs., chpts. in 4 books; co-inventor patented acoustic surface wave device. Mem. Hoover Medal Bd. of Award, N.Y.C., 1986-94, chmn., 1993-94. Fellow IEEE (chmn. tech. com. on personal comms. 1992-94, Best Paper award Sonics Group 1985, Neal Shepherd Best Paper award 1993), Internat. Sci. Radio Union. Office: Polytech Univ 6 Metrotech Ctr Brooklyn NY 11201-3840

BERTONIERE, NOELIE RITA, research chemist; b. New Orleans, Oct. 17, 1936. BS, St. Mary's Dominican Coll., 1959; PhD in Organic Chemistry, U. New Orleans, 1971. Rsch. chemist textiles & food USDA So. Regional Rsch. Ctr., New Orleans, 1960—. Mem. AAAS, Am. Chem. Soc., Am. Assn. Textile Chemists and Colorists, Fiber Soc., Sigma Xi. Achievements include research in cellulose chemistry, durable press cotton fabric, pore size distribution, supramolecular structure of cellulose, photochemistry of small ring heterocycles and carbenes. Office: USDA So Regional Rsch Ctr ARS So Regional Rsch Ctr PO Box 19687 1100 Robert E Lee Blvd New Orleans LA 70179

BERTRAM, FREDERIC AMOS, architect; b. Detroit, Oct. 15, 1937; s. Martin Terrance and Marjorie Constance (Saunders) B. Student, Ctr. for Creative Studies, Detroit, 1957-58; B.Archtl. Engring., Lawrence Inst. Tech., 1962. Registered architect, Mich., Calif., Tex., Fla.; cert. Nat. Council Arch. Rev. Bd. With Detroit City Plan Commn., 1962-63, Louis G. Redstone Assocs., 1963-65, Ziegelman and Ziegelman, 1965-68, Giffels and Rossetti, 1968-69; v.p. design Rossetti Assocs., Detroit, 1969-80; prin. in-charge Rossetti Assocs., Los Angeles, 1980-82; chmn. design juror awards program Delaware Valley Masonry Inst., 1978; chmn. design juror neon sign competition for students Lawrence Inst. Tech., 1978, juror design competition, 1979; juror design competition Masonry Inst. Mich., 1979; lectr. in field; vis. design critic Cranbrook Acad. Art, 1977; pres. Frederic A. Bertram & Assoc., L.A., 1982-84; v.p. dir. ops. RMM Inc., Dallas, 1984-85; v.p., dir. design The Stewart Corp. Architects, Tampa, Fla., 1986-88; pvt. practice Tampa, 1991-93; architect Genesis Group Inc., Tampa, 1993-94, Wanmacher Russell Architects, St. Petersburg, Fla., 1995—. Prin. works, Alcoa Chem. and Metallurgy Bldg., Merwin, Pa. (design), United Airlines Reservation Ctr., Dearborn, Mich. (2 design), Cottonwood Condominiums, Traverse City, Mich. (2 design), Frederic A. Bertram residence, Lake Orion, Mich. (3 design), Gt. Am. Ins. Co. Office Bldg., Birmingham, Mich. (2 design), Ford Motor Land Devel. Office Bldgs., Dearborn, (design), St. John Fisher Coll., Rochester (design), Henry Ford Hosp. Ambulatory Ctr., Dearborn (3 design), Rossetti Assocs. Office Bldg., Detroit (3 design), Henry Ford Hosp. Edn. and Research, Detroit (design), Mfrs. Bank, Detroit (design), Bendix Hdqrs., Southfield, Mich. (design), Bon Secour Hosp., Grosse Pointe, Mich. (3 design), Pressure Vessel, Detroit (design), Washington Blvd Mall, Detroit (design), Monroe City Hall, Mich. (design), Tampa Internat. Airport expansion (design). Served with N.G., 1956-63. Recipient Design award Tampa YMCA-YWCO Fitness Ctr. Fellow AIA (nat. com. on design 1977-80, mem. coms. Detroit, mem. Calif. council), Engring. Soc. Detroit; mem. Tampa Bay AIA. Home: 14810 Rue De Bayonne Apt 2B Clearwater FL 33762-3031

BERTRAM, MANYA M., lawyer; b. Denver; d. Samuel and Ruby (Feiner) Boran; m. Barry Bertram, June 19, 1938; children: H. Neal, Carel. *Husband Barry retired in 1980 as Assistant Insurance Commissioner of the State of Calif. Son H. Neal, Phi Beta Kappa, 1963 Reed College, PhD Physics 1967 Harvard University, is currently a professor at the UC San Diego, Department of Magnetic Recording Graduate Program. Daughter-in-law Ann Pollock Bertram, BA 1983 San Jose State, English Literature. Daughter Carel Bertram, BA 1965 UC Berkeley, Phi Beta Kappa, MA 1988 Art History, University of California at Los Angeles, PhD 1998 Art History, is currently teaching Art History at the University of Texas at Austin. Grandchildren: Alanya, BA Rhetoric, 1996 UC California; Rumeli, BA Arts, 1998 Hampshire College; Seth Aaron, UOP.* JD magna cum laude, Southwestern U., 1962. Ptnr. Most and Bertram, L.A., 1963-83; of counsel Levin, Ballin, Plotkin, Zimring & Goffin, North Hollywood, Calif., 1983-92, Janice Fogg, 1993-97. Former trustee Southwestern U. Sch. Law, former pres. Southwestern U. Sch. Law Alumni Assn.; former bd. advisors Whittier Coll. of Law, L.A., Beverly Coll. Law; commr. Calif. Commn. on Aging, Sacramento, 1977-82; bd. dirs. Jewish Family Svc., L.A. Mem. ABA, Calif. State Bar Assn., L.A. County Bar Assn., Federacion Internac. de Abagados, Iota Tau Tau, B'nai B'rith (life mem.), Hadassah (life mem.). Avocation: geneology.

BERTRAM, PHYLLIS ANN, lawyer, communications executive; b. Long Beach, Calif., July 30, 1954; d. William J. and Ruth A. Bertram; AA, Long Beach City Coll., 1975, BS in Acctg., U. So. Calif., 1977; MBA, Calif. State U., Long Beach, 1978; JD, Western State U., 1982. Bar: Calif. 1982, U.S. Ct. Appeals (9th cir.), U.S. Dist. Ct. Instr., lifeguard City of Long Beach, Calif., 1972-78; sports ofcl. swimming, softball, volleyball, and basketball, 1972—; asst. commr. Met. Conf. Community and Jr. Colls., Long Beach, 1978-84; instr. seamanship, fire sci. and bus. adminstrn. Long Beach City Coll., 1977—; mgmt. cons., 1978—; mgr. Pacific Bell, 1983—, Spl. Access Tariffs, Local Competition Tariffs, Interconnection/Collocation Tariffs, Individual Case Basis Tariffs, Local Competition Tariffs, Long Distance Application Case Mgmt.; instr./lectr. Regulatory Rels./Policy/Requirements; guest lectr. sports officiating camps and tng. sessions. Instr. CPR, water safety, small craft, first aid ARC, 1972—; mem. Rep. Nat. Com. Recipient resolutions Calif. Senate and Assembly, Long Beach City Council; numerous service awards ARC; Ednl. research grantee, City of Long Beach, 1972. Mem. U. So. Calif. Alumni Assn., U. So. Calif. Commerce Assocs., Assn. of MBA Execs., Bay Area Career Women, Inc. (corp. sec., bd. dirs., leadership adv. coun.), So. Calif. Volleyball Ofcls. Assn., Nat. Assn. Sports Ofcls., So. Calif. Basketball Ofcls. Assn., Women's Basketball Ofcls. Assn., Women's Swim Ofcls. Assn. (pres.), So. Calif. Softball Umpires Assn., State Bar Calif., ABA, Fed. Bar Assn. Los Angeles, Internat. Platform Assn., Town Hall Calif., Commonwealth Club of Calif., Los Angeles County Bar Assn., Calif. State U. at Long Beach Alumni Assn., U. So. Calif. Alumni Assn., Delta Theta Phi. Republican. Club: Seal Beach Yacht. Office: Ste 1715 140 New Montgomery St San Francisco CA 94105-3705

BERTRAM, SUSAN, rehabilitation counselor; b. Darlington, S.C., July 7, 1945; d. Ernest and Leigh (Ogburn) Lowry; m. Donald Kent Trout, May 7, 1971 (div. Apr. 1972); m. John David Bertram, Dec. 7, 1980. BFA, U. Ga., 1966; MS, Ga. State U., 1993. Cert. rehab. counselor, nat. cert. counselor, Ga. Social work/counselor State of Ga., Atlanta, 1967-95, rehab. counselor, 1995—; mem. rsch. com. Divsn. Rehab. Svcs., Warm Springs, Ga., 1995—; cert. leader Active Parenting Tng., Atlanta, 1993—. Mem. ACA, Nat. Rehab. Counseling Assn., Ga. Rehab. Assn. Avocations: travel, reading, yoga.

BERTRAND, ANNABEL HODGES, civic worker, artist, calligrapher; b. Birmingham, Ala., Jan. 4, 1915; d. Thomas Edmund and Mae (Crawford) Hodges; m. John Raney Bertrand, Oct. 23, 1942; children: John Thomas, Diana Bertrand Williams, Karen Bertrand Wilson, J'May Bertrand Rivara. BS, Tex. Woman's U., 1935, MA, 1936; postgrad., Columbia U., 1938. Tchr. White Deer (Tex.) Consol. Sch., 1936-37, Tyler (Tex.) Pub. Sch. System, 1938-39; instr. Sam Houston State U., Huntsville, Tex., 1939-42; interim tchr. Portsmouth (N.H.) Pub. Sch., 1943. Bd. dirs. Rome Area Coun. for the Arts, 1980-98, Ga. Coun. for Arts and Humanities, Atlanta, 1979-83, Mental Health Assn. Floyd County, Rome, Ga., 1980-98; active High Mus. Art, Atlanta, 1979-98, Rome Symphony Guild, 1980-98, Friends of Rome/Floyd County Libr., 1985-98, Christian Personhood Book Discussion Group of First United Meth. Ch., 1980-98. Mem. AAUW, United Meth. Women, Rome Music Lovers Club, Sigma Alpha Iota (patroness). Avocations: classical music, college drama and music presentations, travel, reading. Home: 24 College Row Brevard NC 28712-3155

BERTRAND, BETTY HARLEEN, nurse; b. Little Rock, Ark., July 17, 1960; d. Harley Walter and Joyce Elaine (Bryant) Baker; m. Robert K. Bertrand, June 13, 1980; children: Mary, Jessie, Alyssa. AA, Cerro Coso C.C., 1981; ADN, Texarkana Coll., 1989; BSN, U. Ark. Med. Sch., 1994. RN, Tex.; lic. vocat. nurse; cert. low risk neonatal care. Nurse asst. Ridgecrest (Calif.) Cmty. Hosp., 1982-85; lic. vocat. nurse Wadley Regional Med. Ctr., Texarkana, Tex., 1986-89, RN, 1989-92; field supervising nurse HealthCor Home Health, Texarkana, 1992-93; nurse Blankenship Dialysis Ctr., Texarkana, 1993-96; clin. instr. Texarkana Coll., 1996-97, instr. vocat. nursing program, 1997—; nurse St. Michael Health Care Ctr., 1996—. Baptist. Avocations: reading, cross stitching, crochet, parenting, piano. Home: RR 9 Box 679K Texarkana TX 75501-9320

BERTRAND, FREDERIC HOWARD, retired insurance company executive; b. Montpelier, Vt., Aug. 5, 1936; s. George Joseph and Dolores Gertrude (Mallory) B.; m. Elinor Maude Pierce, June 11, 1960; children: Kimberly Sue, Michael Scott, John Frederic (dec.). BSCE magna cum laude, Norwich U., 1958; postgrad., Georgetown U. Law Sch., 1961-63, Carnegie-Mellon U. Sch. Indsl. Adminstrn., 1967-68; J.D., Coll. William and Mary, 1967; D in Bus. Mgmt. (hon.), Norwich U., 1991. Bar: Va. 1967, Vt. 1970; registered profl. engr., Vt. Engr.-adminstr. CIA, Washington, 1960-70; asst. counsel, assoc. counsel, v.p., sr. v.p., bd. dirs. Nat. Life Ins. Co., Montpelier, 1970-83, exec. v.p., chief oper. officer, 1983-85, pres., chief oper. officer, 1985-87, chmn., chief exec. officer, 1987-97, also bd. dirs.; bd. dirs. Chittenden Trust Co., Burlington, Union Mut. Fire Ins. Co., New Eng. Guaranty Ins. Co., Montpelier; bd. dirs. Cen. Vt. Pub. Svcs. Co., Rutland, 1985—, chair, 1997—, Vt. Elec. Transmission Co., 1998—, Catamount Energy Corp., bd. dirs., 1995—, chair, 1997—; civilian aide to Sec. of Army, Washington, 1981-93. Alderman City of Montpelier, 1974-76, pres. city coun., 1975-76, mayor, 1976-78; bd. dirs. Ctrl. Vt. Econ. Devel. Corp., 1985-98; chmn. Vt. Bus. Roundtable, 1995-97, bd. dirs., 1987-98; trustee Norwich U., Northfield, Vt., 1979-85. Recipient Outstanding Alumnus award Norwich U., 1980, Citizen of Yr. award Vt. C. of C., 1992, U.S. Army Disting. Civilian Svc. award, 1993. Mem. Am. Coun. Life Ins. (bd. dirs. 1989-94, chmn. 1993), Vt. Bar Assn., Washington County Bar Assn., Theta Chi, Epsilon Tau Sigma. Republican. Roman Catholic.

BERTRAND, ROBERT SIMEON, manufacturing engineer; b. Waterbury, Conn., Oct. 26, 1946; s. Emile J. and Leannette (Bouffard) B.; m. Lorraine J. Boisvert, May 31, 1969 (div. Mar. 1983); children: Marcus J., Audra L. ASAS, Waterbury State Tech. Coll., 1970; BSMT, Ctrl. Conn. U., 1982. Mfg. engr., tool room foreman Miford Products Corp., Branford, Conn., 1983-85; designer, owner Bert Design, Chesire, Conn., 1985; sr. tooling engr. U.S. Surg., Norwalk, Conn., 1985-88; engring. mgr. O'Hara Metal Products, Brisbane, Calif., 1988-91; sr. tool engr., buyer Ethicon, Inc., Blue Ash, Ohio, 1991-93; sr. mfg. engr. Thomas & Betts, Tulsa, 1994; tooling engring. mgr. AUGAT divsn. Thomas & Betts, Clinton Twp, Mich., 1994-97; sr. procurement engr. avionics and lighting divsn. Allied Signal, Olathe, Kans., 1997—; supplier devel. lean mfg. electonics and avionics sys. divsn Allied Signal, Olathe, 1998—. Mem. Soc. Mfg. Engrs. (sr.), Am. Soc. Metals (sr.). Home: PO Box 860033 Shawnee KS 66286-0033 Office: Allied Signal One Tech Ctr 23500 W 105th St Olathe KS 66061-6615

BERTRAND, WILLIAM ELLIS, public health educator, academic administrator; b. Midland, Tex., May 24, 1944; s. Alvin Lee and Mary Nick (Ellis) B.; m. Jane Trowbridge; children: Katherine, Jacob. BA, La. State U., 1966; PhD, Tulane U., 1972. Instr. to assoc. prof. Delgado C.C., New Orleans, 1966-70; instr. to prof. dept. biostats. and epidemiology Tulane U., New Orleans, 1974—, chmn. dept., 1981-86, postdoctoral fellow, 1972-75, also adj. asst. prof. to adj. prof. sociology dept., 1974-78, Wisner prof. public health, 1986—, v.p. Instnl. Planning Rsch. and Innovation, 1995—; dir. Tulane Internat. Devel. Ctr. and Tulane Ctr. for Internat. Resource Devel., 1988—; chmn. Dept. Internat. Health and Devel., Tulane SPHTM, 1992—; vis. lectr. Sch. Social Work, 1977-80; vis. lectr. Universidad del Valle, Cali, Colombia, 1969-71, 73; dir. and founder Inst. for Study Change in the Americas, New Orleans, 1984-86; co-dir. and prin. investigator Zaire Sch. Pub. Health U. Kinshasa, 1985—; co-prin. investigator Kenya Ministry Health, Nairobi, 1988—, Niger Ministry Health, Niamey, 1988—; prin. investigator Famine Early Warning System, Burkina Faso, Mali, Mauritania, Niger, Sudan, Chad, 1988—. Contbr. numerous articles to profl. publs., book chpts. Mem. State and City AIDS Task Force, New Orleans, 1985. Grantee U.S. Agy. for Internat. Devel., Zaire, 1985, Kenya, 1988, Niger, 1988, Sudan, 1988. Mem. Am. Coll. Epidemiology, Am. Pub. Health Assn., So. Sociol. Soc., Applied Anthrop. Assn., PanAm. Health and Edn. Found. (bd. dirs. 1990—), Delta Omega. Democrat. Baptist. Avocations: tennis, fishing. Office: Tulane U 300 Hebert Hall 6823 Saint Charles Ave New Orleans LA 70118-5698*

BERTSCH, FREDERICK CHARLES, III, business executive; b. Bklyn., Mar. 17, 1942; s. Frederick Charles and Norma Elizabeth (Hodgkins) B.; m. Ana Maria Carmen Natteri, Aug. 20, 1971; children—Frederick C., Ana Cecilia. BA, Wesleyan U., Middletown, Conn., 1965; MBA, U. Pa., 1967. Supr. Ford Motor Co., Dearborn, Mich., 1967-69; cons. Cresap, McCormick & Paget Inc., N.Y.C., 1969-73; dir. corp. devel. IU Internat., Phila., 1973-76; v.p. corp. devel. Enterra Corp., Radnor, Pa., 1976-84, v.p. fin., chief fin. officer, 1985-86; founder F.C. Bertsch & Co., Inc., St. Davids, Pa., 1988—; v.p., CFO Gladwin Corp., Coraopolis, Pa., 1995. Pres. Radnor ABC (A Better Chance), Wayne, Pa., 1984-85, now bd. dirs.; bd. dirs. ARC. Mem. Aronimink Golf Club (Newtown Square, Pa.). Avocations: golf, fishing, gardening. Home and Office: 416 Round Hill Rd Saint Davids PA 19087-4728

BERTUCCIOLI, BRUNO, petrochemical company executive; b. Rome, Italy, Oct. 31, 1954; came to U.S., 1981; naturalized citizen, 1993; s. Giuliano and Meiling (Hwang) B.; m. Barbara Santone, Oct. 3, 1998. Law degree magna cum laude, U. of Rome, 1977. Asst. econ. dept. Italian Fgn. Svc. Dept., Rome, 1975-78; asst. mgr. Ente Nazionale Idrocarburi, Rome, 1978-81; acct. mgr. AGIP USA, N.Y.C., 1982-85, bus. mgr., 1985-87; comml. dir. Enichem USA, N.Y.C., 1987-89; officer, v.p. petrochem. and trading Enichem Am., N.Y.C., 1989—. Author: The Level Club, 1991; cartoonist Oggi 7 Mag.; curator La Mia America, 1995, Italy. Mem. Nat. Petroleum Refiners Assn., Northeastern Petrochemical Assn. Roman Catholic. Avocations: chess, volleyball, antique collecting, writing, painting and drawings. Home: 253 W 73rd St New York NY 10023-2740 Office: Enichem Am 666 5th Ave New York NY 10103-0001

BERTUCELLI, ROBERT EDWARD, accountant, educator; b. Bklyn., Mar. 23, 1948; s. Leo and Gertrude Augusta (Roggenkamp) B.; m. Maryann Marchese, June 13, 1970; children: Nikole, Gina. AAS., Suffolk Community Coll., 1968; BS, C.W. Post Coll., 1970; MS, L.I. U., 1974. CPA, N.Y.; cert. fin. planner, 1989; chartered life underwriter, 1997. Acct. Arthur Young & Co., Westbury, N.Y., 1970-72; sr. tax mgr. Peat, Marwick, Mitchell & Co., Jericho, N.Y., 1972-77; prof. acctg. and taxation C.W. Post Coll., 1977—; pvt. practice, Smithtown, N.Y., 1977-83, Hauppauge, N.Y., 1989-94; ptnr. Bertucelli, Barragato & Co., Smithtown, N.Y., 1983-89, Bertucelli & Malaga, L.L.P., Hauppauge, N.Y., 1994—; lectr. Person Wolinsky Assocs., 1977—. Mem. St. Patrick's Sch. bd., Smithtown, N.Y., 1982-92, pres. 1985-88, 90-92. Recipient Haskins Silver medal N.Y. Soc. CPA's, 1972. Mem. Am. Inst. CPA's, N.Y. Soc. CPA's (author, lectr. 1989—), Nat. Assn. Accts., Estate Planning Coun. (pres. 1996-97), Smithtown C. of C. (treas. 1988-90). Roman Catholic.

BERUBE, JEANNE ANN, state government policy director; b. Milford, Mass., Aug. 7, 1948; d. Eric Francis and Jennie Ann Cameron; children: Cameron, Kate. BS in Indsl. Mgmt., Lowell (Mass.) Tech. Inst., 1971; MS in Mgmt. Sci., Hartford (Conn.) Grad. Ctr., 1997. Bus. mgr. Chariho Sch. Dist., Charlestown, R.I., 1973-74; contr. Cath. Transcript, Hartford, 1975-85; dir. comptroller's office State of Conn., Hartford, 1985—. Sec., treas. parents club Coventry (Conn.) H.S. Parents Club, 1990-93, sch. bldg. subcom., 1988-92. Mem. Govt. Fin. Officers Assn. (standing com. 1998—, award of excellence 1997), Conn. Soc. Govt. Accts. (v.p.), Toastmasters Internat. (pres., area gov.), Assn. Govtl. Accts. (cert. govt. fin. officer), Am. Soc. Pub. Adminstrn. (treas. Conn. chpt.). Office: Office State Comptroller 55 Elm St Rm 219 Hartford CT 06106-1797

BERUBE, MARGERY STANWOOD, publishing executive; b. Middleborough, Mass., Nov. 18, 1943; d. John Peter and Dorothy Cole (Stanwood) Whołan; m. Edgar Roger Berube, Sept. 12, 1967. BA in English, Wilkes Coll., 1965. Creative and prodn. mgr., dir. editorial ops. Med. div. Houghton Mifflin Co., Boston, 1978-81, dir. editorial ops. Reference div., 1982-85, v.p., dir. editorial ops. Trade and Reference div., 1986-87, v.p., dir. editorial art prodn. and mfg. services, 1987-91, v.p., dir. lexical pub., prodn. and mfg. svcs., 1991—. Mem. Bookbuilders (bd. dirs. 1976-80). Avocation: equestrian dressage rider. Office: Hougton Mifflin Co 222 Berkeley St Boston MA 02116-3748

BERUBE, RAYMOND P., federal agency administrator. BSCE, Merrimack Coll., 1968; student, Drexel U., 1975. Registered profl. engr., N.J. Former civil engr. U.S. Dept. Transp., Washington; dep. asst. sec. environ. U.S. Dept. Energy, Washington, 1987—. Recipient Sec. of Energy Gold Medal award, 1996. Office: Dept of Energy Environment Safety & Health 1000 Independence Ave SW Washington DC 20585-0002

BERWANGER, EUGENE HARLEY, history educator; b. Calumet City, Ill., June 8, 1929; s. Henry Nicholas and Cornelia (Benschop) B.; m. Elizabeth A. Kohl, June 12, 1967; children: Anne E., Thomas E. BA, Ill. State U., 1951, MA, 1952; PhD, U. Ill., 1964. Asst. prof. history Ill. Coll., Jacksonville, 1964-67; prof. history Colo. State U., Ft. Collins, 1967—. Bd. editors Pacific Hist. Rev., 1970-73; author: British Foreign Service and American Civil War, 1993, My Diary North and South, 1981, West and Reconstruction, 1980, Frontier Against Slavery, 1967. Cpl. U.S. Army, 1952-54. Office: Colorado State Univ Dept History Fort Collins CO 80523

BERWANGER, KATHLEEN A., secondary school educator; b. Cin., Aug. 25, 1944; d. John A. and Anna Marie (Hollarn) Pfarr; m. Robert H. Gorssheim, July 30, 1966 (div. Oct. 1983); 1 child, Robert John; m. Duane L. Berwanger, June 11, 1988. BA, Edge Cliff Coll., Cin., 1966; MEd, Wright State U., 1989. Cert. tchr., Ohio. Tchr. English Loveland (Ohio) City Schs., 1966-67, 72—, chair dept. English, 1995—; tchr. lang. arts St. Columban, Loveland, 1968-72. Mem. St. Columban Sch. Bd., 1969-71; active various fundraisers St. Columban Ch.; mem. M.A.D.D. Named Outstanding Tchr., Denison U., 1997, Ohio U., 1997. Mem. NEA, Ohio Edn. Assn., Loveland Edn. Assn., Nat. Coun. Tchrs. English (writing judge 1994—), Ohio Coun. Tchrs. English. Avocations: reading, gardening. Home: 8187 Woodruff Rd Cincinnati OH 45255-4536

BERWIND, C. G., JR., manufacturing executive; b. Bryn Mawr, Pa., 1928. Diploma, U. Vt., 1951; MBA, Harvard U., 1953. Chmn., CEO Berwind Corp., Bryn Mawr. Office: Berwind Corp 3000 Centre Sq W 1500 Market St Fl 30W Philadelphia PA 19102-2173*

BERZ, DAVID R., lawyer; b. Chgo., May 21, 1948; m. Sherry Kirschner, Sept. 5, 1970; children: Douglas, Alexander. BA, George Washington U., 1970, JD with honors, 1973. Bar: D.C. 1973, U.S. Supreme Ct. 1977, N.Y. 1985. Mng. ptnr. Weil, Gotshal & Manges, Washington. Author: Environmental Law in Real Estate and Business Transactions, 3 vols., 1992; mem. bd. editors Chem. Waste Litigation Reporter, 1986—; environ. editor Inside Litigation, 1991—; contbr. articles to profl. jours. Bd. dirs. Washington Hebrew Congregation; exec. bd. mem. Washington chpt. Am. Jewish Com.; mem. adv. bd. George Washington Univ. Nat. Law Ctr. Mem. ABA (mem. environ. controls com., corp. banking and bus. law sect., vice chmn. environ. quality control com. sect. adminstrv. law 1978-81), FBA, D.C. Bar Assn., Def. Rsch. Inst. (mem. environ. law com.), U.S. C. of C. (mem. environ. com.). Office: Weil Gotshal & Manges 1615 L St NW Ste 700 Washington DC 20036-5606*

BERZOW, HAROLD STEVEN, lawyer; b. Bklyn., Oct. 22, 1946; s. Julius and Lillian (Hershkowitz) Brzozowsky; m. Lynore Kushner, Aug. 22, 1970; children: Alan, Jason, Rachel. BA, Bklyn. Coll., 1968; JD, Bklyn. Law Sch., 1971. Bar: N.Y. 1972, U.S. Dist. Ct. (so. and ea. dists.) N.Y. 1973, U.S. Ct. Appeals (2d cir.) 1975, U.S. Supreme Ct. 1978. Assoc. Finkel, Nadler & Goldstein, N.Y.C., 1971-77; ptnr. Finkel, Goldstein, Berzow, Rosenbloom & Nash, LLP, N.Y.C., 1977—. Mem. ABA, N.Y. County Bar Assn., N.Y. State Bar Assn., Am. Bankruptcy Inst. Jewish. Home: 15 Acorn Ln Plainview NY 11803-1901 Office: Finkel Goldstein Berzow Rosenbloom & Nash LLP 26 Broadway New York NY 10004-1703

BE SANT, CRAIG, company executive. Pres. TMP Worldwide, Chgo.; dir. mktg. Monster.com, Indpls., 1998—. Office: Monster.com 2611 Waterfront Pkwy Indianapolis IN 46214*

BESANT, LARRY XON, librarian, administrator, consultant; b. Centralia, Ill., Mar. 13, 1935; s. Ben Vern and Marjorie Loyce (Jarboe) B.; m. A. Jean Hofstetter, Dec. 31, 1953; children: Vicki, Lizabeth, Paul, Peter, Mary. A.A., Centralia Jr. Coll., Ill., 1959; B.S. in Chemistry, U. Ill., Urbana, 1961, M.S.L.S., 1962. Asst. librarian Chem. Abstract Assn., Columbus, Ohio, 1962-68; asst. dir. U. Houston Library, 1968-71, Ohio State U. Library, Columbus, 1972-82; dir. libraries Linda Hall Library, Kansas City, Mo., 1982-85; dir. libraries Camden-Carroll Library Morehead (Ky.) State U., Ky., 1985—; library cons. in field; speaker in field. Contbr. numerous articles, revs. to Library Mgmt. Bull., Am. Libraries, other profl. publs. Served with USAF, 1954-57. Mem. ALA, Spl. Librs. Assn. (pres. Ky. chpt. 1996-97), Ky. Libr. Assn., Ky. State Adv. Coun. on Librs. Democrat. Baptist. Avocations: fishing; book collecting (Jack London). E-mail: l.besant@morehead-st.edu. Home: 428 N Wilson Ave Morehead KY 40351-1172 Office: Morehead State U Camden-Carroll Libr Morehead KY 40351

BESCH, EMERSON LOUIS, physiology educator, past academic administrator; b. Hammond, Ind., June 9, 1928; s. Ernest Henry and Carolyn (Dieckmann) B.; m. H. Jean Whitstine, May 28, 1955; children: Karen J., Kevin D., Kathleen L., Kristine A. BS in Biology/Chemistry, S.W. Tex. State U., 1952, MA in Biology/Chemistry, 1955; PhD in Physiology, U. Calif., Davis, 1964. Grad. instr. biology dept. S.W. Tex. State U., San Marcos, 1954-55; research asst., NIH trainee U. Calif., Davis, 1960-64, research physiologist, lectr., 1964-67; research assoc. Pacific Missile Range, USN, Point Mugu, Calif., 1960-64; from assoc. to full prof., head dept. physiology Kans. State U., Manhattan, 1967-74, from assoc. to full prof. mech. engring., 1967-74; prof. mech. engring. U. Fla., Gainesville, 1974-93; prof. physiology U. Fla. Coll. Vet. Medicine, Gainesville, 1974-93, assoc. dean, 1974-87, acting dean, 1980-81, exec. assoc. dean, 1987-88, prof. emeritus, 1993—. Served to capt. USNR. Fellow Aerospace Med. Assn. (exec. council 1985-88, profl. excellence award 1987); mem. Am. Physiology Soc., Soc. for Exptl. Biology & Medicine, Aerospace Physiologist Soc. (pres. 1984-86), Am. Soc. Heating, Refrigerating & Air Conditioning Engring. Achievements include research in environmental physiology and acceleration biology; avocations: painting, stamp collecting, coin collecting, gardening. Home: 15207 Rompel Trail Dr San Antonio TX 78232-4255 Office: U Fla Coll Vet Medicine PO Box 100144 Gainesville FL 32610-0144

BESCH, EVERETT DICKMAN, veterinarian, university dean emeritus; b. Hammond, Ind., May 4, 1924; s. Ernest Henry and Carolyn (Dieckmann) B.; m. Mellie Darnell Brockman, Apr. 3, 1946; children: Carolyn Darnell, Ceryl Lynn, Cynthia Lee, Charlotte Ann, Everett Dickman. D.V.M., Tex. A&M Coll., 1954; M.P.H., U. Minn., 1956; Ph.D., Okla. State U., 1963. Instr. U. Minn., 1954-56; asst. prof. Okla. State U., 1956-64, prof., head dept. vet. parasitology and pub. health, 1964-68; dean Sch. Vet. Medicine, La. State U., 1968-88, prof., 1988-89; sec.-treas. Assn. Am. Vet. Med. Colls., 1974-78, sec. coun. deans, 1976-80, chmn. coun. deans, 1980-81; mem. Nat. Adv. Coun. Health Professions Edn., 1982-86; treas. Am. Vet. Med. Found., 1991-93, v.p., 1993-94, pres., 1994-95, mem., 1995-97; bd. dirs. Coun. Agrl. Sci. and Tech., 1992-95. Contbr. articles to profl. publs., chpts. to books. Served with USN, 1942-48. Mem. AVMA (ho. of dels. 1988-91, exec. bd. 1991-97), Assn. Tchrs. Vet. Pub. Health and Preventive Medicine (pres. 1968), La. Vet.

Med. Assn., Tex. Vet. Med. Assn., Conf. Pub. Health Veterinarians (pres. 1971-72), Am. Assn. Food Hygiene Veterinarians (pres. 1976-77), Am. Assn. Vet. Parasitologists (pres. 1964-65). Research interests: arthropod vectors of disease, internal parasites of ruminants. Home: 1453 Ashland Dr Baton Rouge LA 70806-7838

BESCH, HENRY ROLAND, JR., pharmacologist, educator; b. San Antonio, Sept. 12, 1942; s. Henry Roland and Monette Helen (Kasten) B.; m. Frankie R. Drejer; 1 child, Kurt Theodore. B.Sc. in Physiology, Ohio State U., 1964, Ph.D. in Pharmacology (USPHS predoctoral trainee 1964-67), 1967; USPHS postdoctoral trainee, Baylor U. Coll. Medicine, Houston, 1968-70. Instr. ob-gyn. Ohio State U. Med. Sch., Columbus, 1967-68; asst. prof. Ind. U. Sch. Medicine, Indpls., 1971-73, assoc. prof., 1973-77, prof., 1977, Showalter prof. and chmn. pharmacology and toxicology, 1977—; dir. Ind. State Dept. Toxicology, Indpls., 1991-95; Can. Med. Rsch. Coun. vis. prof., 1979, Swiss Fed. Tech. Inst. vis. prof., 1995; investigator fed. grants, mem. nat. panels and coms.; cons. in field. Contbr. numerous articles pharm. and med. jours.; mem. editorial bds. profl. jours. Fellow Brit. Med. Research Council, 1970-71; Grantee Showalter Trust, 1975—. Fellow Am. Coll. Cardiology; mem. AAAS, Am. Assn. Clin. Chemistry, Am. Coll. Forensic Examiners, Am. Physiol. Soc., Am. Soc. Biochem. Molecular Biology, Am. Soc. Pharmacology and Exptl. Therpeutics, Assn. Med. Sch. Pharmacologists (exec. com. 1985—, pres. 1994-96), Biochem. Soc., Cardiac Muscle Soc., Internat. Soc. Heart Rsch. (exec. com. Am. sect. 1986-92), Nat. Acad. Clin. Biochemistry, N.Y. Acad. Scis., Sigma Xi. Office: Ind U Sch Medicine 635 Barnhill Dr Indianapolis IN 46202-5126*

BESCH, LORRAINE W., special education educator; b. Orange, N.J., June 27, 1948; d. Robert Woodruff and Minnie (Wrightson) B.; m. William Lee Gibson, July 10, 1982. AA in Liberal Arts, Mt. Vernon Coll., 1968; BA in Sociology, U. Colo., 1970; MA in Spl. Edn., U. Denver, 1973. Cert. handicapped thcr., N.J. Elem. resource rm. tchr. Beeville (Tex.) Ind. Sch. Dist., 1973-75; trainable mentally retarded tchr. Kings County Supt. Schs., Hanford, Calif., 1975-78; h.s. resource rm. tchr. Summit (N.J.) Bd. Edn., 1980-81; h.s. resource rm. tchr. Westfield (N.J.) Bd. Edn., 1981-99, head coach field hockey, 1981-83, mem. crisis mgmt. team, 1982-87, in class support tchr. English, 1993-99. Named to Women's Inner Circle Achievement, 1996; recipient Internat. Sash of Academia, ABI, 1997. Mem. AAUW, Nat. Mus. Am. Indian (charter), Nat. Mus. Women in Arts, Nat. Mus. Am. Indian (charter), Smithsonian Mus. (charter), NEA, Coun. Exceptional Children (Learning Disabilities divsn.), N.J. Edn. Assn., Westfield Edn. Assn. (del. 1983-90, tech. com. 1993-94, conf. funds com. 1994-99), Hartford Family Found. (v.p., sec. 1991-97), Wrightson-Besch Found. (sec.-treas. 1994—), Archaeology Conservancy (life), Nat. Trust Historic Preservation, N.J. Hist. Society, Sky Meadows Cir. Avocations: traveling, reading, gardening, tennis. Home: 8 Lone Oak Rd Basking Ridge NJ 07920-1613 Office: Westfield HS 550 Dorian Rd Westfield NJ 07090-3302

BESDINE, RICHARD WILLIAM, medical educator, scientist; b. N.Y.C., Apr. 12, 1940; s. Alan Xerus and Betty (Bronstein) B.; m. Judith Anne Bailey, June 22, 1963 (div. May 1980); children: Sarah Besdine Freedman, Molly Bailey; m. Fox Wetle, July 2, 1981. BS cum laude, Haverford Coll., 1961; MD, U. Pa., 1965. Diplomate Am. Bd. Internal Medicine, Am. Bd. Infectious Disease, Am. Bd. Geriat. Medicine, Nat. Bd. Med. Examiners. Intern Beth Israel Hosp. Medicine, Boston, 1965-66, asst. resident in internal medicine, 1966-67, fellow in immunology and infectious diseases, 1969-72; rsch. fellow in medicine Harvard Med. Sch., Boston, 1969-72, instr. in medicine, 1972-75, asst. prof. medicine, 1975-86, lectr. in medicine, 1986-89; assoc. prof. medicine, cmty. medicine and healthcare U. Conn. Health Ctr. Sch. Medicine, 1986-89, dir. Travelers Ctr. on Aging, assoc. prof. family medicine, 1988—; prof. medicine, cmty. medicine and healthcare U. Conn. Sch. Medicine, 1990—; from asst. to assoc. in medicine Beth Israel Hosp., 1972-75, asst. physician in medicine, 1975-82; assoc. physician in medicine Brigham and Women's Hosp. and Beth Israel Hosps., 1982-88; staff internist Hebrew Rehab. Ctr. for Aged, Roslindale, Mass., 1972-86, dir. geriatric med. edn., 1981-86; attending med. staff John Dempsey Hosp., 1986—, Hebrew Home and Hosp., 1987—, McLean Home and Village, 1987—; mem. cons. med. staff Inst. Living, Newington VA Med. Ctr.; cons., presenter in field; Noble Wiley Jones lectr. U. Oreg. Health Scis. Ctr., Portland, 1980; mem. Harvard-Hastings Project on Ethical Issues in Care of Elderly, 1982-86; vis. prof. U. Toronto Sch. Medicine, 1983, Montreal (Can.) Neurol. Inst., 1984, U. Geneva, 1990, U. Mich., 1991, U. Wis., 1991, Baylor U., 1991, U. Kans. Med. Ctr., 1992, Fallon Clinic and Health Plan, 1992; chair fed. task force on geriatric edn. NIH, 1986; mem. adv. bd. John A. Hartford Found. grant Johns Hopkins U. Sch. Medicine, 1994; chmn. western delegation Seminar on Aging, Singapore, Hong Kong, Taipei and Kuala Lumpur, 1987; mem. spl. adv. group White House Conf. on Aging, 1980-81; mem. task force on reversible dementia in the elderly Nat. Inst. on Aging, 1978-80; dir. health stds. and quality bur., chief med. officer Healthcare Fin. Adminstrn., 1995-97. Co-author: Handbook of Geriatric Care, 1982; editor: Health and Disease in Old Age, 1982, 2d edit., 1988; mem. editl. bd. Geriat. Rev. Syllabus, 1989, 93, 96, assoc. editor, 1991, 93, 96; contbr. chpts. to books and articles to profl. jours. Surgeon USPHS Nat. Ctrs. for Disease Control, 1967-69; bd. dirs. Inst. for Cmty. Rsch., Hartford, 1987—, New Britain Meml. Hosp., 1993, Am. Fedn. for Aging Rsch., 1993—, Am. Geriat. Soc., 1994—, Alzheimers Assn., 1998. Royal Soc. Medicine Found. travelling fellow U. Glasgow, 1972; grantee Geriatric Edn. Ctr., 1983-91, John A. Hartford Found., 1988-94, Charles A. Dana Found., 1988-90, Conn. State Dept. on Aging, 1989-91, Travelers Rsch. Inst. on Health Promotion and Aging, 1990, , Howard and Bush Found. , 1990, Robert Wood Johnson Found., 1991-93, Travelers Found., 1991, 92, 94, NIH Pepper Ctr., 1996. Fellow ACP, Am. Geriat. Soc. (Milo D. Leavitt award 1991), Gerontol. Soc. Am. (Joseph T. Freeman award 1995), Am. Soc. Aging (Pres. award 1997). Home: 157 Main St Farmington CT 06032-2964

BESEN, STANLEY MARTIN, economist; b. Bklyn., Dec. 17, 1937; s. Moe and Sylvia (Forgang) B.; m. Marlene Dublirer, June 10, 1961; children: Roberta Ann, Elizabeth Rebecca. BBA, CCNY, 1958; MA, Yale U., 1960, PhD, 1964. Acting asst. prof. econs. U. Calif.-Santa Barbara, 1962-63; economist Inst. Def. Analyses, 1963-65; mem. faculty Rice U., Houston, 1965-80; prof. econs. Rice U., 1974-79, Cline prof. econs. and fin., 1979-80; co-dir. network inquiry spl. staff FCC, 1978-80; sr. economist Rand Corp., Washington, 1980-92; v.p. Charles River Assocs., Washington, 1992—; vis. Henley prof. law and bus. Columbia U., 1988-89; vis. prof. law and econs., Georgetown U. Law Ctr., 1990-91; mem. task force nat. telecommunications policy making Aspen Inst. Program Communications and Soc., 1977; cons. in field. Author: Misregulating Television: Network Dominance and the FCC, 1984, also articles; co-editor Rand Jour. Econs., 1985-88; mem. editorial bds. profl. jours. Fellow Brookings Instn., 1971-72, NSF, 1973-75. Mem. Am. Econ. Assn. Home: 4918 Western Ave Bethesda MD 20816-1714 Office: Charles River Assocs 600 13th St NW Ste 700 Washington DC 20005-3094

BESHAR, ROBERT PETER, lawyer; b. N.Y.C., Mar. 3, 1928; m. Christine von Wedemeyer, Dec. 20, 1953; children: Cornelia, Jacqueline, Frederica, Peter. AB honors with exceptional distinction, Yale U., 1950, LLB, 1953. Bar: N.Y. 1954. Asst. gen. counsel Waterfront Commn. N.Y. Harbor, 1954-55; law sec. Hon. Charles D. Breitel, Appellate div. 1st dept. N.Y. Supreme Ct., N.Y.C., 1956-58; spl. hearing officer Justice Dept., 1967-68; dep. asst. sec. Commerce; dir. Bur. Internat. Commerce; nat. export expansion coordinator Commerce Dept., Washington, 1971-72; pvt. practice, N.Y.C., 1972—; pres. various family enterprises, 1993—; bd. dirs. Nat. Semicondr. Corp. (audit and dir's. affairs coms., counsel to bd. dirs. 1972-98); mem. bus. adv. panel Nat. Commn. for Rev. of Antitrust Laws, 1978-79; mem. Mcpl. Securities Rulemaking Bd., 1982-85; bd. govs. Fgn. Policy Assn., 1991—. Author: Current Legal Aspects of Doing Business With Sino-Soviet Nations, 1973; editor: Manhattan Auto Study, 1973. Trustee Westchester Coll. Found., 1992—; mem. Planning Bd. of Somers, 1984-97. Scholar of the House, Yale U., 1950. Mem. ABA (chmn. corp. and antitrust law com. 1982-85), N.Y. State Bar Assn., Elizabethan and Gypsy Trail Clubs, Phi Beta Kappa. Home: 120 E End Ave New York NY 10028-7552 Office: 1513 1st Ave at 79th St New York NY 10021-0901 also: PO Box 533 Somers NY 10589-0533

BESHARSE, JOSEPH CULP, cell biologist, researcher; b. Hickman, Ky., Jan. 21, 1944; s. Herschell and June Elizabeth (Bush) B.; m. Janie Iris Robinson, Aug. 21, 1966; children: Joseph Galen, Kari Elizabeth. BA, Hendrix Coll., 1966; MA, So. Ill. U., 1969, PhD, 1973. Asst. prof. Old Dominion U., Norfolk, Va., 1972-75; postdoctoral fellow Columbia U., N.Y.C., 1975-77; asst. prof. Emory U. Sch. Medicine, Atlanta, 1977-80, assoc. prof., 1980-84, prof., 1984-89; prof., chmn. dept. anatomy & cell biology U. Kans. Sch. Medicine, Kansas City, 1989-97; prof., chmn. dept. cell biology, neurobiology and anatomy Med. Coll. Wis., Milw., 1997—; mem. study sect. NIH, Bethesda, Md., 1981-86, 92-96. Mem. editl. bd. Exptl. Eye Rsch., 1985-98, editor retina sect., 1997—; mem. editl. bd. Investigative Ophthalmology, 1987-92, Visual Neurosci., 1990-92; retina sect. editor Exptl. Eye Rsch., 1998—; contbr. more than 90 articles to sci. jours. Rsch. grantee NIH, 1976-98; recipient Rsch. Career Devel. award, 1979-84, Alcon Rsch. award, 1993. M. Democrat. Achievements include advances in understanding the cell biology of photoreceptors in the retina, in the regulation of retinal metabolism and the 24-hour photoreceptor clock (i.e. Circadian clock). Office: Med Coll Wis Dept Cellular Biology and Anatomy Milwaukee WI 53226*

BESHEAR, STEVEN L., lawyer; b. Dawson Springs, Ky., Sept. 21, 1944. A.B., U. Ky., Lexington, 1966, J.D., 1968. Bar: N.Y. 1969, Ky. 1971. Assoc. White and Case, N.Y.C., 1968-70; later ptnr. Beshear, Meng and Green, Lexington; mem. Ky. Ho. of Reps., 1974-79; atty. gen. State of Ky., Frankfort, 1979-83, lt. gov., 1983-87; ptnr. Stites & Harbison, Lexington, 1987—. Bd. editors, Ky. Law Jour., (1967-68.). Mem. Fayette County Bar Assn., Ky. Bar Assn., ABA, Order of Coif, Phi Beta Kappa, Phi Delta Phi, Omicron Delta Kappa. Office: Stites & Harbison 2300 Lexington Fin Ctr 250 W Main St Ste 2300 Lexington KY 40507-1758

BESHEARS, BRENDA K., nursing educator; b. Raymondville, Mo., Sept. 4, 1953; d. Utah G. and Juanita (Medlock) Creek; m. George A. Beshears, Feb. 12, 1972; children: Angie, Kathy. ASN, Hannibal (Mo.) LaGrange Coll., 1985, BSN, 1988; MS, So. Ill. U., 1991. Staff nurse Blessing Hosp., Quincy, Ill.; health educator Family Planning, Hannibal; instr. Hannibal LaGrange Coll.; asst. prof. Blessing-Rieman Coll. Nursing, Quincy, Ill. Mem. ANA, Marion County Cancer Soc. (bd. dirs.). Home: 1204 Walnut St Hannibal MO 63401-4861

BESHEARS, CHARLES DANIEL, insurance executive, retired; b. Vandalia, Mo., Sept. 6, 1917; s. Charles D. and Anabel (Baker) B.; m. Louise Davis Clarke, Sept. 1980; children: Jacqueline, Charles, Scott (dec.), Melanie; stepchildren: Crescente, Maria-Asuncion, Hernan Errazuriz. Grad. exec. program bus. mgmt., UCLA, 1968; advanced mgmt. program, Harvard U., 1971; diplomas in property and casualty ins. and mgmt., Ins. Inst. Am.; grad., Am. Coll. Life Underwriters, 1978. CLU. With Farmers Ins. Group, L.A., 1937-79, v.p. field ops., 1966-68, v.p. charge property and casualty ops., 1968-73; pres., dir. Farmers New World Life Ins. Co., Mercer Island, Wash., 1973-79; dir. Ohio State Life Ins. Co., 1973-79, Investors Guaranty Life Ins. Co., 1973-79; bd. govs., honors. com. Internat. Ins. Soc. Inc. With USAAF, 1942-45. Mem. Am. Soc CLUs, DAV, VFW, Chile Club, Am. Legion. Home: 12257 Sunset Point Cir Wellington FL 33414-5598 also: Casilla 3331 Correo 12, La Reina, Santiago Chile *You can accomplish any goal you want to set for yourself, if the desire is strong enough. Are you willing to pay the price?.*

BESHUR, JACQUELINE E., pet training consultant, writer; b. Portland, Oreg., May 8, 1948; d. Charles Daniel and Mildred (Domreis) Beshears. BA, UCLA, 1970; MBA, Claremont Grad. Sch., 1980; postgrad., City U., Seattle, 1989-90. Dir. and founder L.A. Ctr. for Photog. Studies, 1972-76; precious gem distbr. Douglas Group Holdings, Australia, 1976-78; small bus. owner BeSure Cleaning, 1981-90; animal trainer, exotic livestock farmer, 1990—. Author: Good Intentions Are Not Good Enough, 1992. Dir. County Citizens Against Incineration, 1987—, Ames Lake Protection Com., 1989—. Mem. Bridges for Peace, Nature Conservancy, Wash. Wilderness Coalition, Issaquah Alps Club, Inland Empire Pub. Lands Coun. Republican. Fundamentalist. Office: BeSure Tng PO Box 225 Carnation WA 98014-0225

BESING, RAY GILBERT, lawyer, writer; b. Roswell, N.Mex., Sept. 14, 1934; s. Ray David and Maxine Mable (Jordan) B.; m. Heather McEachern; children: Christopher, Gilbert, Andrew, Paul. Student, Rice U., 1952-54; B.A., Ripon Coll., 1957; postgrad., Georgetown U., 1957; J.D., So. Methodist U., 1960. Bar: Tex. 1960. Ptnr. Geary, Brice, Barron, & Stahl, Dallas, 1960-74; sr. ptnr. Besing, Baker & Glast, Dallas, 1974-77; prin. Law Offices of Ray G. Besing, P.C., Dallas, 1977—; lectr. trial procedures So. Meth. Sch. of Law, 1966-68; guest lectr. comms. law and policy, univs. and industry confs., 1984—; lectr. Bologna Ctr. of Johns Hopkins U., Nitze Sch. Advanced Internat. Studies. *Served as trial attorney representing Carter Electronics in the landmark case of Carterphone vs. AT&T (FCC 1968), opening the telephone equipment market to competition. Represented MCI Telecommunications Corporation in a series of regulatory agency and court cases against AT&T and the Bell Operating Companies, which provided key evidence to MCI and the U.S. Department of Justice in their antitrust suits against AT&T, leading to the 1984 breakup of the AT&T and Bell Telephone System monopolies over equipment and long distance services. Author: The Thirty Years War: The Defeat of the AT&T Monopoly to be published in 2000. Lecturer and adjuct professor on U.S. and European telecommunications history and policy.* Mng. editor, So. Methodist U. Law Jour., 1959-60. Pres. Dallas Cerebral Palsy Found., 1970; bd. dirs. Dallas Symphony, 1972, Dallas Theatre Center, 1971; trustee Ripon Coll., 1969-76; mem. Tex. Gov.'s Transition Team on Telecom., 1982. Tex. Moot Ct. champion, 1958. Mem. Tex. Bar Assn., Dallas Bar Assn., Dallas Jr. C. of C. (v.p. 1964), Sigma Chi. Democrat. Episcopalian (mem. exec. council diocese Dallas, 1969-72). Home and Office: 400 Graham Ave Santa Fe NM 87501-1658

BESOZZI, PAUL CHARLES, lawyer; b. N.Y.C., Aug. 22, 1947; s. Alfio Joseph and Lucy Agnes (Ducibella) B.; m. Caroline Lisa Hesterberg, Oct. 7, 1978; 1 child, Christina Claire. BS cum laude in Fgn. Service, Georgetown U., 1969, JD, 1972; MBA in Bus./Govt. Rels., George Washington U., 1977. Bar: Va. 1972, D.C. 1973, U.S. Ct. Mil. Appeals 1972, U.S. Supreme Ct. 1977, U.S. Ct. Appeals (4th cir.) 1978, U.S. Ct. Appeals (3d cir.) 1996. Assoc. Arnold & Porter, Washington, 1977-80; gen. counsel, minority counsel U.S. Senate Com. on Armed Services, Washington, 1980-84; ptnr. Hennessey, Stambler & Siebert, P.C., Washington, 1984-86, ptnr., Besozzi & Gavin, 1987-93; ptnr., Besozzi, Gavin & Craven, Washington, 1993-95, Besozzi, Gavin, Craven, & Schmitz, 1995-96, Patton Boggs LLP, Washington, 1996—. Contbr. articles and revs. to legal jours. Editor Georgetown Law Jour., 1971-72. Alumni interviewer Georgetown U. Alumni Assn., Washington, 1981—, dir. procurement roundtable, 1991—, Georgetown U. Alumni Assn. (bd. gov., 1993—). Served as capt. JAGC, U.S. Army, 1972-76. Mem. ABA, Fed. Comms. Bar Assn., Phi Beta Kappa, Phi Alpha Theta, Pi Sigma Alpha. Office: Patton Boggs LLP 2550 M St NW Ste 400 Washington DC 20037-1350

BESPALEC, DALE ANTHONY, clinical psychologist; b. Waukegan, Ill., Sept. 21, 1951; s. Anthony Frank Bespalec and Mildred B. (Glogovsky) Etolen; m. Marylou B. Bartholomae, June 23, 1973; 1 child, Christine Marie. BS magna cum laude with honors, Loyola U., 1973, MA, 1975, PhD, 1978. Lic. psychologist, Wis. Staff cons. psychologist Behavior and Mgmt. Cons., Inc., Milw., 1977-79; instr. U. Wis.-Parkside, Racine, 1979; staff psychologist St. Michael Hosp. Mental Health Ctr., Milw., 1979-86, mgr. outpatient, 1986-90; pvt. practice Milw., 1979-88; clinical prof. Wis. Sch. Profl. Psychology, Milw., 1985—, dir. clin. tng., 1990-92; mgr. mental health program Community Meml. Hosp., Menomonee Falls, Wis., 1992-96; sr. staff psychologist Taycheeda Correctional Inst., Fond du Lac, Wis., 1996-97, chief psychologist, 1997—; clin. instr. Med. Coll. Wis., Milw., 1981—; coord. Wis. Psychol. Assn. Diaster Response Team. Contbr. articles to profl. jours. Past v.p. internal devel. Grafton Jaycees; past mem. bd. dirs United Way Ozaukee County; vol. ARC, chair disaster svcs.; active Riveredge Nature Ctr. Fellow NIMH, USPH, 1973-74. Fellow Wis. Psychol. Assn. (mem. adminstrv. coun. 1994-97, mem. divsn. adv. bd. 1999—); mem. APA, Milw. Area Psychologists Assn. (pres. 1994-96), Am. Correctional Assn., Alpha Sigma Nu. Roman Catholic. Avocations: golf, horseback riding, gardening, hunting, historical reenactments. Office: Taycheeda Correctional Inst 751 County Road K Fond Du Lac WI 54935-9099

BESS, RONALD W., advertising executive; b. Bloomington, Ill., July 9, 1946; s. Bloice Monroe and Mary (Trussel) B.; m. Teresa N. Shute, July 22, 1970; children: Daniel, Laura. BS in Mktg., U. Ill., Champaign, 1968, M, 1972. Account exec. Foote, Cone and Belding, Chgo., 1972-75; v.p. account dir. Needham, Harper and Steers, Chgo., 1975-81; sr. v.p. group account dir. DDB Needham, Chgo., 1981-87; pres. Bayer Bess Vanderwarker, Chgo., Foote, Cone & Belding, Chgo. Office: Foote Cone & Belding 101 E Erie St Fl 14 Chicago IL 60611-2850*

BESSE, RALPH MOORE, lawyer; b. Shadyside, Ohio, Nov. 23, 1905; s. Jesse Allman and Hope (Fish) B.; m. Augusta Woodward Mitchell, Apr. 28, 1934; children: Jean Elizabeth Besse Minehart, William Truman, Robert Allen. A.B. magna cum laude, Heidelberg Coll., 1926; J.D., U. Mich., 1929; LL.D., Baldwin-Wallace Coll., 1957, Oberlin Coll., 1962, Case Inst. Tech., 1962, Western Res. U., 1963, Cleve. Marshall Law Sch., 1959; L.H.D., Wilberforce Coll., 1963, Ursuline Coll., 1970. Bar: Ohio 1930. Assoc. Squire, Sanders & Dempsey, 1929-40, ptnr., 1940-48, 70-85; with Cleve. Electric Illuminating Co., 1948-70, pres., 1960-67, chmn. bd., chief exec. officer, 1967-70; chmn. Nat. Machinery Co., 1962-90, bd. dirs., 1962-94. Author: Besse: What Can One Man Do. Contbr. articles to profl. jours. Mem. adv. bd. Ctr. for the Book, Libr. of Congress, 1979; chief U.S. Army Ordinance Cleve. Dist., 1951-62; trustee Nat. History Day, 1980, Ursuline Coll., 1963, 92, John Huntington Art and Poly. Trust, 1966-86, John Huntington Fund for Edn., 1966-86, Heidelberg Coll., 1949-80, Case Western Reserve U., 1970-76, chmn. bd. dirs., 1971-75. Recipient Cleve. medal for pub. service Cleve. C. of C., 1960, Ursula Laurus award Ursuline Coll., 1965, Eisenman award Jewish Community Fedn. Cleve., 1966, Human Relations award NCCJ, 1967, award Cleve. Bus. League, 1967, Univ. medal Case Western Res. U., 1976, Wisdom award of honor Wisdom Soc., 1979, Disting. Service award Ohio Coll. Assn., 1980, Disting. Alumni award U. Mich., 1981, James Dodman Nobel award Coun. Human Rels., 1982; named Father of Community Colls. in Ohio, 1961; Ralph M. Besse chair in bus. established by Heidelberg Coll., 1979, Ralph M. Besse award for teaching excellence established by Cuyahoga Community Coll., 1980; numerous other awards. Fellow Am. Bar Found.; mem. ABA, Ohio Bar Assn., Bar Assn. Greater Cleve. Home: 2701 Ashley Rd Cleveland OH 44122-1922

BESSE, RONALD DUNCAN, publishing company executive; b. Stayner, Ont., Can., Dec. 7, 1938; s. Josiah Reuben and Annie Mae (Buie) B.; m. Barbara Jane Low, Jan. 26, 1963; children: Christopher, Alison. Student, Ryerson Poly. Inst., 1957-60. From sales rep. to v.p. edn. div. McGraw-Hill Ryerson Ltd., Toronto, Ont., Can., 1960-70, pres., CEO, 1973-76; mng. dir., editorial dir. Latin Am. Libros McGraw-Hill Mex., 1970-73; pres. Consol. Graphics Ltd., Toronto, 1976-78; pres., CEO Gage Pub. Ltd., Toronto, 1978-84; chmn., pres., CEO Can. Pub. Corp., Scarborough, Ont., 1984—, 1984—; chmn., CEO Macmillan Can., Gage Distbn. Co., Gage Ednl. Pub. Co., RDB Capital Corp.; bd. dirs. Rogers Comm. Inc., Rogers Media Inc., MDC Inc., Toronto, Luxembourg Cambridge Holding Group, C.I. Mutual Funds. Past bd. govs. The Shaw Festival, Niagara-on-the-Lake; past chmn. Ont. Liberals, Heritage Dinner; active Bd. of Trade. Mem. Can. Publs. Coun., World Pres.' Orgn. (past chmn. Ont. chpt., past internat. dir., chmn.-emeritus Upper Can. chpt.), Internat. Chief Execs. Orgn., Granite Club, Bd. Trade, 4872 Club (past chmn.), The National Club, Muskoka Lakes Golf and Country Club, Ocean Reef Club. Home: 19 Farnham Ave, Toronto, ON Canada M4V 1H6 Office: Can Pub Corp, Can Pub Corp, 164 Commander Blvd, Scarborough, ON Canada M1S 3C7*

BESSER, LAWRENCE WAYNE, corporate accountant; b. Louisville, Feb. 28, 1948; s. Norman George and Dorothy Catherine (Biegert) B.; m. Mary Pamela McAdam, Nov. 22, 1970 (div. Apr. 1985); 1 child, Lawrence W. Jr. BS in Acctg., U. Louisville, 1977. Acct. Kelley Tech. Coatings Inc., Louisville, 1982—, adminstrv. staff, 1983—; head computer dept. Kelley Tech. Coatins, Inc., Louisville, 1984—, head benefits dept., 1985—, EEOC rep., 1987—; documentor Aries Software Co., Louisville, 1986-87. Co. campaign coord. Metro United Way, Louisville, 1985. Fellow Am. Mgmt. Assn., Am. Inst. Profl. Bookkeepers, Common, Ky. Small Systems Assn., mem. investment panel for KTC Profit-Sharing Trust. Democrat. Roman Catholic. Avocations: golf, tennis, stock car racing. Office: Kelley Tech Coatings Inc 1445 S 15th St Louisville KY 40210-1837

BESSEY, PALMER QUINTARD, surgeon; b. Glen Ridge, N.J., Aug. 14, 1944. MD, U. Vt., 1975. Diplomate Am. Bd. Surgeons, Am. Bd. Critical Care Surgery. Intern U. Ala. Hosp., Birmingham, 1975-76, resident in surgery, 1976-81; fellow metabolism and nutrition Brigham and Women's Hosp., Boston, 1981-83; dir. trauma, burns, and surg. critical care Strong Meml. Hosp., Rochester, 1993—; prof. surgery U. Rochester Sch. Medicine and Dentistry, 1993—. Mem. ACS, Assn. Acad. Surgery, Soc Univ. Surgeons, Am. Assn. Surgery Trauma, ASPEN, Soc. Critical Care Medicine, Ctrl. Surg. Assn., Am. Surg. Assn., Am. Bd. Surgery (bd. dirs.), Am. Burn Assn. Office: U Rochester Med Ctr Dept Surgery 601 Elmwood Ave Rochester NY 14642-0001

BESSIE, SIMON MICHAEL, publisher; b. N.Y.C., Jan. 23, 1916; s. Abraham and Ella (Brainin) B.; m. Constance Ernst, Sept. 12, 1945; children: Nicholas, Katherine; m. Cornelia Schaeffer, Dec. 21, 1968. B.A. magna cum laude, Harvard U., 1936. Reporter Newark Star Eagle, 1936; with rsch. dept. RKO-Radio Pictures, 1936-38; editor Market Rsch. Monthly, 1938; free-lance writer Europe, Africa, 1938-39; assoc. editor, war editor, war corr. Look mag., 1940-42; editor Harper & Bros., 1946-52, gen. editor, 1952-59; co-founder Atheneum Pubs., 1959, pres., 1963-75; sr. v.p. Harper & Row, N.Y.C., 1975-81, v.p., 1988-91, also bd. dirs., 1975-87; pres. Joshuatown Pub. Assocs., Lyme, Conn., 1981—; co-pub. Cornelia and Michael Bessie Books, 1981—; cons. editor Counterpoint Press, 1995—; lectr. English, Columbia U., 1953-59; dir. novel workshop New Sch., 1959-63, dir. Franklin book programs, 1963-72; chmn. vis. com. Harvard U. Press, 1972-78, bd. dirs., 1980-91; bd. dirs. Am. Book Pubs. Coun., 1964-69, Ctr. for Book, 1977-81; chmn. trade book div. Assn. Am. Pubs., 1970-72, bd. dirs., 1972-76, chmn., 1974-75, chmn. freedom to read com., 1975-78, internat. freedom to pub. com., 1975—; mem. exec. com. Ctr. for the Book, Libr. of Congress, 1979—, chmn., 1983—. Author: Jazz Journalism, 1938; contbr. numerous articles to mags. Bd. overseers vis. com. dept. history Harvard U., 1964-77; chmn. lit. panel Nat. Arts Council, 1971-74, chmn. spl. projects panel, 1974-81; chmn. bd. advisors Sta. WNET, 1979-83, trustee, 1983-96, life trustee, 1997—; chmn. book com. Alfred P. Sloan Found., 1986-91, mem. tech. book com., 1992—. Served as chief news bur. psychol. warfare br., 1943-44, Algiers, Sicily, Italy; chief psychol. warfare combat team 1944, So. France; dep. dir. USIS, 1944-46, France. Recipient Presdl. Medal of Freedom, 1946, Curtis Benjamin award Assn. Am. Pubs., 1986. Mem. Council Fgn. Relations, Assn. Harvard Alumni (dir. 1974-77), Phi Beta Kappa. Clubs: Century Assn. (N.Y.C.), Harvard (N.Y.C.); Federal City (Washington). Home and Office: 296 Joshuatown Rd Lyme CT 06371-3035

BESSMAN, SAMUEL PAUL, pediatrician, biochemist; b. Newark, Feb. 3, 1921; m. Alice Neuman, July 3, 1945; children: Joel David, Ellen. Student, Coll. William and Mary, 1938-41; M.D., Washington U., St. Louis, 1944. Intern, asst. resident St. Louis Children's Hosp., 1944-45; asst. prof. pediatrics George Washington U., 1947-54; dir. research Children's Hosp., Washington, 1947-54; asso. prof. pediatrics U. Md., 1954-59, prof. pediatric research, 1959-68, prof. biochemistry, 1962-68; prof., chmn. dept. pharmacology and nutrition U. So. Calif., 1968-91, prof. pediatrics, 1969-91, prof. emeritus, 1991—; dir. research Rosewood State Hosp., Md., 1962-68, Jewish Home for Retarded Children, Washington, 1962-68. Founding editor Biochem. Medicine; mem. editorial bd. Analytical Biochemistry. Pres. First Dist. Cmty. Coun., Balt., 1965; trustee Robert Lindner Found.; pres. Molly Towell Found., Alsam Found. Served with USPHS, 1945-47. Recipient Crawford Long award U. Ga., 1963, Creative Scholar award U. So. Calif., 1978, Maimonides award Technion, 1979, Disting. Sci. Achievement award Am. Heart Assn., 1984, Inst. for Advanced Studies award Louis Pasteur Libr. and Sci. Found., 1986, Alumni Achievement award Washington U. Med. Sch., 1994. Fellow AAAS, Am. Acad. Pediat.; mem. Am. Soc. Biol. Chemists, Soc. Pediat. Rsch., Am. Inst. Nutrition, Am. Soc. Pharmacology and Exptl. Therapeutics, Sigma Xi, Alpha Omega Alpha. Achievements include introduction of EDTA treatment of lead poisoning, theoretical basis of hepatic coma, mechanism of insulin action chemistry mental retardation, genetic basis of malnutrition, artificial implantable pancreas, creatine phosphate energy shuttle. Home: 7404 Woodrow Wilson Dr Los Angeles CA 90046-1323

BESSON, LUC, film director; b. Paris, Mar. 18, 1959. Founder Les Films du Loup, Paris, 1982—. Works include: Le Dernier Combat, 1982, Subway, 1984, The Big Blue, 1988, La Femme Nikita, 1990, Atlantis, 1991, The Professional, 1994, The Fifth Element, 1997; and other short films. Office: Seaside Prodns 10202 Washington Blvd Culver City CA 90232-3119

BEST, ALYNDA KAY, conflict resolution mediator; b. Amarillo, Tex., June 20, 1947; d. William Otho and Ruby Jewel (Hamby) Mauldin; m. Paul Wesley Best, Mar. 31, 1978; children: Brett Allison, Trevor William. BA, Tex. Tech. U., 1969; MBA, U. Tex. of Perian Basin, Odessa, 1983. Asst. bus. mgr. Med. Arts Clinic, Lubbock, Tex., 1969-72; fin. supr. Tex. Dept. Human Resources, Lubbock, 1972-79; pvt. practice bus. dir. Odessa, 1979-87; corp. mgr. Midland (Tex.) Emergency Physicians, 1987-95; pres. Conflict Resolution Ctr., Inc., Midland, 1996—. Co-author: (pamphlet) Midland Municipal Water Supply, 1992. Treas. LWV, Odessa/Midland, 1980-82, chmn. nat. res. Midland 1990-93; treas. Hospice of Odessa, 1983-85, Santa Rita PTA, Midland, 1990-92; dir. outreach First Christian Ch., Midland, 1991-93; mem. yearbook com. Midland/Odessa Symphony, 1994; leader Girl Scouts/Boy Scouts, 1986-94; active Midland Cmty. Theatre. Mem. AAUW, Am. Med. Soc., Midland Med. Assn. (excursion coord. 1994-95), Tex. Med. Assn. Aux. (state dist. rep.). Avocations: tennis, painting. Office: Conflict Resolution Ctr Inc 4811 Teakwood Trce Midland TX 79707-1638

BEST, CAROLYN ANNE HILL, middle school education educator; b. Columbia, S.C., Apr. 27, 1951; d. Sidney Sutcliffe Hill and Elizabeth Anne Boylston Hill Matney; m. Ralph Leslie Best, June 29, 1974; 1 child, Leslie Anne. BA in Edn., U. S.C., 1973; MEd, Francis Marion U., Florence, S.C., 1976; postgrad., Francis Marion U., 1996. Tchr. 2d grade Blenheim (S.C.) Pub. Sch., 1973-84; tchr. pre-sch. 1st United Meth. Ch., Bennettsville, S.C., 1985-86; tchr. Bennettsville Mid. Sch., 1988—. Contbr. poetry to River of Dreams, 1994, Best Poems of 1995, Best Poems of 1996, Whispers in the Garden, 1997, Best Poems of the 90's, 1997. Recipient Editor's Choice award Nat. Libr. of Poetry, 1994, 95, 96, Good News award Marlboro County Sch. Sys., Bennettsville, 1996, 97. Mem. NEA, Nat. Coun. Tchrs. of English, Mid. Sch. Assn., S.C. Edn. Assn., Internat. Reading Assn., Internat. Soc. Poets, Nat. Soc. Poets, Famous Poets Soc. (Diamond Homer Trophy 1995), Marlboro County Edn. Assn. Republican. Methodist. Office: Bennettsville Mid Sch 701 Cheraw St Bennettsville SC 29512-2499

BEST, FRANKLIN LUTHER, JR., lawyer; b. Lock Haven, Pa., Dec. 14, 1945; s. Franklin L. and Hazel M. (Yearick) B.; m. Kimberly R., May 1, 1982. BA, Yale U., 1967; JD, U. Pa., 1970; postgrad., Columbia U., 1994. Bar: Pa. 1970. Assoc. MacCoy, Evans & Lewis, Phila., 1970-74; asst. counsel Penn Mut. Life Ins. Co., Phila., 1974-77, asst. gen. counsel, 1978-84, assoc. gen. counsel, 1985-99, corp. counsel, 1999—; counsel, asst. sec. Penn Ins. and Annuity Co., Phila., 1983-96, counsel, sec., 1996—, corp. counsel, 1999—; lectr. Pa. Bar Inst., 1976-84. Author: Pennsylvania Insurance Law, 1991, 2d edit., 1998; contbr. articles to profl. jours. Bd. dirs. Ctr. City South Neighborhood Assn., 1979-80, pres., 1978-79; mem. Com. of Seventy, 1978-84; sec. Washington Sq. Assn., 1977-87; mem. 30th Ward Rep. Exec. Com., 1972-84, West Pikeland Twp. Open Spaces Com., 1987—, chairperson, 1995—, planning commn., 1994—, chairperson, 1996—. Mem. ABA, Internat. Claim Assn. (sec. 1995—, exec. com. 1979-81, 85-88), Phila. Bar Assn., Yale Club of Phila. Baptist. Office: Penn Mut Life Ins Co Independence Sq Philadelphia PA 19172

BEST, GARY ALLEN, special education educator; b. Oceanside, Calif., July 27, 1939; s. Charles Richard and Vivian Elaine (Misner) B.; m. Shirley Joanne Seelhammer, Dec. 18, 1962; 1 child, Joanna Elaine Best Le Fave. BA, Calif. State U., L.A., 1961, MA, 1965; PhD, U. Minn., 1968. Spl. edn. tchr. L.A. Unified Schs., 1961-65; instr. U. Minn., Mpls., 1966-68, Duluth, 1966-68; prof. Wis. State U., Eau Claire, 1966; asst. prof. Calif. State U., L.A., 1968—, chmn. divsn. spl. edn., 1986-91, acting dean, grad. studies, 1986-87, assoc. dean student svcs. Charter Sch. of edn., 1996-98, assoc. dir. tchr. edn. and K-18 programs chancellor's office, 1998—; vis. prof. U. Victoria, B.C., 1970, 74, Western Mich. U., Kalamazoo, 1973; bd. dirs. Calif. State U. Found., Crippled Children's Soc. So. Calif.; mem. spl. edn. adv. com. Calif. Commn. on Tchr. Credentialing. Author: Individuals With Physical Disabilities, 1978; contbr. articles and chpts. to profl. jours. and books on phys. disability and sex edn. for exceptional populations. Registered reader Huntington Rare Books/Manuscript Libr., San Marino, Calif., 1980-81. Recipient Outstanding Prof. award Calif. State U., L.A., 1983, named Disting. Alumnus, 1992; named Alumnus of Yr. Riverside C.C., 1994; Fulbright scholar Taipei, Taiwan, 1991. Mem. Coun. for Exceptional Children (parliamentarian 1991-94, pres. divsn. physically handicapped 1984-85). Office: Calif State U Office Chancellor Office Tchr Edn K-18 Progms 401 Golden Shore Long Beach CA 90802-4275

BEST, GARY THORMAN, commercial real estate broker; b. San Diego, Mar. 11, 1944; s. Roland Elmer and Mildred Mae (Thorman) B.; m. Hollyce Susan Hill, Feb. 22, 1967 (div. Mar. 1973); 1 child, Melissa Anne; m. Georgia Anne Flaherty, May 22, 1973; children: Roland Bryant, Heather Anne. AAS, Pima Community Coll., 1979. CCIM Comml. Investment Real Estate Inst. Sales Mohawk Data Scis. Corp, Tulsa, 1968-69; exec. v.p. Mid-Am. Mgmt. Corp., Tulsa, 1969-73; real estate sales Cragin Lang Free and Smythe, Cleve., 1973-74; land sales Coldwell Banker Comml., Tucson, 1975-80; mgr. sales Coldwell Banker Comml., Cin., Ohio, 1981; resident mgr. Coldwell Banker Comml., Nashville, 1982-83; investment sales Coldwell Banker Comml., Tucson, 1984-85; v.p. Del E. Webb Realty and Mgmt. Co., Tucson, 1986-87; pres. Best Comml. Real Estate, Tucson, 1987-93; sec./treas. Best Asset Mgmt. Svcs., Phoenix, 1993-98, chmn. credit rev. com., 1991-94; with Coldwell Banker Success Realty, Tucson, 1994-97; assoc. broker comml. disvn. Realty Execs. of Tucson, 1997—; regional v.p. Comml. Investment Real Estate Inst., 1992-94, cert. comml. investment mem.; pres. So. Ariz. chpt. Cert. Comml. Investment Mems., Tucson, 1990; mem. New Am. Network, Tucson, 1987-93, mem. adv. bd., 1992-93. Mem. fin. com. Symington for Gov., Tucson, 1990, Kolbe for Congress, Tucson, 1988; adv. bd. Goodwill Industries of Tucson, Tucson Unified Sch. Dist.; dir. Family Counseling Agy., 1995—, treas., 1996-98, 1st v.p., 1998-99, pres., 1999—; chmn. adv. bd. Casa de la Luz, Tucson. Recipient Pres. of Yr. award Civitan Internat., Ariz. dist., Tucson, 1979. Mem. Tucson Bd. Realtors (bd. dirs. 1988-91, v.p. 1992), Ariz. Assn. Realtors (bd. dirs. 1989-91, 92-94, exec. com. 1992), Tucson Econ. Devel. Corp. (bd. dirs., chmn. 1990), Greater Tucson Econ. Coun. (bd. dirs., exec. com. 1990-93), Tucson Met. C. of C. (bd. dirs., chmn. 1993-94, Small Bus. Leader of Yr. award 1989, chmn. 1993-94), Breakfast Club, Rotary. Republican. Avocations: travel, reading, geneology, soccer parent. Office: 6872 E Sunrise Dr Ste 150 Tucson AZ 85750-0723

BEST, HOLLIS G., federal judge; b. 1926. BA, Fresno State Coll., 1948; JD, Stanford U., 1951. Dep. dist. atty. Fresno, Calif., 1951-53; with Manfredo, Best & Forbes, 1953-63, McCormick, Barstow, Sheppard, Coyle & Best, 1963-72; judge Fresno County Superior Ct., 1972-84; assoc. justice 5th appellate dist. Calif. Ct. Appeal, 1984-90, presiding justice, 1990-94; apptd. magistrate judge ea. dist. U.S. Dist. Ct. Calif., 1994. Fax: (209) 372-0324. Office: 1130 O St Fresno CA 93721-2201

BEST, JACOB HILMER (JERRY), JR., hotel chain executive; b. Evanston, Ill., July 21, 1937; s. Jacob Hilmer and Clara (Cornell) B.; m. Janet Patricia Donnelly, June 20, 1959; children: Jacob Hilmer III, Peter B., Julie Donnelly Best Hunt. BS in Hotel Adminstrn., Mich. State U., 1959; postgrad, Stanford U., 1979. From sales rep. to dir. of sales Sheraton Hotels, Chgo., Wash., 1960-62; asst. to owner Camelback Inn, Scottsdale, Ariz., 1963-64; from sales mgr. to exec. v.p. Marriott Hotels, 1964-84; pres. Ramada Inns, Phoenix, 1984-85; pres., CEO, Wyndham Hotels, Dallas, 1985-87, Red Lion Hotels & Inns, Vancouver, Wash., 1987-91, Omni Hotels, Hampton, N.H., 1992-96; ind. cons., 1996-98; COO Tauck Tours, Westport, Conn., 1998—. Named charter mem. Mich. State U. Sch. of Hospitality Hall of Fame, 1995. Mem. Am. Hotel and Motel Assn. Republican. Roman Catholic. Avocations: golf, reading, fishing. Home: PO Box 56 Rancho Santa Fe CA 92067-0056

BEST, JUDAH, lawyer; b. N.Y.C., Sept. 4, 1932; s. Sol and Ruth (Landau) B.; m. Sally Joan Dial, June 29, 1962; 1 child, Stephen Andrew. AB, Cornell U., 1954; LLB, Columbia U., 1959. Bar: N.Y. 1959, D.C. 1961, U.S. Supreme Ct. 1963. Trial atty. Solicitor's Office, U.S. Dept. Labor, Washington, 1960-61; asst. U.S. atty. for D.C., 1961-64; assoc., then ptnr. Chapman, DiSalle & Friedman, Washington, 1964-70; ptnr. Dickstein, Shapiro & Morin, Washington, 1970-80, Steptoe & Johnson, Washington, 1980-87, Debevoise & Plimpton, Washington, 1987—; participant trial advocacy program U. Va. Sch. Law, 1981—. Contbr. articles to profl. publs. Served with U.S. Army, 1954-56. Fellow Am. Coll. Trial Lawyers; mem. ABA (coun., litigation sect. 1977-81, chmn. subcom. on litigation 1982-84, mem. fed. regulation securities com., corp. bank and bus. law sect., pub. contracts sect., vice chmn. ABA Task Force Report on RICO 1983-85, chmn. litigation sect. 1988-89, sect. del. 1989—, mem. standing com. on fed. judiciary 1990-93, chmn. 1996-97, mem. spl. com. on governance 1993-95), Fed. Bar Assn., D.C. Bar Assn., Am. Bar Found., Am. Law Inst., Cosmos Club, Washington Golf and Country Club, City Club of Washington. Home: 2808 Woodland Dr NW Washington DC 20008-2742 Office: Debevoise & Plimpton 555 13th St NW Ste 1100E Washington DC 20004-1163 also: 875 3rd Ave New York NY 10022-6225

BEST, KAREN MAGDALENE, legal secretary; b. Worden, Ill., Oct. 10, 1947; d. Royal H. and Doris (Klausing) Lueker; m. Rodger R. Best, Mar. 29, 1975; 1 child, Jill Marie. Grad. H.S., Edwardsville, Ill., 1965. Claims sec. Madison County Mutual, Edwardsville, 1965-75; legal sec. Young, Welsch, Young & Hall, Danville, Ill., 1975-77, Mudge, Riley & Lucco, Edwardsville, 1977-79, Droste & Price, Mt. Olive, Ill., 1979-95; clk. Wolff Oil Co., Litchfield, Ill., 1995-96; legal sec. Lucco, Brown & Mudge, Edwardsville, 1996-98, Scharf Law Office, Litchfield, Ill., 1998—. Mem. Zion Lutheran Ladies Aid, pres. 1997-99. Lutheran. Avocations: reading, travel. Home: 5324 Niemanville Trl Litchfield IL 62056-4614

BEST, MARY LANI, university program coordinator; b. Hilo, Hawaii, June 3, 1944; d. Stanley Clark and Emma Holokahiki (Martinson) Brooks; m. Leningrad Elarionoff, Aug. 14, 1965 (div. 1981); children: Kimberly Kehaunani, Grad. Ikaika; m. Gary Dean Best, Dec. 7, 1984 (div. 1996). BA, U. Hawaii, Hilo, 1988; MS, Creighton U., 1991. Substitute tchr. Hilo High Sch., 1990; counselor secondary alternative program Westside High Sch., Omaha, 1991; coord. Ctr. for Gifted & Talented Native Hawaiian Children U. Hawaii, Hilo, 1991—. Contbr.: (book) Sociology of Hawaii, 1992; co-editor: Glimpses of Hawaiian Daily Life and Culture, 1994. Active Hale O Na Alii, Hilo, 1988—. Mem. AACD. Republican. Avocations: writing, oil painting, reading, collecting colored liquer crystal. Home: 84 Pukihae St Apt 1104 Hilo HI 96720-2409 Office: U Hawaii 200 W Kawili St Hilo HI 96720-4075

BEST, MELVYN EDWARD, geophysicist; b. Victoria, B.C., Can., Mar. 8, 1941; s. Herbert Best and Irene Jessie (Kelly) MacKenzie; m. Virginia Marie Pignato, July 19, 1970; children: Lisette Anne, Aaron Michael. BSc in Math. and Physics with honors, U. B.C., Vancouver, 1965, MSc in Physics, 1966; PhD in Theoretical Physics, MIT, 1970. Geophysicist mineral exploration Shell Can. Resources Ltd., Calgary, Alta., Can., 1972-77, divsn. geophysicist minerals, 1980-82, mgr. petroleum engring. rsch., 1982-85; head non-seismic rsch. Royal Dutch Shell Exploration and Prodn. Labs., The Hague, The Netherlands, 1978-80; geophys. advisor Teknica Resource Devel. Ltd., Calgary, 1985-86; head basin analysis subdivision Atlantic Geoscience Ctr. Geol. Survey Can., Dartmouth, N.S., 1986-90; dir. Pacific Geosci. Ctr. Geol. Survey Can., Sidney, B.C., 1990-94, sr. rsch. scientist, 1994-97; geophys. cons. Bemex Consulting Internat., Victoria, B.C., 1997—; vis. lectr., rsch. assoc. dept. physics McGill U., Montreal, Que., Can., 1970-72; adj. prof. geology and geophysics, U. Calgary, Alta., Can., 1997—; mem. panel Jeanne d'Arc hydrocarbon resource assessment Can. Govt., 1987-90, mem. petroleum geology working group Office Energy R&D, 1987-92; mem. oil and gas com. Can. Nfld. Offshore Petroleum Bd., 1990-94, com. for coordination of joint prospecting for mineral resources in Asian offshore waters, ofcl. Can. rep., 1992-94; sessional lectr. Ctr. for Earth and Ocean Rsch., U. Victoria, 1995—, adj. prof. earth and ocean scis., 1998—; adj .prof. U. Calgary, 1998—. Author: Resistivity Mapping and Electromagnetic Imaging, 1992; editor: (with J.B. Boniwell) A Geophysical Handbook for Geologists, 1989, (with T.P. Ng) Development and Exploitation Scale Geophysics, 1995. Vol. lectr. Can. Coll. Chinese Studies, Victoria, B.C., 1995-99; vol. Victoria chpt. Habitat for Humanity, 1996-97. Recipient meritorious svc. award Can. Soc. Exploration Geophysicists, Calgary, 1996. Mem. Can. Soc. Exploration Geophysicists (chmn. continuing edn. com. 1982-85, mem. tech. com. 1985 convention, assoc. editor jour. 1986-93, 95—, editor jour. 1993-95), Soc. Exploration Geophysicists (prodn. and devel. geophysics com. 1985-88, geophys. rsch. com. 1988—, organizer workshop 1989, instr. continuing edn. 1985—), Soc. Environ. and Engring. Geophysics (assoc. editor jour. 1995-97, editor 1997—), Assn. Profl. Engrs., Geologists and Geophysicists Alta. (cert.), Calgary Winter Club. Avocations: competitive badminton, squash, tennis, hiking, sailing. Home: 5288 Cordova Bay Rd, Victoria, BC Canada V8Y 2L4 Office: Bemex Consulting Internat, 5288 Cordova Bay Rd, Victoria, BC Canada V8Y 2L4

BEST, PAMELA LAFEUER, secondary school educator; b. Arlington, Va., Feb. 19, 1952; d. Malcolm R. and Christabel P. LaFever; m. Frederick W. Best III; children: Christine, Karin. BS in Edn., Emporia State U., 1978; MBA, Rockhurst Coll., 1985. Receptionist First Va. Bank, Fairfax, 1971-72; sec. Civil Svc. Commn., Washington, 1972-73; nat. sales sec. Diddle-Glaser, Emporia, Kans., 1974-76; bus. edn. tcr. Louisburg (Kans.) H.S., 1978—. Contbr. articles to profl. jours. Recipient 2d pl. Career Virtual Reality award Kans. City Star, 1998, 2d pl. award Kans. Ins. Edn. Found., 1998. Mem. Kans. Bus. Edn. Assn. (presenter 1991—, 1st Pl. Share-an-Idea 1995), Mountain-Plains Bus. Edn. Assn. (1st pl. Share-an-Idea award 1992). Avocations: reading, computers. E-mail: bestp@louisburg.k12.ks.us. Office: Louisburg HS 505 E Amity Louisburg KS 66212

BEST, R. STEPHEN, SR., fire chief. MBA, Regent U. Fire chief Chesapeake (Va.) Fire Dept., 1998—. Office: 304 Albemarle Dr Chesapeake VA 23322

BEST, ROBERT GLEN, geneticist; b. Springfield, Ohio, Jan. 27, 1958; s. Richard Alexander and Ella Marie (Buss) B.; m. Sara Felicia Newton, June 2, 1984; children: Cami DeNeil, Heidi Amber, Adrian Alexander, Joshua Ellis, Christopher Benjamin. BS in Biochemistry, Lehigh U., 1981; MS in Toxicology, N.C. State U., 1983, PhD in Genetics/Toxicology, 1987. Diplomate Am. Bd. Med. Genetics. Med. geneticist, clin. cytogeneticist Richland Mem. Hosp., Columbia, S.C., 1986-89; from acting dir. to assoc. dir. clin. genetics U. S.C., Columbia, 1989-91, dir. clin. genetics, 1991—; assoc. prof. ob-gyn., dir. divsn. clin. genetics; cons. Hybritech Inc., San Diego, 1989—. Grantee March of Dimes, 1990, Ctrs. for Disease Control, 1993-98. Mem. Am. Soc. Human Genetics, Am. Soc. Hematology, European Soc. Human Genetics, Genotoxicity and Environ. Mutagenesis Soc. Avocation: madrigal singing. Home: 101 White Falls Cir Columbia SC 29212-1241 Office: U SC Dept Ob-Gyn Two Med Park # 301 Columbia SC 29203

BEST, ROBERT MULVANE, insurance company executive; b. Newcomerstown, Ohio, May 9, 1922; s. Chester R. and Beatrice (Mulvane) B.; m. Shirley Marie Smith, Nov. 25, 1994; children: Eric, Linda, Grant. BS, Ohio State U., 1947. Agt. Bus. Men's Assurance Co. Am., Columbus, Ohio, 1946-48; mgr. group sales Security Mut. Life Ins. Co., Binghamton, N.Y., 1948-49; asst. supt. agys. Security Mut. Life Ins. Co., Binghamton, 1949-51, dir. sales, 1951-53; asst. mgr. Bus. Men's Assurance Co., Columbus, 1952-61; v.p. in charge agys. Security Mut. Life Ins. Co. N.Y., Binghamton, 1961-66, exec. v.p., 1966-69, pres., 1969—, chief exec. officer, 1972-87, chmn. bd., 1977-90; chmn., chief exec. officer Home Mut. Ins. Co., 1986-89; mem. exec. com. Life Inst. Guaranty Copr., N.Y.C., 1980-89; mem. N.Y. Inst. bd., N.Y.; chmn. bd. trustees bus. coun. Inst. Trust. Trustee Bus. Coun. N.Y. State, Inc.; former dir. Valley Devel. Found., Binghamton; mem. coun. SUNY; bd. govs. Internat. Ins. Seminars; bd. dirs. Twin Tier Home Health Care, Inc., Binghamton; former mem. N.Y. State Bd. Regents, Am. Coun. Life Ins.; chmn. Med. Info. Bur., Inc., Boston, 1989; dir. Greater Broome Cmty. Found., Inc. Lt. (j.g.) USNR, 1942-46. Mem. Am. Soc. CLUs (regional v.p. 1967-70), Am. Council Life Ins. (bd. dir.), Life Ins. Council N.Y. (bd. dir.), Broome County C. of C. (bd. dir. 1970-75, pres. 1974), Empire State C. of C. (former pres., bd. dirs.). Clubs: Binghamton City (bd. dirs. 1969-73); Oteyokwa Lake (Hallstead, Pa.) (pres. 1970-71); Econ. (N.Y.C.). Home: 41A Crestmont Rd Binghamton NY 13905-4117

BEST, ROGER NORMAN, inventor, real estate manager, consultant; b. L.A., Apr. 16, 1949; s. Norman Frank and Muriel Noreen (Atkinson) B.; m. Sheri Lyn Kruyer, Oct. 16, 1982; children: Ryan William, Robert Edward. BA, U. Wash., 1971. Lic. Real Estate Broker, Calif. Musician, entertainer, 1963-69; pres. Best Enterprises, L.A., 1969—; head electronic media svcs. Cedars-Sinai Med. Ctr., L.A., 1971-73; pres. Tazio Prodns., L.A., 1973-76; v.p. Video Disco & Assocs., L.A., 1975-76, DSL Constrn. Corp., L.A., 1977-85; v.p., COO Scott Properties, Inc., L.A., 1978-85; pres., CEO Tazio Properties, Inc., L.A., 1980—. Inventor correctable typewriter ribbon; creator original music videos concept with Visual Music, 1974; featured columnist Apt. Age Mag., L.A., 1989-97. Mem. Van Nuys Airport Adv. Coun., 1987-94. Citation of Appreciation, City of L.A., 1988, 89, 94. Avocations: boating, skiing, flying, target shooting. Office: Tazio Properties Inc 3580 Wilshire Blvd Fl 17 Los Angeles CA 90010-2501

BEST, SUSAN MARIE, artist, educator; b. Peoria, Ill., July 4, 1949; d. Robert H. and Shirley (Critchlow) Coyle; m. David G. Best, Sept. 12, 1970 (div. May 1987); children: Timothy, Molly, Abby, George; m. Richard J. Gualandi, Dec. 20, 1996. BPhar, U. Ill., Chgo., 1972; MA in Fine Arts, Ill. State U., Normal, 1988, MFA, 1991. Grad. pharmacist S&C Drugs, Peoria, 1972, Indian Hosp., Pine Ridge, S.D., 1974-76; instr. art Ill. State U., Normal, 1988-91, Bradley U., Peoria, 1992-93, Ill. Ctrl. Coll., Peoria, 1991-93; artist, 1970—; gallery artist Struve Gallery, Chgo., 1991-93. Exhbn. Contemporary Art Ctr., Oleczyn, Poland. Bd. dirs. St. Thomas Sch., Peoria, 1980-83, Amateur Mus. Club, Peoria, 1982-84; bd. dirs. Peoria Art Guild, 1994—. Recipient Percent for Art award City of New Orleans, 1997, also various awards for art including 2 grants from Ill. Arts Coun. Access Program, 1995; Ill. State U. fellow, 1988-91. Mem. AAUP, AAUW, NOW, Contemporary Arts Ctr. of New Orleans, New Orleans Mus. Art, Chgo. Artists Coalition, Lakeview Art Mus., Sun Found., Planned Parenthood Assn. Democrat. Avocations: skiing, jogging, piano. Studio: 811 1/2 Opelousas Ave New Orleans LA 70114-2429

BEST, WILLIAM ROBERT, physician, educator, university official; b. Chgo., July 14, 1922; s. Gordon and Marian Burton (Shapland) B.; m. Ruth Joanna Stuchlik, Sept. 2, 1944; children: Barbara Ann Best Mulch, Patricia Marian Best Williams. BS, U. Ill., 1945; MD, U. Ill., Chgo., 1947, MS, 1951; postgrad. math. biology, U. Chgo., 1964-65. Diplomate Am. Bd. Internal Medicine, Am. Bd. Hematology. From intern to fellow in hematology then to resident U. Ill. Hosp., 1947-51; asst. prof., assoc. prof. medicine U. Ill. Coll. Medicine, Chgo., 1953-67, prof., assoc. dean, 1972-81; chief Midwest Rsch. Support Ctr., VA Hosp., Hines, Ill., 1967-72, chief staff, 1981-92, sr. health svcs. rschr., 1992—; prof. medicine, assoc. dean for VA affairs Loyola U. Stritch Sch. Medicine, Maywood, Ill., 1981-92; chief staff U. Ill. Hosp., Chgo., 1976-81. Contbr. numerous articles to sci. jours. 1st lt. U.S. Army, 1951-53. Named Alumnus of Yr., U. Ill. Med. Alumni Assn., 1980. Fellow ACP; mem. AMA (br. pres. 1985), Internat. Soc. Hematology, Am. Statis. Assn., AAAS. Episcopalian. Avocations: sailing, computing. Home: 1712 Waverly Cir Saint Charles IL 60174-5869 Office: Midwest Ctr Health Svcs Rsch Edward Hines Jr VA Hosp Hines IL 60141

BESTE, ROBERT CULBERTSON, geologist; b. St. Charles, Mo., July 24, 1949; s. Rebecca Sue Harwerth, Aug. 9, 1987; children: Amy, Zoe, Cassin. BS, S.W. Mo. State U., 1975, postgrad., 1988, 89. Registered profl. geologist, Ark., Mo. Equipment and rd. supr. Ky. Dept. of Parks, Frankfort, 1979-82; with equipment and maintence Mo. Portland Cement, Sugar Creek, Mo., 1982-84; geologist Geol. Cons., St. Louis, 1984-96, Kurtz Concrete Lab., St. Charles, Mo., 1985-88, Triangle Materials Testing and Cons., 1988-93, Lafarge Constrn. Materials, St. Charles, 1993—. Editor: A Location Guide for Rock Hounds in the United States, 1996; author: The Petrography and Stratigraphy of St. Charles Quarry in St. Charles, Mo., 1992, The Petrography and Stratigraphy of Defiance Quarry in Defiance, Mo., 1994; contbr. articles to profl. jours. Capt. U.S. Army Corp. of Engrs., 1975-78. Mem. Soc. of Mining Engrs., Nat. Stone Assn. (rsch. adv. com.), Assn. of Mo. Geologist, Fluoresent Mineral Soc. Home: 2435 Union Rd Saint Louis MO 63125-3457 Office: Lafarge Constrn Materials 2115 S River Rd Saint Charles MO 63303-5714

BESTEHORN, UTE WILTRUD, retired librarian; b. Cologne, Germany, Nov. 6, 1930; came to U.S., 1930; d. Henry Hugo and Wiltrud Lucie (Vincentz) B. BA, U. Cin., 1954, BEd, 1955, MEd, 1958; MS in Library Sci., Western Res. U. (now Case-Western Res. U.), 1961. Tchr. Cutter Jr. High Sch., Cin., 1955-57; tchr., supr. libr. Felicity (Ohio) Franklin Sr. High Sch., 1959-60; with libr. sci. dept. Pub. Libr. Cin. and Hamilton County, 1961-78, with libr. info. desk, 1978-91; ret., 1991; textbook selection com., Felicity-Franklin Sr. High Sch., 1959-60; supr. Health Alcove Sci. Dept. and annual health lectures, Cin. Pub. Library, 1972-77. Book reviewer Library Jour., 1972-77; author and inventor Rainbow 40 marble game, 1971, Condominium game, 1976; patentee indexed packaging and stacking device, 1973, mobile packaging and stacking device, 1974. Mem. Clifton Town Meeting, 1988—; mem. Bookfest 90 com. Pub. Libr. Cin. and Hamilton County. Recipient Cert. of Merit and Appreciation Pub. Library of Cin., 1986. Mem. Cin. Chpt. Spl. Libraries Assn. (archivist 1963-64, 65-70, editor Queen City Gazette bull. 1964-69), Pub. Library Staff Assn. (exec. bd., activities com. 1965, welfare com. 1966, recipient Golden Book 25 yr. service pin, 1986), Friends of the Library, Greater Cin. Calligraphers Guild (reviewer New Letters pub. 1986-88), Delta Phi Alpha (nat. German hon. 1951). Republican. Mem. United Ch. of Christ. Avocations: calligraphy, painting and sketching, writing, photography, violin. Home: 3330 Morrison Ave Cincinnati OH 45220-1440

BESTERMAN, DOUGLAS, composer, orchestrator. Orchestrator Broadway shows: Fosse (Tony Award for best musical 1999), Big, Damn Yankees, King David, A Christmas Carol, Radio City Music Hall Christmas Spectacular; Off-Broadway: weird Romance, Jack's Holiday, Johnny Pye and the Foolkiller, The Gifts of the Magi, Godspell; rochestrated the ballet: But Not for Me; film/TV include: Mulan, Anastasia, Pocahontas, Cinderella; arranger many leading vocalists including Toni Braxton, Kathy Lee Gifford, Jerry Hadley, Patti LuPone, Mandy Patinkin, Chita Rivera. Office: American Guild of Musical Artists 1727 Broadway New York NY 10019-5284*

BESTGEN, WILLIAM HENRY, JR., financial planner; b. Quincy, Mass., June 23, 1947; s. William Henry and Ebba Violet (Fristam) B.; m. Ann Marie Mahoney, Apr. 12, 1975; children: Brad William, Lauren Ann. BA, Northeastern U., 1970. CLU; Chartered Fin. Cons.; Cert. Estate Planner. Fin. planner Bay Fin., Waltham, Mass., 1970—; pres. Yankee Planners, Inc., Middleboro, Mass. Mem. exec. bd. Boston Estate and Bus. Planning Coun. Mem. Am. Soc. CLUs, Nat. Assn. Life Underwriters, Internat. Assn. Fin. Planners, Million Dollar Round Table (life). Republican. Lutheran. Avocations: skiing, boating. Home: 100 Holland Ave Stoughton MA 02072-3251

BESTON, ROSE MARIE, retired college president; b. South Portland, Maine, Sept. 27, 1937; d. George Louis and Edith Mae (Archibald) Beattie; m. John Bernard Beston, Feb. 1, 1970. BA, St. Joseph's Coll., 1961; MA, Boston Coll., 1963; PhD, U. Pitts., 1967; cert. of advanced study, Harvard U., 1978. Mem. faculty St. Joseph's Coll., Maine, 1967-68, SUNY, Oneonta, 1968-69, S.E. Mo. State Coll., 1969-70, U. Queensland and Western Australian Inst. Tech., 1970-76, U. Hawaii, Manoa, 1976-77; assoc. acad. dean Worcester (Maine) State Coll., 1978-80; dean for acad. affairs Castleton (Vt.) State Coll., 1980-84; pres. Nazareth Coll. Rochester, N.Y., 1984-98; ret., 1999; former mem. Neylan Commn., Assn. Cath. Colls. and Univs.; mem. Pres.s' Network of Campus Compact. Contbr. articles to profl. jours. Former mem. bd. govs. Genesee Hosp., Rochester; bd. dirs. Greater Rochester Visitors Bur. Mem. AAUW, Mediaeval Acad. Am., Nat. Assn. Ind. Colls. and Univs., Assn. Commonwealth Lang. and Lit. Studies, Greater Rochester C. of C. (bd. dirs.), Oak Hill Country Club, Phi Delta Kappa.

BESTWICK, WARREN WILLIAM, retired construction company executive; b. Missoula, Mont., June 27, 1922; s. William Andrew and Beatrice Anna (Eddy) B.; m. Glenette Haas, Sept. 11, 1949; children: Sharon Kaye, Carol Eddy, Jan Marie. Student, Glendale Coll., 1941, U. Mont., 1942; BA, U. Wash., 1949, postgrad., 1950. Sr. acct. Frederick & Nelson, Seattle, 1950; contr., bus. mgr. Va. Mason Hosp., Seattle, 1958-64; contr. Bumstead Woolford Co., Seattle, 1964-68; contr., treas. Wash. Asphalt Co., Seattle, 1968-72; exec. v.p., sec., treas. Wilder Constrn. Co., Inc., Bellingham, Wash., 1972-77, pres., COO, CFO, 1977-89, vice-chmn., 1989-92; ret., 1992. Past bd. dirs. Consumers Choice, Bellingham; bd. govs. Va. Mason Med. Ctr., Seattle; past chmn. Area IV adv. bd. Wash. Dept. Commerce and Econ. Devel.; past dir., vice chmn. Mt. Baker Bank, Bellingham; past bd. dirs. adv. bd. Mt. Baker Coun. Boy Scouts Am. Col., pilot USMCR. Decorated DFC (3), Air medal (7). Mem. Assn. Wash. Bus. (past dir.), Whatcom County Devel. Coun. (past dir. and pres.), Bellingham C. of C. (past dir.), Shukson Found. (past dir., pres., bd. dirs.), Marine Res. Officers Assn. (past dir. Seattle), Res. Officers Assn., Marine Corps League, The Beavers (Constrn. hon., emeritus), United for Wash., U. Wash. Alumni Assn., Ret. Officers Assn., Marine Aviation Assn., World Affairs Coun., Wash. Athletic Club (Seattle), Bellingham Golf and Country Club, Bellingham Yacht Club, Rotary (past pres.). Home: 233 N State St Bellingham WA 98225-5323 Home: PO Box 2032 Rancho Santa Fe CA 92067-2032

BETANCOURT, HECTOR MAINHARD, psychology scientist, educator; b. Chile, Sept. 1, 1949; came to U.S. 1979; s. Hector and Eleonora (Mainhard) B.; m. Bernardita Sahli; children: Paul, Daniel. BA, Cath. U., Santiago, Chile, 1976; MA, UCLA, 1981, PhD in Psychology, 1983. From asst. prof. to assoc. prof. psychology Cath. U., Santiago, Chile, 1977-79, 83-85; from assoc. prof. to prof. of psychology Loma Linda U., Riverside, Calif., 1985-93, chmn., 1990-93; prof. psychology Grad. Sch. Loma Linda U., Calif., 1993—; internat. cons. in grad. edn./tng. in psychology, 1997—. Editor Interam. Psychologist, 1982-86; mem. edit. bd. Jour. Cmty. Psychology, 1986-89, Spanish Jour. Social Psychology, 1986—, Conflict and Peace, 1993—, Jour. Personality and Social Psychology, 1997-98; contbr. articles to profl. jours. Recipient Rotary Found. award for Internat. Understanding, Rotary Internat., 1976-77; Fulbright fellow, UCLA, 1979-80. Mem. APA (exec. com. and chmn. task force on ethnicity, divsn. 48 peace psychology 1994-95, pres. 1997-98), Internat. Soc. Polit. Psychology, Internat. Soc. Cross-Cultural Psychology (exec. com. 1984-86), Interam. Soc. Psychology (sec.-gen. 1983-87), Soc. for Psychol. Study Social Issues (U.S. and Can. 1999—), Soc. Personality and Social Psychology. Avocations: internat. politics, literature, philosophy. Office: Loma Linda U Dept Psychology Grad S Loma Linda CA 92350

BETANCOURT L., ANTONIO L., association executive; b. Belen de Umbria, Colombia, Jan. 9, 1944; came to U.S., 1967; s. Angel Maria and Pastora (Lopez) B.; m. Kyoko Kagawa, July 1, 1982; children: Kiantar, Annika, Kyboter, Isaac. Sec. gen. CAUSA Internat., N.Y.C., 1979-89; asst. to pres. New World Comms., N.Y.C., 1980-83; exec. v.p. Internat. Security Coun., Washington, 1984-90; exec. dir. Assn. for the Unity of Latin Am., Washington, 1983—, Summit Coun. for World Peace, Washington, 1981—; dep. sec. gen. Fedn. for World Peace, Washington, 1991—; pres. Young Gruppe, Inc., Washington, 1992—, News & Communication, Inc., 1993—; pres. Group Internat. Arte, Washington, 1996—, World Inst. for Devel. and Peace, 1996—. Exec. editor jour. Global Affairs, 1984-90; exec. dir. conf. procs. Mem. Family Fedn. for World Peace and Unification, N.Y.C., 1996—. Recipient commendation Cath. U., La Plata, Argentina, 1984, Acad. award Mexican Acad. Internat. Law, 1985, Grand Medal of Peace, Dem. People's Republic of Korea, 1996; named hon. citizen Santo Domingo City, 1987. Mem. Am. Fgn. Svc. Assn. (internat. assoc.), Corcoran Gallery, N.Y. Acad. Sci., Oxford Club, Asia Soc., Korea Soc., Wilson Ctr. for Scholars. Avocations: gardening, antique collecting and restoration, hiking, fishing. Home: 6305 Queens Chapel Rd University Park MD 20782-2131 Office: Summit Coun for World Peace 3600 New York Ave NE Washington DC 20002-1947

BETCHEN, STEPHEN J., marital, family and sex therapist; b. Coral Gables, Fla., Oct. 5, 1954; s. Herbert and Millie B.; m. Maria J. Wells, July 12, 1982; children: Jennifer, Melanie. BA, Rutgers U., 1978; MSW, U. Pa., 1981, DSW, 1986. Staff therapist Drenk Guidance Ctr., Mt. Holly, N.J., 1981-85, Marriage & Family Therapy Assocs., Marlton, N.J., 1985-87; sr. therapist, supr. Marriage Coun. Phila., 1986-92; pvt. practice Cherry Hill, N.J., 1992—; postdoctoral fellow N.Y. Hosp.-Cornell Med. Ctr., 1987-88; psychoanalytic fellow Inst. Phila. Assn. Psychoanalysis, 1998-99; clin. assoc. psychiatry U. Pa. Sch. Medicine, 1989-92. Columnist Courier-Post Newspaper, 1992—. Mem. Am. Assn. Marriage & Family Therapists, Am. Assn. Sex Educators, Counselors and Therapists, Soc. Sex Therapy & Rsch., Am. Bd. Sexology, Nat. Assn. Social Workers, Acad. Clin. Sexologists. Office: 1930 Marlton Pike E Ste X114 Cherry Hill NJ 08003-4214

BETHE, HANS ALBRECHT, physicist, educator; b. Strassburg, Alsace-Lorraine, Germany, July 2, 1906; came to U.S., 1935; s. Albrecht Theodore and Anna (Kuhn) B.; m. Rose Ewald, 1939; children: Henry, Monica. Ed. Goethe Gymnasium, Frankfurt on Main, U. Frankfurt; Ph.D., U. Munich, 1928; D.Sc., Bklyn. Poly. Inst., 1950, U. Denver, 1952, U. Chgo., 1953, U. Birmingham, 1956, Harvard U., 1958. Instr. in theoretical physics univs. of Frankfort, Stuttgart, Munich and Tubingen, 1928-33; lectr. univs. of Manchester and Bristol, Eng., 1933-35; asst. prof. Cornell U., 1935, prof., 1937-75, prof. emeritus, 1975—; dir. theoretical physics div. Los Alamos Sci. Lab., 1943-46; Mem. Presdl. Study Disarmament, 1958; mem. Pres.'s Sci. Adv. Com., 1956-60. Author: Mesons and Fields, 1953, Elementary Nuclear Theory, 1957, Quantum Mechanics of One-and Two-Electron Atoms, 1957, Intermediate Quantum Mechanics, 1964; contbr. Handbuch der Physik, 1933, Revs. Modern Physics, 1936-37, Phys. Rev., Astrophys. Jour. Recipient A. Cressy Morrison prize N.Y. Acad. Sci., 1938-40; Presdl. Medal of Merit, 1946; Max Planck medal, 1953; Enrico Fermi award AEC, 1961; Nobel Prize in physics, 1967; Nat. Medal of Sci., 1976; Vannevar Bush award NSF, 1985; Einstein Peace prize Albert Einstein Peace Prize Found., 1993, Oersted prize Am. Assn. Physics Tchrs. Fgn. mem. Royal Soc. London; mem. Am. Philos. Soc., NAS (Henry Draper medal 1968), Am. Phys. Soc. (pres. 1954), Am. Astron. Soc. Office: Cornell U Newman Lab Ithaca NY 14853

BETHEA, LOUISE HUFFMAN, allergist; b. Jackson, Miss., Mar. 27, 1947; d. Theodore G. and Frances (Allen) Huffman; m. Henry L. Bethea, Sept. 15, 1946; children: Mary, Samuel, Sarah. BS, Miss. Coll., Clinton, 1968; MD, U. Miss., 1972. Diplomate Am. Bd. Allergy and Immunology, Am. Bd. Pediatrics. Resident pediatrics U. Miss., Jackson, 1973-75; fellow allergy & immunology U. Fla., 1977-79; pvt. practice Houston, 1983—; instr. pediatrics U. Miss., 1975-77, U. Fla., 1979-80; active Houston Northwest Med. Ctr., 1983—; cons. in field. Fellow Am. Acad. Allergy and Immunology, Am. Coll. Allergy, Am. Acad. Pediatrics. Republican. Episcopalian. Avocations: photography, travel, arts and crafts. Home: 92 Hollymead Dr The Woodlands TX 77381-5121 Office: 17070 Red Oak Dr Ste 107 Houston TX 77090-2615*

BETHEL, MARILYN JOYCE, librarian; b. Detroit, Jan. 14, 1935; d. Thomas Agmey and Mary Helen (Lisek) Hepfner; m. Herschel Earl Bethel, June 20, 1960 (div. Mar. 1969); 1 child, Mary Joyce. BA in Edn., Fla. Atlantic U., 1974; MLS, La. State U., 1975, MEd, 1976; postgrad., Fla. Atlantic U., 1977-78. Cert. reading specialist, Fla. Cons. Fla. Diagnostic and Learning Resources, Ft. Lauderdale, 1979-80; librarian Cocnut Creek (Fla.) Elem. Sch., 1980-82; cons. Fla. Coll. Bus., Pompano, 1982-84; librarian Broward County Librs., Hallandale, Fla., 1983; cataloger Broward County Librs., Ft. Lauderdale, 1983-90; br. head Broward County Librs., Deerfield, 1990-92; librarian Broward County Librs., Pompano, 1992-95, Ft. Lauderdale, 1995—; cons. Fla. Diagnostic and Learning Resources, 1979-80; mem. behavioral objectives writing team Broward County Spl. Edn., 1981. Advisor to periodical Biography Today, 1992—; writer newsletter Exceptional Student, 1979-80. Vol. crisis counselor Sexual Assault Treatment Ctr., Broward County, Fla., 1977-78; lectr., instr. New Covenant Ch., Pompano, 1984-87. With USAF, 1968-69. Recipient Cert. of Appreciation, Bd. County Commrs., Ft. Lauderdale, 1978. Mem. ALA (com. for cataloging for children 1989-95, liaison Freedom to Read 1979-80), Fla. Libr. Assn., Broward County Libr. Assn., Nat. Alzheimers Assn. Republican. Presbyterian. Avocations: floral arranging, snorkeling, swimming, reading. Home: 272 NE 39th Ct Pompano Beach FL 33064-3545 Office: Broward County Librs 100 S Andrews Ave Fort Lauderdale FL 33301-1830

BETHEL, PAULETTE MARTINEZ, retired military officer, counselor; b. New Orleans, Sept. 24, 1952; d. Ernest and Mary Ann (Ferdinand) Carrie; m. Charles Ruffin Burchell, Mar. 3, 1973 (div. 1980); m. Ralph Bethel, Mar. 18, 1984; children: Ralph Alvin, Wendy Taiwai, Kimberly Yvonne, Marc Alexander. BS, La. State U., 1977; MPA, U. Philippines, 1986; MA in Counseling, St. Mary's U., 1996; postgrad., U. Incarnate Word. Lic. profl. counselor. Commd. 2d lt. USAF, 1980, advanced through grades to maj., 1992; officer in charge fo material control USAF, Castle AFB, Calif., 1980-81; asst. opers. support branch chief, stock control officer, stroage and issue officer 3rd supply squadron USAF, Clark Air Base, Philippines, 1981-86; mgr. forward stock program USAF, Wright-Patterson AFB, Ohio, 1986-87, dir. assured distrbn. syss. Logistics Mgmt. Syss. Ctr., 1987-89, airforce supplies syss. analyst Logistics Mgmt. Syss. Ctr., 1990-91; mgr. F100 engine/pacer growht program San Antonio Air Logistics Ctr. USAF, Kelly AFB, Tex., 1991-92; chief spl. opers. sect. Headquarters air Edn. and Tng. Command Directorate of Logistics USAF, Randolph AFB, Tex., 1992-93; chief combat opers support flight 37th supply sq. USAF, Lackland AFB, Tex., 1993-95; ret. USAF, 1995; counselor drug and alcohol Ctrl. Tex. Parole Violator Facility Wackenhut Corrections Corp., San Antonio, 1995-96; therapist GMR Turning Point Ctr., 1996-97; assoc. Counseling Assocs. San Antonio, 1996—; dir. staff devel., therapist ATEX Healthcare, 1997; founder, pres. Betson Cons. Group, 1998—; crisis intervention coun. Rape Crisis Ctr., San Antonio, 1998—; pvt. practice Counseling Assocs. of San Antonio; assoc. marriage and family therapist; crisis intervention counselor Rape Crisis Ctr. Mentor for teenage girls at high risk for pregnancy with Dayton (Ohio) City Pub. Sch. Sys., 1986-90, Edgewood Ind. Sch. Dist., San Antonio, 1991-92. Mem. USAF Women's Officer's Assn. (bd. dirs.), Am. Assn. Marriage and Family Therapists, Child Abuse Prevention Service Speakers Bureau, Amer. Cancer Soc. Speakers Bureau, assoc. mem., volunteer, United Way Prog. Review Team, Alpha Kappa Alpha. Avocations: mentoring, dancing, reading. Home: 11810 Radcliff Ct San Antonio TX 78253-5951

BETHJE, ROBERT, retired general surgeon; b. Braunschweig, Fed. Republic of Germany, Nov. 15, 1922; came to U.S., 1923; s. Robert Paul and Elisabeth Augusta (Lieder) B.; m. Maria Vatral, June 11, 1955; children: Susan Leslie, Robert Eric, Alan Randolph. BS cum laude, CCNY, 1945; MD, N.Y. Med. Coll., 1949. Diplomate Nat. Bd., 1950, Am. Bd. Surgery, 1958. Instr. Biology CCNY, 1946-48; asst. treas. Broome County Med. Soc., Binghamton, N.Y., 1964, v.p., 1965, pres., 1966; pres. med. staff Ideal Hosp., Endicott, N.Y., 1973-76, chief of surgery, 1971-77; chief of surgery Wilson Meml. Hosp., Johnson City, N.Y., 1979-80. Bd. dirs. Broome-Tioga Assn. for Retarded Children, Binghamton, 1983—. Capt. U.S. Army Med. Corps, 1951-53. Fellow Am. Coll. Surgeons; mem. Rotary (Endicott v.p. 1980-81, dir. 1981-84, pres. 1985-86). Avocations: painting, photography, fishing, hunting, gardening. Home: 4 Ivanhoe Rd Binghamton NY 13903-1424

BETHLEN, FRANCIS R., business and economics educator, food distribution engineering specialist; b. Budapest, Hungary, July 2, 1925; came to U.S., 1952; s. Paul and Gabriella (Serenyi) B.; m. Ilona R. Szentimrey, Oct. 7, 1948; children: Anna Maria, Mihaly Antal. BS, Polytechnic U., Budapest, 1947; MS, Cornell U., 1956; PhD, Purdue U., 1962. Teaching asst. dept. agrl. econs. Purdue U., Lafayette, Ind., 1959-61; assoc. prof. econs. SUNY, Plattsburgh, 1961-63, prof., chmn. dept. econs., 1963-69, prof. bus. and econs., 1971-78, prof. mktg., 1981-96; sr. vis. Fulbright prof. dept. econs. Rosario U., Cordoba, Argentina, 1969-70; vis. sr. prof. econs. and mktg. U. Nicaragua, Managua, 1978-79, UN Mgmt. Inst., Arusha, Tanzania, 1979; vis. lectr. Rosario, Argentina, 1987, Budapest, 1989, 90, Moscow, 1990, 91, UFA, Bashkiria, 1992; exec. tng. specialist, Hungary, 1989, 90, 91, 92; internat. mktg. cons., Costa Rica, 1994, 96-97, Argentina, 1995, Hungary, 1996, 97; market extensionist Grange League Fedn., Batavia, N.Y., 1955-59; grad. rsch. asst. Cornell U., Ithaca, N.Y., 1953-56; livestock market specialist Est. San Antonio, Olavarria, Argentina, 1949-52; milling products specialist Aranka Flour Mills, Bicske, Hungary, 1945-48. Contbr. articles to profl. jours. Fulbright scholar, 1969, 70, 78. Mem. Am. Mktg. Assn., Rakoczi Found. (bd. dirs. 1984—), Global Energy Soc., Internat. Econs. Soc., Latin Am. Project Evaluators. Rotary. Knight of St. John of Hospitallers. Home: 4538 Kingsmere Sarasota FL 34235-2627 Office: SUNY Redcay Bldg Beekman St Plattsburgh NY 12901-2701

BETHLEN, ILONA R., designer, educator; b. Budapest, Hungary, Apr. 10, 1921; came to U.S., 1952; d. Dezso and Vilma Gizella (Laszlo) Szentimrey; m. Francis R. Bethlen, Oct. 7, 1948; children: Anna Maria Bethlen LaFontaine, Mihaly Antal. MS, U. Econ. Sci., Budapest, Hungary, 1945; MA, Liszt Acad. Music, Budapest, Hungary, 1947; BA, SUNY, Plattsburgh, 1982. Tchg. asst. Econ. Faculty Jozsef Nador U., Budapest, Hungary, 1943-46; lady driver, trainer Hungarian Horse Racing Assn., Budapest, 1946-48; supplier, artist Gath & Chaves Dept. Stores, Buenos Aires, 1949-52; trainer of standardbreds A. Miller Stables, E. Aurora, N.Y., 1952-56; decorator, art adv. Am. Wallpaper Co., Buffalo, 1956-61; art instr. St. Mary Acad., Champlain, 1962-68; prof. art Coll. Cont. Edn. SUNY, Plattsburgh, 1970-81; gallery mgr. Four Winds Gallery, Burlington, Vt., 1970-77; artist, exhibitor Holt & Renfrew Co., Lupton DuVal Co., others, Toronto and Montreal, 1982—. chairperson disasters ARC, N.Y., 1965-75; bd. dirs., chair edn. progress Joint Coun. Econ. Opportunities, Plattsburgh, N.Y., 1980-88. Named Outstanding Lady-Horse Trainer Buffalo Courier Express, 1952. Mem. AAUW, Rotary (mem. bd. world cmty. svcs. 1985-97, bd. dirs. Sarasota Keys 1997—). Avocations: travel, painting, small gardening.

BETHUNE, GORDON, airline executive; married; 3 children. BS, Abilene Christian U., Dallas; AMP, Harvard U., 1992. Lic. comml. pilot, lic. airframe and power plant mechanic. V.p. engring. and maintenance Braniff and Western Airlines; sr. v.p. ops. Piedmont Airlines; v.p., gen. mgr. Renton div. Boeing Comml. Airplane Group, 1988-94; chmn., CEO Continental Airlines, Inc., Houston, 1994—. Served with USN. Named Aerospace Laureate for comml. air transport Aviation Week & Space Technology, 1996. Office: Continental Airlines Inc PO Box 4607 Houston TX 77210-4607*

BETINIS, EMANUEL JAMES, physics and mathematics educator; b. Oak Park, Ill., Oct. 31, 1927; s. James Emanuel and Ioanna Helen (Kallas) B.; children: Demetrios, Joanna, Markos. BS in Chemistry and Math., Northwestern U., 1950; MS in Applied Math., U. Ill., 1952; MS in Physics, U. Chgo., 1979. Aerodynamicist Northrop Aviation, Hawthorne, Calif., 1953-54; theoretical reactor physicist Atomics Internat., Canoga Park, Calif., 1954-57; applied sci. rep. IBM, Chgo., 1957-61; math. cons. Math. Cons. Svc., Chgo., 1961-81; adj. prof. math. and physics IIT, Roosevelt U., Chgo., 1981-88; mathematician Batelle Meml. Labs., Willowbrook, Ill., 1988-89; asst. prof. physics Elmhurst (Ill.) Coll., 1990—. Contbr. articles to Jour. Geophys. Rsch., Jour. Brit. Interplanetary Soc., Hadronic Jour., Matrix, Lensor Soc. Great Britain. Mem. PTO. With U.S. Army, 1946-47. Fellow Brit. Interplanetary Soc.; mem. Am. Nuclear Soc., Sigma Pi Sigma, Pi Mu Epsilon. Republican. Orthodox. Achievements include patent in golf ball trajectory with lift and drag; research in analytic solution of boundary-value problems in arbitrary geometry, special relativity, quantum mechanical proof of speed of light limitation, analytic solution of 3 dimensional heat conduction equation in arbitrary geometry, nuclear potential and prediction of 470MeV elementary particles, analytic solution of non-linear hydrodynamics equations; development and manufacture of devices for entropy and Biot-Savart physics experiments, calculation of velocity of nucleons in the deuteron, EM theory relativistic time dilation and removal of velocity of light speed limit, Em theory relativistic Schroedinger equations, scattering cross-section for superluminal particles, faster than light quantum mechanics. Office: Elmhurst Coll Dept Physics Box 47 190 Prospect Ave Elmhurst IL 60126-3271

BETLYON, JOHN WILSON, religion educator, archaeologist, clergyman; b. York, Pa., May 5, 1949; s. John Newton and Genevieve June (Gunderman) B.; m. Stephanie Lois Edgerly, May 22, 1976; children—Seth, Frances, Jesse. B.A., Bucknell U., 1971; M.T.S., Harvard U., 1973, Ph.D., 1978. Dir., Carthage Research Inst., Khereddine, Tunisia, 1976-77; minister United Methodist Ch., Port Matilda, Pa., 1977-78; chaplain, asst. prof. N.C. Wesleyan Coll., Rocky Mount, N.C., 1978-80; campus minister Lycoming Coll., Williamsport, Pa., 1980-81; chaplain, assoc. prof. dept. religion Smith Coll., Northampton, Mass., 1981—; numismatist Am. Excavations in Punic Carthage, Tunisia, 1974-79, Umm el-Jimal Project, Jordan, 1984—; fin. dir. Joint Archaeol. Expdn. to Tell El-Hesi, 1978—; adminstrv. dir., numismatist Limes Arabicus Project, Jordan, 1982—; bd. dirs. Higher Edn. Commn., So. New Eng. Conf., United Methodist Ch., 1982—. Author: The Coinage of Phoenicia: The Pre-Alexandrine Period, 1982. Contbr. articles to profl. jours. Bd. dirs. Soc. Organized Against Racism, Boston, 1981—, United Ministries in Higher Edn., Boston, 1982—. Recipient grad. research award Am. Numis. Soc., 1976; Zion research award Am. Schs. of Oriental Research, 1976; Thompson Fund. research award Am. Philos. Soc., 1979; research award Am. Philos. Soc., 1985. Mem. Am. Schs. Oriental Research, Archaeol. Inst. Am. (sec. Western Mass. soc.), Soc. Bibl. Lit. Avocations: cycling; traveling; softball. Home: 63 Dryads Grn Northampton MA 01060-2912 Office: Smith Coll Office of Chaplain Northampton MA 01063

BETSINGER, PEGGY ANN, oncological nurse; b. St. Charles, Mo., Dec. 11, 1939; d. Edward and Dorothy (Brockgrietens) Oelklaus; m. Richard Betsinger, Mar. 17, 1964 (div. Mar. 1986); children: Bryon, Alicia. Diploma, St. John's Hosp. Sch. Nursing, St. Louis U., St. Louis, 1960; student, U. Colo., Colorado Springs, 1973, St. Joseph Coll., 1985. RN, Ohio, Mo.; cert. oncology-chemotherapy nurse. Charge nurse oncology unit Grandview Hosp., Dayton, 1976-81; asst. dir. nurses Alta Nursing Home, Dayton, Ohio, 1982-86; nurse oncology unit De Paul Hosp., St. Louis, 1986—. Vol. nurse ARC, 1971-74. Capt. Nurse Corps, USAF, 1961-64. Mem. Oncology Nursing Soc.

BETT, RICHARD ARNOT HOME, philosophy educator; b. London, June 10, 1957; came to U.S., 1980; s. David Charles Gore and Rosemary Ann (Ball) B.; m. Geraldine Aileen Henchy, May 26, 1986. BA, Oxford (Eng.) U., 1980, MA, 1983; PhD, U. Calif., Berkeley, 1986. Asst. prof. U. Tex., Arlington, 1986-91; vis. asst. prof. Johns Hopkins U., Balt., 1991, asst. prof., 1991-94, assoc. prof. dept. philosophy, 1994—. Author, translator: Sextus Empiricus, Against the Ethicists, 1997; contbr. articles to profl. jours. Recipient jr. fellowship Ctr. for Hellenic Studies, Washington, 1994-95. Mem. Am. Philosophical Assn., Soc. Ancient Greek Philosophy, N.Am. Nietzsche Soc. Office: Johns Hopkins U Dept Philosophy 3400 N Charles St Baltimore MD 21218-2680

BETTENDORF, JERRY, airport administrator. AA, C.C. of Air Force, 1975. Dir. airpark Pinal County Airpark, Ariz., 1980-88; op. supr., airport mgr. Grand Canyon Nat. Park Airport, 1988-91; dir. aviation Laughlin/Bullhead Internat. Airport, Bullhead City, Ariz., 1991—. Staff sgt. USAF, 1969-80. Mem. Assn. Airport Execs. (exec. mem.), Ariz. Airport Assn. (exec. mem.). Office: Laughlin/Bullhead Internat Airport 600 Hwy 95 Bullhead City AZ 86429

BETTERIDGE, FRANCES CARPENTER, retired lawyer, mediator; b. Rutherford, N.J., Aug. 25, 1921; d. James Dunton and Emily (Atkinson) Carpenter; m. Albert Edwin Betteridge, Feb. 5, 1949 (div. 1975); children: Anne, Albert Edwin, James, Peter. A.B., Mt. Holyoke Coll., 1942; J.D., N.Y. Law Sch., 1978. Bar: Conn. 1979, Ariz. 1982. Technician in charge blood banks Roosevelt Hosp., N.Y.C. and Mountainside Hosp., Montclair, N.J., 1943-49; substitute tchr. Greenwich High Sch. (Conn.), 1978-79; intern and asst. to labor contracts office Town of Greenwich, 1979-80; vol. referee Pima County Juvenile Ct., Tucson, 1981-85, judge Pro Tempore Pima County Justice Cts., 1988-91; sole practice immigration law, Tucson, 1982-87; commr. Juvenile Ct., Pima County Superior Ct., Tucson, 1985-87; hearing officer Small Claims Ct., Pima County Justice Cts., Tucson, 1982; mediator Family Crisis Svc., Tucson, 1982-85. Pres. High Sch. PTA, Greenwich, 1970, PTA Council, 1971; mem. Greenwich Bd. Edn., 1971-76, sec., 1973-76; com. chmn. LWV Tucson, 1981, bd. dirs., 1984-85; bd. dirs., sec. Let The Sun Shine Inc., Tucson, 1981—; vol. referee Pima County Superior Ct., 1981-85; lectr. Tucson Mus. Art, 1994—; part time site coord. Elderhostel, Oaxaca, Mex., 1995. Mem. ABA, Conn. Bar Assn., Ariz. Bar Assn., Pima County Bar Assn., Tucson Sr. Acad., Point o'Woods Club. Republican. Congregationalist. Avocation: imports folk art from Oaxaca, Mex. Home and Office: 5320 N Campbell Ave Tucson AZ 85718-4908

BETTI, JOHN ANSO, federal official, former automobile manufacturing company executive; b. Ottawa, Ill., Jan. 6, 1931; s. Louis and Ida (Dallari) B.; m. Joan Doyle, Aug. 22, 1953; children: Diane , Denise, Donna (dec.), Joan. BSMechE, Ill. Inst. Tech., 1952; MS in Engring., Chrysler Inst. Engring., 1954. Registered profl. engr., Mich. Student engr. to asst. chief engr. Chrysler Corp., 1952-62; with Ford Motor Co., 1962-89, from exec. engr. body engring. to v.p., gen. mgr. truck ops., 1962-76; v.p. product devel. Ford of Europe, Inc., Warley, Essex, Eng., 1976-79; also dir. Ford of Europe, Inc.; with N.Am. Automotive Ops., Dearborn, Mich., 1979-84, v.p. powertrain and chassis ops., 1979-83, v.p. mfg. and bus. devel., 1983-84; exec. v.p. tech. affairs and operating staffs Ford Motor Co., Mich., 1985-88; bd. dirs. fin. and exec. coms. Ford Motor Co., Dearborn, Mich., exec. v.p. diversified products ops., 1988-89; undersecretary of def., acquisition and nat. armaments dir. Dept. Def., Washington, 1989-91; instr. Lawrence Inst. Engring., Wayne State U., Detroit, 1953-59; chmn. bd. Ford Motor Co., Caribbean Inc., 1979-84, Ensite Ltd. Can., 1979-84, Ford Aerospace corp., 1988-89, Ford Electronics and Refrigeration Corp., 1988-89; dir. collins & Aikman Corp., 1991-94; mem. dir. compensation com. Breed Tech., 1992-94, Kaysor-Roth Corp., 1993-94. Bd. dirs. Mich. Opera Theatre, 1984-87; trustee Detroit Inst. for Children, 1985-89; mem. nat. adv. com. U. Mich. Engring. Sch., 1985-89; chmn. bd. trustees GMI Engring. and Mgmt. Inst., 1985-89. Recipient Alumni Profl. Achievement award Ill. Inst. Tech., 1980; John Morse Meml. scholar. Mem. NAE, Soc. Automotive Engrs., Lost Tree Club (N. Palm Beach, Fla.), Jupiter Hills Club (Tequesta, Fla.), Tau Beta Pi, Pi Tau Sigma, Alpha Sigma Phi, Beta O mega Nu. E-mail: jbetti@concentric.net.

BETTINGHAUS, ERWIN PAUL, cancer research center administrator; b. Peoria, Ill., Oct. 28, 1930; s. Erwin Paul and Paula (Bretscher) B.; m. Carole Irma Overmier, Apr. 5, 1952; children: Karen Lee, Joyce Anne, Bruce Alan. B.A., U. Ill., 1952, Ph.D., 1959; M.A., Bradley U., 1953. Instr. Mich. State U., East Lansing, 1958-60, asst. prof., 1960-64, assoc. prof., 1964-69, prof., 1969-97; prof. emeritus Mich. State U., East Lansing, 1997—; chmn. dept. communication Mich. State U., East Lansing, 1972-76; dean Coll. Communication Arts and Scis., 1976-96, dean emeritus, 1997—; dep. dir. AMC Cancer Rsch. Ctr., Denver, 1997—; vis. prof. U. Okla., 1970-71. Author: The Nature of Proof, 1971, Persuasive Communication, 1994. Mem. Nat. Cancer Adv. Bd., 1988-94. With U.S. Army, 1953-56. Mem. AAAS, APA, Internat. Comm. Assn. (pres. 1982), Am. Comm. Assn., Assn. for Edn. in Journalism, Assn. Comm. Adminstrn. (pres. 1991). Home: 2170 S Parfet Dr Lakewood CO 80227-1900

BETTIS, JEROME ABRAM, professional football player; b. Detroit, Feb. 16, 1972. Student, U. Notre Dame. Running back L.A. Rams (moved to St. Louis 1995), 1993-94, St. Louis Rams, 1995, Pitts. Steelers, 1996-97; resigned, 1997. Named NFL Rookie of Yr., Sporting News, 1993; selected to Pro Bowl, 1993, 94, 96. Office: Three Rivers Stadium 300 Stadium Cir Pittsburgh PA 15212-5729*

BETTIS, JOHN GREGORY, songwriter; b. Long Beach, Calif., Oct. 24, 1946; s. Wayne Douglas and Nellie Jane (House) B. Songwriter, music pub. Warner/Chappel Music, 1976-82; songwriter, pub. John Bettis Music, Santa Monica, Calif., 1982—. Lyricist: (songs) Yesterday Once More, 1973 (Gold Record), Top of the World, 1974 (Gold Record), Heartland, Can You Stop the Rain, 1991, (Grammy nominee 1991), Promise Me You'll Remember, 1990 (acad. awards nominee 1991), One Moment In Time, 1988 (Emmie 1989), Crazy for You, 1985 (Gold Record), Slow Hand, 1981 (Gold Record), Human Nature, 1983 (Grammy cert.-Album of Yr. 1984); lyricist songs for movies including Say Anything, Star Trek V, Cocktail, Nothing in Common, Godfather Part III; lyricist TV theme songs. Recipient Top TV Series award for Growing Pains, ASCAP, 1986, for Just the Ten of Us, ASCAP, 1987, for Empty Nest, ASCAP, 1990, 34 Gold Records, Rec. Industry Assn. Am., 1970-90, 7 Platinum Records, Rec. Industry Assn. Am., 1970-90, 32 Performance awards ASCAP, 1970-90. Mem. ASCAP (bd. rev. 1982-88, bd. dirs. 1995—), Nat. Acad. Songwriters (bd. dirs. 1980-94, chmn. bd. dirs. 1985-87). Avocations: scuba diving, sailing. Office: John Bettis Music PO Box 668 Sunset Beach CA 90742-0668

BETTISCH, JOHANN, linguist, researcher; b. Temeschburg, Rumania, July 29, 1932; arrived in Germany, 1990; s. Matthias and Maria (Kanyady) B.; m. Katharina Reitter, Oct. 21, 1959; 1 child, Edmond. Diploma in Russian langs., U. Bucharest, 1957; D in Philology, U. Timisoara, Rumania, 1988. Electrotechnician Electromontaj, Timisoara, 1952-55; fgn. lang. tchr. German and Hungarian schs. Resita, 1957-63; sch. inspector County Caras-Severin, Resita, 1963-67; dep. dir. German H.S., Resita, 1967-74; fgn. lang. lectr. Engring Inst. (now named Eftimie Murgu U.), Resita, 1974-82, prodean, 1982-89; owner Trans. Bur., Stuttgart, 1990O. Author: Breviary of Chinese Literature, 1981, Technical English, 1983, Russian Language for Engineers, 1986, Die Technik auf Deutsch, 1988; editor Lang., Lit. and Folklore, 1969-78; inventor solar pump, plug testing device, language continuity electronic testing, among others; contbr. over 150 articles to profl. publs. With Rumanian mil., 1955-57. Recipient award County Caras-Severin Nat. Inventions Saloon, 1987. Mem. N.Y. Acad. Scis., World Esperanto Assn. Avocations: etymology research, esperanto, science fiction. E-mail: jbettisch@aol.com. Home and Office: Weilimdorfer Strasse 157, 70469 Stuttgart Germany

BETTISON, CYNTHIA ANN, museum director, archaeologist; b. St. Louis, Sept. 8, 1958; d. William Leslie and Barbara Ann (Yunker) B. BA in Anthropology and Biology, Pitzer Coll., 1980; MA in Anthropology, Eastern N.Mex. U., 1983; ABD in Anthropology, U. Calif., Santa Barbara, 1986, PhD in Anthropology, 1998. Asst. curator dept. anthropology U. Calif., Santa Barbara, 1988-89, curator dept. anthropology, 1990-91; dir. Western N.Mex. U. Mus., Silver City, 1991—; co-dir. Western N.Mex. U. Archaeol. Field Sch., 1992, 94, 95; lectr. Western N.Mex. U., 1992, 93, adj. asst. prof. dept. social scis., 1994—; various archaeol. positions, 1981—. Contbr. articles to profl. jours. Recipient Conservation Assessment Program grant, 1994-95, NEH, 1994; Gila Nat. Forest grantee, 1992, 94, 95, Mimbres Region Art Coun. mini grantee, 1992, Silver City Lodgers Tax Bd. grantee, Andrew Isabell Meml. Fund grantee U. Calif., 1990, SIMSE grantee, 1994-95, 95-96. Mem. AAUW, Am. Assn. Mus., Am. Anthrop. Assn., Am. Soc. Conservation Archaeology, N.Mex. Mus. Assn., Soc. for Am. Archaeology, Archaeol. Soc. N.Mex., N.Mex. Archaeol. Coun. (sec. 1993-94), Coun. Mus. Anthropology (sec. 1992-94), Mountain Plains Mus. Assn., Univ. Women's Club, Univ. Club, Optimist Club (sec. Silver City chpt. 1992), Silver City Rotary Club, Silver City Grant County C. of C., Chpt. AG PEO, Phi Kappa Phi. Office: Western NM Univ Mus 1000 W College Ave Silver City NM 88061-4158

BETTMAN, GARY BRUCE, lawyer; b. N.Y.C., June 2, 1952; s. Howard G. and Gretel J. (Pollack) B.; m. Michelle Weiner, Aug. 24, 1975; children: Lauren, Jordan, Brittany. BS, Cornell U., 1974; JD, NYU, 1977. Bar: N.Y. 1978, N.J. 1978, U.S. Dist. Ct. (so. and ea. dists.) N.Y. 1979. Assoc. Proskauer Rose, N.Y.C., 1977-80, Gutkin, Miller et al, Milburn, N.J., 1980-81; asst. gen. counsel NBA, N.Y.C., 1981-84, v.p., gen. counsel, 1984-89, sr. v.p., gen. counsel, 1989-93; commr. NHL, N.Y.C., 1993—. Mem. N.Y. State Bar Assn., Assn. of Bar of City of N.Y. (chmn. com. on sports law), N.J. Bar Assn., Sports Lawyers Assn. (bd. dirs. 1985-93, entertainment and sports law com. 1990-93), Phi Kappa Phi. Avocations: skiing, sailing, tennis. Office: NHL 47th Flr 1251 Ave of the Americas New York NY 10020

BETTMAN, JAMES ROSS, management educator; b. Laurinburg, N.C., Sept. 15, 1943; s. Roland David and Virginia Gertrude (Hare) B.; m. Joan Carol Scribner, Dec. 16, 1967; 1 child, David James. BA, Yale U., 1965, MPhil, 1969, PhD, 1969. Prof. mgmt. Grad. Sch. Mgmt., UCLA, 1969-82; IBM rsch. prof. Fuqua Sch. Bus., Duke U., Durham, N.C., 1982-83, Burlington Industries prof., 1983—. Author: An Information Processing Theory of Consumer Choice, 1979, The Adaptive Decision Maker, 1993; co-editor Jour. of Consumer Research, 1981-87; contbr. chpts. to books, articles to profl. jours. Named Scholar/Tchr. of Year Duke U., 1988. Fellow APA, Am. Psychol. Soc.; mem. Assn. Consumer Rsch. (bd. dirs. 1976-79, pres. 1987, fellow in consumer behavior 1992), Inst. Ops. Rsch. and Mgmt. Sci., Am. Mktg. Assn. (Harold M. Maynard award 1979, Paul D. Converse award 1992). Democrat. Episcopalian. Home: 213 Huntington Dr Chapel Hill NC 27514-2419 Office: Duke U Fuqua Sch of Bus Durham NC 27708-0120

BETTNER, BETTY LOU, psychotherapist; b. Chester, Pa.; d. Charles Harry Clark and Esther Virginia (Stevenson) Armstrong; m. Walter Steel Bettner; children: Mark S., Michelle, Matthew C., Todd W. BA cum laude, Neumann Col., 1977; MA, Bowie U., 1979; PhD, Union Grad. Sch., 1989. Cert. Clin. Mental Health Counselor, ACA. Asst. dir. family edn. ctr. Cmty. Col. Phila., 1976-78; instr. Neumann Col., Aston, Pa., 1979-82; dir., family edn. ctr. Springfield (Pa.) Sch. Dist., 1980—; psychotherapist pvt. practice, Media, Pa., 1979—; adv. bd. mem. Children and Youth Svc. of Delaware County, Chester, Pa., 1980—, Child Abuse Prevention of Delaware County, Aston, Pa., 1995—. Author: (with others) Raising Kids Who Can, 1990, Responsibility in the Classroom, 1995, A Parents Guide To Understanding and Motivating Children, 1996, Cinderella, The Sequel, 1997; editor: Adlerian Resource Book, 1989. Mem. ACA, N.Am. Soc. Adlerian Psychology (del. assembly, 1982-92, treas., 1984-86, sec., 1986-88, Disting. Svc. award 1990), Am. Mental Health Counselors Assn., Pa. Counselors Assn. Avocations: quilting, embroidery. Office: 1 Old State Rd Media PA 19063-1574

BETTS, BARBARA LANG, lawyer, rancher, realtor; b. Anaheim, Calif., Apr. 28, 1926; d. W. Harold and Helen (Thompson) Lang; m. Roby F. Hayes, July 22, 1948 (dec.); children: John Chauncey IV, Frederick Prescott, Roby Francis II; m. Bert A. Betts, July 11, 1962; 1 child, Bruce Harold; stepchildren: Bert Alan, Randy W., Sally Betts Joynt, Terry Betts Marsteller, Linda Betts Hansen, LeAnn Betts Wilson. BA magna cum laude, Stanford U., 1948; LLB, Balboa U., 1951. Bar: Calif. 1952, U.S. Supreme Ct. 1978. Pvt. practice Oceanside, Calif., 1952-68, San Diego, 1960—, Sacramento, 1962—; ptnr. Roby F. Hayes & Barbara Lang Hayes, 1952-60; city atty. Carlsbad, Calif., 1969-68; v.p. Isle & Oceans Marinas, Inc., 1970-80, W.H. Lang Corp., 1964-69; sec. Internat. Prodn. Assocs., 1968—, Margaret M. McCabe, M.D., Inc., 1977-78. Co-author: (with Bert A. Betts) A Citizen Answers. Chmn. Traveler's Aid, 1952-53; pres. Oceanside-Carlsbad Jr. Chambrettes, 1955-56; vice chmn. Carlsbad Planning Commn., 1959; mem. San Diego Planning commn., 1959; v.p. Oceanside Diamond Jubilee Com., 1958; candidate Calif. State Legislature, 77th Dist., 1954; mem. Calif. Dem. State Ctrl. Com., 1958-66, co-chmn. 1960-62; co-chmn. 28th Congl. Dist.; alt. del. Dem. Nat. Conv., 1960; co-sponsor All Am. B-24 Liberator Collings Found. Named to Fullerton Union H.S. Wall of Fame, 1986; recipient Block S award Stanford U. Mem. ABA, AAUW (legis. com. 1958-59, local pres. 1959-60, asst. state legis. chmn. 1958-59), DAR (regent Oceanside chpt. 1960-61), DFC Soc. (assoc.), Am. Judicature Soc., Nat. Inst. Mcpl. Officers, Calif. Bar Assn., San Diego County Bar Assn., Oceanside C. of C. (sec. 1957, v.p. 1958, dir. 1953-54, 57-59), Heritage League (2d divsn. 8th Air Force), No. San Diego County Assn. Cs. of C. (sec.-treas.), Bus. and Profl. Women's Club (so. dist. legislation chmn. 1958-59), San Diego C. of C., San Diego Hist. Soc., Fullerton Jr. Assistance League, Calif. Scholarship Fedn. (life), Loyola Guild of Jesuit H.S., Soroptimist Internat. (pres. Oceanside-Carlsbad 1958-59, sec. pub. affairs San Diego and Imperial Counties 1954, pres. pres.'s coun. San Diego and Imperial Counties, Mex. 1958-59), Barristers (Stanford, Sacramento), Disting. Flying Cross Soc. (assoc.), Stanford Mothers, Phi Beta Kappa. Home: 441 Sandburg Dr Sacramento CA 95819-2559 Office: Betts Ranch PO Box 306 Elverta CA 95626-0306 also: 1830 Avenida Del Mundo Coronado CA 92118-4026

BETTS, BARBARA STOKE, artist, educator; b. Arlington, Mass., Apr. 19, 1924; d. Stuart and Barbara Lillian (Johnstone) Stoke; m. James William Betts, July 28, 1951; 1 child, Barbara Susan (dec.). BA, Mt. Holyoke Coll., 1946; MA, Columbia U., 1948. Cert. tchr., N.Y., Calif., Hawaii. Art tchr. Walton (N.Y.) Union Schs., 1947-48, Presidio Hill Sch., San Francisco, 1949-51; free-lance artist San Francisco, 1951; art tchr. Honolulu Acad. Arts, summer 1952, 59, 63, 85, spring 61, 64; libr. aide art rm. Libr. of Hawaii, Honolulu, 1959; art tchr. Hanahauoli Sch., Honolulu, 1961-62, Hawaii State Dept. Edn., Honolulu, 1958-59, 64-84; owner Ho'olaule'a Designs, Honolulu, 1973—. Illustrator: Cathedral Cooks, 1964, In Due Season, 1986; exhibited in Hawaii Pavilion Expo '90, Osaka, Japan, State Found. of Culture and Arts, group shows since 1964, one person shows 1991, 96, 99; represented in Arts of Paradise Gallery, Waikiki, 1990—; traveling exhbns. include Pacific Prints, 1991, Printmaking East/West, 1993-95, Hawaii/Wis. Watercolor Show, 1993-94. Mem. Hawaii Watercolor Soc. (newsletter editor 1986-90), Nat. League Am. Pen Women (art chmn. 1990-92, sec. 1992-94, nat. miniature art shows 1991, 92, 93, 95), Honolulu Printmakers (dir. 1986, 87), Assn. Hawaii Artists. Republican. Episcopalian. Avocations: art, travel, writing, photography. Home: 1434 Punahou St Apt 1028 Honolulu HI 96822-4740

BETTS, BERT A., former state treasurer, accountant; b. San Diego, Aug. 16, 1923; s. Bert A. and Alma (Jorgenson) B.; m. Barbara Lang; children: Terry Lou, Linda Sue, Sara Ellen, Bert Alan, Randy Wayne, LeAnn, John Chauncey, Frederick P., Roby F., Bruce H. BBA, Calif. Western U., 1950. CPA, Calif. Accountant John R. Gillette, 1946-48; ptnr. Gillette & Betts, 1949-50; pvt. accounting practice, 1951-54; ptnr. Betts & Munden, Lemon Grove, Calif., 1954-57; sr. ptnr. Bert A. Betts & Co., 1958-59; treas. State of Calif., 1959-67; prin. Bert A. Betts & Assos., 1967-77; chief exec. officer Internat. Prodn. Assos., 1970-87; dir. Lifetime Communities Inc.; gen. partner Sacramento Met. Airport Properties 4, Ltd., 1970—. Author (with Barbara Lang Betts): A Citizen Answers. Mem. Lemon Grove Sch. Bd., 1954-57; Calif. chmn. Max Baer Heart Fund; state employees chmn. Am. Cancer Soc., 1962-64, bd. dirs. county br., 1963-69, Sacramento County campaign chmn., mem. exec. com., 1965, pres. Sacramento chpt., 1967-68; sponsor All Am. B-24 Liberator Collings Found. Served as 1st lt. USAAF, 1942-45. Decorated D.F.C., Air medal with four clusters; recipient Louisville award Municipal Finance Officers Assn. U.S. and Can., 1963; honored by Calif. Municipal Treas.'s Assn., 1964; inductee Hoover H.S. Hall of Fame, San Diego, 1998. Mem. Nat. Assn. State Auditors, Comptrs. and Treas's Mcpl. Forum N.Y., Calif. Soc. CPAs, San Diego Squadron Air Force Assn. (past vice comdr.), Am. Legion, 2d Air Div. Assn., 8th Air Force Hist. Soc., VFW, Confederate Air Force (col.), Native Sons. Golden West, Internat. B-24 Liberator Club, Foresters, Lemon Grove Masonic Lodge, Calif. Scholarship Fedn. (life), Disting. Flying Cross Soc., Sigma Phi Epsilon, Beta Alpha Psi (hon.), Alpha Kappa Psi (hon.). Presbyn. Clubs: Eagles; Men's (Lemon Grove) (pres.), Lions (Lemon Grove) (treas.); Commonwealth. Home: 441 Sandburg Dr Sacramento CA 95819-2559 also: Betts Ranch East Levee Rd Elverta CA 95626 Home: 1830 Avenida Del Mundo Coronado CA 92118-3018

BETTS, DIANNE CONNALLY, economist, educator; b. Tyler, Tex., Sept. 23, 1948; d. William Isaac and Martine (Underwood) Connally; m. Floyd Galloway Betts Jr., Feb. 14, 1973. BA in History, So. Meth. U., 1976, MA in History, 1980; MA in Econ., U. Chgo., 1986; PhD in Econ., U. Tex., 1991. Affiliated scholar Inst. for Rsch. on Women and Gender/Stanford U., 1993—; economist, tech. analyst, fin. cons. Smith Barney, Dallas, 1994—; mem. women studies coun. So. Meth. U., 1993-94, Fulbright campus interviewing com. mem. 1992-93, pub. rels. and devel. liaison dept. econ., 1990-92, faculty mentor U. honors first year mentoring program,adj. asst. prof. dept. econ. and history So. Meth. U., 1992—, vis. asst. prof. 1990-92, faculty, Oxford, summer 1991-93, adj. instr. dept. history, 1989-90, adj. instr. dept. econ., 1985-89, teaching asst. dept. history, spring 1980; lectr. dept. polit. economy U. Tex., Dallas, summer 1988. Author: Crisis on the Rio Grande: Poverty, Unemployment, and Economic Development on the Texas-Mexico Border, 1994, Historical Perspectives on the American Economy: Selected Reading, 1995; contbr. articles to profl. jours. Rsch. Planning grant NSF, 1992; recipient Marguereta Deschner Teaching award, 1991; Humanities and Scis. Merit scholar, 1978. Mem. Am. Econ. Assn., Am. History Assn., Econ. History Assn., Cliometric Soc., Social Sci. History Assn., N.Am. Conf. on British Studies, Nat. Coun. for Rsch. on Women (affiliate), Omicron Delta Epsilon, Phi Alpha Theta. Home: 6267 Revere Pl Dallas TX 75214-3099 Office: Smith Barney 13455 Noel Rd Ste 1800 Dallas TX 75240-6615

BETTS, DORIS JUNE WAUGH, author, English language educator; b. Statesville, N.C., June 4, 1932; d. William Elmore and Mary Ellen (Freeze) Waugh; m. Lowry Matthews Betts, July 5, 1952; children: Doris LewEllyn, David Lowry, Erskine Moore II. Student, Woman's Coll., U. N.C., 1950-53, U. N.C., 1954; DLitt (hon.), Greensboro Coll., 1987; DLitt, U. N.C., Greensboro, 1990, Queens Coll., 1995; LHD, Erskine Coll., 1994; DHL, Pembroke U., 1995. Newspaperwoman Statesville Daily Record, 1950-51, Chapel Hill (N.C.) Weekly and News-Leader, 1953-54; editorial staff Sanford Daily Herald, 1956-57, N.C. Democrat, 1961-62; editor Sanford (N.C.) News Leader, 1962; lectr. creative writing English dept. U. N.C., Chapel Hill, 1966-74, dir. freshman-sophomore English, 1972-76, assoc. prof., 1974-78, dir. Fellows program, 1975-76, prof., 1978—, asst. dean Honors program, 1979-81, chmn. faculty, 1982-85, Alumni Disting. prof., 1983—, chair faculty, 1980-83; vis. lectr. creative writing Duke U., 1971; staff Ind. U. Summer Writers Conf., 1972, 73; mem. bd. Assoc. Writing Programs, lit. panel Nat. Endowment for Arts, 1979-81, chmn., 1981. Author: (story collections) The Gentle Insurrection, 1954 (G.P. Putnam-U. N.C. Fiction award 1954), The Astronomer and Other Stories, 1966, Beasts of the Southern Wild and Other Stories, 1973 (National Book award nomination 1974); (novels) Tall Houses in Winter, 1957 (Sir Walter Raleigh award 1957), The Scarlet Thread, 1964 (Sir Walter Raleigh award 1965), The River to Pickle Beach, 1972, Heading West, 1981, Souls Raised from the Dead, 1994 (Southern Book Critics award, Southeastern Libr. Assn. award), The Sharp Teeth of Love, 1997, (musical) Violet, 1997; editor: Young Writers at Chapel Hill, 1968; contbr.: Three by Three: Masterworks of the Southern Gothic, 1985, others; appeared in dramatized version of The Ugliest Pilgrim as Violet (Academy award Tex. Film Festival); bibliography in The Home Truths of Doris Betts, 1992. Mem. N.C. Tercentenary Commn., 1961-62, Sanford City Sch. Bd., 1965-71; lit. com. NEA, 1979-82, chair, 1982; mem. ctrl. com. Morehead Found., 1978-93, chair 1992-93; bd. trustees Nat. Humanities Ctr., 1993-96, Union Theol. Seminary, Richmond, Va., 1993-97. Recipient Short Story prize Mademoiselle mag., 1953, N.C. medal for lit., 1975, John Dos Passos award, 1983, medal of merit in short story divsn. Am. Acad. Arts and Letters, 1989, Parker award for lit. achievement, 1982-85, John Caldwell award for svc. to humanities, 1992; Guggenheim fellow, 1958-59, Doctor of Letters (hon.) from Greensboro Coll., Queens Coll., UNC-Pembroke, UNC-Greensboro, Erskine Coll., U. of the South, Carolinian Awd., 1998; Thomas Jefferson Awd., 1999, Judge P.E.N. Hemingway Awds., 1999. Mem. N.C. Writers Assn. Office: U NC Dept English 230 Greenlaw Hall CB # 3520 Chapel Hill NC 27599-3520

BETTS, EDWARD, artist; b. Yonkers, N.Y., Aug. 4, 1920; s. Harrison and Mildred (Waterbury) B.; m. Jane Burke, June 2, 1949 (dec. 1984); children: Peter, John, Wendy; m. Edis Hatch, 1986. BA, Yale U., 1942; MFA, U. Ill., 1952. From instr. to prof. art U. Ill., 1949-84, prof. emeritus, 1984—; assoc. Ctr. for Advanced Study, 1968-69. Watercolor and acrylic painter, 1937—; one-man shows include Contemporary Arts Gallery, N.Y.C., 1953, 55, John Heller Gallery, 1956, 59, Charles Feingarten Gallery, Chgo., 1954, 56-57, Midtown Galleries, N.Y.C., 1961, 65, 68, 72, 76, 89, Krannert Art Mus., U. Ill., 1970; group shows include Corcoran biennial exhbns. Contemporary Am. Painting, 1947, 51, 55, 57, 59, Met. Mus. Am. Painting Today, 1950, Bklyn. Internat. Watercolor Exhbn., 1953, 55, 61, NAD, 1953—, Audubon Artists, Am. Water Color Soc., Calif. Water Color Soc., Bklyn. Mus., 1961, Pa. Acad., 1953-54, 59, 61, Nat. Inst. Arts and Letters, 1962, Water Color USA; Springfield (Mo.) Art Mus., 1963-64, 20th Am. Drawing Ann., Norfolk Mus. Arts and Scis., 1963, Hassam Purchase Fund Exhibit, 1961, 63, Maine 100 Artists of the 20th Century, Colby Coll., 1964; represented in permanent collections Fogg Art Mus., Upjohn Pharm. Co., La Jolla Art Ctr., Indpls. Mus. Art, Stephens Coll. (Mo.), Sandoz Pharm. Co., Atlanta U., St. Lawrence U., Irving Trust Co., N.Y.C., USIA Art in Embassies Program, New Britain Mus. Am. Art, Kans. State U., Rochester (N.Y.) Meml. Art Gallery, Springfield (Mo.) Art Mus., Davenport (Iowa) Mcpl. Gallery, Ball State U., Va. Mus. Fine Arts, Butler Inst. Am. Art, Calif. Watercolor Soc., Tupperware Internat., Orlando, Fla., 1st Nat. Bank Boston, Prudential Life Ins. Co., Newark, also pvt. collections; author: Master Class in Watercolor, 1975, Creative Landscape Painting, 1978, Creative Seascape Painting, 1981, Master Class in Watermedia, 1993. "Creative Lives: Four Maine Artists", Ogunquit Museum of American Art, 1996—. Recipient 1st prize oil painting Brick Store Mus. Exhbn., Kennebunk, Maine, 1949, Arts and Artists Miss. Exhbn., Davenport, Iowa, 1950; Grumbacher award Allied Artists, 1950, Bronze medal of honor, 1956; Audubon Artists award, 1951, 72, Gold medal of honor, 1952; Pennell medal Phila. Water Color Club, 1953, award Portland Mus. Summer Art Festival, 1957, Purchase award Hassam Fund Exhbn., 1966, Winsor and Newton award Ga. Water Color Soc., 1979. Mem. NAD (2d Altman prize 1954, Benjamin Altman prize 1957, 59, 66), Am. Water Color Soc. (Silver medal of honor 1953, 59, Remmey award 1966, Cooper award 1977), Art Students League, Ogunquit Art Assn. (past pres.), Nat. Acad. Design, Am. Watercolor Soc., Century Assn. N.Y.C. Home: 2 Wonderbrook Dr Kennebunk ME 04043-6738

BETTS, HENRY BROGNARD, physician, health facility administrator, educator; b. New Rochelle, N.Y., May 25, 1928; s. Henry Brognard and Marguerite Meredith (Denise) B.; m. Monika Christine Paul, Apr. 25, 1970. A.B., Princeton, 1950; M.D., U. Va., 1954; DSc (hon.), Hamilton Coll., 1992. Diplomate: Am. Bd. Phys. Medicine and Rehab. Intern Cin. Gen. Hosp., 1954-55; resident, teaching fellow NYU Med. Center Inst. Rehab. Medicine (Rusk Inst.), N.Y.C., 1958-63; practice medicine, specializing in phys. medicine and rehab. Chgo., 1963—; staff physiatrist Rehab. Inst. Chgo., 1963-64, assoc. med. dir., 1964-65, med. dir., 1965-86, med. dir., CEO, 1986-94, pres., CEO,, 1994-97, past pres., med. dir., 1997; chmn. Rehab. Inst. Found., 1997; chmn. dept. phys. medicine and rehab. Northwestern U. Med. Sch., 1967-94, prof., 1967—, Manguson prof., 1994-97, assoc. mem. Robert H. Lurie Cancer Ctr., 1993-97; cons. Northwestern Meml. Hosp., Chgo.; mem. adv. bd. Commn. on Future Structure of Vets. Health Care, Dept. Vets. Affairs, 1990-92, Vets. Adv. Com. on Rehab., 1990-96; med. adv. com. Spl. Olympics Internat., 1991—. Contbr. articles to profl. jours. Bd. dirs. Nat. Com. Arts for Handicapped (now called Very Spl. Arts), 1981—, The Hastings Ctr., Nat. Orgn. on Disabilities, Aitken Neurosci. Inst.; chmn. Physicians Against Land Mines; mem. traffic safety adv. coun. Ill. Sec. of State Office, 1992—; mem. adv. coun. on spinal cord and head injuries State of Ill. Dept. Rehab. Svc., 1993—. Recipient Disting. Svc. award Ill. Congress Orgns. Physically Handicapped, 1982, Disting. Svc. award Marine Scholarship Found., Chgo., 1993, Individual Leadership award Infinitec-United Cerebral Palsy, 1994, Disting. Pub. Svc. award Am. Acad. Phys. Medicine and Rehab., 1994, John W. Goldschmidt award for excellence in rehab. Nat. Rehab. Hosp., Washington, 1996, James Brady award Ill. Head Injury Assn., 1989, Disting. Svc. award Nat. Orgn. on Disabilities, 1989, Milton Cohen Disting. Career award Nat. Assn. Rehab. Facilities, 1990, Henry H. Kessler Human Dignity award Kessler Inst. Rehab. Inc., 1992, The Scopus award Am. Friends of the Hebrew U., 1995, The August W. Christmann award for Tech. and Info., City of Chgo. Mayor's Office for People with Disabilities and MOPD Adv. Council, 1995, Hon. diploma for humanitarian svcs. Archeworks, Chgo., 1997, Achievement award Rusk Inst., 1997, Disting. Svc. award Am. Hosp. Assn., 1998; named Physician of Yr., Ill. Gov.'s Com., 1964, Exec. of Yr., Ill. Assn. Rehab. Facilities, 1989—, Disting. Svc. award Am. Hosp. Assn., 1998, Achievement award Risk Inst., 1997, Hon. Diploma for Diplomatic Svcs. Archeworks, 1997, Pub. Svc. award Assn. Acad. Physiatrists, 1998, Disting. Alumnus award Dept. Rehab. Medicine Rusk Inst., NYU Med. Sch., 1998; commended by Ill. Gen. Assembly, 1967; cited for meritorious svc. Pres.'s Com. on Employment of Handicapped, 1965. Mem. Ill. Med. Soc., Assn. Acad. Physiatrists (pres. 1968-69, bd. dirs. 1990-95, Pub. Svc. award 1998), Am. Congress Rehab. Med. (med. adv. com., pres. 1976-77; Gold Key 1984), Mid-Am. Soc. Phys. Med. and Rehab. (pres. 1969), Brain Trauma Found. (bd. dirs. 1990-93), Untied Cerebral Palsy Assn. Greater Chgo. (bd. dirs. 1990—). Home: 1727 N Orleans St Chicago IL 60614-5719 Office: Rehabilitation Inst 345 E Superior St Chicago IL 60611-3015

BETTS, JAMES WILLIAM, JR., financial analyst, consultant; b. Montclair, N.J., Oct. 11, 1923; s. James William and Cora Anna (Banta) B.; m. Barbara Stoke, July 28, 1951; 1 child, Barbara Susan (dec.). BA, Rutgers U., 1946; postgrad. New Sch. for Social Rsch., 1948-49; MA, U. Hawaii, 1957. With Dun & Bradstreet, Inc., 1946-86, svc. cons., 1963-64, reporting and svc. mgr., 1964-65, sr. fin. analyst, Honolulu, 1965-86; owner Portfolio Cons. of Hawaii, 1979—; cons. Saybrook Point Investments, Old Saybrook, Conn., 1979—; owner James W. Betts and Co., 1996—. Contbr. articles to mag. Served with AUS, 1943. Mem. Am. Econ. Assn., Nat. Assn. Bus. Economists, Western Econ. Assn., Atlantic Econ. Soc., Col. Henry Rutgers Soc., Internat. Inst. Forecasters, Transp. Rsch. Forum. Republican. Episcopalian. Office: Portfolio Cons Hawaii 126 Queen St Ste 222 Honolulu HI 96813-4411

BETTS, REBECCA A., lawyer. BA, Dickinson coll., 1972; JD, W.Va. U., 1976. Assoc. Spilman, Thomas, Battle & Klostermeyer, 1976-77; asst. U.S. atty. U.S. Atty.'s Office, 1977-81, chief civil divsn., 1979; founding ptnr. King, Betts & Allen, Charleston, W.Va.; U.S. atty. U.S. Dist. Ct. (So. Dist.), W.Va., 1994—; mem. 4th Cir. adv. com. on rules & procedures, com. for local rules and subcom. on criminal rules for So. Dist. W.Va., mem. civil justice reform act adv. com. Assoc. editor: W.Va. Law Rev. Mem. W.Va. State Bar Assn. (past mem. com. on legal ethics), The Legal Aid Soc. of Charleston (bd. dirs.), Order of the Coif. Office: US Attorney for South Dist WV US Courthouse Rm 4000 300 Virginia St E Charleston WV 25301-2503

BETTS, RICHARD KEVIN, political science educator; b. Easton, Pa., Aug. 15, 1947; s. John Rickards and Cecelia Agnes (Fitzpatrick) B.; m. Adela Maria Bolet, July 25, 1987; children: Elena, Michael, Diego. BA, Harvard U., 1969, MA, 1971, PhD, 1975. Lectr. in government Harvard U., Cambridge, Mass., 1975-76; vis. prof. Harvard U., Cambridge, 1985-88; rsch. assoc. Brookings Instn., Washington, 1976-81, sr. fellow, 1981-90; Shifrin prof. polit. sic., dir. Inst. War and Peace Studies Columbia U., N.Y.C., 1990—; dir. nat. securities studies Coun. on Fgn. Rels., 1996—; mem. staff Senate Select Com. on Intelligence, Washington, 1975-76, NSC, Washington, 1977; adj. prof. Johns Hopkins U., Washington, 1978-85, 88-90; mil. adv. panel Dir. Cen. Intelligence, 1993—; cons. CIA, 1980-91, 93—, Nat. Commn. on Terrorism, 1999; occasion lectr. Nat. War Coll., Fgn. Svcs. Inst., U.S. Mil. Acad. Author: Soldiers, Statesmen and Cold War Crises, 1977 (2d edit. 1991, Lasswell award 1979), Surprise Attack, 1982, Nuclear Blackmail and Nuclear Balance, 1987, Military Readiness, 1995; co-author: The Irony of Vietnam, 1979 (Woodrow Wilson award 1980), Nonproliferation and U.S. Foreign Policy, 1980; editor: Cruise Missiles, 1981, Conflict After the Cold War, 1994. Mem. foreign policy staff Mondale Presidential Campaign, Washington, 1984; mem. Assn. for Retarded Citizens, Bergen County, N.J., 1990—. Recipient Sumner prize Harvard U., 1976, Article award Nat. Intelligence Study Ctr., Washington, 1979, '81. Mem. Coun. on Fgn. Rels., Internat. Inst. for Strategic Studies, Am. Polit. Sci. Assn., Internat. Studies Assn., Soc. for Historians Am. Fgn. Rels., Consortium for Study Intelligence, Coun. Fgn. Rels. (dir. nat. security studies 1996—). Democrat. Avocation: cinema history. Home: 1199 The Strand Teaneck NJ 07666-2020 Office: Columbia U Inst War & Peace Studies 420 W 118th St New York NY 10027-7213

BETZ, EUGENE WILLIAM, architect; b. Dayton, Ohio, Jan. 12, 1921; s. Jesse Earl and Elizabeth Freda (Meyer) B.; m. Marjorie Lois Frank, Oct. 30, 1948; children: Douglas William, Gregory Vincent. BS, U. Cin., 1944. Pres. Eugene W. Betz, Architects, Inc., Dayton, 1956—; Chmn. Bd. Building Standards and Appeals, 1960-63, Kettering Planning Commn., 1957-61. Served with AUS. Recipient Honor award Architects Soc. Ohio, 1967, 71; Award of Merit, 1968, 77, 78; Nation's Sch. Month award Nat. Council Schoolhouse Constrn., 1967; Nat. Citation Am. Assn. Sch. Adminstrs., 1967, 71; Masonry award of excellence, 1976, 78; Outstanding Health Care Facility award UCLA/Columbia U./Archtl. Record, 1980. Mem. AIA (nat. com. architecture for health, 25 Yr. Bldg. award, Dayton Lifetime Excellence in Arch. award), Masons (32nd degree), Rotary. Home and Office: 820 Greenspire Ct Dayton OH 45459-1500

BETZ, HANS DIETER, theology educator; b. Lemgo, Lippe, Germany, May 21, 1931; came to U.S., 1963, naturalized, 1973; s. Ludwig and Gertrude (Vietor) B.; m. Christel Hella Wagner, Nov. 10, 1958; children: Martin, Ludwig, Arnold. Student, Kirchliche Hochschule, Bethel, Fed. Republic Germany, 1951-52, U. Mainz, Fed. Republic Germany, 1952-55, 56-58, Westminster Coll, Cambridge, Eng., 1955-56; Doctor Theologiae, U. Mainz, Fed. Republic Germany, 1957; Habilitation, U. Mainz, 1966. Pastor Evangelical Ch., Rhineland, Fed. Republic Germany, 1961-63; from asst. prof. to prof. Sch. Theology, Claremont Grad. Sch., Calif., 1963-78; prof. N.T. and early Christian lit. U. Chgo., 1978—, Shailer Mathews prof., 1989—, chmn. dept. N.T. and early Christian lit., 1985-94. Author, editor numerous books and articles in German and English, 1959—. Recipient Humboldt Rsch. prize, 1986; Lady Davis fellow Hebrew U., Jerusalem, Israel, 1990, Sackler scholar Tel Aviv U., 1995; NEH rsch. grantee, 1970-83, Am. Assn. Theol. Schs. grantee, 1977, 84. Mem. Soc. Bibl. Lit. (pres. 1997), Studiorum Novi Testamenti Societas (pres. 1999), Chgo. Soc. Bibl. Rsch. (pres. 1983-84). Office: U Chgo 1025 E 58th St Chicago IL 60637-1509

BETZ, RONALD PHILIP, pharmacist; b. Chgo., Nov. 26, 1933; s. David Robert and Olga Marie (Martinson) B.; BS, U. Ill., 1955; MPA, Roosevelt U., 1987; m. Rose Marie Marella, May 18, 1963; children: David Christian, Christopher Peter. Asst. dir. of pharmacy U. Ill., Chgo., 1959-62; dir. pharmacy Mt. Sinai Hosp., Chgo., 1962—; pres. Pharmacy Systems, Inc., 1982-89; teaching assoc. Coll. of Pharmacy, U. Ill., Chgo., 1977-88; adj. clin. asst. prof. pharmacy, U. Ill., 1988—; pres. Pharmacy Svc. and Systems, 1972-81; dir. Ill. Coop. Health Data Systems, 1976-80. Bd. dirs. Howard/Paulina Redevel. Corp., 1983-92 . With U.S. Army, 1956-58. Mem. Am. Soc. Health Sys. Pharmacists, Ill. Pharm. Assn. (pres. 1975), Ill. Acad. Preceptors in Pharmacy (pres. 1972), No. Ill. Soc. Hosp. Pharmacists (pres. 1966), Kappa Psi. Democrat. Lutheran. Contbr. articles in field to profl. jours. Home: 1021 Sussex Dr Northbrook IL 60062-3328 Office: 2750 W 15th Pl Chicago IL 60608-1704

BETZ, WILLIAM ROBERT, chemist; b. Pitts., Dec. 8, 1955; s. Donald Adam and Marie Eileen (Brown) B.; m. Heike Simone Ziegler, Aug. 21, 1992; children: Alexander Robert, Philip William. BS, Pa. State U., 1979. Rsch. chemist Supelco, Inc., Bellefonte, Pa., 1979-85, sr. rsch. chemist, 1986—; speaker in field. Author: (with others) Sampling and Analysis of Airborne Pollutants, 1992; contbr. articles to profl. jours.; patentee in field. Mem. Am. Chem. Soc. Avocations: reading, exercising, traveling. Home: 780 Hillcrest Ave State College PA 16803-3423 Office: Supelco Inc Supelco Park Bellefonte PA 16823

BETZER, ROY JAMES, retired national park service ranger; b. Rapid City, S.D., June 9, 1936; s. Bruce and Virginia Rose (Coppo) B.; m. Jeanette Menegas, Dec. 23, 1962 (div.). BS, Black Hills State Coll., 1959, BS in Edn., 1961; MA, U. S.D., 1966. Nat. pk. svc. ranger, 1992-98, tchr., coll. instr.; Mus. Tech. Living History interpreter U.S. Dept. Army; acting coach San Antonio Performing Arts, Barbizon; actor, cabaret singer, photographer; promotion specialist City of San Antonio. With USN. Avocations: reading, photography, theater, museums, writing. Home: PO Box 840 Stonewall TX 78671-0420

BETZER, SUSAN ELIZABETH BEERS, family physician, geriatrician; b. Evanston, Ill., Aug. 24, 1943; d. Thomas Moulding and Mary Ella (Waidner) Beers; m. Peter Robin Betzer, June 18, 1965; children: Sarah Elizabeth, Katherine Hannah. AB in Biol. Scis. magna cum, Mount Holyoke Coll., 1965; PhD in Oceanography, U. R.I., 1972; MD, U. Miami, 1978. Diplomate Am. Bd. Family Practice, Am. Bd. Geriatrics. Rsch. assoc. dept. marine sci. U. South Fla., St. Petersburg, 1973-74, rsch. scholar, scientist, 1975-76; resident in family practice Bayfront Med. Ctr., St. Petersburg, 1978-81; pvt. practice St. Petersburg, 1982—; clin. asst. prof. dept. family medicine U. South Fla., Tampa, 1982—; cons. physician Fed. Employee Health Clinic, Honolulu, 1981-82. Contbr. articles to profl. jours. Adv. com. St. Petersburg H.S., 1996—; bd. dirs. Fla. Orch., Tampa, 1983-86, 88—, pres., 1985-86, mem. exec. com., 1988—, vice-chair bd. trustees 1996—, founder, chair audience devel. com., St. Petersburg, 1990-94; bd. dirs. Suncoast Ctr. Cmty. Mental Health, St. Petersburg, 1992-93; trustee Bayfront Health Found., 1996—, Bayfront Med. Ctr., Bayfront Health Svcs., 1992-96, vice-chair, 1993-96; vol. physician St. Petersburg Free Clinic, 1979—. Recipient Golden Baton award St. Petersburg Fla. Orch. Guild, 1994; named Woman of Distinction, Suncoast coun. Girl Scouts U.S., 1994, Chmns. award Fla. Orch., 1997. Mem. Am. Acad. Family Physicians (Mead Johnson award 1980), Am. Med. Women's Assn., Fla. Acad. Family Physicians (Dr. of the Day, Fla. Legislature 1995, 96), Mount Holyoke Alumnae Assn. (vol. fund raiser, mem. alumnae honors rsch. com. 1988-91, mem. alumnae devel. com. 1996—), Phi Beta Kappa. Avocations: symphony, birding, cooking, reading. Home: 1830 7th St N Saint Petersburg FL 33704-3322 Office: 461 7th Ave S Saint Petersburg FL 33701-4818

BEUC, RUDOLPH, JR., architect, real estate broker; b. St. Louis, Nov. 7, 1931; s. Rudolph M. and Lillian Ann (Rethemeyer) B.; m. Mildred Hild, Jan. 25, 1968; children: Rudolph III, Ralph M. Archtl. draftsman Bank Bldg. & Equipment Corp. Am., St. Louis, 1950, Hammond & Gorlock, archs., St. Louis, 1957-58; designer Schwarz & Van Hoefen, archs., St. Louis, 1958; arch. George E. Berg Archs., St. Louis, 1958-60; arch. R. Beuc, Archs., Inc., St. Louis, 1960—, pres., also dir., 1960—; pres., dir. Hilterdevco, Inc., St. Louis, 1964—; dir. pub. works Peerless Park, 1967-98. Deacon Webster Groves Presbyn. Ch. With AUS, 1955-57. Mem. AIA, Soc. Am. Registered Archs., Mo. Coun. Archs., Mo. Assn. Bldg. Ofcls. and Insps., Coun. Am. Bldg. Ofcls. Code Adminstrs., Nat. Coun. Archtl. Registration Bds., Am. Legion (past comdr.), Internat. Order Odd Fellows (past grand), Masons, Lions (past pres.), Order Ea. Star, DeMolay, High Twelve (past state pres.), Scottish Rite, Washington U., Westborough Country. Home: 138 W Glendale Rd Saint Louis MO 63119-4060 Office: 142 W Glendale Rd Saint Louis MO 63119-4060

BEUCHERT, EDWARD WILLIAM, lawyer; b. N.Y.C., Feb. 13, 1937; s. August Vincent and Anna (Jaufmann) B.; m. Elizabeth Sadowely, Aug. 5, 1961; children: Edward William Jon, Philip, Suzanne, Alexandra. BA cun laude, Fordham U., 1958; JD cum laude, Harvard U., 1961. Bar: N.Y. 1962. Assoc., then ptnr. and counsel Seward & Kissel, N.Y.C., 1963—; bd. dirs. Cotswold Assn., Inc., v.p., 11979-80, 98-99, pres., 1980-82. Contbr. articles to profl. jours. Bd. dirs. Edgemont Cmty. Coun., Inc., 1984-90, sec., 1984-86, v.p., 1987-90. 1st lt. U.S. Army, 1961-63. Recipient Silver Box award, Edgemont Cmty. Coun., 1998. Mem. ABA, N.Y. State Bar Assn., Assn. of Bar of City of N.Y., Internat. Bar Assn. Republican. Roman Catholic. Home: 53 Inverness Rd Scarsdale NY 10583-3525 Office: 1 Battery Park Plz New York NY 10004-1405

BEUGEN, JOAN BETH, communications company executive; b. Chgo., Mar. 9, 1943; d. Leslie and Janet (Glick) Caplan; B.S. in Speech, Northwestern U., 1965; m. Sheldon Howard Beugen, July 16, 1967. Founder, prin., pres. The Creative Establishment, Inc., Chgo., N.Y.C., San Francisco and Los Angeles, 1969-87, founder, pres. Cresta Communications Inc., Chgo. 1988—; speaker on entrepreneurship for women. Del., White House Conf. on Small Bus., 1979; vice-chmn. Ill. Del. to White House Conf., 1979; trustee Mt. Sinai Hosp. Med. Ctr.; bd. dirs. Chgo. Network; bd. dirs. Chgoland. Enterprise Ctr. Contbr. articles to profl. jours. Recipient YWCA Leadership award, 1985; named Entrepreneur of Yr., Women in Bus. Mem. Nat. Assn. Women Bus. Owners (pres. Chgo. chpt. 1979), Ill. Women's Agenda, Chgo. Assn. Commerce and Industry, Midwest Soc. Profl. Cons., Chgo. Audio-Visual Producers Assn., Chgo. Film Council, Women in Film, Com. of 200, Nat. Women's Forum, Overseas Edn. Fund Women in Bus. Com., Econ. Club of Chgo. Office: The Cresta Group 1050 N State St Chicago IL 60610-7829

BEUGNOT, BERNARD ANDRE HENRI, French literature educator; b. Paris, July 3, 1932; s. Raoul P.H. Beugnot; m. Brigitte L'Hermite, June 11, 1960; children: Marie-Christine, Nicolas, Sophie. Student, Ecole Normale Superieure, Paris, 1954; licence, U. Sorbonne, Paris, 1955, MA, 1956, PhD, 1969; agregation, U. France, Paris, 1958. Prof. Coll. Chartres, France, 1960-62; assoc. prof. French U. Montreal, Que., Can., 1962-69, prof. French lit., 1970—, chmn. French dept., 1965-69, 85-91; prof. emeritus French dept. U. Montreal, Can., 1997—. Mem. editing com. Can. Coun. Humanities, Ottawa, 1970-75, 78-81; editor: J.L.G. Balzac, Entretiens, 1972, 15 other books and over 120 articles on 17th-century and contemporary lit.; co-author (monograph) Boileau, 1973, Manuel Bibliographie, 1982. Lt. inf. French Army, 1958-60. Recipient Prix Halphen Acad. Française, 1974, Ordre Nat. du Mérite Govt. France, 1977, Palmes Academiques Govt. France, 1988. Fellow Royal Soc. Can. Home: 4720 Grosvenor, Montreal, PQ Canada H3W 2L8 Office: U of Montreal, Dept of French, Montreal, PQ Canada H3C 3J7

BEUKEMA, JOHN FREDERICK, lawyer; b. Alpena, Mich., Jan. 30, 1947; s. Christian F. and Margaret Elizabeth (Robertson) B.; m. Cynthia Ann Parke, May 25, 1974; children: Frederick Parke, David Christian. BA, Carleton Coll., 1968; JD, U. Minn., 1971. Bar: Minn. 1971, U.S. Ct. Mil. Appeals 1974, U.S. Dist. Ct. Minn. 1975, U.S. Ct. Appeals (8th cir.) 1981, U.S. Ct. Appeals (fed. cir.) 1984, U.S. Supreme Ct. 1988, U.S. Dist. Ct. (we. dist.) Wis. 1997. Assoc. Faegre & Benson, Mpls., 1971, 75-79, ptnr., 1980—. Vestryman Cathedral Ch. St. Mark, Mpls., 1983-86; bd. dirs. Neighborhood Involvement Program, Mpls., 1986-90, pres., 1989-90; bd. dirs. Ronald McDonald House of Twin Cities, 1991-97, sec., 1995-97. Lt. JAGC, USNR, 1972-75. Mem. ABA, Minn. State Bar Assn., Hennepin County Bar Assn. Republican. Episcopalian.

BEUKERS, KAREN VIOLA (KAREN VIOLA), cardiac nurse; b. Phila., Jan. 26, 1957; d. Frank John and Lovie Kayrene (Lewis) V. RN, Northeastern Hosp. Sch. Nsg., Phila., 1978; RN 1st asst., Del. County Community Coll., Media, Pa., 1988. RN, Pa.; cert. oper. rm. nurse; ACLS. Staff oper. rm. nurse U. Calif., San Diego; asst. head nurse operating rm. Albert Einstein Med. Ctr., Phila.; cardiac oper. rm. nurse, 1st asst. Temple U. Hosp., Phila.; oper. rm. mgr. ortho-neuro, gen. and trauma Sentara Norfolk (Va.) Gen. Hosp., Norfolk, Va.; 1st asst. FoxChase Cancer Ctr., Phila.; lectr. in field; pvt. practice oper. rm. staff nurse, Phila. Mem. Am. Nurses Assn., Assn. Operating Rm. Nurses. Home: 934 Strahle St Philadelphia PA 19111-1412

BEUMER, RICHARD EUGENE, engineer, architect, construction firm executive; b. St. Louis, Feb. 26, 1938; s. Eugene Henry and C. Florence (Braun) B.; m. Judith Louise Rockett, June 25, 1960; children: Kathryn, Karen, Mark. BSEE, Valparaiso U., 1959. Registered profl. engr., Mo., Ill., Ariz., Md., Okla., Ohio, Ga., Va., Mich., D.C., Mass., N.Y., N.C. With Sverdrup Corp. Cos., 1959—; v.p. Sverdrup & Parcel and Assocs., St. Louis, 1974-78; sr. v.p., exec. v.p., dir. Sverdrup & Parcel Assocs., St. Louis, 1979-81; pres. Sverdrup & Parcel Assos., St. Louis, 1982-85; sr. v.p. Sverdrup Corp., 1986-88, exec. v.p., 1989-92, pres., 1993; pres., CEO Sverdup Corp., 1994-95; chmn., CEO Sverdrup Corp., 1996; dir. Sverdrup Corp., St. Louis, 1979—; vice-chmn. Jacobs Engring. Group, Inc., 1999; bd. dirs. Mercantile Bancorp., Aid Assn. for Luths., Valparaiso U., Webster U. Bd. dirs. Downtown St. Louis, Inc., 1982-91; chmn. St. Louis Regional Commerce and Growth Assn., 1998-99; bd. dirs. Jr. Achievement, St. Louis Sci. Ctr.; divsn. chmn. United Way St. Louis, 1980; past chmn. Luth. Med. Ctr., St. Louis; trustee, chmn. St. Louis Luth. High Schs. Recipient Disting. Alumni award Valparaiso U., 1983. Mem. NSPE, Am. Cons. Engrs. Coun. (nat. bd. dirs. 1979-82), Cons. Engrs. Coun. Mo. (pres. 1980), Design Profls. Coalition, Constrn. Industry Pres. Forum, The Moles, St. Louis Elec. Bd. (pres. 1983), Mo. Soc. Profl. Engrs., Univ. Club, Old Warson Club, The Bogey Club. Lutheran. Office: Sverdrup Corp 13723 Riverport Dr Maryland Heights MO 63043-4819

BEUTER, RICHARD WILLIAM, accountant; b. Iowa City, Iowa, Dec. 21, 1942; s. Eugene Richard and Marietta (Lehman) B.; m. Kathleen Louise Jedlicka, June 5, 1965; children: Matthew Jon, Brian Michael. BBA, U. Iowa, 1965. Staff acct. Coopers & Lybrand, South Bend, Ind., 1965-66; staff acct. Coopers & Lybrand, Des Moines, 1966-74, ptnr., 1974-78; ptnr. Price Waterhouse Coopers (formerly Coopers & Lybrand), Indpls., 1978—. Mem. Am. Inst. CPA's (trial bd. Region 7 1987—), Ind. CPA Soc. (ethics com. 1979-82), Hosp. Fin. Mgmt. Assn., Ins. Acctg. Statis. Assn., Crooked Stick Golf Club (Carmel, Ind.), Skyline Club. Roman Catholic. Office: Pricewaterhouse Coopers LLP 2900 1 American Sq Box 82002 Indianapolis IN 46282

BEUTLER, ARTHUR JULIUS, manufacturing company executive; b. LaCrosse, Wis., Sept. 2, 1924; s. Arthur Julius and Augusta Henrietta (Dobe) B.; m. Carolee Yvonne Crawford, Dec. 28, 1952; 1 child, Karen Elizabeth. BSEE, U. Wis., 1948, Grad. in EE, 1968. Registered profl. engr., Wis. Trainee inventor program Gen. Electric Co., Schenectady, N.Y., 1948-51; devel. engr. Gen. Electric Co., Milw., 1951-59, project engr., 1959-61, sr. engr., 1961-64; chief engr. Dings Magnetic Separator Co., Milw., 1964-67; pres., owner Creative Engring. Assocs., Inc., Greendale, Wis., 1967-72, 88—; v.p. mfg. Gettys Mfg. Co., Racine, Wis., 1972-79, v.p. internat., 1979-81; v.p. tech. planning div. motion control div. Gould, Inc. (formerly Gettys Mfg. Co.), Racine, 1981-88; cons. engr. mfg. control systems, robotics. Patentee elec. controls. Served with U.S. Army, 1943-46, PTO. Mem. IEEE (sr., chpt. chmn. 1969-72), NSPE, Soc. Mfg. Engrs. (cert.), Tau Beta Pi, Eta Kappa Nu.

BEUTLER, ERNEST, physician, research scientist; b. Berlin, Sept. 30, 1928; came to U.S., 1936, naturalized, 1943; s. Alfred David and Kaethe (Italiener) B.; m. Brondelle Fleisher, June 15, 1950; children: Steven Merrill, Earl Bryan, Bruce Alan, Deborah Ann. Ph.B., U. Chgo., 1946, B.S., 1948, M.D., 1950; PhD (hon.), Tel Aviv U., Israel, 1993. Intern U. Chgo. Clinics, 1950-51; resident in medicine 1951-53; asst. prof. U. Chgo., 1956-59; chmn. div. medicine City of Hope Med. Ctr., L.A., 1959-78; chmn. dept. clin. rsch. The Scripps Rsch. Inst., La Jolla, Calif., 1978-82, chmn. dept. basic and clin. rsch., 1982-89, chmn. dept. molecular and exptl. medicine, 1989—; clin. prof. medicine U. So. Calif., 1964-79, U. Calif. San Diego, 1979—; mem. hematology study sect. NIH, 1970-74, 89-91; Spinoza Chair U. Amsterdam, 1991. Author 8 books, numerous articles in med. jours.; mem. editorial bds. profl. jours. Adv. com. Blood Products FDA, 1984-88; nat. heart, lung, and blood adv. coun. mem. NIH, 1994-97. Recipient Gairdner award, 1975, Blundell prize, 1985, Nat. Heart, Lung, and Blood Inst. Merit award NIH, 1987, 5th ann. Excellence award Gen. Clin. Rsch. Program, 1993, Nat. Acad. Clin. Biochemistry Lectureship award Kodak Instruments, 1990, Mayo Soley award Western Soc. Clin. Investigation, 1992, City of Medicine award, 1994. Mem. NAS, Am. Acad. Arts and Scis., Assn. Am. Physicians, Am. Soc. Clin. Investigation, Western Assn. Physicians (pres. 1989), Am. Soc. Hematology (mem. exec. com. 1968-72, v.p. 1977, pres. 1979), Am. Soc. Human Genetics (mem. exec. com. 1968-72). Jewish. Achievements include invention of screening tests for galactosemia and other genetic disorders; co-discovery of glucose-6-phosphate dehydrogenase deficiency; origination of X inactivation hypothesis; research on glycolipid disorders. Home: 2707 Costebelle Dr La Jolla CA 92037-3518 Office: The Scripps Rsch Inst 10550 N Torrey Pines Rd La Jolla CA 92037-1000

BEUTLER, FREDERICK JOSEPH, information scientist; b. Berlin, Oct. 3, 1926; came to U.S., 1936, naturalized, 1943; s. Alfred David and Kaethe (Italiener) B.; m. Suzanne Armstrong, Jan. 5, 1969; children—Arthur David, Kathryn Ruth, Michael Ernest. SB, MIT, 1949, SM, 1951; PhD, Calif. Inst. Tech., 1957. Faculty U. Mich., Ann Arbor, 1957—, prof. info. and control engring., 1963-90, prof. emeritus, 1990—, chmn. computer info. and control engring., 1970-71, 77-90, chmn. grad. elect. engring. systems program, 1985-90; vis. prof. Calif. Inst. Tech., 1967-68; vis. scholar U. Calif. at Berkeley, 1964-65. Editorial cons. Math. Rev., 1965-67, 75-88; contbr. articles to profl. jours. and books. Bd. dirs. Ann Arbor Civic Theatre, 1976-78, 91-94. With AUS, 1945-46. NSF rsch. grantee, 1971-75, 76-81, 92-94, Air Force Office Sci. Rsch. grantee, 1970-74, 75-80; NASA grantee, 1959-69. Fellow IEEE (life); mem. Soc. Indsl. and Applied Math. (coun. 1969-74, mng. editor Jour. Applied Math. 1970-75, editor 1984-90, editor Rev. 1967-70), Am. Math. Soc., U. Mich. Retirees Assn. (bd. dirs., sec.-treas. 1994—), Barton Boat Club, Racquet Club of Ann Arbor. Office: Elec Engr and Comp Sci Bldg Univ Michigan Ann Arbor MI 48109-2122

BEUTLER, LARRY EDWARD, psychology educator; b. Logan, Utah, Feb. 14, 1941; s. Edward and Beulah (Andrus) B.; children: Jana, Kelly, Ian David, Gail. BS, Utah State U., 1965, MS, 1966; PhD, U. Nebr., 1970. Diplomate Am. Bd. Clin. Psychology. Asst. prof. psychology Duke U., Ashville, N.C., 1970-71; asst. prof. Stephen F. Austin State U., Nacogdoches, Tex., 1971-73; assoc. prof. Baylor Coll. Medicine, Houston, 1973-79; prof. U. Ariz., Tucson, 1979-90, U. Calif., Santa Barbara, 1990—. Author: Eclectic Psychotherapy, 1983; co-author: Systematic Treatment Selection, 1990; editor Jour. Cons. Clin. Psychology, 1990-96; editor Jour. Clin. Psychology, 1997—. Fellow Am. Psychology Assn., Am. Psychol. Soc. (pres. divsn. psychotherapy, 1997); mem. Soc. Psychotherapy Research (pres. 1986-88). Home: 7602 Hollister Ave Unit 301 Goleta CA 93117-2459 Office: U Calif Santa Barbara Gse Santa Barbara CA 93106

BEUTTENMULLER, RUDOLF WILLIAM, lawyer; b. St. Louis, Dec. 20, 1953; s. Paul A. and Doris R. (Henle) B.; m. Ragina Lee Winters, July 14, 1984. AB cum laude, Princeton U., 1976; JD with distinction, Duke U., 1980. Bar: Tex. 1980, U.S. Dist. Ct. (no. dist.) Tex. 1980. Assoc. Jenkens & Gilchrist, Dallas, 1980-83; ptnr. Gregory, Self & Beuttenmuller, Dallas, 1983-88, Bradley, Bradley & Beuttenmuller, Irving, Tex., 1988-93; dir. Thomas & Self, Dallas, 1994—. Articles editor Duke Law Jour., Durham, 1979-80. Mem. Rep. Nat. Com., Washington, 1984. Mem. ABA, Dallas Bar Assn., Duke Law Alumni Assn., Princeton Alumni Assn. Home: 4417 Amherst Ave Dallas TX 75225-6907 Office: Thomas & Self 5339 Spring Valley Rd Dallas TX 75240-3009

BEVAN, NORMAN EDWARD, religious organization executive; b. Buffalo, N.Y., July 6, 1937; s. Edward Albert and Catherine Irene (Coughlin) B. BA, St. Mary's Sem., Norwalk, Conn., 1961, BD, 1964; lic. in sacred theology, Gregorian U., Rome, 1966; DST, Acad. Alfonsiana, Rome, 1970. Theology prof. Tanzanian Episcopal Conf., Kipalapala, Tanzania, 1971-73; dir. formation Congregation of the Holy Ghost, Chgo., 1973-80; asst. gen. Congregation of the Holy Ghost, Rome, 1980-86; provincial superior Congregation of the Holy Ghost, Pitts., 1985-94; pres. Cath. Theol. Union, Chgo., 1995-97; instr. Holy Ghost Prep. Sch., Bensalem, Pa., 1997—; vocation dir. Congregation of Holy Ghost, 1997—. Roman Catholic. Home: Spiritan Hall 2401 Bristol Pike Bensalem PA 19020

BEVAN, ROBERT LEWIS, lawyer; b. Springfield, Mo., Mar. 23, 1928; s. Gene Walter and Blanche Omega (Woods) B.; m. Ronice Diane Gartin, Jan 25, 1977; children: Matthew Gene, Lisa Ann. AB, U. Mo., 1950; LLB, U. Kansas City, 1957. Bar: Mo. 1957, D.C. 1969. Adminstrv. asst. U.S. Senator T. Hennings Jr., Washington, 1957-60; legis. asst. U.S. Senator E.V. Long, Washington, 1960-69; sr. govt. relations counsel Am. Bankers Assn., Washington, 1970-84; ptnr. Hopkins & Sutter, Washington, 1984-95; of counsel Stinson, Mag and Fizzell, Kansas City, Mo., 1995—. Ghost author: The Intruders, 1967; contbg. editor U.S. Banker, 1985-88. Fieldman Dem. Nat. Com., 1968. Served with U.S. Army, 1946-47, 1951-53. Mem. ABA (bus. law sect., chmn. banking law com. 1988-92, commn. on IOLTA, co-chmn. joint comm. com.), Echequer Club. Avocations: art and antiques. Office: 1201 Walnut St Fl 28 Kansas City MO 64106-2117

BEVAN, TIM, film producer. Prodr. films (with Sarah Radclyffe) My Beautiful Laundrette, 1986, Sammy and Rosie Get Laid, 1987, Paperhouse, 1989; Personal Svcs., 1987, For Queen and Country, 1989, Dark Obsession, 1990, The Tall Guy, 1990, Chicago Joe and the Showgirl, 1990, London Kills Me, 1992, Rubin and Ed, 1992; (with Graham Bradstreet) A World Apart, 1988, Fools of Fortune, 1990; (with Carlos Davis and Anthony Fingleton) Drop Dead Fred, 1991, (with Paul Webster and Ronna B. Wallace) Bob Roberts, 1992; (with Eric fellner) Posse, 1993, Romeo Is Bleeding, 1993, Four Weddings and a Funeral, 1994, The Hudsucker Proxy, 1994, Loch Ness, 1995, Panther, 1995, French Kiss, 1995, Moonlight & Valantino, 1995, Dead Man Walking, 1995, Fargo, 1996, Bean, 1997, The Matchmaker, 1997, The Borrowers, 1997,The Hi-Lo Country, 1997, Elizabeth, 1998 (BAFTA Best British Film, ALFS awd., 1999), The Big Lebowski, 1998, What Rats Won't Do, 1998, Notting Hill, 1999, PLunkett & MacCleane, 1999; For TV Tales of the City, 1993, The Borrowers, 1993, More Tales of the City, 1998. Office: Working Title Films 9333 Wilshire Blvd Beverly Hills CA 90210*

BEVAN, WILLIAM, retired foundation executive; b. Plains, Pa., May 16, 1922; s. William and Elizabeth Merle (Jones) B.; m. Dorothy Louise Chorpening, Feb. 17, 1945; children: William III, Mark Filbert, Philip Ross. AB with honors, Franklin and Marshall Coll., 1942, ScD, 1979; MA, Duke U., 1943, PhD, 1948, LLD, 1972; ScD, Fla. Atlantic U., 1968, Emory U., 1974, U. Md., 1981, Kans. State U., 1987; DHL, So. Ill. U., 1989. Instr. psychology Duke U., 1947, William Preston Few prof. psychology, 1974-92, prof. emeritus, 1992—, provost, 1979-83; instr., then asst. prof. psychology Heidelberg Coll., Tiffin, Ohio, 1946-48; mem. faculty Emory U., 1948-59, prof. psychology, 1958-59; prof. psychology, chmn. dept. Kans. State U., 1959-62, dean arts and scis., 1962-63, v.p. acad. affairs, 1963-66; fellow Center for Advanced Study Behavioral Scis., Stanford, Calif., 1965-66; sr. postdoctoral fellow NSF, 1965-66; v.p., provost Johns Hopkins U., Balt., 1966-70; prof. psychology Johns Hopkins U., 1966-74; exec. officer AAAS, 1970-74, pub. Science, 1970-74; mem. adv. bd. Univ. Coll., U. Md., 1978-86; bd. govs. Research Triangle Inst., 1979-82; v.p. John D. and Catherine T. MacArthur Found., Chgo., 1983-91, ret., 1991; mem. adv. bd. Ctr. Advanced Study U. Va., 1976-89, adv. coun. Sch. Medicine U. Chgo., 1984-89. Editorial adv. bd.: Am. Men and Women of Sci., 12th edit, 1972, Social Sci. Citations Index, 1972-77; contbr. articles to profl. jours. Trustee Human Resources Research Orgn., 1968-88, Franklin and Marshall Coll., 1971-76, Coll. Retirement Equity Fund, 1972-90, Ctr. for Creative Leadership, 1972-79, Bioscis. Info. Svc., 1974-80, Am. Psychol. Found., 1970-77, 83-89, Assn. Advancement of Psychology, 1974-78, William T. Grant Found., 1977-90, HumRRO Internat. Inc., 1985-89, Jackson Meml. Lab., 1986-90. With USNR, 1944-70. Fulbright scholar U. Oslo (Norway), 1952-53. Fellow Am. Psychol. Assn. (pres. 1982), AAAS; mem. Inst. Medicine of Nat. Acad. Sci., Psychonomic Soc., So. Soc. Philosophy and Psychology, History of Sci. Soc., Am. Acad. Arts and Scis., Soc. Exptl. Psychologists, Am. Psychol. Soc., Phi Beta Kappa, Sigma Xi. Clubs: Cosmos (Washington); Century (N.Y.C.). Home: 21 Stoneridge Cir Durham NC 27705-5510

BEVAN, WILLIAM ARNOLD, JR., emergency physician; b. Sault St. Marie, Mich., June 23, 1943; s. William Arnold and Syneva Lois (Martin) B.; m. Martha Lynn Peterson, Dec. 29, 1973; children: Terry Eugene, Brian William, PAtrick Jon. BS, U. Minn., 1966, MD, 1970. Diplomate Am. Bd. Family Practice, Am. Bd. Emergency Medicine. Intern U. Utah, 1970-71; family practitioner Vail Mtn. Med. Profl. Corp., Vail, Colo., 1972-83; emergency physician Vail Valley Emergency Physicians, 1983—; dir. Vail Valley Emergency Dept., 1992—; adviser Western Eagle County Ambulance Dist., 1983—. Trustee Shattuck St. Mary's Sch., Faribault, Minn., 1977—; football coach Battle Mountain H.S., Vail, 1978—. Named Man of Yr. Boy Scouts Am., 1966, 77. Mem. AMA, Rocky Mountain Med. Soc., Colo. Med. Soc. Republican. Lutheran. Home: 0025 Cottonwood Rd Eagle Vail CO 81631 Office: Vail Valley Emergency Dept 181 W Meadow Dr Vail CO 81657-5058

BEVC, CAROL-LYNN ANNE, financial officer; b. Jam, N.Y., Oct. 6, 1952; d. Joseph F. and Dorothea Mae (Kirshe) Bova; m. Frank P. Bevc, May 11, 1974; children: Christine, Elizabeth. Bookkeeper J. Rolfe Davis Ins., Orlando, Fla., 1987-89; CFO Wordwise, Inc., Winter Park, Fla., 1989—. Leader Citrus coun. Girl Scouts U.S.A., 1986-96. Mem. AAUW (pres. Seminole County br. 1985-87, 95-97, bd. dirs., dir. comm. Fla. state 1998—). Avocations: camping, biking. Home: 1511 Black Bear Ct Winter Springs FL 32708-3860 Office: Wordwise Inc 5931 Brick Ct Ste 130 Winter Park FL 32792-9411

BEVC, FRANK PETER, electrical engineer; b. Johnstown, Pa., Mar. 5, 1952; s. Frank Henry and Mildred (Gallo) B.; m. Carol-Lynn Bova, May 11, 1974; children: Christine, Elizabeth. BSEE, U. Pitts., 1973, MBA, 1976. Design engr., program mgr. Westinghouse, Pitts., 1973-83; mgr. tech. projects Westinghouse, Orlando, Fla., 1983-90, mgr. steam sys. engring., 1990-92, mgr. emerging tech., 1992-97; mgr. emerging tech. Siemens Westinghouse, Orlando, 1998—; treas. Gasification Tech. Coun., 1998—; treas. Energy Frontiers Internat., Arlington, Va., 1996-98; bd. dirs. Gasification Techs. Coun. Contbr. articles to profl. jours. Mem. IEEE (sr.), World Energy Congress (mem. tech. bd. 1995-98), Gas Turbine Assn. (v.p. 1992—), Am. Nat. Stds. Inst. (mem. stds. bd. 1974-80), U.S. Advanced Ceramics Assn. (bd. dirs.), Nat. Biomass Industries Assn. Home: 1511 Black Bear Ct Winter Springs FL 32708-3860 Office: Siemens Westinghouse 4400 N Alafaya Trl Orlando FL 32826-2398

BEVELACQUA, JOSEPH JOHN, physicist, researcher; b. Waynesburg, Pa., Mar. 17, 1949; s. Frank and Lucy Ann B.; m. Terry Sanders, Sept. 4, 1971; children: Anthony, Jeffrey, Megan, Peter, Michael, Karen. B.S. in Physics, Calif. State Coll., 1970; postgrad., U. Maine, 1970-72; M.S. in Physics, Fla. State U., 1974, Ph.D., 1976. Diplomate Am. Bd. Health Physics; cert. radiol. shield survey engr.; cert. health physicist (comprehensive and power reactors), sr. reactor operator cert. Teaching/rsch. asst. U. Maine, 1970-72, Fla. State U., 1973-76; rsch. asst. NSF, 1975-76, rsch. assoc., 1976; nuclear engr. Bettis Atomic Power Lab., West Mifflin, Pa., 1973, sr. nuclear engr., 1976-78; ops. rsch.analyst U.S. Dept. Energy, Oak Ridge, 1978-80, chief physicist advanced laser isotope separation program, 1980-83; sr. radiol. engr. GPU Nuclear Corp. (Three Mile Island Sta.-Unit 2), Middletown, Pa., 1983-84; Three Mile Island emergency preparedness mgr. GPU Nuclear Corp., Middletown, Pa., 1984-86, mgr. TMI-2 safety rev. group, 1986-89, dir. radiol. controls TMI-2, 1989; supt. health physics Point Beach Nuclear Plant Wis. Electric Co., Two Rivers, 1989-95; prodn. planning mgr. Point Beach Nuclear Plant, 1995-96; pres., CEO Bevelacqua Resources, Richland, Wash., 1993—; cons. U.S. Dept. Energy's Process Evaluation Bd. of Isotope Separation, Washington, 1981-82. Author: Contemporary Health Physics: Problems and Solutions, 1995, Basic Health

Physics: Problems and Solutions, 1999; contbr. articles to profl. jours. including Physical Rev. Letters. Mem. Rep. Presdl. Task Force, Nat. Rep. Senatorial Com. Recipient Outstanding Performance award Dept. Energy, 1982; grantee USAF, NSF; Von Humboldt fellow U. Hamburg. Mem. Am. Nuclear Soc., Am. Phys. Soc., Am. Acad. Health Physics (profl. devel. com. 1992-94, chmn. 1994, nom. com. 1994-96), Susquehanna Valley Health Physics Soc. (mem. exec. com.), N.Y. Acad. Scis., Soc. Nuclear Medicine, Nuclear Utility Coordinating Group on Emergency Preparedness Implementation, Babcock and Wilcox Owners Group on Emergency Preparedness, Profl. Reactor Operators Soc., Health Physics Soc. (placement com. 1989-92, nominiating com. 1994-97), Am. Bd. Health Physics (vice chmn. comprehensive panel of examiners 1990, chmn. 1991, nat. office mem.), Sigma Pi Sigma. Republican. Lutheran. Club: Oak Ridge Sportsman's. Rsch. on theoretical studies of light nuclei, few nucleon transfer reactions, radiation shielding, laser isotope separation, neutron nuclei, symmetry violations in nuclei, grand unification theories, quark models of nuclear forces, nuclear fuel cycle, laser fusion and gravitational collapse of stars, beta dosimetry, internal dosimetry, health effects of ionizing radiation; nuclear reactor safety, radon health effects and mitigation, radioactive and mixed waste management, applied health physics, internal and external dusimetry. Home and Office: Bevelacqua Resources 343 Adair Dr Richland WA 99352-8563

BEVER, CHRISTOPHER THEODORE, JR., neurologist; b. Washington, Apr. 10, 1949; s. Christopher Theodore and Josephine Jordan (Morton) B.; m. Patricia Ann Thomas, Aug. 23, 1978; children: Erica Jane, Theodore Louis, Katherine Meryl. AB, Washington U., 1971; MD with Distinction in Rsch., U. Rochester, 1975. Intern U. Cin., 1975-76; resident in internal medicine Rutgers Coll. Medicine and Dentistry N.J., Piscataway, 1976-77; resident in neurology Columbia-Presbyn. Med. Ctr., N.Y.C., 1977-80; vis. fellow Coll. Physicians and Surgeons Columbia U., N.Y.C., 1979-80; rsch. assoc. NIH, Bethesda, Md., 1980-82, sr. staff fellow, 1982-84; asst. prof. dept. neurology U. Tenn. Ctr. for Health Scis., Memphis, 1984-87; asst. prof. U. Md., Balt., 1987-92, assoc. prof., 1992-98, prof., 1998—; vis. cons. dept. neurology Nat. Naval Med. Ctr., Bethesda, 1981-84; staff neurologist VA Med. Ctr., Memphis, 1984-87, Univ. Hosp. U. Tenn., 1984-87; cons. neurologist Bapt. Meml. Hosp., Memphis, 1986-87; staff neurologist VA Med. Ctr., Balt., 1987—, U. Md. Hosp., 1987—; co-dir. Mid South Multiple Sclerosis Clinic, Memphis, 1986-87; chief neurology svc. Dept. Vets. Affairs Med. Ctr., Balt., 1990—. Contbr. articles to profl. jours. and chpts. to books; ad hoc reviewer for numerous scientific jours. Fellow U. Rochester Alumni Assn., 1972, 73, NIH, 1979-80, Scottish Rite Com. on Rsch. in Schizophrenia, 1974. Fellow Am. Acad. Neurology; mem. AAAS, Md. Acad. Neurology, Soc. for Neurosci., Internat. Soc. for Interferon Rsch., Soc. for Neurochemistry, Am. Neurol. Assn. Office: U Md Hosp Dept Neurology 22 S Greene St # 46 Baltimore MD 21201-1544

BEVER, MELANIE SUE, credit company manager; b. Reading, Pa., Sept. 11, 1967; d. Franklin Earl Sr. and Betty Mae (Billig) S. BSBA, Shippensburg (Pa.) U., 1989. Mgmt. assoc. Citicorp Credit Svcs., Inc., Hagerstown, Md., 1989-90, unit mgr. data entry, 1990-91, unit mgr. statement processing, 1991-92; unit mgr. payment processing Citicorp Credit Svcs., Inc., Hagerstown, 1992-93, unit mgr. payment mail opening, 1993-95, fin. analyst, 1995-96; sr. mgr. proof and control First Data Merchant Svc., 1996-98, asst. v.p. proof and control, 1998—. Mem. NAFE, Beta Gamma Sigma, Phi Beta Lambda. Lutheran. Avocations: stamp collecting, photography, travel, cooking, reading. Home: 553 W Church St Hagerstown MD 21740-4629 Office: First Data Merchant Svcs One Western Maryland Pkwy Hagerstown MD 21740

BEVERETT, ANDREW JACKSON, marketing executive; b. Midland City, Ala., Feb. 21, 1917; s. Andrew J. and Ella Levonia (Adams) B.; m. Martha Sophia Landgrebe, May 26, 1951; children: Andrew Jackson III, James Edmund, Faye A. BS, Samford U., 1940; MBA, Harvard U., 1942. With United Air Lines, Chgo., 1946-66; dir. aviation econs., sr. mktg. econ. cons. Mgmt. and Econs. Rsch., Inc., Palo Alto, Calif., 1966-71; sr. economist Stanford Rsch. Inst., Menlo Park, 1971-72; pres. Edy's on the Peninsula stores, 1973-78; real estate broker, fin. and tax cons. Saratoga, San Jose, Calif., 1979-99. With USNR, 1942-46. Mem. Nat. Assn. Enrolled Agts., Nat. Assn. Realtors, Pi Gamma Mu, Phi Kappa Phi. Home: 6325 Whaley Dr San Jose CA 95135-1447

BEVERIDGE, ALBERT JEREMIAH, III, lawyer; b. Indpls., Jan. 26, 1935; s. Albert Jeremiah and Elizabeth Lincoln (Scaife) B.; m. Madzy de Kok, June 29, 1962; children: Alexandra, Albert IV, Vanessa. B.A. cum laude, Princeton U., 1957; J.D. cum laude, Harvard U., 1962. Bar: D.C. 1963, N.Y. 1984. Ptnr. Beveridge & Diamond, P.C., Washington, 1974-95, of coun., 1995—; pres. George C. Marshall Found., 1995—; mem. Greater Washington Regional adv. bd. Crestar Bank, 1986—. Bd. dirs. Nat. Symphony Orch., 1969—, pres., 1989-92. 1st lt. U.S. Army, 1957-59. Home: 207 Overhill Dr Lexington VA 24450-1748 Office: George C Marshall Found PO Box 1600 Lexington VA 24450-1600 also: Beveridge & Diamond PC 1350 I St NW Ste 700 Washington DC 20005-7202*

BEVERIDGE, TERRANCE JAMES, microbiology educator, researcher; b. Toronto, Ont., Can., Apr. 29, 1945; s. Fredrick Charles and Doris Elizabeth (Hooks) B.; m. Janice Elizabeth Barnett, Sept. 9, 1970; children: Braden Charles, Jennifer Bree. BS, U. Toronto, 1968, Diploma in Bacteriology, 1969, MS, 1970; PhD, U. Western Ont., 1974. Rsch. assoc. U. Western Ont., London, 1975-78; from asst. prof. to assoc. prof. U. Guelph, Ont., 1978-86, prof., 1986—, Killam prof., 1995-97; vis. prof. Zentrum für Ultrastrucktturforschung, Vienna, Austria, 1984, Biozentrum, Universität der Basel, Switzerland, 1987; dir. Nat. Scis. and Engring. Rsch. Coun. of Can. (NSERC) Gueiph Regional STEM Facility, 1980—. Editor: Metal Ions and Bacteria, 1989, Advances in Bacterial Paracrystalline Surface Layers, 1993; editor Can. Jour. Microbiology, 1982-88, Jour. Bacteriology, 1988-97, Biorecovery, 1987—, Internat. Jour. of Resource and Environ. Biotech., 1994—, Microbiology, 1997—, Arch. Microbiology, 1998—. Recipient Steacie prize Nat. Sci. and Engring. Rsch. Coun. of Can., 1984, Can. Soc. Microbiology award, 1994, Sigma Xi award, 1994. Fellow Royal Soc. Can. (dir. life scis. 1992-95), Am. Acad. Microbiology, Austrian Acad. Sci.; mem. Can. Soc. Microbiologists, Microscopical Soc. Can., Am. Soc. Microbiology (divsnl. award 1984), Electron Microscopic Soc. Am., Nat. Centre Excellence, Can. Bacterial Disease Network, Can. Inst. Advanced Rsch. (assoc. 1988—). Avocations: hiking, cross-country skiing. Office: U Guelph Coll Biol Scis, Dept of Microbiology, Guelph, ON Canada N1G 2W1

BEVERLY, LAURA ELIZABETH, special education educator; b. Glen Jean, W.Va., Nov. 26; d. Sidney and Alma Logan. BA in Elem. Edn., W.Va. State Coll., 1960; MS in Spl. Edn., Bklyn. Coll., 1969; postgrad., Oxford (Eng.) U., 1974, N.Y.U., 1982. Cert. elem./spl. edn. tchr., N.Y. Tchr. Bd. Coop. Ednl. Svcs., Westbury, N.Y., 1966—; mem. adv. bd. Am. Biographical Inst. Inc., Raliegh, N.C., 1985—. Mem. ASCD, Am. Inst. of Parliamentarians, Royal Soc. Health, Phi Delta Kappa. Avocations: reading, traveling. Home: PO Box 346 Glen Jean WV 25846-0346

BEVERLY, SHARON MANNING, women's basketball coach; m. Randy Beverly; 1 child, Preston. Student, Queensborough C.C.; BEd, Queens Coll., 1976, MEd, 1977. Profl. basketball player France, 1977-79; asst. coach Queens Coll., from 1979; women's head basketball coach Fairleigh Dickinson U., 1988—; asst. coach North Team, U.S. Olympic Festival, 1994. Named Coach of Yr., N.J. State Coaches Assn., 1992, NEC, 1992-93. Office: Fairleigh Dickinson U Athletic Comms/Rothman Ctr 1000 River Rd Teaneck NJ 07666

BEVERS, THERESE BARTHOLOMEW, physician, medical educator; b. Amarillo, Tex., Apr. 5, 1960; d. James Oliver Bartholomew and Ruth Ann Berg. BS, Tex. Woman's U., 1981; MD, U. Tex. Health Scis. Ctr., 1987. Intern, then resident U. Tex. Health Sci. Ctr., San Antonio/Bexar County Hosp., 1987-90; physician pvt. practice, Wichita Falls, Tex., 1990-91, Dallas, 1991-94; chief med.dir. Medi Clinic, Houston, 1994-96; asst. prof. clin. cancer prevention, med. dir. cancer prevention ctr. U. Tex., M.D. Anderson Cancer Ctr., Houston, 1996—; mem. expert panel Nat. Comprehensive Cancer Network Breast Screening and Diagnosis Com., Nat. Comprehensive Cancer Network Breast Cancer Prevention Com. Mem. editl. bd. Oncolog, Breast Diseases: A Year Book Quarterly. Mem. AMA (task force on prevention), Am. Acad. Family Physicians, Tex. Acad. Family Physicians (mem. com. health care svcs. 1992-96, mem. com. clin. preventive medicine 1996-98, commr. pub. health and clin. affairs 1998—). Avocations: antiques, decorating, reading. Office: U Tex M D Anderson Cancer Ctr 1515 Holcombe Blvd # 51 Houston TX 77030-4009

BEVERSDORF, ANNE ELIZABETH, astrologer, Jyotishi, author, educator; b. Houston, Tex., Aug. 14, 1949; d. S. Thomas and Norma (Beeson) B. BA, U. Tex., 1972; MLS, Ind. U., 1974. Jyotishi. Founding librarian Social Studies Devel. Ctr. Ind. U., Bloomington, 1975-79, info. specialist, 1980-82; co-founder Ind. Clearinghouse for Computer Edn., Indpls., 1983-86; Calif. mktg. rep. Minn. Ednl. Computing Corp., San Marcos, Calif., 1986-88; pres., chief exec. officer Beversdorf Assocs., Ltd., Vista, Calif., 1988-93; writer, lectr., astrologer Vista, Calif., 1993—; cons. Procter & Gamble Ednl. Services, Cin., 1981-85, Brazil Office of Tech. Edn., Rio de Janeiro, Porto Alegre, 1986; mem. faculty Ind. U., Indpls., 1986, San Diego State U., 1988-91. Contbr. over 30 articles to U.S. and internat. profl. jours. Mem. Am. Coun. Vedic Astrology, Am. Fedn. Astrologers, San Diego Astrol. Soc. Avocations: reading, weaving, needlework, piano music. Home and Office: 1119 Anza Ave Vista CA 92084-4517

BEVERSDORF, DAVID QUENTIN, neurologist, researcher; b. Bloomington, Ind., May 28, 1965; s. Samuel Thomas and Norma (Beeson) B.; m. Sheri Anderson, Dec. 26, 1990. BS, Ind. U., 1987; MD, Ind. U., Indpls., 1992. Med. resident Meth. Hosp. Ind., Indpls., 1992-93; neurology resident Dartmouth-Hitchcock Med. Ctr., Lebanon, N.H., 1993-96; behavioral neurology fellow U. Fla. Coll. Medicine, Gainesville, 1996-98; asst. prof. neurology Ohio State U. Med. Ctr., Columbus, 1998—. Contbr. articles to med. jours., including Lancet, Neurology, Psychiatry Rsch.-Neuroimaging, Jour. Neurology, Neurosurgery and Psychiatry, and Physiology and Behavior. Recipient rsch. grant for autism rsch. Stallone Fund, L.A., 1994. Mem. AMA, Am. Acad. Neurology, Cognitive Sci. Soc., Soc. for Neurosci., Cognitive Neurosci. Soc., Phi Beta Kappa. Office: Ohio State U Med Ctr Dept Neurology 1654 Upham Dr Columbus OH 43210-1250

BE VIER, WILLIAM A., religious studies educator; b. Springfield, Mo., July 31, 1927; s. Charles and Erma G. (Ritter) Be V.; m Jo Ann King, Aug. 11, 1949; children: Cynthia, Shirley. BA, Drury Coll., 1950; ThM, Dallas Theol. Sem., 1955, ThD, 1958; MA, So. Meth. U., 1960; EdD, ABD, Wayne State U., 1968. With Frisco Rlwy., 1943-45, 46-51; John E. Mitchell Co., Dallas, 1952-60; instr. Dallas Theol. Sem., 1958-59; prof. Detroit Bible Coll., 1960-74, registrar, 1962-66, dean, 1964-73, exec. v.p., 1967-74, acting pres., 1967-68; prof., dean edn., v.p. for acad. affairs Northwestern Coll., Roseville, Minn., 1974-81; prof. Northwestern Coll., Roseville, 1981-95, prof. emeritus, 1995—. Editor The Discerner. Bd. dirs. Religion Analysis Svc., Mpls., 1979—, pres., 1989—. With USMC, 1945-46, 50-51; ret. col. Army Res. mem. Res. Officers Assn., Ind. Fund Chs. of Am. (nat. exec. com. 1991-94, v.p. 1993-94), Huguenot Hist. Soc., Bevier-Elting Family Assn., Phi Alpha Theta. Office: Religion Analysis Svc PO Box 22098 Robbinsdale MN 55422-0098

BEVILACQUA, ANTHONY JOSEPH CARDINAL, archbishop; b. Bklyn., June 17, 1923; s. Louis and Maria (Codella) B. Student, Cathedral Coll., Bklyn., 1941-43, Sem. of Immaculate Conception, Huntington, N.Y., 1943-49; JCD, Gregorian U., Rome, Italy, 1956; MA in Polit. Sci, Columbia U., 1962; JD, St. John's U. Sch. Law, 1975. Ordained priest Roman Cath. Ch., 1949; ordained bishop, 1980. Bar: N.Y. 1976, U.S. Dist. Ct. (we. dist.) Pa. 1984, Pa. 1988, U.S. Dist. Ct. (ea. dist.) Pa. 1988, U.S. Supreme Ct., 1989. Asst. pastor Sacred Heart, St. Stephen's Ch., St. Mary's Ch., 1949-50; prof. history Cathedral Prep. Sem., Bklyn., 1950-53; prof. canon law Sem. of Immaculate Conception, Huntington, N.Y., 1968-80; adj. prof. law St. John's U. Sch. Law, Queens, N.Y., 1976-80; successively asst. chancellor, vice-chancellor, chancellor Diocese of Bklyn., 1965-83, dir. Cath. migration and refugee office, 1971-83, ordained aux. bishop, 1980; bishop Diocese of Pitts., 1983-88; archbishop Archdiocese of Phila., 1988—; elevated to cardinal Coll. of Cardinals, 1991; mem. com. pro-life activities, 1989—; mem. com. migration, 1989—; mem. Pontifical Congregation for Causes of Saints, 1991—; mem. Pontifical Coun. "Cor Unum", 1991—. Contbr. articles to profl. jours. Bd. dirs. Mercy Home for Children; chmn. Nat. Coalition for Haitian Refugees. Mem. Canon Law Soc. Am., Pa. Bar Assn., Fellowship of Am. Cath. Scholars. Office: Archdiocese Phila 222 N 17th St Philadelphia PA 19103-1295*

BEVILACQUA, MAURIZIO, member of Canadian parliament; b. Sulmona, Italy, June 1, 1960; m. Elena Cesaroni; 2 children. BA, York U., Toronto. Exec. asst. Members of Provincial and Federal Parliaments, Toronto, Ottawa, Can., 1982-88; mem. parliament Ho. of Commons, Ottawa, 1988—, chmn. standing com. on fin.; opposition critic for employment: youth and disabled, assoc.. opposition critic for energy, mines and resources, 1988-90; mem. standing coms. on Energy, Mines and Resources; Labour, Employment and Immigration and Human Rights and Status of Disabled Persons, 1988-90; parliamentary sec. to Minister of Human Resources Devel., 1995-97; chair of standing com. on Human Resources Devel., 1995-97; chair standing com. on Fin., 1997—. Co-founder Vaughn Comty. of Assns. to Restore Environ. Safety; past pres. Coun. York Student Fedn.; active on many local bds. and in local assns. Office: Can Ho of Commons, Rm 540 N Ctr Block, Ottawa, ON Canada KIA0A6*

BEVILL, TOM, retired congressman, lawyer; b. Townley, AL, Mar. 27, 1921; s. Herman and Fannie Lou (Fike) B.; m. Lou Betts, June 24, 1943; children: Susan B., Donald H., Patricia Lou. BS, U. Ala., 1943, LLB, 1948; LLD(hon.), U. Ala., Tuscaloosa, 1981, Livingston U., 1986; LLD (hon.), U. North Ala., 1991, Troy State U., 1992. Bar: Ala. 1949. Pvt. practice law Jasper, 1948-67; mem. Ala. Ho. of Reps., 1958-66; mem. 90th-104th Congresses from 4th Ala. dist., 1967-97, mem. appropriations com., ret., 1997. Mem. ABA, Ala. Bar Assn., Walker County Bar Assn. (past pres.), Am. Judicature Soc. Home: 411 Ridge Rd Jasper AL 35501

BEVIN, TERESA, educator, psychotherapist, writer; b. Camagüey, Cuba, Dec. 19, 1949; d. Perfecto and Teresa (Larrúa) Rodriguez; m. Julio Enrique Hernández, Feb. 6, 1991 (div. July 1997). AS in Mental Health, Montgomery Coll., 1980; BS in Speech Path., George Washington U., 1982; MA in Speech Pathology, U. Md., 1984, MA in Edn., 1985. Program mgr. youth svcs. YMCA, Silver Spring, Md., 1982-84; program mgr. IPCO Home Health Sys., Silver Spring, 1984-86; prof. Spanish and psychology Montgomery Coll., Takoma Park, Md., 1986—, coord. fgn. langs. dept., 1991—, cons. mental health dept. adv. bd.; asst. to dir. child devel.YWCA, Silver Spring, 1986-87; child specialist outpatient psychiatry dept. Children's Hosp. Nat. Med. Ctr., Washington, 1987-90; psychotherapist Montgomery County Govt. Crisis Ctr., Bethesda, Md., 1990-95; trainer Montgomery County Govt. Social Svcs., 1993—; panelist Univision TV, 1990, 91; presenter NOW and Takoma Park Found. Cmty. Forum, 1994, Am. Inst. for Urban Psychol. Studies, 1994, 95, U. Md., 1995. Author: (novel) Havana Split, 1997, (short stories) Dreams and Other Ailments, 1997; contbg. author: Children in Crisis, 1991, Helping Bereaved Children, 1993. Mem. Internat. Soc. TRaumatic Stress Studies (presenter), Cuban-Am. Cultural Found., Sigma Delta Pi. Democrat. Avocations: writer, singer, musician. Office: Montgomery Coll Takoma Park Campus Takoma Park MD 20912

BEVINGTON, CINDY, reporter; b. Sturgis, Mich., June 22, 1950; d. Fred Haynes and Carol Joan (Nichols) Langley; m. Charles L. Bevington, June 28, 1969; children: Heidi, Scott. Student, Ind. U., Ft. Wayne, 1968, 70, Santa Fe C.C., Gainesville, Fla., 1986. Writer High Springs (Fla.) Herald, 1986-96; staff reporter Evening Star, Angola, Ind., 1993-94, staff writer, 1997—; cmty. leader/host Am. Online-Writers Rms., 1996—; lectr. in field. Chmn. Alachua County Sch. Adv. Coun., Gainesville, 1986-89; mem. impact fees com. Alachua County, 1988; creator city festival Alachua c. of C., 1986-87; spkr. for cts. advising against drunk driving, 1993—; chmn. Mebane Mid. sch. Adv. Com., 1987-91; co-chmn. fundraising com. Mebane Mid. Sch. PTA, 1985-86; team mom Babe Ruth Baseball teams;. Named Vol. of the Yr., Crown region, Fla. Dept. Edn., Tallahassee, 1987; recipient 1st place award for gen. excellence in commentary Fla. Press Club, 1992, 1st place col. writing 1993, for feature writing, 1993, 94, gen. excellence in commentary writing, 1995, pub. svc. writing, 1996, 1st place col. writing Nat. Newspaper assn., 1993, numerous others. Mem. Nat. Newspaper Assn., Nat. Soc. Newspaper Columnists, Hoosier State Press Assn., Soc. Profl. Journalists, Alachua Woman's Club (v.p., corr. sec.), Xi Eta Epsilon (sec. 1997). Home: 1540 South Old US 27 Angola IN 46703-8958 Office: The Evening Star 114 E Broad St Angola IN 46703-1533

BEVINGTON, DAVID MARTIN, English literature educator; b. N.Y.C., May 13, 1931; s. Merle Mowbray and Helen (Smith) B.; m. Margaret Bronson Brown, June 4, 1953; children: Stephen, Philip, Katharine, Sarah. B.A., Harvard U., 1952, M.A., 1957, Ph.D., 1959. Instr. English Harvard U., 1959-61; asst. prof. U. Va., 1961-65, asso. prof., 1965-66, prof., 1966-67; vis. prof. U. Chgo., 1967-68, prof., 1968—, Phyllis Fay Horton prof. in the Humanities, 1985—; vis. prof. N.Y. U. Summer Sch., 1963, Harvard U. Summer Sch., 1967, U. Hawaii Summer Sch., 1970, Northwestern U., 1974. Author: From Mankind to Marlowe, 1962, Tudor Drama and Politics, 1968, Action is Eloquence, Shakespeare's Language of Gesture, 1984; editor: Medieval Drama, 1975, The Complete Works of Shakespeare, 4th edit., 1997, The Bantam Shakespeare, 1988. Served with USN, 1952-55. Guggenheim fellow, 1964-65, 81-82; sr. fellow Southeastern Inst. Medieval and Renaissance Studies, summer 1975; sr. cons. and seminar leader Folger Inst. Renaissance and Eighteenth-Century Studies, 1976-77. Mem. MLA, AAUP, Renaissance Soc. Am., Shakespeare Assn. Am. (pres. 1976-77, 95-96), Am. Acad. Arts and Scis., Am. Philos. Soc. Home: 5747 S Blackstone Ave Chicago IL 60637-1823 Office: Univ Chgo English Dept 5801 S Ellis Ave Chicago IL 60637-5418

BEVINGTON, E(DMUND) MILTON, electrical machinery manufacturing company executive; b. Nashville, Oct. 31, 1928; s. John Laurence and Mary (Halloran) B.; m. Elizabeth Anne Rickey, Sept. 8, 1951 (dec. June 1962); children: Milton, Rickey, Peter; m. Paula Maureen Lawton, Apr. 24, 1965; children: George, Mary-Laurence, Christian, Charles, Justin. Grad., Canterbury Sch., 1945; S.B. in Chem. Engring, Mass. Inst. Tech., 1949; M.B.A., Harvard, 1951. Plant supr. Dewey & Almy Chem. Co. (name changed to W.R. Grace Co., 1954), Cambridge, Mass., 1951-54; marketing research mgr. Dewey & Almy Chem. Co. (name changed to W.R. Grace Co., 1954), 1954-56; merchandising mgr. Westinghouse Electric Co., Staunton, Va., 1956-58; So. zone sales mgr. Westinghouse Electric Co., Atlanta, 1958-59; with The Trane Co., Atlanta and LaCrosse, Wis., 1959—; v.p., gen. mgr. consumer products div. The Trane Co., 1969-70, exec. v.p., 1970-73; chmn., pres. Servidyne Inc., Atlanta, 1974—; bd. dirs. AAA South. Mem. corp. devel. com. MIT, 1978—, bd. dirs. MIT Corp., 1985-91; chmn. Ga. Conservancy, 1989-92, bd. dirs.; bd. dirs. Atlanta coun. Boy Scouts Am., also v.p., 1989-90, pres., 1990-92; bd. dirs. So. region Boy Scouts Am.; pres. Metro Group, 1992-97; bd. dirs. Ga. Dept. Cmty. Affairs, 1988-92. Mem. Pres.' Cir. of NAS, MIT Alumni Assn. (v.p. 1983-85, pres. 1985-86), Tau Beta Pi, Sigma Alpha Epsilon. Clubs: Harvard (N.Y.C. and Boston); Piedmont Driving (Atlanta), Commerce (Atlanta). Home: PO Box 93746 Atlanta GA 30377-0746 Office: 2120 Marietta Blvd NW Atlanta GA 30318-2122*

BEVINGTON, PAULA LAWTON, facilities management consulting executive; b. Cleve., Sept. 25, 1937; d. G(eorge) Albert and Mary Patricia (Walsh) Lawton; m. E(dmund) Milton Bevington, Apr. 24, 1965; children: Milton, Rickey, Peter, George, Mary-Laurence, Christian, Charles, Justin. BA magna cum laude, St. Mary's Coll., Notre Dame, Ind., 1958; JD, Yale U., 1961. Bar: Ga. 1960. Assoc. Sutherland, Asbill & Brennan, Atlanta, 1961-63; vol. various non-profit agys., LaCrosse, Wis., 1971-73, Atlanta, 1965-71, 73—; chmn. Servidyne Systems, Inc., Atlanta, 1980—; bd. dirs. Abrams Industries, Atlanta, Servidyne and Servidyne Systems, Atlanta; mem. adv. bd. Ga. State U. Coll. Law, Atlanta, 1995—. Mem. Jr. League of Atlanta, 1967—, pres., 1980; bd. dirs. Justice Ctr. Atlanta, 1979—, pres. 1999—; bd. dirs., vol. ARC, Atlanta, pres., 1985-86; bd. dirs. World Trade Ctr., Atlanta, 1991—, So. Ctr. for Internat. Studies, 1990—, UNICEF-Atlanta, 1991-99, chair, 1994-96; trustee Oglethorpe U., Atlanta, 1982-91, St. Mary's Coll., 1985-91; mem. Ga. Human Rels. Commn., 1987-99, chair, 1990-98; mem. bd. councilors The Carter Ctr., Atlanta, 1997—. Recipient Disting. Alumna award St. Mary's Coll., 1976, Peace and Justice award Martin Luther King Jr. Ctr., Atlanta, 1987, Brotherhood/Sisterhood award NCCJ, 1994, Outstanding Svc. award Atlanta Legal Aid Soc., 1997; Fulbright scholar, 1963-64. Mem. Rotary Club of Atlanta (dir., pres. 1999-2000), Yale Club (pres. Ga. chpt. 1995-96). Roman Catholic. Avocations: reading, travel, family activities. Home: # B-203 2632 Peachtree Rd NW Atlanta GA 30305 Office: Servidyne Systems Inc 1350 Spring St NW Atlanta GA 30309

BEWKES, EUGENE GARRETT, JR., investment company executive, consultant; b. Norwood, Mass., Sept. 28, 1926; s. Eugene Garrett and Helen (Van Vlaanderen) B.; m. Marjorie Louise Klenk, Aug. 20, 1949; children: Eugene Garrett III, Jeffrey Lawrence, Robert David. BA, Colgate U., 1948; JD, Yale U., 1951; LLD, Colgate U., 1991. Bar: N.Y. 1952. With firm Chapman, Bryson, Walsh & O'Connell, N.Y.C., 1951-55; atty.-adviser also asst. Office Sec. USAF, 1955-57; with Am. Mgmt. Assn., 1957-61, gen. mgmt. div., mgr., 1959-61; gen. counsel, sec., asst. v.p. Reuben H. Donnelley Corp, 1961-67; v.p. law and adminstrn., sec. Canada Dry Corp., 1967-68; v.p. Norton Simon, Inc., N.Y.C., 1968-72; sr. v.p. Norton Simon, Inc., 1972-73, exec. v.p., 1973-77, vice chmn. bd., 1977-81; chmn., pres., chief exec. officer Am. Bakeries Co., 1982-88; cons. Paine Webber Group, Inc., N.Y.C., 1988—, also bd. dirs.; bd. dirs. Interstate Bakeries Corp., numerous Paine Webber mutual funds. Chmn. emeritus bd. trustees Colgate U., Hamilton, N.Y. With USNR, 1945-46. Mem. Yale Club (N.Y.C.), Blind Brook Club, Johns Island Club, Sankaty Club Nantucket, Phi Beta Kappa, Delta Kappa Epsilon, Phi Delta Phi. Home: PO Box 8307 Vero Beach FL 32963-8307 Office: Paine Webber Group Inc 14th Fl 1285 Ave of the Americas New York NY 10019-6096

BEWKES, JEFF, television broadcasting company executive. Exec. v.p., CFO Home Box Office, N.Y.C., until 1991, pres., COO, 1991—, chmn., CEO. Office: HBO Inc 1100 Avenue Of The Americas New York NY 10036-6740*

BEWLEY, DAVID CHARLES, financial planner; b. Lockport, NY, July 12, 1942; s. Charles C. and Marion (W.) B.; m. Donna M. McDowell, Apr. 2, 1977. Student, Syracuse U. CLU; ChFC. Sales mgr. Equitable Life N.Y., Pitts., Pa., 1968-73, Sarasota, Fla., 1973-80; pres. Bewley & Assocs. PA, Sarasota, Fla., 1981—; co-founder, Agri-Planners Fla., Inc., Sarasota, 1983—, Carlisle Benefit Plans, Inc., Sarasota, 1989—. Found. Bd. Boys and Girls Club of Sarasota, Inc. Recipient Bus. of Yr. award Lockport (N.Y.) C. of C., 1991. Mem. Sarasota Assn. Life Underwriters (pres. 1981-82), Sarasota Bay chpt. CLU/ChFC (pres. 1979-80), S.W. Fla. Estate Planning Coun., Million Dollar Round Table (life and qualifying), Ducks Unltd. (co-chair 1987), Field Club, Sarasota U. Club. Episcopalian. Avocations: running, skiing, golf, boating, travel, water fowling. Office: Bewley & Assocs PA 1605 Main St Ste 601 Sarasota FL 34236-5865

BEWLEY, JOHN DEREK, botany researcher, educator; b. Preston, Lancashire, Eng., Dec. 11, 1943; s. Clifford and Marion (Garner) B.; m. Christine E. Nee Kite, Sept. 3, 1966; children: Alexander, Janette Louise. BSc, U. London, 1965, PhD, 1968, DSc, 1983. Asst. prof. U. Calgary, Alta., 1970-73, assoc. prof., 1973-77, prof. biology, 1977-85; prof., chmn. dept. botany U. Guelph, Ont., 1985-90; prof. botany U. Guelph, 1990—, dir. plant biol. program, 1993-94. E.W.R. Steacie Meml. fellow in natural scis. and engring. Rsch. Coun. Can., 1979-81; recipient Career Rsch. Excellence award Sigma Xi, 1993, Disting. Biologist award Can. Coun. Univ. Chairs, 1994. Fellow Royal Soc. Can. (rapporteur plant biology div. 1984-85, convenor 1985-87); mem. Can. Soc. Plant Physiologists (C.D. Nelson award 1978, Gold medal 1992, sec. 1983-85, v.p. 1987-88, pres. 1988-90), Natural Scis. and Engring. Rsch. Coun. Can. (chmn. plant biology grant selection com. 1988-90). Home: 26 Waverley Dr, Guelph, ON Canada N1E 6C8 Office: U Guelph, Dept Botany, Guelph, ON Canada N1G 2W1

BEXTERMILLER, THERESA MARIE LOUISE, architect, computer graphics; b. St. Charles, Mo., Feb. 9, 1960; d. Charles Frederick and Loretta Joan (Unterreiner) B. BArch, Kans. State U., 1983; MFA Computer Graphics/Interactive Media, Pratt Inst., 1990. Lic. architect, N.Y., 1989, Mo., 1990; cert. Nat. Coun. Archtl. Regis., 1996; real estate salesperson, Mo. Grad. architect Mackey/Mitchell, St. Louis, 1983-84, Fleming Corp., St. Louis, 1984-85; project architect, prototype mgr. Casco Corp., St. Louis, 1985-87; architect HBE Corp., St. Louis, 1987-88; freelance architect N.Y.C., 1988-90; with telecomm. Western Union, 1992-93, AT&T Network Systems,

1993-94; computer cons. Alias/Wavefront Software, 1991-97; contract architect M.K.-Ferguson Group, 1994-95, Fru-Con Engring. Inc., St. Louis, 1995-96; prin. TMB Arch./Computer Graphics, 1997—, Le Pique and Orne Architects Inc., 1998—. Active Nat. Trust Historic Preservation, League of Our Lady of Sacred Heart, Assn. Holy Souls, Legion of 1000-W, St. Louis. Mem. Assn. for Computing Machinery-Siggraph, SIG Computer Human Interaction. Roman Catholic. Avocation: computer software. Home: 1120 Blendon Pl Saint Louis MO 63117-1911

BEY, JOAN S., retired public information specialist, writer; b. Boston, Ind., Nov. 30, 1927; d. Frank J. Schoemaker and Lestra J. (Turner) Schoemaker/Kelly; m. John J. Bey, May 8, 1954 (dec. June 1968); children: Anna Marie Bey Witt, Joseph M., John C. Bachelors degree, St. Mary of the Woods Coll., 1949. Reporter, food editor Indpls. Times, 1950-58; freelance pub. rels. profl., cons. Indpls., 1971-90; with pub. info. dept. Ivy Tech. State Coll., Indpls., 1983-97, ret., 1997. Recipient Vesta award Am. Meat Inst., 1952. Mem. Nat. Fedn. Press Women (writing awards 1980s, 90s), Woman's Press Club Ind. (historian 1984—, pres. 1982-84, Kate Milner Rabb award 1986), Soc. Indian Pioneers. Roman Catholic.

BEYER, BARBARA LYNN, aviation consultant; b. Miami, Fla., Feb. 16, 1947; d. Morten Sternoff and Jane (Hartman) B. BA, George Washington U., 1978. Supr. printing office Saudi Arabian Airlines, 1966-67; ops. coord. Modern Air Transport, Miami, Fla., 1968-70; acct. Modern Air Transport, Berlin, 1970-72; rep. Johnson Internat. Airlines, Washington, 1974-75; v.p., bd. dirs. Avmark, Inc., Washington, 1975—, pres., 1989—; chmn., bd. dirs. Avmark Internat., London, 1985—; mng. dir. Avmark Asia Ltd., Singapore, 1988-89, also bd. dirs.; chmn. bd. dirs. Avmark Asia Ltd., Hong Kong, 1989—; pub. Avmark Aviation Economist, London, 1986—; mem. adv. bd. aviation bus. dept. Embry-Riddle Aero. U. Mem. Aviation Space Writers (award 1978, internat. bd. dirs. 1986-88), Nat. Bus. Aircraft Assn., Am. C. of C., Fgn. Corr. Club, Aero Club, Internat. Aviation Club, Nat. Press Club. Avocations: reading, horseback riding, home improvement. Office: Avmark Inc 1600 Wilson Blvd Ste 150 Arlington VA 22209-2505

BEYER, CASEY K., legislative staff member; b. Reno, Jan. 4, 1955. BA, U. Calif., Santa Barbara, 1978; MUP, San Jose U., 1984. Staff aide Rep. Ed Zschau, 1983-86; cons. to hi-tech cos. Silicone Valley, Calif., 1987-88; dist. dir. Rep. Tom Campbell, 1989-92, 1996-97, chief of staff, 1997—; state adminstr. State Senator Tom Campbell, 1993-95. Mem. exec. com. Tax and Fiscal Policy Joint Venture, 1994—, mem. working group, 1994—. Office: Office US Rep Tom Campbell Ste 1C 910 Campisi Way Campbell CA 95008*

BEYER, CHARLOTTE BISHOP, investment management executive; b. N.Y.C., Oct. 16, 1947; d. Edward Morton and Charlote Reid (Handy) Beyer; m. Warren P. Weitman, Jr., July 28, 1967; children: Catherine Scott, Michael Benjamin; m. Keith W. Fiveson, May 31, 1997. BA, CUNY, 1969. With Bankers Trust Co., N.Y.C., 1970-81, v.p. trust svcs. and securities ops., 1979-81; v.p. prin. client svc. and mktg. Wood Struthers & Winthrop Mgmt. Corp. subs. Donaldson Lufkin and Jenrette, N.Y.C., 1985-89; sr. v.p. Wood Struthers & Winthrop Mgmt. Corp. subs. Donaldson Lufkinand Jenrette, N.Y.C., 1987-89; v.p. Lazard Freres Asset Mgmt., N.Y.C., 1989-90; founder Inst. Pvt. Investors, Rsch. and Ednl. Forum, 1990—. Trustee Westover Sch., Middlebury, Conn., 1987—, now pres. bd. trustees. Episcopalian. Office: Inst Pvt Investors 74 Trinity Pl New York NY 10006-2003

BEYER, DONALD STERNOFF, JR., state official; b. Trieste, Free Territory of Trieste, June 20, 1950; came to U.S., 1952; s. Donald Sternoff Sr. and Nancy Prew (McDonald) B.; m. Carolyn Anne McInerney, July 15, 1972 (div.); children: Donald III, Stephanie; m. Megan Carroll, Sept. 19, 1987; children: Clara, Grace. BA in Econs. magna cum laude, Williams Coll., 1972. Pres., v.p. and other positions Don Beyer Volvo, Falls Church, Va., 1974—; lt. gov. Commonwealth of Va., Richmond, 1990-98; urban at large mem. Commonwealth Transp. Bd., Va., 1987-90; chmn. Va. Econ. Bridge Initiative, Va., 1990—. Chmn. Baliles for Gov., No. Va., 1985, Paul Simon for Pres., Va., 1988, Bill Clinton for Pres., Va., 1992; mem. 11th Dist. Dem. Com., Vienna, Va., 1992; Dem. nominee Gov. of Va., 1998. Named Time Mag. Quality Dealer of Yr. for Va., 1991. Mem. Land Rover Alexandria (pres. 1997—). Democrat. Episcopalian. Avocations: golf, skiing, climbing. Office: Don Beyer Volvo 1231 W Broad St Falls Church VA 22046-2117

BEYER, GORDON ROBERT, foreign service officer; b. Chgo., Oct. 13, 1930; m. Mary Paine Winsor, Feb. 22, 1951; children: Theresa Gordon, Hugh Richard, Thomas Paine. AB, Harvard U.; MA, Northwestern U.; postgrad., Nat. War Coll., 1971-72. With Pres.'s Commn. on Vets.' Pensions (Bradley Commn.), 1956; commd. fgn. service officer Dept. State, 1957; officer Am. embassy, Bangkok, 1957-59, Washington, 1959-61; consul Yokohama, Japan, 1961-64; officer Am. embassy, Somalia; consul Am. embassy, Hargeisa, 1964-66, Mogadishu, 1966-67; with Dept. State, Washington, 1967-72; dep. chief of mission Am. embassy, Dar es Salaam, Tanzania, 1972-75; dep. dir. Egyptian desk Dept. State, 1975-77; officer U.S. UN, 1977; dir. Office East African Affairs Dept. State, 1978-80; U.S. Amb. to Uganda, Kampala, 1980-83; with Nat. War Coll., 1983-85; pres. George C. Marshall Found., Lexington, Va., 1985-91; Bd. dirs. Dar es Salaam Internat. Sch., 1972-75, pres., 1974. Author: (monographs) Race and National Security, 1972, Can Low Intensity Conflict be Managed?, 1987, The Marshall Plan: A Contemporary View, 1989, America, Japan and the Atomic Bomb, 1993, The Who?, 1995. Chmn. Rockbridge County Dem. Com., 1997—. 1st lt. USMC, 1953-55. Recipient meritorious honor awards Dept. State, 1967, 75, 82. Mem. Am. Fgn. Service Assn., Cosmos Club (Washington), Harvard Club (N.Y.C.), Dacor Club (Washington). *

BEYER, KAREN HAYNES, social worker; b. Cleve. BA, Ohio State U., 1965; MSW, Loyola U., Chgo., 1969; postgrad. Family Inst., Northwestern U., 1979; MPA, Roosevelt U., 1992; CBA U. Ill. Chgo., 1995. Lic. clin. social worker Ill. With Cuyahoga County Div. Child Welfare, Cleve., 1965, Dallas County Child Welfare Unit, Dallas, 1966; with Luth. Social Svcs. Ill., Chgo., 1967-73; pvt. practice psychotherapy, family mediation, Schaumburg, Ill., 1975-93; therapist Family Svcs. Assn. Greater Elgin (Ill.), 1973-77, dir. profl. svcs., 1977-83; dir. HHS Village of Hoffman Estates, Ill., 1983-93; exec. dir. Larkin Ctr., Elgin, Ill., 1993—. Mem. NASW, Rotary. Unitarian. *Karen Beyer, a licensed clinical social worker, defied a court order to divulge her client's therapy records. The refusal was appealed to the U.S Supreme Court (1996, Jaffee vs. Redmond and the Village of Hoffman Estates). The Supreme Courtmajority decision supported her protection of client privacy and resulted in stronger guarantees of confidentiality in therapy* Office: Larkin Ctr 1212 Larkin Ave Elgin IL 60123-6042

BEYER, LISA, journalist; b. Lafayette, La., 1961. BJ, U. Tex., 1983. Sr. correspondent Asiaweek, Singapore, 1984-88; staff writer, assoc. editor Time Mag., N.Y.C., 1988-91, Jerusalem bur. chief, 1991—. Office: Time Mag Time & Life Bldg Rockefeller Ctr 1271 6th Av New York NY 10020-1393*

BEYER, MARY EDEL, primary education educator; b. Winona, Minn., July 16, 1932; d. Edmund Aloysious and Gertrude Cecilia (Knopick) Edel; m. Argene Lester Beyer, June 7, 1958 (dec. Aug. 1985); children: Jason Edel Beyer, Trudy Edel Beyer, Gerard Edel Beyer, Jeremy Edel Beyer. AS in Edn., Winona State U., 1952, BS, 1967, MS, 1978. Cert. elem. tchr., Minn. Tchr. 1st grade Dodge Ctr. (Minn.) Sch., 1952-55; tchr. 1st grade, kindergarten Dist. 857, Lewiston, Minn., 1955-63; tchr. kindergarten Dist. 861, Winona, 1968-95, Stockton (Minn.) Sch., 1966-70; tchr. Rollingstone Elem. Sch., 1970-95; sch. del. Minn. Edn. Effective Program, 1987-95; pres. Winona Dist. 861 Reading Com. Contbr. to Poland Today Pol-Am. Jour., 1993; celebrity reader Children's Books Reading on the mall, 1990; photographer, writer School News Winona Post, 1985-95; freelance writer. Spencer, cadet mem. USO Group, Winona, 1950-52; leader Girl Scouts-Boy Scouts, 1952-70; mem. Sweet Adelines, 1978—; sings lead Hiawatha Valley Sweet Adelines, sec. 1994-97; apptd. commr. City of Winona Hist. Preservation Commn., 1996—; soprano St. Stanislaus Kostka choir, 1996—. Recipient Pres.'s award Lakeside St. Machines, Winona, 1992, Disting. Svc. award, 1993, Diamond award 4-H Club, Winona, 1995; named Master Knitter Extension Office, Winona, 1985, Ky. Belle of the Blue Grass Gov. of Ky., 1951. Mem. PTA (pres.), Minn. Reading Assn. (del. 1985-95), Polish Heritage Soc. (sec. 1967—), Am. Legion Aux., Knights Columbus (4th degree lady). County Hist. Soc. (mus. vol.), Winona Athletic Club, C. of C. (bus. edn. intern 1995). Avocations: photography, fashion modeling, music, art, doll collecting. Home: 260 W Broadway St Winona MN 55987-5224

BEYER, NORMA WARREN, secondary education educator; b. Bklyn., Dec. 1, 1926; d. Norman Hayden and Catherine Mary Warren; m. Daniel Joseph Beyer, July 10, 1954; children: Catherine Norma, Daniel Joseph Jr., Peter Norman, Maureen Bernadette. BS, CUNY, Bklyn., 1949; MA in Edn., NYU, 1953. Tchr. home econs. N.Y.C. Bd. Edn., Bklyn., 1950—. Bd. dirs. Clearmeadow Civic Assn., East Meadow, 1985—; pres. St. Brigid's Rosary Soc., Westbury, N.Y., 1987-94, 99—; del. U. Fedn. Tchrs., 1989-90. Recipient St. Pius award Diocese of Rockville Ctr., 1975, Leader's Gold medal Nassau County 4H, 1978, Outstanding Community Svc. award Salisbury Rep. Club, 1993, Sr. Elizabeth Ann Seaton medal, 1997. Mem. NAFE, Am. Home Econs. Assn., N.Y.C. Home Econs. Assn. (historian 1978-79), Cath. Tchrs. Assn., Bklyn. Coll., NYU Alumni Assn., Salisbury Rep. Club. Republican. Roman Catholic. Avocations: painting, clothing design and construction, gardening. Home: 251 Clearmeadow Dr East Meadow NY 11554-1211

BEYER, SUSAN KELLEY, school psychologist; b. Eau Claire, Wis., Aug. 30, 1964; d. Frank Albert III and Doris Gertrude (Schafer) Kelley; m. Jason Edel Beyer, Aug. 12, 1995. BS in Psychology, U. Wis., 1987, BS in Dance Edn., 1987; MSEd in Sch. Psychology, U. Wis., Stout, 1989. Lic. sch. psychologist, Minn. Sch. psychologist Tulare County Office of Edn., Visalia, Calif., 1990-93, Hiawatha Valley Edn. Dist., Winona, Minn., 1994—; presenter in field; coach dance team Saint-Sations, 1995—. Big sister YMCA Y-Friends, Winona, 1994—; bd. dirs. Sequoia Melodies Chorus, 1991-93; mem., soloist St. Stanislaus-Kostka Choir, 1995—. Mem. NASP, Minn. Sch. Psychologists Assn., Sweet Adelines Internat. (v.p. Hiawatha Valley chpt. 1997-98, pres. 1998, 1st place small chorus award 1996, mem. Mel-Lynn-Connie Baby quartet 1996-98). Avocations: coaching dance teams, singing, cats, home building. Home: R 3 Box 171B Winona MN 55987-9518 Office: Hiawatha Valley Edn Dist 1410 Bundy Blvd Winona MN 55987-6300

BEYER, SUZANNE, advertising agency executive; b. N.Y.C.; d. Harry and Jennie Hillman; student Nassau Community Coll., 1963-65; grad. Conservatory of Musical Art, N.Y.C., 1947; m. Isadore Beyer; children—Pamela Claire, Hillary Jay. Singer, tchr. piano, N.Y.C., 1947-66; asst. to v.p. media dir. Robert E. Wilson, Advt., N.Y.C., 1967-72; media planner, media buyer Frank J. Corbett div. BBDO Internat., N.Y.C., 1972-77; media planner, media buyer Lavey/Wolff/Swift div. BBDO Advt., N.Y.C., 1977-80, sr. media planner, 1980-83, media supr., 1983-94; media supr. Lyons, Lavey, Nichel, Swift, N.Y.C., 1995-96; pharm. advt. med. media cons., 1996—; soprano Opera Assn. Nassau, 1976—; soprano United Choral Soc., Woodmere, L.I., 1970—, Armand Sodero Chorale, Baldwin, L.I., 1980-86, Rockville Centre Choral Soc., 1986—. Mem. Pharm. Advt. Council, L.I. Advt. Club, Healthcare Bus. Women's Assn. Home: 66 Fonda Rd Rockville Centre NY 11570-2751

BEYER, WERNER WILLIAM, retired English educator; b. Laporte, Ind., Mar. 22, 1911; s. Franz E. W. and Martha L. Beyer; m. Ruth K. Bibos, Nov. 19, 1954; children: Tanya Elena, Mary Deirdre. AB with spl. honors, Columbia Coll., 1934; MA, Columbia U., 1936, PhD, 1945. English sr. master Englewood (N.J.) Sch. for Boys, 1936-41; instr. in English Drew U., Madison, N.J., 1943-45; asst. prof. Rutgers U., New Brunswick, N.J., 1945-48; vis. asst. prof. Columbia U., N.Y.C., 1948; prof. English Butler U., Indpls., 1948-83; vis. prof. Ind. U., Bloomington, 1964-65; dept. head Butler U., 1965-81. Author: Keats and the Daemon King, 1947, Enchanted Forest, 1967, (short stories) Islands Beneath the Moon, 1995; contbr. articles to profl. jours. Cutting fellow, then Lydig fellow, 1941-43, Ford fellow, 1951-52. Fellow Internat. Inst. Arts and Letters (life); MLA, Columbia U. Alumni Assn., Phi Kappa Phi. Avocations: golf, canoeing, theater, opera, travel. Home: 5388 Thicket Hill Ln Indianapolis IN 46226

BEYERLEIN, SUSAN CAROL, educational administrator; b. Royal Oak, Mich., Apr. 23, 1948; d. Jack Frederick and Eleanore Jean Schaper; m. Kerry Norman Beyerlein, July 18, 1970 (div. May 1990); children: Kraig Kerry, Reid Ryan. BS in Elem. Edn., Valparaiso U., 1970; MPA in Ednl. Adminstrn., U. Mich., 1999. Elem. tchr. Warren (Mich.) Consol. Schs., 1970-75; tchr. Adult Edn., Royal Oak, 1979-97; coord. Teen Parent Program, Royal Oak, 1991-98; program supr. Royal Oak Continuing Edn., 1996—; adminstr. Lincoln Early Childhood Ctr., Royal Oak, 1998—; owner, dir. Sue's Summer Swimming, Royal Oak, 1972—; chair com. Royal Oak Adv. Coun., 1994—; mem. Royal Oak Continuing Edn. Adv. Coun., 1994—. Chair Royal Oak Youth Assistance, 1997—; mem. Royal Oak Prevention Coalition, 1992—; chair Royal Oak Family Adv. Com., 1993—. Recipient Cmty. Spirit award Youth Assistance, 1998. Mem. ASCD, Am. Soc. for Pub. Adminstrn., Mich. Assn. for Edn. of Young Children, Mich. Assn. Secondary Sch. Prins., Mich. Assn. Adult and Cmty. Educatorw, Pi Lambda Theta. Lutheran. Avocations: reading, swimming, cross country skiing, dining out. Email: B1Bunch@aol.com. Home: 4209 Manor Ave Royal Oak MI 48073 Office: Lincoln Early Childhood Ctr 1901 E Eleven Mile Rd Royal Oak MI 48067

BEYER-MEARS, ANNETTE, physiologist; b. Madison, Wis., May 26, 1941; d. Karl and Annette (Weiss) Beyer. B.A., Vassar Coll., 1963; M.S., Fairleigh Dickinson U., 1973; Ph.D., Coll. Medicine and Dentistry N.J., 1977. NIH fellow Cornell U. Med. Sch., 1963-65; instr. physiology Springside Sch., Phila., 1967-71; teaching asst. dept. physiology Coll. Medicine & Dentistry N.J., N.J. Med. Sch., 1974-77, NIH fellow dept. ophthalmology, 1978-80; asst. prof. dept. ophthalmology U. Medicine and Dentistry N.J., N.J. Med. Sch., Newark, 1979-85, asst. prof. dept. physiology, 1980-85, assoc. prof. dept. physiology, 1986—, assoc. prof. dept. ophthalmology, 1986—; vis. assoc. prof. dept. ophthalmology and vision sci. U. Wis., Madison, 1995—; cons. Alcon Labs. Contbr. articles in field of diabetic lens and kidney therapy to profl. jours. Chmn. admissions No. N.J., Vassar Coll., 1974-79; mem. minister search com. St. Bartholomew Episcopal Ch., N.J., 1978, fund-raising chmn., 1978, 79; del. Episc. Diocesan Conv., 1977, 78; long range planning com. Christ Ch., Ridgewood, N.J., 1985-87, vestry, 1994-95. Recipient NIH Nat. Rsch. Svc. award, 1978-80, Found. CMDNJ Rsch. award, 1980; grantee Juvenile Diabetes Found., 1985-87, NIH, NEI grantee, 1980-95, Pfizer, Inc. grantee, 1985-89, 93—. Mem. Am. Physiol. Soc., N.Y. Acad. Scis., Soc. for Neurosci., Am. Soc. Pharmacology and Exptl. Therapeutics, Assn. for Rsch. Vision & Ophthalmology, Internat. Soc. for Eye Research, AAAS, The Royal Soc. Medicine, Internat. Diabetes Found., Am. Diabetes Assn., European Assn. Study of Diabetes, Aircraft Owners and Pilots Assn., Sigma Xi. Home: 120 Ely Pl Madison WI 53705-4015

BEYERS, WILLIAM BJORN, geography educator; b. Seattle, Mar. 24, 1940; s. William Abraham and Esther Jakobia (Svendsen) B.; m. Margaret Lyn Rice, July 28, 1968. B.A., U. Wash., 1962, Ph.D., 1967. Asst. prof. geography U. Wash., Seattle, 1968-74, assoc. prof., 1974-82, prof., 1982—, chmn. dept. geography, 1991-95. Mem. Assn. Am. Geographers, Regional Sci. Assn., Am. Econs. Assn., Western Regional Sci. Assn. E-mail: Beyers@u.washington.edu. Fax: 206-543-3313. Home: 7159 Beach Dr SW Seattle WA 98136-2077 Office: U Wash Dept Geography PO Box 353550 Seattle WA 98195-3550

BEYLKIN, GREGORY, mathematician; b. St. Petersburg, USSR, Mar. 16, 1953; came to U.S., 1980; naturalized citizen, 1985; s. Jacob and Raya (Pripshtein) B.; m. Helen Simontov, 1974; children: Michael, Daniel. Diploma in Math., U. St. Petersburg, Leningrad, 1975; PhD in Math., NYU, 1982. Assoc. rsch. sci. NYU, 1982-83; mem. profl. staff Schlumberger-Doll Research, Ridgefield, Conn., 1983-91; prof. dept. applied math. U. Colo., Boulder, 1991—. Contbr. articles to profl. jours. Mem. Am. Math. Soc., Soc. for Indsl. and Applied Math., Soc. Exptl. Geophysicists. Home: 3897 Promontory Ct Boulder CO 80304-1053 Office: U Colo Dept Applied Math PO Box 526 Boulder CO 80309-0526

BEYMAN, JONATHAN ERIC, information officer; b. Newark, Dec. 31, 1955; s. Bernard B. and Miriam (Simon) B.; m. Susan Elizabeth Bleckman, Aug. 23, 1981; children: Michael, Daniel, Max. BS, U. Ct., 1976; MBA, Cornell U., 1981. CPA, Conn. Sr. acct. Arthur Young and Co., N.Y.C., 1976-79; asst. v.p. Chem. Bank, N.Y.C., 1981-84; sr. cons. Am. Mgmt. Systems, N.Y.C., 1985; v.p. Citibank North Am. Investment Bank, N.Y.C., 1985-86; v.p. Lehman Bros., N.Y.C., 1986-88, sr. v.p., 1988-91, mng. dir., 1991-94; chief info. officer and sr. v.p. CUC Internat., Stamford, Conn., 1994-97; co-chief info. officer, exec. v.p. Cendant Corp., Stamford, 1997—. Mem. AICPA. Democrat. Jewish. Avocations: bicycling, reading, running, carpentry. Home: 1 Singing Woods Ct Norwalk CT 06850-1223 Office: CUC Internat 707 Summer St Stamford CT 06901-1026

BEYSTER, JOHN ROBERT, engineering company executive; b. Detroit, July 26, 1924; s. John Frederick and Lillian Edith (Jondro) B.; m. Betty Jean Brock, Sept. 8, 1955; children: James Frederick, Mark Daneil, Mary Ann. B.S. in Engring., U. Mich., 1945, M.S., 1948, Ph.D., 1950. Registered profl. engr., Calif. Mem. staff Los Alamos Sci. Lab., 1951-56; chmn. dept. accel. physics Gulf Gen. Atomic Co., San Diego, 1957-69; pres., chmn. bd. Sci. Applications, Inc., La Jolla, Calif., from 1969, now chmn. bd., chief exec. officer; mem. Joint Strategic Target Planning Staff, Sci. Adv. Group, Omaha, 1978—; panel mem. Nat. Measurement Lab. Evaluation panel for Radiation Research, Washington, 1983—; dir. Scripps Bancorp, La Jolla, 1983. Co-author: Slow Neutron Scattering and Thermalization, 1970. With USN, 1943-46. Fellow Am. Nuclear Soc., Am. Phys. Soc.; mem. NAE. Republican. Roman Catholic. Home: 9321 La Jolla Farms Rd La Jolla CA 92037-1126 Office: Science Applications Inter Corp 10260 Campus Point Dr San Diego CA 92121-1522

BEYTAGH, FRANCIS XAVIER, JR., law educator; b. Savannah, Ga., July 11, 1935. B.A. magna cum laude, U. Notre Dame, 1956; J.D., U. Mich., 1963. Bar: Ohio 1964, U.S. Supreme Ct. 1967, Ind. 1972. Clk. Fuller, Seney, Henry & Hodge, Toledo, 1961; sr. law clk. to Chief Justice Earl Warren, U.S. Supreme Ct., Washington, 1963-64; assoc. Jones, Day, Cockley and Reavis, Cleve., 1964-66; asst. to solicitor gen. U.S. Dept. Justice, Washington, 1966-70; prof. law U. Notre Dame, 1970-74, 75-76; prof., dean U. Toledo Coll. Law, 1976-83; Cullen prof. law U. Houston, 1984-85; prof., dean Ohio State U. Coll. Law, 1985-93, prof., 1993-97; spl. counsel Jones, Day, Reavis & Pogue, Columbus, 1993-96; pres., prof. Fla. Coastal Sch. Law, Jacksonville, 1997-98, prof., 1998—; vis. prof. law U. Va., Charlottesville, 1974-75, U. Mich., 1983-84, So. Meth. U., Dallas, 1997. Editor in chief Mich. Law Rev., 1962-63; author: Supplement to Kauper's Constitutional Law: Cases and Materials, 1977, Constitutional Law: Cases and Materials, 5th edit., 1980, supplements, 1981, 82, 84, Constitutionalism in Contemporary Ireland, 1997; contbr. articles to profl. jours. Served to capt. USNR; ret. Fulbright fellow, 1994. Fellow Am. Bar Found.; mem. ABA, Fla. Bar, Jacksonville Bar Assn., Order of Coif. Home: 49 Marsh Creek Rd Amelia Island FL 32034-6414 Office: Fla Coastal Sch Law 7555 Beach Blvd Jacksonville FL 32216-3000

BEZANSON, KEITH ARTHUR, administrative educational executive; b. Kingston, Ont., Can., May 12, 1941; s. Walter and Eileen B.; m. Monique Ouellet; children: Kathryn, Sarah, Julia. BA, Carleton U., 1964; PhD, Stanford U., 1972. Secondary sch. tchr. Can. Univ. Svcs. Oversears, Nigeria, 1964-66; project dir. Sch. Leavers Rsch. Project, Ghana, East Africa, 1966-72; chief planning officer Can. Internat. Devel. Agy., Africa, 1973-77, regional dir. East Africa, 1977-78, dir. gen. multilateral programs, 1978-81; v.p. Americas br. Can. Internat. Devel. Agy., 1981-85; Can. amb. to Peru and Bolivia Can. Embassy, 1985-88; adminstrv. mgr. Inter-Am. Devel. Bank, 1988-91; pres. Internat. Devel. Rsch. Ctr., Ottawa, Ont., Can., 1991-97; dir. Inst. for Devel. Studies U. Sussex, Brighton, Eng., 1997. Contbr. articles and papers to profl. jours. Decorated Bravery medal Can. Govt., 1981; Ford Found. fellow, 1966-68, Advanced Doctoral fellow Can. Coun., 1969-70. Office: Internat Devel Rsch Ctr, Inst Devel Studies, U Sussex, Brighton BN1 9RE, England

BEZANSON, THOMAS EDWARD, lawyer; b. Hartford, Conn., Aug. 1, 1945; s. Philip Thomas and Lillian (Carlson) B.; m. Janie R. Bezanson, Aug. 10, 1969; children: Philip, Jeffrey. BA, Grinnell, 1967; MA, Rutgers U., 1971, JD, 1974. Bar: N.Y. 1975, U.S. Dist. Ct. (ea. dist.) 1975, U.S. Dist. Ct. (so. dist.) N.Y. 1975, U.S. Ct. Appeals (2d cir.) 1975, U.S. Ct. Appeals (6th cir.) 1980, U.S. Supreme Ct. 1991. Assoc. Chadbourne & Parke, N.Y.C., 1974-81, ptnr., 1981—. Author: 42 Poems, 1993. Bd. dirs. Westchester Philharm., 1992-98, N.Y. Lawyers for the Public Interest, Inc., 1997—. Served in U.S. Army, 1967-69, Thailand. Mem. ABA, N.Y. State Bar Assn., Assn. of Bar of City of N.Y. Office: Chadbourne & Parke 30 Rockefeller Plz New York NY 10112-0002

BEZAR, GILBERT EDWARD, retired aerospace company executive, volunteer; b. Phila., May 24, 1930; s. Abraham Bernard and Leah (Hymowitz) B.; m. Norma Jean Davis, Sept. 4, 1964 (dec. 1968); children: Eric David, Robyn Lisa; m. Elaine R. Spitzer, Jan. 6, 1989. B.S. in Acctg., Temple U., 1951; M.B.A. in Fin. and Mgmt., UCLA, 1957. V.p. Armco-Hitco, Irvine, Calif., 1972-77; v.p. fin. Armco-Nat. Supply Co., Houston, 1977-81; v.p. fin. affairs, treas. Armco, Inc., Middletown, Ohio, 1983-84; v.p. adminstrn. ARMCO Aerospace and Strategic Materials Group, Irvine, 1981-83; v.p. fin. and adminstrn. OCF Aerospace and Strategic Materials Group, Newport Beach, Calif., 1984-88; cons. Exec. Svc. Corps., 1990—; cons. AARP Work Force, 1993—; bd. dirs. Oreg. Metall. Corp., Albany, 1983-97; instr. extension program UCLA, 1957-62, U. Calif. - Irvine, 1963-72. Served to lt. USNR, 1952-55. UCLA teaching fellow, 1955-57. Mem. Fin. Execs. Inst. (v.p. 1982-83), World Affairs Coun., Beta Gamma Sigma. Jewish. Home: 965 Del Mar Ave Laguna Beach CA 92651-3501

BEZEMER, CAL GENE, composer; b. Lynnville, Iowa, Dec. 9, 1936; s. Arie Edward Bezemer and Deana Berdena (Kuipers) Hanen; m. Penelope Kraner, Nov. 14, 1965 (div. June 1969); children: John, Mark, Kristy: 1 adopted child, Christopher. BA in Music Theory-Composition-Piano, Kansas City Conservatory, 1962; grad., Iowa State U., 1965; ThD, Internat. Theol. Sem., 1985. Pvt. practice, 1976—; music dir., pianist Yma Sumac and Herb Jeffries, 1988—; founder, dir. Wholy Cow, 1997—; v.p. Hollywood-Wilshire Symphony, 1978-92, So. Calif. Motion Picture Coun., 1978-92, Hollywood Opera Club, 1978-92. Ptnr. with Leo Savalas, 1997, Dorothy Donnegan, 1997; leader, sideman, Hollywood Bowl, Palladium, Coconut Grove, Music Center, Cinegrill, House of Blues; piano and sax aboard USS Pocono, Admiral's Flagship for Atlantic Fleet; with Al Jarreau, David Sanborn, Debbie Reynolds, Eddie Jefferson, "Scatman" Crothers, Ralph Marterie, Ray McKinley (Glen Miller Band), "Wolfman" Jack, Alan Jones, Four Lads, Art Lund, Gene Bell, Arthur Duncan; columnist Spotlite on Las Vegas (Angel City Jazz Beat). Exec. v.p. Music and Performing Arts Angels, 1978—; assoc. min., organist Internat. Evangelism Crusades, 1983—; v.p. Hollywood Bowl Easter Sunrise Svc. Guild, 1992-95. With USN, 1954-57. Recipient 1st Composers award Matinne Musical Club, 1978. Mem. Am. Soc. Music Arrangers and Composers, Musician's Union, Hollywood Men's Comedy Club, Troupers, Navy League, Am. Legion Film League, Dexter Grey Found. Film Adv. Bd. of Elaine Blythe. Republican. Mem. Christian Ch. Avocations: photography, movies, theater, poetry, reading. Home: 222 S Mariposa Ave Apt 301 Los Angeles CA 90004-5415 Office: Music Angels Prodn 222 S Mariposa Ave Apt 301 Los Angeles CA 90004-5415

BEZOLD, CLEMENT, think tank executive; b. Coral Gables, Fla., 1948. BS, Georgetown U., 1970; PhD, U. Fla., 1976. Asst. dir. Ctr. Govtl. Responsibility, Fla.; vis. scholar The Brookings Inst., 1974-77; pres. Inst. for Alternative Futures, Alexandria, Va., 1977—; pres. Alternative Futures Assocs., 1982—; cons. to local, state, fed. govts. in U.S. and internat., WHO, major corps. including Disney, AT&T, pharm. and health care cos.; tchr. Am. U., U. Fla., Antioch U.; lectr. in field. Author: Anticipatory Democracy (introduction by Alvin Toffler), 1978, others; co-author: (with R. Carlson and J. Peck) The Future of Work and Health, 1985 (Am. Health Mag. book award); editor: (with Erica Mayer) Future Care: Responding to the Demand for Change, 1996. Co-founder Internat. Health Futures Network; bd. dirs. World Future Soc. Office: Inst. Alternative Futures 100 N Pitt St Ste 235 Alexandria VA 22314-3134*

BEZOS, JEFFREY P., multimedia executive. Degree in elec. engring. and computer sci. summa cum laude, Princeton U., 1986. With Bankers Trust Co., N.Y., 1988-90, v.p., 1990; with D.E. Shaw & Co., N.Y., 1990-94, sr. v.p., 1992-94; founder, CEO Amazon.com Inc., Seattle, 1995—; past mem. staff FITEL, N.Y. Mem. Phi Beta Kappa. Office: Amazon com Inc 1200 12th Ave S Seattle WA 98144*

BEZROD, NORMA R., artist; b. Phila., May 17, 1938; d. Samuel Bezrod and Bessie Roffman; m. Arthur J. Cooperman, Aug. 22, 1959 (div. Apr. 1977); 1 child, Seth Alan Cooperman; m. William D. P. Riley, July 1, 1983 (dec. Oct. 1998). BA, Queens Coll., 1960, MS, 1974; EdD, Columbia U., 1986. Lic. fine arts and spl. edn. tchr., N.Y.C.; lic. fine arts tchr., N.Y. Art tchr. N.Y.C. Pub. Schs., 1960-77; exec. dir. art Sr. Ctr., Human Resources Adminstrn., N.Y.C., 1977-78; instr. art edn. Queens (N.Y.) Coll., 1978-79; edn. evaluator, case mgr. N.Y.C. Bd. Edn., 1980-88; cons. N.Y. State Coun. on the Arts, 1977-79. Author: Don't Be Afraid of the Dark, 1977, (series) Lion and Pretty Bird, 1983-85; art critic Good Times, L.I., N.Y., 1971-75. Teaching fellow Queens Coll., 1978-79. Home: PO Box 660125 Flushing NY 11366-0125

BEZRUCHKA, STEPHEN ANTHONY, emergency physician, writer; b. Toronto, Ont., Can., May 9, 1943; s. Jaroslaw and Stella (Pankoff) B.; m. Mary Lynn Hanley, Oct. 6, 1975 (div. 1985); 1 child, Michael; m. Mary Anne Mercer, July 16, 1995; 1 child, Maia Mercer. AM, Harvard U., 1967; MD, Stanford U., 1973; MPH, Johns Hopkins U., 1993. Diplomate Am. Bd. Emergency Medicine. Med. dir. Dhorpatan (Nepal) Health Project, 1974-76; emergency physician various hosps. Wash., 1979—; dir. Surkhet Rural Tng. Ctr. U. Calgary Can. Internat. Devel. Agy., Nepal, 1984-85; dr. travel medicine King County Travel Health CUMC, Seattle, 1987—; affiliate asst. prof. Sch. Pub. Health & Cmty. Medicine, U. Wash., Seattle, 1990—; asst. pub. health officer Kittitas County, Wash., 1994-95; cons. U.S. Dept. State, Nepal, 1993-96; dir. immunization assessment initiative Dept. Health, Wash., 1994-95. Author: Trekking in Nepal, 1972, 7th edit., 1997, The Pocket Doctor, 1988, 3rd edit., 1999, Altitude Illness, 1994, (book and tape) Nepali for Trekkers, 1991. Woodrow Wilson fellow Woodrow Wilson Found., 1966; Nat. Rsch. Coun. Can. fellow, 1966-69; John Hopkins Sch. Hygiene and Pub. Health fellow, 1992-93. Mem. Union Internat. Assns. Alpinism (med. commn., advisory panel), Wilderness Med. Soc., Nepal Med. Assn., King County Med. Soc., Alpine Club of Can. (Am. v.p. 1983-84), Am. Alpine Club. Home: 2030 Bonair Dr SW Seattle WA 98116-1822

BEZUCHA, ROBERT JOSEPH, history educator; b. Racine, Wis., June 6, 1940; s. Robert Donald and Helen Anne (Wacek) B.; m. Jenny L. Kallick, Dec. 14, 1985; children from previous marriage: Thomas Gordon, Margaret Jeanne. BA, Lawrence U., 1962; MA, U. Mich., 1963, PhD, 1968; MA (hon.), Amherst Coll., 1981. Instr. U. Mich., Ann Arbor, 1967-68; asst. prof. Northwestern U., Evanston, Ill., 1968-75; assoc. prof. Syracuse (N.Y.) U., 1975-77; assoc. prof. history Amherst (Mass.) Coll., 1977-81, prof., 1981—, Andrew W. Mellon prof. humanities, 1989-92, George Daniel Olds prof. econs. and social instns., 1996—; cons. Social Sci. Rsch. Coun., N.Y.C., 1978-80, New Eng. Bd. Higher Edn., Boston, 1990—, Nat. Coun., Glimmerglass Opera, 1994—. Author: The Lyon Uprising of 1834, 1974; editor: Modern European Social History, 1972; contbr. articles, essays, revs. to profl. jours. Vice chmn. bd. trustees Westfield (Mass.) State Coll., 1987-92. NEH rsch. grantee, 1973-74; Guggenheim Found. fellow, 1987. Mem. Am. Hist. Assn., Phi Kappa Phi. Home: 74 Overlook Dr Amherst MA 01002-1248 Office: Amherst Coll Dept History Amherst MA 01002-5002

BEZZONE, ALBERT PAUL, structural engineer; b. Sacramento, Calif., June 22, 1931; s. Albert Paul and Angela Edna (Nicolai) B.; m. JoAnn Karslie Walther, Aug. 4, 1951; children: Jeffrey Paul, David Ernest, Judith Eileen. Student, Sacramento City Coll., 1949-50, Calif. State U., 1952-56. Engrng. technician State of Calif., Sacramento, 1950-51; civil engr. County of Sacramento, Calif., 1951-53; with Calif. Dept. Transportation, 1953-93, chief office of structure constrn., structures div., 1977-93; cons. bridge engrng. Sacramento, 1993—. Contbr. articles to profl. jours. Fellow ASCE; mem. Profl. Engrs. in Calif. Govt. Home: 829 Senior Way Sacramento CA 95831-2128 Office: PO Box 942874 Sacramento CA 94274-0001

BHAGAT, PHIROZ MANECK, mechanical engineer; b. Poona, India, Oct. 28, 1948; came to U.S., 1970; s. Maneck Phirozshaw and Khorshed Eduljee (Batliwala) B.; m. Patricia Jane Steckler, Oct. 13, 1979; children: Kay, Sarah. B.Tech., Indian Inst. Tech.-Bombay, 1970; M.S. in Engrng., U. Mich., 1971, Ph.D., 1975. Rsch. fellow in applied mechanics Harvard U., Cambridge, Mass., 1975-77; asst. prof. engrng. Columbia U., N.Y.C., 1977-81, adj. asst. prof., 1981-84; staff engr. Exxon Rsch. & Engrng. Co., Florham Park, N.J., 1981-83, sr. staff engr., 1983—, head sci. computing group, 1988-90; mng. dir. Janus Enterprise Internat., 1992-94. Contbr. articles to profl. jours. K.C., Mahindra scholar, 1970, J.N. Tata scholar, 1970; Horace Rackham predoctoral fellow, 1973-74, 74-75. Mem. AIChE, ASME, N.Y. Acad. Scis., Tau Beta Pi, Sigma Xi. Rsch. devel. of Neural Nets in tech. and bus. applications, pattern recognition and forecasting for business strategies, on application of thermal sciences to model for technicaland business strategies petrochemical processes, science computing, heat transfer, fluid mechanics, thermodynamics, computer modeling, business global computer simulation. Home: 519 Alden St Westfield NJ 07090-3040 Office: Exxon Rsch & Engrng Co Florham Park NJ 07932

BHAGWAN, SUDHIR, computer industry and research executive, consultant; b. Lahore, West Pakistan, Aug. 9, 1942; came to U.S., 1963; s. Vishan and Lakshmi Devi (Arora) B.; m. Sarita Bahl, Oct. 25, 1969; children: Sonia, Sunil. BSEE, Punjab Engrng. Coll., Chandigarh, India, 1963; MSEE, Stanford U., 1964; MBA with honors, Golden Gate U., 1977. Engr. Gaylor Products, North Hollywood, Calif., 1964-68, Burroughs Corp., Pasadena, Calif., 1968-70; engrng. mgr. Burroughs Corp., Santa Barbara, Calif., 1970-78; engrng. mgr. Intel Corp., Hillsboro, Oreg., 1978-81, chmn. strategic planning, 1981-82, gen. mgr., 1983-88; pres., exec. dir., bd. dirs. Oreg. Advanced Computing Inst., Beaverton, 1988-90; strategic bus. mgr. INTEL Corp., Hillsboro, Oreg., 1990-92, gen. mgr. bus. multimedia products, 1992-93, bus. area mgr., 1993-94, dir. internat. mktg., 1995—; spkr. to high tech. industry, Oreg., 1988—; mem. organizing com. Distributed Memory Computing Conf., 1989-90, gen. chmn., 1990-91; chmn. computer tech. adv. bd. Oreg. Mus. Sci. and Industry, 1991-93; bd. dirs. Il-Tracker Inc. Cons. Oreg. Econ. Devel. Dept., 1988-91; bd. dirs. St. Mary's Acad., Portland, 1989-92. Mem. Am. Electronics Assn. (higher edn. com. Oreg. chpt. 1989-90, exec. com. 1990). Avocations: electronics, photography, tennis, art. Home: 13940 NW Harvest Ln Portland OR 97229-3653 Office: INTEL Corp 5200 NE Elam Young Pkwy Hillsboro OR 97124-6497

BHARADWAJ, PREM DATTA, physics educator; b. Gorakhpur, India, May 20, 1931; came to U.S., 1960; s. Ganga Dhar and Bhagwati Devi (Sharma) B.; m. Vidya Wati Sharma, Feb. 14, 1949; children: Rakesh Kumar, Rajnesh Kumar, Vidhu Rani Eranki, Sudha Kar. *Rakesh resides in San Ramon, California with his wife, Madhu, and sons, Amit andAnuj. Both are engineers at Pacific Bell. Rajnesh, an engineer at Inter-Tel Technologies, resides with his wife Suman, an environmental consultant at International Technology Corp. in Hercules, California. Vidhu Eranki, Dr. Bharadwaj's daughter, a sales representative for Sanofi, resides with her husband Sasidhar, a general manager of Moog Controls, England, son Rajiv, and daughter Annu, in East Amherst, New York. Sudhakar, a technical sales manager at i2 Technologies, lives with his wife Medha, a case manager at Cigna Insurance, and daughters Lori and Nina in McKinney, Texas.* BS, NREC Coll. Khurja, India, 1950; MS, Agra (India) Coll., 1952; PhD, SUNY, Buffalo, 1964. Asst. prof. physics B.R. Coll. Agra, 1952-54; lectr. physics GPIC Tehri, Tehri Garhwal, India, 1954-56, Govt. Coll. Meerut, India, 1956-59; asst. prof. physics B.R. Coll. Agra, 1959-60; grad. asst. physics SUNY, Buffalo, 1960-62; from asst. prof. physics to assoc. prof. physics Niagara U., Niagara Falls, N.Y., 1962-66, prof. physics, 1966—, chmn. dept. physics, 1976-86; cons. NSF, 1966-71; reviewer N.Y. State Regents Exams. in Medicine and Dentistry, 1976; summer rsch. participant NSF, La. State U., Baton Rouge, 1965; vis. prof. dept. crystallography Rosewell Park Cancer Inst., Buffalo, N.Y., 1970-71. Co-author: Intermediate Agriculture Physics and Climatology, 1954; contbr. articles to profl. jours. Pres. Sathya Sai Ctr. Buffalo, Amherst, N.Y., 1990-93, Hindi Samaj of Greater Buffalo, Amherst, 1996-97; mem. trust com. Hindu Cultural Soc. Western N.Y., 1999—. Recipient Rajiv Gandhi Nat. Unity award for excellence Govt. India, 1995, Hind Rattan (Jewel of India) award Govt. of India, 1995, others. named Man of Yr. Am. Bio. Mem. India Assn. of Buffalo (co-founder 1961), Hindi Samaj of Greater Buffalo (co-founder 1986), Am. Phys. Soc. Democrat. Hindu. Home: 100 N Parrish Dr Amherst NY 14228-1477 Office: Niagara U Physics Dept Lewiston Rd Niagara Falls NY 14109

BHARDWAJ, ANISH, neuroscientist, medical educator; b. June 3, 1960. Diplomate Am. Bd. Neurology and Psychiatry. Intern Univ. Coll. Hosp., Ibadan, Nigeria, 1984-85; med. officer Sokoto Clinic, Nigeria, 1985-86; rsch. fellow dept. neurology Mt. Sinai Sch. Medicine, N.Y.C., 1987-89, resident in neurology, 1990-92, chief resident in neurology, 1992-93; resident in internal medicine Elmhurst Hosp., Mt. Sinai Sch. Medicine, N.Y.C., 1989-90; neurosci. crit. care fellow Johns Hopkins U. Sch. Medicine, Balt., 1993-95, nat. stroke assn. fellow, 1994-96, instr. depts. neurology, neurol. surgery, anesthesiology and crit. care medicine, 1995-96, dir. neurosci. crit. care fellowship tng. program, asst. prof. depts. neurology, neurol. surgery, anesthesiology and crit. care medicine, 1996—; staff attending neurosci. crit. care unit Johns Hopkins Hosp., Balt., 1995—, asst. prof. Neurology, 1998—. Contbr. articles to profl. jours.; ad hoc reviewer Jour. Cerebral Blood Flow and Metabolism, Crit. Care Medicine; spkr. in field. Fellow Am. Heart Assn. (mem. stroke coun., honorable mention Robert G. Siekert young investigator award in stroke 1995, clinician-scientist award 1996); mem. AMA, Am. Acad. Neurology, Nat. Stroke Assn. (fellowship career devel. award 1994), Soc. for Neurosci., Nigeria Med. Coun. Office: Johns Hopkins U Sch Medicine Meyer Bldg 8-140 600 N Wolfe St Baltimore MD 21287-0005*

BHARGAVA, DINESH, plastic and reconstructive surgeon; b. May 23, 1945; m. Sushma Bhargava, 1973; children: Parul, Nitin. MB, BS, Maulana Azad Med. Coll., New Delhi, India, 1971, M in Surgery, 1973. Rotating intern St. Peter's Hosp., Albany, N.Y., 1974-75; resident U. Rochester, N.Y., 1975-76, 79-81, Westchester County Med. Ctr., Valhalla, N.Y., 1976-79; pvt. practice Cortland, N.Y., 1981—; chief plastic surgery Hudson Valley Hosp., Peekskill, N.Y., Phelps Meml. Hosp., Sleepy Hollow, N.Y. Fellow ACS; mem. AMA, Am. Soc. Aesthetic Surgeons, Liplysis Soc. Am., Rotary Internat., (Ossining chpt.).

BHARGAVA, RAMESHWAR NATH, physicist; b. Allahabad, UP, India, Dec. 25, 1939; came to U.S., 1960; s. Gajadhar Prasad and Rupkanti Bhargava; m. Veena Bhargava, Aug. 15, 1965; children: Sidharth, Amitabh. BS, U. Allahabad, 1957, MS, 1959; PhD, Columbia U., 1966. Fellow IBM Watson Lab., Columbia U., N.Y.C., 1965-66; cons. IBM Watson Rsch. Ctr., Yorktown Heights, N.Y., 1966-67; mem. tech. staff Bell Labs, Murray Hill, N.J., 1967-70; mem. tech. staff Philips Labs, Briarcliff Manor, N.Y., 1970-78, dept. head, 1978-89, assoc. dir., 1989-93; pres. Nanocrystals Tech., Briarcliff Manor, N.Y., 1993—; Organizer symposia and internat. profl. confs.; chmn. Gordon Conf., N.H., 1977. Patentee inventor 3-D TV, Harmonics in High Temperature Superconductors, Doped nanocrystals. Recipient Chancellor's Gold medal U. Allahabad, 1959. Fellow IEEE, Am. Phys. Soc. Home: 5 Morningside Ct Ossining NY 10562-3003 Office: Nanocrystals Tech PO Box 820 Briarcliff Manor NY 10510-0307

BHARTIA, PRAKASH, defense research management executive, researcher, educator; b. Calcutta, West Bengal, India, Jan. 6, 1944; arrived in Can., 1967; s. Benarshi Prasad and Bhagwati Devi (Chirimar) B.; m. Savitri Kanhai, Apr. 27, 1971; children: Sanjay Manish, Anil Manoj. B in Tech. with honors, Indian Inst. Tech., Bombay, 1966; MSc, U. Man., Winnipeg, Can., 1968, PhD, 1971. Assoc. prof. U. Regina, Sask., Can., 1976, asst. dean, 1975-77; def. scientist, chief R&D br. Nat. Defence, Ottawa, Ont., Can., 1977—; head navigation sect. Defence Rsch. Establishment Ottawa, 1981-85; dir. R&D air Defence Hdqrs., Govt. of Can., Ottawa, 1985-86; dir. R&D commnications and space Nat. Defence, Govt. of Can., 1986-89; dir. sonar div. Defence Rsch. Establishment Atlantic, Halifax, 1989-91; dir. radar div. Defence Rsch. Establishment Ottawa, 1991—; chief Defence Rsch. Establishment Atlantic, 1992-97; dir.-gen. Def. Rsch. Establishment, Ottawa, 1997—; adj. prof. U. Ottawa, 1977-96, Daltech, 1997—; dir. Can. Microelectronics Centre, Kingston, 1986-88; mem. elec. engrng. grant selection com. Natural Scis. and Engrng. Rsch. Coun., Ottawa, 1990—, chmn. ind. chair evaluation com., Victoria, 1991; bd. dirs. Tradex Investment Funds, Ottawa, Canadian Ctr. Marine Communication. Author: Microstrip Antennas, 1980, Millimeter Wave Engineering and Applications, 1984, E Plane Integrated Circuits, 1987, Millimeter Wave Microstrip and Printed Circuit Antennas, 1990; author, editor: Microwave Solid State Circuit Design, 1988, Microstrip Lines and Slotlines, 1996; patentee in field. Mem. engrng. adv. com. Queen's U., Kingston, 1989-92, chmn. bd., 1992. Fellow IEEE, Instn. Elec. and Telecommunication Engrs., Royal Soc. of Can.; mem. India Soc. Engrs. Hindu. Home: 164 Palomino Dr, Kanata, ON Canada K2M 1P1 Office: Def Rsch Establish Ottawa, 3701 Carling Ave, Ottawa, ON Canada K1A OZ4

BHARUCHA, JAMSHED, dean; b. July 24, 1956; came to U.S., 1974; s. Jal and Elizabeth Bharucha; m. Shirley Mathews, July 28, 1996. BA with honors, Vassar Coll., 1978; MA, Yale U., 1979; PhD, Harvard U., 1983. Fellow Ctr. Advanced Study in the Behavioral Scis., Stanford, Calif., 1993-94; assoc. dean faculty, John Wentworth prof. Dartmouth Coll., Hanover, N.H., 1997—. Trustee Vassar Coll., Poughkeepsie, N.Y., 1991-99. Rsch. grantee NSF, 1996-99, NIH, 1999—. Mem. Am. Psychol. Soc., Psychonomic Soc., Soc. Music Perception and Cognition. Avocation: active playing violin in amateur chamber groups. E-mail: jbharucha@dartmouth.edu. Office: Dartmouth Coll 6045 Wentworth Hall Hanover NH 03755-3526

BHASIN, MADAN MOHAN, chemical research scientist; b. Lahore, India, June 23, 1938; came to U.S., 1959; s. Late L. Mela Ram and Bahain Devi (Sahni) B.; m. Anand Kumari Chugha, Aug. 5, 1961; children: Madhu Lata, Anoop Kumar. BS with hon., Delhi U., New Delhi, India, 1958; postgrad., Indiana U., 1959-60; PhD, U. Notre Dame, 1964. Chemist Union Carbide Corp., South Charleston, W.V., 1963-69, project scientist, 1969-77, research scientist, 1977-81, group supr., 1981-82, sr. research scientist, group supr., 1982-88, corp. fellow., group supr., 1988—; spkr., lectr. in field. Patentee in field; contbr. articles to profl. jours. Chmn. India Ctr., Charleston, W.V., 1986-96, co-chair, India Heritage Fair, 1996—. Recipient Eugene J. Houdry Award in Applied Catalysis, Catalysis Soc. N. Amer., 1995, Scientific Achievement Awd., Kanawka Valley Section of ACS (Am. Chem. Soc.), 1995, Amer. Chem. Soc. Awd. in Indsl. Chem., 1999, AZKO Nobel. Mem. Am. Chem. Soc. (chmn. summer symposium Indsl. and Engrng. Chem. div. 1986-88, exec. com. mem. 1983-87, chmn. I & EC div. 1990), Catalysis Secretariat (chair 1997), India Assn. (pres. 1979-80). Avocations: photography, tennis, badmington, gardening. Office: Union Carbide Corp Indust Chem Divs PO Box 8361 Charleston WV 25303-0361

BHATHENA, FIRDAUS, software company executive, consultant; b. Bombay, July 17, 1970; came to U.S., 1988; s. Rustom and Manize (Irani) B.; m. Jasmin Palsetia, Jan. 1, 1994. BS, MIT, 1992, MS, 1993. Dir. engrng. Mule Automation Systems, Woburn, Mass., 1993-95; v.p. R & D Kurzweil Ednl. Systems, Waltham, Mass., 1995-96; v.p. R & D, co-founder WebLine Comm. Corp., Burlington, Mass., 1996—. Contbr. articles to profl. jours.; patentee in field. Grad. fellow Tau Beta Pi, 1993. Avocations: marathon running, trekking, music, computers. Office: WebLine Comm Corp 1 Burlington Woods Burlington MA 01803-4539

BHATIA, PETER K., editor, journalist; b. Pullman, Wash., May 22, 1953; s. Vishnu N. and Ursula Jean (Dawson) B.; m. Elizabeth M. Dahl, Sept. 27, 1981; children: Megan Jean, Jay Peter. BA, Stanford U., 1975. Polit. reporter, asst. news editor Spokesman Rev., Spokane, Wash., 1975-77; news editor Dallas Times Herald, 1980-81; asst. news editor San Francisco Examiner, 1977-80, news editor, 1981-85, dep. mng. editor/news, 1985-87; mng. editor Dallas Times Herald, 1987-88; editor York Dispatch, York, Pa., 1988-89; mng. editor The Sacramento Bee, 1989-93; exec. editor The Fresno Bee, 1993; mng. editor The Oregonian, Portland, 1993-97, exec. editor, 1997—; Pulitzer Prize juror, 1992-93, 98-99. Mem. Stanford U. Alumni Assn. (bd. dirs. 1998—), Am. Soc. Newspaper Editors (bd. dirs. 1997—), AP Mng. Editors (bd. dirs. 1991-97), Asian Am. Journalists Assn., Nat. Assn. Minority Media Execs., South Asian Journalists Assn., Investigative Reporters and Editors, Sigma Delta Chi, Theta Delta Chi. Office: The Oregonian 1320 SW Broadway Portland OR 97201-3499

BHATTACHARYA, NANDINI, English educator, researcher, writer; b. Calcutta, India, Oct. 16, 1964; came to U.S., 1987.; d. Gautam and Chandana Bhattacharya. BA, Presidency Coll., Calcutta, 1986; PhD, U. Rochester, 1992. Assoc. prof. Valpariaso (Ind.) U., 1992—. Author: Reading the Splendid Body: Gender and Consumerism in Eighteenth-Century British Writing on India, 1998. Recipient fellowship W.A. Clark Meml. Libr., 1991, Midwest Faculty fellowship Globalization Project, U. Chgo., 1996, Mellon fellowship Huntington Libr., 1997. Mem. MLA. Avocations: reading, writing, tutoring, travel, art viewership. E-mail: Nandini.Bhattacharya@valpo.edu.

BHATTACHARYYA, SHANKAR PRASHAD, electrical engineering educator; b. Rangoon, Burma, June 23, 1946; came to U.S., 1967, naturalized, 1985; s. Nil Kantha and Hem Nalini (Mukherjee) B.; m. Carole Jeanne Colgate, Feb. 10, 1971 (div. Oct. 1985); children: Krishna Lee, Mohadev, Sona Lee. B. Tech., Indian Inst. Tech., 1967; M.S. in Elec. Engrng., Rice U., 1969, Ph.D., 1971. Asst. prof. Fed. U., Brazil, 1971-72, assoc. prof., 1972-76, prof., 1976-80, chmn. elec. engrng., 1978-80; prof. Tex. A&M U., College Station, 1984—, Halliburton prof., 1990, Dresser Industries prof., 1991, Sr. Fulbright lectr., 1989; dir. Systems and Ctrl. Inst., Tex. Engrng. Experiment Sta., 1991-93. Authored 3 Books in the field of automatic control systems; contbr. over 100 articles to profl. jours. NRC resident rsch. fellow NASA, 1974-75, Tex. Engrng. Experiment Sta. fellow, 1989, Boeing-Welliver faculty fellow, 1998; NSF grantee, 1983—. Fellow IEEE (control system soc. assoc. editor 1985—); mem. Soc. Indsl. and Applied Math. Avocation: playing Indian classical music on the sarode. Home: 3214 Westchester Ave College Station TX 77845-7910 Office: Tex A&M U Dept Elec Engrng College Station TX 77843 *You can achieve anything you want if you are truly interested in it—especially in America where opportunities are unlimited.**

BHATTI, NEELOO, environmental scientist; b. New Delhi, Jan. 30, 1955; arrived in Can., 1958, came to U.S., 1982; d. Daljeet Singh and Abnash (Singh) B.; m. James Joseph McAndrew, Sept. 14, 1985. MES, Yale U., 1984, PhD, 1988. Rsch. asst. McGill U., Montreal, Que., Can., 1976-78; teaching asst. Yale U., New Haven, 1983; rsch. intern Cary Arboretum, Millbrook, N.Y., 1983; postdoctoral fellow Argonne (Ill.) Nat. Lab., 1989-90, environ. scientist, 1990-98; environ. effects specialist, cons. World Bank, Washington, 1989—. Author: Dispelling the North American Acid Rain Clouds, 1988, Responding to Threat of Global Warming: Options for Asia and Pacific, 1989, Acid Rain in Asia, 1992; co-editor: Adapting to Climate Change: Assessments and Issues, 1997. F.C.A.C. scholar Govt. Que., 1983-87; Yale U. fellow, New Haven, 1984-88. Mem. Am. Chem. Soc., Am Soc. Foresters, Sigma Xi. Achievements include identification of specific regions within Asia at highest risk from acid deposition; identified basis of pollution problems in Romania, Poland, China; compiled emissions inventory for mercury in Great Lakes region and for SO2 in Asia; assisted in development of climate change strategy for the People's Republic of China. Home: 15425 Purley Ct Lockport IL 60441-9492

BHAUMIK, MANI LAL, physicist; b. Calcutta, India, Jan. 5, 1932; came to U.S., 1959, naturalized, 1968; s. Gunadhar and Lolita (Pramanik) B. B.S., U. Calcutta, 1951, M.S., 1953; Ph.D., Indian Inst. Tech., 1958, DSc (hon.). Fellow U. Calif. at Los Angeles, 1959-63; with Xerox Electro-Optical Systems, Pasadena, Calif., 1961-67, Northrop Corp. Labs., Hawthorne, Calif., 1968-71; research dir. Northrop Corp. Labs., 1971-75; mgr. Laser Tech. Lab., Northrop Research and Tech. Center, 1976-84, sr. staff scientist, 1984-86; lectr. physics Calif. State U., Long Beach, 1967-69. Contbr. articles to profl. jours. Fellow Am. Phys. Soc., IEEE. Patentee in field. Office: Laser Tech Lab PO Box 24050 Los Angeles CA 90024-0050 *A strong and innate belief in basic human goodness has often pulled me out of hostile circumstances where one is likely to lose faith in humanity.*

BHAVSAR, NATVAR PRAHLADJI, artist; b. Gothava, India, Apr. 7, 1934; came to U.S., 1962; s. Prahladji V. and Babu P. B.; m. Janet Brosious, Jan. 15, 1978; children: Shashin, Ajay, Rajeev. AM, Bombay State Higher Art Exam., 1958, Govt. Diploma Art, 1959; BA in Liberal Arts and English Lit, Gujarat U., Ahmedabad, India, 1960; MFA, U. Pa., 1965. Instr. in art U. R.I., 1967, 68, 69. One-man shows include Obelisk Gallery, Boston, 1968, 69, Max Hutchinson Gallery, N.Y.C., 1970, 71, 72, 74, 77, 78, in Houston, 1978, Gallery A. Sydney, Australia, 1970, Gallery Chemould, Bombay, 1970, Kenmore Gallery, Phila., 1963, 74, Kingspitcher Gallery, Pitts., 1977, Gloria Luria Gallery, Bayharbor Fl., 1978, 98, Wichita (Kans.) Art Mus., 1979, 85, Pembroke Gallery, Houston, 1985, 87; Gettler/Pall/Saper, N.Y.C., 1984, Bose-Pacia Modern Gallery, N.Y.C., 1986, ACP Viviane Ehrli Gallery, Zurich, Switzerland, 1997; group shows include Jewish Mus., N.Y.C., 1970, Whitney Mus. Am. Art, 1970 (2), Indpls. Mus. Art, 1970, 78, U. Sydney, 1970, Columbus (Ohio) Gallery Fine Arts, 1971, U. Rochester, 1971, Max Hutchinson Gallery, 1973, Am. Acad. Arts and Letters Art Gallery, N.Y.C., 1973, Ruth S. Schaffner Gallery, Los Angeles, 1974, Reed Coll., 1974, Rockland Ctr. for Arts, West Nyack, N.Y., 1979, Fifth Triennale, New Delhi, India, 1981, Il Sud del Mondo, L'Altra Arte Contemporanea Galleria Civica de Arte Contemporanea, Pizzo, Italy, 1991, Gloria Lurie Gallery, Bay Harbor, Fla., 1978, 92, IlSud del Mondo, L'Attra Contemporanea, Commune di Marsa, Pizzo; Italy, 1991, Angolazioni e Prospettive Della Visione, Nell'Arte Contemporanea, Centro Museografico, Palazzo S.Domenico, Taverna, Italy, 1991, Viviane Ehrli Gallery, Art Cologne (Germany) Internat., 1998; represented in permanent collections Met. Mus. Art, N.Y.C., Boston Mus. Fine Arts, Guggenheim Mus., N.Y.C., Chase Manhattan Bank, N.Y.C., Wichita Art Mus. (Kans.), Herbert F. Johnson Mus. at Cornell U., Australian Nat. Gallery, Canberra, Library of Congress, M.I.T., Ulrich Mus. Art, Wichita, Lannan Found., Power Inst., Sydney, Rose Art Mus. at Brandeis U., U. Mass., Amherst, U. Del., Whitney Mus. Am. Art, N.Y.C., Worcester (Mass.) Mus., Am. express co., N.Y.C., N.B.C., N.Y.C., Olympia and York, Toronto, Readers Digest, N.Y., United Bank of Switzerland, N.Y.C.; monograph Natvar Bhavsar Painting and the Reality of Color (Irving Sandler), 1998. John D. Rockefeller III Fund fellow, 1965-66, Guggenheim Meml. Found. fellow, 1975-76. Subject of profl. articles. Home and Studio: 131 Greene St New York NY 10012-3220

BHUIYAN, MOHAMMAD ALI, university administrator, educator, consultant; b. Dhaka, Bangladesh, Jan. 1, 1959; came to U.S., 1986; s. Nasir Uddin and Luthfunnesa (Khanam) B.; m. Shamima Amin, Aug. 28, 1986; 1 chlid, Muzaffer Ahmed. BSS, U. Dhaka, 1980; MBA, Indian Inst. Mgmt., Bangalore, 1983, Ga. State U., Atlanta, 1988; PhD, U. Fla., 1993. Sales mgr. Brit. Am. Tobacco, Dhaka, 1983-84; lectr. U. Dhaka, 1984-86; grad. rschr. U. Fla., Gainesville, 1989-93; lectr. Morris Brown Coll., Atlanta, 1989; instr. U. Fla., Gainesville, 1992-93; coord. internat. bus. Savannah (Ga.) State U., 1993-96; head dept. bus. Fort Valley (Ga.) State U., 1996-97; asst. dean, prof. Hampton (Va.) U., 1997—. Contbr. articles to profl. jours. Bd. dirs. Better Bus. Bur., Savannah and Macon, Ga., 1994-97, Jr. Achievement, Savannah, 1994-96, ARC, Savannah, 1994-96, Am. Heart Assn., Savannah, 1994-96. Recipient Best Tchr. award Savannah State U., 1994; World Bank fellow, 1986-88. Mem. Acad. of Mgmt., Am. Econ. Assn., Bangladesh Econ. Assn. (life), Am. Assn. Higher Edn., Soc. for Advancement of Mgmt. (life), Acad. Internat. Bus., Rotary club of Savannah (bd. dirs 1995). Avocations: travel, swimming. Home: 1 Captain Ferguson Ln Savannah GA 31411-1703 Office: Hampton U Sch Bus Sch Bus Hampton VA 23668

BHUSHAN, BHARAT, mechanical engineer; b. Jhinjhana, India, Sept. 30, 1949; came to U.S., 1970, naturalized, 1977; s. Narain Dass and Devi (Vati) B.; m. Sudha Bhushan, June 14, 1975; children: Ankur, Noopur. B of Mech. Engrng. with honors, Birla Inst. Tech. and Sci., 1970; MS in Mech. Engrng., MIT, 1971; MS in Mechanics, U. Colo., 1973, PhD in Mech. Engrng., 1976; MBA, Rensselaer Poly. Inst., 1980; DSc, U. Trondheim, Norway, 1990; D of Tech. Scis., Warsaw (Poland) U. Tech., 1996. Mem. rsch. staff dept. mech. engrng. MIT, Cambridge, 1971-72; rsch. asst., instr. dept. mech. engrng. U. Colo., Boulder, 1973-76; program mgr. R&D divsn. Mech. Tech. Inc., Latham, N.Y., 1976-80; rsch. scientist SKF Industries, Inc., King of Prussia, Pa., 1980-81; adv. engr. IBM, Tucson, 1981-85, devel. engr., mgr., 1985-86; sr. engr., mgr. head-disk interface Almaden Rsch. Ctr. IBM, 1986-91; Ohio Eminent scholar, Howard D. Winbigler prof., dir. Computer Microtribiology and Contamination Lab., dept. mech. engrng. Ohio State U., Columbus, 1991—; expert investigator Automotive Specialists, Denver, 1973-76; vis. sr. scientist Royal Norwegian Coun. for Sci. and Indsl. Rsch., U. Trondheim, 1987, USSR Acad. Sci., Moscow, 1989; vis. scholar dept. mech. engrng., chemistry and materials sci. and mineral engrng. U. Calif., Berkeley, 1989; Sony sabbatical chair prof. Sony Corp. Rsch. Ctr., Fujitsuka, Japan, 1997; invited presenter worldwide; spkr. internat. confs. Author: Tribology and Mechanics of Magnetic Storage Devices, 1990, Handbook of Tribology, 1991, Mechanics and Reliability of Flexible Magnetic Media, 1992, Handbook of Micro/Natrotribiology, 1995, 2d edit., 1999, Principles and Applications of Tribology, 1999; editor 13 books; editor-in-chief, founding editor ASME series Advances in Info. Storage Sys., 1991—; editor-in-chief CRC Mechanics and Materials Sci. series; contbr. handbook chpts., tech. papers, numerous articles to profl. jours. Recipient Alfred Noble prize ASCE, IEEE, ASME, AIME, Western Soc. Engrs., 1981, Tech. Excellence award Am. Soc. Engrs. India, 1989, Cert. Appreciation award NASA, 1987, Alexander von Humboldt Rsch. prize for sr. scientists U. Ulm, 1998-99, U. Karlsruhe, 1998-99, Fulbright Sr. Scholar award and guest prof. Tech. U. Vienna, 1999; Ford Found. fellow MIT, 1971; grantee USN, NASA, Dept. Energy, USAF, Franco-Am. Commn. for Edni. Exch. Interfound. grantee Ecole Cen. Lyon, 1999. Fellow ASME (cert. of recognition Design Engring. Conf., Henry Hess award 1980, Burt L. Newkirk award 1983, Gustus L. Larson Meml. award 1986, tribology divsn. Best Paper award, Melville medal for best current original paper 1992), N.Y. Acad. Scis.; mem. NSPE, IEEE (sr.), STLE, Am. Soc. Lubrication Engrs., Am. Acad. Mechanics, Internat. Humanists Soc., Tri-City India Assn., Sigma Xi, Tau Beta Pi, Rotary. Hindu. Avocations: music, photography, hiking, traveling. Home: 10235 Widdington Close Powell OH 43065-9059 Office: Ohio State U 206 W 18th Ave Columbus OH 43210-1189

BIAGI, RICHARD CHARLES, retail executive, real estate consultant; b. Crockett, Calif., Aug. 29, 1925; s. Louis Joseph and Angelina Antonette (Gambaro) B.; m. Emily Annette Gino, Aug. 7, 1949 (dec.); children: Sharon A. Biagi Juhnke, Sandra A. Biagi Ogden; m. Alice C. Mulder, Nov. 26, 1995. BSBA, U. Calif., Berkeley, 1950, cert. in real estate, 1956. Real estate analyst Safeway Stores inc., Oakland, Calif., 1953-58; real estate negotiator Lucky Stores Inc., San Leandro, Calif., 1958-60, div. real estate mgr., 1960-62; mgr. corp. real estate Lucky Stores Inc., San Leandro; v.p. corp. real estate mgr. Lucky Stores Inc., Dublin, Calif., 1963-86; cons. real estate Alamo, Calif., 1986—. Served with USNR, 1943-46, PTO. Mem. Internat. Council Shopping Ctrs. (trustee 1971-76), U. Calif. Bus. Adminstrn. Alumni Assn. (pres. 1970), Calif. Bus. Properties Assn. (bd. dirs. 1972-92), Toastmasters (pres. San Leandro club 1959). Avocations: photography, biking, golf.

BIALER, MARTIN GEORGE, geneticist; b. N.Y.C., June 10, 1952; s. Henry Bialer and Ethel (Raffel) Albert; m. Rachel Sydney Baron, May 5, 1991. BA, Cornell U., 1973; PhD, Med. U. S.C., 1980, MD, 1983. Diplomate Am. Bd. Pediatrics, Am. Bd. Med. Genetics. Intern and resident in pediatrics North Shore U. Hosp., Manhasset, N.Y., 1983-86, assoc. in genetics, 1989—; fellow in genetics U. Va., Charlottesville, 1986-89; asst. prof. pediatrics Cornell U., N.Y.C., 1989-97, NYU Sch. of Medicine, N.Y.C., 1997—. Contbr. articles to Clin. Cardiology, Clin. Chemistry, Am. Jour. Med. Genetics, European Jour. Pediatrics. Muscular Dystrophy Assn. fellow, 1988-89. Fellow Am. Acad. Pediatrics; mem. AMA, Am. Soc. Human Genetics, Am. Coll. Med. Genetics, Nassau Pediatrics Soc., Alpha Omega Alpha. Democrat. Jewish. Office: North Shore U Hosp Dept Pediatrics 300 Community Dr Manhasset NY 11030-3801

BIALKIN, KENNETH JULES, lawyer; b. N.Y.C., Sept. 9, 1929; s. Samuel and Lillian (Kastner) B.; m. Ann Eskind, Aug. 19, 1956; children: Lisa Beth, Johanna. AB, U. Mich., 1950; cert. of attendance, London Sch. Econ., 1952; JD, Harvard U., 1953. Bar: N.Y. 1953, U.S. Dist. Ct. (ea. dist.) N.Y. 1955, U.S. Supreme Ct. 1964, U.S. Dist. Ct. (so. dist.) N.Y. 1972, U.S. Ct. Appeals (2d cir.) 1976. Assoc. Willkie Farr & Gallagher, N.Y.C., 1953-60, ptnr., 1960-88; ptnr. Skadden, Arps, Slate, Meagher & Flom, N.Y.C., 1988—; adj. prof. law NYU, 1967-87; lectr., commentator legal and fin. symposia; mem. N.Y. Stock Exch. Legal Adv. Commn., 1983-92, 98—, chmn. internat. securities subcom., 1989-98; bd. dirs. Citigroup Inc., Travelers Property & Casualty Corp., Oshap Techs., Mcpl. Assistance Corp. City of N.Y., Sapiens Internat., Ltd., Tecnomatix Techs., Ltd.; mem. Adminstrv. Conf. of U.S., 1987-92; chmn. Com. on Fin. Svcs.; vis. com. grad. faculty New Sch. for Social Rsch., 1992—. Editor: The Business Lawyer, 1980; bd. editors Corp. Governance Jour., 1992—; contbr. articles on corp., fin. investment law to profl. jours. Chmn. Conf. Pres. Major Am. Jewish Orgns., 1984-86; chmn. Am.-Israel Friendship League, 1995—; nat. chmn. Anti-Defamation League B'nai Brith, 1982-86; pres. Jewish Cmty. Rels. Coun. N.Y., 1989-92; vice-chmn., dir. Jerusalem Found., Inc., 1975—. Mem. ABA (chmn. fed. regulation securities com. 1974-79, chmn. com. to study fgn. investment in U.S. 1978-80, chmn. ad hoc com. on insider trading regulation 1988—, chmn. sect. corp. banking and bus. law 1981-82, 83), Am. Jewish Hist. Soc. (pres. 1997—), N.Y. County Lawyers Assn. (pres. 1986-88), Am. Bar Retirement Assn. (dir. 1981-84), Coun. Fgn. Rels., Harvard Club. Home: 211 Central Park W New York NY 10024-6020 Office: Skadden Arps Slate Meagher 919 3rd Ave New York NY 10022-3902

BIALO, KENNETH MARC, lawyer; b. N.Y.C., Nov. 21, 1946; s. Walter and Mildred (Miller) B.; m. Katherine Ann Burghard; children: Darren Andrew, Caralyn Alyssa, Jacquelyn Anne, Matthew Joseph Geronimo, Kelsey Elizabeth Ariel. BS, U. Rochester, 1968; JD cum laude (note &comment editor. law review, Order of the Coif, Univ. Scholar), NYU, 1971; LLM, London Sch. Econs., 1973. Bar: N.Y. 1972, U.S. Ct. Appeals (2d cir.) 1974, U.S. Ct. Appeals (fed. cir.) 1988, U.S. Supreme Ct. 1975. Law clk. Hon. L.W. Pierce U.S. Dist. Ct. (so. dist.) N.Y., 1971-72; assoc. Sullivan & Cromwell, N.Y.C., 1973-80; counsel, sr. counsel Exxon Corp., N.Y.C., 1980-90; sr. counsel, chief litigation atty. Exxon Chem. Co., Darien, Conn., 1990-91; ptnr. Baker & Botts, N.Y.C., 1992—; lectr. Practicing Law Inst., N.Y.C., 1982, 88, N.Y. State Bar Assn., 1997. Contbg. editor: Family Legal Guide, 1974; note, comment editor: Law Rev. Univ. Scholar; contbr. articles to profl. jours.; note and comment editor NYU Law Rev. Trustee Village of Larchmont, N.Y., 1991—; mem. PLI Adv. Com. on Litig., 1994—; v.p. bd. dirs. Little League, Larchmont, 1985-94, mem. recreation com., 1987-89; pres., bd. govs. Univ. Club of Larchmont, 1995—. Mem. ABA (litig. sect. task force on client concerns 1994-95, subcom. class action, litig. sect.), N.Y. State Bar (antitrust com., fed. and comml. litig. sect., former chmn. corp. counsel com. 1989-91), Assn. of Bar of City of N.Y. (arbitration com.), Fed. Bar Coun. (com. 2d cir. cts.), Am. Arbitration Assn. (mem. arbitrator's panel), Order of Coif. Avocations: tennis, baseball, opera, symphony. Office: Baker & Botts 599 Lexington Ave New York NY 10022-6030*

BIALOSKY, MARSHALL HOWARD, composer; b. Oct. 30, 1923. Student, Converse Coll., 1942-43, 46, Colo. Coll., 1948; MusB cum laude, Syracuse U., 1949; MusM, Northwestern U., 1950. Asst. prof. music Milton (Wis.) Coll., 1950-54; asst. conductor Milton Coll. Band, 1954; asst. prof. humanities and music U. Chgo., 1956-61; assoc. prof. music and humanities, conductor chorale SUNY, Stony Brook, 1961-64; prof., chmn. dept. fine arts Calif. State U., Dominguez Hills, 1964-77, founding chmn. dept. music, 1977-78, prof. dept. music, 1978-86, prof. emeritus dept. music, 1986—; mem. Calif. State Coll. Employee Assn. Statewide Acad. Coun., 1968-71; mem. Calif. State Coll. Internat. Program Acad. Coun. and Exec. Com., 1967-73; bd. dirs. Monday Evening Concerts, L.A., 1966-77; dir. Saturday Conservatory Music, L.A. chpt., 1967-71; coord. humanities M.A. program Calif. State U., Dominguez Hills; composer-in-residence Chamber Music Conf. and Composer's Forum of the East, Bennington Coll., 1989. Performer various cities, radio stas. and schs. Composer piano music including An Album for the Young, Five Western Scenes, mixed chorus including American Names, A Sight in Camp in the Daybreak Gray and Dim, Women's Chorus including American Poets Suite, At Last, Vocal Music including Two Songs to Poems of Howard Nemerov, folk songs, spirituals, Christmas music, music for wind instruments, string instruments, brass instruments, guitar and percussion instruments. Contbr. articles to jours. Fulbright award, 1954-56; Wurlitzer Found. grantee, 1979, N.Y.C. Meet-the-Composer grantee, 1984, 86; recipient Career Achievement award Profl. Fraternity Assn. Am., 1980. Mem. ASCAP (creative grant award 1976—), Coll. Music Soc., Am. Soc. Univ. Composers (nat. chmn. 1974-77), Nat. Assn. Composers U.S.A. (pres. 1978—), Soc. Composers Inc., Am. Assn. Choral Conductor. Office: Nat Assoc Composer USA PO Box 49256 Los Angeles CA 90049-0256

BIAN, RANDY XINDI, research scientist; m. Shiyuan Zhong, July 1, 1985; 1 child, Jessica. BS, Nanjing (China) U., 1982, MS, 1985; MS, Iowa State U., 1993. Tchg. asst. Nanjing U., 1982-86; lectr. Nanjing Inst. Meteorology, 1987-88; rsch. asst. Iowa State U., Ames, 1989-92; scientist Pacific N.W. Nat. Lab., Richland, Wash., 1993—. Contbr. articles to profl. jours. Mem. AAAS, Am. Geophys. Union, Am. Meteorol. Soc. Avocations: hiking, swimming, chess, travel, fishing. Office: Pacific NW Nat Lab PO Box 999 Richland WA 99352-0999

BIANCHI, CARMINE PAUL, pharmacologist; b. Newark, Apr. 9, 1927; s. Eugene and Constance Jean (DiChiara) B.; m. Judith Holman, June 7, 1957 (dec. Nov. 1989); children: Margaret, Alison, Judith, Joyclyn; m. Eleanor Agatone, Feb. 6, 1993. AB, Columbia U., 1950; MS, Rutgers U., 1953, PhD, 1956; MS (hon.), U. Pa., 1973. Rsch. fellow Bur. Biol. Rsch. Rutgers U., New Brunswick, N.J., 1955-56; USPHS fellow NIH, Bethesda, Md., 1956-58; mem. pharmacology study sect., asst. mem. Inst. for Muscle Disease, N.Y.C., 1959-61; assoc. dept. pharmacology U. Pa. Sch. Medicine, Phila., 1961-62, asst. prof. pharmacology, 1962-66, assoc. prof., 1966-69, prof., 1969-76; prof. pharmacology Thomas Jefferson U., Phila., 1976—, chmn. dept., 1976-87, prof., chmn. emeritus, 1998. Author: Cell Calcium, 1968, Advances in General and Cellular Pharmacology, vol. II, 1977; editor: Protein Metabolism and Biological Function, 1970; (with T. Narahashi) Advances in General and Cellular Pharmacology, vol. I; co-editor: (with George Frank and Henk ter Keurs) Excitation-Contraction Coupling in Skeletal, Cordiac, and Smooth Muscle, 1992. Sgt. M.C., U.S. Army, 1945-47. Mem. AAAS, Am. Pharmacology Soc., N.Y. Acad. Scis., Am. Soc. Zoologists, Biophys. Soc., Am. Chem. Soc., Soc. Gen. Physiology, Phila. Physiol. Soc., Am. Physiol. Soc. Office: Thomas Jefferson U Dept Pharmacology 1020 Locust St Philadelphia PA 19107-6731*

BIANCHI, CHARLES PAUL, technical and business executive, money manager, financial consultant; b. Texarkana, Tex., Sept. 3, 1945; s. Angelo Paul and Jewel Evelyn (LaFayette) B.; m. Stephanie Ellquist, Aug. 11, 1973; children: Charles Brandon LaFayette, Canaan Desiree Ellquist. BA, Dickinson Coll., 1967; M in Bus. Mgmt., Cen. Mich. U., 1976. Cert. fin. planner, registered investment adviser; cert. graphoanalyst. Vol. Peace Corps, 1969-71; employment orientation instr. Pa. Bur. Employment Security, Scranton, 1971-72; mgmt. analyst Defense Logistics Agy., Phila., 1972-75; program, sr. budget analyst Defense Logistics Agy., Alexandria, Va., 1975-78; fed. budget specialist Exec. Office Pres., Office Mgmt. and Budget, Washington, 1978-83; owner, prin. Charles P. Bianchi Fin. Planning and Investment Adv. Services, Arlington, Va., 1984-89; internal cons. Inter-Am. Devel. Bank, Washington, 1983-89; pres. Wealth Conservancy Internat., Inc., Arlington, 1988—, Albany, Oreg., 1990-97; rep. Office Mgmt. and Budget, Am. Assn. Budget and Prog. Analysts, Washington, 1976-77; reg. rep. affiliate Tucker Anthony, R.L. Day, 1987-89. Mem. Inst. Cert. Fin. Planners, Internat. Assn. Fin. Planning, Fin. Analysts Fedn., Internat. Soc. Investment Analysts, Washington Soc. Investment Analysts, Assn. Investment Mgmt. and Rsch., North Va. Soc. Cert. Fin. Planners, Internat. Graphoanalysis Soc., Assn. Returned Peace Corps Vols., North Va. Soc. of Cert. Fin. Planners, Theta Chi. Avocations: musician, military conflict simulation gaming, cross-country skiing, graphoanalysis. Home and Office: 224 N Fillmore St Arlington VA 22201-1228

BIANCHI, MARIA, critical care specialist, adult nurse practitioner, acute care nurse practitioner. Grad., Catherine Laboure Sch. Nursing, 1979, Fitchburg (Mass.) State Coll., 1985; postgrad., Russell Sage Coll., Troy, N.Y.; adult nurse practitioner, Mass. Gen. Hosp., Boston. Cert. post-anesthesia care nurse; critical care clin. specialist. Recovery as mgmt. educator, mktg. and recruitment cons., cons. in critical care nursing; nurse mgr. ICU and post anesthesia ICU, Baystate Med. Ctr., Springfield, Mass., 1980-89; recruitment and sr. faculty St. Francis Med. Ctr. Sch. of Nursing, Hartford, Conn., 1989-92; grad. faculty U. Mass. Med. Ctr., Worcester, 1995-97; per diem nurse practitoner dept. surgery U. Mass. Sch. of Nursing, Amherst, 1995-97, faculty; clin. faculty Am. Internat. Coll., Springfield; rsch. in pain, burn trauma, stress reduction, holistic methods for high risk individuals in maximum security penitentiary and critical care patients; nat. cons. for critical care/post anesthesia issues, pres. TransInternat. Healthcare; nat. lectr. AHI, Balt.; expert witness, Mass. and Conn.; medicolegal cons.; lectr. on critical care and post anesthesia issues, empowerment, acute pain, holistic techniques, medicological documentation, trauma. Mem. AACN, Am. Soc. Post-Anesthesia Nursing (Boston chpt. editl. cons.), Sigma Theta Tau. Office: PO Box 614 Suffield CT 06078-0614

BIANCO, ANTHONY JOSEPH, III, newswriter; b. Oceanside, Calif., May 17, 1953; s. Anthony Joseph Jr. and JoAnn (Reavill) B.; 1 child, Marissa. BA, U. Minn., 1976. Reporter Mpls. Tribune, 1977; bus. editor Willamette Week newspaper, Portland, Oreg., 1978-80; corr. Bus. Week mag., San Francisco, 1980-82; dept. editor Bus. Week mag., N.Y.C., 1982-84, assoc. editor, 1984-85, sr. writer, 1985-92. Author: Rainmaker, 1991, The Reichmanns, 1997. Recipient media award for econ. understanding Amos Tuck Sch., Dartmouth Coll., 1979, award for feature writing Oreg. Newspaper Pubs., 1979, award for excellence in fin. writing N.Y. State Soc. CPA's, 1987, Disting. Editorial Achievement award McGraw-Hill, 1986, Nat. Bus. Book award, Can., 1997. Mem. Soc. Profl. Journalists, N.Y. Fin. Writers Assn. Home: 17 1st St Brooklyn NY 11231-5001

BIANCO, DON CHRISTOPHER, civil servant, retired; b. Steubenville, Ohio, Sept. 26, 1947; s. Dominic Joseph and Anna Mary (Buonaguro) B.; m. Sally Ann Bungart, Dec. 7, 1968 (div. Jan. 1980); 1 child, Celia Z.; m. Cynthia Irene Kuceyski, June 16, 1984. Student, Miami U., Oxford, Ohio, 1965-67; BS in Edn., Ohio State U., 1973. Adminstrv. asst. Ohio Dept. Transp., Columbus, 1973-75; investigator Ohio Div. Consumer Protection, Columbus, 1975-76, Ohio Div. Real Estate, Columbus, 1976; investigator Ohio Div. Unclaimed Funds, Columbus, 1976-82, chief investigator, 1982-98, ret., 1998. Home: 127 Brevoort Rd Columbus OH 43214-3823

BIARD, JAMES ROBERT, electrical engineer; b. Paris, Tex., May 20, 1931; s. James Christopher and Mary Ruth (Bills) B.; m. Amelia Ruth Clark, May 23, 1952; children: James Clark, Jan Elaine; 1 adopted child, Becky Dell. AS, Paris Jr. Coll., 1951; BSEE, Tex. A&M U., 1954, MSEE, 1956, PhD in Elec. Engring., 1957. Sr. engr. Tex. Instruments, Inc., Dallas, 1957-69; v.p. R & D Spectronics, Inc., Richardson, Tex., 1969-78; chief scientist Honeywell Optoelectronics, Richardson, 1978-88, Honeywell Micro Switch, Richardson, 1988—; adj. prof. elec. engring. dept. Tex. A&M U., College Station, 1980—; presenter at nat. and internat. symposia, 1957—. Contbr. over 23 articles to profl. jours. Entertainer for various svc. clubs, radio, TV, bus. and chs., 1957—. Recipient Disting. Alumnus award Tex. A&M U., 1986, Paris Jr. Coll., 1993. Fellow IEEE; mem. Am. PHys. Soc., Nat. Acad. Engring., Sigma Xi, Tau Beta Pi, Eta Kappa Nu, Phi Kappa Phi. Republican. Mem. Ch. of Christ. Achievements include 34 U.S. and 17 foreign patents for gallium arsenide light emitting diode, schottky clamped silicon integrated logic circuits, metal-oxide-semiconductor read only memory, others. Office: Honeywell Micro Switch 830 E Arapaho Rd Richardson TX 75081-2241

BIAS, KIMBERLY VANCE, special education educator; b. Homestead, Fla., June 3, 1968; d. Robert Michael and Linda Vance (Paquet) B. B Specific Learning Disabilities and Elem. Edn., Flagler Coll., 1991; M in Edn. Leadership, U. Ctrl. Fla., 1997. Tchr. spl. edn. Robert E. Lee Mid. Sch., Orlando, Fla., 1991-95, Ocoee (Fla.) Mid. Sch., 1995-96; placement specialist S.W. Mid. Sch., Orlando, 1996-97; tchr. spl. edn. University H.S., Orlando, 1997-98; placement specialist Discovery Mid. Sch., Orlando, 1998-99; asst. prin. Little River Elem., 1999—. Mem. ASCD, Coun. for Exceptional Children, Phi Delta Kappa. Avocations: running, golf, swimming, scuba diving, reading, shopping. Home: 509 Green Spruce Ln Orlando FL 32825-5941

BIASINI, VIRGINIA, social worker; b. N.Y.C., July 5, 1939; d. Albert Eugene and Irene Veronica (Kuzmiak) B. BA, Coll. Mt. St. Vincent, Bronx, N.Y., 1977; MSW, Hunter Coll. CUNY, 1980. Cert. social worker, N.Y., sch. social worker, N.J., clin. hypnotherapist Wellness Inst., Seattle; diplomate Am. Bd. Examiners in Clin. Social Work; lic. clin. social worker, N.J. Office mgr. Wiltwyck Sch. for Boys, N.Y.C., 1963-66; adminstrv. asst. to law ptnr. Acme Quilting Co., Inc., N.Y.C., 1966-73; adminstrv. asst. to chmn. bd. Calvary Hosp., Bronx, 1973-77, oncology social worker, 1977-78, patient rep. program coord., 1978-81; med. social worker Westchester Sq. Med. Ctr., Bronx, 1981-84, sr. social worker, supr., 1984-86; asst. dir. social work dept. Cabrini Med. Ctr., N.Y.C., 1986; dir. social work discharge planning dept. Westchester Sq. Med. Ctr., Bronx, 1986-90; individual, family and group social worker, counselor Kimball-Manchester Ambulatory Care Ctr. div. Kimball Med. Ctr., Whiting, N.J., 1990-96; Kimball field work instr. Med. Ctr. Kean Coll., 1996—, Georgian Ct. Coll., 1997—; instr. field work Union Theol. Sem., 1978-79, Lehman Coll., CUNY, Bronx, 1988-90; mem. adj. faculty Coll. Mt. St. Vincent, 1981-82. Mem. NASW, Acad. Cert. Social Workers, Soc. Social Work Dirs., Nat. Soc. Social Work Dirs., Am. Hosp. Assn. Office: Kimball Med Ctr 600 River Ave Lakewood NJ 08701-5237

BIBART, RICHARD L., lawyer; b. Apr. 10, 1942; m. Lois Ann Rey, Sept. 8, 1963; children: Laurie, Jennifer, Kristen, Ted. BA in Econs., Harvard U., 1964; JD, U. Mich., 1966. Bar: Ohio 1967, U.S. Tax Ct. 1967, U.S. Dist. Ct. (so. dist.) Ohio 1969. Assoc. Porter, Wright, Morris & Arthur, Columbus, Ohio, 1967-72, ptnr., 1972-84; v.p. corp. planning Red Roof Inns., Inc., Hilliard, 1984-86; mgmt. co. pres. Red Roof Inns, Inc., Hilliard, 1986-89, pres., CEO, 1989-91; ptnr. Baker & Hostetler LLP, Columbus, 1991—. Mem. ABA, Ohio Bar Assn., Columbus Bar Assn., Columbus Country Club. Office: Baker & Hostetler LLP 65 E State St Ste 2100 Columbus OH 43215-4215*

BIBB, DANIEL ROLAND, antique painting restorer and conservator; b. Gadsden, Ala., June 10, 1951; s. Cassius Roland and Louise Selma B. Student, Jefferson State, 1969-70, DeKalb Coll., 1971-72. Sales cons. Macy's Antique Gallery, Atlanta, 1973; dir. Collector's Gallery, Atlanta, 1974-76, Connoisseur's Gallery, New Orleans, 1977-79; painting conservator Daniel R. Bibb Fine Painting Conservation & Restoration, Atlanta, 1980—; chief fund raiser Atlanta Rabbit Rescue; researcher for pvt. collectors and museums, Atlanta, 1977-89; listed conservator, New Orleans Museum List of Restorers, New Orleans, 1988. Discovered a lost major painting of Philip IV of Spain, from workshop of Valasquez; exhibited lost painting Atlanta High Mus. Art, 1980; publication of discovered paintin, High Mus. Monthly, 1980; conservator Anglo-Am. Art Mus., Baton Rouge, New Orleans Mus. Art.; owner Fabergè collection on loan to New Orleans Mus. Art, 1996; icon collection touring mus'., Louisiana, Miss. and Alabama, 1998—; writer on various subjects to nat. mags. Fund raiser Am. Heart Assn., Atlanta, 1987, 88, March of Dimes, 1987, 88, Atlanta Rabbit Rescue, 1984—; mem. High Mus. of Art, Atlanta; vol. ARC Disaster Relief Team, Atlanta, 1992, Art Care Art Auction for fight against AIDS, 1992, 93, chmn. Live Auction, 1993. Recipient Design award, Most Authentic Design, Patio Planters of the Vieux Carre, New Orleans, 1977. Mem. Nat. Trust for Historic Preservation. Republican. Baptist. Achievements include raising funds and pub. awareness of animal cruelty. Avocations: antique collecting, collecting Royal portraits, pre-revolutionary Russian icons, porcelain, paintings. Home and Office: Bibb Painting Restoration 807 Summit North Dr NE Atlanta GA 30324-5641

BIBBO, MARLUCE, physician, educator; b. Sao Paulo, Brazil, July 14, 1939; d. Domingos and Yolanda (Ranciaro) B. M.D. U. Sao Paulo, 1963, Sc.D., 1968. Intern Hosps. das Clinicas, U. Sao Paulo, 1963; resident in morphology, 1964-66; instr. dept. morphology and ob-gyn U. Sao Paulo, 1966-68, asst. prof., 1968-69; fellow in cytology U. Chgo., 1969-70, asst. prof. sect. cytology dept. ob-gyn, 1971-73, assoc. prof., 1973-77, assoc. prof. pathology, 1974-77, prof. ob-gyn and pathology, 1978-92; assoc. dir. Cytology Lab., Approved Sch. Cytotech and Cytocybernetics, AMA-Am. Soc. Clin. Pathologists, 1970-91; dir. Cytology Lab., Phila., 1992; prof. pathology and cell biology Thomas Jefferson U., Phila., 1992—, Warren R. Lane prof. pathology & cell biology, 1993—; mem. rsch. com. Ill. divsn. Am. Cancer Soc., 1976-91. Contbr. numerous articles to profl. jours. Fellow Internat. Acad. Cytology (pres.-elect, v.p. 1987, pres. 1992, dep. editor Acta Cytologica, editor 1995), Am. Soc. Clin. Pathologists (coun. on cytopathology); mem. Am. Soc. Cytology (exec. com., pres. 1982-83), U.S. Acad. Pathology, Can. Acad. Pathology, Soc. Analytical Cytology, Coun. Cytopathology. Home: 250 S 9th St Philadelphia PA 19107-5734 Office: Cytology Lab Rm 260 Main Bldg 132 S 10th St Philadelphia PA 19107-5244*

BIBBY, DOUGLAS MARTIN, mortgage association executive; b. Endicott, N.Y., Aug. 24, 1946; s. Dause Leveridge and Virginia (Martin) B.; m. Lorraine C. Creer, Sept. 6, 1969; children: Mariah, Ian. BA in Econs., Denison U., 1968; MBA, U. Tex, 1970. Sr. v.p. J. Walter Thompson Co., N.Y.C., Washington, San Juan, P.R., and Toronto, Can., 1971-82; v.p. Russell Reynolds Assocs., Inc., Washington, 1982-83; sr. v.p. adminstrn. Fed. Nat. Mortgage Assn., Washington, 1983-98; ptnr. The Fin. Group, Potomac, Md., 1999—. Bd. dirs. Martha's Table, 1985—, Arena Stage, 1992—, The Summit Fund of Washington, 1992—. Avocations: tennis, community affairs. Office: The Fin Group 9630 Beman Wood Way Potomac MD 20854

BIBERMAN, LUCIEN MORTON, physicist; b. Phila., May 31, 1919; s. Lewis and Eva (Kerns) B.; m. Anne H. Wilner, Mar. 8, 1941; children: Leslie Biberman Gordon, Judith Biberman Robinson, Candace Biberman Evans. BS, Rensselaer Poly. Inst., 1940; postgrad., Harvard U., 1940-41, Stevens Inst., 1941-42. Phys. chemist Nairn Rsch. Labs., 1942-43; physicist in charge Mayport Magnetic Survey Area, Navy Dept., 1943-44; various positions from physicist in charge phys. measurements group to cons. Aviation Ordnance Dept. and Weapons Devel. Dept. Naval Ordnance Test Sta., 1944-57; assoc. dir. Labs. for Applied Scis. U. Chgo., 1957-63; rsch. staff rsch. and engring. support div. Inst. for Def. Analysis, Alexandria, Va., 1963-71, rsch. staff sci. and tech. div., 1972-96; emeritus, 1996—; vis. prof. dept. elec. engring. U. R.I., 1971-72. Recipient Andrew J. Goodpaster award, 1989, citation U.S. Army Ctr. for Night Vision and Electro Optics, 1990. Fellow IEEE (life), Optical Soc. Am. (emeritus), Soc. Info. Display (emeritus), Soc. Photo-optical Instrumentation Engrs. (emeritus). Home: 5904 Lenox Rd Bethesda MD 20817-6050 Office: Inst for Def Analysis 1801 N Beauregard St Alexandria VA 22311-1772

BIBLE, FRANCES LILLIAN, mezzo-soprano, educator; b. Sackets Harbor, N.Y.; d. Arthur and Lillian (Cooke) B. Student, Juilliard Sch. Music, 1939-47. Artist-in-residence Shepherd Sch. of Music Rice U., Houston, 1975-91. Appeared throughout U.S., Australia, Europe including Vienna Staatsoper, Karlsruhe Staatsoper, Dublin Opera Co., N.Y.C. Opera, NBC-TV Opera, San Francisco Opera, Glyndebourne Opera, San Antonio Opera Festival, New Orleans Opera, Houston Grand Opera, Miami Opera, Dallas Opera; appeared in concer with major symphonies; world premiers (opera): The Ballad of Baby Doe, The Crucible, The Troubled Island, The Dybuk. Named Woman of the Yr. in Opera, Mademoiselle, 1949. Mem. Am. Guild Mus. Artists (past 3d v.p., bd. dirs. 1989-91), Sigma Alpha Iota (hon.), Beta Sigma Pi (hon.). Episcopalian. Home: 2377 Thata Way Hemet CA 92544-7009 *Always try to do your very best with the talent you were given but keep your sense of humor, and don't take yourself too seriously!.*

BIBLE, GEOFFREY CYRIL, tobacco company executive; b. Canberra, Australia, Aug. 12, 1937; s. Cyril Edward Bible and Dorothea Elizabeth (O'Brien) McGrath; m. Sara Curtis Anderson-Emery, Sept. 10, 1965; children—Mary, Tom, Kim. Chartered acct., Australia; cost and mgmt. acct., U.K. Fin. dir. UN, Lebanon and Jordan, 1959-64; budget mgr. ILO, Switzerland, 1965-66; fin. mgr. Esso Med., Switzerland, 1966-68; mgr. corp. planning Philip Morris Europe, Switzerland, 1968-70; mgr. R.W. King & Yuill, Stockbrokers, Switzerland, 1970-76; dir. corp. planning Philip Morris Europe, Switzerland, 1976-78; v.p. Philip Morris Internat., N.Y.C., 1976-81, exec. v.p., 1984-87; , pres., chief exec. officer, 1987-90, 94-95, chmn., 1995—; mgr., dir. Philip Morris Austrlia, Benson Hedges Can., 1981-84; pres., chief auditor officer Kraft Gen. Foods, Glenview, Ill., 1990—. Chmn. Geneva English Sch., 1971-77. Roman Catholic. Office: Philip Morris Co Inc 120 Park Ave New York NY 10017-5592*

BICE, DAVID F., career officer; b. Zanesville, Ohio; m. Charlene Bice. Grad., Pepperdine U.; M in Bus., Ctrl. Mich. U.; grad., Inf. Officer Advanced Course, Ft. Benning, Ga., Nat. War Coll., Royal Marines Commando Course. Enlisted USMC, 1968; advanced through grades to brig. gen. 3rd Marine Expeditionary Forces Hawaii; rifle platoon comdr. 3rd Bn. 1st Marines 1st Marine Divsn.; with 1st Bn. 4th Marines 3rd Marine Divsn., 3rd Bn. 7th Marines 1st Marine Divsn., 1st Tank Bn. 1st Marine Divsn., 3rd Bn. 8th Marines 2nd Marine Divsn., 1986-88, 9th Marine Regiment, 1992-94, 3rd Marine Divsn., Okinawa, Japan, 1994-95; series comdr. Marine Corps Recruit Depot, Paris Island, S.C.; enlisted promotions plans officer manpower dept. Hdqs. Marine Corps; chief European divsn. J-5 The Joint Staff; exch. officer U.K. Royal Marines; comdg. gen. Marine Corps Base Hawaii; dep. comdg. gen. 3rd Marine Expeditionary Forces Hawaii. Decorated Legion of Merit, Nat. Def. medal with Bronze Star, Vietnamese Cross of Gallantry with Silver Star, Vietnam Campaign medal. Office: Dederton Marine Corps Staff HQMC 2 Navy NX Washington DC 20380-

1775 also: Hdqs Marine Corps Divsn Pub Affairs Washington DC 20380-1775*

BICE, MICHAEL DAVID, retail and wholesale executive, marketing consultant, insurance consultant; b. Anderson, S.C., July 18, 1956; s. Johnnie Lee Richard and Virgie Ovaline (Martin) B.; m. Nancy Bice, 1993; children: Ansley Deann Bice, Adam Michael Bice, Kristin Kennedy, Rebekah Kennedy, John WilliamKennedy. Student, U.S. Merchant Marine Acad., 1974, Tri-County Tech. Coll., 1981. Sales rep. Sav-A-Stop, Inc., Roanoke, Va., 1974-75, 76-77, 78-79; with mgmt. dept. Caper House Food Stores, Belton, S.C., 1975; material coord. Jeffrey Mfg., Belton, 1975-76; sales rep. Better Beer and Wine Co., Anderson, 1977-78; with mgmt. dept. Brown Shoe Stores, Anderson, 1979-81; ind. contractor Curtis Products Co., Anderson, 1981-85, sales rep., 1988-89; mgr. Curtis Products Co., Ashland, Va., 1989-91; project coord. Curtis Products Co., Alpharetta, Ga., 1992; CEO B & D Enterprises, Anderson, 1981-85; pres., COO Oriental Sources, Inc., Charlotte, N.C., 1985-87; CEO Jewelry Plus, Anderson, 1985-87; pres. Sales Plus, Anderson, SC, 1988—, Richmond, Va., 1989-91, Ashland, Va., 1989-91; v.p. ops. Maabe Possibilities, Inc., Anderson, 1992-97; comml. mktg. dir., comml. accts. coord. Atlantic Coast Candy, Inc., Anderson, Roswell, Ga., Ashland, Va., 1992-94; v.p. sales, state mgr. Pubrs. Guild of S.C., Taylors, 1994-95; cons. Alliance for Affordable Health Care, S.C., N.C., Ga., 1995-98, cons. for Affordable Health Care, 1996—; gen dir. Amcall, 1995-98; mgr. Bice & Assocs., 1996—; gen. mgr. Southeastern Future Diagnostics, Greer, S.C., 1998—; state referee U.S. Soccer Fedn., FIFA, 1998—; broker AmeriPlan, USA, Greer, 1999—. Ofcl. referee U.S. Soccer Fedn., 1993—. Mem. Nat. H.S. Ofcls. Assn., Nat. Intercollegiate Soccer Ofcls. Assn., S.C. Intercollegiate Soccer Ofcls. Assn., S.C. Upstate Soccer Referee Soc. (sec. 1999—). Avocations: water skiing, snow skiing, fishing, hunting, travel.

BICE, SCOTT HAAS, lawyer, educator; b. Los Angeles, Mar. 19, 1943; s. Fred Haas and Virginia M. (Scott) B.; m. Barbara Franks, Dec. 21, 1968. B.S., U. So. Calif., 1965, J.D., 1968. Bar: Calif. bar 1971. Law clk. to Chief Justice Earl Warren, 1968-69; successively asst. prof., assoc. prof., prof. law., Carl Mason Franklin prof. U. So. Calif., Los Angeles, 1969—; assoc. dean U. So. Calif., 1971-74, dean, 1980—; vis. prof. polit. sci. Calif. Inst. Tech., 1977; vis. prof. U. Va., 1978-79; bd.dirs. Western Mut. Ins. Co., Residence Mut. Ins. Co., Imagine Films Entertainment Co., Jenny Craig, Inc. Mem. editl. adv. bd. Calif. Lawyer, 1989-93; contbr. articles to law jours. Bd. dirs. L.A. Family Housing Corp., 1989-93, Stone Soup Child Care Programs, 1988—. Affiliated scholar Am. Bar Found., 1972-74. Fellow Am. Bar Found. (life); mem. Am. Law Inst., Calif. Bar, Los Angeles County Bar Assn., Am. Law Deans Assn. (pres. 1997-99), Am. Judicature Soc., Calif. Club, Chancery Club, Long Beach Yacht Club. Home: 787 S San Rafael Ave Pasadena CA 91105-2326 Office: U So Calif Sch of Law Los Angeles CA 90089-0071*

BICHA, KAREL DENIS, historian, educator; b. LaCrosse, Wis., Jan. 7, 1937; s. Stephen John and Lauretta Katherine (Horan) B.; m. Roberta Gail Gobar; children: Paul Edwin, Anne Marie. BA, U. Wis., 1958; PhD, U. Minn., 1963. Asst. prof. Colo. State U., Ft. Collins, 1963-64, U. Man., Winnipeg, Can., 1964-66, U. Minn., Morris, 1966-67; assoc. prof. Carleton U., Ottawa, Ont., Can., 1967-69; assoc. prof. Marquette U., Milw., 1969-77, prof., 1977—. Author: American Farmer and the Canadian West, 1968, Western Populism, 1976, Czechs in Oklahoma, 1980, C.C. Washburn and the Upper Mississippi Valley, 1995. Am. Philos. Soc. grantee, 1964, 68, Can. Council grantee, 1966-68, NEH grantee, 1978-80, Bradley Inst. for Democracy and Pub. Values grantee, 1991, 97. Mem. Orgn. Am. Historians, Immigration History Soc. Office: Marquette U PO Box 1881 Coughlin Hall Dept Of Histo Milwaukee WI 53201-1881

BICHETTE, ALPHONSE DANTE, professional baseball player; b. West Palm Beach, Fla., Nov. 18, 1963. Student, Palm Beach C.C. With Calif. Angels, 1988-90, Milw. Brewers, 1991-92; outfielder Colo. Rockies, 1993—. Named Nat. Leagye All-Star Team, 1994-96. Achievements include led nat. leagye in runs batted in (RBI) with (128), hone rums (40), 1995, tied with Tony Gwynn for most hits (197), 1995. Office: Colo Rockies 2001 Blake St Denver CO 80205-2000*

BICHSEL, HANS, physicist, consultant, researcher; b. Basel, Switzerland, Sept. 2, 1924; came to U.S., 1951; s. Paul and Anna Maria Bichsel; m. Sue O. Greenwalt, Sept. 12, 1959; children: Elizabeth Christine, Joseph Oliver. MA, U. Basel, 1951, PhD, 1951. Rsch. asst. Princeton (N.J.) U., 1951-55; rsch. assoc. Rice U., Houston, 1955-57; asst. prof. physics U. Wash., Seattle, 1957-59; affiliate prof. physics U. Wash., Seattle, 1992—; assoc. prof., prof. radiology U. Wash., Seattle, 1969-80; asst. prof., assoc. prof. physics U. So. Calif., L.A., 1959-68; assoc. prof. U. Calif., Berkeley, 1968-69; cons. Internat. Commn. on Radiation Units, Bethesda, Md., 1970—, Los Alamos (N.Mex.) Nat. Lab., 1978-83, IAEA, Vienna, Austria, 1990—; vis. scientist Nat. Inst. Radiol. Scis., Chiba, Japan, 1991-96, U. Sherbrooke Med. Sch., Que., Can.; referee Phys. Rev., Nuclear Instruments and Methods, Physics in Medicine and Biology, also others. Contbr. articles to profl. jours. Fellow Am. Phys. Soc.; mem. Swiss Phys. Soc. E-mail: bichsel@npl.washington.edu. Home and Office: 1211 22nd Ave E Seattle WA 98112-3534

BICK, KATHERINE LIVINGSTONE, scientist, international liaison, consultant; b. Charlottetown, Can., May 3, 1932; came to U.S., 1954; d. Spurgeon Arthur and Flora Hazel (Murray) Livingstone; m. James Harry Bick, Aug. 20, 1955 (div.); children: James A., Charles L. (dec.); m. Ernst Freese, 1986 (dec. 1990). BS with honors, Acadia U., Can., 1951, MS, 1952; PhD, Brown U., 1957; DSc (hon.), Acadia U., 1990. Rsch. pathologist UCLA Med. Sch., 1959-61; asst. prof. Calif. State U., Northridge, 1961-66; lab. instr. Georgetown U., Washington, 1970-72, asst. prof., 1972-76; dep. dir. neurol. disorder program Nat. Inst. Neurol. and Communicative Disorders and Stroke, NIH, Bethesda, Md., 1976-81, acting dep. dir., 1981-83, dep. dir., 1983-87; dep. dir. extramural rsch. Office of Dir. NIH, 1987-90; sci. liaison Centro Studio Multicentrico Internazionale Sulla Demenza, Washington, 1990-95; cons. Nat. Rsch. Coun., Italy, 1991-97, The Charles A. Dana Found., N.Y.C., 1993-98, Edn. Commn. of the States, 1996—. Editor: Alzheimer's Disease: Senile Dementia and Related Disorders, 1978, Neurosecretion and Brain Peptides, Implications for Brain Functions and Neurol. Disease, 1981, The Early Story of Alzheimer's Disease, 1987, Alzheimer Disease, 1994, 2d edit., 1999; contbr. articles to profl. jours. Pres. Woman's Club, McLean, Va., 1968-69; bd. dirs. Fairfax County (Va.) YWCA, 1969-70; pres. Avenel Homeowner's Assn., 1998; pres. Emerson Unitarian Ch., 1964-66; mem. Bethesda Pl. Cmty. Coun., 1992-95, pres., 1993-94; mem. Dana Alliance for Brain Initiatives, 1993—; bd. dirs. Wilmington N.C. Child Advocacy Commn., 1998—. Recipient Can. NRC award Acadia U., 1951-52, NIH Dir.'s award, 1978, Spl. Achievement award NIH, 1981, 83, Superior Svc. award USPHS, 1986, Presdl. Rank award meritorious sr. exec., 1989; Universal Match Found. fellow Brown U., 1956-57, Fed. Exec. Inst. Leadership fellow, 1980. Fellow AAAS; mem. Am. Neurol. Assn., Am. Acad. Neurology, Assn. for Rsch. in Nervous and Mental Disease, Internat. Brain Rsch. Orgn., World Fedn. Neurology Rsch. Group on Dementias (exec. sec. Am. region 1984-86, chmn. 1986-93), Alzheimer's Disease Internat. (mem. scientific and med. adv. bd.), Soc. for Neurosci., Acad. of Medicine (Washington), Dana Alliance for Brain Initiatives.

BICK, RODGER LEE, hematologist, oncologist, researcher, educator; b. San Francisco, May 21, 1942; s. Jack Arthur and Pauline (Jensen) B.; m. Marcella Bick, Mar. 3, 1980 (dec. Feb. 1995); 1 child, Shauna Nicole. MD, U. Calif., Irvine, 1970; PhD, Acad. Medicine, Bialystok, Poland, 1995. Diplomate Am. Bd. Quality Assessment, Am. Bd. Forensic Medicine in Oncology, Hematology, Thrombosis, Hemostasis and Product Liability, Internat. Bd. Thrombosis, Hemostasis & Vascular Medicine, Am. Bd. Pain Mgmt. Med. intern Kern County Gen. Hosp., UCLA, Bakersfield, Calif., 1970-71, internal medicine resident, 1971-72; fellow in hematology-med. oncology Bay Area Hematology Oncology Med. Group, West Los Angeles, Calif., 1974-76; med. staff various hosps., Calif., 1974-77; med. staff, extensive adminstrv. and com. work various hosps., Bakersfield, Calif., 1977-92; med. dir. oncology hematology Presbyn. Comprehensive Cancer Ctr., Presbyn. Hosp., Dallas, 1992-95; staff hematologist/oncologist Bay Area Hematology Oncology Med. Group, Santa Monica, Calif., 1976-77, med. dir. Calif. Coagulation Labs., Inc., Bakersfield, 1977-92, San Joaquin Hematology Oncology Med. Group, 1977-92, Regional Cancer and Blood Disease Ctr. Kern, Bakersfield, 1986-92; asst. clin. prof. to clin. prof. medicine UCLA Ctr. Health Scis., 1976-94, assoc. prof. to prof. allied health profns. Calif. State U., Bakersfield, 1980-92, clin. prof. nursing and health scis., 1982-92; adj. assoc. prof. medicine/physiology, Wayne State U., Detroit; adj. clin. faculty Wesley Med. Ctr. and U. Kans. Med. Sch., Wichita, 1984-86; clin. prof. medicine U. Tex. Southwestern Med. Ctr., 1993—, clin. prof. pathology, 1993—; prof. haematology U. Tasmania Sch. Medicine, 1996; hematology cons. NASA; med. dir. UCLA/Kern Cancer Program, 1991-92, Ctrl. Calif. Heart Inst., 1990-92; invited spkr. and presenter in field, numerous internat. symposia and confs.; dir. numerous workshops in field. Author: Disseminated Intravascular Coagulation and Related Syndromes, 1983, Disorders of Hemostasis and Thrombosis: Principles of Clinical Practice, 1985, 2d. edit., 1992, 3d edit., 1997; guest editor, contbr.: Thrombohemorrhagic Disorders Perplexing to the Hematologist Oncologist, 1992; guest editor: Laboratory Diagnosis of Hemostasis Problems, I, 1994, II, 1995, (monograph) Seminars in Thrombosis and Hemostasis, 1994, Common Bleeding and Clotting Problems for the Internist, 1994; editor-in-chief: Hematology: Princples of Clinical and Laboratory Practice, 2 vols., 1993, Paraneoplastic Syndromes, Hematology Oncology Clinics of North America, 1996; editor: Current Concepts of Thrombosis, 1998; contbr. numerous chpts. to books; author monographs and lab. manuals; contbr. over 250 articles and papers and numerous revs. to profl. jours. and conf. procs.; patentee in field; editor-in-chief Jour. Clin. and Applied Thrombosis/Hemostasis & Vascular Medicine; mem. editl. bd. Am. Jour. Clin. Pathology, Internat. Jour. Haematology. Bd. dirs., exec. com. Bakersfield Symphony Orch., 1988-92. Fellow ACP, Am. Soc. Clin. Pathologists, Assn. Clin. Scientists, Am. Soc. Coagulationists, Internat. Soc. Hematology, Am. Coll. Angiology, Internat. Coll. Angiology, Nat. Acad. Clin. Biochemistry, Am. Heart Assn. (coun. on thrombosis, circulation and atherosclerosis; rsch. and grnat peer rev. com. 1980-86), Am. Geriat. Soc. (founding fellow); mem. AMA, AAAS, Am. Assn. Blood Banks, Am. Soc. Internal Medicine, Am. Soc. Hematology, Internat. Soc. Thrombosis and Haemostasis, Am. Assn. Study of Neoplastic Disease, Am. Assn. Clin. Rsch., Am. Cancer Soc., Internat. Assn. Study of Lung Cancer (founding mem.), Fedn. Am. Scientists, N.Y. Acad. Scis., Calif. Soc. Internal Medicine, Calif. Med. Assn., Calif. Thoracic Soc., Haematology Soc. Australia, Internat. Consensus Com. on Autithrombotic Therapy, numerous others. Lutheran. Avocations: ocean sailing, classical piano, brass musical instruments, photography, target archery, astronomy and astrophotography. Office: 10455 N Central Expy Ste 109 Dallas TX 75231-2215

BICKART, THEODORE ALBERT, university president; b. N.Y.C., Aug. 25, 1935; s. Theodore Roosevelt and Edna Catherine (Pink) B.; m. Carol Florence Nichols, June 14, 1958 (div. Dec. 1973); children: Karl Jeffrey, Lauren Spencer; m. Frani W. Rudolph, Aug. 14, 1982; 1 stepchild, Jennifer Anne Cumming. B Engring. Sci., Johns Hopkins U., 1957, MS, 1958, DEng, 1960; D Univ. (hon.), Dneprodzerzhinst State Tech. U, Ukraine, 19956. Asst. prof. elec. and computer engring. Syracuse (N.Y.) U., 1963-65, assoc. prof., 1965-70, prof., 1970-89, assoc. to vice chancellor for acad. affairs for computer resources devel., 1983-85, dean L.C. Smith Coll. Engring., 1984-89; prof. elec. engring., dean engring. Mich. State U., East Lansing, 1989-98; pres. Colo. Sch. Mines, Golden, 1998—; vis. scholar U. Calif., Berkeley, 1977; Fulbright lectr. Kiev Poly Inst., USSR, 1981; vis. lectr. Nanjing Inst. Tech., China, 1981; hon. disting. prof. Taganrog Radio Engring. Inst., Russia, 1992—; mem. Accreditation Bd. for Engring. and Tch., Engring. Accreditation Commn.; chmn. Engring. Workforce Commn., 1996-98. Co-author: Electrical Network Theory, 1969, Linear Network Theory, 1981; contbr. numerous articles to profl. jours. Served to 1st lt. U.S. Army, 1961-63. Recipient numerous rsch. grants. Fellow IEEE (best paper awards Syracuse sect. 1969, 70, 73, 74, 77, chmn. com. on engring. accreditation activities 1996-98); mem. Am. Soc. Engring. Edn. (v.p. 1997—), Am. Math. Soc., Assn. for Computing Machinery, Soc. for Indsl. and Applied Math., N.Y. Acad. Scis., Ukrainian Acad. Engring. Scis.), Internat. Higher Edn. Acad. Scis. (Russia), Internat. Acad. Informatics (Russia). Avocations: bicycling; hiking; gardening. Home: 1722 Illinois St Golden CO 80401-1836 Office: Colo Sch Mines Office of Pres 1500 Illinois St Golden CO 80401-1887

BICKEL, FLOYD GILBERT, III, investment counselor; b. St. Louis, Jan. 10, 1944; s. Floyd Gilbert and Mary Mildred (Welch) B.; m. Martha Wohler, June 11, 1966; children: Christine Carleton, Susan Marie, Katherine Anne, Jennifer Anne, Laura Elizabeth, Andrew Barrett (dec.). BS in Bus. Adminstrn., Washington U., St. Louis, 1966; MS in Commerce, St. Louis U., 1968. Rschr. Yates, Woods & Co., St. Louis, 1966-67; asst. br. mgr. E.F. Hutton & Co., Inc., St. Louis, 1967-70, v.p. dir. consulting svcs., 1980-88; asst. v.p., resident mgr. Bache & Co., Inc., St. Louis, 1970-72; pres. Donelan-Phelps Investment Advisors, Inc., St. Louis, 1972-80; v.p. Merrill Lynch & Co., St. Louis, 1988—; bd. dirs. Data Rsch. Assocs., Inc, Summit Mktg. Group, Huntleigh Assocs., Eagle RiveR LLC. Mem. City of Des Peres (Mo.), Planning and Zoning Commn., 1975076; chm. St. Louis County Bd. Equalization, 1976-79; pub. safety commr. City of Des Peres, 1977-80, mem. audit and fin. com., 1980-86; mem. State of Mo. Gov.'s Crime Commn., 1981-92; bd. dirs. Villa Duchesne Sch., 1986-92; aldeman City of Huntleigh, 1998—. Mem. Internat. Soc. Cert. Employee Benefit Specialists, St. Louis Soc. Fin. Analysts, Bellerive Country Club, Beaver Creek Club, Cordillera Golf Club, Eagle Springs Golf Club, John M. Olin Bus. Sch. Washington U. Alumni Assn. (pres. 1995-96), John's Island Club. Republican. Roman Catholic. Home: 30 Huntleigh Woods Saint Louis MO 63131-4813 Office: Merrill Lynch & Co 1630 S Lindbergh Blvd Saint Louis MO 63131-3501

BICKEL, JOHN W., II, lawyer; b. Champaign, Ill., Sept. 9, 1948; s. John William and Virginia Bickel; children: Hannah, Molly, Sarah. BS, U.S. Mil. Acad., 1970; JD, So. Meth. U., 1976. Bar: N.Y. 1988, Tex. 1976, U.S. Ct. Appeals (5th and 11th cirs.) 1980, U.S. Supreme Ct. 1983. Assoc. Thompson & Knight, Dallas, 1980-83; ptnr. Brown, Thomas, Karger & Bickel, Dallas, 1983-84; co-mng., co-founder, ptnr. Bickel & Brewer, Dallas, 1984—; co-founding ptnr. Bickel & Brewer Storefront, PLLC, Dallas; adv. mem. Tex. Supreme Ct. Jury Charge Task Force, 1992; mem. com. for qualified judiciary. Mem. exec. bd. So. Meth. U. Sch. Law.; mem. Hiram A. Boaz Soc. So. Meth. U.; mem. Tex. Com.: A Time to Lead--The Campaign for So. Meth. U.; mem. adv. com. Southwestern Ball, 1997—. Fellow Tex. Bar Found., Dallas Bar Found. (sustaining life); mem. ABA, State Bar Tex. (past chmn. litigation com. of environ. and natural resource law sect.), N.Y. Bar Assn., Dallas Bar Assn., Markey/Wigmore Inns of Ct. (Chgo. chpt.), West Point Assn. Grads. (trustee 1997-98, 99—, mem. strategic planning com. 1997—), West Point Soc. North Tex. (bd. dirs.). Office: Bickel & Brewer 4800 Bank One Ctr 1717 Main St Ste 4800 Dallas TX 75201-4651

BICKEL, MINNETTE DUFFY, artist; b. New Bern, N.C., June 24, 1921; d. Richard Nixon and Minnette (Chapman) Duffy; m. William Croft, Jan. 3, 1947; children: Minnette B. Boesel, Susan B. Scioli. Exhibited in one-person shows N.C., statewide portrait exhbns. (two 1st place awards), regional juried shows, (winner three internat. awards); portraits include Gen. Claude Larkin, Tyrone Power, Thomas Graham, James Beckwith, Arthur Rolander, Frederick E. Fox, Senator Jesse Helms, Rachel Carson, R. Bud Dwyer, William Genge, Allison Williams, Dennis O'Connor. Mem. Am. Soc. Portrait Artists (affiliated), Stroke of Genius Gallery, Washington Soc. of Portrait Artists and Portrait Inst. Republican. Website www.portraitartist.com/Bickel. Home: 816 Saint James St Pittsburgh PA 15232-2113 Studio: 809 Bellefonte St Pittsburgh PA 15232-2213

BICKEL, NORA KATHRYN, elementary education educator; b. Slippery Rock, Pa., Oct. 25, 1938; d. Charles DeWitt and Sylvia Irene (Campbell) Wimer; m. Clifford Eugene Bickel, Aug. 25, 1956; children: Diana Sue, Steven Paul, Shirley Eileen. BS, Slippery Rock U., 1968, MEd in Reading, 1970. Elem. tchr. Moniteau Sch. Dist., West Sunbury, Pa., 1967-69; reading specialist Butler (Pa.) Area Sch. Dist., 1969-72, elem. tchr., 1972-97, lead tchr., 1989-97, ret., 1997; cons. State of Pa., Dept. Edn., Divsn. Assessments & Reports; mem. adv. bd. for reading testing div. Pa. Dept. Edn., Harrisburg, 1986—; presenter in field. Mem. NEA, Nat. Coun. Tchrs. English, Internat. Reading Assn., Pa. Edn. Assn., Butler Edn. Assn., Butler County Reading Coun. (pres.), Keystone State Reading Assn. (bd. dirs. 1985—, exec. bd. 1986-98, regional bd. dirs. 1986-98), Grange (past officer Slippery Rock and Pa.). Democrat. Methodist. Avocations: photography, sewing, crafts, reading, crocheting. Home: 3909 William Flynn Hwy Slippery Rock PA 16057-2331

BICKEL, PETER JOHN, statistician, educator; b. Bucharest, Romania, Sept. 21, 1940; came to U.S., 1957, naturalized, 1964; s. Eliezer and P. Madeleine (Moscovici) B.; m. Nancy Kramer, Mar. 2, 1964; children: Amanda, Stephen. AB, U. Calif., Berkeley, 1960, MA, 1961, PhD, 1963; PhD (hon.), Hebrew U. Jerusalem, 1988. Asst. prof. stats. U. Calif., Berkeley, 1964-67, assoc. prof., 1967-70, prof., 1970—, chmn. dept. stats., 1976-79, dean phys. scis., 1980-86, chmn. dept. stats., 1993-97; vis. lectr. math. Imperial Coll., London, 1965-66; fellow J.S. Guggenheim Meml. Found., 1970-71, J.D. and Catherine T. MacArthur Found., 1984-89; NATO sr. sci. fellow, 1974. Author: (with K. Doksum) Mathematical Statistics, 1976, (with C. Klaassen, Y. Ritov and J. Wellner) Efficient and Adaptive Estimation in Semiparametric Models, 1993; assoc. editor Annals of Math. Stats., 1968-76, 86-93; contbr. articles to profl. jours. Fellow J.D. and Catherine T. MacArthur Found., 1984-89. Fellow AAAS (chair sect. U 1996-97), Inst. Math. Stats. (pres. 1980), Am. Statis. Assn.; mem. NAS, Royal Statis. Soc., Internat. Statis. Inst., Am. Acad. Arts and Scis., Royal Netherlands Acad. Arts and Scis., Bernoulli Soc. (pres. 1990). Office: U Calif Dept Stats Evans Hall Berkeley CA 94720

BICKEL, STEPHEN DOUGLAS, insurance company executive; b. Lincoln, Nebr., Dec. 20, 1939; s. Myron Overton and Jane (Sawyer) B.; m. Linda Wall, Apr. 18, 1970; children: Stephanie, Loretta, Valerie. BA, Dartmouth Coll., 1962; LLB, U. Tex., 1965. V.p., actuary Am. Gen. Life Ins. Co., Houston, 1965-80; v.p., actuary Am. Gen. Corp., Houston, 1980-83, sr. v.p., actuary, 1983-87, exec. v.p., 1987-88; pres., chief exec. officer The Variable Annuity Life Ins. Co., Houston, 1988-94, chmn., CEO, 1994-97. Fellow Soc. Actuaries; mem. Acad. Actuaries, Tex. Life Ins. Assn. (chmn. 1995-97), Tex. Life, Accident, Health and Hosp. Svc. Ins. Guaranty Assn. (chmn. 1995-97). Home: 55 Saddlebrook Ln Houston TX 77024-3404

BICKERS, DAVID RINSEY, physician, educator; b. Richmond, Va., Sept. 23, 1941; s. William McKenzie and Helen Virginia (Fitzpatrick) B.; m. Melinda-Lee Jaeger, May 30, 1970; 1 dau., McKenzie Winchester. AB, Georgetown U., 1963; MD, U. Va., 1967. Intern in medicine U. Iowa Hosps., Iowa City, 1967-68; resident in dermatology skin and cancer unit N.Y.U. Med. Center, 1970-73; NIH tng. fellow, guest investigator Rockefeller U., 1971-73, R.J. Reynolds scholar in clin. medicine, asst. prof., asso. physician, 1976-77; asst. prof. dermatology Columbia U. Coll. Physicians and Surgeons, 1973-76; asst. attending dermatologist Presbyn. Hosp., N.Y.C., 1973-76, med. dir., 1997—; prof. dermatology, chmn. dept. Case Western Res. U. Med. Sch., 1977-93, assoc. dean, 1990-93; med. dir. N.Y. Hosp., N.Y.C., 1997—; dir. dermatology svc. U. Hosps., 1977-93, sr. v.p. med. program planning, 1977-89, chief staff, sr. v.p. med. affairs, 1990-93; dir. dermatology svc. Cleve. VA Hosp., 1977-89; mem. gen. medicine A study sect., NIH, 1980-84, chmn., 1982-84; mem. adv. coun. Nat. Inst. Arthritis, Musculoskeletal and Skin Diseases, NIH, 1988-92; Carl Truman Nelson prof. dermatology, chmn. Dept. Coll. Physicians and Surgeons, Columbia U., 1994—; dir. Dermatology Svc. the Presbyn. Hosp., N.Y., 1994—. Author: (with L.C. Harber) Photosensitivity Diseases: Principles of Diagnosis and Treatment, 1981, 2d. edit., 1989, (with Hazen and Lynch) Clinical Pharmacology of Skin Disease, 1984; mem. editorial bd. Jour. Am. Acad. Dermatology, 1979-85, Physicians Drug Alert, 1982—, Today's Therapeutic Trends, 1983—, Photodermatology, 1983-88; assoc. editor Jour. Investigative Dermatol., 1987-97. Served as officer M.C. USAF, 1968-70. Decorated Air Force Commendation medal. Mem. Assn. Am. Physicians, Am. Soc. Clin. Investigation, Am. Soc. Pharmacology and Exptl. Therapeutics, Am. Fedn. Clin. Rsch., Am. Soc. Photobiology, Am. Acad. Dermatology, Am. Dermatol. Assn., Soc. Investigative Dermatology (bd. dirs. 1985-89, sec.-treas. 1989—), Pasteur Club (Cleve.), Med. Strollers (N.Y., 1996), Skin Pharmacology Soc. (sec. 1985-87, pres. 1987-89), Dermatology Found. (sec.-treas. 1984, chmn. bd. 1987-88), Bicontinental Assn. Edn. and Rsch. in Dermatology (founding mem.), German Dermatol. Soc. (hon.), Am. Univ. Beirut (bd. trustees, 1996), Commanderie De Bordeaux, Expert Panel Rsch. Inst. for Fragrance Materials, Am. Bd. of Dermatology (dir. 1997—). Office: Columbia Presbyn Med Ctr AP 1410 161 Fort Washington Ave New York NY 10032-3713

BICKERSTAFF, JEFFERY WAYNE, municipal official; b. Dallas, Aug. 5, 1969; s. Shirley Wayne and Patricia Ann (Anderson) B. AAS, Richland C.C., Dallas, 1991; BS in Geography, Tex. A&M U., 1991, M of Urban Planning, 1994. Cert. Am. Inst. Cert. Planners. Planner City of Garland, Tex., 1994—. Office: City of Garland PO Box 469002 Garland TX 75046-9002

BICKERSTAFF, MINA MARCH CLARK, university administrator; b. Crowley, Tex., Sept. 27, 1936; d. Winifred Perry and Clara Mae (Jarrett) Clark; m. Billy Frank Bickerstaff, June 12, 1954 (div. 1960); children: Billy Mark, Mina Gayle Bickerstaff Basaldu. AA, Tarrant County Jr. Coll., 1982; BBA, Dallas Bapt. U., 1991. Dir. pers. svcs. Southwestern Bapt. Theol. Sem., Ft. Worth, 1976—. Mem. Coll. and Univ. Pers. Assn., Seminary Woman's Club (past treas.), Alpha Chi. Baptist. Avocations: reading, music, genealogy. Office: Southwestern Bapt Theol Sem PO Box 22000 Fort Worth TX 76122

BICKERTON, JANE ELIZABETH, university research coordinator; b. Shrewsbury, Shropshire, Eng., Apr. 16, 1949; came to U.S., 1978; d. Donald Samuel George and Lucy Mary (Hill) B.; m. Anthony Andrew Hudgins, Mar. 18, 1978 (div. Feb. 1995); children: Alexis Kathryn, Samantha Lucy. Grad. health visitor, North London U., 1977; BA, Oglethorpe U., 1980; MA, Ga. State U., 1991; women's health nurse practitioner, Emory U., 1997. RN, Ga., U.K.; cert. family planning nurse, U.K., womens health nurse practitioner. Nurse St. Bartholomews Hosp., London, 1967-72; housing advisor Shelter Housing Aid Ctr., London, 1973-76; owner, dir. Jane Bickerton Fine Arts, Atlanta, 1978-85; curator Ga. State U. Gallery, 1985; co-curator Arts Festival of Atlanta, 1995; coord. rsch. study Emory U., Atlanta, 1995—; co-presenter More Prodns., Ga. State U. Gallery; acting chair Art Papers Inc., chmn., 1990—, art reviewer, 1993—; co-curator bathhouse, billboards, art-in transit Arts Festival Ga., 1995; co-prodr. grant Ga. Humanities Coun., 1989; adj. instr. Atlanta Coll. Art, 1993—; panelist NEA, 1993; nurse Feminist Women's Health Ctr., 1980-90; pers. mgr., asst. mgr. Brit. Pavilion Shop, Expo '92, Spain; visual arts panelist Bur. Cultural Affairs, 1987; juror Arts Festival, Atlanta, 1989. Author: (with John Fletcher) Guide to First-Time House Buyers, 1975; contbg. editor Art Papers, 1981-85; writer: Suns, 1996; exhibited in group shows at Atlanta Coll. Art, 1996=97. Vol. cmty. worker, Guatemala, 1976; mem. adv. com. Arts Festival Atlanta, 1991-93; com. mem. Grady H.S. Parents, Tchrs. and Students Assn.; chmn. com. fine arts Inman Mid. Sch. PTA, 1990-92, Morningside Elem. Sch. PTA, 1986-88; bd. dirs. Pub. Domain, 1992-98; ex-officio bd. dirs. The High Mus. Art, 1996-98. Mem. 20th Century Art Soc. at High Mus. (programming com. mem. 1993, bd. dirs. 1993-98, v.p. 1994-95, pres. 1996-98). Home: 1036 High Point Dr NE Atlanta GA 30306-3235

BICKFORD, JAMES GORDON, banker; b. Huntingdon, Que., Can., 1928; s. Harold Gordon and Jean Forbes (Stark) B.; m. Jetta Goodger-Hill, Aug. 6, 1951. Exec. v.p. Office of Chmn., pres., chief exec. officer Canadian Imperial Bank of Commerce, Toronto, ret.; bd. dirs. CIBC Trust Corp., Toronto. Mem. The Bankers Club (London), Nat. Club (Toronto). Presbyterian. Office: Can Imperial Bank Commerce, Commerce Ct North Ste 2604, Toronto, ON Canada M5L 1A2

BICKFORD, JEWELLE WOOTEN, investment banker; b. Evanston, Ill., Dec. 12, 1941; d. James A. Wooten and Phyllis (Taber) Kades; m. Nathaniel J. Bickford, Feb. 1, 1962; children: Laura C., Emily A. BA, Sarah Lawrence Coll., 1977. Trustee, chair com. on gen. programs and issues Community Svc. Soc., N.Y.C., 1973-77; dir. community bd. assistance unit Office of the Mayor, N.Y.C., 1977-80; v.p. Citibank, N.A., N.Y.C., 1980-84; v.p. Dillon, Read & Co., Inc., N.Y.C., 1984-85, sr. v.p., 1985-88; pres. Tepp, Bickford Fin. Svcs. Inc., 1988-90, Bickford & Ptnrs., Inc., N.Y.C., 1991-94, Bickford Capital Advisors, L.P., 1991-94; mng. dir., head capital markets Rothschild, Inc., N.Y.C., 1994-99, sr. mng. dir., global product head, 1999—; mem. adv. bd. First Womens Bank, 1975-78. Trustee South St. Seaport Theater, chmn. bd., 1978-83; trustee Coro Found., 1982-89, Circle in the Square; bd. dirs. Phoenix House, 1984-95, Citizen Com., 1986-90; trustee, v.p. bd. trustees Fountain House; mem. bus. com. Met. Mus. Art; trustee Randolph Macon Women's Coll., 1998—; mem. adv. bd. Swiss Hotel. Mem. Women's Forum (bd. dirs.). Democrat. Episcopalian. Club: River (N.Y.C.). Home: 969 5th

Ave New York NY 10021-1707 Office: Rothschild Inc Ste 4500 1251 Avenue Of The Americas Fl 51 New York NY 10020-1193

BICKFORD, SHIRLEY VERNA WILLIAMS, retired English educator; b. Washington, May 27, 1934; d. Willie Theodore and Iris (Raiford) Williams; m. Roger G. Bickford, Aug. 21, 1959; children: Janean, Ted, Michael, Iris. BA, Eastern Coll., St. Davids, Pa., 1956; MA, State U. West Ga., Carrollton, 1986. Cert. tchr., Ga. Tchr. English Carrollton (Ga.) Jr. High, 1970-73; min. music Oak Grove Bapt. Ch., Carrollton, 1974-77; tchr. AP English and AP Psychology Ctrl. H.S., Carrollton, 1979-99; ret., 1999. Mem. Nat. Coun. Tchrs. English, Ga. Coun. Tchrs. English. Baptist. Avocations: music, travel.

BICKING, MERLIN KIM LAMBERT, consulting chemist, medical products executive; b. St. Paul, Jan. 9, 1954; s. Zenes J. and Muriel I. (Parson) B.; m. Margaret A. Lambert, Aug. 8, 1981; children: Laura, Linnea, Leah. BS, U. Wis., River Falls, 1976; PhD, Iowa State U., 1982. Asst. prof. SUNY, Buffalo, 1982-85; rsch. scientist Battelle Meml. Inst., Columbus, Ohio, 1985-88; supr. Twin City Testing, St. Paul, 1988-93; cons. ACCTA, Inc., Woodbury, Minn., 1993—; tech. dir. Uroplasty, Inc., Mpls., 1997—; mem. sci. adv. bd. Novamed Med. Mfg., Mpls., 1995—. Contbr. articles to profl. jours. Vol. Kids & Chemistry Program, Woodbury, 1994—. Mem. Am. Chem. Soc., Minn. Chromatography Forum (mem. governing bd. 1991-94), Teltech Expert Network, Assn. Cons. Chemists and Chem. Engrs. Lutheran. Avocations: gardening, baroque trumpet, coaching youth soccer. Office: ACCTA Inc PO Box 25602 Woodbury MN 55125-0602

BICKNELL, BRIAN KEITH, dentist; b. Orlando, Fla., Mar. 8, 1957; s. Keith Arthur and Mary Lou (Papish) B.; m. Gina Rose Smajo; children: Michael Brian, Daniel Keith. BS, U. Notre Dame, 1979, U. Ill., Chgo., 1981; DDS, U. Ill., Chgo., 1983. Practice gen. dentistry Batavia, Ill., 1984—. Fellow Acad. Gen. Dentistry; mem. ADA, Ill. State Dental Soc., Fox River Valley Dental Soc. Roman Catholic. Home: 594 N Van Nortwick St Batavia IL 60510-1119 Office: 109 E Wilson St Batavia IL 60510-2658

BICKNER, BRUCE, food products executive; b. 1943. BBA, De Pauw U., 1965; JD, U. Mich., 1968. Law clk. U.S. Dist. Ct., 1968-70; ptnr. Sidley & Austin, Chgo., 1970-75; with DeKalb (Ill.) Corp., 1975—, v.p., 1976, group v.p., 1980, exec. v.p., dir., 1980, pres., 1986-90, CEO, chmn. bd., 1988-98; CEO, chmn. bd. DeKalb Energy Co., 1988-98, DeKalb Swine Breekers Inc.; co-pres. Monsanto Global Seed Group, Monsanto, Inc., DeKalb, 1998—. Office: Monsanto Global Seed Group 3100 Sycamore Rd Dekalb IL 60115*

BICKS, DAVID PETER, lawyer; b. N.Y.C., Mar. 16, 1933; s. Alexander and Henrietta (Isaacson) B.; m. Marian Ruef, Aug. 24, 1957; children—John Alexander, Jennifer Williams, Caroline Todd, Edward Thomas. A.B., Harvard U., 1955; LL.B., Yale U., 1958. Bar: N.Y. 1959, U.S. Ct. Appeals (2d cir.) 1960, U.S. Dist. Ct. (so. dist.) N.Y. 1961. Asst. U.S. atty. U.S. Dist. Ct. (so. dist.) N.Y., N.Y.C., 1959-61; spl. counsel SEC, N.Y.C., 1961-66; ptnr. LeBoeuf, Lamb, Greene & MacRae L.L.P., N.Y.C., 1966—. Bd. editors Yale Law Jour., 1956-58. Served with U.S. Army, 1958-59. Mem. ABA, N.Y. State Bar Assn. Clubs: Castine Yacht (commodore 1979), Castine Golf (gov. 1984—) (Maine); Harvard of N.Y. (N.Y.C.). Avocation: sailing. Home: 21 E 87th St New York NY 10128-0506 Office: LeBoeuf Lamb Greene & MacRae LLP 125 W 55th St New York NY 10019-5369

BICOFSKY, DAVID MARC, public relations executive; b. Mar. 11, 1947; s. Samuel and Dorothy (Krinsky) B.; m. Catherine Ah Nue Wang, Aug. 30, 1984; children: Robyn Joy, Amanda Lior. AB in Polit. Sci., Hunter Coll., 1969. Reporter, sports writer Herald Statesman, Yonkers, N.Y., 1966-68; copy, layout editor The Record, Hackensack, N.J., 1968-70; editor N.Y. Tel., N.Y.C., 1970-73; pub. rels. supr. AT&T, N.Y.C., 1973-76; dist. staff mgr. pub. rels. N.Y. Tel., 1976-83, div. mgr. pub. rels., 1983-85, dir. editl. svcs., 1985-94; exec. dir. employee comm. NYNEX, 1994-99, retired, 1999; lectr. pub. rels. Trustee Temple Emeth, Teaneck. Mem. Pub. Rels. Soc. Am. (accredited, pres. N.Y. chpt. 1990, nat. bd. dirs. 1993, 94, mem. coll. fellows), Sigma Delta Chi, Tau Epsilon Phi.

BIDART, FRANK, English educator, poet; b. 1939. Faculty mem. dept. English Wellesley (Mass.) Coll., 1972—. Poet: Golden State, 1973, The Book of the Body, 1977, The Sacrifice, 1983, In the Western Night; Collected Poems, 1965-90, 90, Desire, 1997. Recipient Morton Dauwen Zabel award, 1995, Lila Wallace Reader's Digest Found. Writer's Awd., 1993, Rebekka Bobbitt Awd. for Poetry, 1998, Lannan Writer's Awd., 1998. Office: Wellesley Coll Dept English 106 Central St Wellesley MA 02481-8203*

BIDDINGTON, WILLIAM ROBERT, university administrator, dental educator; b. Piedmont, W.Va., Mar. 30, 1925; s. William M. and Sadie (Vogtman) B.; m. Dolores E. Berrett, June 14, 1947; 1 son, William Berrett. Student, Potomac State Coll., 1942-43, Hampden-Sydney Coll., 1943-44; D.D.S. cum laude, U. Md., 1948. Diplomate: Am. Bd. Endodontics. Gen. practice dentistry Balt., 1949-59; instr. Balt. Coll. Dental Surgery, Dental Sch. U. Md., 1949-52, asst. prof., 1952-56, assoc. prof., 1956-59; prof., chmn. dept. endodontics Sch. Dentistry, W.Va. U., Morgantown, 1959-68; asst. dean Sch. Dentistry, W.Va. U., 1966-68, dean, 1968-91, interim v.p. academic affairs, 1979-80, interim v.p. health scis., 1981-82; v.p. Robert C. Byrd Health Scis. Ctr., Morgantown, 1991-92, sr. assoc. v.p., 1992-93, assoc. v.p., 1993—; interim dir. Ctr. on Aging W.Va. U. Sch. Medicine, 1993-95; Mem. at large, sec., vice chmn., chmn. adminstrv. bd., v.p. council deans Am. Assn. Dental Schs., 1974-78, pres., 1983-84. Served with USNR, 1942-46, 48-49. Fellow Am. Coll. Dentists (regent 1983-87, v.p. 1988-89, pres.-elect 1989-90, pres. 1990-91, pres. ACD Found. 1991-92, William John Gies award 1998); mem. ADA (joint commn. on nat. dental exams. 1979-84, commn. on dental health of the coun. on sports medicine of the U.S. Olympic Com. 1980-88, chmn. commn. 1988—, mem. com. on accreditation, coun. on dental edn. 1986-90), W.Va. Dental Assn., Monongahela Valley Dental Soc., Monongahela County Dental Soc. (pres. 1966), Am. Assn. Dental Schs., Internat. Assn. Dental Rsch., Am. Assn. Endodontists, Gorgas Odontological Soc., Psi Omega, Omicron Kappa Upsilon (pres. Supreme chpt. 1965-67). Home: RR 7 Box 720 Morgantown WV 26505-9124 Office: 1157 HSCN PO Box 9001 Morgantown WV 26506-9001

BIDDLE, A. G. W., III (JACK BIDDLE), venture capitalist; b. Chgo., Jan. 24, 1961; s. A.G.W. and Leah Anne (Breen) B.; m. Forée Pendleton McCauley, Apr. 21, 1990; children: A.G.W. IV, Caldwell Knight. BA in Econs., U. Va., 1983. Assoc. Bus. Devel. Ptnrs., Austin, Tex., 1983-85; exec. asst. to CEO, Gartner Group, Stamford, Conn., 1985-86; prin. Vanguard Atlantic, N.Y.C., 1986-90; acting CEO, Decision Tech., Princeton, N.J., 1986-87; pres., CEO, Intercap Systems, Annapolis, Md., 1990-95; gen. ptnr. Novak Biddle Venture Ptnrs., Reston, Va., 1996—; pres. Fubac, Inc., Reston, 1996—; vice chmn. Meridien Emerging Markets, Inc., N.Y.C., 1997—; bd. dirs. Tantivy Comms. Mem. Computer and Comm. Industry Assn. (bd. dirs.), Farmington Country Club, Chevy Chase Club, Annapolis Yacht Club. Please give complete first and middle names. Office: Novak Biddle Venture Ptnrs 1897 Preston White Dr Preston VA 22091

BIDDLE, ALBERT G. W., trade association executive; b. Tulsa, Aug. 14, 1930; s. Albert G. W. and Margaret (Brubeck) B.; m. Stephanie Greher, Mar. 7, 1974; children: Albert G. W., Lisa F., James, Alexandra. BS, U.S. Mil. Acad., 1952. Cons., Booz, Allen & Hamilton, Chgo., 1957-61; dir. diversification H. I. Thompson, Los Angeles, 1961-62; dir. corporate planning Mattel Inc., Los Angeles, 1962-64; pres. Biddle & Assocs., Los Angeles, 1964-68, Decision Resources Corp., Los Angeles, 1968-72, Computer and Communications Industry Assn., Washington, 1972—; founder, dir. Corp. for Open Systems Internat., Alexandria, Va., 1985—; dir., chmn. Esnet, Inc., Washington, 1983—; mem. U.S. Council World Communications Yr., Washington, 1982-83; advisor Office of Tech. Assessment, U.S. Congress, Washington, 1980—; mem. adv. com. ind. sector to sec. Dept. Commerce, Washington, 1982-86; mem. info. tech. adv. com. office mgmt. and budget The White House, 1987—. Mem. adv. bd. J.F. Kennedy Sch. Govt., Harvard, N.Y. and Boston, 1989—. Served to 1st lt. U.S. Army, 1952-55; Korea. Decorated Bronze Star. Republican. Episcopalian. Club: Republican (Washington).

BIDDLE, BRUCE JESSE, social psychologist, educator; b. Ossining, N.Y., Dec. 30, 1928; s. William Wishart and Loureide Jeanette (Cobb) B.; m. Ellen Catherine Horgan; children: David Charles, William Jesse, Jennifer Loureide; m. Barbara Julianne Bank, June 19, 1976. A.B. in Math., Antioch Coll., Yellow Springs, Ohio, 1950; postgrad., U. N.C., 1950-51; Ph.D. in Social Psychology, U. Mich., 1957. Asst. prof. sociology U. Ky., 1957-58; assoc. prof. edn. U. Kansas City, 1958-60; assoc. prof. psychology and sociology U. Mo., Columbia, 1960-66; prof. U. Mo., 1966—, dir. Ctr. Research in Social Behavior, 1966-96; vis. assoc. prof. U. Queensland, Australia, 1965; vis. prof. Monash U., Australia, 1969, vis. fellow Australian Nat. U., 1977, 85, 93. Author: (with R.S. Adams) Realities of Teaching: Explorations with Videotape, 1970, (with M.J. Dunkin) The Study of Teaching, 1974, (with T.L. Good and J. Brophy) Teachers Make a Difference, 1975, Role Theory: Expectations, Identities and Behaviors, 1979, (with D.C. Berliner) The Manufactured Crisis: Myths, Fraud, and the Attack on America's Public Schools, 1995; editor: (with W.J. Ellena) contemporary Research on Teacher Effectiveness, 1964, (with E.J. Thomas) Role Theory: Concepts and Research, 1966, (with P.H. Rossi) The New Media: Their Impact on Education, 1966, (with D.S. Anderson) Knowledge for Policy: Improving Education Through Research, 1991, (with T.L. Good and I.F. Goodson) International Handbook of Teachers and Teaching, 1997. Served with U.S. Army, 1954-56. Fellow APA, Am. Psychol. Soc., Australian Psychol. Soc.; mem. Am. Ednl. Research Assn., Australian Assn. Rsch. Edn., Am. Sociol. Assn., Midwest Sociol. Soc. Home: 924 Yale Columbia MO 65203-1874 Office: U Mo Dept Psychology Rm 210 McAlester Hall Columbia MO 65211

BIDDLE, CATHARINA BAART, artist; m. Livingston L. Biddle, 1973. MFA, George Washington U., Am. U., 1981. Art tchr. Am. Sch., Libya, 1964-66, Washington Pub. Sch. Sys., 1967-73; vol. NEA, 1973-81. Works in mus. and pvt. collections in New York and Wash. D.C. Home: 3050 P St NW Washington DC 20007-3052

BIDDLE, DANIEL R., editor, reporter. Grad., U. Mich. With Cleve. Plain Dealer, 1976-79; reporter Phila. Inquirer, from 1979, asst. city editor, 1991-92, Pa. editor N.J. bur., 1992—, dep. metro. editor. Co-recipient Pulitzer prize for investigative reporting, 1987. Office: Phila Inquirer PO Box 8263 Philadelphia PA 19101-8263*

BIDDLE, DONALD RAY, aerospace company executive; b. Alton, Mo., June 30, 1936; s. Ernest Everet and Dortha Marie (McGuire) B.; m. Nancy Ann Dunham, Mar. 13, 1955; children: Jeanne Kay Biddle Bednash, Mitchell Lee, Charles Alan. Student El Dorado (Kans.) Jr. Coll., 1953-55, Pratt (Kans.) Jr. Coll., 1955-56; BSME, Washington U., St. Louis, 1961; postgrad. computer sci. Pa. State U. Extension, 1963; cert. bus. mgmt. Alexander Hamilton Inst., 1958. Design group engr. Emerson Elec. Mfg., St. Louis, 1957-61; design specialist Boeing Vertol, Springfield, Pa., 1962; cons. engr. Ewing Tech. Design, Phila., 1962-66; chief engr. rotary wing Gates Learjet, Wichita, Kans., 1967-70; dir. engring./R & D BP Chems., Inc. Advanced Materials Div., Stockton, Calif., 1971-93; prin. Biddle & Assocs., Consulting Engrs., Stockton, 1993—; pres., CEO Big Valley Aviation, Inc., Stockton, Calif., 1997—. Guest lectr. on manrated structures, devel. proprietary designs, small bus. devel. to various univs. and tech. socs. Cons. engr. Scoutmaster, counselor, instl. rep. Boy Scouts Am., St. Ann, Mo., 1958-61; mem. Springfield Sch. Bd., 1964. Mem. ASME, ASTM, AIAA, Am. Helicopter Soc. (sec.-treas. Wichita chpt. 1969), Am. Mgmt. Assn., Exptl. Pilots Assn., Soc. for Advancement of Metals and Process Engring. Republican. Methodist (trustee, chmn. 1974-76, 84-86, staff parish 1987-90, fin. 1991-96, video and interiors 1990—). Patentee landing gear designs, inflatable rescue system, glass retention systems, adjustable jack system, cold weather start fluorescent lamp, paper honeycomb core post-process systems. Home: 1140 Stanton Way Stockton CA 95207-2537 Office: Big Valley Aviation Inc ESOP/T 7535 Lindbergh St Stockton CA 95206-3914

BIDDLE, FLORA MILLER, art museum administrator. Pres. Whitney Mus. of Am. Art, N.Y.C., 1978-85, chmn., 1984-95; hon. chmn. Whitney Mus. Am. Art, N.Y.C.; mem. N.Y.C. Art Commn., 1980-90. Author: The Whitney Women and the Museum They Made, 1999. Office: 955 Lexington Ave Ste 9C New York NY 10021-5107

BIDDLE, LIVINGSTON LUDLOW, JR., former government official, author, consultant; b. Bryn Mawr, Pa., May 26, 1918; s. Livingston Ludlow and Eugenia (Law) B.; m. Cordelia Frances Fenton, Mar. 15, 1945 (dec. May 1972); children: Cordelia Frances, Livingston Ludlow IV; m. Catharina Van Beek Baart, Nov. 3, 1973. AB, Princeton U., 1940; LHD (hon.), Mt. St. Mary's Coll., N.Y., 1978; LLD (hon.), Catholic U., 1979; DFA (hon.), U. L.I., 1979, U. Cin., 1979, Providence Coll., 1980, U. Notre Dame, 1980; DL (hon.), Drexel U., 1980. Reporter Phila. Evening Bull., 1940-42; with Am. Field Service, Middle East, North Africa, Italy, France, Germany, 1942-45; spl. asst. to U.S. Senator Claiborne Pell, 1963-65; dep. chmn. Nat. Endowment for Arts, Washington, 1965-67; chmn. div. arts Liberal Arts Coll., Fordham U., Lincoln Center, N.Y.C., 1967-70; spl. asst. to Senator Claiborne Pell, 1973-74; liaison dir. Nat. Endowment for Arts, Washington, 1974-75; chmn. Nat. Endowment for Arts, 1977-81; staff dir. subcom. on edn. arts and humanities U.S. Senate, 1975-77. Author: Main Line, 1950, Debut, 1952, The Village Beyond, 1956, Sam Bentley's Island, 1960, Our Government and the Arts: A Perspective From Inside, 1988. Pres. Children's Service, Inc., Phila., 1960-62; chmn. bd. Pa. Ballet, 1971-72. Decorated Order of Leopold II Belgium, Jubilee medal, Bulgaria; recipient Phila. Athenaeum Best Novel award, 1956. Mem. Chevy Chase Club, Washington Club, Cosmos Club, Century Assn. Club (N.Y.C.). Democrat. Episcopalian. Home: 3050 P St NW Washington DC 20007-3052 *In my work I am seeking to help develop a climate in which the arts may truly flourish for the betterment of mankind.*

BIDDLE, RICHARD B., retired life insurance executive; b. Woodbury, N.J., July 22, 1937; s. Richard and Bertha (Heinz) B.; m. Phyllis Pusey, Sept. 13, 1943; children: Terri, Bonnie, Diana, Richard III. BS, Rider Coll., 1959. Cert. life underwriter. Dist. mgr. Met Life, N.Y.C., 1959-80; field v.p. Great So. Life, Tex., 1980-87; regional brokerage dir. Met Life, 1987-94. Republican. Home: 1926 Moreland Rd Abington PA 19001-1111

BIDDLE, TIMOTHY MAURICE, lawyer; b. San Jose, Calif., Dec. 1, 1940; s. Maurice Francis and Hazel Eda (Bold) B.; m. Florence Elizabeth Hickey, June 15, 1963; children: Elizabeth, Timothy Mark, Matthew, Rebecca. BA in History, Georgetown U., 1962; JD, Cath. U., 1971. Assoc. Jones, Day, Reavis & Pogue, Washington, 1971-77, ptnr., 1977-79; ptnr. Crowell & Moring LLP, Washington, 1979—. Contbr. articles to profl. jours. Capt. USAF, 1962-67. Recipient Disting. Lawyer for 1991 Nat. Coal Assn., 1991. Mem. ABA, Ea. Mineral Law Inst. (trustee), Helicopter Assn. Internat. (bd. dirs., spl. advisor 1990—). Office: Crowell & Moring LLP 1001 Pennsylvania Ave NW Washington DC 20004-2595

BIDELMAN, WILLIAM PENDRY, astronomer, educator; b. L.A., Sept. 25, 1918; s. William Pendry and Dolores (De Remer) B.; m. Verna Pearl Shirk, June 19, 1940; children: Lana Louise Stone, Linda Elizabeth McKinley, Bille Jean Little, Barbara Jo Talley. Student, U. N.D., 1936-37; SB, Harvard, 1940; PhD, U. Chgo., 1943. Physicist Aberdeen Proving Ground, Md., 1943-45; instr., then asst. prof. astronomy Yerkes Obs., U. Chgo., 1945-53; asst. astronomer, then. assoc. astronomer Lick Obs., U. Calif., 1953-62; prof. U. Mich., 1962-69, U. Tex. at Austin, 1969-70; prof. Case Western Res. U., Cleve., 1970-86, prof. emeritus, 1986—; chmn. dept., dir. Warner and Swasey Obs., 1970-75; mem. adv. panel on astronomy NSF, 1959-62; mem. NRC adv. com. on astronomy Office Naval Rsch., 1964-67. Contbr. articles to profl. jours. Mem. Am. Astron. Soc. (councilor 1959-62, participant vis. prof. program 1961-65), Astron. Soc. Pacific (editor publs. 1956-61), Internat. Astron. Union (mem. commns. 29, 45, pres. 1964-67), Phi Beta Kappa. Presbyterian. Achievements include discovery of lines of mercury, krypton and xenon in stellar spectra; discovery of phosphorus stars; co-discovery of barium stars; research in spectral classification, astronomical data and observational astrophysics. Home: 3171 Chelsea Dr Cleveland OH 44118-1256 Office: Case Western Res U Dept Astronomy 10900 Euclid Ave Cleveland OH 44106-1712

BIDEN, JOSEPH ROBINETTE, JR., senator; b. Scranton, Pa., Nov. 20, 1942; m. Jill Tracy Jacobs, June 17, 1977; children: Ashley Blazer, Joseph Robinette, Robert Hunter. BA History, Polit. Sci., U. Del.; JD, Syracuse U., 1968. Bar: Del. 1968. Practice law Wilmington, 1968-72; U.S. senator from Del., 1972—; active New Castle (Del.) County Council, 1970-72; chmn. jud. com., U.S. Senate, 1987-95, mem. 1995—, ranking minority mem., 1995-97; mem. fgn. rels. com., ranking Dem. subcom. European affairs; ranking Dem. subcom. on youth violence; mem. Senate Dem. steering com. and coordination com. Office: 221 Russell Senate Bldg Washington DC 20510-0802*

BIDERMAN, MARK CHARLES, investment banker; b. N.Y.C., Dec. 6, 1945; s. Nathan Bernard and Ruth Leah (Koplik) B.; m. Wendy Lynn Raich, June 7, 1970; children: Robin, Eric. BS, Princeton U., 1967; MBA, Harvard U. Chartered fin. analyst. Rsch. analyst Oppenheimer & Co., Inc., N.Y.C., 1969-87, investment banker, 1987-97; mng. dir. CIBC Oppenheimer Corp., N.Y.C., 1997—. Trustee Congregation Rodeth Sholom, N.Y.C., 1986—, v.p., 1991—. Mem. N.Y. Soc. Security Analysts, Bank and Fin. Analysts Assn. (bd. dirs. 1974-77, pres. 1976-77), Princeton U. Club N.Y. Office: CIBC Oppenheimer Tower World Financial Center New York NY 10281-1003*

BIDLACK, RUSSELL EUGENE, librarian, educator, former dean; b. Manilla, Iowa, May 25, 1920; s. Harold Stanley and Mabel (Thompson) B.; m. Melva Helen Sparks, June 13, 1942; children: Stanley Alden, Martha Sue, Christopher Joel, Harold Wilford. B.A. with honors, Simpson Coll., 1947, Litt.D. (hon.), 1976; A.B. in L.S. with honors, U. Mich., 1948, A.M. in L.S, 1949, A.M. in History, 1950, Ph.D. (L.S.), 1954. Instr. library sci. U. Mich., 1951-56, asst. prof., 1956-60, assoc. prof., 1960-65, prof., 1965-85, dean Sch. Library Sci., 1969-85, prof. and dean emeritus, 1985—. Author: The City Library of Detroit, 1817-1837, 1955, Letters Home, the Story of Ann Arbor's Forty-Niners, 1960, John Allen and the Founding of Ann Arbor, 1962, The Yankee Meets the Frenchman, 1965, The ALA Accreditation Process, 1977, Ann Arbor's First Lady, Events in the Life of Ann I. Allen, 1998. Served to master sgt. AUS, 1941-46. Recipient Beta Phi Mu award for distinguished service to edn. for librarianship, 1977; Melvil Dewey medal creative profl. achievement, 1979; Joseph W. Lippincott award for disting. service to librarianship, 1983. Mem. ALA (chmn. subcom. to rewrite Standards accreditation 1969-72, chmn. com. 1974-76, chmn. Melvil Dewey award jury 1973-74, chmn. Am. Library History Roundtable 1973-74, mem. council 1972-76, chmn. nominating com. 1980-81), Mich. Library Assn. (pres. tech. services sect.), Assn. Library and Info. Sci. Edn. (chmn. deans and dirs. group 1978-79), Mich. Hist. Soc. Home: 1709 Cherokee Rd Ann Arbor MI 48104-4498

BIDLACK, WAYNE ROSS, nutritional biochemist, toxicologist, food scienti; b. Waverly, N.Y., Aug. 12, 1944; s. Andrew L. Bidlack and Vivian Pearl Cowles Williams; m. Wei Wang, July 29, 1995. BS, Pa. State U., 1966; MS, Iowa State U., 1968; PhD, U. Calif., Davis, 1972. Postdoctoral fellow dept. pharmacology U. So. Calif., L.A., 1972-74, asst prof. sch. medicine, 1974-80, assoc. prof., 1980-92, prof., 1992—, asst. dean student affairs, 1988-91, chmn. dept. pharmacology and nutrition, 1991-92; chmn. dept. food sci. and human nutrition Iowa State U., Ames, 1992-95; dean Coll. Agr. Calif. State Poly. U., Pomona, 1995—. Assoc. editor Biochem. Medicine and Metabolic Biology, 1986-87; book reviewer, abstract editor Jour. Am. Coll. Nutrition, 1995—; assoc. editor Environ. Nutritional Interactions, 1996—. Chmn. Greater L.A. Nutrition Coun., 1982-83, So. Calif. Inst. Food Technologists, 1988-89, Toxicology and Safety Evaluation divsn. Inst. Food Technologists, 1989-90, food sci. communicator, 1986-90; chmn. Nat. Coun. Against Health Fraud, 1983-85; mem. expert panel on foods and nutrition, 1989-93. Recipient Outstanding Tchr. Award, U. So. Calif., Sch. Medicine, 1987-88, Meritorious Svc. award, Calif. Dietetic Assn., 1990, Disting. Achievement award, So. Calif. Inst. Food Technologists, 1990, fellow Inst. Food Technologists, 1998. Mem. Soc. Toxicology (chair awards com. food safety sect. 1993-94, chair 1994-95), Nat. Golden Key Soc. (hon.), Gamma Sigma Delta. Republican. Avocations: golf, book collecting. Office: Calif State Polytech U Coll of Agrl 3801 W Temple Ave Pomona CA 91768-2557

BIDWELL, CHARLES EDWARD, sociologist, educator; b. Chgo., Jan. 24, 1932; s. Charles Leslie and Eugenia (Campbell) B.; m. Helen Claxton Lewis, Jan. 24, 1959; 1 son, Charles Lewis. AB, U. Chgo., 1950, AM, 1953, PhD, 1956. Lectr. on sociology Harvard U., 1959-61; asst. prof. edn. U. Chgo., 1961-65, assoc. prof., 1965-70, prof. edn. and sociology, 1970-85, Reavis prof. edn. and sociology, 1985—, chmn. dept. edn., 1978-88, chmn. dept. sociology, 1988-94, dir. Ogburn-Stouffer Ctr., 1988-94. Author books in field; contbr. numerous articles to profl. jours.; editor Sociology of Edn., 1969-72, Am. Jour. Sociology, 1973-78, Am. Jour. Edn., 1983-88. With U.S. Army, 1957-59. Guggenheim fellow, 1971-72. Fellow AAAS; mem. Sociol. Rsch. Assn., Nat. Acad. Edn. (sec.), Phi Beta Kappa. Office: Dept Sociology 5848 S University Ave Chicago IL 60637-1515

BIDWELL, JAMES TRUMAN, JR., lawyer; b. N.Y.C., Jan. 2, 1934; s. James Truman and Mary (Kane) B.; m. Gail S. Bidwell, Mar. 6, 1965 (div.); children: Hillary Day Bidwell Mackay, Kimberley Wade, Cortney E.; m. Katherine T. O'Neil, July 15, 1988. BA, Yale U., 1956; LLB, Harvard U., 1959. Bar: N.Y. 1959. Atty. USAF, Austin, Tex., 1959-62; assoc. Donovan, Leisure, Newton & Irvine, N.Y.C., 1962-68, ptnr., 1968-84; ptnr. White & Case, N.Y.C., 1984-98; sr. counsel Linklaters & Paines, N.Y.C., 1998—. Pres. Youth Consultation Svc., 1973-78; trustee Berkeley Divinity Sch. Mem. ABA, Fed. Bar Assn., N.Y. State Bar Assn., N.Y. County Lawyers Assn. Episcopalian. Office: Linklaters & Paines 1345 Avenue Of The Americas New York NY 10105

BIDWELL, ROBERT ERNEST, inventor; b. Bklyn., Jan. 15, 1926; s. Ernest Martin and Helen (Hamilton) B.; degree in Archtl. Design, Pratt Inst., 1953; m. Patricia Murphy, July 1, 1950; children: Robert Bruce, Kerry Martin, Jane Bidwell Thomassen, James Patrick. Designer, Harrison & Abramovitz, Rockefeller Center, N.Y.C., 1955-58; pres. Robert Bidwell Assos., Farmingdale, N.Y., 1958-68; gen. mgr., dir. design Bioresearch, Inc., Farmingdale, 1968-80; founder, chmn. bd. Bidwell Vineyards and Winery, Cutchogue, N.Y. Inventor, holder 107 patents. Served with AUS, 1944-46. Mem. Soc. Plastic Engrs. (sr.), Am. Soc. Metals, Assn. Advancement Med. Instrumentation, Def. Preparedness Assn., Bidwell Family Assn., U.S. Naval Inst., SAR, L.I. Grape Growers Assn., Rep. Senatorial Inner Circle (Washington). Republican. Mem. Christian Ch. Home: 27 Montrose Pl Melville NY 11747-3403 Office: Bidwell Vineyard Rte 48 Cutchogue NY 11935

BIDWELL, ROGER GRAFTON SHELFORD, biologist, educator; b. Halifax, N.S., Can., June 8, 1927; came to U.S., 1965; s. Roger Edward Shelford and Mary (Bothamly) B.; m. Shirley Mae Rachael Mason, July 1, 1950; children—Barbara, Alison, Roger, Gillian. B.Sc., Dalhousie U., 1947; B.A., Queen's U., 1950, M.A., 1951, Ph.D., 1954. Tech. officer Canadian Def. Research Bd., Kingston, Ont., 1951-56; asst. research officer Nat. Research Council, Halifax, 1956-59; assoc. prof. biology U. Toronto, Ont., 1959-65; prof. biology Case Western Res. U., Cleve., 1965-69; chmn. dept. Case Western Res. U., 1966-68; prof. biology Queen's U., Kingston, Ont., Can., 1969-79, prof. emeritus, 1979—; I.W. Killam research prof. Dalhousie U., Halifax, 1980-85; sr. ptnr. Atlantic Research Assocs. Ltd., Wallace, N.S., 1980-91; exec. dir. Atlantic Inst. Biotech., Halifax, 1985-88; vis. prof. Cornell U., 1961-63; vis. scientist Atlantic Regional Lab., NRC, Halifax, summer 1966, 76; cons. Faculty Edn., Simon Fraser U., 1966; Can. Sci. Exch. visitor to People's Republic of China, 1975, 77. Author: Plant Physiology, 1974, 79; co-editor: Plant Physiology: A Treatise, 1978-90; contbr. over 130 articles to profl. jours., chpts. to textbooks on biochem. mechanisms in plants, protein metabolism, CO_2 metabolism in leaves, photosynthesis and metabolism in marine algae. Active Crime Stoppers, Cumberland region, 1993-97, chmn., 1994-97; mem. several comms. Anglican Diocese N.S.; pres., chmn. bd. Pugwash Coop. Ltd., 1995—. Recipient Queen Elizabeth II Silver Jubilee medal, 1977. Fellow AAAS, Royal Soc. Can.; mem. Canadian Soc. Plant Physiologists (founder, past sec.-treas., pres. 1972-73, Gold medal 1979), Biol. Council Can. (sec. 1973-76), Am. Soc. Plant Physiology. Avocations: bicycling, walking, skiing, bird watching, weaving.

BIDWILL, WILLIAM V., professional football executive; s. Charles W. and Violet Bidwill; m. Nancy Bidwill; children: William Jr., Michael, Patrick, Timothy, Nicole. Grad., Georgetown U. Co-owner St. Louis Cardinals Football Team (now Ariz. Cardinals), 1962-72, owner, 1972—, also chmn., 1972—, pres. Office: Ariz Cardinals PO Box 888 Phoenix AZ 85001-0888*

BIEBEL, CURT FRED, JR., dentist; b. St. Louis, Dec. 7, 1947; s. Curt F. and Jewell (Frank) B.; children: Betheny Doreen, Brendon Matthew. AB in Psychology, U. Mo., Columbia, 1970; DDS, U. Mo., Kansas City, 1974. Assoc. dentist Louis R. Nolan, Inc., St. Louis, 1976-79; gen. practice dentistry Chesterfield, Mo., 1979—. Capt. USAF, 1974-76. Mem. ADA, Greater St. Louis Dental Soc., Chgo. Dental Soc., Country Club of St. Albans, Forest Park Handball Assn., St. Louis Hinder Club. Office: 14378 Wood Lake Dr Chesterfield MO 63017-5714

BIEBEL, PAUL PHILIP, JR., lawyer; b. Chgo., Mar. 24, 1942; s. Paul Philip Sr. and Eleanor Mary (Sweeney) B.; divorced; children: Christine M., Brian E., Jennifer A., Susan E. AB, Marquette U., 1964; JD, Georgetown U., 1967. Bar: Ill. 1967, U.S. Dist. Ct. (no. dist.) Ill. 1967, U.S. Ct. Appeals (6th cir.) 1985, U.S. Supreme Ct. 1972. Asst. dean of men Loyola U., Chgo., 1967-69; asst. state's atty. Cook County State's Atty., Chgo., 1969-75, dep. state's atty., 1975-81; 1st asst. atty. gen. Ill. Atty. Gen., Chgo., 1981-85; pub. defender Cook County Pub. Defender, Chgo., 1986-88; ptnr. Winston & Strawn, Chgo., 1985-86, 88-94, Altheimer & Gray, Chgo., 1994-96; judge Cir. Ct. Cook County, Ill., 1996—. Contbr. articles to profl. publs. Mem. Fed. Bar Assn. (bd. dirs. 1988—, pres. 1994-95), Cath. Lawyers Guild (bd. dirs. 1988—, Cath. Lawyer of Yr. 1988), Ill. Appellate Lawyers, 7th Cir. Bar Assn., Chgo. Bar Assn. (chmn. com. 1991-93), Georgetown Law Alumni Assn. (bd. dirs. 1991-96). Roman Catholic. Avocations: reading, golf. Home: 5415 N Forest Glen Ave Chicago IL 60630-1523 Office: Cir Ct Cook County Child Protection Divsn 1100 S Hamilton Ave Chicago IL 60612-4207

BIEBER, MARK ALLAN, nutrition scientist, researcher; b. Cleve., Sept. 16, 1946; s. Lester and Ethel R. (Rubin) B. BS in Chemistry, U. Pitts., 1968; PhD in Biochemistry, Mich. State U., 1973. Cert. Am. Chem. Soc. Predoctoral trainee NIH, 1968-73; postdoctoral trainee NIH, Bethesda, Md., 1975-77; fell in pediatrics and human nutrition Columbia U. Coll. Physicans and Surgeons, N.Y.C., 1973-77; sr. nutritionist Best Foods, Union, N.J., 1977-79, prin. nutritionist, 1979-83, nutrition rsch. assoc., 1983—; $D, $D; mem. steering com. N.J. Nutrition Coun., 1978-82, Internat. Life Sci. Inst., Washington, 1986—. Contbr. articles to sci. jours. Chmn. bd. Congregation Beth Simchat Torah, 1987-88. Fellow Mataheson Found., 1973-74. Fellow Am. Heart Assn., Am. Coll. Nutrition, Am. Oil Chemists Soc. (pres. N.E. region 1987-88, merit award 1989, chair health and nutrition divsn. 1994-96, chair divsn. coun. 1995-96, mem.-at-large governing bd. 1997-99, sec. 1999—), Am. Soc. for Nutritional Scis., Inst. Food Technologists, Soc. for Nutrition Edn. Democrat. Office: Best Foods 150 Pierce St Somerset NJ 08873-4185

BIEBER-ROBERTS, PEGGY EILENE, communications educator, editor, journalist, researcher; b. Mobridge, S.D., Jan. 8, 1943; d. John J. and Lenora (Schlepp) B. BS, No. State U., Aberdeen, S.D., 1966; MA, U. Wyo., 1984; PhD, U. Wash., 1990. Vol. Peace Corps, Turkey, 1966-68; tchr. secondary pub. schs., Idaho, 1968-69, Pine Ridge (S.D.) Reservation, 1969-71; co-founder Medicine Bow Post weekly newspaper, 1977; legis. reporter various weekly newspapers, Wyo., 1980-82; owner, pub. Capitol Times mag., Cheyenne, Wyo., 1982-84; publisher Skyline West Press, 1983—; lectr. pub. rels. and advt. U. Wash., Seattle, 1986-88; rsch. analyst Elway Rsch./Jay Rockey Co., Seattle, 1989-90; asst. prof. mass media U. Wyo., Laramie, 1990-96; journalism faculty comm. tech. Higher Colls. of Technology, Dubai, United Arab Emirates, 1996-98; polit. campaign mgr. Phil Roberts gubernatorial campaign, Wyo., 1998; asst. prof. journalism and mass comms. Am. U. in Cairo, Egypt, 1999—; indexer McGraw/Hill, Bedford Books, also others, 1988-94. Author, editor hist. almanacs for various states, 1984-87; contbr. articles to profl. jours., chpts. to books. Publicity chmn. Laramie County Dem. Com., Cheyenne, 1982. Recipient 1st Place award for feature writing, Co-1st Place award for editorials Wyo. Press Assn., 1982, Alumni Assn. Faculty Growth award U. Wyo., 1994; named Stout fellow U. Wash., 1990. Mem. Turkish Studies Assn., Internat. Assn. Mass Comm. Rsch., Assn. Ednl. Journalism and Mass Comm., Internat. Comm. Assn., Mid East Studies Assn.

BIECHMAN, JOHN CHARLES, federal agency official; b. Catskill, N.Y., May 18, 1947; s. Sanford I. and Agnes M. (Happ) B.; m. Shelly Leone, Oct. 13, 1979; children: Katherine L., Kerry M. BA, San Jose State U., 1969. Field rep. Rep. Norman Mineta U.S. Ho. of Reps., San Jose, Calif., 1976-78; liaison officer U.S. Dept. HUD, Washington, 1979-81; sr. v.p. govt. affairs Bldg. Owners and Mgrs. Assn., Washington, 1981-87; v.p. Safe Bldgy Alliance, Washington, 1987-90; v.p. for pub. affairs Nat. Assn. Indsl. and Office Parks, Arlington, Va., 1990-92; pres. Potomac Strategies, Alexandria, Va., 1992-93; dep. asst. sec. U.S. Dept. HUD, Washington, 1993—. Mem. coun. City of Morgan Hill, Calif., 1974-78; campaign and transition aide Clinton for Pres., Washington, 1992; mem. Alexandria (Va.) Dem. Com., 1992—; v.p. Alexandria (Va.) Christmas in April. With U.S. Army, 1969-70. Home: 1121 Allison St Alexandria VA 22302-2419 Office: Dept Housing & Urban Devel Congression & Intergov Relation 451 7th St SW Washington DC 20410-0002

BIECK, ROBERT BARTON, JR., lawyer; b. Wiesbaden, Germany, Apr. 13, 1952; s. Robert Barton and Mary-Jean (Boeck) B.; m. Julia A. Dietz, Apr. 20, 1991. Student Rensselaer Poly. Inst., 1970-71; BA in Polit. Sci., U. Nebr., 1974; JD with high honors, Tex. Tech. U., 1977. Bar: Tex. 1977, La. 1977, D.C. 1992, U.S. Dist. Ct. (ea. dist.) La. 1977, U.S. Dist. Ct. (mid. dist.) La. 1978, U.S. Dist. Ct. (we. dist.) La. 1979, U.S. Dist. Ct. (no. and so. dists.) Tex. 1991, U.S. Dist Ct D.C. 1994, U.S. Ct. Appeals (D.C. cir.) 1992, U.S. Ct. Appeals (5th and 11th cirs.) 1981, U.S. Supreme Ct. 1980. Assoc. firm Jones, Walker, Waechter, Poitevent, Carrere & Denegre, New Orleans, 1977-82, ptnr., 1982—. Recipient West Horn Book award West Pub. Co., 1976; Fulbright and Jaworski scholar, 1976. Mem. ABA (litigation sect., bus. law sect., criminal laws com., federal regulation of securities com.), Securities Indusstry Assn., Nat. Soc. Compliance Profls., New Orleans Bar Assn., La. Bankers Assn., 5th Cir. Bar Assn., Order of Coif, Phi Kappa Phi, Phi Delta Phi. Home: 1420 Marengo St New Orleans LA 70115-3815 Office: Jones Walker Waechter Poitevent Carrere & Denegre 201 Saint Charles Ave Ste 5200 New Orleans LA 70170-5100

BIEDERMAN, BARRON ZACHARY (BARRY BIEDERMAN), advertising agency executive; b. N.Y.C.; s. William and Sophye (Groll) B.; m. Susan Howard, Apr. 1, 1967; children: Rachel, David. B.A. with distinction, Cornell U., 1952; MS in Journalism, Columbia U, 1953; postgrad., U. London, 1954. Copy group head Mogul, Williams & Saylor, N.Y.C., 1955-59; sr. writer Lennen & Newell, N.Y.C., 1960-62; v.p., assoc. creative svcs. dir. Cunningham & Walsh, N.Y.C., 1962-64; sr. v.p. Needham, Harper & Steers, N.Y.C., 1964-84; exec. creative dir. Needham, Harper & Steers, 1964-74, mgmt. rep., 1974-79, dir., 1981-84; mng. dir. NH&S Corp. Futures, 1979-80; chmn., chief exec. officer NH&S/Issues & Images, 1981-84; chmn. Biederman & Co., Inc. (name changed to Biederman, Kelly & Shaffer, Inc. 1989), 1984—; chmn. emeritus Biederman, Kelly, Krimstein Ptnrs., 1998; lectr. in field. bd. dirs. Liberty Club, N.Y., 1983-87, Alvin Ailey Dance Theatre, N.Y., 1974. Recipient various advt. awards; Ford Found. fellow Eng., India, 1953-55. Mem. Fin. Comms. Soc. (bd. dirs. 1982-89, pres. 1986-87), Internat. Advt. Assn., Bank Mktg. Assn., Copywriters Club N.Y. (bd. dirs. 1960-64). Club: Liberty (bd. dirs. 1984-86, adv. council 1983-84). Avocations: reading, music, carpentry, gardening, travel. Home: 425 E 58th St Apt 17G New York NY 10022-2300 Office: Biederman Kelly & Shaffer Inc 475 Park Ave S Fl 15 New York NY 10016-6907

BIEDERMAN, DONALD ELLIS, lawyer; b. N.Y.C., Aug. 23, 1934; s. William and Sophye (Groll) B.; m. Marna M. Leerburger, Dec. 22, 1962; children: Charles Jefferson, Melissa Anne. AB, Cornell U., 1955; JD, Harvard U., 1958; LLM in Taxation, NYU, 1970. Bar: N.Y. 1959, U.S. Dist. Ct. (so. dist.) N.Y. 1967, Calif. 1977. Assoc. Hale, Russell & Stentzel, N.Y.C., 1962-66; asst. corp. counsel City of N.Y., 1966-68; assoc. Delson & Gordon, N.Y.C., 1968-69; ptnr. Roe, Carman, Clerke, Berkman & Berkman, Jamaica, N.Y., 1969-72; gen. atty. CBS Records, N.Y.C., 1972-76; sr. v.p. legal affairs and adminstrn. ABC Records, L.A., 1977-79; ptnr. Mitchell, Silberberg & Knupp, L.A., 1979-83; exec. v.p., gen. counsel Warner/Chappell Music Inc. (formerly Warner Bros. Music), L.A., 1983—; adj. prof. Sch. Law Southwestern U., L.A., 1982—; Pepperdine U., Malibu, Calif., 1985-87, Loyola Marymount U., L.A., 1992; lectr. Anderson Sch. Mgmt. UCLA, 1993, U. So. Calif. Law Ctr., 1995-97. Editor: Legal and Business Problems of the Music Industry, 1980; co-author: Law and Business of the Entertainment Industries, 1987, 2nd edit., 1991, 3d edit., 1995. Bd. dirs. Calif. Chamber Symphony Soc., L.A., 1981-92; dir. Entertainment Law Inst. U. So. Calif., 1993—. 1st lt. U.S. Army, 1959. Recipient Hon. Gold Record, Recording Industry Assn. Am., 1974, Trendsetter award Billboard mag., 1976, Gold Triangle award Am. Acad. Dermatology, 1999. Mem. N.Y. Bar Assn., Calif. Bar Assn., Riviera Country Club, Cornell Club. Democrat. Jewish. Avocations: golf, skiing, travel, reading. Home: 2406 Pesquera Dr Los Angeles CA 90049-1225 Office: Warner/Chappell Music Inc 10585 Santa Monica Blvd Los Angeles CA 90025-4921

BIEDERMAN, EDWIN WILLIAMS, JR., petroleum geologist; b. Stamford, Conn., June 30, 1930; s. Edwin Williams and Thelma Frances (Morrow) B.; m. Margaret-Jane Bell White, Aug. 23, 1958; children: Robert, Mary, Jane, James. BA, Cornell U., 1952; PhD, Pa. State U., 1958. Cert. petroleum geologist. Project leader Cities Svc. Co., Tulsa, 1958-68; pres. staff Cities Svc. Co., Cranbury, N.J., 1968-72; asst. dir. Pa. Tech. Assistance program, University Park, Pa., 1972-77, sr. tech. specialist, 1980—; field ctr. dir. NSF Chautauqua Courses, University Park, 1977-80; field ctr. dir. NSF Chautauqua Courses, University Park, 1977-80. Author: Atlas of Oil and Gas Reservoir Rocks From North America, 1986; contbr. articles to profl. jours.; holder 5 patents for geochem. exploration, in situ acidulation of phosphate rock, grate for vertical oil shale kiln, fire retardant foam, lightweight cement for oil wells. With USAF, 1952-54. Pa. State U. scholar 1956-58; am. Assn. Petroleum Geologists grantee 1957; recipient First Place award Project of Yr. Nat. Assn. Mgmt. and Tech. Assistance Ctrs., 1985. Mem. AAAS, Am. Assn. Petroleum Geologists, Soc. Econ. Paleontologists and Mineralogists, Geochem. Soc., Assn. Profl. Geol. Scientists. Achievements include 5 patents for geochemistry exploration, in situ acidulation of phosphate rock, grate for vertical oil shale kiln, fire retardant foam, lightweight cement for oil wells. Office: Pa State U 232 Hosler Bldg University Park PA 16802-5001

BIEDERMAN, JERRY H., lawyer; b. Chgo., July 2, 1946. BA, Stanford U., 1968; JD, U. Chgo., 1971. Bar: Ill. 1971. Mng. ptnr. Neal, Gerber & Eisenberg, Chgo. Mem. ABA (law practice mgmt. sec.) Chgo. Bar Assn. Office: Neal Gerber & Eisenberg 2 N La Salle St Ste 2200 Chicago IL 60602-3801

BIEDERMANN, PAUL FREDERICK, graphic designer; b. Huntington, N.Y., Feb. 11, 1963; s. Manfred Paul and Emily Louise (Galke) B.; m. Glenda Grace Carlos, Sept. 11, 1993; children: Myles, Wyatt. BFA, Washington U., St. Louis, 1985. Graphic designer Handler Group, N.Y.C., 1986-89; art dir. NFL Properties, N.Y.C., 1989-91; creative dir. McGraw-Hill Cos., N.Y.C., 1992—. Designer logos for Pro Bowl, 1990, Quarter Club, 1990, trading cards Proline Portraits, 1990, posters for Am. Bowl, 1990. Recipient various awards for artwork.

BIEDRON, THEODORE JOHN, newspaper advertising executive; b. Evergreen Park, Ill., Nov. 30, 1946; s. Theodore John and Ione Margaret B.; BA in Polit. Sci., U. Ill., 1968; m. Gloria Anne DeAngelo, Nov. 7, 1970; children: Jessica Ann, Lauren. Recruitment advt. mgr. Chgo. Sun-Times, 1968-74; classified advt. mgr. Pioneer Press, Wilmette, Ill., 1974-76, v.p. advt. and promotion, 1993—, sr. v.p. sales and mktg., 1994—, exec. v.p., 1997—; pub. North Shore mag., 1997—; classified mgr., v.p. Lerner Newspapers, Chgo., 1976-79, assoc. pub., 1980-82, advt. dir., 1982-87; v.p., classified advt. mgr. Chgo. Sun-Times, 1987-92. Pres. Northeastern Ill. Univ. Found.; trustee Northlight Theater, 1993-98. Home: 1130 Lake Ave Wilmette IL 60091-1661 Office: Pioneer Press 3701 W Lake Ave Glenview IL 60025-1277

BIEGEL, ALICE MARIE, secondary school educator; b. Blue Island, Ill., Sept. 12, 1947; d. Stanley and Lottie (Matras) Burczyk; m. Peter Leo Biegel, July 27, 1974; children: Kevin, Nicole, Robbie, Ryan. BS in Edn., Chgo. State U., 1968; MS in Edn., Gov.'s State U., 1980. Cert. math. tchr., Ill., Fla. Tchr. algebra Eisenhower High Sch., Blue Island, 1969-71; tchr. algebra and computer edn. Thornton Fractional North & South High Sch., Calumet City, Ill., 1971-76; tchr. geometry, algebra, dir. compensatory edn. Booker High Sch., Sarasota, 1988-90; tchr. algebra, chmn. math dept. Laurel Mid. Sch., Osprey, Fla., 1990-95; algebra tchr., chmn. dept. math. Larel Middle Sch., Osprey, Fla., 1992—; freshmen, jr. sponsor, prom sponsor, fgn. exchange sponsor; developer full yr. curriculum for measurements math course '75. Chmn. pub. rels. and grants com. Jr. League of Sarasota, 1988, 89-90; sponsor H.S. crew team, 1991—. Recipient Tchr. Commendation award State of Ill., 1973. Mem. Nat. Coun. Tchrs. of Math., Sarasota Tchrs. of Math. Club. Roman Catholic. Avocations: scuba diving, interior decorating, boating. Home: 525 Freeling Dr Sarasota FL 34242-1019

BIEGEL, DAVID ELI, social worker, educator; b. N.Y.C., July 3, 1946; s. Jack and Estelle (Lentin) B.; BA, CCNY, 1967; MSW, U. Md., 1970, PhD, 1982; m. Margaret S. Smoot, Jan. 31, 1976 (div.); 1 child, Geoffrey S. Field coord. United Farm Workers, AFL-CIO, Balt., 1971; exec. dir. Junction, Inc., Westminster, Md., 1971-72; dir. office planning and program devel. Cath. Charities, Balt., 1973-76; ctr. assoc., dir. neighborhood and family svcs. project U. So. Calif., Washington Pub. Affairs Ctr., 1976-80; asst. prof. social work U. Pitts., 1980-85, assoc. prof., 1985-86; Henry L. Zucker Prof. social work practice, prof. sociology Mandel Sch. Applied Social Scis., Case Western Reserve Univ., 1987—, co-dir. Ctr. for Practice Innovations, 1991-97; co-dir. Cuyahoga County Cmty. Mental Health Rsch. Inst., 1994—; chair doctoral program Mandel Sch. Applied Social Sci. Case Western Res. U., 1998—. Cons. Vol. VISTA, Raton, N.Mex. and Balt., 1967-70; active Big Bros. Am., Balt., 1974-77. N.Y. State Incentive scholar, 1963-64; VISTA Fellows Program fellow, 1968-70. Fellow Gerontol. Soc. Am.; mem. APHA, NASW, Acad. Cert. Social Workers, Soc. Social Work Rsch. Democrat. Jewish. Co-editor: Innovations in Practice and Service Delivery with Vulnerable Populations Series, Family Caregiving Applications Series; contbr. articles to profl. jours., books; co-author 11 books.

BIEGEL, EILEEN MAE, hospital executive; b. Eau Claire, Wis., Nov. 13, 1937; d. Ewald Frederic and Emma Antonia (Conrad) Weggen; student Dist. One Tech. Inst., 1974, also part time, corr. student U. Wis., Madison; grad. mgmt. seminars; student Upper Iowa U., 1984—; m. James O. Biegel, Oct. 6, 1956; children: Jeffrey Alan, John William. Exec. sec. to pres. Broadcaster Services, Inc., Eau Claire, Wis., 1969-74; exec. sec. to exec. v.p. Am. Nat. Bank, Eau Claire, 1975-77; exec. asst. to pres. Luther Hosp., Eau Claire, 1977—, asst. corporate sec., 1984—; mem. exec. staff, 1985—; asst. corp. sec. Luther Health Care Corp., 1984—; mem. secretarial adv. council Dist. One Tech. Sch. 1975—; corp. sec. Northwest Health Ventures, 1988-92, bd. dirs. State pres. Future Homemakers Am., 1955; mem. governance com. Wis. Hosp. Assn. Cert. profl. sec., 1980; sec. bd. dirs. Chestnut Properties. Mem. Eau Claire Womens Network (founder, mem. steering com.), Profl. Secs. Internat. (chmn. goals and priorities com., pres. Eau Claire chpt. 1982-83), Wis. Hosp. Assn. (gov. com.). Home: 4707 Tower Dr Eau Claire WI 54703-8717 Office: 310 Chestnut St Eau Claire WI 54703-5230

BIEHL, MICHAEL MELVIN, lawyer; b. Milw., Feb. 24, 1951; s. Michael Melvin Biehl and Frieda Margaret (Krieg) Davis. AB, Harvard U., 1973, JD, 1976. Bar: Wis. 1976, U.S. Dist. Ct. (ea. dist.) Wis. 1976. Assoc. Foley & Lardner, Milw., 1976-84, ptnr., 1984—. Author: Medical Staff Legal Issues, 1990; editor: Physician Organizations and Medical Staff, 1996. Mem. Mt. Sinai Med. Ctr. Clin. Investigations Com., Hastings Ctr.; election monitor first multi-party elections in Rep. Ga., 1990; dir. Colorlines Found. for Arts and Culture, Inc., chmn., bd. dirs. Milw. Psychiat. Hosp. and Aurora Behavioral Health Svcs. Mem. ABA, Nat. Health Lawyers Assn., Am. Coll. of Med. Quality, Am. Soc. Law and Medicine. Mem. Unitarian Ch. Home: 10315 N Versailles Ct Mequon WI 53092-5231 Office: Foley & Lardner 777 E Wisconsin Ave Ste 3800 Milwaukee WI 53202-5367

BIEKER, FRED WILLIAM, plastic surgeon; b. May 18, 1933. BA, U. Ill., Chgo.; MD, U. Ill. Pvt. practice Portland, Ore. E-mail: fritz3@micron.net. Address: PO Box 2920 Sun Valley ID 83353-2920

BIEL, LEONARD, JR., urologist; b. N.Y.C., Jan. 17, 1922; s. Leonard and Eleanor Roberta (Abrahams) B.; m. Lynn Arnstein, June 27, 1958; children: Pamela, Alix. AB, Yale U., 1943; MD, N.Y. Med. Coll., 1946. Diplomate Am. Bd. Urology. Intern Paterson (N.J.) Gen. Hosp., 1946-47; resident in surgery Flower and Fifth Ave. Hosps., N.Y.C., 1950-51, Bellevue Hosp., N.Y.C., 1951-52; resident in urology Mt. Sinai Hosp., N.Y.C., 1952-54; pvt. practice N.Y.C., 1954—; asst. attending physician Mt. Sinai Hosp., attending physician Beth Israel North, North Gen. Hosp. Capt. U.S. Army, 1947-49; ETO. Fellow ACS; mem. AMA, N.Y. Acad. Medicine, N.Y. Med. Soc., N.Y. County Med. Soc., Am. Urol. Assn. Avocation: photography. Home and Office: 114 E 90th St New York NY 10128-1550

BIELENSTEIN, HANS HENRIK AUGUST, Oriental studies educator; b. Stockholm, Apr. 8, 1920; came to U.S., 1961; s. Maximilian August Rudolf Gottfried and Elsbeth Margot Erika (von Gruenewaldt) B.; m. Gabrielle Carter Maupin, Jan. 12, 1954; children: Danielle Erika Mary, Andrea Johanna Gabrielle. PhD, Royal U., Stockholm, 1954. Prof. Oriental langs., head Sch. Oriental Studies, Australian Nat. U., Canberra, 1952-61; prof. Chinese history Columbia, 1961—, Dean Lung prof. Chinese, 1985-90, Dean Lung prof. emeritus Chinese, 1990—, chmn. dept. East Asian langs. and cultures, 1969-77. Author books and articles on Chinese history, historiography and demography. Served with Swedish Vol. Corps to Finland, 1939-40. Decorated Finnish War medal with swords and bar; Guggenheim fellow, 1967-68. Mem. Royal Acad. Lit. History and Antiquity (corr. Sweden), Union Club. Home: 304 W 102nd St Apt 3B New York NY 10025-8416

BIELER, CHARLES LINFORD, development director, zoo executive director emeritus; b. East Greenville, Pa., May 19, 1935; s. Frederick William and Emma May (Freed) B.; m. Judith L. Goodwin, Feb. 23, 1963; children: Stewart, Beatriz, Christina. BA, Gettysburg Coll., 1957. Dir. tng. Gen. Motors Corp., 1962-69; mem. staff Zool. Soc. San Diego, 1969—, exec. asst. to dir., 1972-73, dir., 1973-85, dir. devel., 1987—; bd. dirs. San Diego Conv. and Visitors Bur., 1983-88, vice chmn., 1988, chmn., 1989. Bd. dirs. Mercy Hosp. Corp., 1988—. With U.S. Army, 1957-62. Recipient Gettysburg Coll. Disting. Alumni award, 1984. Fellow Am. Assn. Zool. Parks and Aquariums (pres. 1983-84). Home: 1915 Sunset Blvd San Diego CA 92103-1545 Office: San Diego Zoo PO Box 551 San Diego CA 92112-0551

BIELIAUSKAS, VYTAUTAS JOSEPH, clinical psychologist, educator; b. Plackojai, Lithuania, Nov. 1, 1920; came to U.S., 1949, naturalized, 1955; s. Antanas and Anele (Kasparaite) B.; m. Danute G. Sirvydaite, Mar. 12, 1947; children—Linas A., Diana B., Aldona O., Cornelius V. PhD in Psychology, U. Tuebingen, Germany, 1943. Diplomate Clin. Psychology, Diplomate in Marital Family Therapy, Am. Bd. Family Psychology. Asst. prof. U. Munich, Germany, 1944-48; instr. King's Coll., Wilkes-Barre, Pa., 1949-50; mem. faculty Sch. Clin. and Applied Psychology, Coll. William and Mary, 1950-58, prof. psychology, 1953-58, head dept. psychology, 1951-57; assoc. prof. Xavier U., Cin., 1958-60, chmn. dept. psychology, 1959-78, prof., 1960-78, Riley prof. psychology, 1978-88, disting. prof. psychology emeritus, 1988—. Author: zmogus siu dienu problematikoje, 1945, Community Relations Training for Police Supervisors, 1969; H-T-P Research Rev., 1980, CSSS for the H-T-P Drawings, 1981; contbr. articles to profl. jours. Pres., exec. officer Lithuanian World Cmty., 1988-92; exec. v.p. Lithuanian-Am. Cmty., Inc., 1994—; adviser on spl. programs Pres. of Republic of Lithuania, 1995-96. Lt. col. M.S.C., USAR, 1958-65. Recipient Ellis Island medal of honor, 1990. Fellow APA (pres. divsn. 13, 1986, Dist. Svc. award divsn. 36 1998); mem. Ohio Psychol. Assn. (pres. 1978-79, Disting. Svc. award 1980), Soc. Personality Assessment, Internat. Assn. for Study Med. Psychology and Religion (pres. 1972-75), Cin. Acad. Profl. Psychology, Psychologists Interested in Religious Issues (pres. 1971, exec. sec. 1973-75), Cath. Acad. Scis. in the U.S.A. (academician 1987—). Office: Xavier U Dept Psychology Cincinnati OH 45207

BIELINSKI, DANIEL WALTER, management consultant; b. Milw., Feb. 27, 1961; s. Ralph F. and Darlene Joyce (Fitzgerald) B.; m. Christine C. Alaspa, May 11, 1991. BBA summa cum laude in Fin., U. Wis., Milw., 1983; MBA summa cum laude in Fin., Marquette U., Milw., 1988. Cert. ISO 9000 lead auditor. Fin. analyst First Savs. Assn. Wis., Milw., 1983-85, Am. Appraisal Assocs., Milw., 1985-87; teaching asst. Marquette U., 1987-88; fin. cons. Arthur Andersen & Co., Milw., 1988-93; mgmt. cons. Virchow, Krause & Co., Madison, Wis., 1993—. Contbr. articles to profl. pubs.; quoted in profl. publs. Mem. Am. Soc. Quality Control (cert. quality auditor), Christian Businessmen's Com., Beta Gamma Sigma. Home: 1730 Pennsylvania Ave Sun Prairie WI 53590-1771 Office: Virchow Krause & Co 4600 American Pkwy Madison WI 53718-8333

BIELKE, PATRICIA ANNE, psychologist; b. Bay Shore, N.Y., May 11, 1949; d. Lawrence Curtis and Marcella Elizabeth (Maize) Widdoes; m. Stephen Roy Bielke, July 10, 1971; children: Eric, Christine. BA, Carleton Coll., 1971; PhD, U. Minn., 1979. Lic. psychologist, Wis.; cert. marriage and family therapist. Rsch. asst. Nat. Inst. Mental Health, Washington, 1972-74; sch. psychologist Roseville Pub. Schs., St. Paul, 1978-79; psychologist Southeastern Wis. Med. and Social Svcs., Milw., 1979-93; staff psychologist Elmbrook Meml. Hosp., 1986—; pvt. practice Brookfield, Wis., 1991—. Bd. dirs. LWV, Brookfield, 1984-88, Elmbrook Sch. Bd., 1989-99. Mem. APA, Am. Assn. Marriage and Family Therapists. Home: 17455 Bedford Dr Brookfield WI 53045-1301 Office: 700 Pilgrim Pkwy Ste 201 Elm Grove WI 53122-2063

BIELORY, ABRAHAM MELVIN, lawyer, financial executive; b. Modena, Italy, Sept. 20, 1946; came to U.S., 1948; s. Motel and Basia (Spielberg) B.; m. Beverly B. Berkowitz, Jan. 26, 1969; children: Jennifer Rebecca, Debra Elizabeth, David Ethan. BS, N.J. Inst. Tech., 1968; JD, U. Denver, 1973. Bar: N.J. 1974, U.S. Dist. Ct. N.J. 1974, U.S. Supreme Ct. 1979. Field engr. Control Data Corp., Mpls., 1968-69; assoc. Paschon & Feurey, Toms River, N.J., 1973-77, ptnr., 1978; ptnr. VanSicle & Bielory, Toms River, 1978-88, Babcock, Hennes & Bielory, P.C., Bricktown and Toms River, N.J., 1989-96; owner ABEV Fin. Svc., Toms River, 1976—; ptnr. Bielory & Hennes, PC, Bricktown, Toms River, 1996—. V.p. Lakewood Hebrew Day Sch., N.J., 1975-82, pres., 1982-86; trustee Hillel High Sch., Deal, N.J., 1983—; v.p. Congregation Sons of Israel, Lakewood, 1984-86, pres. 1986-88. Sgt. USAF, 1969-73. Fellow ABA; mem. ATLA, N.J. State Bar Assn., Trial Atty. N.J., Ocean County Bd. Realtors, Women's Coun. of Realtors (assoc.), Ocean County Bar Assn. (chmn. ins. com. 1975), Hudson County Bar Assn. (sr. citizen com. 1984), Internat. Lawyers Assn., Jewish War Vets. Republican. Home: 1422 14th St Lakewood NJ 08701-1504

BIELOWICZ, PAUL L., career officer. BA in Polit. Sci., Allegheny Coll., 1970; student, Chanute AFB, Ill., 1971, Squadron Officer Sch., 1975; MPA, U. Okla., 1978; student, Air Command and Staff Coll., 1981, Armed Forces Staff Coll., 1983, Indsl. Coll. Armed Forces, 1987, Def. Sys. Mgmt. Coll., 1993; MA in Procurement and Acquisitions Mgmt., Webster U., 1996. Commd. 2d lt. USAF, 1970, advanced through grades to brig. gen., 1996; flight line maintenance officer detachment 1 374th Tactical Airlift Wing, Ton Son Nhut Air Base, S. Vietnam, 1972; various positions 401st Tactical Fighter Wing, Torrejon Air Base, Spain, 1973-76; stationed at Cannon AFB, N.Mex., 1976-79; various positions Langley AFB, Va., 1979-86, Hdqs. USAF, Pentagon, Washington, 1987-91; stationed at Wright-Patterson AFB, Ohio, 1991-93; dir. tech. and indsl. support directorate San Antonio Air Logistics Ctr., Kelly AFB, Tex., 1993-95, comdr., 1997—; dir. logistics Hdqs. Air Edn. and Tng. Command, Randolph AFB, Tex., 1995-97; comdr. Def. Supply Ctr., Columbus, Ohio, 1997-98. Decorated Legion of Merit with oak leaf cluster, Bronze Star with V device, Small Arms Expert Marksmanship ribbon, Rep. Vietnam Gallantry Cross with Palm, Rep. Vietnam Campaign medal. Office: SAALC/CC 100 Moorman St Kelly A F B TX 78241

BIELSS, OTTO WILLIAM, JR., secondary school educator; b. Weatherford, Tex., Nov. 12, 1933; s. Otto William and Ada Susan (Thomas) B.; m. Patsy Lee Woolsey, Dec. 23, 1958; children: Otto William III, Paul Lee. BA, Hardin-Simmons U., 1954; MS, N. Tex. State U., 1971; postgrad., So. Meth. U., 1957-58, U. Tex., Arlington, 1965-67, U. Tex., Dallas, 1984-87. Engr. Tex. Hwy. Dept., Weatherford, 1954, Gen. Dynamics Corp., Fort Worth, 1956-59; tchr. Tarleton State Coll., Stephenville, Tex., 1959-65; math. tchr. Highland Park High Sch., Dallas, 1965-72, Skyline High Sch., Dallas, 1972-90; travel cons. Travelco, Irving, Tex., 1990-96; asst. prof. math. Paul Quinn Coll., Dallas, 1994—; cluster coord. and dept. chairperson Skyline Math., 1983-90; instr. Dallas County C.C. Dist., various campuses, 1972—;

grader coll. bd. advanced placement exams ETS. Author: Computer Mathematics, 1975; contbr. articles to profl. jours. Vol. various polit. campaigns, Stephenville, Tex., 1959-65, Irving, Tex., 1965—; bd. dirs. council airport noise, Irving, 1982—, Irving Community Concerts, 1991—. Served with U.S. Army, 1954-56, Korea. Grantee NSF, 1961, 67; recipient scholarship Hardin Simmon U., Abilene, Tex., 1951-54. Mem. AAUP, Math. Assn. Am., Greater Dallas Coun. Tchrs. (pres. 1974-76, bus. mgr. 1980-86, nat. rep. 1980-86), Tex. Coun. Tchrs. Math. (bus. mgr. 1980-86, pres. 1988-90), Nat. Coun. Tchrs. Math. (referee jour., rep.), Greater Dallas Tchrs. Math. (pres. 1988-90), Lions (bd. dirs. Irving 1985-87, treas. 1987-89, v.p. 1988-89, pres. 1989-91), Masons, Shriners (bd. dirs. 1988-89, 91, v.p. 1989-90, pres. 1990-91). Methodist. Avocations: photography, camping, gardening. Home: 2609 Trinity St Irving TX 75062-5257

BIEMANN, KLAUS, chemistry educator; b. Innsbruck, Austria, Nov. 2, 1926; came to U.S., 1955, naturalized, 1965; PhD, U. Innsbruck, Austria, 1951. Postdoctoral fellow MIT, Cambridge, 1955-57, instr. in chemistry, 1957-59, asst. prof. chemistry, 1959-62, assoc. prof. chemistry, 1962-63, prof. chemistry, 1963-96, prof. emeritus, 1996—. Author: Mass Spectrometry, 1962; also rsch. publs. in mass spectrometry; assoc. editor Analytical Chemistry, 1985-89; mem. editl. bd. Organic Mass Spectrometry, 1967-75, Biomed. Mass Spectrometry, 1975-85, Fresenius Zeitschrift für Analytische Chemie, 1980-86, Mass Spectrometry Revs., 1981-98, Jour. Protein Chemistry, 1990-96, Jour. Am. Soc. Mass Spectrometry, 1990-96, Protein Sci., 1991-96. Trustee Drug Sci. Found., 1982-88. Recipient Tricentennial medal U. Innsbruck, 1970, Justin Powers award Am. Acad. Pharm. Scis., 1973, N.Y. sect. award Soc. Applied Spectroscopy, 1974, Exceptional Sci. Achievement award NASA, 1977, Fritz Pregl medal Austrian Microchem. Soc., 1977, Maurice F. Hasler award Spectroscopy Soc. Pitts., 1989, J.J. Thomson medal, 1991, P. Edman award, 1992, Assn. of Biomolecular Resource Facilities Beckman award, 1995. Fellow AAAS, Am. Acad. Arts and Scis.; mem. NAS, Am. Chem. Soc. (Field and Franklin award in mass spectrometry 1986), Belgian Chem. Soc. (hon. mem., Gold medal 1962), Am. Soc. for Mass Spectrometry, The Protein Soc. Home: Alton Bay NH 03810 Office: MIT Dept Chemistry Rm 18-587 Cambridge MA 02139-4307

BIEN, JOSEPH JULIUS, philosophy educator; b. Cin., May 22, 1936; s. Joseph Julius and Mary Elizabeth (Adams) B.; m. Françoise Neve, Apr. 8, 1965. BS, Xavier U., MA, 1958; DTC, U. Paris, 1968; postgrad., Laval Univ., 1958, Emory U., 1961-62, U. Edinburgh, 1962; D (hon.), Lucian Blaga U., 1999. Asst. prof. philosophy Univ. Tex., Austin, 1968-73; asso. prof. philosophy Univ. Mo., Columbia, 1973-79; prof. philosophy Univ. Mo., 1979—, chmn. dept. philosophy, 1976-80, 81-83, 1993—; vis. prof. Tex. A&M U., 1980; vis. prof. Dubrovnik Inst. Postgrad. Studies, Yugoslavia, 1983, 84, 85, 89, co-dir., 1990—; Mid-Am. States Univs. Assn. hon. lectr. in philosophy, 1985-86; rsch. assoc. Russian and Slavic Rsch. Ctr., 1989-91; vis. prof. Lucian Blaga U., 1996, Hubei U., 1997, Wichita State U., 1998. Author: History, Revolution and Human Natue: Marx's Philosophical Anthropology, 1984; transl.: (M. Merleau-Ponty) Adventures of the Dialectic, 1973; editor: Phenomenology and the Social Sciences, A Dialogue, 1978, Political and Social Essays by Paul Ricoeur, 1974, Leviathan, 1986, Contemporary Social Thought, 1989, Ethics and Politics, 1992, Philosophical Issues and Problems, 1998. Am. Council Learned Socs. grantee, 1973; Dubrovnik Inst. Postgrad. Studies grantee, 1984; recipient U. Mo. faculty alumni award, 1998. Mem. Soc. Social and Polit. Philosophy (pres. 1979-80, 86-87, 93-94, 97-98), Ctrl. States Philos. Assn. (pres. 1978-79), Ctrl. Slavic Conf. (sec.-tres. 1977, 84), Southwestern Philosophy Soc. (pres. 1997-98). Democrat. Home: 100 W Brandon Rd Columbia MO 65203-3508 Office: Univ Mo Dept Philosophy Columbia MO 65211

BIEN, PETER ADOLPH, English language educator, author; b. N.Y.C., May 28, 1930; s. Adolph F. and Harriet (Honigsberg) B.; m. Chrysanthi Yiannakou, July 17, 1955; children: Leander, Alec, Daphne. Student, Harvard U., 1948-50; BA, Haverford Coll., 1952; MA, Columbia U., 1957, PhD, 1961; postgrad., Bristol (Eng.) U., 1958-59, Woodbrooke Coll., Eng., 1970-71. Lectr. Columbia U., N.Y.C., 1957-58, 59-61; instr. dept. English Dartmouth Coll., Hanover, N.H., 1961-62; asst. prof. Dartmouth Coll., 1963-65, assoc. prof., 1965-68, prof., 1969-97, Geisel prof., 1974-79, Frederick Sessions Beebe '35 prof. in art of writing, 1989-97, prof. emeritus, 1997—; vis. prof. Harvard U., 1983, U. Melbourne, 1983, Woodbooke Coll., 1995; prof. emeritus Dartmouth Coll., 1997—. Author: L.P. Hartley, 1963, Constantine Cavafy, 1964, Kazantzakis and the Linguistic Revolution in Greek Literature, 1972, (with others) Demotic Greek I, 1972, Demotic Greek II, 1982, Nikos Kazantzakis, 1972, Antithesis and Synthesis in the Poetry of Yannis Ritsos, 1980, Three Generations of Greek Writers, 1983, Tempted by Happiness: Kazantzakis' Post-Christian Christ, 1984, Kazantzakis: Politics of the Spirit, Nikos Kazantzakis-Novelist, 1989, Words, Wordlessness, and the Word: Quaker Silence Reconsidered, 1992, (with Darren J.N. Middleton) God's Struggler: Religion in the Works of Nikos Kazantzakis, 1996; translator: The Last Temptation, 1960, Saint Francis, 1962, Report to Greco, 1965 (all by Nikos Kazantzakis), Life in the Tomb (Stratis Myrivilis), 1977, 87; co-editor: Modern Greek Writers, 1972; assoc. editor Byzantine and Modern Greek Studies, 1975-82, Jour. Modern Greek Studies, 1983-89, editor, 1990-99. Trustee Kinhaven Music Sch., Weston, Vt., 1972-78, 81-84, 86-92, pres., 1988-90; trustee Pendle Hill, Wallingford, Pa., 1977-92, 94—, presiding clk., 1983-84, 86; mem. corp. Haverford Coll., 1974—; pres. bd. trustees Hanover Monthly Meeting, Soc. of Friends, 1977-84; chair bd. overseers Kendal at Hanover, 1989-95, chair bd. dirs., 1995-96; trustee Am. Farm Sch., 1998—. Recipient E. Harris Harbison award for disting. teaching Danforth Found., 1968; Fulbright fellow, 1958, 83, 87. Mem. Modern Greek Studies Assn. (pres. 1982-84, mem. exec. com. 1968-85), Yale Club (N.Y.C.). Democrat. Home: 12 Ledyard Ln Hanover NH 03755-2118 also: Terpni 207 Waddell Riparius NY 12862

BIENEN, HENRY SAMUEL, political science educator, university executive; b. N.Y.C., May 5, 1939; s. Mitchell Richard and Pearl (Witty) B.; m. Leigh Buchanan, Apr. 28, 1961; children: Laura, Claire, Leslie. B.A. with honors, Cornell U., 1960; M.A., U. Chgo., 1961, Ph.D., 1966. Asst. prof. politics U. Chgo., 1965-66; asst. prof. politics & internat. affairs Princeton (N.J.) U., 1966-69, assoc. prof., 1969-72, prof., 1972-95, William Stewart Tod prof. politics and internat. affairs, 1981-85, James S. McDonnell Disting. Univ. prof., 1985, dir. Ctr. Internat. Studies, 1985-92, chair dept. politics, 1973-76, dir. African studies progrm, 1977-78, 83-84, dir. rsch. Woodrow Wilson Sch. Pub. & Internat. Affairs, 1979-82, dean; pres. Northwestern U., Evanston, Ill., 1995—; mem. exec. com. Inter-Univ. Seminar on Armed Forces and Soc., 1968-78; cons. U.S. State Dept., 1972-88, Nat. Security Council, 1978-79, World Bank, 1981-89, CIA, 1982-88, Hambrecht & Quist Investment Co., Boeing Corp., Econ Corp., Enserch Corp., Ford Found., Rockefeller Found., John D. and Catherine T. MacArthur Found.; nat. co-dir. Movement for a New Congress, 1970-71; mem. Inst. for Advanced Study, 1984-85, Ctr. Advanced Study in the Behavioral Sciences, 1976-77; vis. prof. Makerere Coll., Kampala, Uganda, 1963-65, Univ. Coll., Nairobi, Kenya, 1968-69, Univ. Ibadan, 1972-73. Editor: World Politics, 1970-74, 78—; author: Tanzania: Party Transformation and Economic Development, 1967, 70, Kenya: The Politics of Participation and Control, 1974, Violence and Social Change, 1968, Armies and Parties in Africa, 1978, Political Conflict and Economic Change in Nigeria, 1985. Grantee Rockefeller Found., 1968-69, 72-73, Seeger fellow, 1989. Mem. Am. Polit. Sci. Assn., Council on Fgn. Relations, Am. Acad. Office: Northwestern U Office of Pres 633 Clark St Evanston IL 60208-1100*

BIENENSTOCK, ARTHUR IRWIN, physicist, educator, government official; b. N.Y.C., Mar. 20, 1935; s. Leo and Lena (Senator) B.; m. Roslyn Doris Goldberg, Apr. 14, 1957; children—Eric Lawrence, Amy Elizabeth (dec.), Adam Paul. B.S., Poly. Inst. Bklyn., 1955, M.S., 1957; Ph.D., Harvard U., 1962; PhD (hon.), Poly. U., 1998. Asst. prof. Harvard U., Cambridge, Mass., 1963-67; mem. faculty Stanford (Calif.) U., 1967—, prof. applied physics, 1972—, vice provost faculty affairs, 1972-77, dir. synchrotron radiation lab., 1978-97; assoc. dir. for sci. Office of Sci. and Tech. Policy, Washington, 1997—; mem. U.S. Nat. Com. for Crystallography, 1983-88, sci. adv. com. European Synchrotron Radiation Facility, 1988-90, 93-96; mem. com. on condensed matter and materials physics NRC, 1996-97. Author papers in field. Bd. dirs. No. Calif. chpt. Cystic Fibrosis Research Found., 1970-73, mem. pres.'s adv. council, 1980-82; trustee Cystic Fibrosis Found., 1982-88. Recipient Sidhu award Pitts. Diffraction Soc., 1968, Disting. Alumnus award Poly. Inst. N.Y., 1977; NSF fellow, 1962-63. Fellow AAAS, Am. Phys. Soc. (gen. councilor 1993-96); mem. Am. Crystallographic Assn., Materials Rsch. Soc. Jewish. Home: 2737 Devonshire Pl NW Ste D Washington DC 20008-3479 Office: Office Sci and Tech Policy Old Exec Office Bldg 17th St and Pennsylvania NW Washington DC 20502

BIENENSTOCK, JOHN, physician, educator; b. Budapest, Hungary, Oct. 6, 1936; s. Maurice and Anne (Horn) B.; m. Dody Sanders, Nov. 24, 1961; children: Jimson Andrew, Adam Sebastian, Robin Anne. MB, BChir, Westminster Med. Sch., London, 1960; postgrad., Harvard Med. Sch., 1964-66, SUNY, Buffalo, 1966-68; MD (hon.), U. Göteborg, Sweden, 1998. Fellow Harvard U. Med. Sch., Boston, 1964-66; Buswell fellow SUNY, Buffalo, 1966-68, asst. rsch. prof. medicine, 1967-68; asst. prof. medicine McMaster U., Hamilton, Ont., Can., 1968-74, assoc. dean rsch., 1972-78, prof. medicine and pathology, 1974—, chmn. dept. pathology, 1978-89, v.p. health scis., 1989-97, dean health scis., 1992-97, univ. prof., 1997—; founder AB Biol. Supply Inc., 1977, Agritech Rsch. Inc., 1980; D.W. Harrington lectr. SUNY, Buffalo, 1986, Rayne vis. prof. U. Western Australia, Perth, 1987; cons. WHO, Geneva, 1970—; also cons. various pharm. cos. Editor: Immunology of Lung, 1984, Mast Cell Differentiation, 1986, Recent Advances in Mucosal Immunology, 1987, Handbook of Mucosal Immunology, 1994, Mucosal Immunology, 1998; contbr. over 350 articles to sci. jours. Chmn. bd. Dundas Valley (Ont.) Sch. Art, 1984-86; chmn., bd. dirs. Can. Red Cross Soc.; chmn. adv. com. nat. blood svcs., 1985-90. Recipient Purkynje medal Assn. Czechoslovak Socs., Prague, 1989, Ross A. McIntyre gold medal U. Nebr., Omaha, 1989, Finkelstein prize Crohn's and Colitis Found., Can., 1996. Fellow RCP (Can.), RCP (London), Royal Soc. (Can.); mem. Swiss Soc. Allergy and Immunology (hon.), Can. Soc. Immunology (pres. 1985-87), Assn. Am. Physicians, Am. Soc. Clin. Investigation, Am. Thoracic Soc., Internat. Union Immunological Socs. (mem. coun.), Soc. Mucosal Immunology (pres. 1990-92), Coll. Internat. Allergologicum (pres. 1998-2002). Jewish. Avocation: painting. Home: 436 Wellington St W # 4.1, Toronto, ON Canada M5V 1E3 Office: McMaster U Fac Health Scis, 1200 Main St W Rm 3N26H, Hamilton, ON Canada L8N 3Z5

BIENIAWSKI, ZDZISLAW TADEUSZ RICHARD, engineering educator emeritus, writer, consultant; b. Cracow, Poland, Oct. 1, 1936; came to U.S., 1978, naturalized; m. Elizabeth Hyslop, 1964; 3 children. Student, Gdansk (Poland) Tech. U., 1954-58; BS in Mech. Engring., U. Witwatersrand, Johannesburg, Republic South Africa, 1961, MS in Engring. Mechanics, 1963; PhD in Rock Engring., U. Pretoria, South Africa, 1968. Prof. mineral engring. Pa. State U., Univ. Park, 1978-96, prof. sci., tech. & society, 1994-96, prof. emeritus, 1996—; pres. Bieniawski Design Enterprises, Prescott, Ariz., 1996—; vis. prof. U. Karlsruhe, Germany, 1972, Stanford U., 1985, Harvard U., 1990, Cambridge (Eng.) U., 1997; chmn. U.S. Nat. Com. on Tunneling Tech., 1984-85; U.S. rep. to Internat. Tunnel Assn., 1984-85. Author: Rock Mechanics Design in Mining and Tunneling, 1984, Strata Control in Mineral Engineering, 1987, Aiming High-A Collection of Essays, 1988, Engineering Rock Mass Classifications, 1989, A Tale of Three Continents, 1991, Design Methodology in Rock Engineering, 1992, Gaudeamus Igitur Poems, 1997; editor: Tunneling in Rock, 1974, Exploration for Rock Engineering, 1976, Milestones in Rock Engring., 1996; contbr. over 160 articles to profl. jours. Recipient Mayor's Proclamation of City of State College Bieniawski Day, 1983. Mem. ASCE (rock mechanics rsch. award 1984). Avocations: genealogy, cosmology, poetry writing, financial planning. Home: The Ranch 3023 Sunnybrae Cir Prescott AZ 86303-5770 Office: PO Box 11205 Prescott AZ 86304-1205

BIENVENU, JOHN CHARLES, lawyer; b. Modesto, Calif., Sept. 11, 1957; s. Robert Charles and Martha Louise (Beard) B.; m. Sarah Luciene Brick, May 10, 1983; children: Reed Charles, Loren John. Student, U. Calif., Berkeley, 1975-78; BA summa cum laude, U. N.Mex., 1985; JD with distinction, Stanford U., 1988. Bar: Calif., 1988, N.Mex., 1990; U.S. Ct. Appeals (9th cir.) 1988, U.S. Ct. Appeals (10th cir.) 1990; U.S. Ct. Fed. Claims, 1991. Assoc. Brobeck, Phleger & Harrison, San Francisco, 1988-90, Rothstein, Walther, Donatelli, Hughes, Dahlstrom & Cron, Santa Fe, N.Mex., 1990-93; prin. Santa Fe, 1993—. Mem. N.Mex. State Bar (legal svcs. com.), Am. Trial Lawyers Assn., ACLU (cooperating atty. N.Mex.). Democrat. Home: 1580 Cerro Gordo Rd Santa Fe NM 87501-6143 Office: PO Box 2455 310 Mckenzie St Santa Fe NM 87501-1883

BIER, LOUIS HENRY GUSTAV, minister; b. Chgo., Jan. 12, 1933; s. Louis Wilfred and Ethel Lea (Laue) B.; m. Helene Mueller, July 29 ,1962; children: Richard Allen, Karen Elizabeth, Lisa Anne. B. of Edn., Chgo. Tchrs. Coll., 1954; B. and M. of Theology, Concordia Sem., 1959; MEd, Boston State Coll., 1962; DRE, Smith Bapt. U., 1987, DD, 1986. Ordained to ministry Luth. Ch. 1959; lic. soc. worker. Vicar Redeemer Luth. Ch., Phila., 1957, 1st Lutheran Ch., Holyoke, Mass., 1957-58; pastor St. Paul's Luth. Ch., West Frankfort, Ill., 1959-61; pastor Trinity Luth. Ch., Boston, 1961-98, eemritus, 1999—; chaplain Boston VA Hosp., 1968—; instr. psychology Boston State Coll., 1967-81; mem. adj. faculty Holy Cross Greek Orthodox Sem., Brookline, Mass1998, 1999; chaplain West Roxbury VA Hosp, 1978-86, The Arbour, Boston, 1969; chaplain German Home for Elderly, Boston, 1962, also trustee, 1971—; bd. dirs. Interfaith Bible Readings, Inc.; circuit counselor Luth. Ch. Mo. Snyod. Incorporator, Faulkner Hosp., 1981; br. pres. A.A.L., 1980; mem. Arboretum dist. Boston coun. Boy Scouts Am., 1976-79, USO Coun. New Eng.; bd. mgrs. Sophia Snow House; served to lt. col. CAP, 1975—; chaplain, col. Mass. State Def. Fort. Recipient Honored Citizen award Kennedy VFW, 1973, Lamb award Luth. Council, 1975, Community Service award Greater Boston Assn. of Retarded Citizens, 1974, George Meany Youth Service award AFL-CIO, 1983, Disting. Eagle Scout award, 1993; Emreson fellow Mil. Chaplains Assn. U.S.A., 1999, Wilson fellow Boy Scouts Am., 1999. Mem. German Soc. Boston (trustee), Luth. Edn. Assn. (life), Mil. Chaplains Assn. (life, treas., v.p., pres.), Assn. of Mental Health Clergy (cert.), Protestant Chaplains Assn., Assn. for Clin. Pastoral Edn., Mass. Chaplains Assn., Concordia Sem. (Servus Ecclesia Christi award). Avocations: swimming, golf, reading. Home: 169 Nahatan St Westwood MA 02090-3607

BIERBAUM, J. ARMIN, petroleum company executive, consultant; b. Oak Park, Ill., June 29, 1924; s. Armin Walter and Harriett Cornelia (Backmann) B.; m. Janith Turnbull, Apr. 17, 1948; children: Steve, Todd, Charles, Peter, Mark. B.S., Northwestern U., 1945, M.S., 1948. Project engr. Am. Oil Co., Ind., 1948-53; sales engr. Universal Oil Products Co., Des Plaines, Ill., 1953-56; tech. dir. Nat. Coop. Refinery Assn., McPherson, Kans., 1956-58; asst. plant mgr., treas., v.p., dir. Gen. Carbon & Chem. Corp., Robinson, Ill., 1958-61; cons. Williston, N.D., 1962-64; v.p. ops. Midland Coops., Inc., Mpls., 1964-72; sr. v.p. ops. Tosco Corp., Los Angeles, 1972-77; pres., chief exec. officer Gary Energy Co., Englewood, Colo., 1977-79, U.S. Ethanol Corp., Englewood, 1979-82; cons., 1983—. Served with USNR, 1942-45. Mem. Am. Inst. Chem. Engrs., Sigma Xi, Phi Epsilon Pi. Office: 7787 S Perry Park Blvd Larkspur CO 80118-9005

BIERI, BARBARA NORMILE, systems analyst, consultant; b. Trenton, N.J., Jan. 4, 1951; d. William Donald and Beatrice Marie (Noon) Normile; m. Paul Daniel Bieri, Apr. 13, 1991. BS in Edn., St. Francis Coll., 1972; postgrad., Pa. State U., 1976, Mercer County C.C., 1983, 85-86. Cert. tchr. elem. and secondary math., N.J., Pa. Tchr. math. and sci. St. Anthony Sch., Trenton, N.J., 1972-77; tchr. math. Cumberland Regional H.S., Seabrook, N.J., 1977-82; programmer N.J. Dept. Human Svcs., Trenton, 1982-84; programmer, analyst Computer Svcs. Group, Trenton, 1984; sr. computer sys. designer Martin Marietta Data Sys., Princeton, N.J., 1984-86; sr. sys. mgr. Storey/Ross/Barker, Inc., Lambertville, N.J., 1987-90; cons. BPN Cons., Hamilton, N.J., 1990-93, MIACO Corp., Landover, Md., 1993-94; sr. sys. analyst Data Based Sys. Internat., Flemington, N.J., 1994—; union rep., negotiating team Cumberland Regional Edn. Assn., Seabrook, N.J., 1980-81; computer tchr. adult edn. West Windsor (N.J.) Plainsboro Adult Edn. Program, 1983-86. Committeewoman Dem. Party, Bridgeton, N.J., 1980. Mem. NAFE, N.J. Novell Users Group, MDBS Users Group, Oracle Users Group, Gamma Sigma Sigma (v.p. 1971-72). Avocations: traveling, needlework, reading. Home: 249 Hobart Ave Hamilton NJ 08629-1622 Office: Data Based Sys 31 Highway 12 Flemington NJ 08822

BIERIG, JACK R., lawyer, educator; b. Chgo., Apr. 10, 1947; s. Henry J. and Helga (Rothschild) B.; m. Barbara A. Winokur; children: Robert, Sarah. BA, Brandeis U., 1968; JD, Harvard U., 1972. Bar: Ill. 1972, U.S. Dist. Ct. (no. dist.) Ill. 1972, U.S. Ct. Appeals (1st-3d, 5th-11th and D.C. cirs.) 1974, U.S. Supreme Ct. 1980. Ptnr. Sidley & Austin, Chgo., 1972—; prof. Ill. Inst. Tech.-Chgo. Kent Coll. Law, 1974—; chmn. legal sect. Am. Soc. Assn. Execs., 1994-95. Contbr. articles to profl. jours. Pres. Neighborhood Justice Chgo., 1983-87; pres. Jewish Vocat. Svc. Mem. Ill. Assn. of Hosp. Attys. (pres. 1991), Chgo. Bar Assn. (bd. govs., 1982-84). Jewish. Club: Standard (Chgo.). Office: Sidley & Austin 1 First Natl Plz Chicago IL 60603-2003

BIERLEY, PAUL EDMUND, musician, author, publisher; b. Portsmouth, Ohio, Feb. 3, 1926; s. William Frederick and Minnie Genieve (Atkin) B.; m. Pauline Jeanette Allison, Sept. 17, 1948; children: Lois Elaine Bierley Walker, John Emerson. B of Aero. Engring., Ohio State U., 1953. Aero. engr. N.Am. Aviation, Columbus, Ohio, 1953-73; engr., data mgr. Ellanef Mfg. Corp., Columbus, 1973-88; tubist Columbus Symphony Orch., 1965-81, Detroit Concert Band, 1973-92; lectr. in field. Author: John Philip Sousa, A Descriptive Catalog of His Works, 1973, John Philip Sousa, American Phenomenon, 1973, rev. edit., 1986 (Deems Taylor award 1986), Office Fun!, 1976, Hallelujah Trombone!, 1982, The Music of Henry Fillmore and Will Huff, 1982, The Works of John Philip Sousa, 1984, Sousa Band Fraternal Society News Index, 1997, also numerous articles, radio and TV copy, concert programs and record jackets; asst. condr., Rockwell Internat. Concert Band, 1961-76; tubist World Symphony Orch., N.Y.C., 1971, Hallelujah Brass Quintet, 1983-92, Brass Band of Columbus, 1984-97, Village Brass, 1993—; editor: Integrity Press, Columbus, 1982—, The Heritage Ency. of Band Music, 1991, supplement, 1996, El Capitan (John Philip Sousa), 1994, Marching Along (John Philip Sousa), 1994. Bd. dirs. Robert Hoe Found., Poughkeepsie, N.Y., 1984—. Served with USAF, 1944-46. Recipient Deems Taylor award ASCAP, 1986, God and Country award Salvation Army, 1995, Ohioana Libr. Assn. Citation, 1996; inductee Wall of Fame, Portsmouth, Ohi, 1994, Columbus Sr. Musicians Hall of Fame, 1997. Mem. Am. Bandmasters Assn. (hon., Edwin Franko Goldman citation 1974), Am. Sch. Band Dirs. Assn. (assoc., A. Austin Harding award 1990), Am. Fedn. Musicians, Sonneck Soc. for Am. Music, Nat. Band Assn., Assn. Concert Bands, Tubists Universal Brotherhood Assn., Windjammers Unltd., John Philip Sousa Found. (Sudler medal 1986), Ohio Hist. Soc., Am. Aviation Hist. Soc., Westerville Hist. Soc., Masons, Phi Beta Mu (Outstanding Contbr. to Bands award 1983). Methodist.

BIERLY, EUGENE WENDELL, meteorologist, science administrator; b. Sept. 11, 1931; m., 1953; 3 children. A.B., U. Pa., 1953; cert., U.S. Naval Postgrad. Sch., 1954; M.S., U. Mich., 1957, Ph.D., 1968. Asst. dept. civil engring. meteorol. labs. U. Mich., Ann Arbor, 1956-60, asst. research meteorologist dept. engring. mechanics, 1960-63, lectr., 1961-63; meteorologist U.S. AEC, 1963-66; dir. meteorology NSF, Washington, 1966-71, coordinator global atmospheric research program, 1971-74, head office climate dynamics, 1974-75, head climate dynamics research sect., 1975-79, dir. div. atmospheric scis., 1979-92; dir. edn. and rsch. Am. Geophys. Union, 1992-98, sr. scientist, 1998—; mem. biol., health and environ. rsch. adv. com. Dept. Energy, 1992—; chmn. adv. cons. bd. Geophys. Inst., U. Alaska, 1993—; chmn. adv. bd. U. Okla. Sch. Meteorology, 1994—; cons. Fla. State U., U. Okla., U. Ariz. Congl. fellow, 1970-71. Fellow AAAS, Am. Meteorol. Soc. (pres. 1984, Charles Franklin Brooks award 1990); mem. Chinese Meteorol. Soc., Am. Geophys. Union, Sigma Xi (presdl. rank merit excellence sr. exec. svc. 1982). Home: 5806 Conway Rd Bethesda MD 20817-3414 Office: AGU Directorate Edn & Rsch 2000 Florida Ave NW Washington DC 20009-1277

BIERMAN, CHARLES WARREN, physician, educator; b. Ada, Ohio, May 27, 1924; s. Linn Carl and Margery (Warren) B.; m. Joan Wingate, May 15, 1952; children: Margot Ellen, Karen Linn, Charlotte Joane, Barbara Anne. MD, Harvard U., 1947. Diplomate Am. Bd. Pediat., Am. Bd. Allergy and Immunology (bd. dirs. 1971-77). Intern Lankenau Hosp., Phila., 1947-48; resident in pediat. Bellevue Hosp., N.Y.C., 1948-49; resident in pediatrics N.Y. Hosp., N.Y.C., 1949-50; fellow in neonatology N.Y. Hosp., 1950, Hosp. Enfants Malades, Paris, 1953-54; resident in allergy U. Wash., Seattle, 1965-67; pvt. practice specializing in pediat. and adult allergy Seattle, 1967-97; mem. staffs Children's Hosp. and Med. Ctr., Univ. Hosp., Harborview Hosp.; instr. pediatrics Cornell Med. Sch., 1949-50; clin. instr. pediatrics U. Wash., Seattle, 1958-59, clin. asst. prof., 1959-62, clin. assoc. prof., 1962-70, clin. prof., 1970—, chief div. allergy dept. pediatrics, 1967-94; hon. rsch. fellow dept. pharmacology, hon. cons. respiratory disease Univ. Coll. London, 1978-79; cons. Wash. State Dept. Social and Health Svcs., 1979-87; gov. Am. Bd. Allergy and Immunology, 1970-78, mem., vice chmn. residency rev. com., 1982-90; vis. prof. pediatrics United Med. Dental Schs., Guy's Hosp., London, 1989. Editor: (with D.S. Pearlman) Allergic Diseases of Infancy, Childhood and Adolescence, 1980, Allergic Diseases from Infancy to Adulthood, 1988, (with D.S. Pearlman, G.G. Shapiro and W. Busse) Allergy Asthma and Immunology, 1995; mem. editl. bd. Pediat., 1972-76, Pediat. in Review, 1977-82, Clin. Revs. in Allergy, 1981-87, Jour. Asthma, Annals of Allergy in Pediat. Allergy; contbr. articles to med. jours. With USN, 1944-46, 50-51, U.S. Army, 1951-52. Fellow Am. Acad. Allergy (exec. com. 1980-83), Am. Acad. Pediatrics (chmn. allergy sect. 1974-76); mem. AMA, Wash. State Med. Assn. (ho. of dels.), Wash. State Pediatrics Assn., Wash. State Allergy Soc., Puget Sound Allergy Soc., Seattle Pediatric Soc., Am. Pediatric Soc., Western Soc. for Pediatric Rsch., Brit. Soc. for Allergy and Clin. Immunology (emeritus). Episcopalian. Home: 4524 E Laurel Dr NE Seattle WA 98105-3839

BIERMAN, GEORGE WILLIAM, technical consulting executive, food technologist; b. Cleve., Mar. 2, 1925; s. George Henry and Esther Josephine (Johnson) B.; m. Nyo Jeanne Iserloth; children: Cynthia, Barbara, Marsha, Jill, Wendy, Mindy, G. Steven, Chris. BS, Rutgers U., 1951; PhD, MIT, 1956. Technician R & D Am. Can Co., Maywood, Ill., 1943-45, Schering Corp., Bloomfield, N.J., 1947-48; tech. dir. Friend Bros., Inc., Malden, Mass., 1951-58; v.p. Herbert V. Shuster, Inc., Boston, 1958-75, pres., Quincy, Mass., 1975-89, vice chmn. bd., 1989-95, sr. scientist, 1995-96; tech. cons. Shuster Labs. Inc., 1996—. Sgt. U.S. Army, 1945-47. Mem. Assn. Smoked Fish Processors (tech. dir. 1968—), Inst. Food Technologists, Nat. Fisheries Inst. (smoked fish com. 1968—). Presbyterian. Avocations: gardening, motorcycling. Home: 19 Curwen Rd Peabody MA 01960-1205 Office: Shuster Labs Inc 5 Hayward St Quincy MA 02171-2493

BIERMAN, JAMES NORMAN, lawyer; b. St. Louis, Nov. 23, 1945; s. Norman and Margaret (Loeb) B.; m. Catherine Best, Apr. 10, 1983; 1 child, James Norman. AB magna cum laude, Washington U., 1967; JD, Harvard Law Sch., 1970. Assoc. Hogan & Hartson, Washington, 1970-72; asst. dean Harvard Law Sch., Cambridge, Mass., 1973-75; assoc. Foley & Lardner, Washington, 1975-79, ptnr., 1979-85, ptnr. in charge, 1985—, mem. mgmt. com., 1989-98. Mng. editor Harvard Jour. Legis., 1969-70. Mem. Civil Rights Reviewing Authority HEW, Washington, 1979-80. Mem. ABA, Fed. Bar Assn., D.C. Bar Assn., Supreme Ct. Bar, Washington Lawyers Com. for Civil Rights and Urban Affairs (bd. dirs.), Phi Beta Kappa, Omicron Delta Kappa, Pi Sigma Alpha, Phi Eta Sigma, City Club (Washington). Home: 906 Peacock Station Rd Mc Lean VA 22102-1021 Office: Foley & Lardner 3000 K St NW Fl 5 Washington DC 20007-5143

BIERMAN, SANDRA LEE, artist; b. Bklyn., N.Y., 1938; d. John Charles Riesberg and Martha Lee Blair; m. Arthur Bierman, Oct. 1, 1983; children: Cheryl, Steven, James. Represented by Moondance Gallery, Santa Fe, N.Mex., 1992-94, Galerie du Bois, Aspen, Colo., 1994-97, Contemporary S.W. Gallery, Santa Fe, 1994—, Merrill Gallery, Denver, 1995—, David Haslam, Boulder, Colo., 1992—, Gallery East, Loveland, Colo., 1996—, Suzanne Brown Gallery, Scottsdale, Ariz., 1997—, Jack Meier Gallery, Houston, Tex., 1997—; instr. workshop Am. Acad. Women Artists, Wickenburg, Ariz., 1997. One-person shows include Nat. Ctr. for Atmospheric Rsch., Boulder, 1992, David Haslam Gallery, 1993, 94, 95, Columbine Gallery, Loveland, Colo., 1995, Contemporary S.W. Galleries, 1996, Lincoln Ctr. for the Arts, Ft. Collins, Colo., 1998, Jack Meier Gallery, 1998; group shows include C.S. Lewis Summer Inst. Show on Tour, 1994, Queens Coll. Art Gallery, Cambridge, Eng., 1994, 99th Nat. Exhbn. Nat. Arts Club, N.Y.C., 1995, 67th Grand Nat. Show, Salmagundi Club, N.Y.C., 1995, Artistes Americaines, Maison du Terroir, Genouilly, France, 1996, Colo. History Mus., 1996, Clymer Mus., Ellensburg, Wash., 1996, Desert Caballeros Mus., Wickenburg, Ariz., 1997, Colo. Gov.'s Invitational Show, Loveland (Colo.) Mus., 1997, 98, 99, Art Expo, N.Y.C., 1998, Art Meets Entertainment, Roar Found., Beverly Hills, Calif., 1998, Palm Desert (Calif) Art Gallery, 1998; works in permanent collections at City of Loveland, CSI

Ltd., Cambridge, Eng., El Pomar Found., Colorado Springs, Colo., Gilford, Inc., N.Y.C., Herzog & Adams, N.Y.C., Harlow Club Hotel, Palm Springs, Calif., Loveland Mus., Telluride Gallery of Fine Art, Colo., Kaiser Permanente, Denver, Kohn Family Trust, Balt., Mfrs.-Hanover trust, N.Y.C., Mayo Women's Clinic, Scottsdale, Penrose Conf., Ctr., Colorado Springs, Philip Chamberlan Inc., Madison, Conn.; featured in Southwest Art Mag., Art Trends Mag., Mountain Living mag., Woman's Mag., Radiance mag., Sun Storm Fine Art Mag., others. Recipient Colo. Gov.'s Purchase award, Loveland, 1988, Best of Show award Western Images, Boulder, 1993, medal of honor award Am. Artists Profl. League, N.Y.C., 1995. Mem. Am. Artist s Profl. League, Nat. Mus. of Women in the Arts, Oil Painters Am., Am. Acad. Women Artists (nominating juror, exec. bd. dirs. 1997—). Studio: 542 Arapahoe Ave Boulder CO 80302-5827

BIERS, MARTIN HENRY, physician; b. Bklyn., Oct. 10, 1931; s. Louis and Sarah (Naidich) Bierfass; m. Elizabeth Jaros Biers, Feb. 11, 1962; children: Eric, Carl, John. BA, NYU, 1951; MD, SUNY, Bklyn., 1955. Cert. in internal medicine and hematology, Am. Coll. Physicians. Intern Kings County Hosp., Bklyn., 1955-56; med. resident Bklyn. Vets. Hosp., 1956-57, Montefiore Hosp., Bronx, N.Y., 1957-58; hematology resident Mt. Sinai Hosp., N.Y.C., 1958-59; pvt. practice White Plains, N.Y., 1961—; attending medicine and chief emeritus hematology dept. White Plains Hosp. Capt. USAF, 1959-61. Mem. Am. Soc. Internal Medicine, N.Y. Med. Soc., Westchester Med. Soc. Office: 15 Chester Ave White Plains NY 10601-5115

BIERSTEDT, PETER RICHARD, lawyer, entertainment industry consultant; b. Rhinebeck, N.Y., Jan. 2, 1943; s. Robert Henry and Betty (MacIver) B.; m. Carol Lynn Akiyama, Aug. 23, 1980 (div. Oct. 1995). AB, Columbia U., 1965, JD cum laude, 1969; cert., U. Sorbonne, Paris, 1966. Bar: N.Y. 1969, U.S. Supreme Ct. 1973, Calif. 1977. Atty. with firms in N.Y.C., 1969-74; pvt. practice cons. legal and entertainment industry, 1971, 75-76, 88—; with Avco Embassy Pictures Corp., L.A., 1977-83; v.p., gen. counsel Avco Embassy Pictures Corp., 1978-80, sr. v.p., 1980-83, dir., 1981-83; gen. counsel New World Entertainment (formerly New World Pictures), L.A., 1984-87, exec. v.p., 1985-87, sr. exec. v.p. Office of Chmn., 1987-88, also bd. dirs.; pres. subs. New World Prodns. and New World Advt. New World Pictures, 1985-88; guest lectr. U. Calif., Riverside, 1976-77, U. So. Calif., 1986, 91, UCLA, 1987, 95, 96; bd. dirs. New World Pictures (Australia) Ltd., FilmDallas Pictures, Inc., Cinedco, Inc. Exec. prodr. (home video series) The Comic Book Greats. Mem. Motion Picture Assn. Am. (dir. 1980-83), Acad. Motion Picture Arts and Scis. (exec. br.), N.Y. State Bar Assn., L.A. Copyright Soc., ACLU. Democrat. Avocations: astronomy, literature, tennis, scuba diving. Home and Office: 2039 N Gramercy Pl Los Angeles CA 90068-3616

BIERWIRTH, JOHN COCKS, retired aerospace manufacturing executive; b. Lawrence, N.Y., Jan. 21, 1924; s. John E. and Alice (Marguerite) B.; m. Marion Moise, June 14, 1946. B.A., Yale U., 1947; J.D., Columbia U., 1950. Bar: N.Y. 1951. Assoc. White & Case, N.Y.C., 1950-53; asst. v.p. N.Y. Trust Co. (now Chase Bank), 1953-57; asst. treas. Nat. Distillers & Chem. Corp., N.Y.C., 1957-58, v.p., 1958-69, head Internat. div., 1963-72, dir., 1966-72, exec. v.p., 1969-72; with Grumman Corp., Bethpage, N.Y., 1972-88, v.p. fin., 1972, pres., 1972, chief exec. officer, 1974-88, chmn. bd., 1976-88. Trustee Adelphi U. Named to L.I. Hall of Fame. Mem. Fgn. Policy Assn. (bd. dirs.), Yale-China Assn. (trustee), Ctr. Marine Conservation (vice-chmn.), Yale Club (N.Y.C.).

BIERY, CHARLES JOHN, SR., accountant; b. Covington, Ky., July 13, 1946; s. William F. and Helen E. (Steffen) B.; m. Jacklyn C. Creamer, Dec. 27, 1946; children: Karen, Charles Jr., David. BA in Bus., Thomas More Coll., 1970. Computer supr. Cin. Bell Telephone Co., 1966-69, acct., 1969-83; acct. Cin. Bell Inc., 1983—; mem. com. Bell Sys.-T/S, N.J., 1979-83. Bd. edn. Diocese of Covington, 1989-92. Sgt. USNG, 1970-76. Named Vol. of Yr. No. Ky. Devel. Dist., 1993-94. Mem. Inst. Mgmt. Accts, KC (state dept. 1992-94, state master 1994—, Vol. of Yr. 1970, 72). Democrat. Roman Catholic. Avocations: cooking, African violets. Home: 307 Florence Ave Newport KY 41071-3206 Office: Cin Bell inc 201 E 4th St Cincinnati OH 45202-4122

BIERY, EVELYN HUDSON, lawyer; b. Lawton, Okla., Oct. 12, 1946; d. William Ray and Nellie Iris (Nunley) Hudson. BA in English and Latin summa cum laude, Abilene (Tex.) Christian U., 1968; JD, So. Meth. U., 1973. Bar: Tex. 1973, U.S. Dist. Ct. (we. dist.) Tex. 1975, U.S. Dist. Ct. (so. dist.) Tex. 1977, U.S. Dist. Ct. (no. dist.) Tex. 1979, U.S. Ct. Appeals (5th cir.) 1979, U.S. Ct. Appeals (11th cir.) 1981, U.S. Supreme Ct. 1981. Atty. Law Offices of Bruce Waitz, San Antonio, 1973-76; mem. LeLaurin & Adams, PC, San Antonio, 1976-81; ptnr. Fulbright & Jaworski, San Antonio, 1981—, head bankruptcy, reorganization and creditors' rights sect., 1990—; policy com. Fulbright & Jaworski, San Antonio, 1996-98; speaker on creditors' rights, bankruptcy and reorganization law; lectr. Southwestern Grad. Sch. Banking, Dallas, 1980, La. State U. Sch. Banking, 1994; presiding officer, U. Tex. Sch. of Law Bankruptcy Conf., 1976, 94, State Bar Tex. Creditors' Rights Inst., 1985, State Bar Tex. Advanced Bus. Bankruptcy Law Inst., 1985, State Bar Tex. Inst. on Advising Officers, Dirs. and Ptnrs. in Troubled Bus., 1987, State Bar Tex. Advanced Creditors Rights Inst., 1988; pres. San Antonio Young Lawyers Assn., 1979-80; mem. bankruptcy adv. com. fifth cir. jud. coun., 1979-80; vice-chmn. bankruptcy com. Comml. Law League Am., 1981-83; mem. exec. bd. So. Meth. U. Sch. Law, 1983-91. Editor: Texas Collections Manual, 1978, Creditor's Rights in Texas, 2d edit., 1981; author: (with others) Collier Bankruptcy Practice Guide, 1993. Del. to U.S./Republic of China joint session on trade, investment and econ. law , Beijing, 1987; designated mem. Bankruptcy Judge Merit Screening Com. State of Tex. by Tex. State Bar Pres., 1979-82; patron McNay Mus., San Antonio; rsch. ptnr. Mind Sci. Found., San Antonio; diplomat World Affairs Coun., San Antonio. Recipient Outstanding Young Lawyer award San Antonio Young Lawyers Assn., 1979. Fellow Soc. of Internat. Bus. Fellow, Am. Coll. Bankruptcy Attys., Tex. Bar Found. (life), San Antonio Bar Found.; mem. Tex. Bar Assn. (chair bankruptcy com. 1982-83, chair corp., banking and bus. law sect. 1989-90), Tex. Assn. Bank Counsel (bd. dirs. 1988-90), San Antonio Young Lawyers Assn. (pres. 1979-80), Plaza Club San Antonio (bd. dirs. 1982—), Zonta (Chair Z club com. 1989-90), Order of Coif. Office: Fulbright & Jaworski 300 Convent St Ste 2200 San Antonio TX 78205-3792 Also: Fulbright & Jaworski 1301 McKinney Ste 5100 Houston TX 77010-3095

BIERY, FRED, judge; b. McAllen, Tex., Nov. 11, 1947; s. Samuel F. and Clara Belle (Martin) B.; m. Marcia Mattingly, May 25, 1989; children: Anna Lisa, Molly. BA, Tex. Luth. Coll., 1970; JD, So. Meth. U., 1973. Bar: Tex., U.S. Dist. Ct. (fed. dist.) Tex. 1974. From assoc. to shareholder Biery, Biery, Davis & Myers, P.C., San Antonio, 1973-78; judge County Ct. Two, San Antonio, 1979-82, 150th Dist. Ct., San Antonio, 1983-88, 4th Ct. of Appeals, San Antonio, 1989-94, U.S. Dist. Ct. (we. dist.) Tex., San Antonio, 1994—. Regent Tex. Luth. Coll., Seguin, 1970—. Served USAR, 1970-76. Recipient Disting. Alumni award Tex. Luth. Coll., 1980; named Outstanding Young Dem., Bexar County Dems., 1978. Mem. ABA, State Bar Tex., San Antonio Bar Assn. (pres. 1987-88, Outstanding Young Lawyer 1980), Am. Inns of Ct. (pres. 1990-92). Avocations: basketball, gardening. Office: US Dist Ct 655 E Durango Blvd 1st Fl San Antonio TX 78206-1102*

BIERY, MARILYN RUTH, organist, conductor, educator, composer; b. Elmhurst, Ill., July 1, 1959; d. Alfred Lewis and Dorothy Jane (Patterson) Perkins; m. James Russell Biery,Aug. 16, 1980; 1 child, Laura Elizabeth. BM in Organ Performance, Northwestern U., 1980, MM, 1982; postgrad., U. Conn., 1994-96; DMA, U. Minn., 1999. Organist, choirmaster St. Andrew's Ch., Meriden, Conn., 1984-86; dir. music ministries Ctr. Ch./First Ch. of Christ, Hartford, Conn., 1986-96; dir. music St. Michael's Cathedral, Springfield, Mass., 1996; co-choir dir., organist Cathedral of St. Paul, St. Paul, 1996—. Composer: (organ pieces) Meditations on the Love of God, 1997, Fruit of the Spirit, 1999; texts author: (anthems) Jesus, Tiny Child, 1988, O Blessed Mary, 1988, O Sacrum Convivium, 1995; arranger, composer I Couldn't Hear Nobody Pray, 1996, others; composer choral text and music Gentle Grace, 1999. Hutchinson scholar, 1997-99. Mem. Am. Guild Organists (assoc., Region I coord. profl. concerns 1992-96, Region VI coord. for profl. concerns 1997—, dir. Nat. Young Artist Competition 1997—), Pi Kappa Lambda. Home: 1548 Pascal St N Saint Paul MN 55108-2329

BIES, ROGER DAVID, cardiologist; b. Athens, Ohio, May 28, 1956; s. Ronald Kenneth and Genivieve H. (Parlow) B.; m. Rhonda Jean Pope; children: Lucas, Tyler, Wade. BA, U. Colo., 1979, MD, 1986. Intern, resident U. Pitts., 1986-89; fellow in cardiology Baylor Coll. Medicine, Houston, 1987-92; asst. prof. medicine U. Colo. Health Scis. Ctr., Denver, 1993—; vis. asst. prof. Inst. Molecular Genetics, Houston, 1993; assoc. dir. cardiology U. Colo. Health Sci. Ctr., 1995—; dir. heart failure/transplant clinic VA Med. Ctr., Denver, 1993—, dir. pacemaker clinic, 1993—; vis. prof. interventional cardiology U. Pitts. Med. Ctr., 1998. Author: A Primer of Molecular Biology, 1992; contbr. articles to profl. jours., chpts. to books. Grantee: VA Rsch. , Am. Heart Assn. Fellow Am. Coll. Cardiology, Soc. Coronary Angiography and Interventions; mem. Am. Fedn. Clin. Rsch. (grantee), Am. Heart Assn, VA Rsch. Office: Ctrl Ariz Heart Specialists 312 N Alma Rd #14 Chandler AZ 85224

BIESELE, JOHN JULIUS, biologist, educator; b. Waco, Tex., Mar. 24, 1918; s. Rudolph Leopold and Anna Emma (Jahn) B.; m. Marguerite Calfee McAfee, July 29, 1943 (dec. 1991); children: Marguerite Anne, Diana Terry, Elizabeth Jane; m. Esther Aline Eakin, Mar. 9, 1992. B.A. with highest honors, U. Tex., 1939, Ph.D., 1942. Fellow Internat. Cancer Research Found., U. Tex., 1942-43, Barnard Skin and Cancer Hosp., St. Louis, also; U. Pa., 1943-44, instr. zoology, 1943-44; temporary research assoc. dept. genetics Carnegie Instn. of Washington, Cold Spring Harbor, 1944-46; research assoc. biology dept. Mass. Inst. Tech., 1946-47; asst. Sloan-Kettering Inst. Cancer Research, 1946-47, research fellow, 1947, assoc., 1947-55, head cell growth sect., div. exptl. chemotherapy, 1947-58, mem., 1955-58, assoc. scientist div., 1959-78; asst. prof. anatomy Cornell U. Med. Sch., 1950-52; assoc. prof. biology Sloan-Kettering div. Cornell U. Grad. Sch. Med. Scis., 1952-55, prof. biology, 1955-58; prof. zoology, mem. grad. faculty U. Tex., Austin, 1958-78; also mem. faculty U. Tex. (Coll. Pharmacy), 1969-71, prof. edn., 1973-78; prof. emeritus zoology U. Tex., Austin, 1978—; cons. cell biology M.D. Anderson Hosp. and Tumor Inst., U. Tex. at Houston, 1958-72; dir. Genetics Found., 1959-78; mem. cell biology study sect. NIH, 1958-63; Sigma Xi lectr. NYU Grad. Sch. Arts and Scis., 1957; Mendel lectr. St. Peter's Coll., Jersey City, 1958; featured spkr. on first Earth Day, Old Westbury Campus of N.Y. Inst. Tech., 1970; Mendel Club lectr. Canisius Coll., Buffalo, 1971; mem. adv. com. rsch. etiology of cancer Am. Cancer Soc., 1961-64, pres. Travis County unit, 1966, mem. adv. com. on personnel for rsch., 1969-73; counsellor Cancer Internat. Rsch. Coop., Inc., 1962-90; mem. cancer rsch. tng. com. Nat. Cancer Inst., 1969-72; gen. chmn. Conf. Advancement Sci. and Math. Teaching, 1966. Author: Mitotic Poisons and the Cancer Problem, 1958; mem. editorial bd. Year Book Cancer, 1959-72; mem. editorial adv. bd. Cancer Rsch., 1960-64, assoc. editor, 1969-72; cons. editor: Am. Jour. Mental Deficiency, 1963-68; mem. editorial bd. The Jour. of Applied Nutrition, 1987-91; contbr. articles to profl. jours. Research Career award NIH, 1962, 67, 72, 77. Fellow N.Y., Tex. acads. scis., AAAS; mem. Am. Assn. Cancer Research (dir. 1960-63), Am. Soc. Cell Biology, Am. Inst. Biol. Scis., Phi Beta Kappa, Sigma Xi (pres. Tex. chpt. 1963-64), Phi Eta Sigma, Phi Kappa Phi. Achievements include provision of early evidence for abnormal chromosome numbers in cancer cells, for occasional excessively multiple-stranded state of cancer chromosomes; demonstration of a direct relation of chromosomal size in mammalian tissues and organs to the local metabolic activity, as evidenced by the local content of B vitamins, of differential toxicity in certain antimetabolites to cancer cells in culture. Home: 2500 Great Oaks Pky Austin TX 78756-2908

BIESTEK, JOHN PAUL, lawyer; b. Chgo., May 28, 1935; s. John P. and Selma (Glick) B.; m. Elizabeth Mary Frer, Dec. 31, 1956; children: Scott, Becky. BS, Loyola U., Chgo., 1957, JD, 1964. Bar: Ill. 1964, U.S. Dist. Ct. (no. dist.) Ill. 1964; registered investment advisor. Sr. ptnr. Biestek & Facchini, Chgo., 1965-74; founding ptnr. John P. Biestek & Assocs., Ltd., Arlington Heights, Ill., 1974—; founder Profl. Retirement Specialists, Inc., 1997. Atty. Wheeling Twp. Rep. Orgn., 1978, fin. chmn., 1982-84; founder, chmn. Arlington Heights Econ. Devel. Commn., 1983-84. Mem. N.W. Suburban Bar Assn. (pres. 1977-78), Arlington Heights C. of C. (pres. 1982-84, dir. and atty. 1972-86, 91-98, Extraordinary Commitment and Leadership award 1984), Bridgeview C. of C. (pres. 1969), Rolling Green Country Club (sec. 1978-81, atty. 1980-84, 90-97, bd. dirs. 1997-98), Rotary (founder Arlington Heights chpt.). Roman Catholic. Home: 16 Dorchester Ct Hawthorn Woods IL 60047 Office: 115 N Arlington Heights Rd Arlington Heights IL 60004-6033

BIESTER, DORIS J., hospital executive. PhD in Nursing and Comty. Orgn., U. Colo., 1994. Pres., CEO Children Hosp., Denver, 1998—. Mem. Urban Peak Assn. (bd. dirs. 1996-98). Office: 1956 E 19th Ave Denver CO 80218

BIGBEE, IVY CAVE, photographer, author; b. Miami, Fla., July 3, 1947; m. James Frederick Spencer, 1966 (dec. Nov. 1969); children: Anthony James, Adam John. BA summa cum laude, U. North Fla., Jacksonville, 1994. Stock photographer SuperStock, Inc., Jacksonville, Fla., 1995—; freelance writer various jours., 1990—, art photographer, poet various jours., 1992—; adj. instr. photography U. North Fla. Author: Optical Allusions: An Art Photographer's Poems, 1997 (Jacksonville Cmty. Found. grant 1996), various monographs; photographer, poet web site, 1997; photographer POW and MIA commemorative stamp, 1995; exhibited in 10 one-woman photography shows. Curator of art, bd. mem. Karpeles Mus., Jacksonville, Fla., 1996—. Episcopalian. E-mail: IBigbee@aol.com.

BIGBIE, JOHN TAYLOR, lawyer, banker; b. Lynchburg, Va., Sept. 12, 1923; s. William Bright and Maria Woodson (Taylor) B.; m. Nadine de Coninck, Oct. 6, 1956; children: Astrid, John Eric. B.A., Princeton U., 1944; J.D., U. Va., 1948. Bar: N.Y. 1950. Assoc. Breed, Abbot & Morgan, N.Y.C., 1948-54; counsel Nat. Assn. Life Underwriters, Washington, 1954-61; v.p., sec., trust officer European-Am. Bank & Trust Co., N.Y.C., 1961-72; European rep. Butlers Bank Ltd., London, 1972-73; also dir.; dep. chmn. Antony Gibbs Fin. Services (C.I.) Ltd., 1974-77; internat. atty. and cons., 1978—. Served to lt. (j.g.) USNR, 1944-46. Mem. S.R., Soc. Colonial Wars, Pilgrims Gt. Britain, White's Club, Lansdowne Club, Bucks Club, Masons (N.Y.C.). Episcopalian. Home: 63 Warwick Square, London SW1V 2AL, England Office: 25 Dover St, London W1X 3PA, England

BIGDA, RUDOLPH A., business and financial consultant; b. Holyoke, Mass., Apr. 27, 1916; s. Alexander and Mary (Sakaske) B.; m. Josephine M. Baginski, June 22, 1946 (dec. July 1976); children: Donald R., Robert A.; m. Ann M. Willette, Dec. 9, 1981. BBA magna cum laude, Bryant Coll., 1935; postgrad., Dartmouth Coll., 1953. Vice pres. Parsons div. Am. Writing Paper Co., Holyoke, 1937-40; contr. F.W. Sickles div. Gen. Instrument Corp., Chicopee, Mass., 1946-54, Hano Bus. Forms Inc., Springfield, Mass., 1954-81; bus. and fin. cons. Palm Bay, Fla., 1981—; instr. Western New Eng. Coll., Springfield, 1974-75; bd. dirs. DRB Comms., Stamford, Conn.; counselor SCORE, Springfield, 1983—. Bd. dirs. Pulaski Heights Old Age Housing, Holyoke. Col. AUS, 1941-46, mem. Res. ret. Recipient alumni award Bryant Coll., 1967. Mem. Inst. of Mgmt. Accts. (pres. Pioneer Valley chpt. 1972-74), Fin. Execs. Inst., Ret. Officers Assn. (pres. Pioneer Valley chpt. 1978-80), Am. Legion, Elks. Republican. Roman Catholic. Avocations: computers, fishing, sports. Home and Office: 280 Berry Ct NE Palm Bay FL 32907-2163

BIGELEISEN, JACOB, chemist, educator; b. Paterson, N.J., May 2, 1919; s. Harry and Ida (Slomowitz) B.; m. Grace Alice Simon, Oct. 21, 1945; children: David M., Ira S., Paul E. A.B., NYU, 1939; M.S., Wash. State U., 1941; Ph.D., U. Calif., Berkeley, 1943. Rsch. scientist Manhattan Dist., Columbia, 1943-45; rsch. assoc. Ohio State U., Columbus, 1945-46; fellow Enrico Fermi Inst., U. Chgo., 1946-48; sr. chemist Brookhaven Nat. Lab., Upton, N.Y., 1948-68; prof. chemistry U. Rochester, N.Y., 1968-78; chmn. dept. U. Rochester, 1970-75; Tracy H. Harris prof. U. Rochester (Coll. Arts and Scis.), 1973-78; v.p. research, dean grad. studies SUNY, Stony Brook, 1978-80; Leading prof. chemistry SUNY, 1978-89, Disting. prof., 1989, Disting. prof. emeritus, 1989—; vis. prof. Cornell U., 1953; NSF sr. fellow, vis. prof. Eidgen Techn. Hochschule, Switzerland, 1962-63; chmn. Assembly Math. and Phys. Scis., NRC-Nat. Acad. Scis., 1976-80. Mem. editorial bd. Jour. Phys. Chemistry, Jour. Chem. Physics. Trustee Sayville Jewish Center, 1954-68. Recipient Nuclear award Am. Chem. Soc., 1958, Gilbert N. Lewis lectr., 1963, E.O. Lawrence award, 1964, Disting. Alumnus award Wash. State U., 1983; John Simon Guggenheim fellow, 1974-75. Fellow AAAS, Am. Phys. Soc., Am. Chem. Soc., Am. Acad. Arts and Sci.; mem. Nat. Acad. Scis. (councilor 1982-85), Phi Beta Kappa, Sigma Xi, Phi Lambda Upsilon. Achievements include research in photochemistry in rigid media, semiquinones, cryogenics, chemistry of isotopes, quantum statistics of gases, liquids and solids. Home: PO Box 217 Saint James NY 11780-0217 *As a youth I became interested in a career in science because it offered the opportunity to test ideas and hypotheses objectively by experiment. This unique aspect of science, which differentiates it from all other branches of learning and knowledge, has been a guiding principle both in my professional and my personal life. My career has included research, teaching, administration and public service.*

BIGELOW, CHARLES CROSS, biochemist, university administrator; b. Edmonton, Alta., Can., Apr. 25, 1928; s. Sherburne Tupper and Helen Beatrice (Cross) B.; m. Elizabeth Rosemary Sellick, Aug. 22, 1977; children: Ann K. Bigelow Siess, David C. B.A.Sc., U. Toronto, 1953; M.Sc., McMaster U., 1955, Ph.D., 1957. Postdoctoral fellow Carlsberg Lab., Copenhagen, 1957-59; assoc. Sloan-Kettering Inst. Cancer Research, N.Y.C., 1959-62; asst. prof. chemistry U. Alta., Can., 1962-64; assoc. prof. U. Alta., 1964-65; vis. prof. Fla. State U., Tallahassee, 1965; assoc. prof. biochemistry U. Western Ont., London, Ont., Can., 1965-69, prof., 1969-74; prof., head biochemistry Meml. U. Nfld., St. John's, Can., 1974-76; dean of sci., prof. chemistry St. Mary's U., Halifax, N.S., Can., 1977-79; dean of sci. U. Man., Winnipeg, Can., 1979-89, dean emeritus, 1990—, prof. chemistry, 1979—; fellow Univ. Coll., 1989, sr. adminstrv. fellow, 1993-94, Univ. Coll. provost 1995-97, sr. scholar, 1997; vis. prof. U. Toronto, 1973-74; vis. scientist Nat. Inst. for Med. Rsch., London, 1984-85; chmn. Ont. Confedn. Univ. Faculty Assns., 1970-71; pres. Can. Assn. Univs. Tchrs., 1972-73. Contbr. articles on protein structure and denaturation to sci. jours. Bd. govs. U. Western Ont., 1972-73, U. Man., 1982-84, Man. Mus. of Man and Nature, 1986-91; bd. mgmt. TRIUMF, Vancouver, 1987-89; pres. N.S. New Democratic party, 1978-79; pres. Man. New Dem. party, 1982-84. Grantee NRC Can., Med. Research Council, Natural Scis. and Engring. Research Council Can. Fellow Chem. Inst. Can.; mem. Can. Biochem. Soc., Am. Chem. Soc., Am. Soc. Biol. Chemists, AAAS, Sigma Xi. Home: 91 Kingston Row, Winnipeg, MB Canada R2M O57 Office: U Man, Univ Coll, Winnipeg, MB Canada R3T 2N2

BIGELOW, DONALD NEVIUS, educational administrator, historian, consultant; b. Danbury, Conn., Aug. 19, 1918; s. Harry R. and Bessie M. (Nevius) B.; m. Louise M. Fournel, Sept. 21, 1957; 1 son, Pierre Nevius. B.A. cum laude, Amherst Coll., 1939, M.A., 1945; Ph.D., Columbia U., 1950. Spl. agt. Inland Marine Ins., North Brit. and Merc. Ins. Co., N.Y.C. and Detroit, 1939-43; with U.S. Engr. Dept., Fairbanks, Alaska, 1942; instr. history Amherst Coll., 1943-45; instr. Columbia U., 1947-50, asst. prof., 1951-55; assoc. prof. Brandeis U., 1955-60; chief lang. and area ctrs. program Office Edn., HEW, Washington, 1961-64; head task force NDEA Title XI Inst. Program, 1964-65, dir. div. ednl. personnel tng., 1965-67, dir. div. program adminstrn., 1967-68; dir. div. coll. programs Bur. Ednl. Personnel Devel., 1968-71; dir. Northeast div. Nat. Ctr. for Improvement Ednl. Systems, 1972-74; spl. asst., assoc. commr. for Instl. Devel. and Internat. Edn., 1974-76; chief grad. tng. Office of Postsecondary Edn., Dept. Edn., Washington, 1976-82; sr. adminstr. The Nat. Faculty, Atlanta, 1985-88; spl. asst. to dep. asst. sec. Office of Postsecondary Edn., U.S. Dept. Edn., Washington, 1988-93, sr. exec. Ctr. Internat. Edn., 1993, program mgr. Dwight D. Eisenhower Leadership Devel. Act of 1992, 1993-96; exec. dir. Javits Fellowship Bd., 1996—, spl. asst. Office Internat. Edn. & Grad. Edn. Office Higher Edn., 1998—; vis. Fulbright prof. Am. civilization U.S. Ednl. Found., India, U. Baroda, U. Lucknow, 1954-55; prof. humanities N.Y. Sch. Music, 1949-56; vis. prof. U. So. Fla., 1969; postdoctoral research fellow George Washington U., 1970-71; lectr. U. Va., 1973; adj. prof. Am. U., 1975; cons. Ford Found., 1957, Carnegie Corp., 1958, U.S. Office Edn., 1959-60; moderator ABC TV series Seminar, 1953-54, PBS WGBH TV series on ethnicity, 1956-57; assoc. dir. com. lang. and area ctrs. Am. Council Edn., 1960-61; book reviewer Nat. Pub. Radio series Options in Education, 1976-77. Author: William Conant Church and the Army and Navy Journal, 1952, (with Joseph Axelrod) Resources for Language and Area Studies, 1960, (with Lyman Legters) Language and Area Centers, 1964, (with others) Non-Western Studies in the Liberal Arts College, 1964; editor: (with Hiram Haydn) Makers of the American Tradition Series, 4 vols., 1953-55, The Annals (The Non-Western World in Higher Education), 1964, The Liberal Arts and Teacher Education: A Confrontation, 1971, Schoolworlds '76, New Directions for Educational Policy, 1976; lectr., contbr. articles to profl. jours. Home: 2901 Q St NW Washington DC 20007-3089 Office: US Dept Edn 400 Maryland Ave SW Washington DC 20202-0001

BIGELOW, GEORGE E., psychology and pharmacology scientist; b. Washington, Aug. 31, 1943. Dir. behavioral pharmacology unit Johns Hopkins U., Balt., Md. Office: Johns Hopkins U Behavioral Pharma Unit 5510 Nathan Shock Dr Baltimore MD 21224-6823

BIGELOW, GORDON STINSON, English educator; b. Springfield, Vt., Sept. 14, 1963; s. Gordon Shoemaker and Beverly (McCarthy) B. AB, Brown U., 1985; MA, U. N.H., 1991; PhD, U. Calif., Santa Cruz, 1998. Tchr. English Haverford (Pa.) Sch., 1985-87; outdoor educator Chewonki Found., Wiscasset, Maine, 1987-88; tchg. asst. U. N.H., Durham, 1989-91, U. Calif., 1991-98; asst. prof. English, Rhodes Coll., Memphis, 1998—; asst. instr., instr. Outward Bound, Rockland, Maine, summers 1990-91. Contbr. articles to profl. jours. Mem. MLA, Am. Conf. Irish Studies, Interdisciplinary 19th Century Studies (conf. organizer Santa Cruz 1995). Office: Rhodes Coll Dept English 2000 N Parkway Memphis TN 38112-1690

BIGELOW, KATHRYN, film director; b. San Carlos, Calif., 1951. Student, San Francisco Art Inst., Whitney Mus. Ind. Study Program, Columbi U. Sch. Film. Director: (films) The Loveless, 1982, Near Dark, 1987, Blue Steel, 1990, Point Break, 1991, Strange Days, 1995, Homicide Life on the Street, 1993, The Set Up, 1998, (TV miniseries) Wild Palms, 1993; script supr. Union City, 1980; author: (screenplays) (with Monty Montgomery) The Loveless, (with Eric Red) Near Dark. Office: First Light care Working title Films 9333 Wilshire Blvd Beverly Hills CA 90210-5408*

BIGELOW, MARGARET ELIZABETH BARR (M.E. BARR), mycology educator; b. Elkhorn, Man., Can., Apr. 16, 1923; d. David Hunter and Mary Irene (Parr) Barr; m. Howard Elson Bigelow, June 9, 1956 (dec.). BA with honors, U. B.C., Vancouver, Can., 1950, MA, 1952; PhD, U. Mich., 1956. Rsch. attaché U. Montreal, Que., Can., 1956-57; instr. U. Mass., Amherst, 1957-65, asst. prof., 1965-71, assoc. prof., 1971-76, prof., 1976-89, prof. emeritus, 1989—. Author: Diaporthales in N.A., 1978, Prodromus to Loculoascomycetes, 1987, Prodromus to Nonlichenized Members of Class Hymenoascomycetes, 1990; contbr. articles to profl. jours. With Can. Women's Army Corps, 1942-46. Mem. Mycol. Soc. Am. (v.p. to pres. 1980-82, editor 1975-80, Disting. Mycologist Award, 1993), Brit. Mycol. Soc., Am. Inst. Biol. Sci. (gen. chmn. ann. meeting 1986). Avocations: gardening, reading. Home and Office: 9475 Inverness Rd, Sidney, BC Canada V8L 5G8

BIGELOW, MARTHA MITCHELL, retired historian; b. Talladega Springs, Ala., Sept. 19, 1921; divorced; children: Martha Frances, Carolyn Letitia. B.A., Montevallo U., 1943; M.A. (tuition fellow, Julius Rosenwald scholar 1943-44, Cleo Hearson scholar, summer 1944, Ency. Brit. fellow 1944-45), U. Chgo., 1944, Ph.D., 1946. Assoc. prof. history Miss. Coll., Clinton, 1946-48, Memphis State U., 1948-49; Assoc. prof. history U. Miss., 1949-50; assoc. curator manuscripts Mich. Hist. Collections, U. Mich., Ann Arbor, 1954-57; prof. history Miss. Coll., 1957-71, chmn. dept. history and polit. sci., 1964-71; dir. Bur. of History, Mich. Dept. State, 1971-90; sec. Mich. Hist. Commn., Mich. Dept. State, state historic preservation officer, 1971-90; coord. for Mich., Nat. Hist. Publs. and Recs. Commn., 1974-90. Contbr. articles profl. publns. Mem. Am. Assn. State and Local History (v.p. 1979-80, pres. 1980-81, fellow summers 1958, 59), Orgn. Am. Historians, Nat. Assn. State Archives and Recs. Assn., So. Hist. Assn., Mich. Hist. Soc., Miss. Hist. Soc. Home: 201 N Jefferson St Clinton MS 39056-4237

BIGELOW, NICHOLAS PIERRE, physicist, educator; b. Princeton, N.J., Dec. 26, 1958; s. Julian Himley and Mary Agnes (Milward) B.; m. Judith Anderson, July 26, 1981; children: Ian, Eric. BS in Elec. Engring. with high honors, Lehigh U., 1980, BS in Physics with high honors, 1981; MS, Cornell

U., 1984, PhD, 1989. Lic. pilot. Mem. tech. staff AT&T Bell Labs., Holmdel, N.J., 1989-91; sr. rsch. assoc. dept. physics and astronomy U. Rochester, N.Y., 1991-92, asst. prof. physics, 1992-97, assoc. prof., 1997—, sr. staff scientist Lab. for Laser Energetics, 1992—; rsch. assoc. Ecole Normale Supèrieure, Paris, 1991-92, vis. prof., 1992-95. Mem. editl. bd. Laser Physics; contbr. chpts. to books, numerous articles to profl. jours. and encys. Alfred P. Sloan Found. fellow, 1993-95; NSF grantee, 1994—; David and Lucile Packard Found. fellow, 1994—. Mem. Am. Phys. Soc., Optical Soc. Am., Tau Beta Pi. Achievements include theoretical and experimental investigations the fields of quantum optics and atomic physics. Office: U Rochester Dept Physics and Astronomy Rochester NY 14627

BIGELOW, PAGE ELIZABETH, public policy professional; b. Louisville, Feb. 9, 1948; d. William Simpson and Page Elizabeth (Smith) B. BA, Wells Coll., 1970; postgrad., NYU, 1971-72, Gen. Theol. Sem., 1971-72. Rsch. asst., libr. Nat. Mcpl. League, N.Y.C., 1970-75, rsch. dir. ethics in govt. project, 1975-80, dir. representation project, 1981-84; sr. assoc. Nat. Civic League (formerly Nat. Mcpl. League), N.Y.C., 1983-87; staff cons. state-city commn. on integrity in govt. N.Y., 1986-87; mem. sr. staff Inst. Pub. Adminstrn., N.Y.C., 1987-95, cons., 1995-97; sr. assoc. Inst. for Dem. Studies, 1996—; v.p., corp. sec. Albanian-Am. Enterprise Fund, 1997—; corp. sec. Am. Bank Albania, 1998—. Author: From Norms of Rules, Regulating the Outside Interests of Public Officials, 1989, Money, Politics and the Public Trust: Gifts, Illegal Gratuities, Bribery, Extortion and Campaign Contributions, 1995; editor: Proceedings of the International Conference on Ethics in Government, 1995. Mem. citizens adv. panel to joint legis. com. on revision and simplification of tax code, N.Y., 1982-86; del. Ednl. Priorities Panel, N.Y.C., 1984-94; mem. Citywide Sch. Bd. Elections Com., N.Y.C., 1985-95. Mem. Coun. on Govtl. Ethics Laws, Jr. League N.Y.C. (corp. sec. 1986-88, 90, Honored Vol. 1990), Albanian Children Fund (corp. sec., 1998—). Episcopalian. Home: 5 Berkeley Rd Maplewood NJ 07040-2511

BIGELOW, ROBERT P., lawyer, arbitrator, mediator, journalist; b. N.Y.C., Jan. 17, 1927; s. Robert R.L. and Doris W.S. (Bissell) B.; m. Katharine W. MacKenty Apr. 14, 1951; children: Katharine R., Robert S., Sanford W., Edward G. AB cum laude, Harvard U., 1950, JD, 1953. Bar: Mass. 1953, N.Y. 1980. Law clk. Supreme Ct. Mass., 1953-54; assoc. Bingham Dana & Gould, Boston, 1954-56; atty., asst. counsel John Hancock Mut. Life Ins. Co., Boston, 1956-66; pvt. practice Woburn and Boston, Mass., 1966-86; of counsel Hennessy Kilburn Killgoar & Ronan, Boston, 1973-84; ptnr. Bigelow & Saltzberg, Woburn, 1980-86; counsel Warner & Stockpole, Boston, 1986-87; sole practice, 1987-91, 95-97; counsel Bird & Bird, London, 1995-97; arbitrator, mediator, 1966—; adj. prof. Dartmouth Coll., 1982-84, Suffolk Law Sch., 1986-92; acting dir. New Eng. Law Inst., 1974-75. Author: (with Susan Nycum)) Your Computer and the Law, 1975, Contracting for Computer Hardware, Software and Services, 1984-95, Computer Contracts, 1987-92; editor Law Office Econs. and Mgmt., 1969-78, Computer Law Svc., 1973-81, Computer Law and Tax Report, 1974-84, Computer Law Newsletter, 1979-87; cons. editor, 1988-91; cons. editor Bull. Computer Law Assn., 1971-97, editor, 1997-98; contbg. editor Cyberspace Lawyer, 1998—, Lawyers Competitive Edge, 1999—; mem. adv. bd. Guide to Computer Law, 1998—; contbr. articles to profl. jours. With U.S. Army, 1945-46, 51-64. Fellow AAAS, Brit. Computer Soc. (life, qualified arbitrator), I.S.P. Can. Info. Processing Soc., Am. Bar Found. (life), Coll. Law Practice Mgmt. (hon.); mem. ABA (editor Computers and the Law 1966, 69, 81, Jurimetrics Jour. 1971-74, Bull. Law, Sci. and Tech. 1977-800, chmn. com. law relating to computers 1979-80, briefs editor Law Practice Mgmt. 1979-91, 93-96), Mass. Bar Assn. (chmn. econs. com. 1969-73, mem. com profl. ethics 1973-79, mem. coun. law practice 1981-84, chmn. bus. law sect. 1984-85), Computer Law Assn. (pres. 1977-79, dir. 1973-84, adv. coun. 1984—), ACM (nat. lectr. 1969-700, chmn. computers and soc. group 1969-71, elections com. 1989-92), Computer Soc. IEEE (sr. mem.), Australian Computer Soc., New Zealand Computer Soc., Soc. Computers and Law (U.K.), Soc. Computers and Law (New South Wales), Authors Guild. Office: 10 Mount Vernon St # 252 Winchester MA 01890-2704

BIGGER, PHILIP JOSEPH, judicial branch official; b. Bronx, N.Y., June 29, 1943; s. Alexander William and Grace (Silvestro) B.; m. Lois Ann Pickell, Oct. 30, 1965; children: Michael, Susan. BA in History, Manhattan Coll., Bronx, N.Y., 1965; MA in History, Wagner Coll., Staten Island, N.Y., 1971. Caseworker N.Y.C. Dept. Social Svcs., Staten Island, 1965-70; probation officer N.Y. State Supreme Ct., Bklyn., 1970-72; probation officer U.S. Dist. Ct, Bklyn., 1972-81, supervising probation officer, 1981-91, dep. chief probation officer, 1991-93, chief pretrial svcs. officer, 1993—. Author: History of the Federal Probation Officers Assn., 1986; contbr. articles to profl. publs. With U.S. Army, 1966-68. Mem. Federal Probation and Pretrial Officers Assn. (v.p. 1991-94, pres. 1995-98). Democrat. Roman Catholic. Avocations: boating, writing. Office: U.S. Pretrial Svcs Agy 225 Cadman Plz E Brooklyn NY 11201-1818

BIGGERS, JOAN NEVILL, social services organization administrator; b. London, Dec. 21, 1924; came to U.S., 1959; became U.S. citizen, 1984; d. Geoffrey Cobbold and Cicely (Midleton) Cobbold Rickwood; m. John D. Biggers, July 24, 1948 (div. 1978); children: David Biggers, Philippa Salzman, Jennifer Wasserman. BSc in Physiology with 1st class honors, London U., 1946, postgrad., 1996-98. Lectr. physiology dept. Bedford Coll. of London U., 1946-48; social worker Dept. Social Svcs., Balt., 1967-70; adminstrv. sec., counselor, rschr. Johns Hopkins U. Hosp., Women's Clinic, Balt., 1970-72; counselor, women's health clinics Peter Bent Brigham Hosp., Boston, 1973-77, founder, dir. dept. patient reps., 1977-81; founder, dir. Hospitality Program, Boston, 1982-89; founder, co-chair Mass. Soc. Patient Reps., Boston, 1978-81, New Beginnings for Widows, Divorced and Single Persons (group leader, pres., 1989-92), Hingham, Mass., 1979-81. Region 4 rep. Episcopal Diocese of Mass., 1994-98; bd. dirs. Brit. Charitable Soc. Named Woman of Yr. on South Shore, Mass., 1993, named Entrepreneur of 1997, S. Shore C of C, Mass. Democrat. Episcopalian. Avocations: writing, painting, tennis, reading, family.

BIGGERS, NEAL BROOKS, JR., federal judge; b. Corinth, Miss., July 1, 1935; s. Neal Brooks and Sara (Cunningham) B.; 1 child, Sherron. BA, Millsaps Coll., 1956; JD, U. Miss., 1963. Sole practice Corinth, 1963-68; pros. atty. Alcorn County, 1964; dist. atty. 1st Jud. Dist. Miss., 1968-75, cir. judge, 1975-84; judge U.S. Dist. Ct. (no. dist.) Miss., Oxford, 1984—. Contbr. articles to profl. jours. Office: US Dist Ct PO Box 1238 911 Jackson Ave Oxford MS 38655-1238

BIGGERS, WILLIAM JOSEPH, retired manufacturing company executive; b. Great Bend, Kans., Mar. 16, 1928; s. William Henry and Frances (Jack) B.; m. Eathil Bonner, Nov. 17, 1956 (div. July 1981); children: Frances, Patricia; m. Diane McLaughlin, Feb. 14, 1983; 1 child, Michael C. B.A., Duke U., 1949. C.P.A., Ga. Pub. acct., 1949-55; sec.-treas. Parker, Helms & Langston, Inc., Brunswick, Ga., 1955-59, Stuckey's, Inc., Eastman, Ga., 1959-60; sec.-treas., v.p. finance Curtis 1000 Inc., 1961-69; v.p. Am. Bus. Products, Inc., Atlanta, 1969-73, chief exec. officer, 1973-88, chmn. bd., 1983-94, chmn. exec. com., 1994-98; bd dirs. Com. Publicly Owned Cos.; former trustee Ga. Coun. Econ. Edn., former mem. listed co. adv. com. N.Y. Stock Exch., Am. Stock Exch. Trustee Berry Coll.; bd. dirs. Atlanta Area coun. Boy Scouts Am. With USNR, 1946, with AUS, 1950-52. Mem. AICPA, NAM, Ga. Soc. CPAs, Fin. Execs. Inst., Am. Mgmt. Assn., Phoenix Soc. Atlanta, Capital City Club, Georgian Club, Marietta Country Club, Highlands Country Club, Rotary, Phi Kappa Psi. *

BIGGERSTAFF, RANDY LEE, academic administrator, sports medicine rehabilitation consultant; b. Buffalo, Feb. 13, 1951; s. Dever Poole and Mary Martha (Smith) B.; m. Sue Ann Knobeloch, Nov. 26, 1977; children: Nicholas Lee, Amy Elizabeth. BS, U. Mo., 1973; MS in Health Mgmt., Lindenwood Coll., 1995. Dist. athletic tng. tchr. Granite City (Ill.) Community Sch. Dist., 1973-77; athletic trainer St. Louis Hummers, Profl. Softball Team, Valley Park, Mo., 1978-79; founder-ptnr., clinic dir. St. Louis Sports Medicine Clinic, Chesterfield, Mo., 1977-82; founder, clin. dir. Iowa Orthopedic Sports Medicine Clinic, Urbandale, 1982-84; clinic dir. St. Louis Orthopedic Sports Medicine Clinic, Chesterfield, 1984-86; ptnr., v.p. St. Louis Rehab. Sports Clinic, Crystal City, Mo., 1986-88; adminstr., regional dir. St. Louis Orthopedic Sports Medicine Clinic, Chesterfield, 1989-90; coord., trainer, cons. St. Luke's Hosp., Chesterfield, 1990-92; v.p. D. P. Biggs Cons. Ltd., Inc., 1992-93; pres. Phoenix Sports Med. Systems, St. Louis, 1993-97; dir. athletic tng. edn., athletic trainer Lindenwood U., 1997; cons. Brentwood & Creve Coeur Skating, St. Louis, 1986—, Gateway Athletics, St. Louis, 1984—; med. coord. Show-Me-Bowl, St. Louis, 1979-82, Summer Biathalon Series, Essex Junction, Vt., 1989—. Contbr. articles to profl. jours. Sec. bd. overseers Lindenwood Coll., St. Charles, Mo., 1992-93, vice chmn., 1993-95, chair, 1995-97, bd. dirs., 1995-97; conference dir. lay spkg. Meth. Ch. Inducted to Mo. Sports Medicine Hall of Fame, 1995, Mo. Sports Hall of Fame, Springfield, 1997. Mem. Nat. Athletic Trainers Assn. (cert., clin. corp. com., treas. M.A.A.T.A. dist. V), Mo. Athletic Trainer Assn. (registered, chair Hall of Fame com. 1991-94), Mid-Am. Athletic Trainers Assn. (treas.). Methodist. Avocations: running, cycling, fitness, hiking, spectator sports. Home: 82 Shirecreek Ct Saint Charles MO 63303-5432 Office: Lindenwood U 209 W Kings Hwy Saint Charles MO 63303

BIGGERT, JUDITH BORG, congresswoman, lawyer; b. Chgo., Aug. 15, 1937; d. Alvin Andrew and Marjorie Virginia (Mailler) Borg; m. Rody Patterson Biggert, Sept. 21, 1963; children: Courtney Ray, Alison Mailler, Rody Patterson, Adrienne Taylor. B.A., Stanford U., 1959; J.D., Northwestern U., 1963. Bar: Ill. 1963, Law clk. to presiding justice U.S. Ct. Appeals (7th cir.), Chgo., 1963-64; sole practice, Hinsdale, Ill., 1964—; rep. Ill. Gen. Assembly, 1993-98, asst. Rep. leader, 1995-98, majority conf. chair, 1995-96; minority spokesperson 81st Dist. Judiciary I Com., 1993-94; mem. gov.'s human svcs. legis. reorgn. task force, from 1996; mem. U.S. Congress from 13th Ill. dist., 1999—, mem. banking and fin. svcs. com., govt. reform com., sci. com. Mem. bd. editors Law Rev., Northwestern U. Sch. Law, 1961-63. Pres. Hinsdale Twp. High Sch. Dist. 86 Bd. Edn., 1983-85; pres. Jr. League Chgo., 1976-78, treas., bd. bd. mgrs., 1966—; chmn. Hinsdale Antiques Show, 1980; pres. Oak Sch. PTA, Hinsdale, 1976-78; pres.-treas. Chgo. jr. bd. Travelers Aid Soc., 1965-70; Sunday sch. tchr. Grace Episcopal Ch., Hinsdale, 1978-80, 82-85; chair, treas., 2d v.p., bd. dirs. Vis. Nurses Assn. Chgo., 1978; bd. dirs. Salt Creek Ballet, 1990—. Recipient Servian award Jr. aux. U. Chgo. Cancer Research Found., Woman of Yr. in Govt., Politics, and Civic Affairs DuPage YWCA, 1995; named one of 100 Women Making a Difference; inductee Hinsdale Ctrl. H.S. Hall of Fame, 1997. Mem. ABA, Ill. Bar Assn., Du Page Assn. Women Lawyers, Coalition Women Legislators. Republican. Office: 508 Cannon House Office Bldg Washington DC 20515-1313 also: 115 W 55th St Ste 100 Clarendon Hills IL 60514-1593*

BIGGIO, CRAIG, professional baseball player; b. Smithtown, N.Y., Dec. 14, 1965. Grad. h.s., Houston. Second base player Houston Astros, 1988—. Named Catcher, The Sporting News Coll. All-Am. Team, 1987; named to Sporting News Silver Slugger Team, 1989, 94, The Sporting News Nat. League All-Star Team, 1994, named to Nat. League All-Star Team, 1991, 92, 94-98; recipient Gold Glove 2d base, 1994-96. Office: Houston Astros PO Box 288 Houston TX 77001-0288*

BIGGLES, RICHARD ROBERT, marketing executive; b. London, Apr. 4, 1946; came to U.S., 1975; s. Thomas Richard and Joan (Ellison) B.; married; children: Kwame, Kwaku, Kwasi. BS, McGill U., Can., 1971; MBA, U. Essex, Eng., 1973. Dir. mktg. MidEast Trading Ltd., London, 1973-74, 1st Devel. Co., Ltd., Accra, Ghana, 1974-75; v.p. mktg. Gulf Coast Corp., Memphis, 1975-80; v.p. mktg. Buckle Internat. AG Inc., Chgo., 1980-87, exec. v.p. mktg., 1987—. Office: Buckle Internat AG Inc PO Box 2522 Chicago IL 60690-2522

BIGGS, ALAN RICHARD, plant pathologist, educator; b. Lewisburg, Pa., June 22, 1953; s. Edgar Harold and Yvonne S. Biggs; m. Lise N. Sade, Oct. 3, 1981; children: Benjamin Jesse Biggs Sade, Skylar Rose Biggs Sade. BS, Pa. State U., 1976, MS, 1978, PhD, 1982. Rsch. scientist Can. Dept. Agr., Vineland, Ont., 1983-89; assoc. prof. W.Va. U., Kearneysville, 1989-95, prof., 1995—. Editor: Defense Mechanisms of Woody Plants Against Fungi, 1992, Cytology, Histology and Histochemistry of Fruit Tree Diseases, 1992; assoc. editor Jour. Phytopathology, 1986-88, Plant Disease, 1994-96; sr. editor Plant Disease, 1998—. Recipient Lee M. Hutchins award, 1993. Mem. AAAS, Am. Phytopath. Soc. (Lee M. Hutchins award 1993). Avocations: photography, bicycling, jazz guitar. Office: WVa U Univ Experiment Farm PO Box 609 Kearneysville WV 25430-0609

BIGGS, ARTHUR EDWARD, retired chemical manufacturing company executive; b. N.Y.C., Jan. 3, 1930; s. Arthur Edward and Pauline (Maier) B.; m. Charlotte Marion Elliott, Sept. 10, 1955; children—Arthur Edward III, William Elliott, Nancy Catherine, Andrew David. B.S. in Acctg. and Fin. Magna cum laude, U. Md., 1951; M.B.A. in Fin. and Prodn. with distinction, Harvard U., 1957. Mgmt. cons. McKinsey & Co., Inc., N.Y.C., 1957-62; asst. controller Mobil Oil Co., N.Y.C., 1963-66, controller, 1966-68; v.p., gen. mgr. plastics div. Mobil Chem. Co., Rochester, N.Y., 1969-73; exec. v.p. Mobil Chem. Co., N.Y.C., 1974-82, pres., 1982-86; chmn. bd. dirs. The Century Group, 1987-91. Vice pres. bd. dirs. Vis. Nurse Svc. N.Y., 1975-88; bd. advisers Pace U., N.Y.C., 1976-88; trustee Quinnipiac Coll., Hamden, Conn., 1982-92, chmn., 1986-90; bd. dirs. Ptnrs. in Care, N.Y.C., 1983-88, chmn., 1983-88; trustee Conn. Conf. Ind. Colls., chmn., 1987-89; trustee Harvard Sch. Bus. 1st lt., pilot USAF, 1951-55. Baker scholar Harvard U., 1957. Mem. Racquet Club Boca Raton, Woodfield Country Club (Boca Raton). Avocation: tennis.

BIGGS, BARBARA CONNER, internist; b. Jackson, Miss., Jan. 14, 1954; d. Robert Alanson Jr. and Lady Rachel (Conner) B.; m. Glenn Blaise Gatipon, May 12, 1990. BA, U. Miss., 1976, MT, ASCP, 1978, MD, 1982. Diplomate Am. Bd. Internal Medicine. Med. technologist U. Miss. Med. Ctr., Jackson, 1978; med. intern Emory U. Hosp., Atlanta, 1982-83, med. resident, 1983-85; physician Prucare HMO, Atlanta, 1985-86; pvt. practice Marietta, Ga., 1986—; vice-chief of med. staff Kennestone Hosp., Marietta, 1995-96, chief of med. staff, 1996-97, bd. trustees, 1995—; bd. dirs. Quality Care Providers, Inc., Atlanta. Presbyterian. Avocations: scuba, sailing, skiing, fishing. Office: 611 Campbell Hill St NW Marietta GA 30060-1301*

BIGGS, BARRY HUGH, lawyer; b. Portland, Oreg., Mar. 24, 1935; s. Hugh Lawry and Elra (Ware) B.; m. Betty Lou Boehm, Aug. 25, 1957; children: Jonathan Hugh, Julianne. BS, U. Oreg., 1956; LLB, Stanford U., 1960. Bar: Wash. 1960. Assoc. Lane Powell Moss & Miller, Seattle, 1960-68; ptnr. Lane Powell Spears Lubersky, Seattle, 1969-92, of counsel, 1992—. Mem. ABA, Wash. State Bar Assn., Tacoma-Pierce County Bar Assn., Seattle Tennis Club, Vashon Island Golf & Country Club, Phi Gamma Delta. Home: 26032 Gold Beach Dr SW Vashon WA 98070-8531

BIGGS, BARTON MICHAEL, investment company executive; b. N.Y.C., Nov. 26, 1932; s. William Richardson and Georgene (Williams) B.; m. Judith Anne Lund, June 12, 1959; children: Wende Hammond, Gretchen G., Barton William. B.A., Yale U., 1955; M.B.A. with distinction, NYU, 1962. Research analyst E.F. Hutton & Co., N.Y.C., 1961-65, asst. to chmn., 1962-65, partner, 1965; co-founder, mng. partner Fairfield Partners, Greenwich, Conn., 1965-73; ptnr., mng. dir. Morgan Stanley & Co., N.Y.C., 1973—, mgr. rsch. dept., 1973-79, 91-93; chmn., CEO Morgan Stanley Asset Mgmt. Co., N.Y.C., 1980—, mem. mgmt. com., 1987—, mem. exec. com., bd. dirs., 1991—; dir. Rand McNally & Co.; chmn. Morgan Stanley Funds. Contbr. articles to profl. jours. Served as 1st lt. USMC, 1955-58. Mem. N.Y. Soc. Security Analysts, Round Hill Club, Field Club (Greenwich), Chevy Chase Club (Washington), Lyford Cay Club (Bahamas). Office: Morgan Stanley Dean Whitter Inv Mng 1221 Ave of the Ames 22d Fl New York NY 10020-1104*

BIGGS, EDMUND LOGAN, college administrator; b. Mattoon, Ill., Dec. 17, 1938; s. Lloyd William and Florence Violet (Fairbanks) B.; 1 child, Lloyd John. BS in Acctg., Kansas State U., 1965; MBA in Mgmt., U. New Haven, 1983; PhD, SUNY, Buffalo, 1991. Computer specialist Union Nat. Bank, Manhattan, Kans., 1963-65, mgmt. trainee, 1965-66; nuclear logistics officer USN, Kirtland AFB, N. Mex., 1967-68, computer programming officer, 1968-69; data automation officer Tan Son Knut, Vietnam, 1969-70; computer systems analyst Stuttgart, Fed. Republic Germany, 1970-72; supply officer USS Sellers, 1973-74; procurement officer def. gen. supply ctr. Richmond, Va., 1974-76; asst. supply/material officer, support force Antarctica, 1976-78; planning and adminstrv. officer, aviation supply officer China Lake, Calif., 1978-79; comptr., commanding officer regional acctg. and disbursing ctr. Subase, New London, Conn., 1980-82; liaison officer def. logistics agy for maj. def. systems Syracuse, N.Y., 1982-83; instr. bus. Erie Community Coll., Buffalo, 1983-86, dept. head banking, ins., real estate, 1986—; adminstr. Structurally Unemployed Retng. Program, Buffalo, 1985—. Mem. VFW, Am. Legion, Optimist Internat., Lions. Roman Catholic. Avocations: antiques, music, cooking, camping. Office: Erie Community Coll 121 Ellicott St Buffalo NY 14203-2601

BIGGS, J. O., lawyer, general industry company executive; b. Kansas City, Mo., Feb. 17, 1925; s. John Olin and Parilee Catherine (Story) B.; m. Marilyn Frances Sweeney, Dec. 27, 1947; children—Melissa Anne, John Kevin, Brian Sweeney. AB, U. Kans., 1947, LLB, 1949. Bar: Kan. bar 1949, Mo. bar 1950, Ia. bar 1953. With legal dept. Kansas City Life Ins. Co., 1950-51; exec. asst. to industry members Regional Wage Stblzn. Bd., 1951-52; dir. labor relations Meredith Pub. Co., 1952-58; with Gustin-Bacon Mfg. Co. (merger into Certain-teed Products Corp. 1966), 1958—, v.p., asst. to pres., 1962-63, pres., chief exec. officer, 1963-66; exec. v.p. Ardmore, Pa., 1966-69; pres. Thermo-Kinetic Corp., 1969-76; mem. firm Wagner, Leek & Mullins, 1976—; cons. in field; sr. v.p., gen. counsel Exec. Hills, Inc., Shawnee Mission, Kans., 1979—. Active Big Bros. of Tucson. Mem. Am., Mo., Kans., Johnson County bar assns., Kansas City Met. Bar Assn., Am. Mgmt. Assn., Sigma Alpha Epsilon, Phi Alpha Phi. Republican. Presbyn. Clubs: Skyline (Tucson), Country (Tucson); Carriage (Kansas City). Home: 8743 Riggs Ln Shawnee Mission KS 66212-1281 Office: 7101 College Blvd Ste 1100 Shawnee Mission KS 66210-1892*

BIGGS, JEFFREY ROBERT, educator; b. New Castle, Pa., May 2, 1941; s. Wallace Robert and Janice Erzinger B.; m. Janet Allen Mathews, May 24, 1969; children: Jennifer Mathews, Jessica Erzinger. BA, Harvard U., 1963; MA, Victoria U., Wellington, New Zealand, 1965; PhD, George Washington U., 1975. With U.S. Consulate Gen., Rio de Janeiro, 1976-78; attache U.S. Embassy, Lisbon, Portugal, 1978-81; dir., pres. bur. inter-Am. affairs Dept of State, Washington, 1981-84; deputy chief of mission Am. Embassy, La Paz, Bolivia, 1985-87; press sec. spkr. of house U.S. Ho. Reps., Washington, 1987-94; sr. advisor Office Nat. Drug Control Policy, Washington, 1995; dir. congl. fellowship program Am. Polit. Sci. Assn., Washington, 1997—. Co-author: Honor in the House: Speaker Tom Foley, 1999. Fulbright fellow, Wellington, New Zealand, 1964-65. Mem. Am. Polit. Sci. Assn., Diplomatic-Consulate Assn. Avocations: fly fishing, hiking, writing. Home: 6406 Kenhowe Dr Bethesda MD 20817 Office: Am Polit Sci Assn 1527 NewHampshire Ave NW Washington DC 20036

BIGGS, JOHN HERRON, insurance company executive; b. St. Louis, July 19, 1936; s. Peter Willis and Lillian (Herron) B.; m. Penelope Frances Parkman, June 13, 1959; 1 child, Henry. AB magna cum laude, Harvard U., 1958; PhD in Econ., Wash. U., 1983. V.p., contr. Gen. Am. Ins. Co., 1970-77; vice chancellor for adminstrn. and fin. Washington U., St. Louis, 1977-85; chmn., pres., chief exec. officer Centerre Trust Co., 1985-89; pres., COO Tchrs. Ins. and Annuity Assn./Coll. Retirement Equities Fund, 1989-93, chmn., pres., CEO, 1993—; bd. dirs. Boeing Co., Ralston Purina Co.; trustee Tchrs. Ins. and Annuity Assn./Coll. Retirement Equities Fund, 1982—; emeritus trustee, former pres. Mo. Bot. Garden; mem. Fin. Acctg. Found., N.Y.C. Partnership. Trustee Washington U., Getty Trust & Fgn. Policy Assn.; chmn. Nat. Bur. Econ. Affairs, Danforth Found., Ch. Pension Fund; bd. dirs., chmn. United Way of N.Y.C. Fellow Soc. Actuaries; mem. Am. Acad. Arts and Scis., Am. Acad. Actuaries (bd. dirs. 1970-73), Bus. Higher Edn. Forum, Westchester Country Club, Sky Club, Harvard Club N.Y., Log Cabin Club, St. Louis Club. Home: 240 E 47th St Apt 23D New York NY 10017-2137 Office: TIAA/CREF 730 3rd Ave New York NY 10017-3206

BIGGS, ROBERT DALE, Near Eastern studies educator; b. Pasco, Wash., June 13, 1934; s. Robert Lee and Eleonora Christine (Jensen) B. B.A. in Edn, Eastern Wash. Coll. Edn., 1956; Ph.D., Johns Hopkins U., 1962. Research asso. Oriental Inst., Univ. Chgo., 1963-64; asst. prof. Assyriology, 1964-67, asso. prof., 1967-72, prof., 1972—. Author: ŠA.ZI.GA: Ancient Mesopotamian Potency Incantations, 1967, Inscriptions from Tell Abu Salabikh, 1974, Inscriptions from al-Hiba-Lagash: The First and Second Seasons, 1976; co-author: Cuneiform Texts from Nippur, 1969, Nippur II: The North Temple and Sounding E, 1978; editor: Discoveries from Kurdish Looms, 1983; assoc. editor: Assyrian Dictionary, 1964-87; editor Jour. Near Ea. Studies, 1972—; mem. editorial bd. Assyrian Dictionary, 1995—. Fulbright scholar Univ. Toulouse, France, 1956-57; fellow Baghdad Sch., Am. Schs. Oriental Rsch., 1962-63, Am. Rsch. Inst. in Turkey, 1972. Mem. Am. Oriental Soc. (pres. Mid. Western br. 1978-79), Archaeol. Inst. Am. (pres. Chgo. soc. 1985-92), Brit. Sch. Archaeology Iraq. Office: U Chgo 1155 E 58th St Chicago IL 60637-1540

BIGGS, THOMAS WYLIE, chemical company executive; b. Seattle, Oct. 28, 1950; s. Ray Wylie and Mildred Virginia (Ramsey) B.; m. Marcia Jean Holts, Aug. 4, 1973; children: Jennifer Tamar, Jordan Wylie. BA, U. Wash., 1972. Chemisty tchr. Samammish High Sch, Bellevue, Wash., 1972-74; sales rep. Litton Industries, Seattle, 1974-75; sales rep. Van Waters & Rogers, Kent, Wash., 1975-80, area chem. mgr., 1988-90, br. mgr., 1990-94; nat. raw materials mgr. Van Waters & Rogers, Kirkland, 1995-97; field sales mgr. Van Waters & Rogers, Kent, Wash., 1980-85; sales mgr. Van Waters & Rogers, South Bend, Ind., 1985-86; mgr. chem. dept. Van Waters & Rogers, Indpls., 1986-88; comml. dir. internat. dept. URECO (subs. Royal Pakhoed Co.), 1997—. 1st lt. USAR, 1973-80. Mem. Chgo. Drug and Chem. Assn., N.W. Paint and Coating Assn., Nat. Petroleum Refiners Assn. Avocations: skiing, golf, travel, fishing. Office: Van Waters and Rogers 6100 Carillon Pt Kirkland WA 98033-7357

BIGHAM, JAMES GEORGE, structural engineer; b. Berwyn, Ill., Aug. 27, 1937; s. James Dellard Bigham and Gladys Marie Zahn. BSCE, U. Notre Dame, 1959. Registered profl. engr., Ill. Bridge engr. Ohio Hwy. Dept., Columbus, Ohio, 1959-62, Goodkind & Odea, Chgo., 1962-63; sales engr. Republic Steel Corp., Oak Park, Ill., 1963-65; structural engr. Army Corps. Engrs., Chgo., 1965-70, New Orleans, 1970-80, Rock Island, Ill., 1980-95; tutor Triton Coll., River Grove, Ill., 1998—; chmn. Sheet Pile Structures-Corps. Engrs., Rock Island, 1980-95. With U.S. Army, 1961. Mem. Structural Engrs. Assn. Ill. Roman Catholic. Avocations: jogging, gardening.

BIGHAM, WANDA RUTH, college president; b. Barlow, Ky., June 19, 1935; d. Herbert Martin and Ada Florene (Baker) Durrett; m. William M. Bigham, Jr., June 7, 1958; children: William M. III, Janet Kaye, Julia Lynn. BME, Murray State U., 1956; MM, Morehead State U., 1971, MHE, 1973; EdD, U. Ky., 1978; cert., Inst. For Ednl. Mgmt. -Harvard U., 1982; LittD (hon.), Loras Coll., 1989. Dir. TRIO programs Morehead (Ky.) State U., 1972-85, assoc. dean acad. affairs, dir. instructional sys., 1982-85, acting dean grad. and spl. acad. programs, 1984-85; exec. asst. to pres. Emerson Coll., Boston, 1985, v.p. for devel., 1986; pres. Marycrest Coll., Davenport, Iowa, 1986-92, Huntingdon Coll., Montgomery, Ala., 1993—. Bd. dirs. Asia-Pacific Fedn. Christian Schs., Internat. Assn. Meth.-Related Schs., Colls. and Univs., Coun. Ind. Colls., Ala. World Affairs Coun., Montgomery, 1994—, Montgomery Symphony Orch., 1993—, Ala. Shakespeare Festival, 1996—, NASCUMC, 1996—, also v.p.; exec. com. Univ. Senate United Meth. Ch., Ctrl. Ala. chpt. ARC, Montgomery, 1995, also v.p.; mem. Leadership Ala., 1994—; co-chair Quad Cities Vision for the Future, Davenport, 1987-92. Recipient Pres.'s award Davenport C. of C., 1988, Women of Spirit and Note award Cmty. Com. of Davenport, 1991, Hope for Humanity award Jewish Fedn. of QC, Rock Island, Ill., 1993; named to Alumni Hall of Fame, Morehead State U., 1988, Disting. Alumna, Murray State Coll., 1988. Mem. Am. Coun. on Edn. (mem. coun. of fellows, bd. dirs. 1994-97, fellow in higher edn. adminstrn. 1983-84), Internat. Assn. Univ. Pres., Montgomery C. of C., Sigma Alpha Iota (Sword of Honor 1956), Phi Kappa Phi, Kappa Delta Pi. Home: 1393 Woodley Rd Montgomery AL 36106-2435 Office: Huntingdon College 1500 E Fairview Ave Montgomery AL 36106-2148

BIGHAM, WILLIAM J., lawyer; b. Bryn Mawr, Pa., July 4, 1949; s. Robert H. and Regina (Schrandt) B.; m. Cindy K. Elkins, Aug. 12, 1972; children: Justin K., Joel M., Meredith E. BBA with honors, Siena Coll., 1971; JD with honors, Rutgers U., 1974. Bar: N.J. 1974, D.C. 1977, U.S. Ct. Appeals (3d cir.) 1983, U.S. Supreme Ct. 1985. Jud. law clk. to Hon. Samuel D. Lenox, Jr. Chancery Divisn. Superior Ct. of N.J., Trenton, N.J., 1974-75; mng. dir., shareholder Sterns & Weinroth, Trenton, 1975—. Mem. ABA, N.J. Bar, D.C. Bar, Mercer County Bar Assn. Roman Catholic. Office: 50 W State St Ste 1400 Trenton NJ 08608-1220

BIGLAN, ANTHONY, medical educator; b. Bklyn., June 6, 1944. BA in Psychology, U. Rochester, N.Y., 1966; MA in Social Psychology, U. Ill., 1968, PhD in Social Psycology, 1971. Rsch. assoc., instr. dept. psychology U. Wash., 1969-72; vis. asst. prof. psychology U. Oreg., 1973-74, asst. prof., 1974-78, rsch. asst., 1977-78; psychologist Behavior Change Ctr., Springfield, Oreg., 1977-82; rsch. scientist Oreg. Rsch. Inst., Eugene, Oreg., 1979—; bd. dirs. Pacific Rsch. Inst., 1992—, bd. chmn., 1994. Contbr. numerous articles to profl. jours. including Jour. Behavioral Medicine, Drugs and Society, The Analyst, others. Bd. dirs. ACLU of Oreg., pres., 1989-91. Nat. Inst. of Drug Abuse grantee, 1991—, Nat. Cancer Inst. grantee, 1995-2000. Home: 2324 W 28th Ave Eugene OR 97405-1426 Office: Oreg Rsch Inst 1715 Franklin Blvd Eugene OR 97403-1983*

BIGLER, HAROLD EDWIN, JR., investment company executive; b. N.Y.C., Apr. 27, 1931; s. Harold Edwin and Elizabeth Augusta (Cutler) B.; m. Lorinda Jennings Bailey, June 21, 1980; children by previous marriage: John Stephen, Diane Elizabeth Bigler Whatley, William Campbell. A.B., Brown U., 1953; M.B.A., Babson Inst., 1957; postgrad., Harvard U. Bus. Sch., 1975. Investment analyst Conn. Gen. Life Ins. Co., 1957-64, asst. sec., 1964, sec., 1964, 2d v.p., 1966-68; v.p. Securities Group, Hartford, 1968-81; chmn. C.G. Investment Mgmt. Co., Inc., 1975-81; pres., dir. Conn. Gen. Fund, Income Fund, Mcpl. Bond Fund, Money Market Fund, Companion Fund, Companion Income Fund, 1975-81; chmn. Bigler Investment Mgmt. Co.; chmn. bd. Bigler Ptnrs., Inc.; gen. ptnr. Crossroads Fund, Crossroads Capital Fund; dir. Conn. Water Service, Inc., Vantage Computer Systems, Inc., various CIGNA mutual funds; chmn. investment adv. com., State of Conn., 1972-78; mem. investment com. Brown U., Providence, R.I., 1968-80; former chmn. Conn. Higher Edn. Student Loan Authority; bd. dirs. New Eng. Asset Mgmt. Co. Inc.; bd. dirs. New Eng. Monthly, Inc. Served as lt. (j.g.) USN, 1953-55. Mem. Am. Council Life Ins. (chmn. securities investment com. 1972-76), Fin. Analysts Fedn. (dir. 1974-76), N.Y. Soc. Security Analysts, Hartford Soc. Fin. Analysts (pres. 1966-67), The Hartford Club, Hartford Golf Club, The Moorings Club (Vero Beach, Fla.). Republican. Home: 14 Thicket Ln West Hartford CT 06107-1320 Office: 190 Farmington Ave Farmington CT 06032-1713

BIGLEY, GEORGE KIM, JR., neurologist; b. Brawley, Calif., Oct. 28, 1951; s. George Kim and Carolyn (Goree) B. BA, U. Calif., San Diego, 1973; MD, U. Chgo., 1977. Diplomate Am. Bd. Psychiatry and Neurology. Intern U. Calif., San Diego, 1977-81, resident in neurology, 1978-81; asst. prof. U. Nev. Sch. Medicine, Reno, 1981-86, assoc. clin. prof., 1986—; practice medicine specializing in neurology Reno, 1986—; mem. bd. med. advisors Multiple Sclerosis Soc., N.Y.C., 1986—, vice-chmn. council profl. adv. com. chmn., 1988—. Bd. trustees No. Nat. Multiple Sclerosis Soc., Reno, 1987—. Mem. Am. Acad. Neurology. Office: Reno Neurol Assocs 85 Rivman Ste 303 Suite 201 Reno NV 89502

BIGLIN, KAREN EILEEN, library director; b. Hastings, Nebr., Apr. 23, 1954; d. James Eugene and Mary Ann (Truhlar) B.; m. Richard Jeffrey, Turnier, Aug. 4, 1979. BA, U. Ariz., 1976, MLS, 1978. Reference libr. No. Ariz. U., Flagstaff, 1978-80, sr. reference libr., 1980-84; reference libr. Tempe (Ariz.) Pub. Libr., 1984; circulation libr. Phoenix Coll., 1984-85; tech. svcs. libr. Scottsdale (Ariz.) C.C., 1985-93, libr. dir., 1993—, pres. faculty senate, 1994-95. Alice B. Good scholar U. Ariz., 1977. Mem. ALA, Ariz. Libr. Assn., Ariz. Online Users Group (pres. 1984-86), Phi Beta Kappa, Phi Kappa Phi, Beta Phi Mu. Avocation: scuba diving. Office: Scottsdale CC 9000 E Chaparral Rd Scottsdale AZ 85250-2614

BIGRAS, BERNARD, Canadian government official; b. Montreal, Que., Can., 1969. BS in Econs., U. Montreal. Chief coun. of the exec. coun. Que. Party of Gouin, 1988-89; treas. Zone of Rosemont; chief of the zone of Rosemont The Election of Benoit Tremblay, 1993; chief coun. of the exec. coun. Que. Block of Rosemont, 1994; dir. Camp du Oui, Rosemont, 1995; with The Nat. Bank, 1990-94; prin. spkr. on environ. and lasting devel. matters Que. Block, Rosemont, 1997; dep., parliament mem. Ho. of Commons, 1997, chmn. caucus, 1998—. Office: Ho of Commons, Edifice de la Confederation, Ottawa, ON Canada K1A 0A6*

BIGUM, RANDALL K. (RANDY), career officer; b. Lubbock, Tex., Dec. 11, 1949. BS in Bus., Ohio State U., 1973; student pilot tng., Williams AFB, Ariz., 1973-74; student F-4 pilot tng., 71st Tactical Fighter Squadron, MacDill AFB, Fla., 1974; student, USAF Fighter Weapons Sch., Nellis AFB, Nev., 1977; student F-15 pilot tng., 58th Tactical Tng. Wing, Luke AFB, Ariz., 1979; student, Squadron Officer Sch., 1980; M in Mil. Art and Sci., Army Command and Gen. Staff Coll., 1985; student, Nat. War Coll., 1993, Syracuse U., 1996. Commd. 2d lt. USAF, 1973, advanced through grades to brig. gen., 1998, various pilot assignments, 1974-77; weapons officer 59th Tactical Fighter Squadron, Eglin AFB, Fla., 1977-79, F-15 instr. pilot, 1979-80; various positions Nellis AFB, 1980-84; air ops. staff officer advanced program office Hdqs. Tactical Air Command, Langley AFB, Va., 1985-88, dep. chief. staff for requirements, 1985-88; ops. officer then comdr. 53rd Tactical Fighter Squadron, Bitburg Air Base, Germany, 1988-91; chief fighter devel. br. Office Undersec. Air Force Acquisition, Pentagon, Washington, 1991-92; comdr. 18th Ops. Group, Kadena Air Base, Japan, 1993-95; exec. officer to dep. comdr. in chief U.S. European Command, Stuttgart-Vaihingen City, Germany, 1995-97; comdr. 4th Fighter Wing, Seymour Johnson AFB, N.C., 1997—. Decorated D.F.C., Legion of Merit, Air medal with three oak leaf clusters, Small Arms Expert Marksmanship Ribbon. Office: 4FW/CC Ste 100 1510 Wright Brothers Ave Seymour Johnson AFB NC 27531-2468

BIHARY, JOYCE, federal judge; b. Detroit, Oct. 24, 1950; d. Paul and Edith (Uden) B.; m. Jonathan W. Lowe, Aug. 22, 1976; children: Jane, Alexis, James Byron. BA, Wellesley Coll., 1972; JD, U. Mich., 1975. Bar: Ga. 1975. Atty. Alston, Miller & Gaines, 1975-77; atty. Rogers & Hardin, 1977-79, ptnr., 1979-87; bankruptcy judge U.S. Dist. Ct., Atlanta, 1987—. Mem. ABA, Ga. Assn. Women Lawyers, Atlanta Bar Assn., Bar Coun. No. Dist. Ga., 11th Cir. Hist. Soc., Joseph Henry Lumpkin Am. Inn of Ct., Southeastern Bankruptcy Law Inst. Office: US Dist Ct US Courthouse 75 Spring St SW Atlanta GA 30303-3309

BIHLDORFF, JOHN PEARSON, hospital director; b. Boston, Aug. 3, 1945; s. Carl Birger and Martha Bowling (McCandless) B.; AB, Harvard U., 1969; MPH, Yale U., 1971; m. Jane Sargent Lyman, Mar. 30, 1968; children: Jennifer, Nathan, David. With McMaster U. Med. Ctr., Hamilton, Ont., Can., 1971-77, assoc. exec. dir., 1975-77; dir. program planning, asst. prof. divsn. med. adminstrn. Vanderbilt U. Med. Ctr. and Sch. Medicine, 1977-78; assoc. hosp. dir., COO U. Conn. Health Ctr.-John Dempsey Hosp., Farmington, Conn., 1978-81; asst. exec. dir. U. Conn. Health Center, Farmington, 1981-82, hosp. dir., 1982-86; pres., CEO St. Luke's Health Found. and Hosp., New Bedford Mass., 1986-91; pres., CEO Newton (Mass.)-Wellesley Hosp. and Newton-Wellesley Health Care Sys., 1991—; chmn. bd. dirs. VHA of Mass., Inc., 1995-97; chmn. bd. dirs. VHA Healthfront, 1995-97; bd. dirs. Tufts Assocs. Health Plan, 1994-96. Home: 107 Elm St Canton MA 02021-1255

BIJUR, ARTHUR WILLIAM, advertising executive; b. N.Y.C., Oct. 7, 1954; s. William Leopold and Hilda (Reis) B.; m. Judy D'Mello, May 22, 1994. BA in Psychology, Hobart Coll., 1977. Pres., exec. creative dir. Cliff Freeman and Ptrs., N.Y.C., 1986—. Recipient numerous advt. awards including Art Dir.'s Club, Clio's, Andy's and Effies, Cannes Lions. Democrat. Created and worked on many well-known advertising campaigns including "Where's the Beef?" for Wendy's Hamburgers, Staples, Little Caesars, Coca-Cola. Office: Cliff Freeman & Partners 375 Hudson St New York NY 10014-3658

BIJUR, PETER I., petroleum company executive; b. N.Y.C.; m. Anne Montgomery; children: Kristin Anne, Matthew Montgomery, David Barrett. BA in Polit. Sci., U. Pitts., 1964; MBA, Columbia U., 1966. Various dist. and regional sales positions Texaco, Inc., 1966-71, mgr. Buffalo sales dist., 1971-73, asst. to sr. v.p. for pub. affairs, 1973-75, staff coord. dept. strategic planning, 1975-77, asst. to exec. v.p. Buffalo sales dist., 1977-80; mgr. Rocky Mountain Refining & Mktg., 1980-81, asst. to chmn. bd., 1981-84; pres. Texaco Oil Trading and Supply Co., 1984, v.p. spl. projects, 1984-86; pres., chief exec. officer Texaco Can. Inc., Don Mills, Ont., 1987-89; chmn. Texaco Ltd., London, 1989-91; pres. Texaco Europe, 1990-92; sr. v.p. Texaco, Inc., White Plains, N.Y., 1992-96, vice chmn. bd., 1996, chmn. bd. dirs., CEO, 1996—; dir. Am. Petroleum Inst., Internat. Paper Co. Trustee Middlebury Coll., NYU Med. Ctr., Mt. Sinai Med. Ctr.; mng. dir. Met. Opera; bd. mgrs. N.Y. Botanical Garden. Fellow Inst. Petroleum, Royal Soc. Arts (London); mem. Bus. Coun., Bus. Roundtable, Conf. Bd., Nat. Petroleum Coun., Coun. Fgn. Rels., Country Club of New Canaan. Office: Texaco Inc 2000 Westchester Ave White Plains NY 10650-0002

BIKALES, NORBERT M., chemist, science administrator; b. Berlin, Jan. 7, 1929; came to U.S., 1946; s. Salomon and Bertha (Bander) B.; m. Gerda V. Bierzonski, Apr. 28, 1951; children: Marguerite Sarlin, Edward A. BS in Chemistry, CCNY, 1951; MS in Chemistry, Polytech. U., 1956; PhD in Chemistry, Poly. U., 1961. Rsch. chemist Am. Cyanamid Co., Stamford, Conn., 1951-62; tech. dir. Gaylord Assocs., Newark, 1962-65; pres. N.M. Bikales & Co., Cons., Livingston, N.J., 1965-76; prof. chemistry, dir. continuing edn. in scis. Rutgers U., New Brunswick and Newark, N.J., 1973-79; dir. polymers program NSF, Washington, 1976-95; head Europe office NSF, Paris, 1995—; trustee Gordon Rsch. Conf., 1990—. Editor Encyclopedia of Polymer Science and Technology, 1962-77; mem. editorial bd. Encyclopedia of Polymer Science and Engineering, 1982-90; contbr. articles to profl. jours., chpts. to books. Pres., Friends of Livingston (N.J.) Libr., 1968-72, Livingston Symphony Orch., 1970-76; judge Internat. Tech. Film '89 Festival, Pardubice, Czechoslovakia, 1989. Recipient award Twp. of Livingston, 1976, Great Medal City of Paris, 1985, Disting. Alumnus award Poly. U., Bklyn., 1986, Disting. Lectr. award Soc. Polymer Sci., Tokyo, 1986, Chevalier des Palmes Academiques award French Govt., 1993, Medal Polish Acad. Scis., 1997, Disting. Svc. award, NSF, 1999. Fellow AAAS, Am. Phys. Soc., N.Y. Acad. Sci.; mem. Am. Chem. Soc. (councilor 1987-89, chmn. polymer divsn. 1983), Internat. Union Pure and Applied Chemistry (titular mem., sec. 1979-87, 93-97, chmn. commn. on recycling of polymers 1993-98, fellow 1998—), Soc. Plastics Engrs. (sr., bd. dirs. 1979-82), Polish Chem. Soc. (hon.), Groupe Français des Polymeres (sci. counselor 1994—). Achievements include 26 patents in materials, chemicals and chemical processes. Office: NSF Am Embassy Paris Psc 116 Box A-211 APO AE 09777-5000 also: NSF Am Embassy, 2 Ave Gabriel, 75382 Paris Cedex 08, France

BIKEL, THEODORE, actor, singer; b. Vienna, Austria, May 2, 1924; came to U.S., 1954, naturalized, 1961; s. Josef and Miriam (Riegler) B.; m. Rita Weinberg, 1967. Student, U. London; grad., Royal Acad. Art, London, 1948; DFA (hon.), U. Hartford, 1992. Apprentice with Habimah Theatre, Tel Aviv, 1942-44, a founder, Tel Aviv Chamber Theatre, 1944-46; theatrical prodns. include A Streetcar Named Desire, London, 1950, The Love of Four Colonels, London, 1950-52, Tonight in Samarkand, N.Y.C., 1954, The Lark, N.Y.C., 1955-56, Rope Dancers, N.Y.C., 1957-58, Sound of Music, N.Y.C., 1959-61, Fiddler on the Roof, various cities, 1968-72, 74, 77, 79, 80, 82-83, 85, 87-96, 98, The Rothschilds (nat. co.), 1972, Jacques Brel is Alive and Well and Living in Paris, various cities, 1974-75, The Good Doctor, various cities, 1975, Zorba, various cities, 1976, 78, Inspector Gen., N.Y.C., 1978, Threepenny Opera, Mpls., 1983, My Fair Lady, Phoenix, 1988-89, She Loves Me, various cities, 1989-90, Sholom Aleichem Lives, 1997, The Disputation, Miami, 1999, The Gathering, N.Y.C., 1999; opera prodns. include La Gazza Ladra, Phila., 1990, Abduction from the Seraglio, Cleve., 1992, Ariadne auf Naxos, L.A. Opera, 1992; motion pictures include African Queen, 1951; The Little Kidnappers, 1951, The Enemy Below, 1957, I Want to Live, 1958, The Defiant Ones, 1958 (Academy award nomination), Blue Angel, 1959, My Fair Lady, 1964, Sands of the Kalahari, 1965, The Russians are Coming, 1966, Sweet November, 1967, My Side of the Mountain, 1969, Darker Than Amber, 1970, The Little Ark, 1971, See You in the Morning, 1989, Shattered, 1991, My Family Treasure, 1993, Crime and Punishment, 1993, Shadow Conspiracy, 1995, Second Chances, 1997; also numerous TV appearances, 1954—; star: TV prodns. The Eternal Light, 1958, Look Up and Live, 1958-60; host-editor: TV prodn. Directions 61, 1961; weekly radio program At Home with Theodore Bikel, 1958-63; concert folk singer, 1955—, rec. artist for, Elektra and Reprise; reader books on tape including The Hope (Herman Wouk), The Glory (Herman Wouk), The Name of the Rose (Umberto Eco); Author: Folksongs and Footnotes, 1960, (autobiography) Theo, 1994. Mem. Nat. Coun. for Arts, 1977-82; founder arts chpt. Am. Jewish Congress, 1961-63, nat. v.p., 1963-70, chmn. governing coun., 1970-80, sr. v.p., hon. chmn. 1980—; del. Democratic Nat. Conv., 1968. Recipient Emmy award, 1988, Lifetime Achievement award Nat. Found. for Jewish Culture, 1997. Mem. AFTRA, SAG, AGMA, Acad. TV Arts and Scis. (gov. 1961-65), AEA (councilor 1961-64, 1st v.p. 1964-73, pres. 1973-82, pres. emeritus 1982—), Am. Coun. Arts (bd. dirs. 1970—), Internat. Fedn. Actors (v.p. 1981-91), Associated Actors and Artists of Am. (pres. 1989—), Acad. Motion Picture Arts and Scis., Am. Fedn. Musicians. Address: Associated Actors & Artists of Am 165 W 46th St Ste 500 New York NY 10036-2501 *If I am a universalist-and I believe myself to be one-I derive my general standard of humanity from a particularist experience. For, above all and before all else, I am a Jew. That, to me, means a heightened awareness of the human condition and the sad-sweet knowledge that where we stand someone has stood before. It means a mode of living and a method of survival. Spiritually and culturally to be a Jew is to be a man on the road from Jerusalem to Jerusalem. I am an American; this is my home and my daily solace. Jerusalem, however, is my hope and my inspiration.*

BIKLEN, PAUL, retired advertising executive; b. Burlington, Iowa, Apr. 2, 1915; s. Fred Ludwig and Lydia (Ruckenbrod) B.; m. Anne Chenoweth, Dec. 30, 1939; children: Stephen C., Douglas P. Writer Gen. Electric Co., 1936-41; pub. relations dir. Kaiser Cargo Inc., Bristol, Pa., 1941-43; advt. exec. Fuller & Smith & Ross Inc., N.Y.C., 1947-52; v.p. N.W. Ayer & Son, N.Y.C., 1952-60; sr. v.p. Ogilvy & Mather, N.Y.C., 1960-72, mng. dir., Malaysia, 1973-75, dir. internat. tng., 1977-87. Author: (with Robert Breth) The Successful Employee Publication, 1946. Bd. dirs. Westport (Conn.) YMCA, 1953-56, Monadnock (N.H.) Hospice, 1993-96, Monadnock Family Svcs., 1997—; mem. Dublin (N.H.) Bd. Adjustment, 1978-86, Dublin Planning Bd., 1989-93. Lt. USN, 1943-45. Mem. Dublin Lake Club, Oriental Club (London). Home: Parsons Rd Dublin NH 03444-0297

BIKLEN, STEPHEN CLINTON, retired student loan company executive; b. Phila., Jan. 27, 1943; s. Paul Frederick and Anne (Chenoweth) B.; m. Britta Jorgensen Anderson, Oct. 21, 1989; children: Robert, Theodore. BA, Brown U., 1964; MBA, U. Pa., 1966. Auditor, acct. Coopers & Lybrand, N.Y.C., 1970-73; fin. analyst, contr. Citibank, N.Y.C., 1973-78; v.p. fin. Citibank N.Y. State, Rochester, 1978-80, bus. mgr. student loans, 1980-92, also bd. dirs.; pres., CEO, Student Loan Corp., Rochester, 1993-97, also bd. dirs.; mem. Nat. Adv. Com. on Student Fin. Assistance, Washington, 1988-96. Lt. USN, 1966-69. Mem. Consumer Bankers Assn. (chmn. edn. funding com. 1988-90, 94-97). Avocations: golf, tennis, stamp collecting.

BILANDIC, MICHAEL A., state supreme court justice, former mayor; b. Chgo., Feb. 13, 1923; s. Matthew and Domenica (Lebedina) B.; m. Heather Morgan, July 15, 1977; 1 son, Michael Morgan. JD, DePaul U., 1948. Bar: Ill. 1949. Master in chancery Cir. Ct. Cook County, Ill., 1964-67; spl. asst. to atty. gen., 1965-68; ptnr. Anixter, Bilandic & Pigott and predecessors, Chgo., 1963-77; acting mayor Chgo., 1976, mayor, 1977-79; ptnr. Bilandic, Neistein, Richman, Hauslinger and Young, Chgo., 1979-84; justice Ill. Appellate Ct., 1984-90, Ill. Supreme Ct., 1990—. Mem. Chgo. City Coun., 1969-76, chmn. com. on environ. control, 1970-74, chmn. fin. com., 1974-76. 1st lt. USMC, 1942-46. Mem. Am., Ill., Chgo. bar assns., Cath. Lawyers Guild. Democrat. Roman Catholic. Office: 160 N La Salle St Fl 20 Chicago IL 60601-3103

BILANIUK, OLEKSA MYRON, physicist, educator; b. Ukraine, Dec. 15, 1926; came to U.S., 1951, naturalized, 1957; s. Petro and Maria (Kunkevytch) B.; m. Larissa T. Zubal, Nov. 14, 1964; children: Larissa, Laada. Student, U. Louvain, 1947-51; M.S., U. Mich., 1953, M.A., 1954, Ph.D., 1957. Postdoctoral fellow U. Mich., 1957-58; rsch. assoc., asst. prof. U. Rochester, 1958-64; assoc. prof. physics Swarthmore Coll., 1964-70, prof., 1970-82, Swarthmore Centennial prof., 1982—; vis. scientist Argentine Atomic Energy Comm., Buenos Aires, 1961-62, Institut de Physique Nucléaire, Orsay, France, spring 1980, Laboratori Nazionali di Frascati, Italy, spring 1984, U. Munich, Germany, fall 1988; vis. prof., cons. Delhi U., summer 1966, Shivaji U., Kolhapur, India, summer 1969, Faculté des Scis., Rabat, Morocco, spring 1978, Kiev U. Ukraine, spring 1994, Inst. Med. Radiology, Kharkiv, Ukraine, summer 1996; Fulbright prof. Lima, Peru, summer 1971, Kinshasa, Zaïre, fall 1975. NSF fellow Max Planck Inst., Heidelberg, Germany, 1967-68, Inst. Physique Nucléaire, Orsay, 1972; NAS exch. scientist Kiev, Ukrainian SSR, 1976. Mem. Am. Phys. Soc., Nat. Acad. Scis. Ukraine, Ukrainian Acad. Arts and Scis. in U.S. (pres. 1998—), Schevchenko Sci. Soc. in U.S., European Phys. Soc., Société Française de Physique, Phi Beta Kappa, Sigma Xi. Research on nuclear structure; with Deshpande and Sudarshan challenged the view that Einstein's relativity precludes the possibility of existence of particles that travel faster than light, 1962. Office: Swarthmore Coll Dept Physics Swarthmore PA 19081 *The most cherished possession of humanity is its spiritual and intellectual heritage. Contributing to the enrichment of this heritage I consider to be a human's loftiest goal.*

BILBO, LINDA SUE HOLSTON, home health nurse; b. Poplarville, Miss., Mar. 20, 1955; d. Theo Gilmore Sr. and Dimple Bernice (Loveless) Holston; divorced; 1 child, Emily LeNore. Diploma, St. Dominic Sch. Nursing, 1976; postgrad., William Carey Coll., 1993-98, BSN, 1998. RN, Miss., La. RN staff nurse med.-surg. Bogalusa (La.) Med. Ctr., 1976-78, Lakeside Hosp., Metairie, La., 1978-80; RN staff nurse ICU/CCU Jo Ellen Smith Hosp., New Orleans, 1980-81; RN staff nurse surgery West Jefferson Hosp., Marrero, La., 1981-82; RN staff nurse home health South Miss. Home Health, Hattiesburg, 1982—; instr. BLS Am. Heart, Miss. Children's Sun. Sch. tchr. 1st Bapt. Ch., 1990-98; active PTA, Poplarville, Miss. 1985-97, Poplarville Band Booster, 1991-97. Named Nat. Essay Contest winner Am. Jour. Nursing, 1993, 94. Mem. Miss. Nurses Assn. Avocations: cooking, swimming, fishing. Home: PO Box 294 Poplarville MS 39470-0294 Office: South Miss Home Health PO Box 16929 Hattiesburg MS 39404-6929

BILBRAY, BRIAN P., congressman; b. Coronado, Calif., Jan. 28, 1951; m. Karen; 5 children. Supr.ctrl. and so. coastal regions San Diego County, Calif.; mem. now 106th Congress from 49th Calif. dist., 1994—; mem. commerce com.; mem. commerce, fin. & hazardous materials, health & environment, oversight & investigations coms. Avocations: sailing, surfing, horseback riding. Office: US Ho of Reps 1530 Longworth HOB Washington DC 20515-0549

BILBRAY, JAMES HUBERT, former congressman, lawyer, consultant; b. Las Vegas, May 19, 1938; s. James A. and Ann E. (Miller) B.; m. Michaelene Mercer, Jan. 1960; children: Bridget, Kevin, Erin, Shannon. Student, Brigham Young U., 1957-58, U. Nev., Las Vegas, 1958-60; BA, Am. U., 1962; JD, Washington Coll. Law, 1964. Bar: Nev. 1965. Staff mem. Senator Howard Cannon U.S. Senate, 1960-64; dep. dist. atty. Clark County, Nev., 1965-68; mem. Lovell, Bilbray & Potter, Las Vegas, 1969-87; mem. Nev. Senate, 1980-86, chmn. taxation com., 1983-86, chmn. interim com. on pub. broadcasting, 1983; 100th-103d U.S. Congresses from 1st Nev. dist.; mem. 100th-103rd Congresses from 1st Nev. dist., 1987-95; mem. fgn. affairs com., 1987-88, mem. house armed svs. com., subcom. procurement, mil. contracts, sea power, mem. small bus. com., chmn. procurement, taxation and tourism subcom., 1989-95; ptnr. Alcalde & Fay, Arlington, Va., 1995—; mem. Spl. Panel on NATO and North Atlantic Alliance, fgn. affairs com., select com. on hunger, 1987-88, select com. on aging, 1988-93, subcoms. Africa, trade exports and tourism, select com. on intelligence, 1993-95; alt. mcpl. judge City of Las Vegas, 1987-89; del. North Atlantic Alliance, 1989-95; bd. visitors U.S. Mil. Acad., West Point, 1995—, vice chmn., 1996-97; mem. adv. bd. Ex-Import Bank of U.S., 1996—. Bd. regents U. Nev. Sys., 1968-72; mem. Nat. Coun. State Govts. Commn. on Arts and Historic Preservation; mem. bd. visitors USAF Acad., 1991-93; mem. Dem. Nat. Com., 1996—. Named Outstanding Alumnus U. Nev., Las Vegas, 1979, Man of Yr. Am. Diabetes Assn., 1989, Man of Yr. Haddassah (Nev.), 1990. Mem. Nev. State Bar Assn., Clark county Bar Assn., U. Nev.-Las Vegas Alumni Assn. (pres. 1964-69, Humanitarian of Yr. 1984), Phi Alpha Delta, Sigma Chi, KC. Democrat. Roman Catholic. Lodges: Elks, Rotary.

BILBY, RICHARD MANSFIELD, federal judge; b. Tucson, May 29, 1931; s. Ralph Willard and Marguerite (Mansfield) B.; m. children: Claire Louise, Ellen M. Moore; m. Elizabeth Alexander, May 25, 1996. BS, U. Ariz., 1955; JD, U. Mich., 1958. Bar: Ariz. 1959. Since practiced in Tucson; law clk. to Chief Judge Chambers, 9th Circuit Ct. Appeals, San Francisco, 1958-59; mem. firm Bilby, Thompson, Shoenhair & Warnock, 1959-79, partner, 1967-79; judge U.S. Dist. Ct., Dist. Ariz., Tucson, 1979-96; chief judge U.S. Dist. Ct., Dist. Ariz., 1984-90, sr. judge, 1996—; conscientious objector hearing officer Dept. Justice, 1959-62; chmn. Pima County Med.-Legal panel, 1968-70; Mem. Tucson Charter Revision Com., 1965-70. Chmn. United Fund Profl. Div., 1968; chmn. Spl. Gift Div., 1970, St. Joseph Hosp. Devel. Fund Drive, 1970; Republican state chmn. Vols. for Eisenhower, 1956; Rep. county chmn., Pima County, Ariz., 1972-74; Past pres. Tucson Conquistadores; bd. dirs. St. Josephs Hosp., 1969-77, chmn., 1972-75. Served with AUS, 1952-54. Fellow Am. Coll. Trial Lawyers; mem. Ariz. Acad., Town Hall (dir. 1976-79). Office: US Dist Ct Rm 426 55 E Broadway Blvd Tucson AZ 85701-1711*

BILCHIK, GARY B., lawyer; b. Cleve., Dec. 7, 1945; s. Hyman M. and Leah (Gitleson) B.; m. Janice Rossen, Dec. 26, 1971; children: Susan, Steven. BBA, Ohio U., 1967; JD cum laude, Ohio State U., 1971. Bar: Ohio 1971, Fla. 1981. Atty., ptnr. Benesch, Friedlander, Coplan & Aronoff LLP, Cleve., 1981—. V.p. Jewish Family Svc., Cleve.; treas. Council Gardens, Cleve. Recipient Danzig Leadership award Jewish Family Svc., 1992. Mem. ABA, Ohio State Bar Assn., Cleve. Bar Assn. Democrat. Home: 25415 Letchworth Rd Cleveland OH 44122-4187 Office: Benesch Friedlander Coplan & Aronoff LLP 2300 American Rd Cleveland OH 44144-2301

BILDERBACK, GEORGE GARRISON, III, chemical dependency counselor; b. Portsmouth, Ohio, Jan. 11, 1964; s. George Garrison Jr. and Jane (Rhodes) B. BSBA in Mgmt. and Fin., Ohio No. U., 1986; BS in Employee Assistance, Franklin U., 1996; postgrad., U. Dayton, 1997—. Cert. Chem. Dependency Coun., Ohio Credentialing Bd.; registered counselor trainee, Ohio. Gen. mgr. Ohio No. U. WONU Radio, Ada, 1985; customer svc. specialist Nationwide Life Ins. Co., Columbus, Ohio, 1986-87, licensing and commn. specialist, 1987-88; rsch. analyst Wausau Ins. Co., Columbus, 1988-89; sr. mktg. specialist Nationwide Life Ins. Co., Columbus, Ohio, 1989-92; regional mktg. dir. Nationwide Life Ins. Co., Portsmouth, N.H., 1992; rsch. analyst Wausau Ins. Co., Columbus, 1988-89; registered rep. MML Investors Svcs., Inc., West Worthington, Ohio, 1993-94; jr. ptnr. Moyer Fin. Group, West Worthington, 1993-94; investment exec. Hamilton Investments Inc., Columbus, 1994-95; co-case mgr. Recovery Assistance, Inc., Westerville, Ohio, 1995-96; counselor Harding Hosp., Worthington, Ohio, 1996-97; intake coord. Stevens House, Columbus, Ohio, 1996-97; case mgr. The Alliance of Children and Family Svcs., 1996—, clin. coord., 1997-98; health info. specialist House of Hope, Inc., 1997—. Dir. local club Civitan Internat., Columbus, 1989-91, 1st v.p. programs, 1991-92, pres., 1994-95. Recipient Transfer Achievement award Franklin U., 1996. Mem. ACA, Employee Assistance Student Assn. (pres. 1996-97), Employee Assistance Profl. Assn. (newsletter editor 1996-98, sec. So. Ohio chpt. 1996—). Republican. Episcopalian. Avocations: golf, skiing, history, painting, reading. E-mail: ggb3@juno.com. Home: 2316 N High St Columbus OH 43202-2902 Office: House of Hope Inc 825 Dennison Ave Columbus OH 43215-1397

BILDERSEE, ROBERT ALAN, lawyer; b. Albany, N.Y., Jan. 22, 1942; s. Max U. and Hannah (Marks) B.; m. Ellen Bernstein, June 9, 1963; 1 child, Jennifer M. A.B., Columbia Coll., 1962, M.A., 1964; LL.B., Yale U., 1967. Assoc. Wolf Block Schorr & Solis-Cohen, Phila., 1967-72; sole practice, Phila., 1972-73; assoc., then ptnr. Fox Rothschild, O'Brien & Frankel, Phila., 1973-80; ptnr. Morgan Lewis & Bockius LLP, Phila., 1980-97; founding ptnr. Bildersee and Silbert, LLP, Phila., 1997—; lectr. Temple U. Sch. Law, Phila., 1978-91; asst. in instrn. Yale U. Law Sch., New Haven, 1966. Author: Pension Regulation Manual, Pension Administrator's Forms and Checklists, 1987; contbg. author: Employee Benefits Handbook, 1982—; editor: Beyond the Fringes; contbr. articles to profl. jours. Woodrow Wilson fellow, 1962. Mem. ABA, Pa. Bar Assn., Phila. Bar Assn. Avocation: wildlife photography. E-mail: erisaplus@aol.com. Office: Bildersee and Silbert LLP 1617 Jfk Blvd Ste 1111 Philadelphia PA 19103-1811

BILECKI, RONALD ALLAN, financial planner; b. Cin., July 15, 1942; s. Allan Frederick and Ruth H. (Parker) B.; m. Judy A. Newberry, Jan. 25, 1964; children: Sherry D. Pavan, Sean P. BA in Chemistry, Calif. State U., 1968. Cert. fin. planner; investment adv. rep. Ins. agt. N.Y. Life Ins., Covina, Calif., 1973-75; asst. mgr. N.Y. Life Ins., Los Angeles, 1975-79; pvt.

practice Rosemead, Calif., 1979-81; pres. Fin. Designs Corp., San Gabriel, Calif., 1981—; fin. planning cons. So. Calif. Edison, Rosemead, 1986—, So. Calif. Gas Co., 1991—, Capital Cities/ABC, 1991—. Mem. Gideons, Covina, 1987. Mem. Internat. Assn. Fin. Planning. Republican. Avocations: chess, jogging, hiking, western dancing. Office: Fin Designs Corp 7220 Rosemead Blvd Ste 206 San Gabriel CA 91775-1377

BILEK, ARTHUR JOHN, criminologist; b. Chgo., Oct. 21, 1929; s. Arthur John and Marcella Agnes (Nohren) B.; m. Angela Concetta Vignola, Oct. 23, 1954 (dec. Feb. 2, 1991); children: Mary Lucille Marcu, Arthur John Bilek III, Judy Ann, Mark Joseph; m. Ellen Holden Clark, Apr. 24, 1993. BS, Loyola U., 1951, MSW, 1953. Cert. protection profl. Chief of police Cook County, Chgo., 1962-67; prof., dept. chair U. Ill., Chgo., 1967-70; chmn. Ill. Law Enforcement Commn., Springfield, Ill., 1968-72; corp. dir. security and safety Hilton Hotel Corp., Beverly Hills, Calif., 1972-74; v.p. Pinkerton's Inc., N.Y.C., 1974-76; corp. dir. security CFS Continental, Chgo., 1976-77; v.p. First Nat. Bank of Chgo., 1978-88; assoc. dir. Northwestern U. Traffic Inst., Evanston, Ill., 1988-96; homicide investigator Cook County Sheriff's Police, Chgo., 1996-98; commr. Nat. Commn. on Criminal Justice, Washington, 1970-72; chmn. Nat. Pvt. Security Adv. Coun., Washington, 1972-74; vice chmn. Edn. and Tng. Sec. of Internat. Assn. Chiefs of Police, 1967-69. Editor: (textbook) Private Security, 1978; co-author: (textbook) Legal Aspects of Private Security, 1980. 1st lt. USAR, 1956-59. Recipient Award of Merit, Gov. of Ill., 1972. Fellow Am. Acad. Forensic Sci.; mem. Northwestern U. Traffic Inst. Alumni Assn., Internat. Banking Security Assn. (hon. mem., chmn. 1982-86). Roman Catholic. Avocations: study of myths and delusions, birding, nature photography. Office: Cook County Sheriff's Police Dept 1401 Maybrook Dr Maywood IL 60153-2414

BILELLO, JOHN CHARLES, materials science and engineering educator; b. Bklyn., Oct. 15, 1938; s. Charles and Catherine (Buonadonna) B.; m. Mary Josephine Gloria, Aug. 1, 1959; children: Andrew Charles, Peter Angelo, Matthew Jonathan. B.E., NYU, 1960, M.S., 1962; Ph.D., U. Ill., 1965. Sr. research engr. Gen. Telephone & Electronics Lab., Bayside, N.Y., 1965-67; mem. faculty SUNY, Stony Brook, 1967-87, asst. prof., 1967-71, assoc. prof., 1971-75, prof. engring., 1975-87, dean, 1977-81; dean Sch. Engring and Computer Sci., prof. mech. engring. Calif. State U., Fullerton, 1986-89; prof. materials sci. and engring., prof. applied physics U. Mich., Ann Arbor, 1989—; vis. prof. Poly. of Milan, 1973-74; vis. scholar King's Coll., London U., 1983; vis. NATO exchange scholar Oxford U., 1986; project dir. synchroton topography project Univ. Consortium, 1981-86; NATO vis. prof. Oxford (Eng.) U., 1998—. Assoc. editor Jour. Materials Sci. and Engring., 1984—. NATO sr. faculty fellow Enrico Fermi Center, Milan, Italy, 1973. Fellow Am. Soc. for Metals; mem. AIME, Am. Phys. Soc., Materials Rsch. Soc. Office: U Mich Dept Material Sci Engring Ann Arbor MI 48109

BILENAS, JONAS, mechanical engineer, educator; b. Kaunas, Lithuania, Dec. 2, 1928; came to U.S., 1949; s. Pranas and Jadvyga (Ambraziejus) B.; m. Dana Melynis, Apr. 17, 1955; children: Jonas V., Andrius R., Laura R. B in Mech. Engring., CCNY, 1955; diploma, Oak Ridge (Tenn.) Sch. Reactor Tech., 1957; PhD, CUNY, 1969. Registered profl. engr., N.Y. Engr. Babcock & Wilcox Co., N.Y.C., 1955-56, Oak Ridge (Tenn.) Nat. Lab., 1956-57; group head Am. Machine & Foundry Co., Greenwich, Conn., 1957-64; group head Grumman Aerospace Corp., Bethpage, N.Y., 1964-72, specialist infrared countermeasures (IRCM) tech., 1972-83, projects mgr. IRCM, 1983-93; retired, 1993; prof. CCNY and CUNY Grad. Ctr., N.Y.C., 1969—; part-time prof. mech. engring. SUNY, Stony Brook, 1988—; mem. program com. Nat. Infrared Countermeasures Symposia, 1990-93. Assoc. editor feature sect. The Engring. Word Jour., 1971—; reviewer of various publs. in field; contbr. articles to profl. jours. Chmn. bd. dirs. Lithuanian Cultural Ctr., Inc., Bklyn., 1995—; mem. platform planning com., del.-at-large Nat. Rep. Senatorial Com., Washington, 1993—. Nuc. scholar U.S. Atomic Energy Commn., 1956-57; recipient citation for infrared suppression advancement Army Sci. Adv. Panel, Carlisle Barracks, Pa., 1972, citation for OV-1 aircraft infrared program, Army Aviation Sys. Command, St. Louis, 1978; recipient best paper award 25th Ann. Infrared Countermeasures Conf., 1987. Mem. ASME (tech. com. on aero. and aerospace heat transfer 1974-80), NSPE, AIAA, Tau Beta Pi, Pi Tau Sigma. Achievements include patents and pioneering work in and devel. of infrared (IR) suppressors and IR countersurveillance equipment for U.S. Army OV-1D Mohawk aircraft, M1 Abrams battle tank, M2 Bradley fighting vehicle, mil. ground installations, and for the USAF Joint-STARS aircraft. Home: 75 Beaumont Dr Melville NY 11747-3431

BILES, CINDY CLEMENTE, academic administrator; b. Endicott, N.Y., July 28, 1954; d. Anthony Dominick and Angeline (DeVita) Clemente; m. Kevin Robert Biles. BS in Biology, SUNY, Binghamton, 1976; MS in Pathology, Duke U., 1979. Electron microscopy technician dept. anatomy Duke U., Durham, N.C., 1979-80, lab. technician dept. physiology, 1980-86; adminstrv. sec. dept. microbiology N.C. Meml. Hosp., Durham, 1986-90; adminstrv. sec. dept. physiology U. N.C., Chapel Hill, 1990-91, adminstrv. sec. dept. nutrition, 1991-92, adminstrv. mgr. Inst. Outdoor Drama, 1992—. Author, designer: Christmas Wishes, 1980; editor (newsletter) U.S. Outdoor Drama. Coord. Nat. Conf. Outdoor Drama, Nat. Outdoor Drama Auditions. Recipient awards for needlework design. Mem. Triangle Western Horseman's Assn. (numerous awards in horseback riding competitions). Avocations: riding and training horses, drawing, painting, reading. Office: U NC Inst Outdoor Drama CB #3240 Chapel Hill NC 27599-3240

BILES, JOHN ALEXANDER, pharmacology educator, chemistry educator; b. Del Norte, Colo., May 4, 1923; s. John Alexander and Lillie (Willis) B.; m. Margaret Pauline Off, June 19, 1943; children: Paula M. (Mrs. Patrick Murphy), M. Suzanne. B.S., U. Colo., 1944, Ph.D. (AEC fellow), 1949. Prof. pharm. chem. Midwestern U., 1949-50; asst. prof. pharm. chem. Ohio State U., 1950-52; asst. prof. pharm. chem. U. So. Calif., L.A., 1952-53, assoc. prof., 1953-57, prof., 1957-98, disting. emeritus prof., 1998—, dean, prof. pharm. scis., 1968-94, John Stauffer dean's chair in pharmacy, 1988-94, John Biles professorship, 1994—; bd. dirs. Marion Merrell Dow; cons. Allergan Pharms., 1953-68, Region IX Bur. Health Manpower Edn., Health Resources Adminstrn., 1973, Region X, 1974, Region VI, 1975, VA Ctrl. Office Pharmacy Svcs.; mem. Nat. Adv. Coun., Edn. for Health Professions, 1970-71, nat. study commn. on pharmacy, 1972-75; mem. adv. panel on pharmacy for study costs of educating profls. Nat. Acad. Scis., Inst. Medicine, 1973; mem. interdisciplinary tng. in health scis. com. Bur. Health Manpower Edn., 1972, post contrn. evaluation com., 1972, health facilities survey com., 1971; mem. adv. coun. Howard U. Coll. Pharmacy, 1985-90; bd. grants Am. Found. for Pharm. Edn., 1996—. Reviewer: Jour. of AMA, 1982-90. Bd. grants Am. Found. Pharm. Edn., 1996—, bd. dirs., 1999—, chmn. bd. grants 1998—; elder Presbyn. Ch., Pacific Palisades, Calif., 1997—. Recipient Lehn and Fink Scholarship award, 1945, S.C. Assos. award for excellence in teaching, 1962. Fellow Acad. Pharm. Scis., Am. Assn. Pharm. Scientists; mem. Am., Cal. Pharm. assns., Am. Cancer Soc. (mem. sci. adv. com. Los Angeles County), Am. Assn. Colls. Pharmacy (study commn. on pharmacy 1973-75, pres. 1990-91), Nat. Adv. Health Svcs. Coun. (bur. health svcs. rsch. 1974), Phi Kappa Phi. Office: U So Calif Sch Pharmacy 1985 Zonal Ave Los Angeles CA 90033-1039

BILES, (LEE) THOMAS, religious organization executive, clergyman; b. Louisville, July 18, 1942; m. Nancy Nanel; children: Stephen Ray, Deron Jay. BA, Howard Payne U., 1964; BD, Southwestern Bapt. Theol. Sem., Ft. Worth, 1967, MDiv, 1973. Ordained to ministry Bapt. Ch., 1962. Pastor Highland Crest Bapt. Ch., Green Bay, Wis., 1967-74, N.W. Bapt. Ch., Milw., 1979-88; dir. missions So. Bapt. Conv., Conn.-R.I., 1974-79; state missions dir. Minn.-Wis. So. Bapt. Conv., 1988-93; exec. dir. Tampa (Fla.) Bay Bapt. Assn., 1993—; moderator Ctrl. Bapt. Assn., Wis., 1969-71, Lakeland Bapt. Assn. Wis., 1981; pres. Minn.-Wis. Pastors and Wives Retreat, 1972, 82, Minn.-Wis. So. Bapt. Fellowship, 1972-73, 81-83. Recipient Disting. Alumni award for Minn. and Wis., Southwestern Bapt. Theol. Sem., 1982, 93, medal of svc. Howard Payne U., 1994. Avocations: jogging, sports, Middle East travel. Home: 4523 Pine Hollow Dr Tampa FL 33624-4547 Office: Tampa Bay Bapt Assn 1060 W Busch Blvd Tampa FL 33612-7707

BILEYDI, SUMER, advertising agency executive; b. Antalya, Turkey, Feb. 7, 1936; came to U.S., 1957; s. Abdurrahman M. and Neriman (Akman) B.; children: Can M., Sera N. BA, Mich. State U., 1961, MA, 1962. Mktg. cons. Export Promotion Ctr., Ankara, 1962; planner Gardner Advt. Agy., St. Louis, 1963-65; planning supr. Batten, Barton, Durstine & Osborn, N.Y.C., 1965-69; assoc. dir. Ketchum, Macleod & Grove, Pitts., 1969-73; sr. ptnr., dir. Carmichael Lynch, Inc., Mpls., 1974-91, sr. ptnr., 1992-98; pres. Manadans/D.W. Thompson, Istanbul, turkey, 1999—; cons. Carmichael-Lynch, Mpls., 1999—; cons. Leading Ind. Advt. Agy. Network, 1987-89, chmn., 1989-91. Contbr. articles to profl. jours. Pres. Turkish Am. Assn., 1974-75. Mem. Am. Mktg. Assn., Advt. Rsch. Found., Advt. Fedn. Minn., Min. Turkish Am. Club. Home: 16670 Baywood Ter Eden Prairie MN 55346-2422 Office: Carmichael Lynch Inc 800 Hennepin Ave Minneapolis MN 55403-1817 Overseas Office: Buyukdere Cad 191, Levent, 80509 Istanbul Turkey

BILEZIKJIAN, EDWARD ANDREW, architect; b. Los Angeles, Mar. 29, 1950; s. Andrew and Alice (Dardarian) B. BSArch, U. So. Calif., 1973, MArch, 1977. Registered architect, Calif. Project mgr. RMA Archtl. Group, Inc., Costa Mesa, Calif., 1977-78; dir. architecture Donald De Mars Assocs., Inc., Van Nuys, Calif., 1978-85; prin. architect EAB Architects, Sepulveda, Calif., 1985-87, Laguna Hills, Calif., 1988—; architect, planner III Trammell Crow Co., Irvine, Calif., 1986-88; prin. architect Fluor Daniel, Inc., Irvine, Calif., 1989—. Chmn. parish coun. Armenian Apostolic Ch. Newport Beach, 1988-91, 94-95. Mem. AIA, Triple-X Fraternity of Calif. (corresponding sec. 1984-85), Nat. Coun. Archtl. Registration Bds. (cert.). Democrat. Mem. Armenian Apostolic Ch.

BILFINGER, THOMAS VICTOR, surgeon, educator; b. Ridgewood, N.J., May 4, 1952; s. Victor Wilhelm and Heidi Erika (Muser) B.; m. Celia Betty Dameron; children: Elizabeth, Christine, Michael. MD, U. Zurich, Switzerland, 1978, ScD, 1979. Intern U. Chgo., 1980-81, rsch. fellow, 1981-82; resident in surgery U. Tex. Med. Br., Galveston, 1982-86, resident in cardiovascular surgery, 1986-88, instr. in surgery, 1988-89; asst. prof. surgery SUNY, Stony Brook, 1989-92, assoc. prof. surgery, 1992—; bd. dirs. cardiovascular intensive care unit SUNY, Stony Brook; rsch. assoc. Neurosci. Inst., SUNY, Old Westbury; sr. rsch. scientist Mind/Body Med. Inst., Harvard med. Sch., Mass.; mem. spl. populations rsch. dept. faculty NIDA, 1994—. Co-author: Evaluation of the Cardiac Surgical Candidate, 1992; mem. editl. bd. Advances in Neuroimmunology; guest editor: Inst. Jour. Cardiology, 1996, 98. Recipient Rsch. grant U. Chgo., 1981, Rsch. grant Eli Lilly, 1989, Rsch. grant NIH, 1991, Career Opportunity Rsch. Tng. award NIMH. Fellow ACS, Am. Coll. Cardiology, Am. Coll. Chest Physicians; mem. Assn. for Acad. Surgery, Soc. Critical Care Medicine, Swiss Soc. Thoracic and Cardiovasc. Surgery, Soc. Thoracic Surgery. Office: SUNY Stony Brook Health Sc Ctr T19 Rm 080 Stony Brook NY 11794

BILGER, BRUCE R., lawyer; b. Balt., Feb. 27, 1952. BA, Dartmouth Coll., 1973; MBA, JD, U. Va., 1977. Bar: Tex. 1977. Mem. Vinson & Elkins, L.L.P., Houston. Mem. Phi Beta Kappa. Office: Vinson & Elkins LLP 2300 First City Tower 1001 Fannin St Houston TX 77002-6760

BILHARTZ, JAMES ROHN, JR., independent oil producer; b. Dallas, Nov. 19, 1955; m. Mary Patricia Callahan, May 21, 1976; children: Jennifer Lauren, James Rohn Daniel III. BS in Petroleum Engring., Tex. A&M U., 1978. Petroleum engr. Tenneco Oil Co., Denver, 1978-80; bus. devel. Tenneco Oil Co., Houston, 1980-81; v.p. JRB Oil & Gas Co., Duncanville, Tex., 1981-93, sr. v.p., 1994—. Bd. trustees Duncanville Ind. Sch. Dist., 1991, v.p., 1992, sec., 1993, v.p. sch. bd., 1994, pres. sch. bd., 1995, 96; pres. Duncanville Ind. Sch. Dist. Found., 1996. Mem. Soc. Petroleum Engrs., Mid Continent Oil and Gas Assn., Tex. Ind. Royalty Producers Orgn. Roman Catholic. Office: JRB Oil & Gas Co 627 Mercury Ave Duncanville TX 75137-2235

BILIRAKIS, MICHAEL, congressman, lawyer, business executive; b. Tarpon Springs, Fla., July 16, 1930; s. Emmanuel and Irene (Pikramenos) B.; m. Evelyn Miaoulis, Dec. 27, 1959; children: Emmanuel, Gus. BS in Engring., U. Pitts., 1959; student, George Washington U., 1959-60; JD, U. Fla., 1963; JD (hon.), Stetson U.; hon. degree, U. Tampa. Bar: Fla. 1964; cert. coll. tchr., Fla. Atty., small businessman Pinellas and Pasco Counties, Fla., 1968—; mem. 98th-104th Congresses from 9th Dist. Fla., 1983—; mem. energy and commerce com., veterans affairs com. Mem. Rep. Task Force on Social Security; co-chmn. Task Force on Infant Mortality; founder, charter pres. Tarpon Springs Vol. Ambulance Service; dir. Greek Studies program U. Fla.; dir. emeritus Juvenile Diabetes and Hospice; mem. Pres.' Coun. U. Fla. Sgt. USAF, 1951-55. Named Citizen of Yr. Greater Tarpon Springs, 1972-73, Man of Yr. United Way, 1989-90. Mem. Am. Legion (comdr. 1977-79), VFW, Amvets, USAF Sgts., NCOA, Air Force Assn., Greater Tarpon Springs C. of C. (past pres., dir.), Pinellas C. of C. (gov.), West Pasco Bar Assn., Am. Judicature Soc., Fla. Bar Assn., Gator Boosters, Fla. Blue Key (hon.), Mason (33 degree), Shriner, Jester, Moose, Elks, Rotary, Eastern Star, Phi Alpha Delta, Sigma Pi. Greek Orthodox. Lodges: Masons; Shriners; Moose; Tarpon Springs Rotary; Elks; Eastern Star; White Shrine of Jerusalem. Office: US Ho of Reps 2369 Rayburn House Ofc Bldg Washington DC 20515*

BILJETINA, RICHARD, natural gas industry executive; b. Austria, Apr. 2, 1947; U.S. citizen, 1959; m. Mary Patricia McCarthy, Oct. 18, 1969; children: Eric, Christine. BSChemE, Ill. Inst. Tech., 1969; MBA, U. Chgo., 1974. From mem. staff to mgr. R & D Inst. Gas Tech., Chgo., 1969-89, asst. v.p., 1989-92, v.p. product tech. R & D, 1992-95, v.p. mktg., 1995—. Contbr. articles to profl. jours. Mgr. Little League, Skokie, Ill., 1978-85; scout master Boy Scouts Am., Skokie, 1980-83. Mem. Automatic Meter Reading Assn., Internat. Assn. Energy Economists. Achievements include patent for novel anaerobic digester.

BILKA, PAUL JOSEPH, physician; b. N.Y.C., Oct. 12, 1919; s. John and Josephine (Hlavaty) B.; m. Madge Ayres Mussey, Dec. 26, 1943. B.S., Trinity Coll., Hartford, Conn., 1940; M.D., Columbia U., 1943; M.S. in Medicine, U. Minn., 1950. Intern Hartford Hosp., 1944-45; fellow in internal medicine Mayo Found, Rochester, Minn., 1947-50; asst. in rheumatology Mayo Clinic, 1949-50; practice medicine specializing in rheumatology Mpls., 1950-91; ret.; clin. prof. medicine U. Minn. Med. Sch.; cons. Mpls. VA Hosp. Author numerous papers in field; also producer films on rheumatology. Served to capt. M.C. AUS, 1945-47. Mem. Am. Coll. Rheumatology (master designation 1992), Nat. Soc. Clin. Rheumatology (pres. 1985-87). Club: Lafayette (Minnetonka, Minn.). Home: 4384 Manitou Rd Excelsior MN 55331-9445

BILL, KAREN S., actress; b. Annapolis, Md., Feb. 22, 1951; d. Charles A. and Orel M. (Heinly) B. BS cum laude, Millersville U., 1973; MEd, Kutztown U., 1976. Tchr. Ephrata (Pa.) Area Sch. Dist., 1973-85; edni. cons. Scribner Educational Pubs. div. Macmillan Pubs., Delran, N.J., 1985-87; telemation and news coord. Sta. WGAL-TV, Lancaster, Pa., 1986-87; actress in indsl. and ednl. tng. videos, 1984—. Appeared in plays including For the Love of Ike, Jacques Brel Is. . ., Carousel, Joseph and the Amazing Technicolor Dreamcoat, Gypsy, The King and I, Annie, Here's Love, Cabaret, Stop the World!, The Roar of the Greasepaint, The Play, Our Town, Sweet Charity, The Philadelphia Story; films include Silence At Bethany, The Whole Truth, Superfights, (film) Girl, Interrupted; TV appearances in commls., news, voice-overs; radio appearances include commls. and voice-overs. Mem. Theater Assn. Pa. Avocation: collecting soundtrack music.

BILL, TONY, producer, director; b. San Diego, Aug. 23, 1940. Student, Notre Dame U. Founder Bill/Phillips Prodns. (with Julia and Michael Phillips), 1971-73; ind. producer, 1973—; bd. govs. Acad. Motion Picture Arts and Scis. Prodr.: Deadhead Miles, Steelyard Blues, 1973, The Sting, 1973, The Sting, 1974, Going in Style, 1979, Hearts of the West, 1975, Harry and Walter Go to New York, 1976, Boulevard Nights, 1979; exec. producer: The Little Dragons, 1978; dir.: The Ransom of Red Chief, 1977, My Bodyguard, 1980, Six Weeks, 1982, Love Thy Neighbor, 1984, Five Corners, 1987, Crazy People, 1990, Untamed Heart, 1993, A Home of Our Own, 1993, Next Door, 1995, Beyond the Call, 1996, Oliver Twist, 1997. Office: Barnstorm Films 73 Market St Venice CA 90291-3603

BILLARD, WILLIAM THOMAS, insurance company executive; b. Peru, Ill., May 14, 1946; s. George Max and Mildred Jean (Kincheski) B.; m. Janice Kay Metcalfe, Aug. 29, 1970; children: Rachelle Lynn, Kimberly Dawn, Bethany Kaye. AA, Ill. Valley Community Coll., 1966; BS in Actuarial Sci., U. Ill., 1969. Asst. mgr. group actuarial CNA Ins. Co., Chgo., 1969-75; dir. actuarial svcs. Delta Dental Plan of Mich., Lansing, 1975-79, v.p., actuary, 1979—; chmn. actuarial com. Delta Dental Plans Assn., Chgo., 1976-80, 84-89, 96—; cons. Delta Dental Plans in Ark., Ind., Kans., Mass., Ohio, Okla., Tenn., Va., Wis., Idaho, Ky., Mo., 1986—. Contbr. articles to profl. publs. Pres. Great Lakes Gymnastics Booster Club, Lansing, 1981-82; coach Okemos (Mich.) Athletic Klub, 1982-89; worker Habitat for Humanity, Lansing-Kalamazoo, 1986—; elder Presbyn. Ch., Okemos, 1987-90; trustee, mem. sch. bd. Lansing Christian Schs., 1992-95, pres., 1994-95. Mem. Am. Acad. Actuaries, Mich. Actuarial Soc., West Mich. Actuarial Club (pres. 1988-96), Walnut Hills Country Club. Avocations: softball, genealogy, golf, singing, weight lifting. Home: 3901 Highwood Pl Okemos MI 48864-3790 Office: Delta Dental Plan of Mich PO Box 30416 Lansing MI 48909-7916

BILLAU, ROBIN LOUISE, engineering and consulting executive; b. Denver, Sept. 19, 1951; d. Emerson Roy and Catherine Louise (Brewster) Billau; m. Edward E. Adams. BA, Western State Coll., 1973; MS, Colo. State U., 1977. Cert. indsl. hygienist. Life sci., indsl. hygienist Mont. Energy Devel. & Rsch. Inst., Butte, 1977-79; indsl. hygiene supr. Mountain States Energy, Butte, 1979-81; asst. prof. Mont. Coll. Mineral Sci. Tech., Butte, 1981-83; indsl. hygiene supr. EG & G Idaho, Idaho Falls, 1983-85, unit mgr., 1985-87, group mgr., 1987-88, sr. tech. adv., 1988-90; cons. environ. mgmt., indsl. hygiene RLB Cons., Inc., Houghton, Mich., 1990-92; mgr. Jason Assocs. Corp., Idaho Falls, Idaho, 1992-94, Lockheed Martin Environ. Systems, Pocatello, Idaho, 1994-95; cons. environ. health and safety Bozeman, Mont., 1996—. Mem. Am. Indsl. Hygiene Assns., Am. Bd. Indsl. Hygiene Idaho Am. Indstl. Democrat. Avocations: skiing, gardening, raising worms and poultry, mountain biking, reading. Home and Office: 174 Quinn Creek Rd Bozeman MT 59715-9635

BILLAUER, BARBARA PFEFFER, lawyer, educator; b. Aug. 9, 1951; d. Harry George and Evelyn (Newman) Pfeffer. BS with honors, Cornell U., 1972; JD, Hofstra U., 1975; MA, NYU, 1982; cert. in risk scis. and pub. policy, Johns Hopkins U., 1999. Bar: N.Y. 1976, Fed. Dist. Ct. N.Y. 1977, U.S. Ct. Appeals (2d cir.) 1978, U.S. Supreme Ct. 1984. Assoc. Bower & Gardner, N.Y.C., 1974-78; sr. trial atty. Joseph W. Conklin, N.Y.C., 1978-80; assoc. dept. head Curtis, Mallet-Prevost, Colt & Mosle, N.Y.C., 1980-82; ptnr. Anderson, Russell, Kill & Olick, N.Y.C., 1982-86, Stroock & Stroock & Lavan, N.Y.C., 1986-90; ptnr., chair environ. and toxic tort practice Keck, Mahin, Cate & Koether, 1990-93; prin. Barbara P. Billauer & Assocs., Lido Beach, N.Y., 1993—; vis. scholar Johns Hopkins U. Sch. Pub. Health, 1998-99; faculty SUNY Stony Brook Med. Sch.; adj. assoc. prof. NYU Grad. Sch., 1982-88; lectr. Rutger's U. Med. Sch.; jud. screening com. Coordinated Bar Assn., 1983-86; mem. spl panel Citywide Ct. Adminstrn. 1982-85; bd. dirs. Weizmann Inst., Am. Com. Co-author: The Lender's Guide to Environmental Law: Risk and Liability, 1993. Fellow Am. Bar Found.; mem. AAAS, ABA (comml. leasing sect. indoor air polution 1990-93), Met. Womens Bar Assn. (v.p. 1981-83, pres. 1983-85, chmn. bd. 1985-87), Nat. Conf. Womens Bar Assn. (bd. dirs., v.p. 1989-95), Internat. Coun. Shopping Ctrs. (environ. com.), Am. Soc. Microbiology, Brit. Occupl. Hygiene Soc., N.Y. Acad. Scis., Am. Soc. Safety Engrs. Environment Personal Injury, Toxic Torts. Office: 146 Eva Dr Lido Beach NY 11561-4818

BILLECI, ANDRE GEORGE, art educator, sculptor; b. N.Y.C., Dec. 2, 1933; s. Salvatore Daniel and Rosaria Grace (Turco) B.; m. Carol Loretta Farinola, Sept. 1, 1956; children—Andrew, John. B.F.A. cum laude, SUNY-Alfred, 1960, M.F.A., 1961. Instr., SUNY Coll. Ceramics-Alfred, 1961-69, asst. prof., 1969-71, assoc. prof., 1971-82, prof. art, 1982-89, prof. emeritus, 1989—; cons. Steuben Glass, N.Y., 1974, Royal Coll. Art, London, 1975, Mary McFadden Inc., N.Y.C., 1978, cons. for India travel/rsch. Corning Mus., 1986, 87, 97, Vitras. s.a., Quetzaltenango, Guatemala, 1988, Argucia & Martinez Crafts, Tegucigalpa, Honduras, 1989, UNICEF, Herat, Afghanistan, 1993, Valley Forge Industries, Harare, Zimbabwe, 1996; award panelist N.Y. State Found. for Arts, 1989; guest speaker 1st Internat. Symposium on Glass Edn., La Granja, Segovia, Spain, 1990; guest lectr. Found for Glass, Barcelona, Spain, 1990. One-man shows include: Am. House Gallery, N.Y.C., 1971, Mus. Contemporary Crafts, N.Y.C., 1970, Corning Mus. Glass, N.Y., 1972, Pilkington Glass Mus., St. Helen's Lancashire, Eng., 1973; represented in permanent collections Nat. Galleries de Prague, Czechoslovakia, Australian Nat. Gallery, Canberra, Mus. Kunsthandwerk, Frankfurt, W.Ger., Lannin Found., Palm Beach, Fla.; commissions include Penn Mutual Life, 1983, E.I. DuPont de Nemours Co., 1985. NSF Travel grantee, India, 1986, research grantee Inst. Glass Sci. and Engring., Greece, 1987. Mem. Internat. Commn. on Glass (com. XVII 1985), Inst. Glass Sci. and Engring., Am. Ceramic Soc., Internat. Sculpture Ctr., AAUP. Home: 801 Islamorada Blvd Punta Gorda FL 33955-1862 Office: SUNY Coll Ceramics Alfred NY 14802

BILLER, GERALDINE POLLACK, curator; b. Milw., Apr. 4, 1933; d. Sidney Samuel and Frieda (Eisenberg) Pollack; m. Joel Wilson Biller, May 1, 1955; children: Sydney Ellen, Andrew John, Charles Benjamin. BS, Northwestern U., 1955; MA, U. Wis., 1991. Tchr. art Va. Sch. System, 1955-56, Internat. Sch., The Hague, The Netherlands, 1959-62; adminstr. internat. rels. program Georgetown U., Washington, 1973-75; freelance graphic designer Washington, Milw., 1978-86; art historian, ind. curator, 1988—; guest curator Latin Am. Women Artists 1915-1995, Milw. Art Mus. pres. bd. dirs. Jewish Family Svcs., Milw., 1991-94, life bd. mem.; bd. mem. Family Svc. Am., Inc., 1998-2000. Home and Office: 4716 N Wilshire Rd Milwaukee WI 53211-1262

BILLER, JOEL WILSON, lawyer, former foreign service officer; b. Milw., Jan. 17, 1929; s. Saul Earl and Mildred (Wilson) B.; m. Geraldine Pollack, May 1, 1955; children—Sydney, Andrew, Charles. B.A., U. Wis., 1950; J.D., U. Mich., 1953; M.A., Northwestern U., 1959. Bar: Wis. 1953. Atty. Milw., 1953-55; vice consul Am. consulate, Le Havre, France, 1956-58; econ. officer Am. Embassy, The Hague, Netherlands, 1959-62; internat. relations officer State Dept., Washington, 1962-66; econ. officer, asst. dir. AID mission, Quito, Ecuador, 1966-69; econ. counselor Am. embassy, Buenos Aires, Argentina, 1969-71; dir. AID mission, Santiago, Chile, 1971-73; spl. asst. to undersec. state for econ. affairs Washington, 1973-74; spl. asst. to dep. sec. state, 1974, dep. asst. sec. state for comml. and spl. bilateral affairs, 1974-76, dep. asst. sec. state for transp., telecommunications and comml. affairs, after, 1976; sr. v.p. Manpower Inc., Milw., 1979-97, sr. v.p., gen. counsel, 1997-98; pvt. practice bus. cons., 1999—. Mem. Am. Fgn. Service Assn., Wis. Bar Assn. Office: Manpower Inc 5301 N Ironwood Rd PO Box 2053 Milwaukee WI 53201-2053

BILLER, JOSE, neurologist; b. Montevideo, Uruguay, Jan. 18, 1948. B in Medicine, A.V. Acevedo Inst., Montevideo, Uruguay, 1965; MD, U. de la Republica, Montevideo, Uruguay, 1974. Diplomate Am. Bd. Psychiatry and Neurology (bd. dirs. 1994—). Intern Columbus Hosp., Chgo., 1976-77; resident neurology Henry Ford Hosp., Detroit, 1977-78; resident neurolgy Loyola U. Hosp., Maywood, Ill., 1978-80; fellow cerebral vascular diseases Bowman Gray Sch. Med., Winston Salem, N.C., 1980-81; asst. prof. neurology Loyola U., Chgo., 1982-84; asst. prof. neurology U. Iowa Coll. Medicine, Iowa City, 1984-87, assoc. prof. neurology, 1987-90, prof. neurology, 1990-91; prof. Northwestern Sch. Medicine, Chgo., 1991-94; dir. stroke program, dir. acute stroke care unit Northwestern Meml. Hosp., Chgo., 1991-94; prof., chmn. dept. neurology Ind. U., 1994—; prof. adhonorem U. of the Republic Sch. of Medicine, Uruguay, 1997—; mem. editl. bd. Stroke, Stroke-Clin. Update, Journal of Stroke and Cerebrovascular Disease, Neurol. Rsch.; Internat. bd. editors: CNS Drugs; cons. physician neurology svc. VA Hosp., Iowa City, 1984-91, staff physician Northwestern Meml. Hosp., Chgo., 1991-94; neurology cons. Rehab. Inst. Chgo., 1991-94; active med. staff Ind. U. Hosps., 1994—, cons. Roudebush VA Med. Ctr., 1994—. Author, co-author of more than 350 articles, book chpts., abstracts; 6 edited books. Fellow ACP, Am. Acad. Neurology, Stroke Coun. Am. Heart Assn.; mem. AMA, N.Y. Acad. Sci., Am. Soc. for Neurology Investigation, Internat. Stroke Soc., Inter-Am. Coll. Physicians and Surgeons, Am. Neurolog. Assn., Am. Heart Assn., Argentinian Neurol. Soc. (hon.), Uruguayan Neurol. Soc. (hon.). Office: Ind U Sch of Medicine Dept

Neurology Emerson Hall 545 Barnhill Dr # 125 Indianapolis IN 46202-5112

BILLER, MORRIS (MOE BILLER), union executive; b. N.Y.C., Nov. 5, 1915; m. Anne Fiefer, Aug. 24, 1940 (dec.); children: Michael, Steven; m. Colee Farris, Jan. 1987. Student, Bklyn. Coll., 1936-38, CCNY, 1946. With U.S. Postal Svc., 1937-92; active Am. Postal Workers Union, Washington, 1937—, N.E. regional coord., 1972-80, pres., 1980—; gen. pres. Manhattan-Bronx Postal Union (N.Y. Metro Area Postal Union), 1959-80; mem. exec. coun. AFL-CIO; bd. dirs. Union Labor Life Ins., Co.; exec. v.p. pub. employee dept. AFL-CIO; pub. mem. fed. adv. council occupational safety and health Dept. Labor. Bd. dirs. Assn. Children with Retarded Mental Devel., United Way Internat.; adv. bd. Cornell U. Trade Union Women Studies Program; adv. council Empire State Coll.; nat. bd. dirs., fed. thrift adv. council A. Philip Randolph Inst.; nat. labor chairperson March of Dimes Telethon; v.p., Muscular Dystrophy Assn. With AUS, 1943-45, ETO. Recipient Disting. Service award N.Y.C. Central Labor Council, 1977; recipient Community Service award N.Y.C. Central Labor Council, 1979, Spirit of Life award City of Hope, 1982, Walter P. Reuther Meml. award Ams. for Democratic Action, 1982. Mem. Combined Fed. Campaign (exec. com.), N.Y.C. Central Labor Council (exec. bd dirs.), Central Labor Council (bd. dirs. central rehab.), Coalition Labor Union Women, Postal, Telegraph and Telephone Internat. (mem. exec. com.), NAACP, A. Philip Randolph Inst. Office: Am Postal Workers Union 1300 L St NW Washington DC 20005-4107*

BILLET, DONALD FRANKLIN, civil engineer, consultant; b. York, Pa., May 26, 1929; s. George Victor and Edna Mae (Daron) B.; m. Joe Ann Moore, May 25, 1955. B in Civil Engring., Syracuse (N.Y.) U., 1951; MS, U. Ill., 1953. Registered profl. engr., Pa., S.C., Ga. Mem. C.E. Corps, USN, 1953-79; civil engr., v.p. Sea Island Engring., Inc., Hilton Head Island, S.C., 1979-89; project design engr. for water and sewer sys. Hussey, Gay, Bell & De Young, Inc., Savannah, Ga., 1989—. Author: Genealogy of Jacob Dellinger, 1733 Immigrant to Pa., 1993, and Billet and Related Families of York, Lancaster and Dauphin Counties, Pa., 1751-97, 1998. Comdr. USN, 1953-79. Mem. SAR (registrar Dr. Mosse chpt. Hilton Head Island 1992-98). Office: Hussey Gay Bell & DeYoung Inc 329 Commercial St Savannah GA 31416

BILLETER, ROBERT JAMES, newspaper publisher; b. Clarksburg, W.Va., Aug. 16, 1926; s. Arch and Mabel Edith (Westfall) B.; m. Eileen Billie Horvath, Apr. 14, 1972; 1 child, William Fletcher. BS, W.Va. U., 1951. Editor Pendleton Times, Franklin, W.Va., 1951-53; copy editor Herald-Dispatch, Huntington, W.Va., 1953-54; reporter The Post, Morgantown, W.Va., 1954-56; copy editor Sun-Telegraph, Pitts., 1956-60; copy editor Post-Gazette, Pitts., 1960-81, night city editor, 1981-85, makeup editor, 1985-91; pub. The Weston (W.Va.) Democrat, 1992—. With U.S. Army, 1945-47. Episcopalian. Avocations: wine tasting, sailing, hiking, skiing. Home: One E 4th St Weston WV 26452 Office: The Weston Democrat 306 Main Ave Weston WV 26452

BILLIAS, GEORGE ATHAN, history educator; b. Lynn, Mass., June 26, 1919; s. Athan O. and Grace (Papadakis) B.; m. Joyce Baldwin, Dec. 28, 1948 (dec.); children: Stephen, Athan, Nancy; m. Margaret Neussendorfer, Aug. 17, 1986. BA magna cum laude, Bates Coll., 1948; MA, Columbia U., 1949, PhD, 1958. Nat. def. historian USAF, 1951-54; instr. U. Maine, 1954-57, asst. prof., 1957-59, assoc. prof., 1959-62; assoc. prof. Clark U., Worcester, Mass., 1962-66; prof. Am. history Clark U., 1966—, Jacob and Frances Hiatt prof. history, 1983-89, Jacob and Frances Hiatt prof. emeritus, 1989—. Author: Massachusetts Land Bankers of 1740, 1959, General John Glover and His Marblehead Mariners, 1960, Elbridge Gerry: Founding Father and Republican Statesman, 1976; editor, contbr.: George Washington's Generals, 1964, Law and Authority in Colonial America: Selected Essays, 1965, The American Revolution: How Revolutionary Was It?, 1965, 4th edit., 1989, Interpretations of American History: Patterns and Perspectives, 2 vols., 1967, 6th edit., 1992, George Washington's Opponents, 1969, The Federalists: Realists or Ideologues?, 1970, American History: Retrospect and Prospect, 1971, Perspectives on Early American History, 1973, American Constitutionalism Abroad, 1990, The Republican Synthesis Revisited: Essays in Honor of George Athan Billias, 1992, George Washington's Generals and George Washington's Opponents, 1993; contbr. numerous articles to profl. jours. With M.C., U.S. Army, 1941-46, ETO. Decorated Bronze Star; Am. Philos. Soc. grantee, 1965; Guggenheim fellow, 1961-62, Am. Coun. Learned Socs. fellow, 1968-69, NEH fellow, 1970-71, 79, 86, Huntington Libr. fellow, 1989-90. Mem. Columbia Seminar in Early Am. History, Inst. Early Am. History and Culture (coun. 1969-72), Am. Hist. Soc., Mass. Hist. Soc., Am. Antiquarian Soc. (honoree symposium and essays volume in field Am. Revolution, The Republican Synthesis Revisited 1989), Phi Beta Kappa. Office: Clark U Dept History Worcester MA 01610

BILLICK, BRIAN, professional football coach; b. Fairborne, Ohio, Feb. 28, 1954; m. Kim Billick; children: Aubree, Keegan. Student, Brigham Young U. Mem. Dallas Cowboys, 1977; asst. coach U. Redlands, 1977-78; grad. asst. Brigham Young U., Provo, Utah, 1978; asst. dir. pub. rels. San Francisco 49ers, 1979-80; coach receivers, tight ends, quarterbacks San Diego State U., 1981-85; offensive coord. Utah State U., 1986-88; asst. coach Stanford (Calif.) U., 1989-91; offensive coord. Minn. Vikings, 1992-98; head coach Balt. Ravens, 1998—. Earned All Western Athletic Conf. honors and honorable mention All-America in 1976 as a tight end, Brigham YOung U. Architect of Minnesota Vikings offense that scored 556 points to break NFL record of 541 points. Office: c/o Baltimore Ravens 11001 Owings Mills Blvd Owings Mills MD 21117*

BILLIG, ETEL JEWEL, theater director, actress; b. N.Y.C., Dec. 16, 1932; d. Anthony and Martha Rebecca (Klebansky) Papa; m. Steven S. Billig, Dec. 23, 1956 (dec. Aug. 1996); children: Curt Adam, Jonathan Roark. BS, NYU, 1953, MA, 1955; student, Herbert Berghof Studio, N.Y.C., 1955-56. Cert. elem. and high sch. tchr. Actress Washington Square Players, N.Y.C., 1950-55, Dukes Oak Theatre, Cooperstown, N.Y., 1955, Triple Cities Playhouse, Binghampton, N.Y., 1956, Candlelight Dinner Playhouse, Summit, Ill., 1970, 73, 77, 79, 90; mng. dir. Theatre 31, Park Forest, Ill., 1971-73; asst. mgr. Westroads Dinner Theatre, Omaha, 1973-76; mng. dir., actress Forum Theatre, 1973, 94; mng. dir., actress, producing dir. Ill. Theatre Ctr., Park Forest, 1976—; mng. dir., actress Goodman Theatre, Chgo., 1987, 95, Ct. Theatre, 1990, Wisdom Bridge Theatre, 1991; dir. drama Rich Ctrl. H.S., Olympia Fields, Ill., 1978-86; del. League of Chgo. Theatres Russian Exchange to Soviet Union, 1989; actress Drury Lane, Oak Brook, Ill., 1989; cons. and lectr. in field. Appeared in films including the Dollmaker, Running Scared, Straight Talk, (TV series) Hawaiian Heat, Missing Persons, Untouchables. V.p. Nat. Coun. Jewish Women, Park Forest, 1968-70; sec. Community Arts Coun., Park Forest, 1984-86; pres. Southland Regional Arts Coun., 1986-92. Recipient Risk Taking award NOW, 1982; grantee Nebr. Arts Coun., 1975, Ill. Arts Coun., 1995, 96, Athena award Matteson Area C. of C., 1997, Abby Found. award, 1997. Mem. AFTRA, SAG, Actors' Equity Assn., League Chgo. Theatres, Ill. Arts Coun. Theatre Panel, Prodrs. Assn. Chgo. Area Theatre (sec. 1988-89), Bus. in the Arts Coun. of C. of C. (charter), Rotary (bd. dirs. Park Forest chpt. 1988-97). Avocations: travel, antiques. Office: Ill Theatre Ctr 400A Lakewood Blvd Park Forest IL 60466-1686

BILLIG, FRANKLIN ANTHONY, chemist; b. L.A., Feb. 11, 1923; s. Frank Henry and Hazel (Rockwell) B.; m. Tetsuko Morinaga, Apr. 23, 1957; 1 child, Patricia Ann Kikuko Billig-Harvey. BS, U. So. Calif., L.A., 1954. CPC, CSS. Sr. rsch. chemist Am. Potash & Chem. Corp., Whittier, Calif., 1954-64; rsch. chemist/lab. mgr./safety officer, Dept. Chemistry U. So. Calif., L.A., 1964—; cons. Flintridge Cons., Inc., Calif., 1980—, Hanson Lab. Furniture, Newberry Park, Calif., 1989; cons./staff assoc. Enterprise Environ. Svcs., L.A., 1981—. Author: Advances in Chemistry, 1959, 61, Organic Synthesis, 1959, Infra Red Spectra of Organic Sulfur Compounds, 1964, Infra Red Spectra of Sulfur Compounds, 1966; patentee in field. Master sgt. USAF, 1942-53, PTO, Korea. Fellow AAAS, L. Pasteur Inst. Advanced Med. Studies, Am. Inst. Chemists; mem. Sigma Xi. Republican. Roman Catholic. Avocations: quantum mechanics, Egyptology, archaeology, geology, paleontology. Home: 12722 Spindlewood Dr La Mirada CA 90638-2735 Office: U So Calif Dept Chemistry University Park Los Angeles CA 90089-1062

BILLIG, FREDERICK STUCKY, mechanical engineer; b. Pittsburgh, Pa., Feb. 28, 1933; s. Thomas Clifford and Melba Helen (Stucky) B.; m. Margaret Rose Pelicano, Nov. 30, 1933; children: Linda Ann Baumler, Donna Marie Bartley, Frederick Thomas, James Richard. B of Engring., Johns Hopkins U., 1955; MS, U. Md., 1958, PhD, 1964. From assoc. engr. to group supr. Applied Physics Lab., Johns Hopkins U., Laurel, Md., 1955-77, asst. dept. supr., 1977-87, assoc. dept. supr., chief scientist, 1987-96; pres., chmn. of bd. Pyrodyne, Inc., New Market, Md., 1996—; lectr. U. Md., College Park, 1965-96, Space Inst., U. Tenn., Tullahoma, 1965-90, UCLA, 1987-89, Purdue U., 1986-93, SUNY, Buffalo, 1987, Va. Poly. Inst. & State U., 1983—; lectr. hypersonics short course, Munich, London, Paris, Rome, 1988; NATO Adv. Group for Aerospace Rsch. Devel. lectr. Ramjet and Ramrocket propulsion system for missiles short course, Monterey, Calif., London, Munich, 1984; mem. consultants panel Project SQUID, Office of Naval Rsch., 1972-74; cons. propulsion directorate USAF Nat. Aerospace Plane Program; bd. dirs. Croft Leominster. Contbr. articles to profl. jours.; mem. editl. bd. Johns Hopkins APL Tech. Digest, 1981-89; patentee (with others) cooled leading edges, fuel injector pilons, high reactivity fuels for supersonic combustion ramjets, a supersonic combustion missile, translating cowl inlet with retractable propellant injection struts, protellant utilization system. Mem. Joint Army-Navy-NASA-Air Force Working Group on Combustion, 1971-74, U.S. nat. com. Internat. Airbreathing Engines Com., 1972-74, chmn., 1980-98, v.p., 1993-98; mem. hypersonic propulsion peer rev. group NASA, 1980; mem. sci. adv. bd. USAF, 1988-92, sci. adv. bd. aerospace vehicles standing panel, 1988-92. Recipient Silver medal Combustion Inst., 1970, Nat. Aerospace Plane Program Pioneer award, 1989, M. M. Bondaruck award USSR Acad. Sci. and Aviation Sport Fedn., Meritorious Civilian Svc. award Dept. Air Force, 1992, Aviation Week and Space Tech.-Aeronautics and Propulsion Laurels award, 1996; elected to Nat. Acad. of Engring., 1995, Engring. Hall of Fame U. Md., 1997. Fellow AIAA (tech. com. on airbreathing propulsion 1966-68, tech. com. on propellants and combustion 1970-72, membership chmn. coun. nat. capital sect. 1971-73, standing com. on membership 1973-84, treas. nat. capital sect. 1973-74, sec. 1974-75, standing com. on publs. 1974-82, bd. dirs. region I 1974-81, v.p. bd. dirs. membership svcs. 1981-82, Hugh L. Dryden lectr. in rsch. 1992); mem. NAE, Combustion Inst., Md. Acad. Sci., Pi Tau Sigma, Phi Kappa Phi. Republican. Avocations: golf, fishing, hunting. Home: 11280 Panorama Dr New Market MD 21774-6732 Office: Pyrodyne Inc 11280 Panorama Dr New Market MD 21774-6732

BILLIG, SHELLEY HIRSCHL, educational research and training consultant; b. Canton, Ohio, June 23, 1951; d. Alex T. and Flora H. Hirschl; m. Stephen M. Billig, Aug. 7, 1977; children: Lisa, Joshua. BA, Boston U., 1973; MA, Tufts U., 1975, PhD, 1978. Prof. U. R.I., Kingston, 1977-78, Northeastern Coll., Boston, 1978-80, Regis Coll., Weston, Mass., 1980-82, Merrimack Coll., N. Andover, Mass., 1982-86; rsch. assoc. N.W. Region Ednl. Lab., Denver, Colo., 1987-88; v.p. RMC Rsch. Corp., Denver, 1988—; mem. editl. bd. JESPAR, Johns Hopkins, Balt., 1995—, adv. bd. Colo. Parent Involvment Ctr., 1995—; prin. investigator Region VIII Comprehensive Ctr. and svc.-learning project lead to establishing Rsch. Network, Kellogg Found. Svc.-Learning Initiative, 1998—. Lead author: Federal Programs and Service-Learning, 1999; contbg. author Parent Involvment in the Middle Grades; contbr. articles to profl. jours. Office: RMC Rsch Corp 1512 Larimer St Ste 540 Denver CO 80202-1620

BILLIG, THOMAS CLIFFORD, publishing and marketing executive; b. Pitts., Aug. 20, 1930; s. Thomas Clifford and Melba Helen S. B.; m. Helen Page Hine, May 14, 1951; children: Thomas Clifford, James Frederick. BSBA summa cum laude, Northwestern U., 1956. Ins. mgr., asst. dir. pers., asst. to chmn. Butler Bros. (now City Products Corp.), Chgo., 1954-59; market rsch. mgr. R.R. Donnelley & Sons, Chgo., 1959-61; pres., dir. Indsl. Fiber Glass Products Corp., Scottville and Ludington, Mich., 1962-69; cons. mass mktg. mgr. Mpls., 1969-71; v.p. Mail Mktg. Systems and Services, St. Paul and Bloomington, Minn., 1971-74; pres., chmn., chief exec. officer Billig Communications (formerly Billig & Assocs.), Duluth, Minn., 1974—; pres. NIARS Corp., Duluth, 1974-85, 95—; also bd. dirs. NIARS Corp.; pres. Fins and Feathers Pub. Co., Mpls., 1977-89; also bd. dirs. Fins. and Feathers Pub. Co., Mpls.; pres., dir. North Coast Mktg. Corp., St. Paul, 1992—; author Nat. Ins. Advt. Regulation Svc., 1972—. Author, pub. NAIC Model Laws, Regulations and Guidelines, 1976-83. Served with USNR, 1948-56. Recipient Samuel Dresner Plotkin award Northwestern U., 1956. Mem. Delta Mu Delta, Beta Gamma Sigma. Office: 1423 N 8th St Superior WI 54880-6664 also: 3390 Lake Elmo Ave N Lake Elmo MN 55042-9799

BILLINGS, CHARLES EDGAR, physician; b. Boston, June 15, 1929; s. Charles Edgar and Elizabeth (Sanborn) B.; m. Lillian Elizabeth Wilson, Apr. 16, 1955; 1 dau., Lee Ellen Billings Kreinbihl. Student, Wesleyan U., 1947-49; M.D., N.Y. U., 1953; M.Sc. (Link Found. fellow), Ohio State U., 1960. Diplomate: Am. Bd. Preventive Medicine. Instr. to prof. depts. preventive medicine and aviation Sch. Medicine Ohio State U., 1960-73, dir. div. environ. health Sch. Medicine, 1970-73, clin. prof. Sch. Medicine, 1973-83, prof. emeritus, 1983—; rsch. scientist indsl. and systems engring., 1992—; med. officer NASA Ames Rsch. Ctr., Moffett Field, Calif., 1973-76; chief Aviation Safety Rsch. Office, 1976-80, asst. chief for rsch. Man-Vehicle Systems rsch. divsn., 1980-83, sr. scientist, 1983-91; chief scientist Ames Rsch. Ctr., 1991-92; cons. Beckett Aviation Corp., 1962-73; surgeon gen. U.S. Army, 1965-77, FAA, 1967-70, 75, 83; mem. NATO-AGARD Aerospace Med. Panel, 1980-86; assoc. advisor USAF Sci. Adv. Bd., 1978-90. Contbr. chpts. to books, numerous articles in field to med. jours. Served to maj. USAF, 1955-57. Recipient Air Traffic Svc. award FAA, 1969, Walter M. Boothby rsch. award, 1972, PATCO Air Safety award, 1979, Disting. Svc. award Flight Safety Found., 1979, John A. Tamisea award, 1980, Laura Taber Barbour Air Safety medal, 1981, Outstanding Leadership medal NASA, 1981, 90, Jeffries Aerospace Med. Rsch. medal AIAA, 1986, Lovelace award NASA Soc. Flight Surgeons, 1996; Ames Rsch. Ctr. fellow, 1989. Fellow AIAA (assoc.), Royal Aero. Soc., Aerospace Med. Assn. (pres. 1979-80); mem. AMA, Internat. Acad. Aviation and Space Medicine, Am. Whippet Club, Midland Whippet Club, RAF Club (Gt. Britain). Home: 1372 Hickory Ridge Ln Columbus OH 43235-1131 Office: 230 Baker ISE Bldg 1971 Neil Ave Columbus OH 43210-1210

BILLINGS, FRANKLIN SWIFT, JR., federal judge; b. Woodstock, Vt., June 5, 1922; s. Franklin S. and Gertrude (Curtis) B.; m. Pauline Gillingham, Oct. 13, 1951; children: Franklin, III, Jireh Swift, Elizabeth, Ann. S.B., Harvard U., 1943; postgrad., Yale U. law Sch., 1945; J.D., U. Va., 1947. Bar: Vt. 1948, U.S. Supreme Ct., 1958. With dept. electronics Gen. Electric Co., Schenectady, N.Y., 1943; bldg. dept. Vt. Marble Co., Proctor, 1945-46; pvt. practice law Woodstock, 1948-52; mem. firm Billings & Sherburne, Woodstock, 1952-66; asst. sec. Vt. Senate, 1949-55, sec., 1957-59; sec. civil and mil. affairs State of Vt., 1959-61; exec. clk. to gov., 1955-57; judge Hartford Mcpl. Ct., 1955-63; mem. Vt. Ho. of Reps., 1961-66, chmn. jud. com., 1961, speaker of ho., 1963-66; judge Vt. Superior Ct., 1966-75; assoc. justice Bar Vt., Montpelier, 1975-83, chief justice, 1983-84; judge U.S. Dist. Ct. Vt., 1984-94, chief judge, 1988-92, sr. ct. judge, 1994—. Active, Town of Woodstock, 1948-72. Served as warrant officer 1st class attached Brit. Army, 1944-45. Decorated Purple Heart; Brit. Empire medal. Mem. Vt. Bar Assn., Delta Theta Phi. Office: US Dist Ct PO Box 598 Woodstock VT 05091-0598

BILLINGS, HAROLD WAYNE, librarian, editor; b. Cain City, Tex., Nov. 12, 1931; s. Harold Ross and Katie Mae (Price) B.; m. Bernice Schneider, Sept. 10, 1954; children: Brenda, Geoffrey, Carol. BA, Pan Am. Coll., 1953; MLS, U. Tex., 1957. Tchr. Pharr-San Juan-Alamo (Tex.) High Sch., 1953-54; catalog librarian U. Tex., Austin, 1954-57; asst. chief catalog librarian U. Tex., 1957-65, chief acquisitions librarian, 1965-67, asst. univ. librarian, 1967-72, asso. dir. gen. libraries, 1972-77, acting dir. gen. libraries, 1977-78, dir. gen. libraries, 1978—; sec. Tex. Bd. Libr. Examiners; mem. adv. com. Tex. Higher Edn. Coordinating Bd. Libr. Formula, 1987-92, acad. support formula adv. com., 1993-94; mem. steering com. Tex-Share Project, 1993-94; trustee Amigos Bibliographic Coun., 1980-83; chmn. Coun. Acad. Rsch. Librs., 1979-81; chmn. rsch. librs. adv. com. Online Computer Libr. Ctr. (OCLC), 1980-82, 87-88, mem. OCLC Users Coun.; bd. dirs. Ctr. Rsch. Librs., Chgo., 1989-96, Assn. Rsch. Librs., 1989-92; mem. Tex. Coun. State Univ. Librs., Assn. Rsch. Librs. Preservation Com., Collection Devel. Com., Coun. on Libr. Resources Preservation and Access Com., Coun. on Libr. Resources/Assn. Am. Pubs. Joint Working Group on Electronic Info., 1993-94; mem. adv. bd. Project Muse-Johns Hopkins U. Press, Balt., 1995—; mem. N.Am. adv. bd. Lit. Online, 1997—; assoc. Tex. Telecomms. Policy Inst., 1996—; mem. coun. on libr. and info. studies area studies materials task force ACLS, 1998—; mem. adv. coun. for Stanford U. Librs., 1998—; project dir. numerous fed. grants. Author: Education of Librarians in Texas, 1956, Edward Dahlberg: American Ishmael of Letters, 1968, A Bibliography of Edward Dahlberg, 1972, The Shape of Shiel, 1865-1896, 1983, The Leafless American, 2d edit., 1986, Magic and Hypersystems, 1990, The Bionic Library, 1991, Supping with the Devil, 1993, The Information Ark, 1994, The Tomorrow Librarian, 1995, Libraries, Language and Change, 1998; editor books in field; contbr. to jours.; mem. editorial bd. Libr. Chronicle, 1970-97. Sec., trustee Littlefield Fund for So. History. Mem. ALA, Tex. Libr. Assn., Assn. Coll. Rsch. Librs. Democrat. Office: U Tex Librs PO Box P Austin TX 78713-8916

BILLINGS, JOHANNA SCHMIDT, journalist, antiques consultant; b. Harrisburg, Pa., Oct. 2, 1964; d. George Frederick and Joan Eileen (Agona) Schmidt; 1 child, Kayleigh. BA in English summa cum laude, Gwynedd-Mercy Coll., Gwynedd Valley, Pa., 1996. Newspaper reporter various newspapers, Pa., 1986-92; freelance journalist Lehigh Valley, Pa., 1993—; co-founder Rose Bowl Collectors, Danielsville, Pa., 1994—; mem. bd. advisors Warman's Price Guide, 1996—; vetter Atlantique City Show, Atlantic City, N.J., 1995—. Author: Collectible Glass Rose Bowls, 1999; regular contbr. Free Press newspaper; columnist Antique Week, Glass Collector's Digest, I Love Cats mag., other mags. and pubsl. Vol. Good Mews, Allentown, Pa., 1996—, Laurie Guthier Lung Transplant Fund, Coopersburg, Pa., 1995-96. Recipient 1st place award for feature series Pa. Newspaper Pubs. Assn., 1992, also numerous photography awards. Mem. Cassell Network of Writers. Libertarian. Office: PO Box 244 Danielsville PA 18038-0244

BILLINGS, JUDITH DIANE, elementary education educator; b. San Jose, Calif., Feb. 11, 1944; d. Milton Edward and Dorothy M. (Dunston) McConnell; m. Gary William Billings, July 11, 1965; children: Keri, Michael, Alyssa Duncan. BA in Edn., San Jose State U., 1965. Cert. K-8 elem. edn. Tchr. 2d and 3d grade Cupertino (Calif.) United Sch. Dist., 1965-67; tchr. pre-sch. Calif. Young World, Sunnyvale, 1969-70; tchr. extended learning Oak Grove Sch. Dist., San Jose, 1972-73; tchr. 2d and 3d grade San Lorenzo Valley Unified Sch. Dist., Ben Lomond, Calif., 1978-87; tchr. 6th grade Redwood Elem., Boulder Creek, Calif., 1991—; homesch. tchr. K-6 Charter 25 San Lorenzo Valley Unified Sch. Dist., 1998-99; supr. student tchrs. U. Calif., Santa Cruz, 1987-89; coord. Life Lab., Santa Cruz, 1990-91. Recipient award Schs. Plus, 1987, 90, Calif. Tchg. Innovations Program, State of Calif., 1984, Golden Apple, 1982. Mem. NEA, San Lorenzo Valley Tchrs. Assn. Home: 1747 Quail Hollow Rd Ben Lomond CA 95005-9581 Office: Redwood Elem Sch 16900 Highway 9 Boulder Creek CA 95006-9626

BILLINGS, PATRICIA JEAN, inventor; b. Clinton, Mo., Feb. 15, 1926; d. Chester Irwin and Zoe Elizabeth (Strieby) Billings; m. William Marlman, June 21, 1949; 1 child, Melanie Ann Runge. Student, Amarillo Coll., 1955. Med. rschr.on Histoplasma capsulation USPHS, 1946-48; rschr. Kansas City T.B. Sanitarium, 1951; med. technologist, 1960-67; tuberculosis rschr. Kansas City County Hosp., 1967-71; Craftcote rschr., 1971-73; pres. Geobond, 1989—; spkr. Simmons Coll., Boston, Fire Materials Conv., Egypt, 1988; interviewed numerous TV shows including The Unbelievable, Gordon Elliott Show, CBS This Morning, Fox 41 News, Am. Chem. Soc., Pub. TV, Boston, Dateline, 1998; inventor Geoboval Construction Material, 2 patents, featured in articles: People Magazine, Wall St. Journ., Automated Builder-internet MIT network (inventor of week). 4 patents. Mem. adv. bd. Mus. History of Women, Washington. Named Inventor of Week, MIT. Home: 8120 Lee Blvd Shawnee Mission KS 66206-1219

BILLINGS, RICHARD BRUCE, economics educator, consultant; b. Waukesha, Wis., Dec. 5, 1938; s. Floyd Henry and Edessa Mary (Burmeister) B.; m. Patricia Christy Barnum, Mar. 31, 1961 (dec. May 1999); children: Stephen Michael, David Christopher. BA in Econs. and Math., U. Ariz., 1962, MA in Econs., 1963; PhD in Econs, Claremont (Calif.) Coll., 1969. Asst. prof. U. Ariz., Tucson, 1965-69; lectr. in econs. U. Ariz., 1970-99, assoc. prof., 1999—; rsch. economist State of Ariz., Phoenix, 1969-70; cons. State of Hawaii, Honolulu, 1984, Bur. Reclamation, Boulder, Colo., 1986, Tucson Water, 1988-89, State of Ariz., Phoenix, 1989. Author: Forecasting Urban Water Demand, 1996; contbr. articles to profl. jours. Pres. Campus Christian Ctr., Tucson, 1971, 75; pres., bd. dirs. 1st United Meth. Ch., Tucson, 1992-94, chair fin. com., 1989-93, 95-99; scoutmaster Boy Scouts Am., Tucson, 1981-86. Mem. Soc. Govt. Economists, Nat. Tax Assn. Democrat. Avocations: hiking, camping, woodworking. Home: 660 N Circle D Way Tucson AZ 85748-3843 Office: U Ariz Dept Econs McClelland Hall 401 Tucson AZ 85721

BILLINGS, RONALD J., dental research administrator. Dir. Eastman Dental Ctr., Rochester, N.Y., 1994—. Office: Univ Rochester Eastman Dental Ctr 625 Elmwood Ave Rochester NY 14620-2913

BILLINGS, THOMAS NEAL, computer and publishing executive, management consultant; b. Milw., Mar. 2, 1931; s. Neal and Gladys Victoria (Lockard) B.; m. Barta Hope Chipman, June 12, 1954 (div. 1967); children: Bridget Ann, Bruce Neal; m. Marie Louise Farrell, Mar. 27, 1982. AB with honors, Harvard U., 1952, MBA, 1954. V.p. fin. and adminstrn. and technol. innovation Copley Newspapers Inc., La Jolla, Calif., 1957-70; group v.p., dir. tech. Harte-Hanks Comm. Inc., San Antonio, 1970-73; exec. v.p. United Media, Inc., Phoenix, 1973-75; asst. to pres., dir. corp. mgmt. systems Ramada Inns, Inc., Phoenix, 1975-76; exec. dir. NRA, Washington, 1976-77; pres. Ideation Inc., N.Y.C., 1977-81; chmn. Bergen-Billings Inc., N.Y.C., 1977-80; pres. The Assn. Svc. Corp., San Francisco, 1978—; pres. Recorder Printing and Pub. Co. Inc., San Francisco, 1980-82; v.p. adminstrn. Victor Techs. Inc., Scotts Valley, Calif., 1982-84; mng. dir. Saga-Wilcox Computers Ltd., Wrexham, Wales, 1984-85; chmn. Thomas Billings & Assocs., Inc., Reno, 1978—, Intercontinental Travel Svc. Inc., Reno, 1983-88, Oberon Optical Character Recognition, Ltd., Hemel-Hemstead, Eng., 1985-86; bd. dirs. 5M Corp., San Francisco, Intercontinental Rsch. Coun., London, Corp. Comm. Coun., Alameda; dir., CEO Insignia Software Solutions group, High Wycombe, Eng., Cupertino, Calif., 1986-89; chmn. Intercontinental News Svc. Inc., London and Alameda, Calif., 1989—; v.p. Cromer Equipment Co., Oakland, Calif., 1991-94; chmn. Newton Group of Cos., Las Vegas, 1993—, Info. Integrity Internat., Inc., Las Vegas, London, 1994—, WordMaster Corp., Reno, 1995—, GolfDoctor!Inc., Las Vegas, 1998—; bd. dirs. Digital Broadcasting Corp., Mountain View, Calif., Lenny's Restaurants Inc., Wichita, Kans., Tymyndr Corp., Dover, Del., Zzyzzyx Corp., Reno, Harrod's Hotel & Casino Corp., Las Vegas, Pandemonium Pictures, Inc., San Mateo, Calif., Bonanza Enterprises, Inc., Virginia City, Nev., Quillmill Ltd., London, Better Betting Systems, Inc., Alameda, Calif., Video Stream, Inc., Cupertino, Calif., ResuMaster Corp., Walnut Creek, Calif., ProcessMaster Corp., Pleasanton, Calif., Enterprise House, Alameda, People Finders, Inc., Walnut Creek, Calif., Chut! Cheri's Chic Chit Choppe, S.A., Laguna Beach, Calif., Waters Equipment Co., Inc., San Francisco, Goldstein Miller and Assocs. Inc., San Bruno, Calif., Silicon World Search Group, Inc., Alameda, Calif., Knickers' Ltd., Reno; speaker and seminar leader; co-inventor Strok-Savr Software, 1994. Bd. dirs. Nat. Allergy Found., 1973—, The Wilderness Fund, 1978—, San Diego Civic Light Opera Assn., 1965-69; chief exec. San Diego 200th Anniversary Expn., 1969; founder, exec. dir. Am. Majority Party, 1993—. The Millenium Three Found., 1996—, The Rememberance Soc., 1996—, People Finders' Inc., 1996—, Corp. Comm. Counsel Inc., 1996—. Served with U.S. Army, 1955-57. Recipient Walter F. Carley Meml. award, 1966, 69. Fellow U.K. Inst. Dirs.; mem. Am. Newspaper Pubs. Assn., Inst. Execs. Inc. (dir.), Inst. Newspaper Fin. Officers, Sigma Delta Chi. Clubs: West Side Tennis, LaJolla Country; Washington Athletic; San Francisco Press; Harvard (N.Y.C.); Elks. Author: Creative Controllership, 1978, Our Credibility Crisis, 1983, Non-Euclidean Theology, 1987, Ruminations on Meta Mentality, 1990, Fixing our Broken System, 1992, (series) The Ethnic Epicure, 1995—; editor: The Vice Presidents' Letter, 1978-92; pub. The Microcomputer Letter, 1982-94, Synthetic Hardware Update, 1987-93, Windows on Tomorrow Magazine, 1994—; editor: Intercontinental News Svc., London and Alameda, Calif., 1985—. Office: PO Drawer I Alameda CA 94501-0262 also: 100 W Grove St Ste 360 Reno NV 89509-4028

BILLINGSLEY, CHARLES CLYDE, musician, composer; b. Clovis, Jan. 7, 1970; s. Colonel Clyde and Judy (Kirkland) B.; m. Jennifer Shae Sullivan, Mar. 27, 1994. BA, Samford U., 1992. Pres., owner Crest Music and Ministry, Birmingham, 1992-94; singer, instrumentalist New Song, Woodstock, Ga., 1994-96; pres., owner Charles Billingsley Concert Ministry, Woodstock, 1996—; singer, featured soloist about 1100 different chs., 1992—. Singer We Wear His Name, People Get Ready, 1994-96 (#1 Hit); writer about 50 songs, 1992—; prodr. 7 albums, 1992—. Mem. Gospel Music Assn. Republican. Baptist. Avocations: racquetball, football. Office: Charles Billingsley Concert Ministry PO Box 440846 Kennesaw GA 30144-9515

BILLINGSLEY, CHARLES EDWARD, retired transportation company executive; b. DeQueen, Ark., Sept. 2, 1933; s. James Glazebrook and Malcolm Elizabeth (Rice) B.; m. Gloria Ann Smith, Sept. 4, 1954; children: Charles M. (dec.), Mark E., Barbara A. BA, U. Okla., 1955, MA, 1960. CPA, Okla. Various mgmt. positions GE, 1959-66; supr. budgets and analysis Pa. R.R., Chgo., 1966-68; contr. ea. region Pa. Cen. R.R., Indpls., 1968; mgr. budgetary adminstrn. Ebasco Industries, N.Y.C., 1968-69; asst. contr. Union Pacific Corp., N.Y.C., 1969-70, Omaha, 1970-88; contr. Union Pacific Corp., Bethlehem, Pa., 1988-90, v.p., contr., 1990-95; sr. v.p. Union Pacific Corp., Bethelehem, Pa., 1995-97. Mem. acctg. adv. com. U. Nebr., Omaha, 1980-83, adv. coun. Coll. Bus., Kans. State U., Manhattan, 1983-87, profl. acctg. coun. U. Iowa, Iowa City, 1985-88, bd. visitors Sch. Acctg., U. Okla., Norman, 1990—. Capt. U.S. Army, 1957. Recipient John P. Begley Disting. Svc. award Creighton U., 1989, John D. DeVries Svc. award Iowa State U., 1989, Outstanding Contbn. award U. Iowa, 1990; named Beta Alpha Psi Acct. of Yr. for Industry, 1993. Mem. AICPA, Okla. Soc. CPAs, Am. Acctg. Assn., Inst. Internal Auditors (bd. dirs. 1980-85, chmn. audit com. 1985), Fin. Execs. Inst., Omaha Club, Delta Tau Delta. Republican. Methodist. Home: 7733 Louis Pasteur Apt 407 San Antonio TX 78229-3472

BILLINGSLEY, FLORENCE ILONA, nurse, case manager; b. Detroit, Dec. 27, 1943; d. John and Doris Fannie (Creighton) B.; 1 child, Marc Todd. LPN, Detroit Practical Nursing Ctr., 1963; ADN, Highland Pk. Cmty. Coll., 1973; BSN, Wayne State U., 1983. RN, Mich.; diplomate Am. Bd. Quality Assurance and Utilization Rev. Physicians; cert. case mgr. Nurse preceptor, staff nurse, charge nurse Harper Hosp., Detroit, 1964-76; pub. health nurse Detroit Health Dept., 1976-86; discharge planning coord. Detroit Receiving Hosp., 1985-86; clin. svcs. mgr. Med. Ctr. Healthcare, Detroit, 1985-88; spl. instr. JTPA Sch. Practical Nursing, Detroit, 1988-89; case mgr. AIDS Consortium of S.E. Mich., Detroit, 1989-90; liaison nurse Renaissance Home Health Care, Oak Park, Mich., 1990-91; alternative health svcs. case mgr. United Am. Healthcare Corp., Detroit, 1991-95; disability mgr. Travelers Ins. Co., Warren, Mich., 1995-99. Vol. for breast and prostate screening programs Mich. Cancer Found., Detroit, 1992—; hospice vol. Hospice of Mich., Detroit, 1993—. Recipient Minority Nurse grant for Grad. Studies in Cmty. Health Nursing, State of Mich., 1989-90. Mem. Mich. Nurses Assn. (del. to conv. 1994-97), Citizens for Better Care, Breast Cancer Resource Task Force, Wayne State U. Alumni Assn., Chi Eta Phi Lambda Chi. Avocations: reading autobiographies, alternative health care, volunteer work.

BILLINGSLEY, JUDITH ANN SEAVEY, oncology nurse; b. Manchester, Conn., Aug. 4, 1947; d. John Frank and Carol Jean (Wood) Seavey; m. Michael Billingsley, June 7, 1969; children: Tamara Lynn, Tara Lynn. Diploma, Hartford Hosp. Sch. Nursing, 1968; student, Coll. of Albemarle, 1985-86, No. Va. C.C., 1990; grad. with honors, George Mason U., 1992. Cert. oncology nurse ANCC, 1995. Staff nurse ICU Manchester Meml. Hosp., 1968-69; staff nurse recovery rm. Burlingame (Calif.) Hosp. and Med. Ctr., 1972-73; staff nurse St. Joseph's Hosp., Atlanta, 1987-89; clin. nurse Alexandria (Va.) Hosp., 1989-91; admissions nurse Hospice of No. Va., 1991-92; neuro-oncology clin. rsch. nurse Winship Cancer Ctr. Emory U. Sch. Medicine, Atlanta, 1992-98; clin. rsch. nurse Blood and Marrow Transplant Group Ga., Atlanta, 1998—. Mem. Golden Key, Sigma Theta Tau, Alpha Chi. Home: 1273 Gray Squirrel Xing Marietta GA 30062-6275

BILLINGSLEY, ROBERT THAINE, lawyer; b. Wichita, Kans., Jan. 9, 1954; s. Thaine Edward and Anita (Moore) B.; m. Anna Barron, Dec. 31, 1983; children: Carol Carothers, Leslie Hope. AB, Coll. of William and Mary, 1976; JD, U. Richmond, 1980. Bar: Va. 1980. Law clk. to presiding justice U.S. Dist. Ct., Roanoke, Va., 1980-81; assoc. McGuire, Woods & Battle, Richmond, Va., 1981-87, Hirschler, Fleischer, Weinberg, Cox & Allen, Richmond, Va., 1987-96; fin. advisr Krammick & Assocs., Fredericksburg, Va., 1996—. Bd. editors The Virginia Lawyer, 1984-86; mem. adv. bd. U. Richmond Law Rev., 1986-97; contbr. articles to profl. publs. Bd. dirs. Bethlehem Ctr., Richmond, 1985-89, United Meth. Found. of Va. Conf., Inc., 1993—, Hanover Indsl. Air Pk. Bus. Assn., 1994-96; mem. adminstrv. bd. Trinity United Meth. Ch., Richmond, 1986-89, trustee, 1988-96, chmn. bd. trustees, 1992-95, chmn. commitment campaign, 1995; team capt. United Way Greater Richmond, 1989, sect. chmn., 1991, divsn. chmn., 1993; team capt. Rappahannock Area United Way, 1998; mem. Leadership Metro Richmond Class, 1992-93; bd. dirs. Arts Coun. of Richmond, Inc., 1994-96, exec. com., 1996; chmn. fin. com. Fredericksburg United Meth. Ch., 1999—; bd. dirs. College Heights Swimming Pool Assn. Mem. ABA (litigation sect., state memnership chmn. young lawyers divsn. 1985-89, state membership chmn. 1989-96), Va. Bar Assn. (com. on alternative dispute resolution), Va. State Bar Assn. (bd. govs. young lawyers conf. 1985-89, spl. com. on professionalism, legal edn., admission to bar), Richmond Bar Assn. (program com., vice chmn. 1990-91, chmn. 1991-92, adminstrn. of justice com. 1992-96), Fredericksburg Bar Assn., William and Mary Alumni Assn. (bd. dirs. Richmond chpt. 1993-95), Richmond Jaycees (bd. dirs. 1984-86), Rappahannock Rotary. Avocations: sports, travel, theatre. Home: 1604 College Ave Fredericksbrg VA 22401-4637 Office: Kramnick & Assocs Ste 100 5444 Jefferson Davis Hwy Fredericksburg VA 22407

BILLINGSLEY, SHIRLEY ANN, writer, poet; b. Center, Tex., Sept. 3, 1953; d. Leonard Waymon and Verna Mae (Moore) B.; m. Willie L. Skinner, Oct. 12, 1980. Diploma, Coastal Coll., Bossier City, La., 1991. Author: articles, poems. Avocations: reading, writing, poetry, spreading God's word. Home: 101 W Shepard Ave # 403 Lufkin TX 75904

BILLINGSLEY, WILLIAM SCOTT, accountant, controller; b. Clearfield, Pa., Mar. 20, 1963; s. William Allen and Janice Marilyn (Bridges) B.; m. Donna Dolphin, June 17, 1989. BS in Acctg., Pa. State U., 1985. CPA, Calif. Cost acct. IBM Corp., Poughkeepsie, N.Y., 1984; staff acct. Arthur Young, Pitts., 1985-88; sr. acct. Ernst & Young, San Diego, 1988-89; contr., acct. Cinema Air Jet Ctr., Inc., Carlsbad, Calif., 1989—. Mem. AICPAs, Pa. Inst. CPAs, Calif. Soc. CPAs. Republican. Presbyterian. Avocations: marathon runner, surfing, snowboarding. Home: 3014 Segovia Ct Carlsbad CA 92009-8352 Office: Cinema Air Jet Ctr Inc 2056 Palomar Airport Rd Carlsbad CA 92008-4863

BILLINGTON, BARRY E., lawyer; b. Bruceton, Tenn., June 24, 1940; s. Charles Raymond and Edith Virginia (Bowles) B.; m. Bonnie Leslie Johnson; Oct. 16, 1971 (div. Mar. 23, 1990); children: Erin Alexis, Barry E., Jr. AB in Econs., Davidson Coll., 1964; JD, Emory U., 1968. Bar: Calif. 1969, Ga. 1971, U.S. Dist. Ct. (ctrl. dist.) Calif. 1969, U.S. Dist. Ct. (no. dist.) Ga. 1971. Assoc. Surr & Hellyer, San Bernardino, Calif., 1968-70; with Mfrs. Life Ins. Co., Atlanta, 1970-71; assoc. Carter, Ansley, Smith & McClendon, Atlanta, 1971-72; of counsel Raiford & Hills, Decatur, Ga., 1972-75; ptnr. Raiford, Hills, Billington & McKeithen, Atlanta, 1975-77, Rich, Bass, Kidd, Witcher & Billington, Decatur, 1977-82, Billington & Beasley, Decatur, 1982-83, Billington & Turner, Atlanta, 1983-85, Barry E. Billington & Associs., Atlanta, 1985—. Editor: Ga. Rep. Party Newsletter, 1968. Rep. publicity dir. San Bernardino County, 1969-79, San Bernardino County for Ronald Reagan Com., 1970; alt. del. Rep. Ctrl. Com. of Calif., 1969-70; chmn. 4th dist. Conservative Caucus, 1977-79; candidate for Ga. Ho. Reps., 52nd dist., 1978, U.S. Congress, 4th dist., Ga., 1980. With U.S. Army Mil. Police Corps, 1958-60. Mem. Atlanta Bar Assn. (spkr.'s com., litigation, family law, criminal law sects. 1974-77), Decatur-DeKalb Bar Assn. (chmn. spkr.'s com. 1977-78), ABA (litigation sect. 1969—), Ga. Trial Lawyers Assn., Assn. Trial Lawyers Am. Home: 878 Sherwood Cir Forest Park GA 30297-3035 Office: 3 Dunwoody Park Ste 103 Atlanta GA 30338-6709

BILLINGTON, DAVID PERKINS, civil engineering educator; b. Bryn Mawr, Pa., June 1, 1927; s. Nelson and Jane Newkirk (Coolbaugh) B.; m. Phyllis Bergquist, Aug. 26, 1951; children: David Jr., Elizabeth Billington Fox, Jane Billington Flucker, Philip, Stephen, Sarah. BS in Engring., Princeton U., 1950; postgrad. (Fulbright fellow), U. Louvain, Belgium, 1950-51, U. Ghent, Belgium, 1951-52; DHL (hon.), Union Coll., 1990; DSc (hon.), Grinnell Coll., 1991; DEng (hon.), Notre Dame U., 1997. Registered profl. engr., N.J. Structural engr. Roberts & Schaefer Co., N.Y.C., 1952-60; assoc. prof. civil engring. Princeton U., N.J., 1960-64, prof. civil engring., 1964—; Gordon Y.S. Wu prof. engring. Princeton U., 1996—; A.D. White prof.-at-large Cornell U., 1987-93; cons. in field. Author: Robert Maillart's Bridges, 1979 (Dexter award 1979), Thin Shell Concrete Structures, 1982, The Tower and the Bridge, 1983, Robert Maillart and the Art of Reinforced Concrete, 1990, The Innovators: The Engineering Pioneers Who Made America Modern, 1996, Robert Maillart: Builder, Designer, Artist, 1997. With USN, 1945-46. Recipient Dana award Charles A. Dana Found., 1990, N.J. Prof. of Yr. award, Carnegie Found., 1995; grantee NEH, 1969-89, NSF, 1963-83, 91-94, NEA, 1977-79; Phi Beta Kappa vis. scholar, 1984-85. Fellow ASCE (3 awards 1956-57, History and Heritage award 1986, George Winter award 1992), Am. Concrete Inst., Am. Acad. Arts and Scis.; mem. NAE, Internat. Assn. for Bridge and Structural Engring., Internat. Assn. Shell Structures, Soc. for History Tech. (Usher prize with J. Doig 1995). Republican. Episcopalian. Home: 45 Hodge Rd Princeton NJ 08540-3011 Office: Princeton U Dept Civil Engring Princeton NJ 08544

BILLINGTON, JAMES HADLEY, historian, librarian; b. Bryn Mawr, Pa., June 1, 1929; s. Nelson and Jane (Coolbaugh) B.; m. Marjorie Anne Brennan, June 22, 1957; children: Susan Billington Harper, Anne Billington Fischer, James Hadley, Jr., Thomas Keator. BA, Princeton U., 1950; D Phil., Oxford (Eng.) U., 1953; LittD (hon.), Lafayette Coll., 1981, U. Pitts., 1988, Williams Coll., 1991, Duke U., 1995; LHD (hon.), LeMoyne Coll., 1982, Rhode Island Coll., 1982, Cath. U. Am., 1983, NYU, 1987, Va. Theol. Sem., 1990, Hood Coll., 1992, U. Scranton, 1992, SUNY, Albany, 1993, Georgetown U., 1993, Bates Coll., 1993, The Am. U., 1995, Mt. Holyoke Coll., 1995; HHD (hon.), Furman U., 1986, Ball State U., 1988; D Pub. Svc. (hon.), George Washington U., 1990; LLD (hon.), Dartmouth Coll., 1990, U. Notre Dame, 1995. Instr. history Harvard U., Cambridge, Mass., 1957-58, fellow Russian Research Ctr., 1958-59, asst. prof. history, 1958-61; assoc. prof. history Princeton (N.J.) U., 1962-64, prof., 1964-73; dir. Woodrow Wilson Internat. Ctr. for Scholars, Washington, 1973-87; Librarian of Congress Libr. of Congress, Washington, 1987—; chmn. Bd. Fgn. Scholarships (Fulbright program), 1971-73, mem. 1973-76; vice-chmn. Atlantic Council's Working Group on the Successor Generation, 1982-86; trustee St. Alban's Sch., 1979-82; dir. Am. Assn. for the Advancement of Slavic Studies, 1968-71; spl. cons. to Chase Manhattan Bank on East-West Matters, 1971-73; vis. rsch. prof. to Inst. History of Acad. Scis. of USSR in Moscow, 1966-67, U. Helsinki, 1960-61, École des Hautes Études en Sciences Sociales, Paris, 1985, 88; vis. lectr. to various univs. in Europe and Asia. Author: Mikhailovsky and Russian Populism, 1958, The Icon and the Axe: An Interpretive History of Russian Culture, 1966, (Serbian transl., 1988), The Arts of Russia, 1970, Fire in the Minds of Men: Origins of the Revolutionary Faith, 1980, (Italian transl., 1986), Russia Transformed: Breakthrough to Hope, Moscow, August 1991, 1992, The Face of Russia, 1998; writer, host: (3-part TV series) The Face of Russia, 1998; mem. adv. bd. Fgn. Affairs, 1974-92, Theology Today, 1974-84; script writer and host of Humanities Film Forum, 1973; contbr. chpts. to books, numerous articles to profl. jours. Trustee John F. Kennedy Ctr. for Performing Arts, Ctr. Theol. Inquiry, Nat. Bldg. Mus., Woodrow Wilson Internat. Ctr. for Scholars, Am. Folklife Ctr.; bd. regents Nat. Libr. Medicine. 1st lt. U.S. Army, 1953-56. McCosh faculty fellow Princeton U., Guggenheim fellow, 1960-61; Rhodes scholar, 1950-53; Fulbright rsch. professor U. Helsinki, 1960-61; decorated Chevalier 1985 and Comdr. 1991 Order of Arts and Letters of France; recipient Gwanghwa medal Republic of Korea, 1991, Woodrow Wilson award Princeton U., 1992, Knight Comdr.'s Cross of Order of Merit, Fed. Republic of Germany, 1996. Mem. Am. Philos. Soc., Am. Acad. Arts and Scis., Cosmos Club, Phi Beta Kappa. Office: The Library of Congress 101 Independence Ave SE Washington DC 20540-0002

BILLINGTON, KEN, lighting designer; b. White Plains, N.Y., Oct. 29, 1946; s. Kenneth Arthur and Ruth (Roane) B. Student, Lester Polakov Studio, Form of Stage Design. Lighting designer: (Broadway prodns.) The Visit, Barrymore Theatre, 1973, Bad Habits, Booth Theatre, 1974, Member of the Wedding, Helen Hayes Theatre, 1975, Wheelbarrow Closers, Bijou Theatre, 1976, Ethel Merman and Mary Martin Together on Broadway, Winter Garden Theatre, 1977, Working, 46th St. Theatre, 1978, Sweeney Todd, Uris Theatre, 1979, Happy New Year, Morosco Theatre, 1980, Copperfield, Am. Nat. Theatre Acad., 1981, Foxfire, Barrymore Theatre, 1982, End of the World, Music Box Theatre, 1984, Grind, Mark Hellinger Theatre, 1985, A Little Like Magic, Lyceum Theatre, 1986, Stardust, Biltmore Theatre, 1987, TRU, Booth Theatre, 1989, Lettice and Lovage, Barrymore Theatre, 1990, The Odd Couple, Belasco Theatre, 1991, Chicago, 1996 (Tony award, 1997), Annie, 1997, Dream, 1997, Caudide, 1997, Footloose, 1998; Lighting designer: (N.Y.C.) The Dream on Monkey Island, St. Mark's Playhouse, 1971, A Meeting by the River, Edison Theatre, 1972, The Government Inspector, Playhouse Theatre, 1973, The Great MacDaddy, St. Mark's Playhouse, 1974, Styne after Styne, Manhattan Theatre Club, 1980, Snoopy, Lambs Theatre, 1982, Talullah, West Side Arts Theatre, 1984, Three Guys Naked from the Waist Down, Minetta Lane Theatre, 1985, Stardust, Theatre-Off-Park, 1986, What the Butler Saw, Manhattan Theatre, 1989, The Lisbon Traviata, Manhattan Theatre Club, 1989, Lips Together, Teeth Apart, Hanhattan Theatre Club, 1991, others, (operas) Simon Boccanegra, Phila. Lyric Opera, 1973, Il Tabarro/Gianni Schicchi, Phila. Lyric Opera, 1974, Anna Bolena, Dallas Civic Opera, 1975, Ashmedai, N.Y.C. Opera, 1976, The Voice of Ariadne, N.Y.C. Opera, 1977, The Merry Widow, N.Y.C. Opera, 1978, La Fanciulla del West, San Francisco Opera, 1979, Silverlake, N.Y.C. Opera, 1980, Willie Stark, Houston Grand Opera, 1981, Candide, N.Y.C. Opera, 1982, Turandot, Vienna State Opera, 1983, Cosi Fan Tutti, Greater Miami Opera, 1984, Madama Butterfly, Houston Grand Opera, 1985, Pagliacci, Greater Miami Opera, 1986, Faust, Seattle Opera, 1987, Marriage of Figaro, Houston Grand Opera, 1988, Orpheus of the Underworld L.A. Opera, 1990, Madama Butterfly, Chgo. Lyric Opera, 1991, Carmen, Houston Grand Opera, 1998, A Little Night Music, 1999, Madame Butterfly, 1999, others.; light designer Radio City Music Hall Christmas Show, 1979—, Concerts Ann-Margret, 1978—, (pub. TV) Showboat, 1989, Berstein At 70, 1988, others. Recipient Illuminating Engring. Soc. of N.Am. Edwin F. Guth Meml. Lighting Design Award of Merit, 1973, Los Angeles Drama Critics award, 1979, 86, Ace award, 1982, Boston Drama Critics award, 1982, 86, Tony award for Lighting Design, 1997. Mem. United Scenic Artists. Presbyterian. Office: 200 W 70th St New York NY 10023-4323*

BILLINTON, ROY, engineering educator; b. Leeds, Eng., Sept. 14, 1935; s. Edwin and Nettie (Billinton); m. Alice Joyce McKenna, July 21, 1956; children—Leslie, Kevin, Michael, Christopher, Jeffrey. B.Sc.E.E., U. Man., 1960, M.Sc., 1963; Ph.D., U. Sask., 1967, D.Sc., 1975. Journeyman electrician McCaine Electric, Winnipeg, Man., Can., 1956; mem. system operation dept. and system planning dept. Man. Hydro, from 1960; asst. prof. to prof., head dept. elec. engring. U. Sask., Saskatoon, 1964—; now assoc. dean pres. PowerComp Assocs., cons. Author: Power System Reliability Evaluation, 1970, (with R. J. Ringlee and A. J. Wood) Power System Reliability Calculations, 1973, (with C. Singh) System Reliability Modelling and Evaluation, 1977; (with R.N. Allan) Reliability Evaluation of Engineering Systems, 1983, Reliability Evaluation of Power Systems, 1984, (with R.N. Allan) Reliability of Large Electric Power Systems, 1988, (with R.N. Allan, L. Salvaderi) Applied Reliability Assessment in Electric Power Systems, 1990, (with W Li) Reliability Assessment of Electric Power Systems Using Monte Carlo Methods, 1994; also articles. Recipient Sir George Nelson award Engring. Inst. Can., 1965-67, Ross medal, 1972, Centennial Disting. Svc. award Can. Elect Assn., 1991; Disting. Researcher award U. Saskatchewan. Fellow IEEE (Outstanding Power Engring. Educator award 1992, McNaughton medal 1994), Royal Soc. Can., Engring. Inst. Can., U.K. Safety and Reliability Soc. Home: 3 McLean Crescent, Saskatoon, SK Canada S7J 2R6 Office: U Sask, Dept Elec Engring, Saskatoon, SK Canada S7N 0W0

BILLITER, FREDA DELOROUS, elementary education educator, retired; b. McAndrews, Ky., Oct. 15, 1937; d. David Wilson and Evalyn May (Puckett) Kendrick; m. William Jefferson Billiter, Sept. 12, 1954; 1 child, Cynthia Delorous. BS in Edn., Ohio U., 1969, MEd, 1987. Cert. elem. tchr., media specialist, reading specialist. Departmental tchr. Ironton (Ohio) City Schs., 1965-66, 3d grade tchr., 1966-67; 2d grade tchr. Portsmouth (Ohio) City Schs., 1969-96. Coord. sec. Scioto County Hist. Soc., Portsmouth, 1980-82; choir mem. Shawnee State U. and Cmty. Choir, Portsmouth, 1973—, Wesley United Meth. Ch. Chancel Choir, Portsmouth, 1985—, Portsmouth Cmty. Chorale, 1993—; mem. Scioto County Hist. Soc. and Nat. Trust. Martha Holden Jennings scholar Ohio U., 1988-89; recipient Cert. of Participation, Portsmouth Area Arts Coun., 1990. Mem. NEA, AAUW, Ohio Edn. Assn., Internat. Reading Assn., S.E. Ohio Coun. Tchrs. English, Scioto County Mus. and Cultural Ctr., Ohio Hist. Soc., Order Ea. Star, Phi Delta Kappa (awards chmn. 1990-91, 94-95), Delta Kappa Gamma (1st v.p. 1990-92, pres. 1992-94), Ohio Bus. and Profl. Women (v.p. 1998—), Kappa Delta Pi (svc. award 1986). Republican. Avocations: reading, singing, piano, sewing. Home: 2890 Circle Dr Portsmouth OH 45662-2445 Office: Wilson Elem Sch 613 Campbell Ave Portsmouth OH 45662-4468

BILLMAN, IRWIN EDWARD, publishing company executive; b. Manhattan, N.Y., July 7, 1940; s. Herman Frank and Ruth (Dutchen) B. BS in Econs, Wharton Sch., U. Pa., 1962. Asst. controller Whelan Drug Co., 1965-66; v.p., treas. Curtis Circulation Co., Phila., 1966-71; exec. v.p., chief operating officer Penthouse, Omni and Forum mags., 1971-81; pres., publisher Oui Mag., N.Y.C., 1981-82; pres. Billman Media Group; ptnr. Mag. Communications Cons.; pres. Global Distribution Svcs., Inc. Mem. Periodical and Book Assn. Am. (pres. 1977-81), Friars, A.C.E.S. Home: PO Box 350 Westhampton NY 11977-0350 Office: PO Box 850 Remsenburg NY 11960-0850

BILLMAN, LARRY EDWARD, writer, director; b. Los Angeles, Oct. 23, 1938; s. Harry Edward and Nina La Vone (Harden) B.; m. Tomoko Katsuko Sekiya, June 19, 1967; children: Sekiya La Vone, Saadia Neva. MBA, Los Angeles City Coll., 1960. Ind. writer, dir., performer, 1958-71; show writer, dir. Walt Disney World/Disneyland, Orlando, Fla. and Anaheim, Calif., 1969-74, mgr. show devel., 1974-79; dir. entertainment Disneyland, Tokyo, 1979-84; dir. spl. projects Disneyland & Walt Disney World, 1984-86; staging dir. Walt Disney's World on Ice Ringling Bros. and Barnum & Bailey Circus, 1986-89; creative dir. entertainment div. Sanrio Puroland, 1990-91, Huis Ten Bosch, 1991-92, Parque Espana, 1992-94; v.p. creative show devel. Walt Disney World, 1994-95; artistic dir. entertainment Tokyo Disney Sea, 1995-98. Writer: Hoop De Doo as performed at Walt Disney World, Tokyo, Disneyland, 1974— (ASCAP Spl. award 1985—), Betty Grable Bio, 1991, Fred Astaire Bio, 1996, Film Choreographers and Dance Directors Encyclopedia, 1996, found., The Acad. of Dance on Film, 1998. Served as pvt. U.S. Army, 1961-63. Mem. ASCAP, Profl. Dancers Soc., Soc. Stage Dir. Choreographers.

BILLMEYER, FRED WALLACE, JR., chemist, educator; b. Chattanooga, Aug. 24, 1919; s. Fred W. and Eleanor (Salmon) B.; m. Annette M. Trzcinski, Aug. 4, 1951; children: Eleanor A., Dean W., David M. B.S., Calif. Inst. Tech., 1941; Ph.D., Cornell U., 1945. With plastics dept. E.I. du Pont de Nemours & Co., 1945-64; lectr. high polymers dept. chemistry U. Del., 1951-64; Vis. prof. chem. engring. Mass. Inst. Tech., 1960-61; prof. analytical chemistry Rensselaer Poly. Inst., Troy, N.Y., 1964-84, prof. emeritus, 1984—; cons. various coms. Internat. Commn. Illumination (CIE), 1964—; mem. U.S. Nat. Com. CIE, 1968—, v.p., 1975-79, mem. for life, 1983—. Author: Textbook of Polymer Chemistry, 1957, Textbook of Polymer Science, 1961, 3d edit., 1984, Synthetic Polymers, 1972, (with Max Saltzman) Principles of Color Technology, 1966, 2d edit., 1981, (with E.A. Collins and J. Bares) Experiments in Polymer Science, 1973, (with R. N. Kelley) Entering Industry, 1975; also articles; editorial adviser: Optical Spectra, 1967-80; editor-in-chief: Color Research and Application, 1976-86. Trustee Munsell Color Found., sec., 1975-83. Recipient Bruning award Fedn. Socs. Coatings Tech., 1977, Deane B. Judd award AIC Internat. Color Assn., 1999. Fellow ASTM (award of merit 1990, Com. on Terminology Members award 1993, Frank W. Reinhart award 1998), AAAS, Am. Phys. Soc., Optical Soc. Am., Soc. Plastics Engrs.; mem. Am. Chem. Soc., N.Y. Soc. Coatings Tech., Inter-Soc. Color Coun. (pres. 1968-70, sec. 1970-82, Macbeth award 1978, Svc. award 1983, Godlove award 1993), Coun. Optical Radiation Measurements (sec. 1979-83), Color Group Bulgaria (hon. mem.), Sigma Xi, Phi Kappa Phi. Home: Apt 218 1786 Union St Niskayuna NY 12309-6394

BILLS, ROBERT E(DGAR), emeritus psychology educator; b. Nutley, N.J., Dec. 15, 1916; s. Willis Minard and Leah Catherine (Condit) B.; m. Annie Tarleton Carley, Dec. 22, 1944; children—Mary Ann Bills Niles, Leah Catherine Bills Hawkins. B.S., Western Ky. U., 1938; M.A., U. Ky., 1946; Ed.D., Columbia U, 1948. Tchr. sci. Breathitt County (Ky.) Bd. Edn., 1938-42; tchr. Anchorage Bd. Edn. (Ky.), 1943-44, prin., 1944-5; critic tchr. sci. U. Ky. Coll. Edn., 1945-46, faculty Coll. Arts and Scis., 1948-56, asst. prof. psychology, 1948-52, assoc. prof., 1952-56, chmn. div. biol. scis., 1950-51; prof. psychology, chmn. dept. Auburn U., 1956-61; prof. ednl. psychology U. Ala., 1961-69, rsch. prof. edn., 1969-79, rsch. prof. emeritus, 1979—, asst. dean rsch., 1961-63, interim dean Coll. Edn., 1963-65, dean, 1965-69, dean emeritus, 1979—; mem. council psychol. resources of South So. Regional Edn. Bd., 1953-56; chmn. Ky. Bd. Examiners Psychologists, 1954-56; vis. prof. U. Fla., 1953, 54, Mich. State U., 1956, U. Wash., 1963; lectr. in field. Bd. dirs. Southeastern Ednl. Corp., 1966-67; sec. Ala. Coalition for Better Edn., 1969-70, pres., 1971-72. Served with U.S. Army, 1943-44; with USCG Aux., 1982—. Recipient Outstanding Prof. award Coll. Edn. U. Ala., 1979; Ednl. Press Assn. award for disting. contbn. to ednl. journalism, 1982. Fellow Am. Psychol. Assn. (sec.-treas. div. 1963-66), Mid-South Edn. Research Assn. (v.p. 1978, pres. 1979), Assn. Supervision and Curriculum Devel. (dir. 1962-64), U.S. Coast Guard Aux (mem. nat. staff 1989—), Sigma Xi, Kappa Delta Pi, Psi Chi, Phi Delta Kappa. Author: Education for Intelligence or Failure?, 1982; contbr. chpts. to books, articles in field to profl. jours. Home: 3448 Tall Pines Cir Tuscaloosa AL 35405-5401

BILLS, ROBERT HOWARD, political party executive; b. North Conway, N.H., Jan. 13, 1944; s. Howard William and Mary Catherine (Jackson) B.; m. Donna Gail Florian; children: Emily Ida, Katherine Mary. Staff writer Weekly People Newspaper, Bklyn., 1970-74, Palo Alto, Calif., 1974-76; nat. sec. Socialist Labor Party, Sunnyvale, 1980—; mem. nat. exec. subcom. Socialist Labor Party, 1976-79. Office: Socialist Labor Party of Am PO Box 218 Mountain View CA 94042-0218

BILLUPS, NORMAN FREDRICK, college dean, pharmacist; b. Portland, Oreg., Oct. 15, 1934; s. John Alexander and Myrtle I. (Morris) B.; m. Shirley Mae Brooks, July 7, 1956; children: Tamra Mae, Timothy Fredrick. Student, Portland State U., 1952-55; BS in Pharmacy, Oreg. State U., 1958, MS in Pharmacy, 1961, PhD (Am. Found. Pharm. Edn. fellow), 1963. Instr. Oreg. State U., 1958-60, grad. asst., 1960-63; asso. prof. pharmacy U. Ky., 1963-73, prof., 1974-77; dean, prof. pharmacy Coll. Pharmacy, U. Toledo, 1977—; pharmacist Ohio, Oreg., Ky., 1961—. Author: American Drug Index, ann, 1977—. Lay leader, chmn. pastor-parish com. local Meth. Ch. Recipient Rsch. Achievement award Am. Soc. Hosp. Pharmacists, 1975, Outstanding Svc. award Ky. Pharm. Assn., 1977; NIH rsch. fellow, 1962-63; Dr. Norman F. Billups Disting. Svc. award established by U. Toledo Pharmacy Alumni Assn., 1992. Mem. Am. Assn. Colls. Pharmacy (Lyman award 1971), Am. Pharm. Assn., Ohio Pharm. Assn. (dir.), Ohio Soc. Hosp. Pharmacists, Toledo Acad. Pharmacy (dir., Pharmacist of Yr. 1997), Coun. Ohio Colls. Pharmacy (chmn. bd. trustees, chmn. coun.), Sigma Xi, Phi Kappa Phi (pres. U. Toledo chpt.), Rho Chi (chpt. advisor, nat. exec. com.), Phi Lambda Sigma (chpt. adv.), Kappa Psi (grand coun. dep., nat. officer), Lambda Kappa Sigma (hon. mem., nat. patron). Office: Univ Toledo Coll Pharmacy 2801 W Bancroft St Toledo OH 43606-3328

BILLY, GEORGE JOHN, library director; b. Rahway, N.J., Apr. 10, 1940; s. George and Marie (Zeleznik) B.; m. Valerie Jean McGreevy, July 19, 1969; children: Margaret, Christine. BA in History, Rutgers U., 1962; MLS, Pratt Inst., 1968; MA in HIstory, Adelphi U., 1973; PhD in History, CUNY, 1982. Ref. libr. Buffalo and Erie County Pub. Libr., 1968-70; acquisitions and ref. libr. Queensborough Community Coll., Bayside, N.Y., 1970-76; reader svcs. libr. U.S. Mcht. Marine Acad. Libr., Kings Point, N.Y., 1977-84, chief libr., 1984—; adj. prof. Palmer Sch. Libr. Info. Sci., C.W. Post/Long Island U., Greenvale, N.Y., 1983—. Author: Palmerston's Foreign Policy: 1848, 1993; compiler booklets in field. Mem. Selection com. Sch. Bd., Manhasset, 1992-94. Charles Freeman Meml. scholar, 1958-62, Buffalo and Erie County Pub. Libr. scholar, 1967-68. Mem. ALA, Assn. Coll. and Rsch. Librs., Spl. Librs. Assn. (transp. divsn.), L.I. Coun. Acad. Libr. Dirs., Nassau County Libr. Assn., Beta Phi Mu. Office: US Mcht Marine Acad 300 Steamboat Rd Kings Point NY 11024-1634*

BILOW, HOWARD L., health care company executive; b. Providence, R.I.. BSBA, Boston U., 1973, MBA, 1975. V.p. corp. mktg. and managed care Fresenius Med. Care, Lexington, Mass., 1990—; bd. dirs. Renaissance Health Care, Inc., Westminster, Co., 1996—. Office: Fresenius Med Care NA 2 Ledgemont Ctr 95 Hayden Ave Lexington MA 02420-9192

BILOW, STEVEN CRAIG, computer and video systems specialist; b. L.A., July 10, 1960; s. Norman and Selma (Rifkin) B.; m. Patricia S. Crabb, Nov. 5, 1989. BFA in Music Composition, Calif. Inst. of the Arts, 1982; cert. logic design/theory, U. So. Calif., 1983; postgrad., Portland State U., 1990—. Cert. tchr. of movement expression, L.A., 1985. Mfg. engr. Hughes Aircraft EDSG, El Segundo, Calif., 1981-85; project engr. electro-optical test systems Hughes Aircraft EDSG, El Segundo, 1985-86; sr. systems analyst Tektronix, Info Display Group, Woodland Hills, Calif., 1986-88; software engr., math. surface representation Interactive Techs. div. Tektronix, Wilsonville, Oreg., 1988-91; sr. tech. support specialist Unix and X Window systems Interactive Techs. div. Tektronix, Wilsonville, Oreg., 1991-95; sr. product specialist video/networking divsn. internat. ops Tektronix Inc., 1995-96, mktg. mgr. video and networking divsn., 1996—; mem. ACM Spl. Interest Group in Computer Graphics, 1988—; keynote spkr. NASA Window System 94, 1994. Composer various electro-acoustic instrumental and choral works, 1978-83; author, editor: Designing For Producibility, 1980, Use Cases, Objects and X, 1993, Managers Guide to the Universal Distributed Desktop, 1995; book rev. editor Jour. Object Oriented Programming, 1991—; contbr. articles, columns and book revs. to profl. jours. Recipient Technical Excellence award, Tektronix, Inc., Wilsonville, 1988, 94. Mem. Object Oriented Programming Sys., Langs., and Applications (exec. com. 1992, 93, 94, 95, sponsor workshop on object-oriented software metrics 1993, 94), IEEE (tech. com. on computer graphics 1985—, tech. com. on super computer applications 1988), Assn. Computing Machinery, Am. Musicol. Soc., Oreg. Master Gardner Assn., Am. Rose Soc., Soc. Motion Picture and TV Engrs. Democrat. Avocations: music, dance, art collecting, stock market, literature. Office: Tektronix Interactive Tech PO Box 500 Beaverton OR 97077-0001

BILSKIE, KATHY, religious order administrator, nun; b. Vincennes, Ind., Aug. 4, 1947; d. Robert Edward and Edna Lillian (Hager) B. BS, Oakland City Coll., 1974; MS in Adminstrn., U. Notre Dame, 1983. Asst. adminstr. St. Joseph's Hosp., Huntingburg, Ind., 1969-83; dir. client svcs. Appalachian Regional Healthcare, Inc., Lexington, Ky., 1983-91; devel. dir. Sisters of St. Benedict, Ferdinand, Ind., 1991—; spkr. Nat. Catholic Devel., Chgo., 1995, St. Mary-of-the-Woods Coll., Terre Haute, Ind., 1993; cons. Nat. Religious Retirement Office, Washington, 1996. Mem. Fund Raising Execs. Louisville, Ky. Planned Giving Coun. Office: Sisters of St Benedict 802 E 10th St Ferdinand IN 47532-9239

BILSKY, EDWARD GERALD, clinical social worker; b. Framingham, Mass., Jan. 31, 1961; s. Morton Edgar and Lois Ruth (Dunn) B. BA in Psychology, BA Sociology cum laude, Boston Coll., 1982; MSW, Simmons Coll. Sch. Social Work, 1991. Lic. ind. clin. social worker. Psychol. student intern Met. State Hosp., Waltham, Mass., 1981-84; family co-therapist Office of Michael A. Sperber, Newton, Mass., 1982; psychol. cons. Mentor, Inc., Cambridge, Mass., 1983-84; mental health worker II St. Elizabeth's Hosp., Brighton, Mass., 1984-85; sr. mental health worker, emergency rm. cons. Metrowest Med. Ctr., 1985-91; clin. social worker Heritage Hosp., 1991-92, dir. admissions, 1992-93, dir. intern tng., 1991-93; clin. social worker Wayland Clin. Assocs., 1991-97; asst. dir. psychiatric emergency svcs. Advocates, Inc., 1993-95; dir. clin. ops. Psychiat. Emergency Svc. Advocates, Inc., 1995-97; dir. mktg. and bus. devel. Behavioral Health Svcs. Divsn., Advocates, Inc., 1997; v.p. ops. Behavioral Health Mgmt. Solutions, Inc., 1993-97; profl. rels. mgr. New England Regional Care Ctr., MCC Behavioral Care, Holyoke, Mass., 1997—. Author: (with others) Managing the Balance: Looking at Work and Home Responsibilities, 1991. Mem. NASW. Home: 5 Blueberry Cir Framingham MA 01701 Office: 300 Whitney Ave Ste 400 Holyoke MA 01040

BILTCHIK, DAVID ELLIS, business consultant; b. N.Y.C., Dec. 16, 1936; s. Isidore and Dorothy Deborah (Turberg) B.; m. Magda Jane Jegher, Aug. 9, 1939; children: Elizabeth Sarah, Christina Deborah. AB, Harvard Coll., 1958. With U.S. fgn. svc. Dept. of State, various locations, 1959-71; with Carnegie Endowment Internat. Peace, Washington, 1971-77; exec. sec. U.S. Dept. Commerce, 1977-78; dep. asst. sec. internat. trade policy U.S. Dept. Commerce, Washington, 1978-81; founding ptnr. Cons. Internat. Group, Inc., Washington, 1981-91, chmn., CEO, 1991—. Pres. Longview Found., Washington, 1994—. With U.S. Army, 1958-59. Mem. Met. Club., St. Albans Tennis Club. Democrat. Jewish. Avocation: tennis. E-mail: CIGROUP@aol.com. Home: 3425 Ordway St NW Washington DC 20016 Office: Cons Internat Group Inc 1616 H St NW Washington DC 20006

BILTONEN, RODNEY LINCOLN, biochemistry and pharmacology educator; b. Ont., Can., Aug. 24, 1937; came to U.S., 1941; s. Frank Emil and Frances Cecilia (Castren) B.; m. Margaret Jane Kobel, Aug. 6, 1960; children—Michael Andrew, Eric Franklin. A.B., Harvard Coll., 1959; Ph.D., U. Minn., 1965. Asst. prof. Johns Hopkins U., Balt., 1966-72; assoc. prof. biochemistry and pharmacology U. Va., Charlottesville, 1972-77, prof., 1977—, assoc. dean, 1979-81, assoc. provost, 1981-84; vis. prof. Gulbenkian Inst., Portugal, 1970-71, U. Lund, Sweden, 1971, Cayetano, Lima, Peru, 1976, U. N.C., Chapel Hill, 1980, CNR, Genoa, Italy, 1993, The Technical U. Denmark, 1995; James Disting. prof. physics St. Francis Xavier U., Antigonish, N.S., 1984; cons. in field. Assoc. editor Biophys. Jour., 1991-95; mem. editl. bd. Chemistry and Physics of Lipids, 1995—; contbr. numerous articles to profl. jours. Recipient G.T. Walker award Sigma Xi, 1965, Huffman Meml. award Calorimetry Conf., 1989; NIH fellow, 1965-66; grantee NSF, 1968—, NIH, 1970—. Mem. Am. Soc. Biol. Chemistry and Molecular Biology, Am. Calorimetry Conf. (chmn. 1976-77), Biophys. Soc. (councilor 1984-86), Am. Chem. Soc., AAAS. Office: Univ Va Dept Pharmacology 1300 Jefferson Park Ave Charlottesville VA 22903-3363

BILYEU, GARY EDWARD, government official; b. Forest City, Iowa, Nov. 9, 1954; s. Roy Marcellus and Norma Jean (Hillesland) B.; m. Lonnie Jo Ann Bartel, Apr. 6, 1974; children: Rachel, Rebekah, Abraham, Deborah. AA, North Iowa Area Cmty. Coll., 1975. Cert. gen. real property appraiser, Iowa. Field appraiser Mason City (Iowa) Assesor, 1976-77, deputy assessor, 1977-80; deputy assessor Cerro Gordo County, Mason City, 1980-82; assessor Story County, Nevada, Iowa, 1982—; assessment adminstrn. specialist IAAO, 1998—. Contbr. articles to profl. jours. Apptd. pub. mem. Legis. Task Force to study Iowa's Sys. of State and Local Taxation, 1997. Mem. Internat. Assn. of Assessing Officers (assessment adminstrn. specialist designation 1998, sect. chair 1995-96). Mem. Assembly of God. Avocations: sports, basketball. Office: Story County 900 6th St Nevada IA 50201-2004

BILZ, LAURIE S., nursing educator; b. Hackensack, N.J., Nov. 27, 1951; d. Richard F. and Lila (Russell) B. AAS, Bergen Community Coll., Paramus, N.J., 1972; BSN, Dominican Coll., 1990; cert. British health care system, Wroxton Coll., Eng., 1990; MSN, Seton Hall U., 1992; MPA, L.I. U., 1994. RN, N.J.; cert. med.-surg. nurse; cert. clin. specialist in med.-surg. nursing. RN Pascack Valley Hosp., Westwood, N.J.; clin. nursing instr. Fairleigh Dickinson U., Teaneck, N.J., 1995—; clin. nursing instr. Bergen C.C., 1993-97. Mem. ANA, N.J. Nurse's Assn., NLN. Home: 509 Bergen Ave Westwood NJ 07675-5244

BINCH, CAROLINE LESLEY, illustrator, photographer; b. Manchester, Eng., June 5, 1947; d. Samuel William and Sybil (Colborne) Binch; children: Joseph, Thomas. Diploma, Salford Tech. Coll., Manchester, 1967. Freelance illustrator Cornwall, Eng. Illustrator: Billy the Great, 1991, Amazing Grace, 1991, Hue Boy, 1993 (Smarties award 1993), Boundless Grace, 1995, Down by the River, 1996, New Born, 1999, Christy's Dream, 1999; illustrator, author: Gregory Cool, 1994, Since Dad Left, 1998. Avocations: music, walking, travel, swimming, outdoors.

BINDENAGEL, JAMES DALE, diplomat; b. Huron, S.D, June 30, 1949; s. Gordon Dean and Patricia Jean (Williams) B.; m. Jean Kathleen Lundfelt, Dec. 26, 1971; children: Annamarie, Carl Jakob. BA, U. Ill, 1971, MPA, 1977. With U.S. Consulate, Bremen, Germany, 1977-79; econ. officer Office Ctrl. European Affairs U.S. Dept. State, Washington, 1980-83, dir. Office Ctrl. European Affairs, 1992-94; polit. officer Am. Embassy, Bonn, Germany, 1983-86, dep. chief mission, 1994-96; acting dir. Can. affairs U.S. Dept. State, 1988-89; dep. chief mission Am. Embassy, Berlin, 1989-90; divsn. chief developing countries and trade orgns. U.S. Dept. State Econ. and Bus. Affairs Bur., 1991; dir. Rockwell Internat., 1991-92; chargé d'affaires, acting amb. Am. Embassy, Bonn, 1996-97; sr. coord. New Transatlantic Agenda German Marshall Fund, 1997-98; dir. Washington Conf. on Holocaust-era Assets, 1998—, spl. envoy, 1999—. Capt. USAR, 1971-74. Congl. fellow Am. Polit. Sci. Assn., 1987-88. Mem. Am. Polit. Sci. Assn. (congl. fellow 1987-88, Nat. Performance award 1998), Am. Coun. on Germany, Coun. on Fgn. Rels., Woodstock Bus. Conf., Pi Sigma Alpha. Roman Catholic. Avocation: tennis, hiking. Office: 202 Northmoor Dr Silver Spring MD 20901-2645

BINDER, BETTYE B., author, lecturer; b. New Rochelle, N.Y., Feb. 12, 1939; d. Alex and Leah (Binder) B.; div. BA, Barnard Coll., 1960; MA in Pub. Law and Govt., Columbia U., 1962. spkr. Whole Life Expo, 1985-97; exec. prodr. Brain and Mind Symposium, L.A., 1992-94. Author: (books) Past Life Regression Guidebook, 1985, 3rd edit., 7th printing, 1999, Past Lives Present Karma Workbook, 1985, Discovering Past Lives and Other Dimensions, 1994, (mini mag.) Who Were You in Past Lives?, 1992, (video) Meditative Techniques, Home Study Guide to Past Life Recall, 1998. Coord. Students for Kennedy-Johnson, N.Y. State, 1960; rschr., writer, Dem. Nat. Com., Washington, 1963-65; assoc. dir. Fight Inflation Together, L.A., 1973-76. Mem. Assn. for Past Life Rsch. and Therapies (bd. dirs. 1991-97, pres. 1993-97). Democrat. Jewish. Avocations: science fiction, ancient history, cats. E-mail: BettyeBinder@netscape.net. Office: PO Box 4011 Culver City CA 90231-4011

BINDER, CHARLES E., federal judge; b. 1949. BA, Western Mich. U., 1971; JD, Duke U., 1974. Law clk. to Hon. Wendell Miles, 1974-76, pvt. practice, 1976-84; magistrate judge U.S. Dist. Ct. (ea. dist.) Mich., Bay City, 1984—. Mem. Fed. Magistrate Judges Assn., State Bar Mich., Bay County Bar Assn. Fax: (517) 894-8819. Office: US Dist Ct Ea Dist Mich Rm 323 1000 Washington Ave Bay City MI 48708

BINDER, DAVID FRANKLIN, lawyer, author; b. Beaver Falls, Pa., Aug. 1, 1935; s. Walter Carl and Jessie Maivis (Bliss) B.; m. Deana Jacqueline Pines, Dec. 25, 1971; children: April, Bret. BA, Geneva Coll., 1956; JD, Harvard U., 1959. Bar: Pa. 1960, U.S. Ct. Appeals (3rd cir.) 1963, U.S. Supreme Ct. 1967. Law clk. to chief justice Pa. Supreme Ct., 1959-61; counsel Fidelity Mut. Life Ins. Co., Phila., 1964-66; ptnr. Bennett, Bricklin & Saltzburg, Phila., 1967-68; mem. Richter, Syken, Ross, and Binder, Phila., 1969-72, Raynes, McCarty, Binder, Ross and Mundy, Phila., 1972—; mem. faculty Pa. Coll. Judiciary; judge pro tempore Phila. Common Pleas Ct., 1991-97; lectr., course planner Pa. Bar Inst.; mem. civil procedural rules com., ad hoc. com. on evidence Supreme Ct. Pa. Author: Hearsay Handbook, 1975, ann. supplements, 2nd edit., 1983, 3rd edit., 1991. Recipient Disting. Alumnus award Geneva Coll., 1981. Mem. ABA, Pa. Bar Assn., Phila. Bar Assn., Assn. Trial Lawyers Am. (lectr.), Pa. Trial Lawyers Assn., Harvard Law Sch. Assn., Am. Bd. Trial Advs., Am. Coll. Trial Lawyers, Union League. Home: 1412 Flat Rock Rd Penn Valley PA 19072-1216 Office: Raynes McCarty Binder Ross and Mundy 1845 Walnut St Ste 2000 Philadelphia PA 19103-4767

BINDER, ELAINE KOTELL, consultant to associations; b. Boston, Oct. 12, 1938; d. Maxwell and Florence (Blumsack) Kotell; m. Richard A. Binder, Aug. 28, 1960; children: Mark Stephen, Jonathan Stuart. AB, Radcliffe Coll., 1960; MA, U. Md., 1975. Tchr. City of Medford, Mass., 1960-62; project dir. Wider Opportunities for Women, Washington, 1971-75, Women's Equity Action League Fund, Washington, 1976-78; mng. ptnr. Binder, Elster, Mendelson, Wheeler, Bethesda, Md., 1978-80; adminstrn. dir. AAUW, Washington, 1980-85; exec. dir. B'nai B'rith Women, Washington, 1985-94; pres. Binder Assocs., Bethesda, 1994—; prin. ptnr. Tecker Consultants, Trenton, N.J., 1994—; cons. Bethesda, 1975-76. Co-author: Careers for Peers, 1973; contbr. articles to profl. jours. Trustee Temple Shalom, Silver Spring, Md., 1974-76; pres., v.p. Montgomery County Commn. for Women, Rockville, Md., 1978-80; commr. Anti-Defamation League, N.Y., 1985—; bd. dirs. Jewish Coun. for the Aging, 1996—. Fellow Am. Soc. Assn. Execs. (bd. dirs. 1990-93, vice chmn. 1994), Greater Washington Soc. Assn. Execs. (com. chair 1989—). Democrat. Jewish. Avocations: music, art, collecting Native American art and artifacts, reading. Office: Tecker Consultants 427 River View Exec Park Trenton NJ 08611 Office: Binder Assocs 6704 Bradley Blvd Bethesda MD 20817-3045

BINDER, GORDON M., health and medical products executive; b. St. Louis, 1935. Degree in elec. engring., Purdue U., 1957; MBA, Harvard U., 1962. Formerly with Litton Industries, 1962-64; various fin. mgmt. positions Ford Motor Co., 1964-69; CFO Sys. Devel. Corp., 1971-81; v.p., CFO Amgen, Thousand Oaks, Calif., 1982-88, CEO, 1988—, chmn. bd., 1990—. Baker scholar Harvard U. Office: Amgen 1 Amgen Center Dr Thousand Oaks CA 91320-1799*

BINDER, HERBERT R., drug store chain executive; b. June 20, 1937; m. Frances Binder, June 26, 1960; children: Marcy, Joel. BS in Pharmacy, U. Toronto, Can., 1960. Owner, pharmacist Parlton Drugs, Toronto, 1962-69; with Shoppers Drug Mart, 1969—; v.p. ops. Shoppers Drug Mart, Willowdale, Can., 1980-84, formerly exec. v.p., 1984-89, pres., also COO, 1989—; bd. govs. Mt. Sinai Hosp.; bd. dirs. Medysis Health Group, Rx Can. Office: Shoppers Drug Mart, 225 Yorkland Blvd, Willowdale, ON Canada M2J 4Y7

BINDER, JAMES KAUFFMAN, computer consultant; b. Reading, Pa., Nov. 20, 1920; s. Paul Burdette and Edna (Kauffman) B.; B.A., Lehigh U., 1941; M.A., Johns Hopkins U., 1952; profl. cert. in systems mgmt. U. Calif.-San Diego, 1976; A.S. in Data Processing, San Diego Evening Coll., 1979, A.A. in Fgn. Lang., 1979; A.A. in Spanish, Mira Costa Coll., Oceanside, Calif., 1981. Instr. English, Notre Dame U., South Bend, Ind., 1948-49; prof. English, Athens (Greece) Coll., 1950-51; CARE rep., Greece, 1951-52; reporter, staff writer Athens News, 1952-53; dir. lang. tng. World Council Chs. Refugee Service, Athens, 1953-54; co-editor Am. Overseas Guide, N.Y., West Berlin, 1957-58; lectr. English, U. Md. Overseas Program, European and Far East divs., 1958-66; successively supr. Cen. Info. Ctr., supt. documents, sr. systems analyst GA Techs., Inc., La Jolla, Calif., 1968-85. Recipient Williams Prize, Lehigh U., 1939, 41; Johns Hopkins U. Grad. Sch. Pres. scholar, 1945-48. Roman Catholic. Clubs: Tudor and Stuart, Automobile of So. Calif. Author: The Correct Comedy, 1951; contbg. translator Modern Scandinavian Poetry, 1948; editor: (with Erwin H. Tiebe) American Overseas Guide, 1958.

BINDER, L(EONARD) JAMES, magazine editor, retired; b. Jackson, Mich., June 21, 1926; s. Leonard George and Ethel Cecile (Lilly) B.; m. Margery Elizabeth Rose, Sept. 6, 1950; children: Timothy James, Michael Paul, Douglas Harold. B.S., Central Mich. U., 1952. Editor Wingfoot Clan, Goodyear Tire & Rubber Co., 1952-54, Wayne (Mich.) Eagle, 1954-55; news editor Pontiac (Mich.) Press, 1955-57; editor, newsman AP, 1957-60; state editor Detroit News, 1960-67; editor-in-chief Army mag., Washington, 1967-93; corr., book reviewer Nat. Observer, 1962-67; v.p. publs. Assn. U.S. Army, 1992-94; ret., 1993. Author: Lemnitzer: A Soldier for His Time, 1997; editor: Front and Ctr., 1991; contbr. articles to various publs. Served with USN, 1944-46; with USAR, 1950-54. Recipient George Washington Honor medal Freedoms Found., 1975, George Washington award editorial, 1974, 76. Mem. Am. Soc. Mag. Editors, Soc. Profl. Journalists, Cosmos Club, Nat. Press Club, Detroit Press Club, Ends of Earth Club, Soc. of Midland Authors. Methodist. Home: 681 N Golden Sands Dr Mears MI 49436-9655 also: 12728 Inverness Way Woodbridge VA 22192-5036

BINDER, MADELINE DOTTI, retail professional; b. Chgo., Oct. 7, 1942; d. Martin and Anne (Sweet) Binder; children: Mark Nathan, Maria Susan. BEd, Nat. Coll. Edn., 1964, MS, 1972, MS in Human Svcs-Counseling, 1993. Tchr. Rochester Schs. (Minn.), 1963-64, Orange County Schs., Orlando, Fla., 1967-68; reading cons. Palatine (Ill.) Schs., 1972-73; instr. Parent Effective Tng., Wilmette, Ill., 1974-76; tchr. Effectiveness Tng., 1974-76; pres. Profls. Diversified, Wilmette, 1976-89; remedial and enrichment reading tchr. Waukegan (Ill.) Pub. Schs., 1986; pres. Lifeline, 1989-90; mgmt. cons. World Wide Diamonds Assn., Schaumburg, Ill., 1979-89; Pearl direct distbr. Amway Corp., Ada, Mich., 1976-94; exec. distbr. NU Skin, 1992; distbr. Emerald-Starlight Internat., 1994—; psychotherapist, 1993-97. Author: Organic Gardening, 1975, The Go-Getters Planner, 1986, Singles Guide to Chicagoland, 1995, 65 Ideas to Assist You in Parenting Your Child During Your Divorce. Leader, Camp Fire Girls, Evanston, Ill., 1963, 75. Ednl. scholar Nat. Coll. Edn., 1971. Mem. Phi Delta Kappa, Alpha Delta Omega. Jewish.

BINDER, MILDRED KATHERINE, retired county public welfare agency executive; b. York, Pa., Jan. 5, 1918; d. Jemie Irving and Emma Jane (Billet) Binder. BA magna cum laude in Sociology, Hood Coll., 1940. Sec., mgr. Stock's Appliances, York, 1940-42; caseworker York County Bd. Assistance, Pa. Dept. Public Welfare, 1942-49, 1953-58, supr., 1949-53, 1958-59, exec. dir., 1959-83. Past mem. exec. com. York County Employment and Tng. Com.; past mem. dept. task forces state Social Service Delivery to Client Info. System, also mem. state ops. rev. bd.; past mem. bd. York County Coun. Alcoholism, 1959-62, Cmty. Progress Coun., 1965-67; co-chmn. Cmty. Dialogue Com., 1968-69; mem. bd. Pre-Paid Health York, Inc., 1979; mem. human svcs. planning coalition United Way, 1978-83, chmn. coun. agy. execs., 1967-71, 1976-78; past mem. consumer adv. couns. Gen. Telephone, Met. Edison; bd. dirs. Literacy Council of York County, 1985-86; mem. York County Human Svcs. Adv. Com., 1983-87; mem. York County Area Agy. on Aging Adv. Com., 1989-95. Named Boss of Yr., Am. Bus. Women, 1973; named in commendations Pa. gov., Pa. Ho. of Reps. Mem. Am. Public Welfare Assn., AAUW (bd. dirs. York br. 1984-96), York County Hist. Soc. (bd. dirs. 1989-97), York Transp. Club (bd. dirs. 1987-91), Coll. Club York (bd. dirs. 1994—), Hood Coll. Club (pres. 1993-97). Home: 1611 W Market St York PA 17404-5416

BINDER, RICHARD ALLEN, hematologist, oncologist; b. Boston, Aug. 26, 1937; s. Harry Aron and Beatrice (Seltzer) B.; m. Elaine F. Kotell; children: Mark Stephen, Jonathan Stuart. BSChemE, Northeastern U., Boston, 1960; MD, Tufts U., Boston, 1964. Diplomate Am. Bd. Internal Medicine, also sub-bds. in Hematology and Med. Oncology. Intern in medicine/resident in medicine New Eng. Med. Ctr., Boston, 1964-66; resident in medicine Columbia Presbyn. Hosp., N.Y.C., 1966-67; fellow in hematology Mt. Sinai Hosp., N.Y.C., 1967-68; instr. Tufts U. Sch. Medicine, 1970-71; asst. prof. Georgetown U., Washington, 1971-75, assoc. clin. prof. medicine, 1975-78, clin. prof. medicine, 1978—; v.p. Inova Health Sys., 1994-95; med. dir. Inova Fairfax Hosp. Cancer Ctr., 1999; assoc. chmn. dept. medicine Inova Fairfax Hosp., 1978—, v.p. med. staff, 1989-91, pres. med. staff, 1992-94, v.p. physician affairs, 1995-96, chmn. cancer steering com., 1997—; bd. dirs. Inova Hosp., Inova Health Sys. Found. Bd., Hospice No. Va.; active Inova Hosps. Bd., 1988-95, Inova Health Sys. Bd., 1992-95, Hospice of No. Va. Bd., 1993—, vice-chmn., 1995-97, chmn. 1998. Editor Hematology Rev.-Family Practice, 1979; contbr. articles to profl. jours. Maj. U.S. Army, 1968-70. Recipient Golden Apple, Georgetown U., 1975, 76, Vicentennial medal Georgetown U., 1991, Excellence in Teaching award Fairfax Hosp., 1994—. Fellow ACP; mem. Am. Soc. Hematology, Am. Soc. Clin. Oncology, Fairfax Hosp. Assn. (bd. dirs. 1988-95), Alumni Assn. Tufts U. (bd. dirs. 1990—), Tufts U. Med. Sch. Alumni Assn. (bd. dirs. 1998—). Home: 6704 Bradley Blvd Bethesda MD 20817-3045 Office: Fairfax Hematology 3289 Woodburn Rd Annandale VA 22003-6800

BINDLEY, WILLIAM EDWARD, pharmaceutical executive; b. Terre Haute, Ind., Oct. 6, 1940; s. William F. and Gertrude (Lynch) B.; children: William Franklin, Blair Scott, Sally Ann. BS, Purdue U., 1961; grad. wholesale mgmt. program, Stanford U., 1966. Asst. treas. Controls Co. Am., Melrose Park, Ill., 1962-65; vice-chmn. E.H. Bindley & Co., Terre Haute, 1965-68; pres., chmn. bd., CEO Bindley Western Industries, Inc., Indpls., 1968—; Scholl scholarship guest lectr. Loyola U., Chgo., 1982; guest lectr. Young Pres. Orgn., Palm Springs, Calif. and Dallas, 1981, 82, 84, Ctr. for Entrepreneurs, Indpls., 1983, Purdue U., West Lafayette, Inc., De Pauw U., Greencastle, Ind., disting. lectr. Georgetown U., Washington, 1989—, mem. adv. bd.; bd. dirs. Key Bank NA, Cleve., Shoe Carnival, Inc.; former owner basketball team Ind. Pacers. State dir. Bus. for Reagan-Bush, Washington and Indpls., 1980; trustee Marian Coll., Indpls., Indpls. United Way, St. Vincent Hosp., Indpls.; bd. dirs. Indpls. Entrepreneurship Acad., Nat. Entrepreneurship Found., U.S. Ski Team, chmn. fin., exec. com. mem.; mem. adv. bd. Rose Hulman Inst. Tech.; mem. pres.'s coun. Purdue U., dean's adv. bd. Named Hon. Ky. Col., 1980, Sagamore of the Wabash, Gov. Orr, State of Ind., 1989, Entrepreneur of Yr., State of Ind., 1992. Mem. Young Pres. Orgn. (area dir., chmn. 1982, award 1983), Nat. Wholesale Druggists Assn. (dir. 1981-84, Svc. award 1984), Purdue U. Alumni Assn. (life), Woodstock Club, Meridian Hills Countryn Club. Republican. Roman Catholic. Avocations: skiing; tennis; golf; boating. Office: Bindley Western Industries Inc Ste 300 10333 N Meridian St Indianapolis IN 46290-1074*

BINES, HARVEY ERNEST, lawyer, educator, writer; b. Winthrop, Mass., Nov. 25, 1941; s. Carl and Lillian (Cooper) B.; m. Joan Carol Paller, Dec. 27, 1964; children: Jonathan W., Joel T., Susanne R., Benjamin E. BS, MIT, 1963; JD, U. Va., 1970. Bar: Mass 1971, Va. 1971, U.S. Dist. Ct. Mass., U.S. Dist. Ct. (ea. dist.) Va., U.S. Ct. Appeals (1st, 3d, 4th, 7th and D.C. cirs.), U.S. Supreme Ct. Law clk. to hon. John D. Butzner Jr. U.S. Ct. Appeals (4th cir.), Richmond, Va., 1970-71; asst. prof. Law Sch. U. Va., Charlottesville, 1971-74, assoc. prof. Law Sch., 1974-76; assoc. Sullivan & Worcester, Boston, 1976-79, ptnr., 1980—; adj. prof. Boston Coll. Law Sch., Chestnut Hill, Mass., 1981-88, bd. dirs., treas. Schweitzer Fellowship, Boston. Author: Law of Investment Management, 1978, 1991. Lt. USNR, 1963-67. Mem. Am. Law Inst., Internat. Bar Assn., Boston Bar Assn. Email: heb@sandw.com. Home: 36 Clarke St Lexington MA 02421-4916 Office: Sullivan & Worcester 1 Post Office Sq Ste 2300 Boston MA 02109-2129

BINES, JOAN PALLER, museum director; b. Indpls., July 8, 1942; d. Ben and Ruth S. Paller; m. Harvey E. Bines, Dec. 26, 1964; children: Jonathan, Joel, Susanne, Benjamin. PhD, U. Va., 1976. Dir. Golden Ball Tavern Mus., Weston, Mass., 1982—. Office: Golden Ball Tavern Mus PO Box 223 Weston MA 02493-0001

BINFORD, GREGORY GLENN, lawyer; b. Canton, Ohio, Oct. 8, 1948; s. Edwin and Helen Marie B. BA, Case Western Res. U., 1970, JD, 1973. Bar: Ohio 1973. Ptnr. Guren, Merritt, Cleve., 1973-84, Benesch, Friedlander, Cleve., 1984—. Mem. men's com. Cleve. Playhouse, 1980—. Mem. ABA, Nat. Health Lawyers Assn., Cleve. Bar Assn. (chair health law sect.), Ohio State Bar Assn. Office: Benesch Friedlander 200 Public Sq 2300 America Bldg Cleveland OH 44114-2378*

BINFORD, JESSE STONE, JR., chemistry educator; b. Freeport, Tex., Nov. 1, 1928; s. Jesse Stone and Eglan Lee (Bracewell) B.; m. Lolita Ramona Fritz, June 8, 1955; children: Lincoln Bracewell, Jason Jolly. BA in Chemistry, Rice U., 1950, MA in Chemistry, 1952; PhD in Phys. Chemistry, U. Utah, 1955. Instr. chemistry U. Tex., Austin, 1955-58; asst. prof. U. of the Pacific, Stockton, Calif., 1958-60, assoc. prof., 1960-61; Fulbright prof., chmn. dept. chemistry Univ. Nacional Autonoma de Honduras, Tegucigalpa, 1968-69; vis. rsch. prof. Thermochemistry Lab., U. Lund, Sweden, 1971, researcher, 1982-83; rsch. fellow Chelsea Coll., U. London, 1983; assoc. prof. U. South Fla., Tampa, 1961-72, prof., 1972—; cons. Fla. consortium AID, Honduras, 1969, Exxon Prodn. Rsch. Co., Houston, 1974; chmn. State Univ. Faculty Senate Coun., Fla., 1972-76; dir. gen. chemistry program U. South Fla., 1978-82, 98—; vis. prof. dept. chem. engring. Rice U., 1993-94, rschr. Cox Lab. for Biomed. Engring., Inst. Bioscis. and Bioengring., 1993-94; mem. Inst. for Biomolecular Sci., U. South Fla., pres. faculty senate, 1999—. Author: (textbook) Foundations of Chemistry, 1977, 2nd edit., 1985; contbr. articles to profl. jours., 1956—. Active bicycle adv. com. Hillsborough County, Tampa, 1975-93, chairperson bicycle adv. com., 1990-93; faculty advisor U. South Fla. Bicycle Club, 1972—; coord. spl. tutoring program Danforth Found., Tampa, 1968. Grantee Petroleum Rsch. Fun, 1960-62, USPHS (NIH), 1966-68, Rsch. Corp., 1986. Mem. AAUP, AAAS, Am. Chem. Soc. (nat. and Fla. sect.), Calorimetry Conf., League of Am. Bicyclists, Golden Key, Sigma Xi, Phi Beta Kappa, Phi Lambda Upsilon,

Sigma Pi Sigma, Omicron Delta Kappa. Avocations: bicycling, travel, reading. Home: 1905 E 111th Ave Tampa FL 33612-6150 Office: U South Fla Dept Chemistry 4202 E Fowler Ave Tampa FL 33620-9951

BING, JONATHAN LLOYD, lawyer; b. Boston, Mar. 13, 1970; s. Richard Newton and Joanne Carol (Goldner) B. BA, U. Pa., 1992; JD, NYU, 1995. Bar: N.Y. 1996, N.J. 1996, D.C. 1996. Law clk. U.S. Dist. Ct. Judge Bruce M. VanSickle, Bismarck, N.D., 1995-96; assoc. Haythe & Curley, N.Y.C., 1996—. Contbr. articles to profl. jours. Recipient Arthur T. Vanderbilt medal NYU Law Sch., N.Y.C., 1995. Mem. ABA, N.Y. State Bar Assn., Assn. of Bar of City of N.Y., N.Y. County Lawyers Assn. Home: 212 E 47th St Apt 29J New York NY 10017-2120 Office: Haythe & Curley Judge Bruce M VanSickle 237 Park Ave New York NY 10017-3140

BING, RICHARD MCPHAIL, lawyer; b. Lewes, Del., Aug. 23, 1950; s. Arden E. and Ellen Louise (Judd) B.; m. Valerie Lynn Wasson, Dec. 18, 1971; children: Jennifer Lynn, Kristin Tyler. BA, U. Richmond, 1972, JD, 1978. Bar: Va. 1979, U.S. Dist. Ct. (ea. and we. dists.) Va. 1979, U.S. Dist. Ct. (we. dist.) Pa. 1990, U.S. Dist. Ct. (no. dist.) N.Y. 1990, U.S. Dist. Ct. (ctrl. dist.) Ill. 1996, U.S. Ct. Appeals (4th cir.) 1979, U.S. Ct. appeals (2d cir.) 1990, U.S. Supreme Ct. 1994, U.S. Dist. Ct. (ctrl. dist.) Ill. 1996. Dir. ins. Bur. of Ins., Richmond, Va., 1978-79; resident gen counsel Va. Gasoline Retailers Assn., Richmond, 1979-83; ptnr. Pearce & Bing, Richmond, 1983-93, Bing & Assocs., P.C., Richmond, 1993—; adj. prof. law J. Sargent Reynolds Community Coll., Richmond, 1984-85. Mem. Henrico County Rep. Com; bd. dirs. Three Chopt PTA, Richmond, 1984-85. Mem. ABA, Va. Bar Assn., Va. Bar, Richmond Bar Assn., Fed. bar Assn., Assn. Trial Lawyers Am., Va. Trial Lawyers Assn., Nat. Lawyers Club, Tcukahoe Jaycees (pres. 1981-82), Bull and Bear Club, Hermitage Country Club, Tobacco Co. Club, The Spider Club (bd. dirs.), Am. Assn. of Franchisees and Dealers, Svc. Sta. Dealers of Am., Inc., Affiliate Attys. Group. Avocations: golf, bicycling, photography. Home: 1701 Habwood Ln Richmond VA 23233-4451 Office: Bing & Assocs PC 300 Arboretum Pl Ste 140 Richmond VA 23236-3465

BINGAMAN, ANNE K., lawyer; b. Jerome, Ariz., July 3, 1943; d. William Emil and Anne Ellen (Baker) Kovacovich; m. Jeff F. Bingaman, Sept. 14, 1968; 1 child, John. BA in History, Stanford U., 1965; gen. course cert. with honors, London Sch. of Econs., England, 1964-65; LLB, Stanford U., 1968. Bar: Calif. 1969, N.Mex. 1969, Ariz. 1969, U.S. Dist. Ct. D.C. 1983. Atty. Brown & Bain, Phoenix, 1968-69, N.Mex. Bur. Revenue, Santa Fe, 1969-70, Modrall, Sperling, Roehl, Harris & Sisk, Albuquerque, 1970, N.Mex. Atty. Gen's. Office, Santa Fe, 1970-72; asst. prof. to assoc. prof. U. N.Mex. Sch. Law, Santa Fe, 1972-76; founding ptnr. Bingaman & Davenport, Santa Fe, 1977-82; ptnr. Brown, Bain & Bingaman, Santa Fe and Washington, 1982-84, Onek, Klein & Farr, Washington, 1984-85, Powell, Goldstein, Frazer & Murphy, Washington, 1985-93; asst. atty. gen. Anti-Trust Div. U.S. Dept. Justice, Washington, D.C., 1993-96; sr. v.p. LCI Internat., McLean, Va., 1997—. Contbr. articles to profl. jours. Mem. exec. com. Stanford Law Sch. Bd. Visitors, 1978-80, 88-90; mem. for N.Mex. of 10th Cir. Jud. Nominating Panel, 1977-80. Ford Found. fellow 1975; recipient Nat. Vol. award Stanford Assocs., 1989. Fellow Am. Bar Found.; mem. ABA, N.Mex. Bar (founder, vice-chair antitrust sect. 1982-85, chair com. to rewrite comm. property & other state laws to conform to ERA), Am. Law Inst. Democrat. Episcopalian. Office: LCI Internat 8180 Greensboro Dr Ste 800 Mc Lean VA 22102-3823*

BINGAMAN, JEFF, senator; b. El Paso, Tex., Oct. 3, 1943; s. Jesse and Beth (Ball) B.; m. Anne Kovacovich, Sept. 13, 1968. BA in Govt., Harvard U., 1965; JD, Stanford U., 1968. Bar: N.Mex. 1968. Asst. atty. gen., 1969; atty. Stephenson, Campbell & Olmsted, 1971-72; ptnr. Campbell, Bingaman & Black, Santa Fe, 1972-78; former atty. gen. State of N.Mex.; now U.S. senator from N.Mex. 106th Congress; mem. armed svcs. com., mem. joint econ. com., mem. Senate Dem. steering and coordination com. State of N.Mex., mem. Senate Den. tech. and comm. com., ranking minority mem., mem. energy and natural resources subcom. of energy prodn. and regulation, mem. labor and human resources com. U.S. Army 1968-74. Democrat. Methodist. Home: PO Box 5775 Santa Fe NM 87502-5775 Office: US Senate 703 Hart Senate Bldg Washington DC 20510

BINGER, WILSON VALENTINE, civil engineer; b. Greenwich, N.Y., Feb. 28, 1917; s. George and Blanche (Wilson) B.; m. Barbara Ridgway, May 19, 1947 (dec. 1984); children: Wilson Valentine, Mary Blanche, Julia Ridgway (Mrs. Nurettin Akgül); m. Jane E. Schwarz, Apr. 24, 1986. AB cum laude, Harvard, 1938, MS in Engring., 1939. Registered profl. engr., N.Y., Ohio. Soils engr. U.S. Army Engrs., Wilmington, Del., 1939-40; soils and found. engr. Gatun 3d Locks project, Panama Canal, 1940-43; soils engr., resident engr. Parsons Brinckerhoff, Hogan & MacDonald, Caracas, Venezuela, 1945-46; chief soils engr. Parsons Brinckerhoff, Hogan & MacDonald, Caracas, Buenos Aires, Argentina, 1948-49; chief soils and found. sect. Isthmian Canal Studies, Panama Canal, 1946-47; chief soils and geology br. Mo. River divsn. U.S. Army Engrs., Omaha, 1947-48; v.p. Porterfield-Binger Constrn. Co., Youngstown, Ohio, 1950-52; regional mgr. Tippetts-Abbett-McCarthy-Stratton, Bogota, Colombia, 1952-56; assoc. ptnr. Tippetts-Abbett-McCarthy-Stratton, N.Y.C., 1957-61, ptnr., 1962-84; chmn., 1975-84, cons. engr., 1985—. Author papers in field. Pres., trustee Chappaqua (N.Y.) Libr., 1967-69; trustee Robert Coll., Istanbul, Turkey, 1970—, vice chmn., 1974-78, sec., 1992—; bd. dirs. Regional Plan Assn., N.Y., 1983-88; chmn. bd. deacons Congl. Ch., 1959-62, trustee, 1985-88. Recipient Disting. Citizen award Warren (Ohio) Met. Area Assn., Steinmetz award Consulting Engr. Mag., Diamond Ann. Lifetime Achievement award N.Y. Assn. Cons. Engrs. Fellow ASCE, Inst. Civil Engrs. (U.K.), Am. Cons. Engrs. Coun. (v.p. 1973-75), N.Y. Acad. Scis.; mem. NAE, Royal Acad. Engring. U.K. (fgn. mem.), Am. Inst. Cons. Engrs. (councillor 1971-73, pres. 1973), NSPE, U.S. Com. Large Dams (mem. exec. com. 1964-69, sec. 1962-78), Internat. Com. Large Dams (v.p. 1978-81), N.Y. Assn. Cons. Engrs. (v.p., dir. 1964-65), Moles, Internat. Road Fedn. (dir. 1975-82, mem. exec. com. 1975-82), Fedn. Internat. des Ingenieurs Conseils (mem. exec. com. 1976-83, treas. 1976-79, v.p. 1980-81, pres. 1981-83), Century Club, Harvard Club (N.Y.C.), Univ. Club, East India Club (London), Phi Beta Kappa. Home: PO Box 225 Chappaqua NY 10514-0225 Office: 44 W 62nd St Apt 26B New York NY 10023-7013

BINGHAM, CHRISTOPHER, statistics educator; b. N.Y.C., Apr. 16, 1937; s. Alfred Mitchell and Sylvia (Knox) B.; m. Carolyn Higinbotham, Sept. 23, 1967. A.B., Yale U., 1958, M.A., 1960, Ph.D., 1964. Research fellow Conn. Agrl. Expt. Sta., New Haven, 1958-64; research assoc. in math. and biology Princeton U., N.J., 1964-66; asst. prof. stats. U. Chgo., 1967-72; assoc. prof. applied stats. U. Minn., St. Paul, 1972-79, prof., 1979—. Contbr. articles to profl. jours. Fellow Am. Statis. Assn., Inst. Math. Stats.; mem. Royal Statis. Soc., Biometric Soc., Soc. Indsl. and Applied Math. Unitarian. Home: 605 Winston Ct Mendota Heights MN 55118-1039 Office: U Minn Dept Applied Stats 1994 Buford Ave Saint Paul MN 55108-6038

BINGHAM, J. PETER, electronics research executive; married; 2 children. BS in Physics cum laude, Polytechnic Inst., N.Y.; MS in Exptl. Physics, U. Md., PhD in Elec. Engring. With RCA Consumer Electronics, David Sarnoff Rsch. Ctr.; exec. v.p., tech. Thomson Consumer Electronics; v.p. engring. Philips Consumer Electronics Co., 1982-91; with Philips Rsch. Philips Electronics N.Am. Corp., 1991; pres. Philips Rsch., 1991—; bd. dirs. Indsl. Rsch. Inst. Recipient David Sarnoff award, RCA Lab. Achievement award; Named in his honor Bingham Peak in Antarctica, Arctic Inst. of North Am. Office: 23 Brookwood Dr Briarcliff Manor NY 10510-2040

BINGHAM, JUNE, author, playwright; b. White Plains, N.Y., June 20, 1919; d. Max J.H. and Mabel (Limburg) Rossbach; m. Jonathan B. Bingham, Sept. 20, 1939 (dec. July 1986); children: Sherry B. Downes, Micki B. Esselstyn, Timothy, Claudia B. Meyers; m. Robert B. Birge, Mar. 28, 1987; 1 stepchild, Robert R. Student, Vassar Coll., 1936-38; BA, Barnard Coll., 1940. Writer, editor U.S. Treasury, Washington, 1943-45; editorial asst. Washington Post, 1945-46; writer Tarrytown (N.Y.) Daily News, 1946. Author: Do Cows Have Neuroses?, Do Babies Have Worries?, Do Teenagers Have Wisdom?, Courage to Change: An Introduction to Life and Thought of Reinhold Niebuhr, 1961, paperback, 1992, U Thant: The Search for Peace, 1970, (play) Triangles, 1986, You and the I.C.U., 1990, (play) Eleanor and Alice, 1996, (with others) The Inside Story: Psychiatry and Everyday Life, 1953, The Pursuit of Health, 1985, (musical) Squanto and Love, 1992, Young Roosevelts, 1993, The Other Lincoln, 1995; contbr. articles to nat. mags., newspapers and profl. jours. Bd. dirs. Barnard Coll., 1970-76, African-Am. Inst., N.Y.C., 1973-90, Riverdale Mental Health Assn., 1983—, Woodrow Wilson Found., Princeton, N.J., 1959-64, 83-89, Lehman Coll. Found., 1983-90, Ittleson Ctr. for Childhood Rsch., 1958-90, Franklin and Eleanor Roosevelt Inst., 1992—; founder T.L.C.; trained liaison comforter Vol. Program of Presbyn. Hosp., N.Y.C. Named Alumna of the Yr., Rosemary Hall, 1976. Mem. Authors Guild (nominating com. 1987-90), Dramatists Guild, PEN, Cosmopolitan Club. Democrat. Avocations: tennis, golf, theatre, movies, reading. Home: 5000 Independence Ave Bronx NY 10471-2804

BINGHAM, PARIS EDWARD, JR., electrical engineer, computer consultant; b. Aurora, Colo., Sept. 26, 1957; s. Paris Edward and Shirley Ann (Blehm) B.; m. Laurie Sue Piersol, May 9, 1981 (div. Sept. 1987); m. Helen Naef, Aug. 7, 1993. BS in Elec. Engring. and Computer Sci., U. Colo., 1979. Mem. tech. staff Western Electric Co., Aurora, 1979-81, system engr., 1981; mem. electronic tech. staff Hughes Aircraft Co., Aurora, 1981-83, staff engr., 1983-86, sr. staff engr., 1986-93, scientist, engr., 1993-94; area systems support engr. Sun Microsystems, Inc., Englewood, Colo., 1994—; cons. RJM Assocs., Huntington, N.Y., 1987-91; cons. Aurora, 1988—. Mem. IEEE, Assn. for Computing Machinery. Republican. Presbyterian. Achievements include research on artificial intelligence applications, distributed networking and computing, next generational software technologies. Office: Sun Microsystems Inc 5251 Dtc Pkwy Ste 500 Englewood CO 80111-2700

BINGHAM, RAYMOND JOSEPH, newborn intensive care nurse; b. Pensacola, Fla., Dec. 4, 1958; s. Joseph Lawson and Barbara June (Hansen) B.; m. Darcy Evelyn Pagones, May 14, 1982; children: John Joseph, Christopher Hansen, Robyn Brady. BA, U. Va., 1985; BSN, Cath. U., 1989. RN clinician, Va.; cert. neonatal intensive care nurse. Staff nurse newborn ICU Georgetown U. Hosp., Washington, 1989-95; staff nurse Fairfax (Va.) Hosp., 1996—; course reviewer Neonatal Network, Petaluma, Calif., 1993-96, reviewer Mother Baby Jour., Petaluma, 1998—. Contbg. editor Jour. Nursing Jocularity, 1996-98; editl. cons. Mother Baby Jour., 1998; contbr. articles to profl. publs. Treas. Stoddert PTA, Washington, 1994. Mem. Nat. Assn. Neonatal Nurses (comm. com. 1995-98), Washington Met. Assn. Neonatal Nurses (comm. com. 1998—). Avocations: running, hiking, writing. Home and Office: 10507 Cambridge Ct Gaithersburg MD 20886-3933

BINGMAN, CHARLES FRANKLIN, public administration educator; b. West Allis, Wis., Sept. 11, 1929; s. Clyde James and Bernice (Hengstler) B. BBA, U. Wis., 1952, MBA, 1956. Mgr. planning and control Nasa-Johnson Space Ctr., Houston, 1962-66; dep. dir. mgmt. programs Office Manned Space Flight Nat. Aero. and Space Adminstrn., Washington, 1967-71; dep. assoc. dir. orgn. mgmt. U.S. Office Mgmt. and Budget, Washington, 1971-76; dep. adminstr. Urban Mass Transp. Adminstrn. U.S. Dept. Transp., Washington, 1976-79, spl. asst. to dep. sec., 1982-83; exec. dir. Pres.'s mgmt. improvement coun. Exec. Office of The Pres., Washington, 1979-80, mgmt. advisor White House Office of Policy Devel., 1980-81; vis. prof. pub. adminstrn. dept. George Washington U., Washington, 1984-97; cons. U.S. and Internat. Govts., 1985—; vis. prof. pub. adminstrn. Washington Ctr. Johns Hopkins U., 1997—. Author: Japanese Government Leadership and Management, 1989, Serving Two Presidents: A History of the Bureau of the Budget, 1992, Revitalizing Federal Management, 1983; contbr. articles to profl. jours. Pres. Woodlake Towers Condo Assn., 1996—. Capt. U.S. Army, 1951-65. U.S. Info. Agy. grantee, 1992. Fellow Nat. Acad. Pub. Adminstrn.; mem. Sr. Execs. Assn. (pres. 1968-69, bd. dirs. 1982-85), Fed. Exec. Inst. Alumni Assn. (bd. dirs. 1983-86), William A. Jump Found. (bd. dirs. 1987—). Republican. Avocations: writing, jogging, hiking, reading. Home: 3100 S Manchester St Apt 815 Falls Church VA 22044-2716

BINIENDA, JOHN J., state legislator; b. Worcester, Mass., June 22, 1947; s. Thaddeus Andrew and Mary Gertrude (O'Coin) B.; children: Julie Ann, John Joseph Jr., Jamie Thaddeus. Student, Quinsigamond C.C., 1965-67; BA, Worcester State Coll., 1970, postgrad., 1970-74. State rep. Dist. 17 Mass. Ho. of reps., 1987—. Mem. Ward 7 Dem. Com., 1987—; mem. Worcester Neighbor Ctr. Mem. Worcester State Coll. Alumni Assn., Am. Legion (Main St. chpt.), Polish Naturalization Ind. Club, Polish Am. Vet. Club, K.C. (3d degree). Address: 41 Circuit Ave E Worcester MA 01603-2150

BINKERT, ALVIN JOHN, hospital administrator; b. Ft. Atkinson, Wis., Oct. 20, 1910; s. John and Clara (Burrow) B.; m. Lucile Latton, June 4, 1939; children: Barbara L., Cynthia R. Binkert Elias. BA, U. Wis., 1931. With Haskins & Sells (CPAs), N.Y.C., 1931-41; comptr. Presbyn. Hosp., N.Y.C., 1941-48, asst. v.p., 1948-54, v.p., gen. mgr., 1954-57, exec. v.p., 1957-70, pres., 1970—, vice chmn. bd., 1975—, also trustee; trustee Sr. Med. Cons.'s, N.Y.C.; lectr. pub. health, adminstrv. medicine Columbia U., 1954—. Trustee Presbyn. Hosp. Mem. Greater N.Y. Hosp. Assn. (past pres., bd. govs.), Hosp. Assn. N.Y. State (past pres., trustee, del.), Am. Coll. Hosp. Adminstrs., Univ. Club, Key Biscayne Yacht Club. Home: 450 E 63rd St Apt 11A New York NY 10021-7934 Office: 622 W 168th St New York NY 10032-3720

BINKLEY, MARILYN ROTHMAN, educational research administrator, researcher; b. N.Y.C., Jan. 27, 1948; d. Edgar and Mollie (Rothenberg) Rothman; B.A., Bklyn. Coll., 1968; M.A., Columbia U., 1971; Ed.D., George Washington U., 1983. Tchr., N.Y.C. Pub. Schs., 1972-77; reading specialist Internat. Sch. Geneva, 1975-77; instr. Marymount Coll. Va., Arlington, 1978-80; edn. cons., Washington, 1980-85; sr. assoc. Office Ednl. Rsch. and Improvement U.S. Dept. Edn.; edn. policy fellow Inst. Ednl. Leadership, 1987-88, nat. rsch. coord. Internat. Assn. for the Evaluation of Edn. Adv., reading literacy study, 1988-95; U.S. coord. Internat. Adult Literacy Study, 1994—; cons. Severn Sch., 1980-83, Dept. Def. Dependent Schs., 1979, Dover Sch. Singapore, 1978, dep. dir. Internat. Life Skills Study, 1998—; nat. project dir. OECD Program for Indicators of Student Achievement, 1998—. Mem. Internat. Reading Assn., Coll. Reading Assn., Nat. Reading Conf., Orton Soc., Assn. Supervision and Curriculum Devel., Am. Ednl. Rsch. Assn., Am. Statistical Assn., Nat. Assn. Ind. Schs., Nat. Coun. Tchrs. English, Nat. Assn. Measurement and Eval., Va. Reading Assn., Md. Reading Assn., Internat. Assn. for the Evaluation of Educational Achievement, Greater Washington Reading Assn., Delta Phi Epsilon, Phi Delta Kappa. Home: 12024 Gatewater Dr Potomac MD 20854-2875 Office: US Dept Edn 555 New Jersey Ave NW Washington DC 20001-2029

BINKS, REBECCA ANNE, communications executive; b. Oak Park, Ill., July 23, 1955; d. Donald Melvin and Elizabeth June (Lobdell) B.; m. Cary Emmett Donham, June 22, 1980; 1 child, Samuel Joseph Donham. Student, Goodman Sch. Drama, Chgo., 1973-76; BA in Liberal Arts, Columbia Coll., Chgo., 1983; MS in Mktg. Comm., Roosevelt U., 1993. Freelance lighting designer, theater tech. Chgo., N.Y.C., 1975-80; retail mgr. Coffee and Tea Exch., Chgo., 1981-84; sales assoc. K&S Photographics, Chgo., 1984-87; supr. client services AGS&R Communications, Chgo., 1987-88; mgr. Meeting Express Systems, Chgo., 1988-90; pres. Binks & Assocs. Inc., Chgo., 1990-95; co-dir. Northside Parents Network, 1996-97; mem. faculty mktg. comm. Columbia Coll., Chgo., 1992-97; mem. faculty English Chgo. State U., 1995—; tchr. travel photography, Chgo., 1987. Designer: (cookbook) Kitchen Angst, 1993; exhibited in group and one-woman shows. Mem. internal communications com. Girl Scouts, Chgo., 1989-91. Mem. NAFE, Chgo. Coun. on Fgn. Rels., Am. Mktg. Assn., Internat. Assn. Bus. Communications, Ancona Sch. Soc. (bd. dirs. 1997—).

BINMOELLER, KENNETH FRANK, physician, surgeon; b. Chgo., Oct. 31, 1956; s. Heinz F. and Chikako Jane (Noya) B.; m. Roswitha Pollinger; children: Eric, Cecile, Timothy, Juliette. BS, Columbia U., 1976; MD, Albert-Ludwigs U., Freiburg, Germany, 1982. Diplomate Am. Bd. Internal Medicine. Intern/resident in internal medicine Baylor Coll. Medicine, Houston, 1984-87; staff physician Honokaa Hosp./Hamakua Infirmary, Hawaii, 1987-88; fellow in gastroenterology Oreg. Health Scis. U., Portland, 1988-90; lectr. gastroenterology U. Nice, France, 1990-91; sr. cons., dept. dir. U. Hamburg, Germany, 1991-97; assoc. prof., dir. endoscopy divsn. gastroenterology U. Calif., San Diego, 1998—. Author: Praxis der Therapeutischen Endoskopie, 1997; editor: Chronic Pancreatitis: An Interdisciplinary Approach, 1997; patentee in field. Mem. Am. Soc. Gastrointestinal Endoscopy, Am. Gastroenterology Assn., Hamburg Med. Soc. Avocations: tennis, hiking, travel. Office: U Calif Divsn Gastroenterology 200 W Arbor Dr San Diego CA 92103-8413

BINNEY, JAN JARRELL, publishing executive; b. Frankfort, Ind., Aug. 16, 1941; d. Robert and Susie (Meek) Jarrell; m. Joseph M. Binney, June 23, 1962; 1 child, Robert J. BS, Purdue U., 1962; MA, Coll. N.J., 1972. Speech-lang. pathologist pub. schs., various locations, 1962-84; pvt. practice speech pathology East Brunswick, N.J., 1982-85; v.p. sales and mktg. The Speech Bin, Inc. Pub., Vero Beach, Fla., 1984—. Editor profl. publs. Deacon Presbyn. Ch., 1985-87, elder, 1987-90; bd. dirs., chpt. chmn. ARC, Indian River Country, Fla. Fellow Am. Speech, Lang. Hearing Assn. (legis. councilor 1981-89, bd. dirs. pub. info. exch. 1987-89, com. on equality 1988-90, bd. dirs. polit. action com.), N.J. Speech, Lang. Hearing Assn. (pres. 1981-82), Exch. Club Indian River (sec. 1998—), Pi Beta Phi Alumnae Club (treas.). Office: The Speech Bin Inc 1965 25th Ave Vero Beach FL 32960-3000

BINNEY, ROBERT HARRY, bank executive; b. London, Oct. 21, 1945; s. Roy and Barbara (Poole) B.; m. Valerie Kay Greene, May 4, 1979; children: Alexandra, Christopher, Nicholas, Paul. MA in Mech. Scis., Cambridge (Eng.) U., 1967; MBA, Manchester (Eng.) Bus. Sch., 1971. Mktg. exec. Rank Xerox, Birmingham, Eng., 1967-69; with Chase Manhattan Bank, various locations, 1971-96; exec. Orion Bank, London, 1971-72; mgr. expansion and diversification Chase Manhattan Bank, N.Y.C., 1972-73; regional dir. expansion and diversification activities Chase Manhattan Bank, Hong Kong, 1973-74; 2nd v.p. Chase Manhattan Bank, London, 1975, exec. dir. Mid. East and Africa Chase Manhattan Ltd. subs., 1975-79, v.p., 1976; mng. dir. Chase Manhattan Asia Ltd. subs. Chase Manhattan Bank, Hong Kong, 1980-83; country mgr. Chase Manhattan Bank, Tokyo, 1983-88; sr. v.p. Chase Manhattan Bank, 1985; sr. banker European fin. industries Chase Manhattan Bank, London, 1988-90, bus. exec. Europe and Mid. East for global securities svc., 1991-96; mng. dir. Eur., Mid. East, Africa cross border custody Citibank, N.A., London, 1996—. Mem. Surrey County Cricket Club. Anglican. Avocations: travel, tennis, bridge. Office: PO Box 200, Cottons Ctr Hays Ln, London SE1 2QT, England

BINNIG, GERD KARL, physicist; b. July 20, 1947; m. Lore Binnig, 1969; 2 children. Diploma in Physics, Goethe U., Frankfurt, Fed. Republic Germany, PhD, 1978. Rsch. staff mem. IBM Zurich Rsch. Lab., 1978—, group leader, 1984—; with Stanford U., 1985-86; hon. prof. physics U. Munich, 1987—; vis. prof. Stanford U., 1986-88; mem. tech. coun. IBM Acad., adv. bd. Bild der Wissenschaft, 1990—. Author: Aus dem Nichts, 1989; mem. editorial bd. Rev. Sci. Instruments, 1990-92. Co-recipient Nobel prize in physics, 1986; recipient physics prize German Phys. Soc., 1982, Otto Klung prize, 1983, Joint King Faisal Internat. prize for sci., Hewlett-Packard Europhysics prize, 1984, Elliot Cresson medal Franklin Inst., 1987, Grosses Verdienstkreuz mit Stern und Schulterband des Verdienstordens, 1987, Minnie Rosen award Ross U., 1988; named to Nat. Inventors Hall of Fame, 1994. Fellow Royal Microscopical Soc. (hon. 1988); Acad. Scis. (fgn. assoc. 1987). Avocations: music, tennis, soccer, golf. Office: IBM Rsch Div Zurich Rsch La, Saumerstrasse 4, Ruschlikon Zürich CH-8803, Switzerland

BINNS, JAMES EDWARD, retired banker; b. Alameda, Calif., Oct. 5, 1931; s. Guy Vivian and Beatrice (Jury) B.; m. Marjean Friesen, Feb. 21, 1951; children: Cheryl Jean Binns Smith, Jana Lee Binns Gualco, Lori LeAnn Binns Mauer. Student, U. Nev., 1950-51; grad., Sch. Bank Audit and Control, U. Wis., 1963, Am. Inst. Banking, 1964. With Sierra Pacific Power Co., Reno, 1948-50; with First Interstate Bank of Nev., Reno, 1951-91; asst. cashier First Interstate Bank of Nev., 1957-63, asst. to cashier, 1963-65, auditor, 1965-84, asst. v.p., 1968-75, v.p., 1975-91; Cameo Jewelry and Loan, Reno, 1992-93; instr. Am. Inst. Banking; past chmn. internal audit com. City of Reno. Mem. Sierra Nevada Cmty. Access TV, Reno Hot August Nights. Mem. AARP (pres., bd. dirs.), Am. Inst. Banking (past pres. Sierra-Nev. chpt., past nat. assoc. coun.), Bank Adminstrn. Inst. (cert. bank auditor, charter pres. chpt., past state dir.), Data Processing Mgmt. Assn. (charter mem. Sierra-Nev. chpt., past pres.), Inst. Internal Auditors (cert. internal auditor, past charter pres. chpt.), Western Indsl. Nev., Masons, Shriners, Elks, Lakeridge Tennis Club, Reno Toastmasters (past pres.), Reno H.S. Alumni Assn. (treas.), E. Campus Vitus (La Plumas Del Oro chpt.), Graegle Tennis Club, Reno C. of C. (mem. spl. events coun.). Home: 1720 Allen St Reno NV 89509-1252 *A true leader must accept all reasonable challenges being fully cognizant that his and the group's success can only be achieved through the combined efforts of all participants.*

BINNS, WALTER GORDON, JR., investment management executive; b. Richmond, Va., June 8, 1929; s. Walter Gordon and Virginia Belle (Matheny) B.; m. Alberta Louise Fry, Apr. 1, 1972; 1 child, Amanda; 1 stepdau., Clarissa. AB, Coll. William and Mary, 1949; AM, Harvard U., 1951; MBA, NYU, 1959. Trainee Chase Nat. Bank, N.Y.C., 1953-54; with GM, N.Y.C., 1954-94, asst. treas., 1974-82, chief investment funds officer, 1982-94, v.p., 1986-94; pres., CEO GM Investment Mgmt. Corp., 1990-94; bd. dirs. Options Clearing Corp., Inc., Equity Fund Latin Am., Commonwealth Equity Fund; investment adv. com. N.Y. State Common Retirement Fund, 1987-94; mem. pension mgrs. adv. com. N.Y. Stock Exch., 1988-94; mem. Gov. Cuomo's Task Force on Pension Fund Investment, 1988-89; mem. adv. com. Pension Benefit Guaranty Corp., 1991-95; mem. adv. com., bd. Chgo. Mercantile Exch., 1988-97, Chgo. Bd. Trade, 1992-93, Commodity Futures Trading Commn., 1992-94; mem. investment adv. com. Va. Retirement Systems, 1994—, Barings/ING Pvt. Equity Ptnrs., 1996—, SUN Asset Mgmt. Ltd., 1997—; mem. fiduciary panel Prudential Ins. Co., 1994-95. Trustee ARC Retirement System, 1987-90, Citizens Budget Commn., N.Y.C., 1982-94, Endowment Assn., Coll. William and Mary, Med. Coll. Va. Found., Maymont Found., Nat. Coun. Econ. Edn., 1982-94, Futures Ind. Assn., 1988-90; bd. dirs. Alcoholism Coun. Greater N.Y., 1982-92; bd. dirs. Cmty. Fund. of Bronxville, Eastchester Tuckahoe, Inc., 1986-92, Friends of Libr. Coll. William and Mary Coll., 1991-97, Fin. Execs. Rsch. Found., 1988-91, Christian Children's Fund, Nat. Coun. on Alcoholism and Drug Dependence, Vellore Christian Med. Coll. & Hosp. Bd.; founder, interim chmn. Friends of Higher Edn. Va., 1997—. Mem. Fin. Execs. Inst. (chmn. com. on employee benefits 1977-80, com. on investment of employee benefit assets 1985-88, treas. 1991-93), Bronxville Field Club, Harvard Club (N.Y.C.), Grolier Club, Commonwealth Club, Westwood Racquet Club, N.Y. Athletic Club, Phi Beta Kappa, Beta Gamma Sigma. Home: 115 Oxford Cir W Richmond VA 23221-3224 also: 120 Central Park S New York NY 10019-1560 Office: PO Box 17308 Richmond VA 23226-7308*

BINO, MARIAL DESOLYN, librarian, educator, psychologist; b. Hurley, Wis., May 11, 1916; d. John and Mary B. BE, U. Wis., 1939, cert. Aeronautics Instr., 1942; MS in Libr. Sci., Columbia U., 1958, MA in Devel. Psychology, 1966. Cert. tchr., Wis. Tchr. elem. schs. Wis., 1940-42, 50-52; aeronautic ground instr. U. Wis., Menomonie, 1942-43; aeronautic ground instr. civil air law U. Wis., Eau Claire, 1943-45; tchr. math., sooc. scis. Arbor Vitae-Woodruff (Wis.) H.S., 1945-46; social worker dept. social svcs. Iron County, Hurley, 1946-50; sch. dist. libr. Hurley Sch. Dist., 1952-91; instr. children's lit. Gogebic C.C., Ironwood, Mich., 1963; vis. lectr. U. Wis., Platteville, summer 1963. Scout leader Girl Scouts Am., Hurley, 1946-50; youth leader ARC, Hurley, 1950-52; mem. City Coun., Hurley, 1982-84. Mem. AAUW, Charles F. Menniger Soc. Avocations: travel, lecturing, reading, writing, swimming.

BINOCHE, JULIETTE, actress; b. Paris, Mar. 9, 1964. Student, Nat. Conservatory of Drama. Appearances in films include Les Nanas, La Vie de Famille, Rouge Baiser, 1985, Rendez-Vous, 1985, Mon beau-Frère a tué ma soeur, Mauvais Sang, 1986, Un tour de Manège, The Unbearable Lightness of Being, 1988, Les amants du Pont-Neuf, 1991, Wuthering Heights, 1992, Damage, 1992, Trois Couteurs: Bleu, 1993, The Horseman on the Roof, 1995, A Couch in New York, 1995, Le Hussard Sur Le Toit, 1995, The English Patient, 1996 (Academy award, 1996), Alice et Martin, 1998, Les Enfants du Siecle, 1999. Recipient Academy award Best Supporting Actress, 1996. *

BINSFELD, CONNIE BERUBE, lieutenant governor; b. Munising, Mich., Apr. 18, 1924; d. Omer J. and Elsie (Constance) Berube; B.S., Siena Heights Coll., 1945, D.H.L. (hon.), 1977; postgrad. Wayne State U., 1966-67; m.

John E. Binsfeld, July 19, 1947; children—John T., Gregory, Susan, Paul, Michael. County commr., Leelanau County, Mich., 1970-74; mem. Mich. Ho. of Reps., 1974-82, asst. rep. leader, 1979-81; del. Nat. Conv., 1980, 88, 92; mem. Mich. Senate, 1982-90, asst. rep. leader, 1979, 81; lt. gov. State of Mich., 1990-98. Mem. adv. bd. Nat. Park System. Named Mich. Mother of Year, Mich. Mothers Com., 1977; Northwestern Mich. Coll. fellow. Mem. Nat. Council State Legislators, LWV, Siena Heights Coll. Alumnae Assn. Republican. Roman Catholic.*

BINSTOCK, ROBERT HENRY, public policy educator, writer, lecturer; b. New Orleans, Dec. 6, 1935; s. Louis and Ruth (Atlas) B.; m. Martha Burns, July 27, 1979; 1 dau., Jennifer. AB, Harvard U., 1956, PhD, 1965. Lectr. Brandeis U., Waltham, Mass., 1963-65, asst. prof., 1965-69, assoc. prof., 1969-72, Stulberg Prof. law and politics, 1972-84, dir. Policy Ctr. Aging, 1979-84; prof. aging, health and soc. Case Western Res. U., Cleve., 1985—; mem. com. on an Aging Soc. Nat. Acad. Scis., Washington, 1982-86. Author: America's Political System, 1st edit., 1972, 2nd edit., 1975, 3rd edit., 1979, 4th edit., 1984, 5th edit., 1991, America's Political System: Urban, State and Local, 1st edit., 1972, 2nd edit., 1975, 3rd edit., 1979, Feasible Planning for Social Change, 1966; editor: The Politics of the Powerless, 1971, Too Old for Health Care?, 1991, Dementia and Aging, 1992, International Perspectives on Aging: Population and Policy Changes, 1982, Handbook of Aging and the Social Sciences, 1st edit., 1976, 2nd edit., 1985, 3d edit., 1990, 4th edit., 1996, The Future of Long Term Care, 1996. Bd. dirs. White House Task Force on Older Ams., 1967-68; chmn. adv. panel Office Tech. Assessment, U.S. Congress, 1982-84 ; tech. adviser, del. White House Conf. on Aging, 1971, 81; trustee Boston Biomed. Research Inst., 1971-84; mem. gov.'s adv. com. Dept. of Elder Affairs Mass., 1974-84; chair, adv. bd. Nat. Acad. on Aging, 1991-95. Recipient Haak-Lilliefors award Mich. State U., 1979, Arthur S. Flemming award Nat. Assn. State Units on Aging, 1988, Key award APHA, 1992, Am. Soc. Aging award, 1994; fellow Ford Found., 1959-69; rsch. grantee NIH, 1968-73. Fellow Gerontol. Soc. Am. (pres. 1976, Donald P. Kent award 1981, Brookdale Prize award 1983); mem. APHA (chair gerontol. health sect. 1996-97). Office: Case Western Res Univ 2040 Adelbert Rd Cleveland OH 44106-4901

BINTLIFF, BARBARA ANN, law librarian, educator; b. Houston, Jan. 14, 1953; d. Donald Richard and Frances Arlene (Appling) Hay; m. Byron A. Boville, Aug. 20, 1977 (div. 1992); children: Bradley, Bruce. BA, Cen. Wash. U., 1975; JD, U. Wash., 1978, MLL, 1979. Bar: Wash. 1979, U.S. Dist. Ct. (ea. dist.) Wash. 1980, Colo. 1983, U.S. Dist. Ct. Colo. 1983. Libr. Gaddis and Fox, Seattle, 1978-79; reference libr. U. Denver Law Sch., 1979-84; assoc. libr., sr. instr. Sch. Law U. Colo., Boulder, 1984-88, assoc. prof., libr. dir., 1989—; legal cons. Nat. Ctr. Atmospheric Rsch., Environ. and Societal Impacts Group, Boulder, 1980; vis. prof. U. Wash., Seattle, 1996. Editor: A Representative Sample of Tenure Documents for Law Librarians, 1988, 2nd edit., 1994, Chapter Presidents' Handbook, 1989, Representatives Handbook, 1990; mem. editorial bd. Legal Reference Svcs. Quarterly, Perspectives: Teaching Legal Research and Writing; contbr. articles to profl. jours. Mem. Am. Assn. Law Librs., Colo. Bar Assn., Colo. Assn. Law Librs. (pres. 1982), Southwestern Assn. Law Librs. (pres. 1987-88, 91-92). Episcopalian. Office: U Colo Law Libr PO Box 402 Boulder CO 80309-0402

BINZEN, PETER HUSTED, columnist; b. Montclair, N.J., Sept. 24, 1922; s. Frederick William and Lucy Beckwith (Husted) B.; m. Elisabeth Virginia Flower, June 12, 1951; children: Lucy Binzen Wildrick, Jennifer Binzen Cardoso, Jonathan Peter, Katherine. B.A. in Polit. Sci, Yale U., 1947; postgrad. (Nieman fellow), Harvard U., 1962. Reporter UP, N.Y.C., 1947, Passaic (N.J.) Herald-News, 1947-50; reporter, editor Phila. Bull., 1951-82; reporter Inquirer, 1982-87, columnist, 1987—. Author: Whitetown U.S.A, 1970, (with Joseph R. Daughen) The Wreck of the Penn Central, 1971, The Cop Who Would Be King, 1977; editor: Nearly Everybody Read It, 1998. Served with U.S. Army, 1943-45. Decorated Bronze Star. Office: Phila Inquirer 400 N Broad St Philadelphia PA 19130-4015

BIOLCHINI, ROBERT FREDRICK, lawyer; b. Detroit, Sept. 22, 1939; s. Alfred and Erma (Barbetti) B.; m. Frances Lauinger, June 5, 1965; children: Robert F., Douglas C., Frances E., Tobin m., Thomas A., Christine M. BA, U. Notre Dame, 1962; LLB, George Washington U., 1965. Bar: Okla., Mich., 1965. Assoc. Doerner, Stuart, Saunders, Daniel, Anderson & Biolchini, Tulsa, 1968-71, ptnr., 1971-94; ptnr. Stuart, Biolchini, Turner & Givray, Tulsa, 1994—; bd. dirs. Pennwell Pub. Co., Lawrence Electronics Inc., Lumen Energy Corp., Bank of The Lakes, Bank of Jackson Hole; chmn. bd. Valley Nat. Bank; mem. Lloyds of London, 1979—; temp. appeals judge Okla. Supreme Ct., 1981—; chmn. Oldfaithful Underwriting, Ltd., 1998—. Bd. dirs. Thomas Gilcrease Mus., past pres., chmn. bd., 1977-80, dir. emeritus, 1980—; bd. dirs., sec., legal clk. Tulsa Ballet Theatre, Inc., 1976-84; trustee, pres. Monte Cassino Endowment, 1978—; chmn. Christ the King Parish Coun., 1974-75; mem. adv. coun. U. Notre Dame Law Sch., 1982—; chmn. Cath. Diocese Tulsa Fund for Future, 1998—; bd. dirs. legal counsel Tulsa Area United Way, 1986—; mem. pres.'s coun. Regis Coll., 1986—. Served as capt. U.S. Army, 1965-67. Mem. Okla. Bar Assn., Mich. Bar Assn., Met. Tulsa C. of C. (bd. dirs. 1992—), Summit Club, Southern Hills Country Club, Club Ltd., Knights of Malta, Knights of the Holy Sepulchre. Roman Catholic. Home: 1744 E 29th St Tulsa OK 74114-5402 Office: First Place Tower 15 E 5th St Ste 3300 Tulsa OK 74103

BIONDI, FRANK J., JR., entertainment company executive; b. N.Y.C., Jan. 9, 1945; s. Frank J. and Virginia (Willis) B.; m. Carol Oughton, Mar. 16, 1974; children: Anne, Jane. BA, Princeton U., 1966; MBA, Harvard U., 1968. Assoc.-corp. fin. Shearson Lehman, Inc., N.Y.C., 1970-71, Prudential Securities, N.Y.C., 1969; prin. Frank J. Biondi Jr. & Assocs., N.Y.C., 1972; dir. bus. analysis Teleprompter Corp., N.Y.C., 1972-73; asst. treas., assoc. dir. bus. affairs Children's TV Workshop, N.Y.C., 1974-78; dir. entertainment program planning HBO, N.Y.C., 1978, v.p. programming ops., 1979-82, exec. v.p. planning and adminstrn., 1982-83, pres., chief exec. officer, 1983, chmn., chief exec. officer, 1984; exec. v.p. entertainment bus. sector The Coca-Cola Co., 1985; chmn., CEO, Coca-Cola TV, 1986; pres., CEO, Viacom Inc, N.Y.C., 1987-96; chmn., CEO, Universal Studios, Inc., Universal City, Calif., 1996-98; pres. Biondi Reiss Capital Mgmt., N.Y.C., 1998—; Bd. dirs. Bank of N.Y., Seagram Co. Ltd., Vail Resorts, Inc., USA Network Inc. Bd. dirs. Leake-Watts Svcs., Yonkers, N.Y., 1975, Mus. TV and Radio, N.Y.C., Claremont Grad. U., Princeton U. Mem. Princeton of N.Y. Club, Edgartown Yacht Club, Game Creek Club (Vail, Colo.). Office: Biondi Reiss Capital Mgmt 1114 Ave of Americas New York NY 10036*

BIONDI, LAWRENCE, university administrator, priest; b. Chgo., Dec. 15, 1938; s. Hugo and Albertina (Marchetti) B. B.A., Loyola U., Chgo., 1962, Ph.L., 1964, M.Div., 1971, S.T.L., 1971; M.S., Georgetown U., 1966, Ph.D. in Socioloinguistics, 1975. Ordained priest Roman Cath. Ch., 1970. Joined Soc. Jesus; asst. prof. sociolinguistics Loyola U., Chgo., 1974-79, assoc. prof., 1979-81, prof., 1982-87, dean Coll. Arts and Scis., 1980-87; pres. St. Louis U., 1987—. Author: The Italian-American Child: His Sociolinguistic Acculturation, 1975, Poland's Solidarity Movement, 1984; editor: Poland's Church-State Relations in the 1980s, 1980, Spain's Church-State Relations, 1982. Trustee Xavier U., 1981-87, Loyola Coll., Balt., 1988-94, Santa Clara U., 1988-98, Kenrick-Glennon Sem., 1988-94, St. Louis U., 1982—, Loyola U., Chgo., 1988-97; bd. dirs. Epilepsy Found. Am., 1985-95, Civic Progress, St. Louis, 1987—, Regional Commerce and Growth Assn., 1987—, Mo. Bot. Gardens, 1987—, St. Louis Zoo, 1994, St. Louis Symphony, 1994, Harry S. Truman Inst. for Nat. and Internat. Affairs, 1987—. Mellon grantee, 1974, 75, 76, 82. Mem. Linguistic Soc. Am., MLA, Am. Anthrop. Assn. Office: St Louis U 221 N Grand Blvd Saint Louis MO 63103-2006

BIONDI, MANFRED ANTHONY, physicist, educator; b. Carlstadt, N.J., Mar. 5, 1924; s. Manfred Anthony and Helen (Flaction) B.; m. Elaine Theresa Leitkam, May 12, 1952; children: David Mark, George Philip. B.S. in Physics, MIT, 1944, Ph.D., 1949. Research assoc. MIT, Cambridge, 1948-49; with Westinghouse Research Labs, Pitts., 1949-60; adv. physicist Westinghouse Research Labs, 1952-57, mgr. physics dept., 1957-60; prof. physics U. Pitts., 1960-86, prof. emeritus, 1987—; also dir. Atomic Scis. Inst., 1968-79; exchange prof. U. Paris, 1976-86; trustee Upper Atmosphere Rsch. Corp.; mem. adv. com. Army Rsch. Office, Durham, N.C., NAS, 1962-64; mem. exec. coun. Fedn. Am. Scientists, 1966-68; mem. adv. panel physics NSF, 1970-72; mem. Army basic rsch. steering com. NRC, 1985-88, chmn., 1987-88. Editorial bd.: Jour. Applied Physics, 1966-68. Served with USNR, 1943-46. Fellow AAAS, Am. Phys. Soc. (chmn. div. electron and atomic physics 1957, chmn. gaseous electronics conf. 1962-64, Davisson-Germer prize 1984); mem. Am. Geophys. Union, Earth and Sky (adv. bd. 1992-94). Home: 1375 Hillsdale Dr Monroeville PA 15146-4444 Office: U Pitts Dept Physics And Astro Pittsburgh PA 15260

BIONDI, MATT, Olympic athlete, swimmer; b. San Diego, Calif., Oct. 8, 1965. Olympic swimmer L.A., 1984, Seoul, Korea, 1988, Barcelona, Spain, 1992. Recipient 8 Olympic Gold medals, 2 Olympic Silver medals, 1 Olympic Bronze medal. Office: USA Swimming One Olympic Plz Colorado Springs CO 80918*

BIONDO, MICHAEL THOMAS, retired paper company executive; b. N.Y.C., Nov. 2, 1928; s. Thomas and Susan (Battaglia) B.; m. Harriet Young, Mar. 1, 1952; children—Sally Ann, Susan, Amy, Michael Thomas. B.A., Adelphi U., Garden City, N.Y., 1950. With St. Regis Paper Co., 1953—, dir. mktg., than v.p. mktg., 1969-78; sr. v.p. packaging and converted products group St. Regis Paper Co., N.Y.C., 1981-84; past bd. dirs. Esselete Inc., Neumetrix Inc.; owner M.T. Biondo Assocs., pvt. investments; past mem. mktg. adv. bd. Columbia U. Grad. Sch. Bus.; past pres. Darien (Conn.) Hist. Soc. Mem. Woodway Country Club (Darien), The Club at Pelican Bay (Fla., vice chmn. bd. govs., past pres.). Home: The Biltmore # 803 8473 Bay Colony Dr Naples FL 34108-6786

BIONDO, RAYMOND VITUS, dermatologist; b. N.Y.C., June 13, 1936; s. Joseph Pernice and Bena Biondo; m. Mary McKinnon, Dec. 24, 1976. BA in Biology, U. No. Colo., 1960; MS in Biochemistry, U. Ark., 1963, BS in Medicine, 1967, MD, 1967. Diplomate Am. Bd. Dermatology. Asst. mgmt. analyst 389th USAF Hosp., Francis E. Warren AFB, Wyo., 1954-58; rsch. trainee NIH at U. Ark., Little Rock, 1961-63; rsch. biochemist VA Hosp., Little Rock, 1963-65; intern U. Cin. Med. Ctr., 1967-68; resident in dermatology U. Ark., Little Rock, 1968-71, asst. clin. prof. dermatology, 1971-90; pres. North Little Rock (Ark.) Dermatology Clinic, 1971-90. Contbr. rsch. articles to profl. publs. Mem. nat. adv. com. on scouting for the handicapped Boy Scouts Am., 1976-81, nat. chmn. med. exploring com., 1981-84, nat. coun., 1977—, nat. exploring com., 1977-92, nat. urban emphasis com. 1990—, nat. Jewish com. on scouting, 1981-84; mem. Ark. Kidney Disease Commn., 1979-83; bd. dirs. Ctrl. Ark. Health Systems Agy., 1984, Congregation B'nai Israel, Little Rock, 1982-84, Jewish Fedn. Ark., 1989-92, Ark Health Care Access Found., 1995—, sec.-treas., 1998-99; founder, pres. Am. Red Magen David for Israel, Ark., 1987-92, 94—. Staff officer USCG Aux. Flotilla and Divsn., 1995. Recipient Outstanding Alumnus award U. No. Colo., 1977, Shofar award, 1992, William H. Spurgeon and Whitney M. Young awards Boy Scouts Am., 1981, Silver Antelope award, 1983, Silver Beaver award, 1977, Nat. Torch of Gold award, 1993, cert. of achievement in cmty. health promotion Ark. Dept. Health, 1983, vol. action award card The White House, 1982, Gov.'s Vol. Excellence award, 1983, 98, Ark. cert. appreciation for pub. svc., 1992, Father Joseph H. Biltz award Ark. Coun. Nat. Conf. of Cmty. & Justice, 1990, 14 Vol. awards U.S. Dept. Vets. Affairs, 1991-99, Vol. Svc. Leadership award, 1999, Nat. Disting. Svc. award Jewish War Vets. of the U.S., 1995, 98, Golden Rule award finalist JC Penney Co./United Way of Pulaski County, 1996, 98, winner, 1999, Olympic Torch Relay nominee, 1996, Spirit of Svc. award Ark. Health Care Access Found., 1996, cert. appreciation City of Little Rock, 1996, Adminstrn. Award of Merit, USCG Aux., 1996, George Washington Honor medal Freedoms Found., 1997, Man of Vol. Achievement award, cert. of achievement for outstanding vol. Ret. and Sr. Vol. Program Ctrl. Ark., 1997, 98, Pres.'s Svc. award nominee, 1997, 98, 99, Intergenerational Vol. award Ark. Aging Svc. Vol. Acad. Coun. Eldercare, 1998, Cmty. Svc. award Sta. KARK-TV, Gov.'s Office and Ark. Divsn. of Volunteerism Dept. of Human Svcs., 1999. Fellow Am. Acad. Dermatology (adv. bd. nat. dermatology program 1973-75); mem. AMA (physicians recognition award 1971-90, cert of appreciation 1984), Ark. Med. Soc. (ho. of dels. 1971—), Ark. Dermatol. Soc. (pres. 1977), Pulaski County Med. Soc., Jewish War Vets U.S. (founder, comdr. Ark. post 436, nat. surgeon 1993-98, nat. vice Boy Scout officer 1993—, nat. White House liaison officer 1993-95, Judge Lawrence Gubow Meml. hon. mention 1989, Cert. of Appreciation Tex. dept. 1991, Cert. of Merit 1992, Chapel of Four Chaplains Legion of Honor 1994, Humanitarian award 1996, Bronze medallion 1997, Sr. Arkansas Hall of Fame Cert. Recognition, 1997, inducted 1998), Congrl. Medal Hon. Soc. (Spl. Contbr. award 1998), Sigma Xi, Alpha Omega Alpha, Golden Key (hon.). Jewish. Home: PO Box 6361 North Little Rock AR 72124-6361

BIR, MICHELLE MARIE, sales executive; b. Canandaigua, N.Y., June 29, 1965; d. Thomas A. and Carol A. (Genecco) B. BS in Econs., Wells Coll., 1987. Merchandiser Bratt-Foster, Syracuse, N.Y., 1988-89; sales exec. 110 Winner Eastman-Kodak Co., Cape Girardeau, Mo., 1989-95; retail rep. Hallmark Cards, Inc., St. Louis, 1995-98; sales rep. Merck Pharm. Co., 1998—. Mem., starter Make-A-Wish Found., Cape Girardeau, 1989. Mem. Am. Women's Econ. Devel. Assn., Cape Girardeau Jaycees. Democrat. Roman Catholic. Avocation: swimming. Home and Office: 518 N Sprigg St Cape Girardeau MO 63701-4812

BIRBARI, ADIL ELIAS, physician, educator; b. Ziguinchor, Senegal, May 26, 1933; s. Elias George and Sophia George (Nasrallah) B.; m. Micheline Michel Ghosn, Feb. 4, 1978; children: Yolande, Sophia. Baccalaureat II, Internat. Coll., Beirut, 1952; BS, Am. U., Beirut, 1955, MD, 1959. Fellow in hypertension Peter Bent Brigham Hosp., Boston, 1963-65, assoc. dir. hypertension lab, 1965-66; asst. prof. medicine and physiology Am. U., Beirut, 1967-72, assoc. prof. medicine and physiology, 1972-77, chmn. dept. medicine, 1999—; prof., chmn. dept. medicine Lebanese U., Beirut, 1987-90; interim chmn. dept. of internal medicine Am. U., Beirut. Author: Kidney and Genetic Diseases, 1986, Manual of Clinical Hypertension; editor-in-chief Lebanese Med. Jour.; contbr. numerous articles to profl. jours. Fellow high blood pressure coun. Am. Heart Assn.; v.p. Lebanese Health Soc., Beirut, 1986; mem. Camille Shamoun Found., Beirut, 1992. Grantee Nat. Coun. Sci. Rsch., 1973-91, European Coun. for BP and Cardiovascular Rsch. Fellow ACP, Internat. Coll. Angiology; mem. Lebanese Assn. Advancement of Sci. (sec. gen. 1974-92), Lebanese Soc. Nephrology and Hypertension (pres. 1975-93, editor-in-chief Jour. 1990-93), Lebanese Hypertension League (pres., editor-in-chief Jour. 1994), Nat. Coun. for Sci. Rsch. (Lebanon), Internat. Soc. Nephrology, Internat./European Soc. Hypertension, Am. Soc. Hypertension, Pan Arab Hypertension Soc. (v.p.), European Coun. Blood Pressure and Cardiovascular Rsch. Avocations: photography, gardening. Office: Am Univ Beirut 850 3rd Ave Fl 18 New York NY 10022-6222

BIRCH, ADOLPHO A., JR., state supreme court justice; b. Washington, Sept. 22, 1932. BA, Howard U., 1956, JD, 1956. Bar: Tenn. 1957. Pvt. practice Nashville, 1958-66, asst. pub. defender, 1964-66, asst. dist. atty., 1966-69; judge Davidson County Gen. Sessions Ct., 1969-78, Tenn. Criminal Ct. (20th jud. dist.), 1978-87; former judge Tenn. Ct. Criminal Appeals; chief justice Tenn. Supreme Ct., Nashville, 1996-97, assoc. justice, 1997—; assoc. prof. Nashville Sch. of Law. Served USNR, 1956-58. Mem. ABA, Nat. Bar Assn., Tenn. Bar Assn., Nashville Bar Assn., Napier Lobby Bar Assn. (past pres.). Office: 401 7th Ave N Ste 304 Nashville TN 37219-1406*

BIRCH, DAVID WILLIAM, college official; b. Crawfordsville, Ind., Oct. 28, 1913; s. Charles Evan and Edna (Vest) B.; m. Elizabeth Marie Casto, Oct. 5, 1946; children: Anthony David, Michael Allen, William Hayes. Student, Trinity Coll., Hartford, Conn., 1956-58; MBA, SUNY, Buffalo, 1966. Engr. Delco-Remy div. Gen. Motors, Anderson, Ind., 1931-51; supt. New Britain (Conn.) Machine Co., 1951-57; plant mgr. Fasteners, Inc., Boston, 1957-60, Curtis Screw Co., Buffalo, 1960-63; ops. mgr. Delevan Elects., East Aurora, N.Y., 1963-66; pres. Essex Recon Corp., Lancaster, N.Y., 1966-78; cons. Anthony, Hayes & Allen, Inc., East Aurora, 1978-80; program chmn. Medaille Coll., Buffalo, 1980-83, bus. mgr., 1983-95, ret., 1995; bd. dirs. Strickler Road Housing Devel., Clarence, N.Y. Author: Wrestle the Angel, 1994. Mem. N.Y. State Orgn. Bursars & Bus. Adminstrs. (bd. dir. 1988-90). Methodist. Avocations: music, lawn care. Home: 212 Hillcrest Rd East Aurora NY 14052-1316

BIRCH, PATRICIA, choreographer, director; b. Englewood, N.J.; d. Abrahan S. and Mary (Levinsohn) B.; m. A. William T. Becker III; children: Jonathan Heath, Alison Becker Hurt, Peter Heath. BA, Bennington Coll. Dancer Martha Graham Co., N.Y.C., West Side Story, 1960. Choreographer, dir. (Broadway and Off-Broadway prodns. music theater and opera stage work) You're A Good Man Charlie Brown, The Me Nobody Knows, A Little Night Music, Grease, Candide, Over Here, Diamond Studs, Pacific Overtures, The Mikado, Gilda Radner, Live From New York, Zoot Suit, They're Playing Our Song, The Cradle Will Rock, Street Scene, In the Time of the Comedian Harmonists, The Happy End, Really Rosie, Raggedy Ann, A Walk on the Wild Side, Elvis, The Mass, The Jumping Frog of Calaveras County, The Gershwin Gala, Club 12, Fanny Hackabout Jones, What About Luv, American Enterprise, Band in Berlin, Parade, Exactly Like You, I Sent A Letter To My Love, The Snow Queen; dir., choreographer videos The Very Thought of You, NBC Olympic Video, Better Not Tell Her, True Colors, Money Changes Everything, Frankie, It's My Party, Beat Street Strut; choreographer videos Harlem Shuffle, She Bop, Jump, concert dance Ballet for The American Ballroom Theater; dir. TV programs Dance in America, Christmas With Flicka, Celebrating Gershwin, Unforgettable, 20th Anniversary, Dancing, Natalie Cole's Untraditional Xmas; music staging/choreographer for TV programs Saturday Night Live, The Gary Shandling Show, Good Sports, The Orchestra, Robert Klein Special, The Oscars, American Music Awards, The Grammys, The Electric Co., The Muppets, Square One, Goldie Hawn Spl., films Grease, Big, Awakenings, Sleeping With the Enemy, Billy Bathgate, Cowboy Way, Used People, the Wild Party, Roseland, Grease II, First Wives Club. Recipient 2 Emmy awards NATAS, 1988, 92, 4 Tony nominations, DGA nomination.

BIRCH, STANLEY FRANCIS, JR., federal judge; b. 1945. BA, U. Va., 1967; JD, Emory U., 1970, LLM in Taxation, 1976. Law clk. to Hon. Judge Sidney O. Smith Jr. U.S. Dist. Ct. (no. dist.) Ga.; mem. firm Greer, Sartain & Carey, Gainesville, Ga., 1974-76, Deal, Birch, Jarrard & Link, Gainesville, 1976-83, Birch, Hartness & Link, Gainesville, 1983-85, Vaughan, Davis, Birch & Murphy, Atlanta, 1985-90; judge U.S. Ct. Appeals (11th cir.), Atlanta, 1990—. Lt. U.S. Army 1970-72. Mem. State Bar Ga., Ga. Bar Found., Atlanta Bar Assn., Gainesville Northeastern Bar Assn., 11th Cir. Hist. Soc., Lawyers Club Atlanta, Ga. Legal History Found., U. Va. Alumni Assn., Emory U. Sch. Law Alumni Assn., Calvert Hall Alumni Assn., Old Warhorse Lawyers Club, Theta Delta Chi. Office: US Ct Appeals 11th Cir 56 Forsyth St NW Atlanta GA 30303-2205*

BIRCHARD, BRUCE, religious organization administrator. BA (high hons.) magna cum laude, Wesleyan Univ., 1967; MA in anthropology, Univ. Chgo., 1968. Coord. disarmament program Phila. Yearly Meeting Friends Peace Com., 1974-84; nat. coord. disarmament program Am. Friends Svc. Com., 1984-92; gen. sec., CEO Friends Gen. Conf., 1992—. Office: Friends Gen Conference 1216 Arch St # 2B Philadelphia PA 19107-2835*

BIRCHER, ANDREA URSULA, psychiatric-mental health nurse, educator, clinical nurse specialist; b. Bern, Switzerland, Mar. 6, 1928; came to U.S., 1947; d. Franklin E. Bircher and Hedy E. Bircher-Rey. Diploma, Knapp Coll. Nursing, Santa Barbara, Calif., 1957; BS, U. Calif., San Francisco, 1961, MS, 1962; PhD, U. Calif., Berkeley, 1966. RN, Calif., Ill. Staff nurse, head nurse Cottage Hosp., Santa Barbara, 1957-58; psychiatric nurse, jr., sr. Langley-Porter Neuropsychiatric Inst., San Francisco, 1958-66; asst. prof. U. Ill. Coll. Nursing, Chgo., 1966-72; prof. U. Okla. Coll. Nursing, Oklahoma City, 1972-93, prof. emeritus, 1993—. Contbr. articles and papers to profl. jours. Recipient award for Outstanding Contributions to Faculty Governance U. Okla. Faculty Senate 1985, 93, others. Mem. AAUP, ANA, AAUW, Am. Psychotherapy Assn. (cert. diplomate), Internat. Soc. for Psychiat. Nursing, Internat. Soc. Psychiat.-Mental Health Nursing, Nat. League for Nursing, N.Am. Nursing Diagnosis Assn., Calif. Assn. of Psychiat. Nurses in Advanced Practice, Ventura County Writers Club, Sigma Theta Tau, Phi Kappa Phi. Republican. Avocations: indoor gardening, cooking, reading, yoga, writing. Home: 1161 Cypress Point Ln Apt 201 Ventura CA 93003-6074

BIRCHFIELD, JOHN KERMIT, JR., lawyer; b. Roanoke, Va., Jan. 8, 1940; s. John Kermit and Christine (Luke) B.; m. Glenys Garnell, Nov. 14, 1964; 1 child, Guthrie Kathryn. B.S. in Econs., Roanoke Coll., 1968; J.D., U. Va., 1971. Bar: N.Y., 1972, U.S. Dist Ct. (so. dist.) N.Y., 1972, U.S. Ct. Appeals (2d cir.), 1972. Assoc. Shearman & Sterling, N.Y.C., 1971-81; ptnr. Holtzmann, Wise & Shepard, N.Y.C., 1981-83; sr. v.p. legal and govtl. affairs, gen. counsel Ga. Pacific Corp., Atlanta, 1983-88; mng. dir. Century Ptnrs., Atlanta, Darien, Conn., 1988—; sr. v.p., gen. counsel, corp. sec. M/A-COM, Boston, 1990-95; bd. dirs. Intermountain Industries, Inc., HPSC, Inc., Dairy Mart Convenience Stores, Inc., Mass. Fin. Compass Group Mutual Funds; chmn. bd. dirs. Display Tech., Inc.; former chmn. bd. dirs. Chas. P. Young Co. Author: How to Borrow on the Eurodollar Market, 1981, The Multinational Joint Venture, 1981. Chmn. adv. bd. Park Pride, 1986-90; bd. dirs., exec. com. Atlanta Ballet, 1984-88, chmn., 1987-88, vice chmn., 1986-87; bd. dirs. Atlanta Music Festival Assn., 1984-90, Friends Piedmont Hosp., 1985-90; bd. dirs., exec. com., treas. Assn. Am.-Indian Affairs, 1983-86; bd. dirs. High Mus. Art, 1986-91, exec. com., 1988-89; bd. visitors Emory U., 1985-88, bd. dirs. Emory U. Mus. Art and Archaeology, 1988-92; bd. dirs., chmn. collections com. Cape Ann Hist. Assn., 1993—; trustee Roanoke Coll., 1988—, Chatham Hall, 1988-94. Mem. ABA, Atlanta Bar Assn., Assn. of Bar of City of N.Y., N.Y. State Bar Assn., Am. Law Inst., Am. Arbitration Assn., Racquet and Tennis Club, India House Club, Piedmont Driving Club, Carlton Club of London, Farmington Country Club, Shenandoah Club, Annisquam Yacht Club, Union Boat Club, Somerset Club. Home: Cranberry Hill 33 Way Rd Gloucester MA 01930-4315

BIRCH-VUJOVIC, JUDITH LEE, writer, lecturer, educator; b. Des Moines, Sept. 11, 1939; d. Robert and Mary Jane Lee (Burch) Stow; m. Tony Warry Anderson, Jan. 9, 1961 (div. Oct. 1968); children: Anthony, Eric, Joby; m. Radojko Vujovic, (dec.). BA, Purdue Calumet U., Hammond, Ind., 1973. Cert. tchr., Ind. Caseworker Lake County Dept. Pub. Welfare, Hammond, Ind., 1973-81; reporter, feature writer, columnist The Times, Hammond, 1981-83, columnist, feature writer, 1991-97; freelance writer, 1983—; facilitator creative writing seminars at schs., librs. and colls. in Ind., Ill., Mich., 1983—. Author: (nonfiction) Profiles In Poverty, 1991, (poems) I, Woman, Take Thee, Life, 1991. Avocations: reading, little theater groups, love of Nature. Home: 6916 Connecticut St Merrillville IN 46410-3638

BIRCK, MICHAEL JOHN, manufacturing company executive, electrical engineer; b. Missoula, Mont., Jan. 25, 1938; s. Raymond Michael and Mildred (Johnson) B.; m. Katherine Royer, Sept. 3, 1960; children: Kevin, Joni Birck Stevenson, Christopher. BSEE, Purdue U., 1960, PhD in Engring. (hon.), 1995; MSEE, NYU, 1962. Mem. tech. staff Bell Tel. Labs., Murray Hill, N.J., 1960-66; dir. engring. Communication Apparatus Corp., Melrose Park, Ill., 1967-68, Wescom, Inc., Downers Grove, Ill., 1968-75; pres. Tellabs, Inc., Lisle, Ill., 1975—; mem. engring. adv. coun. U. Notre Dame, 1983-91; bd. dirs. Profl. Tng. Ctrs., Inc., Hinsdale, Ill., ITW, Glenview, Ill., USF&G, Balt., Molex Inc., Lisle, Ill. Patentee in field. Dir. Purdue Rsch. Found., West Lafayette, 1989—; mem. bus. adv. com. to Rep. Harris Fawell, Washington, 1986—; trustee Benedictine Univ., 1988—; mem. pres.'s coun. Purdue U., 1984—; bd. dirs. Hinsdale Hosp., 1995. Recipient High Tech Entrepreneur award Crain's Ill. Bus., Chgo., 1984, Outstanding Engring. Alumni award Purdue U., 1991, Outstanding Master Entrepreneur award Inc. Mag./Ernst & Young, 1995; named Outstanding Elec. Engring. Alumnus Purdue U., 1995. Mem. Telecommunications Industry Assn. (chmn. pub. rels. 1989-90, bd. dirs., vice-chmn. 1984-91, chmn. 1991), Hinsdale Golf Club, Salt Creek Tennis Club (pres. 1986). Republican. Roman Catholic. Avocations: running, tennis, golf. Office: Tellabs Inc 4951 Indiana Ave Lisle IL 60532-1698*

BIRD, ANTONIA, film director. Motion picture and T.V. dir. Films include Safe, 1993, Priest, 1994 (nominee Best Film British Acad. Awards 1995), Mad Love, 1995, Face, 1997, Ravenous, 1999; T.V. series Inspector Morse, 1987, Thin Air, 1988, TECX, 1990, The Men's Room, 1991, A Masculine Ending. Office: c/o DGA 7920 Sunset Blvd Los Angeles CA 90046*

BIRD, CAROLINE, author; b. N.Y.C., Apr. 15, 1915; d. Hobart Stanley and Ida (Brattrud) B.; m. Edward A. Menuez, June 8, 1934 (div. Dec. 1945); 1 dau., Carol (Mrs. John Paul Barach); m. John Thomas Mahoney, Jan. 5, 1957 (dec. 1981); 1 son, John Thomas. Student, Vassar Coll., 1931-34; BA, U. Toledo, 1938; MA, U. Wis., 1939; LHD (hon.), Keene State U., 1988.

Desk editor N.Y. Jour. Commerce, 1943-44; editl. rschr. Newsweek mag., N.Y.C., 1942-43, Fortune mag., N.Y.C., 1944-46; with Dudley-Anderson-Yutzy, pub. relations, N.Y.C., 1947-68; Froman Disting. prof. Russell Sage Coll., 1972-73; Mather prof. Case Western Res. U., Cleve., 1977. Author: The Invisible Scar, 1966, Born Female, 1968, rev. edit., 1970, The Crowding Syndrome, 1972, Everything a Woman Needs to Know to Get Paid What She's Worth, 1973, rev., 1982, The Case Against College, 1975, Enterprising Women, 1976, What Women Want, 1979, The Two-Paycheck Marriage, 1979, The Good Years, 1983, Second Careers, 1992, Lives of Our Own, 1995; chief writer: The Spirit of Houston, 1978; also articles in nat. mags. Mem. review bd. Dept. State, 1974. Mem. Am. Soc. Journalists and Authors, Am. Sociol. Assn. Home: 1600 S Eads St Apt 1024S Arlington VA 22202-2954

BIRD, DICK, sign painter; b. Mpls., July 10, 1937; s. Earl Edward and Ruth Ann (Brown) B.; m. Kathleen Susan Hilary, Jan. 24, 1959; children: Thomas Richard, Timothy Phillip, Patrick Lawrence. Owner Bird Sign Co., Mpls., 1968-92; sign shop mgr. Holiday Sta. Stores, Bloomington, Minn., 1992-97; tchr. sign painting St. Paul Vo-Tech.; sign and graphic specialist Sign Shop, U. Minn., 1998-99. Author: Freehand Lettering, 1983, The Art of Freehand Pinstriping, 1984, How to Build a Low-Buck Streetrod, 1995. With U.S. Army, 1955-58. Mem. Minn. Street Rod Assn., Nat. Street Rod Assn. Avocations: custom cars, boat building, songwriting, dancing, skiing. Home and Office: 4401 Morgan Ave N Minneapolis MN 55412-1244

BIRD, FRANCIS MARION, JR., lawyer; b. Atlanta, Jan. 14, 1938; s. Francis Marion Sr. and Mary Adair (Howell) B.; m. JoAnn Galvin, Aug. 1994; children from previous marriage: Barbara, Michael. AB, Princeton U., 1959; LLB, Emory U., 1964; LLM, Harvard U., 1966. BAr: Ga. 1964, U.S. Ct. Appeals (3d cir. and 11th cir.), U.S. Dist. Cts. (no. dist. and mid. dist.) Ga. Officer USN, 1959-62; assoc. Jones Bird & Howell, Atlanta, 1964-70, ptnr., 1971-82; ptnr. Alston & Bird, Atlanta, 1982-88; pvt. practice Atlanta, 1988—; dir., sec. Summit Industries, Inc., 1980—. Adv. bd. mem. The Devereux Ctr., Kennesaw, Ga., 1989—. Mem. ABA, State Bar of Ga. (chmn. Standing Com. on Publs. 1977-78), Atlanta Bar Assn. (chmn. small firm/sole practitioner sect. 1995-96), Lawyers Club of Atlanta, Old War Horses Lawyers Club. Avocations: writing, outdoor adventure programs, walking. Home: 110 Montgomery Ferry Dr NE Atlanta GA 30309-2713 Office: 400 Colony Sq NE Ste 1750 Atlanta GA 30361-6307

BIRD, HARRIE WALDO, JR., psychiatrist, educator; b. Detroit, Sept. 21, 1917; s. Harrie Waldo and Ann Josephine (Tossy) B.; m. Della Mae Clemmer, Jan. 4, 1943; children: Harrie Waldo, Kathleen Bird Steinhour, Deborah Bird Hall, Mark Henry, Matthew Alexius, Liza George-Aidan Browning. AB, Yale U., 1939; postgrad., U. Mich. Med. Sch., 1939-41; MD, Harvard U., 1943. Intern Phila. Gen. Hosp., 1943-44; resident Menninger Sch. Psychiatry, Topeka, 1946-48; chief infirmary sect. Winter VA Hosp., Topeka, 1946; psychiatrist Adult Psychiat. Clinic, Detroit, 1949, acting dir., 1950; psychiat. cons. Mich. Epilepsy Center, Detroit, 1950-55; clin. instr. psychiatry Wayne State U., Detroit, 1952-55; assoc. prof. psychiatry U. Chgo., 1955-56; asso. prof. psychiatry U. Mich., Ann Arbor, 1956-63; asst. dean Med Sch., 1959-61; prof. psychiatry, assoc. dean St. Louis U.-Sch. Medicine, 1965-68, clin. prof., 1970-95, clin. prof. emeritus, 1995—, dir. The Family Psychiat. Ctr., 1972-93; ret., 1993, prof. emeritus, 1995—; lectr., cons. in field. Bd. dirs. Mich. Epilepsy Ctr., 1956-63, Wayne County Mental Health Soc., 1956-63, Mich. Epilepsy Assn., 1956-63, El Paso Mental Health Assn., 1969-70, Cranbrook Sch., 1961-63. With M.C., AUS, 1944-46. Recipient Mental Health Inst. award St. John's U., 1966. Fellow Am. Psychiat. Assn. (life); mem. AMA, Am. Family Therapy Assn. (charter), Group for Advancement of Psychiatry, Mo. Med. Soc. (hon.), St. Louis Met. Med. Soc. (life), Ea. Mo. Psychiat. Soc., Phi Beta Kappa.

BIRD, LARRY JOE, professional basketball coach, former professional basketball player; b. West Baden, Ind., Dec. 7, 1956; s. Joe and Georgia B; m. Dinah Mattingly Oct. 1, 1989. Student, Ind. U., 1974, Northwood Inst., West Baden, Ind., 1974; BS, Ind. State U., 1979. Player Boston Celtics, 1979-92, spl. asst. to exec. v.p., 1992-97; head coach Ind. Pacers, 1997—; mem. U.S. Olympic Basketball Team, 1992. Author: (with Bob Ryan) Drive, 1989; actor (film) Blue Chips, 1994. Mem. U.S. Gold Medal team World Univ. Games, Sophia, Bulgaria, 1977, Nat. Basketball Assn. championship team, 1981, 84, 86, Nat. Basketball Assn. All-Star Team, 1980-92; named Collegiate Player of Yr. AP, UPI and Nat. Assn. Coaches, 1978-79; Rookie of Yr. Nat. Basketball Assn., 1980; Most Valuable Player Nat. Basketball Assn. All-Star Game, 1982, Nat. Basketball Assn., 1984-86, Nat. Basketball Assn. Playoffs, 1984, 86. Office: Ind Pacers 300 E Market St Indianapolis IN 46204-2603*

BIRD, LINDA W., realtor; b. Millington, Tenn., Mar. 19, 1952; d. Lawrence F. and Sara Teresa (Kori) Watermolen; m. Dennis Keith Bird, July 29, 1978; children: Kristin Ann, Lauren Elizabeth. BS, Fla. State U., 1974; MEd, Fla. Atlantic U., 1976. Broward County 4H coord. Fla. Cooperative Ext. Svc. U. Fla., Gainesville, 1974-76; sales rep. mgmt. tng. program Proctor and Gamble Distbg. Co., Cin., 1976; with mktg. mgmt. faculty Broward Community Coll., Ft. Lauderdale, Fla., 1978; pub. rels. coord. Port Everglades Authority, Ft. Lauderdale, 1978-80; flight attendant in charge Delta Air Lines, Miami, Fla., 1980-96; pres. Bird Realty, Inc., Ft. Lauderdale, 1984—. Pres. Kids in Distress Aux., 1986-87, Child Care Connection Aux., 1989-90; bd. dirs. Lakes Estates Homeowner Assn., 1982-93; chair Our House Jr. League Greater Ft. Lauderdale, Inc., 1994-95; mem. panel TV show 30 Below, 1972; troop coord. Girls Scouts USA, Pine Crest Sch. Fla. Jr. Coll. Presdl. scholar, Fla. Home Ext. scholar; named one of ten Women of Yr. Thousand Plus Club Am. Cancer Soc., 1986-87. Mem. Fort Lauderdale Panhellenic Assn. (tres. 1978), Delta Delta Delta (pres. 1988-90), Omicron Nu. Democrat. Methodist. Home: 2790 NE 57th Ct Fort Lauderdale FL 33308-2724 Office: Bird Realty Inc 2790 NE 57th Ct Fort Lauderdale FL 33308-2724

BIRD, MARY ALICE, fund raising consultant; b. Hershey, Pa., Mar. 31, 1938; d. George Wilbur and Rachel (Sutcliffe) Hocker; m. John Adams Bird, June 11, 1960; children: Edith Simonton, John Adams Jr., Sarah Hocker. BA in English, Wilson Coll., 1960; MA in Contemporary Letters, U. Tulsa, 1976. Various tchg. positions, 1960-77; dir. career devel. Lake Forest (Ill.) Coll., 1974-75; humanities faculty Tulsa (Okla.) Jr. Coll., 1977-85; program dir. Grace & Holy Trinity Cathedral, Kansas City, Mo., 1985-89; fund raising counsel Ketchum, Inc., Pitts., 1989-92; devel. dir. Farnsworth Art Mus., Rockland, Maine, 1992-95; fund raising counsel Demont & Assocs., Inc., Portland, Maine, 1995—; pvt. practice fund raising cons. Spruce Head, Maine, 1997—; pres. S.W. Region Humanities Assn. of Cmty. and Jr. Colls., 1982-83. Contbr. articles, book revs. and poetry to profl. publs. Nat. bd. mem. Panel Am. Women, Kansas City, 1971-85, The Witness, 1990-95; cmty. grant writer Arts/Humanities Coun. of Tulsa, 1977-85; vol. grant writer various cmty. projects, Tulsa and Kansas City, 1977—; pres. Internat. Visitors Coun., Tulsa, 1984-85; vol. capital campaign cons. various clients, Maine, 1989—; vestry mem., sr. warden St. Peter's Episcopal Ch.; bd. mem., chair devel. com. Georges River Land Trust. Democrat. Avocations: gardening, kayaking, writing, meditation. Home: PO Box 345 Spruce Head ME 04859-0345

BIRD, MARY FRANCIS, secondary education educator; b. Mesilla, N.Mex., July 19, 1941; d. A.D. and Mary Theresa (Veitch) Alexander; m. Willis Monroe Bird Jr., May 3, 1962; children: William Michael, Keith Alexander, Steven Wayne. AA, N.Mex. State U., Farmington, 1977; BS, N.Mex. State U., Las Cruces, 1988. Med. transcriptionist Ctr. for Phys. Therapy and Sports Rehab., Las Cruces, 1988-92; family and consumer scis. tchr. Zia Middle Sch., Las Cruces, 1992—. Bd. sec. Farmington Amateur Baseball Congress, 1977-80; pres. Jr. Women's Club, Farmington, 1979-80; charter sec. Burley (Idaho) Amateur Baseball Assn., 1982-84; chairperson Monument for San Albino Ch., Mesilla, N.Mex., 1992. Recipient Outstanding Svc. award City Coun. and Mayor, Burley, Idaho, 1984; named N.Mex. Outstanding Young Home Economist, N.Mex. Home Econs. Assn., Las Cruces, 1987. Mem. AAUW, Am. Vocat. Assn., Family and Consumer Scis. Avocations: singing, theatre performances, volunteering. Office: Zia Middle Sch 1300 W University Las Cruces NM 88005

BIRD, MARY LYNNE MILLER, professional society administrator; b. Buffalo, Feb. 25, 1934; d. Joseph William and Mildred Dorothy (Wallette) Miller; m. Thomas Edward Bird, Aug. 23, 1958; children: Matthew David, Lisa Bronwen. AB magna cum laude, Syracuse U., 1956; postgrad., Columbia U., 1956-58. Mem. rsch. staff Ctr. for Rsch. in Personality, Harvard U., Cambridge, Mass., 1959-62, Ctr. Internat. Studies, Princeton (N.J.) U., 1962-66, Inst. Internat. Social Rsch., Princeton, 1965, Sch. Internat. Affairs, Columbia U., N.Y.C., 1966-67, Coun. Fgn. Rels., N.Y.C., 1967-69, Twentieth Century Fund, N.Y.C., 1969-72; asst. to pres. World Policy Inst., N.Y.C., 1972-74; dir. devel. Fund for Peace, N.Y.C., 1974-78; dir. fellows program Exec. Council Fgn. Diplomats, N.Y.C., 1978-79; dir. devel. Assn. Vol. Surgical Contraception, N.Y.C., 1979-83; exec. dir. Am. Geog. Soc., N.Y.C., 1983—; cons. Fedn. Am. Scientists, Washington, 1974-75. Trustee Bel Canto Opera Co., N.Y.C., 1975-90; bd. dirs. Finding a Way Project. Maxwell Citizenship scholar Syracuse U., 1952-56. Fellow AAAS; mem. NAS (com. on geography, liaison mem.), Assn. Am. Geographers, Soc. Woman Geographers, Internat. Soc. Spatial Scis. (adv. bd.), Inst. for Current World Affairs (trustee), Nat. Coun. Geog. Edn., 100-Yr. Assn. N.Y., Conf. Latin Americanist Geographers, Planning Com. for Nat. Assessment on Ednl. Progress in Geography, St. David's Soc. (pres.), Colonial Dames Am., Mid-Atlantic club N.Y.C. (bd. dirs.), Princeton Club, Phi Beta Kappa, Phi Kappa Phi, Eta Pi Upsilon. Avocations: singing, sailing. Office: Am Geog Soc 120 Wall St Ste 100 New York NY 10005-3904

BIRD, PETER, geology educator; b. Cambridge, Mass., Sept. 29, 1951; s. George Richmond and Doris (Forgue) B.; m. Jean M. Campbell, Mar. 4, 1972; 1 child, Andrew Campbell. BA in Geol. Scis., Harvard U., 1972; PhD in Earth and Planetary Scis., MIT, 1976. Asst. prof. UCLA, 1976-81, assoc. prof., 1981-85, prof., 1985—. Fellow Geol. Soc. Am., Am. Geophys. Union. Avocations: hiking, photography. Office: UCLA Dept Earth Space Scis Los Angeles CA 90095-1567

BIRD, PHILLIP CRAIG, mortgage company executive; b. Harlan, Iowa, Feb. 22, 1947; s. Victor T. and Dorothy Ann (Book) B.; m. Jane Ann Wilwerding, Aug. 1, 1970; children: Andrea, Sheri, Kelley. Student, U. Nebr., Omaha, 1969-72, Ottawa U., Kansas City, Mo., 1981-82. Lic. real estate broker, Mo. V.p., br. mgr. Iowa Securities/Banco Mortgage/Norwest Mortgage, Omaha, 1971-84; pres. Newport Fin., Kansas City and Overland Park, 1984-87; v.p. 1st Interstate Mortgage, Kansas City, 1987-91; asset mktg. specialist RTC, 1991-94; dir. comml. lending Regional Investment, 1994-96; v.p. Triad Mortgage and Realty Funding Corp., 1996—. Served with U.S. Army, 1966-68. Mem. Nat. Assn. of Indsl. and Office Parks (v.p., sec. 1982-83, bd. dirs. 1984-85, newsletter editor 1982), Comml. Investment div. Johnson County Bd. Realtors (bd. dirs. 1985-87). Republican. Roman Catholic. Club: Milburn Golf & Country Club. Avocations: golf, spectator sports.

BIRD, ROBERT BYRON, chemical engineering educator, author; b. Bryan, Tex., Feb. 5, 1924; s. Byron and Ethel (Antrim) B. Student U. Md., 1941-43; B.S. in Chem. Engring., U. Ill., 1947; Ph.D. in Chemistry, U. Wis., 1950; postdoctoral fellow, U. Amsterdam, 1950-51; DEng (hon.), Lehigh U., 1972, Washington U., 1973, Tech. U. Delft, Holland, 1977, Colo. Sch. Mines, 1986; Sc.D. (hon.), Clarkson U., 1980; ScD (hon.), The Technion U., Israel, 1993; D in engring. sci. (hon.), Eidgenössische Tech. Hochschule, Zürich, Switzerland, 1994; DrEngring (hon.), Kyoto (Japan) U., 1996; ScD (hon.), Tex. A&M U. Asst. prof. chemistry Cornell U., 1952-53, Debye lectr., 1973, Julian C. Smith lectr., 1988; research chemist DuPont Exptl. Sta., summer 1953; mem. faculty U. Wis., 1951-52, 53-57, prof. chem. engring., 1957-92, C.F. Burgess distinguished prof. chem. engring., 1968-72, John D. MacArthur prof., 1982-92, Vilas research prof., 1972-92, chmn. dept., 1964-68; emeritus prof., 1992—; Burgers prof. Technische Univ. Delft, The Netherlands, 1994; vis. prof. U. Calif., Berkeley, 1977, Univ. Catholique de Louvain, Belgium, 1994; D. L. Katz lectr. U. Mich., 1971; W. N. Lacey lectr. Calif. Inst. Tech., 1974; K. Wohl Meml. lectr. U. Del., 1977; W. K. Lewis lectr. MIT, 1982; R. H. Wilhelm lectr., Princeton U., 1991, G. N. Lewis lectr. U. Calif., Berkeley, 1993; Ascher Shapiro lectr. MIT, 1997; lectr. Lectures in Sci. Humble Oil Co., 1959, 61, 64, 66; lecture tour Am. Chem. Soc., 1958, 75, Canadian Inst. Chemistry, 1961, 65; cons. to industry, 1965-90; mem. adv. panel engring. sci. divsn. NSF, 1961-64. Author: (with others) Molecular Theory of Gases and Liquids, 2d printing, 1964, Transport Phenomena, 58th printing, 1999, Spanish edit., 1965, Czech edit., 1966, Italian edit., 1970, Russian edit., 1974, Chinese edit., 1990, Een Goed Begin: A Contemporary Dutch Reader, 1963, 2d edit., 1971, Comprehending Technical Japanese, 1975, Chinese edit., 1985, Dynamics of Polymeric Liquids, Vol. 1, Fluid Mechanics, Vol. 2, Kinetic Theory, 1977, 2d edit., 1987, Reading Dutch: Fifteen Annotated Stories from the Low Countries, 1985, Basic Technical Japanese, 1990, Technical Japanese Supplements: Polymer Science and Engineering, 1995; also numerous rsch. publs.; Am. editor (with others) Applied Sci. Rsch., 1969-86, 89-98; mem. adv. bd. Indsl. and Engring. Chemistry, 1970-72; mem. editl. bd. Jour. Non-Newtonian Fluid Mechanics, 1975—. Served to 1st lt. AUS, 1943-46. Decorated Bronze Star; Fulbright fellow, Holland, 1950, Guggenheim fellow, 1958; Fulbright lectr., 1958, Japan, 1962-63, Sarajevo, Yugoslavia, 1972; recipient Curtis McGraw award Am. Assn. Engring. Edn., 1959, Westinghouse award, 1960, Corcoran award, 1987, Centennial Medallion, 1993, Nat. Medal Sci., 1987. Fellow AIChE (William H. Walker award 1962, Profl. Progress award 1965, Warren K. Lewis award 1974, Founders award 1989, Inst. Lect. award 1992), Am. Phys. Soc., Am. Acad. Arts and Scis.; mem. NAS, NAE, Am. Acad. Mechanics, N.Y. Acad. Scis., Wis. Acad. Scis., Arts and Letters, Am. Assn. Netherlandic Studies, Am. Chem. Soc. (chmn. Wis. sect. 1966, unrestricted rsch. grant Petroleum Rsch. Fund 1963), Soc Rheology, Royal Dutch Acad. Scis. (fgn.), Royal Belgian Acad. Scis. (fgn.), Soc. Chem. Engrs. Japan (hon.), Phi Beta Kappa, Sigma Xi (v.p. Wis. sect. 1959-60), Tau Beta Pi, Alpha Chi Sigma, Phi Kappa Phi, Omicron Delta Kappa, Sigma Tau. Office: U Wis Dept Chem Engring 3004 Engring Hall 1415 Engineering Dr Madison WI 53706-1607

BIRD, THOMAS EDWARD, foreign language and literature educator; b. Rome, N.Y., Mar. 28, 1935; s. Harry J. and Paula W. (Boyce) B.; m. Mary Lynne Miller, Aug. 23, 1958; children: Matthew David, Lisa Bronwen. AB magna cum laude, Syracuse U., 1956; postgrad., Harvard U., 1958-59; MA, Middlebury Coll., 1960; AM, Princeton U., 1965; postgrad., Warsaw U., 1990—. Lectr., assoc. prof. Slavic langs. and lit. Queens Coll., CUNY, Flushing, 1965—; dir., co-dir. Ctr. Jewish Studies, 1996-98; bd. dirs. Pax Romana, Benyumin Shekhter Found., Cymdeithas Madoc, St. David's Soc., St. Nicholas Soc., Soc. of Colonial Wars, chmn. Flag Svc. Com., 1997—. Gen. Soc. of the War of 1812 (pres. New York State Soc.), Soc. of Mayflower Descendants. Author: Patriarch Maximos IV, 1964; editor: Aspects of Religion in the Soviet Union, 1971, The Hard Life of Jura Odcesty, 1980, The 1863 Uprising in Byelorussia, 1980, Skovoroda: An Anthology, 1994; mem. editl. bd. Diakonia, Nationalities Papers, Polish Rev., Zapisy. Served with US Army (Military Intelligence) 1957-62. Recipient George Arents Library award, American Jewish Com. award for interreligious dialogue, Amer. Jewish Com., 1996, Maxwell Citizenship Scholar, 1952-56, NDFL fellow, 1962-65, Woodrow Wilson Fell., 1965, Presdl. Tchg. Awd., 1991. Fellow Soc. for Values in Higher Edn.; mem. AAUP, MLA, Amer. Assn. for Advancement of Slavic Studies, Amer COunc. of Tchrs. of Russ., Columbia U. Faculty Seminars , Belarusan Inst. Arts and Scis., Internatl. Assn. of Belarujan Studies (vice pres.), Polish Inst. Arts and Scis., Russian-American Scholars Assn., Shevchenko Scientific Soc., Ukrainian Acad. Arts and Scis., Hon. Soc. of Cymmrodorion, Dobro Slovo, Club of New York, Phi Beta Kappa, Phi Kappa Alpha. Club: Princeton, Nassau Club of Princeton. Office: Queens Coll CUNY Rufus King Hall 65-30 Kissena Blvd Flushing NY 11367-1597

BIRD, WENDELL RALEIGH, lawyer; b. Atlanta, July 16, 1954; s. Raleigh Milton and R. Jean (Edwards) B. BA summa cum laude, Vanderbilt U., 1975; JD, Yale U., 1978. Bar: Ga. 1978, Ala. 1980, Calif. 1981, Fla. 1982, U.S. Ct. Appeals (2d, 3d, 4th, 5th, 6th, 7th, 8th, 9th, 10th and 11th cirs.) 1979-83, U.S. Supreme Ct. 1983. Law clk. to judge U.S. Ct. Appeals (4th cir.), Durham, N.C., 1978-79, U.S. Ct. Appeals (5th cir.), Birmingham, Ala., 1979-80; pvt. practice San Diego, 1980-82; atty. Parker, Johnson, Cook & Dunlevie, Atlanta, 1982-86; sr. ptnr. Bird & Assocs., P.C., Atlanta, 1986—; adj. prof. Emory U. Law Sch., Atlanta, 1985—; lectr. Washington Non-Profit Tax Conf., 1982—. Author: The Origin of Species Revisited, 2 vols., 1987; contbg. author: Federal Taxation of Exempt Organizations, 1994, CCH Federal Tax Service, 1988—; mem. bd. editors Yale U. Law Jour., 1977-78, others; contbr. articles to profl. jours. Bd. govs. Coun. for Nat. Policy, Washington, 1983—. Recipient Egger prize Yale U., 1978, Vanderbilt U. award, 1972. Mem. ABA (litigation sect., taxation sect., com. on exempt orgns., past chmn. subcom. on religious orgns., past chmn. subcom. on state and local taxes, chmn. subcom. on charitable contbns., sect. on real property probate and trust, com. charitable gifts), Am. Law Inst., Ga. Bar Assn., Fla. Bar Assn., Calif. Bar Assn., Ala. Bar Assn., Assn. Trial Lawyers Am., Phi Beta Kappa. Republican. Avocations: science, skiing, photography, genealogy, piano, architecture. Home: 92 Blackland Rd NW Atlanta GA 30342-4420 Office: Bird & Assocs PC 1150 Monarch Plz 3414 Peachtree Rd NE Atlanta GA 30326-1153

BIRDMAN, JEROME MOSELEY, drama educator, consultant; b. Phila., Dec. 4, 1930; s. Morris Schiowitz and Minerva B.; m. Evanira Pereira Mendes, July 1, 1959; children: Julia, Beatrice. B.S., Temple U., 1956; A.M., U. Ill., 1957, Ph.D., 1970; mem. seminar for Arts Trustees, Harvard U., 1975. Mem. editorial staff Accent Quar. of New Lit., 1957-58; dir. cultural programming for Am. Forces, U.S. Info. Service, Northeast Italy, 1958-61; mem. faculty theatre dept. So. Ill. U., Edwardsville, 1961-71; acad. program officer So. Ill. U., 1972-73; prof. dramatic arts, dean Coll. Fine Arts, U. Nebr., Omaha, 1973-78, Sch. Fine Arts, U. Conn., Storrs, 1978-92; dean emeritus, 1993, consultant, 1993—; adv. bd. Nebr. Alliance for Arts Edn., 1976-78; lectr. USIS, Brazil, 1964; arts commr. Nat. Assn. State Univs. and Land Grant Colls., 1979-89, chmn., 1983-89; panelist NEH, 1976—, Nat. Endowment Arts, 1983—; adv. Conn. Dept. Edn., 1980—; accreditor New Eng. Assn. Schs. and Colls.; cons. to various colls. and univs. in arts adminstrn. Contbr. articles on theatrical art to various profl. publs.; originator exhibit: Artists Who Teach, Washington, 1987; producer or director more than 40 plays, musicals and concerts at universities, 1963-76; translator Six Characters in Search of an Author, U. Mo., 1987-88. Mem. Mayor's Task Force on the Arts, Omaha, 1977-78; bd. dirs. Dance Concert Soc., St. Louis, 1970-73, New Music Circle, 1971-73, Prelude Civic Ballet, Ill., 1971-73, Omaha Opera Co., 1973-75, Omaha Symphony Assn., 1973-78, Stamford Ctr. for the Arts, 1984-89, Met. Arts Council, Omaha, 1976-78, Omaha Children's Mus., 1976-78. Served with U.S. Army, 1952-54. Recipient merit citation Provincia di Vicenza, 1961. Mem. Am. Theatre Assn., Internat. Fedn. Theatre Research, Am. Soc. Theatre Research, Internat. Council Fine Arts Deans, Soc. Theatre Research Great Britain., Societé d'Histoire du Théâtre, Nat. Assn. State Universities and Land-Grant Colls., Am. Theatre Assn./Assn. for Theatre in Higher Edn. Address: 76 Charles Ln Storrs Mansfield CT 06268-2348

BIRD-PORTO, PATRICIA ANNE, personnel director; b. N.Y.C., June 16, 1952; d. Jacques Robert and Muriel (Cooper) Bird; m. Joseph Porto, May 5, 1984; 1 child, Jennifer Ashley. BA, U. So. Calif., 1975; cert. in legal assistantship, U. Calif., Irvine, 1987. Cert. in transp. demand mgmt. Orange County Transit Dist., 1988. Mgr. Bullock's Westwood, West L.A., 1976-78; mgr. ops. Lane Bryant, L.A., 1978-79; supr. employment, dir. personnel May Co. Dept. Stores, 1979-81; adminstr. personnel, dir. benefits Zoetrope Studios, Hollywood, Calif., 1981-82; personnel and ops. analyst Auntie Barbara's, Beverly Hills, Calif., 1982-86; dir. personnel Baylylop, Santa Ana, Calif., 1986-88; pres. Creative Pers. Assocs., 1986-89; owner Flowerman Corona, Del Mar, Calif., 1987—; U.S. dir. human resources UIS, Inc., 1988-93. Co-chair Pro-Wilson Orange County, through 1998. Home: 7 Stardust Irvine CA 92612-3769 Office: 3100 E Coast Hwy Corona Del Mar CA 92625-2301

BIRDSALL, ARTHUR ANTHONY, chemical executive; b. Oneonta, N.Y., Feb. 28, 1947; s. Charles Albert and Mary (Danzi) B.; m. Jane Elaine Fink, Jan. 28, 1967; children: Robert, Thomas, William. AAS in Chemistry, Erie County Tech. Inst., 1966; BS in Chemistry, Saginaw Valley Coll., 1969. Applications engr. Dow Corning Corp., Midland, Mich., 1966-70; product devel. chemist Dow Corning Corp., Elizabethtown, Ky., 1970-71, quality reliability engr., 1971-73; quality assurance supr. Dow Corning Corp., Chgo., 1973-75; product devel. specialist Dow Corning Corp., Midland, Mich., 1975-77; pilot plant mgr. Dow Corning Corp., Freeland, Mich., 1977-80; quality mgr., govt. rels. coord. Dow Corning Ophthalmics, Inc. divsn. Dow Corning Corp., Cosa Mesa, Calif., 1980; quality mgr., govt. rels. coord. Dow Corning Ophthalmics, Inc. divsn. Dow Corning Corp., Midland, 1980-82, mgr. quality/regulatory affairs, 1982-85; corp. mgr. product stewardship Dow Corning Corp., Midland, Mich., 1985-88, program chmn. health environ. and safety bd., 1986-91, product liability issue mgmt. com., 1988-91, mgr. product stewardship, safety and regulatory compliance, 1988-91, European dir. health, environment and regulatory affairs, 1991-96, European dir. health, environ. and regulatory affairs; mem. Dow Corning Europe Environment, Health and Safety Coun., 1992-96, mgr. global product stewardship bus. program, 1996-97, Asia-Pacific environ., health and safety mgmt. advisor, 1996—, dir. global environ., health and safety external affairs, 1999—; cons. ophthalmic device regulations Dow Corning Corp., Midland, 1985; bd. dirs. Contact Lens Inst., also vice-chmn. bd. dirs., 1983-84, treas., 1984-85; chmn. pro-tem ophthalmic device com. Health Industry Mfrs. Assn., Washington, 1982-84, mem. Product Safety Mgmt. Forum; mem. Chem. Industry Dirs. Exch., Material Safety Data Sheet, Electronic Date Interchange Std. Coms., 1986-91; environ, health and safety com. Am. C. of C., Belgium, 1991-96, China, 1998. Co-inventor silicone resins for optical devices, 1977; contbr. articles to profl. jours.; patentee in field. Chmn. Cub Scout Pack com., Midland, 1979; treas. local Parent Tchr. Orgn., Midland, 1977, v.p., 1978, pres., 1979; tchr. Cath. Youth Coun., Midland, 1985; bd. dirs. Blessed Sacrament Sch., 1986-87, mem. edn. commn., 1986-88; mem. adv. bd. Midland County United Way Citizen, 1990-91; mem. panel Midland County United Way, 1999—. Contbr. recipient I.R. 100 award silicone contact lens devel., 1982. Mem. Am. Soc. Quality Control, Regulatory Affairs Profl. Soc., Ctr. European des Silicones (environ. com. 1991-94, mgmt. bd. 1991-96, bd. dirs. 1994-96). Republican. Roman Catholic. Avocations: reading, writing prose and poetry, gardening, collecting art. Home: 2600 Brookwood Dr Midland MI 48640 Office: Dow Corning Corp Mail Stop CO 1272 Midland MI 48686-0994

BIRDSALL, CHARLES KENNEDY, electrical engineer; b. N.Y.C., Nov. 19, 1925; s. Charles and Irene (Birdsall); m. Betty Jean Hansen, 1949 (div. 1977) (dec.); children: Elizabeth (dec.), Anne, Barbara, Thomas, John; m. Virginia Anderson, Aug. 21, 1981. B.S., U. Mich., 1946, M.S., 1948; Ph.D., Stanford U., 1951. Various projects Hughes Aircraft Co., Culver City, Calif., 1951-55; leader electron physics group GE Microwave Lab., Palo Alto, Calif., 1955-59; prof. elec. engring. U. Calif., Berkeley, 1959-91, prof. Grad. Sch., 1994—; founder Plasma Theory and Simulation Group, 1967; founder, 1st chmn. Energy and Resources Com., 1972-74; cons. to industry, Lawrence Livermore Lab. of U. Calif., 1960-86; prof. Miller Inst. Basic Rsch. in Sci., 1963-64; sr. vis. fellow U. Reading (Eng.), summer 1976; rsch. assoc. Inst. Plasma Physics, Nagoya (Japan) U., winter 1981; Chevron vis. prof. energy Calif. Inst. Tech., 1982; area coord. phys. electronics/bioelectronics, 1984-86; joint U.S.-Japan Inst. Fusion Theory vis. prof. Inst. of Plasma Physics, Nagoya U., fall 1988. Author: (with W.B. Bridges) Electron Dynamics of Diode Regions, 1966, (with A.B. Langdon) Plasma Physics via Computer Simulation, 1985, 91, (with S. Kuhn) Bounded Plasmas, 1994. Served with USNR, 1944-46. U.S.-Japan Coop. Sci. Program grantee, 1966-67; Fulbright grantee U. Innsbruck, 1991; recipient Berkeley Citation, 1991. Fellow IEEE (1st recipient Plasma Sci. and Applications award June 1988), AAAS, Am. Phys. Soc.; mem. Sigma Xi, Tau Beta Pi, Eta Kappa Nu. Patentee in field; co-originator many-particle plasma simulations in two and three dimensions using cloud-in-cell methods, 1966. Home: 4050 Valente Ct Lafayette CA 94549-3412 Office: U Calif EECS Dept Cory Hall Berkeley CA 94720

BIRDSALL, NANCY, professional association administrator; b. Feb. 6, 1946. BA in Am. Studies, Am. Coll. of the Sacred Heart, 1967; MA in Internat. Rels., Johns Hopkins U., 1969; PhD in Econs., Yale U., 1979. Social sci. analyst Smithsonian Inst., 1972-76; economist Devel. Econs. Dept., 1979-82; prior holder of various policy and mgmt. positions World Bank, Washington, 1979-93; exec. v.p. Inter-Am. Devel. Bank, Washington, 1993-98; sr. assoc., dir. Politics of Econ. Reform, CArnegie Endowment for Internat. Peace, 1998—; sr. adviser Rockefeller Found., 1988-89; active numerous coms. Nat. Acad. of Scis.; chair bd. dirs. Internat. Ctr. for Rsch. on Women; bd. dirs. Bd. of Population Coun., numerous others. Author numerous publs. on econ. devel. issues. Office: care Carnegie Endowment for Internat Peace 1300 New York Ave NE Washington DC 20036-2103*

BIRDSALL, WILLIAM FOREST, librarian; b. Farmington, Minn., Oct. 30, 1937; s. Herman Elden and Mae Elizabeth (Daugherty) B.; m. Ann

Elizabeth Page, Dec. 20, 1965; children—Sarah, Stephanie, Thomas. B.A., U. Minn., 1955, M.A., 1964; Ph.D., U. Wis., 1973. Reference librarian Iowa State U., Ames, 1961-63; head pub. services Wis. State U., La Crosse, 1965-70; asst. dir. for pub. services U. Man., Winnipeg, Can., 1973-77, assoc. dir. for pub. services 1977-81; univ. librarian Dalhousie U., Halifax, N.S., Can., 1981-97; exec. dir. Novanet, Inc., Halifax, 1998—. Author: Myth of the Electronic Library, 1994, Understanding Telecommunications and Public Policy, 1998; contbr. articles to libr. periodicals. Mem. Atlantic Provinces Library Assn. (pres. 1984), Man. Library Assn. (pres. 1981), Can. Library Assn. (council 1981, 84). Home: 54 Village Crescent, Bedford, NS Canada B4A 1J2 Office: Novanet Inc, 6080 Young St #601, Halifax, NS Canada B3K 5L2

BIRDSONG, ALTA MARIE, volunteer; b. Ft. Worth, July 18, 1934; d. Alton Roy and Artie Marguerite (Bentley) Flowers; m. Kenneth Layne Birdsong, Oct. 18, 1958; children: Suzanne Denise, Jeffrey Layne. BBA in Acctg. magna cum laude, U. North Tex., 1955. Cost engr. Tex. Instruments, Inc., Dallas, 1955-62; part-time acct. Atlanta, 1972—. Mem. DeKalb County Cmty. Rels. Com., 1981-93, chair, 1984-87; mem. Atlanta Regional Com. Adv. Group, 1981-88, Met. Atlanta United Way, 1985—, resource investment vol. sch. age children; chair Sch. Age Child Care Coun., 1987-90; mem. Dekalb County Task Force on Personal Care Homes, Dekalb County Task Force on Domestic Violence; mem. steering com. for bond referendum Dekalb B. Edn.; mem. Vision 2020 Governance Stakeholders ARC, 1994-95; mem. Camp Fire Boys and Girls. Recipient John H. Collier award for Camp Fire, 1991, Luther Halsey Gulick award for Camp Fire, 1993, Frederic E. Ruccius award for Camp Fire, 1993, Mortar Bd. Alumni Achievement award, 1991, Woman of Yr. award Atlanta Alumnae Panhellenic, 1983, Women Who Have Made a Difference award DeKalb YWCA, 1985, Ember award Camp Fire, 1998. Mem. AAUW (divsn. pres. 1987-89, pres. elect 1987-89, mem. v.p. 1984-86, recording sec. 1982-84, assn. nominating com. 1993-97, chair 1995-97, Achievement award 1999), Atlanta Coun. Camp Fire (pres. 1992-94, v.p. 1990-92, region fin. officer 1989-90, region nominating com. chair 1991-92), Atlanta Alumnae Panhellenic (pres. 1978-79, v.p. 1977-78), Freedoms Found. at Valley Force (Atlanta chpt. pres. 1991-92, v.p. 1990-91, v.p. publicity 1988-89, treas. 1985-87, sec. 1983-85, ea.-so. region adv. 1994-97), Nat. Women's Conf., Delta Gamma Alumnae (Atlanta chpt. 1st. v.p. 1985-87, treas. 1972-74, Oxford award 1992). Home: 5241 Manhasset Cv Atlanta GA 30338-3413

BIRDSONG, EMIL ARDELL, clinical psychologist; b. Detroit, Feb. 23, 1943; s. Emil Ardell and Ruby Carolyn (Weaks) B.; m. Beatrice Lee Johnson, Sept. 12, 1981. BA in Psychology, U. Mich., Dearborn, 1968; MA in Psychology, Merrill Palmer Inst., 1981; Psy. S Clin. Edn., Ctr. Humanistic Studies, Detroit, 1988; PhD of Clin. Psychology, Union Inst., Cin., 1994. Lic. psychologist, Mich. Spl. edn. educator Wolf Mid. Sch., Centerline, Mich., 1987-88; intern Ypsilanti (Mich.) Psychiat. Hosp., 1988-90; pvt. practice Detroit, 1994—; clin. supr. Boys & Girls Republic, Farmington Hills, MI, 1999—; grant writer Law Enforcement Assist Act, Mich. With U.S. Army Med. Corps, 1968-70. Named Ky. Col. Gov. of Ky., 1993. Mem. APA, Am. Psychology Soc., Mich. Psychol. Assn., U. Mich. Alumni Assn. (bd. govs., bd. dirs. 1972-73). Democrat. Lutheran. Avocations: chess, genealogical research. Home: 21771 Dexter Ct Warren MI 48089-2826 Office: Boys & Girls Republic 28000 W Nine Mile Rd Farmington Hills MI 48336

BIRDSONG, GEORGE YANCY, manufacturing company executive; b. Suffolk, Va., Nov. 8, 1939; s. William McLemore and Yancey (Brooking) B.; m. Sue Benton, June 10, 1961; children: Anne Cabell, David Jefferson, Charles Randolph. BA, Washington and Lee U., Lexington, Va., 1961; LLB, U. Va., 1964, diploma in basic advanced mgmt., 1968. Bar: Va. 1964. Mem. Godwin & Godwin, Suffolk, 1964-66; sec.-treas. Birdsong Peanuts divsn. Birdsong Corp., Suffolk, 1965—, exec. v.p., 1981-97, pres., 1997—; bd. dirs. Crestar Bank, Suffolk and Norfolk. Dir. Suffolk Redevel. and Housing Authority, 1966-85, chmn., 1966-83; pres. Louise Obici Meml. Hosp. Found., Sufolk, 1980—; chpt. pres. Tri-County Area Planned Parenthood, 1969—; mem. pres.'s adv. coun. Va. Wesleyan Coll., 1971-89, trustee, 1989—; mem. exec. com. Future of Hampton Roads, 1983-96; bd. dirs. Hampton Roads United Way, 1980-84; founding dir. Suffolk YMCA, 1987—; sec., bd. dirs. Suffolk Cmty. Health Ctr., 1992—; bd. dirs. Va. Found. Ind. Colls., 1994—; pres. Suffolk Jaycees, 1968-70. Recipient Disting. Svc. award Suffolk Jaycees, 1971, Order of the Red Triangle YMCA of South Hampton Rd., 1993, Humanitarian award Tidewater chpt. NCCJ, 1997; named 1st Citizen, Suffolk, 1997. Mem. Va. Bar Assn., Suffolk Bar Assn., Va. Mfrs. Assn. (bd. dirs. 1977-79, 87-89), Suffolk C. of C., Suffolk Sports Club, Suffolk Tennis Assn., Elks, Rotary. Methodist. Home: 608 Riverview Dr Suffolk VA 23434 Office: Birdsong Corp 612 Madison Ave Suffolk VA 23434-4028

BIRDWELL, JAMES EDWIN, JR., retired banker; b. Chuckey, Tenn., Apr. 22, 1924; s. James Edwin and Mary Eleanor (Earnest) B.; m. Marilyn Margaretta Gibson, Dec. 20, 1949; children: James Edwin, III, Amy Eleanor, Todd Gibson. A.B., Tusculum Coll., 1949; M.A., Vanderbilt U., 1951. Tchr., coach Doak High Sch., 1948-50; field rep. 3d Nat. Bank, Nashville, 1951-52; trainee Va. Nat. Bank, 1957, v.p., from 1962; chmn., pres. First Am. Bank, Clinton, Tenn., 1973-84; vice chmn. First Am. Nat. Bank, Knoxville, Tenn., 1984-90. Commr. bldgs and grounds Va. Beach, Va., 1970-72; dir. Daniel Arthur Rehab. Ctr., Oak Ridge, 1974-84; dir. Oak Ridge Hosp., 1976-82; dir. Meth. Med. ctr. Found. , Oak Ridge, Tenn., v.p. Roane Anderson Econ. Council, 1976-90; chmn. Clinton Port Authority, 1978—; mem. exec. com. Melton Hill Regional Indsl. Authority, Clinton, Tenn., 1978-95; mem. Anderson County Tax Adv. Bd., 1978—; mem. Indsl. Devel. Bd. Anderson County, 1978—, dir., Coal Creek Mining & Mfg. Co., 1992—; dir. Aveawide Devel. Corp., 1988—. Served with USNR, 1942-46, 52-57. Decorated Air medal. Mem. Am. Bankers Assn., Tenn. Bankers Assn., Robert Morris Assocs., Bank Adminstrn. Inst., Bank Mktg. Assn. Republican. Methodist. Clubs: Oak Ridge Country, Civitan, LeConte. Office: First Am Nat Bank 245 S Main St Clinton TN 37716-3603

BIRELY, WILLIAM CRAMER, investment banker; b. Thurmont, Md., Nov. 13, 1919; s. Victor Morris and Dorothy Grace (Rouzer) B.; m. Luelle Avis Langness, July 21, 1943. Student, Strayer Bus. Coll., 1937-38, Am. U., 1941-42. With Folger, Nolan, Inc., Washington, 1947-52, v.p., 1950-52; gen. partner Rouse, Brewer & Becker, Washington, 1952-55; exec. v.p., treas. Birely & Co., Washington, 1955-62, pres., 1962-67; also dir.; v.p. Mason & Co. (now Legg, Mason, Wood, Walker, Inc.), 1967-70; investment banker Lang & Co., Washington, 1970-85, Chapin, Davis & Co., Balt., 1985-89, Lang Div. Moors & Cabot, Inc., Alexandria, Va., 1989—; v.p., dir. Thurmont (Md.) Bank (now Nations Bank), 1962-73; adv. bd. Farmers & Mechanics Nat. Bank, Thurmont, 1975-76; mem. adv. council SBA, 1962-66. Mem. Bd. Appeals Montgomery County, 1965, Montgomery County Council, 1965-66; treas. Young Republican Club of Montgomery County, 1947, pres., 1948; del. Md. Rep. Conv., 1952, 56, 60; mem. gen. inaugural coms. Eisenhower and Nixon, 1953, 57, Nixon and Agnew, 1968, 72, Reagan and Bush, 1980, 84, Bush and Quayle, 1988. Served with F.A. AUS, 1943-44. Recipient Gov.'s citation for outstanding service to Md. Mem. Am. Legion (life), Huguenot Soc. Washington (life, former v.p.), S.A.R. (life, former nat. trustee), Soc. Mayflower Descendants, Soc. Colonial Wars (life), Soc. War 1812, St. Andrews Soc., Frederick County Hist. Soc. (life), Carroll County Hist. Soc. (life), Washington Hist. Socs. (life), Montgomery County Hist. Soc. (life). Clubs: Bond; Nat. Press; Army and Navy. Home: 900 Ashton Rd PO Box 213 Ashton MD 20861-0213 Office: Lang Div Moors & Cabot Inc 1600 Prince St Ste 113 Alexandria VA 22314

BIRENBAUM, JONATHAN, lawyer; b. Waterbury, Conn., Sept. 12, 1953; s. Bernard and Ethel (Shiller) B. AB, Colgate U., 1975; JD, Union U., 1978. Bar: N.Y. 1979, U.S. Dist. Ct. (so. and ea. dists.) N.Y. 1979, U.S. Supreme Ct. 1984, Conn. 1996. Assoc. Mudge Rose Guthrie Alexander & Ferdon, N.Y.C., 1978-85, prin., 1986-95; ptnr. Paul, Hastings, Janofsky & Walker LLP, 1995—. Mem. ABA, Assn. of Bar of City of N.Y. Office: Paul Hastings et al 1055 Washington Blvd Stamford CT 06901-2216

BIRENBAUM, WILLIAM M., former university president; b. Macomb, Ill., July 18, 1923; s. Joseph and Rose (Whiteman) B.; m. Helen Bloch, Mar. 8, 1951; children: Susan, Lauren Amy, Charles. Dr. Law, U. Chgo., 1949; L.H.D., Columbia Coll., Chgo., 1970. Dean students Univ. Coll., 1955-57; dir. research, conf. bd. Asso. Research Councils, Ford Found. project study post-doctoral internat. ednl. exchanges, 1954-55; asst. v.p. Wayne State U., 1957-61; dean New Sch. Social Research, N.Y.C., 1961-64; v.p., provost Bklyn. Center, L.I. U., 1964-67; pres. Edn. Affiliate, Bedford-Stuyvesant Devel. & Services Corp., Bklyn, 1967-68, S.I. Community Coll., 1968-76; pres. Antioch U., 1976-85. Author: Overlive: Power, Poverty and the University, 1968, Something for Everybody is Not Enough: An Educator's Search for His Education, 1971; Contbg. author: Student Personnel Work in Urban Colleges. Cons. Austrian Ministry Edn., Vienna, 1969; higher edn. adviser Republic of Zambia, 1972; cons. U. Zambia, 1972; faculty Salzburg Seminar in Am. Studies, 1976; founder Nat. Student Assn., 1946-48; chmn. Mich. Cultural Commn., 1960-61; founder, original dir. Detroit Adventure, vol. assn. cultural instns., 1958-61; bd. adv. Bklyn. Acad. Music, 1965—, Bklyn Inst. Arts and Scis; trustee Friends World Coll., Westbury, N.Y., Hasbro Childrens Found., 1985—, Lit. Vols. of N.Y.C., 1986—. Mem. Chgo. Bar Assn., Delta Sigma. Home: 108 Willow St Brooklyn NY 11201-2202

BIRGE, ANNE CONSTANTIN, protective services official; b. Seattle, Sept. 3, 1952. BS, U. Okla., 1977; AS, Valley Coll., 1987. Cert. tchr., Calif. Cmty. svc. officer San Bernardino (Calif.) County Sheriff, 1982-85, dep. sheriff, 1985-89, detective, 1989-95; dist. atty. investigation San Bernardino County Dist. Attys. Office, 1995—; trainer Birge & Assoc., Yucaipa, Calif., 1989; instr. in interviewing and interrogation, hostage negotiations, and stress mgmt. techniques, 1987—. Bd. dirs. Chaffey C.C. Found., Rancho Cucamonga, Calif., 1986-87. Recipient Proclamation award City of Rancho Cucamonga, 1985; named San Bernardino Area C. of C. Law Enforcement Office of Yr., County Sheriff's Dept., 1991. Mem. Calif. Assn. Hostage Negotiators, Women Peace Officers' Assn., Internat. Footprint Assn., Calif. Peace Officers' Assn., Calif. State Sheriffs' Assn., Calif. Dist. Attys. Assn., Calif. Dist. Atty. Investigators' Assn. Episcopalian. Avocations: reading, gardening, hiking. Office: San Bernardino County Dist Attys Office 316 N Mountain View Ave San Bernardino CA 92415-0004

BIRGE, ROBERT RICHARDS, chemistry educator; b. Washington, Aug. 10, 1946; s. Robert Bowen and Dorothy (Richards) B.; m. Constance A. Reed, Aug. 3, 1993; children: Jonathan Richards, David Porter. B.S. in Chemistry, Yale U., 1968; Ph.D. in Chem. Physics, Wesleyan U., Middletown, Conn., 1972. NIH postdoctoral fellow Harvard U., Cambridge, Mass., 1973-75; asst. prof. dept. chemistry U. Calif.-Riverside, 1975-81, chmn. com. on research, 1981-82, assoc. prof. dept. chemistry, 1981-84; Weingart sabbatical fellow Calif. Inst. Tech., Pasadena, 1982-83; prof., head dept. chemistry Carnegie-Mellon U., Pitts., 1984-87, dir. Ctr. Molecular Electronics,, 1984-87; prof. chemistry, dir. W.M. Keck Ctr. Molecular Electronics W.M. Keck Ctr. Molecular Electronics Syracuse (N.Y.) U., 1988—; dir. grad. biophysics program Syracuse (N.Y.) U., 1989-93; rsch. dir. N.Y. State Ctr. for Advanced Tech. in Computer Applications and Software Engring., 1992—; disting. prof. chemistry Syracuse U., 1995—; NATO prof. Advanced Study Inst., Maratea, Italy, 1983; permanent mem. molecular and cellular biophysics study sect. NIH, Bethesda, Md., 1984-89; bd. dirs. West Penn Hosp. Rsch. Found., 1987-88; co-chmn. adv. com. molecular electronics NAS, 1987. Mem. editl. bd. Jour. Nanotech., Brit. Inst. Physics, 1990—, Supramolecular Sci., 1993—, Biocomputing, 1995—; assoc. editor Biospectroscopy, 1993—; regional editor Biosensors and Bioelectronics, 1995—; editl. adv. bd. The Jour. Phys. Chemistry, 1996—; contbr. chpts. to books, more than 180 articles to profl. jours. Treas. council Carnegie Inst. Natural History, Pitts., 1985-87. Served to 1st lt. USAF, 1972-73. Recipient Chancellor's Citation for Exceptional Acad. Achievement, 1996, Nat. Sci. award Am. Cyanamid Corp., 1964; named to Time Digital Top 50 Cyber Elite, Time Inc., 1997; Regents fellow U. Calif., 1976. Mem. Am. Chem. Soc. (Rsch. award 1992), Am. Phys. Soc., Biophys. Soc. Home: 116 Circle Rd Syracuse NY 13210-3046 Office: Syracuse U Dept Chemistry WM Keck Ctr Molecular Elec Syracuse NY 13244

BIRGENEAU, ROBERT JOSEPH, physicist, educator; b. Toronto, Ont., Can., Mar. 25, 1942; came to U.S. 1963; s. Peter Duffus and Isobel Theresa (Meehan) B.; m. Mary Catherine Ware, June 20, 1964; children—Michael, Catherine, Patricia, Michelle. B.Sc., U. Toronto, 1963; Ph.D., Yale U., 1966. Vis. tchr. Benedict Coll., Columbia, S.C., summer 1965; instr. dept. engring. and applied sci. Yale U., New Haven, 1966-67; Nat. Research Council Can. postdoctoral fellow Oxford U., Eng., 1967-68; mem. tech. staff Bell Labs, Murray Hill, N.J., 1968-74; research head scattering and low energy physics dept. Bell Labs, 1975; guest sr. physicist Brookhaven Nat. Lab., Upton, N.Y., 1968—; vis. scientist Riso, Roskilde, Denmark, 1971, 79; prof. physics MIT, Cambridge, 1975—; Cecil and Ida Green prof. physics MIT, 1982—, assoc. dir. Research Lab. for Electronics, 1983-86, head condensed matter atomic and plasma physics, 1987-88, head dept. physics, 1988-91, dean sci., 1991—; cons. Bell Labs., 1977-80, IBM Rsch. Labs., Yorktown Heights, N.Y., 1980-83, Sandia Labs., 1985-92; mem. steering com. Panel on Neutron Scattering, NAS, 1977, mem. core com., major materials facilities com., 1984; co-chmn. Gordon Conf. on Quantum Solids and Fluids, 1979, Gordon Conf. on Condensed Matter Physics, 1986; mem. policy and adv. bd. Cornell High Energy Synchrotron Source, 1980-84, chmn., 1983-84; mem. rev. panel on neutron scattering Dept. Energy, 1980, 82, mem. basic energy scis. adv. com., 1991-95; mem. materials rsch. adv. com. NSF, 1989-90; mem. adv. coun. NEC, 1996—; chmn. DOE panel on rsch. reactor upgrades, 1996, DOE panel on synchrotron sources, 1997. Contbr. articles to profl. jours.; mem. editorial bd. Physical Review. Trustee Assoc. Univs., Inc., 1990-97, Mus. Sci., Boston, 1992—, Argonne Nat. Lab., 1992—, Brookhaven Sci. Assocs., 1998—. Recipient Yale Sci. and Engring. Alumni Achievement award, 1981, Wilbur Lucius Cross medal Yale U., 1986, Oliver E. Buckley Prize Am. Phys. Soc., 1987, B.E. Warren award Am. Crystal Assn., 1988, Magnetism award Internat. Union Pure and Applied Physics, 1997; 48th Richtmyer Meml. lectr. Am. Assn. Physics Tchrs., 1989. Fellow AAAS (exec. coun. 1992-94), Am. Phys. Soc., Am. Acad. Arts Sci. Roman Catholic. Avocations: landscaping; squash; basketball. Office: MIT Rm 6-123 Cambridge MA 02139

BIRINGER, GENE DOUGLAS, music educator, theorist; b. Plainfield, N.J., May 7, 1954; s. Eugene Raymond and Madeline Louise (Naugle) B.; m. Donna Jeanne DiBella, Aug. 15, 1981; children: Ian, Catherine, Claire. BA, Rutgers U., 1979; MusM, U. Ill., Urbana/Champaign, 1980; MPhil, Yale U., 1984, PhD, 1989. Instr. Yale U., New Haven, Conn., 1985-87; asst. prof. Santa Clara (Calif.) U., 1987-90, Tex. Tech U., Lubbock, 1990-95, Lawrence U., Appleton, Wis., 1995—. Author: Schenkerian Theory and Analysis: A Revisionist Approach, 1999. Univ. fellow Yale U., 1982-84; Faculty Tchg. grantee Santa Clara U., 1988; Faculty Tchg. fellow Lawrence U., Appleton, 1997. Mem. Soc. Music Theory, Music Theory Midwest (mem. program com. 1985—), Tex. Soc. Music Theory (mem. exec. com., mem. program com. 1990-95), Phi Beta Kappa, Delta Phi Alpha. Home: 938 E Pacific St Appleton WI 54911-5336 Office: Lawrence U Conservatory of Music Appleton WI 54912

BIRK, JOHN R., marketing/financial services consultant; b. Boston, Aug. 11, 1951; s. Harold F. and Jane Birk; m. Susan Arnold, Feb. 9, 1980; children: John R. Jr., Andrew A. BA in Econs. and English, Colgate U., 1974; Advanced Mgmt. Program, Harvard Bus. Sch., 1991. Sales rep. Procter & Gamble, N.Y.C., 1975-76; dist. field rep. Procter & Gamble, White Plains, N.Y., 1976; unit mgr. Procter & Gamble, Dallas, 1976-78; sales devel. mgr. Pepsi Cola Co., Purchase, N.Y., 1978-80; regional sales mgr. Pepsi Cola Co., San Francisco, 1980-83; dir. sales and mktg. MCI Communications Inc., Atlanta, 1983-84, v.p. sales and mktg., 1984-85; pres., bd. dirs. U.S. Tel. Inc., Dallas, 1985; pres. U.S. Telecom Comms. Svcs. Co., Kansas City, Mo., 1985-86; pres. N.E. div. US Sprint, 1986-87; western group pres. US Sprint, San Francisco, 1987-88; exec. v.p., chief operating officer ADVO-System Inc., Windsor, Conn., 1988-89; pres., COO ADVO Inc., Windsor, 1989-92, also bd. dirs., 1988-92; pres., CEO, dir. Wright Express Corp., South Portland, Maine, 1992-94; chmn. Wright Express Corp., 1994-95; pres., COO Ideon Group Inc. (formerly Safe Card Svcs., Inc.), Jacksonville, Fla., 1995; pres. John R. Birk & Assocs., Ponte Vedra Beach, Fla., 1995—; COO Evercore Ptnrs., 1996—; bd. dirs. T.O. Richardson Mutual Funds, Specialty Products Insulation Inc.; chmn. Aegis Comms. Group, Inc. Bd. dirs. Prevent Blindness, Atlanta, 1984-85, United Way, White Plains, 1986-87, Westchester County Assn., 1986-87, Bay Area Coun., 1987-88, United Way Greater Portland, 1993-95; trustee Found. for Blood Rsch., Inc., 1993-95, Colgate U. Alumni Corp., 1995-99, chmn. pres.'s club, 1997-99. Republican. Roman Catholic. Avocations: tennis, skiing. E-mail: JRBIRK@AOL.com.

BIRK, LEE (CARL BIRK), psychiatrist, educator; b. New Albany, Ind., Feb. 8, 1935; s. Glover McMurtrey and Marie Clyde (Carpenter) B.; m. Emily Perkins Gantt, June 21, 1958 (div. Jan. 1970); children: Elizabeth Waring, Alexandria Lee; m. Ann Harrison Wegner, June 15, 1973 (div. June 1990); children: Lara Blakiston, Jeffrey Lee. Student, Speed Scientific Sch., 1952-53, U. Louisville, 1953-54; BA in Zoology & Chemistry, Valparaiso U., 1956; MD, Johns Hopkins U., 1960. Intern U. Va. Hosp., Charlottesville, 1960-61; resident Harvard Med. Sch., Mass. Mental Health Ctr., Boston, 1961-62, 63-66; instr. psychiatry Harvard Med. Sch., Cambridge, Mass., 1968-69, asst. prof. psychiatry, 1969-73, asst. clin. prof. psychiatry, 1973-76, assoc. clin. prof. psychiatry, 1976—; dir. Learning Therapies, Inc., Newton, Mass., 1971-89, Concord, Mass., 1989-98, Burlington, Mass., 1998—; vis. prof. Inst. Living, Hartford, Conn., 1975; Rhoads lectr. Duke U. Sch. Medicine, 1994. Author/editor: Behavior Therapy in Psychiatry, 1972, Psychoanalysis and Behavior Therapy, 1973, Biofeedback: Behavioral Medicine, 1973; mem. editorial bd. Psychotherapy & Psychosomatics, 1974—, Family Process, 1975-78, 82-83, Jour. of Marital & Family Therapy, 1983-90, Jour. of Psychotherapy Integration, 1989—. Capt. USAF, 1962-63. Mem. Am. Family Therapy Assn., Am. Coll. Psychiatrists, Am. Soc. Clin. Psychopharmacology, Soc. Exploration of Psychotherapy Integration (co-founder). Independent. Avocations: helicopter skiing, whitewater rafting/kayaking. Home and Office: Learning Therapies Inc 8 Hart St Burlington MA 01803

BIRK, ROBERT EUGENE, retired physician, educator; b. Buffalo, Jan. 7, 1926; s. Reginald H. and Florence (Diebolt) B.; m. Janet L. Davidson, June 24, 1950; children—David Eugene, James Michael, Patricia Jean, Thomas Spencer, Susan Margaret. A.B., Colgate U., 1948; M.D., U. Rochester, 1952. Diplomate Am. Bd. Internal Medicine. Intern, resident Henry Ford Hosp., Detroit, 1952-57, chief 2d med. div., 1961-66, asst. to chmn. dept. medicine, 1965-66; practice medicine specializing in internal medicine Grosse Pointe, Mich., 1966-89; sr. active staff St. John Hosp., 1966-89, chief dept. medicine, 1967-70, dir. health edn., dir. grad. med. edn., 1975-86, exec. dir. continuing med. edn., 1975-86; dir. med. affairs St John Ambulatory Care Corp., St. John Home Care Svcs., 1980-89; v.p. clin. affairs St. John Health Corp., 1985-89; assoc. prof. medicine Wayne State U., 1969-89. Contbr. articles to profl. jours. Mem. trustee's coun. U. Rochester, 1973-75, Med. Ctr. alumni coun., 1974-75; bd. trustees St. John Hosp., Macomb Ctr., 1986-89; corp. mem. bd. Boys Clubs Met. Detroit, 1973-89; trustee Mich. Cancer Found., 1980-89, bd. dirs., 1982-85. With U.S. Army, 1943-46. Fellow ACP, Detroit Acad. Medicine; mem. AMA, Assn. Hosp. Med. Edn. (trustee region IV 1986-87), Mich. Assn. Med. Edn. (trustee 1985-86), Am. Soc. Internal Medicine, Am. Acad. Med. Dirs., Alpha Tau Omega. Republican. Episcopalian. Home: 8 Eagle Claw Dr Hilton Head Island SC 29926-1853

BIRKBY, WALTER HUDSON, forensic anthropologist, consultant; b. Gordon, Nebr., Feb. 28, 1931; s. Walter Levy and Margery Hazel (Moss) B.; m. Carmen Sue Gates, Aug. 18, 1955; children: Jeffrey Moss, Julianne. BA, U. Kans., 1961, MA, 1963; PhD, U. Ariz., 1973. Diplomate Am. Bd. Forensic Anthropology (pres. 1985-87, exec. com. 1980-87). Med. and X-ray technician Graham County (Kans.) Hosp., Hill City, 1955-58; phys. anthropologist Ariz. State Mus., Tucson, 1968-85; lectr. anthropology U. Ariz., Tucson, 1981-90, adj. rsch. prof. anthropology, 1990-96, emeritus prof., 1996—; curator phys. anthropology Ariz. State Mus., Tucson, 1985-96; forensic anthropologist Pima County Med. Examiner's Office, Tucson, 1981—, Recovery of Victims of Alfred G. Packer party (1874), Lake City, Colo., 1989; dental cons. USAF Hosp., Davis Monthan AFB, Tucson, 1984-96; human osteologist U. Ariz.-Republic of Cyprus Archaeol. Expdn., 1985-87, Lugnano in Teverina (Italy) Expdn., 1990-91; dir. dept. anthropology masters program in forensic anthropology, 1983-96; cons. to Chief Armed Svcs. Graves Registration Office U.S. Army, 1987-93 97—, UN Internat. Criminal Tribunal for Yugoslavia, 1997-98; mem. disaster mortuary team Nat. Disaster Med. Sys., 1994—. Mem. editorial bd. (jour.) Cryptozoology, 1982—; bd. editors Am. Jour. Forensic Medicine and Pathology, 1992-97; co-author video tng. film Identification of Human Remains, 1980; contbr. articles to profl. jours. Served as sgt. USMCR, 1951-52, Korea. Recipient Achievement medal for meritorious svc. Pima County Sheriff's Dept., 1992, Spl. Recognition award, 1995; NIH fellow U. Ariz., 1966-68. Fellow Am. Acad. Forensic Scis. (exec. com. 1978-81, T. Dale Stewart award in anthropology 1991); mem. Am. Assn. Phys. Anthropologists, Calif. Assn. Criminalists, Ariz. Identification Coun. of the Internat. Assn. for Identification, Ariz. Homicide Investigators Assn., Sigma Xi (pres. local chpt. 1984-85). Republican. Avocations: photography, hunting, fishing. Home: 7349 E 18th St Tucson AZ 85710-4904 Office: Forensic Sci Ctr 2825 E District St Tucson AZ 85714-2081

BIRKELAND, BRYAN COLLIER, lawyer; b. Hibbing, Minn., May 29, 1951; s. Lionel Owen and Peggy Jean (Smith) B.; m. D.J. Loras, Jan. 5, 1974; children: Brett Holton, Blair Leigh, Blake Owen. Student, Washington and Jefferson Coll., 1969-70; BA with high honors, U. Tex., 1973, JD with honors, 1975. Bar: Tex. 1976; ptnr. Jackson Walker, L.L.P., Dallas, 1982—. Moody Found. grantee, 1971. Mem. ABA, IBA, State Bar Tex., Dallas Bar Assn., Order of Coif, Phi Beta Kappa, Phi Kappa Phi, Delta Sigma Rho, Tau Kappa Alpha. Presbyterian. Home: 7639 Southwestern Blvd Dallas TX 75225-7927 Office: Jackson Walker LLP 901 Main St Ste 6000 Dallas TX 75202-3797

BIRKELBACH, ALBERT OTTMAR, retired oil company executive; b. Oak Park, Ill., Feb. 22, 1927; s. August and Ann B.; m. Shirley M. Spandet, Aug. 21, 1948; children: J.A., Lisa M., Grace L. Birkelbach Boland, Ann C. Birkelbach Goren. B.S.Ch.E., U. Ill., 1949. Various engring., supervisory and mgmt. positions Globe Oil & Refining Co., Lemont, Ill., 1949-53, Anderson Prichard Oil Corp., Cyril, Okla., 1953-58, Signal Oil & Gas Co., Los Angeles, 1958-64; mng. dir. Raffinerie Belge de Petroles, Antwerp, Belgium, 1964-74; v.p. Occidental Petroleum Corp., London, Eng., 1972-74; cons. in field, 1974-75; pres. ATC Petroleum Inc., N.Y.C., 1975-81, also dir.; pres. Amorient Petroleum Corp., Laguna Niguel, Calif., 1981-84; mgmt. cons., 1984-87. Served with USCG, 1945-47. Decorated knight Order Leopold Belgium). Mailing Address: PO Box 1151 Carefree AZ 85377-1151

BIRKELUND, JOHN PETER, investment banking executive; b. Chgo., June 23, 1930; s. George R. and Ruth (Olsen) B.; m. Constance I. Smiles, Oct. 25, 1958; children: Gwynne Tibbetts, Elizabeth Oberbeck, Constance Olivia, Diana. AB, Princeton U., 1952. Cons. Booz Allen & Hamilton, Chgo., 1956; v.p. Amsterdam Overseas Corp., N.Y.C., 1956-67; co-founder, chmn., dir. New Court Securities Corp., N.Y.C., 1967-81; pres. Dillon, Read & Co., Inc., N.Y.C., 1981-86, CEO, 1986-93; chmn. SBC Warburg Dillon Read Inc., N.Y.C., 1986-98; sr. advisor Warburg Dillon Read (formerly SBC Warburg Dillon Read Inc.), N.Y.C., 1998—; bd. dirs. Nac Re Corp., Greenwich, Conn.; chmn. Internat. Exec. Svc. Corp., Stamford, Conn., Polish-Am. Enterprise Fund, N.Y.C., Nat. Humanities Ctr., N.C. Bd. fellow Brown U., Providence, 1990—; trustee N.Y. Pub. Libr., N.Y.C., 1990—; chair Thomas J. Watson Inst. for Internat. Studies, Providence. Lt. USNR, 1953-55. Mem. Coun. Fgn. Rels., Phi Beta Kappa, The Links Club, Univ. Club, The Blind Brook Club, Clove Valley Rod and Gun Club. Home: 510 Weed St New Canaan CT 06840-6127 Office: Warburg Dillon Read LLC 535 Madison Ave New York NY 10022-4212

BIRKENHEAD, THOMAS BRUCE, theatrical producer and manager, educator; b. N.Y.C., Dec. 19, 1931; s. Thomas A. and Florence (Morison) B.; m. Susan Leslie Arkin, Dec. 3, 1954 (div. 1983); m. Maria Martins, May 26, 1999; children: Peter Lawrence, David Andrew, Richard James, Alison Jane, Leila Alessandra. BA, Bklyn. Coll. CUNY, 1954, MA, 1958; PhD, New Sch. Social Rsch., 1963. From lectr. to prof. econs. Bklyn. Coll. CUNY, 1957-72, prof., 1972-75; dean Sch. Social Scis., 1972-75; prof. emeritus Bklyn. Coll. CUNY, 1975—; bus. mgr. Theatre II of Glen Cove, N.Y., 1970-74; gen. mgr., cons. Keystone Ctr. of Music and the Arts, 1999. Co-mgr.: Do Black Patent Leather Shoes Really Reflect Up?, Present Laughter, Master Harold and the Boys, Children of a Lesser God, Ain't Misbehavin, Brighton Beach Memoirs, Biloxi Blues, Broadway Bound, Barbara Cook in Concert, Run For Your Wife, Rumors, Lost in Yonkers, Jake's Women, Goodbye Girl: gen. mgr.: Cape Cod Melody Tent, Hyannis, Mass., 1969-71, Twyla Tharp on Broadway, 1980, 81, Joe Egg, 1985, Social Security, 1986,

Long Days Journey Into Night, London and Tel Aviv, 1986, Ain't Misbehavin, N.Y.C., 1988-89, Japan, 1990, Fresh Air Taxi, 1993, Honky Tonk Highway, 1994-96, Dream a Little Dream, 1994-95; co-prodr. 1995 Tony award broadcast, N.H.K. Japan; producer High Mountain Ghost, 1996-98; sec.-treas. Highly Ent., 1995—; mgmt. cons. Keystone Ctr. Performing Arts, 1999. Sponsor U.S. Shooting Team, U.S. Holocaust Meml. Mus., Am. Air Mus., Eng., Carnegie Hall., U.S. Naval Meml. Found. T. Bruce Birkenhead scholarship in performing arts established by Performing Arts Mgmt. Program Bklyn. Coll. Mem. NRA, U.S. Naval Inst., Jimmy Carter Inst., Amnesty Internat., Women in Mil. Svc. for Am., Rover P4 Drivers Gild, W.P. Chrysler Club, Chrysler Products Restorers Club, Vintage Triumph Register, Groucho Club (Eng.), World Jewish Congress. Home: 353 W 44th St Apt 1A New York NY 10036-5416 Office: 12 W 57th St Ste 905 New York NY 10019-3900

BIRKENKAMP, DEAN FREDERICK, editor, publishing executive; b. Litchfield, Ill., May 5, 1956; s. Arnold R. and Virginia Johanna (Droste) B. BA in Anthropology, U. Ill., 1978, MA in Libr. Sci., 1979; cert., Pub. Inst. U. Denver, 1979. Rsch. assoc. law libr. U. Ill., Urbana, 1978-79; editorial asst. Westview Press, Boulder, Colo., 1979-81, mng. editor, 1981-85, exec. editor, v.p., 1985-89, v.p., group dir. editorial acquisitions, 1989-96; v.p., exec. editor Rowman and Littlefield Publs., Boulder, 1996—. Mem. Am. Sociol. Assn., Am. Anthropol. Assn., Am. Edn. Rsch. Assn. Office: Rowman and Littlefield 5370 Manhattan Cir Ste 105 Boulder CO 80303-4250

BIRKENSTOCK, JAMES WARREN, business machine manufacturing company executive; b. Burlington, Iowa, May 7, 1912; s. George Louis and Anna (Flynn) B.; m. Jean Lois Hale, Nov. 30, 1935; children: Robert Hale, Joyce Ann. Student, Burlington Jr. Coll., 1933; B.S. U. Iowa, 1935. With IBM Corp., 1935-72, successively student salesman, jr. salesman, sr. salesman, asst. mgr., St. Louis, br. mgr., Kansas City, spl. sales exec. World Hdqrs., gen. sales mgr., mgr. future demands, spl. adminstrv. asst. corporate ofcls., exec. asst. to pres., exec. dir. product planning and market analysis div., dir. comml. devel., 1935-58, v.p. comml. devel., 1958-70, v.p. corporate relations, 1971-72. Mem. Beta Gamma Sigma, Delta Sigma Pi. Clubs: Country of Fla, Ocean of Fla, Little Club of Fla, Knights of Malta.

BIRKENSTOCK, JOYCE ANN, artist; b. Kansas City, Mo., Oct. 6, 1943; d. James Warren and Jean Lois (Hale) B.; m. Galen Richard Durkin, Sept. 6, 1969; 1 child, Lee Ann Durkin. Portrait artist Portraits South, Raleigh, N.C., 1982-85, Stellers Gallery, Jacksonville, Fla., 1988-96; pub. Arts Uniq, Cookeville, Tenn., 1995—; artist Leanin' Tree Pub., Boulder, Colo., 1990—. Represented in permanent collections at Disney Prodns., Macon, Ga. Hist. Soc., Cornell Mus., Fla. Nat. Bank, Diocese of Palm Beach, Fla., Diocese of Miami, Harid Conservatory, Latner Found., Fairfield U. Recipient Purchase award Disney Prodns., First in Oil Boynton Festival of Arts, Disting. Achievement in Portrait Painting Nat. Portrait Sem., N.Y., Merit award, Best of Show Boca Raton Ctr. for the Arts, M. Grumbacher Silver Medallion Catherine Lorillard Wolfe 85th Ann. N.Y., People's Choice award Human Images Broward Art Guild, Hon. Mention Lighthouse Gallery, Merit award, Best of Show Human Images Exhbn. Broward Art Guild, Best of Portrait Painting award Northlight Books, 1st award for portraiture Artist's mag., 1997. Mem. Am. Soc. of Portrait Artists, Nat. Assn. Women Artists, Portrait Soc. Am., Washington Soc. Portrait Artists (1st Hon. Mention nat. competition 1998), Atlanta Soc. Portrait Artists. Avocations: photography, travel. E-mail: jbart@flinet.com. Home: 11692 N Lake Dr Boynton Beach FL 33436-5543

BIRKERTS, GUNNAR, architect; b. Riga, Latvia, Jan. 17, 1925; came to U.S., 1949, naturalized, 1954; s. Peter and Meria (Shop) B.; m. Sylvia Zvirbulis, July 29, 1950; children: Sven Peter, Andra Sylvia, Erik Gunnar. Diplomingenuer Architekt, Technische Hochschule, Stuttgart, Germany, 1949; D (hon.), Riga Tech. Univ., Latvia, 1990. Designer Perkins & Will, Chgo., 1950-51, Eero Saarinen & Assos., Bloomfield Hills, Mich., 1951-55; prin. chief designer Minoru Yamasaki & Assos., Birmingham, Mich., 1955-59; pres. Gunnar Birkerts & Assos., Inc., Birmingham, 1959; asst. prof. architecture U. Mich., 1961; asso. prof., 1963-69, prof., 1969-90; Graham fellow, 1970; architect in residence Am. Acad. in Rome, 1976; 1st Lawrence J. Plym. disting. prof. architecture U. Ill., 1982; Thomas S. Monaghan architect-in-residence prof. U. Mich., Ann Arbor, 1984; Bruce Alonzo Goff prof. of creative architecture U. Okla., 1990. Prin. works include Schwartz House, Northville, Mich. (First Honor award AIA 1962, Merit award Detroit chpt. AIA 1963, Archtl. Record award 1961), Univ. Reformed Ch., Ann Arbor Mich. (award Ch. Archtl. Guild Am. 1962), Peoples Fed. Savs. & Loan Bank, Royal Oak, Mich., 1963 (Merit award Detroit chpt. AIA 1963), Fisher Adminstrv. Ctr., Detroit (award of merit Mich. Soc. Architects 1967, Merit award Detroit chpt. AIA 1967), Detroit Inst. Arts addition, 1300 Lafayette Apts., Detroit, Tougaloo (Miss.) Coll. (award of honor Mich. Soc. Architects 1974), Vocat.-Tech. Campus, So. Ill. U., Glen Oaks Community Coll. Campus, Centreville, Mich., Lincoln Sch., Columbus, Ind. (AIA Detroit chpt. and nat. Honor awards 1968, 70), Fed. Res. Bank, Mpls. (award excellence Am. Inst. Steel Constrn. 1974, design award Am. Iron and Steel Inst. 1975), IBM Corp. Computer Center, Sterling Forest, N.Y. (honor award Detroit chpt. AIA 1973), Contemporary Arts Mus., Houston (honor award Detroit chpt. AIA 1975), Dance Instructional Facility at Purchase (award honor Mich. Soc. Architects 1977, Honor award Detroit chpt. AIA 1978), Calvary Baptist Ch., Detroit (Honor award Mich. Soc. Architects 1979, award of excellence Am. Inst. Steel Constrn. 1979), IBM Office Bldg., Southfield, Mich. (Honor award Mich. Soc. Architects 1980, energy conservation award Owens Corning Fiberglas Corp. 1977), Duluth Public Libr. (Honor award Mich. Soc. Architects 1981), Fire Sta., Corning, N.Y. (honor award Mich. Soc. Architects 1977), Corning Mus. of Glass, Law Libr. Addition, U. Mich. (award of excellence AIA and ALA 1985), U.S. Embassy bldg., Helsinki, Finland, Coll. of Law bldg., U. Iowa (Award of Honor-Mich. Soc. Architects 1987), Uris Library addition, Cornell U. (honor award Mich. Soc. Architects 1984), Dist. Office Bldg., Green Bay, Wis., Ferguson Residence, Kalamazoo, Mich. (award of honor Mich. Soc. Architects 1986), Chapel & Ednl. Facility, Camp Wildflecken, Fed. Republic Germany (Silver Castle award U.S. Army Corps. Engrs., European div. 1986), St. Peter's Luth. Ch., Columbus, Ind. (award of honor Detroit chpt. AIA 1986, 90), Domino's world hdqrs., Ann Arbor, Mich. (bldg. recognition award Engring. Soc. Detroit 1987, M award for Excellence in Masonry Design Masonry Inst. Mich., 1989), Libr. Addition Conservatory Music Oberlin Coll., Ohio, Prototype Franchise Bldg. Domino's Pizza, Inc. (award of honor Mich. Soc. Architects 1989), Jackson, Mich., Cen. Libr. addition U. Calif., San Diego, Sports Svcs. Bldg. U. Mich., U.S. Embassy, Caracas, Venezuela , Libr. U. Mich., Flint (Design and Constrn. showcase '94 award), Coll. Law Ohio State U., (award of honor AIA Mich., 1995), Kemper Mus. Contemporary Art and Design, Kans. City Mo. (Lighting award, 1995), Ch. Servant, Kentwood, Mich.; exhbns. include Akron Inst. Art, 1954, Sao Paulo (Brazil) Bienniale, 1962, 40 under 40, USA-NY, Architects League, 1965, Mus. Modern Art, N.Y.C., 1971, Notre Dame U., 1973, N.Y. Mus. Modern Art, 1979, Neuberger Mus., Purchase, N.Y., 1981, Am. Acad. and Inst. Arts and Letters, N.Y.C., 1981, U. Ill., 1983, U. Md., College Park, 1985, Saginaw Art Mus., Mich., 1985, Notre Dame U., 1985, Pratt Inst., Bklyn., 1986, NYU, 1986, The Triennale, Milan, Italy, 1986, Judah L. Magnes Mus., Berkeley, Calif., 1986, Nat. Ctr. for Study of Frank Lloyd Wright, Ann Arbor, 1988, St. Peter's Cathedral, Riga, Latvia, 1989, Torino '90, Turin, Italy, 1990, The 3d Belgrade Triennial of World Architects, 1991, The Athenaeum Music and Art Libr., LaJolla, Calif., 1991, Kansas City Art Inst., 1992, Lawrence Tech. U., Southfield, Mich., 1993. Named Young Designer of Year Akron Inst. Art, 1954, Mich. Artist of Yr. Mich. Artrain, 1993; recipient 1st prize Internat. Furniture competition, Cantu, Italy, 1955; 3d prize Internat. competition for Cultural Centre, Belgian Congo; Design award Progressive Architecture mag., 1957, 59, 61, 71; award of excellence Archtl. Record, 1968; Nat. Gold medal Tau Sigma Delta, 1971; Gold medal Detroit chpt. AIA, 1975; Gold medal Mich. Soc. Architects, 1980; Brunner Meml. prize Am. Acad. and Inst. Arts and Letters, 1981; Mich. Art award Arts Found. Mich., 1988, Disting. Prof. Assn. Collegiate Schs. Architecture, 1990. Fellow AIA, Graham Found., Latvian Architects Assn.; mem. Mich. Soc. Architects (Award of Honor 1989), Ch. Archtl. Guild, Hon. Order Ky. Cols. Office: 1830 Tahquamenon Bloomfield Hills MI 48302

BIRKETT, MARY ELLEN, humanities educator; b. Buffalo, Oct. 10, 1946; d. Frank Elliot and Mary Jane (Houck) B.; m. Peter Howe Searl, Jan. 5,

1991. BA, Smith Coll., 1968; MPhil, Yale U., 1971, PhD, 1974. Acting instr. Yale U., New Haven, Conn., 1971-73; instr. Smith Coll., Northampton, Mass., 1973-74, asst. prof., 1974-81, assoc. prof., 1981-89, prof., 1990—. Author: Lamartine and the Poetics of Landscape, 1982; contbr. articles to literary jours., bibliographies. Mem. Phi Beta Kappa. Office: Smith Coll French 84 Green St Northampton MA 01063-1001

BIRKHEAD, GUTHRIE SWEENEY, JR., political scientist, university dean; b. Holden, Mo., Oct. 28, 1920; s. Guthrie Sweeney and Yula Donna (Glass) B.; m. Louise Gartner, Aug. 16, 1952; children—Guthrie Sweeney III, Richard Gartner, Evan Clark. A.A., Jefferson City (Mo.) Jr. Coll., 1940; A.B., U. Mo., 1942, A.M., 1947; M.A., Princeton, 1949, Ph.D in Politics, 1951. Mem. faculty Syracuse U., 1950—, prof. polit. sci., 1960—, chmn. dept., 1959-62, 66-67, dir. met. studies program, 1968-73; asso. dean Maxwell Sch., 1973-77, dean, 1977-88; also dir. pub. adminstrn. programs, 1959-62; dir. research UN Inst. Pub. Adminstrn. for Turkey and Middle East, 1955-56; cons. Pakistan Adminstrv. Staff Coll., Lahore, 1962-64, Ford Found., Pakistan, 1967-68. Co-author: River Basin Administration and the Delaware, 1960, Science and State Government in New York, 1960, Decisions in Syracuse, 1962; Editor: Administrative Problems in Pakistan, 1966, A Look to the North: Canadian Regional Experience, 1974, Education for Public Service, 1980; Contbr. articles to profl. jours. Chmn. pub. finance com. Community Renewal Plan, Syracuse, N.Y., 1970-72; exec. dir. com. local govt. and home rule N.Y. State Constl. Conv., 1967, Syracuse Charter Commn., 1972-74; mem. Nat. Com. Water Quality Policy Nat. Acad. Scis.-NRC, 1974-76; com. to review the metropolitan Washington area water supply study Nat. Acad. Engring/Nat. Research Council, 1977-84. Served with inf. AUS, 1942-46. Fellow Nat. Municipal League, 1952-53. Fellow Nat. Acad. Pub. Adminstrn.; mem. AAAS, Am. Soc. Pub. Adminstrn., Phi Beta Kappa, Sigma Xi. Home: 220 Lockwood Rd Syracuse NY 13214-2035

BIRKHEAD, THOMAS LARRY, minister; b. Owensboro, Ky., Nov. 20, 1941; s. Thomas Butler and Ollie Mae (Brown) B.; m. Melva Jean Young, Oct. 18, 1968; 1 child, David. AB, Western Ky. U., 1963; MDiv, So. Bapt. Theol. Sem., 1968. Ordained to ministry So. Bapt. Conv., 1966. Pastor Mt. Vernon Bapt. Ch., Calhoun, Ky., 1966-69, Sorgho Bapt. Ch., Owensboro, 1969-73, Spottsville (Ky.) Bapt. Ch., 1973-82, Yelvington Bapt. Ch., Maceo, Ky., 1982-86, Ghent (Ky.) Bapt. Ch., 1986-93, Pond Run Bapt. Ch., Beaver Dam, Ky., 1993-98, New Barren Springs Bapt. Ch., Hopkinsville, Ky., 1998—; mem. exec. bd. Ky. Bapt. Conv., Middletown, 1988-91. Co-author: Ghent Baptist Church History 1800-1990, 1990. Asst. moderator exec. bd. Ohio County Bapt. Assn., 1995-96, moderator exec. bd., 1996-97. Mem. Ohio County Ministerial Assn. (v.p. 1994-97, pres. 1997-98), Carroll County Mins. Assn. (treas. 1989-93). Home and Office: 5010 Dogwood Kelly Rd Hopkinsville KY 42240-8889

BIRKHOLZ, RAYMOND JAMES, metal products manufacturing company executive; b. Chgo., Nov. 11, 1936; s. Raymond I. and Mary (Padian) B.; m. Judy Ann Richards, Apr. 23, 1966; children: Raymond J. Jr., Scott C., Matthew R. BSME, Purdue U., 1958; MBA, U. Chgo., 1963. Registered prof. engr., Ill. V.p. apparatus divsn. Gen. Cable Corp., Westminster, Colo., 1973-77; v.p. ops. metals divsn. Ogden Corp., Cleve., 1977-80; v.p. mfg. and engring. Ogden Corp., N.Y.C., 1980-81, pres. indsl. products, 1981-84, v.p., 1984-86; pres., COO Amcast Indsl. Corp., Dayton, Ohio, 1986-90; CEO Hollander Industries Corp., Dayton, Ohio, 1993-94; pres., CEO Republic Storage Systems Co., Inc., Canton, Ohio, 1994—. Home: 4888 Armandale Ave NW Canton OH 44718-2284 Office: Republic Storage Systems Co 1038 Belden Ave NE Canton OH 44705-1454

BIRKMAYER, DONALD TEFFT, college official; b. Troy, N.Y., Mar. 15, 1925; s. Louis Albert and Helen Margaret (Tefft) B.; m. Virginia Abbott, June 19, 1949 (dec. Jan. 1984); children: Carolyn Cox, Richard A., Nancy Kane; m. Madonna Stahl, May 24, 1987. BS im Mgmt. Engring., Rensselaer Poly. Inst., Troy, 1949. Engr. N.Y. State Dept. Transp., Albany, 1949-85; ret., 1985; editor, pub. Intercollegiate Hockey Newsletter, Troy, 1954-94; ret., 1994; coll. hockey adminstr. and announcer Rensselaer Poly. Inst., Troy, 1949—. Staff sgt. C.E., U.S.Army, 1944-46. Recipient cert. of appreciation Ea. Coll. Athletic Conf., 1985; Thomas J. Sheehan Meml. award Rensselaer Poly. Inst., 1985, Alumni Key award, 1986, named to Athletic Hall of Fame, 1995. Avocations: genealogy, local history, travel.

BIRKNER, MICHAEL J., history educator; b. Teaneck, N.J., Mar. 26, 1950; s. John Jules Birkner and Mildred Delores Marsilio; m. Robin Wagner, Oct. 6, 1979; children: Benjamin Michael, Madeline Ann, Joanna Catherine. BA, Gettysburg Coll., 1972; MA, U. Va., 1973, PhD, 1981. Rsch. asst. N.J. Hist. Commn., Trenton, 1977-78; instr. in history Gettysburg (Pa.) Coll., 1978-79, from assoc. prof. to prof., chair dept., 1989—; asst. prof. history U. Ky., Lexington, 1979-81; assoc. editor Papers of Daniel Webster Dartmouth Coll., Hanover, N.J., 1981-83; asst. prof., then assoc. prof. Millersville (Pa.) U., 1985-89. Co-editor: The Governors of New Jersey: Biographical Essays, 1982, Papers of Daniel Webster, Correspondence, 1850-52, 1986; author: Samuel L. Southard: Jeffersonian Whig, 1984, The Transformation of Bergenfield, NJ, 1894-1994, 1994; editor: James Buchanan and the Political Crisis of the 1850's, 1996. Recipient John A. Booth prize N.J. Hist. Soc., 1987, cert. of commendation Am. Assn. State and Local History, 1995; NEH summer fellow, 1989. Mem. Am. Hist. Assn., Orgn. Am. Historians, Pa. Hist. Assn., N.H. Hist. Soc., Soc. Historians of Early Republic, Dwight D. Eisenhower Soc. (pres. 1997-98). Democrat. Roman Catholic. E-mail: mbirkner@gettysburg.edu. Home: 66 E Broadway Gettysburg PA 17325 Office: Gettysburg Coll Dept History Gettysburg PA 17325

BIRKS, NEIL, metallurgical engineering educator, consultant; b. Sheffield, Eng., Oct. 16, 1935; came to U.S., 1978; s. Henry and May (Street) B.; m. Mary Potts; children: Jane C., David J. B Met. with honours, Sheffield U., 1957, PhD in Metallurgy, 1960. Chartered engr. NATO research fellow Max Planck Inst., Gottingen, Fed. Republic Germany, 1960-62; research investigator United Steel Cos., Sheffield, 1962-64; lectr. metallurgy U. Sheffield, 1964-72, sr. lectr., 1972-78; prof. metall. engring. U. Pitts., 1978-98, prof. emeritus, 1999—; cons. in metallurgy, Pitts., 1978-98. Co-author: Introduction to High Temperature Oxidation of Metals, 1983. Fellow Am. Soc. Metals Internat., Inst. Materials London; mem. AIME. Mem. Ch. of England. Home: 840 Ella St Pittsburgh PA 15243-1908 Office: U Pitts 848 Benedum Hall Pittsburgh PA 15261-2208

BIRKY, JOHN EDWARD, banker, consultant, financial advisor; b. Minier, Ill., July 16, 1934; s. John G. and Gertrude K. (Nafziger) B.; m. Susan Becker, Dec. 13, 1937; children: John Brian, Kathleen Debera. BS in Indsl. Adminstrn., U. Ill., 1957; postgrad., Ohio State U., 1957; MBA, Case Western Res. U., 1975. Cert. data processor. Asst. to mgr. Caterpillar Tractor Co., Peoria, Ill., 1957-61; cons. Sutherland Co., Peoria, 1961-63; mgr. United Research Services, San Mateo, Calif., 1963-69; dir. Case Western Res. U., Cleve., 1969-72; v.p. Fed. Res. Bank, Cleve., 1972-79; exec. v.p. Banc Systems Assn., West Lake, Ohio, 1979-83; exec. v.p. Citizens Banking Corp., Flint, Mich., 1983-92, also chmn. auto com., mem. corp. exec. com., 1986-92; fin. planner Bonita Springs, Fla., 1992-98; fin. adviser Amex Fin. Advisors, Inc.; ind. fin. cons. Hopedale, Ill.; bd. dirs. Citizens Bank, Flint, Comml. Nat. Bank, Berwyn, Ill., Citizens Leasing Corp., Grand Rapids, Mich., Flin Inst. Music; chmn. Magicline Inc., 1989-91; speaker various profl. confs. Contbr. articles to banking jours. Mem. Rep. precinct com., Sierra Vista, Ariz., 1964-65; life mem. Pres.'s Task Force, Washington, 1980; advisor automation commn. ARC, Flint, 1987; mem. exec. bd., treas. Flint Inst. Music, 1986-88, vice-chmn.; mem. Am. Bank Adminstrn. Ins.; bd. dirs. Flint Inst. Music; elder, lay pastor First Presbyn. Ch., Flint, 1988-91; bd. dirs. Capt. USAF, 1957-60. Mem. CDP, Am. Bankers Assn., Data Processing Mgmt. Assn., U. Ill. Alumni Assn. (life), Am. Legion, Acacia, Bonita Bay Country Club (Bonita Springs, Fla.), Masons, Shriners, Sun City (Ariz.) Vistoso Golf Club. Republican. Avocations: golf, tennis. Address: 415 NE 2d St Hopedale IL 61747

BIRKY, NATHAN DALE, publishing company executive; b. Lebanon, Oreg., May 29, 1946; m. Tamera St. Clair; children: Jo Marie, Jonathan, David, Michael, Rachel. AB, Ind. Wesleyan U., 1980, MA, 1986. Cen. stores mgr. Evanston (Ill.) Hosp., 1965-67; pres. Cen. Cascade Bldgs., Inc., Salem, Oreg., 1971-78; dir. youth dept. The Wesleyan Ch. World Hdqrs., Marion, Ind., 1980-83; pres. Coachcraft Industries Corp., Brownsville, Oreg.,

1983-87; asst. gen. treas. Internat. Ctr. The Wesleyan Ch., Indpls., 1987-88, gen. pub. Wesley Press, 1988—. Pres. Aumsville Rural Fire Dist., 1977; mem. Linn County Econ. Devel. Com., 1986; mem. gn. bd. adminstrn. The Wesleyan Ch., 1988—; bd. dirs. Protestabt Ch.-Pubs. Assn., 1989; mem. internat. pub. com. World Meth. Coun., 1991—. Mem. Christian Ministries Mgmt. Assn. Avocation: pvt. pilot. Office: Internat Ctr The Wesleyan Ch 8050 Castleway Dr Indianapolis IN 46250-1943*

BIRLE, JAMES ROBB, investment banker; b. Phila., Jan. 25, 1936; s. John George and Mildred C. (Donnelly) B.; m. Mary Margaret McDaniels, Jan. 28, 1961; children—James Robb, Jr., Anne Margaret, Alexandra Lea, John George II. B.S.M.E., Villanova U., 1958. With Gen. Electric Co., San Jose, Calif., 1958; gen. mgr. nuclear energy bus. Gen. Electric Co., San Jose, 1969-77; v.p., gen. mgr. far east business div. Gen. Electric Co., N.Y.C., 1977-81; v.p., gen mgr. air condition div. Gen. Electric Co., Louisville, 1981-82; sr. v.p., group exec. constrn. and engring. svcs. group Gen. Electric Co., Westport, Conn, 1982-85; sr. v.p. corp. trading ops. Gen. Electric Co. N.Y.C., 1985-88; ptnr. The Blackstone Group, N.Y.C., 1988-94; co-chmn., CEO Collins & Aikman Group, N.Y.C., 1988-94; chmn., Resolute Ptnrs., LLC, Greenwich, Conn., 1994—; bd. dirs. Mass. Mut. LIfe Ins. Co., IKON Office Solutions, Inc., Drexel Industries LLC; mem. The Conn. Health and Edn. Facilities Authority, Transparency Internat. Trustee Villanova U. Republican. Avocations: tennis; golf; reading; sailing. Office: Resolute Ptnrs LLC 2 Sound View Dr Greenwich CT 06830-6471

BIRMAN, ALEXANDER, physicist, researcher; b. Moscow, May 23, 1946; came to U.S., 1994; s. Yakov and Rozaliya (Krimerman) B.; m. Emily Freydman, Dec. 25, 1980; children: Igor, Eugene. MSc, Moscow Physico-Tech. Inst., 1970; PhD, Inst. Applied Physics, Moscow, 1975. Sr. rsch. scientist Inst. Applied Physics, Moscow, 1970-85; leading rsch. scientist Astrophysics Corp., Moscow, 1985-93; sr. optical scientist Dicon Fiberoptics, Inc., Berkeley, Calif., 1995—; lectr. Moscow Physico-Tech. Inst., 1987-92. Contbr. articles to profl. jours. Mem. IEEE, Optical Soc. Am., Internat. Soc. for Optical Engring. Achievements include work on theory of waves diffraction in ring lasers; contribution to design of laser and fiber-optic gyroscopes; development of passive fiberoptic components for advanced communication systems. Home: 535 Pierce St Apt 2105 Albany CA 94706-1055 Office: Dicon Fiberoptics 1331 8th St Berkeley CA 94710-1453

BIRMAN, LINDA LEE, elementary education educator; b. Bellingham, Wash., Sept. 2, 1950; d. Ronald L. and Shirley Lee (Smith) Kindlund; m. Steven D. Birman, May 28, 1988; children: Stacy, Michele, Cameron, Colin. BA in Edn., We. Wash. State Coll., 1973; MA in Edn., We. Wash. U., 1978. Cert. elem. and secondary tchr., Wash. Tchr. 2d grade Bellingham, Wash., 1973—; affiliated teaching faculty We. Wash. U., Bellingham, 1992; subject advisory com. Washington State Student Learning Commn. Author Stewart the Skyscraper Falcon, 1997. Mem. NEA.

BIRMAN, VICTOR MARK, mechanical and aerospace engineering educator; b. Leningrad, Russia, Jan. 13, 1950; came to U.S., 1984; s. Mark Samuel and Sima (Pesenson) B.; m. Anna Irene Rabkin, Apr. 9, 1977; children: Michael, Shirley. MS, Shipbuilding Inst., Leningrad, 1973; PhD, Technion, Haifa, Israel, 1983. Engr. Steel Structures Design Inst., Leningrad, 1973-78; grad. teaching asst. Technion, Haifa, 1979-82, rsch. fellow, 1983; engr. Israel Aircraft Industries, Lod, 1984; asst. prof. U. New Orleans, 1984-87, assoc. prof., 1987-89; assoc. prof. U. Mo.-Rolla, St. Louis, 1989-96, prof., 1996—; mem. summer faculty Air Force Office of Sci. Rsch., Wright-Patterson AFB, 1992, 97, NASA Lewis Ctr., 1993-94; vis. scientist Air Force Inst. Tech., 1993, U. Natal (South Africa), 1993. Assoc. editor Composites Part B: Engring., 1991—; translator; reviewer profl. jours., 1989—; contbr. rsch. papers to profl. jours., papers to profl confs. Recipient McDonnell Douglas Faculty Excellence award, 1993-94, 94-95, 95-96, 97-98, Award for Excellence in Rsch., U. New Orleans Alumni Assn., 1987; summer scholar U. New Orleans, 1986. Fellow AIAA (assoc.), ASME (composite materials com., structures and materials com.). Achievements include research in mechanics of composite and smart structures, imperfection-sensitivity, thermoelasticity and buckling of stiffened composite shells, mechanics of ceramic matrix composites and smart composite structures; research for Army Research Office, Office Naval Research, Air Force, Air Force Office of Sci. Rsch., NASA, and industry. Office: U Mo-Rolla Engring Edn Ctr 8001 Natural Bridge Rd Saint Louis MO 63121-4401

BIRMINGHAM, CAROLYN, recreation educator; b. Northhampton, Pa., Oct. 12, 1953; d. William Greason and Phoebe Ann (Thorne) B. BA, U. Rochester, 1975; MA, Ohio State U. 1984, PhD, 1989. Sr. instr. outdoor desegregation program Cleve. Bd. Edn., 1980; dir. sch. camp Cleve. Heights Bd. Edn., 1980; instr. Cleve. Heights Parks & Recreation, 1979-80; outdoor instr. Outward Bound, 1978-85; dir. outdoor adventure Bloomsburg (Pa.) State U., 1981; dir. wilderness program, lect. Earlham Coll., Richmond, Ind., 1981-82; asstantships Ohio State U., Columbus, 1983-87; asst. prof. recreation, coord. program Olivet (Mich.) Coll., 1987-89; asst. prof. recreation Christopher Newport Coll., Newport News, Va., 1989—; cons. in field. Editor: Winds from the Wilderness, 1981; author: Maps and Compass for Pirates and Others; contbr. articles to profl. jours. Vol. Newport News and Norfolk Cities Parks and Recreation, 1989-91, Jamestown Found., 1989-91. Recipient Fellowship Philanthropic Edn. Orgn., Ohio chpt., 1983-85, Grad. Student Alumni Rsch. award Ohio State U., 1989, Faculty Devel. grants Christopher Newport Coll., 1989, 90, 91. Mem. AAHPER and Dance, Va. Alliance for Health, Phys. Edn. and Recreation (chair recreation div.), Nat. Prks and Recreation Assn., Assn. for Experiential Edn. (editor conf. proceedings 1991), Va. Parks and Recreation Assn., Va. Coun. on Outdoor Adventure Edn. (bd. dirs., editor newsletter), Build Carilloneurs N.Am. (chair music exch. com.), Am. Sail Tng. Assn. Avocations: carillon, art, music, outdoor activities, sailing. Office: U Ill 1206 S 6th St Champaign IL 61820-6915

BIRMINGHAM, RICHARD GREGORY, lawyer; b. Buffalo, Aug. 14, 1929; s. William Anthony and Laura Louise (Heinrich) B.; m. Suzanne M. Cannon, May 20, 1961; children: Barbara A. McCarty, Maureen E., Gregory S. BA, U. Notre Dame, 1951; JD, SUNY, Buffalo, 1957. Bar: N.Y. 1957, Del. 1984, Pa. 1993. Law clk. to justices appellate div. N.Y. Supreme Ct. (4th dept.), Rochester, 1957-60; ptnr. Phillips, Lytle, Hitchcock, Blaine & Huber, Buffalo, 1960-84, 90-94, ret., 1994; ptnr. Phillips, Lytle, Hitchcock, Blaine & Huber, Wilmington, Del., 1984-90. Lt. comdr. USN, 1951-54, Korea. Mem. ABA, N.Y. State Bar Assn., Del. Bar Assn., Erie County Bar Assn., Feather Sound Country Club, Rivermont Country Club. Republican. Roman Catholic. Office: 2233 Kingfisher Ln Clearwater FL 33762-3323

BIRMINGHAM, RICHARD JOSEPH, lawyer; b. Seattle, Feb. 26, 1953; s. Joseph E. and Anita (Loomis) B. BA cum laude, Wash. State U., 1975; JD, Seattle U., 1978; LLM in Taxation, Boston U., 1980. Bar: Wash. 1978, Oreg. 1981, U.S. Dist. Ct. (we. dist.) Wash. 1978, U.S. Tax Ct. 1981. Ptnr. Davis Wright Tremaine, Seattle, 1982-93; shareholder Birmingham Thorson & Barnett, P.C., Seattle, 1993—; mem. King County Bar Employee Benefit Com., Seattle, 1986, U.S. Treasury ad hoc com. employee benefits, 1988—. Contbg. editor: Compensation and Benefits Mgmt., 1985—; contbr. articles to profl. jours. Mem. ABA (employee benefits and exec. compensation com. 1982—), Wash. State Bar Assn. (speaker 1984-86, tax sect. 1982—), Oreg. State Bar Assn. (tax sect. 1982—), Western Pension Conf. (speaker 1986), Seattle Pension Round table. Democrat. Avocations: jogging, bicycling, photography. Home: 505 Belmont Ave E Apt 204 Seattle WA 98102-4862 Office: Birmingham Thorson Barnett 3315 Two Union Square 601 Union St Seattle WA 98101-2341

BIRMINGHAM, STEPHEN, writer; b. Hartford, Conn., May 28, 1931; s. Thomas J. and Editha (Gardner) B.; m. Janet Tillson, Jan. 5, 1951 (div.); children: Mark, Harriet, Carey. BA cum laude, Williams Coll., 1950; postgrad., Univ. Coll., Oxford (Eng.) U., 1951. Advt. copywriter Needham, Harper & Steers, Inc., 1953-67. Author: Young Mr. Keefe, 1958, Barbara Greer, 1959, The Towers of Love, 1961, Those Harper Women, 1963, Fast Start, Fast Finish, 1966, Our Crowd: The Great Jewish Families of New York, 1967, The Right People, 1968, Heart Toubles, 1968, The Grandees, 1971, The Late John Marquand, 1972, The Right Places, 1973, Real Lace, 1973, Certain People: America's Black Elite, 1977, The Golden Dream: Suburbia in the 1970's, 1978, Jacqueline Bouvier Kennedy Onassis, 1978, Life at the Dakota, 1979, California Rich, 1980, Duchess, 1981, The Grandes

Dames, 1982, The Auerbach Will, 1983; The Rest of Us, 1984, The LeBaron Secret, 1986, Americas Secret Aristocracy, 1987, Shades of Fortune, 1989, The Rothman Scandal, 1991, Carriage Trade, 1993, The Wrong Kind of Money, 1997; contbr. numerous articles to numerous periodicals. Served with AUS, 1951-53. Mem. New Eng. Soc. of City of N.Y., Phi Beta Kappa. Democrat. Episcopalian. Address: 1247 Ida St Cincinnati OH 45202-1525

BIRNBAUM, AARON S, marketing professional; b. Chgo., June 30, 1969; s. Allan M. and Judith S. Lewin B. BA in Comm., SUNY, Oswego, 1992; MBA, U. Denver, 1996. Field rep. Sigma Alpha Mu Fraternity, Inc., Carmel, Ind., 1992-94; dir. mktg. PULP Comm., Denver, 1994-96; acct. exec. Z Comm., Arlington, Va., 1996-97; pres., CEO Back in the Day, Denver, 1997-98; mktg. mgr. MCI Worldcom, McLean, Va., 1998-99; v.p. strategic mktg. The Coll. Club, San Diego, 1999—; cons. in field. Author: (play) 721 Lancaster, 1990. Vol. Denver children's Mus., 1994-95; mem. U. Denver Grad. Adv. Bd., 1995-96. Mem. Am. Mktg. Assn. Avocations: writing, music. Office: The Coll Club 5353 Mission Ctr Rd Ste 310 San Diego CA 92108

BIRNBAUM, BARRY WILLIAM, special education educator; b. Chgo., Oct. 9, 1952; s. Irving and Beatrice (Factoroff) B. BS, So. Ill. U., 1974; MA, Northeastern Ill. U., 1980; EdD, Nova U., 1991. Cert. secondary spl. edn. tchr., elem. tchr., middle sch. tchr. Tchr. Wood Dale (Ill.) Sch. Dist., 1982-86, Palm Beach (Fla.) Cmty. Schs., Palm Beach County, 1985-93; program prof. Nova U., Ft. Lauderdale, Fla., 1993-95; inclusion specialist Sch. Dist. # 59, Arlington Heights, Ill., 1996-97; prin. Neumann Sch., Chgo.; ednl. svcs. adminstr. South Ctrl. Comm. Svcs., Chgo., 1997-98; prof. spl. edn. Chgo. State U., 1998—. *Barry W. Birnbaum, Ed.D., currently works at Chicago State University as an Assistant Professor in the Department of Special Education. He was named Florida Teacher of the Year in 1991 and IBM/Technology and Learning Teacher of the Year in 1992. He has written a monograph describing technology and special education. He also serves on the Illinois Board of Education Quality Review Team.* Named Fla. Tchr. of Yr., Fla. Assn. for Gifted, 1991, IBM/Tech. and Learning Tchr. of Yr., 1992, Prof. Recognized Spl. Educator in Teaching and Adminstrn., Coun. for Exceptional Children. Mem. Phi Delta Kappa. Democrat. Jewish. Avocations: theater, reading, technology. Home: 5225 W Eddy St Chicago IL 60641-3309 Office: Chgo St Univ Edu Bldg 321 9501 S King Dr Chicago IL 60628-1501

BIRNBAUM, EDWARD LESTER, lawyer; b. Bklyn., Aug. 2, 1939; s. Isaac and Rita (Kuris) B.; m. Madeleine, Apr. 10, 1965; children—Amanda, Jordan. B.A., Queens Coll., CUNY, 1961; LL.B., N.Y.U., 1964. Bar: N.Y. 1964, U.S. Dist. Cts. (so. and ea. dists.) N.Y. 1967, U.S. Ct. Appeals (2d cir.) 1970, U.S. Supreme Ct. 1971, U.S. Dist. Ct. (we. dist.) 1983. Assoc. Korkus & Korkus, N.Y.C., 1964-66, I. Richman, Esq., N.Y.C., 1966-67; ptnr. Herzfeld & Rubin, P.C., N.Y.C., 1967—; lectr. in field; faculty NYU Sch. Continuing Edn., Law and Taxation, 1987—; arbitrator small claims night ct. Contbr. articles on law to profl. jours. Coach Little League Baseball and Little League Basketball; candidate trustee Village of Saddle Rock, town counsel, N. Hempstead, N.Y.; pres., v.p. Village of Saddle Rock Civic Assn.; mem. Liberal Party County com., del. to jud. conv. Mem. ABA, N.Y. State Bar Assn. (chmn. com. on Supreme Ct., ho. of dels.), N.Y. County Bar Assn., Queens County Bar Assn., Nassau County Bar Assn., Am. Arbitration Assn. (arbitrator), Am. Trial Lawyers Assn., N.Y. State Trial Lawyers Assn., N.Y. Bar Found. Home: 70 Shelly Ln Great Neck NY 11023-1822 Office: Herzfeld & Rubin PC 40 Wall St Fl 56 New York NY 10005-2349 *Life is to be lived with understanding and consideration for others and with understanding and consideration from others.*

BIRNBAUM, HENRY, librarian; b. Switzerland, Mar. 7, 1917; came to U.S., 1929, naturalized, 1941; s. Isaac and Fanny (Hauser) B. B.A. magna cum laude in Internat. Relations, U. Colo., 1952; M.S. in L.S, Columbia U., 1954, cert. advanced librarianship, 1973. Personal service mgr. Hoover Mfg. & Sales Co., N.Y.C., 1936-41; adminstrv. asst. Library of Congress Mission in, Europe, 1945-46; library asst. Library Congress, 1946-47; research analyst Office Chief Counsel War Crimes, Nürnberg, Germany, 1947-48; asst. case editor, 1948-49; asst. acquisition div. Bklyn. Coll. Library, 1952-54, catalog librarian, 1954-57, chief circulation librarian, 1957-61; chief librarian Pace U., N.Y.C., 1961-66, dir. librs., 1966-76, Univ. libr., 1977-93, Univ. libr. emeritus, 1994—, sec. senate, 1961-95, Univ. cons., 1994-95; Mem. regents adv. council Task Force on Libraries and Maj. Facilities, N.Y.C.; Regional Plan for Higher Edn., 1972. Author monograph.; Contbr. articles to profl. jours. Trustee N.Y. Met. Reference and Rsch. Libr. Agy. Served with AUS, 1941-45. Pace U. Civic Ctr. Campus Libr. named Henry Birnbaum Libr. in his honor, 1989. Mem. ALA (chmn. ad hoc com. circulation librarians 1959-60, chmn. circulation services discussion group, library adminstrn. div. 1961-62, chmn. planning and action com. circulation service sect. 1968-70), Assn. Coll. and Research Libraries, N.Y. Tech. Services Librarians (chmn. social com. 1958-59), N.Y. Library Club (mem. council 1963-64, 75-78, treas. 1964-66, v.p., pres.-elect 1971-72, pres. 1972-73), Library Assn. City Colls. N.Y. (del. Bklyn. Coll. to exec. council 1956-59), Archons of Colophon (convener 1966-67), N.Y. Hist. Soc., Phi Beta Kappa, Pi Gamma Mu, Delta Phi Alpha. Home: 40 E 10th St New York NY 10003-6221 Office: Pace U NY Campus Pace Pla New York NY 10038

BIRNBAUM, HOWARD KENT, materials science educator; b. N.Y.C., Oct. 18, 1932; s. Jack and Ida (Kornblau) B.; m. Freda Silber, Dec. 25, 1954; children: Elisa, Scott, Shari. BS, Columbia U., 1953, MS, 1955; PhD, U. Ill., 1958. Asst. prof. U. Chgo., 1958-61; assoc. prof. U. Ill., Urbana, 1961-64, prof., 1964—, dir. Materials Rsch. lab., 1987—. Contbr. numerous articles to profl. jours. Fellow AAAS, Am. Phys. soc., Am. Soc. Metals, Materials Soc.; mem. AIME (Inst. Metals lectr. 1984, Mehl Gold medal 1984), NAE, Am. Acad. Arts and Scis. Jewish. Office: U Ill Materials Rsch Lab 104 S Goodwin Ave Urbana IL 61801-2902

BIRNBAUM, IRWIN MORTON, lawyer; b. Bklyn., July 15, 1935; s. Sol N. and Rose (Cohen) B.; m. Arlene R. Burrows, June 8, 1957; children: Bruce J., Leslie R. Birnbaum Ventura, Amy G. Birnbaum Heath. BS in Acctg., Bklyn. Coll., 1956; JD, NYU, 1961. Bar: N.Y. 1962. Budget officer Montefiore Med. Ctr., Bronx, N.Y., 1962-70, v.p., chief fin. officer, 1970-86; counsel Proskauer & Rose LLP, N.Y.C., 1986-89, ptnr., 1989-97; COO Yale Univ. Sch. Medicine, New Haven, Conn., 1997—; bd. dirs. N.Y. Regional Transplant Program, N.Y.C., treas., exec. com.; bd. dirs. FFH/N.E. Ins. Com., MCIC Vt., Inc.; adj. prof. Robert Wagner Sch. Pub. Svc., NYU; lectr. pub. health, health policy, adminstrn. Sch. Medicine Yale U. Editor: Health Care Law Treatise, 1990. Bd. trustees, treas., exec com. Malmonides Med. Ctr., Bklyn., 1988—; sec./treas., exec. com. Hosp. Trustees N.Y. State, 1990-97. Fellow N.Y. Acad. Medicine; mem. Assn. of Bar of City of N.Y. (sec. com. on medicine and law 1989-90, sec. health law com. 1995-96), Am. Acad. Hosp. Attys. (spl. com. in health care systems). Avocations: sailing, tennis, reading, travel. Office: Yale Univ Sch Medicine 333 Cedar St I-209 SHM PO Box 208049 New Haven CT 06520-8049

BIRNBAUM, NORMAN, author, humanities educator; b. N.Y.C., July 21, 1926; s. Silas Jacob and Jean (Bermen) B.; children: Anna, Antonia. B.A., Williams Coll., 1947; M.A., Harvard, 1951, Ph.D., 1958. Editor OWI, 1943-45; teaching fellow Harvard, 1948-52; tutor Adams House, 1949- 52; asst. lectr. London Sch. Econs. and Polit. Sci.; asst. lectr. U. London, 1953-55, lectr., 1955-59; fellow Nuffield Coll., Oxford (Eng.) U., 1959-66; vis. prof. faculty letters and human scis. U. Strasbourg, France, 1964-66; prof. grad. faculty New Sch. Social Research, 1966-68; prof. Amherst Coll., 1968—; mem. Inst. Advanced Study, Berlin, 1975-76; guest fellow Wissenschaftskolleg, Berlin, 1986; Mellon vis. prof. humanities Georgetown U. Law Ctr., 1979-81; prof. Georgetown U., 1981—; cons. NSC, Exec. Office Pres., 1978; vis. prof. Ecole des Hautes Etudes en Scis. Sociales, Paris, 1991; chair scholarly adv. bd. Internat. Inst. Peace, Vienna, 1991—. Author: Sociological Study of Ideology (1940-60), 1962; (with others) Sociology and Religion, 1968, Crisis of Industrial Society, 1969, Towards a Critical Sociology, 1971, Beyond the Crisis, 1977, Social Structure and the German Reformation, 1980, The Radical Renewal, 1988, Searching for the Light, 1993; contbg. editor: Change mag. of Higher Edn., 1970-74; mem. ecitiroal bd. Praxis, 1966—, The Nation, 1978—; editorial cons. Patisan Rev., 1971-83; contbr. articles to profl. jours. Cons. Giovanni Agnelli Found., 1972-75; mem. Wellfleet Psychohistory Conf., 1970—; adviser United Automobile Workers; mem. exec. com. New Democratic Coalition, 1978—, chmn. policy adv. council, 1980-82; mem. nat. exec. com. Dem. Socialist Organizing Com., 1973-77, nat. adv. bd., 1980-82; Mem. founding editorial bd. New Left Rev., London, 1959; sec. com. sociology religion Internat. Sociol. Assn., 1959—, chmn., 1970-74; adviser Democratic Nat. Campaign, 1976, Edward M. Kennedy campaign, 1979, Cranston campaign, 1980, Jackson campaigns, 1980, 1988; adviser, Euro. Socialist parties, 1979—; founding com. Campaign for Am. Future, 1996; Fulbright chair, Univ. Bologna, 1998. Guggenheim fellow, 1971. Mem. Am. Sociol. Assn. (council 1979-82). Office: Georgetown U Law Ctr 600 New Jersey Ave NW Washington DC 20001-2022 *I have always thought that one of the strongest ethical and biological forces propelling us is a concern for our children—for our own children and for the continuation of humanity. This elementary sense of care seems increasingly challenged, by doctrines of callousness and selfishness, poorly disguised as recognition of the sovereignty of the market. It is that sovereignty which threatens us as citizens, and which accounts for the outbursts of hatred and rage we know as the new ethnicity, the new fundamentalism, the new nationalism--all of them, alas,very old.*

BIRNBAUM, S. ELIZABETH, lawyer; b. Ft. Belvoir, Va., Jan. 20, 1958; d. Myron Lionel and Emma Jane (Steiner) Birnbaum. AB, Brown U., 1979; JD, Harvard U., 1984. Bar: Colo. 1984, D.C. 1985, U.S. Dist. Ct. D.C. 1987, U.S. Ct. Appeals (D.C. cir.) 1988, U.S. Ct. Appeals (10th cir.) 1988, U.S. Ct. Appeals (4th cir.) 1990, U.S. Supreme Ct. 1990. Clk. to Justice Dubofsky Supreme Ct. Colo., Denver, 1984-85; assoc. Dickstein, Shapiro & Morin, Washington, 1985-87; counsel to water resources program Nat. Wildlife Fedn., Washington, 1987-91; counsel com. resources U.S. Ho. Reps., Washington, 1991-99; spl. asst. to solicitor U.S. Dept. of Interior, Washington, 1999—. Editor-in-chief Harvard Environ. Law Rev., 1984. Bd. trustees Amphibian Conservation Alliance, 1997-99. Mem. Am. Water Resources Assn., D.C. Bar (steering com. 1994-97, sect. environment, energy and natural resource law). Office: 1849 C St NW Washington DC 20240

BIRNBAUM, SHEILA L., lawyer, educator; b. 1940. B.A., Hunter Coll., 1960, M.A., 1962; LL.B., NYU, 1965. Bar: N.Y. 1965. Legal asst. Superior Ct., N.Y.C., 1965; assoc. Berman & Frost, N.Y.C., 1965-70, ptnr., 1970-72; prof. Fordham U., N.Y.C., 1972-78; prof. NYU, N.Y.C., 1978-86, assoc. dean, 1982-84; ptnr. Skadden, Arps, Slate, Meagher & Flom, 1984—. Author: (with Rheingold) Products Liability, Law, Practice Science, 1974. Mem. N.Y.C. Bar Assn. (mem. exec. com. 1978—, jud. com. 1977), ABA (chmn. product gen. liability, consumer land coms.), Assn. of Bar of City of N.Y. (exec. com. 1978—, 2d century com. 1984-86), Phi Beta Kappa, Phi Alpha Theta, Alpha Chi Alpha. Office: Skadden Arps Slate Meagher & Flom 919 3rd Ave New York NY 10022-3902*

BIRNBAUM, STEVAN ALLEN, investment company executive; b. L.A., Apr. 21, 1943; s. Eugene David and Bessie (Holtzman) B.; m. Barbara Patricia Ostroff, June 29, 1971 (div. Aug. 1991); children: Marc, Jill; m. Bonnie Lynn Baehr, Jan. 2, 1999. BS in Engring., UCLA, 1965; MBA, Harvard U., 1967. Dir. advanced programs Whittaker Corp., L.A., 1967-69; v.p. Hohenberg & Assocs., Beverly Hills, Calif., 1969-74; dir. adminstrv. mgmt. Dames & Moore, L.A., 1974-77; prin. Xerox Venture Capital, L.A., 1977-81; venture capitalist, L.A., 1981-83; ptnr. Oxford Ptnrs., Santa Monica, Calif., 1983-95; pres. Oxcal Venture Corp., Santa Monica, 1981—; founder, bd. dirs. Brentwood Savs. Bank, 1982; bd. dirs. Quintar Corp., Torrance, Calif. Republican. Jewish.

BIRNBERG, JACK, financial executive; b. June 15, 1937; s. Max and Yetta (Halpern) B.; m. Louise Rothstein, June 7, 1959; children: Michael, Steven, John, Jeffrey. BS, Fairleigh Dickinson U., 1959. Acct. firm Scholtz, Simon & Miller, 1960-61; controller, officer Scott, Harvey Co., Inc., 1962-63; pres. M.A. Allan & Co., Inc., Clifton, N.J., 1963-71, dir., 1963-71; chmn. bd. Edios, Inc., 1969-77, Jack Birnberg & Assocs. Inc., pres. NE Regional Assn. Small Bus. Investment Corp.; N.Y., 1970—, Internat. Equities, Ltd., Clifton, 1970-71; chmn. bd., dir. Tappan-Zee Capital Corp., 1973—; exec. com. NE region; chmn. bd. BB Energy Corp., Waldorf Auto Leasing Corp., Waldorf Group, Inc.; dir., chmn. exec. com. Ferdon Equipment Corp.; dir. Tolchin Instruments, N.Y.C., 1970-71, Kraftware Corp., N.Y.C., 1969-71, San Sebastian Gold Mines, 1969-71, Color Canvas, Inc., N.Y.C., 1969-72, Cytoarchectronics, N.Y.C., 1970-72, Tech.-Am. Resources Corp., Paterson, N.J., 1970-71, Joy Footwear Corp., 1974-78, Authenticolor, Inc., 1976-93, Williston Oil Co., 1979-81, Ultra Dynamics Corp., Santa Monica, Calif., 1976-79, Studio Color, 1976-82; mem. Midwest Stock Exchange, 1968-76, Phila.-Balt.-Washington Stock Exchange, 1966-72. Pres., Passaic County Children's Shelter, 1967-68; bd. dirs. Boys Club, Paterson, N.J., 1970-75; chmn. met. div. United Jewish Appeal, 1970; dir. greater Paterson (N.J.) YW-YMHA, 1970-75; bd. dirs. Birnberg Found., 1969—, Barnert Hosp., 1971-91; pres. Daus. Miriam Home for Aged, 1971—, bd. dirs., 1995-97; bd. dirs. Employee Retirement Benefit Assn., 1975—, Barnert Temple, 1976—; chmn. Expo 200 Barnert Temple, 1976—; trustee for various corps., U.S. Bankruptcy Ct. Mem. N.E. Regional Assn. Small Bus. Investment Corps. (pres. 1985-86), Nat. Assn. Small Bus. Investment Corps. (bd. govs. 1985-93). Jewish. Clubs: B'nai B'rith (trustee Greater Clifton chpt. 1962-64); Preakness Hills (N.J.) Country (mem. bd. govs. 1992—, treas. 1994-95); Polo Club of Boca Raton (Fla.). Home: 409 Carriage Ln Wyckoff NJ 07481-2306 Office: 201 Lower Notch Rd Little Falls NJ 07424-1841

BIRNE, CINDY FRANK, business owner; b. Chgo., Nov. 13, 1956; d. Gordon D. and Paula (Feldman) Frank; m. Robert E. Birne, June 27, 1981. BA, Ohio State U., 1979. Creative coord. Point-Comms. divsn. Tracy-Locke Advt., Dallas, 1983; asst. to pres. Tex Schramm Dallas Cowboys, 1984, sales and advt. rep., tour dir., 1985—; sports mktg., comml. endorsements agt. Talent Sports Internat., Dallas; founding mem., exec. dir. QB, Inc.-The Internat. Assn. Profl. Quarterbacks; rep. various high profile athletes; affiliated cons., pub. rels. mgmt. promotion mktg. Burson Marsteller Sports Ptnrs. Internat., Dallas; dir. pub. rels., mktg. Dupree/Miller Literary, Inc.; founder, owner custom corp. promotion pieces, design party invitations and greeting cards Cindy Birne Prodns., Dallas, 1993—. Active Ohio campaign Ronald Reagan for Pres, 1980-81; vol. AHA, Dallas Press Club, Dallas U.S.A. Film Festival, 1980's; vol. Cystic Fibrosis Found., 1990, 92, co-chair All Star-All Sports Fashion Show; event coord. Legends Sports Promotions, Tex. Shoot-Out Classic for Troy Aikman Found.-Juvenile Diabetes Children's Miracle Network, 1993-94; assoc. Thomas Cook Travel Million Dollar Shoot-Out-ARC, 1993; ann. fundraiser Am. Nat. Coun. for Jewish Women; bd. dirs. Golden Acres Nursing Home for Jewish Aged, Dallas, 1993; assoc. Legends Sports Promotions; adv. bd., com. mem. Philanthropy in Tex.; mem. com. for Cystic Fibrosis Tex. Rangers Diamond Ball, 1998; mem. philanthropy com. Tex. Found. Fundraiser for Southwestern Med. Sch. Cornea Eye Transplant Divsn., 1997; mem. com. for cystic fibrosis Tex. Rangers Baseball Assn., 1999; dir. devel. The Cystic Fibrosis Found., 1999.

BIRNE, KENNETH ANDREW, lawyer; b. Englewood, N.J., Apr. 2, 1956; s. Alvin Aaron and Rita May (Gorsky) B.; m. Pamela Beth Ross; children: Jennafer Sara, Allison Francie, Jonathan Ross. BA in Polit. Sci., Ohio State U., 1978; JD, Case Western Res. U., 1981. Bar: Ohio 1981, U.S. Dist. Ct. (no. dist.) Ohio 1981. Sole practice Cleve., 1981-85; ptnr. Peltz & Birne, Cleve., 1985—; instr. Am. Inst. Paralegal Studies, Cleve., 1982-93, pers. dir. Cleve. area, 1984-93; cons. in field. Mem. Ohio Bar Assn., Cleve. Bar Assn. (chmn. practice and procedure clinic 1984-86, vol. Call for Action 1986, meritorious service award 1986), Cuyahoga County Bar Assn., Phi Eta Sigma, Zeta Beta Tau, Phi Delta Phi. Lodge: Masons. Office: Peltz & Birne Midland Bldg Ste 1880 Cleveland OH 44115-1093

BIRNEY, ROBERT CHARLES, retired academic administrator, psychologist; b. Westmont, N.J., May 2, 1925; s. Charles Alexander and Florence (Moore) B.; m. Margaret Ann Momerak, June 18, 1949; children: Reed Charles, Ruth Elizabeth, Barbara Ann, Robert Carl. BA, Wesleyan U., 1950; MA, U. Mich., 1951, PhD, 1955. Mem. faculty Amherst (Mass.) Coll., 1954-67, prof. psychology, 1965-67; dean Sch. Social Scis. Hampshire Coll., Amherst, 1968-70, v.p., 1971-78; dir. planning Colonial Williamsburg (Va.) Found., 1978, v.p. rsch., 1979-86, sr. v.p., 1986-90, ret., 1990; vis. prof. Ruhr U., Fed. Republic Germany, 1966-67; spl. rsch. human motivation. Editor (with Richard Teevan) Van Nostrand Insight Series, 1961-70. Lt. USAAF, 1943-46. Decorated Air medal with 3 oak leaf clusters. Fellow Am. Psychol. Assn.; mem. AAUP, New Eng. Psychol. Assn. (pres. 1975), Cosmos Club, Phi Beta Kappa, Sigma Xi. Home: 103 Walnut Hills Dr Williamsburg VA 23185-3426 Office: Colonial Williamsburg Found S Henry St Williamsburg VA 23185

BIRNEY, WALTER LEROY, religious administrator; b. Garden City, Kans., Apr. 25, 1934; s. Claude David and Mildred Elizabeth (Ferris) B.; m. Iva Lou Mosher, June 18, 1954; children: Mickey, Scotty, Gary, Lorrie, Lindie. BA, Dallas Christian Coll., 1956. Min. First Christian Ch., Benjamin, Tex., 1954-57, Bellaire Christian Ch., San Antonio, 1957-58, Copeland (Kans.) Christian Ch., 1958-84; coord. Nat. Missionary Conv., Copeland, 1966—; dean, promoter Ashland (Kans.) Christian Camp, 1961-84; promoter S.W. Sch. Missions, Copeland, 1973-84. Named Outstanding Alumnus Dallas Christian Coll., 1988. Avocation: long distance running. Office: Nat Missionary Conv PO Box 11 Copeland KS 67837-0011

BIRNKRANT, HENRY JOSEPH, lawyer; b. Phila., Jan. 24, 1955; s. Harry Philip and Myra Arlene (Hendler) B.; m. Lynn Rachel Goldin, Oct. 23, 1983; children: Aviva Michelle, Beth Elana. BA magna cum laude, U. Rochester, 1976; JD, Columbia U., 1979; LLM, NYU, 1983. Bar: D.C. 1979, U.S. Dist. Ct. D.C. 1980; U.S. Ct. Appeals (D.C. cir.) 1980, U.S. Tax Ct. 1984. Assoc. Bergson, Borkland, Margolis & Adler, Washington, 1979-82, Covington & Burling, Washington, 1983-88; assoc. Cole, Corette & Abrutyn, Washington, 1988-90, ptnr., 1991-96; ptnr. Alston & Bird, Washington, 1997—. Author: (with others) Butterworth's International Taxation of Financial Instruments and Transactions, 1989; editor: Columbia Jour. Law and Social Problems, 1979; contbr. articles to profl. jours.; bd. advisors Jour. Internat. Taxation. Mem. ABA (tax section). Home: 5506 Durbin Rd Bethesda MD 20814-1012 Office: Alston & Bird North Bldg 11th Fl 601 Pennsylvania Ave NW Washington DC 20004-2601

BIRNKRANT, SHERWIN MAURICE, lawyer; b. Pontiac, Mich., Dec. 20, 1927. BBA, U. Mich., 1949, MBA, 1951; JD with distinction, Wayne State U., 1954. Bar: Mich. 1955, U.S. Dist. Ct. (ea. dist.) 1960, U.S. Supreme Ct. 1960, U.S. Ct. Appeals (6th cir.) 1966. Mem. Oakland County Bd. Suprs., 1967-68; asst. atty. City of Pontiac, 1956-67, city atty., 1967-83; of counsel Schlussel, Lifton, Simon, Rands, Galvin & Jackier, Southfield, Mich., 1983-90, Sommers, Schwartz, Silver & Schwartz, Southfield, Mich., 1990-95; shareholder Birnkrant & Birnkrant P.C., Farmington Hills, Mich., 1995—. Mem. ABA (chmn. urban, state and local govt. law sect. 1987-88, Mich. chmn. pub. contract law sect. 1979-97, ho. of dels. 1990-93, alternate del. to ho. of dels., 1993-96, vice chmn. coordinating com. for model procurement code for state and local govt. 1974—), State Bar Mich. (chmn. pub. corp. law sect. 1973-74, coun. adminstrv. law sect. 1975-76), Oakland County Bar Assn. (chmn. ethics and unauthorized practices com. 1961-62), Am. Judicature Soc., Mich. Assn. Mcpl. Attys. (pres. 1975, coun. of pres. 1992—). Office: Birnkrant & Birnkrant PC 31555 W 14 Mile Rd Ste 201 Farmington Hills MI 48334-1287

BIRNS, MARK THEODORE, physician; b. Bklyn., Sept. 24, 1949; s. Leon and Naomi B.; m. Ann Krieger, Aug. 15, 1976; children: Samantha Lynn, Michael Eric, Kevin Douglas. BA, Case Western Res. U., 1971; MD, Albert Einstein Coll. Medicine, 1974. Diplomate: Am. Bd. Internal Medicine, Am. Bd. Gastroenterology. Intern Bronx Mcpl. Hosp. Ctr. Albert Einstein Hosps., 1974-75, resident in medicine, 1975-77; fellow in gastroenterology U. Oreg. Health Scis. Ctr., 1977-79; asst. chief gastroenterology Walter Reed Army Med. Ctr., 1979-83; asst. prof. medicine U. Health Scis., 1980-83; emergency physician Shady Grove Adventist Hosp., part time, 1980-83, Frederick Meml. Hosp., Washington, 1980-83; practice medicine specializing in gastroenterology and endoscopic biliary surgery Rockville, Md., 1983—; active staff Shady Grove Adventist Hosp., sec. med. staff, 1986-87, chief gastroenterology sect., vice chmn. dept. medicine, 1988, 89, mem. exec. com., 1990-92, mem. laser com., 1992, 93, 94, 95, mem. OR com., 1996-97; assoc. clin. prof. medicine dept. gastroenterology Georgetown U., Washington, 1988—; active staff Suburban Hosp.; courtesy staff Montgomery Gen. Hosp.; mem. HDO (Health Delivery Orgn.), MAMSI (Mid Atlantic Med. Svcs. Health Plan), 1997—; treas., contract coord. Gastrointestinal Endoscopy Assocs., LLC, 1995—. Major contbg. author: Radiology of the Liver, Biliary Tract, Pancreas and Spleen, 1987. Served to maj. USAR. Fellow ACP, Am. Coll. Gastroenterology; mem. AMA (Physician Recognition award 1978, 81, 84, 87, 90, 93), Am. Gastroent. Assn., Am. Soc. Gastrointestinal Endoscopy (postgrad. edn. com. 1991-92), Md. Soc. Gastrointestinal Endoscopy, Montgomery County Med. Soc. Home: 11413 Twining Ln Rockville MD 20854-1860 Office: 9711 Medical Center Dr Ste 308 Rockville MD 20850-3388

BIRNS, NICHOLAS BOE, educator, editor; b. N.Y.C., May 30, 1965; s. Laurence Richard Birns and Margaret Ann Boe. AB, Columbia U., 1988; MA, NYU, 1990, PhD, 1992. Mem. faculty New Sch. U., N.Y.C., 1995—, Coll. New Rochelle, Bronx, N.Y., 1996—; vis. asst. prof. Western Conn. State U., Danbury, 1992-93; invited lectr. U. Stockholm, 1997-98. Editor: Pow's Notes, 1998—; book rev. editor: Antipodes, 1994—; contbr. articles to profl. jours. Devel. fellow NYU, 1988-89. Mem. Guild of Scholars of Episcopal Ch. Episcopalian. Avocations: baseball, music, following current events. E-mail: nicbirns@interport.net. Home: 205 E 10th St New York NY 10003-7634 Office: New Sch U 66 W 121st St New York NY 10027-6319

BIRO, DAVID ERIC, dermatologist; b. Bklyn., May 22, 1964; s. Laszlo and Dolores (Macchiaroli) B.; m. Daniella Vitale, Sept. 15, 1991. BA, U. Pa., 1986; MD, Columbia U., 1991; PhD, Oxford (Eng.) U., 1993. Diplomate Am. Bd. Dermatology. Intern NYU Med. Ctr., 1991-92; resident in dermatology SUNY Health Sci. Ctr., Bklyn., 1992-95; physician, dermatologist Bay Ridge Skin and Cancer Dermatology, P.C., Bklyn., 1994—; asst. clin. prof. dermatology SUNY Health Sci. Ctr., Bklyn., 1995—. Avocation: writing. Office: Bay Ridge Skin and Cancer Dermatology PC 9921 4th Ave Brooklyn NY 11209-8347

BIRO, KATHY, advertising executive. BS in English Edn., NYU, 1973, MA in Ednl. Adminstrn., 1975; MBA in Mktg. and Fin., Columbia U., 1979. Product devel. mgr. Card Products Divsn. Citicorp, N.Y.C., 1979-81; v.p. Mktg. and Sales, Electronic Banking Chase Manhattan Bank1, N.Y.C., 1981-86; 1st v.p. Nat. Mktg.; dir. Credit Resources Shearson Lehman Hutton, N.Y.C., 1986-89; ptnr. Bank St. Consulting Group, N.Y.C., 1989-90; sr. v.p. Mktg. and Product Mgmt., Global Info. Bankers Trust, N.Y.C., 1990-91; sr. v.p. Mktg. Bronner Slosberg Humphrey, N.Y.C., 1991-99; also bd. dirs. Bronner Slosberg Humphrey, 1991-99; founder, pres. and CEO Strategic Interactive Group, 1995-99; vice chmn. Bronnercom, 1999—. Office: Bronnercom 800 Boylston St Prudential Tower Boston MA 02199*

BIRO, LASZLO, dermatologist; b. Czechoslovakia, May 31, 1929; came to U.S., 1956; s. Sandor and Margaret (Klein) B.; m. Dolores Macchiaroli, July 9, 1961; children: David, Lisa, Deborah, Michele. M.D., Univ. Med. Sch., Debrecen, Hungary, 1953. Diplomate Am. Bd. Dermatology. Intern Kings County Hosp., Bklyn., 1957-58; resident Bellevue Hosp., N.Y.C., 1958-60; pvt. practice medicine specializing in dermatology N.Y.C., 1960-61, Bklyn., 1960—; emeritus dept. dermatology Bklyn. Hosp.; chief dept. dermatology Luth. Med. Ctr.; clin. prof. dermatology SUNY, Downstate Med. Ctr., 1971—. Contbr. articles on skin tumors to profl. jours. Fellow ACP, Am. Acad. Dermatology, N.Y. Acad. Medicine; mem. AMA, Kings County Med. Assn., Bay Ridge Med. Soc. (pres. 1987-88), N.Y. State Dermatol. Soc., Bklyn Dermatol. Soc., Internat. Soc. Tropical Dermatology, N.Y. Acad. Scis., Am. Coll. Cryosurgery (v.p. 1996), Semmelweis Sci. Soc. (pres. 1985). Office: 9921 4th Ave Brooklyn NY 11209-8347

BIRO, SUSAN LORI, lawyer; b. N.Y.C., Jan. 9, 1960; d. Albert Stanley and Marilyn Joy (Fenster) Isaacs; m. John Gregory Biro, May 19, 1985. BA with honors, Purchase Coll., 1980; JD magna cum laude, Washington Coll. Law, 1983. Bar: D.C. 1983, Md. 1984, U.S. Dist. Ct. D.C. 1984, U.S. Tax Ct. 1984, U.S. Ct. Appeals (4th and D.C. cirs.) 1984. Of counsel Silver Freedman & Talf, Washington, 1983-98; judge EPA, Washington, 1998—. Office: Silver Freedman & Talf 1735 I St NW Washington DC 20006-2402

BIRON, CHRISTINE ANNE, medical science educator, researcher; b. Woonsocket, R.I., Aug. 8, 1951; d. R. Bernard and Theresa Priscilla (Sauvageau) B. BS, U. Mass., 1973; PhD, U. N.C., 1980. Rsch. technician U. Mass., Amherst, 1973-75; grad. researcher U. N.C., Chapel Hill, 1975-80; postdoctoral fellow Scripps Clinic and Rsch., La Jolla, Calif., 1980; fellow U. Mass. Med. Sch., Worcester, 1981-82, instr., 1983, asst. prof., 1984-87; vis. scientist Karolinska Inst., Stockholm, 1984; asst. prof. Sch. Medicine Brown U., Providence, 1988-90, assoc. prof., 1990-96, prof., 1996—, Esther Elizabeth Brintzenhoff prof., 1996—, chair Dept. Molecular Microbiology & Immunology, 1999—, dir. grad. program in pathobiology, 1995-99; mem. AIDS and related rsch. study sect. 3 NIH, 1991-93; mem. exptl. immunology study sect. NIH, 1993-97. Assoc. editor Jour. Immunology, 1990-94; bd. editors Proceedings of Soc. for Exptl. Biology and Medicine, 1993-99; contbr. articles, revs. to sci. jours.; sect. editor Jour. Immunology, 1995-99; editor Jour. Nat. Immunity, 1994-98. Leukemia Soc. Am. fellow, 1981, Spl. fellow, 1983, scholar, 1987; grantee NIH, 1985—; rsch. grantee MacArthur Found., 1991-96. Mem. AAAS, Am. Assn. Immunologists (co-chmn. symposium 1990, 94, 95, 96, 98), Am. Soc. Virology, Am. Assn. Immunology (block co-chair nat. meetings 1996—), Sigma Xi. Office: Brown U Biomed Ctr Box G-B618 Providence RI 02912

BIRRELL, STEPHEN REYNOLDS, college administrator; b. Orange, N.J., May 19, 1942; s. Selwyn Lathrop and Elsie Reynolds B.; m. Pauline McNeely, Oct. 29, 1966; children: Rebecca Lynn, Stephanie Susan, Kathleen Reynolds. BA, Williams Col., 1964; MA, Wesleyan U., 1966; MPA, U.N.H., 1980. Dir. student tchg. Brown U., Providence, R.I., 1969-77; coord. tchr. edn. U.N.H., Durham, 1977-82, asst. dir. devel., 1982-84; assoc. dir. devel. Williams Coll., Williamstown, Mass., 1984-91; dir. devel. Amherst (Mass.) Coll., 1991-94, dir. alumni rels. & devel., 1994-95; v.p. for alumni rels. & devel. Williams Coll., Williamstown, Mass., 1995—. With USNR, 1967-69. Home: 265 Bulkley St Williamstown MA 01267-2022 Office: Williams Col Off Alumni Rels and Devel Williamstown MA 02167

BIRREN, JAMES EMMETT, university research center executive; b. Chgo., Apr. 4, 1918; m. Elizabeth S., 1942; children: Barbara Ann, Jeffrey Emmett, Bruce William. Student, Wright Jr. Coll., 1938; BEd, Chgo. State U., 1941; MA, Northwestern U., 1942, PhD, 1947, ScD (hon.), 1985; post-grad., U. Chgo., 1950-51; PhD (hon.), U. Gothenberg, Sweden, 1983; LLD (hon.), St. Thomas U., Can., 1990. Tutorial fellow Northwestern U., 1941-42; research asst. project for study of fatigue Office Sci. Research and Devel., 1942; research fellow NIH, USPHS, 1946-47; research psychologist gerontology unit NIH, 1947-51; research psychologist NIMH, 1951-53, chief sect. on aging, 1953-64; dir. aging program Nat. Inst. Child Health and Human Devel., Bethesda, Md., 1964-65; dir. Gerontology Center; prof. psychology U. So. Calif., 1965-89, Disting. prof. emeritus, 1992—, dean Davis Sch. Gerontology, 1975-86, Brookdale Disting. scholar, 1986-90, dir. Inst. Advanced Study in Gerontology and Geriatrics, 1981-89; dir. Borun Ctr. Gerontol. Rsch. UCLA, 1989-93, assoc. dir. Ctr. on Aging, 1990—; fellow Center for Advanced Study in Behavioral Scis., Stanford, Calif., 1978-79; Green vis. prof. U. B.C., 1979; vis. scientist Cambridge (Eng.) U., 1960-61; Harold E. Jones meml. lectr. U. Calif., Berkeley, 1965; mem. Los Angeles County Bd. Suprs.' Com. on Aging, 1967-69 ; sr. fellow U. So. Calif. Urban Ecology Inst., 1968-70; mem. Dean's Council, U. So. Calif., 1970-86 ; chmn. aging rev. com. Nat. Inst. Aging, 1974-75; program dir. Integration of Info. on Aging: Handbook Project, 1973-76; mem. steering com. Care of Elderly, Inst. of Medicine, 1976-77; bd. dirs. Sears Roebuck Found., 1977-80; chmn. life course prevention research rev. com. NIMH, 1985-87; cons. Roche Seminars on Aging Series, 1980-82. Author: Psychology of Aging, 1964; editor: Handbook of Aging and the Individual, 1959, (with K.W. Schaie) Handbook of the Psychology of Aging, 1996, Encyclopedia of Gerontology, 1996, (with R.B. Sloane) Handbook of Mental Health and Aging, 1992; contbr. articles to books, profl. publs.; bd. collaborators: Gerontologia, 1956-89; asst. editor: Jour. Gerontology, 1956-61, assoc. editor 1961-63, editor-in-chief 1968-74, chmn. publs. com., 1975-78, adv. editl. bd., 1956-69; bd. adv. editors: Devel. Psychobiology, 1967-69; adv. editor: Jour. Human Devel., 1957-58. Mem. adv. com. and del. White House Conf. on Aging, 1995. With USNR, 1943-46; to scientist dir. USPHS Scientist Corps, 1947-65. Recipient award for rsch. on problems of aging CIBA Found., 1956, Stratton award Am. Psychopathol. Assn., 1960, Sr. 65er award Dist. 65 Retail Workers and Dept. Store Union, Sr. 65er award AFL-CIO, 1962, medal for meritorious svc. USPHS, 1965, citation Am. Assn. Ret. Persons, 1970, Am. Pioneers in Aging award U. Mich., 1972, commendation for disting. contbns. to field of gerontology Mayor of L.A., 1968, 74, Merit award Northwestern U. Alumni Assn., 1976, Creative Scholarship and Rsch. award U. So. Calif., 1979, Disting. Educator award Assn. Gerontology in Higher Edn., 1983, Eminent Svc. award Stovall Found., 1984, award of Distinction Am. Fedn. for Aging Rsch., 1986, Sandoz prize for rsch. on aging, 1989, Can. Assn. Gerontology award, 1990, Disting. Emeritus award U. So. Calif., 1992, Pres.'s award Am. Soc. on Aging, 1996; USPHS rsch. fellow, 1946-47. Fellow AAAS, Am. Geriatrics Soc. (founding fellow Western div.), Am. Psychol. Assn. (Disting. Sci. Contbn. award 1968, chmn. membership com. 1969, Disting. Contbn. award Div. Adult Devel. and Aging 1978, pres. div. 1955-56, editor newsletter 1951-55), Gerontol. Soc. (pres. 1961-62, chmn. publs. com. 1974-77, award for meritorious research 1966, Brookdale award 1980); mem. Am. Physiol. Soc., Internat. Assn. Gerontology (chmn. exec. com. 1966-69, chmn. program com. 1968-69), Psychonomic Soc., Western Gerontol. Soc. (dir. 1965—, pres. 1968-69), Golden Key Club, Skull and Dagger Club, Sigma Xi, Phi Kappa Phi. Office: UCLA Ctr on Aging 10945 Le Conte Ave Los Angeles CA 90024-2828

BIRRENKOTT, GLEN P., JR., poultry science educator. Prof. animal and vet. sci. Clemson (S.C.) U. Recipient Purina Mills Teaching award Poultry Sci. Assn., 1992. Office: Clemson U Dept Animal and Vet Sci Clemson SC 29634-0361

BIRSH, ARTHUR THOMAS, publisher; b. Englewood, N.J., Oct. 6, 1932; s. Abraham S. and Mary (Levinsohn) B.; m. Judith Rosenberg, June 29, 1955 (div. 1982); children: Andrew, Philip, Joanne.; m. Joan Alleman, 1983. Grad., Lawrenceville N.J. Sch., 1950; B.A., Yale, 1954. Engaged in sales Western Pub. Co., Poughkeepsie, N.Y., 1956-58; founder Cross Road Press, Hyde Park, N.Y., 1958; pres. Cross Road Press, 1958-60; with Playbill mag., N.Y.C., 1961-92; publisher Playbill mag., 1965-94, chmn., 1993—; group v.p. Metromedia, Inc., 1968-73. Served with AUS, 1954-56. Home: 18 Harbor Island Dr Key Largo FL 33037 Office: Playbill 52 Vanderbilt Ave Fl 11 New York NY 10017-3870 *I have no philosophy, rather a hodge-podge of ideas and beliefs that keep me going; nature is a match for nurture; everybody's scared; love is a condition, not a contract; the stupid or silly things I have done usually seemed smart or important at the time; life is a series of moments—wallowing in the lows extends them—clutching the highs destroys them. Most enduring good things that have happened to me resulted from taking chances and making commitments. Luck beats brains!.*

BIRSH, PHILIP S., publishing executive. Pub., pres. Playbill, N.Y.C., 1985—. Office: Playbill 52 Vanderbilt Ave Fl 11 New York NY 10017-3870*

BIRSTEIN, ANN, writer, educator; b. N.Y.C., May 27, 1927; d. Bernard and Clara (Gordon) B.; m. Alfred Kazin, June 26, 1952 (div. 1982); 1 child, Cathrael. BA, Queens Coll., 1948. Lectr. The New Sch. Queens Coll., N.Y.C., 1953-54; writer-in-residence CCNY, 1960; lectr. The Writers Workshop, Iowa City, 1966, 72; lectr. Sch. Gen. Studies Columbia U., N.Y.C., 1985-87; dir., founder Writers on Writing Barnard Coll., N.Y.C., 1988—; adj. prof. English Hofstra U., L.I., 1980, Barnard Coll., N.Y.C., 1981-93; film critic Vogue mag. Author: Star of Glass, 1950, The Troublemaker, 1955, The Sweet Birds of Gorham, 1966, Summer Situations, 1972, Dickie's List, 1973, American Children, 1980, The Rabbi on Forty-Seventh Street, 1982, The Last of the True Believers, 1988; co-editor: The Works of Anne Frank; past contbg. editor Inside mag.; contbr. to Book World, Confrontation, Connoisseur, Geo, Inside, Mademoiselle, McCall's, N.Y. Times Book Rev., N.Y. Times Travel Sect., The New Yorker, The Reporter, Vogue, Washington Post, among others. Nat. Endowment of Arts grantee, 1983; Fulbright fellow, 1951-52. Mem. PEN (former mem. exec. bd., former chair admissions com.), Authors Guild (former mem. coun.), Phi Beta Kappa (hon.). Democrat. Jewish. Home: 1623 3rd Ave # 27jw New York NY 10128-3638

BIRSTEIN, SEYMOUR JOSEPH, aerospace company executive; b. N.Y.C., May 1, 1927; s. Harry D. and Golde (Lenoff) B.; divorced; 1 child, Diane. BA in Chemistry, NYU, 1947; MS in Phys. Chemistry, Mont. State U., 1948; postgrad., Bklyn. Poly. Inst., 1949-50, Cornell U., 1953. Rsch. chemist Airco, Murray Hill, N.J., 1949-50; br. chief Air Force Cambridge Rsch. Labs., Bedford, Mass., 1951-76; pres. SJB Assoc., Inc., Marlborough, Mass., 1977—. Contbr. articles to profl. jours.; patentee in field. Fellow Am. Inst. Chemists; mem. Am. Chem. Soc., Am. Meteorol. Soc., Sigma Xi. Home and Office: 24 Pippen Rd Marlborough MA 01752-1419

BIRTEL, FRANK THOMAS, mathematician, philosopher, educator; b. New Orleans, Apr. 4, 1932; s. Frank N. and Virginia B.; m. Jane Ella C. Moriarty, Sept. 16, 1964 (dec. 1986); children: Rebecca Anne, Michael Teilhard; m. Margaret S. Bishop, July 28, 1990. B.S., Loyola U. South, 1952; M.S., U. Notre Dame, 1953, Ph.D. in Math., 1960. Sr. mathematician USN Nuclear Power Schs., 1955-57; Instr. Conn. Coll. for Women, New London, 1956-57; lectr. Yale U., 1961-62; asst. prof. Ohio State U., 1960-62; asst. prof. math. Tulane U., 1962-64, assoc. prof., 1964-67, prof., 1967—, Univ. prof., 1981—, spl. asst. to pres., 1975-76, dep. provost, 1976-78, acting dean Grad. Sch., 1978, acting provost, 1978, provost, dean, 1979-81, dir. program of Judeo-Christian Studies, 1982—; vis. prof. U. Nijmegen, Netherlands, 1968-69. Editl. adv. bd. Zygon: The Jour. of Sci. and Religion, 1995—. Trustee New Orleans Mus. Art, 1978-80, 83-86 , St. Mary's Dominican Coll., New Orleans, 1977-86. Yale U. postdoctoral fellow, 1961-62; sr. Fulbright lectr. Eng., Scotland, Germany, Netherlands, 1968-69. Mem. Am. Math. Soc. (assoc. sec. 1977-88). Roman Catholic. Home: 1229 Cadiz St New Orleans LA 70115-3903 Office: Tulane U Math Dept New Orleans LA 70118

BISANZO, MARK THOMAS, sales executive; b. Port Chester, N.Y., Sept. 28, 1941; s. Dominic Daniel and Pauline Ann (Zak) B.; m. Mary Jane Ann Baldino, July 2, 1966; 1 child, Mark Christopher. AAS, Westchester C.C., 1963; BSME, N.Y. Inst. Tech., 1966; MBA, Fordham U., 1972. Instrument engr. Bechtel, N.Y.C., 1966-68, M.W. Kellogg, N.Y.C., 1968-70; sr. controls engr. Power Gas Corp., N.Y.C., 1970-71, Am. Electric Power, N.Y.C., 1971; v.p. Control Assocs., Allendale, N.J., 1971—; mem. adv. bd. Fisher Controls Co., Marshalltown, Iowa, 1997—; bd. dirs. Control Assocs. Pres. Bergen Cath. H.S. Fathers' Club, Oradell, N.J., 1991-94; coach Park Ridge (N.J.) Athletic Assn., 1980-90; mem. Our Lady of Mercy Roman Cath. Ch. Noctornal Adoration Soc., Park Ridge, Middlebury Collegiate Alumni Coll. Parents Alumni Assn. Mem. Soc. Gas Operators, Instrument Soc. Am. (v.p. N.Y. chpt. 1984-85). Avocations: skiing, photography, travel. Home: 67 Degroff Pl Park Ridge NJ 07656-1406 Office: Control Assocs 20 Commerce Dr Allendale NJ 07401-1600

BISBEE, JOYCE EVELYN, utility company manager; b. Portage, Wis., May 15, 1941; d. Orris Dean and Helen Paulina (Golz) B. BS, U. Wis., Stout, 1963; MEd, U. N.C., 1971. Cert. family and consumer sci. Ext. home economist U. Wis., Racine, 1964-68; tchr., dept. chair Oshkosh (Wis.) Pub. Schs., 1963-64, 68-74; mgr. ednl. rels. J.C. Penney, N.Y.C., 1974-78; v.p. Creamer Dickson Basford, PR, N.Y.C., 1978-81; consumer affairs rep. Bklyn. Union, Bklyn., 1983-85, consumer advocate, 1986-92, mgr. consumer outreach and edn., 1992-98; mgr. consumer comm. and advocacy KeySpan Energy, Bklyn., 1998—; mem. consumer affairs com. Bar Assn. City N.Y., 1993-98. Mem. adv. com. N.Y.C. 4-H Youth Program, 1985-96; active East 60s Neighborhood Assn., N.Y.C., 1993—. Recipient Alumni Disting. Svc. award U. Wis.-Stout, 1978. Mem. Am. Gas Assn. (mem. consumer and cmty. affairs com. 1992-96), Am. Assn. Family and Consumer Sci. (v.p. 1977-79), Am. Coun. on Consumer Interests, Soc. Consumer Affairs Profls. in Bus., N.Y.C. Home Economists in Bus. (chair 1985-86, awrd 1993), N.Y. State Utility Consumer Affairs Profls. (chair 1991-92). Lutheran. Avocations: craft shows, cultural performances, cats, travel. Home: 245 E 63rd St New York NY 10021-7456 Office: KeySpan Energy One MetroTech Ctr Brooklyn NY 11201

BISBY, MARK AINLEY, physiology educator; b. Malvern, Eng., Aug. 8, 1946; arrived in Can., 1971; s. Harry and Mary (Alderson) B.; m. Isobel Mary Poulton, July 20, 1968; children: Adam, Luke, Kate. BA, Oxford (Eng.) U., 1968, MA, 1972, PhD, 1972. Asst. prof. U. Calgary, Alta., Can., 1973-77, assoc. prof., 1977-82, prof., 1982-89; prof. physiology Queen's U., Kingston, Ont., Can., 1989—, head dept., 1989-97; dir. programs Med. Rsch. Coun. of Can., Ottawa, Ont., 1997—; adj. prof. Queen's U., Kingston, U. Ottawa, Ont. Contbr. numerous articles to profl. jours. Med. Rsch. Coun. Can. grantee, 1974—, key investigator award Centres of Excellence Programme of Can. Govt. Mem. Can. Physiol. Soc. (sec. 1985-87, pres. 1993), Can. Fedn. Biol. Socs. (pres. 1989-90), Soc. for Neurosci., Internat. Soc. Neurochemistry. Office: Med Rsch Coun, 1600 Scott St, Ottawa, ON Canada K1A 0W9*

BISCARDI, CHESTER, composer, educator; b. Kenosha, Wis., Oct. 19, 1948; s. Chester Frank and Anne Rose (Rizzo) B. Student, Università di Bologna (Italy) and Conservatorio di Musica G. B. Martini, Bologna, 1969-70; BA in English Lit. with honors, U. Wis., 1970, MA in Italian Lit. (Ford Found. fellow), 1972, MM in Composition, 1974; MMA, Yale U., 1976, DMA, 1980. Teaching asst. Italian U. Wis., Madison, 1970-73, ad hoc instr. Italian for reading knowledge, 1973-74, teaching asst. theory, 1973-74; teaching fellow Italian for singers Yale U., New Haven, 1975-76; seminar instr. Fed. Correctional Instn. at Oxford, Wis., summer 1978; faculty mem. music dept. Sarah Lawrence Coll., 1977—; seminar and program faculty Acad. Yr. in N.Y.C., 1984; chmn. dept. music Sarah Lawrence Coll., 1987—, William Schuman chmn. music, 1995—; vis. prof. summer program in Florence at Villa Corsi-Salviati in Sesto Fiorentino with U. Mich., 1987, 94; composer-in-residence U. Wis., 1985, The Chamber Music Conf. and Composers' Forum of the East, Bennington, Vt., 1990. Composer numerous compositions including Tartini, 1972, Turning, 1973, Chartres, 1973, Indovinello, 1974, orpha, 1974, Heabakes: Five Sapphic Lyrics, 1974, they had ceased to talk, 1975, Trusting Lightness, 1975, Tenzone, 1975, Music for the Duchess of Malfi, 1975, Trio, 1976, At the Still Point, 1977, Eurydice, 1978, Mestiere, 1979, Trasumanar, 1980, Di Vivere, 1981, Good-bye My Fancy!, 1982, Music for Witch Dance, 1983, Chêz Vous, 1983, Piano Concerto, 1983, Incitation to Desire, 1984, 93, Tight-Rope, 1985, Piano Sonata, 1986, rev., 1987, Traverso, 1987, No Feeling is the Same as Before, 1988, Companion Piece (for Morton Feldman), 1989, 91, Netori, 1990, Music for an Occasion, 1992, The Gift of Life, 1990-93, Baby Song of the Four Winds, 1994, Guru, 1995, Resisting Stillness, 1996, What a Coincidence, 1997, I Wouldn't Know About That, 1997, Prayers of Steel, 1998, Now You See It, Now You Don't, 1998, The Child Comes Every Winter, 1999. Recipient Prix de Rome, Am. Acad. in Rome, 1976-77; Composer/Librettist grantee Nat. Endowment for Arts, 1977-78, 80-81; Composers' Conf. fellow, Johnson, Vt., 1974, 75; Wis. Arts Bd. grantee, 1976; Nat. Acad. and Inst. Arts and Letters Charles E. Ives scholar, 1975-76; Guggenheim fellow, 1979-80; Mellon Found. grantee, 1979; Am. Music Ctr. grantee, 1980; McDowell Colony fellow, 1981, 84, 92, 94-95, 98; Martha Baird Rockefeller Fund grantee, 1982; Creative Artists Pub. Svc. Program fellow in music, 1983; Japan Found. fellow, 1989-90; N.Y. Found. for Arts Artists fellow in music composition, 1990, 98; Rockefeller Found. Bellagio Study and Conf. Ctr. residency, Lago di Como, Villa Serbelloni, Italy, 1993; Humanities residency The Bogliasco Found., Villa Orbiana, Italy, 1999, others. Mem. Am. Composers Alliance, Am. Acad. in Rome, Am. Music Ctr., Broadcast Music, MacDowell Colony, Century Assn., also others. Home: 542 Ave of Americas Apt 4R New York NY 10011-2011 Office: Sarah Lawrence Coll Music Dept Bronxville NY 10708

BISCEVIC, NANCY LUNSFORD, photographer; b. Cin., Jan. 9, 1937; d. Carlton A. and Lucille P. Lunsford; m. Kamilo R. Biscevic, Aug. 3, 1963 (div. 1981); children: Carlton, Richard, John, Camilla. BAA, U. Cin., 1958. Illustrator GE Co., Cin., 1958-65; tech. illustrator Ate Assocs. Inc., Alameda, Calif., 1981-82, data dept. mgr., 1982-88; desktop publ. supr. Fed. Res. Bank of San Francisco, 1988-89, office adminstr., 1989-95; owner NancyB...Cards, Alameda, 1995—. Organist, choir dir. St. Margaret Mary's Ch., Oakland, Calif., 1977-87. Recipient awards Alameda Photographic Soc., No. Calif. Camera Club Coun., Photographers Forum. Mem. Alameda Photographic Soc., Delta Delta Delta (pres. alumnae chpt. 1961-63). Avocations: photography, walking, piano, drawing. Office: NancyB...Cards PO Box 1038 Alameda CA 94501-0104

BISCHEL, MARGARET DEMERITT, physician, managed care consultant; b. Moorhead, N.D., Nov. 8, 1933; d. Connie Magnus Nystrom and Harriett Grace (Petersen) Zorner; m. Raymon DeMeritt, 1953 (div. 1958); 1 child, Gregory Raymon; m. John Bischel, 1961 (div. 1964); m. Kenneth Dean Serkes, June 7, 1974. BS, U. Oreg., Eugene, 1962; MD, U. Oreg., Portland, 1965. Diplomate Am. Bd. Internal Medicine, Nat. Bd. Med. Examiners. Resident, straight med. intern Los Angeles County/U. So. Calif. Med. Ctr., 1965-68, NIH fellow nephrology, 1968-70, asst. prof. renal medicine, 1970-74; asst. prof., instr. medicine U. So. Calif., 1968-74; instr. nephrology East L.A. City Coll., 1971-74; dir. med. edn. Luth. Gen. Hosp., Park Ridge, Ill., 1974-78, dir. nephrology sect., 1977-80, pres. med. staff, 1974-88; founding mem., med. dir., dir. med. svcs. Luth. Health Plan, Park Ridge, 1983-87; clin. assoc. prof. medicine Abraham Lincoln Sch. Medicine U. Ill., 1975-80; sr. cons. Parkside Assocs., Inc., Park Ridge, 1986-88; pvt. practice Chgo., 1974-88; physician Buenaventura Med. Clinic, Ventura, Calif., 1989-94, med. dir., 1992-94; prin. Apollo Managed Care Cons., Inc., Santa Barbara, Calif., 1988—; trustee Luth. Health Care System, Park Ridge, 1986-90, Unified Med. Group Assn., Seal Beach, Calif., 1993-94; hon. lifetime staff mem. Luth. Gen. Hosp., Park Ridge; mem. formulary com. HealthNet, 1992-94, med. adv. com. TakeCare, 1993-94, quality assurance com. PacifiCare, 1993-94; mem. doctor's adv. network AMA, 1994—. Mem. editl. adv. bd. Managed Behavioral Health Care Man., Credentials and Privileging Manual, Capitation Mgmt. Report; contbr. articles to profl. jours., chpts. to books; editor: Med. Mgmt. Manual, Managed Care Bull. Fellow Am. Coll. Physicians (Calif. (Gov.'s advisor 1993—); mem. Am. Coll. Physicians Execs., Am. Coll. Med. Quality, Nat. Assn. Physician Hosp. Orgns., Nat. Assn. Managed Care Physicians, Sigma Xi. Avocations: real estate, gardening. Office: Apollo Managed Care Consultants Inc 860 Ladera Ln Santa Barbara CA 93108-1626

BISCHOFF, DAVID CANBY, retired university dean; b. Bellefonte, Pa., May 27, 1930; s. Eugen Carl and Jean Stuart (Canby) B.; m. Patricia A. Halfacre, Aug. 15, 1954; children: Cynthia, Steven, Ingrid. B.S., Pa. State U., 1952, Ph.D., 1958; M.S., U. N.C., 1953. Asst. prof. dept. phys. edn. U. Mass., Amherst, 1957-60; asso. prof. U. Mass., 1960-63, prof., 1963—, asso. provost for profl. schs., 1972-79, dep. provost, 1982-84; assoc. chancellor, 1983-92; dean U. Mass. Sch. Phys. Edn., 1973-92; vis. prof. Wesleyan U., 1968-69; bd. dirs. Bay State Games. Past pres. Amherst Community Chest, Amherst Am. Field Service; mem. Amherst Planning Bd., 1958-62; trustee The Hotchkiss Sch., 1990-96; trustee Portland (Maine) Mus. Art. Capt. USAF, ret., 1953-55. Mem. AAHPER, Nat. Coll. Phys. Edn. Assn. (past pres.). Clubs: Algonquin, Hillsboro, Anglers (N.Y.C.). Home: 46 Burbank Farm PO Box 462 Yarmouth ME 04096-0462

BISCHOFF, JOAN, English educator; b. Orange, N.J., Mar. 20, 1943; d. Herbert John and Jeannette Elizabeth (Thomas) B.; m. Egal Feldman, June 14, 1992; stepchildren: Tyla, Auora, Naomi. BS, East Stroudsburg State Coll., 1965; MA, Lehigh U., 1971, PhD, 1975. Cert. tchr., N.J., Pa. English tchr. various pub. schs., Pa., N.J., 1965-70; tchg. asst., fellow in English Lehigh U., Bethlehem, Pa., 1970-74; from instr. to assoc. prof. English Slippery Rock (Pa.) U., 1975-87; from assoc. prof. to prof. English U. Wis., Superior, 1988—. Contbr. articles to profl. jours. Rsch. grantee U. Wis., 1989-92. Mem. MLA. Home: 2019 Weeks Ave Superior WI 54880-6720 Office: Univ Wis Sundquist # 237 Superior WI 54880

BISCHOFF, KENNETH BRUCE, chemical engineer, educator; b. Chgo., Feb. 29, 1936; s. Arthur William and Evelyn Mary (Hansen) B.; m. Joyce Arlene Winterberg, June 6, 1959; children: Kathryn Ann, James Eric. B.S., Ill. Inst. Tech., 1957, Ph.D., 1961. Asst. to assoc. prof. U. Tex., Austin, 1961-67; assoc. prof., then prof. U. Md., 1967-70; Walter R. Read prof. engring. Cornell U., 1970-76, dir. Sch. Chem. Engring., 1970-75; Unidel prof., biomed. and chem. engring. U. Del., 1976-98, emeritus, 1998—, chmn. dept. chem. engring., 1978-82; mem. NRC Bd. on Chem. Scis. and Tech., 1984-86, various coms., 1984—; cons. Exxon Rsch. and Engring., NIH, Gen. Foods Corp., W.R. Grace Co., Koppers Co., DuPont Co. Author: (with D.M. Himmelblau) Process Analysis and Simulation, 1968, (with G.F. Froment) Chemical Reactor Analysis and Design, 1979, 2d edit., 1989; editor: (with R.L. Dedrick and E.F. Leonard) The Artificial Kidney, Proc. 1st. Internat. Symposium Chem. Reaction Engring., 1970, (with R.M. Koros and T.R. Keane) Proc. 9th Symposium, 1986; mem. editorial bd. Advances in Chemistry Series, 1973-76, 78-81, Jour. Bioengring., 1976-80, Jour. Pharmacokin, Biopharmaceutics, 1975-92, Biotech. Progress, 1987—, Advances in Chem. Engring., 1981—. Recipient Ebert prize Acad. Pharm. Scis., 1972, Founders award Chem. Indsl. Inst. Toxicology, 1992, Disting. Alumni award Ill. Inst. Tech., 1996, Profl. Achievement award, 1997; Shell Found. fellow, 1959, NSF fellow, 1960, U. Ghent fellow, 1960-61, NAE fellow. Fellow AAAS, AIChE (dir. 1972-74, chmn. food, pharm. and bioengring. divsn. 1985, chmn. nat. program com. 1978, Profl. Progress award 1976, Food Pharm. and Bioengring. divsn. award 1982, 34th Ann. Inst. lectr. 1982, R.H. Wilhelm award 1987); mem. Am. Inst. Chem. Engr., Am. Chem. Soc., Am. Soc. Artificial Internal Organs, Engrs. Coun. for Profl. Devel. (bd. dirs. 1972-78), Coun. Chem. Rsch. (governing bd. 1981-84, chmn. 1985), Catalysis Soc., AAUP, N.Y. Acad. Scis., Sigma XI, Tau Beta Pi, Phi Lambda Upsilon, Omega Chi Epsilon, Alpha Chi Sigma. Home: Exec House 6100 City Ave #1202 Philadelphia PA 19131

BISCHOFF, LAWRENCE JOSEPH, farmer; b. Connersville, Ind., Jan. 13, 1934; s. Joseph George and Anna M. (Snyder) B.; m. Nancy F. Norman, Sept. 25, 1958 (div. Aug. 1970); children: Ann R., Laura Jo., James Joseph. BS in Agr. and Animal Husbandry, Purdue U., 1954. Machinist, set up man McQuay Norris Mfg. Co., Connersville, 1958-72; owner, operator Bishoff Family Farm, Connersville, 1975—. With U.S. Army, 1956-58. Mem. Nat. FFA Orgn. (life), Am. Legion Post 1 (life), Farm Bur. Coop., Ind. Farm Bur. Inc., Connersville FFA Orgn. (treas. 1952-54), Purdue U. Agr. Alumni (life). Democrat. Roman Catholic. Avocations: basketball, travel. Home and Office: 2360 W Williams Rd Connersville IN 47331-8606

BISCHOFF, MARILYN BRETT, clinical social worker; b. Mt. Vernon, N.Y., Apr. 16, 1930; d. Arthur Cushman and Mary Kathryn (Clark) Brett; m. Walter A. Bischoff, Mar. 25, 1961; children: Holly, Robert. BA magna cum laude, CCNY, 1959; MSW, Columbia U., 1961; D in Social Work, Boston Coll., 1985; cert. in gerontology, U. Mass., Dartmouth, 1995—. Diplomate in clin. social work Am. Bd. Examiners in Social Work. Clin. social worker Providence Child Guidance Clinic, 1961-65, 69-73; pvt. practice clin. social worker Attleboro, Mass., 1994—, Providence, 1965-94; instr. Providence Coll., 1988-89; speaker in field. Active Attleboro (Mass.) Area Mental Health Assn., 1975-94. Columbia Univ. fellow, N.Y.C., 1959-60; Nat. Inst. Mental Health fellow, 1960-61. Mem. NASW (sec.-treas. S.E. Mass. chpt. 1967-68, mem. speaker's bur. R.I. chpt. 1987, diplomate clin. social work), Acad. Cert. Social Workers, R.I. Group Psychotherapy Soc. (chair membership com. 1985-96), Columbia U. Alumni Assn., Attleboro Ski Club, Phi Beta Kappa. Avocations: camping, traveling, photography, sewing, bridge. Home and Office: 10 Norfolk Row Attleboro MA 02703-1629

BISCHOFF, SUSAN ANN, newspaper editor; b. Indpls., July 31, 1951; d. Thomas Anthony and Betty Jean (Coons) B.; m. Jim B. Barlow, June 20, 1975; 1 child, Samantha Lynn. BA, Ind. U., 1973. Rschr.-reporter Congl. Quar., Washington, 1973-74; city desk reporter Houston Chronicle, 1974-75, bus. reporter, 1975-79, asst. bus. editor, 1979-84, bus. editor, 1984-86, asst. mng. editor, 1986—; Houston corr. Kiplinger, Tex. Letter, Washington, 1980-85. Bd. dirs. Houston Chronicle Employees Fed. Credit Union, 1980-87; mem. exec. com. San Jacinto Coun. Girl Scouts U.S., Child Advs.; bd. dirs. U.S. Olympic Festival VII, Houston, 1985-86; bd. dirs. Gulf Coast March of Dimes Birth Defects Found.; mem. class policy Leadership Houston, 1992-94; founding bd. dirs. Greater Houston Women's Found.; mem. exec. com. Gulf Coast affiliate United Way; mem. bd. visitors Anderson Cancer Ctr. U. Tex. Named Outstanding Woman in Houston Journalism YWCA, 1989, Fabulous Femme Greater Houston Women's Found., 1994, Woman of Distinction Crohn's & Colitis Found., 1996; recipient Outstanding Vol. Achievement award Gulf Coast United Way, 1995, Outstanding Media award Nat. Soc. Fund Raising Execs., 1997. Mem. Soc. Profl. Journalists, Am. Assn. Sunday and Feature Editors (dir.), Press Club of Houston Ednl. Found. (founding bd. dirs.). Home: 2929 Buffalo Speedway # 112 Houston TX 77098 Office: Houston Chronicle 801 Texas St Houston TX 77002-2996

BISDIKIAN, CHATSCHIK, electrical engineer; b. Thessaloniki, Greece, Dec. 21, 1960; came to U.S., 1983; s. Chrats and Maria (Kehagian) B.; m. Tung-Yun Teresa Shen, July 7, 1990; children: Eugene Anastasios, Theodore Alexander. 5 yr. diploma, Aristotelion U. Thessaloniki, 1983; MSc, U. Conn., 1985, PhD, 1988. Registered prof. engr., Greece. Rsch., tchg. asst. U. Conn., Storrs, 1983-88; rsch. staff mem. IBM Corp. T.J. Watson Rsch. Ctr., Hawthorne, N.J., 1989—; session organizer, chmn. Internat. Workshop Mobile Comm., 1996. Editl. bd. mem. Telecomm. Sys. Jour., 1993-96, IEEE Network mag., 1999—; contbr. articles to profl. jours. Mem. IEEE (sr.), Phi Kappa Phi, Eta Kapp Nu (Outstanding Young Elec. Engr. award finalist 1995). Achievements include patent for increasing the capacity of data networks. Home: 20 Lawrence St Mount Kisco NY 10549-3302 Office: IBM Corp TJ Watson Rsch Ctr 30 Saw Mill River Rd Hawthorne NY 10532-1507

BISEL, MARSHA MCCUNE, elementary education educator; b. Winchester, Ind., Jan. 27, 1950; d. Floyd Elder and Vista Coral (Rust) McCune; m. Ronald G. Bisel, June 20, 1971; children: Kyle, Brooke, Kam, Robin. BS in Edn. summa cum laude, Taylor U., 1972; MA in Edn., Ball State U., Muncie, Ind., 1975. Life lic. K-8 tchr., Ind. Tchr. Ridgeville (Ind.) Elem. Sch., 1972, basketball coach, 1973-74; basketall coach Deerfield Elem. Sch., Ridgeville, 1972-99, grade level coord. Mem. civic theatre bd. Summer Performance Co., Portland, Ind., 1997-98; bd. dirs. Habitat for Humanity, 1998; active Jay County Girls Little League, Jay County Soccer, Patriot Booster Club, Ch. choir, organist, soloist. Avocations: acting, singing. Home: 6528 S US 27 Portland IN 47371

BISGARD, GERALD EDWIN, biosciences educator, researcher; b. Denver, Aug. 4, 1937; s. Harry Herman and Lucille Margaret (Matson) B.; m. Sharon Kay Cummings, Sept. 9, 1961; children—Jennifer, Kristine, Bradley. B.S., Colo. State U., 1959, D.V.M., 1962; M.S., Purdue U., 1967; Ph.D., U. Wis.-Madison, 1971. Instr., then asst. prof. Purdue U., West Lafayette, Ind., 1962-69; asst. prof., then assoc. prof. U. Wis.-Madison, 1971-77, prof., 1977—, prof./dept. chmn. bioscis., 1980-97; vis. prof. U. Calif.-San Francisco, 1977-78; mem. respiratory and applied physiol. study sect. NIH, 1988-92. Recipient Merit award NIH, 1987; named NIH fellow, 1969-71, Fogarty NIH Sr. Internat. fellow Oxford U., 1993; grantee NIH, 1973—. Mem. Am. Soc. Vet. Physiologists and Pharmacologists (pres. 1982-84), Am. Physiol. Soc., AVMA, Am. Thoracic Soc., Wisc. Assn. Biomed. Reg. Edn. (pres. 1998—). Avocations: sailing; skiing; gardening; hiking. Office: U Wis Sch Vet Medicine 2015 Linden Dr W Madison WI 53706-1100

BISH, L. ANN, retired secondary education educator; b. Schenectady, Apr. 1, 1929; d. Howard P. and Vivian (Townsend) B. BS in Edn., Ohio State U., 1951; MA in Edn., Syracuse (N.Y.) U., 1956. Cert. secondary tchr. Tchr. 6th grade Shaker Hts. (Ohio) Pub. Schs., 1952-54; head resident Syracuse U., 1954-56; dean of women Wilmington (Ohio) Coll., 1956-58; dir. women's housing SUNY, Buffalo, 1958-62; tchr. English, Ken-Ton Pub. Schs., Kenmore, N.Y., 1962-91; tchr. devel. studies Schenectady (N.Y.) County C.C., 1993-95. Mem. cmty. adv. coun. SUNY, Buffalo, 1992-97. Mem. AAUW (pres. Buffalo br. 1989-90, N.Y. State pub. policy dir. 1998—, state bd. dirs.), Mortar Bd., Pi Lambda Theta, Kappa Alpha Theta. Home: 5177 Willowbrook Dr Clarence NY 14031-1476

BISHARA, AMIN TAWADROS, management and consulting firm executive, technical services executive; b. Cairo, Oct. 22, 1944; came to U.S., 1973; s. Tawadros and Fakha (Boules) B.; m. Suzi Guirguis, Aug. 27, 1977; children: James A., Robert A. BSME, Ain Shams U., Cairo, 1968; MSME, Poly. U. N.Y., 1976. Registered profl. engr., N.Y., Tex., Ill., Ariz., Pa., Fla. Field engr. Gen. Engring. Co., Cairo, 1968-71; mech. engr. Engring. Co. for Indsl. Enterprises, Cairo, 1971-73; project engr. Cosentini Assocs., N.Y.C., 1973-76; sr. engr. Ebasco Svcs., Inc., N.Y.C., 1976-79, lead engr., 1979-84; chmn., chief exec. officer PTS Tech. Svcs., Inc., Hurst, Tex., 1985-96; v.p. Metzler & Assocs., 1997-98; sr. mgr. Ernst & Young LLP, 1999—; mem. adv. bd. Entrepreneurship Inst., Ft. Worth, 1990—. lectr. in nuclear industry; strategic and bus. cons. Contbr. articles to profl. publs. Mem. NSPE, ASME Nuc. Air Treatment Sys. (main com.), Masons, Moslah Temple of Ft. Worth. Roman Catholic. Home: 2625 Brookridge Dr Hurst TX 76054-2761

BISHARA, SAMIR EDWARD, orthodontist; b. Cairo, Oct. 31, 1935; s. Edward Constantin and Georgette Ibrahim (Kelela) B.; children: Dina Marie, Dorine Gabrielle, Cherine Noelle. B. Dental Surgery, Alexandria U., Egypt, 1957; diploma in orthodontics, 1967; M.S., U. Iowa, 1970, cert. in orthodontics, 1970, D.D.S., 1972. Diplomate Am. Bd. Orthodontics (pres. Coll. Diplomates 1992). Practice gen. dentistry Alexandria, 1957-68; specializing in orthodontics Iowa City, Iowa, 1970—; fellow in clin. pedontics Guggenheim Dental Clinic, N.Y.C., 1959-60; resident in oral surgery Moassat Hosp., Alexandria, 1960-61; mem. staff Moassat Hosp., 1961-68; asst. prof. dentistry U. Iowa, 1970-73, asso. prof., 1973-76, prof., 1976—; vis. prof. Alexandria U., 1974. Contbr. articles profl. jours., chpts. in books. Fellow Am. Coll. Dentists, Internat. Coll. Dentists; mem. ADA, AAAS, Am. Assn. Orthodontics, Internat. Dental Fedn., Internat. Assn. Dental Research, Am. Cleft Palate Assn., Assn. Egyptian Am. Scholars, Egyptian Orthodontic Soc. (hon.), Columbian Orthodontic Soc. (hon.), Greek Orthodontic Soc. (hon.), Mexican Bd. Orthodontists (hon.), Omicron Kappa Upsilon, Sigma Xi. Home: 1014 Penkridge Dr Iowa City IA 52246-4930 Office: U Iowa Coll Dentistry Orthodontic Dept Iowa City IA 52242

BISHER, JAMES FURMAN, journalist, author; b. Denton, N.C., Nov. 4, 1918; s. Chisholm and Mamie (Morris) B.; m. Lynda Landon; children: Roger, James Furman Jr., Monte. Student, Furman U., 1934-36; A.B. in Journalism, U. N.C., 1938. Editor Lumberton (N.C.) Voice, 1938-39; reporter High Point (N.C.) Enterprise, 1939-40; reporter, state editor Charlotte (N.C.) News, 1940-42, sports editor, 1946-50; sports editor Atlanta Constn., 1950-57, Atlanta Jour., 1957—; columnist The Sporting News, St. Louis; moderator weekly TV show, Football Rev., 1950-68; Vice pres. Bisher Hosiery Mill, Denton, N.C. Author: With A Southern Exposure, 1962, Miracle in Atlanta, 1966, Strange But True Baseball Stories, 1966, Arnold Palmer—The Golden Year, 1971, Aaron, 1974, The College Game, 1974, The Masters, 1976, The Furman Bisher Collection, 1989, Thankful, 1997, Atlanta Half-Century, 1997, also numerous articles; contbr. to: anthologies including Best Sports Stories of Year, 23 times. Chmn. Ga. Christmas Seal campaign, 1961; charter mem. Atlanta-Fulton County Stadium Authority.; bd. dirs. Salvation Army Boys Club, mem. adv. bd. Sarazwen World Open Golf Tournament; mem. Atlanta Sports Coun. Served to lt. USNR Air Corps, 1943-46. Recipient Ga. A.P. Sports Writing award, 18 times; UPI Sports Writing award, 4 times; Turf Writing award Fla. Throughbred Breeders Assn., 1972, 75; Jake Wade award Coll. Sports Info. Dirs. Am., 1979; Sigma Delta Chi awards for best sports commentary, 1982, 93, 90; Bert McGrane award for disting. svc. to coll. football, 1982; N.C. Gov.'s award, 1986; U. N.C. Journalism Hall of Fame, 1985; named Ky. col., 1958, Sportswriter of Yr. Ga. (18 times); hon. Tar Heel, 1961; Disting. Alumnus of Yr. Furman U., 1978; Red Smith award for disting. and meritorious contbn. to art of sportswriting, 1988, Bobby Jones Sportsman of Yr. award, 1994; named to Nat. Sportscasters and Sportswriters Hall of Fame, 1989, Internat. Golf Writers Hall of Fame, 1989, Ga. Sports Hall of Fame, 1990, N.C. Sports Hall of Fame, 1995, Lifetime Achievement in Journalism award PGA in Am., 1996, Ga. Soccer Hall of Fame, 1997, Meml. Golf Journalism award, 1997; sponsor Furman Bisher Acad.-Athletic scholarship Furman U. Mem. Nat. Sportscasters and Sportswriters Assn. (pres. 1974-76), Football Writers Assn. Am. (pres. 1959-60), Golf Writers Assn. Am. (pres. 1992-94), Canongate Golf Club, Legends at Chateau Elan, Capital City Club, Gridiron Club, Chi Psi. Presbyterian. Home: 431 Lester Rd Fayetteville GA 30215-4930 Office: 72 Marietta St NW PO Box 4689 Atlanta GA 30302-4689 *My good fortune in life is not to be confused with success, whose definition yet remains vague to me. Success is some mythical goal clamored and struggled for, and whose pursuit is never-ending. One level leads to a requirement to seek another. Success, in my mind, must be related to the status of that person who achieves happiness, and yet may never have been outside his county.*

BISHOP, ALFRED CHILTON, JR., lawyer; b. Alexandria, Va., Oct. 3, 1942; s. Alfred Chilton and Margaret (Marshall) B.; divorced; 1 son, Alfred Chilton III; m. 2d Catherine Ann Keppel, May 17, 1980. B.A. with distinction, U. Va., 1965, LL.B., 1969; LL.M. in Taxation, Georgetown U., 1974. Bar: N.Y. 1970, U.S. Ct. Appeals (2d cir.), 1970, U.S. Tax Ct. 1971, U.S. Ct. Claims 1971, D.C. 1977. Assoc. Shearman and Sterling, N.Y.C., 1969-70; assoc. trial atty., Office of Chief Counsel IRS, Washington, 1970-74, sr. trial atty., 1974-80, sr. technician reviewer, 1980-81, br. chief, 1981—. Recipient Am. Jurisprudence award 1968, 1968. Mem. ABA (tax sec.), D.C. Bar Assn., Sr. Exec. Service Candidate Network (v.p. 1980-81, pres. 1981-82, dir. 1983), Sr. Exec. Assn., Phi Delta Phi. Episcopalian. Home: 7523 Thistledown Trl Fairfax Station VA 22039-2207

BISHOP, AMELIA MORTON, freelance writer; b. Dallas, Dec. 31, 1920; d. Walter Pierce and Alice (Stanton) Morton; m. J. Ivyloy Bishop, Dec. 18, 1955; children: Dan, Judith. BA, U. Tex., El Paso, 1942; MRE, Southwestern Bapt. Theol. Sem., Ft. Worth, 1953. Reporter Hollywood (Calif.) Citizen-News, 1942-43; in advt. and pub. rels. New Orleans, 1943-48; Tex. state young people's sec. Woman's Missionary Union, Dallas, 1953-56; tchr. Plainview (Tex.) High Sch., 1963-80; instr. Wayland Bapt. U., Plainview, 1957-60, 81-83; freelance writer, 1960—; state v.p. Woman's Missionary Union of Tex., Dallas, 1980-84, state pres., 1984-88, nat. v.p., 1984-88. Author, photographer: The Gift and the Giver, 1984, The Flame and the Candle, 1987, Lenthening Legacy: Eula Mae Henderson, 1998; contbr. numerous articles to publs. Recipient Tex. Bapt. Elder Statesman award Bapt. Gen. Conv. Tex., 1989. Democrat. Avocations: reading, walking, travel. Home: PO Box 163523 Austin TX 78716-3523

BISHOP, ANDRÉ, artistic director, producer; b. N.Y.C., Nov. 9, 1948; s. Andre V. and Felice H. (Francis) Smolianinoff. Attended, Harvard Coll. Artistic dir. Playwrights Horizons, N.Y.C., 1978-92, Lincoln Ctr. Theatre, N.Y.C., 1992—; tchr. NYU, Hunter Coll.; cons. CAPS Playwriting Program. Producer, at Playwright's Horizon, N.Y.C. (plays): March of the Falsettos, The Dining Room, Sister Mary Ignatius Explains It All For You, Isn't It Romantic, Sunday in the Park with George, The Heidi Chronicles (Pulitzer prize 1989), Driving Miss Daisy (Pulitzer prize 1990), Carousel (Tony award 1994), The Heiress (Tony award 1995), A Delicate Balance (Tony award 1996); worked with New York Shakespeare Restival and Am. Place Theatre, N.Y.C. Office: Lincoln Ctr Theater 150 W 65th St New York NY 10023-6903

BISHOP, ANN SHOREY, mental health nurse; b. N.Y.C., Jan. 4, 1947; d. George Heaysman and Clara Bessie (Garrison) Shorey; married; 1 child, George John. Diploma in nursing, Montgomery Hosp. Sch. Nursing, 1967; BSN, U. Pa., 1971; postgrad., Med. Coll. Va., 1976-77. RN, Pa. Staff nurse med.-psychiatry Montgomery Hosp., Norristown, Pa., 1967-69; staff nurse psychiat. med.-surg. Mercer Med. Ctr., Trenton, N.J., 1972-76, Rancocas Valley Hosp., Rancocas, N.J., 1977-79; med., psychiat. mental health and chem. dependency staff nurse Helene Fuld Med. Ctr., Trenton, N.J., 1980—. Mem. Nat. League for Nursing. Mem. Soc. of Friends. Avocations: reading, rail fan, cooking, baking. Office: Helene Fuld Med Ctr 750 Brunswick Ave Trenton NJ 08638-4143

BISHOP, BLAINE ELWOOD, football player; b. Indpls., July 24, 1970. Student, St. Joseph's (Ind.) Coll.; degree in insurance, Ball State U., 1993. Safety Houston Oilers, 1993-97, Tennessee Oilers, 1997—. Named to Pro Bowl, 1995, 96.

BISHOP, BUDD HARRIS, retired museum administrator, artist; b. Canton, Ga., Nov. 1, 1936; s. James M. and Mary E. (Ponder) B.; m. Julia Crowder, Nov. 30, 1968. A.B., Shorter Coll., Rome, Ga., 1958; M.F.A., U. Ga., 1960; student, Arts Adminstrn. Inst. Harvard, 1970. Instr. art Ensworth Sch., Nashville, 1961-63; dir. creative services Transit Advt. Assn., N.Y.C., 1964-66; dir. Hunter Mus. of Art, Chattanooga, 1966-76, Columbus (Ohio) Mus. Art, 1976-87, Samuel P. Harn Mus. Art, U. Fla., Gainesville, 1987-98; vis. lectr. Vanderbilt U., 1962; past pres. bd. Intermuseum Conservation Lab., Oberlin, Ohio. Past trustee Fla. Arts Celebration, Gainesville; mem. Gainesville Art in Pub. Places Trust; mem. faculty Ctr. for Arts and Pub. Policy; bd. dirs. Fla. Assn. Mus. Found., Inc.; mem. nat. adv. bd. Philharm. Ctr. for Arts, Naples, Fla. Recipient gov.'s award Tenn. Art Commn., 1971, 73, Alumni Arts achievement award Shorter Coll., 1979, arts leadership award Columbus Day, 1986, Person of Yr. award in arts Gainesville Sun, 1995, Lifetime Achievement Mus. Svc. award Fla. Assn. Mus., 1997. Mem. Am. Assn. Museums, Assn. Art Mus. Dirs. (past trustee), Southeastern Museums Conf. (James R. Short award 1998), Fla. Art Mus. Dirs. Assn. (Lifetime Achievement award 1998).

BISHOP, C. DIANE, state agency administrator, educator; b. Elmhurst, Ill., Nov. 23, 1943; d. Louis William and Constance Oleta (Mears) B. BS in Maths., U. Ariz., 1965, MS in Maths., MEd in Secondary Edn., 1972. Lic. secondary educator. Tchr. math. Tucson Unified Sch. Dist., 1966-86, mem. curriculum council, 1985-86, mem. maths. curriculum task teams, 1983-86; state supt. of pub. instrn. State of Ariz., 1987-95, gov.'s policy advisor for edn., 1995-97, dir. gov.'s office workforce devel. policy, 1996—; asst. dep. dir. Ariz. Dept. Commerce, 1997—; exec. dir. Gov.'s Strategic Partnership for Econ. Devel., 1997—; mem. assoc. faculty Pima C.C., Tucson, 1974-84; adj. lectr. U. Ariz., 1983, 85; mem. math. scis. edn. bd. NRC, 1987-90, mem. new standards project governing bd., 1991; dir. adv. bd. sci. and engring. ednl. panel, NSF; mem. adv. bd. for arts edn. Nat. Endowment for Arts. Active Ariz. State Bd. Edn., 1984-95, chmn. quality edn. commn., 1986-87, chmn. tchr. crt. subcom., 1984-95, mem. outcomes based edn. adv. com., 1986-87, liaison bd. dirs. essential skills subcom., 1985-87, gifted edn. com. liaison, 1985-87; mem. Ariz. State Bd. Regents, 1987-95, mem. com. on preparing for U. Ariz., 1983, mem. high sch. task force, 1984-85; mem. bd. Ariz. State Community Coll., 1987-95; mem. Ariz. Joint Legis. Com. on Revenues and Expenditures, 1989, Ariz. Joint Legis. Com. on Goals for Ednl. Excellence, 1987-89, Gov.'s Task Force on Ednl. Reform, 1991, Ariz. Bd. Regents Commn. on Higher Edn., 1992. Woodrow Wilson fellow Princeton U., summer 1984; recipient Presdl. Award for Excellence in Teaching of Maths., 1983, Ariz. Citation of Merit, 1984, Maths. Teaching award Nat. Sci. Research Soc., 1984, Distinction in Edn. award Flinn Found., 1986; named Maths. Tchr. of Yr. Ariz. Council of Engring. and Sci. Assns., 1984, named One of Top Ten Most Influential Persons in Ariz. in Field of Tech., 1998. Mem. AAUW, NEA, Nat. Coun. Tchrs. Maths., Coun. Chief State Sch. Officers, Women Execs. in State Govt. (bd. dirs. 1993), Ariz. Assn. Tchrs. Math., Women Maths. Edn., Math. Assn. Am., Ednl. Commn. of the States (steering com.), Nat. Endowment Arts (adv. bd. for arts edn.), Nat. Forum Excellence Edn., Nat. Honors Workshop, Phi Delta Kappa. Republican. Office: Ariz Dept Commerce 3800 N Central Ave Bldg D Phoenix AZ 85012-1908

BISHOP, CALVIN THOMAS, landscape architect, educator; b. Alexander City, Ala., Oct. 11, 1929; s. Isaiah Washington and Flora Bernice (Carlton) B.; m. Lenna Graves, Aug. 28, 1950; children: Leigh Carlton, Beverly Lynn, Lane Amanda. B.Landscape Arch., Auburn U., 1951. Landscape architect John F. Highberger, Memphis, 1949-51; planner Auburn Planning Bd., 1951; landscape architect, designer Ralph Ellis Gunn, Houston, 1952-53; ptnr. Bishop & Walker, Houston, 1953-84; assoc. prof. landscape arch. La. State U., 1965-66; pres. Bishop Wholesale Greenhouses, Inc., Alexander City, Ala., 1982-88; assoc. prof. Miss. State U., Starkville, 1984-97, acting head dept. landscape architecture, 1986, 87-89, assoc. prof. emeritus, 1997—; cons. landscape architecture, 1997—. Works include Am. Rose Center, Shreveport, La. Post adviser Boy Scouts Am., 1971-73; chmn. Gov.'s Houston-Gulf Coast Region-10 Year Goals for Tex. planning com., 1970, Houston Am. Bicentennial Commn., 1973-76; treas. Richmond Elementary PTO, 1975-76; mem. profl. adv. com. Sch. Environ. Design Tex. A.&M. U. Recipient Houston Mcpl. Arts Environ. Design Achievement awards, 1970-72. Mem. Am. Soc. Landscape Architects (pres. S.W. chpt. 1970-71, nat. v.p. 1973-74, 80, pres. 1981-82, coun. fellows 1978—, Nat. Honor award for design, del. to Internat. Fedn. Landscape Architects 1992-93), Houston C. of C., Houston-Auburn U. Alumni Assn. (pres. 1963-64), Pi Kappa Alpha. Baptist. Lodge: Rotary (sgt. at arms 1978-79). Home and Office: 9203 Bonhomme Rd Houston TX 77074-6613 *Man's relationship with gardens go back to the earliest beginnings as a standard for peace and quality of life. Preserving and designing our landscape is a great experience.*

BISHOP, CAROLYN BENKERT, public relations counselor; b. Monroe, Wis., Aug. 28, 1939; d. Arthur C. and Delphine (Heston) Benkert; m. Lloyd F. Bishop, June 15, 1963. BS, U. Wis., 1961; grad., Tobe-Coburn Sch., N.Y.C., 1962. Merchandising editor Co-Ed Mag., N.Y.C., 1962-63; advt. copywriter Woodward & Lothrop, Washington, 1963-65; home furnishings editor Co-Ed Mag., N.Y.C., 1965-68; editor Budget Decorating Mag., N.Y.C., 1968-69; home furnishings editor Family Cir. Mag., N.Y.C., 1969-75; v.p., pub., editorial dir. Scholastic, Inc., N.Y.C., 1975-80; owner Mesa Store Home Furnishings Co., Aspen, Colo., 1980-83; dir. pub. rels. Snowmass Resort Assn., Snowmass Village, Colo., 1983-86; pres. Bishop & Bishop Mktg. Comm., Aspen, 1986-93, Monroe, 1993—; mem. media rels. com. Colo. Tourism Bd., Denver, 1987-90. Author: 25 Decorating Ideas Under $100, 1969; editor: Family Circle Special Home Decorating Guide, 1973. Bd. dirs. Aspen Camp Sch. for the Deaf, 1987-90. Recipient Dallas Market Editorial award Dallas Market Ctr., 1973, Dorothy Dawe award Chgo. Furniture Market, 1973, Guardian of Freedom award, Anti-Defamation League Appeal, 1974. Mem. Rocky Mountain Pub. Rels. Group (chmn. 1991-93), Pub. Rels. Soc. Am. (accredited, small firms co-chair counselors acad. 1992-93), Aspen Writers' Found. (bd. dirs. 1991-93), Tobe-Coburn Alumni Assn., U. Wis. Alumni Assn. Democrat. Office: Bishop & Bishop Mktg Comms 1511 13th Ave Monroe WI 53566-2422*

BISHOP, CHARLES EDWIN, university president emeritus, economist; b. Campobello, S.C., June 8, 1921; s. Fred and Hattie Bess (Wall) B.; m. Dorothy Anderkin, Feb. 13, 1943; children: Susan Ann, Mary Catherine, Charles Edwin. B.S., Berea Coll., 1946; M.S., U. Ky., 1948; Ph.D. (Farm Found. fellow 1948-49), U. Chgo., 1952. Research asst. agrl. econs. U. Ky., 1947-48; research assoc. econs. U. Chgo., 1949-50; mem. faculty N.C. State U., 1950-70, prof. agrl. econs., 1956-70, head dept. agrl. econs., 1957-65, head dept. econs., 1965-66, William N. Reynolds Disting. prof., 1957-70; v.p. U. N.C., Chapel Hill, 1966-70; exec. dir. Agrl. Policy Inst., 1960-66; chancellor U. Md., College Park, 1970-74; pres. U. Ark., Fayetteville, 1974-80, U. Houston System, 1980-86; vis. prof. U. Va., 1961-63; cons. Universidad Agraria, Lima, Peru, 1961-65; mem. Nat. Com. Agrl. Policy, Nat. Planning Assn., 1958-70; agrl. bd. Nat. Acad. Scis., 1963-68; sci. adv. com. to sec. agr., 1962-68; mem. Nat. Manpower Adv. Com., 1962-68; exec. dir. Pres. Johnson's Nat. Adv. Com. on Rural Poverty, 1966-67; mem. food adv. com. Pres. Nixon's Cost of Living Council, 1972; mem. Pres.'s adv. com. White House Conf. on Balanced Nat. Growth and Econ. Devel., 1978. Co-author: Introduction to Agricultural Economic Analysis, 1958. Mem. com. on vet. med. edn. So. Regional Edn. Bd., 1974; trustee Farm Found., 1968-78; bd. dirs. Winthrop Rockefeller Found., 1975-78, Resources for the Future, 1976-90, chmn., 1987-90; co-chmn. bd. Nat. Rural Ctr., 1975-79; mem. Pres.'s Commn. on Agenda for Eighties, 1980; bd. dirs. Houston Industries, 1984-92. Mem. Am. Agr. Econs. Assn. (pres. 1967-68), Am. Econ. Assn., Internat. Assn. Agrl. Econs., Commn. on Cen. European Econ. Devel., Alpha Zeta, Phi Kappa Phi, Gamma Sigma Delta.

BISHOP, CHARLES JOSEPH, manufacturing company executive; b. Gary, Ind., June 22, 1941; s. Charles K. and Angela (Marich) Yelusich; m. Yvonne M. Stazinski, June 8, 1963; children: Stephen, Scott. BS, Purdue U., 1963; PhD, U. Wash., 1969. Mgr. advanced energy systems Boeing Co., Seattle, 1969-77; mgr. systems devel. Solar Energy Research Inst., Denver, 1977-81; v.p. tech. A.O. Smith Corp., Milw., 1981—; mem. adv. bd. S.W. Wis. Rsch. Ctr., Milw., 1987; bd. dirs. Indsl. Rsch. Inst., 1989-92, v.p., 1993, pres. 1995-96. Contbr. articles to profl. jours. Treas. Cedarburg Comty. Scholarship Com., Wis., 1985-91; mem. indsl. liaison coun. U. Wis., Milw., 1985—, U. Wis. Coll. Engring., Madison, 1990-95; mem. Gov.'s Coun. on Sci. and Tech., 1992-94. Recipient Cert. Recognition NASA, 1975. Mem. Univ. Club (Milw.). Republican. Roman Catholic. Avocations: fishing, travel, golf. Office: A O Smith Corp-Corp Tech 12100 W Park Pl Milwaukee WI 53224-3029

BISHOP, CLAIRE DEARMENT, small business owner, former librarian; b. Youngstown, Ohio, Oct. 12, 1937; d. Eugene Howard and Ruth (Bright) DeArment; m. Carl R. Meinstereifel, 1956 (div. 1964; children: Paul, Dawn; m. Olin Jerry Dewberry, Jr., 1974 (div. 1979); m. J. Bruce Bishop, May 6, 1992. BS, Clarion State U., 1967; MLS, Ga. State U., 1977. Cert. libr. media specialist, Ga. Libr. Henry County, Stockbridge, Ga., 1967-69; head libr. Russell H.S., East Point, Ga., 1969-84; engring. libr. Rockwell Internat., Duluth, Ga., 1984-88; rep. Govt. Industry Data Exch. Program, Corona, Calif., 1984-88; libr. Raytheon Co., 1990, Missile Sys. Divsn., Bristol, Tenn., 1988-90; owner, mgr. Claire's Collectibles, rubber stamp store, St. Augustine, Fla. Author newsletter Grin and Stamp It. Sec. San Marco Avenue Mchts. Assn. Mem. St. Augustine IBM Users Group (sec.), Six-Ninety-Six Investment Club (fin. officer), Mensa. Democrat. Avocations: computers, writing, information broker. Home: 238 Ravenswood Dr Saint Augustine FL 32095-3027

BISHOP, CLAUDE TITUS, retired biological sciences research administrator, editor; b. Liverpool, N.S., Can., May 13, 1925; s. Claude Wetmore and Elva (Titus) B.; m. Pierrette Marie Picard, July 8, 1951 (dec. 1975); 1 child, Scot; m. Joan May Marshall, May 5, 1983. B.Sc., Acadia U., Wolfville N.S., 1945, B.A. with honors, 1946; Ph.D. in Chemistry, McGill U., Montreal, Que., 1949; D.Sci. (hon.), U. Western Ont., Can., 1986. Research officer Nat. Research Council Can., Ottawa, Ont., Can., 1949-68, asst. dir. biochem. lab., 1968-72, assoc. dir. div. biol. sci., 1972-78, dir., 1978-87, sec. gen., 1987-90. Author: How to Edit a Scientific Journal, 1984; also articles; asst. editor, co-editor Can. Jour. Chemistry, 1964-69 editor, 1969-70; editor-in-chief Can. Jour. Research, 1969-90. Fellow Royal Soc. Can. Avocations: golf; skiing; music. Home: 63 Holborn Ave, Nepean, ON Canada K2C 3H1

BISHOP, DAVID FULTON, library administrator; b. N.Y.C., Nov. 23, 1937; s. Donald McLean and Clara (Zelley) B.; m. Nancy Driscoll, May 15, 1959; children: Karen McLean, Michael David. MusB, U. Rochester, 1959, postgrad., 1959-60; MS in Library Sci., Cath. U. Am., 1964; postgrad., U. Md., 1967-73. Head serials dept. U. Md. Libraries, College Park, 1967-69, coordinator tech. services, 1969-70, head systems, 1970-73; head cataloger U. Chgo. Libraries, 1973-75, asst. dir. tech. services, 1975-79; dir. libraries U. Ga., Athens, 1979-87; prof., univ. librarian U. Ill., Urbana, 1987-92; univ. libr. Northwestern U., Evanston, Ill., 1992—; trustee Ednl. Comms. (EDUCOM), Washington, 1988-94; bd. dirs. Ctr. for Rsch. Librs., 1992-99; vice-chmn. bd. dirs. Ctr. for Rsch. Librs., 1996-97; chmn. bd. dirs. Ctr. for Rsch. Librs., 1997-98. Mem. ALA, INFORMA (steering com. 1989-93), Assn. Coll. and Rsch. Librs., Coun. on Libr. Resources (proposal rev. com. 1991-95), Coalition for Networked Info. (steering com. 1992-98). Home: 2518 Indian Ridge Dr Glenview IL 60025-1032 Office: Northwestern U Librs Evanston IL 60201

BISHOP, DAVID JOHN, physicist; b. Montgomery, Ala., Oct. 6, 1951; s. Cleo Merton Bishop and Dorothy Johanna Rielly; m. Vanessa Joy Levin, Aug. 22 1982; 1 child, Noah Samuel Bishop. BS in Physics magna cum laude, Syracuse U., 1973; MS in Physics, Cornell U., 1977, PhD, 1978. Postdoctoral mem. tech. staff AT&T Bell Lab., Murray Hill, N.J., 1978-79, mem. tech. staff, 1979-88, head, microstructure physics rsch. dept., 1988-99; head micromechanics rsch. dept. Bell Labs-Lucent Tech., New Providence, N.J., 1999—; adj. prof. physics SUNY, Buffalo. Contbr. to profl. jours. Recipient Bausch and Lomb Hon. Sci. award, 1969. Fellow Am. Phys. Soc.; mem. Phi Beta Kappa. Office: Bell Labs Lucent Techs Rm 1D-231 700 Mountain Ave New Providence NJ 07974*

BISHOP, ELIZABETH SHREVE, psychologist; b. Ann Arbor, Mich., Nov. 18, 1951; d. William Warner Jr. and Mary Fairfax (Shreve) B. AB, U. Mich., 1972; MA, Ohio State U., 1973, PhD, 1976. Lic. psychologist, Mich. Psychologist Franklin County Program for the Mentally Retarded, Columbus, Ohio, 1974, WC Mental Health, Willmar, Minn., 1977-83; chief psychologist Battle Creek (Mich.) Child Guidance Ctr., 1981; dir. psychometrics Meridian Profl. Psychol. Cons., East Lansing, Mich., 1983-92; pres. Arbor Psychol. Cons., Ann Arbor, 1991—. Troop leader Girl Scouts U.S.A., Minn., Mich., Ohio, 1971-87, trainer, 1993—; deacon 1st Congl. Ch., 1996—. Assoc. Univ. London Inst. Edn., 1976. Fellow Am. Orthopsychiat. Assn.; mem. APA, AAUW, Mich. Psychol. Assn., Mich. Women Psychologists, Coun. for Exceptional Children (local pres. 1977-78), Internat. Coun. Psychologists (bd. dirs. 1999—), Internat. Sch. Psychology Assn., LWV (Willmar v.p. 1989-91). Avocations: reading, traveling, birdwatching, photography, music. Home: 1612 Morton Ave Ann Arbor MI 48104-4441 Office: Arbor Psychol Cons 1565 Eastover Pl Ann Arbor MI 48104-6316

BISHOP, GEORGE FRANKLIN, political scientist, educator; b. New Haven, July 26, 1942; s. George Elwood and Mary Bridget (Trant) B.; m. Pama Mitchell, July 15, 1995; 1 child, Kristina. BS in Psychology, Mich. State U., 1966, MA, 1969, PhD, 1973. Instr. multidisciplinary social sci. program Mich. State U., East Lansing, 1972-73; asst. prof. dept. sociology and anthropology U. Notre Dame, Ind., 1973-75; dir. Greater Cin. Survey, 1981-95; rsch. assoc. behavioral sci. lab U. Cin., 1975-77, sr. rsch. assoc. Inst. for Policy Rsch., 1981-93, dir. behavioral scis. lab., 1994-95, assoc. prof. polit. sci., 1982-87, prof., 1987—, dir. grad. cert. program in pub. opinion and survey rsch., 1999—; assoc. dir. Ohio Poll, 1981-95; guest prof. Zentrum für Umfragen, Methoden und Analysen, Mannheim, Germany, 1985, 90, 92; fellow Ctr. for Study of Dem. Citizenship, Dept. Polit. Sci., U. Cin., 1992—, fellow Inst. for Data Scis., 1996—; summer inst. faculty Survey Rsch. Ctr., Inst. for Social Rsch., U. Mich., summer 1993; sr. cons. Burke Mktg. Rsch., Inc., Cin., 1996-98. Sr. editor The Presdl. Debates: Media, Electoral and Policy Perspectives, 1978; sr. author various articles in profl. jours.; mem. editorial bd. Pub. Opinion Quar., 1987-90. Served with U.S. Army N.G., 1960-63. NSF grantee, 1977-84. Mem. AAUP, Midwest Assn. Pub. Opinion Rsch. (pres. 1977-78, Mapor fellow Disting. Scholarship in pub. opinion rsch. 1994), Am. Assn. Pub. Opinion Rsch., Am. Polit. Sci. Assn., World Assn. Pub. Opinion Rsch. (treas. 1983-85). Home: 825 Dunore Rd Cincinnati OH 45220-1416 Office: U Cin Cincinnati OH 45221-0375

BISHOP, GEORGE WILLIAMS, III, supply company executive; b. Williamson, W.Va., May 11, 1936; s. George W. and Dorothy Ann (Scott) B.; BEE, Va. Mil. Inst., 1958; postgrad. U. Va., 1959; m. Nancy Lee Long, Dec. 4, 1976; 1 child, Rebecca Lee; children by previous marriage: George Williams IV, Angela, Brett, Dale Scott. Mgr. elec. div. Buchanan Williamson Supply Co., Grundy, Va., 1962-64, exec. v.p., 1964-77, pres., chmn., 1977-85, dir., 1964-85 ; v.p., gen. mgr. Wingfield & Hundley, Inc., Richmond, Va., 1966-69, pres., 1969-72; chmn. Grundy Coal and Dock Co., 1977-85 , Royal Mgmt. Cons., 1983-86. Served to capt. USAF, 1959-62. Mem. Rotary (local pres. 1965-66). Republican. Presbyterian. Home: 1126 S Federal Hwy Ste 395 Fort Lauderdale FL 33316-1257 Winter Home: 1020 Ponce De Leon Dr Fort Lauderdale FL 33316-1359

BISHOP, GERALD IVESON, pharmaceutical executive; b. Madras, India, Apr. 19, 1935; came to U.S., 1961; s. James Alfred and Muriel Madeleine (Waller) B.; m. Bridget Carey, June 30, 1960; children: Elizabeth, James, Frances, Catherine. BSME, Durham U., Newcastle Upon Tyne, Eng., 1960; MS in Indsl. Engring., MBA, SUNY, Buffalo, 1971. Bus. cons. Associated Indsl. Cons., London, 1964-67; mgr. indsl. engring. Bell Aerospace, Buffalo, 1967-70; exec. asst. to CEO Ayerst Labs. Inc., Rouses Point, N.Y., 1971-76; mgr. I.E. E.R. Squibb & Sons, North Brunswick, N.J., 1977-78; mgr. internat. tech. ops. Johnson & Johnson, New Brunswick, N.J., 1978-92. Mayor Champlain (N.Y.) Cmty., 1975-77. Fellow IEE, Mech. Engrs. (U.K.); mem. Profl. Engrs. Ont., Freemasons (champlain lodge #237). Republican. Avocations: gourmet cooking, shooting, computer technology, travel, reading non-fiction. Home: 877 Penn Estates East Stroudsburg PA 18301-8614

BISHOP, GORDON BRUCE, journalist; b. Paterson, N.J., Jan. 1, 1938; s. Charles E. and Freda Mary (Romyns) B.; m. Jeanne Ann Reed, June 30, 1962; children: Jennifer, Elizabeth. Student, Am. Acad. Dramatic Arts, 1957; BA, Rutgers U., 1967. Reporter, columnist Herald-News, Passaic, N.J., 1959-67; spl. writer Star-Ledger, Newark, N.J., 1969-95; pres., TV prodr. Bishop Pub. Programs, Inc., Eatontown, N.J., 1996—; lectr. Rutgers U., Princeton U. Author: (with Frank Papps) The Purple Canary, 1963, Holding Onto Nothing, 1969, Gems of New Jersey, 1985, Greater Newark: A Microcosm of America, 1989, Gateway to America, 1998; prodr. documentaries including It's My Home for PBS, 1980, Every Day Is Earth Day, 1990, The Baykeeper, 1993, Global War on Pollution, 1994, Gateway to America, 1995; prodr.-collaborator (mus.) Crispus, 1986; columnist N.J. Commerce mag., N.J. Mayors mag., The Patriot N.J., The Courier; syndicated columnist. Environ. commr. Eatontown, N.J., 1973-76; chmn. N.J. Lit. Hall of Fame; dir. Battleship N.J. fundraising campaign, Middletown, N.J., 1998—. Recipient Disting. Pub. Service award N.J. Profl. Soc. Engrs., Nat. Environ. awards Scripps-Howard Found., 1971-75; Nat. Conservation awards Washington Journalism Ctr., 1971-72; Conservation award N.J. Audubon Soc., 1973; named Man of Yr. AABC Congregation, Irvington, N.J.; N.J. Press Assn. awards, 1971-88; N.J. Pub. Health Assn. award, 1987; Mid-Atlantic States Air Pollution Control Assn. Disting. Service award, 1987; named N.J. Journalist of Yr., 1986; Pub. Service award N.J. Profl. Journalism Soc., 1972, 73, 74, 76, 78, N.J. Conf. Mayors award, 1974; Nat. Recycling award Nat. Recycling Assn., 1973; Gold medal N.J. Garden Club, 1980; award Ballew/McFarland Found., 1981, N.J. Agrl. Soc., 1981; Nat. Wildlife Fedn.'s Nat. Conservation Achievement award, 1987, Good Journalism award Nat. Assn. Water Cos., 1992; Inst. Internat. Edn. scholar, U. Manchester, Eng., 1972; Environ. Edn. award N.J. Edn. Assn., 1990, Environ. award Am. Soc. Landscape Architects, 1993, 94. Mem. Rutgers U. Alumni Assn. *The will to live, to learn, and to inspire others flows from a genuine desire to want to work at your best and to share your love with those who seek it. This is our destiny: Work and Love. Without either, you can never realize your full potential as an individual.*

BISHOP, J. JOE, social studies educator; b. St. Petersburg, Fla., May 3, 1962; s. James Joseph and V. Joyce (Marigold) B.; m. Nola Marie Trapp, July 29, 1989; children: Kaia, Courtney, Jim, Katie. AA with Honors, Rainy River Cmty. Coll., International Falls, Minn., 1984; BA cum laude Comms. Theory & Psychology, Winona State U., 1987; MA in Sociology, U. Iowa, Iowa City, 1989, MA in Anthropology, 1995; PhD in Social Studies Edn., U. Iowa, 1999. Tchr. sociology, rsch. asst. U. Iowa, Iowa City, 1987-89, tchg. asst. anthropology, 1991-93, tchg. asst. edn., 1996, project coord., 1996-99, rsch. asst. edn., 1996-97, test item devel., summer 1997, college supr., 1996-98; grad. tchg. fellow U. Oreg., Eugene, 1989-90; adj. prof. Kirkwood C.C., Iowa City, 1990—; presenter in field. Contbr. articles to profl. jours. Mem. Am. Ednl. Rsch. Assn., Am. Anthropological Assn., Am. Sociological Assn., Nat. Coun. Social Studies, Comparative & Internat. Edn. Soc., Soc. Study Symbolic Interaction. Avocation, carpentry.

BISHOP, JAMES DODSON, lawyer, mediator; b. Washington, Sept. 28, 1957; s. James William and Jane Lillian (Dodson) B. BA magna cum laude in Polit. Sci., Lincoln (Pa.) U., 1979; JD, Howard U., Washington, 1982. Bar: Pa. 1985. Dir., atty., Client Arbitration Bd. D.C. Bar, Washington, 1987-93; dir. Archdiocesan Legal Network of Cath. Charities, Washington, 1993—. Mediator, D.C. Superior Ct., Washington, 1987—; lay reader St. Georges Episcopal Ch., Washington, 1984—. Mem. ABA (vice chmn. State and Local Bar Dispute Resolution com., 1986—). Democrat. Episcopalian. Avocation: church activities. Home: 5157 33rd St NW Washington DC 20008-2011 Office: Catholic Charities 1221 Massachusetts Ave NW Washington DC 20005-5302

BISHOP, JAMES FRANCIS, executive search consulting company executive; b. Chgo., Mar. 14, 1937; s. Francis Joseph and Margaret Rose (Nagle) B.; m. Shirley Ann McNulty, Oct. 13, 1962; children: Michael Francis, Noreen Maura, James Francis Jr. BA, Marquette U., 1961, MA, 1965. Spl. agt. Office of Naval Intelligence, Chgo., 1962-65; sr. assoc. Burke & O'Brien Assoc., Inc., N.Y.C., 1965-67, v.p., 1967-74, sr. v.p., 1974-78, pres., 1978-83; pres., CEO Burke, O'Brien & Bishop Assoc., Inc., Princeton, N.J., 1983—. Trustee George St. Playhouse, 1988-93, N.J. Hosp. Assn., 1996—; trustee St. Francis Med. Ctr., Trenton, N.J., 1989—, chmn. bd., 1991-96; chmn., bd. trustees St. Francis Med. Ctr. Found., 1998—; councilman Piscataway, 1968-71. With USMC, 1954-57. Mem. Marquette U. Alumni Assn. (v.p. 1985-87, pres. 87-88). Republican. Roman Catholic. Clubs: Marquette (N.Y.), Springdale Golf Club (Princeton). Home: 33 Richard Ct Princeton NJ 08540-3802 Office: Burke O'Brien & Bishop Assocs 1000 Herrontown Rd Princeton NJ 08540-7716

BISHOP, JAMES FRANCIS, lawyer; b. Oak Park, Ill., Aug. 25, 1940; s. George H. and Helen E. (Newcomb) B.; m. Barbara Anderson; children: Christopher J., Pamela J., Jennifer Lynn. BS, St. Joseph's Coll., Rensselaer, Ind., 1963; JD, Chgo. Kent Coll., 1966. Bar: Ill. 1966, Nev. 1989; cert. food handling specialist, Ill. Trust officer Am. Nat. Bank & Trust Co., Chgo., 1964-67; assoc. Gould & Ratner, Chgo., 1967-73; ptnr. Bishop & Callas, Crystal Lake, Ill., 1973-98, Law Offices of James F. Bishop, Crystal Lake, Ill., 1998—; mem. panel Am. Arbitration Assn. Dir. Adult and Child Rehab. Ctr., Woodstock, Ill., 1974—; vice chmn. McHenry County Sch. Dist. reorganization com., Woodstock, 1985-87, McHenry County Ducks Unltd., Crystal Lake, 1976-89; bd. dirs. No. Ill. Med. Ctr., 1980-82;. Mem. Nat. Solid Waste Assn. Mgmt. (mem. legis. com. 1988), Govt. Refuse Collection and Disposal Assn. (mem. legis. com. 1986-88), McHenry County Bar Assn., Ill. State Bar Assn., Clark County Bar Assn., State of Nev. Bar Assn., Ill. Restaurant Assn. Office: Law Offices of James F Bishop 550 W Woodstock St Crystal Lake IL 60014-3425

BISHOP, JOHN MICHAEL, biomedical research scientist, educator; b. York, Pa., Feb. 22, 1936; married 1959; 2 children. AB, Gettysburg Coll., 1957; MD, Harvard U., 1962; DSc (hon.), Gettysburg Coll., 1983. Intern in internal medicine Mass. Gen. Hosp., Boston, 1962-63, resident, 1963-64; rsch. assoc. virology NIH, Washington, 1964-66, sr. investigator, 1966-68; from asst. prof. to assoc. prof. U. Calif. Med. Ctr., San Francisco, 1968-72, prof. microbiology and immunology, 1972—, prof. biochemistry and biophysics, 1982—; dir. G.W. Hooper Rsch. Found. G.W. Hooper Rsch. Found., 1981—; Univ. prof. U. Calif. Med. Ctr., San Francisco, 1994—; chancellor U. Calif. Med. Ctr., San Francisco, 1998—. Recipient Nobel prize in physiology or medicine, 1989, Biomed. Rsch. award Am. Assn. Med. Colls., 1981, Albert Lasker Basic Med. Rsch. award, 1981, Armand Hammer Cancer award, 1984, GM Found. Cancer Rsch. award, 1984, Gairdner Found. Internat. award, Can., 1984, Medal of Honor, Am. Cancer Soc., 1984; NIH grantee, 1968—. Fellow Salk Inst. (trustee 1991—); mem. NAS, Inst. Medicine, Nat. Cancer Adv. Bd. Achievements include research in biochemistry of animal viruses, replication of nucleic acids, oncogenesis, control of cell growth, and molecular genetics. Office: U Calif Med Ctr Dept Microbiology Box 0552 San Francisco CA 94143-0552

BISHOP, JOYCE ANN, special programs counselor; b. West Mansfield, Ohio, June 16, 1935; d. Frederic J. and Marjorie Vere (Stephens) Armentrout; m. Belinda Lee, Thomas James. AB, Albion Coll., 1956; MA, Western Mich. U., 1969, postgrad., 1972-87. Cert. social worker; lic. profl. counselor. Tchr. phys. edn., health and cheerleading Walled Lake (Mich.) Jr. High Sch., 1956-58; instr. slimnastics adult edn. Milw. Pub. Schs., 1959-65; demonstrator, co. rep. Polaroid Corp., Cambridge, Mass., 1960-81; rsch. asst. fetal electrocardiography Marquette U., Milw., 1962-64; tchr. phys. edn., health and cheerleading Brown Deer (Wis.) High Sch., 1963-65; instr. slimnastics adult edn., instr. volleyball Lakeview High Sch., Battle Creek, Mich., 1966—; dir. student activities, asst. prof. Olivet (Mich.) Coll., 1969-71; transfer counselor spl. programs Kellogg C.C., Battle Creek, 1971—; fin. planner Richard M. Groff Assocs., Inc., 1987. Sec. adult bd. Teens, Inc., 1965-68; bd. dirs. Battle Creek Day Care Ctrs., sec., 1984, pres., 1984-86; founder Battle Creek Breast Cancer Support Group, 1996-99; team capt. United Way Awareness Week, 1984, allocations com. 1985-92; chmn. allocations com. United Way, 1990, 91, 92, 93, United Arts Fund Drive, 1985, chmn., 1986; chair Battle Creek Race for the Cure Survivors, 1996-99; v.p. Southwest Mich. affiliate Susan G. Komen Breast Cancer Found., 1998-99; mem. Battle Creek Leadership Acad. Recipient Master Teaching award Lakeview Schs., 1969, 87. Mem. AAUW, Mich. Assn. Collegiate Registrars and Admissions Officers (pres. 1979-80, historian 1984-87, hon. mem. 1992), Am. Assn. Collegiate Registrars and Admissions Officers (mem. com. 1984-87), Am. Pers. and Guidance Assn., Am. Coll. Pers. Assn., Mich. Pers. and Guidance Assn., Mich. Coll. Pers. Assn., Mich. Assn. Women Deans, Adminstrs. and Counselors, Mich. Assn. Coll. Admissions Counselors, Mich. Occupl. Edn. Assn. (Outstanding Svc. award 1991), Mich. Occupl. Needs Assn. (Spl. Needs Profl. of Yr. 1991), Alpha Chi Omega (selected Outstanding Spl. Needs Profl. in Mich. 1991), Beta Beta Beta. Clubs: Battle Creek Road Runners (v.p. 1983-85), Battle Creek Altrusa, Battle Creek Host Lions Club (asst. sec. 1994-96). Home: 721 Eastfield Dr Battle Creek MI 49015-3823 Office: Kellog Community Coll 450 North Ave Battle Creek MI 49017-3306

BISHOP, JUNE A., secondary education educator; b. Orlando, Fla., June 17, 1950; d. Roy A. and Florence A. (Bensinger) Moyer; m. Perry Charles Bishop, Aug. 18, 1973 (div. June 1986); children: Charly Erin, Tommy Shannon. BA in Math., Fla. State U., 1972; MS in Ops. Rsch., Naval Postgrad. Sch., 1987. Cert. tchr., Fla., Va. Tchr. Orange County Pub. Schs., Orlando, 1972-74; commd. USN, 1976, advanced through grades to lt. comdr., 1985; database mgr., project mgr. Data Processing Svc. Ctr., Pearl Harbor, Hawaii, 1977-79; morale, welfare and recreation officer Naval Activities, U.K. Detachment, Holy Loch, Scotland, 1979-81; logistics plans officer Comdr. in Chief, U.S. Naval Forces Europe, London, 1982-85, Chief Naval Ops., Washington, 1987-90; officer in charge Personnel Support Det., Willow Grove, Pa., 1990-91; instr., exec. asst. U.S. Naval Acad., Annapolis, Md., 1992-94; tchr. math. Garfield H.S., Woodbridge, Va., 1994—. Mem. troop com. Boy Scouts of Am., Annapolis, 1992-94, Lakeridge, Va., 1994-98; treas. Epiphany Luth. Ch., Dale City, Va., 1996-98. Recipient Meritorious Svc. medal, 1990, 94. Mem. Math. Assn. Am., Assn. Women in Math. Avocations: needlework-knitting, crocheting, cross-stitching, crewel, latch hook sewing.

BISHOP, KAY, media educator; b. Grand Forks, N.D., June 16, 1942; d. Arnold Franklin and Louise Thelma (Thompson) Cecka; divorced; children: James C., Jennifer K., Lara G. BA, Fla. State U., 1963, PhD, 1992; MEd, Wash. State U., 1979; MA, U. South Fla., 1984. Cert. media specialist, English tchr., Fla. Media specialist Samoset and Blackburn Elem. Sch., Bradenton, Fla., 1970-71, Bradenton Christian Sch., 1974-84, Palmetto (Fla.) H.S., 1984-92, Sportfield Elem. Sch., Hanau, Germany, 1992-93; reference libr. U. South Fla., Sarasota, 1988-90; libr. Am. Sch. in Switzerland, Montagnala-Lugano, 1993-94; asst. prof. Murray (Ky.) State U., 1994-95, U. So. Miss., Hattiesburg, 1995-97, U. Ky., Lexington, 1997—; chair silver medallion com. Children's Book Festival, U. Miss., 1997—. Contbr. articles to profl. pubs. Mem. Returned Peace Corps Vols., 1965—, Friends of Nepal, 1965—; pres. Manatee (Fla.) Assn. for Media in Edn., 1986-88. Nat. Edn. Assn. title II grantee, 1990-91; Fla. Assn. Media in Edn. scholar, 1990-91. Mem. ALA (conf. com. 1996-97), Am. Assn. Sch. Librs. (nat. rsch. com. 1996—), Assn. Libr. and Info. Sci. Edn., Young Adult Libr. Svcs. Assn. (nat. rsch. com. 1997—), Educators of Libr. Media Specialists (sec.), Internat. Reading Assn., Phi Kappa Phi, Beta Phi Mu. Democrat. Presbyterian. Avocations: reading, swimming. Office: U Ky Sch Libr and Info Sci 502 King Libr S Lexington KY 40506-0039

BISHOP, LEO KENNETH, clergyman, educator; b. Britton, Okla., Oct. 11, 1911; s. Luther and Edith (Scovill) B.; m. Pauline T. Shamburg, Sept. 15, 1935; 1 dau., Linda Paulette. A.B., Phillips U., 1932; L.H.D., 1958; M.A., Columbia U., 1944; M.B.A., U. Chgo., 1957; Litt.D., Kansas City Coll. Osteopathy and Surgery, 1964. Ordained to ministry Christian Ch., 1932; asso. minister Univ. Place Ch., Oklahoma City, 1932-35; minister First Ch., Paducah, Ky., 1935-41, Central Ch., Des Moines, 1941-45; dir. St. Louis office NCCJ, 1945-48; v.p., dir. central div. NCCJ, Chgo., 1949-63; dir. pub. affairs People-to-People, Kansas City, Mo., 1963-66; v.p. Chgo. Coll. Osteopathy, 1966-72; pres. Bishop Enterprises, Colorado Springs, Colo., 1972—; also lectr. Contbr. religious and edni. jours.; Developed: radio series Storm Warning; TV series The Other Guy, 1954. Cons. Community Social Planning Council, Mayor's Race Relations Com., YMCA, St. Louis; Am. del. Conf. World Brotherhood, Paris, 1950; bd. dirs. Am. Heritage Found. Recipient Paducah Jr. C. of C. Most Useful Citizen award, 1937, Distinguished Service award Dore Miller Found., 1958, Freedom Found. of Valley Forge award, 1961; named Chicagoan of Year, 1960. Clubs: Rotary, Union League, Winter Night. Home: 107 W Cheyenne Rd Colorado Springs CO 80906-2550 Office: PO Box 843 Colorado Springs CO 80901-0843

BISHOP, LINDA BAXTER, critical care nurse; b. Wareham, Mass., Mar. 3, 1955; d. Donald E. and Norma L. (Buell) Baxter; m. Eugene E. Bishop, June 2, 1979; 1 child, Heather Rachelle. BSN, U. Va., 1977. Cert. critical care nurse. Staff nurse U. Va., Charlottesville, 1977-79; staff nurse, surg. ICU No. Va. Drs. Hosp., Arlington, 1979-89; staff nurse ICU Self Meml. Hosp., Greenwood, S.C., 1989-92, Augusta Med. Ctr., Fishersville, 1992—. Mem. Sigma Theta Tau.

BISHOP, MARY FERN, editor; b. Ada, Okla., Sept. 12, 1961; d. Thurston A. and Fern Marie (Martin) B. BA, East Ctrl. U., 1983; MS in Mass Comm., Ark. State U., 1985. Reporter Bristow (Okla.) News & Record Citizen, 1985-86; copy editor Daily Oklahoman, Oklahoma City, 1986; instr., asst. prof. East Ctrl. U., Ada, Okla., 1986-95; copy editor Tulsa World, 1995-96, asst. city editor, 1996—; adj. prof. U. Ctr. Okla., 1995; mem. adv. bd. Freedom Info. Okla., Inc., 1993-96. Editor: Mass Communication Law in Oklahoma, 1990. mem. media rels. steering com. Citizens for Econ. Devel., Ada; co-founder So. Okla. Support for HIV, Ada; vol. Meals on Wheels, Ada, Habitat for Humanity, Ada. Mem. Soc. Profl. Journalists, Kappa Tau Alpha. Mem. Christian Ch. (Disciples of Christ). Avocations: canoeing, whitewater rafting. Office: Tulsa World PO Box 1770 Tulsa OK 74102-1770

BISHOP, MAUREEN E., critical care nurse, clinical nurse specialist; b. Watervliet, Mich., Jan. 28, 1957; d. Howard D. and Dolores M. (Kling) B. MSN, Grand Valley State U., 1994; MA, Western Mich. U., 1991. Clin. nurse specialist Lakeland Regional Healthcare Sys., St. Joseph, Mich. Mem. AACN, Nat. Assn. Critical Nurse Specialists, Am. Heart Assn., Sigma Theta Tau, Phi Kappa Phi.

BISHOP, MICHAEL D., emergency physician; b. Anna, Ill., Feb. 10, 1945; m. Mary Susan Wilkens, Dec. 28, 1965; children: Amy Elizabeth, Amanda Marie. AB, GreenvilleColl., 1967; MD, U. Ill., 1971. Diplomate Am. Bd. Emergency Medicine (oral examiner 1980—, dir. 1988-96, mem. exec. com. 1990-95, mem. several bd. coms., sec.-treas. 1991-92, pres.-elect 1992-93, pres. 1993-94). Intern Meth. Hosp. Dallas, 1971-72; emergency physician Bloomington (Ind.) Hosp., 1972—, Morgan County Meml. Hosp., Martinsville, Ind., 1978—, Fayette Meml. Hosp., Connersville, Ind., 1989—, Jackson County Meml. Hosp., Seymour, Ind., 1989—; gen. dir. Immediate Care Ctrs. in Ind., various cities, 1981—; clin. assoc. prof. med. scis. Ind. U., Bloomington, 1980—; pres., CEO Unity Physician Group P.C., Bloomington, Ind., 1971—. Bd. trustee, Sunday sch. tchr. Ellettsville (Ind.) Christian Ch.; bd. dirs. Peoples State Bank, Ellettsville; bd. dirs., sec. Ellettsville Bancshares, Ellettsville Elem. Sch. Bldg. Corp. Fellow Am. Coll. Emergency Physicians (charter, pres. Ind. chpt. 1979-80, nat. councillor 1976-81, 83, mem. nat. multi-hosp./multi-state blue ribbon task force 1981, mem. nat. ins. com. 1976-77, mem. coun. long-range planning com. 1981-82, mem. coun. steering com. 1983-85, chmn. medicare task force 1984-86, chmn. task force on physician payment reform 1986-88, mem. govt. affairs com. 1983-88, 89-93, chmn. 1984-87, 89-93, mem. nat. emergency medicine polit. action com. bd. trustees 1984-88, 89-93, chmn. 1987, 89-93, mem. fin. com. 1987-93, James D. Mills Outstanding Contbn. to Emergency Medicine award 1990, mem. awards com. 1991-93, mem. reimbursement com. 1992—, dir. 1995—, lectr. in field), AHA (mem. Ind. affil. faculty, ACLS), Am. Coll. Physician Execs., Soc. Acad. Emergency Medicine, Christian Med. Dental Soc., Ind. State Med. Assn., Med. Group Mgmt. Assn., Owen Monroe County Med. Soc. Office: Unity Physician Group PC 1155 W 3rd St Bloomington IN 47404-5016*

BISHOP, NANCY STEPHANIE, nurse, health educator; b. San Francisco, July 29, 1942. Diploma in nursing, Jackson Meml. Hosp., 1963; BS in Health Svcs. Adminstrn., Fla. Internat. U., 1979; MS in Human Resources Mgmt., Nova U., 1981; postgrad. in Human Svcs. Adminstrn., U. Sarasota. RN, CNAA. Head nurse Hialeah (Fla.) Hosp., 1964-66; pvt. duty nurse Venice, Fla., 1966-67; staff nurse emergency rm., ICU Onslow Meml. Hosp., Jacksonville, N.C., 1967-68; nursing supr. Hialeah Hosp., Hialeah, 1968-74; adminstr. supr. Venice Hosp., Venice, 1974-79, coord. patient edn., 1979-80, asst. dir. nursing for edn., 1980-81, asst. v.p. for nursing, 1981-85, dir. ednl. svcs., 1985-98; faculty Nat. Louis U., 1998—; affiliate faculty Am. Heart Assn., Fla.; mem. adv. bd., health careers instr. Sarasota (Fla.) County Tech. Inst. Bd. regents Fla. Assn. Direct Vol. Svcs. Mem. Fla. Hosp. Assn., S.W. Fla. Educators, Fla. Soc. Health Edn. & Tng. (bd. dirs. 1992-93). Baptist.

BISHOP, OLIVER RICHARD, state official; b. El Dorado, Kans., Dec. 5, 1928; s. Oliver Harrison and Hazel May (Garabrandt) B.; m. Fuyo Oyake, Aug. 14, 1959; children: Lisa Naomi, Rachel Eri. BS in Pub. Adminstrn. magna cum laude, U. So. Calif., 1963; MS in Econs cum laude, U. S.D., 1971. Cert. planner, office automation profl., assisted housing mgr.; lic. steam engr., Ohio. Commd. 2d lt. USAF, 1956, advanced through grades to maj., 1966, ret., 1971; city mgr. City of Slater, Mo., 1971-73, City of Highland, Ill., 1973-76, City of Napoleon, Ohio, 1976-77; village mgr. Village of Westmont, Ill., 1977-85; revenue and fiscal advisor State of Ill., Chgo., 1985—; planning cons. Bishop's Cons. Services, Westmont, 1985—. Precinct committeeman Rep. Ctrl. com., Dupage County, Ill., 1987-88; candidate for County Bd. Dupage County Dist. 3, 1988; com. chmn. Westmont Planning Commn., 1986-95, 97—; bd. dirs. T.E.A.C.H., Inc., I-Care, Inc. Mem. IEEE, Internat. City Mgmt. Assn., Am. Planning Assn., Am. Inst. Cert. Planners, Govt. Fin. Officers Assn., Office Automation Soc. Internat., Mensa, Intertel, Elks, Masons, Shriners, Pi Sigma Alpha, Omicron Delta Epsilon (pres. Lambda chpt.). Mem. Ch. of Christ. Avocations: philately, photography. Office: Ill Dept Commerce and Community Affairs 100 W Randolph St Ste 3400 Chicago IL 60601-3219

BISHOP, ROB, political party executive. Chmn. Utah State Rep. Party, 1997—. Office: 117 E South Temple Salt Lake City UT 84111-1101*

BISHOP, ROBERT CHARLES, architect, metals and minerals company executive; b. Butte, Mont., June 6, 1929; s. Lester Farragut and Helen Katherine (Bauman) B.; m. B. Jean Rausch, June 29, 1957; children: Desta Fawn Bishop O'Connor, Valerie Dawn. BS in Gen. Engring., Mont. State U., 1958, BArch., 1960. Assoc. architect various firms, Mont., 1960-64; owner, architect R.C. Bishop & Assocs., Butte, Great Falls and Missoula, Mont., 1965-69; owner, chief exec. officer Val-Desta 4M, Butte, 1980—, Val-Desta Mines and Minerals, Louisville, Ky., 1985—; prin. Archtl. Assocs., 1969—; chief exec. officer, pres. Cove-Lock Log Home Mfrs., Inc., Butte, 1968-72, Busy Beaver Enterprises, Great Falls, 1968-72, New Horizon Homes, Missoula, 1968-72; asst. contracts adminstr. Davy-McKee Constrn. Engrs., Butte, 1982-83. Developer 9 major and 2 minor algorithms for mineral prospecting, valid for over 100 areas in Mont. and Idaho; discoverer 100 to 300 million tons of high grade bull quarts and rock crystal, copper and molybdenum, potential world class deposits; discoverer naturally occurring minerals that when infused in a water medium are capable with electrolysis to produce 3.5 times the hydrogen as available from the electrolysis of sea water; co-patentee in field. Advisor, Kiwanis, Jaycees, Nat. Res., 1960-72, Am. Legion, 1976. With U.S. Army, 1953-55. Named One of 2,000 Men of Achievement Melrose Press, 1970, 73. Mem. Internat. Platform Assn., Nat. Hist. Soc. (founding assoc. 1971), Elk Bow Hunting Club (bugle tchr. 1970-84), Butte Mulitlist Club (real estate tchr. 1978-84), Nat. Coun. Archtl. Registeration Bds. (registered architect seismic design 1965—). Presbyterian. Achievements include research in hydraulic trompe technology to retrofit existing hydroelectric generation in a Co-generation format to increase electrical production performance, to reduce fuel consumption and reduce particulate air emissions; research in contaminated waste-water remediation; development of radial dihedral stressed skin roof lens system. Home and Office: 1008 W Galena St Butte MT 59701-1420

BISHOP, ROBERT LYLE, economist, educator; b. St. Louis, June 4, 1916; s. Lyle Austin and Helen (Craden) B.; m. Joan Frances Fiss, Sept. 12, 1942 (dec.). A.B., Harvard, 1937, M.A., 1942, Ph.D., 1949; postgrad., Princeton, 1938-39. Instr. econs. Harvard, 1939-42; mem. faculty Mass. Inst. Tech., 1942—, successively instr., asst. prof., assoc. prof., 1942-57, prof. econs., 1957-86, prof. econs. emeritus, 1986—, head dept. econs. and social sci., 1958-65; dean Sch. Humanities and Social Scis., 1964-73; vis. lectr. Harvard; vis. prof. Brandeis U. Mem. Am. Econ. Assn., Econometric Soc., Am. Acad. Arts and Scis., Phi Beta Kappa. Home: 27 Amherst Rd Wellesley MA 02482-6611 Office: Mass Inst Tech Cambridge MA 02139

BISHOP, ROBERT MILTON, former stock exchange official; b. Elmira, N.Y., June 5, 1921; s. Milton W. and Florence E. (Crofutt) B.; m. Anne Selene Rowan, Oct. 30, 1943; children: Donald M., Anne Selene (Mrs. Donald R. Bennett), Elizabeth M. (Mrs. Thomas H. Speed), Robert Milton, Regina J.M. (Mrs. David P. Bergeland), Rowan J.S. AB, Union Coll., Schenectady, 1943; AM, Trinity Coll., Hartford, Conn., 1955. Asst. dir. pub. relations Union Coll., Schenectady, 1945-47; dir. pub. relations Trinity Coll., 1947-55; mem. staff N.Y. Stock Exchange, 1955-86; dir. dept. mem. firms liaison, asst. dir. dept. mem. firms, 1961-63, v.p., assoc. dir. dept. mem. firms, 1963-65, v.p., dir. dept. mem. firms, 1965-73, sr. v.p. mem. firm regulation and surveillance group, 1973-81, sr. v.p. regulatory svcs. group, 1982-84, sr. v.p. regulatory quality rev. and long-range planning, 1984-86; cons. Lloyds of London, USAID, World Bank, Capital Markets Authorities and Stock Exchs. of Bulgaria, Dominican Republic, Egypt, Jamaica, Kazakhstan, Kenya, Hungary, Morocco, Pakistan, Serbia, Siberia, Singapore, Slovenia, Sri Lanka, Tunisia, Uganda. Author booklets, securities tng. manuals, and model basic rules for a stock exch. Trustee Cathedral Symphony at Cathedral Sacred Heart, Newark, 1984-92, Union Coll., 1989-93. With USAF, 1943-45. Episcopalian. Clubs: India House, Stock Exchange Luncheon, Mohawk. Home: 16 Heritage Ln Scotch Plains NJ 07076-2420 also: 311 E Walnut St Avon Park FL 33825-4044

BISHOP, ROY LOVITT, physics and astronomy educator; b. Wolfville, N.S., Can., Sept. 22, 1939; s. Lovett Grant and Florence May (Jodrey) B.; m. Gertrude Orinda Wellwood, June 3, 1961. B.S., Acadia U., Wolfville, 1961; M.S., McMaster U., 1963; Ph.D., U. Man., 1969. Asst. prof. physics Acadia U., Wolfville, N.S., Can., 1963-72, assoc. prof., 1972-80, prof., 1980-94; head physics dept. Acadia U., 1976-83, 86-92, hon. rsch. assoc., 1994—. Contbr. articles to profl. jours. Recipient Gov. Gen.'s medal Acadia U., 1961; asteroid (6901) Roybishop named in his honor, 1997. Mem. Royal Astron. Soc. Can. (pres. 1984-86, editor Observer's Handbook 1982—, hon. pres. Halifax Ctr. 1998—), Internat. Astron. Union, Can. Astron. Soc., Am. Assn. Physics Tchrs., Blomidon Naturalists Soc. (pres. 1994-97). Avocation: sailing. Home: Avonport, NS Canada B0P 1B0 Office: Acadia U, Dept Physics, Wolfville, NS Canada B0P 1X0

BISHOP, SANFORD DIXON, JR., congressman; b. Mobile, Ala., Feb. 4, 1947; s. Sanford Dixon Sr. and Minne (Slade) B. BA in Political Sci., Morehouse Coll., 1968; JD, Emory U., 1971. Ptnr. Bishop & Buckner, P.C., Columbus, Ga., 1972-92; mem. Ga. Ho. of Reps. from 94th Dist., 1976-90, Ga. State Senate, 1990-92, 103d Congress from 2d Ga. Dist., 1993—; agrl. intelligence com. 105th Congress from 2d Ga. Dist., 1996—; del. Dem. Nat. Conv. 1980, 84, 88; mem. Agrl. Com., Vets. Affairs Com.; chmn. Ga. legis. black caucus. Fellowship, 1971-72; named Man of the Yr. Men's Progressive Club Columbus, Ga., 1977, Black Georgian of the Yr., 1983, Most Influential Black Men in Ga.; recipient Outstanding Legis. award Ga. NOW, 1983-84, Legis. Svc. award, Ga. Mcpl. Assn., 1984, 86, Friend of the Children award Child Adv. Coalition. Mem. ABA, Nat. Bar Assn., Ga. Bar Assn., Ala. Bar Assn., Am. Judicature Soc., Shriners, Masons (32 degree), Phi Delta Phi, Pi Sigma Alpha, Kappa Alpha Psi. Democrat. Baptist. Office: US Ho of Reps 1433 Longworth Bldg Ofc Washington DC 20515-1002 also: Albany Towers 235 W Roosevelt Ave Ste 216 Albany GA 31701-2374*

BISHOP, SID GLENWOOD, union official; b. Gladehill, Va., Nov. 11, 1923; s. Clarence Glenwood and Lillian Helen (Onks) B.; m. Carol Faye Miller, Mar. 2, 1990. Grad., U.S. Naval Trade Sch., 1942; cert. in labor rels., Concord Coll., Athens, W.Va., 1961. Telegraph operator Virginian R.R., 1946-47, C & O R.R., 1947-62; local chmn. Order R.R. Telegraphers, 1960-62; gen. chmn. C & O-Virginian R.R.'s, 1962-68; 2d v.p. Transp.-Communication Employees Union, St. Louis, 1968-69; v.p. transp. com. divsn. Brotherhood Ry. and Airline Clks., Rockville, Md., 1969-73; asst. internat. v.p. Brotherhood Ry. and Airline Clks., Rockville, 1973—; mem. subcom. Labor Rsch. Adv. Coun., Dept. Labor, 1975, mem. com. on productivity, tech., growth Bur. Labor Statistics, 1975-77. With USN, 1941-46. Mem. AFL-CIO, Can. Labor Congress, Hunting Hills Homeowners Assn., VFW, Chantilly Nat. Golf and Country Club, Elks, Masons, K.T., Shriners. Home and Office: 676 NE 28th Ave Okeechobee FL 34972-3323

BISHOP, SIDNEY WILLARD, lawyer; b. Denver, Oct. 28, 1926; s. Sidney W. and Helen (Marihugh) B.; m. Betty Lou Dolan, May 10, 1947; children—Linda, Thomas, Nancy, Joan, Ann, Mary, Elizabeth, Sidney Willard III, Jane. BS, Regis U., Denver, 1949; J.D., U. Denver, 1950. Bar: Colo. 1950, Calif. 1958. With January & Yegge, Denver, 1949-50; dep. dist. atty. Cheyenne County, Colo., 1951-56; pvt. practice Cheyenne Wells, Colo., 1950-56; with Prudential Ins. Co. Am., Los Angeles, 1956-61, 64-68; asst. counsel law dept., 1958-61, asst. gen. solicitor, 1964-66, dir. govt. relations, 1966-68; gen. counsel Am. Ins. Assn., N.Y.C., 1968-70; with firm Svenson & Garvin, Van Nuys, Calif., 1970-73; sr. v.p., gen. counsel Beneficial Standard Life Ins. Co., 1973-91; of counsel Adams, Duque, L.A., 1991-96, Beckman, Davis, Smith & Ruddy, L.A., 1996—; confidential asst. to postmaster gen. U.S., 1961, asst. postmaster gen. bur. facilities, 1962-63, dep. postmaster gen., 1963-64. So. Calif. vice chmn. Statewide Water Devel. Com., 1959-60. Served with USNR, 1944-46. Office: 601 S Figueroa St Ste 2600 Los Angeles CA 90017-5713

BISHOP, (INA) SUE MARQUIS, psychiatric and mental health nurse educator, researcher, administrator; b. Charleston, W.Va., Sept. 30, 1939; d. Harold Edwin and Ina Mabel (Walkup) Marquis; m. Randal Young Bishop, Feb. 27, 1960: children: Jon Marquis, Heather Suzanne. RN, Norton Infirmary Sch. Nursing, 1960; BSN, Murray State U., 1963; MSN, Ind. U., 1967, PhD, 1983. RN, Ky., Ind., Fla., N.C. Ind. staff nurse psychiatry Norton Infirmary, Louisville, 1960-61; head nurse obstetrics, nursing supr. Murray (Ky.) Gen. Hosp., 1961-62; primary care nurse, crisis counselor infirmary Murray State U., 1962-63; staff nurse, clin. instr. Madison (Ind.) State Hosp., 1963-65; instr. through assoc. prof. Ind. U. Sch. Nursing, Indpls., 1967-89, developer child/adolescent psychiat., mental health nursing program, 1982-83, chairperson grad. dept., 1983-89; prof., asst. dean Coll. of Nursing U. South Fla., Tampa, 1989-91; dean Coll. Nursing U. N.C., Charlotte, 1992-95; dean U. N.C. Coll. of Nursing and Health Professions, Charlotte, 1995—; pvt. practice marital and family therapy, 1975-89; cons. in field. Founding editor-in-chief Jour. of Child and Adolescent Psychiatric and Mental Health Nursing, 1987-91; contbr. articles to profl. jours. Bd. dirs. Carolinas blood svcs. region ARC, 1997—. NIHM trainee Ind. U., 1965-67, USPHS profl. nurse trainee Ind. U., 1977-78; recipient Youth Advocacy award Ind. Advs. for Child Psychiat. Nursing, 1987, Disting. Svc. award Ind. U. Sch. Nursing Alumni Assn., 1989, Nat. Youth Advocacy award Advs. for Child Psychiat. Nursing, 1990. Fellow Am. Acad. Nursing; mem. ARC (bd. dirs. 1997—), Am. Nurses Assn., Psychiat. Mental Health Nursing Coun., Soc. for Edn. and Rsch. in Psychiat. Mental Health Nursing (pres. 1988-90), Am. Assn. Marital and Family Therapy, So. Nursing Rsch. Soc., So. Piedmont Alzheimer's Assn. (bd. dirs. 1999—), New South Hospice of Charlotte and Lincoln County (bd. dirs. 1995—), Sigma Theta Tau.

BISHOP, SUSAN KATHARINE, executive search company executive; b. Palm Beach, Fla., Apr. 3, 1946; d. Warner Bader Bishop and Katharine Sue (White) McLennan; m. Robert Uchitel, Dec. 27, 1973 (div. 1979); 1 child, Rachel. B.A., Briarcliff Coll., 1968; M.B.A., Fordham U., 1985. Actress N.Y.C., 1968-72; producer, hostess Sta. KIMO-TV, Anchorage, 1972-74; dir. programming Visions Pay TV, 1974-79; recruiter Joe Sullivan & Assocs., N.Y.C., 1980-82; prin. Johnson, Smith & Knisely, 1982-88; ptnr. Schmitt Bishop Tolette, N.Y.C., 1989-91; pres. Bishop Ptnrs., Ltd., N.Y.C., 1991—. Mem. Cable TV Adminstrn. and Mktg. Soc., Women in Cable, Assn. Exec. Search Cons. (bd. dirs.). Office: Susan Bishop Assocs 708 3rd Ave New York NY 10017-4201

BISHOP, THOMAS WALTER, French language and literature educator; b. Vienna, Austria, Feb. 21, 1929; came to U.S., 1940, naturalized, 1944; s. Martin M. and Katherine (Abeles) B.; m. Muriel Hausman, June 30, 1950 (div. 1967); children: Jeffrey Bishop (dec.), Katherine; m. Helen Gary, Dec. 15, 1967. AB, NYU, 1950; AM, U. Md., 1951; postgrad., U. Paris, 1950-51; PhD, U. Calif., Berkeley, 1957. Asst. in French U. Calif., Berkeley, 1951-55; instr. NYU, 1956-59, asst. prof., 1959-61, assoc. prof., 1961-64, prof., 1964—, Florence Gould prof. French lit., 1975—, dir. La Maison Française, 1959-64, chmn. dept. French, 1966—; chmn. Ctr. for French Civilization and Culture, 1978—; vis. prof. Ecole des Hautes en Scis. Sociales, Paris, 1980, 87, 94, 99, Harvard U., 1995; cons. NEH, 1980—. Author: Pirandello and the French Theater, 1960, rev. edit., 1970, L'Avant-Garde Théâtrale: French Theater Since 1950, 1970, rev. edit., 1975, Huis Clos de Jean-Paul Sartre, 1975, Beckett, 1976, 2d edit., 1985, Le Passeur d'Océan, 1989, From the Left Bank, 1997; co-editor: Samuel Beckett-Cahier de l'Herne, 1976, 85. Trustee French Inst.-Alliance Française N.Y., 1971—, Lycée Francais, N.Y.C., 1989—; bd. dirs. French-Am. Found., 1976-86. Decorated chevalier Legion d'Honneur, commandeur Order Nat. du Merite, officer Ordre des Arts et Lettres, officer Palmes Academiques; recipient Obie award, 1979, Grand Prix de l'Academie Francaise, 1993; Fulbright fellow, 1965. Fellow N.Y. Inst. Humanities; mem. MLA, PEN, Beckett Soc. (pres. 1986-88). Office: NYU 19 University Pl New York NY 10003-4556

BISHOP, TILMAN MALCOLM, state senator, retired college administrator; b. Colorado Springs, Jan. 1, 1933; B.A., M.A., U. No. Colo.; m. Pat Bishop, 1951; 1 son, Barry Alan. Retired adminstr., dir. student services Mesa State Coll., Grand Junction, Colo.; mem., pres. pro tem Colo. Senate. World series com. Nat. Jr. Coll. Baseball. Served with U.S. Army. Mem. Am. Sch. Counselors Assn., Nat. Assn. for Counseling and Devel., Colo. Assn. for Counseling and Devel. Republican. Methodist. Lodges: Elks, Lions. Avocations: fishing, small game hunting. Office: State Capitol Bldg Denver CO 80203 Home: 2697 G Rd Grand Junction CO 81506-8367

BISHOP, VIRGINIA WAKEMAN, retired librarian and humanities educator; b. Portland, Oreg., Dec. 28, 1927; d. Andrew Virgil and Letha Evangeline (Ward) Wakeman; m. Clarence Edmund Bishop, Aug. 23, 1953; children: Jean Marie Bishop Johnson, Marilyn Joyce. BA, Bapt. Missionary Tng. Sch., Chgo., 1949, Linfield Coll., McMinnville, Oreg., 1952; MEd, Linfield Coll., McMinnville, Oreg., 1953; MA in Librarianship, U. Wash., 1968. Ch. worker Univ. Bapt. Ch., Seattle, 1954-56, 59-61, pre-sch. tchr. parent coop presch., 1965-66; libr. N.W. Coll., Kirkland, Wash., 1968-69; undergrad. libr. U. Wash., Seattle, 1970; libr., instr. Seattle Cen. Community Coll., 1970-91. Leader Totem coun. Girl Scouts U.S., 1962-65; pres. Wedgwood Sch. PTA, Seattle, 1964-65; chair 46th Dist. Dem. Orgn., Seattle, 1972-73; precinct com. officer Dem. Party, 1968-88, 96—; candidate Wash. State Legislature, Seattle, 1974, 80; bd. dirs. Univ. Bapt. Children's Ctr., 1989-95, chair, 1990-95; vol. Ptnrs. in Pub. Edn., 1992-96. Recipient Golden Acorn award Wedgwood Elem. Sch., 1966. Mem. LWV of Seattle (2d v.p. 1994-96), U. Wash. Grad. Sch. Libr. and Info. Sci. Alumni Assn. (1st v.p. 1986-87, pres. 1987-88). Baptist. Avocations: swimming, hiking, reading. Home: 3032 NE 87th St Seattle WA 98115-3529

BISHOP, WARNER BADER, finance company executive; b. Lakewood, Ohio, Dec. 13, 1918; s. Warner Brown and Gladys (Bader) B.; m. Katherine Sue White, Dec. 15, 1944; children: Susan, Judith, Katharine, Jennifer; m. Barrie Osborn, Feb. 4, 1967 (div. Dec. 1980); children: Wilder, Brooks.; m. Susan Bragg Howard, June 3, 1982. A.B., Dartmouth, 1941; M.B.A., Amos Tuck Grad. Sch., 1942; grad. Advanced Mgmt. Program, Harvard U., 1955. With Archer-Daniels-Midland Co., Cleve., 1946-59; successively sales rep., export mgr., sales mgr., divisional gen. mgr., asst. v.p. Archer-Daniels-Midland Co., 1946-56, v.p., 1956-59; pres. Fed. Foundry Supply Co., 1957-59, Wyodak Clay & Chem. Co., 1957-59, Basic, Inc., until 1963, Union Fin. Corp., Cleve., 1963-74; pres. Union Savs. Assn., 1963-74, chmn., 1970—; chmn., pres. Transohio Financial Corp., Cleve., 1974-85; dir. Blue Cross-Blue Shield Ohio, Med. Cons. Imaging Co.; trustee Med. Cleve. Mut.; dir. Med. Life Ins. Co.; sec. Foundry Ednl. Found., 1956-60. Contbr. articles to trade jours. Gen. campaign mgr. Cleve. Area Heart Soc., bd. chmn., 1960-61; mem. corp. Fenn Coll.; Bd. dirs. Ohio Heart Soc.; chmn. Highland Redevel. Corp., 1963-68; pres. Council High Blood Pressure; dir. Am. Heart Soc., 1963-68, 1964-69. Served to lt. USNR, 1942-45; comdg. officer escort vessels. Clubs: Union (N.Y.C.); Meadow (Southampton, N.Y.); Chagrin Valley Hunt, Union, Kirtland Country, Tavern (Cleve.); Bath and Tennis, Everglades (Palm Beach, Fla.). Home: 300 S Ocean Blvd Penthouse B Palm Beach FL 33480 also: One Bratenahl Pl #1504 Bratenahl OH 44108

BISHOP, WAYNE STATON, lawyer; b. Tarboro, N.C., Oct. 30, 1937; s. Lionel Lyston and Lelia Ruth (Staton) B.; children: John, Jeffrey, Scott. AB, U. N.C., 1959, JD, 1964. Bar: D.C. 1964, U.S. Supreme Ct. 1968. Atty. appellate litigation NLRB, Washington, 1964-68; practiced in Washington, 1968—; co-founder Bishop & Wallace, 1994; chmn. The Linkage Group, Washington, 1994—; mem. adv. com. U.S. Trade Rep., 1984—; medm. adv. bd. Inter-Am. Mgmt. Edn. Found., 1992—. Co-author: Authorization Cards and the National Labor Relations Board, 1969. Transition ofcl. Office Pres.-elect Reagan, 1980; nat. dir. Presdl. Campaign Reagan-Bush, 1980. Mem. ABA, FBA, D.C. Bar Assn. Office: 4515 Foxhall Cres NW Washington DC 20007-1056

BISHOP, WILLIAM PETER, research scientist; b. Lakewood, Ohio, Jan. 18, 1940; s. William Hall and Ethel Laverle (Evans) B.; m. Sarah Gilbert, Sept. 1, 1963. BA in Chemistry with honors (Nat. Merit scholar), Coll. Wooster, Ohio, 1962; PhD (NDEA fellow), Ohio State U., 1967. Resident research assoc. Ohio State U., 1967-69; mem. staff Sandia Labs., Albuquerque, 1969-75; head nuclear waste program NRC, Washington, 1975-78; dep. dir. environ. observation div. NASA, 1978-81, dep. dir. life scis. div., 1981-83; dep. asst. adminstr. satellites NOAA, 1983-85, acting asst. adminstr. satellites and info. services, 1985-87; v.p. SAIC, Washington, 1987-89; v.p. for rsch. Desert Rsch. Inst., Las Vegas, Nev., 1989-94; assigned to U.S. Dept. of Energy, 1995—; mem. Nat. Acad. Com. Earth Studies, 1989-91, Task Group on Priorities in Space Rsch., 1990-94; chair Adv. Commn. on Geoscis. NSF, 1994-97. Author articles in field. Trustee Keystone (Colo.) Ctr., 1986-95, Nev. Devel. Authority, 1989-95, Univ. Corp. for Atmospheric Rsch., 1991-97; bd. dirs. Opportunities Industrialization Ctrs., Albuquerque, 1974-75, Cave Rsch. Found., 1967-74. Recipient Meritorious Service award NRC, 1977; Spaceship Earth award NASA, 1981; Meritorious Service award U.S. Dept. Commerce, 1985. Fellow Nat. Speleological Soc. (conservation editor bull. 1974-78), Am. Astron. Soc. (v.p. tech. 1987-88); mem. AAAS, Am. Geophys. Union, AIAA, N.Mex. Acad. Scis., Sigma Xi, Phi Lambda Upsilon. Office: US Dept Energy DP 60 Washington DC 20585

BISHOP, WILLIAM THURMOND, federal judge; b. 1939. BA, The Citadel, 1961; LLB, U. S.C., 1964. Bar: S.C. Pvt. practice, Columbia, S.C., 1968-87; bankruptcy judge for S.C., U.S. Bankruptcy Ct., Columbia, 1987—. With U.S. Army, 1965-68. Office: US Bankruptcy Ct 1100 Laurel St Columbia SC 29201-2423

BISHOP, WILLIAM WADE, advertising executive; b. Mt. Vernon, N.Y., Apr. 17, 1939; s. Kenneth Farrington and Dorothea (Renz) B.; m. Jacqueline Kenton, May 21, 1966; children: William Jr., Christopher. BA, Ohio Wesleyan U., 1961. Account exec. Ogilvy & Mather, Grey, BBDO, N.Y.C., 1964-72; v.p. Ted Bates, N.Y.C., 1972-74; category mgr. Gen. Foods Corp., White Plains, N.Y., 1974-79; mng. dir. Mktg. Corp. Am., Westport, Conn., 1979-80; exec. v.p. MCA Advt., N.Y.C., 1980-84, pres., chief exec. officer, 1984-86; pres., chief exec. officer MCA Communications Group, 1986-89; pres. Ally & Gargano, N.Y.C., 1986-89; chmn., chief exec. officer CHC Advt., 1989-92; CEO CHC Advt. and M.E.D. Comms., 1992—; pres., CEO Ryan Direct, Westport, Conn., 1992-94; dir. South Beach Beverages, 1995—; chmn., CEO Sierra Comms. Group, 1995—. Served with USMC, 1962-68. Mem. Salem Golf Club. Republican. Congregationalist. Avocations: lacrosse, tennis, golf. Office: Sierra Comm 15 River Rd Wilton CT 06897-4065

BISHOP-GRAHAM, BARBARA, secondary school educator, journalist; b. Angwin, Calif., Apr. 22, 1941; d. Will Francis and Esther Clara (Blisserd) Bishop; children: Gregory Mark, Steven Bishop. BA in Journalism, U. Hawaii, 1975, BA in English, 1975, BA in Art History, 1975, BFA in Painting and Drawing, 1975; nat. cert. in journalism, Kans. State U., 1994; MA in Tech. Curriculum & Instrn., Calif. State U., Sacramento, 1999. Cert. tchr., Hawaii. Photography instr., art tchr. Hawaii Sch. for Girls, Honolulu, 1974-76; substitute tchr. English State Dept. Edn., Oahu, 1977-78; English and grammar instr. Hawaii Sch. for Bus., Honolulu, 1979-80; media dir., exec. asst., historian Oriental Treasures and Points West, Honolulu, 1981-82; legal asst. Goodsill, Anderson, Quinn, Honolulu, 1983-84; lang. arts and photography tchr. Lodi (Calif.) H.S., 1984-88, writing and lang. arts tchr., 1988-93, journalism adviser, 1993-95, lang. arts tchr., 1993-96, Brit. lit. tchr., 1996—; mem. curriculum coun. Lodi Unified Sch. Dist., 1989-92, 97—; liaison to PTSA Lodi H.S., 1991-92, mentor tchr., 1991-94, 97—; student literary mag. advisor Lodi H.S., 1989—. Sportswriter Oakland Tribune, 1957-60, Author Three Poems, 1998; contbr. articles to profl. publs. Fundraiser chmn. Big Bros. of Am., San Francisco, 1967; media dir. Clements (Calif.) Cmty. Cares, 1985-89. Recipient Edn. Contbn. award Masons 1988-92, 20th Century Achievement award Am. Biographical Inst., 1999; grantee Nat. Endowment of Arts, rsch. Japanese Lit. 1989; social rschr. grantee Brazil, U. So. Calif., 1992, grantee, 1992; grantee S. Joaquin County Office Edn., 1996-97; champion Hawaii State barrel racing, 1980. Mem. NEA, Calif. Tchrs. Assn. (Calif. state tchrs. coun. rep. 1996-97), Lodi Edn. Assn. (conf. fund chair 1989-97). Republican. Seventh-Day Adventist. Avocations: writing, dressage riding and showing, growing and testing roses. Office: Lodi HS 3 S Pacific Ave Lodi CA 95242-3020

BISHOPRIC, KARL, investment banker, real estate executive, advertising executive; b. Greensboro, N.C., Jan. 5, 1925; s. James Robert Karl and Frances (Farrell) B.; m. Rose Anne Straub, Mar. 4, 1944 (div. Jan. 1972); children—Robert Lewis, James Nelson (dec.), Bruce Graham; m. Carmen Deruth Dunlop, May 26, 1973. B.A., U. N.C., 1945. With Houck & Co., Roanoke, Miami, Va., Fla., 1946-54; pres. Houck & Co., Miami, Fla., 1948-54, Bishopric-Green-Fielden, Inc., Miami, N.Y.C., 1954-68; chmn. bd. Bishopric-Green-Fielden, Inc., 1968-73, Lando-Bishopric, Inc., 1973-74; chmn., dir. Advt. & Marketing Internat. Network, Inc., 1972-74; pres. Miami Nat. Bank, 1974-75; assoc. Oscar E. Dooly Assos., Inc., 1974-76; prin. 1st Equity Financial Corp., 1975—; pres. 1st Equity Properties, Inc., 1976—; v.p., dir. Fundamental Mgmt. Corp., 1986-89. Pres. United Fund Dade County, 1967-68, trustee, 1963—; chmn. Port Action Com., 1969-71; bd. dirs. Community TV Found. S. Fla., 1965-67, v.p., 1969-72; mem. citizens bd. U. Miami, 1968—, pres. citizens bd., 1982-83, trustee, 1983-85; bd. dirs. Econ. Soc. S. Fla., 1969-73, Urban Coalition Greater Miami, 1968-72, Fla. Philharmonic Orchestra Found., 1992—, Miami Lighthouse for the Blind, 1993—; bd. dirs. Urban League Greater Miami, 1956-65, pres., 1956-60; chmn. budget leaders conf. United Funds and Community Councils Am., 1968; trustee Lowe Art Mus., 1973-86. Served to lt. (j.g.) USNR, 1944-46. Recipient Printer's Ink Silver medal. Mem. Greater Miami C. of C. (dir. 1971-74, trustee 1976—), Alpha Delta Sigma, Beta Theta Pi. Home: 600 Biltmore Way Coral Gables FL 33134-7541 Office: 1st Equity Corp Fla 444 Brickell Ave Ste P6 Miami FL 33131-2466

BISHOPRIC, SUSAN EHRLICH, public relations executive; b. N.Y.C.. AAS, Fashion Inst. Tech., 1965. Exec.-in-tng. Bloomingdales, Abraham & Strauss; merchandise coord. Seventeen mag.; publicity dir. Germaine Monteil Cosmetiques; account exec. Rowland Co., 1968-69, account supr., 1969-73, v.p., 1973-75, sr. v.p., creative dir., 1975-78, exec. v.p., 1979-81; pub. rels. dir. Susan Gilbert & Co., 1984-86; head pub. rels. divsn. Beber Silverstein & Ptnrs., 1986-89; founder, pres. Bishopric Agy., Coral Gables, Fla., 1989—. Office: Bishopric Agy 400 Viscaya Ave Coral Gables FL 33134-7160

BISKUPIC, JOAN, reporter; b. Chgo., 1956. BA, Marquette U., 1978; MA, U. Okla., 1986; JD, Georgetown U., 1993. Reporter, State Capital bur. chief Tulsa Tribune, Okla., 1985-87; Washington corrs., 1987-88; legal affairs reporter Congressional Quarterly, 1989-92; Supreme Ct. reporter The Washington Post, Washington, 1992—. Office: The Washington Post 1150 15th St NW Washington DC 20071-0001*

BISNETTE, DENA LYNN, journalist; b. Concordia, Kans., Mar. 13, 1959; d. John Eddie and Dorothy (Haidinger) B.; m. Joseph A. Gilliam, Mar. 13, 1988. AA, Jones County Jr. Coll., Ellisville, Miss., 1979; BA in English, U. So. Miss., 1981; MS in Criminal Justice, U. So. Miss. Long Beach, 1990. Reporter Laurel (Miss.) Leader-Call, 1982-84; writer, photographer Sea Coast Echo, Bay St. Louis, Miss., 1984-90; freelance journalist, photographer Bay St. Louis, 1990—; owner, tailor Another Time Sewing, Pass Christian, Miss., 1990-99. Contbr. articles to various mags. Mem. Soc. Profl. Journalists, Highlands and Islands Assn., Gulf Coast Writer's Assn. Roman Catholic. Avocations: music, herb gardening, clothing designing, dogs.

BISPING, BRUCE HENRY, photojournalist; b. St. Louis, Apr. 27, 1953; s. Harry and Marian B.; m. Joan M. Berg, Sept. 29, 1984; children: Erin Elizabeth Giovanna, Trevor Thomas. B.J., U. Mo., Columbia, 1975. Summer intern Cleve. Press, 1974, The Virginian/Pilot-Ledger Star, Norfolk, 1975; staff photojournalist Mpls. Tribune, 1975-82, Mpls. Star and Tribune, 1982—; freelance photographer Black Star Pub. Co., N.Y.C., 1975—, Sporting News, St. Louis, Underwater USA, Business Week, Time, U.S. News World Report, Newsweek, Am. Illustrated, N.Y. Times, Los Angeles Times, other nat. and local publs.; past mem. faculty Mo. Photojournalism Workshop. Mem. Nat. Press Photographers Assn. (assoc. dir. Region 5 1981-82, dir. Region 5 1983-86, rep. to exec. com. 1984, Nat. Newspaper Photographer of Year award 1976, Regional Newspaper Photographer of Year award 1977, citation for dedication to profession 1985), Twin Cities News Photographers Assn. (pres. 1979-80), Profl. Assn. Diving Instrs. (open water instr. rating), Oldsmobile Club of Am. (bd. dirs. Minn. Club, news editor). Office: Mpls Tribune 425 Portland Ave Minneapolis MN 55488-1511

BISSELL, ALLEN MORRIS, engineer, consultant; b. Orange, N.J., Sept. 13, 1935; s. Chester Wright and Leila Allen (Morris) B.; m. Olivia Smith (dec. 1990); children: Leila Morris, William Emerson; m. Barbara Clement, June 1, 1991. BS in Naval Sci., U.S. Naval Acad., 1960; BSME, Naval Postgrad. Sch., 1966; MS in Computer Systems, George Washington U., 1973. Registered profl. engr., Md., Va.; diplomate Am. Coll. Forensic Engrng. and Tech. Commd. ensign USN, 1960, advanced through grades to capt., 1981, commanding officer USS Seneca, 1966-68; adviser Vietnam Naval Acad., Nha Trang, Republic Vietnam, 1969-70; engrng. instr. Naval Acad. Faculty, 1970-73; commanding officer USS Hoist, then USS McCandless, 1974-77, chief engr. USS Forrestal, 1978-80; commanding officer Naval Data Automation Ctr. USN, Norfolk, Va., 1980-83; ret. USN, 1983; sr. engr. and contract mgr. Vitro Labs., 1984-88; v.p. Trident Engring. Assocs., Annapolis, Md., 1988-90; pres. Allen M. Bissell, Inc. Cons. Engrs., Chevy Chase, Md., 1990—, Design Construct Internat., Inc., Cons. Engrs., Chevy Chase, 1995—; cons. Trident Engring. Assocs., 1971—; lectr. Kapos Assocs., Rosslyn, Va., 1990—; pres. Design Construct Internat., Inc., 1992—. Co-author: SHipboard Damage Control, 1973; designer waste water treatment machinery. Mem. Md. Rep. party, 1989-95, Fairness in Taxation, 1991. Decorated Bronze Star medal, Legion of Merit. Mem. ASME, NSPE, NAS (naval pollution study group, mechanical design task group leader). Episcopalian. Avocation: rebuilding sports cars.

BISSELL, GEORGE ARTHUR, architect; b. L.A., Jan. 31, 1927; s. George Arthur and Ruby Zoe (Moore) B.; m. Laurene Conlon, Nov. 21, 1947; children: Teresa Ann, Thomas Conlon, William George, Robert Anthony, Mary Catherine. BArch, U. So. Calif., 1953. Registered architect, Calif. Ptnr. Bissell Co., Covina, Calif., 1953-57, Bissell & Durquette, A.I.A., Pasadena, Calif., 1957-61; owner George Bissell, A.I.A., Laguna Beach, Calif., 1961-72; ptnr. Riley & Bissell, A.I.A., Newport Beach, Calif., 1967-72; pres. Bissell/August, Inc., Newport Beach, 1972-83, Bissell Architects, Inc., Newport Beach, 1983—. Bd. dirs. Newport Ctr. Assn., 1973-78, Lido Isle Community Assn., Newport Beach, 1985-87, Hamilton Cove Assn., 1991-92. With U.S. Mcht. Marine, 1944-46. Fellow AIA (pres. Orange County chpt. 1975, Calif. coun. 1978, nat. bd. dirs. 1980-83, Progressive Arch. award 1974, Nat. AIA Honor award 1978, 98, Merit award Calif. Coun. 1988); mem. Newport Harbor Yacht Club, Lido Isle Yacht Club. Avocations: sailing, skiing, travel. Home: 108 Via Havre Newport Beach CA 92663-4905 Home (summer): Hamilton Cove 27 Camino de Flores Catalina Island CA 90704 Office: Bissell Architects 446 Old Newport Blvd Newport Beach CA 92663-4211

BISSELL, JAMES DOUGAL, III, motion picture production designer; b. Charleston, S.C., Aug. 6, 1951; s. James Dougal Sr. and Elizabeth McPherson (Jones) B.; m. Teresa Ann Atkinson, June 1, 1974 (div. Sept. 1987); m. Martha Wynne Snetsinger, Oct. 22, 1995; children: James Dougal, Alexander Wynne, Elizabeth Wynne. BFA in Theatre, U. N.C., 1973. Art dir. various TV movies, L.A., 1976-81; prodn. designer E.T. The Extra-Terrestrial, L.A., 1981, Twilight Zone-The Movie, L.A., 1982, The Falcon and The Snowman, Mexico City, 1983-84; prodn. designer, 2d unit dir. The Boy Who Could Fly, Vancouver, B.C., Can., 1985, Harry and the Hendersons, L.A., 1986; prodn. designer Someone to Watch Over Me, L.A. and N.Y.C., 1986-87, Twins, L.A. and Santa Fe, 1988—; visual cons. St. Elmo's Fire, Hollywood, 1984; title co-designer Amazing Stories, Hollywood, 1985; art dir. The Last Starfighter, Hollywood, 1983; prodn. designer, 2nd unit dir. Always, L.A., Libby Mt., Epharata, Wash., 1989; prodn. designer Arachnophobia, Venezuela, Cambria, Calif., L.A. Prodn. designer Rocketeer, 1990, The Pickle, N.Y.C. and L.A., Dennis the Menace, Chgo., 1992, Blue Chips, L.A., Chgo., New Orleans, 1993, Jumanji, Vancouver, New Eng., 1994-95, Tin Cup, Tucson, Houston, 1995, My Fellow Americans, L.A., Asheville, N.C. Nominee Prodn. Design award Brit. Acad. Film Arts, London, 1982. Mem. Soc. Motion Picture and TV Art Dirs., Dir.'s Guild Am., Acad. Motion Picture Arts and Scis.

BISSELL, JOHN HOWARD, marketing executive; b. Bklyn., July 8, 1935; s. Donald Henry and Lillian (Eckberg) B.; m. Joan Becker, Sept. 7, 1963; children: John Edward, Mary Katherine. BA in Polit. Sci., Yale U., 1956. Brand mgr. Procter and Gamble, Inc., Cin., 1960-71; v.p., new products mktg. Frito-Lay, Inc., Dallas, 1971-80; v.p. mktg. The Stroh Brewery Co., Detroit, 1980-85, sr. v.p., spl. products div., 1985-91; pres. Stroh Foods, Inc. subs. The Stroh Brewery Co., Detroit, 1985-91; mng. ptnr. cons. div. Gundersen Ptnrs., L.L.C., Bloomfield Hills, Mich., 1991—. Chmn. corp. funds campaign Sta. WTVS, Detroit, 1986; exec. bd. dirs. Detroit coun. Boy Scouts Am., 1983—. Served as 1st lt. USAF, 1957-59. Mem. Adcrafters, Birmingham Athletic Club, Yale Club (N.Y.C.). Republican. Presbyterian. Home: 3310 Morningview Ter Bloomfield Hills MI 48301-2472

BISSELL, JOHN W., federal judge; b. Exeter, N.H., June 7, 1940; s. H. Hamilton and Sarah W. B.; m. Caroline M.; July 15, 1967; children—Megan L., Katharine W. AB, Princeton U., 1962; LLB, U. Va., 1965. Law clk. U.S. Dist. Ct., N.J., 1965-66; assoc. Pitney, Hardin & Kipp, Newark and Norristown, N.J., 1966-69, ptnr., 1972-78; asst. U.S. atty. N.J., 1969-71; judge Essex County, N.J., 1978-81, N.J. Superior Ct., 1981-82, U.S. Dist. Ct. N.J., Trenton and Newark, 1983—. Office: US Dist Ct Federal Square PO Box 999 Newark NJ 07101-0999

BISSELL, MARK, consumer products company executive. CEO Bissell, Grand Rapids, Mich., 1990—. Office: Bissell Inc 2345 Walker Ave NW Grand Rapids MI 49544-2597*

BISSELL, PHIL (CHARLES P. BISSELL), cartoonist; b. Worcester, Mass., Feb. 1, 1926; s. Ralph Kenneth and Dorothy Earle (Pennell) B.; m. Beverly Barrows, Sept. 17, 1948; children: Steven Barrows, Christopher William. Student, Sch. Practical Art, Boston, 1946-48; hon. degree, Art Instrn. Sch., Mpls., 1971. Theatrical and editl. sports cartoonist Christian Sci. Monitor, 1949-53; sports cartoonist Boston Globe, 1953-65; sports and editl. cartoonist Worcester Telegram and Evening Gazette, 1967-75; sports cartoonist Boston Herald, 1975-77; editl. cartoonist Lowell (Mass.) Sun, 1980-87; illustrator, cartoonist Cartoon Corner Syndicate, Rockport, Mass., 1987—; cons. D.C. Graphics, Lexington, Mass., 1987—; originator football helmet logo New England Patriots, 1960; portrait artist City of Lowell Bridge Placque, 1982. Represented in permanent collections Basketball Hall Fame, Springfield, Mass., Football Hall of Fame, Canton, Ohio, Baseball Hall of Fame, Cooperstown, N.Y., Internat. Swimming Hall of Fame, Ft. Lauderdale, Fla., Dwight D. Eisenhower Meml. Libr., Abilene, Kans.; cartoonist: (book) Sportspot, 1978, World Ency. of Cartooning, 1980, Tall Tales from Tall Ships, 1992. Recipient N.Am. Racing Assn. award, 1958, Scarlet Quill award Boston U., 1976, Hockey award Mass. Bay Chiefs, 1981. Mem. Baseball Writers Assn. Am. Home: 5 Shetland Rd Rockport MA 01966-1911 Office: Cartoon Corner 5 Shetland Rd Rockport MA 01966-1911 *Humor and laughter can hold mankind together, and if you can share it with your fellow-man, I feel it's a successful day's work!.*

BISSET, JACQUELINE, actress; b. Weybridge, Eng., Sept. 13, 1946. Student, French Lycée, London. Made film debut in: The Knack, 1965; other motion pictures include Cul de Sac, 1965, Two for the Road, 1965, Casino Royale, 1966, The Sweet Ride, 1967, The Detective, 1967, Bullitt, 1968, The First Time, 1968, Airport, 1969, The Grasshopper, 1968, The Mephisto Waltz, 1969, Believe in Me, 1971, The Life and Times of Judge Roy Bean, 1972, Stand Up and Be Counted, 1972, The Thief Who Came to Dinner, 1972, Day for Night, 1972, Murder on the Orient Express, 1974, The Spiral Staircase, 1974, End of the Game, 1974, St. Ives, 1975, The Deep, 1975, Le Magnifique, 1973, Sunday Woman, 1974, The Greek Tycoon, 1976, Secrets, 1969, Who is Killing the Great Chefs of Europe?, 1976, Amo Non Amo, 1979, When Time Ran Out, 1979, Rich and Famous, 1980, Inchon, 1979, Class, 1983, Under the Volcano, 1984, High Season, 1986, Hoffman's Honger, 1993, Les Marmottes, 1993, East & West: Paradise Lost, 1993, Crimebroker, 1993, La Cérémonie, 1995, Once You Meet a Stranger, 1996, The Honest Courtesan, 1996, Let the Devil Wear Black, 1998; appeared in TV films Anna Karenina, 1984, Forbidden (Home Box Office), 1985, Choices, 1985, miniseries Napoleon and Josephine, 1987; La Maison de Jade, 1988, Wild Orchid, 1989, Scenes From The Class Struggle in Beverly Hills, 1989, The Maid, 1990, Rossini Rossini, 1990, Leave of Absence, 1994, September, 1996, End of Summer, 1996, Steve McQueen: The King of Cool, 1998, Witch Hunt, 1998, Brittanic, 1999. Address: care William Morris Agency 151 S El Camino Dr Beverly Hills CA 90212-2704 also: care VMA, 10th Ave George, V 75008 Paris London*

BISSETT, BARBARA ANNE, steel distribution company executive; b. Cleve., Sept. 27, 1950; d. George Jr. and Helen (Kirkwood) B.; m. Kerry Mark Kitchen, Oct. 6, 1979; children: Mark Jeffrey, Lauren Brooke. BFA, U. Denver, 1974. Inside sales rep. Bissett Steel Co., Cleve., 1977-78, inside sales mgr., 1978-80, v.p., 1980-88, pres., 1988—; mentor strategic planning course Greater Cleve. Growth Assn., 1987-95; bd. dirs. Cleve. Cuyahoga County Port Authority. Bd. dirs. Greater Cleve. Growth Assn. Govt. Affairs, 1994—; bd. trustees Enterprise Devel., Inc., 1994—, Playhouse Sq. Found., 1996—. Mem. Am. Soc. Metals, Steel Svc. Ctr. Inst. (v.p. programming young leadership forum 1989, pres. 1991-93, bd. dirs. No. Ohio chpt., v.p. 1994, pres. north Ohio chpt. 1995-97), Coun. Smaller Enterprises (leadership coun. 1989—, bd. dirs. 1990—, first vice chair 1996, chair 1998—), Assn. Women in Metals Industries, Women's City Club. Republican. Presbyterian. Home: 1994 Coes Post Run Cleveland OH 44145-2059 Office: 9005 Bank St Cleveland OH 44125-3425

BISSETTE, SAMUEL DELK, astronomer, artist, financial executive; b. Wilson, N.C., Aug. 10, 1921; s. Zachariah Coye and Annie Wright (Rice) B.; m. Ruby Graham Raynor, Sept. 8, 1943; children: Judy Sabra, David Coye. Student pub. schs., various coll. courses. With Peoples Fed. Savs. and Loan Assn., Wilmington, N.C., 1939-89, pres., chief exec. officer, 1959-77, chmn. bd., 1973-89, dir., 1954-89; visual artist, 1972—; one-man exhbns. FDIC Gallery, Washington, 1978, St. John's Mus. Art, Wilmington, N.C., 1974, 81, 84, Raleigh Civic Center, 1977, N.C. Mus. Art, 1978, 82d Ann. U.S. Open Watercolor Exhbn., N.Y.C., 1982, Discovery Pl., Charlotte, N.C., 1994; commd. by Wachovia Bank to execute 40 paintings Portrait of North Carolina, 1976; originated mosaic murals for Belk-Beery Co., Wilmington, 1979; originated exhbn. N.C. Circa 1900, 1983; traveling tour N.C. Mus., 1984-87; originated 35 piece exhbn. Images From the Microworld, 1991 (gift to Wake Forest U. 1997); created 60 painting exhbn. The Universe According to Earth, given to U.N.C., Wilmington, 1993; originator astromicroscopy, astrophotomicrography for astronomy, 1994; author: A Guide to Astromicroscopy, 1994, An Astromicroscopy Study of the Southern Hemisphere Sky, 1995. Trustee N.C. Mus. Art, Raleigh, 1980-85; chmn. N.C. Artists Exhbn., 1979. Served with USAAF, 1941-45. Mem. N.C. Watercolor Soc. (v.p. 1980), N.C. Art Soc. (dir. 1974-82), St. John's Mus. Art (pres. 1973-74). Republican. Baptist. Clubs: Cape Fear (pres. 1978), Cape Fear Country, Carolina Yacht (Wilmington). Address: 1939 S Live Oak Pky Wilmington NC 28403-5321

BISSETTE, WINSTON LOUIS, JR., lawyer, mayor; b. Statesville, N.C., Sept. 18, 1943; s. Winston Louis and Rubye (Goode) B.; m. Sara Oliver, Aug. 21, 1965; children: W. Louis III, Thomas Anderson. BA, Wake Forest U., 1965; JD, U. N.C., Chapel Hill, 1968; MBA, U. Va., 1970. Bar: N.C. 1968. Asst. v.p. Wachovia Bank & Trust Co., Winston-Salem, N.C., 1970-74; v.p., treas. Western Carolina Bank, Asheville, N.C., 1974-76; ptnr. McGuire, Wood & Bissette, P.A., Asheville, 1976—. Mayor City of Asheville, 1985-89, mem. city coun., 1983-89; co-chmn. I-26 corridor Assn., 1987—; chmn. West N.C. Devel. Assn., 1995-98; regional adv. coun. HUD, 1986-90; mem. Gov.'s Task Force on Urban Transp., 1986, Yr. of the Mtns. Commn., 1995-97; chmn. Asheville Sports Com., 1991-97, Buncombe County Econ. Devel. Commn., 1997—, Asheville Cmty. Betterment Found., 1992; bd. trustees Wake Forest U., 1996—, Western Carolina U., 1995—; chmn. Advantage Asheville, 1996—; sec.-treas. Grove Arcade Pub. Mkt. Found., 1992—; bd. dirs. Mission-St. Joseph's Health Sys., Inc., 1996-99. Mem. ABA, N.C. Bar Assn., Asheville Area C. of C. (pres. 1991-92), Wake Forest U. Alumni Assn. (pres. 1992-93), Country Club of Asheville, Civitan Club. Republican. Presbyterian. Avocations: golf, running. Home: 321 Old Toll Rd Asheville NC 28804-3716 Office: McGuire Wood & Bissette PA 48 Patton Ave PO Box 3180 Asheville NC 28802-3180

BISSINGER, FREDERICK LEWIS, retired manufacturing executive, consultant; b. N.Y.C., Jan. 11, 1911; s. Jacob Frederick and Rosel (Ensslin) B.; m. Julia E. Stork, Aug. 4, 1935 (dec. Dec. 1989); children: Frederick Louis, Elizabeth Julia; m. Barbara S. Simmonds, Dec. 4, 1993. ME, Stevens Inst. Tech., 1933, MS in Chemistry, 1936; JD, Fordham U., 1938. Bar: D.C. 1937, N.Y. 1939, Ohio 1943, U.S. Supreme Ct. 1943. Instr. chemistry Stevens Inst. Tech., Hoboken, N.J., 1933-36; assoc. Pennie, Davis, Marvin & Edmonds, N.Y.C., 1936-42; counsel, bus. cons. Pennie, Davis, Marvin & Edmonds (name now Pennie & Edmonds), N.Y.C., 1976—; with Indsl. Rayon Corp., Cleve., 1942-61, v.p. charge rsch., 1948-57, group v.p. mktg. and rsch., 1957-59, v.p., gen. mgr., 1959-60, pres., chief exec. officer, 1960-61; group v.p. Midland-Ross Corp., Cleve., 1961-62; v.p., dir., mem. exec. com. Stauffer Chem. Co., N.Y.C., 1962-65; v.p. Allied Chem. Corp., N.Y.C., 1965-66, exec. v.p., 1966-69, pres., chief oper. officer, 1969-74, vice chmn., 1974-76, also bd. dirs.; bd. dirs. Selas Corp. Am. Chmn. emeritus bd. trustees Steven Inst. Tech.; trustee emeritus Fordham U.; mem. N.Y. State Econ. Devel. Bd., 1975. Mem. AAAS, Am. Chem. Soc., Soc. of Chem. Industry (Am. sect.), Societe de Chimie Industrielle, Chemists Club, Sky Club, Sakonnet Golf Club, Met. Club. Home: 9 W Irving St Chevy Chase MD 20815-4218

BISSINGER, MARK CHRISTIAN, lawyer; b. Steubenville, Ohio, June 4, 1957; s. Emerson Melvin and Nancy (Osbun) B.; m. Julie Furber, Sept. 28, 1985; children: Lucas Christian, Nathan Kenneth. BS in Civil Engring., Purdue U., 1979; JD, U. Cin., 1983. Bar: Ohio 1983, U.S. Dist. Ct. (so. dist.) Ohio 1983, U.S. Ct. Appeals (6th cir.), Ky. 1993. Assoc. Dinsmore & Shohl, Cin., 1983-90, ptnr., 1990—; spkr. Ohio Continuing Legal Edn., Cin., 1990—; lectr. Nat. Bus. Inst., 1990—; commn. cert. attys. as splsts. Supreme Ct. Ohio; mem. Supreme Ct. Ohio's Bd. Bar Examiners. Pres. Ctr. for Comprehensive Alcoholism Treatment, Cin., 1989-92; bd. mem. Community Operation Devel. Inc., Cin., 1991—, Five Mile Chapel Soc., Cin., 1989—. Named Order of Coif, Cin., 1983. Mem. ABA, Cin. Bar Assn., Ohio Bar Assn., No. Ky. Bar Assn., Ky. Bar Assn. Avocations: family, travel, sports. Office: Dinsmore & Shohl 255 E 5th St Cincinnati OH 45202-4700

BISSLER, RICHARD THOMAS, mortician; b. Ravenna, Ohio, Nov. 23, 1953; s. Richard Samuel and Ruth Marion (Cowan) B.; m. Jane H. Vair, Aug. 23, 1975; children: Stephanie Ann, Carlie Jane. BS in Mortuary Sci., U. Minn., 1976; grad., Nat. Found. Funeral Svc. Mgmt., 1983. Lic. funeral dir. and embalmer Ohio; cert. crematory operator Cremation Assn. N.Am. Funeral svc. asst. Bissler & Sons Funeral Home, Kent, Ohio, 1970-74, mortician, 1976—, corp. sec., 1983-86, corp. sec.-treas., 1986-88, pres., 1988—; bd. dirs. Home Savs. Bank, Kent; bd. dirs., treas. NSM Ins. Co. Ltd. Trustee Kent Free Libr., 1986—, St. Patrick's Sch. Endowment Fund, 1994—, Nat. Selected Morticians Ins. Trust, 1995—; past bd. dirs., pres. Portage County A.C.S., Kent; past treas. NEO-SIDS Found., Akron, Ohio, 1990; mem. adult edn. adv. com. Kent City Schs.; steering com. Portage County Hospice; devel. com. United Christian Ministries, 1996-98; mem. Vision 2000 com. City of Kent; mem. Kent Bus. and Edn. adv. com. Recipient Disting. Svc. award Kent Jaycees, 1986. Mem. Nat. Funeral Dirs. Assn., Ohio Embalmers Assn., Ohio Funeral Dirs. Assn., Nat. Selected Morticians (meeting chair 1989), Funeral Ethics Assn., Kent Area C. of C. (dir. 1985-89, Outstanding Bus. Person award 1992), Order of the Golden Rule, Kent Rotary (dir. 1991-93, pres. 1995-96), K.C. Republican. Roman Catholic. Avocations: golf, photography, travel. Office: Bissler & Sons Funeral Home 628 W Main St Kent OH 44240-2212

BISSON, CLAUDE, retired chief justice of Quebec; b. Three Rivers, Que., Can., May 9, 1931; s. Roger Bisson and Marcelle Morin; m. Louisette Lanneville, Oct. 12, 1957; children: Alain, Marie, Louis. BA, Laval U., 1950, Licentiate in Laws, 1953. Bar: Que. 1954. Pvt. practice Three Rivers, 1954-69; judge Superior Ct. Dist. Montreal, Que., 1969-80, Ct. of Appeal, Province of Que., Montreal, 1980-96; also chief justice of Que., 1988-94; counsel McCarthy Tetrault, Montreal, 1996—. Decorated officer The Order of Canada, 1999. Mem. Can. Bar Assn., Que. Garrison Club, Quebec City. Home: 6150 Du Boise Ave # 7K, Montreal, PQ Canada H3S 2V2 Office: McCarthy Tetrault, 1170 Peel St, Montreal, PQ Canada H3B 4S8

BISSON, ROGER, middle school educator; b. Biddeford, Maine, Oct. 16, 1944; s. Napoleon and Simonne (Desrochers) B.; m. Janet Elizabeth Gerace, Aug. 9, 1969. BA in Biology, St. Michael's Coll., Winooski, Vt., 1969; MEd in Adminstrn. and Planning, U. Vt., 1991; tech. edn. cert., Lyndon State Coll., 1991. Cert. Sci. tchr. grades 7-12, tech. edn. tchr. grades 7-12, prin. grades K-12. 5th and 7th grade tchr. Sacred Heart Sch., Sharon, Mass., 1964-66; algebra I, French I and II and Latin I tchr. Notre Dame H.S., Fitchburg, Mass., 1966-68; 7th and 9th grade sci. tchr. Meml. Jr. and Sr. H.S., Bellingham, Mass., 1968-79; sci. and tech. edn. instr. grades 6, 7, 8 Folsom Sch., South Hero, Vt., 1979—; mem. info. tech. com. Grand Isle Supervisory Dist., North Hero, Vt., 1985—; tech. edn. cons. Alburg (Vt.) Elem. Sch., 1992—; sch.-to-work lead tchr. New Am. Sch.-Folsom, South Hero, 1992—, sci. lead tchr., 1994—; mem. tchr./bus. internship program Vt. Math. Coalition, Montpelier, summer 1994; initiator Electronic Portfolio Project 6, 7, 8, 1994—, Student/Bus. Internship Program, 1994—; presenter Nat. Ednl. Computing Conf., Boston, spring 1994, Vt. Fest '94, Fairlee, Vt., fall 1994, Sch.-to-Work Initiative Conf., Burlington, summer 1996, Regional Edn. Television Network Conf., Burlington, fall 1997, Vt. Fest '98 Info. Tech. Conf. Contbr. articles to profl. jours.; presenter in field. Initiator Grand Isle County Networking Initiative, Grand Isle County, Vt., 1991, Grand Isle County Peer Coaching Program, Grand Isle County, 1991. Recipient Sch.-to-Work Initiative Gov.'s Office, 1995, award Lake Champlain Regional C. of C., 1996, Vocat. Edn. award Grand Isle Rotary Club, 1998; co-recipient IBM Test Flight 1991 award, Essex Junction, Vt., 1992. Mem. ASCD, NEA, NSTA, Vt. Edn. Assn., Vt. Sci. Tchrs. Assn., Vt. Tech. Edn. Assn., Grand Isle Supervisory Union (bldg rep., negotiator, grievance com., past pres.), Vt. State Technology Coun., Vt. Inst. Sci., Math. and Technology. Roman Catholic. Avocations: woodworking, furniture refinishing, carpentry, computer technology, fine dining. Office: Folsom Sch 75 South St South Hero VT 05486-4913

BISSON, TERRY BALLANTINE, author, editor; b. Madisonville, Ky., Feb. 12, 1942; s. Max Willis and Martha (Ballantine) B.; m. Deirdre Holst (div. 1969); children: Nathaniel, Peter, Zöe; m. Judy Yost Jensen, 1971; children: Kristen, Gabriel, Welcome. Student, Grinnell Coll., 1960-62; BA, U. Louisville, 1964. Participant univ. and lit. confs.; keynote speaker ann. conf. So. Humanities Coun., Huntsville, Ala. Author: (novels) Wyrldmaker, 1981, Talking Man, 1987, Fire on the Mountain, 1988, Voyage to the Red Planet, 1990, Pirates of the Universe, 1996; (novels pub. in Germany, Italy, Russia, Japan,and U.K.); (young adult biography) Nat Turner, Slave Revolt Leader, 1988; Bears Discover Fire and Other Stories, 1993; creator No-Frills Books, 1981; co-author: Car Talk with Click and Clack, The Tappet Brothers, 1991, A Green River Girlhood, 1990; co-editor: Hauling up the Morning, 1990; contbr. short fiction to Playboy, Omni, others. Recipient Hugo award World Sci. Fiction Conf., 1991, Mayor's award for excellence City of Owensboro, Ky., 1991, Phoenix award Deep South Conf., 1993, Theodore Sturgeon award U. Kans., 1991. Mem. Authors Guild, Sci. Fiction Writers Am. (Nebula award 1990). Office: care Susan Ann Protter Lit Agt 110 W 40th St Rm 1408 New York NY 10018-3616*

BISSONNETTE, JEAN MARIE, elementary school educator, polarity therapist; b. Millinocket, Maine, May 4, 1942; d. Frederick Joseph and Ella Lucia (Michaud) B. B.Diploma, Scolasticat Notre Dame, Rimouski, Que., Can., 1960-61; teaching diploma St. Joseph Coll., Cross Point, Que., 1962; BS, Gorham State Coll., 1967; MS, U. So. Maine, 1976. Joined Sisters of Holy Rosary Roman Catholic Ch., 1957-64, Edn. coordinator parish ch., Yarmouth, Maine, 1969-71; Cath. Youth Orgn. adviser Sacred Heart Parish, Yarmouth, 1972-73, parish coun., 1991-94, 98-01, vice-chair, 1994-95, parish coun. by-laws, 1994-95, worship/spirituality chair, 1990-95; elem. tchr. Rowe Sch., Yarmouth, 1967-92, Yarmouth Elem. Sch., 1992-95; cons. Holistic Ctr., Lewiston, Maine, 1982-85; mem. Spiritual Direction, Concordia, Kans., 1985. Author: Oceanography, 1969; Death/Dying for Children, 1985. Contbr. articles to profl. jours. Trustee Yarmouth Hist. Soc., 1976; instr. adult phys. fitness Town of Yarmouth, 1979-90; mem. Yarmouth Chem. Free Teenagers, 1985. Recipient Brevet du CJN award Naturaliste du Can., 1963; Maine Oceanography Com. grantee, 1970; Maine Wellness Conf. Leadership award, 1986-90, Maine Council Econ. Edn. fellow, 1972. Mem. Yarmouth Profl. Com. (chmn. 1973-76). Club: Volksmarch (So. Maine). Avocations: canoeing; camping. Home: PO Box 101 54 Anderson Ave Yarmouth ME 04096-8300 Office: WH Rowe School St Yarmouth ME 04096

BISTER-BROOSEN, HELGA, German linguistics educator; b. Krefeld, Germany, July 22, 1947; came to U.S., 1975; d. Heinz and Helene Broosen; m. Klaus Bister, June 4, 1971 (div. Jan. 1985); m. Roland Willemyns, Sept. 30, 1991. MA, U. Münster, Germany, 1971; MAT, U. Cologne, Germany, 1973; PhD in Germanic Linguistics, U. Calif., Berkeley, 1986. Tchr. middle sch. and h.s., Cologne, 1971-76; tchg. asst. U. Calif., Berkeley, 1980-86; lectr. U. San Francisco, 1985-86; lectr. Germanic linguistics U. N.C., Chapel Hill, 1986-88, asst. prof., 1988-94, assoc. prof., 1995—, asst. chair, supr. tchg. assts., dir. undergrad. lang. prog., 1986—; vis. prof. U. Duisburg, Germany, 1992, 97. Author monographs; co-author textbook Spektrum. Grammatik im Kontext, 1992, also workbook/lab. manual, instr.'s resource manual; editor books. Recipient rsch. and travel grants. Mem. MLA, AATG, GAL, IVG. Office: U NC Chapel Hill Dept Germanic Langs 438 Dey Hall Chapel Hill NC 27599-3160

BISTLINE, F. WALTER, JR., lawyer; b. Lakeland, Fla., Sept. 30, 1950; s. Frederick Walter and Mary Carolyn (Stansell) B.; m. Rabun Huff, Mar. 18, 1972. B.A., Emory U., 1972; J.D., Boston U., 1975. Bar: N.Y. 1976, Tex. 1979. Assoc. firm White & Case, N.Y.C., 1975-79; assoc. Johnson & Gibbs, P.C., Dallas, 1979-81, ptnr./shareholder, 1981-95; ptnr. Porter & Hedges, L.L.P., Houston, 1995—; lectr. So. Meth. U. Sch. of Law, 1991. Contbr. articles to profl. jours. Office: Porter & Hedges LLP 3500 NationsBank Ctr 700 Louisiana St Houston TX 77002-2700

BISWAS, DHRUBES, electrical engineer; b. Durgapur, India, Sept. 11, 1964; ž; s. Samaraesh and Mamata (Chakraborty) B. B Tech. in Elec. Engring., Indian Inst. Tech., 1987; MSEE, U. Ill., 1991, PhD, 1992. Mgr. processing & devel. Northeast Semicondr. (EG&G), East Fishkill, N.Y., 1992-93; rsch. assoc. Cornell U., Ithaca, N.Y., 1993-94; prin. engr. AMP Inc., Clarksburg, Md., 1994-97; mgr. gallium arsenide molecular beam epitaxy materials Alpha Industries, Woburn, Mass., 1997-99; mgr. advanced materials Anadigics, Warren, N.J., 1999—. Mem. IEEE, Materials Rsch. Soc., Lasers and Electooptics Soc., Electron Devices Soc., Tau Beta Pi, Phi Kappa Phi. Avocations: volleyball, hiking, writing poetry, car racing. Home: 70 Bedford St Burlington MA 01803-3657 Office: Anadigics 35 Technology Dr Warren NJ 07059

BISWAS, LINDA JOYCE, midwife; b. Lancaster, Pa., June 12, 1951; d. John Millhouse and Julia Louise (Moore) Kilheffer; m. Harold Biswas, Feb. 27, 1987 (div. Aug. 1994); children: Adina Bornini, John Abram. RN, St. Josephs Hosp. Sch. Nursing, 1972; cert. nurse midwife, Frontier Sch. of Midwifery, 1978. RN, Pa., N.J.; cert. family nurse practitioner, Pa.; cert. nurse midwife, Pa., N.J. Staff RN in ICU/CCU St. Joseph's Hosp., Lancaster, Pa., 1972-74; missionary nurse, midwife/RN/family nurse practitioner Churches of God Mission, Bangladesh, 1974-90; staff nurse midwife Tricenter Midwifery Svcs., Huntingdon, Pa., 1990-92, Rhoades Family Health Svcs., Quarryville, Pa., 1984, 92-93, Shore Meml. Hosp., Somers Point, N.J., 1993—. Author, translator: Training Manual for Village Health Promoters, 1983. Mem. Am. Coll. of Nurse Midwives. Republican. Mem. Chs. of God. Home: 6 Woodlot Ct Somers Point NJ 08244-1600 Office: Shore Meml Hosp Prenatal Clinic 1 E New York Ave Somers Point NJ 08244-2387

BITENSKY, SUSAN HELEN, law educator; b. N.Y.C., Jan. 3, 1948; d. Reuben Bitensky; m. Elliott Lee Meyrowitz, Apr. 17, 1982; 1 child, William N. BA magna cum laude, Case Western Res. U., 1971; JD, U. Chgo., 1974. Bar: Pa. 1974, U.S. Dist. Ct. (we. dist.) Pa. 1974, U.S. Ct. Appeals (3d cir.) 1975, U.S. Ct. Appeals (2d cir.) 1977, N.Y. 1979, U.S. Dist. Ct. (so. and ea. dists.) N.Y. 1979, Mich. 1988. Asst. gen. counsel United Steelworkers Am., Pitts., 1974-77; assoc. Cohen, Weiss and Simon, N.Y.C., 1977-81; assoc. counsel N.Y.C. Bd. Edn., Bklyn., 1981-87; assoc. prof. law Detroit Coll. Law at Mich. State U., 1988-93, prof. law, 1993—. Contbg. author: Children's Rights in America: UN Convention on the Rights of the Child Compared with U.S. Law; contbr. articles to profl. jours. Mem. ABA, Phi Beta Kappa. Office: Detroit Coll Law at Mich State U 447 Law College Bldg East Lansing MI 48824-1300

BITER, RICHARD M., federal official. BS in Transp., Tri-State U., Angola, Ind. Transp. specialist ICC, Chgo., Washington, Atlanta, San Francisco, from 1975; regional dir. ICC, Phila., to 1996; dep. dir. Office of Intermodalism, U.S. Dept. Transp., Washington, 1996—, acting dir., 1998—. Recipient numerous Spl. Achievement and Recognition awards from govt. and pvt. orgns. Office: US Dept Transp Office of Intermodalism Washington DC 20090

BITHER, MARILYN KAYE, emergency nurse, educator; b. Spokane, Wash., Sept. 3, 1941; d. Orville Christopher and Harriet Frances (Bolen) Shiek; m. Richard Eugene Bither, Nov. 11, 1959; children: Bruce Allen, Michele Rae. Diploma, Deaconess Hosp. Sch. Nursing, 1962; cert. in teaching, Humboldt State U., 1984. RN, Calif.; cert. emergency nurse; cert. ACLS, PALS, and BLS instr.; cert. paramedic instr. Crit. care/obstetrics/emergency staff nurse Seaside Hosp., Crescent City, Calif., 1963-80; staff nurse, interim nurse mgr. emergency dept. St. Joseph Hosp., Eureka, Calif., 1980-95; emergency nurse, educator Redwood Meml. Hosp., Fortuna, Calif., 1992—, critical care nurse, 1992-93; telenurse emergency svcs. Gen. Hosp., Eureka, 1992-95; health direct nurse Brim Healthcare, Portland, Oreg., 1995—; EMT instr. Coll. of the Redwoods, Eureka, 1983-93, emergency/critical care cons., 1984-88, emergency med. systems coord., 1987-93; vocat. edn. EMT II, mobile ICU nurse instr. Humboldt County Office Edn., Eureka, 1988-92, vocat. edn. paramedic instr., 1990-95; mem. EMT II curriculum task force Calif. EMS Authority, Sacramento, 1985-86; mem. Calif. affiliate faculty in ACLS/PALS Am. Heart Assn., 1987-95; cons. in field. Author, editor ednl. programs in field. CPR instr. Am. Heart Assn., Humboldt County, 1980-95; 1st aid instr. Nat. Safety Coun., Western Region, 1992-95; U.S. del. to Russia and Eastern Europe tour People to People Internat., 1991. Named State Officer, Calif. Jaycees, 1977-78, Nurse of Yr. Humboldt Nurses Interest Group, 1992; recipient Star of Life award Northcoast Emergency Med. Svcs., 1987. Mem. Emergency Nurses Assn. (prehosp. task force 1987-88), Order of Eastern Star. Republican. Methodist. Avocations: sewing, creative writing, walking, bicycling. Home: 22815 NE 121st St Vancouver WA 98682-9748 Office: Brim Healthcare 305 NE 102nd Ave Portland OR 97220-4170

BITNER, JOHN HOWARD, lawyer; b. Indpls., Feb. 27, 1940; s. Harry M. Jr. and Jeanne B. (Eshelman) B.; m. Vicki Ann D'Ianni, 1961; children: Kerry, Holly, Robin. AB in English and History, Northwestern U., 1961; JD cum laude, Columbia U., 1964. Bar: Ill. 1964. Assoc. Bell, Boyd & Lloyd, Chgo., 1964-71, ptnr., 1972—, chair of corp. and secs. dept., 1988—, vice chmn. of firm, 1992—. Contbr. articles to profl. jours.; editor Columbia Law Rev. Mem. St. Gregory Episcopal Sch. Bd.; mem. bd. visitors Columbia Law Sch. Mem. ABA, Ill. Bar Assn., Chgo. Bar Assn., Union League, Mid-Day Club, Glen View Club, Legal Club, Delta Upsilon, Phi Delta Phi. Presbyterian. Avocations: tennis, reading, scuba. Home: 2329 Lincolnwood Dr Evanston IL 60201-2048 Office: Bell Boyd & Lloyd Three First Nat Plz Chicago IL 60602

BITNER, JOHN WILLIAM, banker; b. Jersey Shore, Pa., July 6, 1948; s. John W. and Gertrude Elizabeth (Brownlee) B. BS in Econs., Lebanon Valley Coll., Annville, Pa., 1970; MBA, Boston Coll., Chestnut Hill, Mass., 1983. V.p. Commonwealth Bank, Williamsport, Pa., 1970-78, Neworld Bank, Boston, 1978-81; fixed income mgr. Digital Equipment Co., Maynard, Mass., 1981-84; sr. v.p. Ea. Bank, Malden, Mass., 1984—. Author: Successful Bank Asset/Liability Management, 1992; fin. columnist The Salem Evening News; contbr. articles to profl. jours. Past pres. Boys and Girls Club Greater Salem; mem. adv. bd. Mystic Valley Elder Svcs. Kellogg fellow, 1973-75. Mem. Fin. Analysts Fedn., Boston Security Analysts Soc., North Shore C. of C. (econ. devel. com.), Rotary.

BITNER, WILLIAM LAWRENCE, III, retired banker, educator; b. Harrisburg, Pa., Dec. 25, 1930; s. William Lawrence, Jr. and Anna (Horstick) B.; m. Wylla Mae Bowman, June 9, 1956; children: Lizabeth Anne, Lynne Ellen Bitner Ackner. BS in Edn., Pa. State U., Bloomsburg; MA, Rutgers U.;

PhD in Adminstrn., NYU. Tchr. Scotch Plains High Sch., N.J., 1956-57; asst. supt. schs. Scotch Plains Sch. Dist., 1958-61, Plainview Sch. Dist., N.Y., 1961-63; supt. schs. Glen Falls Sch. Dist., N.Y., 1963-72; assoc. commr. edn. N.Y. State Edn. Dept., Albany, 1972-76; sr. v.p. 1st Nat. Bank Glen Falls, 1976, pres., CEO, 1977-93; pres., CEO Evergreen Bancorp, Inc., 1980-93; ret., 1993; pres. Assoc. for Advancement of Internat. Edn., Dept. State, 1971-73; bd. dirs. Sandy Hill Corp., Hudson Falls, N.Y., N.Am. Med. Instrument Corp. Pres., chmn. bd. trustees, bd. dirs. Glens Falls Family YMCA, 1984-85; bd. trustees Hyde Collections, Glens Falls, 1963-88, chmn. bd., 1985-88; trustee Albany Med. Coll., 1977-85; bd. dirs. Glens Falls Hosp., 1988—, Lake Champlain Cancer Rsch. Orgn., Inc., Burlington, Vt., 1988—; chmn. Cmty. Lending Corp. N.Y., 1991-92; pres.-elect N.Y. State Coun. of Sch. Supts., 1971-72; dir. N.Y. State Health Care Trustees, 1998—. Recipient Dean John W. Withers Meml. award NYU Alumni Assn., 1964, Disting. Svc. award Bloomsburg U. Pa., 1972, Nat. PTA Life Membership, Adirondack coun. PTA, 1972, Outstanding Sch. Adminstr. award N.Y., 1976, Fgn. Lang. Tchrs. Assn., 1975, Spl. award Human Resources Sch., 1975, Disting. Svc. award Glens Falls YMCA, 1992; Charles F. Kettering Found. fellow Carleton Coll., 1966; named one of Outstanding Young Men in Am., N.Y. Jaycees, 1966. Mem. N.Y. State Coun. Sch. Dist. Adminstrs. (hon. life), N.Y. State Bankers Assn. (pres. 1989-90), Ind. Bankers Assn. N.Y. State (pres. 1984-85, Disting. Svc. award 1991), East Lake Woodland Country Club, Glens Falls Country Club, Univ. Club (N.Y.C.). Republican. Avocations: golf, squash. Home: 54 Wincrest Dr Queensbury NY 12804-1345 also: 4902 Turtle Creek Trl Oldsmar FL 34677-1969

BITONDO, DOMENIC, engineering executive; b. Welland, Ont., Can., June 7, 1925; came to U.S., 1950, naturalized, 1956; s. Vito Leonard and Vita Maria (Gallipoli) B.; m. Delphine May Dicola, June 11, 1949; children—Michael, Annamarie, David, Marisa. BS, U. Toronto, 1947, MS, 1948, PhD, 1950. Aerodynamist, Aerophysics div. N.Am. Aviation Co., Downey, Calif., 1950-51; project engr. to chief of aerodynamics Aerophysics Devel. Corp., Santa Barbara, 1951-59; staff engr. Northrup Corp., Hawthorne, Calif., 1959-60; head test planning and analysis TRW Systems, Inc., El Segundo, Calif., 1960-61; dept. head aeromechanics dept. Systems Research and Planning div., founder, dir. Advanced Ballistic Reentry Systems Program (ABRES) Aerospace Corp., El Segundo, 1961-63; dir. engring. Aerospace Systems div. Bendix Corp., Ann Arbor, Mich., 1963-69; engring. mgr. Apollo lunar sci. expts., 1966; dir., gen. mgr. Bendix Research Labs., Southfield, Mich., 1969-79; exec. dir. research and devel. Bendix Corp., Southfield, Mich., 1979-80; pres. Bitondo Assocs. Inc., Ann Arbor, 1980—; Gordon N. Patterson lectr. U. Toronto, 1976; trustee Central Solar Energy and Research Corp., Detroit, 1978-80; dir. Continental Controls Corp., San Diego.; Def. Research Bd. Can. asst., 1948, NRC asst., 1947. Contbr. tech. articles to profl. jours. Mem. AIAA, NRC (mem. com. on mgmt. tech.), NAS (mem. task force to Indonesia in methodology of tech. planning), Mich. Energy Resource Rsch. Assn. (trustee 1978), Nat. Mgmt. Assn. (Gold Knight award), Indsl. Rsch. Inst. (emeritus). Office: 5 Manchester Ct Ann Arbor MI 48104-6562

BITRAN, JACOB DAVID, internist; b. Thessaloniki, Greece, Sept. 23, 1947; came to U.S., 1952; s. David Jacob and Martha (Faratzi) B.; m. Linda Sue Androw, Dec. 26, 1970; children: Lauren, Dina. BS, U. Ill., Chgo., 1968, MD, 1971. Diplomate Am. Bd. Internal Medicine with subspecialties in med. oncology, hematology. Intern in medicine Michael Reese Med. Ctr., Chgo., 1971-72, resident in internal medicine, 1973-75, clin. asst. prof. medicine, 1977-81, clin. assoc. prof. medicine, 1981-84; resident in pathology Rush Presbyn. St. Luke's Med. Ctr., Chgo., 1972-73; fellow in hematology/oncology U. Chgo., 1975-77, assoc. prof. medicine, 1984-88, prof. medicine, 1988-91; dir. divsn. hematology/oncology Luth. Gen. Hosp., Park Ridge, Ill., 1991—; prof. medicine U. Ill., Chgo., 1996-98; mem. sci. adv. bd. Lederle Labs., Wayne, N.J., 1986-89. Editor: Lung Cancer, 1988. Fellow ACP, Am. Coll. Chest Physicians; mem. Am. Assn. for Cancer Rsch. (program chmn. 1988-89), Am. Soc. Clin. Oncology (program chmn. 1990-91). Democrat. Achievements include development of usable chemotherapy regimen for non small cell lung cancer that has been in clinical use since 1976; exploration of dose intensive chemotherapy in breast cancer. Avocations: tennis, rowing. Office: Lutheran General Hospital 1700 Luther Ln Park Ridge IL 60068-1270

BITTEL, MURIEL HELENE, managing editor; b. N.Y.C., Mar. 22; d. Ernest Henry and Helen Minnie (Seibel) Albers; m. Robert Gifford Walcutt, June 15, 1946; children—Lynn Lowell Walcutt, Mark James Walcutt, Judith Anne Walcutt; m. Lester Robert Bittel, May 8, 1973. B.A., Douglass Coll. Feature writer Daily Home News, New Brunswick, N.J.; editor Fawcett Pubs., N.Y.C., 1940-46; pub. relations dir. Electrovox/Walco Inc., East Orange, N.J., 1946-62; mng. editor Acad. Hall Pubs., Bridgewater, Va., 1974—. Mng. editor: Ency. Profl. Mgmt., 1978; Handbook Profl. Mgrs., 1985, A Surprise in Every Corner, 1994, Island Adventures, 1995. Home: 106 Breezewood Ter Bridgewater VA 22812-1433

BITTEN, MARY JOSEPHINE, quality consultant, municipal official; b. Brighton, Mich., May 20, 1942; d. William Frederick and Josephine Grace (Wright) Belz; m. Gerald A. Bitten, (div. Dec. 1982); children: Joann, Mark, Scott. Student, Howell High Sch., 1960; BBA, Cleary Coll., 1997. Bookkeeper Bitten Brothers, Brighton, Mich., 1963-67; v.p. Holiday Of Hartland (Mich.), 1977-88; acct. Taylor Bldg., Detroit, 1978-79; pres. Mar-Bar Ins., Brighton, Mich.; real estate mgr. C-21, Howell, Mich., 1979-86; township clk. Township of Brighton, Mich., 1987-90; self-employed builder Brighton, Mich., 1986—; cons., 1990—; pres. Merry Maids 707, Inc., 1990-95; bus. cons. quality engring. QS-900, 1992&. Mem. Republican Women, dir. Livingston County Clks., treas. Livingston County Township Assn., 1988, chmn. Brighton Township Recycling, 1988, Mich. Township Assn., Brighton Area C. of C. Lutheran. Home: 59 Old US 23 Hwy Brighton MI 48116

BITTENBENDER, ROBERT A., state official; b. Berwick, May 27, 1941; s. G. Clair and Mildred (Moser) B.; m. Kathie Hamsher; children: Robin Deardorff, Reed; stepchildren: Tammy Hamsher, David Hamsher. BS, Albright Coll., 1963; MA in Govt. Adminstrn., U. Pa., 1970. Various positions Office of the Budget/DGS, 1963-79, dep. sec. for the budget, 1979-83, sec. of the budget, 1983-87, exec. dir. senate appropriations com., 1988-95, appt. sec. of the budget, 1995—; mem. State Employees Retirement Bd.; past trustee Albright Coll. Named Disting. Alumni award Albright Coll., 1982. Mem. Nat. Assn. State Budget Officers (hon. life). Office: Budget Office 238 Main Capitol St Harrisburg PA 17101-1808

BITTER, JOHN, university dean emeritus, musician, businessman, diplomat; b. N.Y., Apr. 8, 1909; s. Karl and Marie Agnes (Schevill) B.; m. Dorothy Michelson, 1934; 1 dau., Ursula; m. Barbara Pinion, Feb. 22, 1947; children: Robin Simonetta, Noel Lesley, Marietta. Grad., Curtis Inst. Music, Phila., 1931. Condr. Jacksonville (Fla.) Symphony Orch., 1934-36, Fla. State Symphony, 1936-39; asso. condr. Leopold Stokowski's All Am. Youth Orch., 1940-41; condr. symphony orch. U. Miami, 1940-59, dean sch. music, 1951-63, dean emeritus, 1980—; asst. to pres., lectr. humanities, 1963-64; v.p. Keyes Investment Group, 1982—; condr. summer symphony, 1951-63; guest condr. Berlin Philharmonic Orch., Berlin Staatsoper, Hamburg Philharmonic, Radio Italiana, others, 1946-67; Realtor Keyes Co., 1978—; Consul for Germany in, Miami, 1969-78; adj. prof. Fla. Internat. U., 1989, U. Miami, 1990; lectr. Urania Forum, Berlin, 1990—. Bd. trustees Miami Lighthouse for the Blind, 1995. Maj. AUS, 1942-46. Decorated Bronze Star; officer's cross Order of Merit Fed. Republic of Germany, 1972; recipient Allied Arts prize for composition, 1969; Nat. Sales Achievement awards, 1968-72; Steuben award, City of Berlin, 1985. Mem. Nat. Assn. Schs. Music (v.p. 1959), Nat. Speakers Assn., Phi Mu Alpha Sinfonia (hon.), Phi Kappa Phi. Home: 770 NE 69th St Apt 4B Miami FL 33138-5763 *"Use your eyes as if tomorrow you would be struck blind. Use your ears, listen to the harmonies of nature, the sounds of symphonies, as if tomorrow you would become deaf. Taste and touch with relish and enjoyment. Revel in beauty and make the most of every sense.". . . Helen Keller. I add: the mind and spirit will follow.*

BITTER, SHLOMO ABRAHAM, systems integration company executive; b. Tel Aviv, Jan. 4, 1954; came to U.S., 1979; m. Henni Katz, July 18, 1978; 3 children. BS in Computer Sci. and Math., Bar-Ilan U., Israel, 1979; MS in Computer Sci., Columbia U., 1981. Various mgmt. positions Crystal Brands Inc., N.Y.C., 1980-89, v.p. MIS, 1989-92; corp. v.p. info. sys. Donna Karan, N.Y.C., 1992-93; v.p., CIO Starter Corp., New Haven, 1993-94; dir. tech. svcs. Computer Generated Solutions Inc., N.Y.C., 1995—. Lt. Israel Def. Forces, 1972-76. Avocations: traveling, reading. Home: 14424 70th Rd Flushing NY 11367-1718 Office: Computer Generated Solutions 1675 Broadway New York NY 10019-5820

BITTERMAN, MARY GAYLE FOLEY, broadcasting executive; b. San Jose, Calif., May 29, 1944; d. John Dennis and Zoe (Hames) Foley; m. Morton Edward Bitterman, June 26, 1967; 1 child Sarah Fleming. BA, Santa Clara U., 1966; MA, Bryn Mawr Coll., 1969, PhD, 1971. Exec. dir. Hawaii Pub. Broadcasting, Honolulu, 1974-79; dir. Voice of Am., Washington, 1980-81, Dept. Commerce, Honolulu, 1981-83, E.-W. Ctr. Inst. Culture and Comm., Honolulu, 1984-88; cons. pvt. practice, Honolulu, 1989-93; pres., CEO KQED, Inc., San Francisco, 1993—; Bd. dirs. Bank of Hawaii, Honolulu, 1984—, McKesson Corp., San Francisco, 1995—; trustee Am.'s Pub. TV Stas., 1997—; vice chmn. TIDE 2000, Tokyo, 1984-93. Producer: (film) China Visit, 1978; contbr. numerous articles on internat. telecomms. to various pubs. Bd. dirs. United Way, Honolulu, 1986-93; chmn. Kuakini Health System, Honolulu, 1991-94. Recipient Candle of Understanding award Bonneville (Utah) Internat. Corp., 1985; named hon. mem. Nat. Fedn. Press Women, 1986. Fellow Nat. Acad. Pub. Info.; mem. Pacific Forum, CSIS (bd. govs.), Bay Area Coun. (bd. dirs.), World Affairs Coun. (bd. dirs.). Office: KQED Inc 2601 Mariposa St San Francisco CA 94110 Address: 229 Kaalawai Pl Honolulu HI 96816-4435

BITTERMAN, MELVIN LEE, real estate developer; b. Yankton, S.D., Dec. 9, 1938; s. Edward Phillip and Amanda Bertha (Moke) B.; m. Constance Winfried Mann, Nov. 7, 1970; 1 child, Janet Amanda. BA, N. Tex. State U., 1967. Librarian City of Glendale, Calif., 1967-71; sales rep. Allstate Ins. Co., Glendale, 1971-86; property mgr./developer Glendale, 1986—. With U.S. Army, 1961-64. Mem. Rotary (sec. 1985), Alpha Beta Alpha. Republican. Roman Catholic. Avocations: amateur radio, fishing, tennis, trap shooting, ping pong. Address: 1400 Beaudry Blvd Glendale CA 91208-1708

BITTERMAN, MORTON EDWARD, psychologist, educator; b. N.Y.C., Jan. 19, 1921; s. Harry Michael and Stella (Weiss) B.; m. Mary Gayle Foley, June 26, 1967; children—Sarah Fleming, Joan, Ann. B.A., NYU, 1941; M.A., Columbia U., 1942; Ph.D., Cornell U., 1945. Asst. prof. Cornell U., Ithaca, N.Y., 1945-50; assoc. prof. U. Tex., Austin, 1950-55; mem. Inst. for Advanced Study, Princeton, N.J., 1955-57; prof. Bryn Mawr Coll., Pa., 1957-70, U. Hawaii, Honolulu, 1970—; dir. Békésy Lab. Neurobiology, Honolulu, 1991—. Author: (with others) Animal Learning, 1979; editor: Evolution of Brain and Behavior in Vertebrates, 1976; co-editor: Am. Jour. Psychology, 1955-73; cons. editor Jour. Animal Learning and Behavior, 1973-76, 85-88, Jour. Comparative Psychology, 1988-92. Recipient Humboldt prize Alexander von Humboldt Found., Bonn, W.Ger., 1981; Fulbright grantee; grantee NSF, Office Naval Research, NIMH, Air Force Office Sci. Research, Deutsche Forschungsgemeinschaft. Fellow Soc. Exptl. Psychologists (Warren medal 1997), Am. Psychol. Assn., AAAS; mem. Psychonomic Soc. Home: 229 Kaalawai Pl Honolulu HI 96816-4435 Office: Univ Hawaii Bekesy Lab of Neurobiology 1993 E West Rd Honolulu HI 96822-2321

BITTERWOLF, THOMAS EDWIN, chemistry educator; b. New Orleans, Jan. 19, 1947; s. Alvin John and Naomi Mae (Hendrix) B.; m. Caroline Elizabeth Means, May 25, 1968; children: Heidi Elizabeth, Katharine Naomi. BS, Centenary Coll., 1968; PhD, W.Va. U., 1976. Commd. ensign USN, 1973, advanced through grades to comdr., 1987; instr. Naval Nuclear Power Sch., Orlando, Fla., 1973-77, U.S. Naval Acad., Annapolis, Md., 1977-82; resigned USN, 1982; asst. prof. U.S. Naval Acad., Annapolis, Md., 1982-85, assoc. prof., 1985-88; assoc. prof. chemistry U. Idaho, Moscow, 1988-91, prof. chemistry, dir. teaching enhancement, 1991-96, assoc. dean coll. letters scis., 1996-98; exit stds. commr. Idaho High Schs., 1998—. Contbr. articles to refereed jours. Mem. AAAS, Am. Chem. Soc., Royal Soc. Chemistry, Sigma Xi. Methodist. Avocation: theater. Home: PO Box 8188 Moscow ID 83843-0688 Office: U Idaho Dept Chemistry Moscow ID 83844-2343

BITTLE, EDGAR H., lawyer; b. Des Moines, Feb. 26, 1942; s. Harold A. and Ruth (Davis) B.; m. Barbara Paul, May 21, 1966 (div. Dec. 1982); children: Bradford, Wendy, Deborah, Mark; m. Barbara Bowman Madden, June 18, 1983; children: Stephen Madden, Patrick Madden. BA, Cornell U., 1964; JD, U. Mich., 1967. Bar: Iowa, U.S. Dist. Ct. (so. dist.) Iowa, U.S. Ct. Appeals (8th cir.), U.S. Supreme Ct. Assoc. to ptnr. Herrick, Langdon, Belin & Harris, Des Moines, 1967-79; ptnr. Ahlers, Cooney, Dorweiler, Haynie, Smith & Allbee, P.C., Des Moines, 1979—; gen. counsel Iowa Assn. Sch. Bds., 1973-97. Contbr. numerous articles to profl. jours. State rep. Iowa Ho. Reps., 1973-76. Mem. ABA (urban, labor and employment law, adminstrv. law and banking sects.), Am. Mgmt. Assn., Iowa State Bar Assn., Nat. Sch. Bd. Assn. (chair 1981-82), Iowa Coun. Sch. Attys., Polk County Bar Assn., Nat. Assn. Bond Lawyers, Nat. Assn. Coll. and U. Attys. Office: Ahlers Cooney Dorweiler Haynie Smith & Allbee PC 100 Court Ave Ste 600 Des Moines IA 50309-2200

BITTLE, POLLY ANN, nephrology nurse, researcher; b. Orlando, Fla., Jan. 15, 1963; d. James T. and Maybell (Wendel) B. ADN, Valencia Community Coll., Orlando, 1984, AA, 1986; BSN, U. South Fla., 1987. Cert. in CPR, emergency cardiac care, ACLS. Clin. rsch. coord. nephrology, hypertension, cardiothoracic surgery U. South Fla. Coll. Medicine, Tampa, 1987—; interim dir. nursing U. South Fla. Dialysis Ctr., Tampa, 1994-95, asst. dir., 1996—. Contbr. articles to profl. jours. Governing body mem. U.S. Dialysis Ctr., 1996—. Mem. Am. Heart Assn., Am. Nephrology Nurses Assn., Fla. Nurses Assn., Sigma Theta Tau, Phi Theta Kappa.

BITTMAN, WILLIAM OMAR, lawyer; b. Milw., Aug. 6, 1931; s. Omar A. and Lyda (Schneider) B.; m. Carole Jean Chiletti, Aug. 25, 1956; children: Michael John, Barbara Bittman Jensen, Mary Elizabeth Bittman McGee, William Omar, Robert James, Julie Anne, Carrie Lynn. B.S., Marquette U., 1956; student, Law Sch., 1956-57; J.D., DePaul U., 1959. Bar: Ill. bar 1960, D.C. bar 1967. With Dept. Justice, 1960-67; spl. atty. Dept. Justice, Washington, 1965-67; ptnr. Hogan & Hartson, Washington, 1967-74; ptnr. firm Pierson, Ball & Dowd, Washington, 1974-88, chmn., 1987-88; ptnr. Reed, Smith, Shaw and McClay, 1989—; chief prosecutor in govt. trial of James R. Hoffa, 1964, of Robert G. Baker, 1967; chief trial counsel to former sec. of labor Raymond J. Donovan, 1986-87. Named one of Chgo.'s 10 outstanding young men, 1964; recipient Sustained Outstanding Performance award Dept. Justice, 1964, Spl. Act. Meritorious Achievement award, 1967. Mem. Am., Fed., D.C., Ill. bar assns. Roman Catholic. Home: 9116 Bradley Blvd Rockville MD 20854-4605 Office: 1100 East Tower 1301 K St NW Washington DC 20005-3317

BITTNER, RONALD JOSEPH, computer systems analyst, magician; b. Schenectady, N.Y., July 30, 1954; s. Richard John and Catherine (Stepnowski) B.; m. Elayne Louise Simpson, May 14, 1983; 1 child, Krysten Elayne. AS in Chemistry, Orange County C.C., Middletown, N.Y., 1978; BA in Bus. Mgmt., Herbert Lehman Coll., Bronx, N.Y., 1983. Internal cons. Internat. Paper Co., Tuxedo, N.Y., 1978-87; systems analyst McGraw-Hill News, N.Y.C., 1987-89; sr. systems analyst Orange County Info. Svcs., Goshen, N.Y., 1989-91, Columbia Tristar Home Video, N.Y.C., 1991-93; MIS mgr. Post Perfect, N.Y.C., 1993-94, Warner Bros., N.Y.C., 1994—; cons. in magic Shawnee Playhouse, Poconos, Pa., 1985. Contbr. articles to newspapers and mags., 1980-88. Mem. Variety Club Internat., Soc. Am. Magicians (pres. 1985-87, assembly pres. 1993—, Magician of Yr. award 1995), Internat. Brotherhood of Magicians, Acad. Magical Arts, Microcomputer Mgrs. Assn. (program coord.). Avocations: scuba diving, underwater photography, cooking, bowling, chess. Home: 186 Forest Rd Wallkill NY 12589-4712

BITZEGAIO, HAROLD JAMES, retired lawyer; b. Coalmont, Ind., Jan. 29, 1921; s. Nicholas Gilbert and Dora Belle (Burns) B.; m. Betty Jean Law, Apr. 15, 1950; children: Judith L. Bitzegaio Wallin, Gail Ann Bitzegaio Wright, Susan R. Bitzegaio Denyer, James R., Jane E. BS, Ind. State U., 1948; JD, Ind. U., 1953; grad., Ind. Jud. Coll., 1980. Bar: Ind. 1953, U.S. Dist. Ct. (so. dist.) Ind. 1953, U.S. Ct. Appeals (7th cir.) 1956. Sole practice Terre Haute, Ind., 1953-58, 81-97; judge Vigo Superior Ct., Terre Haute, 1959-80; of counsel Anderson & Nichols Law Office. Editor, contbr.: Indiana Pattern Jury Instructions, 1966. Mem. Ind. Adv. Com. Civil Rights, Indpls., 1961-70, Mayor's Com. Civil Rights, Terre Haute, 1967-68; bd. dirs. Wabash Valley Council Boy Scouts Am., Terre Haute, 1960-80. Served to lt. comdr. USN, 1941-46, PTO. Decorated D.F.C. with gold star, Air medal with two gold stars, Purple Heart; named Sagamore of the Wabash, Gov. of Ind., 1990. Mem. ABA, Ind. Bar Assn., Terre Haute Bar Assn., Ind. Judges Assn. (bd. mgrs. 1961-80, pres. 1977-78), Ind. U. Law Alumni Assn. (pres. 1973-74, recipient disting. service award 1974), VFW (life), Nat. Rifle Assn. (life), Ducks Unltd. (nat. trustee, emeritus). Democrat. Club: Terre Haute Country (bd. dirs. 1974-76). Home and Office: 2703 E Springhill Dr Terre Haute IN 47802-8406

BITZER, DONALD LESTER, electrical engineering educator, retired research laboratory administrator; b. East St. Louis, Ill., Jan. 1, 1934; s. Jess L. and Marjorie (Look) B.; m. Maryann Drost, July 2, 1955; 1 son, David. B.S., U. Ill., 1955, M.S., 1956, Ph.D., 1960; PhD (hon.), MacMurray Coll. Mem. faculty U. Ill.-Urbana, 1955—, asst. prof., 1960-63, assoc. prof., 1963-67, prof. elec. engring., 1967—, dir. Computer-Based Edn. Research Lab., 1967-89; disting. prof. rsch. N.C. State U., 1989—; cons. in field. Contbr. articles to profl. jours.; pioneer PLATO-large computer-based edn. system; co-inventor plasma display panel. Recipient Indsl. Rsch. 100 award, 1966, Bobby Connelly Meml. award Miami Valley Computer Assn., 1973, Recognition award Soc. for Info. Display, 1979, Edn. award Am. Fedn. Info. Processing Socs., 1989, Elec. Engring. Disting. Alumni award U. Ill., 1992; named laureate Lincoln Acad of Ill., 1982; Internat. Engring. Consortium fellow, 1994. Fellow AAAS, IEEE, Assn. Devel. Computer-Based Instrnl. Sys., Internat. Engring. Consortium; mem. NAE (Vladimir K. Zworykin award), Data Processing Mgmt. Assn. (Computer Sci. Man of Yr. award), Am. Soc. Engring. Edn. (Chester Carlson award), Nat. Acad. Engring. Home: 104 Christofle Ln Cary NC 27511-6473 Office: NC State U Computer Sci Dept PO Box 8206 Raleigh NC 27695-8206

BIVANS, MAURITA W., school administrator; b. Del., July 31, 1944; d. Harvey and Wilson (Thompson) Yarber; m. Lorenzo A. Bivans, June 22, 1968; children: Lorenzo Jr., Lamont. BA in Arts and Scis., Rutgers State U., 1966, MEd, 1984, EdD, 1993. Cert. elem. tchr., sch. adminstr./supr. Tchr. elem. edn. Berlin Twp. Schs., West Berlin, N.J., 1966-89, dir. spl. svcs., 1989-97; asst. supt. Washington Twp. Pub. Schs., 1997—; adj. prof. Trenton State Coll., Ewing, N.J., 1995-96. Mem. Berlin Twp. Mcpl. Alliance Anti-Drug Program, 1990—, Marlton Track Program, Evesham Twp., 1990-94. Named Tchr. of Yr. Berlin Twp. Schs., Govs. Recognition Com., 1989; Dr. Martin Luther King Jr. scholar, 1990. Mem. ASCD, CEC, N.J. Assn. for Supervision and Curriculum Devel., N.J. Assn. Pupil Svcs. Adminstrs., N.J. Assn. Sch. Adminstrs., Rutgers U. Grad. Alumni Assn., Kappa Delta Pi.

BIVENS, CONSTANCE ANN, retired elementary education educator; b. Madison, Ind., June 26, 1938; d. Nelson and Virginia (Cole) B. BS, George Peabody Coll. for Tchrs., now Vanderbilt U., 1960, MA, 1966; EdD, Nova Southeastern U., Ft. Lauderdale, Fla., 1982. Cert. educator. Tchr. Broward County Schs., Ft. Lauderdale, Fla., 1960-61, 65-97, Jefferson County Schs., Louisville, Ky., 1961-62, Ft. Knox (Ky.) Schs., 1962-64, Madison (Ind.) Consol. Schs., 1964-65; ret., 1997; chmn. K-Adult Coun., Nova Schs., Ft. Lauderdale, 1976-78; cons. 1978-80. Author: Boots, Butterflies, and Dragons, 1982. Mem. Hollywood Hills United Meth. Ch., 1966—, mem. Sing in Chancel Choir, pres. Sunday Sch. class, 1991-94, Walk to Emmaus, 1990, 91-92; active Children's Cancer Caring Ctr. Inc., Broward County chpt., 1986—, Hollywood Hist. Soc., Zool. Soc. Fla. Mem. AAUW, NEA, Hist. Madison, Inc., Jefferson County Hist. Soc., Internat. Order King's Daus. and Sons, Irish Cultural Inst., Ft. Lauderdale Lawn Bowling Club, Delta Kappa Gamma Soc. Internat. (internat. expansion com. 1986-88, chmn. internat. program of work com. 1988-90, internat. rep. World Confedn. Orgns. of Tchg. profession 1989, chmn. S.E. regional conf. 1991, internat. nominations com. 1992-96, chmn. 1994-96, hdqrs. adminstrv. com. 1997—; 1st v.p. Mu State 1993-95, Mu State pres. 1995-97, Sara Ferguson Achievement award 1990, internat. convention credentials com. 1998, chmn. Mu state achievement award com. 1999—). Republican. Methodist. Avocation: travel. Home: 5516 Arthur St Hollywood FL 33021-4608

BIVENS, DONALD WAYNE, lawyer, judge; b. Ann Arbor, Mich., Feb. 5, 1952; s. Melvin Donley and Frances Lee (Speer) B.; children: Jody, Lisa. BA magna cum laude, Yale U., 1974; JD, U. Tex., 1977. Bar: Ariz. 1977, U.S. Dist. Ct. Ariz. 1977, U.S. Ct. Appeals (9th cir.) 1977, U.S. Ct. Appeals (fed. cir.) 1984, U.S. Supreme Ct. 1982. Ptnr. Meyer, Hendricks & Bivens, P.A., Phoenix, 1977—; judge pro tem Maricopa County Superior Ct., Ariz., 1987—, Ariz. Ct. Appeals, Phoenix, 1999—; bd. dirs. Ctr. for Law in Pub. Interest, Phoenix, 1983-85. Note & Comment editor Tex. Law Rev., Austin, 1976-77. Pres. Ariz. Young Dems., 1980-82, Scottsdale Men's League, 1980-82; v.p., bd. dirs. Phoenix Symphony Assn., 1980-86; bd. dirs. Scottsdale Arts Ctr. Assn., 1981-84, Planned Parenthood Cen. and No. Ariz., 1989-92; adv. bd. Ariz. Theater Co., 1987-88. Recipient Consul award U. Tex. Sch. Law, 1977, Three Outstanding Young Men award Phoenix Jaycees, 1981. Mem. ABA (coun. litigation sect. 1995-98, chmn. computer litigation com. 1989-92, resource devel. com. litigation sect. 1992—, tech. task force 1998—, state del. to Ho. of Dels. 1999—), Am. Bar Found., Ariz. Bar Found., State Bar Ariz. (bd. govs. 1993-2000, pres. 1998-99—, peer rev. com. 1992—), Ariz. Trial Lawyers Assn., Maricopa County Bar Assn. (bd. dirs., chmn. Trial Adv. Inst. 1986-87, Mem. of Yr. 1998), Thurgood Marshall Inn of Ct. (pres. 1992-93). Democrat. Avocations: music, theater. Home: 4929 E Cochise Rd Paradise Valley AZ 85253-1044 Office: Meyer Hendricks & Bivens PA 3003 N Central Ave Ste 1200 Phoenix AZ 85012-2915

BIVENS, LYNETTE KUPKA, elementary education educator; b. Chgo., June 1, 1950; d. Walter Edward and Agnes (Berry) Kupka; m. William Joseph Bivens, Sept. 29, 1973; 1 child, Tia Lyn. BE, Govs. State U., 1990, MA in Math. Edn., 1994; grad., Nat. Staff Devel. Coun. Acad., 1998. Cert. elem. tchr., Ill. Tchr. math. Brooks Jr. High, Harvey, Ill., 1990-97; tchr. gifted OW Huth Mid. Sch., Matteson, Ill., 1997—; adj. prof. math edn., Governor's State U., 1998—. Fellow Nat. Coun. Tchrs. Math., Ill. Coun. Tchrs. Math.; mem. Ill. Computing Educators, Nat. Staff Devel. Coun., Mid. Level Sci., Math, Tech. Network. Democrat. Avocations: fine needlework, reading, photography, computers and technology. E-mail: Lk-Bivens@Govst.edu.

BIVINS, SUSAN STEINBACH, systems engineer; b. Chgo., June 5, 1941; d. Joseph Bernard and Eleanor Celeste (Mathes) S.; BS, Northwestern U., 1963; postgrad. U. Colo., 1964, U. Ill., 1965, UCLA, 1971; m. James Herbert Bivins, June 7, 1980. With IBM, 1967-94, support mgr. East, White Plains, N.Y., 1977-78, systems support mgr., western region, L.A., 1978-81, br. market support mgr., 1981-84, mgr. IBM ops. and support L.A. Summer Olympics, 1984; mgr. IBM office supporting devel. FAA air traffic control system for 1990's, 1984-88, mgr. complex systems mktg., 1988-89, acct. devel. mgr. aerospace engring. and mfg., 1989-91, mgr. cons. and outsourcing indsl. sector trading area, 1991-92, cons. orgn. task forces, 1992-93; project exec. IBM Integrated Sys. Solutions Corp., 1993-94; exec. dir. BDM Internat. Inc., 1995—; pres. Jastech, 1986—. Vol. tchr. computer sci. Calif. Mentally Gifted Minor Programs; vol. L.A. Youth Motivation Task Force; dir. pub. rels. Lake of the Ozarks Jazz Festival, 1993-95; bd. dirs. Greater Lake Area Arts Coun., 1993-95. Mem. Systems Engring. Symposium, Pi Lambda Theta. Developed program to retrieve data via terminal and direct it to any appropriate hardcopy device, 1973. Office: BDM Internat 1501 Bdm Way # 3a522 Mc Lean VA 22102-3204

BIVONA, VIRGINIA SIENA, acquisitions editor; b. Cleve., May 16, 1931; d. Vincent James Sr. and Virginia Catherine (Johnson) Siena; divorced; children: Mark, Lawrence, Stephanie, Matthew, Elizabeth. Attended, Western Res. U., 1950-53. Advt. dir. Am. Direct Mail Mktg., Dallas, 1981-78; pres. Tex. Grid Systems, Inc., Richardson, 1982-93; gen. mgr. Tex. Grid Systems (div. Visu-Com Inc.), Balt., 1993-96; acquisitions editor Rep. of Texas Press, 1997—. Author: Notes from a Chameleon, 1984, 99, Dirty Dining, A Cookbook for Lovers, 1991, Top Texas Chefs Favorite Recipes, 1999he History Forgot, 199, Ida Mae Tutweiler & The Traveling Tea Party, 1999. Vol. Hist. Preservation League, Dallas, 1987—. Mem. Noetic Sci. Inst., Dallas Ft. Worth Writers Workshop, Nat. Mus. Women in Arts. Avocations: cooking, camping, walking, painting, rock-hound. Home: 13820

Methuen Green St Dallas TX 75240-5829 Office: Woodware Publishing Inc. 2320 Los Rios Blvd. Plano TX 75240

BIX, BRIAN, law educator; b. Mpls., Aug. 1, 1962; s. Harold Charles and Helen (Helman) B. BA, Washington U., St. Louis, 1983; JD, Harvard U., 1986; DPhil, Oxford (Eng.) U., 1991. Bar: Mass. 1994, Conn. 1995. Jud. clk. to Justice A. Handler N.J. Supreme Ct., Trenton, 1986-87; jud. clk. to Judge S. Reinhardt 9th Circuit Ct. of Appeals, L.A., 1987-88; lectr. in law Kings Coll., U. London, 1991-93; jud. clk. to Justice Benjamin Kaplan Mass. Appeals Ct., Boston, 1993-95; assoc. prof. law Quinnipiac Law Sch., Hamden, Conn., 1995-98, prof., 1998—; vis. prof. of law George Wash. Law Sch., 1999. Author: Law, Language and Legal Determinacy, 1993, Jurisprudence: Theory and Context, 1996, 2d edit., 1999; editor: Analyzing Law, New Essays in Legal Theory, 1998. Mem. Am. Law Inst. Office: Quinnipiac Law Sch 275 Mount Carmel Ave Hamden CT 06518-1950

BIXBY, FRANK LYMAN, lawyer; b. New Richmond, Wis., May 25, 1928; s. Frank H. and Esther (Otteson) B.; m. Katharine Spence, July 7, 1951; children—Paul, Thomas, Edward, Janet. AB, Harvard U., 1950; LLB, U. Wis., 1953. Bar: Ill. 1953, Wis. 1953, Fla. 1974. Since practiced in Chgo.; ptnr. firm Sidley & Austin, 1963-97, counsel, 1998—. Editor-in-chief Wis. Law Rev, 1952-53; mem. editorial bd. Chgo. Reporter, 1973-89. Trustee MacMurray Coll., Jacksonville, Ill., 1973-85; bd. dirs. Chgo. Urban League, 1962—, v.p., 1972-86, gen. counsel, 1972—, chmn. 1986-89; bd. dirs. Community Renewal Soc., 1973-86, Voices for Ill. Children, 1987-90; chmn. trustees Unitarian Ch., Evanston, Ill., 1962-63; bd. dirs. Spencer Found., 1967—, chmn. 1975-90; mem. dist. 202 bd. edn. Evanston Twp. High Sch., 1975-81, pres., 1977-79. Recipient Man of Year award Chgo. Urban League, 1974. Mem. ABA, Ill. Bar Assn., Wis. Bar Assn., Fla. Bar Assn., Chgo. Bar Assn., Chgo. Coun. Lawyers, Chgo. Coun. Fgn. Rels., Order of Coif, Harvard Club (pres. 1964-65), Mid-Day Club., Phi Beta Kappa. Home: 505 N Lake Shore Dr Apt 4607 Chicago IL 60611-3409 Office: Sidley & Austin 1 First Natl Plz Chicago IL 60603-2003*

BIXBY, HAROLD GLENN, manufacturing company executive; b. Lamotte, Mich., July 14, 1903; s. Charles Samuel and Laura (Schenk) B.; m. Pauline Elizabeth Summy, July 3, 1928; children: Mary Louise and Richard Glenn (twins). A.B., U. Mich., 1927, LL.D. (hon.), 1972. Began in accounting dept. Ex-Cell-O Corp., Detroit, 1928; asst. sec. Ex-Cell-O Corp., 1929, controller, 1933, sec., treas. and dir., 1937, became v.p., treas., dir., 1947, pres., gen. mgr., 1951-70, chmn. bd., chief exec. officer, 1970-72, chmn. bd., 1972—, chmn. exec. com., 1973-79. Bd. dirs., hon. trustee Kalamazoo Coll., Harper Hosp., Detroit. Mem. Greater Detroit C. of C., Tau Kappa Epsilon. Clubs: Economic, Detroit Athletic, Detroit Golf. Home and Office: 16351 Rotunda Dr Ste 357 Dearborn MI 48120-1159

BIXBY, WALTER E., insurance company executive; b. Kansas City, Mo., Feb. 12, 1932; s. Walter E. Sr. and Angeline Inez (Reynolds) B.; m. Mary Martha Musser (div. 1982); children: Ann, Robert Phillip, Walter E. III. BS in Bus. Adminstrn., U. Mo., 1953. Field tng. Kansas City (Mo.) Life Ins. Co., 1956-57, agt., 1957-58, asst. v.p., 1958-63, v.p., 1963-64, v.p., dir. agys., 1964-65, adminstrv. v.p., 1965-87, exec. v.p., 1987-90, pres., 1990-98, also bd. dirs.; vice chmn. bd. Kansas City Life Ins. Co., 1974—; chmn. bd. dirs. Sunset Life Ins. Co., Olympia, Wash., Old Am. Ins. Co.; bd. dirs. United Mo. Bank of Kansas City; treas. J.B. Reynolds Found., Kansas City, Mo. Bd. dirs. Heart of Am. Coun. Boy Scouts Am., Knasas City, Mo., Kansas City Art Inst.; mem. Cross and Cockade Soc. of WWI Aero Historians, Wetherby, West Yorkshire. Served to 1st lt. USAF, 1953-55. Mem. Am. Coun. Life Ins., U. Mo. Alumni Assn., MENSA, Carriage Club, Kansas City Country Club, Univ. Club (Kansas City, Mo.). Libertarian. Avocations: reading, history, science, political philosophy, model airplanes, old movies, sports. Home: 400 W 49th Ter Apt 1800 Kansas City MO 64112-2303 Office: Kansas City Life Ins Co 3520 Broadway St Kansas City MO 64111-2565

BIXLER, MARGARET TRIPLETT, former manufacturing executive; b. Bluffton, Ohio, Sept. 15, 1917; d. Ray Leon and Etta Mabel (Lantz) Triplett; m. Roland M. Bixler, July 1, 1939; children: Katharine, David. AB, U. Mich., 1939; MA, U. New Haven, 1982. Sec. of bd. J-B-T Instruments, Inc., New Haven, 1940-76, chmn. of bd., 1976-91; ret., 1992. Author: Winds of Freedom, 1991, 2d edit., 1995.

BIZIOU, PETER, cinematographer. Cinematographer: (films) Bugsy Malone, 1978, Monty Python's Life of Brian, 1979, Time Bandits, 1981, Pink Floyd-The Wall, 1982, Another Country, 1984 (Cannes award best artistic contbn.), 9 1/2 Weeks, 1986, A World Apart, 1988, Mississippi Burning, 1988 (Academy award best cinematography 1988, British Acad. award 1989, award British Soc. Cinematographers 1989), Rosencrantz and Guildenstern Are Dead, 1991, City of Joy, 1992, Damage, 1992, In the Name of the Father, 1993, Road to Wellville, 1994, Richard III, 1995, The Truman Show, 1997.

BIZUB, BARBARA L., elementary school educator; b. Newark, Jan. 14, 1947; d. Anthony Edward and Mary Travers Petti; m. William Joseph Bizub, Aug. 27, 1966; children: William Anthony, Melissa Catherine Bizub. BA in Elem. Edn., Kean Coll., 1975, MA in Early Childhood Edn., 1985. Cert. tchr. N-8. Tchr. grade one Roselle (N.J.) Bd. Edn., 1975-76, Title VII reading specialist, grades 1-4, 1976-78, tchr. second grade, 1978-79, kindergarten tchr., 1979—; cons. whole lang. Roselle Bd. Edn., 1993-94; guest spkr. 31st Ann. Reading Conf./Kean Coll., Union, N.J., 1994; guest lectr. Kean Coll., 1996, 98, 99; materials presenter 28th Ann. Reading Conf., Rutgers U., 1996; workshop presenter N.J. Assn. for Edn. of Young Children, 1997, 98. Co-author: Family Life Curriculum, K-7, 1985-89; pilot tchr. Whole Lang. Initiative, Roselle, 1993. Recipient A-Plus for Kids Grant, A-Plus for Kids, 1994, 96. Mem. Nat. Coun. Tchrs. English (guest spkr. 1994), Internat. Reading Assn., Ctrl. Jersey Tchrs. of Whole Lang., N.J. Assn. Kindergarten Educators, Ctrl. Jersey Tchrs. Whole Lang., Phi Kappa Phi. Roman Catholic. Avocations: reading, fly fishing, aerobics, cooking, antiquing. Office: Roselle Bd Edn 710 Locust St Roselle NJ 07203-1919

BIZUB, JOHANNA CATHERINE, library director; b. Denville, N.J., Apr. 13, 1957; d. Stephen Bernard and Elizabeth Mary (Grizzle) B.; m. Scott Jeffrey Smith, 1992. BS in Criminal Justice, U. Dayton, 1979; MLS, Rutgers U., 1984. Law libr. Morris County Law Libr., 1981-83, Clapp & Eisenberg, Newark, 1984-86; dir. libr. Sills Cummis, 1986-94; libr. dir. Montville (N.J.) Twp. Pub. Libr., N.J., 1994-97; libr. dir. law dept. Prudential Ins. Co. Am., Newark, 1997—. Mem. ALA, N.J. Law Librs. Assn. (treas. 1987-89, v.p./pres.-elect 1989-00, pres. 1990-91), Am. Assn. Law Librs. (pvt. law librs. SIS, vice chair 1992-93, chair 1993-94, past chair 1994-95), N.J. Libr. Assn., Assoc. Libr. of Morris County (v.p. 1995, pres. 1996, treas. 1997-01), Spl. Libr. Assn. N.J. (treas. 1990-92), Am. Legion Aux. (treas. Rockden unit 175 1983-93). Democrat. Roman Catholic. Home: 11 Elm St Rockaway NJ 07866-3108 Office: Prudential Ins Co Am 22 Plz 751 Broad St Newark NJ 07102-3714

BIZZI, EMILIO, neurophysiologist, educator; b. Rome, Feb. 22, 1933; came to U.S., 1963, naturalized, 1982; s. Vittorio and Anna (Galeazzi) B.; m. Jane Stockton Shaw, Aug. 9, 1941. MD summa cum laude with highest honors, U. Rome, 1958. Postdoctoral trainee Inst. Med. Pathology, U. Siena, Italy, 1958-60; postdoctoral trainee Inst. Physiology, U. Pisa, Italy, 1960-63; rsch. assoc. neurophysiol. lab., dept. zoology Washington U., St. Louis, 1963-64; vis. assoc. sect. physiology, lab. clin. sci. NIMH, Bethesda, Md., 1964-66; rsch. assoc. dept. psychology MIT, Cambridge, 1966-67; lectr. dept. psychology MIT, 1967-68, assoc. prof. neurophysiology, 1969-72, prof. neurophysiology, 1972-80, Eugene McDermott prof. brain scis. and human behavior, 1980—; dir. Whitaker Coll., MIT, 1983-88, chmn. dept. Brain and Cognitive Scis., 1986-97; mem. adv. bd. Biomed. Engring. Ctr. for Clin. Instrumentation. Contbr. numerous chpts., articles, abstracts to profl. publs.; editorial bd. Brain Theory Newsletter, 1980—, Jour. Motor Behavior, 1981—, Jour. Neurobiology, 1981—. Recipient Alden Spencer award Columbia U. Coll. Physicians and Surgeons, 1978, Whitaker Health Scis. award MIT, 1978, Hermann von. Helmholtz award 1992; Found. for Rsch. in Psychiatry fellow, 1978—. Mem. NAS, AAAS, Internat. Brain Rsch. Orgn., Am. Acad. Arts and Scis., Italian Nat. Acad., Am. Acad. Clin. Neurophysiol., Am. Physiol. Soc., Soc. Neurosci. Office: MIT Dept Brain & Cognitive Scis Cambridge MA 02139-4307

BJALAND, LEIF, artistic director, conductor. MusM, U. Mich. Prof. Yale U.; music dir. Yale Symphony Orch.; affiliate artist asst. condr. San Francisco Symphony Orch., 1986-90; condr. Chgo. Symphony Orch., 1988; resident condr., artistic coord. New World Symphony, 1989; artistic dir., condr. Fla. W. Coast Symphony, 1997—; condr. San Francisco Symphony Youth Orch.; guest condr. Arkon Symphony, Anchorage Symphony, Cin. Symphony, Des Moines Symphony, Detroit Symphony, Fla. Philharm., Ft. Wayne Philharm., Fresno Philharm., Grant Pk. Music Festival Chgo., La. Philharm., Nat. Symphony, R.I. Philharm., Rochester Philharm., San Jose Symphony, Santa Rosa Symphony, Va. Symphony, Utah Symphony, Pacific Music Festival Orch., Sapporo Symphony; opera condr. Fla. Grand Opera, 1993-94, 95-96, 97, Opera Co. the Philippines. Office: Fla W Coast Symphony 709 N Tamiami Trail Sarasota FL 34236

BJERKAAS, CARLTON LEE, technology services company executive; b. Fergus Falls, Minn., Apr. 17, 1948; s. Jay Oscar and Anna Marie (Bangert) B.; children: Kristopher Scott, Eric Stefan, Todd Philip. BS, U. N.D., 1970; MS, MIT, 1977; MPA, Auburn U., Montgomery, Ala., 1983. Commd. 2d lt. USAF, 1970, advanced through grades to col., 1992; weather forecaster Weather Detachment, Homestead AFB, Fla., 1971-73; flight examiner Weather Reconnaissance Squadron, Andersen AFB, Guam, 1973-75; radar rsch. meteorologist A.F. Geophysics Lab., Hanscom AFB, Mass., 1976-82; chief support br. operational requirements & testing Hdqrs. Mil. Airlift Command, Scott AFB, Ill., 1983-85; chief aerospace environ. requirements Hdqrs. A.F. Systems Command, Andrews AFB, Md., 1985-87; comdr. Weather Detachment, Lajes Field, Azores, Portugal, 1987-89; asst. chief of staff Hdqrs. Air Weather Svc., Scott AFB, 1989-91, dir. resource mgmt., 1991-92, dir. program mgmt., integration, 1992-94; dir. sys. and comm., 1994-95, dir. tech., plans and programs, 1995—; sr. scientist Hdqrs. Air Weather Svc., Scott AFB, Ill., 1995-96; divsn. mgr. Sci. Applications Internat. Corp., O'Fallon, Ill., 1996—. Contbr. articles to profl. jours. Com. chmn. Boy Scouts Am., O'Fallon, Ill., 1991-92; coach, referee youth sports, O'Fallon, 1989—; chmn. Sch. Bd., Lajes Field Azores, 1988-89; mem. Sch. Dist. Com., Lajes Field Azores, 1987. Fellow Am. Meteorol. Soc.; mem. AAAS, ASPA, N.Y. Acad. Scis., Acad. Polit. Sci., Air Weather Assn., Air Lift and Tanker Assn., Phi Beta Kappa, Sigma Xi, Phi Eta Sigma, Pi Alpha Alpha. Methodist. Avocations: computers, soccer coaching, Boy Scouts. Office: Science Applications Intl Corp 619 W Highway 50 O'Fallon IL 62269-1942

BJERKNES, MICHAEL LEIF, dancer; b. Oak Park, Ill., Dec. 6, 1956; s. Christian Edward and Barbara Ann (Sirkin) B.; m. Pamela Booth Mitchell, July 15, 1979; children: Philip, Anna, Alexandra. Student, Rosary Coll., 1970-73; M in Internat. Mgmt., U. Md., 1997. Dancer Joffrey II, N.Y.C., 1973-74; soloist Chgo. Ballet, 1974-76, Houston Ballet, 1976-78, Joffrey Ballet, N.Y.C., 1978-79, 79-82; union rep. Joffrey Ballet, 1980-82, workshop tchr., 1982—, tchr. sch., 1983-85; repetiteur Washington Ballet, 1989-90; guest ballet master Universal Ballet, 1994—; guest tchr. Md. Youth Ballet, 1997—; quality leader GE Info. Svcs., 1997—, pres., bd. dirs. Am. Dance Inst., 1999—. Prin. dancer Royal Winnipeg (Manitoba, Can.) Ballet, 1979, Milw. Ballet, 1984, Washington Ballet, 1985-90; guest artist No. Ballet Theatre, Manchester, Eng., 1981, Minn. Dance Theatre, 1982-85, Chamber Ballet, 1984, Ballet Chgo., 1990, Tulsa Ballet Sch., 1991, Universal Ballet, 1991; tchr. various ballet schs. U.S., 1972-79, Ruth Page Found., Chgo., 1982-84, Washington Sch. Ballet, 1986-93; ballet master Universal Ballet, Seoul, 1990-95, Washington Ballet, 1993-96; choreographer Universal Ballet, 1993; vol. project devel. mgr. Internat. Exec. Svc. Corps, 1997, Chgo. Dance Masters, 1997, 98; quality mgr. GE, 1997-99; v.p. Tech. Leaders, Inc., 1999. Mem. Am. Guild Musical Artists (bd. dirs. 1980-81), Can. Actor's Equity.

BJONTEGARD, ARTHUR MARTIN, JR., foundation executive; b. Lynn, Mass., Mar. 23, 1938; s. Arthur M. and Irma W. (Cook) B.; m. Wilma Joy Golding, Oct. 15, 1966; children—Arthur M., Karla Kristin. B.A., Duke U., 1959; J.D., U. Va., 1962; postgrad., Stonier Grad. Sch. Banking, Rutgers U., 1966; grad. advanced mgmt. program, Harvard U. Sch. Bus., 1974. Bar: N.J. 1962, S.C. 1967. Bank examiner U.S. Treasury Dept., Richmond, Va., 1962-66; trust officer S.C. Nat. Bank, Columbia, 1966-74; sr. v.p. S.C. Nat. Bank, 1974-81; pres. S.C. Nat. Corp., Columbia, 1981-84; vice-chmn. S.C. Nat. Corp., 1984-92; pres. Ind. Colls. and Univs. of S.C. Inc., 1992—; commr. Columbia Housing Authority, 1995—. Pres. United Way of the Midlands, Columbia, 1984-85, S.C., 1986-87, Univ. Assocs., Columbia, 1984-85, Friday Luncheon Club, Columbia, 1984, Spring Valley Ednl. Found., 1986—, Ctrl. Carolina Community Found., 1990-96; chmn. Columbia Community Resl. Coun., 1984, Fedn. of the Blind, 1992—. Named Vol. of Yr., Urban League, Columbia, 1984; recipient Order of Palmetto award, S.C. Gov., 1992. Mem. S.C. Bar Assn., Palmetto Soc., Thomas Jefferson Soc., S.C. C. of C., Forest Lake County Club, Palmetto Club, Spring Valley Country Club. Episcopalian. Avocations: tennis; swimming; spectator sports. Office: Ind Colls and Univs of SC PO Box 12007 Columbia SC 29211-2007

BJORK, GORDON CARL, economist, educator; b. Seattle, Dec. 15, 1935; s. Gordon E. and Florence E. (Bloomberg) B.; m. Susan Jill Serman, Dec. 29, 1960; children: Katharine, Rebecca, Susannah, Anders. AB, Dartmouth Coll., 1957; BA (hon.), Oxford U., 1959, MA, 1963; PhD, U. Wash., 1963. Lectr. econs. U. B.C., Vancouver, Can., 1962-63; asst. prof. econs. Carleton U., Ottawa, Ont., 1963-64; assoc. prof. econs. Columbia U., N.Y.C., 1964-68; pres. Linfield Coll., McMinnville, Oreg., 1968-74; prof. econs. Oreg. State U., Corvallis, 1974-75; Lovelace prof. econs. Claremont McKenna Coll., Claremont Grad. Sch., Calif., 1975—; Henry Walker disting. vis. prof. bus. enterprise U. Hawaii, 1985-86; vis. prof. econs. Nottingham (Eng.) U., 1990. Author: Private Enterprise and Public Interest: The Development of American Capitalism, 1969, Life, Liberty and Property: The Economics and Politics of Land Use Planning and Environmental Control, 1980, Stagnation and Growth in the American Economy, 1985, The Way It Worked and Why It Won't: Structural Change and the Slowdown of U.S. Economic Growth, 1999. Lt. USCGR, 1960-68. Rhodes scholar, 1957; Battelle Inst. fellow, 1975. Mem. Phi Beta Kappa. Republican. United Ch. of Christ. Home: 4609 Vista Buena Rd Santa Barbara CA 93110 Office: Claremont McKenna Coll Claremont Grad Sch Dept Econs Claremont CA 91711 *An educator teaches by what he is and what he does. My objective, as a teacher, is to mold the values and conceptual framework of the next generation.*

BJORK, ROBERT DAVID, JR., lawyer; b. Evanston, Ill., Sept. 29, 1946; s. Robert David and Lenore Evelyn (Loderhose) B.; m. Linda Louise Reese, Mar. 27, 1971; children: Heidi Lynne, Gretchen Anne. BBA, U. Wis., 1968; JD, Tulane U., 1974. Bar: La. 1974, U.S. Dist. Ct. (ea. dist.) La. 1974, U.S. Ct. Appeals (5th cir.) 1974, U.S. Dist. Ct. (mid. dist.) 1975, U.S. Supreme Ct. 1977, U.S. Dist. Ct. (we. dist.) 1978, U.S. Ct. Appeals (11th cir.) 1981, Calif. 1983, U.S. Dist. Ct. (no. dist.) Calif. 1983, U.S. Dist. Ct. (ea. dist.) Calif. 1984. Ptnr. Adams & Reese, New Orleans, 1974-83; assoc. Crosby, Heafey, Roach & May, Oakland, Calif., 1983-85; ptnr. Bjork, Lawrence, Poeschl & Kohn, Oakland, 1985—; instr. paralegal studies Tulane U., New Orleans, 1979-82. Mem. Tulane U. Law Rev., 1973-74; editor Med. Malpractice newsletter, 1983—. Bd. dirs. Piedmont (Calif.) Coun. Camp Fire, 1984-92, pres., 1987-89; treas. Couhig Congl. Com., New Orleans, 1980-82; bd. dirs. Camp Augusta Trust, 1990—. Lt. USNR, 1968-71. Mem. ABA, Internat. Assn. Def. Counsel, Calif. Bar Assn., La. Bar Assn. (chmn. young lawyers sect. 1982-83), Am. Soc. Law and Medicine. Home: 1909 Oakland Ave Piedmont CA 94611 Office: Bjork Lawrence Poeschl & Kohn 483 9th St Oakland CA 94607-4024

BJORK, ROBERT ERIC, language professional educator; b. Virginia, Minn., Feb. 19, 1949; s. George Emanual and Alice Celinda (Sandberg) B. BA, Pomona Coll., 1971; MA, UCLA, 1974, PhD, 1979. Adj. lectr. Writing Programs and Medicine UCLA, 1979-83; asst. prof., assoc. prof. English Ariz. State U., Tempe, 1983-89, prof., 1989—; vis. scholar St. Catharine's Coll. Cambridge U., 1997; dir. Ariz. Ctr. Medieval Renaissance Studies, 1994—. Author: Old English Verse Saints' Lives, 1985; editor: Cynewulf: Basic Readings, 1996, A Beowulf Handbook, 1997; transl. Lars Hård Trilogy, 1983-85, Holme Trilogy, 1989-90, Only a Mother, 1991; co-editor Studies in Scandinavian Lit. and Culture, 1992—; gen. editor Modern Scandinavian Lit. in Translation, 1984-94; dir., gen. editor Medieval and Renaissance Texts and Studies, 1996—. Recipient Tchg. award Burlington No. Found., 1988. Mem. Internat. Assn. U. Profs. English, Medieval Acad. Am. (dir. data project), Renaissance Soc. Am. (coun.). Office: Ariz State Univ Ctr Medieval Renaissance Tempe AZ 85287

BJORKHOLM, JOHN ERNST, physicist; b. Milw., Mar. 22, 1939; s. Jack W. and Marion B. (Anderson) B.; m. Mary J. Durbin, June 20, 1964; children—Kristin E., Laura J. BSE in Engring. Physics highest honors, Princeton U., 1961; MS, Stanford U., 1962, PhD in Applied Physics, 1966. Mem. tech. staff Electronics Rsch. Lab. AT&T Bell Labs., Holmdel, N.J., 1966-83, disting. mem. tech. staff, 1983-94, cons. in applied physics, 1994-96; prin. scientist components rsch. Intel Corp., Santa Clara, Calif., 1996—. Contbr. numerous articles to profl. jours.; patentee in field. Chmn. Gordon Rsch. Conf. on Nonlinear Optics and Lasers, 1977; comptr. Conf. on Lasers and Electro-Optics, 1989-91; trustee Princeton U., 1991-95. NSF fellow, 1961-62, Howard Hughes fellow, 1962-65. Fellow Am. Phys. Soc., Optical Soc. Am. (dir.-at-large 1988-90, fin. and investment com. 1988-91, exec. com. 1990, treas. 1992-96); mem. IEEE (sr.), NRC (com. on atomic, molecular and optical sci. 1988-91). Home: 408 Cabonia Ct Pleasanton CA 94566-6381 Office: Intel Corp L-395 7000 East Ave # L-395 Livermore CA 94550-9516

BJORKMAN, OLLE ERIK, plant biologist, educator; b. Jonkoping, Sweden, July 29, 1933; came to U.S., 1964; s. Erik Gustaf and Dagmar Kristina (Svensson) B.; m. Monika Birgit Waldinger, Sept. 24, 1955; children: Thomas N.E., Per G.O. MS, U. Stockholm, 1957; PhD, U. Uppsala, 1960; DSc, U. Uppsala, Sweden, 1968. Asst. scientist dept. genetics and plant breeding U. Uppsala, 1956-61; rsch. fellow Swedish Natural Sci. Rsch. Coun., 1961-63; postdoctoral fellow Carnegie Instn. Wash., Stanford, Calif., 1964-65, mem. staff, 1966—; assoc. prof. biology by courtesy Stanford (Calif.) U., 1967-77, prof. biology by courtesy, 1977—; vis. fellow Australian Nat. U., Canberra, 1971-72, 78; advisor to pres. Desert Rsch. Inst., Nev., 1980-81; vis. sci. Australian Inst. Marine Sci., 1983; sci. advisor Kettering Found., 1976-77; mem. panel world food and nutrition study NRC, 1976; com. carbon dioxide effects Dept. Energy, 1977-82; competitive grants panel Dept. Agr., 1978; numerous other coms. and panels. Co-author: Experimental Studies of the Nature of Species V, 1971, Physiological Processes in Plant Ecology, 1980; mem. editorial bd. Planta, 1993—; contbr. articles to profl. publs. Recipient Linneus prize Royal Swedish Physiographic Soc., 1977. Fellow Am. Acad. Arts and Scis., AAAS; mem. NAS, Am. Soc. Plant Physiologists (Stephen Hales award 1986), Australian Acad. Sci. (Selby award 1987), Royal Swedish Acad. Scis., Australian Soc. Plant Physiologists. Home: 3040 Greer Rd Palo Alto CA 94303-4007 Office: Carnegie Inst Dept Plant Biology 260 Panama St Stanford CA 94305-4101

BJORNDAHL, DAVID LEE, electrical engineer; b. Rock Island, Ill., June 19, 1927; s. Richard Gideon and Olive Muriel (Winter) B.; m. Clara Mae Buck, Feb. 16, 1952; children: William, Jay, Jan, Jill. PhD in Elec. Engring., Purdue U., 1956. Sr. engr. Litton Guidance & Control Systems, Beverly Hills, Calif., 1956-58; project engr. Litton Guidance & Control Systems, Woodland Hills, Calif., 1958-62, dir. advanced programs, 1962-66; mgr. Martin-Marietta, Denver, 1966-67; dir. advanced programs Litton Aero. Products, Woodland Hills, 1967-74; v.p. engring. Litton Aero. Products, Moorpark, Calif, 1974-86, chief scientist, 1986-93; ret., 1993; part-time cons., Chatsworth, Calif., 1993—. Contbr. articles to profl. jours. Mem. Sigma Chi, Eta Kappa Nu. Republican. Achievements include design of various electronic navigation systems for aircraft. *

BJORNDAL, ARNE MAGNE, endodontist; b. Ulstein, Norway, Aug. 19, 1916; s. Martin I. and Anne Bjorndal; m. Katharine G. Benson, Jan. 12, 1952; children: Katharine, Kari, Lee. BS, State Coll., Volda, 1939; DDS, U. Oslo, 1947, U. Iowa, 1954; MS, U. Iowa, 1956. Diplomate Am. Bd. Endodontics. Instr. Coll. Dentistry U. Oslo, 1948-50, 51-53; intern Forsyth Dental Infirmary, Boston, 1950-51, NIDR, 1960; mem. faculty U. Iowa, Iowa City, 1954—, prof., 1964—, founder, head dept. endodentics, 1956-80; vis. prof. U. Alexandria, Egypt, 1978. Author: Anatomy and Morphology of Human Teeth, 1983. Maj. USNG, 1963-70. Decorated King Haakon VII medal (Norway); Fulbright scholar, 1950-51. Fellow Am. Coll. Dentists; mem. ADA (Svc. Fgn. Countries award 1979), Iowa Dental Assn. (life), Am. Assn. Endodontics, N.Y. Acad. Sci., Optimists, Elks, Omicron Kappa Upsilon. Republican. Lutheran. Home: 2510 Bluffwood Cir Iowa City IA 52245-3543 Office: Coll Dentistry U Iowa Iowa City IA 52242

BJORNSON, EDITH CAMERON, foundation executive, communications consultant; b. Orlando, Fla., Sept. 12, 1937; d. Hilliard Francis and Edith Muriel (McBride) Cameron; m. Carroll N. Bjornson, Jan. 11, 1963; children: Lisa Carol, Karl Cameron (dec.). BA, U. Fla., Gainesville, 1953, MA, 1956; profl. cert., Ecole de Cuisine LaVerenne, Paris, 1983. Copywriter Sta. WGGG, Gainesville, Fla., 1953-54; exec. asst. Actors' Studio, N.Y.C., 1956-58; prodn. asst. Omnibus, N.Y.C., 1958-59; assoc. prodr. Robert Saudek Assocs., N.Y.C., 1958-60, ABC News Adlai Stevenson Reports, N.Y.C., 1960; asst. gen. mgr. Sta. WNDT-TV, N.Y.C., 1960-63; co-prodr. The Open Mind, N.Y.C., 1963-69; dir. local programming Telepromter, Inc., N.Y.C., 1979-80; corporate v.p. programming Westinghouse Broadcasting and Cable, N.Y.C., 1980-83; cons. Sta. WNYC-TV, N.Y.C., 1984-86; v.p., sr. program officer The Markle Found., N.Y.C., 1986-98; mem. working group Carter Commn. on Radio and TV, Atlanta, 1992-96; mem. strategic planning bd. Conn. Pub. TV; bd. dirs. N.Y. New Media Assn., N.Y.C., 1998—; bd. dirs. Conn. Pub. TV and Radio, 1999; cons. in new media profit and non-profit orgns. Project advisor: (computer software) Voyager Co., 1993, SimHealth, 1994, (Internet software, multi-player online games) ReInventing America, 1995, President '96; contbr. articles to profl. jours. Vice chmn. bd. dirs. HealthCare Chaplaincy, N.Y.C., 1989-96; bd. dirs. Pro-Natura USA, N.Y.C., 1995—; life trustee Health Care Chaplaincy, N.Y.C., 1997. Recipient Emmy award Acad. TV. Arts and Scis., 1960. Mem. Internat. Assn. Culinary Profls., Night Kitchen (computer software developers bd. dirs. 1996-98), Ocean Reef Club, Mortar Board, Delta Gamma. Republican. Avocation: cooking. Home: 34 E Lyon Farm Dr Greenwich CT 06831-4349

BLACHER, RICHARD STANLEY, psychiatrist; b. N.Y.C., May 24, 1924; s. Charles and Bernardine (Zolotorofe) B.; m. Sara-Lee Rudolph, July 4, 1960 (dec. 1970); 1 child, Lisa; m. Marjory May Popky, Oct. 27, 1985. BA, Brown U., 1945; MD, U. Rochester, 1948; cert. in psychoanalysis, N.Y. Psychoanalytic Inst., 1963. Diplomate Am. Bd. Psychiatry and Neurology. Clin. asst. attending psychiatrist Mt. Sinai Hosp., N.Y.C., 1955-66, assoc. attending psychiatrist, 1966-74; assoc. clin. prof. Mt. Sinai Sch. Medicine, N.Y.C., 1967-74; clin. prof. Tufts U. Sch. Medicine, Boston, 1974-85, prof. psychiatry, 1985—, lectr. in surgery, 1977—; psychiatry lectr. Boston U. Sch. Medicine, 1995—; bd. dirs. Internat. Consortium for Study of Neurol. and Psychol. Reactions to Cardiac Surgery, 1980—. Editor: The Psychological Experience of Surgery, 1987; editl. bd. Found. of Thanatology, N.Y.C., 1988—, Wiley Series in Psychiatry, N.Y.C., 1987—; contbr. over 50 articles to profl. jours. Pres. Tenafly (N.J.) Nature Ctr. Assn., 1972; mem. steering com. Greater Boston Physicians for Social Responsibility, Cambridge, Mass., 1983-92; trustee Boston Civic Symphony Orch., 1993—. Fellow Am. Psychiat. Assn. (life); mem. Am. Psychoanalytic Assn., Internat. Psychoanalytic Assn., Am. Psychosomatic Soc., Am. Coll. Psychoanalysts, N.Y. Psychoanalytic Soc., Boston Psychoanalytic Soc. Jewish. Avocations: birding, natural history. Home and Office: 50 Plainfield St Newton MA 02468-1618

BLACHLY, JACK LEE, lawyer; b. Dallas, Mar. 8, 1942; s. Emery Lee and Thelma Jo (Budd) B.; m. Lucy Largent Rain, Jan. 15, 1972; 1 son, Michael Talbot. BBA, So. Meth. U., 1965, JD, 1968. Bar: Tex. 1968, U.S. Ct. Appeals (5th cir.) 1969, U.S. Supreme Ct. 1975, U.S. Tax Ct. 1977. Trust officer First Nat. Bank in Dallas, 1968-70; ptnr. firm Reese & Blachly, Dallas, 1970-71; assoc. firm Rain Harrell Emery Young & Doke, Dallas, 1971-76; staff atty. Sabine Corp., Dallas, 1976-77, mgr. legal dept., 1977-80, v.p., gen. counsel, 1980-89; asst. gen. counsel Pacific Enterprises Oil Co. USA (merger Sabine Corp. and Pacific Enterprise Oil Co. USA), Dallas, 1989-90; pvt. practice Dallas, 1990—. Mem. Tex. Bar Assn., Dallas Bar Assn., Dallas Gun Club, Northwood Club. Baptist. Office: 16012 Red Cedar Trl Dallas TX 75248-3901

BLACHMAN, MICHAEL JOEL, lawyer; b. Portsmouth, Va., Aug. 16, 1944; s. Zalmon I. and Rachel G. (Grossman) B.; m. Paula D. Levine, Nov. 23, 1969; children: Dara R., Erica Dale. BS, Am. U., 1966; JD, U. Tenn., 1969. Bar: Va. 1969, U.S. Dist. Ct. (ea. dist.) Va. 1971, U.S. Supreme Ct. 1974, U.S. Ct. Appeals (4th cir.) 1977. Asst. commonwealth's atty. Commonwealth of Va., Portsmouth, 1970-72; assoc. Bangel, Bangel & Bangel, Portsmouth, 1972-77, ptnr., 1977—; chmn. Portsmouth Juvenile Adv. Com., 1975-78. Mem. Va. Dem. Steering Com. 1980-85; vice chmn. Indsl. Devel. Authority and Port and Indsl. Commn., Portsmouth, 1987-89, chmn. 1989-93; bd. dirs. United Jewish Fedn. Tidewater, 1980—, v.p. 1989—. With USCGR, 1966-72. Recipient Young Leadership award United Jewish Fedn. Tidewater, 1983. Mem. ABA, Assn. Trial Lawyers Am., Va. Bar Assn., Va. Trial Lawyers Assn. (v.p. 1985-88, pres. 1989-90), So. Trial Lawyers Assn. (bd. dirs. 1991—), Portsmouth Bar Assn., Portsmouth C. of C., Kiwanis (bd. dirs. Portsmouth club 1973-75), B'nai B'rith. Jewish. Avocations: tennis, travel, reading. Office: Bangel Bangel & Bangel PO Box 760 Portsmouth VA 23705-0760

BLACHMAN, MORRIS J., dean, management consultant; b. Portsmouth, Va., May 16, 1939; s. Julian M. and Ella (Caplan) B.; m. Leslie Neiman, Dec. 26, 1961 (div. 1983); children: Aliza, Karen; m. Penny Lee Siegel, May 27, 1984; children: Max, Julia. BA, Brandeis U., 1961; MA, U. S.C., 1968; PhD, NYU, 1976. Tchr. history Woodrow Wilson H.S., Portsmouth, Va., 1961-62; asst. dir. Ibero-Am. Lang. and Arts Ctr. NYU, N.Y.C., 1972-73; instr., asst., assoc. prof. U. S.C., Columbia, 1973-96, asst. dean continuing med. edn. and faculty devel., 1996—; pres. M.J. Blachman & Assocs., Inc., Columbia, 1986—; cons. Daniel Mgmt. Ctr., U. S.C., 1993—. Co-author: Drug War Politics: The Price of Denial, 1996, Confronting Revolutions, 1986; contbr. articles to profl. jours. Program dir. Leadership S.C., Columbia, 1979-81; bd. dirs. Columbia Jewish Fedn., 1988—, Columbia Jewish Cmty. Ctr., 1988—, Jewish Family Svcs., 1996—. 1st lt. USAF, 1962-66. Decorated Bronze Star; recipient Cert. of Appreciation, U.S. Dept. State, 1983, Outstanding Svc. award Jewish Family Svcs., Columbia, 1997, Spl. Cmty. Svc. award Columbia Jewish Fedn., 1994. Mem. Alliance for Continuing Med. Edn., L.Am. Studies Assn., Internat. Studies Assn. Democrat. Jewish. Avocations: reading, travel. Home: 117 Park Shore Dr W Columbia SC 29223-6026 Office: 3555 Harden Sta Ext #100 Columbia SC 29203

BLACK, ALLEN DECATUR, lawyer; b. Pitts., July 27, 1942; s. Gerald Richard and Amy Elizabeth (Haymaker) B. AB, Princeton U., 1963; LLB magna cum laude, U. Pa., 1966. Bar: D.C. 1967, Pa. 1971, U.S. Supreme Ct. 1975. Law clk. to Hon. John Minor Wisdom, New Orleans, 1966-67; trial atty. Dept. Justice, 1967-68; asst. prof. law U. North Dakota, Grand Forks, 1971; practice comml. and antitrust litigation law, ptnr. firm Fine, Kaplan & Black, Phila., 1975—; lectr. in law Rutgers U., 1972-77, Temple U., 1978, U. Pa., 1985. Served with JAGC USN, 1968-71. Fellow Am. Coll. Trial Lawyers; mem. Am. Law Inst. (mem. coun.), Pa. Bar Assn., Phila. Bar Assn., Phila. Art Alliance. Republican. Episcopalian. Office: 1845 Walnut St Philadelphia PA 19103-4708

BLACK, ANDERSON DUANE, writer, business consultant; b. Jackson, Mich., May 15, 1928; s. Walter Ward and Mary Christmas (Anderson) B.; m. Sheila Eiko Ueda, Dec. 26, 1962. BS, Northwestern U., 1954; MA, U. Hawaii, 1959, MBA, 1979. Instr. U. Hawaii, Honolulu, 1959-62; mgr. Castle & Cooke, Inc., Honolulu, 1963-84; pres. A.D. Black Assocs., Lanai City, Hawaii, 1984—; adminstr. Lanai Cmty. Hosp., Lanai City, Hawaii, 1989-92. Author: (play) Tsunami!, 1960, (play) Year of the Great Poy Shortage, 1961, Golden Children of Hawaii, 1987. Bd. dirs. State Comprehensive Health Planning Coun., Honolulu, 1969-75; pres., bd. dirs. Pacific and Asian Affairs Coun., Honolulu, 1964-70; chair Hawaii Campaign Spending Commn., 1997—. Recipient Pacific House award Pacific and Asian Affairs Coun., 1969. Mem. Lanai City Lions Club (pres. 1963—), Lions Internat. (state sec. dist. 50 1983-84). Avocations: flying, travel. Home: 1634 Makiki St Apt 102 Honolulu HI 96822-4437 Office: AD Black Assocs PO Box 765 Lanai City HI 96763-0765

BLACK, ARTHUR LEO, biochemistry educator; b. Redlands, Calif., Dec. 1, 1922; s. Leo M. and Marie A. (Burns) B.; m. Trudi E. McCue, Nov. 11, 1945; childrenA;3 Teresa Townsend, Janet Carter, Patti Tleimat. BS, U. Calif., Davis, 1948, PhD, 1951. Faculty physiol. chemistry Sch. Vet. Medicine U. Calif. at Davis, 1951—, prof., 1962—, prof. emeritus, 1991—, chmn. dept. physiol. scis., 1968-75; cons. NIH, 1970-72, U.S. Dept. Agr., 1977-80; chmn. Nutritional Scis. Tng. Com., 1971-72. Contbr. papers to profl. jours. Served to 1st lt. USAAF, 1943-46. Recipient Sci. Faculty award NSF, 1958; Acad. Senate Disting. Teaching award U. Calif., Davis, 1977; Research grantee NSF; Research grantee NIH, 1952—. Fellow Am. Inst. Nutrition (Borden award 1963); mem. Am. Soc. Biol. Chemists, Am. Physiol. Soc., Am. Soc. for Nutritional Scis., Sigma Xi, Phi Beta Kappa, Phi Zeta. Home: 891 Linden Ln Davis CA 95616-1763 Office: U Calif Dept Molecular Bioscis Davis CA 95616

BLACK, B. R., retired educational administrator, consultant; b. Tampa, Fla., Apr. 6, 1942; s. R.C. and Gladys (Gaines) B.; m. Katy Black, Apr. 2, 1987; children: Amy Christine, Dale Rainer. AA, Marion (Ala.) Inst., 1962; BA, Fla. State U., 1964; MEd, Rollins Coll., 1974; EdD, Nova U., Ft. Lauderdale, Fla., 1988. Tchr. biology, chmn. sci. dept., asst. prin. high sch., 1970-85; supr. MIS, Sch. Bd. Polk County, Bartow, Fla., 1985-86, supr. instrnl. computing, 1986-93, dir. instrnl. tech., 1993-97; ret., 1997; ednl. cons. Instrnl. Tech. Rsch., Crawfordville, Fla., 1997—; presenter numerous workshops and confs. Author: Trouble Shooting Microcomputers; mem. nat. editl. adv. bd. Electronic Learning, 1989-92. Capt. U.S. Army, 1964-70. Mem. ASCD (ednl. futurists network 1989-95), Fla. Coun. Instnl. Tech. Leaders (sec. 1995—), Fla. Instnl. Computing Suprs. (bd. dirs. 1988-90, state chmn. 1989), Fla. Assn. for Computers in Edn., Fla. Assn. Ednl. Data Systems, Fla. ASCD, Internat. Soc. for Tech. in Edn., Phi Delta Kappa. Home: 343 River Plantation Rd Crawfordville FL 32327-1517 Office: Instrnl Tech Rsch 343 River Plantation Rd Crawfordville FL 32327-1517

BLACK, BARBARA ANN, publisher; b. Eureka, Calif., Dec. 11, 1928; d. William Marion and Letitia (Brunia) Black; m. Vinson Brown, June 18, 1950 (dec Dec. 1991); children: Tamara Pinn, Roxana Hodges, Keven Brown. BA, Western State Coll., Gunnison, Colo., 1950. Cert. tchr., Colo. Editor/proofreader Naturegraph Pubs., Los Altos, Calif., 1950-53; co-owner, mgr. Naturegraph Pubs., San Martin, Calif., 1953-60, Healdsburg, Calif., 1960-76; owner/mgr. Naturegraph Pubs., Happy Camp, Calif., 1976—. Author: Barns of Yesteryear, 1993; co-author: Sierra Nevada Wildlife, 1996, The Californian, 1999. Mem. Am. Booksellers Assn. Baha'i Faith. Avocations: gardening, backpacking, animal training.

BLACK, BARBARA ARONSTEIN, legal history educator; b. Bklyn., May 6, 1933; d. Robert and Minnie (Polenberg) A.; m. Charles L. Black, Jr., Apr. 11, 1954; children—Gavin B., David A., Robin E. BA, Bklyn. Coll., 1953; LLB, Columbia U., 1955; MPhil, Yale U., 1970, PhD, 1975; LLD (hon.), N.Y. Law Sch., 1986, Marymount Manhattan Coll., 1986, Vt. Law Sch., 1987, Coll. of New Rochelle, 1987, Smith Coll., 1988, Bklyn. Coll., 1988, York U., Toronto, Can., 1990, Georgetown U., 1991. Assoc. in law Columbia U. Law Sch., N.Y.C., 1955-56; lectr. history Yale U., New Haven, 1974-76, asst. prof. history, 1976-79, assoc. prof. law, 1979-84; George Welwood Murray prof. legal history Columbia U. Law Sch., N.Y.C., 1984—, dean faculty of law, 1986-91. Editor Columbia Law Rev., 1953-55. Active N.Y. State Ethics Commn., 1992-95. Recipient Fed. Bar Assn. prize Columbia Law Sch., 1955. Mem. Am. Soc. Legal History (pres. 1986-90), Am. Acad. Arts and Scis., Am. Philos. Soc., Mass. Hist. Soc., Supreme Ct. Hist. Soc., Selden Soc., Century Assn. Office: Columbia U Sch Law 435 W 116th St New York NY 10027-7201

BLACK, BRUCE D., judge. BA, Albion Coll., 1969; JD, U. Mich., 1971. Judge U.S. Dist. Ct. N.Mex., 1996—. Office: 333 Lomas Blvd NW Albuquerque NM 87102

BLACK, CAROLE, broadcast executive; b. Cin.. BA in English lit., Ohio State U. With Procter & Gamble, Cin.; account supr., sr. v.p., mgmt. rep. DDB Needham, Chgo., 1983-86; v.p. worldwide mktg. home video Walt Disney Co., 1986-88, sr. v.p. mktg., TV, 1988-94; pres., gen. mgr. NBC 4, L.A., 1994-99; pres., CEO Lifetime TV, 1999—. Office: KNBC 3000 W Alameda Ave Burbank CA 91523-0002

BLACK, CATHLEEN PRUNTY, publishing executive; b. Chgo., Apr. 26, 1944; d. James Hamilton and Margaret (Harrington) B. BA, Trinity Coll., 1966. Advt. sales rep. Holiday mag., N.Y.C., 1966-69, Travel & Leisure mag., N.Y.C., 1969-70, New York mag., 1970-72; advt. dir. Ms. mag., 1972-75, assoc. pub., 1975-77; assoc. pub. New York mag., 1977-79, pub., 1979-83; pres. USA Today, 1983, pub., 1984-91; exec. v.p. mktg. Gannett Co., Inc., from 1985, also bd. dirs.; pres., CEO Newspaper Assn. Am., Reston, Va., 1992-95; pres. Hearst Mags., N.Y.C., NY, 1996—. Office: Hearst Mags 959 8th Ave New York NY 10019-3795*

BLACK, CHARLES CATUS, industrial company executive; b. Yonkers, N.Y., May 10, 1952; s. Harold Edward and Channel Catus (Streigh) B. BA, Princeton U., 1963; MA, Harvard U., 1965, PhD, 1970. Office mgr. No. Lights, N.Y.C., 1970-72, divsn. mgr., 1972-75, v.p. ops., 1975-80; pres. Blackstone Industries, East Brewster, N.Y., 1981—. Author: Management: A Cat and Mouse Game, 1985, Marketing: The Early Bird May Not Get the Worm, 1988. Mem. Internat. Feline Soc. Office: Blackstone Industries 28 RD 1 Patterson NY 12563

BLACK, CLANTON CANDLER, JR., biochemistry educator, researcher; b. Tampa, Fla., Nov. 27, 1931; s. Clanton Candler Black and Cora (Winfred) Eady B.; m. Betty Louise Dantzler, Apr. 10, 1952; children—Marjorie Kay, Clanton Candler III, Julia Renee. B.S.A., U. Fla., 1953, M.S.A., 1957, Ph.D., 1960. NIH postdoctoral fellow Cornell U., Ithaca, N.Y., 1960-62; C. F. Kettering Found. fellow Kettering Research Lab., Antioch Coll., Yellow Springs, Ohio, 1962-63, staff scientist, asst. prof., 1963-67; prof. biochemistry U. Ga., Athens, 1967—, research prof. biochemistry/molecular biology, 1982—; Fulbright-Hays scholar to USSR, 1976; cons. plant biochemistry, physiology Internat. Atomic Energy Agy. Nat. Agr. U., Lima, Peru, 1981—. Editor: CO2 Metabolism and Plant Productivity, 1976, Net Carbon Dioxide Assimilation in Higher Plants, 1972, Handbook of Biosolar Resources, Vol. IA, IB, 1982. Served to cpl. U.S. Army, 1953-55. Recipient Merit award Bot. Soc. Am., 1981, Alex Laurie award Am. Soc. Hort. Sci., 1984. Fellow AAAS; mem. Am. Soc. Plant Physiology (sec.-treas., v.p., pres. 1975-79), Am. Soc. Biol. Chemists, Russian Soc. Plant Physiology (hon.), Sigma Xi, Phi Kappa Phi, Phi Sigma, Gamma Sigma Delta. Baptist. Home: 250 Southview Dr Athens GA 30605-1434 Office: U Ga Biochem and Molecular Bio Dept Life Scis Bldg Athens GA 30602

BLACK, CLIFFORD MERWYN, academic administrator, sociologist, educator; b. Lafayette, Ohio, Mar. 6, 1942; s. Richard Allen and Ivaloo Mae (Mosher) B.; m. Janet Ruth Knecht, Aug. 3, 1963; 1 child, Jonathan Andrew. BA, Adrian Coll., 1963; MDiv, Meth. Theol. Sch., 1966; PhD, Northwestern U., 1972. Cert. clin. sociologist; lic. profl. counselor. Asst. prof. Wilberforce (Ohio) U., 1973-74, The Ohio State U., Mansfield, 1974-78; instr. U. North Tex., Denton, 1978-79, asst. prof., 1979-83, sociology program dir., 1982-83, assoc. prof., 1983-89, chair Ctr. for Pub. Svc., 1984-86, chair dept. sociology, 1986-87, assoc. dean Sch. Cmty. Svc., 1986-88, 91-92, acting dean Sch. Cmty. Svc., 1988-90, prof., 1989-92; prof. Tex. A&M Internat. U., Laredo, 1989-92, dean Sch. Edn. and Arts and Scis., 1992-94, dean Coll. of Arts and Humanities, 1994-96, dir. Interant. Justice Ctr., 1996—; cons. Denton County Sheriff's Dept., Denton, 1984-89; mem. state coordinating bd. com. on Two Yr. Coll. Curriculum, 1986-89. Author: (book) Alternative Sentencing: Electronically Monitored Correction Supervision, 1992; contbg. editor for Clin. Sociology Newsletter, 1983-84; mem. editorial bd. Sociol. Practice, 1984-89; contbr. numerous articles to profl. jours. Pres. Sam Houston Elem. PTA, Denton, 1985-86; trustee Denton Ind. Sch. Dist., 1986-89; mem. United Way Bd., Laredo, 1994-95. Mem. Nat. Clin. Sociology Assn. (v.p. 1984-86, certification bd. mem. 1984-90, nat. certifier 1985-92, nat. program chair for ann. meeting 1984-85), Clin. Sociology Assn. Tex. (pres. 1982-84), Nat. Sociol. Practice Assn. (exec. bd. 1990-91), Nat. Sociol. Practice Assn. (certification bd. 1990-91), Am. Sociol. Assn. (sect bd. 1981-84, sociol. practice sect. sec./treas. 1981-84), Southwestern Sociol. Assn. (chair com. on professions 1983-86), Am. Criminology Soc., Acad. Criminal Justice Scis. Avocations: field archaeology, walking, reading, writing, drawing. Home: 8506 Callow Ct Laredo TX 78045-1983 Office: Tex A&M Internat U 5201 University Blvd Laredo TX 78041-1900

BLACK, CONRAD MOFFAT, publishing corporate executive; b. Montreal, Aug. 25, 1944; s. George Montegu and Jean Elizabeth (Riley) B.; m. Barbara J.E. Amiel. BA, Carleton U., 1965; LLL, Laval U., 1970; MA in History, McGill U., 1973; LLD (hon.), St. Francis Xavier U., 1979, McMaster U., 1979; LittD (hon.), U. Windsor, 1979; LLD (hon.), Carleton U., 1989. Chmn., co-owner Ea. Twps. Pub. Co., Ltd., Knowlton, Que., 1966—; chmn. Sterling Newspapers Ltd., Vancouver, 1971—; pres., chmn. exec. com. Argus Corp. Ltd., 1978-79; chmn. bd., chmn. exec. com. Argus Corp. Ltd., Toronto, 1979—, CEO, 1985; chmn. The Ravelston Corp. Ltd., 1978; chmn. Hollinger, Inc., 1985, CEO, 1987; chmn., CEO Telegraph Group Ltd., 1987; chmn. Saturday Night Mag. Ltd., 1987; dep. chmn. Am. Pub. Co., 1987; chmn. and CEO Hollinger Internat. Inc.; chmn., CEO Southam Inc., 1994—, dir.; bd. dirs. EdperBrascan Ltd., Can. Imperial Bank of Commerce, Ltd., The Spectator (1828) Ltd., Inc., UniMedia, Inc., Jerusalem Post Publs. Ltd., Sotheby's Holdings Inc.; mem. adv. bd. Nat. Interest, Washington, Gulfstream Aerospace Corp., Coun. Fgn. Rels. Author: Duplessis, 1977, reprinted as Render Unto Caesar, 1998, A Life in Progress, 1993. Patron Malcolm Muggeridge Foun. Decorated officer Order of Can., apptd. to Privy Coun. of Can., 1992. Mem. Trilateral Commn., Americas Soc. (chmn.'s coun.), Internat. Inst. for Strategic Studies, Bilderberg Meetings (steering com.), Toronto Club, York Club, Toronto Golf Club, Granite Club, Univ. Club (Montreal), Mt. Royal Club (Montreal), Everglades Club, Beach Club (Palm Beach), Athenaeum, Beefsteak, Whites (London), Garrick (London). Office: Hollinger Inc 10 Toronto St, Toronto, ON Canada M5C 2B7 also: Telegraph Group Ltd, Canary Wharf, 1 Canada Sq, London E14 5DT, England also: Hollinger Internat 712 5th Ave New York NY 10019

BLACK, CONSTANCE JANE, artist; b. Norwood, Mass., Oct. 15, 1929; d. William Arthur Broadley and Julia Abigail Eells; m. Carl Burton Black, Sept. 9, 1950; children: Melanie, Laura Black Simmons, Carl David. AA, Vesper Geroge Sch. Art, 1950. Author: (poetry) Litany of Days, 1998; one-woman show at Pen & Brush Inc., N.Y.C., 1998. Mem. Pen & Brush Inc. (Hors Concours award 1999), Provincetown Art Assn. and Mus. (bd. dirs. 1992-98). Mem. Baha'i Faith. Avocations: music, crafts, computers. E-mail: ejblack@capecod.net. Home: 6 Priscilla Alden Rd Provincetown MA 02657

BLACK, CORA JEAN, evangelist, wedding consultant; b. Mt. Pleasant, Pa., July 30, 1941; d. Alfred John and Ruby Isabel (Waugaman) B.; m. Arthur Byron Everett, Mar. 27, 1974. Student, Greensburg Bus. Coll., 1962, Moody Bible Inst., 1966; DD, Internat. Bible Inst., 1972; postgrad., Seton Hill Coll., 1986. Ordained evangelist; notary public. Advt. display silk-screen artist West Penn Power Co., Greensburg, Pa., 1962-63; missionary to W.I. Gospel Light Ministry, New Stanton, Pa., 1964; pers. dir., Pa. state chair Assn. Internat. Gospel Assemblies of DeSota, Mo., 1970-80; founder, pres. America for Christ Ministry, New Stanton, 1974—; owner, founder Sea-Jay's All Faith Wedding Chapel, New Stanton, 1979—; coord. Holy Land tours, 1971-83; mem. Kathryn Kuhlman Concert Choir, Pitts., 1955-62; owner Sea-Jay All Pet Hotel, New Stanton. Author of Christian literature; composer of published and recorded Gospel music including Christ is Coming! Are You Ready?, America for Christ, and The Joy of Life; weekly radio broadcasts. Mem. BMI, AIGA (internat. pub. rels. dir., Pa. chmn. for Women in Christ), Am. Psychotherapy Assn. (cert.), Am. Acad. Bereavement, Ctrl. Westmoreland C. of C., Westmoreland Hist. Soc., New Stanton Hist. Soc. (sec.-treas. 1995—), Am. Assn. Christian Counselors (charter, counselor), Pa. Assn. Notaries, Internat. Platform Assn., DAR, Assn. Internat. Gospel Assemblies (pub. rels. dir. for U.S. and 40 some countries), Tri-State Gospel Music Assn. (treas. 1998—). Republican. Avocations: travel, photography, decorating and designing, painting, animals. Home: 440 N Center Ave PO Box 192 New Stanton PA 15672-0192 Office: Sea-Jays 440 N Center Ave New Stanton PA 15672-9416

BLACK, CREED C., JR., lawyer; b. Nashville, Mar. 2, 1951. BA magna cum laude, Yale U., 1973; JD cum laude, U. Pa., 1976. Bar: Pa. 1976, U.S. Supreme Ct. 1989. Law clk. to Hon. Herbert A. Fogel U.S. Dist. Ct. (ea. dist.) Pa., 1976-77; trial atty. criminal divsn. U.S. Dept. Justice, Washington, 1977-78; spl. asst. to U.S. atty. ea. dist. Va., 1978; mem. organized crime and racketeering sect. Cleve. Strike Force, 1978-80, Phila. Strike Force, 1980-82; atty. Ballard Spahr Andrews & Ingersoll, Phila., 1982-96; pvt. practice Phila., 1996—. Mem. ABA, Fed. Bar Assn., Phila. Bar Assn., Nat. Assn. Criminal Def. Lawyers, Order of Coif. Office: 1700 Market St Ste 2632 Philadelphia PA 19103-3903*

BLACK, CREED CARTER, newspaper executive; b. Harlan, Ky., July 15, 1925; s. Creed Carter and Mary (Cole) B.; m. Mary C. Davis, Dec. 28, 1947 (div. 1976); children: Creed Carter, Steven D., Douglas S.; m. Elsa Goss, Dec. 9, 1977; 1 child, Michelle. BS with highest distinction and honors in Polit. Sci., Northwestern U., 1949; MA, U. Chgo., 1952; LLD (hon.), Davidson Coll., 1991; LHD (hon.), Ctr. Coll., 1996. Reporter Paducah (Ky.) Sun-Democrat, 1942-43, 46; editor Daily Northwestern, 1947; copy editor Chgo. Sun-Times, 1949, Chgo. Herald-Am., 1950; editl. writer Nashville Tennessean, 1950-57, exec. editor, 1957-59; v.p., exec. editor Savannah (Ga.) Morning News and Savannah Evening Press, 1959-60, Wilmington (Del.) Morning News and Evening Jour., 1960-64; mng. editor Chgo. Daily News, 1964-68, exec. editor, 1968-69; asst. sec. for legislation HEW, 1969-70; editor Phila. Inquirer, 1970-77; chmn., pub. Lexington (Ky.) Herald-Leader, 1977-88; pres., trustee Knight Found., Miami, Fla., 1988-98. With 100th Inf. divsn. AUS, WWII, ETO. Decorated Bronze Star; recipient Northwestern U. Alumni medal, 1973. Mem. Newspaper Assn. of Am., So. Newspaper Pubs. Assn. (pres. 1987—), Am. Soc. Newspaper Editors (pres. 1983), Nat. Conf. Editl. Writers (pres. 1962), Riviera Country Club, Kappa Tau Alpha, Lambda Chi Alpha. Methodist. Home: 11044 SW 77th Court Cir Miami FL 33156-3766

BLACK, DANIEL HUGH, retired secondary school educator; b. Arab, Ala., July 4, 1947; s. Lehmon Ray and Lillian Geneve (Divine) B. BS, U. Ala., Tuscaloosa, 1970; MEd, Ala. A&M U., 1976; PhD, Vanderbilt U., 1981; MA, St. John's Coll., Annapolis, Md., 1988. Social studies tchr., advanced placement govt. tchr. Grissom High Sch., Huntsville, Ala., 1970-98; adj. instr. history Calhoun C.C., 1982—, Ala. A&M U., 1989-94, Great Books in the Western World, U. Ala., Huntsville; essay reader advanced placement Am. govt. and politics exam. Ednl. Testing Svc., 1991-96. Mem. NEA, Ala. Edn. Assn., Huntsville Edn. Assn., Nat. Trust for Hist. Preservation (master class James Madison and Federalist Papers 1989), Phi Delta Kappa. Home: 1019 Old Monrovia Rd NW Apt 232 Huntsville AL 35806-3505 Office: Virgil I Grissom High Sch Bailey Cove Huntsville AL 35802

BLACK, DAVID, writer, educator, producer; b. Boston, Apr. 21, 1945; s. Henry Arnold and Zelda Edith (Hodosh) B.; m. Deborah Hughes Keehn, June 22, 1968 (div. 1994); children: Susannah Haden, Tobiah Samuel McKee; m. Barbara Weisberg, June 20, 1996. BA cum laude, Amherst Coll., 1967; MFA, Columbia U., 1971. Free-lance writer, 1971—; writer-in-residence Mt. Holyoke Coll., South Hadley, Mass., 1982-86. Author: Minds, 1982, Like Father, 1978 (Notable Book of Yr. N.Y. Times, 1978, One of 7 Best Novels of Yr. Washington Post), Peep Show, 1986, An Impossible Life, 1998; (non-fiction) Ekstasy, 1975, The King of Fifth Avenue (Notable Book of Yr. N.Y. Times 1981), Murder at the Met, 1984 (Edgar award nomination), Medicine Man, 1985, The Plague Years, 1986 (Nat. Mag. award reporting Nat. Assn. Sci. Writers award); (play) An Impossible Life, 1990 (Book of Yr. award Foreward Mag. 1998); (screenplay) The Confession, 1999; contbr. articles and stories to popular mags.; author screenplays for Disney, Martin Bregman, Michael Douglas, Highgate, M.G.M., Paramount, Interscope, Tristar, Castle Rock, Belative, Warners, others; miniseries for Chris-Rose/CBS/Viacom; writer teleplays Death and the Lady, Miami Vice, Hill Street Blues, Gideon Oliver, Law and Order (nominee Golden Globe 1992, nominee Edgar, 1992, 99, Emmy nominee 1992, 98), H.E.L.P., others; exec. prodr., creator The Cosby Mysteries, Under Fire, The Good Policeman, Legacy of Lies; story editor Hill Street Blues, 1986-88, Miami Vice, 1987-88; prodr. The Lou Gossett Show, 1988; co-creator and supervising prodr. The Nasty Boys; supervising prodr. H.E.L.P., 1989-90; supervising prodr. Law and Order, 1990-92, cons. prodr., 1997—; contbg. editor Rolling Stone, 1986-89. Recipient Atlantic Firsts award Atlantic Monthly, 1973, Playboy's Best Article of Yr. award Playboy mag., 1979, Nat. Assn. Sci. Writers award, 1985, hon. mention for Best Essay of Yr., 1986, Giorgi award, Cert. Merit, ABA, 1998; grantee Nat. Endowment Arts, 1979; nominee for Best Episodic Drama of Yr. Writers Guild ann. awards, 1988. Mem. Mystery Writers Am. , PEN, Internat. Assn. Mystery Writers, Authors Guild, Writers Guild East, Williams Club, Century Assn., SAG, Players, Explorer's Club. Jewish/Unitarian. Office: care Todd Feldman/ICM 8942 Wilshire Blvd Beverly Hills CA 90211-1934

BLACK, DAVID CHARLES, astrophysicist; b. Waterloo, Iowa, May 14, 1943. BS, U. Minn., 1965, MS, 1967, PhD in Physics, 1970. Fellow NAS, 1970-72; rsch. scientist theoretical astrophysics Ames rsch. ctr. NASA, Houston, 1972—, chief scientist space sta. NASA, 1985—; dir. Lunar & Planetary Inst., Houston, 1988—. Mem. AAAS, N.Y. Acad. Sci. Achievements include research in theoretical studies of the formation and evolution of stars and planetary systems, interpretation of rare gas isotopic data from meteorites and lunar samples. Office: Lunar & Planetary Inst 3600 Bay Area Blvd Houston TX 77058-1113*

BLACK, DAVID EVANS, sculptor, painter; b. Gloucester, Mass., May 29, 1928; s. John Weston Jr. and Doris Grey (Merchant) B.; m. Karlita Kunz Black, June 21, 1953; children: Eric, Ann Margo. BA, Wesleyan U., Middletown, Conn., 1950; MA, Ind. U., 1954. Instr. to prof. Ohio State U., Columbus, 1954-84, prof. emeritus, 1984—; artist Columbus, 1954—; juror Wexner Ctr. for Arts Architecture Competition, Ohio State U., Columbus, 1982. Sculptor: pub. projects, New Arcadia, Mich., 1987 (nat. competition award 1988), Windpoint, Japan, 1985 (1st prize internat competition 1985), Jetty, Belmont, Calif, 1990 (nat. competition award 1990), Sonora, Tucson, 1991 (nat. competition award 1990), Flyover, Wright Bros. Meml., Dayton, Ohio, 1996 (internat. competition award 1994), Cin., 197, Hammond, Ind., 1999, Cedar Rapids, 1999. Cpl. U.S. Army, 1951-53. Fulbright fellow to Florence, Italy, U.S. Govt., 1962-63; artist individual grantee Nat. Endowment for Arts, 1965, fellow to Berlin, German Govt., Deutsche Akademische Austauschdienst, Berlin, 1970-72. Avocations: travel, collecting oriental art, photography. Home and Office: 1066 Lincoln Rd Columbus OH 43212-3234

BLACK, DENISE LOUISE, secondary school educator; b. Ft. Sill, Apr. 16, 1950; d. Nelson Arthur and Virginia Mary (Smith) Taber; m. Robert Paul Black, Aug. 12, 1972; children: Paula Ann, Jennifer Lea. AA, C.C. of Allegheny County, Boyce campus, 1970; BS, Slippery Rock State Coll., 1972; MA, Ea. Mich. U., 1978. Cert. guidance and counselor. Adult edn. tchr. ecology and physiology Huron Valley Schs., Milford, Mich., 1973-74; tchr. gen. biology and earth sci. Howell (Mich.) Pub. Schs., 1974-75; adult edn. tchr. life sci. Holly (Mich.) Area Schs., 1978-80, Hartland (Mich.) Consol. Schs., 1978-86; tchr. biology Walled Lake (Mich.) Consol. Schs., 1988—, Hartland Consol. Schs., 1990—. Coach, Milford Youth Athletic Assn., 1973-85; leader 4-H Club; Huron Valley Horse Com.; youth advisor Mich. State Rabbit Breeders Assn., 1990-92. Mem. Assn. Suprvision and Curriculum Devel., Nat. Assn. Biology Tchrs., Mich. Assn. Biology Tchrs., Mich. Adult Curriculum Connection (bd. dirs.), Mich. Sci. Tchrs. Assn., Beta Beta Beta, Phi Kappa Phi, Phi Theta Kappa. Methodist. Home: 2576 Shady Ln Milford MI 48381-1438

BLACK, D(EWITT) CARL(ISLE), JR., lawyer; b. Clarksdale, Miss., Aug. 17, 1930; s. DeWitt Carlisle Sr. and Alice Lucille (Hammond) B.; m. Ruth Buck Wallace, June 6, 1970; children: Elizabeth B. Smithson, D. Carl Black III. BA, Miss. Coll., 1951, LLB, 1963; MPA, Princeton U., 1953; LLM in Taxation, NYU, 1965. Bar: Miss. 1963, U.S. Dist. Ct. (so. dist.) Miss. 1963, U.S. Ct. Appeals (5th cir.) 1965. Rsch. asst. Pub. Affairs Rsch. Coun., Baton Rouge, 1956-57; asst. mgr., dir. rsch. Miss. Econ. Coun., Jackson, 1957-64; ptnr. Butler, Snow, O'Mara, Stevens & Cannada, Jackson, 1965-98, of counsel, 1999—; chair Miss. Tax Inst., Jackson, 1987. Treas. New Stage Theatre, Jackson, 1965-69; pres. Miss. Symphony Orch. Assn., Jackson, 1985-86, Miss. Symphony Found., Jackson, 1989-92. Cpl. U.S. Army, 1953-55. Fellow Am. Coll. Tax Counsel; mem. Miss. Bar Assn. (chair tax sect. 1989-90), Univ. Club, River Hills Club. Episcopalian. Avocations: fishing, reading. Home: 1704 Poplar Blvd Jackson MS 39202-2119 Office: 1700 Deposit Guaranty Plz Jackson MS 39201

BLACK, DONNA RUTH, lawyer; b. Yuma, Ariz., Sept. 13, 1947; d. Roy Welch and Rosalie Edith (Harrison) B.; m. Jeffrey A. Charlston, May 2, 1981; children: Gavin Lewis, Trevor Elias. BA in History with honors, U.

Ariz., 1969; JD, UCLA, 1975. Bar: Calif. 1975, D.C. 1979, U.S. Dist. Ct. (ctrl. dist.) Calif., 1975, U.S. Dist. Ct. (no. dist.) Calif. 1987, U.S. Dist. Ct. (ea. dist.) Calif. 1989, U.S. Ct. Appeals (8th cir.) 1978, U.S. Ct. Appeals (9th cir.) 1983, U.S. Supreme Ct. 1994. Equity ptnr. Baker & Hostetler, L.A., 1975-95; equity ptnr. Manatt, Phelps & Phillips, L.A., 1995—. Author/editor: California Environmental Law Handbook. Mem. ABA (chmn. sect. natural resources, energy and environ. law, mem. nominating com. ho. of dels., chmn. sect. officers' conf. adv. com.), State Bar Calif., Los Angeles County Bar Assn., UCLA Law Alumni Assn. (bd. dirs. 1996—, v.p. 1998—, pres. 1999). Avocations: music, art, travel, poetry, writing. Home: 1130 Tower Rd Beverly Hills CA 90210-2131 Office: Manatt Phelps & Phillips 11355 W Olympic Blvd Los Angeles CA 90064-1614

BLACK, EILEEN MARY, elementary school educator; b. Bklyn., Sept. 20, 1944; d. Marvin Mize and Anne Joan (Salvia) B. Student, Grossmont Coll., El Cajon, Calif., 1964; BA, San Diego State U., 1967; postgrad., U. Calif., San Diego, Syracuse U. Cert. tchr., Calif. Tchr. La Mesa (Calif.)-Spring Valley Sch. Dist., 1967—. NDEA grantee Syracuse U., 1968; recipient 30 Yrs. Svc. award La Mesa-Spring Valley Sch. Dist., 1997. Mem. Calif. Tchrs. Assn., Greenpeace, San Diego Zoological Soc., Wilderness Soc. Roman Catholic. Avocations: reading, baseball, walking. Home: 9320 Earl St Apt 15 La Mesa CA 91942-3846 Office: Lemon Ave Elem Sch 8787 Lemon Ave La Mesa CA 91941-5459

BLACK, ELWOOD C., councilman. City councilman Indpls., 1992—. Democrat. Office: City Coun Bldg 200 E Washington St Ste 241 Indianapolis IN 46204-3310*

BLACK, GEORGIA ANN, educational administrator; b. DeSoto, Mo., Feb. 3, 1945; d. Walter Vernon and Mabel (Luebbers) Hardin; m. Gary R. Black Sr., Jan. 9, 1965; children: Gary Jr., Nancy, Walter, Kelly. AS, Mineral Area Coll., 1966; BS in Elem. Edn., U. Mo., 1969; M.Adminstrn. and Supervision, Southeast Mo. State U., 1979. Cert. tchr., Mo., Tex., supervision and mid-mgmt. Tchr. 4th grade Sacred Heart Sch., Festus, Mo., 1964-65; tchr. math. 7-8th grades Athena Sch., DeSoto, Mo., 1969-71, Spring Br. Ind. Sch. Dist., Houston, 1971-74; tchr. math. 7-9th grades Cen. R-111 Sch. Dist., Flat river, Mo., 1974-84; tchr. math. 7-8th grades El Paso (Tex.) Ind. Sch. Dist., 1984-91; asst. prin. Clardy Sch., 1991-93; curriculum and instrn. facilitator El Paso (Tex.) Ind. Sch. Dist., 1993—. Sponsor Math. Club, 1990; campaign coord. U.S. Senate Race, St. Francois County, Mo., 1976. Named Tchr. of Yr. MacArthur Faculty, 1989-90. Mem. Greater El Paso Coun. Tchrs. Math. (treas. 1986-90). Avocation: reading.

BLACK, HILLEL MOSES, publisher; b. N.Y.C., Apr. 8, 1929; s. Isidore and Ida (Feldstein) B. B.A., U. Chgo., 1949, M.English and Fgn. Langs., 1952. Copy boy N.Y. Times, N.Y.C., 1952-53; reporter AP, Pitts., Newark and Phila., 1954-58; freelance writer N.Y.C., 1959-65; editor Saturday Evening Post, N.Y.C., 1966-67; sr. editor William Morrow & Co., N.Y.C., 1967-77, editor-in-chief, 1977-82; pub. gen. books div. Macmillan Pub. Co., N.Y.C., 1983-87; pub. Richardson, Steirman & Black, N.Y.C., 1987-88; pres. Birch Lane Press, 1989—; editorial dir. Carol Pub. Group, N.Y.C., 1989—. Author: The Watch Dogs of Wall Street, Buy Now, Pay Later, The American Schoolbook. Mem. Century Assn., Pubs. Club. Office: Carol Pub Group 120 Enterprise Ave Secaucus NJ 07094-1902

BLACK, JAMES DAVID, woodcarver, English educator, editor, poet; b. Fluvanna County, Va., July 26, 1942; s. Clarke Ogden and Helen Mae (Kidd) B.; m. Melinda Cauley Goodwin, Aug. 3, 1974; 1 child, Joshua David. BS, U. Va., 1965, MEd, 1967; PhD, Rockwell U., 1984. Mgr. Newcomb Hall Book Store, Charlottesville, Va., 1965-67; counselor Culpeper (Va.) County Schs., 1967-68; tchr. psychology James Madison U., Harrisonburg, Va., 1968-70; tchr. English Louisa County (Va.) Schs., 1971-97; owner, profl. woodcarver So. Comfort Crafts, Louisa, Va., 1995—. Poetry editor English Jour.; author poems; contbr. articles to profl. jours. Scoutmaster Explorer Post 3, Louisa, 1973-82; mem., program chair Louisa Friends of Libr., 1989. Mem. Nat. Coun. Tchrs. English (poetry editor), Va. Assn. Tchrs. English (secondary mem.-at-large 1992, sec. 1995), Louisa Rotary (various positions), Phi Delta Kappa. Republican. Mem. United Methodist Ch. Home and Office: 3798 Goldmine Rd Louisa VA 23093-5431

BLACK, JAMES ISAAC, III, lawyer; b. Lakeland, Fla., Oct. 26, 1951; s. James Isaac Jr. and Juanita (Feemster) B.; m. Vikki Harrison, June 15, 1973; children: Jennifer Leigh, Katharine Ann, Stephanie Marie. BA, U. Fla., 1973; JD, Harvard U., 1976. Bar: Fla. 1976, N.Y. 1977, U.S. Tax Ct. 1984. Assoc. Sullivan & Cromwell, N.Y.C., 1976-84, ptnr., 1984—. Mem. ABA, N.Y. State Bar Assn. (persons under disability com. trusts and estates law sect. 1984-90), Assn. of Bar of City of N.Y. (sec. 1980-81, trusts estates and surrogates ct. com. 1980-83), Scarsdale Golf Club. Home: 23 Chesterfield Rd Scarsdale NY 10583-2205 Office: Sullivan & Cromwell 125 Broad St Fl 28 New York NY 10004-2489

BLACK, JAMES ROBERT, industrial engineer; b. Davenort, Iowa, Feb. 17, 1948; s. Robert James and Anne Louise (Johnson) B.; m. Mary Ann O'Malley, June 5, 1971; 1 child, Robert Joseph. BS in Indsl. Engring., Iowa State U., 1970, MS, 1971; MBA, U. Chgo., 1976. Indsl. engr. Inland Steel Co., East Chicago, Ind., 1971-76, sr. indsl. engr., 1976-77; indsl. engring. supr. Clark Equipment Co., Jackson, Mich., 1977-78; indsl. engring. mgr. Harrison plant Graphic Sys. divsn. Rockwell Internat., Rockford, Ill., 1978-83; corp.supr. adminstrv. work mgmt. Kohler Co., Wis., 1983-87; mgr. mfg. svcs. Frigidaire Co.-Wet Products, Jefferson, Iowa, 1987-91, assembly ops. mgr., 1991-93; Kaizen facilitator Frigidaire Co.-Wet Products, Webster City, Iowa, 1993, paint process mgr., 1993, plant engring. mgr., 1993-95; mfg. cons. Ctr. for Indsl. Rsch. and Svc., Iowa State U., 1995—; pres. James R. Black & Assocs., 1997—; co-leader, guest lectr. Am. Mgmt. Assn., 1979-80; mem. adv. coun. Iowa State U. Ctr. Indsl. rsch. and Svc., 1992-94; mem. planing com. Iowa conf. Mfg., 1991-93, chmn., 1993. Contbr. articles to profl. jours. Cons. Project Bus. divsn. Jr. Achievement, 1980; chmn. pack com. Cub Scouts, Boy Scouts Am., 1980-83, Webelos leader, 1982-83, asst. scoutmaster, 1983-84, scoutmaster, 1984-88, dist. vice chmn., 1984-86, dist. scouting chmn., 1986-88; asst. soccer coach, 1981-83, coach, 1984-85. Fisher Governor scholar, 1968-69, Maytag scholar, 1969-70. Mem. Inst. Indsl. Engrs. (sr.; treas. 1979-80, pres. 1980-81, bd. dirs. 1989-91, v.p. 1991-92), Am. Soc. for Quality, Assn. for Mfg. Excellence, Mainstream Living and Story County Devel. Ctr. (phonathon co-chmn. 1993-95, bd. dirs. 1994—, treas. 1995-97, v.p. 1997—), Kohler Engring. and Tech. Orgn. (program chmn. 1986, chmn. 1987) K.C., Phi Kappa Phi, Tau Beta Pi, Gamma Epsilon Sigma, Psi Chi, Beta Gamma Sigma. Home: 900 Vermont Cir Ames IA 50014-3060 Office: CIRAS/Iowa State U 2501 N Loop Dr Ste 500 Ames IA 50010-8614

BLACK, SIR JAMES (WHYTE), pharmacologist; b. June 14, 1924. MB, ChB, U. St. Andrews; MD (hon.), U. Edinburgh, 1989; DSc (hon.), U. Glasgow, 1989. Asst. lectr. physiology U. St. Andrews, 1946; lectr. physiology U. Malaya, 1947-50; sr. lectr. U. Glasgow Vet. Sch., 1950-58; with ICI Pharms. Ltd., 1958-64; head biol. rsch., dep. rsch. dir. Smith, Kline & French, Welwyn Garden City, 1964-73; prof., chmn. dept. pharmacology Univ. Coll., London, 1973-77; dir. therapeutic rsch. Wellcome Rsch. Labs., 1978-84; prof. analytical pharmacology King's Coll. Hosp. Med. Sch., U. London, 1984—; chancellor Dundee (Scotland) U., 1992—. Decorated Knight, 1981; recipient Nobel prize for medicine, 1988. Fellow Royal Coll. Physicians, Royal Soc. (Mullard award 1978); mem. Royal Coll. Vet. Surgeons (hon. assoc.). Office: U Dundee, Chancellors Office, Dundee DD1 4HN, Scotland

BLACK, JERRY BERNARD, lawyer; b. Bklyn., Sept. 16, 1940; s. Paul A. and Esther (Rosenberg) B.; m. Joyce Fenmore, Nov. 29, 1975; children: Abigail B., Andrew S. AB, Harvard U., 1962, LLB, 1965. Bar: N.Y. 1966, U.S. Supreme Ct. 1976. Assoc. Cravath, Swaine & Moore, N.Y.C., 1966-77; asst. sec., sr. counsel Revlon, Inc., N.Y.C., 1978-83; v.p., dep. gen. counsel Hertz Corp., N.Y.C., 1984-86; ptnr. Hill, Betts & Nash, N.Y.C., 1987-90, Wilson, Elser, Moskowitz, Edelman & Dicker, LLP, N.Y.C., 1990—. Mem. ABA (loan documentation subcom. of comml. fin. svcs. com. 1995), Assn. of Bar of City of N.Y. (com. inter-Am. affairs 1973-75), N.Y. State Bar Assn. Home: 149 E 73rd St New York NY 10021-3592 Office: Wilson Elser Moskowitz Edelman & Dicker 150 E 42nd St New York NY 10017-5612

BLACK, JOHN SHELDON, lawyer; b. New Haven, Oct. 19, 1948; s. Samuel Paul West and Betty (Lohman) B.; m. Darcy A. Howe, Nov. 24, 1984; children: Kathryn Anne, Andrew Alden. BA, Colo. Coll., 1970; JD, Duke U., 1973. Bar: Mo. 1973, U.S. Supreme Ct. 1977, U.S. Ct. Appeals (10th cir.) 1982, U.S. Ct. Appeals (8th cir.) 1989. Assoc., then ptnr. Swanson, Midgley, Gangwere, Kitchin & McLarney, LLC, Kansas City, Mo., 1973—; trustee Mo. Bar Found., 1994—; mem. Gov.'s Commn. to Review Mo. Jud. Sys., 1993-97. Sec. Lyric Opera Kansas City, 1990-92. Fellow Am. Bar Found.; mem. ABA (mem. ho. dels. 1994—), Mo. Bar Assn. (mem. bd. govs. 1981-94, v.p. 1990-91, pres. 1992-93), Lawyers Assn. Kansas City (pres. 1986-87). Episcopalian. Home: 434 W 56th St Kansas City MO 64113-1203 Office: Swanson Midgley et al 922 Walnut St Ste 1500 Kansas City MO 64106-1809*

BLACK, JOHN W., federal judge. AB, Coll. of William and Mary, 1962; LLB, U. Tex., 1965. Pvt. practice Brownsville, Tex., 1965-92; magistrage judge U.S. Dist. Ct. (so. dist.) Tex., Brownsville, 1992—. Fax: (956) 548-2598. Office: US Dist Ct So Dist Tex 234 Fed Bldg 500 E 10th St Brownsville TX 78520

BLACK, KAREN, actress; b. Park Ridge, Ill., July 1, 1942; d. Norman A. and Elsie (Reif) Zeigler; m. Charles Black (div.); m. Robert Burton (div. 1974); m. L. Minor Carson, July 4, 1975; 1 son, Hunter. Ed., Northwestern U.; studied with, Lee Strasberg. Appeared on Broadway in The Playroom, 1965, Keep it in the Family, 1968; films include debut You're a Big Boy Now, 1969, Hard Contract, 1969, Easy Rider, 1969, Five Easy Pieces, 1970, A Gunfight, 1971, Portnoy's Complaint, 1972, Rhinoceros, 1974, The Outfit, 1974, The Great Gatsby, 1974, The Day of the Locust, 1975, Nashville, 1975, Family Plot, 1976, Crime and Passion, 1976, Burnt Offerings, 1976, Capricorn One, 1978, In Praise of Older Women, 1979, Killer Fish, 1979, The Last Word, 1979, Valentine, 1979, Miss Right, 1980, Come Back to the Five and Dime, Jimmie Dean, Jimmie Dean, 1982, Growing Pains, 1982, Breathless, 1983, Killing Heat, 1984, Martin's Day, 1985, Invaders From Mars, 1986, Cut and Run, 1986, New York Crossing, 1996, Dinosaur Valley Girls, 1996, Crimetime, 1996, Children of the Corn: The Gathering, 1996, Stir, 1997, Dogtown, 1997, Conceiving Ada, 1997, Men, 1997, Light Speed, 1998, Felons, 1998, Fallen Arches, 1998; TV film The Strange Possession of Mrs. Oliver, 1977, Bury the Evidence, 1998, Spoken in Silence, 1999, Mascara, 1999. Recipient N.Y. Film Critics award for best supporting actress, 1970. *

BLACK, KENNETH, JR., retired insurance executive and educator, author; b. Norfolk, Va., Jan. 30, 1925; s. Kenneth and Margaret Virginia (Wolf) B.; m. Mabel Llewellyn Folger, Sept. 20, 1948; children—Kenneth III, Kathryn Anne. A.B., U. N.C., 1948, M.S., 1951; Ph.D., U. Pa., 1953. Ptnr. Colonial Ins. Agy., Chapel Hill, N.C., 1948-50; instr. U. Pa., 1952-53; chmn. ins. dept. Ga. State U., 1953-69, Regents' prof. ins., 1959-92, C.V. Starr prof. internat. ins., 1984-92, Regent's prof. emeritus, 1992—, dean Coll. Bus. Adminstrn., 1969-84; dean emeritus Coll. Bus. Adminstrn. Internat. Ins. Soc., Inc., 1992—, pres., CEO, 1988-92, vice chmn., bd. dirs., 1992—; bd. dirs. Scudder Varible Life Investment Fund, Boston. Author: (with Russell) Human Behavior and Life Insurance, 1963, rev. edit., 1993, Human Behavior and Property and Liability Insurance, 1964, (with Keir and Surrey) Cases in Life Insurance, 1965, (with Huebner and Webb) Property and Liability Insurance, 1968, 4th edit., 1996, (with Russell) Human Behavior in Business, 1972, Understanding and Influencing Human Behavior, 1981, (with Skipper) Life Insurance, 12th edit., 1994; editor: Jour. Fin. Svc. Profls., 1959—; ins. series for Prentice Hall, Inc., 1959—. Vice chmn. Pres.'s Commn. R.R. Retirement, 1971-73; trustee Village of St. Joseph, 1969-80; exec. dir., trustee Ednl. Found., Inc., 1969-96. Served with USN, 1944-46. Recipient Solomon S. Huebner gold medal Am. Coll., 1985, Laureate Ins. Hall Fame, 1993, Order of the Golden Fleece, UNC, 1948. Mem. Am. Risk and Ins. Assn. (pres. 1964), Phi Beta Kappa, Beta Gamma Sigma, Omicron Delta Kappa, Alpha Kappa Psi. Roman Catholic. Home: 1762 Nancy Creek Blf NW Atlanta GA 30327-1912

BLACK, KIRK J., television executive; b. Ohio, Aug. 23, 1966. BA in Comm., Bowling Green State U., 1988. Local sales mgr. WNCN, Raleigh, N.C., 1994-96; gen. mgr. WIBW-TV, Topeka, Kans., 1996—. Mem. Nat. Assn. Broadcasters, Kans. Assn. Broadcasters, KTNDA. Office: WIBW-TV PO Box 119 Topeka KS 66601-0119*

BLACK, LARRY DAVID, library director; b. Section, Ala., Mar. 3, 1949; s. Haskin Byron and Mima Jean (Holcomb) B.; m. Mary Frances Patterson, Aug. 29, 1971; 1 child, Amy Susan. BA in History & Polit. Sci., U. Ala., 1971, MLS, 1972; M in Pub. Adminstrn., Ohio State U., 1981. Asst. dir. Bedsole Library Mobile (Ala.) Coll., 1972-73; dir. Baldwin County Libr. System, Summerdale, Ala., 1973-76; dir. libr. svc. Troy State U., Bay Minette, Ala., 1976-77; dir. main libr. Columbus Met. Libr., Ohio, 1977-83, asst. exec. dir., 1983-84, exec. dir., 1984—. Mem. Ohio Libr. Assn., Am. Soc. Pub. Adminstrs. Democrat. Club: Cen. Ohio Corvette (Columbus). Avocations: woodworking, gardening, restoration of old Corvette automobiles and Harley-Davidson motorcycles. Home: 7381 Seeds Rd Orient OH 43146-9608 Office: Columbus Met Libr 96 S Grant Ave Columbus OH 43215-4702*

BLACK, LEONARD JULIUS, retail store consultant; b. Bethlehem, Pa., Apr. 26, 1919; s. Morris and Reba I. (Perlman) B.; m. Betty Glosser, June 21, 1942; children: Susan Eiseman, Jodie Lichtenstein. BS, U. Pa., 1941; LLD, St. Francis Coll. With Glosser Bros., Inc., Johnstown, Pa., 1946-86; mdse. mgr. ready to wear Glosser Bros., Inc., 1954-59, exec. v.p. stores and supermarkets, 1959-69, pres., CEO, 1969-86, also bd. dirs.; cons. staff Coopers & Lybrand. Past bd. dirs. Conemaugh Valley Meml. Hosp., Greater Johnstown Com., Johnstown Econ. Devel. Com.; bd. dirs. Johnstown Area Regional Industries. Lt. comdr. USNR, 1942-46. Mem. Palm Beach Civic Assn., Citizens Assn. Palm Beach, Sunnehanna Country Club, High Ridge Country Club. Republican. Home and Office: 2780 S Ocean Blvd Palm Beach FL 33480-5581

BLACK, LISA HARTMAN (LISA HARTMAN BLACK), actress, singer; b. Houston, June 1; m. Clint Black, Oct. 20, 1991. Grad., High Sch. Performing Arts, Houston. TV series: Tabitha, 1977-78, High Performance, 1983, Knots Landing, 1982-86, 2000 Malibu Rd., 1993; TV Movies: Murder at the World Series, 1977, Where the Ladies go, 1980, Gridlock (also released as The Great American Traffic Jam), 1980, Beverly Hills Cowgirl Blues, 1985, Roses Are for the Rich, 1987, Full Exposure: The Sex Tapes Scandal, 1989, The Operation, 1990, The Take, USA, 1990, Fire! Trapped on the 37th Floor, 1991, Not of This World, 1991, Red Wind, 1991, The Return of Elliot Ness, 1991, Without a Kiss Goodbye, 1993, Search for Grace, 1994, Someone Else's Child, 1995, Have You Seen My Son?, 1996, Out of Nowhere, 1997, Still Holding On: The Legend of Cadillac Jack, 1998; TV mini-series: Jacqueline Susann's Valley of the Dolls, 1981, Judith Krantz's Dazzle, 1995; films: Deadly Blessing, 1981, Where the Boys Are, 1984, also recorded Hold On I'm Comin', 1979, Til My Heart Stops, 1988; prodr. Have You Seen My Son?, 1996; TV guest appearances include Police Woman, 1974, Vega$, 1978, On Stage America, 1984, The Hitchhiker, 1983, Matlock, 1986. Office: Hartman-Black Enterprises 8489 W 3rd St Los Angeles CA 90048-4124*

BLACK, MARTIN PATRICK, urban planner; b. Buffalo, N.Y., May 30, 1962; s. Patrick John and Michaelee Suzanne (Zankl) B.; m. Mary Ann Marchlewski, Aug. 10, 1985; children: Joshua Martin, Jacob Matthew. BA in German, Psychology, U. Buffalo, 1982, MS in Environ. Studies, 1984; MPA in Coastal Mgmt., U. W. Fla., 1985. Rsch. assoc. Environ. Studies Ctr., Amherst, N.Y., 1982-84, W. Fla. Regional Planning Coun., Pensacola, 1984-85; v.p. planning Gaines & Assocs., Inc., Pensacola, 1985-87; planner, market analyst Baskerville-Donovan, Inc., Pensacola, 1987-89; freelance cons. Pensacola, 1987-89; zoning supt. City of Fort Walton Beach, Fla., 1989; land use adminstr. Tallahassee/Leon County, Fla., 1989-95; utility svc. mgr. City of Tallahassee, 1995-97; dir. planning, zoning, bldg. and pub. works Town of Longboat Key, Fla., 1997—; devel. adv. bd. Innovation Park, Tallahassee, 1990-97; expert witness U.S. Dist. Ct. (no. dist.) Fla., 1991—, Fla. Cir. Ct. (2d cir.), 1990—; guest lectr. Fla. State U., 1991-95, Fla. A&M U., 1993-94, Internat. Right of Way Assn., 1993. Den leader Boy Scouts Am., Tallahassee, Fla., 1996-97, Sarasota, 1997—; gov. appointee Geographic Adv. Coun., Fla., 1997—. Recipient Merit award Historic Preservation Bd. Tallahassee, 1994. Mem. Am. Inst. Cert. Planners (cert.), Am. Planning Assn. (lobbying corr. 1990—), Urban Land Inst. (assoc.), Fla. Planning Assn. (dir. 1985-87). Republican. Lutheran. Home: 4496 Golden Lake Dr Sarasota FL 34233-1978 Office: Town of Longboat Key 610 General Harris St Longboat Key FL 34228-1412

BLACK, MAUREEN, realty company executive; b. Manchester, Eng., Feb. 4, 1937; came to U.S., 1957, naturalized, 1962; d. William Henry and Kathleen Mary (Cleaver) Jackson; grad. Felt and Tarrant Comptometer Sch., Eng., 1953; student Alamogordo br. N.Mex. State U., 1959-60, 62-63; m. Charles J. Dugan, Nov. 1979; 1 dau., Karen Elizabeth Black. Office mgr., personnel dir. J.C. Penney Co., Alamogordo, 1958-66; exec. sec. to project mgr. Re-entry System div. Gen. Electric Co., Holloman AFB, 1967-68; soc. editor, columnist Alamogordo Daily News, 1968-73; regional corr. El Paso (Tex.) Times, 1968-75; free lance writer and photographer; script writer Film Unit 505, Alamogordo, 1971; realtor asso. Shyne Realty, Alamogordo, 1975-77, West Source Realtors, 1977-80; owner, broker Hyde Park West Realty Co., 1980—. Pres., Alamogordo Music Theatre, 1971-72. Mem. planning com. tourism, recreation, convs. Gov. of N.Mex., 1965; mem. N.Mex. State Film Commn., 1973-74; life mem. Aux. of Zia Sch. for Handicapped Children, pres. Aux., 1975-76, 80-82; mem. Zia Sch. Bd., 1988-89, v.p., 1991-92; pres. Zia Found., 1988-89, 91-92, v.p. Zia Found. 1994-96. Recipient service award Nat. Found., March of Dimes, 1971; Americanism medal DAR, 1972; named Career Woman of Yr., Alamogordo chpt. Am. Bus. Women's Assn., 1971. Mem. Alamogordo C. of C. (chmn. convs. and motion picture com. 1965—), Nat. Assn. Realtors, Realtors Assn. N.Mex., Internat. Realtors Assn. Alamogordo Bd. Realtors (chmn. public relations com., v.p. 1981-82, pres. 1983-84), N.Mex. Opera Guild. Home: 1206 Desert Eve Dr Alamogordo NM 88310-5503 Office: PO Box 2021 Alamogordo NM 88311-2021

BLACK, NOEL ANTHONY, television and film director; b. Chgo., June 30, 1937; s. Samuel Abraham and Susan (Quan) B.; children: Marco Eugene, Nicole Alexandra. BA, UCLA, 1959, MA, 1964. Ind. fil, TV dir., 1966—; asst. prof. grad. program Inst. Film and TV, Tisch Sch. of Arts, NYU, 1992-93. Dir. (TV films) Trilogy: The American Boy, 1967 (Outstanding Young Dir. award Monte Carlo Internat. Festival of TV, Silver Dove award Internat. Cath. Soc. for Radio and TV), I'm a Fool, 1977, Mulligan's Stew, 1977, The Golden Honeymoon, 1979, The Electric Grandmother, 1981 (George Foster Peabody award 1982), The Other Victim, 1981, prime Suspect, 1981, Happy Endings, 1982, Quarterback Princess, 1983, Deadly Intentions, 1985, Promises to Keep, 1985, A Time to Triumph, 1985, My Two Loves, 1986, Conspiracy of Love, 1987, The Town Bully, 1988, Hollow Boy, 1991, (short films) Skaterdater, 1966 (Grand Prix award Cannes XX Film Festival, Grand Prix Tech. Cannes XX Internat. Film Festival, awards Cork Film Festival, Silver medal Moscow Internat. Film Festival, others), Riverboy, 1967 (Lion of St. Mark awrad Venice Internat. Film Festival, 1st prize Vancouver Internat. Film Festival), (feature films) Pretty Poison, 1968, Mirrors, 1974, A Man, A Woman and A Bank, 1978; screenwriter, exec. prodr. Mischief, 1984. Mem. Writers Guild Am., Dirs. Guild Am., Acad. Motion Picture Arts and Scis., Acad. TV Arts and Scis. Office: Starfish Prodns 126 Wadsworth Ave Santa Monica CA 90405-3510

BLACK, PAGE MORTON, civic worker; b. Chgo.; d. Alexander and Rose Morton; m. William Black, Mar. 27, 1962. Student, Chgo. Mus. Coll. Singer, pianist, Pierre Hotel, N.Y.C., Warwick Hotel, One Fifth Ave. Sherry Netherland Hotel; singer radio show and comml. Chock Full o' Nuts Corp.; rec. artist Atlantic Records, Den Records; co-founder Page and William Black Post-Grad. Sch. Medicine, Mt. Sinai Med. Sch., 1965—; chmn., mem. exec. bd. Parkinsons' Disease Found., Columbia U. Med. Ctr. (mem. adv. coun.); mem. nat. vis. coun. Columbia U. Health Scis. Faculties; hon. chmn. Chock Full O' Nuts Corp., 1983-90; active Columbia Presbyterian Health Scis. Adv. Coun.; founding mem. ASPCA. Recipient Ann. award Parkinsons' Disease Found., 1987, Police Athletic League, 1992, Mahattan Mag. award, 1992, Lifetime Achievement award Parkinson's Disease Found., 1997, Dean's award for Disting. Svc., Columbia U. Coll. Physicians & Surgeons, 1998. Home: Premium Pt New Rochelle NY 10801

BLACK, PAUL HENRY, medical educator, researcher; b. Boston, Mar. 11, 1930; s. Samuel Louis and May (Goldberg) B.; m. Sandra Merkin, June 2, 1962; children: Scott, Marc, Jeffrey. AB, Dartmouth Coll., 1952; MD, Columbia U., 1956. Diplomate Am. Bd. Internal Medicine. Intern Mass. Gen. Hosp., Boston, 1956-57, resident in medicine, 1957-58, clin. and rsch. fellow, 1958-60, resident in medicine, 1960-61; sr. asst. surgeon Lab. Infectious Diseases USPHS Nat. Inst. Allergy and Infectious Diseases, NIH, Bethesda, Md., 1961-63; sr. surgeon Lab. Infectious Diseases USPHS Nat. Inst. Allergy and Infectious Diseases, U. Glasgow Inst. Virology, Scotland, 1963-64, Nat. Inst. Allergy and Infectious Diseases, NIH, Bethesda, Md., 1964-67; asst. prof. medicine Harvard U. Med. Sch., Boston, 1967-70, assoc. prof. medicine, 1970-80; asst. physician Mass. Gen. Hosp., Boston, 1967-70, assoc. physician, 1970-80, hon. physician, 1980—; dir. Hubert H. Humphrey Cancer Rsch. Ctr. Boston U., 1979-83; chmn., prof. microbiology, research prof. surgery, prof. medicine Boston U. Sch. Medicine, 1979-96, prof. emeritus, 1996—; cons. Roswell Park Meml. Inst., Buffalo, 1976-80, Monsanto Chem. Corp., St. Louis, 1976-82, Collaborative Research, Inc., Lexington, Mass., 1984-90, Nat. Cancer Adv. Bd. Subcom. on the Evaluation of Cancer Ctrs., Bethesda, 1975-80; sci. cons. U.S.-Israel Binat. Sci. Found., Jerusalem, Israel, 1974—; mem. NIH Study Sect. Virology, 1968-72, Tumor Virus Detection Segment, Spl. Virus Cancer Program, Bethesda, 1972-76; mem. subcom. on environ. carcinogens, Am. Cancer Soc. Task Force on Cancer Prevention, 1975-82 , sci. adv. bd. Worcester Found. for Exptl. Biology, Mass., 1976-78, sci. adv. bd. Dartmouth-Hitchcock Med. Ctr., Hanover, N.H., 1976-80, Gov.'s Task Force on AIDS, Commonwealth of Mass., Boston, 1983—; chmn. spl. virus cancer program contract rev. com., Nat. Cancer Inst., 1977-79. Author monograph; contbr. articles to profl. jours., chpts. to books. Nat. Cancer Inst. grantee, 1967-87. Fellow AAAS; mem. Am. Soc. Clin. Investigation, Infectious Diseases Soc., Am. Soc. Microbiology, Am. Soc. Virology, Am. Assn. Med. Sch. Microbiology Chmn., Soc. Gen. Microbiology, Sigma Xi. Democrat. Jewish. Home: 21 Dawes Rd Lexington MA 02421-5926 Office: Boston U Sch Medicine 80 E Concord St Boston MA 02118-2307

BLACK, PERCY, psychology educator; b. Montreal, Que., Can., Jan. 6, 1922; s. Ovido and Rose (Vasilevsky) B.; m. Virginia Arne, June 21, 1951; children—Deborah, David, Elizabeth, Jonathan. B.S., Sir George Williams Coll., Montreal, 1944; M.Sc., McGill U., 1946; Ph.D., Harvard U., 1953. Instr. in Social Scis. U. Ky., 1948-49; rsch. asst. in Race Rels. U. Chgo., 1950-51; rsch. assoc. in Child Psychology U. Minn., 1949-50; Asst. prof. psychology U. N.B., Fredericton, 1951-53; vis. scholar Univ. Coll., London, 1953-54; dir. research Social Attitude Survey, Yonkers, N.Y., 1955-67; prof. emeritus in Psychology Pace U., Pleasantville, N.Y., 1967—; Contbg. author: Societies Around the World, 2 vols., 1953; author: The Mystique of Modern Monarchy, 1953; contbr. articles to profl. jours. Fellow AAAS; mem. APA, Am. Psychol. Soc., B'nai B'rith. Home: 29 Cross Hill Ave Yonkers NY 10703-1422 Office: Pace U Psychology Dept Pleasantville NY 10570-2799

BLACK, PERRY, neurological surgeon, educator; b. Montreal, Oct. 2, 1930; came to U.S., 1959, naturalized 1979; s. Ovido and Rose (Vasilevsky) B.; children: Daniel Ovid, Julie Miriam, Amy Rose. BSc, McGill U., Montreal, 1951, MD, CM, 1956. Intern, then asst. resident in medicine and gen. surgery Jewish Gen. Hosp., Montreal, 1956-58; asst. resident in neurology Montreal Neurol. Inst., 1958-59; resident in neurosurgery Johns Hopkins Hosp., Balt., 1959-63, neurosurgeon, 1964-79; NIH fellow in physiology Johns Hopkins U. Sch. Medicine, 1961-62, instr. neurol. surgery, 1964-67, asst. prof., 1967-69, assoc. prof., 1969-79, asst. prof. psychiatry, 1967-70, assoc. prof., 1970-79; prof. Hahnemann U. Sch. Medicine, Phila., 1979-94, chmn. dept. neurosurgery, dir. pain treatment program, 1979-94, dir. brain tumor program, 1983-94; prof. neurosurgery Med. Coll. Pa. and Hahnemann U., 1994—, dir. malignant brain tumor program, 1995—; dir. neurosurgery in the brain Tumor Ctr., Med. Coll. Pa. and Hahnemann U., Phila.; dir. child head injury project dept. neurol. surgery Johns Hopkins Hosp., 1963-79; dir. lab. neurol. scis., chmn. ctrl. rsch. authority Friends Med. Sci. Rsch. Ctr., Balt., 1972-79, hon. dir., 1979—; mem. neurology study sect. NIH, 1973-77; coun. neurosurg. rep. Johns Hopkins Med. Sch., 1977-78, coun. vice chmn., 1978-79. Editor: Drugs and the Brain, 1969, Physiological Correlates of Emotion, 1970, Brain Dysfunction in Children: Etiology, Diagnosis, and

Management, 1981; contbr. articles to profl. jours. Bd. dirs. Epilepsy Assn. Central Md., 1966-77, chmn. profl. adv. bd., 1973-75; mem. com. of fifty Epilepsy Found. Am., 1970-76, state coordinator for Md., 1973-76. Recipient Residents Paper award So. Neurosurg. Soc., 1963, Volvo award World Fedn. of Neurosurgical Socs., 1985. Mem. AAAS, Congress Neurol. Surgeons (chmn. sci. and edn. com. 1969-72, chmn. sci. program com. 1971-72, editor newsletter 1972-75, mem. exec. com. 1972-75, mem. nominating com. 1975-77, chmn. internat. com. 1975-81, assoc. editor jour. 1976-82, editor jour. internat. neurosurgery 1976-87, Disting. Svc. award 1977), AMA, AAUP, Am. Assn. Neurol. Surgeons (Harvey Cushing Soc., mem. subcom. on continuing edn. 1974-78), Am. Pain Soc., Soc. Neurol. Surgeons, Am. Soc. Stereotactic and Functional Neurosurgery, Soc. for Neurosci., Rsch. Soc. Neurol. Surgeons, Am. Epilepsy Soc., Am. Neurol. Assn., Internat. Assn. for Study of Pain, Philadelphia County Med. Soc., Phila. Neurol. Soc. (2nd v.p. 1982-83), Pa. Neurosurg. Soc. (mem. coun. 1989—, sec., treas. 1990, pres. 1992), Mid-Atlantic Neurosurg. Soc. Office: Hahnemann Univ Hosp Dept Neurosurgery Broad & Vine Mail Stop 455 Philadelphia PA 19130-1192*

BLACK, PETE, retired state legislator, educator; b. Ansbach, Germany, Sept. 16, 1946; came to U.S., 1948; s. Howard and Kadi (Fietz) B.; m. Ronda Williams, July 12, 1970; 1 child, Darin. BS, Idaho State U., 1975, MEd, 1998. Cert. elem. tchr. Tchr. Pocatello (Idaho) Sch. Dist., 1975—; mem. Idaho Ho. Reps., Boise, 1983-96, asst. minority leader, 1987-96; tech. tng. specialist Sch. Dist. 25, 1996—; mem. edn. tech. coun.; mem. adv. coun. chpt. II ESEA. Bd. dirs. Arts for Idaho. With USNR, 1964. Mem. NEA, Idaho Edn. Assn. (bd. dirs.), Idaho Libr. Assn. (state libr. bd.). Democrat. Home: 2249 Cassia St Pocatello ID 83201-2059 Office: Idaho House of Reps Statehouse Mail Boise ID 83720

BLACK, RHONDA STOUT, special education educator; b. Salt Lake City, Feb. 5, 1960; d. Doyle and Afton Glenna (Nebeker) Stout; m. Richard Terrell Black, Mar. 25, 1989. BS in Child-Family Devel. magna cum laude, U. Utah, 1982, BS in Psychology magna cum laude, 1982, MS in Spl. Edn., 1991, EdD in Occupl. Studies, 1996. Behavior specialist, instr. Columbus Community Ctr., Salt Lake City, 1984-85, program mgr. occupational skill tng., 1985-93; rsch. asst. U. Ga., Athens, 1993-96; asst. prof. U. Hawaii, Honolulu, 1996—. Faculty scholar U. Utah, 1980-81; recipient postdoctoral scholarship COMRISE, 1999. Mem. Am. Vocat. Assn., Am. Ednl. Rsch. Assn., Nat. Assn. Vocat. Spl. Needs Pers., Coun. for Exceptional Children (tchr. edn., career devel. divsn. and mental retardation), Phi Beta Kappa, Phi Eta Sigma, Phi Kappa Phi, Phi Delta Kappa, Omicron Theta Tau. Democrat.

BLACK, RICHARD A., community college president; b. Mar. 29, 1944; m. Jo Ann Black, 1974; 2 children. BS in Math., S.E. Mo. State U., 1966; MEd, U. Mo., Columbia, 1967, postgrad., 1971-73; postgrad., Harvard U., 1995. Instr. math. Ritenour Sr. H.S., Overland, Mo., 1966-69; adminstrv. assoc., asst. dean for continuing edn. St. Louis C.C. at Meramec, 1973-79, asst. and assoc. dean for continuing edn., 1979-86, dean of instrn., 1986-91, pres., 1992—. Bd. dirs. Higher Edn. Ctr. St. Louis. Served with U.S. Army. Mem. Mo. C.C. Assn. (trustee 1989-92, pres. adminstrv. sect.), St. Louis Conf. on Edn., St. Louis Symphony Soc., Kirkwood Area C. of C., St. Loius Art Mus., Mo. Hist. Soc., Kirkwood Rotary. Avocations: music, golf, photography, microcomputers, travel. Home: 148 Saylesville Dr Chesterfield MO 63017-3456 Office: Saint Louis Community College at Meramec 11333 Big Bend Rd Kirkwood MO 63122-5799*

BLACK, RICHARD BRUCE, business executive, consultant; b. Dallas, July 25, 1933; s. James Ernest and Minerva Iantha (Braden) B.; children: Kathryn Braden, Paula Anne (dec.), Erica Lynn. BS in Engring., Tex. A&M U., 1954; MBA, Harvard U., 1958; postgrad., Northwestern U., 1960-62; PhD (hon.), Beloit Coll., 1967. With Vulcan Materials Co., Birmingham, Ala., 1958-62; v.p. fin. Warner Electric Brake & Clutch Co., Beloit, Wis., 1962-67, dir., 1973-85; pres. automotive group, exec. v.p. corp. Maremont Corp., Chgo., 1967-72, pres. corp., COO, 1972-76, pres., chmn., CEO, 1976-79; pres., CEO, dir. Alusuisse of Am., Inc., N.Y.C., 1979-81; chmn., CEO, dir. AM Internat., Inc., Chgo., 1981-82; owner R. Black & Assocs., 1983—; chmn. ECRM, Boston, 1983—; pres., dir. Oak Technology, Inc., Sunnyvale, Calif., 1998—; bd. dirs. Gabelli Funds, Inc., Gen. Scanning Corp., Morgan Group Inc., Benedetto Gartland, Inc., Grand Eagle Cos., Inc.; lectr. econs. Beloit (Wis.) Coll., 1964-67. Author: (with Jack Pierson) Linear Polyethylene-Propylene: Problems and Opportunities, 1958. Trustee Beloit Coll., Am. Indian Coll. Fund., N.Y.C., Teton Sci. Sch., Bard Coll. Ctr. for Curatorial Studies, Inst. for Advanced Study, Princeton, N.J., Snake River Conservancy Found. 1st lt. USAF, 1954-56. Recipient Flame of Hope Lifetime Achievement award, Am. Indian Coll. Fund, 1998. Mem. Am. Alpine Club, Harvard Club (N.Y.C.).

BLACK, RICHARD W., director, financial aid; b. Mt. Vernon, Ohio, Sept. 19, 1941; s. John Wilson and Helen (Harrington) B.; m. Donna M. Arganbright, Mar. 15, 1975; children: Jason, Alaska, Alex, Alycia. BA, Harvard Coll., 1963; MA, Tufts U., 1968. Asst. dir. fin. aid Tufts U., Medford, Mass., 1965-68; dir. fin. aid. Washington Tech. Inst., Washington, 1968-70; edn. program specialist U.S. Office Edn., Washington, 1970-74; dir. fin. aid Georgetown U., Washington, 1974-79; coord. fin. aid Harvard U., Cambridge, Mass., 1979-83; dir. fin. aid U. Calif., Berkeley, 1983--, interim exec. dir. admissions and enrollment, 1998--; chmn. Grad. and Profl. Fin. Aid Coun., 1983-84; vice chmn. Grant Adv. Com., Calif. Student Aid Commn., 1995--. Author: The Complete Family Guide to College Financial Aid, 1995. Democrat. Office: U Calif-Berkeley Office of Financial Aid 201 Sproul Hall Berkeley CA 94720

BLACK, RILLA ALMA, violinist, library assistant, poet; b. Quincy, Ill., June 23, 1920; d. Frank and Georgia Eleanor (Stewart) Darnell; m. Albert Black, Nov. 9, 1944 (dec. Aug. 1998); children: Diana, Linda, Robert. BA, Culver-Stockton Coll., Canton, Mo.; MA in English, Chapman Coll., Orange, Calif., 1991; student, Eastman Sch. Music, Rochester, N.Y., 1943-44. Cert. tchr., Ill. Tchr. Bowen (Ill.) H.S., 1942-43; libr. asst. Orange County Pub. Libr., Santa Ana, Calif., 1977-91. Contbr. poetry to anthologies. Mem. Chapman Symphony, Orange, Calif., concertmaster, 1958. Mem. Internat. Soc. Poets, Am. Collegiate Poets Anthology. Listed in Nat. Libr. Poetry Selection: Outstanding Poets of 1998.

BLACK, RITA ANN, communications executive; b. Newark, Sept. 2, 1950; d. Henry and Mary (Solomon) Black; m. David Joseph Franus, Dec. 30, 1973. B.A. in English, U. Rochester, 1972; M.S. in Journalism, Columbia U., 1975. Accredited bus. communicator. Sr. editor Book Prodn. Industry, mag., New Canaan, Conn., 1972-74, 75-76; mgr. publs. AAUP, N.Y.C., 1976-78; sr. communication specialist Ciba-Geigy Corp., Ardsley, N.Y., 1978-80, mgr. internal communication, 1980-84; exec. speechwriter IBM Corp., Armonk, N.Y., 1984-86, sr. info. rep., 1986-88; program adminstr. U.S. media rels., 1988-90; program mgr. corp. media rels., 1990-91; sr. program adminstr. corp. image advt., 1991-92; nat. mktg. mgr. Deloitte & Touche LLP, Wilton, Conn., 1993—. Mem. Pub. Relations Soc. Am. (Bronze Anvil award 1996), Internat. Assn. Bus. Communicators (dir. 1982-84, Gold Quill 1983, 84, Dist. I award of excellence 1982), Phi Beta Kappa. Office: Deloitte & Touche LLP 10 Westport Rd Wilton CT 06897-4522

BLACK, ROBERT ALLEN, lawyer; b. Ocala, Fla., Aug. 15, 1954; s. Allen Harrison and Rose Marie (Dupree) B. BA, U. Tex., El Paso, 1977; JD summa cum laude, Tex. Tech U., 1980. Bar: Tex. 1980, U.S. Ct. Appeals (5th and 11th cirs.) 1980, U.S. Supreme Ct. 1985. Ptnr. Mehaffy & Weber, Beaumont, Tex., 1980—; mng. ptnr. Mehaffy & Weber, 1998—; adj. prof. law Lamar U., Beaumont, Tex., 1981-84. Case note editor Tex. Tech Law Rev., 1979-80; editor Jefferson County Bar Jour., 1991-93. Pres. Humane Soc. S.E. Tex., Beaumont, 1983-89; bd. dirs. YMCA, Beaumont, 1985-87, Beaumont Cmty. Players, 1989-91; host TV show Pets on Parade, Beaumont, 1986-87; mem. Beaumont City Planning and Zoning Commn., 1987-90; mem. Beaumont Hist. Landmark Commn., 1989-90. Named one of Outstanding Young Men of Am., Jaycees, 1982. Mem. ABA, Jefferson County Bar Assn. (treas. 1994-95, v.p. 1995-96, pres.-elect. 1996-97, pres. 1997-98)), Tex. Bar Assn., Am. Contract Bridge League (bd. govs. 1992-96, pres. unit 201, 1991-93, 94-96). Democrat. Avocations: book collecting, tennis, history. Home: 601 22nd St Beaumont TX 77706-4915 Office: Mehaffy & Weber 2615 Calder St Beaumont TX 77702-1986

BLACK, ROBERT CHARLES, author, lawyer; b. Detroit, Jan. 4, 1951; s. Robert Charles and Eileen Lois (Perry) B. BA, U. Mich., 1973; JD, Georgetown U., 1977; MA, U. Calif., Berkeley, 1984, SUNY, Albany, 1996. Bar: Calif. Rsch. atty. Mich. Ct. Appeals, Detroit, 1977-78, San Francisco, 1978-82; tchg. assoc. U. Calif., Berkeley, 1982-85; law intern ACLU, L.A., 1985; rsch. atty. SMH, Inc., Somerville, Mass., 1985-87; tchg. asst. SUNY, Albany, 1991-92; adj. prof. Coll. St. Rose, Albany, 1994; cons. The Police Found. Author: The Abolition of Work and Other Essays, 1986, Friendly Fire, 1992, Beneath the Underground, 1994, Anarchy After Leftism, 1997. Regents fellow U. Calif., Berkeley, 1982, 83; Hindelaang fellow SUNY, 1989. Mem. State Bar Calif., Phi Beta Kappa, Phi Eta Sigma. Office: PO Box 3142 Albany NY 12203-0142

BLACK, ROBERT COLEMAN, judge, lawyer; b. Greenville, Ala., July 3, 1934; s. James Monroe and Mabel (Coleman) B.; m. Carolyn Musselwhite, Dec. 20, 1960; children: Elizabeth Anne, Robert C., Carolyn Jane. B.S. in Commerce and Bus. Adminstrn, U. Ala., 1960, LL.B., 1961. Bar: Ala. 1961. Law clk. to justice Ala. Supreme Ct., 1961-62; partner firm Hill, Hill, Carter, Flanco, Cole & Black, Montgomery, Ala., 1968—; spl. asst. atty. gen. Ala. Hill, Hill, Carter, Flanco, Cole & Black, 1969-79; judge Circuit Ct., 1979—; prof. law Jones Law Sch., Montgomery; instr. bus. law U. Ala. at Montgomery, Auburn U.; lectr. continuing legal edn. Ala. Bar Assn.; faculty Ala. Jud. Coll. City chmn. March of Dimes, 1966; Bd. dirs. March of Dimes Found., 1966-67, Montgomery YMCA, St. James Parrish Sch.; trustee Ala. Indsl. Sch. Served with USMCR, 1954-57. Mem. Ala. Bar Assn., Montgomery County Bar Assn. (chmn. exec. com. 1969-70, pres. 1971), Phi Delta Phi, Beta Gamma Sigma. Office: 425 S Perry St Montgomery AL 36104-4235

BLACK, ROBERT DURWARD, television producer; b. Flint, Mich., June 6, 1952; s. Joseph Perrin and Lois Jane (Hamilton) B. BA, Wheaton (Ill.) Coll., 1974; cert. bus. adminstrn., U. Ill., Chgo., 1991. Sr. account exec. NCR Corp., 1982-84; contr. Bob Horsley's, Inc., 1974-82, v.p., gen. mgr., 1984-87; pres., prodr. weekly ecumenical TV broadcast 30 Good Minutes, 1987—. Office: Chgo Sunday Evening Club 200 N Michigan Ave Chicago IL 60601-5909

BLACK, ROBERT FREDERICK, former oil company executive; b. Mansfield, Ohio, Jan. 9, 1920; s. Judson Ammi and Pauline (Remy) B.; m. Conita Fay McCoslin, June 25, 1944; children: Ronald Gregory, Peggy Lynn. Student, Miami U., Oxford, Ohio, 1946-47. Asst. mgr. Warner Bros. Theatres, Mansfield, 1935-42; asst. treas. Red Arrow Freight Lines, Inc., Houston, 1947-56; contr., sec. Cactus Petroleum Inc., Houston, 1956-62; project contr. Del E. Webb Corp., Clear Lake City, Tex., 1962-65; treas. Mitchell Energy & Devel. Corp., The Woodlands, Tex., 1965-82. With USAAC, 1942-46, CBI. Named to Honorable Order of Ky. Colonels. Mem. Fin. Execs. Inst. (life, past bd. dirs. Houston chpt.), CBI Vets Assn., DeMolay Alumni Assn., Burma Star Assn., Sun City West Hi 12 Club (past pres.), Sun City West Ohio Club, Sun City West Recreational Vehicle Club, Masons (life, treas. Sun City West Lodge, grand organist Grand Lodge of Ariz. 1997-98). Republican. Home: #193 11596 W Sierra Dawn Blvd Surprise AZ 85374-9722

BLACK, ROBERT L., JR., retired judge; b. Cin., Dec. 11, 1917; s. Robert L. and Anna M. (Smith) B.; m. Helen Chatfield, July 27, 1946; children: William C., Stephen L., Luther F. AB, Yale U., 1939; LLB, Harvard U., 1942. Bar: Ohio 1946, U.S. Ct. Appeals (6th cir.) 1947, U.S. Supreme Ct. 1955. pvt. practice, Cin., 1946-53; ptnr. Graydon, Head & Ritchey, Cin., 1953-72; judge Ct. Common Pleas, Cin., 1973-77, Ct. Appeals, Cin., 1977-89, vis. and assigned judge, 1989-92; mem. jury instrns. com. Ohio Jud. Conf. 1973—, chmn. 1986-92. Councilman Village Indian Hill (Ohio), 1953-65, mayor, 1959-65; mem. standing com. Diocese of So. Ohio, Episcopal Ch., 1958-64, lay del. to gen. assembly, 1966, 69; vestryman, warden Indian Hill Episcopal Ch.; chmn. Cin. Human Rels. Commn., 1967-70. Served to capt. U.S. Army, 1942-45. Decorated Bronze Star. Mem. Cin. Bar Assn., Ohio Bar Assn., ABA, Am. Judicature Soc., Nat. Legal Aid and Defender Assn., Phi Beta Kappa. Republican. Episcopalian. Clubs: Queen City, Camargo, Commonwealth (Cin.). Contbr. articles on law to profl. jours. Home: 5900 Drake Rd Cincinnati OH 45243-3306

BLACK, ROBERT LINCOLN, pediatrician; b. Los Angeles, Aug. 25, 1930; s. Harold Alfred and Kathryn (Stone) B.; m. Jean Wilmott McGuire, June 27, 1953; children: Donald J., Douglas L., Margaret S. A.B., Stanford U., 1952, M.D., 1955. Diplomate: Am. Bd. Pediatrics. Intern Kings County Hosp., Bklyn., 1955-56; resident and fellow Stanford U. Hosp., 1958-62; practice medicine specializing in pediatrics Monterey, Calif., 1962—; Clin. prof. Stanford U., 1962—; cons. Calif. Dept. Health, Sacramento, 1962—; mem. Calif. State Maternal, Child, Adolescent Health Bd., 1984-93. Author: (with others) California Health Plan for Children, 1979. Bd. dirs. Lyceum of Monterey Peninsula, 1963—; mem. Monterey Peninsula Unified Sch., 1965-73, pres., 1968-70; mem. Mid-Coast Health System Agy., Salinas, Calif., 1975-80, pres., 1979-80; bd. dirs. Carmel Bach Festival, Calif., 1972-81. With USAF, 1956-58. Fellow Am. Acad. Pediatrics; mem. Calif. Med. Assn., Monterey County Med. Soc., Inst. Medicine Nat. Acad. Sci. Democrat. Home: 976 Mesa Rd Monterey CA 93940-4612 Office: 920 Cass St Monterey CA 93940-4507

BLACK, ROBERT PERRY, retired banker, executive; b. Hickman, Ky., Dec. 21, 1927; s. Burwell Perry and Veola (Moore) B.; m. Mary Rives Ogilvie, Oct. 27, 1951; children: Patty Rives, Robert Perry. BA, U. Va., 1950, MA, 1951, PhD, 1955. Research assoc. Fed. Res. Bank, Richmond, Va., 1954-55, assoc. economist, 1956-58, economist, 1958-60, asst. v.p., 1960-62, v.p., 1962-68, 1st v.p., 1968-73, pres., 1973-92; part time instr. U. Va., 1953-54; asst. prof. U. Tenn., 1955-56; lectr. U. Va., 1956-57, J. Boone Aiken vis. prof. banking Francis Marion Coll., Florence, S.C., 1991; mem. Gov.'s Adv. Bd. Revenue Estimates, 1976-92, Va. Econ. Recovery Commn., 1991-92; mem. adv. bd. Health Corp. Va., 1981-93; mem. bd. govs. Capital Area Assy., 1989-93, mem. exec. com., 1989-93; bd. dirs. Media Gen. Corp., Winchester Evening Star, Inc., Rockingham Publ. Co., T. Rowe Price's Fixed Income Mutual Funds, 1993-98. Contbr. articles to profl. jours. Past dir. Ctrl. Richmond Assn.; former trustee Collegiate Schs., past chmn.; mem. Assn. for Preservation of Va. Antiquities, 1971—; chmn. Main to the James Devel. Com., 1971-73; adv. coun. Robert E. Lee coun. Boy Scouts Am., 1977-78; bd. dirs. Retreat Hosp., 1988-98; past pres. United Way Greater Richmond, active Corp. Divsn., 1986; bd. dirs., mem. exec. com., treas., chmn. fin. com. Downtown Devel. Unltd., 1975-86; chmn. adv. com. Ctr. Banking Edn., Va. Union U., 1977-79; trustee E. Angus Powell Endowment for Am. Enterprise, 1980-88, Acad. for Econ. Edn., 1990-94; mem. adv. bd. Ctr. for Advanced Studies, U. Va., 1986-94; mem. Forum Club, 1987—; bd. dirs. Va. United Meth. Homes, Inc., 1990-94, v.p., 1991-92, chmn., 1992-94; mem. Gov.'s Com. on Def. Conv. and Econ. Adjustment, 1992-94; dir. Va. Biotech. Rsch. Park, 1992-94. With AUS, 1946-47. Recipient George Washington Honor medal award Freedoms Found., Valley Forge, 1978, Brotherhood citation NCCJ, 1991, J. Curtis Hall award for outstanding svc. Va. Coun. Econ. Edn., Outstanding Svc. award Ctrl. Richmond Assn., 1991, Silver Hope award Ctr. Va. chpt. Nat. Multiple Sclerosis Soc., 1992, Disting. Citizen award Robert E. Lee coun. Boy Scouts Am., 1993, Robert P. Black Rsch. Professorship in Econs. at U. Va. established by friends, 1993. Mem. Va. Inter-Govt. Inst. (bd. dirs. 1986-93), Country Club Va. (bd. dirs. 1980-85, 88, v.p. 1981-83, pres. 1983-85), The Commonwealth Club, Foundry Golf Club, Raven Soc., Phi Beta Kappa (past pres. Richmond chpt.), Beta Gamma Sigma, Alpha Kappa Psi, Kappa Alpha. Methodist. Home: 10 Dahlgren Rd Richmond VA 23233-6104

BLACK, RONNIE DELANE, religious organization administrator, mayor; b. Poplar Bluff, Mo., Oct. 26, 1947; s. Clyde Olen and Leona Christine Black; m. Sandra Elaine Hulett, Aug. 27, 1966; 1 child, Stephanie. BA, Oakland City (Ind.) Coll., 1969; M Div, So. Bapt. Theol. Sem., 1972. Ordained to ministry Gen. Assn. of Gen. Bapts., 1967. Pastor Gen. Bapt. Ch., Fort Branch, Ind., 1972-78; stewardship dir. Gen. Bapt. Hdqrs., Poplar Bluff, Mo., 1978-97, exec. dir., 1997—; councilman City of Poplar Bluff, 1985-97, mayor, 1990-92, 95-96. Office: Gen Bapts 100 Stinson Dr Poplar Bluff MO 63901-8736

BLACK, ROSA VIDA, writer, educator; b. Lovell, Wyo., Sept. 18, 1903; d. Robert John Bischoff and Rose Ann Jensen; m. Clinton Melford Black, June 4, 1925 (dec. May 1989); children: Harvey, Jean, Homer, John, Evelyn, Merrill, Francis, Carol. Student, U. Wyo., 1922-24, U. Utah, 1946. Tchr. Converse Sch. Dist., Douglas, Wyo., 1922-23, Granite Sch. Dist., Salt Lake City, 1946, Granger Camp Daus. of Utah Pioneers, Salt Lake City, 1950—; speech dir. Kearns 13th ward L.D.S. Ch. Young Women Mut. Improvement Assn., 1968, pres., 1924-25; writer, narrator script Kearns North Stake Relief Soc. Singing Mothers Concert, 1967, 68; lectr. on womanhood and patriotic subjects to girls' groups; writer, presenter tribute to builders of Lovell Canal, 1993; program chmn. Basin (Wyo.) Woman's Club, 1942. Author: Mother of the Year, 1969, Mother Stood Tall, 1971, Open Door to the Heart, 1986, Meet My Wonderful Family, 1993, Pioneer Stories of Yesterday for Children of All Ages of Today and Tomorrow, 1997; (essays) I Believe, 1996; (histories) Under Granger Skies, 1963 (award), Proud of Kearns, 1979 (award), Lovell, Our Pioneer Heritage, 1986, Pioneer Stories of Yesterday for Children of Today and tomorrow, 1997; co-author: Living Testimonies, Personal Histories, 1967. Panel advisor PTA, Salt Lake City, 1950; judge of election Rep. Party, Lovell, 1924; reader Relief Soc., Granger, Utah, 1953, pres., 1934-41, organist, 1957-60, social sci. tchr., 1952-54, theology tchr., 1954; mem. Young Women Orgn., pres., 1944; missionary, Australia, 1971-73, Nauvoo, Ill., 1975-77; asst., planner children's parade, Laramie, Wyo., 1932; counselor Stake Relief Soc., Laramie, 1931; pres. Children's Primary Orgn., Basin, Wyo., 1941-42. Recipient Cert. of Merit, Am. Mothers com., 1969. Mem. Daus. of the Utah Pioneers (capt. 1968—, pres. 1988-89, tchr. 1992—). Democrat. Mormon. Avocations: reading, writing, visiting with friends and family. Office: Daus of Utah Pioneers 330 N Main St Salt Lake City UT 84103-1632

BLACK, RUBY L., nursing educator; b. York, Ala., Sept. 7, 1950; d. James D. and Mary D. Lindsey; m. Frank S. Black, Mar. 16, 1974; children: Piper Lindsey, Jason Bennett. BSN, Tuskegee Inst., 1973; MSN, Tex. Women's U., 1978; postgrad., U. Memphis, 1996—. Staff nurse Cleve. Clinic, 1973-74; staff nurse, asst. head nurse Ben Taub Hosp., Houston, 1975-78; asst. prof. Murray (Ky.) State U., 1978-84; clin. specialist VA Med. Ctr., Jackson, Miss., 1985-87; assoc. prof. nursing U. Tenn., Martin, 1988—; mem. N.W. Tenn. Health Coun., Union City, 1996—. Mem. adv. bd. Martin (Tenn.) Jr. H.S., 1991-93; 1st aid vol. Martin Primary and elem. Schs., 1991—; bd. dirs. Interfaith Ctr., Martin, 1995—; bd. dirs. Tenn. Nurses Found., Nashville, 1996-97, N.T. Med. Credit Union, Martin, 1989-92; vice chair ch. coun. McCabe United Meth. Ch., Martin, 1994—. Mem. Nurses Assn. (bd. dirs. dist. 10 1988—, nominating com. 1993-94, pres. 1990-91, v.p., sec. 1994—, Nurse of Yr. Dist. 10 1997), Tenn. Pub. Health Assn., Faculty Women's Club (v.p. 1991-92, pres. 1992-93), Sigma Theta Tau (chpt. pres. 1982-84, Outstanding Mem. 1983). Home: 104 Shadow Wood Cv Martin TN 38237-8148 Office: U Tenn Martin Dept Nursing Martin TN 38238

BLACK, SAMUEL HAROLD, microbiology and immunology educator; b. Lebanon, Pa., May 1, 1930; s. Harold William and Beatrice Irene (Steckbeck) B.; m. Elisabeth Martha Zandveld, Aug. 16, 1961 (dec. Aug. 1997); children: Vicki Ann, Alisa Jo. Student, Hershey Jr. Coll., 1948-50; B.S., Lebanon Valley Coll., 1952; postgrad., U. Pa., 1952-54; M.S., U. Mich., 1958, Ph.D., 1961. NSF fellow Tech. U. Delft, The Netherlands, 1960-61; instr. U. Mich., Ann Arbor, 1961-62; asst. prof. Baylor Coll. Medicine, Houston, 1962-67, assoc. prof., 1967-71; assoc. prof. Mich. State U., East Lansing, 1971-73, prof., 1973-75; prof. microbiology and immunology Tex. A&M U., College Station, 1975—, head dept. med. microbiology and immunology, 1975-90, asst. dean for curriculum and undergrad. med. edn., 1985-87, interim dean Coll. Medicine, 1987-88, assoc. dean Coll. Medicine, 1988-91, prof. humanities in medicine, 1998—; lectr. U. Houston, 1964-66; vis. prof. Swiss Fed. Inst. Tech., Zurich, 1969-70. Served with M.C., U.S. Army, 1954-56. Recipient citation Lebanon Valley Coll. Alumni Assn., 1981. Fellow Am. Acad. Microbiology; mem. Am. Soc. Microbiology, Am. Soc. Cell Biology, Soc. Gen. Microbiology, Electron Microscope Soc. Am., Soc. Invertebrate Pathology. Home: 1205 King Arthur Cir College Station TX 77840-4827 Office: Tex A&M U Coll Medicine Dept Humanities in Medicine Immunology College Station TX 77843

BLACK, SARAH JOANNA BRYAN, secondary school educator; b. Port Arthur, Tex., Sept. 30, 1948; d. Foster Paul and Evelyn June (Whetsel) Bryan; m. David Lee Black, Nov. 26, 1971; children: Bryan Joseph, Kelley Allison, David Neal. BA, U. Tex., 1971. Tchr. math. Robert E. Lee H.S., Baytown, Tex., 1971-87, Lee Coll., Baytown, 1987—; tchr. math., chair dept. math. Ross S. Sterling H.S., Baytown, 1987—. Pres. Svc. League, Baytown, 1980; pres. Peter McKenney Soc. C.A.R., Baytown, 1984; treas. PTA of Stephen F. Austin Elem., Baytown, 1984; mem. John Lewis chpt. DAR, Baytown, 1980—, Colonial Dames, Tex., 1980—; treas. East League Little League, Baytown, 1986; treas. Grace Meth. Ch. Women, Baytown, 1985; mem. Cedar Bayou Meth. Ch., 1988-90; pres. Cedar Bayou PTO, 1988; historian Sterling PTSO, 1989. Named Secondary Tchr. of Yr., GCC Ind. Sch. Dist., 1991; recipient Tex. Excellences award Outstanding H.S. Tchr., U. Tex. Ex-Student Assn., 1993, Seminole Pipeline Tchg. Achievement award, 1995. Mem. Baytown Classroom Tchrs. (treas.), Baytown Edn. Assn., San Jacinto Coun. Math. Tchrs., Nat. Coun. Tchrs. of Math., Tex. Execs. (bd. dirs.), Welfare League, Bay Area Panhellenic (rush chmn.), Alpha Xi Delta (area rush chmn.), Alpha Delta Kappa, Delta Kappa Gamma. Republican. Methodist. Home: 3702 Autumn Ln Baytown TX 77521-2707 Office: 300 W Baker Rd Baytown TX 77521-2301

BLACK, STEPHEN FRANKLIN, lawyer; b. N.Y.C., Nov. 28, 1944; s. Theodore Russell Black and Zelma (Carmel) Bernstein; m. Laurie N. Bromberg, June 25, 1967 (div. Oct. 1988); children: Hilary F., Jane S., Katharine L.; m. Anne M. Richmond, Oct. 14, 1989. AB magna cum laude, Harvard U., 1965; JD magna cum laude, U. Mich., 1968; MLitt, Oxford (Eng.) U., 1970. Bar: D.C. 1969. Ptnr. Wilmer, Cutler & Pickering, Washington, 1970—; chmn. exec. coun. lawyers com. The Shakespeare Theatre, 1996—, mem. Guild bd., 1997—; dir. Am. Soc. for Legal History, 1979-82. Author: Internal Corporate Investigations, 1985, Der Zivilprozess in Den Vereinigten Staaten, 1986, Complying With Foreign Corrupt Practices Act, 1997; contbr. articles to profl. jours. Marshall scholar, 1968. Home: 1605 22nd St NW Washington DC 20008-1921 Office: Wilmer Cutler & Pickering 2445 M St NW Washington DC 20037-1487

BLACK, STEPHEN L., lawyer; b. Cin., Ohio, Dec. 3, 1948. AB magna cum laude, Harvard U., 1971, JD, 1974. Bar: Ohio 1974, U.S. Ct. Appeals (6th cir.). Law clerk to Hon. George Edwards U.S. Ct. Appeals (6th cir.), 1974-75; mayor City of Indian Hill, Ohio, 1995—; now ptnr. Graydon, Head & Ritchey, Cin. Mem. Ohio State Bar Assn., Cin. Bar Assn. Office: Graydon Head & Ritchey 1900 5th Third Ctr 511 Walnut St Cincinnati OH 45202-3157*

BLACK, SUSAN, public relations consultant; b. N.Y.C., Feb. 24, 1953; d. Owen Joseph and Joan Anne (Gorman) B.; m. John Berard, May 23, 1992; 1 child, Alexander Black Mitchell. BA, Conn. Coll., 1974. Asst. editor Continental Ins., N.Y.C., 1975-76; pub. affairs officer Citibank, N.Y.C., 1976-78; mgr. Gen. Signal, Stamford, Conn., 1978-81; account exec., v.p., sr. v.p. Hill and Knowlton, N.Y.C., 1981-91; prin. Dilenschneider Group Inc., N.Y.C., 1991-98; pub. rels. cons. San Francisco, 1998—.

BLACK, SUSAN HARRELL, federal judge; b. Valdosta, Ga., Oct. 20, 1943; d. William H. and Ruth Elizabeth (Phillips) Harrell; m. Louis Eckert Black, Dec. 28, 1966. BA, Fla. State U., 1965; JD, U. Fla., 1967; LLM, U. Va., 1984. Bar: Fla. 1967. Atty. U.S. Army Corps of Engrs., Jacksonville, Fla., 1968-69; asst. state atty. Gen. Counsel's Office, Jacksonville, 1969-72; judge County Ct. of Duval County, Fla., 1973-75; judge 4th Jud. Cir. Ct. of Fla., 1975-79; judge U.S. Dist. Ct. (mid. dist.) Fla., Jacksonville, 1979-90, chief judge, 1990-92; judge U.S. Ct. Appeals (11th cir.) Fla., Jacksonville, 1992—; faculty Fed. Jud. Ctr.; mem. U.S. Judicial Conf. Com. on Judicial Improvements; bd. trustees Am. Inns. Ct. Found. Trustee emeritus Law Sch. U. Fla.; past pres. Chester Bedell Inn of Ct. Mem. Am. Bar Assn., Fla. Bar Assn., Jacksonville Bar Assn. Episcopalian. Office: US Dist Ct PO Box 53135 311 W Monroe St Jacksonville FL 32201-3135*

BLACK, THEODORE HALSEY, retired manufacturing company executive; b. Jersey City, Oct. 22, 1928; s. Theodore Charles and Mary (Carroll) B.; m. Marilyn Rigsby, 1979; children: Deborah, Theodore Jr., Susan, Zelda, Carol, Brian. BSEE, U.S. Naval Acad., Annapolis, 1953; postgrad., Harvard U., 1974. Salesman, sales mgr. Ingersoll-Rand Co., N.Y.C., 1957-

67, gen. mgr. turbo products divsn., 1967-72, v.p., 1972-87; from pres., COO to chmn., CEO Ingersoll-Rand Co., Woodcliff Lake, N.J., 1988-93; ret., 1993; pres., CEO Dresser-Rand Co., Corning, N.Y., 1987-88; bd. dirs. Gen. Pub. Utilities, Parsippany, N.J., Best Foods, Englewood Cliffs, N.J., McDermott Internat., New Orleans. Capt. USMC, 1946-49, 53-59. Recipient Naval Aviator award USN, Corpus Christi, Tex., 1955. Roman Catholic. Avocations: hunting, fishing, tennis, golf. Office: Ingersoll-Rand Co 200 Chestnut Ridge Rd Westwood NJ 07675-7700

BLACK, THOMAS DONALD, retired religious organization administrator; b. Mercer, Pa., Feb. 7, 1920; s. Harry Alexander and Bessie (Gilkey) B.; m. Frances Anna Greenan, Mar. 1, 1923; children: David Alan, Donald Francis, Joseph Harry, Timothy John (dec.). BA, Grove City Coll., 1942, DD, 1955; MDiv, Pitts.-Xenia Theol. Sch., 1945; MST, Temple U., 1954. Ordained to ministry United Presbyn. Ch. N.Am., 1945. Founding pastor Creston Hills United Presbyn. Ch., Oklahoma City, 1945-50; pastor Blvd. United Presbyn. Ch., Phila., 1950-54, Am. Ch. in London, 1973-76; exec. sec. United Presbyn. Bd. Fgn. Mission, Phila., 1954-58; assoc. gen. sec. Commn. on Ecumenical Mission and Relations United Presbyn. Ch.-U.S.A., N.Y.C., 1958-70, gen. sec. Commn. on Ecumenical Mission and Relations, 1970-72, assoc. gen. dir. Program Agy., 1977-84; exec. dir. Gen. Assembly Council Presbyn. Ch. (USA), N.Y.C. and Atlanta, 1985-87; acting assoc. gen. sec. Nat. Coun. Chs. in U.S.A., 1989-90; interim dir. U.S. Office World Coun. Chs., N.Y.C., 1991-92; chmn. bd. dirs. Christian Lit. Fund, Geneva, 1964-69, Ravemcco, Lit-Lit, N.Y.C., 1962-66. Author: Merging Mission and Unity, 1986; contbr. articles and pamphlets to mission and ch. publs. Interim assoc. Riverside Ch., 1992-93; pastoral assoc. Abington Presbyn. Ch., 1994-98. Home: Rydal Park 617H 1515 The Fairway Rydal PA 19046-1435 *We want to be appreciated for what we are, but uncertain of being accepted, we try to justify our lives by what we have accomplished. God accepts us for what we are.*

BLACK, W. L. RIVERS, III, lawyer; b. Biloxi, Miss., Sept. 2, 1952; s. William L. Jr. and Virginia (Howell) B.; m. Lisa A. Paige, Feb. 25, 1981 (div.); children: Jordanna, Caitlin; m. Elaine Kusulos, Apr. 25, 1993; children: Aristide, Hallie. BPA, U. Miss., 1974, JD, 1977; LLM in Marine Law, U. Wash., 1982; LLM in Internat. Law, U. Brussels, 1983. Bar: Miss. 1977, U.S. Ct. Mil. Appeals 1980, Wash. 1982, U.S. Ct. Appeals (9th cir.) 1983, U.S. Ct. of Internat. Trade, 1998. Instr. U. Md., Scotland and Italy, 1978-81; ptnr. Lane Powell Spears Lubersky, Seattle, 1983—. Mem. editl. bd. Maritime Law Reporter. With USN, 1977-81, Morocco, Scotland; capt. JAGC, USNR, 1983—. Mem. Seattle-King Bar Assn. (chair maritime sect. 1987-88), Inter-Pacific Bar Assn. (chair maritime law com. 1994-96), Asia-Pacific Lawyers Assn. (chair maritime com. 1986-89), Maritime Law Assn. of U.S., Washington Athletic Club, Naval Club (London). Methodist. Avocation: sailing. Office: Lane Powell Spears Lubersky 1420 5th Ave Ste 4100 Seattle WA 98101-2338

BLACK, WALTER EVAN, JR., federal judge; b. Balt., July 7, 1926; s. Walter Evan and Margaret Luttrell (Rice) B.; m. Catharine Schall Foster, June 30, 1951; children: Walter Evan III, Charles Foster, James Rider. A.B. magna cum laude, Harvard U., 1947, LL.B., 1949. Bar: Md. 1949. Assoc. Hinkley & Singley, Balt., 1949-53; ptnr. Hinkley & Singley, 1957-67; asst. U.S. atty. Dist. Md., Balt., 1953-55; U.S. atty. Dist. Md., 1956-57; ptnr. Clapp, Somerville, Black & Honemann, Balt., 1968-82; U.S. dist. judge Dist. Md., Balt., 1982—, chief judge, 1991-94; sr. status, 1994—; Sec.-treas. Parkwood Cemetery Co., Balt., 1967-82; also dir.; sec. So. Mech. Inc., Balt., 1971-82; also dir.; pres. Charles T. Brandt Inc., Balt., 1972-82; also dir. Chmn. Bd. Municipal and Zoning Appeals, Balt., 1963-67; mem. Jail Bd., Balt., 1971-73, Atty. Grievance Commn., 1978-82, Rev. Bd., 1975-78, chmn., 1975-76; mem. Gov.'s Commn. to Revise Annotated Code, 1975-82. Alt. Md. del. Republican Nat. Conv., 1960; chmn. Rep. City Com., Balt., 1962-66; Md. del. Rep. Nat. Conv., 1964; Bd. dirs. Balt. Urban League, 1963-69, 76-82; bd. dirs. Union Meml. Hosp.; dir. Hosp. for Consumptives of Md. Mem. Bar Assn. Balt. City, ABA, Md. Bar Assn., Rule Day Club, Lawyers' Round Table. Baptist. Office: US Dist Ct 101 W Lombard St Ste 404 Baltimore MD 21201-2626

BLACK, WILFORD REX, JR., state senator; b. Salt Lake City, Jan. 31, 1920; s. Wilford Rex and Elsie Isabell (King) B.; m. Helen Shirley Frazer; children: Susan, Janet, Cindy, Joy, Peggy, Vanna, Gayle, Rex. Student schools in Utah. Locomotive engr. Rio Grande R.R., 1941-81; mem. Utah Senate, 1972-96, speaker Third House, 1975-76, majority whip, 1977-78, minority leader, 1981-90; chmn., vice chmn. United Transp. Union, 1972-78; sec. Utah State Legis. Bd., United Transp. Chmn. bd. Rail Operators Credit Union, 1958-87; mission pres. Rose Park Stake Mormon Ch., high priest group leader Rose Park 9th Ward, 1980-83, 10th Ward, 1996—, mem. Rose Park Stake High Council, 1957-63. Served with U.S. Army, 1942-45. Recipient various awards r.r and legis. activities. Democrat. Office: 826 N 1300 W Salt Lake City UT 84116-3877

BLACK, WILLIAM GORDON, pension consultant; b. Winnipeg, Man., Can., Aug. 9, 1927; s. William Fotheringham and Mary Teresa (Douglas) B.; children: Sandra, Perelandra, Andra-Lee, Gordon. Grad. in acctg., U. Man., 1949. Chartered acct. Sr. acct. William Gray & Co., Winnipeg, 1944-50, Peat, Marwick, Mitchell, Winnipeg and Montreal, 1951-54; treas. Kingsway Transports, Montreal, Que., Can., 1955-60; with Can. Steamship Lines, Montreal, 1961-81, successively sec.-treas., comptroller, v.p. fin., sr. v.p.; sr. v.p., dep. chmn. The CSL Group Inc., Montreal, 1981-92, also bd. dirs.; bd. dirs. Can. SS Lines Inc. Mem. Inst. Chartered Accts. Man., Inst. Chartered Accts. Que., Pension Investment Assn. Can., Assn. Can. Pension Mgmt., Beaconsfield Golf Club. Office: CSL Group Inc 759 Victoria Sq. Montreal, PQ Canada H2Y 2K3

BLACK, WILLIAM REA, lawyer; b. N.Y.C., Nov. 4, 1952; s. Thomas Howard and Dorothy Chambers (Dailey) B.; m. Kathleen Jane Owen, June 24, 1978; children: William Ryan, Jonathan Wesley. BSBA, U. Denver, 1978, MBA, 1981; JD, Western State U., Fullerton, Calif., 1987. Bar: Calif., U.S. Ct. Appeals (fed. cir.), U.S. Dist. Ct.; lic. real estate broker. Bus. mgr. Deere & Co., Moline, Ill., 1979-85; dir. Mgmt. Resource Svcs. Co., Chgo., 1985-86; sr. v.p. Geneva Corp., Irvine, Calif., 1986-91; pvt. practice Newport Beach, Calif., 1991-92; gen. counsel Sunclipse, Inc., 1992-98; spl. counsel Amcor, Ltd., 1992-98; dir. gen. Amcor de Mex., S.A. de C.V., 1993-98; secretario KHL de Mex. S.A. de C.V., 1995-98; CEO Kuroi Kiku Corp., Kuroi Ryu Corp., First Reconnaissance Co.; exec. v.p., dir., gen. counsel, sec. LL Knickerbocker Co., Inc., 1997-99, Mann-Craft, Inc., Pyraponic Industries, Arkenol Asia, Inc.; dir. Anle Paper Co.; sec. Krasner Group, TCJC, Inc., Charisma Mfg. Co., Inc., KGI Fashions, Inc., Dermasci. Labs., Inc., Raymark Container, Inc., Georgetown Collection, Inc., Magic Attic Press, Inc., The LL Knickerbocker Co. (Thailand), Ltd., Harlyn Internat. Co., Ltd., S.L.S. Trading Co., Ltd., Am. Employers Def., Inc., United Studios Self Def., Inc. Mng. editor Western State U. Law Rev., Fullerton, 1984-87. Instr. Pai Lum Kung Fu Karate, Hartford, Conn., 1970-75, U.S. Judo Assn., Denver, 1975-80, United Studios Kenpo, L.A., 1995—. Recipient Am. Jurisprudence award Bancroft-Whitney Co., 1984, 85, 86; Pres.'s scholar full acad. merit scholarship, 1983. Mem. ABA, Am. Soc. Appraisers, Inst. Bus. Appraisers, Assn. Productivity Specialists, Am. Employment Law Coun., Profls. in Human Resources Assn., Am. Mgmt. Assn., Orange County Bar Assn., L.A. County Bar Assn., Mu Kappa Tau. Avocations: karate (2d degree black belt), skiing, scuba, golf. Office: Ste 350 369 San Miguel Dr Newport Beach CA 92660

BLACKADAR, ALFRED KIMBALL, meteorologist, educator; b. Newburyport, Mass., July 6, 1920; s. Walter Lloyd and Harriett (White) B.; m. Beatrice J. Fenner, Mar. 23, 1946; children: Bruce Evan, Russell Lloyd, Thomas Alan. AB, Princeton U., 1942; PhD, NYU, 1950. From instr. to asso. prof. NYU, 1946-56; lectr. climatology Columbia U., 1953-55; mem. faculty Pa. State U., 1956—, prof. meteorology, 1961—, prof. emeritus, 1985—, head dept., 1967-81; mem. exec. com. Univ. Corp. Atmospheric Rsch., 1965-68; mem. exec. com. divsn. earth scis. NRC, 1966-69; mem. Internat. Commn. on Dynamical Meteorology, 1978-94, chair working group A, 1978-85; vis. prof. Christian-Albrechts U., Kiel, Germany, 1985-95. Editor: Meteorological Research Revs., 1957; exec. editor: Weatherwise, 1981-95. Sec. Univ. Christian Assn., 1964-68. Served to maj. USAAF, 1942-46. Recipient Sr. Scientist award Alexander von Humboldt Found., 1973. Fellow AAAS, Am. Meteorol. Soc. (sec. 1965-69, pres. 1971-72, editor monographs, Charles F. Brooks award 1969, Cleveland Abbe award 1986, chmn. publs. commn. 1978-84, chair com. on awards 1989-90), Am. Geophys. Union, Deutsche Meteorologische Gesellschaft (fgn. mem.), North Plainfield (N.J.) Hall of Fame. Baptist. Home: 805 W Foster Ave State College PA 16801-3938 Office: Pa State U 503 Walker Bldg University Park PA 16802-5013

BLACKBOURN, DAVID GORDON, history educator; b. Spilsby, Eng., Nov. 1, 1949; s. Harry and Pamela Jean (Youngman) B.; m. Deborah Frances Langton; 2 children; BA with honors, Cambridge U., Eng., 1970, PhD, 1976. Rsch. fellow Jesus Coll., Cambridge, 1973-76, Inst. European History, Mainz, Fed. Republic Germany, 1974-75; lectr. Queen Mary Coll., U. London, 1976-79, Birkbeck Coll., U. London, 1979-85; reader in history Birkbeck Coll., 1985-89, prof. history, 1989-92; prof. history Harvard U., Cambridge, Mass., 1992-97, Coolidge prof., 1997—; vis. Kratter prof. history Stanford (Calif.) U., 1989-90; guest lectr. U.S., Eng., Italy, Yugoslavia, Fed. Republic Germany, 1976—, ann. lect. German Hist. Inst., London, 1998; mem. acad. adv. bd. Inst. for European History, Mainz, 1995—; hist. cons. Channel 4 TV (U.K.), History Channel (U.S.). Author: Class, Religion and Local Politics in Wilhelmine Germany, 1980, (with G. Eley) The Peculiarities of German History, 1984, Populists and Patricians: Essays in Modern German History, 1987, (edited with R.J. Evans) The German Bourgeoisie, 1991, Marpingen: Apparitions of the Virgin Mary in Bismarckian Germany, 1993 (Am. Hist. Assn. prize for best book), The Long Nineteenth Century: A History of Germany, 1780-1918, 1998. Numerous appearances on Brit. Broadcasting System, 1977—. Contbr. articles to profl. jours. Gov. Goodrich Sch., London, 1983-86. Alexander von Humboldt Found. fellow, 1984-85; German Acad. Exchange grantee, 1977, John Simon Guggenheim Meml. Found. fellow, 1994-95. Fellow Royal Hist. Soc.; mem. German History Soc. (com. 1981-85, sec. 1979-81), German Hist. Inst. (London) (com. 1983-92), Inst. for European History (Mainz, Germany). Avocations: writing, reading, jazz, politics, classical music.

BLACKBURN, ALEXANDER LAMBERT, author, English literature educator; b. Durham, N.C., Sept. 6, 1929; s. William Maxwell and Elizabeth Cheney (Bayne) B.; m. Jane Allison, 1957 (div. 1974); children: David Alexander, Philip William Rhodes; m. Inés Dölz, Oct. 14, 1975. BA, Yale U., 1951; MA, U. N.C., 1956; PhD, Cambridge (Eng.) U., 1963. Instr. Hampden-Sydney (Va.) Coll., 1960-61, U. Pa., Phila., 1963-65; lectr. U. Md., RAF, Upper Heyford, England, 1967-73; prof. English U. Colo., Colorado Springs, 1973-95; prof. emeritus, 1996—. Author: The Cold War of Kitty Pentecost, 1979, The Myth of the Picaro, 1979, A Sunrise Brighter Still: The Visionary Novels of Frank Waters, 1991, Suddenly a Mortal Splendor, 1995; editor: The Interior Country: Stories of the Modern West, 1987, Higher Elevations: Stories from the West, A Writers' Forum Anthology, 1993; editor-in-chief Writers' Forum, vols. 1-21, 1974-95; author essays, revs. and articles. 1st lt. U.S. Army, 1951-53. Recipient Chancellor's award U. Colo., 1994, Faculty Book award, 1993, Am. Acad. Poets award, 1959. Mem. Authors Guild, Colo. Authors League, Western Lit. Assn., Rocky Mountain MLA, PEN West, Coun. Lit. Mags. and Presses. Avocations: watercolor. Home: 6030 Twin Rock Ct Colorado Springs CO 80918-3239

BLACKBURN, ELIZABETH HELEN, molecular biologist; b. Hobart, Australia, Nov. 26, 1948; 1 child. BS, U. Melbourne, Australia, 1970, MS, 1971; PhD in Molecular Biology, Cambridge (Eng.) U., 1975; DSc (hon.), Yale U., 1991. Fellow in biology Yale U., New Haven, 1975-77; fellow in biochemistry U. Calif., San Francisco, 1977-78; from asst. prof. to prof. molecular biology U. Calif., Berkeley, 1978-90; prof. U. Calif., San Francisco, 1990—, chairperson Dept. Microbiology and Immunology, 1993—, prof., chair microbiology and immunology. Recipient Eli Lilly award in microbiology, 1988, NAS award in molecular biology, 1990. Mem. AAAS (elected 1991), NAS (fgn. assoc. 1993), Am. Soc. Cell Biology (pres. 1998), Royal Soc. London. Office: U Calif Micro & Immunol Box 0414 San Francisco CA 94143-0414*

BLACKBURN, HENRY WEBSTER, JR., retired physician; b. Miami, Fla., Mar. 22, 1925; s. Henry Webster and Mary Frances (Smith) B.; m. Nelly Paula Trocme, Jan. 10, 1951 (div. 1984); children: John Keith, Katherine Ann, Heidi Elizabeth; m. Stacy Richardson, Sept. 1, 1991. Student, Fla. So. Coll., Lakeland, 1942-43; BS, U. Miami, 1947; MD, Tulane U., 1948; MS, U. Minn., 1957; Dr honoris causa, U. Kuopio, Finland, 1988; DSc (hon.), Tulane U., 1999. Intern Chgo. Wesley Meml. Hosp., 1948-49; resident in medicine Am. Hosp. Paris, 1949-50; med. officer in charge USPHS, Austria, Fed. Republic Germany, 1950-53; med. fellow U. Minn., Mpls., 1953-56; retired Divsn. Epidemiology, 1996; med. dir. Mut. Svc. Ins. Co., St. Paul, 1956; asst. prof. physiol. hygiene U. Minn., 1958-61, assoc. prof., 1961-68, prof., 1968—, lectr. medicine, 1956—, dir. lab. phsyiol. hygiene Sch. Pub. Health, 1972—, prof. medicine, 1972—, chmn. div. epidemiology, 1983-90, Mayo prof. pub. health, 1990-96; vis. prof. U. Geneva, 1970; mem. adv. coun. Nat. Heart, Lung and Blood Inst., 1989-93; mem. com. on diet and health NRC, 1986-89; Ancel Keys lectr., 1991; mem. food adv. com. FDA, 1995—. Author: Cardiovascular Survey Methods, 1968, On the Trail of Heart Attacks in Seven Countries, 1995, "P.K." Irreverent Memoirs of a Preacher's Kid; mem. editl. bd. numerous jours.; contbr. articles to profl. jours. Lt. (j.g.) USNR, 1942-50, capt. USPHS inactive res. Recipient Thomas Francis award in epidemiology, 1975, Naylor Dana award in preventive medicine, 1976, Louis Bishop award in cardiology, 1979, Gold Heart award Am. Heart Assn., 1990, Rsch. Achievement award Am. Heart Assn., 1992; Mayo chair in pub. health, 1988. Fellow APHA, Am. Coll. Cardiology, Am. Epidemiol. Soc.; mem. AAAS (chmn. med. sect.), Belgian Royal Acad. Medicine, Am. Heart Assn. (dir. 1971-74), Internat. Soc. Cardiology (coun. epidemiology 1971-74, chmn. 1986-91), Internat. Epidemiol. Soc., Alpha Omega Alpha, Phi Kappa Phi, Delta Omega. E-Mail: blackburn@epivat.epi.umn.edu. Home: 1525 Kaltern Ln Minneapolis MN 55416-3507 Office: U Minn Div Epidemiology 1300 S 2nd St Minneapolis MN 55454-1075

BLACKBURN, JOHN GILMER, lawyer; b. Opelika, Ala., Oct. 21, 1927; s. John A. and Vera (Isley) B.; m. Phyllis Blackburn, May 12, 1951; children: Gay Blackburn Maloney, Allison Blackburn Akins, Lisa Blackburn Ayerst. BS in Acctg., Auburn U., 1950; JD, U. Ala., 1954; LLM in Taxation, NYU, 1956. Bar: Ala. 1954. Sole practice Decatur, Ala., 1955-79; ptnr. Blackburn, Maloney & Schuppert, P.C., Decatur, 1979—; lectr. various tax seminars. Mayor, City of Decatur, 1962-68; mem. exec. com. Ala. Dems.; chmn. Auburn U. Found.; chmn. Ala. Rev. Com. on Higher Edn. With U.S. Army, 1946-47, to 1st lt., 1951-52, ETO. Mem. ABA (com. on life ins., cos. sect. taxation), Ala. Bar Assn. (chmn. tax sect.). Methodist. Lodge: Kiwanis. Office: PO Box 1469 Decatur AL 35602-1469

BLACKBURN, JOHN LESLIE, small business owner; b. Malta Bend, Mo., Dec. 21, 1924; s. Clarence Oliver and Vivian (Mitchener) B.; m. Gloria Bullington, June 10, 1950; 1 child, Holly. BS, Mo. Valley Coll., 1950; MEd, U. Colo., 1952; PhD, Fla. State U., 1969. Counselor to men Fla. State U., Tallahassee, 1952-56; from asst. dean of men to dean student devel. U. Ala., Tuscaloosa, 1956-69, v.p. devel., 1978-90; vice chancellor student affairs U. Denver, 1969-74, vice chancellor univ. resources, 1974-78; pres. Blackburn Ednl. Techs., Tuscaloosa, 1990—; gen. sec. Am. Assn. of U. Administrators, Tuscaloosa, Ala., 1993-97; interim dir. Challenge 21, Tuscaloosa, 1998—; mem. Model City Mayor's Adv., Denver, 1970-73, Nat. Adv. Coun. on Extension and Continuing Edn., Washington, 1976-78; cons. to sec. HEW, Washington, 1976. Contbr.: Pieces of Eight, 1978. Sgt. AUS, 1943-46, CBI. The Blackburn Inst. was created in his honor by U. Ala., 1995, John L. Blackburn Exemplary award in his honor by AAUA, 1991. Mem. AAUA (pres. 1977-79), Am. Coun. on Edn. (acad. affairs commn. 1970-73), Nat. Assn. Student Pers. Adminstrn. (pres. 1973-74), Nat. Inst. Rsch. and Devel. (founder 1974). Home: 1601 St Andrews Dr Tuscaloosa AL 35406-2058 Office: Blackburn Ednl Techs PO Box 2615 Tuscaloosa AL 35403-2615

BLACKBURN, JOHN OLIVER, economist, consultant; b. Miami, Fla., Sept. 13, 1929; s. Elmer E. and Proxie (Hughes) B.; m. Jeanne Elise Miles, Nov. 29, 1957; children: Katherine Elise, John Parkinson, David Laurence. AB, Duke U., 1951; postgrad., U. Miami, 1951-52; PhD, U. Fla., 1959. CPA, Fla. From asst. prof. econs. to prof. Duke U., 1959-81, provost, 1970-71, chancellor, 1971-76; asst. prof. bus. adminstrn. Am. U., Beirut, 1961-62; vis. prof. Davidson Coll., 1983. Author: The Renewable Energy Alternative, 1987, Solar Florida: A Sustainable Energy Future, 1993. Bd. dirs. Fla. Conservation Found., U.S. Found. of Univ. of the Valley of Guatemala, Orlando Philharmonic Orch., United Arts of Ctrl. Fla.; bd. visitors Nicholas Sch. Environ. Duke U. With USNR, 1952-55. Mem. Archs., Designers and Planners for Social Responsibility, Phi Beta Kappa. Democrat. Mem. United Ch. of Christ. Home: 221 Shell Pt E Maitland FL 32751-5843

BLACKBURN, RICHARD WALLACE, lawyer; b. Detroit, Apr. 21, 1942; s. Wallace Manders and E. Jean (Beetham) B.; m. Dede Frances Reid, Aug. 29, 1964; children: David Thomas, Jeffrey Manders, Megan Louise. Student, Baldwin-Wallace Coll., 1960-62; A.B., Mich. State U., 1964; J.D., George Washington U., 1967; grad. advanced mgmt. program, Harvard Bus. Sch., 1988. Labor atty. Chesapeake & Potomac Telephone Co., Washington, 1967-70; gen. corp. atty. Chesapeake & Potomac Telephone Co., Richmond, Va., 1970-74; regulatory atty. AT&T, N.Y.C., 1974-76; gen. atty. New Eng. Telephone Co., Boston, 1976-81; v.p., gen. counsel New Eng. Telephone Co., 1981—; exec. v.p., gen. counsel, sec. Duke Energy, Charlotte, N.C. Dir. New Eng. Legal Found., 1988; mem. Concord (Mass.) Zoning Bd. Appeals, chmn., 1984, 87; trustee Mass. Eye and Ear Infirmary. Mem. Fed. Communications Bar Assn., Am. Bar Assn., Newcomen Soc. N.Am., Boston Bar Assn. Republican. Episcopalian. Office: Duke Energy Corp 422 S Church St PO Box 1244 Charlotte NC 28201*

BLACKBURN, ROBERT MCGRADY, retired bishop; b. Bartow, Fla., Sept. 12, 1919; s. Charles Fred and Effie Frances (Forsythe) B.; m. Mary Jeanne Everett, Nov. 16, 1943 (dec. May 1977); children: Jeanne Marie (Mrs. Ramon Cox), Robert M., Frances Lucille; m. Jewell Haddock, Sept. 9, 1978. B.A., Fla. So. Coll., 1941; M.Div., Emory U., 1943, LL.D., 1973; D.D. (hon.), LaGrange Coll., 1961. Ordained to ministry Methodist Ch., 1943; pastor United Methodist Ch., Boca Grande, Fla., 1943-44; asso. pastor First Methodist Ch., Orlando, Fla., 1946-48, Mt. Dora, Fla., 1948-53, DeLand, Fla., 1953-60, Jacksonville, Fla., 1960-68; sr. pastor First Methodist Ch., Orlando, 1968-72; bishop United Meth. Ch., Raleigh, N.C., 1972-80, Va. Conf., 1980-88; Mem. program council United Methodist Ch., 1963-72; del. to Meth. Gen. Confs., 1968, 70, 72. Trustee Randolph-Macon Coll., Randolph-Macon Woman's Coll., Randolph-Macon Acad., Va. Wesleyan, Shenandoah Coll. and Conservatory of Music, Ferrum Coll. Served as chaplain U.S. Army, 1944-46. Home: 8431 Mizner Cir E Jacksonville FL 32217-4326

BLACKBURN, ROGER LLOYD, lawyer; b. Mobile, Ala., Mar. 18, 1946; s. Rogers Hammock and Louise (Megahee) B.; m. Linda McNulty, Mar. 29, 1969. BA, U. Fla., 1968, JD, 1971. Bar: Fla. 1971, U.S. Dist. Ct. (so. dist.) Fla. 1972, U.S. Tax Ct. 1979. Ptnr. Blackwell, Walker & Gray, Miami, Fla., 1971-76, Leesfield & Blackburn, P.A., Miami, 1976-92; pvt. practice North Ctrl. Fla., 1992—; of counsel Hicks & Anderson, P.A., Miami, 1995—. Mem. ATLA, Fla. Bar Assn., Dade County Bar Assn. (bd. dirs. 1974-86), Acad. Fla. Trial Lawyers (bd. dirs. 1985-91, exec. com. 1989-91), Dade County Trial Lawyers Assn. (pres. 1985-86), Am. Bd. Trial Advocates (pres. Miami chpt. 1991-92, nat. bd. dirs., chmn. seminar com., diplomate), Eighth Jud. Cir. Bar Assn., U. Fla. Law Ctr. Assn. (trustee 1986-95, trustee emeritus 1995—), U. Fla. Coll. Law Alumni Coun. (pres. 1984), Fla. Acad. Cert. Mediators, Fla. Blue Key. Democrat. Office: 100 Biscayne Blvd Miami FL 33132-2304

BLACKBURN, SADIE GWIN ALLEN, executive; b. San Angelo, Tex., Oct. 14, 1924; d. Harvey Hicks Allen and Helen (Harris) Weaver; m. Edward Albert Blackburn Jr., Feb. 25, 1946; children: Edward III, Catherine Ledyard, Robert Allen. BA, Rice U., 1945, MA, 1975. Bookkeeper, trust dept. State Nat. Bank, Houston; tchr. elem. sch. Galveston, Tex.; mng. ptnr. Storey Creek Partnership, Houston, 1989—; spl. projects dir. San Jacinto; dir. master plan State Historial Park; lectr. in landscape design history. Co-author: Houston's Forgotten Heritage, 1822-1914, 1991; contbr. articles to gardening publs. Newsheet chmn. Jr. League, Galveston, 1950-53, art chmn., Houston Jr. League, 1957-58, mental health study com., 1959-61, 2d v.p., 1962-63, provisional chmn., 1962-63, interview chmn., 1963-64; adv. bd. Bayou Bend Gardens chmn. Mus. Fine Arts, 1973-74, Bayou Bend adv. com., 1987-89; v.p. Mental HEalth Assn., 1957-62; asst. treas. Child Guidance Assn., 1962-65; mem. Rice U. Hist. Commn., 1974-75; pres. River Oaks Garden Club, Houston, 1975-76; mem. adv. com. Bayou Bend Gardens, 1991—. Recipient Sweet Briar Disting. Alumna award, 1991. Mem. Garden Club Am. (zone chmn. 1977-79, founders fund vice chmn. 1979-80, dir. 1980-82, rec. sec. 1982-84, v.p. 1984-86, archive co-chmn. 1986-87, 1st v.p. 1987-89, pres. 1989-91), Nat. Wildflower Rsch. Ctr. (bd. dirs.), Nat. Parks and Conservation Assn. Bd. (v.p. 1995-97, sec. 1997-99), San Jacinto Mus. History (pres. bd. 1975-77). Republican. Episcopalian. Avocations: gardening, fishing, hunting, bridge, golf. Home: 1030 Potomac Houston TX 77057-1916

BLACKBURN, SHARON LOVELACE, federal judge; b. 1950. BA, U. Ala., 1973; JD, Samford U., 1977. Law clk. to Hon. Robert Varner U.S. Dist. Ct. Ala., 1977-78; staff atty. Birmingham Area Legal Svcs., 1979; asst. U.S. atty. U.S. Atty's. Office, 1979-91; judge U.S. Dist. Ct. (no. dist.) Ala., Birmingham, 1991—. Mem. Birmingham Bar Assn. Office: US Dist Ct 730 US Courthouse 1729 5th Ave N Birmingham AL 35203-2000

BLACKBURN, TERENCE LEE, dean; b. Pitts., Pa., July 13, 1948; s. Glenn E. and Ruby E. (Fornof) B.; m. Catherine T. Dwyer, Sept. 7, 1974; children: Allegra, Brandon. BA, Duquesne U., 1970; JD, Columbia U., 1973. Bar: Ohio 1973, N.Y. 1975, N.J. 1994. Asst. atty. gen. Ohio Atty. Gen. Office, Columbus, 1973-75; assoc. Aranow Brodsky et al, N.Y.C., 1975-78, Kronish Lieb et al, N.Y.C., 1978-82; v.p., gen. counsel First Nat. Properties, N.Y.C., 1982-88; prof. law Law Sch. Seton Hall U., Newark, 1988-97; acting dean Sch. Diplomacy Seton Hall U., South Orange, N.J., 1997—. Contbr. articles to profl. jours. Capt. U.S. Army, 1973. Fulbright scholar Coun. Internat. Exch. Scholars, 1995. Office: Seton Hall U Sch Diplomacy 400 S Orange Ave South Orange NJ 07079-2697

BLACKBURN, THOMAS HAROLD, English language professional, educator; b. Englewood, N.J., May 28, 1932; s. Harold L. and Alice A. (Benton) B.; m. Ann Sharon Leigh, June 15, 1963; children: Adam Leigh, Benton. B.A., Amherst Coll., 1954; B.A. (Rhodes scholar), Jesus Coll., Oxford U., 1956, M.A., 1961; Ph.D., Stanford, 1963. Instr. Swarthmore (Pa.) Coll., 1961-63, asst. prof., 1963-68, asso. prof., 1968-75, prof. English lit., 1975-92, dean, 1975-81, Centennial prof., 1992—; vis. lectr. Bryn Mawr Coll., 1964; vis. tutor St. Edmund Hall, Oxford, 1971. Contbr. articles to profl. jours. Pres. bd. dirs. Swarthmore Pub. Libr., 1976-85; bd. dirs. Swarthmore Swim Club, 1981-87, v.p., 1985, pres., 1986; councilman Swarthmore Borough Coun., 1986-93, v.p., 1988-90, pres., 1990-93. Am. Council Learned Socs. fellow, 1965. Mem. MLA, Milton Soc. Am., Renaissance Soc., Nat. Coun. Tchrs. English, Am. Rhodes Scholars, Coll. Conf. on Comm. and Composition, Phi Beta Kappa. Home: 801 Yale Ave Apt 1001 Swarthmore PA 19081-1816*

BLACKBURN, WILLIAM STANLEY, lawyer; b. Nashville, Nov. 7, 1951; s. William Hodge and Margaret Virginia (Ware) B.; m. Laura Ross Wilson, July 23, 1983; children: William, Margaret. BS in Economics, Auburn U., 1973; JD, U.Va., 1976. Assoc. Kilpatrick & Cody (now Kilpatrick Stockton, LLP), Atlanta, 1976-82, ptnr., 1982—; co-chair Bus. Transactions Group, 1996—. Notes Editor Va. Law Review, 1975-76, mem. editorial bd., 1974-75. Sec. Boys and Girls Clubs of Metro Atlanta, Inc., 1984—, mng. bd. dirs., 1982—, mem. exec. com., 1984—; chmn. legal divsn. Fulton County, Am. Heart Assn., 1981; mem. Leadership Atlanta, 1983-84; sec. Young Men's Round Table, High Mus. Art, 1984-85, pres., 1985-86, mem., 1983-86; group chmn. United Way Atlanta, 1984, account exec.; bd. dirs. Japan-Am. Soc. Ga., 1986-90. Fellow Am. Coll. Investment Counsel; mem. ABA (sect. bus. law, com. legal opinions 1992—, Young Lawyers Sect. banking law subcom. 1980-81), State Bar Ga. (corp. banking law sect., sec. sect. 1998, legal opinions com. 1991—, chair 1992—, Younger Lawyers sect. long range planning com. 1979-80, pub. com. 1979-80, credit union com. 1980-81), Atlanta Bar Assn. (courts com. 1982-83, co-chmn. joint task force mcpl ct. City of Atlanta 1982-83, law day com. 1984), Can. Am. Soc. Atlanta (bd. dirs. 1998—), Cobb County C. of C. (internat. bus. coun. 1984—), Lawyers Club Atlanta, Piedmont Driving Club, Capital City Club, Nine O'Clocks, Order of Coif, Phi Kappa Phi, Omicron Delta Kappa, Phi Eta Sigma, Omicron Delta Epsilon. Avocation: golf. Home: 2595 Habersham Rd NW

Atlanta GA 30305-3557 Office: Kilpatrick Stockton LLP 1100 Peachtree St NE Ste 2800 Atlanta GA 30309-4501*

BLACKBURN, WYATT DOUGLAS, insurance executive; b. Amarillo, Tex., July 6, 1954; s. Wyatt W. and Marjorie C. (Wyre) B.; m. Deborah L. Garland, Feb. 28, 1987; children: Wyatt Woodrow, Taylor Lynne. BBA, W. Tex. State U., 1976. Staff acct. Harvey, Messenger & Co. CPA's, Amarillo, 1974-77; audit mgr. Martin W. Cohen & Co. CPA's, Dallas, 1977-78; sr. v.p. adminstrv. ops., 1978-88, sr. v.p., CFO, 1988-94, sr. v.p., COO, 1995-97, exec. v.p., COO State Nat. Cos., Fort Worth, 1997—; bd. dirs. State & County Mut. Fire Ins. Co., State Nat. Ins. Co., State Nat. Life Ins. Co., Tex. Mem. AICPA, Tex. Soc. CPAs, Omicron Delta Epsilon. Home: 1028 Diamond Blvd Southlake TX 76092-6208 Office: State Nat Cos 8200 Anderson Blvd Fort Worth TX 76120-3620

BLACKER, HARRIET, public relations executive; b. N.Y.C., July 23, 1940; d. Louis and Rebecca (Siegel) B.; m. Roland Algrant, Aug. 6, 1970 (div. Jan. 1981); m. Matthew E. Harlib, Aug. 25, 1988. B.A., U. Mich., 1962. Exec. dir. publicity Random House, N.Y.C., 1974-79; East Coast v.p. Pickwick Maslansky Koenigsberg, N.Y.C., 1980-81; v.p. pub. relations Putnam Pub. Group, N.Y.C., 1981-85; pres. Harriet Blacker, Inc., N.Y.C., 1986-90; ptnr. Blacker Hunter Pub. Rels. Inc., N.Y.C., 1990-93; pres. Blacker Communications, N.Y.C., 1993—. Mem. Publishers Publicity Assn. (sec. 1973-75, treas. 1982-83, pres. 1983-85), Women's Media Group. *

BLACKETER, JAMES RICHARD, artist; b. Laguna Beach, Calif., Sept. 24, 1931; s. Cleo Toby and Ida Hattie (Renter) B.; children: Susan Elizabeth Glover, Mary Jane Kelsey; m. Frances Kay Smith, July 18, 1977. Owner Blacketer Sign Co., Laguna Beach, 1950-53; designer/art dir. Fed. Sign and Signal Corp., Santa Ana, Calif., 1953-73; owner The Studio Antiques, Laguna Beach, 1973-95. Exhibited in group shows at Showcase 21, L.A., 1959, The Studio Gallery, Laguna Beach, Ferguson Gallery, La Jolla, Long Beach Art Mus., Porth Gallery, Laguna Beach, Pasadena Art Mus., Los Angeles County Fair, Laguna Beach Art Festival, Fresno Art Mus., Ebell Club, L.A., Wells Gallery, Laguna Beach, others; represented in permanent collections at Norton Simon Art Mus., Laguna Beach Art Assn., South Coast Med. Ctr. Bd. dirs. festival of Arts, Laguna Beach, 1965-66. Recipient Nat. Award for Outdoor Advertising, Nat. Elec. Sign Assn., 1970, 71, 72, Nat. Award for Design, Nat. Interscholastic Art Assn., Pitts., 1950, Calif. Award for poster design Am. Legion, State of Calif., 1946; winner various painting awards, 1950—. Mem. Laguna Beach Art Assn. (art dir. 1968-69, bd. dirs. 1969-70). Avocations: antique and art collecting, antique automobiles, designing historical home interiors. Home: 266 Canyon Acres Dr Laguna Beach CA 92651-1106

BLACKEY, EDWIN ARTHUR, JR., geologist; b. Tamworth, N.H., Oct. 19, 1927; s. Edwin Arthur and Flora (Whipple) B.; m. Patricia Ann Matthews, Jan. 22, 1955; children: Mark Edwin, Janet Angove. BS, U. N.H., 1951; postgrad. Worcester (Mass.) Poly. Inst., 1955-56. Geologist, N.E. divsn. Corps Engrs., Waltham, Mass., 1951-72, divsn. geologist, 1972-82, cons. engrng. geologist, 1982—. Chmn., Hist. Dists. Commn. Sudbury (Mass.); trustee Sudbury Hist. Soc., pres., 1988-89; mem. Earth Removal Bd. Sudbury; past pres. Sudbury Jr. Ski Program. Served with AUS, 1946-47. Cert. geologist, Maine. Recipient Meritorious Civilian Svc. award C.E., 1983, Johnston Svc. award, 1996. Mem. Assn. Engrng. Geologists (nat. chmn. bldg. codes com., nat. bd. dirs., 1982, dir. New Eng. sect., chmn. New Eng. sect. 1982-85, nat. exec. dir. 1987-97, dir. mission to USSR 1990, Eastern Europe 1992), Am. Geologic Inst. Episcopalian. Club: U.S. Eastern Ski. Address: 62 King Philip Rd Sudbury MA 01776-2363

BLACKEY, PAMELA ANN CONLEY, medical/surgical nurse; b. Norwalk, Conn., Mar. 23, 1964; d. Elton B. Jr. and Olga (Mitaly) C. Diploma in nursing, NHVTC/M, 1983, AS in Nursing, 1989. Cert. med.-surg. nurse. Camp nurse Camp Young Judaea, Amherst, N.H.; nurse Cath. Med. Ctr., Manchester, N.H., Nurses Across Am., Boynton Beach, Fla.; nurse surg. spl. care unit Darmouth Hitchcock Med. Ctr., Lebanon, N.H. Home: 1026 Long St Webster NH 03303

BLACKFORD, JOHN, magazine editor; b. Norfolk, Va., Feb. 8, 1944; s. Frank Robertson and Polly (Baldwin) B.; m. Anne Little; children: David, Jacob. BA, U. N.C., Chapel Hill, 1967; postgrad., Temple U., 1977-78. Book editor Rodale Press, Emmaus, Pa., 1978-82; editor Software Retailing, Dover, N.J., 1983-84, Computer Dealer, Dover, 1984-86; exec. editor Personal Computing, Hasbrouck Heights, N.J., 1986-90; editor-in-chief Computer Shopper, N.Y.C., 1991—. Co-author: Build Your Harvest Kitchen, 1982. Recipient Jesse H. Neal award for best feature article Computer Dealer mag., 1984. Mem. IEEE, Computer Press Assn., Nature Conservancy. Avocations: landscape photography, old-time country music, internet surfing, sci. fiction. Office: Computer Shopper/Ziff Davis 28 E 28th St New York NY 10016*

BLACKFORD, ROBERT NEWTON, lawyer; b. Cin., Feb. 5, 1937; s. Robert Criley and Virginia Pendleton (Yowell) B.; m. Margaret Ann Williams, July 22, 1961; children: William Pendleton, John Whitner. BSBA, U. Fla., 1960; JD, Emory U., 1968. Bar: Fla. 1968, Ga. 1968. Mem., dir. Maguire, Voorhis & Wells, P.A., Orlando, Fla., 1972-98, sec., treas., 1972-95; ptnr. Holland & Knight LLP, Orlando, 1998—; dir. Hughes Supply, Inc., Orlando, 1970—, sec., 1972-96, asst. sec., 1996-98; dir., sec. Princeton Fin. Corp., 1987-94. Mem. Orlando Mcpl. Planning Bd., 1969-75, Orlando Downtown Devel. Bd., 1972-77, chmn., 1975-77, bd. dirs. Crime Commn., Inc., 1985-88; mem. Orange County's Refuse Disposal Citizens Coordination Com., 1988-90, Orange County Solid Waste Adv. Bd., 1992-96; mem. neighborhood concerns com. Orlando Naval Tng. Ctr. Base Closing Commn., 1994-96; trustee Chelsey G. Magruder Found., Inc., 1981—, pres., 1982-85, 92-94, sec., 1998—; trustee Orlando Mus. Art, 1980-82, 85-91, pres. 1985-86, chmn. bd., 1986-87, v.p. 1989-91; ruling elder First Presbyn. Ch., Orlando, 1989—, tchr., 1970—. Mem. ABA, Fla. Bar Assn., Ga. Bar Assn., Orange County Bar Assn., Orlando Area C. of C. (pres. 1980, chmn. bd. dirs. 1981), Orange County Hist. Soc. (bd. dirs. 1980-83), Country Club Orlando (bd. dirs. 1994-97, sec. 1994-96). Democrat. Home: 2931 Nela Ave Orlando FL 32809-6178 Office: Holland & Knight LLP 200 S Orange Ave Ste 2600 Orlando FL 32801

BLACKHAM, ANN ROSEMARY (MRS. J. W. BLACKHAM), realtor; b. N.Y.C., June 16, 1927; d. Frederick Alfred and Letitia L. (Stolfe) DeCain; m. James W. Blackham Jr., Aug. 18, 1951; children: Ann C., James W. III. AB, St. Mary of the Springs Coll., 1949; postgrad., Ohio State U., 1950. Mgr. br. store Filene & Sons, Winchester, 1950-52; broker Porter Co. Real Estate, Winchester, 1961-66; sales mgr. James T. Trefrey, Inc., Winchester, 1966-68; pres., founder Ann Blackham & Co. Inc., Realtors, Winchester, Mass., 1968—. Mem. bd. econ. advisors to Gov., 1969-74; participant White House Conf. on Internat. Cooperation, 1965; mem. Presdl. Task Force on Women's Rights and Responsibilities, 1969; mem. exec. coun. Mass. Civil Def., 1965-69; chmn. Gov.'s Commn. on Status of Women, 1971-75; regional dir. Interstate Assn. Commn. on Status of Women, 1971-74; mem. Gov. Task Force on Mass. Economy, 1972; mem. Gov.'s Jud. Selection Com., 1972, Mass. Emergency Fin. Bd., 1974-75; mem. bd. registration Real Estate Brokers & Salesman Commonwealth of Mass., 1991-94, chmn. 1994—; bd. visitors Ohio Dominican Coll., 1995—; corporator, trustee Charlestown Savs. Bank, 1974-84; corporator Winchester Hosp., 1983—; dir. Winchester Hosp. Found., 1998—; mem. Winchester 350th Anniversary Commn.; mem. design rev. commn. Town of Winchester; bd. dirs. Phoenix Found., Bay State Health Care, Mass. Taxpayers Found., Speech and Hearing Found., Baystate Health Mgmt., Realty Guild Inc., (v.p. 1995-96, pres. 1997, 98, bd. dirs. 1996, 97, 98, 99); mem. regional selection panel White House Fellows, 1973-74; mem. com. on women in svc. U.S. Dept. Def., 1977-80; 2d v.p. Doric Dames, 1971-74, bd. dirs., 1974—; dep. chmn. Mass. Rep. State Com., 1965-66, 96—; sec. Mass. Rep. State Conv., 1970, del., 1960, 62, 64, 66, 70, 72, 74, 78, 90, 98; state vice chmn. Mass. Rep. Fin. Com., 1970; alt. del.-at-large Rep. Nat. Conv., 1968, 72, del., 1984; Rep. State Committeewoman, 1996—; pres. Mass. Fedn. Rep. Women, 1964-69; v.p. Nat. Fedn. Rep. Women, 1965-79; pres. Scholarship Found., 1976-78, Mass. Fedn. Women's Clubs; dir.; alumnae liaison The Beaumont Sch. for Girls. Recipient Pub. Svc. award Commonwealth of Mass., 1978, Merit award Rep. Party, 1969, Pub. Affairs award Mass. Fedn. Women's Clubs, 1975; named Civic Leader of Yr., Mass. Broadcasters, 1962; recipient Bus. Owner of Yr. award New England Women Bus. Owners, 1995. Mem. Greater Boston Real Estate Bd. (hon., bd. dirs.), Eastern Middlesex Bd. Realtors (life mem. multi million dollar club), Mass. Assn. Realtors (bd. dirs.), Nat. Assn. Realtors (women's coun.). Brokers Inst. (cert.), Coun. Realtors (cert., pres. 1983-84), Winchester C. of C. (bd. dirs.), Greater Boston C. of C., Nat. Assn. Women Bus. Owners, ENKA Soc., Rotary Internat., Tequesta Fla. Country Club, Capitol Hill Club, Ponte Vedra Club, Winchester Boat Club, Winchester Country Club, Wychmere Harbor Club, Womens City Club, Boston Coll. Club, Winton Club (sec., bd. dir.), Hyannis Yacht Club, Boston Coll. Club. Home: 60 Swan Rd Winchester MA 01890-3747 Office: Ann Blackham & Co Inc 9 Thompson St Winchester MA 01890-2903

BLACKIE, SPENCER DAVID, physical therapist, administrator; b. Endicott, N.Y., Sept. 27, 1946; s. Norman and June (Spencer) B.; m. Bonnie Jean Randall Moulton, June 11, 1967 (div. Apr. 1985); children: Rhonda, Randy, Brenda; m. Sharon Joan Clingman, May 10, 1986; children: Kristen, Sean, Alex. BS, Loma Linda U., 1968; MA, U. So. Calif., 1973; MS, Boston U., 1980. Cert. in manual therapy, clin. specialist in orthop. phys. therapy. Clin. dir. Loma Linda (Calif.) U. Med. Ctr., 1972-74; dir. rehab. svcs. New Eng. Meml. Hosp., Stoneham, Mass., 1974-84, Mt. Carmel Hosp., Colville, Wash., 1984-92, Regina Med. Ctr., Hastings, Minn., 1992—. Mem. Pool Com., Hastings, 1994; chmn. Parks and Recreation Bd., Colville, 1991-92. Capt. U.S. Army, 1969-71. Cmty. Fitness grantee Perrier Mineral Waters, Stoneham, 1978; decorated U.S. Army commendation medal. Mem. Am. Phys. Therapy Assn., Am. Occupl. Therapy Assn., Am. Acad. Orthop. Manual Phys. Therapy, Am. Soc. Hand Therapists, Minn. and Wis. Occupl. Therapy Assn., Rotary. Seventh-Day Adventist. Avocations: bicycling, classical guitar, karate, hiking/backpacking. Office: Regina Med Ctr 1175 Nininger Rd Hastings MN 55033-1056

BLACKISTONE, KEVIN, sports columnist. Sports columnist Dallas Morning News, 1990—. Office: The Dallas Morning News 508 Young St Dallas TX 75202-4828*

BLACKLEDGE, DAVID WILLIAM, academic administrator; b. Cin., Mar. 10, 1930; s. William Clinton and Helen Louise (Van Curen) B.; m. Diana Marjorie Wiley, June 5, 1953; children: David Noel, William Dean, Alan Keith, Naomi Karen. BS, Purdue U., 1953; MA, Rutgers U., 1965; grad., Nat. War Coll., 1975. Commd. 2d lt. U.S. Army, 1953, advanced through grades to col., 1974; asst. prof. mil. sci. Rutgers U., New Brunswick, N.J., 1961-64; instr. Am. history U. Md.-Far East Div., Bangkok, 1967-68; dir. nat. security studies U.S. Army War Coll., Carlisle, Pa., 1978-83; dir. fin. aid Dickinson Sch. Law, Carlisle, 1983-94, dir. admissions and fin. aid, 1984-94, exec. asst. to the dean, 1994—. Bd. dirs. Carlisle area United Way, 1983-86, Sarah Todd Retirement Home, Carlisle, 1989-95. Decorated Legion of Merit with oak leaf cluster. Mem. Rotary. Office: Dickinson Sch Law 150 S College St Carlisle PA 17013-2899

BLACKLER, ANTONIE WILLIAM CHARLES, biologist; b. Portsmouth, Eng., Oct. 19, 1931; came to U.S., 1964; s. Leslie Guy and Florence (Harris) B.; m. Rochelle Lois Melkin, Mar. 12, 1970; children—Mia Samantha, Joshua Harris. B.S. in Zoology, U. Coll., London, 1953, Ph.D., 1956. Professeur extraordinaire U. Geneva, Switzerland, 1961-64; prof. zoology Cornell U., Ithaca, N.Y., 1964—. Mem. Internat. Soc. Devel. Biology, Am. Soc. Devel. Biology. Research on origins of sex. Home: 14 Nottingham Dr Ithaca NY 14850-8704 Office: Cornell U Genetics Biotech Bldg Ithaca NY 14853

BLACKLOW, ROBERT STANLEY, physician, medical college administrator; b. Cambridge, Mass., June 24, 1934; s. Leo Alfred and Clara Edna (Cumenes) B.; m. Winifred Young, Dec. 7, 1958; children: Stephen Charles, Kenneth Lawrence, David Alan. A.B. summa cum laude, Harvard U., 1955, M.D. cum laude, 1959; DSc (hon.), Kent State U., 1998. Intern Peter Bent Brigham Hosp., Boston, 1959-60; resident Peter Bent Brigham Hosp., 1960-61, 63-64, 67-68; instr. Harvard U., 1967-70, asst. prof. medicine, 1970-76, asso. prof., 1976-78, asst. to dean faculty of medicine, 1969-73, asso. dean, 1973-78; prof., internal medicine Rush Med. Coll., 1978-85, dean, 1978-81; v.p. for med. affairs Rush-Presbyn.-St. Luke's Med. Center, Chgo., 1978-81; prof. medicine Jefferson Med. Coll., Phila., 1985-92, sr. assoc. dean, 1985-92; pres., dean Northeastern Ohio Univs. Coll. Medicine, 1992—, prof. community medicine, prof. medicine, 1992—; mem. sci. adv. com. Nat. Fund for Med. Edn., 1981-84, Nat. Cancer Inst., 1986-95; bd. dirs. Nat. Resident Matching Program, 1993—, pres.-elect, 1994-95, pres. 1995-96, treas., 1998-99. Editor: Signs and Symptoms, 1971, 6th edit., 1983; mem. editl. bd. Jour. Med. Humanities, 1997—. Trustee Chestnut Hill Sch., Newton, Mass., 1970-79, Belmont (Mass.) Hill Sch., 1973-79, Chgo. chpt. ARC, 1979, Greater Akron (Ohio) Musical Assn., 1993—, mem. exec. com., 1998—; mem. Ill. Health Svc. Corps Task Force, Ill. Dept. Pub. Health, 1980; corporator Belmont Hill Sch., 1978—. Served with USPHS, 1961-63. Fellow Inst. Medicine Chgo., ACP, Chgo. Soc. Internal Medicine; mem. AAAS, N.Y. Acad. Scis., Assn. Am. Med. Colls., Assn. Acad. Health Ctrs., Harvard Musical Assn., Portage Country Club (Akron), Phi Beta Kappa, Sigma Xi, Alpha Omega Alpha. Clubs: Longwood Cricket (Boston), Badminton and Tennis (Boston), Harvard (Boston); Harvard (N.Y.C.); Cliff Dwellers (Chgo.), Harvard (Chgo.) (bd. dirs.), Literary (Chgo.); Franklin Inn (Phila.); Germantown Cricket (Phila.), Twin Lakes Country Club. Home: 1150 Pin Oak Dr Sugar Bush Knolls OH 44240-6254 Office: Northeastern Ohio Univs Coll Medicine PO Box 95 Rootstown OH 44272-0095

BLACKMAN, DANNY, religious organization administrator. Dir. General Services of the Pentecostal Free Will Baptist Ch., Dunn, N.C., 1993. Office: The Pentecostal Baptist Ch PO Box 1568 Dunn NC 28335-1568*

BLACKMAN, DAVID LEE, research scientist; b. Chgo., Jan. 4, 1948; s. Sol and Carol Edith (Rothman) B. BS in Maths., U. Ariz., 1973; student, Laney Coll., Oakland, Calif., 1977-79; MS in Chemistry, San Francisco State U., 1983. Lic. technician. Rsch. cons. Detox Assn., San Bernadino, Calif., 1973-74; peer counselor Laney Coll., 1977-79; lectr. San Francisco State U., 1979-83; staff rsch. assoc. U. Calif., Berkeley, 1984—; speaker PEW Found., N.Y., 1989. Author: Flourescent Spectroscopy..., 1983; contbr. articles to prof. jours. Mem. adv. bd. P.P. Land Conservancy, Berkeley, 1984-86; bd. dirs. Cmty. Svcs. United, Berkeley, 1985-86; vol. No. Alameda ARES/RACES, Berkeley, 1992-95. NSF grantee, 1989, 91. Mem. AAAS, Am. Assn. Physics Tchrs., Am. Radio Relay League, Co-op. Am., N.Y. Acad. Sci., Golden Gate Nat. Park Assn., Sierra Club, Mensa. Democrat. Jewish. Avocations: photography, computers, water coloring, swimming, non-linear dynamics. Home: 307 W 2nd St Phoenix OR 97535

BLACKMAN, DAVID MICHAEL, lawyer; b. Oakland, Calif., Jan. 29, 1943; s. Sidney Joshua and Pauline (Golson) B.; m. Ardis Blackman; children: Jeremy, Rebekah, Kyra, Stephanie. BA cum laude, San Francisco State U., 1968; JD, U. Calif., Davis, 1972. Bar: Calif. 1972, U.S. Dist. Ct. (ea. dist.) Calif. 1972, U.S. Tax Ct. 1974, U.S. Ct. Appeals (9th cir.) 1987; cert. Am. Bd. Profl. Liability Attys., Nat. Bd. Trial Advocacy. Dep. atty. gen. State of Calif., Sacramento, 1972-73; staff State Pub. Defender, Sacramento, 1978-79; ptnr. Blackman & Blackman, Sacramento, 1973—; adj. prof. U. Calif., Davis., 1982-84; arbitrator Am. Arbitration Assn.; judge pro-tem Superior Ct.; lectr. in field; founding sponsor Civil Justice Found.; mem. Dept. of Ins. Task Force on Consumer Complaints and Unfair Practices. Author practice manuals. Mem. ATLA, Calif. Trial Lawyers Assn. (Chpt. Pres. of Yr. award 1988), Sacramento County Bar Assn. (coun. 1978-80), Capitol City Trial Lawyers Assn. (pres. 1988). Home: 3585 Montclair Rd Cameron Park CA 95682-9031 Office: Blackman & Blackman 7750 College Town Dr Ste 300 Sacramento CA 95826-2361

BLACKMAN, JOHN CALHOUN, IV, lawyer; b. Monroe, La., Dec. 13, 1944; s. John Calhoun Blackman III and Marie (Collens) Bernstein; m. Paula Perry, Aug. 19, 1966 (div. Mar. 1986); children: Carrie Marie, Caroline Frances, Mary Winston; m. Judy Swayze, Apr. 19, 1986. BA, La. State U., 1966, JD, 1969. Bar: La. 1969, U.S. Ct. Appeals (5th cir.) 1969, U.S. Tax Ct. 1972, U.S. Supreme Ct. 1976. Ptnr. Hudson, Potts & Bernstein, Monroe, 1969-79, Blackman, Arnold & Pettway, Monroe, 1979-88, Jones, Walker, Waechter, Poitevent, Carrere & Denegre, Baton Rouge, 1988—; adj. prof. law La. State U., Baton Rouge, 1990-93; mem. Bank One La. N.A., Baton Rouge Regional Bd.; mem. com. of 100 econ. devel., 1993—; mem. trust code com. Lat. State Law Inst., 1982—, reporter bus. trust code com., 1994—. Mem. La. State U. Found.; mem. adv. commn. Estate Planning and Adminstrn. Cert., 1994-99, chmn., 1998-99. Fellow Am. Bar Found., Am. Coll. Trusts and Estates Counsel (employee benefits com.), Am. Coll. Tax Counsel; mem. ABA (litigation task force, employee benefits com., taxation sect.), La. Bar Assn. (cert. tax specialist, cert. estate planning and adminstrn. specialist, chmn. taxation sect. 1976-77, chmn. liaison com. with dist. dir. IRS 1981-82, liaison com. with regional commrs. office), Estate Planning Coun. N.E. La. (pres. 1975-76, qualified for appt. as mediator under La. Mediation Act), Country Club of La. Republican. Episcopalian. Office: Jones Walker et al 8555 United Plaza Blvd Fl 5 Baton Rouge LA 70809-2260

BLACKMAN, KENNETH ROBERT, lawyer; b. Providence, May 19, 1941; s. Edward and Beatrice (Wolf) B.; m. Meryl June Rosenthal, June 7, 1964; children: Michael, Susan, Kevin. AB, Brown U., 1962; LLB, Columbia U., 1965, MBA, 1965. Bar: N.Y. 1966. Law clk. to U.S. Dist. Judge, 1965-66; ptnr. Fried, Frank, Harris, Shriver & Jacobson, N.Y.C., 1966—. Mem. ABA, N.Y. Bar Assn., Assn. Bar City of N.Y., Phi Beta Kappa, Beta Gamma Sigma. Office: Fried Frank Harris Shriver & Jacobson 1 New York Plz Fl 22 New York NY 10004-1980

BLACKMAN, LEE L., lawyer; b. Phila., Aug. 28, 1950; s. Harold H. and Mary Elizabeth Blackman; m. Kathryn M. Forte, Oct. 5, 1979; 1 child, Shane Forte. BA, U. So. Calif., 1973, JD, 1975. Bar: Calif. 1975, U.S. Dist. Ct. (ctrl. dist.) Calif. 1975, U.S. Ct. Appeals (9th cir) Calif. 1977, U.S. Supreme Ct. 1980, U.S. Dist. Ct. (ea. dist.) Calif. 1984, U.S. Dist. Ct. (no. dist.) Calif. 1988. Atty. Kadison, Pfaelzer, Woodard, Quinn & Rossi, L.A., 1975-81, assoc., ptnr., 1981-87; ptnr. McDermott, Will & Emery, L.A., 1987—; arbitrator L.A. Superior Ct., 1986-90; judge pro tem Superior Ct. State of Calif., 1986-92; speaker in field. Mem. editl. adv. bd. Airport Noise Report, 1989-99; article editor ABA Health Litig. Reporter, 1996-97. Mem. ABA, State Bar of Calif., Legion Lex Inn of Ct. (master bencher 1989—). Office: McDermott Will & Emery 2049 Century Park E Ste 3400 Los Angeles CA 90067-3208

BLACKMAN, ROBERT IRWIN, real estate developer and investor, lawyer, accountant; b. N.Y.C., May 16, 1928; s. Sol and Selma (Landsman) B.; m. Sally Miller, Sept. 14, 1950; children: Meryl Amy, Michael Roger. BS cum laude, Rutgers U., 1948; JD, N.Y. Law Sch., 1950. Bar: N.Y. 1951. Instr. corp. fin. Sch. Bus. Adminstrn., Rutgers U., Newark, 1948; pub. acct. Sol Blackman & Co., N.Y.C., 1948-50; pvt. practice law Robert I. Blackman, N.Y.C., 1951-66; ptnr. Blackman, Lefrak and Blackman, CPA's, N.Y.C., 1963-73, Blackman, Lefrak, Galgey, Meyerson & Feld, N.Y.C., 1966-73; of counsel Blackman, Lefrak, Feld & Fisher, N.Y.C., 1973-76; v.p., head dept. real estate investment ops. Mass. Mut. Life Ins. Co., Springfield, P.R., 1976-78; pres. Kidder Peabody Realty Corp., 1978-80; v.p. corp. fin. Kidder Peabody & Co., N.Y.C., 1978-80; sr. v.p. Cadillac Fairview Corp., Toronto, Ont., Can., 1980-83; exec. v.p. Cadillac Fairview Urban N.E., Inc., N.Y.C., 1980-83; pres. The Best of Bklyn. Properties, Inc., Bklyn., 1987—; exec. v.p. fin., dir. Trust Mortgage Corp., San Juan, P.R., 1971-76; trustee TMC Mortgage Investors, Boston, 1973-76; bd. dirs. owners and builders divsn. Real Estate Bd. N.Y. Capt. USAR, 1957-60. Mem. AICPA, ABA, N.Y. State Soc. CPA's. N.Y. Soc. Attys.-CPA's (bd. dirs. 1966-70), Beta Gamma Sigma, Phi Delta Phi, Phi Epsilon Pi, Heights Casino Club (Bklyn. Heights, N.Y.), Wyantenuck Country Club (Gt. Barrington, Mass.). Home: Bushnell Rd Hillsdale NY 12529 Office: Best of Bklyn Properties 1 Tiffany Pl # 514 Brooklyn NY 11231-2900

BLACKMAN, ROBERT R., JR., career officer. Grad., Cornell U., 1970, Basic Sch., Amphibious Warfare Sch., Marine Corps Command and Staff, 1985. Commd. 2nd lt. USMC, 1970, advanced through grades to brig. gen., 1996; platoon comdr., co. exec. officer 1st Bn. 4th Marines; series comdr., dir. sea sch. Marine Corps Recruit Depot, San Diego, 1972-75; S-3A, rifle co. comdr. 3rd Bn. 1st Marines; with 3rd Marines Divsn.; S-3 2nd Bn. 4th Marines; plains officer Officer Assignment Br. Hdqs. Marine Corps; S-3A, S-3 Air-Ground Exch. Program MAG-26; with 2nd Marine Divsn.; exec. officer 8th Marines; with 3rd Bn. 8th Marines, 22nd MEU; fellow in nat. security affairs Kennedy Sch. Govt.; with Ops. Divsn. Hdqs. Marine Corps, 1990; comdg. gen. 2nd Marine Divsn., Camp Lejeune, N.C., 1999—. Office: 2nd Marine Divsn PSC Box 20003 Camp Lejeune NC 28542-0003 also: Hdqs Marine Corps Divsn Pub Affairs Washington DC 20380-1775*

BLACKMAR, CHARLES BLAKEY, state supreme court justice; b. Kansas City, Mo., Apr. 19, 1922; s. Charles Maxwell and Eleanor (Blakey) B.; m. Ellen Day Bonnifield, July 18, 1943 (dec. 1983); children: Charles A. (dec.), Thomas J., Lucy E. Blackmar Alpaugh, Elizabeth S., George B.; m. Jeanne Stephens Lee, Oct. 5, 1984. AB summa cum laude, Princeton U., 1942; JD, U. Mich., 1948; LLD (hon.), St. Louis U., 1991. Bar: Mo. 1948. Pvt. practice law Kansas City; ptnr. Swanson, Midgley, Jones, Blackmar & Eager, and predecessors, 1952-66; profl. lectr. U. Mo. at Kansas City, 1949-58; prof. law St. Louis U., 1966-82, prof. emeritus; judge Supreme Ct. Mo., 1982-89, 1991—, chief justice, 1989-91, sr. status, 1992; spl. asst. atty. gen. Mo., 1969-77, labor arbitrator, active sr. judge, 1992—; chmn. Fair Pub. Accommodations Commn. Kansas City, 1964-66; mem. Commn. Human Rels. Kansas City, 1965-66. Author: (with Volz and others) Missouri Practice, 1953, West's Federal Practice Manual, 1957, 71, (with Devitt) Federal Jury Practice and Instructions, 1970, 3d edit., 1977, (with Devitt, Wolff and O'Malley) 4th edit., 1988-92; contbr. numerous articles on probate and corp. law to profl. publs. Mem. Jackson County Rep. Com., 1952-58; mem. Mo. Rep. Com., 1956-58. 1st lt., inf. AUS, 1943-46. Decorated Silver Star, Purple Heart. Mem. Am. Law Inst., Nat. Acad. Arbitrators, Mo. Bar (spl. lectr. insts.), Disciples Peace Fellowship, Scribes (pres. 1986-87), Order of Coif, Phi Beta Kappa. Mem. Disciples of Christ Ch. Home: 2 Seaside Ln Apt 402 Belleair FL 33756-1989

BLACKMER, DONALD LAURENCE MORTON, political scientist; b. Boston, July 6, 1929; s. Alan Rogers and Josephine (Bedford) B.; m. Joan Dexter, Aug. 25, 1951; children: Stephen, Alexander, Katherine. AB magna cum laude, Harvard U., 1952, AM, 1956, PhD, 1967. Sheldon traveling fellow Harvard U., 1952-53; exec. asst. to dir. Ctr. for Internat. Studies, MIT, Cambridge, 1956-61; asst. dir. Ctr. for Internat. Studies, MIT, 1961-68, lectr., 1960-61, asst. prof. polit. sci., 1961-67, assoc. prof., 1967-73, prof., 1973-95; prof. emeritus, 1995—; assoc. dean Sch. Humanities and Social Sci., 1973-81; dir. Program in Sci., Tech. and Soc., 1977-81, head dept. polit. sci., 1981-88; research asso. West European studies Harvard U., 1973—. Author: Unity in Diversity: Italian Communism and the Communist World, 1967, (with Annie Kriegel) The International Role of the Communist Parties of Italy and France, 1975; co-author, editor: (with Max F. Millikan) The Emerging Nations: Their Growth and United States Policy, 1961, (with Sidney Tarrow) Communism in Italy and France, 1975. With U.S. Army, 1953-55. Home: 42 King Ln Concord MA 01742-4942 Office: MIT E53-373 Cambridge MA 02139

BLACKMON, WILLIE EDWARD BONEY, lawyer; b. Houston, Apr. 16, 1951; s. A.L. and Florence (Joseph) B. BBA in Mktg., Tex. A&M U., 1973; JD, Tex. Southern U., 1982. Bar: Nebr. 1984, Mich. 1985, U.S. Dist. Ct. (ea. dist.) Mich., 1984, U.S. Ct. Mil. Appeals 1984, U.S. Supreme Ct. 1987, Tex. 1989, U.S. Dist. Ct. (no. dist.) Tex. 1990, U.S. Dist. Ct. (so. dist.) Tex. 1993. Terr. sales mgr. Gillette Co., 1977-79; sales and mktg. coord. Drilco divsn. Smith Internat., 1973-77; legal intern Gulf Coast Legal Found., Houston, 1982; intern/ind. counsel City of Detroit, 1982-84; judge advocate USAF, Ellsworth AFB, Offutt AFB, S.D., 1984-89, USAFR, Reese AFB, Randolph AFB, Tex., 1989-94; dep. staff judge advocate Tex. Air N.G., Ellington Field, Tex., 1994—; asst. criminal dist. atty., Lubbock County, Tex., 1990-91; asst. criminal dist. atty., Harris County, Tex., 1991-92; pvt. practice, Houston, 1992-97; assoc. mcpl. judge City of Houston, 1995-97, mcpl. judge, 1997—; admissions liaison officer USAF Acad., 1990—; internat. election supr. Orgn. for Security and Coop. in Europe (OSCE), Bosnia, 1997; adj. instr. Judge Advocate Gen.'s Sch. Air Univ., Maxwell AFB, Ala., 1996, 97; guest spkr., lectr. Tex. Tech. U., U. Nebr., Creighton U., Tex. A&M U., Tex. So. U. Named to Tex. A&M U. Athletic Hall of Fame, 1994. Mem. ABA, NAACP, State Bar Tex., Nebr. Bar Assn., State Bar Mich., Nat. Bar Assn. (Living Legend award 1990), Tex. assn. African Am. Lawyers, Houston Lawyers Assn., Wolverine Bar Assn., Am. Judges Assn., Tex. Mcpl. Cts. Assn., , Mexican-Am. Bar Assn., Houston Bar Assn., Tex. Coalition Black Dems., Aggie Officers Assn., Masons. Baptist. Avocations: scuba diving, skiing, hiking, biking, dancing. Home: 8766 Pattibob St Houston TX 77029-3333 Office: 1400 Lubbock St Ste 214 Houston TX 77002-1526

BLACKMORE, JAMES HERRALL, clergyman, educator, author; b. Warsaw, N.C., Feb. 15, 1916; s. Willie Richard and Martha Janie (Sansbury) B.; m. Ruth May Lillick, Jan. 26, 1945; children: Julia, John. BA cum laude, Wake Forest Coll., 1937; BD, Colgate Rochester Div. Sch., 1940; postgrad., Duke U., 1940-41, U. Iowa, 1949; PhD, U. Edinburgh, 1951. Ordained to ministry Bapt. Ch., 1940. Dir. religious edn. Parsells Ave. Bapt. ch., Rochester, N.Y., 1938-40; pastor King (N.C.) Bapt. Ch., 1941-43, Masonboro Bapt. ch., Wilmington, N.C., 1947-49, First Bapt. Ch., Spring Hope, N.C., 1951-61; dir. pub. rels. Southeastern Bapt. Theol. Sem., Wake Forest, N.C., 1963-69, dir. publs., spl. instr., 1969-83, prof. assoc. div. studies, 1983-84; editor Outlook, 1963-84; vis. prof. Southeastern Bapt. Theol. Sem., 1985-96. Author: The Cullom Lantern, A Biography of W.R. Cullom, 1963, A Preacher's Temptations, 1966, A reticule, A Collection of Short Stories and Essays, 1969, Sermons of Warsaw, 1975, Conversations About Jesus, 1977, The Wayfarer, 1977, A Flight of Sparrows, 1978, Sermons at Masonboro, 1978, Biblical Orientation, 1981, Sermons at Spring Hope, 1983, Second Acts, 1984, The A.C. Reid Legacy, 1988, Reflections on the Temptations of Christ, 1992, others; contbr. articles to religious and learned jours., also to encys. Sec. bd. dirs. Bibl. Recorder, 1959-62; chmn. hist. com. Bapt. State Con., N.C. 1970-72. Served to maj. chaplain AUS, 1943-46. Mem. Bapt. Pub. Rels. Assn., Lions, Kappa Delta Alpha, Chi Eta Tau. Home: 209 S Wingate St Wake Forest NC 27587-2531

BLACKNER, BOYD ATKINS, architect; b. Salt Lake City, Aug. 29, 1933; s. Lester Armond and Anna (McDonald) B.; m. Elizabeth Ann Castleton, June 4, 1955; children: Catherine Blackner Philpot, David, Elizabeth, Genevieve Blackner Tayler. B.Arch., U. Utah, 1956, B.F.A., 1956. Registered architect, Fla., Utah, Wyo. Asst. landscape architect Nat. Park Service, Mt. Rainier, Wash., 1956; job capt. Cannon, Smith & Gustavson, Salt Lake City, 1957, Hellmuth, Obata & Kassabaum, St. Louis, 1958-59, Caudill, Rowlett & Scott, Houston, 1959-60; project architect Victor A. Lundy, Sarasota, Fla., N.Y.C., 1960-63; pvt. practice architecture Salt Lake City, 1963—; lectr. Salt Lake C.C., 1995; mem. adv. coun., vis. juror, critic Grad. Sch. Architecture, U. Utah, 1983-99; grad. program dept. landscape architecture and environ. planning Utah State U., 1977-92; mem. region 8 adv. panel archtl. and engrng. svcs. GSA, 1977-78. Featured in (book) Sarasota School of Architecture, 1995; mem. editorial adv. bd.: Symposia mag, 1977-83; contbr. articles to mags. Vice chmn. Utah Advanced Gift Heart Fund drive, 1964; co-chmn archtl. div. United Fund drive, 1964; mem. Salt Lake City City Walls Com., 1976-77, Salt Lake City Council for Arts, 1977-78, Utah Gov.'s Adv. Com. Low Income Housing, Utah Rev. Panel Emergency Energy Conservation Programs; adv. bd. Utah Citizens for Arts, Utah Soc. Autistic Children; mem. dinner exec. com. Nat. Jewish Hosp., Nat. Asthma Ctr., Denver, 1983; bd. dirs. Utah State Div. History, Utah State Hist. Soc., 1989-97; mem. Gov.'s Strategic Initiatives for History Task Force, 1991. Recipient Danforth Honor award, 1951, also numerous AIA awards including regional design awards for U. Utah Library Fountain, 1970, Westminster Coll. Fountain Plaza, 1972, Nat. award for Kearns/Daynes/Alley Annex, 1978, Western Mountain Region Hist. award of merit for Daynes/Kearns/Alley Annex, 1977, Am. Assn. Sch. Adminstrs. Exhibit award for Wilson Elementary Sch. Green River, Wyo., 1974, Award merit Producers' Council, Inc., 1978, award Nat. Lincoln Arc Welding Found., 1978, Urban Design award 3d Ann. Program, 1979, award of honor We. Mountain Region for HUD Low Income Housing Project, Salt Lake City Housing Authority, 1988, ACI award for Seven Canyon's Fountain, Liberty Park, Salt Lake City, 1994, Cmty. Svc award Salt Lake Found., 1995, Brownstone Bldg. Hist. Renovation award Salt Lake City Downtown Alliance Award Program, 1996, Honors in Arts award Salt Lake Area C. of C., 1997, Disting. Alumnus award U. Utah Founders Day Award Ceremony, 1997, people of vision award Prevent Blindness Utah, 1998, others. Fellow AIA (bd. dirs. Utah chpt. 1968, 71, sec. 1972-73, chmn. regional conf. 1974, pres. 1975-76; chmn. jury for Wyo. chpt. design awards program 1974, regional rep. to housing com., nat. honor award jury 1979, recorder nat. conv. 1982, speaker West Mountain region conf. 1991); mem. Salt Lake Area C. of C. (v.p. 1980-81, chmn. bd. 1982-83), U. Utah Alumni Assn. (bd. dirs. 1987-90), Salt Lake Swim and Tennis Club, Alta Club (bd. dirs. 1985-89, sec. 1991-92, pres. 1994-95), Rotary (treas. Salt Lake City club 1976-77, pres. 1979-80, v.p. 1987, pres. found. 1990-92). Home and Studio: 1460 Military Way Salt Lake City UT 84103-4455

BLACKNEY, ARTHUR BRUCE, Middle East defense and aviation consultant; b. London, Nov. 29, 1934; s. Roy Belsham and Winifred Emma (Treble) B.; m. Valerie Florence Laws, Aug. 20, 1960; children: Karen Jane, Sarah Louise. Postgrad. Cert. Advanced Study Engring., Cambridge (U.K.) U., 1968; MBA with distinction, Westminster U., London, 1985, MA, 1988. European engr.; chartered engr. Commd. Royal Air Force, 1961-85, advanced through ranks to group capt., 1980; chief engr. RAF Brize Norton, Oxford, Eng., 1977-79; head maint. analysis and computing establishment Royal Air Force Swanton Morley, Norfolk, Eng., 1979-82; asst. dir. Ministry of Def., London, 1982-85; dir. adminstrn. and pers. Forsyte Kerman, London, 1985-87; gen. mgr. Airwork Ltd., Muscat, Oman, 1988-92; bus. strategy advisor Airwork Ltd., Bournemouth, Eng., 1992-93; internat. bus. mgr. Short Bros. Plc, Bournemouth, Eng., 1993-94; Middle East defense and aviation cons. Blackney Consultancy Svcs. Ltd., Oxford, 1994—. Chmn. Brit. Scholarships for Oman, Muscat, 1991-92. Fellow Instn. of Mech. Engrs., Inst. of Mgmt., Royal Geog. Soc., Royal Soc. of Arts. Ch. of Eng. Avocations: local history, genealogy, mountaineering, family activities. Home: The Cottage, Swan Ln, Burford Oxfordshire OX18 4SH, England Office: Blackney Consultancy Svcs, The Tannery, Burford Oxfordshire OX18 4DQ, England

BLACKNEY, GARY, university football coach; b. Astoria, N.Y., Dec. 10, 1944; m. Lauretta Blackney; children: Debbie, David, Kyle, Gary Jr. BS, U. Conn., 1967. Asst. coach U. Conn., Storrs, 1968-70; asst. coach defensive backs Brown U., Providence, R.I., 1970-72; asst. coach offensive backs R.I. U., Kingston, 1973-74; defensive backs coach U. Wis., Madison, 1975-76, defensive coord., 1977; defensive backs coach UCLA, 1978-79; asst. coach defense, defensive coord., defensive backs Ohio State U., Columbus, 1984-90; head coach Bowling Green (Ohio) U., 1991—. Named Coach of Yr., Mid Am. Conf., 1991, 92. Mem. Am. Football Coaches Assn. (bd. trustees, 1996—, Coach of Yr. Midwest Region 1991, 92). Office: Bowling Green U. Perry Stadium Bowling Green OH 43403*

BLACKSHEAR, A. T., JR., lawyer; b. Dallas, July 5, 1942; s. A.T. and Janie Louise (Florey) B.; m. Stuart Davis Blackshear. B.B.A. cum laude, Baylor U., 1964, J.D. cum laude, 1968. Bar: Tex. 1968, U.S. Ct. Appeals (5th cir.) 1970, U.S. Tax Ct. 1970; C.P.A., Tex. Acct. Arthur Andersen & Co., Dallas, 1964-66; assoc. Fulbright & Jaworski, Houston, 1969-75; ptnr. Fulbright & Jaworski, 1975—, chmn. exec. com., 1992—. Trustee Baylor Coll. Medicine, Meml./Hermann Healthcare Sys.; bd. dirs. Ctrl. Houston, Inc. Mem. ABA, State Bar Tex., Houston Bar Assn., Houston Ctr. Club, Coronado Club, Houston Country Club. Baptist. Office: Fulbright & Jaworski 1301 Mckinney St Fl 51 Houston TX 77010-3031

BLACKSHEAR, CORNELIUS, federal judge; b. 1939. BS, CUNY, 1971; JD, Fordham U., 1977. Bar: N.Y. With N.Y.C. Policy Dept., 1962-79; asst. U.S. trustee, U.S. trustee for so. dist. N.Y., N.Y.C., 1979-85; bankruptcy judge for so. dist. N.Y., U.S. Bankruptcy Ct., N.Y.C., 1985—. With USN, 1959-62. Mem. ABA, Nat. Conf. Bankruptcy Judges, Bankruptcy Lawyers Bar Assn., N.Y. State Bar Assn., Malcolm B. Allen Black Bar Assn. Office: US Bankruptcy Ct US Customs House One Bowling Green 6th Fl New York NY 10004-1408

BLACKSON, BENJAMIN F(RANKLIN), clinical social worker; b. Newark, Del., Nov. 4, 1933; s. Benjamin Franklin and Lulu Etta (Taylor) B.; m. Sirletta Fordelma Belcher, Feb. 28, 1957 (dec. Aug. 1990); children: Benita, Barbara. BS, Trenton State Coll., 1972; MSW, MBA, Rutgers U., 1975; MSW advanced cert., U. Pa., 1980; D of Human Service, The Fielding Inst., 1988. Bd. cert. diplomate in clin. social work; cert. social work. Commd. USAF, 1952, advanced through grades to maj., 1975, air traffic contr., 1952-69, multi engine pilot, 1957; clin. social worker USAFR, 1975-85, ret., 1985; mem. Blackson Enterprises, Bordentown, N.J., 1969-81; CEO B.E. Inc., Bordentown, 1975—. vice-chmn. Bordentown Recreation Com., 1973. Fellow Am. Orthopsychiat. Assn.; mem. Acad. Cert. Clin. Social Worker, Nat. Assn. Social Workers (clin. chmn. N.J. 1978-80), Nat. Fedn. Socs. for Clin. Social Work, Am. Assn. Sex Edn. Counselors and Therapists. Avocation: oper. real estate. Home and Office: 200 Mary St Bordentown NJ 08505-1816

BLACKSTOCK, JERRY B., lawyer; b. Monticello, Ga., Mar. 9, 1945; s. J.B. and Eugenia (Jones) B.; m. Margaret Owen, June 10, 1967; children: Towner Anson, Michael Owen, Kendrick. BA, Davidson Coll., 1966; JD, U. Ga., 1969. Bar: Ga. 1969, U.S. Ct. Appeals (5th cir.) 1970, U.S. Supreme Ct. 1978, U.S. Ct. Appeals (11th cir.) 1981, U.S. Ct. Appeals (fed. cir.) 1984. Trial ptnr. Powell, Goldstein, Frazer & Murphy, Atlanta, 1969—; adj. prof. law Emory U., Atlanta, 1975-81; mem. adv. bd. Jour. Intellectual Property Law, U. Ga. Sch. Law, 1992-98; chair Ga. Jud. Qualifications Commn., 1994—. Author: Georgia Appellate Practice Handbook, 1977, Preparation of a Lawsuit for Trial, Pre-Trial Practice, Appellate Practice, 1980, (with others) Georgia Lawyers Basic Practice Handbook, 2d edit. Pres. parents coun. Trinity Sch. Inc., 1981-82; pres. parents club Woodward Acad. Lower Sch., 1986-88, bd. dirs., treas., Woodward Acad. Upper Sch., 1988-91, v.p., 1991-92, pres., 1992-94; chmn. Ga. Athlete Agt. Regulatory Commn., 1989-99; chmn. bd. dirs. Pastoral Counseling Svc. Atlanta; trustee Ga. Legal History Found.; mem. Leadership Ga., 1980; mem. Leadership Atlanta, 1990, exec. com., 1991-92; trustee Riverside Mil. Acad., 1996—; bd. dirs. Fed. Defender Program Inc., Ga., 1993—. Fellow Am. Bar Found., Am. Coll. Trial Lawyers, Internat. Acad. Trial Lawyers, Ga. Bar Assn. (editor-in-chief jour. 1984-85, bd. govs. 1982-98, exec. com. 1990-95, intellectual property law, computer law and gen. practice and trial law sects.), Ga. Bar Found.; mem. ATLA (intellectual property litigation sect.), ABA (patent, trademark and copyright, sci. and tech., tort and ins. practice and litigation sects.), So. Trial Lawyers Assn., Ga. Trial Lawyers Assn., Atlanta Bar Assn. (editor-in-chief Atlanta Lawyer 1972-73), Am. Law Inst., Atlanta Legal Aid Soc. (adv. bd. 1979-86), Atlanta Lawyers Club, Ga. Def. Lawyers Assn. (bd. dirs. 1989-91, dir. Trial Acad. 1987), Am. Bd. Trial Advs. (diplomate, bd. dirs. 1990—, state exec. com. 1985—), Am. Arbitration Assn. (arbitrator, comml. and constrn. panels, Ga.-Ala. adv. com. for large complex cases), Licensing Execs. Soc., Inc., Am. Intellectual Property Law Assn., Computer Law Assn., Davidson Coll. Atlanta Alumni Assn. (pres. 1982-83), Bleckley Am. Inn of Ct. (master of the bench), Commerce Club, Old War Horse Lawyers Club, Cherokee Town and Country Club, 191 Club. Methodist. Avocation: running. Fax: 404-572-6999. E-mail: jblackst@pgfm.com. Home: 3364 Chatham Rd NW Atlanta GA 30305-1140 Office: Powell Goldstein Frazer & Murphy 191 Peachtree St NE Fl 16 Atlanta GA 30303-1740

BLACKSTOCK, LEROY, lawyer; b. El Reno, Okla., Apr. 19, 1914; s. Herbert Austin and Ethel Mae (Gwin) B.; m. Virginia Lee Lowman, Dec. 29, 1939; children: Craig, Priscilla, Birch, Lore, Trena. Grad., Draughon's Bus. Inst., Tulsa, 1933; LL.B., U. Tulsa, 1938. Bar: Okla. 1938. With Phillips Petroleum Co., Tulsa, 1933-41; asst. credit mgr. Phillips Petroleum Co., 1939-41; practiced in Tulsa, 1941-74; counsel Blackstock & Montgomery; dir., gen. counsel Tulsa Homebuilders Assn., 1959-68; dir. Fourth Nat. Bank, Tulsa, 1969-76, Owasso 1st State Bank, Okla., 1967-70; pres. Skelly Stadium Corp., 1964-70; pres., trustee Gt. Western Investment Trust; mem. nat. adv. com. Practising Law Inst., 1969-70; pres. Jud. Reform Inc., 1966-70; lectr. law office mgmt., econs. U. Tulsa Coll. Law, 1970-75; chmn. Okla. Coun. on Jud. Complaints, 1974-84; pres. Tulsa Sci. Center, 1968-73; chmn. Tulsa U. Law Schs. Com., 1960-74, Citizens Adv. Com. County Commrs., 1963-66; pres., bd. dirs. Tulsa County Bar Found., 1962-66; patron Okla. Bar Found., trustee, 1966; mem. Gov.'s Acad. for State Govt., 1966-68; chmn. Okla. Supreme Ct. Bar Com., 1966. Author: Managing Partner Approach, Paper Dolls and Lawyers' Fees. Pres. Tulsa council Camp Fire Girls, 1971-72; pres. Tulsa Baptist Laymen's Corp., 1962-66; Bd. dirs. Tulsa County Mental Health Assn., 1963-70, Tulsa Psychiat. Found., 1964-67; pres. Tulsa County Legal Aid Soc., 1961-62, bd. dirs., 1958-66. Served with USNR, 1943-46. Recipient Disting. Citizens award Okla. Psychol. Assn., 1963; Disting. Alumni award U. Tulsa, 1969, 78; Disting. Alumni award Tulsa U. Coll. Law, 1978; Boss of Year award Tulsa County Assn. Legal Secs., 1978. Fellow Am. Coll. Probate Counsel; mem. ABA (ho. dels. 1965-67, mem. spl. com. on nat. coordination of disciplinary enforcement 1969-72, standing com. profl. discipline 1973-77), Okla. Bar Assn. (bd. govs. 1965-67, pres. 1966), Tulsa County Bar Assn. (pres. 1962, Outstanding Atty. award 1961), World Assn. Lawyers (charter mem.), Tulsa County Hist. Soc. (founding mem.), Photog. Soc. Am., Soc. Amateur Cinematographers, Phi Alpha Delta. Republican. Baptist (chmn. deacons 1962, chmn. bldg. com. 1951-53). Club: Petroleum (dir. 1974-77). Home: 7213 S Atlanta Tulsa OK 74136 Office: 320 S Boston Ave Ste 2000 Tulsa OK 74103-4709

BLACKSTOCK, VIRGINIA LEE LOWMAN (MRS. LEROY BLACKSTOCK), civic worker; b. Bixby, Okla., July 2, 1917; d. Joseph Arthur and Winifred (Lundy) Lowman; student Tulsa Coll. Bus., 1935-37; m. Leroy Blackstock, Dec. 29, 1939; children—Vincent Craig, Priscilla Gay (Mrs. Richard S. Kurz), Burch Lee, Lore Anne (Mrs. Dwight Mitchell), Trena Jan (Mrs. Frank Dale). Legal sec. law firm, Tulsa, 1937-41. Chmn. program Internat. Students in Tulsa, 1955-65; mem. Tulsa Council Camp Fire Girls, 1963-66; mem. youth com. Tulsa Philharmonic Soc., 1969-70; now mem. women's assn.; pres. Eliot Elementary P.T.A., 1961-62, Edison High Sch. P.T.A., 1971-72; mem. Tulsa Opera Guild. Co-chmn. Democratic precinct No. 132, 1960-67. Mem. Tulsa County Bar Aux. (pres. 1954-55, sec. 1962-63, chaplain 1966-67). Baptist. Clubs: Petroleum. Home: 7213 S Atlanta St Tulsa OK 74136

BLACKSTON, BRENDA JOYCE, computer software company manager; b. Columbia, S.C., Apr. 7, 1953; d. Walter Edward and Dorothy Nell (Stephens) Blackston; children: Sasha, Ashley. BA in Edn., U. S.C., 1975, MEd, 1981, PhD, 1984. Cert. elem. reading tchr., reading coord., reading supr., elem. prin., supt., S.C. Tchr. S.C., 1975-81; coord. field placement U. S.C., Columbia, 1982-83, prof. edn., 1983-89; chpt. I and Edn. Improvement Act dir. Georgetown (S.C.) Sch. Dist., 1984-90; sales rep. Computer Curriculum Corp., Sunnyvale, Calif., 1990-93, regional mgr., 1993—. Contbr. articles to profl. jours. Mem. NAFE, Internat. Reading Assn., S.C. Internat. Reading Assn. (pres.-elect, pres. 1989-90, com. chair blue ribbon edn. com. 1989), Phi Delta Kappa. Avocations: reading, walking on the beach.

BLACKSTONE, DARA, music educator; b. Norwich, Conn.; d. Dan and Barbara B.; m. Shigeru Hayashi, June 1995. BS, U. Conn., 1977, MusM, 1980, DPhil, 1996. Grad. asst. U. Conn., Storrs, 1978-80, 84-85; choir dir. 1st Bapt. Ch., Mansfield, Conn., 1979-87; tchr., choral dir., drama dir. Tolland (Conn.) H.S., 1979-96; lectr., conductor U. Conn., 1985-87; cons., vocal coach, conductor pvt. practice, 1978—. Bd. dirs. North Stonington Citizens Land Alliance. Mem. Am. Choral Dirs. Assn. (life), Music Edn. Nat. Conf. Avocations: hiking, canoeing, skiing, skydiving, travel.

BLACKSTONE, PATRICIA CLARK, banker, psychotherapist; b. Louisville, June 30, 1952; d. Robert Phillips and Jeanne Orr (Rice) Clark; m. Patrick H. Thorpe, June 8, 1974 (div. March 1981); m. William M. Blackstone II, Nov. 2, 1985. BA, Indiana U., 1974; MEd, U. North Tex., 1990. Cert. counselor. Mgr. Citizens Fidelity Bank & Trust Co., Louisville, 1974-77; pers. mgr. Am. Gen. Corp., Houston, 1977-81; asst. v.p. human resources MCorp (name now BANK ONE), Dallas, 1983-87, 90; v.p. adminstrn. Tex.-PCS Industries, Inc., Dallas, 1987-89; mgr. employment and tng. First Nat. Bank Pa., Erie, Pa., 1990-92; asst. v.p., mgr. Banc One Corp., Akron, Ohio, 1992-96, 98—, Cleve., 1996-98; cons. First Am. Bankshares, Washington, 1987, Interstate Battery Co. Am., Dallas, 1987, Guaranty Fed. Savs. Bank, Dallas, 1989, BANK ONE, Tex., 1990, Lake Erie Presbytery, Erie, Pa., Greater Akron Musical Assn., 1995, Door and Hardware Inst., 1996; cert. instr. Main Event Mgmt. Corp., Sacramento, 1977-81. Author: Code of Ethics and Harassment-Free Workplace Guide, 1993; co-author: (with William M. Blackstone II) Preparing for Christian Marriage, 1987. Ruling elder edn. Preston Hollow Presbyn. Ch., Dallas, 1987-90, First Presbyn. Ch. Covenant, Erie, Pa., 1992-93; mem. Dallas Mus. Art, 1985-87, The 500, Inc., Dallas, 1986, Akron Symphony Guild, 1994-96; v.p. membership, bd. dirs. Jr. League of Akron, 1996-97, pres.-elect, 1998, pres., 1999—; mem. Vol. Ctr., Akron, 1993-96; mem. women's bd. Akron Child Guidance Ctr., 1997—; bd. dirs. Northeast Ohio chpt. Coun. Nat. Assn. Investors Corp. Fellow Life Mgmt. Inst.; mem. ACA, ASTD (bd. dirs. Erie Tri-State chpt.), Soc. Human Resources Mgmt. (designated Sr. Profl. in Human Resources 1990), Am. Inst. Banking (bd. dirs. Erie/Crawford chpt.). Democrat. Office: Banc One Mgmt Co 50 S Main St Akron OH 44308-1828

BLACKTON, CHARLES S(TUART), history educator; b. N.Y.C., Oct. 27, 1913; s. James Stuart and Paula Hunt (Hilburn) B.; m. Mary Jane Porri, Aug. 16, 1938 (dec. Aug. 1975); children: John Stuart, Susan Porri Blackton Tallman; m. Margaret Rosalind Hando (Baroness Delacourt-Smith), Dec. 21, 1978. B.A., UCLA, 1936, M.A., 1937, Ph.D, 1939. Teaching fellow UCLA, 1937-39; asst. prof. Adams State Coll., Colo., 1939-42; from instr. to assoc. prof. history Colgate U., Hamilton, N.Y., 1946-57, prof., 1957-74, Russell Colgate prof., 1974-82, Russell Colgate prof. emeritus, 1982—, dir. social scis. div., 1961-70; mem. nat. selection com. Inst. Internat. Edn., 1954-56, chmn. India, Australia and Japan coms., 1956-58, mem. selection com. for Australia, 1983; cons., referee Nat. Endowment for the Humanities, 1975-81. Contbr. articles to profl. jours. Served as lt. USNR, 1943-46. Recipient award in Pacific History Am. Hist. Soc., 1940; grantee Social Sci. Research Council, 1951; Fulbright grantee, 1952-53; Fulbright lectr., 1963-64; vis. fellow U. Sri Lanka, 1971, 74, 78. Clubs: Army and Navy (Washington); Hamilton. Home: Hantana Farm PO Box 267 Hamilton NY 13346-0267

BLACKWELDER, BRENT FRANCIS, environmentalist; b. Buffalo, Jan. 4, 1943; s. Francis Winfield and Evelyn Hellen B.; m. Teresa Ann Stotzer, Apr. 5, 1975; children: Matthew, Laura. AB summa cum laude, Duke U., 1964; MA in Math., Yale U., 1966; PhD in Philosophy, U. Md., 1975. Chmn. math. dept. Philander Smith Coll., Little Rock, 1966-68; founder Environ. Policy Ctr., Washington, 1972; chmn., founder Am. Rivers, Washington, 1973-85; founder, staff mem. Environ. Policy Inst., Washington, 1974—; v.p. Friends of the Earth, Washington, 1989-94, pres., 1994—; bd. mem. 20/20 Vision, Washington, 1990—, Am. Rivers, Washington, 1973-93. Author: Water Conservation, 1982, Bankrolling Successes I, 1988, II, 1995. Pres. Plan Takoma, Takoma Park, Washington, 1977-83; bd. mem. League Conservation Voters, 1980-97, chmn., 1981-91. Grad. fellow NSF, 1964, Woodrow Wilson fellow, 1964. Episcopalian. Avocations: canoeing, golf, piano, magic, squash. Home:: 3517 Rodman St NW Washington DC 20008-3118 Office: Friends of the Earth 1025 Vermont Ave NW Ste 300 Washington DC 20005-6303

BLACKWELDER, RICHARD E(LIOT), entomologist, zoology educator, archivist; b. Madison, Wis., Jan. 29, 1909; s. Eliot and Jean (Bowersock) B.; m. Ruth MacCoy, Jan. 4, 1935 (dec. Nov. 1989). PhD, Stanford U., 1934. W.R. Bacon fellow Smithsonian Instn., Washington, 1935-38; asst. curator Am. Mus. Nat. History, N.Y.C., 1939-41; assoc. curator U.S. Nat. Mus., Washington, 1941-56; assoc. prof. St. John Fisher Coll., Rochester, N.Y., 1956-58; prof. So. Ill. U., Carbondale, 1958-77; archivist Marquette U., Milw., 1978—; co-founder, bd. dirs. Soc. Systematic Zoology, 1950-65; Timothy Hopkins lectr. Stanford U., Palo Alto, Calif., 1956. Author: Taxonomy, 1967, Diversity of Animals, 1980; compiler: (concordance) A Tolkien Thesaurus, 1990, also entomol. and zool. reference books; contbr. monographs, articles to encys. and profl. jours. Recipient various acad. awards. Mem. Cosmos Club, Sigma Xi. Home: 3120 Independence St Cape Girardeau MO 63703-5043

BLACKWELL, CECIL, science association executive; b. Enterprise, Miss., Oct. 29, 1924; s. George Dewey and Neely (Baggett) B.; m. Louise McLendon, May 27, 1944; children—Cecil Carl, Donna Lynn, Gregory Dale. B.S., Miss. State U., 1951; M.S., U. Md., 1955; postgrad., U. Ark., 1953-54. Asst. horticulturist Truck Crops Br. Expt. Sta., Crystal Springs, Miss., 1951; research asst. U. Md., College Park, 1951-52; instr., jr. horticulturist U. Ark., 1952-54; extension horticulturist U. Ga., 1954-56, head extension hort. dept., 1956-59; hort. editor Progressive Farmer, Birmingham, Ala., 1959-65; exec. dir. Am. Soc. Hort. Sci.; pub. Jour. Am. Soc. Hort. Sci., HortScience, St. Joseph, Mich., 1965-74, Mt. Vernon, Va., 1974-79, Alexandria, Va., 1979-88; exec. dir. emeritus Am. Soc. Hort. Sci., 1989—; cons., writer, 1989—. Author: (with L.A. Niven) Garden Book for the South, 1961. Served with USAAF, 1944-46. Decorated Air medal; Gen. Edn. Bd. fellow Rockefeller Found., 1951-52. Fellow Am. Soc. Hort. Sci.; mem. AAAS, Internat. Soc. Hort Sci., Am. Inst. Biol. Scis., Royal Hort. Soc. (hon.), Alpha Zeta. Mem. Ch. of God. Address: 300 County Rd 475 Meridian MS 39301-8729 *My parents imparted to me self-confidence, and instilled in me an insatiable hunger for learning and an abiding love and respect for my fellow man and for God. To whatever degree my life and my career have been a success, it has been motivated by a compelling desire to be of service to mankind and to be a creative, productive, useful member of society.*

BLACKWELL, DAVID H., statistics educator; b. Centralia, Ill., Apr. 24, 1919; s. Grover and Mabel (Johnson) B.; m. Ann Madison, Dec. 27, 1944; children—Ann, Julia, David, Ruth, Grover, Vera, Hugo, Sara. A.B., U. Ill., 1938, A.M., 1939, Ph.D., 1941, D.Sc. (hon.), 1965; D.Sc. (hon.), Mich. State U., 1967, Carnegie-Mellon U., 1981. Instr. stats. So. U., 1942-43; instr. stats. Clark Coll., 1943-44; asst. prof. stats. Howard U., Washington, assoc. prof., prof.; prof. dept. stats. U. Calif.-Berkeley, 1954—. Author: (with M.A. Girshick) Theory of Games and Statistical Decision, 1984. Recipient Von Neumann Theory prize Ops. Rsch. Soc. Am.- The Inst. Mgmt. Sci. Fellow Inst. Math. Stats. Am. Statis. Assn., Ops. Rsch. Soc. Am.-Inst. Mgmt. Scis. Home: 3021 Wheeler St Berkeley CA 94705-1826 Office: U Calif-Berkeley Dept Statistics 367 Evans Hall # Mc3860 Berkeley CA 94720-3860*

BLACKWELL, DAVID JEFFERSON, retired insurance company executive; b. Towson, Md., Mar. 17, 1927; s. Jefferson Davis and Salome Lucille (Love) B.; m. Joan Lou Mumma, June 16, 1949; children—David Jefferson, Robert Allen. Student, U. Minn., 1944, Yale U., 1945; B.A., Haverford Coll., 1949. Assoc. dir. Prudential Ins. Co., Newark, Mpls., 1949-67; exec. dir. Ednl. Testing Service, Princeton, N.J., 1967-70; 2d v.p. Mass. Mut. Life Ins. Co., Springfield, 1970-71, v.p., 1971-76, sr. v.p., 1976-81, exec. v.p., 1981-87; pres., chief exec. officer Ins. Systems Roundtable, Inc., Hartford, Conn., 1987-88, David J. Blackwell & Assocs., Woodstock, Vt., 1988-98; ret., 1998; treas., chmn. mgmt. advisory com. Amdahl Users Group, 1977; instr. ins. U. Minn., 1958-64. Mem. exec. bd. Pioneer Valley coun. Boy Scouts Am., 1970-75; v.p. Springfield Thetre Arts Assn., 1974-79; trustee Bay Path Jr. Coll., 1974-87; bd. dirs. Ottauquechee Health Svc., 1988; bd. dirs., vice chmn. Woodstock Area Coun. on Aging, 1993-99. With U.S. Army, 1944-46. Mem. Coll. Life Underwriters, Woodstock Country Club, Rotary (bd. dirs.). Republican. Episcopalian (mem. vestry). Home: PO Box 534 Woodstock VT 05091-0534

BLACKWELL, GARLAND W(AYNE), retired military officer; b. Roxboro, N.C., July 8, 1956; s. Garland and Mattie (Wright) B.; m. Juanita M. Downell, Dec. 6, 1996. BSBA, U. N.C., 1978; MBA, N.Mex. Highlands U., 1982; JD, Willamette U., 1998. CPA, cert. internal auditor. Commd. 2d lt. USAF, 1978, advanced through grades to major, 1990; dep. acctg. and fin. officer 1606 Air Base Wing USAF, Kirtland AFB, N.Mex., 1979-82; staff auditor Air Force Audit Agy., Vandenberg AFB, Calif., 1982-83, Torrejon AB, Spain, 1983-85; audit office chief Air Force Audit Agy., Castle AFB, Calif., 1985-89; audit mgr. Air Force Audit Agy., Norton AFB, Calif., 1989-92; comptroller 432 Fighter Wing USAF, Misawa AB, Japan, 1992-94; controller N.C. Ctrl. U., 1997-98, U. San Diego, 1999—. Active Caring By Sharing Maranatha Community Ch., L.A., 1989-92; bd. dirs. project alpha March of Dimes, San Bernadino, Calif., 1990-91; bd. dirs. Portland Habilitation Ctr., 1996-97. Decorated Commendation medal (3), Meritorious Svc. medal (2), Nat. Defense medal; named one of Outstanding Young Men Am., 1984, 86, 88, Most Eligible Bachelor Ebony Mag., 1989. Mem. Nat. Assn. Cert. and Univ. Bus. Officers, Tax Profls., Inst. Inte rnal Auditors, Am. Soc. Mil. Comptrollers (chpt. v.p. 1986-88), Nat. Black Masters in Bus. Adminstrn. Assn. (life), Air Force Assn., Tuskegee Airmen, Inc., Alpha Phi Alpha (life, chpt. v.p. 1981-82). Avocations: reading, travel, beach. Home: 9117 Outinda St Spring Valley CA 91977

BLACKWELL, J. KENNETH, state official; b. Feb. 28, 1948. BS, Xavier U., Cin., 1970, MEd, 1971. Treas. State of Ohio, Columbus, 1994-98, sec. of state, 1999—. Office: State of Ohio Sec of State 30 E Broad St Fl 14 Columbus OH 43266-0418*

BLACKWELL, JOHN, polymers scientist, educator; b. Oughtibridge, Sheffield, Eng., Jan. 15, 1942; came to U.S., 1967; s. Leonard and Vera (Brook) B.; m. Susan Margaret Crawshaw, Aug. 5, 1965; children: Martin Jonathan,

Helen Elizabeth. BSc in Chemistry, U. Leeds, Eng., 1963, PhD in Biophysics, 1967. Postdoctoral fellow SUNY-Syracuse Coll. Forestry, 1967-69; vis. asst. prof. Case Western Res. U., Cleve., 1969-70; asst. prof. Case Western Res. U., 1970-74, asso. prof., 1974-77, prof. macromolecular sci., 1977—; chmn. dept., 1985-95; F. Alex Nason prof., 1991—; vis. prof. Kennedy Inst. Rheumatology, London, 1975, Centre National de Recherche Scientifique, Grenoble, France, 1977, U. Frieburg, Fed. Republic Germany, 1982; chmn. Gordon Conf. on Liquid Crystalline Polymers, 1992; cons. in field. Author: (with A.G. Walton) Biopolymers, 1973; mem. editorial bd. Macromolecules, 1989-92; adv. bd. Jour. Macromolecular Sci.-Physics, 1986—; internat. adv. bd. Acta Polymerica, 1992—; contbr. articles to profl. jours. Recipient award for disting. achievement Fiber Soc., 1981, Sr. Scientist award Alexander von Humboldt Found., Max Planck Inst. for Polymer Rsch., Mainz, Fed. Republic Germany, 1991, Rsch. Career Devel. award, 1973-77. Fellow Am. Phys. Soc. (exec. com. divsn. high polymer physics 1986-90, vice chmn. 1987-88, chmn. 1988-89); mem. Am. Chem. Soc. (chmn. cellulose divsn. 1999, Anselm Payen award 1999), Am. Crystallography Soc. (chmn. fiber diffraction spl. interest group 1993-94), Biophys. Soc. (chmn. biopolymer subgroup 1975-76), Fiber Soc. Episcopalian. Home: 2951 Attleboro Rd Shaker Heights OH 44120-1815 Office: Case Western Res U Dept Macromolecular Sci Cleveland OH 44106-7202

BLACKWELL, JOHN WESLEY, securities industry executive, consultant; b. Evanston, Ill., Sept. 17, 1941; s. John Dakin Huggins and Mary Louise (Alger) Wells; m. Karen Alice Kralowetz, Dec. 19, 1964; children: Thomas Wesley, Julie Louise, Evan Stewart. BA, Mich. State U., 1964, MBA, 1965. V.p. A.G. Becker, N.Y.C., 1975-80; v.p. Drexel Burnham Lambert Inc., N.Y.C., 1980-82, 1st v.p., 1982-83, sr. v.p., 1983-89; cons., 1989—. Dist. leader United Way, Bronxville, N.Y., 1974, exec., Habitat for Humanity of Collier County. Mem. HideAway (Marco Island, Fla.), Island Country Club (Marco Island). Avocations: private investment, skiing, tennis, scuba, riding, golf. Home: Les Falls 870 S Collier Blvd Marco Island FL 34145-6100 Office: Orion Cons 870 S Collier Blvd PHB Marco Island FL 34145

BLACKWELL, MENEFEE DAVIS, lawyer; b. Lexington, Mo., Feb. 17, 1916; s. Horace F. and Berrien (Menefee) B.; m. Mary Louise Harris, Apr. 25, 1942; 1 son, Stephen M. (dec.). A.B., U. Mo., 1936; J.D., U. Mich., 1939. Bar: Mo. 1939. Pvt. practice Kansas City, now retired; ptnr. Blackwell, Sanders, Matheny, Weary & Lombardi, now retired. Bd. dirs. Greater Kansas City Community Found., 1986-93, Chas. R. Cook and Minnie K. Cook Found., Starlight Theatre Assn., Jacob L. and Ella C. Loose Found., pres. 1989-91; trustee William Rockhill Nelson Trust and Nelson Gallery Found., 1957-91, Louetta M. Cowden Found., Jacob L. and Ella C. Loose Found., Midwest Rsch. Inst.; bd. govs. Am. Royal Assn. Maj. AUS, 1942-46, WWII. Decorated Silver Star, Bronze Star with 2 clusters, Purple Heart. Mem. ABA, Mo. Bar Assn., Kansas City Bar Assn., Kansas City Country Club, Kansas City Club, River Club, Order of Coif, Phi Beta Kappa, Phi Delta Theta, Phi Delta Phi. Episcopalian. Home: 1215 W 57th Ter Kansas City MO 64113-1171 Office: 2300 Main St Kansas City MO 64108-2416

BLACKWELL, MICHAEL SIDNEY, broker, financial services executive; b. Ft. Bragg, N.C., June 14, 1957; s. Cedric Lee Jr. and Susan Olivia (Womack) B.; m. Janet Marie Thomas, Apr. 29, 1986; children: Sydney Marie, Catherine Leigh. Student, La. State U., 1981; BS Mktg., LaSalle U., 1993, MBA, 1994. Cert. fund specialist; registered fin. cons. From sales mgr. to nat. mktg. dir. various corps., 1977-92; v.p. Alliance Fin. Svcs., Atlanta, 1992-95, also bd. dirs., 1992-95; pres. United Securities Alliance, Atlanta, 1992-95, also bd. dirs., 1992-95; sr. v.p., spl. cons. to chmn. World Mktg. Alliance, Inc., Norcross, Ga., 1995—; mng. dir. WMA Consumer Svcs. Inc., Norcross, 1995—; adj. faculty mem. Kent Coll., Mandeville, La., LaSalle U.; bd. dirs. 10X, Inc., Shreveport, La., Legacy, Inc., Baton Rouge. Mem. Internat. Assn. Fin. Planning, Nat. Eagle Scout Assn., Inst. Cert. Fund Specialists, Internat. Assn. Registered Fin. Cons. Republican. Baptist. Avocations: family, golf. Office: World Mktg Alliance Ste 400 400 Perimeter Ctr Terraces Atlanta GA 30346

BLACKWELL, PAUL EUGENE, SR., army officer; b. York, S.C., Aug. 19, 1941; s. Paul Webb and Ruby Mae (Hartness) B.; m. Janet Gail Glenn, June 23, 1963; 1 child, Paul Eugene Jr. BS, Clemson (S.C.) U., 1963, MS, 1965; postgrad., Clemson (S.C.) U., 1970-72; LLD, Clemson (S.C.) U., 1992. Commd. 1st lt. U.S. Army, 1963, advanced through grades to lt. gen., 1994; comdr. 1st Bn., 4th inf., 3d inf. divsn. U.S. Army, Aschaffenburg, W. Ger., 1980-82; ops. officer 9th Inf. Div. U.S. Army, Ft. Lewis, Wash., 1983-85; chief staff 9th Inf. Div. U.S. Army, Ft. Lewis, 1985-86, comdr. 1st Brigade, 9th Inf. Div., 1986-88; dep. dir. ops. Nat. Mil. Command Ctr., Joint Staff U.S. Army, Washington, 1988-89; asst. div. comdr. 3d Armored Div., Germany, 1989-91; comdg. gen. 2d Armored Div., Garlstedt, Germany, 1991-92; comdr. 24th Inf. Div., Ft. Stewart, Ga., 1992-94; dep. chief staff ops. Dept. Army, Washington, 1994-96. Ruling elder Presbyn. Ch., Puyallup, Wash., 1985-88, Beth Shiloh Presbyn. Ch., 1998—, supt. 1997—. Decorated DSM with oak leaf cluster, Silver Star with oak leaf cluster, Legion of Merit with oak leaf cluster, Bronze Star with V device with eight oak leaf clusters, Purple Heart, Air medal, Army Commendation medal with V device and three oak leaf clusters, others. Mem. 82d Airborne Div. Assn., 9th Inf. Div. Assn. (pres. 1986-88), Marine Corps Assn., Assn. of U.S. Army, Tiger Brotherhood (hon.), Am. Ordnance Assn., Octofoil Assn., 3d Armored Div. Assn., 2d Armored Div. Assn., 24th Inf. Div. Assn., Assn. U.S. Army, DAV, Masons, Shriners, Ft. Stewart Skeet Club, Phi Kappa Phi, Gamma Sigma Delta, Alpha Zeta, Alpha Tau Alpha. Avocations: hunting, skeet shooting, running. Home: 650 N Shiloh Rd York SC 29745-8378

BLACKWELL, SAMUEL EUGENE, state legislator; b. Superior, Wyo., Aug. 31, 1930; s. Thomas Eugene and Panzey Fay (Dazey) B.; m. Beverly Joan Nottingham, Jan. 10, 1953; children: Michael, Nyla, Holly. Grad., high sch. Operator Hallaburton Co., Rock Spring, Wyo., 1956-65, FMC of Wyo., Green River, 1965-92; mem. Wyo. Legislature, Cheyenne, 1982-94. Served to cpl. U.S. Army, 1949-52, Korea. Mem. Elks, Am. Legion. Democrat. Home: 610 Donalynn Dr Rock Springs WY 82901-7309

BLACKWELL, THOMAS FRANCIS, lawyer; b. Detroit, Nov. 25, 1942; m. Sandra L. Kroczek; children: Robert T., Katherine M. BA, U. Notre Dame, Ind., 1964; JD, U. Mich., 1967. Bar: Mich and U.S. Dist. Ct. (we. and ea. dists.) Mich. 1968, U.S. Ct. Appeals (6th cir.) 1969. Assoc. Smith, Haughey, Rice & Roegge, Grand Rapids, Mich., 1967-71, ptnr., 1971—, treas., 1979-85, 89—, exec. com., 1985-89; spl. asst. atty. gen. State of Mich., 1972-82. Fellow Mich. State Bar Found.; mem. ABA, State Bar Mich., Grand Rapids Bar Assn., FBA, Products Liability Adv. Coun., Mich. Def. Trial Attys., Peninsular, Kent Country Club. Office: Smith Haughey Rice & Roegge 250 Monroe Ave NW Ste 200 Grand Rapids MI 49503-2251

BLACKWELL, WILLIAM ALLEN, electrical engineering educator; b. Ft. Worth, May 17, 1920; s. Charles Clarence and Lilly (Hartsfield) B.; m. Sherry LaRue Tibbets, June 1, 1949; children: David Allen, Rebecca Rae. BSEE, Tex. Tech. Coll., 1949; MS, U. Ill., 1952; PhD, Mich. State U., 1958. Project engr. Gen. Dynamics Corp., 1959-61; prof. elec. engring. So. Meth. U., 1961, Okla. State U., 1961-66; prof. elec. engring., head dept. Va. Poly. Inst. and State U., Blacksburg, 1966-81, prof., 1981-88, prof. emeritus, 1988—; vis. prof. U.S. Mil. Acad., West Point, N.Y., 1981-82. Author: (with H.E. Koenig) Electromechanical System Theory; Mathematical Modeling of Physical Networks, 1968; (with L.L. Grigsby) Introductory Network Theory, 1985; contbr. articles to profl. jours. With. USAAF, 1941-45. Named Disting. Alumnus Elec. Engring. Alumni Assn. U. Ill, 1979, Disting Engineer award Tex. Tech U., 1990. Fellow IEEE (Centennial medal 1984, Region 3 Outstanding Educator award 1986); mem. Am. Soc. Engring. Edn., Lions (pres. Blacksburg 1979-80, 1997-98). Home: 403 Lucas Dr Blacksburg VA 24060-3622

BLACKWELL, WILLIAM ERNEST, broadcast industry executive; b. Rocky Mount, N.C., Apr. 1, 1932; s. Rosser I. and Ellen W. (Wilkinson) B.; BS, Davidson Coll., 1954; MBA, U. N.C., 1958; m. Elizabeth Levitan, Feb. 22, 1973. Security analyst Jefferson Standard Life Ins. Co., Greensboro, N.C., 1958-66, asst. treas., 1966-69, 2d v.p., 1969-81; v.p. corp. devel. Jefferson-Pilot Corp., Greensboro, 1981-83, sr. v.p. corp. devel., 1983-85, exec. v.p., 1986-91; pres. Jefferson-Pilot Comm. Co., 1991-97. Served in U.S. Army, 1954-56. Mem. Inst. Chartered Fin. Analysts, N.C. Soc. Fin. Analysts, Nat. Assn. Life Underwriters. Office: Jefferson-Pilot Corp PO Box 3384 Greensboro NC 27402-3384

BLACKWOOD, GARY LYLE, author; b. Meadville, Pa., Oct. 23, 1945; s. Roy William and Susie Esther (Stallsmith) B.; m. Judith Ann McPeak, Feb. 23, 1971 (div. May 1973); m. Jean Ann Lantzy, Oct. 3, 1977; children: Gareth, Giles, Tegan. BA, Grove City Coll., 1967. Playwright-in-residence Mo. So. State Coll., Joplin, 1989-93, 97. Author: (juvenile novels) Wild Timothy, 1987, The Dying Sun, 1989 (Best Young Adult Novel Friends of Am. Writers 1990), The Shakespeare Stealer, 1998, (ALA Notable Children's Book); (stage play) Dark Horse, 1993 (winner Ferndale Repertory Theater play competition 1993). Home: 6031 County Road 105 Carthage MO 64836-3368

BLAD, BLAINE L., agricultural meteorology educator, consultant; b. Cedar City, Utah, Apr. 2, 1939; s. Carl Hamblin and Loueda (Allan) B.; m. Virginia Jean Blackham, Feb. 14, 1964; children: Debra Jean, Sheryl Kay, Colleen, Kenneth L., Stephen L., Kirk L., Kerry Kim. BS, Brigham Young U., 1964; MS, U. Minn., 1968, PhD, 1970. NDEA fellow U. Minn., St. Paul, 1964-67, technician, 1966-70, rsch. asst., 1967-70; asst. prof. U. Nebr., Lincoln, 1970-76, assoc. prof., 1976-82, prof., 1982—, head dept. agrl. meteorology, 1987-97, dir. Sch. Natural Resource Scis., 1997—; assoc. dir. Gt. Plains Regional Ctr. for Global Environ. Change, 1992—; cons. NASA, Houston, 1978-80, Standard Oil Co. Ohio, Cleve., 1983-86. Author: Microclimate: Biological Environment, 1983; sect. editor: International Crop Science, 1992; assoc. editor Agronomy Jour., 1981-87. Scoutmaster Cornhusker coun. Boy Scouts Am., 1976-94. Fellow Am. Soc. Agronomy (chair div. 1976-77); mem. Crop Sci. Soc. Am., Gamma Sigma Delta (chair membership com. 1992). Mem. LDS Ch. Avocations: sports, reading, camping, fishing, hunting. Home: 1933 Twin Ridge Rd Lincoln NE 68506-2358 Office: U Nebr Sch Natural Resource Scis 302 Biochemistry Hall Lincoln NE 68583-0758 *There is awe, majesty, wonder and beauty in Nature—God's handiwork. Take time to watch a thunderstorm, see the sun rise and set, hike a trail, fish a river or lake and do it with friends and loved ones.*

BLADE, MELINDA KIM, archaeologist, educator, researcher; b. Jan. 12, 1952; d. George A. and Arline A. M. (MacLeod) B. BA, U. San Diego, 1974, MA in Tchg., MA, 1975, EdD, 1986. Cert. secondary tchr., Calif.; cert. C.C. instr., Calif.; registered profl. historian, Calif. Instr. Coronado Unified Sch. Dist., Calif., 1975-76; head coach women's basketball U. San Diego, 1976-78; instr. Acad. of Our Lady of Peace, San Diego, 1976—, chmn. social studies dept., 1983—, counselor, 1984-92, co-dir. student activities, 1984-87, coord. advanced placement program, 1986-95, dir. athletics, 1990; mem. archaeol. excavation team U. San Diego, 1975—, hist. researcher, 1975—; lectr., 1981—. Author hist. reports and rsch. papers; editor U. San Diego publs. Vol. Am. Diabetes Assn., San Diego, 1975—; coord. McDonald's Diabetes Bike-a-thon, San Diego, 1977-78; bd. dirs. U. San Diego Sch. Edn. Mem. ASCD, Nat. Coun. Social Studies, Calif. Coun. Social Studies, Soc. Bibl. Archeology, Assn. Scientists and Scholars, Internat. for Shroud of Turin, Medieval Acad. Am., Medieval Assn. Pacific, Am. Hist. Assn., Register of Profl. Archaeologists, San Diego Hist. Soc., Phi Alpha Theta (sec.-treas. 1975-77), Phi Delta Kappa. Office: Acad Our Lady of Peace 4860 Oregon St San Diego CA 92116-1340

BLADEN, EDWIN MARK, lawyer, judge; b. Detroit, Feb. 2, 1939; s. Philip and Ruth Sara (Millstein) B.; m. Paula Dee Maskin, Sept. 2, 1962; children: Philip, Sara, Jeffrey. BA, Wayne State U., 1962, JD, 1965. Asst. atty. gen. State of Mich., Lansing, 1965-86; mng. atty. Moran & Bladen, Lansing, 1987-93; pvt. practice, East Lansing, Mich., 1994-97; adminstrv. law judge USCG, 1999—. Author: Consumer Law of Michigan, 1978. Mem. Dem. Polit. Reform Comm., Mich., 1968. With U.S. Army Security, 1957-60, Korea. Recipient Alexander Freeman scholarship Wayne State U., Detroit, 1962-65. Mem. State Bar Mich. (chmn. anti-trust sect., treas./sec. 1990-94), Nat. Assn. Fraud Units (pres. 1985-86). Office: 1314 Fairoaks Ct East Lansing MI 48823-1810

BLADEN, LAURIE ANN, women's health nurse; b. Van Wert, Ohio, June 28, 1962; d. Arnold Hugh and Evelyn Martha (Woods) Kirchenbauer; m. David C. Bladen, Apr. 24, 1982; children: Maureen, Nathan, Olivia. ADS in Nursing, Lima Tech. Coll., 1981; BSN, N.Y. Regents Coll., 1983. Staff nurse pediatrics Mercer Cmty. Hosp., Coldwater, Ohio, 1981-85, coord. pediatric unit, 1985-87, house supr., 1987-90, staff nurse obs-gyn., 1990-93, coord. JACHO, 1992—; ind. nurse evaluator Ohio Nurse Testing Svc., Columbus, 1993-95; chair retention com. Mercer City Hosp., 1993-94. Author: CNOR Handbook for Success, 1994. Avocations: reading, family. Home: 3085 Slavik Rd Coldwater OH 45828-8720 Office: Mercer Cmty Hosp 800 W Main St Coldwater OH 45828-1613

BLADES, HERBERT WILLIAM, diversified consumer products company executive; b. Dubuque, Iowa, Apr. 27, 1908; s. Walter and Nellie (Quilliam) B.; m. Jane Larison Marshall, June 1, 1933; children—John William, William Stoddard. B.S., Northwestern U., 1931. Gen. mgr. John Wyeth and Bro., Can., Ltd., 1935-38; v.p., gen. mgr. Kolynos Co., 1938-43; asst. to pres. Am. Home Products Corp., 1943-46, exec. v.p., 1960—, also dir.; exec. v.p. Wyeth Labs. div., 1946-56, pres., 1956-71, chmn. bd., 1971-73; dir. Carlo Erba, S.p.A., Milan, Italy, Provident Mutual Life Ins. Co. Phila., Phila. Nat. Bank, Phila.; Cons. White House Conf. on Aging, 1961; dir. Pa. Plan to Develop Scientists Med. Research.; Bd. dirs. Bryn Mawr (Pa.) Hosp., Pharm. Mfrs. Assn. Found., Inc.; bd. mgrs. Wistar Inst. Recipient Order of Honneur et Merite Republic Haiti, 1959. Mem. Pharm. Mfrs. Assn. (dir.), Delta Upsilon. Presbyn. (elder, trustee). Clubs: Racquet (Phila.); St. Davids (Wayne). Home: Villa 37 1400 Waverly Rd Gladwyne PA 19035-1254 Office: Am Home Products Corp PO Box 8299 Philadelphia PA 19101-8299

BLADES, JOHN MICHAEL, museum director; b. Decatur, Ill., Jan. 19, 1952; s. Robert Ray and Beverly Ann B.; m. Sandra Jean Barghini, Feb. 11, 1995; 1 child, Erin R. BS, Calif. Poly. State U., 1981; postgrad., Tex. Christian U., 1981-84; cert., U. Calif., Berkeley, 1994. From guide supr. to head pub. affairs office Hearst Castle, San Simeon, Calif., 1986-95; instr. Cuesta Coll., San Luis Obispo, Calif., 1987-90; exec. dir. Henry M. Flagler Mus., Palm Beach, Fla., 1995—; grant reviewer Inst. Mus. & Libr. Svcs., D.C., 1996—; chmn. long range planning com. Palm Beach County Cultural Coun., West Palm Beach, Fla., 1996—, mktg. com., 1995—; presenter, lectr. in field. Contbr. articles and photographs to profl. jours. Pres. Mozart Festival, San Luis Obispo, 1993; chmn. Cultural Execs. Coun., Palm Beach County, 1996—; bd. dirs. Cambria (Calif.) C. of C., 1994-95, Ctrl. Coast Tourism Coun., San Luis Obispo, 1993-95. Sgt. USAF, 1970-74. Mem. Am. Assn. Mus. (pub. rels. com., com. on audience rsch. and evaluation, treas-sec. historic house profl. interest com. 1996—, accreditation reviewer 1999), Am. Assn. Museums, Fla. Art Mus. Dirs. Assn. Republican. Episcopalian. Avocations: sailing, salt water aquariums, collecting antiquities. Fax: (561) 655-2826. E-mail: blades@emi.net. Home: PO Box 705 Palm Beach FL 33480-0705 Office: Henry M Flagler Mus PO Box 969 Palm Beach FL 33480-0969

BLAGG, JAMES W., prosecutor; m. Nancy Sanford; 3 children. BA in Govt., St. Mary's U., Tex., 1968, JD, 1972. Bar: Tex. 1972. Asst. dist. atty. Bexar County, Tex., 1973-80; asst. U.S. Atty., 1981-84; chief criminal divsn. U.S. Atty. for Western Dist. Tex., 1984-85, first asst., 1984-85, U.S. atty., 1996—; pvt. practice law, 1985-95. Served to capt., inf. U.S. Army. Recipient Prosecutor of Yr. award Texans' War on Drugs, 1984. Office: US Atty Western Dist Tex 601 NW Loop 410 Ste 600 San Antonio TX 78216-5597*

BLAGOJEVICH, ROD R., congressman; b. Chgo.; s. Rade and Millie (Govedarica) B.; m. Patti Blagojevich; 1 child, Amy. BA in History, Northwestern U., 1979; JD, Pepperdine U., 1983. Past pvt. practice Chgo.; past asst. state atty. Cook County, Ill.; elected Ill. State House, 1992; mem. Ill. Ho. of Reps., 1996—, 105th and 106th Congresses from 5th Ill. dist., 1997—; pvt. practice atty. Office: US Ho of Reps 331 Cannon House Off Bldg Washington DC 20515 also: 4064 N Lincoln Ave Chicago IL 60618-3038 also: 11 W Conti Pkwy Fl 3D Elmwood Park IL 60707-4505

BLAHD, WILLIAM HENRY, physician; b. Cleve., May 11, 1921; s. Moses and Rae (Lichtenstader) B.; m. Miriam Weiss, Jan. 29, 1971; children—Andrea Margery, William Henry, Karen Ruth. Student, Western Res. U., 1939-40, U. Ariz., 1940-42; M.D., Tulane U., 1945. Diplomate Am. Bd. Nuclear Medicine (chmn. 1982, v.p. 1986-97, pres. 1998—), Am. Bd. Internal Medicine (bd. govs. 1981). Resident in pathology and internal medicine VA Wadsworth Med. Center, 1948-52, ward officer metabolic research ward, 1951-52, asst. chief radioisotope service, 1952-56; chief nuclear medicine dept. VA Wadsworth Med. Center, Los Angeles, 1956-97, dir. nuclear medicine dept., 1997—; prof. dept. medicine U. Calif., Los Angeles; mem. ACGME residency rev. com. for nuclear medicine, 1979-97, chmn., 1991-97; mem. Joint Rev. Com. on Ednl. Programs in Nuclear Medicine Tech., 1986-93; mem. subcom. on naturally occurring and accelerator produced radioactive materials Com. on Interagency Radiation Rsch. and Policy Coordination, 1988-92; cons. nuclear medicine; mem. adv. com. on human uses radioisotopes Calif. Dept. Health Svcs.; mem. HEW Interagy. Task Force on Ionizing Radiation, 1978; dir. nuclear medicine Mt. Sinai Hosp., L.A., 1955-76, Valley Presbyn. Med. Ctr., Van Nuys, Calif., 1959-85, St. Joseph Hosp. Med. Ctr., Burbank, Calif., 1958-83. Author 3 textbooks on nuclear medicine. Contbr. numerous articles to med. jours. Served with U.S. Army, 1946-48. Grantee Muscular Dystrophy Assn. Am., 1965-69, Nat. Cancer Inst., 1973-76. Fellow ACP, Am. Coll. Nuclear Physicians (bd. regents 1974-80); mem. Soc. Nuc. Medicine (trustee 1966-74, pres. 1977-78, Disting. Scientist award No./So. Calif. chpts. 1975, Disting. Sci. award Western Regional chpts. 1995), Health Physics Soc. (pres. So. Calif. chpt. 1964-66), Calif. Med. Assn. (mem. sci. bd. 1975-81, chmn. adv. bd. nuclear medicine 1976-84), Am. Bd. Med. Spltys., COCERT, Soc. Exptl. Biology and Medicine, AMA, Los Angeles County, Calif. med. assns., Western Assn. Physicians, Am. Fedn. Clin. Research, Nat. Assn. VA Chiefs Nuclear Medicine (pres. 1985-87), Western Soc. Clin. Research, Alpha Omega Alpha. Office: Nuclear Med Dept VA Greater LA Healthcare 691/W115 11301 Wilshire Blvd Los Angeles CA 90073

BLAHUT, RICHARD EDWARD, electrical and computer engineering educator; b. Orange, N.J., June 9, 1937; s. Edward John and Julia Anna (Chamer) B.; m. Barbara Ann Krachenfels, Aug. 30, 1958; children: Gregory, Kenneth, Janice, Jeffrey. B.S. in Elec. Engring., MIT, 1960; M.S. in Physics, Stevens Inst. Tech., Hoboken, N.J., 1964; Ph.D. in Elec. Engring., Cornell U., 1972. Engr. Kearfott (GPI), Little Falls, N.J., 1960-64, IBM, Owego, N.Y., 1964-94; courtesy prof. elec. engring. Cornell U., 1974-94; prof. elec. and computer engring. U. Ill., Urbana, 1994—, adj. prof. elec. engring., 1986-94; sys. cons. Ioptics Corp., Bellview, Wash. Author: Theory and Practice of Error Control Codes, 1983, Fast Algorithms for Digital Signal Processing, 1985, Principles and Practice of Information Theory, 1987, Digital Transmission of Information, 1990. IBM fellow, 1980. Fellow IEEE (pres. info. theory group 1982, editor Transactions on Info. theory, Alexander Graham Bell award 1998), NAE. Republican. Roman Catholic. Home: 1502 Bridge Point Ln Champaign IL 61822-9272 Office: U Ill Coordinated Sci Lab Urbana IL 61801

BLAIKIE, WILLIAM, government official; b. Transcona, Can., June 19, 1951. BA, U. Winnipeg, 1973; MDiv, U. Toronto, 1977. Ordained minister United Ch., 1978. Mem. parliament/house leader New Dem. Party of Can., Ottawa, Ont., 1979—, NDP critic for internat. trade. Office: House of Commons, Rm 214 West Block, Ottawa, ON Canada K1A 0A6*

BLAIN, CHARLOTTE MARIE, physician, educator; b. Meadeville, Pa., July 18, 1941; d. Frank Andrew and Valerie Marie (Serafin) B.; student Coll. St. Francis, 1958-60, DePaul U., 1960-61; M.D., U. Ill., 1965; m. John G. Hamby, June 12, 1971 (dec. May 1976); 1 son, Charles J. Hamby. Intern, resident U. Ill. Hosps., Chgo., 1967-70; practice medicine specializing in internal medicine, Elmhurst, Ill., 1969—; instr. medicine U. Ill. Hosp., 1969-70; asst. prof. medicine Loyola U., 1970-71; mem. staff Elmhurst Meml. Hosp., 1970—; clin. asst. prof. Chgo. Med. Sch., 1978-95, U. Ill. Med. Sch., 1995—, Rush Med. Coll., 1997—. U. Ill. fellow in infectious diseases, 1968-69. Bd. dirs. Classical Symphony. Diplomate Am. Bd. Family Practice, Am. Bd. Internal Medicine. Fellow A.C.P., Am. Acad. Family Practice; mem. AMA, Am. Soc. Internal Medicine, Am. Profl. Practice Assn., AAAS, Royal Soc. Medicine, DuPage Med. Soc. Roman Catholic. Club: Univ. (Chgo.). Contbr. articles and chpts. to med. jours. and texts. Home: 320 Cottage Hill Ave Elmhurst IL 60126-3302 Office: 135 Cottage Hill Ave Elmhurst IL 60126-3330

BLAIN, PETER CHARLES, lawyer; b. Milw., Nov. 15, 1949; s. Emile Octave and Mary Catherine (Usalis) B.; m. Katherine Stauber, June 12, 1971; children: Thomas Peter, Timothy Charles, Katherine Elizabeth, Peter James. BS, Wis. State U., Stevens Point, 1971; JD, Georgetown U., 1978. Bar: Wis. 1978. Budget analyst VA, Washington, D.C., 1974-78; atty. Reinhart, Boerner, Van Deuren, Norris & Rieselbach S.C., Milw., 1978—; chmn. Wis. State Bar Insolvency Sect., 1995-97; lectr. U. Wis., Milw., 1984—. Contbr. articles to profl. jours. 2d Lt. U.S. Army, 1972-74. Listed Best Lawyers in Am., Woodward/White, 1987—. Mem. Milw. Bar Bankruptcy Sect. (prog. chmn. 1984-85, sect. chmn. 1986-87, co-chair bankruptcy sect. bench/bar com. 1998—). Democrat. Roman Catholic. Avocation: reading. Office: Reinhart Boerner Van Deuren Norris & Rieselbach SC 1000 N Water St Ste 1800 Milwaukee WI 53202-6650

BLAINE, BARRY RICHARD, library director; b. Mount Pleasant, Pa., Aug. 14, 1950; s. Frederick Edward Sr. and Gwendolyn Newill Blaine. BS, Clarion U. of Pa., 1972; MLS, U. Pitts., 1976. Cert. pub. librarian, sch. librarian, Pa. Temp. asst. librarian Portage (Pa.) Area H.S. Dist., 1972-73; temp. sch. librarian Lackawanna (N.Y.) City Sch., 1974-75; temp. part-time librarian Mt. Pleasant Pub. Libr., 1976; librarian Hempfield Pub. Libr., Irwin, Pa., 1978-79; head librarian Uniontown (Pa.) Pub. Libr., 1979-94, Brownsville (Pa.) Free Pub. Libr., 1994—. Mem. Pa. Libr. Assn. Avocations: reading, gardening. Office: Brownsville Free Pub Libr 100 Seneca St Brownsville PA 15401

BLAINE, CHARLES GILLESPIE, retired lawyer; b. N.Y.C., Mar. 12, 1925; s. James G. and Marion (Dow) B.; m. Gloria Beckwith, Dec. 16, 1944 (div. 1985); children: Cathryn D. Blaine Muzzy, Susan B. Blaine Nesbitt, Charles Gillespie; m. Patricia Stapleton Griffis, May 25, 1985. Grad., St. Paul's Sch., 1943; student, Amherst Coll., 1946; LL.B., U. Va., 1948. Bar: N.Y. 1949. Pvt. practice Buffalo, 1949-93; of counsel Phillips, Lytle, Hitchcock, Blaine & Huber, 1994, ret., 1994; pres., dir. Legal Aid Bur. Buffalo, 1967-68. Author: Federal Regulation of Bank Holding Companies, 1973. Bd. edn. City of Buffalo, 1970-73; bd. dirs. SUNY Coll. Buffalo, 1965-82, chmn., 1980-82; bd. dirs. SUNY Coll. of Buffalo Found., 1984-90; bd. dirs. Salvation Army, 1961-63, Children's Aid Soc., 1967-72, Buffalo Fine Arts Acad., 1970-73; bd. dirs., treas. State Communities Aid Assn., N.Y.C., 1984-90; chmn. men's adv. com. coun. Boy Scouts Am., 1967-68; dir. Buffalo Coun. World Affairs, 1983-90. pres., 1989-90; chancellor Episcopal Diocese Western N.Y., 1975-92. Lt. (j.g.) USNR, 1943-46. Mem. ABA, N.Y. State Bar Assn. (chmn. banking, corp. and bus. law sect. 1966-67), Erie County Bar Assn., Assn. of Bar of City of N.Y., Am. Law Inst., Buffalo and Erie County Hist. Soc., Grosvenor Soc., Buffalo Club, Marshall Club, Lawyers Club Buffalo, Crag Burn Club. Episcopalian. Home: 1775 N Davis Rd East Aurora NY 14052-9440 Office: Phillips Lytle Hitchcock Blaine & Huber 3400 Marine Midland Ctr Buffalo NY 14203-2887

BLAINE, DAVIS ROBERT, valuation consultant executive; b. Gary, Ind., Oct. 30, 1943; s. Jack Davis and Virginia Sue (Mintzer) B.; m. Karen Ellen Levenson, Dec. 28, 1981; children: Davis Justin, Tristan D., Brittara K., Whitney K. B.A., Dartmouth Coll., 1965; M.B.A., U. Mich., 1969. Founder, sr. v.p. Am. Valuation Cons., Chgo., 1971-78, chmn. bd., 1978; exec. v.p. Valuation Research, Chgo., 1978-80; pres. Valuation Research, Los Angeles, 1980-83; sr. v.p. Arthur D. Little Valuation, Inc., Woodland Hills, Calif., 1983-87; owner, chmn. bd. Olesen, 1989-92; founder, chmn. bd. The Mentor Group Inc., Los Angeles, 1981—; founder, pres. ICS Corp., Chgo., 1976-82, v.p. bd., 1982-87. Served to lt. (j.g.) USNR, 1966-68. Mem. Beta Theta Pi.

BLAINE, EDWARD H., health science administrator, educator; b. Farmington, Mo., Jan. 30, 1940; s. Theodore Warren and Tessa Ella (McClanahan) B.; m. Susan Irene Cring (div. 1992); children Jennifer, Marquis Edward. AB, U. Mo., 1962, MA, 1967, PhD, 1970, DSc (hon.),

1989. Player Green Bay Packers, Green Bay, Wisc., 1962-63, Phila. Eagles, Phila., Pa., 1963-67; asst. prof. physiology U. Pitts., 1973-77; dir. renal Pharmacology Merk Inst., West Point, Pa., 1977-86; sr. dir. G.D. Searle Rsch. & Devel., St. Louis, 1986-92; dir. Dalton Cardio-Vascular Rsch. Ctr., U. Mo., Columbia, Mo., 1992—; adv. com. NIH, Bethesda, Md., 1974-86; adv. bd. Global Interaction, Phoenix, Ariz., 1991-93. Contbr. to profl. jours. Deans adv. bd. grad. divsn. U. Mo., Columbia, 1988-92; chmn. Searle-St. Louis United Way, 1990; exec. com. U. Mo. Development Coun., 1993-94; bd. dirs. Mo. Found. for Med. Rsch., Columbia, Mo., 1993—; pres. Varsity M Assn. U. Mo., 1993-94. Named All Am. UPI/Look Mag., 1961; recipient Rsch. Career Development award NIH, 1975. Mem. Am. Soc. Hypertension (v.p. 1992-94), Am. Physiological Soc., Am. Soc. Pharm. Exptl. Therapeutics, Endocrine Soc. Avocations: canoeing, scuba, hiking, skiing. Home: 4 E Clarkson Rd Columbia MO 65203-3520 Office: Univ of Missouri Dalton Cardiovascular Rsch Ctr Columbia MO 65211

BLAINE, ROBERT VIRGIL, principal; b. Kansas City, Mo., July 29, 1942; s. Virgil L. and Angel (Bezingue) B.; m. S. Kay Harris, Aug. 14, 1965; children: Sabra, Robert H., Ryan L. BS, Mo. U., 1964, MEd, 1965, DEd, 1975. Tchr., asst. prin. North Kansas City (Mo.) H.S., 1965-76; prin., dir. Blue Springs (Mo.) H.S., 1976-88; prin. Raytown (Mo.) South H.S., 1988-98; adj. prof. Ctrl. Mo. State U., 1998—. Contbr. articles to profl. jours. Mem. Mo. Gov.'s Commn. on Performance, 1994-96. Named Outstanding Mo. Prin. Mo. Interscholastic Press Assn., 1979; recipient In Honor of Excellence award Nat. Assn. Secondary Sch. Prins./Burger King, 1984. Mem. ASCD, Nat. Assn. Secondary Sch. Prins. (pres. 1992-93, bd. dirs. 1987-91, Outstanding Mo. Secondary Prin. 1984), Mo. Assn. Secondary Sch. Prins. (pres. 1985-86), Phi Delta Kappa. Methodist. Avocations: trout fishing, outdoor cooking, reading. Home: 1305 SW Mic O Say Dr Blue Springs MO 64015-5427 Office: Raytown South HS 8211 Sterling Ave Raytown MO 64138-2647

BLAINE, STEVEN ROBERT, lawyer; b. Tulsa, Aug. 24, 1969; s. Kent Robert and Barbara Ellen (Loftus) B. BA, Bellarmine Coll., 1992; JD, U. Dayton, 1995. Bar: Ky. 1995. Contract atty. Brown, Todd & Heyburn, PLLC, Louisville, 1996—. Mng. editor Dayton Intellectual Property Law Jour., 1994-95. Ky. Gov.'s scholar. Mem. ABA, Ky. Bar Assn., Fed. Bar Assn., Louisville Bar Assn. Avocations: tennis, yoga, Celtic music, Impressionist art, Woody Allen films, all things Celtic. E-Mail: blainesr@iglou.com. Home: 747 Yorkwood Pl Louisville KY 40223-3555

BLAIR, ANDREW LANE, JR., lawyer, educator; b. Charleston, W.Va., Oct. 10, 1946; s. Andrew Lane and Catherine (Shaffer) B.; m. Catherine Lynn Kessler, June 21, 1969; children—Christopher Lane, Robert Brook. B.A., Washington & Lee U., 1968; J.D., U. Denver, 1972. Bar: Colo. 1972, U.S. Dist. Ct. Colo. 1972, U.S. Ct. Appeals (10th cir.) 1972. Assoc., Dawson, Nagel, Sherman & Howard, Denver, 1972-78; ptnr. Sherman & Howard, Denver, 1978—; lectr. U. Denver Law Sch., 1980-83, U. Colo., Colorado Springs, 1984, U. Colo. Law Sch., Boulder, 1991. Author: Uniform Commercial Code sects. for Colorado Methods of Practice, 1982. Contbr. articles to profl. jours. Mem. ABA, Colo. Bar Assn. Democrat. Methodist. Home: 1111 Humboldt St Denver CO 80218-3123 Office: Sherman & Howard 633 17th St Ste 2900 Denver CO 80202-3665

BLAIR, BONNIE, former professional speedskater, former Olympic athlete; b. Cornwall, N.Y., Mar. 18, 1964; d. Charlie and Eleanor Blair; m. David Cruikshank; 1 child, Grant B. Cruikshank. Student, Mont. Tech. Univ. Mem. U.S. Olympic Team, Sarajevo, Yugoslavia, 1984; Gold medalist, 500m Speedskating, Bronze medalist 1,000m Calgary Olympic Games, 1988; Gold medalist, 500m Speedskating Albertville Olympic Games, 1992, Gold medalist, 1000m Speedskating, 1992; Gold medalist, 500m Speedskating Lillehammer Olympic Games, 1994, Gold medalist, 1000m Speedskating, 1994; pro tour speedskater, 1994-95. Recipient James E. Sullivan award for Outstanding U.S. amateur athlete, 1993, Sportswoman of the Year, Sports Illustrated, 1994. 1st American woman in any sport to win gold medals in consecutive Winter Olympics; 1st American speedskater to win a gold medal in more than one Olympics.Most decorated female Olympian of all time -- five gold medals, six total. Office: Advantage Internat Mgmt Inc # 1500 1751 Pinnacle Dr Ste 1500 Mc Lean VA 22102-3833*

BLAIR, C. JACKSON, school administrator; b. Winchendon, Mass., June 4, 1943; s. Charles Louis and LaVilla Janette (Orr) B.; m. Pamela Beth Smithberger, June 15, 1968; children: C. Jackson II, Mark John Huffman, Scott Buffington, Anne Pamela MacGregor. BA, Allegheny Coll., 1965. Sr. v.., asst. to the CEO J. Henry Schroeder Bank & Trust Co., N.Y.C., 1978-84; sr. v.p. Corroon & Black Corp., N.Y.C., 1984-90; v.p. for external affairs RGNS, Rabun Gap, Ga., 1991-94; headmaster Christchurch (Va.) Sch., 1994-96; dir. instnl. advancement, dean of admissions Gilmour Acad., Gates Mills, Ohio, 1996-98; dir. devel. The Winchenden (Mass.) Sch., 1998—; pres. U.S. Fund for Leadership Devel., Southport, Conn., 1989—; pres. Jackson Blair Cons., Winchendon; mem. world bus. adv. bd. Am. Grad. Sch. Internat. Mgmt., Glendale, Ariz., 1980-84. Chmn. Stamford (Conn.) Chamber Orch.; bd. dirs. Conn. Grand Opera, Greater Bridgeport (Conn.) Symphony; mem. exec. com., bd. dirs. World Affairs Coun. Pitts., 1966-76. Recipient Eidemiller award for outstanding citizenship, 1991; named to Outstanding Young Men of Am., 1964. Mem. Univ. Club of Pitts. Republican. Avocations: international affairs, international travel, reading history and biography, bridge. Home: 518 Central St Winchendon MA 01475-1237

BLAIR, CHARLES LEE, physician; b. Stamford, Conn., May 1, 1954; s. Charles Francis Jr. and Mae E. (Gallmoyer) B.; m. Ellen Jill Weiss; children: Eric Charles, Melanie Alison, Hayley Grace. BA, U. Vt., 1976; MD, U. Conn., 1981. Diplomate in psychiatry and geriatric psychiatry Am. Bd. Psychiatry and Neurology. Resident in psychiatry U. Conn. Sch. Medicine, Farmington, 1981-85, asst. clin. prof. psychiatry, 1985-93, assoc. clin. prof. psychiatry, 1993—; John C. Leonard fellow Hartford (Conn.) Hosp., 1985-86, dir. psychiat. edn., 1988-90; pvt. practice Hartford, 1985—; mem. psychiatry residency tng. com. U. Conn. Sch. Medicine, Farmington, 1983-84, 88-90. Rock Sleyster Meml. scholar AMA, 1980-81. Mem. APA, Conn. Psychiat. Soc., Hartford County Med. Assn., Hartford Psychiat. Soc. (treas. 1991-92, sec. 1992-93, program chair 1993-94, pres. 1994-95), Phi Beta Kappa. Home: 149 Steele Rd West Hartford CT 06119-1047 Office: 100 Retreat Ave Ste 612 Hartford CT 06106-2528

BLAIR, CHARLIE LEWIS, elementary school educator; b. Troy, Ala., Dec. 22, 1940; s. James Horace and Dollie Rosa (Cannon) B.; m. Doshia Mae Anderson, mar. 31, 1962; children: Duane Alan, Mark Lewis. AAS, C.C. of Air Force, 1980; AS, U. S.C. Sumter, 1988; BA in Edn., Coastal Carolina Coll., 1989; MEd, U. So. Miss., 1995. Cert. elem. edn. educator, K-12 adminstr. Sgt. USAF, 1958-86; tchr. Lemira Elem. Sch., Sumter, S.C., 1989-90, High Hills Mid. Sch., Sumter, 1990-96; asst. principal Lakewood H.S., Sumter, S.C., 1996—. Mem. Disabled Am. Vets., 1989—, Am. Legion, Columbia, S.C., 1989—. Named Dean's Honor Student U. S.C. Sumter, 1988, Pres.'s Honor Student U. S.C. Sumter, 1989, to Nat. Dean's List U. S.C. Sumter, 1987-89. Mem. NEA, ASCD, Nat. Assn. of Secondary Sch. Prinicpals, Palmetto State Tchrs. Assn., S.C. Edn. Assn., U. S.C. Sumter Edn. Assn. (pres. 1988-89), Kappa Delta Pi, Phi Kelta Kappa. Baptist. Avocations: woodworking, auto repair, upholstery, reading, music.

BLAIR, DAVID CHALMERS LESLIE, composer, writer; b. Long Beach, Calif., Apr. 8, 1951; s. David Chalmers Leslie and Eleanor LaVerne (Kramer) B. Student, Long Beach City Coll., 1976-78; BA in French, cert. tchr. ESL, Calif. State U., Long Beach, 1979; postgrad., U. de Provence, Aix-en-Provence, France, 1979-80. Author: Death of an Artist, 1982, Vive la France, 1993, Death of America, 1994, Mother, 1998; composer, writer and recorder of 101 albums including Her Garden of Earthly Delights, Sir Blair of Rothes, Europe, and St. Luke Passion. Leader Libertarian Party Chippewa Valley, Wis., 1994-97; candidate Wis. State Assembly-67th Dist., 1996. Avocations: the arts, marksmanship, travel. Home: 19331 105th Ave Cadott WI 54727-5529

BLAIR, DAVID WILLIAM, mechanical engineer; b. Santa Barbara, Calif., Oct. 5, 1929; s. David Sutherland and Norah Mildred (Higgins) B.; m. Rosemary Constance Miles, Jan. 30, 1954; children: Karen E., Barbara A., M. Maria, Amanda M., David B. O., Rachel P. BS, Oreg. State U., 1952; MS, Columbia U., 1954, PhD, 1961. From asst. to instr. mech. engring. Columbia U., N.Y.C., 1952-58; rsch. assoc. Princeton (N.J.) U., 1958-61; rsch. scientist AeroChem Rsch. Labs., Princeton, 1961-62; postdoctoral fellow Royal Norwegian Coun. Indsl. and Engring. Rsch., Kjeller, Norway, 1962-63; assoc. prof. Polytechnic Inst. Bklyn., 1963-69; engring. assoc. Corp. Rsch. Labs. Exxon Rsch. and Engring. Co., Linden, N.J., 1969-83; pres. Princeton Sci. Enterprises, Inc., 1985—. Contbr. articles to Handbook of the Engring. Scis., AIAA Jour., Jour. Quantitative Spectroscopy and Radiative Transfer, Environ. Sci. and Tech.; patentee for multi-stage process for combusting fuels containing fixed-nitrogen chemical species, efficient high temperature radiant furnace, conductive polymer ignitors. Mem. Princeton Twp. Com., 1975-82, Princeton Joint Commn. on Civil Rights, 1975-87, Princeton Consol. Commn., 1995-96. Mem. ASME, AIChE, Am. Phys. Soc., Combustion Inst., Tau Beta Pi, Sigma Tau, Phi Kappa Phi, Pi Mu Epsilon, Pi Tau Sigma. Democrat. Achievements include patent for multi-stage process for combusting fuels containing fixed-nitrogen chemical species, efficient high temperature radiant furnace, and conductive polymer ignitors. Home and Office: Princeton Sci Enterprises Inc 1108 Kingston Rd Princeton NJ 08540-4132

BLAIR, DENNIS CUTLER, career officer; m. Diane Blair; children: Duncan, Pamela. BA, U.S. Naval Acad.; postgrad., Oxford U., Eng. Commd. ensign USN, advanced through grades to vice adm.; comdr. USS Cochrane, Yokosuka, Japan, 1984-86, Naval Sta. Pearl Harbor, 1989-90, Kitty Hawk Battlegroup, 1993-95; assoc. dir. Ctrl. Intelligence Mil. Support, 1995-96; mem. staff NSC; dir. Joint Staff, 1996-99; comdr. in chief U.S. Pacific Command, Camp H.M. Smith, Hawaii, 1999—. Decorated Legion of Merit with 3 gold stars, Def. Disting. Svc. medal with 2 oak leaf clusters; Rhodes scholar Oxford U.; White Ho. fellow; Naval Ops. fellow. Office: Comdr in Chief US Pacific Command Box 64028 Camp HM Smith HI 96861-4028

BLAIR, EDWARD MCCORMICK, investment banker; b. Chgo., July 18, 1915; s. William McCormick and Helen Haddock (Bowen) B.; m. Elizabeth Graham Iglehart, June 28, 1941; children: Edward McCormick, Francis Iglehart. Grad., Groton Sch., 1934; B.A., Yale U., 1938; M.B.A., Harvard U., 1940. With William Blair & Co., Chgo., 1946—; ptnr. William Blair & Co., 1950-61, mng. ptnr., 1961-77, sr. ptnr., 1977—. Bd. dirs. George M. Pullman Ednl. Found.; trustee Coll. of Atlantic, Bar Harbor, Maine; life trustee U. Chgo., Rush-Presbyn.-St. Luke's Med. Ctr., Chgo., Art Inst. Chgo. Lt. comdr. USNR, 1941-46. Home: PO Box 186 Sheridan Rd Lake Bluff IL 60044 Office: William Blair & Co 222 W Adams St Chicago IL 60606-5307

BLAIR, EDWARD PAYSON, theology educator; b. Woodburn, Oreg., Dec. 23, 1910; s. Oscar Newton and Bertha (Myers) B.; m. Vivian Krisel, Sept. 13, 1934; children: Phyllis, Sharon. BA, Seattle Pacific U., 1931; S.T.B., N.Y. Theol. Sem., 1934; PhD, Yale U., 1939. Ordained to ministry Free Meth. Ch., 1939; transferred to Meth. Ch., 1950. Prof. Bible Seattle Pacific U., 1939-41, dean Sch. of Religion, 1940-41; prof. Old Testament N.Y. Theol. Sem., N.Y.C., 1941-42; prof. Bibl. interpretation Garrett-Evang. Theol. Sem., Evanston, Ill., 1942-60, Harry R. Kendall prof. New Testament interpretation, 1960-71, adj. prof. New Testament interpretation, 1971-75; lectr. in field; archaeol. excavator in Israel at Anata, 1936, Herodian Jericho, 1951, Mt. Gerizim, 1966, 68. Editor Bibl. Rsch., 1964-65; co-editor, author (with others): Illustrated Family Encyclopedia of Living Bible, 1967; author: Jesus in the Gospel of Matthew, 1960, Deuteronomy and Joshua, 1964, Abingdon Bible Handbook, 1975, Illustrated Bible Handbook, 1987. Two Brothers' fellow Yale U., Jerusalem, 1935-36; recipient citation Laymen's Nat. Bible Com., 1975; named Alumnus of Yr., Seattle Pacific U., 1981. Mem. Am. Schs. of Oriental Rsch., Am. Acad. Religion, Soc. Bibl. Lit. Home and Office: 299 N Heather Dr Camano Island WA 98292 *The biblical perspectives on God, Jesus Christ, and the world and its inhabitants, while expressed in the language and thought forms of antiquity, yet offer the best insights available for meaningful living in our own difficult times.*

BLAIR, FRED EDWARD, social services administrator; b. Huntington, W.Va., Oct. 6, 1933; s. Fred E. and Pearl Amy (King) B.; m. Lois Ann Thomas, Aug. 16, 1958; children: Lesli Winifred, Annlyn Paige, Carter Thomas. BBA, Marshall U., 1955; MA, U. Iowa, 1965. Cert. healthcare exec. Adminstrv. asst. Jefferson Med. Coll. Hosp., Phila., 1964-66; asst. adminstr. Barberton (Ohio) Citizen Hosp., 1966-67; sr. asst. adminstrn. U. Ala. Hosp. and Clinics, 1967-68; exec. dir. Ohio Valley Med. Ctr., Wheeling, W.Va., 1969-83; pres. Ohio Valley Health Svcs. and Edn. Corp., 1983-86; pres., chief exec. officer United Care Inc. (formerly Peoples Community Hosp. Authority), Wayne, Mich., 1986-90; pres. Blair Ltd., Inc., 1991—; Instr. health services mgmt. U. Ala., Birmingham; dir. W.Va. Hosp. Service, Inc. (Blue Cross); preceptor health adminstrn. George Washington U., Med. Coll. Va. Bd. dirs. W.Va. Health Systems Agy., treas., 1978; bd. dirs. W.Va. Heart Assn., Wheeling Country Day Sch.; mem. exec. com. W.Va. Regional Med. Program; elder Vance Meml. Presbyn. Ch.; usher First Presbyn. Ch., Birmingham, Mich. Fellow Am. Coll. Healthcare Adminstrs.; mem. Am. Coll. Healthcare Execs., Am. Hosp. Assn., W.Va. Hosp. Assn., Nat. League Nursing, Am. Assn. Mental Health Adminstrs., Am. Pub. Health Assn., Mich. Hosp. Assn. (legis. and pub. policy com., svc. corp. com., HAPAC team, com. on govt. relations), S.E. Mich. Health Council (vice chair com. on health facilities planning, trustee). Club: Rotary.

BLAIR, GARY, women's collegiate basketball coach; b. Aug. 10, 1945; m. Nan Smith; children: Matt, Paige. BS in Health & Phys. Edn., Tex. Tech. U., 1972, MA in Phys. Edn., 1974. Head coach Stephen F. Austin Coll., 1985-93, U. Ark., Fayetteville, 1993—. Office: U Ark Women's Athletics Dept 131 Barnhill Arena Fayetteville AR 72701

BLAIR, GRAHAM KERIN (KERRY BLAIR), lawyer; b. Aug. 20, 1951; s. Joseph William and Ruth Marilyn (Shore) B.; m. Melanie Ann Offield, Sept. 12, 1998; children: Elizabeth, Austin. BA, So. Meth. U., 1973; JD, U. Tex., 1976. Bar: Tex. 1976, U.S. Ct. Appeals (5th cir.) 1977, U.S. Dist. Ct. (so. dist.) Tex. 1977. Assoc. Bracewell & Patterson, Houston, 1976-79; ptnr., co-chmn. litigation sect. Chamberlain, Hrdlicka, White, Williams & Martin, Houston, 1979-82; sr. ptnr. Norton & Blair, Houston, 1982-93; shareholder, head Houston litigation group Verner, Liipfert, Bernhard, McPherson and Hand, Chartered, Houston, 1993—; author, lectr. on banking and constrn. litigation and alternative dispute resolution procedures; dir. advocacy, bd. advs. U. Tex. Sch. Law, Austin, 1976. *Mr. Blair has over twenty-three years of experience and leadership in complex business litigation, successfully representing clients in disputes alleging damages in the hundreds of millions of dollars. His clients have included major oil and gas companies, insurers, energy developers, large banks and borrowers, public universities, hotel owners, construction and manufacturing concerns, public ac counting and law firms. Kerry Blair's articles and comments have been featured in the Wall Street Journal, ABA Journal, The American Banker, National Law Journal, The Texas Lawyer and various other domestic and international newspapers and business journals.* Contbr. articles to profl. jours. Lt. USNR, 1973-76. Fellow Houston Bar Found.; mem. ABA, Tex. Bar Found., Houston Bar Assn. (mem. adminstrn. justice com.), State Bar Tex., Alpha Tau Omega. Republican. Methodist. Address: Verner Liipfert Bernhard McPherson and Hand Chtd 1111 Bagby St Fl 47 Houston TX 77002-2551

BLAIR, HARRY WALLACE, political science educator, consultant; b. Washington, Mar. 25, 1938; s. James Newell and Greta (Flintermann) B.; m. Barbara Ann Shailor, Dec. 26, 1981; 1 child, Emily Rebecca. AB in History, Cornell U., 1960; MA in Polit. Sci., Duke U., 1966, PhD in Polit. Sci., 1970. Instr. polit. sci. Colgate U., 1968-70; asst. prof. polit. sci. Bucknell U., Lewisburg, Pa., 1970-77, assoc. prof., 1977-83, prof., 1983—, chair dept., 1982-85, 88-90; vis. fellow Ctr. for Internat. Studies, Cornell U., 1972-73, vis. assoc. prof. rural sociology and rsch. assoc., spring-summer 1979, vis. assoc. prof., 1980-81, vis. prof. rural sociology, fall 1987; rsch. assoc. So. Asian Inst., Sch. Internat. Affairs, Columbia U., spring-summer 1974; social analyst Bur. Sci. and Tech., Office of Rural Devel., U.S. Agy. for Internat. Devel., 1981-82, sr. social sci. analyst Ctr. for Devel. Info. and Evaluation, 1992-94, sr. democracy advisor Bur. for Policy and Program Coord., Ctr. for Devel. Info. and Evaluation, 1995, 96-97; vis. fellow Sch. Forestry and Environ. Studies, Yale U., spring-summer 1986. Contbr. articles to books and profl. jours. Lt. U.S. Army, 1961-63. Office: Bucknell Univ Dept Polit Sci Lewisburg PA 17837

BLAIR, JAMES PEASE, photographer; b. Phila., Apr. 14, 1931; s. Jacob Jackson and Dorothy Flagg (Pease) B.; m. Patricia Carol Wohlgemuth, Aug. 13, 1964; children: Matthew Ward, David Alexander. BS, Ill. Inst. Tech., 1954. Reporter, film photographer Sta. WIIC-TV, Pitts., 1958-59; freelance photojournalist, 1959-62, 94—; staff photographer Nat. Geog. Soc., Washington, 1962-94; ret., 1994; instr. Rochester Inst. Tech., 1978, Internat. Ctr. of Photography, N.Y.C., 1992, Maine Photographic Workshops, 1988-99 disting. vis. prof. U. Mo., 1992. Photographer: Listen With The Eye, 1964, As We Live And Breathe, 1971, Our Threatened Inheritance, 1984, Wooden Fences, 1997; one-man shows in, Pitts., 1962, New Haven, 1977, Washington, Teheran, 1975, St. Louis, 1990. Lt. (j.g.) USN, 1954-56. Poynter fellow Yale U., 1977; recipient Overseas Press Club Best Photog. Reporting from Abroad award, 1977. Mem. White House News Photographers Assn., Am. Soc. Picture Profls., Nat. Press Photographers Assn., Cosmos Club. Home: 1411 30th St NW Washington DC 20007 also: 27 Washington St Middlebury VT 05753-1214

BLAIR, JOHN, consulting scientist; b. Budapest, Hungary, Dec. 5, 1929; came to U.S., 1950, naturalized, 1955; s. Eugene I. and Helen (Benedek) B.; m. Constance Smith Drown, Sept. 10, 1955; children: David E., Jennifer C. BS, MIT, 1954, MS, 1955, ScD, 1960. With Pacific Semiconductors, Inc., Culver City, Calif., 1955-57; elec. engring. faculty MIT, 1957-66; dir. corp. rsch. Raytheon Co., Lexington, Mass., 1966-94; prin. JBX Techs., Inc., Wayland, Mass., 1994—; mem. energy R&D and nat. progress The White House, 1961; mem. Army Sci. Bd., Dept. Army, Washington, 1978-84, 86-90; rep. Indsl. Rsch. Inst., 1977-94, emeritus, 1994—; mem. adv. bd. Coll. Engring., U. Ill., Urbana, 1986—; mem. dean's adv. coun. Coll. Engring., U. Mass., Amherst, 1978-94; mem. vis. com. Sch. Elec. Engring. and Computer Sci., Poly. U., Bklyn., 1991—; mem. adv. bd. Ctr. for Intelligent Controls, MIT-Harvard U.-Brown U., 1987-94; mem. industry and univ. govt. com. U. Calif., Berkeley, 1970-74, chmn., 1974; mem. vis. com. on elec. engring. and computer sci. MIT, 1970-73, mem. vis. com. on ocean engring., 1991-95, lectr. ocean engring., 1995-98; external rev. com. Materials Sci., Los Alamos Nat. Lab., 1995—; adv. com. Ctr. for Engring. Sci. Advanced Rsch., Oak Ridge Nat. Lab., 1995—; army sci. bd. Dept. of the Army, Washington, 1997—; sci. advisor Idaho Nat. Engring. and Environ. Lab., 1998—. State industry adv. coun. MIT Sea Grant Coll. Program, 1970—; mem. Nat. Sea Grant Rev. Panel, NOAA, Dept. Commerce, 1979-85. Recipient citation Sec. of Army, 1991; Ford Found. fellow, 1960-61. Mem. Cosmos Club. Home: 25 Moore Rd Wayland MA 01778-1417

BLAIR, JOYCE ALLSMILLER, computer science educator; b. Louisville, Aug. 29, 1951; d. Freeman A. and Margaret J. (Schmidt) Allsmiller; m. James R. Blair, Aug. 7, 1971 (dec. Sept. 1992); 1 child, Sherry. BS, Ea. Ky. U., 1973; MS, U. Ky., 1975; PhD, Vanderbilt U., 1991. Asst. prof. computer sci. U. Ky., Lexington, 1975-81, Ea. Ky. U., Richmond, 1981-86; prof. Belmont U., Nashville, 1988—; dir. honors program Belmont U., Nashville, 1993-96. Mem. Assn. for Computing Machinery (treas. Mid S.E. chpt. 1994—). Mem. Christian Ch. (Disciples of Christ). Office: Belmont U 1900 Belmont Blvd Nashville TN 37212-3757*

BLAIR, KAREN ELAINE, respiratory care practitioner, health educator; b. Arnold, Pa., Nov. 9, 1958; d. William Alpheus and Elizabeth Margaret (Koepp) Blair. AAS, Pa. State U., 1979; BS, Indiana U. of Pa., 1987; MEd, Pa. State U., 1996, doctoral student in health, 1999. Cert. pulmonary technologist; registered respiratory therapist. Instr. health edn. Pa. State U., New Kingston; coord. pulmonary rehab. dept., health club dir. Pa. State U., New Kensington; pulmonary rsch. technician U. Pitts.; gym supr. Pa. State U., New Kensington; respiratory therapist, instr., trainer CPR Western Pa. Hosp., Pitts.; level 1 coach U.S. Volleyball Assn.; spkr. in field. Named Outstanding Alumni, Pa. State U., 1993. Mem. APHA, AAHPERD (chair cmty. health Pa. chpt., v.p. health divsn., 1998-99, Health Edn. Profl. 1998), NAFE, AAUW, Am. Sch. Health Assn., Pa. Sch. Health Assn., Health Educators Inst., Am. Assn. Respiratory Care, Pa. Soc. Critical Care Medicine, Nat. Soc. for Cardiopulmonary Tech., Pa. State U. Alumni Assn. v.p. chpt. 1991-94, bd. dirs. 1991-96, exec. com.), Soc. for Clin. Data Mgmt. Sys., Pa. Soc. Pub. Health Edn., Pa. Pub. Health Assn., Biology Club. Home: 1907 Kenneth Ave New Kensington PA 15068-4224

BLAIR, LINDA DENISE, actress; b. Westport, Conn., Jan. 22, 1959; d. James Fredrick and Elinore (Leitch) B. Student pub. schs., Westport, Conn. Model, then actress on TV commls. Film appearances include: The Sporting Club, 1970, The Way We Live Now, 1969, The Exorcist, 1973, Airport '75, 1974, Sweet Hostage, 1975, Exorcist Part II: The Heretic, 1977, Roller-Boogie, 1979, Double Blast, 1993, Sorceress, 1994, Scream, 1996, Prey of the Jaguar, 1996; TV appearances include: Born Innocent, 1974, Sarah T.—Portrait of a Teenage Alcoholic, 1974, Victory at Entebbe, 1976, Stranger in Our House, 1978, Hell Night, 1981, Chained Heat, 1983, Night Patrol, 1985, Savage Streets, 1985. Recipient Golden Globe, also Peoples Choice awards for Exorcist, 1974; plaque for Sarah T.; 3 Bravo mag. Favorite Actress awards; South America's Favorite Actress award, 1977. Mem. AFTRA, Screen Actors Guild, Am. Horse Shows Assn. Address: c/o David Shapira & Assocs 15301 Ventura Blvd Ste 345 Sherman Oaks CA 91403*

BLAIR, LOUIS HELION, foundation executive; b. Richmond, Va., Feb. 9, 1939; d. Jean Bichier and Jean Blair Helion; m. Suzanne Sessoms Lemon, June 1, 1982; 1 child, Robert. BEE, U. Va., 1961; MEE, MIT, 1962, degree elec. engring. (hon.), 1963; LLD (hon.), William Jewell Coll., 1993; DSc (hon.), Baker U., 1994. Sr. rsch. staff Urban Inst., Washington, 1969-76; policy analyst Office of Sci. and Tech. Policy, Washington, 1976-79; staff mem. U.S. Radiation Policy Coun., Washington, 1979-81, U.S. Senate Commerce Com., Washington, 1981-83; cons. Washington and Paris, 1983-89; exec. sec. Truman Scholarship Fedn., Washington, 1989—. Mayor, coun. mem. City of Falls Ch., 1969-74; mem. Solid Waste Adv. Group, State of Va., 1971-72. Fellow Nat. Acad. of Pub. Adminstrn. Avocations: French cooking. Office: Truman Scholarship Found 712 Jackson Pl NW Washington DC 20006-4901

BLAIR, MARDIAN JOHN, hospital management executive; b. Rock Springs, Wyo., Dec. 30, 1931; s. Edmund B. and Bernice A. (Mardian) B.; m. Joan Alece Peters, June 20, 1954; children: Michael, Robyn, Douglas, Beth Ann, John. BS in Bus., Union Coll., Lincoln, Nebr., 1954; MA in Bus. Orgn., U. Nebr., Lincoln, 1958; MS in Hosp. Adminstrn., Northwestern U., 1961. Staff auditor Peat, Marwick, Mitchell & Co., 1958; acct. Hinsdale (Ill.) Sanitarium and Hosp., 1958-59; coordinator devel. Hinsdale (Ill.) San. and Hosp., 1959, asst. to adminstr., 1959, asst. adminstr., 1960-63, adminstr., 1963-70; pres. Portland (Oreg.) Adventist Hosp., 1970-76, N.W. Med. Found., Portland, 1972-79, Fla. Hosp., Orlando, 1979-84; pres., CEO Adventist Health Sys. Sunbelt, 1984—; Bd. dirs. Premier, Inc. Bd. dirs. Oakwood Coll., So. Adventist U., Southwestern Adventist U.; bd. overseers Rollins Coll. Crummer Sch. Bus., Union Coll., Lincoln, Nebr. Fellow Am. Coll. Hosp. Adminstrs., Am. Coll. Healthcare Adminstrs.; mem. Am. Hosp. Assn., Assn. Adventist Health Care Execs., Adventist Healthcare Assn. (cabinet mem.), Fla. Hosp. Assn. Home: 1132 Dorchester St Orlando FL 32803-1012 Office: Adventist Health Sys 111 N Orlando Ave Winter Park FL 32789-3675

BLAIR, MARGARET MENDENHALL, research economist, consultant; b. Bartlesville, Okla., Nov. 8, 1950; d. Harold Leroy and Mary Winifred (Simmons) Mendenhall; m. Forrest Randall Blair, May 29, 1971 (div. Sept. 1979); m. Roger Lisle Conner, June 22, 1991; 1 child, Elizabeth LeeAnn Conner. BA, U. Okla., 1973; postgrad., Harvard U., 1982-83; MA, MPhil, PhD, Yale U., 1989. Reporter Houston Chronicle, 1973-75; reporter, bur. mgr. Fairchild Publs., Houston, 1975-77; corr. Bus. Week, Houston, 1977-79, bur. chief, 1979-82; economist Fed. Res. Bank N.Y., N.Y.C., 1985; rsch. asst. Yale U., New Haven, 1985-86, lectr., 1986-87; rsch. assoc. Brookings Instn., Washington, 1987-94, sr. fellow, 1995—; dir. Brookings Project on Corps. and Human Capital, 1996—; co-dir. Brookings Project on Intangible Sources of Value, 1998—; mem. adj. faculty U. Md. Coll. Bus. and Mgmt., 1993-94; vis. prof. Georgetown U. Law Ctr., 1996—; mem. steering com., rapporteur Woodstock Seminar Series on Bus. Ethics, Washington, 1989—; mem. subcoun. on capital allocation Competitiveness Policy Coun., 1993-96; rapporteur Salzburg (Austria) Seminar on Internat. Fin. Markets, 1989; mem. steering com. time horizons project Coun. on Competitiveness, Washington, 1990; mem. Task Force on Restructuring America's Labor Market

Instns., MIT/Sloan Sch. Mgmt., 1997—. Author: The Deal Decade Handbook, 1993, Ownership and Control: Rethinking Corporate Governance for the Twenty-first Century, 1995; editor: The Deal Decade: What Takeovers and Leveraged Buyouts Mean for Corporate Governance, 1993, Wealth Creation and Wealth Sharing: A Colloquium on Corporate Governance and Investments in Human Capital, 1996, Employees' Role in Corporate Governance, 1999, The New Relationship Human Capital in the American Corporation, 1999; contbr. numerous articles to profl. jours. Vol. Big Sisters Washington Met. Area, 1989-92; organizer neighborhood watch group, Washington, 1990; mem. bd. advisors Ctr. for Cmty. Interest, 1993-98. Univ. fellow Yale U., 1983-86, Leo Model fellow Brookings Instn., 1987-88; rsch. grantee Boston U. Mfrs. Roundtable, 1990, Columbia U. Instnl. Investor Project, 1994, Alfred P. Sloan Found., 1995, 96. Mem. Am. Econ. Assn., Am. Law Econs. Assn. Avocations: ballet, spelunking, cooking. Office: Brookings Instn 1775 Massachusetts Ave NW Washington DC 20036-2188

BLAIR, MARGARET WHITMAN, writer, researcher; b. Chgo., Apr. 25, 1951; d. Morton Robert and Frances (Pornes) Whitman; m. Robert Morris Blair, July 30, 1978; children: Matthew, David. BA, Am. U., 1973, MA, 1979. Tchr. English Japan, 1973-74, Peace Corps, Thailand, 1975-77; adminstrv. asst. LWV, Washington, 1977-78; journalist Bus. Internat., Washington, 1980-82; journalist, editor Bur. Nat. Affairs, Washington, 1982-84; writer, trade specialist Am.-Israel Pub. Affairs Com., Washington, 1984-85; journalist, editor Washington Tariff & Trade Letter, Rockville, Md., 1986-88; freelance writer Rockville, 1988—; lectr. writing hist. fiction Smithsonian. Author: (children's book) Brothers at War, 1997, House of Spies, 1999, (monographs) Israel's Agricultural Achievements, 1987, U.S.-Israel Free Trade Area, 1984; host, co-prodr.: (TV show) Out of the Past, 1995—; contbr. articles to profl. jours. Vol. PTA, Rockville, 1996—. Recipient Excellence in reporting series Nat. Press Club, 1987. Mem. Washington Ind. Writers (chmn. screenwriters group 1996-97, bd. dirs.), Golden Radio Buffs of Md. (hon.). Jewish. Office: White Mane Pub PO Box 152 Shippensburg PA 17257-0152

BLAIR, PATRICIA WOHLGEMUTH, economics writer; b. N.Y.C., Nov. 30, 1929; m. James P. Blair, Aug. 13, 1964; children: David A., Matthew W. BA with honors, Wellesley Coll., 1950; MA, Haverford Coll., 1952. Officer U.S. Agy. Internat. Devel., New Delhi, 1953-55, 63-64; editor Carnegie Endowment for Internat. Peace, N.Y.C., 1956-63, Devel. Digest, Nat. Planning Assn., Washington, 1965-68; staff assoc. Commn. on Internat. Devel., World Bank, Washington, 1969-70; ind. cons., writer, editor, 1970—. Editor: Health Needs of the World's Poor Women, 1980; contbr. articles to profl. publs. Mem. adv. com. Unitarian-Universalist Holdeen India Fund, Washington, 1984—; bd. dirs. Equity Policy Ctr., Washington, 1980-85. Mem. Soc. Internat. Devel. (internat. governing coun. 1975-79), Assn. Women in Devel., Asia Soc., UN Assn. Home and Office: 27 Washington St Middlebury VT 05753-1214

BLAIR, PHYLLIS E., artist, sculptor, illustrator; b. N.Y.C., Oct. 5, 1922; d. Franz Joseph and Marian Jane (Burke) Emmerich; m. Thomas Slingluff Blair, Sept., 17, 1946; children: Joan Dix, George Dike, Hadden Slingluff. Student, Skidmore Coll., 1940-42, Art Students League, 1945, Westminster Coll., 1970-72, Bennington Coll., 1989. Asst. art dept. Skidmore Coll., Saratoga Springs, N.Y., 1940-42; art illustrator & engring. draftsman GE, Schenectady, N.Y., 1942-44, Bell Labs., N.Y.C., 1944-46; elem tchr. Clinton, Tenn., 1946-47. One-woman shows include Hoyt Inst. Fine Arts, New Castle, Pa., 1971, 93, Butler Inst. Am. Art, Youngstown, Ohio, 1982, Westminster Coll., New Wilmington, Pa., 1983, Butler Inst. Am. Art, Salem, Ohio, 1994. Art curator Human Svcs. Ctr., New Castle, 1968-89, Jameson Meml. Hosp., 1978—, Almira Home, New Castle, 1990; founding mem. Nat. Mus. of Women in the Arts, Washington. Recipient Benjamin Rush award Pa. Med. Soc., 1991. Mem. Hoyt Inst. Fine Arts (chair art com. & permanent collection 1967—, trustee 1967—, Blair Sculpture Walkway named in her honor 1996), Am. Heart Assn. (Disting. Svc. award 1978). Avocations: golf, painting, sculpting. Summer Home: 2906 Ola Plank Rd New Castle PA 16105

BLAIR, REBECCA SUE, English educator, lay minister; b. Terre Haute, Ind., Mar. 26, 1958; d. Albert Eldon and Genevieve Virginia (Smith) B.; m. Richard Volle Van Rheeden, May 27, 1989. BA in English magna cum laud, U. Indpls., 1980; MA in Medieval Lit. with honors, U. Ill., Springfield, 1982; MA, Ind. U., 1986, PhD, 1988. Grad. asst. U. Ill., Springfield, 1980-82; dir. English language tng. Ind. U., Bloomington, 1982-83, assoc. instr., 1982-88; assoc. prof., chmn. dept. English Westminster Coll., Fulton, Mo., 1989—; dir. writing assessment Westminster Coll., Fulton, 1989—; vis. prof. Webster U., St. Louis, Mo., 1988-89; writing assessment cons. Pepperdine U., Malibu, Calif., 1995, numerous colleges and univs., 1989—; mem. exec. com. of the faculty Westminster Coll.; mem. Assessment Com., College-Wide Budget Com., Profl. Stds. Com., Pers. Com., Dean's Cabinet Coun. of Chairs and Dirs., Edn. Task Force, Task Force to Reorganize the Acad. Area, Enrollment Svcs. Task Force; women's studies rep. Mid-Mo. Am. Coun. of Univs.; faculty sponsor Alpha Chi Scholastic Hon. Soc.; faculty organizer awareness of rape/domestic violence Take Back the Night Rally. Author: The Other Woman: Women Authors and Cultural Stereotypes in American Literature, 1988; author conf. papers, articles; presenter workshops, seminars; spkr. in field. Bd. dirs. Am. Cancer Soc., Callaway County, Mo., 1989-92; mem. pastor nominating com. First Presbyterian Ch., Fulton, Mo., 1990-91, elder, 1990—, session mem., elected mem., 1990-93, 97-2000, chmn. nominating com., 1993-94, chmn. music search com., 1994-95; pulpit supply Mo. Union Presbytery, 1995—, mem. com. on ministry, 1997-2000, stated clk., 1997—; mem. Greater Mo. Focus on Leadership, 1992; vol. Habitat for Humanity, Fulton, 1993—; bd. dirs., founding mem. Coalition Against Rape and Domestic Violence, Fulton, 1995-97; bd. dirs. Friends of the Libr., Fulton, 1995-98, pres., 1997-98; sec. Fulton Art League, 1996—. Named Outstanding Faculty Mem., Westminster Coll., Fulton, 1991-92, Panhellenic Faculty Mem. of Year, Westminster Coll., 1996-97. Mem. Nat. Coun. for Rsch. on Women, Nat. Coun. Tchrs. of English, Am. Studies Assn., Midwest Modern Lang. Assn., Modern Lang. Assn., Writing Prog. Adminstrs., Coll. Composition and Comm., Fulton C. of C. (vol. 1992-96), Kiwanis (bd. dirs. 1990—, founder Circle K Club 1994, v.p. 1995-96, pres.-elect 1996-97, pres. 1997-98). Presbyterian. Avocations: gourmet cooking, reading, trains, writing. Home: 711 Jefferson St Fulton MO 65251-1878 Office: Westminster Coll 501 Westminster Ave Fulton MO 65251-1230

BLAIR, RICHARD BRYSON, lawyer; b. Athens, Ohio, Oct. 1, 1945; s. Richard Holmes and Doris Ruth Blair; m. Ellen A. Riehl, Aug. 24, 1968; children: Heather Ann, Heidi Lynn, Richard Holmes II, Molly Jane. BA, Franklin and Marshall Coll., 1967; JD, Ohio Northern U., 1970. Bar: Ohio 1970, U.S. Dist. Ct. (no. dist.) Ohio 1972. Assoc. Roth and Stephens, Youngstown, Ohio, 1970-75; ptnr. Roth and Stephens, Youngstown, 1976-77; ptnr., v.p. Roth, Stephens, Blair and Co. LPA, Youngstown, 1977—, Roth, Blair, Roberts, Strasfeld & Lodge, LPA, Youngstown. Bd. dirs. Greater Youngstown Coalition of Christians, 1994-98, co-chmn., 1996-98; trustee, mem. bd. edn. Eagle Hts. Acad. Mem. Ohio Bar Assn., Mahoning County Bar Assn., Internat. Assn. Ins. Counsel, Ohio Assn. Civil Trial Attys., Def. Rsch. Inst., Nat. Assn. R.R. Trial Counsel. Avocations: family, church activities, golf, sailing, jogging. Home: 253 Wildwood Dr Youngstown OH 44512-3340 Office: Roth Blair Roberts Strasfeld & Lodg LPA 1100 Bank 1 Bldg Youngstown OH 44503

BLAIR, ROBERT, animal science administrator, educator, researcher; b. Beith, Ayrshire, Scotland, May 29, 1933; s. Samuel and Mary (McBeth) B.; m. Moreen McGhie, Apr. 5, 1958; children—Rosalind M.J., Robert S. B.Sc., U. Glasgow, 1956; Ph.D., U. Aberdeen, 1960; D.Sc., U. Sask., 1983. Prin. sci. officer Agrl. Research Council, Edinburgh, Scotland, 1966-75; dir. nutrition Swift Can. Co. Ltd., Toronto, Ont., Can., 1976-78; mem. faculty U. Sask., Saskatoon, Can., 1978-84, prof. animal sci., 1984; prof. animal sci. U. B.C., Vancouver, Can., 1984-98, head dept., 1984-91, prof. emeritus, 1998—. mem. subcom. on vitamin tolerance NRC, Washington, 1984-87; cons. life scis. office Fedn. Am. Socs. Exptl. Biology, Bethesda, Md. Co-editor in chief: Animal Feed Science and Technology, Amsterdam, Netherlands; Contbr. chpts. to books, articles to profl. jours. Decorated Knight Lufsensic Ursinius Order (The Netherlands). Fellow Agrl. Inst. Can.; mem. World Assn. Animal Prodn. (pres. 1988-93), Nutrition Soc. U.K., Nutrition Soc. Can., Am. Inst. Nutrition, Am. Soc. Animal Sci., Can. Soc. Animal Sci. (pres. western br. 1985-87). Home: 4384 Quesnel Dr, Vancouver, BC Canada V6L 2X6 Office: U BC Dept Animal Sci, 2357 Main Mall Ste 248, Vancouver, BC Canada V6T 1Z4

BLAIR, ROBERT ALLEN, business executive, lawyer; b. Suffolk, Va., June 25, 1946; s. Thomas Francis Jr. and Ossie (Southern) B.; m. Linda Britt, Dec. 27, 1970; children: Robert Allen II, Thomas Edward. BA in Math., Coll. William and Mary, 1968; JD, U. Va., 1973. Bar: Mass. 1974, U.S. Dist. Ct. Mass. 1974, U.S. Ct. Appeals (D.C. cir.) 1976, U.S. Dist. Ct. D.C. 1980. Assoc. Goodwin, Procter & Hoar, Boston, 1973-74; assoc. Surrey & Morse, Washington, 1974-78, ptnr., 1979-81; mng. ptnr. Anderson, Hibey & Blair, Washington, 1981-95; ptnr., chair govt. practice group Manatt, Phelps & Phillips, 1995-99; co-chmn., gen. counsel GlobalOptions, LLC, Washington, 1999—; dir. Palmer Tech. Services, Inc., Washington, 1983-93. Mem. editorial bd. Law Rev. U. Va., 1971-73. Chmn. bd. Inst. on Terrorism and Subnat. Conflict, Washington, 1982-95; co-counsel Citizens for Dem. Alternatives in 1980, Washington, 1979-81; mem. adv. panel on fgn. policy, def. and arms control Dem. Nat. Com., Washington, 1982-85; mem. drafting team for fgn. policy, def. and arms control issue workshop Dem. Nat. Conf., Phila., 1982, mem. bus. coun., 1988-90, 94—, mng. trustee, 1994-95; mem. Senate Dem. Roundtable, Washington, 1983—; mem. Senate Dem. Leadership Circle, Washington, 1983—; vice chmn. Potomac Group, Washington, 1983-84, chmn., 1984-85; mem. adv. council Dem. Platform Com., Washington, 1984; spl. counsel 1984 Dem. Nat. Conv., San Francisco, 1984; spl. counsel to nat. fin. chmn. Dem. Nat. Com., Washington, 1984-85, mem. fin. bd. dirs., 1983-85, 88; mem. Nat. Dem. Club, Senate Dem. Majority Trust, 1992—; vice chmn. Washington Fgn. Affairs Soc., 1984-87; mem. Gov.'s Econ. Adv. Council, Va., 1986-94; commr. Va. Port Authority, Commonwealth Va., 1991-96, vice chmn. finance/planning com., 1992-94, chmn., 1994-96; chmn. S Corp. Assn., Washington 1996—, chmn. reform project, 1993-96; advisory bd. Thomas Jefferson Program Pub. Policy William and Mary, 1996—; bd. dirs. Everybody Wins, 1997—, Youth Leadership Inst., Washington, 1984-86. Named to Outstanding Young Men Am., U.S. Jaycees, 1976. Mem. ABA, Univ. Club (Washington). Home: 4936 Rodman St NW Washington DC 20016-3239 Office: GlobalOptions LLC 1615 L St NW Ste 1350 Washington DC 20036

BLAIR, ROBERT C., federal judge. Judge Hawaii Dist. Ct. (1st cir.), Honolulu. Office: Kauikeaouli Hale 11th Fl 1111 Alakea St Honolulu HI 96813-2801

BLAIR, ROBERT CARY, insurance company executive. BS, Butler U., Indpls., 1961. From mgmt. chmn. and trainee to dir., CEO Westfield Cos., 1961—. Office: Westfield Cos 1 Park Cir Westfield Center OH 44251

BLAIR, ROBERT NOEL, artist; b. Buffalo, Aug. 12, 1912; s. Charles Francis and Grace Ethylin (McGonegal) B.; m. Jeannette Kenney, Aug. 8, 1943; children: Jeanne Elizabeth (dec.), David Francis, Bruce Allen. Student, Albright Art Sch., 1931, Sch. Mus. Fine Arts, 1931-33, Art Inst. Buffalo, 1937, U. Buffalo, 1951. Painted Western N.Y., No. Vt. subjects, 1933-43; instr. Art. Inst. Buffalo, 1939-42, dir., 1945-49; instr. Buffalo Mus. Sci., 1939-42, U. Buffalo, 1952. Contbg. author: Water Colorists at Work, 1972; contbr. painting of Vt. in color to Vermont Life Mag., spring 1988, watercolor to Met. Mus. books, 1991; one-man shows Buffalo, 1937-41, 45, 53, N.Y.C., 1938-41, 53, 62, Albright Art Gallery, Buffalo, 1942, 54-55, U. Ala., 1944, others, paintings exhibited Internat. Water Color Exhibit. Bklyn., Art Inst., Chgo., exhbns. Nat. Gallery, Washington, Fleming Mus., Vt., State U. Coll., Buffalo, 1966, Burchfield Art Ctr., State U. Coll., Buffalo, 1985, others; painter murals, Fifth area Chapel, Fort McClellan, Ala., 1943, Post Hosp., 1944, Bethlehem Steel Plant, Lackawanna, 1947, Olean (N.Y.) House, Unitarian Ch., East Aurora, N.Y., Lake View Hotel, Lake View, New York, works in permanent collection, Nat. Mus. History and Art, Taiwan, Niagara U., Colgate U., Met. Mus., N.Y.C., Munson Williams Proctor Inst., Utica, Dubuque and Bryn Mawr art assos., Butler Art Inst., Ford Motor Co., U. State N.Y., 100 paintings and drawings of World War II in Burchfield Art Ctr., SUNY, Buffalo, 1986; 42 paintings and 2 drawings of the Battle of the Bulge and Army glider action included in U.S. Army art collection. Served with AUS, 1942-45. Awarded water color prize Western N.Y. exhibit, 1940-44, 1947-51; Guggenheim fellow, 1946-51; Silver and Gold medals Buffalo Soc. Artists, 1947, 50; Ala. Water Color Soc., 1947; water color prize Art Inst. Chgo., 1948; watercolor prize N.Y. State Exhbn., 1950; Waugh prize Buffalo Soc. Artists Ann., 1951, 54; gold medal, 1955, 57-68; silver medal, 1956, 62, 69; water color prize 2d Spring Art Exhibit, Buffalo, 1957; 1st watercolor prize Youngstown (Ohio) Nat., 1953; 1st watercolor prize Western N.Y. Exhbn., 1963; 1st watercolor prize Chautauqua Nat. Exhibit, 1963; watercolor prize Balt. Water Color Club, 1954; Buffalo Soc. Artists ann. painting prize, 1958, 62-65, 70; watercolor prize, 1959; gold medal, 1972; Silvermine Guild watercolor prize, 1958; drawing prize Indsl. Niagara Art Exhbn.; 1st painting prize Cooperstown N.Y. Nat. Exhbn., 1970, water color prize, 1989; 1st Watercolor prize White Mountain Art Festival, Sholow, Ariz., 1970; watercolor prize Chautauqua Nat. Exhbn., 1972; Watercolor award West Tex. Watercolor Nat., 1985 others. Mem. Am. Water Color Soc., Patteran Soc., Buffalo Soc. Artists. *Over 48 years I have been a painter. Each time I paint I try to do better. So in a way each time is more difficult—a greater challenge. Sometimes it seems one is starting all over again with the latest painting. To be an artist you must be born again, every day.*

BLAIR, ROBIN ELISE FARBMAN, financial and management consultant, accountant; b. Detroit, Jan. 22, 1951; d. Aaron A. and Marie A. (Prager) Farbman; m. Charles E. Manley, 1996. B.A., Mich. State U., 1974; postgrad. Wayne State U., 1976, Pace U., 1985, New Sch. for Social Rsch., 1992-93. Drama critic Lansing State Jour., Mich., 1974; asst. editor Gale Research Co., Detroit, 1974-77; copy chief Ballantine Books, Random House, N.Y.C., 1977-79; fin. mgr. and adminstr. Ark Restaurants Corp., N.Y.C., 1980-83; owner, pres., acct., cons., Robin Blair Acctg. Services, N.Y.C., 1984—. Mem. NAFE, AAUW, N.Y. SBA. Democrat. Unitarian. Avocations: writing; piano. Address: 59 W 76th St New York NY 10023-1543

BLAIR, SANDRA JEAN, author, publisher; b. Denver, Apr. 14, 1938; d. Harold Eugene Blair and Elizabeth Mae (Alexander) Blair Dodd. Student, Phoenix Coll., 1969. Tchr. Arthur Murray Studio, Denver, 1956-57; supr. Dales Dance studio, Denver, 1958-60; with New Eng. Advt.-Dow, Denver, 1960-65; owner, mgr. Copper Penny Bar, Phoenix, 1965-71; tchr., salesperson Bobby Ball Agy., Phoenix, 1976-78; salesperson KMOG Radio, Payson, Ariz., 1982-84; owner Inspired Pub. Co., Payson, 1994—. Author/editor: It Is Time to Try Paradise, 1995. Mem. Payson Lightworker Assn., Payson Area Writers Soc. (sec.-treas. 1993-96), Ariz. Psychic Alliance, Payson Love Corp., Payson Tennis Club (pres. 1984-92). Avocations: golf, sailing, scuba diving, tennis, pool.

BLAIR, SLOAN BLACKMON, lawyer; b. Groesbeck, Tex., Nov. 3, 1929; s. Sloan and Rosamond (Blackmon) B.; m. Eleanor Cuthrell, Nov. 17, 1953; children: Deborah, Mary Emily. BA, U. Tex., 1951, LLB, 1953. Bar: Tex., U.S. Dist. Ct. (no. dist.) Tex., U.S. Ct. Appeals (5th cir.), U.S. Supreme Ct. Assoc. Cantey, Hanger, Johnson, Scarborough & Gooch, Ft. Worth, 1956-58; atty. Sinclair Refining Co., Chgo., 1958-60; assoc. Cantey, Hanger et al., Ft. Worth, 1960-62; ptnr. Cantey & Hanger, Ft. Worth, 1962—. Contbr. case notes to Tex. Law Rev. Bd. dirs. Goodwill Industries Ft. Worth, 1960's; mem. Ft. Worth Arts Coun., Tex. Heritage, Inc., Ft. Worth, State Bar Grievance Com., Ft. Worth, mid. 1960's, Tex. Bd. Law Examiners, Austin, 1977-83. Lt. (j.g.) USNR, 1953-56. Fellow Tex. Bar Found.; mem. ABA, Tex. Bar Assn., Tarrant County Bar Assn. (bd. dirs. 1970's), Phi Delta Phi. Republican. Methodist. Avocations: reading, history, travel. Office: Cantey & Hanger 801 Cherry St Ste 2100 Fort Worth TX 76102-6898

BLAIR, THOMAS DELANO, inspector general Smithsonian Institution; b. Plum Branch, S.C., Apr. 8, 1946; s. Richard and Evangeline B.; m. Frances V. Veney, 1973; children: Jayson T., Todd J. BS in Bus. Adminstrn., S.C. State Coll., 1967; MBA, U. Md., 1978. CPA, Md., Cert. Internal Auditor. Asst. bank examiner FDIC, Balt., 1967, 71; auditor U.S. Army Audit Agy., Linthieum Hghts., Md., 1971-72, Dept. Defense, Arlington, Va., 1973-74; supr. mgmt. analyst U.S. Gen. Acctg. Office, Washington, 1974-79; dir. office of inspector gen. Johnson Space Ctr. Nat. Aero. and Space Adminstrn., Goddard Space Fligt Ctr., Washington, Greenbelt, Md., 1979-84; regional mgr. Office of Inspector Gen., U.S. Dept. Vet. Affairs, Atlanta, 1984-90; inspector gen. Smithsonian Instn., Washington, 1990—. Mem. AICPA, Assn. Govt. Accts., Fed. Investigators Assn., Inst. Internal Auditors. Office: Smithsonian Instn 955 L'Enfant Pla Ste 7600 Washington DC 20560-0905

BLAIR, TIMOTHY DANIEL, quality assurance specialist; b. Balt., Aug. 16, 1963; s. Francis Daniel and Mary Catherine (Grimm) B.; m. Catherine Elizabeth Park, Jan. 25, 1984; children: Daniel Park, Samantha Leigh, Mary Catherine Bahme. Grad., Catonsville Sr. H.S., Balt., 1982. Mgr. Pizza Hut of Md., Inc., Howard County, 1986, Sorrento's West, Balt., 1987-89, Marriott Family Restaurants, Washington, 1989-91; specialist Alpharma USPD, Balt., 1991—. Sec. Drexelwoods Homeowners Assn., Balt., 1987-98. Republican. Roman Catholic. Avocations: cooking, fishing, reading, computers. E-mail: CrashTB@aol.com. Office: Alpharma USPD 7205 Windsor Blvd Baltimore MD 21244-2654

BLAIR, VIRGINIA ANN, public relations executive; b. Kansas City, Mo., Dec. 20, 1925; d. Paul Lowe and Lou Etta (Cooley) Smith; m. James Leon Grant, Sept. 3, 1943 (dec. July 1944); m. Warden Tannahill Blair, Jr., Nov. 7, 1947; children: Janet, Warden Tannahill, III. BS in Speech, Northwestern U., 1948. Free-lance writer, Chgo., 1959-69; writer, editor Smith, Bucklin & Assocs., Inc., Chgo., 1969-72, account mgr., 1972-79, account supr., 1979-80, dir. pub. relations, 1980-85; pres. GB Pub. Rels., 1985—; judge U.S. Indsl. Film Festival, 1974, 75; instr. Writer's Workshop, Evanston, Ill., 1978; dir. Northwestern U. Libr. Coun., 1978-91, dir. alumnae bd., 1986—, John Evans Club bd., 1990-98. Emmy nominee Nat. Acad. TV Arts & Scis., 1963; recipient Service award Northwestern U., 1978, Creative Excellence award U.S. Indsl. Film Festival, 1976, Gold Leaf merit cert. Family Circle mag. and Food Coun. Am., 1977, Cert. of Excellence for superior achievement in media rels. N.Am. Precis Syndicate, 1997. Mem. Pub. Rels. Soc. Am. (counselors acad.), Am. Advt. Fedn. (lt. gov. Ill. 6th dist.), Women's Advt. Club Chgo. (pres.), Publicity Club Chgo., Nat. Acad. TV Arts & Scis., John Evans Club (bd. dirs.), Woman's Club Evanston (pres.), Zeta Phi Eta (Svc. award 1978, 93), Alpha Gamma Delta, Philanthropic and Ednl. Orgn. (Ill. chpt. pres.. dist. pres.). Author dramas (produced on CBS): Jeanne D'Arc: The Trial, 1961; Cordon of Fear, 1961; Reflection, 1961; If I Should Die, 1963; 3-act children's play: Children of Courage, 1967. Home and Office: 463 Highcrest Dr Wilmette IL 60091-2357

BLAIR, WARREN EMERSON, retired federal judge; b. Chgo., June 23, 1916; s. Henry Allan and Mae Idella (Spratt) B.; m. Madeline Mary Sheehan, 1947 (dec. 1997). J.D., DePaul U., 1940; M.B.A., George Washington U., 1958. Bar: Ill. bar 1940, Republic of Korea bar 1951, U.S. Supreme Ct. bar 1954, Ohio bar 1954, N.Y. State bar 1964. Mem. firm Blair, Chiara & Blair, Chgo., 1940-42; atty. SEC, Cleve., 1947-54; chief enforcement atty. trading and exchanges div. SEC, Washington, 1954-60; asst. regional adminstr. SEC, N.Y.C., 1960-64; adminstrv. law judge SEC, Washington, 1964-70; chief adminstrv. law judge SEC, 1970-94; mem. Adminstrv. Conf. U.S., 1972-74. Served to 1st lt. U.S. Army, 1942-46; to capt. 1950-52, ETO, Korea. Decorated Silver Star, Purple Heart with oak leaf cluster. Mem. ABA, Fed. Bar Assn., Am. Judicature Soc., Fed. Adminstrv. Law Judges Conf., Pi Gamma Mu, Delta Kappa Epsilon. Home: 2440 Virginia Ave NW Washington DC 20037

BLAIR, WAYNE M, lawyer; b. Spokane, Washington, Oct. 17, 1942. BS in Elec. Engr., U. Washington, 1965, JD, 1968. Bar: Wash. 1968. Asst. corp. counsel City of Seattle, 1968. With USAF, 1968-72. Recipient Helen M. Geisness award, 1987. Mem. ABA, Seattle-King County Bar Assn. (trustee 1981-83, pres. 1987-88), Washington State Bar Assn. (pres.), Am. Judicature Soc., Phi Delta Phi. Office: Seattle-King County Bar Assn 320 Central Bldg Seattle WA 98104 also: 5800 Columbia Ctr 701 5th Ave Seattle WA 98104-7016*

BLAIR, WILLIAM DRAPER, JR., conservationist; b. Charlotte, N.C., May 3, 1927; s. William D. and Mary-Eula (Mason) B.; m. Jane Fraser Coleman, June 25, 1949; children—Jane C. Blair Gelston, Elizabeth Blair Jones. BA, Princeton U., 1949. Successively reporter, Korean war corr., European corr. Balt. Sunpapers, 1949-53; successively asst. editor, corr., London, chief Bonn (Germany) bur., chief Paris bur. Newsweek mag., 1953-59; with State Dept., Washington, 1959-62, dir. Office Media Services, 1962-70, dep. asst. sec. for pub. affairs, 1970-80; pres. The Nature Conservancy, 1980-87; mem. Nat. Wetlands Policy Forum, 1987-88. Author: Katharine Ordway: The Lady Who Saved the Prairies, 1989. Served with USMCR, 1945-46. Recipient Meritorious Honor award Dept. State, 1964, Superior Honor award, 1967, Disting. Honor award, 1980, Paul Bartsch award Audubon Naturalist Soc., 1987, Chevron Conservation award, 1987, Disting. Svc. award Am. Forestry Assn., 1989. Mem. The Nature Conservancy (gov. 1972-80, chmn. bd. govs. 1975-77, trustee Maine chpt. 1987-94, Oak Leaf award 1988), Audubon Naturalist Soc. Ctrl. Atlantic States (dir. 1966-73, pres. 1968-70), Metropolitan Club, 1925 F St Club, Chevy Chase Club (Washington). Address: 5006 Warren St NW Washington DC 20016-4370

BLAIR, WILLIAM GRANGER, retired newspaperman; b. Chgo., Nov. 17, 1925; s. William Mitchell and Martha (Granger) B.; m. Sue Cunningham, Apr. 19, 1952 (div.); children: Robert, Bruce (dec.), Laura; m. Ellen Lopin, Sept. 29, 1970. AB in English cum laude, Princeton U., 1950. Reporter Kansas City (Mo.) Star, 1950-52; mem. staff N.Y. Times, 1953-90; fgn. corr., Paris, 1956-62, London, 1965-67, bur. chief, Jerusalem, 1962-65, mgr. employee communications, 1968, mgr. pub. relations, 1969-70, dir. pub. relations, 1970-73, broadcast corr., 1973-79, met. reporter, 1980-90. Served with USMCR, 1943-46, PTO. Mem. reporting team whose news coverage of regional flood helped to earn Pulitzer award for The Kansas City Star, 1952; corr. in France and Algeria when N.Y. Times won 1st Pulitzer prize awarded specifically to a fgn. news staff for internat. reporting, 1958. Mem. Ivy Club. Home: 320 E 52nd St New York NY 10022-6708

BLAIR, WILLIAM MCCORMICK, JR., lawyer; b. Chgo., Oct. 24, 1916; s. William McCormick and Helen (Bowen) B.; m. Catherine Gerlach, Sept. 9, 1961; 1 son, William McCormick III. A.B., Stanford U., 1940; LL.B., U. Va., 1947. Bar: Ill. 1947, D.C. 1972. Assoc. firm Wilson & McIlvaine, Chgo., 1947-50; adminstrv. asst. to Gov. Adlai E. Stevenson of Ill., 1950-52; ptnr. firm Stevenson, Rifkind & Wirtz, Chgo., 1955-61, Paul, Weiss, Rifkind, Wharton & Garrison, N.Y.C., 1957-61; U.S. ambassador to Denmark, 1961-64, to Philippines, 1964-67; gen. dir. John F. Kennedy Ctr., 1968-72; ptnr. firm Surrey & Morse, Washington, 1978-84; of counsel Surrey & Morse, 1984-86. Bd. dirs. Am.-Scandinavian Found., N.Y.C.; v.p. bd. dirs. Albert and Mary Lasker Found., N.Y.C., 1968-98. Capt. USAAF, 1942-46. Decorated Bronze Star U.S.; officer Order of Crown, Belgium; Order of Sikatuna, Philippines; comdr. cross Order of Dannebrog 1st class, Denmark). Mem. Am. Coun. Ambs. (vice chmn., pres. 1985-89), Soc. Animal Protective Legis. (trustee), Phi Delta Phi. Office: 2510 Foxhall Rd NW Washington DC 20007-1123

BLAIS, HELEN CHRISTINE, daycare operator; b. Augusta, Maine, Mar. 7, 1937; d. Henry and Wanda Tuttle; m. Alfred J. Taylor, July 2, 1955 (dec. Jan. 1996); children: Maryann Chapman, David E. Taylor, Cathy Taylor (dec.), Debbie M. Stickney; m. Maurice P. Blais, Dec. 28, 1996. Grad. h.s., Augusta. Registered daycare operator; notary public. Sec. auto repair bus. Chelsea, Maine, 1975-95; owner, operator Taylor's Daycare, Chelsea, 1995—; founder Chelsea CANE, 1992. Author: Chelsea, Maine History Vol. I, Vol. II, 1996. CPR instr., Chelsea; bd. dirs. Chelsea Planning Bd.; com. mem. 911 Enhancement Com., Chelsea, Chelsea Budget Com.; mem. Chelsea Homecoming Assn. Recipient Cert. of Honor, Town of Chelsea, 1995. Mem. East Kennebec Pomona Grange (#25), Chelsea Sorbornate Grange (#215, chaplain). Roman Catholic. Avocations: crocheting, knitting, sewing, cooking, research. Home: Outer Hosp St RR 2 Box 116 Augusta ME 04330-9607

BLAIS, ROBERT HOWARD, lawyer; b. Muskegon, Mich., May 14, 1955. BA with high honors, Mich. State U., 1977; JD cum laude, U. Notre Dame, 1980. Ptnr. Bogle & Gates, Seattle, 1988-93; shareholder Gores & Blais, Seattle, 1993—; adj. prof. estate and tax planning Seattle U., 1982-83; chairperson Wash. State U. Planned Giving Adv. Bd., 1989-96. Mem. ABA, Wash. State Bar Assn. (real property, probate and trust coun. 1987-88), , Seattle-King County Bar Assn., Estate Planning Coun. Seattle (pres. 1996-

97), Am. Coll. Trust and Estate Counsel. Office: Gores & Blais 1420 5th Ave Ste 2600 Seattle WA 98101-1357

BLAIS, ROGER NATHANIEL, physics educator; b. Duluth, Minn., Oct. 3, 1944; s. Eusebe Joseph and Edith Seldina (Anderson) B.; m. Mary Louise Leclerc, Aug. 2, 1971; children: Christopher Edward, Laura Louise. BA in Physics and French Lit., U. Minn., 1966; PhD in Physics, U. Okla., 1971; cert. in computer programming, Tulsa Jr. Coll., 1981; cert. in bus., UCLA, 1986. Registered profl. engr., Okla. Instr. physics Westark C.C., Ft. Smith, Ark., 1971-72; asst. prof. physics and geophys. scis Old Dominion U., Norfolk, Va., 1972-77; asst. prof. engring. physics U. Tulsa, 1977-81, assoc. prof., 1981-98, prof., 1998—; assoc. dir. Tulsa U. Artificial Lift Projects, 1983—, chmn. physics, 1986-88, vice-provost, 1989-92, provost, v.p. acad. affairs, 1998—. Contbr. articles to profl. jours. Fellow Instrument Soc. Am. (dir. test measurement divsn. 1995-97); mem. AAAS, AAUP, NSPE, Am. Phys. Soc., Am. Geophys. Union, Soc. Petroleum Engrs., Am. Assn. Physics Tchrs., Am. Soc. Engring. Edn., N.Y. Acad. Scis., Iron Wedge Soc., Phi Beta Kappa, Sigma Xi, Sigma Pi Sigma, Tau Beta Pi, Phi Kappa Phi. Home: 5348 E 30th Pl Tulsa OK 74114-6314 Office: U Tulsa Office of Provost 600 S College Ave Tulsa OK 74104-3126

BLAISDELL, CHARMARIE JENKINS, historian, educator; b. Phila., Jan. 23, 1934; d. Edward Cope Jenkins and June Franklin (Blaisdell) Jenkins; m. Robert Howard Webb, Sept. 12, 1953 (div. Feb. 1974); children: Kristin Blaisdell Webb, Margaret Henderson Webb. BA, Boston U., 1955; MA, Tufts U., 1964, PhD, 1970. Asst. prof. Boston Coll., Chestnut Hill, Mass., 1970-71; asst. prof. history Northeastern U., Boston, 1971-72, assoc. prof., 1977—; bd. dirs. History Making Prodns., Boston, 1987—, pres., 1997—; bd. dirs. Boston Oral History Ctr., 1996—. Contbr. chpts. to books, articles to profl. jours. Cmty. mediator Marblehead (Mass.) Mediation Svcs., 1995—. Recipient award in Tchg. Excellence, Northeastern U., 1991, 99. Mem. Am. Hist. Assn., Sixteenth Century Studies Assn. (pres. 1975), New Eng. HJist. Assn. (exec. com.), Blaisdell Rsch. Assocs. (founder, prin.). Quaker. Avocations: community theater, sailing, skiing. Home: 70 Pleasant St Marblehead MA 01945-3346 Office: Northeastern U Dept History ME 249 Boston MA 02115

BLAISDELL, ELENA MARIE MARMO, artist, printer; b. N.Y.C., May 3, 1951; d. Albert John and Evelyn (Musto) Marmo; m. Mark John Blaisdell, Aug. 18, 1998; 1 child, Lisa Nicole. AA in Liberal Arts, Inverhills C.C., Inver Grove Heights, Minn., 1988; student, U. Minn., postgrad. Advt. artist Barbizon Corp., N.Y.C., 1968-71; greeting card artist Norcross Inc., N.Y.C., 1971-72; TV artist, promotion specialist Hubbard Broadcasting, Mpls., 1975-80; freelance media artist L.A., 1980-81; designer, artist Mills Enterprises, White Bear Lake, Minn., 1981-83; printer, quality control specialist Taylor Corp., Mankato, Minn., 1998—; calendar painting honorarium Glaxo-Wellcome, N.Y.C., 1999. Illustrator children's book: Once Upon A Time, 1995; contbr. art to Expressions, Art Buyers Guide, Nat. Art Internat. web gallery. Vol. spkr. on stroke recovery. Mem. Minn. Arts Bd., Very Spl. Arts. Roman Catholic. Avocations: knitting, crocheting, organ, mandolin, singing. Home: 6420 Carleda Way Inver Grove Heights MN 65076

BLAISING, CRAIG ALAN, religious studies educator; b. San Antonio, Sept. 28, 1949; s. Claude Lawrence and Mildred Helen (Craig) B.; m. Diane Sue Garrison, May 31, 1975; children: Emily Grace, Jonathan Craig. BS, U. Tex., 1971; ThM, Dallas Theol. Sem., 1976, ThD, 1979; PhD, U. Aberdeen, Scotland, 1988. Lic. to ministry So. Bapt. Conv., 1972. Adj. prof. dept. religion U. Tex., Arlington, 1978; asst. prof. systematic theology Dallas Theol. Sem., 1980-85, assoc. prof., 1985-89, acting dept. chmn., 1988-89, prof., 1989-95; prof. So. Bapt. Theol. Sem., 1995-96, Joseph Emerson Brown prof. Christian theology, 1996—, assoc. v.p. acad. adminstrn., 1999—. Co-author: Progressive Dispensationalism, 1993; co-editor: Dispensationalism, Israel and the Church: The Search for Definition, 1992; contbr.: Bible Knowledge Commentary, 1985, Evangelical Dictionary of Theology, 1985, Handbook of Evangelical Theology, 1993, Encyclopedia of Early Chritianity, 1997, Three Views on the Millennium and Beyond, 1999; contbr. articles to religious jours. Rotary Found. fellow U. Aberdeen, 1978-79. Mem. Evang. Theol. Soc. (regional pres. 1986-87), Dispensational Study Group (pres. 1988-90), Am. Acad. Religion, Soc. Bibl. Lit., N.Am. Patristic Soc., Soc. for Study of Ea. Orthodoxy and Evangelicism, Tau Beta Pi. Office: So Bapt Theol Sem 2825 Lexington Rd Louisville KY 40280-0001

BLAKE, ANN BETH, psychologist; b. Hibbing, Minn., Dec. 31, 1944; d. James Edward Foutz and Betty Helen (Blake) Smith; adopted d. Edmund Carl Drinkwitz; m. John Peter Hennes, June 10, 1978 (div. Nov. 1979). AA, Hibbing State Jr. Coll., 1964; PhB, U. N.D., 1966; MEd, U. Wash., 1978, PhD, 1983. Lic. psychologist, Wash. House staff Seattle Children's Home, 1966-67; caseworker, case reviewer Wash. Dept. Social and Health Svcs., Everett and Seattle, 1967-75; group and individual facilitator Human Alternatives N.W., Seattle, 1975-79, 84; teaching asst. in curriculum and instrn. U. Wash., 1978-80; contract counselor Luth. Social Svcs., 1982-84; counselor Highland Community Coll., Midway, Wash., 1984; therapist Thurston-Mason Community Mental Health Ctr., Olympia, Wash., 1984-87; asst. prof. psychology St. Martin's Coll., Lacey, Wash., 1987-90, pres. faculty, 1988-89; pvt. practice Olympia, 1987—; grad. field advisor Antioch Coll., Seattle, 1985-90, Vt. Coll., Montpelier, 1989-93, Union Grad. Sch., 1995—; part-time faculty Centralia Coll., 1993-95; program co-dir. City U., 1995-97; program coord. Antioch U., Seattle, 1997—, faculty coord. com., 1999—. Mem. APA, Deschutes Psychol. Assn. (treas. 1985-87), Jungian Psychotherapists Assn. (pres. 1998-99). Democrat. Avocations: biking, embroidery, meditation. Home: PO Box 1245 Olympia WA 98507-1245 Office: PO Box 1245 Olympia WA 98507-1245

BLAKE, BUD (JULIAN WATSON), cartoonist; b. Nutley, N.J., Feb. 13, 1918; s. George Wilbur and Hazel (Metcalfe) B.; m. Doris Gaskill, Jan. 4, 1941; children: Julian G., Mariana. Student, Nat. Acad. Design, 1935-36. Sketch artist, art dir., exec. art dir. Kudner Agy., N.Y.C., 1937-43, 46-54. Cartoonist: Ever Happen To You, syndicated by King Features; also free lance cartooning for various mags. and ads, 1954-65; cartoonist: syndicated comic strip Tiger, 1965—; Paperback cartoon books include Tiger, Tiger Turns On; others. Served with inf. AUS, 1943-46. Mem. Nat. Cartoonists Soc. (Best Humor Strip award 1971, 78), Newspaper Features Council. Home and Office: PO Box 146 Damariscotta ME 04543-0146

BLAKE, CATHERINE C., judge; b. Boston, July 27, 1950; d. John Ballard and Jean Place (Adams) B.; m. Frank Eisenberg, June 22, 1974; 3 children. BA magna cum laude, Radcliffe Coll., 1972; JD cum laude, Harvard Law Sch., 1975. Bar: Mass. 1975, Md. Ct. Appeals 1977, U.S. Ct. Appeals (4th cir.) 1977, U.S. Dist. Ct. Md. 1977, D.C. 1979. Assoc. Palmer & Dodge, Boston, 1975-77; asst. U.S. atty. Dist. of Md., Balt., 1977-83, first asst. U.S. atty., 1983-85, 86-87, U.S. atty. (court-appointed), 1985-86; U.S. magistrate judge U.S. Dist. Ct. Md., Balt., 1987-95, U.S. dist. ct. judge, 1995—. Mem. Fed. Bar Assn., Md. Bar Assn., Nat. Assn. of Women Judges, Fed. Judges' Assn. Office: US Courthouse 101 W Lombard St Ste 1034 Baltimore MD 21201-2603

BLAKE, D. STEVEN, lawyer; b. Saginaw, Mich., June 2, 1940. BA, Mich. State U., 1963; JD, U. Calif., Davis, 1971. Bar: Calif. 1972. Sr. ptnr. Downey, Brand, Seymour & Rohwer, Sacramento, 1971—; adj. prof. law U. Pacific, 1998—. Co-author: California Real Estate Finance and Construction Law, 1995. Mem. ABA (bus. law sect.), Am. Arbitration Assn. (arbitrator), State Bar Calif. (chair corp. com., sect., fin. instns. com., bus. law sect., panelist, presenter numerous seminars Calif. State Bar Continuing Edn. Bar 1981-91, co-chair corps. com. bus. law sect. 1997), Yolo County Bar Assn. Office: Downey Brand Seymour & Rohwer 555 Capitol Mall Ste 1050 Sacramento CA 95814-4601

BLAKE, DARLENE EVELYN, political worker, consultant, educator, author; b. Rockford, Iowa, Feb. 26, 1947; d. Forest Kenneth and Violet Evelyn (Fisher) Kuhlemeier; m. Joel Franklin Blake, May 1, 1975 (dec. Jan. 1989); 1 child, Alexander Joel. AA, North Iowa Area Community Coll., Mason City, 1967; BS, Mankato (Minn.) State Coll., 1969; MS, Mankato (Minn.) State U., 1975. Cert. profl. tchr., Iowa; registered art therapist. Tchr. Bishop Whipple Sch., Faribault, Minn., 1970-72; art therapist C.B. Wilson Ctr., Faribault, 1972-76, Sedgwick County Dept. Mental Health, Wichita, Kans., 1976-79; cons. Batten, Batten, Hudson & Swab, Des Moines, 1979-81; pres. J.F. Blake Co., Inc., Des Moines, 1990—; polit. cons. to Alexander Haig for Pres., 1987-88; mgmt. tng. specialist Comms. Data Svcs., Inc., Des Moines, 1988-90, exec. mgr. customer svc. spl. interest fulfillment div., 1990-92; mem. nat. adv. bd. Alexander Haig for Pres., 1987-88; cert. cons. assoc. Drake, Beam, Morin, Inc., Des Moines, 1993—; coord. staff devel. U. Iowa Hosps. and Clinics, Iowa City, 1998—. Exhibited in one-woman show at local libr., 1970. Mem. U.S. Selective Svc. Bd. 26 and 27, Polk County, Iowa, 1981-98; sustaining mem. Rep. Nat. Com.; Rep. cand. Polk County Treas., Des Moines, 1982; chmn. Polk County Rep. Party, 1985-88; commr. Des Moines Commn. Human Rights and Job Discrimination, 1984-89; mem. Martin Luther King Scholarship Com., 1986-88; mem. Iowa State Bd. Psychology Examiners, 1983-90; mem. 5th Dist. Jud. Nominating Commn., 1990-96, Iowa Supreme Ct. Jud. Nominating Commn., 1996—; mem. State Jud. Nominating Commn, 1996—; active Des Moines Sister Cities Commn., 1997-98. Mem. Am. Art Therapy Assn., Iowa Art Therapy Assn. (pres. elect 1984-85, founder), Des Moines Garden Club (pres. 1984-85), Polk County Rep. Women (pres. elect 1983-85). Lutheran. Avocations: sewing, gardening, fine arts, music, reading. Home and Office: 15 Woodland Hts NE Iowa City IA 52240-9136

BLAKE, EDWARD STEPHENS, secondary education educator; b. Rome, N.Y., June 8, 1948; s. James Stanley and Katherine Elizabeth (Stephens) B.; m. Kathleen Marie Leonard, Aug. 30, 1983; children: Devin Patrick, Cara Elizabeth. AA, Hudson Valley C.C., Troy, N.Y., 1968; BS, SUNY, Oswego, 1970; MS, SUNY, Cortland, 1976. Permanent cert. tchr., N.Y. Tchr. Whitesboro (N.Y.) Mid. Sch., 1970—. E-mail: eblake@whitesboro-middle.moric.org. Office: Whitesboro Mid Sch 75 Oriskany Blvd Whitesboro NY 13492

BLAKE, FRANK BURGAY, librarian, writer; b. N.Y.C., Feb. 10, 1924; s. Francis Gilman and Marguerite (Burgay) B.; m. Filomena Yolanda Ciaccio, Dec. 15, 1962; children: Anthony Francis, Robert Burgay. BS, U. Minn., 1947; BS in Med. Record Libr. Sci., St. Louis U., 1948; MS, NYU, 1951; diploma, Air U., 1960; postgrad., Cornell U., 1962. Staff U.S. Army Hosp., Ft. Ord, Calif., 1964-65; med. record libr. County of Tulare, Visalia, Calif., 1966-69, Winnebago (Wis.) Mental Health Inst., 1970-81; preceptor ind. study program in mental health adminstrn. U. Minn., 1977; exec. dir. Medica, Inc., Tulare, 1968-70; cons. med. record program evaln. Herzing Insts., Inc., Milw., 1971-73, Interboro Gen. Hosp., Bklyn., 1949-50; with Kings County Hosp. Ctr., Bklyn., 1949-54, Met. Hosp., N.Y., 1954-55, VA Hosp., N.Y.C., 1956-58, 2500th USAF Hosp., Mitchel AFB, Hempstead, N.Y., 1958-60, St. Francis Hosp., Bronx, N.Y., 1960-63, Rahway (N.J.) Hosp., 1963-64, Bur. Correctional Health Svcs., Madison, Wis., 1981-82, Clovis (Calif.) Meml. Hosp., 1969-70, and many others; mem. med. stenographer program, 1971-72; bd. advisers med. record technician program Moraine Park Tech. Inst., Fond du Lac, Wis., 1974-78, bd. dirs. Oshkosh Com. on Aging, 1988—; sec. Coalition Wis. Aging. Groups, 1990-92; mem. adj. faculty Fox Valley Technical Coll., Appleton, Wis., 1998. Author: Medical and Dental Capabilities at Correctional Institutions in Wisconsin, 1982, Medical Terminology Source Book, 1983, An Instructional Manual for the Problem Oriented Medical Record in Correctional Institutions, 1984; contbr. articles to profl. jours. Mem. AARP (pres. Winnebago chpg. 45, vice-chmn. Wis. state legistlative com. 1993-95, work force cons. 1991-93, Health Care Am. spkr. 1993-94, award for Health Care Am. Forums 1993-94, Leadership award 1994, Meritorious Svc. award 1995), Am. Assn. Med. Records Librs., AAAS, Coalition of Wis. Aging Groups (state sec. 1990), Am. Assn. Med. Records Librs., AAAS, Coalition of Wis. Aging Groups (state sec. 1990), Am. Pub. Health Assn., Am. Mgmt. Assn., Internat. Platform Assn., Northeastern Assn. Med. Record Librs. (v.p. 1970-71), Candlelight Club. Home: 2020 Wisconsin St Oshkosh WI 54901-2290 Office: PO Box 1581 Oshkosh WI 54902-1581

BLAKE, GEORGE ALAN, JR., non-profit association executive, consultant; b. Niles, Mich., Jan. 8, 1956; s. George Alan Blake and Inez Edna (Ewert) Brock; m. Kathryn Jean Sanders, Mar. 2, 1979 (div. Nov. 1985); m. Audrey Ann Paxton, June 30, 1986; children: Amanda Sue Blake, Alexander Xavier Blake. BS, So. Ill. U., 1983; MS, U. So. Calif., 1988; PhD in Mgmt., Brighton U., 1996. Process cons., GM; cert. psyc. technician, AAPT. Commd. USMC, 1974, advanced through grades to staff sgt., 1984, resigned, 1984; sales trainer GM, Pontiac, Mich., 1985-86; systems engring. devel. profl. Electronic Data Systems, Pontiac, 1985-86; mktg. info. systems adminstr. Mastic Corp., South Bend, Ind., 1987-89; instr. Apollo Coll., Tucson, Ariz., 1989-90; mgmt. info. system mgr. Hutronix Mfg., Tucson, 1990; database mgr. Dames & Moore Environ. Cons., tucson, 1990-91; psychiatric technician Tucson Psychiatric Inst./Charter Hosp., Tucson, 1986-94; assoc. prof. Tucson U., 1993-94; pres. Am. Assn. Psychiatric Technicians, West Chicago, 1991—; bus./mgmt. cons. AAPT Solutions, Niles, Mich.; reviewer Chronical Guidance Publs., Moravia, N.Y., 1994—; reviewer/writer NTC Pub. Group, Chgo., 1995—; interviewee Bus. Mktg. Mag., 1988. Editor: A Textbook for Psychiatric Technicians, 1995, Outline of Knowledge for Psychiatric Technicians, 1993; author: (curriculum) Social Research Methods/History of Psychology, 1993, (monograph) Occupational Report for Psychiatric Technicians, 1994. Chmn. behavioral health legis. com. Ariz. Coalition of Human Svcs., 1993-94, supervisory com., Mastic Employees Fed. Credit Union, South Bend, Ind., 1987-89. Staff Sgt. USMC, 1974-84. Mem. Mental Health Assn. (v.p. 1993-94, registered lobbiest, 1993-94), Tucson Pima County Job Club (bd. dirs. 1992-93), Tucson Assn. Vol. Adminstrs., Am. Assn. of Psychiat. Technicians (pres. 1991—). Unitarian Universalist. Avocations: books, Latin, entrepreneurs, philosophy, lectrs./learning. Office: AAPT 336 Johnson Rd Ste 2 Michigan City IN 46360

BLAKE, GEORGE ROWLAND, soil science educator, water resources research administrator; b. Provo, Utah, Mar. 14, 1918; s. Samuel Henry and Annie Matilda (Bevan) B.; m. Kathryn M. Sumsion, Feb. 26, 1941; children: Carla Paul (dec.), Rowland, Lorraine Blake Phillips, Henry; m. Helen M. Patten, May 25, 1985. B.A., Brigham Young U., 1943; Ph.D., Ohio State U., 1949. Missionary LDS Ch., Germany, 1937-39; with FBI, Washington, 1941-42; research fellow, teaching asst. Ohio State U., Columbus, 1946-49; asst. prof., asst. research specialist Rutgers U., New Brunswick, N.J., 1949-55; assoc. prof. dept. soil sci. U. Minn., St. Paul, 1955-60, prof., 1960-84, dir., prof. emeritus, 1984—, dir. Water Resources Research Ctr., 1979-84; NSF sr. postdoctoral fellow, Braunschweig, Fed. Republic of Germany, 1962-63; Fulbright guest prof. U. Hohenheim, Fed. Republic of Germany, 1970-71; Ford Found. cons., Chile, 1967; guest prof. U. Kesthely, Hungary, 1974, U. Warsaw, Poland, 1981; USAID cons., Morocco, 1979-88; adj. prof. Institut Agronomique et Veterinaire Hassan II Rabat Morocco, 1982-88; guest prof. Humboldt U., Berlin, German Dem. Republic, 1986; Benson Inst. cons., Guatemala, 1990, 94. Contbr. articles to profl. jours. Pub. affairs vol. LDS Ch., Frankfurt, Germany, 1996-97. Recipient Georgicon award U. Kesthely, 1974, Müncheberg Plaque Acad. of Sci., German Dem. Republic., Spl. Emeritus Recognition award Brigham Young U. Emeritus Assn., 1996. Fellow Am. Soc. Agronomy, Soil Sci. Soc. Am.; mem. Internat. Soc. Soil Sci., Soil Sci. Soc. Am., Soil Conservation Soc. Am., Sigma Xi, Gamma Sigma Delta, Omicron Delta Kappa. Home: 2215 N 1400 E Provo UT 84604-2103

BLAKE, JEFF, professional football player; b. Daytona Beach, Fla., Dec. 4, 1970; s. Emory Blake. Student, East Carolina U. With N.Y. Jets, 1992-93; quarterback Cin. Bengals, 1994—. Selected to Pro Bowl, 1995. Home: 3685 Winding Lake Cir Orlando FL 32835-2659 Office: Cin Bengals One Bengals Dr Cincinnati OH 45204*

BLAKE, JOHN EDWARD, retired car rental company executive; b. Chgo., Aug. 9, 1933; s. Edward Aloysius and Laura (Schlichter) B.; m. Joan Patricia Kautz, Aug. 28, 1965; children: Kathryn, John, Amy. LLB, De Paul U., 1959. Bar: Ill. 1960. Supr. property U.S. Gypsum, Chgo., 1960-66; real estate rep. Ford Motor Co., Dearborn, Mich., 1966-68; mgr. real estate Roadway Express, Akron, Ohio, 1968-70; dir. properties Hertz Corp., N.Y.C., 1970-76, staff v.p., 1976-84, v.p., 1984-87; sr. v.p. Hertz Corp., Park Ridge, N.J., 1987-96; ret., 1996. Mem. bd. trustees Cath. Community Svcs., Archdiocese of Newark. Mem. Am. Assn. Airport Execs. (assoc.), Internat. Assn. Corp. Real Estate Execs. (chmn. bd. dirs. 1993-95, chmn. bd. trustees 1995-98, sr. advisor 1998). *With age hopefully comes wisdom and an ability to live within one's limitations while nurturing one's talents.*

BLAKE, JONATHAN DEWEY, lawyer; b. Long Branch, N.J., June 14, 1938; s. Edgar Bond and Haven (Johnstone) B.; m. Prudence Anne Rowsell, Dec. 22, 1964 (div. June 1977); children: Juliet Haven, Deborah Anne, Susanna Rowsell; m. Elizabeth L. Shriver, Dec. 9, 1977; children: Jonathan Shriver-Blake, Molly Shriver-Blake. BA magna cum laude, Yale U., 1960, LLB cum laude, 1964; BA, MA, Oxford U., Eng., 1962. Bar: D.C. 1965, U.S. Supreme Ct. 1973, U.S. Dist. Ct. D.C. 1965, U.S. Dist. Ct. Md. 1985, U.S. Ct. Appeals (D.C. cir.) 1965, U.S. Ct. Appeals (2d cir.) 1973. Assoc. Covington & Burling, Washington, 1964-72, ptnr., 1972—, chmn. mgmt. com., 1996—; tchr. Howard U., Washington, 1965-70, U. Va., Charlottesville, 1965-70. Contbr. articles to profl. jours. Pres. Great Falls Citizens Assn., Va., 1967-68; exec. com., bd. dirs. Deerfield Acad, Mass., 1980-85. Rhodes scholar, 1960; recipient Gordon Brown prize, 1959. Mem. ABA (chair internat. telecomm. com. 1993-99), Fed. Comm. Bar Assn. (pres. 1980-85). Home: 4926 Hillbrook Ln NW Washington DC 20016-3208 Office: Covington & Burling PO Box 7566 1201 Pennsylvania Ave NW Washington DC 20044-7566

BLAKE, LAURA, architect; b. Berkeley, Calif., Dec. 26, 1959; d. Igor Robert and Elizabeth (Denton) B. BA in Art History, Brown U., 1982; MArch, UCLA, 1985. With The Ratcliff Architects, Berkeley, 1986-90; architect IDG Architects, Oakland, Calif., 1990-92; assoc. ELS/Elbasani & Logan Architects, Berkeley, 1992—. Organizer charity ball Spinsters San Francisco, 1988, sec., 1988-89, mem. adv. bd., 1989-92; mem. San Francisco Jr. League, 1991—. Recipient Alpha Rho Chi bronze medal, 1985. Mem. AIA, Soc. Calif. Pioneers. Republican. Episcopalian. Avocations: travel, photography, sport, the arts. Office: ELS/Elbasani & Logan Architects 2040 Addison St Berkeley CA 94704-1190

BLAKE, MARY ELLEN, medical/surgical and home care nurse, educator; b. N.Y.C.; d. Patrick R. and Mary A. (Goggin) Flynn; m. Gerald J. Blake; children: Gerald, Regina, Lynn, Laura. RN, St. Vincent's Hosp., N.Y.C.; BSN, St. Peter's Coll., Englewood, N.J., 1987; grad., Fairleigh Dickinson U. Staff nurse Englewood (N.J.) Hosp.; continuing edn. instr. Holy Name Hosp., Teaneck, N.J., 1987-90; edn. cons. Palisades Gen. Hosp., North Bergen, N.J., 1990—. Mem. Sigma Theta Tau. Office: Valley Home Care Essex Rd Paramus NJ 07047

BLAKE, NORMAN, hotel executive; b. N.Y.C.; m. Karen Blake; 3 children. MA, Purdue U., 1966, PhD (hon.), 1995. Various planning, mktg. and info. sys. positions GE, 1967-74, 76-79; exec. v.p. Top Inc., 1974, pres., 1975; v.p., gen. mgr. comml. and indsl. financing divsn. GE Credit Corp., 1979-81, exec. v.p. financing ops., 1981-84; chmn., CEO Heller Internat. Corp., Chgo., 1984-90; chmn., pres., CEO USF&G, Balt., 1991-97, Promus Hotel Corp., Memphis, 1997—; bd. dirs. St. Paul Cos., Enron Corp., Owens Corning; chair task force Bus. and Edn. Serving Together, Balt.. Office: Promus Hotel Corp 755 Crossover Ln Memphis TN 38117-4900

BLAKE, NORMAN PERKINS, JR., finance company executive; b. N.Y.C., Nov. 8, 1941; s. Norman Perkins and Eleanor (Adams) B.; m. Karen Cromwell, Sept. 12, 1965; children: Kellie, Kimberly, Adam. BA, Purdue U., 1966, MA, 1967. With GE, 1967-74, 76—; mgr. strategic planning ops., plastics bus. div. GE, Pittsfield, Mass., 1976-78, mgr. bus. devel. consumer products and services sector, 1978-79; staff exec. GE, Fairfield, Conn., 1979; v.p., gen. mgr. comml. and indsl. fin. div. GE Credit Corp., Stamford, Conn., 1979-81, exec. v.p. financing ops., 1981-84; chmn. and chief exec. officer Heller Internat. Corp., Chgo., 1984-90, pres., 1984-90; chmn., chief exec. officer Heller Fin., Inc., Chgo., until 1990, Heller Overseas Corp., Chgo., 1984-90; now chmn., CEO, pres. U.S. Fidelity & Guaranty Co., Baltimore, 1990-98; chmn., pres. Fidelity & Guaranty Ins. Underwriters., Balt., 1990-98; vice chmn. St. Paul Cos., Marco Island, Fla., 1990-98; chmn., pres., CEO Promus Hotel Corp., Memphis, 1998—; with Top, Inc., Troy, Mich., 1974-76, pres., 1976; bd. dirs. Owens/Corning Fiberglas. Office: Promus Hotel Corp 755 Crossover Ln Memphis TN 38117-4900*

BLAKE, PETER JOST, architect; b. Berlin, Sept. 20, 1920; came to U.S., 1940, naturalized, 1944; Student, U. London, 1938; student in architecture, Regent St. Poly., London, 1939, U. Pa., 1941; BArch, Pratt Inst., 1949. Apprentice to Serge Chermayeff, Architect, London, 1938-39, George Howe, Oskar Stonorov and Louis Kahn, Architects, Phila., 1940-42; curator dept. architecture and indsl. design Mus. Modern Art, N.Y.C., 1948-50; assoc. editor Archtl. Forum, N.Y.C., 1950-61, mng. editor, 1961-64, editor-in-chief, 1965-72; ptnr. Peter Blake & Julian Neski, Architects, N.Y.C., 1956-60, James Baker & Peter Blake, Architects, N.Y.C., 1964-71; contbg. editor New York mag., N.Y.C., 1968-76; editor-in-chief Architecture Plus, N.Y.C., 1972-75; chmn. Sch. Architecture, Boston Archtl. Ctr., 1975-79; chmn. dept. architecture and planning Cath. U. Am., Washington, 1979-86, prof. architecture, 1986-91; prin. Peter Blake Architect, Washington, 1979-93; prof. emeritus Cath. U. Am., Washington, 1991—; vis. critic, lectr. Harvard U., Cambridge, Mass., Yale U., New Haven, Cornell U., Ithaca, N.Y., Washington U., St. Louis, Tulane U., New Orleans, Pratt Inst., Cooper Union, New Sch. for Social Rsch., Bennington Coll., Columbia U., N.Y.C., Ill. Inst. Tech., U. Mich., Ann Arbor, also schs. of architecture in Hamburg, Aachen, Hanover, Braunschweig, and West Berlin, Fed. Republic of Germany, Vienna, Zurich, Halifax, N.S., Can., Maracaibo, Venezuela, Milan, and Hong Kong; chmn. Alcoa Conf. on Future of Housing, Boca Raton, Fla., 1957; chmn. Internat. Design Conf., Aspen, Colo., 1962, bd. dirs., 1965-73, advisor to bd., 1974-91; chmn. adv. panel on quality of Iranian housing, urban devel. and new town planning Shah of Iran, 1976; mem. U.S. del. Internat. Conf. on Theater Design, Berlin, 1960; participant Internat. Conf. on Urban Design, New Delhi, 1965, U.S./Yugoslav Conf. on Housing, Zagreb, 1974, Iran Internat. Congress on Architecture, Persepolis, 1974, U.S. del. Helsinki Cultural Forum, Budapest, Hungary, 1985; spkr. at seminar in Chandigarh, India, 1994. Author: The Master Builders, 1960, God's Own Junkyard, 1964, Form Follows Fiasco, 1977, No Place Like Utopia, 1993; contbr. articles to mags. and newspapers; important works include Hollis Unitarian Ch., Queens, N.Y., offices and warehouse, Queens, Temple Emanu-El, Livingston, N.J., Ford Found. Ideal Theater, Darrow Sch. Libr., New Lebanon, N.Y., Berlin-Tegel Airport Project, Manistee (Mich.) Town Planning Project, Max Planck Inst. Project, Berlin, Rehab. Ctr., Binghamton (N.Y.) State Hosp., Roundabout Theater, Stage One, N.Y.C., Neely Exptl. Theatre, Vanderbilt U., Nashville, P.R. Traveling Theatre, N.Y.C., Apt. Bldg., I.B.A., St. Lukas Ch., West Berlin; collaborator with Kevin Roche in Dept. State competition design new U.S. Embassy in Berlin, 1995. Served with AUS, 1943-47, ETO. Recipient Howard Myers award for archtl. journalism, 1960; Graham Found. Advanced Studies in Fine Arts fellow, 1962, several grants; Ford Found. grantee, 1960; disting. design fellow Nat. Endowment for Arts, 1984. Fellow AIA (Architecture Critics medal 1975). Office: 474 W 238th St Apt 3A Bronx NY 10463-2027

BLAKE, RAN, jazz pianist, composer; b. Springfield, Mass., Apr. 20, 1935; s. Philip Randall and Alison (Powers) B. BA, Bard Coll., 1960. tchr. New Eng. Conservatory, Boston, 1967—, chmn. third stream jazz program, 1973—; faculty Hartford Conservatory Music, 1972-75; music columnist Morningsider, 1960-62; contbr. articles to profl. jours. Appearances include, Monterrey Festival, 1962, Antibes (France) Music Festival, 1963, Lake Como (Italy) Jazz, 1977, Nancy (France) Jazz Pulsations Festival, 1977, New Eng. Life Hall, Boston, 1977, Contemporary Music Festival, So. Meth. U., 1977, Peabody Conservatory, Johns Hopkins U., 1978, U. Mass., 1978, 79, Mexico City, 1978, Bogota, Colombia, 1978, Buenos Aires, Argentina, 1978, Mendoza, Argentina, 1978, Rosario, Argentina, 1978, Tucuman, Argentina, 1978, Festival d'Anjou, Angers, France, 1978, Harvard U., 1978, N.Y.C., 1978, Lulu White's, Boston, 1978, Fisk U., 1979, Vanderbilt U., 1979, Ala. Sch. Fine Arts, 1979, Jonathan Swift's, Boston, 1979, 80, 82, New Eng. Conservatory, 1979, 80, 81, 82, 83, U. Mass., 1979, Black Beans Studio, N.Y.C., 1979, Northwestern U., Evanston, Ill., 1979, Am. Embassy, Winnipeg, Man., Can., 1979, Brandon (Man.) U., 1979, Painted Bride Arts Center, Phila., 1979, McGill U., 1979, U. Que., 1979, Sweet Basil's, N.Y.C., 1979, Theatre du Ranelagh, Paris, 1980, Ch. of the Covenant, Boston, 1980, Milan, Italy, 1980, West Bank Cafe, N.Y.C., 1980, Berlin Jazz Festival, 1980, U. Padua, Italy, 1980, Bunratty's, Boston, 1981, Rome, 1981, Third Stream Festival, Boston, 1982, St. Botolph Club, Boston, 1982, Merkin Concert Hall, N.Y.C., 1983, Kivik, Sweden, 1983, Nuclear Freeze Concert, Boston, 1983, Fed. Res. Bank, Boston, 1983, Fontbonne Coll., St. Louis, 1983, Am. Conservatory Music, 1983, Jazz Showcase, 1983, New Eng. Conservatory, 1984, numerous others; appeared on TV shows, Flemish TV, radio, 1963, 66-

67, concerts in ten European countries; rec. artist: (with Jeanne Lee) Newest Sound Around, 1962, reissued, 1980; R.B. Plays Solo Piano, 1966, The Blue Potato and Other Outrages, 1969, Breakthru, 1975, Wende, 1976, Open City, 1977, Crystal Trip, 1977, Take One, 1978, Take Two, 1978, Rapport, 1978, Realization of a Dream, 1978, Third Stream Today, 1979, Film Noir, 1980, Third Stream Recompositions, 1980, Improvisations with Jaki Byard, 1982, Duke Dreams, 1982, Portfolio of Doktor Mabuse, 1983, Ran Blake: Suffield Gothic, 1984, Short Life of Barbara Monk, 1986, You Stepped out of a Cloud, 1989, The Compleat Ran Blake, 1989, That Certain Feeling, Epistrophy, 1991, Masters From Different Worlds, 1994, Round About, 1994, Duke Dreams: The Legacy of Strayhorn Ellington, 1994, Unmarked Van, 1997, (with Anthony Braxton) A Memory of Vienna, 1997; subject of numerous articles; arts columnist: Bay State Banner, 1974—. Active Am. Com. For Democracy in Greece, 1967. Recipient RCA Album First prize Germany, 1963, Prix Billie Holiday, 1980; Guggenheim fellow, 1982, Nat. Endowment Arts fellow in Jazz Composition, 1982, Mass. Arts Found. fellow, 1982, MacArthur Fellowship Found. award, 1988. Mem. AAUP, NARAS, Met. Cultural Alliance, Mass. Council Arts and Humanities, Am. Assn. Music Therapy, World Jazz Soc., Assoc. Musicians Greater N.Y., Music Critics Assn., Coll. Music Soc., Film Soc. N.Y.

BLAKE, RICHARD F., transistor devices company executive; b. Medford, Mass., Oct. 9, 1924; s. Earl Clement and Mary Bella (Munro) B.; m. Patsy Ruth McCoy, June 6, 1950 (div. June 1976); children: Hallie P., Richard P.; m. Wanda Joanna Wright, June 28, 1980. BSEE, tulane U., 1948. Test engr. Gen. Electric, Schenectady, N.J., 1948-49; instr. elec. engring. U. Ala., Tuscaloosa, 1949-51; project engr. Naval Rsch. Lab., Washington, 1951-54; prin. engr. Emerson Rsch. Lab., Washington, 1954-56; mgr. electronic Walter Kidde, Allwood, N.J., 1956-60; CEO Transistor Devices, Cedar Knolls, N.J., 1960—. Author: Static Relay, 1958; inventor in field. Pres. Morris Ctr. YMCA, Cedar Knolls, 1978-82. Mem. Naval Ad Hoc Power Supply Com., Tau Beta Pi. Avocations: sailing, grandchildren's activities. Office: Transistor Devices 85 Horsehill Rd Cedar Knolls NJ 07927-2097

BLAKE, ROBERT (MICHAEL GUBITOSI), actor; b. Nutley, N.J., Y, Sept. 18, 1933; m. Sondra Kerry (div.); 2 children. Appeared in "Our Gang" comedy series movie shorts as Micky Gubitosi; film appearences as Bobby Blake include I Love You Again, 1940, Andy Hardy's Double Life, Sheriff of Las Vegas, 1942, 1942, China Girl, 1942, Mokey, 1942, Salute to the Marines, 1943, Slightly Dangerous, 1943, The Big Noise, 1944, Lost Angel, 1944, Tuscon Raiders, 1944, Marshal of Reno, 1944, Meet the People, 1944, The San Antonio Kid, 1944, Vigilantes of Dodge City, 1944, Cheyenne Wildcat, 1944, Colorado Pioneers, 1945, Great Stage Coach Robbery, 1945, Dakota, 1945, The Horn Blows at Midnight, 1945, Lone Texas Ranger, 1945, Marshal of Laredo, 1945, Phantom of the Plains, 1945, Pillow to Post, 1945, The Woman in the Window, 1945, Sante Fe Uprising, 1946, Sheriff of Redwood Valley, 1946, Sun Valley Cyclone, 1946, Conquest of Cheyenne, 1946, A Guy Could Change, 1946, Home on the Range, 1946, Humoresque, 1946, California Gold Rush, 1946, In Old Sacramento, 1946, Out California Way, 1946, Stagecoach to Denver, 1946, Homesteaders of Paradise Valley, 1947, The Last Round-Up, 1947, The Marshal of Cripple Creek, 1947, Oregon Trail Scouts, 1947, The Return of Rin Tin Tin, 1947, Rustlers of Devil's Canyon, 1947, Vigilantes of Boomtown, 1947, The Treasure of the Sierra Madre, 1948, The Black Rose, 1950, Apache War Smoke, 1952, Treasure of the Golden Condor, 1953, The Veils of Bagdad, 1953, The Rack, 1956, Screaming Eagles, 1956, Three Violent People, 1956, Wagon Wheels Westward, 1956; film appearences as Robert Blake include Eros, 1950, Rumble on the Docks, 1956, The Tijuana Story, 1956, The Beast of Budapest, 1958, Revolt in the Big House, 1958, Battle Cry, 1959, Pork Chop Hill, 1959, The Purple Gang, 1960, Town Without Pity, 1961, PT 109, 1963, The Greatest Story Ever Told, 1965, This Property Is Condemned, 1966, In Cold Blood, 1967, Tell Them Willy Boy Is Here, 1969, Ripped Off, 1971, Corky, 1972, Electra Glide Is Blue, 1973, Busting, 1974, Coast to Coast, 1980, Second-Hand Hearts, 1981, Money Train, 1995, Lost Highway, 1996; TV appearences include Baretta, 1975-78, Blood Feud, 1983, Heart of a Champion: The Ray Mancini Story, 1985, Judgement Day: The John List Story, 1993 (Best Actor Emmy nominee 1993); creator, exec. prodr., actor: The Big Black Pill, 1981, The Monkey Mission, 1981; exec. prodr., actor: Of Mice and Men, 1981, Murder 1, Dancer 0, 1983, Helltown, 1985. Office: ICM 8942 Wilshire Blvd Beverly Hills CA 90211 Address: 40 West 57th St New York NY 10019*

BLAKE, ROBERT PHILIP, human services administrator, music therapist; b. Indpls., Dec. 19, 1950; s. Robert Cameron and Marian Elsie (Barkman) B.; m. Marva Lynn Basye, July 13, 1971 (div. Feb. 1983); 1 child, Heidi Kai; m. Lois Ann Bleifus, Nov. 20, 1983 (div. Mar. 1996); children: Stephanie Fawn, Robert Joseph; m. Susan Christine Seebode, July 25, 1998; 1 child, Joshua Rey. AA, Cabrillo Coll., 1971; BA, Ind. U., 1973; MA, Goddard Coll., 1979; PhD, Walden U., 1996. Registered music therapist, 1979; cert. therapeutic recreation specialist, 1979; lic. mental health profl., Wash., 1988—. Music therapist Meth. Hosp., Indpls., 1973-76; recreation therapist VA Med. Ctr., Seattle, 1979-80, Fairfax Hosp., Kirkland, Wash., 1979-80; clin. program dir. Peninsula Community Mental Health Ctr., Port Angeles, Wash., 1980-94; exec. dir. Alaska Ctr. for Children and Adults, Fairbanks, 1995-99; student performer, composer Up With People, Tucson, 1967-70; founder, dir. People Helping People, Indpls., 1974-77, The Logos Musical, Port Angeles, 1987-95; 1st exec. dir. Wash. Assn. County Designated Mental Health Profls., Seattle, 1981-82; involuntary treatment coord., Clallam County, Wash., 1983-94; presenter internat. workshops Assn. Care of Children in Hosps., Nat. Welfare Ministeries, Am. Pers. Guidance Assn., 1974-79; exec. dir. The Logos Corp., 1987-95. Author: (book) Gut Reaction: Music Therapy, 1979, Milestones: The History of Logos, 1990, Building Toward the Year 2000: You Can't Buy It, You Have to Build It, 1991—; composer, producer (album) Reaching Out, 1977, (cassette) Touch the Intrinsic, 1989, Winds of Change, 1991; Ind. Health Careers Gov.'s award, 1974. treas. Arctic Alliance, 1996-98, v.p., 1998; chmn. Alaska-Cmty. Partnerships for Access, Solutions and Success, 1997-98. Am. Humanist Educators Assn. Div. grantee, 1989. Mem. Up With People Internat. Alumni (rep. cast C-1968-69), Fairbanks Sunriser's Rotary Club (internat. youth exch. dir.). Democrat. Baptist. Avocations: recording studio, exotic birds and animals, music camp, timber farm, international performing group director. E-mail: drúblake@mosquitonet.com. Home: PO Box 72300 Fairbanks AK 99707-2300 Office: Alaska Ctr for Children and Adults 1020 Barnette St Fairbanks AK 99701

BLAKE, ROBERT ROGERS, psychologist, behavioral science company executive; b. Brookline, Mass., Jan. 21, 1918; s. Charles B. and Margaret B.; m. Mercer Blain, Sept. 4, 1941; children—Brooks Blake, Cary Blake. B.A., Berea Coll., 1940; M.A., U. Va., 1941; Ph.D., U. Tex., 1947; LLD, Berea Coll., 1992. Diplomate Am. Bd. Profl. Psychology. Prof. psychology U. Tex., 1947-62; pres. Sci. Methods, Inc., Austin, Tex., 1961-81, chmn., 1982—; lectr. U. Reading, Eng; clin. psychologist Tavistock Clinic, London; lectr., rsch. assoc. Harvard U.; mem. hon. faculty of behavioral sci. Inst. Bus. Adminstrn. and Mgmt., Tokyo. Author: numerous books including Group Dynamics: Key to Decision Making, 1961, The Managerial Grid, 1964, 30th Anniversary re-release, 1994, Managing Intergroup Conflict in Industry, 1964, Corporate Darwinism, 1966, Corporate Excellence Through Grid Organization Development, 1968, Building a Dynamic Corporation Through Grid Organization Development, 1969, The Marriage Grid, 1971, How to Assess the Strengths and Weaknesses of a Business Enterprise, 1972, The Grid for Supervisory Effectiveness, 1975, Consultation, 1976, Diary of an OD Man, 1976, Making Experience Work: The Grid Approach to Critique, 1978, The New Managerial Grid, 1978, Making Experience Work: The Grid Approach to Critique, 1978, The Social Worker Grid, 1979, The New Grid for Supervisory Effectiveness, 1979, The Versatile Manager: A Grid Profile, 1980, Grid Approaches to Managing Stress, 1980, Role Playing: A Practice Manual for Group Facilitators, 1980, The Grid for Sales Excellence, 1980, Grid Approaches for Managing Stress, 1980, The Real Estate Sales Grid, 1980, The Academic Administrator Grid: A Guide to Developing Effective Management Teams, 1981, Synergogy: An Instrumented Team Learning Approach, 1981, Productivity: The Human Side, 1981 (Book of Yr. award Am. Mgmt. Assn. for Productivity 1982), Grid Approaches for Managerial Leadership in Nursing, 1981 (Book of Yr. award Am. Jour. Nursing 1982), The Secretary Grid, 1983, Synergogy: A New Strategy for Education Training and Development, 1984 (Book of Yr. award div. instructional devel. Assn. Ednl. Communications and Tech. 1985, Most Recommended Bus. Book award for Exec. Achievement The Libr. Jour. 1985, Human Resources Devel. Hall of Fame award Tng. mag. 1987, Outstanding Contbn. to Field Human Resource Devel. award Univ. Assocs. 1988), Solving Costly Organizational Conflicts, 1984, The Managerial Grid III, 1985, Executive Achievement: Making It at the Top, 1986, Spectacular Teamwork, 1987, GridWorks: An Approach that Increases Employee Participation and Promotes Esprit de Corps, 1987, Change by Design, 1989, Leadership Dilemmas-Grid Solutions, 1991, Solution Selling: The Grid Science Approach, 1994. Served with USAAF (personnel cons. Aviation Psychol. Program), 1942-45. Fulbright scholar, 1949-50; Korzbyski Meml. Address spkr., 1961, 82; Frederick J. Gaudet Meml. lectr., 1986; recipient Human Resource Devel. Hall of Fame award Tng. Mag., 1982, award for Outstanding Contbn. to field human resource devel. Univ. Assocs., 1988, Lifetime Achievement award Internat. Assn. Conflict Mgmt., 1994. Fellow APA; mem. Inst. Gen. Semantics (trustee). Home: 3700 Hampton Rd Austin TX 78705-1826 Office: Sci Methods Inc PO Box 195 Austin TX 78767-0195

BLAKE, STEWART PRESTLEY, retired ice cream company executive; b. Jersey City, Nov. 26, 1914; s. Herbert P. and Ethel (Stewart) B.; m. Helen Davis, Nov. 16, 1982; children by previous marriage: Nancy Blake Yanakakis, Benson Prestley. Student, Trinity Coll., 1934-35, LL.D., 1976; PhD, Western New Eng. Coll., 1980, Springfield Coll., 1982; PhD (hon.), Path Bay Coll., 1993, Quinnipiac Coll., 1993. Co-founder Friendly Ice Cream Corp., 1935, chmn., to 1979. Past chmn. bd. trustees Bay Path Coll., Longmeadow, Mass. Clubs: Colony (Springfield), Longmeadow Country, Sailfish Point Yacht (Stuart). Home: 700 Hall Hill Rd Somers CT 06071-1058

BLAKE, WILLIAM L., airport company executive; b. Chgo., Apr. 5, 1938. BS, U. Ill., Champagne, 1960; JD, Georgetown U., 1966. Dir. Ill. div. aeros. Capital Airport, Springfield, 1992—. Office: Ill Div Aeros Capital Airport 1 Langhorne Dr Springfield IL 62707-8415

BLAKE-INADA, LOUIS MICHAEL, cardiologist, researcher; b. Osaka, Japan, June 4, 1956; came to U.S., 1959; s. Edward Kneeland, Sr. and Setsuko (Inada) Blake. BA in Biochemistry and Molecular Biology, U. Calif., Santa Barbara, 1979; MD, Case Western Res. U., 1983. Diplomate Am. Bd. Internal Medicine, Am. Bd. Nuc. Medicine. Intern in gen. surgery Letterman Army Med. Ctr., San Francisco, 1983-84; resident in internal medicine Sch. Medicine Stanford U., Calif., 1988-90, resident in nuc. medicine, 1990-92, chief resident in nuc. medicine, 1991-92; fellow in cardiology Calif. Pacific Med. Ctr., San Francisco, 1992-93; fellow in cardiology, cardiac imaging U. Calif., San Francisco, 1993-95; fellow in invasive cardiology U. N.Mex. Health Sci. Ctr., 1997-98; asst. prof. medicine (cardiology), asst. prof. radiology U. Nev. Sch. of Medicine, Reno, 1998—. Contbr. articles to med. jours. including Am. Jour. Radiology, Jour. Nuc. Medicine, others; contbr. editor Jour. Am. Coll. Cardiology, 1993-95. Capt. U.S. Army, 1979-88. Evelyn Neizer rsch. fellow Stanford U., 1992, Prof. of the Year, UMV of Nevada sch. of med., 1999. Fellow Am. Coll. Angiology; mem. ACP, Am. Coll. Cardiology, Am. Coll. Nuc. Physicians, Am. Heart Assn. (coun. on cardiovascular radiology), Am. Heart Assn. (coun. on vascular biology), Soc. Nuc. Medicine, Assn. Military Surgeons of the U.S. Republican. Roman Catholic. Avocations: stocks and bonds, skiing, running, piano, languages. Home: 1855 Joy Lake Rd Reno NV 89511-8718 Office: U Nev Sch of Med Reno NV 89557

BLAKELY, EDWARD JAMES, economics educator; b. San Bernardino, Calif., Apr. 21, 1938; s. Edward Blakely and Josephine Elizabeth (Carter) Proctor; m. Maaike C. Vander Sleesen, July 1, 1971; children: Pieta C., Brette D. BA, U. Calif., Riverside, 1960; MA, U. Calif., Berkeley, 1964; MBA, Pasadena Nazerene Coll., 1967; EdD in Edn. and Mgmt., UCLA, 1971. Mgr. Pacific Telephone Co., Pasadena, Calif., 1960-65; exec. dir. Western Community Action Tng., Los Angeles, 1965-69; spl. asst. U.S. Dept. State, Washington, 1969-71; asst. chancellor, assoc. prof. U. Pitts., 1971-74; assoc. dean and prof. applied econs. and behavioral scis. U. Calif., Davis, 1974-77; asst. v.p. U. Calif., Berkeley, 1977-85, prof., chmn. dept. city and regional planning, 1985—; expert advisor Orgn. Econ. Cooperation and Devel., asst. to Mayor Elihu Harris, City of Oakland. Author: Rural Communities in Advanced Industrial Society, Community Development Research, Taking Local Development Initiative, Planning Local Economic Development SAGE, 1988, Separate Societies: Poverty and Inequality in U.S. Cities (Paul Davidoff award 1993), 1992, Fortress America: Gated Communities in the U.S., 1998. Chmn. fin. com. Pvt. Industry Council of Oakland (Calif.), 1978-85; vice chmn. Ecole Bilingue Sch., Berkeley, 1982-85, chmn., 1988—; chmn. bd. Royce Sch., Oakland, Calif., 1988—; sec., treas. Econ. Devel. Corp., Oakland, 1983; expert advisor Orgn. Econ. Corp. and Devel., Paris, 1986; apptd. to pres. trust Pres. Bill Clinton, 1997—; mayoral candidate City of Oakland, Calif., 1998. Served to 1st lt. USAF, 1961-63. Recipient San Francisco Found. award, 1991, Paul Davidoff award, 1993; Guggenheim fellow, 1995-96, fellow Urban Studies Australian Inst. Urban St., 1985, German Acad. Exch., 1984; Fulbright St. scholar Internat. Exch. of Scholars, 1986, John Simon Guggenheim fellow, 1995-96; named to Athlete Hall of Fame, U. Calif. Riverside Alumni Press, 1992, 125th Anniversay Prof. U. Calif. at Riverside Berkeley Campus, 1992; apptd. by Pres. Bill Clinton to the Pres. Trust, 1997. Mem. Cmty. Devel. Soc. (bd. dirs. 1980-84, svc. award 1983, disting. svc. award 1990), Calif. Local Econ. Devel. (standing com. 1980-81), Am. Planning Assn. (accreditation com.), Am. Assn. Collegiate Schs. of Planning, Nat. Assn. State and Land Grant Colls. (exec. com. 1987), Phi Delta Kappa, Lambda Alpha. Club: Rueful Order. Home: 652 Orange Grove Ave # 0 South Pasadena CA 91030-2353 Office: Univ So Calif Sch Urban Reg Planning & Devel Los Angeles CA 90089-0042

BLAKELY, JOHN T., lawyer; b. Beloit, Wis., May 26, 1944; s. Walter Edwin and Virginia (Treleaven) B.; m. Ellen Ford, Dec. 27, 1968 (div. Apr. 1988); children: Sara, Ford; m. Pamela Rose Westmoreland, Mar. 16, 1991. BA, Duke U., 1966; JD, U. Mich., 1969. Bar: Fla., U.S. Ct. Appeals (11th cir.), U.S. Dist. Ct. (mid. dist.) Fla., U.S. Supreme Ct.; bd. cert. personal injury lawyer; bd. cert. Nat. Bd. Trial Advocacy. Instr. law U. Wis., Madison, 1969-70; assoc. Carlton, Fields, Ward et al., Tampa, Fla., 1970-73; ptnr. Johnson, Blakely, Pope, Bokor, Ruppel & Burns, P.A., Clearwater, Fla., 1973—. Mem. ABA, ATLA, Fla. Bar (bd. cert. civil trial law), Acad. Fla. Trial Lawyers, Nat. Bd. Trial Advocacy. Office: Johnson Blakely Pope Et Al 975 6th Ave S Naples FL 34102-6753

BLAKEMAN, ROYAL EDWIN, lawyer; b. N.Y.C., June 9, 1923; s. Jesse Herbert and Edythe Roslyn (Siegel) B.; m. Edith Hughes, Sept. 1, 1945; children: Carol, Elizabeth, Forrest. BA, Hofstra Coll., 1942; LLB cum laude, NYU, 1947. Bar: N.Y. 1947, U.S. Dist. Ct. (so. dist.) N.Y. 1956, U.S. Ct. Appeals (2d cir.) 1972, Calif. 1973, U.S. Supreme Ct. 1973. Pvt. practice Lindenhurst, N.Y., 1947-51; assoc. Jack J. Katz, N.Y.C., 1951-53, Marshall Bratter, Greene & Klein, N.Y.C., 1953-55; ptnr. Marshall, Bratter, Greene, Allison & Tucker (specializing in theatrical law), N.Y.C., 1955-81; of counsel Pryor, Cashman, Sherman & Flynn, N.Y.C., 1981-91, Robert M. Blakeman & Assocs., Valley Stream, N.Y., 1991—; gen. counsel Nat. Acad. Rec. Arts and Scis.; officer, dir. Mark Goodson Prodns. Mem. editorial bd. TV Quar. Mem. TV com. Anti Defamation League, N.Y. Served to chief petty officer U.S. Maritime Service, 1942-46. Recipient George M. Esterbrook Disting. Service award Hofstra Alumni Assn., 1966. Mem. Nat. Acad. TV Arts and Scis. (pres., bd. govs. N.Y.C. chpt.; past nat. pres., trustee), Nat. Youth Council, Nat. Acad. Rec. Arts and Scis. (gen. counsel). Club: Dad's (Long Beach) (pres. 1955). Avocations: golf, bridge, music. Home: 750105B Lido Blvd Long Beach NY 11561-5236 Office: Robert M Blakeman & Assocs 108 S Franklin Ave Valley Stream NY 11580-6105

BLAKEMORE, CLAUDE COULEHAN, banker; b. Los Angeles, Apr. 26, 1909; s. Claude Payne and Agnes C. (Coulehan) B.; m. Violet E. Alt, Aug. 27, 1937; children: Susan Blakemore Daniels, Bruce A. Student, UCLA, 1928-29, U. Iowa, 1929; grad., Stonier Sch. Banking, Rutgers U., 1951. With First Nat. Bank Santa Ana, Calif., 1930-41; comptroller of currency, asst. nat. bank examiner, 1941-42; bank examiner Fed. Res. Bank San Francisco, 1942-45; with First Nat. Bank San Diego, 1945-70, sr. v.p., 1962-64, pres., 1964-70, chief exec. officer, 1966-70; pres, chief exec. officer So. Calif. First Nat. Corp., 1969-71; pres., trustee USF Investors; dir. Rice, Hall, James & Assos., Percy H. Goodwin Co., Western Bldg. Spltys. Bd. dirs. San Diego County Med. Rehab. Center Assn.; bd. dirs., pres. San Diego County council Boy Scouts Am.; bd. dirs., treas., chmn. bd. San Diego Hall of Sci.; bd. dirs. San Diego Symphony. Mem. Am. Bankers Assn. (exec. council), Calif. Bankers Assn. (pres., dir.), Sigma Pi. Home: 1822 Altamira Pl San Diego CA 92103-1202

BLAKENEY, ALLAN EMRYS, Canadian government official, lawyer; b. Bridgewater, N.S., Can., Sept. 7, 1925; s. John Cline and Bertha (Davies) B.; m. Mary Elizabeth Schwartz, 1950 (dec. 1957); m. Anne Louise Gorham, May 1959; children: Barbara, Hugh, David, Margaret. BA, Dalhousie U., 1945, LLB, 1947, LLD (hon.); BA (Rhodes scholar), Oxford U., 1949, MA, 1955; DCL (hon.), Mount Allison U.; LLD (hon.), York U., Toronto, U. Western Ont., London, 1991, U. Regina, 1993, U. Sask., 1995. Bar: N.S. 1950, Sask. 1951. Queen's counsel, 1961; sec. to govt. fin. office Govt. Sask., 1950-55; chmn. Sask. Securities Commn., 1955-58; ptnr. Davidson, Davidson & Blakeney, Regina, Sask., 1958-60, Griffin, Blakeney, Beke, Koskie & Lueck, Regina, 1964-70; premier of Sask., 1971-82; Mem. Sask. Legislature, 1960-88; Officer of the Order of Can., 1992; leader of the opposition Sask. Legislature, 1970-71, 82-87; prof. Osgoode Hall Law Sch., York U., 1988-90, U. Sask., 1990—; minister of edn., Sask., 1960-61, provincial treas., 1961-62, minister pub. health, 1962-64; mem. Royal Commn. on Aborginal Peoples, 1991-93. Home: 1752 Prince of Wales Ave, Saskatoon, SK Canada S7K 3E5 Office: U Saskatchewan Coll Law, 15 Campus Dr, Saskatoon, SK Canada S7N 5A6

BLAKENEY, KAREN ELIZABETH, social work administrator, consultant; b. Evanston, Ill., June 27, 1953; d. Elwood Francis and Irene Loretta (Filloon) Garlick; m. Lawrence Ray Blakeney, Sept. 6, 1975 (div.); life ptnr. Ydalia Granado; children: Jesse Alan, Aaron Paul. Cert. in Christian edn., Angeles Bible Coll., L.A., 1972; BA in Anthropology, Calif. State U., Long Beach, 1978; MS in Counseling Psychology, Mt. St. Mary's Coll., LA., 1992; cert. in non-profit mgmt., U. So. Calif., 1998. Commd. pastor Hosanna Ministries, 1994. Archaeologist VTM Corp., Vandenburg AFB, Calif., 1979-81; archaeologist, Arroyo Grande, Calif., 1981-82; acct. Airport Datsun/Volvo, Santa Maria, Calif., 1982-83; adminstrn. mgr. Concord Sys., Reseda, Calif., 1983-86; ins. broker Prudential Ins. Co., Torrance, Calif., 1986-87; mgr. legal compliance dept. G.J. Sullivan Cos., L.A., 1987-92; psychotherapy intern Hosanna Ministries, Santa Monica, Calif., 1990-95; children's social worker Dept. Children and Family Svcs., L.A., 1994-96; dir. social work Internat. Foster Family Agy., Carson, Calif., 1996-97; dir. youth svcs. L.A. Gay and Lesbian Ctr., Hollywood, Calif., 1997—; lectr. Calif. Poly. Inst. Archaeol. Field Sch., Mission San Antonio de Padua, 1978-81; co-founder, exec. dir. Inst. for trauma Intervention, L.A., 1993-96. Author: (poetry) Sacred Journey, 1995. Bd. dirs. Art To Grow On, San Pedro, Calif., 1992-94, Desert Stream Ministries/AIDS Resource Ministry, L.A., 1985-91; mem. parent-tchr. adv. bd. Park Western Elem. Sch., San Pedro, 1993-94; dir. mem. Consortium for Homeless Youth Svcs., Hollywood, 1997—; rep. L.A. County Sci. Planning Area Dist. 4 Coun., 1999—. Mem. Calif. Assn. Marriage and Family Therapists, Calif. Stat U.-Long Beach Anthropology Alumni Assn. (alumni bd. 1984-85) . Avocations: artist, writing. Office: LA Gay and Lesbian Ctr 1625 Schrader Blvd Hollywood CA 90028-6213

BLAKESLEE, DIANE PUSEY, financial planner; b. West Chester, Pa., Apr. 12, 1933; d. Norman S. and Leona (Ruth) Pusey; m. Earle B. Blakeslee, June 11, 1954; children: Samuel N., Barbara Blakeslee Porteous, David E., Ruth D. Blakeslee Overton. BA, Hood Coll., 1988. CLU; cert. fin. planner. Dist. mgr. Tchrs. Mgmt. and Investment Corp., Newport Beach, Calif., 1972-78, Walt Becker, Inc., Fresno, Calif., 1978-80; pres. Blakeslee & Blakeslee, San Luis Obispo, Calif., 1980—. Author: (column for Sr. Mag. and syndicated for radio) Dollars and Sense; co-editor: How to Survive on $50,000 to $150,000 a Year, 1984; host monthly TV program Welcome to The World of Financial Planning, 1984-87. Bd. dirs., treas. Pvt. Industry Coun., 1979-84; bd. dirs., treas. Child Devel. Ctr., 1980-83; bd. dirs. Cuesta Coll. Found., 1985—; bd. dirs., 1st v.p. San Luis Obispo Art Assn.; 1st v.p. San Luis Obispo Estate Planning Coun.; bd. dirs. Cert. Fin. Planners Bd. of Standards, Ethics and Profl. Rev., 1993-97; regent Coll. Fin. Planning, 1980-85; chmn. planned giving com. Cuesta Coll., 1984-86, pres. found. Named bd. mem. of Yr., Econ. Opportunity Coun., San Luis Obispo County, 1983, Woman of Achievement of Yr. cen. Calif. region Bus. and Profl. Women, 1985-86, Nat. Cert. Fin. Planner of Yr., 1986; recipient Disting. Alumni award George Sch., 1991. Mem. Internat. Assn. Fin. Planners, Inst. Cert. Fin. Planners (chmn. pub. relations, bd. dirs. 1978-82), Nat. Life Underwriters Assn., Bur. Nat. Affairs Tax Mgmt. (bd. advisors 1986—). Republican. Mem. Soc. of Friends. Club: Womens' Network (San Luis Obispo). Avocations: hiking, gardening, sketching. Home: 88 Country Club Dr San Luis Obispo CA 93401-8908 Office: Blakeslee & Blakeslee 299 Madonna Rd San Luis Obispo CA 93405-5430

BLAKESLEE, EDWARD EATON, lawyer, insurance executive; b. N.Y.C., July 23, 1921; s. Edward Eaton and Ada Rainbow (Harris) B.; m. Janice Callaghan, Mar. 19, 1944; children—Edward, David. LLB cum laude, NYU, 1947, LLM in Taxation, 1957; grad. exec. program in bus. adminstrn., Columbia U., 1966. Bar: N.Y. 1947. Atty. Mut. Life Ins. Co. N.Y., 1947-69, 2d v.p., gen. solicitor, 1969-73, v.p., gen. solicitor, 1973, gen. counsel, 1974-85; gen. counsel, bd. dirs. Am. Life Ins. Co. of N.Y., 1986-88; mng. dir., chief exec. officer Sargasso Mut. Ins. Co., Ltd., Hamilton, Bermuda, 1986-93, also bd. dirs.; pres. Securities Investors Indemnification Co., Ltd., Hamilton, Bermuda, 1989-90; spl. counsel Rosenman & Colin, 1990-92; of counsel Shea & Gould, 1992-94, Werner & Kennedy, 1994—; assessor Ins. Marketplace Stds. Assn., 1997—. With AC U.S. Army, 1943-46. Mem. ABA, N.Y. State Bar Assn., Assn. Bar City of N.Y., Assn. Life Ins. Counsel, NYU Alumni Fedn. (dir. emeritus), NYU Law Alumni Assn., Univ. Club. Home: 495 Birchtree Rd Oradell NJ 07649-1303 Office: 1633 Broadway New York NY 10019-6708

BLAKESLEE, WESLEY DANIEL, lawyer, consultant; b. Wilkes-Barre, Pa., May 28, 1947; s. Daniel Leo and Anne Blakeslee; m. Georgia Carroll Croft, July 28, 1973; children—Jaime Kiersten, Christopher Justin, Shaun Michael. B.S., Pa. State U., 1969; J.D. (hon.), U. Md.-Balt., 1976. Bar: Md. 1976, U.S. Dist. Ct. Md. 1977, U.S. Tax Ct. 1984. Systems analyst NASA, Greenbelt, Md., 1969-76; assoc. Semmes, Bowen & Semmes, Balt., 1976-78; assoc. Dulany & Davis, Westminster, Md., 1978-83, ptnr., 1983; sole practice, Westminster, 1984—; Assoc. Gen. Couns., Johns Hopkins Univ., 1999—, lectr., dir. computer devel. U. Md. Law Sch., Balt., 1984-89. Contbg. author, editor; Maryland District Court Practice, 1981, revised 1983. Author: Understanding Computers, 1984. Contrbg. author: Computers, 1984. Rep. Carroll County, Md. State Employment and Tng. Council, 1980-82; bd. dirs. Carroll County chpt. Am. Heart Assn., Westminster 1981-87; bd. mgrs. Carroll County YMCA, 1987-95; bd. govs. Md. Law Sch. Fund, Balt., 1982—. Mem. ABA, Fed. Bar Assn. (treas. Balt. chpt. 1984-90), Md. Bar Assn. (young lawyers sect. council 1982-84, Outstanding Service award 1984, litigation sect. coun. 1982—, Chair 1995), Carroll County Bar Assn. (treas. 1984), Order of Coif, Delta Theta Phi, Carroll County Dem. Club, Westminster Rotary. Roman Catholic. Home: 980 Hook Rd Westminster MD 21157-7335 Office: 104 E Main St Westminster MD 21157-5003

BLAKLEY, BENJAMIN SPENCER, III, lawyer; b. DuBois, Pa., Sept. 1, 1952; s. Benjamin Spencer Jr. and Mary Jane (Campney) B.; m. Kathleen M. Ellermeyer, Oct. 20, 1989; children: Benjamin Spencer IV, Kevin Charles, Kyra Jane. BA, Grove City Coll., 1974; JD, Duquesne U., 1977. Bar: Pa. 1977. Ptnr. Blakley, Jones & Mohney, DuBois, 1977—; pub. defender Clearfield (Pa.) County, 1977-84; instr. Pa. State U., DuBois, 1979-85. Mem. adv. bd. Salvation Army Pa. Corp., DuBois, 1978-98, chmn., 1988-91; mem. DuBois Area Youth Aid Panel, 1984-87; mem. Citizens for Effective Govt., DuBois, 1985-97; trustee DuBois Vol. Fire Dept., 1986-87, treas., 1987-90; mem. DuBois Ednl. Found., 1990—, Cath. Counseling and Adoption Svcs., 1996—; bd. dirs. DuBois Sr. and Cmty. Ctr., 1992-97. Mem. Pa. Bar Assn., Clearfield County Bar Assn., DuBois Vol. Fire Dept. Relief Assn. (pres. 1998). Democrat. Methodist. Office: Blakley Jones & Mohney PO Box 6 90 Beaver Dr Du Bois PA 15801-2440

BLAKLEY, JOHN CLYDE, telecommunications consultant; b. Bogota, Colombia, Sept. 14, 1955; came to U.S., 1964; s. Arthur C. and Dorothy M. (Balcome) B.; m. Jean M. Padden, May 21, 1983. BS, U. Miami, 1977, MEd, 1979. Notary at large, Fla. Mgr., adminstrv. asst. U. Miami Student Union, Coral Gables, Fla., 1977-79; mgr. Aladdins Castle, Inc., South Miami, Fla., 1979-80; adminstrv. mgr., cons. Lexow Brackins, CPA's, Hollywood, Fla., 1981-84; firm adminstr., cons. Lexow, Brackins, Koffler,

CPA's, Hollywood, 1985-89; firm adminstr., computer mgr. Dohan/Simon, CPA's, Miami, 1989-92; product mgr. Expert Software, Inc., 1992-93, IS mgr., 1993-96; sr. cons. Trien & Assocs., 1996—; pres. Miami Apple Users Group, 1983; cons. YMCA, 1983. Chmn. Multiple Sclerosis Project Dance Marathon, Coral Gables, 1977-79; coord. United Way Miami, 1975-79. Recipient Whitten award Assn. Coll. Unions, 1977, Outstanding Leadership award C. of C., 1973, Outstanding Vol., United Way, 1975, Outstanding Alumni award U. Miami, 1986, 92. Mem. Assn. Acctg. Adminstrs., Fla. Inst. CPA's, Assn. Coll. Unions Internat. (chmn. region 6, 1975-77), U. Miami Young Alumni Club (bd. dirs., pres.), U. Miami Alumni Assn. (bd. dirs.), Hurricane Club, Gold Coast Macintosh Computer Club (bd. dirs.). Home: 11501 SW 92nd Ct Miami FL 33176 Office: Trien & Assocs PO Drawer 402488 Miami Beach FL 33140-0488

BLALOCK, ANN BONAR, policy analyst, evaluation researcher; b. Parkersburg, W.Va., Apr. 16, 1928; d. Harry and Fay (Conley) Bonar; m. Hubert Blalock, Jr., 1951 (dec. 1991); children: Susan Blalock Lyon, Kathleen Blalock McCarrell, James W.; m. Gerhard E. Lenski, 1996. AB, Oberlin Coll., 1950; MA, U. N.C., 1954; MSW, U. Wash., 1978. Pvt. cons. Admiralty Inlet Consulting, Hansville, Wash. Sr. author: Introduction to Social Research, 2d edit., 1982; co-editor: Methodology in Social Research, 1968; editor: Evaluation Forum, 1986-97, Evaluating Social Programs, 1990. Recipient research award Partnership for Employment and Tng. Careers. Mem. NASW (past pres. Wash. State chpt.), Am. Eval. Assn. (past com. chair), Assn. Pub. Policy Analysis and Mgmt. Home: PO Box 409 Hansville WA 98340-0409

BLALOCK, BRENDA GALE, city official; b. Marble Valley, Ala., Oct. 24, 1948. City clk. City of Montgomery, Ala., 1997—. Office: Office of City Clerk 103 N Perry St Montgomery AL 36104*

BLALOCK, SHERRILL, investment advisor; b. Newport News, Va., June 9, 1945; d. David Graham and Martha Lee (Bennett) B.; m. Jonathan L. Smith, Oct. 27, 1985; 1 child, Graham C.G. BA, Smith Coll., 1967. Chartered fin. analyst. Investment broker Legg Mason & Co., Washington, 1968-77, Blyth Eastman Dillon, Washington, 1977-80; portfolio mgr., mng. dir. Mitchell Hutchins, N.Y.C., 1980-88; gen. ptnr., portfolio mgr. Weiss Peck & Greer, N.Y.C., 1988-95; gen. ptnr. Delphi Asset Mgmt., N.Y.C., 1995-98; founder, mng. mem. Chesapeake Asset Mgmt., N.Y.C., 1998—. Mem. investment com. Diocese of N.Y. of Episcopal Ch., 1992—, trustee Estate and Property of Diocesan Conv. of N.Y., 1996—; trustee Cathedral of St. John the Divine, 1998—. Mem. Washington Soc. Investment Analysts, Inst. Chartered Fin. Analysts. Office: Chesapeake Asset Mgmt 1 Rockefeller Plz Rm 1210 New York NY 10020-2002

BLAN, KENNITH WILLIAM, JR., lawyer; b. Dec. 15, 1946; s. Kennith William and Sarah Shirley (Shane) B.; 1 child, Noah Winton; m. Lyndy r. Ervin, Sept. 1, 1995. BS, U. Ill., 1968, JD, 1971. Bar: Ill. 1972, U.S. Supreme Ct. 1978. With Office State's Atty., Vermilion County, Ill., 1971-72; atty. Chgo. Title & Trust Co., 1972; assoc. Graham, Meyer, Young, Welsch & Maton, Ill., Chgo., Springfield, Danville, 1972-74; pvt. practice Danville, 1975—; spl. asst. atty. gen. Ill., 1974-76; atty. City of Georgetown, Ill., 1985-92, Village of Belgium, Ill., 1987-89, Village of Westville, Ill., 1988-91. Contbr. chpts. to books. Chmn. Vermilion County Young Rep. Club, 1975-77; founding sponsor Civil Justice Found.; mem. Christian Businessmen's Com., Christian Legal Soc. Capt. CAP. Mem. ABA, ATLA, Ill. Bar Assn., Vermilion County Bar Assn., Lawyer-Pilots Bar Assn., Ill. Trial Lawyers Assn. (bd. mgrs.), Ind. Trial Lawyers Assn., Am. Soc. Law and Medicine, Christian Legal Soc., Gideons Internat., Aircraft Owners and Pilots Assn., Elks. E-mail: blanlaw@aol.com. Office: PO Box 1995 Danville IL 61834-1995

BLAN, OLLIE LIONEL, JR., lawyer; b. Ft. Smith, Ark., May 22, 1931; s. Ollie Lionel and Eva Ocie (Cross) B.; m. Allen Conner Gillon, Aug. 19, 1960; children: Bradford Lionel, Elizabeth Ann, Cynthia Gillon. A.A., Ft. Smith Jr. Coll., 1951; LL.B., U. Ark., 1954. Bar: Ark. 1954, Ala. 1959, U.S. Dist. Ct. (no. dist.) Ala. 1959, U.S. Dist.Ct. (mid. and so. dist.) Ala. 1960, U.S. Ct. Appeals (5th cir.) 1960, U.S. Ct. Appeals (11th cir.) 1982, U.S. Supreme Ct. 1991. Rsch. analyst Ark. Legis. Coun., 1954-55; law clk. to judge U.S. Dist. Ct. (no. dist.) Ala., Birmingham, 1959-60; assoc. Spain, Gillon & Young, Birmingham, Ala., 1960-64; ptnr. Spain & Gillon and predecessor firms, Birmingham, Ala., 1965—; tchr. Am. Inst. Banking, 1965-68; speaker Ala. Inst. Continuing Edn., 1978—. Contbr. articles to legal jours. Treas. Jefferson County Hist. Assn., 1972-81, vice chmn., 1981-86, chmn., 1986-93; mem. Jefferson County Rep. Exec. Com., 1973-76; mem. Briarwood Sch. Bd., Birmingham, 1982-86; chmn. Here's Life Birmingham, 1986-88. Capt. USMCR, 1955-58, ret. Mem. ABA, Am. Bd. Trial Advocates, Ark. Bar Assn., Ala. Bar Assn. (com. on admissions and legal edn. 1971-74, com. jud. office 1972-76, com. ins. programs, bd. bar commrs. 1987-92), Birmingham Bar Assn. (exec. com. 1986-89), Ala. Def. Lawyers Assn. (v.p. 1983-84, 91-93, bd. dirs. 1988-91, sec.-treas. 1993-94, pres. elect. 1994-95, pres. 1995-96), Am. Coun. Life Ins., Internat. Assn. Def. Counsel (chmn. accident, health and life ins. com. 1987-90, Ala. state rep. 1996—), Def. Rsch. Inst. (Ala. state rep. 1996—), Summit Club (charter). Baptist. Home: 2100 English Village Ln Birmingham AL 35223-1729 Office: Spain & Gillon LLC 2117 2nd Ave N Birmingham AL 35203-3705 *My desire has been to achieve the highest standard in whatever area of life I am thrust, guided by principles of ethics and Christianity.*

BLANC, MAUREEN, public relations executive. Ptnr. Blanc & Otus Pub. Rels., Inc., San Francisco. Office: Blanc & Otus Pub Rels Inc 135 Main St Fl 12 San Francisco CA 94105-1812

BLANC, PETER (WILLIAM PETERS BLANC), sculptor, painter; b. N.Y.C., June 29, 1912; s. Edward H. and Martha Elliott (King) B. BA, Harvard U.; LLB, St. Johns U.; postgrad., Corcoran Sch. Art.; MA, Am. U. Assoc. Pennie, Davis, Marvin & Edmonds, N.Y.C., 1935-44; instr. Am. U., Washington, 1950-53. One-man shows include Washington Pub. Libr., 1950, Passedoit Gallery, 1951, 53, 58, Albert Landry Galleries, N.Y., 1960, La Galeria Escondida, Taos, 1955, Hudson River Mus., 1961, 65, Associated Artists Gallery, Washington, 1962, Amel Gallery, N.Y.C., 1964, Ft. Worth Art Mus., 1966, Thomson Gallery, N.Y.C., 1969, Benson Gallery, Bridgehampton, N.Y., 1969, Southampton Coll., 1971, Avanti Galleries, N.Y.C., 1974, Elaine Benson Gallery, Bridgehampton, 1979, Goat Alley Gallery, Sag Harbor, N.Y., 1984, 86, 91, Benton Gallery, Southampton, N.Y., 1988, Art House Odeon, Sag Harbor, 1993, Clayton & Liberatore Gallery, Bridgehampton, 1995, 97; group shows include Corcoran Gallery, 1948, 51, Whitney Mus. Am. Art, 1952, City Art Mus., St. Louis, 1951, Washington Water Color Club, 1949, 51, 52, Riverside Mus., 1950, 54, 58, 64, New Sch. for Social Rsch., 1956, Springfield Mus. Art, 1952, Nat. Collection Fine Art, Washington, 1953, Balt. Mus. Art, 1953, Bklyn. Mus., 1955, Fogg Mus. Art, 1959, NYU, 1960, St. Paul Gallery, 1961, Internat. Gallery N.Y., 1961, Fort Worth Art Mus., 1963, Assoc. Art Gallery, Washington, 1961, Hudson River Mus., 1965, Parrish Art Mus., Southampton, 1965, Benson Gallery, Bridgehampton, 1966-67, 77, Daniels Gallery, N.Y.C., 1965, East Hampton Guild Hall, N.Y.C., 1966-67, 73, Southampton Coll., 1967-72, Iona Coll., N.Y., 1968, Mercy Coll., N.Y., 1970, Ashawagh Hall, Springs, N.Y., 1971-77, 80, 82-87, 89, 91, 92, 93, Artists Equity Assn., N.Y.C., 1975, N.Y. Artists-Union Carbide Gallery, N.Y.C., 1975, 77, Art Guild, N.Y.C., 1976, Abe Rattner Ctr. for Arts, Sag Harbor, 1979, Guild Hall Mus., East Hampton, 1980, 86, 87, 89, Rattner Meml. Studio, Sag Harbor, 1980, Jacob K. Javits Fed. Bldg., N.Y.C., 1983, Old Jail Art Ctr., Albany, Tex., 1984, Lever House, N.Y.C., 1985, Goat Alley Gallery, Sag Harbor, 1983-98, Gallery Art 54, N.Y.C., 1986, Taos Arts Festival, N. Mex., 1986, Benton Gallery, Southampton, N.Y., 1987-90, Westbeth Galleries, N.Y.C., 1988-91, Lexington Ave. Armory, Artists of the Hamptons, N.Y.C., 1992, Art House Odeon, Sag Harbor, 1992, 93, Broome Street Gallery, N.Y.C., 1992, 93. Aaron Galleries, Chicago, 1994 Millenium Gallery, E. Hampton, 1995—, Clayton-Liberatore Gallery, Bridgehampton, N.Y., 1996-97. Lt. U.S. Army, 1944-46. Recipient awards Corcoran Gallery Art, 1949, awards Soc. Washington Artists, 1951, 53, awards Washington Water Color Club, 1949, 52. Mem. Spiral Group, N.Y. Artists Equity Assn. (dir. 1963-70), Artists Guild Washington (pres. 1951-53), Soc. Washington Artists, Proto-V Group, Am. Soc. Contemporary Artists, Artists' Alliance East Hampton. Home: PO Box 138 87 Jermain Ave Sag Harbor NY 11963-3405 Other: 161 W 75th St New York NY 10023-1801

BLANC, ROGER DAVID, lawyer; b. N.Y.C., Dec. 26, 1945; s. Robert Smith and Ara Jeanne (Ponchelet) B.; m. June Chunchin Ku, Sept. 17, 1972; children: David Jung-Wei, Gregory Jung-Lee, Cynthia Jung-Lin. BA, Yale U., 1967; JD, Columbia U., 1970. Bar: N.Y. 1971. Ptnr. Willkie Farr & Gallagher, N.Y.C.; lectr. various profl. orgns. Contbr. articles to profl. jours. Mem. Bd. Edn., Chappaqua, N.Y., 1985-90; dir. Yale Alumni Schs. Com. of Westchester, 1994—. Mem. ABA, Assn. of Bar of City of N.Y. (chmn. subcom. on market regulation, com. on fed. regulation of securities ABA 1993—), Nat. Assn. Securities Dealers, Inc. (mem. legal adv. bd. 1997—). Clubs: University (N.Y.C.); Whippoorwill (Armonk, N.Y.). Office: Willkie Farr & Gallagher 787 Seventh Ave New York NY 10019-6099*

BLANCHARD, BRUCE, environmental engineer, government official; b. Ft. Stotsenburg, Philippines, Dec. 26, 1932; s. Wendell and Marcella (Palmer) B.; m. Mary Josie Cain, July 31, 1992; children: Wendell, Laura, Renee. BS in Civil Engring., MTI, 1957, MS in Civil Engring., 1964; honor. grad., Commd. and Gen. Staff Course, Ft. Leavenworth, Kans., 1980. Teaching and rsch. asst. MTI, 1957-59, asst. lacrosse coach, 1958-59, 64; hydraulic engr. Bur. Reclamation, Dept. Interior, Denver, 1959-60, 60-61; water resources planning engr. Phoenix, 1961-66; sr. staff specialist Water Resources Coun., Washington, 1966-69; environ. specialist Office of Sec. Dept. Interior, Washington, 1970-71; dir. Office Environ. Project Rev., Washington, 1971-89; dep. dir. U.S. Fish and Wildlife Svc., Dept. of Interior, Washington, 1989-97; spl. asst. for tribal self-governance Office of Sec. of Interior, 1997—. Editor: The Nation's Water Resources, 1968. With U.S. Army, 1961-66; col. Md. N.G., 1967-85. Decorated Army Commendation medal, Army Meritorious Svc. medal, Army Achievement medal; recipient Commendation medal State of Md., 1976, 78, 79, Meritorious Svc. medal State of Md., 1983, Meritorious Svc. medal Dept. Interior, 1985, Disting. Svc. medal, 1999. Mem. ASCE, AAAS, Am. Geophys. Union, Am. Water Resources Assn., N.G. Assn. U.S., Soc. Am. Mil. Engrs., U.S. Armor Assn., Am. Soc. Pub. Adminstrs., Sr. Execs. Assn. Explorers Club, Phi Gama Delta. Home: 80 Observatory Cir NW Washington DC 20008-3611

BLANCHARD, CARY, football player; b. Fort Worth, Nov. 5, 1968; m. Mindy Blanchard; children: Blake, Bayli. Student, Okla. State U. Kicker Indpls. Colts, 1995—. Named to Pro Bowl, 1996.

BLANCHARD, CHARLES ALAN, lawyer, former state senator; b. San Diego, Apr. 14, 1959; s. David Dean and Janet (Laxson) B. BS, Lewis & Clark Coll., 1981; M of Pub. Policy, Harvard U., 1985, JD, 1985. Bar: Ariz. 1987, U.S. Dist. Ct. Ariz. 1988, U.S. Ct. Appeals (D.C. cir.) 1988, U.S. Ct. Appeals (9th cir.) 1988, U.S. Supreme Ct. 1994. Law clk. to hon. Harry T. Edwards Washington, 1985-86; law clk. to hon. Sandra Day O'Connor U.S. Supreme Ct., Washington, 1986-87; assoc. ind. counsel Ind. Counsel James McKay, Washington, 1987-88; atty. Brown & Bain, P.A., Phoenix, 1988-97; state senator State of Ariz., Phoenix, 1991-95; dir. Office of Legal Counsel Office of Nat. Drug Control Policy, Washington, 1997—; adj. prof. Ariz. State U. Coll. Law, 1996; chmn. Senate Judiciary Com., Phoenix, 1991-93; Dem. candidate U.S. Congress, 1994. Contbr. articles to profl. jours. Bd. dirs. Florence (Ariz.) Immigrant and Refugee Rights Project, 1990-97, Homeless Legal Assistance Project, Phoenix, 1992-97, Tempe Comty. Action Agy., 1994-97, ABA Com. on Immigration Law, 1996-98, ABA Com. on Substance Abuse, 1998—, Luth. Vol. Corps., Washington, 1986-88; state committeeman Ariz. Dem. Party, Phoenix, 1991-97; chmn. Ariz. Dem. Leadership Coun., Inc., 1992-97. Recipient Disting. Svc. award Ariz. Atty. Gen., 1992; Toll fellowship Coun. of State Govts., 1991; named Disting. Young Alumni Lewis and Clark Coll., 1987. Mem. ABA. Home: 2500 Q St NW Apt 405 Washington DC 20007-4348 Office: Office of Nat Drug Control Policy Exec Office of the Pres Washington DC 20503

BLANCHARD, DANIELLE RENÉ, music educator; b. Pontiac, Mich., Feb. 25, 1961; d. Richard Ford and donna Erle (Marvin) B. BS, Oakland U., 1983; MEd, Vander Cook Coll. Music, 1992. Cert. continuing tchr., Mich. Instr. Will-O-Way Apprentice Theatre, Bloomfield Hills, Mich., 1981-83, Oakland U., Rochester, Mich., 1984-87; assoc. dir., vocal coach Vocal Arts Acad., Rochester, 1983—; instr. Clarkston (Mich.) Cmty. Sch., 1988—; performer, dir. numerous nightclub acts, plays, musicals, revs., Detroit and Chgo., 1979—; cons., clinician D.B. Assocs., Waterford, Mich., 1983—; vocalist/arranger John Gaiaier Assocs., Troy, Mich., 1984—; staff clinician Music Unltd. Workshop Svcs., Clarkston, 1984—; bd. dirs. EverGreen Morning press, clarkston. Vocalist, arranger albums The Rosary Tapes, 1994 (3 Grammy award nominations); vocalist children's albums (8 Grammy award nominations); co-author: (play) The Gig Is Up, 1985; performer Montreux Jazz Festival, Detroit, 1989. Named WDIV Tchr. of Yr., Post-Newsweek, 1995. Mem. NARAS, Mich. Sch. Vocal Music Assn. (bd. dirs. 1989—, supr. 1993), Music Educators Nat. Conf., Clarkston Edn. Assn. (pub. rels. chair). Avocations: photography. composition, lapidary. Office: DB Assocs 1360 Nancywood Dr Waterford MI 48327-2041

BLANCHARD, DAVID LAWRENCE, aerospace executive, real estate developer, consultant; b. Taulbee, Ky., Feb. 13, 1931; s. Charles Lorraine and Gwyndolyn (Johnson) B.; m. Allene Irma Horne, June 28, 1958; children: Leslie Ruth, David Lawrence Jr. AB in Religion, Ind. Wesleyan U., 1953; MS in Physics, U. Louisville, 1959; PhD in Applied Physics, Cath. U. Am., 1971. Instr. U. Louisville, 1955-57, Ind. Wesleyan U., 1957-58; rschr. Naval Ordnance Lab., White Oak, Md., 1958-64; aerospace rschr., engr. NASA Goddard Space Flight Ctr., Greenbelt, Md., 1964-71, supr., mgr., 1971-79, sr. exec., 1979-81; staff cons., dir. rsch. Ford Aerospace Corp., Houston and Detroit, 1981-84; chief engr. Ford Aerospace, Houston, 1984-85; dir., exec. dir. space programs Ford Aerospace, Seabrook, Md., 1985-90; pres. Loral AeroSys, Seabrook, Md., 1990-96, Lockheed Martin Space Mission Systems, 1996-97; founder, prin. COGENT, LLC., Kennewick, Wash., 1997—; NASA rsch. fellow Eidgenossische Technische Hochschule, Zurich, Switzerland, 1974-75; rsch. advisor NRC, Greenbelt, Md., 1979-80; mem. pres.'s adv. coun. Ind. Wesleyan U., 1998—; mentor for small start up businesses Dingman Sch. Entrepreneurship, 1997—. Patentee fuze arming device. Chmn., charter mem. bus. and industry steering com. DuVal Aerospace Magnet Sch., Prince Georges County Schs. Seabrook, 1989-92, mem. bus. and industry adv. com. on sci. and tech., 1989-91; charter mem. bd. Opportunity Skyway, 1990-97; trustee, chmn. fin. com. Houghton Coll., N.Y., 1987-96, trustee, 1997—; charter mem., bd. trustees Md. Space Bus. Roundtable, 1989-97, pres., 1991-93; bd. visitors U. Md. Univ. Coll., 1994—, U. Md. Found., 1996—; charter mem., bd. trustees World Hope Internat., 1996—; bd. dirs. Willard J. Houghton Found., 1987—, chair bd., 1997—. With U.S. Army and USAR, 1957-64. Recipient Exceptional Svc. award NASA, 1968, Exceptional Performance award, 1973. Fellow Washington Acad. Scis., AIAA (assoc.); mem. Sigma Xi, Sigma Pi Sigma. Lutheran. Achievements include research in gravity-gradient stabilization experiment on 1500 foot antenna array in low earth orbit.

BLANCHARD, EDMOND P., Canadian government official; b. Campbellton, N.B., Can., May 31, 1954; s. John E. and Mary Rita (Hughes) B. B in Commerce, Dalhousie U., Halifax, N.S., Can., 1975; LLB, Dalhousie U., Halifax, N.S., 1978. Assoc. Tingley and Humphrey, Campbellton, 1979; ptnr. Tingley, Humphrey & Blanchard, Campbellton, Humphrey & Blanchard, Campbellton, 1989; min. of state for mines & energy Province of N.B., 1989-91, atty. gen., min. of justice, regional devel. corp. and intergovtl. affairs, 1991-94, min. of justice, atty. gen., 1994-95, min. of fin., min. of state for quality, 1995—, also chmn. bd. of mgmt. cabinet com.; MLA for Campbellton Riding Can., 1999—. Active Liberal Party-Campbellton, N.B., 1987—. Mem. Law Soc. N.B., Can. Bar Assn. Roman Catholic. Home: 4 Yorsdun Ct, Campbellton, NB Canada E3N 3N9 Office: Dept of Finance, 113 Roseberry St, CN Bldg 2nd Fl Rm 221, Campbellton, NB Canada 83N 2G6*

BLANCHARD, ERIC ALAN, lawyer; b. 1956. BBA, U. Mich., 1978; JD, Harvard U., 1981. Bar: Ill. 1981. Atty. Schiff, Hardin & Waite, 1981-86; corp. atty. Dean Foods Co., Franklin Park, Ill., 1986-88, gen. coun., sec., v.p., pres. dairy divsn., 1988—. Office: Dean Foods Co 3600 N River Rd Franklin Park IL 60131-2185*

BLANCHARD, GEORGE SAMUEL, retired military officer; b. Washington, Apr. 3, 1920; s. George S. and Elizabeth (Blanchard) B.; m. Beth Howard, June 9, 1944; children: Kate E. (Mrs. Ronald Hausner), Marylou C. (Mrs. John Hennessey), Deborah E. (Mrs. Eberhard Roell), Blythe H. (Mrs. Charles Watkins). Student, Am. U., 1938-40; BS, U.S. Mil. Acad., 1944; MS, Syracuse U., 1948; grad. Advanced Mgmt. Program, Harvard, 1966. Commd. 2d lt. AUS, 1944, advanced through grades to gen., 1975; served as co. comdr. and staff officer Europe, 1944-47; adviser Taiwan, 1955-57; with 82d Airborne Div. U.S., 1958-60, Korea, 1961-62, Vietnam, 1966-68; comdr. 82d Airborne div. Ft. Bragg, N.C., 1970-72; mem. Pentagon staff, 1962-66, 68-70, comdg. gen. VII Corps U.S. Army Europe, 1973-75, comdr. in chief U.S. Army Europe, 1975, ret., 1979; past pres. World USO, Gen. Analysis, Inc.; bd. dirs. Atlantic Coun. U.S. Contbr. to Ency. Brit. Vice chmn. Literacy Coun. Moore County. Decorated D.S.M. with 3 oak leaf clusters, Silver Star with oak leaf cluster, D.F.C., Bronze Star with oak leaf cluster. Mem. Assn. U.S. Army, Ret. Officers Assn. (past pres.), VFW, U.S. Soc. French Legion of Honor, Nat. Mil. Families Assn. Episcopalian.

BLANCHARD, J. A., publishing executive. CEO Deluxe Corp., St. Paul. Office: Deluxe Corp 3680 Victoria St N Saint Paul MN 55126-2906*

BLANCHARD, JAMES ARTHUR, engineer, computer systems specialist, financial planner; b. Evanston, Ill., Oct. 26, 1949; s. Arthur Knights and Verna Eloise (LeMann) B.; m. Debra Kathleen Smith, July 10, 1976; children: Andrew, Charles, Kenneth. BSCE, Northwestern U., 1972; MBA, U. Chgo., 1987. Registered profl. engr., Ill. Trainee DeLeuw, Cather and Co., Chgo., 1969-72; trainee Chgo. Transit Authority, 1972-74, procedural analyst, 1974-78, supt. capital program support, 1978-90, dir. capital program support, 1990-92, mgr. capital investment support, 1992—; mem. Chgo. Area Transp. Study Unified Work Program com., 1981; prin. Strategic Info. Solutions, 1997; planner Lincoln Fin. Advisors, 1998. Bd. dirs. Morton Grove (Ill.) Baseball Assn., 1991-97; active Marquette U. Parents Assn., Park View Sch. Parents Assn. Mem. Mensa, Beta Gamma Sigma. Roman Catholic. Avocations: investment analysis, gardening, travel, baseball, fine dining. Home: 8517 Austin Ave Morton Grove IL 60053-2928

BLANCHARD, LEONARD ALBERT, management consultant, writer; b. New Britain, Conn., July 30, 1947; s. Albert Edward and Sophie Marian (Lemanski) B.; children: Sarah Maddin Henniger, Henry Wyche Hunter. BA in English cum laude, Washington & Lee U., 1969; MA, Emory U., 1974, PhD, 1975. Instr. English, coach Oak Ridge (N.C.) Mil. Inst., 1969-71, St. Mark's Sch., Dallas, 1974-75; instr. English El Centro Coll., Dallas, 1975-79; writer, developer, liaison Southland Corp., Dallas, 1979-87; dir. devel. Franchise Group Internat., Little Rock, 1987-88; cons. Len Blanchard, Sarasota, Fla., 1988—; v.p. human resources Harken Internat., Bedford, Tex., 1989-90; mgmt. cons. Tropical Breeze Inn, Sarasota, 1996—. Author essays and poems, including An American Passion, 1999. Mem. Acad. Am. Poets, Libr. Congress Assocs., Washington & Lee U. Alumni Assn. Democrat. Avocations: swimming, hiking, classical music. Office: PO Box 17312 Sarasota FL 34276-0312

BLANCHARD, LOUIS A., medical/surgical nurse, educator; b. Chgo., Dec. 28, 1924; s. Glenkern A. and Luella (Sheehan) B.; m. Hedy H. Blanchard, Aug. 3, 1963. Diploma in Nursing, U. Ill.-Cook County Sch., Chgo., 1953; BS in Psychology and Biology, Roosevelt U., Chgo., 1964; MEd, Xavier U., Cin., 1971; BSN with honors, Fla. Internat. U., 1979. RN, Fla. Charge nurse cystoscopic surg. Mercy Hosp., 1956; supr. o.r. St. Anne's Hosp., 1955-57; staff nurse Nat. Hosp. for Nervous Disease, Queen's Square, Holborn, London, Eng., 1958-60; DON Soverign Nursing Home, Chgo., 1967; instr. Fox River Pavillion Psychiat. Hosp., Chgo., 1969-73; instr. in anatomy and med.-surg. nursing Ravenswood Med. Ctr. Sch. of Nursing, Chgo., 1969-73; pvt. duty nurse Miami, Fla., 1979-92; bd. dirs. Nurse's Ofcl. Registry, Miami, 1974-79. Donor Hedy Blanchard nursing award Fla. Internat. U., 1990. Recipient cert. of appreciation Nurse's Ofcl. Registry, 1979, Fla. Internat. U. Alumni Assn., 1982. Mem. ANA, Fla. Nurses Assn. (treas. 5th dist. 1989-90), Xavier Alumni Assn., Sigma Theta Tau, Tau Delta Phi.

BLANCHARD, RICHARD EMILE, SR., management services executive, consultant; b. Thompson, Conn., July 13, 1928; s. Lionel A. and Bernadette L. (Jolicoeur) B.; m. Lorraine Patricia Lachapelle, July 3, 1954; children: Michele Welling, Richard E., Danielle Wornstaff, Marie Blanchard Oser, Robert Allen, Janine. BS in Biology, Providence Coll., 1952; postgrad., U. Conn. Sch. Law, West Hartford, 1952-53. Cert. mgmt. cons. Chemist Charles Pfizer Co., Inc., N.Y.C., 1953-56, med. salesman, 1956-60, coll. rels. mgr., 1960-63, pers. mgr., 1963-67; dir. manpower and orgn. devel. Sky Chef divsn. Am. Airlines, N.Y.C., 1967-70; dir. manpower ARA Svcs., Inc., Phila., 1970-72, v.p., 1972-76; v.p. pers. Jerrico, Inc., Lexington, Ky., 1976-78; chmn., CEO Career Mgmt., Inc., C.M. Temporary Svcs., C.M. Mgmt. Svcs., Lexington, 1978—; cons. pers. svcs. Bd. dirs. Ky. Higher Edn. Coun., Bluegrass United Way, 1978—, Jr. Achievement, 1979—, Better Bus. Bur., 1985—, United Way of the Bluegrass, 1998—, U. Ky. Small Bus. Devel. Ctr., Ky. Econ. Devel. Coun.; v.p. Bluegrass Ednl. Work Coun., 1980—, Bluegrass Better Bus. Bur., 1990—, bd. dirs., past pres.; chmn. adv. bd. U. Ky. C.C., 1987—; divsn. chmn. United Way, 1990, 92—; bd. dirs., vice-chmn. Human Rights Commn., 1991-94; co-chmn. bd. dirs. Bluegrass MS Soc., 1996; mem. adv. bd. C.C. divsn. U. Ky., Muscular Dystrophy Bluegrass Coun. With USN, 1946-48. Mem. Inst. Mgmt. Cons., Am. Mgmt. Assn., Am. Soc. Pers. Assocs. (past pres. N.Y. chpt.), Nat. Assn. Temporary Svcs., Ind. Temporary Svcs. Assn., Ky. Assocs. Temporary Svcs. (past pres.), Ky. State C. of C. (bd. dirs.), Lexington C. of C. (bd. dirs. 1996—), Lexington Country Club, Exec. Fitness and Sports Ctr., Lexington Tennis Club, Rotary (bd. dirs. 1996—). Republican. Roman Catholic. Home: 16279 Edgemont Dr Fort Myers FL 33908-3658 Office: Career Mgmt Inc CM Staffing Svcs 698 Perimeter Dr Ste 200 Lexington KY 40517-5114

BLANCHARD, RICHARD FREDERICK, construction executive; b. Orange, N.J., Feb. 8, 1933; s. William F. and Dorothy Dew (Wright) B.; m. Jill Isles, Nov. 23, 1985. BA, Dartmouth Coll., 1955; MBA, Harvard U., 1957. Apprentice Wm. Blanchard Co., Newark, 1958-62, estimator, 1962-65; project mgr. Wm. Blanchard Co., Springfield, N.J., 1965-72, pres., 1972—. V.p. Newark Mus., 1986—. With U.S. Army, 1957-58. Mem. Bldg. Contractors Assn. N.J. (trustee 1986—), N.J. State C. of C. (bd. dirs. 1980-88). Presbyterian. Avocations: mountain climbing, skiing.

BLANCHARD, TOWNSEND EUGENE, retired service companies executive; b. Du Quoin, Ill., Jan. 30, 1931; s. Townsend and Anna Belle (Jackson) B.; m. Norma Louise Barr, Dec. 18, 1960; children: John Barr, Susan Melody, Jayne Ann Blanchard Reishus, Stephen Eugene. BS, U. Ill., 1952; MBA, Harvard U., 1957. Cons. Ill. Sch. Bond Svc., Monticello, 1958-62; co-founder, treas., chief fin. officer Americana Nursing Ctrs., Monticello, 1962-75; v.p. fin., treas., CFO, chief of staff Cenco, Inc., Chgo., 1975-79; sr. v.p., CFO DynCorp., McLean, Va., 1979-97; bd. dirs. Landmark Sys., Inc., DynCorp, 1987—; chmn. Employee Stock Ownership Plan; bd. trustees DynCorp, 1997—. Elder Presbyn. Ch.; bd. dirs. Combined Health Appeal, 1986-96; bd. advisors Cameron Glen Care Facility, 1989-92. Lt. USNR, 1952-55. Decorated Spl. Commendation letter. Mem. Fin. Execs. Inst. (chpt. pres. 1988-89, nat. v.p. and bd. dirs. 1991-94), Internat. Platform Assn., U. Ill. Alumni Club, Harvard U. Bus. Sch. Club, Harvard Club Washington, Econ. Club Chgo., Am. Legion, Delta Sigma Phi (trustee nat. found. 1982-89, pres. nat. found. 1988-89, Harvey W. Herbert award 1975, Mr. Delta Sig award 1988). Home and Office: 1222 Aldebaran Dr Mc Lean VA 22101-2305

BLANCHARD, WILLIAM GRAHAM, film educator; b. Montgomery, Ala., Dec. 18, 1944; s. Harry and Elizabeth Isabell (Graham) B.; m. Janice Ann, June 12, 1970 (dec. Dec. 1996); 1 child, Anthony. BA, Mich. State U., 1967; MA, U. So. Calif., L.A., 1970. Film lab. technician Capital Film Lab., Lansing, Mich., 1968; cinematographer Walt Disney Prodns., Burbank, Calif., 1969-70; film producer Mich. State U., East Lansing, Mich., 1970-75; film producer, prof. Lansing Community Coll., 1975—; ind. film maker. Producer (films) The Soo Locks (Ann Arbor Film Festival award 1979, Big Muddy Film Festival award 1979, Balt. Internat. Film Festival award 1979), Va. Commonwealth U. award 1979, Sinking Creek Festival award 1979), A Difference of Rights, 1980, The Afternoon (Cine Golden Eagle award 1964), (video tapes) Last Watch for Steam, 1989, Wheelchair User's Guide to Mackinac Island and the Straits Area, 1991 (several awards); cinematographer (TV shows) Snow Bear, 1969, Mountain Born, 1970. E-Mail bblancha@lansing.cc.mi.us. Home: 2011 Cumberland Rd Lansing MI

48906-3771 Office: Lansing Community Coll 3661 Art Program PO Box 40010 Lansing MI 48901-7210

BLANCHARD, WILLIAM HENRY, psychologist; b. St. Paul, Mar. 25, 1922; Charles Edgar and Ethel Rachel (Gurney) B.; m. Martha Ida Lang, Aug. 11, 1947; children: Gregory, Marcus, Mary Lisa. Diploma in Sci., Mason City Jr. Coll., 1942; BS in Chemistry, Iowa State U., 1944; PhD in Psychology, U. So. Calif., 1954. Lic. clin. psychologist, Calif. Shift chemist B.F. Goodrich Chem. Co., Port Neches, Tex., 1946-47; court psychologist LA. County Gen. Hosp., 1954-55; psychologist, dir. rsch. So. Reception Ctr. and Clinic Calif. Youth Authority, Norwalk, 1955-58; social scientist Rand Corp., 1958-60, Sys. Devel. Corp., 1960-70; mem. faculty Calif. State U.-Northridge, L.A., 1970; assoc. prof. UCLA, 1971; faculty group leader urban semester U. So. Calif., L.A., 1971-75; sr. rsch. assoc. Office of the Chancellor Calif. State U., UCLA, L.A., 1975-76; sr. fellow Planning Analysis and Rsch. Inst., Santa Monica, 1976-96; pvt. practice psycchologist Calif., 1976-96; clin. assoc. dept. psychology U. So. Calif., 1956-58. Author: Rousseau and the Spirit of Revolt, 1967, Aggression American Style, 1978, Revolutionary Morality, 1984, Neocolonialism American Style, 1996; contbr. articles to profl. jours. Mem. com. on mental health West Area Welfare Planning Coun., L.A., 1960-61; commr. Bd. Med. Examineres, psychology exam com. State of Calif., 1969; v.p. Parents and Friends of Mentally Ill Children, 1968-69, pres., 1966-68, trustee, 1968-69. Mem. APA, AAAS, Internat. Soc. Polit. Psychology. Home: 4307 Rosario Rd Woodland Hills CA 91364-5546

BLANCHET, BERTRAND, archbishop; b. Montmagny, Que., Can., Sept. 19, 1932; s. Louis and Alberta (Nicole) B. B.A., Coll. Ste-Anne-de-la Pocatiere, 1952; L.Th., Laval U., 1956, D.Sc., 1975. Ordained priest Roman Catholic Ch., 1956, consecrated bishop, 1973; tchr. biology Coll. and Coll. d'Enseignement Gen. et Profl., La Pocatiere, 1963-73; bishop of Gaspe Que., 1973-92; archbishop of Rimouski, 1992—. Mem. Chevaliers de Colomb, Rimouski. Address: CP 730, 34 Eveche Ouest, Rimouski, PQ Canada G5L 7C7

BLANCHET, JEANNE ELLENE MAXANT, artist, educator, performer; b. Chgo., Sept. 25, 1944; d. William H. and L. Barbara (Martin) Maxant; m. Yasuo Shimizu, Apr. 28, 1969 (div. 1973); m. William B. Blanchet, Aug. 21, 1981 (dec. May 1993). BA summa cum laude, Northwestern U., 1966; MFA, Tokyo U., 1971; MA, Ariz. State U., 1978; postgrad., Ill. State U., 1979-80; PhD, Greenwich U., 1991. Instr. Tsuda U., Kodaira, Japan, 1970-71; free-lance visual, performing artist various cities, U.S., 1973—; artist in residence YMCA of the Rockies, Estes Park, Colo., 1976-81 summers; prof. fine arts Rio Salado Coll., Surprise, Ariz., 1976-91; lectr. Ariz. State U. West, Sun City, 1985-93; evaluator several arts couns. including Ariz. Humanities Coun., 1993, Ariz. Humanities Coun. Scholar's SPkrs. Bur., 1998—; Prescott Melodrama ragtime pianist, 1993, 94; artist with Performing Arts for Youth, 1994—. Selected for regional, state, nat. juried art shows, 1975—, mus. and gallery one-woman shows of computer art, 1988—; author: Original Songs and Verse of the Old (And New) West, 1987, A Song in My Heart, 1988, Reflections, 1989, The Mummy Story, 1990; contbr. articles to newspapers, profl. jours. Founding mem. Del Webb Hosp. Woodrow Wilson fellow, 1966; ADA B.C. Welsh scholar, 1980; recipient numerous art, music awards, 1970—, major computer art awards in regional, nat., and internat. shows, 1990—. Mem. Nat. League Am. Pen Women (sec. chpt. 1987, v.p. 1988, pres. 1990-92, pres. Colo. chpt. 1996-97), Ariz. Press Women (numerous awards in original graphics and writing 1980s, 90s), Nat. Fedn. Press Women, Northwestern U.'s John Evans Club, Henry W. Rogers Soc., P.E.O. (rec. sec. chpt. BV 1998—), Phi Beta Kappa. Avocations: computers, ragtime piano, hiking, parapsychology. Home and Office: 6735 E Greenway Pky # 1048 Scottsdale AZ 85254 *To live is to think, to create.*

BLANCHET-SADRI, FRANCINE, mathematician; b. Trois-Rivieres, Quebec, Can., July 25, 1953; came to U.S., 1990; d. Jean and Rolande (Delage) B.; m. Fereidoon Sadri, July 28, 1979; children: Ahmad, Hamid, Mariamme. BSc in Math., U. Quebec a Trois-Rivieres, Can., 1976; MS, Princeton U., 1979; PhD, McGill U., 1989. Rsch., tchg. asst. U. Quebec, Trois-Rivieres, Quebec, Can., 1974-76; lectr. U. Quebec, 1976; rsch. asst. Princeton (N.J.) U., 1978; lectr. U. Tech. Isfahan, Iran, 1982-84, McGill U., Montreal, Quebec, 1988-89; assoc. prof. U. N.C., Greensboro, 1990—. Contbr. articles to profl. jours. Recipient Rsch. Excellence award 1991; Natural Scis. and Engring. Coun. Can. postgrad. fellow, 1976-80, Fonds pour la Formation de Chercheurs et L'aide a la Rsch. fellow, 1985-87, Natural Scis. and Engring. Rsch. Coun. Can. fellow, 1990; New Faculty grantee U. N.C., Greensboro, 1990-91, NSF grantee, 1991—. Mem. Am. Math. Soc., Assn. for Computing Machinery. Achievements include discovery that the dot-depth of a generating class of aperiodic monoids is computable. Office: U NC Dept Math Scis PO Box 26170 Greensboro NC 27402-6170

BLANCHETT, CATE, actress; b. Melbourne, Australia, May 14, 1969. Grad., Nat. Inst. Dramatic Art, Australia, 1992. With Sydney Theatre Co., Belvoir St. Theatre Co. Appeared in theatre prodns., including Top Girls, Kafka Dances (New Comer award Sydney Theatre Critics Circle 1993), Oleanna (Rosemont Best Actress award), Hamlet, 1995, Sweet Phoebe, The Tempest, The Blind Giant is Dancing; actress (TV appearances) Heartland, Bordertown, G.P., Police Rescue; actress (films) Parklands, 1996, Paradise Road, 1997, Thank God He Met Lizzie, 1997 (Best Performance by an Actress in Supporting Role award Australian Film Inst. 1997), Oscar and Lucinda, Elizabeth, 1998 (Nominated Oscar 1999, Nominated Best Performance by an Actress in a Leading Role award Brit. Acad. Awards 1999, Best Actress award Broadcast Film Critics Assn. Awards 1999, Best Actress award Chgo. Film Critics Assn. Awards 1999, Best Performance by an Actress in a Motion Picture award Golden Globe 1999, Best Actress in Motion Picture award Golden Satellite Awards 1999, Actress of Yr. 1999, Nominated Screen Actors Guild award 1999), Talented Mr. Ripley, 1999, Ideal Husband, 1999, Pushing Tin, 1999. Office: care Robyn Gardiner, PO Box 128, Surry Hills 2010 NSW, Australia*

BLANCHETTE, OLIVA, philosophy educator; b. Berlin, N.H., May 6, 1929; s. Delphis and Odelia (Morneau) B.; m. Dorothy M. Kennedy, May 25, 1975; children: Nicole Elizabeth, Frances Kathleen. A.B. in Philosophy, Boston Coll., 1953, M.A., 1958; Licentiate in Philosophy, Coll. St. Albert de Louvain, Belgium, 1954; Licentiate in Sacred Theology, Weston Coll., 1961; Ph.D. in Philosophy, U. Laval, Que., Can., 1966. Prof. Latin, Greek and English Boston Coll. High Sch., 1954-57; instr. philosophy Boston Coll., 1964-65, asst. prof., 1965-67, asso. prof., 1967-74, prof., 1974—; dean Sch. of Philosophy, 1968-73; dir. Inst. for Social Thought. Author: Initiative in History: A Christian-Marxist Exchange, 1967, For a Fundamental Social Ethic: A Philosophy of Social Change, 1973, The Perfection of the Universe According to Aquinas: A Teleological Cosmology, 1992; contbr. articles on philosophy of history, metaphysics, philosophy of religion, and social ethics to scholarly jours. Mem. Hegel Soc. Am., Metaphys. Soc. Am., Internat. Soc. Metaphys. Home: 28 Florence St Natick MA 01760-2121 Office: Boston Coll Chestnut Hill MA 02167

BLANCHETTE, ROBERT WILFRED, business executive, lawyer; b. New Haven, July 7, 1932; s. Wilfred H. and Dora R. (deJordy) B.; m. Marna Madelaire Nielsen, May 17, 1969; children: Pierre de Jordy, Valerie Claude. BA, U. Conn., 1953; Woodrow Wilson fellow, Fulbright scholar, U. Grenoble, France, 1953-54; LLB cum laude, Yale U., 1957. Bar: Conn. 1957, D.C. 1977. Ptnr. firm Adams, Blanchette & Evans, 1957-62; gen. counsel N.Y., N.H. & H. R.R., 1963-68; gen. atty. New Eng. Penn Cen. Co., 1969-70; exec. dir. America's Sound Transp. Rev. Orgn., Washington, 1969-70; counsel to bd. trustees Penn Cen. Transp. Co., Phila., 1970-74, trustee, 1974—, chmn. bd. trustees, chief exec. officer, 1975-78; ptnr. firm Alston, Miller & Gaines, Washington, 1976-81; adminstr. Fed. R.R. Adminstrn., Washington, 1981-83; pres., chief exec. officer The TGV Co., Washington, 1983-89; pvt. practice law Washington, 1983—; of counsel Verner, Liipfert, Bernhard, McPherson & Hand, Washington, 1989-90; v.p. law, gen. counsel Assn. of Am. R.R.s, Washington, 1990-97; atty. pvt. practice, 1997—; tutor Yale U., 1961-68. Editor-in-chief: Yale Law Jour. Trustee Assumption Coll., Worcester, Mass., 1981—. 1st lt. USAF, 1958-60. Mem. ABA, D.C. Bar Assn., Order of Coif. Roman Catholic. Clubs: Yale (N.Y.C.); Columbia Country (Chevy Chase, Md.). Home: 5315 Falmouth Rd Bethesda MD 20816-2916

BLANCK, RONALD RAY, hospital administrator, internist, career officer; b. Lancaster, Pa., Oct. 8, 1941; s. Harvey Ray and Mildred Catherine (Smith) B.; m. Donna Rae Ault, Sept. 17, 1971; children: Jennifer, Susan. BS, Juniata Coll., 1963; DO, Phila. Coll. Osteo. Medicine, 1967; DSc in Osteopathy (hon.), New Eng. Coll. Osteo. Medicine, 1982; LLD (hon.), Phila. Coll. Osteo. Medicine, 1991. Diplomate Am. Bd. Internal Medicine. Intern Lancaster Osteo. Hosp., 1967-68; resident in internal medicine Walter Reed Army Gen. Med. Ctr., 1970-73; commd. capt. U.S. Army, 1968, advanced through grades to lt. gen., 1996; gen. med. officer U.S. Army, Vietnam, 1968-69, Ft. Myer, Va., 1969-70; asst. chief gen. med. svc. Walter Reed Army Med. Ctr., Washington, 1973-74, asst. chief dept. medicine, 1974-76; asst. dean student affairs Sch. Medicine Uniformed Svcs. U., Bethesda, Md., 1976-79; chief dept. medicine Brooke Army Med. Ctr., San Antonio, Tex., 1979-82; chief med. corps career activities office Army Med. Dept. Pers. Support Act, Washington, 1982-85; comdr. U.S. Army Hosp., Berlin, 1986-88, Army Regional Med. Ctr., Frankfurt, Germany, 1988-90; dir. prof. svcs., chief med. corps affairs Office of Surgeon Gen., Fall Church, Va., 1990-92; comdr. Walter Reed Army Med. Ctr., Washington, 1992-96; surgeon gen., comdr. MECOM U.S. Army, Falls Church, Va., 1996—; asst. prof. clin. medicine Georgetown U., Washington, 1972-78; clin. instr. medicine Howard U., Washington, 1975-77; assoc. prof. medicine USUHS, Bethesda, 1976-; clin. assoc. prof. medicine U. Tex., San Antonio, 1979-80, clin. prof. medicine, 1980-82; USUAS Bethesda, Md. Disting. Prof. Military Medicine, 1998—. Guest editor Osteopathic Annals, 1981; mem. editorial adv. bd. History of Medicine in Vietnam, 1981. Trustee Assn. Mil. Osteo. Physicians and Surgeons, Boca Raton, Fla., 1992, U.S. Soldier's and Airmen's Home, Washington, 1992; advisor bd. regents Uniformed Svcs. U. Health Scis., Bethesda, 1992; bd. dirs. Nat. Med. Vets. Soc., Chgo., 1993. Decorated Bronze Star, Legion of Merit, Def. Superior Svc. medal; recipient Founder's award Tex. Coll. Osteo. Medicine, 1991. Fellow Am. Coll. Physicians (gov.); mem. AMA (alt. del.), Am. Acad. Physician Execs., Am. Osteo. Assn., Assn. Mil. Surgeons U.S. (John Shaw Billings award 1976), Berlin Internat. Med. Soc., Assn. Mil. Osteo. Physicians and Surgeons, Soc. Med. Cons. Armed Forces (assoc.). Episcopalian. Avocations: reading, jogging. Office: The Surgeon Gen 5109 Leesburg Pike # 6 Falls Church VA 22041-3208

BLANCO, JOSEFA JOAN-JUANA (JOSSIE BLANCO), social services administrator; b. Havana, Cuba, Jan. 31, 1954; came to U.S., 1962; d. Oscar Manuel and Josefa (Rodriguez) B.; m. John Franklin Hurt III, Nov. 18, 1979 (div. June 1985); children: John Franklin IV, Jeaninne Bernadette; 1 child, Richard Manuel Tejeda. BA in Psychology and Religion, Fla. Internat. U., 1975, MA in Sch. Psychology, 1976, postgrad. in pub. adminstrn., from 1983; MS in Human Resource Adminstrn., Villanova U., 1979; PhD in Adminstrn., West Coast U. Lic. tchr., Fla.; tng. lic. clin. and child care svcs. Psychometrician Mailman Ctr. for Child Devel., U. Miami, 1975-76; supr. adoptions Health and Rehabilitative Svcs. Fla., Miami, 1972-75, 76-80; instr. psychology Draughons Jr. Coll., Memphis, 1980-81; spl. project dir. Children's Psychiat. Ctr., Miami, 1981-84; exec. dir. Community Habilitation Ctr., Miami, 1984-86; shelter dir. Miami Bridge, Inc., Miami, 1986-89; regional dir. Luth. Ministries Fla., Ft. Lauderdale, 1989-90; exec. dir. Residential Pla. at Blue Lagoon Inc., Miami, 1990; grant writer, researcher, speaker at confs., 1990—; instr. Dade County Pub. Sch. System, 1991—; health ctr. adminstr. Dade County Pub. Health Dept. State of Fla. Dept. Health and Rehab. Svcs., 1992-94; instr. Dade County Pub. System, 1994—; instr. psychology Fla. Nat. Coll., 1998—, acad. adv., 1999—; facilitator nat. confs. Nat. Justice Dept. Bd. dirs. S.E. Region Com. To Study AIDS and AIDS Prevention; mem. Adult Congregate Living Facility. Recipient award for svc. to runaways Fla. Network, 1989, plaque for work with troubled youth Friends Fla. Network, 1989; Miami Herald scholar, 1969. Mem. Residential Child Car Assn. (bd. dirs., chmn. advocacy com.), Fla. Network Youth and Family Svcs. (quality assurance com., tng. com.), NAFE. Republican. Roman Catholic. Avocations: water sports, tennis. Address: 10521 SW 48th St Miami FL 33165-5649

BLANCO, KATHLEEN BABINEAUX, lieutenant governor; m. Raymond; 6 children. With La. State Legis. Dist. 45, 1984-88, mem. house edn. com., mem. house transp., hwys., and pub. works com.; mem. house edn. com., mem. house transp., hwys., and pub. works com. Pub. Svc. Commn., La., 1988-94, chair, 1993-95; lt. gov. State of La., 1995—. Address: PO Box 44243 Baton Rouge LA 70804-4243*

BLANCO, LAURA, film producer; b. Havana, Cuba, July 3, 1956; came to U.S., 1960; d. Lauro and Marina (Mardones) B.; m. Robert F. Shainheit, June 30, 1988. Asst. box office treas., press agt. Zev Bufman Entertainment, Inc., Orlando, St. Petersburg, Fla., 1978-83; press agt. Kool Jazz Festival and Heritage Fair, Orlando, 1982; producer La. World Exposition Inc., New Orleans, 1983-84, Festival Ventures, Inc., Miami, Fla., 1985-86; producer/dir. hispanic events Festival Prodns., Inc., N.Y.C., 1986-87; pres. Blanco Shainheit Prodns., Blanco Shainheit Music, N.Y.C., 1988—; ptnr. unanimo, 1992—. Prodr. (short film) The Summer of My Dreams, 1994, La Ciudad, 1995, (feature film, award winner Havana Film Festival, 1998), Perdida, 1998. Bd. dirs. Artists Community Fed. Credit Union, 1988-90. Mem. ASCAP, Am. Latin Music Assn. Avocation: collecting arts and crafts period furnishings and pottery, Lat. Am. art.

BLANCO, LUCIANO-NILO, physicist; b. Havana, Cuba, May 28, 1932; s. Luciano and Maria Teresa (Zayas) B.; m. Noemi de los A. Vitier, Dec. 16, 1956; 1 child, Marina Margarita. Student, U. Havana, 1949-54; fellow, Pa. State U., MIT, 1954-55; PhD in Physics, U Havana, Acad. Scis., 1962, 63. Inspector Chas. Martin Co. of Cuba, Havana, 1953-54; researcher Co. Rayonera Cubana, Matanzas, 1955-59; rsch. scientist Comision de Fomento Nacional, Havana, 1959-63; instr., physics prof. U. Havana, 1959-65; dir., rsch. physicist Acad. Scis., Havana, 1963-70; dir. phys. lab. and operation rsch. Avon, SA, Madrid, 1970-76; rsch scientist, mem. faculty physics U. Miami, Coral Gables, Fla., 1976-94; prof. physics, dir. Inst. Theoretical Rsch., Coral Gables, Fla., 1990—; sci. advisor Internat. Yrs. of the Quiet Sun, Havana, 1964-65; cons. Clean Energy Rsch. Inst. U. Miami, Coral Gables, 1980—; cons. physicist, U.S.A., Spain, 1970—. Editor: Energias No-Convencionales, 1983; editor Boletin de Geofisica, 1965-67, EnergyNotes and EnergyLetters, 1990-94; contbr. articles to profl. jours. Fellow Fgn. Ops. Adminstrn. and U.S. Weather Bur., Washington, 1954, Clean Energy Rsch. Inst., Coral Gables, 1982. Mem. Am. Phys. Soc., Internat. Energy Soc. (pres. 1982-95), N.Y. Acad. Scis., Royal Instn. Gt. Britain, Sigma Xi. Achievements include research in solar-terrestrial relationships, neutrino physics and astrophysics, fundamental principles in energy, theoretical physics, biophysics. Office: Inst Theoretical Rsch PO Box 248514 Miami FL 33124-8514

BLAND, ANNIE RUTH (ANN BLAND), nursing educator; b. Bennett, N.C., Oct. 14, 1949; d. John Wesley and Mary Ida (Caviness) Brown; m. Chester Wayne Bland; 1 child, John Wayne; stepchildren: Jason Tyler, Adam Mathew. BSN, East Carolina U., Greenville, N.C., 1971; MSN, U. N.C., Chapel Hill, 1978; postgrad., U. S.C., 1996—. RN, N.C.; cert. clin. specialist in adult psychiat./mental health nursing; cert. BLS instr. Staff nurse VA Med. Ctr., Durham, N.C., 1974-75, 77-80; psychiat. clin. instr. Duke U. Med. Ctr., Durham, 1980-82, asst. head nurse, 1982-90, staff nurse, 1993—; psychiat. clin. nurse specialist John Umstead Hosp., Butner, N.C., 1990-93; psychiat. head nursing instr. Alamance C.C., Graham, N.C., 1994-96. Asst. Sunday sch. tchr. Mt. Hermon Bapt. Ch., Durham, 1994, 96-97. Capt. USN, 1971-74, USNR, 1974-97, ret. 1997. Recipient award for nursing excellence Great 100 Orgn., Raleigh, N.C., 1991, Letter of Appreciation Am. Heart Assn., Chapel Hill, 1992. Mem. ANA, N.C. Nurses Assn. (sec. dist. 11, 1981), Naval Res. Assn., Assn. Mil. Surgeons U.S., U. N.C. Chapel Hill Alumni Assn. and Sch. Nursing, East Carolina U. Alumni Assn. and Sch. Nursing, Nat. Alliance for Mentally Ill, Epilepsy Found., Res. Officers Assn. U.S. Baptist. Avocations: tennis, swimming, water skiing, snow skiing. Home: 2534 New Hope Ch Rd Chapel Hill NC 27514 Office: U South Carolina Sch of Nursing CB #7460 Carrington Hall Chapel Hill NC 27599-7460

BLAND, FREDERICK AVES, architect; b. Galveston, Tex., Dec. 21, 1945; s. David and Florence (Aves) B.; m. Morley Ann Thomson, Dec. 21, 1968; 1 child, Chloe Thomson. BA, Yale U., 1968, MArch, 1972. Registered architect, N.Y., Conn., Fla., Va. Assoc. Beyer Blinder Belle, Architects & Planners, N.Y.C., 1974-77, dir. design, 1977-79, ptnr., 1979—; chief architect Yale Archeol. project Royal Abbey St. Denis, Paris, 1970-80. V.p. Bklyn. Heights Assn., 1981-86, pres., 1992-94; panel mem. N.Y. State coun. on Arts, 1985-86; exec. com. Friends of Edn., Mus. of Modern Art; trustee Bklyn. Botanic Garden, 1993—, chmn. horticulture com., 1996—, exec. com., 1996—, vice-chmn., 1999—; bd. trustees Bklyn. Hist. Soc.; v.p. N.Y. Found. Architecture, 1998, pres., 1999. Mem. AIA (nat. com. on design, coll. of fellows, jury of fellows 1995-97), Am. Inst. Cert. Planners, Mcpl. Art Soc. N.Y., Heights Casino Club (bd. govs. 1981-87, pres. 1987-90), Rembrandt Club, Yale Club (N.Y.C.). Democrat. Episcopalian. Home: 26 Pierrepont St Brooklyn NY 11201-7209 also: 30 Wallace Rd Stony Creek CT 06405-5730 Office: Beyer Blinder Belle Architects 41 E 11th St Fl 2 New York NY 10003-4673

BLAND, GILBERT TYRONE, foodservice executive; b. Fredericksburg, Va., Mar. 10, 1955; s. Robert Edward and Ruth Elizabeth (Bumbry) B.; children: Robert David, Allison Michelle, Elizabeth Caroline. BS, James Madison U., 1977; MBA, Atlanta U., 1979. Banking officer Continential Ill. Bank, Chgo., 1979-83; v.p. Independence Bank, Chgo., 1983-85; pres. Tymark Enterprises Inc., Norfolk, Va., 1985—; chmn. The Tycorp Group, Norfolk, Va., 1995—; owner, franchisee Burger King, No. Va., 1985—, Pizza Hut, Va. and Greensboro, N.C., 1995—; pres. Burger King Minority Franchise Assn., Miami, Fla., 1988-92; bd. dirs. Nat. Franchise Assn., Miami, 1988-92, Burger King Diversity Action Coun., 1992-96 (charter mem.), S.E. Region Internat. Pizza Hut Franchise Holders Assn., 1996-98; marketing adv. com. Burger King, 1992-98; State of Va. Small Bus. Financing Authority, Richmond, 1990—. Chmn., exec. com., bd. advisors Old Dominion Univ. Sch. Bus., Norfolk, 1990, Va. Marine Sci. Mus. Found., Virginia Beach, 1991; trustee James Madison U. Found., 1992; bd. dirs. Hampton U. Bus. Adv. Ctr., Greater Norfolk Corp., Senatra Hosp. Norfolk, Chamber Group Plans, Inc., Norfolk State U. Athletic Found.; exec. bd. Tidewater Coun. Boy Scouts of Am. Recipient James W. Mclamore Outstanding Svc. Leadership award Burger King Franchise Assn., 1992, Community Svc. award Alpha Kappa Alpha, 1990, Norfolk Community Hosp., 1991; Burger King Endowed scholar James Madison U., 2992. Mem. Beta Gamma Sigma. Baptist. Avocations: biking, chess, swimming. Office: Tymark Enterprises Inc 223 E City Hall Ave Ste 401 Norfolk VA 23510-1716

BLAND, JOHN L., lawyer; b. Wichita Falls, Tex., Sept. 20, 1944. Student, Vanderbilt U.; BA, U. Tex., 1967, JD with honors, 1969. Bar: Tex. 1969. Mem. Bracewell & Patterson, LLP, Houston, 1969—. Mem. State Bar Tex., Houston Bar Assn., Phi Delta Phi. Office: Bracewell & Patterson LLP 2900 S Tower Pennzoil Pl 711 Louisiana St Houston TX 77002-2781*

BLAND, J(OHN) RICHARD, lawyer; b. Denver, Oct. 30, 1946; s. Harry Edward and Julia Lenora (Bjelland) B.; m. Carole Jeanne Martin, Aug. 25, 1968. BS, Augustana Coll., 1968; JD, Drake U., 1971. Bar: Iowa 1971, Minn. 1971, U.S. Supreme Ct. 1976. Assoc. Meagher & Geer PLLP, Mpls., 1971-75, ptnr., 1975—; lectr. Minn. Inst. of Legal Edn., Mpls., 1985—. Fellow Am. Coll. Trial Lawyers; mem. Minn. Bar Assn., Minn. Def. Lawyers Assn. (bd. dirs. 1986-88). Home: 17225 5th Ave N Plymouth MN 55447-3593 Office: Meagher & Geer PLLP 33 S 6th St Ste 4200 Minneapolis MN 55402-3722

BLAND, MARYBETH, volunteer, artist; b. Queens, N.Y., Aug. 24, 1956; d. John Domminck Bland and Lorraine E. Groser; m. Anthony Paul O'Leary, May 1, 1981. BA, L.I. U., 1978; alcohol studies cert., Seattle U., 1983. Cert. chem. dependency counselor, Wash. Resident counselor Resource Found., Stanwood, Wash., 1977-80; mental health worker Alderwood Inn, Mountlake Terrace, Wash., 1980; team leader Ruth Dykeman Ctr., Burien, Wash., 1980-84; counselor Pt. Job Around, Seattle, 1985-86; adolescent program coord. Intercept, Federal Way, Wash., 1986-90. Bicycle pedestrian adv. com. City of Olympia, 1995-98; advisor for bike pedestrian safety and edn. com., Olympia, 1997—; diversity panelist The Olympian, Olympia, 1998—; vol. Stream Team, Olympia, 1996—. Recipient Cert. of Appreciation Alcohol Drug Helpline, 1991, Recognition award Olympia City Coun., 1998. Mem. Esperanto League of N.Am. Avocations: playing harmonica, swimming, Esperanto, reading, bird watching. Home: 606 Lilly Rd NE #523 Olympia WA 98506

BLAND, TERESA P., financial analyst, consultant; b. N.Y.C., Oct. 19, 1957; d. Richard James and Janet (Myers) B. BA in Art History and Comparative Lit., Fordham U., 1989. Adminstrv. asst. Juilliard Sch., N.Y.C., 1988-90; bursar Grad. Sch. Figurative Art, N.Y.C., 1990-91; registrar Cunningham Dance Found., N.Y.C., 1993-94, fin. officer, 1994-95; contr. Stephen Gaynor Sch., N.Y.C., 1995-96; internal controls analyst Office of the Comptr., City of N.Y., 1998—; archivist Found. for Dance Promotion, N.Y.C., 1996. Vol. KAPOW. Charlotte W. Newcombe Found. scholar, 1988, 89. Mem. Film Soc. Lincoln Ctr., Mus. Modern Art, Fordham U. Alumni Fedn. Democrat. Avocations: opera, ballet, cinema, travel, museums. Home: 3900 Greystone Ave Riverdale NY 10463-1944 Office: Comptr's Office Mcpl Bldg One Centre St New York NY 10007

BLANDA, SANDI, artist; b. N.Y., Jan. 30, 1949; m. Robert S. Blanda, Feb. 24, 1973; children: Jaime, Elyse. BA, Queens Coll., 1971. Folk artist Great Neck, N.Y., 1983—. Designer sea shell mosaics in octagonal mahogany cases "Sailor's Valentine"; exhbns. include Sailor's Valentine Gallery, Nantucket, Mass., 1984—, Quester Gallery, Stonington, Conn., 1994—, Bailey-Matthews Shell Mus., Sanibel, Fla., 1996—, The Christina Gallery, Martha's Vineyard, Mass., 1997—, Stephanie Hoppen Ltd., London, 1997—, others. Recipient numerous 1st and 2nd prizes for folk art, Sanibel Shell Fair, 1990-98, L.I. Shell Show, 1990. Home: 18 Oxford Blvd Great Neck NY 11023-2239

BLANDER, MILTON, chemist; b. Bklyn., Nov. 1, 1927; s. Benjamin and Yetta (Schwartzman) B.; children: Benjamin, Alice, Kathryn, Daniel, Joshua. BS, CUNY, 1950; PhD, Yale U., 1953. Rsch. assoc. Cornell U., Ithaca, N.Y., 1953-55; chemist Oak Ridge (Tenn.) Nat. Lab., 1955-62; chemist, group leader Rockwell Internat. Sci. Ctr., Thousand Oaks, Calif., 1962-71; sr. chemist, group leader Argonne (Ill.) Nat. Lab., 1971-97; founder Quest Rsch., South Holland, Ill., 1995—. Recipient Materials Rsch. award U.S. Dept. Energy, 1984, Alexander von Humboldt award. Fellow AAAS, Meteoritical Soc.; mem. Metall. Soc., Am. Chem. Soc., Electrochem. Soc. (Max Bredig award 1987), Norwegian Acad. Tech. Scis. Office: Argonne Nat Lab 9700 S Cass Ave Argonne IL 60439

BLANDFORD, DICK, electrical engineering and communications educator. Chmn. dept. elec. engring. and computer sci. U. Evansville, Ind., 1994—. Office: U Evansville Dept Elec Engring/Computers 1800 Lincoln Ave Evansville IN 47722*

BLANDFORD, ROGER DAVID, astronomy educator; b. Grantham, Eng., Aug. 28, 1949; s. Jack George and Janet Margaret (Evans) B.; m. Elizabeth Kellett, Aug. 5, 1972; children: Jonathan, Edward. BA, Magdalene Coll., Cambridge U., 1970; MA, PhD, Cambridge U., 1974. Rsch. fellow St. John's Coll., Cambridge U., 1973-76; asst. prof. astronomy Calif. Inst. Tech., Pasadena, 1976-79, prof., 1979-89, Richard Chace Tolman prof. theoretical astrophysics, 1989—; mem. Inst. Advanced Study, Princeton, 1974-75. Contbr. articles to profl. publs. W.B.R. King scholar, 1967-70; Charles Kingsley Bye fellow, 1972-73; Alfred P. Sloan research fellow, 1980, Guggenheim fellow, 1988—. Fellow Royal Soc., Royal Astron. Soc., Cambridge Philos. Soc.; mem. Am. Astron. Soc. (Warner prize 1982, Heineman prize 1998), Am. Acad. Arts and Scis. Office: Calif Inst Tech Dept Astrophysics Pasadena CA 91125

BLANE, HOWARD THOMAS, research institute administrator; b. De Land, Fla., May 10, 1926; s. Chesley Thomas and Olive Henrietta (Van Heest) B.; children: Benjamin, Eva. BA cum laude, Harvard U., 1950; MA, Clark U., 1951, PhD, 1957. Instr. Harvard Med. Sch., Cambridge, Mass., 1957-66, asst. clin. prof., 1966-70; assoc. prof. U. Pitts., 1970-72, prof., 1972-86; rsch. prof. SUNY, Buffalo, 1986—; dir. Rsch. Inst. Addictions, Buffalo, 1986-96; cons. Nat. Inst. on Alcohol Abuse and Alcoholism, Washington, 1970—; v.p. Health Edn. Found., Washington, 1975—; bd. dirs. Rsch. Found. for Mental Hygiene, Albany, N.Y., 1986-96; principal investigator numerous grants. Author: The Personality of the Alcoholic, 1968; editor:

Frontiers of Alcoholism, 1970, Youth, Alcoholism and Social Policy, 1979, Psychological Theories of Drinking and Alcoholism, 1987. Clark U. scholar, Worcester, Mass., 1950-51. Fellow APA, Am. Psychol. Soc.; mem. APHA, AAAS, Rsch. Soc. on Alcoholism. Office: Rsch Inst on Addictions 1021 Main St Buffalo NY 14203-1016

BLANK, ARTHUR M., home and lumber retail chain executive; b. 1942. Acct. Arthur Young & Co., N.Y.C., 1963-67; with Daylin Inc., Los Angeles, 1967-74; v.p., treas. Handy Dan Home Improvement Ctrs. Inc., Los Angeles, 1974-78; with Home Depot Inc., Atlanta, 1978—, now pres., chief oper. officer, asst. sec., also bd. dirs. Office: Home Depot Inc 2455 Paces Ferry Rd NW Atlanta GA 30339-4024*

BLANK, FLORENCE WEISS, literacy educator, editor; b. Bridgeport, Conn.; d. Maurice Herbert and Henrietta Helen (Shapiro) Weiss; m. Bernard Blank, Apr. 10, 1965 (dec. Aug., 1989). Student Journalism, English, Psychology, Richmond Profl. Inst.; student, U. Richmond, Northwestern U., Va. Union U., 1967, 73, 74, U. Wis., Milw., 1971, Va. Commonwealth U., 1973, D.C. Tchrs. Coll., 1975. Tchr. adult edn. dept. Richmond (Va.) Pub. Sch. System, 1952-77; project dir., tchr. tng. and edn. dir., tchr. Right to Read Fed. Grant, D.C., 1976-79; in-svc. tchr. tng. U. D.C., Washington, 1975-87; cons.-tchr. in-svc. tchr. tng. program Durham (N.C.) City Schs., 1983-87; tchr. adult edn. dept. Henrico County (Va.) Pub. Schs., 1987—; dir., condr. numerous in-svc. tng. seminars, classes for elem. and secondary sch. and adult edn. tchrs. in Va., D.C., Md.; tchr. of ESL classes in evening sch.; tchr., spl. com. tng. program for Chesapeake and Ohio Ry., Richmond, 1955-59; tchr. spl. class for postal and fed. employees at Phyllis Wheatley YWCA, Richmond, 1968; dir., tchr. Weiss Reading Inst., Richmond, 1960-76. Co-author: (with Carolyn W. Guertin) Sound Skill Builder, 1976; editor-in-chief: Sure Steps to Reading and Spelling, 1976, The Science of Reading and Spelling. Mem. Am. Assn. for Adult and Continuing Edn., Learning Disabilities Assn., The Learning Disabilites Coun. of Richmond, Altrusa Internat. Inc. of Capital City of Va. Avocations: creative writing, English lang. rsch., composer, lyricist. Home: 5309 W Grace St Richmond VA 23226-1113

BLANK, LEONARD, psychologist; b. N.Y.C., May 10, 1927; s. Samuel Blank; m. Bernice Bukaretsky, Nov. 3, 1953 (dec. Aug. 1991); children: Jordan, Rona, Lyda. BA, Bklyn. Coll., 1949, MA, 1952; PhD, NYU, 1955; postgrad., Stanford U., 1957, NYU, 1967. Dir. insts. and agys. N.J. Dept. Mental Hygiene, Trenton, 1961-65; pvt. practice Kingston, N.J., 1961—; assoc. prof. psychology Rutgers U., New Brunswick, N.J., 1965-70; clin. prof. psychiatry Robert Wood Johnson Med. Sch., Piscataway, N.J., 1977—; dir. N.J. Inst. Psychotherapy, Princeton, N.J., 1980—. Author: The Diogenese Group, 1997, Psychological Evaluations and Psychotherapy, Psychology of Everyday Life, 1960, Changing Behavior, 1996; software developer: Princeton Medical Index, 1990; co-editor: Confrontation, Sourcebook of Training in Clinical Psychology. Fellow: APA, Am. Group Psychotherapy Assn., Am. Assn. Marriage and Family; mem. Am. Acad. Psychotherapy. Office: PO Box 557 Kingston NJ 08528-0557

BLANK, MARION SUE, psychologist; b. N.Y.C., Dec. 20, 1933; d. Morris David and Tillie Jean (Sherman) Hersch; m. Martin Blank, July 3, 1955; children: Donna, Jonathan, Ari. BA, CCNY, 1955, MS in Edn, 1956; PhD, Cambridge (Eng.) U., 1961. Asst. prof. Albert Einstein Coll. Medicine, 1965-70, asso. prof., 1970-73; prof. dept. psychiatry Rutgers Med. Sch., Piscataway, N.J., 1973-83; mem. adj. faculty dept. psychiatry Columbia Coll. Physicians and Surgeons, N.Y.C., 1980-83; dir. reading disabilities rsch. inst., pvt. practice, cons., 1983—; Nat. Tour lectr. Speech Pathology Assn. Australia, 1996. Author: Teaching Learning in the Preschool - A Dialogue Approach, Preschool Language Assessment Instrument, 1978, (with Rose and Berlin) The Language of Learning, 1978, (with Marquis and Klimovitch) Directing School Discourse, 1994, Directing Early Discourse, 1995, Sentence Master, 1990-96, (with Berlin) A Parent's Guide to Educational Software, 1991, (with Marquis and Klimovitch) Directing School Discourse, 1994, Directing Early Discourse with Marquis and Klimovitch, 1995. Pinsent-Darwin fellow, 1960; recipient award of commendation N.J. Speech and Hearing Assn., 1979, Spl. Edn. award Software Pubs. Am., 1990, N.J., USPHS Career Devel. award, 1965-73; named N.J. nominee Kleffner Lifetime Svc. award Am. Speech Lang. Hearing Assn., 1994, 95. Fellow APA; mem. Assn. for Children with Learning Disabilities. Home: 157 Columbus Dr Tenafly NJ 07670-1635 *It is heartening, albeit at times difficult, to live in a period of revolutionary change for women.*

BLANK, MATTHEW C., broadcast company executive; m. Susan McGuirk; children: Meredith, Gordon. Degree, U. Pa.; MBA, Baruch Coll. Past sr. v.p. consumer mktg. Home Box Office; exec. v.p. mktg. Showtime Networks, Inc. (Showtime, The Movie Channel, Fliz, Showtime Extreme, Showtime en Español, Showtime Event TV), N.Y.C., 1981-91, pres., COO, 1991—, past CEO, also chmn. bd. dirs.; bd. dirs., mem. exec. com. Sundance Ch. Showtime Networks, Inc. (Showtime, The Movie Channel, Fliz, Showtime Extreme, Showtime en Español, Showtime Event TV); Bd. dirs. Comedy Central, Phoenix Pictures. Trustee Rheedlen Ctrs. Children and Families; bd. dirs. Walter Kaitz Found., mem. exec. com.; active Nat. Minorities in Cable, Cable Positive, others. Recipient Vanguard award for mktg., 1991, Chmn.'s award Cable TV and Mktg., 1991, Friends of Children award Rheedlen Ctrs. Children and Families, 1996, Fairness award Gay and Lesbian Alliance Against Defamation, 1997. Mem. NCCJ (mem. exec. bd. dirs.), Nat. Acad. Cable Programming (bd. govs.), Nat. Cable TV Assn. (bd. dirs.), Pub. Edn. Needs Civic Involvement in Lng. (bd. dirs.), Cable in the Classroom (bd. dirs.). Office: care Showtime Networks Viacom Inc 1515 Broadway New York NY 10036*

BLANK, MYRON NATHAN, theater executive; b. Des Moines, Aug. 30, 1911; s. Abraham Harry and Anna (Levy) B.; m. Jacqueline Navran, Oct. 22, 1935; children: Beverly, Alan, Steven. BA, U. Mich., 1933. With Cen. States Theatre Corp., Des Moines, 1933—, pres., 1950—; founder Raymond Blank Hosp. for Children, 1978, A.H. & Theo Blank Performing Arts Ctr.; mem., chmn. trust com. Iowa Des Moines Nat. Bank, 1950-82. Salvage chmn. War Prodn. Bd. Polk County, 1940-42; past bd. dirs. Salvation Army, Child Guidance Ctr., YMCA; built Raymond Blank Lodge and Sick Bay, Camp Mitigwa Boy Scout Camp, Anna Blank Hosp. for Child Guidance Ctr., A.H. Blank Park Zoo; chmn. Des Moines United Way dr., 1976; endowed permanent chair for gifted and talented children, U. Iowa, permanent scholarship, Weitzmann Inst., Israel; pres. Greater Des Moines Com., 1953, pres. of Theatre Owners of Amer., 1957, 58; bd. dirs. NATO, Iowa Meth. Hosp., Des Moines C. of C., Simpson Coll., Des Moines Club, Wakonda Club; hon. chmn. Variety Club Telethon, 1999. Lt. comdr. USN, 1943-46. Recipient Brotherhood award NCCJ, 1976, Am. Humanitarian award Variety Club Am., 1980, The Iowa award Nat. Soc. for Fund Raising Execs., Disting. Alumni award U. Iowa, 1990, Jr. Achievement Laureate award, 1997. Mem. Theatre Owners Am. (pres. 1955, chmn. bd. dirs. 1956-57). Jewish. Avocations: golf, hunting, fishing. Office: Cen States Theatre Corp 414 Insurance Exchange Des Moines IA 50309-2321

BLANK, WILLIAM RUSSELL, mathematics educator; b. Utica, N.Y., Aug. 7, 1916; s. William Nicholas and Marguerite Dorothy (Pugh) B.; m. Elizabeth Jeanette Roman, Sept. 12, 1942; children: William Keith, Marvin Darryl, Ronald Paul. BA, Union Coll., Nebr., 1939; MA, U. Nebr., 1953. Cert. tchr. math., physical sci., N.Y. Tchr. math., sci. Staatsburg (N.Y.) Union Sch., 1941-42, Fresno (Calif.) Union Acad., 1946-48; instr. math. Union Coll., Lincoln, Nebr., 1948-50; tchr., dept. head Whitesboro (N.Y.) Cen. Sch., 1950-78; adj. faculty Mohawk Valley Community Coll., Utica, 1956—. Sgt. U.S. Army, 1942-45. Recipient awards NSF, 1957, 58, 59, 60. Mem. Ret. Tchrs. Assn., VFW, Am. Legion, IBM Magicians Club, SAM Magician Club, Pi Mu Epsilon, Phi Delta Kappa, Nat. Coun. Tchrs. Math. Avocations: traveling, reading, music, ch. functions. Home: 34 Burr Ave New York Mills NY 13417

BLANKE, RICHARD BRIAN, lawyer; b. St. Louis, Oct. 28, 1954; s. Robert H. and Phyllis I. (Kessler) Schaffler. BA, U. Pa., 1977; JD, U. Mo., 1980. Bar: Mo. 1980, U.S. Dist. Ct. (ea. and we. dists.) Mo. 1980. Ptnr. Blanke & Assocs., St. Louis County, Mo., 1980-90, Uthoff, Graeber, Bobinette & O'Keefe, St. Louis, 1991—; lawyer; b. St. Louis, Oct. 28, 1954; s. Robert H. and Phyllis I. (Kessler) Schaffler. BA, U. Pa., 1977; JD, U. Mo., 1980. Bar: U.S. Dist. Ct. (ea. and we. dists.) Mo. 1980, Mo. 1980. Ptnr. Blanke & Assocs., St. Louis County, Mo., 1980-90, Uthoff, Graeber, Bobinette & O'Keefe, St. Louis, 1991—. Mem. ABA, Assn. Trial Lawyers Am., Mo. Bar Assn., Mo. Assn. Trial Attys., St. Louis Met. Bar Assn. Mem. ABA, ATLA, Mo. Bar Assn., Mo. Assn. Trial Attys., St. Louis Met. Bar Assn. Office: Uthoff Graeber Bobinette & O'Keefe 906 Olive St Ste 300 Saint Louis MO 63101-1426

BLANKENAU, GAIL SHAFFER, writer; b. Chadron, Nebr., Apr. 27, 1959; d. Gordon Carlyle and Marian Caroline (Crites) Shaffer; m. Donald Gerard Blankenau, Dec. 28, 1985; children: Aleksander, Philip, Lauren. BA in French and English, U. Nebr., 1981; MA in Internat. Policy, Monterey Inst. Internat. Stds., 1983; cert. in bus. French, U. Bordeaux, France, 1981. Project mgr. Dept. Agrl. Econs., Lincoln, Nebr., 1985-90; freelance writer Lincoln, 1990—; part-time proofreader Gen. Reporting Svc., Lincoln, 1993—; mem. nat. task force on instrnl. tech. Coop. Ext., 1987-90. Co-author: (booklet) Cash Flow Planning Interactive Videodisc 2.0, Setting Up the System, Cash Flow Planning Interactive Videodisc Program Workbook; contbr. articles to profl. jours. and popular mags. Bd. dirs. women's ministries 1st Plymouth Congl. Ch., Lincoln, 1986-87; mem. Nebr. worship com. Eastridge Presbyn. Ch., Lincoln, 1996—; mem. Cantores Fideles Women's Choir, 1996—, New Eng. Hist. and Geneal. Soc., Boston, 1997—; life mem., genealogist's helper Alden Kindred, 1995—. Recipient CINDY award, 1990, 2d pl. award Reader's Digest Manuscript Competition, 1994. Mem. Soc. Children's Writers and Illustrators, Nebr. Writers Guild, Children of the Am. Revolution (sr. v.p. 1989-92, state v.p. 1990-92), Wahoo Women's League (co-pres. 1990-91), Guilford Keeping Soc., Jr. League of Lincoln, Lincoln Legal Aux. Avocations: music, genealogy. Home: 4601 Christopher Ct Lincoln NE 68516-2878

BLANKENBEKER, JOAN WINIFRED, communications, computer, and information management executive; b. Phila., Dec. 4, 1945; d. Henry Charles Ayton and Winifred M. Ayton Jacobs; m. Cleon Jerry Blankenbeker, Oct. 10, 1969; children: Robert Edgar, Jennifer Ellen. BA in History, Memphis State U., 1968; MS in Human Resource Mgmt., U. Utah, 1976. Hdqrs. squadron sect. comdr. Tactical Air Command Langley AFB, Hampton, Va., 1981-85; exec. asst. to dep. chief of staff Hdqs. Allied Forces, North (NATO), Oslo, 1985-88; chief pers. affairs Air Edn. and Tng. Command, Randolph AFB, Tex., 1988-91; dir., dep. dir., pers. programs, chief Dep. Chief of Staff for Pers. Hdqrs., San Antonio, 1988-91; comdr., dep. comdr. 3750 Support Group Sheppard AFB, Wichita Falls, Tex., 1991-92; dir. info. mgmt. Hdqs. Air Edn. and Tng. Command, San Antonio, 1992-95; dep. dir. comm. and info. Air Edn. and Tng. Command, San Antonio, 1996-98; dir. adminstrn. Design Divn., 1998—; voting mem. Air Force Info. Mgmt. Policy Coun., San Antonio, 1992-96; bd. dirs. Air Force AFIT Info. Resource Mgmt., San Antonio; cons. Retiree Activities, 82 Tng. Wing, Sheppard AFB, Wichita Falls, 1991-92; chmn. hazardous waste subcom. Sheppard AFB, Wichita Falls, 1991-92. Leader Girl Scouts U.S., New Braunfels, Tex., 1992-95; mem. Broad Investment Group of New Braunfels, 1996—. Ret. Col. USAF. Named Air Tng. Command Mil. Sr. Pers. Mgr. of Yr., Comdr. ATC, Randolph AFB, 1989, Randolph AFB Most Outstanding Fed. Woman, Fed. Women's Program, 1989, Tactical Air Command's Outstanding Sr. Adminstrv. Officer, Comdr. TAC, Langley AFB, 1983, Command Falcon award HQ Air Edn. and Tng., 1998. Mem. Armed Forces Comm. and Electronic Assn., New Braunfels C. of C., Beta Sigma Phi (pres., v.p., sect.-treas. 1969—). Republican. Episcopalian. Avocations: stained glass, snow skiing, reading, gardening. E-mail: jblank@mailgw.dot.state.tx.us. Home: 2686 River Oaks Dr New Braunfels TX 78132-3245 Office: Tex Dept Transp Design Divn 125 E 11th St Austin TX 78701-2409

BLANKENFELD, BEVERLY (B. J. BLANKENFELD), real estate professional; b. Brown County, Ind., Oct. 17, 1944; d. Albert H. and Kathryn M. (Stogdill) Cross; children from a previous marriage: Brian, Lynn, Jackie; m. Richard Blankenfeld, Aug. 1995. Student, House of James Beauty Coll., 1961-62; grad. real estate course, Bloomington, Ind. Lic. real estate agent, Ind. Cosmetologist Bloomington, 1964-77, real estate professional, 1977—; sales mgr. Rod Figg Realtors, Bloomington, 1986-89; sales mgr. F.C. Tucker/Bloomington, 1989-90, dir. affiliate svcs., 1990-91; realtor Century 21 All Seasons Realtors, Bloomington, 1991—. Pres. Monroe County Plan Commn., Bloomington, 1991-92; v.p. Bd. Zoning Appeals, 1989; served on Monroe County Commn., 1988-94. Mem. Am. Bus. Women Assn. (treas., pres., recording sec., Woman of Yr. 1986), Bloomington Bd. Realtors (past treas., Realtor of Yr. 1985), Ind. Assn. Realtors (state pub. rels. chair, Disting. Citizen award), Nat. Assn. Realtors (pub. rels. com.), Bloomington C. of C. (Athena award Bus. Woman of Yr. 1989). Republican. Home: 3845 Tamarron Dr Bloomington IN 47408-2820 Office: Copenhaver & Assoc Inc New Homes Tamarron/Barr Pl 3845 Tamarron Dr Bloomington IN 47408

BLANKENHEIMER, BERNARD, economics consultant; b. N.Y.C., July 6, 1920; s. Benjamin and Anna (Barach) B.; m. Rosalind Drescher, Dec. 4, 1943; children—Alan Howard, Susan Leslie. B.A., Bklyn. Coll., 1941; postgrad., N.Y. U., 1941-42; M.A. in Econs, George Washington U., 1950. With U.S. Dept. Commerce, 1942-76, jr. economist European div., 1942, asst. economist, 1945-47, internat. economist Africa sect. Brit. Commonwealth div., 1948-50, chief African sect. Africa-Near East div., 1950-61, dep. dir. Africa div., 1961, dir., 1962-68; dep. dir. Office Import Programs U.S. Dept. Commerce, Washington, 1970-72; dir. Office Import Programs U.S. Dept. Commerce, 1973-76; U.S. Fgn. Service sr. comml. officer Am. consulate gen. Johannesburg, Republic South Africa, 1968-70; dir. U.S. Trade Mission to, Liberia, Ghana, Sierra Leone, Guinea, 1960, Mission to, Kenya, Uganda, Tanganyika, 1963; adviser U.S. del. 22d session GATT, Geneva, 1965; mem. U.S. observer del. UN Econ. Commn. for Africa Symposium on Industrialization, Cairo, 1966; mem. 9th Sr. Seminar in Fgn. Policy Dept. State, 1966-67; observer U.S. del. Unctad III, Santiago, Chile, 1972; mem. U.S. del UNESCO Meeting of Experts, Geneva, 1973, Internat. Rubber Study Group meetings, Geneva, 1973, 74, Djakarta, Indonesia, 1975; mem. U.S. del. to 5th Internat. Tin Conf. Negotiations, Geneva, 1975, Unctad Confs. on Tungsten and Copper, Geneva, 1976, Unctad Consultation on Copper, Geneva, 1976; asst. dir. econ. cons. services Wolf & Co., 1976-78; v.p. Econ. Cons. Services, Inc., Washington, 1978-79; lectr. African studies Johns Hopkins Sch. Advanced Internat. Studies, 1957-62, Am. U. Sch. Bus. Adminstrn., 1967, Howard U., 1962-68. Contbr. articles to govtl., profl. jours. Served with AUS, 1942-45. Recipient silver medal for distinguished authorship Dept. Commerce, 1960, spl. achievement award, 1972, 75. Fellow African Studies Assn., Royal Geog. Soc. Home and Office: 5633 Willow Creek Ln Delray Beach FL 33484-6908

BLANKENSHIP, DOLORES MOOREFIELD, principal, music educator, retired; b. Atlanta, June 4, 1929; d. Albert Talmadge and Willie Mae (Cole) Moorefield; divorced; 1 child, Diane Lee. BME, Northwestern U., 1951; MA, Ohio State U., Columbus, 1958. Cert. music tchr., secondary principal, Ohio. Vocal music tchr. Hoke Smith High Sch., Atlanta, 1951-52; vocal instr., tchr. Reynoldsburg (Ohio) Sch., 1952-53; substitute music tchr. various public schs., El Paso, Tex., 1953; vocal music tchr. Columbus (Ohio) Public Schs., 1956-73, asst. prin., 1973-86, prin., 1986-94. Adv. bd. Capital Area Humane Soc., Columbus, 1987-94; pres. Altrusa, Columbus, 1973, 87; mem. Columbus Mus. of Arts; vol. Wexner Ctr. for Arts, 1994-99; mem. planning com. Columbus Arts Festival, 1994-99; vol. FACTLIVE Columbus Pub. Sch.; docent Columbus Symphony Orch., 1995; AARP coord. Capital City Task Force, 1997-99. Mem. Nat. Middle Sch. Adminstr. Assn. (Ohio chpt., Columbus chpt. pres. 1990-91), Columbus Adminstr. Assn. (exec. bd. 1989-91), Ohio Assn. Deans, Adminstr., Counselors (treas. 1988-90). Avocations: reading, jazz music, movies, plays, travel. Home: 1291 Hanford Sq Columbus OH 43206-3668

BLANKENSHIP, DWIGHT DAVID, business owner; b. Ashland, Ky., Mar. 18, 1944; s. David Earl and Dorthy Irene (King) B.; m. Joyce Eddy, Mar. 1, 1969 (div. Oct. 1984); children: Dwight W., Cheryl L. Grad. high sch., Ashland, Ky. Owner, mgr. Royal Pool, Sarasota, Fla., 1970-72, Am. Indian Jewelry, Sarasota, Fla., 1972-78, Daves Enterprises, Big Pine Key, Fla., 1978-86, D & D Enterprises, Ocala, Fla., 1986—, Master Mktg. Prodn. Co., Bradenton, Fla., 1987—, Gold Designs, Bradenton, Fla., 1987-90. Avocations: swimming, lapidary, stone setting, goldsmith. Home: 6716 26th St W Bradenton FL 34207-5705 also: Gold Designs/Master Mktg 1304 53rd Ave W Bradenton FL 34207-2861

BLANKENSHIP, EDWARD G., architect; b. Martin, Tenn., June 22, 1943; s. Edward G. and Martha Lucille (Baldridge) B. BArch, Columbia U., 1966, MSc in Architecture, 1967; MLitt in Arch., Cambridge U., U.K., 1971. Registered architect, N.Y., Calif. Sr. v.p. Landrum & Brown, Inc., Los Angeles. Author: The Airport-Architecture, Urban Integration, Ecological Problems, 1974. William Kinne fellow, 1966; alt. Fulbright fellow to Eng., 1967. Mem. AIA. Episcopalian. Clubs: United Oxford and Cambridge U., Meadow (Southampton), Am. Friends of Cambridge U. Home: 2508 Buckland Ln Northbrook IL 60062 Office: 1021 W Adams St Chicago IL 60607-2911

BLANKENSHIP, JAY RANDALL, social services executive; b. Daytona Beach, Fla., Aug. 12, 1955; s. Manuel Elmore and Jane Ruth (Hayes) B.; m. Ellen Mary Abrams, Apr. 30, 1983; children: Jennifer, Leah. BS in Wildlife Biology, U. Wis., Stevens Point, 1977; MSW Adminstrn., U. Wis., Milw., 1987. Cert. ind. social worker, Wis. Outdoor edn. tchr. Pinewood Acad., Eagle River, Wis., 1977-78; wildlife biologist U.S. Peace Corps, Montserrat, West Indies, 1978-80; youth cmty. conservation project dir. Jewish Cmty. Ctr., Milw., 1981; camp dir. Children's Outing Assn., Milw., 1982-89, exec. dir., 1990—; founder Camp for Kids, Milw. Author: The Wildlife of Montserrat, 1990. Mem. Milw. Rotary, Milw. Jewish Coun. Cmty. Rels., Hillel Found. Jewish. Avocations: golf, fishing, skiing. Home e-mail: jblank@execpc.com. Office e-mail: coa@execpc.com. Home: 4313 N Maryland Ave Milwaukee WI 53211-1650 Office: Children's Outing Assn 909 E North Ave Milwaukee WI 53212-3492

BLANKENSHIP, JENNY MARY, public relations executive, publisher, editor-in-chief; b. Mpls., Nov. 15, 1955. AA in bus., Weatherford Coll.; cert. paralegal, Southern Meth. U.; BBS in Mktg., U. Tex., BBA in Journalism; PhD, So. Meth. U., 1998. Mktg. coord. Fingerhut Corp., Minnetonka, Minn.; pub. rels. coord. Family Svcs. Inc, Ft. Worth, Tex.; pres. Gloss Mgmt. Inc, Weatherford, Tex.; editor The Shorthorn, Arlington, Tex.; v.p., editor Randy Keck & Co., Boston; editor-in-chief Community Press, Hico, Tex.; dir. pub. affairs Hico Chiropractic; pub. Tex. Spotlight; promoter Dallas Cowboy Legends Event, 1997; dir. pub. rels. Hope Inc., Mineral Wells, Tex.; dir. Randy Keck & Co.; fundraising cons. WICI, Waco, Tex., instr. seminars Ctr. for Profl. & Exec. Devel. U. Tex; promoter Dallas Cowboy Legends, 1997. Author: Poetry of the Old Testament, 1987, The Business of Life, 1988, Do Over, 1994, The Brains, The Club and The Sneak, 1999, Shadows of Hate, 1999; pub. Tex. Spotlight. Vol. merit badge counselor, dist. officer, dist. tng. chair Boy Scouts Am. Recipient Best Layout, Column, Page award Columbia U., 1987, 90, Best Upstart Weekly in the State award Southwest Journalism Conf., 1994, Best Sports award South Tex. Press, 1995, Best Layout award South Tex. Press, 1995. Mem. Women In Communication, Inc. (Best Feature award, Best Advt. Campaign, 1991, Best Broadcast Feature award, 1990), MENSA, NAFE (com. mem), Soc. Profl. Journalists, United Meth. Women (pres.), Kiwanis. Methodist. Avocations: painting, singing, collecting headwear. Fax: (254) 364-2746. E-mail: texspot@email.com. Office: Tex Spotlight PO Box 308 Hico TX 76457-0308

BLANKENSHIP, ROBERT EUGENE, chemistry educator; b. Auburn, Nebr., Aug. 25, 1948; s. George Robert and Jane (Kehoe) Leech; m. Elizabeth Marie Dorland, June 26, 1971; children: Larissa Dorland, Samuel Robert. BS, Wesleyan U., Nebr., 1970; PhD, U. Calif., Berkeley, 1975. Postdoctoral fellow Lawrence Berkeley Lab., Berkeley, 1975-76, U. Washington, Seattle, 1976-79; asst. prof. Amherst (Mass.) Coll., 1979-85; assoc. prof. Ariz. State U., Tempe, 1985-88, prof., 1988—, dir. Ctr. Study of Early Events in Photosynthesis, 1988-91. Editor Anoxygenic Photosynthetic Bacteria, 1995, Editor-in-chief Photosynthesis Rsch., 1988-99; cons. editor Advances in Photosynthesis, 1991-98; contbr. 150 articles to sci. jours. Recipient Alumni award Nebr. Wesleyan U., 1991, Disting. Rsch. award Ariz. State U., 1992, Mentoring award Ariz. State U., 1998. Mem. AAAS, Am. Chem. Soc., Union of Concerned Scientists, Internat. Soc. of Photodynthesis Rsch. Democrat. Avocations: bicycling, hiking, camping, cooking, travel. Home: 13824 S Canyon Dr Phoenix AZ 85048-9085 Office: Ariz State U Dept Chemistry And Bio Tempe AZ 85287-1604

BLANKENSHIP, SAMUEL MAX, physicist; b. Pulaski, Va., Aug. 3, 1943; s. William McKinley and Frances Adeline (Smythers) B.; m. Arvila Anne Corwin, 1964 (div. 1973); 1 child, Corwynn; m. Brenda Dale Allen, 1980; 1 child, Hannah. BS, U. S.C., 1965, PhD, 1975. Postdoctoral fellow U. Calif., Irvine, 1975-76; prin. rsch. scientist Ga. Inst. Tech., Atlanta, 1976—, head Mission Analysis br., 1985-89, dir. advanced programs office spl. projects, 1990—, coord. program in microflyers, 1994-98, dir. T&E Rsch. and Edn. Ctr., 1995—, dir. Space Tech. Advanced Rsch. Ctr., 1997—, GTRI fellow, 1999—; cons. MEI, Huntsville, Ala., 1991-92. Author: Backpacking Guide to Southern Mountains, 1974, 2d edit., 1975; editor: Roles for Georgia Tech and Other Universities in Meeting National challenges, 1992. Capt. USAF, 1967-71. GTRI fellow, 1999. Mem. AAAS, Am. Phys. Soc., Internat. T&E Assn. (southeastern v.p. 1996—, Atlanta chpt. pres. 1992-93, chmn. ann. symposium 1995, 99), Sigma Xi, Phi Beta Kappa, Mu Alpha Theta. Achievements include research on first computer-based low energy neutrino experiment; discovered relationship between expected-value and Monte Carlo modeling paradigms. Office: Georgia Inst of Tech T&E Rsch and Edn Ctr Atlanta GA 30332

BLANKFORT, LOWELL ARNOLD, newspaper publisher; b. N.Y.C., Apr. 29, 1926; s. Herbert and Gertrude (Butler) B.; m. April Pemberton; 1 child, Jonathan. BA in History and Polit. Sci., Rutgers U., 1946. Reporter, copy editor L.I. (N.Y.) Star-Jour., 1947-49; columnist London Daily Mail, Paris, 1949-50; copy editor The Stars & Stripes, Darmstadt, Germany, 1950-51, Wall St. Jour., N.Y.C., 1951; bus., labor editor Cowles Mags., N.Y.C., 1951-53; pub. Pacifica (Calif.) Tribune, 1954-59; free-lance writer Europe, Asia, 1959-61; co-pub., editor Chula Vista (Calif.) Star-News, 1961-78; co-owner Paradise (Calif.) Post, 1977—; co-owner Monte Vista (Colo.) Jour., Ctr. (Colo.) Post-Dispatch, Del Norte (Colo.) Prospector, 1978-93, Plainview (Minn.) News, St. Charles (Minn.) Press, Lewiston (Minn.) Jour., 1980—, Summit (Colo.) Sentinel, New Richmond (Wis.) News, 1981-87, Yuba City Valley Herald, Calif., 1982-85, TV Views, Monterey, Calif., 1982-87, Summit County Jour., Colo., 1982-87, Alpine (Calif.) Sun, 1987-93. *Mr. Blankfort has received many awards including Best Editorials in California, non-dailies; 1st or 2nd place seven consecutive years, California Newspaper Publishers Association; Best Editorial in the United States, National Newspapers Association; Best Editorial U. S. suburban newspapers, Suburban Publishers Newspapers of America; Headliner of the Year, San Diego Press Club; John Swett Award, California Education Association; and Citizen of the Year, Sweetwater Education Association. Special Media Award, National Conference of Christians and Jews. Mr. Blankfort is a widely traveled writer. He has interviewed many heads of state including Fidel Castro in Cuba, Li Peng and Li Xiannin in China, and Benezir Bhutto in Pakistan.* Columnist, contbr. articles on fgn. affairs to newspapers. Active Calif. Dem. Ctrl. Com., 1963. Recipient awards Best Editls. in Calif., non-dailies, 1st or 2nd place seven consecutive years (Calif. Newspaper Pub. Assn.), Best Editl. in U.S. (Nat. Newspaper Assn.), Best Editl. U.S. Suburban Newspapers (Suburban Pubs. Newspapers Am.), Headliner of Yr. (San Diego Press Club), John Swett award (Calif. Edn. Assn.) and Citizen of the Yr. (Sweetwater Edn. Assn.), Spl. Media award (Nat. Conf. Christians and Jews), for articles on South America; named Outstanding Layman of Yr., Sweetwater Edn. Assn., 1966, Citizen of Yr., City of Chula Vista, 1976, Headliner of Yr., San Diego Press Club, 1980. Mem. ACLU (pres. San Diego chpt. 1970-71), Calif. Newspaper Pubs. Assn., World Affairs Coun. San Diego (pres. 1996—), Ctr. Internat. Policy (bd. dirs. 1991—), Internat. Ctr. Devel. Policy (nat. bd. 1985-90), UN Assn. (pres. San Diego chpt. 1991-93, nat. coun. 1992-97, nat. bd. 1997—), World Federalist Assn. (nat. bd. 1992—, pres. San Diego chpt. 1984-86), Soc. Profl. Journalists, East Meets West Found. (nat. v.p. 1992-98), Inst. of the Ams. (assoc. 1989—, mem. internat. coun. 1994—). Achievements include widely travelled writer: more than 100 nations on all continents. Has interviewed many heads of state including Fidel Castro in Cuba, Li Peng and Li Ziannin in China, Benezir Bhutto in Pakistan, Kim Dae Jung in Korea. Home: Old Orchard Ln Bonita CA 91902 Office: 315 4th Ave Ste S Chula Vista CA 91910-3816

BLANKINSHIP, HENRY MASSIE, management consultant; b. Providence, Sept. 27, 1949; s. Ernest Randolph and Henrietta (Massie) B.; m. Linda Ferber, Jan. 17, 1981; children: John Byron, Kevin Mark, Sara Jane. Tech. mgr. Dept. of Navy, Washington, 1972-98; mgmt. cons.,

1998—. Nat. corr. Karate Illustrated Mag., 1976-79. Head Karate instr. YMCA, Fairfax County, Va.; police spl. teams cons., Fairfax County. Recipient Outstanding Navy Civilian Svc. award, 1976-82, 84, 86, 88-95, Gold Wreath USN, 1977, Navy Spl. Acts award, 1983; named Ea. Region Karate Champion. Mem. Am. Mgmt. Assn., Nat. Assn. Combative Arts, Self Def. Sys. Internat. (Soke-Dai successor), Internat. Fedn. Jujutsuans, U.S. Kickboxing Assn., U.S. Karate Assn., Internat. Martial Arts Assn. (pres.), Taifung Martial Arts Assn. (chair bd. dirs.). Republican. Avocation: karate (black belt 6th degree). Office: Navy Pers & Manpower Data Systems Mgmt PO Box 1610 Arlington VA 22210-0910

BLANKLEY, WALTER ELWOOD, manufacturing company executive; b. Phila., Sept. 23, 1935; s. George William and Martha Emily (McCord) B.; m. Rosemary Deniken, Aug. 16, 1958; children: Stephen Michael, Laura Ann. BSME, Princeton U., 1957. Mgr. planning Ametek Hunter Spring, Hatfield, Pa., 1965-66, gen. mgr., 1966-69; asst. to pres. Ametek, Inc., San Francisco, 1969-71; v.p. Ametek, Inc., Watsonville, Calif., 1971-78, group v.p., 1978-82, sr. v.p., 1982-90; pres., chief exec. officer Ametek, Inc., Paoli, Pa., 1990-93; dir. Kinark Corp., Tulsa, 1988-90; chmn., CEO Ametek, Inc., Paoli, 1993—; bd. dirs. Amcast, Dayton, Ohio, CDI, Phila.; trustee Mfr.'s Alliance for Productivity and Innovation, Inc., 1995—. Mem. ASME (adv. bd. 1991-95), Alu,inum Extruders Coun. (pres. 1974-76, bd. dirs. 1992—), Tech. Coun. Greater Phila. (bd. dirs. 1992—). Office: Ametek Inc Station Sq Paoli PA 19301-1307

BLANKS, NAOMI MAI, retired English language educator; b. Trezevant, Tenn., June 22, 1917; d. Hubbard Tazewell and Clara Clyde (Smith) Williamson; m. Jeff J. Blanks Jr., June 19, 1936 (dec.); children: Barbara, Jeff III, George (dec.). Student, Lambuth Coll., Jackson, Tenn., 1934-35; BA, Bethel Coll., McKenzie, Tenn., 1961; MA, George Peabody Coll., Nashville, 1966. Tchr. lang. arts Trezevant (Tenn.) Jr. High Sch., 1957-60; tchr. English McKenzie (Tenn.) High Sch., 1961-68; assoc. prof. English Bethel Coll., McKenzie, 1968-85; ret.; cons. lang. arts Harcourt Brace Jovanovich. Reviewer biography: T.S. Eliot: A Life, 1986, Waldo Emerson, 1982. Bd. dirs. Carroll County Devel. Ctr., Huntingdon, Tenn., 1976-88. NEH seminar grantee, 1980; NDEA fellow, 1965; recipient Alumni Svc. award, Bethel Coll., 1984, Tchr. of the Yr., 1975, 84. Mem. AAUP, So. Assn. Sec. Schs. and Colls. (evaluation com.), Delta Kappa Gamma (chpt. pres. 1970-72, Ky. col. 1985). Democrat. Methodist. Avocations: nature lover, birder. Home: PO Box 186 Trezevant TN 38258-0186

BLANTON, EDWARD LEE, JR., lawyer; b. nr. Hope Mills, N.C., Oct. 31, 1931; s. Edward Lee and Margaret M. (Bullard) B.; m. Cathleen Estelle Edwards, Aug. 13, 1960; children: Edward Lee III, Cathleen Estelle, Margaret Ellyn. BS, Davidson Coll., 1953; MA, Vanderbilt U., 1954; LLB, U. Md., 1960. Bar: Md. 1960. Tchr. math. Balt. City schs., 1956-59; law clk. to judge Washington, 1960-62; practice in Balt., 1962-65, 69—; ptnr. Adelberg, Rudow & Blanton, 1969-72, Blanton & McCleary, 1973-93; asst. atty. gen. State Md., Balt., 1965-68; chmn. subcom. drafting revision Md. election laws Md. Legis. Coun., 1966-67; chmn. subcom. drafting revision Md. income tax laws Hughes Commn., 1966-67. Bd. dirs. United Christian Citizens, 1971-92, pres., 1974-75; pres. Ctrl. Balt. Ecumenical Sch. Christian Edn., 1971-74, Hist. Long Green Valley, Inc., 1980-86, Ctr. for Prevention of Child Abuse, 1991-96; mem. State Rep. Ctrl. Com., 1982-86; mem. citizens adv. com. Charles H. Hickey Sch., 1983-91, chmn., 1987-91; mem. Ctrl. Towson Com. Christian Businessmen, Balt. Coun. Fgn. Affairs; v.p., dir. Long Green Valley Conservancy, Inc., 1995-98; trustee com. Presbyn. Ch., Balt., St. James Acad., Monkton, Md., 1989-95, Egenton Home, Balt.; Rep. nominee for Atty. Gen. of Md., 1990. 1st lt. AUS, 1954-56; capt. Md. N.G., 1957-62. Mem. Nat. Lawyers Assn., Bar Assn. Balt. County, Newcomen Soc. N.Am., Christian Legal Soc., Long Green Valley Assn. (pres. 1979-89), Center Club, Masons, Delta Theta Phi. Presbyterian (elder). Home: Avondell Glen Arm MD 21057 Office: 404 Allegheny Ave Baltimore MD 21204-4255

BLANTON, FAYE WESTER, legislative staff member; b. Tallahassee, Nov. 9, 1946. Staff asst. govtl. efficiency com. Fla. Senate, Tallahassee, asst. to dir. mgmt. staff, asst. sec., sec., 1996—. Advisor, counselor Girls State, Boys State, YMCA Youth Legislature, Silver-Haired Legislature. Mem. Am. Soc. Legis. Clks. and Secs. Fax: 850-487-5174. Home: 1217 Lowry Dr Tallahassee FL 32312 Office: Fla Senate The Capitol Ste 405 404 S Monroe St Tallahassee FL 32399-1100

BLANTON, HOOVER CLARENCE, lawyer; b. Green Sea, S.C., Oct. 13, 1925; s. Clarence Leo and Margaret (Hoover) B.; m. Cecilia Lopez, July 31, 1949; children: Lawson Hoover, Michael Lopez. JD, U. S.C., 1953. Bar: S.C. 1953. Ordained deacon, Bapt. Ch. Assoc. Whaley & McCutchen, Columbia, S.C., 1953-66; ptnr. McCutchen, Blanton, Rhodes and Johnson and predecessors, Columbia, 1967—; dir. Legal Aid Service Agy., Columbia, chmn. bd., 1972-73. Gen. counsel S.C. Rep. Conv., 1962; del. Rep. State Conv., 1962, 64, 66, 68, 70, 74; bd. dirs. Midlands Cmty. Action Agy., Columbia, vice chmn., 1972-73; bd. dirs. Wildewood Sch., 1976-78; mem. Gov.'s Legal Svcs. Adv. Coun., 1976-77, Commn. on Continuing Legal Edn. for Judiciary, 1977-84, Commn. on Continuing Lawyer Competence, 1988-92, Commn. on Continuing Legal Edn. and Specialization, 1992-98, sec. 1995, chmn., 1996-99. Mem. ABA. S.C. Bar (ho. of dels. 1975-76, chmn. fee disputes bd. 1977-81), Richland County Bar Assn. (pres. 1980), S.C. Def. Trial Attys. Assn., Def. Rsch. Inst., Assn. Def. Trial Attys. (state chmn. 1971-77, 80-95, exec. coun. 1977-80), Am. Bd. Trial Advs. (pres. S.C. chpts. 1989), Toastmasters Club (pres. 1959), Palmetto Club, Phi Delta Phi. Home: 3655 Deerfield Dr Columbia SC 29204-3730 Office: 1414 Lady St Columbia SC 29201-3304

BLANTON, JACK SAWTELLE, oil company executive; b. Shreveport, La., Dec. 7, 1927; s. William Neal and Louise (Wynn) B.; m. Laura Lee Scurlock, Aug. 20, 1949; children: Elizabeth Louise Blanton Wareing, Jack Sawtelle Jr., Eddy Scurlock. BA, U. Tex., 1947, LLB, 1950. Bar: Tex. 1950. With Scurlock Oil Co., Houston, 1950-88, v.p., 1956-58, pres., 1958-83, chmn. bd., 1983-88; pres. Eddy Refining Co., Houston, 1988—; chmn. bd. trustees Houston Endowment, Inc.; pres. Eddy Refining Co.; bd. dirs. Pogo Producing Co., Burlington No. Santa Fe, Inc. Past chmn. bd. trustees St. Luke's United Meth. Ch., Houston; past chmn. bd. regents U. Tex. System, 1985-89; past vice chmn., bd. dirs. Meth. Hosp., Houston. Mem. Nat. Petroleum Coun., Mid-Continent Oil and Gas Assn. (past pres.) Houston C. of C. (life), Sons Republic of Tex. (past pres. San Jacinto chpt.), Sam Houston Meml. Assn., Nat. Tennis Assn., U.S. Lawn Tennis Assn., Tex. Ind. Oil Producers and Refiners, Ex-Students Assn. U. Tex. (past pres.), Greater Houston Partnership (chmn. 1985-86), Delta Kappa Epsilon, Phi Delta Phi, Phi Alpha Delta. Clubs: Houston (Houston) (past pres.), River Oaks Country (Houston); El Dorado Country (Palm Springs, Calif.). Office: Eddy Refining Co 700 Louisiana St Ste 3920 Houston TX 77002-2731 office: Houston Endowment Inc 600 Travis St Ste 6400 Houston TX 77002-3000

BLANTON, JOHN ARTHUR, architect; b. Houston, Jan. 1, 1928; s. Arthur Alva and Caroline (Jeter) B.; m. Marietta Louise Newton, Apr. 10, 154 (dec. 1976); children: Jill Blanton Milne, Lynette Blanton Rowe, Elena Diane. BA, Rice U., 1948, BS in Architecture, 1949. With Richard U. Neutra, L.A., 1950-64; pvt. practice architecture Manhattan Beach, 1964—; lectr. UCLA Extension, 1967-76, 85, Harbor Coll., Los Angeles, 1970-72. Archtl. columnist Easy Reader newspaper, 1994-96; designed nine bldgs. included in L.A.: An Architectural Guide; works featured in L'architettura mag., 1988; design philosophy included in American Architects (Les Krantz), 1989. Mem. Capital Improvements Com., Manhattan Beach, 1966, city commr. Bd. Bldg. Code Appeals; chmn. Zoning Adjustment Bd., 1990, Planning Commn. 1993-99. With Signal Corps, U.S. Army 1951-53. Recipient Best House of Yr. award C. of C., 1969, 70, 71, 83, Preservation of Natural Site award, 1974, design award, 1975, 84. Mem. AIA (contbr. book revs. to jour. 1972-76, Red Cedar Shingle/AIA nat. merit award 1979). Office: John Blanton AIA Architect 1456 12th St # 4 Manhattan Beach CA 90266-6113

BLANTON, LAWTON WALTER, retired dean; b. Perry, Fla., Oct. 25, 1914; s. Lawton Walter and Minnie Florelle (Truesdale) B.; BS, U. Fla., 1936, MS, 1941; postgrad. U. Chgo., 1949, Columbia, 1951-53. Rsch. assoc. U. Fla., Gainesville, 1941-42, asst. prof. math., 1942-53; asst. dean students Coll. City N.Y., 1955-57; dir. admissions Montclair Coll., Upper Montclair, N.J., 1957-61, dean students, 1961-80, ret., 1980. Lawton W. Blanton Hall named in his honor Montclair State Coll., 1982. Mem. Am. Assn. Higher Edn., Nat. Assn. Student Pers. Adminstrs., Am., N.J. pers. and guidance assns., N.Y. Schoolmasters, Eastern Assn. Coll. Deans and Advisers of Students, N.J. State Coll. Chief Student Affairs Officers (pres. 1977-78), Nat. Collegiate Honors Council, Am. Hort. Soc., Am. Hemerocallis Soc., Am. Plant Life Soc., Am. Rhododendron Soc. Home: 1 Oak Cres Little Falls NJ 07424-2414

BLANTON, LEWIS M., federal judge; b. 1934. AB, St. Louis U., 1958; JD, U. Mo., 1965. Bar: Mo. Atty. Thompson, Walther & Shewmaker, St. Louis, 1965-69, Blanton, Rice & Sickal, Sikeston, Mo., 1969-71, Robison & Blanton, Sikeston, 1971-78; assoc. judge Cir. Ct. of Scott County, Mo., 1979-91; magistrate judge U.S. Dist. Ct. (ea. dist.) Mo., Cape Girardeau, 1991—. Contbr. articles to profl. jours. Mem. ABA, Mo. Bar, Scott County Bar Assn., Cape Girardeau County Bar Assn., Bar Assn. Met. St. Louis, Fed. Magistrate Judges Assn. Office: 111 US Courthouse 339 Broadway St Cape Girardeau MO 63701-7330

BLANTON, ROGER EDMUND, mechanical engineer; b. Sherman, Tex., Apr. 20, 1955; s. Ray Edwin Blanton and Shirley Warlene (Ball) Gallion; m. Brenda Kay, Oct. 22, 1976; children: Ryan E., Rachel E., Rebekah E. BSME with honors, U. Tulsa, 1980, postgrad., 1981—. Registered profl. engr., Okla. Sr. project engr. John Zink Co., Tulsa, 1980-84; sr. applications engr., sr. oil console engr. Dresser-Rand, Broken Arrow, Okla., 1984-90; dir. incineration divsn. Radco, Tulsa, 1990-92; mgr. Vapor Recovery Callidus Tech., Tulsa, 1992-96; bus. mgr. total vapor control mgmt. Asia-Pacific John Zink Co., Tulsa, 1996—; mem. mech. engring. adv. bd. U. Tulsa. Deacon 1st Bapt. Ch., Tulsa, 1989. Mem. ASME, NSPE, Tau Beta Pi. Republican. Baptist. Achievements include development of solutions to unique hazardous waste incineration problems; development and design of specialty burners and incinerators; testing of destruction efficiency for hazardous waste incineration; co-development of unique carbon adsorption gasoline vapor recovery system. Home: 7186 S 75th East Ave Tulsa OK 74133-2817 Office: John Zink Co 11920 E Apache St Tulsa OK 74116-1300

BLANTON, W. C., lawyer; b. LaRue County, Ky., Apr. 13, 1946; s. Crawford and Lillian (Phelps) B. BS in Math., Mich. State U., 1968, BA in Social Sci., 1968; MEd, U. Vt., 1970; JD, U. Mich., 1975. Bar: Ind. 1975, U.S. Dist. Ct. (no. and so. dists.) Ind. 1975, U.S. Ct. Appeals (7th cir.) 1977, Minn. 1996, U.S. Dist. Ct. Minn. 1996. Residence hall dir. U. Wis., Madison, 1970-72; assoc. Ice Miller Donadio & Ryan, Indpls., 1975-81, ptnr., 1982-94; ptnr. Popham, Haik, Schnobrich & Kaufman, Ltd., 1995-97, Oppenheimer Wolff & Donnelly LLP, Mpls., 1997—. Mem. ABA. Democrat. Avocations: skiing, travel, bridge. Office: Oppenheimer Wolff & Donnelly LLP 3400 Plaza VII 45 S 7th St Ste 3400 Minneapolis MN 55402-1609

BLANTZ, THOMAS EDWARD, Roman Catholic priest, educator; b. Massillon, Ohio, June 18, 1934; s. Raymond Lawrence Blantz and Katherine Jeanette Chance. AB, U. Notre Dame, 1957; STL, Gregorian U., 1961; PhD, Columbia U., 1968. Ordained priest, Roman Cath. Ch., 1960. Asst. prof. U. Notre Dame, 1968-76, univ. archivist, 1969-78, v.p. student affairs, 1970-72, assoc. prof., 1976-94, prof., 1994—. Author: Priest in Public Service, 1982, George N. Shuster, 1993; contbr. articles to profl. jours. Trustee U. Notre Dame, 1970—. Mem. Am. Hist. Assn., Orgn. of Am. Historians, Am. Cath. Hist. Assn. Avocation: stamp collecting. E-mail: Thomas.E.Blantz.1@nd.edu. Home: PO Box 927 Notre Dame IN 46556 Office: U Notre Dame Dept of History Notre Dame IN 46556

BLASCHKE, RENEE DHOSSCHE, alderman; b. San Antonio, Oct. 4, 1938; d. Raoul Albert Emil and Lillian Lenore (Parker) Dhossche; m. Kenneth Blaschke; children: Kenneth, Rex, Rochelle. Office mgr. Smithville (Tex.) Hosp., 1958-68; mgr., buyer Ken's Rexall Pharmacy, Smithville, 1976-92, ret., 1992; owner Creations by Renee; tax assessor, collector City of Smithville, 1968-76, alderman, 1977-82, 94-98, mayor, 1998—; gardening cons. Past pres. region X, bd. dirs. Tex. Mcpl. League; trustee, chmn. fin., chmn. adminstrv. bd. 1st United Meth. Ch., Smithville; active Boy Scouts Am., Girl Scouts U.S.; chmn. Smithville Bicentennial Commn., Smithville Sesquicentennial Commn., Smithville Centennial Com., bd. dirs. Keep Tex. Beautiful, Tex. Urban Forestry Coun., Smithville CFC, 1994-97, Smithville Econ. Devel. Bd., 1994-97; Smithville Tree Bd., Smithville Tree City USA, Keep Smithville Beautiful; sec.-treas. Trees for Tex. Gov.'s Task Force-Earth Day, 1990; mem. devel. bd. Seton Hosp., 1979—. Named Garden Club Woman of Yr., State Fair Tex., 1993. Mem. Am. Pharm. Assn. Aux., Tex. Pharm. Assn. Aux., Tex. Garden Clubs (pres. 1991-93, life mem.), Nat. Coun. State Garden Clubs (master flower show judge, landscape design critic, presenter seminars, design cons.), U. Tex. Ex-Students (past pres.), Smithville Garden Club (pres.), Smithville C. of C. (city hostess, bd. dirs., chmn. econ. devel. bd. 1994—, pres. 1996—). Avocations: oil painting, needlepoint, bridge, gardening.

BLASCHKE, TERRENCE FRANCIS, medicine and molecular pharmacology educator; b. Rochester, Minn., Oct. 4, 1942; s. Robert Elmer and Carmella Ann (Seeby) B.; m. Jeannette F. Martin, June 8, 1968; children: Anne, John. BS in Math. cum laude, U. Denver, 1964; MD, Columbia U., 1968. Diplomate Am. Bd. Internal Medicine, Nat. Bd. Med. Examiners. Intern in medicine UCLA Ctr. for Health Scis., 1968-69, asst. resident, 1969-70; clin. assoc. metabolism br. Nat. Cancer Inst., NIH, Bethesda, Md., 1970-72; clin. rsch fellow div. clin. pharmacology dept. medicine U. Calif. Med. Ctr., San Francisco, 1972-74; asst. prof. medicine (clin. pharmacology) Stanford (Calif.) U. Sch. Medicine, 1974-81, asst. prof. pharmacology, 1978-81, assoc. prof. medicine (clin. pharmacology) and pharmacology, 1981-91, prof. medicine (clin. pharmacology)-molecular pharmacology, 1991—; bd. govs. Am. Bd. Clin. Pharmacology, 1990-92; vis. worker div. molecular pharmacology Nat. Inst. for Med. Rsch., London, 1980-81, Ctr. for Biopharm. Scis., U. Leiden and dept. med. info. scis. Erasmus U., The Netherlands, 1990; mem. Medi-Cal drug use rev. bd. Calif. Dept. Health Svcs., 1993-96; chmn. generic drugs adv. com. FDA, 1990-94; mem. bd. sci. advisors Merck Sharp and Dohme Rsch. Labs., Rahway, N.J., 1986-90; mem. pharmacology study sect. NIH, 1979-83; faculty of medicine Moi U., El Doret, Kenya; vis. prof. Ctr. Drug Devel. Sci., Georgetown U., 1997-98; spl. govt. employee FDA, 1997—. Mem. editl. bd. Drug Therapeutics: Concepts for Physicians, 1978-81, Rational Drug Therapy, 1984-85, Clin. Pharmacology and Therapeutics, 1981—, Drug Interaction Facts, 1983-87, Drug Metabolism and Disposition, 1994—; assoc. editor Ann. Rev. Pharmacology and Toxicology, 1989—. Officer USPHS, 1970-72. Recipient faculty devel. award in clin. pharmacology Pharm. Mfrs. Assn. Found.; Burroughs-Wellcome scholar. Mem. ACP, AAAS, Am. Soc. for Clin. Pharmacology and Therapeutics (chmn. liaison com. for clin. pharmacology 1985-89, sci. program com. 1986-87, pres. 1988-89, assoc. sec.-treas. 1990-92, chmn. long range planning com. 1992-94), Am. Soc. Pharmacology and Exptl. Therapeutics (exec. com. clin. pharmacology divsn. 1986-89), Am. Fedn. Clin. Rsch., Western Soc. Clin. Investigation, Western Assn. Physicians, Western Pharmacology Soc., Phi Beta Kappa, Alpha Omega Alpha. Office: Stanford U Med Ctr Div Clin Pharmacology S-009 300 Pasteur Dr Stanford CA 94305-5130

BLASCO, ALFRED JOSEPH, business and financial consultant; b. Kansas City, Mo., Oct. 9, 1904; s. Joseph and Mary (Bevacqua) B.; m. Kathryn Oleno, June 28, 1926; children: Barbara Blasco Lowry, Phyllis Blasco O'Connor. Student, Kansas City Sch. Accountancy, 1921-25, Am. Inst. Banking, 1926-30; Ph.D. (hon.), Avila Coll., 1969. From office boy to asst. controller Commerce Trust Co., Kansas City, Mo., 1921-35; controller Interstate Securities Co., Kansas City, 1935-45; v.p. Interstate Securities Co., 1945-53, pres., 1953-61, chmn. bd., 1961-68; sr. v.p. ISC Fin. Corp., 1968-69, hon. chmn. bd., 1970-77, pres., 1979-88; chmn. bd. Red Bridge Bank, 1966-72; Mark Plaza State Bank, Overland Park, Kans., 1973-77; spl. lectr. consumer credit Columbia U., N.Y.C., 1956, U. Kans., Lawrence, 1963-64. Contbr. articles to profl. jours. Pres. Cath. Community Library, 1955-56; Mem. Fair Public Accomodations Com., Kansas City, Mo., 1964-68; ward committeeman, 1972-76; pres., hon. bd. dirs. Baptist Med. Ctr., 1970-74; chmn. bd. dirs. St. Anthony's Home, 1965-69; chmn. bd. trustees Avila Coll., 1969-89. Decorated papal knight Equestrian Order Holy Sepulchre of Jerusalem, 1957, 58 knight comdr., 1964, knight grand cross, 1966, knight of collar, 1982, lt. No. Lieutenancy U.S., 1970-77, vice gov.-gen., 1977-82; named Bus. Man of Yr. State of Mo., 1957, Man of Yr. City of Hope, 1973; recipient Community Svc. award Rockne Club Notre Dame, 1959, wisdom award of honor, 1979; Brotherhood award NCCJ, 1979. Mem. Soc. St. Vincent de Paul (pres. 1959-67), Am. Indsl. Bankers Assn. (pres. 1956-57), Am. Inst. Banking (chpt. pres. 1932-33), Bank Auditors and Controllers Assn. (chpt. pres. 1928-29), Fin. Execs. Inst. (chpt. pres. 1942-43), Nat. Assn. Accts. Clubs: Rotary, Kansas City, Hillcrest Country, Serra (pres. 1959-60).

BLASE, NANCY GROSS, librarian; b. New Rochelle, N.Y.; d. Albert Philip and Elsie Wise (May) Gross; m. Barrie Wayne Blase, June 19, 1966 (div.); 1 child, Eric Wayne. BA in Biology, Marietta (Ohio) Coll., 1964; MLS, U. Ill., 1965. Info. scientist brain info. svc. Biomed. Libr., UCLA, 1965-66; libr. Health Sci. Libr., U. Wash., Seattle, 1966-68, Medlars search analyst, 1970-72, coord. Medline, 1972-79, head Natural Scis. Libr., 1979—; mem. libr. adv. com. Elizabeth C. Miller Libr., Ctr. for Urban Horticulture, Seattle, 1986-90. Contbr. articles to profl. jours. NSF fellow interdept. tng. program for sci. info. specialists U. Ill., 1964-65. Mem. Am. Soc. for Info. Sci. (pres. personal computer spl. interest group 1993-94, chair constn. and bylaws com. 1994-97, chair Spl. Interest Group/Med. Info. Sys. 1998-99, rsch. grantee Pacific N.W. chpt. 1984-85), Internat. Tng. in Comm. (pres. Pacific N.W. region 1994-95), Phi Beta Kappa (pres., of Univ. of Wash. chpt. 1993-97), Bet Chaverim (pres. 1998—). Avocations: walking, golf, reading. Home: 10751 Durland Ave NE Seattle WA 98125-6945 Office: U Wash Natural Scis Libr PO Box 352900 Seattle WA 98195-2900

BLASI, ALBERTO, Romance languages educator, writer; b. Buenos Aires, Jan. 21, 1931; s. Alberto B. and Emma (Raffo) B. Diploma en Letras, U. Buenos Aires, 1957, Licenciado en Letras, 1965; D. Letras, U. La Plata, 1976; postgrad. (fellow), U. Iowa, 1975. Sr. lectr. U. Buenos Aires, 1965-69; prof. U. Rosario, Argentina, 1969-73; vis. writer U. Iowa, 1974-75; assoc. prof. Spanish Bklyn. Coll., CUNY, 1975-79, prof. modern langs, 1979—; prof. Spanish CUNY Grad. Sch., 1979—. Author: Los Fundadores, 1962, Introducción a Lucio López, 1965, La tarea del cuento en Fin de Siglo, 1968, Güiraldes y Larbaud: Una amistad creadora, 1970, Manuel Podestá, 1982; editor: La gran aldea, 1965, Fin de Siglo, 1968, Essays on Lucio Victorio Mansilla, 1981, Movimientos literarios del siglo XX en Iberoamérica: Teoría y práctica, 1982, Don Segundo Sombra, 1983, 2d edit., 1996; contbr. articles to profl. jours. Recipient French Govt. award Bourse de Marque, 1972, Soc. Argentine Writers Book award, 1960, CUNY rsch. award, 1980-83, 99-2000, Argentine Found. for the Arts award, 1966, 69, Municipality of Buenos Aires Book award, 1967. Mem. PEN Club Internat., Internat. Assn. Hispanists, Internat. Comparative Lit. Assn. Office: Brooklyn Coll Dept Modern Languages Brooklyn NY 11210

BLASIER, COLE, political scientist; b. Jackson, Mich., Mar. 16, 1925; s. Stewart Parnell and Helen (Cole) B.; m. Martha Hiett, Sept. 20, 1947; children: Peter Cole, Martha Hamilton. AB, U. Ill., 1947; postgrad., U. Mex., 1947; AM, Columbia U., 1950, cert. Russian Inst., 1950, PhD in Polit. Sci., 1955. Career fgn. svc. officer U.S. Dept. State, Belgrade, Yugoslavia, 1951-54, Bonn, Federal Republic of Germany, 1954-57, Washington, 1957-60, Moscow, 1958; exec. asst. to pres., sec. bd. trustees Colgate U., Hamilton, N.Y., 1961-63; prof. polit. sci. U. Pitts., 1964-88; chief hispanic div. Libr. Congress, Washington, 1988-93; sr. rsch. assoc. North-South Ctr. U. Miami, Coral Gables, Fla., 1993-95; dir. ctr. Latin Am. studies U. Pitts., 1964-74; adv. bd. Handbook Latin Am. Studies, 1972-88; exchange scholar Polish Inst. Internat. Affairs, Warsaw, Poland, 1975, Inst. Latin Am., Moscow, 1979; U.S. chmn. U.S./USSR Exchange in Latin Am. Studies, 1980-86; mgmt. cons. project to revive ancient libr., Alexandria, Egypt, 1993; mgmt. cons., Vladivostok, Russia, 1999; adj. prof. Georgetown U., 1993—; field work in Russia and Germany, 1996. Author: The Hovering Giant, U.S. Responses to Revolutionary Change in Latin America, 1976, rev., 1985, The Giant's Rival, The USSR and Latin America, 1983, rev., 1987, Cuba in the World, 1979, The End of the Soviet-Cuban Partnership, Cuba After the Cold War, 1993, Clinton in Latin America, 1994, Dilemmas in Promoting Democracy, 1995, North South Center, Russia's Institute of Europe, 1996; editor U. Pitts. Press Latin Am. series, 1968-91. Pres. UN Assn. Pitts., 1985. Lt. (j.g.) USNR, PTO, 1943-46. Fellow Rotary Santiago Chile 1947-48, Kennan Inst. Woodrow Wilson Ctr., 1978, Fulbright, Buenos Aires, Argentina, 1986, Heinz Endowment, 1988; Rockefeller Found. grantee, Cali, Colombia, 1963-64; decorated Knighthood of Isabel la Catolica (Spain), 1993. Mem. Lat. Am. Studies Assn. (pres. 1986-87), Am. Polit. Sci. Assn. Home: 4287 Embassy Park Dr NW Washington DC 20016-3605

BLASINGAME, BENJAMIN PAUL, electronics company executive; b. State College, Pa., Aug. 1, 1918; s. Ralph Upshaw and Sue Mae (Combs) B.; m. Ella Mae Perry, Aug. 29, 1942 (dec.); children—Nancy J. Blasingame Wambach, James P., Margaret A. Blasingame Kramer, John R.; m. Margaret A. Timmons, Mar. 21, 1992. B.S. in Mech. Engring., Pa. State U., 1940; Sc.D. in Aero. Engring., M.I.T., 1950. Commd. 2d lt. USAAF, 1941; advanced through grades to col. USAF, 1955; head astronautics dept. U.S. Air Force Acad., 1958-59; resigned, 1959; gen. mgr. electronics div. Gen. Motors Corp., 1959-70; mgr. Milw. operation Delco Electronics div., 1970-72, Santa Barbara operation,, 1972-79. Author: Astronautics, 1964. Bd. dirs. Santa Barbara Cottage Hosp., 1977-87; chmn. Santa Barbara Metro, Nat. Alliance Bus., 1972-75; trustee Santa Barbara Found., 1982-93, pres., 1992-93; mem. adv. bd. Leonard Ctr. for Enhancement Engring. Edn., Pa. State U., 1993-97; dir. Santa Barbara Bank and Trust, 1984-94. Decorated Legion of Merit; recipient Public Service award NASA, 1969, Public Service medal, 1973. Mem. AIAA, Nat. Acad. Engring., N.Y. Acad. Scis., Internat. Acad. Astronautics, Santa Barbara C. of C. (bd. dirs. 1977-79). Unitarian. Club: La Cumbre Country. Patentee in field. Home: 517 Carriage Hill Ct Santa Barbara CA 93110-2022 *Any list of the characteristics of a good manager must include knowledge of what is being managed. To think otherwise is to claim that an orchestra leader need not be a musician.*

BLASIOTTI, ROBERT VINCENT, accountant, consultant; b. Phila., Nov. 15, 1949; s. Vincent Mario Blasiotti and Hilda (Romani) Greer; m. Katheryn Phyllis Ombres, Dec. 15, 1973 (div. Apr. 1982); m. Gilda Maria Cipriani, June 17, 1988; children: Melissa, Gabriella, Robert Jr. BS, Pa. State U., 1971, MBA, 1973. CPA, Pa. Jr. acct. Goldenberg, Rosenthal & Co., Phila., 1971-73, sr. acct., 1973-75; mgr. acctg. Gross & Co., Jenkintown, Pa., 1975-77; owner Blasiotti & Co., West Chester, Pa., 1977—; CPA, advisor Big Bros. Chester County, West Chester, 1985—; cons. Presdl. Adv. Coun., 1984; fin. advisor Exton Sq. Mall Merchants Assn., 1978-89; bd. advisors Med-Trans, Inc., 1982-84. Mem. Big Bros.-Big Sisters Chester County, 1978—; trustee Rep. Presdl. Task Force, 1982—; mem. coun. St. Maximilian Kolby Ch., 1994-97; bd. advisors Our Lady's Missionaries of Eucharist, 1999—. Served from 2d lt. to capt. U.S. Army, 1971-79. Mem. C. of C., Jaycees (chmn. 1980-84), Italian Social Club (fin. sec. 1992-96), KC (treas. 1994, dep. grand knight 1995, grand knight 1996, trustee 1997—), Lions (treas. 1980-81), Men of Malvern. Roman Catholic. Avocations: philately, numismatology, golf, horticulture, fishing. Office: Blasiotti & Co 933 S High St Ste B West Chester PA 19382-5489

BLASS, JOHN PAUL, medical educator, physician; b. Vienna, Austria, Feb. 21, 1937; s. Gustaf and Jolan (Wirth) B.; m. Birgit Annelise Knudsen, Dec. 20, 1960; children: Charles, Lisa. AB summa cum laude, Harvard U., 1958; PhD, U. London, 1960; MD, Columbia U., 1965. Postdoctoral fellow Am. Cancer Soc., Columbia U., 1962-63; intern Mass. Gen. Hosp., Boston, 1965-66; resident in medicine Mass. Gen. Hosp., 1966-67; research assoc. Nat. Heart and Lung Inst., Bethesda, Md., 1967-70; asst. prof. psychiatry and biol. chemistry UCLA, 1970-76, assoc. prof., 1976-78; mem. staff UCLA Hosps. Clinics, 1970-78; Winifred Masterson Burke prof. neurology, prof. medicine Cornell U. Med. Center, 1978—; attending neurologist N.Y. Hosp.; mem. NBS-1 rev. com. NIH, 1981-84; councilor Nat. Inst. Aging, 1986-89; chmn. Nat. Adv. Panel on Alzheimers's Disease U.S. Congress, 1987-91, mem., 1993-96. Editl. bd. Jour. Neurochemistry, 1981-86, Neurochem. Rsch., 1984-86, Neurochem. pathology, Neurobiol. Aging, Jour. Neurol. Scis., 1990—; assoc. editor Jour. Am. Geriatric Soc., 1982-87, Age, 1993—, Yearbook of Neurology and Neurosurgery, 1992—; co-editor: Caring for Alzheimer's Patients, 1990, Familial Alzheimer's Disease, 1989, Treatment of Alzheimer's Disease, 1989, Principles of Geriatrics and Gerontology, 2d edit. 1990, 3d edit. 1994; contbr. articles to profl. jours. Mem. sci. adv. bd. Will Rogers Inst., 1981-97, Allied Signal Aging Award Com., 1993-95. Served as asst. surgeon USPHS, 1967-70. Marshall scholar, 1958-60. Mem. Soc.

Neurosci. (chmn. social issues com.), Biochem. Soc., Am. Soc. Biol. Chemists, Am. Soc. Neurochemistry (council, chmn. public policy com.), Internat. Soc. Neurochemistry (council, chmn. clin. com.), Am. Soc. Clin. Investigation, Am. Geriatrics Soc., Am. Fedn. Aging Rsch. (v.p., chmn. research com. 1982-87, pres. 1994-96), Assn. Alzheimers and Related Disease (sci. adv. bd. 1982-86), Am. Chem. Soc., Phi Beta Kappa, Sigma Xi, Alpha Omega Alpha. Jewish. Home: 1 Orchard Pl Bronxville NY 10708-2509 Office: Burke Med Rsch Inst 785 Mamaroneck Ave White Plains NY 10605-2523

BLASS, NOLAND, JR., retired architect; b. Little Rock, May 28, 1920; s. Noland and Isabel (Ringelhaupt) B.; m. Elizabeth Weitzenhoffer, Oct. 21, 1947; children: Elizabeth Victoria, Wendy Blass Dilivio. BArch., Cornell U., 1941. Registered architect, Ark. Designer-prin. Blass Chilcote Carter Gaskin Bogart & Norcross, Little Rock, 1946-71; pres. Blass Chilcote and ptnrs. and predecessor firms, 1972-90, ret., 1990; bd. dirs. Ottenheimer Found., Little Rock, 1985—; mem. Fifty for the Future, Little Rock, 1965— (pres. 1985-87). Prin. works include Worthen Bank bldg., 1969, Supreme Ct. bldg. State of Ark., 1972, Edn. Lab. for Med. Scis., U. Ark., 1974; one-man exhbn. of miniature bronze sculpture at Temple Gallery, San Miguel de Allende, Mex., 1994. Pres. Ark. Arts Center, 1972; mem. Little Rock Planning Commn., 1960-69; pres. Pulaski Met. YMCA, 1967-68; mem. Gov.'s Inauguation Com., 1971; pres. Ark. Orch. Soc., 1976; trustee A.I.A. Ednl. Endowment Fund; bd. dirs. Levi Hosp., Mid-Am. Arts Alliance, 1980—; pres. Levi Found., 1983; trustee Ark. Orch. Fedn., 1990. Served with AUS, 1941-45. Fellow AIA (pres. Ark. br. 1958-59, Ark. Gold medal 1989); mem. Masons (33 degree), Tau Beta Pi, Zeta Beta Tau. Democrat. Jewish. Avocation: collecting Japanese inro. Home: 34 Riverpoint Little Rock AR 72202-1411 Office: GHN 303 W Capitol Ave Little Rock AR 72201-3531

BLASS, WALTER PAUL, consultant, management educator; b. Dinslaken, Germany, Mar. 31, 1930; s. Richard B. and Malvi (Rosenblatt) B.; m. Janice L. Minott, Apr. 2, 1954; children: Kathryn, Christopher, Gregory. BA, Swarthmore Coll., 1951; postgrad., Princeton U., 1951-52; MA, Columbia U., 1953. Asst. laos and cambodia desk ofcr. ICA, Wash., 1957-58; gen. mgr. R.B. Blass Co., Deal, NJ, 1958-61; economist AT&T, N.Y.C., 1961-65; country dir. Peace Corps., Afghanistan, 1966-68; asst. v.p. revenue requirement studies NY Telephone Co., N.Y.C., 1968-70; dir. corp. planning AT&T, 1970-82, dir. strategic planning, 1982-85; ret., 1985—; Pres., Strategic Plans, Unltd., Warren, N.J., 1985—. Exec. Fellow-in-Residence Martino Grad. Sch. Bus. Adminstrn., Fordham U., N.Y.C., 1986-90; cons. McKinsey & Co., Telecom. Authority Ireland, McDonnell Douglas, Heller Fin., Inc.; lectr. in field; vis. prof. U. Grenoble, France, 1988, Ecole Superieure de Commerce, Chambery and Grenoble, France, 1989—. Trustee Guilford Coll., 1975—, chmn. planning com., 1992-99, vice chmn. tchrs. and officers com., 1999—. Co-author: The Strategic Planning Handbook, 1982, Handbook of Strategic Planning, 1986. Lt., j.g., USNR, 1953-56, Woodrow Wilson Found., sr. fell., 1974-85. Mem., N.Y. Acad. Scis., Soc. Values in Higher Edn. (dir. 1983-86), Am. Econ.Assn., Nat. Assn. Bus. Economists, The Planning Forum (dir. 1972), Royal Econ. Soc. Home and Office: 6 Casale Dr Warren NJ 07059-6703

BLATE, MICHAEL, author, lecturer; b. Queens, N.Y., June 24, 1938; s. Martin Stanley and Sylvia (Lax) B.; m. Bonnie Gloria Baker, Oct. 18, 1958 (div. 1962); children: Laurie Sue, Keith Martin; m. Barbara Gail Watson, June 21, 1998. Student, U. Miami, Oxford, Ohio, 1957, U. Miami, Coral Gables, Fla., 1959, U. Fla., 1962, Broward C.C., Davie, Fla., 1962. Registered principal, investment adviser. V.p. Western Water Co., Inc., Hollywood, Fla., 1959-65, Marina Products Mfg., Inc., Ft. Lauderdale, Fla., 1963-87; investment counsel pvt. practice, Davie, Fla., 1965-67; founder, reg. prin. officer M. Blate & Co., Davie, Fla., 1967-69; advisor Nova Convertible Inv. Fund, Ft. Lauderdale, Fla., 1969-88; founder, CEO Falkynor Communications, Davie, Fla., 1974-87; CEO Falkyn, Inc., Davie, Fla., 1987—; Author, radio-TV guest columnist The G-Jo Inst., Davie, Fla., 1975—; spokesperson, columnist, journalist, The G-Jo Inst., Hollywood, Fla., 1975—. Author: The Natural Healer's Acupressure Handbook Vol. I, II, 1978, How to Heal Yourself Using Hand Acupressure, How to Heal Yourself Using Foot Acupressure, Acugenics: Beat Stress in Five Minutes, The Tao of Health: The Way of Total Well-Being, 1982, When the Market Makes a Bottom, Vendanta for the 21st Century, 1995, The Master of G-Jo Acupressure Home-Study Certification Program, 1995, The Instructor of G-Jo Acupressure Home-Study Certification Program, 1995, G-Jo Ear Acupressure, 1996, Sanjeevini ("Prayer-in-a-Bottle") Operator's Kit, 1996, Neti Yoga and the Seven Ultimate Secrets, 1997, A Yogi Explains the Bhagavad Gita: Enlightenment for the New Millennium, 1998, The Acugenics Longevity and Wellness Special Report, 1998, Better Sex with Acugenics, 1998, Better Sleep With Acugenics, 1998, Better Eyesight With Acugenics, 1998, Dynamic Nutrition! The Acugenics Way of Eating for Pleasure and Health, 1998, Lifelong Fitness With Acugenics, 1998, Lose Weight Easily With Acugenics, 1998, Stop Smoking (and Other Addictions) With Acugenics, 1998, How To Relieve Allergies With Acugenics, 1998, How To Relieve Arthritis With Acugenics, 1998, How To Relieve Back Pain With Acugenics, 1998, How To Relieve Colds and Influenza With Acugenics, 1998, How To Relieve Depression With Acugenics, 1998, How To Relieve Constipation With Acugenics, 1998, How To Relieve Diarrhea With Acugenics, 1998, How To Relieve Headaches and Migraines With Acugenics, 1998, How To Relieve Indigestion With Acugenics, 1998, How To Relieve Menopause With Acugenics, 1998, Better Vision With Acugenics, 1998, others; columnist: Healthy & Natural Mag., Wolfe's Digest of Alternative Medicine, Townsend Letter for Doctors and Patients, American Survival Guide. Dir. United Fund of Broward County, Ft. Lauderdale, Fla., 1961; officer, dir. Jaycees, Hollywood, Fla., 1959-60; mem. Rotary Internat., W. Hollywood, Fla., 1968-70; founder, Vegetarian Gourmet Soc., Davie, Fla., 1982-88, Sathya Prema Charitable Found. Recipient Jaycee Key Man of Qtr. and Yr. awards, Hollywood, Fla., 1961, Kinsa Nat. Photographer's awards, Eastman Kodak, Fla., N.Y.C., N.Y., 1973-75. Avocations: yachting, traveling, photography, organic fruit farming, Oriental studies and philosophies. Office: The G Jo Institute PO Box 1460 Columbus NC 28722-1460

BLATT, HAROLD GELLER, lawyer; b. Detroit, Apr. 8, 1934; s. Henry H. and Berdye (Geller) B.; m. Elaine K. Greenberg, July 9, 1960; children—Lisa K., James G., Andrew N. B.S., Washington U., St. Louis, 1955, LL.B., 1960; LL.M., NYU, 1961. Bar: Mo. 1960. Ptnr. Bryan Cave, St. Louis, 1961—; dir. Artex Internat., Highland, Ill. Trustee Webster U., St. Louis, 1982-97, Washington U. Med. Ctr., St. Louis, 1983-96, Barnes-Jewish, Inc., 1993—; chmn. Jewish Hosp., St. Louis, 1983-88. 1st lt. U.S. Army, 1955-57. Mem. ABA, Mo. Bar Assn., Noonday Club (St. Louis), St. Louis Club.

BLATT, MORTON BERNARD, medical illustrator; b. Chgo., Jan. 9, 1923; s. Arthur E. and Hazel B. Student Central YMCA Coll., 1940-42, U. Ill., 1943-46. Tchr., Ray-Vogue Art Schs., Chgo., 1946-51; med. illustrator VA Center, Wood, Wis., 1951-57, Swedish Covenant Hosp., Chgo., 1957-76; med. illustrator Laidlaw Bros., River Forest, Ill., 1956-59; cons., artist health textbooks, 1956-59; illustrator Standard Edn. Soc., Chgo., 1960; art editor Covenant Home Altar, 1972-83, Covenant Companion, 1958-82. Served with USAAF, 1943-44. Mem. Art Inst. Chgo. Club: Chgo. Press. Illustrator: Atlas and Demonstration Technique of the Central Nervous System; also numerous med. jours.; illustrator, designer Covenant Hymnal, books, record jackets. Address: 373 Eliseo Dr Greenbrae CA 94904-1326

BLATT, PHILIP MARK, hematologist, educator; b. Suffern, N.Y., Oct. 19, 1943; s. Kurt Bernard Blatt and Frieda (Einstoss) Richter; m. Paula Marie Breen, Feb. 15, 1981; 1 child, Rebecca Emily. BA, U. Pa., 1965; MD, Washington U., St. Louis, 1969. Diplomate Am. Coll. Physicians; Lic. N.C., Del. Resident U. N.C., Chapel Hill, 1969-72; Fellow U. Utah, Salt Lake City, 1972-73; Fellow U. N.C., Chapel Hill, 1973-75, from instr. to dir. Hemophila Ctr., 1974-82; from provisional mem. to prof. Medicine & Pathology Depts. Christianna Care Health Sys., Newark, 1982—, assoc. dir. hematology lab., 1983-97, dir. hematology and coagulation labs., 1997—; clin. assoc. prof. Thomas Jefferson Med. Ctr., Phila., 1982—; dir. Hemophilia Ctr. Med. Ctr. Del., Newark, 1982—. Contbr. articles to profl. jours. Mem. Internat. Soc. Thrombosis-Hemostasis, World Fedn. Hemophilia, Am. Soc. Hematology, Am. Soc. Lab. & Clin. Medicine, So. Soc. Clin. Investigation. Avocations: tennis, squash, basketball fan, reading.

BLATT, RICHARD LEE, lawyer; b. Oak Park, Ill., May 24, 1940; s. B. Lee Gray and Madelyn Gertrude (Bentley) B.; m. Carol Milner Jenkinson, May 21, 1965 (div. Dec. 1984); children: Christopher Andrew Lee, Katherine Lee, Susannah Lee; m. Carolyn Elizabeth LeBlanc, Jan. 31, 1987; 1 child, Jennifer Lee DeNux Blatt. BA, U. Ill., 1962; JD, U. Mich., 1965. Bar: Ill. 1968, U.S. Dist. Ct. (no. dist.) Ill. 1968, U.S. Ct. Appeals (7th cir.) 1968, U.S. Supreme Ct. 1974, U.S. Dist. Ct. (so. dist.) Ill. 1977, U.S. Ct. Appeals (4th cir.) 1987, N.Y. 1989, U.S. Ct. Appeals (3rd cir.) 1990, U.S. Dist. Ct. (ea. and so. dists.) N.Y., 1998. Assoc. Peterson, Lowry, Rall, Barber & Ross, Chgo., 1968-75; ptnr. Peterson, Ross, Schloeb & Seidel, Chgo., 1975-91, Peterson & Ross, Chgo., 1991-94; sr. ptnr. Blatt, Hammesfahr & Eaton, Chgo., 1994—. Author: (with Robert G. Schloerb, Robert W. Hammesfahr, Lori S. Nugent) Punitive Damages: A Guide to the Insurability of Punitive Damages in the United States and Its Territories, 1988, (with Robert W. Hammesfahr and Lori S. Nugent) Punitive Damges: A State-by-State Guide to Law and Practice, 1991 (in Japanese 1995). Capt. inf. USAR, 1965-67, Korea. Fellow Chartered Inst. Arbitrators; mem. ABA, Ill. State Bar Assn., Soc. Mayflower Desc. State Ill., N.Y. State Bar Assn., Chgo. Bar Assn., Chgo. Club, Racquet Club Chgo., Phi Beta Kappa, Phi Kappa Phi. Home: 70 E Cedar St Apt 1101 Chicago IL 60611-1179 Office: Blatt Hammesfahr & Eaton 333 W Wacker Dr Ste 1900 Chicago IL 60606-1226

BLATT, SIDNEY JULES, psychology educator, psychoanalyst; b. Phila., Oct. 15, 1928; s. Harry and Fannie (Feld) B.; m. Ethel Shames, Feb. 1, 1951; children: Susan, Judith, David. B.S., Pa. State U., 1950, M.S., 1952; Ph.D., U. Chgo., 1957; postgrad., Western New Eng. Inst. for Psychoanalysis, 1972. Postdoctoral fellow Neuropsychiat. Inst. of U. Ill. Med. Ctr., Psychiat. and Psychosomatic Inst. of Michael Reese Hosp., New Eng., 1957-59; instr. Univ. Coll. U. Chgo., 1959-60; mem. faculty Yale U., New Haven, 1960—, prof. psychology and psychiatry, 1974—; mem. faculty Western New Eng. Inst. for Psychoanalysis, 1975—; Sigmund Freud prof. psychoanalysis, Ayala and Sam Zacks prof. of art history Hebrew U., 1988-89; Fulbright sr. rsch. fellow, 1988-89; mem. NIMH Rsch. Fellowship Rev. Panel, 1966-69, NIMH Psychology Tng. Rev. Panel, 1969-74. Author: (with J. Allison and C. Zimet) Interpretation of Psychological Tests, 1968, 2d edit., 1988, (with C. M. Wild) Schizophrenia: A Developmental Analysis, 1976, (with E.S. Blatt) Continuity and Change in Art: The Development of Modes of Representation, 1984, (with Z.V. Segal) The Self in Emotional Distress, 1993, (with R. Q. Ford) Therapeutic Change: An Object Relations Perspective, 1994. Recipient award for disting. contbns. to rsch. Assn. Med. Sch. Profs. Psychology; named Disting. Practitioner of Psychology, Nat. Acad. Practice, 1983; Found. Fund Rsch. in Psychiatry fellow, 1961-64. Mem. APA, AAAS, AAUP, Soc. Personality Assessment (pres. 1984-86, Bruno Klopfer and Marguerite R. Hertz awards for disting. contbns. to personality assessment). Office: Yale U 25 Park St New Haven CT 06519-1110

BLATT, SOLOMON, JR., federal judge; b. Sumter, S.C., Aug. 20, 1921; s. Solomon and Ethel (Green) B.; m. Carolyn Gayden, Sept. 12, 1942; children: Gregory, Sheryl Blatt Hooper, Brian. AB, U. S.C., 1941, LLB, 1946, LLD (hon.), 1987; LLD (hon.), The Citadel, 1990, Coll. of Charleston, 1992. Bar: S.C., 1946. Ptnr. Blatt & Fales, Barnwell, S.C., 1946-71; judge U.S. Dist. Ct. S.C., Charleston, 1971-86, chief judge, 1986-90; sr. judge U.S. Dist. Ct. S.C., 1990—. Office: US Dist Ct SC PO Box 835 Charleston SC 29401*

BLATTER, FRANK EDWARD, travel agency executive; b. Denver, Jan. 9, 1939; s. Anthony John and Irene Marie (Tobin) B.; m. Barbara E. Drieth, Sept. 6, 1959; children: Dean Robert, Lisa Kay Faircloth, Paul Kelly. BS, Regis U., Denver, 1961; grad., Colo. Sch. Banking, 1966, Sch. Bank Adminstrn., 1973. CPA, Colo. Acct. McMahon, Maddox & Rodriguez (C.P.A.s), Denver, 1960-63, United Bank Denver, 1963-65; with United Banks Colo., Inc., Denver, 1965-86; pres. Cath. Cmty. Svcs., Denver, 1987, Premiere Travel and Cruises, Denver, 1988—. Mem. nat. adv. coun. and devel. com., chmn. ann. funds coun. Regis U.; chmn. adv. coun. Camp Santa Maria; crusade chmn. Am. Cancer Soc., Denver. Mem. AICPA, Tax Execs. Inst. (past pres. Denver), Colo. Soc. CPAs, Fin. Execs. Inst. (dir.), Bank Adminstrn. Inst. (dir.), Arrowhead Golf Club. Roman Catholic. Office: 3900 S Wadsworth Blvd Ste 475 Denver CO 80235-2207

BLATTMACHR, JONATHAN GEORGE, lawyer; b. Warner Robins, Ga., Apr. 7, 1945; s. George Gustav and Janet Elizabeth (Tice) B.; m. Betsy Eloise Masters, Aug. 15, 1970; children: Jonathan, Jeffrey. AB, Bucknell U., 1967; JD cum laude, Columbia U., 1970. Bar: N.Y. 1973, U.S. Dist. Ct. (so. and ea. dists.) N.Y. 1973, U.S. Tax Ct. 1983, Calif. 1987, Alaska 1988, U.S. Ct. Appeals (9th cir.) 1989, U.S. Supreme Ct. 1989. Assoc. Simpson Thacher & Bartlett, N.Y.C., 1970-77; ptnr. Milbank, Tweed, Hadley & McCloy, N.Y.C., 1977—; lectr. law Columbia U. Sch. Law, 1979-90; adj. prof. law NYU Sch. Law, 1983, 87—; former mem. adv. bd. NYU Inst. on Fed. Taxation; former regent, fellow, former chairperson estate & gift tax com. Am. Coll. Trusts & Estates Counsel; mem. L.I. Tax and Estate Planning Coun.; mem. fin. and estate planning bd. CCH Inc. Author: Wealth Preservation and Protection for Closely-Held Business Owners (And Others), 1993; co-author: Carryover Basis Under the 1976 Tax Reform Act, 1977, Income Taxation of Estates and Trusts, 1978, 80, 85, 89; former editor The Chase Rev.; former editor Probate Notes; bd. editors Trusts and Estates; editor-in-chief Conspectus Current. Chair N.Y. Iola Fund. Capt. USAR, 1970-72. Decorated Army Commendation medal. Mem. ABA (former chairperson com. on marital deduction-estate planning real property probate and trust law sect., former chairperson com. on generation-skipping transfer taxation, real property, probate & trust law sect.), N.Y. State Bar Assn. (former chairperson trusts & estates law sect., chairperson interest on lawyer account adv. com., former chairperson surrogate's cts. com. trusts & estates law sect.), Assn. of Bar of City of N.Y. Office: Milbank Tweed Hadley & McCloy 1 Chase Manhattan Plz Fl 47 New York NY 10005-1413

BLATTNER, FLORENCE ANNE, music educator; b. Rockford, Ill., Nov. 27, 1935; d. Keith F. and Grace L. (Turney) Perkins; m. Lewis Olof Blattner, Mar. 28, 1959; children: Gloria Grace Blattner Mundt, Gayle Mary Blattner Ludwig. BA, Carroll Coll., 1958; studied with, Vladimir Levitski, 1984-95, Weekly and Arganbright, U. Ind, 1993, 98, Joanne Tierney, 1996—. Libr. Racine (Wis.) Pub. Schs., 1958-60, elem. substitute tchr., 1961-62, elem. and jr. high tchr., 1962; pvt. practice piano instr. Indpls., 1970-78; data processor OMS Internat., Greenwood, Ind., 1978; pvt. practice piano and theory instr. Des Moines, 1980-83; piano and theory instr. Prelude Piano Studio, Apple Valley, Minn., 1983—. Duettist concerts of duet lit., Grace Luth. Ch., 1996, Christ United Meth., 1996, 99, White Bear Lake, Minn., 1996, Racine, 1996, 98, Mall of Am., Bloomington, Minn., 1996, 97, 98, Apple Valley, 1997. ch. pianist, accompianist, 1970—; vol. Rep. Party-Minn., Apple Valley, 1992, 94, 96, 98. Mem. Nat. Assn. Music Tchrs., Minn. Music Tchrs. (assoc. cer. mem., state ensemble festival chair 1994-97, mem. cert. com. 1997—), South Suburban Music Tchrs. Assn. (1st v.p. 1995-97, pres. 1998—). Avocations: canoeing, hiking, traveling, reading.

BLATTNER, ROBERT A., lawyer; b. Lima, Ohio, July 9, 1934; s. Simon James and Estelle Leila (Aarons) B.; m. Judith Reinfeld, Feb. 5, 1964 (div. July 1980); children: Wendy Lynn, Lauren Jill; m. Eileen Savransky, Dec. 18, 1983. BA, Northwestern U., 1956; LLB, Case Western Reserve U., 1959. Bar: Ohio, Ill., U.S. Supreme Ct. Assoc. Hribar & Conway, Euclid, Ohio, 1960-62, Ulmer & Berne, Cleve., 1962-65; exec. dir. Ohio State Legal Svcs., Columbus, Ohio, 1965-67; gen. counsel, dir. real estate Sawyer Bus. Colls., Evanston, 1967-72; assoc. Guren Merritt Feibel Sogg & Cohen, Cleve., 1972-75, ptnr., 1975-84; ptnr. Benesch, Friedlander, Coplan & Aronoff, Cleve., 1984-93; shareholder Kaufman & Cumberland Co., L.P.A., Cleve., 1994—. Author: Consumer Affairs, 1973, The Construction Loan Process, 1979, Real Estate Financing, 1978, Acquisition, Development and Financing of a Commercial Complex-A Case Study, 1982; contbr. articles to profl. jours. Pres. Am. Jewish Com., Cleve., 1980-82, officer, 1976-80, chmn. adv. com., 1998—; v.p. Criminal Justice Coord. Com., Cleve., 1980-84, Cleve. Play House, 1988-92, bd. dirs., 1978—, pres., 1992-94, chmn., 1994-96, v.p., 1996—. Recipient Max Freedman Young Leadership award, Cleve., 1974. Mem. ABA, Nat. Assn. Bond Lawyers, Ohio State Bar Assn., Cleve. Bar Assn. (chmn. real estate com. 1978-79, chmn. real estate law insts. 1979, 87). Jewish. Avocations: tennis, golf, classical music, reading. Office: Kaufman & Cumberland Co LPA 25 W Prospect Ave Ste 1500 Cleveland OH 44115-1049

BLATTNER, WOLFRAM GEORG MICHAEL, meteorologist; b. Nuremberg, Germany, Sept. 28, 1940; came to U.S., 1969; s. Richard and Margarete (Zirngibl) Blattner; m. Brunhilde Klara Wey, Oct. 31, 1969; children: Michelle (dec.), Paul. Diploma in meteorology, U. Mainz, Germany, 1968. Rschr. NATO, Hanscom Field, Mass., 1968-69; project scientist Radiation Rsch. Assocs., Ft. Worth, 1969-83, dir. atmospheric optics, 1983-85; engring. specialist, Electro-Optics LTV, Dallas, 1985-90; sr. analyst Mission Analysis Loral Vought Systems, Dallas, 1990-96; project mgr. studies and analysis Lockheed Martin Vought Systems, Dallas, 1996—; cons. SciTec, Inc., Princeton, N.J., 1983-92. Contbg. author: Radiation in the Atmosphere, 1977; contbr. articles to profl. jours. Mem. referee com. U.S. Soccer Fedn., Chgo., 1990—. Mem. Am. Meteorol. Soc. Roman Catholic. Achievements include research in twilight radiation and radiative transfer. Home: 611 Joyce St Weatherford TX 76086-9563 Office: Lockheed Martin Vought Sys MS WT-52 PO Box 650003 Dallas TX 75265-0003

BLATZ, LINDA JEANNE, marketing professional; b. N.Y.C., Dec. 8, 1950; d. William Edmund and Jeanne Grace (Hyman) B. BS, U. Md., 1972. Mgr. sales Milliken & Co., N.Y.C., 1972-81; retail market mgr. Greenwood Mills Mktg. Co., N.Y.C., 1981-89; dist. mgr. Steelcase Inc., N.Y.C., 1989-94, tng. cons., 1994-95, team leader, 1995—. Contbr. articles to profl. jours. Mem. N.Y.C. Ballet Guild; corr. sec. PEO; mem. jr. com. N.Y.C. Ballet; v.p. membership, bd. mgrs. exec. com. N.Y. Jr. League (Outstanding Vol. award 1991-92); nominating dir. Assn. Jr. Leagues Internat., 1997, centennial adv. bd., 1999—. Recipient Outstanding Vol. of the Yr. award N.Y. Jr. League, 1992. Mem. AAUW, U. Md. Alumni Assn., Am. Woman's Econ. Devel. Corp., East River Rowing Club, Alpha Gamma Delta. Congregationalist. Avocations: ballet, aerobic dancing, swimming, reading. Home: 2 Tudor City Pl New York NY 10017-6800 Office: 4 Columbus Cir New York NY 10019-1100

BLAU, BARRY, marketing executive, financial investor; b. N.Y.C., Oct. 4, 1927; s. Emanuel B. and Henrietta Marsha (Moses) B.; m. Eileen Diane Lefkowitz, Aug. 28, 1948; children: Shawn, Peter, Emily, Juliet. With Huber Hoge & Sons, N.Y.C., 1952-57, Sullivan, Stauffer, Caldwell & Bayles, 1958-67, 1958-67, O&M Direct Response, 1958-67, 1968-77; founder Blau Mktg. Techs. Group, 1958-67, 1978-98. Mem. Birchwood Country Club. Jewish. Office: MHI Assoc 9 Bayberry Rdg Westport CT 06880-1713

BLAU, FRANCINE DEE, economics educator; b. N.Y.C., Aug. 29, 1946; d. Harold Raymond and Sylvia (Goldberg) B.; m. Richard Weisskoff, Aug. 1969 (div. 1972); m. Lawrence Max Kahn, Jan. 1, 1979; children: Daniel Blau Kahn, Lisa Blau Kahn. BS, Cornell U., 1966; AM, Harvard U., 1969, PhD, 1975. Vis. lectr. Yale U., New Haven, 1971; instr. econs. Trinity Coll., Hartford, Conn., 1971-74; research assoc. Ctr. for Human Resource Research, Ohio State U., Columbus, 1974-75; asst. prof. econs. and labor and indsl. relations U. Ill., Urbana, 1975-78; assoc. prof. U. Ill., 1978-83, prof., 1983-94; Frances Perkins prof. indsl. and labor rels. Cornell U., 1994—; cons. law firms, 1979, 81-83, EEOC, 1981-85, U.S. Commn. on Civil Rights, 1976, 20th Century Fund Task Force on Working Women, 1970-71; mem. Nat. Acad. Scis. Panel on Technology and Women's Employment, 1984-86; mem. Nat. Acad. Scis. Panel on Pay Equity Rsch., 1985-89; rsch. assoc. Nat. Bur. Econ. Rsch., Cambridge, Mass., 1988—. Author: Equal Pay in the Office, 1977, (with Marianne Ferber) The Economics of Women, Men and Work, 1986, 2d edit., 1992, (with Marianne Ferber and Anne Winkler) The Economics of Women, Men and Work, 3rd edit., 1998; editor Jour. Labor Econs., 1992-95; assoc. editor Jour. Econ. Perspectives, 1994—; mem. editorial bd. Social Sci. Quar., 1978-94, Signs: Jour. Women in Culture and Soc., 1979—, Women and Work, 1984—, Indsl. Rels., 1989-97; bd. editors Am. Econ. Rev., 1998—; editor (with Ronald Shrenburg) Gender and Family Issues in the Workplace, 1997; contbr. articles to profl. jours. Recipient Burlington Northern faculty achievement award, 1993; Harvard U. fellow, 1966-68; U.S. Dept. Labor grantee, 1977-80. Mem. Am. Econ. Assn. (v.p. 1993), Indsl. Rels. Rsch. Assn. (exec. bd. 1987-89, pres. 1997), Midwest Econ. Assn. (v.p. 1983-84, pres. 1991-92, exec. com. 1990-93), Population Assn. Am. Office: Cornell U Sch Indsl & Labor Rels Ithaca NY 14853-3901

BLAU, HARVEY RONALD, lawyer; b. N.Y.C., Nov. 14, 1935; s. David and Rose (Kuchinsky) B.; m. Arlene Joan Garrett, Mar. 21, 1964; children: Stephanie Elizabeth, Melissa Karen, Victoria Gayle. A.B., N.Y.U., 1957, LL.M., 1965; JD, Columbia U., 1961. Bar: N.Y. 1961. Practiced in N.Y., after 1961; sr. partner firm Blau, Kramer, Wactlar & Lieberman, Jericho, N.Y., 1966—; law sec. to U.S. Dist. Judge Cooper So. Dist. N.Y., 1962-63; asst. U.S. atty. So. Dist. N.Y., 1963-66; chmn. Griffon Corp., Aeroflex Corp.; bd. dirs. Nu Horizons Electronics Corp., Reckson Assocs. Realty Corp., Benjamin N. Cardozo Sch. Law. Trustee Village of Old Westbury. Served to capt. JAGC, AUS, 1958-66. Mem. Fed. Bar Assn., Assn. of Bar of City of N.Y., Bar Assn. of Nassau County. Home: 125 Wheatley Rd Old Westbury NY 11568-1210 Office: Griffon Corp 100 Jericho Quadrangle Jericho NY 11753-2708

BLAU, HELEN MARGARET, molecular pharmacology educator; b. London, May 8, 1948; (parents Am. citizens); d. George E. and Gertrude Blau; m. David Spiegel, July 25, 1976; children: Daniel Spiegel, Julia Spiegel. BA in Biology, U. York (Eng.), 1969; MA in Biology, Harvard U., 1970, PhD in Biology, 1975. Predoctoral fellow dept. biology Harvard U., Cambridge, Mass., 1969-75; postdoctoral fellow div. med. genetics U. Calif. Dept. Biochemistry and Biophysics, San Francisco, 1975-78; asst. prof. dept. pharmacology Stanford (Calif.) U., 1978-86, assoc. prof. dept. pharmacology, 1986-91, prof. dept. molecular pharmacology, 1991—, chair dept. molecular pharmacology, 1997—, Donald E. and Delia B. Baxter prof., 1999—; co-chmn. various profl. meetings. Mem. editorial bd. 10 jours. including Jour. Cell Biology, Somatic Cell Molecular Genetics and Exptl. Cell Rsch., Molecular and Cellular Biology; contbr. articles to profl. jours. Mem. ad hoc molecular cytology study sect. NIH, 1987-88; mem. five-yr. planning com genetics and teratology br. NICHHD/NIH, 1989. Recipient Rsch. Career Devel. award NIH, 1984-89, SmithKline & Beecham award, 1989-91, Women in Cell Biology Career Recognition award, 1992, Excellence in Sci. award FASEB, 1999; Mellon Found. faculty fellow, 1979-80, William H. Hume faculty scholar, 1981-84; grantee NIH, NSF, Muscular Dystrophy Assn., march of Dimes, 1978—; Yvette Mayent-Rothschild fellow for vis. profs. Inst. Curie, Paris, 1995. Fellow AAAS; mem. NAS (del. to China 1991), Am. Soc. for Cell biology (nominating com. 1985-86, program com. 1990), Soc. for Devel. Biology (pres. 1994-95). Avocations: skiing, swimming, hiking, music, theatre. Office: Stanford U Sch Medicine Molecular Pharmacology Dept Stanford CA 94305-5332

BLAU, MONTE, retired radiology educator; b. N.Y.C., June 17, 1926; s. Samuel and Rose (Cohen) B.; m. Guitta Drimer, June 30, 1946; children: Saul, Hannah. BS in Chemistry, Poly. Inst. Bklyn., 1948; PhD in Phys. Chemistry, U. Wis., 1952. Rsch. chemist Geochronometric Lab., Yale U., 1952-53; with div. neoplastic diseases Montefiore Hosp., N.Y.C., 1953-54; cancer rsch. scientist Roswell Park Meml. Inst., Buffalo, 1954-75; prof., chmn. dept. nuclear medicine SUNY, Buffalo, 1975-83; vis. prof. radiology Harvard Med. Sch., Boston, 1983-90; mem. USP adv. panel on radiopharms.; chmn. med. adv. com. N.Y. State bur. Radiol. Health; chmn. isotopes adv. com. Los Alamos Nat. Lab. Mem. editorial bd. Jour. Nuclear Medicine. With USN, 1944-46. Mem. Soc. Nuclear Medicine (v.p. 1964, pres. 1972), Am. Chem. Soc., Am. Assn. Physicists in Medicine. Home: PO Box 605 South Wellfleet MA 02663-0605

BLAU, MOROCAI, plastic surgeon; b. Regar, Russia, May 27, 1945; m. Rose Ann; children: Tamar, Gabriel, Daniel. MD, U. Tel Aviv, 1972. Diplomate Am. Soc. Plastic and Reconstructive Surgery; bd. cert. plastic surgery. Surg. intern, plastic surgery resident Belinson Hosp., Tel Aviv U. Med. Sch., 1972-74; straight surg. intern Albert Einstein Med. Sch., Bronx, N.Y., 1974-75; resident gen. surgery Albert Einstein Med. Sch., Bronx, 1975-78, resident plastic surgery, 1978-79, chief resident plastic surgery, 1979-80; pvt. practice plastic surgery White Plains, N.Y., 1983—; attending plastic surgeon White Plains Hosp., St. Agnes Hosp., Westchester Cmty. Med. Ctr., 1980—. Art work exhibited San Francisco, N.Y.C., Tel Aviv, Europe, 1981—. Officer Israel Army Svc., 1963-66. Mem. N.Y. Med. Soc., Westchester Med. Soc. Home: 12 Greenridge Ave White Plains NY 10605-1238

BLAU, PETER MICHAEL, sociologist, educator; b. Vienna, Austria, Feb. 7, 1918; came to U.S., 1939, naturalized, 1943; s. Theodor I. and Bertha

(Selka) B.; m. Judith R. Fritz, July 31, 1968; 1 dau., Reva T.; 1 dau. by previous marriage, Pamela L. AB, Elmhurst Coll., 1942, LLD, 1973; PhD, Columbia, 1952; MA, Cambridge U., 1966. Mem. faculty Wayne State U., 1949-51, Cornell U., 1951-53; asst. prof. sociology U. Chgo., 1953-58, assoc. prof., 1958-63, prof., 1963-70; prof. Columbia U., N.Y.C., 1970-88; Quetelet prof. sociology Columbia, N.Y.C., 1977-88; Disting. prof. SUNY, Albany, 1978-81; Robert Broughton Disting. rsch. prof. U. N.C., Chapel Hill, 1988—; Social Sci. Rsch. Coun. predoctoral fellow, 1948-49; fellow Ctr. Advanced Studies Behavioral Scis., 1962-63; sr. postdoctoral fellow NSF, 1962-63; Pitt prof. Am. history and instns. Cambridge (Eng.) U., 1966-67; fellow Netherlands Inst. for Advanced Study, 1975-76; Guggenheim fellow, 1985-86; bd. dirs. Social Sci. Rsch. Coun., 1966-69. Author: The Dynamics of Bureaucracy, 1955, rev. edit., 1963, 73, Bureaucracy in Modern Society, 1956, (rev. (with M.W. Meyer), 1971, 87, (with W.R. Scott) Formal Organization, 1962, Exchange and Power in Social Life, 1964, (citation classic); (with Otis Dudley Duncan) The American Occupational Structure, 1967 (Sorokin award Am. Sociol. Assn., citation classic); (with Richard A. Schoenherr) The Structure of Organizations, 1971, The Organization of Academic Work, 1973, On the Nature of Organizations, 1974, Inequality and Heterogeneity, 1977 (Disting. Scholarship award Am. Social. Assn.); (with Joseph E. Schwartz) Crosscutting Social Circles, 1983, Stuctural Contexts of Opportunities, 1994; editor: Approaches to the Study of Social Structure, 1975, (with R. K. Merton) Continuities in Structural Inquiry, 1981, 1983, Am. Jour. Sociology, 1961-67. With AUS, 1943-45. Decorated Bronze Star; recipient Commonwealth award, 1981, Irwin award, 1986; FACS Econs. fellow, 1997. Fellow Am. Acad. Arts and Scis.; mem. NAS, AAUP, Am. Philos. Soc., Am. Sociol. Assn. (pres. 1973-74), Internat. Sociol. Assn. Office: Univ NC Sociology Dept Chapel Hill NC 27514

BLAUFOX, MORTON DONALD, physician, educator; b. N.Y.C., July 19, 1934; s. Emanuel and Elizabeth (Rosenblum) B.; m. Paulette Goldberg, Dec. 20, 1958; children: Laurie Beth, Ellen Ruth, Andrew David. Student, Harvard U., 1952-55; M.D., SUNY, 1959; Ph.D., U. Minn., 1964. Diplomate Am. Bd. Internal Medicine, Am. Bd. Nuclear Medicine (bd. dirs. 1985-91). Intern Jewish Hosp. of Bklyn., N.Y.C., 1959-60; fellow in medicine Mayo Found. Med. Edn. and Research, Rochester, Minn., 1960-64; advanced research fellow Am. Heart Assn., 1964-66; research fellow in medicine Harvard Med. Sch., Boston, 1964-66; asst. in medicine and radiology Peter Bent Brigham Hosp., Boston, 1964-66; asst. prof. radiology, also assoc. in medicine Albert Einstein Coll. Medicine, Bronx, N.Y., 1966-71; dir. sect. nuclear medicine Albert Einstein Coll. Medicine, 1966-76, dir. unified dept., 1976-82, chmn. unified dept., 1982—, assoc. dir. clin. research center, 1968-72, assoc. prof. radiology, 1971-76, prof. radiology, 1976—, assoc. prof. medicine, 1972-78, prof. medicine, 1978—; asst. attending physician Bronx Mcpl. Hosp. Center, 1966-71, assoc. attending, 1972, attending physician, 1972—; dir. div. nuclear medicine Montefiore Med. Center, 1976-82, chmn. dept. nuclear medicine, 1982—; cons. kidney disease control program USPHS, 1967-72; me. adminstrv. coun. nuclear medicine VA, 1972-73; mem. panel on radiopharms. U.S. Pharmacopeia, 1970-76; mem. hypertension adv. com. N.Y.C. Dept. Health, 1975-76; mem. Am. Bd. Nuclear, 1984-90; treas. exec. com. Am. Bd. Nuclear Medicine, 1987-89, chmn., 1990; mem. clin. trials rev. com. Nat. Heart, Lung and Blood Inst., 1988-92, reviewer ready rsch., 1992—; mem. subcom. on non-pharmacologic therapy of Joint Nat. Com. on Detection Evaluation and Treatment of High Blood Pressure, 1991-92; mem. Brookhaven Linac Isotope Producer Users' adv. com. Brookhaven Nat. Lab., 1992-96; mem. internat. liaison com. World Fedn. Nuclear Medicine and Biology, 1992-94; active Coun. Cardiovascular Radiology; hon. prof. medicine Shanxi U. Med. Sch., China, 1997. Editor: (with others) Seminars in Nuclear Medicine, 1970—, Evaluation of Renal Function and Disease with Radionuclides, 1972, 2d edit., 1989, Procs. Internat. Symposium, 1972, 75, 80, 87, 90, PDR for Nuclear Medicine and Radiology, 1971-80, Unilateral Renal Function Studies, 1978, (with others) Secondary Hypertension: Current Diagnosis and Management, 1981, Non-Pharmacologic Therapy of Hypertension, 1987, Newer Diagnostic Methods in Nephrology and Urology, 1986; mem. editl. bd. Radionuclides in Nephrology, 1980, also editor: editl. bd. Jour. Nuclear Medicine, 1973-81, Nephron, Uroradiology, 1978—, Jour. Nuclear Medicine and Allied Sci., 1982—, Nuclear Medicine Comm., 1979—, Renal Failure, 1985-89, Am. Jour. Hypertension, 1987—; assoc. editor: Barnet's Pediatrics, 1972; sect. editor for diagnostics and techniques Current Opinions in Nephrology and Hypertension, 1992-96; contbr. The Merck Manual, 14th, 15th and 16th edits., 1982-91, Merck Manual Medical Information, home edit., 1997; co-author: Blood Pressure Measurement: An Illustrated History, 1998; contbr. articles to profl. jours. Recipient Edward Nobel Found. award, 1963, Albert Lasker pub. health service award, 1980. Fellow ACP, Am. Nephrology Soc., Am. Coll. Nuclear Physicians, Coun. on High Blood Pressure Rsch., Coun. Cardiovascular Radiology, N.Y. Acad. Medicine (libr. com. 1985—, chmn. sect. on nuclear medicine 1993-95, chmn. ad hoc com. artifact collection, chmn. history of medicine adv. com. 1995—); mem. AMA, Am. Heart Assn., Am. Physiol. Soc., Am. Fedn. Clin. Rsch., Am. Soc. Hypertension (membership com.), Soc. Nuclear Medicine (pres. Greater N.Y. chpt. 1975-76, chmn. acad. coun. 1976-77, exec. and sci. coms., chmn. publ. com. 1979-82, trustee, Berson-Yalow award 1989), Ind. Soc. Nuclear Medicine (Sarabhai Oration 1989), Internat. Soc. Nephrology, Internat. Hypertension Soc., Coun. on High Blood Pressure Rsch. (med. adv. bd.), N.Y. Med. Soc., Med. Collectors Assn. (pres. 1983—), Swiss Soc. Nuclear Medicine (hon., corr.), Sigma Xi. Research on hypertension, renal function and evaluation of renal function with radioisotopes, renal blood flow and renin secretion. Home: 101 Drake Smith Woods Ln Rye NY 10580-4316 Office: Montefiore Med Park 1695A Eastchester Rd Bronx NY 10461-2374 *My life has been directed toward the acquisition, clarification and dissemination of knowledge in the health sciences. The use of such goals to help train young people embarking on a career, with honesty and integrity, has been a particularly rewarding experience.*

BLAUSER, JEFFREY MICHAEL, professional baseball player; b. Los Gatos, Calif., Nov. 8, 1965. Student, Sacramento City Coll. With Atlanta Braves, 1984-97, Chgo. Cubs, 1997—; mem. Nat. League All-Star Team, 1993. Recipient Silver Slugger award, 1997; named to N.L. All Star Team, 1997. Achievements include played in World Series, 1991, 92. Office: care Chgo Cubs Wrigley field 1060 W Addison St Chicago IL 60613-4305*

BLAVAT, JERRY (GERALD JOSEPH BLAVAT), radio and television personality, actor; b. Phila., July 3, 1940; s. Louis Blavat and Lucille Capuano; children: Kathi, Geraldine, Stacy, Deserie. Grad. high sch., Phila. Dancer Bandstand TV show, Phila., 1953-55; record promoter Cameo/Parkway Records, Phila., 1956-59; road mgr., mgr. various rock and roll groups including Danny and the Juniors, also Don Rickles, 1957-59; night club performer, live radio show host various clubs, radio stas., Phila., 1959-62; disc jockey radio stas. including Stas. WCAU, WFIL, WCAM, WPGR, WSSJ, WTKU, WPAZ, Phila., Delaware Valley, 1962—; program dir. Geator Gold Radio Network, Pa., N.J., Del., Md., and N.J., 1989—; owner night club Memories, Margate, N.J., 1970—; mem. nominating com. Rock & Roll Hall of Fame, Phila., 1988—. TV appearances include The Monkees, Mod Squad, Joey Bishop Show, Tonight Show, Mike Douglas Show, Pat Boone Show, Merv Griffin Show; movie appearances include Baby, It's You, 1983, Desperately Seeking Susan, 1985, Cookie, 1989; producer, host TV shows Discophonic Scene, 1965-66, Jerry Blavat Show, 1966-70, On the Air with the Geator, 1991—, Backstage with Blavat, 1992—; producer over 30 record albums of collections/anthologies; rec. artist 5 pop singles; contbr. articles, biographies, liner notes to profl. jours., programs and record albums. Bd. dirs., performer Hero Scholarship Fund, Phila., 1963-70; bd. dirs. Police Athletic League, Phila., 1966-70; fundraiser numerous schs., chs., founds., and pub. TV. Inductee Phila. Rock & Roll Hall of Fame, 1986, installed in permanent exhibit Rock and Roll Hall of Fame, Mus. of Radio and Records, 1998; inductee Phila. Music Alliance Walk of Fame, 1993. Mem. AFTRA, SAG, Am. Guild Variety Artists, Nat. Music Found. (adv. bd. 1989—). Avocations: horseback riding, swimming, reading, native American history. Office: Celebrity Showcase PO Box 25010 Philadelphia PA 19147-0210

BLAYDES, JUNE LOUISE, volunteer; b. Indpls., June 16, 1929; d. Charles Edwin Chalfin and Freda Viola Huls (Stinger) Comer; m. Louis Justus Schulz, Feb. 7, 1948 (dec. May 1974); children: Louis K., Judy A Schulz-Merriman, Larry L.; m. Fred Blaydes, Apr. 9, 1976. Grad. H.S., Indpls. Realtor Louis Schulz Co., Indpls., 1961-71; pres., owner Floral Concepts Co., Indpls., 1981-90. Pres. Christian Mothers PTA, Christ the King Sch., Indpls., 1955-63; vol. St. Vincent's Hosp., Indpls., 1974-76, Indpls. Speech and Hearing Ctr., Inpls., 1979-84; choir mem. Christ the King Ch., Inpls., 1994—; bd. dirs. Coburn Place Safe Haven, Indpls., 1996—. Named Vol. of the Month, WMYS (1430) Radio, Indpls., 1997. Mem. Riviera Club, Women of the Moose. Republican. Roman Catholic. Avocations: family activities, travel, mall walkers group, Euchre club, bridge club. Home: 6727 Limerick Ct Indianapolis IN 46250-4415

BLAYDES, SOPHIA BOYATZIES, English language educator; b. Rochester, N.Y., Oct. 16, 1933; d. James George and Helene (Bougdanos) Boyatzies; m. David Fairchild Blaydes, June 4, 1961; children: Stephanie Anne, Jeffrey Glenn. B.A., U. Rochester, 1955; M.A., Ind. U., 1958, Ph.D., 1962. Teaching asst. English Ind. U., 1955-62; instr. to asst. prof. Am. Thought and Lang. dept. Mich. State U., 1962-65; instr. to prof. English W.Va. U., Morgantown, 1966—, chair faculty senate, 1990-91, coord. program for sr. and retired faculty, 1994—; pres. Carolinas Symposium for British Studies, 1990-91; co-dir. Lit. Discussion Group for Sr. Citizens, 1978—; mem. faculty Elderhostel, 1985, 87, 88, 90, 94; mem. ctrl. exec. com. Folger Inst., 1992—; chair faculty senate, bd. advisors W.Va. U., 1990-91, rep. to adv. coun. to bd. trustees, 1993—; state del. to the 1995 White House Conf. on Aging; bd. trustees Univ. Sys., 1998—. Author: Christopher Smart as a Poet of His Time: A Re-Appraisal, 1966, (with others) Sir William Davenant, 1981, Sir William Davenant: An Annotated Bibliography, 1986; editor: (with others) Selected Papers from the W.Va. Shakespeare and Renaissance Association, 1976, The Literary Discussion Group, 1982, 85; contbr. chpts. to books, articles to profl. jours., encys., dictionaries, bibliographies. Mem. cen. exec. com. Folger Inst., 1992—. Recipient Disting. Manuscript award Mich. State U., 1965, Gerontology Ctr. award, 1983; named Disting. West Virginian, W.Va. Gov., 1995; grantee W.Va. Found., 1973, W.Va. Humanities, 1980; W.Va. U. Senate rsch. grantee, 1984, 89; Folger fellow, 1981, Folger grantee, 1988, 91; recipient Sigma Tau Delta Outstanding Tchg. award, 1996. Mem. Am. Soc. 18th Century Studies, MLA, W.Va. Assn. Coll. English Tchrs. (pres. 1977), Shakespeare and Renaissance Soc. W.Va. (chmn. 1978, 84), Carolinas Symposium on Brit. Studies (chair program 1989, pres. 1990, conf. chair 1993). Home: 652 Bellaire Dr Morgantown WV 26505-2421 Office: W Va U PO Box 6296 Morgantown WV 26506-6296

BLAYDES, STEPHANIE ANNE, policy analyst; b. East Lansing, Mich., Aug. 6, 1963; d. David Fairchild and Sophia (Boyatzies) B. BA in Philosophy, Gettysburg Coll., 1985. Staff asst. to Majority Whip Tom Foley U.S. House Reps., Washington, 1986-87, staff asst. to Majority Whip Tony Coelho, 1987-89, spl. asst. to Hon. Robert E. Wise Jr., 1989-93, mem. svcs. advisor House info. sys., 1993-94; sr. health program analyst health svcs. financing Dept. Def., Washington, 1995; sr. program analyst Dept. Def. Policy & Planning Coord. Of Health Affairs, Washington, 1996—; program analyst policy & planning coordination Dept. Def., Washington, 1996-98; dep. dir. mktg., analysis & materials, comm. & customer svc. Tricare Mgmt. Activity, OASD Health Affairs, Falls Church, Va., 1998—. Vol. Bob Wise for Congress, Washington, 1989-93; mem. host com. Kids County dinner Stewart B. McKinney House, Washington, 1993—; vol. cons. Doug Costle for U.S. Senate, Washington, 1994. Democrat. Greek Orthodox. Home: 955 Windwhisper Ln Annapolis MD 21403 Office: Tricare Mgmt Activity OASD 5111 Leesburg Pike Ste 622 Falls Church VA 22041

BLAYLOCK, JAMES CARL, clergyman, librarian; b. Guntown, Miss., Jan. 27, 1938; s. Carl Houston and Katie Lee (Pugh) B.; m. Jo Ann Enlow, May 3, 1962; children: Jacquelyn Ann, John Thomas. AA, Southeastern Bapt. Coll., Laurel, Miss., 1962; BTh, N.Am. Theol. Sem., Jacksonville, Tex., 1964; BA, U. Tex., Tyler, 1976; MRE, Bapt. Missionary Sem., Jacksonville, 1977; MSLS, Tex A&M U., 1980. Ordained to ministry Bapt. Ch., 1962. Pastor Mt. Pleasant Ch., Bedias, Tex., 1962-64, Buena Vista Ch., Timpson, Tex., 1964-70, 1st Bapt. Ch., Maydelle, Tex., 1970-86, Corinth Ch., Jacksonville, Tex., 1986—; asst. dir. Bapt. News Svc., Jacksonville, 1969-88, dir., 1988-99; asst. editor Directory and Handbook of Bapt. Missionary Assn., Jacksonville, 1969-88, editor, 1988-99; libr. Bapt. Missionary Assn. Theol. Sem., Jacksonville, 1972—. Editor Mt. Olive Evangel, 1965-70; author: History of 1st Bapt. Ch. Maydelle, Tex., 1986, Buena Vista Bapt. Ch., 1986, Glimpses from the Past, 1988. Mem. Am. Theol. Libr. Assn., ALA, Tex. Libr. Assn. Home: 625 W Kickapoo St Jacksonville TX 75766-4621 Office: Bapt Missionary Assn Theol Sem 1530 E Pine St Jacksonville TX 75766-5407

BLAYLOCK, MOOKIE (DARON OSHAY BLAYLOCK), professional basketball player; b. Garland, Tex., Mar. 20, 1967. Student, Midland (tex.) Coll., Oklahoma Coll. Guard N.J. Nets, 1989-92, Atlanta Hawks, 1992—. Named to NBA All-Defensive First Team, 1994. Office: Atlanta Hawks South Tower One CNN Ctr Ste 405 Atlanta GA 30303*

BLAYLOCK, NEIL WINGFIELD, JR., applied statistics educator; b. Ft. Smith, Ark., Aug. 18, 1946; s. Neil Wingfield Sr. and Phyllis Catherine (Brown) B.; m. Naomi Josephine Smith, Aug. 25, 1968; children: Neil Wingfield III, Scott Allen, Adrian Philip, Paul Alexander. BA in Math., St. Mary's U., 1968; MS in Stats., U. Tex., San Antonio, 1987. Cert. tchr., Tex. High sch. math. tchr. San Antonio Ind. Sch. Dist., 1968-70; sr. engr. Martin Marietta Aerospace Corp., Orlando, Fla., 1972-79; staff analyst S.W. Rsch. Inst., San Antonio, 1979O; evening faculty mem. U. Tex., San Antonio, 1987—, St. Mary's U., San Antonio, 1996—. Contbr. articles to profl. jours. Com. chmn. Boy Scouts Am., San Antonio, 1982-93, asst. scoutmaster, 1993-96. Fellow AIAA (assoc., chmn. S.W. Tex. sect. 1983, dep. dir. region IV 1991-95, nat. membership com. 1991—, bd. dirs. 1995—, Spl. Svc. award 1984, 95, 96, Disting. Achievement award 1989), Hypervelocity Impact Soc. (co-founder, nat. membership chmn. 1988-92), Am. Statis. Assn. Roman Catholic. Achievements include development of specialty military devices, quantitative risk mgmt. techniques, regression techniques for nondimensional scale modeling experiments, advanced devel. of nonnuclear Pershing missile, explosion safety and protection. Home: 7111 Moss Creek Dr San Antonio TX 78238-2725 Office: SW Rsch Inst 6220 Culebra Rd San Antonio TX 78238-5100 *Died Oct. 27, 1998.*

BLAZEJOWSKI, CAROL, sports team executive, retired basketball player. With N.J. Gems, 1980-81. Named Women's Basketball Player of Yr., 1978, Converse Women's Player of Yr., 1977. Achievements include All-Am. selection, 1976, 77, 78, single season and career women's basketball scoring records, 1976, member World Univ. Gold Medal team, Mexico City, 1979, Pan Am. Silver Medal team, 1979, leading scorer Women's Basketball League, 1980-81. Office: New York Liberty 2 Penn Plaza New York NY 10121 Office: c/o Basketball Hall of Fame PO Box 179 Springfield MA 01101-0179

BLAZEK, F. DOUGLAS, surgeon; b. Pitts., Apr. 18, 1960; s. Frank V. and N. Jean (Saunders) B.; m. Robin E. Falconer, May 17, 1986; children: Cody D., Clayton J., Cooper N. BS in Sci., Pa. State U., 1981; MD, Jefferson Med. Coll., 1983. Diplomate Am. Bd. Surgery. Resident in surgery Akron (Oho) Gen. Med. Ctr., 1983-88; pvt. practice, High Point, N.C., 1988—; mem. active staff High Point Regional Hosp., 1988—, med. dir. ICU, 1990-94; reviewer Peer Rev. Orgn. N.C.; mem. faculty Advanced Laparoscopic Tng. Ctr., Marietta, Ga., 1991-92; bd. dirs., pres., founding mem. Cornerstone Health Care, 1995—. Bd. dirs. High Point-Thomasville chpt. ARC, 1990-93; mem. adult adv. cocm. med. explorers post Boy Scouts Am., 1990-91; mem. Challenge: High Point Class of 1992; mem. capital campaign steering com. Habitat for Humanity, 1992-93. Fellow ACS; mem. N.C. Med. Soc. (del. 1991-93), Guilford County Med. Soc. (bd. censors 1992-95), Mensa, Kiwanis (chmn. major emphasis 1990-91). Republican. Methodist. Office: Cornerstone Health Care PA 624 Quaker Ln Ste 101C High Point NC 27262-3832

BLAZEK, STEVEN JOSEPH, investment company executive, sales executive; b. Marshalltown, Iowa, June 6, 1966; s. James Frank and Mary Anne (Heil) B.; m. Regina Michele Irvine, Dec. 29, 1991; 1 child, Beau Irvine Blazek. BBA in Fin., Iowa State U., 1988. Investment rep. AmerUS Investments, Des Moines, 1989-96, v.p., sales mgr., 1996—; asst. v.p., bank mgr. AmerUS Bank, Des Moines, 1991-96. Avocations: running, rock climbing, mountain biking, reading. Home: 2729 NW 73d Ave Ankeny IA 50021 Office: AmerUS Investments 418 6th Ave Des Moines IA 50309-2407

BLAZEK, WAYNE JOSEPH, auditor; b. Masontown, Pa., Mar. 21, 1950; s. Joseph Edward and Helen (Kurella) B.; m. Rebecca Cayce, Aug. 23, 1975; 1 child, John Franklin. AS in Welding Tech., Fayette Tech. Sch., 1969; AS in Mech. Design, Fayette Inst. Commerce and Tech., 1971; cert. in indsl. mgmt., Emporia State U., 1979. Registered lead assessor; quality sys. lead auditor. From sr. draftsman to mech. inspector Bechtel Power Corp., Gaithersburg, Md., 1971-74; sr. nuclear designer Ebasco Svcs. Inc., Norcross, Ga., 1974-75; welding engr. Kaiser Engrs. Inc., Moscow, Ohio, 1975-77; quality control welding coordinator, then quality control tng. coordinator Daniel Internat., Strawn, Kans., 1977-80; auditor quality assurance, vendor rep. Houston Light and Power Co., 1980-81; quality assurance engr. Perini Corp., Framingham, Mass., 1981-83; lead quality assurance engr. Pub. Svc. Elec. and Gas Co., Hancock Bridge, N.J., 1983-85, lead engr. quality assurance procurement, 1985-95, sr. staff engr. quality assurance procurement, 1990-95; mgr. registration audits Vikar Assocs., Boothwin, Pa., 1995-97; Registar Accrediation Bd./Internat. Registar Cert. Auditors lead auditor Quality Mgmt. Inst., Springfield, Pa., 1997—. Mem. IEEE, Am. Welding Soc., Am. Soc. Quality Control, Jaycees, NRA, Ducks Unltd., U.S. TAG 176. Democrat. Roman Catholic. Avocations: hunting, fishing, travel, gunsmithing, gun restoration. Home: 49 Adams St Swedesboro NJ 08085-1569 Office: Quality Mgmt Inst 900 W Sproul Rd Ste 103 Springfield PA 19064-1217

BLAZEK-WHITE, DORIS, lawyer; b. Easton, Md., Nov. 17, 1943; d. George W. and Nola M. (Buterbaugh) Defibaugh; children: Christine T., Judson M.; m. Thacher W. White. BA, Goucher Coll., 1965; JD, Georgetown U., 1968. Bar: D.C. 1969, Virgin Islands 1969, U.S. Ct. Appeals (3d cir.) 1969, U.S. Ct. Appeals (D.C. cir.) 1971, Md. 1979. Gen. practice with Judge Warren H. Young, U.S. Virgin Islands, 1968-70; assoc. Covington & Burling, Washington, 1970-76, ptnr., 1976—. Mem. Am. Coll. Trust and Estate Counsel. Office: Covington & Burling PO Box 7566 1201 Pennsylvania Ave NW Washington DC 20044

BLAZER, DAN GERMAN, psychiatrist, epidemiologist; b. Nashville, Feb. 23, 1944; s. Dan German and Mary Elizabeth (Owsley) B.; m. Sherrill Walls, Aug. 19, 1966; children: Dan German III, Natasha Leigh. BA, Vanderbilt U., 1965; MD, U. Tenn., 1969; MPH, U. N.C., 1979, PhD, 1980. Diplomate, Am. Bd. Psychiatry and Neurology. Fellow Montefiore Hosp. and Med. Ctr., N.Y.C., 1975-76; asst. prof., assoc. prof., then prof. psychiatry Duke U. Med. Ctr., Durham, N.C., 1976—, J.P. Gibbons prof. of psychiatry, 1990—; interim chair of psychiatry Duke U. Med. Ctr., 1990-93; dean of med. edn. Duke U., 1992—; prof. cmty. and family medicine Duke U. Med. Ctr., 1986—; chair, bd. dirs. Am. Geriatrics Soc., N.Y., 1983—; bd. dirs. ret. persons svcs. Am. Assn. Ret. Persons, Alexandria, Va., 1987-92, pres. Psychiat. Rsch. Soc., Salt Lake City, 1988; chmn. epidemiology and disease control study sect. NIH, Bethesda, Md., 1988—. Author: Depression in Late Life, 1993, Freud vs. God, 1998, Introduction to Clinical Research in Psychiatry, 1998, Life is Worth Living, 1987; editor: Textbook of Geriatric Psychiatry, 1996. Mem. Brooks Ave. Ch. of Christ, Raleigh, N.C., 1982. Recipient Rsch. Career Devel. award, NIMH, 1977, Alex Haley award, East Tenn. Bapt. Hosp., Knoxville, 1986, Disting. Svc. award, U. N.C. Sch. Pub. Health, Chapel Hill, 1989, Milo Leavitt award Am. Geriatric Soc., 1997. Fellow Am. Psychiat. Assn., Am. Coll. Psychiatrists, So. Psychiat. Assn., Gerontol. Soc. Am., Am. Psychopathol. Assn.; mem. Inst. of Medicine, Nat. Acad. Scis. Democrat. Avocations: hiking, reading. Office: Duke U Med Ctr PO Box 3005 Durham NC 27715-3005

BLAZEY, JUDITH LEISTON, school district administrator; b. Rochester, N.Y., Mar. 6, 1941; d. Emanuel R. and Julia (Nicoletti) Leiston; m. John T. Blazey, May 11, 1963; children: John T. II, James R., Jeffrey S. BS, SUNY, Brockport, 1962, MS, 1987, CAS, 1988. Cert. sch. dist. adminstr., sch. adminstr. and supr. English dept. coord. Palmyra (N.Y.)-Macedon High Sch., 1979-82, 84-88, 89-91, tchr., 1962-63, 64-66, 1972-95, ret., 1995; dist. English/lang. arts coord. Palmyra Macedon Cen. Sch., 1988-89; adj. instr. SUNY Finger Lakes Cmty. Coll., Canandaigua, N.Y., 1982-86. Mem. Nat. Coun. Tchrs. English, N.Y. State English Coun., Delta Kappa Gamma.

BLAZEY, MICHAEL ALAN, educator; b. Rochester, N.Y., Jan. 5, 1952; s. Charles Henry and Kathryn Blazey; m. Jennifer Anne Nestegard, July 6, 1991; children: Amanda Rose, Lauren Olivia. BA, U. Oreg., 1974; MS, S.D. State U., 1977; PhD, Pa. State U., 1984. Recreation supt. Brookings (S.D.) Parks and Recreation, 1974-77; instr. Kans. State U., Manhattan, 1977-79; recreation dir. Ketchikan (Alaska) Parks and Recreation, 1979-80; grad. asst. Pa. State U., University Park, 1980-83; instr. Western Carolina U., Cullowhee, 1983-84; assoc. prof. Wash. State U., Pullman, 1984-90; assoc. prof., chair dept. Calif. State U., Long Beach, 1990—; cons. Queen Mary, Long Beach, 1989-92; rsch. proposal cons. Am. Assn. Ret. Persons Andrus Found., Washington, 1993-96; cons. Calif. Parks and Recreation, Sacramento, 1993, Wash. Tourism Devel., Olympia, 1985-90, Landermann-Moore and Assocs., Anacortes, Wsh., 1995—, L.A. City Atty.'s Office. Contbr. articles to profl. jours. Mem. Housing and Cmty. Devel. Citizen Participation Com., La Habra, Calif., 1995-98, La Habra Planning Commn., 1998—; bd. dirs. United Meth. Ch. Campus Ministry, Long Beach, 1991—. Named Glenn E. Robinson lectr. S.D. State U., 1991; recipient Rsch. award Am. Assn. Ret. Persons/Andrus, 1988. Mem. Nat. Recreation and Parks Assn., Calif. Parks and Recreation Soc., World Leisure and Recreation Assn., Soc. Park and Recreation Educators (comm. chmn. 1995-96), Am. Assn. Higher Edn. Avocations, gardening, bicycling, in-line skating, home improvement, travel. Office: Calif State U 1250 N Bellflower Blvd Long Beach CA 90840-0001

BLAZINA, JANICE FAY, transfusion medicine physician; b. Youngstown, Ohio, Apr. 20, 1953; d. Joseph and Cordelia Evelyn (Mitchell) B. BS, Youngstown State U., 1975; MD, Ohio State U., 1978. Diplomate Am. Bd. Pathology. Resident in anat. and clin. pathology U. Ala. Med. Ctr., Birmingham, 1978-82; assoc. pathologist various hosps., Bryan, Tex., 1982-83, High Plains Bapt. Hosp., Amarillo, Tex., 1983-84; fellow in blood banking Baylor U. Med. Ctr., Dallas, 1984-85; asst. prof. dept. pathology Ohio State U., Columbus, 1985-93, asst. prof. Sch. Allied Med. Professions, 1987-93; asst. dir. transfusion svc. Ohio State U. Hosp., 1985-89, assoc. dir., 1989-90, dir., 1990-93, med. dir. histocompatibility, paternity, apheresis and phlebotomy svcs., 1987-93, divsn. med. tech., 1987-93; asst. med. dir. Carter Blood Ctr., Ft. Worth, 1993-95, med. dir., 1995-96. Contbr. articles to profl. publs. Grantee: Bremer Found., 1987. Mem. AMA, Am. Soc. Apheresis, Am. Soc. Histocompatibility and Immunogenetics, Am. Assn. Blood Banks (insp. 1987—), Am. Med. Womens Assn., Ohio Assn. Blood Banks (trustee 1990-93, sec. 1992-93), Ohio Acad. Sci., Grad. Women Sci., Assn. Women Sci. Cen. Ohio (v.p. 1989-90, pres. 1990-91). Mem. Church of Christ. Avocations: gardening, cats, African violets.

BLAZING, MICHAEL AUGUST, internist; b. 1961. MD, U. Calif., San Francisco, 1987. Postdoctoral fellow Duke U. Med. Ctr., now asst. prof. medicine, 1991—. Recipient Clinician-Scientist award Am. Heart Assn., 1995-96. Home: 2113 Carriage Way Chapel Hill NC 27514-9466 Office: Duke U Med Ctr Dept Cardiology Box 3126 Durham NC 27710*

BLAZZARD, NORSE NOVAR, lawyer; b. St. Johns, Ariz., July 8, 1937; s. Howard N. and Viola (Greer) B.; m. Mary Elizabeth Jecker, June 15, 1958; children—Howard Norse, Mary Catherine; m. Judith A. Hasenauer, July 2, 1977. AB, Stanford U., 1959; JD, U. Calif., Hastings 1962; CLU. Bar: Calif. 1963, U.S. Dist. Ct. (no. dist.) Calif. 1966, Conn. 1974, U.S. Dist. Ct. Conn. 1975, U.S. Supreme Ct. 1975, U.S. C.t Appeals (D.C. cir.) 1977, U.S. Ct. Appeals (2d cir.) 1978, Fla. 1993. Counsel, Calif. Western Life Ins. Co., Sacramento, 1966-70; sr. v.p., gen. counsel NARE Life Svc. Co., Palo Alto, Calif., 1970-74; pres. Blazzard, Grodd & Hasenauer, P.C., Westport, Conn., 1974—; chmn. ins. products task force Fin. Products Standards Bd., 1988-89; chmn. Nat. Assn. Variable Annuities, 1994. Bd. govs. Norwalk Symphony, 1979. Capt. JAGC, U.S. Army, 1692-66. Mem. ABA, Calif. Bar Assn., Fed. Bar Assn., Conn. Bar Assn., D.C. Bar Assn., Fla. Bar Assn., Am. Soc. CLU's (pres. Fairfield County chpt. 1977-79). Republican. Mormon.

BLEAKLEY, PETER KIMBERLEY, lawyer; b. Franklin, Pa., Aug. 19, 1936; s. Rollin R. and Marion (St. James) B.; m. Mary B. DeRosa; children: Jennifer A., Sarah A., Nicholas D. B.A., U. Va., 1958, LL.B., 1962. Bar: Va. 1962, D.C. 1966, U.S. Ct. Appeals (2d cir.), U.S. Ct. Appeals (3d cir.),

U.S. Ct. Appeals (5th cir.), U.S. Ct. Appeals (6th cir.), U.S. Ct. Appeals (7th cir.), U.S. Ct. Appeals (8th cir.), U.S. Ct. Appeals (9th cir.), U.S. Ct. Appeals (D.C. cir.), U.S. Supreme Ct. Trial atty. Fed. Trade Commn., Washington, 1962-66; trial atty. Dept. Justice, Washington, 1966; assoc. Arnold & Porter, Washington, 1966-70, ptnr., 1971—. Fellow Am. Coll. Trial Lawyers; mem. ABA. Democrat. Avocations: tennis, skiing, bicycling, golf. Home: 3103 Hawthorne St NW Washington DC 20008-3540 Office: Arnold & Porter 555 12th St NW Washington DC 20004-1206

BLECHER, CAROL STEIN, oncology clinical nurse specialist; b. Bronx, N.Y., July 5, 1947; d. Ludwig and Hedwig (Merkel) Stein; m. Niles Blecher, Mar. 20, 1971; children: Herbert B., Phillip J., Martin D. BSN, N.Y. Univ., 1969; MS, Rutgers Univ., 1989. Staff nurse asst. head nurse Mt. Sinai Hosp., N.Y.C., 1969-71; per diem nurse Orthopedic Surgeon, L.I., N.Y., 1972-77; staff nurse per diem Parkway Hosp., Forest Hills, N.Y., 1974-77; staff nurse Union (N.J.) Hosp., 1981-83, head nurse med./surg./oncology, 1983-88; patient care coord. D-7 Oncology Newark (N.J.) Beth Israel Medical Ctr., 1988-89; oncology clinical coord. Union Hosp., 1989-96; adminstrv. dir. clin. svcs. Hematology and Oncology Assocs. of N.J., Pa., Union, N.J., 1996-97; IMPACT ctr. coord. Response Oncology Inc., Bayonne, N.J., 1997—. Contbg. author Safe Handling of Cytotoxic Drugs, 1997; contbr. chpt. to book. Mem. Am. Acad. Medical Adminstrs., Oncology Nursing Soc. (SIG coord. 1993-95, SIG com. 1995—), North Central N.J. Chpt. Oncology Nursing Soc. (treas. 1991-93), Upstate N.J. chpt. Oncology Nursing Soc., N.J. Nurses Assn., Sigma Theta Tau. Democrat. Jewish. Avocations: cooking, reading, crossword puzzles. Home: 615 Wyoming Ave Elizabeth NJ 07208-1536 Office: IMPACT Ctr of Bayonne Bayonne Hosp Bayonne NJ 07002

BLECHMAN, R. O., artist, filmmaker; b. Bklyn., Oct. 1, 1930; s. Samuel and Mae Blechman; m. Moisha Kubinyi, Mar. 3, 1960; children: Nicholas, Max. BA, Oberlin Coll., 1952. Freelance illustrator N.Y.C., 1953—, freelance producer, designer animated films, 1975—; pres. R.O. Blechman, Inc., N.Y.C., 1978—, The Ink Tank, N.Y.C., 1979—. Author, illustrator: The Juggler of Our Lady, 1952, Onion Soup, 1963, Behind the Lines, an autobiography and anthology, 1980, The Life of Saint Nicholas, 1996, The Book of Jonah, 1997; exhibited one-man shows, Gallery Delpire, Paris, 1968, Graham Gallery, N.Y.C., 1978, ITC Gallery, 1981, Galerie Bartsch & Chariau, Munich, 1982, 92; represented in permanent collections, Mus. Modern Art, N.Y.C., Chase Manhattan Bank; executed murals, Mus. Natural History, U.S. Pavilion Expo '67, Folger Shakespeare Library.; films include The Juggler of Our Lady, 1958, Abraham and Isaac, 1971, Exercise, 1974, Simple Gifts, 1978, No Room at the Inn, 1978 (Clio award 1968, 69, 73), L'Histoire du Soldat, 1984 (Emmy award 1984). Trustee Swann Found. Mem. Alliance Graphique Internat., Am. Inst. Graphic Arts, Graphic Artists Guild. Office: The Ink Tank 2 W 47th St New York NY 10036-3319

BLECK, THOMAS FRANK, architect; b. Waukegan, Ill., Aug. 13, 1929; s. Henry Bernard and Edna (Kilbert) B.; m. Virginia Eleanore Pavlik, June 16, 1951; children: Thomas G., James H., Catherine Bleck Muschler, Marilynn Bleck Cobbs, Robert F., Susan M. Gibbs, Linda M. Mai, John W., Charles D. BS in Archtl. Engring., U. Ill., 1951. Lic. architect, Ill., Wis., N.J., Tex., Mass. Pvt. practice architecture Waukegan, 1956—; cons. Six Flaggs Corp., Ocean Spray Cranberries Inc. prin. works include mcpl. bldgs., librs., fire stas., chs., schs. Mem. AIA, Nat. Council Archtl. Registration Bds. Republican. Roman Catholic. Avocations: skiing, fishing, traveling, hiking. Home: 10330 W Yorkhouse Rd Waukegan IL 60087-2402 Office: 1321 Glen Rock Ave Waukegan IL 60085-6231

BLECK, VIRGINIA ELEANORE, illustrator; b. Waukegan, Ill., Dec. 22, 1929; d. George William and Eugenia (Van Honder) Pavlik; m. Thomas Frank Bleck, June 16, 1951; children: Thomas G., James H., Catherine Bleck-Muschler, Marilynn Bleck-Cobbs, Robert F., Susan M. Bleck-Gibbs, Linda Bleck-Mai, John W., Charles D. U. Ill. Art Inst. Chgo., 1947-50, Student, 1947-50. Free lance artist Waukegan, 1950-86; artist Merrill-Chase Galleries, Chgo., 1972-77, Hallmark Cards Inc., Kansas City, Mo., 1977—; owner, operator Bleck Tree Farms, Waukegan, Green Oaks and Grayslake, Ill., 1972—. Republican. Roman Catholic. Avocations: conservation, hiking, travel, forestry. Home and Office: 10330 W Yorkhouse Rd Waukegan IL 60087-2402

BLECKE, ARTHUR EDWARD, principal; b. Oak Park, Ill., Sept. 21, 1926; s. Paul Gerard and Mathilda (Ziebell); m. June Audrey Eckholm, Jan. 22, 1949; children: William, Robert, Carol. B.S. in Phys. Edn., U. Ill., 1950; M.Edn., Loyola U., 1967. Tchr., coach Buckley High Sch., Ill., 1951-52, Paxton High Sch., Ill., 1952-53, Luther High Sch. North, Chgo., 1953-65, also dept. chmn.; asst. coach football and basketball Elmhurst Coll., Ill., 1965-66; dean, prin. Antioch Community High Sch., Ill., 1966-91; cons. in field; lectr. Contbr. articles to profl. jours. Mem. sanitary dist. Village of Lindenhurst, Ill., 1968-92; planning commn., 1967-77; chmn. long range planning com. and bldg. com. Bella Vista Luth. Ch. Served with U.S. Army, 1945. Recipient Hon. Mention Those Who Excel, Ill. State Bd. Edn., 1980; named Prin. of Yr. for Ill. Nat. Assn. of Secondary Sch. Prins., The Coun. of Chief State Sch. Officers, and the Burger King Corp., 1987. Mem. Lindenhurst Sanitary Dist. (pres. 1968-92), Ill. Prins. Assn. (dir. 1980-81, 83-84, herman graves award, 1991), Nat. Assn. Secondary Sch. Prins. Lutheran. Avocations: Golf; model building; model railroading.

BLEDSOE, DREW, professional football player; b. Ellensburg, Wash., Feb. 14, 1972. Student, Wash. State U. Quarterback New Eng. Patriots, 1993—. Selected to Pro Bowl, 1994. Holds NFL single season record for most passes attempted (691), 1994, single game record for most passes completed (45), most passed attempted without an interception (70), Nov. 13, 1994, vs. Minn. Vikings; led NFL in total passing yards (4,555), 1994. Office: c/o New Eng Patriots Foxboro Stadium 60 Washington St Foxboro MA 02035-1354*

BLEDSOE, MARY LOUISE, medical, surgical nurse; b. Sylacauga, Ala., May 21, 1935; d. Thomas Franklin and Beulah Mae (Vines) Borden; m. Ralph Johnson Bledsoe, June 28, 1958; children: Lynn, Steve, Johnny. LPN, N.F. Nunnelley Tech. Sch., Childersburg, Ala., 1971; AA, Alexander City (Ala.) Jr. Coll., 1989; BSN, Jacksonville (Ala.) State U., 1991. RN, Ala. Pediatric nurse Sylacauga Hosp., 1971-90; med./surg. staff nurse Coosa Valley Med. Ctr., Sylacauga, 1991-92, med./surg. chg. nurse, 1993-94; med./surg. staff nurse Coosa Valley Bapt. Med. Ctr., Sylacauga, 1994-96, charge nurse, 1996-98; retired, 1998. Musician/choir dir. Rising Star Bapt. Ch., Sylacauga, 1985-93, Mt. Olive Bapt. Ch., Childersburg, 1993-96. 1Mem. ANA, Ala. State Nurses Assn., Phi Theta Kappa. Baptist. Avocations: music, sewing, craftwork. Home: 980 Coaling Rd Sylacauga AL 35151-6112

BLEDSOE, SUSAN MCCALLUM, operations manager, stockbroker; b. Mineola, N.Y., Mar. 23, 1942; d. John Hamilton and Elaine Plitt McCallum; m. William Anthony Bledsoe, Feb. 19, 1966; children: Braden, Thomas Ruffin. AB, Vassar Coll., 1964. Licensed stockbroker, Ga. Asst. underwriter First Boston Corp., N.Y.C., 1964-65; from office mgr. to stockbroker Raymond James Financial Svcs., Atlanta, 1981-95, stockbrocker, 1995—. Bd. trustees Vassar Coll.; pres. Alumni Assn., Poughkeepsie, N.Y., 1998—, The Ga. Conservancy, Atlanta, 1997—; chair bd. dirs., chair Friends of Atlanta/Fulton Pub. Libr., 1990-92. Recipient Govs. Vol. award Ga. 5th Dist., 1979. Democrat. E-mail: smbled@mindspring.com. Home: 3631 Tuxedo Rd NW Atlanta GA 30305 Office: Raymond James Financial Svcs 455 E paces Ferry Rd Atlanta GA 30305

BLEDSOE, TOMMY DALTON, minister; b. Carrollton, Ga., July 23, 1942; s. Johnson Dalton and Mary Doris (Cooley) B.; m. Donna Lee Shores, June 25, 1966; children: Tommy D. Jr., Jonathan Lee, Jennifer Leigh. AB in English, Ga. State Coll., 1964; ThM, New Orleans Bapt. Theol. Sem., 1967; MEd in Counseling, Ga. State U., 1972, PhD, 1980. Ordained to ministry So. Bapt. Conv., 1966; lic. marriage and family therapist, Ga., S.C. Assoc. pastor Temple Bapt. Ch., New Orleans, 1968; pastor Mt. Ararat Bapt. Ch., Gaffney, S.C., 1969-70, Arbor Heights Bapt. Ch., Douglasville, Ga., 1973-77; cons. to min. counseling 1st Bapt. Ch., Douglasville, 1977-81; interim pastor Adairsville (Ga.) Bapt. Ch., 1983-84; pastor Unity Bapt. Ch., Newnan, Ga., 1984-86; counselor The Living Ctr., Douglasville, 1986-88; pastor 1st Bapt. Ch., Soperton, Ga., 1988-90, Wrens (Ga.) Bapt. Ch., 1990-94; psychologist Dept. Mental Health, Anderson, S.C., 1994—; tchr. Ctr. Hill Elem. Sch., Atlanta, 1970-74; counselor David T. Howard High Sch., Atlanta, 1974-76, Frederick Douglass High Sch., Atlanta, 1976-84; dir. Pastoral Counseling Assocs., 1982-86; asst. prof. continuing edn. Mercer U., Douglasville, 1985-86; with acad. support office Reinhardt Coll., Waleska, Ga., 1988; adj. faculty Christianity dept. Brewton-Parker Coll., Mt. Vernon, Ga., 1989—; moderator Hephzibah Bapt. Assn., 1991-92; v.p. Hephzibah Bapt. Ministers' Fellowship. Contbr. articles to profl. jours. Mem. AACD, Daniell Bapt. Mins.' Assn. (v.p. 1988-89, pres. 1989-90), Treutlen County Ministerial Alliance (moderator 1988-90), Daniell Bapt. Assn. (vice-moderator 1989-90), Am. Assn. for Marriage and Family Therapy (clin.), Ga. Assn. for Marriage and Family Therapy (editor newsletter 1984-86), Kiwanis. Avocations: music, fishing, drawing, cycling. Address: 5375 Victoria Fls Grovetown GA 30813-5201

BLEE, FRANCIS J., municipal official; b. Absecon, N.J., May 29, 1958; m. Kathy; children: Samantha, Francesca. BA in Polit. Sci., Dickinson Coll., 1980; DC, Life Chiropractic Coll., Marietta, Ga., 1985. Jr. h.s. tchr. St. Nicholas Sch., 1980; chiropractor Absecon, N.J., 1985—; mem. Absecon City Coun., N.J., 1991-95, pres., 1992-93; mem. N.J. Gen. Assembly, Egg Harbor Twp., N.J., 1995—, mem. assembly appropriations com., assembly health com., 1996—, mem. commn. on capital budgeting and planning. Bd. trustees Absecon Edn. Found.; past bd. trustees Atlantic Mental health Orgn.; bd. dirs. CARING Med. Day; past varsity head coach Absecon Blue Devils Youth Football Team; past head coach St. Augustine Prep Cross Country and Track Teams; active The 200 Club of Cape May and Atlantic County; vice-chair Task Force on Reorgn., Capitol Commn. Assembly. Mem. Absecon Kiwanis (past bd. dirs.). Achievements include World Natural Powerlifting Fedn. Nat. and Internat. champion, 1994, 95. Office: NJ Legis Offices 6814 Tilton Rd Unit H Egg Harbor Township NJ 08234-4490*

BLEEKER, BERNARD MARTIN, designer, graphic; b. St. Cloud, Minn., July 17, 1947; s. Benjamin Kekrops and Malene Karen (Moklev) B.; m. Jeannette Marie Lamourea, Dec. 10, 1992. BS, St. Cloud State U., 1974. Pres., CEO Resplendency Endeavors, Inc., Mpls., 1988—. Author: (poem) Minnesota Winter: A Remembrance, 1997. Co-capt. Block Club, 1996—. Mem. Am. Swedish Inst., Neighborhood Revitalization Program Environ. Com. Lutheran. Avocations: reading, exercise. Home: 1076 18th Ave SE Minneapolis MN 55414-2551

BLEIBERG, LEON WILLIAM, surgical podiatrist; b. Bklyn., June 9, 1932; s. Paul Pincus and Helen (Epstein) B.; m. Beth Daigle, June 7, 1970; children: Kristina Noel, Kelley Lynn, Kimberly Ann, Paul Joseph. Student, L.A. City Coll., 1950-51, U. So. Calif., 1951, Case Western Res. U., 1951-53; DSc with honors, Temple U., 1955; D in Podiatric Medicine, Pa. Sch. Podiatric Medicine, 1965; PhD, U. Beverly Hills, 1970. Served rotating internship various hosps., Phila., 1954-55; resident various hosps., Montebello, L.A., 1956-58; surg. podiatrist So. Calif. Podiatry Group, Westchester (Calif.), L.A., 1956-75; health care economist, researcher Drs. Home Health Care Svcs., 1976—; chmn. bd. Unltd. Healthcare, Metro Manila, Philippines; v.p. pub. rels. Bilboa Wellness Found., Upland, Calif.; CEO Med. Trianon, Newbury Park, Calif.; dir. biomechanics dept. Anit-Aging and Rejuvenation Clinic, Torrance, Calif.; podiatric cons. U. So. Calif. Athletic Dept., Morningside and Inglewood (Calif.) High Schs., Internet Corp., Royal Navy Assn., Long Beach, Calif. Naval Sta.; exec. cons. Thomas Med. Group, Pomona, Calif., 1995, Cardiotel, Van Nuys, Calif., 1995; lectr. in field; healthcare affiliate Internat. divsn. CARE/ASIA, 1987; pres. Medica, Totalcare, Cine-Medics Corp., Strategic World-Wide Health Care Svcs.; exec. dir. Internat. Health Trust, developer Health Banking Program; adminstr. Orthotic Concepts, 1993; prof. health care econs. and med. rehab. Global U., Ontario, Calif., chmn. dept. health care econs., chmn. dept. biomechanics and phys. rehab.; CEO Integrated Wellness Ctrs.; exec. dir. wellness divsn. Crown Golden Eagles; mem. nat. leadership Temple U., Phila.; exec. dir. The Med. Trianon. Producer (films) The Gun Hawk, 1963, Terrified, Day of the Nightmare; contbr. articles to profl. jours. Hon. Sheriff Westchester 1962-64; commd. mem. Rep. Senatorial Inner Circle, 1984-86; co-chmn. health reform com. United We Stand Am., Thousand Oaks, Calif.; mem. exec. coun. State of Calif., United We Stand Am.; active 1st Security and Safety, Westlake Village, Calif., 1993—; lt. comdr. med. svcs. corps Brit.-Am. Sea Cadet Corps, 1984—; track coach Westlake High Sch., Westlake Village; exec. sec. Nat. Coalition Parents for Anti-Drug/Violence Corp., Inc. L.A. World Affairs Coun.; county inspector U.S. Election Com., Calif.; exec. sec. Nat. Coalition of Parents Against Drug Abuse and Violence. With USN, 1955-56. Recipient Medal of Merit, U.S. Presdl. Task Force. Mem. Philippine Hosp. Assn. (Cert. of Appreciation 1964, trophy for Outstanding Svc. 1979), Calif. Podiatry Assn. (hon.), Am. Podiatric Med. Assn. (hon.), Acad. TV Arts and Scis., Royal Soc. Health (Eng.), Western Foot Surgery Assn., Am. Coll. Foot Surgeons, Am. Coll. Podiatric Sports Medicine, Internat. Coll. Preventive Medicine, Hollywood Comedy Club, Sts. and Sinners Club, Westchester C. of C., Hals Und Beinbruch Ski Club, Beach Cities Ski Club, Orange County Stamp Club, Las Virgenes Track Club, Masons, Shriners. Fax: (805) 499-8877. Home: 55 N Wendy Dr Newbury Park CA 91320

BLEICH, MICHAEL ROBERT, healthcare administrator and consultant; b. Columbus, Wis., Mar. 8, 1952; s. David Arthur and Lorraine Mary (Hanson) B.; children: Kirsten, Kara, Kaitlin. Diploma, St. Luke's Hosp. Sch. Nursing, Racine, Wis., 1976; BSN, Milton (Wis.) Coll., 1979; MPH, U. Minn., 1987; PhD, U. Nebr., 1998. RN, Wis., Nebr.; cert. advanced nursing adminstr. V.p. patient svcs. St. Mary's Med. Ctr., Racine, 1979-88; assoc. prof. Mt. Senario Coll., Ladysmith, Wis., 1982-90; cons. on nursing and healthcare Quality Healthcare Resources, Inc., Chgo., 1989-94; v.p. patient care svcs. Bryan Meml. Hosp., Lincoln, Nebr., 1990-96; cons. healthcare systems and leadership pvt. practice, Lincoln, 1996-98; internal cons. clin. sys. and performance improvement Health Midwest Johnson County, Overland Pakr, Kans., 1998—; cons. healthcare systems and leadership, 1996—. Editor: (with M. Bratton) Information Management and Computers, 1990; contbg. author: Documenting Care, 1991, Encyclopedia of Nursing Quality Assurance, 1991, Commitment to Excellence: Developing a Professional Nursing Staff, 1987; contbg. author: Leading and Managing, 1995, Quality Management in Nursing and Health Care, 1996; mem. editorial bd. Jour. Nursing Care Quality; contbr. articles to profl. jours. Named Nebr. Nurse of Yr., Nebr. Nurses Assn., 1993; W.K. Kellogg fellow; recipient Johnson & Johnson-Wharton Fellowship for Nurse Execs., 1997. Mem. ANA, Am. Orgn. Nurse Execs., N. Am. Nursing Diagnosis Assn. (co-chair membership), Nat. League for Nursing (Nebr. pres. 1995-97), Acad. Human Resource Devel., Sigma Theta Tau. Home: 8215 W 123d Terrace Overland Park KS 66213

BLEICHER, SAMUEL ABRAM, lawyer; b. Omaha, June 21, 1942; s. David Bernard and Rachael (Faigin) B.; m. Beatrice Koretsky, June 16, 1965 (dec. Nov. 12, 1995); children: Leo, Zena; m. Emily Blair Chewning, May 17, 1997. BA, Northwestern U., 1963; JD, Harvard U., 1966. Bar: Nebr. 1966, Ohio 1972, D.C. 1979, Va. 1989, Md. 1991. Prof. law U. Toledo Coll. Law, 1966-76; dep. dir. for regulation and enforcement Ohio EPA, 1972-75; issues generalist Carter-Mondale Presdl. Campaign, Atlanta, 1976; policy analyst Carter-Mondale Transition Planning Group, Washington, 1976-77; spl. asst. to adminstr. NOAA Dept. Commerce, Washington, 1977, dir. Office Ocean Mgmt., 1977-78, dep. asst. adminstr., 1978-80, dep. gen. counsel, 1980-81; of counsel Blank, Rome, Comisky & McCauley, Washington, 1981-85; ptnr. Frank, Bernstein, Conaway & Goldman, Tysons Corner, Va., 1985-90; prin. Miles & Stockbridge P.C., Washington, 1990—. Contbr. articles to profl. publs. Democrat. Jewish. Office: Miles & Stockbridge 1400 16th St NW Ste 400 Washington DC 20036-2216

BLEIER, CAROL STEIN, writer, researcher; b. N.Y., Jan. 31, 1942; d. Shelley and Ruth (Brown) Stein; m. Michael Bleier, Oct. 9, 1966; children: Thomas, Lisa, Mark. BA in English Lit., Syracuse U., 1963; MLS, U. Pitts, 1986. Pub. info. specialist IRS, Washington, 1964-68; columnist Springfield (Va.) Ind., 1977-78; mktg. cons. Greater Pitts. Mus. Coun., 1986-88; pub. rels. dir. Greater Pitts. Literacy Coun., 1988-89; writer, 1985—. Author: (corp. history book) To Good Health and Life: L'Chaim A History of Montefiore Hospital of Pittsburgh, 1898-1990, 1997; co-author: (corp. history book) The Ketchum Spirit: A History of Ketchum Communications Inc., 1992; contbg. author: Encyclopedia of Library History, 1994; contbr. articles to periodicals. Mem. ALA, Beta Phi Mu. Democrat. Jewish. Avocations: reading, travel. Home: 214 Lynn Haven Dr Pittsburgh PA 15228-1821

BLEIER, MICHAEL E., lawyer. BA, U. Tulsa, 1962; JD, Georgetown U., 1965. Bar: Pa, D.C. Atty. Office of Gen. Counsel, Bd. Govs. Fed. Reserve System, 1971-78, sr. counsel, 1979-81, asst. gen. counsel, 1981-82; mng. counsel Mellon Bank Corp., Pitts., 1982-88, asst. gen. counsel, 1989-91, dep. gen. counsel, 1991-92, gen. counsel, 1992—, sr. mgmt. com. Mem. Am. Bankers Assn. (vice chmn. bank counsel com. 1996—), Lawyers Coun. Bankers Roundtable (chmn. 1993-98). Office: Mellon Bank Corporation 19th flr One Mellon Bank Ctr Pittsburgh PA 15258

BLEIFELD, STANLEY, sculptor; b. Bklyn., Aug. 28, 1924; s. Benjamin and Rose (Molshatsky) B.; m. Naomi Kaplan Ruby, Sept. 5, 1949; children: Becky Paula, Emily Harriet. BFA, Tyler Sch. Fine Arts, Phila., 1949; BSEd, Temple U., 1949, MFA, 1950; D of Fine Arts (hon.), Lyme Acad. Fine Arts, Conn., 1997. fellow Tyler Sch. Fine Arts, Temple U., 1967—. One-person shows Peridot Gallery, N.Y.C., 1963, 65, 68, Fairfield (Conn.) U., 1967, FAR Gallery, N.Y.C., 1971, 73, 77, New Britain Mus. Art (Conn.), 1974, Kenmore Gallery, Phila., 1967, Franz Bader Gallery, Washington, 1987, 91; exhibited in group shows Internat. Art Festival, Newport, R.I., 1964, Am. Fedn. Arts, 1966, 67, Conn. Commn. on Arts, 1972, Parrish Art Mus., Southampton, N.Y., 1968, others; represented in permanent collections Mus. of City of N.Y., Fairfield (Conn.) U., New Britain Mus. Art, Tampa Bay Art Ctr., Fla., Temple U., Phila., Westmoreland Mus., Pa., Pa. State Mus., U. Edinburg (Scotland), L.B. Johnson Libr., Tex.; executed relief sculptures The Prophets, Vatican Pavilion, N.Y. Worlds Fair, 1964-65, Magic Carpet, Kokomo Pub. Libr., 1970, Family of Acrobats, Civic Ctr., Orlando, Fla., 1973, Alberta Family, Century Gardens, Calgary, Can., 1981, Father McGivney Meml. KC Internat. Hdqrs., New Haven, 1982; sculptor U.S. Navy Meml., Washington, 1982—, Jacksonville, Fla., 1988, Great Lakes, Ill., 1997, San Diego, Calif., 1998, Henry C. Singleton, Sr. Monument, Key West, Fla., 1994, Marine Relief, Brookgreen Gardens, S.C., 1996; designer Medal of Liberty ACLU, 1984; dir. Bleifeld Sculpture Group, New Canaan, Conn., 1966—; instr. Silvermine Guild Art, New Canaan, Conn., 1963-66, asst. prof. art Western Conn. State Coll., New Haven, 1953-55. Served with USNR, 1944-46. Recipient Shikler award Nat. Acad. Design, 1977, Meiselman prize, 1997, 98, Tiffany fellow, 1965, 67. Fellow Nat. Sculpture Soc. (pres. 1991-93, chmn. editl. bd. Sculpture Rev., treas. 1994, Bronze medal 1970, 94, John Gregory award 1964, Proskauer award 1977, Hexter award 1980, 98, Henry Hering award 1990, Silver medal 1991, Chilmark award 1994); mem. Artists Equity, NAD (academician, coun.), Fedn. Internationale de la Medaille, Century Assn. Jewish. Avocation: tennis. Home: 27 Spring Valley Rd Weston CT 06883-1546

BLEIL, WALTER G., lawyer; b. Phila., July 6, 1950. BA, Villanova U., 1972; JD, Harvard U., 1975. Bar: Pa. 1975. Ptnr. Reed Smith Shaw & McClay, Pitts., 1985-97, Doepken Keevican & Weiss, Pitts., 1997—. Office: Doepken Keevican & Weiss USX Tower 600 Grant Ste 58 Pittsburgh PA 15219-2703

BLEILER, CATHERINE ANN, financial executive; b. Allentown, Pa., Aug. 17, 1952; d. Richard Herbert and Joyce May (Stephens) Souilliard; m. Wiliam Thomas Bleiler, Mar. 20, 1971; children: Michelle Lynn, Craig William. AA, Lehigh County C.C., Schecksville, Pa., 1981; BA, Muhlenberg Coll., Allentown, Pa., 1986; MBA, Moravian Coll., Bethlehem, Pa., 1991. Cert. mgmt. acct. Acct. Fin. Am., Allentown, 1981-84; mgmt. info. analyst Chrysler First, Allentown, 1984-87; dir. fin. planning Nations Credit, Allentown, 1987-92, dir. mgmt. planning and reports, 1992-94, divsn. contr., 1994-95, dir. risk mgmt., 1995; dir. bus. planning and analysis Tokai Fin. Svcs., Berwyn, Pa., 1996; fin. mgr. dist. Qualex, Inc., Allentown, 1997—. Recipient mgmt. devel. program award Am. Fin. Svcs. Assn., Chapel Hill, N.C., 1991. Mem. Inst. Mgmt. Accts. Presbyterian. Home: 1989 Orchard Ave Allentown PA 18104-1228

BLEILER, EVERETT FRANKLIN, writer, publishing company executive; b. Boston, Apr. 30, 1920; s. Joseph Eugene and Rose Caroline (Mayor) B.; m. Ellen Haas, May 12, 1956; children: Richard, John, Constance, Dorothy. AB cum laude, Harvard U., 1942; MA, U. Chgo., 1951; Diploma, U. Leiden, The Netherlands, 1952. Freelance writer, 1952-55; advt. mgr. Dover Publs., N.Y.C., 1955-60, mng. dir., 1960-65, exec. v.p., 1965-78; editorial cons. Charles Scribners Sons, N.Y.C., 1978-83. Author more than 60 books including The Checklist of Fantastic Literature, 1948, Essential Japanese Grammar, 1963, Best Tales of Hoffmann, 1967, Mother Goose's Melodies, 1970, Eight Dime Novels of the Victorian Period, 1974, Wagner, The Wehrwolf by G. W. M. Reynolds, 1975, Seventeenth Century Floral Engravings of Emanuel Sweerts, 1976, Richmond, Exploits of a Bow Street Runner, 1976, (under name Liberte E. LeVert) Prophecies and Enigmas of Nostradamus, 1979; A Treasury of Victorian Detective Stories, 1979, A Treasury of Victorian Ghost Stories, 1981, Science Fiction Writers, 1982, The Guide to Supernatural Fiction, 1983, Supernatural Fiction Writers, 1985, Science-Fiction: The Early Years, 1991, Science-Fiction: The Gernsback Years, 1998, others; co-author: (with Wendell C. Bennett) Northwest Argentine Archeology, 1948, (with Guy Stern) Essential German Grammar, 1961. Sgt. U.S. Army, 1942-46. Recipient World Fantasy award World Fantasy Com., Providence, 1978, World Fantasy award (lifetime), London, 1988, Pilgrim award Sci. Fiction Rsch. Assn., 1984, Pres.'s award World Sci. Fiction Assn., 1986, Locus award for best non-fiction book, 1992; named to N.J. Literary Hall of Fame, 1979; Kt. Comdr., Order of Star, Realm of Redonda; Fulbright fellow, 1952. Democrat. Home: 4076 Interlaken Beach Rd Interlaken NY 14847-9632

BLENCOWE, PAUL SHERWOOD, lawyer; b. Amityville, N.Y., Feb. 10, 1953; s. Frederick Arthur and Dorothy Jeanne (Ballenger) B.; m. Mary Frances Faulk, Apr. 11, 1992; 1 child, Kristin Amanda. BA with honors, U. Wis., 1975; MBA, U. Pa., 1976; JD, Stanford U., 1979. Bar: Tex. 1979, Calif. 1989. Assoc. Fulbright & Jaworski, Houston, 1979-86; assoc. Fulbright & Jaworski, London, 1986-87, ptnr., 1988-89; ptnr. Fulbright & Jaworski L.L.P., L.A., 1989—. Editor: China's Quest for Independence: Policy Evolution in the 1970s, 1980; editor-in-chief Stanford Jour. of Internat. Law, 1978-79; contbr. articles on U.S. securities and corp. law to profl. jours. Mem. ABA, The Calif. Club, Phi Beta Kappa, Phi Kappa Phi, Beta Theta Pi. Office: Fulbright & Jaworski LLP 865 S Figueroa St Fl 29 Los Angeles CA 90017-2543

BLENDON, ROBERT JAY, health policy educator; b. Dec. 19, 1942; s. Edward and Theresa B.; m. Marie C. McCormick, Dec. 31, 1977. BA, Marietta (Ohio) Coll., 1964; MBA, U. Chgo., 1966; MPH, Johns Hopkins U., 1967, DSc, 1969. Fellow Ind. U. Med. Ctr., Indpls., 1965-66; instr. dept. med. care and hosps. Johns Hopkins U. Sch. Hygiene and Pub. Health, Balt., 1969-70, also asst. to assoc. dean for health care programs Sch. Medicine, 1969-70, asst. prof. dept. med. care and hosps., 1970-71; asst. dir. planning and devel. Office of Health Care Programs, Johns Hopkins Med. Instns., Balt., 1970-71; spl. asst. for health affairs to dep. undersec. for policy coordination HEW, Washington, 1971-72; and spl. asst. for policy devel. to asst. sec. to health and sci. affairs, 1971-72; sr. v.p. Robert Wood Johnson Found., Princeton, N.J., to 1987; prof. health policy and polit. analysis Harvard U. Sch. Pub. Health and Kennedy Sch. of Govt., Boston, 1987—; dep. dir. health policy Harvard U.; vis. lectr. Princeton U., 1972-87; sr. policy analyst com. on health svcs. industry Cost of Living Coun., Washington, 1971; bd. dirs. Johns Hopkins Hosp. and Health Sys. Mem. editorial bd. Jour. of Am. Med. Assn., 1992—. Mem. Council Fgn. Relations, Inst. Medicine, Nat. Acad. Scis. Home: 478 Quinobequin Rd Newton MA 02468-2127 Office: Harvard U Sch Pub Health 677 Huntington Ave Boston MA 02115-6028

BLENKARN, KENNETH ARDLEY, mechanical engineer, consultant; b. Amarillo, Tex., May 19, 1929; m. 1952. BA, Rice U., 1951, BS, 1952, MS, 1954, PhD in Mech. Engring., 1960. Instr. mechanical engring. Rice U., 1952-54; rsch. engr. Amoco Prod. Co., 1954-57, sr. rsch. engr., 1960-63, staff rsch. engr., 1963-68, rsch. assoc., 1968-72, rsch. supr., 1972-76, rsch. dir., 1976-86, cons., 1986—. Mem. Nat. Acad. Engring. Home: 9115 E 37th Ct Tulsa OK 74145-3414

BLENKINSOPP, JOSEPH, biblical studies educator; b. Bishop Auckland, Durham, Eng., Apr. 3, 1927; came to U.S., 1968; s. Joseph William and

Mary (Lyons) B.; m. Irene H. Blenkinsopp, Mar. 30, 1968 (div. 1991); children: David, Martin; m. Jean Porter, July 10, 1993. BA with honors in History, U. London, 1948; STL, Internat. Theologate, Turin, Italy, 1956; Licentiate in Sacred Scripture in Bibl. Studies, Bibl. Inst., Rome, 1958; DPhil in Bibl. Studies, Oxford (Eng.) U., 1967. Lectr. Internat. Theologate, Romsey, Eng., 1958-62, Heythrop Coll., Oxford U., 1965; vis. asst. prof. Vanderbilt U., Nashville, 1968, Chgo. Theol. Sem., 1968-69; assoc. prof. Hartford (Conn.) Sem. Found., 1969-70; assoc. prof. bibl. studies U. Notre Dame, Ind., 1970-75, prof., 1975-85, John A. O'Brien prof., 1985—; rector Ecumenical Inst., Tantur, Israel, 1978; coord. excavation Capernaum (Israel) Excavation, 1980-87. Author: Prophecy and Canon, 1977 (nat. religious book award 1977), History of Prophecy in Israel, 1983, 2d edit., 1996, Wisdom and Law in the Old Testament, 1983, 2d edit., 1995, The Pentateuch, 1992, Sage, Priest, Prophet: The Intellectual Tradition in Ancient Israel, 1995. Grantee NEH, Oxford U., 1982-83. Mem. Am. Acad. Religion, Soc. Bibl. Lit. (editl. bd. 1987-90), Cath. Bibl. Assn. (pres. 1990), Soc. O.T. Studies, Assn. Jewish Studies. Roman Catholic. Office: U Notre Dame 181 Decio Hall Notre Dame IN 46556-5644

BLENKO, WALTER JOHN, JR., lawyer; b. Pitts., June 15, 1926; s. Walter J. and Ardis Leah (Jones) B.; m. Joy Kinneman, Apr. 9, 1949; children: John W., Andrew W. BS, Carnegie-Mellon U., 1950; JD, U. Pitts., 1953. Bar: Pa. 1954. Pvt. practice law Pitts., 1954—; ptnr. Eckert, Seamans, Cherin & Mellott, Pitts., 1984-93, of counsel, 1993—; mem. adv. bd. dept. mech. engrng. Carnegie-Mellon U., 1992—. Active Churchill Vol. Fire Co., 1970-82; charter and hon. mem. Wilkinsburg Emergency Med. Svc.; sec. Hampton Twp. Zoning Hearing Bd., 1991-92, vice-chmn., 1993; mem. Hampton Twp. Sch. Bd., 1993-97, pres. 1996. With U.S. Army, 1944-46, ETO. Decorated Bronze Star; recipient Disting. Svc. award Carnegie-Mellon U. Alumni Assn., 1993. Fellow Am. Coll. Trial Lawyers; mem. ASME, Pa. Bar Assn., Allegheny County Bar Assn., Assn. Bar of City of N.Y., Pitts. Intellectual Property Law Assn. (pres. 1977-78), Engrs. Soc. Western Pa., Internat. Patent and Trademark Assn., Carnegie-Mellon U. Alumni Assn. (exec. bd. 1996—, exec. com. 1997—), Duquesne Club, Univ. Club, Princeton Club (N.Y.), Rolls-Royce Owners Club (bd. dirs. 1982-84, v.p. publs. 1984-87, treas. 1987-89). Avocation: old cars. Home: 4073 Middle Rd Allison Park PA 15101-1207 Office: Eckert Seamans Cherin & Mellott 600 Grant St Pittsburgh PA 15219-2702

BLESCH, K(ATHY) SUZANN, small business owner; b. Evansville, Ind., Dec. 14, 1951; d. Robert Lee McBride and E. Jean (Oliver) Schumacher; m. Larry J. Blesch, Aug. 17, 1974; children: Nicholas R., Spencer A., Clayton W. Grad. Grad. Realtors Inst., Ind. U., 1979; cert. residential specialist, Nat. Assn. Realtors, 1980. Waitress, hostess Skyway & Pete's, Evansville, Ind., 1971-73; operator, asst. mgr. Stecklers T.A.S., Evansville, 1969-71; salesperson, broker Midwest Realty, Evansville, 1973-78; broker, owner Blesch Realty, Evansville, 1978-80; broker, salesperson Brand Realty, Evansville, 1980-83; owner, operator Nick Nackery Pl., Evansville, 1985—. Bd. dirs. Hope of Evansville, 1976-79. Mem. Nat. Costumers Assn. Avocations: family, reading. Home and Office: 201 E Virginia St Evansville IN 47711-5529

BLESSEN, KAREN ALYCE, free lance illustrator, designer; b. Columbus, Nebr.. BFA, U. Nebr., 1973. Freelance illustrator, 1973-86; designer Dallas Morning News, 1986-89, freelance illustrator, designer, 1989—; owner, illustrator Karen Blessen Illustration, Dallas, 1989—. Illustrator: Be An Angel, 1994. Recipient Pulitzer Prize for explanatory journalism, 1989; awards from N.Y. Art Dirs. Club, Soc. Newspaper Design, Dallas Press Club; commd. by Absolut to represent Tex. in Absolut Statehood series. Home and office: Karen Blessen Illustration 6327 Vickery Blvd Dallas TX 75214-3348

BLESSING, GARY ALBERT, technical communications executive; b. Dayton, Ohio, Oct. 14, 1956; s. Richard A, and Janet A. (Geary) B.; m. Janice J. Caya, Feb. 15, 1990. Student Elec. Engrng., Ohio State U., 1983; student Electronics, Cleve. Inst. Electronics, 1986. Technician Graphics Scanning Corp., Buffalo, 1984-87; tech. mgr. Mobile Comms. of Am., Buffalo, 1987-90, Profl. Comms., Inc., Buffalo, 1990-95, USA Mobile, 1995-96; engrng. supr., facilities mgr. Marine Midland Roof Project Arch Comms. Inc., Buffalo, 1996—; marine roof mgr. Omni Am., 1997—. Mem. World Future Soc. Avocations: stock market, wood working, bicycle riding and racing, numismatics. Office: Arch Comms Inc 2870 Niagara Falls Blvd Buffalo NY 14228-2020

BLESSING, MAXINE LINDSEY, secondary education educator; b. Skirum, Ala., Mar. 27, 1920; d. John Amos and Lizzy Maude (Croft) Lindsey; m. Alvin Reed Blessing, June 24, 1939; 1 child, Deanna Dawn Blessing Gilbert. BS in Secondary English Edn., Jacksonville (Ala.) U., 1956; postgrad., Auburn U., 1974-75. Tchr. DeKalb County (Ala.) Schs., 1943-97; ret., 1997; Beta Club sponsor Crossville (Ala.) H.S., 1960—, drama dir. jr. and sr. plays, 1960—, interim counselor. Sunday sch. tchr., pianist, organist Skirum Bapt. Ch., Crossville. Mem. AAUW, NEA, Nat. Coun. Tchrs. English, Ala. Coun. Tchrs. English, Ala. Edn. Assn., DeKalb County Edn. Assn. (mem. English textbook com. 1988-89), Ea. Star (worthy matron 1944-45), Skirum Cmty. Club (various coms.). Democrat. Baptist. Avocations: music, church and community activities, bridge, reading, attending plays. Home: 2314 County Road 46 Dawson AL 35963-3400 Office: Crossville HS PO Box 38 Crossville AL 35962-0038

BLESSING, SCOTT FRANCIS, marketing executive; b. Reading, Pa., Dec. 17, 1957; s. Theodore Robert and Mary Catherine (Brailer) B. BSBA, Shippensburg U., 1979; MBA, St. Joseph's U., Phila., 1994. Dir. nat. mktg. and promotions Dolfin Corp., Shillington, Pa., 1979-82, asst. v.p. sales, 1982-84; mdse. mgr. VF Corp., Wyomissing, Pa., 1985-88, dir. mktg., 1988-92; exec. v.p. Medalist Apparel, Inc., Reading, Pa., 1992-95; pres., COO Performance Sports Apparel, Inc., Reading, 1995—. Vol. Big. Bros./Big Sisters Berks County, Reading, 1981-90, v.p., 1983-85; bd. dirs. youth svcs. YMCA of Reading and Berks County, 1990-96. Recipient Outstanding Svc. to Children award Big Bros.-Big Sisters Berks County, 1980-88. Mem. Reciprocity Club (Reading) Splash Club (pres. 1989-92), Sigma Tau Gamma. Republican. Roman Catholic. Avocations: water polo, swimming. Home: 105 Colleen Ct Wyomissing PA 19610-1043

BLESSINGER, TIMOTHY LOUIS, secondary school educator; b. Jasper, Ind., Feb. 7, 1953. B in Secondary Edn., St. Bernard Coll., 1975; M in Secondary Edn., Ind. State U., 1980. Lic. secondary sch. tchr., Ind. English tchr. Heritage Hills Mid./H.S., Lincoln City, Ind., 1975—; coach Heritage Hills Mid./H.S., Lincoln City, 1975-86, advisor h.s. yearbook, 1982—; mem. ISTEP and standards com. Ind. Dept. Edn., Indpls., 1996—; owner Blessinger Internat. Pub. House, Inc. Author: Lincoln: The Kentuckiana years, 1997, Lincoln, Illinois Prairie Years, 1997, Lincoln: Washington, D.C., Years, 1997, The Seven Homes of Lincoln, 1999. Recipient Nat. Medal of Patriotism Am. Police Hall of Fame, Miami, Fla., 1996. Mem. NEA, North Spencer Reading Coun. (pres. 1977-78), Ind. State Reading Coun., Internat. Reading Assn., Ind. Coun. Tchrs. of English, Nat. Coun. Tchrs. of English, Nat. Mid. Sch. Assn. Avocations: art collecting, reading, writing, photography, sports. Home: RR 2 Box 303A Dale IN 47523-9545 Office: PO Box 1776 Hwy 162 Lincoln City IN 47552

BLETHEN, FRANK A., newspaper publisher; b. Seattle, Apr. 20, 1945. B.S. in Bus., Ariz. State U. Pub. Walla Walla Union-Bulletin, Wash., 1975-79; pub., circulation mgr. Seattle Times Newspaper Co., 1985—; chmn. Walla Walla Union-Bull., Yakima (Wash.) Herald Republic, Blethen Maine Newspapers, Portland, Augusta, Waterville; pres. Blethen Corp. Mem. pres.' adv. bd. Wash. State U. and U. Wash.; campaign chair United Way King County, 1996, 97, bd. dirs., 1996—; bd. dirs. Md. Inst. for Minority Journalism Edn., 1994—. Recipient Pulitzer prize (3) for best newspaper reporting and investigative reporting, 1997, Nat. Reports, 1991, Ida B. Wells award for lifetime achievement in advancement of minority employment, 1997, Leadership Conf. on Civil Rights Chairperson's award for spl. merit, 1999, Edward R. Murrow award Wash. State U., 1998, Weldon B. Gibson Disting. Vol. award Wash. State U., 1998; named to WAsh. State Hall of Journalistic Achievement, 1998. Mem. Nat. Assn. of Minority Media Execs., Am. Newspaper Pubs. Assn. (bd. dirs., chmn. telecomm. com.), Sigma Delta Chi. Office: Seattle Times Fairview Ave N & John St PO Box 70 Seattle WA 98111-0070

BLETHEN, SANDRA LEE, pediatric endocrinologist; b. San Mateo, Calif., May 16, 1942; d. Howard Albion and Laura Katherine (Wolf) B.; m. Fred I. Chasalow, Nov. 26, 1966. SB in Biochemistry, U. Chgo., 1961; PhD in Biochemistry, U. Calif., Berkeley, 1965; MD, Yeshiva U., 1975. Diplomate Am. Bd. Pediatrics. Fellow biochemistry Brandeis U., Waltham, Mass., 1965-68; instr. biochemistry U. Calif., San Diego, 1968-69; asst. prof. San Francisco State U., 1969-71; resident in pediatrics Columbia Presbyn. Med. Ctr., N.Y.C., 1975-77; fellow pediatric endocrinology U. N.C., Chapel Hill, 1977-79; asst. prof. pediatrics Washington U., St. Louis, 1979-84; assoc. prof. pediatrics SUNY, Stony Brook, 1985-96; assoc. attending pediatrician L.I. Jewish Med. Ctr., New Hyde Park, N.Y., 1984-90; attending pediatrician Univ. Hosp., Stony Brook, 1991-96; cons. Genentech, Inc., South San Francisco, Calif., 1985-96, sr. endocrinologist, 1996—, assoc. dir. product experience, 1997—, sr. clin. scientist, 1999—; cons. Genentech, Inc., South San Francisco, Calif., 1985-96, , assoc. dir. product experience, 1997—; cons. Diagnostic Systems Labs., Webster, Tex., 1989-96. Mem. editl. bd. Steroids, 1990—, Jour. of Endocrinology and Metabolism, 1995-98; contbr. 89 articles to profl. jours. Predoctoral fellow NSF, 1961-63, Postdoctoral fellow USPHS, 1965-67. Mem. Am. Pediatric Soc. (program com. 1994), Endocrine Soc., Lawson Wilkens Pediatric Endocrine Soc. (membership chair 1994-95), Soc. for Pediatric Rsch., Phi Beta Kappa, Alpha Omega Alpha. Avocation: sailing. Office: Med Affairs Genentech Inc 1 Dna Way South San Francisco CA 94080-4918

BLETHEN, SHIRLEY E., dialysis nurse, administrator; b. Lewiston, Maine, Oct. 14, 1950; d. John Elwell and Katri Maria (Kyllonen) Waterman; m. Harold B. Blethen, May 20, 1972; children: Amy, Janet, Joseph, Jeffrey. Diploma, Mercy Hosp. Sch. Nursing, Portland, Maine, 1972. Cert. nephrology nurse. Charge nurse, pediatrics Henrietta Goodall Hosp., Sanford, Maine, 1972-79; staff nurse Wm. W. Backus Hosp., Norwich, Conn., 1979-85, clin. coord., 1985-91; nurse mgr. Wm. W. Backus Hosp., Norwich, 1991-94; staff nurse Ctrl. Conn. Dialysis Ctr., 1994—, nurse mgr., 1994-96; charge nurse Diablo Renal Svcs., Walnut Creek, Calif., 1996-98, Antioch, Calif., 1998—. Mem. Am. Nephrology Nurses Assn.

BLETHYN, BRENDA ANNE, actress; b. Ramsgate, Kent, England, Feb. 20, 1946. Actress Royal Nat. Theater, U.K., 1975-89. Appeared in films, including The Witches, A River Runs Through It, Secrets & Lies (Best Actress award Cannes Film Festival, 1996, Golden Globe award, Acad. award nominee), Music From Another Room, In the Winter Dark, Girls Night, Little Voice, Night Train; television includes Outside Edge (Best Comedy Actress award British Comedy Awards, 1994), Grown-Ups, The Buddha of Suburbia, The Bullion Boys, The Imitation Game; Broadway shows include Absent Friends (Outstanding New Talent award Theater World Awards, 1991). Office: ICM 8942 Wilshire Blvd Beverly Hills CA 90211-1934*

BLETTNER, JAMES DONALD, engineering company executive; b. Indpls., May 8, 1924; s. Joseph Anthony Blettner and Dorothea C. (Daum) Linville; m. Margaret P. Falkenroth, Aug. 22, 1948; 1 child, Dale Thomas. BEE, Purdue U., 1949. Registered profl. engr., Ind. Prodn. engr. Brown Rubber Co., Lafayette, Ind., 1949-52; tooling engr. Brown Rubber Co., Lafayette, 1952-55, head research div., 1955-58; supt. job shop Leaman Machines, Lafayette, 1958-60; pres. Blettner Engrng. Co., Fairland, Ind., 1961—. Patentee in field. Elder St. James Luth. Ch., Lafayette, 1983-85. Served with USAF, 1943-46. Republican. Club: Power Squadron Stuart (Fla.). Avocations: sailing, fishing, swimming, golf. Home: PO Box 3062 Jensen Beach FL 34958-3062

BLEVEANS, JOHN, lawyer; b. Danville, Ill., Mar. 29, 1938; s. Edward Harold and Angelita (Robinson) B.; m. Luanna Harrison Burdick, Aug. 17, 1962; children: Lincoln Edward, Melanie Catherine. BA, Trinity U., 1960; LLB, U. Tex., 1965. Bar: Tex. 1965, D.C. 1967, U.S. Supreme Ct. 1969, Ill. 1971. Mem. gen. counsel's office Acacia Mut. Life Ins. Co., Washington, 1967-68; trial and appellate atty., civil rights div. U.S. Dept. Justice, Washington, 1966-67, 69-70; exec. dir. Washington Lawyers' Com., Civil Rights Under Law, 1970-71; chief counsel Lawyers' Com., Civil Rights Under Law, Cairo, Ill., 1971-72; assoc. Mayer, Brown & Platt, Chgo., 1972-74, ptnr., 1974-83, 91-92; sr. v.p., assoc., gen. counsel Continental Ill. Nat. Bank and Trust Co. of Chgo., 1983-89; dep. gen. counsel Continental Bank N.A., Chgo., 1989-91; ptnr. Mayer, Brown & Platt, Chgo., 1991-92; of counsel Arthur Andersen & Co., Chgo., 1992-95, Hong Kong, 1996-97; of counsel Arthur Andersen & Co., Sydney, Australia, 1995-96. Alderman City of Evanston, Ill., 1981-89; chmn. Evanston Zoning Bd. Appeals, 1991-92. Capt. USNR ret. Mem. Tex. Bar Assn., D.C. Bar Assn., Nat. Ski Patrol, Law Club Chgo., Univ. Club. Office: 8634 W Diggin Hill Rd Hanover IL 61041-9520

BLEVINS, DALE GLENN, agronomy educator; b. Ozark, Mo., Aug. 29, 1943; s. Vernon Henry and Edna Gertrude (Payne) B.; m. Brenda Jo Graves, Aug. 27, 1967; 1 child, Jeremy. BS in Chemistry, S.W. Mo. State U., 1965; MS in Soils, U. Mo., 1967; PhD in Plant Physiology, U. Ky., 1972. Postdoctoral fellow botany dept. Oreg. State U., Corvallis, Oreg., 1972-74; asst. prof. botany U. Md., College Park, 1974-78; assoc. prof. agronomy dept. U. Mo., Columbia, 1978-86, prof., 1986—. Mem. Am. Soc. Plant Physiology, Am. Soc. Agronomy, Crop Sci. Soc. Am. Office: Univ Mo Dept Agronomy 1-87 Agriculture Bldg Columbia MO 65211*

BLEVINS, JAMES RICHARD, English educator, academic administrator; b. Shady Valley, Tenn., Feb. 1, 1934; s. Paul Clarence and Viola (Price) B.; m. Barbara Kennedy, July 1, 1960. BA, David Lipscomb Coll., Nashville, 1956; MA, PhD, Vanderbilt U., 1969. From asst. prof. to prof. English U. So. Ind., Evansville, 1966—, dean Sch. Liberal Arts, 1988—. Prodr. New Harmony (Ind.) Theatre, 1988—, Lincoln Theatre, Lincoln City, Ind., 1989—. Bd. dirs. Ind. Humanities Coun., Indpls., 1983-88, chmn., 1986-88; bd. dirs. Fedn. State Humanities Coun., Washington, 1986-88. Recipient Mayors Art award Arts Coun. Southwestern Ind., 1995. Democrat. Avocations: bridge, tennis, theater. Office: U So Ind 8600 University Blvd Evansville IN 47712-3534

BLEVINS, JEFFREY ALEXANDER, lawyer; b. Forest Hills, N.Y., June 18, 1955; s. William E. and Mary J. Blevins; m. Pamela A. Manos, Nov. 26, 1983 (div. Mar. 1995); 1 child, Mary; m. Diane L. Banno, June 12, 1999. BA, Denison U., 1977; JD, DePaul U., 1981. Bar: Ill. 1981, U.S. Dist Ct. (no. dist.) Ill. 1981, U.S. Dist. Ct. (we. dist. Wis. 1984, U.S. Ct. Appeals (7th cir.) 1984, U.S. Supreme Ct. 1990. Personnel specialist Comerica Bank, Detroit, 1979-80; assoc. Bell, Boyd & Lloyd, Chgo., 1981-88, ptnr., 1988—; lectr., author Ill. Inst. Continuing Legal Edn., 1989. Editor in chief DePaul Law Rev., 1980. Mem. Ill. State Bar Assn. (labor and employment coun. 1992-95), Chgo. Bar Assn., Mid-day Club, Union League Club, Omicron Delta Epsilon. Republican. Lutheran.

BLEVINS, PATRICIA M., state legislator. Mem. Del. State Sen., 1992—. Office: 209 Linden Ave Elsmere Wilmington DE 19805-2515 Office: Del State Senate Legislative Hall Dover DE 19903*

BLEVINS, THOMAS E., college administrator, educator; b. Welch, W.Va., Mar. 8, 1949; s. Casper Claude and Bessie Oliv (Shumate) B.; m. Brenda Louise Mabry Lamastus, Mar. 27, 1971 (div. Oct. 1980); children: Tracy, James, Matthew; m. Betty Ruth Rader, May 23, 1992. BS, Bluefield (W.Va.) State Coll., 1971; MA, Marshall U., 1973; CAGS, Va. Tech. U., 1980, EdD, 1986. Cert. tchr., W.Va. Tchr., asst. prin. Elkhorn Jr. H.S., Powhatan, W.Va., 1971-74; tchr., media ctr. dir. Northfork (W.Va.) H.S., 1974-77; coord. audiovisual svcs. Bluefield State Coll., 1977-84, dir. instrnl. tech., 1984—, dir. tchr. edn., 1990-96, prof. edn. and English, 1988—, dir. ctr. for extended learning and acad. computing, 1996—; mem. adv. panel W.Va. Humanities Found., Charleston, 1978-81; mem. tech. implementation planning team State Coll. and Univ. System of W.Va., Charleston, 1995-96. Recipient Edgar Dale award W.Va. Ednl. Media Assn./Assn. Ednl. Comms. and Tech., 1984. Mem. Assn. for Ednl. Comms. and Tech. (cert. com., accreditation com.), W.Va. Ednl. Media Assn. (pres. 1982-84), W.Va. C.C. Assn. (bd. dirs. 1995—), W.Va. Satellite Network, W.Va. Higher Edn. Instrnl. TV Consortium, Rotary of Bluefield (chair Rotoract and Rotary Info. 1995—), Elks. Democrat. Avocations: woodworking, reading, swimming. Home: 2339 Verdun Hts Bluefield WV 24701-4727 Office: Bluefield State Coll 219 Rock St Bluefield WV 24701-2100

BLEVINS, WILLIAM EDWARD, management consultant; b. Pocahontas, Va., Oct. 18, 1927; s. Howard Muncey and Elsie Jane (Wire) B.; m. Mary Hester Jenkins, Aug. 25, 1951; children—Jeffrey Alexander, Jennifer Lynn McEldowney, Bradley Edward. AB, Marshall Coll., 1951; MPA, CCNY, 1960. Personnel mgr. Equitable Life, N.Y.C., 1951-66; asst. v.p., dir. mgmt. devel. Nat. Bank Detroit, 1966-69, v.p., dir. personnel, 1969-74, sr. v.p., dir. personnel, 1974-91; sr. v.p., dir. human resources NBD Bancorp, Inc., Detroit, 1980-92; pres. WEB Communications Co., Detroit, 1993—; bd. dirs. Blue Cross & Blue Shield Mich., Detroit, 1980-92, Human Resources Coun. AMA, 1979-84, 87-92, Detroit Exec. Svc. Corps., 1993-96, Ctrl. Mich. Health Plan, Inc., 1997. Trustee Bon Secour Hosp., Grosse Point, Mich., 1975-84, St. John's Bon Secour Sr. Cmty., 1989—, chmn., 1995—; bd. dirs. Oxford Inst., 1987-89, bd. dirs. Holy Cross Hosp., 1996-98; mem. corp. adv. bd. Am. Heart Assn., 1995-98. Recipient Outstanding Alumnus award Marshall U., 1976, Hall of Fame award Lambda Chi Alpha, 1996. Mem. Am. Bankers Assn. (bd. dirs. 1974-75), Am. Inst. Banking (bd. dirs., bd. regents, chmn. 1983-90), Am. Soc. Employers (bd. dirs. 1970-94, treas. 1970-90, vice chmn. 1991-92, chmn. 1992-94), Alpha Bank Pers Group (founder, chmn. 1972-74, 86), Mich. Pers. Indsl. Rels. Group (chmn. 1980-92), Bank Adminstr. Inst. (human resources commn. 1983-88), Detroit Athletic Club, Country Club Detroit. Republican. Office: WEB Comms Co 551 Fisher Rd Grosse Pointe MI 48230-1214 *How lucky I am to live in the USA. It offers a fine education to those who want it; meaningful jobs to those who prepare and strive, a wonderful place for romance, an ideal place to raise a family. I have been truly blessed with lots of help along the way.*

BLEWETT, DAVID LAMBERT, English literature educator; b. Calgary, Alta., Can., Dec. 18, 1940; s. John and Sydney Catherine (Cole) B. BA with honors, U. Man., Winnipeg, 1962, MA, 1963; PhD, U. Toronto, Ont., Can., 1971. Lectr. McMaster U., Hamilton, Ont., Can., 1969-71, asst. prof., 1971-77, assoc. prof., 1977-84, prof., 1984—. Author: DeFoe's Art of Fiction, 1979, The Illustration of Robinson Crusoe: 1719-1920, 1995, Japanese trans., 1998; editor: Roxana, 1982, Amelia, 1987, Moll Flanders, 1989, Roderick Random, 1995; editor Eighteenth-Century Fiction, 1988—. Grantee Social Scis. and Humanities Rsch. Coun. Can., 1989-90, 96—. Mem. Am. Soc. for Eighteenth-Century Studies, Can. Assn. for Eighteenth-Century Studies Assn. Can. Univ. Tchrs. English, Can. Assn. Univ. Tchrs., Internat. Assn. U. Profs. of English, Royal Soc, Lit., Reform Club, McMaster U. Faculty Assn. (pres. 1992-93). Avocations: travel, music. Home: 390 Wellesley St E # 16, Toronto, ON Canada M4X 1H6 Office: McMaster U, Dept English, Hamilton, ON Canada L8S 4L9

BLEWETT, ROBERT NOALL, lawyer; b. Stockton, Calif., July 12, 1915; s. Stephen Noall and Bess Errol (Simard) B.; m. Virginia Weston, Mar. 30, 1940; children: Richard Weston (dec.), Carolyn Blewett Lawrence. LLB, Stanford U., 1936, JD, 1939. Bar: Calif. 1939. Dep. dist. atty. San Joaquin County, 1942-46; practice law Stockton, 1946-98; ptnr., pres. Blewett & Allen, Inc., Stockton, 1971—. Chmn. San Joaquin County chpt. ARC, 1947-49; v.p. Goodwill Industries, 1967-68; vice chmn. Stockton Sister City Commn., 1969-70; adv. bd. bus. adminstrn. dept. U. Pacific; trustee San Joaquin Pioneer and Haggin Galleries. Fellow Am. Coll. Estate and Trust Counsel, Am. Bar Found.; mem. ABA, Am. Judicature Soc., Am. Law Inst., State Bar Calif. (mem. exec. com. on conf. of dels. 1969-72, vice chmn. 1971-72), Order of the Coif, Rotary (pres. 1987-88), Yosemite Club, San Francisco Banker's Club, Masons, Shriners, Delta Theta Phi, Theta Xi. Republican. Home: 3016 Dwight Way Stockton CA 95204-1809 Office: 141 E Acacia St Stockton CA 95202-1400

BLEWETT, STEPHEN DOUGLAS, journalism educator, public relations consultant; b. Bremerton, Wash., Feb. 21, 1942; s. Wesley Edgar and Christina (Ball) B.; m. Judith Marie Mohr, June 17, 1967; children: Mark Joseph, Christina Marie, Susan Renee. BA in Journalism, Ea. Wash. U., 1969, MA in English, 1981. Newspaper reporter/editor The Spokesman-Rev., Spokane, Wash., 1970-73; pub. rels. coord. Wash. Water Power Co., Spokane, 1973-88; prof./program dir. Ea. Wash. U., Spokane, 1988—; prin. Comm. Concepts, Spokane, 1989—; mem. cmty. adv. bd., mktg. com. Jr. League Spokane, 1996-98. Author: A History of The Washington Water Power Company: 1889-1989, 1989, (with Jeffrey L. Stafford) Hitting the Bricks: A College Student's Practical Guide to Finding Work as a Communication Professional, 1995, (one act play) Pancakes to Go, 1985; cons. editor Inland, 1993-96; contbr. articles to profl. jours. Active Spokane Pub. Rels. Coun., 1995—, mktg. com. Cath. Diocese Found., 1996—. With USAF, 1961-65. Recipient Max award of merit Spokane Advt. Fedn., 1982, 83 85, cert. excellence for spl. events United Way of Am., 1983. Mem. Internat. Assn. Bus. Communicators (accredited, bd. dirs., past pres. Metro Spokane chpt. 1982-95, ethics com. 1992-95, award of merit 1985, Gold Quill award of merit 1986), Pacific Northwest Assn. Journalism Educators (past pres.), Immaculate Heart Retreat Ctr. Dirs. Club. Democrat. Roman Catholic. Avocations: golf, reading, church activities. Office: Ea Wash U 705 W 1st Ave Spokane WA 99201-3909

BLEWITT, GEORGE AUGUSTINE, physician, consultant; b. Pittston, Pa., May 8, 1937; s. George Augustus and Virginia (Wills) B.; m. Anne Katherine Mullahy, June 16, 1962; children: George, Mary Katherine, John, Patrick. B.S., King's Coll., Wilkes-Barre, Pa., 1958; M.D., Thomas Jefferson U., Phila., 1962. Diplomate Am. Bd. Internal Medicine. Intern Phila. Gen. Hosp., 1962-63; resident Phila. VA Hosp., 1963-66; fellow Thomas Jefferson U., Phila.; clin. instr. Stanford U. Sch. Medicine, Calif., 1967-75; staff physician Palo Alto VA Hosp., Calif., 1973-75; clin. prof. medicine Jefferson Med. Coll., 1977-80; assoc. dir. clin. services Smith, Kline & French, Phila., 1976-78; med. dir. Menley & James Labs., Phila., 1978, v.p. research devel., 1978-80; assoc. med. dir. Bristol-Myers Products, N.Y.C., 1980-81, v.p., med. dir., 1981-82, v.p., dir. research devel., 1982-91, v.p. sci. resources, 1991-93; pres. George A. Blewitt, M.D. & Assocs., Inc., Doylestown, Pa., 1993—; adj. prof. U. Calif., Santa Barbara, 1989—, Jefferson Med. Coll., Phila., 1993—. Served to maj. USAR, 1963-71. Fellow ACP; mem. AMA, Am. Soc. Nephrology, Am. Heart Assn., Pa. Med. Assn. Home and Office: 2 Aster Ct Doylestown PA 18901-2618

BLEWITT, THOMAS M., federal judge; b. 1949. BA, U. Scranton, 1972; MPA, Marywood Coll., 1979; JD, Temple U., 1983. Bar: Pa. 1983. Spl. investigator Pa. Bur. Consumer Protection, Harrisburg, 1972-80; assoc. Law Office Marshall E. Anders, Scranton, Pa., 1983-84; asst. dist. atty. Lackawanna County, Scranton, 1984-86; asst. fed. pub. defender for mid. dist. Pa. Office Pub. Defender, Scranton, 1986-92; assoc. Lenahan & Dempsey, Scranton, 1988-89; magistrate judge for mid. dist. Pa., U.S. Magistrate Ct., Scranton, 1992—. Office: US Magistrate Ct 417 Fed Bldg 235 N Washington Ave Scranton PA 18503-1512

BLEY, ANN, program analyst; b. N.Y.C., July 12, 1954; d. Albert Vincent and Autilia (Eliseo) Rizzo; m. Elmer Raymond Bley; 1 child, Shannon Kathryn Bley. BA cum laude, U. Mich., 1976; MBA cum laude, Boston U., 1978. Mgmt. analyst U.S. Army Tank-Auto. Command Force Devel. Div., Warren, Mich., 1979-85; Program, Budget analyst PM Abrams Tank Systems, Warren, Mich., 1985-91; program analyst PM Combat Mobility Sys., DSA, Tacom, Warren, Mich., 1991—. Contributed to professional publications and others. Protegee to Dep. Asst. Sec. Plans, Programs, Policy, Dept. of Army, 1995-96; registration chair Mich. Women's Vote 96; mem. exec. bd. Common Cause of Mich., 1998—. Mem. Federally Employed Women (regional compliance chair 1996-98, chpt. pres. 1995-97, Nat. award for compliance activities 1993, nat. tng. program chair 1985), Am. Soc. Mil. Comptrs., Performance Mgmt. Assn., Beta Gamma Sigma, business honors soc. Avocations: boating, travel. Home: 31080 Mckinney Dr Franklin MI 48025-1313 Office: US Army Tank Auto Command PM Combat Mobility Sys AMSTA-DSA-CM-G Warren MI 48397-5000

BLEY, CARLA BORG, jazz composer; b. Oakland, Calif., May 11, 1938; d. Emil Carl and Arlene (Anderson) Borg; m. Paul Bley, Jan. 27, 1959 (div. Sept. 1967); m. Michael Mantler, Sept. 29, 1967 (div. 1992); 1 dau., Karen. Student public schs., Oakland. mem. adv. bd. Jazz Composers Orch. Assn. Freelance jazz composer, 1956—, pianist, Jazz Composers Orch., N.Y.C., 1964—, European concert tours, Jazz Realities, 1965-66; founder, WATT, 1973—, toured Europe with Jack Bruce Band, 1975; leader, Carla Bley Band, touring, U.S. and Europe, 1977—; composed, recorded: A Genuine Tong Funeral, 1967, (with Charlie Haden) Liberation Music Orch., 1969; opera Escalator Over the Hill, 1970-71 (Oscar du Disque de Jazz

1973), Tropic Appetites, 1973; composed: chamber orch. 3/4, 1974-75; film score Mortelle Randonnèe, 1983; recorded: Dinner Music, 1976, The Carla Bley Band: European Tour, 1977, Musique Macanique, 1979, (with Nick Mason) Fictitious Sports, 1980, Social Studies, 1980, Carla Bley Live!, 1981, Heavy Heart, 1984, I Hate to Sing, 1985, Night Glo, 1985, Sexted, 1987, Duets, 1988, Fleur Carnivor, 1989, The Very Big Carla Bley Band, 1991, Go Together, 1993, Big Band Theory, 1993, Songs with Legs, 1995, Goes to Church, 1996, Fancy Chamber Music, 1998, Are We There Yet?, 1999. Named winner internat. jazz critics poll Down Beat mag., 1966, 71, 72, 78, 79, 80, 83, 84; Best Composer of Yr., Down Beat Readers' Poll, 1984, composer/arranger of yr., 1985-92; Guggenheim fellow, 1972; Cultural Coun. Found. grantee, 1971, 79; Nat. Endowment for the Arts grantee, 1973, Oscar du Disque de Jazz (for Escalator Over the Hill) 1973; named Best in Field Jazz Times critics poll, 1990, Best Arranger, Downbeat Critics Poll, 1993, 94, Best Arranger, Downbeat Readers' Poll, 1994; recipient Prix Jazz Moderne from Academie du Jazz for The very Big Carla Bley Band album, 1992. Office: Watt Works PO Box 67 Willow NY 12495-0067

BLEZNICK, DONALD WILLIAM, Romance languages educator; b. N.Y.C., Dec. 24, 1924; s. Louis and Gertrude (Kleinman) B.; m. Rozlyn Burakoff, June 15, 1952; children—Jordan, Susan. BA, CCNY, 1946; MA, U. Nacional de Mex., 1948; PhD, Columbia U., 1954. Instr. romance langs. Ohio State U., 1949-55; prof. Pa. State U., 1955-67; prof. U. Cin., 1967—, head dept., 1967-72; instr. Romance langs.; vis. prof. Hebrew U., Jerusalem, 1974. Bibliographer, MLA Internat. Bibliography, 1966-81; rev. editor Hispania, 1965-73, editor, 1974-83, editor's adv. coun., 1984—, El Ensayo Espanol del Siglo Veinte, 1964, Historia del Ensayo Espanol, 1964, Duelo en el Paraiso (Goytisolo), 1967, Madrugada (Duero Vallejo), 1969, (with W.T. Pattison) Representative Spanish Authors, 1971, Quevedo, 1972, Variaciones interpretativas en torno a la nueva narrativa hispanoamericana, 1972, Directions of Literary Criticism in the Seventies, 1972, Sourcebook for Hispanic Literature and Language, 1974, 3d expanded edit., 1995, Homenaje a Luis Leal, 1978, Studies on Don Quixote and other Cervantine Works, 1984, Critical Edition of La Diana (Jorge Montemayor), 1990, The Thought of Contemporary Spanish Essayists, 1993, Studies in Honor of Donald W. Bleznick, 1995; founder, exec. editor Cin. Romance Rev., 1982-88; field editor: Twayne Spanish Literature Series, 1981—; contbr. articles to profl. jours., Ency. Americana. With CIC, 1946-47. Decorated Knight's Cross Order Civil Merit (Spain), 1977; Am. Philos. Soc. rsch. grantee, 1964; Downer fellow CCNY, 1947-48; U. Cin. Taft rsch. and publ. grantee, 1972, 75, 78, 83, 88, 89, 92; named 1 of 15 outstanding scholars in Spanish lit. in Cuadernos Salmantinos de Filosofia, Salamanca, Spain, 1977; recipient Rieveschl award for excellence in rsch. U. Cin., 1980, award Hispania, U. So. Calif., 1983; fellow U. Cin. Grad. Sch., 1984. Mem. AAUP, Am. Assn. Tchrs. Spanish and Portuguese (exec. com. 1975—, award 1984, v.p. 1992, pres. 1993, Honored for Outstanding Career 1995, disting. svc. award 1997), MLA, Los Ensayistas (adv. bd. 1976—), Comediantes, Midwest Modern Lang. Assn., Conf. Editors of Learned Jours. (exec. com. 1978-79), Celestinesca, Cervantes Soc. Am., Phi Beta Kappa (pres. Delta chpt. of Ohio 1971-72, 86-87), Sigma Delta Pi (state dir. Ohio 1968-74, Order of Don Quijote 1970, v.p. Midwest 1975-83, Jose Martel award 1980), Phi Sigma Iota (hon. pres. 1998), Kappa Delta Pi. Home: 2444 Madison Rd Apt 1806 Cincinnati OH 45208-1255 Office: U Cin Dept Romance Langs Cincinnati OH 45221

BLICKENSTAFF, DANNY JAY, retired civilian military employee; b. Hagerstown, Md., Mar. 2, 1946; s. Daniel Webster and Mildred Elmira (Greenwalt) B.; m. Jean Ann McSwain, Oct. 10, 1965 (div. 1977); children: Ramona Glynn, Andrea Mae, Camellia Kay; m. Sharon Elizabeth Ward, Aug. 26, 1978. BA, U. Md., 1975, MBA, 1979. Electronics technician U.S. Naval Ordnance Lab., White Oak, Md., 1964-71; R & D electronics lab. supr. U.S. Dept. Transp., McLean, Va., 1971-81; program analyst U.S. Army Hdqs. 7th Signal Command, Ft. Ritchie, Md., 1981-86; program/ops. rsch. analysis officer U.S. Army Hdqs. 7th Signal Command, Ft. Ritchie, 1986-93; program mgr. Def. Info. Svc. Agy., Ft. Ritchie, 1993-96, security specialist, 1996-99; ret., 1999. Active Totem Pole Playhouse, Fayettville, Pa., 1976, Washington County Assn. Retarded Citizens, Hagerstown, Md., 1986. Mem. NRA, Md. Christmas Tree Assn. Republican. Mem. Brethren Ch. Avocations: live theater, travel, gardening, raising Christmas trees and llamas. Home: 16345 Mount Tabor Rd Hagerstown MD 21740-1030

BLICKENSTAFF, KATHLEEN MARY, lawyer, mental health nurse, nursing educator; b. Greenville, Ohio, Oct. 24, 1950; d. Donald Edward and Mary Ann (Subler) Berger; m. Daniel E. Blickenstaff, June 10, 1972 (div. Mar. 1988); children: Benjamin Arin, Amanda Marie, Kathryn Megan. BS, Ohio State U., 1972, MS, 1973, sch. nurse cert., 1990; JD, Capital U. Law Sch., 1998. Cert. sch. nurse grades K-12. Cons. cmty. educator S.W. Cmty. Mental Health Ctr., Columbus, 1973-77; patient and cmty. educator Daniel E. Blickenstaff, DDS, Inc., Columbus, 1977-86; staff nurse Riverside Meth. Hosp., Columbus, 1986-90; clin. instr. Columbus (Ohio) State C.C., 1989; asst. prof. Capital U., Columbus, 1989-96; assoc. prof. Capital U., 1996—; mem. cmty. svcs. com. Mid Ohio Dist. Nurses Assn., Columbus, 1990—, bd. dirs., 1991-94. Leader Girl Scouts, Grandview Heights, Ohio, 1989-93; bd. dirs. H.S. PTO, Grandview Heights (Ohio) City Schs., 1990-93, treas. H.S. PTO, 1990-92, co-chair oper. levy, 1991. Mem. ABA, ANA, Ohio Nurses Assn., Am. Assn. Nurse Attys., Ohio State Bar Assn., Columbus Bar Assn., Sigma Theta Tau. Republican. Roman Catholic. Avocations: quilting, sewing, gardening. Home: 1138 Westwood Ave Columbus OH 43212-3240 Office: Capital Univ 2199 E Main St Columbus OH 43209-2394

BLICKLE, PETER, German educator; b. Ravensburg, Germany, Sept. 26, 1961; came to U.S., 1984; s. Ernst and Hedwig (Wetzel) B.; m. Jaimy Gordon, Dec. 23, 1988. BA in Classics and English, We. Mich. U., 1987; MA in Comparative Lit., U. Mich., 1989, PhD in German Lit., 1995. Tchg. asst. German U. Mich., Ann Arbor, 1988-89, 91-95, lectr. German, 1995-96; asst. prof. German Western Mich. U., Kalamazoo, 1996—. Author: Maria Beig und die Kunst der scheinbaren Kunstlosigkeit, 1997; translator from the German (with Jaimy Gordon) Lost Weddings, 1990. Mem. MLA, Am. Assn. Tchrs. of German, German Studies Assn., Literarisches Forum Oberschwaben, Mich. Acad. Sci., Arts, and Letters. Home: 1803 Hazel Ave Kalamazoo MI 49008-2843 Office: Dept Fgn Langs and Lits Western Mich Univ Kalamazoo MI 49008-5091

BLICKWEDE, DONALD JOHNSON, retired steel company executive; b. Detroit, July 20, 1920; s. Frederic H. and Laura L. (Johnson) B.; m. Meredith Lloyd, Aug. 23, 1943; children: Karen (Mrs. Kimball J. Knowlton), Jon Frederic. B.S., Wayne U., 1943; postgrad., Stevens Inst. Tech., 1943-45; Sc.D., Mass. Inst. Tech., 1948; postgrad. in bus. adminstrn., Harvard, 1969. Metallurgist Curtiss Wright Corp., 1943-45; head high temperature alloys br. Naval Research Lab., 1948-50; research engr. Bethlehem Steel Corp., Pa., 1950-52; div. head Bethlehem Steel Corp., 1952-63, v.p., 1964-82; Campbell Meml. lectr. Am. Metal Congress, 1968, William Park Woodside Meml. lectr., 1969, Zay Zeffries Meml. lectr., 1970; Andrews Meml. lectr. Porcelain Enamel Inst., 1972. Fellow Am. Soc. Metals (hon., pres. 1983); mem. AIME, Am. Acad. Engring., Am. Iron and Steel Inst. (chmn. gen. rsch. com. 1971-73), Indsl. Rsch. Inst. (pres. 1975), Iron and Steel Inst. Japan (hon., Yukawa Meml. lectr. 1984), Green Valley Country Club. Home: 891 Cotonia Green Valley AZ 85614

BLIDBERG, D. RICHARD, marine engineer; b. Manchester, N.H., Jan. 26, 1945. BS, U. N.H., 1972. Technician Woods Hole Oceanograph. Inst., 1968; mgr. Subsea Surveys, ORE Inc., 1972-76; dir., assoc. dir. Marine Systems Engring. Lab. U. n.H., 1976-93; prin. investigator NSF/Nat. Oceanic & Atmospheric Adminstr. Advan. Rsch. Proj. Agy., Office Naval Rsch., 1976—; assoc. edn. Inst. Elec. and Electronics Engrs. J. Oceanograph. Engr., 1982—; dir., owner Autonomous Undersea Syss. Inst., Lee, N.H.; trustees Assn. Unmanned Vehicle Systs., 1983-90, Autonomous Undersea Syst. Inst., 1993; panel mem. Nat. Rsch. Coun. Marine Bd. Study undersea Vehicles, 1992—. Mem. IEEE, ACM, Assn. Unmanned Vehicle Systems, Marine Technol. soc. Office: Autonomous Undersea Syss Inst 86 Old Concord Tpke Lee NH 03824-6728*

BLILEY, THOMAS JEROME, JR., congressman; b. Chesterfield County, Va., Jan. 28, 1932; s. Thomas J. and Carolyn F. Bliley; m. Mary Virginia Kelley, June 22, 1957; children: Mary Vaughan, Thomas Jerome III. B.A., Georgetown U., 1952. Pres. Joseph W. Bliley Funeral Home, 1972-80; mem. 97th-104th Congresses from 3rd (now 7th) Va. dist., Washington, D.C., 1981—; former ranking minority mem. D.C. com., now chmn. House Commerce Com.; vice-mayor Richmond City Council, 1968-70, mayor, 1970-77; past bd. dirs. Nat. League Cities; past pres. Va. Mcpl. League. Past bd. dirs. Crippled Children's Hosp.; past bd. dirs. St. Mary's Hosp.; bd. visitors Va. Commonwealth U.; bd. govs. Va. Home for Boys. Served with USN. Republican. Roman Catholic.

BLIM, RICHARD DON, retired pediatrician; b. Kansas City, Mo., Nov. 8, 1927; s. Miles G. and Latha Mae (Daniels) B.; m. Myrle Rae Blim, Apr. 12, 1952; children: Richard David, Carol Rae, John Miles. BA, U. Kans., 1949, MD, 1953. Diplomate Am. Bd. Pediatrics. Intern U. Kans., 1953-54, resident in pediatrics, 1954-56; practice medicine specializing in pediatrics; pres. Pediatric Assocs., Kansas City, Mo., 1956-89; dir. med. affairs St. Lukes Hosp., Kansas City, 1989-99; Peter T. Bohan lectr. U. Kans., Kansas City, 1978; Max Seham lectr. U. Minn., Mpls., 1982; mem. editorial bd. Mo. Medicine, 1978-92, Pediatric Annals, 1982-92, Pediatric News, 1983-92, Health Care Mgmt. Rev.; mem. VHA Phys. Leadership Coun. Bd. dirs. Marillac Spl. Sch. for Children, 1976-79 . Served to sgt. U.S. Army, 1946-48, PTO. Named Outstanding Med. Alumnus U. Kans. Sch. Medicine, 1978; recipient Clifford G. Grulee award, 1984, Katherine Berry Richard MD award Children Mercy Hosp., 1997. Fellow Am. Acad. Pediatrics (pres. 1980-81, exec. bd. 1973-80, chmn. Mo. chpt. 1964-67); mem. AMA, Inst. Medicine of NAS, Jackson County Med. Soc. (pres. 1976), S.W. Pediatric Assn. (pres. Kansas City 1963), Mo. Med. Assn., Metro. Med. Soc. (merit award 1996), Coun. Med. Specialties Soc. (rep., exec. bd. 1974-80), Kans. U. Med. Alumni (pres. 1973), Loch Lloyd Club, Alpha Omega Alpha. Republican. Presbyterian. Home: 100 W 172d St Belton MO 64012

BLINDER, ABE LIONEL, management consultant; b. Osage, Iowa, Nov. 7, 1909; s. Heimer and Fanny (Zellner) B.; children: Henry David, Jonathan. Ph.B., U. Chgo., 1931. Circulation mgr. Apparel Arts, Chgo., 1932-33, Esquire, Inc., Chgo., 1933-36; circulation dir. Esquire, Inc., 1936-45, dir., 1945-84, v.p., 1945-51, exec. v.p., 1952-61, pres., 1961-77, chmn. bd., 1977-80, chmn. internat. ops., treas., 1980-84, cons., 1984-89. Bd. dirs. Alliance for Resident Theatres, N.Y.C. Mem. Phi Beta Kappa. Clubs: Harmonie (N.Y.C.); Metropolis Country. Home: 5 Horseguard Ln Scarsdale NY 10583-2310

BLINDER, ALBERT ALLAN, judge; b. N.Y.C., Nov. 27, 1925; s. William and Sarah (Gold) B.; m. Meredith Zaretzki, Nov. 16, 1961 (dec.); 1 son, Adam Z.; m. Joan Goodman, Jan. 20, 1985. A.B., N.Y. U., 1944, postgrad., 1944-45; J.D., Harvard U., 1948. Bar: N.Y. 1949, U.S. Dist. Ct. (so. dist.) N.Y. 1953, U.S. Ct. Appeals (2d cir.) 1953; U.S. Supreme Ct. 1967. Asst. U.S. atty. so. dist. N.Y., 1950-53; asst. dist. atty. County of Bronx, N.Y., 1954-60; ptnr. Saxe, Bacon & O'Shea, N.Y.C., 1960-64; ptnr. Blinder, Steinhaus & Hochhauser, N.Y.C., 1965-73; judge N.Y. State Ct. Claims, N.Y.C., 1973-96; jud. hearing officer N.Y. State Supreme Ct., 1996—; asst. counsel N.Y.C. Bd. High Edn., 1953-54; research counsel N.Y. Commn. on the Law of Estates, 1965; assoc. counsel N.Y. Commn. Revision of Penal Law, 1966-70; asst. counsel N.Y. Commn. on Eminent Domain, 1970-73; rsch. asst. N.Y. Commn. State Ct. System, 1971-73. Mem. ABA, Internat. Bar Assn., N.Y. State Bar Assn., Assn. Bar City N.Y., N.Y. County Lawyers Assn., Am. Arbitration Assn. (mem. nat. panel arbitrators 1965-73). Assoc. editor: Am. Criminal Law Quarterly, 1968-70; mem. adv. bd. Am. Criminal Law Quarterly, 1969-70. Office: 115 Broadway New York NY 10006

BLINDER, JANET, art dealer; b. L.A., Sept. 21, 1953; d. Joseph and Margaret (Nadel) Weiss; m. Martin S. Blinder, Dec. 10, 1983. Founder Nationwide Baby Shops, Santa Monica, Calif., 1976-82; adminstr. Martin Lawrence Ltd. Editions, Van Nuys, Calif., 1982-90; art dealer L.A., 1990—. Mem. benefit com. AIDS Project L.A., 1988, prin. sponsor ann. fundraiser, 1990; mem. benefit com. Art Against AIDS, L.A., 1989; patron, sponsor Maryvale Orphanage, Rosemead, Calif., 1984—; patron Scottsdale Ctr. for the Arts. Recipient Commendation for Philanthropic Efforts City of L.A. Mayor Tom Bradley, 1988. Mem. Mus. Modern Art, Whitney Mus. Am. Art, Guggenheim Mus., Palm Springs (Calif.) Mus. Art, Mus. of Contemporary Art, Scottsdale (Ariz.) Ctr. for the Arts.

BLINDER, MARTIN S., business consultant, art dealer; b. Bklyn., Nov. 18, 1946; s. Meyer and Lillian (Stein) B.; m. Janet Weiss, Dec. 10, 1983. BBA, Adelphi U., 1968. Account exec. Bruns, Nordeman & Co., N.Y.C., 1968-69; v.p. Blinder, Robinson & Co., Westbury, N.Y., 1969-73; treas. BHB Prodns., L.A., 1973-76; pres. Martin Lawrence Ltd. Edits., Van Nuys, Calif., 1976-94, chmn., 1986-94, bd. dirs., 1994—; pres., dir. Corp. Art Inc., Visual Artists Mgmt. Corp., Art Consultants Inc.; pres., owner, founder MSB Fine Art, Phoenix, 1994—; lectr. bus. symposia. Contbr. articles to mags. and newspapers; appeared on TV and radio. Mem. Dem. Nat. Com.; mem. benefit com. AIDS project, L.A., 1988; bd. dirs. Very Spl. Arts, 1989—, chmn. visual arts Internat. Very Spl. Arts Festival, 1989; patron Guggenheim Mus., N.Y.C., Mus. Modern Art, N.Y.C., L.A. County Mus. Art, L.A. Mus. Contemporary Art (hon. founder), Whitney Mus. Am. Art, Palm Springs Mus. Art, Hirschhorn Mus., Washington, Skirball Mus., L.A., Diabetes Found. of City of Hope, B'nai B'rith Anti-Defamation League, Very Spl. Arts, Scottsdale (Ariz.) Ctr. for the Arts, Scottsdale Mus. Contempory Art; mem. Citizens for Common Sense; bd. dirs., pres. Rsch. Found. for Crohns Disease; mem. benefit com. Art Against AIDS, 1989; co-chair artists com. for Don't Bungle the Jungle Companions of Arts and Nature, 1989; prin. sponsor, ann. fundraiser AIDS Project, L.A., 1990. Read into Congl. Record, 1981, 83, 86, 88, 91; recipient resolution of commendation L.A. City Coun., 1983, State of Calif. resolution for contbn. to arts in Calif., 1983, Merit award Republic Haiti for contbn. to arts, 1985, U.S. Senate commendation, 1983, County of L.A. Bd. Suprs. resolution for contbn. to arts in So. Calif., 1983, Gov. of R.I. resolution for contbns. to arts, 1985, commendation County of Los Angeles-Supr. Ed Edelman, 1991, commendation for contbns. to the arts and the healing arts City of L.A., 1991, commendation for contbns. to arts and philanthropy Mayor David Dinkins, N.Y.C., 1992; Nov. 18, 1985 declared Martin S. Blinder Day in L.A. in his honor by Mayor Tom Bradley, spl. award San Diego Youth and Cmty. Svcs., Bruin Bear award for helping to establish Blinder Rsch. Found., 1994. Mem. Fine Art Pub.'s Assn. (bd. dirs. 1990-94), Med. Art Assn. at UCLA.UCLA. Office: MSB Fine Art 9135 N 70th St Scottsdale AZ 85253-1961

BLINDER, RICHARD LEWIS, architect; b. N.Y.C., June 14, 1935; s. Maxwell E. and Mona (Wittlin) B.; m. Ellen Rifkind, June 18, 1958; children—Michael, Karen. B.S. in Architecture, U. Cin., 1959; M.Arch., Harvard U., 1960. Registered architect, N.Y., N.J., Fla., D.C., Md. Designer Bellevue Hosp. Project, N.Y.C., 1961-64; project architect Victor Gruen, Architect, N.Y.C., 1964-66, assoc., 1966-68; ptnr. Beyer Blinder Belle, N.Y.C., 1968—; trustee 7th Regiment Armory Conservancy, chmn. Fitch Charitable Trust, 1988—. Trustee Montclair Art Mus., 1993—; mem. Mcpl. Arts Soc., N.Y.C., 1975—, Montclair Bd. Adjustment, N.J., 1977-80; trustee Adult Sch. Montclair, 1979-82; chmn. Montclair Redevel. Agy., 1980-84. Recipient Preservation Honor award Nat. Trust for Hist. Preservation, 1980, Tucker award of excellence Bldg. Stone Inst., 1983, Bard award City Club N.Y., 1984, Disting. Achievement award B'nai Brith, 1988, Disting. Alumnus award U. Cin., 1991. Fellow AIA (Disting. Architecture award N.Y. chpt., Design award 1988, Honor award 1988, Presdl. Design award 1988, Nat. AIA Firm award 1995); mem. Real Estate Bd. N.Y. Inc. (zoning com.), Harvard Club (N.Y.C.). Home: 91 Lloyd Rd Montclair NJ 07042-1731 Office: Beyer Blinder Belle 41 E 11th St Fl 2 New York NY 10003-4673*

BLINDER, SEYMOUR MICHAEL, chemistry educator; b. N.Y.C., Mar. 11, 1932; s. Morris and Ida (Styszynskaya) B.; m. Frances Ellen Bryant, July 8, 1978; children: Michael Ian, Stephen Earl, Matthew Bryant, Amy Rebecca, Sarah Jane. A.B., Cornell U., 1953; M.A., Harvard U., 1955, Ph.D., 1958. Sr. physicist Applied Physics Lab., Johns Hopkins U., 1958-61; asst. prof. chemistry Carnegie Inst. Tech., 1961-62; vis. prof. Harvard U., 1962-63; prof. chemistry U. Mich., 1963—. Author: Advanced Physical Chemistry, 1969, Foundations of Quantum Dynamics, 1974; Mem. bd. editors: Jour. Am. Chem. Soc., 1978-80; contbr. research articles to profl. jours. Guggenheim fellow, 1965-66; NSF sr. postdoctoral fellow, 1970-71. Mem. AAAS, Am. Phys. Soc., Philos. Soc. Washington, Phi Beta Kappa. Home: 1240 Ferdon Rd Ann Arbor MI 48104-3635 Office: U Mich Dept Chemistry Ann Arbor MI 48109-1055

BLINKEN, DONALD, ambassador, investment banker; b. N.Y.C., Nov. 11, 1925; s. Maurice Henry and Ethel (Horowitz) B.; m. Vera Evans, Oct. 15, 1975; 1 child, Antony John. B.A. magna cum laude, Harvard U., 1947. Cons. Marks & Spencer, Ltd., London, 1950-51; pres. Exchange Trading Corp., N.Y.C., 1952-53; v.p. Stein's Stores, Inc., N.Y.C., 1953-58, E.M. Warburg & Co., Inc., 1961-72; sr. v.p., chmn. exec. com. E.M. Warburg, Pincus & Co., Inc., N.Y.C., 1970-81, mng. dir., 1981-86, dir., 1987-94; U.S. amb. Budapest, Hungary, 1994-97; mem. adv. com. on internat. econ. policy Dept. of State, 1998—. Author: Wooi Tariffs and American Policy, 1948; chmn. publ. com. Commentary, 1984-87. Co-chmn. Concerned Citizens for Arts N.Y. State, 1972-82; pres. Bklyn. Acad. Music, 1971-76, Mark Rothko Found., 1976-88; mem. trustees' council Nat. Gallery Art, 1984-94; trustee SUNY, 1976-90, chmn. bd., 1978-90; bd. dirs. N.Y. Philharmonic Soc., 1986-94, vice chmn. 1989-94; mem. U.S. 2d Circuit Nominating Panel, 1979; trustee Manville Personal Injury Settlement Trust, 1986-91; trustee N.Y. Pub. Libr., 1990-94; dir. Inst. Internat. Edn., 1990-94; trustee Isamu Noguchi Found., 1987-94; bd. overseers Nelson Rockefeller Inst. of Govt., 1985-94; chancellor Coun. of Cen. European U., 1998—; mem. adv. bd. Sch. Internat. and Pub. Affairs, Columbia U., 1998—. With USAAF, 1944-45. Mem. Century Assn. Club, River Club (N.Y.C.), Coun. Fgn. Rels., Coun. Am. Ambs. Home: 435 E 52nd St New York NY 10022-6445 Office: 466 Lexington Ave New York NY 10017-3140

BLINKEN, ROBERT JAMES, manufacturing and communications company executive; b. N.Y.C., Apr. 18, 1929; s. Maurice Henry and Ethel (Horowitz) B.; m. Jeanne Pagnucco, Mar. 5, 1955 (div. Jan. 1967); children: Robert James, Rachel; m. Allison Matsner, Dec. 14, 1967; children: Anna, Ingrid. Grad., Horace Mann Sch., N.Y.C., 1946; B.A. cum laude, Harvard U., 1950. Pres. Teleprinter Corp., Paramus, N.J., 1953-61; v.p. Mite Corp., New Haven, 1961-63, pres., 1963-75; chmn. Mite Corp., 1975-85, Comm. Network Enhancement, Mountainside, N.J., 1986—; trustee Jewish Assn. Svc. to Aged, Albright Inst. Archeol. Rsch. Served to 1st lt. USAF, 1950-53. Office: 230 Park Ave Fl 26 New York NY 10169-2699

BLINN, CYNTHIA LEES, middle school educator; b. Boston, Jan. 26, 1960; d. Wayne Lowry and Evelyn Elizabeth (Spencer) Lees; m. John Bayard Blinn, Oct. 18, 1958. BS in Edn., Lesley Coll., Cambridge, Mass., 1992; postgrad., Emerson Coll., Boston, 1993—. Lic. tchr., Mass. Ednl./writing program cons. Mass. Dept. Corrections, 1993-96; freelance writer/editor Am. Correctional Assn., Lanham, Md., 1995-97; gifted/talented program asst., writing tchr. Ottoson Mid. Sch., Arlington, Mass., 1993-96, 8th grade English lang. arts tchr., 1997—; book reviewer Voice of Youth Advocates Mag., Lanham, Md., 1994—; tchr. cons. Boston Writing Project, 1996—; ednl. tour cons. EF Ednl. Tours, Cambridge, Mass., 1995—. Author: ABLE MINDS: Using Literature to Transform Behavior, 1995, rev., 1998; editor: Maternal Ties: A Selection of Programs for Female Offenders, 1997; contbr. articles to profl. jours. Vol. writer, fundraiser AIDS Action Com., Boston, 1985-95; vol. literacy tutor Harvard Adult Lit. Initiative, Greater Boston area, 1988-92, Laubach Lit. Internat., 1983-85; host family for inner city youth The Fresh Air Fund, N.Y.C., 1995-96, rep. Mass. Tchrs. Assn., 1997—; vol. mentor Just A Start House, 1998—. Boston Writing Project grantee, 1996. Mem. NEA, Correctional Ednl. Assn., Educators for Social Responsibility, Nat. Writers Union, Am. Correctional Assn., Mass. Tchrs. Assn., Found. for Children's Books, Tchrs. and Writers Collaborative. Home: 27 Bryant St Woburn MA 01801-5621 Office: Ottoson Middle Sch 63 Acton St Arlington MA 02476-6012

BLINN, JOHN ROBERT, secondary school educator; b. Apr. 8, 1946. BS in Journalism, Bowling Green U., 1968, BS in Edn., 1970; MA in Journalism, Ohio State U., 1969; PhD in Mass Comm., Ohio U., 1982. Tchr. English, journalism Toledo (Ohio) Pub. Schs.; publs. advisor, 1970—. Address: 525 N Summit St Bowling Green OH 43402-2037

BLISH, EUGENE SYLVESTER, trade association administrator; b. Denver, Oct. 9, 1912; s. George Joseph and Lillian Lenox (O'Neill) B.; m. Susan M. Monti, Feb. 21, 1950; children: Eugene A., Mary, Susan Blish Clarke, Julia Blish Gordon. BSC, U. Notre Dame, 1934. Advt. dir. Colo. Milling and Elevator Co., Denver, 1934-45; advt. and mktg. cons., Denver, 1945-57; asst. exec. dir. Am. Sheep Producers Council, Denver, 1957-74; merchandising rep. Nat. Potato Bd., Denver, 1974-87. Mem. alumni bd. dirs. U. Notre Dame, 1947-49. Mem. Soc. Mayflower Desc., Barnstable Hist. Soc. (Mass.). Clubs: Denver Athletic, Mt. Vernon Country, Denver Notre Dame. Home and Office: 1370 Madison St Denver CO 80206-2613

BLISH, JOHN HARWOOD, lawyer; b. Racine, Wis., May 9, 1937; s. Wesley Wainwright and Lois Margaret (Jensen) B.; m. Edith Josephine Smith, Aug. 5, 1961; children: Geoffrey Harwood, Catherine Elizabeth. AB, Brown U., 1959; JD, U. Mich., 1965. Bar: R.I. 1965, U.S. Dist. Ct. R.I. 1967, U.S. Ct. Appeals (1st cir.) 1973, U.S. Ct. Appeals (Fed. cir.) 1985. Assoc. Edwards & Angell, Providence, 1965-73, ptnr., 1973-86, Blish & Cavanagh, Providence, 1986—. Bd. overseers Moses Brown Sch., Providence, 1978-81; bd. dirs., past pres. Sophia Little Home, Cranston, R.I.; trustee, past pres. Providence Country Day Sch., East Providence, R.I. Served to lt. j.g. USN, 1959-62. Fellow Am. Coll. Trial Lawyers; mem. R.I. Bar Assn., ABA, Am. Judicature Soc., Assoc. Alumni Brown U. (past bd. dirs., sec.), Univ. Club (trustee, past pres.), Brown of R.I. Club (trustee, past pres., Providence), Acoaxet Club (Westport, Mass.), Order of Coif, Phi Delta Phi. Home: 66 Catlin Ave Rumford RI 02916-2329 Office: Blish & Cavanagh 30 Exchange Ter Ste 8 Providence RI 02903-1765

BLISS, DONALD TIFFANY, JR., lawyer; b. Norwalk, Conn., Nov. 24, 1941; s. Donald Tiffany and Marina (Popova) B.; m. Nancy Arnold, Sept. 14, 1974; children: Evan Hale, Bion Northam. J.D., Harvard U., 1966. Bar: N.Y. 1969, D.C. 1971, U.S. Dist. Ct. D.C. 1975, U.S. Ct. appeals (D.C. cir.) 1971, 84, U.S. Supreme Ct. 1975. Peace Corps atty. Micronesia, 1966-67; legis. counsel Congress of Micronesia, 1968; cons. judiciary Am. Samoa, 1968; assoc. firm LeBoeuf, Lamb, Leiby & McCrae, N.Y.C., 1969; asst. to sec. HEW, 1969-72; spl. asst. to adminstr. EPA, 1972-73; exec. sec. AID, 1973-74; dep. gen. counsel U.S. Dept. Transp., 1975-77, acting gen. counsel, 1976-77; ptnr. firm O'Melveny & Myers, Washington, 1979—; mem. Maritime Adv. Com., 1984-85; pres. Harvard Law Sch. Assn. D.C., 1985-86; chmn. Transp. Sect. FBA, 1987-90; mem. interior task force Grace Commn.; nat. pres. The Ripon Soc. Recipient spl. citation HEW, 1972, 73; Pres.'s Cert. Exec. Mgmt., 1973; Superior Achievement award Dept. Transp., 1976; trustee Studio Theatre, Landon Sch. (ex-officio), Arts for the Aging (1st v.p.); pres. Dara's Canine Found., Inc. Mem. ABA (gov. com. air and space forum), Fed. Bar Assn., D.C. Bar Assn. (co-chmn. sect. adminstrv. law and agy. practice, 1988-90), Harvard Club, City Club D.C, Chevy Chase Club. Author: Drug Testing and Federal Employees: Lessons from the Transportation Experience, 1988, Economic Deregulation and Safety: Are They Compatible, 1989, A Challenge to U.S. Aviation Leadership: Launching the New Era of Global Aviation, 1991, Supreme Court Preemption Analysis: Differentiating the Hamiltonians and Jeffersonians, 1993. Home: 6732 Newbold Dr Bethesda MD 20817-2223 Office: O'Melveny & Myers 555 13th St NW Ste 500W Washington DC 20004-1159

BLISS, KATHERINE ELAINE, Latin American history educator; b. Dallas, Aug. 26, 1968; d. Robert Harms and Juliee Dixie (Fuselier) B. AB in History, Harvard-Radcliffe Coll., Cambridge, 1990; AM in History, Harvard U., 1990; PhD in History, U. Chgo., 1996. Lectr. U. Chgo., 1995; asst. prof. U. Mass., Amherst, 1996—. Interviewer Harvard Club Schs. Comm., Chgo., 1993-96; vol. Centro Edn. y Cultura, Chgo., 1993, Clínica Infantil, Ticumán, Marelos, Mex., 1994. Jacob K. Javits fellow U.S. Dept. Edn., 1990-95, Dissertation fellow Mellon Found., 1995-96. Mem. Am. Hist. Assn., L.Am. Studies Assn., Cong. L.Am. History, Phi Beta Kappa. Avocations: backpacking, oil painting, creative writing, cooking. Office: U Mass Dept History Herter Hall Amherst MA 01003

BLISS, LEE, English language educator; b. Buffalo, Aug. 9, 1943; d. Charles Perry and Louise (Ramseyer) B. PhD, U. Calif., Berkeley. Asst. prof. U. Calif., Santa Barbara, 1977-82, prof., 1988—; vis. asst. prof. Scrips Coll., Pomona, Calif., 1972-73; part time lectr. UCLA, 1973-75; vis. assoc. prof. Claremont Grad. Sch., Pomona, 1980. Author: The World's Perspective, 1983, Francis Beaumont, 1987. Summer fellow NEH, 1974, Folger fellow, 1992-93. Mem. MLA, Renaissance Soc. Am., Shakespeare Assn. Am., Malone Soc. Office: U Calif Dept English Santa Barbara CA 93106

BLISS, MARIAN ALICE, information systems professional; b. Burlington, Wis., Feb. 15, 1943; d. Charles Homer and Mabel Alice (Mantz) Jackson; m. Robert L. McDill, Feb. 13, 1965 (div.); children: Kimberly Ann, Scott Daniel; m. Erlan Shelly Bliss, Nov. 17, 1982. BA, U. Colo., 1965; MBA, Golden Gate U., 1985; MS in Systems Mgmt., U. Denver, 1991. Cert. Inst. for Cert. Computer Profls.; cert. Project Mgmt. Inst., project mgmt. profl. Cardiopulmonary technician Rancho Los Amigos Hosp., Downey, Calif., 1965-66; cardiology technologist William Beaumont Hosp., Royal Oak, Mich., 1966-67; pulmonary technologist Dallas County Hosps., 1967-68; with Pacific Bell, 1980-96, account exec., 1985; sys. design analyst Pacific Bell, San Ramon, Calif., 1986, staff analyst, 1988-90, sr. systems analyst, 1988-90, mgr. software configuration mgmt., 1990-92; graphical user interface devel. Pacific Bell, 1993, info. sys. project mgr. on line text retrieval, 1994, project mgr. phase 1 data warehouse, 1995, project mgr. strategic sys. engring., 1996—; Y2K program mgmt., software devel. & implementation cons. Interim Tech., 1997—. Treas. Greenbrook Sch. PTA, Danville, 1978, pres., 1979. Mem. AAUW. Episcopalian. Avocations: golf, bridge, photography. Home: 357 Conway Dr Danville CA 94526-5511 Office: 444 Market St Ste 760 San Francisco CA 94111-5327

BLISS, ROBERT HARMS, lawyer; b. Paris, Tex., Nov. 20, 1940; s. Jack Edward and Ruth Eugenia (Harms) B.; m. Juliee Dixie Fuselier, Dec. 29, 1964; 1 child, Katherine Elaine. B.A., U. Colo., 1964; J.D., U. Tex., 1967. Bar: Tex. 1967; cert. civil trial specialist, mediator-arbitrator, spl. master. Since practiced in Dallas; assoc. Johnson, Bromberg, Leeds & Riggs, 1967-72; ptnr. Bliss, Danner & Bishop, 1972-74; individual practice, 1974; pres. Bliss & Hughes, P.C., Dallas, 1978-88; pvt. practice Robert Harms Bliss P.C., 1988-98; mem. faculty advanced real estate law State Bar Tex., 1985, 92-93, 95, 97; ptnr. Glast, Phillips & Murray, PC, 1998—; mem. faculty CLE series So. Meth. U. Sch. Law, Dallas, 1989, 92, 94, 97, 98, 99; mem. faculty Mortgage Lending Inst., U. Tex. Sch. Law, 1994, 97, 98, 99. Contbr. articles to profl. jours. Bd. dirs. Dallas Symphony Orch. Guild, Dallas Classic Guitar Soc.; mem. Gov.'s Task Force on Immigration, 1983-84, Tex. Real Estate Commn., 1983-87; adv. bd. Tex. Real Estate Rsch. Ctr., Tex. A&M U., 1985-87; ch. adv. Episcopal Diocese Dallas. Mem. ABA, State Bar Tex. (adv. coun. real estate, probate and trust sect.), Dallas Bar Assn. (past chmn. real property sect.), Tex. Coll. Real Estate Attys. (bd. dirs.), Assn. Atty.-Mediators (pres.), Soc. Profls. in Dispute Resolution, U. Tex. Teaching Quiz-Masters Assn., Phi Delta Phi. Home: 29 Ashton Ct Dallas TX 75230-1977 Office: 13355 Noll Rd LB 48 2200 One Galleria Tower Dallas TX 75240-6657

BLISS, RONALD GLENN, lawyer; b. Buckeye, Ariz., Mar. 22, 1943; s. Glenn Francis Bliss and Jessie Marie (Waymire) Harrington; m. Charlene Wallace, Sept. 18, 1965; children: Erik, Jason. BS, USAF Acad., 1964; JD, Baylor U., 1976. Bar: Tex. 1976, U.S. Dist. Ct. (so. dist.) Tex. 1977, (no. dist.) Tex. 1981, (we. dist.) Tex. 1985, U.S. Ct. Appeals (5th cir.) 1979, (11th cir.) 1982, (D.C. cir.) 1982, U.S. Supreme Ct. 1980. Capt., fighter pilot USAF, U.S., Vietnam, 1964-74; prisoner of war Vietnam, 1966-73; assoc. Fulbright & Jaworski, Houston, 1976-84, ptnr., 1984—; mem. adv. com. So. Dist. Tex., 1992; chmn. Tex. Aerospace Commn., 1995-96. Contbr. to profl. jours. Pres. Norchester Club Inc., 1980; bd. dirs. Athletic Club Houston, 1984-85; bd. govs. Houston Center Club, 1987—, cert. mediator. Mem. ABA, Tex. Bar Assn., Am. Intellectual Property Law Assn., Houston Intellectual Property Law Assn., Licensing Exec. Soc., 4th Allied POW Wing. Office: Fulbright & Jaworski LLP 1301 Mckinney St Ste 5100 Houston TX 77010-3031*

BLISS, WILLIAM STANLEY, JR., corporate financial and marketing consultant; b. Evanston, Ill., Aug. 23, 1932; s. William S. and Virginia B.; m. Beverly Jean Bailer, June 27, 1959; children: William Bailer, Susan Blair. B.S. in Physics, Miami U., Oxford, Ohio, 1954; M.B.A., Harvard U., 1961. With Leeds & Northrup Co., North Wales, Pa., 1965-79; mfg. dir. Leeds & Northrup Co., North Wales, 1972-75, dir. indsl. relations, 1975-79; pres. Wollard Airport Equipment, Inc., Miami, Fla., 1980-94; mktg. cons., 1994—. Pres. North Pa. United Way, Lansdale, 1976-79, v.p., 1973-76; vestryman Ch. of the Messiah, Gwynedd, Pa., 1974-80; bd. dirs. Jubilee Ctr. South Broward, Inc., 1998—. Served to lt. USN, 1954-59. Mem. Theta Chi (pres.). Republican. Episcopalian.

BLISSETT, WILLIAM FRANK, English literature educator; b. East End, Sask., Can., Oct. 11, 1921; s. Ralph Richardson and Gladys (Jones) B. BA, U. B.C., 1943; MA, U. Toronto 1946, PhD, 1950. Lectr dept. English U. Toronto, 1946-50, prof. English, 1965-87, prof. emeritus, 1987; assoc. prof. dept. English U. Sask., 1950-57, prof., 1957-60; prof., head dept. English Huron Coll., London, Ont., 1960-65. Author: The Long Conversation, 1981; editor: Editing Illustrated Books, 1980; editor U. Toronto Quar., 1965-76; adv. bd.: Ency. of Shakespeare and Music, 1991, Chesterton Rev., 1984—; co-editor: Spenser Ency., 1982-90; joint editor: A Celebration of Ben Jonson, 1974; subject of book: Craft and Tradition: Essays in Honour of William Blissett, 1990. Huron Coll. hon. fellow, 1966; Royal Soc. Can. fellow, 1979. Mem. Internat. Assn. Univ. Profs. English, Renaissance Soc. Am., David Jones Soc. Anglican. Home: 36 Castle Frank Rd Apt 212, Toronto, ON Canada M4W 2Z7 Office: Univ Coll, Univ Toronto, Toronto, ON Canada M5S 1A1

BLISSITT, PATRICIA ANN, nurse; b. Knoxville, Tenn., Sept. 23, 1953; d. Dewitt Talmadge and Imogene (Bailey) B. BSN with high honors, U. Tenn., 1976, MSN, 1985; postgrad., U. Wash., 1996—. RN; cert. in case mgmt.; cert. trauma nurse core course, ACLS, pediat. advanced life support. Staff nurse neurosci. unit City of Memphis Hosp., 1976-78, head nurse neurosci. unit, 1978-79; physician's asst. Dr. John D. Wilson, Columbus, Miss., 1979-81; staff nurse med.-surg.-trauma ICU U. Tenn. Meml. Hosp., Knoxville, 1982-83; staff nurse neurosci. ICU Bapt. Meml. Hosp., Memphis, 1985-86, clin. nurse specialist neurosci., 1986-94, trauma coord., 1991-93, neuro case mgr., 1993-94; staff nurse neurosurg. ICU Harborview Med. Ctr., Seattle, 1994—; nurse cons. neurosci. VA Hosp., Memphis, 1986; mem. adv. com. Tenn. Bd. Nursing Practice. Author: (with others) Critical Care Nursing in Clinics of North America, 1990, Jour. Neurosci. Nursing, 1986, 92, 96, Guidelines for Critical Care Nursing; abstractor: Nursing SCAN in Critical Care, 1995—; contbr. articles to sci. jour., chpt. to book; mem. editl. cons. bd. Focus on Critical Care, 1990-92. WSNF, WSNA scholar, 1998, AANN scholar, 1999. Mem. ANA (mem. coun. med.-surg. nurses, mem. coun. clin. nurse specialists), Am. Assn. Neurosci. Nurses (cert. neurosci. nurse, pres. local chpt. 1989-90, treas. local chpt. 1987-89, mem. neurosci. nursing test devel. com. Am. Bd. Neurosci. Nursing 1996—, nat. lectr., mem. and chair resource devel. com., mem. continuing edn./ann. sci. program com., program/seminar chairperson local chpt. 1990-93, mem. nurse practice com., chairperson patient edn. project 1991-92, mem. program/seminar com., program/seminar chairperson mid-South chpt. 1990-93, chairperson nat. resource devel. com. 1992-94, pres. local chpt. 1995-98, editor local chpt. newsletter 1998—), AACN (life, cert. critical care nurse, lectr., mem. CCRN corp. exam. devel. com. 1989-92, NTI spkr. 1992, editl. cons. bd. 1990-92, pres.-elect Greater Memphis area chpt. 1989-90, pres. 1990-91, immediate past pres., chairperson nat. critical care awareness week 1990-93, chpt. cons. Region II 1991-93, chpt of yr. com. chairperson 1992-94, chairperson-elect Puget Sound chpt. program 1995-96, chairperson program com. 1996-97, editor elect newsletter Puget Sound chpt. 1997-98, mem. program com. 1997—, newsletter editor Puget Sound chpt. 1998-99, pres.-elect 1999—), Am. Assn. Spinal Cord Injury Nurses, Wash. Nurses Assn., Tenn. Nurses Assn. (mem. com. on practice 1992-93), Tenn. Nursing Congress (pres. 1990-94), Am. Assn. Neurol. Surgeons (assoc.), Western Inst. Nursing, Sigma Theta Tau. Methodist. Avocation: music. Home: 1105 Spring St Apt 405 Seattle WA 98104-3514

BLITCH, RONALD BUCHANAN, architect; b. New Orleans, May 14, 1953; s. James Buchanan and Hilda Goodspeed (Mouledoux) B. BArch magna cum laude, U. Notre Dame, 1976. Lic. architect. Architect Blitch Architects, Inc., New Orleans, 1970—, pres., 1977—. Bd. dirs. St. Elizabeth's Home, New Orleans, 1982—; pres. adv. bd., 1989-90; bd. dirs. Holy Cross Sch., New Orleans, 1984—, pres. 1994; bd. regents Our Lady of the Holy Cross, 1993, East Jefferson Hosp. Found., Metairie, La., 1985—, chmn. 1989; Chmn. architects seletion bd. State of La., 1994; with La. State Bd. Archtl. Examiners, 1994. Prin. works include Vatican Pavilion 1984 World's Fair; contbr. articles to profl. jours. Recipient Exec. of Yr. award Greater New Orleans Exec. Assn., 1988, Living and Giving award Juvenile Diabetes Found., 1990, Vol. Activist award St. Elizabeth's Guild, 1993, Role Model award Young Leadership Coun., 1995. Mem. La. Architects Assn. (bd. dirs. 1979-83, pres. 1990, 93, honor award 1980, 84, 85, 86, 87, 88 honor award of excellence 1982, 84, 85, 86, 87), AIA (sec. New Orleans chpt. 1983-85, com. on architecture for health, design for aging com. 1990—, newsletter editor; nat. honor award 1984, 85, 93, 94, honor award of excellence 1985, 86), Nat. Council Archtl. Registration Bds., Acad. Architecture Health (v.p. design 1994), Am. Hosp. Assn., Am. Assn. Homes for Aging, Greater New Orleans Execs. Assn. (dir. 1978—), Notre Dame Club (pres. 1984-85), Mercedes Benz Club (bd. dirs. 1982-85), Serra (trustee 1984-85), Rotary (bd. dirs. 1988—), Met. Area Com., Tau Beta Pi, Tau Sigma Delta. Republican. Roman Catholic. Home: PO Box 665 Abita Springs LA 70420-0665 Office: Blitch/Knevel Architects Inc 757 Saint Charles Ave New Orleans LA 70130-3780*

BLITMAN, HOWARD NORTON, construction company executive; b. N.Y.C., Dec. 9, 1926; s. Charles H. and Anna (Palestine) B.; m. Maureen Lefcort-Winter, 1975. CE, Rensselaer Poly. Inst., 1950; MA, New Sch. Social Research, 1973. Registered profl. engr., N.Y., N.J., Conn., Mass., S.C. Field engr. Drier Structural Steel Co., N.Y., 1950-51; design engr. Blitman & Tischler, N.Y.C., 1952-60; project engr. Blitman Constrn. Corp., N.Y.C., 1960-61; coordinator Blitman Constrn. Corp., 1961-62, exec. v.p., 1962-69, pres., 1969-81; pres., dir. Blitman Bldg. Corp., 1981—; mem. housing com. State Constnl. Conv., 1968; mem. N.Y.C. Commn. Investigation Water Main Breaks. Mem. sch. bd. Mt. Pleasant Cottage Sch., Union Free Sch. Dist., Pleasantville, N.Y.; pres., bd. dirs. Jewish Child Care Assn. N.Y.; v.p. bd. dirs. Beth Israel Med. Ctr.; mem. coun. Rensselaer Poly. Inst.; chmn. archtl. rev. bd. Town of Scarsdale, N.Y., trustee 1989-93; trustee Village of Scarsdale, 1989, dep. mayor, 1992—; mem. Planning Bd. Scarsdale, 1994—, chmn., 1998—. 2d lt. Chem. Corps AUS, 1944-47; 1st lt., 1951-53. Recipient Norman Tishman Human Relations award, 1967. Mem. NSPE (chmn. profl. engrs. in constrn., pres. 1997, chmn. 1996-97; nat. treas. 1999—) ASCE, N.Y. State Soc. Profl. Engrs. (pres. 1978, pres. N.Y. chpt. 1974-75), ASME, Harmonie Club (N.Y.C.), Masons (N.Y.C.). Home: 3 Elmdorf Dr Scarsdale NY 10583-4203

BLITT, RITA LEA, artist; b. Kansas City, Mo., Sept. 7, 1931; d. Herman Stanley and Dorothy Edith (Sofnas) Copaken; m. Irwin Joseph Blitt, Apr. 18, 1951; 1 child, Chela Connie. *Rita Blitt's husband, Irwin Blitt, is a former vice president of the International Council of Shopping Centers and past president of the Jewish Community Campus of Kansas City which he helped found in 1986. Their daughter, Chela, is a free lance journalist, having co-produced Contragate/Undercurrents for Pacifica radio beginning in 1984, produced Zeroing In for KPFA radio, Berkeley, California, 1989, written many articles for newspapers and magazines, and produced the 1996 video Sisters and Daughters Betrayed: The Trafficking of Women. Chela is the mother of Dorianna Blitt, born in 1996.* Student, U. Ill., 1948-50; BA, Kansas City U., 1952; postgrad., Kansas City Art Inst., 1952-54. Freelance painter, sculptor Leawood, Kans., 1958—. *In 2000, Rita Blitt: Drawings, Paintings and Sculpture will be published in conjunction with a traveling exhibit which will include the showing of dancing hands: Visual Arts of Rita Blitt followed by a workshop which encourages everyone to "let their hands dance on paper with one hand or two".* Author: Nessie the Sculpture, 1978; collaborations with dancers and musicians such as dancer/choreographer David Parsons, 1996, and cellist Yehuda Hanani, 1986; creator of words and paintings for internat. distributed posters "Kindness is Contagious, Catch It!", led to the founding of the Kindness Program sponsored by The Stop Violence Coalition; One-woman exhbns. include Unitarian Gallery, Kansas City, Mo., 1965, Spectrum Gallery, N.Y.C., 1969, Angerer Gallery, Kansas City, Mo., 1974, Battle Creek (Mich.) Civic Art Ctr., 1975, Harkness Gallery, N.Y.C., 1977, Martin Schweig Gallery, St. Louis, 1977, Gargoyle Gallery, Aspen, Colo., 1978, Tumbling Waters Mus., Montgomery, Ala., 1978, St. Louis U., 1980, Leedy-Voulkos Gallery, Kansas City, Mo., 1987, Joy Horwich Gallery, Chgo., 1987, Goldman Gallery, Haifa, Israel, 1989, Bet Shmuel, Jerusalem, 1989, Goldman Kraft Gallery, Chgo., 1990, Singapore Nat. Mus., 1991, Albrecht-Kemper Mus., St. Joseph, Mo., 1991, Aspen (Colo.) Inst., 1992, Foothills Art Ctr., Golden, Colo., 1992, Mackey Gallery, Denver, 1992, U. Ill., Urbana, 1994, Kennedy Mus. U. Ohio, Athens, 1994, Krasl Art Ctr., St. Joseph, Mich., 1994, Baker U., Baldwin, Kans., 1995, Ctrl. Exch., Kansas City, Mo., 1995, Atchison (Kans.) Muchnik Gallery, 1996, Marines Meml. Theater, San Francisco, 1997, Resourceful Women, San Francisco, 1997, City Ctr., N.Y., 1998; group exhbns. include Kansas City (Mo.) Mus., 1959, Ringling Mus., Sarasota, Fla., 1967, Springfield (Mo.) Mus., 1967, Joslyn Mus., Omaha, 1972, Doug Drake Gallery, Kansas City, 1975, Conry Gallery, Kansas City, Mo., 1976, Cyvia Gallery, New Haven, 1977, Gargoyle Gallery, Aspen, Colo., 1979, Putney Gallery, Aspen, 1979, Carrefour Gallery, N.Y.C., 1979, Elaine Benson Gallery, Bridgehampton, N.Y., 1980, Tall Grass Fine Arts Gallery, Kansas City, Mo., 1980, 81, Art and Design Gallery, N.Y.C., 1982, Winter Manhattan (Kans.), Streker, Gallery, 1983, Joanne Lyons Gallery, Aspen, 1984, Banaker Gallery, 1987, 88, Andrea Ross Gallery, Santa Monica, Calif., 1990, LA 90, L.A., 1990, Eva Cohon, Chgo., 1995, Obere Galerie, Berlin, 1995, Din Deutsches Inst., Berlin, 1995, Dance Aspen, Colo., 1997; permanent collections include Albrecht-Kemper Mus., St. Joseph, Mo., Ga. Inst. Tech., JFK Libr., Cambridge, Mass., Kennedy Mus. Ohio U., Athens, Nat. Mus. Singapore, Skirball Mus., L.A., Spertus Mus., Chgo., Kansas City (Mo.) Children's Mus., Kennedy Mus., Ohio U., Ga. Tech. Ctr. for the Arts, and other numerous pvt. and pub. collections; sculptures in numerous pub. places including, Calif., Ill., Kans., Mo., Md., N.J., N.Y., Japan, Singapore. Mem. Soc. Fellow The Nelson Gallery Found., The Aspen Inst.; bd. dirs. Trio Found.; mem. The Stop Violence Coalition; rsch. assoc. The Internat. Rsch. on Jewish Women. Mem. Internat. Sculpture Ctr., Kansas City Artists Coalition. Avocations: music, dance, travel, hiking.

BLITZ, STEPHEN M., lawyer; b. N.Y.C., July 29, 1941; s. Leo and Dorothy B.; m. Ellen Sue Mintzer, Sept. 23, 1962; children: Catherine Denise, Thomas Joseph. B.A., Columbia U., 1962, B.S. in Elec. Engring., 1963; LL.B., Stanford U., 1966. Bar: Calif. 1967, U.S. Dist. Ct. (cen. dist.) Calif. 1967, Colo. 1996. Law clk. to judge U.S. Dist. Ct. Central Dist. Calif., 1966-67; ptnr. Gibson, Dunn & Crutcher, L.A., 1967-96, Denver, 1996—; adj. prof. law U. West Los Angeles Sch. Law, 1978-80, dir. pub. counsel, 1981-83, 94-96. Mem. ABA, L.A. County Bar Assn. (exec. com. 1986-96, chmn. 1994-95, real property sect.), Order of Coif. Office: Gibson Dunn & Crutcher 1801 California St Ste 4100 Denver CO 80202-2641

BLITZER, CHARLES, educational administrator; b. N.Y.C., Aug. 10, 1927; s. Max and Grace (Rosenberg) B. AB, Williams Coll., 1947; MA, Harvard U., 1949, PhD, 1952; LLD (hon.), Smith Coll., 1989. Instr. polit. sci. Yale U., 1950-54, asst. prof., 1954-60; exec. assoc. Am. Council Learned Socs., N.Y.C., 1960-65; dir. edn. Smithsonian Instn., Washington, 1965-68, asst. sec. for history and art, 1968-83; pres., dir. Nat. Humanities Ctr., Research Triangle Park, N.C., 1983-88; dir. Woodrow Wilson Internat. Ctr. for Scholars, Washington, 1988-97, dir. emeritus, 1997—; lectr. New Sch. for Social Rsch., N.Y.C., 1960-61; vis. prof. CUNY, 1964-65; adv. bd. Ctr. for Electronic Texts in the Humanities, 1991—; bd. trustees Archives Am. Art, 1988—. Author: (with C.J. Friedrich) The Age of Power, 1957, An Immortal Commonwealth, 1960, The Age of Kings, 1967. Staff dir. Nat. Commn. on Humanities, 1963-64; mem. adminstrv. com. for Dumbarton Oaks, Harvard, 1968-75, mem. adv. bd., 1975-85, chmn., 1978-85; mem. Indo-U.S. Sub-Commn. on Edn. and Culture, 1974-96, chmn., 1989-92; mem. vis. com. Rsch. Ctr. Linguistics and Semiotic Studies, Ind. U., 1980-86, 90—; mem. vis. scholar com. Phi Beta Kappa, 1979-90, mem. senate, 1982-91, 97—, v.p., 1991-94, pres., 1994-97; alderman City of New Haven, 1955-60; bd. dirs. Ctrl. Atlantic Regional Edn. Lab., 1966-68; chmn. Coun. Internat. Exch. Scholars, 1972-78, mem., 1978-81; mem. nat. adv. bd. Libr. of Congress Ctr. for the Book, 1983—; trustee Exploratorium, 1977-90, hon. trustee, 1990—; trustee Smith Coll., 1979-89, Hartwick Coll., 1998—, Asian Cultural Coun., 1984-91, Hirshhorn Mus. and Sculpture Garden, Smithsonian Instn., 1982-89, Am. Acad. for Liberal Edn., 1996—; bd. visitors Duke U. Press, 1986, Wake Forest U., 1984-87; mem. vis. com. Sackler Gallery, Smithsonian Instn., 1985-94, chmn., 1989-94; bd. dirs. Coun. Basic Edn., 1989-94, Am. Philos. Soc., 1988—, U.S.-New Zealand Coun., 1992—; mem. Am. adv. bd. U. London, 1993—; mem. acad. com. U.S. Holocaust Meml. Mus., 1980—, chmn. publs. subcom., 1993—. Rockefeller Found. fellow, 1955-56; Huntington Library research grantee, 1957. Mem. Cosmos Club, Century Club (N.Y.C.). Home: 617 A St NE Washington DC 20002-6029

BLITZER, JUDI RAPPOPORT, bank executive; b. N.Y.C., Feb. 24, 1949; d. Murray Benjamin and Jeannette (Srebnick) Rappoport; m. David Mayers Blitzer, June 8, 1973; children: Mark Rappoport Blitzer, Julie Rappoport Blitzer. BA in Polit. Sci., Brown U., 1970. Mng. dir., head corp. mergers and aquisitions The Chase Manhattan Bank, N.Y.C., 1970—. Mem. benefit com. Paper Bag Players, N.Y.C., 1988—. Home: 320 West End Ave New York NY 10023 Office: The Chase Manhattan Bank 270 Park Ave 28th Fl New York NY 10017

BLITZ-WEISZ, SALLY, speech pathologist; b. Buffalo, Nov. 9, 1954; d. Isaac and Paula (Goldstein) Blitz; m. Andrew Weisz, Dec. 16, 1984; 1 child, Naomi Ariel Weisz. BA in Speech Pathology, Audiology, SUNY, Buffalo, 1976, MA in Speech Pathology, 1978; MS Sch Counseling, pupil pers credential, U. LaVerne, 1991. Lic. speech/lang. pathologist, Calif. Speech, lang. pathologist Lang. Devel. Program, Tonawanda, N.Y., 1978-82, Bailey and Drown Assocs., La Habra, Calif., 1982-83; speech, lang. specialist, cons. Pasadena (Calif.) Unified Schs., 1983-94, L.A. Unified Schs., 1996—. Active Anti-Defamation League, San Fernando Valley, 1985-86; mem. 2d Generation Holocaust Survivors, Los Angeles, 1986—. Recipient Excellence in Studies award Temple Shaarey Zedek, Buffalo, 1968. Mem. Am. Speech-Lang.-Hearing Assn. Democrat. Club: Jewish Young Adults. Lodge: B'nai Brith. Avocations: exercise workouts, bicycling. Home: 11671 Amigo Ave Northridge CA 91326-1849 Office: L A Unified Sch Dist Mid City-SESU Los Angeles CA 90051

BLIVEN, BRUCE, JR., writer; b. L.A., Jan. 31, 1916; s. Bruce and Rose (Emery) B.; m. Naomi Horowitz, May 26, 1950; 1 son, Frederic Bruce. AB, Harvard U., 1937. Reporter Manchester (Eng.) Guardian, 1936, corr., 1940-42; editorial asst. New Republic mag., 1937-38; editorial writer N.Y. Post, 1939-42; contbr. New Yorker (other nat. mags.), 1946—; tchr. Writers Conf. Ind. U., 1955, 66. Author: The Wonderful Writing Machine, 1954, Battle for Manhattan, 1956, Under the Guns, 1972, Book Traveller, 1975, Volunteers, One and All, 1976, The Finishing Touch, 1978, New York: A Bicentennial History, 1981, (juveniles) The Story of D-Day, 1956, 50th anniversary edit., 1994, The American Revolution, 1958, From Pearl Harbor to Okinawa, 1960, From Casablanca to Berlin, 1965, (with Naomi Bliven) New York: The Story of the World's Most Exciting City, 1969. Pvt. to capt. F.A. AUS, 1942-45. Decorated Bronze Star with oak leaf cluster. Mem. Authors Guild, P.E.N., Soc. Am. Historians, Century Assn. Office: care The New Yorker 20 W 43rd St New York NY 10036-7400

BLIVEN, NAOMI, book reviewer; b. N.Y.C., Dec. 28, 1925; d. Frederic and Minnie (Goodfriend) Horowitz; m. Bruce Bliven, Jr., May 26, 1950; 1 son, Frederic Bruce. A.B., Hunter Coll., 1945. Mem. editorial staff New Republic, 1945-47, Random House, 1949-54; book reviewer New Yorker mag., 1958—. Author: On Her Own, 1989, (with Bruce Bliven, Jr.) New York: The Story of the World's Most Exciting City, 1969. Mem. P.E.N. (exec. bd.), The Authors Guild, Phi Beta Kappa. Office: care The New Yorker 20 W 43rd St New York NY 10036-7400

BLIZNAKOV, EMILE GEORGE, biomedical research scientist; b. Kamen, Bulgaria, July 28, 1926; came to U.S., 1961, naturalized, 1966; s. George P. and Paraskeva B. MD, Faculty of Medicine, Sofia, Bulgaria, 1953. Dir. Regional Sta. for Hygiene and Epidemiology; chief dist. dept. health Pirdop, Bulgaria, 1953-55; staff scientist, microbiologist Rsch. Inst. for Epidemiology and Microbiology, Ministry Health, Sofia, 1955-59; vis. scientist Gamaleya Research Inst. Epidemiology and Microbiology, Acad. Med. Scis., Moscow, 1958-59; sr. staff scientist, prof. life scis. New Eng. Inst., Ridgefield, Conn., 1961-81; dir. personnel New Eng. Inst., 1968-74, v.p., 1974-76, pres., 1976-81; exec. dir. research and devel. Libra Research, Rockville, Md., 1981-83; pres., sci. dir. Lupus Rsch. Inst., Rockville, Md., Ridgefield, Conn., 1981-88; biomed. rsch. cons., 1988—; cons. to indsl., pharm. pub., and pub. rels. firms in U.S., Europe and Japan; lectr. in fields. Author med. books; contbr. articles to profl. jours.; patentee in fields. Fannie E. Rippel Found. grantee, 1972-80; G.M. McDonald Found. grantee, 1972-81; Whitehall Found. grantee, 1971-75; Wallace Genetic Found. grantee, 1972-81. Fellow Royal Soc. Tropical Medicine and Hygiene (London); mem. AMA, AAUP, AAAS, Inflammation Rsch. Assn. (USA), Internat. Soc. for Infectious Diseases, Internat. Soc. Chronobiology, Interam. Soc. Chemotherapy, Am. Fedn. Clin. Rsch., Am. Soc. Microbiology, Am. Coll. Toxicology, Am. Soc. Neurochemistry, Internat. Assn. Biomed. Gerontology, Am. Aging Assn., Reticuloendothelial Soc., Bioelectromagnetic Soc., N.Y. Acad. Scis. Home and Office: 2801 N Course Dr Apt H-205 Pompano Beach FL 33069-3061

BLIZNAKOV, MILKA TCHERNEVA, architect; b. Varna, Bulgaria, Sept. 20, 1927; came to U.S., 1961, naturalized, 1966; d Ivan Dimitrov and Maria Kesarova (Khorozova) Tchernev; m. Emile G. Bliznakov, Oct. 23, 1954 (div. Apr., 1974). Architect-engr. diploma, State Tech. U., Sofia, 1951; Ph.D., Engring.-Structural Inst., Sofia, 1959; Ph.D. in Architecture, Columbia U., 1971. Sr. researcher Ministry Heavy Industry, Sofia, 1950-53; pvt. practice architecture Sofia, 1954-59; assoc. architect Noel Combrisson, Paris, 1959-61; designer Perkins & Will Partnership, White Plains, N.Y., 1963-67; project architect Lathrop Douglass, N.Y.C., 1967-71; assoc. prof. architecture and planning Sch. Architecture, U. Tex., Austin, 1972-74; prof. Coll. Architecture, Va. Poly. Inst. and State U., Blacksburg, 1974—; prin. Blacksburg, 1975—; bd. dirs. founder Internat. Archives Women in Architecture, Va. Poly. Inst. and State U., The Parthena award, 1994. Prin. works include Speedwell Ave. Urban Renewal, Morristown, N.J., 1967-69, Wilmington (Del.) Urban Renewal, 1968-70, Springfield (Ill.) Ctrl. Area Devel., 1969-71, Arlington County (Va.) Redevel., 1975-77; author: (with others) Utopia e Modernitá, 1989, Reshaping Russian Architecture, 1990, Russian Housing in the Modern Age, 1993, Nietzsche and Soviet Culture, 1994, New Perspectives on Russian and Soviet Artistic Culture, 1994, Signs of Times, Culture and the Emblems of Apocalypse, 1998, Women Architects in Eastern Europe: The Contributions of the Bulgarians, 1997, International Archive of Women in Architecture, 1997. William Kinne scholar, summer 1970, vis. scholar Inst. Advanced Russian Studies, The Wilson Ctr. of Smithsonian Instn., 1988; NEA grantee, 1973-74, Am. Beautiful Found. grantee, 1973, Internat. Rsch. and Exch. Bd. grantee, 1984-93; Fulbright Hays rsch. fellow, 1983-84, 91, 99; recipient Parthend award, 1994. Mem. Internat. Archive Women in Architecture (founder, chair bd. dirs.), Am. Assn. Tchrs. Slavic and East European Langs., Soc. Archtl. Historians, Nat. Trust Hist. Preservation, Am. Assn. Advancement of Slavic Studies, Assn. Collegiate Schs. of Planning, Inst. Modern Russian Culture (chairperson architecture, co-founder, dir.), Assn. Collegiate Schs. of Architecture. Home: 2813 Tall Oaks Dr Blacksburg VA 24060-8109 Office: Coll Architecture Va Poly Inst And State Blacksburg VA 24061

BLIZZARD, ALAN, artist; b. Boston, Mar. 25, 1939; s. Thomas and Elizabeth B. Student, Mass. Coll. Art; M.A., U. Ariz.; M.F.A., U. Iowa, 1963. Instr. in art U. Iowa; vis. asst. prof. art Albion Coll., U. Okla.; asso. prof. UCLA; now prof. painting Scripps Coll. and; Claremont Grad. Sch. Represented in permanent collections Bklyn. Mus., Met. Mus. Art, N.Y.C., Art Inst. Chgo., Denver Art Mus., La Jolla (Calif.) Mus. Art, Ashland U., Columbia U., McGeorge Sch. Law, Pomona Coll., Sacramento State U., Pitzer Coll., Fluor Corp., Kouri Capital Corp., N.Y.C. Office: Scripps Coll Art Dept Claremont CA 91711

BLOBEL, GÜNTER, cell biologist, educator; b. Waltersdorf, Silesia, Germany, May 21, 1936. MD, U. Tübingen, Germany, 1960; PhD in Oncology, U. Wis., 1967. Intern Germany, 1960-62; fellow lab. cellular biology Rockefeller U., 1967-69; asst. prof. cell biology Rockefeller U., N.Y.C., 1969-73, assoc. prof., 1973-76, prof., 1976—; investigator Howard Hughes Med. Inst., 1986—; founder, pres. Friends of Dresden, Inc. Contbr. articles to profl. jours. and chpts. to books. Recipient Gairdner Found. award, 1982, Warburg medal German Biochem. Soc., 1983, Wilson medal Am. Soc. Cell Biology, 1986, U.D. Mattia award Roche Inst. Molecular Biology, 1986, Louisa Gross Horwitz prize Columbia U., 1987, Waterford Biomedical Sci. award, 1989, Albert Lasker Basic Med. Rsch. award, 1993, King Faisal internat. prize for sci., 1996, Mayor's award for Excellence in Sci. and Tech., 1997. Mem. Nat. Acad. Scis. (U.S. Steel award in molecular biology 1978, Richard Lounsbery award 1983), Am. Acad. Arts and Scis.,

Japan Biochem. Soc. (hon.), Am. Soc. Cell Biology (pres. 1990), German Soc. Cell Biology (hon.), Am. Philos. Soc., European Molecular Biol. ORgn. (assoc.). Office: Rockefeller U Cell Biology Lab 66th and York Ave New York NY 10021-6339

BLOCH, ALAN NEIL, federal judge; b. Pitts., Apr. 12, 1932; s. Gustave James and Molly Dorothy B.; m. Elaine Claire Amdur, Aug. 24, 1957; children: Rebecca Lee, Carolyn Jean, Evan Amdur. B.S. in Econs, U. Pa., 1953; J.D., U. Pitts., 1958. Bar: Pa. 1959. Indsl. engr. U.S. Steel Corp., 1953; practice law Pitts., 1959-79; judge U.S. Dist. Ct. (we. dist.) Pa., Pitts., 1979-96, sr. judge, 1997—; mem. Jud. Conf. U.S. Com. on Ct. Security, 1987—; chmn. joint task force on death penalty representation Supreme Ct. Pa.-Ct. Appeals; past mem. Rule 11 task force Ct. Appeals (3d cir.). Contbr. articles to legal publs. Vice chmn. Stadium Authority Pitts., 1970-80; bd. dirs. St. John's Gen. Hosp., Pitts., 1975-80. Served with AUS, 1953-55. Mem. Am. Bar Assn., Acad. Trial Lawyers Allegheny County, Phi Delta Phi. Jewish. Club: River. Office: US Dist Ct We Dist US Post Office and Courthouse 700 Grant St Rm 837 Pittsburgh PA 15219*

BLOCH, BOBBIE ANN, nurse, educator. BSN, Wayne State U., 1969; MSN, U. Calif. San Francisco, 1976; PhD in Curriculum and Instrn., U. Toledo, 1992. Asst. prof. nursing U. Mich. Sch. Nursing, Ann Arbor, 1976-82; edn. specialist Community Health Nursing U. Mich. Hosps. Ambulatory Care, Ann Arbor, 1982-83; asst. prof. nursing Gerontol. Nursing Dept., Med. Coll. Ohio Sch. Nursing, Toledo, 1983-85; dir. edn. and tng. Calvert Meml. Hosp., Prince Frederick, Md., 1993-95; dir. edn. Lorien Nursing and Rehab. Ctr., Columbia, Md., 1995-97, Hebrew Home Greater Washington, Rockville, Md., 1997-99, AIMM for Health, Hyattsville, Md., 1999—. Contbr. articles to profl. jours. Recipient Wash. State Nurses Assn. Cert. Recognition award for Outstanding Book, 1983, Am. Jour. Nursing Pub. Book of Yr. awards for Publication in 1983. Mem. ANA, ASTD, Md. Nurses Assn., Internat. Soc. Performance and Instrn., Nat. Nursing Staff Devel. Orgn., Sigma Theta Tau. Home: Apt 347 11140 Rockville Pike Rockville MD 20852

BLOCH, ERICH, retired electrical engineer, former science foundation administrator; b. Sulzburg, Germany, Jan. 9, 1925; came to U.S., 1948, naturalized, 1952; s. Joseph and Tony B.; m. Renee Stern, Mar. 4, 1948; 1 child, Rebecca Bloch Rosen. Student, Fed. Poly. Inst., Zurich, Switzerland, 1945-48; BSEE, U. Buffalo, 1952; hon. degrees, U. Mass., George Washington U., Colo. Sch. Mines, SUNY Buffalo, U. Rochester, Oberlin Coll., U. Notre Dame, Ohio State U., Rensselaer Poly. Inst., 1989, Washington Coll., 1989, CUNY, N.Y.C., 1991; hon. degree, Poly. U., Bklyn., N.Y., 1993. With IBM, 1952-84; v.p. gen. mgr. IBM, East Fishkill, N.Y., 1975-80; v.p. tech. personnel devel. IBM, Armonk, N.Y., 1980-84; mem. com. computers in automated mfg. NRC, 1980-84; dir. NSF, Washington, 1984-90; fellow Coun. on Competitiveness, 1990—; prin. Washington Adv. Group, 1998—; past vis. disting. prof. George Mason U.; bd. dirs. Motorola Inc., Convex Computers, Quality Edn. for Minorities Network, Telogy Network. Patentee in field. Recipient U.S. medal of tech., 1985, Computer World/Smithsonian award for innovation, 1991, Swedish Royal Order of the Polar Star, NAE Buche award statesmanship tech. Fellow IEEE (Founder's award 1990, Computer Pioneer awards 1993, 94), AAAS; mem.NAE (Arthur M. Bueche award 1997), Am. Soc. Mfg. Engrs. (hon., Eugene Merchant Mfg. medal ASME and Soc. Mfg. Engrs.), Am. Soc. Engring. Edn., Royal Swedish Acad. Engring. Scis., Japan Acad. Engring. E-mail: ebloch@theadvisorygroup.com.

BLOCH, FRANK SAMUEL, law educator; b. Jan. 16, 1945; s. Felix Jacob and Lore Clara (Misch) B.; m. Melissa Roth, Mar. 12, 1972; children: Julia Devi, Sara Shanti. BA, Brandeis U., 1966, MA, 1971, PhD, 1978; JD, Columbia U., 1969. Bar: Calif. 1970, Tenn. 1980, U.S. Dist. Ct. (no. dist.) Calif. 1971, U.S. Ct. Appeals (7th cir.) 1976, U.S. Dist. Ct. (mid. dist.) Tenn. 1980, U.S. Ct. Appeals (6th cir.) 1983. Assoc. atty. Calif. Rural Legal Assistance, Madera, Calif., 1971-72, directing atty., 1972-73; lectr. in law, clin. fellow U. Chgo., 1974-79; assoc. prof. law Vanderbilt U., Nashville, 1979-86, prof., 1986—, dir. clin. edn., 1979—; pres. Legal Svcs. of Mid. Tenn., Inc., 1991-92, 95-96; cons. Internat. Social Security Assn., 1993—; cons. Adminstrv. Conf. of U.S., 1988-93. Rsch. fellow Internat. Social Security Assn., 1992-93; Fulbright grantee, 1986. Mem. ABA, Nat. Acad. Social Ins., Nashville Bar Assn., Nat. Legal Aid and Defender Assn. Democrat. Jewish. Home: 1119 Park Ridge Dr Nashville TN 37215-4515 Office: Vanderbilt U Sch Law 131 21st Ave S Nashville TN 37203

BLOCH, HENRY WOLLMAN, tax preparation company executive; b. Kansas City, Mo., July 30, 1922; s. Leon Edwin and Hortense Bienenstok; m. Marion Ruth Helzberg, June 16, 1951; children: Robert, Thomas M., Mary Jo, Elizabeth Ann. BS, U. Mich., 1944; D of Bus. Adminstrn. (hon.), Avila Coll., Kansas City, Mo., 1977, U. Mo., Kansas City, 1989; LLD (hon.), N.H. Coll., 1983, William Jewell Coll., Liberty, Mo., 1990. Ptnr. United Bus. Co., 1946-55; chmn., past CEO H & R Block, Inc., Kansas City, 1955—, also dir.; bd. dirs. Commerce Bancshares, Inc., Kansas City, CompuServe, Inc., Valentine Radford Advt.; chmn. Midwest Rsch. Inst. Past trustee Clearinghouse for Midcontinent Founds.; past bd. dirs. Menorah Med. Ctr.; bd. dirs., past pres. Menorah Med. Ctr. Found.; former mem. pres.'s adv. coun. Kansas City Philharmonic Assn.; chmn., dir. H & R Block Found.; pres. of trustees U. Kansas City, Nelson-Atkins Mus. Art, trustee, dir., past chmn. bus. coun.; former trustee Am. Mus. Assn.; past bd. dirs. Jewish Fedn. and Coun. Greater Kansas City; dir., past pres. Civic Coun. Greater Kansas City; gen. chmn. United Negro Colls. Fund, 1986; bd. dirs. St. Luke's Hosp., Internat. Rels. Coun., Kansas City Cmty. Found.; former mem. bd. dirs. Coun. of Fellows of Nelson Gallery Found., Am. Jewish Com.; former mem. bd. govs. Kansas City Mus. History and Sci.; bd. dirs. Midwest Rsch. Inst., vice chmn.; bd. dirs. Kansas City Symphony, past dir.; bd. dirs. Greater Kansas City Community Found.; gen. chmn. Heart of Am. United Way Exec. Com., 1978; past met. chmn. Nat. Alliance Businessmen; former mem. bd. regents Rockhurst Coll.; former mem. bd. chancellor's assocs. U. Kans. at Lawrence; former mem. bd. dirs. Harry S. Truman Good Neighbor Award Found.; bd. dirs. Internat. Rels. Coun.; bd. dirs., v.p. Kansas City Area Health Planning Coun.; past pres. Found. for a Greater Kansas City; dir. Mid-Am. Coalition on Health Care, St; Luke's Found.; trustee Jr. Achievement of Mid-Am.; vice chmn. corp. fund Kennedy Ctr. 1st lt. USAAF, 1943-45. Decorated Air medal with 3 oak leaf clusters; named Mktg. Man of Yr. Sales and Mktg. Execs. Club, 1971, Chief Exec. Officer of Yr. for svc. industry Fin. World, 1976, Mainstreeter of Decade, 1988, Entrepreneur of Yr., 1986; recipient Disting. Exec. award Boy Scouts Am., 1977, Salesman of Yr. Kansas City Advt. Club, 1978, Civic Svc. award Hyman Brand Hebrew Acad., 1980, Golden Plate award Am. Acad. Achievement, 1980, Chancellor's medal U. Mo.-Kansas City, 1980, Pres.'s trophy Kansas City Jaycees, 1980, W.F. Yates medal for disting. svc. in civic affairs William Jewell Coll., 1981, bronze award for svc. industry Wall Street Transcript, 1981, Disting. Missourian award NCCJ, 1982, Lester A. Milgram Humanitarian award, 1983, Hall of Fame award Internat. Franchise Assn., 1983; named to Bus. Leader Hall of Fame Jr. Achievement, 1980; honoree Sales and Mktg. Execs. Internat. Acad. of Achievement, 1991. Mem. Greater Kansas City C. of C. (past pres.), C. of C. Greater Kansas City (Mr. Kansas City award 1978), Acad. Squires, Golden Key Nat. Honor Soc. (hon.), Oakwood Country Club, River Club, Carriage Club, Kansas City Country Club. Jewish. Office: H&R Block Inc 4400 Main St Kansas City MO 64111-1812

BLOCH, HERBERT, classicist, medievalist, historian, educator; b. Berlin, Germany, Aug. 18, 1911; came to the U.S., 1939, naturalized, 1946; s. Ludwig and Alice (Gutmann) B.; m. Clarissa Coolidge Holland, Nov. 23, 1943 (dec. Aug. 1958); children: Anne Coolidge, Nini; m. Ellen Cohen, Aug. 25, 1960 (dec. May 1987). Dottore in Lettere, U. Rome, 1935, diploma di Perfezionamento, 1937; LLD, U. Cassino, Italy, 1989. Instr. Greek and Latin Harvard U., Cambridge, Mass., 1941; asst. prof. Greek and Latin Harvard U., Cambridge, 1942-47, assoc. prof. Greek and Latin, 1947-53, prof. Greek and Latin, 1953-73, Pope prof. Latin lang. and lit., 1973-82, Pope prof. Latin lang. and lit. emeritus, 1982—; with excavation Ostia, Italyž, 1938-39; mem. Inst. for Advanced Study, Princeton, N.J., 1953-54; prof.-in-charge Sch. Classical Studies, Am. Acad. Rome, 1957-59; mem. bd. Syndics Harvard U. Press, Cambridge, 1961-65; trustee Loeb Classical Libr. Harvard U., Cambridge, 1964-73, sr. fellow Soc. of Fellows, 1964-79. Author: I bolli laterizi e la storia edilizia romana, 1948, 2d edit., 1968, Supplement to Volume XV1 of the Corpus Inscriptionum Latinarum Including Complete Indices to the Roman Brick-Stamps, 1948, 2d edit., 1967, Monte Cassino in the Middle Ages, 3 vols., 1986 (Haskins medal The Medieval Acad. Am. 1988, Praemium Urbis, Rome, 1987), The Atina Dossier of Peter the Deacon of Monte Cassino. A Hagiographical Romance of the Twelfth Century, 1998. Recipient Fulbright award, Italy, 1950-51; Guggenheim fellow, 1950-51; fellow for ind. study and rsch. NEH. Fellow Am. Acad. Arts and Scis., Med. Acad. Am. (pres. of fellows 1990-93); mem. Am. Philological Assn. (dir. 1959-64, 66-70, v.p. 1966-68, pres. 1968-69), Am. Philos. Soc., Deutsches Archaeologisches Inst., Pontificia Accademia Romana di Archeologia (hon.), Zentraldirektion der Monumenta Germaniae Historica (corr.), Finnish Acad. Sci. and Letters, Premio Cultori di Roma, Rome, 1999. Home: 524 Pleasant St Belmont MA 02478-3201

BLOCH, JULIA CHANG, foundation administrator, former bank executive, educator; b. Chefoo, Peoples Republic of China, Mar. 2, 1942; came to U.S., 1951, naturalized, 1962; d. Fu-yun and Eva (Yeh) Chang; m. Stuart Marshall Bloch, Dec. 21, 1968. BA, U. Calif., Berkeley, 1964; MA, Harvard U., 1967, postgrad. in mgmt., 1987; DHL (hon.), Northeastern U., Boston, 1986. Vol. Peace Corps, Sabah, Malaysia, 1964-66, tng. officer East Asia and Pacific region, Washington, 1967-68, evaluation officer, 1968-70; mem. minority staff U.S. Senate Select Com. on Nutrition and Human Needs, Washington, 1971-76, chief minority counsel, 1976-77; dep. dir. Office of African Affairs, U.S. Internat. Comm. Agy., Washington, 1977-80; fellow Inst. Politics, Harvard U., Cambridge, Mass., 1980-81; asst. adminstr. Bur. for Food for Peace and Voluntary Assistance, AID, Washington, 1981-87, asst. adminstr. Bur. for Asia and Near East, 1987-88; assoc. U.S.-Japan Rels. Program, Ctr. for Internat. Affairs, Harvard U., Cambridge, Mass., 1988-89; amb. to Kingdom of Nepal, 1989-93; group exec., v.p. Bank Am., San Francisco, 1993-96; pres. The U.S.-Japan Found., 1996-98; dir. Am. West Airlines, 1994—, Penn Mutual Life Ins., 1997; trustee Eisenhower Exchange Fellowship, 1995—, U.S. China Rels. Com., 1998—; U.S. Senate rep. World Conf. on Internat. Women's Yr., Mex., 1975; advisor U.S. Del. to Food and Agr. Orgn. Conf., Rome, 1975; rep. Am. Council Young Polit. Leaders, Peoples Republic China, 1977; charter mem. Sr. Exec. Svc., 1979; head U.S. del. Biennial Session World Food Programme, Rome, 1981-86, Devel. Assistance Com. Meeting on Non-Govtl. Orgns., Paris, 1985, Intergovtl. Group on Indonesia, The Hague, The Netherlands, 1987, World Bank Consultative Group Meeting, Paris, 1987, mem. exec. women in govt., 1988-93, mem. coun. fgn. rels., 1991—; mem. com. to visit art mus. Harvard U., 1989—; mem. U.S. Nat. Com. for Pacific Econ. Cooperation, 1984—; mem. adv. bd. Women's Campaign Fund, 1976-78, trustee, bus. leadership circle, 1994—; exec. bd. mem. Internat. Ctr. for Rsch. on Women, 1974-81; mem. presdl. adv. coun. Peace Corps, 1988-89; founder Women Fgn. Policy Group, 1990; mem. Am. Himalayan Found. Bd., 1994, Am. Refugee Com. Bd., 1993—; vis. prof. internat. rels. Peking U., 1998. Author: A U.S.-Japan Aid Alliance, 1991; co-author: Chinese Home Cooking, 1986; mem. Nat. Presdl. Debate Forum, 1987-92; mem. nat. adv. coun. Experiment in Internat. Living, 1981-83; commr. Asian Art Mus., San Francisco, 1994. Hon. Fulbright fellow, 1996, Wildrow Wilson fellow, 1999; recipient Hubert Humphrey award for internat. svc., 1979, Humanitarian Svc. award AID, 1987, Leader for Peace award Peace Corps, 1987, Asian Am. Leadership award, 1989, Brotherhood/Sisterhood award Nat. Conf. on Christians and Jews, 1996; named Outstanding Woman of Color, Nat. Inst. for Women of Color, 1982, Woman of Distinction, Nat. Conf. for Coll. Women Student Leaders and Women of Achievement, 1987, Disting. Pub. Svc. award Nat. Assn. Profl. Asian Pacific Am. Women, 1989; Ford Found. Study fellow for internat. devel. Harvard U., 1966, Paul Harris award Rotary, 1992, Award of Honor Narcotic Enforcement Assn., 1992. Mem. Orgn. Chinese Am. Women (founder, chair 1977—, bd. dirs., Woman of Yr. 1987), Asia Soc. (pres. coun. 1989, trustee 1994), Am. Studies Ctr. (vice-chair), Prytannean Honor Soc., Coun. Fgn. Rels., Mortar Bd., Cosmos Club. Republican. Avocations: ceramics, gourmet cooking, collecting art.

BLOCH, KONRAD EMIL, biochemist; b. Neisse, Germany, Jan. 12, 1912; came to U.S., 1936, naturalized, 1944; s. Frederick D. and Hedwig (Streimer) B.; m. Lore Teutsch, Feb. 15, 1941; children—Peter, Susan. Chem. Engr., Technische Hochschule, Munich, 1934; Ph.D., Columbia U., 1938. Asst. prof. biochemistry U. Chgo., 1946-50, prof., 1950-54; Higgins prof. chemistry Harvard U., Cambridge, Mass., 1954-82, prof. emeritus, 1982—. Recipient Nobel prize in physiology and medicine, 1964, Ernest Guenther award in chemistry of essential oils and related products, 1965, Nat. Medal of Sci., 1988. Fellow AAAS; mem. Am. Chemistry Soc. (Fritsche award 1964), Am. Soc. Biol. Chemists (pres. 1967), Nat. Acad. Scis., Am. Philos. Soc., Royal Sci. (fgn.). Office: Harvard U Dept Chemistry/Chem Biology 12 Oxford St Cambridge MA 02138-2902*

BLOCH, KURT JULIUS, physician; b. Germany, Oct. 17, 1929; s. Max and Mathilde B.; m. Margot Bendit, June 25, 1953; children: Kenneth D., Donald B. BS, CCNY, 1951; MD, NYU, 1955. Diplomate Am. Bd. Internal Medicine, Am. Bd. Allergy and Immunology, subspecialties Rheumatology, Diagnostic Lab. Immunology. Intern, asst. resident Bellevue Hosp., N.Y.C., 1955-57; resident in medicine Mass. Gen. Hosp., Boston, 1960-61, physician, 1974—, chief clin. immunology and allergy units, 1976—; instr. medicine Harvard Med. Sch., Boston, 1965-68, asst. prof., 1968-70, assoc. prof., 1970-74, prof., 1974—; sr. investigator Arthritis Found., 1964-69. Contbr. articles to profl. jours. With USPHS, 1957-60. Mem. Am. Soc. Clin. Investigation, Am. Assn. Physicians. Achievements include research on the biologic functions of antibodies, mechanisms of inflammation of the intestine, and the immunobiology of sensorineural hearing loss. Office: Mass Gen Hosp Clin Immunology and Allergy Units Boston MA 02114

BLOCH, PAUL, public relations executive; b. Bklyn., July 17, 1939; s. Edwin Lionel and Antoinette (Greenberg) B. B.B. Polit. Sci., UCLA, 1962. Publicist Rogers & Cowan, Beverly Hills, Calif., 1962-70, v.p., 1970-75, sr. v.p., ptnr., 1975-83, exec. v.p., sr. ptnr., 1983—, also vice chmn., co-chmn. Asst. Am. Cancer Soc., United Way, Am. Diabetes Assn., UNICEF, 1975—; adv. council Orange County Sheriff's Dept., 1980—. Served with U.S. Army, 1957. Recipient Les Mason award Publicity Guild Am., 1991. Mem. Publicists Guild of Am. (award for publicity campaign for Brian's Song 1972), Country Music Assn. Office: Rogers & Cowan 1888 Century Park E Fl 5 Los Angeles CA 90067-1702 *I wouldn't trade my life for the world.*

BLOCH, PETER, editor. Editor Penthouse Mag., N.Y.C. Office: Penthouse Mag General Media 11 Penn Plz 12t5h Fl New York NY 10172-0003*

BLOCH, RALPH JAY, professional association executive; b. N.Y.C., Sept. 21, 1942; s. Alexander and Catherine (La Bue) B.; m. Patricia Ann Cassone, Aug. 18, 1963 (div.); 1 child, Marci Suzanne; m. Helen Lightstone, June 19, 1988. BS, UCLA, 1965. Sales rep. Lowell Wood Co., L.A., 1967-68; mgr. Home Furniture, L.A., 1968-72; co-owner, gen. mgr. Home Furniture, 1972-78; pres. Concepts III, Inc., Greenville, S.C., 1978-79; from western exec. v.p. to mktg. v.p. Nat. Home Furnishings Assn., 1979-83; pres., owner The Access Group, Inc., Chgo., 1984—. Mem. Chgo. Soc. Assn. Execs., Am. Soc. Assn. Execs. Avocations: backpacking, hiking, sailing, cooking. Office: The Access Group Inc 35 E Wacker Dr Ste 500 Chicago IL 60601-2105*

BLOCH, RICHARD ISAAC, labor arbitrator; b. East Orange, N.J., June 15, 1943; s. Jacques Henry and Hannah (Levi) B.; m. Susan Low, July 11, 1966; children: Rebecca Low, Michael Low. A.B., Dartmouth Coll., 1965; J.D., U. Mich., 1968, M.B.A., 1974. Bar: Mich. 1969, D.C. bar 1975. Assoc. firm Seyfarth, Shaw Fairweather & Geraldson, Chgo., 1968; lectr. U. Mich. Grad. Sch. Bus. Adminstrn., 1969-71; asst. prof. law U. Detroit, 1971-75; prin. Richard I. Bloch, P.C. (labor arbitrator), Washington, 1969—; vis. prof. law Wayne State U., 1974, George Washington U., 1983; adj. prof. Am. U., 1978, Georgetown U. Law Ctr., 1989, 90; chmn. fgn. svc. grievance bd. Dept. State, 1977-80; chief umpire United Mine Workers and Bituminous Coal Operators Assn., 1980-81; permanent arbitrator Maj. League Baseball, 1983-85, arbitrator Nat. Hockey League, Electric Boat Co., Metal Trades Coun., Nat. Football League; permanent arbitrator Alcoa and United Steelworkers Am. Author: Arbitration of Discipline Cases, 1979, Labor Agreement in Arbitration, 1983, Interest Arbitration, 1986; contbr. articles to law jours. Mem. Dartmouth Coll. Alumni Council, 1974-77. Mem. ABA, Mich. Bar Assn., D.C. Bar Assn., Indsl. Rels. Rsch. Assn., Nat. Acad. Arbitrators (bd. govs.). Home and Office: 4335 Cathedral Ave NW Washington DC 20016-3560

BLOCH, ROSEMARIE, artist, musician; b. Cin., July 28, 1940; d. Henry William and Claire Mary Steigerwald; m. Arthur Leroy Bloch, May 19, 1962; children: James Kenneth, Diana, Karl. Cert., Art Acad. Cin., 1962. instr. spl. svcs. U.S. Army, Ft. Dix, N.J., 1968-69, Germany, 1971; artist-in-residence Madeira (Ohio) H.S., 1990-91; mem. exec. coun. Art Acad. Cin. Alumni, 1992-94. Exhibited paintings in one-woman shows at Pub. Libr. Hamilton County, 1990, Civic Garden Ctr., Cin., 1994, Middletown Fine Arts Ctr., 1995, 98, Mercy St. Theresa Ctr., Mariemont, Ohio, 1997, Mt. St. Mary's Coll., Emmitsburg, Md., 1999, others. Mem. Little League baseball com., Germany, 1971-72; vol. ARC, U.S. Armed Forces, Germany, 1972-73; active Boy Scouts Am. Mem. Cin. Art Club, Middle Town Fine Arts Ctr. Avocations: musician, gardener. Email: rosebloch@yahoo.com. Home: 2258 Chapel Rd Okeana OH 45053-9738

BLOCH, STUART MARSHALL, lawyer; b. Detroit, Nov. 5, 1942; s. A. Howard and Pauline Betty (Rappaport) B.; m. Julia Chang, Dec. 21, 1968. AB, U. Miami, 1964; LLB, Harvard U., 1967. Bar: Mich. 1968, D.C. 1968. Ptnr. Ingersoll and Bloch, Washington, 1972—; chmn. Real Estate Reporter, Ltd., Washington, 1978—. Author: A Periodical Guide to FIRREA, 1989, The Workout Game, 1987, 90, The Liability Game, 1988; editor State Digest of Land Sales, 1977—, D.C. Real Estate Reporter, 1979—; fellow Salzburg Seminar, 1988. Chmn. Land Devel. Inst., Washington, 1974—; trustee Arena Stage, 1983, Black Student Fund, Washington, 1983; major gifts chmn. Harvard U. Law Sch., 1983; 25th reunion chmn. U. Miami, 1989; pres. Internat. Found. for Timesharing, 1983; mem. corp. Northeastern U., Boston, 1983; mem. bd. individual vol. svc. Jewish Nat. Fund, 1994. Recipient spl. citation Am. Land Devel. Assn., 1980; citation D.C. City Coun., 1982, Jewish Nat. Fund Tree of Life award, 1991. Mem. ABA, D.C. Bar Assn., Mich. Bar Assn., Univ. Club (Washington). Office: Ingersoll & Bloch 1300 N St NW Washington DC 20005-3600

BLOCK, ALLAN JAMES, communications executive; b. Oct. 1, 1954; s. Paul Jr. and Marjorie (McNab) B. BA, U. Pa., 1977. Coord. electronic tech. planning Toledo Blade Co., 1981-83, dir. electronic planning, 1984-85; dir. mktg. Buckeye Cablevision Inc., Toledo, 1985-87; v.p. cablevision and TV Blade Communications, Inc., Toledo, 1987-88, exec. v.p., 1989, mem., chief exec. com., co-CEO, 1989—, vice-chmn. bd., 1990—; pres. Blade Cablevision Co., 1987—, Blade Broadcasting Co., 1987—; bd. dirs. Toledo Blade Co., Blade Comms., Inc., P.G. Pub. Co. Bd. dirs. C-SPAN, 1991—; trustee Med. Coll. Ohio, 1991—. Mem. Toledo Club, Met. Club (N.Y.C.), Penn Club (N.Y.C.), Duquesne Club (Pitts.). Home: 235 14th St Toledo OH 43624 Office: Blade Communications Inc 541 N Superior St Toledo OH 43660-0001

BLOCK, ALVIN GILBERT, journal executive editor; b. Moline, Ill., Sept. 15, 1946; s. Sylvan Emory Block and Pauline (Kutten) Salzman; m. Sarah Cannon Michael, June 17, 1977 (div. 1984); m. Ellen Marie Chapman, Jan. 19, 1992; children: Will Chapman, Thomas Chapman. BA, Bradley U., 1968. Editl. asst. Playboy mag., Chgo., 1970; exec. Salzman & Co., Davenport, Iowa, 1971-74; editor Ketchum (Idaho) Tomorrow, 1975-77; reporter Idaho Statesman, Ketchum, 1978-80; freelance writer, Sacramento, 1980-82; mng. editor Calif. Jour., Sacramento, 1983-94, editor, columnist, 1995—; co-editor Calif. Polit. Almanac; editor Calif. Govt. and Politics Annual; v.p., exec. editor State Net, 1996—; commentator Sta. KXPR-FM, Sacramento, 1985-88. Councilman City of Ketchum, 1979. With U.S. Army, 1969-74. Recipient award for column Idaho Newspaper Assn., 1975, Soc. Profl. Journalists, 1995. Avocations: baseball, military history, railroading. Home: 1133 Marian Way Sacramento CA 95818-3718 Office: Calif Jour 2101 K St Sacramento CA 95816-4920

BLOCK, AMANDA ROTH, artist; b. Louisville, Feb. 20, 1912; d. Albert Solomon and Helen (Bernheim) Roth; m. Gordon J. Wolfe, June 16, 1931 (div. 1947); 1 child, Joseph G. Wolf; m. Maurice Block, Jr., July 15, 1949. Student, Smith Coll., 1930-31, U. Cin., 1933, Art Acad. Cin., 1933-40, Ind. U.; BFA, Purdue U., 1960. Instr. Herron Sch. Art, Ind. U. Purdue U., Indpls., 1969-73; instr. lithography Indpls. Art Ctr., 1974; adv. bd. Indpls. Art League Found., 1979-81. One-woman shows, 1444 Gallery, Indpls., 1962, Sheldon Swope Art Gallery, Terre Haute, Ind., 1963, 73, Park Avenue Gallery, Indpls., 1964, Harriet Crane Gallery, Cin., 1965, Talbot Gallery, Indpls., 1967, Merida Gallery, Louisville, 1967, Herron Mus. Art, Indpls., 1969, Editions Ltd. Gallery, Indpls., 1972, 79, Franklin (Ind.) Coll., 1973, Tucson Mus. Sch., 1977, Indpls. Art League, 1992; two-woman shows, Jason Gallery, N.Y.C., 1964, Orange County Coll., Middletown, N.Y., 1964, Washington Gallery, Frankfort, Ind., 1975, Edits. Ltd. Gallery, Indpls., 1983; exhibited in group shows, Chgo. Art Inst., 1941, Butler Inst. Am. Art, Youngstown, Ohio, Burr Gallery, N.Y.C., Hanover Coll., Wabash, Ind., De Pauw U., Soc. Am. Graphic Artists AAA Gallery, Purdue U., Istan Gallery, Tokyo, Phila. Print Club, Pa. Acad. Fine Arts, 1969, Imprint Gallery, San Francisco, 1972, Van Straaten Gallery, Chgo., 1973, McNay Inst., San Antonio, 1972, Pratt Graphics, N.Y.C., 1976, Ind. State Mus., 1976, Indpls. Mus. Art, 1977, Tucson Mus. Art, 1978, internat. traveling exhbn., Soc. Am. Graphic Artists, 1974-75, traveling exhbn., 1977, 78; represented in permanent collections, Continental Ill. Bank, Chgo., De Pauw U., Ind. State Coll., Terre Haute, Ind., Med. Soc., Indpls., Sheldon Swope Art Gallery, Stevens Coll., Boston Public Library, USIA, Lafayette (Ind.) Art Center, Lippman Assos., architects, Indpls., J.B. Speed Mus., Louisville, IBM Bldg., Indpls., Phila Mus. Art, Bklyn. Mus., Cin. Art Mus., N.Y. Public Library, Columbua U. Gallery, N.Y.C., Biodynamics Inc., Indpls., Fidelity Bank, Carmel, Ind., Tuscon Mus. Art, Indpsl. Mus. Art. Recipient award Ben and Beatrice Goldstein Found., N.Y.C., 1971. Mem. Soc. Am. Graphic Artists. Jewish. Home: 947 Tiverton Ave Apt 1237 Los Angeles CA 90024-3012

BLOCK, BARBARA ANN, biology educator; b. Springfield, Mass., Apr. 25, 1958; d. Merrill and Myra (Winograd) B. BA, U. Vt., 1980; PhD, Duke U., 1986. Postdoctoral fellow U. Pa., Phila., 1986-88; asst. prof. organismal biology U. Chgo., 1988-93; asst. prof. biol. sci. Stanford U., 1993-97, assoc. prof., 1997—. Contbr. articles to profl. jours. Recipient Presdl. Young Investigator award NSF, 1989; MacArthur fellow, 1996, Pew Conservation fellow, 1997. Mem. AAAS, Am. Soc. Zoologists, Biophys. Soc. Democrat. *

BLOCK, DENNIS JEFFREY, lawyer; b. Bronx, N.Y., Sept. 1, 1942; s. Martin and Betty (Berger) B.; m. Lauren Elizabeth Troupin, Nov. 27, 1967; children: Robert, Tracy, Meredith. BA, U. Buffalo, 1964; LLB, Bklyn. Law Sch., 1967. Bar: N.Y. 1968, U.S. Dist. Ct. (ea. dist.) N.Y., U.S. Dist. Ct. (so. dist.) N.Y., U.S. Ct. Appeals (2d, 3d, 5th, 6th, 7th, 8th, 9th, 10th and 11th cirs.), U.S. Supreme Ct. Br. chief SEC, N.Y.C., 1967-72; assoc. Weil, Gotshal & Manges, L.L.P., N.Y.C., 1972-74, ptnr., 1974-98; ptnr. Cadwalader, Wickersham & Taft, N.Y.C., 1998—. Co-author: The Business Judgment Rule: Fiduciary Duties of Corporate Directors and Officers, Law & Business, Inc., 1987, 5th edit., 1998; co-editor: The Corporate Counselor's Desk Book, 1982, 5th edit., 1999; contbr. articles to profl. jours. Chmn. major gifts lawyers div., United Jewish Appeal Fedn., 1987-89, chmn. lawyers div., 1989-91. Mem. ABA (coun. litigation sect., com. on corp. laws sect. bus. law), Assn. of Bar of City of N.Y., Am. Law Inst.

BLOCK, EMIL NATHANIEL, JR., military officer; b. Newark, Ohio, Oct. 3, 1930; s. Emil Nathaniel and Louise Jeanette (Palmer) B.; m. Marian Lou Davis, June 9, 1956; children: Eric, Emil Darin. BS, US Naval Acad., 1956; MSE in Instrumentation, U. Mich., 1961, MSE in Aero. and Astronautical Engring, 1961; MS in Bus. Adminstrn, George Washington U., 1966. Commd. 2d lt. U.S. Air Force, 1956, advanced through grades to maj. gen., 1979; spl. asst. for B-1 matters, dep. chief staff for research and devel. Hdqrs. USAF, Washington, 1976-78; chief of staff mil. airlift command, dir. Air Force C-X task force, Scott AFB, Ill., 1978-80; dir. plans Hdqrs. USAF, Pentagon, Washington, 1980-81; pres. Blime, Inc., 1981—. Decorated D.S.M. (2), Legion of Merit (3), D.F.C., Bronze Star, Meritorious Service medal (2), Air medal (5); Jimmy Doolittle fellow, 1978. Mem. Air Force Assn.

BLOCK, FRANCESCA LIA, writer; b. Hollywood, Calif., Dec. 3, 1962; d. Irving Alexander and Gilda Rona (Klein) B.; m. Chris Schuette. BA in English Lit., U. Calif., Berkeley, 1986. Author: Weetzie Bat, 1989 (ALA

Best Book award 1989), Witch Baby, 1991 (Sch. Libr. Jour. Best Book award), Cherokee Bat and the Goat Guys, 1992 (ALA Best Book awar, N.Y. Times Book Rev. Notable Book), Ecstasia, 1993, Missing Angel Juan, 1993 (ALA Best Book award 1993), Primavera, 1994, The Hanged Man, 1994, Baby Be Bop, 1995 (Pub.'s Weekly Best Book award 1995, ALA Best Book award 1995), Girl Goddess # 9, 1996, Dangerous Angels, 1998, I Was A Teenage Fairy, 1998; co-author: (with Hillary Carlip) Zine Scene, 1998, Violet and Claire, 1999. Mem. Phi Beta Kappa. Democrat. Jewish. Office: Artist's Agy 230 W 55th St Apt 29D New York NY 10019-5206

BLOCK, FRANKLIN LEE, retired lawyer; b. Wilmington, N.C., Nov. 24, 1936; s. Charles Morris and Hannah (Solomon) B.; m. Wendy Barshay, June 14, 1959; children: Steven, Amy, Ellen. BS, The Citadel, 1959; JD, Wake Forest U., 1976. Bar: N.C. 1976. Pvt. practice Wilmington, N.C., 1978-81; ptnr. Block & Trask, Wilmington, 1981-95, Block, Crouch, Keefer and Huffman, 1996-98; ret., 1998; mem. N.C. Senate, 1987-92; U.S. magistrate (part-time) Eastern Dist. N.C., 1977-86. V.p. pres. Cape Fear United Way, Wilmington, 1982-83, pres. 1985. Capt. U.S. Army, 1959-61. Mem. ABA, N.C. Bar Assn., N.C. Acad. Trial Lawyers, Masons. Democrat. Jewish. Address: 322 Causeway Dr Wrightsville Beach NC 28480-1911

BLOCK, FREDERIC, judge; b. Bklyn., June 6, 1934; s. Norman Louis and Florence (Ferman) B.; m. Estelle Lenora Kaufman, Dec. 18, 1960; children: Neil M., Nancy L. AB, Ind. U., 1956; LLB, Cornell U., 1959. Bar: N.Y. 1959, U.S. Supreme Ct. 1967, U.S. Ct. Appeals (2nd cir.) 1971, U.S. Dist. Ct. (ea. and so. dists.) N.Y. 1975. Law clk. appellate div. N.Y. State Supreme Ct., Albany, 1960-61; ptnr. Block & Hamburger, Smithtown, N.Y.; U.S. Dist. Ct. Judge Bklyn.; lectr. Cornell U. Law Sch., Ithaca, N.Y., 1984—. Composer mus. show Professionally Speaking, 1986. Counsel edn. com. N.Y. State Constl. Conv., 1967; mem. Suffolk County Charter Rev. Commn., N.Y., 1968-70. Named Man of Yr., Cystic Fibrosis Found., 1984. Fellow Am. Bar Found., N.Y. Bar Found.; mem. N.Y. State Bar Assn. (spl. counsel 1981, v.p. 1983-86), Suffolk County Bar Assn. (pres. 1979-80, Pres.'s award 1985), N.Y. State Assn. Sch. Attys. (pres. 1982), N.Y. State Conf. Bar Leaders (chmn. 1980-82). Avocation: musical composition. Home: 15 Stern Dr Prt Jefferson NY 11777-1162 Office: US Dist Ct 225 Cadman Plz E Brooklyn NY 11201-2741*

BLOCK, HERBERT LAWRENCE (HERBLOCK), editorial cartoonist; b. Chgo., Oct. 13, 1909; s. David Julian and Tessie (Lupe) B. Student, Lake Forest (Ill.) Coll., 1927-29, LLD (hon.), 1957; LittD (hon.), Rutgers U., 1963; LHD, Williams Coll., 1969, Haverford Coll., 1977, U. Md., 1977; LHD (hon.), Colby Coll., 1986; student, Art Inst. Chgo. (part time classes). Editl. cartoonist: Chgo. Daily News, 1929-33, NEA Svc., 1993-43, U.S. Army, 1943-45; editl. cartoonist: The Washington Post, 1946—; author: the Herblock Book, 1952, Herblock's Here and Now, 1955, Herblock's Special for Today, 1958, Straight Herblock, 1964, The Herblock Gallery, 1968, Herblock's State of the Union, 1972, Herblock Special Report, 1974, Herblock On All Fronts, 1980, Herblock Through the Looking Glass, 1984, Herblock At Large, 1987, Herblock: A Cartoonist's Life, 1993, Bella And Me: Life in the Service of a Cat, 1995; designer U.S. postage stamp commemorating 175th anniv. of Bill of Rights, 1966. Recipient Pulitzer prize in cartooning, 1942, 54, 79, Am. Newspaper Guild award, 1948, Heywood Broun award, 1950, Sidney Hillman award, 1953, Reuben Outstanding Cartoonist award Nat. Cartoonists Soc., 1957, Lauterbach award for svc. to civil liberties, 1959, Florina Lasker award N.Y. Civil Liberties Union, 1960, Bill of Rights Day award, 1966, Power of Print award, 1977, 4th Estate award Nat. Press Club, 1977, Overseas Press Club citation, 1979, NEA award for human rels., 1970, ACLU award, 1981, World Hunger Media award, 1984, People for Am. Way 1st Amendment award, 1985, Elijah Parish Lovejoy award, 1986, Hubert H. Humphrey Civil Rights award, 1987, Franklin Roosevelt Freedom medal Franklin Delano Roosevelt Four Freedoms Found., 1987, World Humor award Workshop Libr. on World Humor, 1988, Overseas Press Club award, 1988, Outstanding Consumer Media Svc. award Consumer Fedn. of Am., 1989, Good Guy award Nat. Woman's Polit. Caucus, 1989, Population Inst. Global Media award, 1990, Maggie award Planned Parenthood Fedn. of Am., Inc., 1991, 92, 97, Pres.'s award Am. Lung Assn., 1993, Robert F. Kennedy Spl. Recognition Book award, 1994, Presl. Medal of Freedom, 1994, Thomas Nast award Overseas Press Club, 1995, Lifetime Achievement award Reporters Com. for Freedom of Press, 1995; inducted into The Cartoon Hall Fame, Boca Raton, Fla., 1997, N.T. "Pete" Shields award Ctr. to Prevent Handgun Violence, 1998. Fellow Am. Acad. Arts and Scis., Sigma Delta Chi (awards 1949, 50, 52, 57); mem. Phi Beta Kappa (hon.). Office: Washington Post 1150 15th St NW Washington DC 20071-0002

BLOCK, ISAAC EDWARD, professional society administrator; b. Phila., Aug. 8, 1924; s. Louis Emanuel and Stella Florence (Goodman) B.; m. Marline Beryl Lewin, June 16, 1957; children—Nancy Anne, Kathie Sue, Stephen Edward. BS in Physics, Haverford Coll., 1944; MA in Math., Harvard U., 1947, PhD in Math., 1952. Math. cons. Philco Corp., Phila., 1951-54; mgr. computer ctr. Burroughs Corp., Phila., 1954-59; mgr. engring. computer ctr. Univac div. Sperry Rand Corp., Phila., 1959-61; mgr. applied math. systems Univac div. Sperry Rand Corp., Blue Bell, Pa., 1961-64; tech. advisor Auerbach Corp., Phila., 1964-65; mgr. Auerbach Info. Inc., Phila., 1965-67, v.p., gen. mgr., 1967-72; v.p., dir. product planning and devel. Auerbach Pub. Inc., Phila., 1972-76; mng. dir. Soc. for Indsl. and Applied Math., Phila., 1976-94, cons., 1994—; sec., 1951-53, chmn. pubs. com., 1954-63, v.p., 1964-74, council, 1957-65, trustee, 1971-75, chmn. bd. trustees, 1974-75; lectr. Computation Lab, Wayne State U., summers 1954-55. Served with USNR, 1944-45. Fellow AAAS; mem. Assn. Computing Machinery, Am. Math. Soc., Phi Beta Kappa, Sigma Xi. Avocations: photography, music. Home: 7904 Cobden Rd Laverock PA 19038-7255

BLOCK, JAMES A., hospital administrator, pediatrician; b. Dayton, Ohio, 1940. Grad., Haverford Coll., 1962; MD, NYU, 1966. Chief ambulatory svcs. Surgeon General's Comprhensive Health Planning office; assoc. dir. Community Health Svc. Health Svcs. and Mental Health Adminstrn. USPHS; intern pediatrics Strong Meml. Hosp., Rochester, N.Y., 1966-67; resident pediatrics and ambulatory medicine Strong Meml. Hosp. U. Rochester, 1969-71; pediatrician, head ambulatory svcs. Genesee Hosp., 1971-79; pres. Rochester Area Hosps. Corp., N.Y., 1979-85; asst. to pres., then pres., CEO U. Hosps. Cleve., 1985-86, 86-92; pres., CEO Johns Hopkins Hosp., Johns Hopkins Health System, Balt., 1992-97; adj. prof. Health Policy Case Western Reserve U., 1991; faculty Hosp. Fin. Mgmt. Assn., Am. Assn. Med. Colls.; chmn. RHN bd. ops. com.; mem. gov's commn. ambulatory Care Cost Containment, N.Y. State, 1977—; HCFA Physician Discussion Group; adj. prof. pediatrics Johns Hopkins U. Sch. Medicine; adj. prof. health policy Johns Hopkins Sch. Hygiene and Pub. Health; cons. in field; speaker in field; bd. dirs. MMI Cos., Inc., Greater Balt. Com.; del. Coun. Teaching Hosps. Assn. Am. Med. Colls.; sr. cons. UN Found., N.Y.C., 1998—. Editorial adv. bd. Jour. Ambulatory Care Mgmt.; contbr. articles to profl. jours. Campaign cabinet United Way; mem. Lombardi Task Force Hosp.; bd. dirs. Robert Wood Johnson Found. Community Hosp. Med. staff Primary Group Practice program (past), sr. program cons. 1974-82, Unicef, Mercantile Bankshares Inc., Omna Inc., Soc. Med. Adminstrs.; trustee Johns Hopkins U., Johns Hopkins Health System/ Johns Hopkins Hosp. Health fellow Nat. Urban Coalition, 1971-72. Mem. APHA, AMA, Am. Acad. Med. Dirs., United Way (corp. mem.), Ambulatory Pediatric Assn., Med. Adminstrs. Conf. Home: 1207 Malvern Ave Baltimore MD 21204-6721

BLOCK, JOHN DOUGLAS, auction house executive; b. Princeton, N.J., May 3, 1948; s. S. Lester and Ruth (Harris) B.; m. Hilary Cushing, June 22, 1985; children: Alexander, Brooke. BA, Princeton U., 1970. Vice chmn., dir. internat. jewels N.Am. & S.Am. Sotheby's, N.Y.C., 1970-94, v.p. H&S Am., 1994—, also bd. dirs. Mem. The Millbrook Golf and Tennis Club. Avocations: travel, collecting art and antiques, equestrian sports. Office: Sothebys N Am 1334 York Ave New York NY 10021-4806

BLOCK, JOHN ROBINSON, newspaper publisher; b. Toledo, Oct. 1, 1954; s. Paul Jr. and Marjorie Jane (McNab) B. BA, Yale U., 1977. Reporter AP, Miami, Fla., 1977-78, N.Y.C., 1978-80; Washington corr. The Toledo Blade, 1980-82; European corr. The Toledo Blade, London, 1982—; Sunday editor The Toledo Blade, 1983-85, asst. mng. editor, 1985-87, exec. editor, 1987-89; co-pub., editor-in-chief The Blade, Toledo, 1989—; co-pub. Pitts. Post-Gazette, 1989—, editor-in-chief, 1993—; v.p., bd. dirs. P.G. Pub. Co., Pitts.; exec. v.p., bd. dirs. Blade comm., Inc., Toledo. Chmn. City Mgr.'s Hist. Preservation Com., Toledo, 1983-85; chmn. airport com. Toledo-Lucas County Port Authority, 1994-97. Mem. Am. Soc. Newspaper Editors, Soc. Profl. Journalists. Clubs: Nat. Press (Washington), Yale (N.Y.C.), Belmont Country (Perrysburg, Ohio). Home: 725 Devonshire St Pittsburgh PA 15213-2905 Office: Blade Communications Inc 541 N Superior St Toledo OH 43660-0001 also: Pitts Post-Gazette 34 Blvd Of The Allies Pittsburgh PA 15222-1204*

BLOCK, JOHN RUSLING, former secretary of agriculture; b. Galesburg, Ill., Feb. 15, 1935; children: Hans, Cynthia, Christine, Savannah. B.S., U.S. Mil. Acad., 1959. Farmer Gilson, Ill., 1960-77; dir. Ill. Dept. Agr., Springfield, 1977-81; sec. agr. U.S. Dept. Agr., Washington, 1981-86; pres. Food Distbrs. Internat., Falls Church, Va., 1986—. Served to 2d lt. U.S. Army, 1958-60. Named Outstanding Young Farmer Am. Jaycees, 1969. Mem. Ill. Farm Bur., Knox County Farm Bur. Office: Food Distributors Internat 201 Park Washington Ct Falls Church VA 22046-4519

BLOCK, JULES RICHARD, psychologist, educator, university official; b. N.Y.C., Nov. 23, 1930; s. Jules Irving and Elizabeth (Shinkle) B.; m. Elizabeth Ehrenstein, Dec. 21, 1952 (div. Nov. 1978); m. Patricia Clark, Feb. 29, 1980; children—Cheryl, Janet. B.A., Hofstra Coll., 1952; Ph.D., N.Y. U., 1962. Lectr. Hofstra U., Hempstead, N.Y., 1956-60, instr., 1960-62, asst. prof., 1962-66, assoc. prof., 1966-70, prof., 1970-79, chmn. dept. psychology, 1968-78, exec. dir. research and resource devel., 1976-85, asst. to pres. for info. systems, 1985-87, v.p. planning and liaison, 1987—; rsch. asst. Human Resources Rsch. and Tng. Inst., Albertson, N.Y., 1957-59, rsch. assoc., 1959-61, dir. rsch., 1961-71; pres. Instrumental Psychol. Methods, Hempstead, Inst. for Rsch. and Evaluation, Hempstead; v.p. Y&B Assocs., Hempstead, 1983-98, pres., 1998—. Contbr. articles to profl. jours. Mem. Nassau County Youth Bd., 1968-70; Exec. dir. Initial Teaching Alphabet Found., 1965-72. Served with USNR, 1952-56. Recipient award for outstanding research in rehab. Nat. Rehab. Council, 1969. Mem. Am. Psychol. Assn. Home: 33 Primrose Ln Hempstead NY 11550-4633 Office: Hofstra U Off of VP Planning & Liasion Hempstead NY 11550

BLOCK, KERRY REAGAN, special education educator; b. St. Louis, Jan. 25, 1963; s. David and Delores (Kornblum) B. BS, U. Wyo., 1985; MEd, U. No. Colo., 1992, EdD, 1996. Tchr. Denver Acad., 1985-92; asst. prof. spl. edn. Chadron (Nebr.) State Coll., 1995-98, Met. State Coll. Denver, 1998—. Mem. NEA, Coun. Exceptional Children, Am. Coun. Rural Edn. Home: 1481 Hwy 103 Idaho Springs CO 80452

BLOCK, LAWRENCE, author; b. Buffalo, June 24, 1938; s. Arthur Jerome and Lenore Harriet (Nathan) B.; m. Loretta Kallett, Mar. 10, 1960 (div. 1973); children: Amy Jo Block Reichel, Jill Diana, Alison Elspeth; m. Lynne Wood, Oct. 2, 1983. Student, Antioch Coll., 1955-59. Editor Scott Meredith Lit. Agy., N.Y.C., 1957-58; editor Whitman Pub. Co., Racine, Wis., 1964-66; free lance writer, 1957—; pres., seminar leader Write for Your Life, N.Y.C. and Ft. Myers Beach, Fla., 1983-88; instr. Hofstra U., Hempstead, N.Y., 1981. Author: (novels) Mona, 1961, Death Pulls A Doublecross, 1962, The Girl with the Long Green Heart, 1965, The Thief Who Couldn't Sleep, 1966, The Cancelled Czech, 1966, Deadly Honeymoon, 1967, Tanner's Twelve Swingers, 1967, Two for Tanner, 1968, Tanner's Tiger, 1968, Here Comes A Hero, 1968, After The First Death, 1969, The Specialists, 1969, Such Men Are Dangerous, 1969, Me Tanner, You Jane, 1970, No Score, 1970, Ronald Rabbit Is A Dirty Old Man, 1971, Chip Harrison Scores Again, 1971, Five Little Rich Girls, 1976, The Topless Tulip Caper, 1975, The Sins of the Fathers, 1976, In the Midst of Death, 1976, Time to Murder and Create, 1977, Burglars Can't Be Choosers, 1977, The Burglar in the Closet, 1978, The Burglar Who Liked to Quote Kipling (Nero Wolfe award), 1979, Ariel, 1980, The Burglar Who Studied Spinoza, 1980, A Stab in the Dark, 1981, Eight Million Ways to Die, 1982, The Burglar Who Painted Like Mondrian, 1983, When the Sacred Ginmill Closes (Japanese Maltese Falcon award), 1986, Random Walk, 1988, Out on the Cutting Edge, 1989, A Ticket to the Boneyard, 1990, A Dance at the Slaughterhouse, 1991, A Walk Among the Tombstones, 1992, The Devil Knows You're Dead, 1993, The Burglar Who Traded Ted Williams, 1994 (German Marlowe award), A Long Line of Dead Men, 1994, The Burglar Who Thought He Was Bogart, 1995, Even the Wicked, 1997, The Burglar in the Library, 1997, Hit Man, 1998, Tanner on Ice, 1998, Everybody Dies, 1998, The Burglar in the Rye, 1999; (nonfiction) Writing the Novel From Plot to Print, 1979, Telling Lies For Fun and Profit, 1981, Write for Your Life, 1985, Spider, Spin Me a Web, 1988; (with Delbert Ray Krause) Swiss Shooting Talers and Medals, 1965; (with Cheryl Morrison) Real Food Places, 1981; (with Harold King) Code of Arms, 1981, (with Ernie Bulow) After Hours, 1994; (short story collections) Sometimes They Bite (trophy 813 Societe of France), 1983, Like A Lamb to Slaughter, 1984, Some Days You Get The Bear, 1993, Ehrengraf for the Defense, 1994, One Night Stands, 1999; contbg. editor Writer's Digest, 1976-90; contbr. stories to various mags. including Cosmopolitan, Playboy, mystery mags. Named Suspense Writer of Yr., Romantic Times, 1984, Grand Maitre du Roman Noir, Calibre 38, 1996. Fellow Flat Earth Soc. of Can. (U.S. plenipotentiary 1971—), Va. Ctr. for the Creative Arts; mem. The Players, Mystery Writers Am. (Edgar Allan Poe award 1985, 92, 94, 98, Grand Master award 1994), Pvt. Eye Writers Am. (pres. 1984, Shamus award 1983, 85, 96), Internat. Assn. Crime Writers, Internat. Narcotics Enforcement Officers Assn., Internat. Assn. for Study of Organized Crime, Crime Writers Can., Crime Writers Assn. (U.K.), Crime Writers of Norway. E-Mail: LawBloc@aol.com.

BLOCK, M. JULIANN MCCARTHY, school psychologist; b. Lewistown, Mont., Jan. 5, 1957; d. John Joseph and Helen Patricia (Ryan) McCarthy; m. David William Block, Jan. 8, 1993; step-children: Will Jacob, Bret Roman. BA, Carroll Coll., 1979; MA, U. Mont., 1983, 84. Cert. tchr., sch. psychologist, Ariz.; nat. cert. sch. psychologist. English tchr. Garfield County H.S., Jordan, Mont., 1979-81; sch. psychologist Cassia County Joint Sch. Dist., Burley, Idaho, 1984-85, Ednl. Svc. Dist. #112, Vancouver, Wash., 1985-92, Chandler (Ariz.) Unified Sch. Dist., 1992-94, Fountain Hills (Ariz.) Unified Sch. Dist., 1994-98, Flaggstaff Unified Sch. Dist., 1998—. Del. Wash. Dem. Party Clark County, Olympia, 1992. Mem. ASCD, Nat. Assn. Sch. Psychologists. Roman Catholic. Avocations: music, theater, golf, cooking, hiking. Home: PO Box 61 Flagstaff AZ 86002-0061 Office: Marshall Elem Sch 850 N Bonito Flagstaff AZ 86001

BLOCK, MARTIN, lawyer; b. N.Y.C., July 14, 1937; s. Leonard and Rose (Tenzer) B.; m. Linda Zuckerman, Dec. 25, 1965 (div. 1979); children: Sarin, Bryson; m. Ann Block, July 15, 1990. Student Bklyn. Coll., 1959-61, NYU, 1962-63; LL.B., Bklyn. Law Sch., 1965. Bar: N.Y. 1965, U.S. Dist. Ct. (so. and ea. dists.) N.Y. 1966, U.S. Ct. Appeals (2d cir. 1979). Assoc. Seymour L. Colin, N.Y.C., 1965-70; assoc. then ptnr. Queller, Fisher, Block & Wisotsky, N.Y.C., 1970-85; ptnr. Sanders, Sanders, Block & Woycik, P.C. 1985—; instr. Hofstra U. Trial Adv. Program, 1994—; guest lectr. Lawline-Cable TV, N.Y.C., 1984. Served as staff sgt. USNG, 1959-64. Recipient Cert. in Civil Trial Adv. Nat. Bd. Trial Adv., 1993. Mem. ATLA, Nassau County Bar Assn. (chair Plaintiffs Roundtable com.), Assn. Trial Lawyers of City of N.Y., N.Y. State Trial Lawyers Assn. (lectr. 1984), Nassau-Suffolk Trial Lawyers Assn. (treas. 1998 sect., bd. dirs. 1994-97), Pres. Club, Am. Arbitration Assn. Democrat. Jewish. Office: Sanders Sanders Block & Woycik PC 100 Herricks Rd Mineola NY 11501-3652

BLOCK, MELVIN AUGUST, surgeon, educator; b. Evansville, Ind., July 2, 1921; s. August William and Alma (Klutey) B.; m. Marcia Jean Jacobs, May 28, 1955; children: Deborah Ann, Christopher Reed. B.S., Ind. U., 1942, M.D., 1944; Ph.D., U. Minn., 1953. Intern Ind. U. Med. Center, 1945; resident Mayo Clinic, Rochester, Minn., 1948-54; chmn. dept. surgery Henry Ford Hosp., Detroit, 1975-79, Scripps Clinic Med. Group, La Jolla, Calif., 1980-87; clin. prof. surgery U. Mich. Med. Sch., 1970-80, U. Calif., San Diego Med. Sch., 1980-93. Contbr. numerous articles to profl. jours. Served to capt. M.C. AUS, 1945-47. Fellow Royal Coll. Surgeons Can.; mem. ACS (past gov.), Am., Central, Western (past pres.) surg. assns., Am. Thyroid Assn., Am. Gastroenterology Assn., Soc. Surg. Alimentary Tract, Soc. Head and Neck Surgeons, Soc. Internationale de Chirurgie, AMA, Calif., San Diego county med. socs., Acad. Surg. Detroit (past pres.), Detroit Surg. Soc. (past pres.), Internat. Assn. Endocrine Surgeons, Am. Assn. Endocrine Surgeons, Sigma Xi, Alpha Omega Alpha. Home: 4575 Excalibur Way San Diego CA 92122-1513 Office: Scripps Clinic Med Group 10666 N Torrey Pines Rd La Jolla CA 92037-1027 *Time is our most valuable possession. It is limited qualitatively and quantitatively. This realization should be implied in most actions.*

BLOCK, MICHAEL DAVID, minister; b. Albuquerque, Jan. 19, 1958; s. Isaac Edward and Lucy Mac (Waide) B.; m. Rebecca Lynn Hart, June 30, 1979; 1 child, Nathanael David. BA, Wayland Bapt. U., 1980; MDiv, Southwestern Bapt. Sem., 1983, PhD, 1990. Ordained to ministry Bapt. Ch., 1982. Min. music Finney Bapt. Ch., Plainview, Tex., 1978-79, Date St. Bapt. Ch., Plainview, Tex., 1979-80; pastor Levita Bapt. Ch., Gatesville, Tex., 1984-85, 1st Bapt. ch., Comanche, Okla., 1985-91, Crestwood Bapt. Ch., Oklahoma City, 1991-96, First Bapt. Ch., Monett, Mo., 1996—; lectr. Ministry Tng. Inst., Okla. Bapt. U., 1992-96. Basketball coach Youth Sports League, Duncan, 1989-90. Mem. Comanche C. of C. (coord. Christmas food baskets 1986-90), Mullins Bapt. Assn. (sec., dir. missions, search com. 1987-88, moderator 1987-89, chmn. budget com. 1990-91), Capital Bapt. Assn. (vice moderator 1992-94, chair com. on coms. 1994-95, pers. com. 1994-96, exec. com. 1992-94, continuing edn. com. 1992-94), Ministerial Alliance. Republican. Office: 412 4th St Monett MO 65708-2015 *The call of life is to walk with God. The challenge of life is to live in obedience to God. The change of life is to influence others toward God.*

BLOCK, MICHAEL KENT, economics and law educator, public policy association executive, former government official, consultant; b. N.Y.C., Apr. 2, 1942; s. Philip and Roslyn (Klein) B.; m. Carole Arline Polansky, Aug. 30, 1964 (div.); children: Robert Justin, Tamara Nicole; m. Olga Vyborna, Dec. 1, 1996. A.B., Stanford U., 1964, A.M., 1969, Ph.D., 1972. Research analyst Bank of Am., San Francisco, 1965-66; research assoc. Planning Assocs., San Francisco, 1966-67; asst. prof. econs. U. Santa Clara, 1969-72; asst. prof. econs. dept. ops. research and adminstrv. sci. Naval Postgrad. Sch., Monterey, Calif., 1972-74, assoc. prof., 1974-76; research fellow Hoover Instn., Stanford U., 1975-76, sr. research fellow, 1976-87; dir. Center for Econometric Studies of Justice System, 1977-81; ptnr. Block & Nold, Cons., Palo Alto, Calif., 1980-81; assoc. prof. mgmt., econs. and law U. Ariz., Tucson, 1982-85, prof. econs. and law, 1989—; mem. U.S. Sentencing Commn., Washington, 1985-89; exec. v.p. Cybernomics, Tucson, 1991—; pres. Goldwater Inst. for Pub. Policy, Phoenix, Ariz., 1992—; sr. policy adviser State of Ariz. Gov. Symington, 1996-97; mem. Ariz. Residential Utility Consumer Bd., 1995-96, chmn. Ariz. Constl. Def. Coun., 1994-97, Ariz. Juvenile Justice Adv. Coun., 1996-97; seminar dir. Econ. Devel. Inst./ World Bank, 1992-95; cons. in field. Author: (with H.G. Demmert) Workbook and Programmed Guide to Economics, 1974, 77, 80, (with James M. Clabault) A Legal and Economic Analysis of Criminal Antitrust Indictments:, 1955-80; contbr. articles to profl. publs. Fellow NSF, 1965, Stanford U. Fellow Progress and Freedom Found.; mem. Am. Econ. Assn., Phi Beta Kappa. Office: U Ariz Econ Dept McClelland Hall Tucson AZ 85721

BLOCK, NEAL JAY, lawyer; b. Chgo., Oct. 4, 1942; s. William Emanual and Dorothy (Harrison) B.; m. Frances Keer Block, Apr. 19, 1970; children: Jessica, Andrew. BS, U. Ill., 1964; JD, U. Chgo., 1967. Bar: Ill. 1967, U.S. dist. Ct. (no. dist.) Ill. 1967, U.S. Ct. Appeals (3d and 6th cirs.) 1968, U.S. Claims Ct. 1990, U.S. Ct. Appeals (Fed. cir.) 1991. Atty., advisor U.S. Tax Ct., Washington, 1967-69; assoc. Baker & McKenzie, Chgo., 1969-74, ptnr., 1974—, client credit dir., 1989—; adj. prof. law Kent Law Sch., Ill. Inst. Tech., Chgo., 1986-90. Mem. ABA, Chgo. Bar Assn. (chmn. fed. tax com. 1983-84), Ill. State Bar Assn., AICPA (honorable mention award 1964), Ill. Soc. CPA's. (silver medal 1964, Leading Ill. Atty. 1997). Office: Baker & McKenzie 1 Prudential Pla 130 E Randolph St Ste 3700 Chicago IL 60601-6342

BLOCK, NED, philosophy educator; b. Chgo., Aug. 22, 1942; s. Eli William and Blanche (Rabinowitz) B.; m. Susan Carey, May 17, 1970; 1 child, Eliza. SB in Physics and Philosophy, MIT, 1964; postgrad. in philosophy, St. John's Coll., Oxford U., Eng., 1964-66; PhD, Harvard U., 1971. Asst. prof. philosophy MIT, Cambridge, 1971-77, assoc. prof., 1977-83, prof., 1983-96, chair dept. philosophy, 1989-95; prof. philosophy NYU, 1996—; mem. faculty NEH Inst. on Philosophy of Psychology, summer 1981, 93; grant reviewer NSF, Can. Coun.; pres. Soc. for Philosophy and Psychology, 1978-79; chair MIT Press Cognitive Sci. Rev. Bd., 1992-95; vis. rschr. Ecole Poly., Paris, 1995-96. Adv. editor Contemporary Psychology; mem. editorial bd. Cognition, Cognition and Brain Theory, Cognitive Sci.; mem. adv. editorial bd. Lang. and Cognitive Processes, Mind and Lang. Philos. Studies; mem. bd. editorial advisors Behavioral and Brain Scis.; contbr. articles to profl. jours. (selected as one of 10 best Philosophers' Ann., 1983, 90, 95). Grantee U.S. Nat. Com. for Internat. Union History and Philosophy Sci., 1979, 83, NEH, 1979-82, NSF, 1985-86, 1988-90, Am. Council Learned Socs., 1988-89; fellow Old Dominion Found., 1973-74, Sloan Found., 1980-81, Guggenheim Found., 1984-85; sr. fellow Ctr. for Study Lang. and Info. at Stanford U., 1984-85; NIH postdoctoral fellowship, 1970-71; conf. on his work, U. Barcelona, 1993. Home: 37 Washington Sq W New York NY 10011-9181 Office: NYU Dept Philosophy Main Bldg 100 Washington Sq E New York NY 10003-6688

BLOCK, PAUL ALAN, novelist, editor; b. N.Y.C., Mar. 2, 1951; s. Murray Harold and Estelle (Kleckner) B.; m. Amy Morton Lent, Apr. 14, 1973 (div. Feb. 1984); children: Kiva Lent Block, Ueyn Lent Block; m. Constance Patricia Orcutt, Mar. 3, 1990. Student, SUNY, Binghamton, 1969-71; BA, Empire State Coll., 1973. Copy editor San Pedro (Calif.) News-Pilot, 1978-79; asst. city editor The Knickerbocker News, Albany, N.Y., 1979-81; editor-in-chief Book Creations, Inc., Canaan, N.Y., 1981-93, cons. editor, 1993—; editl. dir. Skyward Pub., Dallas, 1997—; copy desk chief Times Union, Albany, 1998—. Author: San Francisco, 1988, The Deceit, 1989, Beneath the Sky, 1993, Darkening of the Light, 1994, Song of the Mohicans, 1995, The Calling, 1996; author under pseudonym Hank Mitchum: Durango, 1985, Mesa Verde, 1986, Royal Coach, 1987; author under pseudonym Justin Ladd: The Peacemaker, 1988; author under pseudonum Donald Clayton Porter: Creek Thunder, 1995, Medicine Shield, 1996; author (screenplay for PBS series) Chickenfeed. V.p. New Lebanon (N.Y.) Sch. Bd., 1986-88. Mem. Writers Guild of Am. West, Western Writers of Am. Avocations: collecting and restoring antique typewriters, extensive travel.

BLOCK, PHILIP DEE, III, investment counselor; b. Chgo., Feb. 14, 1937; married; 2 children. BS in Indsl. Adminstrn. with high honors, Yale U., 1958. Trainee and engr. Inland Steel Co., Chgo., 1958-60, raw materials coordinator, 1961-65, gen. mgr. purchases, 1966-72, gen. mgr. corp. planning, 1973-76; v.p. materials and services Inland Steel Container, Chgo., 1977-79, v.p. purchases, 1980-85; v.p. Capital Guardian Trust Co., Chgo., 1986—. Bd. dirs. Children's Meml. Hosp.; trustee Chgo. Hist. Soc., Shedd Aquarium Soc. With USAR, 1959-64. Home: 1430 N Lake Shore Dr Chicago IL 60610-6658 Office: Capital Guardian Trust Co 1 First Natl Plz Ste 2544 Chicago IL 60603-2003

BLOCK, RICHARD RAPHAEL, lawyer, economic development arbitrator; b. Phila., Nov. 9, 1938; s. Harry and Ida (Brandes) B.; m. Joanne Kramer, July 1, 1943 (div. Jan. 1973); 1 child, Jeffrey. AB, Dickinson Coll., 1959; LLB cum laude, U. Pa., 1962. Bar: Pa. 1963, N.J. 1980, D.C. 1982. Assoc. Folz & Bard, Phila., 1963-64; ptnr. Melzer & Schiffrin, Phila., 1964-75, Beitch & Block, Phila., 1975-90; dir. community rels. Dist. Atty. of Phila., 1991-96; chief tech. officer Phila. Dept. of Commerce, 1996—; chmn. hearing com Disciplinary Bd. Supreme Ct. Pa., 1982-90. Contbg. author: Handbook of Pennsylvania Courts, 1970, Divorce Mediation, 1985, Prenuptial Agreements, 1989, Encyclopedia on Matrimonial Practice, 1991; assoc. editor U. Pa. Law Rev.; contbr. articles to profl. jours. Vice pres. Am. Jewish Congress, Phila., 1975; campaign mgr. Elect Joan Specter to City Coun., Phila., 1978, 82, 86. Mem. Pa. Bar Assn. (arbitrator Inter-Atty. Dispute Resolution 1987—, speaker 1988) Am. Arbitration Assn., Phila. Coll. Judiciary (lectr. 1984). Republican. Avocations: horse racing, computers, music.

BLOCK, ROBERT CHARLES, nuclear engineering and engineering physics educator; b. Newark, Feb. 11, 1929; s. George and Sue (Ehrenkranz) B.; m. Rita Adler, June 28, 1952; children: Keith, Robin. BSEE, Newark Coll. Engring., 1950; MA in Physics, Columbia U., 1953; PhD in Nuclear Physics, Duke U., 1956. Elec. engr. Nat. Union Radio Corp., W. Orange, N.J., 1950-51, Bendix Aviation Co., Teterboro, N.J., 1951; physicist Oak Ridge Nat. Lab., 1955-66; prof. nuclear engring. and sci. Rensselaer Poly. Inst., 1966-96, head dept. nuclear engring. and engring. physics, 1987-93, 1987-93, assoc. dean engring. for acad. & student affairs, 1993-96; prof. emeritus, 1997—; founder, v.p., treas. Becker, Block & Harris Inc., 1981-92; vis. scientist Atomic Energy Rsch. Establishment, Harwell, Eng., 1962-63, Am. Inst. Physics, 1961-67; vis. prof. Kyoto (Japan) U., 1973-74; vis. physicist Brookhaven Nat. Lab., 1975, mem. vis. com. nuclear energy dept., 1982-86; cons. Gen. Electric Co., 1968-79; cons., mem. nuclear cross sect. adv. com. AEC, 1969-72; mem. U.S. Nuclear Data Com., 1972-74, NRC panel on low and medium energy neutrons, 1977; dir. Gaerttner Linac Lab., 1974—; vis. faculty Sandia Nat. Lab., 1986. Co-author chpt. in books. Recipient Glenn Murphy award Am. Soc. Engring. Edn., 1991, William H. Wiley Disting. Faculty award Rensselaer Poly. Inst., 1995; Japanese Ministry Edn. rsch. grantee, 1973-74. Fellow Am. Nuclear Soc.; mem. AAAS, AAUP, IEEE, Am. Phys. Soc., Sigma Xi, Sigma Pi Sigma, Phi Beta Tau, Tau Beta Pi. Research on neutron physics, radiation effects in electronics, and radiation applications. Home: 114 3rd St Troy NY 12180-4037 Office: Rensselaer Poly Inst Gaerttner LINAC Lab 110 8th St Troy NY 12180-3522

BLOCK, ROBERT I., psychologist, researcher, educator; b. Newark, N.J., Jan. 30, 1951; s. Milton and Harriet (Safier) B. BA with honors, Shimer Coll., 1969; MS, Harvard U., 1972, Rutgers U., 1977; PhD, Rutgers U., 1981. Teaching asst. psychology dept. Rutgers U., New Brunswick, N.J., 1975-76; psychologist Lafayette Clinic, Detroit, 1982-84; rsch. assoc. psychiatry dept. Wayne State U., Detroit, 1982, instr., 1982-84; assoc. rsch. scientist dept. anesthesia U. Iowa, Iowa City, 1984-88, asst. prof. dept. anesthesia, 1988-94, assoc. prof. dept. anesthesia, 1994—; cons. State of Mich., Lafayette Clinic, Detroit, Hoffmann La-Roche, Inc.; reviewer Psychopharmacology and Anesthesiology; mem. faculty senate Sch. of Medicine, Wayne State U., Detroit, 1982-84. Contbr. articles to Anesthesiology, Brit. Jour. Anaesthesia, Psychopharmacology, Pharmacol. Biochem. Behavior. Fellow Rutgers U.; grantee Nat. Inst. on Drug Abuse, 1987-91, 93—. Mem. AAAS, Collegium Internat. Neuro-Psychopharmacologicum, Am. Psychol. Assn. Achievements include research on effects of nitrous oxide, benzodiazepines, marijuana, and other drugs on human associative processes, memory, and cognition. Home: 2029 Waterford Dr Coralville IA 52241-2734 Office: U Iowa Dept Anesthesia Westlawn Bldg Iowa City IA 52242

BLOCK, ROBERT N., federal judge. Apptd. magistrate judge cen. dist. U.S. Dist. Ct. Calif., 1995. Fax: (213) 894-6860. Office: 1006 US Courthouse 312 N Spring St Los Angeles CA 90012-4701

BLOCK, RUTH, retired insurance company executive; b. N.Y.C., Nov. 7, 1930; d. Albert and Celia (Shapiro) Smolensky; BA, Adelphi U., 1952; m. Norman Block, April 5, 1952. With Equitable Life Assurance Soc. of U.S., 1952-87, v.p., planning officer, 1973-77, sr. v.p. in charge individual life ins. bus., 1977-80, exec. v.p. individual ins. bus.'s, 1980-87, duties expanded to include group life and health bus.'s, chief ins. officer, 1984-87; chmn., chief exec. officer Equitable Variable Life Ins. Co., 1980-84; bd. dirs. Amoco Corp., Ecolab Inc., (40) ACM Mut. Funds; trustee Life Underwriter Tng. Coun., 1983-85; vis. exec. Mobil Co. U. Iowa, 1978. Bd. dirs. Stamford (Conn.) YWCA, 1977-80, Donaldson, Lufkin & Jenrette, 1983-86, Avon Products, 1985-91, St Lukes Cmty. Svcs., 1991-94; nat. chmn. Equitable United Way, 1978. Recipient Disting. Alumni award Adelphi U. Sch. of Bus., 1979, Catalyst award 1983, WEAL award, 1983, N.Y.C. YMCA award. Mem. Nat. Assn. Securities Dealers (gov. at large 1982-84), Com. of 200, Womens Econ. Round Table, Rsch. Bd.(emeritus), Bus. Execs for Nat. Security, Women's Forum N.Y. and Conn. Office: PO Box 4653 Stamford CT 06907-0653

BLOCK, SANDRA LINDA, special education educator; b. Inglewood, Calif., Aug. 29, 1947; d. Milton and Anne (Leiderman) Berenbaum; divorced; 1 child, Rina Ann Hunter. BS, U. So. Calif., 1969. Cert. tchr., Calif. Tchr. L.A. Unified Sch. Dist., 1969-87; mentor tchr. Calif.; comty. tchr. Irvine, Calif., 1987—. Mem. AAUW. Democrat. Jewish. Avocations: reading, traveling. Home: 4 Del Rey Irvine CA 92612-2961

BLOCK, STANLEY HOYT, pediatrician, allergist; b. N.Y.C., Oct. 28, 1943; s. Julius and Zilla Augustus (Friedman) B. BA, U. Chgo., 1963; MD, Yale U., 1966. Diplomate Am. Bd. Pediatrics, Am. Bd. Allergy and Immunology. Intern Children's Hosp. of Phila., Mass., 1966-67; resident Babies Hosp., Columbia Presbyn. Med. Ctr., N.Y.C., 1967-69; pediatrician, allergist pvt. practice Lynn and Lowell, 1971-77; med. dir. Providence (R.I.) Ambulatory Health Care Found., 1977—. Major U.S. Army, 1969-71. Recipient Tchg. award in pediatrics R.I. Hosp. House Officers Assn., 1982, Dr. Charles L. Hill award for Pub. Svc., R.I. Med. Soc., 1995. Fellow Am. Acad. Pediatrics, Am. Acad. Allergy, Asthma and Immunology, R.I. Soc. of Allergy (former pres., sec.); mem. R.I. Med. Soc. Avocations: hiking, cross country skiing. Office: Providence Ambulatory Health Care Found 375 Allens Ave Providence RI 02905-5010*

BLOCK, WILLIAM, newspaper publisher; b. N.Y.C., Sept. 20, 1915; s. Paul and Dina (Wallach) B.; m. Maxine Horton, Mar. 23, 1944; children: William Jr., Karen Block Johnese, Barbara Block Burney, Donald. AB, Yale U., 1936. With circulation, other depts. Toledo Blade, 1937-39, asst. to gen. mgr., 1939-41; co-pub. Pitts. Post-Gazette and Toledo Blade, 1941-87, pub., 1987-89; chmn. PG Pub. Co., Pitts., 1989—; chmn. bd. dirs. Blade Comm., Inc. Bd. dirs. Gateway to Music Inc.; trustee emeritus Am. Assembly; sponsor Allegheny Conf. on Community Devel. Capt. AUS, 1941-46; served in mil. govt., Korea, 1945-46. Mem. Internat. Press Inst., Am. Soc. Newspaper Editors, Soc. Profl. Journalists, Am. Newspaper Assn. *

BLOCK, WILLIAM K., JR., newspaper executive; b. New Haven, Nov. 28, 1944; s. William and Maxine (Horton) B.; m. Carol Pauline Zurheide, Aug. 1, 1970; children: Diana, Nancy, Katherine. BA, Trinity Coll., Hartford, Conn., 1967; JD, Washington and Lee U., 1972. Bar: Pa., U.S. Supreme Ct. Staff mem. Red Bank (N.J.) Register and Toledo Blade, 1972-77; advtg. mgr. Red Bank (N.J.) Register, Shrewsbury, N.J., 1977-79, sales mgr., 1979-80; pub. Red Bank (N.J.) Register, 1980-82; dir. ops. Toledo Blade Co., 1983-84, v.p. ops., 1984-86, v.p., gen. mgr., 1986-87, pres., 1987—, co-pub., 1990—; co-pub. Pitts. Post Gazette, 1990—; v.p. Blade Communications, Inc., Toledo, 1987-88, pres., 1989—. V.p. Toledo Sesquicentennial Commn., 1986-87, Inland Press Assn.; bd. dirs. Toledo Symphony, Maumee Valley Hist. Soc.; pres. Read for Literacy, Inc. With U.S. Army, 1968-70, Vietnam. Mem. Toledo Country Club, Toledo Club. Avocations: reading, tennis, travel, fishing. Office: Blade Communications Inc 541 N Superior St Toledo OH 43660-0001

BLOCK, WILLIAM KENNETH, lawyer; b. N.Y.C., Oct. 23, 1950; s. Louis and Catherine Veronica (Kerr) B. BA, Colgate U., 1973; JD, Union U., Albany, N.Y., 1976. Bar: N.Y. 1977. Gen. counsel N.Y.C. Tax Commn., 1978-81; asst. commn. fin. N.Y.C. Dept. Fin., 1981-84, dep. commr. fin., 1984-89; assoc. Schwartz, Weiss, Steckler & Hoffman, P.C., N.Y.C., 1989-91; pvt. practice, William K. Block, P.C., N.Y.C., 1992—; adj. lectr. real estate NYU, 1992—. Contbr. articles on real property tax law and procedure to profl. jours. Mem. ABA, Internat. Assn. Assessing Officers (chmn. met. jurisdiction coun. 1987-88, presdl. citation 1986, McCareen award 1988), N.Y. State Assessors Assn., N.Y. State Bar Assn., New York County Bar Assn. (com. on City of N.Y., real property com., govt. counsel com.), Real Estate Rev. Bar Assn., dir. 1995—), Assn. Bar City of N.Y. (com. on tax certiorari), Real Estate Bd. N.Y. (com. on taxation). Democrat. Roman Catholic. Home: 115 E 34th St Apt 20K New York NY 10016-4631 Office: 295 Madison Ave Fl 38 New York NY 10017-6304

BLOCK, ZENAS, management consultant, educator; b. N.Y.C., Dec. 7, 1916; s. Joshua and Celia (Kaplow) B.; m. Lillian Bialek, June 12, 1938 (dec. 1985); children: Richard, Karen Block Chase Graubard), Margaret Block Walker; m. Janet Andre, Aug. 13, 1988. BS, CCNY, 1938; postgrad., Bklyn. Poly. Inst., 1939-41. Chemist Clairol Inc., N.Y.C., 1938-39; chief chemist Am. Dietaids Co., Yonkers, N.Y., 1938-48; dir. labs. DCA Food Industries, N.Y.C., 1948-55, v.p. rsch., 1955-60, pres. bakery divsn., 1960-64, group v.p., 1964-71, exec. v.p., 1971-77, vice chmn. bd., 1977-79, also bd. dirs.; chmn. bd. dirs. Nisshin DCA Foods Inc., Tokyo, 1975-79, DCA Industries Ltd., Eng., 1976-79; bd. dirs. IMPAC Group; founder, pres. Haystack Cable Vision Inc., Lakeville, Conn., 1978-80, v.p. and pres., 1980-82; adj. lectr. Grad. Sch. Bus. Adminstrn., U. Conn., 1979-81; clin. prof. NYU, 1984-91, adj. prof. entrepreneurship grad. divsn. Stern Schs. Bus., NYU, 1991—, founder, assoc. dir. Ctr. for Entrepreneurial Studies, 1984-89; adj. prof. mgmt. Lally Sch. Mgmt., Rensselaer Poly. Inst., 1991-92, 97-98, vis. prof., 1996-97, curriculum cons., 1997-99. Author: It's All on the Label, 1981; (with I.C. MacMillan) Corporate Venturing: Creating New Businesses Within the Firm, 1993; mem. editorial bd. Jour. Bus. Venturing; contbr. articles to acad. and profl. jours.; patentee food processing field. Bd. dirs. N.Y.C. Mission Soc., 1983-87, Salisbury Family Svcs., 1983-87; trustee Salisbury Assoc., 1992-95; mem. bd. fin. Town of Salisbury, 1996—. Home and Office: PO Box 530 Salisbury CT 06068-0530

BLODER, LISA W., critical care nurse, mental health nurse; b. Birmingham, Ala., June 28, 1965; d. James A. and Audrey E. (Bryant) Weeks; m. Harald K. Bloder, Mar. 25, 1989; 1 child, Amanda. AS in Emergency Medicine, Trenholm St. Tech., 1984; ASN, Jefferson State Jr. Coll., 1987. RN, Ala., Fla.; cert. case mgr. Staf nurse Humana Hosp. East Mongtomery (Ala.); nurse mgr., dir. case mgr., dir. clin. assessment ctr. Laurel Oaks Hosp., Orlando, Fla., 1988-95; case mgr., dir. case mgmt. Ctrl. Fla. region Integrated Health Svcs. of Orlando, 1995-97; adminstr. IHS Hospice of Fla., Montverde and Orlando, 1997-98; case mgr. CarELink Ptnrs. Inc., Orlando, 1998—. Mem. Case Mgmt. Soc. Am., Hospice and Palliative Nurses Assn. Home: 16012 Four Lakes Ln Montverde FL 34756-3017

BLODGETT, ELSIE GRACE, association executive; b. Eldorado Springs, Mo., Aug. 2, 1921; d. Charles Ishmal and Naoma Florence (Worthington) Robison; m. Charles Davis Blodgett, Nov. 8, 1940; children: Carolyn Doyel, Charleen Bier, Lyndon Blodgett, Daryl (dec.). Student Warrensburg (Mo.) State Tchrs. Coll., 1939-40; BA, Fresno (Calif.) State Coll., 1953. Tchr. schs. in Mo. and Calif., 1940-42, 47-72; owner, mgr. rental units, 1965—; exec. dir. San Joaquin County (Calif.) Rental Property Assn., Stockton, 1970-81; prin. Delta Rental Property Owners and Assocs., 1981-82; propr. Crystal Springs Health World, Inc., Stockton, 1980-86; bd. dirs. Stockton Better Bus. Bur. Active local PTA; Girl Scouts U.S., Boy Scouts Am.; bd. dirs. Stockton Goodwill Industries; active Vols. in Police Svc., 1993; capt. Delaware Alpine Neighborhood Watch, 1994—. Named (with husband) Mr. and Mrs. Apt. Owner of San Joaquin County, 1977. Mem. Nat. Apt. Assn. (state treas. women's div. 1977-79), Calif. Ret. Tchrs. Assn. Republican. Methodist. Lodge: Stockton Zonta. Home and Office: 2285 W Mendocino Ave Stockton CA 95204-4005

BLODGETT, FORREST CLINTON, economics educator; b. Oregon City, Oreg., Oct. 6, 1927; s. Clinton Alexander and Mabel (Wells) B.; m. Beverley Janice Buchholz, Dec. 21, 1946; children: Cherine Eiline Klein, Candis Melis, Clinton George. BS, U. Omaha, 1961; MA, U. Mo., 1969; PhD, Portland State U., 1979. Joined C.E. U.S. Army, 1946, commd. 2d lt., 1946, advanced through grades to lt. col., 1965, ret., 1968; engring. assignments U.S. Army, Japan, 1947-49, U.K., 1950-53, Korea, 1955-56, Alaska, 1958-60, Vietnam, 1963; staff engr. 2d Army Air Def. Region U.S. Army, Richards-Gebaur AFB, Mo., 1964-66; base engr. Def. Atomic Support Agy., Sandia Base, N.Mex., 1966-68; bus. mgr., trustee, asst. prof. econs. Linfield Coll., McMinnville, Oreg., 1968-73, assoc. prof., 1973-83, prof., 1983-90, emeritus prof. econs., 1990—; pres. Blodgett Enterprises, Inc., 1983-85; founder, dir. Valley Community Bank, 1980-86, vice chmn. bd. dirs., 1985-86. Commr., Housing Authority of Yamhill County (Oreg.), chmn., 1980-83; mem. Yamhill County Econ. Devel. Com., 1978-83; bd. dirs. Yamhill County Found., 1983-91, Oreg. Internat. Coun., 1995—. Decorated Army Commendation medal with oak leaf cluster; recipient Joint Service Commendation medal Dept. of Def. Mem. Soc. Am. Mil. Engrs. (pres. Albuquerque post 1968), Am. Econ. Assn., Western Econ. Assn. Internat., Nat. Ret. Officers Assn., Res. Officers Assn. (pres. Marion chpt. 1976), SAR (pres. Oreg. soc. 1985-86, v.p. gen. Nat. Soc. 1991-93), Urban Affairs Assn., Soc. for The History of Tech., Am. Law and Econs. Assn., Pi Sigma Epsilon, Pi Gamma Mu, Omicron Delta Epsilon (Pacific NW regional dir. 1978-88), Rotary (pres. McMinnville 1983-84). Republican. Episcopalian. Office: Linfield Coll 1300 NE 16th Ave #1020 Portland OR 97232-1487

BLODGETT, FRANK CALEB, retired food company executive; b. Janesville, Wis., Apr. 22, 1927; s. Frank Caleb Pickard and Dorothy (Korst) B.; m. Jean Ellen Fountain, June 23, 1951; children: Caleb J., Barbara F., David K. Grad., Beloit Coll., 1950; postgrad., Advanced Mgmt. Program, Harvard U., 1969. 1st v.p., dir. Frank H. Blodgett Inc., Janesville, 1947-61, pres., dir., 1961-62; with Gen. Mills Inc., Mpls., 1961-92, v.p., dir. mktg., 1967-69, gen. mgr., v.p., 1969-73, group v.p., 1973-76, exec. v.p., 1976-80, vice chmn., 1981-92, chief fin. and adminstrv. officer, 1985-92, dir., 1980-92; ret., 1992; bd. dirs. Medtronic, Inc., Reliastar Fin. Corp. and subs., Northwestern Nat. Life Ins. Co., HealthSpan Health Sys. Corp.; dir. Waldorf Corp., 1993—. Trustee Gen. Mills Found., 1980-92, Washburn Child Guidance Ctr., 1972-75, Beloit Coll., 1976—, Nutrition Found., 1980-84; bd. dirs. Cereal Inst., 1970-76, chmn., 1973-74; bd. dirs. Abbott Northwestern Hosp. With USN, 1944-46, PTO. Recipient Disting. Svc. citation Beloit Coll., 1990. Mem. Millers Nat. Fedn., Young Millers Orgn. (past pres.), U.S. C. of C. (bd. dirs. 1982-88), Greater Mpls. C. of C. (bd. dirs. 1975-76), Phi Kappa Psi (trustee alumni bd. Beloit 1961-62), Phi Eta Sigma. Home: 688 Hillside Dr Wayzata MN 55391-9643

BLODGETT, GEOFFREY THOMAS, history educator; b. Hanover, N.H., Oct. 13, 1931; s. Harold William and Dorothy Ardis (Briggs) B.; m. Jane McCall Taggart, Dec. 22, 1954; children: Lauren, Barbara, Sally. AB, Oberlin Coll., 1953; AM, Harvard U., 1956, PhD, 1961. Instr. Oberlin (Ohio) Coll., 1960-62, asst. prof., 1962-66, assoc. prof., 1966-68, prof. history, 1968-88, Danforth prof. history, 1988—, chair history dept., 1969-73, 82. Author: The Gentle Reformers, 1966, Oberlin Architecture, 1985 (Western Res. award 1986); contbr. articles on polit. and archtl. history to profl. jours. Mem. City Planning Commn., Oberlin, 1970-73; chair City Historic Preservation Commn., Oberlin, 1974-80. Lt. (j.g.) USN, 1953-55, Korea, Japan. Rsch. fellow Social Sci. Rsch. Coun., 1959-60, Am. Coun. Learned Socs., 1973-74, NEH, 1980-81. Mem. Orgn. Am. Historians, Oberlin Hist. Improvement Orgn., Soc. Archtl. Historians (Western Res. chpt.). Democrat. Avocation: architectural photography. Home: 273 Oak St Oberlin OH 44074-1517 Office: Oberlin Coll Dept History Rice Hall Oberlin OH 44074

BLODGETT, JULIAN ROBERT, small business owner; b. Honolulu, Nov. 21, 1919; s. Harry Hoagland and Esther Julia (Lyons) B.; m. Eleanor Anne Fischer, Nov. 4, 1941 (dec. 1983); children: Eric, Julie, Byron, Paul. BA, UCLA, 1940. Stock clk. Northrop Aircraft Co., Hawthorne, Calif., 1941-42; spl. agt. FBI, Washington, 1942-44, 46-57, Standard Oil Calif., San Francisco, 1945-46; gen. mgr. Western Indsl. Security Co., L.A., 1961-63; chief bur. investigation L.A. Dist. Atty., 1957-61; owner, operator Julian R. Blodgett Investigations, L.A., 1961—, Grey Fox Ltd., 1995—. Chmn., commr. L.A. City Housing Authority, 1963-65. Mem. Former Agts. FBI. Office: PO Box 49658 Los Angeles CA 90049-0658

BLODGETT, MARK STEPHEN, legal studies educator, author; b. St. Louis, Sept. 21, 1954; s. Warren Harding and Anna Helen (Stroska) B. BBA, U. Ga., 1976, MBA, 1978; JD, St. Louis U., 1983; postgrad., Harvard U., Cambridge U. Bar: Ga. 1983 (inactive). Law clk. to presiding judge State Ct. of Cobb County, Marietta, Ga., 1983-84; assoc. Law Firm, Atlanta, 1984-86; assoc. prof. legal studies Suffolk U., Boston, 1994—; asst. prof. legal studies Ga. State U., 1987-93, assoc. prof., 1994—. Co-author: International Dimensions of the Legal Environment of Business, 1995; editor Am. Bus. Law Jour.; contbr. articles to acad. jours. Regional dir. Am. Cancer Soc., Ga., 1987-89, v.p., 1989-90, pres., 1990-91. Mem. ABA, Am. Soc. Internat. Law, Acad. Legal Studies in Bus. (pres. internat. sect. 1996), Acad. Internat. Bus., Soc. Bus. Ethics. Episcopalian. Avocations: languages, athletics. Home: 90 Gainsborough St Unit 302E Boston MA 02115-6542 Office: Suffolk U Beacon Hill 8 Ashburton Pl Ste 631 Boston MA 02108-2770

BLODGETT, OMER WILLIAM, electric company design consultant; b. Duluth, Minn., Nov. 27, 1917; s. Myron O. and Minnie (Foster) B.; m. Dorothy B. Sjostrom, June 11, 1949; 1 child, Robert W. B.Metall.Engring. with distinction, U. Minn., 1941, M.E., 1976; DSc (hon.), Le Tourneau U., 1995. Registered profl. engr., Ohio. Welding supt. Globe Shipbldg. Co., Superior, Wis., 1941-45; sales engr. Lincoln Electric Co., Cleve., 1945-54; design cons., then sr. design cons. Lincoln Electric Co., 1954—; condr. seminars Australian Inst. Steel Constrn., Australia, 1971, 75, 78, New Zealand, 1975, South African Inst. Steel Constrn., 1981, Republic of China, 1985, London, 1986, 88, Brazil, 1988, Tokyo, 1992, Istanbul, Turkey, 1993. Author: Design Weldments, 1963, Design of Welded Structures, 1966, also papers. Fellow ASCE (hon.), ASME, Am. Welding Soc. (lectr. 1968, A.F. Davis silver medal 1962, 73, 80, 83, Higgins award 1983); mem. Sigma Xi, Tau Beta Pi. Home: 2013 Aldersgate Dr Cleveland OH 44124-3807 Office: 22801 Saint Clair Ave Cleveland OH 44117-2524

BLODGETT, RUTH, medical executive. MS, Northwestern U. COO Berkshire Med. Ctr., 1994—. Mem. Am. Coll. Health Care Execs. Office: 725 North St Pittsfield MA 01201

BLODGETT, TODD ALAN, publisher, marketing executive; b. Iowa City, Sept. 10, 1960; s. Gary Burl and Sandy Jean (Hodgson) B.; m. Linda Marie Reuber. BA in Journalism, Drake U., 1983. Fin. dir. Senator Roger W. Jepsen Re-election Com., Des Moines, 1983-84; staff asst. Reagan-Bush Inaugural Com., Inc., Washington, 1984-85; editorial asst. White House Staff News Summary, Washington, 1985-86; acct. exec. J.L. Whitehead & Assoc., Washington, 1986-87; domestic policy advisor Bush-Quayle '88 Com., Washington, 1987-88; sr. policy advisor analyst Rep. Nat. Com., Washington, 1989-90; campaign advisor Blodgett for Iowa Legislature campaign, Mason City, Iowa, 1992-92, also re-election advisor; CEO Rep. Victory Strategists, Inc. Contbr. editor American Conservative, 1991—; assoc. pub. Slick Times Mag., 1993-96; exec. editor Firearms & Preparedness Mag., 1996-98; contbr. articles to popular mags.; regularly nterviewed on Am. politics on BBC. Mem. The Conservative Network, Washington, 1985—; sustaining mem. Rep. Ctrl. Com. of Iowa, Des Moines, 1983; mem. Lincoln Club of Iowa, Des Moines, 1988—. Mem. NRA (life), Ducks Unltd., Reagan Appointees Alumni Assn. (mem.), Kennedy-Warren Residents Assn. (pres. 1989-92), U.S. C. of C., Univ. Club of Washington, D.C., Sigma Alpha Epsilon. Presbyterian. Avocations: hunting, snow and water skiing, numismatics, gun collecting, skeet shooting. Fax: (202) 319-9867. Home: 8239 The Midway Annandale VA 22003-3716 Office: Rep Victory Strategists Inc Ste 32 3133 Connecticut Ave NW Washington DC 20008-5104

BLODGETT, WARREN TERRELL, public affairs educator; b. Ranger, Tex., Sept. 15, 1923; s. William Serle Sr. and Alice Louise (Furman) B.; m. Dorothy Jean Chapin, Mar. 7, 1946; children: Robert Harold, William Arthur, Katherine Ann. BA, Baylor U., 1943; MS Pub. Adminstrn., Syracuse U., 1947. Research assoc. U. Tex., Austin, 1947-50, assoc. dir. policy rsch inst., 1982-90, Mike Hogg prof. urban mgmt., 1982-95, Mike Hogg prof. emeritus in urban mgmt., 1995—; personnel dir. City of Austin, 1950-52, adminstrv. asst. to city mgr., 1952-55, asst. city mgr., 1955-60; city mgr. City of Waco, Tex., 1960-63, City of Garland, Tex., 1963-64; adminstrv. asst. to gov. State of Tex., Austin, 1964-69; prin. in charge govt. cons. Peat, Marwick and Mitchell, Austin, 1969-82; cons. Tex. Dept. Water Resources, Austin, 1984-86, Legis. Audit Com., Austin, 1984-85; Tex. Com. Economy and Efficiency in Govt., Austin, 1985-87, Tex. Office of Speaker, Austin, 1985-87. Chmn. bd. Tex. Mcpl. Retirement System, 1961-62. Served to 1st lt. U.S. Army, 1943-46. Mem. Nat. Acad. Pub. Adminstrn., Internat. City Mgmt. Assn. (fund for profession 1986-89, chmn. Found. 1980-84), Internat. City-County Mgmt. Assn. ((Disting. Svc. award 1993), Nat. Civic League (hon. life dir. 1989, chmn. 1986-87, vice chmn. 1987-88), Austin Area Urban League (treas. 1985-87). Democrat. Mem. Christian Ch. Avocation: tennis. Home and Office: 1801 Lavaca St Austin TX 78701-1338

BLOEDE, MERLE HUIE, civic worker; b. Brady, Tex., May 4, 1921; d. Hulon William and Anna (Lohn) Huie; student San Angelo Bus. Coll., 1944; m. Victor G. Bloede III, Mar. 11, 1945; children—Dee Anna Smith Willis, Victor G. IV, Susan Lohn Quaid. Asst supr. Office Censorship, San Antonio, 1942-43, Patroness North Shore Hosp., Manhasset, N.Y., 1954-56, 67-68; vol. Waldorf Sch. Scholarship Fund, Garden City, N.Y., 1957; asst. treas., exec. bd., mem. art com. Meml. Sloan-Kettering Cancer Ctr. Soc., N.Y.C., chmn. pub. relations com., 1982-83 Mem. North Shore So. Soc. (pres. 1963-65). Republican. Mem. Community Reformed Ch. Clubs: Sands Point (N.Y.) Golf, Flower Hill Garden (chmn. community service com. 1967), Delray Dunes (Fla.) Golf and Country. Home: 4923 King Palm Cir Boynton Beach FL 33436-5902 also: 19 Duke Of Gloucester Manhasset NY 11030-3209 also: Cow Creek Rnch Lohn TX 76852

BLOEDE, VICTOR CARL, lawyer, academic executive; b. Woodwardville, Md., July 17, 1917; s. Carl Schon and Eleanor (Eck) B.; m. Ellen Louise Miller, May 9, 1947; children—Karl Abbott, Pamela Elena. A.B., Dartmouth Coll., 1940; J.D. cum laude, U. Balt., 1950; LL.M. in Pub. Law, Georgetown U., 1967. Bar: Md. 1950, Fed. Hawaii 1958, U.S. Supreme Ct. 1971. Pvt. practice Balt., 1950-64; mem. Goldman & Bloede, Balt., 1959-64; counsel Seven-Up Bottling Co., Balt., 1958-64; dep. atty. gen. Pacific Trust Ter., Honolulu, 1952-53; asst. solicitor for ters. Office of Solicitor, U.S. Dept. Interior, Washington, 1953-54; atty. U.S. Justice, Honolulu, 1955-58; assoc. gen. counsel Dept. Navy, Washington, 1960-61, 63-64; spl. legal cons. Md. Legislature, Legis. Council, 1963-64, 66-67; assoc. prof. U. Hawaii, 1961-63, dir. property mgmt., 1964-67; house counsel, dir. contracts and grants U. Hawaii System, 1967-82; house counsel U. Hawaii Research Corp., 1970-82; legal counsel Law of Sea Inst., 1978-82; legal cons. Rsch. Corp. and grad. rsch. divsn. U. Hawaii, 1982-92; spl. counsel to Holifield Congl. Commn. on Govt. Procurement, 1970-73. Author: Hawaii Legislative Manual, 1962, Maori Affairs, New Zealand, 1964, Oceanographic Research Vessel Operations, and Liabilities, 1972, Hawaiian Archipelago, Legal Effects of a 200 Mile Territorial Sea, 1973, Copyright-Guidelines to the 1976 Act, 1977, Forms Manual, Inventions: Policy, Law and Procedure, 1982; writer, contbr. Coll. Law Digest and other publs. on legislation and pub. law. Mem. Gov.'s Task Force Hawaii and The Sea, 1969, Citizens Housing Com. Balt., 1952-64; bd. govs. Balt. Cmty. YMCA, 1954-64; bd. dirs. U. Hawaii Press, 1964-66, Coll. Housing Found., 1968-80; appointed to internat. rev. commn. Canada-France Hawaii Telescope Corp., 1973-82, chmn., 1973, 82; co-founder, incorporator First Unitarian Ch. Honolulu. Served to lt. comdr. USNR, 1942-45, PTO. Grantee ocean law studies NSF and NOAA, 1970-80. Mem. ABA, Balt. Bar Assn., Fed. Bar Assn., Am. Soc. Internat. Law, Nat. Assn. Univ. Attys. (founder & 1st chmn. patents & copyrights sect. 1974-76). Home: 635 Onaha St Honolulu HI 96816-4918

BLOEMBERGEN, NICOLAAS, physicist, educator; b. Dordrecht, The Netherlands, Mar. 11, 1920; came to U.S., 1952, naturalized, 1958; s. Auke and Sophia M. (Quint) B.; m. Huberta D. Brink, June 26, 1950; children: Antonia, Brink, Juliana. BA, Utrecht U., 1941, MA, 1943; PhD, Leiden U., 1948; MA (hon.), Harvard U., 1951; D of Sci. (hon.), Laval U., 1987, U. Conn., 1988, U. Hartford, 1991, Moscow State U., 1997; LHD (hon.), U. Mass., Lowell, 1994, U. Ctrl. Fla., 1996, N.C. State U., 1998. Teaching asst. Utrecht U., 1942-45; research fellow Leiden U., 1948; mem. Soc. Fellows Harvard U., 1949-51, assoc. prof., 1951-57, Gordon McKay prof. applied physics, 1957—, Rumford prof. physics, 1974, Gerhard Gade univ. prof., 1980, prof. emeritus, 1990; vis. prof. U. Paris, 1957, U. Calif., 1965, Collège de France, Paris, 1980; Lorentz guest prof. U. Leiden, 1973; Raman vis. prof. Bangalore, India, 1979; Fairchild Disting. scholar Calif. Inst. Tech., 1984; von Humboldt Sr. Scientist, Munich, Fed. Republic Germany; hon. prof. Fudan U., Shanghai, People's Republic of China; Disting. Vis. Prof. CREOL, U. Ctrl. Fla., 1995. Author: Nuclear Magnetic Relaxation, 1948, Nonlinear Optics, 1965, Encounters in Magnetic Resonance, 1996, Encounters in Nonlinear Optics, 1996; also articles in profl. jours. Recipient Buckley prize for solid state physics Am. Phys. Soc., 1958, Dirac medal U. New South Wales (Australia), 1983, Stuart Ballantine medal Franklin Inst., 1961, Half Moon trophy Netherlands Club N.Y., 1972, Nat. medal of Sci., 1975, Lorentz medal Royal Dutch Acad., 1978, Frederic Ives medal Optical Soc. Am., 1979; von Humboldt sr. scientist award Munich, 1980, von Humboldt medal, 1989, Nobel prize in Physics, 1981; Guggenheim fellow, 1957. Fellow Am. Phys. Soc., Am. Acad. Arts and Scis., IEEE (Morris Liebmann award 1959, Medal of Honor 1983), Indian Acad. Scis. (hon.); mem. Optical Soc. Am. (hon.), Nat. Royal Dutch Acads. Scis., Nat. Acad. Engring., Am. Philos. Soc., Deutsche Akademie der Naturforscher Leopoldina, Koninklyke Nederlandse Akademie von Wetenschappen (corr.), Paris Acad. Scis. (fgn. assoc.), Royal Norwegian Soc. Scis. and Letters (fgn.). Office: Harvard U Div Applied Scis Pierce Hall Cambridge MA 02138

BLOEMER, ROSEMARY CELESTE, bookkeeper; b. St. Louis, Jan. 26, 1930; d. Edward J. and Leslie F. (McCreary) Walsh; m. Edward H. Bloemer,

Sept. 4, 1948; children: Stephen, Diane, Janet. Cert. in court reporting, Bayside Coll., San Francisco, 1948; student, U. Mo., St. Louis, 1949-51, 83. Profl. singer Harvey Kincer Band, St. Louis, 1945-49; teller Roosevelt Savs. & Loan, 1967; income tax sec. Boatmen's Nat. Bank, St. Louis, 1968-73; sec. psychology dept. Washington U., St. Louis, 1978; beverages contr. Chase-Park Plaza Hotel, St. Louis, 1977-81; owner Bloemer Tax Svc., St. Louis, 1975—; legal sec. Lickhalter Law Office, St. Louis, 1970-88, Law Office of James K. Steitz, St. Louis, 1981-83; bookkeeper, tax advisor Mo. Hwy. Patrol Assn., Inc., St. Louis, 1981-83; bookkeeper, tax acct. Mo. State Hwy. Patrol Civilian Employees Assn., St. Louis, 1983-92; acct. Clarion Hotel, St. Louis, 1986, Bel-Air Hilton Inn, St. Louis, 1984-85; consignment standard stock machine screws, contr. accounts receivable Consol. Aluminum Co., 1973-75; sec. to 5 fin. specialists Cmty. Devel. Agy., St. Louis, 1980-81; tax preparer H&R Block, 1991-95; mem. team of reporters Price Waterhouse, 1990-96. Arbitrator, shopper, speaker Better Bus. Bur. St. Louis, 1980—; sec. to pres. Bd. Higher Edn., Christian Ch., 1975-77; vol. in choir Shrine of St. Joseph, St. Louis. Mem. Nat. Soc. Tax Profls., Nat. Assn. Tax Practitioners, Am. Soc. Notaries; Internat. Platform Assn. Roman Catholic. Avocations: gardening, sewing. Home and Office: 1435 Trampe Ave Saint Louis MO 63138-2541

BLOEMSMA, MARCO PAUL, investor; b. Heemstede, The Netherlands, July 20, 1924; s. Philippus and Wilhelmina Geertruida (Bonebakker) B.; LLM, Leyden U., 1948; m. Mieke Harten, Sept. 23, 1955; children: Marco Reinier, Barbara Patricia, Michiel Alexander. Lawyer firm van der Feltz, Voûte & Riechelmann, 1948-49; assoc., then ptnr. Blackstone, Rueb & van Boeschoten, 1951-72; pres. C. Harten Holding B.V., The Hague, 1972-85; bd. dirs. Mauritshuis Found.; positions formerly held include chmn. KTI-Group, Ten Doesschate-group, Euroma Holding; dir., pres., chmn. Patino-group; chmn. Lips United-group, ICL Nederland B.V., Auto-Palace-group, Bloemsma Holding B.V., Nebim Handelmaatschappy B.V.; bd. dirs. Mobil Chemie B.V., Ambac B.V., Volvo Bedryfswagens B.V., Ned. Mij. Mijnbouwkundige Werken N.V., Polak & Schwarz N.V., Lockheed Europe N.V., Vulcaansoord N.V., Merck Sharp en Dohme Nederland N.V., Rockwool Lapinus B.V., Svenska Metallverken/Granges Nederland B.V., Winthrop Europe N.V., Packard Instruments Europe N.V., Foster Grant Europe N.V., Anchor Found. (Verolme). Author nat. reports on fiscal and corp. subjects. Served with Dutch Naval Reserve, 1949-51. Hon. Ky. col. since 1962. Clubs: Cercle Interalliée (Paris), Cercle Litteraire (Lausanne). Home: 5 Ave de Crousaz, 1010 Lausanne Switzerland

BLOESCH, DONALD GEORGE, theologian, writer, educator; b. Bremen, Ind., May 3, 1928; s. Herbert Paul and Adele Josephine (Silberman) B.; m. Brenda Mary Jackson, Nov. 23, 1962. BA, Elmhurst coll., 1950; BD, Chgo. Theol. Sem., 1953; PhD, U. Chgo., 1956; DDiv, Doane Coll., 1983. Ordained to ministry Evang. & Reformed Ch., 1953. Prof. theology U. Dubuque Theol. Sem., 1957-93, emeritus prof. theology, 1993—; vis. prof. religion U. Iowa, Iowa City, 1982, Ont. Theol. Sem., Toronto, Can., 1984, 92. Author: Essentials of Evangelical Theology, 2 Vols., 1978, 79, The Ground of Certainty, 1971, Freedom for Obedience, 1987, A Theology of Word and Spirit, 1992, Holy Scripture, 1994, God the Almighty, 1995, among others; contbr. numerous articles to profl. jours. Fellow Am. Assn. Theol. Schs., 1963-64, 90, World Coun. Chs., 1956-57, Inst. for Advanced Christian Studies, 1978. Mem. Am. Theol. Soc. (pres. Midwest divsn. 1974-75), Karl Barth Soc. N.Am. Republican. United Ch. of Christ. Avocations: gospel and country music, swimming, piano playing. Home: 2185 St John Dr Dubuque IA 52002-2751 Office: U Dubuque 2000 University Ave Dubuque IA 52001-5050

BLOM, DANIEL CHARLES, lawyer, investor; b. Portland, Oreg., Dec. 13, 1919; s. Charles D. and Anna (Reiner) B.; m. Ellen Lavon Stewart, June 28, 1952; children: Daniel Stewart (dec.), Nicole Jan Heath. BA magna cum laude, U. Wash., 1941, postgrad., 1941-42; JD, Harvard U., 1948; postgrad., U. Paris, 1954-55. Bar: Wash. 1949, U.S. Supreme Ct. 1970. Tchg. fellow speech U. Wash., 1941-42; law clk. to justice Supreme Ct. Wash., 1948-49; since practiced in Seattle; assoc. Graves, Kizer & Graves, 1949-51; gen. counsel Northwestern Life Ins. Co., 1952-54; ptnr. Case & Blom, 1952-54; assoc., ptnr., of counsel Ryan, Swanson & Cleveland, 1956—; exec. v.p., gen. counsel Family Life Ins. Co., 1977-85, spl. counsel, 1985-91; vice chmn. Wash. Bd. Bar Examiners, 1970-72, chmn., 1972-75; mem. industry adv. com. Nat. Assn. Ins. Commrs., 1966-68; pres. Wash. Ins. Coun., 1971-73, gen. counsel, 1975-78; mediator Arbitration Forums, Inc. Editor Wash. State Bar Jour., 1951-52; assoc. editor The Brief, 1975-76; author: Life Insurance Law of the State of Washington, 1980, Banking and Insurance, Deregulatory Cross-Currents, 1985, Hostile Insurance Company Takeovers: New Frontier of the Law, 1990, Administrative Finality Under the Washington Insurance Code, 1991, Business and Professionalism, 1994, The Civility Problem, 1995, Technics and the Civilization of Law Practice, 1997, Varieties of Regulatory Experience, 1998. Chmn. jury selection Wash. Gov.'s Writer's Day Awards, 1976; bd. dirs. Crisis Clinic; trustee Bush Sch., 1971-79, v.p., 1976-77; trustee, v.p. Frye Mus., Seattle, 1976-82, World Affairs Coun. Seattle, 1972-94, Friends of Seattle Pub. Libr., 1982-87; bd. visitors U. Wash. Libr., 88-92, Friends of U. Wash. Librs., bd. dirs., 1991-95, pres., 1991-92. 2d lt. AUS, 1942-45, PTO. Decorated Bronze Star; Rhodes scholarship finalist, 1949. Mem. ABA (vice chmn. com. on life ins. law, sect. tort and ins. practice 1971-76, chmn. 1976-78, sect. program chmn. 1978-79, mem. coun. 1979-83, chmn. pub. rels. com. 1981-83, chmn. com. on profl. independence of the lawyer 1984-85, chmn. com. on scope and correlation 1985-86, chmn. com. on handbook and bylaws 1987-88, chmn. hist. com. 1991-94, del. ABA to Union Internat. Des Avocats 1986-91, policy coord. tort and ins. practice sect. 1986-90), Wash. Bar Assn. (award of merit 1975, chmn. legal edn. liason com. 1977-78), Seattle Bar Assn., Union Internat. Des Avocats (v.p. 1987-92), N.Am. Found. for Internat. Legal Practice (dir. 1987-95, pres. 1987-89, chmn. 1990-95), Am. Judicature Soc., Assn. Life Ins. Counsel, Harvard Law Sch. Assn., Am. Coun. Life Ins. (legis. com. 1982-85), Am. Arbitration Assn., Found. UIA (coun. 1990-97), Fedn. Regulatory Counsel, (dir. 1995-97), Harvard Assn. Seattle and Western Wash. (trustee 1976-77), Phi Beta Kappa, Tau Kappa Alpha. Home: 100 Ward St # 602-3 Seattle WA 98109-5613 Office: Ryan Swanson & Cleveland 1201 3rd Ave Ste 3400 Seattle WA 98101-3034

BLOMDAHL, SONJA, artist; b. Waltham, Mass., Sept. 8, 1952. BFA, Mass. Coll. Art, 1974; postgrad., Orrefors Glass Skolen, Sweden, 1976. Ptnr. Berkshire Blown Glass Works, Stockbridge, Mass., 1974-76, Glass Eye Studios, Seattle, 1979-83; owner, operator glass bowling studio Seattle, 1983—; bd. adv. Pratt Fine Arts Ctr., Seattle; tchg. asst. Pilchuck Sch., Stanwood, Wash., 1978-81; instr. glass blowing Pratt Fine Arts Ctr., Seattle, 1980-84; summer instr. Summervail Workshop, Vail, Colo., 1983-84, Pilchuck Sch., Stanwood, 1985, Appalachian Ctr., Smithville, Tenn., 1986, Haystack Mountain Sch., Deer Isle, Maine, 1988, 92. One-person shows include Traver Sutton Gallery, Seattle, 1981-85, 87, Leedy Voulkos Gallery, Kansas City, Mo., 1986, 91, Edgewood Orchard Galleries, Fish Creek, Wis., 1989, William Traver Gallery, Seattle, 1989-92, 94, Maveety Gallery, Gleneden Beach, Oreg., 1991, The Glass Gallery, Bethesda, Md., 1992, Daniel Saxon Gallery, L.A., 1992, Corning Mus. of Glass at the Hermitage, Leningrad and Moscow, 1989-90, Cheney Cowles Mus., Spokane, Wash., 1991, Boise (Idaho) Art Mus., 1991, Internat. Exhibit Glass Kanazawa, Japan, 1992, Whatcom Co. Mus, Bellingham, Wash., 1992-93, King County Arts Commn., Seattle, 1993; commd. Everett Pub. Libr., Wash. Visual Artists Fellow grantee Nat. Endowment Arts, 1986, Artist's Trust Fellow grantee, 1987. Office: c/o William Traver Gallery 110 Union St Seattle WA 98101-2099*

BLOME, DENNIS H., United States marshal. BA in Criminal Justice and Psychology, Mt. Mercy Coll., 1980. Dept. mgr. Cedar Rapids (Iowa) C. of C., 1966-71; from dep., sgt., lt., capt. to sheriff Linn County, Cedar Rapids, 1984-94; U.S. marshall apptd. by Pres. Clinton Dept. Justice, Cedar Rapids, 1994—. Office: Fed Bldg Rm 320 101 1st St SE Cedar Rapids IA 52401-1202*

BLOMGREN, RONALD WALTER, business executive; b. Chgo., May 18, 1934; s. Carroll L. and Geraldine (Traver) B.; m. Jorja Lembke, Jan. 5, 1947 (dec.); children: Lisa Blomgren Moseley, Ronald Walter, Jr., Justin Chasen; m. Diane L. Crescenzo, June 15, 1996; children: Hannah M., Oliver; stepchildren: Ryan, Devin, Dillon. Student, N.C. State U., 1956. Salesman Dixie Yarns, Chattanooga, 1956-57; exec. Milliken & Co., N.Y.C., 1957-77; group v.p. Texfi Industries, N.Y.C., 1977-79; v.p. Werner Mgmt., N.Y.C., 1979-81; exec. v.p. Jesse Jeans & Kim, N.Y.C., 1981-83; with Office of Chmn. J.P. Stevens & Co., N.Y.C.; dir. retail, new bus. devel. E.I. DuPont de Nemours & Co., 1989-95; mng. dir. "The Principles" mgmt. and cons. film prodn., spl. event mktg., advt. and promotion; bd. dirs. Double Eagle Mfg. Co.; pres., COO West Indian Sea Island Trading Ltd.; v.p. mktg., bd. dirs. Haven TV & Home Enterprises Inc. Trustee Mus. Theater Workshop, N.Y.C., 1988—; elder local Presbyn. Ch.; cubmaster. Republican. Avocations: skiing, tennis, golf, sailing.

BLOMQIST, CARL GUNNAR, cardiologist; b. Båraryd, Sweden, Dec. 31, 1931; came to U.S., 1965, naturalized; s. Arvid Elias and Karin Johanna (Hullman) B.; m. Joan Barre Bakula, 1961; children: Mary Jennifer, Peter Carl. BM, U. Lund, Sweden, 1954, MD, 1960; PhD, Karolinska Inst., Stockholm, 1967. Rsch. fellow in cardiovasc. epidemiology U. Minn. Med. Ctr., Mpls., 1960-61; resident Karolinska Inst., 1962-65; mem. faculty U. Tex. Med. Ctr., Southwestern Med. Sch., Dallas, 1966—, prof. medicine and physiology, 1976—, dir., 1993-98, prof. cardiology, 1998—; mem. rsch. study com. Am. Heart Assn., 1970-73; mem. applied physiology study sect. NIH, 1974-78; mem. space biology and medicine com. NAS, 1986-90. Author articles in field; mem. editl. bd. profl. jours. Grantee NIH; Grantee NASA; established investigator Am. Heart Assn. Fellow Am. Coll. Cardiology, Am. Coll. Sports Medicine; mem. Internat. Acad. Astronautics, Am. Heart Assn. (fellow coun. epidemiolo), Aerospace Med. Assn. (Luis H. Bauer Founders award 1995), Am. Physiol. Soc. Home: 4229 Willow Grove Rd Dallas TX 75220-1935 Office: Southwestern Med Sch Div Cardiology Dallas TX 75235

BLOMQUIST, CARL ARTHUR, medical and trust company executive, insurance executive; b. L.A., Feb. 2, 1947; s. Carl Arthur and Delphine Marie (Forcier) B.; m. Diane Leslie Nunez, May 5, 1973 (div. Dec. 1979); 1 child, Kristin; m. Patricia Marie Johnson, Feb. 3, 1984 (div. Dec. 1988), m. Sharon Elaine Fromwiller, Oct. 14, 1995. BS, U. San Diego, 1969; MPH, UCLA, 1973. Auditor Naval Area Audit Svc., San Diego, 1969-71; trainee USPHS, Washhington, 1971; asst. adminstr. Northridge (Calif.) Hosp., 1973-76; asst. adminstr. fin. and facilities St. Vincent Med. Ctr., L.A., 1976-77; asst. v.p. 1st Interstate Mortgage, Pasadena, Calif., 1977-79; chief exec. officer Coop. Am. Physicians/Mut. Protection Trust, L.A., 1979-94; spl. dep. Calif. ins. commr. Exec. Life Ins. Co., L.A., 1991-94, acting CEO, 1991-92; prin. Carl A. Blomquist Cons., Playa Del Rey, Calif., 1994-95; mgr., CEO Head Injury Rehab. Svcs., LLC, 1995—; mem. instl. review bd. Motion Picture Hosp. Woodland Hills, Calif., 1993—; bd. dirs. Risk Mgmt. Assurance Corp., Dallas, 1996—; profl. adv. com. L.A. Posada Home Health, Pasadena, 1996—. Mem. Calif. Health Facilities Financing Authority, Sacramento, 1981—; co-chmn. Adv. Commn. on Malpractice Ins., Calif. Senate, Sacramento, 1984-92, mem. Commn. on Cost Containment in State Govt., 1984—; bd. dirs. Chaminade Coll. Prep. Sch., West Hills, Calif., 1988. Journalism grantee Helms Found., 1965. Mem. Am. Coll. Healthcare Execs., Am. Hosp. Assn., President's Assn. of Am. Mgmt. Assn., Health Care Execs. So. Calif., Hosp. Coun. So. Calif., UCLA Health Care Mgmt. Alumni Assn. (bd. dirs. 1987-94), Case Mgmt. Soc. Am., Am. Congress of Rehab. Med., Big Brothers Am. Republican. Roman Catholic. Avocations: sailing, skiing, golf. Office: Carl A Blomquist Cons 6641 Vista Del Mar Playa Del Rey CA 90293-7545

BLOMQUIST, DAVID WELS, journalist; b. Detroit, June 16, 1956; s. August Wels and Sally Lou (Ball) B. AB, U. Mich., 1976; AM, Harvard U., 1978. Tchg. fellow Harvard U., Cambridge, 1978-82; asst. sr. tutor Harvard U., 1981-82; supervising sect. editor CBS Inc., N.Y.C., 1982-84; staff writer The Record of Hackensack, N.J., 1984-86, state polit. corr., 1986-89, chief polit. writer, 1990-92, chief Trenton bur., 1992-94; dir. The Record Poll, Hackensack, 1992-98, dir. online devel., 1998-99; dir. new media Detroit Free Press, 1999—. Author: Elections and the Mass Media, 1982; contbr. articles to profl. jours. Mem. Am. Polit. Sci. Assn. (edn. com. 1984-86), N.J. Legis. Corrs. Club (pres. 1992), Harvard Club of N.Y., Nat. Press Club Washington. Avocations: music, ballet. Office: Detroit Free Press 600 W Fort St Detroit MI 48226

BLOMQUIST, ROBERT OSCAR, insurance company executive; b. Passaic, N.J., Aug. 19, 1930; s. Oscar and Adeline Louise (Hotaling) B.; m. Audrey M. Korn, Apr. 4, 1954; children: Dana C., Carin E. BA, Allegheny Coll., Meadville, Pa., 1952; MS, Columbia, 1953. With Chase Manhattan Bank, N.Y.C., 1957-76; gen. mgr. Chase Manhattan Bank, U.K., 1970; regional exec. Chase Manhattan Bank, U.K., Scandinavia, Africa, 1971; sr. v.p., group exec. Chase Manhattan Bank, Europe and Africa, 1971-74, Nat. Banking Group, 1975-76; pres., dir. Chase Manhattan Leasing Corp., Chase Nat. Svcs. Corp., Chase Manhattan Realty Leasing Corp., 1974-76; chmn. Chase Banks-Internat., Chgo., L.A. and Houston, 1974-76; pres., dir. Franklin State Bank, Somerset, N.J., 1976-80; vice chmn., dir. Mercantile Bank, N.A., St.Louis, 1980-87; exec. v.p., chief credit officer Integra Fin. Corp., Pitts., 1988-93; chmn. bd. dirs. Luth. Brotherhood Life Ins. Co., Mpls., 1993—; bd. dirs. Robert Morris Assocs., 1987-88. Contbr. articles to profl. jours. Bd. dirs. Luther N.W. Sem., St. Paul, 1982-85; trustee Thiel Coll., Greenville, Pa., 1988—. Lt. USNR, 1954-59. Mem. Kelly Greens Country Club (Ft. Myers, Fla.), Univ. Club (St. Louis), Mpls. Club, Duquesne Club (Pitts.). Home: 16151 Kelly Woods Dr Fort Myers FL 33908-3146 Office: Luth Brotherhood 625 4th Ave S Ste 100 Minneapolis MN 55415-1665*

BLOMSTROM, BRUCE A., healthcare executive; b. Salem, Mass., July 4, 1937; m. Anne Blomstrom; children: Jeffrey, Kristin. BS, MIT, 1959, MS in Indsl. Mgmt., 1962. Asst. sec. Ministry of Commerce and Industry, Govt. of Uganda, Kampala, 1962-64; regional dir., Far East dir., internat. product mgmt., Libby McNeil & Libby, Chgo., 1965-73; dir. corp. planning, exec. mng. dir. Nippon Abbott; gen. mgr. South Africa Abbott Labs., North Chicago, Ill., 1973-82; v.p. Alpha Therapeutic, L.A., 1982-84; v.p.corp. devel. Whittaker Corp., L.A., 1984-85; pres., CEO Guardian Products divsn. Sunrise Med., Arleta, Calif., 1985-90; pres., CEO, dir. Clinishare, Inc. divsn. Unihealth, Chatsworth, Calif., 1991-97; pres., dir. NMC Homecare divsn. Fresenius Med. Care, 1997—; pres., dir. Unihealth Investment, Burbank, Calif., 1995-97; bd. dirs. Cedaron, Davis, Calif. Contbr. articles to profl. jours. Mem. alumni fund bd. MIT, 1996—; bd. dirs., v.p. Pasadena (Calif.) Symphony Assn., 1985-97; mem. Pacific Coun. on Internat. Policy, L.A., 1996—. 1st lt. USAR, 1959-67. Mem. Calif. Assn. for Health Svcs. at Home (legis. com. 1992-97), San Marino (Calif.) City Club (bd. dirs. 1994-96), Japan Am. Soc., Delta Tau Delta. Avocations: tennis, swimming, travel, foreign affairs.

BLOND, STUART RICHARD, newsletter editor; b. L.A., Sept. 1, 1953; s. Elmer George and Anne G. Blond; m. Stella Pyrtek, July 28, 1986. BA in Art, Calif. State U., 1977. Editor, v.p. advt. Packard Automobile Classics, Fords, N.J., 1988—; sales Packard Industries, Boonton, N.J., 1989—. Editor (newsletter) The Cormorant News Bulletin, 1988—. Home and Office: 84 Hoy Ave Fords NJ 08863-1938

BLONDEAU, JACQUES PATRICK ADRIEN, reinsurance company executive; b. La Bourboule, France, Apr. 7, 1944; s. Marcel and Suzanne (Bacon) B.; m. Claude Pierrard, June 18, 1968; children: Sophie, Guillaume. Student, Lycée Janson de Sailly, Paris, 1964-65; Hautes Etudes Commerciales, Paris, 1968. Group controller Pechiney France, 1975-80; sr. v.p. Pechiney Corp., U.S., 1980-84; mng. dir. Pechiney Australia, 1984-88; pres. Howmet Resources, France, 1984-88, SCOR, France, 1989—; chmn., CEO SCOR, Paris, 1994—; pres. SCOR US, 1989-94; chmn., CEO SCOR, Paris, 1994—. Mem. Wall St. Club. Avocations: tennis, skiing. Home: 179 Blvd Pereire, 75017 Paris France Office: SCOR Immeuble SCOR, 1 Ave du President Wilson, 92074 Paris DefCedex, France

BLONDIN, JOAN, nephrologist educator; b. Beaumont, Tex., Nov. 28, 1936; d. Joseph Albert and Ona Mae (Williamson) B. BS, La. Tech U., 1959; MNS, Cornell U., 1961; MD, La. State U., 1969. Diplomate Am. Bd. Internal Medicine. Instr. U. Ala., Tuscaloosa, 1961-62; rsch. assoc. Cornell U., Ithaca, N.Y., 1962-63; asst. specialist La. State U., Baton Rouge, 1963-65; intern Barnes Hosp., St. Louis, 1969-70, resident, 1970-72; postdoctoral fellow Washington U., St. Louis, 1972-74, asst. prof., 1974-78; ptnr. Nephrology Cons., Monroe, La., 1978—; assoc. prof. La. State U., Shreveport, 1978-98; adj. prof. human ecology La. Tech. U., 1988; active staff St. Francis Med. Ctr., 1978—, North Monroe Community Hosp., 1984—; adj. prof. Coll. Pharmacy, Northeast La. U., 1996. Contbr. articles to profl. jours. Bd. dirs. Central Bank; bd. trustees Nat. Kidney Found. of La., 1988-97; mem. La. Bd. Regents, 1989-94, chmn., 1992; med. dir. North La. Dialysis Ctr., 1992-97, Ruston Kidney Ctr. Fellow La. Cancer Society, 1966, NIH, 1968; recipient Disting. Svc. award La. Dietetic Assn., 1998. Mem. AAAS, ACP, End Stage Renal Disease (chmn. quality consensus com. 1994-96), Internat. Soc. Nephrology, Am. Soc. Internal Medicine, Am. Soc. Nephrology, Am. Soc. Tropical Medicine and Hygiene, Am. Soc. Parenteral and Enteral Nutrition, Am. Heart Assn. (coun. on hypertension), Renal Physicians Assn. (bd. dirs., fin. com. 1991-94, chmn. quality care com.), N.Y. Acad. Scis., La. Med. Soc. (del. 1988—), Ouachita Med. Soc. (pres.-elect 1998-99, pres. 1999—), Sigma Xi, Alpha Omega Alpha, Phi Kappa Phi, Omicron Nu. Republican. Episcopalian. Avocations: music, needlepoint, reading. Home: 301 Country Club Rd Monroe LA 71201-2562 Office: Nephrology Cons 711 Wood St Monroe LA 71201-7549

BLONDIN-ANDREW, ETHEL, Canadian government official; b. Fort Norman, Mar. 25, 1951; d. Cecilia Modeste, adopted d. Joseph and Maire Therese Blondin; children: Troy, Tanya, Timothy. BEd, U. Alta., 1974. Tchr. Tuktoyaktuk, Ft. Franklin, Ft. Providence, 1974-81; tchr. lang. spl. dept. edn. Yellowknife, 1981-84; tchr. U. Calgary & Arctic Coll., 1983; mgr., then acting dir. Pub. Svc. Commn., Canada, 1984-86; sec. state tng. and youth Can. Canada, 1993-97, sec. state children and youth, 1997—; mem. bd. dirs. Arctic Inst. N.Am., Nat. Steering Ctr., Aboriginal Lang. Policy Dvel.; chair Indigenous Lang. Devel. Rev. Ctr. Recipient Culture and Heritage Preservation award MLA, 1987, Hilroy Scholar award R.C. Hill Char. Found., 1982. Office: Human Resources Devel Canada, Pl du Portage 2 Phase IV, 140 Promenade du Portage, Hull, PQ Canada K1A 0J9

BLONIGEN, BRUCE ALOYSIUS, economics educator; b. St. Cloud, Minn., Aug. 28, 1966; s. Victor Aloysius and Delores Christina B.; m. Denice Ann Gray, Jan. 8, 1994. BA, Gustavus Adolphus Coll., 1988; MA, U. Calif., Davis, 1992, PhD, 1995. Admissions counselor Gustavus Adolphus Coll., St. Peter, Minn., 1988-90; asst. prof. U. Oreg., Eugene, 1995—. Contbr. articles to profl. jours. Grantee NSF, 1998—. Mem. Am. Econ. Assn., Phi Beta Kappa. Office: U Oreg Dept Econs Eugene OR 97403

BLONSKY, EUGENE RICHARD, neurologist; b. Dec. 28, 1934. BA, Harvard U., 1955; MD, Northwestern U., 1959. Dir. Ctr. for Pain Studies, Rehab. Inst., Chgo., 1981-93, Pain and Rehab. Clinic of Chgo., 1993—; assoc. prof. neurology Northwestern U. Med. Sch., Chgo., 1977—. E-mail: e-blonsky.nwu.edu. Office: 455 Sheridan Rd Glencoe IL 60022-1713

BLOOD, ARCHER KENT, retired foreign service officer; b. Chgo., Mar. 20, 1923; s. Francis Earle and Hazel Mary (Brown) B.; m. Margaret Lloyd Millward, May 14, 1948; children: Shirley, Barbara, Peter, Archer. BA, U. Va., 1943; postgrad., Army War Coll., 1962-63; MA, George Wash. U., 1963. Commd. fgn. service officer Dept. State; vice consul Thessaloniki, Greece, 1947-48, Munich, Germany, 1949-50; 2d sec. Athens, Greece, 1950-52; vice consul Algiers, 1953; 2d sec. Bonn, Germany, 1953-55; consul Dacca, 1960-62; pers. officer Dept. State, 1963-65; dep. chief of mission Kabul, 1965-68; polit. counselor Athens, 1968-70; consul gen. Dacca, 1970-71; dep. dir. personnel Dept. State, Washington, 1972-74; dep. comdt. Army War Coll., 1974-77; dep. chief of mission Am. embassy, New Delhi, India, 1977-80; chargé d'affaires Am. embassy, New Delhi, 1980-81; vis. prof., diplomat-in-residence Allegheny Coll., 1982-90, prof. emeritus, 1990—. Served with USNR, 1944-46. Recipient Christian A. Herter award, award for disting. civilian service Sec. Army. Mem. Phi Beta Kappa. Presbyterian.

BLOOD, BRIAN ELLIS, artist; b. Weymouth, Mass., Jan. 7, 1962; s. George Ellis and Madeline Blood. Degree in comml. art, Vesper George Sch. of Art, Boston, 1982; BFA, Acad. of Art Coll., San Francisco, 1993, MFA, 1999. Instr. Acad. of Art Coll., 1993—. Recipient award of excellence Nat. Oil Painters of Am., Chgo., 1996, 2d pl. award Yosemite Renaissance, Yosemite Nat. Pk., 1997. Mem. Pastel Soc. of West Coast (award of merit 1996), Oil Painters of Am., Calif. Arts Club. Democrat. Roman Catholic. E-mail: bbfineart@aol.com. Home: 1612 Hyde St Apt C San Francisco CA 94109 Office: Acad of Art Coll 625 Sutter St San Francisco CA 94102

BLOOD, ROBERT ALVIN, sculptor; b. Jan. 7, 1924. Student, Pa. Acad. Fine Arts. Artist-in-residence Schenectady (N.Y.) Mus., 1961-68; curator Contemporary Sculpture at Chesterwood, Stockbridge, Mass., 1988. Prin. works exhibited at St. Pius X Ch., Londonville, N.Y., St. Helen's Cath. Ch., Schenectady, Cathedral of Immaculate Conception, Albany; ne-woman shows include Ten Broeck Mansion, Albany, 1998, So. Vt. Art Ctr., Mass., Vt., 1998, 99; group shows include Schenectady Mus., 1971, SUNY Gallery, Albany, 1981, 86, Albany Inst., 1985, Gledhill Nursery, West Hartford, Conn., 1993, Williamsville Inn, Stockbridge, Mass., 1996, So. Vt. Art Ctr., Manchester, 1997, 98, Kingston (N.Y.) Area Libr., 1997, others. Home: 1218 Regent St Schenectady NY 12309-5829

BLOODWORTH, A(LBERT) W(ILLIAM) FRANKLIN, lawyer; b. Atlanta, Sept. 23, 1935; s. James Morgan Bartow and Elizabeth Westfield (Dimmock) B.; m. Elizabeth Howell, Nov. 24, 1967; 1 child, Elizabeth Howell. AB in History and French, Davidson Coll., 1957; JD magna cum laude with 1st honors, U. Ga., 1963. Bar: Ga. 1962, U.S. Supreme Ct. 1971. Asst. dir. alumni and pub. relations Davidson Coll., N.C., 1959-60; assoc. Hansell & Post, Atlanta, 1963-68, ptnr., 1969-84; ptnr. Bloodworth & Nix, Atlanta, 1984-95, Bloodworth & McSwain, Atlanta, 1996—; counsel organized crime com. Met. Atlanta Commn. on Crime, 1965-67; asst. sec., counsel Met. Found. Atlanta, 1968-76. Bd. dirs. Atlanta Presbytery, 1974-78; trustee Synod of S.E., Presbyn. Ch. in U.S.A., Augusta, Ga., 1982-87; trustee Big Canoe Chapel, Ga., 1983-86, 88-91, chmn. bd. trustees, 1985-86, 90-91; mem. pres.'s adv. coun. Presbyn. Homes, 1989—; mem. president's adv. coun. Thornwell Home and Sch. for Children, 1998—. elder North Ave Presbyn. Ch., Atlanta. 1st lt. Intelligence Corps, USAR, 1957-59. Recipient Jessie Dan MacDougal Scholarship award U. Ga. Found., 1963, Outstanding Student Leadership award Student Bar Assn., U. Ga., 1963. Fellow Am. Coll. Trust and Estate Counsel; mem. ABA, State Bar Ga., Atlanta Bar Assn., Atlanta Estate Planning Coun., North Atlanta Estate Planning Coun., Capital City Club, Lawyers Club, Sphinx Club, Gridiron Club, Phi Beta Kappa, Phi Kappa Phi, Omicron Delta Kappa, Alpha Tau Omega (pres. chpt. 1957), Phi Delta Phi (grad. of yr. 1963, pres. chpt. 1963). Republican. Presbyterian. Home: 3784 Club Dr NE Atlanta GA 30319-1108 Office: 706 Monarch Plz 3414 Peachtree Rd NE Atlanta GA 30326-1113

BLOODWORTH, GLADYS LEON, educator; b. Natchitoches, La., July 9, 1946; d. Rudolph and Mary (LeRoy) Leon; m. John Edward Bloodworth, Aug. 14, 1971; children: John, Jeremy. BA, Southern U., Baton Rouge, 1968; MA, Calif. State U., Dominguez Hills, 1989. Lang. arts tchr. grades 6-10 Natchitoches Parish Schs.; categorical program adviser L.A. Unified Schs., mentor tchr., 1988-91, coord. gifted coord., 1988. Named Outstanding Math Tchr., 1987-88. Mem. NEA, United Tchrs. L.A., Calif. Tchrs. Assn., Women in Edml. Leadership, Kappa Kappa Iota. Methodist.

BLOODWORTH, J(AMES) M(ORGAN) BARTOW, JR., physician, educator; b. Atlanta, Feb. 21, 1925; s. J.M. Bartow and Elizabeth (Dimmock) B.; m. G. Jean Stone, Nov. 26, 1947; children: Lowell Ann, Joyce Lynn, Elizabeth Carol; m. Joan G. Wiltgen, July 8, 1972; children: Allison Joan, Ellen Lucy. Student, Emory U., 1942-43, 44-48, MD, 1948; student, Stanford U., 1943-44. Intern, then asst. resident pathology Columbia-Presbyn. Med. Ctr., N.Y.C., 1948-50; instr. pathology Columbia U., 1949-50; asst. resident medicine U. Iowa Hosp., 1950-51; mem. faculty Ohio State U. Coll. Medicine, 1951-62, prof. pathology, 1960-62; chief divsn. pathologic anatomy Ohio State U. Hosp., 1954-61; pathologist Columbus State Hosp., 1954-57; prof. pathology and lab. medicine U. Wis., Madison, 1962-95, prof. emeritus, 1995—; chief lab. svc. Madison VA Hosp., 1962-89, pathologist, 1989-95. Editor: Endocrine Pathology, 1968, 2d edit., 1982, 3rd edit., 1996; contbr. numerous articles to publs. in field. Served with AUS, 1941-45. Recipient Fight for Sight citation Am. Assn. Rsch. in Ophthalmology, 1964. Mem. AMA, Wis. Med. Assn., Am. Assn. Clin. Endocrinologists (charter), Dane County Med. Soc., Wis. Soc. Pathologists (pres. 1977-79), Am. Soc. Investigative Pathologists, Histochem. Soc., Am. Diabetes Assn. (Lilly award 1963, Profl. Svc. award Wis. affiliate 1982), So. Wis. Diabetes Assn., Am. Heart Assn., Wis. Heart Assn., Soc. Exptl. Biology and Medicine, Internat.

Acad. Pathology, Am. Soc. Clin. Pathology, Am. Assn. Neuropathologists, Nat. Soc. Med. Rsch., Am. Soc. Cell Biology, Gyro Internat. Club (pres. Columbus chpt. 1962, pres. Madison chpt. 1980, 95). Home: 4514 Crescent Rd Madison WI 53711-4721

BLOODWORTH, SANDRA GAIL, artist, arts administrator; b. Charleston, Miss., Nov. 22, 1950; d. Deward Dupree and Eva Pauline (Early) B. BSEd, Miss. Coll., 1972; MA, U. Miss., 1973; MFA, Fla. State U., 1980. Devel. assoc. Studio in a Sch., N.Y.C., 1987-88; mgr., Arts For Transit Met. Transp. Authority, N.Y.C., 1988-92, dep. dir., Arts For Transit, 1992-96, dir., Arts For Transit, 1996—; mem. adv. bd. N.Y. Transit Mus., Bklyn., Fine Art Dept./FIT, N.Y.C.; vis. artist Berkshire Sch. of Contemporary Art, North Adams, Mass. Author: (catalogue) Art en Route: MTA Arts for Transit, 1994. Office: Arts for Transit Met Transp Authority 347 Madison Ave New York NY 10017-3706

BLOODWORTH, WILLIAM ANDREW, JR., academic administrator; b. San Antonio, Sept. 9, 1942; s. William Andrew Sr. and Ellan Oma (Gatliff) B.; m. Julia Ann Rankin, Nov. 27, 1964; children: Nicole, Paul William. BS, Tex. Luth. Coll., 1964; MA, Lamar U., 1967; PhD, U. Tex., 1972; grad., Harvard Inst. Ednl. Mgmt., 1989. Tchr. Boerne (Tex.) and Port Neches (Tex.) pub. schs., 1964-67; asst. instr. U. Tex., Austin, 1969-72; asst. prof. English E. Carolina U., Greenville, N.C., 1972-77, assoc. prof., 1977-82, prof., 1982-90, chmn. English dept., 1982-88, acting vice chancellor for acad. affairs, 1987-89; provost, v.p. for acad. affairs Cen. Mo. State U., Warrensburg, 1990-93; pres. Augusta (Ga.) State U., 1993—. Author: Upton Sinclair, 1977, Max Brand, 1993; contbr. articles to profl. publs., chpts. to books. Mem. Am. Assn. Higher Edn., Rotary, Phi Kappa Phi (chpt. pres. 1989-90), Phi Delta Kappa. Avocations: running, writing. Home: 819 Kamel Cir Augusta GA 30909-2709 Office: Augusta State U Office of the Pres Augusta GA 30904-2200

BLOOM, ADAM I., psychologist; b. Bklyn., May 18, 1964; s. Jeffrey and Eileen (Tannenbaum) B.; m. Michelle Longo, Mar. 23, 1991; 1 child, Matthew. BA in Psychology, SUNY, Oneonta, 1986; MS in Ednl. and Sch. Psychology, CUNY, Bklyn., 1988; D in Psychology, Yeshiva U., 1993. Lic. psychologist, N.Y.; cert. sch. psychologist, N.J., N.Y. Psychology extern Jewish Bd. Child and Family Svcs., Bklyn., 1986-87; psychologist in tng. N.Y.C. Bd. Edn., S.I., 1987-88, sch. psychologist, 1988-92, 93-94; clin. psychology intern Montefiore Med. Ctr., Albert Einstein Coll. Medicine, Bronx, N.Y., 1992-93; psychologist Mental Health Assn. Westchester (N.Y.), Inc., 1994-97; assoc. clinic dir. Mental Health Svcs./Family Ct., N.Y.C., 1997—; tchg. asst. SUNY, Oneonta, 1986; leader Support Group for Parents of Children with Tourette's Syndrome, 1995—; pvt. practice psychology, White Plains, N.Y., 1995—; consulting psychologist Spectrum Behavioral Health, Poughkeepsie, N.Y., 1996—; spkr. in field. Mem. APA, Nat. Assn. Sch. Psychologists (cert.), Nat. Register Health Svc. Providers in Psychology, N.Y. Assn. Sch. Psychologists, Westchester County Psychologists Assn., Westchester Tourette's Syndrome Assn. (v.p. 1994—), Kappa Delta Pi. Avocations: lifeguard instructing, tennis, swimming. Office: 62 Waller Ave White Plains NY 10605-1408

BLOOM, ALFRED HOWARD, college president; b. N.Y.C., Feb. 27, 1946; s. Alfred H. and Martha (Berrol) B.; m. Margaret Hennigan, Aug. 22, 1971. BA, Princeton U., 1967; PhD, Harvard U., 1974. Asst., assoc. prof. Swarthmore (Pa.) Coll., 1974-86, assoc. provost, 1985-86, pres., 1991—; dean of faculty, v.p. acad. affairs Pitzer Coll., Claremont, Calif., 1986-90, exec. v.p., 1990-91; pres. Swarthmore (Pa.) Coll., 1991—. Author: The Linguistic Shaping of Thought, 1981; contbr. articles to profl. jours. Fulbright-Hayes fellow, 1968, Rsch. grantee SSRC, 1978, 81, NEH, 1975, 86. Mem. Assn. for Asian Studies. Avocations: study of langs. and cultures, intercultural gastronomy. Office: Swarthmore Coll Office of Pres 500 College Ave Ste 2 Swarthmore PA 19081-1390

BLOOM, BARRY MALCOLM, pharmaceutical consultant; b. Roxbury, Mass., Aug. 12, 1928; s. Morris and Ann (Levine) B.; m. Joan Martha Ensign, June 27, 1956; children: Catherine, Brian, Joanna. SB, MIT, 1948, PhD, 1951, postgrad., 1967; D of Humane Letters (hon.), Conn. Coll., 1992. Rsch. chemist Pfizer, Inc., Groton, Conn., 1952-63, dir. medicinal chems. and rsch., 1963-71, pres. cen. rsch. div., 1971-90, v.p. rsch., 1971-90, corp. mgmt. com., 1984-93, sr. v.p. R&D, 1990-92, exec. v.p. R & D, 1992-93; cons. pvt. practice, 1993—; bd. dirs. Cubist Pharms., Inc., Neurogen Corp., Vertex Pharms., Inc., Incyte Pharms., Inc., Catalytica Pharms., Microbia, Congl. Commn. on Fed. Drug Approval Process, PMA Commn. on Drugs for Rare Diseases; cons. U.S. Congress Office Tech. Assessment, 1976-77; mem. Conn. Tech. Adv. Bd., 1985-90. Mem. editorial bd. Ann. Reports in Medicinal Chemistry, 1968-70; patentee in field. Bd. mgrs. Lawrence and Meml. Hosp. NRC postdoctoral fellow U. Wis., 1952; Poly. Inst. Tech. fellow N.Y.C., 1980; recipient Spl. Achievement award CT Innovations, Inc., 1997. Mem. Am. Chem. Soc. (chmn. div. medicinal chemistry 1967), Conn. Acad. Sci. and Engring., Pharm. Mfrs. Assn. (chmn. R&D sect. 1976). Home and Office: Mackintosh Rd Lyme CT 06371

BLOOM, BENJAMIN S., education educator; b. Lansford, Pa., Feb. 21, 1913; married; 2 children. BA, Pa. State U., 1935, MS, 1935; PhD, U. Chgo., 1942; LHD (hon.), Rutgers U., 1970, Ohio State U., 1983, U. San Diego, 1990; Docteur Honoris Causa, U. Liege, Belgium, 1992. Rsch. worker Pa. State Relief Orgn., 1935-36, Am. Youth Commn., 1936-38; rsch. asst. Coop. Study in Gen. Edn., 1939-40; rsch. asst. bd. examinations U. Chgo., 1943-59, coll.-univ. examiner, 1943-59, from instr. to disting. svc. prof., 1943-70, Charles Swift Disting. Svc. prof. emeritus, 1970—; prof. edn. Northwestern U., Evanston, Ill., 1983-89; vis. prof. edn. UCLA, summer 1968; Jacks disting. vis. prof. edn. Stanford U., 1969-70; edn. advisor Govt. of India, 1957-59, Govt. of Israel, 1963, 68, others; chmn. R & D com. Coll. Entrance Examinations Bd., Nat. Labs. Early Childhood Edn.; mem. adv. com. R & D ctrs. U. Ga., UCLA, U. Pitts., Sci. Rsch. Assocs., evaluation Rsch. Ctr. U. Va.; mem. panel to select edn. R & D ctrs. U.S. Office Edn., mem. adv. com. on R & D ctrs. and regional labs.; chmn. Invitational Conf. on Testing Problems, 1967; vice chmn. Meeting of Experts on Curriculum of Gen. Edn., UNESCO, Moscow, 1968; dir. Internat. Seminar Advanced Tng. in Curriculum Devel., Sweden, summer 1971. Author: Evaluation in Secondary Schools, 1958, Evaluation in Higher Education, 1961, Stability and Change in Human Characteristics, 1964, Human Characteristics and School Learning, 1976, All Our Children Learning: A Primer for Parents, Teachers and other Educators, 1980, Developing Talent in Young People, 1985; (with J. Axelrod et al.) Teaching by Discussion, 1948, (with G.G. Stern and M.I. Stein) Methods in Personality Assessment, 1956, (with D. Krathwohl and others) Taxonomy of Educational Objectives: Handbook I, Cognitive Domain, 1956, vol. II, The Affective Domain, 1964, (with L. Broder) Problem-solving Processes of College Students, 1958, (with F. Peters) Use of Academic Prediction Scales for Counseling and Selecting College Entrants, 1961, (with A. Davis and R. Hess) Compensatory Education for Cultural Deprivation, 1965, (with others) Handbook on Formative and Summative Evaluation of Student Learning, 1971, (with MESA student group) The State of Research on Selected Alterable Variables in Education, 1980, (with G.F. Madaus and J.T. Hastings) Evaluation to Improve Learning, 1981, (with Soshlak and others) Developing Talent in Young People, 1985; assoc. editor: International Study of Achievement in Mathematics, A Comparison of Twelve Countries, vols. I and II, 1966; editorial cons. Irish Jour. Edn., Internat. Jour. Eductional Scis., Jour. Applied Social Psychology, Sch. Rev., Jour. Educational Psychology; contbr. numerous chpts. to books and articles to profl jours. Recipient John Dewey award John Dewey Soc., 1968, Tchrs. Coll. medal for disting. svc. Columbia U., 1970, award for disting. contbns. to edn. Am. Educational Rsch. Assn. and Phi Delta Kappa, 1970, special medals and awards from govts. of Belgium, Israel and Finland; named Disting. Alumni fellow Pa. State U., 1973; fellow Ctr. Advanced Study in the Behavioral Scis., 1959-60. Fellow APA (Thorndike Meml. award 1972); mem. Internat. Assn. Evaluation of Educational Achievement (founding mem., mem. coun. 1959—), Internat. Curriculum Assn. (founding mem., mem. coun. 1972—), U.S. Nat. Acad. Edn., Am. Educational Rsch. Assn. (pres. 1965-66), Phi Delta Kappa, Psi Chi. Office: U Chgo Sch Edn Judd Hall 5835 S Kimbark Ave Chicago IL 60637-1635*

BLOOM, BRUCE, hotel executive; b. Cleve., May 1947. Devel. and franchising positions Perkin's Restaurant (divsn. Holiday Corp.), Internat. Dairy Queen; v.p. franchising Marriott Family Restaurants, Roy Rogers div. Marriott Corp.; v.p. devel. Krystal Co.; sr. v.p., brand mgr. Fairfield In by Marriott, Washington, 1997—; guest spkr., panelist, writer in field. Mem. Internat. Franchise Assn. (bd. dirs., chmn. franchise rels. com.), Nat. Assn. Corp. Real Estate Execs. (past pres. restaurant coun.). Office: Fairfield Inn by Marriott Dept 955.03 1 Marriott Dr Washington DC 20058

BLOOM, CLAIRE, actress; b. London, Feb. 15, 1931; d. Edward Max and Elizabeth (Grew) B.; m. Rod Steiger, Sept. 19, 1959 (div. Jan. 1969); 1 child, Anna Justine; m. Philip Roth, Apr. 29, 1990 (div. Mar. 1995). Student, Badminton Sch., Bristol, Eng., Fern Hill Manor, New Milton, Eng., Guildhall Sch. Music and Drama, London. Disting. vis. prof. Hunter Coll., N.Y.C., 1989-90. Appeared as Ophelia, Stratford-Upon-Avon, 1948; plays include Ring Around the Moon, London, 1949-51, Romeo and Juliet, also as Juliet in Old Vic tour of U.S.; film roles in limelight Richard III, 1956, Alexander the Great, 1956, The Brothers Karamazov, 1958, Look Back in Anger, 1958, The Brothers Grimm, 1962, The Chapman Report, 1962, The Haunting, 1963, 80,000 Suspects, 1963, Alta Infidelita, 1963, Il Maestro di Vigeuono, 1963, The Outrage, 1964, The Spy Who Came in from the Cold, 1965, The Illustrated Man, 1969, Three into Two Won't Go, 1969, A Severed Head, 1971, A Doll's House, 1973, Islands in the Stream, 1976, Clash of the Titans, 1981, Always, 1984, Sammy and Rosie, 1987, Crimes and Misdemeanors, 1989, Mad Dogs and Englishmen, 1994, Daylight, 1995; Broadway prodns. include Rashomon, 1959; other theatre appearances include Duel of Angels, London, 1958, Altona, Royal Court Theatre, London, 1960, Ivanov, London, 1964, A Doll's House, Hedda Gabler, 1971, Vivat! Vivat Regina!, 1972; N.Y. appearance The Innocents, 1976; London appearances A Doll's House, 1973, A Streetcar Named Desire, 1974, Rosmersholm, 1977, The Cherry Orchard, 1981, These are Women, 1982-83, When We Dead Awaken, 1990, Daughters, Wives and Mothers, 1991, Silenced Voices, 1992, Women in Love, 1993, The Cherry Orchard, 1994, Long Days Journey into Night, 1996, Electra, 1998; many roles Brit. and U.S. TV including In Praise of Love, 1975, A Legacy, 1975, Henry VIII, 1979, Hamlet, 1979, The Ghost Writer, 1983, Cymbeline, 1983, King John, 1983, Brideshead Revisited, 1981, Shadowlands, 1984, Time and the Conways, 1985, miniseries Queenie, 1987, Anastasia, 1987, Shadow in the Sun, 1988, The Camomile Lawn, 1991, The Mirror Crack'd, 1992, Remember, 1993, Village Affairs, 1994, Family Money, 1996, When the Dead Man Heard, 1997; author: Limelight and After, 1982, Leaving A Doll's House, 1996. Recipient Evening Standard award, London, 1974, Brit. Film and TV award, London, 1984. Office: Marion Rosenberg Agy 8428 Melrose Pl West Hollywood CA 90069-5308

BLOOM, DAVID ALAN, pediatric urology educator; b. Buffalo, July 26, 1945; m. Martha Lichty, June 8, 1980. BS, Rensselaer Poly. Inst., 1967; MD, SUNY, Buffalo, 1971. Diplomate Am. Bd. Surgery, Am. Bd. Urology (exam. com. 1992-96), Nat. Bd. Med. Examiners. Intern UCLA, 1971-72, resident in surgery, 1972-75, chief resident, 1975-76, resident in urology, 1976-77, sr. resident, 1978-79, chief resident, lectr., 1979-80; vis. fellow, registrar Inst. Urology and St. Peter's Hosp., U. London, 1977-78; asst. prof. surgery U. Mich., Ann Arbor, 1984-86, assoc. prof., 1986-93, prof., 1993—, chief pediatric urology, 1984—; cons. urology surgery br. Nat. Cancer Inst., NIH, Bethesda, Md., 1982, Naval Regional Med. Ctr., Portsmouth, Va., 1983, Walter Reed Army Med. Ctr., Washington, 1985, VA Hosp., Ann Arbor, 1985; cons. pediat. urology Henry Ford Hosp., Detroit, 1986; locum in urology Gt. Ormond Street Hosp. for Sick Children and Inst. urology, Shaftesbury Hosp., London, 1986; asst. prof. surgery, then assoc. prof. Uniformed Svcs. U. Health Scis. Sch. Medicine, Bethesda, 1980-84, clin. assoc. prof., 1985, assoc. prof. pediat., 1984; presenter and cons. in field. Author: (with McGuire, Catalona and Lipshultz) Advances in Urology, 1995-97; mem. editl. bd. Urology, 1992—, Jour. Endourology, 1997—, Contemporary Urology, 1997—, British Jour. Urology, 1999—; reviewer Jour. Endourology, 1992-98, Jour. Pediatric Surgery, 1992-98, Jour. Urology, 1988-98, Surgery, 1992-98, So. Jour. Medicine, 1995-97, Clin. Pediat., 1995-98, European Urology, 1996-98, Fertility & Sterility, 1997; contbr. articles to profl. jours. Lt. col. M.C., U.S. Army, 1980-84; mem. USAR. Fellow ACS (motion picture com. 1996); mem. AMA, Am. Acad. Pediat. (exec. com. sect. on urology 1989-93, historian 1993-98); Am. Assn. Clin. Urologists, Halsted Soc. (photographer, dir. 1999—), Longmire Surg. Soc., Reed M. Nesbit Soc., Soc. for Pediatric Urology, Soc. Genitourinary Reconstructive Surgeons, Soc. Univ. Urologists, Uniformed Svcs. U. Surg. Assocs., Nat. Urologic Forum (sec.-treas. 1995), European Assn. Urology, Soc. Internat. Urology. Office: U Mich 1500 E Medical Center Dr Ann Arbor MI 48109-0005

BLOOM, DAVID RONALD, retail drug company executive; b. Toronto, Can., Apr. 20, 1943; s. Samuel and Tillie B.; m. Molly Rosenbloom, May 8, 1966; children: Corinne, Michael. BSc in Pharmacy, U. Toronto, 1967. Pharmacist Plaza Drugs, Toronto; assoc. Shoppers Drug Mart Ltd., Toronto, dir. ops., v.p. ops., exec. v.p. ops., pres. cen. Ont. and Man. regions, pres., chief exec. officer, 1983-86, chmn., CEO, 1986—, also chmn. bd. dirs.; bd. dirs. IMASCO Ltd.; chmn. Koffler Inst. Pharmacy Mgmt. Bd. dirs. Sick Kids Hosp., Toronto; adv. coun. York U. Faculty Adminstrv. Studies, Nat. Assn. Chain Drug Stores. Mem. Can. Assn. Chain Drug Stores, Chief Execs. Orgn. Office: Shoppers Drug Mart, 225 Yorkland Blvd, Willowdale, ON Canada M2J 4Y7

BLOOM, FLOYD ELLIOTT, physician, research scientist; b. Mpls., Oct. 8, 1936; s. Jack Aaron and Frieda (Shochman) B.; m. D'Nell Bingham, Aug. 30, 1956 (dec. May 1973); children: Fl'Nell, Evan Russell; m. Jody Patricia Corey, Aug. 9, 1980. AB cum laude, So. Meth. U., 1956; MD cum laude, Washington U., St. Louis, 1960; DSc (hon.), So. Meth. U., 1983, Hahnemann U., 1985, U. Rochester, 1985, Mt. Sinai U. Med. Sch., 1996, Thomas Jefferson U., 1997, Washington U., 1998. Intern Barnes Hosp., St. Louis, 1960-61; resident internal medicine Barnes Hosp., 1961-62; research asso. NIMH, Washington, 1962-64; fellow depts. pharmacology, psychiatry and anatomy Yale Sch. Medicine, 1964-66, asst. prof., 1966-67, asso. prof., 1968; chief lab. neuropharmacology NIMH, Washington, 1968-75; acting dir. div. spl. mental health NIMH, 1973-75; commd. officer USPHS, 1974-75; dir. Arthur Vining Davis Center for Behavioral Neurobiology; prof. Salk Inst., La Jolla, Calif., 1975-83; dir. div. preclin. neurosci. and endocrinology Scripps Rsch. Inst., La Jolla, 1983-89, chmn. dept. neuropharmacology, 1989—; mem. Commn. on Alcoholism, 1980-81, Nat. Adv. Mental Health Coun., 1976-80; chmn. scientific adv. bd. Pharmavene, Inc.; bd. dirs. Alkermes, Inc.; mem. sci. adv. bd. Neurocrine, Inc., 1993—, Neurobiol. Tech. Inc., 1994-98, Health Care Ventures, Inc., 1998—. Author: (with J.R. Cooper and R.H. Roth) Biochemical Basis of Neuropharmacology, 1971, 7th edit., 1996, (with Lazerson and Hofstadter) Brain, Mind and Behavior, 1984, (with Lazerson) 2d edit., 1988, (with W. Young and Y. Kim) Brain browser, 1989; editor: Peptides: Integrators of Cell and Tissue Function, 1980, Progress in Brain Research, vol. 199, 1994, vol. 100, 1997, (with D.J. Kupfer) Neuro-Psychopharmacology: The Fourth Generation of Progress, 1994, Handbook of Chemical Neruoanatomy, 1997, The Primate Nervous System, 1997, vol. II, 1998; co-editor: Regulatory Peptides, 1979-90, (with M. Randolph) Funding Health Sciences Research, 1990; assoc. editor: Biological Psychiatry, 1993-95; editor-in-chief Science, 1995—. Trustee Wash. U., 1998—. Recipient A. Cressy Morrison award N.Y. Acad. Scis., 1971, A.E. Bennett award for basic rsch. Soc. Biol. Psychiatry, 1971, Arthur A. Fleming award Science mag., 1973, Mathilde Solowey award, 1973, Biol. Sci. award Washington Acad. Scis., 1975, Alumni Achievement citation Washington U., 1980, McAlpin Rsch. Achievement award Mental Health Assn., 1980, Lectr.'s medal College de France, 1979, Steven Beering medal, 1985, Janssen award World Psychiat. Assn., 1989, Passerow Found. award, 1990, Herman von Helmholtz award, 1991, Pythagora award, 1994, Presdl. award Soc. for Neurosci., 1995, Golgi prize U. Brescia, 1996; Disting. fellow Am. Psychiat. Assn., 1986; named scientist of the yr. Achievement Rewards for Coll. Scientists, 1996, Gold medal Soc. Biol. Psychiatry, 1997. Fellow AAAS (bd. dirs. 1986-90), Am. Coll. Neuropsychopharmacology (mem. coun. 1976-78, chmn. program com. 1987, pres. 1988-89, Hoch award 1998); mem. NAS (chmn. sect. neurobiology 1979-83), Inst. Medicine (mem. coun. 1986-89, 93-95), Am. Philos. Soc., Am. Acad. Arts and Scis., Soc. Neurosci. (sec. 1973-74, pres. 1976), Am. Soc. Pharmacology and Exptl. Therapeutics, Am. Soc. Cell Biology, Am. Physiol. Soc., Am. Assn. Anatomists, Rsch. Soc. Alcoholism (chmn. program com. 1985-87, pres.-elect 1989-91, pres. 1991-93), Swedish Acad. Sci. (fgn. assoc. 1989). Home: 628 Pacific View Dr San Diego CA 92109-1768 Office: The Scripps Rsch Inst 10666 N Torrey Pines Rd La Jolla CA 92037-1027

BLOOM, HAROLD, humanities educator; b. N.Y.C., July 11, 1930; s. William and Paula (Lev) B.; m. Jeanne Gould, May 8, 1958; children: Daniel Jacob, David Moses. B.A., Cornell U., 1951; Ph.D., Yale U., 1955; L.H.D., Boston Coll., 1973, Yeshiva U., 1976, U. Bologna, 1997, St. Michael's Coll., 1998, U. Rome, 1999. Mem. faculty Yale U., 1955—, prof. English, 1965-77, DeVane prof. humanities, 1974-77, prof. humanities, 1977—, sterling prof. humanities, 1983—; vis. prof. Hebrew U., Jerusalem, 1959, Breadloaf Summer Sch., 1965-66, Soc. for Humanities, Cornell U., 1968-69; vis. Univ. prof. New Sch. Social Research, N.Y.C., 1982-84; Charles Eliot Norton prof. of poetry Harvard U., 1987-88; Berg prof. English, NYU, 1988—. Author: Shelley's Mythmaking, 1959, The Visionary Company, 1961, Blake's Apocalypse, 1963, Commentary on Blake, 1965, Yeats, 1970, The Ringers in the Tower, 1971, The Anxiety of Influence, 1973, Wallace Stevens: The Poems of Out Climate, 1977, A Map of Misreading, 1975, Kabbalah and Criticism, 1975, Poetry and Repression, 1976, Figures of Capable Imagination, 1976, The Flight to Lucifer: A Gnostic Fantasy, 1979, Agon: Towards a Theory of Revisionism, 1981, The Breaking of the Vessels, 1981, The Strong Light of the Canonical, 1987, Freud: Transference and Authority, 1988, Poetics of Influence: New and Selected Criticism, 1988, Ruin the Sacred Truths, 1988, The Book of J, 1990, The American Religion, 1992, The Western Canon, 1994, Omens of Millennium, 1996, Shakespeare: The Invention of the Human, 1998, How to Read and Why, 1999; editor, introducer Chelsea House Modern Critical Views and Interpretations, 1984—. Recipient John Addison Porter prize Yale U., 1955; Newton Arvin award, 1967; Melville Cane award Poetry Soc. Am., 1970; Zabel prize Am. Inst. Arts and Letters, 1982, Christian Gauss prize Phi Beta Kappa, 1989; Guggenheim fellow, 1962; Fulbright fellow, 1955; MacArthur prize fellowship, 1985. Mem. Am. Acad. Arts and Letters (Gold medal 1999), Am. Philos. Soc. Home: 179 Linden St New Haven CT 06511-2407 *Most instances of religion are mere manifestations of religiosity, which is endemic in our nation, where nine of ten say that God loves them. Spinoza observed that we should love God without expecting that God would love us in return.*

BLOOM, JACK SANDLER, investment banker; b. Boston, Mar. 20, 1957; s. Joseph and Inez (Sandler) B.; m. Jennifer Kingson, May 14, 1964; 1 child, Valerie. BA, Harvard U., 1979; MBA, MIT Sloan Sch., 1983. V.p. Allied Ventures, N.Y.C., 1983-85, Kaufman & Co., Boston, 1985-88; pres. Bloom & Co. (now Alpha Capital Corp.), N.Y.C., 1988—; mng. dir. corp. fin. Commonwealth Assocs., 1994-95; pres. Auto Am., 1996—. Office: Bloom & Co 950 3rd Ave Ste 2600 New York NY 10022-2705

BLOOM, JACOB A., lawyer; b. Bklyn., Apr. 10, 1942. BA, Columbia U., 1963, LLB, 1966. Bar: Calif. 1968. Sr. ptnr. Bloom, Hergott, Cook, Diemer & Klein, Beverly Hills, Calif. Champion Moot Ct. Office: Bloom Hergott Cook Diemer & Klein 150 S Rodeo Dr Fl 3 Beverly Hills CA 90212-2410*

BLOOM, JANE MAGINNIS, emergency physician; b. Ithaca, N.Y., June 22, 1924; d. Ernest Victor and Miriam Rebecca (Mansfield) M.; m. William Lee Bloom, Mar. 31, 1944; children: David Lee, Jan Christopher, Carolyn Wells, Eric Paul, Joseph William, Robert Carl, Mary Catherine, Thomas Mark, Patrick Martin (dec.), Arthur Emerson. BS, U. Mich., 1968, MD, 1974. Diplomate Am. Bd. Internal Medicine, Am. Bd. Emergency Medicine. Rotating intern Wayne County Gen. Hosp., Eloise, Mich., 1974-75; resident in internal medicine St. Mary's Hosp., Rochester, 1975-77; emergency physician Emergency Physicians Med. Group, Ann Arbor, 1986—. Fellow Am. Coll. Emergency Physicians (life); mem. AMA, Mich. State Med. Soc., Am. Coll. Medicine, Am. Med. Womens Assn., Am. Assn. Women Emergency Physicians, Washtenaw County Med. Soc., Am. Coll. Emergency Physicians. Avocations: bird watching, planting trees, classical music, walking. Home and Office: 537 Elm St Ann Arbor MI 48104-2515

BLOOM, JOHN PORTER, historian, editor, administrator, archivist; b. Albuquerque, Dec. 30, 1924; s. Lansing Bartlett and Maude Elizabeth (McFie) B.; m. Eva Louise Platt, 1954 (div.); children: Katherine Elizabeth Bloom Jassen, John Lansing, Susan Marie; m. Nancy Jo Tice, July 30, 1968. AB, U. N.Mex., 1947; AM, George Washington U., 1949; PhD, Emory U., 1956; cert. in pre-meteorology, Reed Coll., 1944. Mem. faculty No. Ga. Coll., 1950-51, Brenau Coll., 1952-56, U. Tex., El Paso, 1956-60; historian, mus. planner, editor Nat. Park Service, Washington, 1960-64; editor Territorial Papers of the U.S., 1964-80; sr. specialist western history Nat. Archives, Washington, 1964-80; dir. Holt-Atherton Pacific Ctr. Western Studies, Stockton, Calif., 1981-84; editor Pacific Historian, U. Pacific, Stockton, 1981-84; program com. chmn. Conf. History Am. West, Santa Fe, 1961, 71; cons. NEH div. pub. programs Nat. Hist. Publs. and Records Commn., Va. History and Mus. Fedn., 1976-79; mem. adv. bd. Capitol Studies, U.S. Capitol Hist. Soc., 1971-73. Editor: monograph The American Territorial System, 1973, Territorial Papers of the U.S., 1969, 71; editor, co-editor: monograph Soldier and Brave and other vols., 1963; book reviewer, contbr. articles to profl. jours. Chmn. Fairfax County Hist. Commn., 1972-73; active Cultural Heritage Bd., Stockton, Calif., 1982-85; bd. dirs. Gateway Inc., Alexandria, Va., 1971-75; sheriff Potomac Corral of the Westerners Internat., 1974; bd. dirs. Joseph Priestley Chapel Assocs. Inc., 1978-81. Served with USAAF, 1943-45. So. Fellowships Fund fellow, 1955-56. Mem. We. History Assn. (hon., life, pres. 1974, v.p. 1973, mem. Ray Allen Billington award com. 1979-82, Spl. Svc. award), Westerners Internat. Inc. (pres. 1981-83, bd. dirs. 1988-95), Westerners Soc. (Golden Spike award 1969), Coun. Am.'s Mil. Past (bd. dirs. 1982-96), Orgn. Am. Historians, Ea. Nat. Pks. and Monuments Assn., So. Hist. Assn., Pioneer Am. Soc., Rio Grande Hist. Found., Mus. N.Mex. Assn., Hist. Soc. N.Mex. (bd. dirs., 1st v.p. 1999—, mem. editl. adv. bd. N.Mex. Hist. Rev. 1998—). E-mail: jbloom@zianet.com. Home: 5620 Real del Norte Las Cruces NM 88012-7268

BLOOM, JULIAN, artist, editor; b. Cleve., May 6, 1933; s. John Bernard and Lillian Judith (Finkel) B.; m. Shirley Ann Harper, Nov. 29, 1954; children: Sandra Layne Walker, Andrea Sue Wells. AA, Cypress Coll., 1972; student, U. LaVerne (Calif.), 1983-86. Lab tech. Harvey Aluminum, Torrance, Calif., 1956-64, foreman, 1964-66; sr. draftsman Northrop Corp., Anaheim, Calif., 1966-67; designer Northrop Aircraft, Anaheim, Calif., 1967-69, facilities engr., 1969-81, design to corp. cost designer, 1982-84; mfg. engring. mgr. Northrop Aircraft, Anaheim, 1984-85, mfg. mgr., 1985-92; artist, owner Realistic Watercolors, Cypress, 1992—; instr. watercolor Huntington Beach Art Ctr., 1997—, City of Cypress, 1998—. Featured in The Best of Watercolor, 1995; columnist Event Newspapers, 1998—. Co-chmn. Cypress (Calif.) Cultural Arts Planning Com., 1993-95; pres. Cypress Art Art League, 1993-96; commr. Cypress Cultural Arts, 1999—. Served with U.S. Army, 1954-56. Fellow Am. Artists Profl. League (Signature award 1993); mem. Nat. Watercolor Soc. (assoc. mem. 1989—, editor newsletter 1994-97), Watercolor West (bd. dirs. 1999—). Republican. Jewish. Avocations: travel, computers, photography. Home and Office: 4522 Cathy Ave Cypress CA 90630-4212

BLOOM, KATHRYN RUTH, public relations executive; d. Morris and Frances Sondra (Siegel) B. BA, Douglass Coll.; MA, U. Toronto, Can. Dir. spl. projects United Jewish Appeal, N.Y.C., 1973-78; mgr. pub. affairs Bristol-Myers-Squibb Co., N.Y.C., 1978-86; mgr. pub. rels. pharm. and nutritional Bristol-Myers Squibb Co., N.Y.C., 1986-90, dir. pharm. and rsch. communications, 1990-91; dir. communications Biogen, Inc., Cambridge, 1992—. Mem. N.Y.C. com. Women's Campaign Fund, 1984-91; v.p., bd. dirs. N.Am. Conf. on Ethiopian Jewry, N.Y.C., 1985-93; overseer Boston Lyric Opera; dir. Jewish Vocat. Svc. of Boston, 1995-97. Mem. Women Execs. in Pub. Relations, The Boston Club, Phi Beta Kappa. Office: Biogen Inc 14 Cambridge Ctr Cambridge MA 02142-1481

BLOOM, LAWRENCE STEPHEN, retired clothing company executive; b. New Rochelle, N.Y., Apr. 30, 1930; s. Hyman and Eleanor (Bursch) B.; m. Mary Ann Hendricks, Aug. 15, 1959; children: Mark, Julie. B.S. in Commerce and Fin, Bucknell U., Lewisburg, Pa., 1952. Trainee Gimbels, N.Y.C., to 1954; with Warnaco Inc., 1954-90; former chmn. Warnaco Men's Knitwear (Puritan, Thane and Hathaway Knitwear), Altoona, Pa.; bd. dirs. Woolknit Assocs., Nat. Sportwear and Outerwear Assocs.; chpt. chair Svc. Corps of Retired Execs. Served with AUS, 1952-54. Home: 340 Deer Run Road Hollidaysburg PA 16648-3110

BLOOM, LEE HURLEY, lawyer, public affairs consultant, retired household products manufacturing executive; b. N.Y.C., June 21, 1919; s.

Harry and Harriet (Bresel) B.; m. Mary Louise Tolan, Dec. 15, 1945; children: Daniel, Louise, Douglas. B.S., MIT, 1940; LL.B., Harvard U., 1943. Bar: Mass. 1947, N.Y. 1951. Atty. legal div. Lever Bros. Co., N.Y.C., 1947-67; v.p., sec., gen. counsel Lever Bros. Co., 1968-70, adminstrv. v.p., dir., 1970-82; pres. Unilever U.S., Inc., 1978-82, vice chmn., 1982-83; Donald L. Wilson prof., Grinnell Coll., Iowa, 1986. Chmn. bd. Larchmont (N.Y.) chpt. ARC, 1961-63; Mem. Town of Mamaroneck (N.Y.) Republican Com., 1957-69; mem. Mamaroneck Planning Bd., 1959-69; mem. Mamaroneck Town Bd. 1969-85, dep. supr., 1982-83; coordinator N.Y. State Sch. and Bus. Alliance for Yonkers Pub. Schs., 1987-93; chmn. Ctr. for Performing Arts Lehman Coll., 1987-93. Served to lt. comdr. USNR, 1941-46. Mem. Soap and Detergent Assn. (dir. 1971-83, vice chmn. 1978-79, chmn. 1980-82), Assn. Pvt. Enterprise Edn. (exec. com. 1985-93), Internat. C. of C. (trustee U.S. coun. 1978-86, exec. com. 1980-86, vice chmn. 1982-85, sr. trustee 1987—), UN Assn. U.S.A. (pres. so. N.Y. state divsn. 1989-93). Home and Office: 22 Myrtle Blvd Larchmont NY 10538-1823

BLOOM, LEONARD, language educator; b. Bklyn., Mar. 28, 1937; s. Meyer and Lena (Brown) B.; m. Barbara Dee Shepse, Aug. 16, 1964; children: Felicia, Erica. BA, Bklyn. Coll., 1958; MA, Fla. State U., 1960; PhD, U. Pitts., 1967. Cert. secondary sch. tchr., N.Y., Conn. Tchg. fellow Spanish Fla. State U., Tallahassee, 1958-60, U. Pitts., 1962-64; Spanish and French tchr. N.Y.C. Pub. Sch. Sys., 1960-61; prof. Spanish Duquesne U., Pitts., 1963-67; chmn., prof. U. Bridgeport, Conn., 1967-0; tchr. of Spanish New Canaan (Conn.) Pub. Schs., 1991-94; adj. prof. Albertus Magnus Coll., New Haven, 1994—; mktg. dir. Bodvin Inc., Fairfield, Conn., 1975-96; translator, interpreter Revlon Internat., Eastchester, N.Y., 1983-85; instr. Spanish City of New Haven, 1995-97; instr. in music and history Elderhostel, Sarasota, Fla., 1998. Editor Jour. Basque Studies in Am.; contbr. articles to profl. jours. V.p. Probus Club, Fairfield, 1981-83; instr. Greater Bridgeport (Conn.) Jewish Cmty. Ctr., 1992-94, New Haven Police and Fire Depts., 1996-97. Grad. tchg. fellow Fla. State U., 1958; Mellon fellow, 1962; recipient award Sigma Delta Pi, 1960, 84. Mem. Am. Assn. Tchrs. Spanish and Portuguese (co-organizer, planner seminar 1977-78), Soc. Basque Studies in Am. (v.p. 1983-91, program com.), Conn. Orgn. Lang. Tchrs. (conf. coord. 1984-85). Avocations: classical music, foreign films, wine, travel, walking. Home: Apt 1715 4134 Central Sarasota Pkwy Sarasota FL 34238-6600 Office: Soc Basque Studies Am 19 Colonial Gdns Brooklyn NY 11209-5403

BLOOM, MICHAEL ANTHONY, lawyer; b. Phila., Sept. 4, 1947; s. Edward Bloom and Edythe (Weiss) Barbour; m. Debra Sue Lobis, Aug. 15, 1971; 1 child, Alexis Rachael. AB, Dickinson U., 1969; JD, Villanova U., 1974. Bar: Pa. 1974, U.S. Dist. Ct. (ea. dist.) Pa. 1974, U.S. Tax Ct. 1976, U.S. Ct. Appeals (3d cir.) 1977, U.S. Ct. Appeals (4th cir.) 1979, U.S. Supreme Ct. 1980. Assoc. Pelino, Wasserstrom, Chucas & Monteverde, Phila., 1974-77, Wasserstrom & Chucas, Phila., 1977-79; ptnr. Wasserstrom, Chucas, Sirlin & Bloom, Phila., 1980-82, Cohen, Shapiro, Polisher, Shiekman and Cohen, Phila., 1982-88, Morgan, Lewis & Bockius, Phila., 1988—; chmn. Hearing Commn. Disciplinary Bd., Pa. Supreme Ct., 1987-89; co-founder, past chmn., mem. steering com. Ea. Dist. Pa. Bankruptcy Conf., Phila., 1989, 94-95. Contbr. articles to profl. jours. Bd. dirs. Jewish Community Ctrs. of Greater Phila., 1987-91; bd. dirs., pres. Gershman YM-YWHA, Phila., 1987-90; co-chmn. Share Our Strength, Phila, 1987-90; v.p., bd. dirs. Pa. Ballet Asssn., 1987—; mem. adv. bd. Pa. Vol. Lawyers for Arts, 1990—. Recipient Fidelity award Fidelity Bank, Phila., 1983, Joseph and Sylvia Daroff award Jewish Y's and Community Ctrs., Phila., 1984. Fellow Am. Bar Found., Pa. Bar Found.; mem. ABA (com. on counsel responsibility sect. bus. law 1990), Am. Bankruptcy Inst., Pa. Bar Assn. (chmn. legal ethics and profl. responsibility com. 1985-91, com. on specialization 1989—, publs. com. 1986—, ho. of dels. 1983—, co-chair, mem. com. Amicus Curiae Brief com. 1991-94, Spl. Achievement award 1986, 87, 88), Phila. Bar Assn. (bd. govs. 1982-84, chmn. spl. com. on ethics in govt. 1988—). Avocation: middle and long distance running. Office: Morgan Lewis & Bockius 1701 Market St Philadelphia PA 19103-2903*

BLOOM, MYER, physicist, educator; b. Montreal, Que., Can., Dec. 7, 1928; s. Israel and Leah (Ram) B.; m. Margaret Holmes, May 29, 1954; children—David, Margot. B.Sc., McGill U., 1949, M.Sc., 1950; Ph.D., U. Ill., 1954; D (hon.), Tech. U. Denmark, 1994. Research fellow U. Leiden, 1954-56; faculty U. B.C., Vancouver, 1956—; assoc. prof. U. B.C., 1960-63, prof. physics, 1963-93; D (hon.) Concordia U., 1995. Recipient Steacie prize, 1967, Jacob Biely prize, 1968, Gold medal Can. Assn. Physicists, 1973, Sci. Coun. of B.C. Chmn.'s award for career achievement, 1992, Izaak Walton Killam Meml. prize in natural sci., 1995; Alfred P. Sloan fellow, 1961-65; John Simon Guggenheim fellow, 1964-65; Izaak Walton Killam Meml. scholar, 1978-79. Fellow Royal Soc. Can., Am. Phys. Soc., Can. Inst. for Advanced Rsch. Research in structure and molecular motion in biological and model membranes, nuclear magnetic resonance. Home: 5669 King's Rd, Vancouver, BC Canada V6T 1K9

BLOOM, ROBERT, language professional educator; b. N.Y.C., May 28, 1930; s. Michael and Fannie (Hecker) B.; m. Gloria Loebenson, Aug. 29, 1953; children: Claudia, Madeline, Jonathan. BA, NYU, 1951; MA, Columbia U., 1952; PhD, U. Mich., 1960. Asst. prof., assoc. prof. English U. Calif. Berkeley, 1960-72, prof. English, 1972—. Author: The Indeterminate World: A Study of the Novels of Joyce Cary, 1962, Anatomies of Egotism: A Reading of the Last Novels of H.G. Wells, 1977; contbr. articles to profl. jours. Lt. j.g. U.S. Coast Guard, 1952-54. Bruern fellow in Am. Civilization U. Leeds, 1963. Mem. Modern Lang. Assn., Phi Beta Kappa. Avocations: playing piano, cycling, music, reading. Office: Univ Calif Dept English Berkeley CA 94720

BLOOM, ROBERT H., advertising executive. Chmn. bd., CEO Publicis/ Bloom, Inc., N.Y.C. Office: Publicis/Bloom Inc 304 E 45th St New York NY 10017-3425*

BLOOM, RUTH ELSA, educator, administrator; b. Phila., Jan. 13, 1954; d. George and Signe Elizabeth (Andersen) Kulp; m. David Allen Bloom, Oct. 4, 1975; children: Amy Elizabeth, Lisa Catherine. BS, Millersville U., 1975; MEd, Kutztown U., 1983; elem. prin. cert., Lehigh U., 1987. Cert. elem. prin., elem. tchr., special edn. Elem. tchr. Brandywine Heights Area Sch. Dist., Topton, Pa., 1975-88, elem. adminstrv. asst., 1987-88, elem. prin., 1988-92; tchr. Brandywine Heights Sch. Dist., Topton, Pa., 1992—; coord., dir. Chpt. 1 Fed. Program, Topton, 1987-92, Pa. State Testing Program, Topton, 1987-89. Trustee Brandywine Libr., Topton, 1989—, pres. bd., 1993, 94, 95, 96, 97, 98; mem. elem. edn. adv. com. Kutztown U., 1989-92; cadette leader, 1992-95, sr. leader Girl Scouts U.S., 1995—; lead housing supr. Olympic Village, Atlanta, 1996; asst. resident camp dir. Mosey Wood, Great Valley U.S. Girl Scouts. Grantee Ednl. Tech., 1986; recipient Outstanding Girl Scout Leader award Great Valley Coun., Girls Scouts USA, 1998. Avocations: violinist, gardening. Office: Brandywine Heights Sch Dist Weis St Topton PA 19562

BLOOM, SHERMAN, pathologist, educator; b. Bklyn., Jan. 26, 1934; s. Philip and Sadie (Kaplan) B.; m. Miriam Fishman, Feb. 11, 1960; children: Naomi, Stephanie. BA, NYU, 1955, MD, 1960. Diplomate Am. Bd. Anat. Pathology. Intern in medicine Kings County Hosp., Bklyn., 1960-61; fellow in exptl. pathology, resident in anatomic and clin. pathology NYU Med. Ctr. and Bellevue Hosp., N.Y.C., 1961-65; instr. pathology NYU Sch. Medicine, 1965-66; asst. prof. U. Utah Coll. Medicine, Salt Lake City, 1966-70, assoc. prof., 1970-72; assoc. prof. U. South Fla. Coll. Medicine, Tampa, 1973-76, prof. pathology, 1976-77; prof. pathology George Washington U. Coll. Medicine, Washington, 1977-88; prof., chmn. dept. pathology U. Miss. Med. Ctr., Jackson, 1988—; cons. Sci. Rev., NIH; mem. cardiovascular study sect. NSF, FDA; dir. coun. on cardiovascular and geriatric health Amer Coll. Nutrition, 1998-01; bd. dirs. Scientists Ctr. Animal Welfare, pres. elect, 1987, pres., 1988. Mem. editorial bd. Jour. Am. Coll. Nutrition, 1982, Am. Jour. Cardiovascular Pathology, 1985; assoc. editor Cardiovascular Pathology, 1990; contbr. numerous articles to profl. publs. Del. Utah State Dem. Party, 1968. NIH fellow, 1962; Dilthey Found. fellow, 1982. Fellow Am. Coll. Nutrition; mem. Internat. Acad. Pathologists, Am. Physiol. Soc., Am. Assn. Pathologists, Internat. Soc. Heart Research, Soc. Cardiovascular Pathology (pres. 1986-87). Jewish. Home: 4433 Wedgewood St Jackson MS 39211-6219

BLOOM, STEPHEN G, journalist, educator; b. Orange, N.J., Aug. 19, 1951; s. Jerome and Marian Louise (Grossner) B.; m. Iris Bonny Frost, Oct. 11, 1987; 1 child, Michael. AB, U. Calif., Berkeley, 1973. News editor Latin Am. Daily Post, Rio de Janeiro, 1979-81; staff writer Dallas Morning News, 1981-84, L.A. Times, 1984-85; feature writer San Jose (Calif.) Mercury News, 1986-87; sr. writer Sacramento Bee, 1987-91; press sec. Mayor Frank Jordan, San Francisco, 1992; prof. journalism U. Iowa, Iowa City, 1993—. Contbr. articles to various newspapers and profl. jours. Columbia U. vis. scholar, 1995; recipient Bronze award Soc. Am. Travel Writers, 1996. Avocations: playwriting, short-fiction writing. Office: Sch Journalism U Iowa Iowa City IA 52242

BLOOM, STEPHEN JOEL, distribution company executive; b. Chgo., Feb. 27, 1936; s. Max Samuel and Carolyn (Gumbiner) B.; m. Nancy Lee Gillan, Aug. 24, 1957; children: Anne, Bradley, Thomas, Carolyn. B.B.A., U. Mich., 1958. Salesman, then gen. mgr. Cigarette Service Co., Countryside, Ill., 1957-65, pres., chief exec. officer, 1965—; exec. v.p., chief exec. officer S. Bloom, Inc., Countryside; pres., dir. Intercontinental Cons. Corp., Balt., chmn. bd., 1978—; v.p. Philip Morris USA; dirs. Amerimark Fin. Corp. Fin. chmn. DuPage County Rep. Com., 1976; mem. Chgo. Crime Commn. Named Man of Yr. Chgo. Tobacco Table, 1972; named to Tobacco Industry Hall of Fame, 1985. Mem. Nat. Automatic Mdsg. Assn. (Minuteman award 1974), Nat. Assn. Tobacco Distbrs. (chmn. nat. legis. com. Young Exec. of Yr. award, dir. 1978), Ill. Assn. Tobacco Distbrs., Young Pres. Orgn., Chgo. Pres. Orgn., Morningside Rancho Mirage Club (pres. 1996-97). Lodge: Rotary. Home: 3 Hamil Ln Clarendon Hills IL 60514-1462 Office: 7512 S County Line Rd Hinsdale IL 60521-6961

BLOOM, STEPHEN MICHAEL, magistrate judge, lawyer; b. San Francisco, June 10, 1948; s. Alan I. and Wilma (Morgan) B.; m. Rebecca J. Nelson, June 19, 1976; children: Benjamin Jacob, Molly Marie, John Robert. Student, Dartmouth Coll., 1966-68; BA in English, Stanford U., 1970; student, Calif. State U., Sacramento, 1973-74; JD, Willamette Coll. Law, 1977. Bar: Oreg. 1977, U.S. Dist. Ct. Oreg. 1979. Adminstrv. asst. Calif. Dept. Edn., Sacramento, 1973-74; atty. Joyce & Harding, Corvallis, Oreg., 1977-78; dep. dist. atty. Umatilla County, Pendleton, Oreg., 1978-79; atty. Morrison & Reynolds, Hermiston, Oreg., 1979-81, Kottkamp & O'Rourke, Pendleton, 1981—; appointed U.S. magistrate, 1988. Bd. dirs. Edn. Svc. Dist., Pendleton, 1982-89. Lt. (j.g.) USN, 1970-72. Mem. ABA, Oreg. Bar Assn., Rotary (pres. 1990-91, bd. dirs. 1991). Avocation: sailing. Office: US Dist Ct PO Box 490 Pendleton OR 97801-0490 also: Kottkamp & O'Rourke 331 SE 2nd St Pendleton OR 97801-2224*

BLOOMBERG, LAWRENCE S., securities executive, art collector; b. Montreal, Que., Can., May 28, 1942; s. Sol and Sylvia Bloomberg; m. Frances Bloomberg; children: Debra, Bonnie, Jonathon. B of Commerce, Sir George Williams U., 1963; MBA, McGill U., 1965; LLD (hon.), Concordia U., 1996. Chartered fin analyst. Dir. Cinram Ltd., other pvt. cos., 1965-76; various mgmt. positions including head of rsch., v.p., dir. Instnl. Equity Sales, Nesbitt Thomson and Co., 1965-76, v.p., dir., 1975-79; founding mem. 1st Marathon Securities, Ltd., 1979; pres., CEO, dir. 1st Marathon Inc., 1984-99; past mem. Young Pres.'s Orgn.; past mem bd. govs. Toronto Stock Exch.; founding mem. Concordia's Faculty of Commerce and Adminstrn. Bus. Adv. Com.; bd. dirs. Cinran Ltd. Bd. govd., vice chmn. Mt. Sinai Hosp., chmn. The Best Medicine campaign; mem. budget and fin. com., Baycrest Ctr. for Geriatric Care; trustee Simon Wiesenthal Ctr., Inc.; co-chmn. toronto's 1994 United Jewish Appeal/Operation Exodus Campaign; active United Way campaigns; past gov. Jr. Achievement of Can.; mem. Rector's Cir., Concordia U., founding mem. Faculty of Commerce and Adminstrn. Bus. Adv. Com.; bd. dirs. Toronto Internat. Film Festival Group, Royal Ont. Mus. Found.; mem. Can. Inst. Internat. Affairs; former bd. dirs. Toronto Stock Exch. Recipient Human Rels. award Can. Coun. Christians and Jews. Mem. XPO, World Pres.'s Orgn., Bus. Coun. on Nat. Issues, C.D. Howe Inst., Rector's Cir. of Concordia U., Investment Dealers Assn. of Can. (bd. dirs., exec. com.). Avocations: running, golf. Office: First Marathon Inc 2 First Canadian Pl, Toronto, ON Canada M5X 1J9*

BLOOMBERG, MICHAEL RUBENS, finance and information services company executive; b. Boston, Feb. 14, 1942; divorced; 2 children. Graduate, Johns Hopkins U., 1964, Harvard U., 1966. Processing clerk Salomon Brothers, 1966; gen. ptnr. sys. devel. Salomon Brothers, N.Y.C.; pres. founder Bloomberg L.P., N.Y.C., 1981—; pub. Bloomberg Business News, N.Y.C.; gen. mgr. Bloomberg Television, Bloomberg Radio, Sta. WBBR-AM 1130, N.Y.C.; pub. Bloomberg Mag./Bloomberg Personal Mag., Princeton, N.J., Bloomberg Personal, Skillman, N.J. Chmn. bd. trustees Johns Hopkins U.; trustee Big Apple Circus, Ctrl. Park Conservancy, Met. Mus. Art, H.S. Econs. And Fin., Inst. Advanced Study, Lincoln Ctr. Performing Arts, Jewish Mus., N.Y. Police and Fire Widows' and Children's Fund, Spence Sch., Prep for Prep, S.L.E. Found., U.S. Ski Team Ednl. Found., Serpentine Gallery, London. Mem. U.S. C. of C. (trustee). Office: Bloomberg LP 499 Park Ave 15th Fl New York NY 10022-1240

BLOOMBERG, STU, broadcast executive. Chmn. ABC Entertainment. Office: ABC Inc Exec Ste 2040 Avenue Of The Stars Los Angeles CA 90067-4785*

BLOOMER, HAROLD FRANKLIN, JR., lawyer; b. N.Y.C., Nov. 4, 1933; s. Harold Franklin and Allene (Cress) B.; m. Mary Jane Lloyd, July 16, 1955 (div. June 1976); children: Sarah Allene, Margaret Gail, Leslie Lloyd; m. Freya Donald, Nov. 30, 1985; children: Katharine Roma, Alice Donald. AB, Amherst Coll., 1956; LLB, Columbia U., 1967. Bar: Conn. 1967, N.Y. 1968, U.S. Dist. Ct. Conn. 1968, U.S. Dist. Ct. (so. and ea. dists.) N.Y. 1974, U.S. Ct. Appeals (2d cir.) 1974. Assoc. Debevoise, Plimpton, Lyons & Gates, N.Y.C., 1967-77; counsel Burlington, Underwood & Lord, Jeddah, Saudi Arabia, 1977-78; chief internat. counsel Saudi Rsch. & Devel. Corp., London, 1978-80; counsel Morgan, Lewis & Bockius LLP, London and N.Y.C., 1980-81, ptnr., 1981—; adj. prof.Pepperdine U. Sch. Law, London, 1985. Mem. Rep. Town Meeting, Greenwich, Conn., 1964-74, 92—, chmn. pub. works com., 1971-74, chmn. land use com., 1998—; mem. Rep. Town Com., Greenwich, 1973-74; trustee San. Products Trust, Riverside, Conn., 1965-74. Lt. (j.g.) USNR, 1957-60. Kent scholar Columbia U., 1965-66, Stone scholar Columbia U., 1966-67. Mem. ABA, Am. Arbitration Assn. (panel of arbitrators 1990—), Assn. of Bar of City of N.Y., Riverside Yacht Club. Republican. Episcopalian. Avocations: sailing, canoeing, skiing, biking, running. Office: Morgan Lewis & Bockius LLP 101 Park Ave New York NY 10178

BLOOMER, WILLIAM ARTHUR, security industry executive; b. Bellaire, Kans., Jan. 23, 1933; s. James Charles and Nettie Alice (Baker) B.; m. Sharon Sue Vernon, May 30, 1954; children: Leigh Anne, Jeffrey Alan, Brenda Sue. BS in Edn., Emporia (Kans.) State U., 1955; MS in Mgmt., Rensselaer Poly. Inst., 1970. Commd. 2d lt. USMC, 1955, advanced through grades to brigadier gen., 1981, ret., 1986; exec. v.p. Am. Protective Svcs., Inc., Arlington, Va., 1986—; chmn. RNC Liquid Assets Fund, L.A. City councilman City of Irvine, Calif., 1990-93, pub. safety commr., 1986-88; chmn. bd. govs. Rep. Assocs. Orange County, Calif., 1989; fin. commr. City of Irvine, 1989-90. Decorated 2 Legions of Merit, Disting. Flying Cross, Bronze star, 17 Air medals, Kuang Hua medal (Republic of China); named Disting. Alumnus Emporia State U., 1985. Mem. Soc. Experimental Test Pilots (assoc.), Am. Soc. Indsl. Security. Methodist. Avocations: golf, glider flying, personal computing. Home: 9203 Cross Oaks Ct Fairfax Station VA 22039-3337 Office: Am Protective Svcs Inc 1911 Fort Myer Dr Ste 302 Arlington VA 22209-1603*

BLOOMFIELD, DANIEL KERMIT, college dean, physician; b. Cleve., Dec. 14, 1926; s. Joseph Bernard and Henrietta (Namen) B.; m. Frances Aub, June 10, 1955; children: Louis, Ruth, Anne. B.S., U.S. Naval Acad., 1947; M.S., Western Res. U., 1954, M.D., 1954. Intern Beth Israel Hosp., Boston, 1954-55; resident Beth Israel Hosp., 1955-56, Mass. Gen. Hosp., Boston, 1956-67; research fellow chemistry Harvard U., 1957-59; hon. asst. registrar cardiology Nat. Heart Hosp., London, 1959-60; sr. instr. medicine Western Res. U., Cleve., 1960-64; sr. clin. instr. medicine Western Res. U., 1964-70; dir. cardiovascular research Community Health Found., Cleve., 1964-66; assoc. medicine Mt. Sinai Hosp., Cleve., 1966-69; prof. medicine U. Ill. Sch. Medicine, Urbana, 1970-96; dean Coll. Medicine U. Ill.-Urbana, 1970-84; prof. emeritus, 1996—; Investigator Am. Heart Assn., 1960-64. Pres. Champaign-Urbana Jewish Fedn., 1985-88, Cen. Ill. Jewish Fedn., 1988-92; bd. dirs. Planned Parenthood, 1988-89. With USN, 1947-50. Recipient citation for contbns. to med. edn. Ohio Heart Assn., 1964. Mem. Alpha Omega Alpha. Home: 103 E Michigan Ave Urbana IL 61801-5027

BLOOMFIELD, KEITH MARTIN, management executive; b. Bronx, N.Y., Sept. 11, 1951; s. Monroe Louis and Shirley B. (Mason) B.; BA, Windham Coll., 1973; MS, Syracuse U., 1974; m. Adrienne Donna Young, Sept. 2, 1979. Personnel/cons. Automatic Data Processing Inc., Clifton, N.J., 1975-78; cons. European Am. Bank, N.Y.C., 1978-79; cons. Consol. Edison N.Y., 1979-81; div. mgr. Pepsi-Cola Mgmt. Inst., Purchase, 1981-87; cons. Pepsi-Cola Co., Purchase, 1981-87; sr. program mgr. Learning Internat., Stamford, Conn., 1987-89; v.p. ops. Ctr. for Media Arts, N.Y.C., 1989-92, Krauthammer Internat., 1992-93, Rollins Hudig Hall, 1994-95; dir. human resources Lincoln Tech. Inst., West Orange, N.J., 1995—; chmn. Eastchester Cable TV Adv. Com. Mem. Syracuse U. Alumni. Contbr. short stories to various publs.; writer stage and screen plays. Home: 260 Garth Rd Scarsdale NY 10583-4051

BLOOMFIELD, LOUIS AUB, physicist, educator; b. Boston, Oct. 11, 1956; s. Daniel Kermit and Frances (Aub) B.; m. Karen Shatkin, Aug. 28, 1983; children: Elana, Aaron. BA in Physics, Amherst Coll., 1979; PhD in Physics, Stanford U., 1983. Postdoctoral physicist AT&T Bell Labs., Murray Hill, N.J., 1983-85; asst. prof. U. Va., Charlottesville, 1985-91, assoc. prof., 1991-96, prof, 1996—. Author: (Book) How Things Work: The Physics of Everyday Life. Recipient Alumni Tchr. award U. Va., 1992, Pres.'s Rsch. prize, 1994; named Presdl. Young Investigator NSF, 1986, Young Investigator Office of Naval Rsch., 1988, Va. Outstanding Faculty award, 1998; Alfred P. Sloan fellow, 1989. Fellow Am. Phys. Soc. (Apker award 1980). Jewish. Office: Univ of Va Dept Physics Charlottesville VA 22901

BLOOMFIELD, LOUISE ANNE, editor; b. Rome, Mar. 9, 1955; came to U.S., 1955; d. Theodore Robert and Margery A. (Wald) B. BA, Oberlin Coll., 1976. Editor William Heinemann Ltd., London, 1978-84, Grove's Dictionaries of Music, N.Y.C., 1984-85; freelance editor, translator N.Y.C., 1985-89; editor, then mng. editor Macmillan Co. (now Atlas Editions Inc.), N.Y.C., 1990-94, exec. editor Collier's Ency., 1995-98; editl. svcs. mgr. Aspen Law & Bus. Rev., N.Y.C., 1998—. Office: Aspen Law & Bus Rev 36th Fl 1185 Avenue of the Americas New York NY 10036

BLOOMFIELD, MAXWELL HERRON, III, history and law educator; b. Galveston, Tex., Aug. 17, 1931; s. Maxwell Herron and Violet Clemons (Turner) B.; m. Helen Lorraine Anderson, Sept. 11, 1965. BA, Rice U., 1952; LLB, Harvard U., 1957; PhD in History, Tulane U., 1962. Bar: Tex. 1957. Lectr. Tulane U., 1961-62; instr. Ohio State U., 1962-66; asst. prof. history Cath. U. Am., Washington, 1966-68, assoc. prof., 1968-74, prof., 1974—, chmn. dept. history, 1977-80, prof. law, 1985-98, prof. emeritus, 1998—; vis. prof. U. Va., 1973. Author: Alarms and Diversions: The American Mind Through American Magazines, 1967, American Lawyers in a Changing Society, 1776-1876, 1976; (with John McWilliams and Carl Smith) Law and American Literature, 1983; mem. editl. bd. Md. Hist. Mag., 1974-75, Capitol Studies, 1979-80, Legal Studies Forum, 1985-96. With U.S. Army, 1952-54. Am. Bar Found. fellow, 1968-69, Project '87 fellow, 1981; ABA grantee, 1979-80. Mem. State Bar Tex., Am. Soc. Legal History, Am. Hist. Assn., Am. Cath. Hist. Assn., Orgn. Am. Historians, Phi Beta Kappa. Democrat. Roman Catholic. Home: 1913 Saratoga Dr Hyattsville MD 20783-2102 Office: Cath U Am Columbus Sch Law Washington DC 20064

BLOOMFIELD, SARA, museum director. Exec. dir. U.S. Holocaust Memorial Museum, Washington, D.C. Office: US Holocaust Meml Council Public Programs 100 Raoul Wallenberg Pl SW Washington DC 20024-2126

BLOOMFIELD, STEVEN B., think-tank executive. Dir. Fellows Program Weatherhead Ctr. for Internat. Affairs Harvard U., Cambridge, Mass.; acting exec. dir. Weatherhead Ctr. for Internat. Affairs Harvard U. Office: Weatherhead Ctr for Internat Affairs 1731 Cambridge St Rm 622 Cambridge MA 02138*

BLOOMGARDEN, KATHY FINN, public relations executive; b. N.Y.C., June 9, 1949; d. David and Laura (Zeisler) Finn; m. Zachary Bloomgarden; children: Rachel, Keith, Matthew. BA, Brown U., 1970; MA, Columbia U., PhD. Pres. Rsch. & Forecasts, N.Y.C.; pres., dir. Ruder-Finn, Inc., N.Y.C., 1988-98, pres., 1998—. Mem. comms. com. Brown U., Providence. Mem. Pub. Rels. Soc. Am., Am. Mgmt. Assn. (bd. dirs.), Coun. Fgn. Rels. Jewish. Home: 1043 North Ave New Rochelle NY 10804-3628 Office: Ruder Finn 301 E 57th St New York NY 10022-2900*

BLOOMQUIST, DENNIS HOWARD, lawyer; b. Mpls. Sept. 18, 1942; s. Howard Richard and Ingrid Marit (Brostrom) B.; m. Shirley Anne Ruemele, Aug. 22, 1964; children—Michael Dennis, Eric William. B.A., Albion Coll., Mich., 1964; M.B.A., Mich. State U., 1965; J.D. cum laude, Wayne State U., 1968; LL.M., NYU, 1975. Bar: Mich. 1968, U.S. Dist. Ct. (ea. dist.) Mich. 1968, N.Y. 1971, Va. 1995. Assoc. Parsons, Tennent, Hammond, Hardig & Ziegelman, Detroit, 1968-70, Alexander and Green, N.Y.C., 1970-73; tax counsel Mobil Oil and Mobil Corp., N.Y.C., 1973-81, gen. counsel Mobil Land Devel. Corp., N.Y.C., 1981-88, real estate and land devel., Mobil Corp., 1984-88, asst. gen. tax counsel, Fairfax, Va., 1988—; lectr. continuing legal edn. Mem. ABA, Bar Assn. Mich., N.Y. State Bar Assn. Congregationalist. Home: 11136 Rich Meadow Dr Great Falls VA 22066-1417 Office: 3225 Gallows Rd Fairfax VA 22037-0002

BLOOMQUIST, KENNETH GENE, music educator, university bands director; b. Boone, Iowa, Dec. 29, 1931; s. Carl Arvid and Alma Florence (Lindahl) B.; m. Carole Ann Murphy, Feb. 14, 1954; children: Leslie Ann, Laurie Kathleen, Daniel John. BS in Music Edn., U. Ill., 1953, MusM, 1957. Band dir. Urbana (Ill.) Pub. Schs., 1956-57; band dir., supr. music Taylorville (Ill.) Pub. Schs., 1957-58; asst. band dir., trumpet tchr. U. Kans., Lawrence, 1958-68, dir. bands, 1968-70; dir. bands Mich. State U., East Lansing, 1970-78, 88-93, dir. Sch. Music, 1978-88; dir. bands, 1988-93; dir. bands emeritus Mich. State U., East Lansing, 1993; guest band condr., U.S., Europe, Asia, 1968—; condr. fgn. tours, 1964, 75, 76, 78, 85, 92, 95; cons. adjudicator of music, U.S., Europe, Mex., Taiwan, Indonesia, Japan, Thailand, Korea. Contbr. articles to profl. jours., others. Pres. Music Boosters Okemos (Mich.) Pub. Schs., 1970-72; bd. dirs. Lansing Symphone Orch., 1978-84, Okemos Community Ch., 1984-87. Sgt. U.S. Army, 1953-55. Recipient Alumni award U. Ill., 1966. em. Nat. Band Assn. (nat. pres. 1980-82), Am. Band Masters Assn. (nat. pres. 1995-96), Coll. Band Dirs. Assn., Music Educators Nat. Conf., Phi Mu Alpha. Avocations: golf, bridge, tennis, travel, reading.

BLOOMQUIST, RODNEY GORDON, geologist; b. Aberdeen, Wash., Feb. 3, 1943; s. Verner A. and Margaret E. (Olson) B.; m. Linda L. Lee, Dec. 19, 1964 (div. July 1968); m. Bente Brisson Jørgensen, Aug. 4, 1977; 1 child, Kira Brisson. BS in Geology, Portland State U., 1966; MS in Geology, U. Stockholm, 1970, PhD in Geochemistry, 1977. Rschr. U. Stockholm, 1974-77; asst. prof. Oreg. Inst. Tech., Klamath Falls, 1978-80; geologist Wash. State Energy Office, Olympia, 1980-96; sr. scientist Wash. State U., Olympia, 1996—; vis. prof. Internat. Sch. Geothermics, Pisa, Italy, 1990—; adj. prof. Evergreen State Coll., Olympia, 1996—; cons. U.S. Dept. Energy, Washignton, 1990, Govt. of Can., 1984, Aesa-Stal Geoenergy, Lund, Sweden, 1985-86, City and County of San Francisco, 1988-89, Lake County, Calif., 1992, San Francisco State U., 1993, Internat. Geoenergy Consortium, Springfield, Mo., 1996-98, Portland GE, 1997-98, GeothermEx, Oakland, Calif., 1998. Author: Regulatory Guide to Geothermics, 1991; mem. editl. bd. Geothermics, 1985-88; also numerous books and articles. Smitts fellow, Sweden, 1974, Royal Rsch. fellow, Sweden, 1975-77; rsch. grantee U. Stockholm, 1975-77. Mem. Geothermal Resources Coun. (bd. dirs. 1985-92, pres. 1989, pres. Pacific N.W. sect. 1982-85), Internat. Dist. Energy Assn. (western sect. bd. dirs. 1990—, bd. dirs. 1994-97, chmn. com. gov. rels. 1997—), Internat. Geothermal Assn. (bd. dirs. 1988-92, 95—, chmn. edn. com. 1988—), N.Am. Dist. Heating and Cooling Inst. (bd. dirs. 1986-88), Am. Blade Smith Soc. (bd. dirs. 1989—). Democrat. Lutheran. Avocations: skiing, backpacking, fishing, hunting. Office: Wash State Univ 925 Plum St SE Olympia WA 98501-1529

BLOOR, W(ILLIAM) SPENCER, electrical engineer, consultant; b. Trenton, N.J., Oct. 16, 1918; s. W. Harry and Evva (Averre) B.; m. Barbara P. Walters, Jan. 19, 1952; children: William G., Robert S. B.S. in Elec. Engring, Lafayette Coll., 1940, D.Eng. (hon.), 1981. With Leeds & Northrup Co., 1940-81; product market devel. mgr. Leeds & Northrup Co., Phila., 1966-68; engring. coordination mgr. Leeds & Northrup Co., North Wales, Pa., 1968-69; mgr. steam and nuclear power systems Leeds & Northrup Co., 1969-81; cons. in pvt. practice, 1981—; cons. staff Beacon Rsch. Found., Beaver Coll., Franklin Inst., past chmn. com. on sci. and arts. Served to lt. USN, 1943-46. Named Engr. of Yr. Delaware Valley, 1980. Fellow IEEE, Instrument Soc. Am. (v.p. publs. 1968-70, pres. 1974, chmn. history com., mem. IEEE Lamme medal com. 1989-91); mem. NAE , Phi Beta Kappa, Tau Beta Pi, Eta Kappa Nu. Presbyterian. Design and application of control and monitoring systems for electric power generating stations. Home and Office: 401 Meadowbrook Dr Huntingdon Valley PA 19006-6820

BLOSER, DIETER, radiologist; b. Yugoslavia, Aug. 17, 1944; came to U.S., 1947, naturalized, 1954; s. Peter and Eva Helen Bloser; A.B., Princeton U., 1966; M.D., Case Western Res. U., 1970; m. Deborah Pierce Forbes, Nov. 25, 1967; children—Peter Forbes, Timothy Philip. Intern dept. medicine U. Hosps. of Cleve., 1970-71, resident in radiology, 1971-72, 74-76, chief resident, 1975-76; practice medicine specializing in radiology, Parma, Ohio, 1976—; mem. staff Parma Community Gen. Hosp., 1976—, chief nuclear medicine, 1977—, chief radiology, 1984—; pres. Parma Radiologic Assocs, Inc., 1990—. Gen. Hosp. Bd. dirs. Cleve. chpt. Juvenile Diabetes Found., 1986-90; active Am. Diabetes Assn., 1985—; trustee Case Western Reserve U. Sch. Med Alumni Assn., 1985-89. Served to lt. comdr. USN, 1972-74. Diplomate Am. Bd. Radiology. Mem. Am. Coll. Radiology, Radiol. Soc. N. Am., Ohio Radiol. Soc., Cleve. Radiol. Soc. (pres.-elect 1986-87, pres. 1987-88), Am. Inst. Ultrasound in Medicine, Cleve. Acad. Medicine, AMA, Ohio Med. Assn., Princeton Alumni Assn. (schs. com.), Phi Beta Kappa, Alpha Omega Alpha. Lutheran. Home: 18185 Windswept Cir Chagrin Falls OH 44023-2439 Office: Parma Community Hosps 7007 Powers Blvd Cleveland OH 44129-5495

BLOSKAS, JOHN D., financial executive; b. Waco, Tex., July 13, 1928; s. George and Alvina (Schrader) B.; m. Anna Louise Nelson, Feb. 7, 1955; children: Suzzanne (dec.), John D., Kenneth Douglas. Exec. sec. Waco Jr. C. of C., 1953-55; assoc. editor Mexia (Tex.) Daily News, 1955-56; dir. publicity Valley C. of C., Weslaco, Tex., 1956-57; religion editor Houston Chronicle, 1957-58; v.p. pub. rels. annuity bd. So. Bapt. Conv., Dallas, 1984-92, v.p., endowment officer annuity bd., 1984-90; v.p. Lady Love Cosmetics, Dallas, 1984-90; retired, 1990, fin. mgmt. cons., 1990—; chmn. Greenville (Tex.) Airport adv. bd. Author: Staying in the Black, Financially, Living Within Your Means; editor: THe Years Ahead. Served with USNR, 1945-49, 50-51. Mem. Southern Bapt. (past pres.), Tex. Bapt. Assn. (past pres.), Pub. Rels. Assn., Pub. Rels. Soc. Am. (accredited), Religious Pub. Rels. Coun., Sales and Mktg. Execs., Bapt. Devel. Officer's Assn., Assn. Bapt. Found. Execs., Dallas Estate Planning Coun., Fellowship Christians in Arts, Media and Entertainment. Home: 7508 Blossom Ln Frisco TX 75034-5470 Office: PO Box 1192 Frisco TX 75034-1192

BLOSSER, HENRY GABRIEL, physicist; b. Harrisonburg, Va., Mar. 16, 1928; s. Emanuel and Leona (Branum) B.; m. Priscilla May Beard, June 30, 1951 (div. Oct. 1972); children: William Henry, Stephan Emanuel, Gabe Fawley, Mary Margaret; m. Mary Margaret Gray, Mar. 16, 1973 (dec. Jan. 1995); m. Amy June Conley, May 11, 1995 (div. Feb. 1997); m. Lois Pearlena Lynch, Oct. 17, 1998. BS, U. Va., 1951, MS, 1952, PhD, 1954. Physicist Oak Ridge (Tenn.) Nat. Lab., 1954-56, group leader, 1956-68; assoc. prof. physics Mich. State U., East Lansing, 1958-61, prof., 1961-90, Univ. Disting. prof., 1990—, dir. Cyclotron Lab., 1961-89; cons. Harper Hosp., Detroit, 1983—, Ion Beam Applications, Belgium, 1996—, others; adj. prof. radiation oncology Wayne State U., Detroit, 1996—. Bd. dirs. Midwest Univs. Rsch. Assocs., 1960-63. With USNR, 1946-48. predoctoral fellow NSF, 1953-54, sr. postdoctoral fellow, 1966-67; Guggenheim fellow, 1973-74. Fellow Am. Phys. Soc. (Bonner prize 1992); mem. Sigma Xi, Phi Beta Kappa, Kappa Alpha. Home: 2350 Emerald Forest Cir East Lansing MI 48823-7200 Office: Mich State U Nat Cyclotron East Lansing MI 48824-1321

BLOSSER, PAMELA ELIZABETH, metaphysics educator, counselor, minister; b. Norman, Okla., Dec. 12, 1946; d. William Bernard and Emma Elizabeth (Armbrister) Carpenter; m. William Richard Stewart, June 10, 1969 (div. Apr. 1979); m. Paul Gerald Blosser Jr., Sept. 24, 1994. BA, Tex. Christian U., 1969; DDiv, Interfaith Ch. Metaphysics, Windyville, Mo., 1992; DMetaphysics, Sch. Metaphysics, Windyville, 1994; degree with honors, Maria Montessori Tng. Divsn., London, 1977. Ordained to ministry Interfaith Ch. of Metaphysics, 1992; cert. in counseling. Dir. metaphysics ctrs. Sch. Metaphysics, various locations, 1979-89; directress Golden Moments Montessori, Columbia, Mo., 1987-89; instr. metaphysics Sch. Metaphysics, various locations, 1977-89; readings coord. Sch. Metaphysics, Windyville, 1989—, dir. printing, 1989—, instr. metaphysics, 1991—; min. of music Interfaith Ch. Metaphysics, Windyville, 1990—, min., 1995—; dir. Coll. Prep. Camp for Children, Sch. Metaphysics, Windyville, 1990—; mem. ordination bd. Interfaith Ch. of Metaphysics, 1993—; bd. govs. Sch. of Metaphysics, 1997—. Author: (books of essays) Power of Structure, 1988, Total Recall, 1993, Motivation: From Existence to Fulfillment, 1997; contbr. articles to profl. jours. Mem. Dallas County Homemakers (sec.-treas. 1995-96), Homemaker Club Windyville (v.p. 1995, 98, pres. 1996, 99). Rep[illegible]lican. Avocations: reading, playing Celtic harp. Home: HC 1 B[illegible] 15 Windyville MO 65783-9703 Office: Sch of Metaphysics HC 1 B[illegible] 15 Windyville MO 65783-9703

BLOSSMAN, ALFRED RHODY, JR., banker; b. Madisonville, La., Oct. 21, 1931; s. Alfred Rhody and Mabel (Perrin) B.; m. Royanne Elaire Hurd, Dec. 28, 1957; children: Alfred Rhody III, Roy Edward, Gary Bennett, Christopher Hurd, David Quintin, John Eric. *A.R. Blossman III, BA Southeastern U. and is partner in appraisal firm. Murphy Blossman, married to Trish, is father of A.R. IV, James Niklaus, Jon Justice. Roy Edward, BA Finance, JD, is partner in law firm Carver, Darden, Koretsky, Tessier, Finn, Blossman & Areaux, L.L.C, married to Michelle and father of Roy Edward II, Rebeckah Elaire. Gary Bennett, BA Accounting, is president of Parish National Bank, married to Donna, and father of Lauren Adele, Amber Royanne. Christopher Hurd, BA General Business, married Allison and is father of Christopher Hurd II, Clayton Hunter. David Quintin, BA Accounting, is CPA, president of Abita Brewing, Inc., and married to Caroline. John Eric, BSCEng, is Project Engineer at Cofelxip Stena Offshore, Inc.* AB in Gen. Bus., La. State U., 1955. Pres. Blossman Hydratane Gas, Inc., Covington, La., 1963-67; chmn. First Nat. Corp., First Nat. Bank, Covington, 1968-84; pres., CEO, First Nat. Bank, 1980-84, Parish Nat. Bank, Covington, 1992—; chmn. Parish Nat. Bank, Bogalusa, La., 1968-92; pres., CEO Parish Nat. Bank, Covington, 1992-96, CEO, 1997—. Mem. Phi Delta Theta. Republican. Roman Catholic. Home: 10 Blossman Ln Covington LA 70433-4707 *My formula for life is shaped by the moral and ethical guidelines of my religious faith and my own personal code of ethics. Thank God, strong self discipline has made that possible, as well as channelling my enthusiasm for whatever role I have played; being it business, or hobby; educational, military service, parent or grandparent, in a positive direction.*

BLOSSOM, BEVERLY, choreographer, dance educator; b. Chgo., Aug. 28, 1926; d. Theodore and Florence (Pfeiffer) Schmidt; m. Roberts Blossom, 1966 (div.); 1 child, Michael. BA, Roosevelt U., 1950; MA, Sarah Lawrence, 1953. Dancer Alwin Nikolais Co., N.Y.C., 1952-62; instr. Adelphi U., L.I., N.Y., 1964-66; prof. dance dept. U. Ill., Urbana, 1967-90. Choreographer Festival Theatre, Krannert Ctr., Urbana, Radio Show, 1985, Quick-Step, 1985, Heartbeat, 1985, Interlude from Veranda, 1985; choreographer: Rehearsal for a Class Act, 1983, You Are Still With Me, Fred, 1983, Ordinary Heartbreak, 1984, Egg, 1984, Weatherwatch, 1986, Potpourri, 1986, Eye of the Beholder, 1986, Russian Tea Room, 1986, Entitled, 1987, Grass Widow, 1987, Inch, 1987, Castles in Spain, 1988, Swansong, 1989, ...Exit, 1990, The Cloak, 1990, Onward, 1991, Shards, 1993, Dead Monkey, 1996, Cynicism, 1996, more. Choreography grantee Nat. Endowment for the Arts, 1986, 87, 88, 89, 90, 92, 93, 94, 95, Ill. Arts Coun. Choreography grantee, 1980, 81, 82; recipient Bessie award, 1993. Mem. Am. Guild of Musical Artists (cert.), Screen Actors Guild (cert.), Union of Profl. Employees (cert.).

BLOTNER, NORMAN DAVID, lawyer, real estate broker, corporate executive; b. Boston, Dec. 6, 1918; s. Leon and Sarah B.; m. Helen I. Whitman (dec.), Aug. 13, 1954; 1 son, James B. McClain (dec.). AB, Harvard U., 1940, JD, 1947. Bar: N.Y. 1948. Mem. firm Spiro, Felstiner, Prager & Treeger, N.Y.C., 1947-52; with Lane Bryant Inc., N.Y.C., 1953-82; sr. v.p., gen. counsel, sec., dir. Lane Bryant Inc., 1968-82, ret., 1982. Bd. dirs. Better Bus. Bur. Met. N.Y., until 1982. With USNR, 1941-46. Mem. Assn. of Bar of City of N.Y., Harvard Varsity Club, New Rochelle Tennis Club. Republican. Home: 140 Overlook Rd New Rochelle NY 10804-4139 also: 2784 S Ocean Blvd Palm Beach FL 33480-5506

BLOUCH, TIMOTHY CRAIG, food company executive; b. Lebanon, Pa., June 26, 1954; s. Charles and Elaine (Krick) B.; m. Donna Joyce Walmer, June 18, 1977. AA, Harrisburg Area Community Coll., 1974; BBA, Pa. State U., 1977, MBA, 1991. Prodn. supr. Kraft, Inc., Allentown, Pa., 1977-78; prodn. supr. Hershey (Pa.) Chocolate USA, 1978-82, mgr. inbound and fleet ops., 1982-83, mgr. inbound ops., 1983-84, mgr. transp. rates, 1984-86, mgr. traffic services, 1986-90, transp. planning mgr., 1990-93, mgr. transp. planning and rates, 1993—. Republican. Avocations: tennis, fine arts. Office: Hershey Chocolate USA 19 E Chocolate Ave Hershey PA 17033-1314

BLOUET, BRIAN WALTER, geography educator; b. Darlington, Eng., Jan. 1, 1936; came to U.S., 1966, naturalized, 1982; s. Raymond Walter and Marjorie Hannah Blouet; m. Olwyn Mary Salt, July 30, 1970; children—Andrew, Helen, Amy. B.A. with honors, U. Hull, Eng., 1960, Ph.D., 1964. Lectr. U. Sheffield, Eng., 1964-69; vis. assoc. prof. U. Nebr., Lincoln, 1966-67, assoc. prof., 1969-75, prof., 1975-83, chmn. dept. geography, 1976-81, dir. Ctr. Gt. Plains studies, 1979-83; head dept. geography Tex. A&M U., College Station, 1983-89; Huby prof. geography, Reves scholar in residence Coll. William and Mary, 1989—. Author: The Story of Malta, 1967, 72, 76, 81, 94, Halford Mackinder: A Biography, 1987; editor: (with O.M. Blouet) Latin America, 1981, 93, 97, Origins of Academic Geography in the United States, 1981. Served with Royal Air Force, 1955-57. Fellow Royal Geog. Soc., Ctr. Gt. Plains Studies; mem. Assn. Am. Geographers. Office: Coll William & Mary Govt Dept Williamsburg VA 23187-8795

BLOUGH, ROY, retired economist; b. Pitts., Aug. 21, 1901; s. Silas S. and Mary (Wertz) B.; m. Marie Goshorn, May 19, 1923; children: Richard, William, Donald. AB, Manchester Coll., 1921, LLD, 1944; AM, U. Wis., 1922, PhD, 1929; LHD, Columbia U., 1954. Asst. prof. history and econs. Manchester Coll., North Manchester, Ind., 1922-24, assoc. prof., 1924-25; assoc. prof. U. Cin., 1932-38; dir. tax rsch. U.S. Dept. Treasury, 1938-46, asst. to sec., 1944-46; prof. econs. and polit. sci. U. Chgo., 1946-52, on leave, 1950-52; mem. Coun. Econ. Advisers to Pres., 1950-52, Tax. Adv. Mission to Turkish Govt., 1949; prin. dir. Dept. Econ. Affairs UN, 1952-55; prof. internat. bus. Columbia U., N.Y.C., 1955-66; S. Sloan Colt prof. banking and Internat. fin. Columbia U., 1966-70, S. Sloan Colt prof. emeritus, 1970—; disting. vis. prof. fin. U. Fla., 1972; Nixon vis. prof. econ. policy Whittier Coll., 1973; mem. UN Tax Adv. Mission to Govt. of Peru, 1957, 59, UN Adv. Mission to Govt. of Chile, 1959; cons. Com. for Econ. Devel., 1965-73. Author: (with others) Facing the Tax Problem, 1937, Federal Taxing Process, 1952, International Business Environment and Adaptation, 1966, Economic Problems and Economic Advice, 1978, Studies in the Taxation of Foreign Source Income, 1979; editor: Nat. Tax Jour., 1947-50; contbr. articles to profl. jours. Mem. Am. Econ. Assn. (v.p. 1954), Nat. Tax Assn., Am. Fin. Assn., Coun. on Fgn. Rels., UN Assn. U.S.A., Cosmos (Washington). Home: 10450 Lottsford Rd Apt 335 Mitchellville MD 20721-2744

BLOUIN, FRANCIS XAVIER, JR., history educator; b. Belmont, Mass., July 29, 1946; s. Francis X. and Margaret (Cronin) B.; m. Joy Alexander; children: Benjamin, Tiffany. AB, U. Notre Dame, 1967; MA, U. Minn., 1969, PhD, 1978. Asst. dir. Bentley Library U. Mich., Ann Arbor, 1974-75, assoc. archivist Bentley Library, 1975-81, dir. Bentley Library, 1981—, asst. prof. history and library sci., 1979-83, assoc. prof., 1983-89, prof., 1989—. Author: The Boston Region..., 1980, Vatican Archives: An Inventory and Guide to Historical Documentation of the Holy See, 1998; editor Intellectual Life on Michigan Frontier, 1985, Archival Implications Machine..., 1980. Trustee Much. Student Found., 1986-91; dir. Am. Friends of Vatican Libr., 1981—. Fellow Soc. Am. Archivist (mem. governing council 1985-88); mem. Orgn. Am. Historians, Hist. Soc. Mich. (trustee 1982-88, pres. 1987-88), Assn. Records Mgrs. and Adminstrs., Internat. Council on Archives. Office: U Mich Bentley Hist Libr 1150 Beal Ave Ann Arbor MI 48109-2113

BLOUNT, BENROE WAYNE, physician; b. Augusta, Ga., Feb. 8, 1950; s. Benroe and Loreen Moellering B.; m. Merry Teresa Van Dam, Feb. 14, 1974 (dec. May 8, 1974); m. Young Hui Cho, Nov. 23, 1976; children: Teresa Jana, Daniel Paul. BS, U.S. Mil. Acad., 1972; MA, U. Calif., Berkeley, 1975; MD, U. Miami, 1983; MPH, U. Wash., 1990. Commd. 2d lt. U.S. Army, 1972, advanced through grades to lt. col., 1987, retired, 1994; intern, resident DeWitt Army Hosp., Alexandria, Va., 1983-86; divsn. chief, dept. vice chair Emory Sch. Medicine, Atlanta, 1994—. Contbr. articles to profl. jours., chpts. to books. Independent. Avocation: church. Office: Divsn Family Medicine Ste 818A 490 Peachtree St NW Atlanta GA 30308

BLOUNT, CHARLES WILLIAM, III, lawyer; b. Independence, Mo., Nov. 14, 1946; s. Charles William and Mary Marguarette (Van Trump) B.; m. Susan Penny Smith Turner, Dec. 20, 1969 (div. Nov., 1987); children: Charles William IV, Chaille Elizabeth; m. Bonnie M. Harp., Jan. 1, 1991. BS in Journalism, U. Kans., 1968; JD cum laude, U. Toledo, 1981. Bar: Mo. 1981, U.S. Dist. Ct. (we. dist.) Mo. 1981, Tex. 1985, U.S. Dist. Ct. (no. dist.) Tex. 1988, U.S. Ct. Appeals (5th cir.) 1995, U.S. Supreme Ct. 1997; cert. in civil appellate law Tex. Bd. Legal Specialization. Litigation assoc. Shugart, Thomson & Kilroy, Kansas City, Mo., 1981-84, Hughes & Luce, Dallas, 1984-87; litigation assoc. Simpson & Dowd L.L.P., Dallas, 1987-91, ptnr., 1991-94; mem. Dowd & Blount, Dallas, 1994-99; ptnr. Perry-Miller & Blount, L.L.P., Dallas, 1999—. Bd. govs. U. Toledo Coll. Law, 1980-81; trustee Episcopal Diocese We. Mo., Kansas City, 1983-84; mem., chmn. com. Boy Scouts of Am., Kansas City, 1983-84, Richardson, Tex., 1984-92. 1st lt. U.S. Army, 1968-72. Mem. Phi Kappa Phi, Phi Kappa Tau (pledge pres., social chmn., activities chmn., 1965—). Avocations: music, reading. Office: Perry-Miller & Blount LLP Ste 675 LB 45 3300 Oaklawn Ave Dallas TX 75219

BLOUNT, JAMES ROBERT, military career officer; b. Columbus, Ohio, Dec. 13, 1958; s. Robert and Beatrice Louise Blount; m. Kelle Ann Bush, Jan. 2, 1978; children: Daniel O., Natalie M. AA in Criminal Justice, Rollins Coll., 1980; BA in Bus. Adminstrn. and Acctg., Nat. U., 1984; student, USN-Office Candidate Sch., 1984-85, USN-Surface Warfare Sch., 1985, 92; ministerial cert. studies, Berean Coll., 1988; MA in Nat. Security Affairs, Naval Postgrad. Sch., 1991. Commd. 1st lt. USN, 1984, advanced through grades to lt. comdr.; mine countermeasures officer USS Leader USN, Charleston, S.C., 1985-87; exec. asst., navigator, legal officer USS Pensacola USN, Little Creek, Va., 1987-89; combat cargo officer, weapons officer USS Racine USN, Long Beach, Calif., 1992-93; 1st lt. USS Durham USN, San Diego, 1993; ops. officer, comdr. mine countermeasure squadron one USN, Ingleside, Tex., 1994-95; instr., co. officer, tng. officer, facilities mgr. U.S. Naval Acad., Annapolis, Md., 1995-98; comdg. officer Mil. Entrance Processing Sta. U.S. Naval Acad., Oklahoma City, 1999—. Youth leader various chs., Seaside, Calif., Rockport, Tex., Annapolis; martial arts instr. various recreation ctrs., Charleston, Monterey, Calif., Long Beach. Cpl. USMC, 1977-78, sgt. USMC, 1981-84; with USN, 1979-81. Mem. Fed. Exec. Bd. Avocations: martial arts, weight lifting, running, scuba diving. Home: 1340 SW 108th Pl Oklahoma City OK 73170

BLOUNT, KERRY ANDREW, defense analyst; b. Lubbock, Tex., Sept. 1, 1949; s. Andrew William Blount and Evelyn Ruth (Caldwell) Anderson; m. Barbara Jean Massey, May 21, 1971; children: Tanis Andra, Zeitel Elizabeth. BA in Internat. Studies, West Tex. State U., 1971; MA in Russian Area Studies, Georgetown U., 1973; grad. in Soviet studies, U.S. Army Russian Inst., Garmisch, Germany, 1984. Commd. 2d lt. U.S. Army, 1971, advanced through grades to maj., 1982; comdr. Counterintelligence Spl. Ops., Frankfurt, Germany, 1975-77; intelligence analyst Intelligence Ctr. Pacific, Honolulu, 1978-81; diplomatic courier U.S. Dept. State, Helsinki, Finland, 1983; intelligence instr. Brit. Intelligence Ctr., Ashford, Eng., 1984-86; sr. intelligence analyst Army Intelligence and Threat Analysis Ctr., Washington, 1986-89; resigned U.S. Army, 1989; sr. def. analyst Sci. Applications Internat. Corp., Denver, 1989-94, mgr. C2 warfare program, 1994-97; sr. def. analyst SRS Techs., Las Vegas, Nev., 1997—. Contbr. articles to profl. jours. Mem. bd. elders S.E. Ch. of Christ, Aurora, Colo., 1995-97. Mem. Armed Forces Comm. and Electronics Assn., Assn. of U.S. Army. Avocations: choral music, drama productions.

BLOUNT, MICHAEL EUGENE, lawyer; b. Camden, N.J., July 9, 1949; s. Floyd Eugene and Dorothy Alice (Geyer) Durham; m. Janice Lynn Brown, Aug. 22, 1969; children: Kirsten Marie, Gretchen Elizabeth. BA, U. Tex., 1971; JD, U. Houston, 1974. Bar: Tex. 1974, Ill. 1980, D.C. 1981, U.S. Ct. Appeals (D.C. cir.) 1978, U.S. Ct. Mil. Appeals 1975, U.S. Supreme Ct. 1977. Atty. advisor Office of Gen. Counsel SEC, Washington, 1977-78, legal asst. to chmn., 1978-79; assoc. Gardner, Carton & Douglas, Chgo., 1980-84; ptnr. Arnstein, Gluck, Lehr, Barron & Milligan, Chgo., 1984-86, Seyfarth, Shaw, Fairweather & Geraldson, Chgo., 1987—; trustee Assn. Securities Exchange Commn. Alumni. Served as lt. JAGC, USN, 1974-77. Mem. ABA (fed. regulation of securities com.), Chgo. Bar Assn., Order of Barons, Phi Alpha Delta (chpt. treas. 1973.), Univ. Club (Chgo.). Home: 1711 Galloway Dr Barrington IL 60010-5737 Office: Seyfarth Shaw Fairweather & Geraldson 55 E Monroe St Ste 4200 Chicago IL 60603-5863

BLOUNT, ROBERT HADDOCK, corporate executive, retired naval officer; b. Miami, Fla., Dec. 8, 1922; s. Uriel and Aleve Sadie (Haddock) B.; m. Jeannette Mae Barclay, May 13, 1951 (dec. 1998); children: Barbara Mae, Jennifer. B.E.E., MIT, 1947; M.S. in Systems Engring, George Washington U., 1970; student, Naval War Coll., 1958-59. Commd. ensign USNR, 1946; transferred to U.S. Navy, 1947, advanced through grades to rear adm., 1973; comdr. submarines, service in MTO, PTO, Scotland, Panama; chief staff, aide to comdr. Submarine Flotilla 6, 1970-72; comdr. Naval Sta., Naval Base Charleston, S.C., 1972-73; comdr. U.S. Naval Forces, So. Command; also comdt. 15th Naval Dist. Ft. Amador, C.Z., 1973-75; dir. undersea and strategic warfare div. Office Chief Naval Ops. Washington, 1975-77; dep. dir. research, devel., test and evaluation OPNAV, 1977-78, comdr. Operational Test and Evaluation Force, 1978-82, ret., 1982, pvt. industry cons., 1986-90; ret. Va. Ops. div. EDO Corp., 1990. Pres. C.Z. council Boy Scouts Am., 1974. Decorated D.S.M., Meritorious Service medal with star, Navy Expeditionary medal; recipient Scroll of Honor Navy League, 1974. Mem. Naval Submarine League, U.S. Naval Inst., Norfolk Yacht and Country Club, Rotary. Address: 1516 Blanford Cir Norfolk VA 23505-1706

BLOUNT, STANLEY FREEMAN, marketing educator; b. Detroit, June 12, 1929; s. Harry Alfred and Thelma (Freeman) B.; m. Constance Parker, Aug. 30, 1957; children—Jeffrey Parker, Lori Maria. B.A., Wayne State U., 1952, M.A., 1959; Ph.D., Northwestern U., 1962. Account exec. Jam Handy Corp., Detroit, 1952-54; marketing mgr. Chrysler Corp., Detroit, 1954-58; instr. Northwestern U., 1961-62; asst. prof. U. Ill., 1962-63; assoc. prof. Kent State U., 1963-67; prof., dept. chmn. State U. N.Y. at Albany, 1967—, chmn. ednl. policies council, 1970—; disting. vis. prof. U. of Americas, Mexico, 1966; dir. Femtec Inc.; exec. dir. U. Albany Found. Chmn. subcom. legis. affairs N.Y. State affiliate Am. Heart Assn., 1974—. Served with AUS, 1946-48. Named Outstanding Faculty Mem. Kent State U., 1964. Mem. Sigma Xi, Gamma Theta Upsilon. Clubs: Essayons, Audubon, Phalanx. Research on environment analysis and preception, digitized land use mapping, land use and resource mgmt. Home: 11 Pheasant Ln Delmar NY 12054-4109 Office: SUNY at Albany Sch Business Albany NY 12222

BLOUNT, WINTON MALCOLM, JR., manufacturing company executive; b. Union Springs, Ala., Feb. 1, 1921; s. Winton Malcolm and Clara B. (Chalker) B.; m. Carolyn Self Blount, Dec. 22, 1981; children: Winton Malcolm III, Thomas A., S. Roberts, Katherine Blount Miles, Joseph W. Student, U. Ala., 1939-41; LHD (hon.), Judson Coll., 1967, Amherst Coll., 1990; HHD (hon.), Huntingdon Coll., 1969; LLD, Birmingham-So. Coll., 1969; DCL, U. Ala., 1969, DSci., 1971; D. in Pub. Svc., Seattle-Pacific Coll., 1971; PhD (hon.), Rhodes Coll., Samford U., Washington and Jefferson Coll., Troy State U.; DCS (hon.), St. John's U., 1983. Pres., chmn. bd. Blount Bros. Corp., Montgomery, Ala., 1946-68; postmaster gen. U.S. Washington, 1969-71; chmn. exec. com. Blount, Inc., Montgomery, Ala., from 1973, chmn. bd., CEO, 1974-90, 91-93, chmn. bd., 1990-91, 93—; mem. Pres.'s Cabinet, Washington, 1969-71. Chmn. Ala. Citizens for Eisenhower, 1952; Southeastern dir. Nixon-Lodge, 1959-60; bd. dirs. United Appeals Montgomery; bd. dirs. Montgomery YMCA, also life mem.; former trustee So. Rsch. Inst.; trustee Rhodes Coll., former chmn. bd.; trustee emeritus U. Ala.; bd. visitors Air U., Maxwell AFB, Ala., 1971-73; mem. adv. coun. U.S. Army Aviation Mus., Ft. Rucker, Ala.; trustee So. Ctr. Internat. Studies. With USAAF, 1942-45. Named One of 4 Outstanding Young Men Ala., 1956, Man of Yr., Montgomery, 1961, Citizen of Yr., Montgomery Advertiser, 1987; recipient citation for disting. svc. City of Montgomery, 1966, Ct. Honor award Montgomery Exch. Club, 1968, Nat. Brotherhood award NCCJ, 1970, Silver Quill award Am. Bus. Press, 1971, Charles Frankel prize NEH, 1991, Disting. Svc. to Arts award Nat. Govs. Assn., 1992, Disting. Svc. award Rhodes Coll., 1993. Mem. Am. Mgmt. Assns. (trustee), Bus. Coun., Conf. Bd., NAM (Golden Knight Mgmt. award Ala. coun. 1962), Am. Enterprise Inst., U.S. C. of C. (nat. pres. 1968), Ala. C. of C. (pres. 1962-65), Newcomen Soc. N.Am., Rotary. Home: 5801 Vaughn Rd Montgomery AL 36116-1106 Office: Blount Internat Inc Box 949 4520 Executive Park Dr Montgomery AL 36116-1621*

BLOUNT, WINTON MALCOLM, III, investment executive; b. Albany, Ga., Dec. 14, 1943; s. Winton Malcolm Jr. and Mary Katherine (Archibald) B.; m. Lucy Durr Dunn, June 6, 1970; children: Winton Malcolm IV, K. Stuart, William, Judkins. Student, U. Ala., 1962-63; B.A., U. South, 1966; M.B.A., U. Pa., 1968. With Blount Bros. Corp., Montgomery, Ala., 1968-73, project mgr., 1972-73; with Mercury Constrn. Corp., Montgomery, 1973-77; pres. Mercury Constrn. Corp., 1975-77; chief exec. officer, chmn. bd. Benjamin F. Shaw Co., Wilmington, Del., 1977-80; pres., chief operating officer Blount Internat., Ltd., Montgomery, 1980-83, pres., chief exec. officer, 1983-85; chmn., chief exec. officer Blount Internat., Ltd., 1985-87; sr. v.p. Blount Inc., 1985-87; vice chmn., 1987-89; chmn., chief exec. officer Winton Blount III & Assocs., 1989—; chmn., chief exec. officer Wright Plastics Co., 1989—, Cobb Pontiac-Cadillac & Royal Motor Co., 1990—, Blount-Strange Ford, Lincoln, Mercury, 1991—; bd. dirs. Dunn Constrn. Co., Birmingham, Ala. Mem. fin. com. Ala. Rep. Com., 1980-82; chmn., 1999—; bd. dirs. So. Rsch. Inst., 1995—, Montgomery YMCA, Episcopal High Sch., 1988-89, 95—, Ala. Pub. Affairs Rsch. Coun., 1979-83, Bus. Coun. Ala.; active Tukabatchee Area coun. Boy Scouts Am., 1980-83; bd. visitors U. Ala. Coll. Commerce and Bus. Adminstrn., 1983-88; mem. bd. control Com. of 100; mem. bd. Leadership Ala., 1989-93, 95—, chmn. bd., 1997-98, Ala. Coun. Econ. Edn. Mem. Chief Execs. Orgn., World Pres.'s Orgn.), Montgomery C.

of C. (dir. 1981-88), Del. C. of C. (dir. 1979-80), NAM (dir. 1982-85). Episcopalian. Office: PO Box 230039 Montgomery AL 36123-0039

BLOUSTEIN, PETER EDWARD, entertainment management consultant, producer; b. N.Y.C., June 19, 1937; s. Francis Jerome and Jean (Pinsky) B.; m. Ariadne Natalie Jeon, June 17, 1962; children: Arlyn Sofia, Rachel Jean. AA, Boston U., 1957. Stage mgr. Radio City Music Hall, N.Y.C., 1959-63; advance dir. Time-Life Inc., N.Y.C., 1963; stage mgr. N.Y. Worlds Fair, N.Y.C., 1964; script analyst and dir. various studios L.A., 1964-69; mgr. Walt Disney, L.A. and Orlando, 1969-78; dir. entertainment Walt Disney World, Orlando, 1978-84; producer PremierCruise Lines/NCL, Miami/Cape Canaveral, Fla., 1984-88; producer various dinner theatres Orlando, 1984—; producer Entertainment Lotte World, Seoul, Korea, 1989—; cons. in entertainment PEB Assocs., Inc., Windermere, Fla., 1988—; producer AmeriFlora '92, 1990—; entertainment cons. to Opryland, 1990—; owner World Famous Rocket Belt; dir. reopening Navy Pier, Chgo., 1995; producer Fable Fantasy Parade Samsung Corp., Korea, 1996, 97, 98; cons. Walt Disney Entertainment; pres. Am. Gladiators Orlando Live!, 1996; pres. Gladco Corp., 1996. Producer opening celebration Jr. Olympics, Tampa, 1990; dir. opening Alamo Dome, 1993, Olympic Festival, 1993; producer, dir. Parade at World Expo, Taejon, Korea, 1993; hosp. visitor Congregation of Liberal Judaism, Winter, Park, Fla., 1988, bd. dirs., 1974-76; pres. Theme Park Mgmt. Inst., 1991—. With U.S. Army, 1960-66. Jewish. Avocations: reading, travel, sports.

BLOUT, ELKAN ROGERS, biological chemistry educator, university dean; b. N.Y.C., July 2, 1919; s. Eugene and Lillian B.; m. Joan E. Dreyfus, Aug. 27, 1939; children: James E., Susan L., William L.; m. Gail A. Ferris, Mar. 29, 1985; 1 child, Darya L.M. A.B., Princeton U., 1939; Ph.D., Columbia U., 1942; A.M. (hon.), Harvard U., 1962; D.Sc. (hon.), Loyola U., 1976. With Polaroid Corp., Cambridge, Mass., 1943-62, successively rsch. chemist, assoc. dir. rsch., 1948-58, v.p., gen. mgr. rsch., 1958-62; rsch. assoc. Harvard U., 1950-52, 56-60, lectr. on biophysics, 1960-62, prof. biol. chemistry, 1962-90, Edward S. Harkness prof. biol. chemistry, 1964-90, Edward S. Harkness prof. emeritus, 1990—, head dept. biol. chemistry, 1965-69; dean for acad. affairs Harvard Sch. Pub. Health, 1978-89, chmn. dep. environ. sci. and physiology, 1986-88, dir. div. biol. scis., prof., 1987-91; prof. emeritus Harvard Sch. of Pub. Health, 1991—; rsch. assoc. Children's Hosp. Med. Ctr., Boston, 1950-52, cons. chemistry, 1952—; mem. conseil de surveillance Compagnie Financière du Scribe, 1975-81; trustee Bay Biochem. Rsch., Inc., 1973-83; mem. exec. com. divsn. chemistry and chem. tech. NRC, 1972-74, mem. assembly of math. and phys. scis., 1979-82; mem. sci. adv. com. Ctr. for Blood Rsch., Inc., 1972-92, emeritus trustee, 1992—, also mem. bd. dirs.; mem. rsch. adv. com. Children's Hosp. Med. Ctr., 1976-80, 84-90, chmn., 1987-90; mem. sci. adv. com. Mass. Gen. Hosp., 1968-71, Rsch. Inst., Hosp. for Sick Children, Toronto, Ont., Can., 1976-79; mem. adv. coun. dept. biochem. scis. Princeton U., 1974-83, chmn. adv. coun. program in biology, 1983-95; mem. vis. com. dept. chemistry Carnegie-Mellon U., 1968-72; bd. visitors Faculty Health Scis., SUNY, Buffalo, 1968-70; overseer Boston Mus. Sci.; trustee Boston Biomed. Rsch. Inst., 1990—, v.p., 1990-94; bd. govs. Weizmann Inst. Sci., Rehovot, Israel, 1978—; bd. dirs. Nat. Health Rsch. Found., ESA, Inc.; bd. dirs., sec.-treas. Nat. Acads. Corp.; gen. ptnr. Gosnold Investment Fund Ltd. Partnership, 1985-95; bd. dirs., investment mgr. Auburn Investment Mgmt. Corp., 1985—; sci. advisor Affymax Rsch. Inst., 1988-95; sr. adviser sci. FDA, 1991—; mem. sr. adv. bd. The Ency. of Molecular Biol., 1991; mem. coun. visitors Marine Biol. Lab., 1992—; pres., trustee Inst. for Internat. Vaccine Devel., 1997—. Mem. adv. bd. Jour. Polymer Sci, 1956-62; mem. editl. bd. Biopolymers, 1963-85, hon. founding editor, 1985—; mem. editorial bd. Am. Chem. Soc. Monograph Series, 1965-72, Internat. Jour. Peptide and Protein Rsch., 1978-89; mem. editl. adv. bd. Macromolecules, 1967-70, Jour. Am. Chem. Soc., 1978-82; contbr. articles to profl. jours. Recipient Princeton Class of 1939 Achievement award, 1970, Nat. Med. Sci. award , 1990, John Phillips award Phillips Exeter Acad., 1998; NRC fellow Harvard U., 1942-43. Fellow AAAS (fin. com. 1977-84, com. on investments 1984—, chmn. budget com. 1988-92, treas. 1992-98), N.Y. Acad. Arts and Scis., Optical Soc. Am. (past pres. New Eng. sect.); mem. NAS (treas. 1980-92, treas. emeritus 1992—, fin. com. 1976—, adv. com. USSR and Eastern Europe 1979-84, mem. com. sci. engring. and pub. policy 1992-95, audit com. 1994—), Inst. Medicine, Russian Acad. Scis. (fgn.), Am. Chem. Soc. (nat. councillor 1958-61, Ralph F. Hirschmann award 1991), The Chem. Soc., Am. Soc. Biol. Chemists (fin. com. 1973-82), Biophys. Soc., Commn. on Phys. Scis., Math., and Resources of NRC, Internat. Orgn. Chem. Scis. in Devel. (coun. 1981—, chmn. fin. com. 1982—, v.p., treas. 1985—, bd. dirs. 1985—), Fedn. Am. Socs. Exptl. Biology (investments adv. com. 1981-85). Achievements include patents in field. Home: 1010 Memorial Dr Apt 12A Cambridge MA 02138-4856 Office: Harvard U Med Sch Dept Biol Chemistry Molecular Pharmacology Boston MA 02115

BLOW, GEORGE, lawyer; b. Chgo., Oct. 4, 1928; s. George Waller and Katharine Rowland (Cooke) B.; m. Sarah Wendel Kuhn, Nov. 4, 1957; children: Mary Allmand Blow Prevost, George Rowland, Wendel Matthiessen. AB cum laude, Harvard U., 1950; JD, U. Va., 1953. Bar: Va. 1953, D.C. 1954, U.S. Ct. Appeals (D.C. cir.) 1954, U.S. Dist. Ct. D.C. 1954, U.S. Ct. Mil. Appeals, 1955, U.S. Supreme Ct. 1956, U.S. Ct. Appeals (4th cir.) 1961, U.S. Ct. Appeals (fed. cir.) 1982. Assoc. Covington & Burling, Washington, 1953-63; ptnr. Patton, Boggs & Blow, Washington, 1963-93; mem. adv. coun. Internat. Human Rights Law Group, Washington, 1988-98. Mem. Com. of 100 on Fed. City, Washington, 1984—, trustee, 1985-87; bd. dirs. Washington Inst. Fgn. Affairs, 1976-98, Sheridan-Kalorama Hist. Assn., Washington, 1987-89. Mem. D.C. Bar, Va. State Bar, Soc. of Cincinnati in State of Va., Soc. Colonial Wars, Met. Club Washington, Order of Coif, Phi Delta Phi.

BLOW, STEVE, newspaper columnist. Metro columnist Dallas Morning News, 1978—. Office: The Dallas Morning News 508 Young St PO Box 655237 Dallas TX 75265-5237*

BLOWER, JOHN GREGORY, special education educator; b. Orange, Calif., Mar. 18, 1952; s. James Girard and Juanita Mae (Pierce) B.; 1 child, Becky Renee. BS in Psychology, Pacific Christian, 1975; MEd in Spl. Edn., Idaho State U., 1982. Assoc. minister edn. 1st Christian Ch., Santa Ana, Calif., 1972-75; spl. edn. tchr. Fremont County Schs., St. Anthony, Idaho, 1977—; vice chmn., con. People for Spl. People, St. Anthony, 1986—. Program coord. Idaho Spl. Olympics, St. Anthony, 1978—, bd. dirs., Boise, 1982-88, chmn. bd. dirs., Boise, 1987-88. Mem. Coun. for Exceptional Children, Nat. Edn. Assn. Office: South Fremont High Sch 855 S Bridge St Saint Anthony ID 83445-2034

BLOYD, BEVERLY, nurse; b. McCook, Nebr., Jan. 16, 1952; d. Ernest and Doris (Shaw) Fimple; m. Monte R. Bloyd, Apr. 7, 1973; children: Sarah, Douglas, Rebecca. Diploma, Mary Lanning Sch. Nursing, 1973; BS in Nursing, Kearney State Coll. Nursing, 1990; MA in Mgmt., Bellevue U., 1998. Dir. subacute nursing Mary Lanning Meml. Hosp., Hastings, Nebr. Mem. ANA (cert. in med.-surg. nursing), Orthopaedic Nurse's Assn., Nat. Orthopaedic Nurses Assn. (cert.), Assn. Rehab. Nurses. Home: 1203 E 9th St Hastings NE 68901-4144

BLOYD, STEPHEN ROY, environmental manager, educator, consultant; b. Alameda, Calif., Aug. 17, 1953; s. William Allen and Alice Louella (Scott) B. Grad. high sch., Reedley, Calif., 1971. Cert. environ. mgr., Nev.; registered hazardous substances specialist. Reagent tech. Tenneco Corp., Gold Hill, Nev., 1982; environ. tech. Pierson Environ. Drilling, Modesto, Calif., 1982-84; pres. Bloyd and Assocs., Dayton, Nev., 1986—. Author: Hazardous Waste Site Operations for General Site Workers, 1992; editor: (newsletter) Pumper, 1991. Firefighter Dayton Vol. Fire Dept., 1975, capt., 1976-78, chief, 1978-83, tng. officer, 1984-96; mem. Silver City (Nev.) Fire Dept., 1996—; coord. Ctrl. Lyon County Hazardous Materials, 1997—; asst. prof. Dodd/Beals Fire Protection Tng. Acad. U. Nev., Reno, 1990-96; instr. chemistry hazardous materials Nat. Fire Acad., Emmitsburg, Md., 1989—, instr. hazardous materials incident mgmt., 1996—; mem. bylaw com. Dayton Regional Adv. Coun., 1989. Named Firefighter of Yr., City of Dayton, 1992. Mem. NRA, Nat. Environ. Tng. Assn., Nat. Environ. Health Assn., Nev. State Firemen's Assn. (1st v.p. 1992-93, 2d v.p. 1991-92, pres. 1993-94, chmn. hazardous materials com. 1987-93, legis. com. 1991, bylaws com. 1986), Nev. Fire Chief's Assn., Internat. Platform Assn., Soc. Nat. Fire Acad. Instrs. Libertarian. Avocations: fishing, motorcycles, firearms, camping, reading. Office: PO Box 113 Silver City NV 89428-0113

BLUCHER, PAUL ARTHUR, lawyer; b. Youngstown, Ohio, Aug. 1, 1958; s. Arthur E. and Lillian L. (McQuillan) B.; m. Brenda Lee Kilgore, Aug. 25, 1990. AS with honors, Youngstown State U., 1984, BS magna cum laude, 1986; JD, U. Pitts., 1990. Bar: Fla. 1990, U.S. Dist. Ct. (mid. dist.) Fla. 1997, U.S. Ct. Appeals (11th cir.) 1998. Police officer Mahoning County Sheriff, Youngstown, 1979-85, police detective, 1985-87; assoc. Brigham, Moore, et al., Sarasota, Fla., 1990-96; ptnr. Brigham, Moore, et al., Sarasota, 1996-97; sole practice law Sarasota, 1997—. Mem. allocations & admissions com. United Way, Sarasota, 1996— (Pathfinder Club Recognition award 1996); mem. Amyotrophic Lateral Sclerosis Assn. 1995—. Mem. ABA (state and local gov. com. 1990-99, real property sect. condemnation com. 1999—), Fla. Bar Assn. (stress mgmt. com. 1997—, young lawyers 1990-95, eminent domain com. 1990—), Fla. Restaurant Assn. Democrat. Roman Catholic. Avocations: scuba diving, boating, flying. E-mail: pblucher@fifthamendment.com. Office: 1800 2nd St Ste 803 Sarasota FL 34236-5986

BLUDER, LISA, women's collegiate basketball coach; b. Appleton, Wis., Apr. 16, 1961; m. David; 1 child, Hannah Marie. Grad., No. Iowa U., 1983. Head coach women's basketball St. Ambrose U., 1983-90, Drake U., Des Moines, 1990—. Vol. Iowa Habitat for Humanity. Named Converse coach of yr. NAIA, 1990; named coach of yr. Mo. Valley Conf., 1995. Mem. Women's Basketball Coaches Assn. (Kodak All-Am. selection com., midwest regional adv. com. NCAA divsn. 1 women's tournament, dist. V coach of yr. 1995). Office: Drake Ctr 1421 27th St Des Moines IA 50311*

BLUE, JAMES GUTHRIE, retired veterinarian; b. Flora, Ind., Oct. 22, 1920; s. Van C. and Florence A. (Guthrie) B. AB, Wabash Coll., 1943; postgrad., Northwestern U., 1943; DVM, Ohio State U., 1950; AA in Labor Negotiation/Rels., L.A. Trade Tech. Coll., 1989. Pvt. practice cons., 1950-80; field vet. City of L.A., 1980—, acting chief vets., 1992, chief vets., 1992-95; rsch. project cons. Calif. State U. Northridge, 1980-87; pro med. svcs. sec.-negtiator AFSCME, L.A., 1983-96; sec. Ariz. Bd. Vet. Med. Examiners, 1973-79. Mem. wellness com. Drug Free Work Place, 1989-99. Lt. comdr. USN, 1943-46, USNR, 1946-65. Mem. AMVA, N.Y. Acad. Scis., Am. Soc. Lab. Animal Practitioners, L.A. World Affairs Coun., San Diego Vet. Med. Assn., So. Ariz. Vet. Med. Assn., Calif. Vet. Med. Assn. (environ. and pub. health ecology com. 1986-99, state ethics com. 1986-98, wellness com. 1988-99), So. Calif. Vet. Med. Assn. (coun. mem., polit. action com., continuing edn. com. 1980-99), Am. Legion, Navy League, Shriners, Mil. Order World War, U.S. Naval Rsch. Assn., Navy League Coun. Tucson, Rep. Club Tucson (treas. 1996-99), Res. Officers Assn. Republican. Home: 2121 E 2nd St Tucson AZ 85719-4928

BLUE, J(OHN) RONALD, evangelical mission executive; b. Milw., Sept. 4, 1935; s. Earl R. and Wretha J. (Teater) B.; m. Elizabeth F. Wood, Sept. 7, 1962; children: Elisa, Laurie, David. BA, U. Nebr., 1957; cert. contact lens fitter, Ohio State U., 1960; ThM, Dallas Theol. Sem., 1965; PhD, U. Tex., Arlington, 1983. Contact lens fitter Ohio State U., Columbus, 1960-61; field dir. C.Am. Mission, Guatemala, Salvador, Guatemala, Salvador and Spain, 1965-75; dept. chmn. Dallas Theol. Sem., 1975-92; pres. CAM Internat., Dallas, 1992—; bd. dirs. Outreach, Inc., Grand Rapids, Mich.; mem. adv. bd. Proclamation, Inc., Dallas, 1992—, v.p. bd. Interdenominational Foreign Missions Assn., 1998—, edit. bd. Evangelical Missions Quaterly. Contbg. author: Walvoord: A Tribute, 1982, Bible Knowledge Commentary, 1983, 85, Essays in Honor of J.D. Pentecost, 1986, Devotions for Kindred Spirits, 1995, Basic Theology Applied, 1996. Lt. USN, 1957-59. Mem. Pi Epsilon Pi, Theta Xi. Republican. Avocation: travel. Home: 3504 Halifax Dr Arlington TX 76013-1909 Office: CAM Internat 8625 La Prada Dr Dallas TX 75228-5034

BLUE, JOSEPH EDWARD, physicist; b. Quitman, Miss., Sept. 29, 1936; s. Edward Lee and Allie Belle (Corley) B.; m. Neva Rosetta Deal, Apr. 14, 1962; children: Tracy Marie, Gina Lynn. BS in Physics, Miss. State U., 1961; MS in Engring. Sci., Fla. State U., 1966; PhD in Mech. Engring., U. Tex., 1971. Physicist Navy Mine Def. Lab., Panama City, Fla., 1961-68; rsch. sci. engr. U. Tex., Austin, 1968-71; rsch. physicist Naval Rsch. Lab., Orlando, Fla., 1971-73, Meas br. head, 1973-81, supt., 1981-95; dir. Naval Undersea Warfare Ctr. Divsn. Newport Underwater Sound Ref. Detachment, Orlando, Fla., 1995-96; v.p. Leviathan Legacy Inc., Orlando, Fla., 1996—. Author: (with others) Benchmark Papers in U/W Acoust, 1975; contbr. articles to Jour. Acoustical Soc. Am. Fellow Acoustical Soc. Am. Democrat. Methodist. Achievements include patents for low frequency acoustic source, color sonar display, time internal to pulse height converter, device for alerting manatees to danger from boats; research in resonant scattering, parametric depth sounder using water's nonlinearity, substantial sound pressure from tow-powered sources, and manatee hearing. Office: Leviathan Legacy Inc 3313 Northglen Dr Orlando FL 32806-6338

BLUE, MONTE LYNN, college president; b. Ft. Worth, Feb. 25, 1945; s. Bert Leonard and Mary Lee (Cooper) B.; m. Sheryl Doris O'Connor, July 1, 1966; children: Michelle Denea, Laura Lynn. BA, North Tex. State U., 1967, MA, 1972; EdD, U. Houston, 1979. Illustrator Gen. Dynamics, Ft. Worth, 1967-71; instr. advt. art, Cen. Campus San Jacinto Jr. Coll., Pasadena, Tex., 1971-74, dist. dir., instr. media, 1975-79, dean student services, South Campus, 1979-81, dean student services, Cen. Campus, 1981-83, pres., 1983—; bd. dirs. Deer Park Edni. Found.; bd. dirs. Southeast Econ. Devel. Coun., 1995—, chmn. bd., 1997-98; moderator Bd. of Southmore Med. Ctr.; speaker numerous presentations to various community, civic and profl. groups. Contbr. articles to profl. jours.; speaker numerous presentations to various community, civic and profl. groups. Vice chmn. bd. dirs. San Jacinto YMCA, Pasadena, 1986-87, chmn., 1987-88. Named Outstanding Alumni, Ft. Worth Ind. Sch. Dist., 1984. Mem. Am. Assn. Community Jr. Colls., Am. Assn. Higher Edn., Nat. Orgn. on Legal Problems in Edn., Assn. Tex. Colls. and Univs., Tex. Pub. Community Jr. Coll. Assn., LaPorte/Bayshore C. of C. (bd. dirs. 1987-89, pres. 1989), Nat. Soc. Painters in Casein and Acrylic, Rotary (local pres. 1986-87), Phi Theta Kappa (hon. mem. Mu Omicron chpt., Hall of Honor 1985). Democrat. Baptist. Lodge: Rotary (local pres. 1986-87). Avocation: painting. Office: San Jacinto Coll Cen 8060 Spencer Hwy Pasadena TX 77505-5903

BLUE, ROBERT LEE, secondary education educator; b. Columbiaville, Mich., Apr. 23, 1920; s. Arthur Floyd and Elma (Ellis) B.; BA, Mich. State U., 1941; MA, U. Mich., 1952; m. Dorothy L. Seward, July 15, 1961. Tchr., Chesaning (Mich.) H.S., 1941-42, 45-57; prin. Ricker Jr. H.S., Saginaw, Mich., 1957-59, Buena Vista H.S., Saginaw, 1960-69; asst. prof. secondary edn. Central Mich. U., Mt. Pleasant, 1969—. Bd. dirs. Hartley Edn. Nature Camp, 1957-69; pres. Saginaw County Assn. Ret. Sch. Pers., Mich. Assn. Ret. Sch. Pers. (chmn. awards com., Disting. Svc. award 1995). With U.S. Army, 1942-45. Decorated Bronze Star. Mem. NEA (life), Mich. Edn. Assn., Assn. Tchr. Educators, Mich. Assn. Tchr. Educators, Nat. Assn. Secondary Sch. Prins., Mich. Assn. Secondary Sch. Prins., Mich. PTA (hon. life), Am. Legion, Mich. Hist. Soc., Saginaw County Hist. Soc., Lapeer County Hist. Soc., Optomist, Pit and Balcony, Masons, Phi Delta Kappa. Republican. Methodist. Author: Footsteps Into The Past, A History of Columbiaville, 1979, also articles. Home: 1437 Lathrup Ave Saginaw MI 48603-4787 Office: 3037 Davenport Ave Saginaw MI 48602-3652

BLUEFARB, SAMUEL MITCHELL, physician; b. St. Louis, Oct. 15, 1912; s. Sol and Pauline (Brown) B.; m. Grace Parsons, Jan. 1, 1944; 1 son, Richard Alan; m. Leah Rose Vendig Pollock, Jan. 24, 1968; children—Fred, Nancy Pollock. B.S., U. Ill., 1936; M.D., 1937. Diplomate Am. Bd. Dermatology and Syphilology. Intern Cook County Hosp., Chgo., 1937-38; resident Bellevue Hosp., N.Y.C., 1939-41; practice medicine specializing in dermatology, 1941-78; sr. attending dermatologist, chmn. dept. Cook County Hosp., 1952-58; attending dermatologist VA Lakeside Hosp., 1954-78; sr. attending staff Chgo. Wesley Meml. Hosp., Passavant Hosp.; prof., chmn. dept. dermatology Northwestern U. Med. Sch., 1962-78; prof. dermatology U. South Fla., 1985-88; chmn. dept. dermatology Bay Pines VA Hosp., Fla., 1984-87. Author books and articles. Fellow Am. Acad. Dermatology and Syphilology (dir. 1969), ACP; mem. AMA, Ill. Med. Soc. (past pres. dermatol. sect.), Chgo. Med. Soc., Soc. Investigative Dermatology, Chgo. Dermatol. soc. (past pres.), Am. Dermatol. Assn., Noah Worcester Dermatology Soc. Home: 1250 Park Ave W Highland Park IL 60035-2265

BLUESTEIN, BARBARA ANN, librarian; b. Pitts., Feb. 3, 1952; d. Griffith and Mary Jane (Thompson) Ray; m. Michael Richard Bluestein, Aug. 26, 1973; children: Matthew Alan, Jeremy Micah. BS in Edn., Miami U., Oxford, Ohio, 1974; MEd, Xavier U., 1977. Permanent tchg. cert. ednl. media grades 7-12, Ohio. Libr. Princeton H.S., Cin., 1974-89, head libr., 1989—. Den leader pack 72 Boy Scouts Am., Cin., 1990-95, merit badge counselor, 1992—, sch. night coord., 1994-97. Named Key Leader Boy Scouts Am.-Dan Beard Coun., Cin., 1994; recipient Meritorious Svc. award Boy Scouts Am.-Dan Beard Coun., Cin., 1995, Dist. Award of Merit, 1997. Mem. DAR, Reviewers Young Adult Lit. (v.p. 1997-99, pres. 1999—). Avocations: reading, swimming, waterskiing. Home: 3249 Braewood Dr Cincinnati OH 45241-3184 Office: Princeton HS 11080 Chester Rd Cincinnati OH 45246-3802

BLUESTEIN, EDWIN A., JR., lawyer; b. Hearne, Tex., Oct. 16, 1930; s. Edwin A. and Frances Grace (Ely) B.; m. Marsha Kay Meredith, Dec. 21, 1957; children: Boyd, Leslie. B.B.A., U. Tex., 1952, J.D., 1958. Bar: Tex. 1957, U.S. Ct. Appeals (5th cir.) 1960, U.S. Dist. Ct. (so. dist.)Tex. 1959, U.S. Dist. Ct. (ea. dist.)Tex. 1965, U.S. Supreme Ct. 1967, U.S. Ct. Appeals (11th cir.) 1982. Law clk. U.S. Dist. Ct., Houston, 1958-59; assoc. Fulbright & Jaworski, Houston, 1959-65, participating atty., 1965-71, ptnr., 1971-97; head admiralty dept. Fulbright & Jaworski, 1984-93; sr. ptnr. Fulbright & Jaworski, Houston, 1990-97; of counsel Fulbright & Jaworski, 1998—; mem. permanent adv. bd. Tulane Admiralty Law Inst., New Orleans, 1983—; mem. planning com. Houston Marine Ins. Seminar, 1970-76; lectr. profl. seminars. Assoc. editor: American Maritime Cases; contbr. articles to profl. jours. Mem. Tex. Coastal Mgmt. Adv. Com., Austin, 1975-78; bd. dirs. Barbour's Cut Seafarers Ctr., 1992—, Houston Internat. Seafarers Ctr., 1993—. Served with U.S. Army, 1952-54. Recipient Yachtsman of Yr. award Houston Yacht Club, 1978; Eagle Scout, Boy Scouts Am., 1944. Mem. Tex. Bar Found., Maritime Law Assn. U.S. (mem. exec. com. 1980-83), Houston Mariners Club (pres. 1970), Southeastern Admiralty Law Inst. (dir. 1983-85, Houston C. of C. (chmn. ports and waterways com. 1978-79), Propeller Club U.S., Theta Xi (chpt. pres. 1952). Methodist. Club: Houston Yacht (commodore 1979-80). Home: 603 Bayridge Rd La Porte TX 77571-3512 Office: Fulbright & Jaworski 1301 Mckinney St Houston TX 77010-3031

BLUESTEIN, HOWARD BRUCE, meteorology educator; b. Chelsea, Mass., Oct. 8, 1948. BSEE, MIT, 1971, MSEE, 1972, MS in Meteorology, 1972, PhD in Meteorology, 1976. Asst. prof. meteorology U. Okla., Norman, 1976-83, assoc. prof., 1983-90, prof., 1990—; vis. asst. prof. meteorology U. Okla., Norman, 1976-79. Author: Synoptic-Dynamic Meteorology in Midlatitudes, Vol. I, 1992, Vol. II, 1993, Tornado Alley, 1999. Named Okla. Prof. of Yr., Coun. Advancement and Support of Edn., 1989. Fellow Am. Meteorol. Soc. (chair severe local storms com. 1993-95). Avocations: photography, internat. folkdancing. Office: U Okla Sch Meteorology 100 E Boyd St Rm 1310 Norman OK 73019-1000

BLUESTEIN, STEVE FRANKLIN, comedian, writer; b. Boston, Jan. 15, 1947; s. Bernard Benjamin Bluestein and Leona (Rubenstein) Grell. BS in Speech, Emerson Coll., 1968. Comedian various night clubs, TV shows and films, nationwide, 1972—; writer Norman Lear, Playboy, Sid and Marty Kroft, L.A., 1976; screenwriter Warner Bros., L.A., 1981; writer Bernstein/Hovis Prodns., L.A., 1984—; v.p. Camden Air Care. Photographs on exhibit Alexander Gallery, Studio City, Calif., 1988; segment producer, writer Fox TV Totally Hidden Video; writer Candid Camera, 91 edit., Writers Guild Am. West Award Show, 1994-95, (pilot) The Seagulls, 1997; co-host: Surprise Decorator. Active Big Bros. of Greater L.A., 1979—. Mem. AFTRA, SAG, Writers Guild Am. Democrat. Avocation: photography.

BLUESTEIN, VENUS WELLER, retired psychologist, educator; b. Milw., July 16, 1933; d. Richard T. and Hazel (Beard) Weller; m. Marvin Bluestein, Mar. 7, 1954. BS, U. Cin., 1956, MEd, 1959, EdD, 1966. Diplomate Am. Bd. Examiners in Profl. Psychology. Psychologist-in-tng. Longview State Hosp., Cin., 1956-58; sch. psychologist Cin. Pub. Schs., 1958-65; asst. prof. psychology U. Cin., 1965-70, assoc. prof., 1970-79, prof., 1979-93, prof. emerita, 1993—, dir. sch. psychology program, 1965-70, co-dir. sch. psychology program, 1970-75, dir. undergrad. studies, 1976-91, dir. undergrad. advising, 1991-93; cons. child psychologist. Sec., U.S. exec. com. rsch. Children's Internat. Summer Villages, 1964-68; chmn. Ohio Interuniv. Coun. Sch. Psychology, 1967-68. Editor Ohio Psychologist, 1961-68, co-editor, 1972-79; contbr. articles to profl. publs. Vol. Hmilton County Parks, 1982—, vol. naturalist, 1995—; vol. educator Cin. Zoo, 1983—. Recipient George B. Barbour award, 1985. Fellow Am. Acad. Sch. Psychology; mem. AAUP, APA, Ohio Psychol. Assn. (citation 1972, Disting. Svc. award 1968), Cin. Psychol. Assn. (sec. 1961-62), Sch. Psychologists Ohio, Forum for Death Edn. and Counseling, Kappa Delta Pi, Sigma Delta Pi, Psi Chi (award for outstanding mentor 1985, award for outstanding contbns. to undergrad. psychology students 1994). Avocations: horseback riding, wildlife photography. Office: U Cin Dept Psychology ML 376 Cincinnati OH 45221

BLUESTONE, DAVID ALLAN, pediatrician; b. Pitts., Apr. 9, 1938; s. Sam Bluestone and Sarah Cohen Sager; m. John Sidlow, Oct. 12, 1957 (div. 1980); children: Daniel, Bradley, Deborah; m. Leslie Florence Widson Kaplan, May 26m 1983. BA, Hamilton Coll., 1959; MD, U. Pitts., 1963. Diplomate Am. Bd. Pediatrics. Pediatric intern Health Ctr. Hosps. U. Pitts., 1963-64; pediatric resident Children's Hosp., Pitts., 1964-65, L.A., 1967-68; pediatrician Med. Arts Pediatric Med. Group, Inc., L.A., 1968—. Lt. Med. Corps USNR, 1965-67. Mem. AMA, Calif. Med. Assn., Los Angeles County Med. Assn., L.A. Pediatric Soc., Phi Delta Epsilon (pres. 1982-83, assoc. regional gov. 1994—), Zeta Phi. Avocations: travel, photography. Office: Med Arts Pediatric Med Group Inc 6221 Wilshire Blvd Ste 215 Los Angeles CA 90048-5201

BLUESTONE, JEFFREY ALLEN, immunology educator, researcher; b. Ft. Sill, Okla., Apr. 8, 1953; s. Jules Henry Bluestone and Blanche Pomerantz; m. Leah Marcy Rosenkrantz, Sept. 9, 1979; children: David Benjamin, Sarah Beth. BS with high honors, Rutgers U., 1974, MS, 1976; PhD, Cornell U., 1980. Sr. staff fellow Nat. Cancer Inst., Bethesda, Md., 1980-84, sr. investigator, 1984-87; assoc. prof. U. Chgo., 1987-91, prof., 1991-95, Charles B. Higgins prof., 1995—, dir. Ben May Inst. Cancer Rsch., Daniel K. Ludwig prof., 1995—; mem. sci. adv. bd. Howard Hughes Med. Inst., 1999; mem. sci. adv. bd. Alexion Pharm., New Haven, Conn., 1995—, MedImmune Corp., Gaithersburg, Md., 1995—; founding scientist XCyte Therapies, Seattle, 1997—; mem. Nat. Coun. on Aging-NIH, Bethesda, 1996—, U.S.-Japan Coop. Rsch. Coun.-NIH, Bethesda, 1997—; lectr., spkr. in field. Sect. editor: Jour. Immunology, 1989-93, dep. editor, 1997—; editor: (immunogenetics sect.) Immunologic Rsch., 1990—; assoc. editor: Transplantation, 1991—, Jour. Immunotherapy, 1992-95, Immunity, 1996—, Immunol. Rev., 1996—; transmitting editor: Internat. Immunology, 1996—; mem. editl. bd.: Thymus, 1994-97, Current Opinions in Immunology, 1995—; contbr. numerous rev. chpts. and rsch. papers to profl. publs. Recipient Am. Cancer Soc. Faculty Rsch. award, 1989-94; Gould Found. Faculty scholar 1987-89, Markey Found. Faculty scholar, 1987-88; Guggenheim fellow, 1997. Mem. Am. Assn. Immunologists, Am. Diabetes Assn., Transplantation Soc., Chgo. Assn. Immunology (pres. 1992-94). Office: U Chgo MC1089 5841 S Maryland Ave Chicago IL 60637-1463

BLUFORD, GUION STEWART, JR., engineering company executive; b. Phila., Nov. 22, 1942; s. Guion Stewart and Lolita Harriet (Brice) B.; m. Linda M. Tull, Apr. 7, 1964; children: Guion Stewart, James Trevor. B.S. in Aerospace Engring., Pa. State U., 1964; grad., Squadron Officers Sch., 1971; M.S. in Aerospace Engring., Air Force Inst. Tech., 1974, Ph.D. in Aerospace Engring., 1978; D.Sc. hon., Fla. A&M U., 1983; MBA, U. Houston, 1987; DSc (hon.), Tex. So. U., Va. State U., Morgan State U., Stevens Inst. Tech., Tuskegee U., Bowie (Md.) State Coll., Thomas Jefferson U., Chgo. State U., Georgian Ct. Coll., Drexel U., Kent State U. Commd. 2d lt. U.S. Air Force, 1965, advanced through grades to col., 1983; F-4C fighter pilot 12 Tactical Fighter Wing U.S. Air Force, Cam Ranh Bay, Vietnam, 1966-67; T-38 instr. pilot 3630 Flying Tng. Wing U.S. Air Force, Sheppard AFB, Wichita Falls, Tex., 1967-72; chief aerodynamics and airframe br. Air Force Flight Dynamics Lab., Wright-Patterson AFB, Dayton, Ohio, 1975-78; NASA astronaut Johnson Space Ctr., Houston, 1978-93; retired U.S. Air Force, 1993; v.p., gen. mgr. div. engring. svcs. Fed. Data Corp., Bethesda, Md., 1993—. Decorated USAF Command Pilot Astronaut Wings, Air Force Commendation medal, Air medal with 9 oak leaf clusters, Def. Superior Svc. medal, Legion of Merit; recipient Mervin E. Gross award Air Force Inst. Tech., 1974, Disting. Nat. Scientist award Nat. Soc. Black Engrs., 1979, Group Achievement award NASA, 1980, Disting. Alumni award Pa. State U. Alumni Assn., 1983, 85, 91, 92, Space Flight medal NASA, 1983, Pa. Disting. Svc. medal, 1984, NASA Exceptional Svc. medal, 1992, NASA Disting. Svc. Medal, 1994, Def. Meritorious Svc. medal, Nat. Intelligence medal of achievement. Fellow AIAA; mem. Nat. Rsch. Coun. Aeronautics and Space Engring. Bd., Tau Beta Pi. Christian Scientist. Office: Fed Data Corp 3005 Aerospace Pkwy Cleveland OH 44142-1003

BLUH, CYNTHIA HUBBARD, insurance company executive; b. Greenwich, Conn., Aug. 3, 1937; d. Walter Prescott and Kathryn Elizabeth (Brown) Hubbard; m. George Kenneth Bluh, Mar. 23, 1932; children: Geoffrey, Alexandra, Joshua, Rebecca. BA, U. Colo., 1960; MEd, U. Mass., 1972; cert. advanced grad. studies, Springfield (Mass.) Coll., 1976. Registered securities dealer; cert. tchr., guidance counselor, Mass. Tchr. Seattle Opportunities Industrialization Ctr., 1967-69; tchr. Union 38 Conway (Mass.) Grammar Sch., 1970-75; acct. exec. Metlife, Holyoke, Mass., 1977—; dir., chmn. bd. Engineers House Co., Ltd., 1991—; bd. dirs. Engrs. House Ltd. Inn and Apts., Antigua, West Indies. Mem. Conway Hist. Conway Hist. Commn., 1968—; regional coord. West of Boston Territory Unitarian Universalist Svc. Com., Cambridge, Mass., 1986—. Fellow Life Underwriter Tng. Coun., Life Underwriters Assn., 1987. Mem. Pioneer Valley Assn. Life Underwriters (sec. 1984—). Democrat. Avocations: travel, geneology, music, hiking. Office: Met Life Ins Co 330 Whitney Ave Holyoke MA 01040-2751

BLUHER, GREGORY, computer scientist, mathematician; b. Odessa, Ukraine, May 9, 1960; came to U.S., 1979; s. Froim and Alla (Shvetz) Blyukher; m. Antonia Rose Wilson, May 25, 1986; children: Andrew Emmanuel, Julia Elizabeth, Sarah Elena. MA in Math. with honors, Johns Hopkins U., 1983; PhD in Math., Princeton U., 1988; MS in Computer Sci., UCLA, 1992. Asst. prof. The Coll. of N.J., Trenton, 1987-88, Whittier (Calif.) Coll., 1988-89; programmer The Software Toolworks, L.A., 1989-90; rschr. computer sci. dept. UCLA, 1990-92; staff programmer IBM, San Jose, 1992-93; project leader ORACLE, Redwood City, Calif., 1993-95; sr. computer scientist Dept. of Def., Washington, 1995—. Translator: Introduction to the Classical Theory of Abelian Functions, 1990. Interviewer alumni coun. Johns Hopkins U., Balt., 1985-89. IBM scholar, 1983. Mem. IEEE-Computer Soc., Assn. Computing Machinery, Phi Beta Kappa. Home: PO Box 252 Simpsonville MD 21150-0252

BLUHM, BARBARA JEAN, communications agency executive; b. Chgo., Mar. 5, 1925; d. Maurice L. and Clara (Miller) B. Student Coll. William and Mary, 1943-45; BS, U. Wis., 1947. Exec. tng. program Carson Pirie Scott & Co., Chgo., 1947-52; home economist Lever Bros. Co., Chgo., 1952-57; field rep. The Merchandising Group, Chgo., 1957-62; v.p. The Merchandising Group, N.Y.C., 1962-82, pres., 1982-87, chmn., 1987-90. Publicity chmn. James Lenox House Assn., N.Y.C., 1980-90; vol. Venice Hosp., Venice Little Theatre; sec. Coll. Club of Venice; mem. Venice Art League, Venice Symphony. Mem. Venice Yacht Club, Venice Golf and Country Club, Venice Hist. Preservation League. Republican. Presbyterian. Home: 1470 Colony Pl Venice FL 34292-1550

BLUHM, GENE ELWOOD, trade journal editor and publisher; b. Cleve., June 6, 1920; s. Elmer Karl and Helga (Johansen) B.; m. Florence Ethel Slingo, Oct. 6, 1942; children: Gary Gene, Judy Edith. Student, Western Res. U., Cleve., 1939-41, 46-48; real estate cert., Cleve. C.C., 1978. Lic. realtor, Ohio. Reporter Cleve. Press, 1939-41; radio broadcaster WHK, WERE, WJW, others, Cleve., 1948-70; editor Properties Mag., Cleve., 1947-98, pub., 1989-98; mem. pub. rels. com. Midtown Corridor, Cleve., 1980's. Editor: Polka Parade, 1951; editor, pub.: My Confidential Golf Progress Book, 1973; author series Properties Mag., 1963 (award winning); contbr. articles to profl. jours. Councilman Mayfield Village, Ohio, 1970s; cubmaster Cub Scout Pack 139, Hillcrest Area, Cleve., 1950s; organizer Indian Guides and Indian Princess Tribes Hillcrest YMCA, Lyndhurst, Ohio, 1950s-60s; program chmn. Mayfield Twp. Hist. Soc., Hillcrest Area, 1980s. Master 1st sgt. USAF, 1942-45. Mem. Cleve. Area Bd. Realtors (pub. rels. com. 1970s, chmn. Spkrs. Bur. 1970s, chmn. Pres. Ball 1970s, Affiliate of Yr.), Soc. Profl. Journalists, Press Club, Masons (chaplain). Avocations: creative writing, public speaking, music, golf, radio.

BLUHM, MYRON DEAN, sales professional; b. St. Joseph, Ill., Dec. 7, 1934; s. Lorenz E. and Etta (Sieberns) B.; m. Lucinda Ann Meade, June 27, 1954; children: Kathie S. Alblinger, Mitchell D., Beth A.Russell. Student, Ill. Comml. Coll., 1954, Dale Carnegie U., 1966. Franchise sales mgmt. Mr. Steak Embers & Char Steak, Urbana, Ill., 1966-71; sales mgr. McCurdy Seed, Fremont, Iowa, 1974-86, Crow's Seed, Milford, Ill., 1986-94, Sams/Hockaday Ins., Decatur, Ill., 1994—. Named Agt. of the Year life Ins. Co. 1962, Gen. Mgr. of the Year, 1963, Shaklee Sales Coord., 1973—. Mem. Jaycees, Moose, Lions. Lutheran. Home: 5531 San Luis Dr Fort Myers FL 33903-1319 Office: Sams Hockaday & Assocs 120 W Prairie Ave Decatur IL 62523-1219

BLUHM, WILLIAM THEODORE, political scientist, educator; b. Newark, Oct. 13, 1923; s. Frederick Theodore and Charlotte Catherine (Walz) B.; m. Eleanor Elizabeth Kearns, Apr. 22, 1950; children: Catherine Elizabeth, Susanna Marie, Andrew Edward Frederick. B.A., Brown U., 1948; M.A., Tufts U., 1949; Ph.D., U. Chgo., 1957. Instr. polit. sci. U. Rochester, 1952-53, asst. prof., 1957-63, assoc. prof., 1963-67, prof., 1967-92, prof. emeritus, 1993—; instr. polit. sci. Brown U., 1953-57; cons. C.H. Beck Verlag, Munich, 1966-70. Author: Theories of the Political System, 1965, Building an Austrian Nation: The Political Integration of a Western State, 1973, Ideologies and Attitudes, 1974, Force or Freedom?: The Paradox in Modern Political Thought, 1984; co-author: The World of the Policy Analyst, 1990, 2d edit. 1997; editor: The Paradigm Problem in Political Science, 1982; contbr. articles profl. jours. Served with Signal Corps AUS, 1943-46. Decorated Bronze Star Medal; U. Rochester research grantee, 1963-64, 68-69; Fulbright research fellow to Austria, 1965-66; NSF summer grantee, 1967, 68; U. Rochester Bridging fellow, 1980-81; Nat. Endowment for Humanities grantee, 1976. Mem. Am. Polit. Sci. Assn., Sigma Nu. Democrat. Roman Catholic. Office: U Rochester Dept Polit Sci Rochester NY 14627

BLUITT, KAREN, software engineering director; b. N.Y.C., Oct. 25, 1957; d. James Bertrand and Beatrice (Kaufman) B.; m. Kenneth Mark Curry, Nov. 24, 1979 (div. Dec. 1991). BS, Fordham U., 1979; MBA, Calif. State Poly. U., 1982; postgrad., George Mason U. Software engr. Hughes Aircraft Co., Fullerton, Calif., 1979-81; microprocessor engr. Beckman Instruments Co., Fullerton, 1981-82, Singer Co., Glendale, Calif., 1982-83; sr. software engr. Sanders Assoc., Nashua, N.H., 1983-85; software project mgr. GTE Corp., Billerica, Mass., 1985-86; sr. software engr. Wang Labs., Lowell, Mass., 1986-87; project task leader Vanguard Rsch., Lexington, Mass., 1987-88; program mgr. Applied Rsch. & Engring., Bedford, Mass., 1989-91, Sparta, McLean, Va., 1992-93; prin. software engr. Sci. Applications Internat., Arlington, Va., 1993-94; tech. mgr. CACI, Arlington, 1994, Booz-Allen & Hamilton, Vienna, Va., 1995, MRJ Tech. Solutions, Inc., Fairfax, Va., 1996-97, Softek Systems, Inc., Fairfax, 1998—. 1st lt. USAF, 1979-88. Scholar Gov. N.Y. Scholarship Com., 1975-79, Beta Gamma Sigma, 1978—. Mem. IEEE, AAUW, Am. Women in Sci., Am. Brokers Network, Assn. Computing Machinery, Data Processing Mgmt. Assn., Soc. Women Engrs., Wash. Soc. of Engrs. Office: Softek Sys Inc 4114 Legato Rd Fairfax VA 22033-4002

BLUM, ARTHUR, social work educator; b. Cleve., May 25, 1926; s. Rebecca (Pivowar) Blum; m. Lenore Sharrie Secord, Dec. 26, 1954; children: Alex, Joel. AB, Western Res. U., 1950, MS in Social Adminstrn., 1952, DSW, 1960. Group worker Cleve. Jewish Community Ctr., 1952, Cleve. Child Guidance Ctr., 1954-58; project dir. Case Western Res. U., Cleve., 1958-60, prof. social work, 1960—, Grace Longwell Coyle chair, 1987—; prof. Smith Coll., Northampton, Mass., 1961-63; cons. Bellefaire Regional Treatment Ctr., Cleve., 1962-85, City of East Cleve., 1967-70, Jewish Welfare Fedn., Cleve., 1968-72, Fedn. Community Plannning, Cleve., 1976-78, 20 other human svcs. agys., 1960—; vis. prof. Tel Aviv U., 1971-72, 79-80. Editor: Healing Through Living, 1971, Aging and Care Giving, 1990, Innovations in Practice and Service Delivery, 1999; contbr. numerous articles to profl. jours. Sgt. U.S. Army, 1945-46, with Med. Svcs. Corp, 1952-54. Recipient Outstanding Alumnus award Case Western Res. U., 1968. Mem. AAUP, Nat. Assn. Social Workers, Coun. Social Work Edn., Assn. Group Workers. Democrat. Jewish. Avocations: camping, sailing, racquetball, gardening. Office: Case Western Res U Sch Applied Social Scis Univ Circle Cleveland OH 44106

BLUM, BARBARA DAVIS, investor; b. Hutchinson, Kans.; d. Roy C. and Jo (McKinnon) Davis; children: Devin, Hunter, Ragan, Davis. Student, U. Kans.; BA, Fla. State U., 1960, MSW, 1961. Faculty Pediat. Psychiatry Clinic, U. Kans. Med. Ctr., Lawrence, 1961-63; acting adminstr. Suffolk County (N.Y.) Mental Health Clinic, Huntington, L.I., 1963-65; founder, ptnr. Mid-Suffolk Ctr. for Psychotherapy, Hauppage, L.I., N.Y., 1965-67; v.p. Restaurant Assocs. Ga., Inc., Atlanta, 1967-75; dep. adminstr. U.S. EPA, Washington, 1977-81; mem. Pres.'s Interagy. Coordinating Coun.; chmn., pres., CEO Abigail Adams Nat. Bancorp and Adams Nat. Bank, Washington, 1983-98; CEO BDB Investment Partnership, 1998—; chair U.S./Japan Environ. Agreement, 1977; head 1st U.S. Environ. Del. to China, 1978; chmn. Environ. Policy Inst., 1981-84; sr. advisor UN Environ. Program, 1981-84; bd. dirs. Washington Bd. Trade; chair Ctr. for Policy Alternatives; trustee Fed. City Coun.; nat. adv. coun. U.S. SBA. Chmn. D.C. Econ. Devel. Fin. Corp.; founder Leadership Washington; del. UN Mid Decade Conf. on Women, 1980; bd. dirs. Kaiser Permanente Mid Atlantic; dep. dir. Carter-Mondale U.S. presdl. campaign, 1976, Carter/Mondale Transition Team, Washington, 1976-77; panelist Clinton-Gore Econ. Conf., Little Rock and Atlanta; presdl. appointee bd. dirs. Inst. for Am. Indian Art; trustee Southeastern U. Decorated comdr.'s cross Order of Merit W. Ger.; recipient Disting. Service award Federally Employed Women, 1978, Spl. Conservation award Nat. Wildlife Fedn., 1976, Orgn. of Yr. award Ga. Wildlife Fedn., 1974, Disting. Service award Americans for Indian Opportunity, 1978. Mem. Washington Women's Forum, Internat. Women's Forum, Cosmos Club, Econs. Club. Democrat.

BLUM, BETTY ANN, footwear company executive. Student, Vanderbilt U. Various positions Zayre Dept. Store, Framingham, Mass., 1970-75; divsn. pres. Mootsie Tootsies, pres. Jones N.Y., exec. v.p. Maxwell Shoe Co., Hyde Park, Mass., 1976-88, exec. v.p., 1988—; mem. bd. women's study group Brandeis U., 1998. Trustee Dana Farber Cancer Inst., 1998; dir. 210 Internat. Found., 1991.

BLUM, DAVID ELIAS, neurlogist; b. L.A., Oct. 27, 1955; s. John and Elsie Blum; m. Eve G. Blum, Aug. 7, 1983; children: Ben, Alex. BA, Cal Tech, 1977; MA, UCLA, 1981; MD, U. Calif., San Diego, 1985. Co-dir. epilepsy program Barrow Neurol. Inst., Phoenix, 1991—. Office: Barrow Neurol Inst 350 W Thomas Rd Phoenix AZ 85013

BLUM, GERALD HENRY, department store executive; b. San Francisco, 1926; s. Abe and Mildred (Loewenthal) B.; children: Shelley, Todd, Ryan, Derek. A.B., Stanford U., 1950. Mdse. trainee Emporium, San Francisco, 1950-51; with Gottschalks Inc. (formerly E. Gottschalk & Co., Inc.), Fresno, Calif., 1951-98, v.p., 1954-63, exec. v.p., 1963-82, pres., sec., 1982-94, ret., 1998, also vice chmn. bd. dirs. Bd. dirs. Fresno Conv. Bur., 1954—, pres., 1985-87; bd. dirs. Better Bus. Bur., Fresno, 1954-77, Blue Cross, Calif. 1972-85; mem. adv. com. Fresno County Arts Ctr., 1982-85, bd. dirs., 1958-66, v.p. 1961; chmn., Fresno County, 1957, Foundation Bd., (Washington), CARE, 1988—; mem. Area VII Calif. Vocat. Edn. Com., 1972-75, Mayor's Bi-Racial Com., 1968-69; founding v.p. Jr. Achievement, Fresno County, 1957-63; bd. dirs. Fresno Boys Club, 1958-62, Central Calif. Employers Coun., 1956-62, treas. 1958; bd. dirs. Fresno Philharm. Orch., 1954-58, Salvation Army, Fresno, 1956-67, Youth Edn. Svc., 1956-57, Fresno County Taxpayers Assn., 1954, San Joaquin Valley Econ. Edn. Project, 1953; bd. dirs., bus. adv. coun. Fresno City Coll., 1955-57; trustee Valley Children's Hosp., 1955-57, United Crusade, Fresno, 1952-62; pres. bus. adv. coun. Calif. State U., Fresno, 1998—. With USAFF, 1944-47, PTO. Recipient Disting. Svc. award Fresno Jaycees, 1959; winner World's Championship Domino Tournament, 1969, 86, 88. Mem. Nat. Retail Fedn. (dir. 1978-94), Calif. Retailers Assn. (dir. 1964-94), Fresno C. of C. (dir. county, city 1955-57, Boss of Yr., Jr. C. of C. 1980), Nat. Secs. Assn. (Boss of Yr. 1978), Fresno County Stanford U. Alumni Assn. (pres. 1952), Pres. Club of Calif. State U., Rotary (v.p. Fresno club 1962). Clubs: Univ. Sequoia Sunnyside, San Joaquin Country, Downtown (Fresno) (pres. 1978). Office: Blum Consulting 9 River Park Pl E Ste 380 Fresno CA 93720-1530

BLUM, JACOB JOSEPH, physiologist, educator; b. Bklyn., Oct. 3, 1926; s. Paul and Anna (Brown) B.; m. Ruth Marsey, June 3, 1960; children: Mark, Douglas, Lisa, Laura. BA, NYU, 1947; MS, U. Chgo., 1950, PhD, 1952. Mem. staff Naval Med. Rsch. Inst., Bethesda, Md., 1953-56; chief biophysics sect. gerontology br. NIH, Balt., 1958-62; prof. physiology Duke U., Durham, N.C., 1962—, James B. Duke prof., 1980-97, James B. Duke prof. emeritus, 1997—. With AUS, 1945-46. Merck postdoctoral fellow, 1952, Guggenheim fellow, 1969, Fogarty sr. internat. fellow, 1992. Mem. Am. Physiol. Soc., Soc. Protozoologists (pres. 1991). Home: 2525 Perkins Rd Durham NC 27706-2518

BLUM, JOAN KURLEY, fundraising executive; b. Palm Beach, Fla., July 27, 1926; d. Nenad Daniel and Eva (Milos) Kurley; m. Robert C. Blum, Apr. 15, 1967; children: Christopher Alexander, Martha Jane, Louisa Joan, Paul Helmuth, Sherifa. BA, U. Wash., 1948. Cert. fund raising exec. U.S. dir. Inst. Mediterranean Studies, Berkeley, Calif., 1962-65; devel. officer U. Calif. at Berkeley, 1965-67; pres. Blum Assocs., Fund-Raising Cons., San Anselmo, Calif., 1967-92, The Blums of San Francisco, 1992—; mem. faculty U. Calif. Extension, Inst. Fund Raising, S.W. Inst. Fund-Raising U. Tex., U. San Francisco, U.K. Vol. Movement Group, London, Australasian Inst. Fund Raising. Contbr. numerous articles to profl. jours. Recipient Golden Addy award Am. Advt. Fedn.; Silver Mailbox award Direct Mail Mktg. Assn., Best Ann. Giving Time-Life award, others; decorated commdr. Sovereign Order St. Stanislas. Mem. Nat. Soc. Fund-Raising Execs. (dir.), Nat. Assn. of Hosp. Devel., Women Emerging., Rotary (San Francisco), Fund Raising Inst. (Australia), Tahoe Yacht Club. Office: 202 Evergreen Dr Kentfield CA 94904-2708 also: Ste 103, 781 Pacific Hwy, Chatswood NSW 2067, Australia

BLUM, JOHN ALAN, urologist, educator; b. Bklyn., Feb. 2, 1933; s. Louis J. and Pauline (Kushner) B.; m. Debra Merlin Ackerman, June 30, 1957; children: Louis Jeffrey, Alfred Merlin, Jacqueline. AB, Dartmouth, 1954; MD, NYU, 1958; MS, U. Minn., 1965. Diplomate Am. Bd. Urology. Intern, U. Minn. Hosp., Mpls., 1958-59, resident, 1959-64; practice medicine, specializing in urology, Chgo., 1964-66, Mpls., 1966-67, San Diego, 1969—; chmn. dept. urology Mt. Sinai Hosp., Chgo., 1965-66; asst. prof. urology U. Minn., Mpls., 1967; assoc. clin. prof. urology U. Calif., San Diego, 1969—; chief of staff Hillside Hosp., San Diego, 1989-92; chmn. dept. surgery, div. urology Mercy Hosp., San Diego, 1991-93; mem. staff Scripps Hosp., La Jolla, Calif., 1969—; adj. assoc. prof. uro-pathology Uniform Svcs. U. of Health Sci., Behtesda, Md., 1988—. Bd. dirs. Vietnam Vet. Leadership Program. Capt. USNR, 1967-93, Vietnam, ret. 1993. Fellow ACS; mem. Am., Calif. med. assns., Am. Urol. Assn., San Diego Urol. Soc. (pres. 1991-93), San Diego Surg. Soc. (pres. 1977), Phi Beta Kappa, Sigma Xi, Alpha Omega Alpha, San Diego Yacht Club. Research in devel. of silicone rubber for urinary tract. Home: 890 Cornish Dr San Diego CA 92107-4247 Office: 4060 4th Ave Ste 310 San Diego CA 92103-2120

BLUM, JOHN MORTON, historian; b. N.Y.C., Apr. 29, 1921; s. Morton Gustave and Edna (LeVino) B.; m. Pamela Louise Zink, June 28, 1944; children: Pamela, Ann, Thomas Tyler. AB, Harvard U., 1943, MA, 1947, PhD, 1950, LLD (hon.), 1980; MA, Cambridge (Eng.) U., 1963; DHL (hon.), Trinity Coll., 1970; LLD (hon.), Colgate U., 1978. Research assoc., then asst. prof. history, assoc. prof. M.I.T., 1948-57; prof. history Yale U., 1957-95, ret., 1995; Pitt prof. Cambridge U., 1963-64; Harmsworth prof. Oxford U., 1976-77. Author: Joe Tumulty and the Wilson Era, 1951, The Republican Roosevelt, 1954, Woodrow Wilson and the Politics of Morality, 1956, From the Morgenthau Diaries, Vol. I, 1959, Vol. II, 1965, Vol. III, 1967, Yesterday's Children, 1959, The Promise of America, 1966, Roosevelt and Morgenthau, 1970, V Was for Victory, 1976, The Progressive Presidents, 1980, Years of Discord, 1991, Liberty Justice Order, 1993; assoc. editor: (with Elting E. Morison) Letters of Theodore Roosevelt (8 vols.), 1951-54; editor: The National Experience, 1963, The Price of Vision, 1973; Public Philosopher, 1985. Trustee Buckingham Sch., 1954-56, Hotchkiss Sch., 1964-70; mem. Andover Alumni Council, 1957-60. Served from ensign to lt. USNR, 1943-46. Harvard U. fellow, 1970-79. Mem. Am. Acad. Arts and Scis., Mass. Hist. Assn., Century Assn., Phi Beta Kappa. Home: 313 St Ronan St New Haven CT 06511-2327

BLUM, JON H., dermatologist; b. Detroit, Aug. 9, 1944; s. David and Hedwig B.; m. Rosie Jacobs, June 25, 1967; children: Michael, Steven, Suzanne. BS, Wayne State U., 1965, MD, 1969. Diplomate Am. Bd. Dermatology. Intern Beaumont Hosp., Royal Oak, Mich., 1969-70; med. resident Henry Ford Hosp., Detroit, 1970-71; dermatology resident Henry Ford Hosp., 1971-74; dermatologist Farmington Hills, Mich., 1974—; staff physician, William Beaumont Hosp.; cons., Internat. Hair Route, Mississauga, Ontario, Can., 1980—; clin. asst. prof. dermatology, Wayne State U., Detroit, 1976—. Author: (with others) Electrolysis, 1984. Mem. Am. Acad. Dermatology, Mich. Dermatology Soc., Mich. State Med. Soc., Oakland County Med. Soc. Avocation: computers. Office: Jon H Blum MD Ste 330 32905 W 12 Mile Rd Farmington Hills MI 48334-3345

BLUM, JUNE, artist, curator; b. N.Y.C., Dec. 10, 1929; d. Henry Charles and Elsie Druiett; m. Maurice C. Blum (dec.). MA, Bklyn. Coll., 1959; attended, Bklyn. Mus. Art Sch., Pratt Graphic Art Ctr., New Sch. Social Rsch. Curator contemporary art Suffolk Mus., Stony Brook, N.Y., 1971-75; curator at large Cocoa Beach, 1975—; dir. Women for Art, Cocoa Beach, Fla., 1976—; dir. mus. Individual Mus., Cocoa Beach, Fla., 1980—. One-person shows include Bronx Mus., 1975, NN Gallery, Seattle, 1977, Nassau County Mus. Fine Arts, Roslyn, N.Y., 1980, Brevard C.C., Melbourne, Fla., Cocoa, Fla., 1984, King Performing Art Ctr. Gallery, Melbourne, 1990, SOHO 20 Artists, N.Y.C., 1998, Mus. Art and Sci., Melbourne, 1998; exhibited in group shows including Bklyn. Mus., 1975, Queens Mus., Flushing, N.Y., 1976, Nassau County Mus. Fine Art, Bklyn., 1980, Brevard Mus., Cocoa, 1995, Mus. at Stony Brook, 1996; author: Metamorphosis of June Blum, 1976, Betty Friedan Series, 1976, Female Connection, 1978, A Woman's Space, 1980. Art chairperson, v.p. Cocoa Beach Libr., 1992—, mem. time capsule com., 1998; art chairperson Brevard Commn. Women, 1985. Recipient Anne Eisner Putnam Meml. prize Nat. Acad. Nat. Assn. Women Artists, N.Y.C., 1968, honorable mention White Mountain Festival Arts, Jefferson, N.H., 1977. Mem. Womens Caucus Art, Coll. Art Assn., East Ctrl. Fla. Women Caucus Art (pres. 1980—). Home: 120 Boca Ciega Rd Cocoa Beach FL 32931-2602

BLUM, MARGARET D., federal agency administrator. BA, U. Fla. Tchr.; with fuel supply ctr. U.S. Dept. Def.; with hdqs. staff U.S. Coast Guard; dir. Office Maritime Labor and Tng. U.S. Dept. Transp., Washington, 1991-92, dir. Office of Acquisitions, 1993-94, assoc. adminstr. port, intermodal and environ. activities, 1994—. Office: Ports Intermodal & Environ Activities US Dept Transp 400 7th St SW Rm 7214 Washington DC 20590*

BLUM, MELVIN, chemical company executive, researcher; b. N.Y.C., Jan. 8, 1936; s. Paul Henry and Dora (Schneiderman) B.; m. Paula Linda Weiss, July 11, 1969; 1 child, Lara Joyce. BS, Columbia U., 1957, MA, 1959; PhD, Duke U., 1964, Burlington Inst., 1970. Sales mgr. Nuclear Corp. Am., Burbank, Calif., 1960-62; pres. Atomergic Chemetals Corp., Farmingdale, N.Y., 1963—, Burlington Sci. Corp., Farmingdale, 1974—; v.p. Am. Roland Chem. Co., S.I., N.Y., 1984—. Author: Handbook of Rare Elements, Encyclopedia of Chemical Technology, Strategic Metal Investments, (mag.) DMSO Reporter. Capt. USAFR, 1959-65. Mem. Am. Chem. Soc., Am. Soc. Metals, Am. Nuclear Soc., Am. Inst. Physics, N.Y. Acad. Scis., Chemists Club. Home: 1385 Lyon Pl Wantagh NY 11793-2919 Office: Atomergic Chemetals Corp 222 Sherwood Ave Farmingdale NY 11735-1718

BLUM, RICHARD ARTHUR, writer, media educator; b. Bklyn., July 28, 1943; w. Albert Elias and Eve (Griboff) B.; m. Barbara Fierstein, Sept. 16, 1967 (div. 1986); children: Jason Robert, Jennifer Rebecca; m. Ilene Shatoff, Sept. 2, 1995. BA, Fairleigh Dickinson U., 1965; MS, Boston U., 1968; PhD, U. So. Calif., 1977. Producer, dir., fellow Sta. WGBH-TV, Boston, 1965-67; program exec., writer, assoc. exec. producer Columbia Pictures-TV, L.A., 1968-74; instr. to asst. prof. U. Tex., Austin, 1974-78; sr. program officer NEH, Washington, 1978-82; sr. exec. producer Rainbow Programming Svc., N.Y.C., 1982; vis. faculty Harvard U., Cambridge, Mass., 1984-86; asst. prof. U. Md., College Park, 1984-88, assoc. prof., dir. RTUF Writing Program, dir. undergrad. studies, 1989-92; dir. TV and Film Writing Inst., U. Md., College Park, 1991-92; prof., dir. motion picture divsn. U. Ctrl. Fla., Orlando, 1993-95, prof. film dept., 1996—; mem. faculty Am. Film Inst. Workshops, 1982-86, The Writers Ctr., Bethesda, 1982-92. Author: Television Writing: From Concept to Contract, 1980, rev. edit., 1984, American Film Acting: The Stanislavski Heritage, 1984, Working Actors: The Craft of TV, Film and Stage Performance, 1989, (with Richard Lindheim) Primetime: Network TV Programming, 1987, (with Richard Lindheim) Inside Television Producing, 1991, Television and Screenwriting, 1995, 3d edit., 1995; screenwriter (with Frank Tavares) The Elton Project, 1992, Desert Fire, 1987. (with A. Gerson) Sonja's Men, 1991; screenwriter MODE VIII, 1998; screenwriter, co-prodr. TAL, 1999. Judge Nicholl Screenwriting fellowships Acad. Motion Picture Arts and Scis., 1986-89, Corp. Pub. Broadcasting awards, 1988-90; bd. mem. Ctrl. Fla. Film Coun., 1992-95, Fla. Inst. for Film Edn., 1992-95, Ind. Prodrs. Project, Enzian Theatre-Fla. Film Festival Grants, 1995. Recipient Creative and Performing Arts award U. Md., 1986, Arts and Humanities award, 1987, Ford Found. award, 1988. Mem. Broadcast Edn. Assn., Univ. Film and Video Assn. Home: 3338 Hadleigh Crest Orlando FL 32817-2051 Office: U Ctrl Fla Film Dept PO Box 163120 Orlando FL 32816-3120

BLUM, RICHARD HOSMER ADAMS, educator, writer; b. Ft. Wayne, Ind., Oct. 7, 1927; s. Hosmer and Imogene (Heino) B. A.B. with honors magna cum laude, San Jose State Coll., 1949; Ph.D., Stanford U., 1951. Research dir. Calif. Med. Assn., San Francisco, 1956-58, San Mateo County (Calif.) Mental Health Service, San Mateo, 1958-60; lectr. Sch. Criminology, U. Calif., Berkeley, 1960-62; mem. faculty Stanford (Calif.) U., 1962-78, prof. dept. psychology, 1970-75, prof. dept. gynecology and obstetrics, 1982-97; mem. faculty Stanford (Calif.) U. Law Sch., 1975-78; chmn. bd. Am. Lives Endowment, Portola Valley, Calif., 1979—; chmn. Intern. Rsch. Group on Drug Legis. and Programs, Geneva, 1969-78; pres. Bio-Behavioral Rsch. Group, Inc., Palo Alto, 1964-87; owner/operator Shingle Mill Ranch, 1964—; vis. fellow Wolfson Coll. U. Cambridge, 1984; vis. prof. social and polit. sci. U. Cambridge, 1997-98. Author 21 books in field of health, criminology, public policy, psychology; author 7 books of Fiction. Served in U.S. Army, 1951-53, Korea. Fellow APHA, AAAS, APA, Am. Psychol. Soc., Am. Sociol. Assn., Soc. Advanced Legal Studies (hon., life); mem. Archaeol. Inst. Am., Sigma Xi, Cosmos Club, Athenaeum Club, San Francisco Univ. Club. Unitarian. Home and Office: PO Box 620482 Woodside CA 94062-0482

BLUM, SARAH LEAH, nurse psychotherapist; b. Atlantic City, N.J., Dec. 5, 1939; d. David and Diana (Fedner) B.; m. Joseph J. McGoran, Aug. 24, 1970 (div. 1986); children: Lorna Hope Marie, Sean-David Justin. BSN, Seattle U., 1971; M in Nursing, U. Wash., 1976. Cert. clin. specialist. Nurse Atlantic City Hosp., 1960-62, Kaiser Found. Hosp., L.A., 1963-66; instr. nursing North Idaho Coll., Coeur D'Alene, 1972-74; pvt. practice Federal Way, Wash., 1977-85, Auburn, Wash., 1985—; nurse psychotherapist Christian Counselling Svc., Tacoma, 1977-83; founder The Found. for Planetary Healing; creator Drums, Dreams & Re-Membering; cons. in field; presenter workshops. Contbr. articles to profl. jours. Creator Healing Day, 1985. Capt. Nurse Corps, U.S. Army, 1966-71, Vietnam. Fellow Am. Orthopsychiatric Assn.; mem. ANA, Nat. Nursing Hon. Soc., Internat. Transactional Analysis Assn., Inst. Developmental Edn. and Psychotherapy (bd. dirs. 1989-93, chair profl. membership com. 1991-94), Vietnam Veterans of Am. (bd. dirs. 1983-85, 1st woman mem.). Avocations: music, cross-country skiing, sailing. Home and Office: 303 O St NE Auburn WA 98002-4645

BLUM, VICKY JOLENE, medical/surgical nurse; b. Defiance, Iowa, Aug. 6, 1951; d. Merle B. and Marjie E. (Schumacher) Greer; m. Michael J. Blum, July 10, 1971; children: Jennifer, Jason, Jared. RN, Jennie Edmundson Sch. Nursing, Council Bluffs, Iowa, 1988. Staff nurse med./surg. Jennie Edmundson Meml. Hosp. Mem. ANA, Iowa Nurses Assn. Office: Jennie Edmundson Meml Hosp 933 E Pierce St Council Bluffs IA 51503-4626

BLUMBERG, AVROM AARON, physical chemistry educator; b. Albany, N.Y., Mar. 3, 1928; s. Samuel and Lillian Ann (Smith) B.; m. Eleanor Leah Simon, Aug. 5, 1955 (dec. Sept. 1967); 1 child, David Martin; m. Judith Anne Kohlhagen, Mar. 9, 1969; children: Susan Margaret, Jonathan Samuel. BS in Chemistry, Rensselaer Poly. Inst., 1949; PhD in Phys. Chemistry, Yale U., 1953. Fellow glass sci. Mellon Inst., Pitts., 1953-59, fellow polymer sci., 1959-63; from asst. to assoc. prof. phys. chemistry DePaul U., Chgo., 1963-75, prof., 1975—, head div. natural scis. and math., 1966-82, chmn. dept. chemistry, 1986-92; vis. lectr. chemistry dept. U. Pitts., 1957-58; cons. in field. Author: Form and Function, 1972; contbr. articles to profl. jours. Participant scientists and speakers program Mus. Sci. and Industry, Chgo., 1985—; Dem. precinct capt., Evanston, Ill., 1970-78. Mem. Am. Chem. Soc. (speakers program Chgo. sect. 1983—), Royal Soc. Chem. London, Arms Control Assn., Sigma Xi. Jewish. Avocations: music, reading, art, travel, cooking. Home: 1240 S State St Chicago IL 60605-2405 Office: DePaul U Dept Chemistry 2320 N Kenmore Ave Chicago IL 60614-3210

BLUMBERG, BARBARA SALMANSON (MRS. ARNOLD G. BLUMBERG), retired state housing official, housing consultant; b. Bklyn., Oct. 2, 1927; d. Sam and Mollie (Greenberg) Salmanson; m. Arnold G. Blumberg, June 19, 1949 (dec. June 1989); children: Florence Ellen Schwartz, Martin Jay, Emily Anne. BA, De Pauw U., 1948; postgrad., New Sch. for Social Rsch., N.Y.C. Mem. pub. rels. dept. Nate Fein & Co., N.Y.C., 1948-51; freelance pub. rels. cons., 1960—; councilwoman North Hempstead, N.Y., 1975-82; adviser to energy com. N.Y. State Assembly, N.Y.C., 1982-84; dir. spl. needs housing Divsn. Housing and Cmty. Renewal, State of N.Y., 1984-89, ret., 1989; mem. bd. visitors Pilgrim State Hosp. Pres. UN Assn. Great Neck, N.Y., 1967-69, chmn. China Study Workshop, 1966-67; pres. Shalom chpt. Hadassah, 1955-57; exec. v.p. Lakeville PTA, Great Neck, 1963-65, Great Neck South Jr. H.S., 1965-66; co-chair UNICEF, Great Neck, 1968-70, spkrs. bur., 1971—; v.p. Herricks Cmty. Life Ctr., 1976-77, B'nai B'rith, Lake Success, N.Y.; coord. 6th Congl. Dist., N.Y. McGovern for Pres.; bd. dirs. New Dem. Coalition Nassau, Am. Jewish Congress, Day Care Coun. Nassau County, Citizens Sch. Com., Great Neck; active Reform Dem. Assn. Great Neck; platform com. Nassau Dem. Com.; del. Dem. Nat. Conv., 1992; adv. com. to spkr. N.Y. State Assembly; resource coun., housing devel. com. Cmty. Advocates; chair North Hempstead Housing Authority; trustee L.I. Power Authority, 1994-96. Recipient award Anti-Defamation League, New Hyde Park, N.Y., 1975, Alumni award DePauw U., 1977, Hadassah New Life award, 1980, Women's Pole of Honor, North Hempstead, 1994. Mem. North Shore Archeol. Assn. (chmn. study group), Women in Comm., Internat. Platform Assn., L.I. Womens Network (co-convenor), Interfaith Nutrition Network (v.p.), Cmty. Advocates (bd. dirs.), Mental Health Assn. Nassau County (bd. dirs.), North Shore NAACP, N.Y. Alumni Club DePauw U. (trustee), Alpha Lambda Delta. Home: 12 Birch Hill Rd Great Neck NY 11020-1309

BLUMBERG, BARUCH SAMUEL, academic research scientist; b. N.Y.C., July 28, 1925; s. Meyer and Ida (Simonoff) B.; m. Jean Liebesman, Apr. 4, 1954; children: Anne, George, Jane, Noah. BS, Union Coll., Schenectady, 1946; MD, Columbia U., 1951; PhD, Oxford (Eng.) U., 1957; 20 hon. doctoral degrees. Intern, then resident Columbia div. Bellevue Hosp., N.Y.C., 1951-53; fellow in medicine Columbia-Presbyn. Med. Ctr., N.Y.C., 1953-55; chief geog. medicine and genetics sect. NIH, Bethesda, Md., 1957-64; assoc. dir. clin. rsch. Fox Chase Cancer Ctr., Phila., 1964-86, v.p. population oncology, 1984-89, Fox Chase disting. scientist, 1989—; sr. advisor to pres. Fox Chase Cancer Ctr.; univ. prof. medicine and anthropology U. Pa., 1977—; master Balliol Coll., Oxford (Eng.) U., England, 1989-94; George Eastman vis. prof. Oxford U., 1983-84; Raman vis. prof. Indian Inst. Scis., Bangalore, 1986; Ashland vis. prof. U. Ky., Lexington, 1986, 87; disting. vis. Nat. U. Singapore, 1992; vis. prof. U. Otago, Dunedin, New Zealand, 1994; James W. McLaughlin vis. prof. U. Tex.; vis. prof. dept. medicine Stanford U. Med. Ctr.; sr. advisor to pres. Fox Chase Cancer Ctr., 1989—; fellow Ctr. Advanced Study Behavioral Scis., Stanford U., Calif.; Larry Lokey disting. vis. prof. human biology Stanford U. Contbr. articles to profl. jours. Lt. USNR, 1943-46. Recipient Albion O. Berstein, M.D. award Med. Soc. State of N.Y., 1969, Grand Sci. award Phi Lambda Kappa, 1972, Ann. award Eastern Pa. br. Am. Soc. Microbiology, 1972, Passano award Williams & Wilkens Co., 1974, Modern Medicine Disting. Achievement award, 1975, Internat. award Gairdner Found., 1975, Karl Landsteiner Meml. award Am. Assn. Blood Banks, 1975, Nobel prize in physiology or medicine, 1976, Scopus award Am. Friends of Hebrew U., 1977, Strittmatter award Philadelphia County Med. Soc., 1980, Disting. Service award Pa. Med. Soc., 1982, Zubrow award Pa. Hosp., 1986, Achievement award Sammy Davis Jr. Nat. Liver Inst., 1987, John P. McGovern award Am. Med. Writers Assn., 1988, Gov.'s Award in the Scis. Commonwealth of Pa., 1989, John Blundell award Brit. Blood Transfusion Soc., 1989, Gold Medal award Can. Liver Found. and Can. Assn. Study of Liver, 1990, Showa Emperor Meml. award Japan, 1994; elected to Nat. Inventor Hall of Fame, 1993. Fellow ACP, Royal Coll. Physicians; mem. NAS, AAAS, Inst. Medicine of NAS, Am. Acad. Arts and Scis. (inst. medicine), Assn. Am. Physicians, Am. Soc. Clin. Investigation, Am. Soc. Human Genetics, Explorers Club N.Y., Athenaeum (London). Office: Fox Chase Cancer Ctr 7701 Burholme Ave Ste 2 Philadelphia PA 19111-2497

BLUMBERG, DAVID RUSSELL, librarian; b. Balt., July 27, 1956; s. Stanley Edward and Norma Ray (Bennett) B.; m. Eleanor K. Wang, June 7, 1989. BA, Loyola Coll., Balt., 1978; MLS, U. Md., Balt., 1984. Lic. profl. libr., Md. Correctional libr. State of Md., Balt., 1984-85; assoc. libr. Enoch Pratt Free Libr., Balt., 1979-83, libr. supr., 1985—. Bd. dirs. Santa Claud Anonymous, Balt., 1983—; chmn. Balt. Rep. Com., 1986-98; program dir. Ind. Rep. Coalition, Balt., 1991—; pres. Roland Park Civic League, Balt., 1997—; bd. dirs. Md. Leadership Coun., sec., 1996—. Named New Mem. of Yr., Balt. Jr. Assn. Commerce, 1985, Mem. of Yr., 1986; Man of Yr., Balt. Rep. Com., 1987. Mem. Md. Libr. Assn. (pres. spl. svcs. divsn. 1987-88, 92-93), Kiwanis (pres. Hamden-Midtown 1996-97, lt. gov. Dist. 12 1999—). Jewish. Avocations: collecting movie posters, reading, paperweights. Home: 5405 Falls Road Ter Baltimore MD 21210-1906

BLUMBERG, DONALD FREED, management consultant; b. Phila., Jan. 30, 1935; s. Harry and Sara (Freed) B.; B.A., U. Pa., 1952, B.E.E., 1957, M.B.A., 1958, postgrad., 1963; m. Judith Toplin, June 16, 1960; children—Michael, Susan. Sr. planner IBM Corp., 1960-61; dir. planning and research services Pa. Research Assocs., 1962-65; dir. ops. research and long range planning Philco Ford Corp., 1965-68; mgr. mgmt. sci. div. Sci. Mgmt. Corp., 1968; v.p. Computer Scis. Corp., 1969; pres., chief exec. officer D.F. Blumberg & Assocs., Inc., Ft. Washington, Pa., 1969—, sole practice, 1973—, chmn. Blumberg Shaw Cons., Ltd., London, 1988—; instr. U. Pa.; lectr. Am. Mgmt. Assn., Temple U., 1993-94. Mem. Upper Dublin Twp. Govt. Study Commn., 1974-75; acting prin. dep. asst. sec. def. Dept. Def., 1975; mem. bd. dirs. U. Pa. Engring. Sch. Author: (book) Managing Service As A Strategic Profit Center (award McGraw Hill). Pres. Enclave High Rise Condominium. Served to 1st lt., AUS, 1959-60. Mem. Inst. Mgmt. Scis., Ops. Research Soc. Am., IEEE, Inst. Dirs., Assn. Field Service Mgrs. (Del. Valley chpt. chair). Democrat. Jewish. Contbr. over 450 articles on field service, strategic and service management long range planning and applications of mgmt. sci. techniques to profl. jours. Home: 1922 Audubon Dr Dresher PA 19025-1902 Office: D F Blumberg & Assoc Inc 1300 Virginia Dr Ste 110 Fort Washington PA 19034-3221

BLUMBERG, EDWARD ROBERT, lawyer; b. Phila., Feb. 15, 1951. BA in Psychology, U. Ga., 1972; JD, Coll. William and Mary, 1975. Bar: Fla., 1975, U.S. Dist. Ct. Fla., 1975, U.S. Ct. Appeals, 1975, U.S. Supreme Ct., 1979. Assoc., Knight, Peters, Hoeveler & Pickle, Miami, Fla., 1977-76; ptnr. Deutsch & Blumberg, P.A., Miami, 1978—; adj. prof. U. Miami Sch. Paralegal Studies. Author: Proof of Negligence, Mathew Bender Florida Torts, 1988. Mem. ABA (ho. of dels. 1997—), ATLA, Dade County Bar Assn., Fla. State Bar (bd. govs., pres. elect 1996-97, pres. 1997-98), Acad. Fla. Trial Lawyers, Nat Bd. Trial Advocacy (cert. civil trial adv.), Fla. Bar Found. (bd. dirs. 1996—). Office: Deutsch & Blumberg PA 100 Biscayne Blvd Fl 28 Miami FL 33132-2304

BLUMBERG, GERALD, lawyer; b. N.Y.C., July 25, 1911; s. Saul and Amelia (Abramowitz) B.; m. Rhoda Shapiro, Jan. 7, 1945; children: Lawrence, Rena, Alice, Leda. A.B. cum laude, Cornell U., 1931; J.D. cum laude, Harvard, 1934. Bar: Mass. 1934, N.Y. 1934. Pvt. practice N.Y, 1934—; mem. firm Gerald & Lawrence Blumberg LLP; instr. econs. Cornell U., 1931; mem. Harvard Legal Aid Bur., 1934. Bd. dirs., v.p., exec. com. Am. Com. Weizmann Inst. Sci.; internat. bd. govs. Weizmann Inst. Sci., 1982—. Mem. ABA, N.Y. State, Westchester, Yorktown bar assns., Phi Beta Kappa, Phi Kappa Phi. Home: 1305 Baptist Church Rd Yorktown Heights NY 10598-5810 Office: Gerald & Lawrence Blumberg LLP 521 5th Ave New York NY 10175-0003

BLUMBERG, GRACE GANZ, law educator, lawyer; b. N.Y.C., Feb. 16, 1940; d. Samuel and Beatrice (Finkelstein) Ganz; m. Donald R. Blumberg, Sept. 9, 1959; 1 dau., Rachel. B.A. cum laude, U. Colo., 1960; J.D. summa cum laude, SUNY, 1971; LL.M., Harvard U., 1974. Bar: N.Y. 1971, Calif. 1989. Confidential law clk. Appellate Div., Supreme Ct., 4th Dept., Rochester, N.Y., 1971-72; teaching fellow Harvard Law Sch., Cambridge, Mass., 1972-74; prof. law SUNY, Buffalo, 1974-81, UCLA, 1981—; reporter Am. Law Inst., Prins. of the Law of Family Dissolution. Author: Community Property in California, 1987, rev. edit., 1999, Blumberg's California Family Code Annotated (ann.); contbr. articles to profl. jours. Office: UCLA Sch Law Box 951476 Los Angeles CA 90095-1476

BLUMBERG, JOEL MYRON, cardiologist; b. N.Y.C., Oct. 17, 1940; s. Howard Godfrey and Lily Ruth (Goldberg) B.; B.A., DePauw U., 1962; M.D., N.Y. U., 1966; m. Judith Ellen Green, Aug. 23, 1964; children—Amy, Hillary, Michelle. Intern, N.Y. U.-Bellevue Med. Center, N.Y.C., 1966-67, resident in internal medicine, 1969-71; fellow in cardiology Cornell U.-N.Y. Hosp., 1971-73; pvt. practice internal medicine and cardiology, Greenwich, Conn., 1973—; attending staff Greenwich Hosp., 1973—, coronary care cons., 1973—; physician to out-patients N.Y. Hosp., 1973-77; clin. instr. Cornell U. Med. Coll., 1971-77; clin. asst. prof. Yale Sch. Medicine, 1975—; lectr. in preventive cardiology to civic groups. Trustee, Temple Sholom, Greenwich, Conn.; bd. visitors DePauw U., bd. incorporators Greenwich Hosp. Diplomate Am. Bd. Internal Medicine. Fellow A.C.P., Am. Coll. Cardiology, Am. Coll. Chest Physicians, Am. Heart Assn. (council on clin. cardiology); mem. Am. Soc. Internal Medicine, N.Y. Heart Assn., Greenwich, Fairfield County, Conn. State med. socs. Club: B'nai B'rith (Stamford, Conn.). Contbr. articles to profl. jours. Home: 59 Old Stone Bridge Rd Cos Cob CT 06807-1511 Office: 2 1/2 Deerfield Dr Greenwich CT 06831-5335

BLUMBERG, JUNE BETH, artist; b. Abington, Pa., May 14, 1959; d. Frederick Blumberg and Elin (Brunswick) Binder. A of Gen. Studies, Montgomery Community Coll., 1985; BFA, Moore Coll. of Art, Phila., 1991. Stats. clk. Crime Prevention Assn., Phila., 1980-81; workshop tchr. Jefferson Hosp. Evening Program, Phila., 1986-87; art asst. Mildred Greenberg, Phila., 1988-89; vis. artist Moore Coll. of Art & Design, Phila., 1990; admission rep. Franklin Inst., Phila., 1990-92; rsch. scientist, artist Phila., 1979—; sec. fellowship Pa. Acad. Fine Art, 1995, 96. Shows include Nexus Art Gallery, Phila., 1979, Moore Coll. Art & Design, Phila, 1985-90, upper Saddle Cultural Ctr., N.J., 1986, Art Ctr. N.J., Milford, 1986, Ky. Highlands Mus., Ashland, 1988, Studio Arts Ctr. Internat., Florence, Italy, 1989, Palette and Chisel Acad. Fine Arts, Chgo., 1990, West Bend Gallery, Wis., 1990, Rittenhouse Fine Arts Ann., Phila., 1985-87, 90, Pen and Brush Club, N.Y.C., 1987, 89, 90, Clinton St. Gallery, Schenectady, N.Y., 1990, Pa. Acad. Fine Arts, Phila., 1991, 93, Phila. Print Club, 1991-97, Reno Gazette Jour. Bldg., Nev., 1991, Woodmere Art Mus., Phila., 1991, 92, 98, Axis Gallery, Phila., 1992, Artcetera, Auburn, Calif., 1992, Dellora Norris Cultural Ctr., St. Charles, Ill., 1992, Gallery Cedar Hollow, Malvern, Pa., 1993, 479 Gallery, Phila., 1993, City Hall, Phila., 1993, Art Initiatives, N.Y.C., 1993, 94, Border Book Store, Phila., 1994, 95, Mills Pond House, St. James, N.Y., 1994, Nat. Arts Club, N.Y.C., 1994, Highwire Gallery, Phila., 1993, 94, The Police Bldg. Gallery, N.Y.C., 1995, Internat. Platform Assn., Washington, 1995, Riverbank Arts, Stockton, N.J., 1997, The Bear and Koala Tea Co., Bordentown, N.J., 1998, Main Line Art Ctr., Haverford, Pa., 1998, Phila. Sketch Club, 1998, N.Y. Law Sch., N.Y.C., 1998, Cmty. Arts Ctr., Wallingford, Pa., 1999, Cumberland County Coll., Vineland, N.J., 1999, Wilmington Pub. Libr., 1999. Tutor Homeless Shelter, 1986. Recipient scholarship, 1983-85, Spl. Merit award Pen and Brush Club, 1990. Mem. NAFE, APHA, World Affairs Coun., Pastel Soc. West Coast, The Internat. Platform Assn. (Best of Show 1995), Toastmasters, Phi Theta Kappa. Democrat. Avocations: politics, reading, swimming, philosophy. Address: PO Box 148 Bala Cynwyd PA 19004-0148

BLUMBERG, MARK STUART, consultant; b. N.Y.C., Nov. 16, 1924; s. Sydney N. and Mollie (Leshrowitz) B.; m. Luba Monasevitch, 1952; children: Bart David, Eve Luise; m. 2d Elizabeth R. Conner, 1974. Student, Johns Hopkins U., 1942-43, Harvard U., 1943-44; D.M.D., Harvard U., 1948, M.D., 1950, student Sch. Public Health, 1955. Intern, children's med. service Bellevue Hosp., N.Y.C., 1950-51; ops. analyst Johns Hopkins U. Ops. Research Office, Chevy Chase, Md., 1951-54; exchange analyst Army Ops. Research Group (U.K.), West Byfleet, Eng., 1953-54; staff Occupational Health Program, USPHS, Washington, 1954-56; asso. ops. analyst to dir. health econs. program Stanford (Calif.) Research Inst., 1956-66; asst. to v.p. adminstrn. to dir. health planning, office of the pres. U. Calif., Berkeley, 1966-70; corp. planning advisor to dir. spl. studies Kaiser Found. Health Plan, Inc., Oakland, Calif., 1970-94; dir. Kaiser Found. Health Plan of Conn., Hartford, 1982-94, Kaiser Found. Health Plan Mass., 1987-94; cons. risk adjusted measures Oakland, 1994—; various times cons. Pan Am. Health Orgn., Calif. State Dept. Mental Hygiene, Carnegie Commn. on Higher Edn., various agys. HHS. Contbr. writings to profl. publs. Vol. Grenfell Med. Mission, Harrington Harbour, Que., Can., summer 1948; mem. tech. adv. com. AB 524 State of Calif., 1992—. Served with USNR, 1943-45; with USPHS, 1954-56. Mem. Ops. Research Soc. Am. (past mem. council, Health Applications sect.), Hosp. Mgmt. Systems Soc. (charter), Inst. of Medicine of Nat. Acad. Scis., Am. Public Health Assn., Soc. for Epidemiologic Research.

BLUMBERG, MICHAEL ZANGWILL, allergist; b. Phila., July 29, 1945; s. Jerome Blumberg and Vivian Rose (Liebman) Steiger; m. Barbara Sue Gurman, June 9, 1973; children: Jessica Lynn, Jason Mark. AB, Brandeis U., 1967; MD, Jefferson Med. Coll., 1971; MSHA., Va. Commonwealty U., 1998. Bd. cert. pediatrics, allergy and immunology. Intern, resident N.Y. Hosp., Cornell U. Med. Ctr., 1971-73; fellow in allergy and immunology Nat. Jewish Hosp.-U. Colo. Med. Ctr., 1973-75; chief allergy sect. major Scott Air Force Base, Ill., 1975-77; physician-ptnr. Va. Allergy and Asthma Assocs., Richmond, 1977—, mng. ptnr., 1998—; asst. clin. prof. pediatrics Med. Coll. Va., Richmond, 1977—; chief of allergy Children's Hosp. of Richmond, 1987—; ptnr. Clin. Rsch., Richmond, 1998—; med. advisor Rhone Poulenc Rorer, Allen Hansburys, Glaxo, Marion Merrell Dow Inc. Contbr. articles and abstracts to profl. jours.; contbg. editor: Review in Allergy, 1978; mem. editl. bd. Jour. Asthma, 1996—. Bd. dirs. Jewish Cmty. Ctr., Richmond, 1984-87; exec. com. pres., bd. dirs., chmn. quality assurance, bd. govs. Beth Shalom Home Va., Richmond, 1987—; bd. dirs. endowment fund, mem. budget com. Jewish Fedn. Fellow Va. Allergy Soc. (program dir. 1989-90), Am. Coll. Allergy, Asthma and Immunology (pub. rels. com.), Coll. Chest Physicians, Am. Acad. Pediatrics; mem. Am. Coll. Allergy Sports Medicine (practice stds. com. 1994-95), Am. Acad. Allergy, Asthma and Immunology (mem. managed care com.), Am. Thoracic Soc., Friends of Brandeis Athletics, Masons, Phi Kappa Phi (mem. Va. Commonwealth U. chpt. 1999). Jewish. Avocations: American history, aerobic exercise. Home: 1602 Swansbury Dr Richmond VA 23233-4628 Office: Va Allergy and Asthma Assocs 7605 Forest Ave Ste 103 Richmond VA 23229-4936

BLUMBERG, NAOMI, symphony musician, educator; b. Chgo.; married. Student, Northwestern U., Juilliard Sch. Music; B in Mus. Edn., Roosevelt U., Chgo.; studied with Karl Fruh, Dudley Powers, Bernard Greenhouse, Frank Miller, Claus Adam. Cellist Oregon Symphony, Portland, 1965—; prin. cellist West Coast Chamber Orchestra, 1980-90, North Coast Chamber Orchestra, 1972-77; cellist Portland Opera Orchestra, 1973-84, prin. cellist, 1979-80; private instr. Community Mus. Ctr., Portland, 1965—, dir., coach chamber mus. program, 1985—; founder and cellist Trio Encore, 1992—; instr. U. Portland, Pacific U., Portland State U.; adjudicator OMTA Syllabus, and others. Recipient Gruber award Chamber Mus. Am., 1993. Mem. MNTA, Am. String Tchrs. Assn., Oregon Cello Soc. (cofounder, pres. 1984-96). Office: Community Music Ctr 3350 SE Francis St Portland OR 97202-3066*

BLUMBERG, PETER STEVEN, manufacturing company executive; b. Bklyn., Feb. 18, 1944; s. Howard G. and Lily G. (Goldberg) B.; m. Judith E. Pauly, Apr. 22, 1967; children: Ann Pauly, Matthew Edward, Heather Rebecca, Emily Jessica. BS, U. Va., 1967. Salesman Coll. House, Inc., Westbury, N.Y., 1967-71; sales mgr. Coll. House, Inc., Westbury, 1971-76, gen. mgr., 1977-78; sec.-treas. Sch. Tchrs. Supply Corp., Westbury, N.Y., 1979—; pres. College House, Richmond, Va., 1979—. Rsch. assoc. Fred Hutchinson Cancer Rsch. Ctr., Seattle; active Nat. Right-to-work Legal Def. Found., United Jewish Appeal-Operation Exodus, World Jewish Congress, Leukemia Soc. Am., Coalition to Stop Gun Violence, Handgun Control, Inc., Simon Wiesenthal Ctr. Holocaust Studies, Ams. Against Union Control of Govt., Jewish Chautaquqa Soc., Hebrew Immigrant Aid Soc.; charter supporter U.S. Holocaust Meml. Coun. Mem. Nat. Assn. Coll. Stores, Imprinted Sportswear Assn., Screenprinting & Graphic Imaging Assn. Internat., U. Va. Alumni Assn. (life), Hurrycanes Running Club. Jewish. Home: 817 Colony Bluff Pl Richmond VA 23233 Office: 1400 Chamberlayne Ave Richmond VA 23222

BLUMBERG, PHILIP FLAYDERMAN, real estate developer; b. Miami, Fla., Nov. 10, 1957; s. David and Lee (Dickens) B.; m. Lina Esther Waingortin, Apr. 13, 1986; children: David, Peter, Douglas. BBA, U. N.C., 1979; MBA, Harvard U., 1983. Pres. Am. Ventures Corp., Miami, Fla., 1979—; mng. ptnr. Banyan Reach ltd., Cutler Ridge, Fla., 1979; pres. Realdata Info. Systems, Inc., Miami, 1984, Am. Ventures Realty Corp., Miami, 1985, Am. Ventures Realty Investors, Miami, 1990; chmn. exam. com. Profl. Savs. Bank, Coral Gables, Fla., 1985-87. Trustee Colony Performing Arts Theatre, Miami Beach, Fla., 1985; mem. U. Miami Venture Coun., Coral Gables, 1984; co-chmn. Japan-Miami Bus. Coun., 1987-94; trustee Beacon Coun., 1988—, bd. dirs. 1997—; bd. dirs. Downtown Devel. Authority, City of Miami, 1988-94, exec. com., 1992—, chmn. transp. com., 1988—; bd. dirs. Dade County Task Force on Empowerment & Enterprise Zones, 1993—, Brickell Area Assn., 1988—; mem. bd. trustees Temple Israel, 1989-93; chmn. Orange Bowl Spl. Events Com., 1993—; adv. coun. Orange Bowl Com., 1994—; chmn. Olympic Soccer Organizing Com., South Fla., 1993-96; bd. dirs. Dade County Transit 2020 Coalition, 1993—; mem. Tampa Bay Partnership, 1995—; mem. State of Fla. Wages Coalition for Dade and Monroe Counties, 1997—, Joint Edn. Partnership Bd. Dirs., 1997—. Mem. Japan-Am. Soc. South Fla. (bd. dirs. 1988-89), Japan Soc. South Fla. (bd. dirs. 1990-94), Fla. C. of C. (bd. dirs. 1997—), Greater Miami C. of C. (bd. govs. 1992—, exec. com. vice chmn. for bus. and industry/econ. devel. 1994-97), Greater Miami Fgn. Trade Zone (bd. dirs. 1996—), Greater Miami C. of C. (chmn. welfare reform task force 1996—, chmn. internat. econ. group 1997-98, first vice chmn. 1998—), Miami Dade Cmty. Coll. Found. (bd. dirs. 1998—), Miami-Dade County Empowerment Zone Task Force. Home: 10440 SW 53rd Ave Coral Gables FL 33156-3414 Office: Am Ventures Corp 255 Alhambra Cir Ste 1100 Coral Gables FL 33134-7400

BLUMBERG, PHILLIP IRVIN, law educator; b. Balt., Sept. 6, 1919; s. Hyman and Bess (Simons) B.; m. Janet Helen Mitchell, Nov. 17, 1945 (dec. 1976); children: William A.M., Peter M., Elizabeth B., Bruce M.; m. Ellen Ash Peters, Sept. 16, 1979. AB, Harvard U., 1939, JD, 1942; LLD (hon.), U. Conn., 1994. Bar: N.Y. 1942, Mass. 1970. Assoc. Willkie, Owen, Otis, Farr & Gallagher, N.Y.C., 1942-43, Szold, Brandwen, Meyers and Blumberg, N.Y.C., 1946-66; pres., chief exec. officer United Ventures Inc., 1962-67; pres., chief exec. officer, trustee Federated Devel. Co., N.Y.C., 1966-68, chmn. fin. com., 1968-73; prof. law Boston U., 1966-74; dean U. Conn. Sch. Law, Hartford, 1974-84, prof. law, 1984-89, dean and prof. law emeritus, 1989—; bd. dirs. Verde Exploration Ltd.; mem. legal adv. com. to bd. dirs. N.Y. Stock Exch., 1989-93; advisor corp. governance project, restatement of suretyship and restatement of agy. Am. Law Inst.; vis. lectr. U. Brabant, Tilburg, Netherlands, 1985, U. Internat. Bus. and Econs., Beijing, 1989, U. Sydney, 1992, Jagiellonian U., Cracow, Poland, 1992. Author: Corporate Responsibility in a Changing Society, 1972, The Megacorporation in American Society, 1975, The Law of Corporate Groups: Procedure, 1983, The Law of Corporate Groups: Bankruptcy, 1985, The Law of Corporate Groups: Substantive Common Law, 1987, The Law of Corporate Groups: General Statutory Law, 1989, The Law of Corporate Groups: Specific Statutory Law, 1992, The Multinational Challenge to Corporation Law, 1993, The Law of Corporate Groups: State Statutory Law, 1995, The Law of Corporate Groups: Enterprise Liability, 1998; mem. editl. bd. Harvard Law Rev., 1940-42, treas., 1941-42; contbr. articles to profl. jours. Trustee Black Rock Forest Preserve, Inc.; trustee emeritus Conn. Bar Found. Capt. USAAF, 1943-46, ETO. Decorated Bronze Star. Mem. ABA, Conn. Bar Assn., Am. Law Inst., Hartford Club, Harvard Club (Boston), Army & Navy Club (Washington), Phi Beta Kappa, Delta Upsilon. Home: 791 Prospect Ave Apt B-5 Hartford CT 06105-4224 Office: U Conn Sch Law 65 Elizabeth St Hartford CT 06105-2213

BLUMBERG, SHERRY HELENE, Jewish education educator; b. Mar. 7, 1947. BA in Drama Edn., U. Ariz., 1969; MA in Librarianship, San Jose State U., 1973; MA in Jewish Edn., Hebrew Union Coll., L.A., 1976, PhD in Jewish Edn., 1991. Sr. reference specialist Stanford (Calif.) U. Libr., 1969-73; dir. edn. B'nai Israel, Sacramento, 1976-79, Temple Israel, Long Beach, Calif., 1979-85; assoc. prof. Jewish edn. Hebrew Union Coll.-Jewish Inst. Religion, N.Y.C., 1985-99; vis. assoc. prof. Jewish edn. Gratz Coll., York, Pa., 1999; dir. edn. Temple Shalom, Milw., 1999—. Author: God: The Eternal Challenge, 1980, A Teacher's Guide To Rooftop Secrets and Other Stories of Anti-semitism, 1987; co-author: Death, Burial and Mourning in the Jewish Tradition, 1978, Divorce in the Jewish Tradition, 1979, Teaching Jewish Theology, Spirituality and Gode, 1999. Mem. ASCD, Internat. Seminar on Religion, Edn. and Values, Assn. Profs. and Rschrs. in Religious Edn. (mem. nat. bd. 1993—), Religious Edn. Assn. (exec. bd. 1991—, acting pres. 1995-96, pres. 1999—), Union Am. Hebrew Congregations (exec. bd. commn. Jewish edn. 1997—), Assn. Supervision and Curriculum Devel. Office: Congregation Shalom Jewish Inst Religion 7630 N Santa Monica Blvd Milwaukee WI 53217

BLUME, JOHN AUGUST, consulting civil engineer; b. Gonzales, Calif., Apr. 8, 1909; s. Charles August and Vashti (Rankin) B.; m. Ruth Clarissa Reed, Sept. 14, 1942 (dec. 1984); m. Jene Frances Osborn, Aug. 28, 1985. A.B., Stanford, 1932, C.E., 1934, Ph.D., 1966. Constrn. engr. San Francisco-Oakland Bay Bridge, 1935-36; individual practice civil and structural engring. San Francisco, 1945-57; pres. John A. Blume & Assocs., San Francisco, 1957-81, chmn., sr. cons., 1980-85; now pvt. cons. Hillsborough, Calif.; past mem., chmn. adv. council Sch. Engring., Stanford U.; past chmn. adv. com. Earthquake Engring. Research Center, U. Calif. at Berkeley.; cons. prof. civil engring. Stanford U. Author: A Machine for Setting Structures and Ground into Forced Vibration, 1935, Structural Dynamics in Earthquake Resistant Design, 1958, A Reserve Energy Technique for the Design and Rating of Structures in the Inelastic Range, 1960, Dynamic Characteristics of Multistory Buildings, 1969; co-author: Design of Multistory Reinforced Concrete Buildings for Earthquake Motions, 1961, An Engineering Intensity Scale for Earthquakes and Other Ground Motion, 1970, The SAM Procedure for Site-Acceleration-Magnitude Relationships, 1977; Contbr. articles to profl. jours. John A. Blume Earthquake Engring. Center at Stanford U. named in his honor. Mem. Nat. Acad. Engring., Structural Engrs. Assn. Calif. (pres. 1949), Cons. Engrs. Assn. Calif. (pres. 1959), ASCE (hon.; pres. San Francisco sect. 1960, Moisseiff award 1953, 61, 69, Ernest E. Howard award 1962), Seismol. Soc. Am. (medal 1986), N.Y. Acad. Scis. (hon. life), Soc. Am. Mil. Engrs., Internat. Assn. Earthquake Engring. (hon.), Earthquake Engring. Research Inst. (hon.; pres. 1977-81, medal 1991), Sigma Xi, Tau Beta Pi. Home and Office: 85 El Cerrito Ave Hillsborough CA 94010-6805

BLUME, JUDY SUSSMAN, author; b. Elizabeth, N.J., Feb. 12, 1938; d. Rudolph and Esther (Rosenfeld) Sussman; m. John M. Blume, Aug. 15, 1959 (div. Jan. 1975); children: Randy Lee, Lawrence Andrew; m. George Cooper, June 6, 1987; 1 stepchild, Amanda. B.A. in Edn., NYU, 1960; LHD (hon.), Kean Coll., 1987, Endicott Coll., 1995. Author: (fiction) including The One in the Middle is the Green Kangaroo, 1969, Iggie's House, 1970, Are You There God? It's Me, Margaret (selected as outstanding children's book 1970), Freckle Juice, 1971, Then Again, Maybe I Won't, 1971, It's Not the End of the World, 1972, Tales of a 4th Grade Nothing, 1972, Otherwise Known as Sheila the Great, 1972, Deenie, 1973, Blubber, 1974, Forever, 1975, Starring Sally J. Freedman as Herself, 1977, Superfudge, 1980, Tiger Eyes, 1981, The Pain and the Great One, 1984, Just As Long As We're

Together, 1987, Fudge-A-Mania, 1990, Here's to You, Rachel Robinson, 1993, others; (adult novels) Wifey, 1977, Smart Women, 1984, Summer Sisters, 1998; (other writings) Letters to Judy: What Kids Wish They Could Tell You, 1986,; exec. producer (25 min. film) Otherwise Known As Sheila The Great, Barr Films, 1988. Founder, trustee The Kids Fund, 1981. Recipient Carl Sandburg Freedom to Read award Chgo. Pub. Libr., 1984, The Civil Liberties award ACLU, 1986, John Rock award Ctr. for Population Options, 1986, Margaret A. Edwards for lifetime achievement ALA, 1996, numerous Children's Choice award, U.S.A., Europe, Australia. Mem. Authors Guild (bd. dirs.), Nat. Coalition Against Censorship (adv. bd.), Soc. Children's Book Writers (bd. dirs.). Jewish. Office: care William Morris Agy 1325 Ave of Ams New York NY 10019

BLUME, LAWRENCE DAYTON, lawyer; b. Kansas City, Mo., July 7, 1948; s. Dayton G. and Meredith L. (Bruns) B. BA, U. Ariz., 1970; JD, U. Mo., 1974. Bar: Mo. 1974, D.C. 1989, U.S. Dist. Ct. (we. dist.) Mo. 1974, U.S. Ct. Appeals (fed. cir.) 1984, U.S. Supreme Ct. 1978, U.S. Tax Ct. 1980, U.S. Ct. Internat. Trade 1981, N.Y. 1996. Ptnr. Swanson, Midgley, Gangwere, Clarke & Kitchin, Kansas City, 1974-80; prin. Miller & Blume, P.C., Washington, 1980-89; ptnr. Graham & James, Washington, 1989—, D.C. mng. ptnr., 1992-94; N.Y. mng. ptnr. Graham & James LLP, N.Y.C., 1994-98, firm chmn., 1998—; lectr. Nat. Assn. Fgn. Trade Zones, Washington, 1981—, Am. Assn. Exporters and Importers, N.Y.C., 1984—, various colls., univs. and trade groups, 1980—; prin. instr. Seminar on Internat. Bus. Transactions and Litigation Techniques. Mem. ABA, Inter-Am. Bar Assn. (sr.), Internat. Trade Bar Assn., Am. Assn. Exporters and Importers, Nat. Dem. Club, Order of Barristers. Democrat. Office: Graham & James LLP 885 3rd Ave Ste 2100 New York NY 10022-4834

BLUME, MARSHALL EDWARD, finance educator; b. Chgo., Mar. 31, 1941; s. Marshall Edward Blume and Helen Corliss (Frank) Gilbert; m. Loretta Ryan, June 25, 1966; children—Christopher, Caroline, Catherine. SB, Trinity Coll., Hartford, Conn., 1963; MBA, U. Chgo., 1965, PhD, 1968; MA (hon.), U. Pa., 1970. Lectr. applied math. Grad. Sch. Bus., U. Chgo., 1966, instr. bus. fin. and applied math., 1967; lectr. fin. U. Pa., Phila., 1967, asst. prof., 1968-70, assoc. prof., 1970-74, prof., 1974-78, Howard Butcher prof., 1978—, chmn. dept., 1982-86, assoc. dir. Rodney White Ctr., 1978-86; prin. Prudent Mgmt. Assocs., 1982—; dir. Rodney White Ctr., 1986—; mem. U.S. Compt. Gen. adv. bd. on Oct. 1987 stock market crash, 1987-88; prof. fin. European Inst., Brussels, 1975-76, New U. Lisbon, Portugal, 1982; vis. prof. Stockholm Sch., spring 1976, U. Brussels, 1975. Author: Mutual Funds and Other Institutional Investors, 1970, The Changing Role of the Individual Investor, 1978, The Structure and Reform of the U.S. Tax System, 1985, Revolution on Wall Street: The Rise and Fall of the New York Stock Exchange, 1993; editor: Encyclopedia of Investments, 1982, The Complete Guide to Investment Opportunities, 1984; assoc. editor Jour. Fin. and Quantitative Analysis, 1967-76, Jour. Fin. Econs., 1976-81, Jour. of Portfolio Mgmt., 1985—; mng. editor Jour. Fin., 1977-80, assoc. editor, 1985-88, Jour. of Fin. Income, 1990—. Contbr. articles to profl. publs. Trustee Trinity Coll., Hartford, Conn., 1980-86, Rosemont (Pa.) Sch., 1991-93; commr. Bi-Partisan Commn. on Pa. Pension Fund Investments, 1989-93. Mem. Am. Fin. Assn. (officer 1977-80), Am. Econs. Assn., Fin. Economist Roundtable, New Castle (Pa.) Sailing Club, NASD (chmn. econ. adv. bd. 1998). Home: 204 Woodstock Rd Villanova PA 19085-1419 Office: U Penn Rodney L White Ctr Fin Rsch 3250 Steinberg Hall Philadelphia PA 19104

BLUME, MARTIN, physicist; b. Bklyn., Jan. 13, 1932; s. Julius and Frances (Cohen) B.; m. Sheila Bierman, June 12, 1955; children—Frederick, Janet. A.B., Princeton U., 1954; A.M., Harvard U., 1956, Ph.D., 1960. Fulbright rsch. fellow Tokyo U., 1959-60; rsch. assoc. Atomic Energy Rsch. Establishment, Harwell, Eng., 1960-62; with Brookhaven Nat. Lab., Upton, N.Y., 1962—; sr. physicist Brookhaven Nat. Lab., 1970—, head solid state physics, dep. chmn. physics dept., 1975-79, assoc. dir., 1981-84, dep. dir., 1984-96; editor-in-chief Am. Phys. Soc., Ridge, N.Y., 1997—. NSF grantee, 1973-78; E.O. Lawrence award Dept. of Energy, 1981. Fellow Am. Acad. Arts and Scis., Am. Phys. Soc., AAAS, N.Y. Acad. Scis.; mem. Phi Beta Kappa, Sigma Xi. Home: 284 Greene Ave Sayville NY 11782-3003 Office: Brookhaven Nat. Lab. Physics Dept Bldg 510 Upton NY 11973 also: Am Phys Soc One Research Rd Ridge NY 11961

BLUME, PAUL CHIAPPE, lawyer; b. Omaha, Oct. 11, 1929; s. Herman Alexander and Marie (Simoni) B.; m. Mary Lou Higgins, June 28, 1958; children—Nancy, Julia, Paul II, William. BS in Commerce, Loyola U., Chgo., JD. Bar: Ill. 1957. Legal sect. mgr. Aldens Inc., 1957-58; assoc. Lord, Bissell & Brook, 1959-63, of counsel, 1983—; v.p., gen. counsel Nat. Assn. Ind. Insurers, Des Plaines, Ill., 1963-83, Ill. Ins. Info. Svc., 1987-96, Ill. Ins. Conf., Chgo., 1984-96; pres. Ins. Briefs, Inc., 1984—. Capt. U.S. Army, 1951-53. Mem. Ill. State Bar Assn., Chgo. Bar Assn., Fedn. Ins. Counsel, Turnberry Country Club (Crystal Lake, Ill.). Office: 115 S La Salle St Chicago IL 60603-3801

BLUME, PETER FREDERICK, museum director; b. Syracuse, N.Y., June 5, 1946; s. Edward Frederick and Charlotte (Murray) B.; m. Karolyn Waller Vreeland, Oct. 4, 1980 (div. 1998); 1 child, Susanna. BFA, Syracuse U., 1967, postgrad., 1972-73; postgrad., Attingham Summer Sch., Eng., 1976, Mus. Mgmt. Inst., Berkeley, Calif., 1986. Curator Allentown (Pa.) Art Mus., 1974-84, dir., 1984—; mem. museums panel Pa. Council on Arts, Harrisburg, 1983-87. Author exhbn. catalogs. Mem. Hist. Archtl. Rev. Bd., Allentown, 1978-83; acquisitions com. Hist. Bethlehem (Pa.) Inc., 1982—; mem. Old Allentown Preservation Assn., 1977—. Served with U.S. Army, 1967-73. Rockefeller Found. fellow Met. Mus. Art, N.Y.C., 1973-74. Mem. Assn. Art. Mus. Dirs., Am. Assn. Mus., Mid-Atlantic Mus. Conf. Lodge: Rotary. Home: 1411 W Hamilton St Apt 6B Allentown PA 18102-4256 Office: Allentown Art Mus PO Box 388 Allentown PA 18105-0388

BLUME, RICHARD STEPHEN, medical company executive, physician; b. Jan. 23, 1958. BS in Engring., Columbia U., 1980; MD, N.Y. Med. Coll., 1984; MPH, Rutgers U., 1991. Med. officer U.S. Army, 1984-89; intern Walter Reed Army Med. Ctr., 1984-85; chief resident Occupl. Medicine Rutgers, Piscataway, N.J., 1990-91; v.p. Sandler Occupl. Medicine Assocs., Melville, N.Y., 1991—; founder, pres. SelfTest, Inc., Northport, N.Y., 1998—. Fellow Am. Coll. Preventive Medicine; mem. Tau Beta Pi, Alpha Omega Alpha. E-mail: selftest1@aol.com. Home: 18 Beach Ave Northport NY 11768

BLUMEL, JOSEPH CARLTON, university president; b. Kansas City, Mo., Mar. 3, 1928; s. Joseph F. and Lillian M. (Spinner) B.; m. Priscilla Bryant, June 16, 1961; children—Christina, Carolyn. B.S., U. Nebr., 1950, M.A., 1956; Ph.D., U. Oreg., 1965; LL.D. (hon.), U. Hokkaido, Japan, 1976. Prof. econs. Portland (Oreg.) State U., 1968, dean undergrad. studies, assoc. dean faculty, 1968-70, v.p. acad. affairs, 1970-74, pres., 1974-86, pres. emeritus, disting. sr. prof., 1986—. Served with U.S. Army, 1951-53. Mem. Phi Kappa Phi, Alpha Kappa Psi, Beta Gamma Sigma. Home: 9580 SW Melnore St Portland OR 97225-4137

BLUMENAU, IRIS WARECH, nursing consultant; b. Newark, Dec. 12, 1928; m. William Blumenau, Aug. 20, 1949 (dec.); 1 child, Bonnie Kaplan. Diploma, Newark Beth Israel Hosp., 1949; BA, Jersey City State Coll., 1975. Office mgr., bus. adminstr. Ctr. for Dermatology, P.A., West Orange, N.J., 1952-89; ret., 1989; pvt. cons. setting up and running med. office, 1989—.

BLUMENAUER, EARL, congressman; b. Portland, Oreg., Aug. 16, 1948. BA, Lewis and Clark Coll., 1970, JD, 1976. Asst. to pres. Portland State U., 1971-73; mem. Oreg. Ho. of Reps., 1973-79; county commr. Multnomah County, Portland, 1979-87; mem. Portland City Coun., 1987-96, 104th-106th Congresses from 3d Oreg. dist., 1996—; mem. transp. com., 1996—; mem. water resources and the environment com. Avocations: bicycling, running. Office: US House of Reps 1406 Longworth HOB Washington DC 20515-3703 also: 516 SE MorrisonSte 250 Portland OR 97214

BLUMENFELD, CHARLES RABAN, lawyer; b. Seattle, May 24, 1944; s. Irwin S. and Freda I. (Raban) B.; children: David, Lisa. BA, U. Wash., JD, 1969. Bar: Wash. 1969, U.S. Dist. Ct. (we. dist.) Wash. 1969, U.S. Ct. Appeals (9th cir.) 1975, U.S. Supreme Ct. 1979, U.S. Dist. Ct. D.C. 1981, U.S. Ct. Appeals (D.C. cir.) 1981. Legis. counsel U.S. Senator Henry M. Jackson, Washington, 1969-72; ptnr. Bogle & Gates, Seattle, 1973-99, Perkins & Coie, Seattle, 1999—. Mem. ABA (sect. natural resources, energy and environment). Office: Perkins & Coie 1201 3rd Ave 48th Fl Seattle WA 98101-3099*

BLUMENFELD, JEFFREY, lawyer, educator; b. N.Y.C., May 13, 1948; s. Martin and Helen Kay (Smith) B.; m. Laura Madeline Ross, June 11, 1970; children: Jennifer Ross Blumenfeld, Joshua Ross Blumenfeld. AB in Religious Thought cum laude, Brown U., 1969; JD, U. Pa., 1973. Bar: D.C. 1973. Asst. U.S. atty. U.S. Atty. for D.C., Washington, 1975-79; trial atty. Antitrust div. U.S. Dept. of Justice, Washington, 1973-75, sr. trial atty. U.S. versus AT&T staff, 1979-82, asst. chief spl. regulated industries, 1982-84, chief U.S. versus AT&T staff, 1984; ptnr. Blumenfeld & Cohen, Washington, 1984—; v.p., gen. counsel Rhythms Net Connections, 1997—; adj. prof. Georgetown U. Law Ctr., Washington, 1983—. Bd. dirs. Charles E. Smith Jewish Day Sch., Washington, 1991-93. Democrat. Jewish. Office: Blumenfeld & Cohen 1615 M St NW Ste 700 Washington DC 20036-3214

BLUMENFELD, ROCHELLE S. REZNIK, artist; b. Pitts., June 19, 1936; d. Lawrence S. and Rose (Fairman) Reznik; m. Irving L. Blumenfeld, Dec. 3, 1955; children: Harold E., Beth A., Louis C. Student, Carnegie Mellon U.; student of, Samuel Rosenberg. Exhibited in one and two person shows at Regent House, Pitts., 1962, Arts and Crafts Ctr., Pitts., 1966, Pitts. Plant for Art, 1973, 75, 80, 83, Wellsboro Artmobile, 1967, Carnegie Mus. of Art, Pitts., 1971, Gallery G., Pitts., 1987, Jewish Cmty. Ctr., Pitts., 1997, Pitts. Theol. Sem., 1999, others; group exhbns. include Regent House, Carnegie Mus. of Art, Three Rivers Arts Festival, Pitts., Pitts. Plan for Art, Assoc. Artists of Pitts., Associated Artist Exhbn., Dunferline, Scotland, Copley Soc., Boston, Westmoreland Mus. Art, Greensburg, Pa., Americans in Paris, Paris; represented in collections at U. Pitts., Nat. Steel Co., Carnegie Mus. of Art, Mellon Bank, Pitts., Humble Oil Co., Enjay, N.J., Blue Cross of Western Pa., Pitts., Beth Israel Synagogue, Greenville, S.C., Allegheny Steel Co., Pitts., Blount Inc., Montgomery, Ala., others; subject of articles. Recipient numerous awards for art works. Mem. Assoc. Artists of Pitts., Pitts. Ctr. for the Arts, Am. Guild Judaic Art.

BLUMENFELD, WARREN JAY, writer, educator; b. N.Y.C., May 27, 1947; s. Howard and Blanche (Mahler) B. BA in Sociology and Music, San Jose State U., 1969; MEd, Boston Coll., 1974; postgrad., U. Mass., Amherst, 1994—. Cert. spl. edn., secondary tchr., Mass. Founder, dir. Nat. Gay Student Ctr., Washington, 1971-73; tchr. Perkins Sch. for the Blind, Watertown, Mass., 1973-80; features editor Gay Cmty. News, Boston, 1980-81; diversity workshop facilitator Office Tng. and Devel. U. Mass., Amherst, 1995-96, also at colls., high schs. and bus., 1971—; tchg. asst. Sch. Edn., U. Mass., 1996—. Author: AIDS and Your Religious Community, 1991; co-author: Looking at Gay and Lesbian Lfe, 1988; editor: Homophobia: How We All Pay the Price, 1992; editor-in-chief Jour. Gay, Lesbian and Bisexual Identity, 1994—; co-prodr. Cambridge Documentary Films, 1980-82. Recipient Making a Difference award Boston Mag., 1993, James Baldwin Lit. award Boston Gay and Lesbian Polit. Alliance, 1994; U. Mass. grantee, 1996. Mem. Am. Ednl. Rsch. Assn. (Book award 1989), Nat. Gay and Lesbian Task Force, Editors of Learned Jours., Nat. Writers Union. Jewish. Avocation: playing violin. Home: PO Box 929 Northampton MA 01061-0929

BLUMENFELD-KOSINSKI, RENATE, French educator; b. Apr. 10, 1952. BA, Rutgers U., 1975; PhD, Princeton U., 1980. Assoc. prof. Columbia U., N.Y.C., 1989-93; assoc. prof. U. Pitts., 1994-98, prof. French, 1998—.

BLUMENGOLD, JEFFREY GENE, health care financial and reimbursement expert; b. Dec. 25, 1950; s. Irving and Marjorie (Freeman) B.; m. Vivienne Colletti, Oct. 15, 1972; children: Stacey, Craig. BBA, Bernard M. Baruch Coll., 1973, CUNY, 1973; MBA, CUNY, 1976. CPA, N.Y., N.J. Asst. mgr. royalty acctg. MacMillan Pub. Corp., N.Y.C., 1973-74; tchr. acctg. Port Richmond H.S., S.I., 1974-75; dir.-provider audit dept. Empire Blue Cross and Blue Shield, N.Y.C., 1976-77, 78-88; acct. Pannell, Kerr, Foster & Co., N.Y.C., 1977-78; dir. fin. Cath. Med. Ctr. Bklyn. and Queens, 1988-91; ptnr. in charge of health care svcs. M.R. Weiser & Co. LLP, N.Y.C., 1991—; former vice chmn. bd. Ctr. for Home Health Devel., 1995-97; bd. dirs. HomeHealth Assembly of N.J.; adj. prof. acctg. Coll. S.I., CUNY, N.Y. Inst. Tech. With USAR, 1972—. Mem. AICPA, Inst. Mgmt. Accts., Healthcare Fin. Mgmt. Assn. (prin. and practices bd. 1999—), Nat. Prins. and Practices Bd., Nat. Assn. Home Care-Fin. Mgrs. Forum, N.Y. State Soc. CPA's (former chmn. health care instns. com.), Am. Acctg. Assn. Office: care MR Weiser & Co LLP 399 Thornall St Edison NJ 08837-2236

BLUMENKRANZ, MARK SCOTT, surgeon, researcher, educator; b. N.Y.C., Oct. 23, 1950; s. Edward and Helene (Cymberg) B.; m. Recia Kott, June 10, 1975. AB, Brown U., 1972, MD, 1975, MMS, 1976; postgrad., Stanford U., 1975-79, U. Miami, 1979-80. Intern, resident Stanford (Calif.) U. Med. Ctr., 1975-79; fellow Bascom Palmer Eye Inst. U. Miami, Fla., 1979-80; asst. prof. Bascom Palmer Eye Inst., Miami, 1980-85; assoc. prof. Wayne State U., Detroit, 1985-92; clin. prof. Stanford U., 1992—, dir. of retina, 1992—, chmn. dept. ophthalmology, 1997—; assoc. examiner Am. Bd. Ophthalmology. Mem. edit. bd. Ophthalmology, Retina; contbr. chpts. to books and articles to profl. jours.; inventor ophthalmic devices. Mem. bd. overseers Brown U. Sch. Medicine. Recipient Visual Scis. medal in Visual Scis. Rosenthal Found., 1990, Heed award Heed Found., 1988, Manpower award Rsch. to Prevent Blindness. Mem. Am. Acad. Ophthalmology (mem. preferred practice com., others), Macula Soc. (chmn. rsch. com. 1986-90), Assn. Rsch. in Vision and Ophthalmology (chmn. retina sect. 1987-90), Retina Soc. (mem. membership com.), Maimonodes Soc. (mem. exec. com.). Avocations: tennis, sailing, electronic music, fitness. Office: Stanford Univ Dept Ophthalmology Boswell A-157 Stanford CA 94305 also: 1225 Crane St Menlo Park CA 94025-4257

BLUMENSHINE, MAHLON, banker; b. Washington, Ill., May 11, 1928; s. Mahlon and Mabel Mae (Schick) B.; m. Carolyn Sue Longden, June 26, 1960; children: J. Wesley, Bradley Ward, Blake Alan. Standard Banking degree, So. Ill. U., 1967; Grad. Banking degree, U. Wis., 1974. V.p. Community Bank, East Peoria, Ill., 1956-75; pres., trust officer Sunnyland Bank, Washington, Ill., 1975—; also bd. dirs. Sunnyland Bank. Alderman City of Washington, Ill., 1979-83; treas. Dist. 50 Schs., Washington, 1983-87; past chmn. Easter Seal Drive, Heart Fund Drive, Cancer Fund Drive. Served as cpl. U.S. Army, 1950-52. Mem. Am. Inst. Banking (pres. cen. Ill. chpt. 1957-58), Washington C. of C., Am. Legion, VFW. Republican. Methodist. Lodge: Kiwanis. Avocations: stamp and coin collecting, gardening, golf. Home: 910 Hampton Rd Washington IL 61571-1258 Office: Sunnyland Bank Box 99 Washington IL 61571

BLUMENTHAL, ANNA CATHERINE, English educator; b. Providence, R.I., Feb. 7, 1952; d. Andrew J. and Marion (Allen) Sabol; m. Robert A. Blumenthal, Aug. 22, 1973; 1 child, Rachel A. BA, Univ. Rochester, 1974; M in Eng., Washington Univ., 1976, PhD, 1986. Asst. prof. Eng. Morris Brown Coll., Atlanta, 1989-93; asst. prof. Eng. Morehouse Coll., Atlanta, 1993-97, assoc. prof. Eng., 1997—; referee for articles, 1994; invited speaker at confs., 1992, 93, 97. Contbr. articles to profl. jours. Named Activity Dir. (with Joan Hildenbrand), U.S. Dept. Edn., 1991-93. Mem. MLA, South Atlantic MLA, College Lang. Assn., Nat. Coun. Tchrs. Eng., Ga. Coun. Tchrs. Eng., Philogical Assn. Carolinas. Office: Morehouse Coll Dept Eng 830 Westview Dr SW Atlanta GA 30314-3773

BLUMENTHAL, CARLENE MARGARET, vocational-technical school educator; d. Carl and Helen (Chervenak). BA, U. Ill., 1959; MA, Chgo. State U., 1969; student, No. Ill. U., Oxford, Eng., Nat. Louis U. Cert. in secondary lang. arts, social studies. Tutor Triton Coll., River Grove, Ill.; tchr. bus. English Robert Morris Coll., Chgo.; developer vocat. and bus. English curriculum Chgo. Pub. Schs.; participant Nat. Louis U. Right-o-Soar Project, 1990; presenter in field. Contbr. articles to profl. jours. Del. Dem. Nat. Conv., 1996. Tchr.-Sponsor of Yr., VFW, Ill., 1993; grantee U. Chgo., 1990, 91, 93; Mellon fellow, 1992-94, Annenberg fellow, 1995. Mem. NAFE, Am. Vocat. Assn., Nat. Coun. Tchrs. English (panel chair conv. 1996), Ill. Assn. Tchrs. English (workshop presenter 1995), Ill. Vocat. Assn. (affiliate mem. bd. dirs. 1997, del. Nat. Women's Rights Conv.), Ill. Fedn. Tchrs., Ill. Assn. for Advancement of Black and Vocat. Educators (workshop presenter 1992, bd. dirs. 1997), Chgo. Tchrs. Union (3 coms., workshop presenter 1994), Coalition Labor Union Women, Phi Delta Kappa (tchr. task force 1996). Home: 5649 W Leland Ave Chicago IL 60630-3221

BLUMENTHAL, EILEEN FLINDER, writer, theater educator; b. N.Y.C., Jan. 12, 1948; d. Philip and Diane (Flinder) B. BA, Brown U., 1968, MA, 1968; PhD, Yale U., 1978. Prof. theater arts Rutgers U., 1977—. Author: Julie Taymor: Playing with Fire, 1998, (USITT award), Joseph Charkin; contbr. articles, theater revs to newspapers, profl. jours. recipient George Jean Nathan award, 1988-89; Guggenheim fellow, NEH fellow. Mem. PEN, Am. Theater Critics Assn. Office: Theater Arts Dept Mason Gross Sch Arts Walters Hall Rutgers U 2 Chapel Dr New Brunswick NJ 08901-8527

BLUMENTHAL, FRITZ, printmaker, painter; b. Mainz, Germany, June 16, 1913; came to U.S., 1938, naturalized, 1944; s. Albert and Recha (Feibelmann) B.; m. Marianne Leiter, Mar. 31, 1947; children: John Frederick, Stephanie Ann. Student, U. Frankfort, Germany, 1931, U. Freiburg, Germany, 1932, U. Wurzburg, Germany, 1932-36; M.D., U. Bern, Switzerland, 1937. One-man shows: Albany Inst. History and Art, N.Y., 1952, Gutenberg Mus., Mainz, 1964, Kunstverein, Ulm, W.Ger., 1965, Kenneth Taylor Gallery, Nantucket, Mass., 1965, others; group shows: Audubon Artists, N.Y.C., 1945, Print Club Phila., 1960-72, Herbert E. Feist Gallery, N.Y.C., 1972, Pratt Graphic Ctr., 1974-77, U. Del. invitational: Disting. Mid-Atlantic Artists, 1980, Weintraub Gallery, N.Y.C., 1984, The Mt. Aramah Exhibition: The Art of Rockland and Orange, Arden, N.Y., 1986, Sragow Gallery, N.Y.C., 1988, Nat. Mus. Am. Art, Washington, 1988-89, 97, McNay Art Inst., San Antonio, 1989, Bibliothèque Nationale, Paris, 1992, Mus. Fine Arts, Boston, 1990-91, others; represented in permanent collections: Met. Mus. Art, N.Y.C., Nat. Gallery of Art, Washington, Nat. Mus. Am. Art, Washington, Smithsonian Instn., Washington, Stedelijk Mus. Amsterdam, Netherlands, Victoria and Albert Mus., London, Yale U. Art Gallery, Nat. Pinacothek, Athens, Greece, Bklyn. Mus., Mus. and Library, Lincoln Ctr., N.Y. Public Library, Mus. Modern Art, N.Y.C., Mus. Fine Arts, Boston, Bündner Kunstmuseum, Chur, Switzerland, Bibliothèque Nationale, Paris, The Israel Mus., Jerusalem, Tel Aviv Mus. Art, Morgan Guarantee Trust Co., N.Y.C., Gutenberg Mus., Mainz, Fed. Republic Germany, Kunstverein, Ulm, Fed. Republic Germany, St. Louis Art Mus., Mus. de les Arts Grafiques Barcelona, Spain, Mus. Nacional d'Art de Catalunya, Barcelona, Fogg Mus. Art, Harvard U., Cambridge, Mass., Staatliche Graphische Sammlung, Munich, Germany, Staatsgalerie Moderner Kunst, Munich, Herbert F. Johnson Mus. Art Cornell U., The Minn. Inst. Arts, Meml. Art Gallery U. Rochester, others; commns. include 48 program cover designs for Greater Middletown Arts Coun. and N.Y. State Coun. on Arts; author poetry pub. literary mags., analyzed in Deutsche Exilliteratur seit 1933 vol. 2, 1989; subject of books Das Neue Mainz: Fritz Blumenthal (Werner Spanner), 1964, The Art of Monoprint (La Liberté and Mogelon), 1974, others. Recipient First Prize in Painting Nantucket Art Assn., Mass., 1961. Home: 864 Silver Lake Scotchtown Rd Middletown NY 10941-1119

BLUMENTHAL, HAROLD JAY, microbiologist, educator; b. N.Y.C., Jan. 21, 1926; s. Louis Jacques and Rose (Peck) B.; m. Doris Ceren, June 18, 1950; children—Robert Martin, Steven Mark, David Alan. B.S., Ind. U., 1947; M.S., Purdue U., 1949, Ph.D., 1953. Postdoctoral fellow Inst. Cancer Research, Phila., 1953; research assoc. Rackham Arthritis Research unit U. Mich., 1954-56, instr. microbiology, 1954-56, asst. prof., 1956-62, assoc. prof., 1962-65; prof. dept. microbiology Stritch Sch. Medicine, Loyola U., Chgo., 1965-94; prof. emeritus, 1994—; chmn. dept. Stritch Sch. Medicine, Loyola U., 1965-86; mem. adv. panel NSF, 1961-63, dir. summer program, 1963-64; mem. adv. com. Nat. Acad. Scis., 1966-75; mem. biol. com. Argonne U. Assn.-Argonne Nat. Lab., 1972-75, chmn., 1973; vis. prof. Catholic U. Chile, 1972. Author: (with W.W. Yotis and T. Hashimoto) Appleton & Lange's Review of Microbiology, 1989, 3d edit., 1997; contbr. chpts. to books. Served with AUS, 1944-46. AEC fellow, 1952, Am. Cancer Soc. fellow, 1953, NIH fellow, 1963-64. Mem. AAAS, AAUP, Am. Soc. Microbiology (mem. council 1977-81, mem. com. on edn. 1959-71, chmn. 1961-64, mem. found. microbiology lectures com. 1983-86), Am. Acad. Microbiology (vis. prof.), Am. Inst. Biol. Scis. (mem. vis. high sch. biologist program 1959-64), Ill. Soc. Microbiology (pres. 1976, Tanner-Shaughnessy Merit award 1981), Am. Chem. Soc., Fedn. Am. Scientists, Sigma Xi. Office: Loyola U Stritch Sch Medicine 2160 S 1st Ave Bldg 105 Maywood IL 60153-3304*

BLUMENTHAL, HERMAN BERTRAM, accountant; b. Phila., Sept. 30, 1916; s. Bertram and Florence (Wax) B.; m. Elaine J. Belsinger, May 25, 1941; children—Bonni Ann, Herman Bertram III. Student, Oxford U., Birmingham U., Eng., Edinburgh U., Scotland; B.S., Wharton Sch., U. Pa., 1938. CPA, Pa. Pres. Harlan Products, Inc., Phila., 1958-65; sr. ptnr. Shestack, Blumenthal & Stein (C.P.A.'s), Phila., 1964-88; former lectr. Cambridge U., Eng. Mem. nat. panel arbitrators Am. Arbitration Assn. Sec., Greater Phila. Council of Temple Brotherhoods; chmn. bd. trustees Montgomery County Community Coll., 1969-77; bd. dirs. Elkins Park Free Library, Montgomery County March of Dimes; nat. bd. dirs. Assn. Community Coll. Trustees, 1976-82. Served to capt. USAAF, 1940-46, ETO. Mem. Mensa (internat. treas. 1970-76), B'nai Brith (trustee), Triple Nine Soc. Clubs: Ivy Hill Bridge (past pres.), Masons. Home: 1001 Chateau Twr 7050 Sunset Dr S Saint Petersburg FL 33707-2899

BLUMENTHAL, HERMAN THEODORE, physician, educator; b. N.Y.C., Apr. 8, 1913; s. Samuel and Jennie (Price) B.; m. Eleonore Gottlieb, Aug. 18, 1940 (dec. 1972); children: Daniels S., Frederic A.; m. Margaret B. Phillips, May 29, 1974; children: Edward P., Shana P. B.S., Rutgers U., 1934; M.S., U. Pa., 1936; Ph.D., Washington U., St. Louis, 1938, M.D., 1942. Resident in pathology Jewish Hosp., St. Louis, 1942-43; dir. labs of various hosps., 1945-65; asso. prof. pathology St. Louis U., 1947-52, adj. prof. community medicine, 1975—; mem. faculty Washington U., 1965—, research prof. gerontology, 1965—; dir. Midwest Med. Lab., 1965-82. Author: (with J.G. Probstein) Pancreatitis—A Clinical-Pathological Correlation, 1954; Editor: Cowdry's Arteriosclerosis—A Survey of the Problem, 2d edit, 1967, Medical Aspects of Gerontology, 1962, Interdisciplinary Topics in Gerontology, Vols. 1-8, 1968-71, Handbook of Diseases of Aging, 1981, Dilman's Elevational Hypothalmic Mechanisms in Aging and Disease, 1981; Contbr. articles on aging, transplanation, endocrinology, cancer, pathology to profl. jours.; editor Handbook of Diseases of Aging, 1983. Served to maj. M.C. AUS, 1942-45. Mem. Soc. Exptl. Biology and Medicine, Am. Heart Assn., Am. Diabetes Assn., Am. Assn. Cancer Research, Soc. Pathologists and Bacteriologists, Am. Soc. Exptl. Pathology, Gerontol. Soc., AAUP, Sigma Xi. Home: 6203 Washington Ave Saint Louis MO 63130-4847

BLUMENTHAL, JEFFREY MICHAEL, lawyer; b. Putnam, Conn., Apr. 5, 1960; s. Bernard Saunders and Sheila (Molans) B.; m. Catherine Gallo, Sept. 20, 1987; children: Matthew Samuel, Scott Benjamin. BA summa cum laude, U. Hartford, 1981; JD, U. Va., 1985. Bar: Mass. 1985, Conn. 1986, U.S. Dist. Ct. Conn. 1986, U.S. Dist. Ct. (so. and ea. dists.) N.Y. 1988. Law clk. to Chief Judge T.F. Gilroy Daly, U.S. Dist. Ct. for Conn., 1985-87; assoc. Debevoise & Plimpton, N.Y.C., 1987-89; atty. for law and regulatory affairs Aetna Life & Casualty Co., Hartford, Conn., 1989-90, counsel, 1990-96; counsel Aetna/U.S. Healthcare, Hartford, 1996-98; corp. bus. unit year 2000 project mgr. Aetna, Inc., Hartford, 1998—. Mem. Defense Rsch. Inst., 1997—, Economic Development Comm., 1996—, vice-chair, 1999—; bd. dirs. Main St. Partnership, 1996-97, co-chair Economic Restructuring Comm., 1996-97, co-dir. Hartford Area Mediation Program, 1991-93, mem.; mem. mediation program Weaver High Sch., Hartford; com. mem. State of Conn. Study of Mediation Programs, 1992-93; chmn. Town of Simsbury Recycling Com., 1993-94; mem. Conn. Lawyers Clearinghouse on Affordable Housing, 1990-92; mem. bd. visitors U. Hartford Coll. Arts and Scis., West Hartford, Conn., 1989-90. Hardy C. Dillard legal writing fellow U. Va., 1983-84. Mem. Raven Soc. Office: Aetna Inc 151 Farmington Ave Rm RE2L Hartford CT 06156-0002

BLUMENTHAL, KAREN, newspaper executive. Bus. editor Dallas Morning News, 1992-94; dep. bur. chief Dallas bur. The Wall St. Jour., 1994-96, bur. chief Dallas bur., 1996—. Office: The Wall St Jour 1201 Elm St Dallas TX 75270-2102*

BLUMENTHAL, MICHAEL CHARLES, writer, educator; b. Vineland, N.J., Mar. 8, 1949; s. Julius Ernst and Betty Blumenthal; m. Cynthia Mae Curtner, Oct. 2, 1982 (div. May 1984); m. Isabelle Germaine Leconte, Dec. 2, 1989; 1 child, Noah Gabriel. BA, SUNY, Binghamton, 1969; JD, Cornell U., 1974. Assoc. prof. English Harvard U., Cambridge, Mass., 1983-88, dir. creative writing, 1988-92; sr. Fulbright prof. Eotvos Lorand U., Budapest, Hungary, 1992-95; vis. prof. U. Haifa, Israel, 1996-97; vis. writer S.W. Tex. State U., San Marcos, 1997-98; disting. vis. poet Wichita (Kans.) State U., 1999; writer, editor Time-Life Books, Alexandria, Va., 1977-80; spl. asst. to chmn. NEH, Washington, 1980-81; prodr., dir. West German TV, Washington, 1981-83; Bingham poet-in-residence U. Louisville, 1982; sr. editor Cen. European U. Press, Budapest, 1988-92. Author: Laps, 1984 (Juniper prize 1994), The Wages of Goodness, 1992, Weinstock Among the Dying, 1993 (Ribelow prize 1994), When History Enters the House, 1998. Bd. dirs. Ptnrs. in Edn., Austin, Tex., 1998—, MacDowell Colony, Peterborough, N.H., 1985-88; trustee Am. U. Ctr. Aix-en-Provence, France, 1992—. NEA fellow, 1984, Ingram-Merrill fellow, 1985, Guggenheim fellow, 1988-89, Fulbright fellow, 1992-95. Mem. Internat. PEN, Acad. Am. Poets (Peter I. B. Lavan award 1986), Poets and Writers, N.Y. Bar Assn. Avocations: skiing, swimming, hiking, language study, translation. E-mail: mcblume@ibm.net. Home: 3311 Merrie Lynn Ave Austin TX 78722

BLUMENTHAL, RALPH HERBERT, natural science educator; b. N.Y.C., Feb. 24, 1925; s. Max and Celia (Sametsky) B.; m. Renee Cohen, Jan. 31, 1948; children: David S., Robert I., Meryl A. Orlando. BA, Bklyn. Coll., 1945, MA, 1949; PhD, NYU, 1956. Jr. engr. Hamilton Radio Corp., N.Y.C., 1945; lectr. physics Bklyn. Coll., 1946-48; physicist, project leader Naval Supply Activities, Bklyn., 1948-52; physicist, supr. test group Picatinny Arsenal, Dover, N.J., 1952; lectr. physics Bklyn. and Queens Colls., 1952-54; instr. physics CCNY, N.Y.C., 1954-61; assoc. mem. tech. and mgmt. staff Sperry Gyroscope Co., New Hyde Park, N.Y., 1958-63; sr. staff physicist Grumman Aerospace Corp., Bethpage, N.Y., 1963-70; adj. assoc. prof. physics Queensborough C.C., Queens, 1970-81; physics tchr. Sewanhaka H.S., Elmont, N.Y., 1970-88; adj. assoc. prof. physics Adelphi U. H.S. Program, 1976-87; adj. assoc. prof. natural sci. Hofstra U., Hempstead, N.Y., 1988—. Co-author: College Physics: A Programmed Aid, 4 vols., 1967, Spanish edit. (Fisica Basica), 1973; contbr. articles to profl. jours. Fellow AAAS; mem. Am. Phys. Soc. Avocations: history of science, bicycling, travel. Home: 15 Bonnie Dr Westbury NY 11590-2803 Office: Hofstra U Chemistry Dept Hempstead NY 11550

BLUMENTHAL, RICHARD, state attorney general; m. Cynthia Blumenthal; 4 children. BA, Harvard Coll.; JD, Yale U., 1973. Law clk. Justice Harry A. Blackmun, 1974-75; U.S. atty. State of Conn., 1977-81, former rep., 1984-87, senator, 1987-90, state atty. gen., 1991—. Sgt. USMCR. Office: Atty Gen Office 55 Elm St Hartford CT 06106-1797*

BLUMENTHAL, RICHARD CARY, construction executive, consultant; b. Bklyn., Dec. 18, 1951; s. Mervin Harold and Barbara June Blumenthal; m. Ginnilyn Hawkins; children: Aaron Joseph, Meredith Taylor. BS, U. N.H., 1974. Planner RECON Assocs., Hamilton, Mont., 1976-77; project mgr. Grizzly Mfg., Hamilton, 1977-78; profl. carpenter Ed Brown Constrn., Bainbridge Island, Wash., 1978-79; pres. Richard Blumenthal Constrn., Inc., Bainbridge Island, 1979—; instr. Bainbridge Island Community Sch., 1993—. Mem. pk. bd. coun. City of Winslow, 1989-90; bd. dirs. Bainbridge Island Pub. Libr., 1992-99; mem. Land Use Profls. Forum, 1992—; mem. advisory com. Bainbridge Island Park & Rec. Gymnastics Com., 1993-98. Mem. Ind. Bus. Assn., C. of C. Avocations: bicycling, hiking, rock climbing, music. Home and Office: 330 Nicholson Pl NW Bainbridge Island WA 98110

BLUMENTHAL, RONNIE, lawyer; b. Passaic, N.J., Nov. 27, 1944; d. Paul and Marga (Stern) B. BA, George Washington U., 1966, JD, 1969. Bar: D.C. 1969. Gen. atty. EEOC, Washington, 1969-71, spl. asst. to commr., acting chmn., 1971-78, sr. atty., 1978-82, dir. spl. svcs. staff, 1982-85, dir. compliance programs, 1985-91, acting dir. Office of Communications-Legis. Affairs, 1991-92; spl. asst. U.S. atty. Dept. Justice, Washington, 1992, dir. Office Fed. Ops., 1992—; legis. fellow U.S. Senate, 1982; chmn. Performance Review Bd., Exec. Resources Bd. Mem. ABA, D.C. Bar Assn., Fed. Bar Assn., Exec. Women in Govt., Womens Bar Assn. Home: 3701 Connecticut Ave NW Washington DC 20008-4556 Office: EEOC 1801 L St NW Rm 5001 Washington DC 20036-3811

BLUMER, DENNIS HULL, lawyer; b. Dayton, Ohio, Sept. 23, 1940; s. Robert Howard and Mary Eleanor Hull B.; m. Alice Painter Howard, Oct. 30, 1965; children: Mackenzie Hughes, Alexandra Paige. BA, Yale Coll., 1962, JD, 1965. Asst. to pres. Ctrl. State U., Wilberforce, Ohio, 1965-66; asst. to v.p. for adminstrn. U. Wis. Sys., Madison, 1966-68, spl. asst. to pres., 1968-71; exec. asst. to pres. U. Md., College Park, 1971-95; v.p., gen. counsel George Washington U., Washington, 1995—. E-mail: olmdhb@ogc.gwu.edu. Home: 2801 Davenport St NW Washington DC 20008 Office: George Washington U Ste 525 2100 Pennsylvania Ave NW Washington DC 20052

BLUMER, DONNA, councilwoman. Councilwoman City of Dallas, 1993—. Office: Dallas City Coun 1500 Marilla St Rm 5fn Dallas TX 75201-6300*

BLUMER, FREDERICK ELWIN, philosophy educator; b. Glencoe, Okla., Sept. 16, 1933; s. Edward H. and Eva Marie (Forbes) B.; m. Ann Louise Anderson, June 9, 1956; children—Frederick Edward, William Robert. BA, Millsaps Coll., 1955; BD, Emory U., 1958, PhD, 1962; postgrad., Georg August U., Goettingen, Germany, 1960-61. Ordained to ministry United Meth. Ch., 1962; chaplain, instr. philosophy and religion Nebr. Wesleyan U., Lincoln, 1962-63, asst. prof., 1963-65, assoc. prof., 1965-67, prof., 1967-76, v.p. acad. affairs, 1967-70, provost, v.p. acad. affairs, 1970-76; pres. Lycoming Coll., Williamsport, Pa., 1976-89; Moll prof. faith and life Baldwin-Wallace Coll., Berea, Ohio, 1989—; dean, dir. Graz (Austria) Ctr., 1972-73; mem. univ. senate United Meth. Ch., 1980-88, 93-97, pres., 1980-88, chmn. Commn. on Theol. Edn.; exec. com. Commn. Ind. Colls. and Univs. Pa., 1978-81, treas., 1988-89. Editor: Nebr. Wesleyan Univ. Press, 1967-76; Contbr. articles to profl. jours. Dir. edn. Lincoln United Way, 1971; bd. dirs. N.E. Lincoln YMCA, 1968-71, Lincoln Symphony Orch., 1971-76, Williamsport/Lycoming United Way, 1976-83; bd. mgrs. Williamsport Hosp., 1982-89; chmn. Found. Ind. Colls. Pa., 1987-88; bd. dirs. Pine Street Found., 1982-86, Lycoming Found., 1985-89. Recipient Pres.'s award Nebr. Wesleyan U., 1966; Cokesbury fellow, Dempster fellow, Rockefeller doctoral fellow Emory U. Mem. Nat. Assn. Schs., Colls., Univs. of United Meth. Ch. (pres. 1987-89), Williamsport-Lycoming C. of C. (dir., exec. com. 1976-85), Phi Kappa Phi, Pi Gamma Mu, Theta Phi, Omicron Delta Kappa. Republican. Home: 20798 Burgandy Dr Cleveland OH 44136-5602 Office: Baldwin-Wallace Coll Dept Religion Berea OH 44017-2088

BLUMKIN, LINDA RUTH, lawyer; b. N.Y.C., Aug. 25, 1944; d. Louis and Edith (Fortus) Blumkin. A.B. cum laude, Barnard Coll., 1964; LL.B. cum laude, Harvard U., 1967, LL.M., 1973. Bar: N.Y. 1968, U.S. dist. ct. (so. dist.) N.Y. 1969, U.S. Ct. Apls. (2nd cir.) 1969, U.S. Supreme Ct. 1982. Assoc. Fried, Frank, Harris, Shriver & Jacobson, N.Y.C., 1967-71, ptnr., 1979—; lectr. Boston U., 1971, asst. prof. mgmt., 1972-73; assoc. Breed, Abbott & Morgan, N.Y.C., 1973-77; asst. dir. Bur. Competition FTC, 1977-79. Mem. ABA, N.Y.C. Bar Assn. Office: Fried Frank Harris Shriver & Jacobson 1 New York Plz Fl 24 New York NY 10004-1901

BLUMMER, KATHLEEN ANN, counselor; b. Iowa Falls, Iowa, Apr. 17, 1945; d. Arthur G. and Julia C. (Ericson) Thorsbakken; m. Terry L. Blummer, Feb. 13, 1971 (dec. 1980); 1 child, Emily Erica. AA, Ellsworth Coll., Iowa Falls, 1965; BA, U. Iowa, 1967; postgrad., Northeastern Ill. U., 1969-70, U. N.Mex., 1980—; MA, Western N.Mex. U., 1973. Asst. buyer Marshall Field & Co., Chgo., 1967-68; social worker Cook County Dept. Pub. Aid, Chgo., 1968-69; tchr. Chgo. Pub. Schs., 1968-69; student fin. aid counselor Western N.Mex. U., Silver City, 1971-72; family social worker, counselor Southwestern N.Mex. Svcs. to Handicapped Children and Adults, Silver City, 1972-74; career edn. program specialist Galluo McKinley County (N.Mex.) Schs., 1974-76; dir. summer sch. Loving (N.Mex.) Mcpl. Schs., 1977; counselor, dept. chmn. Carlsbad (N.Mex.) Pub. Schs., 1977-82; counselor Albuquerque Pub. Schs., 1982—. Mem. AAUW (topic chmn. Carlsbad chpt., v.p. Albuquerque chpt.), N.Mex. Personnel and Guidance Assn., Theos Club, Highpoint Swim and Racquet Club (Albuquerque), Elks. Democrat. Lutheran.

BLUMOFE, ROBERT FULTON, motion picture producer, association executive; b. N.Y.C.; s. Julius and Fannie (Rosenstein) B.; children: Robert David, Joanna Beth. A.B., J.D., Columbia U. Bar: N.Y., Calif. Mem. legal dept. Paramount Pictures, Hollywood, Calif., 1946-52; producer TV films Revue Prodns. of MCA, Inc., Hollywood, 1952-53; v.p. charge prodn. and West Coast ops. United Artists Corp., Hollywood, 1953-66; ind. motion picture producer Hollywood, 1966—; guest lectr. univs.; mem. steering com. U. So. Calif. Film Conf.; v.p., trustee, chmn. exec. com. Motion Picture and TV Fund, recipient medallion of honor, 1968; dir. Am. Film Inst., West, Beverly Hills, Calif., 1977-81. Films include Yours, Mine and Ours, 1968, Pieces of Dreams, 1969, Bound for Glory (best picture nomination Acad. Motion Picture Arts and Scis., Christopher award), 1976 (Film Adv. Bd. award). Co-chmn. United Jewish Welfare Fund, 1959; So. Calif. chmn. Am.-Israel Cultural Found., 1963; bd. dirs. Los Angeles Philharmonic, 1964-70; pres. Permanent Charities Com., 1974-75. Served to 1st lt., ordnance AUS, 1943-45. Recipient Samuel Goldwyn Founders award Permanent Charities Com. Entertainment Industries, 1978; John Jay Disting. Alumni award Columbia Coll., 1981. Mem. John Jay Assos., Harlan Fiske Stone Assos., Acad. Motion Picture Arts and Scis. (bd. govs. 1978—), Am. Film Inst., Producers Guild Am. Home: 1100 Alta Loma Rd West Hollywood CA 90069-2455

BLUMRICH, JOSEF FRANZ, aerospace engineer; b. Steyr, Austria, Mar. 17, 1913; s. Franz and Maria Theresia (Mayr) B.; m. Hildegard Anna Schmidt-Elgers, Nov. 7, 1935; children: Michael Sebastian, Christoph, Stefan. BS in Aero. and Mech. Engring., Ingenieurschule Weimar (Germany), 1934. Engr., Gothaer Waggonfabrik A.G., Gotha, Germany, 1934-44; ct. interpreter U.S. Mil. Ct., Linz, Austria, 1946-51; dep. chief hydraulics dept. United Austrian Iron and Steel Works, Linz, 1951-59; structural design engr. Army Ballistic Missile Agy., Huntsville, Ala., 1959-61; chief structural engring. br. G.C. Marshall Space Flight Ctr., NASA, Huntsville, 1961-69, chief systems layout br., 1969-74; cons. in field, 1974—. Served with German Army, 1944-45. Recipient Apollo Achievement award NASA, 1969, Exceptional Service medal, 1972. Author: The Spaceships of Ezekiel, 1974; Kasskara, 1979; editorial cons. on space sci. and rocketry Scribner-Bantam English Dictionary, 1977; contbr. articles to profl. jours.; patentee in field. Mem. N.Y. Acad. Scis. Home: PO Box 433 Estes Park CO 80517-0433

BLUMROSEN, ALFRED WILLIAM, law educator; b. Detroit, Dec. 14, 1928; s. Sol and Frances (Netzorg) B.; m. Ruth L. Gerber, July 3, 1952; children: Steven Marshall, Alexander Bernet. BA, U. Mich., 1950, JD, 1953. Bar: Mich. 1953, N.J. 1961, N.Y. 1981. Sole practice Detroit, 1953-55; mem. faculty Rutgers Law Sch., Newark, 1955—, prof., 1961—, acting dean, 1974-75, Herbert J. Hannoch scholar, 1984, Thomas A. Cowan prof., 1986—; dir. fed.-state rels., chief conciliations U.S. EOOC, 1965-67, cons. to chmn., 1977-79; advisor U.S. Dept. Justice, HUD, 1968-72, U.S. Dept. Labor, 1995-96; of counsel Kaye, Scholer, Fierman, Hays & Handler, N.Y.C., 1979-82; dir. Ford Found. intentional discrimination project Rutgers U., Law Sch., 1998—. Author: Black Employment and the Law, 1971, Modern Law: The Law Transmission System and Equal Employment Opportunity, 1993; contbr. articles to profl. jours. Fulbright scholar, South Africa, 1993, Rockefeller Inst. Resident scholar Bellagio Conf. Ctr., 1995. Mem. ABA (Ross essay prize 1983), Internat. Soc. for Labor Law and Social Security, Indsl. Relations Rsch. Assn., Order of Coif. Office: Rutgers U Sch Law 15 Washington St Newark NJ 07102-3105

BLUMROSEN, RUTH GERBER, lawyer, educator, arbitrator; b. N.Y.C., Mar. 7, 1927; d. Lipman Samuel and Dorothy (Finklebrand) Gerber; m. Alfred William Blumrosen, July 3, 1952; children: Steven Marshall, Alexander B. BA in Econs., U. Mich., 1947, JD, 1953. Bar: Mich. 1953, U.S. Supreme Ct. 1967, U.S. Ct. Appeals (3d cir.). pvt. practice law, Detroit, 1953-55; cons. civil rights litigation, 1958-65; acting chief advice and analyses, acting dir. compliance EEOC, Washington, 1965; asst. dean Howard U., Washington, 1965-67; consul to chmn. EEOC, 1979-80; expert EEO HHS, Washington, 1980-81; assoc. prof. Grad. Sch. Mgmt., Rutgers U., Newark, 1972-87; adj. prof. Rutgers Law Sch., 1994—; resident scholar Rockefeller Found., Bellagio, Italy, 1995. Adviser, N.J. Commn. on Sex Discrimination in the Statutes, 1983-85; commr. N.J. Gov.'s Study Commn. on Discrimination in Pub. Works Procurement and Constrn. Contracts, 1990-93. Gen. advisor, Rutgers Law Sch. Intentional Discrimination Proj., three year study of employment discrimination funded by The Ford Found.-1998—, Fulbright scholar So. Africa, 1993. Mem. ABA, Fed. Bar Assn., Indsl. Rels. Rsch. Assn., Nat. Com. Pay Equity. Author: (with A. Blumrosen) Layoff or Worksharing: The Civil Rights Act of 1964 in the Recession of 1975; (with A. Blumrosen, et. al.) Downsizing and Employee Rights, 50 Rutgers Law Review 943, 1998; The Duty to Plan for Fair Employment Revisited: Worksharing in Hard Times, 1975; Wage Discrimination, Job Segregation and Title VII of Civil Rights Act of 1964, 1979; Wage Discrimination and Job Segregation: The Survival of a Theory, 1980; An Analysis of Wage Discrimination in N.J. State Service, 1983; Worksharing, STC and Affirmative Action in Shorttime Compensation: A Formula for Worksharing; Remedies for Wage Discrimination., 1987. Office: 15 Washington St # 915 Newark NJ 07102-3105

BLUMSTEIN, ALFRED, urban and public affairs educator; b. N.Y.C., June 3, 1930; m. Dolores Reguera, Jan. 26, 1958; children: Lisa, Ellen, Diane. BS in Engring. Physics, Cornell U., 1951, PhD in Ops. Rsch., 1960; MS in Stats., U. Buffalo, 1954; JD (hon.), John Jay Coll., 1996. Prin. ops. analyst Cornell Aeronautical Lab., Buffalo, 1951-61; rsch. staff Inst. Def. Analyses, Arlington, Va., 1961-69; dir. sci. and tech. task force Pres.'s Commn. Law Enforcement and Adminstrn. Justice, Washington, 1966-67; J. Erik Jonsson Univ. prof. urban sys. and ops. rsch. H. John Heinz III Sch. Pub. Policy and Mgmt. Carnegie-Mellon U., Pitts., 1969—, dean, 1986-93, dir. Nat. Consortium on Violence Rsch., 1996—; overseas fellow Churchill Coll. Cambridge U., 1983—; chmn. various panels NRC Com. Rsch. Law Enforcement and Adminstrn. Justice, 1982-86, chmn. com., 1980-83; mem. NRC Commn. Behavioral and Social Scis. and Edn., 1994—. Mem. editl. bd. Ops. Rsch. Letters, Jour. Rsch. in Crime and Delinquency, Evaluation Rev., Jour. Criminal Justice, Sci. Commn. of Internat. Soc. of Criminology, 1985-91, others; co-editor Cambridge Criminology Series; contbr. articles to profl. jours. Chmn. Pa. Commn. Crime and Delinquency, Harrisburg, 1979-90; mem. Pa. Commn. on Sentencing, 1986-96; bd. dirs. Police Found., 1990-96; nat. adv. com. Inst. Rsch. on Poverty at U. Wis., 1989-94. Fellow AAAS, Am. Soc. Criminology (pres. 1991-92, Sutherland award 1987); mem. NNAE, Ops. Rsch. Soc. Am. (pres. 1977-78, Kimball medal 1985, Pres.'s award 1993), Am. Statis. Assn., Inst. Ops. Rsch. and Mgmt. Scis. (pres. 1996), Law and Society Assn., The Inst. Mgmt. Scis. (pres. 1987-88), Internat. Fedn. Operational Rsch. Socs. (v.p. N.Am. 1992-94), Consortium of Social Sci. Assns. (pres. 1999—), Cosmos Club, Omega Rho (hon.). Home: 1455 Wightman St Pittsburgh PA 15217-1260 Office: Carnegie-Mellon U H John Heinz III Sch Pub Policy Mgmt Pittsburgh PA 15213

BLUMSTEIN, EDWARD, lawyer; b. Phila., Aug. 24, 1933; s. Isaac and Mollye (Rodofsky) B.; m. Susan Perloff, Aug. 13, 1983; 1 child, Daniel Blumstein. BS in Econs., U. Pa., 1955; JD, Temple U., 1958. Bar: U.S. Dist. Ct. (ea. dist.) Pa. 1959, U.S. Ct. Appeals (3rd cir.) 1959. Sole practice Phila., 1959-85; ptnr. Blumstein, Block & Pease, Phila., 1985—; adj. prof. Sch. Law Temple U., 1994—. Gen. Counsel to North American Ski Journalists Assn. With U.S. Army, 1958-64. Mem. ABA, Pa. Bar Assn., Phila. Bar Assn. (bd. govs. 1984-85, past chmn. family law sect. 1984). Assn., Phila. Trial Lawyers Assn., Acad. Family Mediators and Family Mediation Assn. Del. Valley (pres. 1990-91). Republican. Jewish. Lodge: B'nai B'rith.. Avocations: skiing, sailing, reading, photography. Office: Blumstein Block & Pease 1518 Walnut St Fl 4 Philadelphia PA 19102-3419

BLUMSTEIN, JAMES FRANKLIN, legal educator, lawyer, consultant; b. Bklyn., Apr. 24, 1945; s. David and Rita (Sondheim) B.; m. Andree Kahn, June 25, 1971. BA in Econs., Yale U., 1966, MA in Econs., LLB, 1970. Bar: Tenn. 1970, U.S. Ct. Appeals (6th cir.) 1970, U.S. Dist. Ct. (mid. dist.) Tenn. 1971, U.S. Supreme Ct. 1974, N.Y. 1985. Instr. econs. New Haven Coll., 1967-68; pre-law adviser office of dean Yale U., New Haven, 1968-69; sr. pre-law adviser office of dean Yale U., 1969-70, asst. in instrn. law shc., 1969-70; asst. prof. law Vanderbilt U., Nashville, 1970-73; assoc. prof. Vanderbilt U., 1973-76, prof., 1976—, spl. advisor to chancellor for acad. affairs, 1984-85; assoc. dir. Vanderbilt Urban and Regional Devel. Ctr., 1970-72, dir. ctr., 1972-74; sr. rsch. assoc. Vanderbilt Inst. for Pub. Policy Studies, 1976-85, sr. fellow, 1985—, dir. health policy ctr., 1995—; Commonwealth Fund fellow, vis. assoc. prof. law and policy scis. law sch. Duke U. and Inst. of Policy Scis. and Pub. Affairs, 1974-75; adj. prof. health law med. sch. Dartmouth U., scholar-in-residence intermittently, 1976-78; John M. Olin vis. prof. Sch. Law, U. Pa., 1989; elected mem. Inst. Medicine NAS, 1990—; cons. law, health policy, civil and voting rights, land use, state taxation, torts; lectr. in field. Editor: (with Eddie J. Martin) The Urban Scene in the Seventies, 1974, (with Benjamin Walter) Growing Metropolis: Aspects of Development in Nashville, 1975, (with Lester Salamon) Growth Policy in the Eighties (Law and Contemporary Problems Symposium), 1979; (with Frank A. Sloan and James M. Perrin) Uncompensated Hospital Care: Rights and Responsibilities, 1986, (with Frank A. Sloan and James M. Perrin) Cost, Quality, and Access in Health Care: New Roles for Health Planning in a Competitive Environment, 1988; (with Frank A. Sloan) Organ Transplantation Policy: Issues and Prospects, 1989, (with Frank A. Sloan) Antitrust and Health Care Policy (Law and Contemporary Problems Symposium), 1989, (with Clark C. Havighurst and Troyen A. Brennan) Health Care Law and Policy, 1998, bd. Jour. Health Politics, Policy and Law, 1981—; mem. pub.'s adv. bd. Nashville Banner, 1982-98; contbr. articles to profl. jours., op-ed articles to newspapers. Mem. Health Econs. Task Force, Middle Tenn. Health Sys. Agy., 1979; mem. adv. bd. LWV, 1979-80; mem. Nashville Mayor's Commn. on Crime, 1981; cons. Leadership Nashville, 1977—, Tenn. Motor Vehicle Commn., 1986-87, Leadership Music, 1989—; panelist Am. Arbitration Assn., 1977—; chmn. Tenn. adv. com. U.S. Commn. on Civil Rights, 1985-91, mem., 1991-97; sec. Martin Luther King Jr. Holiday Com., State of Tenn., 1985-87; bd. dirs. Jewish Fedn. Nashville and Middle Tenn., 1981-90, mem. exec. com., 1988-90, chmn. cmty. rels. com., 1980-82, chmn. campus com., 1987-89; chmn. Yale Alumni Schs. Com. Middle Tenn., 1983—; mem Tenn. Gov.'s Task Force Medicaid, 1992-94; mem. adv. panel Office Tech. Assessment study of defensive medicine and use of med. tech., 1991-94; chmn. task force cost containment and med. malpractice Rand Corp., 1991-92; active Inst. Medicine Com. on Adequacy of Nursing Staffing, 1994-96; mem. adv. com. on The Records of Congress, 1997—. Bates Jr. fellow, 1968-69; grantee Ford Found./Rockefeller Found. Population Program, 1970-73, Health Policy grantee HCA Found., 1986-90; grantee State Justice Inst., 1991—, Robert Wood Johnson Found., 1994—; nominated Adminstr., Office Info. and Regulatory Affairs, Office Mgmt. and Budget, 1990; named One of Outstanding Young Men in Am. U.S. Jaycees, 1971; recipient award Univ. Rsch. Coun., 1971-72, 73-74, 79-80, 94-95, Earl Sutherland prize achievement in rsch. Vanderbilt U., 1992, Paul J. Hartman award Outstanding Prof., 1982. Mem. ABA (sec. sect. legal edn. and admissions to bar 1982-83, chmn. subcom. on state and local taxation com. on corp. law and taxation sect. on corp., banking and bus. law 1983—, mem. accreditation com. sect. legal edn. and admissions to bar 1983-89, mem. com. on state and local taxation sect. on taxation 1983—), NAS (inst. of medicine), Assn. Am. Law Schs. (chmn. law, medicine and health care sect. 1987-88, mem. exec. com. 1988-92, 2d vice chmn. sect. local govt. law 1976-78, mem. sect. coun. 1980-86), Tenn. Bar Assn., N.Y. State Bar Assn., Nashville Bar Assn. (Liberty Bell award 1987), Hastings Ctr., Assn. for Pub. Policy Analysis and Mgmt., Assn. Yale Alumni (del.), Yale U. Law Sch. Alumni Assn. (exec. com. 1985-88), Univ. Club (Nashville). Home: 2113 Hampton Ave Nashville TN 37215-1401 Office: Vanderbilt U Law Sch 21st Ave S Nashville TN 37240

BLUMSTEIN, SUSAN BENDER, fundraiser; b. Phila., Dec. 20, 1943; d. Israel Boris and Lillian (Zebooker) B.; m. Allan Blumstein, Oct. 3, 1967; children: Eve, Zachary. BA, U. Pa., 1965. Exec. v.p. Am. Friends Israel Philharmonic Orch., N.Y.C., 1981-89; asst. v.p. devel. Jewish Theol. Sem., N.Y.C., 1989-94; rep. World ORT Union, 1994-96; v.p. devel. Manhattan Sch. Music, N.Y.C., 1996—; cons. Nat. Found. Jewish Culture, N.Y.C., 1989, Israel Bonds, N.Y.C., 1990, Internat. Mendelssohn-Stiftung, Leipzig, Germany, 1993, JCCA, N.Y.C., 1994. Chair U.S.A. Women's Lecture Series, N.Y., 1990-92; mem. St. Petersburg Philharm., 1997—.

BLUM-VEGLIA, CHERYL ANN, accountant; b. Elizabeth, N.J., Jan. 5, 1966; d. Kenneth Peter and Mary Jo (Faccone) B. BA in Acctg. and Fin., Muhlenberg Coll., 1988. CPA, Pa. Auditor Deloitte & Touche, Parsippany, N.J., 1988-91; internal auditor N.J. Hwy. Authority, Woodbridge, 1991-96. vol. Inst. for Children with Cancer and Blood Disorders. Mem. N.J. Soc. CPA's. Pa. Inst. CPAs, Muhlenberg Coll. Alumni Amb. Assn. Roman Catholic. Avocations: swimming, shopping, dancing, family.

BLUNDELL, WILLIAM EDWARD, journalist, consultant; b. N.Y.C., Sept. 23, 1934; s. W. Edward and Anne Elizabeth (Dur) B.; m. Gayle Swango, Oct. 19, 1957; children: Bonnie, Scott. BS, Syracuse U., 1956; postgrad., U. Kans., 1959-61. Reporter Dallas bur. Wall Street Jour., 1961-63; reporter N.Y. bur. Wall Street Jour., N.Y.C., 1963-65, page one writer, 1965-68; chief L.A. bur. Wall Street Jour., 1968-78, nat. corr., 1978-89; news editor Wall Street Jour., L.A., 1989-90; cons., major newspapers, 1991—; Nat. pres. Ind. Assn. Pubs. Employees, 1965-67. Co-author: Swindled: Great Business Frauds of the 70s, 1976; author: Storytelling Step by Step, 1985, The Art and Craft of Feature Writing, 1989; editor (anthology) The Innovators, 1967. Served to 1st lt. AUS, 1957-59. Recipient Berger award for distinguished met. reporting Columbia U., 1966; Roy Howard award for pub. service Scripps-Howard Found., 1974; Disting. feature writing award Am. Soc. Newspaper Editors, 1982. Mem. Zeta Psi. Episcopalian. Home and Office: 2100 Emmons Rd Cambria CA 93428-4512*

BLUNDELL, WILLIAM RICHARD CHARLES, electric company executive; b. Montreal, Apr. 13, 1927; s. Richard C. and Did Aileen (Payne) B.; m. Monique Audet, Mar. 20, 1959; children: Richard, Emily, Michelle, Louise. BA in Sci., U. Toronto, 1949. Registered profl. engr., Ont. Sales engr. Can. Gen. Electric Co., Toronto, 1949-51, travelling auditor, 1951, various fin. positions, 1951-66, treas., 1966-68, v.p.-fin., 1968-70, v.p., exec. consumer div., 1970-72; v.p., exec. apparatus div. Can. Gen. Electric Co., Lachine, Que., 1972-79; pres., chief exec. officer Camco Inc., Weston, Ont., 1979-83; pres., chief operating officer Can. Gen. Electric Co. Ltd., Toronto, 1983-84; chmn., chief exec. officer Gen. Electric Can. Inc., 1985-90; ret., 1991; chmn. Mfrs. Life Ins. Co., 1994-98; bd. dirs. Alcan Aluminum Ltd., Swiss Bank (Can), Export Devel. Corp., Seaside Cable TV, Purolator Courier Ltd., Sceptre Investment Counselling Ltd., Kasten Chase Applied Rsch. Ltd., ISG Techs., Inc., Triple Crown Electronics Inc. Apptd. Officer of Order of Can., 1997. Home: 45 Stratheden Rd, Toronto, ON Canada M4N 1E5

BLUNK, FORREST STEWART, lawyer; b. Doniphan, Mo., July 22, 1913; s. Forest Stanley and Margaret Anna (Stewart) B.; m. Mary Williams, July 10, 1971; children—Scott Stewart, Sally Jo. B.A., U. Wyo., 1936; J.D., U. Wyo., 1940. Bar: Ill. bar 1946, Colo. bar 1953. Asso. firm Vogel & Bunge, Chgo., 1946-50; assoc. January & Yegge, Denver, 1953-55; ptnr. Blunk and Johnson, Denver, 1955—; pres., dir. Williams Land & Livestock Co., Tie Siding, Wyo. Served with AUS, 1941-46, ETO. Mem. Fed., Am., Ill., Wyo., Colo., 5th Dist., 10th Circuit bar assns., Colo. Def. Bar Assn. (pres. 1969-70), Lawyer-Pilots Bar Assn., Internat. Assn. Ins. Counsel, Denver Bar, Am. Bd. Trial Advs. (pres. Colo. chpt. 1974-75, nat. sec. 1975-76), Legal Club Chgo. Republican. Clubs: Masons, Elks, Rotary, Ft. Collins Country, Denver Athletic. Home: 1829 Elim Ct Fort Collins CO 80524-2205 Office: 2696 S Colorado Blvd Suite 595 Denver CO 80222

BLUNT, ROY D., congressman; b. Niangua, Mo., Jan. 10, 1950; s. Leroy and Neva (Letterman) B.; m. E. Roseann Ray; children: Matthew Roy, Amy Roseann, Andrew Benjamin. BA, S.W. Bapt. U., 1970; MA, S.W. Mo. State U., 1972. Tchr. Marshfield (Mo.) High Sch., 1970-73; instr. Drury Coll., Springfield, Mo., 1973-82; clk. Greene County, Springfield, 1973-85; sec. of state State of Mo., Jefferson City, 1985-93; pres. Southwest Bapt. U., 1993-96; mem. 105th-106th Congresses from 7th Mo. dist., 1997—; mem. Fed. Election Commn. Adv. Panel; del. Atlantic Treaty Assn. Conf., 1987; mem. Congressional Com. on Commerce, 1999—, Internat. Rels., 1997-98, Ho. Reps. Steering Com., 1997; del. Nat. Hist. Publs. and Records Commn., 1997—. Author: (with others) Missouri Election Procedures: A Layman's Guide, 1977; Voting Rights Guide for the Handicapped. Bd. dirs. Ctr. for

Democracy; mem. Mo. Mental Health Advocacy Coun., 1998-99; mem. exec. bd. Am. Coun. of Young Polit. Tchrs., 1998-99; chmn. Mo. Housing Devel. Commn., Kansas City, 1981, Rep. State Conv., Springfield, 1980; chmn. Gov.'s Adv. Coun. on Literacy; co-chmn. Mo. Opportunity 2000 Commn., 1985-87; Rep. candidate for lt. gov. of Mo., 1980; active local ARC, Muscular Dystrophy Assn., others. Named One of 10 Outstanding Young Americans U.S. Jaycees, 1986, Springfield's Outstanding Young Man Jaycees, 1980, Mo.'s Outstanding Young Civic Leader, 1981. Mem. Nat. Assn. Secs. of State (chmn. voter registration and edn. com., sec., v.p. 1990). Am. Coun. Young Polit. Leaders. Baptist. Lodges: Kiwanis, Masons. Office: US Ho of Reps 217 Cannon Ho Office Bldg Washington DC 20515-2507

BLUSH, STEVEN MICHAEL, nuclear scientist, safety consultant; b. Parkville, Mo., June 1, 1948; s. William Edwin Blush and Jeanne Arlene Harrington; m. Joanna Ann Henderson; children: Paul Henderson Blush, Sarah Courtney Blush.. BA in Anthropology, U. Calif., 1970; postgrad., Boston Coll., San Francisco State U. Investigator Korean-Am. relations, subcommittee on internat. orgns. U.S. House Of Representatives, Washington, 1977-79; task group leader, investigator, Three Mile Island subcommittee on Nuclear Regulation U.S. Senate, Washington, 1979-80; chief investigator Pres. Nuclear Safety Oversight Com., Washington, 1980-81; pvt. cons., 1981-83; sr. study dir. of nuclear safety-related policy issues NRC, NAS, NAE, Inst. Med., Washington, 1984-90; spl. cons. to the sec. of energy U.S. Dept. Energy, Washington, 1989-90, dir. Office of Nuclear Safety, 1990-93; pres. Steve Blush Cons., Inc., Beverly Hills, Calif., 1993—; mem. nuclear rev. and audit group Ill. Power Co., 1993-97; cons. U.S. Senate Com. on Energy and Natural Resources, 1994-95, Dept. Energy, 1995—, Boston Edison Co., 1997, Commonwealth Edison Co., 1996, Osborn Maledon, 1998—; nuclear safety specialist Scientech, Inc., Washington, 1995—; tech. advisor NOVA, Frontline; rschr. Nuclear Control Inst. Adolph Kersten scholar Univ. Calif., 1966. Mem. Senior Exec. Svc.

BLUST, LARRY D., lawyer; b. Bushnell, Ill., Feb. 16, 1943. BS with high honors, U. Ill., 1965, JD with high honors, 1968. Bar: Ill. 1968; CPA, Ill. Mem. Jenner & Block, Chgo.; mem. Ill. Bd. CPA Examiners, 1978-81. Contbr. articles to profl. jours. Mem. ABA (tax sect., partnerships com. 1975-80, 1982-85), Ill. State Bar Assn., Order of the Coif. Office: Jenner & Block 1 E Ibm Plz Fl 4000 Chicago IL 60611-7603*

BLUTE, PETER I., transportation executive, former congressman; b. Jan. 28, 1956; m. Roberta Crudale, 1986; children: James, Daniel. BA cum laude in Polit. Sci., Boston Coll., 1978. Sports promotion/mktg.; mktg. rep. Burdett Sch., Boston; campaign worker for U.S. Senate candidate U.S. Senator Elliot Richardson, Boston, 1984; advisor Mass. Civic Interest Coun./Citizens for Limited Taxation, Boston; mem. Mass. State Rep. from 11th Dist., Worcester, 1986-93, 103d Congress from 3d Mass. Dist., 1993-96; exec. dir., CEO Massport, Boston, 1996—; mem. transp. and infrastructure com., govt. reform and oversight com. Mem. Civic Interest Coun. Mem. KC, Young Reps. Roman Catholic. Office: Mass Port Authority Ste 200 S One Harborside Dr East Boston MA 02128-2909

BLUTH, B. J. (ELIZABETH JEAN CATHERINE BLUTH), sociologist, aerospace technologist; b. Phila., Dec. 5, 1934; d. Robert Thomas and Catherine Cecelia (Boxman) Gowl; m. Thomas Del Bluth, Aug. 20, 1960 (dec. Aug. 6, 1980); children: Robert Thomas, Richard Del. B.A. in Sociology (Washington semster fellow), Bucknell U., 1953; M.A., Fordham U., 1960; Ph.D., UCLA, 1970. Teaching fellow in methods of social research Fordham U., 1957-58; reading instr. St. Margaret's High Sch., Tappahannock, Va., 1958-59; instr. history, civics and English, Rosary High Sch., San Diego, 1959-60; successively instr., asst. prof. sociology Immaculate Heart Coll., Los Angeles, 1960-65; prof. sociology Calif. State U., Northridge, 1965-87; grantee NASA Ames Research Ctr., Moffett Field, Calif., 1982-83; grantee space sta. program NASA, Washington, 1983-87; aerospace technologist system engring. div. space sta. program office NASA, Reston, Va., 1987-90, spl. asst. to dep. program dir. space sta. freedom program and ops., 1990-94; spl. tech. asst. to dir. edn. divsn., mgr. edn. evaluation NASA, Washington, 1994—, program mgr. on-line edn. evaluation program, 1994—; cons. Immaculate Heart Cmty., L.A., 1967-69; engring. rsch. NASA Space Sta. design Boeing Aerospace Co., 1982-83; mem. Presdl. Citizens Adv. com. on Space, Coun. Nat. Space Policy, Nat. Tech. Com. on Soc. & Tech., UN team on relevance of space activities to econ. and social devel.; professor emeritus Calif. State U., 1987—; computational scis. and informatics inst. dir.'s search com. George Mason U., 1992-93. Editor: (with others) Search for Identity Reader, vol. I and II, 1973, (with S.R. McNeal) Update on Space, vol. I, 1961, Parson's General Theory of Action, 1982, Space Station Habitability Report, 1983, Soviet Space Station Analog, 1983, Space Station Human Productivity Study NASA, 1986, Russian Mir Space Station Analog, 1993; contbr. articles to profl. jours. Recipient Alpha Omega faculty awards, 1966, 74, disting. teaching award Calif. State U., Northridge, 1968, NASA superior accomplishment award, 1990, NASA, performance awards 1991-94; Inst. Advancement in Teaching and Learning fellow, Calif. State U., 1974. Fellow Am. Astronautical Soc.; mem. AIAA (chpt. award for outstanding program 1980), Am. Sociol. Assn., L5 Soc., Brit. Interplanetary Soc., Inst. Social Sci. Study of Space (acad. adv. bd.), Space Studies Inst., Internat. Acad. Astronautics (com. on space econs. and benefits), Phi Beta Kappa. Republican. Office: NASA Code FE Edn Div 300 E St SW Washington DC 20546-0005 *To seed the universe with intelligence you must: never give up, no matter how little progress you see day-to-day for it's the "big picture" where the changes show up; always concentrate on the practical, no matter how enticing theories appear; never forget that ideas and systems and institutions are nothing more than ideas, and ideas can change—that is the true vehicle to freedom. Always reach beyond the horizon, knowing that horizons have no limit save that of our imagination.*

BLUTH, DON, animator, director, screenwriter; b. El Paso, Tex., Sept. 13, 1938. Student, Brigham Young U. Animator Walt Disney Studios, 1956, 71-79, Filmation, 1967, Sullivan Studios, 1986—; co-founder, dir. (with Gary Oldman and John Pomery) Don Bluth Prodns., 1979-85. Animation dir.: Robin Hood, 1973, The Rescuers, 1977, Pete's Dragon, 1977, Xanadu, 1980; dir., prodr., story adapter: The Secret of Nimh, 1982, All Dogs Go To Heaven, 1989; dir., prodr.: Am American Tail, 1986, The Land Before Time, 1988, Rock-a-Doodle, 1992, Thumbelina, 1993, A Troll in Central Park, 1994, The Pebble and the Penguin, 1994; dir., prodr., story adapter, lyricist: (TV) Banjo the Woodpile Cat. Office: Fox Animation Studios 2747 E Camelback Rd Phoenix AZ 85016-4322*

BLUTTER, JOAN WERNICK, interior designer; b. London, July 6, 1929; naturalized, 1948; d. Samuel and Bertha (Cohn) Wernick; m. Melvyn Blutter, Oct. 29, 1948; children: Janet Lesley Shiff, Steven. Pres. Blutter Shiff Design Assocs., Chgo., 1955—; partner Designers Collaborative, San Francisco, 1975—; design cons. Exec. House Ltd., Chgo.; bd. dirs. Fashion Group. Contbr.: articles to Interior Design; others. Mem. Women's Bd. United Cerebral Palsy. Fellow Am. Soc. Interior Designers (nat. dir., past pres. Ill. chpt., nat. bd. dirs., past nat. sec., nat. chmn. industry 1978-79, nat. chmn. Design Internat. Program 1981-82, Gold Key award, Design award, Presdl. award); mem. Mchts. and Mfrs. Club, Art Inst. Chgo., Mus. Contemporary Art. Home: 340 W Diversey Pky Chicago IL 60657-6241 Office: Blutter/Shiff Design Assoc 1648 Merchandise Mart Chicago IL 60654

BLY, CHARLES ALBERT, nuclear engineer, research scientist; b. Winchester, Va., Jan. 11, 1952; s. Theodore and Nancy Irma (Fisher) B.; m. April Marie Monnen, July 24, 1976. BS in Nuclear Engring., U. Va., 1978, MS in Nuclear Engring., 1983; student, Nat. Acad. Nuclear Tng., 1992-93; postgrad. in nuclear engring., U. Va., 1994—, cardiovasc. rsch. tng., 1999—. Nuclear reactor operator Nuclear Reactor Facility of the U. Va., Charlottesville, 1977-80, sr. reactor operator, 1980-83, rsch. engr., 1981-83; vis. engr. Brit. Nuclear Fuel Ltd. Springfields Works, Preston Lancashire, England, 1983; nuclear engr. Comml. Nuclear Fuel div. Westinghouse Electric, Pitts., 1983-92, Beaver Valley Power Sta. Duquesne Light Co., Shippingport, Pa., 1992-94; lead prof. Oak Ridge (Tenn.) Nat. Lab. Am. Tech. Inst., 1994-95; nuclear reactor staff Nuclear Reactor Facility of U. Va., Charlottesville, 1995-99; staff U. Va. Health Svcs. Cardiovasc. Gene Therapy Lab., Charlottesville, 1999—. Contbr. numerous articles to profl. jours. Candidate Shenandoah County (Va.) Bd. of Supervisor, 1975; mem. Ad Hoc Com. to Prevent Extension of I-66 Hwy. Through George Washington Nat. Forest, Strasburg, Va., 1979, Ad Hoc Com. to Preserve the Pitts. Aviary, 1991. Mem. ASME, IEEE, ASTM, AAAS, Am. Nuc. Soc., Am. Phys. Soc., ASM Internat., Assn. Energy Engrs., The Engring. Soc., Profl. Engr.'s Soc., Fedn. Am. Scientists, Engr.'s Soc. Western Pa., N.Y. Acad. Scis., Internat. Platform Assn. Democrat. Lutheran. Achievements include invention of fusion and hybrid fission/fusion nuclear fuel rod, combined cycle steam turbine, gas turbine nuclear power plants, neutron flux driven cold fusion in palladium; discovery of neutrino-driven nucleon fission chain reactions/nucleon decay chain reactions; discovery of graviton-driven fermion fission chain reactions; development of Bohr model of nucleons; development of Bohr model of gravitation; development of a generalized Bode's Law; development of a fundamental subatomic particle rest mass correlation. Home: 777 Mountainwood Rd Apt D Charlottesville VA 22903-6507 Office: U Va Nuclear Reactor Facility Charlottesville VA 22903-2442

BLY, JAMES CHARLES, JR., financial services executive; b. Kane, Pa., Jan. 24, 1952; s. James Charles Bly Sr. and Dorothy Rose Hau Smith; m. Laurie Ann Ramadon, June 6, 1987; children: Alana W., Bridget R., James C. III, Chase N. BA, St. Bonaventure U., 1973. CLU, ChFC. Mgmt. trainee Conn. Gen. Life, Washington, 1974-76; rep. CIGNA Fin. Svcs., McLean, Va., 1976-79; mng. exec. Integrated Resources Equity Corp., N.Y.C., 1980-82; pres. Source Capital, Ltd., Pitts., 1982—; chmn., CEO Source Cos., LLC, 1998—; mem. adv. bd. John J. Kirlin, Inc., Rockville, Md., 1980—, Royal Bank of Can., Global Fin. Svcs., Network, 1991-97, Internat. Advisors Network, Ltd., 1998—; bd. dirs. Holgate Toy Co., Kane, Pa., Liberty-Pitts. Sys., Inc., Orr Felt Co., Piqua, Ohio. Author: Business Preservation Trusts, 1991. Active Rep. Nat. Com. Mem. Am. Soc. CLUs and ChFCs, Family Firm Inst., Nat. Assn. Life Underwriters, Nat. Assn. Securities Dealers, Internat. Assn. for Fin. Planning, Estate Planning Coun. (Pitts.), World Affairs Coun., Y Group, Duquesne Club, The Stonedale Guns, Edgeworth Club, St. James Club, Sewickley Heights Golf Club. Republican. Avocations: music, automobiles, history, travel. Home: Spanish Tract Rd Sewickley PA 15143 Office: Source Capital Ltd 1 Gateway Ctr # 1800 Pittsburgh PA 15222-1435

BLY, MARK JOHN, dramaturg, playwriting educator; b. Sioux Falls, S.D., Feb. 1, 1949; s. Myrle S. and Lois L. Bly. BA, U. Minn., 1974; MA, Boston Coll., 1977; MFA, Yale U., 1980. Script reader Yale Repertory Theater, New Haven, 1977-80, assoc. artistic dir., 1992—; assoc. literary mgr. Arena Stage, Washington, 1980-81; dramaturg, literary mgr. The Guthrie Theater, Mpls., 1981-89; artistic assoc., dramaturg Seattle Repertory Theatre, 1989-92; co-chair dramaturgy and dramatic criticism dept. Yale Sch. Drama, New Haven, 1992-97, chair playwriting dept., 1992—. Editor: The Production Notebooks, 1996; contbg. editor Yale's Theater Mag., 1985-93, 98—, advisory editor, 1993-98; contbr. articles to profl. jours. and books. Mem. Literary Mgrs. and Dramaturgs Am. (regional v.p. 1989-90, v.p. for comm. 1991-92). Avocation: paleontology. Office: Yale Univ Sch Drama PO Box 208244 New Haven CT 06520-8244

BLY, ROBERT, poet; b. Madison, Minn., Dec. 23, 1926; s. Jacob Thomas and Alice (Aws) B.; m. Carolyn McLean, June 24, 1955 (div. 1979); children: Mary, Bridget, Noah Matthew Jacob, Micah John Padma.; m. Ruth Ray, June 27, 1980. Student, St. Olaf Coll., 1946-47; AB, Harvard, 1950; MA, U. Iowa, 1956. Editor, pub. Fifties Press (became Sixties, Seventies, Eighties, now Nineties), Madison, 1958—; Co-chmn. Am. Writers vs. Vietnam War, 1966—. Author: (poems) Silence in the Snowy Fields, 1962, (with William Duffy and James Wright) The Lion's Tail and Eyes: Poems Written Out of Laziness and Silence, 1962, The Light Around the Body, 1967 (Nat. Book award 1968), Chrysanthemums, 1967, Ducks, 1968, The Morning Glory, 1969, The Teeth Mother Naked at Last, 1971, (with William E. Stafford and William Matthews) Poems for Tennessee, 1971, Christmas Eve Service at Midnight at Sr. Michael's, 1972, Water Under the Earth, 1972, The Dead Seal Near McClure's Beach, 1973, Sleepers Joining Hands, 1973, Jumping Out of Bed, 1973, The Hockey Poem, 1974, Point Reyes Poems, 1974, Old Man Rubbing His Eyes, 1975, The Loon, 1977, This Body is Made of Camphor and Gopherwood, 1977, Visiting Emily Dickinson's Grave and Other Poems, 1979, This Tree Will Be Here for a Thousand Years, 1979, The Man in The Black Coat Turns, 1981, Finding an Old Ant Mansion, 1981, Four Ramages, 1983, The Whole Moisty Night, 1983, Out of the Rolling Ocean, 1984, Mirabai Versions, 1984, In The Month of May, 1985, A Love of Minute Particulars, 1985, Selected Poems, 1986 (L.A. Times Poetry award nominee 1986), Loving a Woman in Two Worlds, 1987, The Moon on a Fencepost, 1988, The Apple Found in the Plowing, 1989, What Have I Ever Lost By Dying?, 1992, Meditations on the Insatiable Soul, 1994, Morning Poems, 1997; (non-fiction) A Broadsheet Against the New York Times Book Review, 1961, Talking All Morning: Collected Conversations and Interviews, 1980, The Eight Stages of Translation, 1983, The Pillow and the Key, 1987, A Little Book on the Human Shadow, 1988, American Poetry: Wildness and Domesticity, 1990, Iron John: A Book About Men, 1990, Remembering James Wright, 1991, The Sibling Society, 1996; editor: The Sea and the Honeycomb, 1966, A Poetry Reading Against the Viet Nam War, 1967, Forty Poems Touching Upon Recent History, 1970, Leaping Poetry, 1975, News of the Universe, 1980, Ten Love Poems, 1981, The Fifties and the Sixties, 10 vols., 1982, The Winged Life: The Poetic Voice of Henry David Thoreau, 1986, The Rag and Bone Shop of the Heart: Poems for Men, 1992, The Darkness Around Us is Deep: Selected Poems of William Stafford, 1993, The Soul Is Here for Its Own Joy, 1995; translator (from Swedish) The Story of Gösta Berling (Selma Lagerlöf), 1962, I Do Best Alone at Night (Gunnar Ekelöf), 1968, Twenty Poems of Tomas Tranströmer), 1972, Night Vision (Tomas Tranströmer), 1972, Friends, You Drank Some Darkness: Three Swedish Poets, Matinson, Ekelöf and Tranströmer, 1975, (from Norwegian) Knut Hamsun Hunger, 1967, Twenty Poems of Rolf Jacobsen, 1977, Twenty Poems of Olav H. Hauge, 1987, (from German) Twenty Poems of Georg Trakl, 1961, Selected Poems of Rainer Maria Rilke, 1980, (from Spanish) Twenty Poems of Cesar Vallejo, 1963, Forty Poems of Juan Ramon Jimenez, 1967, Twenty Poems of Pablo Neruda, 1967, Lorca and Jimenez: Selected Poems, 1973, Time Alone: Selected Poems of Antonio Machado, 1983, (with Lewis Hyde) (from Spanish) Twenty Poems of Vincente Aleixandre, 1977, (from Spanish) (prose) The Eight Stages of Translation, 1983, A Little Book on the Human Shadow, 1986, American Poetry: Wildness and Domesticity, 1990, Remembering James Wright, 1991, (from French) Ten Poems of Francis Ponge, 1990, Ten Poems of Robert Bly Inspired by the Poems of Francis Ponge, 1990, (from Rajasthani) Mirabai Versions, 1993, (from Hindi and English) The Kabir Book: 44 of the Ecstatic Poems of Kabir, 1977. Served with USNR, 1944-45. Recipient award Nat. Inst. Arts and Letters, Nat. Book award in poetry, 1968; Fulbright grantee, 1956-57; Amy Lowell fellow, 1964-65; Guggenheim fellow, 1965-66, 72-73; Rockefeller Found. fellow, 1967. Mem. Am. Acad. Arts and Letters. Address: 1904 Girard Ave S Minneapolis MN 55403-2945*

BLY, ROBERT MAURICE, lawyer; b. Connersville, Ind., Oct. 31, 1944; s. Karl H. and Faye Virginia (DeHoff) B.; m. Ann Patrice Gleason, Aug. 24, 1968; 1 child, Thomas Robert. BS, Ball State U., 1966; JD, U. Tenn., 1973. Bar: Ill. 1973, Ind. 1974, U.S. Dist. Ct. (so. dist.) Ind. 1974, U.S. Dist. Ct. (no. dist.) Ind. 1978, U.S. Supreme Ct. 1981, Tenn. 1991, U.S. Dist. Ct. (ea. dist.) Tenn. 1992. Pub. sch. tchr. pub. schs., Ind., 1966-71; regional counsel's staff Chgo. (Ill.) Title & Trust Co., 1973-75; dep. prosecutor Porter County Ind., Valparaiso, 1975-76; pvt. practice law Valparaiso and Kokomo, Ind., 1976-91, Knoxville, 1992—; adj. instr. Ind. U., Kokomo, 1987-91; del. Ho. of Dels., Ind. Bar Assn., Indpls., 1988; founder Southeast Estate Planning Inst.; guest lectr. in field. Columnist Fairfield Glade Sun, 1993-94; contb. author: Generations Planning Your Legacy, 1999. Pres. Vols. in Cmty. Svc., Kokomo, 1980-85; del. Ind. State Rep. Conv., Indpls., 1986; mem. Nat. Rep. Senatorial Com., Washington, 1993-96. Fellow Esperti Peterson Inst. for Wealth Strategies, Offshore Inst., Mid South Estate Planning Forum (founding mem., pres. 1997—); mem. Nat. Network Estate Planning Attys., Tenn. Bar Assn. (tax, probate and trusts sect.). Episcopalian. Avocations: collecting and restoring classic automobiles, traveling. Office: 9111 Cross Park Dr Ste D200 Knoxville TN 37923-4521

BLYNN, GUY MARC, lawyer; b. Bklyn., May 26, 1945; s. S. Jerry and Viola T. Vogel Blynn; children: Daniel Scott, Harlan Sterling, Aaron Seth. BS in Econs. cum laude, U. Pa., Wharton Sch. of Fin. Commerce, 1967; JD cum laude, Harvard U., 1970. Bar: N.C., N.Y., U.S. Ct. of Appeals for Fed. Cir., U.S. Ct. of Appeals for the 2d Cir., U.S. Dist. Cts. for the Middle Dist. of N.C., Southern and Eastern Dist. N.Y. Assoc. Kaye, Scholer, Fierman, Hays & Handler, N.Y.C., 1970-78; assoc. counsel R.J. Reynolds Industries Inc., Winston Salem, N.C., 1978-79; sr. counsel RJR Nabisco Inc., Winston Salem, N.C., 1979-86; dep. gen. counsel R.J. Reynolds Tobacco Co., Winston Salem, N.C., 1986-1989, v.p., dep. gen. counsel, sec., 1989—; lectr. Wake Forest U. Sch. of Law, 1980-93; cons. Dept. Commerce, 1987-90. Contbr. articles to profl. jours. Chmn. Brand Names Edn. Found., 1988-94; bd. dirs. N.C. Vol. Lawyers for the Arts, 1985-91, pres., 1987-91. Mem. ABA, Am. Arbitration Assn. (panel of arbitrators 1975-95), Carolina Patent Trademark & Copyright Law Assn. (v.p. 1979-80, pres. 1980-81), Am. Intellectul Property Law Assn. (chmn. taxation and fin. matters com. 1991-92), Am. Bar Assn. Forum Com. on Entertainment And Sports Industries, Assn. of Bar of City Of N.Y. (chmn. com. on trademarks and unfair competition 1975-78, subcommittee on patent and trademark office practice 1976-77), Anti-Defamation League (N.C. regional adv. bd. 1987—, chmn. elect 1991-93, chmn. 1993—, vice chmn. 1990-91), U.S. Trademark Assn. (bd. dirs. 1982-90, v.p. 1984-85, exec. v.p. 1985-86, pres., chmn. 1986-87). Home: PO Box 20383 Winston Salem NC 27120-0383 Office: R J Reynolds Tobacco Co 401 N Main St Winston Salem NC 27101-3818

BLYTH, JEFFREY, journalist; b. Chester-Le-Street, Durham, Eng., Mar. 20, 1926; came to U.S., 1957; m. Myrna Blyth, Nov. 1962; children: Jonathan, Graham. Fgn. corr. London Daily Mail, 1951-71; radio journalist BBC/SABC, N.Y.C., 1971-95; editor-in-chief Interpress, N.Y.C., 1972—. Pres. Fgn. Press Assn., N.Y.C., 1969-71. Mem. Overseas Press Club, London Press Club. Office: Interpress 400 Madison Ave Rm 1704 New York NY 10017-1997

BLYTH, JONATHAN J., legislative staff member. BA in Govt., Franklin and Marshall Coll., 1989; MPA, George Washington U., 1993. Intern Senator Alfonse D'Amato, 1986, GOPAC, 1987; profl. devel. staff Dept. of Navy Naval Facilties Engring. Command, 1989-90; legis. corr., sys. mgr. Congressman Robert S. Walker, 1990-93; sr. legis. asst. Congressman Richard W. Pombo, 1993-95; chief of staff, legis. dir. Congressman William J. Martini, 1995-97; legis. asst. Senator James Jeffords, 1997-98; legis. dir. Congressman Bob Barr, 1998—. Office: 101 N Carolina Ave SE Washington DC 20003

BLYTH, MYRNA GREENSTEIN, publishing executive, editor, author; b. N.Y.C., Mar. 22, 1939; d. Benjamin and Betty (Austin) Greenstein; m. Jeffrey Blyth, Nov. 25, 1962; children: Jonathan, Graham. B.A., Bennington (Vt.) Coll., 1960. Sr. editor Datebook mag., N.Y.C., 1960-62, Ingenue mag., N.Y.C., 1963-68; book editor Family Health mag., 1968-71; book and fiction editor, then assoc. editor Family Circle mag., N.Y.C., 1972-78; exec. editor Family Circle mag., 1978-81; editor-in-chief Ladies' Home Jour., 1981—, pub. dir., sr. v.p., 1987—, editor-in-chief, pub. dir.; editor-in-chief, pub. dir. More Mag., 1998—; freelance writer, contbr. mags. Author: (novels) Cousin Suzanne, 1975, For Better and For Worse, 1978; contbr. articles to New Yorker mag., New York mag., Redbook mag., Cosmopolitan mag., Reader's Digest. Bd. dirs. Child Care Action Campaign, N.Y.C., 1989—; mem. nat. adv. bd. Susan G. Komen Breast Cancer Found.; active The Communitarians, Nat. Commn. on Am. Jewish Women. Recipient Headliner award Women in Comms., Inc., 1992, Human Rels. award Am. Jewish Com.'s Pub. Divsn., 1992. Mem. Am. Soc. Mag. Editors (exec. com. 1989—), N.Y. Women in Comm., Inc. (past pres., Amb. of Excellence, Matrix award 1988), Women's Media Group, Authors League, Overseas Press Club (bd. govs.). Office: Ladies' Home Jour 125 Park Ave Fl 20 New York NY 10017-5529

BLYTHE, WILLIAM LEGETTE, II, editor, writer; b. Washington, May 13, 1957; s. William Brevard and Gloria (Nassif) B.; m. Joan Elizabeth Kubisch. BA with honors, U. N.C., 1979; MFA, U. Ala., Tuscaloosa, 1986. Editor The Black Warrior Rev., Tuscaloosa, 1983-84; writer-in-residence St. Albans Sch., Washington, 1986-87; with Esquire mag., N.Y.C., 1987-97, assoc. fiction editor, lit. editor, monthly columnist; contbg. editor Harpers, Mirabella, N.Y.C. Editor: Why I Write, 1998; co-editor: (anthology) Lust, Violence, Sin, Magic, 1993; guest editor Bookforum; contbr. short stories, articles and revs. to Best Am. Short Stories, N.Y. Times Book Rev., Esquire, Mirabella, The New Yorker, Outside, Spin, Utne Reader, Epoch, Carolina Quar., Mo. Rev., also others. N.C. acad. scholar U. N.C., 1975-79; dean's fellow U. Ala., 1982, 83. Office: Mirabella Mag 1633 Broadway Fl 44 New York NY 10019-6708

BOADLE-BIBER, MARGARET CLARE, physiology educator; b. Melbourne, Australia, Jan. 18, 1943; came to U.S., 1967; d. Campbell Dean and Constance Ellen (Browne) Boadle; m. Thomas Ulrich Leonard Biber, Oct. 8, 1969; 1 child, Eric Gustav Nicholas. BS, U. Coll. London, 1964; DPhil, Oxford (Eng.) U., 1967. Rsch. assoc. pharm. dept. Yale U. Sch. Medicine, New Haven, Conn., 1968-69, instr. pharm. dept., 1969-71, asst. prof. pharm. dept., 1971-75; assoc. prof. physiology dept. Va. Commonwealth U., Richmond, 1975-87, prof. physiology dept., 1987—, interim chair, 1991-93, chair, 1993—. Contbr. articles to profl. jours. Mem. Am. Soc. Neurochemistry, Am. Soc. Pharm. & Exptl. Therapeutics, Soc. Neurosci. Office: Va Commonwealth U 1101 E Marshall St Richmond VA 23298-0551

BOADT, LAWRENCE EDWARD, priest, religion educator; b. L.A., Oct. 26, 1942; s. A. Loren and Eleanor (Power) B. MA in Religious Studies, St. Paul's Coll., Washington, 1968; STL, Cath. U. Am., 1971, MA in Semitic Langs., 1972; SSL, Pontifical Bibl. Inst., Rome, 1974, SSD, 1976. Ordained priest Roman Cath. Ch., 1969. Priest St. Andrew's Parish, Clemson, S.C., 1969-70, St. Susanna Parish, Rome, 1971-75; aux. staff St. Paul the Apostle Parish, N.Y.C., 1975-86, Good Shepherd Parish, N.Y.C., 1986—; publ., pres. Paulist Press., Mahwah, N.J., 1997—; prof. of the Bible Washington Theol. Union, Silver Spring, Md., 1976-97, prof. emeritus, 1997—. Editor: Toward Understanding the New Testament, 1978, Ezekiel's Oracle Against Egypt: A Literary and Philological Study, 1980, Jeremiah XXVI-LII, Zephaniah, Habakkuk and Nahum, 1983, Reading the Old Testament: An Introduction, 1985, An Introduction to Wisdom and the Book of Proverbs, 1986; editor-in-chief Theol. Inquiries; pub. editor Cath. Bibl. Quar., 1978-84; assoc. editor New Cath. World; contbr. articles to religious jours. Recipient Best Old Testament Book of Yr. Bibl. Archaeology Soc., 1986. Mem. Cath. Bibl. Assn. (regional pres. 1979-80, nat. pres. 1995-96), Am. Sch. Oriental Rsch., Soc. Bibl. Lit. (regional sec. 1984-90), Am. Acad. Religion. Office: Paulist Press 997 Macarthur Blvd Mahwah NJ 07430-2096

BOAK, JOSEPH GORDON, cardiologist; b. Indpls., Aug. 19, 1942; s. Joseph and Anne (Bates) B.; m. Marilyn Romanski, Oct. 3, 1942; children: Joseph Jr., Marshall. BA, Hamilton Coll., 1964; MD, U. Pa., 1970. Diplomate Am. Bd. of Med. Examiners, Am. Bd. Internal Medicine, Am. Bd. Cardiovascular Diseases. Intern Cook County Hosp., Chgo.; resident Rush Presbyn. Med. Ctr., Chgo., 1970-73; assoc. in medicine U. Ill. Med. Ctr., Chgo., 1971-73; instr. Temple U. Hosp. and Med. Sch., Phila., 1973-75; head cardiac clinic Jersey Shore Med. Ctr., Neptune, N.J., 1977-90; chief cardiac lab. Jersey Shore Med. Ctr., Neptune, 1979-84; clin. asst. prof. medicine Grad. Hosp. U. Pa., Phila., 1981—; attending physician Freehold (N.J.) Area Hosp., 1982—; clin. asst. prof. medicine Rutgers U., New Brunswick, N.J., 1983—; chief cardiology sect. Freehold Area Hosp., 1986—; chmn. cardiology dept. Jersey Shore Med. Ctr., Neptune, N.J., 1978—; founder Assoc. Cardiology Monmouth County, Neptune City, N.J., 1980-86; mem. intensive care com. Freehold Hosp., 1985—; mem. constn., bylaws com., mem. exec. com. Jersey Shore Med. Ctr., Neptune, 1990, chmn. cardiac surg. task force, 1988-89. Contbr. articles to profl. jours. Cardiology fellow Temple U. Hosp., 1973-75. Fellow Am. Coll. Physicians, Am. Coll. Cardiologists; mem. Am. Soc. Internal Medicine, Monmouth County Med. Soc., N.J. Med. Soc., Am. Heart Assn. Presbyterian. Clubs: Monmouth Boat, Spring Lake Bath and Tennis. Office: Monmouth Cardiologists Assocs 2102 Corlies Ave Neptune NJ 07753-6141

BOAL, DEAN, retired arts center administrator, educator; b. Longmont, Colo., Oct. 20, 1931; s. Elmer C. and L. Mildred (Snodgrass) B.; m. Ellen Christine TeSelle, Aug. 23, 1957; children: Brett, Jed. B.Music, B.Music Edn., U. Colo., 1953; M.Music, Ind. U., 1956; D. Musical Arts, U. Colo., 1959. Mem. faculty Hastings (Nebr.) Coll., 1958-60; head piano dept. Bradley U., Peoria, Ill., 1960-66; dean, pianist Peabody Conservatory, Balt., 1966-70; prof. piano, chair music SUNY, Fredonia, 1970-73; pres. St. Louis Conservatory, 1973-76; dir. radio sta. KWMU, St. Louis, 1976-78; v.p., gen.

mgr. Sta. WETA-FM, Washington, 1978-83; dir. arts and performance programs Nat. Pub. Radio, Washington, 1982-89; pres. Interlochen (Mich.) Ctr. for the Arts, 1989-95; pres. emeritus, 1995—. Author: Concepts and Skills for the Piano, Book I, 1969, Book II, 1970, Interlochen: A Home for The Arts, 1998; contbr. articles to profl. jours. Mem. adv. bd U. Colo. Coll. Music, 1987—; trustee Alma Coll., 1992-95. Served with U.S. Army, 1953-55. Woodrow Wilson teaching fellow, 1983-89; recipient Disting. Alumnus award in Profl. Music Univ. Colo., 1987. Mem. Eastern Public Radio Network (chmn. 1979-82), Coll. Music Soc., Pi Kappa Lambda, Mu Phi Epsilon, Phi Mu Alpha. Presbyterian.

BOARD, JOSEPH BRECKINRIDGE, JR., political scientist, educator; b. Princeton, Ind., Mar. 5, 1931; s. Joseph Breckinridge and Rachel Eleanor (Unthank) B.; children from previous marriage: Ian Robert, Annika Caroline, Amanda Anne; m. Mary Squire, Jan. 1, 1998. AB with highest honors, Ind. U., 1953, JD, 1958, PhD, 1962; BA (Rhodes scholar 1953-55), Oxford (Eng.) U., 1955, MA, 1961; PhD (hon.), Umea U., Sweden, 1973. Teaching fellow govt. Ind. U., 1955-58, lectr. govt., 1958; asst. prof. polit. sci. Elmira Coll., 1959-61; asso. prof. polit. sci., chmn. dept. Cornell Coll., 1961-64; prof. polit. sci., chmn. dept. Union Coll., Schenectady, 1964—; Robert Porter Patterson prof. govt. Union Coll., 1973—, chmn. faculty, 1983-85; pres. Paralegals-Plus Assocs., Inc., 1986—; acad. visitor London Sch. Econs. and Polit. Sci., 1972-73; adj. prof. Albany Law Sch., 1974—; scholar-in-residence Sch. Law Indiana U., 1999—; acting prof., chmn. dept. polit. sci. U. Umea, 1979; vis. prof. U. Paris (Sorbonne), 1987; mem. Rhodes Scholarship Selection Com. Nebr., 1961-62, Iowa, 1963-64, N.Y., 1991, 92; mem. regional selection com. for Woodrow Wilson Fellowships, 1966—; mem. exec. coun. Iowa Conf. Polit. Scientists, 1963-65; spl. adv. coll. and univ. affairs Young Citizens for Johnson, 1964; cons. Nat. Endowment Humanities, 1968, N.Y. State Dept. Edn., 1968; mem. polit. sci. adv. com. Fulbright-Hays Program, 1969-73; assoc., adv. com. for Western Europe Council for Internat. Exchange of Scholars; chmn. Scandinavian peer rev. com. Linkages Project; mem. U.S. Com. on NATO Fellowships; cons., co-host Nobel Prize broadcast Nat. Pub. Radio, 1976; vis. fellow Oriel Coll., Oxford, 1994—; acad. assoc. The Atlantic Coun.; chair bd. advisors Trans-nat. Rsch. Project on Effects of European Unification. Author: The Government and Politics of Sweden, 1970. Bd. advisers Schenectady Salvation Army; trustee, treas. Schnectady County Community Coll.; trustee Oriel Coll. (Oxford U.), Devel. Trust, 1991—. Fulbright lectr. Sweden, 1968-69; Central Am. fellow Asso. Colls. Midwest, 1962; NDEA postdoctoral fellow in Portuguese, 1963; recipient Disting. Svc. award SUNY Bd. Trustees Comty. Colls., 1997. Mem. Am. Assn. Rhodes Scholars, Am. Polit. Sci. Assn., AAUP, Ind. Bar, Am. Arbitration Assn., Am-Scandinavian Found. (com. on fellowships 1981—), Northeastern Polit. Sci. Assn. (exec. Council 1972), Soc. for Advancement Scandinavian Studies (exec. council 1972), Soc. Letters (Lund U.), Acacia, Phi Beta Kappa. Democrat. Episcopalian. Home: 3319 River Rd Arlington VT 05250-8998 Office: Union Coll Political Sci Dept Schenectady NY 12308

BOARDMAN, DAVID, newspaper editor; m. Barbara Winslow; children: Emily, Madeline. BS in Journalism, Northwestern U., 1979; M in Comm., U. Wash., 1983. Copy editor Football Weekly, Chgo., 1977-79; reporter Anacortes (Wash.) American, 1979-80, Skagit Valley Herald, Mt. Vernon, Wash., 1980-81; reporter, copy editor The News Tribune, Tacoma, 1981-83; copy editor The Seattle Times, 1983, editor, reporter, 1984, nat. editor, 1984-86, local news editor, 1986-87, asst. city editor, 1987-90, regional editor, 1990-96, metro. editor, 1997—, asst. mng. editor, 1997—; vis. faculty Poynter Inst. Media Studies, St. Petersburg, Fla. Recipient Goldsmith Prize in Investigative Reporting JFK Sch. Govt. Harvard U., 1993, Worth Bingham prize, 1993, Investigative Reporters and Editors award, 1993, AP Mng. Editors Pub. Svc. award, 1992, 1st place nat. reporting Pulitzer Prize, 1990, lead editor Pulitzer Prize in investigative reporting, 1997; finalist Pulitzer Prize, 1993, 98, 99; fellow Japan-IBCC fellowship Ctr. Fgn. Journalists, 1995. E-mail: dboardman@seattletimes.com. Office: The Seattle Times PO Box 70 1120 John St Seattle WA 98109-5321

BOARDMAN, EUNICE, retired music educator; b. Cordova, Ill., Jan. 27, 1926; d. George Hollister and Anna Bryson (Feaster) Boardman. B. Mus. Edn., Cornell Coll., 1947; M. Mus. Edn., Columbia U., 1951; Ed.D., U. Ill., 1963; DFA (hon.), Cornell Coll., 1995. Tchr. music pub. schs., Iowa, 1947-55; prof. music edn. Wichita State U., Kans., 1955-72; vis. prof. mus. edn. Normal State U., Ill., 1972-74, Roosevelt U., Chgo., 1974-75; prof. mus. edn. U. Wis., Madison, 1975-89, dir. Sch. Music, 1980-89; prof. music, dir. grad. program in music edn. U. Ill., Urbana, 1989-98; ret. Author: Musical Growth in Elementary School, 1963, 6th rev. edit., 1996, Exploring Music, 1966, 3d rev. edit., 1975, The Music Book, 1980, 2d rev. edit., 1984, Holt Music, 1987, Dimensions of Musical Thinking, 1989. Mem. Soc. Music Tchr. Edn. (chmn. 1984-86), Music Educators Nat. Conf. Avocations: reading; handwork. Office: U Ill 3000 Music Urbana IL 61801

BOARDMAN, GREGORY DALE, environmental engineer, educator; b. Montpelier, Vt., Dec. 12, 1950; s. Theodore Robert and June Irene (Rogers) B.; m. Gail Cynthia Bedell, June 6, 1970 (div. Dec. 1986); children: Heather Eve, Kristina Marie, Jessica Anne; m. Shelley Ann Mitchell, Aug. 28, 1987; 1 child, Courtney Dale. MS, U. N.H., 1973; PhD, U. Maine, 1976. Registered profl. engr., Va.; diplomate of environ. engring. Asst. prof. civil engring. Va. Poly. Inst. and State U., Blacksburg, 1976-83, assoc. prof., 1983-98, prof., 1998—; mem. bd. Dept. Commerce, Richmond, Va., 1987-94; cons. to numerous cos., 1976—. Author 2 manuals; contbr. numerous articles to profl. jours., chpts. to books. Chmn. Montgomery County Cmty. Shelter, Va., 1986-91, chmn. of program, 1990-91; mem. planning commn. Town of Blackburg, 1989-93. Rsch. grantee EPA, NIH, NOAA, Water Rsch., numerous others, 1976—. Mem. ASCE (coms.), Soc. Environ. Toxicology and Chemistry, Water Environ. Fedn., Internat. Assn. on Water Quality, Assn. Environ. Engring. Profs., Am. Assn. Textile Chemists and Colorists, Sigma Xi, Tau Beta Pi, Phi Kappa Phi. Achievements include research on industrial waste treatment and development of short-term toxicity tests. Office: Va Poly Inst and State U Dept Civil/Environ Engring 417 NEB Blacksburg VA 24061

BOARDMAN, JOHN MICHAEL, mathematician, educator; b. Manchester, Eng., Feb. 13, 1938; came to U.S., 1969, naturalized, 1973; s. William Edgar and Carrie (Brown) B.; m. Jacqueline O'Brien Schulman, 1967 (div. 1977); children: Susan, Andrew. B.A., Trinity Coll., Cambridge U., 1961, Ph.D., 1965. Vis. lectr. U. Chgo., 1966-67; asst. lectr. U. Warwick, Eng., 1967-68; assoc. prof. Johns Hopkins U., Balt., 1969-72; prof. Johns Hopkins U., 1972—. Author: Singularities of Differentiable Maps, 1967, (with R.M. Vogt) Homotopy Invariant Algebraic Structures on Topological Spaces, 1973, Modular Representations on the Homology of Powers of Real Projective Space, 1993; (with D.C. Johnson and W.S. Wilson) Unstable Operations on Generalized Cohomology, 1995. Served with RAF, 1956-58. Sci. Rsch. Coun. fellow, 1964-66; NSF grantee, 1970-88. Mem. Am. Math. Soc. Quaker. Home: 6217 Northwood Dr Baltimore MD 21212-2802 Office: Johns Hopkins U Dept Math 3400 N Charles St Baltimore MD 21218-2680

BOARDMAN, MARK SEYMOUR, lawyer; b. Birmingham, Ala., Mar. 16, 1958; s. Frank Seymour and Flora (Sarinopoulos) B.; m. Cathryn Dunkin, 1983; children:Wilson Paul, Joanna Christina. BA cum laude, U. Ala., 1979, JD, 1982. Bar: Ala. 1982, U.S. Dist. Ct. (no. dist.) Ala. 1982, U.S. Ct. Appeals (11th cir.) 1983, U.S. Supreme Ct. 1987. Assoc. Spain, Gillon, Riley, Tate & Etheredge, Birmingham, 1982-84; ptnr. Porterfield, Scholl, Bainbridge, Mims and Harper, P.A., Birmingham, 1984-93, Boardman Carr & Weed, P.C., Birmingham, 1993—. Pres. Holy Trinity Holy Cross Greek Orthodox Cathedral, 1991, 92, sec., 1987, asst. treas., 1986, treas., 1988, 89, v.p., 1990, 96, 97, 98, 99, bd. auditors, 1994; mem. coun. Greek Orthodox Diocese of Atlanta, 1992-95; mem. Shelby County (Ala.) Work Release Commn., sec., 1996. Mem. ABA, Ala. State Bar, Shelby County Bar Assn. (treas. 1992-93, sec. 1994, v.p. 1995, pres. 1996), Birmingham Bar Assn. (co-chmn. econs. of law com. 1997, local bar liaison com. 1997), Am. Jud. Soc., Ala. Def. Lawyers Assn., Def. Rsch. Inst., Ala. Claims Assn., Order of Barristers, Phi Beta Kappa, Delta Sigma Rho-Tau Kappa Alpha, Pi Sigma Alpha. Greek Orthodox. Home: 1915 Wellington Rd Birmingham AL 35209-4026 Office: Boardman Carr & Weed PC PO Box 59465 Birmingham AL 35259-9465

BOARDMAN, MAUREEN BELL, community health nurse; b. Hartford, Conn., June 11, 1966; d. Jack Russell and Mary Elizabeth (Brumm) Bell; m. Byron Earl Boardman, June 4, 1988; 1 child, Meghan Elizabeth. BSN, U. Maine, Orono, 1988; MSN, U. Tenn., 1991. ACLS; cert. family nurse practitioner. Charge nurse med.- surg. divsn. Scott County Hosp., Oneida, Tenn., 1988-89, employee health nurse, 1989-92; RN team leader Oneida Home Health, 1989, Quality Home Health, Oneida, 1989-90; family nurse practitioner Straightfork Family Care Clinic, Pioneer, Tenn., 1992-96, Huntsville (Tenn.) Family Care Clinic, 1996—; mem. child abuse rev. team Dept. Human Svcs., Huntsville, Tenn., 1993—; adj. prof. Coll. Nursing U. Tenn., 1997. Med. advisor, liaison Scott County (Tenn.) Sch. Systems Sci. Fair Com., 1992—; bd. dirs., editor newsletter Appalachian Arts Coun., Oneida, 1993—, v.p., 1996-98, del., 1997; com. on health policy TNA, 1998—. Mem. Tenn. Nurses Assn. (del. to conv. 1994, 95, 96, 97, com. on health policy 1998—), Sigma Theta Tau (sec. Gamma Chi chpt. 1996—). Roman Catholic. Avocations: reading, biking, swimming, dancing. Home: 119 Hillcrest Dr Oneida TN 37841-6659 Office: Huntsville Family Care Clinic 641 Baker Hwy Huntsville TN 37756-4127

BOARDMAN, RICHARD JOHN, lawyer; b. Newton, Mass., Mar. 28, 1940; s. Raymond Everett and Miriam Lucile (Temperley) B.; 1 child, Lawrence Luke. BA, U. Mass., 1962; JD, U. N.D., 1965; LLM, Yale U., 1966. Bar: N.D. 1965, Mo. 1970, U.S. Dist. Ct. (ea. dist.) Mo. 1970, U.S. Ct. Appeals (8th cir.) 1970, U.S. Supreme Ct. 1968. Asst. prof. law Cath. U. of Am. Law Sch., Washington, 1966-69; assoc. dir., atty. Legal Aid Soc., St. Louis, 1969-74; asst. prof. of comm. med. St. Louis U. Med. Sch., 1974-78; pvt. practice, 1978—; pres. Lafayette Title Co., 1980—; v.p. Gateway Legal Svcs., St. Louis, 1997—; bd. dirs. Bar Plan Title Ins. Co. Pres. Singer Inst., St. Louis, 1982-85; bd. dirs. Kids in the Middle, Inc., St. Louis, 1980-82, Places for People, Inc., St. Louis, 1973-75. Mem. ABA, ACLU, Mo. Ind. Title Assn., Mo. Bar Assn. (subcom. chair property com. 1988-90, chair property law com. 1996-98), St. Louis Met. Bar Assn. (co-chair title ins. sect., 1990—, chair real property sect. 1987-89), Am. Land Title Assn., Nat. Network Estate Planning Attys. (charter). Office: 4526 S Grand Blvd Saint Louis MO 63111-1039

BOARDMAN, ROBERT A., lawyer; b. 1947. BA, Muskingum Coll., 1969; JD, Case Western Reserve U., 1972. Bar: Ohio 1972, Colo. 1976. Assoc. atty. Roetzel & Andress, 1972-75, atty., 1975-83; asst. gen. coun., sec. Manville Corp., Denver, 1983-87, v.p., sec., 1988-90; sr. v.p., gen. coun. Navistar Internat. Transp. Corp., Chgo., 1990—. E-mail Address: RABG@NAVISTAR.com. Office: Navistar Internat Transp Corp 455 N Cityfront Plaza Dr Chicago IL 60611-5503*

BOARDMAN, SEYMOUR, artist; b. Bklyn., Dec. 29, 1921; s. Joseph and Bessie (Warren) B. BSS, CCNY, 1942; postgrad., Ecole des Beaux-Arts, Paris, 1946-47, Atelier Fernand Leger, 1948, Art Students League, N.Y.C., 1949-50, Ecole de la Grande Chaumiere, 1950-51. One-man shows, Galerie Mai, Paris, 1951, Martha Jackson Gallery, N.Y.C., 1955, 56, Stephen Radich Gallery, N.Y.C., 1960-61, 62, A.M. Sachs Gallery, N.Y.C., 1965, 67, 68, Dorsky Gallery, N.Y.C., 1972, Aaron Berman Gallery, N.Y.C., 1978, Anita Shapolsky Gallery, N.Y.C., 1987, 91, Anderson Gallery, Buffalo, 1994; group shows include, Carnegie Internat., Pitts., 1955, Whitney Mus. Am. Art, 1955, 61, 67, Nebr. Art Assn., 1956, Kunsthalle, Basel, Switzerland, 1964, Santa Barbara Art Mus., 1964, Albright-Knox Gallery, Buffalo, 1967, Cornell U., 1971, Anita Shapolsky Gallery, N.Y.C., 1986, David Anderson Gallery, Buffalo, 1991-92; represented in permanent collections, Whitney Mus. Am. Art, Guggenheim Mus., Walker Art Ctr., Mpls., Santa Barbara Mus. Art, NYU. Served with USAAF, 1942-46. Longview Found. grantee, 1963; Guggenheim Found. fellow, 1972-73; Adolph and Esther Gottlieb Found. grantee, 1979, 83; Pollock-Krasner Found. grantee, 1985-86, 91, 98. Address: 234 W 27th St New York NY 10001-5905

BOARDMAN, WILLIAM PENNIMAN, lawyer, banker; b. Columbus, Ohio, June 22, 1941; s. John King and Eleanor Susan (Penniman) B.; m. Nancy Louise Staby, Apr. 10, 1971; children: Abigail Blair, Anna Neel, Elizabeth Penniman. B.A., Washington and Lee U., 1963, JD summa cum laude, 1969. Bar: Ohio 1969. Mgmt. trainee 1st Nat. City Bank, N.Y.C., 1963-64; ptnr. Porter, Wright, Morris & Arthur, Columbus, 1969-81; gen. counsel, exec. v.p. BancOhio Nat. Bank, Columbus, 1981-84; gen. counsel BancOhio Corp., Columbus, 1981-84; v.p. Banc One Corp., Columbus, 1984-88, sr. v.p., 1988-90, exec. v.p., 1990-93, sr. exec. v.p., 1993-98; sr. exec. v.p. Banc One Corp., Chgo., 1998—; bd. dirs. Visa Internat., Checkfree Corp., Electronic Payment Sys.; chmn. bd. Visa USA, 1998—. Trustee Washington and Lee Univ., 1993—; trustee Columbus Sch. for Girls, 1981, v.p., pres.-elect, 1986-88, pres., 1988-90. 1st lt. arty. U.S. Army, 1964-66, Korea. Republican. Episcopalian. Clubs: Rocky Fork Hunt and Country (trustee 1983-89, v.p. 1986, pres. 1987), The Columbus Club (bd. dirs. 1990-96, pres. 1994-96), The Golf Club (New Albany, Ohio). Office: Bank One Corp First National Plz Chicago IL 60670-0897

BOARMAN, GERALD L., principal. EdD, Southeastern U., 1983. Prin. Eleanor Roosevelt H.S., Greenbelt, Md.; chief ednl. adminstr. Eleanor Roosevelt Cmty. Schs. Adv. bd. Washington Post Prin.'s Inst. Named Md. State Prin. of Yr., 1995-96; recipient Md. Guidance Counselor Adminstr. of Yr. award, 1991, Md. Music Educator of Yr. award for adminstr., 1993, Milken Nat. Edn. award, 1995-96, Disting. Educator award, Washington Post, 1997-98. Mem. ASCD, Am. Assn. Secondary Adminstrs., Nat. Assn. Secondary Sch. Prins., Nat. Sch. Pub. Rels. Assn. (adv. bd.), Md. Assn. Secondary Sch. Prins. (pres. 1999). Office: Eleanor Roosevelt HS 7601 Hanover Pky Greenbelt MD 20770-2099

BOARMAN, MARJORIE RUTH, manufacturing company executive, consultant; b. Lakeland, Fla., Apr. 14, 1953; d. Hugh Francis and Nancy Addair (McCracken) Roberts; m. Edward F. Moore, June 28, 1975 (div. 1986); children: Kulani Anne, Brittany Elizabeth; m. James Louis Boarman, Feb. 5, 1987; 1 child, Joshua; stepchildren: Steven, Christina, Paulette. BS in Edn., Fla. State U., 1975; MEd, U. Hawaii/Manoa, 1978. Cert. tchr., Fla., Mo. Substitute tchr. KCCA Preschs., Honolulu, 1975; tchr. Hickam Day Care Ctr., Hickam AFB, Hawaii, 1975-77; tchr., sales rep. Grolier Interstate Inc., Honolulu, 1977; tchr. Kiddie Kollege Presch., Hickam AFB, 1977-79, Our Lady of Sorrows Schs., St. Louis, 1979-80; program dir. Clayton (Mo.) YWCA, 1981-82; cons. Parent Talk Svcs., Phoenix, 1983-85; tchr. Polk County Schs., Polk City, Fla., 1986-89; co-owner Boarman Built Inc., Green Ridge, Mo., 1989—. Co-creator: Bon Voyage board game, 1992. V.p. Green Ridge 2000 Team, 1995—; leader, coord. Camp Fire Boys and Girls, Lakeland, 1988—; bd. dirs. Boswell PTA, Auburndale, 1991-92, Windsor R-1 Sch. Bd., 1999—, Henry County R-1 Sch. Bd., 1999—, Mo. Womens Coun., 1998—. Mem. NAFE, Auburndale C. of C. (bd. dirs. 1991-92), Green Ridge C. of C. (bd. dirs. 1994-96), Sedalia Bus. and Profl. Women (2nd v.p. membership chmn. 1994-95, 1st v.p. issues mgmt. chmn. 1995-96, pres.-elect 1996-97, State Individual Devel. award, pres. 1997-98, dir. 1998—), Windsor C. of C. (bd. dirs. 1999—), Kappa Delta Pi. Republican. Pentecostal. Avocations: swimming, raquetball, camping, travel, sewing, gardening. Office: Boarman Built Inc 128 S Main St Ste A Windsor MO 65360

BOAS, FRANK, lawyer; b. Amsterdam, North Holland, The Netherlands, July 22, 1930; came to U.S., 1940; s. Maurits Coenraad and Sophie (Brandel) B.; m. Edith Louise Bruce, June 30, 1981 (dec. July 1992); m. Jean Scripps, Aug. 6, 1993. AB cum laude, Harvard U., 1951, JD, 1954. Bar: U.S. Dist. Ct. D.C. 1955, U.S. Ct. Appeals (D.C. cir.) 1955; U.S. Supreme Ct. 1958. Atty. Office of the Legal Adviser U.S. State Dept., Washington, 1957-59; pvt. practice, Brussels and London, 1959-79; of counsel Patton, Boggs & Blow, Washington, 1975-80; pres. Frank Boas Found., Inc., Cambridge, Mass., 1980—. Mem. U.S. delegation to UN confs. on law of sea, Geneva, 1958, 60; vice chmn. Commn. for Ednl. Exch., Brussels, 1980-87; mem. vis. com. Harvard Law Sch., 1987-91, Ctr. for Internat. Affairs, 1988—; dir. Found. European Orgn. for Research and Treatment of Cancer, Brussels, 1978-87, Paul-Henri Spaak Found., Brussels, 1981—, East-West Ctr. Found., Honolulu, 1990—, Law of the Sea Inst., Honolulu, 1992-97, Pacific Forum CSIS, Honolulu, 1996—, Honolulu Acad. Arts, 1997—; hon. sec. Am. C. of C. in Belgium, 1966-78. With U.S. Army, 1955-57. Decorated Officer of the Order of Leopold II, comdr. Order of the Crown (Belgium), comdr. Order of Merit (Luxembourg); recipient Tribute of Appreciation award U.S. State Dept., 1981, Harvard Alumni Assn. award, 1996. Mem. ABA, Fed. D.C. Bar Assn., Pacific and Asian Affairs Coun. (pres.), Honolulu Com. Fgn. Relations, Pacific, Outrigger Canoe (Honolulu), Travellers (London), Am. and Common Market (Brussels pres. 1981-85), Honolulu Social Sci. Assn. Home: 4463 Aukai Ave Honolulu HI 96816-4858

BOAS, NANCY M., curator; b. Chgo.; d. Arthur Magid and Eva (Blum) Witcoff; m. Roger Boas; children: John, Christopher, Anthony, Lucy. AB, Sarah Lawrence Coll. Guest curator Fine Arts Mus., San Francisco, 1989; adj. curator Fine Arts Mus., 1993—, co-curator, 1995; lectr. in field. Author: The Society of Six California Colorists, 1997. V.p. San Francisco Art Commn., 1989-92. Home: 3329 Washington St San Francisco CA 94118 Office: Fine Arts Mus Am Art Dept San Francisco CA 94118

BOASBERG, LEONARD W., reporter; b. Omaha, Mar. 27, 1923; s. William and Nell (Levin) B.; m. Lore Metzger, Dec. 12, 1946; children: Mark, Daniel, Judith. BA, Yale U., 1948; MA, U. Nebr., 1963. Editor Jewish Press, Omaha, 1948-52; owner Live Wire Cleaners, Omaha, 1952-64; polit. columnist Omaha Sun Newspapers, Omaha, 1958-68; editorial page editor Harrisburg Patriot & Evening News, Pa., 1964-69; assoc. dir. info. Pa. House of Reps., Phila., 1969-70; mem. editorial bd. Phila. Inquirer, Phila., 1971-84, cultural arts reporter, 1984—. Contbr. articles to profl. jours. Served to capt. U.S. Army Intelligence, 1942-46, China, Japan. Recipient 9 awards. Mem. Soc. Profl. Journalists, Sigma Delta Chi. Democrat. Jewish. Avocations: French, Italian, Japanese, Chinese and Am. langs., culture, history and politics. Home: 349 Saunders Dr Wayne PA 19087-5406 Office: Phila Inquirer 400 N Broad St Philadelphia PA 19130-4099

BOAT, RONALD ALLEN, business executive; b. Dayton, Ohio, Nov. 16, 1947; s. Robert Mallory and Elvetta June (Smith) B. Student, Naval Acad./Army Sch. Music, Norfolk, Va., 1968-69, Ariz. State U., 1966-68. Pres. Prodn. Svcs., Phoenix, 1968—, Greek Specialties Corp., Phoenix, 1980-94; v.p. Am. Baby Boomers, San Diego, 1984-93; co-founder, v.p. Internat. Food Network, San Diego, 1985-90; founder, pres. AMC Food Svcs. Corp., 1991-94; pres. The Natural Light Co., 1994-96; ind. prodr. Intel, Honeywell, Best Western, Sperry, Phoenix, 1985—, Phoenix Health Plan, B.P.I., Maricopa Refining Co., P.A.R. Techs., Profitmax, Cycle-Masters, Continental Homes, Framatome, PMH Found., Coldwell Banker, KareMor Internat., Crowne Plaza Hotels, Continental Homes, Phoenix Suns, Arkitekton, Framatome, Rockridge Technologies; mem. Lund Team Real Estate Adv. Bd., 1991-95; bd. dirs. Lund Real Estate Corp., 1990-95. Founder, pres. Group AMC, Inc., 1995—. With U.S. Army, 1968-71. Named Outstanding sales rep. Club Am., Dallas, 1972-73, Top Distbr. Club Am., Dallas, 1973; recipient Top Restaurant award Am. Heart Assn., Phoenix, 1988, Best of Phoenix restaurant award, 1991. Mem. Am. Radio Relay League, Internat. Platform Assn., Phi Mu Alpha Sinfonia. Republican. Avocations: amateur radio, music, travel. E-mail: ronb@psavideo.com. Office: P S A 14628 N 48th Way Scottsdale AZ 85254-2203

BOAT, THOMAS FREDERICK, physician, educator, researcher; b. Pella, Iowa, Sept. 7, 1939; s. Bert Reuben and Anne Marie (Schoenbohm) B.; m. Barbara Mary Walling, June. 9, 1962; children: Sarah Elizabeth, Mary Barbara, Anne Christine. BA, Cen. Coll., Pella, 1961; MS, U. Iowa, 1965, MD, 1966. Diplomate Am. Bd. Pediat., Am. Bd. Pediat. Pulmonology. Resident in pediat. U. Minn., Mpls., 1966-68; clin. assoc. NIH, Bethesda, Md., 1968-70; fellow in pediat. pulmonology Case Western Res. U., Cleve., 1970-72, instr. pediat., 1972-73, asst. prof., 1973-76, assoc. prof., 1976-81, prof., 1981-82; prof., chmn. dept. pediat. U. N.C., Chapel Hill, 1982-93; chmn. dept. pediat. U. Cin. Sch. Medicine, 1993—; dir. Cin. Children's Hosp. Rsch. Found., 1993—; prin. investigator Pediat. Pulmonary Specialized Ctr. Rsch., NIH, 1991-93; chmn. Am. Bd. Pediat., 1994. Editor Current Opinions in Pediat., 1990-93; mem. editl. bd. Lung Rsch. jour. Bd. dirs. Ronald McDonald House, Chapel Hill, 1985-88, Cystic Fibrosis Found., chmn. rsch. devel. program, 1983—. Lt. comdr. USPHS, 1968-70. Fellow Am. Acad. Pediat.; mem. Am. Pediat. Soc. (pres.-elect 1999), Am. Thoracic Soc. (chmn. pediat. assembly 1983-84), Assn. Med. Sch. Pediat. Dept. Chairs (pres.-elect 1994-97, pres. 1997-99). Office: Children's Hosp Med Ctr 3333 Burnet Ave # 3301 Cincinnati OH 45229-3026

BOATMAN, DEBORAH ANN, hospice nurse; b. Muskogee, Okla., Sept. 8, 1955; d. John and Joanne Everitt; children: Will Boatman, Jeb Boatman. BA in Psychology, Northeastern State U., Tahlequah, Okla., 1981; BSN, U. Okla., 1985. RN, Okla.; cert. RN in hospice ANCC. Oncology staff nurse St. Francis Hosp., Tulsa, 1985; staff nurse St. John Hospice, Tulsa, 1986, St. Francis Hospice, Tulsa, 1986-94, Hospice of Okla. County, Oklahoma City, 1994—. Mem. Oncology Nursing Soc., Hospice Nurses Assn., Golden Key.

BOATMAN, ELIZABETH ARTLE, information systems specialist, municipal official; m. Steve Boatman, Apr. 6, 1996; 1 child, Zach. BS in Computer Sci., Youngstown State U., 1982. Database adminstr. Nat. Steel Corp., Pitts., 1982-85, Ciba Geigy Corp., Ardsley, N.Y., 1985-87; mgr. br. cons. svcs. IBM, Chgo., 1987-94; dir. cons. svcs. ShowCase Corp., Chgo., 1994-95; bus. practice leader, mgmt. cons. practice Blackwell Cons. Svcs., Chgo., 1995-97; dir. Mayor's Office Bus. and Info. Mgmt. City of Chgo., 1996-97; chief info. officer dept. bus. and info. svcs., 1997—. Office: Bus & Info Svcs Richard J Dailey Ctr 50 W Washington St Rm 2700 Chicago IL 60602-1328*

BOATWRIGHT, CHARLOTTE JEANNE, hospital marketing and public relations executive; b. Chattanooga, Dec. 12, 1937; d. Clifton Jentry and Veltina Novella (Braden) Blevins; m. Robert W. Boatwright; children: Lynn Kay, Janis Ann, Karen Jean, Mary Ruth, Melody Susan, April Celeste. Diploma, Erlanger Sch. Nursing, Chattanooga, 1963; BS, U. Tenn., Chattanooga, 1976, MEd, 1981; PhD, Columbia Pacific U., San Rafael, Calif., 1987. RN, Tenn.; cert. domestic violence counselor; diplomate Nat. Assn. Forensic Counselors, Nat. Bd. Addiction Examiners; cert. mediator Mediation Assn. Tenn. Surgeon's asst. William Robert Fowler, M.D., Chattanooga, 1963-64; instr. med.-surg. nursing Baroness Erlanger Hosp. Sch. Nursing, 1964-67, instr. fundamentals nursing, 1971-74, chmn. dept. mental health-psychiat. nursing, 1977-81; staff nurse Meml. Hosp., Chattanooga, 1967-68, nursing supr., 1968-70; dir. inservice edn. Hutcheson Med. Ctr., Ft. Oglethorpe, Ga., 1970-71; youth work cons. Sewanee Dist. Episcopal Chs., Chattanooga, 1975-76; dir. spl. projects North Park Hosp., Chattanooga, 1984-87, dir. mktg. and pub. rels., 1987—; pres. CBB Comms.; freelance writer. mem. dept. youth work Episcopal Diocese Tenn., 1975-77, mem. violence in soc. resource team; condr. adult ch. sch. groups St. Martin's Episcopal Ch., Chattanooga; vice chmn. Brynewood Park Cmty. Assn., 1985, 86; founder, chairperson Domestic Violence Coalition of Greater Chattanooga, 1994; bd. dirs. Family Violence Shelter Com., Sexual Abuse Resource Ctr., Coalition Against Family Violence Greater Chattanooga. Recipient Liberty Bell award Chattanooga Bar Assn., 1997. Mem. Am. Coll. Healthcare Execs. (nominee), Tenn. Hosp. Assn., Tenn. Soc. for Hosp. Mktg. and Pub. Rels., Chattanooga Press Assn., Chattanooga C. of C., U. Tenn. Alumnae Assn., Columbia Pacific U. Alumnae Assn. Republican. Avocations: music, reading, gardening, travel.

BOAZ, DAVID DOUGLAS, foundation executive; b. Mayfield, Ky., Aug. 29, 1953; s. Seth Thomas Jr. and Martha Elizabeth (Pruitt) B. BA, Vanderbilt U., 1975. Exec. dir. Young Am.'s Found., Sterling, Va., 1975-76; editor New Guard Mag., Sterling, 1976-78; exec. dir. Council for a Competitive Economy, Washington, 1978-80; research dir. Clark for Pres. Com., Washington, 1980; v.p. Cato Inst., Washington, 1981-89, exec. v.p., 1989—; bd. dirs. Ctr. for Ind. Thought, N.Y.C., Women's Freedom Network; bd. regents Congl. Schs. Va., 1991—. Author: Libertarianism: A Primer, 1997; co-editor: Beyond the Status Quo, 1985, An American Vision, 1989, Market Liberalism: A Paradigm for the 21st Century, 1993; editor: Left, Right and Babyboom, 1986, Assessing the Reagan Years, 1988, The Crisis in Drug Prohibition, 1990, Liberating Schools: Education in the Inner City, 1991, The Libertarian Reader, 1997; contbr. to books and newspapers. Mem. Free Press Assn. Office: Cato Inst 1000 Massachusetts Ave NW Washington DC 20001-5400

BOAZMAN, FRANKLIN MEADOR, financial consultant; b. Dallas, Dec. 31, 1939; s. Howard Clark and Mary Elinor (Meador) B.; m. Tommie Sharon Cope, July 15, 1961 (div. Feb. 1974); children: Michael Louis, Terry Ann; m. Dianne Codone, Nov. 19, 1988. MBA, Tulane U., 1984. V.p. ops. Indsl. Uniform & Towel Co., Dallas, 1963-70; pres. Visual Presentations,

Inc., Dallas, 1970-74; gen. mgr. Aratex Services, Inc., New Orleans, 1974-82, group mgr., 1982-86; pres. New Orleans Cons. Group, Ltd., 1985—. Mem. Met. Rep. Businessmen's Fedn. of New Orleans. Office: New Orleans Cons Group Ltd 401 Focis St Metairie LA 70005-3435

BOBBIE, WALTER, theatrical director; b. Scranton, Pa.. Postgrad., Catholic U. dir. City Ctr. Encore series, plays include Fiorello!, For Whom the Southern Belle Tolls, Durang Durang, Nude Nude Totally Nude, A Grand Night for Singing, Chicago, Footloose; actor plays including Guys and Dolls, Assassins, Getting Married, Anything Goes, Cafe Crown, Driving Miss Daisy, I Love My Wife, A History of the American Film, Grease!, also films and TV; radio actor Prairie Home Companion. Recipient Tony, Drama Desk and Outer Crits Circle awards for direction of Chicago. *

BOBBITT, CURTIS WAYNE, English educator; b. Muncie, Ind., Dec. 12, 1951; s. Stanley Curtis and Nancy Joan Bobbitt. BA in English, Ind. U., 1974, MS in Secondary Edn., 1976; PhD in Brit. and Am. Lit., Ball State U., 1989. Tchr. English Connersville (Ind.) H.S., 1974-77, Palmyra (Wis.) H.S., 1978-79; doctoral fellow Ball State U., Muncie, Ind., 1982-87; asst. prof. English Coll. of Great Falls, Mont., 1987-90; assoc. prof. English U. Great Falls, Mont., 1990-98, prof. English, 1998—; dir. writing program U. Great Falls, 1992—. Mem. Disciples of Christ. Avocations: reading, bicycling. E-mail: cbobbitt@ugf.edu. FAX: 406-791-5992. Office: Univ Great Falls 1301 20th St Great Falls MT 59405

BOBBITT, JAMES MCCUE, chemist; b. Charleston, W.Va., Jan. 18, 1930; s. James Sterling and Grace (McCue) B.; m. Jane Ann Hickman, Mar. 15, 1952; children: John Sterling, Ann, Laura. B.S., W.Va. U., 1951; Ph.D., Ohio State U., 1955. Instr. chemistry U. Conn., 1956-59, asst. prof., 1959-63, assoc. prof., 1963-68, prof., 1968-92, prof. emeritus, 1992—, acting head dept., 1976-77, head dept., 1977-82; postdoctoral fellow Wayne State U., 1955-56; NSF fellow U. Zurich, Switzerland, 1959-60; guest prof. U. East Anglia, 1964-65, U. Kiel, Germany, 1968, Tohoku U., Japan, 1971, 86, La Trobe U., Australia, 1971-72. Author: Thin Layer Chromatography, 1963, (with R.J. Gritter and A.E. Schwarting) Introduction to Chromatography, 1968, rev. edit., 1985. Mem. Am. Chem. Soc., Phi Beta Kappa, Sigma Xi, Phi Lambda Upsilon. Democrat. Congregationalist. Home: 88 Atwoodville Rd Mansfield Center CT 06250-1104 Office: U Conn Chem Dept Storrs Mansfield CT 06268*

BOBBITT, JOHN MAXWELL, surgeon, medical educator; b. Jan. 20, 1927. MD, U. Mich., 1952. Intern, then resident in surgery U. Mich., Ann Arbor, 1952-57; clin. assoc. prof. surgery Med. Sch. Marshall U., Huntington, W.Va., 1972-80. Contbr. numerous articles on nautical rsch. to popular publs., 1985—. Elected to W.Va. Ho. Dels., 1966, 68. Home: 69 Queens Ct Newport News VA 23606

BOBBITT, JUANITA MARILYN CRAWFORD, international organization executive; b. N.Y.C., Sept. 4, 1938; d. Philip Theodore and Lillian Beatrice (Nelson) Crawford; 1 child, Edmund Michael. BA in Romance Lang., CUNY, Bklyn., 1959; MA in Econ., NYU, 1982; MPA, Harvard U., 1984. Pub. adminstrn. officer UN, N.Y.C., 1974-84, econ. affairs officer, 1984-92, sr. pub. adminstrn. officer, 1992-97, head gender adv. svcs. unit, 1998, internat. devel. cons., 1999—. Contbr. articles to profl. jours. Exec. com. St. George's Cmty. Devel. Corp., Bklyn., 1994-99; rep. provincial coun. Episcopal Ch., 1993-96. Mem. ASPA (exec. com., sect. internat. comparative adminstrn.), Harvard Club (N.Y.C. chpt., program com. 1991—), Tri-State J.F. Kennedy Alumni Assn., (exec. com. 1987—), Delta Sigma Theta (pres. Bklyn. chpt. 1966-68, chair internat. com. 1993—, nat. projects com. 1973-74). Episcopalian. Avocations: reading, walking, dancing, arts. Office: UN One United Nations Plz New York NY 10017

BOBBITT, PHILIP CHASE, lawyer, educator, writer; b. Temple, Tex., July 22, 1948; s. Oscar Price and Rebekah Luruth (Johnson) B.; m. Selden Anne Wallace (div. 1990). AB, Princeton U., 1971; JD, Yale U., 1975; PhD, Oxford U., 1983, MA, 1984. Bar: Tex. 1977, U.S. Supreme Ct. 1989. Law clk. to Judge Henry Friendly U.S. Ct. Appeals (2d cir.), 1975-76; asst. prof. law U. Tex., Austin, 1976-79, prof., 1979—, Cooper K. Ragan Regents prof., 1988-89, Baker & Botts prof., 1989-96, mem. univ. com., 1979-80, A.W. Walker chair in law, 1996—; assoc. counsel to Pres. U.S., 1980-81; legal counsel U.S. Senate Select Com. on Secret Mil. Assistance to Iran and Nicaraguan Opposition, 1987-88; dir. for intelligence Nat. Security Coun., 1997-98, sr. dir. critical infrastructure, 1998—; mem. faculty Salzburg Seminar, 1987; vis. fellow Internat. Inst. Strategic Studies, 1981-82; jr. rsch. fellow Nuffield Coll., Oxford U., 1982-84, rsch. fellow, 1984-85, Anderson sr. rsch. fellow, 1985-91, mem. modern history faculty, 1984-91; counselor on internat. law U.S. Dept. State, Washington, 1990-93, Woodrow Wilson Ctr. for Internat. Scholars, 1994; sr. rsch. fellow King's Coll./U. London, 1994—. Author: Democracy and Deterrence, 1988; (with Guido Calabresi) Tragic Choices, 1979, Constitutional Fate, 1982; (with Lawrence Freedman and Gregory Treverton) Nuclear Strategy, 1988, Constitutional Interpretation., 1991. Trustee Princeton U. Mem. Am. Law Inst., Internat. Inst. Strategic Studies (London), Austin Coun. Fgn. Affairs (pres. 1983—), Coun. Fgn. Rels. (N.Y.C.), Adminstrv. Conf. U.S. (spl. com. on ethics in govt.), Tex. Philos. Soc., Yale Club, Century Assn., Met. Club (Washington). Democrat. Baptist. Office: U Tex Law Sch 727 E 26th St Austin TX 78705-3224

BOBCO, WILLIAM DAVID, JR., consulting engineering company executive; b. Chgo., Aug. 11, 1946; s. William David and Eleanor Josephine (Dvojack) B.; m. Donna Domenica DiFrancesca, Sept. 13, 1969; 1 child, Christina Marie. BS in Engring., U. Ill., Chgo., 1969; MBA in Prodn. Mgmt., U. Chgo., 1983. Prodn. mgr. Am. Can Co., Maywood, Ill., 1972-73; with Footlik & Assocs., Evanston, Ill., 1973—; exec. v.p. Footlik & Assocs., Evanston, 1986—; mem. indsl. adv. bd. U. Ill. Coll. Engring., Chgo., 1992—, chmn. alumni devel. com., 1991-95, mem. dean selection com., 1994. Vol. Art Inst. of Chgo., 1983-84; mem. facilities and grounds com. St. Giles Parish, 1995—, co-chair, 1997—, treas. golf com., 1997—. Mem. ASME (bd. dirs. Chgo. sect. 1984—, vice chmn. 1991, newsletter editor 1987—, chmn. Chgo. sect. 1992-94, region VI rep. to A World in Motion K-12 tng. program, SAE (co-sponsor 1993), Engring. Alumni Assn. U. Ill. chgo. (pres. 1984-88, bd. dirs. 1975—), U. Ill. Alumni Assn. (bd. dirs. 1985-91, nominating com. 1991, Loyalty award 1988, Constituent Leadership award 1991, Disting. Svc. award 1994). Roman Catholic. Avocations: travel, art, music. Office: Footlik & Assocs 2521 Gross Point Rd Evanston IL 60201-4928

BOBENHOUSE, NELLIE YATES, insurance company executive; b. Spickard, Mo., May 3, 1936; d. Joseph Howard and Nellie Elizabeth (Tuttle) Yates; m. Lewis L. Griffin, Apr. 22, 1956 (div. Jan. 1964); 1 child, Elizabeth Anne Griffin Van Blarcom; m. Robert A. Bobenhouse, Aug. 28, 1965. Student, St. Joseph (Mo.) Jr. Coll., 1955, Grandview Coll., 1980. Sec. News-Press & Gazette, St. Joseph, 1954-56; sec., bookkeeper Wilson's Locker & Ins., Spickard, Mo., 1956-60, Oyler's Locker, Spickard, 1960-64; sec. Equitable of Iowa Agy., Des Moines, 1964-68, agy. office supr., 1968-94. City clk. City of Spickard, 1959-60; support group leader, co-founder Chronic Fatigue Syndrome Soc., Des Moines, 1988—; bd. dirs. Iowa Chronic Fatigue Syndrome/CFIDS Assn., Cedar Rapids, 1991; mem. Des Moines Women's Club, 1994—. Fellow Life Mgmt. Inst.; mem. Ins. Women Des Moines (com. chmn. 1975), P. Buckley Moss Soc., Beta Sigma Phi (sec.-treas. 1958-60, Woman of Yr. 1959), PEO (G.Y. chpt.), 1998—. Republican. Disciple of Christ. Avocations: gardening, antique cars, quilting, bridge. Home: 905 59th St West Des Moines IA 50266-7516

BOBER, LAWRENCE HAROLD, retired banker; b. N.Y.C., Mar. 29, 1924; s. Michael N. and Julia (Verschleiser) B.; m. Natalie S. Birnbaum, Aug. 27, 1950; children: Stephen, Marc, Elizabeth. B.S., NYU, 1949; postgrad., Grad. Sch. Bus. Adminstrn., 1949-50. With Hanover Bank (now Chase Bank), 1941-87, asst. sec., 1950-52, asst. treas., 1953-55, asst. v.p., 1955-60, v.p., 1960-71, sr. v.p. (North Am. div.-II), 1971-87; bd. dirs. Fab Industries, Inc. Dir., past chm. The Renesselaerville Inst.; past vice chmn., bd. fellows Brandeis U.; pres. Congregation Emanuel of Westchester; dir. Cobblefield Homeowners Assn. White Plains, N.Y. 1st lt. USAAF, 1942-45. Decorated D.F.C. with two oak leaf clusters, Air medal with three oak leaf clusters; recipient Human Relations award Am. Jewish Com., 1968, Community Service award Nat. Jewish Hosp. and Research Center, 1980, Community Service award Am. Jewish Congress, 1988. Home: 7 Westfield Ln White Plains NY 10605-5459

BOBER, PHYLLIS PRAY, humanities educator, art historian; b. Portland, Maine, Dec. 2, 1920; d. Melvin Francis and Lea Arlene (Royer) Pray; m. Harry Bober, Aug. 11, 1943 (div. June 1973); children: Jonathan Pray, David Hall. BA, Wellesley Coll., 1941; MA, NYU Inst. Fine Arts, 1943, PhD, 1946; LHD (hon.), U. Rome, 1993. From instr. to lectr., curator Wellesley (Mass.) Coll., 1947-49, 51-54; tchg. assoc. Sch. Arch. MIT, Cambridge, Mass., 1951-53; rsch. assoc. NYU Inst. Fine Arts, N.Y.C., 1954-73; chair, founder dept. fine arts Univ. Coll. NYU, 1967-73; prof. fine arts NYU, 1970-73; dean Grad. Sch. Arts and Scis. Bryn Mawr (Pa.) Coll., 1973-80, prof. history of art, prof. classical/Near Ea. archaeology, 1973-91, Leslie Clark prof. in humanities, 1987-91, prof. emerita, 1991—; founder, dir. Census of Antique Works of Art Known to the Renaissance, Warburg Inst., U. London, 1947-84; staff mem. NYU Excavations in Samothrace, 1948, 49, 72; mem. Grad. Record Exam. Bd., Princeton, N.J., 1976-80; rep. to ACLS (Amer. Counc. of Learned Societies), 1982-88; Mellon vis. prof. of fine arts U. Pitts., 1986; co-dir. NEH Summer Seminar for Coll. Tchrs., Rome, 1990; vis. prof. Dept. Edn. Am. Acad., Rome, 1999. Author: Drawings After the Antique by Amico Aspertini, 1957; co-author: Renaissance Artists and Antique Sculpture, 1986, 90, The Rotunda of Arsinoe, vol. III, 1992, Art, Culture and Cuisine, 1999; contbr. articles to profl. jours. Bd. dirs. Med. Coll. Pa. (now Allegheny U. of the Health Scis.), 1979—; pres. Pa. Assn. Grad. Schs., 1977-78, Northeastern Assn. Grad. Schs., 1978-79; Dem. committeewoman, 1986-94. Sr. fellow Soc. for Humanities, Cornell U., 1984, corr. fellow German Archaeol. Inst., 1958—, fellow Accademia dei Lincei Rome, 1996—, Guggenheim fellow, 1979-80, hon. fellow Warburg Inst., U. London, 1993—; Appleton Eminent scholar in the Arts, Fla. State U., 1998. Mem. Coll. Art Assn. (bd. dirs. 1982-90, pres. 1988-90), Renaissance Soc. Am. (bd. dirs. 1982-85, pres. 1983-84), Archaeol. Inst. Am., Internat. Assn. Classical Archaeology, Dames d'Escoffier Culinary Historians of Boston, Italian Art Soc., Culinary Soc. Phila., Amer-Italy Soc., Am. Philosophical Soc. Unitarian Universalist. Avocations: cooking, doll house miniatures, ecology. Home: 29 Simpson Rd Ardmore PA 19003-2812 Office: Bryn Mawr Coll Bryn Mawr PA 19010

BOBINS, NORMAN R., banker. Vice chmn. Exch. Nat. Bank Chgo., 1969-90; formerly vice chmn. LaSalle Nat. Bank, Chgo.; now pres., ceo LaSalle Nat Bank (now LaSalle Bank, N.A.), Chgo., 1990—. Office: LaSalle Bank NA 135 S La Salle St Fl 3 Chicago IL 60603-4174*

BOBINSKI, GEORGE SYLVAN, librarian, educator; b. Cleve., Oct. 24, 1929; s. Sylvan and Eugenia (Sarbiewski) B.; m. Mary Lillian Form, Feb. 20, 1953; children-George Sylvan, Mary Anne. BA, Case Western Res. U., 1951, MS in Libr. Sci., 1952; MA, U. Mich., 1961, PhD, 1966. Rsch. asst. Bus Info. Bur., Cleve. Pub. Libr., 1954-55; asst. dir. Royal Oak (Mich.) Pub. Libr., 1955-59; dir. librs. State U. Coll. at Cortland, N.Y., 1960-67; prof., asst. dean Sch. Libr. Sci. U. Ky., 1967-70; prof., dean Sch. Info. & Libr. Studies SUNY, Buffalo, 1970—; Fulbright-Hays lectr. in libr. sci. U. Warsaw, Poland, 1977; trustee Western N.Y. Libr. Rsch. Coun., 1971-87, pres., 1972, 82; vis. scholar Jagiellonian U., Krakow, Poland, 1992, 97. Author: A Brief History of the Libraries of Western Reserve University, 1826-1952, 1955, Carnegie Libraries, Their History and Impact on American Public Library Development, 1969, Dictionary of American Library Biography, 1978, also articles. Mem. N.Y. Gov.'s Commn. on Librs., 1990—. With AUS, 1952-54. Recipient Meritorious Svc. medal Jagellonian U., Krakow, Poland, 1997. Mem. ALA (mem. pub. com., mem. coun.), N.Y. Libr. Assn., Assn. Am. Libr. Schs. (chmn. coun. of deans 1985-86). E-mail: bobonski@gcsu.buffalo.edu. Home: 69 Little Robin Rd Buffalo NY 14228-1125 Office: SUNY Buffalo Sch Info and Libr Studies Baldy Hall Buffalo NY 14260

BOBISUD, LARRY EUGENE, mathematics educator; b. Midvale, Idaho, Mar. 16, 1940; s. Walter and Ida V. (Bitner) B.; m. Helen M. Meyer, June 15, 1963. B.S., Coll. of Ida., 1961; M.A., U. N.M., 1963, Ph.D., 1966. Vis. mem. Courant Inst. Math. Scis., N.Y.C., 1966-67; prof. math. U. Idaho, Moscow, 1967—. Contbr. articles to profl. jours. Mem. Am. Math. Soc. Home: 860 N Eisenhower St Moscow ID 83843-9581 Office: Univ Idaho Dept Math Moscow ID 83844-1103

BOBLETT, MARK ANTHONY, civil engineering technician; b. Beckley, W.Va., Jan. 21, 1959; s. Murriel Garner and Meredith Genevieve (Sheppard) B.; m. Susan Renee Walker, June 26, 1982; children: Miranda Lauren, Adrienne Lisbeth. AS in Civil Engring. Tech., W.Va. Inst. Tech., 1983, AS in Bldg. Constrn. Tech., 1983. Quality control technician Pittsburgh Testing Lab., Houston, 1984, Elmo Greer & Sons, Beckley, 1984-86; quality control coord. Green Constrn. Co., Beckley, 1986-88; assoc. agt. Nationwide Ins., Beckley, 1987-88; lab. mgr. Law Engring. Inc., Raleigh, N.C., 1988-96; founder Tech IV Corp., Raleigh, 1997—. Baptist. Home: 111 Triple Crown Run Louisburg NC 27549-9010 Office: PO Box 150 Bunn NC 27508

BOBO, GENELLE TANT (NELL BOBO), office administrator; b. Paulding County, Ga., Oct. 31, 1927; d. Richard Adolph and Mary Etta (Prance) Tant; m. William Ralph Bobo, May 1, 1948; children: William Richard, Thomas David (dec.). AS, Berry Coll., Mt. Berry, Ga., 1947. Exec. sec. Macon (Ga.) Kraft Co., 1951-54; med. sec. Drs. Loveman & Fleigleman, Louisville, 1954-55; tchr. Fulton County Schs., Palmetto, Ga., 1960-68; exec. sec. Rayloc, Atlanta, 1968-70; adminstrv. coord. U. Ga., Athens, 1970-77; assoc. to dir. Mission Svc. Corps, Home Mission Bd. So. Bapt. Conv., Atlanta, 1977-94; rschr., writer Sta. 11-TV, Atlanta, 1989. Author: Driven by a Dream, 1992. Philanthropy chmn. Exec. Women, Inc., Atlanta, 1968-69; mem. adv. coun. Baylor U., Waco, Tex., 1993—. Mem. NAFE. Baptist. Avocations: public speaking, teaching, music, sewing, reading. Home: 87 Vickers Rd Fairburn GA 30213-1139 Office: 4200 N Point Pkwy Alpharetta GA 30022-4174

BOBO, LEN DAVIS, musician; b. Vicksburg, Miss., Feb. 1, 1949; s. Samuel Redus and Eugenia (Causey) B.; m. Pamela Jeannine Moore, Apr. 13, 1974; children: Celeste Nichole, Brittany Noelle. AA, Hinds Jr. Coll., 1969; MusB, Miss. Coll., 1971; MusM, U. Tenn., 1975. Consecrated diaconal minister Meth. Ch. Dir. music Lakewood United Meth. Ch., No. Little Rock, Ark., 1976-79; music instr. U. Ark., Little Rock, 1975-90; ch. organist Pulaski Heights United Meth. Ch., Little Rock, 1979-93; music instr., coll. organist Hendrix Coll., 1983-98; minister of music First United Meth. Ch., Maumelle, Ark., 1993-94; instr. computer sci. The Anthony Sch., Little Rock, Ark., 1994-96; assoc. dir. music, organist, dir. Music and Arts Inst. First Presbyn. Ch., Pine Bluff, Ark., 1996—; vis. instr. music U. Ctrl. Ark., Conway, 1998—; cons. in field. Composer (organ solo) Psalm 23, 1973, Praise to the Lord, 1977, Enchamatics, 1987, Fantasie pourle Trompette en chamade, 1990, (choral piece) The Lord's Prayer, 1979, (vocal solo) The Magnificat and Nunc Dimitis, 1979. Organist Ark. Celebration of 150 Yrs. Statehood, 1986. Sgt. Ark. Air N.G., 1974-76. Recipient Disting. Alumnus, Dept. Music, Miss. Coll., 1997. Mem. Am. Guild Organists, Fellowship Meth. Musicians (pres. 1978-79), Presbyn. Assn. Musicians, Nat. Fedn. Music Clubs (pres. Hot Springs chpt. 1981-82, Ark. Ch. Musician of Yr. award 1986), USCG Aux., Kiwanis. Avocations: boating, fishing, photography, biking. Home: 335 Stonecastle Dr Brandon MS 39047 Office: Covenant Presbyn Ch 400 Ridgewood Rd Jackson MS 39211

BOBRICK, EDWARD A., federal judge; b. 1935. JD, DePaul U., 1964. Magistrate judge U.S. Dist. Ct. (no. dist.) Ill., 1990—. Office: US Dist Ct 1822 Dirksen Bldg 219 Dearborn St Chicago IL 60604-1702

BOBRICK, STEVEN AARON, marketing executive; b. Denver, Apr. 11, 1950; s. Samual Michael and Selma Gertrude (Birnbaum) B.; m. Maria Diane Boltz, Oct. 5, 1980. Attended, U. Colo., 1968-72. Registered apt. mgr. Owner Bobrick Constrn., Denver, 1969-72; with Bell Mtn. Sports, Aspen, Colo., 1972-75; mgr. Compass Imports, Denver, 1975-80, Aurora (Colo.) Bullion Exch., 1980-81; contr. Bobrick Constrn., Aurora, 1981-85; appraiser Aurora, 1985—; property mgr. Aurora (Colo) Cmty. Mental Health, 1989-98, active real estate and constrn., facilities mgr., 1989-98; exec. mgmt. asst. E-470 Pub. Hwy. Authority, 1998, mktg./pub. rels. web master, 1998—. Co-author: Are You Paying Too Much in Property Taxes, 1990. Coun. mem. City of Aurora, 1981-89; chmn. Explore Commercial Opportunities, Aurora, 1986-89, bd. dirs.; bd. dirs. Adam County Econ. Devel. Commn., Northglenn, Colo., 1985-89; vice chair Aurora Urban Renewal Authority, 1982-89; chmn. Aurora Enterprise Zone Found., 1991—; bd. dirs. Aurora Community Med. Clinic, 1987-88. Avocations: skiing, mountain biking, exercise. Office: 7600 E Orchard Rd Ste 370 Aurora CO 80011

BOBROFF, HAROLD, lawyer; b. Bronx, N.Y., Apr. 29, 1920; s. Max and Mary (Platofsky) B.; m. Marion Hemendinger, Nov. 25, 1945; children: Caren Spital, Fredric Jon. B.B.A., City U. N.Y., 1947; J.D., N.Y. Law Sch., N.Y.C., 1951. Bar: N.Y. State 1952. Ptnr. Bobroff & Olonoff (C.P.A.s), 1949-51, 52; auditor U.S. Army Audit Agy., N.Y.C., 1951-89; ptnr. Bobroff, Olonoff & Scharf, Attys., N.Y.C.; chief dep. county atty. Nassau County, N.Y., 1962-63; chief counsel joint legis. com. on ins. N.Y. State Legislature, 1965-67; pvt. practice Woodmere, N.Y., 1989—; chief counsel com. on intergovt. relations N.Y. State Constl. Conv., 1967. Fin. sec. Nassau County Dem. Com., 1973; former chmn. bd. Trustees Nassau Community Coll.; former pres., trustee Temple Sinai of L.I.; former v.p. N.Y. Fedn. Reform Synagogues; trustee UHAC; former comdr. Jewish War Vets Post. Served with AUS, 1942-45. Decorated Bronze Star medal with oak leaf cluster, Presdl. Unit citation with oak leaf cluster; Belgium Fouraggere; Honored by United Jewish Appeal Fedn. Mem. B'nai B'rith. Lodge: Masons. Home and Office: 795 Hampton Rd Woodmere NY 11598-2518

BOBROW, MARC ADAM, auditor, accountant; b. Dec. 26, 1968. BA in Sociology, Brandeis U., 1991; MBA in Acctg., U. Conn., 1997. Program dir. Camp Ramah in New Eng., Palmer, Mass., 1987-95; wilderness instr. Hurricane Island Outward Bound, Yulee, Fla., 1992-93, Pathfinders, Inc., Corrales, N.Mex., 1993-94; audit auditor PricewaterhouseCoopers, Hartford, Conn., 1997—. Email: marc.a.bobrow@us.pwcglobal.com. Home: 130 Palisado ave Windsor CT 06095 Office: 100 Pearl St Hartford CT 06103

BOBROW, MICHAEL LAWRENCE, architect; b. N.Y.C., Apr. 18, 1939; s. Jack and Ruth (Gureasko) B.; m. Julia Dessery Thomas, Mar. 24, 1980; children by previous marriage: Elizabeth, Erica, David; 1 stepchild, Leslie Thomas. BArch, Columbia U., 1963. Registered arch. Calif. Sr. arch. Office Surgeon Gen./U.S. Air Force, Washington, 1963-66; dir. arch. Med. Planning Assoc., Malibu, Calif., 1966-72; founder, chmn., design ptnr. Bobrow/Thomas & Assocs., L.A., 1972—; founder, coord. programs in health complex facilities design UCLA Grad. Sch. Arch. and Urban Planning, 1972-80; adj. prof. UCLA Grad. Sch. Pub. Health, deans adv. bd.; chmn. UCLA, Columbia U. Internat. Hosp. Design Competition; trustee Otis Coll. Art & Design; chmn. bd. Arts and Arch. Mag. Prin. works include City of Hope Nat. Med. Ctr., Cook County Hosp., Prototype Campus Calif. State U., Channel Islands, Motion Picture and TV Hosp., Cedars Sinai Med. Ctr., Otis Coll. Art & Design, VA L.A. Clinic, St. Lukes Med. Ctr., Camp Pendleton Naval Hosp., Shriners Hosp., UCLA Arroyo Bridge, Beckman Rsch. Lab., others; contbr. articles to profl. jours. Pres. The Friends of the Schindler House, L.A., 1978-79; dir. Am. Hosp. Assn. Ann. Design Inst.; chmn. strategic planning and design com. Westwood Village Bus. Improvement Dist.; chmn. Hosp. Coun. So. Calif. Seismic Design Inst., 1994. Named one of Outstanding Architects Under 40, Bldg. Design and Constrn. Mag., 1978; recipient Preservation award L.A. Conservancy to the Friends of Schindler House, 1982. Fellow AIA (co-chmn. com. on arch. for health spl. task force on capital reimbursement 1983—, Nat. and Regional Design awards); mem. Beverly Hills Tennis Club. Office: Bobrow/Thomas & Assocs 1001 Westwood Blvd Los Angeles CA 90024-2902*

BOBROW, SUSAN LUKIN, lawyer; b. Cleve., Jan. 18, 1941; d. Adolph and Yetta (Babkow) Lukin; m. Martin J. Bolhower, Nov. 28, 1986 (div. Dec. 1988); children from previous marriage: Elizabeth Bobrow Pressler, Erica, David. Student, Antioch Coll., Yellow Springs, Ohio, 1958-61; BA, Antioch Coll., L.A., 1975; JD, Southwestern U., L.A., 1979. Bar: Calif. 1980. Pvt. practice Beverly Hills, Calif., 1983-88; assoc. Schulman & Miller, Beverly Hills, 1988-89; staff counsel Fair Polit. Practices Commn., Sacramento, Calif., 1990-96; sr. counsel Calif. State Lottery, Sacramento, 1996-98, Employment Tng. Panel, Sacramento, 1998—; panel for paternity defense L.A. Superior Ct., 1984. Exhibited paintings at Death and Trasnfiguration Show, Phantom Galleries, Sacramento, 1994; exhibited photography U. Calif.-Davis Women's Art Collaborative, Phantom Galleries, Sacramento, 1997, Camera Arts, Sacramento, 1998, Viewpoint Gallery Exhibit, Sacramento, 1998. Bd. dirs. San Fernando Valley Friends of Homeless Women and Children, North Hollywood, Calif., 1985-88, Jewish Family Svcs., 1997; mem. adv. bd. Project Home, Sacramento Interfaith Svc. Coun., 1990-91; v.p. cmty. affairs B'nai Israel Sisterhood, Sacramento, 1991-93; bd. dirs. Sacramento Jewish Family Svcs., 1997-98. Recipient commendation Bd. Govs. State Bar of Calif., 1984. Mem. Inst. Noetic Scis., Sacramento Inst. Noetic Scis. (steering coun. 1994), Los Angeles County Bar Assn. (Barristers com. on adminstrn. of justice 1985), Sacramento County Bar Assn. (com. on profl. responsibility 1993-94, alt. del. to state bar conv. 1991), Sacramento Women Artists, Sacramento Valley Photographic Arts Ctr. Democrat. Office: Employment Tng Panel 1100 J St Sacramento CA 95814

BOCCARDI, LOUIS DONALD, news agency executive; b. Bronx, N.Y., Aug. 26, 1937; s. Louis and Delphine Boccardi; m. Joan M. Quinlan, Jan. 18, 1964; children—Susan, Lynn, Paul, Mark, Lauren. B.A., Fordham Coll., 1958; B.S., Columbia U. Grad. Sch. Journalism, 1959. Reporter/desk editor N.Y. World Telegram & Sun, 1959-64; asst. mng. editor N.Y. World Jour. Tribune, 1966-67; asst. gen. news editor AP, N.Y.C., 1967-69, mng. editor, 1969-73, v.p., exec. editor, 1973-85, pres., 1985—, now pres., CEO; mem. Pulitzer Prize bd.; bd. visitors Columbia U. Sch. Journalism, Northwestern U. Medill Sch. Mem. nat. adv. bd. Media Studies Ctr. Recipient Alumni Achievement award Fordham Coll., 1967, Outstanding Alumnus award Fordham U., 1968. Mem. Am. Soc. Newspaper Editors (Disting. Svc. mem.). Office: Associated Press 50 Rockefeller Plz Fl 6 New York NY 10020-1666

BOCCHINO, FRANCES LUCIA, retired oil company official; b. Bronx, N.Y., July 5, 1944; d. Pasquale and Mary Ruth (Lacerenza) B. Grad. high sch., Bklyn., 1962. Various positions Texaco Inc., N.Y.C., 1965-86; sr. analyst exec. dept. Texaco Inc., Harrison, N.Y., 1987-90, transfer agt., 1990-95; comms., 1995—. Active Whitestone (N.Y.) Taxpayers Assn. Mem. Corp. Transfer Agts. Assn. Republican. Roman Catholic. Home: 15-15 150th St Whitestone NY 11357-2530 Office: Northern Intelligence Agy 3333 New Hyde Park Rd New Hyde Park NY 11042-1205

BOCCHINO, LISA, magazine editor; b. Rego Park, N.Y., July 28, 1967; d. Sabino Anthony and Cathleen (Bilardello) Rizzo; m. Frank Bocchino, Apr. 25, 1992; 1 child, Emily. BA in English and Psychology, Washington U., St. Louis, 1989. Editl. asst. Heat Treating Fairchild Publs., N.Y.C., 1990, dept. editor Metal Ctr. News, 1990-92; mng. editor ID Mag. Bill Comm., N.Y.C., 1992-96; copy editor ID Mag., 1996—. Home: 7573 Thornlee Dr Lake Worth FL 33467-7855 Office: Bill Communications 355 Park Ave S New York NY 10010-1789

BOCCI, RAYMOND PERRY, auditor; b. Cleve., June 17, 1942; s. Perry and Ann (Legoski) B.; m. Barbara Lynn Steffen, June 30, 1973; children: Christopher, Brian. BS, Kent State U., 1965; MS, Roosevelt U., 1983. CPA, Ill.; cert. internal auditor; cert. fraud examiner. Internal auditor Kennecott Copper Corp., Shaker Heights, Ohio, 1971-73; sr. internal auditor, sr. budget analyst Brunswick Corp., Skokie, Ill., 1973-78; audit mgr. Allied Products, Chgo., 1978-81, Allstate Enterprise Mortgage, Deerfield, Ill., 1981-84; regional audit mgr. Coldwell Banker Real Estate, Chgo., 1981-92; audit dir. Homart Devel. and Gen. Growth Properties, Chgo., 1992—. Mem. AICPA, Ill. CPA Soc., Inst. Internal Auditors (bd. dirs. N.W. Chgo. chpt. 1995-97). Avocation: travel. Office: Gen Growth Properties 110 N Wacker Dr Chicago IL 60606-1511

BOCCIA, BARBARA, lawyer; b. Bklyn., Dec. 16, 1957; d. Daniel and Marie Boccia. BS with honors, U. Tenn., 1980; JD, U. of the Pacific, 1983. Bar: Calif. 1983, D.C. 1983. Litigation lawyer, ptnr. Mullen & Filippi, San Francisco, 1983-86; litigation lawyer Jones, Brown, Clifford & McDevitt, San Francisco, 1987-88; litigation lawyer, mng. lawyer Crymes, Hardie & Heer, San Francisco, 1988-89; pvt. practice Daly City, Calif., 1989-92; sr. trial atty., supervising atty. Akin & Carmody, San Francisco, 1992-94; prin. Law Office of Barbara Boccia, Inc., Daly City, Calif., 1994—; arbitrator, corp. cons., writer, educator, speaker in field. Vol. Hotline and Spks. Bur., San

Francisco AIDS Found., 1987-90; mem. founding bd. dirs. Northeast Ark. Regional AIDS Network; HIV instr. ARC, 1991. Named One of Outstanding Young Women in Am., 1980. Mem. San Francisco Bar Assn., Indsl. Claims Assn., Ins. Edn. Assn., Queen's Bench, Italian Welfare Agy. Avocations: jogging, basketball, aerobics, writing, being a mom. Office: PO Box 2210 Daly City CA 94017-2210

BOCCIA, JUDY ELAINE, home health agency executive, consultant; b. San Diego, Aug. 29, 1955; d. Robert Garrett and Jerry Athalee (Carruth) Stacy; 1 child, Jennifer Lynn. BSN, Calif. State U., San Diego, 1978. RN, Calif.; lic. pub. health nurse, Calif. Staff nurse Univ. Hosp., U. Calif., San Diego, 1978-80, 81-82, Moffitt Hosp., San Francisco, 1980-81, Humana Huntington, Huntington Beach, Calif., 1982-84; intravenous and hospice vis. nurse Town & Country Nursing, Garden Grove, Calif., 1984-85; vis. nurse Vis. Nurse Assn., Orange, Calif., 1985-86; v.p. Doctors and Nurse Med. Mgmt., Newport Beach, Calif., 1986-89; dir. nursing HMSS, So. Calif., 1989-90; pres. Premier Care, Irvine, 1990-91, Homelife Nursing & Staffbuilders, Lake Forest, Calif., 1991—; cons., Calif., 1987—; pres., adminstr. Homelife Nursing-Staff Builders, O.C., 1991-97; AIDS educator; presenter in field; guest radio spkr. Mem. Oncology Nursing Soc., Intravenous Nurse Soc., Calif. Nurses Assn. Methodist. Avocations: singing, walking with daughter, gardening. Home: 19 Stone Pine Aliso Viejo CA 92656-2131 Office: 19 Stone Pine Aliso Viejo CA 92656

BOCCIA ROSADO, ANN MARIE, paralegal; b. San Pedro, Calif., Apr. 23, 1958; d. Franklin S. and Julia (Mattera) Boccia; m. Robert Daniel Rosado. AA, Harbor Coll., 1983; paralegal cert., Continental Tech. Inst., L.A., 1986. Invoicing/sales rep. Bronson of Calif., Gardena, 1976-78; traffic mgr. GSC Athletic Equipment, San Pedro, 1978-81; exec. legal sec. Stein, Shostak, Shostak & O'Hara, L.A., 1981; paralegal, computer adminstr. Stolpman, Krissman, Elber, Mandel & Katzman LLP, Long Beach, Calif., 1981—; cons. San Pedro Chiropractic Ctr., 1989-96; instr. Michaels Stores, Inc., 1997—. Recipient Presdl. award Calif. Trial Lawyers Assn., 1988; named Legal Sec. of the Yr., 1998. Mem. Nat. Paralegal Assn., Assn. Trial Lawyers Am., L.A. Trial Lawyers Assn. (speaker 1989-92, moderator 1991, voter registration com. 1988-89, Ann. Law Day participant 1991-92), L.A. Paralegal Assn., Long Beach Legal Secs. Assn. (chmn. benefits 1995—, treas. 1998, v.p. 1999). Democrat. Roman Catholic. Avocations: computer programming, walking, reading, boating, needlepoint. Office: Stolpman Krissman Elber Mandel & Katzman LLP 19th Flr 111 W Ocean Blvd Fl 19 Long Beach CA 90802-4632

BOCHCO, STEVEN, screenwriter, television producer; b. N.Y.C., Dec. 16, 1943; s. Rudolph and Mimi B.; m. Barbara Bosson; 2 children. BA., Carnegie Tech., 1966. Scriptwriter, editor, prodr. Universal Studios, L.A., 1966-78; writer, prodr. MTM Enterprises, Studio City, 1978-85, Twentieth Century Fox, L.A., 1985-87; chmn. CEO Steven Bocho Prodns., L.A., 1987—. Writer: (films) (with Harold Clements) The Counterfeit Killer, 1968, (with Michael Cimino and Deric Washburn) Silent Running, 1972; co-writer: (TV series) Columbo, 1971-78, McMillan and Wife, 1971-76, Griff, 1973-74, Delvecchio, 1976-77, McMillan, 1977, Turnabout, 1979, (TV movie) Double Indemnity, 1973, Uneasy Lies the Crown, 1990; co-writer, prodr.: (TV series) Paris, 1979-80, Bay City Blues, 1983-84, (TV pilots) The Invisible Man, 1975, Richie Brockelman: Missing Twenty-four Hours, 1976, (TV movies) Lieutenant Schuster's Wife, 1972, Vampire, 1979, Columbo: Uneasy Lies the Crown, 1990; co-creator, exec. prodr., writer: (TV series) Hill Street Blues, 1981-86 (Emmy award best drama series 1981, 82, 83, 84, Emmy award best writing in drama series 1981, 82, Golden Globe award best drama series 1982, 83), L.A. Law, 1986-87 (Emmy award best drama series 1987, 89, Emmy award best writing in drama series 1987, Golden Gobe award best drama series 1987, 88), Hooperman, 1987-89, Doogie Howser, M.D., 1989-93, Cop Rock, 1990, Civil Wars, 1991-93, NYPD Blue, 1993—(Golden Globe award best drama series 1994, Outstanding Drama Series Emmy award, 1995), Byrds of Paradise, 1994, Murder One 1995-96, Public Morals; creator, exec. cons: (TV series) Capitol Critters, 1992. Office: PO Box 900 Beverly Hills CA 90213-0900*

BOCHERT, LINDA H., lawyer; b. East Orange, N.J., May 13, 1949. BA, U. Wis., 1971, MS, 1973, JD, 1974. Bar: Wis. 1974. Dir. environ. protection unit Wis. Atty. Gen. Office, 1978-80; exec. asst. to the secy. Wis. Dept. Natural Resources, 1980-91; ptnr., coord. environ. practice group Michael, Best & Friedrich, Madison, Wis., 1991—. Mem. ABA, Wis. State Bar Assn., Legal Assn. for Women. Office: Michael Best & Friedrich PO Box 1806 Firstar Plaza 1 S Pinckney St Madison WI 53701-1806

BOCHETTO, GEORGE ALEXANDER, lawyer; b. Bklyn., Oct. 7, 1952; m. Paula Agins, Aug. 6, 1987; children: David, Evan. BA, SUNY, Albany, 1975; JD cum laude, Temple U., 1978. Bar: Pa. 1978, N.Y. 1995, U.S. Dist. Ct. (ea. dist.) Pa. 1979, U.S. Supreme Ct. 1992, U.S. Tax Ct. 1986. Pvt. practice, 1979-90; assoc. Pelino & Lentz, P.C., Phila., 1978-79, Monteverde & Hemphill, P.C., Phila., 1990-93, Bochetto & Lentz, P.C., Phila., 1993—. Contbr. articles to profl. jours. Bd. dirs. Pa. Spl. Olympics, 1986—; mem. Rep. State Com., Pa., 1992—; appt. Pa. State Athletic Commr. Gov. Ridge, 1995—. Mem. ABA, Pa. Bar Assn., Phila. Bar Assn. (subcom. chairperson profl. responsibility com. 1978—). Avocations: amateur boxing, boating, sports. Office: Bochetto & Lentz PC 1524 Locust St Philadelphia PA 19102-4401

BOCHNER, HART, actor; b. Toronto, Ont., Can., Oct. 3, 1956. BA in English, U. Calif. San Diego, La Jolla, 1978. Appeared in films Islands in the Stream, 1975, Breaking Away, 1978, Rich and Famous, 1980, The Wild Life, 1984, Making Mr. Right, 1986, Die Hard, 1988, Apartment Zero, 1988, Fellow Traveller, 1989, Mr. Destiny, 1990, Mad at the Moon, 1991, The Innocent, 1992, The Breakup, 1997, Anywhere But Here, 1998; TV miniseries Haywire, 1979, East of Eden, 1980, Having It All, 1982, Sun Also Rises, 1984, War and Remembrance, 1986-87 (Emmy award 1989), And the Sea Will Tell, 1990, Complex of Fear, 1992, Children of the Dust, 1994; dir. (short film) The Buzzz, 1992, PCU, 1993, High School High, 1995-96.

BOCHNER, MEL, artist; b. Pitts., 1940. B.F.A., Carnegie Inst. Tech., 1962. Former instr. Sch. Visual Arts, N.Y.C. One-man shows Galerie Heiner Friedrich, Munich, Galerie Konrad Fischer, Dusseldorf, Germany, Ace Gallery, Los Angeles, 1969, Galleria Sperone, Torino, Italy, 1970, Galleria Toselli, Milan, Italy, 1970, Mus. Modern Art, N.Y.C., 1971, Galerie Sonnabend, Paris, 1972, 73, 74, 78, Sonnabend Gallery, N.Y.C., 1972, 73, 76, 80, 82, 83, Lisson Gallery, London, 1972, Univ. Art Mus., Berkeley, Calif., 1974, Balt. Mus. Art, 1976, Bernier Gallery, Athens, 1977, Gallerie Schema, Milan and Florence, Italy, 1978, Galerie Art in Progress, Dusseldorf, Germany, 1979, Daniel Weinberg Gallery, San Francisco, 1981, Centre Internat. de Creation Artistique, 1982, Abbaye de Senanque, Gordes, France, 1982, Yarlow Salzman Gallery, Toronto, 1983, Daniel Weinberg Gallery, San Francisco, 1983, Pace Editions, N.Y.C., 1983; group shows include Finch Coll. Mus. Art, 1967, Paula Cooper Gallery, N.Y.C., 1968, Seattle Art Mus., 1969, Mus. Modern Art, N.Y.C., 1970, Museo Civico D'Arte Moderna, Turin, Italy, 1970, Gallery Nachst St. Stephen, Innsbruck, 1971, Spoleto Festival, Itlay, 1972, Documenta V. Kassel, Germany, 1972, Sonnabend Gallery, N.Y.C., 1972, 77, 81, Kunstmuseum, Basel, Switzerland, 1972, Fogg Mus., Harvard U., Cambridge, Mass., 1973, Seattle Art Mus., Seattle, 1973, Whitney Mus. Am. Art, N.Y.C., 1973, Princeton Art Mus., 1974, Art Inst. Chgo., 1974, Mus. Modern Art, N.Y.C., 1975, Am. Drawings' Mus., Leverkusen, 1975, Art Gallery Ont., 1975, Mus. Modern Art, N.Y.C., 1976, Chgo. Art Inst., 1976, Fort Worth Mus., 1976, Detroit Inst. Art, 1976, Whitney Mus. Am. Art, N.Y.C., 1977, 83, Mus. Contemporary Art, Chgo., 1977, Phila. Mus. Art, 1978, Leo Castelli Gallery, 1978, Whitney Mus. Am. Art, N.Y.C., 1979, Palazzo Reale, Milan, Italy, 1979, W Centre Georges Pomipdou, Beauborg, Paris, 1979, MIT, 1980, Beaubourg Centre Nationale d'Art et de Culture, 1981-82, Centre Georges Pompidou, 1981-82, Chgo. Art Inst., 1982, Yale U. Art Gallery, 1982, Janet Steinberg Gallery, Sonnabend Gallery; represented in permanent collections Los Angles County Mus., Mus. Nat. d'Art Moderne, Paris, Whitney Mus. Am. Art; film Walking a Straight Line Through Grand Central Station, 1965, N.Y.C. Windows, 1965, Dorothea in Fifteen Positions Stasis, 1970; contbr. articles to profl. jours. recipient Acad.-Inst. award for art, 1990. Office: care Sonnabend Gallery 420 W Broadway New York NY 10012-3764*

BOCHY, BRUCE, professional sports team manager, coach; b. Landes de Boussac, France, Apr. 16, 1955; m. Kim B.; children: Greg, Brett. Coach San Diego Padres, 1993-94, mgr., 1994—. Office: San Diego Padres PO Box 2000 San Diego CA 92112-2000*

BOCK, CAROLYN A., author, consultant, trainer, small business owner; b. Jan. 25, 1942; d. Wilfred Ignatius and Marcella Mary (Birkemeier) Gerschutz; m. Donald Charles Bock, Sept. 7, 1974 (dec. Nov. 1997); 1 child, Jonathon Edward. Student, Notre Dame Coll., 1960-62, John Carroll U., 1962-66. With sales and purchasing depts. Schaffer Diversified Corp. and other cos., Cleve., 1962-74; columnist, writer, 1979—; owner Dynmic Living Assocs., Westlake, 1986—. Author: Authors, Artists and Auras, 1988, Gerschutz family history, 1989. Co-founder, trustee Cmty. Action Team, Westlake, 1980-85; trustee, co-founder Westlake Arts Coun., 1983-84, pres., 1984-85; chmn. Morning Sem., Rocky River, Ohio, 1981-85; pres. Westlake PTA Coun., 1980-82, Parkside Jr. High PTA, Westlake, 1983-84; active Boy Scouts, Clague Playhouse, Westlake Hist. Soc., 1985-98, Westfield Ctr. Hist. Soc. Recipient Outstanding Svc. award Boy Scouts Am., 1980; named hon. life mem. Ohio PTA, 1982. Mem. Medina County Area C. of C., Soc. Profl. Journalists. Unitarian Universalist. Avocations: travel, reading, cooking, gardening. Home: Box 240 Lodi OH 44254 also: 9183 S Leroy Rd Westfield Center OH 44251

BOCK, EDWARD JOHN, retired chemical manufacturing company executive; b. Ft. Dodge, Iowa, Sept. 1, 1916; s. Edward J. and Maude (Juday) B.; m. Ruth Kunerth, Aug. 9, 1941; children: Barbara, Edward, Nancy, Roger. M.S. in Mech. Engring, Iowa State U., 1940. With Monsanto Co., St. Louis, 1941—, asst. gen. mgr. inorganic chems. div., 1958-60, v.p., gen. mgr., 1960-65, v.p. adminstrn., mem. exec. com., dir., 1965-68, pres., CEO, chmn. corp. mgmt. and exec. coms., dir., 1968-72; chmn. bd., CEO, Cupples Co., St. Louis, 1975-85; cons.; bd. dirs. Harbour Group Ltd. Past chmn. bd. trustees Deaconess Hosp.; past trustee Ladue Chapel; bd. govs. Iowa State U. Found. Recipient Silver Anniversary All-Am. Football award Sports Illustrated, 1963; Anston Marston award Iowa State U., 1972; Significant Sig award, 1971; named to All Am. Football Team, 1938; elected to Nat. Football Found. Hall of Fame, 1970, 1st elected to Iowa State U. Athletic Hall of Fame, 1997. Mem. ASME, Sigma Chi, Tau Beta Pi. Clubs: St. Louis, Old Warson Country (pres. 1972), Bogey, Arnold Palmer's Bay Hill. Home and Office: 2232 Clifton Forge Dr Saint Louis MO 63131-3107

BOCK, FRANK JOSEPH, information systems specialist; b. Rochester, N.Y., Sept. 4, 1958; s. John Henry and Irene (Kaiser) B.; m. Aline Maria Caubergs, Aug. 26, 1984. Degree in philosophy, Cath. U. of Louvain, PhD in Philosophy, 1991. Asst. dean Cath. Univ. of Louvain (Belgium), 1984-91; rsch. assoc. SBR & Co., Washington, 1992; career counselor Bernard Haldane & Assoc., Washington, 1992-94; dir. info. systems & devel. resources Leukemia Soc. of Am. Rsch. Found., Washington, 1993-94; assoc. dir. rsch. fund devel. Leukemia Soc. of Am., N.Y.C., 1994-96, nat. project mgr., 1996-97, assoc. nat. dir. info. technology, 1997—. Mem. Assn. Profl. Rschrs. Advancement, Nat. Psychol. Assn. Psychoanalysis. Office: Leukemia Soc Am 600 3rd Ave New York NY 10016-1901

BOCK, JERRY (JERROLD LEWIS), composer; b. New Haven, Nov. 23, 1928; s. George Joseph and Rebecca (Alpert) B.; m. Patricia Faggen, May 28, 1950; children: George Albert, Portia Fane. Student, U. Wis., 1945-49, L.H.D. (hon.), 1985. Writer: score for high sch. mus. comedy My Dream, 1945; score for original coll. musical Big as Life, 1948; wrote: songs for TV show Admiral Broadway Revue, also Show of Shows, 1949-51; composer songs, Camp Tamiment, summers 1950, 51, 53; writer: continuity sketches Mel Torme show, CBS, 1951, 52; writing staff: Kate Smith Hour, 1953-54; writer: original songs for night club performers, including night club revue Confetti; wrote: songs for Wonders of Manhattan (hon. mention Cannes Film Festival 1956); composer: music for Broadway show Catch a Star, 1955, Mr. Wonderful, 1956, (collaborated with Sheldon Harnick on) The Body Beautiful, 1958, Fiorello, 1959 (Pulitzer prize, Drama Critics award, Antoinette Perry award), Tenderloin, 1960, She Loves Me, 1963, revival, 1990, Fiddler on the Roof, 1964, Silver Anniversary prodn. nat. tour, 1989-90, revival, 1990-91, 93, The Apple Tree, 1966, The Rothschilds, 1972, revival, 1990-91; London prodn. of She Loves Me, 1964, off-Broadway, 1982, Jerome Robbins Broadway, 1989; London prodn. of Fiddler on the Roof, 1964 (Tony award), Warsaw prodn., 1985, Fiorello, Goodspeed Opera House, summer 1985, (film) A Stranger Among Us, 1992; wrote series of children's songs now pub. under title Sing Something Special; also recorded album, N.Y. Bd. Edn., radio broadcasts, 1961—. Recipient 9 Tony awards Best Musical of Yr. Fiddler on the Roof, 1964, Johnny Mercer award Songwriters Hall of Fame, 1990, Olivier award Best Musical Revival for She Loves Me, 1994; named to Theatre Hall of Fame, 1990. Mem. Broadcast Music Inc. (adv. panel), Nat. Found. Advancement in Arts (endowment group).

BOCK, JOHN LOUIS, architect; b. Richmond, Va., Aug. 17, 1945; s. Paul Hevener and Byrd (Johnson) B.; m. Carol Ann Chiocca, Feb. 5, 1983. Student Va. Poly. Inst., 1963-65; BS, Richmond Profl. Inst., 1968. Draftsman, G. Richard Brown, Architect, 1964-66; project capt. J. Henley Walker, Jr., Architect, 1966-69; tchr. mech. drawing Chesterfield County Schs., 1969-70; project architect J. Henley Walker, Jr., Architect, 1970-76, Harry S. Cruickshank, Architect, Richmond, 1976-77, Edward F. Sinnott & Son, Architect, Richmond, 1977-78; v.p., sec. Ernie Rose, Inc., Architects, Richmond, Va., 1978-91, also dir.; owners John L. Bock Architect, Mechanicsville, Va., 1991—. Mem. Constrn. Specifications Inst. (dir. Richmond chpt. 1981, 91, 93, 94, v.p. chpt.; award 1981, 83, chmn. scholarship found. 1996-98), Ducks Unltd. (chmn. Mechanicsville chpt. 1983-87, nat. sponsor 1983-91, Spl. award Va. com. 1986, Distng. Service award 1988). Episcopalian. Home: 8044 Shady Knoll Ln Mechanicsville VA 23111-2262

BOCK, RUSSELL SAMUEL, author; b. Spokane, Wash., Nov. 24, 1905; s. Alva and Elizabeth (Mellinger) B.; m. Suzanne Ray, Feb. 26, 1970; children: Beverly A. Bock Wunderlich, James Russell. B.B.A., U. Wash., 1929. Part-time instr. U. So. Calif., UCLA, 1942-50; with Ernst & Ernst, CPAs, Los Angeles, 1938, ptnr., 1951-69; cons. Ernst & Young, 1969—. Author: Guidebook to California Taxes, annually, 1950—, Taxes of Hawaii, annually, 1964—; also numerous articles. Dir., treas. Cmty. TV So. Calif., 1964-74; dir., v.p. treas., So. Calif. Symphony-Hollywood Bowl Assn., 1964-70; bd. dirs. Cmty. Arts Music Assn., 1974-76, 78-84, Santa Barbara Symphony Assn., 1976-78, Santa Barbara Boys and Girls Club, 1980-93, UCSB Affiliates, 1983-85, Santa Barbara Civic Light Opera, 1995-97. Mem. Am. Inst. C.P.A.s (council 1953-57, trial bd. 1955-58, v.p. 1959-60), Calif. Soc. C.P.A.s (past pres.), Los Angeles C. of C. (dir. 1957-65, v.p. 1963), Sigma Phi Epsilon, Beta Alpha Psi, Beta Gamma Sigma. Clubs: Birnam Wood Golf, Santa Barbara Yacht. Office: 300 Hot Springs Rd Apt 190 Santa Barbara CA 93108-2069

BOCK, WALTER JOSEPH, zoology educator; b. N.Y.C., Nov. 20, 1933; s. Paul and Anne (Kalsch) B.; m. Katharine Lippitt, June 29, 1957; children: Katharine Rose, Susan Ruth, Walter David. B.S., Cornell U., 1955; M.A., Harvard U., 1957, Ph.D., 1959. NSF postdoctoral fellow Universität Frankfurt Main, 1959-61; asst. prof. dept. zoology U. Ill., 1961-64, assoc. prof., 1964-65; asst. prof. dept. biol. scis. Columbia U., 1965-66, assoc. prof., 1966-73, prof., 1973—; research asso. Am. Mus Natural History, 1965—. Author: (with J.J. Morony and J. Farrand) Reference List of the Birds of the World, 1975; Contbr. articles to profl. jours. Pres. Tenafly (N.J.) Nature Center, 1977-80; permanent sec. Internat. Ornithol. Com., 1986-98; pres. 23rd Internat. Ornithological Congress, 2002. NSF grantee, 1962-79. Mem. Am. Ornithologists Union (Coues award 1975), Am. Soc. Zoologists, Am. Soc. Naturalists (treas. 1978-80), Soc. Study Evolution, Soc. Systematic Biology, AAAS, Brit. Ornithologists Union, Deutschen Ornithologen-Gesellschaft. E-mail: wb4@columbia.edu. Home: 114 Hudson Ave Tenafly NJ 07670-1004 Office: Columbia U Dept Biological Scis New York NY 10027 *Humans are not independent of the earth's environment in which they live and of their evolutionary history. As a scholar, I hope to learn about evolutionary and ecological mechanisms; as a teacher I hope to pass this knowledge on to others; and as a person I hope to preserve and enjoy the beauty of nature that exists about us.*

BOCKELMAN, CHARLES KINCAID, physics educator; b. San Francisco, Nov. 29, 1922; s. Bernhardt Jacob and Ruth Gladys (Kincaid) B.; m. Elizabeth Button, June 15, 1950 (div. July 1, 1978); 1 child, Faith; m. Christina DiGiusto, Feb. 16, 1991. PhB, U. Wis., 1947, PhD, 1951; MA, Yale U., 1965. Rsch. assoc. MIT, Cambridge, 1951-55; prof. physics Yale U., New Haven, 1955-93, prof. emeritus, 1993—. Trustee Associated Univs., 1970-88, Assn. Univs. for Rsch. in Astronomy, 1978-85. Fellow Inst. Theoretical Physics, 1958, Guggenheim, 1971; vis. fellow Nat. U. Mexico, 1964. Fellow Am. Phys. Soc. Home: 22 Mount Nebo Rd Newtown CT 06470-2471

BOCKELMAN, JOHN RICHARD, lawyer; b. Chgo., Aug. 8, 1925; s. Carl August and Mary (Ritchie) B. Student, U. Wis., 1943-44, Northwestern U., 1944-45, Harvard U., 1945, U. Hawaii, 1946; BSBA, Northwestern U., 1946; MA in Econs., U. Chgo., 1949, JD, 1951. Bar: Ill. 1951. Atty.-advisor Chgo. ops. office AEC, 1951-52; asso. firm Schradzke, Gould & Ratner, Chgo., 1952-57, Brown, Dashow & Langeluttig, Chgo., 1957-59, Antonow & Weissbourd, Chgo., 1959-61; partner firm Burton, Isaacs, Bockelman & Miller, Chgo., 1961-69; pvt. practice Chgo., 1970—; prof. bus. law Ill. Inst. Tech., Chgo., 1950-82; lectr. econs. DePaul U., Chgo., 1952-53; bd. dirs., sec. Arlington Engring. Co.; bd. dirs., v.p., Universal Distbrs., Inc. Pres. 1212 Lake Shore Dr. Condo Assn., Chgo., Near North Assn. of Condo Pres., Chgo. Served with USNR, 1943-46. Mem. ABA, Ill. Bar Assn., Chgo. Bar Assn., Cath. Lawyers Guild Chgo., Lake Point Tower Club, Barclay Ltd. Club, Whitehall Club, Internat. Club, Anvil Club (East Dundee, Ill.), Univ. Club (San Diego), Tavern Club (Chgo.), Phi Delta Theta. Home: 1212 N Lake Shore Dr Chicago IL 60610-2371 Office: 104 S Michigan Ave Ste 808 Chicago IL 60603-5906

BOCKHOP, CLARENCE WILLIAM, retired agricultural engineer; b. Paullina, Iowa, Mar. 28, 1921; s. Fred Henry and Sophie Dorothea (Laue) B.; m. Virginia Buhman, July 9, 1949; children—Barbara Lucille, Nancy Jeanne, Bryan William, Karl David. B.S. in Agrl. Engring, Iowa State U., 1943, M.S. in Agrl. Engring, 1955, Ph.D. in Agr. Engring. and Theoretical and Applied Mechanics, 1957. Mgr. service and edn. Stewart Co., Dallas, 1948-53; mem. faculty Iowa State U., Ames, 1953-57, 60-80, prof. agrl. engring., 1960-80, head dept. agrl. engring., 1962-80; prof., head dept. agrl. engring. U. Tenn., 1957-60; head dept. agrl. engring. Internat. Rice Research Inst., Los Banos, The Philippines, 1980-86; vis. prof. U. Ghana, 1969-70. Gen. reporter, VIth Internat. Congress Agrl. Engring., Lausanne, Switzerland, 1964; Author articles in field. Served to capt. AUS, 1943-48. Fellow Am. Soc. Agrl. Engrs. (chmn. Tenn. sect. 1958-59, chmn. mid-central sect. 1960-61, chmn. Iowa sect. 1963-64, chmn. edn. and research div. 1966-67, dir. 1973-75); mem. Am. Soc. Engring. Edn. (chmn. agrl. engring. div. 1966-67), Sigma Xi, Gamma Sigma Delta, Phi Kappa Phi, Phi Mu Alpha, Tau Beta Pi. Lutheran. Address: 424 Hide A Way Ln E Lindale TX 75771-5215

BOCKIAN, DONNA MARIE, data processing executive; b. N.Y.C., June 4, 1946; d. Forrest Mager and Mary C. (Lovelace) Hastings; m. James Bernard Bockian, Sept. 16, 1984; children: Vivian Shifra, Adrian Adena, Lillian Tova. BA in Psychology, Vassar Coll., 1968; diploma in systems analysis NYU, 1978. Computer programmer RCA, N.Y.C., 1968-71; systems analyst United Artists Corp., N.Y.C., 1971-78; project leader Bradford Nat. Corp., N.Y.C., 1978-81; project mgr. Mfrs. Hanover Trust, N.Y.C., 1981-83; project mgr. Chem. Bank, N.Y.C., 1983-86; mgr. fin. systems Salomon Bros., N.Y.C., 1986-87; v.p. James B. Bockian and Assocs., 1987-93; mgr. systems quality assurance GAB Bus. Svcs., Inc., Parsippany, N.J., 1989-91; mgr. bus. systems GAB Bus. Svcs., Inc., Parsippany, N.J., 1991-93; mgmt. cons. ADIA Info. Techs., Inc., Piscataway, N.J., 1994; assoc. Data Mgmt. and Integration Svcs., Merrill Lynch & Co., Inc., 1995-96, cons. info. mgmt. svcs., 1996-97, asst. v.p. 1997—. Mem. Assn. Women in Computing (exec. com. 1982-83), Data Adminstrn. Mgmt. Assn. N.Y., Vassar Club (N.Y.C., Jersey Hills). Avocation: photography. Office: Merrill Lynch & Co 400 Atrium Somerset NJ 07883

BOCKIAN, JAMES BERNARD, computer systems executive; b. Jersey City, Sept. 16, 1941; s. Abraham and Evelyn (Skner) B.; m. Donna M. Hastings; children: Vivian Shifra, Adrian Adena, Lillian Tova. BA, Columbia U., 1963; MPA, U. Mich., 1965; MA, Yale U., 1967. Vice-consul, 3d sec. Embassy Dept. State, Washington, 1957-61; sr. systems analyst J.C. Penney Co., N.Y.C., 1961-67; mgr. systems svcs., head dept. systems projects McDonnell Douglas Automation Co., East Orange, N.J., 1967-76; prin. JBBA, Inc. (formerly James B. Bockian & Assocs., Inc.), Morristown, N.J., 1976—; v.p. MIS Thomas Cook, Inc., 1980-83, exec. cons. to Thomas Cook Group; lectr. in field. Author: Management Manual for Systems Development Projects, 1979, Project Management for Systems Development, 1981, AT&T User Guide to Information Systems Development, 1980; contbr. articles to profl. jours. Mem. N.Y. Acad. Scis., Internat. Assn. Cybernetics, Assn. Computing Machinery, Data Processing Mgmt. Assn., Am. Mgmt. Assn., Systems and Procudures Assn., Yale Club (N.Y.C.). Home: 26 Farmhouse Ln Morristown NJ 07960-3032 Office: JBBA Inc Olde Frg E Ste 26-5B Morristown NJ 07960

BOCKIUS, RUTH BEAR, nursing educator; b. Groffdale, Pa., Dec. 19, 1925; d. Weidler Romaine and Ruth Mary (Jacoby) Bear; m. Thomas B. Bockius Jr., Dec. 15 1945; children: Donna Ruth, Dawn Eileen. AA, Phoenix Coll., 1970; BSN, Ariz. State U., 1973, MEd, 1978. Instr. nursing Glendale (Ariz.) Community Coll.; coord. health edn. Samaritan Health Svcs., Phoenix; dir. patient/community edn. Maryvale Samaritan Hosp., Phoenix, edn. dir., ret., 1994. Grantee Fed. Nursing; AMA scholar, 1st Nat. Bank scholar. Mem. Am. Soc. Hosp. Edn. and Tng., Am. Hosp. Assn., Phi Theta Kappa, Phi Kappa Phi.

BOCKSERMAN, ROBERT JULIAN, chemist; b. St. Louis, Dec. 20, 1929; s. Max Louis and Bertha Anna (Kremen) B.; m. Clarice K. Kreisman, June 9, 1957; children: Michael Jay, Joyce Ellen, Carol Beth. BSc, U. Mo., 1952; postgrad., Far East Intelligence Sch, Tokyo, 1954; MSc, U. Mo., 1955. Chemist Sealtest Corp., Peoria, Ill., 1955-56; prodn. mgr. Allan Drug Co., St. Louis, 1957-59; rsch. chemist Monsanto Co., St. Louis, 1960-65; purchasing agt. Monsanto Co., Sauget, Ill., 1966-67; founder, pres. Pharma-Tech Industries, Inc., Union, Mo., 1967-84; tech. dir. Overlock-Howe Consulting Group, St. Louis, 1984-85; founder, pres. Conatech Consulting Group, Chesterfield, Mo., 1985—; sec., mem. industry packaging adv. com. Sch. of Engring., U. Mo., Rolla, 1979—; adj. prof. dept. food sci./nutrition U. Mo., Columbia; adj. prof. dept. engring. mgmt. U. Mo., Rolla; vis. lectr. U. Mo., Clayton, Northwestern U., Evanston, Ill. Tech. reviewer Jour. Inst. of Packaging Profls., Jour. Packaging Tech., Mo. Waste Control Scholarship Grants and Research, Medical Device and Diagnostic Industry Jour., Medical Plastics and Biomaterials Publication. (editorial adv. bd.); panelist (Help Desk Column) Medical Device and Diagnostic Industry mag. Mem. Mo. Waste Control Coalition; mem. stormwater engring. com. City of Creve Coeur, Mo.; nat. mem. Libr. Congress, Mo. Hist. Soc. With U.S. Army, 1952-54, Korea. Small Bus. Innovation rsch. grantee. Mem. ASTM, Am. Coll. Forensic Examiners, Cons. Packaging Engring. Coun., Inst. Packaging Profls. (cert. packaging profl.), Am. Technion Soc., Inst. Food Technologists Arrangements (St. Louis), Nat. Forensic Ctr., Teltech Resource Network, Am. Chem. Soc., Am. Plastics Coun., Mo. Acad. Scis., N.Y. Acad. Sci., Acad. Sci. St. Louis, Assn. Cons. Chemists and Chem. Engrs., Am. Nutraceutical Assn., Nat. Dir. Expert Witnesses, Sigma Xi. Achievements include research on toxicological effects of additives from packaging materials upon foodstuffs, on biological and photo degradation of polymers, on technology of form/fill/seal packaging engineering, new sterilization technologies for medical devices and pharmaceuticals, barrier properties of polymer films, toxicology of chemical dusts and fumes, and food irradiation effects on humans. Home: 54 Morwood Ln Creve Coeur MO 63141-7621 Office: Conatech Cons Group 287 N Lindbergh Blvd Creve Coeur MO 63141-7849

BOCKSTEIN, HERBERT, lawyer; b. N.Y.C., Jan. 27, 1943; s. Stanley Joseph and Sylvia (Tannenbaum) B.; m. Bonnie Sue Ritt, Sept. 2, 1967 (div.); children: Andrew, Jana; m. Nadine Bernstein, June 27, 1988. BA, NYU, 1963, JD cum laude, 1971; MBA, Cornell U., Ithaca, N.Y., 1966. Bar: N.Y. 1972, Mo. 1979. Assoc. Stroock & Stroock & Lavan, N.Y.C., 1971-78, Stolar, Heitzmann & Eder, St. Louis, 1978-80, Finley, Kumble, Wagner, Heine, Underberg, Manley & Casey, N.Y.C., 1980-83; ptnr. Finley, Kumble, N.Y.C., 1983-87, Myerson & Kuhn, N.Y.C., 1988-89, Ashinoff, Ross & Korff, N.Y.C., 1989-90, Newman Tannenbaum, N.Y.C., 1990-96, Tenzer Greenblatt, N.Y.C., 1996—. Mem. ABA, N.Y. State Bar Assn., Estate

Planning Coun. N.Y.C., Order of Coif. Avocations: tennis, golf. Home: 18 Old Mill Ln Ardsley NY 10502-1528 Office: Tenzer Greenblatt LLP 405 Lexington Ave New York NY 10174-0002

BOCK-TOBOLSKI, MARILYN ROSE, artist, art educator; b. South Bend, Ind., Jan. 21, 1941; d. Francis John and Mildred Irene (Moser) Bock; m. James Joseph Tobolski, Sept. 1, 1962; children: Erica Francis, Jessica Moser, Melina Jamie. BS in Fine Arts, Ind. U., 1964; postgrad. in Painting, Mich. State U., 1965-66; MS in Fine Arts, U. St. Francis, 1975. Art instr. Ft. Wayne (Ind.) Cmty. Schs., Northwest Allen County Sch. Sys., South Bend (Ind.) Cmty. Sch. Corp.; assoc. faculty drawing and painting dept. continuing edn. Ind. U.-Purdue U., Ft. Wayne, Ind., 1975-85, Sch. Fine and Performing Arts, 1978-89, 91-92, Sch. Edn., 1983-85, 89-90, women's art history and cross-disciplinary courses Dept. Women's Studies and Ind. U., Purdue U. Sch. Fine & Performing Arts IUPU, 1996, 97, 98, 99; drawing instr. Dept. Parks and Recreation, Ft. Wayne, 1989-96; guest artist gifted and talented visual art programs, mentor program Ft. Wayne Cmty. Schs., 1991, art dept. Northwest Allen Schs., Fort Wayne, 1986, 87, 88, 89, 90, Metro Sch. Sys., Wabash, Ind., 1986, 87, Bunche Elem. Sch., Ft. Wayne, 1994, 95, 96; mem. panel Matter, Mind, Spirit Exhbn. Nat. Mus. Women in Arts, Indpls., 1999. One woman exhbns. include Del. Cmty. Coll., Media, Pa., 1970, Tri-State Coll., Angola, Ind., 1971, Ft. Wayne (Ind.) Mus. Art, 1972, Manchester (Ind.) Coll., 1973, Watsons-Crick Gallery Purdue U., West Lafayette, Ind., 1975, Lakeview Gallery St. Francis Coll., Ft. Wayne, 1975, 83, Artlink Contemporary Artspace, Ft. Wayne, 1979, St. Mary's Coll., Notre Dame, Ind., 1982, Thomas Smith Fine Art Gallery, Ft. Wayne, 1985, Canterbury Art Ctr. Gallery, Ft. Wayne, 1988, Allen County Pub. Lib. Galleries, Ft. Wayne, 1993; group exhbns. include South Bend (Ind.) Art Ctr., 1961, 76, 91, Lansing (Mich.) Cmty. Gallery, 1968, Ball State U., Muncie, Ind., 1973, 74, 76, 82, Ind. U.-Purdue U., Ft. Wayne, 1974, 75, 77, 78, 81, 88, Ft. Wayne Mus. Art, 1975, 77, 78, 79, 83, 86, 87, Linker Gallery, Ft. Wayne, 1977, Ind. State Mus., Indpls., 1978, 80, Artlink Contemporary Artspace, Ft. Wayne, 1978, 79, 80, 81, 83, 85, 86, 87, 88, 95, 98, 99, 1st Presbyn. Ch. Gallery, Ft. Wayne, 1977, 81, Lakeview Gallery U. St. Francis, Ft. Wayne, 1978, 89, Unitarian Gallery, Ft. Wayne, 1979, Anderson (Ind.) Coll., 1980, A. Montgomery Ward Gallery U. Ill., Chgo., Indpls. Art League, 1991, J. Barrett Galleries, Toledo, 1982, Indpls. Mus. Art, 1983, Radsdall Gallery U. Ky., Lexington, 1984, Liturgical Visual Art Exhibit, Chgo., 1984, Cryna Internat. Gallery, Chgo., 1984, Wehrle Art Gallery Ohio Dominican Coll., Columbus, 1986, Thomas Smith Fine Art Gallery, Ft. Wayne, 1986, 87, Indpls. Press Club,1986, Artemisia Gallery, Chgo., 1986, Canterbury Art Ctr., Ft. Wayne, 1987, Schumacher Gallery, Columbus, 1987, Johnson Humrickhouse Mus., Coshocton, Ohio, 1989, J. Beck Gallery, Ft. Wayne, 1989, Rapp Gallery, Louisville, Ky., 1990, Vincennes (Ind.) U., 1992, Allen County Pub. Lib., Ft. Wayne, 1983-86, 92, 94, 95, 96, Reynolds-Heller Gallery, Columbus, 95, Lakeland Art Assn., Warsaw, Ind., 1996; represented in numerous private and pub. collections Ft. Wayne Mus. Art, Lincoln Nat. Corp., Ft. Wayne; executed paintings for St. Vincent De Paul Ch., Ft. Wayne, Ind., Crosier Ctr., Ft. Wayne, Downtown on the Landing, Ft. Wayne, others; featured in Art Insight, The Communicator, News-Sentine, Arts Ind., The Indianapolis NE, NUVO and others. Recipient award of Excellence Schumacher Gallery, 1987. Mem. Soc. Layerists in Multi Media, Artlink Contemporary Gallery (panel mem. 1979-82, 84-88). Roman Catholic. Avocations: film, books, anthropology, mythology, psychology. Home and Studio: 11534 Cherrywood Dr Fort Wayne IN 46845-9665

BOCKUS, HERMAN WILLIAM, JR., artist, educator, writer; b. Frazee, Minn., Feb. 21, 1915; s. Herman William and Emma (Kimmerle) B.; m. Janet Davidson Fisher, Jan. 15, 1944; children: Genevieve, Kim, William, Heidi, Jill. BBA, U. Minn., 1937, BS, 1948, MEd, 1949. Salesman Food Warehouse, New Ulm, Minn., 1937-39; interpreter U.S. Govt., Colon, Canal Zone, 1939-42; art tchr. Highlands U., Las Vegas, N.Mex., 1948; art prof. Pasadena City Coll., 1950-75, head dept. art, 1965-66; tech. writer Calif. Inst. Tech., Pasadena, 1960-64. author: Advertising Graphics, 1969, 4th edit. 1986, Checklist for Better Tennis, 1973, Designers Notebook, 1977, Life Science Careers, 1991, Boys, 1995, The Universe, 1999. Capt. USMC, 1942-45. Recipient Cert. of Merit, L.A. Art Dirs. Show, 1965. Avocation: tennis. Home: 1943 Coolidge Ave Altadena CA 91001-3505

BOCKWOLDT, TODD SHANE, nuclear engineer; b. Spirit Lake, Iowa, July 31, 1967; s. Larry Ray and Gale Glee (Bobzien) B.; m. Margery Pitzer, June 9, 1990. BS in Nuclear Engring., Ga. Tech, 1989, MS in Nuclear Engring., 1990. Lic. profl. engr., 1999. Grad. rsch. asst. Ga. Inst. Technology, Atlanta, 1989-90; S5W (submarines) and A1G (carriers) fleet reactor engr. DOE/USN Naval Reactors Hdqrs., Arlington, Va., 1990-95; asst. naval reactors rep. DOE/USN Norfolk Naval Shipyard, Portsmouth, Va., 1995-98; control drive mechanism design engr. naval reactors hdqs. DOE/USN, Arlington, Va., 1998—; tech. program chmn. Am. Nuclear Soc. Student Conf., Atlanta, 1988; nuclear engring. rep. Mech. Engring. Student Adv. Com., Ga. Tech, 1988-89. Lt. USN, 1990—. Scholar NROTC, 1985-89, MCDAC, 1985-89, Am. Soc. Naval Engrs. scholar, 1987-89; recipient Gold medal Soc. Am. Mil. Engrs., 1988, Ga. Tech Honor award Soc. Am. Mil. Engrs., 1989, Outstanding Coll. Students of Am. award, 1989. Mem. Am. Nuclear Soc. (grad. scholar 1989-90), Tau Beta Pi, Mensa, Alpha Nu Sigma. Lutheran. Home: 20887 Chippoaks Forest Cir Sterling VA 20165-2446

BOCSKOR, NANCY LEAH, political consultant; b. Dayton, Ohio, Sept. 20, 1957; d. Andrew Michael and Phyllis (Moberly) B. BA, Otterbein Coll., 1979. Legis. dir. Congressman Newt Gingrich, Washington, 1979-81; pub. affairs Nat. Rep. Congl. Com., Washington, 1981-83; dep. dir. Nat. Rep. Senatorial Com., Washington, 1983-85; exec. dir. Nebr. Rep. Party, Lincoln, 1985-87; field rep. Dole for Pres. Campaign, Lincoln, 1987-88; account exec. Welch Assocs., Arlington, Va., 1988-89; chief staff Congressman Jon Kyl, Washington, 1989-90; pvt. practice cons. Arlington, 1990—; lectr. Rep. Nat. Com., Washington, 1991—, George Washington U., Washington, 1995—, Am. U., Washington, 1995—, U. Md., Coll. Pk., 1997—, Yale U., 1997—. Author: Campaign Encyclopedia, 1991, revised edit., 1997; editor: PAC Encyclopedia, 1996, rev. edit., 1998. Bd. dirs. Friends of Rabbits, Alexandria, Va., 1997—. Named Rising Polit. Star Campaigns and Elections Mag., 1996. Mem. Nat. Assn. Rep. Campaign Profls. Avocations: needlework, travel. E-mail: Bocskor@aol.com.

BOCZKAJ, BOHDAN KAROL, structural engineer; b. Kowel, Poland, Nov. 14, 1930; came to U.S., 1973, naturalized, 1979; s. Walenty and Anna (Sarnecka) B.; m. Teresa Marcela Bioniosek, Aug. 23, 1955; 1 child, Boleslaw. MS in Civil Engring., Tech. U. of Silesia, Gliwice, Poland, 1962; PhD, Tech. U. Lodz (Poland), 1969. Registered profl. engr., Pa. Asst. prof. Tech. U. of Silesia, 1969-73, Tech. U., Rzeszow, Poland, 1970-71; sr. engr. Dravo Engrs., Pitts., 1973-83; vis. prof. Birzeit U., West Bank, Israel, 1984-86; prin. engr. Schneider Engrs., Bridgeville, Pa., 1986-88; design engr. Rust Internat., Pitts., 1988-90; prin. engr. S.E.I. Engrs. and Cons., Pitts., 1990-91; cons., 1992-94; specialist Hoogovens Tech. Svcs., 1995-97; civil engring. mgr. CV Engring., Pitts., 1997; structural engring. cons., 1998—. Contbr. articles on prestressed concrete and theory of plates, concrete fatigue, structure on mine subsiding area to profl. jours.; co-author: Defense of Poland-Today and Tomorrow, 1993, Vision of Poland, 1995. Teaching grantee Fulbright Found. Coun. for Internat. Exch. of Scholars, Birzeit U., 1985-86. Mem. ASCE, Polish Inst. Arts and Scis. in Am. Roman Catholic. Achievements include patent on Coke Oven Machinery. Home: 728 Riehl Dr Pittsburgh PA 15234-2511

BOCZKO, STANLEY, urologist; b. June 9, 1949. MD, Albert Einstein Coll. Medicine, Bronx, N.Y., 1973. Pvt. practice urology N.Y.C., 1978—.

BODA, VERONICA CONSTANCE, lawyer; b. Phila., Oct. 8, 1952; d. Louis Paul and Helen Ann (Zwigaitis) B. AB, Wilson Coll., 1974; JD, Vt. Law Sch., 1978; LLM in Taxation, Villanova U., 1989. Bar: Pa. 1978, U.S. Dist. Ct. (ea. dist.) Pa. 1982, U.S. Tax Ct. 1984. Staff atty. Cape-Atlantic Legal Services, Atlantic City, 1978-79; sole practice Phila., 1980—; tchr. Am. Inst. for Paralegal Studies, Phila., 1982-86; instr. bus. adminstrn. program Pa. State U., Media, Pa., 1987-88; ins. agt. Prudential Ins. Co., Wayne, Pa., 1985-86; ins. broker V C Boda & Co., Phila., 1986—. Author: (with others) Newberg on Class Actions, 1985; editor Women Lawyers Jour., 1993-97; contbr. articles to profl. jours. Bd. dirs. Emergency Aid of Pa. Found., 1994-96; bd. dirs. Colonial Phila. Hist. Soc., 1983, pres., 1984-89. Mem. Nat. Assn. Women Lawyers (treas., pres.), Phila. Bar Assn. (chair com. real estate sect. 1984-86). Democrat. Roman Catholic. Avocations: tennis, gardening, chess, theater, art. Office: PO Box 1587 Philadelphia PA 19105-1587

BODAH, WILLIAM T., federal judge; b. 1938. BS, Ohio U., 1961; JD, Ohio State U., 1964. Asst. atty. gen. U.S. Atty. Gen.'s office, Columbus, 1964-65, 66-67; atty. Capital Fin. Corp., Columbus, 1965-66, East Ohio Gas Co., Cleve., 1967-72; assoc. Manchester, Bennett, Powers & Ullman, Youngstown, Ohio, 1972-85; bankruptcy judge U.S. Dist. Ct. (no. dist.) Ohio, Youngstown, 1985—. Author: A Local Rules Guide for Ohio Northern District Bankruptcy Court, 1988, A Few Useful Provisions — The Adoption of the Bill of Rights, 1991, Thew Parameters of the Non-Plan Liquidating Chapter 11: Refining the "Lionel" Standard, 1992; contbr. articles to legal jours. Fellow Am. Coll. Bankruptcy; mem. Nat. Conf. Bankruptcy Judges, Am. Bankruptcy Inst., John H. Clarke Am. Inn of Ct., Phi Delta Phi. Fax: (330) 746-0480. Office: US Dist Ct No Dist Ohio 125 Market St Ste 218 Youngstown OH 44503

BODANSKY, DAVID, physicist, educator; b. N.Y.C., Mar. 10, 1924; s. Aaron and Marie (Syrkin) B.; m. Beverly Ferne Bronstein, Sept. 7, 1952; children: Joel N., Daniel M. BS, Harvard U., 1943, MA, 1948, PhD, 1950. Instr. physics Columbia U., N.Y.C., 1950-52, assoc., 1952-54; mem. faculty U. Wash., Seattle, 1954—, assoc. prof. physics, 1958-63, prof., 1963-93, prof. emeritus, 1993—, chmn. dept., 1976-84. Co-author: (with Fred H. Schmidt) The Energy Controversy: The Fight over Nuclear Power, 1976, (with others) Indoor Radon and Its Hazards, 1987, Nuclear Energy: Principles, Practices, and Prospects, 1996; editl. bd.: Rev. Sci. Instruments, 1967-69. With AUS, 1943-46. Sloan Research fellow, 1959-63; Guggenheim fellow, 1966-67, 74-75. Fellow Am. Phys. Soc. (chair Panel on Pub. Affairs 1995), AAAS; mem. Am. Assn. Physics Tchrs., Am. Nuc. Soc., Health Physics Soc., Phi Beta Kappa. Research in nuclear physics, nuclear astrophysics and energy policy. Office: U Wash Dept Physics Seattle WA 98195-1560

BODANSKY, ROBERT LEE, lawyer; b. N.Y.C.. BA cum laude, Syracuse U., 1974; JD with honors, George Washington U., 1977; cert. postgrad. studies, Ctr. Internat. Legal Studies, Salzburg, Austria, 1978. Bar: Md. 1978, D.C. 1978, U.S. Dist. Ct. Md. 1978, U.S. Ct. Appeals (D.C. cir.) 1980, U.S. Dist. Ct. D.C. 1980, U.S. Ct. Appeals (4th cir.) 1981, U.S. Supreme Ct. 1982. From assoc. to ptnr. Feldman, Krieger, Goldman & Tish, Washington, 1978-83; ptnr. Feldman, Bodansky & Rubin, Washington, 1984-95; prin. Freer, McGarry, Bodansky & Rubin PC, Washington, 1995-97; ptnr. Nixon Peabody LLP (formerly Nixon, Hargrave, Devans & Doyle), Washington, 1997—; advisor internat. bus. law and taxation programs McGeorge Sch. Law, Sacramento, Calif., 1985—. Author: Special Problems of Subcontractors and Suppliers, 1987. Legal advisor Parkwood Resident's Assn., Kensington, Md., 1984; bd. dirs. Ridgeleigh Residents' Assn., 1987—, Congregation Har Shalom, 1989-91; tchr. Adas Israel Congregation, Washington, 1975-91. Mem. ABA (chmn. subcom. internat. and foreign bus. law young lawyers div. 1978-80), Md. State Bar Assn., D.C. Bar Assn. Office: Nixon Peabody LLP 1 Thomas Cir NW Ste 700 Washington DC 20005-5802

BODANSZKY, MIKLOS, chemist, educator; b. Budapest, Hungary, May 21, 1915; came to U.S., 1957, naturalized, 1964; s. Lajos and Maria (Friedner) B.; m. Agnes A. Vadasz, Apr. 21, 1950; 1 child, Eva. Diploma in chem. engring, Tech. U. Budapest, 1939, DSc, 1949. Sr. lectr. Tech. U. Budapest, 1950-56; research assoc. Cornell U. Med. Coll., 1957-59; sr. research assoc. Squibb Inst. Med. Research, New Brunswick, N.J., 1959-66; prof. chemistry and biochemistry Case Western Res. U., Cleve., 1966-83; Charles Frederic Mabery prof. research in chemistry Case Western Res. U., 1978-83, prof. emeritus, 1983—. Author: Peptide Synthesis, 1966, 2d edit., 1976, Principles of Peptide Syntheses, 1984, 2d edit, 1993, The Practice of Peptide Synthesis, 1984, 2d edit., 1994, Peptide Chemistry, 1988, 2d edit., 1993, The World of Peptides, 1991; editorial bd. Jour. Antibiotics, 1971-87, Internat. Jour. Peptide Protein Rsch., 1978-89. Recipient Pierce award, 1977; Morley medal, 1978; A. von Humboldt award, 1979. Mem. Am. Chem. Soc., Am. Soc. Biol. Chemistry, Hungarian Acad. Scis. (fgn.). Research in Nitrophenyl ester method of peptide synthesis, 1954; first synthesis gastrointestinal hormone secretin, 1966; synthesis vasoactive intestinal peptide, 1973.

BODDIE, DON O'MAR, recording company executive, producer, recording artist; b. St. Louis, Nov. 22, 1944; s. George Palmer and Lucille (Owens) Johnson-Boddie; m. Martha Lee Brown, Oct. 11, 1970 (div. Dec. 1979); children: Don O'Mar, Anthony, Shawn, Shellie. BS in Bus. Mgmt. Tarkio Coll., 1988; BS in Mgmt., 1988, St. Louis Music Inst., 1968. Rec. artist Bamboo Records, St. Louis, 1966-70; producer, writer Puzzletown Prodns., St. Louis, 1970-77, James Earl World Prodns., East St. Louis, Ill. and Memphis, 1975-79, Hi Records, Memphis, 1975-79, Motown Records, Los Angeles, 1976-78; owner, producer, writer, artist Chrome Records, St. Louis, 1978—; cons. Archway Studios, St. Louis, 1970-85, Music Assocs. in Mo. Corp, Jefferson City, Mo., 1978—, JD Mgmt., St. Louis, 1978—; v.p. Scorpio Prodns., Pine Lawn, Mo., 1980-82, music producer, 1980-84. Producer: Lets Be Lovers, 1985 (Heritage award), The Legend, 1986 (Heritage award); rec. artist Can't Stop the Fire, 1987 (Heritage award), New Thing Between Us (charted Top 5 on Midwest Survey 1990, 91), True Love (charted Top 5 on Midwest Survey 1990, 91); host, presenter Gateway Music Awards Ceremony, 1991; headliner for Cigarettes/Salem Spirit Festival, 1985; featured performer Shock Wave Music TV Show, Friends of The Black Music Society Gateway Awards Lacledes Landing, 1991. Recipient Named New R&B Rec. Artist of Yr. Gateway Music Award, 1990, 91. Mem. entertainment com. to elect Irene Smith, St. Louis, 1982., Music Assocs. Mo. (pres. 1986—),St Louis Bd. od Edn. State Mo., 1991, Chpt. 1 reading tchr. (basic skills), 1995, secondary edn. gen. edn. devel. (ABE), sr. master tchr. Adult Basic Edn., 1997, 98, music dir., Clay Cmty. Edn.Ctr. Democrat. Roman Catholic. Avocations: basketball, martial arts. Office: Chrome Records 6112 Hancock Ave Saint Louis MO 63134-2116

BODDIE, LEWIS FRANKLIN, obstetrics and gynecology educator; b. Forsyth, Ga., Apr. 4, 1913; s. William F. and Luetta T. (Sams) B.; m. Marian Bernice Claytor, Dec. 27, 1941; children: Roberta Boddie Miles, Lewis Jr., Bernice B. Jackson, Pamela, Kenneth, Fredda, Margaret. BA, Morehouse Coll., 1933; MD, Meharry Med. Sch., 1938. Diplomate Am. Bd. Ob-Gyn (proctor parti exam Los Angeles area 1955-63). Intern Homer-Phillips Hosp., St. Louis, 1938-39, resident in ob-gyn, 1939-42; mem. attending staff Grace Hosp., Detroit, 1944-48, Parkside Hosp., Detroit, 1944-48, Los Angeles County Gen. Hosp., 1952-79; sr. mem. attending staff Queen of Angels Hosp., Los Angeles, 1964-91, chmn. dept. ob-gyn, 1968-70; asst. clin. prof. U. So. Calif. Sch. Medicine, L.A., 1953-79, asst. clin. prof. emeritus, 1979—; assoc. clin. prof. U. Calif., Irvine, 1956-81; sec. Verndro Med. Corp., 1952-90. vice chmn. bd. mgrs. 28th St. YMCA, Los Angeles 1960-75; steward African Meth. Episc. Ch., Los Angeles, 1949—. Fellow ACS (life), Am. Coll. Ob-Gyn (life), Los Angeles Ob-Gyn Soc. (life): mem. Los Angeles United Way (priorities and allocations coms., 1985-95, standards com. 1987-95, new admission com. 1988-95), Children's Home Soc. (bd. dirs. 1952-89, trustee 1989—, v.p. 1963-68, pres. 1968-70), Child Welfare League Am. (bd. d irs. 1969-76). Republican.

BODDIE, REGINALD ALONZO, lawyer; b. New Haven, June 14, 1959; s. Gladys Geraldine (Harrell) B. BA, Brown U., 1981; JD, Northeastern U., 1984. Bar: N.Y., U.S. Dist. Ct. (ea. and so. dists.) N.Y. 1986, D.C. 1987, U.S. Ct. Appeals (2d cir.) 1989, U.S. Supreme Ct. 1990. Staff atty. Legal Aid Soc., N.Y.C., 1984-86, Harlem Legal Svcs., N.Y.C., 1986-88; asst. counsel Ctr. for Law and Social Justice Medgar Evers Coll. CUNY, 1988-95; pvt. practice Law Offices of Reginald A. Boddie, N.Y.C., 1995—; arbitrator Lemon Law, N.Y. Atty. Gen. and Am. Arbitration Assn., N.Y.C., 1986-94. Founder, pres., exec. dir. United Youth Enterprises, Inc., New Haven, 1976—; founder, dir. Coll. Prep. program Ctrl. H.S., Providence, 1980-81; bd.dirs. Claremont Neighborhood Ctrs., Inc., Bronx, N.Y., 1994-96; vol. instr. ARC, New Haven, 1975-90; bd. dirs. Boys and Girls' Clubs of Union County, Union, N.J., 1996-98. Recipient Good Citizenship award Civitan Internat. Club, New Haven, 1977, 2 commendations Brown U., 1981, Outstanding Cmty. Svc. award New Haven Police Dept., 1984, Cmty. Svc. award Pub. Sch. 21, Bklyn., 1993, others. Mem. N.Y. State Bar Assn., N.Y.C. Bar Assn., Bklyn. Bar Assn. Office: Ste 2035 19 Fulton St Rm 408 New York NY 10038-2100

BODDIGER, GEORGE CYRUS, insurance corporate executive, consultant; b. Polo, Ill., July 5, 1917; s. George E. and Bertha Belle (Billig) B.; m. Wilma Helen Ray, May 23, 1943; children: Nancy Boddiger Estrada, Jean Boddiger Johnstone, Kathryn Boddiger Jones. B.S., U. Ill., 1939; M.B.A. with distinction, Harvard U., 1943. CLU. Various positions Mut. of Omaha, Omaha, 1952-59; pres., dir. Pacific Fidelity Life Ins. Co., Los Angeles, 1959-71, Equitable Life Ins. Co., Washington, 1971-82; vice chmn., dir. Gulf United Corp., Washington, 1982-84; bd. dirs., dir. Premier Parking Corp.; adv. bd. DCG Corp. Mem. U. Ill. Found., Pres.'s Coun.; bd. dirs. Nat. Multiple Sclerosis Soc.; pres. emeritus Internat. Fedn. Multiple Sclerosis Socs., pres., 1983-85; elder Potomac Presbyn. Ch. With AUS, 1943-46. Recipient Hope Chest award Nat. Multiple Sclerosis Soc., Bess Goodman Humanitarian award, Lifetime Achievement award Internat. Fedn. Multiple Sclerosis Socs. Fellow Life Mgmt. Inst.; mem. Harvard Bus. Sch. Club Washington (chmn., dir.), Sigma Alpha Epsilon. Clubs: Congressional Country (Bethesda, Md.); Met. (Washington). Office: 415 Russell Ave Apt 908 Gaithersburg MD 20877-2842

BODE, BARBARA, foundation executive, Internet consultant, entrepreneur; b. Evanston, Ill.; d. Carl and Margaret Emilie (Lutze) B. B.A. magna cum laude, U. Md., MA; scholar, Ludwig-Maximillians-Universitat, Munich; English Speaking Union scholar, U. London; Bundesrepublik scholar, Goethe Institut, Lubeck, W. Ger.; postgrad. NDEA fellow, UCLA. Woodrow Wilson teaching fellow N.C. Central U., Durham; pres. Children's Found., Washington, 1970-86, Council on Founds., 1986-89; v.p. Coun. Better Bus. Bur., 1990-95; exec. dir. Coun. Bettter Bus. Bur. Found., 1990-95; founder Campaigns Online, Washington, 1998—. Bd. dirs. Children's Found., Rainbow TV Works, Nat. Com. for Responsive Philanthropy, Disability Rights, Edn. and Def. Fund Partnership, Women's Campaign Fund, 1984-88; founding mem. Women of Washington, 1992—, Leadership Washington, class of 1994, 94—; trustee The Richmond Found. Woodrow Wilson Nat. Found. fellow, 1963-64. Mem. Women and Founds. Corp. Philanthropy, Washington Regional Assn. Grantmakers, Consulting Women, DC Webgirls. Episcopalian. Home: 1661 Crescent Pl NW Washington DC 20009-4074 Office: Campaigns Online Ste 508 1661 Crescent Pl NW Apt 508 Washington DC 20009-4049

BODE, RICHARD ALBERT, retired financial executive; b. Oak Park, Ill., July 26, 1931; s. Charles John and Esther (Burgert) B.; m. Marjorie Ann Lane, July 28, 1962; children—Anne, Julie, John, Ellen, Mary Elizabeth. Student, Loras Coll., 1949-51; BSC, DePaul U., 1953; MBA, U. Detroit, 1960. CPA, Ill. With Baumann, Finney & Co. (pub. accountants), Chgo., 1953-56; staff accountant Nat. Tea Co., Chgo., 1956- 58; divisional controller Nat. Tea Co., Detroit, 1958-62; asst. controller Eagle Food Centers, Rock Island, Ill., 1962-63; comptroller Brinks, Inc., Chgo., 1963-68; treas. Brinks, Inc., 1968-69, v.p., treas., 1970-78; v.p. fin. DLM, Inc., Allen, Tex., 1978-89; adv. coun. Govt. Acctg. Stds., 1996-99. Mem. Village Hinsdale Plan Commn., 1969-75, Plano Bd. Adjustments, 1988-90, Plano City Coun., 1990—, dep. mayor pro tem, 1995-96, mayor pro tem, 1996-97; sec.-treas. Allen Indsl. Found., 1983-88; bd. dirs. Plano Homeowners Coun., 1984-90, pres., 1987-88; mem. Regional Transp. Coun., 1993—; mem. adv. coun. Tex. Mcpl. Retirement Sys., 1996—. Mem. Ill. C.P.A. Soc. (dir. 1976-78). Home: 2032 Switzerland Plano TX 75025

BODE, WALTER ALBERT, editor; b. St. Louis, Nov. 12, 1950; s. George Albert and Madeline (Nuckles) B.; m. Carmela La Gamba, 1995; 1 child, Willy. BA, Princeton U., 1973; MA, U. Calif., Davis, 1981. Editorial asst. Lit. Guild, N.Y.C., 1981-82; editorial asst., asst. editor Viking Press, N.Y.C., 1982-86; editor, sr. editor Grove Press, N.Y.C., 1986-90, editor-in-chief, 1990-93; freelance editor, 1993-94; sr. editor Harcourt Brace and Co., N.Y.C., 1994—. Avocations: cooking. Office: Harcourt Brace & Co 15 E 26th St New York NY 10010*

BODEA, ANDY S., bank executive; b. Cluj, Romania, June 19, 1962; came to U.S., 1985, naturalized, 1990; s. Aurel and Maria Bodea; m. Joanna I. Chromely, Feb. 25, 1993; 1 child, Julia S. BA, U. Calif., Berkeley, 1988; MS, Harvard U., 1990, PhD, 1994. Engr. aide Adelberg Labs., Encino, Calif., 1985-86; engr. Lawrence Berkeley Lab., Berkeley, Calif., 1987-88; cons. Sch. Bus. Adminstrn. Harvard U., Cambridge, Mass., 1989-91, cons. program on info. rsch. policy, 1991-92; cons. McKinsey & Co., N.Y.C., 1992-93; mgr. Monitor Co., Cambridge, 1993-95; mgr. strategy and corp. bus. devel. GE, Fairfield, Conn., 1995-97; mgr. acquisition integration, quality and product devel. GE Capital Svcs., Stamford, Conn., 1996-98; v.p., team leader GE Capital Merchant Banking Group, N.Y.C., 1998—. Recipient Pres'. Undergraduate Fellow U. Calif., 1986; Univ. scholar Harvard U., 1988-90. Mem. Coun. Fgn. Rels., Fgn. Policy Assn., UN Assn. Avocations: tennis, golf, music. Office: GE Capital-Mcht Banking Group 335 Madison Ave Fl 12 New York NY 10017-4669

BODEN, GUENTHER, endocrinologist; b. Ludwigshafen, Germany, Jan. 8, 1935; came to U.S., 1965; s. Alwin and Irma (Godelman) B.; m. Irene Ulrike Dingeldein, Dec. 12, 1970; children: Karin, Stephanie, Eric, Dirk. MS, Heidelberg U., Germany, 1956; MD, Munich U., 1959. Intern City Hosp. Hamburg, Germany, 1960-62; rsch. fellow in biochemistry U. Tübingen, Germany, 1963-65; rsch. fellow in medicine P.B. Brigham Hosp., Boston, 1965-67; resident physician Rochester (N.Y.) Gen. Hosp., 1967-70; rsch. prof. biochemistry Temple U. Sch. Medicine, Phila., 1986—, prof. medicine, 1977—; chief div. endocrinology/metab. Temple U. Sch. Medicine, Phila., 1987—, dir. gen. clin. rsch. ctr., 1989—. Mem. editl. bd. Jour. Clin. Endocrine Metabolism, 1985-88, Clin. Diabetes, 1995—, Am. Jour. Physiology, 1998—; contbr. articles to profl. jours. Rsch. grantee NIH, 1973—, Am. Diabetes Assn., 1985—; recipient Rochester N.Y. Diabetes award Rochester Acad. Medicine, 1970. Fellow ACP; mem. Am. Diabetes Assn., Am. Soc. Clin. Investigation, Am. Endocrin Soc. Office: Temple Univ Hosp 3401 N Broad St Philadelphia PA 19140-5189

BODENHEIMER, SALLY NELSON, reading educator; b. Bedford, Ind., Aug. 31, 1939; d. Paul Edwin Sr. and Sarah Kathryn (Scott) Nelson; m. Robert Edward Bodenheimer, June 24, 1961; children: Robert Edward, Marc Alan, Bryan Lee. BS, U. Tenn., Knoxville, 1961, postgrad.; postgrad., Northwestern U., Carson Newman Coll., Johnson Bible Coll. Cert. tchr. K-3, 1-9, K-12, music. Interni Crow Island Elem., Winnetka, Ill., 1961-62; tchr. 1st grade Wilmot Elem Sch., Deerfield, Ill., 1962-63, Vestal Elem. Sch., Knoxville, 1981-82; 7th grade math. tchr. Knox County Schs., Doyle Middle Sch., Knoxville, 1982-83; kindergarten tchr. Mt. Olive Sch., Knoxville, 1983-93, chpt. I lang, reading, reading recovery tchr., 1993—, chpt. I Lang. Reading, Reading Recovery, 1993-95, tchr. kindergarten, 1995—. Recipient Knoxville Arts Coun. Art in Edn. award, Golden Apple award Knoxville News Sentinel, Outstanding Environ. Edn. award. 21st Century Classroom. Mem. NEA, ASCD, Tenn. Edn. Assn., Knox County Edn. Assn., Smoky Mountain Reading Assn., Internat. Reading Assn., Nat. Coun. Tchrs. Math., Smoky Mountain Math. Educators Assn., Nat. Sci. Tchrs. Assn., Music Educators Nat. Conf., East Tenn. Foxfire Tchrs. Network (steering com.), Greater Knoxville C. of C. (leadership edn., Best Tchr. award 1989, Best award 1996), Delta Kappa Gamma, Pi Lambda Theta, Sigma Alpha Iota. Home: 3335 Tipton Station Rd Knoxville TN 37920-9565

BODENSTEIN, IRA, federal government lawyer; b. Atlantic City, Nov. 9, 1954; s. William and Beverly (Grossman) B.; m. Julia Elizabeth Smith, Mar. 9, 1991; children: Sarah Rose, George William, Jennie Kathryn. Student, Tel Aviv U., 1974-75; BA in Govt., Franklin & Marshall Coll., 1977; JD in Econs., U. Miami, 1980. Bar: Ill. 1980, U.S. Dist. Ct. (no. dist.) Ill. 1980, U.S. Ct. Appeals (7th cir.) 1982, Fla. 1983. Assoc. James S. Gordon Ltd., Chgo., 1980-85, mem., 1985-89; mem. Portes, Sharp, Herbst & Fox, Ltd., Chgo., 1990-91; shareholder Towbin & Zazove, Ltd., Chgo., 1991-93; ptnr. D'Ancona & Pflaum, Chgo., 1993-98; U.S. trustee Region 11, Chgo., 1998—. Pres., bd. dirs., benefit chmn. Gus Giordano Jazz Dance, Chgo., 1990—; treas. Chgo. Pub. Art Group, 1995-99. Mem. ABA (bus. law sect., rep. young lawyers divsn. dist. 15, 1986-87, ann. meeting adv. com. 1990, spkr. spring meeting 1996, 97), Chgo. Bar Assn. (bd. dirs. young lawyers sect. 1985-87, chmn.-elect 1987-88, chmn. 1988-89, antitrust com., chmn. athletics com. 1984-85, bd. mgrs. 1990-92, chmn. pub. affairs and media rels. com., chmn. assn. meetings com., memberships com. 1996, cert. of appreciation 1984-93, 96-97). Democrat. Jewish. Home: 2848 W Wilson Ave Chicago IL 60625-3743 Office: Office US Trustee 227 W Monroe St Ste 3350 Chicago IL 60625

BODENSTEINER, CAROL A., public relations executive; b. Maqouketa, Iowa, Oct. 11, 1948. BA in Speech and English, U. No. Iowa, 1972. Tchr. Waterloo Cmty. Sch., 1972-73; editor Am. Soybean Assn., 1973-77; acct. exec. Freiberg-Frederick & Assoc., 1977-79; acct. exec. CMF&Z, 1979-81, acct. supr., 1982-83, acct. group mgr., 1983-87, v.p., assoc. mng. dir., 1987-88, sr. v.p., assoc. mng. fir., 1988-89, exec. v.p. gen. mgr., 1989-90, pres., pub. rels., 1990—. Mem. Pub. Rels. Soc. Am. (nat. mem. com., 1991, Cedar Valley devel. chair., 1981), Counselors Acad., Nat. Agrl. Mktg. Assn. Office: CMF&Z Pub Rels 600 E Court Ave Des Moines IA 50309-2021*

BODEY, BELA, immunomorphologist; b. Sofia, Bulgaria, Jan. 18, 1949; came to U.S., 1985, naturalized, 1994; s. Joseph and Rossitza (Derebeeva) B.; m. Victoria Psenko, Aug. 29, 1979; children; Bela Jr., Vivian. MD, Med. Acad., Sofia, 1973; PhD in Immuno-Biology, Inst. Morphology, Bulgarian Acad. Sci., Sofia, 1977. Lic. physician, exptl. pathologist, embryologist, immuno-morphologist, thymologist, exptl. oncologist. Asst. prof. Semmelweis Med. U., Budapest, 1977-80; prof. Inst. Hematology, Budapest, 1980-83; rsch. assoc. Tufts U., Boston, 1985; rsch. fellow immuno-pathology Mass. Gen. Hosp./Harvard U., Boston, 1986; rsch. fellow Childrens Hosp. L.A., 1987-90, rsch. scientist, 1991-92; asst. prof. rsch. pathology, Sch. of Medicine Univ. Southern Calif., 1992—, prof. pathology Sch. Medicine, 1995—; vis. prof. Alexander von Humboldt Found., Ulm, Fed. Republic Germany, 1984. Mem. Am. Assn. Cancer Rsch., Am. and Can. Acad. Pathology, French Soc. Cell Biology, French Soc. Electronmicroscopy, Internat. Soc. Exptl. Hematology, Internat. Soc. Comparative Oncology, N.Y. Acad. Scis., Free Masons. Roman Catholic. Avocations: travel, swimming, dancing. Home: unit 1 8000 Canby Ave Bldg 4 Reseda CA 91335 Office: U So Calif Sch Medicine 2011 Zonal Ave Los Angeles CA 90033-1034

BODEY, RICHARD ALLEN, minister, educator; b. Hazelton, Pa., Nov. 27, 1930; m. Ruth Lois Price, 1955; children: Bronnlyn Beth Spindler, Richard Allen Jr. Student, Muhlenberg Coll., 1948; AB, Lafayette Coll, 1952; MDiv, Princeton Theol. Sem., 1955; postgrad., U. Toronto, 1961, Gannon Coll., 1963, Winona Lake Sch. Theology, 1963; ThM, Westminster Theol Sem., 1972; D Ministry, Trinity Evang. Div. Sch., 1984, Seabury-Western Theol. Sem., 1985. Ordained to ministry Presbyn. Ch. U.S.A., 1955. Pastor Marshall Meml. Presby. Ch., Lebanon, Ill., 1955-56; instr. Bible McKendree Coll., Lebanon, Ill., 1956; pastor 3d Presbyn. Ch., North Tonawanda, N.Y., 1956-62; instr. Buffalo Bible Inst., 1961; pastor 1st Presbyn. Ch., Corry, Pa., 1962-64, Dales Meml. United Presbyn. Ch., Phila., 1964-66; prof. preaching, chmn. Practical Theol. Dept. Reformed Theol. Sem., Jackson, Miss., 1966-73; interim pastor 1st Presbyn. Ch., Hazlehurst, Miss., 1967-68; stated supply pastor Presbyn. Ch., Union Church, Miss., 1970-73; head of staff 1st Assoc. Reformed Presby. Ch., Gastonia, N.C., 1973-79; dir. Gastonia Sch. Bibl. Studies, N.C., 1979; assoc. prof. practical theol. Trinity Evang. Divinity Sch., Deerfield, Ill., 1979-87, prof., 1987-95; chaplain Civitan, 1975; dir. continuing edn. Trinity Evang. Divinity Sch., 1982-87, DMin coord. and examiner, 1989-96; instr. preaching Moody Bible Inst. Corr. Sch., Chgo., 1982-86; vis. instr. Westminster Theol. Sem., Phila., 1987-88, lectr., 1990, cons. in continuing edn., 1990-91, DMin examiner, 1994-96; instr. North Chgo. Theol. Inst., 1991-94; vis. faculty Columbia (S.C.) Internat. U. and Seminary, 1991; seminar leader Nat. Conf. on Preaching, 1990-94; Bible conf. and retreat spkr. Author: You Can Live Without Fear of Death, 1980; editor, contbr. Good News for All Seasons: 26 Sermons for Special Days, 1987, Inside the Sermon: Thirteen Preachers Discuss Their Methods of Preparing Messages, 1990, The Voice from the Cross: Seven Sermons on the Last Words of Our Lord, 1990, If I Had Only One Sermon to Preach, 1994; editor: Voices, 1980-88, The Lamb of God, 1994; co-editor: Come to the Banquet, 1998; contbr. to Ency. of Christianity, 1962-72, Ministers Manual, 1974, 82, Zondervan Pictorial Bible Ency., Baker Ency. of Bible, 1988, Handbook of Contemporary Preaching, 1993, The Complete Library of Christian Worship, 1996; contbr. articles to profl. jours.. Chmn. Here's Life Metrolina, Gastonia Area, 1976; founding bd. chmn. Gastonia Evang. Assn., 1978-79, Gaston Christian Sch., 1979; chmn. planning com. Evang. Affirmations, 1989. Recipient Porter Bible prize Lafayette Coll., 1950, David Fowler Atkins Jr. prize, 1952, Gastonia Evang. Assn. award, 1979. Mem. Am. Acad. Ministry (charter). Avocation: travel, collecting miniature cathedrals and cottages, reading, music. *To me life's highest meaning and deepest satisfaction lie in a personal relationship with Jesus Christ as divine Saviour and Lord. My supreme aim and motive are to honor Him in everything I do. I can think of no worthier pursuit, no more challenging goal, for anyone in any age.*

BODIE, BELIN FREDERICK, dermatologist; b. Normal, Ill., Sept. 24, 1948; s. Belin Vorhees and Thelma Louise B.; m. Judy Joy Hester, July 12, 1980; children: Joy Elizabeth, Brandon Frederick. BS, Rhodes Coll, 1970; MD, U. Ala., 1974. Diplomate Am. Bd. Pediatrics, Am. Bd. Dermatology. Intern U. South Ala., 1974-75, resident, 1975-77; resident U. Ala., Birmingham, 1977-80; pvt. practice Mobile. Mem. Rotary, Alpha Omega Alpha, Phi Beta Kappa, Omicron Delta Kappa. Home: 4606 Kingswood Dr S Mobile AL 36608 Office: Spring Hill Dermatology Clinic 4300 Old Shell Rd Mobile AL 36608

BODINE, BRETT, professional race car driver; b. Chemung, N.Y., Jan. 11, 1959; m. Diane Bodine; 1 child, Heidi. Professional race car driver NASCAR Winston Cup races, 1986—; winner 1990 First Union 400, 1990. Office: c/o NASCAR 1801 W Internat Speedway Daytona Beach FL 32114 also Office: Brett Bodine Racing 304 Performance Rd Mooresville NC 28115-9592*

BODINE, GEOFF, professional race car driver; b. Chemung, N.Y., Apr. 18, 1949; children: Matthew, Barry. Profl. race car driver NASCAR, 1979—; owner, driver, 1993—. Recipient Busch Pole award, 1996; won Daytona 500, 1986, Internat. Race of Champions, 1987, Winston Select, 1994; named Rookie of Yr., NASCAR, 1982. Office: c/o Bessey Motorsports 11881 Vance Davis Dr Charlotte NC 28269-7694 Office: c/o NASCAR PO Box 2875 Daytona Beach FL 32120-2875*

BODINE, JAMES FORNEY, retired civic leader; b. Villanova, Pa., June 16, 1921; s. William Warden and Angela (Forney) B.; m. Jean G. Guthrie, June 25, 1949; children: Jane G., Margaret F., Murray G., Tracy W. B.A., Yale U., 1944; M.B.A., Harvard U., 1948. With First Pa. Bank, Phila., 1948-78; v.p. First Pa. Bank, 1958-63, sr. v.p., 1963-65, exec. v.p., 1965-68, sr. exec. v.p., dir., 1968-72, pres., 1972-77; pres. First Pa. Corp., 1974-78; sec. of commerce Commonwealth of Pa., 1979-80; mng. partner Urban Affairs Partnership, 1980-87. Home: 401 Cypress St Philadelphia PA 19106-4206 Office: 1207 Chestnut St Philadelphia PA 19107-4102

BODINE, JOHN JERMAIN, pastor; b. Jamestown, N.Y., Jan. 21, 1941; s. Henry B. Lathrop and Josephine (Waring Bodine) Ward; Wilhelmina Thea Bijlefeld, Sept. 15, 1984; children: Melissa Heather, Courtney Joy. BA, St. John's Coll., 1963; BD, Hartford Sem. Found., 1967, PhD, 1973. Ordained to ministry United Ch. Christ, 1970. Asst. dean Hartford Sem. Found., Hartford, Conn., 1971-74; asst. dir. Macdonald Ctr. Study Islam, Hartford, 1974-77; pastor, tchr. Congl. Ch. Henniker (N.H.), 1979-83, Newent Congl. Ch., Lisbon, Conn., 1983-87, Stratham (N.H.) Community Ch., 1987—; scribe Rockingham Assn., United Ch. Christ, N.H., 1990—; chmn. HIV/AIDS Working Group, United Ch. Christ, N.H., 1990-93; mem. Task Force Homosexuality, Conn., 1985-87, Coun. Ch. Soc., United Ch. Christ, N.H., 1980-83, trustee N.H. conf., 1992-98, mem. exec. com. N.H. conf., 1994—, mem. nominating com., 1998—, mem. budget and fin. com., 1998—, pres., 1999—. Contbr. articles to profl. jours. Chmn. safety programs, Conn. Red Cross, Hartford, 1972-79; mem. Child Abuse Task Force, Concord, N.H., 1981-83; mem., bd. dirs. N.H. SPCA, 1996; bd. dirs. Pastoral Counseling Ctr., Durham, N.H., 1993—; signator Portsmouth N.H. Covenant of Conscience; trustee Wiggin Meml. Libr., Stratham, 1999—. Campus Ministry fellow, Danforth Found., 1964-65, traveling fellow Hartford Sem. Found., 1966; recipient Thompson prize Hartford Found., 1966, Tyler prize, 1966. Office: Stratham Community Ch Emery Ln Stratham NH 03885

BODINE, LAURENCE, lawyer, editor, marketer; b. Kissimmee, Fla., Nov. 4, 1950; s. Cornelius and Tatiana (Krupenin) B.; 1 child, Theodore Laurence. Student, Universitat Munchen, Munich, Germany, 1970-71; BA, Amherst Coll., 1972; JD, Seton Hall U., 1981. Bar: Wis. 1981, U.S. Dist. Ct. (we. dist.) Wis. 1981. Reporter The Star-Ledger, Newark, 1973-76, N.Y. Daily News, N.Y.C., 1976-78; reporter, asst. editor Nat. Law Jour., N.Y.C., 1978-81; assoc. Stafford, Rieser, Rosenbaum & Hansen, Madison, Wis., 1982; assoc. editor ABA Jour., Chgo., 1982-85, editor, pub., 1986-89; pub. Lawyers Alert, 1989-91; dir. comm. Sidley & Austin, Chgo., 1991—, adminstr. LawMarketing Listserv online discussion group, 1996—; legal malpractice columnist Ill. Legal Times, 1995-96. Co-author: Trial Manual for Proving Hedonic Damages, 1992, author supplement, 1995; mng. editor newsletter The Legal View, 1991-96; law columnist Mag. Week, 1989-92; profl. responsibility columnist Lawyers Weekly U.S.A., 1993-96; editor Acctg. Liability Alert, 1998-99. Mem. Legal Mktg. Assn. (bd. dirs. Chgo. chpt. 1995, 97-98). Office: Sidley & Austin One First National Plz Chicago IL 60603

BODINSON, HOLT, conservationist; b. East Orange, N.J., Nov. 14, 1941; s. Earl Herdien and Hermine (Holt) B. BA, Harvard, 1963; m. Ilse Marie Maier, Feb. 29, 1970. Sr. asso. Am. Conservation Assn., Inc., N.Y.C., 1966-70; dir. Office of Policy Analysis, N.Y. State Dept. Environ. Conservation, Albany, 1970-71, dir. div. ednl. services, 1971-77; dir. Ariz.-Sonora Desert Mus., 1977-78; exec. dir. Safari Club Internat./Safari Club Internat. Conservation Fund, Tucson, 1980-89; conservation dir. Safari Club Internat., Tucson, 1991-94, dir. wildlife and govtl. affairs, 1994-96; committeeman, Montgomery Twp. Conservation Commn., 1967-70; sec. N.Am. del. Conseil Internat. de la Chasse et de la Conservation du Gibier, 1988—; gen. sec. World Hunting and Conservation Congress, 1988; dir. Internat. Wildlife Mus., 1991-96; nat. sec. United Conservation Alliance, 1994-96. Served with arty. AUS, 1964-66. Mem. Stony Brook-Millstone Watershed Assn. (dir.), Safari Club Internat. (dir. Ariz. chpt.), N.Y. Outdoor Edn. Assn. (dir.), Outdoor Writers Assn. of Am., N.Y. State Rifle and Pistol Assn. (dir.). Episcopalian. Club: Harvard of So. Ariz. (pres.). Author: (with Clepper and others) Leaders in American Conservation, 1971. Contbg. editor Jour. Environmental Edn., 1968-94; dir. Conservationist mag. 1971-77, N.Y. State Environment newspaper, 1971-74. Home: 4525 N Hacienda Del Sol Tucson AZ 85718-6619 Office: 5683 N Swan Rd Tucson AZ 85718-4565

BODKIN, HENRY GRATTAN, JR., lawyer; b. L.A., Dec. 8, 1921; s. Henry Grattan and Ruth May (Wallis) B.; m. Mary Louise Davis, June 28, 1943; children: Maureen L. Dixon, Sheila L. McCarthy, Timothy Grattan. B.S. cum laude, Loyola U., Los Angeles, 1943, J.D., 1948. Bar: Calif. 1948. Pvt. practice Los Angeles, 1948-51, 53-95; ptnr. Bodkin, McCarthy, Sargent & Smith (predecessor firms), L.A.; of counsel Sullivan, Workman & Dee, L.A., 1995—. Mem. L.A. Bd. Water and Power Commrs., 1972-74, pres., 1973-74; regent Marymount Coll., 1962-67; trustee Loyola-Marymount U., 1967-91, vice chmn., 1985-86. With USNR, 1943-45, 51-53. Fellow Am. Coll. Trial Lawyers; mem. Calif. State Bar (mem. exec. com. conf. of dels. 1968-70, vice chmn. 1969-70), California Club, Riviera Tennis Club, Tuna Club, Chancery Club (pres. 1990-91), Phi Delta Phi. Republican. Roman Catholic. Home: 956 Linda Flora Dr Los Angeles CA 90049-1631 Office: Sullivan Workman & Dee 800 S Figueroa St Fl 12 Los Angeles CA 90017-2521

BODKIN, RUBY PATE, corporate executive, real estate broker, educator; b. Frostproof, Fla., Mar. 11, 1926; d. James Henry and Lucy Beatrice (Latham) P.; m. Lawrence Edward Bodkin Sr., Jan. 15, 1949; children: Karen Bodkin Snead, Cinda, Lawrence Jr. BA, Fla. State U., 1948; MA, U. Fla., 1972. Lic. real estate broker. Banker Barnett Bank, Avon Park, Fla., 1943-44, Lewis State Bank, Tallahassee, 1944-49; ins. underwriter Hunt Ins. Agy., Tallahassee, 1949-51; tchr. Duval County Sch. Bd., Jacksonville, Fla., 1952-77; pvt. practice realty Jacksonville, 1976—; tchr. Nassau County Sch. Bd., Jacksonville, 1978-83; sec., treas., v.p. Bodkin Corp., R&D/Inventions, Jacksonville, 1983—; assoc. Brooke Shields Innovative Designer Products, Inc., Kendall Park, N.J., 1988-92. Author: 100 Teacher Chosen Recipes, 1976, Bodkin Bridge Course for Beginners, 1996, Class Conscious, 1999; published poet. Mem. Jacksonville Symphony Guild, 1985—; mem. Southside Bapt. Ch. Recipient 25 Yr. Svc. award Duval County Sch. Bd., 1976, Tchr. of Yr. award Bryceville Sch., 1981, Edn., Volunteerism, Employment award finalist, 1973. Mem. Am. Contract Bridge League, Nat. Realtors Assn., Southside Jr. Woman's Club, Garden Club Sweetbriar (bd. dirs.), Riverside Woman's Club Jacksonville (bd. dirs. 1991-92), UDC (Martha Reid chpt. #19), Fla. Edn. Assn. (pres. problems com. 1958), Duval County Classrooms Tchrs. (v.p. membership 1957), Woman's Club Jacksonville Bridge Group, Fla. Ret. Tchrs. Assn., Fla. Realtors Assn., N.E. Fla. Realtors Assn., Jacksonville Geneal. Soc. (practicing genealogist, family historian 1986—), Friday Musicale of Jacksonville, San Jose Golf Country Club, Jacksonville Sch. Bridge. Baptist. Avocations: reading, writing, genealogy, photography, club bridge, walking, travel. Home: 1149 Molokai Rd Jacksonville FL 32216-3273 Office: Bodkin Jewelers & Appraisers PO Box 16482 Jacksonville FL 32245-6482

BODKIN, THOMAS WILLIAM, architectural engineer; b. Phila., Sept. 11, 1968; s. James Thomas and Margaret Rose (Begley) B. BS in Archtl. Engring., Pa. State U., 1992. Carpenter Mike Mullin Constrn., Richboro, Pa., 1989-93. 1st lt. USMC, 1993-98. Mem. Golden Key, Phi Alpha Epsilon. Roman Catholic. Avocations: flying (multi-engine instrument rating), carpentry, weightlifting. Home: 38 Harvest Rd Warminster PA 18974-1315

BODLEY, HARLEY RYAN, JR., editor, writer, broadcaster; b. Dover, Del., Nov. 24, 1936; s. Harley Ryan and Mildred Olivia (Carver) B.; m. Patricia Jean Hall, Dec. 4, 1981. B.A., U. Del., 1959; postgrad., Am. U., 1960. Sports editor Del. State News, Dover, 1959-60; sports dir. Radio WDOV, Dover, 1958-62; sports writer News-Jour. Papers, Wilmington, Del., 1960-63; night sports editor News-Jour. Papers, 1963-67, asst. sports editor, 1967-71, sports editor, 1971-82; baseball editor USA Today, Washington, 1982—; discussion leader Am. Press Inst., Reston, Va., 1967-76; TV host Sta. WHYY-TV, Wilmington, 1967-74; columnist The Sporting News, St. Louis, 1978-83; commentator NBC-TV, Baseball: An Inside Look, 1987, USA Today: The TV Show, 1988-89; USA Today Radio Report, 1987-89; baseball analyst CNN, 1989—; commentator and host Baseball Sunday, United Syndications Radio Network, 1988-90; commentator CBS Radio Network baseball pre-game, 1990—. Author: I Learned To Fly, So Can You, 1967; The Team That Wouldn't Die, 1981, Countdown to Cobb, 1985; writer Best Sports Stories, 1967-71, 1977-79, 1982, 1985. Flight safety counselor FAA, Phila., 1968-72. Served as sgt. U.S. Army N.G. 1956-64. Named Sportswriter of Yr., Nat. Sportscasters and Sportswriters Assn., 1961, 63, 65, 67-70, 73-75, 78-79; recipient Best of Gannett award Gannett Co., Inc., 1981; Mark Twain award AP, 1980; 25th Year award Baseball Commr., 1983. Mem. AP Sports Editors (pres. 1981-82, Best Sports Story award 1981, 1st place award 1982), Baseball Writers Assn. Am. (Phila. chpt. chmn. 1977-78), Wilmington Sportswriters and Broadcasters (pres. 1963 sec-treas. 1965-83), Sigma Delta Chi (Top Sports award 1982). Episcopalian. Clubs: Wilmington Country; Northeast Yacht. Avocations: golf; pilot; boating. Office: USA Today 1000 Wilson Blvd Ste 600 Arlington VA 22209-3905 also: care Athletes & Artists 421 7th Ave New York NY 10001-2002

BODMAN, RICHARD STOCKWELL, telecommunications executive; b. Detroit, Apr. 9, 1938; s. Henry Taylor and Marie Louise (McMillan) B.; m. Karna Small; children: Taylor Stockwell, James Martyn. B.S. in Engring, Princeton, 1959; M.S. in Indsl. Mgmt, Mass. Inst. Tech., 1961. CPA, Calif. With Touche Ross & Co., San Francisco, 1961-71, ptnr., 1967-71; asst. sec. for mgmt. and budget U.S. Dept. Interior, Washington, 1971-73; asst. treas. E.I. duPont de Nemours & Co., Inc., Wilmington, Del., 1973-75, product mgr., 1975, mgr. mktg., 1976, asst. comptroller, 1977-78; sr. v.p. fin. and corp. devel. Communications Satellite Corp., Washington, 1978-80; pres., chief exec. officer Comsat Gen. Corp., Washington, 1980-82; pres. Satellite TV Corp., Washington, 1982-84, Washington Nat. Investment Corp., 1985-90; sr. v.p. corp. strategy and devel. AT&T Co. Inc., Basking Ridge, N.J., 1990-96; mng. gen. ptnr. AT&T Ventures, Washington, 1996—; bd. dirs. Tyco Internat., Inc., Young & Rubicam, Inc., 1996-99, ISS Group, Inc., Reed Elsevier. Bd. dirs. San Francisco Spring Opera Co., 1965-68, Del. Art Mus., 1975-77; mem. ctrl. selection com. Morehead Found. U. N.C., Chapel Hill, 1972-82; trustee BoyClubs Am., 1983-89, USN Meml. Found., 1991-92, Morristown Meml. Hosp., 1992—. Mem. Bohemian Club, Chevy Chase Country Club, Knickerbocker Club, Burning Tree Club, Met. Club. Home: 27587 Riverbank Dr Bonita Springs FL 34134-2645 also: 4930 Loughboro Rd NW Washington DC 20016 Office: 2 Wisconsin Cir Chevy Chase MD 20815-7003

BODMAN, SAMUEL WRIGHT, III, specialty chemicals and materials company executive; b. Chgo., Nov. 26, 1938; s. Samuel W. Jr. and Lina (Lindsay) B.; m. M. Diane Barber, July 31, 1997; children: Elizabeth L., Andrew M., Sarah H. BSChemE, Cornell U., 1961; ScD, MIT, 1964. Tech. dir. Am. R & D, Boston, 1964-70; prof. MIT, Cambridge, Mass., 1964-70; v.p. Fidelity Venture Assn., Boston, 1970-74; pres. Fidelity Venture Assocs., 1974-77; chmn. Fidelity Venture Assn., 1977; pres. Fidelity Mgmt. & Rsch. Co., Boston, 1976-86; pres., COO FMR Corp., 1982-86; exec. v.p., dir. Fidelity Group Mut. Funds, 1980-86; pres., COO Cabot Corp., Boston, 1987-88, chmn., CEO, also bd. dirs., 1988—, now chmn., CEO; bd. dirs. Westvaco, Inc., N.Y.C., John Hancock Mut. Life Ins. Co., Cabot Oil & Gas Corp., Houston, Security Capital Group Inc. Trustee, mem. exec. com. MIT, Cambridge; trustee Isabella Stewart Gardner Mus., Boston, New England Aquarium, Boston. Episcopalian. Office: Cabot Corp 75 State St Ste 13 Boston MA 02109-1806

BODNAR, ELISABETH M., occupational health consultant; b. Bridgeport, Conn., Apr. 21, 1927; d. James Peter and Elisabeth Ilona (Szabo) B. Diploma in nursing, St. Francis Hosp., Hartford, Conn., 1947; BS, Sacred Heart U., 1977; MA, Fairfield U., 1980. RN, Conn.; cert. occupational health nurse, audiometric & occupational hearing conservation. Health svc. administr. McKesson & Robbins Inc., Fairfield, Conn.; occupl. health tech. cons. Liberty Mutual Ins. Co., Wallingford, Conn.; ret.; cons. in field. Contbr. articles to profl. jours. Bd. dirs. Fairfield U.; health adv. coun. Harvard/Boston U. Ednl. Resource Ctr. Named Conn. Schering Occupational Health Nurse, 1977. Mem. Am. Assn. of Occupational Health Nurses (pres. 1985-89, bd. dirs. 1980-89), Northeast Region Occupational Health Nurses, Conn. state, So. Conn. Assn., Sigma Theta Tau (Mu Delta chpt.).

BODNAR, JACKIE SUE, molecular biologist, geneticist; b. Provo, Utah, Oct. 11, 1972; d. Jack Earl and Suzanna (Steele) Perry; m. James D. Bodnar, Aug. 27, 1994. Student, U. Utah, 1988; BS, Brigham Young U., 1993; postgrad., UCLA, 1996—. Lab. technician Brigham Young U., Provo, 1990-1993; computer scientist, programmer Lawrence Livermore (Calif.) Nat. Labs., 1992, molecular biology rsch. scientist, 1993; rsch. scientist new tech. and automation Incyte Pharm., Inc., Palo Alto, Calif., 1994-96. Mem. Mapleton (Utah) Youth City Coun., 1989. Mem. AAAS, Assn. Women in Sci., Am. Soc. Biochemistry and Molecular Biology, Fedn. Am. Socs. Exptl. Biology (contbr. articles to jour.). Avocations: reading, fossil collecting, painting, poetry. Office: UCLA Rm 47-123 CHS Box 951679 Los Angeles CA 90095

BODNAR, PETER O., lawyer; b. Queens, N.Y., Mar. 19, 1945; s. John and Edith (Schultz) B. BA in Govt., NYU, 1966; JD, Fordham U., 1970. Bar: N.Y. 1971, U.S. Dist. Ct. (so. dist.) N.Y. 1973. Confidential law sec. to Hon. Evans V. Brewster Family Ct. and County Ct. Westchester County, N.Y., 1970-73; pvt. practice White Plains, N.Y., 1973-77; ptnr. Bodnar & Greene, P.C., White Plains, N.Y., 1977-80, Bender & Bodnar, White Plains, N.Y., 1980-98; prin. Law Offices of Peter O. Bodnar, White Plains, NY, 1998—; pres., CEO P.A.J. Am. Ltd./The Olo Corp., 1990-97, Organica, USA, Inc., 1998—. Trustee Village of Ossining, N.Y., 1975-77. Fellow Am. Acad. Matrimonial Lawyers; mem. ABA (family law sect.), N.Y. State Bar Assn. (family law sect.), Westchester County Bar Assn. (family law sect., exec. com. 1992—). Office: 140 Grand St White Plains NY 10601-4831

BODNER, EMANUEL, industrial recycling company executive; b. Houston, July 25, 1947; s. Eugene and Eve (Pryzant) B.; m. Jennifer L. Holt, Sept. 13, 1981; children: Jessica Elyse, Jeremiah. BBA, U. Tex., 1969. V.p. Bodner Metal & Iron Corp., Houston, 1969-95, pres., 1995—. Contbr. articles to profl. jour. Bd. dirs. Tex. Coun. on Disabilities, 1986-90; mem. Tex. Legis. Coun., Citizens Adv. Commn. Study of Vocat. Rehab., 1970-72; mem. removal of archtl. barriers com. Tex. Rehab. Assn., 1971; mem. handicapped access program task force Tex. Dept. Human Resources, 1978-79; bd. dirs. Tex. Rehab. Commn., 1985-91, bd. sec., 1990-91; mem. Tex. Gov.'s Com. on Employment of the Handicapped, vice chmn. employment devel. sub-com., 1981-82; mem. new leadership exec. com. State of Israel Bonds, 1984; mem. Resource Group serving Tex. Task Force on Waste Mgmt. Policy, 1988; pres. Gulf Coast chpt. Inst. of Scrap Recycling Industries, 1989-91, chmn. conv., 1987-89; mem. solid waste fee team Tex. Water Commn., 1990-91; mem. Keep Tex. Beautiful; mem. steering com. Clean Houston Recycling Coun., 1991-92; apptd. chmn. long range planning com. Tex. State Bd. Physician Asst. Examiners, 1994-99, chmn., 1998-99; co-chair com. Beth Yeshurun Religious Sch., 1995-98. Hatan Torah honoree Beth Yeshurun Religious Sch., 1998; bd. resolution award Tex. Rehab. Commn., 1991. Mem. Inst. Scrap Recycling Industries (bd. dirs. 1989-91, nat. pub. rels. com., nat. fgn. trade com., bd. dirs. Gulf Coast chpt. 1977-84, chmn. bd. dirs. 1991-93, Pres.'s plaque Gulf Coast chpt. 1991, chmn. chpt. pub. rels. com. 1978-83, editor Gulf Coast Reporter, 1978-85, sec. Gulf Coast chpt. 1984-85, treas. 1985, 2d v.p. 1986-87, chmn. membership com. 1986-87, vice chmn. 1992—, 1st v.p. and chair conv. com. 1987—, pres. 1989-91, chmn. conv. 1987-89, Outstanding award 1985, vice chmn. chpt. pres. com. 1990-91, vice chmn. membership com. 1990-91, chmn. bd. 1991-93), Ex-Students Assn. U. Tex., Shriners, Masons (32d deg.), Alpha Epsilon Pi (life). Jewish. Office: Bodner Metal & Iron Corp 3660 Schalker Dr Houston TX 77026-3525

BODNER, JOHN, JR., lawyer; b. Dover, N.J., May 4, 1927; s. John and Anna (Kushman) B.; m. Anne Potter; children: John Edward, Brit-Marie, Anne Kristin, Peter Andrew. Student, Cornell U., 1946-50; JD, Northwestern U., 1953; MLA, Johns Hopkins U., 1969. Bar: D.C. 1954. Bigelow teaching fellow U. Chgo. Law Sch., 1953-54; atty. Dept. Justice, Washington, 1954-56; assoc. Howrey & Simon, Washington, 1956-64, ptnr., 1964—; law lectr. various univs. With U.S. Army, 1945-46. Mem. ABA, FBA, D.C. Bar Assn., Met. Club. Roman Catholic. Home: 4707 Reservoir Rd NW Washington DC 20007-1906 Office: Howrey & Simon 1299 Pennsylvania Ave NW Ste 1 Washington DC 20004-2420

BODNER, SUSAN R., marketing and communications executive; b. N.Y.C., Apr. 20, 1949; d. Milton Meyer and Muriel Ruby (Walash) Swersky; m. Lawrence Bodner, Oct. 25, 1970 (div. June 1975); children: Jennifer Lynn Bodner, Jason Ross Bodner. BA in Edn., U. Md., 1970; BA in English, 1971; paralegal cert., Barry Coll., 1980; MBA, Ga. State U., 1980. Tchr. devel. curriculum Solomon Shecter Hillel Community Day Sch., North Miami Beach, Fla., 1974-77; English tchr. Hebrew Acad. Atlanta, 1977-78; life underwriter, estate planner Life Va. Ins., Atlanta, 1978-79; paralegal, probate and estate mgmt. Abrams, Anton Robbins, Resnick, Schneider & Mager, Hollywood, Fla., 1980-81; svc. cons. mktg. dept. Southern Bell, Ft. Lauderdale, Fla., 1981-83; dir. community rels. The Jewish Home, Atlanta, 1984-87; dir. mktg. and comm. svcs. The United Jewish Fedn. Metrowest, Whippany, N.J., 1988-95; exec. dir. mktg. and comm. Jewish Fedn. Greater Phila., 1995—; pub.'s rep. The Jewish Pub. Group-The Jewish Exponent, 1995—; pubs. rep., adminstr. The Metrowest Jewish News, Whippany, 1988-95; cons. strategic mktg., comms. and pub. rels. for philanthropic orgn. and beneficiary agys., Whippany, 1988-95; pub. Metrosource, community resource book, 1990—, Inside Quar., lifestyle mag., 1994. Life mem. Nat. Coun. Jewish Women, Millburn-Shorthills, 1984—; mem. Nat. United Jewish Appeal, adv. bd. Nat. Direct Mktg. Ctr., Nat. Mktg. Planning Adv. Group. Mem. NAFE, N.J. Press Women (state and nat. comm. award 1990, 91, 92, 93, 94), N.J. Exec. Women, Pub. Rels. Soc. Am., Am. Mktg. Assn. Office: Jewish Fedn Greater Phila 226 S 16th St Philadelphia PA 19102-3348

BODNEY, DAVID JEREMY, lawyer; b. Kansas City, Mo., July 15, 1954; s. Daniel F. and Retha (Silby) B.; m. Sarah Hughes; children: Christian Steven, Anna Claire. BA cum laude, Yale U., 1976; MA in Fgn. Affairs, U. Va., 1979, JD, 1979. Bar: Ariz. 1979, U.S. Dist Ct. Ariz. 1980, U.S. Ct. Appeals (9th cir.) 1980, U.S. Supreme Ct. 1983. Legis. asst., speechwriter U.S. Senator John V. Tunney, Washington, 1975-76; sr. editor Va. Jour. of Internat. Law, 1978-79; assoc. Brown and Bain PA, Phoenix, 1979-85, ptnr., 1985-90; gen. counsel New Times, Inc., Phoenix, 1990-92; ptnr. Steptoe & Johnson, Phoenix, 1992—; vis. prof. Ariz. State U., Tempe, 1985, 94—. Co-author: Libel Defense Resource Center: 50-State Survey, 1982—. Bd. dirs. Ariz. Ctr. for Law in the Pub. Interest, Phoenix, 1983—, pres., 1989-90; chmn. Yale Alumni Schs. Com., Phoenix, 1984-87; vice chmn. City of Phoenix Solicitation Bd., 1986-88, chmn., 1988-90; bd. dirs. Children's Action Alliance, 1995—, v.p., 1998—; mem. adv. panel on Civil Liberties to

White House Commn. on Aviation Safety and Security, 1997. Mem. ABA (forum com. on communication law 1984—, concerned correspondents network com. 1979—), Ariz. Bar Assn. Democrat. Clubs: Yale (bd. dirs. Phoenix club 1979—), Ariz. Acad. Office: Steptoe & Johnson 40 N Central Ave Ste 2400 Phoenix AZ 85004-4453

BODOFF, JOSEPH SAMUEL UBERMAN, lawyer; b. Bryn Mawr, Nov. 2, 1952; s. Bernard David and Ruth Irma (Uberman) B. BS, Pa. State U., 1974; JD, Villanova U., 1977. Bar: Pa. 1977, U.S. Dist. Ct. (ea. dist.) Pa. 1979, U.S. Ct. Appeals (3d cir.) 1980, U.S. Supreme Ct. 1988, Mass. 1987, U.S. Dist. Ct. Mass. 1988, U.S. Ct. Appeals (1st cir.) 1988, R.I. 1998, U.S. Dist. Ct. R.I. 1999. Jud. law clk. Phila. County Ct. of Common Pleas, 1977-79; assoc. Pincus, Verlin, Hahn & Reich, Phila., 1979-86; ptnr. Kaye, Fialkow, Richmond & Rothstein, Boston, 1986-91, Gaston & Snow, Boston, 1991, Warner & Stackpole, Boston, 1991-94, Hinckley, Allen & Snyder, Boston, 1994-98, Shechtman & Halperin, Boston, 1998—; dir. Am. Bankruptcy Inst., Alexandria, Am. Bd. of Certification, Alexandria, Coun. of Cert. Bankruptcy Specialists; co-chair ABI Unsecured Trade Creditor com., Alexandria, 1993-98, ABI Creditors' Com. Manual Task Force, 1993-94, chair ABI Task Force on Preferences, 1995-97; chair NACM Bankruptcy and Insolvency Group, Portland, 1998—. Author: Cramdown: The Ultimate Chapter 11 Threat, 1992, (with others) Bankruptcy Business Acquisitions, 1998; contbr. articles to profl. publs. Mem. Mus. Coun. of Mus. of Fine Arts, Boston, 1997-99. Mem. ABA, Am. Bankruptcy Inst. (dir. 1995—), Coun. of Cert. Bankruptcy Specialists (dir. 1995—), Am. Bd. of Certification (dir. 1996—), Boston bar Assn., Nat. Assn of Credit Mgmt. Avocations: skiing, tennis, wine collecting, piano. Home: 64 Forest St Chestnut Hill MA 02467-2930 Office: Shechtman & Halperin 265 Franklin St Boston MA 02110-3113

BODOVITZ, JAMES PHILIP, lawyer; b. Evanston, Ill., Aug. 20, 1958; s. Philip Edward and Dosha (Laurman) B. BS, U. So. Calif., 1980, JD, 1984. Bar: N.Y. 1985, D.C. 1989, Calif. 1990. Assoc. Shearman & Sterling, N.Y.C., 1984-89, San Francisco, 1989-92; br. chief divsn. broker-dealer enforcement U.S. Securities Exch. Commn., N.Y.C., 1992-96; v.p., counsel law dept. The Equitable Life Assurance Soc. of U.S., N.Y.C., 1996—. Mem. ABA, Assn. Bar City N.Y. (Thurgood Marshall award 1998). Democrat. Office: The Equitable Cos 12th Fl 1290 Ave of Americas New York NY 10104

BODSWORTH, FRED, author, naturalist; b. Port Burwell, Ont., Can., Oct. 11, 1918; s. Arthur John and Viola (Williams) B.; m. Margaret Neville Banner, July 8, 1944; children: Barbara (Mrs. Edward Welch), Nancy (Mrs. Richard Hannah), Neville. Student pub. schs., Port Burwell. Reporter St. Thomas (Ont.) Times-Jour., 1940-43; reporter, editor Toronto (Ont.) Daily Star, 1943-46; staff writer, editor Maclean's Mag., Toronto, 1947-56; novelist, 1956—; organizer, leader numerous natural history tours. Author: Last of the Curlews, 1954, 2d edit., 1995, The Strange One, 1960, The Mating Call, 1961, The Atonement of Ashley Morden, 1964, The Sparrow's Fall, 1967 (also pub. in Eng., fgn. translations), The Pacific Coast, Illustrated Natural History of Canada series, 1970; (with others) Wilderness Canada, 1970; editor: Illustrated Natural History of Canada series, 1980-81. Bd. dirs. Natural Sci. of Can., 1980-88; hon. bd. dirs. Long Point Bird Obs., 1970—; chmn. bd. trustees James L. Baillie Meml. Fund for ornithol. field research, 1975-88. Mem. Fedn. Ont. Naturalists (hon. life, pres. 1964-66), Internat. PEN, Writers Union of Can. Clubs: Ornithological, Field Naturalists (past pres.), Brodie (Toronto). Address: 294 Beech Ave, Toronto, ON Canada M4E 3J2

BOE, DAVID STEPHEN, musician, educator, college dean; b. Duluth, Minn., Mar. 11, 1936; s. Egbert Thomas and Beatrice Ella (Steen) B.; m. Sigrid North, July 23, 1961; children: Stephen, Eric. B.A. magna cum laude, St. Olaf Coll., Northfield, Minn., 1958; M.Mus., Syracuse (N.Y.) U., 1960. Asst. prof. music U. Ga., 1961-62; mem. faculty Oberlin (Ohio) Coll. Conservatory Music, 1962—, prof. organ and harpsichord, 1976—, dean, 1976-90; dir. music, organist First Lutheran Ch., Lorain, Ohio, 1962—; organ recitalist U.S. and Europe, 1962—; mem. advanced placement music com. Coll. Entrance Exam. Bd., 1980-83; vis. prof. Fla. State U., 1991, U. Notre Dame, 1991-92. Fulbright scholar W. Ger., 1960-61. Mem. Nat. Assn. Schs. Music (trustee, sec. 1981-87), Phi Beta Kappa, Pi Kappa Lambda. (nat. pres. 1986-90). Office: Oberlin Coll Conservatory Music Oberlin OH 44074

BOE, GERARD PATRICK, health science association administrator, educator; b. Washington, Jan. 20, 1936; s. Harold David and Bernice Virginia (Lemon) B.; m. Irene Margaret Dazevedo, Oct. 24, 1959 (div. Jan. 1988); children: Steven Alan, Christine Ann; m. Charlotte Greene Hudson, Dec. 30, 1989. BS in Biology, W.Va. Wesleyan Coll., 1958; MS in Clin. Pathology, Ohio State U., 1969; PhD in Edn. and Mgmt., Tex. A&M U., 1976. Commd. 2d lt. U.S. Army, 1963, advanced through grades to lt. col.; health care adminstr., 1963-81, ret., 1981; adminstrv. dir. Ga. Radiation Therapy Ctr., Augusta, 1981-83; pres. Profl. Mgmt. Cons., Augusta, 1983-89; exec. dir. Am. Med. Technologists, Park Ridge, Ill., 1989—; faculty Webster U., So. Ill. U., 1980—. Contbr. articles to profl. jours. Recipient cert. of appreciation ARC, 1976, Pres.' award Augusta chpt. Internat. Mgmt. Coun., 1989. Mem. Soc. Armed Forces Med. Lab. Scientists (Pres.' award 1982), Nat. Clearing House for Licensure, Enforcement and Regulation, Clin. Lab. Mgmt. Assn., Inst. Cert. Profl. Mgrs. (cert., bd. regents 1990—), Am. Soc. Clin. Pathologist (cert.). Republican. Methodist. Avocations: coins, stamps, racquetball, sports. Office: Am Med Technologists 710 Higgins Rd Park Ridge IL 60068-5737*

BOECKMAN, ROBERT KENNETH, JR., chemistry educator, organic chemistry researcher; b. Pasadena, Calif., Aug. 26, 1944; s. Robert Kenneth Sr. and Orletta Christine (Brinck) B.; m. Mary Helen Delton, June 19, 1976. BS, Carnegie Inst. Tech., 1966; PhD, Brandeis U., 1971. NIH fellow Columbia U., N.Y.C., 1970-72; from asst. prof. to prof. chemistry Wayne State U., Detroit, 1972-79; prof. chemistry U. Rochester, N.Y., 1980—; cons. Eastman Kodak, 1986—, Ricerca Inc., Painesville, Ohio, 1983—, Novartis Pharms. Inc., East Hanover, N.J., 1982—, Procter & Gamble Pharm., cin., 1990—, Rhône-Poulenc Rorer, 1992—. Mem. editl. bd. Organic Syntheses, 1988-96; assoc. editor Jour. Organic Chemistry, 1997—; contbr. articles to profl. jours. Recipient career devel. award NIH, 1976-81, award for acad. achievement Probus Club, 1979; fellow A.P. Sloan Found., 1976-80. Fellow Japanese Soc. for Promotion Sci. (Von Humboldt Rsch. Prize for Sr. Scientists 1992-93, Marshal Gates scholar 1996—); mem. Am. Chem. Soc., Royal Soc. Chemistry, Deutscher Chemiker Gesellschaft, Sigma Xi, Oakhill Country Club Rochester. Republican. Roman Catholic. Avocations: golf, basketball. Office: U Rochester Hutchinson Hall Dept of Chemistry Rochester NY 14627

BOECKMANN, H. F., automotive executive. CEO, owner, pres. Galpin Motors, North Hills, Calif. Office: Galpin Motors Inc 15505 Roscoe Blvd North Hills CA 91343-6598*

BOEDEKER, BEN HAROLD, anesthesiologist, educator; b. Jackson, Wyo., Mar. 17, 1953; s. Harold Steven and Eva Andra (Andrews) B.; m. Lisa Carol Mau, June 26, 1988; children: Kirsten, David. BS, Colo. State U., 1976, DVM, 1979; PhD, Georgetown U., 1988; MD, John Byrns Sch. Med., 1987. Diplomate Am. Bd. Anesthesiology, Specialty Qualifications in Pain Mgmt., Am. Bd. Clin. Pharmacology, Nat. Bd. Med. Examiners. Advanced through ranks to lt. col. USAF, 1979-96; resident in internal medicine Georgetown U., Washington, 1987-88; chief gen. med. Kirk Army Health Clin., Aberdeen Proving Ground, Md., 1988-90; resident in anesthesiology Walter Reed Army Med. Ctr., Washington, 1990-93, chief combat anesthesia, 1993-94, staff anesthesiologist, 1993-96; dir. pain mgmt. and rehab. svcs. VAMC, Columbia, Mo., 1996—; adj. faculty Acad. Health Scis. Ft. Sam Houston, Tex., 1995—; adj. asst. prof. anesthesiology Uniformed Svc. U., Bethesda, Md., 1994-96; pres. Intellimed Biorsch., Wheatland, Wyo., 1992—; assoc. prof. anesthesia and perioperative medicine U. Mo. Student editor Med. Student, 1982-86; contbr. articles to profl. jours., chpts. to books. Pres. Casper (Wyo.) Coll. Young Reps., 1971-73; vol. fireman Dubois (Wyo.) Fire Dept., 1971-76; vol. ambulance attendant Dubois Vol. Ambulance, 1971-76; treas. students for Reagan, Honolulu, 1984. Mem. Am. Coll. Clin. Pharmacology, Am. Soc. Anesthesiology (cert. appreciation 1993, 94, Burroughs Welcome scholar 1992), Am. Pain Soc., Soc. Ambulatory Anesthesia, Am. Soc. Regional Anesthesiology, Wyo. Soc. Roman Catholic. Avocations: fishing, hunting. Home: 1307 Dunbar Dr Columbia MO 65203-5165 Office: VAMC Anesthesia Dept 124 500 Hospital Dr Columbia MO 65212

BOEDER, THOMAS L., lawyer; b. St. Cloud, Minn., Jan. 10, 1944; s. Oscar Morris and Eleanor (Gile) B.; m. Carol-Leigh Coombs, Apr. 6, 1968. BA, Yale U., 1965, LLB, 1968. Bar: Wash. 1970, U.S. Dist. Ct. (we. dist.) Wash. 1970, U.S. Dist. Ct. (ea. dist.) Wash. 1972, U.S. Ct. Appeals (9th cir.) 1970, U.S. Supreme Ct. 1974, U.S. Ct. Appeals (D.C. cir.) 1975, U.S. Ct. Appeals (10th cir.) 1993. Litigation atty. Wash. State Atty. Gen., Seattle, 1970-72, antitrust div. head, 1972-76, chief, consumer protection and antitrust, 1976-78, also sr. asst. atty. gen. and criminal enforcement, 1979-81; ptnr. Perkins Coie, Seattle, 1981—. Served with U.S. Army, 1968-70, Vietnam. Mem. ABA (antitrust sect.), Wash. State Bar Assn. (antitrust sect.). Lutheran. Office: Perkins Coie 1201 3rd Ave Fl 40 Seattle WA 98101-3000

BOEDO, STEPHEN, mechanical engineer, consultant; b. Buffalo, Apr. 10, 1960; s. Gordon Eugene and Florence Frances (DeGeorge) B.; m. Sharon Lee Lindahl, Aug. 16, 1986; children: Stephen Matthew, Emily Frances. BA summa cum laude, SUNY, Buffalo, 1983; MS, Cornell U., 1986, PhD, 1995. Sr. engr. Borg-Warner Automotive, Ithaca, N.Y., 1986-92, staff engr., 1996—; sr. tech. analyst Fed.-Mogul Corp., Ann Arbor, Mich., 1992-96; adj. instr. Tompkins-Cortland C.C., Dryden, N.Y., 1988-92; self-employed cons., Ithaca, 1986—; guest lectr. on mech. design various univs. Reviewer various jours., 1986—; contbr. articles to profl. jours.; patentee in field. Mem. ASME, Soc. Automotive Engrs., Cornell Soc. Engrs., Phi Beta Kappa. Avocations: soccer, chess, astronomy. Office: Borg Warner Automotive 770 Warren Rd Ithaca NY 14850-1291

BOEGEHOLD, ALAN LINDLEY, classics educator; b. Detroit, Mar. 21, 1927; s. Alfred Lindley and Katherine Eleanore (Yager) B.; m. Julie Elizabeth Marshall, Apr. 3, 1954; children: Lindley, Alan M. Jones, David, Alison. AB in Latin, U. Mich., 1950; AM in Classical Philology, Harvard U., 1954; student, Am. Sch. Classical Studies, Athens, Greece, 1955-57; PhD in Classical Philology, Harvard U., 1958. From instr. to asst. prof. dept. classics U. Ill., Champaign-Urbana, 1957-60; from asst. prof. to prof. dept. classics Brown U., Providence, R.I., 1960—; dir. summer session Am. Sch. Classical Studies, Athens, 1963-64, 74, 80, vis. prof., 1968-69; dir. Ancient studies program Brown U., 1985-91, chmn. dept. classics, 1966-71, acting chmn., 1973-74; vis. lectr. history Harvard U., 1967; vis. prof. classics Yale U., 1971, U. Calif., Berkeley, 1978; mem. com. to evaluate dept. classics Swarthmore Coll., 1972, U. Va., 1982, 88, coms. humanities and history Yale U. Coun., 1982-87; interim pres., v.p. and sec. Naragansett Soc. Archaeol. Inst. Am.; vice-chmn. mng. com. Am. Sch. Classical Studies, 1985-90, chmn., 1990-98; invited lectr., spkr. in field. Editor: (with A.C. Scafuro) Athenian Identity and Civic Ideology, 1993; author, editor: Agora XXVIII, Law Courts at Athens, 1995; author: When A Gesture was Expected. A Selection of Examples from Archaic and Classical Greek Literature, Printon, 1999; translator: In Simple Clothes (by Constantine Cavafy); mem. bd. advisors Am. Jour. Archaeology, 1981-85; interim referee papers and books to numerous assns. and presses; contbr. articles to profl. jours. Active ACLU, Amnesty Internat., Providence Athenaeum, Mass. Audubon Soc., Common Cause; trustee Gennadius Libr., Am. Sch. Classical Studies, Athens. Cpl. U.S. Army. Thomas Day Seymour fellow Am. Sch. Classical Studies Athens, 1955-56, Rsch. fellow, 1974-75, Rsch. fellow Agora Excavations, 1980-81, Charles Eliot Norton fellow Am. Sch. Classical Studies Athens (Harvard U.), 1956-57, Howard fellow Brown U., 1964-65, Sr. fellow NEH, 1980-81; grantee Am. Coun. Learned Socs., 1964-65. Fellow Explorers Club; mem. Am. Assn. Ancient Historians, Am. Philol. Assn., Archaeol. Inst. Am. (various coms.), Classical Assn. New Eng. (exec. com. 1968-70), Aegean Inst. (bd. advisors 1976-95), Inst. Nautical Archaeology (bd. dirs. 1973-82). Office: Brown Univ 48 College St Providence RI 02912-9021

BOEGEL, NICK NORBERT, accountant, lawyer; b. West Bend, Wis., Mar. 14, 1972; s. Kenneth and Portia (Steahl) B. BSBA, Boston U., 1994; MBA, Ind. U., 1997, JD, 1998. Bar: Ind. 1998; CPA, Ind. Assoc. ins. tax cons. Pricewaterhouse Coopers, Indpls., 1998—. Mem. Ind. bar. Avocations: golf, fishing, hunting, billiards, darts. Home: 10603 Brixton Ln Fishers IN 46038

BOEHEIM, JIM, college basketball coach; b. Lyons, N.Y., Y, Nov. 17, 1944. BA in Social Sci., Syracuse U., 1966, M in Social Sci. Full-time asst. basketball coach Syracuse (N.Y.) U., 1972-76, head basketball coach, 1976—; mem. coaching staff U.S. basketball team Goodwill Games, Seattle, 1991 (silver medal), World Championships, Argentina (bronze medal), World Univ. Games, 1989. Hon. chmn. Kidney Found.; active orgns. Multiple Sclerosis, Cystic Fibrosis, Children's Miracle Network, Make-A-Wish, Pioneer Ctr. for Blind and Disabled, Lighthouse, People in Wheelchairs, Easter Seals, Spl. Olympics. Named Dist. II Coach of Yr., Nat. Assn. Basketball Coaches, 1980, 84, 87, 89, 92, 94, U.S. Basketball Writers Assn., 1979, 80, 91; named Big East Conf. Coach of Yr., 1984, 91; elected Syracuse Univ. Letterwinner of Distinction, 1988; inducted into Syracuse Sports Hall of Fame, 1991; named Best Golfer in Coll. Basketball, 1989; recipient Syracuse Mayor's Achievment award, 1980. Office: Syracuse Univ Basketball Dept Manley Field House Syracuse NY 13244-5020*

BOEHLERT, SHERWOOD LOUIS, congressman; b. Utica, N.Y., Sept. 28, 1936; s. Sherwood John and Elizabeth Monica (Champoux) B.; divorced; children: Mark C. Brooks, Tracy Boehlert Suk, Leslie; m. Marianne Willey Phillips, July 10, 1976; 1 stepchild, Laura Brooke Drahzal. B.S. in Pub. Relation, Utica Coll., Syracuse U., 1961. Mgr. pub. relations Wyandotte Chems. Corp., Mich., 1961-64; chief of staff Rep. Alexander Pirnie, Washington, 1964-73, Rep. Donald J. Mitchell, 1973-79; exec. Oneida County, 1979-82; mem. 98th-104th Congresses from 25th (now 23rd) N.Y. dist., Washington, 1983—, mem. permanent select com. on intelligence; mem. sci. com.; del. North Atlantic Assembly; mem. N.E.-Midwest Congl. Coalition; co-chmn. N.E. Agr.; chmn. Fire Svcs. Caucus, Minor League Baseball Caucus. Author: Telling the Congressman's Story The Voice of Government, 1968. Bd. dirs. Utica Coll. Found. Served with U.S. Army, 1956-58. Republican. Lodge: Rotary. Office: Ho of Reps 2246 Rayburn Bldg Washington DC 20515-3223 also: Alexander Pirnie Fed Bldg Rm 200 10 Broad St Utica NY 13501-1233

BOEHLKE, CHRISTINE, public relations executive; b. Dover, N.J., Dec. 29, 1946. BA in Creative Writing, U. Pa., 1968. Acct. supr. D.J. Edelman, 1978-79, group v.p., 1979-81; v.p. client svcs. mgr. Burson-Marsteller, Chgo., 1981-83; v.p., gen. mgr. Burson-Marsteller, San Francisco, 1983-85; v.p., mgr. northern calif. Burson-Marsteller, 1985-86, sr. v.p. western regional mgr., 1986-87; prin. Phase Two Strategies, San Francisco, 1987—. Mem. Pub. Rels. Soc. Am. (counselor's acad.), Commonwealth Club of Calif. Office: Phase Two Stategies 170 Columbus Ave Ste 300 San Francisco CA 94133-5160*

BOEHLKE, WILLIAM FREDRICK, public relations executive; b. Chgo., Dec. 16, 1946; s. William Fredrick and Cynthia Charlotte (Blackmore) B.; m. Christine Ann Chervenak, July 19, 1969. Student, Wharton Sch. Bus., Phila., 1965-69. Pres. and CEO Data Solve Corp., Chgo., 1981-84, Lati Corp. Inc., San Francisco, 1985-89, Phase Two Strategies Inc., San Francisco, 1989—. Contbr. articles to profl. jours. Mem. IEEE, USR/Group, Assn. Computing Machinery, Pub. Rels. Soc. Am. Avocation: computer software tech. Office: Phase Two Strategies Inc 170 Columbus Ave San Francisco CA 94133-5119

BOEHM, BARRY WILLIAM, computer science educator; b. Santa Monica, Calif., May 16, 1935; s. Edward G. and Kathryn G. (Kane) B.; m. Sharla Perrine, July 1, 1961; children: Romney Ann, Tenley Lynn. BA, Harvard U., 1957; PhD, UCLA, 1964. Programmer, analyst Gen. Dynamics, San Diego, 1955-59; head infosci. dept. Rand Corp., Santa Monica, 1959-73; chief scientist TRW Def. Sys. Group, Redondo Beach, Calif., 1973-89; dir. infosci. and tech. office Def. Advanced Rsch. Agy. Dept. Def., Arlington, Va., 1989-92, dir. software and computer tech. office, dir. def. rsch. and engring., 1992; TRW prof. software engring., dir. Ctr. for Software Engring. U. So. Calif., L.A., 1992—; co-chmn. Fed. Coordinating Coun. Sci., Engring. and Tech. High Performance Computing WG, Washington, 1989-91; chmn. DOD Software Tech. Plan WG, Arlington, 1990-92, NASA G & C/Infosystems Adv. Com., Washington, 1973-76; guest lectr. USSR Acad. Sci., 1970. Author: ROCKET, 1964, Software Engineering Economics, 1981; co-author: Characteristics of Software Quality, 1978, Software Risk Management, 1989; co-editor: Planning Community Information Utilities, 1972. Recipient Warnier prize Soc. Software Analysts, 1984, Freiman award Internat. Soc. Parametric Analysts, 1988, Award for Excellence Office of Sec. of Def., 1992. Fellow ACM (Disting. Rsch. award in Software Engring. 1997), NAE, AIAA (chair TC computers 1968-70, Information Sys. award 1979), IEEE (gov. bd. computer sci. 1981-82, 86-87). Office: U So Calif Computer Sci Dept Los Angeles CA 90089-0781

BOEHM, DAVID ALFRED, publisher, producer; b. N.Y.C., Feb. 6, 1914; s. Alfred and Frances (Ehrlich) B.; m. Sylvia Link, Sept. 18, 1965 (dec. 1977); children: Suzanne, Diana, Lincoln, Emily, David Lee; m. Janet Barnes, July 14, 1994. A.B., Columbia Coll., 1934. Editor Standard Stats Co., 1936-38; pres. Printed Arts Co., 1938-41; asst. prodn. mgr. McGraw-Hill Book Co., 1941-44; editor Cupples & Leon Pubs., 1944-45; sales mgr. Greenberg-Publisher, 1945-49; founder, pres., now chmn. Sterling Pub. Co., N.Y.C., 1949—; editor, pub. Sterling Pub. Co. (Guinness Book of World Records), 1960-90; pres. Printed Arts Co., 1958-86, Bold Face Books, Inc., 1958-80, World Record Films, 1975-90, Guinness Mus. of World Records and Exhibit Halls, Inc., 1976-84, David A. Boehm Prodns. Inc., 1979-94; founder, editor Guinness Mag., 1981-82; chmn. Lit. Tours, Inc., 1981-84. Author 21 books on stamp collecting, games, fgn. countries, humor, book publishing. Office: Sterling Pub's Co 387 Park Ave S Fl 5 New York NY 10016-8810*

BOEHM, EDWARD GORDON, JR., university administrator, educator; b. Washington, Jan. 30, 1942; s. Edward and Catherine (Murray) B.; m. Regina Ellen Evans, June 25, 1966; children: Evan Arnold, Andrew Edward. BS in Edn., Frostburg State U., 1964; MEd, The Am. U., 1970, D of Higher Edn., 1977. Dir. univ. devel., dean for student devel., assoc. dean/dir. admissions, instr. Coll. Arts & Scis. The Am. U., Washington, 1968-79; assoc. vice chancellor acad. affairs, asst. prof. edn., dean admissions Tex. Christian U., Ft. Worth, 1979-89; sr. v.p., asst. prof. Coll. Edn., exec. dir. Found. Marshall U., Huntington, W.Va., 1989-95; pres. Keystone Coll., La Plume, Pa., 1995—; mem. adv. coun. Tandy Tech. Scholars, Ft. Worth, 1989—; trustee, mem. com. The Coll. Bd., N.Y.C., 1987-91. Contbr. book chpt.: Student Services and the Law, 1988; contbr. articles to profl. jours. Bd. dirs., v.p. Boys & Girls Club, Huntington, 1989-95, Tri-State coun. Boy Scouts Am., Huntington, 1989-95; bd. dirs., pres. United Way River Cities, Huntington, 1989-95; bd. dirs. Leadership W. Va., Charleston, 1992-95, Leadership Tri-State, Ironton, Ohio, 1991-95; bd. dirs. Tyler Hosp., 1995—, Waverly Cmty. House, 1996—; mem. Leadership Wilkes-Barre Exec. Program, Class of '96, Leadership Lackawanna Exec. Program, Class of '96, N.E. Regional Cancer Inst. Adv. Bd.; pres. bd. dirs. Pa. Assn. of Nonprofit Orgns., 1998; mem. nonprofit adv. bd. Nonprofit Resource Ctr., U. Scranton, 1998—; bd. mem. Tyler Meml. Hosp. Cmty. Health Care Vision Task Force, 1999—. Named W.Va. Outstanding Fundraising Exec., Nat. Soc. Fundraising Execs., 1993, Citizen of Yr., Herald Dispatch, 1993, Disting. West Virginian, 1995; recipient Cir. of Excellence in Fundraising award Coun. for Advancement and Support of Edn., 1993; John Deaver Drinko Acad. fellow Marshall U. Mem. Huntington C. of C., Lawrence County C. of C., Greenup County C. of C., Engrs. Club Huntington, Huntington Rotary Club (bd. dirs. 1989-95). Avocations: tennis, soccer, history, golf, hiking. Home: 29 College Ave La Plume PA 18440 Office: Keystone Coll One College Green La Plume PA 18440-0200

BOEHM, ERIC HARTZELL, information management executive; b. Hof, Germany, July 15, 1918; came to U.S., 1934, naturalized, 1940; s. Karl and Bertha (Oppenheimer) B.; m. Inge Pauli, June 5, 1948; children: Beatrice (dec.), Ronald James, Evelyn (dec.), Steven David. B.A., Wooster (Ohio) Coll., 1940, Litt.D. (hon.), 1973; M.A., Fletcher Sch. Law and Diplomacy, 1942; Ph.D., Yale U., 1951. With Dept. Air Force, 1951-58; chmn. bd. ABC-CLIO, Santa Barbara, Calif., 1960—, European Bibliog. Ctr., CLIO Press, Ltd., Oxford, Eng., 1970—; pres. Internat. Sch. of Info. Mgmt., 1987-94, chmn., 1994—; chmn. bd. dirs. Internat. Acad. at Santa Barbara, 1970-88, Internat. Sch. Info. Mgmt.; pub. Environ. Studies Inst., 1971—, Info. Inst., 1980—; cons. on bibliography, information systems. Author: We Survived, 1949; microfilm Policy-making of the Nazi Government, 1969; editor Historical Abstracts, 1955-83, cons., 1983—; editor America: History and Life, 1964-83, cons., 1983—; editor Bibliographies on International Relations and World Affairs, an Annotated Directory, 1965, Blueprint for Bibliography, a System for Social Sciences and Humanities, 1965, Clio Bibliography Series, 1973—; co-editor Historical Periodicals, 1961, 2d edit., 1983-85; pub. Advanced Bibliography of Contents: Political Science, 1969—, ART Bibliographies: Modern, 1972—, Environ. Periodicals Bibliography, 1972—; bd. advisors Info. Strategy, The Exec.'s Jour., 1984—; contbr. articles to profl. jours. Bd. dirs. UN Assn., Santa Barbara, 1973-77, Santa Barbara's Adv. Bd. Internat. Relationships (Sister Cities), 1974, Friends of Public Library, Friends of U. Calif. at Santa Barbara Library; mem. affiliates bd. U. Calif.-Santa Barbara; vice chmn. New Directions Found., 1984-88; adv. bd. Nuclear Age Peace Found., 1985—. With USAAF, 1942-46. Recipient Disting. Alumnus award Wooster Coll., 1990. Mem. AAAS, Am. Soc. Info. Sci., Assn. Bibliography in History (v.p. 1986, pres. 1987), Calif. Library Soc., Nat. Trust Historic Preservation, Santa Barbara Com. Fgn. Rels., Am. Friends of Wilton Park, Santa Barbara C. of C. (dir. 1980-84), Univ. Club, Rotary, Phi Beta Kappa. Home and Office: 800 E Micheltorena St Santa Barbara CA 93103-2220

BOEHM, FELIX HANS, physicist, educator; b. Basel, Switzerland, June 9, 1924; came to U.S., 1952, naturalized, 1964; s. Hans G. and Marquerite (Philippi) B.; m. Ruth Sommerhalder, Nov. 26, 1956; children: Marcus F., Claude N. MS, Inst. Tech., Zurich, 1948, PhD, 1951. Research assoc. Inst. Tech., Zurich, Switzerland, 1949-52; Boese fellow Columbia U., 1952-53; faculty Calif. Inst. Tech., Pasadena, 1953—, prof. physics, 1961—, William L. Valentine prof., 1985-94, William L. Valentine prof. emeritus, 1995—; Sloan fellow, 1962-64; NSF sr. fellow Niels Bohr Inst., Copenhagen, 1965-66, CERN, Geneva, 1971-72, Laue-Langevin Inst., 1980. Recipient Humboldt award, 1980, 84. Fellow Am. Phys. Soc. (Tom W. Bonner prize 1995); mem. Nat. Acad. Scis. Research on nuclear physics, nuclear beta decay, neutrino physics, atomic physics, muonic and pionic atoms, parity and time-reversal. Home: 2510 N Altadena Dr Altadena CA 91001-2836 Office: Calif Inst Tech Mail Code 161 33 Pasadena CA 91125

BOEHM, P. DIANN, elementary education educator; b. Tulsa, Apr. 13, 1954; d. George Mural and Mabel Adella (Harris) Floyd; m. John Charles Boehm, Jr., June 2, 1979; children: Rachel Rebbecca, John Patrick, Katherine Louise. BS in Edn., George Mason U., 1981. Cert. elem. tchr., Tex. Tchr. 4th grade Internat. Sch., Manila, Philippines, 1981-82; tchr. prekindergarten Resurrection Episc. Ch., Austin, Tex., 1982-83; tchr. 9th grade St. Louis Cath. Sch., Austin, 1983-84; tchr. 4th grade St. John's Sch., Houston, 1984-85; tchr. kindergarten St. Thomas Cath. Sch., Austin, 1986-87; tchr., tech. coord. St. Andrew's Episc. Sch., Austin, 1989—; prin., coord. High Tech Schoolhouse, Tex.; tchr. HHC, Austin, 1991—; keynote speaker Fla. State Computer Conf.,1991—; cons. Scholastic pubs. Author: (book) The Internet Schoolhouse, A Teacher's Best Friend; contbr. articles on tech. in edn. to various pubs. Chair person bd, Episc. Ch. Women, St. David's Episc. Ch., 1989—, chair person United Thank Offering, 1991—. Named Tex. Tchr. of Yr. in Tech., Tex. Dept. Edn., 1992, Apple Disting. Educator. Mem. Tex. Ctr. Edn. Technology (hon. mention 1991, '92), VITAL (Leadership in Tech. award 1992). Republican. Avocations: singing, crocheting, biking. Office: Internet Schoolhouse 58 Saint Stephens School Rd Austin TX 78746-3231

BOEHM, ROBERT FOTY, mechanical engineer, educator, researcher; b. Portland, Oreg., Jan. 16, 1940; s. Charles Frederick and Lufteria (Christie) B.; m. Marcia Kay Pettibone, June 10, 1961; children—Deborah, Robert Christopher. B.S. in Mech. Engring., Wash. State U., Pullman, 1962, M.S., 1964; Ph.D., U. Calif., Berkeley, 1968. Registered profl. engr., Calif. With Gen. Electric Co., San Jose, Calif., 1964-66; mem. faculty U. Utah, Salt Lake City, 1968-90, prof. mech. engring., 1976-90, chmn. dept., 1981-84; Nat. Sandia Labs., Albuquerque, 1984-85; prof. U. Nev., Las Vegas, 1990—, chmn. mech. engring. dept., 1990-96, univ. sys. sr. liaison to Dept. Energy, 1994-95, dir. rsch. Coll. Engring., 1999—; mem. Utah Solar Adv. Com., Utah Energy Conservation and Devel. Coun., 1980-88; dir. Energy Rsch. Ctr., 1994—. Author: Design Analysis of Thermal Systems, 1987; editor:

Direct Contact Heat Exchange, 1988, Developments in the Design of Thermal Systems, 1997; tech. editor Jour. Solar Energy Engring., 1980-84; contbr. articles to profl. jours. Named Utah Engring. Educator of Yr., Utah Engrs. Coun., 1988, Disting. Tchr., U. Utah, 1989; recipient UNLV Barrick Sr. Rsch. award, 1994. Fellow ASME; mem. ASHRAE, Am. Soc. for Engring. Edn., Internat. Solar Energy Soc., Corvair Soc. Am., Vintage Chevrolet Club Am., Sigma Xi. Home: 4999 Mesa View Dr Las Vegas NV 89120-1216 Office: U Nev Mech Engring Dept PO Box 454027 Las Vegas NV 89154-4027

BOEHM, STEVEN BRUCE, lawyer; b. N.Y.C., May 22, 1954; s. Henry and Irene (Jonas) B. BA, Rutgers U., New Brunswick, N.J., 1975; JD, Rutgers U., Newark, 1978. Bar: N.J., 1978, D.C., 1982, U.S. Dist. Ct. N.J., U.S. Dist. Ct., D.C. Enforcement atty. SEC, Washington, 1978-81, atty. office gen. counsel, 1982, counsel to the commr., 1982-83; assoc. Sutherland Asbill & Brennan, LLP, Washington, 1983-87, ptnr., 1988—. Philip J. Levin scholar Rutgers U., 1975-78. Mem. ABA (corp., banking and bus. law com.), D.C. Bar Assn., Phi Beta Kappa, Pi Sigma Alpha. E-Mail:sboehm@sablaw.com. Office: Sutherland Asbill & Brennan LLP 1275 Pennsylvania Ave NW Washington DC 20004-2404

BOEHM, TONI GEORGENE, seminary dean, nurse; b. New Kensington, Pa., Dec. 28, 1946; d. Sylvio Chipoletti and Eula Gene (Smittle) Fox; m. Raymond Stawinski, Dec. 11, 1965 (div. Sept. 1978); 1 child, Michelle Stawinski Ivy; m. Jay Thomas Boehm, Apr. 28, 1983; children: Jonathon, Kimberly, Allison Cole, Amanda. Diploma, Allegheny Valley Sch. Nursing, Natrona Heights, Pa., 1967; family nurse practitioner cert., U. Kans., 1976; BA in Edn., Ottawa (Kans.) U., 1978; MSN, U. Mo., Kansas City, 1981; grad., Unity Sch. of Christianity, Unity Village, Mo., 1989; PhD in Religious Studies, Am. World U., 1997. Ordained to ministry Assn. of Unity Chs.; cert. occupl. health nurse. Nurse Allegheny Valley Hosp., Natrona Heights, 1967-74; head nurse, dir. nursing Truman Med. Ctr., Kansas City, Mo., 1974-78; mgr. med. Hallmark Card Inc., Kansas City, Mo., 1978-85; sr. staff specialist ANA, Kansas City, Mo., 1985-87; dean of adminstrn. Unity Sch. Christianity, 1987—; nat. spkr. and freelance writer for ministry and self-unfoldment. Author: The Spiritual Intrapreneur, 1996. Mem. nat. steering com. for fundraising Unity Sch. of Christianity; mem. women's coun. U. Mo. Recipient scholarships. Mem. ANA, NCCJ, Mo. Nurses Assn. (bd. dirs. 1975-85), U. Mo. Sch. Nursing Alumni Assn., Assn. Unity Chs. (urban curriculum com. 1987—, ministerial edn. com. 1987—, field licensing com. 1990). Republican. Avocations: travel, reading, music, writing. Home: 430 N Winnebago Dr Lk Winnebago MO 64034-9321 Office: Unity Sch Christianity Lees Summit MO 64065

BOEHM, WERNER WILLIAM, social work educator; b. Oberlangenstadt, Germany, June 19, 1913; came to U.S., 1937, naturalized, 1944; s. Karl and Bertha (Oppenheimer) B.; m. Bernice Roseburg Brower, June 5, 1948 (dec. Dec. 1983); 1 child, Andrew; m. Laurie Horn, Feb. 2, 1986. LL.B., U. Dijon, France, 1936, D.L., 1937; M.S.W., Tulane U., 1941, LHD (hon.), 1992, LLD (hon.), 1994. Prof. social work U. Minn., 1952-63, dir., coordinator U.S. and Canadian social work curriculum study, 1955-58; dean Grad. Sch. Social Work, Rutgers U., 1963-72, disting. prof., 1972-81, emeritus prof., 1981—; dir. Center for Internat. and Comparative Social Welfare, 1973-81; vis. Disting. prof. Seton Hall U., 1984-87; v.p. Minn. Welfare Conf., 1954-55; bd. dirs. U.S. Com. on Internat. Social Work, 1955-61, 76-92; vice chmn. commn. 10th Internat. Conf. Social Work, Italy, 1961; rep. 10th Internat. Conf. Social Work (11th Conf.), Brazil, 1962; mem. continuing edn. tng. rev. com. NIMH, 1969-72; chmn. Commn. I, XVth Internat. Conf., Manila, 1970; Sr. Fulbright travel grant Italo-U.S. Com. on Edn1. Exchange in Social Welfare, Rome, 1969; sr. Fulbright appointment, Italy, 1971; vis. scholar Nat. Inst. Social Work Tng., London, 1972-73; U.S. rep. commn. on social devel. XVIII Internat. Conf. on Social Welfare, San Juan, 1976; lectr. internat. meetings Ger., France, 1975-80, 82, Australia, 1983, Israel, 1998. Author: Objectives of the Social Work Curriculum of the Future, 1959, The Social Casework Method in Social Work Education, 1959; author U.S. report for, 19th and 20th Internat. Confs. on Social Welfare, 1978, 80, also seven monographs in field; adv. editor: Social Work Series, Harper & Row, Pubs., 1963-83; editor-in-chief: Internat. Social Work, 1975-81; contbr. articles to profl. jours., chpts. to books. Mem. Gov.'s Council on Aging, 1960; mem. N.J. Crime Commn., 1966-68; mem. nat. exec. council Am. Jewish Com., 1984—, mem. nat. affairs com., 1986—. Recipient Cassidy Meml. rsch. award U. Toronto, 1959, Disting. Alumnus award Tulane U., 1981, medal Rutgers U., 1983, Lifetime Achievement award Coun. Social Work Edn., 1995; named Social Worker of Yr., Nat. Assn. Social Workers, 1983. Mem. AAAS, NASW (chmn. commn. on edn. 1965-67, bd. dirs., exec. com. 1966-67), Internat. Coun. Social Welfare (bd. dirs. U.S. com. 1979-89), Coun. Social Work Edn. (exec. com. 1967-69, chmn. commn. on ednl. svcs. 1968-72, commn. internat. social work 1978-82, com. on inquiry N.J. chpt. 1986-92, del. 1986, Lifetime Achievement award 1995), Nat. Commn. Social Work Careers (bd. dirs.), Nat. Conf. Social Welfare (1st v.p. 1969-70), N.J. Welfare Coun. (exec. com. 1964-70), N.J. Assn. Social Workers (Social Work Pioneer 1992), Cosmos Club. Home: 21 Carpender Rd New Brunswick NJ 08901-1501 Office: Rutgers U Sch Social Work 536 George St New Brunswick NJ 08901-1167

BOEHMER, RAQUEL DAVENPORT, television producer, newsletter editor; b. Bklyn., Feb. 24, 1938; d. John Joralemon Davenport and Fanny (Barberis) Allison; m. Peter Joseph Boehmer; children: Kristian Ludwig, Louisa, Timothy Joralemon. BA, Wells Coll., 1959. Radio producer Maine Pub. Broadcasting Network, Bangor, 1977—; developer, editor consumer newsletter Seafood Soundings, Monhegan, Maine, 1986-92; columnist, editor newsletter New Monhegan Press, Monhegan, Maine, 1989-96, chief editor, 1995—; speaker Seafare, L.A., 1986; keynote speaker Beyond Wells Day, Wells Coll., Aurora, N.Y., 1988; pres. bd. dirs. Monhegan Artists' Residency Corp., 1995—. Writer, prodr. (radio commentary) Whole Foods for All People, 1977-91; prodr., host (TV cooking program) Different Kettle of Fish, 1984; prodr./host TV cooking program Great Tastes of Maine, Maine Pub. TV, 1996; author: A Foraging Vacation, 1982, Raquel's Maine Guide to New England Seafoods, 1988, Raquel's Maine Guide to Northeast Winter Vegetables, 1993. Writer legislation, Maine legis., 1985, 87, 91; treas. Monhegan Plantation, 1970-72, chair bicentennial com., 1976; chair Monhegan Sch. Bd., 1973-74; co-chair Monhegan Solid Waste Com., 1988-98; commr. Maine State Liquor and Lottery Commn., 1996—; mem. edn. task force Nat. Alcohol Beverage Control Assn., 1998—. Recipient Pub. Svc. award Maine Nutrition Coun., 1987, Alumnae award Wells Coll., 1992; named Gt. New Eng. Cook, Yankee mag., 1986. Mem. Women's Fisheries Network (bd. dirs. N.E. chpt. 1992-94, sec. to nat. bd. dirs. 1994-97, v.p. 1997-98, pres. nat. bd. dirs. 1998—), Nat. Alcohol Beverage Control Assn. (edn. task force 1998—), Colonial Dames Am., Women's Strike for Peace. Avocations: foraging, second fiddle playing. E-mail: raquel@monhegan.com. Home and Office: 10 Lobster Cove Rd Monhegan ME 04852

BOEHNE, EDWARD GEORGE, banker; b. Evansville, Ind., May 15, 1940; s. Edward John and Lucy Naomi (Strieter) B.; m. Patricia Graffis, Jan. 24, 1960; children: Lisa Elena, Edward Mark. BS, Ind. U., 1962, MBA, 1963, MA, 1967, PhD in Econs, 1968; LLD (hon.), Widener U., 1989. Economist Fed. Res. Bank, Phila., 1968-70, rsch. officer, economist, 1970-71, v.p., dir. rsch., 1971-73, sr. v.p., 1973-81, pres., 1981—; tchr. Bradley U., 1963-65, Ind. U., 1965-67, Temple U., 1969-70. Chmn. Pa. Hosp., 1993-97; chmn. University City Sci. Ctr.; bd. dirs. Global Interdependence Ctr. Recipient Lieber award Ind. U., 1967, Gov.'s citation for outstanding svc. to Pa., 1978, Whitney Young Leadership award 1986, Stephen Girard award, 1987. Mem. Am. Econ. Assn., Nat. Assn. Bus. Economists. Office: Fed Res Bank Phila PO Box 66 10 Independence Mall Philadelphia PA 19106-1521

BOEHNEN, DANIEL A., lawyer; b. Mitchell, S.D., Aug. 5, 1950; s. Lloyd and Mary Elizabeth (Buche) B.; m. Joan Bensing, May 22, 1976; children: Christopher, Lindsey. BS in Chem. Engring. cum laude, Notre Dame U., 1973; JD, Cornell U., 1976. Bar: Ill, U.S. Dist. Ct. (no. dist.) Ill., U.S. Ct. Appeals (7th and fed. cirs.), U.S. Supreme Ct. Atty. Allegretti, Newitt, Witcoff & McAndrews Ltd., Chgo., 1976—, assoc., 1982—; ptnr., exec. officer Allegretti & Witcoff, Ltd., Chgo., 1986—, bd. dirs., 1993-96; founder, mng. ptnr. McDonnell Boehnen Hulbert & Berghoff, Chgo., 1996—. Acrive Northbrook Caucus, Ill., 1980—; bd. dirs. Mitchell (S.D.) Prehist. Indian Village Soc., 1983—; commr. Northbrook Planning Commn., 1993—. Mem. ABA, AIPLA, Cornell Law Assn. Chg. (chmn.), Fed. Cir. Bar Assn. (bd. dirs.). Avocations: skiing, photography, scuba diving. Office: McDonnell Boehnen Hulbert & Berghoff 300 S Wacker Dr Chicago IL 60606-6680

BOEHNER, JOHN A., congressman; b. Reading, Ohio, Nov. 17, 1949; m. Deborah Gunlack, 1973; children: Lindsay M., Tricia A. BS, Xavier U., 1977. Pres. Nucite Sales, Inc.; mem. Ohio Ho. of Reps., 1984-90; mem. 102nd-105th Congresses from 8th Ohio dist., Washington, D.C., 1991—, chmn. subcom. on employer-employee rels., 1998—; exec. com. mem. Nat. Rep. Congl. Com.; chmn. Ho. Rep. Conf. Com.; mem. Ag. Com., Ho. Oversight Com. Active Ohio Farm Bur. Mem. KC, Cin., Dayton, Middletown C. of C. Roman Catholic. Republican. Office: US Ho of Reps 1011 Longworth Bldg Washington DC 20515-3508

BOEHNER, LEONARD BRUCE, lawyer; b. Council Bluffs, Iowa, Apr. 19, 1930; s. Bruce and Flora (Kruse) B. AB, Harvard U., 1952, JD, 1955. Bar: N.Y. 1956, U.S. Dist. Ct. (so. dist.) N.Y. 1963, U.S. Ct. Appeals (2d cir.) 1963, U.S. Supreme Ct. 1964. Assoc. Dewey, Ballantine, Bushby, Palmer & Wood, N.Y.C., 1959-66; ptnr. Clare & Whitehead, N.Y.C., 1966-73, Morris & McVeigh LLP, N.Y.C. 1973—. Served to lt. USN, 1955-59. Mem. Assn. Bar City N.Y. Club: Union (N.Y.C.). Office: Morris & McVeigh 767 3rd Ave New York NY 10017-2023

BOEKE, EUGENE H., JR., construction executive; b. Birmingham, Ala., Oct. 7, 1925; s. Eugene Herman and Lillian (Rogers) B.; m. Joy Weller, Aug. 11, 1951. BS in Arch., Ga. Inst. Tech., 1949. From engr. to v.p. Beers Constrn. Co., Atlanta, 1949-91, v.p. emeritus, 1992—; bd. dirs. Bon Enterprises, Tulsa; mem. Concrete Adv. Bd. Ga., 1972—. Active Boy Scouts Am. With U.S. Army, 1943-46. Recipient Silver Beaver award Boy Scouts Am., 1975. Mem. Am. Concrete Inst. (hon., 318 bldg. code for reinforced concrete 1977-95, Roger H. Corbetta award 1988), Reinforced Concrete Rsch. Coun., Am. Soc. for Concrete constrn. (pres. 1993-95), Gombe Soc., Am. Arbitration Assn. Baptist. Home: PO Box 11062 Big Canoe GA 30143-0185 Office: Beers Constrn 70 Ellis St NE Atlanta GA 30303-2499

BOEKELHEIDE, KIM, pathologist; b. Iowa City, 1952. MD, Duke U., 1980. Diplomate Am. Bd. Pathology, Am. Bd. Anatomy and Clin. Pathology. Resident Duke U. Med. Ctr., Durham, N.C., 1980-84; asst. prof. Brown U., Providence, 1984-90, assoc. prof., 1990-95, prof., 1995—. Burroughs Wellcome scholar in toxicology Soc. Toxicology, 1994. Office: Brown U Box G-B518 Divsn Bio & Medicine Providence RI 02912

BOEKELHEIDE, VIRGIL CARL, chemistry educator; b. Cheslea, S.D., July 28, 1919; s. Charles F. and Eleonor (Toennies) B.; m. Caroline Barrett, Apr. 7, 1924; children: Karl, Anne, Erich. AB magna cum laude, U. Minn., Mpls., 1939, PhD, 1943. Instr. U. Ill., Urbana, 1943-46; asst. prof. to prof. U. Rochester, 1946-60; prof. dept. chemistry U. Oreg., Eugene, 1960—. Contbr. articles to profl. jours. Recipient Disting. Achievement award U. Minn., 1967; recipient Alexander von Humboldt award W.Ger. Govt., 1974, 82, Centenary Lectureship Royal Soc. G.B., 1983, Coover award Iowa State U., 1981; Disting. scholar designate U.S.-China Acad. Sci., 1981; Fulbright Disting. prof. Yugoslavia, 1972. Mem. NAS, Pharm. Soc. Japan (hon.). Home: 2017 Elk Ave Eugene OR 97403-1788 Office: U Oreg Dept Chemistry Eugene OR 97403

BOEKER, PAUL HAROLD, non-profit organization official, diplomat; b. St. Louis, May 2, 1938; s. Victor W. and Marie Dorothy (Bernthal) B.; m. Margaret Macon Campbell; children: Michelle Renee, Kent Elliott, Katherine Madison. AB magna cum laude, Dartmouth Coll., 1960; postgrad., Princeton U., 1961; MA in Econs., U. Mich., 1967. Joined Dept. State, 1961; vice consul Duesseldorf, Germany, 1962-63; 2d sec. Am. Embassy, Bogotá, Colombia, 1964-66; mem. White House Task Force on Internat. Devel., 1969; dir. Office Devel. Fin., Dept. State, 1970; 1st sec. Am. Embassy, Bonn, Germany, 1971-73; mem. policy planning staff Dept. State, 1974, dep. asst. sec. state for internat. fin. and devel., 1975, sr. dep. asst. sec. state for econ. and bus. affairs, 1976; ambassador to Bolivia, 1977-80; dir. Fgn. Service Inst., Washington, 1980-81; mem. Sec.'s Planning Council, Washington, 1983-84; ambassador to Jordan, 1984-87; pres. Inst. of the Ams., U. Calif., San Diego, 1988—. Author: Lost Illusions: Latin America's Struggle for Democracy; editor: Latin America's Turnaround, 1993. Recipient Arthur S. Fleming award for outstanding young people in fed. service, 1976, Presdl. Disting. Service award, 1985, 87. Mem. Am. Acad. Diplomacy, Coun. on Fgn. Rels.

BOELENS, PATRICIA ANN, accountant, nurse; b. Grinnell, Iowa, May 21, 1943; d. Harold Willis and Mary Louise (Phipps) Andes; m. William Carl Laubengayer, Aug. 15, 1963; children: Karl E., Kevin E.; m. Francis Raymond Boelens, Sept. 19, 1992; stepchildren: Kristina M., Kirk M. Diploma in nursing, St. Lukes Hosp., Cedar Rapids, Iowa, 1965; BSN, Coe Coll., 1976; AAS in Acctg. Tech., Kirkwood C.C., Cedar Rapids, 1987. Staff nurse Cedar Rapids, 1974-77; dir. nursing North Brook Manor Care Ctr., Cedar Rapids, 1977-78; staff nurse Linn County Pub. Health, Cedar Rapids, 1979-81; staff acct. Jean E. Kruse, CPA, Cedar Rapids, 1987-88; office mgr. Gordon Mollman, PA, Cedar Rapids, 1988-89; staff acct. Cindy Davis & Assocs., Moline, Ill., 1990-93, Watts & Assocs., Moline, Ill., 1993-94, AAA Iowa, Bettendorf, 1994-95, On With Life, Inc., Ankeny, Iowa, 1996—; spkr. continuing edn. workshops for various orgns., 1977-79; Iowa Nurses Assn. rep. Iowa Health Sys. Agy., Iowa City, 1979-83. Chair vol. adv. com. Linn County Coun. on Aging, Cedar Rapids, 1978-81. Nominee Nurse of Yr., Jour. Gerontol. Nursing, 1978. Mem. ANA (Iowa del. 1982), Iowa Nurses Assn. (continuing edn. rev. panel 1976-78, 3d v.p. 1978-80), Inst. Mgmt. Accts. (treas. Illowa chpt. 1992-94), Nat. Assn. Tax Practitioners, Kiwanis (com. chair Moline chpt. 1991-94), Phi Theta Kappa, Sigma Theta Tau. Home: 209 13th St SW Altoona IA 50009-2403 Office: On With Life Inc 715 SW Ankeny Rd Ankeny IA 50021-9798

BOELTER, PHILIP FLOYD, lawyer; b. Independence, Iowa, Mar. 25, 1943; s. Floyd Joseph and Eileen R. (Wilson) B.; m. Linda Lee Franck, June 7, 1964; children: Carrie Lynn, John Philip. BS in Indsl. Engring., Iowa State U., 1965; JD, U. Iowa, 1968. Ptnr. Dorsey & Whitney, Mpls., 1968—. Trustee Gustavus Adolphus Coll., 1996—. Mem. Mpls. Athletic Club (treas. 1992, sec. 1993, v.p. 1994, pres. 1995). Lutheran. Avocations: landscape gardening, skiing, fishing, reading, volleyball. Office: Dorsey & Whitney 220 S 6th St Ste 2200 Minneapolis MN 55402-1498

BOELZNER, GORDON, orchestral conductor; b. Inglewood, Calif., July 6, 1937; s. Gordon Dix and Angie Irene (Ketchum) B. Student, Eastman Sch. Music, 1954-57; BMus, Manhattan Sch. Music, 1958; pvt. studies with Arturo Benedetti Michelangeli, Italy, 1957. Condr., solo pianist N.Y.C. Ballet Orch., 1958—, now mus. dir., 1984—; guest appearances as piano soloist and condr. orchs. in Am. and Europe. Performance include Interplay, Tschaikovsky Piano Concerto #2, Allegro Brillante, Tarantella, The Four Temperaments, Davidsbundlertanze; piano Ballets include Dances At a Gathering, In The Night; conducted The Nutcracker, Symphony In C., A Midsummer Night's Dream. Office: NYC Ballet NY State Theatre 20 Lincoln Center Plz New York NY 10023-6913*

BOENNING, HENRY DORR, JR., investment banker; b. Phila., Oct. 16, 1914; s. Henry Dorr and Clara Virginia (Smith) B.; m. Clare Huston Miller, Feb. 18, 1946; m. Sara Ann Perkins, Aug. 19, 1964. B.S., U. Pa., 1935; postgrad., Harvard Bus. Sch., 1935-37. Partner Boenning & Co., Phila., 1946-70; v.p. Boenning & Scattergood, Inc., 1970—, also dir.; dir. Fluid Energy Process and Equipment, Hatfield, Pa. Served from 2d lt. to maj. AUS, 1939-46. Mem. Phi Gamma Delta. Home: 936 Rock Creek Rd Bryn Mawr PA 19010-1923 Office: 4 Tower Bridge 200 Barr Harbor Dr Fl 3D West Conshohocken PA 19428

BOENSCH, ARTHUR CRANWELL, lawyer; b. Charleston, S.C., Nov. 9, 1933; s. Frank Neville and Mary Alice (Cranwell) B.; m. Katherine Hume Lucas, June 16, 1956; children: Arthur Cranwell, Katherine Breland, Alice Metzendorf, Frances Murdaugh, Benjamin; m. 2d, Annelle Yvonne Beach, July 27, 1979. BS in Gen. Engring., U.S. Naval Acad., 1956; JD, U. S.C., 1970. Bar: S.C. 1970, U.S. Dist. Ct. (so. dist.) Ga. 1970, U.S. Dist. Ct. S.C. 1971. Ptnr. Ackerman & Boensch, Walterboro, S.C., 1970-73, Bogoslow & Boensch, Walterboro, S.C., 1973-75; pvt. practice Walterboro, S.C., 1976—; city recorder, mcpl. ct. judge, Walterboro, 1973-78. Chmn. Colleton County Alcohol and Drug Abuse Commn., 1991-96; dist. chmn. Boy Scouts Am., 1988-95, mem. exec. bd. Coastal Carolina coun., 1978—; vestryman St. Jude's Episcopal Ch.; lay rector Cursillo Episcopal Diocese of S.C., 1989; del. Episcopal conv. Diocese of S.C., 1995-96, 98-99, standing com., 1997—. Lt. Comdr. USN, 1956-57. Recipient Silver Beaver award and Dist. Merit award Boy Scouts Am., 1982; James West fellow, 1996. Mem. S.C. Bar Assn. (chmn. lawyers caring about lawyers com. 1989-91), Rotary, Phi Alpha Delta. Address: PO Box 258 Walterboro SC 29488-0003

BOER, F. PETER, chemical company executive; b. 1941. AB, Princeton U., 1961; PhD, Harvard U., 1965. With Tex Div. Lab. Dow Chem. Co., 1965-78, dir; v.p., mgr. R & D Am. Can Co., 1978-83; v.p., pres. rsch. div., corp. tech. group W.R. Grace & Co., from 1983; sr. v.p., until 1989, exec. v.p., until 1995; pres., chief exec. officer Tiger Scientific Inc.; adj. prof. Sch. Mgmt. and chem. engring. Yale U. Mem. Nat. Acad. Engring. Office: Tiger Scientific Inc 47 Country Rd S Village Of Golf FL 33436

BOERGERS, DAVID PAUL, energy executive; b. Buffalo, May 22, 1945; m. Mary Lang; children: Kathleen, Patrick. BS in Math., Niagara U., 1967; JD, Cath. U., Washington, 1972. Bar: D.C. 1972. Atty. Office of Gen. Counsel in hydroelectric licensing Fed. Energy Regulatory Commn., Washington, 1972, acting sec.; legal advisor to chmn. on hydroelectric and elec. issues Fed. Energy Regulatory Commn., 1990-92. Office: Fed Energy Regulatory Commn Office of Sec 888 1st St NE Washington DC 20426-0002

BOERINGER, GRETA, librarian; b. Vermillion, S.D., Jan. 19, 1960; d. James Leslie and GraceNocera B. BA, Susquehanna U., 1981; JD, Tulane U., 1985; MS in Libr. & Info. Sci., U. N.C., 1989. Bar: La. 1985. Reference documents computer libr. U. Ark., Little Rock, 1989-92; fed. depository libr. inspector U.S. Govt. Printing Office, Washington, 1992-96; legal reference specialist Law Libr. Congress Reading Room, Washington, 1996-97; reference documents, non-print libr. Pace U., White Plains, N.Y., 1997—; cmty. legal resources network libr. CUNY Law Sch., Flushing, N.Y., 1999—. Democrat. Mem. Soc. of Friends. Avocation: acting Shakespeare. Fax: 914-422-4139. E-mail: gboeringer@law.pace.edu. Office: Pace U Law Sch Libr 78 N Broadway White Plains NY 10603-3710

BOERNER, RALPH E. J., forest soil ecologist, plant biology educator; b. Bklyn., Oct. 2, 1948; s. Kurt Heinz and Erika Annalisa (Tappe) B.; m. Elizabeth Ann Wrobel, May 29, 1982; 1 child, Annalisa Marie. BS in Biology, SUNY, Cortland, 1970; MS in Biology and Marine Sci., Adelphi U., 1972; MPh in Botany, Rutgers U., 1974, PhD, 1980. Grad. tchg. asst. Adelphi U., Garden City, N.Y., 1970-72; environ. sci. N.Y. Dept. Environ. Protection, Huntington, N.Y., 1972; grad. tchg. asst., rsch. fellow Rutgers U., New Brunswick, N.J., 1972-74, 78-80; asst. prof. Burlington County Coll., Pemberton, N.J., 1974-78; asst. prof. Ohio State U., Columbus, 1980-86, assoc. prof., 1986-93, prof., 1993—, chair dept. evolution, ecology and Organismal Biology, 1990—; vis. prof. U. de Concepcion, Chile, 1987; cons. Columbus-Franklin County Met. Parks Commn., 1982—, Ohio Dept. Natural Resources, 1983—, The Nature Conservancy, 1988—, Denison U., 1991; contbr. papers to various profl. meetings. Mem. editl. bd. Mycorrhiza; contbr. articles and revs. to profl. jours. Bd. trustees The Nature Conservancy, 1987-95, also chair sci./land protection com., mem. strategic planning com. Predoctoral fellow NSF, 1972; grantee Columbia Gas Corp., 1982-85, Ohio Dept. Natural Resources, 1982-83, 85-86, 86-87, 88, 89-90, 91-92, 92-93, 93-94, Columbia-Franklin County Met. Parks Dist., 1984-89, NSF, 1986-89, 87-88, 89-90, 90-92, Tinker Found., 1987, USDA Forest Svc., 1993; recipient Alumni award for disting. tchg. Ohio State U., 1989, Oak Leaf award The Nature Conservancy, 1992. Fellow AAAS; mem. Am. Inst. Biol. Scis., Acad. Tchg., Ecol. Soc. Am. (mem. Buell Award com. 1981-86, chmn. 1982-85, mem. program com. 198-688, mem. awards com. 1983-86, chmn. local arrangements ann. meeting 1987, mem. profl. ethics com. 1994—), Internat. Assn. Ecology, Internat. Assn. Landscape Ecology, Natural Areas Assn., So. Appalachian Bot. Club, Soil Ecology Soc. Am., Torrey Bot. Club (mem. Hervey Award com. 1980), Sigma Xi. Home: 2759 Chester Rd Columbus OH 43221-3327 Office: Ohio State U Dept Plant Biology 1735 Neil Ave Columbus OH 43210-1220*

BOERNER, SHEILA GERTRUDE, secondary education educator; b. St. Paul, Dec. 10, 1946; d. William Thomas and Ardis Gwendolyn (Rice)Fahey; m. Ronald Ralph Boerner, June 5, 1971; children: James, Kevin, Brian, Sharleen, Anne, Cyndi. BS, U. Minn., 1968; MA, U. Nebr., 1973. Cert. tchr., Nebr. English tchr. North Platte (Nebr.) Sr. H.S., 1968-74, St. Patrick's Jr.-Sr. H.S., North Platte, 1994—. Mem. Nat. Coun. Tchrs. English. Roman Catholic. Avocations: reading, writing poetry, walking. Home: 1802 Birchwood Rd North Platte NE 69101-5910 Office: St Patrick's Jr-Sr HS PO Box 970 North Platte NE 69103-0970

BOERNER-NILSEN, JO M., real estate trainer; b. Wayne, Okla., Apr. 17, 1944; d. James Olman and Virgie M. (Jones) Whitaker; m. Buddy Dennis Boerner, July 3, 1964 (div. 1987); children: Christopher Alexander, James Dennis, Edward Floyd. Grad., Realtor Inst. Okla. State U., 1979. Cert. residential specialist. Assoc. Abide Realtors, Oklahoma City, 1976-83; br. mgr. Merrill Lynch Realtors, Oklahoma City, 1983-86; dir. career devel. Marolyn Pryor & Assocs., Oklahoma City, 1986-87; nat. tng. dir., v.p. Long & Foster Realtors, Fairfax, Va., 1987—, v.p., 1998—; regional v.p. Women's Coun. of Realtors, Chgo., 1987; bd. dir. Oklahoma City Bd. Realtors, 1984-85; instr. Realtors Inst. Okla. State U., 1987. Contbr. articles to profl. jours. Bd. govs. Wednesday's Child Found., Oklahoma City, 1987; mem. Allied Arts Coun., Oklahoma City, 1985-87, Realtors Polit. Action Com., Okla., 1984-87. Recipient State of Excellence award Okla. State Gov., 1987, Omega Tau Rho medal. Mem. Nat. Women's Coun. of Realtors (gov. bd. 1985-87), Nat. Assn. Realtors, Women's Coun. of Realtors (pres. 1985, gov. 1986), Va. Assn. Realtors, Siga Internat. (trustee 1982-83), Toastmasters. Republican. Avocations: travel, writing. Office: Long & Foster Realtors 11351 Random Hills Rd Ste 100 Fairfax VA 22030-7409

BOERRIGTER, GLENN CHARLES, educational administrator; b. Hickman, Nebr., Aug. 25, 1932; s. John Anthony and Ruth (Hupel) B.; m. Carol Marie Dunker, June 13, 1959; children: Dean Glenn, Kay Anne. AB, Nebr. Wesleyan U., 1953; MEd, U. Nebr., 1957, DEd, 1960. Prin., tchr. Daykin, Nebr., 1953-55; prin., supt. Atkinson, Neb., 1955-58; instr. U. Nebr., 1958-60; asst. prof. edn. No. State Tchrs. Coll., Aberdeen, S.D., 1960-61; edn. specialist sch. adminstrn. U.S. Office Edn., Washington, 1961-63, coordinator research, 1963-65, chief adminstrn. studies br., 1965-67, dir. div. elementary and secondary research, 1968-71, chief applied studies br., 1971-72, chief research br., 1972-78, chief program improvement br., 1978-89, dep. dir. div. nat. programs, 1990-94; ret., 1994; cons. ednl. research matters colls., univs., pub. schs. State Dept. Edn. (profit and non-profit groups, also various fgn. govts.). Contbr.: chpt. to Elementary Teacher Education, 1971; also articles profl. jours. Recipient Superior Service award U.S. Office Edn., 1971. Mem. NEA, Am. Ednl. Research Assn., Am. Vocat. Assn., Am. Vocat. Research Assn., Phi Delta Kappa. Presbyterian (elder). Home: PO Box 427 Arlington NE 68002-0427

BOERS, TERRY JOHN, sportswriter, radio and television personality; b. Harvey, Ill., Sept. 13, 1950; s. John and Ruth (Rubottom) B.; m. Carolyn Grace Imgruet, Feb. 20, 1971; children: John, Joseph, Cary, Chris. BJ, No. Ill. U., 1972. Sports editor Sun-Jour. Newspapers, Lansing, Ill., 1972-73; asst. sports editor Star Publs., Chicago Heights, Ill., 1973-78; sports copy editor Detroit Free Press, 1978-80; sports copy editor Chgo. Sun-Times, 1980-82, beat reporter, 1982-88, 90-92, columnist, 1988-90; panelist program The Sportswriters, Sta. WGN-Radio, Chgo., 1988-92; panelist cable TV program Sportsfire, 1990-91, 94-97, co-host, 1990-91; co-host afternoon program Sta. WSCR, Chgo., 1992—; sports columnist Arlington Heights Daily Herald, 1994-98. Author articles for sports mags. Recipient 1st Pl. award for column Ill. AP Sports Editors, 1988, Peter Lisagor award, 1989. Office: Sta WSCR-AM 4949 W Belmont Ave Chicago IL 60641-4332

BOERSEMA, DAVID BRIAN, philosopher, educator; b. Ft. Monroe, Va., Dec. 23, 1951; s. Munroe Eskel and Waneeta Diana (Wren) B. BA, Hope Coll., Holland, Mich., 1973; MA, Mich. State U., 1978, PhD, 1985. Instr. Jackson (Mich.) C.C., 1977-78, Mich. State U., East Lansing, 1979-82, Delta Coll., Midland, Mich., 1982-84; asst. prof. Pacific U., Forest Grove, Oreg., 1985-91, assoc. prof., 1991-97, prof. philosophy, 1997—, Douglas C. Strain prof. of natural philosophy, chair, 1990—. Contbr. articles to profl. jours.

Recipient S.S. Johnson award for tchg. Pacific U., 1994, Arthur and Lois Graves award Pomona Coll., 1994; J.J. Malone Faculty fellow Nat. Coun. on U.S.-Arab Relations, 1992; George F. Baker scholar, 1972. Mem. AAAS, History of Sci. Soc., Philosophy of Sci. Soc., Sigma Xi. Office: Pacific Univ 2043 College Way Forest Grove OR 97116-1797

BOERSMA, P. DEE, zoology educator; d. Henry W. (dec.) and Vivian (Anspach) B. BS, Ctrl. Mich. U., 1969; PhD, Ohio State U., 1974. Asst. prof. Inst. Environ. Studies, U. Wash., Seattle, 1974-80, assoc. prof., 1980-88, prof. environ. studies, 1988-93, prof. zoology, 1988—, adj. prof. women's studies, 1993—, assoc. dir., 1987-93, acting dir., 1990-91; mem. sci. adv. com. for outer continental shelf Environ. Studies Program, Dept. Interior, 1980-83; prin. investigator Magellanic Penguin Project, N.Y. Zool. Soc., 1982—; Evans vis. fellow U. Otago, New Zealand, 1995, Pew fellow in conservation adn the environ., 1997—. Contbr. articles to profl. jours. Mem. adv. U.S. del. to UN Status Women Commn., N.Y.C., 1973, UN World Population Conf., Romania, 1974; mem. Gov. Lowry's Task Force on Wildlife, 1993; sci. adv. EcoBios, 1985-95; bd. dirs. Zero Population Growth, 1975-82, Washington Nature Conservancy, 1995-98, bd. adv. Walt Disney World Animal Kingdom, 1993—, bd. dirs. Perigrine Fund, 1995—, bd. dirs. Bullitt Found., 1997—; mem. scholar diplomatic program Dept. of State, 1977. Recipient Outstanding Alumni award Cen. Mich. U., 1978, Matrix award Women in Comm., 1983; named to Kellogg Nat. Leadership Program, 1982-85; recipient Top 10 Outsiders of Yr. award Outside Mag., 1987, Outstanding Centennial Alumni award Ctrl. Mich. U., 1993; sci. fellow The Wildlife Conservation Soc., 1982—. Fellow Am. Ornithol. Union (regional rep. Pacific seabird group 1981-85); mem. AAAS, Ecol. Soc. Am., Wilson Ornithol. Soc., Cooper Ornithol. Soc., Soc. Am. Naturalists, Soc. for Conservation Biology (bd. govs. 1991-94, pres. elect 1995-97, pres. 1997-99). Club: Gopher Brokers (Seattle pres. 1982-83). Office: U Wash Dept Zoology PO Box 351800 Seattle WA 98195-1800

BOES, LAWRENCE WILLIAM, lawyer; b. Bklyn., Aug. 3, 1935; s. Lawrence and Elizabeth (Schaefer) B.; m. Joan Mary Elward, Oct. 2, 1965; children: Lawrence, Siobhan, Thomas. AB, Columbia Coll., 1961; JD, Columbia U., 1964. Bar: N.Y. 1965, U.S. Dist. Ct. (ea. dist.) N.Y. 1968, U.S. Dist. Ct. (so. dist.) N.Y. 1968, U.S. Ct. Appeals (2d cir.) 1971, U.S. Ct. Appeals (8th cir.) 1974, U.S. Supreme Ct. 1974, U.S. Ct. Appeals (9th cir.) 1982, U.S. Ct. Appeals (3d cir.) 1988. Law clk. to judge U.S. Ct. Appeals (2d cir.), 1964-65; assoc. Reavis & McGrath, N.Y.C., 1965-70, ptnr., 1970-88; ptnr. Fulbright & Jaworski L.L.P., N.Y.C., 1989—. Revs. editor Columbia Law Rev., 1963-64. Mem. Village of Westbury Code Rev. Commn., N.Y., 1983—, chmn., 1991—. Cpl. U.S. Army, 1958-60. Pulitzer scholar N.Y.C. Bd. Edn., 1954; nat. scholar Columbia U., 1962. Mem. ABA, N.Y. State Bar Assn., Bar Assn. Nassau County (chair 1998—, profl. ethics com.), Univ. Glee Club N.Y.C. (sec. 1998—). Avocations: gardening, baseball, glee club singing. Office: Fulbright & Jaworski LLP 666 5th Ave New York NY 10103

BOESCH, DIANE HARRIET, elementary education educator; b. Erie, Pa., July 3, 1942; d. William Jacob and Dorothy Gertrude (Call) B. BS, Edinboro (Pa.) State U., 1964; MA, Kent (Ohio) State U., 1968; postgrad., So. Ill. U., Carbondale, 1969, CUNY, 1972, Norwalk State Tech. Coll., 1979, Northeastern U., Boston, 1982, Fla. State U., 1988. Tchr. math. Iroquois Area Sch. Dist., Erie, 1964-67; grad. asst. Kent State U., 1967-68; tchr., writer Comprehensive Sch. Math. Project, Carbondale, Ill., 1968-70; tchr. math. Weston (Conn.) Pub. Schs., 1970—, dept. chmn. math., 1989—; dir. Weston Tchr. Ctr., 1983-84; condr. workshops on math. and writing, Conn., 1970—. Contbr. articles to profl. publs. Vol. nat. elections, Erie, 1960, West Haven, Conn., 1972. Recipient Celebration of Excellence award Conn. State Dept. Edn., 1988, Presdl. award NSF, 1990. Fellow Conn. Acad. for Edn. in Math. and Sci.; mem. NEA, Nat. Coun. Tchrs. Math., Conn. Educator Talent Pool, Conn. Edn. Assn., Weston Tchr. Assn., Coun. Presdl. Awardees in Math., Pi Mu Epsilon, Kappa Delta Pi. Republican. Lutheran. Avocations: genealogy, writing, music, reading, Atlanta Braves baseball. Office: Hurlbutt Elem Sch 9 School Rd Weston CT 06883-1696

BOESCH, FRANCIS THEODORE, electrical engineer, educator; b. N.Y.C., Sept. 28, 1936; s. Victor and Margaret (Wright) B. B.S., Poly. Inst. N.Y., 1957, M.S., 1960, Ph.D., 1963. Instr., then asst. prof. elec. engring. Poly. Inst. N.Y., 1957-63; mem. mil. research staff Bell Telephone Labs., 1963-68, mem. research staff, 1969-79; prof. elec. engring. and computer sci., dept. head Stevens Inst. Tech., Hoboken, N.J., 1979-88; dean of faculty Stevens Inst. Tech., Hoboken, 1988-93; prof. elec. engring., 1993—; McKay prof. elec. engring. and computer sci. U. Calif., Berkeley, 1968-69. Author: Large-Scale Networks, 1976; editor-in-chief: Networks, 1970-81; editor: Graph Theory, 1978-81; contbr. articles to profl. jours. Vice pres. Fair Haven (N.J.) Little League, 1974; scoutmaster Fair Haven council Boy Scouts Am., 1973-78, dist. commnr. Monmouth council, 1978-80. Fellow IEEE, N.Y. Acad. Scis.; mem. Assn. Computing Machinery, Am. Math. Soc., Sigma Xi, Eta Kappa Nu. Home: 16-02 Everett Ter Fair Lawn NJ 07410-2410 Office: Stevens Inst Tech Castle Point Sta Hoboken NJ 07030

BOESE, GERALDINE FLORENCE, nurse administrator; b. Bklyn., May 12, 1939; d. Jack and Florence (Masamino) Cardullo. AA in Nursing, Fairleigh Dickinson U., 1960; BS, Mercy Coll., 1986. Cert. nursing adminstr. Staff nurse Mount Sinai Hosp., N.Y.C., 1960-61, Englewood (N.J.) Hosp., 1961-64; asst. head nurse N.J. Coll. Medicine, Jersey City, 1964-66; head nurse, acting supr. Mt. Sinai Hosp., N.Y.C., 1966-68; sr. adminstrv. supr. Phelps Meml. Hosp., North Tarrytown, N.Y., 1969-85; asst. dir. field ops. Rain Home Attendant, Bronx, N.Y., 1985-86; dir. br. svcs. U.S. Home Care, Bronx, 1986-87; dir. clin. svcs. Kimberly Quality Care, New Rochelle, N.Y., 1987-92; corp. dir. nursing Unltd. Care Inc., White Plains, N.Y., 1992-94; co-owner, founder, adminstr. Forget-Me-Not Tng., Inc., White Plains, N.Y., 1994—. Recipient Amita Nursing award, 1969, Nurse award N.Y. State Legislature, 1992; named Dir. Clin. Svcs. of Yr. Lower N.Y. Region, 1990. Mem. N.Y. State Nurses Assn. Office: Forget-Me-Not Tng Inc 199 Main St Ste 211 White Plains NY 10601-3204

BOESE, GILBERT KARYLE, cultural organization executive; b. Chgo., June 24, 1937; s. Carl H. and Winifred A. Boese; m. Lillian R. Boese; children: Ann Carroll, Peter Austin, Sara Elisabeth. B.A., Carthage (Ill.) Coll., 1959; M.S., No. Ill. U., 1965; Ph.D.; NIMH trainee 1970, Johns Hopkins U., 1973. Instr. biology Thornton Community Coll., Harvey, Ill., 1965-67; asst. prof. biology Elmhurst (Ill.) Coll., 1967-69; dep. dir. Chgo. Zool. Park, Brookfield, Ill., 1971-80; dir. Milw. County Zool. Gardens, Milw., 1980-89; pres. Zool. Soc. Milw. County, Milw., 1989—, Found. for Wildlife Conservation, 1993—; tech. cons. Belize Zoo and Tropical Edn. Ctr.; founder Birds without Borders Aves Sin Frontera internat. program; dir. Miller Brewery Friends of the Field. Bd. dirs. Dian Fossey Gorilla Found., mem. internat. coordinating com., pres., 1997—; bd. dirs. Lewa Conservancy Kenya; mem. wetlands acquisition com. Pewaukee Lake, Wis. Fellow Royal Geog. Soc., Am. Assn. Zool. Parks and Aquariums (bd. dirs.); mem. Bird Feeder Soc., Hemmingway Soc., Adventurers Club. Office: Zool Soc Milw County 10005 W Bluemound Rd Milwaukee WI 53226-4346

BOESE, LILLIAN R., performing company executive. Exec. dir. Milw. Ballet. Office: Milwaukee Ballet 504 W National Ave Milwaukee WI 53204-1792

BOESE, SANDRA JEAN, publishing executive; b. Ely, Minn., July 31, 1940; d. John Frank and Millie Jean (Prebeg) Simonick; m. Lee Robert Boese Sr., June 15, 1963; children: Lee Robert Jr., Joy Karin. BA in Speech and Elem. Edn., Marquette U., 1962. Elem. tchr., 1962-67; pub., editor Classroom Connections, Inc., Merced and Sacramento, 1988—, also chmn. bd.; pres. Calif. State Bd. Edn., Sacramento, 1984-86; exec. dir. Teen Talk Radio Show, 1994—. Trustee Merced City Sch. Dist., 1975-83; commr. Calif. Post-Secondary Edn. Commn., Sacramento, 1983; bd. dirs. Far-West Lab., San Francisco, 1984, The Achievement Coun., San Francisco, 1985. Recipient Commendation of Exemplary Svc. award Calif. State Senate, 1983, Cert. of Appreciation, Calif. State Dept. Edn., 1983; named Woman of Distinction Soroptimist Internat., 1987. Mem. AAUW (Woman of Distinction 1986), Calif. Sch. Bds. Assn. (bd. dirs. del. assembly, 1978-81, chmn. conf. 1979-80, founder chmn. polit. action com. 1982-83, Outstanding Svc. award 1982, Spl. Recognition 1986), Merced City C. of C. (pres. 1985-86, Athena award 1988), Nat. Assn. State Bds. Edn. (bd. dirs. 1984-86), Assn. Marquette U. Women (Mary Neville Bielefeld award 1986). Republican. Roman Catholic. Avocations: painting, decorating, wardrobe design, jogging. Office: Classroom Connections Inc 2824 Park Ave Ste C Merced CA 95348

BOESE, TED C., furniture designer; b. Oshkosh, Wis., Aug. 14, 1931; s. Walter Paul and Bertha Alma (Meyer) B.; m. Paula C. Schriefer, July 19, 1958; children: Tania, Eric, Lori. Grad. high sch., Detroit, 1949. Apprentice woodworker Splty. Cab, Detroit, 1950-52; ptnr. Boese Wood Products, Detroit, 1954-76; owner, pres. Penta Assoc., Petoskey, Mich., 1976-96, retired, 1996. Inventor needle guard for syringe, 1989. Sgt. U.S. Army, 1952-54, Korea. Avocations: computer programs, CADD layouts of furniture and furniture design. Home and Office: 7920 10 Mile Rd NE Rockford MI 49341-8304

BOESEL, CHARLES MATHER, communications professional. BA in Polit. Sci. and Comm., DePauw U., 1986. With Rep. Nat. Com., 1986-87, Commn. on the Bicentennial of the U.S. Constn., 1987, Victory '88/1988 Rep. Nat. Conv., 1987-89, U.S. Dept. Edn., 1989-90, Premier Concierge, Inc., 1990-91; spokesperson U.S. Dept. Labor, 1991-93; chief spokesman Office of U.S. Rep. Thomas J. Bliley, Jr., 1993-95; comm. dir. Office of U.S. Senator Mike DeWine, 1995—. Office: 140 Russell Senate Office Washington DC 20510-3503

BOESEL, MILTON CHARLES, JR., lawyer, business executive; b. Toledo, July 12, 1928; s. Milton Charles and Florence (Fitzgerald) B.; m. Lucy Laughlin Mather, Mar. 25, 1961; children: Elizabeth Boesel Sagges, Charles Mather, Andrew Fitzgerald. BA, Yale U., 1950; LLB, Harvard U., 1953. Bar: Ohio 1953, Mich. 1953. chmn., bd. dirs. Michabo, Inc.; bd. dirs. Fifth Third Bank of Northwestern Ohio. Lt. USNR, 1953-56. Episcopalian. Clubs: Toledo Country; Leland Country (Mich.). Sawgrass Country (Fla.). Home: 5520 S Citation Rd Toledo OH 43615-2154

BOESHE, BARBARA LOUISE, real estate executive; b. Phila.; d. Raymond Gerard and Gilda (Nicotera) Lepone; children: Diedrich R., Alison Dru, Tyson Phillip. BS, Temple U., 1963. Lic. real estate broker, N.J. Sales person Sofroney Real Estate, Sea Isle City, N.J., 1978-88; office mgr. Hoey Real Estate, Sea Isle City, 1988-93; pres. Farina & Boeshe Real Estate Co., Sea Isle City, 1994—; ptnr., developer Boeshe-Federico, Sea Isle City, 1986-90. Vice chmn. bd. adjustment, Sea Isle City, 1982-86, active Mayor's Adv. Com., 1985-86, Parking Authority, 1984-85; committeewoman Rep. County Com., Sea Isle City, 1982-85, 89-90, alt. Rep. city leader, 1991-92, 1992—; v.p. Cape May County Planning Bd., 1992-94, chairperson, 1994—. Recipient, 5 Million dollar Gold Awd., Greater Wildwood Cape May County Bd. Realtors, 1998. Mem. Sea Isle City C. of C. (bd. dirs., sec. 1986-89, treas. 1989-90, v.p. 1991-92, pres. 1992-95), Greater Wildwood/Cape May County Bd. Realtors (million dollar award 1982-88, 92-95, 2-1/2 million dollar award 1989-91, 2-1/2 million dollar award 1996, 97). Roman Catholic. Home: 13 74th St Sea Isle City NJ 08243-1326 Office: Farina & Boeshe Real Estate Co 4315 Landis Ave Sea Isle City NJ 08243-1828

BOESKIN, BRYAN EDWARD, public administrator; b. Norman, Okla., May 5, 1964; s. Dan Edward and Catherine Kennedy Reyes B. BA in Polit. Sci., History, U. Okla., 1991; MA in Polit. Sci., Calif. State U., L.A., 1995. Adminstr. aid City of La Mirada, Calif., 1993-95; adminstr. analyst City of Santa Clarita, Calif., 1995-97; mgmt. analyst City of Arcadia, Calif., 1997—. Mem. Municipal Mid Mgrs. Assn. So. Calif. Sgt. U.S. Army, 1984-87. Mem. Am. Soc. Pub. Adminstrs. Fax: 626-359-7028. E-mail: bboeskin@excite. Home: 327 Genoa Unit B Monrovia CA 90106 Office: City of Arcadia 11800 Goldring Rd Arcadia CA 91066

BOESPFLUG, JOHN FRANCIS, JR., lawyer; b. 1944. AB, Whitman Coll., 1966; JD, U. Wash., 1969. Bar: Wash. 1969. Of counsel Bogle & Gates, Bellevue, Wash., 1994—. Mem. ABA. Office: Bogle & Gates 10500 NE 8th St Ste 1500 Bellevue WA 98004-4398

BOETTCHER, ARMIN SCHLICK, lawyer, banker; b. East Bernard, Tex., Apr. 12, 1941; s. Clem C. and Frances Helene (Schlick) B.; m. Virginia Nan Barkley, Apr. 13, 1963; children: Lynn Frances, Laura Anne. BBA, U. Tex., Austin, 1963, JD, 1967. Various positions personal trust dept. Republic Bank Houston, 1967-75, sr. v.p., trust officer, head trust dept., 1975-82; exec. v.p., dir. Union State Bank, East Bernard, 1988-98; exec. vice pres. First Prosperity Bank, East Bernard, 1998—. Bd. dirs. Whispering Oaks Civic Club, 1980-85, pres., 1981. Mem. Houston Bus. and Estate Planning Council, Houston Bar Assns., U. Tex. Ex-Students Assn. (life), Meml. Forest Club (dir. 1981-83), Sigma Chi. Methodist. Office: First Prosperity Bank Bldg PO Box 40 Easr Bernard TX 77435

BOETTCHER, HAROLD PAUL, engineer, educator; b. Eagle, Wis., July 24, 1923; s. Emil Ernst and Henrietta (Seefeld) B.; m. Dorothy Strandberg, Feb. 1, 1948; children—David Paul, John Harold, Mark Alan. B.S., U. Wis., 1947, M.S., 1950, Ph.D., 1954. Registered profl. engr., Wis. Instr. mechanics U. Wis., Madison, 1946-54; research dir. electric motor lab. A.O. Smith Corp., Milw., 1954-61; assoc. prof. U. Wis., Milw., 1961-65, prof., 1965-88, prof. emeritus, 1988—, chmn. dept., 1965-69, 74-77. Served with USN, 1944-46. Mem. IEEE (sr.), Am. Soc. Engring. Edn., Sigma Xi. Home: W230S3411 Milky Way Rd Waukesha WI 53189-7941 Office: U Wis Milwaukee WI 53201

BOETTCHER, NORBE BIROSEL, chemist; b. Manila, June 6, 1932; d. Dionisio Martinez and Filomena (Cuaresma) Birosel; m. Robert Arnold Boettcher, June 6, 1961; 1 child, Heidi Noriko. BS in Chemistry, Philippine Women's U., 1953; postgrad., U. Iowa, 1955-57. Chemist, rsch. and devel. Lawry's Foods, Inc., L.A., 1957-61; chemist, quality control, rsch. and devel. Sunsweet Products, San Jose, Calif., 1964-68; teaching asst., rsch. chemist Coe Coll., Cedar Rapids, Iowa, 1969-77; chemist, rsch. and devel. Penford Products Co., Cedar Rapids, 1977-92, analytical chemist customer lab. svc., 1992-98, ret., 1998. Mem. Brucemore, Inc., Cedar Rapids, Met. Opera Guild, N.Y.C. Mem. AAAS, AAUW, Cedar Rapids Art Mus., Philippine-Am. Club (social chmn. 1987-89, pres. Linn County, Iowa 1989-91, bd. dirs. 1992—), Iowa Poetry Assn. Republican. Roman Catholic. Research in ring reactions on chlorophyll A and starch content in paper by HPLC. Avocations: poetry, music, travel. Home: 348 7th St Marion IA 52302-3325 Office: Penford Products Co 1st St SW Cedar Rapids IA 52406

BOEX, JAMES RICHARD, academic administrator, medical researcher; b. Cambridge, N.Y., Mar. 8, 1948; s. Lewis Francis and Harriet Clare (Fremont) B.; m. Susan Thorne, Jan. 1976 (div. May 1989); children: Leendra, Lewis, Christian, Allison, Noelle; m. Denise Dawn Gibson, Apr. 25, 1992. BA, SUNY, Buffalo, 1970; MBA, Kent State U., 1991. Asst. dean NEOUCOM, Rootstown, Ohio, 1977-83, assoc. dean, spl. asst. to pres., 1983-93, dir. office health svcs., 1993—; edn. asst. Roswell Pk. Med. Inst., Buffalo, 1972-77. Contbr. articles to profl. jours. Mem. Assn. Hosp. Med. Edn. (bd. dirs. 1986-90), Health Pub. Network (mem. steering com. 1996). Avocations: gardening, photography. E-mail: jrb@neoucom.edu. Office: NEOUCOM 4209 State Rte 44 Rootstown OH 44272

BOFAY, FRED, university administrator. B in Civil Engring., Miss. State U.; MS in Structures, U. Ky.; PhD, Va. Poly. Inst. Asst. dean for engring. edn., dir. civil engring. program Vanderbilt U.; chmn. dept. civil engring., assoc. dean acad. affairs W.Va. U.; dean Engring. Coll. Wayne State U., 1986-95; pres. N.Y.C. Tech. Coll., Bklyn., 1998—; vis. prof. U. Liverpool, Eng., U. Wales Univ. Coll., Cardiff, U. Autonoma Met., Azcapotzalco, Mex.; dir. Greenfield Coalition, 1996; presenter in field. Author 2 textbooks; contbr. numerous tech. and profl. papers to profl. jours. Recipient Centennial medallion Am. Soc. for Engring. Edn., Civil Engring. Divsn.'s George K. Waldin award, Gold award Detroit's Affiliate Coun. Office: 300 Jay St Brooklyn NY 11201-1909

BOFF, KENNETH RICHARD, engineering research psychologist; b. N.Y.C., Aug. 17, 1947; s. Victor and Ann (Yunko) B.; m. Judith Marion Schoer, Aug. 2, 1969 (dec. Apr. 1997); children: Cory Asher, Kyra Melissa. BA, CUNY, 1969, MA, 1972; MPhil, Columbia U., 1975, PhD, 1978. Research scientist Human Resources Lab., Wright Patterson AFB, Ohio, 1977-80; sr. scientist Armstrong Aerospace Med. Rsch. Lab. (now Armstrong Lab.), Wright Patterson AFB, Ohio, 1980—, dir. design tech., 1980-91; dir. human engring. div. Armstrong Aerospace Med. Rsch. Lab. (now Armstrong Lab.), 1991-97; chief scientist, human effectiveness directorate Air Force Rsch. Lab., 1997—; project custodian Internat. Air. Standard Coordination Com., Washington, 1984; chmn. com. Tri-Service Human Factors Tech. Adv. Group, Washington, 1984—; chair human factors com. NATO Adv. Group Aerospace R&D, Paris, 1992—; chair human sys. tech. panel Dept. Def., 1994-97; U.S. coord. NATO Rsch. and Tech. Orgn. Human Factors, 1997—. Editor: Handbook of Perception and Human Performance, 1986, Human Engineering Data Compendium, 1988, System Design: Behavioral Perspectives on designers, Tools and Organizations, 1987; contbr. articles to profl. jours. Travel grantee Rank Prize Found., Cambridge, Eng., 1984; named Air Force Scientist of the Quarter, 1989; recipient Patent award for rap-com display tech., 1989, Human Factors Soc. award for best publ., 1989. Mem. IEEE, Human Factors Soc., Am. Psychol. Assn. (div. 21 engring. psychology). Avocations: computers, photography. Home: 6510 Shadow Wynd Cir Dayton OH 45459-2343 Office: Armstrong Lab Human Engring Divsn Wright Patterson AFB OH 45433

BOGAARD, WILLIAM JOSEPH, lawyer; b. Sioux City, Iowa, Jan. 18, 1938; s. Joseph and Irene Marie (Hensing) B.; m. Claire Marie Whalen, Jan. 28, 1961; children: Michele, Jeannine, Joseph, Matthew. BS, Loyola Marymount U., L.A., 1959; JD with honors, U. Mich., 1965. Bar: Calif. 1966, U.S. Dist. Ct. (ctrl. dist.) Calif. 1966. Ptnr. Agnew, Miller & Carlson, L.A., 1970-82; exec. v.p., gen. counsel 1st Interstate Bancorp, L.A., 1982-96; vis. prof. securities regulation and banking Mich. Law Sch., Ann Arbor, 1996-97; lectr. securities regulation and corps. U. So. Calif. Law Sch., L.A., 1997—; mem. Calif. Commn. on Jud. Nominees Evaluation, 1997-99. Mem. city coun., mayor City of Pasadena, Calif., 1978-86, 99—. Capt. USAF, 1959-62. Mem. ABA, Calif. State Bar, Los Angeles County Bar Assn. (Corp. Counsel of Yr. award 1988). Avocations: jogging, French and Spanish languages, hiking. Office: U So Calif Law Sch 699 Exposition Blvd # 442 Los Angeles CA 90007-4003

BOGAN, ELIZABETH CHAPIN, economist, educator; b. Morristown, N.J., Aug. 22, 1944; d. Daryl Muscott and Tirzah (Walker) Chapin; m. Thomas Rockwood Bogan, June 5, 1965; children: Nathaniel Rockwood, Andrew Allerton. AB, Wellesley Coll., 1966; MA, U. N.H., 1967; PhD, Columbia U., 1971. Mem. faculty Fairleigh Dickinson U., Madison, N.J., 1971-92, prof. econs., 1982-92; chmn. merit scholarship com. Farleigh Dickinson U., Madison, N.J., 1981-82, reviewer univ. press; mem. faculty Princeton (N.J.) U., sr. lectr. in econs., 1992—; vis. prof. Princeton U., 1991. author articles and macroecons. text. Recipient Outstanding Tchr. award Fairleigh Dickinson U., 1979, 86, 87, Richard Quandt award for tchg. econs. Princeton U., 1997; NSF fellow, Pres'. fellow, Earhart fellow Columbia U., 1968-71. Mem. AAUP, Am. Econ. Assn., Ea. Econ. Assn., Atlantic Econ. Soc. Congregationalist. Clubs: Wellesley, Beacon Hill. Home: 41 Windermere Ter Short Hills NJ 07078-2254 Office: Princeton U 109 Fisher Pl Princeton NJ 08540

BOGAN, MARY FLAIR, stockbroker; b. Providence, July 9, 1948; d. Ralph A.L. and Mary (Dyer) B.; B.A., Vassar Coll., 1969. Actress, Trinity Sq. Repertory Co., R.I., Gretna Playhouse, Pa., Skylight Comic Opera, Milw., Cin. Playhouse, Playmakers' Repertory, N.C.; mem. nat. co. No Sex, Please, We're British; also TV commls., 1970-77; account exec. E.F. Hutton & Co., Inc., Providence, 1977-88; account v.p. Paine Webber, 1986-97, v.p. investments Prudential Securities, Providence, 1997—; econ. reporter Sta. WPRI-TV, 1982-85, Sta. WJAR-TV, 1987—. Recipient Century Club award, 1980, 81, 82, 83, 85; Blue Chip Sales award, 1983, 85, Pacesetter Sales Award, 1986-90. Named. Woman of the Yr. Profl. Bus. and Rep. Women's Assn. Mem. Barker Players, Univ. Club, Brown Faculty. Home: 18 Cooke St Providence RI 02906-2023 Office: Prudential Securities 900 Fleet Center 50 Kennedy Plz Providence RI 02903-2393

BOGARD, CAROLE CHRISTINE, lyric soprano; b. Cin.; d. Harold and Helen Christina (Whittlesey) Geistweit; m. Charles Paine Fisher, Dec. 30, 1966; children: Christine, Pamela. Student, San Francisco State U. Debuts include: Despina in Cosi fan Tutte (Mozart), San Francisco, 1965, Poppea in Coronation of Poppea (Monteverdi), Netherlands Opera, 1971; other appearances include, Boston Opera, N.E.T., orchs. Boston, Madrid, Minn., Phila., Pitts., San Francisco, summer festivals, Mostly Mozart, N.Y., Tanglewood, Carmel, Aston Magna, Gt. Barrington, Mass., appeared in concerts throughout Europe and with Smithsonian Chamber Players, 1976—; recorded numerous albums including 1st rec. of songs of John Duke for his 80th birthday, 1979, recital of Groupe des Six; premiered songs of Dominic Argento in, Holland, 1978, songs of Richard Cumming (in collaboration with Donald Gramm); regular participant rec. and scholarly projects, Smithsonian Instn.; judge regional auditions, Boston; tchr., with emphasis on technique as taught in last Century. Mem. Sigma Alpha Iota. Home: 161 Belknap Rd Framingham MA 01701-3886 *In my career, I've stuck to old-fashioned principles - trying to use my talent according to the standards which place singing technique on a level with the most taxing instruments. I sing for sincere acclaim and demand for my talent and my music, avoiding repertoire which would abuse my voice. I have refrained from pushing myself through "arranged" magazine articles about my hobbies and insipid appearances on TV talk shows. I have done my best rather than my most - by choice.*

BOGARD, LAWRENCE JOSEPH, lawyer; b. Champaign, Ill., July 12, 1952; s. Morris Ray and Norma Jean (Shingleton) B.; m. Rebecca Lynn Jackson, May 6, 1978; children: Caitlyn Elizabeth, Peter Jackson. AB, Vassar Coll., Poughkeepsie, N.Y., 1974; JD, Georgetown U., 1977. Bar: D.C. 1977. Atty. U.S. Customs Svc., Washington, 1977-80; assoc. Cladouhos & Brashares, Washington, 1980-84; atty. U.S. Dept. Commerce, Washington, 1984; ptnr. Rose, Schmidt, Hasley & Disalle, Washington, 1984-88, McKenna & Cuneo, Washington, 1988-98, Neville, Peterson & Williams, Washington, 1998—; faculty Practicing Law Inst., 1984, 92; mem. U.S.-Can. Free Trade Agreement Ch. 19 Dispute Resolution Roster, 1991-94, panelist, 1992, panel chair 1993; mem. NAFTA Dispute Resolution Roster, 1994—. Author: (with others) Commerce Speaks on Antidumping, 1984, Treatment of Non-Market Economies Under U.S. Antidumping and Countervailing Duty Law: A Petitioner's Perspective, 1992; supervisory editor Customs Law and Administration, 1998—. Mem. ABA, D.C. Bar Assn., Ct. Internat. Trade Bar Assn. Democrat. Presbyterian. Office: Neville Peterson & Williams 1233 20th St NW Washington DC 20036-2304

BOGARDUS, CARL ROBERT, JR., radiologist, educator; b. Hyden, Ky., June 26, 1933; s. Carl Robert and Jeannette Wanda (Eversole) B.; m. Norma Gail Shields, June 24, 1956; children—Carl Robert III, Cynthia Gail. B.A., Hanover Coll., 1955; M.D., U. Louisville, 1959. Diplomate: Am. Bd. Radiology, Am. Bd. Nuclear Medicine. Intern Penrose Cancer Hosp., Colorado Springs, Colo., 1959-60; resident Penrose Cancer Hosp., 1960-63; mem. staff U. Okla. Med. Center, 1963-95, prof. emeritus dept. radiation therapy; dir. Okla. Cancer Treatment Ctr., Midwest City; cons. Okla. hosps.; pres. Cancer Care Network, Inc. Author: Practical Applied Physics of Radiology and Nuclear Medicine, 1969; contbg. author: Benign and Malignant Tumors of the Bladder, 1971, Radiation Biology for the Physician, 1973; Contbr. profl. jours. Fellow Am. Coll. Radiology (bd. chancellors, sec.-treas. 1987-91, pres. 1991-92); mem. Okla. Soc. Nuclear Medicine (charter pres. 1966), Am. Soc. Therapeutic Radiology (nat. sec. 1968-70, treas. 1987-88, pres. 1989-90), S.W. Regions Soc. Nuclear Medicine, Okla. Radiol. Soc. (treas. 1970, pres. 1974-75, counselor to Am. Coll. Radiology 1976-85), Okla. County Radiol. Soc. (pres. 1974). Home: 3224 Lamp Post Ln Oklahoma City OK 73120-5621 Office: 230 N Midwest Blvd Midwest City OK 73110-4321

BOGART, CAROL LYNN, writer, media consultant; b. Lakewood, Ohio, Mar. 9, 1949; d. Lloyd William and Evelyn Mary (Overmyer) B.; 1 child, Michael Lloyd. BLS, Bowling Green State U., 1973; grad.training prog., Nat. Theater Conservatory, Denver, 1992. Reporter, anchor Sta. WNEP-TV, Scranton, Pa., 1975-76; reporter Sta. WXIA-TV, Atlanta, 1976-79; reporter, fill-in morning anchor Sta. WLS-TV, Chgo., 1979-82; anchor, reporter Sta. KMGH-TV, Denver, 1982-89; media cons., video producer, voice-over and on-camera talent Bogart Inc., Denver, 1989-93, Tiffin, Ohio, 1997—; reporter, field prodr., writer Stas. WOIO-WUAB-TV, Cleve., 1995-96; radio host Sta. WTTF, Tiffin, 1996; lifestyles editor, columnist Advertiser-Tribune, Tiffin, OH, 1998—; columnist, informed investorphotographer

Kostech Corp., Reno, 1998—; lifestyles editor, columnist, photographer The Advertiser-Tribune, Tiffin, 1998—; talk show host TV 21, Fremont, Ohio, 1996-97; N.W. Ohio stringer AP, 1998—; propr. Paradise Farm Nature Ctr.; corr. The Toledo Blade, 1998—; guest speaker various schs. and univs., Denver, 1982-93, Cleve. 1994-96, Tiffin, 1997—. contr. Country Living Mag. Vol. pet therapy, grief counseling, advocate for children with AD(H)D. Mem. AFTRA, SAG, Nat. Assn. Broadcast Engrs. and Techs., Tiffin C. of C., Ohio Farm Bur., Optimists, Toastmasters. Avocations: breeder of Basset hounds and Himalayan cats, gardening, investing, photography, real estate development.

BOGART, JUDITH SAUNDERS, public relations executive; b. Batesville, Ind., Nov. 16, 1936; d. David Rodman and Anne Eva (Kohles) Saunders; m. William Robert Bogart, Oct. 22, 1971. BA, Baldwin-Wallace Coll., 1958. Dir. pub. rels. Greater Cin. Girl Scout Coun., 1958-61, Nation's Capital Girl Scout Coun., Washington, 1963-65, Gt. Rivers Girl Scout Coun., Washington, 1965-68; account rep. Edn. Funds Inc., Providence, 1967-68; dir. cmty. rels. Cin. Human Rels. Commn., 1968-76; cmty. rels. cons. Cin., 1976-77; v.p. pub. rels. Jewish Hosp. Cin., 1977-85; exec. v.p. Diversified Communicatons Inc., Cin., 1985-88; pres. Judith Bogart Assocs., Cin., 1989-91; dir. pub. rels. Sive/Young & Rubicam, Cin., 1991-96. Pres. Gt. Rivers coun. Girl Scouts U.S., 1984-87, bd. dirs., 1987—; bd. dirs. Nat. Coun. Internat. Visitors, Washington, 1988-95, chmn., 1991-93; trustee Cin. Internat. Visitors Ctr., 1981-87; co-chmn. pub. rels. Greater Cin. Bicentennial, 1985-88; mem. planning bd. United Way, Cin., 1987—; mem. cmty. rels. bd. Xavier U., Cin., 1983—, chmn., 1991—; bd. dirs. Family Svc. Cin. Area, 1995—; chmn. bd. WGUC Cmty. Bd., 1993—; pub. rels. chair Kids Voting S.W. Ohio, 1996—; pres. Cin.-Kharkiv Sister City Project, 1999—. Named Career Woman of Achievement, YWCA, 1983. Fellow Pub. Rels. Soc. Am. (accredited, nat. pres. 1983, pres. Cin. chpt. 1976, Outstanding Mem. 1977); mem. Women in Comms., Inc. (nat. headliner 1982, nat. pub. rels. com., Outstanding Woman in Comms. 1976), N.Am. Pub. Rels. Coun. (pres. 1989), Bankers Club (bd. govs. 1995—, Inst. for Cmty. Capacity Bldg., bd. dirs. 1995—).

BOGART, KEITH CHARLES, neurologist; b. Lorain, Ohio, Apr. 12, 1936; s. Lloyd William and Evelyn (Overmyer) B.; m. B. Diane Seigel, June 8, 1967; children: Keith Charles Jr., Catherine Michelle; m. Alice Craib, July 21, 1976; 1 child, Matthew William. BA, Ohio State U., 1958, MD, 1961. Diplomate Am. Bd. Psychiatry and Neurology, Am. Bd. Qualification in EEG, Am. Bd. Neurorehabilitation. Asst. prof. neurology U. Wis., Madison, 1968-69, Creighton U., Omaha, Nebr., 1975-78; chmn. neurology Gunderson Clinic, Lacrosse, Wis., 1969-75; clin. neurologist Mansfield (Ohio) Neurology, Inc., 1978-99; med. dir. rehab. unit Mansfield Gen. Hosp., 1988-91; med. dir. SCCI Hosp., Mansfield, 1998; cons. neurology VA Hosp., Omaha, 1977-78. Bd. dirs. Boy Scouts Am., Mansfield, 1986. Served to lt. comdr. USPHS, 1963-65. Fellow Am. Acad. Neurology, Am. EEG Soc. (mem. lab. accreditation bd. 1984-87); mem. AMA (Physician's Recognition award 1969, 72, 77, 82, 86, 87, 88, 91, 94, 97), Ctrl. Assn. EEGers (pres. 1977-78), Nebr. Epilepsy League (pres. 1976-78), Wis. Med. Soc. (chmn. neurology sect. 1975), Wis. Neurol. Soc. (pres. 1973), Richland County Med. Soc. (pres. 1988, sec.-treas. 1986—), Knights of Magic (pres. 1986-87, Magician of Yr. 1984, 85, 86), Internat. Brotherhood Magicians (v.p. ter. 1986-91, Presdl. citation 1988), Inner Magic Circle (assoc.), Internat. Platform Assn., Rotary. Avocations: professional magician, travel, golf, reading. Home: 3 Sprunt Pond Hilton Head SC 29928 Office: Mansfield Neurology Inc 222 Marion Ave Mansfield OH 44903-2100

BOGART, LOUISE BERRY, education educator; b. N.Y.C., July 15, 1942; d. Herbert George and Flora Louise (Porcelli) Berry; m. Burton Stanley Bogart, Aug. 29, 1965; children: Samuel Isaac, Jonathan Douglas. BA, Kans. State U., 1964; MEd, Coll. Notre Dame, Belmont, Calif., 1973; postgrad., U. Hawaii-Manoa, 1991—. Cert. Montessori tchr.; cert. pvt. tchr., Hawaii; cert. tchr., prin., Ohio; cert. neurolinguistic profl., neurolinguistic master. Field advisor, sr. program dir., day camp dir. Kaw Valley Girl Scout Coun., Topeka, 1964-65; field advisor Seal of Ohio Girl Scout Coun., Columbus, 1966-67; elem. tchr. St. Joseph Mntessori Sch., Columbus, 1970-78; pre-kindergarten tchr. Maryknoll Grade Sch., Honolulu, 1978-80; head tchr. elem. classes Montessori Cmty. Sch., Honolulu, 1980-83; asst. prof. edn. Chaminade U. of Honolulu, 1982-92, assoc. prof. edn., 1993—, acting chair dept. edn., 1988-90, dept. chair, 1994-96, Montessori Program dir., 1986-92. Active Girl Scouts U.S., Honolulu, 1978—. Eisenhower grantee U.S. Dept. Edn., 1989-90, 90-91, 91-92, 93-94, 95-96, others. Mem. ASCD, Am. Montessori Soc. (vice chair 1987-91), Montessori Assn. Hawaii (v.p. 1980-81), Nat. Assn. Edn. of Young children, Hawaii Assn. Edn. of Young Children, Hawaii Coun. Tchrs. Math., Internat. Inst. Peace Educators, World Coun. for Curriculum and Instrn. Home: 1131 Kaumoku St Honolulu HI 96825-1303 Office: Chaminade U Honolulu 3140 Waialae Ave Honolulu HI 96816-1510

BOGART, PAUL, film director; b. N.Y.C., Nov. 21, 1919; s. Benjamin and Molly (Glass) B.; m. Alma Jane Gitnick, Mar. 22, 1941; children: Peter Gareth, Tracy Katherine, Jennifer Jane. Ed. pub. schs., N.Y.C. Puppeteer, actor Berkeley Marionettes, 1946-48; stage mgr., assoc. dir. NBC, 1950-52; freelance dir. film and TV, 1952—; lectr. New Sch. Social Research, 1960, ANTA, 1960, Memphis State U., 1968-84 , U. Calif., Irvine, 1979, UCLA, 1979, Loyola Marymount, 1981, Tisch Film Sch., NYU, 1991. TV prodns. include U.S. Steel Hour, Kraft Theatre, Armstrong Circle Theatre, Goodyear Playhouse, Hallmark Hall of Fame, 1953-60, The Defenders, 1963 (Emmy award 1964-65), Dear Friends (Emmy award 1967-68), Shadow Game (Emmy award 1969-70), Ages of Man, 1965, Final War of Ollie Winter, 1966, All in the Family, 1975-79 (Emmy awards 1977-78), The Golden Girls (Emmy award 1985-86), The War Widow (PBS), The Shady Hill Kidnapping (PBS), Weekend (PBS), Nutcracker: Money, Madness and Murder, 1987, Natica Jackson, 1987; films include Marlowe, 1968, Halls of Anger, 1969, Skin Game, 1971, Class of '44, 1973, Mr. Ricco, 1975, Oh, God! You Devil, 1984, The Canterville Ghost, 1986, Torch Song Trilogy, 1988, Broadway Bound, 1991, The Heidi Chronicles, 1995. Served with USAAF, 1944-46. Recipient Christopher award 1955, 73, 75, Human Arts award Community Relations Conf. So. Calif., 1964, Humanitas award, 1977-78, Golden Globe award, 1977, So. Calif. Motion Picture Council award, 1979, Film Adv. Bd. award, 1979, Homage award Eurofipa D'Honneur, Cannes Film Festival, 1991. Mem. Dirs. Guild Am. (nat. dir. 1962, 79, 80-81, 87, awards 1977-78), Writers Guild Am., Am. Film Inst., Acad. Motion Picture Arts and Scis. (bd. govs. 1979-81), Acad. TV Arts and Scis., Soc. Stage Dirs. and Choreographers. Office: 1900 Ave Of Stars Ste 1040 Los Angeles CA 90067-4401

BOGART, REBECCA A., musician, educator; b. Palo Alto, Calif., Sept. 6, 1960. BSBA summa cum laude, U. Calif., Berkeley, 1981; MusM in Piano Performance, San Francisco Conservatory, 1985. Tchr., owner Rebecca Bogart Piano Studio, various, 1977—; rsch. analyst First Deposit Corp., San Francisco, 1982-87; concert pianist, 1983—; group mgr. Preeman Music, Arcadia, Costa Mesa, Mission Viego, San Diego, 1993. Recipient prize Carmel Music Soc. Competition, 1986, Pacific Internat. Piano Competition, 1987, 2 prizes San Francisco Bay Area Keyboard Arts Competition, 1996, Ibla Grand Prize Internat. Comp., Ragusa, Sicily, 1998; Alfred Hertz fellow U. Calif., Berkeley, 1986, Montalvo fellow Villa Montalvo Ctr. Arts, Saratoga, Calif., 1989. Mem. Chamber Music Am., Music Tchrs. Nat. Assn. (cert.), Music Tchrs. Assn. Calif. (v.p. Alameda County br. 1996-98), Phi Beta Kappa. Avocations: cooking, gardening.

BOGART, WILLIAM HARRY, lawyer; b. Sayre, Pa., Mar. 5, 1931; s. Harry M. and Luella C. Bogart; AB, Duke U., 1953; AAA, The Hague Acad. Internat. Law, 1962; JD, Syracuse U., 1963; m. Karin Rudolph, Dec. 12, 1962 (div. Dec. 1987); children: Barbara, Silke. Bar: N.Y., 1964. Mem. firm Ali, Gerber, Parr & Bogart, Syracuse, N.Y., 1966-67, Bogart & Andrews, Syracuse, 1967-77; mem. firm Bogart & Assocs., P.C., Syracuse, 1977—; cons. in field to various govts, fin. instns., ednl. instns.; lectr. in field. Contbr. articles to profl. jours. Drafted civil rights laws for Czechoslovak Constn. Mem. missionary com. Presbyterian Ch., 1974-77; active with Acad. Scis. and Russian Govt. drawing comml., ins. and banking laws. Served with USMC, 1951-52. Mem. ABA, Am. Arbitration Assn., N.Y. State Bar Assn., N.Y. State Trial Lawyers Assn., Onondaga County Bar Assn., Assn. of Attenders and Alumni, Lawyers Intergroups, World Ct., Assn. Atty. and Advocates, UN Assn., Univ. Club, Army and Navy Club, Witte Soc. Dem Hague Club, Masons (32d degree). Democrat. Home: 110 E Lake Rd Skaneateles NY 13152-9110 Office: 1600 State Tower Bldg 109 S Warren St Syracuse NY 13202

BOGDAN, JOANN, retail executive. Chief acctg. officer, contrl. Dayton Hudson Corp., Mpls. Office: Dayton Hudson Corp 777 Nicollet Mall Fl 13 Minneapolis MN 55402-2055

BOGDANOFF, JOHN LEE, aeronautical engineering educator; b. East Orange, N.J., May 25, 1916; s. Paul George and Louise (Oswald) B.; m. Ruth Franklin Brown, Sept. 9, 1945; children: Sue Carol, Paul Lawson. B.M.E., Syracuse U., 1938; S.M., Harvard U., 1939; Ph.D., Columbia U., 1950. Asst. project engr. Wright Aero. Corp., Paterson, N.J., 1939-46; instr. civil engring. Columbia U., 1946-50; faculty Purdue U., Lafayette, Ind., 1950—; prof. engring. scis. Purdue U., from 1953; now prof. emeritus, former head Purdue U. (Sch. Aero., Astronautics and Engring. Schs.); treas. Kozin-Bogdanoff & Assos.; cons. to industry, 1950; past v.p., dir. Midwest Applied Sci. Corp., Lafayette. Author articles in field. Fellow ASME, AAAS; mem. Am. Phys. Soc., Nat. Acad. Engring., Sigma Xi. Research in dynamics, vibration, fatigue, wear, cumulative damage theory, application of stochastic processes to engring. problems. Home: 327 Laurel Dr West Lafayette IN 47906-2151 Office: Sch Aero Astronautics Engring Purdue U West Lafayette IN 47907*

BOGDANOVICH, MICHELE L., legislative staff member; b. St. Louis, May 26, 1955. BA, George Washington U., 1977. Staff aide Nat. League Cities, Washington, 1978; legis. aide Rep. William L. Clay, Washington, 1979-89, legis. dir., 1989—. Office: Office Rep William L Clay 2306 Rayburn House Office Washington DC 20515*

BOGDANOVICH, PETER, film director, writer, producer, actor; b. Kingston, N.Y., July 30, 1939; s. Borislav and Herma (Robinson) B.; m. Polly Platt, 1962 (div. 1970); children: Antonia, Alexandra; m. L.B. Straten, 1988. Owner The Holly Moon Co., Inc., L.A., 1992—. Actor Am. Shakespeare Festival, Stratford, Conn., 1956, N.Y. Shakespeare Festival, 1958, (TV episode) Northern Exposure, 1993; dir., producer off-Broadway plays: The Big Knife, 1959, Camino Real, Ten Little Indians, Rocket to the Moon, 1961, Once in a Lifetime, 1964; film feature-writer for Esquire, N.Y. Times, Village Voice, Cahiers du Cinema, L.A. Times, N.Y. Mag., Vogue, Variety, others, 1961—; films: The Wild Angels (2d unit dir., co-writer, actor), 1966; Targets (dir., co-writer, producer, actor), 1968, The Last Picture Show (dir., co-writer, N.Y. Film Critics award, Brit. Acad. award 1971), 1971, Directed by John Ford (dir., writer, interviewer), 1971, What's Up, Doc? (dir., co-writer, producer, Writer's Guild Am. award 1972), 1972, Paper Moon (dir., producer, Silver Shell, Mar del Plata, Spain), 1973, Daisy Miller (dir., producer, Best Dir. Brussels Festival 1974), 1974, At Long Last Love (dir., writer, producer), 1975, Nickelodeon (dir., co-writer), 1976, Saint Jack (dir., co-writer, actor, Pasinetti award, Critics prize Venice Festival 1979), 1979, They All Laughed (dir., writer), 1981, Mask (dir.), 1985, Illegally Yours (dir., producer), 1988, Texasville (dir., producer, writer), 1990, Noises Off (dir., exec. producer), 1992, The Thing Called Love (dir.), 1993; author: The Cinema of Orson Welles, 1961, The Cinema of Howard Hawks, 1962, The Cinema of Alfred Hitchcock, 1963, John Ford, 1968, Fritz Lang in America, 1969, Allen Dwan: The Last Pioneer, 1971, Pieces of Time: Peter Bogdanovich on the Movies, 1973, enlarged, 1985, The Killing of the Unicorn: Dorothy Stratten: 1960-80, 1984, (with Orson Welles) This Is Orson Welles, 1992; editor: A Year and a Day Engagement Calendar, 1991—; co-dir., writer, interviewer: The Great Professional: Howard Hawks, 1967; weekly network commentator CBS This Morning, 1987-89; dir. (TV series episode) Fallen Angels, 1995, Painted Word, 1995. Mem. Dirs. Guild of Am., Writers Guild of Am., Acad. Motion Picture Arts and Scis. also: care Martin Baum and Rick Nicita CAA 9830 Wilshire Blvd Beverly Hills CA 90212-1804*

BOGDON, GLENDON JOSEPH, orthodontist; b. Green Bay, Wis., Sept. 23, 1935; s. Joseph Frank and Anne Marie (Jacklin) B.; m. Susanne Ellen Daley, Aug. 8, 1959; 1 child, Amy Sue. BS, St. Norbert Coll., DePere, Wis., 1957; DDS, Marquette U., 1971, MS in Clin. Dentistry, 1973. Officer IRS, Chgo., 1958; social worker Cath. Welfare Bur., Milw., 1958-59; tchr. secondary sch. So. Door County Schs., Brussels, Wis., 1959-67; practice dentistry specializing in orthodontics Milw., 1973—. Writer fitness column Cath. Herald; contbr. articles to profl. jours.; patentee in field. Served with U.S. Army, 1957-58. Mem. Greater Milw. Dental Assn. (Continuing Edn. award 1971-73), Wis. Dental Assn. (Continuing Edn. award 1971-74, 79-81, ADA (Continuing Edn. award 1976-78), Royal Soc. Health, Wis. Soc. Orthodontists, Midwestern Soc. Orthodontists, Am. Assn. Orthodontists, World Fedn. Orthodontists, Spitfire Soc., Am. Running and Fitness Assn., Orthodontic Ctrs. of Am. Democrat. Roman Catholic. Avocations: bread baking, jogging. Office: 3044 S 92nd St Milwaukee WI 53227-3678

BOGDONOFF, MORTON DAVID, physician, educator; b. N.Y.C., Dec. 8, 1925; s. M. Myron and Minnie (Alpher) B.; m. Jano Segal, July 1, 1951 (div. 1971); children—Reid, Ladd, Jesse, Drue; m. Mary Patton Welt, May 9, 1975. MD, Cornell U., 1948. Diplomate: Nat. Bd. Med. Examiners, Am. Bd. Internal Medicine. Intern, jr. asst. resident, sr. asst. resident dept. medicine N.Y. Hosp., N.Y.C., 1948-50; sr. asst. surgeon USPHS, Nat. Heart Inst., Johns Hopkins U., Balt., 1950-52; sr. asst. resident dept. medicine Duke Hosp., 1952-53, Eli Lilly Research fellow div. endocrinology and metabolism, 1953-54, chief resident dept. medicine, 1954-55; attending physician, chief metabolic div. Durham VA Hosp., 1955-56, cons., 1959-62; asso. prof. clin. medicine Med. Sch. U. Miami, 1956-57; assoc. dept. medicine Duke U., 1955-56, asst. prof. medicine, 1957-59, asso. prof., 1959-62, prof. med., 1962-69, asst. dean grad. med. edn., 1967-69; prof., chmn. dept. internal medicine U. Ill., Chgo., 1970-75; prof. medicine to prof. emeritus Med. Coll. Cornell U., 1975-95, 95—; cons. Ft. Bragg Hosp., 1959-62, VA Hosps., Fayetteville, Durham, West-Side, Chgo.; mem. study sect. health svcs. rsch. NIH, 1966-70, Commonwealth Fund, 1985-94, Cath. Med. Ctr., 1990-94, Nat. Med. Fellowships, 1987—. Editor: clin. Rsch., 1959-64; chief editor: Archives of Internal Medicine, 1967-77, New Developments in Medicine, 1986-90; sci. editor: Drug Therapy, 1978-94; contbr. articles to profl. jours. Fellow Center Advanced Study Behavioral Scis., Stanford, 1977-78. Fellow A.C.P.; mem. Am. Fedn. Clin. Research (past pres.), Am., So., Central socs. clin. investigation, Assn. Am. Physicians, AAAS (chmn. Sect. N 1981-82), Endocrine Soc., Psychosomatic Soc. (past nat. councillor), Soc. Exptl. Biology and Medicine, AMA, Harvey Soc., Alpha Omega Alpha. Office: NY Hosp/Cornell Med Ctr 525 E 68th St New York NY 10021-4885

BOGE, ARNOLD JOSEPH, builder, contractor; b. North Buena Vista, Iowa, Oct. 19, 1949; s. Norbert William and Loretta Marie (Dean) B.; m. Susan Diane Shultz, May 10, 1969; children: Diane, Matthew, Laura; m. Carol Marie Urbain, June 28, 1980; children: Renae, Kayln. AS, North Iowa Area C.C., Mason City, 1981. Crane operator White Farm Equipment Co., Charles City, Iowa, 1972-73; constrn. foreman Merrill Masonry Inc., Brevard, N.C., 1973-77; owner Boge Constrn., Ionia, Iowa, 1977—; supr. Chickasaw County, New Hampton, Iowa, 1987—. Dir. 1st Jud. Dist. Corrections, Waterloo, Iowa, 1987—; mem. Chickasaw County Rep. Ctrl. Com., 1986-97. With U.S. Army, 1969-71. Recipient State of Iowa Gov.'s Vol. award, 1989. Mem. VFW (comdr. 1989-91), Lions. Republican. Roman Catholic. Avocations: hunting, fishing, travel. Home: 2160 Amherst Pl Ionia IA 50645-9439 Office: Chickasaw County PO Box 311 New Hampton IA 50659-0311

BOGE, WALTER EDWARD, retired army civilian official, private consultant; b. Queens, N.Y., May 1, 1937; s. Edward August and Elizabeth (Weis) B.; m. Lucille Dodson, Feb. 1, 1964; children: William August, Matthew Stephen, Christopher Adam. BSCE, CCNY, 1960; MSCE, Purdue U., 1973. Registered engr.-in-tng., N.Y. Project engr. U.S. Army Enging. Topographic Lab., Ft. Belvoir, Va., 1960-71, chief spl. project br., 1971-76, mgr. spl. programs, 1976-80, chief sys. studies div., 1980-83, dir. Geog. Scis. Lab., 1983, tech. dir., 1983-96; dir. U.S. Army Topographic Engring. Ctr., Alexandria, Va., 1990-96; chmn. tri-svc. panel on battlespace environment Dept. Def., Washington, 1993—. Contbr. articles to profl. jours. Pres. Collingwood Springs Civic Assn., Fairfax County, Va., 1980, chmn. edn. com., 1982—; pres. Riverside Gardens Recreation Assn., Fairfax County, 1981. Recipient comdr.'s award for leadership U.S. Army Topographic Enging. Lab., 1975, Presdl. Meritorious Exec. award, 1991, 96, Dept. Army Exceptional Civilian Svc. award, 1996. Mem. Am. Soc. Photogrammetry and Remote Sensing (nat. bd. dirs. 1963-94), Chi Epsilon, Phi Kappa Phi. Roman Catholic. Avocations: bridge, hunting.

BOGEN, ANDREW E., lawyer; b. L.A., Aug. 23, 1941; s. David and Edith B.; m. Deborah Bogen, Oct. 10, 1970; children: Elizabeth, Michael. BA, Pomona Coll., Claremont, Calif., 1963; LLB, Harvard U, 1966. Assoc. Gibson, Dunn & Crutcher, L.A., 1966-73, ptnr., 1973—. Trustee Exceptional Children's Found., L.A., 1976-89; bd. dirs. St. Anne's Maternity House, 1990—. Office: Gibson Dunn & Crutcher 333 S Grand Ave Ste 4400 Los Angeles CA 90071-3197

BOGEN, EUGENE M., federal judge. Magistrate judge U.S. Dist. Ct. (no. dist.) Miss., Greenville, 1995—. Fax: (601) 332-6881. Office: US Dist Ct (no dist) Miss 305 Main St Rm 364 Greenville MS 38701

BOGENSBERGER, JOAN HELEN HESS, school administrator, consultant; b. Ft. Collins, Colo., Aug. 18, 1939; d. Eugene Vernon and Margaret Rose (Mantey) Hess; m. Robert R. Bogensberger, Aug. 20, 1960; children: John Andrew, Margaret Rose, Helen Marie. BA, Colo. State Coll., Greeley, 1961; MA, Western Wash. U., 1976; postgrad. U. Wash., 1964. Cert. tchr., Wash. Tchr., elem. schs. South Cen. Sch. Dist., Seattle, Wash., 1960-68; vol. music tchr. Immaculate Comception Sch., Mt. Vernon, 1968-71; libr. Mt. Vernon Christian Sch., 1971-76; founder, tchr., prin. Floyd Paxton Sch., Mt. Vernon, 1977—; chair program state edn. conv. Wash. Fedn. Ind. Schs., 1989-90; cons. in field; developer art curriculum; v.p. Skagit Community Band Bd. Wash. State Homeschs. V.p. Skagit Performing Arts Coun., IDEAS, Spokane, 1997. Mem. ASCD, Internat. Reading Assn., Nat. Coun. Tchrs., Assn. Childhood Edn., Tau Beta Sigma, Delta Omicron. Roman Catholic. Office: Floyd Paxton Elem Sch 1340 Avon Allen Rd Mount Vernon WA 98273-8204

BOGENSCHUTZ, J. DAVID, lawyer; b. Covington, Ky., May 15, 1944; s. John Francis and Virginia Margaret (Dugan) B.; m. Mary H. McCleary, Oct. 24, 1981; children: Kathleen, Emily. BA, Miami U., Oxford, Ohio, 1966; JD, U. Cin., 1969. Bar: Ohio 1969, U.S. Dist. Ct. (so. dist.) Ohio 1970, U.S. Ct. Appeals (6th cir.) 1971, Fla. 1971, U.S. Dist. Ct. (so. dist.) Fla. 1972, U.S. Ct. Appeals (5th cir.) 1980, U.S. Dist. Ct. (mid. dist.) Fla. 1981, U.S. Ct. Appeals (4th and 11th cirs.) 1981, U.S. Dist. Ct. (ea. dist.) Wis. 1989. Instr. Criminal Justice Inst. Nova U., 1977; instr. Broward County Criminal Justice Inst., 1972; asst. solicitor County of Broward, 1971, chief asst. state's atty., 1974-77; ptnr. Bogenschutz & Dutko, P.A., Ft. Lauderdale, Fla.; mem. Gov.'s Com. on Criminal Justice Standards and Goals, 1975-76; mem. bench bar liaison com. U.S. Dist. Ct. (so. dist.) Fla., 1985—. Mem. ATLA, NACDL, Broward County Bar Assn. (criminal law sect. chmn. 1980-81, exec. com. 1981-86, sec., treas. 1985-86), Ohio Bar Assn., Fla. Bar Assn. (criminal law sect., grievance com. 17th jud. cir. 1982-84), Fed. Bar Assn., Greene County Bar Assn., Fla. Pros. Atty.'s Assn., Nat. Dist. Atty.'s Assn. Democrat. Roman Catholic. Office: Bogenschutz & Dutko PA Colonial Bank Bldg 600 S Andrews Ave Ste 500 Fort Lauderdale FL 33301-2851

BOGER, DALE L., chemistry educator; b. Hutchinson, Kans., Aug. 22, 1953; s. Lester W. and Elizabeth (Korkish) B. BS in Chemistry, U. Kans., 1975; PhD in Chemistry, Harvard U., 1980. Asst. prof. U. Kans., Lawrence, 1979-83, assoc. prof., 1983-85; assoc. prof. Purdue U., West Lafayette, Ind., 1985-87, prof., 1987-91; Richard and Alice Cramer chair chemistry Scripps Rsch. Inst., La Jolla, Calif., 1991—. Recipient Career Devel. award NIH, 1983-88; NSF fellow, 1975-78, Alfred P. Sloan fellow, 1985-89; Searle scholar, 1981-84. Mem. Am. Chem. Soc. (A.C. Cope scholar 1989, Aldrich creative work in organic synthesis 1999), Internat. Soc. Het. Chemistry (Katritky award 1997). Home: 2819 Via Posada La Jolla CA 92037-2205 Office: Scripps Rsch Inst 10550 N Torrey Pines Rd La Jolla CA 92037-1000

BOGER, DAN CALVIN, statistical and economic consultant, educator; b. Salisbury, N.C., July 9, 1946; s. Brady Cashwell and Gertrude Virginia (Hamilton) B.; m. Gail Lorraine Zivna, June 23, 1973; children: Gretchen Zivna, Gregory Zivna. BS in Mgmt. Sci., U. Rochester, 1968; MS in Mgmt. Sci., Naval Postgrad. Sch., Monterey, Calif., 1969; MA in Stats., U. Calif., Berkeley, 1977, PhD in Econs., 1979. Cert. cost analyst, profl. estimator. Rsch. asst. U. Calif., Berkeley, 1975-79; asst. prof. econs. Naval Postgrad. Sch., Monterey, 1979-85, assoc. prof., 1985-92, prof., 1992—, chmn. dept. command, control and comm., 1995—, chmn. dept. computer sci., 1997—, chmn. dept. info. warfare, 1997—, dean divsn. computer and info. scis. and ops., 1997—; bd. dirs. Evan-Moor Corp.; cons. econs. and statis. legal matters CSX Corp, others, 1977—. Assoc. editor The Logistics and Transp. Rev., 1981-85, Jour. Cost Analysis, 1989-92; mem. editl. rev. bd. Jour. Transp. Rsch. Forum, 1987-91; contbr. articles to profl. jours. Lt. USN, 1968-75. Flood fellow Dept. Econs. U. Calif., Berkeley, 1975-76; dissertation rsch. grantee A.P. Sloan Found., 1978-79. Mem. IEEE, Internat. Coun. on Sys. Engring., Am. Econ. Assn., Am. Statis. Assn., Econometric Soc., Inst. for Mgmt. Sci. and Ops. Rsch. (sec., treas. mil. applications soc. 1987-91), Sigma Xi. Home: 27 Cramden Dr Monterey CA 93940-4145 Office: Naval Postgrad Sch Code CC Monterey CA 93943

BOGER, DAVID L, librarian; b. Dec. 15, 1953. BA Humanities and Religion, Texas Wesbryan Coll., Fort Worth, TX, 1977; MLA, North Texas State Univ., Denton, TX, 1980. Librarian Boyce Ditto Public Library, Mineral Weals, TX, 1980-87, asst. dir., 1988—. Home: 4928 El Campo Ave Apt 213 Fort Worth TX 76107

BOGER, GENA CECILE, school psychologist; b. Highland, Ill., Mar. 27, 1953; d. Alvis Gene and Mary Thelma (Willeford) Zeller; m. Thomas Gene Boger, Aug. 11, 1973; children: Janna Lynn, Emily Michelle. BA, So. Ill. U., Edwardsville, 1975, MS, 1977. Cert. sch. svc. pers., Ill. Sch. psychologist Belleville (Ill.) Area Spl. Edn. Dist., 1978-91, East Alton (Ill.) Elem. Schs., 1991—. Village trustee Village of South Roxana, Ill., 1975-78; coleader Brownie troop Girl Scouts U.S., South Roxana, 1986-87; coach Youth Baseball League, Roxana, Ill., 1995-97. Recipient Those Who Excel award Ill. State Bd. Edn., 1996. Mem. NEA, Ill. Edn. Assn., Nat. Assn. Sch. Psychologists, Ill. Sch. Psychologists Assn. (Sch. Psychology Practitioner of Yr. 1989), So. Ill. Psychol. Assn. Free Methodist. Avocations: volunteer school booster clubs, sports, music, reading, gardening. Home: 4816 Oak Ridge Dr East Alton IL 62024-2808 Office: Tri Dist Spl Svcs 501 E Lorena Ave Wood River IL 62095-2123

BOGER, LAWRENCE LEROY, university president emeritus; b. DeKalb County, Ind., Sept. 26, 1923; s. Lester Elmer and Lazeal (Witt) B.; m. Frances June Wilbur, Sept. 2, 1945; children: Richard Lee, Judith Ann. BS, Purdue U., 1947; postgrad., Harvard U., U. Chgo.; MA, Mich. State U., 1948, PhD, 1950. Faculty dept. agrl. econs. Mich. State U., 1948-77, beginning as instr., successively asst. prof., assoc. prof., 1948-54, prof., head dept., 1954-69, dean Coll. Agr. and Natural Resources, 1969-76, univ. provost, 1976-77; pres. Okla. State U., Stillwater, 1977-88, ret., 1989; cons. U.S. Crop Reporting Service, Dept. Agr., 1953-56, Bur. Census and Statis. Reporting Service, 1965-68; cons. village devel. program for Pakistan govt. Ford Found., 1957, 64, 67; cons. programs econ. assistance Nat. U. of Colombia, S.Am., Kellogg Found., 1959; mem. Nat. Com. on Use of Electronic Data Processing in Farm Mgmt.; dir.-at-large Central Bank for Coops., FCA, 1967-71; mem. joint univ. adv. com. U. Nigeria, 1965-68; mem. Okla. Commn. for Superconducting Supercollider, 1987; guest lectr. Govt. of Taiwan, 1979. Mem. Spl. Commn. on Land Use Planning, 1971-73; chmn. Gov.'s Oil and Gas Task Force, 1973; del. White House Conf. on Nutrition, 1969, Chgo. Foothills Conf. on Inflation, 1974, Pres.'s Conf. on Inflation, Washington, 1974; mem. Gov.'s Council on Sci. and Tech., 1983-87; mem. Okla. Futures, 1987-88; trustee Nat. 4-H Council, 1981-88, Scroggs Scholarship Found.; bd. dirs. State Fair Okla., Omniplex, Okla. Acad. State Goals, 1986-88, Mid-Am. Rsch. Inst., 1986-88; mem. blue ribbon com. U.S. Farm Export Edn. Project, 1980-82; chmn. Commn. on County Govt. Personnel Edn. and Tng., 1982-88, Okla. UN Day, 1986; mem. Benedum Panel on Agr., W.Va., 1984; mem. bd. sci. and tech. for internat. devel. NRC, 1984-86; mem. com. to evaluate the possibility of football championship Coll. Football Assn., 1987; mem. hon. bd. dirs. Okla. Spl. Olympics, 1987-88; trustee Kirksville Coll. Osteo. Medicine, 1989-98; mem. adv. bd. Okla. State U. Coll. Osteo. Medicine, 1994—; mem. policy adv. bd. Resources For The Future, Nat. Ctr. Food and Agr. Policy, 1989—, chmn. 1992—, Okla. State Univ. Found. bd. govs., 1992—, trustee, 1992-97. Mem. Am. Agrl. Econs. Assn. (v.p. 1960-61, found. bd. 1988-91), Am. Osteo. Assn. (bur. profl. edn.

1994—, coun. on internat. osteo. med. ednl. affairs 1997—), Internat. Assn. Agrl. Econs. (Am. coun., participant conf. USSR 1970), Am. Statis. Assn., Mid-Am. State Univs. Assn. (chmn. 1980-81), Okla. State C. of C. (bd. dirs), Stillwater C. of C. (bd. dirs), Blue Key, Sigma Xi, Alpha Zeta, Omicron Delta Kappa, Pi Mu Epsilon, Phi Kappa Phi. Home: 5015 Woodland Dr Stillwater OK 74074-1347 Office: Okla State U 313 Pub Info Bldg Stillwater OK 74078

BOGER, RICHARD EDWIN, JR., minister; b. Atlanta, May 13, 1952; s. Richard Edwin and Marie Yoder (Leonard) B.; m. Jill Roberta Howard, Apr. 26, 1980; 1 child, John Michael Howard. AB, Lenoir-Rhyne Coll., 1973, Hamma Sch. Theology, 1975; MDiv, Pacific Luth. Theol. Sem., 1978. Ordained to ministry Evang. Luth. Ch. Am., 1980. Vesper intern Vesper Soc., San Leandro, Calif., 1975-76; coord. vols. Care Network, San Leandro, 1978; intern Christ Our Shepherd, Peachtree City, Ga., 1979-80; pastor Luth. Ch. of Our Savior, Jacksonville, N.C., 1980-90, Nazareth Luth. Ch., Rural Hall, N.C., 1990—; counselor Neighborhood Ch. Clinic, Springfield, Ohio, 1974; pastoral counselor Eden Hayward (Calif.) Pastoral Counseling Svc., 1975-76; mem. Jacksonville Ministerial Assn., 1980-81, Onslow County Ministerial Fellowship, 1984; mem. worship com., music com. N.C. Synod Luth. Ch. in Am., 1982, 84-86, 94, 97-99; assoc. N.C. Chaplains Assn., 1984; pres. Forsyth Luth. Coun., 1992. Pub. Nazareth Luth. Ch. Home Page, 1995. Bd. dirs. ARC, Jacksonville, 1981-89. Mem. Soc. of the Holy Trinity (founding mem.), Alban Inst., Forsyth Luth. Area Pastors (coord. 1996—), Forsyth Luth. Coun., Rural Hall-Stanleyville Mins. Assn. (pres. 1995-97), United Ministry Rural Hall (bd. dirs. 1994—, sec. 1997). E-mail: rbogerjr@aol.com. Office: St Thomas Net Ministry PO Box 17072 Winston Salem NC 27116 *Ours is the God who died. No other religion can make that claim. When we fully accept the fact that God became man and then died for us out of love, then and only then do we begin to live.*

BOGGESS, JERRY REID, protective services official; b. Murray, Utah, Feb. 1, 1944; s. Reid and Clara (Thompson) B.; m. Portia Stevens, Aug. 19, 1967; children: Bart, Blake, Trent. BSME, U. Utah, 1967; grad. Exec. Devel. Program, UCLA, 1982. Registered profl. engr., Calif. Apprentice pipe fitter, shop fabricator, then engr., gen. mgr. Western Automatic Sprinkler Co., Salt Lake City, 1962-68; br. mgr. Grinnell Fire Protection Systems, Salt Lake City, 1968-71; dist. gen. mgr. Grinnell Fire Protection Systems, L.A., 1971-81, corp. v.p., gen. mgr., 1981-83; exec. v.p. Grinnell Fire Protection Systems, Exeter, N.H., 1989—; pres. Tyco Fire & Safety Svcs. (formerly Grinnell Fire Protection Systems), Exeter, N.H., 1996—, Cosco Fire Protection, L.A., 1983-89; v.p., sec., proprietary dir. Grinnell Sistemas de Protección contra Incendio, s.a. de c.v., L.A., 1981-83; edn. trade advisor Glendale (Calif.) Community Coll.; mem. Calif. Profl. Engr. Rev. Bd. Dist. chmn. Boy Scouts Am., Calif, N.H.; active ch. orgn.; mem. Fire Sprinkler Adv. Bd., So. Calif. Mdem. Nat. Fire Protection Assn., Nat. Fire Sprinkler Assn. (bd. dirs.), Am. Soc. Prof. Engrs. (vice-chmn. sect.), Soc. Fire Protection Engrs. (pres.), Theta Tau. Home: 671 S Ocean Blvd Boca Raton FL 33432-6220 Office: Tyoc Fire & Safety Svcs 1 Town Center Rd Boca Raton FL 33486*

BOGGESS, THOMAS PHILLIP, III, graphics arts company executive; b. Greenville, Ky., Jan. 22, 1921; s. William C. and Gertrude Lucille (Lumpkins) B.; grad. high sch.; m. Ann Marie Mossner, Sept. 1, 1942; children—Thomas Phillip IV, Nancy L. Vice-pres. Alfred Mossner Co., Chgo., 1945-70, pres., chief exec. officer, 1970—, also dir.; treas., dir. Blue Printers Supply Corp., Chgo. Chmn. zoning bd. of appeals, Village of River Forest, Ill., 1950—; mem., past bd. dirs. Westchester (Ill.) Bible Ch. Served with USNR, 1942-45. Decorated Purple Heart, Bronze Star (5). Mem. Blue Print Club of Chgo. (pres. 1957-62), Disabled Am. Vets. Club: Oak Park Country. Home: 335 Gale Ave River Forest IL 60305-2015 Office: 137 N Wabash Ave Chicago IL 60602-1910*

BOGGS, CHRISTOPHER B., accountant, auditor; b. Oxford, Ohio, Feb. 3, 1966; s. Robert E. and Betty J. (Bulleit) B.; m. Karla E. Cooper, May 1, 1993. BS in Acctg., Miami U., Oxford, Ohio, 1988. CPA, Ohio, Ind. CPA Crowe Chizek, Indpls., 1989—. Mem. AICPA, Ohio CPA Soc., Ind. CPA Soc. Democrat. Presbyterian. Avocations: golf, boating, home restoration. Office: Crowe Chizek PO Box 40977 3815 River Crossing Pky Indianapolis IN 46240-0977

BOGGS, CORINNE CLAIBORNE (LINDY BOGGS), former congresswoman; b. Brunswick Plantation, La., Mar. 13, 1916; d. Roland Philomen and Martha Corinne (Morrison) Claiborne; m. Thomas Hale Boggs, Jan. 22, 1938 (dec.); children: Barbara Boggs Sigmund (dec.), Thomas Hale Jr., Corinne Boggs Roberts, William Robertson (dec.). BA, Sophie Newcomb Coll., Tulane U., 1935, LLD (hon.); LittD, U. St. Thomas; DPub Svc. (hon.), Trinity Coll., Washington, 1975; hon. degree, St. Mary of Woods; LLD, Loyola U., Notre Dame U., Wesleyan U., Cath. U. Law Sch., Xavier U., St. Mary's Coll., St. Thomas Aquinas Coll., Univ. New Orleans, Our Lady of Holy Cross Coll., Notre Dame Sem., Coll. of St. Elizabeth. Tchr. history and English St. James Parish, La., 1936-37; elected to 93d Congress to fill vacancy caused by death of husband, 1973; re-elected to 94th-101st Congresses from 2d La. Dist., 1973-91; ret., 1991; ambassador to Rome Tulane U., New Oleans; mem. appropriations com. majority mem. from Ho. of Reps., Am. Revolution Bicentennial Adminstrn. Bd., chmn. Commn. Ho. of Reps. Bicentenary; mem. campaign com. Dem. Nat. Com., 1974; first chairwoman Dem. Nat. Conv., 1976; mem. Com. on Bicentennial of U.S. Constn. Pres., Dem. Congl. Wives Forum, 1954, Womans Nat. Democratic Club, 1958-59, Congl. Club, 1971-72; co-chmn. Inaugural Balls for Presidents John F. Kennedy, 1961, Lyndon Johnson, 1965; mem. Nat. Hist. Publs. and Records Com.; bd. dirs. La. Council for Music and Performing Arts; hon. bd. dirs. Met. New Orleans chpt. Nat. Found. March of Dimes; bd. advisers. CLOSE-UP and Presdl. Classroom; regent emeritus Smithsonian Instn.; mem. president's council Tulane U. Recipient Weiss Meml. award NCCJ, 1974; Nat. Oak award La. Assn. Ind. Colls. and Univs., Disting. Service medal Saint Mary's Dominican Coll., 1976, Humanitarian award AMVETS Nat. Aux., Torch of Liberty award B'nai B'rith, 1976, Gala IV award Birmingham So. U., 1976, Eleanor Roosevelt Humanitarian award, 1977, E. Roosevelt Centennial award, 1984, 1st woman recipient Disting. Alumna award Tulane U., 1986; 1st woman recipient VFW Congl. award, 1986; bldg., rm. in U.S. Capitol bldg., energy bldg. Tulane U., U.S. Vets. Hosp. Unit, New Orleans, Challenger Space Ctr. and Mission Control Ctr., Baton Rouge, and dam named in her honor. Mem. Nat. Soc. Colonial Dames, LWV, Internat. Fedn. Cath. Alumni, Internat. Women's Forum. Avocations: flower arranging, dancing. Address: Office of the President Ambassador Corinne Clairborne Boggs Tulane Univ New Orleans LA 70118-5665*

BOGGS, DANNY JULIAN, federal judge; b. Havana, Cuba, Oct. 23, 1944; s. Robert Lilburn and Yolanda (Pereda) B.; m. Judith Susan Solow, Dec. 23, 1967; children: Rebecca, David, Jonathan. A.B., Harvard Coll., Cambridge, Mass., 1965; J.D., U. Chgo., 1968; LLD (hon.), U. Detroit Mercy, 1994. Dep. commr. Ky. Dept. Econ. Security, 1969-70; legal counsel, adminstrv. asst. Gov. Ky., 1970-71; legis. counsel to Rep. legislators Ky. Gen. Assembly, 1972; asst. to solicitor gen. U.S. Dept. Justice, Washington, 1973-75; asst. to chmn. FPC, Washington, 1975-77; dep. minority counsel Senate Energy Com., Washington, 1977-79; of counsel Bushnell, Gage, et al., Washington, 1979-80; spl. asst. to Pres. White House, Washington, 1981-83; dep. sec. U.S. Dept. Energy, Washington, 1983-86; judge U.S. Ct. Appeals (6th cir.), Cin., 1986—; mem. adv. com. on appellate rules Jud. Conf. U.S., 1991-94, com. on automation and tech., 1994—. Mem. vis. com. U. Chgo. Law Sch., 1984-87, 99—; del. Republican Nat. Conv., 1972; staff dir. energy subcom. Rep. Platform Com., 1980; trustee Lexington Sch., 1999—. Mem. ABA, Ky. Bar Assn., Mont Pelerin Soc., Phila. Soc., Order of Coif, Phi Delta Phi. Office: US Ct Appeals US Courthouse 601 W Broadway Rm 220 Louisville KY 40202-2238

BOGGS, GEORGE ROBERT, academic administrator; b. Conneaut, Ohio, Sept. 4, 1944; s. George Robert and Mary (Mullen) B.; m. Ann Holladay, Aug. 8, 1969; children: Kevin Dale, Ian Asher, Micah Benjamin. BS in Chemistry, Ohio State U., 1966; MA in Chemistry, U. Calif., Santa Barbara, 1968; postgrad. in ednl. adminstrn., natural scis., and edn., Calif. State U., 1969-72; PhD in Ednl. Adminstrn., U. Tex., 1984. Cert. standard teaching specialization in jr. coll. teaching, C.C. supvr., C.C. chief adminstrv. officer. Instr. chemistry Butte Coll., Oroville, Calif., 1968-85, divsn. chmn. nat. sci. and allied health, 1972-81, assoc. dean of instrn., 1981-85; pres., supt. Palomar C.C. Dist., San Marcos, Calif., 1985—; speaker SCCCIRA, Calif., 1985; adj. instr. Austin (Tex.) C.C., 1982; guest lectr. Calif. State U., Chico, 1970, 83, 84, panelist, 1975; tchg. asst. U. Calif., Santa Barbara, 1966-68, Ohio State U., 1965-66; mem. numerous coms. for colls. and univs., Calif., 1968—; cons. U. Calif., Berkeley, 1995—, U. Wis., Madison, 1997—, Pellissippi State Tech. Coll., 1995, El Camino Coll., 1994, U. Hawaii C.C., 1994, Dept. Nat. Edn., Rep. South Africa, 1993, San Joaquin Delta C.C. Dist., 1986, Marin C.C. Dist., 1985. Contbr. articles to profl. jours.; cons. editl. adv. bd. Jour. Applied Rsch. in the C.C., 1993—; mem. editl. bd. C.C. Rev., 1997—. Presenter Nat. Conf. Teaching Excellence and Conf. of Pres.'s, 1983, 93, 95, presenter, mem. coordinating com., 1984, chmn. steering com., 1985; presenter Profl. and Orgl. Devel. Network, 1984; ad hoc com. CPEC/FIPSE/Chancellor's Office, 1984; mem. steering com. Learning Assessment Retention Com., 1983—, pres.-elect 1985-86; mem. instl. research design team No. Calif. Higher Edn. Council, 1984, mission charrette writing team, 1985. Richardson fellow 1982-83; scholar Gen. Ohio State U., 1963, Stadium Dormitory, 1962-65, Scholastic R., 1962, Nat. Honor Soc., 1962; recipient Stanley A. Mahr Cmty. Svc. award Past Pres.' Coun. San Marcos C. of C., Calif., 1994, cert. of Achievement in Recognition of Leadership Excellence and Cmty. Svc. Congress of U.S. Ho. of Reps., 1994, San Diego Hall of Success, 1988, Pacific Region CEO award Assn. C.C. Trustees, Victoria, B.C., Can., 1993, Recognition award Nat. Coun. for Rsch. and Planning Mgmt., 1997, Marie Y. Martin CEO award Assn. C.C. Trustees, 1996, Harry Buttimer Disting. Adminstrs. award Assn. Calif. C.C. Trustees, 1994; named hon. elder Nat. Coun. on Black Am. Affairs, 1993; proclamation of Jan. 14, 1994 as Dr. George R. Boggs Day in Vista, Calif., 1994. Mem. NSF (mem. adv. com. to directorate for edn. and human resources 1995-97, evaluator 1992, 93, 98), Nat. Rsch. Coun. (mem. undergrad. sci. edn. com. 1993-95, chmn. subcom. tchg. and learning 1993-95), Assn. Calif. Coll. Tutorial and Learning Assistance (presenter 1984), Calif. Assn. C.C. (conf. presenter 1984, com. on research 1985—), Assn. Calif. C.C. Adminstrs. (commn. membership devel. 1985), C.C. League Calif. (bd. dirs. 1990-92, presenter confs. 1990-98), Faculty Assn. Calif. C.C., Calif. C.C. Chief Exec. Officers' Assn, San Diego and Imperial Counties C.C. Assn., Am. Assn. Cmty. and Jr. Colls. (presenter 1989, 90, 91, 94, 95, bd. dirs. 1990-95, fed. rels. com. 1990-91, 94-95, chair elect 1993—, chair bd. dirs. 1993-94, exec. com. 1993-95, chair bd. nominating com. 1994-95), So. Calif. C.C. Chief Exec. Officers Assn. (sec., treas. 1990—), Phi Kappa Phi, Upsilon Pi Upsilon (pres. 1965-66), Phi Rho Pi. Lodge: Rotary (pres. Durham club 1980-81, dist. sec. Calif., 1983-84, various other offices and com. positions held locally and nationally). Home: 521 Cassou Rd San Marcos CA 92069-9711 Office: Palomar Coll 1140 W Mission Rd San Marcos CA 92069-1415

BOGGS, GEORGE TRENHOLM, lawyer; b. Charleston, S.C., Apr. 17, 1947; s. Edwin and Laura (Blair) B.; m. Emilie Louise von Thelen, Sept. 6, 1975; children: George T. Jr., Blair M. AB, Princeton U., 1969; JD, U. Va., 1974. Bar: Va. 1974, D.C. 1975. Tchr., Taft Sch., Watertown, Conn., 1969-71; mem. Dickstein Shapiro Morin and Oshinsky LLP, Washington, 1974—, ptnr., 1980—. Mem. ABA, Internat. Bar Assn., Va. Bar Assn. Republican. Episcopalian. Editor: (with John M. Paxman) The United Nations: A Reassessement, 1973. Office: Dickstein Shapiro Morin & Oshinsky LLP 2101 L St NW Washington DC 20037-1526

BOGGS, JACK AARON, banker, municipal government official; b. Easley, S.C., July 4, 1935; s. Walter Benston and Bessie Mae (Jones) B.; m. Isabel Thomas Brown, July 7, 1965; children—James Brenston, Renee Chaplin, Edward Cunningham, Donn Lester. BS in Bus. Econs, U.S.C., 1964; grad., Sch. Banking, U. Wis., 1974. Chartered bank auditor certified internal auditor. Sec.-treas. Cedarpoint Farms Corp., Columbia, S.C., 1963-67; auditor S.C. Nat. Bank, Columbia, 1967-76; pres. S.C. Automated Clearing House Assn., 1976—; mem. 5th dist. ops. adv. com. Fed. Res. Bank of Richmond, 1997—; instr. S.C. Bankers Sch., 1972-80; sec., treas. Five Star Pubs., 1986-88; bd. dirs. NACHA, Inc., 1989—; vice chmn. ACH Exec. Dirs. Group, 1989-90, chmn., 1991-93. Mem. town coun., Town of Arcadia Lakes, S.C., 1977-85, mayor, 1985-89, chief of police, 1990-91; treas. S.C. Fedn. Older Ams., 1982-84. With USNR, 1952-60, Air N.G., 1960-63. Mem. Nat. Assn. Accts., Inst. Internal Auditors (bd. govs. 1971-74, pres. 1973-74, internat. rsch. com. 1972-75, internat. membership com. 1976), Data Processing Mgmt. Assn., Bank Adminstrn. Inst. (1st award 1972), S.C. Ducks Unltd. (treas. 1984-92, 98—, state chmn. 1992-94), Sigma Delta Pi, Chi Psi. Democrat. Unitarian. Home: 804 Arcadia Lakes Dr Columbia SC 29206-1321 Office: SC Automated Clearing House Assn PO Box 1787 Columbia SC 29202-1787 *It's not who you are; it's what you do that counts.*

BOGGS, JAMES ERNEST, chemistry educator; b. Cleve., June 9, 1921; s. Ernest Beckett and Emily (Reid) B.; m. Ruth Ann Rogers, June 22, 1948; children: Carol, Ann, Lynne. AB, Oberlin Coll., 1943; MS in Chemistry, U. Mich., 1944, PhD, 1953. Rsch. chemist Manhattan Dist. Project, Linde Air Products, Tonawanda, N.Y., 1944-46; asst. prof. dept. chemistry Eastern Mich. U., Ypsilanti, 1949-52; instr. U. Mich. at Ann Arbor, 1952-53; mem. faculty dept. chemistry U. Tex., Austin, 1953—, assoc. prof., 1958-66, prof., 1966-98; emeritus prof., 1998—; asst. dean Grad. Sch. U. Tex., Austin, 1958-67, dir. Center for Structural Studies, 1969-79, acting dir. Inst. Theoretical Chemistry, 1979-81; program officer for theoretical and computational chemistry NSF, 1991-94; founder, organizer series Austin Symposia on Molecular Structure, 1966—; chmn. subcom. on theoretical chemistry Internat. Union Pure and Applied Chemistry, 1995—; internat. lectr. in field. Mem. editl. bd. Jour. Molecular Structure; contbr. numerous articles to profl. jours. Mem. World Assn. Theoretical Chemists, Am. Chem. Soc., Am. Phys. Soc., Nat. Acad. Scis. (India), Phi Beta Kappa, Sigma Xi, Phi Lambda Upsilon, Gamma Alpha. Research in structural chemistry, microwave spectroscopy, quantum chemistry. Home: 4603 Balcones Dr Austin TX 78731-5221

BOGGS, JOHN STEVEN, sales and development executive; b. Indpls., Apr. 7, 1960; s. William Joseph and Bernadine Ann (Hague) B.; m. Mellissia M. Chentnik, Jan. 25, 1997. BS, U. Indpls., 1982. Outside and inside salesperson Mutual Pipe and Supply Co., Indpls., 1982-94; councilman City of Greenwood, 1988-95; pres. Greenwood City Coun., 1991; sales and bus. devel. Stephen Jacobs & Co., Inc., Indpls., 1994—; COO Protential Learning & Performance, LLC, Indpls., 1996—; pres. Lofts of Valle Vista Homeowners Assn., Greenwood, 1985-88. Rep. precinct committeeman, 1987-95; Greenwood Rep. City chair, 1995; chmn. Johnson County Solid Waste Mgmt. Dist., 1991-95. Office: Stephen Jacobs & Co Inc 10585 N Meridian St Ste 220 Indianapolis IN 46290-1067

BOGGS, JOSEPH DODRIDGE, pediatric pathologist, educator; b. Bellefontaine, Ohio, Dec. 31, 1921; s. Walter C. and Birdella Z. (Coons) B.; m. Donna Lee Shoemaker, June 12, 1964; 1 son, Joseph Dodridge. A.B., Ohio U., 1941, Litt.D., 1966; M.D., Jefferson Med. Coll., 1945. Intern Jefferson Med. Coll. Hosp., Phila., 1945-46; resident Peter Bent Brigham Hosp., Boston, 1946-48; asso. pathologist Peter Bent Brigham Hosp., 1947-51; instr. pathology Harvard Med. Sch., Boston, 1948-51; with Children's Meml. Hosp., Chgo., 1951—; dir. labs. Children's Meml. Hosp., 1951—; prof. pathology Northwestern U., Chgo., 1952-92, prof. emeritus, 1992—; dir. BSP Ins. Co., Phoenix. Contbr. articles to profl. jours. Mem. med. adv. bd. Ill. Dept. Corrections, Springfield, 1971-77; bd. dirs. Blood Systems Inc., Phoenix, 1972-94, Community Hosp., Evanston, Ill., 1958-61, Lorretto Hosp., Chgo., 1971-72; chmn. Chgo. Regional Blood Program, 1978-80; bd. dirs. Ben Venue Labs., 1985—. Capt. M.C., U.S. Army, 1948-51. Mem. Am. Soc. Study of Liver Disease, N.Y. Acad. Scis., Midwest Soc. Pediatric Research, Inst. Medicine, Ill. Soc. Pathologists (pres. 1965), Ill. Assn. Blood Banks (pres. 1969-70). Office: 1448 N Lake Shore Dr Chicago IL 60610-6655

BOGGS, MARCUS LIVINGSTONE, JR., publisher, novelist, editor; b. Birmingham, Ala., Dec. 10, 1947; s. Marcus Livingstone and Sarah Alice (McFarland) B.; m. Elizabeth Ruth Bell, June 12, 1977. A.B., Princeton U., 1970. Editor Oxford Univ. Press, N.Y.C., 1977-83, Harcourt Brace Jovanovich, San Diego, 1983—. Author: Scissors, Paper, Stone, 1981, Echos and Silences of Proposed Trilogy. Mem. Amnesty Internat., Sierra Club. Club: Sierra. Office: Westview Press Inc 5500 Central Ave Boulder CO 80301-2877*

BOGGS, RALPH STUART, retired lawyer; b. Toledo, June 6, 1917; s. Nolan and Sarah (MacPhie) B.; m. Mary Frances Sharp Wiggins, Sept. 7, 1940; children: Sally Ann Boggs Bashore, William S., Robert A. A.B., Denison U., 1939; LL.B., U. Mich., 1942. Bar: Ohio 1942, U.S. Supreme Ct. 1960. Spl. agt. FBI, 1942-45; practiced in Toledo, 1946-99; ptnr. Boggs, Boggs & Boggs (P.A.), 1946-87; of counsel Eastman and Smith, 1987-98; ret. Mem. Maumee Bd. Edn., 1953-69, Maumee Recreation Com., 1954-69; life mem. Toledo adv. com. Salvation Army, pres., 1981-83; pres. Maumee Men's Rep. Club, 1947-48; former chmn. bd. trustees Presbytery of Maumee, Inc.; trustee, sec. Masonic Toledo Trust, 1986-97, Stevenson Theatre Trust, 1997—; asst. sec. Otis Avery Browning Masonic Meml. Fund, 1987-97. Named to Toledo H.S. Athletes Hall of Fame, 1995—. Mem. ABA, Ex-FBI Agts. Soc., Ohio Bar Assn., Lucas County Bar Assn., Toledo Bar Assn., Masons (33 degree), Shriners, Heather Downs Country Club (Toledo) (past pres., dir.), Sigma Chi (life). Presbyterian (elder). Home: 5916 Cresthaven Ln Apt B416 Toledo OH 43614-1200 *Education, preparation and perseverance are essential to attaining success.*

BOGGS, ROBERT NEWELL, editor; b. Denver, Sept. 14, 1930; s. John Irwin and Rowena Opal (Newell) B.; m. Gwendolyn Carol Lee, June 18, 1955; children: Kerrie Kim Hanley and Kristie Kay Barszcz (twins), Kevin Clarke, Karole Lee Johns. BS in Mech. Engring., U. Colo., 1958. Design engr. Denver Equipment Co., 1958-59; application engr., writer Gates Rubber Co., Denver, 1959-63; asst. editor Design News, Denver, after 1963, then assoc. editor, sr. editor, 1971, mng. exec. editor, 1971-90; so. tech. editor Design News, Chapel Hill, N.C., 1990-95; ret., 1995; co-founder Busy B Ceramics, 1975; owner December Crafters; founder, pres. The Bridge Ctr., Inc., 1996—. Pres. Franklin Assn. Childhood Edn., Denver, 1969, Cherrywood Ridge Civic Assn., 1969-71, mem. adv. bd., Marshfield, Mass., 1975-77. With USAF, 1950-54. Mem. ASME, Am. Soc. Bus. Press Editors (founding pres. chpt. 1974-75, dir. 1979-82, 1st v.p. 1983-84), Marshfield Civic Assn. (founding pres. 1973-75). Office: 602 Jones Ferry Rd Carrboro NC 27510-2165

BOGGS, ROBERT WAYNE, healthcare administrator; b. St. Helena, Calif., Sept. 17, 1941; s. Wayne Cress Boggs and Ann (Stevenson) Isham; m. Donna F. Ferguson, Nov. 24, 1967; children: Jacquelin, Ryan. BS, Fresno State U., 1964; PhD, U. Calif., Davis, 1970. Bd. cert. nutritionist. Staff mem. Procter & Gamble, Cin., 1970-73, sect. head, 1973-76, assoc. dir., 1976-83, dir., 1983-99; cons. RWB Mgmt. Sys., 1999—; mem. adv. bd. U. Cin., 1991-94, mem. pharm. sci. bd., 1987—; exec. sec. Procter Found., 1982-95; bd. dirs. Cin. Riverhawks, 1997—. Mem. St. Xavier H.S. Athletic Bd., 1991-93; pres. Glendale Youth Sports, 1989, Christ Ch. Glendale, 1988; v.p. Team Cin., 1993; mem. adv. bd. Cin. Classics, 1995. Mem. Am. Inst. Nutrition (adv. bd. 1988-91), Nutrition Today Soc. Avocations: soccer, equestrian events, tractor restoration.

BOGGS, STEVEN EUGENE, lawyer; b. Santa Monica, Calif., Apr. 28, 1947; s. Eugene W. and Annie (Happe) B. BA in Econ., U. Calif., Santa Barbara, 1969; D of Chiropractic summa cum laude, Cleveland Chiropractic, L.A., 1974; PhD in Fin. Planning, Columbia Pacific U., 1986; JD in Law, U. So. Calif., 1990. Bar: Calif. 1990, U.S. Dist. Ct. (cen. dist.) Calif. 1990, Hawaii 1991, U.S. Ct. Appeals (9th cir.); CFP; lic. chiropractor Hawaii, Calif.; lic. radiography X-ray supr. and operator. Faculty mem. Cleveland Chiropractic Coll., 1972-74; pres. clinic dir. Hawaii Chiropratic Clinic, Inc., Aiea, 1974-87; pvt. practice Honolulu, 1991—; mem. faculty Hawaii Pacific U., 1997-99; cons. in field; seminar presenter 1990—. Contbr. articles to profl. jours. Recipient Cert. Appreciation State of Hawaii, 1981-84. Fellow Internat. Coll. of Chiropractic; mem. ABA, Am. Trial Lawyers Assn., Consumer Lawyers of Hawaii, Am. Chiropractic Assn., Hawaii State Chiropractic Assn. (pres. 1978, 85, 86, v.p. 1977, sec. 1979-84, treas. 1976, other coms., Valuable Svc. award 1984, Cert. Appreciation 1986, Cert. Achievement 1986, Chiropractor of Yr. 1986, Outstanding Achievement award 1991), Consumer Lawyers of Hawaii (bd. dirs.). Democrat. Avocations: sailing, scuba, snorkling, boogie boarding, bicycling. Office: 1188 Bishop St Ste 1705 Honolulu HI 96813-3307

BOGGS, THOMAS HALE, JR., lawyer; b. New Orleans, Sept. 18, 1940; s. Thomas Hale and Corinne (Claiborne) B.; m. Mary Barbara Denechaud, Dec. 27, 1960; children—Hale, Elizabeth, Douglas. A.B., Georgetown U., 1961, LL.B., 1965. Bar: D.C. 1965, U.S. Ct. Appeals 1966, U.S. Supreme Ct. 1971. Economist Joint Econ. Com., U.S. Congress, 1961-65; spl. asst. to dir. Office Emergency Planning, 1965-66; practice in Washington, 1966—; mem. firm Patton Boggs, L.L.P., 1966—; Presdl. Commn. on Exec. Exch., 1979-81; Presdl. del. Independence of Solomon Islands, 1978, Trade Mission to People's Republic of China, 1979. Co-author: Private Trade Barriers in the Atlantic Community, 1964, Corporate Political Activity, 1984. Dem. candidate for U.S. Ho. of Reps. 8th Dist. Md., 1970; mem. Charter Commn., Dem. Nat. Com., 1973; trustee Fed. City Coun., Chesapeake Bay Trust, The Keystone Ctr. Mem. Am. Judicature Soc., ABA (com. chmn.), Martime, Fed. Bar Assns., Delta Theta Phi. Home: 6 E Kirke St Chevy Chase MD 20815-4217 Office: Patton Boggs LLP 2550 M St NW Ste 500 Washington DC 20037-1350*

BOGGS, WADE ANTHONY, professional baseball player; b. Omaha, June 15, 1958; m. Deborah Bertercelli; children: Meagann, Brett. Student, Hillsborough C.C., Fla. Baseball player Boston Red Sox, 1976-92, N.Y. Yankees, 1992-97, Tampa Bay Devils, 1997—. Mem. Am. League All-Star Team, 1985-96, Sporting News Am. League All-Star Team, 1983, 85-88, 91, 94, Sporting News Am. League Silver Slugger Team, 1983, 86-89, 91, 93-94; named Am. League Gold Glove, 1994; Am. League records held: most consecutive 200 hit seasons (7), 1983-89, highest rookie year aver. (349), 1982, most singles in a season (187), 1985. Achievements include played in World Series, 1986. Office: Tampa Bay Devil Rays One Tropicana Drive Saint Petersburg FL 33705*

BOGGS, WILLENE GRAYTHEN, property manager, oil and gas broker, consultant; b. Vancouver, Wash., Mar. 10, 1939; d. William Louis and Zorah (Williams) Graythen; m. Ray Buck Glasgow, Feb. 8, 1964 (div. June 1969); m. Harry Maurice Boggs, May 23, 1993. BA in History, Centenary Coll., 1975; postgrad., La. State Law Sch., 1984, S.E. La. U., 1989. Tchr., educator St. Tam Parish Sch. Bd., Lacombe, La., 1964-65; abstractor St. Tam Parish Legal News, Covington, La., 1965-66, Kansas City Title Ins. Co., New Orleans, 1966-69, Lawyers Title Ins. Corp., New Orleans, 1975-77, Frawley, Wogan, Miller & Co., New Orleans, 1977-79; owner, mgr. Idea House and Sweet Home Antiques, Metairie, La., 1973-76; owner, mgr., abstractor, oil and gas broker Willene Glasgow & Assocs., Metairie, 1969-73; owner, mgr., abstractor Willene Glasgow & Assocs., Covington, La., 1979-93; pres. WCV Mgmt., Inc., Nashville, 1993-94, Charlotte, N.C., 1997—; asst. to art dir. Bascom-Louise Gallery, Highlands, N.C., 1996; legal asst. Poyner & Spruill, LLP, Charlotte, 1998. Author: Decoupage and Related Crafts, 1972; contbg. writer Times-Picayune, New Orleans, 1989, LAD News, 1998-99. Bd. dirs. Air, Water and Earth Inst., Covington, 1989; bd. dirs., pres. Pontchartrain Area Recycling Coun., Inc., Covington, 1989, 90, 91, 92, 93; mem. Citizens Adv. Com. on Solid Waste, 1988, 89, 90, 91, 92; coord. Pontchartrain Area Recycling Conv., 1988; fund raiser March of Dimes, Am. Cancer Soc., Arthritis Found., others, 1986—; pres. Mount Lori Home Owners Assn., Highlands, N.C., 1998-99. Named hon. sec. state State of La., 1987. Mem. AAUW (conf. chmn. 1988-89, 92-93, chmn. Ednl. Found. 1989-91, Mem. of Yr. award Covington-Mandeville br. 1989, v.p. membership 1991-93), Petroleum Landman's Assn., Covington C. of C. (legis. chmn. 1988—, Mem. of Yr. award 1988), Art League of Highlands (membership chmn. 1996, publicity chmn. 1997), Highlands-Cashiers Garden Club (v.p. 1997), Metrolina Paralegal Assn., N.C. Bar Assn. Legal Asst. Divsn. Avocations: fine arts, arts and crafts, restoring antique furniture, collecting antique toys. Home and Office: 7212 Rock Island Rd Charlotte NC 28278-6512

BOGGS, WILLIAM O., English educator; b. Erie, Pa., Oct. 19, 1950; s. Charles Hayes and Mildred Agnes (Terrill) B.; m. Patricia R. Campbell, Mar. 7, 1992; stepchildren: Jarret Snyder, Cherish Snyder. BS in Edn., Edinboro U. of Pa., 1972, MA in English, 1974; DA in English, Carnegie Mellon U., 1981. Asst. prof. English Frostburg (Md.) U., 1980-81, W.Va. U., Morgantown, 1981-82; assoc. prof. English Robert Morris Coll., Pitts., 1982-89; prof. English Slippery Rock (Pa.) U., 1989—; adj. prof. English Waynesburg (Pa.) Coll., 1981. Author: Swimming in Clean Water, 1989, Eddy Johnson's American Dream, 1992, The Man Who Never Comes Back, 1995. Committeeman Butler (Pa.) County Rep. Party, 1990-92. Recipient award Am. Acad. Poets, 1978-79. Mem. Masons. Office: Slippery Rock U Dept English Slippery Rock PA 16057

BOGHANI, ASHOK BALVANTRAI, consulting firm executive; b. Bombay, Aug. 8, 1949; came to U.S., 1970; s. Balvantrai Pranlal and Charusheela (Kapadia) B.; m. Meera Kapadia, May 30, 1977; children: Ami, Amar. B of Tech., Indian Inst. Tech., Bombay, 1970; MS, MIT, 1971, M in Mech. Engring., 1973, ScD, 1974. Staff engr. Foster-Miller, Waltham, Mass., 1974-77, project mgr., 1977-79; sr. cons. Arthur D. Little, Inc., Cambridge, Mass., 1979-90, dir., 1990—, v.p., 1994—, leader N.Am. transp. and automotive practice, 1998—; mem. transp. hazmat com. Transp. Rsch. Bd., Washington, 1987-94; mem. Benefits, Evaluation and Assessment com., Intelligent Vehicle Hwy. Systems Am., Washington, 1992-96. Contbr. articles to profl. jours. Recipient cert. of recognition NASA, 1976, 78. Mem. ASME, Soc. Automotive Engrs., Indus Entrepreneurs-Atlantic (charter mem.),. Democrat. Avocations: photography, travel, hiking, music. Home: 3 Sawmill Rd Acton MA 01720-5835 Office: Arthur D Little Inc Acorn Park Cambridge MA 02140

BOGHOLTZ, WILLIAM E., minister; b. L.A., Mar. 25, 1959; s. Wilhelm E. and Elizabeth F. (Caulfield) B.; children: Rebekah Ann, Matthew James; m. Maria M. Sanchez, Sept. 25, 1998. BA, Wagner Coll., 1981; MDiv, Luth. Theol. Sem., 1985; D in Ministry, Grad. Theol. Found., Donaldson, Ind., 1999. Ordained to ministry Luth. Ch. in Am., 1985. Intern/vicar Bethel Luth. Ch., Auburn, Mass., 1983-84; pastor Holy Trinity Luth. Ch., York Springs, Pa., 1985-88, Atonement Luth. Ch., S.I., N.Y., 1989-91, Our Saviour Luth. Ch., S.I., 1991—; coord./host pastor S.I. Liberian Refugee Ministry, 1997—; adj. instr. Wagner Coll., S.I., 1993-97; mem. Christian edn. com. and parish life commn. Ctrl. Pa. synod Luth. Ch. in Am., 1986-87; mem. bishop's com. for ecumenical affairs Lower Susquehanna synod Evang. Luth. Ch. in Am., 1988, stewardship com. Metro N.Y. synod, 1990-92; tchr. religion Trinity Luth. Sch., S.I., 1990-94, 97-98; convenor, mem. S.I. Luth. Ministerium, 1989-91; chairperson Adams County Migrant Ministry, Gettysburg, Pa., 1986-88; chmn. adv. bd. Luth. Cmty. Svc., N.Y.C., 1989-94; chmn. bd. dirs. Luth. Social Svcs., N.Y.C., 1996—; sec. bd. dirs. Luth. Social Svcs., N.Y.C., 1992-96; bd. dirs. Luth. Family and Cmty. Svcs., N.Y.C., 1992—, sec., 1994—. Editor, pub. booklet Churches of Oakwood/Richmondton, S.I., 1990; mem. editl. bd. Bride of Christ, 1993-96. Bd. dirs. United Way Adams County, 1985-87. Mem. Ecumenical Soc. Blessed Virgin Mary, Luth. Liturgical Renewal, S.I. Clergy Assn. (treas. 1990-91). Office: Our Saviour Luth Ch 549 Bard Ave Staten Island NY 10310-3015

BOGHOSIAN, PAULA DER, computer business consultant; b. Watervliet, N.Y., Nov. 19, 1933; d. Harry and Osgi (Piligian) der B. BS magna cum laude, Syracuse U., 1964, MS, 1967; postgrad., SUNY, Oswego, 1972, SUNY, Albany, 1974. Cert. profl. sec. Asst. prof. Cazenovia (N.Y.) Coll., 1964-73; instr. Bd. of Coop., Syracuse, N.Y., 1973-76, dir. bus. careers, 1976-92; cons. computer bus., prin. Syracuse, 1984—. Zonta scholar, 1964; Jessie Smith Noyes grantee Syracuse U., 1965. Mem. Assn. Info. Systems Profl. (com. chmn.), Bus. Tchrs. Assn. of N.Y. State, Adminstrv. Mgmt. Soc., Eastern Bus. Tchrs. Assn., Assn. for Supervision and Curriculum Devel., Assn. of Am. Jr. Colls., Assn. of Am. U. Profs., Nat. Assn. for Armenian Studies and Rsch. Harvard U., Internat. Tng. Communications (v.p. 1985-86), Delta Pi Epsilon, Beta Gamma Sigma, Phi Kappa Phi, Pi Lambda Theta, Sigma Lamda Delta. Republican. Mem. Armenian Apostolic. Avocations: music, golf, water colors, designer, travel. Home and Office: 3181 Bellevue Ave Apt B6 Syracuse NY 13219-3156

BOGHOSIAN, VARUJAN YEGAN, sculptor; b. New Britain, Conn., June 26, 1926; s. Mesrop and Baidzar (Saylandzian) B.; m. Marilyn Cummins, Sept. 1, 1953; 1 dau., Heidi. Student, Conn. Tchrs. Coll., 1946-48, Vesper George Sch. Art, 1948-50; B.F.A., Yale U., 19—, M.F.A., 1959; M.A. (hon.), Brown U., 1965, Dartmouth Coll., 1969. Instr. art U. Fla., 1958-59, Pratt Inst., 1961, Yale U., 1962-64; asst. prof. art Cooper Union Coll., 1959-64; asso. prof. Brown U., 1964-68; artist-in-residence Dartmouth Coll., 1968, prof. art, 1968—, George Frederick Jewett prof. art, 1983—; sculptor in residence Am. Acad. in Rome, 1966-67, 75. Artist woodcut portfolios Orpheus, 1951, The River Styx, 1971; numerous one-man shows including Stable Gallery, N.Y.C., 1963, 64, 65, 66, Cordier and Ekstrom, N.Y.C., 1969, 71, 73, 75, 77-80, 82, 84, 87-89, Arts Club of Chgo., 1970, Claude Bernard Gallery, N.Y.C., 1991, Norton Gallery Art, Palm Beach, Fla., 1993; group shows include Berry Hill Galleries, N.Y.C., 1996, Obelisk Gallery, Rome, 1953, Mus. Modern Art, N.Y.C., 1956, Hanover Gallery, London, 1966, retrospective Hood Mus., Hanover, N.H., 1989; represented in numerous permanent collections including, Mus. Modern Art, N.Y.C., Whitney Mus. Am. Art, N.Y.C., Met. Mus. N.Y.C., Addison Gallery Am. Art, Andover, Mass., Worcester Art Mus., Phoenix Art Mus. Chmn. bd. MacDowell Colony. With USN, 1944-46. Recipient award Nat. Inst. Arts and Letters, 1972; Fulbright grantee, Italy, 1953; U.S. Dept. State specialists grantee, 1961; fellow Howard Found., 1966, John Simon Guggenheim Found. fellow, 1985. Mem. NAD, Am. Acad. Arts and Letters (St. Botolph award 1991), Century Assn. (N.Y.C.), St. Botolph Club (Boston). Club: Century (N.Y.C.). Office: Darmouth Coll HB 6081 Visual Studies Office Hanover NH 03755

BOGIS, NANA EILEEN, librarian; b. Phila., Feb. 4, 1938; d. Herman B. and Rose L. Bogis. BA, Temple U., 1960; MLS, Drexel U., 1966. Cataloger Bucks County Libr., Doylestown, Pa., 1966-68; head cataloger Montgomery County Libr., Norristown, Pa., 1968-69; dir. Mt. Holly (N.J.) Pub. Libr., 1970-74, Monroe Twp. Pub. Libr., Williamstown, N.J., 1974—; adj. prof. Drexel U., Phila., 1967-69; cons. CBG Video Circuit, Williamstown, 1985—, Chipshape, Williamstown, 1989—. Mem. ALA, Am. Film Inst., N.J. Libr. Assn. Avocations: cinema, theatre, opera, travel. E-mail: nbogis@buyrite.com. Office: Free Pub Libr Monroe Twp 306 S Main St Williamstown NJ 08094

BOGLE, JOHN CLIFTON, investment company executive; b. Montclair, N.J., May 8, 1929; s. William Yates, Jr. and Josephine (Hipkins) B.; m. Eve Sherrerd, Sept. 22, 1956; children: Barbara, Jean, John Clifton, Nancy, Sandra, Andrew. AB magna cum laude, Princeton U., 1951; LhD (hon.), Widener U., 1997. With Wellington Mgmt. Co., Phila., 1951-74, asst. to pres., 1954-62, sec., adminstrv. v.p., 1962-66, exec. v.p., 1966-67, pres., CEO, 1967-74; founder, sr. chmn. Vanguard Group Investment Cos. (Wellington Fund, Windsor Fund, others), Valley Forge, Pa., 1974—; former bd. dirs., mem. exec. com. CGU; bd. dirs., chmn. corp. objectives com. Mead Corp. Author: Bogle on Mutual Funds: New Perspectives for the Intelligent Investor, 1993, Common Sense on Mutual Funds: New Imperatives for the Intelligent Investor, 1999; subject of biography: John Bogle and the Vanguard Experiment: One Man's Quest to Transform the Mutual Fund Industry, by Robert Slater, 1996; numerous articles to profl. jours., chpts. to books. Chmn. bd. trustees Blair Acad.; bd. dirs. Nat. Constn. Ctr., Am. Indian Coll. Fund.; former mem. adv. coun. econs. dept. Princeton U.; dir. Independence Standards Bd. Mem. Nat. Assn. Securities Dealers (investment cos. com. 1967-74, long-range planning com. 1973-74), Investment Co. Inst. (gov. 1969-81, chmn. 1969-70), Securities and Exch. Commn. (market oversight and fin. svcs. adv. com.), Merion Cricket Club (Haverford), Merion Golf (Ardmore). Office: Vanguard Group PO Box 2600 Valley Forge PA 19482-2600

BOGLE, RONALD E., academic administrator; b. Oklahoma City, June 28, 1952; s. J. Robert and Kathleen Gladys (Birdsall) B.; m. Kathleen Marie Donovan, July 14, 1979; children: Kevin Donovan, Erin Kathleen. Student spl. studies, Austrian-Am. Inst., Vienna, 1974; BS, Baker U., 1974; postgrad., U. Kans., 1979-81. Asst. dean admissions Baker U., Baldwin, Kans., 1974-79; mktg. and pub. rels. dir. Gould/Evans Partnership, Lawrence, Kans., 1979-81; mktg. and pub. rels. v.p. HTB Inc., Oklahoma City, 1982-88, Oklahoma City C. of C., 1989-91; adminstr. mktg. and devel. Okla. Med. Ctr., Oklahoma City, 1991-94; v.p. univ. advancement Oklahoma City U., 1994-98; v.p. external affairs U. Ctrl. Okla., Edmond, 1998—. Pres. Oklahoma City Bd. of Edn., 1995—; mem. steering com. Murrah Meml. Task Force, Oklahoma City, 1996-98; chmn. Okla. Task Force on Charter Schs., Oklahoma City, 1995; chmn., exec. dir. Nat. Govs. Assn. ann. meeting, Tulsa, Okla., 1993; chmn. Jr. League cmty. adv. bd., Oklahoma City, 1995-96; bd. dirs. Coun. for Great City Schs., 1993-97, Arts Coun. Okla., 1994—, Bus. Circle for the Arts, 1998—. Nominee Paragon award, Leadership Oklahoma City, 1996. Mem. Okla. Acad. for State Goals (mem. exec. com. 1994—), Rotary Club. Avocations: piano and vocal music, hiking, family, church. Home: 3001 Willow Brook Rd Oklahoma City OK 73120-5724

BOGNER, NORMAN, novelist, screenwriter, playwright; b. Bklyn., Nov. 13, 1935; s. Manny and Rose (Schwartz) B.; m. Felice Gordon, Nov. 15, 1959 (div. June 1974); children: Jonathan Scott, Nicholas Sean, Alexander Evan; m. Bettye Jean Strong McCartt, Feb. 14, 1991. BA cum laude, Syracuse U., 1957; postgrad., NYU, New Sch. for Social Rsch., Columbia U., The Sorbonne, Paris. Editl. mgr. Jonathan Cape, London, 1961-65; story editor ABC-TV Armchair Theatre, 1965-68; writer. Author: (novels) In Spells No Longer Bound, 1961, Spanish Fever, 1963, Divorce, 1966, Seventh Avenue, 1967, The Madonna Complex, 1968, Making Love, 1971, The Hunting Animal, 1973, Snowman, 1977, Arena, 1979, California Dreamers, 1981, To Die in Provence, 1998, Honor Thy Wife, 1999, (screenplay) Privilege, 1967, (plays) The Match, 1965, The Waiters, 1967. Email: nbogner@earthlink.net.

BOGORAD, BARBARA ELLEN, psychologist; b. N.Y.C.; d. Albert Lyon and Miriam Ida (Serlin) B. BA, CUNY, 1969; MS, Rutgers U., 1972, Yeshiva U., 1981; PsyD, Yeshiva U., 1983. Lic. psychologist, N.Y.; diplomate Am. Bd. Profl. Psychol., 1992, Am. Bd. Forensic examiners, Am. Bd. Psychol. Specialities, Am. Bd. Disabilities; cert. psychopathologist; master addictions counselor. Psychotherapist South Shore Ctr. Psychotherapy, Merrick, N.Y., 1978-82; psychology intern Birch Ctr. Exceptional Children, Queens, N.Y., 1980-81; clinical intern Long Island Jewish Hosp., Glen Oaks, N.Y., 1981-82; clin. intern South Oaks Hosp., Amityville, N.Y., 1982-83; staff psychologist St. John's Episc. Hosp., Far Rockaway, N.Y., 1984-86, St. Charles Hosp., Port Jeff, N.Y., 1987-88; pvt. practice Amityville, 1985-94; staff psychologist South Oaks Hosp., Amityville, 1988-94, dir. sexual abuse recovery program, 1991-94; pvt. practice Massapequa, N.Y., 1994—; speaker in field; radio and TV appearances 1990—. Vol. crisis relief worker Nassau and Suffolk counties, N.Y., 1990—. Fellow Am. Acad. Sch. Psychology; mem. APA, Am. Acad. Experts Traumatic Stress, Ea. Psychol. Assn., N.Y. State Psychol. Assn., Nassau County Psychol. Assn., Suffolk County Psychol. Assn., Am. Assn. Psychiat. Svcs. Children, Psychologists in Hosp. Practice, Am. Profl. Soc. Abuse of Children, Nat. Assn. Childcare Resource and Referral Agys. (aux.). Avocations: photography, gardening, travel, choral singing. Office: 627 Broadway Massapequa NY 11758-5031

BOGORAD, LAWRENCE, biologist, educator; b. Tashkent, U.S.S.R., Aug. 29, 1921; came to U.S., 1922; s. Boris and Florence (Bernard) B.; m. Rosalyn G. Sagen, June 29, 1943; children—Leonard Paul, Kiki M. Lee. B.S., U. Chgo., 1942, Ph.D., 1949. Instr. botany U. Chgo., 1948-51, asst. prof. dept. botany, 1953-57, assoc. prof., 1957-61, prof., 1961-67; prof. biology Harvard U., Cambridge, Mass., 1967-92; chmn. dept. biology Harvard U., 1974-76; dir. Maria Moors Cabot Found. Harvard U., Cambridge, Mass., 1976-87; Maria Moors Cabot prof. biology Harvard U., 1980-92, prof. emeritus, 1992—; vis. investigator Rockefeller Inst., N.Y.C., 1951-53; mem. com. on sci. and pub. policy NAS, 1977-81; mem. NAS-NAE-IOM com. on sci. engring. and pub. policy, 1990-92; mem. Assembly of Life Scis., NRC, Space Studies Bd., 1995-98; mem. joint coun. on food and agrl. scis. Dept. Agr., 1978-82. Assoc. editor Bot. Gazette, 1958; mem. editl. com. Ann. Rev. Plant Physiology, 1963-67, Ann. Rev. Cell Biology, 1984-88; mem. editl. bd. Plant Physiology, 1965-66, Biochimica Biophysica Acta, 1967-69, Jour. Cell Biology, 1967-70, Jour. Applied and Molecular Genetics, 1981-85, Plant Molecular Biology, 1981-85, Plant Cell Reports, 1981-85; editor, chmn. editl. bd. Proc. Nat. Acad. Scis., 1991-95. Served with AUS, 1943-46. Merck fellow, 1951-53; Fulbright fellow, 1960; recipient Career Research award NIH, 1963. Fellow Am. Acad. Arts and Scis.; mem. NAS (chmn. botany sect. 1974-77, mem. coun. 1989-92, editor procs., chmn. editl. bd. Procs. 1991-95), AAAS (bd. dirs. 1982-86, pres. 1986-87, chmn. bd. 1987), Am. Philos. Soc., Am. Soc. Biol. Chemistry, Am. Soc. Cell Biology, Am. Soc. Plant Physiologists (pres. 1968-69, Stephen Hales award 1982), Royal Danish Acad. Scis. and Letters (fgn.), Soc. Devel. Biology (pres. 1984). Office: Harvard U Dept Molecular/Cellular Bio 16 Divinity Ave Cambridge MA 02138-2020

BOGOSIAN, ERIC, actor, writer; b. Boston, Apr. 24, 1953; s. Henry and Edwina B.; m. JoAnne Bonney, Oct. 1990. Student, U. Chgo., 1971-73; BA, Oberlin Coll., 1976. Founder, dir. The Kitchen, N.Y.C. Actor, writer: (theatre, off-broadway debut) Men Inside, 1982, Voices of America, 1982, (dir., design supr.) FunHouse, 1983, Drinking in America (Drama Desk award for outstanding solo performance 1986), 1986, Talk Radio, 1987, Sex, Drugs, Rock & Roll, 1990, Pounding Nails in the Floor with My Forehead, 1994, SubUrbia, 1994, Griller, 1998; (film) (Cinemax spl.) Drinking in America, 1986, Talk Radio, 1988, Sex, Drugs, Rock & Roll, 1991, Dolores Claiborne, 1995, Under Siege 2, 1995; TV show appearances: The Twilight Zone, Miami Vice, Law & Order, Larry Sanders Show, Witchhunt, 1994: TV movie appearances: The Caine Mutiny Court Martial, 1988; author: Sex, Drugs, Rock & Roll, 1990, Pounding Nails in the Floor with my Forehead, 1994, Notes from Underground, 1993, (play and film) subUrbia, 1994; author, creator (with Steven Spielberg) (TV series) High Incident, 1996, (voice) Arabian Knight, 1995, The Substance of Fire, 1996, (voice) Beavis and Butthead do America, 1996, Office Killer, 1997, Deconstructing Harry, 1997, Gossip, 1999. Recipient Obie, 1986, 90, 94, Drama Critics Circle award; grantee Nat. Endowment for Arts, Berlin Film Fest Silver Bear award, 1988. Mem. SAG, AFTRA, Writer's Guild, Actor's Equity. *

BOGUCKI, PETER IGNATIUS, archaeologist; b. Phila., Mar. 11, 1954; s. Alfred and Jadwiga (Kulpinska) B.; m. Virginia Creeden, Dec. 10, 1978; children: Caroline, Marianna. BA, U. Pa., 1974; MA, Harvard U., 1977, PhD, 1981. Lectr. in anthropology U. Mass., Boston, 1982-83; dir. studies Forbes Coll. Princeton (N.J.) U., 1983-94, asst. dean sch. engring. and applied sci., 1994—; lectr. Archaeol. Inst. Am., 1990-91. Author: Early Neolithic Subsistence and Settlement in the Polish Lowlands, 1982, Forest Farmers and Stockherders: Early Agriculture and its Consequences in North-Central Europe, 1988, The Origins of Human Society, 1999; editor: Case Studies in European Prehistory, 1993; mem. editl. adv. bd. Environ. Archaeology jour.; contbr. articles to profl. jours. Grantee Nat. Geographic Soc., 1989, 90. Mem. Nat. Acad. Advising Assn., Am. Soc. Engring. Edn., European Assn. Archaeologists, Soc. Am. Archaeology, Internat. Coun. Archaeozoology, Assn. for Environ. Archaeology, Sigma Xi. Office: Princeton U Sch Engring Applied Sci Princeton NJ 08544

BOGUE, ALLAN GEORGE, history educator; b. London, Ont., Can., May 12, 1921; married; 3 children. B.A., U. Western Ont., 1943, M.A., 1946; Ph.D., Cornell U., 1951; LL.D., U. Western Ont., 1973; D.Fil (hon.), U. Uppsala, 1977. Lectr. econs. and history, asst. librarian U. Western Ont., 1949-52; from asst. prof. to prof. history U. Iowa, 1952-64, chmn. dept., 1959-63; prof. history U. Wis.-Madison, 1964-68, chmn. dept., 1972-73, Frederick Jackson Turner prof. history, 1968-91; mem. hist. adv. com. Math. Soc. Sci. Bd., 1965-71; Scandinavian-Am. Found. Thord-Gray lectr., 1968; mem. Council Inter-Univ. Consortium Polit. Research, 1971-73, 89-91; vis. prof. history Harvard U., 1972; dir. Social Sci. Research Council, 1973-76. Author: Money at Interest, 1955, From Prairie to Corn Belt, 1963; co-author, editor: The West of the American People, 1970; co-author, contbr.: The Dimensions of Quantitative Research in History, 1972; co-editor, contbr.: American Political Behavior: Historical Essays and Readings, 1974; co-editor: The University of Wisconsin: One Hundred and Twenty Five Years, 1975; author: The Earnest Men, 1981, Clio and the Bitch Goddess, Quantification in American Political History, 1983, The Congressman's Civil War, 1989; co-editor: The Jeffersonian Dream: Studies in the History of American Law Land Policy and Development, 1996, Frederick Jackson Turner, 1998. Social Sci. Rsch. Coun. fellow, 1955, 66, Guggenheim fellow, 1970, H.E. Huntington Libr. fellow, 1991, 93, Sherman Fairchild Disting. fellow Calif. Inst. Tech., 1975, Ctr. for Advanced Study in the Behavioral Scis. fellow, 1985, NEH fellow, 1985. Fellow Agr. Hist. Soc. (pres. 1963-64); mem. Orgn. Am. Historians (pres. 1982-83), Am. Hist. Assn., Econ. Hist. Assn. (pres. 1981-82), Social Sci. Hist. Assn. (pres. 1977-78), Nat. Acad. Scis., Western Hist. Assn. (hon. life). Office: U Wis Dept History Madison WI 53706

BOGUE, ANDREW WENDELL, federal judge; b. Yankton, S.D., May 23, 1919; s. Andrew S. and Genevieve Bogue; m. Florence Elizabeth Williams, Aug. 5, 1945; children—Andrew Stevenson, Laurie Beth, Scott MacFarlane. B.S., S.D. State U., 1941; LL.B., U. S.D., 1947. Bar: S.D. 1947. States atty. Turner County, S.D., 1952-67; judge 2d Jud. Cir., S.D., 1967-70; judge U.S. Dist. Ct. S.D., Rapid City, 1970—, chief judge, from 1980, sr. judge, 1985—. Mem. S.D. Bar Assn., Fed. Judges Assn. Episcopalian. Office: US Courthouse Fed Bldg Rm 244 515 9th St Rapid City SD 57701-2626*

BOGUES, TYRONE CURTIS (MUGGSY BOGUES), professional basketball player; b. Balt., Jan. 9, 1965; m. Kimberly Bogues; children: Tyeisha, Brittany, Tyrone Jr. Student, Wake Forest U., 1983-87. Guard Washington Bullets, 1987-88, Charlotte (N.C.) Hornets, 1988-97, Golden State Warriors, Oakland, Calif., 1997—. Founder "Reading and Roundball" charity basketball game, Balt.; dir. numerous basketball camps. Recipient Inspirational Trophy Jim Thorpe Pro Sports Awards, 1995; number retired at Wake Forest; all-time leader assists and steals Atlantic Coast Conf., assist to turnoer ratio NBA, assists Charlotte Hornets; named Belt/WBTV Hornets Player of Yr., 1993-94. Avocations: softball, golf. Office: Golden State Warriors 1011 Broadway Oakland CA 94607

BOGUS, CARL THOMAS, law educator; b. Fall River, Mass., May 14, 1948; s. Isidore E. and Carolyn (Dashoff) B.; m. Dale Shepard, Sept. 5, 1970 (div. 1987); children: Elizabeth Carol, Ian Troy; m. Cynthia J. Giles, Nov. 5, 1988; 1 child, Zoe Churchill. AB, Syracuse U., 1970, JD, 1972. Bar: Pa. 1973, U.S. Dist. Ct. (ea. dist.) Pa. 1973, U.S. Ct. Appeals (3d cir.) 1976, U.S. Supreme Ct. 1977. Assoc. Steinberg, Greenstein, Gorelick & Price, Phila., 1973-79, ptnr., 1979-83; assoc. Mesirov, Gelman, Jaffe, Cramer & Jamieson, Phila., 1983-84, ptnr., 1985-91, assoc. prof. Roger Williams U. Sch. Law, 1996—; vis. prof. Rutgers U. Sch. Law, Camden, 1992-96; mem. bd. Visitors Coll. Law, Syracuse U., N.Y., 1976—; mem. nat. adv. panel Violence Policy Ctr., 1993—. Contbr. articles to profl. jours. Bd. dirs. Handgun Control, Inc., 1987-89, bd. govs., 1992-93; bd. dirs. Ctr. to Prevent Handgun Violence, 1989-92, Lawyers Alliance for Nuclear Arms Control, 1987-89. Mem. ABA (Ross Essay award 1991), Syracuse Law Coll. Assn. (exec. sec. 1979-83, 2d v.p. 1983-85). Democrat. Jewish. Office: Roger William U Sch Law 10 Metacom Ave Bristol RI 02809-5103

BOGUTZ, JEROME EDWIN, lawyer; b. Bridgeton, N.J., June 7, 1935; s. Charles and Gertrude (Lahn) B.; m. Helene Carole Ross, Nov. 20, 1960; children: Marc Lahn, Tami Lynne. BS in Fin., Pa. State U., 1957; JD, Villanova U., 1962. Bar: Pa., U.S. Dist. Ct. (ea. dist.) Pa., U.S. Ct. Appeals (3d cir.), U.S. Supreme Ct. Assoc. Dash & Levy, Phila., 1962-63, Abrahams & Loewenstein, Phila., 1963-64; dep. dir., chief of litigation Community Legal Svcs., Phila., 1964-68, dir., 1968-78; emeritus, 1978—; pvt. practice law Phila., 1968-71; ptnr. Bogutz & Mazer, Phila., 1971-81, Fox Rothschild O'Brien & Frankel, Phila., 1981-98; judge Pro Tem Phila. Ct. Common Pleas, 1992—; ptnr. Christie, Pabarue, Mortensen & Young, P.C., Phila., 1998—; adj. clin. prof. law Villanova (Pa.) U., 1969-72, lectr., 1987—, bd. consultors Law Sch., 1983—; pres. Internat. Mobile Machines, Phila., 1980-81, Interdigital Comm., 1980-81, also bd. dirs. ABA-JAD Lawyers Conf., 1987-92,em. exec. coun., 1986-92, vice chmn., 1987-88, chmn., 1989-90, chmn. nominating com., 1989-90, mem. long range planning com., 1989-90; bd. dirs. Jefferson Park Hosp., Phila. Bd. dirs. Am. Friends of Hebrew U., 1988-93, chmn. exec. com., 1991-93, pres., 1993-95, chmn. bd. 1995-98, chair steering com., pres. Pa. Futures Commn. on Justice in the 21st Century, 1993—, chmn. of bd., 1993-97. With USAR, 1956-60. Fellow Am. Bar Found. (life), Pa. Bar Found. (life, pres. 1986-88, bd. dirs. 1983—, lifetime dir. 1991—), Am. Judicature Soc. (life, bd. dirs. 1990—); mem. ABA (ho. of dels. 1980-84, 86-96, credentials and admissions com. 1987-88, nominating com. 1992, 93, chair ABA/JAD bench bar com., vice chmn. lawyer's conf. 1987-89, chair 1988-90, co-chair mid-yr. meeting com. 1987-88, planning com., conf. sect. officers, 1988-90, bd. mem. consortium on legal svcs. and pub. 1987-91, mem. disaster relief task force, bd. dirs., commr., chmn. ABA Commn. on Advt. 1988-91), Pa. Bar Assn. (pres. 1985-86, bd. dirs. 1983-90, chair Governance Com., 1996-98), Phila. Bar Found. (pres. 1981), Phila. Bar Assn. (v.p. 1978, pres.-elect 1979, chancellor 1980, sec. 1975-78, trustee 1979—), Pa. Bar Trust (chair 1993—), Pa. House of Dels. (life; chair governance com. 1996-98), Nat. Met. Bar Leaders (founder, pres. 1979-82, pres. emeritus 1983—), Nat. Conf. Bar Pres. (exec. coun. 1981-84), Phila. C. of C. (bd. dirs. 1980-83). Republican. Jewish. Avocations: golf, sailing. Home: 110 S Somerset Ave Ventnor City NJ 08406-2848 Office: Christie Pabarue Mortensen & Young 10th Fl 1880 Jfk Blvd Fl 10 Philadelphia PA 19103-7424

BOGY, DAVID B(EAUREGARD), mechanical engineering educator; b. Wabbaseka, Ark., June 4, 1936; s. Jesse C. and Dorothy (Duff) B.; m. Patricia Lynn Pizzitola, Mar. 28, 1961; children: Susan, Rebecca. B.S., Rice U., 1959, M.S., 1961; Ph.D., Brown U., 1966. Mech. engr. Shell Devel. Co., Houston, 1961-63; asst. prof. mech. engring. U. Calif., Berkeley, 1967-70, assoc. prof., 1970-75, prof., 1975—, chmn. dept. mech. engring., 1991—, founder, dir. computer mechanics lab., William S. Floyd, Jr. Disting. prof., 1993—; cons. IBM Rsch., 1972-83; mem. nat. com. on theoretical and applied mechanics NRC. Served with C.E. U.S. Army, 1961-62. Fellow ASME (exec. com. tribology div.); mem. IEEE (sr.), NAE. Research on static and dynamic elasticity, fluid jets and mechanics of computer disk files and printers. Home: 8531 Buckingham Dr El Cerrito CA 94530-2533 Office: U Calif 6189 Etcheverry Hall Berkeley CA 94720-1740

BOH, IVAN, philosophy educator; b. Dolenji Lazi, Yugoslavia, Dec. 13, 1930; s. France and Marija (Mihelic) B.; m. Magda Kosnik, Aug. 30, 1957; children: Boris, Marko. B.A., Ohio U., 1954; M.A., Fordham U., 1956; Ph.D., U. Ottawa, Ont., Can., 1958. Instr. Clarke Coll., Dubuque, Iowa, 1957-59; asst. prof. Clarke Coll., 1959-62; vis. asst. prof. U. Iowa, 1962-63; Fulbright research fellow U. Munich, Germany, 1964-65; asso. prof. Mich. State U., 1966-69; prof. philosophy Ohio State U., Columbus, 1969-95, prof. emeritus, 1995—; rsch. in Spanish librs., 1972-73; MUCIA exch. prof. Moscow State U., 1979-80; Fulbright sr. rsch. fellow U. Ljubljana (Yugoslavia), 1982-83; Irex and Fulbright sr. rsch. fellow U. Halle-Wittenberg, German Dem. Republic, and Jagiellonsky U. (Poland), 1986-87. Author: Epistemic Logic in the Later Middle Ages, 1993; contbr. articles to profl. jours. Recipient Evans Latin prize Ohio U., 1954. Mem. Am. Philos. Assn., Am. Catholic Philos. Assn., Medieval Acad. Am. Home: 6171 Middlebury Dr E Columbus OH 43085-3374 Office: Ohio State U Dept Philosophy Columbus OH 43210

BOH, ROBERT HENRY, civil engineer, construction company executive; b. New Orleans, Sept. 15, 1930. BS in Civil Engring., Tulane U., 1951, MS in Civil Engring., 1953. Civil engr. Boh Bros. Constrn. Co., New Orleans, 1951; mem. faculty dept. civil engring. Tulane U., 1952-53, civil engr., 1953-55; civil engr. Boh Bros. Constrn. Co., 1955—, bd. dirs., v.p., treas., 1960—, pres., CEO, 1967-93, chmn. bd. dirs., 1986—; vis. lectr. civil engring., 1959-68; mem. adv. bd. The Times-Picayune. Mem. New Orleans Bus. Coun., Metrovision Econ. Devel. Coun., Com. of 100 for Econ. Devel. of State of La.; immediate past chmn. bd. adminstrs. Tulane U. Edn. Fund, 1988-93; chmn. bd. dirs. Chamber/New Orleans and the River Region, 1985. Mem. ASCE, NSPE, La. Engring. Soc., Associated Gen. Contractors Am. (life dir.New Orleans dist. past pres.), Associated Gen. Contractors La. (dir., past pres.). Office: Boh Bros Construction Co PO Box 53266 New Orleans LA 70153-3266

BOHAN, THOMAS LYNCH, lawyer, physicist; b. Terre Haute, Ind., Feb. 12, 1938; s. Richard Timothy and Anna Elizabeth (Lynch) B.; m. Linda Ann Sian, Nov. 26, 1960 (div. Dec. 1981); children: Richard Michael, Cecilia Anne, John Charles; m. Rhonda Beth Berg, July 4, 1987. BS in Physics, U. Chgo., 1960; MS in Physics, U. Ill., 1964, PhD in Physics, 1968; JD, Franklin Pierce Law Ctr., 1980. Bar: Maine 1980, Mass. 1980, U.S. Dist. Ct. Maine 1980, U.S. Patent Office 1980, U.S. Ct. Appeals (1st cir.) 1992, U.S. Ct. Appeals (2nd cir.) 1994, U.S. Supreme Ct., 1996. Research assoc. U. Ill., Urbana, 1968-69; asst. prof. physics Bowdoin Coll., Brunswick, Maine, 1969-76; assoc. Sunenblick, Fontaine and Reben, Portland, Maine, 1980-82; ptnr. Med. and Tech. Cons., Portland, 1982-86, sole propr., 1986—; propr. Thomas L. Bohan & Assoc., Portland, 1985—. Editor (with A. Damask) Forensic Accident Investigation: Motor Vehicles-1, 1995; editor Forensic Accident Investigation: Motor Vehicles-2, 1997; contbr. articles to profl. jours. Chmn. Community Devel. Com., Brunswick, 1976-78; organizer, treas., pres. Peaks Island Land Preserve, Inc., 1994-97. Research grantee Am. Heart Assn., 1970-76, The Research Corp., 1972-74, NSF/NATO, 1967; fellow Tex. Instruments, 1965; Fulbright scholar, Peru, 1972-73. Fellow Am. Acad. Forensic Sci. (chair engring. sci. sect. 1997-98, bd. dirs. 1999—); mem. AAAS, Am. Chem. Soc., Am. Phys. Soc., Cumberland County Bar Assn., Maine Trial Lawyers Assn. Sigma Xi. Home: 54 Pleasant Ave Peaks Island ME 04108-1188 Office: Med & Tech Cons and Thomas L Bohan & Assocs. 371 Fore St Portland ME 04101-5010

BOHANAN, DAVID JOHN, management consultant; b. Utica, N.Y., Dec. 13, 1946; s. Clifton Ralph and Florence Susan Bohanan; m. Judith Ann Petrocci, July 31, 1977; children: Luke, Jacob. BFA in Ceramics and Painting, Alfred U., 1968; BS in Commerce, U. Md., 1979; MBA in Mgmt., Boston U., 1981. Pub. R&R in the Med Mediterranean Pubs. Srl., Vicenza, Italy, 1974-81; pvt. practice fin. cons. Jersey City, 1981-86; bus. cons. S&B Practice Mgmt. Assocs., Greenbrook, N.J., 1986—; fin. planner Fin. Found., Inc., Greenbrook, N.J., 1986-98; rep. Nathan & Lewis Securities, Inc., N.Y.C., 1982-93, Cadaret, Grant & Co., Syracuse, N.Y., 1994—. Capt. F.A., U.S. Army, 1968-74. Decorated Bronze Star with oak leaf cluster. Republican. Home: 10 Saw Mill Rd Lebanon NJ 08833-4618 Office: S&B Practice Mgmt Assocs 314 Us Highway 22 Green Brook NJ 08812-1700

BOHANNAN, JULES KIRBY, printing company executive; b. Richmond, Va., June 21, 1917; s. Jules Kirby and Essie (Lambertson) B.; m. Lucyann Davis, June 28, 1941; children: Judy, Jay Kirby. Student, Syracuse U., 1946; BA, Kennedy-Western U., 1991. From order dept. staff to asst. mgr. Standard Salesbook Co., Inc., N.Y.C., 1936-49; mgr., dir. Standard Salesbook Co. Inc., 1949-51, v.p., 1950; exec. v.p. Newport Bus. Forms Co. Inc., Hampton, Va., 1951-59; pres. Newport Bus. Forms Co. Inc., 1960-62, dir., 1962-88; pres. Office Supply Inc., Hopewell, Va., 1950-62; ptnr. Paperconverters, Ltd., 1995—; bd. dirs. Printing Plates Inc. Chmn. safety com. Boy Scouts Am., 1958—; chmn. budget com. United Fund; chmn. bd. Tri-City Literacy Coun. With USNR, 1941-45. Mem. N.A.M. (mktg. com.), Nat. Ordnance Assn., Sales Execs. Club, Toastmasters, James River Country Club, Williamsburg Country Club. Episcopalian.

BOHANNAN, PAUL JAMES, anthropologist, writer, former university administrator; b. Lincoln, Nebr., Mar. 5, 1920; s. Hillory and Hazel (Truex) B.; m. Laura Marie Smith, May 15, 1943 (div. 1975); 1 child, Denis Michael; m. Adelyse D'Arcy, Feb. 28, 1981. B.A., U. Ariz., 1947; B.Sc., Oxford U., Eng., 1949, Ph.D., 1951. Lectr. social anthropology Oxford (Eng.) U., 1951-56; asst. prof. anthropology Princeton (N.J.) U., 1956-59; prof. Northwestern U., Evanston, Ill., 1959-75, U. Calif., Santa Barbara, 1976-82; prof., dean social scis. and communications U. So. Calif., Los Angeles, 1982-87, prof. emeritus, 1987—. Author: Justice and Judgement, 1957, Africa and Africans, 1964, 4th edit., 1995, Divorce and After, 1970, We, the Alien, 1991, How Culture Works, 1995. Served to capt. U.S. Army, 1941-45. Decorated Legion of Merit. Mem. Am. Anthrop. Assn. (pres. 1979-80), Am. Ethnol. Soc. (dir. 1963-66), African Studies Assn. (pres. 1963-64), Social Sci. Research Council (dir. 1962-64).

BOHANNON, JEAN ANDREA, research company executive; b. Washington, June 1, 1932; d. Alonzo and Tina (Holtyclaw) B.; m. (dec. Dec. 1984); children: Jean, June. Student, Thomas Edison Coll., 1976; PhD, Rutgers U., 1980; MA, 1986; postgrad., NYU, 1990-94. Sales staff Fuller Brush Co., Newark, 1970-75, Avon, Newark, 1975-79, Studio Girl, Calif., 1970, Blair Cosmetics, Calif.; pres. Bohannon Rsch. Co., Newark, 1988—; presenter and spkr. in field. Author: Jean, the Success, Mary, Now Its Time, Education and the Vast Era It Encompasses, Future Perspectives, New Perspectives, Short Stories by Bohannon, The Return to the Jungle, The Rite of the Bohannon, How I Solved My Financial Problems. Mem. Urban League Guild (hon.), Sierra Club, Apple Club. Democrat. Roman Catholic. Avocations: stamp collecting, reading, art. Home: 853 S 13th St Newark NJ 07108-1315 Office: Mid City Duplication Broad St Newark NJ 07102

BOHANNON, LINDA SUE, special education educator; b. L.A., July 19, 1954; d. Hearold Eugene and Ruth Ella (Sanders) Paisley; divorced; children: David Eugene, Jamie Lyn. AS, Mt. San Antonio C.C., Walnut, Calif., 1974; AA, Antelope Valley C.C., Lancaster, Calif., 1990; BA, Calif. State U., Northridge, 1992; MA, Chapman U., Orange, Calif., 1994. Cert. tchr. Calif., learning handicapped tchr., Calif.; cert. resource program specialist. Paraeducator L.A. County Office of Edn., Downey, Calif., 1987-93; tchr. Westside Sch. Dist., Lancaster, Calif., 1993-96, Lancaster Sch. Dist., Lancaster, 1996—; dir. Awana Girls Club, Leona Valley, Calif., 1993-95; advisor Calif. Jr. Scholarship Fedn., Lancaster, 1994-96. Mem. Christian Educators Assn., Calif. Educators Assn., Calif. Assn. Resource Specialists. Republican. Avocations: visual arts, sculpture, gardening, nat. parks. Office: New Vista Mid Sch 753 E Avenue K12 Lancaster CA 93535-4710

BOHANNON-KAPLAN, MARGARET ANNE, publisher, lawyer; b. Oakland, Calif., July 6, 1937; d. Thomas Morris and Ruth Frances (Davenport) Bohannon; m. Melvin Jordan Kaplan, Feb. 2, 1961; children: Mark Geoffrey, Craig Andrew, Stephen Joseph, David Benjamin, Jonathan Michael. *Ms. Bohannon-Kaplan is the niece of the late David D. Bohannon, a noted community planner and developer who was well known for his contributions to civic affairs in northern California. Husband, Melvin J. Kaplan, has been a philanthropist and entrepreneur since 1962. He is an alumnus of MIT and the University of California at Berkeley and is currently an investment banker concerned primarily with commercial real estate. Entrepreneurial sons founded two real estate companies and a software company. Combined contributions to the community include service in the Coast Guard, Air Force, Fire Department, and in the fields of health, education and law.* Student, Smith Coll., 1955-56, U. Cin., 1956; B.A. in Philosophy, U. Calif.-Berkeley, 1960; LL.B., LaSalle Extension U., 1982, Coll. Fin. Planning, 1985. Bar: Calif. 1982. Engaged in property mgmt., real estate investment Kaplan Real Estate, Berkely and San Francisco, 1961-77; investment exec. Wellington Fin. Group, San Francisco, 1977—; cons. fin. planning and law San Francisco and Carmel, Calif., 1982—; pres. Wellington Publs., Carmel, 1983—, Exec. Advt., Carmel, 1983—; talk shor host stations KNRY, KIEZ, 1999. *Ms. Bohannon-Kaplan has concentrated on pro-bono activities since 1984 when she began promoting social security reform. She directs the 501(c) 3 Harry Singer Foundation whose mission is to promote responsibility nationally. Projects include annual essay contests, online activities (www.singerfoundation.org) and Another Way, which focuses on three undervalued assets (the young, the old and new technology) on local problems. It engages the educational system in experiential learning and efficiently locates and connects resources in a community. Another Way is NOT a new program; it enhances existing programs and encourages people to assume responsibility.* Carmel, 1983—. Author: Another Way, 1997, (pseudonym Helen P. Rogers), Everyone's Guide to Financial Planning, 1984, Social Security: An Idea Whose Time Has Passed, 1985, The American Deficit: Fulfillment of a Prophecy?, 1988, The Election Process, 1988, The Deficit: 12 Steps to Ease the Crisis, 1988, (series) Taking A Stand On, 1991, Alternatives, 1992; editor: What Role if Any, Should Government's Role be Regarding Child Care in the United States?, 1991, What if Any, Should Governments Role Be Regarding Health Care in the United States, 1992, What Role Does, And What Role Should Media Play in Choosing Our Candidates for National Office?, 1993, Doesn't Anyone Care About the Children?, 1994, Responsibility: Who Has It and Who Doesn't and What That Means to The Nation, 1994, 97, White Hats: People Who Try To Make A Difference, 1994, Governments Struggling with Limited Resources, 1995, Should Government Intervene to Help Children and Teens In Trouble, If so How?, 1996, Excerpts From the Harry Singer Foundation High School Essay Contests, 1996-99. Co-founder The Harry Singer Found., Carmel, Calif., 1988; ind. candidate for U.S. Senate, 1992. Dir. Singer Online internat. programs, 1993—. Mem. ABA, Calif. Bar Assn., Calif. Real Estate Assn., Internat. Assn. Fin. Planners, Inst. Cert. Fin. Planners, Ind. Sector, Philanthropy Round Table Civicus. Club: Commonwealth (San Francisco). Office: PO Box 223159 Carmel CA 93922-3159

BOHANON, KATHLEEN SUE, neonatologist, educator; b. Mpls., 1951. BA summa cum laude, U. Minn., 1973, MD, 1977. Diplomate Am. Bd. Pediats., Am. Bd. Neonatal-Perinatal Medicine. Commd. 2d lt. USAF, 1973, advanced through grades to col., 1995; resident in pediats. Case Western Res. U., Cleve., 1977-80; gen. pediatrician USAF, 1980-85; fellow in neonatology Wilford Hall Med. Ctr., San Antonio, 1985-87; neonatologist, dir. neonatal ICU USAF Med. Ctr., Wright-Patterson AFB, Ohio, 1987-95, chmn. dept. pediat., 1995-98, chief med. staff, 1998—; asst. clin. prof. pediats. U. N.D. Sch. Medicine, Grand Forks, 1981-82; assoc. Wright State U. Sch. Medicine, Dayton, Ohio, 1987—, Uniformed Svc. U. Health Scis., Washington, 1988—; mem. com. Infant Bio-Ethics Com., Dayton, 1990—. Mem. Am. Acad. Pediats. Office: 74th MDG/SGH 4881 Sugar Maple Dr Wright Patterson AFB OH 45433

BOHANON, LUTHER L., federal judge; b. Ft. Smith, Ark., Aug. 9, 1901; s. William Joseph and Artelia (Campbell) B.; m. Marie Swatek, July 17, 1933; 1 son, Richard L. LLB, U. Okla., 1927; LLD (hon.), Oklahoma City U., 1991. Bar: Okla. 1927, U.S. Supreme Ct. 1937. Gen. practice law Seminole, Okla. and Oklahoma City, 1927-61; judge U.S. Dist. Ct. Okla. (no., ea., and we. dists.), 1961-74, sr. judge, 1974—. Mem. platform com. Democratic Nat. Conv., 1940. Served to maj. USAAF, 1942-45. Recipient citations and awards including citation from Okla. Senate and Ho. of Reps., 1979, Okla. County Bar Assn. and Jour. Record award, 1987, Humanitarian award NCCJ, 1991; Luther Bohanon Am. Inn of Ct. named in his honor Am. Inn of Ct. XXIII/U. Okla., 1991. Mem. U.S. Dist. Judges Assn. (10th cir.), Fed. Judges Assn., Okla. Bar Assn., Oklahoma County Bar Assn., Oklahoma City C. of C., Sigma Nu, Phi Alpha Delta. Methodist. Clubs: Mason (Shriner, 32 deg.), K.T, Jester, Kiwanis, Com.of 100, Men's Dinner Club. Home: 1617 Bedford Dr Oklahoma City OK 73116-5406 Office: US Dist Ct PO Box 1514 200 NW 4th St Ste 2001 Oklahoma City OK 73102-3028

BOHANON, RICHARD LEE, federal bankruptcy judge; b. Oklahoma City, Feb. 9, 1935; s. Luther L. and Marie F. (Swatek) B.; m. Ann L. Eddleman; children: Christopher, David, Philip. A.B., Dartmouth Coll., 1957; LL.B., Okla. U., 1960; LL.M., N.Y.U., 1962. Bar: Okla. 1960, U.S. Ct. Appeals (10th cir.) 1961, U.S. Supreme Ct. 1976. Ptnr., Bohanon & Barth, Oklahoma City, 1964-79, Andrews, Davis, Legg, Bixler, Milsten & Price, Oklahoma City, 1979-82; judge U.S. Bankruptcy Ct., Western Dist. Okla., Oklahoma City, 1982—. Mem. Nat. Conf. Bankruptcy Judges (bd. of govs.). Office: US Ct House 201 Dean A Mcgee Ave Oklahoma City OK 73102-3416

BOHI, LYNN, state legislator; b. Cleve., Feb. 20, 1947; m. Charles W. Bohi. BA, Olivet Coll., 1970; postgrad., Plymouth State U. State rep. Vt. Ho. of Reps., 1989-90, 93-94, 1995-96, 97-98; chair local govt. com., 1997-98. Active Conn. River Joint Commn. Upper Valley River Subcom., Human Svcs. Coun., 1987-89, United Way Upper Valley, 1981-88, Hartford Recycles, Workforce Investment Bd., Adult Edn. Coun.; trustee EarthRight, 1991-94. Mem. No. Light Quilting Guild, Hartford Garden Friends. Address: 156 Manning Dr White River Junction VT 05001-8075

BOHL, ALLEN, coach; m. Sherry Helen Akers; children: Brett Allen, Nathan Gregory, Heide Cherie. B, Bowling Green, 1970; M, Southern Miss., 1973; PhD, Ohio State, 1978. Math tchr., asst. football and basketball coach New Carlisle-Bethel; teaching asst. Ohio State; instr. elec. Keesler Air Force Base; athletic adminstr. Ohio State; dir. athletics Fresno State. Named Outstanding Young Man of Am. U.S. Jaycees, 1979. Mem. Cen. Ohio Racquetball Assn. (pres. 1979-81), Airman of Yr. award, 1972. Office: Fresno State 5305 N Campus Dr Fresno CA 93740-8020*

BOHLE, ROBERT HENRY, journalism educator; b. Oak Park, Ill., June 24, 1947; s. William Henry and Vivian Grace (Frasier) B.; m. Suzanne Egan, Mar. 12, 1994; children: Cameron Jay, Christopher Robert. BA in English cum laude, Calif. State U., Long Beach, 1970, MA in English lit., 1972; PhD in Comm., U. Tenn., 1984. Sports reporter and copy desk, copy clk., news copy clk. Long Beach Ind., 1968-72; tchr. English and journalism Monache High Sch., Porterville, Calif., 1972-74; instr., acting chmn. Orange Coast Coll., Costa Mesa, Calif., 1974-76; instr. Palomar Coll., San Marcos, Calif., 1976, Coll. of the Sequoias, Visalia, Calif., 1976-83; assoc. prof. Sch. of Mass Comm., Va. Commonwealth U., Richmond, 1983-95; prof. dept. Comms. and Visual Arts U. North Fla., Jacksonville, 1995—; spkr. and presenter workshops and seminars; publ. and internet cons. Author: From News to Newsprint, 2d edit., 1992, Publication Design for Editors, 1990, (with others) Color in American Newspapers, 1986; contbr. numerous articles to profl. jours. Recipient Presdl. Citation Coll. Media Advisers, Inc., 1983, Outstanding Young Man in Am. award U.S. Jaycees, 1982, Gannett Found. Graduation scholarship, 1982; Freedom Forum Prof.'s Publ. grantee, 1992. Mem. Assn. for Edn. in Journalism and Mass Comm. (editl. adv. bd. Journalism and Mass Comm. Educator 1988—), Soc. Newspaper Design (mem. edn. com. 1985—, contbg. editor Design jour. 1993-95), Kappa Tau Alpha, Phi Kappa Phi. Avocations: soccer, hiking, canoeing, golf, bicycling, fishing.

BOHLE, SUE, public relations executive; b. Austin, Minn., June 23, 1943; d. Harold Raymond and Mary Theresa (Swanson) Hastings; m. John Bernard Bohle, June 22, 1974; children: Jason John, Christine K. BS in Journalism, Northwestern U., 1965, MS in Journalism, 1969. Tchr. pub. high schs Englewood, Colo., 1965-68; account exec. Burson-Marsteller Pub. Relations, Los Angeles, 1969-73; v.p., mgr. pub. relations J. Walter Thompson Co., Los Angeles, 1973-79; founder, pres. The Bohle Company, L.A., 1979—; former exec. v.p. Ketchum Pub. Rels., L.A.; free-lance writer, instr. communications Calif. State U. at Fullerton, 1972-73; instr. writing Los Angeles City Coll., 1975-76; lectr. U. So. Calif., 1979—. Contbr. articles to profl. jours. Dir. pub. rels. L.A. Jr. Ballet, 1971-72; pres. Panhellenic Advisers Coun., UCLA, 1972-73; mem. adv. bd. L.A. Valley Coll., 1974-75, Coll. Communications Pepperdine U., 1981-85, Sch. Journalism U. So. Calif., 1987-95, Calif. State U., Long Beach, 1988-93; bd. visitors Medill Sch. Journalism Northwestern U., 1984—. Recipient Alumni Svc. award Northwestern U., 1995; Univ. scholar, 1961-64, Panhellenic scholar, 1964-65; named to Hall of Achievement, Medill Sch. Journalism, 1997, charter mem. Hall of Fame. Fellow Pub. Rels. Soc. Am. (bd. dirs. L.A. chpt. 1981-90, v.p. 1983, pres. 1989, del. nat. assembly 1980, 94, 95, 96, co-chmn. long-range strategic com. 1990, pres.'s adv. coun. 1991, exec. com. Counselors Acad. 1984-86, sec.-treas. 1990, chmn. 1992, sec. Coll. Fellows 1993, vice chair 1994, chmn. 1995, Silver Anvil award 1994)); mem. Pub. Rels. Orgn. Internat. (U.S. founder, bd. dirs. 1994—), World Com., Women in Comm., Shi-ai, Delta Zeta (editor The Lamp 1966-68, Woman of Yr. award 1993), Kappa Alpha Tau. Office: 1999 Avenue Of The Stars Los Angeles CA 90067-6022

BOHLEN, JEFFREY BRIAN, protective services official; b. Blue Island, Ill., Mar. 7, 1961; s. Albert John and Andrea Lee (Mangano) B.; m. Joan Mary Zarlengo, Sept. 8, 1985; children: Jeffrey Brian Jr., Ashley Marie, Lindsey Marie, Bradley John. Student, Governor's State U., 1995, Prairie State Coll., 1995—. Steel inspector Century Steel, Chicago Heights, Ill., 1979-80; asphalt supr. Chicago Heights St. Dept., 1980-84; police officer Chicago Heights Police Dept., 1984—, cons., lectr., 1990—; owner Creative Customwear, 1998—; owner World champ Sports Cards, Chicago Heights, 1990-94; lectr. Nat. Law Enforcement Inst., Santa Rosa, Calif., 1997—. Author: (booklet) Gang Identification, 1993, (book) Where Have Our Children gone, 1995. Bd. dirs. Chicago Heights Small Fry Basketball, 1995—. Recipient Outstanding Achievement award Sch. Dist. # 170, 1995, Sch. Dist. # 206, 1995, Operation: CHANGE, 1995, Ill. Ho. Rep. Flora Ciarlo, 1995. Mem. Nat. Tactical Officers Assn., Midwest Gang Officer Assn. Avocations: golf, collecting sports cards, travel. Office: Chicago Heights Police Dept 1601 S Halsted St Chicago Heights IL 60411-3584

BOHLI, HARRY JOHN, JR., structural engineer, consultant; b. Balt., Dec. 16, 1951; s. Harry John Sr. and Wanda Ann (Cholewczynski) B.; divorced; children: Harry John III, James Philip. AA, Harford Coll., Bel Air, Md., 1971; BS in Civil Engring., U. S.C., 1974. Registered profl. engr., Tex., Tenn., N.C. Structural engr. TVA, Knoxville, Tenn., 1974-86, Contract Engr., Garland, Tex., 1986—; pres. Harry J. Bohli, Jr., P.E., Garland, 1996—. Mem. ASCE, NSPE, Tex. Soc. Profl. Engrs., Dallas-Fort Worth U. S.C. Alumni Club (asst. dir. 1995—). Avocations: swimming, numismatics. Home: 1721 Highgate Pl Garland TX 75044-6855 Office: PO Box 450238 Garland TX 75045-0238

BOHLINGER, LEWIS HALL, state government official; b. Little Rock, July 8, 1942; s. Lewis Hall Bohlinger and Helen Elisa (Reid) Bragg; m. Kathleen Ann Klein, Jan. 30, 1967; children: Lewis Hall, Reid Watson. BS, Southeastern La. U., 1965; MS, Tulane U., 1970, ScD, 1975. Rsch. asst. Delta Primate Rsch. Ctr., Covington, La., 1965-69; health physicist La. Bd. Nuclear Energy, Baton Rouge, 1971-80; asst. adminstr. La. Nuclear Energy Divsn., Baton Rouge, 1980-87; dep. asst. sec. La. Office of Environ. Affairs, Baton Rouge, 1983-89; asst. sec. La. Office of Air Quality, Baton Rouge, 1984-86; dep. sec. La. DEQ, Baton Rouge, 1987-88; adminstr. La. Radiation Protection Divsn., Baton Rouge, 1989-94, La. Hazardous Waste Divsn., Baton Rouge, 1994-96; dep. sec. La. Dept. Environ. Quality, Baton Rouge, 1996—; adj. asst. prof. Tulane U., New Orleans, 1988—; chair Cen. Interstate Low Level Radioactive Waste Compact Commn., 1983-89, 91, chmn./mem. various state and fed. tech. coms. Grantee USPHS, 1969-71. Mem. Am. Nuclear Soc., La. Environ. Health Assn., Health Physics Soc., La. Air and Waste Mgmt. Assn., Delta Omega Soc. Home: 11930 Parkbrook Ave Baton Rouge LA 70816-4672 Office: LA Dept Environ Quality PO Box 82263 Baton Rouge LA 70884-2263

BOHLKE, GARY LEE, lawyer, playwright; b. Yakima, Wash., Mar. 9, 1941; s. Francis Douglas and Laura Mae (Bianchi) B. BA, U. Wash., 1963; JD, Am. U., 1966; LLM, U. London, 1967; diploma, London Inst. World Affairs, 1967. Bar: DC 1967. Assoc. Mason, Fenwick & Lawrence, Washington, 1967-70; atty., adv. U.S. C.E., Washington, 1972-74; ast. solicitor environ. law U.S. Dept. Interior, Washington, 1974-83; sr. atty. environ. protection U.S. Dept. Interior, 1983-86; assoc. gen. counsel litigation and enforcement Farm Credit Adminstrn., 1988-90; dir. Ackerson & Feldman Chartered, 1991-93; ptnr. Semmes, Bowen & Semmes, 1993-97; mem. mgmt. com. Internat. Law Practice Group, 1995-97; prin. Oppenheimer, Wolff, Donnelly & Bayth (and predecessor firm), 1997-98; shareholder Ablondi, Foster, Sobin & Davidow PC, 1998—. Author: (plays) Echoes, 1988, The Crime Tetraology consisting of Double Cross, 1982, Obsession, 1984, Judgment, 1985, Act of Justice, 1987; (novel) Forever a Stranger, 1990, (screenplay) Double Cross, 1992. Vice chmn. com. on environ. and transp., Washington; advisor Neighborhood Comm. 4C, 1980-88. Mem. ABA, D.C. Bar Assn. (chmn. environ. law com. 1977-78). Lutheran. Home: 1716 Eutaw Pl Baltimore MD 21217-3730 Office: 1150 18th St NW Ste 900 Washington DC 20036

BOHM, FRIEDRICH (FRIEDL) K.M., architectural firm executive. Degree in architecture, U. Vienna; M in City and Regional Planning, Ohio State U. With NBBJ, Columbus, Ohio, 1975—, mng. ptnr., 1987-97, pres., chmn., 1997—; hon. consul to Austria; advisor internat. policy Prime Min. Austria; bd. dirs. Huntington Nat. Bank, M/I Homes. Recipient Disting. Alumnus award Ohio State U., numerous design awards and recognitions; named Entrepreneur of Yr., INC. mag., 1992; Fulbright scholar. Fellow AIA. Office: NBBJ 1555 Lake Shore Dr Columbus OH 43204-3825*

BOHM, GEORG G. A., physicist; b. Brünn, Czechoslovakia, Oct. 7, 1935; came to U.S., 1966; s. Gustav Anton and Olga B.; m. Marga L. Girak; children: Astrid, Alexander. BSEE, U. Vienna, Austria, 1957, PhD in Physics, 1962, postgrad., 1962-64. Scientist Max-Planck Inst. Physikalische Chemie, Göttingen, Germany, 1972-75; group leader, mgr. Firestone Tire & Rubber Corp., Westbury, N.Y., 1967-72; asst. dir. rsch. lab. Firestone Tire & Rubber Corp., Akron, Ohio, 1973-93; dir. rsch. Bridgestone/Firestone, Akron, 1993—; bd. dirs. Bridgestone Firestone Rsch. Inc.; vis. prof. IAEA, Vienna, 1964-66; adv. panel Nat. Acad. Sci., Washington, 1994-95; adv. bd. Ctr. Molecular & Microstructure Composits Case Western U./Akron U., 1990-94. Mem. editl. bd. Jour. Rubber Chemistry & Tech., 1982-85; contbr. articles to profl. jours.; patentee in field. Mem. Am. Chem. Soc. Avocations: chess, tennis, golf. Office: Bridgestone/Firestone Rsch 1200 Firestone Pkwy Akron OH 44317-0002*

BOHM, HENRY VICTOR, physicist; b. Vienna, Austria, July 16, 1929; came to U.S., 1941, naturalized, 1946; s. Victor Charles and Gertrude (Rie) B.; m. Lucy Margaret Coons, Sept. 2, 1950; children: Victoria Rie, Jeffrey Ernst Thompson. AB, Harvard U., 1950; MS, U. Ill., 1951; PhD, Brown U., 1958. Jr. physicist GE, 1951, 53-54; teaching, research asst. Brown U., 1954-58, research assoc., summer 1958; staff mem. Arthur D. Little, Inc., Cambridge, Mass., 1958-59; asso. prof. physics dept. Wayne State U., Detroit, 1959-64; acting chmn. physics dept. Wayne State U., 1962-63, prof., 1964-93; prof. emeritus Wayne State U., Detroit, 1993—; v.p. for grad. studies and research Wayne State U., 1968-71, v.p. for spl. projects, 1971-72, provost, 1972-75, on leave, 1978-83, interim dean Coll. Liberal Arts, 1984-86; pres. Argonne Univs. Assn., 1978-83; vis. prof. Cornell U., 1966-67, U. Lancaster, Eng., summer 1967, Purdue U., winter, 1977, Rensselaer Poly. Inst., winter 1992; cons.-examiner commn. on instns. higher edn. N. Central Assn. Colls. and Schs., 1971-80, mem. commn., 1974-78. Bd. dirs. Center for Research Libraries, Chgo, 1970-75, chmn., 1973; bd. overseers Lewis Coll., Ill. Inst. Tech., 1980-83. Lt. USNR, 1951-53. Fellow Am. Phys. Soc. Office: Wayne State U Dept Physics Detroit MI 48202

BOHME, DIETHARD KURT, chemistry educator; b. Boston, June 20, 1941; s. Kurt F. and Maria (Kiesel) B. B.Sc., McGill U., 1962, Ph.D., 1965. Asst. prof. dept. chemistry York U., Downsview, Ont., 1970-74; assoc. prof. York U., Ont., Ont., 1974-77, prof. chemistry, 1977—; disting. rsch. prof. chemistry York U., Ont., 1994—; dir. grad. program in chemistry York U., 1979-85, chmn. dept. chemistry, 1985-90; mem. chemistry grant selection com. Nat. Scis. and Engring. Research Council of Can., Ottawa, 1983-86. Contbr. articles to profl. jours. NAS-NRC postdoctoral rsch. assoc., 1965-67; A.P. Sloan fellow, 1974, sr. scientist vis. fellow U. Warwick, Eng., 1978, Killam rsch. fellow, 1991-93; recipient Rutherford Meml. medal in chemistry Royal Soc. Can., 1981, A.v. Humboldt rsch. award, 1990, John C. Polanyi award in Phys. and Theoretical Chemistry, 1998. Fellow Chem. Inst. Can. (phys. chemistry divsn. exec. 1980-83, Noranda lectr. in phys. chemistry 1983), Royal Soc. Can.; mem. Am. Soc. Mass Spectrometry, Am. Chem. Soc. Home: 38 Alberta Dr, Concord, ON Canada L4K 4X5 Office: York U Dept Chemistry, 4700 Keele St, Toronto, ON Canada M3J 1P3

BOHMONT, DALE WENDELL, agricultural consultant; b. Wheatland, Wyo., June 7, 1922; s. J.E. and Mary (Armann) B.; m. Marilyn J. Horn, Mar. 7, 1969; children: Dennis E., Craig W. B.S., U. Wyo., 1948, M.S., 1950; Ph.D., U. Nebr., 1952; M.P.A., Harvard U., 1959. Registered investment adv., SEC. Pub. sch. tchr. Rock River, Wyo., 1941-42; from research asst. to head plant scis. U. Wyo., 1946-60; assoc. dir. expt. sta. Colo. State U., 1961-63; dean, dir. agr. U. Nev., Reno, 1963-82, dean, dir. emeritus, 1982—; pres. Bohmont Cons. Inc., 1982—; mem. Brucheum Group, Waynesboro, Va., 1984; cons. Devel. & Resources Corp., N.Y.C., 1968—, Fredriksen, Kamine & Assocs., Sacramento, 1976, Nev. Agrl. Found., 1986—; pres. Enide Corp., Reno, 1974-80, Thermal Dynamics Internat., 1983-87, Cryabis, Inc., Reno, 1993-95; co-chmn. rsch. planning West Divsn. Agr. Expt. Stas., 1975; mem. exec. com., coun. adminstrv. heads agr. Nat. Assn. State Univ. Land Grant Colls., 1975. Author: Golden Years of Agriculture in Nevada, 1989; contbr. articles to profl. jours.; mem. editorial bd.: Crops and Soils, 1962—. Pres. Dale W. and Marilyn Horn Found., 1998—. Served with USAAF, 1942-45. Fellow AAAS, Agronomy Soc.; mem. Western Soc. Weed Scis. (hon.), Western Crop Sci. Soc. (pres. 1962-63), Nat. Expt. Sta. Dirs. Assn. (chmn. 1967-68), Am. Range Mgmt. Soc., Farm House (dir. 1962—), Weed Soc. Am. (hon.), Sigma Xi, Gamma Sigma Delta (pres. 1964-66), Alpha Zeta, Alpha Tau Alpha, Phi Kappa Phi. Lodge: Lions (v.p. 1985-86, pres. 1986-87 bd. dirs. 1985—). Home: 280 Island Ave Reno NV 89501-1844 *There is nothing that has been done that could not have been done better; therefore, there is always room for improvement and always room at the top.*

BOHN, BARBARA ANN, laboratory director; b. St. Louis, Nov. 24, 1943; d. Arthur John Joseph and Eleanor Caroline (Kinsman) B. BS in Med. Tech., Loyola U., New Orleans, 1965; MBA, Old Dominion U., 1984. Med. technologist Broward Gen. Med. Ctr., Ft. Lauderdale, Fla., 1965-66; microbiologist Duke U. Hosp., Durham, N.C., 1966-71; tech. lab. coord. Harvard Cmty. Health Plan, Cambridge, Mass., 1971-77; tech. lab. dir. Louise Obici Meml. Hosp., Suffolk, Va., 1977-89; lab. mgr. Orlando (Fla.) Health Care Group, 1989-91; tech. lab. dir. Metpath of Fla., 1992-93; tech. cons. ASCP; planning analyst, chmn. Diagnosis Related Group task force, 1983-85; dir. adv. bd. Western Tidewater Area Health Edn. Com., 1983-87, bd. dirs., sec. Edmarc, Inc., Suffolk, 1985-86, pres., bd. dirs., dir. 1986-87. Mem. Am. Soc. Clin. Pathologists (assoc., program chmn. workshops Boston 1977), Clin. Lab. Mgmt. Assn. (fin. chmn. 1983), Hosp. Purchasing Svc. (pres. lab. com. 1983), Am. Hosp. Assn. (adv. bd.), Soc. for Hosp. Planning and Mktg. (adv. bd.), Beta Beta Beta. Avocations: piano, tennis, published poet. Address: 3635 Whitehall Dr Bldg 1-404 West Palm Beach FL 33401-1088

BOHN, CHARLOTTE GALITZ, retired real estate executive; b. Chgo., Aug. 7, 1930; d. Chester Charles and Sarah Madelyn (McCarthy) B; m. Robert Allan Galitz, Nov. 25, 1955; children: Charles Robert, Thomas Allan, Madelyn Clare, (div. Sept. 1965). Student, Northwestern U., 1955, City Coll., Chgo., 1989. Lic. real estate salesperson, N.C. Lab. tech. Kraft Foods Rsch. Lab., Glenview, Ill., 1950-56; researcher data processing control Kemper Ins. Co., Chgo., 1967-70; jr. acct. Tractor Supply Co., Chgo., 1970-75; real estate salesman MGM Realty Co., Chgo., 1975-81, 85-88, Prime Realty, 1989-98; broker Bohn Real Estate Agy, Raleigh, N.C., 1981-85; founder, pres. Pvt. Rsch., Chgo., 1985; ret., 1998; researcher zoning map City of Raleigh, 1980-81; bd. dirs. Off-Campus Writers Workshop. Contbr. various rsch. projects and sci. proposals. Vol. Chgo. Boys' Club; treas. churchwomen of St. Mary's, Crystal Lake, Ill.; vol. lifeguard Easter Seal Soc.-Multiple Sclerosis, Raleigh, 1983-84, PTA, 1967-77; bd. dirs. Off-Campus Writer's Workshop; chair grammar sch. 50th reunion, 1994; scholarship judge Mensa, Chgo., 1995, 96, 99. Recipient Adviser Emblem of Merit award Jr. Achievement, 1955. Mem. AAAS, Smithsonian Inst. (assoc.), Nat. Trust Hist. Preservation, Raleigh C. of C., Jaycee Aux. (restaurant mgr.), Chgo. N. Side Realty Bd., Nat. Geog. Soc., Wilson Ctr. Assn., Mensa (nominating), Am. Assn. Ret. Persons, Irish Am. Heritage Ctr., Libr. Congress (assoc. charter), Chgo. Cath. U. Club. Roman Catholic. Avocations: textiles, sports, antiques, music, poetry. Home: 6126 W Roscoe St Chicago IL 60634-4145 Office: Private Rsch 6126 W Roscoe St Chicago IL 60634-4145

BOHN, DENNIS ALLEN, electrical engineer, executive; b. San Fernando, Calif., Oct. 5, 1942; s. Raymond Virgil and Iris Elouise (Johnson) B.; 1 child, Kira Michelle; m. Patricia Tolle, Aug. 12, 1986. BSEE with honors, U. Calif., Berkeley, 1972, MSEE with honors, 1974. Engring. technician GE Co., San Leandro, Calif., 1964-72; research and devel. engr. Hewlett-Packard Co., Santa Clara, Calif., 1973; application engr. Nat. Semicondr. Corp., Santa Clara, 1974-76; engring. mgr. Phase Linear Corp., Lynnwood, Wash., 1976-82; v.p. rsch. and devel., ptnr. Rane Corp., Mukilteo, Wash., 1982—; founder Toleco Systems, Kingston, Wash., 1980. Suicide and crisis ctr. vol., Berkeley, 1972-74, Santa Clara, 1974-76. Served with USAF, 1960-64. Recipient Am. Spirit Honor medal USAF, 1961; Math. Achievement award Chem. Rubber Co., 1962-63. Editor: We Are Not Just Daffodils, 1975; contbr. poetry to Reason mag.; tech. editor Audio Handbook, 1976; contbr. articles to tech. jours.; columnist Polyphony mag., 1981-83; 2 patents in field. Fellow Audio Engring. Soc.; mem. IEEE, Tau Beta Pi. Office: Rane Corp 10802 47th Ave W Mukilteo WA 98275-5098

BOHN, JAMES FRANCIS, physical education educator; b. Pitts., July 14, 1950; s. William L. and Rita (Graham) B.; children: J. Matthew (dec.), Stephanie. BS, Slippery Rock State U., 1972, postgrad., 1979. Cert. tchr., Pa. Tchr. South Fayette Twp., McDonald, Pa., 1972—; instr. Community Coll. of Allegheny County, Pitts., 1975; evaluator Middle States Assn. of Secondary Schs. and Colls., 1980-81. Dir. Bethel Park (Pa.) Girls Softball Assn., 1991-93. Recipient Gift of Time Tribute, Am. Family Inst., 1992. Mem. AAHPERD, NEA, Nat. Assn. Sport and Phys. Edn., Pa. Edn. Assn., South Fayette Edn. Assn. Home: 5600 Libr Rd 17A Bethel Park PA 15102-3722

BOHN, PAUL BRADLEY, psychiatrist, psychoanalyst; b. Santa Monica, Calif., Apr. 11, 1957; m. Pamela Summit, Nov. 17, 1990. BA in Pharmacology, U. Calif., Santa Barbara, 1980; MD, U. Calif., Irvine, 1984; postgrad. in Psychoanalysis, L.A. Psychoanalytic Inst., 1988-93; PsyD, Grad. Inst. Contemporary Psychoanalysis, 1995. Diplomate Am. Bd. Psychiatry and Neurology, added qualifications in addiction psychiatry. Psychiat. resident UCLA, 1984-88, assoc. dir. anxiety disorders clinic, 1989-95; assoc. clin. prof. psychiatry, 1989—; dir. social anxiety clinic UCLA, 1993-95; fellow U. So. Calif., L.A., 1988-89; v.p. Pacific Psychopharmacology Rsch. Inst., Santa Monica, 1990—; pvt. practice psychiatry Santa Monica, 1988—; expert reviewer, Med. Bd. Calif.; diplomate Am. Bd. Addiction Psychiatry, 1997. Grantee Ciba-Geigy, Santa Monica, 1992. Fellow Am. Psychiat. Assn.; mem. So. Calif. Psychiat. Assn., Anxiety Disorders Assn. of Am., Obsessive Compulsive Found. Office: 2730 Wilshire Blvd Ste 325 Santa Monica CA 90403-4747

BOHN, RALPH CARL, educational consultant, retired educator; b. Detroit, Feb. 19, 1930; s. Carl and Bertha (Abrams) B.; m. Adella Stanul, Sept. 2, 1950 (dec.); children: Cheryl Ann, Jeffrey Ralph; m. JoAnn Olvera Butler, Feb. 19, 1977 (div. 1990); stepchildren: Kathryn J., Kimberly J., Gregory E.; m. Mariko Tajima, Jan. 27, 1991; 1 child, Thomas Carl; 1 stepchild, Daichi Tajima. BS, Wayne State U., 1951, EdM, 1954, EdD, 1957. Instr. part-time Wayne State U., 1954-55, summer 1956; faculty San Jose (Calif.) State U., 1955-92, prof. div. tech., 1961-92, chmn. dept. indsl. studies, 1960-69, assoc. dean ednl. svc., 1968-70, dean continuing edn., 1970-92, prof. emeritus, 1992—; cons. Calif. State U. Sys., 1992—; cons. quality edn. sys. USAF, 1992—; dir. nat. program on non-collegiate sponsored instrn. Calif. State Univ. Sys., 1995—, Calif. State U. Inst., 1997-99; guest summer faculty Colo. State Coll., 1963, Ariz. State U., 1966, U. P.R., 1967, 74, So. Ill. U., 1970, Oreg. State U., 1971, Utah State U., 1973, Va. Poly. Inst. & State U., 1973, U. Idaho, 1978; cons. U.S. Office of Edn., 1965-70, Calif. Pub. Schs., 1960, Nat. Assessment Ednl. Progress, 1968-79, ednl. div. Philco-Ford Corp., 1970-73, Am. Inst. Rsch., 1969-83, Far West Labs for Ednl. Rsch. Devel., 1971-86; mem. adv. bd. Ctr. for Vocat. and Tech. Edn., Ohio State U., 1968-74; dir. project Vocat. Edn. Act, 1965-67, NDEA, 1967, 68; co-dir. Project Edn. Profession Devel. Act, 1969, 70; mem. commn. coll. and univ. contracts Western Assn. Schs. and Colls, 1976-78, chmn. spl. com. on off-campus instrn. and continuing edn., 1978-88; chmn. continuing edn. accreditation visit U. Santa Clara, 1976; mem. accreditation team for Azusa Pacific Coll., 1975, Portland State U., 1975, 95, Brigham Young U., 1976, 86, 96, Columbia Coll., 1977, Western Wash. U., 1978, 88, Wash. State U., 1980, 90, 99, Chapman Coll., 1980, Calif. State U., Fullerton, 1981, Westminster Coll., 1983, Columbia U., 1983, Boise State U., 1984, 94, U. Hawaii, Hilo, 1984, U. Oreg., 1987, 97, U. Mont., 1989, Calif. Poly. U., Ponona, 1990, North Island Naval Air Sta., USN, 1990, U. Calif., Irvine, 1991, Western Conservative Bapt. Sem., Oreg., 1992, US Naval Sta., Hawaii, 1992, West Coast U., 1995, Norfolk Military Educ. Stations, 1996; U. Utah, 1997, Utah State U., 1997; Golden Gate U., 1997; vice chmn. accreditation team U. Guam, 1978, Pepperdine U., 1979, U. LaVerne, 1980, Azusa Pacific Coll., 1981, Nat. U., 1987, Loma Linda U., 1988, 91; chmn. accreditation team Azusa Pacific Coll, 1977, Calif. Coll. Podiatric Medicine, 1982, So. Ill. U., Carbondale, 1983, Northrup U., 1984, Cogswell Coll., 1986, chmn. of spl. USAF visitation to George AFB, 1986; chair of accreditation visits Calif. State U., Chico, 1987, Chapman Coll., 1987, Hawaii Loa Coll., 1990, Myrtle Beach Air Force Base, S.C., 1990, U. Hawaii, 1991, Homestead AFB, Fla., 1992, Nellis AFB, Nev., 1992, West Coast U., Calif., 1992, Langley AFB, 1992, Seymour Johnson AFB, N.C., 1992, 1998; Shaw AFB, S.C., 1993, 99, Tustin Marine Corps Air Sta., Calif., 1993, El Toro Marine Corps Air Sta., Calif., 1993, Yokota Air Base, Japan, 1993, Holloman AFB, 1993, Mountain Home AFB, 1994, Jacksonville NAS, 1994, Cecil NAS, 1994, Mayport NS, 1994, Rota NAS, 1994, Edwards AFB, 1994, Little Rock AFB, 1995, Fort Hood U.S. Army, 1995; Howard AFB, Panama, 1997; Hickman AFB, Hawaii, 1998; Iwakuni Marine Air Base, Japan, 1999; Camp Butler Marine Corps. Base, Okinawa, 1999, Kadena Naval Station, Ikinawa, Japan, 1999. Author: (with G.H. Silvius) Organizing Course Materials for Industrial Education, 1961, Planning and Organizing Instruction, 1976; (with A. MacDonald) Power-Mechanics of Energy Control, 1970, 2d edit., 1983, The McKnight Power Experimenter, 1970, (with A. MacDonald), Power and Energy Technology, 1989, (with A. MacDonald): Energy Technology: Power and Transportation, 1992; (with others) Basic Industrial Arts and Power Mechanics, 1978, Technology and Society: Interfaces with Industrial Arts, 1980, Fundamentals of Safety Education, 3d edit., 1981, (with others) Energy, Power and Transportation Technology, 1986, (with A. MacDonald) Energy Technology, Power and Transportation, 1991; editor (with Ralph Norman) Graduate Study in Industrial Arts, 1961; indsl. arts editor Am. Vocat. Jour., 1963-66; editor Jour. Indsl. Tchr. Edn., 1962-64. Lt. (j.g.) USCGR, 1951-53, capt. Res. ret. Recipient award Am. Legion, 1945; Wayne State U. scholar, 1953. Mem. NEA, Nat. Assn. Indsl. Tech. (bd. accreditation), Am. Indsl. Arts. Assn. (pres. 1967-68, Ship's citation 1971), Am. Coun. Indsl. Art Tchrs. Edn. (pres. 1964-66, Man of Yr. award 1967), Nat. Univ. Continuing Edn. Assn. (chair accreditation com. 1988-91), Nat. Assn. Indsl. Tchr. Educators (past v.p.), Calif. Indsl. Edn. Assn. (State Ship's citation 1971), Am. Drive Edn. Assn., Nat. Fluid Power Soc., Am. Vocat. Assn. (svc. awards 1966, 67), N.Am. Assn. for Summer Sessions (v.p. western region 1976-78), Luth. Acad. Scholarship, Calif. Employees Assn. (pres. San Jose State Coll. chpt. 1966-67), Western Assn. Summer Session Adminstrs. (newsletter editor 1970-73, pres. 1974-75), Calif. C. of C. (edn. com 1969-77), Industry-Edn. Coun. Calif. (bd. dirs. 1974-80), Sci. and Human Values, Inc. (bd. dirs. 1974—, chmn. bd. 1976—), Tahoe Tavern (bd. dirs. 1987-91, chmn. bd. 1988-90), Seascape Lagoon Homeowners Assn. (bd. dirs. 1988-95, chmn. 1989-95), Nat. Gold Key Honors Soc. (hon. life). Home and Office: 713 Clubhouse Dr Aptos CA 95003-5431

BOHN, ROBERT HERBERT, lawyer; b. Austin, Tex., Sept. 2, 1935; s. Herbert and Alice B.; m. Gay P. Maloy, June 4, 1957; children: Rebecca Shoemaker, Katherine Bernat, Robert H., Jr.. BBA, U. Tex., 1957, LLB, 1963. Bar: Tex. 1963, Calif. 1965. Ptnr. Boccardo Law Firm, San Jose, Calif., 1965-87, Alexander & Bohn, San Jose, 1987-91; Bohn, Bennion & Niland, 1992-97, Bohn & Bohn, 1998—; spkr. Calif. Continuing Edn. of Bar; judge pro tem Superior Ct. of Calif., San Jose, 1975-96. Mem. Consumer Attys. Calif., Am. Bd. Trial Advocates, ATLA, Santa Clara County Bar Assn., Calif. State Bar Assn., Trial Lawyers Pub. Justice, Santa Clara County Trial Lawyers Assn. (pres.), Roscoe Pound Found., Million Dollar Advocates Forum, Lawyers Arbitration Mediation Svc. (pres.), Commonwealth Club Calif., Silicon Valley Capital Club, Exec. Golfers (dir. gen.), Texas Cowboys Assn., Phi Gamma Delta. Home: 14124 Pike Rd Saratoga CA 95070-5380 Office: 152 N Third St Ste 200 San Jose CA 95112

BOHNEN, MICHAEL J., lawyer; b. Buffalo, Mar. 9, 1947; s. Joyce B. Oppenheim, June 19, 1969; children—Sharon, Deborah. B.A., Harvard U., 1968, J.D., 1972. Bar: Mass. 1972. Assoc. Nutter, McClennen & Fish, LLP, Boston, 1972-80, ptnr., 1980—; lectr. Boston U. Law Sch., 1981-85. Pres., Solomon Schechter Day Sch., Newton, 1980-82; pres. Jewish Community Rels. Council, Boston, 1991-93; chmn. Combined Jewish Philanthropies, 1993-95, New Jewish H.S., 1995—; vice chmn. Jewish Coun. for Pub. Affairs., 1995-99. Co-author: Mass. Corporate Forms, 1990. Mem. Boston Bar Assn. (chmn. corp. law com. 1997-99). Home: 60 Nathan Rd Newton MA 02459-1105 Office: Nutter McClennen & Fish LLP One International Pl Boston MA 02110

BOHNEN, ROBERT FRANK, hematologist, oncologist, educator; b. Huntington, N.Y., Jan. 3, 1941; s. Oscar and Sarah Leah (Piel) B.; m. Mollyn Villareal, June 20, 1965; children: Sharon Kay, Scott Owen David, Paul Alan. BS in Zoology, Syracuse U., 1961; MD, Columbia U., 1965. Diplomate Am. Bd. Internal Medicine, Am. Bd. Med. Oncology, Am. Bd. Hematology. Intern Buffalo (N.Y.) Gen. Hosp., 1965-66; resident in medicine SUNY, Buffalo, 1968-69; resident in medicine U. Utah, Salt Lake City, 1969-70, clin. hematology fellow, 1970-71, med. oncology fellow, 1971-72; physician hematology and med. oncology Cons. Med. Group, Carmichael and Roseville, Calif., 1972-91, Cancer Treatment Ctr. Merle West Med. Ctr., Klamath Falls, Oreg., 1991—; instr. medicine and hematology/oncology U. Calif., Davis, Sacramento, 1973-77, asst. clin. prof. medicine and hematology/oncology, 1977-83; clin. instr. dept. family medicine Oreg. Health Scis. U., Portland, 1994—; sr. staff Mercy Am. River Hosp., Carmichael, Calif., Mercy San Juan Hosp., Carmichael, Roseville (Calif.) Cmty. Hosp.; courtesy staff Sutter Cmty. Hosp. Sacramento; active staff Merle West Med. Ctr., Klamath Falls; med. dir. Hospice Roseville, Calif.; prin. investigator No. Calif. Oncology Group Clin. Trials; med. adv. bd. Vis. Nurses Assn.; lectr. and presenter in field. Contbr. articles to profl. jours. Chmn. Greater Sacramento Cancer Coun. Clin. Trials Com./No. Calif. Oncology Group Outreach Com.; bd. dirs., sec. Greater Sacramento Cancer Coun.; chmn. prof. edn. com., bd. dirs. Tri-County chpt. Am. Cancer Soc.; soloist Sacramento Valley Concert Choir, Klamath Chorale; active Masterworks Chorus; cast member Linkville Players and Ross Ragland Theater Prodns., Klamath Falls, 1991—; choir dir. Sacred Heart Ch., Klamath Falls, 1992—. Med. Oncology fellow Am. Cancer Soc., U. Utah Med. Ctr., 1971-72. Mem. Am. Soc. Clin. Oncology, S.W. Oncology Group, Radiation Therapy Oncology Group, Nat. Surg. Adjuvant Breast Program, Phi Beta Kappa. Democrat. Roman Catholic. Avocations: musical theater, photography, choral singing and directing. Office: Cancer Treatment Ctr Merle West Med Ctr 2610 Uhrmann Rd Klamath Falls OR 97601-1123

BOHNENKAMPER, KATHERINE ELIZABETH, library science educator; b. Wichita, July 20, 1955; d. William Eugene and Emily Jane (Yount) Miller; m. David Allen Bohnenkamper, May 29, 1994; 1 child, Daniel William. BS in Edn., Emporia State U., 1977; MEd, Wichita State U., 1981; MA, Kans. State U., 1988; MLS, Emporia State U., 1990. Tchr. high sch. Brown County Pub. Schs., Horton, Kans., 1978-79; substitute tchr. Wichita Pub. Schs., 1979-81, 86-90, tchr. jr. high sch., 1981-86; libr. Kans State Hist. Soc., Topeka, 1990-91; asst. prof. libr. sci. Drury Coll., Springfield, Mo., 1991—. Instr. 1st aid & CPR ARC, Wichita and Springfield, 1976—. Recipient Arnie H. Richards Meml. scholar Sch. Libr. and Info. Mgmt. Emporia State U., 1990. Mem. Mo. Libr. Assn. (officer-reference coun. 1995-98), Springfield Area Libr. Assn. (v.p. 1995-97), DAR (chpt. historian 1982-84, 94-98), Order Eastern Star. Presbyterian. Avocations: church choir, travel, reading, photography. Home: 1022 E Greenwood St Springfield MO 65807-3713 Office: FW Olin Libr Drury Coll 900 N Benton Ave Springfield MO 65802-3712

BOHNHOFF, DAVID ROY, agricultural engineer, educator; b. Plymouth, Wis., June 10, 1956; s. Roy Arthur and Jean Audrey (Manneck) B.; m. Rhonda Kay Johanning, July 2, 1982; children: Benjamin, Christian, Aaron. BS in Agrl. Engring., U. Wis., Platteville, 1978; MS in Agrl. Engring., U. Wis., Madison, 1985, PhD in Agrl. Engring., 1988. Registered profl. engr., Wis. Design engr. Gehl Co., West Bend, Wis., 1979-80; dairy farmer Galmset Farms, Plymouth, Wis., 1981-82; rsch. asst. agrl. engring. dept. U. Wis., Madison, 1982-87, lectr. agrl. engring., 1987-88, asst. prof. agrl. engring., 1988-93, assoc. prof. agrl. engring., 1993-95; divsn. rsch. and product devel. mgr. Lester Bldg. Systems, Lester Prairie, Minn., 1995-96; assoc. prof. biological sys. engring. U. Wis., Madison, 1996—; mem. Midwest Plan Svc., Ames, Iowa, 1988-95, chmn., 1993-94, mem. constrn. sect. com. 1993-95, chmn. task force, 1990, mem. design and constrn. com., 1988-94. Contbr. articles, reports to profl. jours. Youth soccer coach Regent Soccer Club, Madison, 1989-94, Madison 56ers Soccer Club, 1994-95, youth basketball coach YMCA, Madison, 1994; youth softball coach Madison Area Sch.-Cmty. Recreation League, Madison, 1994; Cub Scout den leader Boy Scouts Am., Madison, 1991-92; project leader 4-H Club, Madison, 1992-95, Glencoe Cmty. Recreational Soccer coach, 1996. Named Outstanding Recent Alumnus U. Wis.-Platteville, 1993, Young Engr. of Yr. ASAE Wis. Sect., 1994; named to Nat. Rural Builder Hall of Fame Rural Builder, 1996. Mem. Am. Assn. Agrl. Engring. (chmn. structures com. 1994-96, post and pole design com. 1991-97; mem. various coms., chmn. Wis. sect. 1991-92, program chair 1990-91, sec.-treas. 1989-90, 97-98, nominating com. 1988-89, tech. reviewer trans. and Jour. Applied Engring. in Agr., Outstanding Paper award 1992, Superior Paper award 1997), Nat. Frame Builders Assn. (mem. rsch. & edn. com., Bernon C. Perkins award 1996), Alpha Gamma Rho (alumni sec. Beta Gamma chpt. 1980, pres. 1980-81), Alpha Zeta, Gamma Sigma Delta. Lutheran. Avocations: all sports, woodworking, playing cards. Home: 5931 Schroeder Rd Madison WI 53711-2573 Office: U Wis Agrl Engring Dept 460 Henry Mall Madison WI 53706-1533

BOHO, DAN L., lawyer; b. Chgo., Sept. 18, 1952; s. Lawrence M. and Genevieve A. (Zurek) Boho; m. Sheri L. Krisco, Sept. 10, 1977; children: Courtney, Ashley. BA, Loyola U., Chgo., 1974, JD, 1977. Bar: Ill. 1977, Fed. Trial Bar 1977. Sr. ptnr., group leader litigation group Hinshaw & Culbertson, Chgo., 1977—. Mem. Fedn. Ins. and Corp. Counsel, Ill. Soc. Trial Lawyers (bd. dirs.), Def. Rsch. Inst., Assn. Def. Trial Attys., Ill. Def. Coun., Advs. Soc., Ill. Bar Assn. (past del. assembly), Polish Am. Assn. (past chmn. bd. dirs.), Japan Am. Soc. (bd. dirs.), Travelers and Immigrants Aid (bd. dirs.), Trial Lawyers Club (past pres. Chgo. chpt.), Phi Alpha Delta (past pres. Webster chpt.). Avocations: travel, tennis, skiing.

BOHOSKEY, BERNICE FLEMING, mineral-land owner, writer; b. Seattle, Feb. 9, 1918; d. Wilfred R. and Katherine E. (Emmeluth) Blair; stepdau. E. Charles Fleming; m. Woodward Bohoskey, Aug. 6, 1942 (dec. 1979); children: Charles W., Katherine A., Michael J., Constance E. Student, Mills Coll., Oakland, Calif., 1935-36, Cornish Sch. Arts, Seattle, 1936-38. Model various newspapers. mags., 1936-38; splty. dancer Earl Carroll's Vanities; actress various radio shows, stage plays and movies, Hollywood, Calif.; ptnr. Yakima Sheep Co. Composer: (hymn) Blessed Trinity, 1948, (song) God's on His Throne, 1948, (song) Just Give Me the Merry-Go-Round, 1949; contbr. articles to profl. jours. Founder, pres. Young First Voters Groups, 1940; spkr., organizer, Yakima County, Wash.; pres. Young Reps. Club, Wash., 1940. Mem. Jr. League (sustaining). Republican. Charismatic Christian.

BOHR, AAGE NIELS, physicist, educator; b. June 19, 1922; s. Niels and Margrethe (Nörlund) B.; m. Marietta Bettina Soffer (dec. 1978); 3 children: m. Bente Meyer Scharff, 1981. Ph.D., U. Copenhagen, Denmark, 1954; D honoris causa, Manchester U., 1961; hon. degrees, Oslo U., 1969, Heidelberg U., 1971, Trondheim U., 1972, Uppsala U., 1975. Jr. sci. officer Dept. Sci. and Indsl. Research, London, 1943-45; research assoc. Inst. Theoretical Physics U. Copenhagen, 1946—, prof. physics, 1956—; dir. Niels Bohr Inst., 1962-70; mem. bd. Nordita, 1958-74, dir., 1975-81. Author: Rotational States of Atomic Nuclei, 1954; (with Ben R. Mottelson) Nuclear Structure, Vol. 1, 1969, Vol. 2, 1975. Recipient Dannie Heineman prize, 1960; Pope Pius XI medal 1963; Atoms for Peace award, 1969; H.C. Ørsted medal, 1970; Rutherford medal, 1972; John Price Wetherill medal, 1974; Nobel prize in physics, 1975; Ole Römer medal, 1976. Mem. Danish, Norwegian, Yugoslavian, Polish, Swedish acads. scis., Royal Physiograph. Soc. Lund, Sweden, Am. Acad. Arts and Scis., Nat. Acad. Scis. (U.S.), Deutsche Akademie der Naturforscher Leopoldina, Am. Philos. Soc., Finska Vetenskaps-Societeten, Pontifical Acad. Achievements include research in nuclear physics and quantal physics in general. Office: Niels Bohr Inst, Blegdamsvej 15-17, DK-2100 Copenhagen Denmark

BOHRMAN, DAVID ELLIS, television news producer; b. Hollywood, Calif., Apr. 30, 1954; s. Stanford Mervyn and Ardelle Joyce (Coleman) B.; m. Catherine Marie Leuchs, June 9, 1976; children—Amber Catherine, Harrison Zerr. B.A. in French, Stanford U., 1976, B.S. in Phys. Sci., 1976; M.S. in Journalism, Columbia U., 1978. Producer KNXT, CBS, Los Angeles, 1978-80; field producer ABC News Nightline, N.Y.C., 1980-81, sr. producer, 1981-82; sr. producer ABC World News Tonight, 1982-84, ABC Polit. Broadcasts and Spl. Events, 1984-88, exec. prodr. ABC News Interactive, 1988-91, creator, exec. prodr. World News Now, 1991-93, combined unit World News Now, World News This Morning, Good Morning America News, 1992-93; exec. prodr. spl. events NBC News, 1993—. Patentee in field. Recipient Emmy award Nat. Acad. TV Arts and Sci., 1982, 87, 92, 94. Golden Mike awards Radio TV News Assn., 1979, Los Angeles Press Club award, 1979, Valley Press Club award, Nat. Assn. Working Women award, 1979, Dupont, Peabody, Polk awards for Nightline, Mac World Superstacks award, 1989, 90, Mac User award, 1991, Christopher award, Arthur Ashe award, 1995. Avocation: computers. Office: NBC News 30 Rockefeller Plz Fl 2 New York NY 10112-0036

BOHRNSTEDT, GEORGE WILLIAM, educational researcher; b. Arcadia, Wis., Sept. 28, 1938; s. Russell Gail and Agnes (Brecht) B.; m. Josephine Orlanda, Aug. 11, 1962 (div. 1973); children—Elizabeth (dec.), Brian, Matthew; m. Jennifer Lou Cain, Sept. 28, 1980; 1 child, Kassandra. Student, Winona State Coll., 1956-58; B.S., U. Wis., 1960, M.A., 1963, Ph.D., 1966. Research assoc. U. Wis., Madison, 1966-69; assoc. prof. Mpls., 1969-73, chmn. dept. sociology, 1970-73; prof. Ind. U., Bloomington, 1973-88, chmn. dept. sociology, 1982-86, dir. Inst. Social Research, 1974-79; sr. v.p., dir. Am. Inst. for Rsch., Palo Alto, Calif., 1988-96, sr. v.p. for rsch., 1996—. Author: (with others) Statistics for Social Data Analysis, 3d edit., 1994; Basic Social Statistics, 1991; editor: Sociological Methodology, 1970; editor Sociol. Methods and Rsch., 1971-79, 84-87, Social Psychology Quar., 1980-82. Served to U.S. Army, 1962. Fellow NSF, 1963, NIMH, 1964-66, Ctr. for Advanced Studies in Behavioral Scis., 1986-87; Found. for Child Devel. Belding scholar, 1976-77. Mem. Am. Sociol. Assn., Psychometric Soc., Am. Statis. Assn., Soc. Exptl. Social Psychologists. Avocation: jazz musician. Office: Am Insts Rsch Behavioral Scis John C Flanagan Rsch Ctr PO Box 1113 Palo Alto CA 94302-1113

BOICE, CRAIG KENDALL, management consultant; b. Portland, Oreg., June 25, 1952; s. Charles A. and Audrey (Larson) B.; m. Jacinta E. Remedios, Nov. 21, 1979. BA summa cum laude, Beloit Coll., 1973; MA, Yale U., 1974, M.Phil., 1976, M in Pub. and Pvt. Mgmt., 1979. Instr. fellow philosophy Yale U., New Haven, 1978-79; economist Overseas Pvt. Investment Corp., Washington, 1978; sr. cons. Coopers and Lybrand, Washington and London, 1979-81; v.p. ops. Internat. Licensing Network, N.Y.C., 1981-82; pres., chmn., chief exec. officer Boice Dunham Group, N.Y.C., 1983—; adj. asst. prof. NYU, 1984—. Cons. Lake Placid Olympic Organizing Com., (N.Y.), 1979, New Haven Homesteading Program, 1979. Mem. Am. Mktg. Assn., Assn. Energy Engrs., Automated Meter Reading Assn., Computer and Automated Sys. Assn., Soc. Mfg. Engrs., Strategic Leadership Forum, World Future Soc., Geospatial Info. & Tech. Assn. Democrat. Office: Boice Dunham Group 30 W 13th St New York NY 10011-7912

BOICE, JOHN DUNNING, JR., epidemiologist, science administrator; b. Bklyn., Dec. 20, 1945; s. John Dunning and Irene Ellen (Gesso) B.; m. Jennifer Rex, Dec. 14, 1974; children: John Dunning III, James Brittin, Jason Adams, Justin Rex. BS, U. Tex., El Paso, 1967; MS, Rensselaer Poly. Inst., 1968, Harvard U., 1973; ScD, Harvard U., 1977. Rsch. asst. Schellenger Rsch. Lab., El Paso, Tex., 1965-67, Texas Instruments, Midland, Tex., 1966, Linear Accelerator Lab, Troy, N.Y., 1968-69; commd. 2d lt. USPHS, 1969, advanced through grades to capt., 1983; physicist Bur. Radiol. Health, Woburn, Mass., 1969-72; epidemiologist FDA, Rockville, Md., 1972-76; chief radiation epidemiology Nat. Cancer Inst., Bethesda, Md., 1977-96; sci. dir. Internat. Epidemiology Inst., Rockville, Md., 1996—, Internat. Commn. on Radiation Protection, 1997—, Nat. Coun. Radiation Protection Measurements, 1979—; del. UN Sci. Com. on Effects of Atomic Radiation, 1993—. Author: Epidemiologic Analysis, 1979; author, editor: Radiation Carcinogenesis, 1982, Multiple Primary Cancers, 1985; author monograph. Recipient Gorgas medal Assn. Mil. Surgeons U.S., 1994, E.O. Laurence awrd Dept. of Energy, 1994. Mem. Nat. Coun. Radiation Protection and Measurements. Mem. Ch. of Christ. Achievements include rsch. on cancer producing effects of ionizing radiation; exposures occurring in med., environ., mil., and occupl. settings. Office: Internat Epidemiology Inst 1500 Research Blvd Rockville MD 20850-3127*

BOIMAN, DONNA RAE, artist, art academy executive; b. Columbus, Ohio, Jan. 13, 1946; d. George Brandle and Donna Rae (Rockwell) Hall; m. David Charles Boiman, Dec. 8, 1973 (div. Aug. 1990). BS in Pharmacy, Ohio State U., 1969; student, Columbus Coll. Art & Design, 1979-83. Registered pharmacist, Ohio. Pharmacist, mgr. various retail stores, Cleve., 1970-73, Columbus, 1973-77; owner L'Artiste, Reynoldsburg, Ohio, 1977-81; pres. Cen. Ohio Art Acad., Reynoldsburg, 1981-90, Art Acad. Ctrl. Ohio, Reynoldsburg, 1990—; owner Big Red Designs, Reynoldsburg, 1989—; pub. rels. mgr. Freedom Farm Equestrian Ctr., Pataskala, Ohio, 1991—; design dir., v.p. Sterling Automotive Mgmt., Inc.; cons. to Mayor City of Reynoldsburg, 1986-87, webmaster; owner Ctrl. Ohio Art Graphics/Design/Website Design. Represented in permanent collections including Collector's Gallery Columbus Mus. Art, Gallery 200, Columbus Art Exch., The Huntington Collection, Dean Witter Reynolds Collection, Zanesville Art Ctr., Mt. Carmel East Hosp., Columbus, Corp. 2005, Radisson Hotels, Mich. and Ohio, Fifth 3d Bank, Bexley, Ohio, On Line Computer Libr., Dublin, Ohio, Columbus Torah Acad.; author: Anatomy Made Easy: Draw, Color and Learn, Anatomy and Structure: A Guide for Young Artists, 1988. Mem. Columbus Better Bus. Bur. Recipient John Lennon Meml. Award for the Arts, Internat. Art Challenge com., 1987. Mem. Pa. Soc. Watercolorists, Nat. Soc. Layerists in Multimedia, Columbus Art League, Cen. Ohio Watercolor Soc. (pres. 1983-84), Am. Quarter Horse Assn., Ohio Quarter Horse Assn., Allied Artists of Am. (assoc.), Licking County Art Assn., Nat. Wildlife Fedn., Ohio State U. Alumni Assn., Ohio State U. Pharmacy Alumni Assn. (charter), Mid-Ohio Dressage Assn., U.S. Dressage Fedn., Ohio Arabian Horse Assn., Internat. Arabian Horse Assn., Arabian Sport Assn., Inc., Columbus Auto Dealers Assn. Avocations: showing horses, skiing, white water river running, judging figure skating. Office: Cen Ohio Art & Graphics PO Box 209 7315 E Main St Reynoldsburg OH 43068-2105

BOIME, ALBERT ISAAC, art history educator; b. St. Louis, Mar. 17, 1933; s. Max and Dorothy (Rubin) B.; m. Myra Block, June 23, 1964; children: Robert, Eric. A.B., UCLA, 1961; M.A., Columbia U., 1963, Ph.D., 1968. Instr. social history of art Columbia U., 1966-67; assoc. prof. SUNY, Stony Brook, 1967-72; prof., chmn. dept. SUNY, Binghamton, 1972-74, prof., 1974-78; prof. social history of art UCLA, 1978—; art historian in residence Coll. Creative Studies, U. Calif.-Santa Barbara, 1973; judge NEH, Washington, 1975; mem. adv. council N.Y. Acad. Art, N.Y.C., 1981—. Author: The Academy and French Painting in the 19th Century, 1971, Thomas Couture and the Eclectic Vision, 1981, the Social History of Modern Art: Vol. 1: Art in an Age of Revolution, 1987, Hollow Icons: The Politics of Sculpture in Nineteenth Century France, 1987, Vincent Van Gogh: Sternennacht, 1989, The Art of Exclusion: Representing Blacks in the Nineteenth Century, 1990, The Social History of Modern Art Vol. 2: Art in an Age of Bonapartism, 1990, The Magisterial Gaze: Manifest Destiny and American Landscape Painting (ca. 1830-1865), 1991, The Art of the Macchia and the Risorgimento, 1993, The Odyssey of Jan Stussey in Black and White, 1995, Art and the French Commune, 1995, Violence and Utopia: The Work of Jerome Boime, 1996, The Unveiling of the National Icons: A Plea for Patriotic Iconoclasm in a Nationalist Era, 1998. Served with AUS, 1955-58. Am. Council Learned Socs. fellow, 1970-71; Guggenheim fellow, 1974-75, 84-85; Regents fellow Smithsonian Institution, 1989-90. Mem. Coll. Art Assn., Soc. Fellows Am. Acad. at Rome. Office: UCLA Dept Art 405 Hilgard Ave Los Angeles CA 90095-9000 *I am grateful for this opportunity to join with my listing the memory of my dear brother, Jerome Philip Boime, whose rare, provocative mind inspired me with the sheer joy of intellectual pursuit. Whatever present success I may have, I owe to my capacity to thoroughly enjoy my work, to exult in ideas and the unboundedness of scholarly activity, and to commit this love to my developing engagement with political, philosophical and social issues.*

BOISE, AUDREY LORRAINE, education educator; b. Hackensack, N.J., Feb. 12, 1933; d. Paul George and Lillian Rose (Goedecker) B. BA, Wellesley (Mass.) Coll., 1955; MA, Fairleigh Dickinson U., 1977. Cert. tchr. K-8, learning disabilities, supervision. Tchr. Township of Berkeley Heights (N.J.), 1958-67; learning cons. Borough of New Providence (N.J.), 1978-82, 1986—, Scotch Plains/Fanwood (N.J.), 1984-86; instr. Fairleigh Dickinson U., Madison, N.J., 1983, 1975-76; several other short-term teaching positions; supr. student tchrs., 1975-78; lectr. on fgn. countries and U.S. History, N.J., 1967—; travel agt. (part-time) 1972—. Mem. Rep. Nat. Com. Campaign Coun., Nat. Rep. Senatorial Com., Washington, Rep. Presdl. Task Force, Washington, Rep. Presdl. Legion of Merit, N.J. State Rep. Com., Trenton, Nat. Fedn. Rep. Women, Washington. Mem. NEA, AAUW, N.J. Assn. Learning Cons., Assn. for Children with Learning Disabilities, N.J. Edn. Assn., Internat. Platform Assn., Fortnightly Club, Hist. Soc. Summit. Methodist. Avocations: travel, photography. Office: New Providence Bd Edn Dept Spl Svcs 356 Elkwood Ave New Providence NJ 07974-1838

BOISSEAU, JERRY PHILIP, financial services company executive; b. Plattsburgh, N.Y., June 5, 1939; s. Augustine Arthur and Genevieve Francis (Poland) B.; m. Linda Gael Cummings Aug. 18, 1961; children: Gregory Philip, Lisa Michele. B of Gen. Studies, U. Nebr., 1970; MEd in Adminstrn., Fitchburg State Coll., 1978; MBA, Western New Eng. Coll., 1981. Cert. fin. planner; lic. registered prin.; registered investment advisor. Enlisted U.S. Army, 1961, commd. 2d lt., 1963, advanced through grades to lt. col., 1979, ret., 1981; account exec. Prudential-Bache Securities, Springfield, Mass., 1981-87; pres. Arlington Beach Co., Seaside Park, N.J., 1987-91, resigned, 1991; lectr. Ocean County Coll., 1991—; adj. faculty mem. Coll. For Fin. Planning, Denver, 1992—; instr., lectr. U. Mass., Amherst, 1982-87, Greenfield (Mass.) C.C., 1983-86; owner, mgr. Amherst Fin. Svcs., Toms River, N.J., 1987—; mem. bd. trustees Cmty. Med. Ctr. Found.; bd. dirs. Ocean Harbor House, treas., 1998—; bd. dirs. Ocean County YMCA, sec., 1998—; bd. dirs., organizer Shore Cmty. Bank, 1996—. Past pres. parish coun. St. Catharines of Siena Ch., Seaside Park; ocean devel. adv. com. Children's Specialized Hosp., 1994-97. Mem. KC (4th degree), Inst. CFPs, Internat. Assn. Fin. Planners (pres. Ctrl. N.J. chpt. 1991-93, registry adv. coun. 1991-93, practitioners adv. coun. 1993-95), Letip of Ocean County (pres. 1993-94), Ctrl. N.J. Estate and Fin. Planning Coun., Toms River C. of C., Toms River Country Club, Seaside Park Yacht Club (treas. 1995-96), Rotary (pres. Amherst 1986-87, Paul Harris fellow; bd. dirs. Ctrl. Ocean Club, pres. 1997-98). Republican. Roman Catholic. Home: PO Box 591 Seaside Park NJ 08752-0591 Office: PO Box 1959 Toms River NJ 08754-1959

BOISSEAU, RICHARD ROBERT, lawyer; b. Phila., Sept. 6, 1944; s. Robert Bartholomew and Anne Cecilia (Tierney) B.; m. Jo-Ann Elizabeth Tompkins, Jan. 20, 1970; children: Richard Andrew, Thomas, Kristen. BS cum laude, Drexel U., 1968; JD cum laude, Temple U., 1974. Bar: Ga. 1974, U.S. Dist. Ct. (no. dist.) Ga. 1974, U.S. Ct. Appeals (4th cir.) 1980, U.S. Ct. Appeals (11th cir.) 1981, U.S. Supreme Ct. 1984, U.S. Ct. Appeals (9th cir.) 1986. Ptnr. Kilpatrick Stockton LLP, Atlanta, 1974—. Contbg. author: How Arbitration Works, 1987, 93, 97; contbr. articles to numerous profl. publs. Bd. dirs. Vis. Nurse Health Sys., Atlanta, 1976—. Mem. Ga. Bar Assn., Atlanta Bar Assn. Republican. Roman Catholic. Avocations: golf, running. Office: Kilpatrick Stockton LLP 1100 Peachtree St NE Ste 2800 Atlanta GA 30309-4501

BOISSEVAIN, BENJAMIN MATHEW, investment banker; b. Palo Alto, Calif., July 4, 1960; s. Thijs and Angie Boissevain. BS, BA, U. Calif., Berkeley, 1984; JD, NYU, 1987. Assoc. White & Case, N.Y.C., 1987-90; sr. mgr. Girocredit, Vienna, Austria, 1990-94; asst. dir. Barclays Bank, BZW, N.Y.C., 1994-96; founder, mng. dir. E Technologies Internat., N.Y.C., 1996-97; bd. dirs. Rhizome Internet, LLC, N.Y.C. Panel mem. World Wide Web Artists Consortium, N.Y., 1997. Mem. N.Y. New Media Assn., MIT Enterprise Forum (bd. dirs., chmn. digital media com. 1997). Avocations: chess, skiing, tennis. Fax: 212-475-1101. Office: E Technologies Internat. Assocs., LLC Ste 725 611 Broadway New York NY 10012

BOISVERT, LAURIER JOSEPH, communications executive; b. Legal, Alta., Can.; married with three children. Honors Degree in Commerce, Carleton U., Ottawa, 1981. Tech. tng. supr. Bell Can., 1964-72, Telesat, Gloucester, Ont., Can., 1972-73; mgr. Telesat, Gloucester, 1973-75, dir. Earth Sta. Ops., 1982-84; dir. network svcs. ops. Telesat, Ottawa, 1984-88, v.p. network svcs. ops., 1988-93; pres., COO Telesat, 1993, CEO, pres., 1993—; also bd. dirs.; pres., CEO TMI Comm., Inc.; bd. dirs. PT. Pasific Satelit Nusantara, Comm. Rsch. Coun., Asian Broadcasting Comm. Network Ltd. (ABCN), Telecomm. Access Partnerships (TAP), TMI Comm., Inc. Office: Telesat Canada, 1601 Telesat Ct, Gloucester, ON Canada K1B 5P4

BOK, DEAN, cell biologist, educator; b. Douglas County, S.D., Nov. 1, 1939; s. Kryn Arie and Rena (Van Zee) B.; m. Audrey Ann Van Diest, Aug. 21, 1964; children: Jonathan, Jeremy, James. B.A., Calvin Coll., 1960; M.A., Calif. State U., Long Beach, 1965; Ph.D., UCLA, 1968. Sci. instr. Valley Christian High Sch., Cerritos, Calif.; prof. neurobiology and Dolly Green prof. ophthalmology UCLA; asso. dir. Jules Stein Eye Inst., 1972-80; Wellcome vis. prof. biomed. scis., 1994. Recipient disting. teaching awards UCLA, sr. sci. investigator award Rsch. To Prevent Blindness Inc., 1986, 95, Disting. Alumnus award Calif. State U., 1986, Calvin Coll., 1990; grantee Nat. Eye Inst., Nat. Retinitis Pigmentosa Soc.; William and Mary Greve internat. rsch. scholar Rsch. To Prevent Blindness Inc., 1982. Fellow AAAS; mem. Nat. Eye Inst. (bd. sci. counselors 1980-82, MERIT award 1987-96), Assn. Research in Vision and Ophthalmology (trustee 1978-82, Friedenwald award 1985, Alcon award 1985), Am. Soc. Cell Biology. Home: 2135 Kelton Ave Los Angeles CA 90025-5705 Office: UCLA Los Angeles CA 90024

BOK, DEREK, law educator, former university president; b. Bryn Mawr, Pa., Mar. 22, 1930; s. Curtis and Margaret (Plummer) B.; m. Sissela Ann Myrdal, May 7, 1955; children: Hilary Margaret, Victoria, Tomas Jeremy. B.A., Stanford U., 1951; J.D., Harvard U., 1954; M.A., George Washington U., 1958. Fulbright scholar Paris, 1954-55; faculty Harvard U. Law Sch., Cambridge, Mass., 1958—, prof., 1961—, dean, 1968-71; pres. Harvard U., Cambridge, 1971-91; 300th anniversary univ. prof. Harvard U., 1991—. Editor: (with Archibald Cox) Cases and Materials on Labor Law, 1962; author: (with John T. Dunlop) Labor and the American Community, 1970, Beyond the Ivory Tower: Social Responsibilities of the Modern University, 1982, Higher Learning, 1986, Universities and the Future of America, 1990, The Cost of Talent, 1993, (with William G. Bowen) The Shape of the River, 1998; contbr.: In the Public Interest, 1980, The State of the Nation, 1997. Bd. dirs., nat. chmn. Common Cause, 1999—, Overseas Cts. Inst. Music, 1997—. Fellow Ctr. for Advanced Studies in the Behavioral Scis., 1991-92. Fellow Am. Acad. Arts and Scis., mem. Inst. Medicine, Am. Philos. Soc., Phi Beta Kappa. Office: Harvard U JFK Sch of Govt Cambridge MA 02138

BOK, JOAN TOLAND, utility executive; b. Grand Rapids, Mich., Dec. 31, 1929; d. Don Prentiss Weaver and Mary Emily (Anderson) T.; m. John Fairfield Bok, July 15, 1955; children: Alexander Toland, Geoffrey Robbins. AB, Radcliffe Coll., 1951; JD, Harvard U., 1955. Bar: Mass. 1955. Assoc. Ropes & Gray, Boston, 1955-61; pvt. practice Boston, 1961-68; atty. New England Electric Sys., Westborough, Mass., 1968-73, asst. to pres., 1973-77, v.p., sec., 1977-79, vice chmn., 1979-84, pres., CEO, 1988-89, chmn., 1984-98, chmn. emeritus, 1998—; bd. dirs. Avery Denison Corp., John Hancock Mut. Life Ins. Co., Solutia, Inc., New England Elec. Sys. Bd. dirs. Nat. Osteoporosis Found.; trustee Libr. of Boston Athenaeum, Urban Inst., Worcester Found. for Biomed. Rsch., Woods Hole (Mass.) Oceanog. Instn.; past pres. bd. overseers Harvard U.; mem. corp. Mass. Gen. Hosp. Fellow Am. Bar Found.; mem. Boston Bar Assn., Am. Acad. Arts and Scis., Phi Beta Kappa. Unitarian. Home: 53 Pinckney St Boston MA 02114-4801 Office: NEES Co 22 Beacon St Boston MA 02108-3703

BOK, JOHN FAIRFIELD, lawyer; b. Boston, Aug. 30, 1930. AB magna cum laude, Harvard U., 1952, LLB magna cum laude, 1955. Bar: Mass. 1955, N.Y. 1982, Pa. 1984. Assoc. firm Ropes & Gray, Boston, 1957-62, 64-69; counsel to devel. adminstr. Boston Redevel. Authority, 1962-64; ptnr. firm Csaplar & Bok, Boston, 1969-90, Gaston & Snow, Boston, 1990-91; of counsel Foley, Hoag & Eliot, Boston, 1991—; instr. law Boston Coll. Law Sch., part-time 1974-75; lectr. Practicing Law Inst., 1974, New Eng. Law Inst., 1973. Editor Harvard Law Rev., 1954-55. Pres. Cambridge St. Comty. Devel. Corp., 1972-75, Citizens Housing and Planning Assn., 1968-70, Met. Cultural Alliance, 1973-75, Beacon Hill Civic Assn., 1959-61, Beacon Hill Nursery Sch., 1964-65, Peddock's Island Trust, 1982-85, Mus. Wharf, 1989—, Boston Ballet, 1991-94, Peter Faneuil Devel. Group, Inc., 1992—, Mass. Hort. Soc., 1995—; v.p. The Comty. Builders, Inc., 1969-97, pres. 1998—; chmn. Boston Children's Mus., 1976-78, Mass. Housing Partnership, 1985-92, Social Policy Rsch. Group Inc., 1985-92, Boston Mcpl. Rsch. Bur., 1979-81, bd. dirs. and/or officer Boston Neighborhood Housing Svcs., 1974-76, Boston Waterfront Devel. Corp., 1970-85, Archtl. Conservation Trust for Mass., 1978-92, Wheelock Coll., 1980-97, Strawberry Banke, Inc., 1981-86, Met. Boston Housing Partnership, Inc., 1984-95, Cambridge Coll., 1984—, Boston Housing Authority monitoring com., 1984-90, The Boston Harbor Assn., 1984-92, Back Bay Assn., 1988-92, Hist. Mass., 1989—, African Am. Meeting House, 1993—; mem. Boston Archives and Records Advt. Commn., 1988—, Comty. Music Ctr., 1995—, Island Alliance, 1995—, Light Boston!, 1995—. Fulbright-Hays scholar, 1976. Mem. ABA, Mass. Bar Assn., Boston Bar Assn. (chmn. land use com. 1971-74), Phi Beta Kappa. Home: 53 Pinckney St Boston MA 02114-4801 Office: Foley Hoag & Eliot 1 Post Office Sq Boston MA 02109-2170

BOK, SISSELA, philosopher, writer; b. Stockholm, Dec. 2, 1934; d. Gunnar and Alva (Reimer) Myrdal; m. Derek Bok, May 7, 1955; children—Hilary, Victoria, Tomas. BA, George Washington U., 1957, MA, 1958, LHD (hon.), 1986; PhD, Harvard U., 1970; LLD (hon.), Mt. Holyoke Coll., 1985; LHD (hon.), Clark U., 1988, U. Mass., 1991, Georgetown U., 1992. Lectr. Simmons Coll., Boston, 1971-72; lectr. Harvard-MIT Div. Health Scis. and Tech., Cambridge, 1975-82, Harvard U., Cambridge, 1982-84; assoc. prof. philosophy Brandeis U., Waltham, Mass., 1985-89, prof. philosophy, 1989-92; fellow Ctr. for Advanced Study, Stanford, Calif., 1991-92; Disting. fellow Harvard Ctr. Population and Devel. Studies, Cambridge, Mass., 1993—; mem. ethics adv. bd. HEW, 1977-80; bd. dirs. Population Coun., 1971-77; mem. Pulitzer Prize Bd., 1988-97, chmn., 1996-97. Author: Lying: Moral Choice in Public and Private Life, 1978 (Melcher award, George Orwell award), Secrets: On the Ethics of Concealment and Revelation, 1982, Alva: Ett kvinnoliv, 1987, A Strategy for Peace, 1989, Alva Myrdal: A Daughter's Memoir, 1991 (Melcher award), Common Values, 1996, Mayhem: Violence as Public Entertainment, 1998; mem. editl. bd. Ethics, 1980-85, Criminal Justice Ethics, 1980—, Contention, 1990-96, Common Knowledge, 1991—, (with others) Euthanasia and Physician-Assisted Suicide, 1998. Bd. dirs. Inst. for Philosophy and Religion, Boston U.; mem. Pulitzer Prize Bd., 1989-97. Recipient Abram L. Sachar Silver medallion Brandeis U., 1985, Radcliffe Coll. Grad. Soc. medal, 1993, Barnard Coll. medal of distinction, 1995, centennial medal Harvard Grad. Sch. Arts & Scis., 1998. Fellow Hastings Ctr. (dir. 1976-84, 94-97); mem. Am. Philos. Assn.

BOKENKOTTER, THOMAS STEPHEN, clergyman; b. Cin., Aug. 19, 1924; s. Anthony and Bertrude (Wessel) B. S.T.L., Angelicum, Rome, 1951; PhD in History, Louvain, Belgium, 1954. Ordained priest Roman Cath. Ch., 1950. Prof. ch. history Athenaeum of Ohio, Cin., 1960-80; pastor Assumption Ch., Cin., 1980—; adj. prof. theology Xavier U., Cin., 1980—; dir. Over Rhine Soup Kitchen, Cin., 1976—; chmn. Tom Geiger Guest House, Cin., 1990—. Author: (book) Concise History of Catholic Church, 1977, Dynamic Catholicism, 1992, Church and Revolution, 1998. Mem. Am. Cath. Hist. Assn. Home: 4512 Hector Ave Cincinnati OH 45227-2711

BOKOR, BRUCE H., lawyer; b. Tampa, Fla., Sept. 18, 1947. BSBA with honors, U. Fla., 1969, JD with honors, 1972; LLM in Taxation, NYU, 1973. Bar: Fla. 1972, U.S. Tax Ct. 1974, U.S. Supreme Ct. 1977. Atty. Johnson, Blakely, Pope, Bokor, Ruppel & Burns, P.A., Tampa; pres. Pinellas County Estate Planning Coun., 1980. Editor-in-chief U. Fla. Law Rev., 1971-72. Fellow Am. Coll. Trust and Estate Counsel, Am. Coll. Tax Counsel; mem. ABA,, Fla. Bar (chmn. tax sect. 1987-88, exec. coun. 1973—), Am. Law Inst., Clearwater Bar Assn., Order of Coif, Phi Kappa Phi, Beta Gamma Sigma, Blue Key. Office: PO Box 1100 100 N Tampa St Ste 1800 Tampa FL 33602*

BOLAN, THOMAS ANTHONY, lawyer; b. Lynn, Mass., May 30, 1924; s. Thomas J. and Margaret (Cremin) B.; m. Marie T. Gerst, Nov. 25, 1950; children: Sean, Douglas, Mary, Jacqueline, William. BA summa cum laude, St. John's U., 1952, LLB summa cum laude, 1950, LLD (hon.), 1985. Bar: N.Y. 1951. Assoc. Burroughs & Brown, N.Y.C., 1951-53; asst. U.S. atty. Dept. Justice, N.Y.C., 1953-57; assoc. Roy M. Cohn, N.Y.C., 1957-59; with Saxe, Bacon & Bolan, N.Y.C., 1960-71, counsel, 1972-87; ptnr. Bolan, Lang, Biancone, Tiffenberg, PC, N.Y.C., 1987-89; pres. Thomas A. Bolan, PC, N.Y.C., 1989—; lectr. law St. John's U., 1957-61; pres., chmn. bd. 5th Ave. Coach Lines, N.Y.C., 1967-68, Championship Sports, Inc., N.Y.C., 1961—; treas., exec. dir. Feature Sports, Inc., 1959-61; chmn. bd. Merc. Nat. Bank, Chgo., 1967-68, Gateway Nat. Bank, Chgo., 1966-67; sec. Balt. Paint and Chem. Corp., N.Y.C., 1966-68, TelePro Industries Inc., N.Y.C., 1966-68; sec., dir. B.S.F. Co., N.Y.C., 1966-68, Defiance Industries, N.Y.C., 1966-68; v.p. Am. Steel and Pump Corp., N.Y.C., 1966-68, WRNJ Assocs., Atlantic City, 1961-68, Harrisburg Broadcasting Co., Palmyra, Pa., 1966-68; sec., treas., dir. Berwick Broadcasting Corp., Reading, Pa., 1967-68; dir. Overseas Pvt. Investment Corp., 1982-86. Bd. editors Nat. Law Jour., 1983-90; contbr. articles to profl. jours. Co-chmn. N.Y. Reagan Fin. Com., 1980, N.Y. Reagan-Bush Campaign Com., 1984; founder law chmn. Conservative Party, N.Y. State, 1962—; chmn. E. Side Conservative Club, N.Y.C., 1973—; v.p. Crusade for Am., Rockville Ctr., N.Y., 1957-62; bd. regents St. Francis Coll., Bklyn., 1968—; treas. Ednl. Reviewer, 1960—; pres. Cambria Heights (N.Y.) Parish Coun., 1968-70; pres., dir. Pro Ecclesia Found., 1972-73; trustee Cambria Heights Boys Club Assn., 1968-72, St. John's U., 1987-98, emeritus, 1999—; v.p., dir. Heiser Found., 1955-73; mem. Com. to Restore Internal Security, 1979-96; mem. Coun. for Nat. Policy, 1983—, Internat. Policy Forum, 1988—; mem. Am. Coun. on Germany, 1983—, U.S. Commn. for UNESCO, 1983-85; bd. visitors Eureka Coll., 1983—, Inst. for Italian Heritage & Culture St. John's U., 1992—; nat. adv. coun. Actors Youth Fund, 1982—; mem. U.S. Senator Alfonse D'Amato's Jud. Screening Com., 1980-98; pres., bd. dirs. Global Leadership Inst., 1986—; pres., trustee Nat. Rev. Inst., 1992—, Found. for Study of Nat. Civic and Internat. Affairs, 1993—; dir. Narnia Catechetical and Cultural Ctr., Inc., 1991—, Am. Friends of James Joyce, 1998—; mem. N.Y. State Vets. Adv. Coun., 1989-91. With USAF, 1943-45. Decorated Air medal with 5 oak leaf clusters; recipient Medal of Honor the 52d Assn., 1981, Bella V. Dodd Meml award N.Y. County Conservative Party, 1981, Ann award Bronx County Conservative Party, 1984, Charles Edison award Conservative Party N.Y. State, 1987, Disting. Svc. award Nat. Cath. War Vets, 1985, Celtic Cross award, 1997, Cross for Conspicuous Svc. State of N.Y. 1989, Ann. Heritage award Bklyn.-Queens Conservative Party, 1991, Madison award St. John's U. Sch. Law, 1991, Annual award Nat. Traditionalist Caucus, 1994, Pietas medal St. John's U., 1997. Mem. Cath. Lawyers Guild, Internat. Assn. Jurists, Am. African Affairs Assn. (sec., bd. dirs. 1975—), Cath. War Vets. (Queens County judge adv. 1965—, nat. judge adv. 1984—, Svc. award Queens County chpt. 1968, 77, 90, elected to nat. order St. Sebastian 1981), Ret. Officers Assn. (Knickerbocker chpt.) , Eighth Air Force Hist. Soc., Knights of Malta. Office: 521 5th Ave Fl 10 New York NY 10175-1099

BOLAND, CATHERINE A. BENNING, quality assurance specialist; b. Red Bank, N.J.; d. William A. and Teresa A. Benning; m. Brian J. Boland, Apr. 24, 1993. BSN, Rutgers U., Newark, 1985. RN, N.J.; cert. nursing adminstr. Community health nurse All Health Care, Inc., Middletown, N.J., 1985-86; utilization rev. nurse Marlboro (N.J.) State Hosp., 1985-91; quality assurance specialist Div. Devel. Disabilities, Trenton, N.J., 1991-92, Div. Mental Health and Hosp's. Bur. of Licensing and Inspection, Trenton, 1992-98; housing specialist divsn. mental health svcs. Office of Dep. Dir., 1999—. Mem. Sigma Theta Tau.

BOLAND, CHRISTOPHER THOMAS, II, lawyer; b. Scranton, Pa., June 10, 1915; s. Patrick J. and Sarah (Jennings) B.; m. Nora Cusick, Jan. 23, 1943; m. Cornelia Bingham, Mar. 1, 1980. BSS cum laude, Georgetown U., 1937; LL.B., Harvard, 1940. Staff dir. Spl. Senate Com. on Atomic Energy, 1945-47; staff dir., counsel Joint Senate-House Com. on Atomic Energy, 1947; pvt. practice Washington, 1947—; sr. ptnr. Gallagher, Boland, Meiburger & Brosnan, Washington, 1955-93, sr. counsel, 1994—; utility specialist Dept. Energy. Served to lt. col., intelligence USAAF, 1941-45. Mem. ABA, D.C. Bar Assn., Fed. Energy Bar Assn. (pres. 1970), Congressional Country Club (pres. 1974), Harvard Club (Washington), Burning Tree Club (Bethesda, Md.), Rehoboth Beach (Del.) Country Club. Home: 5309 Cardinal Ct Spring Hill Bethesda MD 20816 Office: 1023 15th St NW Ste 900 Washington DC 20005-2602

BOLAND, GERALD LEE, health facility financial executive; b. Harrisburg, Pa., Apr. 2, 1946; s. Vincent Harry and Alice Jane (Geiste) B.; m. Sandra Elaine Welch; 1 child, Peter Alexander. BS, Lebanon Valley Coll., 1968. Acctg. trainee Armstrong Cork Co., Millville, N.J., 1968; payroll supr., plant ops. acct., 1969-70; sr. fin. acct. Lancaster (Pa.) Gen. Hosp., 1970-71, mgr. gen. acctg., 1972; corp. acctg. mgr. HMW Industries, Inc., Lancaster, 1972; corp. controller Fleck-Marshall Co. subs. Gable Industries, Lancaster, 1973-74, sec.-treas., 1974-75; contr. Dominion Psychiat. Treatment Ctr., Falls Church, Va., 1975-76; contr., dir. fin. Miller & Byrne, Inc., Rockville, Md., 1976-79; v.p. internal auditing Medlantic Healthcare Group, 1979-88; v.p. ops. Kapner, Wolfberg & Assocs., Van Nuys, Calif., 1988-89; dir. acctg. Providence Hosp., 1989-95, asst. controller, 1995—. Mem. Am. Acctg. Assn., Nat. Assn. Accts., Hosp. Fin. Mgmt. Assn., Eastern Fin. Assn., Am. Hosp. Assn., Am. Mgmt. Assn., Fin. Mgmt. Assn., Inst. Internal Auditors. Home: 13021 Silver Maple Ct Bowie MD 20715-1933

BOLAND, JAMES FRANCIS, JR., naval officer, helicopter pilot; b. Jersey City, N.J., June 16, 1951; s. James Francis and Evarista (Monahan) B.; m. Susan Dorsey O'Dea, June 26, 1976; children: Brian Thomas, Brendan Timothy. BS, U.S. Nava. Acad., 1973; MS in Nat. Security Strategy, U.S. Nat. War Coll., 1994. Commd. ensign USN, 1973, advanced through grades to capt., 1994; fleet pilot, various ships U.S. Atlantic Fleet, 1973-86; commdg. officer Helicopter Anti-Submarine Squadron Light-32, Norfolk, Va., 1989-90; air officer USS Inchon, 1990-92; comdg. officer Helicopter Anti-Submaraine Squadron Light 30 Norfolk, 1992-93; comdr. U.S. Naval Base, Guantanamo Bay, Cuba, 1994-95; comdr. naval forces Joint Task Force 160, Guantanamo Bay, Cuba, 1994-95; dir. shore safety programs Naval Safety Ctr., Norfolk, 1995-98; chief plans divsn. Maritime Def. Zone Atlantic, 1998—; flight comdr. USN-Royal Navy Exch. Program, Portland, Dorset, U.K., 1981-83. Mem. U.S. Naval Inst. (life), Naval Helicopter Assn. (regional dir. 1992-93, regional v.p. 1989-90), Assn. Naval Aviation, Chesapeake Bay Found. Roman Catholic. Avocations: military history, foreign affairs, American literature, recreational boating and swimming. Office: Naval Safety Ctr 375 A St Norfolk VA 23511-4303

BOLAND, JANET LANG, judge; b. Kitchener, Ont., Can., Dec. 6, 1924; d. George William and Miriam Janet (Geraghty) Lang; m. John Brown Boland, Oct. 1, 1949; children: Michael, Christopher, Nicholas. B.A., Waterloo Coll., 1946; law degree, Osgoode Hall, 1950; hon. doctorate of law, Sir Wilfred Laurier U. Bar: Ont. 1976, named Queen's counsel 1965. Mem. firm White, Bristol, Beck & Phipps, Toronto, Ont., 1959-69; partner firm Lang Michener, Toronto, 1969-72; county ct. judge Toronto, 1972-76; judge Supreme Ct. of Ont., Toronto, 1976—; co-chmn. Penal Reform for Women Joint Com., 1956-58. Mem. Jr. League Toronto (hon. pres.), Can. Women's Sr. Golf Assn. Roman Catholic. Office: 164 Inglewood Dr, Toronto, ON Canada M4T 1H7

BOLAND, JOHN KEVIN, bishop. ordained priest June 14, 1959. Appointed Bishop Savannah Diocese, 1995—. Office: Catholic Pastoral Center 601 E Liberty St Savannah GA 31401-5196*

BOLAND, JOSEPH ANTHONY, state official; b. Terre Haute, Ind., July 26, 1943; s. Joseph Wayne and Dorothy Jean (Kloster) B.; m. Phyllis Ann Porter, May 14, 1977; children: Matthew, Peter, David, Nathan. AB, Ind. State U., 1973; Assoc. Cert., Word Faith Fellowship Bible In, Paris, Ill., 1995. Reporter/columnist Terre Haute Star, 1969-82; asst. minister Rock Run Ch., Rosedale, Ind., 1995-97; equipment scheduler Ind. Dept. Transp., Crawfordsville, 1981—. Bd. dirs. Crisis Pregnancy Ctr. of Wabash Valley, Terre Haute, 1990-95. With USNR, 1965-67. Office: Ind Dept Transp 291 W 300 N Crawfordsville IN 47933-9088

BOLAND, MARGARET CAMILLE, financial services administrator, consultant; b. Washington, Feb. 20, 1929; d. Harvey Alvin and Margaret Estelle (Head) Jacob; m. Robert Edgar Hollingsworth, July 14, 1960 (div. July 1980); children: William Lee, Robert Edgar Hollingsworth Jr., Barbara Camille, Bradford Damion; m. James Aldo Boland, Sept. 12, 1998. AA, Va. Intermont Coll., 1949. Bookkeeper Fred A. Smith Real Estate, Washington, 1949-53; adminstrv. asst. mgr. Airtronic, Inc., Bethesda, Md., 1953-61; pers. adminstr. Sears Roebuck, Washington, 1973-74; adminstrv. mgr., communication mgr. Garvin GuyButler Corp., San Francisco, 1980-88, exec. sec., pers. mgr., 1989-95, adminstrv. cons., ret., 1996; adminstrv. cons., Concord, Calif.; assoc. Robert Hollingsworth Nuclear Cons., Walnut Creek, Calif., 1975-79. Bd. dirs. Civic Arts, Walnut Creek, 1975-98; bd. dirs., mem. pub. rels. com. Valley Art Ctr., Walnut Creek, 1997—. Recipient Spl. Recognition award AEC, 1974. Mem. Internat. Platform Assn., Commonwealth Club, Beta Sigma Phi (pres. 1954). Democrat. Presbyterian. Avocations: travel, art appreciation, investments, hiking, reading. Home: 1160 Rockledge Ln # 7 Walnut Creek CA 94595

BOLAND, RAYMOND JAMES, bishop; b. Tipperary, Ireland, Feb. 8, 1932; came to U.S., 1957; Ed., Nat. U. Ireland and All Hallows Sem., Dublin. Ordained priest Roman Cath. Ch., Dublin, 1957. Vicar gen., chancellor of Washington archdiocese; ordained bishop Birmingham, Ala., 1988-93; transferred as bishop Kansas City, St. Joseph, Mo., 1993—. Address: PO Box 419037 Kansas City MO 64141-6037*

BOLAÑOS, ANITA MARIE, lawyer; b. Berwyn, Ill., Apr. 20, 1964; d. Jose M. and Anita Marie (Loycano) Bolaños. AB, U. Mich., 1986; JD, DePaul U., 1989. Bar: Ill. 1990. Ptnr. Schiller DuCanto & Fleck, Chgo., 1990—. Fellow Am. Acad. Matrimonial Lawyers; mem. ABA, Ill. Bar Assn. Roman Catholic. Avocations: running, piano. Office: Schiller DuCanto & Fleck 200 N La Salle St Ste 2700 Chicago IL 60601-1099

BOLANOS, MICHAEL TEMPLETON, new media executive; b. Denville, N.J., Jan. 29, 1965; s. Henry and Jean Mary (Chardi) B. Mng. dir. Bell and Barter Theater/Arts Ctr., Rockaway, N.J., 1981-83; pres. The Musicom Corp., N.Y.C., 1981—, U.S./Soviet Exch. Initiative, 1985-86; prior. Hart-

Bolanos and Assocs., N.Y.C., 1987-88; pres. Global Programming Inc., N.Y.C., Tokyo, 1990-93; pres., CEO Entertainment Drive LLC, N.Y.C., 1995—; artistic coord. U.S./Soviet Exchange Initiative; mem. bd. Friends of Am. Theatre Wing, 1991-92; cons. NHK-TV, Tokyo, Fujisankei Group, Osaka, Japan, 1989-91, CompuServe, Columbus, Ohio, 1993-91. Creator/reporter Kidcast, KAMR-TV, Amarillo, Tex., 1975-76; co-creator, patentee eDrive Movie Viewer, 1994; creator Entertainment Drive (eDrive) on CompuServe, 1994 (Visionary Citation award Smithsonian/Computerworld 1995), eDrive Japan on NiftyServe, 1997; creator Offcl. Cindy Crawford website, 1998, StarClubs.com; creator, exec. prodr. www.cindy.com., the Ofcl. Cindy Crawford Web site. Artist coord. Rally for Soviet Jewry, Coalition to Free Soviet Jews, 1987; exec. prodr. on-line coverage of telethon Muscular Dystrophy Assn., 1994-95, exec. prodr. on-line chat Artists' Rights Found., 1995. Recipient Cyber 60 award N.Y. Mag., 1995, CyberStar award Virtual City Mag., 1996. Mem. The Japan Soc. (concert prodr. 1987), Am. Acad. Children's Entertainment (bd. outside advisors), Actor's Fund Am. (Inner Cir.), Internet Content Coalition, Young Entrepreneurs Assn., N.Y. New Media Assn., Sales and Mktg. Execs. N.Y., Assn. for Interactive Media. Avocations: acting, singing, travel, Japanese language and art. Office: Entertainment Drive 225 E 24th St New York NY 10010-3842

BOLANOS, ROLANDO D., protective services officer; b. 1952. AA in Criminal Justice, Union Coll., Cranford, N.J.; BS in Criminal Justice, Fla. Internat. U., MPA. Police officer Jersey City Police Dept., 1973-77; spl. agt. South Region Ops. Bur., Miami, Fla., 1977-80, spl. agt. supr., 1980, asst. spl. agt. in chg., 1980-82; bur. chief Fla. dept. Law Enforcement, Miami, 1982-87; chief of police Hialeah (Fla.) Police Dept., 1987—; adj. prof. Fla. Internat. U., 1993—; lectr. in field. Bd. dirs. YMCA, Hialeah, Simon Bolivar Inst. of Violence. With U.S. Army, 1970-73. Recipient Cert. of Appreciation, Ho. of Reps., State of Fla., 1982, Meritorious Svc. award Fla. Dept. Law Enforcement, 1986; recognized as Outstanding Fla. Law Enforcement Officer of 1979, Ho. of Reps., State of Fla. Mem. FBI Nat. Acad. Grad. Assocs., Fla. Police Chiefs Assn., Dade County Assn. Chiefs of Police (past pres.), Internat. Assn. Chiefs of Police, Miami-Dade Criminal Justice Inst. (bd. dirs.), Hialeah Latin C. of C., Internat. Pers. Mgmt. Assn., Hialeah Miami Springs North West Dade C. of C. Office: Hialeah Politce Dept 5555 E 8th Ave Hialeah FL 33013-1342*

BOLAS, GERALD DOUGLAS, art museum administrator, art history educator; b. Los Angeles, Nov. 1, 1949; s. Norman Theodore and Elizabeth Louise (Douglas) B.; m. Deborah Jean Wohletz, Nov. 25, 1978; children: Ellen Claire, John David. BA, U. Calif.-Santa Barbara, 1972, MA, 1975; PhD, CUNY, 1998. Tchg. asst. U. Calif.-Santa Barbara, 1973-74; NEH mus. intern Yale U. Art Gallery, New Haven, 1975-76, asst. to dir., 1976-77; dir. Washington U. Gallery of Art, St. Louis, 1977-88, Portland (Oreg.) Art Mus., 1988-92, Ackland Art Mus. at U. N.C., Chapel Hill, 1994—; adj. asst. prof. art history Washington U., 1982-88, U. N.C., Chapel Hill, 1994—; advisor Mo. Arts Coun., St. Louis, 1981-82; field reviewer Inst. Mus. Svcs., Washington, 1980-83; panelist NEA, 1989, NEH, 1990, 95, N.C. Arts Coun., 1995; bd. dirs. Asian Art Soc. of Washington U., 1983-88; mem. No. Calif. adv. com. Archives of Am. Art; active Lake Oswego Arts Commn., 1993-94. Author: Illustrated Checklist of Washington University Collection, 1981; contbr. to (books): Ketav: Flesh and Word in Israeli Art, 1996, Paris in Japan: The Japanese Encounter with European Painting, 1987; also contbr. articles to other publs.; numerous catalog forewords. Organizer numerous exhbns. Fellow Winterthur Mus. 1993, Smithsonian Instn., 1993. Mem. Coll. Art Assn., Assn. Art Mus. Dirs. Office: Ackland Art Mus Campus Box 3400 U NC Chapel Hill NC 27599-3400

BOLCH, CARL EDWARD, JR., corporation executive, lawyer; b. St. Louis, Feb. 28, 1943; s. Carl Edward and Juanita (Newton) B.; m. Susan Bass; children: Carl, Allison, Natalie, Melanie, Jordan. BS in Econs, U. Pa., 1964; JD, Duke U., 1967. Bar: Fla. 1967. CEO, chmn. bd. dirs. RaceTrac Petroleum,Inc., Atlanta, 1967—. Edition editor: Close Corporations, 1967. Mem. ABA, Fla. Bar Assn., Soc. Ind. Gasoline Marketers (pres. 1987-89), Nat. Assn. Convenience Stores (bd. dirs. 1994—). Office: RaceTrac Petroleum Inc PO Box 105035 300 Technology Ct Atlanta GA 30348-5035 also: RaceTrac Petroeleum Inc 300 Technology Ct Smyrna GA 30082-5235*

BOLCOM, WILLIAM ELDEN, musician, composer, educator, pianist; b. Seattle, May 26, 1938; s. Robert Samuel and Virginia (Lauermann) B.; m. Fay Levine, Dec. 23, 1963 (div. 1967); m. Katherine Agee Ling, June 8, 1968 (div. 1969); m. Joan Clair Morris, Nov. 28, 1975. BA, U. Wash., 1958; MA, Mills Coll., 1961; postgrad., Paris Conservatoire de Musique, 1959-61, 64-65; D of Mus. Art, Stanford U., 1964; D of Music (hon.), San Francisco Conservatory, 1994, Albion Coll., 1995; studied with, Berthe Poncy Jacobson, 1949-58, John Verrall, 1951-58, Leland Smith, 1961-64, Darius Milhaud, 1957-61; George Rochberg, 1966. Acting asst. prof. music dept. U. Wash., Seattle, 1965-66; lectr., asst. prof. music Queens Coll., CUNY, Flushing, 1966-68; vis. critic music theater Drama Sch., Yale U., 1968-69; composer in residence Theater Arts Program, NYU, N.Y.C., 1969-71; asst. prof. U. Mich. Sch. Music, Ann Arbor, 1973-78, assoc. prof., 1973-77, prof., 1977-93, Ross Lee Finney disting. prof. composition, 1993—; mem. jury Nat. Endowment for Arts, 1976-77, 84, 85. Composer: 6 symphonies, 1957, 64, 79, 86, 89, 97, String Quartets 1-8, 1950-65, String Quartet #9 (Novella), 1972, String Quartet #10, 1988, Décalage for cello and piano, 1961-62, Fantasy-Sonata for piano, 1960-62, Concertante for Flute, Oboe, Violin, and Orch, 1960, cabaret opera Dynamite Tonite, 1960-63, rev., 1966, Octet, 1962, Concerto-Serenade for Violin and Strings, 1964, 12 Etudes for Piano, 1959-66, Fives, Double Concerto for Violin, Piano and Strings, 1966, Morning and Evening Poems (Cantata), 1966, Session I for Chamber Ensemble, 1965, Session II for violin and viola, 1966, Session III for clarinet, violin, cello, piano, percussion, 1966, Session IV for chamber ensemble, 1967, Black Host for organ, percussion and taped sounds, 1967, Piano Rags, 1967-74, cabaret opera Greatshot, 1967-69, Praeludium for vibraphone and organ, 1969, Dark Music for timpani and cello, 1970, Duets for Quintet, 1970, Unpopular Songs, 1969-71, Hydraulis for organ, 1971, Commedia for chamber orch, 1971, Whisper Moon (chamber ensemble), 1971, Frescoes for two pianists, 1971, Seasons for solo guitar, 1974, Open House, song cycle on poems by Roethke, 1975, Piano Concerto, 1975-76, Piano Quartet, 1976, Revelation Studies for Carillon, 1976, Mysteries for Organ, 1976, score for stage works Puntila (Brecht), 1976, Man is Man (Brecht), 1977, Beggar's Opera (posthumous collaboration with Darius Milhaud), 1978, Violin Sonatas, 1956, 78, 92, 94, 12 Gospel Preludes for Organ, 1979, 81, 84, Humoresk for organ and orch., 1969, Brass Quintet, 1979, 24 Cabaret Songs, 1963-96, Aubade for Oboe and Piano, 1982, Songs of Innocence and of Experience (Blake), 1956-82, Violin Concerto in D, 1983, Lilith (saxophone, piano), 1984, Abendmusik, 1977, Little Suite of Dances in E flat for clarinet and piano, 1984, Orphée-Sérénade, 1984, Fantasia Concertante for viola, cello and orch., 1985, Capriccio for Violoncello and Piano, 1985, orchestral dance suite Seattle Slew, 1986, 12 New Etudes for Piano, 1977-86 (recipient Pulitzer Prize, 1988), Spring Concertino for Oboe and Chamber Orch., 1986-87, Five Fold Five for woodwind quintet and piano, 1985-87, Clarinet Concerto, 1990, (musical) Casino Paradise (libretto Arnold Weinstein), 1986-90, Fairy Tales for viola, cello, bass, 1987-88, Sonata for Violoncello and Piano, 1989, (song cycle on Am. women poets) I Will Breathe a Mountain, 1989-90, The Mask (chorus and piano), 1990, Recuerdos for two pianos, 1991, opera McTeague (libretto A. Weinstein and R. Altman), 1990-92, Lyric Concerto for flute and orch., 1993, Trio for clarinet, violin and piano, 1993, Sonata for 2 pianos in one movement, 1993, Suite for play Broken Glass by Arthur Miller, 1994, Let Evening Come (soprano, viola, piano), 1994, A Whitman Triptych, (mezzo-soprano and orchestra), 1995, GAEA Concertos 1-3 for Left Hand and Orch., 1996, Second Piano Quartet, 1995, Briefly It Enters, 1996 (voice and piano), Fanfare for the Detroit Opera House, 1996 (brass), Nine Bagatelles, 1996 (piano), Spring Trio, 1996 (piano trio), Turbulence-A Romance, 1996 (2 voices and piano); pianist in recs: (with Gerard Schwarz) Cornet Favorites, (with Clifford Jackson, baritone) An Evening with Henry Russell, (with mezzo-soprano Joan Morris) Other Songs of Leiber and Stoller, (with Joan Morris and Max Morath) These Charming People, (with Joan Morris) The Girl on the Magazine Cover, (with Joan Morris) Songs of Ira and George Gershwin, (with Joan Morris and Lucy Simon) The Rodgers and Hart Album, (with Joan Morris and Max Morath) More Rodgers and Hart, (with Joan Morris) Silver Linings (anthology of Jerome Kern), (with Joan Morris) Blue Skies (anthology of Irving Berlin), (with Joan Morris) Black Max (Bolcom cabaret songs with A. Weinstein poetry), (with Joan Morris) Lime Jello: An American Cabaret, (with Joan Morris) Night & Day (anthology of Cole Porter), (with Joan Morris) Let's Do It, (with Sergiu Luca) Works for Violin and Piano (by Bolcom), (with Joan Morris) After the Ball, Vaudeville, Songs of the Great Ladies of the Musical Stage, Wild About Eubie, (with Joan Morris and Clifford Jackson and chorus) Who Shall Rule This American Nation: Songs of Henry Clay Work, (with Joan Morris and Robert White) Orchids in the Moonlight and The Carioca (songs of Vincent Youmans); recs. Bolcom's 4th Symphony (Grammy nominee 1987), Violin Concerto, 5th Symphony, Fantasia Concertante (Am. Composers Orch.), 10th String Quartet (Stanford String Quartet), 1st and 3rd Symphonies, Seattle Slew Suite (Louisville Orch.), Orphée-Sérénade (Grammy nominee 1994), others; solo recordings include Heliotrope Bouquet, Pastimes and Piano Rags, Bolcom Plays His Own Rags, Piano Music of George Gershwin, Piano Music of Darius Milhaud, Bolcom: 12 Etudes, Euphonic Sounds (Scott Joplin anthology); author: (with Robert Kimball) Reminiscing with Sissle and Blake, 1973, Trouble in the Music World, 1988; editor book of essays: The Aesthetics of Survival by George Rochberg, 1982; contbr. to Grove's Dictionary, 6th edit; contbg. editor: Annals of Scholarship. Recipient Kurt Weill award, 1963, William and Noma Copley award, 1960, Marc Blitzstein Award for Excellence Am. Acad. Arts and Letters, 1965, N.Y. State Coun. award, 1971, Nat. Endowment for Arts award, 1974, 79, 82-84, Koussevitzky Found. award, 1974, 93, Henry Russel award, U. Mich., 1977, Mich. Arts Coun. award, 1986, Gov.'s Arts award, 1987, Pulitzer Prize in Music, 1988, Citation of Merit U. Mich. Sch. Music Alumni Assn., 1989, Disting. Achievement award U. Wash., 1993, Alfred I. Du Pont award, 1994, Henry Russel lectr., U. Mich., 1997; Guggenheim Found. fellow, 1964, 68; Rockefeller Found. grantee, 1965, 69, 72. Mem. Am. Acad. Arts and Letters, Am. Music Ctr., Am. Composer Alliance, Am. Repertory Theatre (bd. dirs.), Grant Pk. Concerts Chgo. (bd. dirs.), Charles Ives Soc. (bd. dirs.), Delta Omicron (nat. patron), Azazels. Home: 3080 Whitmore Lake Rd Ann Arbor MI 48105-9649 Office: U Mich Sch Music 2243 Moore Bldg Ann Arbor MI 48109

BOLDEN, BETTY, labor relations administrator. Various positions including assoc. dep. Sec. of Labor, Dept. of Labor, Washington; chair Fed. Svc. Impasses Panel, Washington, 1995—; part-time dealer out-of-print books, 1988—. Office: Fed Labor Rels Authority Fed Svc Impass Panel 607 14th St NW Washington DC 20005-2000

BOLDEN, CHARLES F., JR., career officer; b. Columbia, S.C.; m. Alexis Walker; children: Anthony Che, Kelly.l. BS, U.S. Naval Acad., 1968; MS in Sys. Mgmt., U. So. Calif., 1977; grad., U.S. Naval Test Pilot Sch., Patuxent River, Md., 1979; various hon. doctorates. Commd. 2nd lt. USMC, 1968, advanced through grades to dep. comdg. gen., 1997, naval aviator, 1970; stationed at VMA (AW)-533 USMC, Nam Phong, Thailand, 1972-73; marine corps officer selection, recruiting officer USMC, L.A., 1973-75; various assignments at Marine Corps Air Sta. USMC, El Toro, Calif., 1975-78; stationed at Sys. Engring. and Strike Aircraft Test Director Naval Air Test Ctr., ordnance test pilot in A-6E, EA-6B and A-7C/E aircraft; dep. commandant U.S. Naval Acad., Annapolis, Md.; asst. wing comdr. 3rd Marine Aircraft Wing, Miramar, Calif., 1995-97; dep. comdg. gen. First Marine Expeditionary Force Marine Forces Pacific, 1997—; astronaut on Space Shuttle Columbia NASA, 1986, pilot of Space Shuttle Discovery, 1990, comdr. of Space Shuttle Atlantis, 1992, asst. dep. adminstr., 1992-94. Decorated 2 Legion of Merit awards, D.F.C., Air medal. Address: Hqrs Marine Corps Divsn Pub Affairs Washington DC 20380-1775*

BOLDEN, THEODORE EDWARD, denist, educator, dental research consultant; b. Middleburg, Va., Apr. 19, 1920; s. Theodore D. and Mary E. (Jackson) B. A.B., Lincoln U., 1941, LL.D. (hon.), 1981; D.D.S., Meharry Med. Coll., 1947; M.S. (John Hay Whitney Found. opportunity fellow), 1951, Ph.D. (USPHS fellow), 1958. Diplomate: Am. Bd. Oral Medicine, Am. Bd. Oral Pathology. Instr. operative dentistry, pedodontics and periodontics Meharry Med. Coll., 1948-49; chmn. oral pathology (Sch. Dentistry), 1962-77, dir. rsch., 1962-75, assoc. dean, 1965-70; asst. prof. gen. and oral pathology Seton Hall Coll. Medicine and Dentistry, 1957-60, assoc. prof., 1960-62; prof. gen. and oral pathology, dean coll. Coll. Medicine and Dentistry of N.J.-N.J. Dental Sch., Newark, 1977-88; acting chmn. gen. and oral pathology Univ. Medicine and Dentistry of N.J.-N.J. Dental Sch., 1979-80; prof. dept. oral pathology, biology and diagnostic scis. Coll. Medicine and Dentistry of N.J.-N.J. Dental Sch., 1988-90, prof. emeritus, 1991—; cons. dental rsch. Colgate-Palmolive Co., 1991—; trustee Am. Fund for Dental Health. Author: (with John Manhold, Jr.) Outline of Pathology, 1960, Dental Hygiene Examination Review Book, 4th edit, (with E. Mobley and E. Chandler), 1982, 1 and 1 = 1 It Really Do!!!, 1987, My Po Son don gon and Broke His Neck...And Mama Too!, 1990, The Tiger is Loose, 1992, Memories and Thanks, 1995, Big Mama, 1996, Angie Threw/Throws A Partie, 1997, Jovita's F.P.L., 1997, 55 Years Ain't So Baaaaaaaaad, 1997, Celebration Time, 1997, Louise Epperson---Lady Extraordinaire---We Salute You, 1998. Chmn. adv. health com. Montclair (N.J.) Health Dept., 1959-60, commr. urban redevel., Town of Montclair, 1960-62; trustee Neighborhood Council, 1987—. Served to sgt. U.S. Army, 1942-43, 51-52. Fellow Am. Acad. Oral Pathology, Am. Acad. Oral Medicine, Internat. Coll. Dentistry; mem. Nat. Dental Assn. (editor quar. 1974-82), Pan-Tenn. Dental Assn. (statistician 1977-91, historian 1983-91), Capital City Dental Soc., Ewell Neil Dental Soc., Internat. Assn. Dental Rsch., Sigma Xi, Omicron Kappa Upsilon, Kappa Sigma Pi. Baptist. Home: 29 Montague Pl Montclair NJ 07042-2808

BOLDOSSER, RANDY RICHARD, management consultant, communications equipment company executive; b. Pottstown, Pa., July 5, 1957; s. Randall Kermit and Regina Eleanor (Stofko) B.; m. Nancy June Shilay, June 13, 1981; children: Katherine Ann, Christina Dawn. BSEE, Lehigh U., 1979, MS in Computer Sci., 1983, MS in Mfg. Sys. Engring., 1986; MBA, Columbia U., 1992. Engr. Western Electric, Allentown, Pa., 1979-82; mem. tech. staff AT&T Bell Labs., N.J. & Pa., 1983-86; project mgr. AT&T Bell Labs., Warren, N.J., 1987-91; product mgr. AT&T Network Systems, Warren, 1992-93; mgr. strategic planning AT&T, Bridgewater, N.J., 1993-96; dir. info. tech. Shilay Assocs. Inc., Wantagh, N.Y., 1993—; mgr. bus. mgmt., wireless design Lucent Techs. Inc., Whippany, N.J., 1996—. Contbg. author: Prentice-Hall Handbook of Advanced Manufacturing Methods, 1986. Mem. IEEE (chair comm. soc. tech. com. 1995-96), Am. Philatelic Soc. Republican. Episcopalian.

BOLDRA, SUE ELLEN, social studies educator, business owner; b. McPherson, Kans., Sept. 9, 1949; d. Herman Glenn and Betty Rose (Krehbiel) Holloway; m. Carl Sterling Boldra, Dec. 19, 1970; children: Jeremy, Brandon, Amber, Chelsea. BA in History and English, McPherson Coll., 1971; MS in Polit. Sci., Ft. Hays State U., 1977. Tchr. English Canton (Kans.)-Galva Mid. Sch., 1971-72; tchr. English and social studies Felten Mid. Sch., Hays, Kans., 1972-90; tchr. social studies Hays H.S., 1990—; edn. instr. Ft. Hays State U., summer 1995—; adj. prof. ednl. adminstrn. and counseling Ft. Hays State U., Hays, 1995—. Mem. Hays City-Ellis County Planning Comm., Hays, 1995, sec., 1996-97, vice-chmn., 1997-98, precinct com. chairwoman, 1996—. Republican. Home: 2405 General Custer Rd Hays KS 67601-2321 Office: Hays HS 2300 E 13th St Hays KS 67601-2646

BOLDT, DAVID RHYS, journalist; b. N.Y.C., Nov. 27, 1941; s. Joseph Raymond and Margaret (Nutting) B.; m. Feresheh Sarshar, June 11, 1967 (dec. 1989); 1 son, Thomas Arash; m. Kelly Clark, July 27, 1991. B.A., Dartmouth Coll., 1964. Staff writer The Wall Street Jour., N.Y.C., 1964-65; staff writer Los Angeles bur. The Wall Street Jour., 1967-69; staff reporter The Washington Post, Washington, 1969-72; with Phila. Inquirer, 1973—; editor The Inquirer mag., 1976-86, dep. editor editorial page, 1986-87, editor editorial page, 1987-94, columnist, 1994—; chmn. Met. Sunday Newspapers editorial adv. bd., 1985-86; instr. Temple U., 1974-80. Editor: The Founding City, 1976. Served to 1st lt. U.S. Army, 1965-67. Recipient Pulitzer Prize for local reporting (as part of Inquirer staff), 1980, Overseas Press Club citation for excellence, 1980. Unitarian. Home: 7809 Winston Rd Philadelphia PA 19118-3532 Office: Phila Inquirer PO Box 8263 Philadelphia PA 19101-4099*

BOLDT, MICHAEL HERBERT, lawyer; b. Detroit, Oct. 11, 1950; s. Herbert M. and Mary Therese (Fitzgerald) B.; m. Margaret E. Clarke, May 25, 1974; children: Timothy (dec.), Matthew. Student, U. Detroit, 1968-70; B.A., Wayne State U., 1972; J.D., U. Mich., 1975. Bar: Ind. 1975, U.S. Dist. Ct. (so. dist.) Ind. 1975, U.S. Ct. Appeals (7th cir.) 1979, U.S. Supreme Ct. 1980, U.S. Ct. Appeals (D.C. cir.) 1983. Assoc. Ice, Miller, Donadio & Ryan, Indpls., 1975-81, ptnr., 1982—; bd. dirs. Star Alliance, Inc. Contbr. articles to profl. jours. Mem. ABA, Ind. State Bar Assn., Indpls. Bar Assn., Highland Golf and Country Club, Skyline Club. Office: Ice Miller Donadio & Ryan Box 82001 1 American Sq Indianapolis IN 46282-0001

BOLDT, OSCAR CHARLES, construction company executive; b. Appleton, Wis., Apr. 20, 1924; s. Oscar John and Dorothy A. (Bartmann) B.; m. Patricia Hamar, July 9, 1949; children: Charles, Thomas, Margaret. BSCE, U. Wis., 1948. Pres. O.J. Boldt Constrn. Co., Appleton, 1950-79, CEO, chmn. bd. dirs., 1979-84; chmn. bd. dirs. The Boldt Group Inc., Appleton, 1984—; sec. W.S. Patterson Co., 1963-89, also bd. dirs., 1963-97; trustee Lawrence U., 1981—; bd. dirs. M&I Bank, L.A., Midwest Express. Chmn. bd. dirs. Cmty. Found. for Fox Valley Region, 1991-93; pres. Appleton YMCA, 1955-57, Appleton Meml. Hosp., 1975-76; bd. dirs. United Health Wis., 1990-99; co-chmn. fund drive Fox Cities United Way, 1994. 2d lt. USAAF, 1943-45. Recipient Disting. Svc. award Appleton Jaycees, 1960, Disting. Engr. award U. Wis., 1985, Walter Rugland Cmty. Svc. award, 1988, Master Entrepreneur award Ernst and Young, 1991, Renaissance award, 1991, Regent's award St. Olaf's Coll., 1993, N.E. Wis.'s Sales amd Mktg. Mag. Exec. of Yr. award, 1994, Disting. Alumni award U. Wis. Alumni Assn., 1999; Paul Harris fellow, 1979. Mem. Appleton Area C. of C. (pres. 1967), Appleton Rotary (pres. 1975-76, Vocat. Svc. award 1977, Paul Harris fellow), Riverview Country Club (pres. 1968-69). Republican. Presbyterian. Home: 1715 W Reid Dr Appleton WI 54914-5175 Office: The Boldt Group Inc PO Box 373 2525 N Roemer Rd Appleton WI 54911-8623

BOLDUC, ERNEST JOSEPH, association management consultant; b. Lawrence, Mass., June 11, 1924; s. Ernest Joseph and Ernestine (Mercier) B.; m. Grace Gaydis, June 23, 1945; children: Philip, Richard, Stephen. BS in M.E, Northeastern U., 1948. Cert. Assn. Exec. Market devel. rep. Kawneer Co., Boston and N.Y.C., 1950-55; market devel. rep. Kaiser Aluminum, N.Y.C., 1955-58; exec. sec. Com. Tool Steel Producers Am. Iron and Steel Inst., N.Y.C., 1958-66; exec. dir. Nat. Council Paper Industry for Air and Stream Improvement, N.Y.C., 1966-83; prin. EJB Assocs., Armonk, N.Y., 1983—; lectr. in assn. mgmt., meeting planning; coord. program USAID for Mongolian C. of C. trade devel. delegation touring U.S., 1993; cons. to U.S. Dept. Commerce in Albania on assn. mgmt. project, 1995; cons. to World Environment Ctr. projects, Slovakia, Rumania, Bulgaria, Ukraine; cons. USAID-PEM Project, Haiti, 1998. Author: Curtain Wall Do's and Don'ts, 1955, Planning the Successful Meeting, 1959, The Art of Budgeting For Associations, 1980, The Three P's of Running Meetings, 1990; editor Tool Steel Trends, 1961-66. Vol. exec. Internat. Exec. Svc. Corps in Botswana, 1990, in Bulgaria, 1992; trustee No. Castle Hist. Soc., 1990-92; cons. to USAID Mission in Ghana, Africa on assn. mgmt. project, 1992; vol. advisor Citizens Democracy Corp in Bulgaria, 1995; vol. speaker Am. Cancer Soc. on prostate cancer, 1998—. Decorated Air medal with 3 oak leaf clusters; recipient Man of Yr. award N.Y. Producers Coun., 1955, W. Erwin Story citation Northeastern U., 1991, Vol. Recognition award Am. Cancer Soc. 1998. Mem. Am. Soc. Assn. Execs. (life; awards com. 1978-80, internat. com. 1992), N.Y. Soc. Assn. Execs. (life; dir. 1979-80, chmn. govt. rels. com. 1979-81, presdl. citation 1987, Disting. Svc. award 1993), Meeting Planners Internat. (bd. dirs. N.Y. chpt. 1979-80), Am. Arbitration Assn. (panel arbitrators). Office: 2 Sunrise Pl Armonk NY 10504-1444

BOLDUC, JEAN PLUMLEY, journalist, education activist; b. Hartford, Conn., Aug. 13, 1958; d. Peter Winslow and Elizabeth Josephine (Hamann) Plumley; m. Richard Allen Bolduc, Jan. 25, 1978; children: Brian Richard, Robert Allen. BA, U. N.C., 1994. Mktg. analyst Ctrl. Carolina Bank, Durham, N.C., 1984-87; computer trainer/cons. On Site Svcs., Chapel Hill, N.C., 1987-91; pres. Pub. Edn. Press, Inc., Hillsborough, N.C., 1994—; coord. safe schs. program Orange County Sheriff's Dept., Hillsborough, N.C., 1995-96; exec. dir. The Odyssey Project, Hillsborough, 1996-97; owner Pen & Inc. New Media Pub. and Editl. Svcs., Hillsborough, 1997—; mem. adv. bd. Project Graduation, Hillsborough, 1995-96; lit. jour. advisor Orange County Schs., Hillsborough, 1995-96. Chair Orange County Human Rels. Commn., 1989-91, Orange County Safe Schs. Task Force, 1993-95; chair subcom. Blue Ribbon Task Force on African-Am. Student Achievement, Chapel Hill Schs., 1991; pres. AIDS Svc. Agy., Inc., Chapel Hill, 1990-91, Sycamore Presch., Inc., Chapel Hill, 1993-94. Recipient Key to Chapel Hill for cmty. svc. Chapel Hill Town Coun., 1991. Home: 5519 Hideaway Dr Chapel Hill NC 27516-9517 Office: Pen & Inc PO Box 1561 Hillsborough NC 27278-1561

BOLE, GILES G., physician, researcher, medical educator; b. Battle Creek, Mich., July 28, 1928; s. Giles Gerald, Sr. and Kittie Belle B.; m. Elizabeth J. Dooley, May 11, 1985; children: David Giles, Elizabeth Ann. BS, U. Mich., Ann Arbor, 1949, MD, 1953. Diplomate Am. Bd. Internal Medicine. Resident in internal medicine U. Mich., Ann Arbor, 1953-56, fellow rheumatology Rackham arthritis research unit, 1958-61, asst. prof. internal medicine, 1961-64, assoc. prof. internal medicine, 1964-70, prof. internal medicine, 1970—; physician-in-charge Rackham Arthritis Research Unit, Ann Arbor, 1971-86, chief rheumatology div., 1976-86; assoc. dean clin. affairs, sr. assoc. dean Med. Sch. U. Mich., Ann Arbor, 1986-88, exec. assoc. dean Med. Sch., 1988-90, interim dean Med. Sch., 1990-91, dean Med. Sch., 1991-96, dean emeritus Med. Sch., 1996—; dir. U. Mich. Arthritis Ctr., Ann Arbor, 1977-86; bd. govs. Am. Bd. Internal Medicine, 1979-83, chmn. rheumatology com., 1979-83. dir. U. Mich. Arthritis Ctr., Ann Arbor, 1977-86; bd. govs. Am. Bd. Internal Medicine, 1979-83, chmn. rheumatology com., 1979-83; mem. physician payment rev. commn. Office Tech. Assessment, U.S. Congress. Capt. M.C., USAF, 1956-58. Recipient Borden Academic Achievement award U. Mich., 1953; Postdoctoral Research fellow Arthritis Found., 1961-63. Mem. Am. Fed. Clin. Rsch. (chmn. Midwest sect. 1967-68), Cen. Soc. Clin. Rsch. (pres. 1976-77), Am. Rheumatism Assn. (pres. 1980-81). Home: 6015 W Ellsworth Rd Ann Arbor MI 48103-9609 Office: U Mich Med Sch M 7300 Med Sci I 1301 Catherine Rd Ann Arbor MI 48109-0600

BOLEN, DAVID B., ambassador, former corporation executive; b. Dec. 23, 1923; m. Betty Gayden; children: Cynthia, Myra, David B. BS, U. Colo., 1950, MS, 1950; MPA, Harvard U., 1960; student, Nat. War Coll. Joined Fgn. Service, 1950; adminstrv. asst. Monrovia, Liberia, 1950-52; econ. asst. Karachi, Pakistan, 1952-55; detailed internat. economist Dept. Commerce, Washington, 1955-56, State Dept., 1957-58; desk officer for Afghanistan, 1958-59; detailed advanced econ. studies Harvard, 1959-60; econ. officer Accra, Ghana, 1960-62; staff asst. Washington, 1962-64; officer-in-charge Nigerian affairs, 1964-66, detailed Nat. War Coll., 1966-67; econ. and comml. officer, econ. counselor Bonn, Germany, 1967-72; econ.-comml. counselor Belgrade, 1972-74; ambassador to Botswana, Lesotho and Swaziland, 1974-76; dep. asst. sec. state for African affairs U.S. Dept. State, Washington, 1976-77; ambassador to German Democratic Republic, 1977-80; assoc. dir. internat. affairs E.I. duPont de Nemours & Co., Inc., Wilmington, Del., 1981-89; cons. E.I. duPont de Nemours & Co., Inc., 1989-94. Contbg. editor: World Economic Problems and Policies, 1965. Mem. preliminary investigatory com. Del. Ct. on the Judiciary, 1990-92; mem. polit. sci. vis. com. MIT, 1983-88; trustee U. Del., 1983-92; bd. dirs. Med. Ctr. Del., Del. Coun. Econ. Edn., U.S. Coun. on Internat. Bus., 1981-89, Internat. Mgmt. Devel. Inst., 1981-89, Pacific Basin Trade and Econ. Coun., 1981-89, U.S.-USSR Trade and Econ. Coun., 1981-89, U.S.-German Dem. Republic Trade and Econ. Coun., 1981-89, Coun. Fgn. Rels., U.S.-Yugoslav Econ. Coun., 1986-90, U. Colo. Found., Inc., 1990-96; mem. U. Colo. Bus. Dean's Adv. Coun., 1992-98; dir. Denver Com. on Fgn. Rels., 1994-99; mem. U.S. Olympic track and field team, 1948; advisor Berlin Sculpture Fund, 1997—. Recipient Robert Russell Meml. award, 1948, Norlin Disting. Alumni award U. Colo., 1969; named to Hall of Honor, 1969, Alumni of Century, 1976; recipient Disting. Service award U. Colo., 1983. Mem. Am. Coun. on Germany (chmn. Denver chpt. 1995-99), Nat. War Coll. Alumni Assn., Fgn. Serv. Assn., Wilmington World Affairs Coun. (dir. 1981-92), Internat. Amateur Athletic Assn., Wilmington Club, U. Colo. Alumni Assn., Harvard Alumni Assn. Home: 3940 Greenbriar Blvd Boulder CO 80303-7046

BOLEN, ERIC GEORGE, biology educator; b. Plainfield, N.J., Nov. 24, 1937; s. Wilbur Fraser and Doris (Wicks) B.; m. Rebecca Ann Woodhull, Aug. 20, 1967 (div. Jan. 1981); children: Brent F., Staci L.; m. Elizabeth Ann Danek, May 27, 1986. BS, U. Maine, Orono, 1959; MS, Utah State U., 1962, PhD, 1967. Instr. biology Tex. A&M U., Kingsville, 1965-66; asst.

prof. dept. range & wildlife mgmt. Tex. Tech U., Lubbock, 1966-73, assoc. dean grad. sch., 1978-88; dean grad. sch. U. N.C., Wilmington, 1988-94, prof. biology, 1988—; Asst. dir. Welder Wildlife Found., 1973-78. Co-author: (coll. textbooks) Wildlife Ecology and Management, 1984, 4th edit., 1999, Waterfowl Ecology and Management, 1994, Ecology of North America, 1998; contbr. over 180 articles to profl. jours., ency. Named Disting. Alumnus, U. Maine, 1991; recipient Achievement award Utah State U., 1997. Mem. Am. Ornithol. Union., Wilson Ornithol. Soc., Cooper Ornithol. Soc., Southwestern Assn. Naturalists, Wildlife Soc. Office: Univ NC Dept Biol Scis 601 S College Rd Wilmington NC 28403-3201

BOLENDER, JAMES HENRY, tire and rubber manufacturing executive; b. New Boston, Ohio, Nov. 26, 1937; s. James Harold and Lucille Virgie (Grooms) B.; m. Nancy Jo Paull, Feb. 3, 1970; 1 child, Shawn O. BS, Ohio U., 1959. Contr. Firestone Tire and Rubber Co., Valencia, Venezuela, 1971-73, Bethune, France, 1973-76; mgr. corp. acctg. Firestone Tire and Rubber Co., Akron, Ohio, 1976-80, asst. contr., 1980-81, group v.p. fin., 1981-82, v.p., contr., 1982-88, internat. sr. v.p., 1988-91; v.p., CFO Jetstream Power Internat. Inc., Holmesville, Ohio, 1992-98. Trustee Akron Urban League and Community Ctr., 1979-81, Akron Svc. Ctr., 1982-86, Akron Gen. Med. Ctr., 1986-87. Office: Jetstream Power Internat Inc 8224 County Road 245 Holmesville OH 44633-9724

BOLENDER, TODD, choreographer; b. Canton, Ohio, 1914. Student, Hanya Holm, N.Y.C.; enrolled, Sch. American Ballet, N.Y.C., 1936. Joined Lincoln Kirstein's Ballet Caravan, 1937; formed Am. Concert Ballet; choreographed 1st ballet, 1943; also danced with Ballet Theatre, 1944 and Ballet Russe de Monte Carlo, 1945, joined Ballet Soc., 1946; prin. dancer N.Y.C. Ballet, 1948-61; dir. ballet cos. of opera houses of Cologne and Frankfurt; numerous nat. and internat. freelance choreography assignments, 1952-80; artistic dir. State Ballet of Mo., Kansas City, 1981-96, artistic dir. emeritus, 1996. Recipient Mo. Arts Coun. awrd, 1987, W.F. Yates for disting. svc. William Jewell Coll., 1995. Office: State Ballet Mo 706 W 42nd St Kansas City MO 64111-3191

BOLENE, MARGARET ROSALIE STEELE, bacteriologist, civic worker; b. Kingfisher, Okla., July 11, 1923; d. Clarence R. and Harriet (White) Steele; m. Robert V. Bolene, Feb. 6, 1948; children: Judith Kay, John Eric, Sally Sue, Janice Lynn, Daniel William. BS, U. Okla., 1946. Technican bacteriology dept. Okla. Dept. Health, Oklahoma City, 1946-48; asst. bacteriologist Henry Ford Hosp., Detroit, 1948-49; bacteriol. cons., also asst. bus. mgr. Ponca Gynecology and Obstetrics, Inc., 1956-92, ret. Organizing dir. Bi-Racial Coun., 1963; lay adviser Home Nursing Svc., 1967-68; mem. exec. bd. PTA, 1956-71; active various cmty. drives; sponsor Am. Field Svc.; patron Ponca Playhouse; bloodmobile vol. ARC; vol. Helpline; Rep. precint organizer, 1960. Mem. AAUW (treas. 1964-66), DAR (life, sec.-treas. 1961-67, 1st vice regent 1972-73, chpt. treas. 1974-84, chpt. chaplain 1991—, state schs. chmn. 1990-94), Kay-Noble County Med. Aux. (treas. 1957-58, 66-67), Ponca City Art Assn., Pioneer Hist. Soc., Okla. Heritage Assn., Okla. Hist. Soc., Friends Cultural Ctr., Mus. Found., Inc. (publicity chmn.), Friends Md. Mansion, Daus. Founders and Patriots (life, state pres. 1980-84, registrar 1993—), Nat. Huguenot Soc. (corr. sec.), Hereditary Order First Families Mass. Daus. Am. Colonists (chpt. regent 1982-84, state flag chmn. 1990-92), Magna Charta Dames (treas. Okla. chpt. 1984, life), Plantagenet Soc., Order Colonial Physicians and Chirurgiens (life), Ancient and Honorable Arty. Co. Women Descs. Okla. Ct. (life, treas. 1983-84, registrar 1986—), Dames of Ct. of Honor, Colonial Dames of 17th Century, Daus. of Colonial Wrs (registrar 1998—), Colonial Daus. 17th Century, U. Okla. Assn. (life), Ponca City Music Club, Red Rose Garden Club (pres. 1983-84, treas. 1993-95), Twentieth Century Club (rec. sec. 1992-94, treas. 1999—), Wall St. Ladies Investment Club, Lambda Tau, Phi Sigma, Alpha Lambda Delta. Presbyterian (elder 1983-86, trustee 1998—). Home: 2116 Juanito Ave Ponca City OK 74604-3813

BOLER, JOHN, manufacturing executive; b. 1934. CEO Boler Co., Itasca, Ill., 1978—. Office: Boler Co 500 Park Blvd Itasca IL 60143-3121*

BOLES, DEBORAH ANN, gerontology nurse; b. Milw., July 1, 1953; d. William Bernard Sweeney Jr. and Ann (Hallead) Sweeney Nelson; children: Joanna, Catherine, Angeline, Elisabeth. BSN with distinction, Orvis Sch. Nursing, Reno, 1987. RN, Calif.; cert. gerontol. nurse. Staff nurse post surg. fl. St. Mary's Regional Med. Ctr., Reno, 1987-90; staff nurse med. fl. St. Francis Regional Med. Ctr., Santa Barbara, Calif., 1990-92, charge nurse transitional care unit, clin. nurse, 1992-95; staff nurse IV Cottage Care Ctr., 1994; clin. resource nurse, charge nurse, transitional care unit Cottage Hosp., Santa Barbara, 1995—; instr. BCLS cmty. class coord.; affiliate faculty BCLS AHA Infection Control Liaison. Mem. Phi Kappa Phi. Home: 431 E Micheltorena St Santa Barbara CA 93101-1124

BOLES, ERIC PAUL, staffing company executive; b. Albany, Ky., July 10, 1965; s. Don Howard and Doris L. (Claborn) B.; m. Tabitha Hope Appleby, Oct. 22, 1992 (div. Aug. 1995). AA in Computer Sci., U. Ky., 1990; Real Estate Cert., Cumberland Real Estate Acad., N.C., 1986; cert. paralegal, So. Career Inst., 1989; BS in Computer Sci., Am. Inst. Computer Sci., 1997. Cert. network engr. Network suport splst. Long John Silvers, Lexington, Ky., 1990-92; network engr. Pomeroy Computer Resources, Lexington, 1992-95; MIS mgr. Studio Plus Hotels, Lexington, 1995-97; v.p. Alliance Staffing, Lexington, 1997-98; owner, pres. Techsource Inc., Lexington, 1998—; co-owner Consig4u, 1999—. With U.S. Army, 1983-85. mem. Soc. Human Resources, Lexington (Ky.) C. of C., Masons, Disabled Am. Vets. Home and Office: 1023 Creekford Dr Weston FL 33326

BOLES, JOHN, professional baseball coach, manager; b. Chgo., Aug. 19, 1948; m. Rosemary Boles; children: Blake, Kevin. Head baseball coach St. Xavier Coll., Chgo., 1973-79, U. Louisville, 1980-81; mgr. Gulf Coast League White Sox, 1981-85; dir. player devel. Kansas City Royals, 1986-89; field coord. Montreal (Can.) Expos, 1989-90, dir. player devel., 1990-91; dir. player devel. Fla. Marlins, Miami, 1991-95, v.p. player devel., 1995-98, mgr., 1998—. Office: c/o Florida Marlins 2267 NW 199th St Miami FL 33056*

BOLES, JOHN P., bishop; b. Boston, 1930. Student, Boston Coll. Ordained priest Roman Cath. Ch., 1955. Titular bishop Nova Sparsa and aux. bishop Boston, 1992—. Office: 307 Bowdoin St Dorchester MA 02122-1834

BOLES, ROGER, otolaryngologist; b. Oakland, Calif., Jan. 13, 1928; s. Albert and Julia Boles; m. Marianna Reeves, June 16, 1956; children: Martin Reeves, Melissa. AB, Stanford U., 1949; postgrad., Denver U., 1950-52; MD with distinction, George Washington U., 1956. Diplomate Am. Bd. Otolaryngology, Am. Bd. Med. Specialties. Intern Fitzsimmons Army Hosp., Denver, 1956-57; asst. resident through sr. clin. instr. Mich. U. Hosp., Ann Arbor, 1959-63, faculty dept. otorhinoloaryngology, 1963-74, prof., 1973-74; prof., chmn. otolaryngology U. Calif. San Francisco Sch. Medicine, 1974-89; pres. med. staff U. Calif., San Francisco, 1982-83, prof. otolaryngology, 1989-98, prof. emeritus otolaryngology, 1998—, ret., 1998; cons. for otolaryngology to Surgeon Gen., USAF, 1975-85; mem. staff San Francisco Gen. Hosp., 1984—, Childrens Hosp. San Francisco (bd. dirs. 1987-91); cons. in otolaryngology Va. Hosp., Ann Arbor, Wayne County Hosp., Eloise, Mich., So. Mich. Prison, Jackson, Fed. Penitentiary, Milan, Mich., 1963-74, Letterman Gen. Hosp., Presidio of San Francisco, U.S. Naval Hosp., Oakland, Calif., 1974-93, Kaiser Hosp., Oakland, 1975, Va. Hosp., San Francisco; bd. dirs. Council Med. Splty. Socs., 1981-82, sec., 1982-83; bd. dirs. Am. Acad. Otolaryngology-Head and Neck Surgery, 1981-88, coord. for continuing med. edn., 1980-83, pres., 1987; mem. Accreditation Coun. for Continuing Med. Edn., 1986-92, chmn., 1990; chmn. PEPP com., 1988-89, 90, vice chmn., 1989, residency rev. com. for otolaryngology; Marshall-Hale Hosp., San Francisco, 1975-83, bd. dirs., 1983-87; mem. Am. Bd. Med. Specialties, 1984-89, exec. com., 1988-89; vis. prof. various univs.; participant in confs., convs., workshops, seminars, insts. Contbr. chpts. to books, numerous revs., articles and abstracts to profl. lit. Served with M.C., AUS, 1956-59. Fellow ACS (chmn. adv. coun. for otolaryngology 1977-80, adv. com. for continuing med. edn. 1982-83), Am. Laryngol. Soc.; mem. AMA (ho. dels. 1975-82, bd. editors archives otolaryngology 1975-85, mem. reference com. on ins. and med. svc. 1978, adv. com. for continuing med. edn. 1981-87), Am. Acad. Opthalmology and Otolaryngology (assoc. sec. com. on continuing edn. 1974-80, chmn. manuals editorial com. 1977-80, mem. at large exec. com. div. otolaryngology 1977-78, mem. interspecialty cooperation com. med. specialty socs. 1978-88), Am. Acad. Facial Plastic and Reconstructive Surgery (co-chmn. standards com. 1977-80, med. edn. com. 1979-81—), Soc. Univ. Otolaryngologists (sec.-treas. 1973-80, chmn. com. on undergrad. curriculum 1969-74, mem. exec. council 1968-79, pres. 1978), Council Acad. Socs.-Assn. Am. Med. Colls., Assn. Acad. Depts. Otolaryngology (vice chmn. subcom. Nat. Cancer Inst. liaison com. 1977-81, chmn. edn. nominating coms. 1978-79), Am. Bronco-Esophagological Assn. (mem. council 1981-82), Am. Bd. Otolaryngology (bd. dirs. 1974-91, exec. com. 1981-88, mem. various coms. 1974-91, chmn. ad hoc com. for nomination process for membership on bd. dirs. 1976-77, pres. 1986-88), Am. Council Otolaryngology (mem. subcom. on hearing 1976-80, research adv. com. 1977-81, pres. 1978-79), Am. Laryngol., Rhinological and Otolaryn. Soc. (mem. editorial bds. transactions 1978-88, mem. council 1982-88, pres. 1986-87, historian 1994—), Am. Soc. for Neck and Head Surgery, Otosclerosis Study Group, Am. Tinnitus Assn. (sci. adv. bd. 1978-81), Pacific Coast Oto-Opthal. Soc., Soc. Med. Cons. to Armed Forces, Calif. Med. Assn. (program co-chmn. sects. on allergy and otolaryngology, neurology and otolaryngology 1977-78, chmn. adv. council of otolaryngology 1979-80), Calif. Otolaryn. Soc. (pres. 1978-80), U. Calif. San Francisco Sch. Medicine Alumni-Faculty Assn. (pres. 1978-79), Am. Otological Soc., Am. Laryngol. Assn. (council 1983-84), San Francisco Med. Soc. (bd. dirs. 1983-90, treas. 1989-90), Royal Coll. Surgeons in Ireland (hon.), U. Mich. Med. Ctr. Alumni Assn. (bd. govs. 1983). Office: Univ Calif San Francisco Dept Otolaryngology 400 Parnassus Ave # A-717 San Francisco CA 94122-2721 Home: PO Box 620203 Woodside CA 94062-0203

BOLES, THOMAS LEE, medical technician; b. Chgo., Sept. 6, 1946; s. Millard Martin and Gayle Alberta (Salley) B. BS, N.M. State U., 1971; MA, Calif. State U., Long Beach, 1989. Mech. engr. U.S. Army Engr. Dist., Ft. Worth, 1972-74; aerospace engr. Naval Air Rework Facility North Island, San Diego, 1974-80; mech engr. 11th Coast Guard Dist., Long Beach, 1980-83; EEG/magnetoencephalography technician VA Med. Ctr., Albuquerque, 1990-91; EEG technician Gerald Champion Hosp., Alamogordo, N.M., 1992-99; cons. HydroNuc. Corp., Albuquerque, 1971. Vol. docent, exhibitor Toy Train Depot, Alamogordo, 1993—; active Sierra Club, N.M., Tex., Calif., 1967-96. Mem. Am. Soc. Electroneurodiagnostic Technicians. Democrat. Methodist. Avocations: choral singing, art, writing, model railroading.

BOLEY, ANDREA GAIL, secondary school educator; b. Lewistown, Pa., July 27, 1956; d. Robert Banks and Marjorie Katheryn (Shearer) Henry; m. Richard C. Shiley, m. May 13, 1978 (dec. June 1996); 1 child, Evan Andrew; m. Daniel M. Boley, Feb. 6, 1999. BS in Music Edn., Indiana U. of Pa., 1978; Jr. High Sci. Cert., Brevard Community Coll., Melbourne, Fla. Choral dir./tchr. S.W. Jr. High Sch., Brevard County Sch. Dist., Palm Bay, Fla., 1988—. Contbr. articles to profl. jours. Named Stone Middle Sch. tchr. of the Yr., 1984-85. Mem. ASCD, AAUW, Music Educators Nat. Conf., Fla. Music Educators Assn. (bd. dirs.), Fla. Vocal Assn., Brevard Fedn. Tchrs., Am. Fedn. Tchrs., Tri-M (Fla. chmn.), Nat. Tri-M Adv. Com. Home: 1255 Sapulpa Rd SW Palm Bay FL 32908

BOLEY, BRUNO ADRIAN, engineering educator; b. Gorizia, Italy, May 13, 1924; came to U.S., 1939, naturalized, 1945; s. Orville F. and Rita (Luzzatto) Bolaffio; m. Sara R. Kaufman, May 12, 1949 (dec. Sept. 1983); children: Jacqueline Boley Acquaviva, Daniel L. B.C.E., CCNY, 1943, D.Sc. hon., 1982; M. in Aero. Engring., Poly. Inst. Bklyn., 1945, D.Sc. in Aero. Engring., 1946. Asst. dir. structural research, aero. engring. dept. Poly. Inst. Bklyn., 1943-48; engring. specialist Goodyear Aircraft Corp., 1948-50; assoc. prof. aero. engring. Ohio State U., 1950-52; assoc. prof. civil engring. Columbia U., 1952-58, prof., 1958-68, dir. postdoctoral preceptor program, 1962-68; Joseph P. Ripley prof. engring., chmn. theoretical and applied mechanics Cornell U., Ithaca, N.Y., 1968-72; dean Technol. Inst., Walter P. Murphy prof. Northwestern U., Evanston, Ill., 1973-86, dean emeritus, Walter P. Murphy prof. emeritus, 1986—; prof. civil engring. and engring. mechanics Columbia U., N.Y.C., 1987—; mem. adv. com. George Washington U., Princeton U., Yale U., Cornell U., FAMU/FSU Inst. Engring., Duke U., Lehigh U., Nat. Cheng Kung U., Republic of China, Istanbul Tech. U., Rowan Coll. N.J.; mem. sci. adv. coun. Internat. Ctr. for Mech. Sics., Udine, Italy, 1980—, Istanbul Tech. U.; chmn. Midwest Program for Minorities in Engring., 1975-82; bd. govs. Argonne Nat. Lab., 1983-86; bd. advisors Who's Who in Sci. and Engring. Author: Theory of Thermal Stresses, 1960, High Temperature Structures and Materials, 1964, Thermoinelasticity, 1970, Crossfire in Professional Education, 1976; also articles, numerous tech. papers; editor-in-chief: Mechanics Research Communications; bd. editors Jour. Thermal Stresses, Bull. Mech. Engring. Edn., Internat. Jour. Computers and Structures, Internat. Jour. Engring. Sci., Internat. Jour. Fracture Mechanics, Internat. Jour. Mech. Engring. Scis., Internat. Jour. Solids and Structures, Jour. Applied Mechanics, Jour. Structural Mechanics Software, Letters in Applied and Engring. Sci., Nuclear Engring. and Design. Recipient Disting. Alumnus award Poly. Inst. N.Y., 1974, Townsend Harris medal, 1981, commendation Ill. Ho. of Reps., 1986, Theodore von Karman medal ASCE, 1991, Outstanding Scholar award Sigma Xi, 1996, Lagrange Lectr. award Accademia Nazionale dei Lincei, Rome, 1996; NATO fellow, 1964-65, NSF fellow, 1965, Japan Soc. Promotion of Sci. Rsch. fellow, 1987. Fellow AIAA, AAAS, Am. Acad. Mechanics (pres. 1974, Disting. Svc. medal 1987), Am. Soc. Engring. Edn.; mem. ASME (hon., exec. com., pres. applied mechanics divsn. 1975, bd. govs. 1984-86, Worcester Reed Warner medal 1991), NAE (life, chmn. task force engring. edn. 1979-80, edn. adv. bd. 1982-86, editl. bd. The Bridge 1986-90, membership com. 1984-88, awards com. 1993-95, chair 1996), Soc. Engring. Scis. (pres. 1975, Disting. Svc. medal 1987, life), Assn. Chairmen Depts. Mechanics (founder, pres. 1970-72), Internat. Assn. Structural Mechanics in Reactor Tech. (chmn. 1977, adv.-gen. 1979—), Thermal Stress Congress (advisor-gen. 1997), Internat. Union Theoretical and Applied Mechanics (sec. Congress com. 1976-96, bur. 1988-96, treas. 1992-96, personal mem. Gen. Assembly 1980—, treas. 1992—), Am. Soc. Engring. Edn. (project bd. 1987, Centennial award 1993), N.Y. Acad. Scis. (Outstanding Educator of Am. 1971), U.S. Nat. Com. Theoretical and Applied Mechanics (chmn. 1975-79, personal mem. Gen. Assembly 1980—), Ill. Coun. Energy Rsch. and Devel. (chmn. 1979-84), Engring. Found. (conf. com. 1986-88). Home: 310 W 106th St New York NY 10025-3429

BOLGER, DAVID P., bank executive; b. Aug. 23, 1957. BS in Acctg./Fin., Marquette U., 1979; MM in Fin., Northwestern U., 1980. Credit analyst Am. Nat. Bank & Trust Co., Chgo., 1980-82, comml. banking officer, 1982-89, sr. v.p., CFO, 1989-92, exec. v.p., 1992-93, exec. v.p., treas., 1993-94, pres., 1996-98; mng. dir. Banc One, Chgo., 1998—. Bd. dirs. Mercy Hosp. & Med. Ctr., Impulse Theatre Co., Fist Non-Profit Ins. Co.; active United Way/Crusade of Mercy. Mem. Chgo. Hist. Soc., Execs. Club Chgo., Robert Morris Asscos. Office: Banc One 66 Commerce St Chicago IL 60603-3403*

BOLGER, ROBERT JOSEPH, retired trade association executive; b. Phila., Aug. 9, 1922; s. Harold Stephen and Edna (Adams) B.; m. Helen Siegfried, May 22, 1954; children: Robert, Mary T., Cynthia A., Ann M., Catherine B., David A. BS, Villanova U., 1943; postgrad., Northwestern U., 1945-46, U. Pa., 1946-47, U. Geneva, 1948-49; DS in Pharmacy (hon.), Mass. Coll. Pharmacy, 1983. Salesman Container Corp., Phila., 1947; supr. sales Kraft Food Co., Phila., 1949-52; overseas mgr., dir. retail relations Smith, Kline Beckman Corp., Phila., 1952-62; asst. to exec. v.p. Nat. Assn. Chain Drug Stores, Inc., Arlington, Va., 1962-67, pres., 1967-87, ret., 1987; founder, developer Robert J. Bolger Assocs., 1988—; bd. dirs. Barr Labs., Pomona, N.Y., 1988—, Am. Pharm. Inst., Washington, 1988—, Am. Found. Pharm. Edn., Gen. Computer Corp., Twinsburg, Ohio, 1992—; bd. dirs. Nat. Drug Trade Conf., pres., 1974-82. Co-author: Chain Drug Retailing, 1980. Bd. dirs. Alexandria (Va.) Hosp., Nat. Council on Patient Info. and Edn. Served to lt. comdr. USNR, 1943-45, 46, PTO. Decorated Air medal; named Man of Yr. Cosmetic and Toiletry sect. United Jewish Appeal, 1972, Chain Exec. of Yr., Chain Drug Rev., 1979; recipient Torch of Learning award Am. Friends of Hebrew U., 1987, Chain Drug Rev. Bd. Lifetime Achievement award, 1988, Robert B. Begley award for contbns. to chain drug industry, 1988. Mem. Am. Pharm. Assn., Com. of 100, U.S. C. of C., Cen. Council Nat. Retail Assns. (chmn.), Am. Retail Fedn. (bd. dirs.), Nat. Assn. Retail Druggists, Joint Commn. Pharmacy Practitioners, Pharmacists Against Drug Abuse (bd. dirs. 1986—), Am. Soc. Assn. Execs. (life), Nat. Assn. Execs. Club (bd. dirs.), Am. Druggist Bd. Advisers, Key Exec. Industry Council, Alexandria Chief Execs. Clubs: Belle Haven Country (Alexandria). Author: Chain Drug Retailing, 1981. Home and Office: 7705 Maid Marian Ct Alexandria VA 22306-2718

BOLGER, STEPHEN GARRETT, English and American studies educator; b. Phila., Apr. 27, 1927; s. Stephen Joseph and Marjorie Louise (Carroll) B.; m. Mary Patricia Whalen, Sept. 3, 1951; children: Christine, Patricia, Elizabeth, Garrett, Cecilia, Madeleine. BA, U. Notre Dame, 1950; MA, U. Pa., 1951, PhD, 1971. Instr. English Georgetown U., Washington, 1953-58; prof. English and Am. studies Rosemont (Pa.) Coll., 1958—. Author: Irish Character in American Fiction 1830-1860, 1976. Served with USNR, 1944-46. Recipient Disting. Teaching award Lindbach Found., 1983, Teaching Excellence award Sears-Roebuck Found., 1990. Mem. Am. Conf. for Irish Studies. Democrat. Roman Catholic. Avocations: music, astronomy. Home: 42 Airdale Rd Bryn Mawr PA 19010-1601 Office: Rosemont Coll Rosemont PA 19010

BOLGER, VIRGINIA JOAN, nursing administrator; b. N.Y.C.; d. Vincent and Lillian (Stryker) Cerrato; m. Lawrence Bolger; children: Wayne, Debra, Susan, Robert. AAS in Nursing, Suffolk County C.C., 1973; BSN, L.I. U., 1975, MPS in Health Care Adminstrn., 1977. Head nurse Patchogue (N.Y.) Nursing Ctr., 1973-74, Ross Nursing Home, Brentwood, N.Y., 1977-78; dir. nursing & health care Svcs. Little Flower Children Svcs., Wading River, N.Y., 1974-77, 78—; com. mem. spl. edn. Little Flower Sch. Dist. Past chairperson Health Care Coords. Diocese of N.Y. Named to Dean's List Suffolk Community Coll. Mem. Profl. Nursing Assn. Suffolk County. Home: 109 Carroll Ave Ronkonkoma NY 11779-4232 Office: Little Flower Children's Svc North Wading River Rd Wading River NY 11792

BOLIAN, GEORGE CLEMENT, health care executive, physician; b. New Orleans, May 24, 1930; s. George William and Effie (McQuaid) B.; m. Patricia Ruth Green, July 27, 1957 (div. 1984); children—Mark Geoffrey, Gregory Wayne; m. Patricia Ann Morrison, Mar. 26, 1984; children—Joshua Sean, Zachary Ryan. B.A., U. Chgo., 1950, Harvard U., 1952; M.D., Tulane U., 1957. Diplomate Am. Bd. Psychiatry and Neurology. Intern Nassau County Med. Ctr., East Meadow, N.Y., 1957-58; resident psychiatry and child psychiatry U. Cin., 1958-62; instr., asst. prof. U. Wash., Seattle, 1965-70; dir. dept. psychiatry Children's Orthopaedic Hosp. and Med. Ctr., Seattle, 1968-70; assoc. prof. U. Hawaii, Honolulu, 1970-86; dir. community mental health ctr. Queen's Med. Ctr., Honolulu, 1971-83, sr. v.p., 1976-83, pres., 1983-86; practice medicine, Nashville, 1986-87; assoc. prof., acting dir. child and adolescent psychiatry Vanderbilt U., Nashville, 1987-89, dir. resident edn., 1988-93; vice chmn. dept. psychiatry, 1988—; chmn. Med. Sch. Acad. Programs Vanderbilt U., Nashville, 1993—. Contbr. numerous articles to profl. jours. Served to capt. U.S. Army, 1962-65. Fellow Am. Psychiat. Assn. (life), Am. Acad. Child Psychiatry, Am. Orthopsychiat. Assn. (life); mem. AMA. Home: 6002 Hickory Valley Rd Nashville TN 37205-1306 Office: Vanderbilt U Med Ctr Nashville TN 37232

BOLICH, GREGORY GORDON, humanities educator; b. Spokane, Wash., July 7, 1953; s. Glenn Gordon and Joanne G. (Stinger) B.; m. Barbara Jo Ranson, Apr. 8, 1976; children: April Louise, Alicia Layne, Amanda Larissa, Arielle Liron. BA in Philosophy and Religion, Seattle Pacific U., 1974, M of Christian Ministries in Ednl. Psychology, 1975; MA in Religion, Western Evang. Sem., 1977, MDiv in Christian Thought, 1978; PhD in Ednl. Leadership, Gonzaga U., 1983; PhD in Psychology, Union Inst., 1993. Mem. faculty Inland Empire Sch. of the Bible, Spokane, 1975-76; adminstr. First Evang. Free Ch., Spokane, 1978-79; pres. Christian Studies Inst., Cheney, 1979-89; grad. asst. research Gonzaga U., Spokane, 1981-83, staff mem. Ctr. for Research, 1981-83; psychology and religious studies faculty Cleve. Community Coll., 1993—; adj. faculty Grad. Schy. Union Inst., 1993—, Ea. Wash. U., 1985-93; doctoral rsch. asst. Gonzaga U., 1984-86; mentor Fuller Sem., Pasadena, Calif., 1984; v.p. faculty senate Cleve. C.C., 1997-98, honors program coord., 1997—; exec. dir. Adult Survivors of Abuse, 1991-94. Author: Karth Barth and Evangelicalism, 1980, Authority and the Church, 1982, The Christian Scholar, 1986; co-author: Introduction to Religion, 1988, God in the Docket, 1992, Serving Human Experience: The Boundary Metaphor, 1993, Psycho's Child: The Story of Psychology, 1998; also religious articles to profl. jours. and mags. Active Friends of Seven, Spokane, 1985-89, United Ministries in Higher Edn., Spokane, 1985-93; assoc. mem. YWCA, Spokane, 1984-85. Mem. APA, Bibl. Archaeology Soc., Internat. Thespian Soc., Soc. Bibl. Lit., N.W. Soc. Patristic and Koine Studies (v.p. 1986), Theology Forum (exec. officer 1981-84), Internat. Soc. for Traumatic Stress Studies, Alpha Kappa Sigma. Democrat. Jewish. Avocations: basketball, tennis, theatre. Office: Social Studies Dept Cleve CC Shelby NC 28150 *I call religion that region where the ordinary and the extraordinary meet and intermingle. Within its bounds are light, life, and laughter.*

BOLICK, JAN MARIE, art educator; b. Abilene, Tex., Nov. 10, 1968; d. William Doug and Patricia Lynn Metcalf; m. Kyle Wayne Bolick, July 3, 1993. BFA, Midwestern State U., 1993; B in Art Edn. magna cum laude, Wichita State U., 1997. Cert. tchr., Kans. Art educator Bluestem Sch. Dist., Leon, Kans., 1997—. Avocation: creating art work. Home: 10054 SW Eagle Rd Augusta KS 67010

BOLIE, VICTOR WAYNE, engineering educator emeritus; b. Silverton, Oreg., July 23, 1924; m. Earleen Mercia Dale, Mar. 12, 1945. BS in Physics, Iowa State U., 1949, MS in Math., 1950, PhD in Math., Physics, Elec. Engring., 1952; BA in Chemistry, Coe Coll., 1957; MA in Physiology, Stanford U., 1959. Registered profl. engr., Okla., N.Mex. Rsch. adminstr. Collins Radio Co., 1952-57; assoc. prof. Iowa State U., 1957-58, prof., chmn. biomed. engring., 1959-63; rsch. adminstr. Rockwell Internat. Corp., 1963-66; prof. elec. engring. U. Ariz., 1966-67; chaired prof. Okla. State U., 1967-71; chmn. dept. elec. and computer engring. U. N.Mex., Albuquerque, 1971-76, prof. elec. and computer engring., 1976-95, prof. emeritus, 1995—; team mem. Engring. Coll. Accred. Bd. Engring. & Tech., 1969-76. Author over 90 publs. in field; mem. editorial bd. Biomed. Engring. Trans. IEEE, 1967-70; dir. 33 MS and PhD theses; 38 patents, 2 copyrights. 1st lt., multi-engine pilot, instr., USAF, 1942-47. NSF sr. postdoctoral fellow, 1958-59; recipient Gold Ring Highest Acad. Achievement award USAF, 1944, Rsch. Dir. award Morris Animal Found., 1961, Disting Rsch. Svc. award U. N.Mex., 1988, Cert. Recognition Los Alamos Nat. Lab., 1988. Fellow IEEE (nat. chmn. joint com. on engring. in medicine and biology, 1964-65); mem. NSPE, Am. Physiol. Soc., Air Force Assn., Res. Officers Assn., Sigma Xi, Phi Kappa Phi.

BOLIN, BERT RICHARD JOHANNES, atmospheric physicist, research meteorologist; b. Nyköping, Sweden, May 15, 1925; s. Richard and Karin Lovisa (Johansson) B.; m. Ulla Karin Frykstrand, June 7, 1952 (div. 1979); children: Dan, Karina, Göran. BS, U. Uppsala, 1946; MS, U. Stockholm, 1949, PhD in Meteorology, 1956. Assoc. prof. U. Stockholm, 1956-61, prof., 1961-90; scientific dir. European Space Rsch. Orgn., Paris, 1965-67; dir. Internat. Meteorol. Inst., 1961-91; scientific advisor to Swedish Prime min./vice prime min. Stockholm, 1986-91; chmn. joint orgn. com. GARP WMO, Geneva, 1967-70; vice chmn. Swedish Natural Sci. Rsch. Coun., 1977-80; chmn. intergovtl. panel on climate change WMO/UNEP, Geneva, 1988-97. Contbr. articles to profl. jours. Recipient OMI prize World Met. Orgn., 1981, Tyler prize U. So. Calif., 1988, Grüne Rosette Köber Stiftung, 1990, Milkankovic medal European Geophys. Soc., 1993, Blue Planet prize Asahi Glass Found., 1995, Environ. prize U. Lund, 1995, Swedish Royal medal, size 12, 1997, award for sci. co-op AAAS, 1998, Climate Protection award EPA US, 1998, Grole Environ. Leadership award GEF, World Bank, 1999. Mem. Royal Swedish Acad. Scis., Swedish Acad. Engring. Scis., Russian Acad. Scis., U.S. Nat. Acad. Scis., N.Y. Acad. Scis. Mem. Social Dem. Party. Avocations: choir singing, outdoor life. Home: Kvarnåsvägen 6, 18451 Österskär Sweden

BOLIN, DANIEL PAUL, music educator; b. Indpls., Apr. 11, 1948; s. Gillespie Green and Myrtle Genell (Runner) B.; m. Marilyn Jo McBride Rader, Aug. 8, 1970 (div. Mar. 1984); children: John William, Douglas Patrick; m. Jane Ann Crecelius, Oct. 29, 1987. BM, Butler U., 1970, MM, 1975, secondary adminstrn. cert., 1981; postgrad., U. Mich., summer 1976; EdD, Ind. U., 1988. Cert. music tchr., secondary sch. adminstr., supt., Ind. Band dir., gen. music orch. dir., asst. band dir. Wood H.S., Indpls., 1970-72; orch. dir., asst. band dir. Manual H.S., Indpls., 1972-73, band dir., 1973-74; band dir., chmn. fine arts dept. Lebanon (Ind.) H.S., 1974-77; band and choir dir., chmn. music dept. Southport H.S., Indpls., 1977-83, asst. prin., 1983-87; dir. secondary edn. Met. Sch. Dist. Perry Twp., Indpls., 1987-89, dir. pers. and student svcs., 1989-91, interim supt., 1992-93, asst. supt., 1991-95; prof., chair music dept. Butler U., Indpls., 1995—; facilitator I.U. Project LEAD, 1988-89; chmn. ISSMA Contest Manual Revision Com., 1982; sec. ISMA-NISBOVA Merger Com., 1978-81; bd. dirs. ISSMA, 1981-84; dir. BallState U. Mid-Am. Music Clinic, 1982, 83; mem. staff Ind. U. Music Clinic, 1974; chmn. Indpls. All-City H.S. Band, 1974; music dir. Eli Lilly Co., 1974; guest condr. Anthaneum Orch., 1974, Ctrl. Ind. Youth Wind Ensemble, 1980, Ind. All Region Jr. High Band, 1981; marching band com. ISMA, 1975, mem. music selection com., 1978; mem. camp staff Purdue U. Band Camp, 1981; co-founder, co-dir. Gt. Lake Music Camps, Inc., 1981—; coord. Ind. State Band, Orch. and Choir Finals, 1985-88; guest condr., host U.S. Army Field Band, 1986, 88, 89, 93, 95, 97, U.S. Marine Band, 1989, 94; guest condr. USAF Band of the Rockies. Conferee White House Conf. for Drug-Free Am., 1987-88; mem. program bd. Young Audiences of Ind., 1992—, bd. dirs., 1994—, chmn. bd., 1996—; coord. awards ceremonies X Pan-Am. Games, 1987; v.p. bd. dirs. Indpls. Chamber Orch., 1997. Performance scholar Butler U. Mem. Am. Sch. Band Dirs. Assn. (Stanbury award 1979), Am. Assn. Sch. Adminstrs., Music Educators Nat. Conf., Ind. Music Educators Assn., Ind. Assn. for Supervision and Curriculum Devel., Ind. Assn. Pub. Sch. Supts. (charter), Ind. All-State Music Festivals Assn. (bd. dirs. 1978-81, facilities coord. 1979-80, sec. 1980-81), Ind. State Sch. Music Assn., Ind. Sch. Music Assn., Northern Ind. Sch. Band, Orchestra, & Vocal Assn., Phi Delta Kappa, Pi Lambda Theta, Phi Kappa Lambda, Phi Mu Alpha, Kappa Kappa Psi. Avocations: music, travel, historical readings. Office: Butler U Coll Fine Arts 4600 Sunset Ave Indianapolis IN 46208-3487*

BOLIN, RICHARD LUDDINGTON, industrial development consultant; b. Burlington, Vt., May 13, 1923; s. Axel Birger and Eva Madora (Luddington) B.; m. Jeanne Marie Brown, Dec. 18, 1948; children: Richard Luddington, Jr., Douglas, Judith, Barbara, Elizabeth. BSChemE, Tex. A&M U., 1947; MSChemE, MIT, 1950; postgrad. advanced mgmt. program Harvard Bus. Sch., 1969. Jr. rsch. engr. Humble Oil & Refining Co., Baytown, Tex., 1947-49; staff mem. Arthur D. Little, Inc., Cambridge, Mass., 1950-56, Caribbean office mgr. San Juan, 1957-61, gen. mgr., Mex., 1961-72; pres. Internat. Parks, Inc., Flagstaff, Ariz., 1973-94, chmn., 1995—; bd. dirs. Parque Indsl. de Nogales, Nogales, Sonora, Mex.; dir. The Flagstaff Inst., 1976—, Secretariat World Export Processing Zones Assn., 1985—; mem. adv. bd. Lowell Obs., Flagstaff, 1993-94. With U.S. Army, 1942-46. Mem. Univ. Club of Mex.*For 17 years resident in Latin America for ADL, Richard Bolin assisted in the development of Puerto Rico's "Operation Bootstrap" and conducted the 1964 study for the Mexican government to create Mexico's "Maquiladora" export factories, now 3000 in number employing directly over 1,000,000 workers, most in 107 private industrial parks. Convinced of the efficiency of the modern "export processing zone" (EPZ) to lead poor countries out of poverty, he founded International Parks, Inc. in 1973 and The Flagtaff Institute in 1976 and directs the latter's project, the World Export Processing Zones Association (WEPZA), with 150 EPZs active in 50 countries* Office: PO Box 986 Flagstaff AZ 86002-0986

BOLIN, VERNON SPENCER, microbiologist, consultant; b. Parma, Idaho, July 9, 1913; s. Thadeus Howard Bolin and Jennie Bell Harm; m. Helen Epling, Jan. 5, 1948 (div. 1964); children: Rex, Janet, Mark; m. Barbara Sue Chase, Aug. 1965; children: Vladimir, Erik. BS, U. Wash., 1942; MS, U. Minn. 1949. Teaching asst. U. Minn.-Mpls., 1943-45; rsch. assoc. U. Utah, Salt Lake City, 1945-50, fellow in surgery, 1950-52; rsch. virologist Jensen-Salsbery Labs., Inc., Kansas City, Mo., 1952-57; rsch. assoc. Wistar Inst. U. Pa., 1957-58; rsch. virologist USPHS, 1958-61; founder Bolin Labs., Phoenix, 1959—, also bd. dirs. Contbr. articles to profl. jours. Served with U.S. Army, 1931-33. Mem. N.Y. Acad. Scis., Phi Mu Chi. Home: 36629 N 19th Ave Phoenix AZ 85027-9143

BOLIN, VLADIMIR DUSTIN, chemist; b. Inglewood, Calif., Feb. 25, 1965; s. Vernon Spencer and Barbara Sue (Chase) B.; m. Elizabeth Lynne Boswood, May 18, 1985; children: Ragnar Spencer, Roark Morgan. BS, U. Ariz., 1987. Chemist, microbiologist Bolin Labs., Inc., Phoenix, 1987-93; bd. dirs., pres. Aerotech Labs., Inc., Phoenix, 1993—, pres., 1993—; pres. Kalmar Labs., Inc., Phoenix, 1993—, also bd. dirs.; v.p. lab ops. Aqualab Inc., Phoenix, 1996—; bd. dirs., pres. Kalmar Labs., Inc., Phoenix; bd. dirs. Aqualab Inc., v.p., 1996—; bd. dirs. Ariz. Indoor Quality Coun., v.p. 1995—. Mem. ASTM, AAAS, Am. Water Works Assn. (pres.), Assn. Official Analytical Chemists, Am. Soc. Microbiolgoy, Am. Chem. Soc., N.Y. Acad. Scis. Home: 2020 W Lone Cactus Dr Phoenix AZ 85027-2624 Office: Aerotech/Kalmar Labs Inc 2020 W Lone Cactus Dr Phoenix AZ 85027-2624

BOLING, EDWARD JOSEPH, university president emeritus, educator; b. Sevier County, Tenn., Feb. 19, 1922; s. Sam R. and Nerissa (Clark) B.; m. Carolyn Pierce, Aug. 8, 1950; children: Mark Edward, Brian Marshall, Steven Clark. BS in Accounting, U. Tenn., 1948, MS in Stats., 1950; EdD in Ednl. Adminstrn, Vanderbilt U., 1961; LLD (hon.), U. Richmond, 1984. With Wilby-Kinsy Theatre Corp., Knoxville, Tenn., 1940-41, Aluminum Co. Am., 1941-42; instr. statistics U. Tenn., 1948-50; research statistician Carbide & Carbon Chem. Corp., Oak Ridge, 1950; supr. source and fissionable materials accounting Carbide & Carbon Chem. Corp. (K-25 plant), 1951-54; budget dir. Tenn., 1955-59; commr. finance and adminstrn., 1959-61; v.p. U. Tenn., 1961-70, pres., 1970-88, pres. emeritus, 1988—, univ. prof., 1988-92; mem. So. Regional Edn. Bd., 1957-61, 70-81, 83-90, 92-96, mem. exec. com., 1974-75, 79-81, vice chmn., 1986-88; mem. Edn. Commn. of States, 1970-82; trustee, chmn. Am. Coll. Testing Program, 1983-85; dir. emeritus Allied Signal Corp., CSX, N.A. Philips, United Foods, Home Fed. Bank. Author: (with D. A. Gardiner) Forecasting University Enrollment, 1952, Methods of Objectifying The Allocation of Tax Funds to Tennessee State Colleges, 1961. Mem. Nat. Govs. Conf. Good Will Tour to Brazil and Argentina, 1960; Mem. com. on taxation Am. Council on Edn. Served with AUS, 1943-46, ETO. Mem. Am. Statis. Assn., Assn. Higher Edn., Nat. Assn. Land-Grant Colls. (com. on financing higher edn.), Am. Coll. Pub. Rels. Assn. (trustee chmn. com. taxation and philanthropy), Am. Coun. on Edn., Knoxville C. of C. (bd. dirs., chmn. bd. 1989-91), Tenn. Resource Valley (dir., chmn. bd. 1991-92, chmn. supr. com. 1992—, chmn. 21st century jobs initiative), Am. Legion, Phi Kappa Phi (Scholarship award 1947), Beta Gamma Sigma (charter pres. Alpha chpt. 1948), Phi Delta Kappa, Omicron Delta Kappa, Beta Alpha Psi. Democrat. Office: U Tenn System Andy Holt Towers Ste 731 Knoxville TN 37996

BOLING, JOSEPH EDWARD, numismatist, retired military officer; b. San Antonio, Oct. 17, 1942; s. Jack Leroy and Judy Alice (Atwood) B.; m. Helen-Louise Phelps, June 11, 1964 (div. 1984); children: L. Margaret, David A., Evan J. BS in Metallurgy, MIT, 1964; MBA, U. Wash., 1973; grad., Japanese Nat. Def. Coll., 1984. Commd. 2d lt. U.S. Army, 1964, advanced through grades to col., 1987; dep. chief staff computer architecture U.S. Army, Heidelberg, Germany, 1989-92; asst. dep. dir. Worldwide Mil. Command Control System Def. Communications Agy., Reston, Va., 1985-89; retired U.S. Army, 1992. Author: (with others) WWII Military Currency, 1978, WWII Remembered History in Your Hands, A Numismatic Study, 1995, (also editor) Paper Money of the 20th Century: Japan Vol. 1 1979, Japan Vol. 2, 1988. Fellow Am. Numismatic Soc. (life, East Asian coinage com. 1985—), Royal Numismatic Soc.; mem. Internat. Bank Note Soc. (life, pres. 1986-90, treas. 1993—), Am. Numismatic Assn. (life, chief judge 1991-93, 95—, dir. judges' familiarization-cert. seminar 1986—, medal of merit 1991, Howland Wood award 1995), Pacific N.W. Numismatic Assn. (sec. 1994-96, sec.-treas. 1996—), Numismatic Lit. Guild, Assn. U.S. Army. Republican. Episcopalian. Avocation: research and publishing on Japanese numismatics. Address: PO Box 4718 Federal Way WA 98063-4718

BOLING, JUDY ATWOOD, civic worker; b. Madras, India, June 19, 1921 (parents Am. citizens); d. Carroll Eugene and Marion Frances (Ayrer) Atwood; m. Jack Leroy Boling, Apr. 8, 1941 (dec. July 1988); children: Joseph Edward, Jean Ann, James Michael, John Charles. AA, San Antonio Jr. Coll., 1940; student Rogue Community Coll., Grants Pass, Oreg., 1978-79, So. Oreg. State Coll., Ashland, 1982—. Contbr. articles to profl. jours. First aid instr. ARC, various locations, 1940-65, chmn. vols., Calif., 1961-62, Eng., 1964-65; den mother cub scouts Boy Scouts Am., Monterey, Calif., 1951-52; active Girl Scouts U.S., 1953—, coun. pres., Winema (Oreg.) Coun., 1971-73, 79-82, historian, 1990—, del. to nat. coun., 1966, 72, 81, cons. for nat. pubs., 1971, 79; Sunday sch. tchr. Base Chapel, Pyote, Tex., 1949-51, choir dir., 1951; Sunday sch. adminstr. Base Chapel, Morocco, 1954-55; Sunday sch. tchr. Hermon Free Meth. Ch., L.A., 1956-57; active United Way campaign, 1967-84, Childrens Festival, 1974-88; former liaison with local people in Japanese-Am., Franco-Am., Anglo-Am. orgns.; mem., patron Rogue Craftsmen Bd., Grants Pass, 1972-85, sec., 1972-78, v.p., 1978-85; bd. dirs. Rogue Valley Opera Assn., 1978-85, sponsor/mem., 1978—; bd. dirs. Community Concert, 1979-88, 92-97, mem. Grants Pass Friends of the Symphony, 1989— (bd. dirs. 1992—); vol. RSVP, 1982—; historian Josephine County Rep. Women, 1982-86, treas., 1986-94, 98, sec., 1994-96; elected Rep. precinct committeeperson, 1991—; sustaining mem. Sta. KSYS pub. TV; mem. Sta. KSOR pub. radio; frequent pub. speaker. Recipient Thanks badge Girl Scouts U.S., 1957, 60, 73, Girl Scouts Japan, 1959, U.K. Girl Guides, 1982; others; cert. of appreciation USAF, 1959, City of Hagi, City of Fukuoka (Japan), Gov. of Fukuoka Prefecture; 2 citations Internat. Book Project; Oreg. Vol. award Sen. Packwood, 1983; Community Woman of Year award Bus. and Profl. Women, 1984, Nat. award Juliette Gordon Low World Friendship medal Girl Scouts Am., 1995. Mem. P.E.O. (DC, Oreg. chpt.) Josephine County Hist. Soc. (bd. dirs. 1991—), So. Oreg. Resources Alliance, Am. Host Found., Friends of Libr., Grants Pass Art Mus., Knife and Fork Club (bd. dirs. 1994-97), Phi Theta Kappa. Address: 3016 Jumpoff Joe Creek Rd Grants Pass OR 97526-8778

BOLING, PATRICIA ANN, political science educator, researcher, writer; b. Ft. Sill, Okla., Feb. 14, 1953; d. Victor LeRoy and Dorothy Mildred (Collins) B.; m. Mark Campbell Tilton, Sept. 21, 1981; children: Ellen, Clio, Andrew. BA in Politics, U. Calif., Santa Cruz, 1975; MA in Polit. Sci., U. Calif., Berkeley, PhD, 1984. Teaching asst. U. Calif., Berkeley, 1977-80, teaching assoc., 1981-82; asst. prof. Trinity U., San Antonio, Tex., 1984-86; freelance writer, researcher Tokyo, 1986—; spl. research fellow Social Sci. Research Inst., Internat. Christian U., Tokyo, 1988—. Sponsor Campub NOW, Young Democrats, Trinity U., 1985-86. Summer research fellowship Trinity U., 1985, 86; grad. fellowship U. Calif., Berkeley, 1981-82. Democrat. Clubs: Internat. Friendship (Tokyo). Avocations: swimming, hiking, cross-country skiing, Japanese culture.

BOLING, ROBERT BRUCE, physical education educator; b. Hammond, Ind., July 28, 1939; s. Kermit W. and Linda E. (Swan) B.; m. Nancy Carol Adams, Dec. 4, 1965. BS, Murray State U., 1964, MS, 1965; PhD, U. So. Miss., 1972. Tchr., coach Casey (Ill.) High Sch., 1965-66, Trigg County High Sch., Cadiz, Ky., 1966-67, Christian County High Sch., Hopkinsville, Ky., 1967-69; tchr. Miss. State U., Mississippi State, 1975—. Author: KINES: Kinesiology in an Interactive New Educational Strategy, 1992. Mem. AAHPERD, Miss. AAHPERD, Am. Coll. Sports Medicine. Baptist.

BOLINGER, ROBERT STEVENS, banker; b. Mt. Union, Pa., July 22, 1936; s. J. Morrow and Nell E. (Stevens) B.; m. Reba M. Fleisher, June 17, 1962; children: Todd Wesley, Steven Morrow, Mark Andrew. AB, Dartmouth Coll., 1958, MBA, 1962. From auditor to asst. sec. Irving Trust Co., N.Y.C, 1962-66; asst. v.p. Wall St. divsn. Irving Trust Co., N.Y.C., 1966-70, v.p. regional credit officer, 1970-71, v.p., 1972-75; pres., CEO, dir. Farmers First Bank, Lititz, Pa., 1976—, Susquehanna Bancshares, Inc., Lititz, 1982—; pres. Susquehanna Bancshares East, Inc., 1997—; chmn. bd. dirs. Susquehanna Bancshares South Inc.; pres., CEO, bd. dirs. Susque Bancshares Life Ins. Co., Inc.; dir. Donegal Group, Inc., Atlantic States Ins. Co., So. Ins. Co. Va., Econ. Devel. Co. Lancaster County, Pioneer Ins. Co., Ohio; dir. Del. Am. Ins. Co. Bd. dirs. United Way of Lancaster County, Pa., 1977-84, Linden Hall Sch. Girls, Lititz, 1982-92, Bank Adminstrn. Inst., Chgo., 1989-93, Lancaster (Pa.) Gen. Hosp. Found. Lt. (j.g.) USN, 1958-61; lt. comdr. USNR, 1961-72. Mem. Lancaster C. of C. and Industry (dir., treas. 1978-80), Hamilton Club, Bent Creek C. of C., Masons. Republican. Presbyterian. Office: Susquehanna Bancshares Inc 26 N Cedar St Lititz PA 17543-1514

BOLITHO, LOUISE GREER, educational administrator, consultant; b. Wenatchee, Wash., Aug. 13, 1927; d. Lon Glenn and Edna Gertrude (Dunlap) Greer; m. Douglas Stuart, June 17, 1950 (div. Dec. 1975); children: Rebecca Louise, Brian Douglas. BA, Wash. State U., 1949. With Stanford (Calif.) U., 1967-91, adminstrv. asst. physics labs., 1974-77, mgr. ctr. for research in internat. studies, 1977-84, law sch. fin. and adminstrv. services dir., 1984-86; computer cons., Palo Alto, Calif., 1984—; acting mgr. Inst. for Internat. Studies, 1987-88, fin. analyst, 1988-91. Mem. Peninsula vols., Menlo Park, Calif., 1986-94; budget com. chmn., bd. dirs. Mid-Peninsula Support Network, Mountain View, Calif., 1984-86; chairperson active older adults com. YMCA; pres. 410 Sheridan Ave. Homeowners Assn., 1989-93, treas., 1993-99, sec., 1999—; treas. Friends of Music Stanford U., 1999—. Mem. AAUW (bd. dirs. 1987-88). Home and Office: 410 Sheridan Ave Apt 445 Palo Alto CA 94306-2020

BOLIVAR, FRANCISCO, biochemist; b. Mexico City, Mar. 7, 1948; s. Jose and Carmen (Zapata) B.; children: Francisco, Paulina, Jose. Degree in chemistry, Nat. Autonomous U. Mex., Mexico City, 1971, M Biochemistry, 1973, PhD in Biochemistry, 1975; D Honoris Causa, U. Lieje, Belgium, 1994. Assoc. rschr. Nat. Autonomous U. Mex., full rschr. level I, 1977-83, full rschr. level III, 1983—, chmn. molecular biology dept., 1980—, dir. genetic engring. ctr., 1982—; dir. biotech. inst. Nat. Autonomous U. Mex., Cuernacava, Mex., 1991. Editor jour. Gene, 1982—; contbr. more than 120 articles to profl. jours. Recipient Nat. prize in sci. Pres. of Mex., 1992, Prince of Asturias prize in sci. Govt. of Spain, 1991, Manuel Noriega prize in Sci. OAS, 1988, others. Mem. Am. Soc. Microbiology, Academia Investigacion Cientifica, Mex. Colegio Nacional. Office: UNAM Inst Biotech, PO Box 510-3, Cuernavaca 62271, Mexico

BOLKER, HENRY IRVING, retired chemist, research institute director, educator; b. Montreal, Que., Can., Feb. 19, 1926; s. Abraham Isaac and Mary (Ballon) B.; m. Estelle Ruth Samuels, Nov. 22, 1953; 1 dau., Louise Ellen. BA, Queen's U., Kingston, Ont., Can., 1948; MA, Queen's U., 1950; PhD, Yale U., 1952. Rsch. chemist DuPont of Can., Ltd., Kingston, Ont., 1954-60; rsch. chemist Pulp and Paper Rsch. Inst. Can., Pointe Claire, Que., 1960-67, sect. head, 1967-77, div. dir., 1977-80, asst. dir. rsch., 1980-81, assoc. dir. rsch., 1981-83, dir. rsch., 1984-86, dir. acad. affairs, 1987-90; exec. dir. Nat. Network of Ctrs. of Excellence on Mech. Pulps, 1990-93; rsch. assoc. McGill U., Montreal, 1962-91. Author: Natural and Synthetic Polymers, 1974; contbr. articles to profl. jours.; patentee in field. Pres. Youth Sci. Found., Ottawa, 1965-66; sec. Lakeshore Chamber Music Soc. Ste. Anne de Bellevue, Que., 1973-74; pres. Lakeshore Dog Tng. Assn., Pointe Claire, 1975-77; chmn. Pointe Claire Cultural Centre, 1978-80. Fellow Internat. Acad. Wood Sci. (sec.-treas. 1989-92), Chem. Inst. Can. (chmn. 1979-81, v.p. 1986-87, pres. 1987-88, Montreal medal 1984), Sigma Xi; mem. Am. Chem. Soc., Can. Pulp and Paper Assn. Home: 110 Spartan Cres, Pointe Claire, PQ Canada H9R 3R5

BOLL, CHARLES RAYMOND, engine company executive; b. Columbus, Ind., Mar. 29, 1920; s. Charles Raymond and Hestella (Snyder) B.; m. Mary Genevieve Lortz, Nov. 6, 1943; children: Charles Raymond III, Cynthia Ann. B.S. in Elec. Enging, Purdue U., 1941. With Cummins Engine Co., Inc., Columbus, 1941-89; sales engr. Cummins Engine Co., Inc., 1941-42; asst. regional mgr. Cummins Engine Co., Inc., Cleve., 1947; mgr. engine sales Cummins Engine Co., Inc., 1948-52, gen. sales mgr., 1953-55, v.p. sales, 1955-60, exec. v.p. mktg., 1960-64, pres. Internat. div., 1965-66, exec. v.p., 1965-85, also bd. dirs., 1956-88, dir. emeritus, 1988—. 1st lt., Signal Corps, AUS, 1943-46. Named Outstanding Elec. Engr., Purdue U., 1992. Mem. Soc. Automotive Engrs. Home: 2940 Washington St Columbus IN 47201-2946

BOLLAG, JEAN-MARC, soil biochemistry educator, consultant; b. Basel, Switzerland, Feb. 19, 1935; came to U.S., 1965, naturalized, 1975; s. Marcel and Renee (Levy) B.; m. Brigitte Gertrud Baumgartner, Apr. 26, 1960; children: Daniel, Gideon, Roni, Judith. Ph.D., U. Basel, 1959. Grad. research asst. Bot. Inst., U. Basel, 1956-59; postdoctoral research assoc. Weizmann Inst. Sci., Rehovot, Israel, 1963-65, Cornell U., Ithaca, N.Y., 1965-67; asst. prof. soil microbiology Pa. State U., University Park, 1967-71, assoc. prof., 1971-77, prof., 1977—; vis. sci. CIBA-Geigy, Basel, 1975-76; dir. Ctr. for Bioremediation and Detoxification; cons. to fed. agys., chem. cos. Co-editor Soil Biochemistry Series; contbr. numerous articles in environ. microbiology and microbial control of soil pollution to profl. publs. Recipient Badge of Merit, Polish Ministry Agr., 1977, Research award Gamma Sigma Delta, 1982; Julius Baer fellow Weizmann Inst. Sci., 1963-65. Fellow Soil Sci. Soc., Am. Soc. Agronomy (Environ. Quality Rsch. award 1995), Am. Acad. Microbiology; mem. AAAS, Internat. Soc. Soil Sci., Am. Soc. Microbiology, Am. Chem. Soc., Internat. Humic Substances Soc. Democrat. Home: 368 Bradley Ave State College PA 16801-6322 Office: Penn State Ctr for Bioremediation & Detox 129 Land Water Research University Park PA 16802-4900

BOLLBACK, ANTHONY GEORGE, minister; b. N.Y.C., Aug. 27, 1922; s. Anthony J. and Elizabeth Ann (Balzer) B.; m. Evelyn Watson, Aug. 14, 1943; children: James, Joy, Judith, Jonathan. Diploma, Nyack Coll., 1943. Ordained to ministry Christian and Missionary Alliance, 1945. Pastor Christian and Missionary Alliance, Coudersport, Pa., 1943-46, Chatham, N.J, 1950-52, Honolulu, 1970-77, Silver Spring, Md., 1978-85; missionary Christian and Missionary Alliance, China, 1947-49, Japan, 1952-57, Hong Kong, 1958-70; supt. western dist. Christian and Missionary Alliance, Omaha, 1985-93; interim pastor Kapahulu Bible Ch., Honolulu, 1994, First Alliance Ch., Orlando, 1996; trustee Crown Coll., St. Bonifacious, Minn., 1985-93; pres. Evang. Missions Fellowship, Hong Kong, 1967-70, Oahu Assn. Evangelicals, Honolulu, 1974-76; dir. Okoboji Lakes Bible & Missionary Conf. Ctr., Arnolds Park, Iowa, 1994-96. Author: To China and Back, 1991, Jack and Jenny mystery series: Smugglers in Hong Kong, 1997, Capture of the Twin Dragon, 1997, Mystery of the Counterfeit Money, 1998, Rescue at Cripple Creek, 1999. Mem. Nyack Coll. Alumni Assn. (pres. 1983-84). Republican.

BOLLE, DONALD MARTIN, retired engineering educator; b. Amsterdam, The Netherlands, Mar. 30, 1933; came to U.S., 1955, naturalized, 1961; s. Maarten C. and Petronella (Kramer) B.; m. Barbara June Girton, Nov. 29, 1957; children—Alan Martin, Thomas Raymond, John Kenneth, Cornelis Adrianus. BS, Durham U., Eng., 1954; PhD, Purdue U., 1961; MA (hon.), Brown U., 1966. Asst. prof. elec. engring. Purdue U., 1961-62; NSF postdoctoral fellow dept. applied math. and theoretical physics Cambridge (Eng.) U., 1962-63; asst. prof. engring. Brown U., 1963-66, asso. prof., 1966-70, prof., 1970-80; Chandler-Weaver chair elec. engring. Lehigh U., Bethlehem, Pa., 1980-81; dean Lehigh U. (Coll. Engring. and Applied Sci.), 1981-88; sr. v.p. acad. affairs Poly. U., Bklyn., 1988-91, prof., 1991-99, v.p. adminstrn., 1995-96; Richard Merton vis. prof. Technische Hochschule, Braunschweig, Germany, 1967; cons. in field. Fellow IEEE, AAAS, IEE (U.K.); mem. ACLU, Sigma Xi, Tau Beta Pi, Eta Kappa Nu. Home: 6448 Eichler Cir Coopersburg PA 18036-1382 Office: Poly Univ Rt 110 Farmingdale NY 11735

BOLLE, ROBERT L., lawyer, administrator; b. Grand Rapids, Oct. 23, 1943. BA, U. Mich., 1965; JD, Wayne State U., 1968; LLM, NYU, 1969, LLM in Taxation, 1970. Gen. counsel Interstate Commn. Potomac River Basin, Rockville, Md., 1992—, acting dir., 1997-98. Mem. Human Rights Commn. Minn., 1972-74. Mem. State Bar Assn., Miss. State Bar Assn., D.C. State Bar Assn. Minn. Office: Interstate Commn Potomac River Basin 6110 Executive Blvd Ste 300 Rockville MD 20852*

BOLLENBACH, STEPHEN FRASIER, entertainment executive; b. Los Angeles, July 14, 1942; s. Walter and Betty (Mason) B.; m. Suzanne Weimer, Apr. 13, 1963 (div. Dec. 1969); m. Barbara May Christeson, Dec. 31, 1970; children: Christopher, Keat. BS in Fin., UCLA, 1965; MBA, Calif. State U., 1968. CFO D.K. Ludwig Group, N.Y.C., 1977-80; chmn., CEO S.W. Savs. & Loan, Phoenix, 1980-82; sr. v.p. fin., treas. Marriott Corp., Washington, 1982-86; sr. v.p., CFO, dir. Holiday Corp., Memphis, 1986-90, Promus Cos., Memphis, 1990; exec. v.p., CFO Marriott Corp., Washington, 1992-93; pres., CEO Host Marriott Corp., Washington, 1993-95; sr. exec. v.p., CFO Walt Disney Co., Burbank, Calif., 1995—; bd. dirs. Carr Realty Corp., Washington, Mid-Am. Apt. Cmtys., Inc., Memphis, Am. West Airlines, Phoenix; mem. adv. bd. CFO Mag., Boston. Office: Hilton Hotels Corporation P.O.Box 5567 Beverly Hills CA 90210-5567

BOLLENBACHER, HERBERT KENNETH, steel company official; b. Wilkinsburg, Pa., Apr. 16, 1933; s. Curtis W. and Ebba M. (Frendberg) B.; m. Nancy Jane Cercena, June 29, 1957; children: Mary E., Kenneth E. AB, U. Pitts., 1960, MEd, 1963. Cert. safety profl. Staff asst. tng. J & L Steel Co., Pitts., 1963-66; mgr. tng., devel. and accident prevention Textron Corp., Pitts., 1966-72; supr. safety Copperweld Steel Co., Warren, Ohio, 1972-75, mgr. safety, security, 1975-78, mgr. human resources conservation, 1978-94; exec. v.p. Charles Mgmt., Inc., 1994—; mem. adj. faculty Pa. State U. mem. Eastminster Presbytery Com. on Ministry; bd. dirs. Trumbull County Prison Ministry. Served with U.S. Army, 1954-56. Mem. Am. Soc. Safety Engrs. (past pres. Ohio-Pa. chpt., Ohio Safety Profl. of Yr. 1983-84, 92-93), Ohio Soc. Safety Engrs. (state chaplain), Am. Iron and Steel Inst. (chmn. safety task force), Mfrs. Assn. Eastern Ohio and Western Pa. (safety chmn. 12 yrs.; safety profl. of yr. award 1984, coordinator Ohio seat belt coalition 1986, Gov.'s spl. recognition award), Gov.'s Traffic Safety Coun., 1989, Trumbull Camp Gideons Internat. (past pres.), Ohio Gideons (area coordinator, membership cabinet), Rotary (Paul Harris fellow, pres., benefactor, Ideal of Svc. in Workplace award), Boy Scouts Am. (western reserve coun., loss prevention com.). Presbyterian (elder). Author suprs. monthly discussion guide, article for tech. publ. Avocations: softball; volleyball; reading. Office: Charles Mgmt Inc 24850 Aurora Rd Cleveland OH 44146-1761 *Personal philosophy: The chief end of man is to glorify God and be a blessing to your fellow men.*

BOLLER, PAUL FRANKLIN, JR., retired American history educator, writer; b. Spring Lake, N.Y., Dec. 31, 1916; s. Paul Franklin and Grace (Hall) B. BA, Yale U., 1939, PhD, 1947; DLitt, Tex. Wesleyan U., 1993. From asst. to full prof. So. Meth. U., Dallas, 1948-66; prof. U. Mass., Boston, 1966-76; Lyndon Johnson prof. history Tex. Christian U., Ft. Worth, 1976-83, prof. emeritus, 1983—; vis. prof. U. Tex., Austin, 1963-64. Author: (with J. Tilford) This Is Our Nation, 1961, George Washington and Religion, 1963, Quotemanship, 1967, American Thought in Transition, 1865-1900, 1967, American Transcendentalism, 1830-1860, 1974, Freedom and Fate in American Thought, 1978, Presidential Anecdotes, 1981, Presidential Campaigns, 1984, (with R. Story) A More Perfect Union, 1984, (with R.L. Davis) Hollywood Anecdotes, 1987, Presidential Wives, 1988, (with J. George) They Never Said It, 1989, Congressional Anecdotes, 1991, Memoirs of an Obscure Professor, 1992, Not So!, 1995. Lt. (j.g.) USN, 1942-46. Mem. Tex. Inst. Letters, Authors Guild, Phi Alpha Theta, Phi Beta Kappa. Democrat. Avocations: music, films, hiking, jogging, swimming. Office: Tex Christian Univ Box 297260 Fort Worth TX 76129

BOLLER, RONALD CECIL, glass company executive; b. Cleve., Mar. 12, 1939; s. Ernest Russell and Rose B.; m. Marilyn L. Emery, Oct. 14, 1967 (div. 1982); children: Lori J., Lisa L. BS, Purdue U., 1962; MBA, U. Chgo., 1970. Engr. system sales and application Leeds & Northrup Co., North Wales, Pa., 1965-68; with Owens-Ill., Inc., Toledo, 1970—, dir. planning, rsch. and analysis, 1977-78, mgr. corp. real estate, 1978-80, mgr. portfolio mgmt. and benefit funds, treasury, 1980-81, dir. benefit fin., treasury, 1981-88, v.p., dir. risk and benefit fin., 1988-90, v.p. investments, 1991—. Pres. Great Lakes Credit Union, Toledo, 1976-77, Harbor Capital Advisors, 1989—; trustee Toledo Mus. Art, 1990—, Toledo Cmty. Found., Inc. 1992—; investment com. Mercy Health Ptnrs., 1991—. Office: Harbor Capital Advisors One SeaGate Toledo OH 43666-0001

BOLLES, CHARLES AVERY, librarian; b. Pine Island, Minn., Aug. 10, 1940; s. Arthur Marston and Clarice Ione (Figy) B.; m. Marjorie Elaine Hancock, May 177, 1964; children: Jason Brice, Justin Brian. BA, U. Minn., 1962, MA in Libr. Sci., 1963, PhD in Libr. Sci., 1975. Catalog and serials librarian U. Iowa, Iowa City, 1964-67; asst. prof. Emporia (Kans.) State U., 1970-76, dir. Sch. Libr. Sci., 1978-80; dir. libr. devel. divsn. Kans. State Libr., 1976-78; state librarian State of Idaho, Boise, 1980—. Mem. MLA, Chief Officers State Libr. Agys., Western Coun. State Librs. (chmn. 1985-86, 98—), Pacific N.W. Libr. Assn. (pres. 1990-91), Idaho Libr. Assn. Office: Idaho State Libr 325 W State St Boise ID 83702-6014

BOLLES, DONALD SCOTT, lawyer; b. Buffalo, Dec. 17, 1936; s. Theodore H. and Marie (Heth) B.; m. Jean Waytulonis Oct. 24, 1963 (dec. May 1983); children: Scott, Matthew; m. Geraldine Novinger, Feb. 14, 1988. BA,

Alfred U., 1960; JD cum laude, U. San Diego, 1970. Bar: Calif. 1971, U.S. Dist. Ct. (so. and no. dists.) Calif. 1971. Ptnr. Hutton, Foley, Anderson & Bolles, Inc., King City, Calif., 1971-95, Anderson & Bolles, Inc., King City, Calif., 1995—; prof. Monterey Coll. Law, Calif. Editor lead articles San Diego Law Rev., 1969-70. Trustee Mee Meml. Hosp., King City, 1974-78, chmn., 1978-80; chmn. King City Recreation Commn., 1974-77; candidate mcpl. ct. judge primary and gen. election, Monterey County, Calif., 1986; sec., founding mem. bd. dirs. Project Teen Ctr. Inc., 1986-90; bd. dirs. Sun St. Ctrs., 1991-99, Monterey Coll. Law, 1995—; pres. Corral de Tierra Homeowners Assn., 1996-98. Served to capt. U.S. Army, 1961-67, Vietnam. Decorated Combat Infantryman's badge, Army Commendation medal. Mem. Monterey County Bar Assn. (exec. com. 1985-86). Republican. Club: Toastmasters (King City) (pres. 1972-74). Lodge: Lions (pres. 1975-76, sec. 1984-86 King City club). Avocations: application of computer science to practice of law, tennis, golf, bridge, choir. Home: Apt 18 23799 Monterey Salinas Hwy Salinas CA 93908-9328 Office: Anderson & Bolles Inc PO Box 26 523 Broadway St King City CA 93930-3230

BOLLES, SUSAN, production designer; b. Boston, May 25, 1960; d. Peter Piper and Jacqueline Maoria (Gilmore) B. BA in Theater, U. Mass., 1982; MFA, NYU, 1985; cert., L'Univ. Cath. L'ouest, Angiers, France, 1980. vis. lectr. Tisch Sch. of Arts NYU, 1997. Prodn. designer (feature films) The Suburbans, Myth of Fingerprints, His & Hers, Illtown, Denise Calls Up, Me & the Mob, Wide Sargosso Sea (AD), (short films) Master of the Manor, Where or When, Tourist Season, Afterimages, Afterlife of Grandpa, One Sunday Afternoon, Two Scoops for Slugger, Timothy's Adventures, (TV) The Kids' Choise Awards, House of Buggin', The MTV Beach House, The Rolonda Show, Inside the Comedy Mind, Night After Night, Turn It Up!, The Ben Stiller Show, Remote Control, also numerous Tn spls. and pilots. Recipient Broadcast Designers' award, 1989, 90. Mem. United Scenic Artists local 829 (exam judge 1986—, exam. com. 1991—), Soc. Motion Picture and TV Art Dirs. local 876. Democrat. Unitarian. Avocation: art collecting. Fax: (213) 629-4692.

BOLLICH, ELRIDGE NICHOLAS, investment executive; b. Eunice, La., Sept. 10, 1941; s. Nicholas Joseph and Caroline (Manuel) B.; m. Shirley Anne Yackel, July 14, 1973; children: Jennifer, Brian, Sandra. BBA in Fin., Tex. A&M U., 1963. Registered rep. N.Y. Stock Exchange. Asst. v.p. Rotan Mosle, Houston, 1969-74, v.p., 1975-86; 1st v.p. Rotan Mosle Paine Webber, Houston, 1986-88, Smith Barney, Houston, 1988-97; sr. v.p. Paine Webber, Houston, 1997—; dir. devel. bd. Nat. Commerce Bank, Houston, 1987-88. Cubmaster Boy Scouts Am., Houston, 1987-91; mem. troop com. troop 642 Boy Scouts Am., 1992—. 1st lt. U.S. Army, 1963-65, Vietnam, capt. USAR, 1967-69. Mem. VFW, Houston Security Dealers, Stock and Bond Club, Houston Racquet Club, KC. Roman Catholic. Avocations: hunting, tennis, plays, coaching boys and girls basketball, Boy Scouts. Office: Paine Webber Inc 5 Post Oak Park Ste 900 Houston TX 77027-3414

BOLLIGER, EUGENE FREDERICK, retired surgeon; b. Detroit, Sept. 19, 1923; s. Eugene Hans and Julia Frederick (Larson) B.; m. Lois Ann Doan, Dec. 16, 1946; children: Mark, Glen, Cynthia. MD, U. Mich., 1946. Diplomate Am. Bd. Surgery. Intern, then surg. resident Grace Hosp., Detroit, 1947-52; ward surgeon Madigan Army Hosp., Ft. Lewis, Wash., 1952-54; asst. chief surgery 2d Gen. Hosp., Munchweiler, Germany, 1954-55; chief surgery U.S. Army Hosp., Pirmasson, then Wurzburg, Germany, 1955-57; attending surgeon Northwestern Hosp., Mpls., 1957-58; chief of surgery Dickey County Meml. Hosp., Ellendale, N.D., 1958-82; surgeon SHARE HMO, Mpls., 1982-87; chief of surgery Mid-Dakota Hosp., Chamberlain, S.D., 1988-91, Gregory (S.D.) Community Hosp., 1991-94; retired, 1994; surg. cons. West Holt Hosp., Atkinson, Nebr., 1992-94, St. Anthony's Hosp., O.Neill, Nebr., 1992-94; real estate cons. Westin-Reid, Mpls., 1987-88. Major U.S. Army, M.C., 1949-57. Fellow ACS; mem. AMA. Republican. Lutheran. Avocations: piano, singing, woodworking, former pilot.

BOLLING, LANDRUM RYMER, retired academic administrator, writer, consultant; b. Parksville, Tenn., Nov. 13, 1913; s. Landrum Austin and Carrie Mae (Rymer) B.; m. Frances Morgan, July 6, 1936; children: Roger Landrum (dec.), Brian Austin, David Morgan, Rebecca Lucy, Daniel Wade, Sarah Middleton. BA, U. Tenn., 1933; MA, U. Chgo., 1938; LLD, Valparaiso U., Wabash Coll., Oberlin Coll., Alderson-Broadus Coll., Beloit Coll., Rose-Hulmann Poly. Inst., Haverford Coll., Waseda U. (Japan), Ind. State U., Ea. Nazarene Coll., Denison U., Campbell Coll., Ind. U.; LHD, Anderson Coll., Ind. Tech. Coll., Earlham Coll. Adminstrv. asst. personnel div. TVA; also housing mgr. Town of Norris, editor Norris News, 1933-36, freelance writer, 1936-37; instr. polit. sci. Brown U., 1938-40; assisted in orgn. Community Service Inc., Yellow Springs, Ohio; also editor and pub. Yellow Springs News, 1940-41; instr. to assoc. prof. polit. sci. Beloit Coll., 1942-46; war corr. Mediterranean Theater, 1944-45; fgn. corr. Berlin and Central Europe, 1946-48; prof. polit. sci. Earlham Coll., 1948-58, gen. sec., 1955-58, pres., 1958-73; exec. v.p. Lilly Endowment, 1973-75, pres., 1975-77; chmn. Council on Founds., 1978-81; research prof. of diplomacy Georgetown U., Washington, 1981-83; pres. The Ecumenical Inst. (Tantur), Jerusalem, 1983-89; sr. fell. Ctr. of Internatl. Policy, Wash.; sr. adv. Conflict Mgmt. Grp., Cambridge; journalistic, editorial assignments, N.Y., Europe, 1949, 52-53; sr. counsellor Mercy Corps Internat., 1989—; sr. fellow Ctr. for Internat. Policy, 1991—; sr. advisor Conflict Mgmt. Group, 1992—. Author: City Manager Government in Dayton, 1940; co-author: (Settel et al) This is Germany, 1950, Search for Peace in the Middle East, 1970; editor: Reporters Under Fire, 1985; contbr.: Private Diplomacy with the Soviet Union, 1987, Conflict Resolution: Track II Diplomacy, 1987. Mem. Gov. of Ind. Commn. on Post High Sch. Edn., 1968; mem. Pres.'s Commn. on 25th Anniv. UN, 1970; chmn. Internat. Quaker Working Party on Middle East Peace, 1968; mem. Am. del. Soviet-Am. Talks, Dartmouth Conf., 1974, 76, 78, 79; life mem. bd. dirs. Earlham Coll., Richmond, Ind.; bd. dirs. Haverford (Pa.) Coll., 1980-85, Youth for Understanding, Friendship Force; co-sec. DeBurght Conf. on East/West Dialogue on Human Rights, 1988—. Recipient Founder's Day medal U. Tenn. Knoxville, 1997. Mem. Assn. Am. Colls. (bd. dirs.), Gt. Lakes Colls. Assn. (chmn. bd. dirs. 1962-64), Ind. Conf. Higher Edn. (pres. 1961-62), Council Fgn. Relations. Mem. Soc. of Friends. Clubs: Century (N.Y.C.); Cosmos (Washington). Office: Ctr for Internat Policy 1755 Massachusetts Ave NW Washington DC 20036-2102 also: Conflict Mgmt Group 9 Waterhouse St Cambridge MA 02138-5756 also: Mercy Corps Internat 1730 Rhode Island Ave Washington DC 20036

BOLLINGER, DON MILLS, retired grocery company executive; b. Seymour, Ind., Mar. 7, 1914; s. Don Albert and Hannah (Mills) B.; m. EmmyLou Groub, Nov. 5, 1938; children: Linda Bollinger McCoy, Thomas R., Barbara Bollinger Flaherty. AB, DePauw U., 1936; MBA, U. Pa., 1938. With Seymour Woolen Mills, Ind., 1938-51, pers. mgr., 1945-51; with John C. Groub Co. Inc., Seymour, 1951-99, chmn., sr. exec. officer, 1980-84, chmn., chief exec. officer, 1984-91, chmn., 1991-99, also bd. dirs.; chmn. bd. Fidelity Fed. Savs. & Loan (merged with Home Fed. Savs. Bank 1990), Seymour, until 1987; pres., bd. dir. Dotto Inc., 1984—. Pres. Jackson County United Fund, Seymour, 1961-64; officer ARC Jackson County, 1941-43, 72-77, chmn. 75-76, 76-77; bd. dirs. Jackson County Juvenile Home, Brownstown, Ind., 1978-92, pres., 1983-84. Recipient Man and Boy award Boys' Clubs Am., 1963, Svc. to Mankind award, La Sertoma, 1977; named Boss of Yr., Seymour Jaycees, 1964; inducted into DePauw U. Athletic Hall of Fame, 1991. Mem. Ind. Retail Coun. (bd. dirs. exec. com. 1977-94), Seymour C. of C. (pres. 1968, Citizen of Yr. award 1987), Ind. State C. of C. (bd. dirs. 1984-92), Washington C. DePauw Soc. Republican. Methodist. Club: Seymour Country. Lodges: Elks, Rotary (pres. 1962-63). Home: 660 Braewick Rd Seymour IN 47274-1430 Office: John C Groub Co Inc Freeman Field Ave A & D St Seymour IN 47274

BOLLINGER, KENNETH JOHN, aerospace engineer, computer and space scientist; b. Warren AFB, Wyo., Nov. 6, 1954; s. John Henry and Charleen Edna (Wallick) B.; m. Christine Faye Ferguson, May 11, 1973; children: Kelly Raun, Orion Grant, Sara Selene. BS, Calif. Poly. U., 1987. Ops. engr. AER Voyager project, dep. team chief Magellan project Jet Propulsion Lab., Pasadena, Calif., 1986-89; asst. mgr., PDS Rings Node NASA Ames, Moffett Field, Calif., 1993-98; web svcs. mgr. NASA Ames, Moffett Field, 1998—, project mgr., lunar prospector, space directorate; pres. Web Frontiers, Space Frontiers San Jose, Calif., 1993—. Mem. Amateur Radio Civil Emergency Svc., 1988. Mem. Amateur Radio Club, NASA Ames.

BOLLINGER, LEE CARROLL, law educator; b. 1946. B.S., U. Oreg., 1968; J.D., Columbia U., 1971. Law clk. to Judge Wilfred Feinberg U.S. Ct. Appeals (2nd cir.), 1971-72; law clk. Chief Justice Warren Burger U.S. Supreme Ct., 1972-73; asst. prof. law U. Mich., 1973-76, assoc. prof., 1976-78, prof., 1978-94, dean, 1987-94; provost Dartmouth Coll., 1994-96, prof. govt., 1994-96, pres. U. Mich., 1997, prof. law, 1997—; rsch. assoc. Clare Hall, Cambridge U., 1983. Author: (with Jackson) Contract Law in Modern Society, 1980; The Tolerant Soc., 1986, Images of a Free Press, 1991. Fellow Am. Acad. Arts and Scis. Recipient Rockefeller Humanities fellowship. Office: U Michigan 2074 Fleming Adminstrn Bldg Ann Arbor MI 48109-1340

BOLLINGER, MICHAEL, artistic director; b. St. Louis, July 1, 1954; s. Rollie Bollinger and Blanche (Bush) Easley; m. Dee J. Rodd, Sept. 6, 1980; children: Tanner Michael, Allison Jeanette. Student, Webster U., 1972-73, U. Mo., 1973-74, U. Mo., St. Louis, 1974-75; BFA, Webster U., 1978. Producing dir., founder Mainstage Theatre, Lake of the Ozarks, Mo., 1978-84; artistic producing dir. Arrow Rock (Mo.) Lyceum Theatre, 1980—; dir. Lyceum Airwaves Theatre, 1985-88; guest instr. acting Mo. Baptist Coll., St. Louis, Stephens Coll., Columbia, Mo. Valley Coll., Marshall, mem. theatre adv. panel Mo. Arts Coun., St. Louis, 1987-90; co-prodr. Mo. State Theatre Conf., St. Louis; mem. citizens adv. bd. KBIA-PBS Radio; adv. com. Inter-Act; Teen to Teen Theatre, Columbia, 1992-93; adjudicator Am. Coll. Theatre Fest, Ruston, La., 1992, Tenn. Arts Commn. Artist Fellowship, Nashville, 1994, Am. Coll. Theatre, 1997. Prodr., dir., actor more than 150 plays and musicals, including 6 world premieres. Facilities chmn. cultural planning com. Columbia Com. on the Arts, 1993-95; adjudicator Prelude awards, Indpls., 1993, 96, Am. Assn. Cmty. Theatre Festival, Ill., 1997. Recipient Mo. Arts award Mo. Arts Coun., 1983, 94, Outstanding Young Men of Am. award U.S. Jaycees, 1983. Mem. Actors Equity Assn. Liberal. Baptist. Avocations: raising children, photography, outdoor activities, history. Office: Arrow Rock Lyceum Theatre High St Arrow Rock MO 65320

BOLLINGER, PAMELA BEEMER, health facilities administrator; b. Chgo., Apr. 7, 1947; d. Eldred Harlan and Shirley Pearl (Olsen) Beemer; m. Gary Allen Bollinger, Aug. 23, 1969. BS, Millikin U., 1969. Med. technologist Rush-Presbyt. St. Luke's Med. Ctr., Chgo., 1969-70, exec. technologist, 1975-77; hematology supr. Meml. Hosp. DuPage County, Elmhurst, Ill., 1970-75; chief med. technologist U. Tex.-M.D. Anderson Hosp., Houston, 1977-88; lab. dir. Northeast Med. Ctr. Hosp., Humble, Tex., 1988-93; regional field svc. mgr. Corning Clin. Lab., Irving, Tex., 1994—; cons. Technicon Instruments Corp., Tarrytown, N.Y., 1984-88, Coulter Electronics, Inc., Hialeah, Fla., 1978-83. Contbg. author: Clinical Laboratory Annual, 1984, Phlebotomy Handbook, 1984, Clinical Hematology: Principles, Procedures, Correlations, 1988. Vol. Ponderosa Forest Civic Assn., Houston, 1985, Muscular Dystrophy Assn., Houston, 1980-81. Mem. Am. Soc. Clin. Pathology (cert.), Am. Soc. Med. Tech. (Joseph J. Kleiner meml. award 1985), Tex. Soc. Med. Tech. Avocations: interior design, fashion consulting, reading. Home: 5037 Albany Dr Plano TX 75093-5076 Office: Baylor Univ Med Ctr 3600 Gaston Ave Dallas TX 75246-1800

BOLLMAN, MARK BROOKS, JR., communications executive; b. Meriden, Conn., Aug. 24, 1925; s. Mark B. and Esther (Stevens) B.; m. Barbara Ann Smith, July 8, 1928; children—Mark Brooks, III, Richard N., Steven A. A.B., Princeton U., 1949; M.B.A., Harvard U., 1951. Sr. v.p. Benton & Bowles Inc., N.Y.C., 1968-70; exec. v.p. Diners Club Inc., N.Y.C., 1970-72; corp. v.p. Magnavox Co., N.Y.C., 1972-75; pres. McDonald & Little Inc., Atlanta, 1975-77; sr. v.p., sr. ptnr., dir. N.W. Ayer and Ptnrs., N.Y.C., 1977-95; pres. M & B Communications, 1978—. Served with AUS, 1944-46. Decorated Purple Heart. Republican. Episcopalian. Clubs: Clinton (Conn.); Stanwich (Greenwich, Conn.). Home: 20 Rockwood Ln Greenwich CT 06830-3815

BOLLUM, FREDERICK JAMES, biotechnology executive; b. Ellsworth, Wis., June 14, 1927; s. Frederick Edward and Helen (Buchholz) B.; m. Joan Bachman, July 18, 1948 (div. Sept. 1974); children: Thomas, Jane, Barbara, Susan. B.A., U. Minn., 1949, Ph.D., 1956. Postdoctoral fellow U. Wis., Madison, 1956-58; biochemist Oak Ridge Nat. Lab., 1958-65; prof. biochemistry U. Ky., Lexington, 1965-77; prof. Uniformed Services U. Health Scis., Bethesda, Md., 1977-89; chmn. dept. biochemistry Uniformed Services U. Health Scis., 1977-81; pres. Supertechs Inc, 1989—; vis. prof. Univ. de Santiago, Chile, 1969, U. Calif. Med. Center, San Francisco, 1973, Johns Hopkins Med. Sch., Balt., 1983; cons. NIH, 1969-73, 75-77, Am. Cancer Soc., 1972-72. Mem. editorial bd.: Jour. Biol. Chemistry, 1966-69, Biochemistry, 1977-80. Served with USCGR, 1945-46; Served with USNR, 1951-53. Recipient K.A. Forster prize Mainz, 1974, Merit award NIH, 1986; USPHS fellow, 1956-58, 72-73. Fellow AAAS; mem. Am. Chem. Soc., Am. Soc. Biol. Chemists, Sigma Xi. Club: Cosmos (Washington). Discoverer of mammalian DNA polymerase and terminal transferase. Home: 10213 Sundance Ct Potomac MD 20854-4052 Office: Supertechs Inc 9610 Med Cte Dr Ste 101 Rockville MD 20850

BOLLUYT, LINDA BETH, library director; b. Aug. 5, 1948. BS, Northwestern Coll., Orange City, Iowa, 1970. Elem. tchr. Glidden (Iowa)-Ralston Cmty. Sch., 1970-72; dir. Spirit Lake (Iowa) Pub. Libr., 1980—. E-mail: publib@spirit-lake.ki2.ia.us.

BOLMAN, RALPH MORTON, III (CHIP BOLMAN), cardiac surgeon; b. Ft. Wayne, Ind., Dec. 6, 1946; s. Ralph Morton and Jean (Bonham) B.; m. Ceeya Patton, Oct. 10, 1975; children: Paige, Melissa. BA, Williams Coll., 1969; MD, St. Louis U., 1973. Diplomate Am. Bd. Surgery, Am. Bd. Thoracic Surgery. Resident in surgery Duke U., Durham, N.C., 1973-80; resident in thoracic surgery U. Minn., Mpls., 1980-82, asst. prof. surgery, 1982-84; assoc. prof. surgery Washington U. Sch. Medicine, St. Louis, 1984-88; prof. surgery, chief cardiovasc. & thoracic surgery U. Minn., Mpls., 1989—; dir. cardiac surgery Health Ptnrs., Mpls., 1995—; bd. govs. U. Minn. Health Sys., Mpls., 1994-97; bd. dirs. Preferred One, Mpls. Bd. dirs. United Network of Organ Sharing, Richmond, Va., 1988-90. Mem. Am. Surg. Assn., Am. Assn. Thoracic Surgery, Internat. Soc. Heart & Lung Transplantation (bd. dirs. 1994-95), Soc. Univ. Surgeons. Avocations: fly fishing, cycling, running, hiking, reading. Office: U Minn Box 207 MNHC 420 Delaware St SE Minneapolis MN 55455-0374*

BOLOGNESI, DANI PAUL, virologist, educator; b. Forgaria, Italy, Mar. 19, 1941; s. Carlo and Marina (Iem) B.; m. Sarah Sampson, Aug. 1, 1964; children: James, Michael. B.S., Rensselaer Poly. Inst., 1963, M.S., 1965; Ph.D. in Virology, Duke U., 1967. Rsch. assoc. dept. surgery Duke U., 1967-68; NIH postdoctoral fellow Max-Planck Institut für Virusforschung, Tübingen, Fed. Republic Germany, 1968-71; asst. prof. surgery, microbiology and immunology Duke U., Durham, N.C., 1971-72; assoc. prof. surgery, assoc. prof. microbiology and immunology Duke U., 1972-77, prof. surgery, prof. microbiology and immunology, 1977-84, James B. Duke prof. exptl. surgery, 1984—, dir. AIDS Ctr. for Rsch., 1989—; CEO Trimeris Corp., Durham, N.C., 1998—; cons., mem. med. and sci. adv. com. Leukemia Soc. Am.; mem. NIH Virology Study Sect.; mem. Bd. Sci. Counselors, chmn. subcom. on AIDS. Editor AIDS Research and Human Retroviruses, 1987—; mem. editorial bd.: Cancer Research, 1978—, Virology, 1978—. Mem. Sigma Xi. Home: 17 Harvey Pl Durham NC 27705-5628 Office: Duke U Med Ctr 204 Sorf Bldg PO Box 2926 Durham NC 27710*

BOLOGNESI, GIANCARLO, linguist, orientalist, educator; b. Milan, Italy, Oct. 20, 1923; s. Pietro and Maria (Conti) B. Degree, Cath. U., Milan, 1945. From asst. lectr. to prof. Linguistics Cath. U., Milan, 1946—, dir. Linguistics Inst., 1954—, vice chancellor, 1972-80, pres. acad. scis., 1985-90; pres. Linguistics Soc., Milan, 1983—; conservator Libr. and Picture Gallery, Milan, 1977—; bd. dirs. Cultural Found. "Ambrosianeum", Milan, 1981—; v.p. Acad. Scis., Milan, 1991—. Author: Origins of Iranian Loanwords in Armenian, 1960, Aelfrics's Latin Grammar, 1967, Linguistic Philological Oriental Writings, 1990, G. Leopardi and Armenian, 1994, The Progymnasmata of Theon, 1997, Byron and Armenian, 1997, On the Indo-European Consonant System, 1998; editl. bd. mem. Annual of Armenian Linguistics, 1980—. Recipient Gold medal Min. Edn., 1975. Mem. Internat. Soc. Armenian Studies, Soc. Lexicol. Computing (exec. com. 1987—), Nat. Virgilian Acad., Nat. Acad. Scis. of Armenia, Rotary Club (pres. 1985-86, Paul Harris fellow 1987). Avocations: travel, photography. Home: via Santa Croce 10, 20122 Milan Italy Office: Cath Univ, Largo A Gemelli 1, 20123 Milan Italy

BOLOGNIA, JEAN LYNN, academic dermatologist; b. Hammond, Ind., July 1, 1954; d. John Paul and Jo Ann (Dill) B.; m. Dennis Lawrence Cooper, Aug. 25, 1985. BA summa cum laude, Rutgers U., 1976; MD cum laude, Yale U., 1980. Diplomate Nat. Bd. Med. Examiners, Am. Bd. Dermatology. Intern, resident in internal medicine Yale-New Haven Hosp., 1980-82, resident in dermatology, 1982-85; rsch. fellow dermatology Yale U. Sch. Medicine, New Haven, 1985-87, asst. prof. dermatology, 1987-93, assoc. prof. dermatology, 1993-97, prof. dermatology, 1997—, dir. residency tng. program, 1994—; mem. coalition for dermatol. care women Am. Acad. Dermatology/Soc. Investigative Dermatology/Women's Dermatol. Soc., Schaumburg, Ill., 1994-98, chair 1997-98; med. coun. Skin Cancer Found., N.Y.C., 1995—; mem. grad. med. edn. com. Yale New Haven Hosp., 1996—; lectr. more than 20 univs. and internat. meetings. Author: (book chpt.) Harrison's Principles Internal Medicine, 1990, 94, 97; contbr. articles to profl. jours. including Nature, Jour. Investigative Dermatology, Archives Dermatology; mem. editl. bd. Jour. Women's Health, Pigment Cell Rsch., Current Opinion in Dermatology. Recipient Individual Nat. Rsch. award Nat. Inst. Cancer, 1987-89; rsch. fellow Dermatology Found., 1985. Mem. Am. Acad. Dermatology (melanoma/skin cancer com. 1995-99, regulatory guidelines 1994-96, interdisciplinary edn. com. 1996—, environment coun. 1997—, manpower com. 1998—, intersoc. liaison coun. 1997-98, bd. dirs. Sulzberger Inst. 1998—, audit com. 1999—), Am. Dermatol. Assn., Soc. for Investigative Dermatology (resident/fellow program com. 1996—), Am. Bd. Dermatology (in-house tng. exam com. 1996-99), Women's Dermatol. Soc. (networking com. 1996-99, chair, 1996-98, audit com. 1998—, bd. dirs. 1999—, newsletter editor 1999—), Assn. Profs. Dermatology, Dermatology Found. (med. and sci. com. 1997—), Pan Am. Soc. for Pigment Cell Rsch. (coun. 1998—), Med. Dermatology Soc. (pres.-elect 1999). Achievements include patent for enhancing depigmentation therapy; research in depigmentation therapy, characteristics of nevi and melanoma, disorders of pigmentation. Avocations: gardening, collecting antiques. Office: Yale U Sch Medicine 500 LCI 333 Cedar St New Haven CT 06510-3289

BOLOKER, ROSE L., school psychologist; b. Bklyn., Mar. 18, 1951; d. Charles and Frances (Frey) B. BS in Psychology with honors, Bklyn. Coll., 1984; MS in Edn., Bklyn. Coll., CUNY, 1986. Cert. sch. psychologist. Sch. psychologist N.Y.C. Bd. Edn., Bklyn., 1986—, field trainer, 1990—; co-dir. Biofeedback Tng. Inst., Bklyn., 1987-88. Bd. dirs., crew chief, tng. officer Flatlands Vol. Ambulance Corps, Bklyn., 1975-82. Mem. Nat. Assn. Sch. Psychologists, N.Y. Assn. Sch. Psychologists, Assn. Applied Psychophysiology and Biofeedback, Kappa Delta Pi. Home: 2163 E 23rd St Brooklyn NY 11229-3645 Office: NYC Bd Edn CSE Dist 19 301 Vermont St Brooklyn NY 11207-3511

BOLOMEY, ROGER HENRY, sculptor; b. Torrington, Conn., Oct. 19, 1918; s. Henry Albert and Ida (Vurlod) B.; m. Alice Susanne Ryser, June 11, 1948; children: Florence Susanne, Yvonne Marguerite. Student, Acad. Fine Arts, Florence, Italy, 1947, U. Lausanne, Switzerland, 1947-48, Calif. Coll. Arts and Crafts, Oakland, 1948-50. Prof. Herbert H. Lehman Coll., CUNY, 1968-75; prof., chmn. dept. art Calif. State U. at Fresno, 1975-83; painter, 1948-60, sculptor, 1960—; mem. adv. bd. Mus. No. Ariz. Art Inst., Flagstaff, 1976-78, Nat. Sculpture Conf., U. Kans., Lawrence, 1971-80. Chosen to execute 2 large sculptures for state office bldg., Albany, N.Y., 1967, sculpture for, new Nassau County Supreme Ct. Bldg., 1968, Lehman High Sch., Bronx, N.Y., 1969, Eastridge Mall, San Jose, Cal., 1970, N.Y. State Office Bldg., Hauppauge, N.Y., 1973, others.; one-man shows including, Bolles Gallery, San Francisco, 1960, Royal Marks Gallery, N.Y.C., 1964, 65, numerous group exhbns., 1960—, including, 66th Arm. Exhbn., Chgo. Art Inst., 1962, Salon de Mai, Paris (France) Mus. Art, 1963, 64, Whitney Mus., 1964, Larry Aldrich Mus., Ridgefield, Conn., 1964, Carnegie Inst. Internat. Exhbn., 1964, Whitney Mus., 1964, 66, Highlights, 1964-65, Larry Aldrich Mus., 1965, Quatrieme Expn. Suisse de Sculpture, Bienne, Switzerland, 1966, Amerikanische Kunst aus Schweizer Besitz, St. Gallen, Switzerland, 1966, Contemporary Am. Painting and Sculpture, U. Ill. at Urbana, 1967; represented permanent collections, Mus. Modern Art, San Francisco Mus. Modern Art, Whitney Mus., Slädlische Kunsthalle, Mannheim, W.Ger., Larry Aldrich Mus., Bundy Art Gallery, Waitsfield, Vt., San Francisco Art Inst., Oakland Mus., Los Angeles County Mus., U. Calif. Mus. Art, Berkeley, Chase Manhattan Bank, N.Y.C., also numerous pvt. collections; curator: Forgotten Dimension. Recipient 1st prize, commn. for large mural San Jose (Calif.) State Coll. competition, 1962, 1st prize, purchase award Bundy Art Gallery competition, 1963, Sculpture prize 84th Ann. competition San Francisco Art Inst., 1965. Hon. fellow Royal Acad. Fine Arts (Hague, Netherlands); mem. San Francisco Art Inst., Am. Fedn. Arts. First to use polyurethane from its fluid form as a medium of art. Address: 6968 Sweetwater Ct Boulder CO 80301-3836 *My ultimate goal is to live a fully creative life with the hope that what I do and the way I live will stimulate others to do the same.*

BOLOOKI, HOOSHANG, cardiac surgeon; b. Langeh, Iran, Mar. 28, 1937; came to U.S., 1960, naturalized, 1976; s. Hossein and Fatima (Arjomand) B.; m. C. Joanne McDonald, Aug. 30, 1975; children: Hooshang Michael, Cyrus William, Andrew John. BS cum laude, Alborz Coll., Tehran, 1954; MD, Tehran U., 1960. Intern, resident in surgery Kings County Hosp.; asst. instr. SUNY Med. Center, Bklyn., 1961-67; resident in thoracic and cardiovascular surgery Jackson Meml. Hosp. and U. Miami Sch. Medicine, 1967-69; faculty U. Miami (Fla.) Med. Sch., 1969-77, prof. surgery, 1977—; attending surgeon, dir. adult cardiac surgery Jackson Meml. Hosp., 1969—; dir. cardiopulmonary transplant program U. Miami Jackson Meml. Hosp., 1986-98; cons. VA Hosp., Miami, 1977-90; mem. adv. panel cardiovascular surgery Ethicon Inc., Davis & Geck Co., Inc. Author: Clinical Application of Intra-Aortic Balloon Pump, 1976, 3d edit., 1998, Medical Examination Review, Thoracic Surgery, 2d edit., 1972, 3d edit. Vol. 18, 1981, Cardiovascular Surgery, Vol. 38, 1981; contbr. articles to profl. jours. Recipient Research Career Devel. award NIH, 1972-77, grantee, 1972-75; recipient Grand award U. Tex. Med. Br., 1968. Fellow ACS, Royal Coll. Surgeons Can., Am. Coll. Cardiology, Am. Coll. Chest Physicians; mem. AMA (cert. merit), Am. Surg. Assn., Am. Assn. Thoracic Surgery, Soc. Univ. Surgeons, Am. Heart Assn., Fla. Heart Assn. (cert. of merit), Fla. Thoracic Soc., Soc. for Thoracic Surgeons, So. Thoracic Surg. Assn. (membership com. 1985-87, chmn. 1989, v.p. 1991), Soc. Internat. de Chirugie, Internat. Cardiovascular Soc., Soc. Vascular Surgery, Internat. Soc. Heart & Lung Transplantation, Soc. Acad. Surgeons, David Park Racquet Club, Ski Club. Republican. Moslem. Office: U Miami Sch Med Thoracic Cardio Surgery R-114 Miami FL 33101

BOLOTIN, LORA M., retired business owner, electronics executive; b. Dallas; d. Joseph and Bertha Marshall; m. M. L. Bolotin, June 21, 1953; children: Linda Susan, Scott Evan, Kent Carter. BA in Edn., Roosevelt U., 1952; postgrad., UCLA, 1980, Calif. State U., Northridge, 1988. Cert. tchr., Ill. Tchr. Chgo. Bd. Edn., 1952-55; v.p. Bolotin Assocs., Inc., Woodland Hills, Calif., 1973-83, pres., 1984-96, ret. Art Inst. of Chgo. scholar, 1946; recipient 2 Sterling Silver Art medals, Am. Legion, 1946, 47. Avocations: travel, sailing, reading, painting.

BOLOTOWSKY, ANDREW ILYITCH, flutist, composer; b. N.Y.C., Aug. 20, 1949; s. Ilya Yulevitch and Meta (Cohen) B. Studied with William Kincaid, Phila., 1963-67; studied with Elaine Schaffer, N.Y.C., 1967; studied with Jean-Pierre Rampal, France, 1967; BA, New Sch. Social Rsch., 1971. 1st flute Pan Am. Orch., 1982—; flutist Am. Festival of Microtonal Music, N.Y.C., 1983—, Downtown Music Ensemble, N.Y.C., 1983-84, 92-94, Downtown Music Prodns., 1983—; 1st flute Philharm. Symphony Westchester, 1987-90; with Am. Landmark Festivals, 1973—; baroque flutist Muse, 1987—, Am. Landmark Festival Concerts, 1973—; performer over 2500 concerts, U.S.a., 1967—; vis. artist Beloit (Wis.) Coll., 1970-73; mime and flute in concert, 1974-84; Delbarton Baroque Ensemble, 1978-81; Criterion Concerts Guggenheim Mus., N.Y.c., 1979; artist N.Y. Com. for Young Audiences, N.Y.C., 1980-87; artist in residence summer mus. theater workshop NYU, 1981; pres. SoHo Baroque Opera Co., N.Y.C., 1983—, Laurel Arts Festival, Jim Thorpe, Pa., 1991, 92, 93, 94. Rec. artist 6 Serenades by Fernando Carulli, 1978, 20th Century Music for Flute and Guitar, 1978, Music for Flute and Mime, 1982, Behavioral Drift by Franz Kamin, 1980, What The Wind Told, 1979, Scribble Music Sampler by Franz Kamin, 1983,

Poetry Music Quilts by Beth Anderson, 1982, Mark Steven Brooks: Compositions 1973-87, 1987; recs. include Pitch, Vol. I No. 3, 1988-89, Indian Summer by Tui St. George Tucker, Opus 1 records No. 107, Timepieces by Rita Falbel, 1991, Between the Keys, Newport Classic CD, 1992, Open Secrets (by Jackson Maclow), 1993 XICD, The Music of Frank Wigglesworth, CRI CD 733, Raj Kapoor's CD Kathmandu Embrace, 1997, Crayon (Jackson Maclow issue), 1997, Melody Sumner Carnahan The Time IS Now, Frog Peak Music CD, 1998, Johnny Reinhard's Raven, Stereo Soc. CD, 1999, Judith St. Croix's Vision of Light and Mystery, Sonic Muse CD, 1999, also others; editor Flute Charts for "Pitch", vol. I number 4, 1990; live performances on radio and tv including Stas. WBAI, WQXR, WNYC New Sounds, WKCR, WFUV, NBC, CBS, NYC-TV; extra (films) Eyewitness, 1980, Godfather III, 1990. Grantee Carnegie Recital Hall, Tully Hall Criterion Found., 1976, 77, 78, 79, Meet the Composer, 1978, 80. Avocations: study of earlier flute systems, walking tours, Russian literature. Office: PO Box 492 New York NY 10003

BOLSTER, ARCHIE MILBURN, retired foreign service officer; b. Ames, Iowa, Apr. 9, 1933; s. Horace Goodwin and Ella Schimpf B.; m. Ann Dorcas Matthews, Mar. 22, 1959; children: Christopher, Matthew, Amy. B.A. in Internat. Relations, U. Va., 1955; M.A. in Pub. Policy and Adminstrn., U. Wis., 1972. Commd. fgn. service officer Dept. State, 1958; assigned Phnom Penh, Cambodia, 1959-60, Tabriz, Iran, 1961-63, Tehran, Iran, 1964-66, 74-76; assigned Bur. Intelligence and Research, 1966-68, Office Fuels and Energy, 1969-71; consul gen. Antwerp, Belgium, 1978-81; dep. dir. Div. Office Security Assistance and Sales, 1981-83; dep. chief Aviation Negotiations Div., 1983-84; spl. projects officer Bur. Refugee Programs, 1984-86; Freedom of Info. Act reviewer, 1984-94, 97—; mem. White House Counsel's Iran-Contra Task Force, 1987-90; mem. staff U.S.-Iran Claims Tribunal, The Hague, Netherlands, 1994-96. Chmn. editorial bd.: Fgn. Service Jour, 1971. Pres. Williamsburg Civic Assn., Arlington, Va., 1969-70. Served with USNR, 1955-58. Mem. Am. Fgn. Svc. Assn., Assn. Part-Time Profls. (bd. dirs., v.p. 1989-91). Home: 2738 N Lexington St Arlington VA 22207-1437

BOLSTER, ARTHUR STANLEY, JR., history educator; b. Bismarck, N.D., Jan. 30, 1922; s. Arthur S. and Gertrude (Pierce) B.; m. Elizabeth Barker Winkfield, Oct. 8, 1949; children: Stephen Clark, Gregory Pierce. A.B., Dartmouth, 1943; M.A., Harvard, 1947, Ph.D., 1954. Tchr. history Grosse Pointe (Mich.) High Sch., 1952-57, Pelham (N.Y.) High Sch., 1957-59; mem. faculty Harvard U., Cambridge, Mass., 1959—; prof. edn. Harvard U., 1967-82, prof. emeritus, 1982—. Author: James Freeman Clarke, Disciple to Advancing Truth, 1954. Served to lt. USNR, 1943-46. Mem. New Eng. History Tchrs. Assn. (pres. 1968-69, Kidger award 1970), Phi Beta Kappa. Mem. United Ch. of Christ (deacon). Home: 587 Laconia Cir Lake Worth FL 33467-2662 Office: Harvard U Grad Sch Edn Longfellow Hall Cambridge MA 02138

BOLSTER, JACQUELINE NEBEN (MRS. JOHN A. BOLSTER), communications consultant; b. Woodhaven, N.Y.; d. Ernest William Benedict and Emily Claire (Guck) Neben; student Pratt Inst., Columbia U.; m. John A. Bolster, May 8, 1954. Promotion mgr. Photoplay mag., 1949-53; merchandising mgr. McCall's, N.Y.C., 1953-64; dir. promotion and merchandising Harper's Bazaar, N.Y.C., 1964-71; dir. advt. and promotion Elizabeth Arden Salons, N.Y.C., 1971-76; dir. creative services Elizabeth Arden, Inc., 1976-78, dir. communications Elizabeth Arden Salons, 1978-87, communication cons., 1987—. Recipient Art Director's award 1961, 66. Mem. Fashion Group, Fashion Execs. Roundtable, Inner Circle, Advt. Women N.Y. (life), Women's Nat. Rep. Club (life). Episcopalian. Home and Office: 8531 88th St Woodhaven NY 11421-1308 also: Halsey Neck Ln Southampton NY 11968

BOLSTER, RONALD HUGH, company executive; b. Pitts., Oct. 17, 1939; s. Herbert Louis and Janet Donaldson Bolster; m. Patricia Marie Lebec, Sept. 16, 1961. HVAC tech., Gateway Tech., 1973. Cert. HVAC contractor. Technician Dual Refrigeration, Pitts., 1972, McDonald Heating, Pitts., 1973-74; pres., treas. Bolster-Dehart, Pitts., 1974—. Choir mem. St. John's Ch., Pitts., 1939-68, Wexford, Pa., 1968-97, Perry Hwy. Ch., Pitts., 1997-99. Staff sgt. U.S. Army, 1961-66. Mem. ACCA, N.H. Builders Assn., N.H. Chamber. Democrat. Lutheran. Office: Bolster-Dehart Inc 333 Rochester Rd Pittsburgh PA 15237

BOLSTER, WILLIAM LAWRENCE, broadcast executive; b. Waterloo, Iowa, Nov. 28, 1943; s. William and Mildred Bolster; m. Eileen Madigan; children: Bill, Brian, Barry. Grad., Loras Coll. With Am. Blackhawk Broadcasting Co., Waterloo, 1967-73, v.p., 1973-83; v.p., gen. mgr. Sta. KWWL-TV div. Am. Blackhawk Broadcasting Co., Waterloo, 1977-83, Sta. KSDK-TV, St. Louis, 1983-89; former pres. Multimedia Broadcasting Co.; pres., CEO CNBC, Fort Lee, N.J.; pres. NBC4-TV, N.Y.C., 1991-96; pres. NBC Lafin Am. Mem. bd. regents Briar Cliff Coll.; trustee St. Louis U., NBC-TV Affiliate; bd. dirs. Regional Plan Assn.; mem. adv. bd. TV Bur.; mem. TV Operators Caucus Bd. Named Man of Yr. Variety Club, 1983; recipient 1st Media award for outstanding coverage and fin. assistance to black community NAACP, St. Louis, Ellis Island Gold medal of achievement. Mem. NATAS (pres., bd. dirs. St. Louis chpt. 1987), Nat. Assn. Broadcasters (children's TV com.), Waterloo C. of C. (bd. dirs.). Office: CNBC Nat Broadcasting Co Inc 2200 Fletcher Ave Fort Lee NJ 07024-5005

BOLSTERLI, MARGARET JONES, English educator, farmer; b. Watson, Ark., May 10, 1931; d. Grover Clevel and Zena (Cason) Jones; m. Mark Bolsterli, Dec. 30, 1953 (div. Dec. 1964); children: Eric, David. BA with honors, U. Ark., 1952; MA, Washington U., St. Louis, 1953; PhD, U. Minn., 1967. Asst. prof. Augsburg Coll., Mpls., 1967-68; prof. English, U. Ark., Fayetteville, 1968-93, prof. emeritus, 1993—, dir. Ctr. for Ark. and Regional Studies, 1984-87; Fulbright lectr., Portugal, 1986; vis. rsch. fellow Yale U., 1997-98; bd. dirs. Ark. Humanities Coun., 1992-94. Author: The Early Community at Bedford Park, 1977, Vinegar Pie and Chicken Bread, 1982, Born in the Delta, 1991, A Remembrance of Eden, 1993; contbr. articles and stories to Jour. Modern Lit., So. Quar., others. NEH Younger Humanist grantee, 1970-71; Ark. Endowment for Humanities grantee, 1980, 81. Mem. MLA (pres. women's caucus), South Cen. MLA. Democrat.

BOLT, BRUCE ALAN, seismologist, educator; b. Largs, Australia, Feb. 15, 1930; came to U.S., 1963; naturalized, 1972; s. Donald Frederick and Arlene (Stitt) B.; m. Beverley Bentley, Feb. 11, 1956; children: Gillian, Robert, Helen, Margaret. BS with honors, New Eng. U. Coll., 1952; MS, U. Sydney, Australia, 1954, PhD, 1959, DSc (hon.), 1972. Math. master Sydney (Australia) Boys' High Sch., 1953; lectr. U. Sydney, 1954-61, sr. lectr., 1961-62; research seismologist Columbia U., 1960; dir. seismographic stas. U. Calif., Berkeley, 1963-89, prof. seismology, 1963-93, prof. emeritus, 1993—, chmn. acad. senate Berkeley divsn., 1993-94; mem. com. on seismology NAS, 1966-72, chmn. nat. earthquake obs. com., 1979-81; earthquake and wind forces com. VA, 1971-75; mem. Calif. Seismic Safety Commn., 1978-93, chmn., 1984-86; earthquake studies adv. panel U.S. Geol. Survey, 1979-83, U.S. Geodynamics Com., Am. Geophys. Union, 1979-84; seismic adv. bd. Calif. Dept. Transp., 1994—; pres. Consortium Strong Motion Sys. Inc., 1999—. Author, editor textbooks on applied math., earthquakes, geol. hazards and detection of underground nuclear explosions. Recipient H.O. Wood award in seismology, 1967-72, Alquist Silver medal Calif. Earthquake Safety Found., 1995; Fulbright scholar, 1960; Churchill Coll. Cambridge overseas fellow, 1980, 91. Fellow Am. Geophys. Union (mem. geophys. monograph bd. 1971-78, chmn. 1976-78), Geol. Soc. Am., Calif. Acad. Scis. (trustee 1981-92, 1998—, pres. 1982-85, Fellows medal 1989), Royal Astron. Soc. (assoc.); mem. Nat. Acad. Engring. (IDNDR com. 1992-94), Seismol. Soc. Am. (editor bull. 1965-70, bd. dir. 1965-71, 73-76, pres. 1974-75), Internat. Assn. Seismology and Physics Earth's Interior (exec. com. 1964-67, v.p. 1975-79, pres. 1980-83), Earthquake Engring. Rsch. Inst. (Dist. Lectr. 1998), Calif. Univs. Rsch. Earthquake Engring. (sec. 1988-91), Australian Math. Soc., Chit Chat Club, Bohemian Club, U. Calif. Berkeley Faculty Club (pres. 1996—). Achievements include research on dynamics, elastic waves, earthquakes, reduction geophys. observations; inferences on structure of earth's interior; cons. on seismic hazards. Home: 1491 Greenwood Ter Berkeley CA 94708-1935

BOLT, DAWN MARIA, real estate agent, financial adviser; b. Bklyn., June 12, 1949; d. Gulick Arthur B. and Georgette Helen (Werner) Bolt-Wiggs; widowed; children: Robert B. Williams, Wesley A. Williams. BA, Bklyn. Coll., 1971. Cert. fin. planner; chartered fin. analyst. Fin. analyst Blyth Eastman Dillon, N.Y.C., 1971-77; rating agy. analyst Fitch Investors Svc., N.Y.C., 1977-78; bank analyst Merrill Lynch, N.Y.C., 1978-80; fin. analyst Moodys Investors Svc., N.Y.C., 1980-86; real estate sales agt. J.R. Silvers Realty, N.Y.C., 1987-95, Coldwell Banker Hunt Kennedy, N.Y.C., 1995-98; pvt. practice fin. planning, 1998—. Avocations: bowling, tennis, skiing, reading. Office: Coldwell Banker Hunt Kennedy 1200 Lexington Ave New York NY 10028-1426

BOLT, THOMAS, writer, artist; b. Washington, Nov. 21, 1959; m. Sophie Claire Forrester, Nov. 1, 1991. BA, U. Va., 1982. Author: (poetry) Land, 1982, Out of the Woods, 1989, Dark Ice, 1993.; contbg. editor BOMB, 1989—. Recipient Yale Younger Poets prize Yale U. Press, 1988, Rome prize for lit. Am. Acad. Arts and Letters, 1993, Peter I. B. Lavan Younger Poet award Acad. Am. Poets, 1993, Elizabeth Matchett Stover Best Poem award, 1994; Ingram Merrill fellow, 1991, Artists fellow N.Y. State Found. for the Arts, 1997. Fellow Am. Acad. Rome, 1994. Office: 110 Suffolk St New York NY 10002-3309*

BOLT, THOMAS ALVIN WALDREP, lawyer; b. Anderson, S.C., Dec. 1, 1956; s. Thomas Alvin Waldrep Jr. and Jane Gray (Sullivan) Thompson; m. Jenifer Smith, Sept. 2, 1989; 1 stepchild, Royce Stevenson Ward. BA in Govt. and English, Wofford Coll., 1978; postgrad., U. S.C., 1980-81, JD, 1982. Bar: V.I., 1983. Asst. to Gov. Exec. Office of Gov., Columbia, S.C., 1979; exec. asst. S.C. Senate, Columbia, 1979-80; legal clk. S.C. Pub. Svc. Commn., Columbia, 1981; legis. asst. S.C. Ho. of Reps., Columbia, 1981-82; asst. to atty. gen. Office of Atty. Gen., Columbia, 1982; asst. legis. counsel Legis. of V.I., St. Thomas, V.I., 1983-87; counsel to pres. Legis. of V.I., 1987, counsel to the majority, 1987-88; counsel to the commn. U.S. V.I. Law Revision Commn., St. Thomas, 1988-91; pvt. practice Tom Bolt & Assocs. P.C., St. Thomas, V.I., 1991—; intern UN, N.Y.C., 1976; commr. Nat. Conf. Commrs. on Uniform State Laws, Chgo., 1988—, chmn. drafting com. on Money Svc. Bus. Act, 1996—; prof. law U. V.I., St. Thomas; tchr. history All Saints Cathedral Sch., 1983; mem. bd. advisors V.I. Bus. Jour., 1994-98. Editor: Revised United States Virgin Islands Criminal Code, 1988-91. State committeeman S.C. Dem. Com., Columbia, 1980-83, vice chmn., 1980-82; territorial committeeman V.I. Dem. Com., St. Thomas, 1988-92; mem. Friends of Denmark, LWV, St. Thomas Arts Coun., V.I. Youth Multi-Svc. Ctr.; treas. Coun. on Alcoholism St. Thomas-St. John, 1992-93; sec. St. Thomas Hist. Trust, 1987-88; pres. Blackbeard's Hill Neighborhood Assn., 1988—; bd. dirs. Friends of Baa, Pub. Libr ., 1994—, pres., 1995—. Frank Hoke Leadership scholar Delta Sigma Phi, 1976, Am. Legion scholar, 1978-82. Mem. ABA (ho. of dels. 1989—, drafting com. 1992-96, house com. state and local bar assns. 1996—, Am. Law Inst. com. on continuing profl. edn. 1992-95, membership com. 1989—, sect. on adminstrv. law and regulatory practice, vice chmn. state adminstrv. law com. 1990—, sect. on internat. law and practice Caribbean law com. 1990—, real estate interest group sect. on law practice mgmt., sect. on urban, state and local govt.; govt. ops. com., young lawyers divsn., vice chmn. cmty. law week com., exec. subcom., govt. lawyers com.), Attys. Liability Protection Soc. (bd. dirs. 1995—), Am. Law Network (bd. dirs.), V.I. Bar Assn. (bd. govs. 1988, 90—, chmn. com. legis. and law reform 1987-93), St. Thomas-St. John C. of C., Rotary (sgt. arms 1991-92, bd. dirs. St. Thomas II chpt. 1987-89, 90-92, clk. consistory bd. dirs. 1991-93. Mem. Reformed Ch. Am. Avocations: travel, sailing, hist. preservation. Home: Morning Star Beach Saint Thomas VI 00802 Office: Corporate Pl Royal Dane Mall Charlotte Amalie VI 00802

BOLT, WILLIAM J., military officer. BA in Econs., U. Notre Dame, 1962; Master's degree, U. Va., 1976; grad., Armed Forces Staff Coll., Army War Coll. Commd. 2d lt. U.S. Army, 1962, advanced through grades to lt. gen.; dep. comdg. gen. TRADOC, 1997—. Decorated Disting. Svc. medal, Legion of Merit (3), Bronze Star (3). Office: The Joint Staff Bldg 116 30 Harrison St Fort Monroe VA 23651

BOLTANSKI, CHRISTIAN, painter, photographer; b. Paris, Sept. 6, 1944; s. Etienne and Annie (Lauran) B. Profl. photographer and artist Paris, 1969—. One-man shows include Sonnabend Gallery, N.Y.C., 1973, 75, 79, 82, Musée d'Art Moderne, Paris, 1970, 76, (retrospective) 1981, Mus. Modern Art, Oxford, 1973, Israel Mus., Jerusalem, 1973, Louisiana Mus., Hamleback, Denmark, 1974, Centre Nat. d'Art Contemporian, Paris, 1974, Kunsthalle, Kiel, Fed. Republic of Germany, 1975, Centre d'Art Contemporain, Geneva, 1975, Landesmuseum, Bonn, Fed. Republic of Germany, 1976, Mus. Contemporary Art, La Jolla, Calif., 1977, Galleria Bruno Soletti, Milan, 1977, Musée de Peinture, Calais, 1980, Carpenter Art Ctr., Harvard U., Cambridge, Mass., 1980, Centre Georges Pompidou, Paris, 1984, Kunsthaus, Zurich, Switzerland, 1984, Galerie Crousel-Hussenot, Paris, 1985, Kunstverein, Munich, 1986, Photographer's Gallery, London, 1986, Mus. Contemporary Art, Chgo., 1988, Centro de Arte Reina Sofia, Madrid, 1988, Maria Goodman Gallery, N.Y.C., 1988, 90, Galerie Ghislaine Hussenot, Paris, 1989, Vancouver Art Gallery, 1989, Mus. Contemporary Art, Basle, 1989, Jean Bernier Gallery, Athens, 1989, Marika Malacorda Gallery, Geneva, 1989, Univ. Art Mus., Berkeley, Calif., 1989, Israel Mus., Jerusalem, 1989, Foksal Mus., Warsaw, Poland, 1989, Galerie des Beaux Arts, Brussels, 1990, Kaufmann Gallery, Basle, 1990, Whitechapel Gallery, London, 1990, Mus. de Grenoble, France, 1990, Inst. Contemporary Arts, Nagoya, 1990, 1990, Kunsthalle, Hamburg, Germany, 1991, Lisson Gallery, London, 1991; group shows include Documenta 5, Kassel, Germany, 1972, Venice Biennale, 1980, Westkunst, Cologne, Fed. Republic of Germany, 1981; represented in permanent collections Musée d'Art Moderne, Paris, Kunsthalle, Hamburg, Neue Gallerie, Aachen, Germany, Louisiana Mus., Hamleback, Boymans-van Beuningen Mus., Rotterdam, The Netherlands, Mus. Fine Arts, Lodz, Poland, Israel Mus., Jerusalem, Art Inst. Chgo., Fine Art Houston, Galerie Ghislaine Husseno, Paris, others; author: Reconsitutions des Gestes, 1971, 10 Portraits Photographiques, 1972, Album Photographique, 1972, Inventaire, 1973, Quelques Interpretations, 1974, 10 Regles et Technique, 1975, Les Morts pour Rire, 1975; (with others) Modellbilder, 1976. Recipient Grand Prix nat. de peinture, 1990. Home: 146 blvd Camélinat, 92240 Malakoff France also: care Marian Goodman 24 W 57th St New York NY 10019-3918

BOLTON, CARILE ORVILLE BOGY, auditor, accountant; b. Kingston, Jamaica, Aug. 30, 1962; s. Neville and Nicole (Roth) B.; m. Nandy Seuratton, Sept. 1984; children: Perry, Harry. BS in Acctg., St. John's U., 1983; MBA, Pace U., 1987. FLMI. Auditor Am. Internat. Group, N.Y.C., 1984-90; internal audit mgr. and system analyst Delaware Charter, Wilmington, 1990-94; pres. Cobb Entertainment, Inc., Newark, Del., 1994—. Author/illustrator more than 15 children's books, 1995-96; inventor toys; creator more than 25 amusement park rides, 1990-96; composer more than 15 songs; creator movies and ednl. computer games for children. Avocations: tennis, soccer. Home: 115 Woodshade Dr Newark DE 19702-1413

BOLTON, (MARGARET) ELIZABETH, artist, poet; b. Cranston, R.I., Sept. 7, 1919; d. James Ewart and Pamela (White) Hill; m. Archer Leroy Bolton Jr., Nov. 29, 1941; children: Wendy, Daria, Pamela, James. Student, Colby Sawyer Coll., 1936-39. Sec. Dr. Augustus Thorndike, Boston, 1939-41; sec. rehab. orgn. Mass. Gen. Hosp., Boston, 1950-51; sec. Nat. Acad. Scis., Washington, 1957-60, Mitre Corp. Electronics, Burlington, Mass., 1961-62; exec. sec. Manpower, Burlington, 1961-69; sec. RCA, Burlington, 1962-63; substitute tchr. art pub. high schs., various cities, Mass., 1970-81. Exhibited in various group shows (1st prize 1979, 80); poetry pub. in New Voices, 1981, Golden Treasury of Great Poems, 1989, Vol. II, 1989, Summer Treasury of Poems of America, 1992, Fall Treasury of Poems of America, 1992. Mem. Friends of the Libr., 1986—, Exeter Area Art Assn. Recipient 2d prize Newburyport Art Assn., 1977, 1st prize Nashua Art Assn., 1986, Award of Merit Certs. (2) World of Poetry, 1988, Golden Poet award, 1989, Golden Poet award World of Poetry, 1992. Mem. Christian Ch. Avocations: music, singing, writing, photography, bicycling, bird watching. Home: 12 Glen Dr Hampstead NH 03841-2242

BOLTON, JOHN ROBERT, lawyer, former government official; b. Balt., Nov. 20, 1948; s. Edward Jackson and Virginia (Godfrey) B.; m. Gretchen Brainerd, Jan. 1986; 1 child, Jennifer Sarah. BA summa cum laude, Yale U., 1970, JD, 1974. Bar: D.C. 1975, U.S. Dist. Ct. D.C. 1975, U.S. Ct. Appeals (D.C. cir.) 1975, U.S. Ct. Appeals (4th cir.) 1977, U.S. Ct. Appeals (3d cir.) 1978, U.S. Supreme Ct. 1978, U.S. Ct. Appeals (5th and 11th cirs.) 1981, U.S. Ct. Appeals (10th cir.) 1983, U.S. Ct. Appeals (1st, 6th, 7th, 8th and 9th cirs.) 1988, U.S. Ct. Appeals (2d cir.) 1989. Assoc. Covington & Burling, Washington, 1974-81, ptnr., 1983-85; legal cons. The White House, Washington, 1981; gen. counsel Agy. for Internat. Devel., Washington, 1981-82, asst. adminstr., 1982-83; exec. dir. com. on resolutions Rep. Nat. Com., Washington, 1983-84; asst. atty. gen. legis. affairs U.S. Dept. Justice, Washington, 1985-88, asst. atty. gen. civil div., 1988-89; asst. sec. internat. orgn. affairs bur. U.S. Dept. State, Washington, 1989-93; ptnr. Lerner, Reed, Bolton & McManus (and predecessor firms), Washington, 1993—; adj. prof. George Mason U. Law Sch., 1994—; pres. Nat. Policy Forum, Washington, 1995-96; sr. v.p. Am. Enterprise Inst., Washington, 1997—. Contbr. articles to profl. jours. Mem. Phi Beta Kappa, Pi Sigma Alpha. Republican. Lutheran. Office: 1150 17th St NW Washington DC 20036-4603

BOLTON, KENNETH ALBERT, management consultant; b. Mar. 6, 1941; s. Albert and Myrtle (Nelting) B.; m. Maryanne Lavelle; 1 child, Katharine. BS in Indsl. Engring., Pa. State U., 1978. Registered profl. engr., Calif. With GE, Allentown, Pa., 1961-63; system mgr. GE, Phila., 1963-72; mgr. MCS Mgmt. Internat., Washington, 1972-80, Coopers & Lybrand, Phila., 1980-82; dir. cons. Worden & Risberg, Phila., 1982-83; v.p. mktg. Laminated, Inc., Hatfield, Pa., 1983-86; pres. Mgmt. Internat., Phila., 1986-90, Wm. P. Bolton, Inc., Phila., 1990—. Contbr. articles to profl. jours. Advisor Jr. Achievement, Media, Pa., 1970; mem. adv. bd. Salvation Army. Mem. NSPE, am. Arbitration Assn. (panel of arbitrators), Phila. C. of C. (bd. dirs. 1975, lobbyist small bus. com. 1978), Union League Phila., St. George's Club Bermuda. Republican. Avocations: golf, computers, antiques. Home: 5900 Atlantic Ave Ventnor City NJ 08406-2862 Office: Mgmt Internat 100 S Dorset Ave Ventnor City NJ 08406-2834

BOLTON, KEVIN MICHAEL, human resources executive; b. Boston, Oct. 10, 1951; s. Thomas James and Winifred Agnes (Burke) B.; m. Lynn Thompson, May 30, 1976; children: Neil, Philip, Madeleine. B. Gen. Studies, U. Mich., 1973. CLU; cert. assoc. in risk mgmt. Ins. Inst. Am. Sous-chef Club Switzerland, Fairbanks, Alaska, 1974-76; sales rep. Travelers Ins. Cos., Phoenix, 1977-78; assoc. Third Party Adminstrs., Phoenix, 1979-80; mgr employee benefits, pensions, ERISA reporting, 401K plans Dial Corp., Phoenix, 1981-86; sr. dir. compensation and benefits Greyhound Lines, Inc., Dallas, 1987-92; v.p. pers. liability mgmt. Pittston Coal Mgmt. Co., Lebanon, Va., 1992-94; pres. Human Resources Consulting, Dallas, 1994—; speaker Nat. Employee Benefit Inst., Soc. Ins. Rsch., IF of Employee Benefit Plans. Mem. Greater Phoenix Affordable Health Care Consortium, 1985-87. Mem. Internat. Found. Employee Benefit Plans (bd. dirs. 1988—, new product devel. com. 1988—), Am. Soc. CLU & ChFC, U. Mich. Alumni Soc., Tex. Longhorns Soccer Club (mgr.). Avocation: soccer. Home and Office: 6622 Tulip Ln Dallas TX 75230-4153

BOLTON, ROBERT FLOYD, construction executive; b. Dunlap, Iowa, Oct. 18, 1942; s. Russel J. And Mary Jane (Lacey) B.; m. Mary Louise Hartman, May 15, 1988. Lic. residential/comml. gen. bldg. contractor. Sole practice farming Dunlap, Iowa, 1967-72; supr. Phillips Constrn. Co., Cottonwood, Ariz., 1972-84; contractor Bolton Bldg. and Devel. Co., Sedona, Ariz., 1984—; cons. in field. With U.S. Army, 1964-66. Mem. Nat. Assn. Home Builders, Am. Soc. Home Inspectors, C. of C., VFW, Meth. Mens Fellowship Club. Republican. Methodist. Avocations: reading, hiking, woodworking. Home & Office: 90 Evening Glow Pl Sedona AZ 86351-7912

BOLTON, ROBERT HARVEY, banker; b. Alexandria, La., June 19, 1908; s. James Wade and Mary (Calderwood) B.; m. Elsie Elizabeth McLundie (dec. Mar. 1987); children: Robert Harvey Jr., Elizabeth McLundie (Mrs. Robert Conery Hassinger), Mary Calderwood (Mrs. James Kelly Jennings Jr.); m. Abigail Crow Goodwin. BS, U. Pa., 1930. With credit dept. Guaranty Trust Co., N.Y.C., 1930-32; asst. cashier Rapides Bank & Trust Co., Alexandria, 1932-36, cashier, 1936-43, v.p., 1943-47, exec. v.p., 1947-56, pres., 1956-86, chmn., 1986-90, sr. chmn., 1990—, also bd. dirs.; bd. dirs. New Orleans br. Fed. Res. Bank Atlanta., 1979-81, First Commerce Corp., New Orleans; nat. bd. dirs. Robert Morris Assocs., 1943-45; La. rep. to Conf. State Bank Suprs., 1964-71. Mem. La. State U. Found., Pineville, devel. bd., Pres.'s club, bd. dirs. James C. Bolton Libr., Alexandria; fin. steering com. Attakapas coun. Boy Scouts Am., 1971-84; chmn. Rapides Parish chpt. ARC, 1943, Alexandria Little Theatre, 1942; hon. chmn. La. Coll. Quality Edge Dr. '95; bd. dirs. Rapides United Givers, Indsl. Devel. Bd. Ctrl. La.; mem. exec. com. Ctrl. Cities Devel. Com., Coun. for Better La., 1970—, Bus. and Indsl. Devel. Corp. La., 1971-73; mem. La. Bapt. Conv. Fedn. Bd., 1994-95; deacon Emmanuel Bapt. Ch., chmn. fin. com., chmn. Every Mem. Canvass, 1937-74; mem. citizen's adv. com. La. Spl. Edn. Ctr., La. Pub. Broadcasting; chmn., mem. St. Francis Cabrini Hosp. Found. Bd.; mem. Pub. Affairs Rsch. Coun. Recipient Disting. Svc. award Jr. C. of C., 1943, Humanitarian of Yr. award Arthritis Found., 1990, Disting. Svc. award La. Nat. Guard, Disting. Citizen award Boy Scouts Am., 1991, Outstanding Citizen award YWCA, 1992, Disting. Svc. award Trustees La. Coll., 1993, Rapides Arts & Humanities Cultural Advocate award, 1994. Mem. VFW, Am. Bankers Assn. (pres. state bank divsn. 1955), Mortgage Bankers Assn. (mem. Washington com. 1962-74), La. Bankers Assn. (pres. 1980, mem. legis. study com. 1950—, mem. fed. affairs com. 1971—), La. Mortgage Bankers Assn. (pres. 1952, mem. legis. com. 1970-74), U.S. C. of C. (mem. fin. com. 1964-71), Alexandria-Pineville C. of C. (pres. 1965, chmn. aviation com. 1972-84, military affairs com., econ. devel. com.), Am. Legion, Boston Club, Internat. House Club (New Orleans), Confrerie du Tastevin Club, Masons, Rotary (pres. Alexandria chpt. 1942, Govs. Choice award 1993-94). Home: 3200 Parkway Dr Alexandria LA 71301-4757 Office: Rapides Bank & Trust Co 400 Murray St PO Box 31 Alexandria LA 71309-0031

BOLTON, ROGER EDWIN, economist, educator; b. Dover, Pa., Nov. 23, 1938; s. Oscar Jacob and Edna Irene (Hughes) B.; m. Julia Carolyn Gooden, June 27, 1964; children: Christopher, Jonathan. AB, Franklin and Marshall Coll., 1959; PhD, Harvard U., 1964. Instr. Harvard U., Cambridge, Mass., 1964-66; asst. prof. econs. Williams Coll., Williamstown, Mass., 1966-69, assoc. prof., 1969-74, prof., 1974—, William R. Kenan Jr. prof., 1992-94, Edward Dorr Griffin prof., 1986-91, chmn. dept., 1975-76, 79-81, dir. Ctr. Humanities and Social Scis., 1985-87, chair faculty steering com., 1991-92; vis. prof. Wellesley Coll., 1977, U. Pa., 1981-82; George A. Miller vis. prof. U. Ill., 1988; disting. vis. prof. U. Wis., Madison, 1989; vis. prof. Clark U., 1993; mem. assoc. staff Brookings Instn., 1965-68; sr. economist Curran Assocs., 1973-75; rsch. assoc. Joint Ctr. for Urban Studies, 1979-81. Author: Defense Purchases and Regional Growth, 1966; co-author: Regional Diversity, 1981; editor: Defense and Disarmament, 1966; co-editor Internat. Regional Sci. Rev., 1985-89: mem. editl. bd. Annals Regional Sci., Can. Jour. Regional Sci., Growth and Change; mem. editorial bd., book rev. editor Jour. Regional Sci.; also numerous articles. Mem. Berkshire County Regional Planning Commn., Mass., 1980-81, 82-88, clk., 1983-85, vice-chmn., 1985-87; mem. Williamstown Planning Bd., 1983-86, chmn., 1985-86; bd. dirs. No. Berkshire Indsl. Park and Devel. Corp., chmn., 1986-88. Recipient Outstanding Contbn. to Planning award, 1989; Woodrow Wilson fellow, 1959-60, Danforth fellow, 1959-64. Mem. Am. Econ. Assn., Regional Sci. Assn. (councillor 1988-91), Planning History Group, Assn. Am. Geographers, Am. Fin. Assn., Fin. Mgmt. Assn., Regional Studies Assn. Home: 30 Grandview Dr Williamstown MA 01267-2528 Office: Williams Coll Dept Econs Fernald House Williamstown MA 01267

BOLTON-HOLIFIELD, RUTHIE, basketball player; b. McClain, Miss., May 25, 1967; d. Linwood and Leola Bolton; m. Mark Holifield. B of Exercise Physiology, Auburn U., 1989. Basketball player C.A. Faenza, Italy, 1993, Erreti Faenza, Italy, 1994-95, Sacramento Monarchs, 1997—; mem. U.S.A. Women's Nat. Basketball Team. Lead singer Antidum Tarantula, Italy. 1st lt. USAR. Recipient gold medal 1994 Goodwill Games, 1994, World Championship Qualifying Team FIBA World Championship, 1993, World Univ. Games, 1991, U.S. Olympic Fesitval, 1986; bronze medal World Championship, 1994; named USA Basketball's Female Athelete of Yr., 1991, 1st Am. woman to play profl. basketball in Hungary and Sweden, 1990-91; named to NCAA 1989 Mideast Region All-Tournament Team, 1988, 89, NCAA Final Four All Tournament Team, 1988, SEC All-Academic Team, 1988, 89, All-SEC second team, 1989; earned SEC All-Tournament Team honors, 1988, All-WNBA 1st team, 1997, named first ever WNBA player of week, 1997, mem. gold medal winning Olympic team Atlanta, 1996, mem. U.S. Basketball Women's Nat. Team, 1995-96. Office: Sacramento Monarchs One Sports Pkwy Sacramento CA 95834*

BOLTZ, CHRISTINE, community health and emergency nurse; b. Lansdale, Pa., Sept. 12, 1958; d. Philip T. and Dorothy May (Trumbauer) B. BSN, Cedar Crest Coll., Allentown, Pa., 1980; MA in Human Resources Devel. Mgmt., Webster U., 1993; MS in Nursing Informatics, U. Md., 1998. RN, Md.; cert. trauma nurse, ACLS instr., nursing adminstr., in nursing informatics. Commd. ensign USN, 1980, advanced through grades to comdr., 1996; emergency room staff nurse Naval Hosp., Beaufort, S.C., 1984-87; emergency room/ward charge nurse U.S. Naval Br. Hosp. Sigonella, 1987-88; quality assurance coord. U.S. Naval Branch Hosp. Sigorella, 1988-89; nursing div. head acute care clinic Naval Station, Norfolk, Va., 1989-90; divsn. officer med-surg. ward Fleet Hosp. 5, Jubail, Saudi Arabia, 1990-91; nursing div. officer ob/gyn. clinic Br. Med. Clinic, Norfolk, 1991-92; nursing dept. head br. med. clinic Naval Air Sta., Bermuda, 1992-94; nursing divsn. officer ob-gyn. clinic Nat. Naval Med. Ctr., Bethesda, Md., 1994-97; nursing informatics officer Naval Med. Ctr., San Diego, 1999—. Mem. Assn. Women's Health, Obstet. and Neonatal Nurses, Am. Acad. Ambulatory Nursing, Emergency Nurses Assn., Am. Med. Informatics Assn., Sigma Theta Tau, Phi Kappa Phi. E-mail: cboltz@concentric.net.

BOLTZ, GERALD EDMUND, lawyer; b. Dennison, Ohio, June 1, 1931; s. Harold E. and Margaret Eve (Hecky) B.; m. Janet Ruth Scott, Sept. 19, 1959; children: Gretchen Boltz Fields, Eric Scott, Jill Marie. BA, Ohio No. U., 1953, JD, 1955. Bar: Ohio 1955, U.S. Supreme Ct. 1964, Calif. 1978, U.S. Dist. Ct. (cen. dist.) Calif. 1978. Asst. atty. gen. State of Ohio, 1958; atty. spl. investigations unit SEC, 1959-60, legal asst. to commr., 1960-61, sr. trial and spl. counsel, Denver, 1961-66, regional adminstr., Ft. Worth, 1967-71, regional adminstr., Los Angeles, 1972-78; ptnr. Fine, Perzik & Friedman, Los Angeles, 1979-83, Rogers & Wells, Los Angeles, 1983-92, Bryan Cave, 1992—. Co-author: Securities Law Techniques. Served with U.S. Army, 1955-57. Recipient SEC Disting. Service award, 1971. Mem. ABA, Fed. Bar Assn., Los Angeles Bar Assn., Ohio Bar Assn., Calif. Bar Assn. Republican. Presbyterian (elder). Club: Calif. Yacht (Marina Del Rey, Calif.). Avocations: sailing, bridge, piano. Home: 1105 Centinela Ave Santa Monica CA 90403-2316 Office: Bryan Cave 120 Broadway Ste 300 Santa Monica CA 90401-2386

BOLTZ, MARY ANN, aerospace materials company executive, travel agency executive; b. Far Rockaway, N.Y., Jan. 12, 1923; d. Thomas and Theresa (Domanico) Caparelli; m. William Emmett Boltz; children: Valerie Ann Boltz Austin, Beverly Theresa, Cynthia Marie Boltz O'Rourke. Grad. high sch., Lawrence, N.Y., 1941. Publicist CBS, N.Y.C., 1943-48; mgr. Coast-Line Internat. Distbrs. Ltd., Lindenhurst, N.Y., 1961-80, v.p., 1980-86, pres., 1987-90, CEO, 1990—; chief exec. officer Air Ship 'N Shore Travel, Woodmere, N.Y. and Marco Island, Fla., 1978—; pres. Bangor Realty, 1975. Formerly radio and TV editor local publs., writer Gotham Guide mag. Sec. Inwood Civic & Businessmen's Assn., 1952-64, pres., 1964-66, chmn. bd., 1967-68; pres. Lawrence Pub. Schs. System PTA, 1956-58; pres., life mem. Cen. Coun. PTA, 1958-60; founder Inwood Civic Scholarship Fund, 1964; v.p. Econ. Opportunity Coun., Inwood; mem. fundraising bd. yearly ball St. Joachim Ch., Cedarhurst, N.Y.; gift chmn. L.I. Bd. Boys Town of Italy; bd. dirs. Marco Island Cancer Fund Dr.; dir., promoter Marco Island Philharmonic Symphony; dir. polit. campaign William Sieffert, Oceanside, N.Y.; chmn. 30 yr. reunion Class of 41, 1971, 50 yr. reunion, 1991, 55th yr. Lawrence H.S. reunion Class of 1938, 39, 40, 41, 42; asst. chmn. 50 yr. reunion Class of 42, 1991, Lawrence H.S. 55th Reunion Class of 1941, 1996; fundraiser Stecker and Horowitz Sch. Music Dinner Com., 1978, Am. Bus. Women's Assn., Long Island charter chptr., Rockville Centre, N.Y., 1990-92, United Fund, Red Feather Ball, 1992. Recipient award Nassau Herald Newspaper, Cedarhurst, Inwood Civic Assn., PTA Life Membership award, 25 Yr. Silver Medallion Boys Town of Italy, gold medal, 1995, Citizen of Yr. Bronze Plaque award Inwood Civic Assn., 1996; named Woman of the Year Boys Town of Italy, 1997. Mem. Am. Bus. Women's Assn. (L.I. charter chpt.), Nissoquogue Golf Club, Sun 'N Surf Beach Club, Island Country Club (Marco Island, Fla.), Desert Mountain Country Club. Republican. Roman Catholic. Home: 149 Hempstead Ave Rockville Centre NY 11570-2904 Office: Coast-Line Internat Distbrs 274 Bangor St Lindenhurst NY 11757-3633

BOMAN, JOHN HARRIS, JR., retired lawyer; b. Anniston, Ala., Mar. 8, 1910; s. John Harris and Myrtle (Creen) B.; m. Marie Askew, Aug. 17, 1935 (dec. Jan. 1996); children: John Harris, Scott A., Proctor C.; m. Catherine Strateman, Feb. 1, 1997. AB, Marquette U., 1930; JD, U. Mich., 1933. Bar: Ga. 1933. Pvt. practice, 1933-91; assoc. firm Crenshaw & Hansell, 1933; sr. mem. Hansell & Post, 1939-89; cons. Jones, Day, Reavis & Pogue, 1989-91; ret., 1992; pres. bd. Atlanta Legal Aid Soc., 1956; sec. Met. Atlanta Community Found., 1952-77. Gen. counsel Atlanta Area coun. Boy Scouts Am., 1947-94, Woodruff Arts Ctr.; trustee Atlanta Lawyers Found., W.I.H. and Lula E. Pitts Found. Lt. comdr. USNR, World War II. Recipient Silver Beaver award Boy Scouts Am. Fellow Am. Bar Found.; mem. ABA, Ga. Bar Assn., Atlanta Bar Assn., Lawyers Club Atlanta (pres. 1950), State Bar Ga., Am. Law Inst., Capital City Club (Atlanta), Commerce Club (Atlanta). Methodist. Home: 3497 Paces Valley Rd NW Atlanta GA 30327-3201 Office: Jones Day Reavis & Pogue 3500 Suntrust Plaza 303 Peachtree St NE Ste 3500 Atlanta GA 30308-3242

BOMBA, JOHN GILBERT, civil engineer, consultant; b. Yorktown, Tex., Feb. 8, 1932; s. Vincent Englebert and Regina Bertha (Ibrom) B.; m. Jane Killingsworth, June 9, 1958; children: Anne K., Marian R. Thomas, Beatrice J., Norma J. Ohlenbusch. BS in petroleum engr., Tex. A&M, 1954, postgrad. civil, 1959; postgrad. structural, U. Tulsa, 1965. Registered profl. engr. Tex., Okla., La. Jr. engr Collins Construction Co., Port Lavaca, Tex., 1954, 56-61; civil engr. Sigler, Clark & Assocs., Weslaco, Tex., 1961-64; sr. engr. Williams Brothers Co., Tulsa, Okla., 1964-68; dir. of marine svcs. William Brothers Engr. Co., Tulsa, 1968-78; sr. project mgr. R.J. Brown & Assocs., The Hague, The Netherlands, 1978-82; chief engr. R.J. Brown & Assocs. Ltd., Singapore, 1982-88, R.J. Brown & Assocs. of Am., Houston, 1988-93, Kvaerner R.J. Brown, Houston, 1993—. Editor: Proceedings of Workshop Pipeline Research Needs, 1997; contbr. numerous articles to profl. jours. With U.S. Army Signal Corp., 1954-56. Fellow Am. Soc. Civil Engrs. (chmn. exec. com. pipeline divsn. 1977, 78, chmn. pipeline rsch. com., 1995-97), Houston Marine Tech. Soc. (mem. exec. coun. 1996—). Republican. Roman Catholic. Home: 9834 Moorberry Ln Houston TX 77080-6402 Office: Kvaerner RJ Brown 7001 Corporate Dr Ste 200 Houston TX 77036-5139

BOMBARDIERI, MERLE ANN, psychotherapist; b. Atlanta, Mar. 16, 1949; d. Sol and Sadie (Drucker) Malkoff; m. Rocco Anthony Bombardieri, Jr., Aug. 22, 1971; children: Marcella, Vanessa. B.A. in Psychology, Mich. State U., 1971; M.S.W., San Diego State U., 1976. Cert. clin. social workers, Mass., clin. hypnosis Am. Soc. Clin. Hypnosis; Diplomate Nat. Assn. Social Workers, Am. Bd. Examiners in Clin. Social Work. Crisis intervention worker and trainer Listening Ear, East Lansing, Mich., 1969-71; tchr. English as 2d lang. Instituto Brasil Estados Unidos, Rio de Janeiro, 1971-73; supr. infant unit Married Student Day Care Ctr., Mich. State U., East Lansing, 1973-74; psychotherapist/family life educator Family Svc. Assocs., San Diego, 1975-77; psychotherapist Dade Wallace Mental Health Ctr., Nashville, 1977-78; psychotherapist/workshop leader Met. Beaverbrook Mental Health Ctr., Waltham, Mass., 1980-81; pvt. practice psychotherapy, Acton-Belmont, Mass., 1982—; clin. dir. Resolve, Inc., infertility orgn., Belmont, 1982-84; clin. cons., 1984—; cons. HealthData Internat., Westport, Conn., 1983—, Open Door Soc., Newton, Mass., 1983—, First Day Film Corp., 1985—, Mass. Dept. Social Svcs., 1987; sec. Boston Fertility Soc., 1995, others; psychology seminar leader; radio and TV appearances. Author: The Baby Decision, 1981, (cassettes) Your Mind's Own Medicine, 1998; founder, editor, pub. Wellspring newsletter; contbr. articles to profl. and med. jours. N.Y. State Regents scholar, 1967; NIMH trainee, 1970. Mem. Acad. Cert. Social Workers, Phi Beta Kappa, Phi Kappa Phi. Home: 4 Broadview Rd Acton MA 01720-4202 Office: 33 Bedford St Lexington MA 02420-4430

BOMBERGER, JOHN HENRY AUGUSTUS, pediatrician; b. Wheeling, W.Va., June 12, 1929; s. John H.A. and Anna Laura (Gottwals) B.; div. 1975; children: Debra Ann, John H.A. IV. BS, Trinity Coll., Hartford, Conn., 1951; MD, Temple U., 1956. Diplomate Am. Bd. Pediat. Intern U.S. Naval Hosp., Phila., 1956-57; resident in pediat. U.S. Naval Hosp. and Children's Hosp. of Phila., 1957-59; physician Phila. and Jacksonville (Fla.) Naval Hosp., 1956-62, Children's Hosp., Phila., 1962—, Delaware County Meml. Hosp., Drexel Hill, Pa., 1964—; pvt. practice Drexel Hill, 1964-85; med. dir. Mirmont Rehab. Ctr., Lima, Pa., 1985-87, Alcoholism & Addiction Ctr., Delaware County Meml. Hosp., Drexel Hill, 1985-89. Lt. comdr. USN, 1955-62. Mem. Am. Med. Soc. on Alcoholism & Drug Dependencies (cert. 1987), Am. Acad. Family Physicians, Polyologists Med. Club (Phila. sec.-treas. 1968-88). Republican. Episcopalian. Avocations: stamp collecting, music, sports. Home: 17-11 Valley Rd Drexel Hill PA 19026-5407

BOMBERGER, RUSSELL BRANSON, lawyer, writer; b. Lebanon, Pa., May 1, 1934; s. John Mark and Viola (Aurentz) B.; divorced; children—Ann Elizabeth, Jane Carmel. BS, Temple U., 1955; MA, U. Iowa, 1956, M.A., 1961, PhD, 1962; MS, U. So. Calif., 1960; LLB, JD, LaSalle U.; grad., U.S. Marine Corps Command and Staff Coll., 1987, U.S. Naval War Coll., 1991. Bar: Calif. 1970, U.S. Supreme Ct. 1975. Mem. editorial staff Phila. Inquirer, 1952-54; lectr. U. Iowa, 1955-57, U. So. Calif., 1957-58; asst. prof. U.S. Naval Postgrad. Sch., Monterey, Calif., 1958-62; assoc. prof. U.S. Naval Postgrad. Sch., 1963-75, prof., 1975-89, prof. emeritus, 1989—; practice law, 1970—; free lance writer, 1952—, communications cons., 1963—; safety cons. internat. program U. So. Calif. Inst. Safety and Systems Mgmt., 1983—; cons. Internat. Ctr. for Aviation Safety, Lisbon, 1984—. Author: (novel) The Alternate Candidate, (broadcast series) The World of Ideas, (motion picture) Strokes and Stamps, (stage play) Closely Held; abstracter-editor: Internat. Transactional Analysis Assn. Capt. USNR, 1966-94. Decorated Meritorious Civilian Svc. medal, 1989; Am. Psychol. Found. fellow Columbia U., 1954-55, CBS fellow U. So. Calif., 1957-58. Office: PO Box 8741 Monterey CA 93943-8741

BOMBIERI, ENRICO, mathematician, educator; b. Milan, Italy, Nov. 26, 1940; came to U.S., 1977; s. Carlo and Luisa (Cambi) B.; m. Susan Russell, Jan. 21, 1967; 1 child, Donata. PhD, U. Milan, 1963. Prof. math. U. Cagliari, Italy, 1965, U. Pisa, Italy, 1966-74, Scuola Normale Superiore, Pisa, 1974, Inst. Advanced Study, Princeton, N.J., 1977—. Recipient Fields medal Internat. Math. Union, Vancouver, Can., 1974. Mem. Am. Acad. Arts and Scis., Acad. Nazionale Delle Scienze Italy, Acad. Nazionale dei Lincei (corr. mem.; Feltrinelli prize 1976, Balzan prize 1981). Office: Inst Advanced Study Sch Mathematics Olden Ln Princeton NJ 08540*

BOMBOY, JOHN DAVID, mathematics educator; b. Somerset, Pa., May 22, 1953; s. David E. and Betty (Smith) B.; m. Nancy L. Dutrow, Apr. 22, 1978; children: Amanda Joy (dec.), Amy Lynn (dec.). BS, Clarion State Coll., 1975, MS, 1980. Cert. secondary tchr., Ohio, Pa. Math. tchr. East Palestine (Ohio) City Schs., 1975-77; math. tchr. Marion Center (Pa.) Area Schs., 1977—, dir. athletics, 1982—, dir. cmty. svcs., 1998—. Mem. Pa. State Athletic Dir.'s Assn. (exec. com.), Nat. Interscholastic Athletic Adminstrs. Assn. (cert. athletic adminstr.), Pa. Interscholastic Athletic Assn., Assn. Wrestling Ofcls., Am. Sport Edn. Program Instrs., Dist. 6 Athletic Dirs. Assn. (treas. 1994—), Appalachian Conf. (sec.-treas. 1987—). Republican. Lutheran. Avocations: bowling, volleyball, collecting license plates, wrestling referee. Home: 306 Highland Dr Home PA 15747-9607 Office: Marion Ctr Area High Sch PO Box 156 Marion Center PA 15759-0156

BOMER, ELTON, state official; b. July 30, 1935; m. Ginny Bomer; 2 children. BBA in Bus. Mgmt., U. Houston, 1959. Computer sales and mktg. mgr. IBM Corp., 1965-74; mem. Tex. Ho. Reps., Austin, 1981-85; mem. bd. dirs. Sprint/United Telephone Midwest Corp., 1985-95; sr. v.p. East Tex. Nat. Bank, Palestine, Tex., 1990-95; mem. Tex. Ho. of Reps., Austin, 1991-95; commr. ins. Tex. Dept. Ins., Austin, 1995-99; sec. of state State of Tex., 1999—. Named to Tex. Monthly 10 Best Legislators List, 1993. Office: Sec. of State PO Box 12887 Austin TX 78711-2887*

BOMES, STEPHEN D., lawyer; b. Providence, Jan. 15, 1948; s. Edward and Lillian L. (Dick) B.; m. Barbara Jean Thomas, Feb. 4, 1989; 1 child, Laura Alexandria. BS, Boston U., 1968; JD, U. Calif., Hastings, 1971; postgrad., Columbia U., 1974; LLM, NYU, 1975. Bar: Calif. 1972, N.Y. 1975, Fla. 1975, D.C. 1975, U.S. Dist. Ct. (no. and cen. dists.) Calif. 1972, U.S. Ct. Appeals (2d and 9th cirs.). Assoc. Milbank, Tweed, Hadley & McCoy, N.Y.C., 1975-79, London, 1979-81; ptnr. Brobeck, Phleger & Harrison, San Francisco, 1981-93, Loeb and Loeb, L.A., 1994-96, Heller Ehrman White & McAuliffe, L.A., 1997—; instr. NYU 1973-75; adj. asst. prof. CUNY, 1974; bd. dirs. Brazil Soc. No. Calif., Pan. Am. Soc. Author: The Dead Hand: The Last Grasp, 1976, (with W.F. Johnson) Real Estate Transfer, Development and Finance, Cases and Materials, 1975; co-editor: Commercial Agency and Distributions in Europe, 1992. Trustee and counsel 1066 Found. NYU fellow, 1973-75; included in Euromoney's Guide to the World's Leading Banking Lawyers. Mem. L.A., Assn. of Bar of City of N.Y., Internat. Bar Assn., Jonathan Club. Office: Heller Ehrman et al 601 S Figueroa St Fl 40 Los Angeles CA 90017-5704*

BOMGARDEN, STANLEY RALPH, minister; b. Freeport, Ill., Nov. 4, 1946; s. Ralph George and Dorothy Lorraine (Heeren) B.; m. Theresa Jane McCarten, June 7, 1969 (div. 1976); children: Peter, Elizabeth; m. Sylvia Ann Stone Maurer, June 27, 1986; stepchildren: Timothy Maurer, Jane Parks, Sarah DeHahn. BA, Cen. Coll., Pella, Iowa, 1969; MDiv, Western Theol. Sem., Holland, Mich., 1972; postgrad., U. Iowa, 1975-78, Grad. Theol. Found., 1998—. Ordained to ministry Ref. Ch. Am., 1975, Presbyn. Ch. (U.S.A.), 1988. Pastor 1st Ref. Ch., Rotterdam Jct., N.Y., 1973-75; assoc. pastor 1st Bapt. Ch., Iowa City, 1977-78; pastor 1st Presbyn. Ch., Beebe, Ark., 1988-91, Meml. Presbyn. Ch., Dayton, Ind., 1991—; counselor Highland Community Coll., Freeport, 1979-81; dir. Christian edn. 2d Presbyn. Ch., Freeport, 1983-87; guest lectr. Ark. State U., Beebe, 1989-91; program coord. Freeport Area Ch. Coop., 1984-87; moderator witness com. Presbytery of Ark., 1990-91; moderator com. on ministry Presbytery of Wabash Valley, 1996-98. Illustrator: The Server's Book of the Mass, 1987; contbg. editor Festivals mag.; mem. editorial bd. newsletter Body and Soul; contbr. stories and articles to profl. jours. Mem. Lions (pres. Beebe club 1990-91). Democrat. Home: 294 Conjunction St Dayton IN 47941 Office: Meml Presbyn Ch PO Box 186 Dayton IN 47941-0186

BOMMER, TIMOTHY J, lawyer; b. Columbus, Ohio, Dec. 9, 1940; s. Thomas F. and Susan L. (Proper) B.; m. Sandra K. Bartlett, May 16, 1964; children: Breton J., Kevin A., Melissa K. BA, U. Wyo., 1963, JD, 1970. Bar: Wyo. 1970, Colo. 1970. Dep. county and pros. atty., 1970-74; ptnr. Ranck & Bommer, Jackson, 1970-77; magistrate judge U.S. Dist. Ct., Jackson, 1976—; sole practice Jackson, 1977—. Chmn. fee arbitration com. Wyo. State Bar, 1980-84; mem. Wyo. Jud. Nominating Commn., 1984-88. Mem. ABA, ATLA, Am. Bd. Trial Advocates, Wyo. Trial Lawyers Assn. Republican. Episcopalian. Avocations: boating, hunting, fishing, skiing. Office: PO Box 1728 Jackson WY 83001-1728

BOMSTEIN, ALAN CHARLES, construction company executive; b. Balt., July 29, 1945; s. David Arthur and Dorothy Ruth (Seidel) B.; m. Nancy Sue Auerbach, Dec. 24, 1968; children: David, Joshua. Student, U. Md., 1962-66. V.p. Page Corp. div. U.S. Home Corp., Silver Spring, Md., 1967-72; nat. dir. mktg. U.S. Home Corp., Clearwater, Fla., 1973-74; pres. Creative Contractors, Inc., Clearwater, 1975—; bd. dirs., vice-chmn. 1st Nat. Bank Fla. (formerly known as Citizens Bank), Clearwater; bd. dirs. BayCare Health Sys., 1997—, treas., chmn. fin. com., 1997—; bd. dirs. F.N.B. Corp., Hermitaga, Pa. Dir., chmn. long range planning com. Ruth Eckerd Hall Performing Arts Ctr. and Theatre, Clearwater, 1982-87; bd. govs. Morton Plant Hosp., Clearwater, 1988-94, mem. planning com., 1984, chmn., 1988-90, fin. com. 1990—, audit com., chmn., 1990-92, ad hoc Long Range Planning Com., 1990-94, chmn. bd. trustees, 1992-94; pres. Tampa Bay Forum, 1984-87; chmn. Clearwater Housing Devel. Corp., 1982—; chmn. Clearwater Downtown Devel. Bd., 1983-84, 88—; participant Leadership Fla., 1983—; bd. dirs. Clearwater Marine Sci. Ctr., 1985-87, Clearwater Progress Inc., 1984-86, North Suncoast Bd. Fla. Orch., 1983-85, Fla. Aquarium, Tampa, 1987-90, Fla. Orch., 1988-89, Pinellas Sports Authority, appointed by County Commn., 1990—, sec., treas., 1992—; advisor Clearwater Phillies Baseball Club, 1985-87; gov.'s appointee Fla. Constrn. Lic. Bd., 1988-89; v.p. Pinellas County Jewish Fedn., 1987-88, bd. dirs. 1986-89; apptd. Pinellas County Bd. Adjustments, 1993—, chmn., 1996-97; apptd. Fla. 6th Cir. Jud. Nominations Com., 1994—, Clearwater High Speed Rail Commn., 1994—; trustee U. South Fla., 1996—; mem. Pinellas County Charter Rev. Commn., 1998—. Named Young Profl. of 1979 Building Design and Constrn. mag., 1979; recipient Liberty Bell award Clearwater Bar Assn., 1985, Community Service award, Award of Excellence in Archtl. Constrn. Fla. Chpt. AIA, 1984. Mem. Greater Clearwater C. of C. (bd. govs. 1980—, pres. 1985-86, Bilgore award 1991, Mr. Clearwater award 1991), Pinellas Suncoast C. of C. (exec. com. 1985-89, bd. govs. 1983-89, vice chmn. 1987-88), Jr. League of Clearwater-Dunedin (mem. adv. bd. 1987-90), Assoc. Gen. Contractors (bd. dirs. 1990-92), The Clearwater Club (bd. dirs. 1991-94), Rotary, Belleair Country Club. Republican. Jewish. Avocations: photography, boating, golfing, video. Office: Creative Contractors Inc 620 Drew St Clearwater FL 33755-4108

BONA, CHRISTIAN M., dentist, psychotherapist; b. Breslau, Schlesien, Germany, Apr. 24, 1937; arrived in Sweden, 1951; s. Humbert Serafin and Ingeborg Jenny (Holmgren) B.; m. Eva Tengblad, June 10, 1962 (div. 1980); children: Christian Georg, Richard Rolf, Henrik Nils; m. Monica Siv Karlsson, Jan. 26, 1982. DDS, Dental High Sch., Malmoe, Sweden, 1962; PhD in Acupuncture, U. Gothenburg, Sweden, 1986; cert. Traditional Chinese Medicine, U. Beijing, 1987. Asst. prof. Dental High Sch., Gothenburg, 1972-76; head dental health dept. Eriksbergs Mer. Verkstads AB, Gothenburg, 1972-78; head dental health and psychotherapy dept. Tandhalsovarden Mariaplan, Gothenburg, 1984—; sec. Swedish Dental Assn., Gothenburg, 1968-72, Swedish Soc. Clin. Hypnosis, Gothenburg, 1979-81, pres., 1981-84; cons. U. Computeraided Adminstrn., Gothenburg, 1972-78, U. Dental Practice Adminstrn., 1976-78. Author: Dental Psychotherapy and Hypnosis, 1986. Apptd. grand hospitaller, 1996—, mem. high coun. Sovereign Order St. John in Denmark. Mem. German-Sweden Assn. (treas. 1968-71), Partille Sailing Club (founder 1976, pres. 1976-81), Fram Sailing and Yacht Club (bd. dirs. 1981-86), Knight of Sovereign Order Hosp. St. John Jerusalem in Denmark, St. Eskil of the Order of St. John (treas. 1995—). Avocations: sailing, down-hill and cross-country skiing, photography. Office: Tandhalsovarden Mariaplan, Mariagatan 11 B, 41471 Göteborg Sweden

BONA, FREDERICK EMIL, public relations executive; b. Union City, N.J., Mar. 3, 1939; s. Henry C. and Clementina A. Bona; m. Doris L. Hurlbert, May 27, 1961; children: Lauri Paporello, Dawn Rizzo, Christine Cabana, F.A. (Rick). BS in Mktg., Fairleigh Dickinson U., 1962. Press rels. rep. W.R. Grace & Co., N.Y.C., 1962, mgr. press rels., 1970, dir. press rels., 1980, v.p. corp. communications div., 1983, dep. group exec., 1985, v.p., 1987-94; prin. The Dilenschneider Group, Inc., N.Y.C., 1994-95, LS Comms., Inc., N.Y.C., 1995—. Dep. communications mgr. Pvt. Sector Survey on Cost Control (Grace Commn.), Washington, 1982-85. Mem. Overseas Press Club (bd. govs. 1988-91, 94-97), Pub. Rels. Soc. N.Y. Roman Catholic. Office: LS Communications Inc 17 Devon Rd Boonton NJ 07005-9305

BONA, JERRY LLOYD, mathematician, educator; b. Little Rock, Feb. 5, 1945; s. Louis Eugene and Mary Eva (Kane) B.; m. Pamela Anne Ross, Dec. 23, 1966; children: Rachael Elizabeth, Jennifer Dani'el. BS in Applied Math. and Computer Sci., Washington U., St. Louis, 1966; PhD in Math., Harvard U., 1972. Rsch. fellow U. Essex, Colchester, Eng., 1970-72; L. E. Dickson instr. U. Chgo., 1972-73, from asst. prof. to assoc. prof. to prof., 1973-86; prof. Pa. State U., University Park, 1986-90, Raymond Shibley prof., 1990-95, acting chmn., 1990-91, chmn., 1991-95; CAM prof. math. and physics U. Tex., Austin, 1995—; rsch. fellow Harvard U. dept. math., 1970, 73; U.K. Sci. and Engring. Rsch. Coun. sr. vis. fellow Fluid Mechanics Rsch. Inst., U. Essex, 1973, 74, 75, 77, 78; vis. rsch. assoc. Brookhaven Nat. Lab., 1976, 77; NAS exch. visitor to Poland, 1977; vis. prof. Centro Brasileiro Pesquisas Fisicas, Rio de Janeiro, 1980, Math. Rsch. Ctr., 1980-81, U. Brasilia, 1982, Lab. Anvendt Matematisk Fysik, Danish Tech. Sch., 1982, Inst. Math. and its Applications, U. Minn., 1985, 88, 90, 91; rsch. prof. Applied Rsch. Lab., Pa. State U., 1986-95; prof. invité U. Paris-Sud, Ctr. d'Orsay, 1982, 86-87, 88, 89, 92, l'Inst. Nat. Sci. Rsch.-Oceanology, U. Que., 1982-87, Ecole Normale Superieure de Cachan, 1990-91, dir. rsch. CNRS, 1995, U. Bordeaux, 1995; invited prof. Inst. Pure and Applied Math., Rio de Janeiro, 1991, 92, 93, Acad. Sinica, Beijing, 1991, 96, Math. Scis. Rsch. Inst., Berkeley, Calif., 1994, U. de Paris Nord, Math. Lab. Villetaneuse, 1993, 95, 99, U. Oxford, 1995; invited spkr. ann. meeting Am. Phys. Soc., Notre Dame, 1979; invited spkr. Am. Math. Soc. meeting, Mpls., 1984, San Francisco, 1995; invited spkr. Internat. Biennial Fluid Mechanics Meeting, Blazjewko, Poland, 1979, Internat. Congress of Mathematicians, Helsinki, 1978; Britton lectr., McMaster U., 1986, SIAM ann. meeting, San Diego, 1989, Porcelli lectr. LSU, 1993, Taft lectr. U. Cin., 1996; chmn. Com. Applied Math. U. Chgo., 1981-86; mem. College Coun., U. Chgo., 1981-84, College Curriculum Com, 1984-86, Governing Com., Phys. Scis. Collegiate Divsn., 1985-86, Univ. Disciplinary Com., 1986, Penn State U. task force on undergrad. edn., 1989-91, hon. degree recepient recommendation com., 1994-95 ; mem. scientific adv. com. basic rsch. math. scis. U.S. Army Rsch. Office, 1979-82, review com. divsn. math. and computer sci. Argonne Nat. Lab., 1984-90, chmn., 1985-89; mem. review panel, site visit team NSF Sci. and Tech. Ctrs., 1988; mem. NATO postdoctoral fellowships review panel, 1991; mem. ABET evaluating team, 1992; chmn. proposal review panel Dept. Energy, 1993; co-dir. Math. Edn. Reform Network, 1993—; mem. vis. com. U. Ill. dept. math., Chgo., 1993, MIT dept. math., 1993-97, CUNY Brooklyn Coll. dept. math., 1994, U. N.C. dept. math., 1996; mem. forum post secondary edn. Math. Scis. Edn. Bd., 1994—; chmn. nat. vis. com. N.Y. Collab. for Excellence in Tchr. Prep. in Math., Sci., Tech., 1996—. Mem. editl. bd. Siam J. Math. Anal., 1979—, editor-in-chief, 1987-92; mem. editl. bd. 15 profl. jours.; contbr. more than 100 papers to profl. jours. Grantee W. M. Keck Found., 1989, NSF, 1972—; NSF grad. fellow Harvard U., 1966-70; Woodrow Wilson fellow Harvard U., 1966-67. Fellow AAAS (nat. com. chair 1994-97); mem. Soc. for Indsl. and Applied Math. (com. mng. editors 1987-92, com. on coms. and appointments 1988-95, vis. lectr. 1992—, rep. to AAAS sect. com. on math. 1994-97, nat. com. chair 1987-92, Am. Math. Soc. (nat. com. chair 1989-96, 99—, mem. com. to select Steele prize winner 1984-87, adv. com. on newsletter on collegiate math. edn. 1987-88, bd. judges for Nat. Sci. and Engring. Fair 1990, 1991, chmn. liaison com. AAAS 1990-92, com. on edn. 1992-96, chmn. subcom. grad. and postdoctoral edn. 1993-95, univ. lectr. series com. 1994—, chmn., 1999—, nomination com. 1995-98, chmn. nomination com. 1995-96), Math. Assn. Am. (com. on undergrad. program in math. 1987-91, subcom. on maj. in math. scis. 1989-90, subcom. on calculus reform and 1st 2 yrs. 1989-91, rep. to AAAS sect. com. on math. 1993-96, program of cons. 1994—), Tau Beta Pi. Achievements include setting up a fluid mechanics lab in math. depts.; helping to organize interdisciplinary programs in science, engineering, economics, finance, computer science and mathematics. Office: U Tex Dept Math Austin TX 78712

BONACORSI, GREGORY JAMES, mechanical engineer; b. Lawrence, Mass., Dec. 16, 1955; s. Dominic and Elaine Mary (Maloney) B.; m. Jody Michele St. Germain, Aug. 16, 1980 (div.); children: Jaime Michele, Jacquelyn Arlyne. BSME, U. N.H., 1978; MSME, Northeastern U., 1984. Registered profl. engr., Mass., N.H. Pvt. practice carpenter Salem, N.H., 1972-78; with engring. devel. program Aircraft Engine Bus. Group, Gen. Electric Co., Lynn, Mass., 1978-80, evaluation engr., 1981-89; program mgr. GE, Lynn, Mass., 1989-94; prin. cons. Gas Turbine Svcs., Salem, 1994—; ind. bldg. cons., Methuen, Mass., 1983—. Bd. dirs. Colonial Village Condo Assn., Methuen, 1986-88. Recipient Sanford A. Moss award, 1987, Managerial award Gen. Electric Co., 1987. Republican. Roman Catholic. Avocations: carpentry, computers, fishing, family activities, gardening. Home: 7 Dana Rd Salem NH 03079-3481

BONACORSI, MARY CATHERINE, lawyer; b. Henderson, Ky., Apr. 24, 1949; d. Harry E. and Johanna M. (Kelly) Mack; m. Louis F. Bonacorsi, Apr. 23, 1971; children: Anna, Kathryn, Louis. BA in Math., Washington U., St. Louis, 1971; JD, Washington U., 1977. Bar: Mo. 1977, Ill. 1981, U.S. Dist. Ct. (ea. dist.) Mo., U.S. Dist. Ct. (so. dist.) Ill., U.S. Ct. Appeals (8th cir.), U.S. Supreme Ct. Ptnr. Thompson Coburn, St. Louis, 1977—; chairperson fed. practice com. eastern dist., St. Louis, 1987—, eight cir. jud. conf. com., St. Louis, 1987—. Mem. ABA, Assn. Trial Lawyers of Am., Mo. Bar Assn., Met. St. Louis Bar Assn., Order of Coif. Office: Thompson Coburn One Mercantile Ctr Saint Louis MO 63101

BONACQUIST, HAROLD FRANK, JR., lawyer; b. Schenectady, N.Y., June 14, 1948; s. Harold F. Sr. and Janice (Piper) B.; m. Lucy Carol Walters, Jan. 14, 1984; 1 child, Lucy Piper. BA, Cornell U., 1971; JD cum laude, Albany (N.Y.) Law Sch., 1974. Bar: N.Y., 1975. Litigation assoc. Lynn &

Lynn, P.C., Albany, 1974-75, Weil, Gotshal & Manges, N.Y.C., 1976-81; legal rsch. clerk appellate divsn. 3d dept. Albany, 1975-76; counsel Offices of Willard DaSilva, Garden City, N.Y., 1981-82; counsel Traub, Bonacquist & Fox, N.Y.C., 1995—, mem., 1982-95; mem. Leaf, Sternklar & Drogin, N.Y.C., 1987-88; lectr. N.Y. State Commn. Corrections, Albany, 1973-74; legal writing instr. Albany Law Sch., 1973-74; mediator U.S. Bankruptcy Ct. So. Dist., N.Y.C., 1994—. Comments editor Albany Law Rev., 1973-74; contbr. articles to profl. jours. V.p., nat. legal advisor The Holiday Project, San Francisco, 1984-87; com. mem. The Presbyn. Ch., Mt. Kisco, N.Y., 1994—. Mem. Justinian Soc. Republican. Home: 19 Sun Valley Dr North Salem NY 10560-1049 Office: Traub Bonacquist & Fox 655 3rd Ave New York NY 10017-5617

BONADUCE, JUDITH, medical/surgical nurse, community health nurse; b. Phila., June 17, 1950; d. Mario and Julia (Giacchetti) Bonaduce; children: Julia, Jennifer, James, Janine. AAS in Liberal Arts, Del. County Community Coll., Media, Pa., 1987, AAS in Nursing, 1989; BSN, Villanova U., 1995; postgrad., Widener U., 1995—. Nurses aide Fitzgerald-Mercy Hosp., Darby, Pa.; companion to elderly Dunwoody Retirement Village, Newtown Sq., Pa.; nurse Misericordia Hosp., Phila., 1990-91; staff nurse Liberty Home Health, 1990-95, weekend supr., 1995-96; dir. patient care svcs. Maxim Healthcare Svcs., 1996-98; mgr. call ctr. consumer physician referral line U. Pa. Health Sys., 1998—; spkr. cmty. and ch. orgns. Mem. Sigma Theta Tau. Home: 1024 Lamb Rd Clifton Heights PA 19018-2910

BONANNI, MARC A., English language educator, newscaster; b. Easton, Pa., Apr. 26, 1969; s. Joseph A. Bonanni and Connie J. (Scagliotta) Christiansen. BA, Temple U., 1991; cert. in edn., East Stroudsburg U., 1992, MEd, 1998. Cert. english tchr., Pa.; lic. FCC. News reporter Sta. WEST/WLEV, Easton, 1989—; english tchr. Easton Area H.S., 1993—; cons. Coll. Bd., Phila., 1995—. Mem. Pa. Edn. Assn., Easton Area Edn. Assn., Pop Culture Assn. Am., World Lit. Soc. (Univ. Okla. chpt.), Nat. Coun. Teach English. Democrat. Avocations: film studies, music, photography. Home: 2709 Broad St Easton PA 18045 Office: Easton Area HS 2601 William Penn Hwy Easton PA 18045-5267

BONAPART, ALAN DAVID, lawyer; b. San Francisco, Aug. 4, 1930; s. Benjamin and Rose B.; m. Helen Sennett, Aug. 20, 1955; children—Paul S., Andrew D. A.B. with honors, U. Calif., Berkeley, 1951, J.D., 1954. Bar: Calif. 1955, U.S. Tax Ct. 1965, U.S. Supreme Ct. 1971. Assoc. Bancroft & McAlister (formerly Bancroft, Avery & McAlister), San Francisco, 1959-62; ptnr. Bancroft & McAlister, San Francisco, 1962-93, Bancroft & McAlister, A Profl. Corp., 1993—; past trustee Bancroft and McAlister Found.; mem. adv. com. Heckerling Estate Planning Inst., U. Miami, Fla., 1974-87, 92—, mem. faculty, 1974, 91—; past dir. Myrtle V. Fitchen Trust. Mem. ABA, Am. Coll. Trust and Estate Counsel, Nat. Acad. Elder Law Attys., Inc., Bar Assn. San Francisco, State Bar Calif. (cert. in estate planning, probate and trust law Bd. Legal Specialization 1991). Office: Bancroft & McAlister PC 601 Montgomery St Ste 900 San Francisco CA 94111-2612

BONAR, DANIEL DONALD, mathematics educator; b. Murraysville, W.Va., July 7, 1938; s. Nelson Edward and Ada Polk Bonar; m. Martha Dolores Baker, Aug. 8, 1966; 1 child, Mary Martha. BSChemE, W.Va. U., 1960, MS in Math., 1961; PhD in Math., Ohio State U., 1968. Instr. Denison U., Granville, Ohio, 1965-66; asst. prof. Denison U., Granville, 1966-68, 69-71, assoc. prof., 1971-77, prof., 1977—, George R. Stibitz disting. prof. math. and computer sci., 1995, chair dept. math and computer sci., 1971-77, 96-97; asst. prof. Wayne State U., Detroit, 1968-69; vis. asst. prof. Ohio State U., Columbus, 1968. Author: On Annular Functions, 1971; contbr. articles to profl. jours. Active Granville Sch. Bd., 1973-79, pres., 1979; active Licking County Joint Vocat. Sch. Bd., Newark, Ohio, 1974-79, Granville Devel. Bd., 1974-79, Granville Found., 1996—. Inducted into W.Va. U. Chem. Engring. Dist. Alumni Acad., 1999. Mem. Nat. Coun. Tchrs. Math., Math. Assn. Am. Democrat. Methodist. Avocations: checkers, puzzles, local history buff, farming, traveling. E-mail: bonar@denison.edu. Home: 237 W Elm St Granville OH 43023 Office: Dept Math and Computer Sci Denison Univ Granville OH 43023

BONASSI, JODI, artist, marketing consultant; b. L.A., Aug. 22, 1953; d. Julian and Sara (DeNorber) Feldman; m. Raymond Gene Bonassi, June 7, 1986; 1 child, Spencer. Student, Otis Art Inst., L.A., 1972, Calif. State U., L.A., 1983-85, Calif. State U., Northridge, 1985-86. participating artist Concern Found. and World Cup Soccer Gala Event for Cancer Rsch., Beverly Hills, Calif., 1994; lectr., guest spkr. L.A. Pub. Libr., Canoga Park, 1999; mem. adv. bd. Park LaBrea Art Coun. Artist: Creative With Words Publications, 1987; artist, pub. various greeting cards, 1994—; one-woman shows include Pt. Adesa Gallery, Rancho Mirage, Calif., 1996, Showtime TV Film Trust Me, 1997, Orlando Gallery, 1999; exhibited in group shows at Bowles-Sorokko Gallery, Beverly Hills, 1994, ChaChaCha, Encino, Calif., 1994—, Lyn/Bassett Gallery, L.A., 1994, Topanga (Calif.) Canyon Gallery, 1994, Hartog Fine Art Gallery, L.A., 1995, Charles Hecht Gallery, Tarzana, Calif., 1995, New Canyon Gallery, Topanga, 1995, Made With Kare, West Hills, Calif., 1995, Gail Michael Collection, Northridge, 1995, Mythos Gallery, Burbank, 1995-96, Nicole Brown Simpson Found., 1996, Orlando Gallery, Sherman Oaks, Calif., 1998, West Gallery, U. Calif., Fullerton, 1998, The Century Gallery at Mission Coll., 1998, Orlando Gallery, 1998-99; represented in pvt. collections; illustrator All About Us, 1996; featured in various articles and art revs. Art tchr. K-12 West Valley Christian Ch. Schs., 1997—. Recipient Best Banner 2d prize L.A. County Mus. Art, Park LaBrea Arts Couns. for PLB/LACMA Family Art Fund, 1997, World Peace Tour, 1997, Orlando Gallery, Spl. Judges Art award Park LaBrea Art Coun., 1998, L.A. County Mus. of Art. Mem. Calif. Women Bus. Owners, L.A. Mcpl. Art Gallery Registry, So. Calif. Women's Caucus for Art, Soc. Children's Bookwriters and Illustrators. Avocations: hiking, reading, swimming. Studio: 22647 Ventura Blvd Ste 160 Woodland Hills CA 91364-1416

BONAVENTURA, LEO MARK, gynecologist, educator; b. East Chicago, Ill., Aug. 1, 1945; s. Angelo Peter and Wanda D. (Kelleher) B.; student Marquette U., 1963-66; M.D., Ind. U., 1970; married; children—Leo Mark, Dena Anne, Angela Lorena, Nicole Palmira, Leah Michelle, Adam Xavier. Intern in surgery, Cook County Hosp., Chgo., 1970-71; resident in ob-gyn., Ind. U. Hosps., 1973-76, fellow in reproductive endocrinology and infertility, 1976-78; asst. prof. ob-gyn., Ind. U., 1976—, asst. head sect. reproductive endocrinology and infertility, 1978-80, head sect., 1980-81. Served with USN attached to USMC, 1971-73. Named Intern of Yr., Cook County Hosp., 1971. Diplomate Am. Bd. Obstetrics and Gynecology, Am. Bd. Reproductive Endocrinology and Infertility. Mem. Central Assn. Ob-Gyn., Am. Coll. Obstetricians and Gynecologists, Am. Fertility Soc., Can. Fertility Soc., Soc. Reproductive Endocrinologists, Soc. Reproductive Surgeons. Roman Catholic. Contbr. articles to profl. jours. Office: 8091 Township Line Rd Indianapolis IN 46260-2495

BONAZZI, ELAINE CLAIRE, mezzo-soprano; b. Endicott, N.Y.; d. John Dante and Zina (Rossi) B.; m. Jerome Ashe Carrington, Sept. 21, 1963; 1 step-son, Christopher. B.M. (George Eastman scholar), Eastman Sch. Music. Artist-in-residence SUNY, Stonybrook; former mem. faculty Peabody Conservatory; vis. prof. Eastman Sch. Music, Rochester, N.Y., 1979; more operatic premieres than any other living Am. singer; frequent judge major nat. and internat. competitions. Debuts, Santa Fe Opera, 1958, Opera Soc. Washington, 1960, N.Y.C. Opera, 1965, Opera Internacional, Mexico City, Mexico, 1966, Mini-Met, 1973, Europe, West Berlin Festival opera, 1961, Spoleto (Italy) Festival, 1974, Castel Franco Festival Venetian Music, Venice, Italy, 1975, Berlin Bach Festival, 1976, Netherlands Opera, 1978, Minn. Opera, 1985, Artpark Festival, 1987, Opera Theater of St. Louis, 1988, New Orleans Opera, 1988, Paris, 1979, Spoleto-Charleston Festival, 1981, Edmonton Opera Can., 1990, New Orleans Opera, 1990, Winnipeg Opera, 1993; frequent Libr. of Congress concerts; title role in Pique Dance, Washington Opera, Rostropovich conducting, 1989, in Vanessa, Opera Theatre of St. Louis, 1988, Carlson's Midnight Angel, Opera Theatre of St. Louis, 1993, Glimmerglass Opera La Calisto, 1995; currently leading roles with N.Y.C. Opera; soloist, with most major Am. orchs., Canadian Broadcasting Corp., BBC NET Opera Theatre, NBC, ABC, CBS TV networks, recs. on, Candide, Columbia, Vanguard, CRI, Folkways, Vox, Grenadilla, Pro Arte and Nonesuch Records; over 40 world premiers of major works by leading composers with major orchs. and opera cos. Named 1 of 6 honored alumni 50th Anniversary Year, Eastman Sch. Music, 1971, Trustees Council U. Rochester, 1976, Recital in honor of 75th Anniversary of Eastman Sch. of Music, 1996; formerly William Matheus Sullivan grantee; recipient Concert Artists Guild award, 1960. Mem. Mu Phi Epsilon. Chosen by Stravinsky, Hindemith, Menotti, Chavez, Rorem, Thomson, Argento, Pasatieri, Diamond for premieres of their works, master classes Europe and U.S.; more operatic premieres than any other living American singer. Home: 650 W End Ave New York NY 10025-7355 Office: care Trawick Artists 1926 Broadway New York NY 10023-6915 *In performing great music one tries to be honest as well as inventive-in communicating emotion. And one tries to remain true to the intentions of the composer. It can be a frustrating task requiring infinite patience and infinite care, but what joy for the performer when at last he can touch the heart of the listener.*

BONCHER, MARY, talent agent; b. Green Bay, Wis., Jan. 19, 1946; d. Anthony Peter and Bernice Mary (Lannoye) Williams; m. Joseph Phillip Boncher, Jan. 7, 1967; children: Yvette, Noelle. Diploma, Rosemary Bischoff Sch. Modeling, Milw., 1965. Dir. Mary Boncher Model Agy. & Sch. Ltd., Bloomington and St. Charles, Ill., 1970-80, Mary Boncher Model Agy. Ltd., St. Charles, 1980-84, Mary Boncher Model Mgmt. Ltd., Chgo., 1985-91; ptnr. ARIA Model & Talent Mgmt. Ltd., Chgo., 1992—, sec., treas.; fashion reporter TV and radio Men's Fashion Assn., N.Y.C., 1975-80, Eleanor Lambert's Am. Designer, N.Y. Fashion Press, N.Y.C., 1975-80; fashion corr. Green Bay Daily News, 1975-76. Lector Cath. mass, 1983-90, 92—; registered lobbyist, Ill.; mem. Rep. Nat. com., 1994—. Mem. Am. Security Coun. (nat. adv. bd.), Ams. for Responsible TV and Radio, Ill. Creative Cmty. (pres. 1996-98). Republican. Roman Catholic. Office: ARIA Model & Talent Mgmt Ltd 1017 W Washington St Ste 2C Chicago IL 60607-2100

BONCHEV, DANAIL GEORGIEV, chemist, educator; b. Burgas, Bulgaria, Feb. 20, 1937; s. Georgi Nikolov and Penka Danailova Bonchev; m. Pravdolyuba Vladimirova, Oct. 31, 1960 (div. 1983); 1 child Adelina Boncheva-Karakoleva; m. Dimitrina Kostova Kostova, June 10, 1984; 1 child, Elina. BS in Chem. Engring., High Inst. Chem. Tech., Sofia, Bulgaria, 1960; PhD in Quantum Chemistry, Acad. Scis., Sofia, Bulgaria, 1970; DSc in Math. Chemistry, State U., Moscow, 1984. Chem. engr. Chem. Komninat, Dimitrovgrad, Bulgaria, 1960-63; asst. prof. chemistry High Inst. Chem. Tech. (name now Assen Zlatarov U.), Burgas, Bulgaria, 1963-72, assoc. prof., head dept phys. chemistry, 1973-91, prof. chemistry, 1987—, dean inorganic chemistry faculty, 1987-91; head lab. math. chemistry Bulgarian Acad. Scis., Sofia, 1986-91; rector, founder Free Univ., Burgas, Bulgaria, 1991-94; referee internat. jours. in theoretical chemistry. Author: Information-Theoretical Characterization of Chemical Structures, 1983, (textbook) Structure of Matter, 1979, Physical Chemistry, 1994, Chemical Reaction Networks, 1996; editor: (series) Mathematical Chemistry, Graph Theoretical Approach to Chemical Reactivity; mem. editl. bd. Jour. Math. Chemistry, 1987-93, MATCH, 1989—, SAR and QSAR in Environ. Rsch., 1994—; contbr. over 160 articles to internat. sci. jours. Decorated Cyril and Methodius order II, State Coun. Bulgaria, Sofia, 1987. Mem. Internat. Soc. Math. Chemistry (officer), Am. Chem. Soc., World Assn. Theoretical Organic Chemistry, N.Y. Acad. Scis., Bulgarian Acad. Scis. (corr.). Achievements include contbns. to characterization of molecular topology, molecular branching, cyclicity, centrality; in deriving the properties of chem. elements (transactinids), compounds, polymers and crystals from their structure; in the classification, coding, and complexity of chemical compounds and mechanisms of chemical reactions, in developing chemical information theory, etc. Office: Tex A&M U Marine Scis Mitchell Campus Galveston TX 77553-1675 also: Assen Zlatarov U, 8010 Burgas Bulgaria

BOND, ALMA HALBERT, psychoanalyst, author; b. Phila., Feb. 6, 1923. BA in Psychology (with honors), Temple U., 1944; MA in Psychology, NYU, 1951; PhD in Devel. Psychology, Columbia U., 1961. Diplomate Am. Bd. Psychotherapy. Pvt. practice psychoanalysis pvt. practice, N.Y.C., 1953-91; tng. analyst Inst. Psychoanalytic Tng. and Rsch., N.Y.C., 1963—. Author: Who Killed Virginia Woolf, A Psychobiography, 1989, America's First Woman Warrior: The Courage of Deborah Sampson, 1992, Dream Portrait, 1992, Is There Life After Analysis?, 1993, On Becoming a Grandparent, 1994, Profiles of Key West, 1996, the Autobiography of Maria Callas, a Novel, 1998; sr. writer CAYO mag.; contbr. Key West Citizen, Solaris Hill, Tropic Keys, Time Out, Remember. Lt. USN, 1944-46. Recipient Honors in Psychology Temple U., 1944, Winner Am. Literary Press Contest, 1993, Runner up First Novel Contest, 1995, Hemingway award. Mem. Internat. Psychoanalytic Assn. Home: 606 Truman Ave # 1 Key West FL 33040-3284 Office: 606 Truman Ave # 1 Key West FL 33040-3284

BOND, AUDREY MAE, real estate broker; b. New Orleans, June 17, 1932; d. Melvin and Ann Thomas (Freeman) Respert; m. Robert M. Bond, Aug. 16, 1975; children: Betty Lee, Deborah Huggins. AA, Oxnard (Calif.) Coll., 1977. Lic. real estate broker, Calif. Benefit authorizer Dept. HEW, San Francisco, 1955-75; pvt. practice realty, 1977-88; owner/broker A. Bond Realty, Oxnard, Calif., 1988—. Bd. dirs. Luth. Sem., 1992—; sec.-treas. Channel Islands confs. Evang. Luth. Ch. in Am., 1989—; chmn. fellowship com. Our Redeemer Luth Ch., Oxnard; mem. Venturaa County Bd. Suprs.; alt. mem. Assessment Appeals Bd. No. 1, 1994—. Named Realtor of Yr., Oxnard Harbor Assn. Realtors, 1996. Mem. Profl. Coll. Women's Orgn. (v.p.), Nat. Assn. Ret. Fed. Employees (1st v.p.), Calif. Bd. Realtors, Nat. Bd. Realtors, Oxnard Harbor Bd. Realtors (trustee 1992, chmn. membership com. award 1990), African Am. C. of C. Tri Counties (treas. 1994—), Zonta Internat., Xi Tau (pres. parliamentarian 1995-97).

BOND, CHRISTOPHER SAMUEL (KIT BOND), senator, lawyer; b. St. Louis, Mar. 6, 1939; s. Arthur D. and Elizabeth (Green) B.; 1 child, Samuel Reid. BA with honors, Princeton U., 1960; LLB, U. Va., 1963. Bar: Mo. 1963, U.S. Supreme Ct. 1967. Law clk. to presiding chief justice U.S. Ct. of Appeals (5th cir.), Atlanta, 1963-64; assoc. Covington & Burling, Washington, 1965-67; pvt. practice law Mexico, Mo., 1968; asst. atty. gen., chief counsel consumer protection div. State of Mo., 1969-70, gov., 1973-77, 81-85; auditor, 1971-73; ptnr. Gage & Tucker, Kansas City, 1985-87; U.S. senator from Mo., 1987—, chmn. small bus. com. 104th Congress; mem. appropriations com., 1991—, chmn. subcom. on VA, HUD and ind. appropriations agys., 1991—, subcom. on def., 1993—, subcom. on fgn. ops., 1999—, subcom. on transp., 1995—; budget com., 1989—, environment and pub. works com., 1995—, subcom. on drinking water, fisheries and wildlife, 1995—; chmn. small bus. com., senate Rep. policy com.; pres. Gt. Plains Legal Found., Kansas City, Mo., 1977-80; chmn. Rep. Gov.'s Assn., Midwestern Gov.'s Conf., chmn. con. on econ. and community devel., 1981-83, chmn. con. on energy and environment, 1983-84. Republican. Presbyterian. Office: US Senate 3274 Russell Senate Bldg Washington DC 20510*

BOND, ENRIQUETA CARTER, science administrator; b. Buenos Aires, May 22, 1939; d. James Prescott and Harriette Mortley (Bovard) Carter; m. Langhorne Bond, Aug. 26, 1962; children: Langhorne Carter, Prescott McCook. AB in Zoology and Physiology, Wellesley Coll., 1961; MA in Biology and Genetics, U. Va., 1963; PhD in Biology and Biochem. Genetics, Georgetown U., 1969. Asst. prof., acting chmn. biology Chatham Coll., Pitts., 1970-73; asst. prof., dept. exec. dept. med. scis. So. Ill. U., Springfield, 1974-78; staff officer Nat. Acad. Scis., Inst. of Medicine, Washington, 1979-80, divsn. dir., 1981-88, exec. officer, 1989-94; pres. Burroughs Wellcome Fund, Durham, N.C., 1994—; bd. regents Nat. Libr. Medicine, Bethesda, Md., 1996—; bd. sci. counselors Nat. Ctr. Infectious Diseases, Atlanta, 1997—; bd. mem. health sci. policy Inst. Medicine, Washington, 1994-97. Contbr. articles to profl. jours. Bd. dirs. N.C. Biotech Ctr., Research Triangle Park, N.C., 1995—, pres., 1998; bd. dirs. Rsch. Triangle Found., 1996—; mem. leadership coun. Rsch. America!, Alexandria, Va., 1996—. Recipient Profl. Staff award Nat. Acad. Sci., 1985. Mem. AAAS, APHA, Inst. Medicine (mem. coun. 1999—), Am. Soc. Microbiology, Soc. for Advancement of Women's Health Rsch. (sec. bd. dirs. 1995—), Sigma Xi. Episcopalian. Avocations: needlepoint, reading. Office: Burroughs Wellcome Fund 4709 Creekstone Dr Ste 100 Durham NC 27703-8472

BOND, FRANCES CURTIS, retired editor; b. Chgo., Feb. 9, 1909; d. Vine Harlan Sr. and Frances Lay (Watson) Curtis; m. Bradford Austin Bond, Mar. 8, 1940 (dec. Nov. 1991); 1 child, David Bradford. *Mayflower descendant from Thomas Rogers, who arrived in Plymouth, Massachusetts, 1620. Great-grandfather, Nathan Whitney Watson, first resident of Chicago suburb Hyde Park, 1835. Grandfather, Nathan Whitney Watson II, traveled by covered wagon from Chicago to California and back in 1852, became American Express Company agent until retirement. Great-grandfather, Nelson Lay, co-founded Kewanee, Illinois, 1854. Mother, Frances Watson Curtis was the first woman city treasurer of Rochester, Indiana, 1931-1936. Grandson, Ross David Bond, named International Technical Manager/Konica Business Technologies, Inc.'s Mexican and Latin American operations, 1998. Son, David Bradford Bond (deceased 10/23/96) was a Math teacher, Knox College.* B Journalism, U. Mo., 1932. Editor Nutrilite News Mytinger & Casselberry, Inc., Long Beach, Calif., 1948-58; dir. pub. info. and cmty. rels. Long Beach Commn. on Econ. Opportunities, 1967-77; cmty. editor Long Beach Rev. mag., 1978-90; ret., 1990. Bd. dirs., historian Ch. Women United, Long Beach, 1996; mission coord. United Meth. Women, Long Beach, 1996; mem. adminstrv. bd. Grace United Meth. Ch., Long Beach, 1996; former bd. dirs., exec. com. Pacific Coast Press Club; former adv. coun. com. on aging United Way; former mem. Calif. Atty. Gen.'s Adv. Com. on Consumer Info. and Crime Prevention for Sr. Citizens; former bd. dirs., sec. Calif. Dirs. Aging Programs; former mem. adv. bd. Sr. Opportunities and Svcs. Elderly Nutrition Program; former mem. adv. bd. Long Beach Children's Mus.; former bd. dirs. Internat. Cmty. Coun. of Calif. State U., Long Beach, Long Beach Ballet; former bd. dirs., exec. com. South Bay Indian Svcs., NAACP, Long Beach, Pacific Coast Press Club. Recipient 4 1st Pl. and 3 2d Pl. awards Internat. Indsl. Publs. Contest, 1951, Blue Pencil award for Outstanding Govt. Publs., Fed. Editors Assn., 1974, 75, 1st and 2d Pl. award Calif. Cmty. Action Exec. Dirs. Assn., 1976, Merit award Pacific Coast Press Club, 1988, Mission Recognition award United Meth. Ch., 1990; named Safe Driver of Yr. Long Beach, Nat. Safety Coun., 1963, Vol. of Mo., Long Beach Sr. Ctr., 1991, Lay Person of Yr., Grace United Meth. Ch., 1996. Mem. DAR (life, bd. dirs. Susan B. Anthony chpt. 1989-90), NAACP (life), Fulton County Hist. Soc. (life), Ind. Hist. Soc., Soroptomist Internat. (life, Soroptomist of Long Beach Hall of Fame 1997), Soc. Mayflower Descendants. Democrat. Avocation: photography. Home: 1625 Appleton St Apt 3C Long Beach CA 90802-4026

BOND, GEORGE CLEMENT, anthropologist, educator; b. Knoxville, Tenn., Nov. 16, 1936; s. J. Max and Ruth Elizabeth (Clement) B.; m. Alison Murray, Sept. 21, 1940; children: Matthew, Rebecca, Jonathan, Sarah. BA, Boston U., 1959; MA, London Sch. Econs., 1962, PhD, 1968. Lectr. U. East Anglia, Norwich, Eng., 1966-68; asst. prof. Columbia U., N.Y.C., 1968-74, assoc. prof. Tchrs. Coll., 1974-80, prof., 1980—, dir. Inst. African Studies, 1989—. Author: Politics of Change in a Zambia Community, 1976; editor: African Christianity, 1979, Social Stratification and Education, 1981, The Social Construction of the Past, 1994, AIDS in Africa and the Caribbean, 1997; contbr. articles to scholarly publs. Home: 229 Larch Ave Teaneck NJ 07666-2345 Office: Columbia U Inst of African Studies 420 W 118th St New York NY 10027-7213*

BOND, GORMAN MORTON, ornithologist, researcher; b. Elkridge, Md., Apr. 6, 1921; s. Morton Bradley Bond and Mary Agnes (Soper) Olfky; m. Leona Steinberg, Apr. 9, 1957; 1 child, Alissa. BA, George Washington U., 1963. Ornithologist U.S. Fish and Wildlife Svc., Washington, 1948-55; exhibits planner, birds Smithsonian Inst., Washington, 1956-63, rsch. asst. to sec., 1964-81; ret., 1981; instr. Dist. of Columbia Literacy Program, 1977-78. Staff sgt. USAAF, 1943-45. Decorated Air medal; recipient Smithsonian documentary film award, 1963, Merit Badge counselor Boy Scouts Am., 1974-75. Mem. Am. Ornithologists Union (chmn. archives com. Washington 1969-79), Nat. Audobon Soc. (editor bird census 1953-59), Biol. Soc. Washington (corr. sec. 1950-55). Avocations: birdwatching, photography. Home: 7361 Swan Point Way Columbia MD 21045-5010

BOND, HAROLD H., poet; b. Boston, Dec. 2, 1939; s. Khorin and Ovsanna (Avakian) B.; m. Ruth Thomasian, June 6, 1981 (div. Oct. 1985). AB in English-Journalism, Northeastern U., 1962; MFA in Creative Writing, U. Iowa, 1967. Asst. editor Horizon House, Dedham, Mass., 1962-65, Allyn and Bacon, Boston, 1967-69; copy editor Boston Globe, 1969-71; editor Ararat mag., N.Y.C., 1969-70; tchr. Cambridge Ctr. for Adult Edn., 1968—; founder, dir. Seminars in Poetry Writing, 1978—. Author: The Northern Wall, 1969, Dancing on the Water, 1970, The Way It Happens to You, 1979, Arveste II, 1962, The Young American Poets, 1968, Ararat: A Decade of Armenian-American Writing, 1969, the New Yorker Book of Poems, 1969, Speaking for Ourselves: American Ethnic Writing, 1969, 75, Eleven Boston Poets, 1970, East Coast Poets, 1971, Getting Into Poetry, 1972, New Voices in American Poetry, 1973, Outside/Inside, 1973, Shake the Kaleidoscope: A New Anthology of Modern Poetry, 1973, Armenian-North American Poets: An Anthology, 1974, The Blacksmith Anthology, 1975, Writing a Poem, 1975, Armenian-American Poets: A Bilingual Anthology, 1976, Traveling American with Today's Poets, 1977, I Sing the Song of Myself: Autobiographical Poems, 1978, The Writing Experience, 1979, Anthology of Magazine Verse and Yearbook of American Poetry, 1981, The Aspect Anthology: A Ten-Year Retrospective, 1981, Poems: A Celebration, 1982, Ararat: 25th Anniversary Anthology, 1985, Despite This Flesh: The Disabled in Stories and Poems, 1985, Toward Solomon's Mountain: Poetry of the Disabled Experience, 1986, Light Year '87, 1986, Sutured Words: Contemporary Poetry About Medicine, 1987, The Villanelle: EThe Evolution of a Poetic Form, 1988, Introduction to Special Education: Teaching in an Age of Challenge, 1992, And What Rough Beast: Poems at the End of the Century, 1999 (with others) 3X3, 1969; contbr. poetry to publs. Recipient First prize Armenian Allied Arts Assn., 1963, 64, 65, Kansas City Star awards, 1967, 68, Award PEN of Am., 1975, 77, 86, The Authors League of Am., 1975, 78, 86; fellowship Nat. Endowment for the Arts, 1976. Avocations: antiques, classic cars, photography, classical music. Home: 11 Chestnut St Melrose MA 02176

BOND, JOAN, elementary school educator; b. Americus, Ga., Dec. 24, 1945; d. Doyle Holden and Frances (Brown) B. BS in Elem. Edn., U. Ga., 1975, MEd, 1979, EdS, 1982. Clk. emergency room St. Mary's Hosp., Athens, Ga., 1963-64; receptionist, asst. Office Dr. Shu-Yun T. Tsao, Athens, 1964-66; tchr. remedial reading Danielsville (Ga.) Elem. Sch., 1975-76, primary tchr., 1975—. Tchr., dir. presch. Hull (Ga.) Bapt. Ch., 1970-84, asst. tchr. adult class, 1985—; mem. honor roll com. Danielsville Elem. Sch. PTO, 1990-92. Mem. Profl. Assn. Ga. Educators. Democrat. Avocations: beach activities, U. Ga. football, basketball and gymnastics fan. Home: 999 Glenn Carrie Rd Hull GA 30646-4210 Office: Danielsville Elem Sch PO Box 67 Danielsville GA 30633-0067

BOND, JON ROY, political science educator; b. Chickasha, Okla., Dec. 30, 1946; s. Henry Lee and Othelle (Payne) B.; m. Patricia Anne Garner (div. Apr. 1989); 1 child, Lynn Elizabeth Bond; m. Wanda Karon Martin Frazier, July 11, 1992; children: Mika Karon Frazier, Monika Kara Frazier. BA, Okla. State U., 1969, MA, 1973; PhD, U. Ill., 1978. Prof. polit. sci. Tex. A&M U., 1976—. Co-author: Pres. in the Legislative Arena, 1990; co-editor: Jour. of Politics, 1993-97; contbr. articles to profl. jours. Precinct chair Brazos County Democratic Party, College Station, 1984-87. Mem. Am. Polit. Sci. Assn., Midwest Polit. Sci. Assn. (exec. coun. 1992-95), Southern Polit. Sci. Assn., Pi Sigma Alpha (exec. coun. 1994-98). Democrat. Methodist. Home: 1412 Frost St College Station TX 77845-5630 Office: Tex A&M U Dept Polit Sci College Station TX 77843

BOND, JULIAN, civil rights leader; b. Nashville, Jan. 14, 1940; s. Horace Mann and Julia Agnes (Washington) B.; m. Pamela S. Horowitz, Mar. 17, 1990; children by previous marriage: Phyllis Jane, Horace Mann, Michael, Jeffrey, Julia. BA, Morehouse Coll., 1971; LLD (hon.), Dalhousie U., 1969, U. Bridgeport, 1969, Wesleyan U., Conn., 1969, U. Oreg., 1969, Syracuse U., 1970, Eastern Mich. U., 1971, Tuskegee Inst., 1971, Howard U., 1971, Morgan State U., 1971, Wilberforce U., 1971, Patterson State Coll., 1972, N.H. Coll., 1973, Detroit Inst. Tech., 1973; DCL (hon.), Lincoln (Pa.) U., 1970. A founder Com. Appeal for Human Rights, 1960, exec. sec., 1961; a founder Student Nonviolent Coordinating Com., 1960, communications dir., 1961-66; reporter, feature writer Atlanta Inquirer, 1960-61, mng. editor, 1963; mem. Ga. Ho. of Reps., from Fulton County, 1965-75, Ga. State Senate, 1975-87; vis. prof. history and politics Drexel U., 1988-89; Pappas fellow U. Pa., 1989; vis. prof. Harvard U., fall 1989, 91; prof. U. Va., fall 1990, 1993—, Am. U., 1991—, Williams Coll., fall 1992. So. corr. Reporting Racial Equality Wars; narrator Parts 1 and 2, Eyes on the Prize. Bd. dirs. So. Conf. Edn. Fund, Robert F. Kennedy Meml. Fund, So. Regional Coun., Coun. for Liveable World, Ctr. for Community Change; pres. emeritus So. Poverty Law Ctr.; chmn. bd. dirs. NAACP, 1998—. Barred from Ho.

because of Vietnam statements, 1966; U.S. Supreme Ct. ruled his Constl. rights were violated, 1966. Office: 5435 41st Pl NW Washington DC 20015-2911

BOND, MICHELE DENISE, early childhood educator; b. Schenectady, Jan. 4, 1966; d. William James Jr. and Marlene Elizabeth (Wayto) B. BS, Russell Sage Coll., 1988, BA in Creative Arts in Therapy, 1988; MS in Reading, SUNY, Albany, 1992. Remedial reading asst. tchr. Waterford (N.Y.)-Halfmoon Elem. Sch., 1988-89; 2d grade tchr. The Doane Stuart Sch., Albany, 1989-91, kindergarten tchr., 1991-94; kindergarten tchr. Schalmont Ctrl. Schs., Schenectady, 1994—; pvt. tutor, 1988—; classroom supr./habilitation specialist Oswald D. Heck Devel. Ctr., Niskayuna, N.Y., summer 1989. Choral accompanist, singer Russell Sage Coll. Community Chorus, Troy, N.Y., 1990-92; singer Burnt Hills Oratorio Soc., Burnt Hills, N.Y., 1995—, Mohawk Valley Chorus, Amsterdam, N.Y., 1998. Home: 2202 Hugh St Schenectady NY 12306-4415

BOND, MYRON HUMPHREY, investment executive; b. Chickasha, Okla., Jan. 12, 1938; s. Reford and Jane Embick (Humphrey) B.; m. Janice Wootten, July 1, 1961; children: Richard Allen, Lori Elizabeth. BS in Petroleum Engring., U. Okla., 1961, MS in Petroleum Engring., 1965. Registered profl. engr., Okla. Staff engr. Exxon, Houston, 1960-68; sr. v.p. Paine Webber, Inc., Dallas, 1968—; pres., chmn. Four Bees Ranch Inc., 1989—; dir. Am. Pub. Communications, Inc., 1991-92. Bd. dirs. Dallas Epilepsy Assn., 1980-82, Dallas Campfire Girls, 1980-82. Lt. (s.g.) USN, 1961-64. Mem. Nat. Assn. Securities Dealers (prin., mem. Dist. 6 com. 1994-96), Dallas C. of C., Dallas Country Club, Brook Hollow Golf Club. Republican. Presbyterian. Avocations: sports, ranching. Home: 4536 Belfort Pl Dallas TX 75205-3619 Office: Paine Webber 5956 Sherry Ln Ste 1100 Dallas TX 75225-6595

BOND, NELSON LEIGHTON, JR., health care executive; b. Glen Ridge, N.J., Apr. 17, 1935; s. Nelson Leighton and Dorothy Louise (Minsch) Hudson B.; m. Susan Priscilla McDonald, June 7, 1958 (div. May 1981); children: Sally Louise, Nelson Leighton III, Trevor Paul, Elizabeth Bond Brennan, Susan Bond Kearney; m. Gwendolen Nash Gorman, July 24, 1982. BA, Lehigh U., 1957; MBA, Harvard U., 1966. Dist. mgr. McGraw Hill, Inc., N.Y.C., 1957-64; assoc. McKinsey and Co., Inc., N.Y.C., 1966-68; fin. analyst Drexel Harriman Ripley, Inc., N.Y.C., 1968-69; instl. salesman Faulkner Dawkins and Sullivan, N.Y.C., 1969-70; v.p. Alex Brown and Sons, Balt., 1970-77; pres., dir. Blood Pressure Testing, Inc., Reisterstown, Md., 1977—; pres. Consumer Micrographics, Inc., Balt., 1980-83; pres. Medscreen, Inc., Balt., 1987-89, also bd. dirs.; mng. dir. Offutt Securities, Inc., 1987-98, Bond & Assocs., Reisterstown, Md., 1991-99; chmn., pres., chief exec. officer, bd. dirs. Power Source, Inc., Reisterstown, 1991-99, The Green Spring Group, Inc., Reisterstown; pres. Maidstone Acquisition Co., LLC, 1998—. Pres. Parents' Club St. Paul's Sch., Brooklandville, Md., 1978-79. 1st lt. USAR, 1958-60. Foote, Cone and Belding fellow Harvard U., 1965. Republican. Episcopalian. Avocations: golf, history, travel. Office: Bond & Assocs PO Box 1053 Reisterstown MD 21136-7053

BOND, NILES WOODBRIDGE, cultural institute executive, former foreign service officer; b. Newton, Mass., Feb. 25, 1916; s. George Wood and Clara Mehitabel (Bonney) B.; m. Julia Rice Folsom, June 25, 1940 (dec. Sept. 1986); children: Ellen Dudley, Nancy Kenneth; m. Pamela Guest Bird, Sept. 17, 1988. A.B., U. N.C., 1937; A.M., Fletcher Sch. Law and Diplomacy, Medford, Mass., 1938. U.S. fgn. service officer, 1939-68; vice consul Havana, Cuba, 1939-40, Yokohama, Japan, 1940-41; 3d sec., vice consul Madrid, Spain, 1942-45; 2d sec., 1945-46; adviser to U.S. delegation to 4th session Econ. and Social Council, 1947; 2d sec., vice consul Bern, Switzerland, 1947; 1st sec. and consul, 1947; asst. chief div. N.E. Asian affairs Dept. State, 1947-49, officer in charge Korean affairs, 1949-50; adviser to U.S. delegation to 4th session UN Gen. Assembly, 1949; 1st sec. Office of U.S. Polit. Adviser to Supreme Comdr. Allied Powers, Tokyo, Japan, 1950; acting chmn. Allied Council for Japan, 1952; counselor embassy Tokyo, 1952, Seoul, Korea, 1953-54, Rome, Italy, 1956-58; dir. Office UN Polit. and Security Affairs, Dept. State, 1954-56; counselor of embassy, vis. lectr. Bologna Center, Johns Hopkins U., 1957-58; research fellow Ctr. for Internat. Affairs, Harvard, 1958-59; minister-counselor embassy Rio de Janeiro, Brazil, 1959-63; coordinator interdeptl. seminar Dept. State, 1963; minister, consul gen. São Paulo, Brazil, 1964-68; sec. bd. trustees Corcoran Gallery Art, Washington, 1973-86; pres., bd. dirs. Brazilian-Am. Cultural Inst., 1976-86; mem. ct. sys. study com. D.C. Bar, 1979-81, exec. dir. fee arbitration bd., 1981-87; exec. dir. Project Orbis, 1972; adviser São Paulo Bienal, 1969; dir. internat. exhbns. com. Am. Fedn. Art, 1976-77. Author: poetry Arcanum, 1965, Elegos, 1967, Dreams From a Wintry Night, 1993. Decorated commendatore Al Merito della Repubblica Italiana, grand officer Order So. Cross (Brazil). Mem. Univ. Club, Army and Navy Club (Washington), Harvard Club (N.Y.C.). Interned in Japan upon outbreak of war, repatriated on S.S. Gripsholm, Aug. 1942. Home: 35 Sill Ln Old Lyme CT 06371-1132

BOND, PETER DANFORD, physicist; b. Providence, Jan. 30, 1940; s. Douglas D. and Helen H. (Cannon) B.; m. Sandra E. Salim, Aug. 3, 1968; children: Jennifer, Colin; stepchildren: Anthony Shane, John Shane. BA, Harvard U., 1962; MA, Western Res. U., 1963; PhD, Case Western Res. U., 1969. Rsch. assoc. Stanford U., Palo Alto, Calif., 1969-72; asst. physicist Brookhaven Nat. Lab., Upton, N.Y., 1972-74, assoc. physicist, 1974-76, physicist, 1976-86, sr. physicist, 1986—, assoc. chmn. physics dept., 1986-87, dep. chmn., 1987-97, chmn., 1987-97, interim dep. dir., 1997-98, interim dir., 1997-98, spl. asst. to dir., 1998—, sr. policy analyst office sci. and tech. policy, 1999—; chmn. exec. com. Holifield Heavy Ion Rsch. Facility, 1981; mem. program adv. com. Super Heavy Ion Linear Accelerator, 1977-81, chmn., 1981; mem. program com. on heavy ions SUNY, Stony Brook; mem. panel to rev. maj. nuclear physics facilities Dept. Energy, 1987; mem. siting panel for Gammasphere, 1989; reviewer physics program SUNY Grad. Sch.; mem. physics divsn. adv. com. Oakridge Nat. Lab., 1992-97; mem. com. of visitors to NSF, 1994; mem. nuclear sci. adv. com. to Dept. Energy/NSF, 1994-97; mem. dean's adv. com. MIT/Lab. Nuclear Sci., 1994—. Contbr. numerous articles to profl. jours. FOM fellow (the Netherlands), 1983-84. Fellow AAAS, Am. Phys. Soc. (nuclear physics div. 1977-79, program com. 1989-90); mem. Sigma Xi. Avocation: athletics. Home: 7 Simpson Pl Stony Brook NY 11790-1744 Office: Brookhaven Nat Lab Directors Office Bldg 460 Upton NY 11973

BOND, RICHARD LEE, lawyer, state senator; b. Kansas City, Kans., Sept. 18, 1935; s. Clarence Ivy and Florine (Hardison) B.; m. Sue S. Sedgwick, Aug. 23, 1958; children: Mark, Amy. BA, U. Kans., 1957, JD, 1960. City atty. Overland Park, Kans., 1960-62; adminstrv. asst. to Congressman Robert Ellsworth, Washington, 1961-66, Congressman Larry Winn, Washington, 1967-85, Congressman Jan Meyers, Washington, 1986; chmn. bd. dirs. Home State Bank, Kansas City, 1983-94; ptnr. Bennett, Lytle, Wetzler et al, Prairie Village, Kans., 1986-89; senator State of Kans., Topeka, 1985—, senate pres., 1997—; vice chmn. Guaranty Bank and Bancshares, Kansas City, Kans., 1995—. Republican. Presbyterian. Avocations: gardening, tennis, hunting, fishing. Home: 9823 Nall Ave Shawnee Mission KS 66207-2915

BOND, THOMAS MOORE, JR., labor mediation and arbitration executive; b. Louisville, Ky., Dec. 17, 1930; s. Thomas Moore and Louise Elleanor (Jones) B.; m. Kathryn Keith, Apr. 10, 1950 (dec.); children: Gilbert, Louise, Lela; m. Ethel Ayako Kuramitsu, Aug. 15, 1965; children: Thomas Toshiro, Richard, Jane, Julian Horace. BS in Econs., Ind. U., 1953. Bus. agt. organizer Hosp. Workers, San Francisco, 1961-65; internat. rep. organizer Svc. Employees' AFL-CIO, Louisville, Ky., 1965-70; exec. dir. Union Am. Physicians, San Francisco, 1973-78; owner Thomas Moore Bond Group, Berkeley, Calif., 1979—; pvt. practice labor mediator and arbitrator. Editor: The Negro Conservative, 1981. Bd. dirs. adv. com. for paralegal tng. Merritt Coll., Oakland, Calif., 1983; mem. labor commn. City of Berkeley, 1986-88, 91. 1st lt. inf. U.S. Army, 1946-50. Mem. Indsl. Rels. Rsch. Assn., Soc. Fed. Labor Rels. Profls., Inst. Advanced Law Study. Republican. Congregationalist. Office: Thomas Moore Bond Group 2123 1/2 5th St Berkeley CA 94710-2208

BOND, THOMAS ROSS, television assistant director; b. Dallas, Sept. 16, 1926; s. Ashley Ross and Margaret (Sauter) B.; m. Pauline Francis Goebel, Apr. 18, 1953; 1 child, Thomas Ross. BA, L.A. State Coll., 1951. Actor Hal Roach Studios, Culver City, Calif., 1932-40, Warner Bros., Burbank, Calif., 1937, MGM, Culver City, 1938, KFWB Radio, Hollywood, Calif., 1937; asst. dir. KFSN-TV, Fresno, Calif., 1975—; producer Emmanuel Luth. Ch., North Hollywood, 1959-72. Appeared in films including Our Gang Comedies, 1932-40, Superman, 1946-48. With USN, 1945-46. Republican. Lutheran. Home: 14704 Road 36 Madera CA 93638-8434 Office: KFSN-TV 1777 G St Fresno CA 93706-1688

BOND, VICTORIA ELLEN, conductor, composer; b. L.A., May 6, 1945; d. Philip and Jane (Courtl) B.; m. Stephan Peskin, Jan. 27, 1974. B Mus. Arts, U. So. Calif., L.A., 1968; M Mus. Arts, Juilliard Sch. Music, 1975, D Mus. Arts, 1977; DFA (hon.), Washington and Lee U., 1992, Hollins Coll., 1995, Roanoke Coll., 1995. Condr., composer; mem. N.Y. State Coun. Arts Music Panel, 1987-90; bd. dirs. N.Y. Women Composers. Guest condr. Cabrillo Music Festival, Calif., 1974, White Mountains Music Festival, N.H., 1975, Aspen (Colo.) Music Festival, 1976, Shenandoah Music Festival, W.Va., 1977, Colo. Philharm., 1978, Houston Symphony, 1979, 86, Buffalo Philharm., 1979, Pitts. Symphony, 1980, N.W. Chamber Orch., Seattle, 1980, Anchorage Symphony, 1980, 82, Ark. Symphony, 1981, Hudson Valley Philharm., N.Y., 1981, Newton Symphony, Boston, 1982, Hartford Symphony, 1982, RTE Symphony, Dublin, Ireland, 1983, Albany Symphony Orch., 1984-85, Houston Symphony Orch., 1986, Richmond Symphony Orch., 1987, Williamsburg Symphony Orch., Greenville Symphony Orch., Des Moines Symphony Orch., Utah Symphony Orch., Cape Cod Symphony Orch., Tallahassee Symphony Orch., Va. Symphony Orch, 1988-90, Shanghai Symphony, 1993, 94, Erie (Pa.) Philharmonic, 1995, Amarillo (Tex.) Symphony, 1996, Opera Carolina, N.C., 1997, 99, Harrisburg (Pa.) Opera, 1997, 98, 99, Wuhan Symphony, China, 1997, 99, Hunan Symphony, Changsha, China, 1998; music dir. New Amsterdam Symphony Orch., N.Y.C., 1978-80, Pitts. Youth Symphony Orch., 1978-80, Empire State Youth Orch., 1982-86, Southeastern Music Ctr., 1983-84, Bel Canto Opera, 1983-86, Roanoke (Va.) Symphony Orch., 1986-95; artistic dir. Bel Canto Opera Co., 1986-88, artistic adv., Wuhan Symphony (China), 1997—, Opera Roanoke, 1989-95; Exxon/Arts Endowment condr., Pitts. Symphony, 1978-80, artistic dir., Harrisburg Opera, 1998—; recs. include Twentieth Century Cello, Two American Contemporaries, The Frog Prince, An American Collage, Live from Shanghai, Victoria Bond: Compositions, The American Piano Concerto; commd. by Pa. Ballet, 1978, Jacob's Pillow Dance Festival, 1979, Am. Ballet Theater, 1981, Empire State Inst. Performing Arts, 1983, 84, Stage One, Louisville, 1986, Ga. State U., 1986, L'Ensemble, 1990, Renaissance City Winds, 1990, Audubon String Quartet, 1990, Women's Philharm., San Francisco, 1993, Va. Explore Park and The Shanghai Symphony, 1994, D Day Found., 1994, Linda Plaut, 1994, The Billings (Mont.) Symphony, The Elgin (Ill.) Symphony. Bd. dirs. Am. Music Ctr. Recipient Victor Herbert award 1977, Perry F. Kendig award, 1988, ASCAP Composition award 1973—; Nat. Inst. for Music Theater grantee in opera conducting N.Y.C. Opera, 1985, Martha Baird Rockefeller grantee, 1978-79, Meet-The-Composer grantee in Composition, 1973—; Juilliard scholar, 1972-77; Juilliard fellow, 1975-77, Aspen Music Festival fellow, 1973-76; named Exxon/Arts Endowment Conductor, 1978-80, Woman of Yr. in Va., 1990, 91; featured on NBC Today show, 1990, profiled in C.S. Monitor, 1987, Wall Street Jour., 1987, other mags. and shows. Mem. ASCAP (awards 1975—), Am. Symphony Orch. League, Am. Fedn. Musicians, Condrs. Guild (bd. dirs. 1994—), Internat. Alliance Women in Music, N.Y. Women Composers, Conductor's Guild (bd. dirs. 1994—), Mu Phi Epsilon. Avocations: horseback riding, sailing, hiking. *I believe that our life's work is in sharing our talents and gifts with others. Our own happiness and fulfillment are in direct proportion with the amount we give of ourselves.*

BOND, WILLIAM HENRY, librarian, educator; b. York, Pa., Aug. 14, 1915; s. Walter Loucks and Ethel (Bossert) B.; m. Helen Elizabeth Lynch, Dec. 6, 1943 (dec. Jan. 1999); children: Nancy Barbara, Sally Lynch. A.B., Haverford Coll., 1937; M.A., Harvard, 1938, Ph.D., 1941. Research fellow Folger Shakespeare Library, 1941-42; asst. to librarian Houghton Library, Harvard, Cambridge, Mass., 1946-48; curator manuscripts Houghton Library, Harvard, 1948-64, librarian, 1965-82; lectr. bibliography Harvard, 1964-67, prof., 1967-86, librarian, prof. emeritus, 1986—; asst. keeper manuscripts Brit. Mus., 1952-53; Sandars reader in bibliography Cambridge (Eng.) U., 1981-82. Author: Thomas Hollis of Lincoln's Inn, a Whig and His Books, 1990; editor: (Christopher Smart) Jubilate Agno, 1954, Supplement to Census of Medieval and Renaissance Manuscripts in the United States, 1962, The Houghton Library, 1942-67, 1967, Records of a Bibliographer, 1967, 18th Century Studies in Honor of Donald F. Hyde, 1970, (with Hugh Amory) The Printed Catalogues of the Harvard College Library 1723-1790, 1996. Trustee Emerson Meml. Assn., 1964-89, Concord (Mass.) Free Pub. Library, 1966-71; trustee Historic Deerfield (Mass.) Inc., 1965-91, hon. trustee, 1991—, v.p., 1985-88. Served to lt. USNR, 1943-46. Guggenheim fellow, 1982-83. Mem. Bibliog. Soc. Am. (pres. 1974-75), Bibliog. Soc. London (hon. sec. for Am. 1964-93), Grolier Club, Am. Antiquarian Soc. (councillor 1970-91, hon. councillor 1991—), Mass. Hist. Soc., Colonial Soc. Mass. (pres. 1981-93, hon. mem. 1994—), The Johnsonians, Phi Beta Kappa. Home: 109 The Valley Rd Concord MA 01742-4900 Office: Houghton Library Cambridge MA 02138

BOND, WILLIAM JENNINGS, JR., air force officer; b. Boyce, La., Mar. 12, 1953; s. William Jennings and Iris Elizabeth (Chenault) B.; m. Karen Lynne Lloid, May 20, 1975 (dec. Aug. 1980); m. Mary Dean Clark, Nov. 19, 1983; 1 child, William Seth. B in Music Edn., Northwestern State U. La., 1974, MusM, 1978; MS in Adminstrn., Ctrl. Mich. U., 1992; grad., Joint Mil. Intelligence Coll., 1994; postgrad., Nova Southeastern U.; grad., Armed Forces Staff Coll. Choral dir. Fairview (La.) H.S., 1975-80; commd. 2d lt. USAF, 1980, advanced through grades to maj., 1991; comdr. sect. squadron 23d Civil Engrs., Alexandria, La., 1983-85; tng. flight comdr. USAF Officer Tng. Sch., San Antonio, 1985-87, chief student adminstrn., 1987-88; missile crew evaluator comdr. 321st Missile Wing, Grand Forks, 1990-92; mem. missile combat crew 448th Missile Squadron, Grand Forks, 1988-90, instr., evaluator flight comdr., 1992—, internat. treaty implementation officer, 1992-93; chief, mil. prodn. analysis br. Def. Intelligence Agy., Washington, 1994-96; mem. Bosnian task force Office Sec. of Def., Washington, 1997—. Vol. fireman Town of Boyce, La., 1968-71; res. police officer Natchitoches (La.) Police Dept., 1973; combined fed. campaign dir. USAF Officer Tng. Sch., 1986; trustee, choral dir. Calvary Bapt. Ch., Emarado, N.D., 1992; choral dir. South Run Bapt. Ch., Springfield, Va., 1993-97. T.H. Harris Edn. scholar State of La., 1971-74. Mem. NRA, ASPA, Am. Mgmt. Assn., Nat. Mil. Intelligence Assn., Acad. Mgmt., Kiwanis Internat., Sigma Iota Epsilon. Republican. Avocations: shooting sports, photography. Home: 201 Ridgefield Dr Bossier City LA 71111-2370

BOND, WILLIAM L., career officer; b. Roseburg, Oreg.. Commd. U.S. Army, advanced through grades to brig. gen., 1998; comdg. gen. Simulations, Tng. and Instrumentation Command, Orlando, Fla., 1998—. Office: Simulations Tng and Instrumentation Command 12350 Research Pky Orlando FL 32826-3276

BONDAR, RICHARD JAY LAURENT, biochemist; b. N.Y.C., Sept. 4, 1940; s. Kelliher H. and Helen (Halper) B.; m. Enid Sue Teicher, Dec. 21, 1961; children: Randal, Karen. BS, McGill U., Montreal, Que., Can., 1962; MS, Calif. Inst. Tech., 1965; PhD, U. Calif., Riverside, 1969. Tech. dir. Worthington Biochem. =Corp., Freehold, N.J.; prin. devel. chemist Beckman, Brea, Calif.; mgr. Abbott Labs, South Pasadena, Calif.; v.p. Internat. Medication Systems, South El Monte, Calif.; mgr. pharm. devel. Banner Pharmacaps, Chatsworth, Calif.; mgr. quality control lab. 3M Pharmaceuticals, Northridge, Calif. Contbr. over 30 refereed articles to profl. jours. Fellow Am. Inst. chemists; mem. Am. Chem. Soc., Am. Assn. Pharm. Scientists, Sigma Xi.

BONDAREFF, WILLIAM, psychiatry educator; b. Washington, Apr. 29, 1930; s. Leon and Gertrude Bondareff; children by previous marriage: Hyla, Sarah; m. Rita Haber Kassoy, Jan. 2, 1988. BS in Zoology, George Washington U., 1951, MS in Zoology, 1952; PhD in Anatomy, U. Chgo., 1954; MD, Georgetown U., 1962. Diplomate Am. Bd. Psychiatry and Neurology with added qualifications in geriatric psychiatry. Rsch. assoc., instr. anatomy U. Chgo., 1955; rotating intern USPHS Hosp., Balt., 1962-63; resident in psychiatry Northwestern Meml. Hosp. Inst. Psychiatry, Chgo., 1978-80; asst. prof. anatomy Northwestern U., Evanston, Ill., 1963-65, assoc. prof., 1965-69, prof., 1969-78, chmn. dept. anatomy, 1970-78; prof. psychiatry and gerontology U. So. Calif., L.A., 1981—; mem. staff U. So. Calif. Univ. Hosp., L.A., 1991—; mem. attending staff L.A. County/U. So. Calif. Med. Ctr., L.A., 1981—; mem. Hosp. Good Samaritan, L.A., 1981—; mem. staff Norris Cancer Hosp., 1987—; physician/cons. VA Hosp., Downey, Ill., 1969-80, Jewish Home for Aged, Reseda, Calif., 1981-90; vis. staff mem. medicine Passavant Pavilion Northwestern Meml. Hosp., 1972-80; dir. div. geriat. psychiatry U. So. Calif., 1981—; dir. U. So. Calif.-St. Barnabas Alzheimer Disease Ctr., 1985—; acting dir. dept. Gerontology Research Inst. Andrus Gerontology Ctr.-U. So. Calif., 1982; staff psychiatrist Los Angeles County Hosp., 1981—; past holder various com. offices Northwestern U. Editor Mechanisms of Aging and Devel., 1970—; assoc. editor Am. Jour. Anatomy, 1970-76; mem. editorial Bd. Alzheimer Disease and Associated Disorders-An Internat. Jour., 1985—, Neurobiology of Aging, 1980—; The Jour. of Gerontology, 1981-84, Internat. Rev. Jour. of Psychiatry, 1988—; contbr. articles to profl. jours. Mem. sci. adv. bd. Alzheimer's Disease & Related disorders Assn. L.A., bd.dirs., 1989—; mem. rsch. rev. com. treatment, devel. and assessment Nat. Inst. Mental Health, 1987-92. Served with USPHS, 1955-63. USPHS fellow, 1955, U. Cambridge Clare Hall vis. fellow, 1980, Hughes Hall vis. fellow, 1988; scholar Allergy Found., 1960, U. Chgo., 1953; recipient Career Devel. award Nat. Inst. Neurol. Disease and Blindness, 1966-69, Sesquicentennial award Hobart and William Smith Colls., 1972, Sandoz prize Internat. Assn. Gerontology, 1983, Alzheimer Disease and Related Disorders Assn. award, 1984; Fulbright Lectr., U. Goteborg, Sweden, 1967-68. Fellow AAAS (councilor 1970-74), Am. Psychiat. Assn. (geriatrics task force 1981), Gerontol. Soc.; mem. Am. Assn. Anatomists (chmn. local com. ann. meeting 1969), Electron Microscope Soc. Am., Am. Soc. Cell Biology, Am. Acad. Neurology (chmn. neuroanatomical scis. sect. 1971-77), Soc. Neurosci., Assn. Anatomy Chmn. (councilor 1975-77), Am. Assn. Geriat. Psychiatry (program com. 1984—, bd. dirs. 1985-89), So. Calif. Psychiat. Soc., Internat. Psychogeriat. Assn., Cajal Club, Cosmos Club, Sigma Xi. Office: U So Calif Sch Medicine MOL 203 1237 N Mission Rd Los Angeles CA 90033-1018

BONDARENKO, HESPERIA AURA LOUIS, entrepreneur; b. Detroit, June 24, 1929; d. Arthur and Lola (Papadopoulou) Louis; m. William Bondarenko, Dec. 28, 1950; children: Marc, Fernande, Leif. Student, UCLA, 1962-64. Cert. comml. artist; cert. tchr., Ala. Designer Ernst Kern Co., Detroit, 1946-49, J.W. Knapp Co., Lansing, Mich., 1950-53; dir. interior visual mechandising Pizitz, Inc., Birmingham, Ala., 1968-75; photo stylist Bondarenko Photography, Birmingham, 1982-87; owner So. Postage Svcs., Birmingham, 1969—; designer Mich. Bell Tel., Detroit, 1952-53, Festival of Arts-Greece, Birmingham, 1969, Festival of Arts-Israel, Birmingham, 1972; designer display animation Horn's, Pitts., 1949. Dir. voter registration LWV, Birmingham, 1966-68; mem. Birmingham Mus. Art, 1988—, Nat. Mus. Women in Arts, 1989—. Mem. Internat. Assn. Postage Vendors, Ala. Retail Assn.

BONDAROOK, NINA, public relations consultant; b. N.Y.C., Sept. 19, 1955; d. Peter and Lydia Bondarook; m. Earl S. Belofsky, Apr. 14, 1989. BA in Journalism, Ariz. State U., 1977; MS in Applied Comm., U. Denver, 1990. Account mgr. Waggener Edstrom PR, Bellevue, Wash., 1996—. Mem. Pub. Rels. Soc. Am., Soc. Profl. Journalists. Office: Waggener Edstrom Strategic PR 11400 SE 8th St Ste 250 Bellevue WA 98004

BOND-BROWN, BARBARA ANN, musician, educator; b. Kansas City, Mo., July 1, 1955; d. John Bartley, Jr. and Tressie Laverne (Nichols) Bond; m. Lance Elliott Brown, Mar. 11, 1979. Student, Ctrl. Mo. State U., 1973-74, 75-77, U. Mo., 1974, William Jewell Coll., 1975; studies with Karen Halverhout, Prarie Village, Kans., 1995—. Dist. accompanist Kansas City Pub. Schs., 1979-82; ind. music tchr. Independence, Mo., 1982-84; ind. music tchr., accompanist San Francisco, 1984-92; ind. music tchr. Barbara Bond-Brown Music Studio, Lee's Summit, Mo., 1992—. Mem. Kans. City Music Tchrs. Assn. (v.p. achievement auditions 1994—, v.p. fall festival 1994—, chmn. pre-coll. honors auditions 1995—), Mo. Music Tchrs. Assn. (chmn. honors auditions 1993—, officer 1995—), Music Tchrs. Nat. Assn., Federated Music Tchrs. Avocations: reading, writing, cooking, traveling. Home and Studio: 906 SE 5th Ter Lees Summit MO 64063-4343

BONDE, LINDA MERILYN, elementary school educator; b. Faribault, Minn., June 29, 1955; d. Gary Robert and Merilyn Eunice (Jackson) Hanson; m. Steven Earl Bonde, June 27, 1981; children: Marcus S.,Kyle D., Angella L. BS, St. Cloud State U., 1977. Cert. tchr., Minn. Chpt. 1 tchr. Cannon Falls (Minn.) Elem. Sch., 1977-79, tchr. grade 6, 1979—. Home: 18537 Kane Ave Nerstrand MN 55053-2800 Office: Cannon Falls Area Elem Sch 1020 Minnesota St E Cannon Falls MN 55009-2242

BONDE, COUNT PEDER CARLSSON, investment company executive; b. Stockholm, Sept. 2, 1923; came to U.S., 1992; s. Carl Gustaf and Ebba (Wallenberg) B.; m. Ylva M. Jenssen, June 18, 1948 (div. Jan. 1956); children: Johan, Ulrika, Hans; m. J. Madeleine Rouchier, Sept. 27, 1957 (div. May 1988); m. Clarissa Leggett, July 2, 1989; children: Helena, Amelie, Sophia. Student exam, Sigtunaskolan, Sigtuna, Sweden, 1942; res. officer, Royal Horse Guard, Cavalry, Stockholm, 1946; Lic.Jur., Uppsala U., 1948. Asst. judge Dist. Ct. Askim, Göteborg, Sweden, 1948-51; banking trainee U.S., France, Germany, 1952-56; from asst. v.p. to exec. v.p. Stockholms Enskilda Bank, 1957-71; dep. chief exec. Skandinaviska Enskilda Banken, Stockholm, 1972-73, Salén Shipping Group, Stockholm, 1973-76; spl. rep. Skandinaviska Enskilda Banken, Zürich, Switzerland, 1977; pres., CEO Banque Scandinave en Suisse, Geneva, 1978-82; exec. vice-chmn. Investor AB, Providentia AB, Stockholm, 1983-91; vice-chmn. Investor AB, Stockholm, 1992-93; bd. dirs., vice-chmn., chmn. Alfa-Laval AB, Stockholm, 1961-91; vice-chmn. Stora AB, Falun, Sweden, 1985-91, Skandia Ins. Group AB, Stockholm, 1985-92, Astra AB, Sodertalje, Sweden, 1987-92; chmn. Forestal Valdivia, Santiago, Chile, 1991-94, Investor Internat. AB, Washington, 1993-98; chmn. European-Am. Bus. Coun., Washington. Governing bd. Nat. Cathedral Sch. for Girls, Washington, 1999—; adv. bd. Korn/Ferry Internat., L.A. Capt. Cavalry, Sweden, 1952-76. Decorated Knight Royal Order of Vasa, 1972, The King's Gold Medal, 1994, grand officer Portuguese Order of Henry the Seafarer by Pres. of Portugal, 1991, grand cross Order of St. Gregorius the Great by His Holiness the Pope, 1991, grand cross Order of Leopold II by H.M. the King of the Belgians, 1994; named Lord in Waiting, Ct. of His Majesty the King of Sweden. Mem. Royal Bachelors Club (Göteborg), Royal Swedish Yacht Club, Met. Club, Nat. Press Club, Chevy Chase Club. Home: Oak View 3201 36th St NW Washington DC 20016-3143

BONDERMAN, DAVID, company executive. CEO Tex. Pacific Group, Ft. Worth. Office: Tex Pacific Group 201 Main St Ste 2420 Fort Worth TX 76102-3105*

BONDI, BERT ROGER, accountant, financial planner; b. Portland, Oreg., Oct. 2, 1945; s. Gene L. and Elizabeth (Poynter) B.; m. Kimberley Kay Higgins, June 18, 1988; children: Nicholas Stone, Christopher Poynter. BBA, U. Notre Dame, 1967. CPA, Colo., Calif., Wyo. Sr. tax acct. Price Waterhouse, Los Angeles, 1970-73; ptnr. Valentine Adducci & Bondi, Denver, 1973-76; sr. ptnr. Bondi & Co., Englewood, Colo., 1976—; 50 for Colo.-1998 dir. Citizens Bank. Bd. govs. Met. State Coll. Found.; bd. dirs. Am. Cancer Soc. Denver; mem. adv. bd. Jr. League of Denver. Served with U.S. Army, 1968-70. Mem. C. of C., Community Assns. Inst., Govt. Fin. Officers Assn., Colo. Soc. Assn. Execs. (edn. com.), Home Builders Assn., Am. Inst. CPAs, Colo. Soc. CPAs, Wyo. Soc. CPAs, Rotary (Denver), Notre Dame Club, Metropolitan Club (Denver), Castle Pines Country Club. Roman Catholic. Home: 49 Glenalla Pl Castle Rock CO 80104-9026 Office: Bondi & Co 44 Inverness Dr E Englewood CO 80112-5410

BONDI, JOSEPH CHARLES, JR., education educator, consultant; b. Tampa, Fla., Aug. 15, 1936; s. Joseph C. and Virginia B.; m. Patsy L. Hammer, Aug. 6, 1960; children: Pamela, Beth, Bradley. B.S., U. Fla., 1958, M.Ed., 1964; Ed.D., U. Fla. 1968. Tchr., adminstr. Hillsborough County (Fla.) Pub. Schs., 1958-65; instr. U. South Fla., Tampa, 1965-66, asst. prof., 1966-68, assoc. prof., 1968-74, prof. edn., 1974—; ptnr. Wiles, Bondi & Assocs., edn. cons.; cons. in field, South Africa, Hong Kong, China, Taiwan, Can., Am. Internat. Schs. Author 17 textbooks including Developing Middle Schools, 1972, Curriculum Development, 1979, 5th edit., 1997, Practical Politics for School Administrators, 1981, The Essential Middle School,

1981, 93, Supervision: A Guide to Practice, 4th edit., 1996. Councilman City of Temple Terrace, Fla., 1970-74, mayor, 1974-78; ruling elder Presbyn. Ch. With USNR, 1958-63. Mem. Fla. ASCD (pres.), Am. Edni. Rsch. Assn. Democrat. Office: U South Fla Coll Edn Tampa FL 33620

BONDINELL, STEPHANIE, counselor, former educational administrator; b. Passaic, N.J., Nov. 22, 1948; d. Peter Jr. and Gloria Lucille (Burden) Honcharuk; m. Paul Swanstrom Bondinell, July 31, 1971; 1 child, Paul Emil. BA, William Paterson U., 1970; MEd, Stetson U., 1983. Cert. elem. educator, Fla.; guidance counselor grades K-12, Fla. Tchr. Bloomingdale (N.J.) Bd. Edn., 1971-80; edn. dir. Fla. United Meth. Children's Home, Enterprise, 1982-89; guidance counselor Volusia County Sch. Bd., Deltona, Fla., 1989—; coord. sch. improvement svcs., Deltona Lakes, 1996-98. Sec. adv. com. Deltona Jr. High Sch., 1984-88; sec. Deltona Jr. PTA, 1982; vice-chmn. adv. com. Deltona Mid. Sch., 1988, chmn., 1989-91, chmn., 1991-92; mem. Deltona High Adv. Com., 1995-96; mem. secondary sch. task force Volusia County Sch. Bd., 1986—; mem. Volusia County Rep. Exec. Com., Rep. Presdl. Task Force; mem. state adv. bd. Fla. Future Educators Am., 1991-92; coord. sch. improvement svcs. Deltona Lakes, 1996-98; dist. chmn. Volusia County Fla. Future Educators Am., 1990—. Acad. scholar Becton, Dickinson & Co., N.J., 1966; N.J. State scholar, 1966-70; named girls state rep. Am. Legion, N.J., 1966, Tchr. of Yr. Deltona Lakes, 1991, 95; recipient Vol. Svc. award Volusia County Sch. Bd., Deland, 1985, Outstanding Ednl. Partnership award S.W. Volusia C. of C., 1998. Mem. ASCD, AAUW, Coun. Exceptional Children, Divsn. for Learning Disabilities, Fla. Assn. Counseling and Devel., N.J. Edn. Assn., Volusia Tchrs. Orgn., Internat. Platform Assn., Deltona Civic Assn., Deltona Rep. Club (v.p. 1991), 4 Townes Federated Rep. Women's Club (sec., v.p.), Stetson Univ. Alumni Assn. Avocations: painting, creative writing, dancing. Home: 1810 W Cooper Dr Deltona FL 32725-3623 Office: Volusia County Sch Bd 2022 Adelia Blvd Deltona FL 32725-3976

BONDOC, ROMMEL, lawyer; b. Pomona, Calif., June 23, 1938; s. Nicholas Rommel and Gladys Sue (Buckner) B.; m. Ariel Guiberson, Aug. 20, 1960 (div. 1963); m. Alberta Linnea Young, Dec. 13, 1967; children—Daphne, Patience, Margaret, Nicholas. A.B., Stanford U., 1959, J.D., 1963. Bar: Calif. 1964, U.S. Ct. Appeals (9th cir.) 1965, U.S. Supreme Ct. 1969. Assoc. Melvin Belli, San Francisco, 1964-66, Vincent Hallinan, San Francisco, 1966-69; sole practice, San Francisco, 1969—. Mem. San Francisco Bar Assn. (judiciary com. 1982-85), No. Calif. Criminal Trial Lawyers Assn. (bd. dirs. 1972—, pres. 1978-79), Calif. Attys. for Criminal Justice (bd. dirs. 1975-80). Democrat. Methodist. Home: 509 Canyon Rd Novato CA 94947-4330 Office: 819 Eddy St San Francisco CA 94109-7701

BONDS, BARRY LAMAR, professional baseball player; b. Riverside, Calif., July 24, 1964; s. Bobby B. Student, Ariz. State U. With Pitts. Pirates, 1985-92, San Francisco Giants, 1992—. Named MVP Baseball Writers' Assn. Am., 1990, 1992, 1993, Maj. League Player Yr. Sporting News, 1990, Nat. League Player Yr. Sporting News, 1990, 91, mem. Sporting News Coll. All-Am. team, 1985, mem. All-Star team, 1990, 1992-96; recipient Gold Glove award, 1990-94, 96, Silver Slugger award, 1990-96. Led Nat. League in intentional walks, 1992-94. Office: San Francisco Giants Candlestick Point 3 Com Park San Francisco CA 94124*

BONDS, GEORGIA ANNA, writer, lecturer; b. N.Y.C., Dec. 30, 1917; d. Alex Matthews and Mattie Ethel (Stephens) Arnett; m. Alfred Bryan Bonds Jr., Feb. 23, 1939; children: Anna Belle, Alfred Bryan III, Alexandra Burke, Stephen Arnett. BA, U. N.C., Greensboro, 1938; MA, La. State U., 1940; postgrad., U. N.C., 1940-42, Baldwin-Wallace Coll., 1960s. Editl. asst. The So. Rev., Baton Rouge, 1938-39; editor Abstracts of Theses La. State U., Baton Rouge, 1940; editl. asst. pub. sch. curricula State of La., 1941; free-lance writer, lectr., 1943—; editor dist. newspaper United Meth. Ch., Cleve., 1979-91; lectr. on Egyptian days and ways, 1956-70, internat. concerns, 1970-85, Cherokee Indian heritage, 1985—. Editor: (English transl.) Wheat Growing in Egypt, 1954; author: The Lake Erie Girl Scout Council, the First Seventy-five Years, 1987; contbr. articles to popular mags. Active Girl Scouts USA, 1928—, leader, organizer troop 1, Cairo, 1953-55, mem. Lake Erie coun., Cleve., 1956—, leader, organizer Mounted troop, 1957-80, coun. bd. dirs., 1966-70, 79-87, coun. pres., 1979-84, mem. nat. coun., 1966-72, 78-83, troop leader internat. encampment, 1968, condr. world tour nat. and internat. ctrs., 1972, world conf. asst., 1984, organizer troops, Volgograd, Russia, 1991—; mem. Dist. United Meth. Women, Cleve., 1956—, bd. dirs., 1965-78, pres., 1974-78, com. on dist. superintendency, 1977-81, chair, 1978-81, mem. World Meth. coun., London, 1966; mem. Ch. Women United in Ohio, 1960—, state bd. dirs., 1966-72; active YWCA, Little Rock, 1950—, bd. dirs., 1950-53, bd. dirs. Cleve. chpt., 1977-79; active Philanthropic Ednl. Orgn., 1950—, bd. dirs. Ohio state chpt., 1965-71, pres., 1971. Recipient Outstanding and Dedicated Svc. award Girl Scouts of Lake Erie Coun., 1979, Thanks Badge, 1971, Thanks Badge II, 1997, World Friendship and Understanding Through Girl Scouting award Girl Scouts of Lake Erie Coun., 1984, award of honor for fund raising S.W. Gen. Hosp. Found., 1996. Mem. AAUW (bd. dirs. 1984-89), Baldwin-Wallace Coll. Women's Club (hon. life mem.), Order of Ea. Star, Delta Zeta, Kappa Phi, Phi Beta Kappa (Cleve. assn. bd. dirs. 1964-69, pres. 1968). Avocations: swimming, travel. Home: PO Box 768 Berea OH 44017-0768

BONDS, JOHN WILFRED, JR., lawyer; b. Jackson, Tenn., May 6, 1943; s. John Wilfred Sr. and Louise (Robinson) B.; m. Mary Anne Hatchett, July 18, 1969; children: Kathleen Lucile, Mary Julia. BS, U.S. Air Force Acad., 1965; JD, Vanderbilt U., 1973. Bar: Ga. 1973. Commd. 2nd lt. USAF, 1965; advanced through grades to capt. USAF, Vietnam, Thailand, 1965-70; resigned USAF, 1970; assoc. Sutherland, Asbill & Brennan, Atlanta, 1973-79, ptnr., 1979—. Editor in chief Vanderbilt Law Rev., 1973. Mem. ABA, Ga. Bar Assn., Atlanta Bar Assn., Lawyers Club Atlanta, Order of Coif. Presbyterian. Office: Sutherland Asbill & Brennan 999 Peachtree St NE Atlanta GA 30309-3996

BONDS, SOPHIA JANE RIDDLE, geriatrics, medical/surgical nurse; b. Prentiss County, Miss., July 28, 1937; d. Cleatis Ross and Nona Exie (Palmer) Riddle; m. Joseph Luther Bonds, Sr., Jan. 21, 1956; children: Theresa Regina Bonds Peters, Joseph Luther, Jr., Michael Timothy, Sheila Elaine Bonds Ryan, Terry Jane Bonds Lee. LPN, Northeast Miss. Jr. Coll., 1968, ADN, 1980. RN, Miss. Asst. head nurse Magnolia Hosp., Corinth, Miss.; head nurse Aletha Lodge, Booneville, Miss.; supr. Alcorn County Care Inn, Corinth; staff nurse swingbed Bapt. Meml. Hosp., Booneville; mem. Miss. State Dept. Health, Gero Psyche Booneville, Miss. Bapt. Meml. Hosp. Mem. ANA.

BONDURANT, EMMET JOPLING, II, lawyer; b. Athens, Ga., Mar. 16, 1937; s. John Parnell and Mary Claire (Brannon) B.; m. Jane E. Fahey, Aug. 12, 1990; children by previous marriage: Emmet Jopling III, Katherine Elizabeth, Melissa Eileen, Christopher Scott, Miles Stephen. A.B. cum laude, U. Ga., 1958, LL.B. magna cum laude, 1960; LL.M., Harvard U., 1962. Bar: Ga. 1959. Law clk. to Judge Clement Haynsworth, Jr. U.S. Ct. Appeals, 4th Circuit, 1960-61; assoc. Kilpatrick, Cody, Rogers, McClatchey & Regenstein, Atlanta, 1962-68; ptnr. Kilpatrick, Cody, Rogers, McClatchey & Regenstein, 1968-77; ptnr. firm Bondurant, Mixson & Elmore and predecessor, Atlanta, 1977—; vis. lectr. in antitrust law U. Ga., spring 1971; pres. Atlanta Legal Aid Soc., 1972-73; vice chmn. Ga. Gov.'s Commn. on Criminal Justice Standards and Goals, 1974. Contbr. articles on antitrust and reapportionment, right to counsel, bankruptcy, and local govt. issues to profl. jours.; co-editor: Antitrust Law Developments, 1974. Mem. Joint Atlanta-Fulton County Citizens Adv. Com. on Consolidation, 1969; chmn. Atlanta Charter Commn., 1971-72; co-chmn. Com. for Sensible Rapid Transit, Atlanta, 1971-72. Named 1 of 5 Outstanding Young Men of 1970, Atlanta Jaycees, 1992 Ga. Trial Lawyer of the Year, Am. Bd. Trial Advocates (Ga. Chpt.); recipient Good Govt. award, LWV Atlanta-Fulton County, 1980, Durfee award, Calif. Western Sch. Law, 1984. Fellow Am. Bar Found.; mem. ABA (exec. com. atlanta lawyers com. for civil rights), Ga. Bar Assn., Atlanta Bar Assn. (exec. com. 1975-81, Leadership award 1992), State Bar Ga. (chmn. sect. antitrust law 1972-73, chmn. jud. sys. comm. 1991—), Am. Law Inst., Am. Coll. Trial Lawyers, Am. Acad. Appellate Lawyers, Am. Judicature Soc., Ga. Law Sch. Alumni Assn. (pres. 1996-97), Lawyers Club Atlanta (sec. 1971-72), Phi Beta Kappa, Phi Delta Phi, Phi Kappa Phi, Kappa Alpha. Methodist. Home: 2930 Habersham Rd NW Atlanta GA 30305-2846 Office: Bondurant Mixson & Elmore Ste 3900 1201 W Peachtree St NW Atlanta GA 30309-3417

BONDURANT, STUART, physician, educational administrator; b. Winston-Salem, N.C., Sept. 9, 1929; s. Stuart Osborne Bondurant; m. Susan Haughton Ehringhaus, May 5, 1991; children from previous marriage: Stuart, Margaret Lynn, Nancy Vance. BS, Duke U., 1952, MD, 1953; DSc (hon.), Ind. U., 1980. Intern Duke Hosp., Durham, N.C., 1953-54; resident in internal medicine Duke Hosp., 1954-55; resident Peter Bent Brigham Hosp., Boston, 1958-59; asst. prof. medicine Ind. U. Sch. Medicine, Indpls., 1959-61; assoc. prof. Ind. U. Sch. Medicine, 1961-66, prof., 1966-67; assoc. dir. Ind. U. Cardiovascular Research Ctr., 1961-67; chief med. br. artificial heart-myocardial infarction program NIH, Bethesda, Md., 1966-67; prof. medicine, chmn. dept., physician in chief Albany Med. Ctr. Hosp., N.Y., 1967-74; pres., dean Albany Med. Coll., 1974-79; prof. medicine U. N.C., Chapel Hill, 1979—, dean Sch. Medicine, 1979-94, interim dean, 1996-97; dir. Ctr. for Urban Epidemiology Studies N.Y. Acad. Medicine, N.Y.C., 1994-96. Contbr. articles to med. jours. Recipient Disting. Alumnus award Duke U. Sch. Medicine, 1974, Merit award Am. Heart Assn., 1975, Thomas Jefferson award U. N.C.-Chapel Hill, 1998; Citizen Laureate U. Found., Albany, 1979. Master ACP (regent, pres. 1980); fellow Am. Soc. Clin. Investigation (v.p. 1974), Assn. Am. Physicians (pres. 1985-86), Inst. of Medicine, Assn. Am. Med. Colls. (exec. com. 1977, chmn. coun. deans 1979-81, chmn. 1993-94), Royal Coll. Physicians Edinburgh, Royal Coll. Physicians London. Office: U NC Sch Medicine CB # 7000 Office of Dean Chapel Hill NC 27599-7000

BONDY, PHILIP KRAMER, physician, educator; b. N.Y.C., Dec. 15, 1917; s. Eugene Lyons and Irene (Kramer) B.; m. Sarah B. Ernst, Mar. 18, 1949; children: Jonathan L., Jessica, Steven M. AB, Columbia U., 1938; MD, Harvard U., 1942; MA (hon.), Yale U., 1961. Intern Peter Bent Brigham Hosp., Boston, 1942-43; mem. staff Grady Meml. Hosp., Atlanta, 1943, 46-48, chief resident in medicine, 1947-48; mem. faculty Emory U., 1947-48, 49-52, asst. prof. medicine, 1951-52; Alexander Browne Coxe fellow physiol. chemistry Yale U., New Haven, 1948-49, mem. faculty, 1948-49, 52-74, 77-88, prof. medicine, 1961, 77-88, prof. emeritus, 1988—, C.N.H. Long prof. medicine, 1965-74, chmn. dept. internal medicine, 1965-72, assoc. dean for vets. affairs, 1983-89, chmn. com. outpatient svcs., 1960-62; chmn. med. divsn. Royal Marsden Hosp., 1972-77; Cancer Rsch. Campaign prof. Inst. Cancer Rsch., London; cons. Ludwig Inst. Cancer Rsch., Zurich, Switzerland, 1972-77; assoc. chief of staff for rsch. West Haven VA Med. Ctr., 1977-83, chief of staff, 1983-89; mem. med. vis. com. Brookhaven Nat. Labs., 1969-73, chmn., 1973; mem. program project com. NIH-Nat. Inst. Arthritis and Metabolic Disease, 1964-68, chmn., 1966-68; mem. exptl. biol. sect. breast cancer task force NIH-Nat. Cancer Inst., 1973-76; mem. adv. coun. NIDDK, 1990-94; mem. planning com. Med. Rsch. Svc. VA, 1985-88, chmn., 1986-88; mem. N.E. region planning com. VA. Editor-in-chief Jour. Clin. Investigation, 1957-62, Yale Jour. Biology and Medicine, 1978-92; editor: Diseases of Metabolism, 6th, 7th, 8th edits, Yearbook of Endocrinology and Metabolism, 1963-64; editorial bd. Conn. Medicine, 1959-61, Yearbook of Medicine, 1954-84, Medicine, 1963-85, Merck Manual, 1969—, Clinics in Endocrinology and Metabolism, 1973-84, Cancer Topics, 1975-79. Sec. libr. bd. City of Woodbridge, Conn., 1960-67; sec. bd. dirs. Southbury Tng. Sch. Found.; sec., bd. trustees Southbury Tng. Sch.; mem. governor's Coun. on Mental Retardation, Conn., 1997—. Capt. M.C., AUS, 1943-46. Recipient Edward Sutliffe Brainard prize Columbia U., 1938, Sigma Xi prize Emory U., 1949, Rsch. Career award NIH, 1962, 66. Fellow AAAS (chmn. sect. N on med. sci. 1979), Royal Coll. Physicians, Royal Soc. Medicine (v.p. sect. oncology 1975-77); mem. ACP (master), Endocrine Soc. (councillor 1964-67, mem. publs. com. 1965-72, chmn. 1968-72), Assn. Am. Physicians, Assn. Physicians Gt. Britain and Ireland, Am. Soc. Clin. Investigation, Am. Fedn. Clin. Rsch., Nat. Assn. VA Chiefs of Staff (mem. exec. com. 1986-88), Soc. Exptl. Biology and Medicine, Interurban Clin. Club, Inst. Cancer Rsch. (London, hon.). Home: 9 Chestnut Ln Woodbridge CT 06525-1701

BONE, ROBERT WILLIAM, writer, photojournalist; b. Gary, Ind., Sept. 15, 1932; s. Robert Ordway and Georgia Juanita (Clapp) B.; m. Sara Ann Cameron, Aug. 14, 1965; children: Christina Ann, David Robert. BS in Journalism, Bowling Green State U., 1954. Editor, tng. literature The Armor Sch., Ft. Knox, Ky., 1954-56; reporter, photographer Middletown (N.Y.) Daily Record, 1956-59, San Juan (Puerto Rico) Star, 1959-60; news editor Popular Photography Mag., N.Y.C., 1960-62; editor-in-chief Brazilian Bus. Mag., Rio de Janeiro, 1962-63; picture editor Time-Life Books, N.Y.C., 1963-68; sr. writer Fielding's Travel Guide to Europe, Mallorca, Spain, 1968-71; staff writer Honolulu Advertiser, 1971-84; free-lancer Honolulu, 1984—; stringer Time-Life News Svc., 1981-86. Author: Maverick Guide to Hawaii, 1977, Maverick Guide to Australia, 1979, Maverick Guide to New Zealand, 1981, Fielding's Alaska and the Yukon, 1989; travel editor Honolulu mag., 1985-88, R.S.V.P. mag., 1988-89. 1st lt., U.S. Army, 1954-56. Named to Journalism Hall Fame Bowling Green State U., 1990. Mem. Soc. Am. Travel Writers, Am. Soc. Mag. Photographers. Democrat. Home and Office: 1053 Lunaai St Kailua HI 96734-4633

BONEAU, C. ALAN, psychology educator, researcher; b. Cin., Feb. 2, 1926; s. Charles A. and Virginia Louise (Kircher) B.; m. Ann Mallin, Sept. 2, 1955; children: Denise Lynn, Jonathan Alan, Paul Charles. BA in Psychology with high honors, U. Cin., 1950, MA in Psychology, 1951; PhD in Exptl. Psychology, Duke U., 1957. Supr. employment testing aircraft gas turbine div. Gen. Electric Co., 1952-53; grad. asst., rsch. asst., univ. fellow Duke U., Durham, N.C., 1953-57, USPHS postdoctoral rsch. fellow, 1957-58, asst. prof., 1958-62, asst. to dean, 1962-64, assoc. prof., 1962-66; ednl. affairs officer Am. Psychol. Assn., 1966-71, dir. programs and planning, 1971-76, exec. officer, 1974-75; sr. assoc. Devel. Assocs., Inc., Arlington, Va., 1977-78; prgram mgr. Essex Corp., Alexandria, Va., 1978-80; prof. psychology George Mason U., Fairfax, Va., 1980-98, chair psychology dept., 1980-82, emeritus prof., 1998—; rsch. prof. Krasnow Inst. for Advanced Studies, 1998—; mem. faculty senate Duke U., 1962-64; cons. in field, 1976-80; rsch. psychologist Army Rsch. Inst., 1980-89. Contbr. articles to profl. jours. Treas. Sci. Manpower Commn., 1976. With USN, 1944-46. USPHS spl. postdoctoral fellow Stanford U., 1965-66, citation classic recognition Current Contents, 1986. Fellow AAAS, APA (cons. editor Jour. Applied Psychology 1981-86, exec. com. editor newsletter 1981, rep. to Coun. Social Sci. Assns. 1975-76, liaison to Nat. Adv. Mental Health Coun.), Soc. for Gen. Psychology (pres. 1987), Am. Psychol. Soc., Washington Acad. Sci.; mem. Psychonomic Soc., Soc. for Computers in Psychology, Soc. for Studying Unity Issues in Psychology (pres. 1987-88), Phi Beta Kappa, Sigma Xi. Office: Dept of Psychology George Mason U Fairfax VA 22030

BONELLI, ANTHONY EUGENE, former university dean; b. Detroit, June 17, 1934; s. Anthony Emile and Ruby (Hughey) B.; m. Charlotte Schattel, Dec. 28, 1957; children—Stella Elizabeth, Anthony Eugene, John Christopher. B.Mus., Coll.-Conservatory of Music, U. Cin., 1956, M.Mus., 1958; Ph.D., Eastman Sch., 1970. Instr. piano and theory Del Mar Coll., Corpus Christi, Tex., 1958-60, asst. prof., 1960-63, assoc. prof., 1963-65, prof., 1965-69, chmn. music theory dept., 1960-65, dean divsn. fine arts, chmn. dept. music, 1965-69; mem. faculty Eastman Sch. Music, 1963-64; prof. music, chmn. divsn. music So. Meth. U., Dallas, 1969-74, dean Meadows Sch. Arts, 1978-96; Thomas James Kelly prof. music, dean Coll.-Conservatory of Music, U. Cin., 1974-78; pres. Dallas Symphony Assn., 1993—. Contbr. articles to profl. jours. Pres. Corpus Christi Arts Council, 1967-69; bd. dirs. Corpus Christi Symphony, 1965-69, Dallas Symphony, 1970-74, 78—, Cin. Symphony Orch., Cin. Ballet Co., Cin. Opera Co., Cin. Chamber Music Soc., KERA, Channel 13, Dallas Opera; mem. NEA Task Force, 1978, Tex. Commn. on Arts, 1980. Mem. Nat. Assn. Schs. Music (nat. sec. 1975-78, exec. com.), Coll. Music Soc., Music Tchrs. Nat. Assn., Music Educators Nat. Conf., Internat. Council Fine Arts Deans (pres. 1978-80), Dallas Civic Music Assn. (pres. elect 1980, pres. 1981-82), Pi Kappa Lambda (pres. 1980—). Episcopalian. Office: Dallas Symphony Assn 2301 Flora St Ste 300 Dallas TX 75201-2413*

BONER, DONALD LESLIE, information systems executive; b. Lawton, Okla., June 3, 1944; s. Jessie Edward and Violet (Cravens) B.; m. Carol Ann Stevens, Oct. 25, 1966 (div. June, 1973); children: Freda L., Zirque M.; m. Suellen Jackson, Dec. 1, 1973. *Son, bassist Zirque was four times winner of "New Talent Deserving Wider Recognition" nomination from Downbeat magazine. He has recorded with Paul Voudourie, Chris Spears and Ralf Illenberger. Daughter Freda, a drummer, is a founding member of the Blake Babies and other bands. She has appeared on MTV and on Late Night with Conan O'Brien. Wife Suellen has been recognized by federal and state agencies for working with the disabled.* Student, Area Vocat. Tech. Sch., Nashville, Tenn., 1967, Tenn. Inst. Broadcasting, Nashville, 1969; AS, Ind. Vocat. Tech. Coll., Indpls., 1983. Acting dir. Near East Side Community Orgn., Indpls., 1971-74; sgt. Marion County Sheriff's Dept., Indpls., 1975-76; acquisition mgr. Colonial Discount, Indpls., 1977-80; community organizer Christamore House, Indpls., 1978-79; pres., co-founder Smoner Investment Co., Indpls., 1979-80; sgt. Pinkerton, Inc., Indpls., 1980-82; computer programmer Group VI Marketing, Indpls., 1982-83; dir. product devel., operation mgr. Adman, F.A.S., Indpls., 1983—; freelance programmer Programmers Guild, Indpls., 1980-82. Author: 5 computer games, 1980-82. Mem. adv. com. Purdue U. Dept. of Computer Tech. Industry; dcampaign coord. Small Claims Ct. judge, Indpls., 1974; mem. Dem. precinct com., Indpls., 1974-78. Recipient Caspar award Community Svc. Coun., Indpls., 1972, first prize for winemaking, Ind. State Fair, 1975. Mem. Nat. Assn. for Computing Machinery (bd. dirs. cen. Ind. chpt. 1986-87, vice chmn. 1987-88, chmn. 1988-89), Indpls. Computer Soc., IEEE Computer Soc., Cellar Master Club (treas. Indpls. 1975-91). Avocations: wine making, video, music, theatre. Home: 516 E 15th St Indianapolis IN 46202-2634 Office: Adman F.A.S. VNU Bus Info Sys Inc 151 N Delaware St Ste 1750 Indianapolis IN 46204-2512

BONERZ, PETER, actor, director; b. Portsmouth, N.H., Aug. 6, 1938; s. Christopher Andrew and Elfrieda Anne (Kern) B.; m. Rosalind Ditrapani, Dec. 14, 1963; children: Eric, Eli. B.S., Marquette U., 1960. Instr. UCLA, 1991-94. Stage actor: The Premise, The Committee, White House Murder Case, Story Theatre; film actor: Funnyman, Medium Cool, Catch-22, The Serial, Man in the Moon; dir. TV series The Bob Newhart Show, Murphy Brown, Friends, Newsradio, Home Improvement, the Hughley's. Served with AUS, 1961-63. Recipient award for comedy directing Dirs. Guild Am., 1992, Emmy nomination, 1993, Dirs. Guild nomination, 1994, Cable Ace nomination, 1996.

BONESIO, WOODROW MICHAEL, lawyer; b. Hereford, Tex., Dec. 27, 1943; s. Harold Andre and Elizabeth (Ireland) B.; m. Michaele Ann Dougherty; children: Elizabeth Eaton, Jo Kristin, William Michael. B.A., Austin Coll., 1966; J.D., U. Houston, 1971. Bar: Tex. 1971, U.S. Dist. Ct. (we., no., so., and ea. dists.) Tex. 1973, U.S. Ct. Appeals (5th cir.) 1973, U.S. Ct. Appeals (11th cir.) 1981. Law clk. to U.S. dist. Judge Western Dist. Tex., San Antonio, 1971-73; ptnr. Akin, Gump, Strauss, Hauer & Feld, Dallas, 1973-92, Kuntz & Bonesio LLP, Dallas, 1992—; speaker profl. confs. Democratic precinct chmn. Dallas County; ruling elder, First Presbyterian Ch., Dallas, 1999—; bd. dirs. Grace Presbytery Devel. Bd., 1986-88. Fellow Tex. Bar Found.; mem. ABA, Fed. Bar Assn., Am. Judicature Soc., Dallas Bar Assn., Tex. Bar Coll., Dallas Bar Found., Dallas Assn. Def. Counsel, Order of Barons, Austin Coll. Alumni Assn. (bd. dirs. 1983), U. Houston Law Alumni Assn. (chpt. pres. 1982), Vocal Majority (bd. dirs. 1990—), Soc. for Preservation and Encouragement Barber Shop Quartet Singing in Am. (internat. chorus champions 1975, 79, 82, 85, 88, 91, 94, 97), Lake Highlands Exch. Club, Phi Alpha Delta. Office: Kuntz & Bonesio LLP 1717 Main St Ste 4050 Dallas TX 75201-4639

BONESSA, DENNIS R., lawyer; b. Uniontown, Pa., Jan. 15, 1948; s. Arthur V. and Josephine A. (Sierzega) B.; m. Bernadine Kopec, May 1, 1976; children: Dirk Arthur, Andrew Edward. BA, Pa. State U., 1969; JD, Georgetown U., 1972. Bar: Pa., U.S. Dist. Ct. (we. dist.) Pa., U.S. Ct. Appeals (3rd cir.), U.S. Tax Ct. Ptnr. Reed, Smith, Shaw & McClay, Pitts., 1972—. Mem. Pa. Bar Assn., Allegheny County Bar Assn. Office: Reed Smith Shaw & McClay PO Box 2009 Pittsburgh PA 15230-2009

BONESTEEL, MICHAEL JOHN, lawyer; b. L.A., Dec. 22, 1939; s. Henry Theodore Samuel Becker and Kathleen Mansfield (Nolan) B.; children: Damon Becker, Kirsten Kathleen; m. Susan Elizabeth Schaff, June 1, 1980. AB in History, Stanford U., 1961; JD, U. So. Calif., 1966. Bar: Calif. 1967, U.S. Dist. Ct. (cen. and so. dists.) Calif. 1967, U.S. Dist. Ct. (no. dist.) Calif. 1969, U.S. Dist. Ct. (ea. dist.) Calif. 1983, U.S. Supreme Ct. 1989. Assoc., Haight, Brown & Bonesteel and predecessors , Santa Monica, Calif., 1967-71, ptnr. 1972—. Fellow Internat. Acad. Trial Lawyers, Am. Coll. Trial Lawyers; mem. ABA, State Bar Calif., Am. Soc. Most Venerable Order of Hosp. St. John of Jerusalem, L.A. County Bar Assn., Def. Rsch. Inst., Assn. of So. Calif. Def. Counsel, Bel Air Bay (Santa Monica) Club, L.A. Country Club, Mil. and Hospitaller Order of St. Lazarus of Jerusalem Grand Priory of Am. Episcopalian. Office: Haight Brown & Bonesteel 1620 26th St Ste 4000N Santa Monica CA 90404-4013

BONET, FRANK JOSEPH, lawyer; b. N.Y.C., Apr. 6, 1937; s. Frank and Alexandra (Roots) B.; m. Mary Ellen Mathews, July 14, 1962; children—Catherine Ann, Frank Joseph, Elizabeth Mary, Jean Marie. B.A. magna cum laude, St. John's U., 1958, LL.B. (assoc. editor law rev.), 1961. Bar: Tex. 1961. With Horn & Hardart Co., N.Y.C., 1961-72, corp. sec., head corp. legal dept., 1969-72; real estate atty. J.C. Penney Co., Inc., 1972-77; sr. S.W. regional real estate atty. J.C. Penney Co., Inc., Dallas, 1977-89, mng. atty. real estate dept., 1989-91, also asst. corp. sec.; mng. atty. JCP Realty, Inc., Dallas, 1992-94; chief real estate counsel J.C. Penney Co., Inc., Dallas, 1994-98; lectr. Internat. Coun. Shopping Ctrs. Contbr. articles profl. jours. Mem. N.Y. State Bar, State Bar Tex. Home: 1909 Deerfield Dr Plano TX 75023-5110 Office: 6501 Legacy Dr Plano TX 75024-3612

BONETT, EDWARD JOSEPH, JR., law clerk, public housing manager; b. Phila., Oct. 27, 1963; s. Edward J. Sr. and Lucia (Celia) B.; m. Jennifer Baldino, Nov. 15, 1992. BS, Drexel U., 1985; MBA, Villanova U., 1992; postgrad., Temple U., 1997—. Svc. rep. Phila. Housing Authority, 1987-89, adminstrv. technician, 1989-93, policy planner II, 1994-95, relocation mgr., 1995-98. Author, editor (newsletter) Tomorrows Dawn, 1995—. Com. mem. Dem. Party, Phila., 1986-88; mem. St. Richard Pastoral Coun., Phila., 1995-97, Bella Vista Cmty. Assn., Phila., 1984-91; eucharistic min. St. Paul/ St. Richard Parish, Phila., 1991—. Recipient Cmty. Svc. Palumbo Recreation Ctr., 1983. Mem. St. Thomas More Soc., Nat. Assn. of Housing and Redevelopment Offcls. Roman Catholic. Avocations: baseball, playing trumpet, reading. Home: 1726 W Oregon Ave Philadelphia PA 19145-4726

BONEVAC, DANIEL ALBERT, philosopher, author; b. Pitts., Jan. 20, 1955; s. Daniel Paul and Katherine Dawn (Dryer) B.; m. Beverly Ann Burford, Aug. 14, 1976; children: Marian Dawn, Melanie Elizabeth. BA, Haverford Coll., 1975; MA, U. Pitts., 1977, PhD, 1980. Asst. prof. philosophy U. Tex., Austin, 1980-85, assoc. prof., 1985-92, prof., 1992—, chmn. dept. philosophy, 1991—. Author: (books) Reduction in the Abstract Sciences, 1982 (Johnsonian prize Jour. of Philosophy), Deduction, 1987, The Art and Science of Logic, 1990; editor: Today's Moral Issues, 1992; co-editor: Beyond the Western Tradition, 1992, Understanding Non-Western Philosophy, 1993; mem. editl. bd. Am. Philos. Quar. Sr. fellow Tex. Pub. Policy Found., Austin, 1995—. Grantee NSF, 1986-88. Mem. Am. Philos. Assn. (Johnsonian prize 1980), Soc. for Exact Philosophy, Nat. Assn. Scholars. Republican. Presbyterian. Office: Univ Tex Dept Philosophy Austin TX 78712*

BONEY, JEW DON, councilman; s. J. Don and Clara (Payne) B. Student, U. Tex. Ordained minister Bapt. Ch., 1981. Prodr., host TV and radio talk shows; councilman City of Houston, 1996—, mayor pro-tem, 1998—; mem. aviation, competetive bidding, coun. rules, ethics, fiscal affairs, internat. trade, neighborhood planning and protection, pub. health and redevel. and revitalization coms., chair subcom. on Africa and Caribbean Houston City Coun.; cons./strategic planner leadership devel. tng. for cmty.-based orgns.; prodr./host Pacifica Radio Sta. KPFT-TM program "From the Frontline", 1989-95, KYOK Radio program "From the Frontline", 1993-95. Counselor, adminstrv. cons. Over the Hill, Inc., 1988-89; chmn. Houston chpt. Nat. Black United Front, 1985-95, Coalition to Free Clarence Lee Brantley, 1987-91; pastor House of the Lord Bapt. Ch., 1986-87; project dir. Computerized Edn. Project, 1984-86; cons., cmty. organizer Houston Interfaith Sponsoring Com., 1981-82; chmn., founder Campaign to Save the Children; chmn. Houston Voter Edn. Project; co-chmn., charter mem. Harris County Minorities and Law Enforcement Coalition, Houston Pub. Action Com.; founding mem. Afro-Am. Players, U. Tex., 1972; vol. cons. U.S. Dept. Justice, 1978-95; Allen Pkwy. Village steering com. Houston Housing Authority, 1985; weekend steering com. Congl. Black Caucus, 1981, others.

Recipient Disting. Svc. award Houston tchrs. Assn., 1976, Cert. of Cmty. Recognition KMJQ Majic 102 FM, 1983, Cert. of Recognition for Outstanding Cmty. Svc. Brentwood Bapt. Ch. Bus. and Profl. Men's Unit, 1984, Disting. Svc. award Over the Hill, Inc., 1985, Great Achievement award New Testament Bapt. Ch., 1985, Humanitarian award Nat. Coun. Negro Women, 1985, Cmty. Svc. award Nat. Assn. Black Social Workers and Nat. Assn. of Blacks in Criminal Justice, Outstanding Cmty. Svc. award Over the Hill, Inc., 1986, Spl. award Unaited Negro Coll. Fund, 1987, Civil Rights/Human Rights Leadership award So. Christian Leadership Conf. and Amnesty Internat., 1987, Martin Luther King Jr. award for civil rights Houston br. NAACP, 1988, Cmty. Svc. award Houston Bus. and Profl. Men's Club, 1990, Houston Peace and Justice award Houston Peace Network, 1990, Pres.'s award Houston br. NAACP, 1990, Silver award for outstanding ministry and cmty. svc. Harris County Coun. of Orgns., 1991, Cert. of Recognition for Outstanding Cmty. Svc. Internat. Assn. Black Profl. Fire Fighters, 1992, NCNW-DIH Disting. Svc. award, 1996, African Am. Lesbian and Gay Alliance Barbara Jordan award, 1996, Mickey Leland Leadership award Houston Black Fire Fighters, 1996, The H.S. of Meteorology and Space Sci. Leadership award, 1997, Blacks in Govt. award, 1997, Order of the Niger award The Nigerian Found., 1997. Mem. Black United Front (chmn. Houston chpt.), Houston Voter Edn. Project, Campaign to Save the Children. Avocations: hiking, creative writing, bicycling, travel, computer technologies. Office: PO Box 1562 Houston TX 77251-1562

BONFANTE, LARISSA, classics educator; b. Naples, Italy; came to U.S., 1939, naturalized, 1951; d. Giuliano and Vittoria (Dompé) B.; m. Peter B. Warren, Sept. 1950 (div. 1962); children: Sebastian Raditsa, Alexandra Bonfante-Warren; m. Leo Ferrero Raditsa, May 2, 1973. Student, Radcliffe Coll., 1950, U. Rome, 1951; BA, Barnard Coll., 1954; MA, U. Cin., 1957; PhD, Columbia U., 1966. Mem. faculty NYU, 1963—, prof., 1978—, chmn. dept. classics, 1978-84, 87-90; cons. in field. Author: Etruscan Dress, 1975, Out of Etruria, 1981, Reading the Past, Etruscan, 1990, (with Giuliano Bonfante) The Etruscan Language, 1983 (transl. into Italian 1985, into Romanian 1995); editor: Etruscan Life and Afterlife: Handbook of Etruscan Studies, 1986 (transl. into Romanian 1996), (with Francesco Roncalli) Antichità dall'Umbria a New York, 1991, (with Judith Sebesta, ed.) The World of Roman Dress, 1994, Corpus Speculorum Etruscorum, N.Y. The Metropolitan Museum of Arts, 1997; translator: Chronology of the Ancient World (E.J. Bickerman) 1986, The Plays of Hrotswitha of Gandersheim, 1979; also articles. Mem. Archaeol. Inst. Am. (gov. bd. 1982-88), Istituto di Studi Etruschi (fgn.), German Archaeol. Inst. (corres. mem.). Home: 50 Morningside Dr New York NY 10025-1739 Office: NYU Classics Dept 25 Waverly Pl New York NY 10003-6701

BONFIELD, ANDREW JOSEPH, tax practitioner; b. London, Jan. 26, 1924; came to U.S., 1946; s. George Willliam and Elizabeth Agnes B.; m. Eleanor Ackerman, Oct. 16, 1955; children: Bruce Ian, Sandra Karen. Gen. mgr. Am. Cushion Co., L.A., 1948-50, Monson Calif. Co., Redwood City, 1951-58; mfrs. mktg. rep. Monson Calif. Co., San Francisco, 1958-62; tax practitioner, bus. cons. Redwood City, 1963—, San Jose, Calif., 1963—, Los Gatos, Calif., 1963—, Carmel, Calif., 1963—, Kihei, Hawaii, 1963—. Past treas., dir. Northwood Park Improvement Assn.; exec. bd. Santa Clara County Coun. Boy Scouts Am., 1971—, past coun. pres., mem. Nat. coun.; mem. Santa Clara County Parks and Recreation Commn., 1975-81, 82-86, mem. County Assessment Appeals Bd., 1978-86, Hawaii Bd. Taxation Review, 1992-98. With Brit. Royal Navy, 1940-46. Decorated King George VI Silver Badge; recipient Silver Beaver award, Vigil honor award Boy Scouts Am.; enrolled to practice before IRS. Mem. Nat. Assn. Enrolled Agts., Calif. Soc. Enrolled Agts., Hawaii Assn. Pub. Accts., Royal Can. Legion (past state parliamentarian, past state 1st vice comdr.), Rotary (pres. San Jose E. 1977-78, pres Kihei-Wailea 1993-94), Los Gatos Masons, Aloha Temple Shriners of Honolulu (amb.). Home: 181 Hacienda Carmel Carmel CA 93923

BONFIELD, ARTHUR EARL, lawyer, educator; b. N.Y.C., May 12, 1936; s. Louis and Rose (Lesser) B.; m. Doris Harfenist, June 10, 1958; 1 child, Lauren. BA, Bklyn. Coll., 1956; JD, Yale U., 1960, LLM, 1961, postgrad. (sr. fellow), 1961-62. Bar: Conn. 1961, Iowa 1966. Asst. prof. U. Iowa Law Sch., 1962-65, assoc. prof., 1965-66, prof., 1966-69, Law Sch. Found. prof., 1969-72, John Murray prof., 1972—, assoc. dean for research, 1985—; summer vis. prof. law U. Mich., 1970, U. Tenn., 1972, U. N.C., 1974, Hofstra U., 1977, Lewis and Clark U., 1984; gen. counsel spl. joint com. state adminstrv. procedure act Iowa Gen. Assembly, 1974-75; spl. counsel adminstrv. procedure exec. br. State of Iowa, 1975; chmn. com. constl. law Nat. Conf. Bar Examiners Multi-State Bar Exam, 1977—; reporter 1981 Model State Adminstrv. Procedure Act, Nat. Conf. Commrs. Uniform State Laws, 1979-81; cons. Ark. State Constl. Conv., 1980; chmn. Iowa Gov.'s Com. State Pub. Records Law, 1983; Iowa commr. Nat. Conf. Commrs. on Uniform State Laws, 1984-2000; chmn. Iowa Gov.'s Task Force on Uniform Adminstrv. Rules, 1985-92, Iowa Gov.'s Task Force Team on Regulatory Process, Rule Making, and Rules Rev., 1999—. Prin. draftsman Iowa Civil Rights Act, 1965, Iowa Fair Housing Act, 1967, Iowa Adminstrv. Procedure Act, 1974, Iowa Open Meetings Act, 1978, Iowa Civil Rights Act, 1978, Amendments to Iowa Public Records Law, 1984, Amendments to Iowa Administrative Procedure Act, 1998; author: State Administrative Rule Making, 1986, State and Federal Administrative Law, 1989; contbr. numerous articles to law jours. Recipient Outstanding Service to Civil Liberties award Iowa Civil Liberties Union, 1974, Hancher Finkbine Outstanding Faculty Mem. award U. Iowa, 1980, Faculty Excellence award Iowa Bd. Regents, 1995, Outstanding Law Sch. Tchg. award U. Iowa, 1996; named Frederick Klocksiem fellow Aspen Inst. Humanistic Studies, summer 1978. Mem. ABA (chmn. divsn. state adminstrv. law 1976-80, coun. 1980-84, chmn. sect. 1987-88, sect. adminstrv. law and regulatory practice), Am. Law Inst., Iowa State Bar Assn. (chmn. com. adminstrv. law 1971-85, coun. sect. adminstr. law 1990-93, 94-97, 98-99, reporter and mem., task force on state adminstrv. law reform 1994-96, Pres. award Outstanding Svc. to Bar and Public 1996), Am. Coun. Learned Soc. (del. from Assn. Am. Law Schs. 1984-94). Home: 206 Mahaska Dr Iowa City IA 52246-1606 Office: U Iowa Sch Law Iowa City IA 52242

BONFIGLIO, THOMAS ALBERT, pathologist, educator; b. Rochester, N.Y., Oct. 17, 1942; s. Charles P. and Minnie C. (Argentiere) B.; m. Mary Barat Rice, July 2, 1966; children: Susan Marie, Amy Elizabeth, Megan Lynn. BS magna cum laude, St. John Fisher Coll., 1964; MD, U. Rochester, 1969. Diplomate Am. Bd. Pathology; cert. Nat. Bd. Med. Examiners, Internat. Bd. Cytopathology, N.Y.S. lab. dir.; lic. Ohio, N.Y. Intern in pathology U. Hosps. Cleve., 1969-70, resident in pathology, 1969-71; tchg. fellow pathology Case Western Res. U., 1969-71; chief resident in pathology Strong Meml. Hosp., Rochester, N.Y., 1971-72; instr., pathology fellow U. Rochester Med. Ctr., 1971-72, asst. prof. pathology, 1972-76, assoc. dir. cytopathology lab., assoc. dir. sch. cytotech., 1973-76, acting dir. surg. pathology, divsn., dir. cytopathology lab., 1975-76; asst. prof. pathology Case Western Reserve U., 1976-77; asst. pathologist, chief divsns. cytopathology and surg. pathology Mt. Sinai Hosp., Cleve., 1976-77; assoc. prof. pathology U. Rochester Med. Ctr., 1977-84, prof. pathology, 1984-89, prof., acting chmn. dept. pathology and lab. medicine, 1989-90, prof., chair dept. pathology and lab. medicine, 1990-97, clin. prof. pathology, 1997—; cons. pathology Rochester Gen. Hosp., 1978—, Genesee Hosp., 1979-97; attending pathologist, dir. surg./pathology unit, 1984-85, Strong Meml. Hosp., attending pathologist, dir. anatomic pathology divsn., 1985-97, pathologist in chief, 1989-97; sr. attending pathologist, head pathology divsn. Genesee Hosp., 1997—; mem. Cytotechnologist Exam. Com., 1980-83, Biol. Stain Commn., 1981-91, cytopathology exam com. Am. Bd. Pathology, 1984-89, spl. ad hoc com. cytopathology N.Y. State Dept. Health, 1988, others; v.p. Intersoc. Pathology Coun., 1988, pres., 1989; bd. dirs. Univs. Assoc. Rsch. and Edn. in Pathology; presenter papers, abstracts; participant, invited spkr., dir., panelist numerous workshops, meetings, seminars, confs., teleconfs. in field; vis. prof., guest lectr. Med. Coll. Ohio, Toledo, 1980, Dartmouth-Hitchcock Med. Ctr., Hanover, N.H., 1982, William Beaumont Army Med. Ctr., El Paso, 1984, Med. U. N.J., Newark, 1984, New Eng. Deaconess Hosp., Boston, 1985, Henry Ford Hosp., Detroit, 1989, Loyola U. Sch. Medicine, Chgo., 1990, St. Francis Hosp., Hartford, Conn., 1991, Marshall U. Sch. Medicine, Huntington, W.Va., 1991, U. Iowa Sch. Medicine, Huntington, W.Va., 1991, U. Iowa Sch. Medicine, Iowa City, 1991, U. Mass. Sch. Medicine, 1994. Author: Cytopathologic Interpretation of Transthoracic Fine-Needle Biopsies, 1983, (with others) Histologic Typing of Female Genital Tract, 1994; editor: Gynecologic Cytopathology, 1997, Fine Needle Aspiration of Subcutaneous Organs and Masses, 1996; mem. editl. bd. Human Pathology, 1982—, Am. Jour. Clin. Pathology, 1985—, Lab. Medicine, 1984-90; mem. N.Am. rev. bd., editl. adv. bd. ACTA Cytologica; contbr. articles to profl. jours.; author video Cytopathology of Fine Needle Biopsies of the Abdomen, 1985. Fellow Am. Soc. Clin. Pathologists (v.p. 1990-91, pres.-elect 1991-92, pres. 1992-93, clin. pathologists commn. on continuing edn., Disting. Svc. award 1988, bd. dirs. 1985-94, chmn. nominating com. 1988, 92, rsch. and devel. com. 1985-89, chmn. quality assurance steering com. 1987-92, dep. commr. commn. on continuing edn. 1984-90, chmn. coun. cytopathology 1983-84, coun. on cytopathology 1979-84), Coll. Am. Pathologists, Internat. Acad. Cytology (sci. program com. 1988-89, terminology com. 1992); mem. AMA, Am. Soc. Cytology (Cert. of Merit for outstanding svcs. 1987, Papanicolaou award 1991, v.p. 1984-85, pres.-elect 1985-86, pres. 1986-87, chmn. sci. program com. 1982-84, exec. com. 1980-88, numerous others), Am. Soc. Investigative Pathology, Arthur Purdy Stout Soc. Surg. Pathologists, Assn. Dirs. Anatomic and Surg. Pathology (coun. 1989-95), Assn. Pathology chmn., Internat. Soc. Gynecol. Pathologists, Monroe County Med. Soc., N.Y. State Soc. Pathologists, Rochester Area Assn. Pathologists (v.p. 1978-79, pres. 1979-80), U.S. and Can. Acad. Pathology, Alpha Omega Alpha. Roman Catholic. Avocations: fishing, boating. Home: 3666 NiBawauka Beach Canandigua NY 14424 Office: Genesee Hosp Dept Pathology 224 Alexander St Rochester NY 14607-4055

BONGIORNO, JAMES WILLIAM, electronics company executive; b. Westfield, N.Y., Apr. 2, 1943; s. Samuel Salvatore and Marjorie Ruth (Hardenburg) B. Student public schs. Profl. musician, 1961-65; engr. Hadley Labs., Pomona, Calif., 1965-66, Marantz Co., Woodside, N.Y., 1966-67; chief engr. Rectilinear Research Corp., Bklyn., 1967-68; profl. musician, writer Popular Electronics, also Audio mag., 1968-71; dir. engring. Dynaco Inc., Phila., 1972, S.A.E. Inc., Los Angeles, 1973-74; founder, pres. Gt. Am. Sound Co. Inc., Chatsworth, Calif., 1974-77; founder, 1977; pres. Sumo Electric Co. Ltd., West Hollywood, Calif., 1977—; ind. electronic cons. Patentee class A audio amplifier, FM IF-detector. Recipient State of Art Design award Stereo Sound mag., Tokyo, 1976, 80. Mem. Audio Engring. Soc., Am. Fedn. Musicians. Republican. Home and Office: PO Box 4835 Santa Barbara CA 93140-4835 *Aside from the fact that my lifetime goal has always been to design the world's finest amplifier, I also wanted it to be affordable by as many people as possible. I am happy that I have achieved this goal as there are a lot more poor people than rich people.*

BONGIORNO, JOSEPH JOHN, JR., electrical engineering educator; b. Bklyn., Aug. 3, 1936; s. Joseph John and Mildred Rose (LoPinto) B.; m. Carol Marie Olsen, Nov. 22, 1958; children: James Michael, Peter Joseph, Richard Edward, Cathryn Mary. BEE, Poly. Inst. Bklyn., 1956, MEE, 1958, DEE, 1960. Asst. prof. Poly. Inst. N.Y., Bklyn., 1960-64, assoc. prof., 1964-74, prof., 1974-96, prof. emeritus, 1996—; cons. Unisys (formerly Sperry Systems Mgmt.), Gt. Neck, N.Y., 1963-93. Contbr. articles to profl. jours. Mem. St. Aidan's Parish Sch. Bd., Williston Park, N.Y., 1967-70, 73-76, pres. 1975-76. Rsch. grantee NSF, Washington, 1972, 82, 85, Army Rsch. Office, Durham, N.C., 1993. Fellow IEEE (Control Systems Soc. best paper award 1977). Roman Catholic. Home: 36 Park Ave Williston Park NY 11596-1628 Office: Poly U Rte 110 Farmingdale NY 11735

BONHAG, THOMAS EDWARD, insurance company executive, financial consultant, financial planner; b. Bronxville, N.Y., Jan. 19, 1952; s. Herman Arthur and Anne Elizabeth (Sage) B.; m. Noreen Patricia Early, Apr. 24, 1976 (div. Dec. 1981); m. Cornelia Hackett Lyons, Oct. 8, 1983. BS, Fordham U., 1973; MBA, St. John's U., 1979; postgrad., Am. Coll., 1979-84. CLU; cert. fin. planner, chartered fin. cons. Field sales rep. Colgate-Palmolive Co., N.Y.C., 1973-74; employee relations officer Chase Manhattan Bank, N.Y.C., 1974-78; agt., dist. mgr. Equitable Life Assurance Soc., N.Y.C., 1979-83; v.p. northeastern region mktg. Equitable Life Assurance Soc., Edison, N.J., 1984-90; sr. v.p. Kornreich Life Assocs., Inc., N.Y.C., 1990-94; CEO, Winged Keel Group, Inc., N.Y.C., 1994-95; CEO, Equitable Life, N.Y.C., 1995, dir. advanced planning/markets, 1995-98; mng. dir. The deBart Group, Inc., N.Y.C., 1999—; fin. cons. Am. Geriatrics Soc., N.Y.C., 1983-86. Mem. Hoboken (N.J.) Environ. Com., 1983-90; mayoral appointee citizens' budget adv. com. Twp. of Cranford, N.J., 1991-92; mem. Cranford Bd. Edn., 1991-94, pres., 1992-94. Mem. Am. Soc. CLUs, Nat. Assn. Life Underwriters, Inst. Cert. Fin. Planners, Assn. for MBA Execs., Estate Planning Coun. N.Y.C. Libertarian. Roman Catholic. Avocations: golf, walking, bicycling. Home: 406 Monmouth Ave Spring Lake NJ 07762-1131

BONHAM, CLIFFORD VERNON, retired social work educator; b. Paradise, Calif., July 11, 1921; s. Leon C. and Mary M. (Horn) B.; m. Vesta H. Williamson, May 4, 1956; children: William Robert Rohde (stepson), Larry Dean, Tami Marie. Student, San Francisco State U., 1948-49; BA, U. Calif., Berkeley, 1951, MSW, 1953. Lic. clin. social worker, marriage and family counselor, Acad. Cert. Social Workers. Parole agt. Calif. State Dept. Youth Authority, 1953-59, rsch. interviewer, supervising parole agt., 1959-64; field instr. Grad. Sch. Social Work, Calif. State U., Fresno, 1964-67; assoc. prof. Grad. Sch. Social Work, Calif. State U., 1967-74, prof., 1974-91, prof. emeritus social work, 1991—, field sequence coord., 1971-80; assoc. coord. field program Grad. Sch. Social Work, 1967-71, coord. field program, Fresno, 1971-80; counselor Suicide Prevention Program, Fresno, Calif., 1964-70; cons. Fresno County Domestic Rels., 1967-70, Fresno County Pub. Defenders' Office, 1986-88; commr. Fresno County Juvenile Justice Commn., 1971-81; mem. state legis. com. on housing felons, 1980; social work cons. various hosps., Fresno, 1971-89; mem. Dept. Youth Authority Youth Justice Task Force, 1986-88. Bd. dirs. Piedmont Pines Assn., Oakland, Calif., 1960-64; mem. Fresno County Emergency Housing Bd., 1970-72; mem. adv. com. on Correctional Edn., 1989-90; mem. Correctional Bd. Edn., 1991-92; mem. Madera County Mental Health Bd., 1991-93. With USN, 1940-46. Mem. NASW, Calif. Probation and Parole Assn. (regional v.p. 1973-74), Soc. Clin. Social Workers, Assn. Advancement of Social Work with Groups. Democrat. Unitarian. Home: PO Box 1284 Oakhurst CA 93644-1284

BONHAM, HAROLD FLORIAN, research geologist, consultant; b. L.A., Sept. 1, 1928; s. Harold Florian and Viola Violet (Clopine) B.; m. Sally Mae Reimer, Sept. 6, 1952; children: Cynthia Jean Kimball, Douglas Craig, Gary Stephen. AA in Physics, U. Calif. Berkeley, 1951; BA in Geology, UCLA, 1954; MS in Geology, U. Nev., 1963. Geologist So. Pacific Co., 1955-61; mining geologist Nev. Bur. Mines and Geology, Reno, 1963-93, acting dir., state geologist, 1993-95; cons. geologist, 1996—; cons. UN, Can., Australia, Peoples Republic of China, 1980-90; cons. in field. Contbr. articles to profl. jour. V.p. Palomino Valley Gen. Improvement Dist., Nev., 1986-88. With USN, 1946-49, PTO. Fellow Geol. Soc. Am., Soc. Econ. Geologist, Assn. Exploration Geochemists (councillor 1988-94); mem. Geol. Soc. Nev. Republican. Avocations: reading, computers, photography. oenology. Home: 2100 Right Hand Canyon Rd Reno NV 89510-9396

BONHAM, (ANDREW) KENT, legislative staff member; b. Morristown, N.J., Mar. 1, 1972. Student, London Sch. Econs.; grad., Colby Coll., 1994. Hansard scholar. Office: 346 Russell Senate Office Washington DC 20510-2705

BONHAM, RUSSELL AUBREY, chemistry educator; b. San Jose, Calif., Dec. 10, 1931; s. Russell Aubrey and Margaret Florence (Wallace) B.; m. Miriam Anne Dye, Mar. 23, 1957; children: Frances, Margaret, Anne. BA, Whittier Coll., 1954; PhD, Iowa State U., 1958. Instr. Ind. U., Bloomington, 1958-60; postdoctoral fellow Naval Rsch. Lab., 1960; asst. prof. math. U. Md., 1960; asst. prof. chemistry Ind. U., Bloomington, 1960-63, assoc. prof., 1963-65, prof. chemistry, 1965-95, prof. emeritus, 1996—; rsch. prof. chemistry Ill. Inst. Tech., Chgo., Ill., 1995—. Co-author: High Energy Electron Scattering, 1974; mem. editorial bd.: The Jour. of the Brazilian Chem. Soc., 1989—; contbr. over 175 articles and papers to profl. jours. Recipient Fulbright fellowship U. Tokyo, 1964-65, Guggenheim fellowship, 1964-65, Humboldt prize, 1977, 81, grant NSF, 1993—. Fellow Am. Phys. Soc., AAAS; mem. Am. Phys. Soc., Am. Crystallographic Assn., Am. Chem. Soc., Sigma Xi. Achievements include research on electron impact cross section measurements of molecular species of interest to low pressure processing plasmas. Office: Ill Inst Tech Dept Biol Chem Phys Scis 3101 S Dearborn Chicago IL 60616

BONHAM-CARTER, HELENA, actress; b. Eng., May 26, 1966. Ed., Westminster. TV appearances include A Pattern of Roses, Miami Vice, A Hazard of Hearts, The Vision, Arms and the Man, Beatrix Potter, Dancing Queen, Fatal Deception, A Dark Adapted Eye; films include Lady Jane, A Room with a View, Maurice, Francesco, The Mask, Getting It Right, Hamlet, Where Angels Fear to Tread, Howard's End, Mary Shelley's Frankenstein, A Little Loving, Mighty Aphrodite, Margaret's Museum, 1994, Portraits Chinois, 1995, Twelfth Night, 1995, Wings of a Dove, 1996, Revengers Comedies, 1996, Keep the Aspidistra Flying, 1997, The Theory of Flight, 1997, Fight Club, 1998. Office: Adam Isaccs United Talent 9560 Wilshire Blvd Beverly Hills CA 90212 also: Conway Van Gelder, 18-21 Jermyn St, London SW1Y 6HP, England

BONHAM-YEAMAN, DORIA, law educator; b. Los Angeles, June 10, 1932; d. Carl Herschel and Edna Mae (Jones) Bonham; widowed; children: Carl Q., Doria Valerie-Constance. BA, U. Tenn., 1953, JD, 1957, MA, 1958; EdS in Computer Edn., Barry U., 1984. Instr. bus. law Palm Beach Jr. Coll., Lake Worth, Fla., 1960-69; instr. legal environment Fla. Atlantic U., Boca Raton, 1969-73; lectr. bus. law Fla. Internat. U., North Miami, 1973-83, assoc. prof. bus. law, 1983—. Editor: Anglo-Am. Law Conf., 1980; Developing Global Corporate Strategies, 1981; editorial bd. Attys. Computer Report, 1984-85, Jour. Legal Studies Edn., 1985—. Contbr. articles to profl. jours. Bd. dirs. Palm Beach County Assn. for Deaf Children, 1960-63; mem. Fla. Commn. on Status of Women, Tallahassee, 1969-70; mem. Broward County Democratic Exec. Com., 1982—; pres. Dem. Women's Club Broward County, 1981; mem. Marine Coun. of Greater Miami, 1978-94, Svc. award, 1979. Recipient Faculty Devel. award Fla. Internat. U., Miami, 1980; grantee Notre Dame Law Sch., London, summer 1980. Mem. AAUW (pres. Palm Beach county chpt. 1965-66), U.S. Coun. for Internat. Bus., No. Dade C. of C., Acad. Legal Studies in Bus., Alpha Chi Omega (alumnae club pres. 1968-71), Tau Kappa Alpha. Episcopalian. Office: Fla Internat U Coll Bus Adminstrn Bus Law Dept North Miami FL 33181

BONIEY, EMILY ANN, critical care nurse, anesthesist nurse; b. Weirton, W.Va., Mar. 27, 1965; d. Joseph and Mary (Kopa) B. ADN, W.Va. No. Community Coll., 1986; BSN, Duquesne U., 1988; MSN in Anesthesia, U. Pitts., 1991. RN, Pa. Staff nurse post-anesthesia ICU Presbyn. U. Hosp., Pitts., staff nurse anesthesist. Recipient U.S. Achievements Acad. award. Mem. Am. Assn. Nurse Anesthetists, Am. Assn. Critical Care Nurses, Phi Eta Sigma, Phi Theta Kappa.

BONIFAY, CAM, professional sports team executive; b. St. Petersburg, Fla., Feb. 12, 1952. B Indsl. Mgmt., Ga. Tech., 1974. Profl. baseball player St. Louis Cardinals, 1974-75; scout Cin. Reds, 1976-78, St. Louis Cardinals, 1978-80; scouting supr. Southeast U.S. and Latin Am., 1982-87; nat. scout to dir. of scouting Pitts. Pirates, 1988-90, asst. gen. mgr., 1990-93, sr. v.p., gen. mgr., 1993—; h.s. tchr., basketball, baseball, and football coach, Macon Ga. *

BONIFAZI, STEPHEN, chemist; b. Hartford, Conn., Oct. 31, 1924; s. Camillo and Carrie (Mortensen) B.; BS, Trinity Coll., Hartford, 1947; post-grad. Okla. U., 1943-44, Rensselaer Poly. Inst., 1955-58; m. Joan Rose Dunlop, Dec. 19, 1959; 1 dau., Karen Stephanie. Sr. chemist Pratt & Whitney Aircraft Co., East Hartford, Conn., 1950-56, supr. chemistry, 1956-58, project chemist, West Palm Beach, Fla., 1958-63, gen. supr. chemistry, 1963-78, fuels and lubricants specialist, 1978-86, cons. 1986—. Served with inf. AUS, 1943-45; ETO. Decorated Bronze Star medal. Mem. ASME, ASTM, Am. Chem. Soc., Am. Soc. Lubrication Engrs., Am. Soc. Mech. Engrs., Internat. Assn. for Hydrogen Energy, Coordinating Research Council, Sigma Pi Sigma. Contbr. articles to sci. jours. Home and Office: 237 Eagleton Lake Blvd Palm Bch Gdns FL 33418-8059

BONILLA, BOBBY (ROBERTO MARTIN ANTONIO BONILLA), professional baseball player; b. N.Y.C., Feb. 23, 1963. Student, N.Y. Tech. Coll. With Chgo. White Sox, 1985-86, Pitts. Pirates, 1981-85, 1986-91; with N.Y. Mets, 1991-95; with Balt. Orioles, 1995-96; traded to Fla. Marlins, Miami, 1997-98; outfielder N.Y. Mets, 1999—. Named to Sporting News Nat. League All-Star Team, 1988, 90-91, All-Star team, 1988-91, 93; recipient Silver Slugger award, 1988, 90-91. Office: NY Mets Pro Player Stadium 123-10 Roosevelt Ave Flushing NY 11368*

BONILLA, DAISY ROSE, parochial school English language educator; b. N.Y.C., May 9, 1964; d. Frank J. and Aurea (Rivera) B. A in Computer Sci. cum laude, Bayamon U., 1984; BA in Edn. summa cum laude, Caribbean U., 1991, MA in TESOL. Cert. tchr. secondary English. Data entry clk. Dept. Health, San Juan, 1987-91; tchr. English Colegio Santa Rosa, Bayamon, P.R., 1991-92, Disciples of Christ Acad., Bayamon, 1992-95, Colegio Marista, Guaynabo, 1995—. Recipient Hostos medal Tchr.'s Assn., 1991, Outstanding Internship award Phi Delta Kappa, 1991. Mem. ASCD, Nat. Coun. Tchrs. English. Home: 17 Calle 12 Bayamon Gardens Bayamon PR 00957-1719

BONILLA, HENRY, congressman, broadcast executive; b. Jan. 2, 1954; m. Deborah Knapp; children: Alicia, Austin. BJ, U. Tex. Reporter KTVV, Austin, Tex., 1976-78; reporter, prodr. KENS-TV News, 1978-80; asst. Press sec. for Gov. Dick Thornburgh, Phila., 1981; news producer WABC-TV, N.Y.C., 1982-85; asst. news dir. WTAF-TV, Phila., 1985-86; TV exec. prodr. KENS-TV, San Antonio, 1986-89; mem. appropriations com. 103rd-105th Congress from 23rd Tex. dist., Washington, D.C., 1993—; mem. appropriations, labor, edn. and nat. security coms. Bd. v.p. San Antonio Crimestoppers; mem. adv. bd. United Way Vol. Ctr.; mem. adv. coun. Univ. Tex. Women's Athletics Dept., San Antonio Mus. Assn. Mex. Splendors Media; bd. dirs. Careers Info. and Referral Svc., San Antonio Pub. Library Found. Recipient San Antonio Hispanic C.of C. Leadership award, 1989, Corp. Community Svc. award, 1990. Republican. Home: 19 Sanctuary Dr San Antonio TX 78248-1666 Office: US Ho of Reps 1427 Longworth Bldg Washington DC 20515-4323

BONILLA-FELIX, MELVIN A., pediatrician, educator; b. San Juan, P.R., June 20, 1962. MD, U. Puerto Rico, 1986. Cert. pediat., pediat. nephrology, 1993. Intern U. San Juan Pediat. Hosp., 1986-87, resident in pediat., 1987-89; fellow in pediat. nephrology St. Louis Childrens, 1992; asst. prof. pediat. U. Tex., Houston, 1992—. Recipient Minority Scientist Devel. award Am. Heart Assn., 1995-96. Mem. Am. Assn. Pediat. Office: Univ PR Med Scis Campus Dept Pediat PO Box 365067 San Juan PR 00936-5067

BONIN, DO, basketball coach; b. New Iberia, La., Aug. 18, 1955. BS, Northwestern State U., Natchitoches, La., 1977, MS, 1983. Head coach Dodson H.S., 1977-84; asst. coach Pineville H.S., 1984-87; head coach Leesville H.S., 1987-92; asst. basketball coach Fordham U., Bronx, 1993-94; head women's basketball coach Nicholls State U., Thibodaux, La., 1994—. Office: Nicholls State Univ Women's Athletics Dept PO Box 2032 Thibodaux LA 70310*

BONIN, GREGORY, umpire; b. Lafayette, La., June 15, 1955; children: Samuel, Benjamin. Grad., Southwestern La. U. Umpire Fla. State League, Tex. League, Internat. League, Colombian Winter League, Dominican Republic Winter League, Nat. League, 1986—. Avocations: fishing, golfing, hunting. Office: Nat League 350 Park Ave New York NY 10022 Office: Umpires Union 1735 Market St Philadelphia PA 19103

BONIN, PAUL JOSEPH, real estate and banking executive; b. Malden, Mass., Mar. 6, 1929; s. Honoré Auguste and Yvonne Adrienne (Vuillaumié) B.; m. Annette Kagey, Jan. 19, 1968; children: Adam Spencer, Christopher Paul, Page Alexandra. Student, Bentley Coll., 1948-50, NYU, 1950-52, New Sch. for Social Rsch., 1962. Lic. real estate broker, N.Y. Acct. Henry W.T. Mali & Co., N.Y.C., 1951-58; budget contr., asst. account exec., developer budget control system Young & Rubicam, N.Y.C., 1958-60; v.p. Wm. Alfred White, Inc., N.Y.C., 1960-65; pres. Bonin & Barringer, Inc., N.Y.C., 1964-65; v.p. Wm. B. May & Co., Previews, Inc., N.Y.C., 1965-69; dir. acquisitions Nationwide Real Estate Co., N.Y.C., 1969-74; v.p. Landauer Assocs., Inc., N.Y.C., 1974-79, Citibank, N.A., N.Y.C., 1979-82; pres. Assocs. Mgmt., Inc., Dallas, 1982-84; dir. acquisitions The Hendrix Cos., N.Y.C., 1984-85, The Ziegelman Orgn., N.Y.C., 1985-86; sr. v.p. Crossland Svs. Bank, Bklyn., 1987-89; pres. asset mgmt. group Team Cos., N.Y.C., 1989-93;

asset valuation rev. team leader, portfolio mgr. FDIC, Franklin, Mass., 1990—; asset mgr. Shell Pension Fund of The Hague, The Netherlands, Electricity Coun. of Eng., London, N.Y.C.; real estate cons. Pan Am World Airways, N.Y. State Dept. Housing and Cmty. Renewal. With USN, 1946-48. Mem. Mortgage Bankers Assn., Nat. Assn. Realtors (cert. property mgr.), Inst. Real Estate Mgmt. Roman Catholic. Avocations: tennis, skiing. Home: 2 Old River Rd Barrington RI 02806-1614 Office: FDIC 101 E River Dr East Hartford CT 06108-3285

BONIN, RAYMOND, member of Canadian parliament; b. Sudbury, Ontario, Can., Nov. 20, 1942. BA, Laurentian U. Mem. staff Air Canada; prof. Cambrian U.; mem. parliament Canadian Ho. of Commons, Ottawa, 1993—; chair standing com. on Transport, past vice chair then chair standing com. on Aboriginal Affairs and No. Devel.; past mem. standing com. on Human Resources Devel. Past mem. Laurentian Hosp. Bd., Social Svcs. Bd. City of Sudbury; founding mem. Crime Stoppers Sudbury, past mem. of parish coun. Office: Can Ho of Commons, 416 W Block, Ottawa, ON Canada K1A0A6 Other Office: 2-1475 Hwy 69 N, Val Caron, Canada*

BONIN, SUZANNE JEAN, artist; b. Oakland, Calif., Nov. 12, 1955; d. Charles Freeman and Dorice Ruth (Brown) B.; m. Donald George Winchester, May 16, 1986 (div. Nov. 1990); m. Joseph Bogusis, Nov. 2, 1996. Grad. h.s., Alton, N.H. Owner, mgr. Bonin Gallery, Wolfeboro, N.H., 1983-94, Bonin Studio, Wolfeboro, N.H., 1994—; spl. needs art instr. Kingswood Regional Sch. System, Wolfeboro, 1982. Designer logo Audubon Soc. of N.H., 1982; exhbn. The Art Place, Wolfeboro. Charter mem. Gov. Wentworth Arts Coun., Wolfeboro, 1980, vol., 1980—; donor N.H. Public TV, Durham, N.H.; initiator of art collection for silent auction Hospice, Wolfeboro, 1982—; mem. Cmty. Ch. of Alton, 1962—. Mem. League of N.H. Craftsmen, Washington Area Printmakers, No. N.H. Arts Alliance. Avocations: gardening, fishing, swimming, cross-country skiing, basketball. Home: 713 Beach Pond Rd Wolfeboro NH 03894-4530 Office: Bonin Studio PO Box 801 Wolfeboro NH 03894-0801

BONINI, WILLIAM EMORY, geophysics educator; b. Washington, Aug. 23, 1926; s. John Emory and Thelma (Scrivener) B.; m. Rose Rozich, Dec. 4, 1954; children: John Allen, Nancy Mara, James Prior, Jennifer Adra. B.S. in Engring, Princeton, 1948, M.S., 1949; Ph.D., U. Wis., 1957. Mem. faculty Princeton, 1953-96, prof. civil and geol. engring., 1966-70, George J. Magee prof. geophysics and geol. engring., 1970-96; prof. emeritus, 1996—; chmn. water resources program Princeton, 1971-74, chmn. geol. engring. program, 1973-96; ret., 1996. Author articles in field. Pres. Yellowstone-Bighorn Research Assn., Red Lodge, Mont., 1959-60, 71-73, v.p., 1966-71, 85-87. Served with USNR, 1945-46. Nat. Acad. Sci. exchange scientist to Yugoslavia, 1974; NSF sr. postdoctoral fellow U. Newcastle upon Tyne, Eng., 1963-64. Fellow Geol. Soc. Am. (sec.-treas. geophysics div. 1981-83, chmn. geophysics div. 1985-86); mem. Am. Assn. Petroleum Geologists, Soc. Exploration Geophysicists, Nat. Assn. Geosci. Tchrs. (councilor-at-large 1981-83, v.p. 1983-84, pres. 1984-85), Sigma Xi (v.p. Princeton chpt. 1988-89, pres. 1989-90). Research on gravity and magnetic anomalies and crustal structure, seismic crustal studies, geophys. exploration engring. and groundwater studies, environmental geology. Home: 74 Robert Rd Princeton NJ 08540-5333

BONINO, FERNANDA, art dealer; b. Torino, Italy, Jan. 5, 1927; came to U.S., 1963; d. Francesco Pogliani and Marina Collino; m. Alfredo Bonino, July 29, 1925 (dec. Jan. 1981). M in Art, U. Italy, Torino, 1942. Dir. Galeria Bonino Ltd., N.Y.C., 1963-90, dir., pres., 1981—. Mem. Art Dealers Assn. Am. Office: Galeria Bonino Ltd 48 Great Jones St New York NY 10012-1133

BONIOR, DAVID EDWARD, congressman; b. Detroit, June 6, 1945; s. Edward John and Irene (Gaverluk) B.; children: Julie, Andy. BA, U. Iowa, 1967; MA in History, Chapman Coll., Calif., 1972. Mem. Mich. Ho. of Reps., 1973-77; minority whip 95th-105th Congresses from 12th (now 10th) Mich. Dist., 1977—; mem. com. on rules, House Majority Whip, 1991—. Author: The Vietnam Veteran: A History of Neglect, 1984. Served in USAF, 1968-72. Democrat. Roman Catholic. Office: US Ho of Reps 2207 Rayburn Bldg Washington DC 20515-2210*

BONIS, JOSEPH JOHN, financial executive; b. Mt. Vernon, N.Y., Apr. 16, 1953; s. John Joseph and Frances Helen (Controvich) B.; m. Betty Ann Conroy, Sept. 22, 1984; 1 child, Elizabeth Anne. BS, Villanova U., 1975; MBA, Fairleigh Dickinson U., 1986. CPA, N.Y. Sr. acct. Deloitte & Touche, N.Y.C., 1975-79; asst. contr. Fed. Paper Bd. Co., Inc., Montvale, N.J., 1979-88; dir. fin. sys. The Haagen-Daz Co., Teaneck, N.J., 1988-90; v.p. fin. & adminstrn. Chep USA, Park Ridge, N.J., 1990-96; CFO The Hardardt Group, Parsippany, N.Y., 1996-97; sr. v.p. fin., CFO O'Sullivan Menu Pub., Carlstadt, N.J., 1997—. Office: O'Sullivan Menu Pub 110 Triangle Blvd Carlstadt NJ 07072-2701

BONIS, LASZLO JOSEPH, business executive, scientist; b. Budapest, Hungary, May 31, 1931; came to U.S., 1957; s. Joseph and Ilona (Hunvald) B.; m. Eva Markovich, July 31, 1955 (div. 1981); children: Andrea Christine, Peter Anthony Laszlo; m. Cheryl E. Olsen, Dec. 28, 1985. DM Ing. Mech. Engring., U. Tech. Sci., Budapest, 1953; MSc in Metallurgy, MIT, 1959, postgrad., 1959-60. Registered profl. engr., Calif., Mass.; cert. chemist Nat. Cert. Commn. Assoc. dir. material research Electronics, Inc., Budapest, 1953-56; prof. U. Tech. Sci., 1953-56; rsch. asst. MIT, Cambridge, 1957-60; exec. v.p., tech. dir. Ilikon Corp., Natick, Mass., 1960-62, pres., tech. dir., 1962-74; mgmt. cons. Tech. Fin. and Mktg., Inc., Natick, Mass., 1974—; pres., chmn., tech. dir. Composite Container Corp., Medford, Mass., 1977-88; pres. T.F.M. Cons., Dover, Mass., 1988—. Editor: (4 vols.) Fundamental Phenomena in the Material Science; contbr. articles to profl. jours.; patentee in field. Bd. dirs. The Opera Co., Boston, 1962-85, pres., 1966-85; pres. Boston Arts Coun., 1974—, Boston Opera House, 1991-94. Recipient Muse award Pub. Action for the Arts, 1984, George Washington award Am. Hungarian Found., 1984, Golden Door award Internat. Inst., 1980; named One of Outstanding Young Men of Greater Boston C. of C., 1966. Fellow Am. Inst. Chemists; mem. N.Y. Acad. Scis., MIT Club. E-mail: dr.bonis@tfmconsultants.com. Office: TFM Cons 52 Haven St Dover MA 02030-2131

BONJEAN, CHARLES MICHAEL, foundation executive, sociologist, educator; b. Pekin, Ill., Sept. 7, 1936; s. Bruno and Catherine Ann (Dancey) B. BA, Drake U., 1957; MA, U. N.C., 1959, PhD in Sociology, 1963. Mem. faculty U. Tex., Austin, 1963—; Hogg prof. sociology U. Tex., 1974—, chmn. dept., 1972-74; exec. assoc. Hogg Found., 1974-79, v.p., 1979-93; exec. dir. Hogg Found., 1993—; sociology editor Chandler Pub. Co., 1967-73, Crowell Pub. Co., 1973-77, Dorsey Press, 1979-88, Wadsworth Pub. Co., 1988-93; mem. coun. Intern-Univ. Consortium Polit. and Social Rsch., 1972-76; mem. steering com. Coun. Social Sci. Jour. Editors, 1975-81; 2d v.p. Conf. S.W. Found., 1984-85, 1st v.p., 1985-86, pres., 1986-87; exec. com. Grantmakers Evaluation Network, 1994-98; mem. exec. com. Grantmakers in Health, 1995-98, bd. dirs., 1995-98; chmn. rsch. com. Coun. Founds., 1991-94, bd. dirs., 1998—; mem. adv. com. Am. Sociol. Found., 1992-97, chmn., 1995-97. Co-author: Sociological Measurement, 1967, Sociology: A Core Text with Adapted Readings, 1990; co-editor: Blacks in the United States, 1969, Planned Social Intervention, 1969, Community Politics, 1971, Political Attitudes and Public Opinion, 1972, The Idea of Culture in the Social Sciences, 1973, Social Science in America, 1976, The Mexican Origin People in the United States, 1985, Community Care of the Chronically Mentally Ill, 1989, Mental Health Research in Texas, 1990; editor Social Sci. Quar., 1966-94; cons. editor Am. Jour. Sociology, 1974-76, The Am. Sociologist, 1990-96; contbr. to profl. jours. Bd. dirs. Lake Travis Ednl. Found., 1986-91. Recipient tchg. excellence award U. Tex. Students Assn., 1965, Alumni Disting. Svc. award Drake U., 1979; Sigma Delta Chi scholar, 1957. Mem. Am. Sociol. Assn. (chmn. cmty. sect. 1976-78, publs. com. 1978-81, chmn. 1979-81, pres. sect. on orgns. 1983-84, chmn. dist. scholarship com. 1992-84, coun. 1985-88, exec. office and budget com. 1994-97), Southwestern Sociol. Assn. (pres. 1972-73), Southwestern Social Sci. Assn. (exec. com. 1966-97, v.p. 1992-93, pres.-elect 1993-94, pres. 1994-95), Philos. Soc. Tex. Home: 16310 Clara Van St Austin TX 78734-3928 Office: U Tex Austin TX 78713-7998

BONKO, LARRY WALTER, columnist, writer, radio personality; b. McAdoo, Pa., June 5, 1934; s. John and Mary C. (Zuber) B.; m. Annemarie C. Bonko, Feb. 17, 1957; children: C. Mark, L. Dirk. Sports columnist Daily Press, Newport News, Va., 1957-61; columnist The Virginian-Pilot, Norfolk, 1961—. Author: Sinners and Showoffs, 1975. Corr., USN, 1953-57. Office: The Virginian-Pilot Landmark Comm Inc 150 W Brambleton Ave Norfolk VA 23510-2075

BONN, ETHEL MAY, psychiatrist, educator; b. Cin., Oct. 14, 1925; d. Stanley Ervin and Ethel May (Cliffe) B. BA, U. Cin., 1947; MD, U. Chgo., 1951. Asst. chief, then chief women's neuro-psychiat. services VA Hosp., Topeka, 1956-61, chief north service, 1961-62; assoc. dir. for clin. services Ft. Logan Mental Health Ctr., Denver, 1962-67, dir., 1967-76; clin. instr. psychiatry U. Colo. Sch. Medicine, 1963-76; field rep. Joint Commn. on Accreditation of Hosps., 1976-78; assoc. clin. prof. psychiatry UCLA Sch. Medicine, 1978-81; chief of quality assurance VA Med. Ctr.-Brentwood, L.A., 1978-81; chief psychiatry service VA Med. Ctr., Albuquerque, 1981-89; assoc. prof. psychiatry U. N.Mex. Sch. Medicine, 1981-89; prof. emeritus psychiatry sch. medicine U. N.Mex., 1989—; cons. Fitzsimons Army Hosp., Denver, 1963-67, U. Calif. Dept Biobehavioral Scis., Los Angeles, 1978-81, VA Hosps., Ft. Lyon, Colo., Sheridan, Wyo., Tuscaloosa, Ala., 1963-67. Contbr. chpts. to books, articles to profl. jours. Recipient Dirs. commendation, VA, 1962, 81, 89, Psychiat. Adminstrs. award Am. Assn. Psychiat. Adminstrs., 1976. Fellow Am. Coll. Psychiatrists (emeritus), Am. Psychiat. Assn. (life; program com. insts. for hosp. and cmty. psychiatry 1977-81), Am. Coll. Mental Health Adminstrn. (founding), Am. Coll. Utilization Rev. Physicians; mem. AMA, Am. Hosp. Assn. (chmn. psychiat. sect. 1972-74). Avocations: travel, gardening, oil and watercolor painting, collecting rocks and minerals, photography. *My life has been most satisfying thanks to my parents, teachers, mentors, colleagues, and friends. I have been able to do what I wanted to do, professionally and personally: delivering quality to my work and relationships.*

BONN, THEODORE HERTZ, computer scientist, consultant; b. Phila., May 27, 1923; s. Norman Eugene and Matilda (Rickliss) B.; m. Edith Jeanette Sindell, Apr. 7, 1946; children: Suzanne, Miriam, Matthew. BSEE, U. Pa., 1943, MSEE, 1947. Rsch. asst. U. Pa., Phila., 1943-47; sr. engr. Eckert Mauchly Computer Corp., Phila., 1947-49; chief sonar components U.S. Naval Air Devel. Ctr., Johnsville, Pa., 1949-50; chief engr. rsch. and peripheral devel. UNIVAC, Blue Bell, Pa., 1950-64; dir. applied rsch. and standards Honeywell Info. Svc., Waltham, Mass., 1964-70; dir. Computer Rsch. Lab. Sperry Rsch. Ctr., Sudbury, Mass., 1970-83; mgr. C3I Systems Dept. Sperry Corp., Waltham, 1983-85; pres. Bonn Cons., Falmouth, Mass., 1985-90. *Mr. Bonn's most widely used technical innovation is the Nickel-Cobalt-Phosphorus-alloy for magnetic recording in disc files. He invented the megacycle magnetic amplifiers used as the pulse amplifiers in the popular Univac Solid State 80/90. As a research manager he was an early proponent of data compression, and vigorously supported the work of Lempel, Cohn and Welch, performed under his supervision. In the IEE Computer Society, Mr. Bonn started Computer Magazine, which is the highly successful prototype of a large number of magazines subsequently started by other technical disciplines in the IEEE.* Contbr. articles to profl. jours.; holder 45 patents in electronics field. Fellow IEEE (vice chmn. computer soc., chmn. tech. program com. Spring Joint Computer Conf., 1969, exec. com., fin. com., U.S. Activities bd. 1980-81, v.p. publs. 1980-82, bd. dirs. 1982-84, ednl. activities bd. 1984, Richard E. Merwin award Computer Soc. 1987). Jewish. Avocations: tennis, photography, music, travel, reading. Home: 98 Shoreland Path East Falmouth MA 02536 Home (winter): HA213 1601 Pelican Point Dr Sarasota FL 34231-6793

BONNABEAU, RAYMOND C., physician; b. Hempstead, N.Y.. BS, Fordham U., 1955; MD, N.Y. State Coll. Medicine, 1959; PhD, U. Minn., 1967. Diplomate Am. Bd. Surgery, Am. Bd. Thoracic Surgery. Intern U. Minn. Hosps., 1959-60; resident in surgery U. Minn. Med. Ctr., 1960-66; physician to U. Minn. Antarctic expdn., 1960-61; instr. surgery U. Minn. Med. Ctr., 1966-67, asst. prof. surgery, 1967-68; asst. prof. surgery Cornell U. Med. Coll., N.Y.C., 1968; surgery instr. W.Va. U. Sch. Medicine, 1971-72, asst. prof. surgery, 1972-75; clin. asst. prof. surgery U. Minn., 1975-79, clin. assoc. prof. surgery, 1979-98, clin. prof. surgery, 1998—; instr. Gustavus Adolphus Sch. Nursing, Bethesda Luth. Med. Ctr., St. Paul, 1981-83, mem. faculty, 1980-84, staff surgeon, 1975-87, surg. dir. spl. care unit, 1977-85, chief of surgery, 1982-84, dir. med. edn., 1984-86; bd. dirs. Inver Hills C.C.; asst. attending surgeon Clarksburg (W.Va.) VA Med. Ctr., 1972-75; staff surgeon VA Hosp., Mpls., 1985-90; dir. emergency med. preparedness Dept. Vets. Affairs, Washington, 1990-91. Contbr. more than 100 articles to profl. jours. Acting bd. dirs. Stagecrafters, Bridgeport, W.Va., 1975, Na Fianna Irish Players, 1995—, Ft. Sam Houston Med. Field Svc., 1969, 95th EVAC Hosp., Rep. of Vietnam, 1969-70, Dept. of Surg., Spec. Treatment Ctr., Ft. Gordon, 1970-71, Chief of Surg., 350 Evacuation Hosp., 1973-75, 5501st US Army Hosp., Ft. Snelling, 1975-77, Chief of Profl. Svcs., Deputy Commander, 5501st US Army Hosp., Ft. Snelling, 1977-81, Commander 73D Combat Support Hosp., 1982-85, Commander, 5501 US Army Hosp., Ft. Snelling, 1985-89, Commander, 30th Hosp. Ctr., Ft. Sheridan, 1989-90, Deputy Surgeon Gen. for Mobilization and Reserve Affairs, 1990-94, ret., 1994. Decorated Disting. Svc. medal, Legion of Merit, Bronze Star, numerous service medals, Army Commendation medals, Nat. Def. Medal with bronze star, Antarctic Svc. medal, Vietnam Svc. medal with two bronze stars, Humanitarian Svc. medal, Vietnam Campaign medal, Vietnamese Cross of Gallantry with palm unit citation, Order Mil. Merit, Order of the 88th. Fellow ACS, Southeastern Surg. Congress; mem. AMA, Am. Polar Soc., Am. Soc. Med. History, Assn. for Acad. Surgery, Assn. of the U.S. Army, Assn. Mil. Surgeons of the U.S., Soc. Internat. d'Histoire de la Medicine, Minn. Surg. Soc., Minn. Heart Assn., Res. Officers Assn., Dept. W.Va. Res. Officers Assn. (surgeon 1974-75), Soc. Thoracic Surgeons, Harrison County Med. Soc., Ramsey County Med. Soc., Twin City Thoracic and Cardiovasc. Surg. Soc., Am. Coll. Chest Physicians (pulmonary surg. com.), Royal Soc. Medicine (London), Internat. Coll. Surgeons, N.Am. Soc. Pacing and Electro-Physiology, Minn. History Medicine Soc., St. Paul Surg. Soc., History Sci. Soc., N.Y. Acad. Sci., VFW, Vietnam Vets. Am., Am. Legion, Lions. Office: One Veterans Dr Minneapolis MN 55417-2300

BONNARD, RAYMOND, theater director; b. Chambersburg, Pa., May 13, 1951; m. Ricki Whitacre, Jan. 22, 1977; children: Christopher David, Alexander Whitacre. BS cum laude, Indiana (Pa.) U., 1973; MFA cum laude, Ohio U., 1976. Prodn. mgr. Mo. Reparatory Theatre, Kansas City, 1978-79; assoc. prodr. Tiffany's Attic Theatre, Waldo Astoria Theatre, Kansas City, 1979-81; prodn. stage mgr. Folly Theatre, Kansas City, 1981; mng. dir. Del. Theatre Co., Wilmington, 1981-84; producing dir. Studio Arena Theatre, Buffalo, 1984-95; asst. prof. U. Mo., Kansas City, 1978-79; respondent Am. Coll. Theatre Festival. Active Buffalo Fin. Planning Comm., Leadership Buffalo. Mem. League Regional Theatres (exec. com. 1988-91), Theatre DIst. Assn. (v.p. 1993—).

BONNEAU, SUE ELLEN, advancement researcher; b. Seymour, Ind., Aug. 1, 1959; d. C. Frederick and Mary Bea (Pollard) Miller; m. Phillip R. Bonneau, Dec. 26, 1981; children: Jeffrey Alan, Kyle Andrew. BS in Journalism, Ball State U., 1981. With Ball State U., Muncie, Ind., 1987-88, prospect rsch. specialist, 1988—. Mem. fin. com. Yorktown (Ind.) United Meth. Ch., 1996-97; vol. Oakhurst Gardens, Muncie, 1995—; bd. dirs. No. Ind. United Meth. Found., 1998—. Mem. Assn. Prospect Rschrs. Advancement (bd. dirs. 1992-97, pres. Ind. chpt. 1997), Master Gardeners. Avocations: cycling, gardening. Office: Ball State U 2800 W Bethel Ave Muncie IN 47306-0002

BONNELL, PAMELA GAY, library administrator; b. Monterey, Calif., Feb. 2, 1948; d. Dewey L. and Marlyce I. (Hanson) Scoggins; m. Chrisman E Bonnell, Mar. 2, 1974 (div. 1983); m. Vernil S. Henerson, June 18, 1966 (div. 1971), 1 child, V. Samuel Henderson III; m. Hugh R. McElroy, Nov. 10, 1990 (div. 1996). BA, Cameron U., Lawton, Okla., 1972; MLS, U. Okla., 1972-73. Libr. Met. Libr. System, Oklahoma City, 1974-75, Office of the City Mgr., Dallas, 1977-80; dir. audience devel. Dallas Symphony Orch., 1980-81; libr. Dallas Morning News, 1981-83; libr. mgr. Plano (Tex.) Pub. Libr. System, 1983-91; dir. libr. svcs. Waco-McLennan County Libr. System, Waco, Tex., 1992—. Author: Fund Raising for Small Libraries, 1983; contbr. chpt. to book, articles to profl. jours. Gala chmn. Easter Seal Soc., Dallas, 1988; bd dirs. Women's Shelter, Plano, Tex., 1991; pres. Townbluff Homeowners Assn., Plano, 1984-90, Hippodrome Theatre Guild, 1996; trustee Dallas Symphony Orch., 1981; trea. YWCA, 1995-96; exec. bd. Am. Heart Assn., 1997—. Recipient SIRS Intellectual Freedom award Tex. Libr. Assn., 1990, Telecomms. Excellence award Ctrl. Tex. Edn., 1997. Mem. ALA (councilor-at-large 1990-99, pres. Intellectual Freedom Round Table 1993-94, constn. and bylaws chair 1994-97, Shirley Olofson Meml. award 1974, Cert. of Spl. Thanks 1986, John Phillip Immroth award 1990), Freedom to Read Found., Tex. Mcpl. Libr. Dirs. (pres. 1994-95), Tex. Libr. Assn. (chmn. Adminstrs. Roundtable 1994-95), Ctrl. Tex. Women's Allience (bd. dirs. 1992-96), Leadership Waco Alumni Assn., Rotary, Jr. League, Am. Heart Assn. (exec. bd. 1997—). Avocations: reading, travel. Home: 2334 Melissa Dr Waco TX 76708-3068 Office: Waco-McLennan County Libr Sys 1717 Austin Ave Waco TX 76701-1741

BONNELL, WILLIAM CHARLES, secondary education educator; b. L.A., Aug. 28, 1959. BA in English and History, San Francisco State U., 1983, MA in Classics, 1986; Diploma in Theology, Oxford (Eng.) U., 1992. Cert. English, history, Latin tchr., Calif. Tchr. English and Latin San Mateo (Calif.) Union Dist. High Sch., 1986—. Contbr. articles to profl. jours. Scholar Rotary Internat., 1991-92. Mem. Am. Classical League, Calif. Classical Assn. (sec. 1996—), Classical Assn. of Mid. West & South, Dickens Fellowship. Anglican. Office: San Mateo High Sch 506 N Delaware St San Mateo CA 94401-1781

BONNER, BESTER DAVIS, school system administrator; b. Mobile, Ala., June 9, 1938; d. Samuel Matthew and Alma (Davis) Davis; m. Wardell Bonner, Nov. 28, 1964; children: Shawn Patrick, Matthew Wardell. BS, Ala. State Coll., 1959; MS in Library Sci., Syracuse U., 1966; PhD, U. Ala., 1982. Cert. tchr. Librarian Westside High Sch., Talladega, Ala., 1959-64; librarian, tchr. lit. Lane Elem. Sch., Birmingham, Ala., 1964-65; head librarian Jacksonville (Ala.) Elem. Lab. Sch., 1965-70; asst. prof. library media Ala. A&M U., Huntsville, 1970-74; adminstv. asst. to pres. Miles Coll., Birmingham, 1974-78, chmn. div. edn., 1978-85; specialist media Montgomery County Pub. Schs., Md., 1987-88; dir. libr. and media svcs. div. curriculum and ednl. tech. Dist. of Columbia Pub. Schs., 1988—; forum leader Nat. Issues Forum, Domestic Policy Assn. U. Ala., Birmingham, 1983-84; mem. Libr. Svcs. Construction Act Adv. Com. Contbr. writer The Developing Black Family, 1975. Chmn. ethics commn. St. Ala., Montgomery 1977-81; radiothorn site coordinator United Negro Coll. Fund, Birmingham 1981. Mem. ALA, Ala. Instructional Media Assn. (pres. dist. II 1971-72), Assn. Women Deans and Adminstrs., Com. 100, D.C. Assn. Sch. Librs., D.C. Libr. Com., Am. Assn. Sch. Librs., Nat. Assn. State Ednl. Profls. Democrat. Methodist. Avocations: writing, speaking, consulting, piano. Home: 9601 Burgess Ln Silver Spring MD 20901-4701

BONNER, BILLY EDWARD, physics educator; b. Oak Grove, La., Dec. 12, 1939; s. James Wilbur and Julia (Deer) B. BS, La. Tech. U., 1961; MA, Rice U., 1963, PhD, 1965. Prin. scientific officer Rutherford High Energy Lab., Didcot, Berkshire, England, 1966-70; postdoctoral fellow U. Calif., Davis, 1971-72; physicist Los Alamos (N.Mex.) Nat. Lab., 1972-85; scientific assoc. CERN, Geneva, 1983-84; prof. physics Rice U., Houston, 1985—, chmn. dept. physics, 1986-91, dir. Bonner Nuclear Lab., 1987—. Editor 3 books; contbr. articles to profl. jours. Avocations: squash, fishing, cooking. Office: Rice Univ Bonner Nuclear Labs Houston TX 77005-1892

BONNER, FRANCIS TRUESDALE, chemist, educator, university dean; b. Salt Lake City, Dec. 18, 1921; s. Walter Daniel and Grace (Gaylord) B.; m. Evelyn Hershkowitz, Jan. 17, 1946 (dec. 1990); children: Michael David, Joan Alisa (dec.), Rachel Pearl; m. M. Jane Carlberg, Dec. 31, 1994. B.A., U. Utah, 1942; M.S., Yale U., 1944, Ph.D., 1945. Chemist Manhattan Project S.A.M. Labs. Columbia U., 1944-46; chemist Clinton Labs., Oak Ridge, 1946-47; scientist Brookhaven Nat. Lab., Upton, N.Y., 1947-48; research collaborator Brookhaven Nat. Lab., 1958-88; asst. prof. chemistry Bklyn. Coll., 1948-54; Carnegie vis. fellow Harvard, 1954-55; research phys. chemist Arthur D. Little, Inc., Cambridge, Mass., 1955-58; prof. dept. chemistry SUNY-Stony Brook, 1958—, chmn. dept., 1958-70, dean for internat. programs, 1983-86, prof. emeritus, 1992—; cons. editor Addison-Wesley Pub. Co., Reading, Mass., 1956-77; Rockefeller Found. adviser on curriculum, instl. devel. Universidad Del Valle, Cali, Colombia, 1961-62, 64, Ford Found. adviser, 1968; Ford Found. adviser to Universidad de Antioquia, Medellin, Colombia, 1962-64; dir. N.Y. Met. Area Center Chem. Edn. Materials Study, 1961-62; mem. com. for chemistry Coll. Entrance Exam. Bd., 1962-63; mem. adv. council on Coll. Chemistry, 1967-70; mem. coll. proficiency exam. com. chemistry N.Y. State Edn. Dept., 1963-64, 66-70; NSF sr. postdoctoral fellow Service des Isotopes Stables, Centre d'Etudes Nucleaires de Saclay, Gif-Sur-Yvette, France, 1964-65; vis. scientist Swiss Fed. Inst. for Water Resources and Water Pollution Control, Swiss Fed. Inst. Tech., Zurich, 1973, Kings Coll. U. London, 1987; Nat. Acad. exchange visitor, Romania, 1975; mem. grants adv. panel Fund for Overseas Grants and Edn., 1968-76; bd. dirs. Research Found. State U. N.Y., 1976-88. Author: (with Melba Phillips) Principles of Physical Science, 1957, 2d edit., 1971; Contbr. articles profl. jours. Mem. Ind. Rev. Panel for Decommissioning of Shoreham Nuclear Power Sta., 1992-95; mem. bd. edn. Ctrl. Sch. Dist. 6, Huntington, N.Y., 1968-72. Fellow AAAS; mem. N.Y. Acad. Scis., Am. Chem. Soc., Geochem. Soc., Am. Geophys. Union, AAUP, Sigma Xi. Home: PO Box 2063 Setauket NY 11733-0707 Office: State U NY Dept Chemistry Stony Brook NY 11794

BONNER, JACK, public relations company executive; b. Phila., Nov. 19, 1948; s. Frank and Marilyn (Ruskin) B. B.S., U. Ariz., 1971. Dir. Office Community Affairs, City of Tucson, 1972-77; with press office Rep. Nat. Com., Washington, D.C., 1977-79; press. sec. U.S. Senator John Heinz, Washington, 1979-80, exec. asst., 1980-82; exec. v.p. John Adams and Assocs., Washington, 1982-84; pres. Bonner and Assocs., Washington, 1984—; adj. prof. Am. Univ. Sch. of Pub. Policy; adj. prof. Am. U. Sch. Pub. Affairs, Washington; speaker on corp. grassroots campaigns to numerous orgns., including ABA, Pub. Affairs Coun., others.

BONNER, JACK WILBUR, III, psychiatrist, educator, administrator; b. Corpus Christi, Tex., July 30, 1940; s. Jack Wilbur and Irldene (Turner) B.; m. Myra Lynn Taylor; children: Jack Wilbur, IV, Katherine Lynn, Shelley Bliss. AA, Del Mar Coll., Corpus Christi, 1960; BA with honors, U. Tex., Austin, 1961; MD, S.W. Med. Sch., U. Tex., Dallas, 1965. Diplomate Am. Bd. Psychiatry and Neurology. Intern U. Ark. Med. Center, 1965-66; resident Duke U. Med. Center, 1966-69; assoc. in psychiatry Highland Hosp. div. Duke U. Med. Center, Asheville, N.C., 1971, asst. prof. psychiatry, 1972-80, dir. outpatient services, 1972-75, med. dir., 1975-81; chmn. bd. dirs., chief exec. officer, med. dir. Highland Hosp., Asheville, N.C., 1981-92; med. dir. The Oaks Psychiat. Health Sys., Austin, Tex., 1992-93; exec. med. dir. The Oaks Psychiat. Health System, Austin, Tex., 1993-94; med. dir. Behavioral Health Svcs., Greenville (S.C.) Hosp. Sys., 1994—, adminstr. Behavioral Health Svcs.., 1996—; asst. clin. prof. Duke U. Med. Ctr., Durham, N.C., 1982-87, asst. cons. prof. psychiatry, 1987—; clin. assoc. prof. U. N.C. Sch. Medicine, Chapel Hill, 1986-92, Quillen-Dishner Coll. Medicine, Johnson City, Tenn., 1989-92, U. Tex. Health Sci. Ctr., San Antonio, 1993-94, U. S.C. Sch. Medicine, Columbia, 1995—. Author: (with others) The Psychology of Discipline, 1983, Unmasking the Psychopath: Antisocial Personality and Related Syndromes, 1986; contbr. articles to profl. jours. Chmn. bd. dirs. The Highland Found., 1980-93; bd. dirs. Western N.C. Med. Peer Rev. Found., 1975-78; trustee La Amistad Found., Maitland, Fla., 1985-95, N.C. Symphony, 1987-92. Fellow Am. Psychiat. Assn. (trustee 1999—), So. Psychiat. Assn. (v.p. 1984-85, chmn. bd. regents 1988-89, pres.-elect 1991-92, pres. 1992-93), Am. Coll. Psychiatrists (treas. 1992-95, 2d v.p. 1999—); mem. AMA, Nat. Assn. Psychiat. Health Sys. (trustee 1989-94, 1st v.p. 1990-91, pres.-elect 1991-92, pres. 1991-93), Am. Group Psychotherapy Assn., Nat. Acads. Practice, Buncombe County (N.C.) Med. Soc. (pres.-elect 1982, pres. 1983), N.C. Psychiat. Assn. (pres.-elect 1981-82, pres. 1982-83), Nat. Anorexic Aid Soc. (nat. anorexia adv. coun. 1979-86), So. Med. Assn. (sec. sect. on neurology, neurosurgery and psychiatry 1977-80, chmn.-elect 1980-81, chmn. 1981-82), Ctrl. Neuropsychiat. Hosp. Assn. (councillor 1981-85, pres.-elect 1982-83, pres. 1983-84), Group Advancement Psychiatry (treas. 1991-99, pres.-elect 1999—), U. Tex. Southwestern Med. Sch. Alumni Assn. (bd. dirs. 1988-95, pres. 1989-91), Benjamin Rush Soc., Phi Theta Kappa. Home: 4 Brookside Way Greenville SC 29605-1212 Office: Greenville Hosp Sys Behavioral Health Svcs 701 Grove Rd Greenville SC 29605-5601

BONNER, JOHN TYLER, biology educator; b. N.Y.C., May 12, 1920; s. Paul Hyde and Lilly Marguerite (Stehli) B.; m. Ruth Anna Graham, July 11, 1942; children: Rebecca, Jonathan Graham, Jeremy Tyndall, Andrew Duncan. Grad., Phillips Exeter Acad., 1937; BSc, Harvard U., 1941, MA, 1942, PhD (Jr. fellow 1942, 46-47), 1947; DSc (hon.), Middlebury Coll., 1970. Asst. to assoc. prof. Princeton U., 1947-58, prof., 1958-90, emeritus prof., 1990—, chmn. dept. biology, 1965-77, 83-84, 87-88; lectr. embryology Marine Biol. Lab., Woods Hole, Mass., 1951-52; spl. lectr. U. London, 1957, Bklyn. Coll., 1966; Arnold Bernhard vis. prof. Williams Coll., 1989; Raman prof. Indian Acad. Scis., 1990; trustee Biol. Abstracts, 1958-63; mem. bd. editors Princeton U. Press, 1965-68, 71, trustee, 1976-82. Author: Morphogenesis, 1952, Cells and Societies, 1955, The Evolution of Development, 1958 The Cellular Slime Molds, 1959, rev. edit., 1967, The Ideas of Biology, 1962, Size and Cycle, 1965, The Scale of Nature, 1969, On Development, 1974, The Evolution of Culture in Animals, 1980, (with T.A. McMahon) On Life and Size, 1983, The Evolution of Complexity, 1988, Researches on Cellular Slime Moulds, 1991, Life Cycles, 1993, Sixty Years of Biology, 1996; also sci. papers; editor: Growth and Form, 1961. Evolution and Development, 1981; assoc. editor Am. Scientist, 1961-69; mem. editl. bd. Am. Naturalist, 1958-60, 66-68, Jour. Gen. Physiology, 1962-69, Growth, 1955-89, Differentiation, 1976-90, Oxford Surveys in Evolutionary Biology, 1982-93. Pvt. to 1st lt. USAC, 1942-46; staff aero. med. lab. Wright Field, Dayton, Ohio. Sheldon traveling fellow Panama, 1941; Rockefeller traveling fellow France, 1953; Guggenheim fellow Scotland, 1958, 71-72; recipient Selman A. Waksman award for contbns. to microbiology Theobold Smith Soc.; NSF sr. postdoctoral fellow, 1963. Fellow Am. Acad. Arts and Scis., Indian Acad. Scis. (hon.); mem. NAS, Am. Soc. Naturalists, Soc. Growth and Devel., Am. Philos. Soc., Phi Beta Kappa, Sigma Xi.

BONNER, MICHAEL DAVID, adult education educator, researcher; b. N.Y.C., May 1, 1952; s. Francis Truesdale Bonner and Evelyn Hershkowitz; m. Daniela Gobetti. AB, Harvard U., 1974; MA, Princeton U., 1984, PhD, 1987. Lectr. Cornell U., Ithaca, N.Y., 1987-88; asst. prof. U. Mich., Ann Arbor, 1989-95, assoc. prof., 1995—, dir. Ctr. Mid. Eastern and N. African Studies, 1997—. Author: Aristocratic Violence and Holy War, 1996. Mem. Am. Oriental Soc., Middle East Studies Assn. Office: U Mich Rm 4640 1080 S University Ave Ann Arbor MI 48109-1106

BONNER, ROBERT CLEVE, lawyer; b. Wichita, Kans., Jan. 29, 1942; s. Benjamin Joseph and Caroline (Kirkwood) B.; m. Kimiko Tanaka, Oct. 11, 1969; 1 child, Justine M. BA, Md. U., 1963; JD, Georgetown U., 1966. Bar: D.C. 1966, Calif. 1967, S. Ct. Appeals (4th, 5th, 9th, 10th cirs.), U.S. Supreme Ct. Law clk. to judge U.S. Dist. Ct., L.A., 1966-67; asst. U.S. atty. U.S. Atty's Office (cen. dist.) Calif., L.A., 1971-75, U.S. atty., 1984-89; judge U.S. Dist. Ct. (cen. dist.) Calif., L.A., 1989-90; ptnr. Kadison, Pfaelzer, et al, Los Angeles, 1975-84; dir. Drug Enforcement Adminstrn., Washington, 1990-93; ptnr. Gibson, Dunn & Crutcher, L.A., 1993—; chair Calif. Commn. on Jud. Performance, 1997—. Served to lt. comdr. USN, 1967-70. Fellow Am. Coll. Trial Lawyers, Fed. Bar Assn. (pres. Los Angeles chpt. 1982-83). Republican. Roman Catholic. Office: Gibson Dunn & Crutcher 333 S Grand Ave Ste 4400 Los Angeles CA 90071-3197

BONNER, ROBERT WILLIAM, lawyer; b. Vancouver, B.C., Can., Sept. 10, 1920; s. Benjamin York and Emma Louise (Weir) B.; m. Barbara Newman, June 16, 1942; children: Barbara Carolyn (Mrs. Massie), Robert York, Elizabeth Louise (Mrs. McPhee). B.A. in Econs. and Polit. Sci, U. B.C., 1942, LL.B., 1948. Bar: B.C. 1948, created Queen's counsel 1952. With firm Clark Wilson White Clark & Maguire, Vancouver, 1948-52; atty. gen. Province of B.C., 1952-68; sr. v.p. adminstrn. MacMillan Bloedel Ltd., 1968-70, exec. v.p. adminstrn., 1970-71, vice chmn., 1971-72, pres., chief exec. officer, 1972-73, chmn. bd., 1973-74, ret., 1974; chmn. B.C. Hydro & Power Authority, 1976-85; ptnr. Bonner & Fouks, 1974-84, Robertson, Ward, Suderman, Vancouver, 1985-89, Ward & Co., Vancouver, 1989—. Mem. B.C. Legislature, 1952-69; mem. Energy Supplies Allocation Bd., bd. dirs. Served to maj. Royal Canadian Army, 1942-45; lt. col. Res. (ret.). Mem. Canadian Bar Assn., Law Soc. B.C. (life bencher), Delta Upsilon. Mem. Social Credit Party. Clubs: Mason, Vancouver; Union (Victoria). Home: 5679 Newton Wynd, Vancouver, BC Canada V6T 1H6 Office: Ward & Co, 804-1112 W Pender St, Vancouver, BC Canada V6E 2S1

BONNER, SHIRLEY HARROLD, business communications educator; b. Pitts., July 22, 1929; d. William DeWitt Jr. and Erma Dorothy (Ruppert) Harrold; m. Joseph A. Bonner, Apr. 21, 1956; children: Margaret Leslie, Joseph Edward. BS in Edn., U. Pitts., 1951, MEd, 1971, PhD, 1981. With Gulf Oil Corp., Pitts.; tchr. Three Rivers Bus. Sch., Pitts., Antwerp (Belgium) Internat. Sch., Duff's Bus. Sch., Pitts., C.C. of Allegheny County, Pitts., Learning Ctr. Chatham Coll., 1994—; pres. Chatham Coll. literacy bd., 1997—. Author: Margaret of Austria, Governess of the Low Countries, 1507-1530, 2 vols.; contbr. articles to The Balance Sheet. Past bd. dirs. Am. Protestant Ch. of Antwerp; pres. Chatham Coll. Adult Literacy Bd., 1997-00. Mem. AAUW (pres. DuBois area br. 1967-69), Assn. for Bus. Communication, World Affairs Coun Pitts. (consul), Delta Zeta. Republican. Avocations: travel, mysteries, biographies. Home: 403 Denniston Ave Pittsburgh PA 15206-4411

BONNER, THOMAS NEVILLE, history and higher education educator; b. Rochester, N.Y., May 28, 1923; s. John Neville and Mary (McGowan) B.; children by previous marriage: Phillip Lynn, Diana Joan; m. Sylvia M. Firnhaber, Dec. 28, 1984. AB, U. Rochester, 1947, MA, 1948; PhD, Northwestern U., 1952; LLD, U. N.H., 1974, U. Mich., 1979. Acad. dean William Woods Coll., 1951-54; prof. history, chmn. dept. social sci. U. Omaha, 1955-62; Fulbright lectr. U. Mainz, Germany, 1954-55; prof., head history dept. U. of Cin., 1963-68, v.p. acad. affairs, provost, 1967-71; pres. U. N.H., Durham, 1971-74, Union Coll.; chancellor Union U., Schenectady, 1974-78; pres. Wayne State U., Detroit, 1978-82, disting. prof. history and higher edn., 1983-97; vis. scholar Ariz. State U., Tempe, 1997—; vis. prof. U. Freiburg, Fed. Republic Germany, 1982-83. Author: Medicine in Chicago, 1957, 91, The Kansas Doctor, 1959; (with others) The Contemporary World, 1960, Our Recent Past, 1963, American Doctors and German Universities, 1963, 87, To the Ends of the Earth: Woman's Search for Education in Medicine, 1992, Becoming a Physician: Medical Education in Great Britain, France, Germany and the United States, 1750-1945, 1995; editor, translator: Journey Through the Rocky Mountains, 1959. Democratic candidate for Congress, 1962; legis. aide to Senator McGovern, 1962-63. Served with Radio Intelligence Corps AUS, 1942-46, ETO. Guggenheim fellow, 1958-59, 64-65. Mem. Am. Hist. Assn., Orgn. Am. Historians, Am. Assn. for History Medicine, Phi Beta Kappa, Pi Gamma Mu, Phi Alpha Theta. Home: 10970 E San Salvador Dr Scottsdale AZ 85259-5726

BONNER, WALTER JOSEPH, lawyer; b. N.Y.C., Nov. 18, 1925; s. Walter John and Marie Elizabeth (Guerin) B.; m. Maureen O'Malley; 1 child, Justin R.; children from previous marriage: Kevin P., Keith M., Barbara A., Susan E. A.B. cum laude, Cath. U. Am., 1951; J.D., Georgetown U., 1955. Bar: U.S. Supreme Ct., D.C., Va. Law clk. to judge U.S. Ct. Appeals D.C. Circuit, 1954-55; judge U.S. Dist. Ct., Washington, 1955-56; asst. U.S. dist. atty. for D.C., 1956-60; ptnr. firm Michaels, Wishner & Bonner, Washington; adj. prof. Georgetown U. Law Ctr., 1957-58, 67-83. Trustee Lawrence E. Dean Meml. Scholarship Fund, Georgetown U. Med. Ctr. Served with USNR, 1943-85, capt. Res. ret. Fellow Am. Coll. Trial Lawyers; mem. ABA, Fed. Bar Assn., Bar Assn. of D.C., Va. State Bar, Va. Trial Lawyers Assn., Res. Officers Assn., Naval Res. Lawyers Assn., Naval Res. Assn., Phi Delta Phi. Clubs: Officers and Faculty (U.S. Naval Acad.). Office: 1140 Connecticut Ave NW Ste 900 Washington DC 20036-4009

BONNER, WILLIAM ANDREW, chemistry educator; b. Chgo., Dec. 21, 1919; s. Francis Augustus and Celestine Louis (Horine) B.; m. Cyrena Nelson, June 1944 (div. Mar. 1960); children: Randolph, Joseph, Jay, Teresa; m. Norma Carmen Loyola, Apr. 1961; children: Constance, Candace. BS, Harvard U., 1941; PhD, Northwestern U., 1944. Instr. chemistry Northwestern U., Evanston, Ill., 1945-46; instr. chemistry Stanford (Calif.) U., 1946-47, from asst. prof. to prof. chemistry, 1947-83, prof. emeritus chemistry, 1983—. Author: (with A.J. Castro) Essentials of Modern Organic Chemistry, 1965; contbg. author numerous rsch. papers and revs. Guggenheim Found. fellow (Switzerland), 1953. Mem. Am. Chem. Soc., Internat. Soc. for the Study of Origins of Life. Democrat. Avocations: photography, painting, gardening, hiking. Home: 626 Hawthorne Ave Los Altos CA 94024-3120 Office: Stanford U Dept Chemistry Stanford CA 94305

BONNER, WILLIAM P., physician; b. Gaffney, S.C., May 21, 1948; children: Lil, Ann. BS in Pre-med., Clemson U., 1970; MD, Med. U. S.C., 1974. Diplomate Am. Bd. Family Practice, Am. Bd. Geriatric Medicine. Resident in family practice Greenville (S.C.) Hosp. Sys., 1974-76, chief resident, 1976-77, staff, 1977—; staff St. Francis Health Sys., Greenville, 1977—; pvt. practice Greenville, 1977—; staff Gree. Mem. AMA, Am. Acad. Family Practice, S.C. Acad. Family Practice, Greenville County Med. Soc. (treas. 1990-92, sec. 1992, pres.-elect 1993).

BONNET, JOHN DAVID, physician, medical facility administrator; b. Champaign, Ill., Feb. 22, 1928; s. James Herbert and Anne Eleanor (Lautenslager) B.; m. Beverly Bennett, June 26, 1949; children: David Gregory, James Vinvent, Peter Alan. BS, U. Ill., 1948; MD, Johns Hopkins U., 1952; MS, U. Minn., 1958. Diplomate Am. Bd. Internal Medicine. Intern Johns Hopkins Hosp., 1952-53; resident internal medicine Mayo Clinic, 1953-54, 56-58; cons. hematology and oncology Scott and White Clinic, Temple, Tex., 1958-93; lectr. in medicine Tex. A&M U., Temple, 1974-80, prof. medicine Health Sci. Ctr., 1980-93; med. dir. Temple Cmty. Free Clinic, 1993—; prin. investigator S.W. Oncology Group, San Antonio, 1963-93. Trustee Scott & White Meml. Hosp., Scott, Sherwood and Brindley Found., 1970-93, Ctrl. Cmtys. Mental Health Mental Retardation, Temple, 1990. Capt. USAF, 1954-56. Nat. Cancer Inst. grantee, 1963-93. Fellow ACP; mem. AMA (mem. ho. of dels. 1980-94), Am. Soc. Clin. Oncology, Am. Soc. Hematology. Republican. Presbyterian. Avocations: hiking, golf, farming.

BONNEVILLE, RICHARD BRIGGS, retired petroleum exploration and production executive; b. Chgo., July 15, 1942; s. Alfred Briggs and Grace Estelle (Burke) B.; B.S. in M.E., U. Notre Dame, 1964; M.B.A., Harvard U., 1967; m. Mary Ann E. Pittman, July 17, 1976; children: Ann M., John B. Project engr. Hamilton Standard div. United Technologies, 1964-65; asst. to pres. Strathmore Paper div. Hammermill Paper, Springfield, Mass., 1966; mgr. planning Union Oil Co., Schaumburg, Ill., 1967-72; asst. to exec. v.p. Santa Fe Industries, Inc., Chgo., 1972-77, mgr. planning, 1977-79, dir. planning, 1979-84; corp. sec. Santa Fe So. Pacific Corp., 1984-88;, v.p. planning, Santa Fe Energy Resources, Inc., Houston, 1988-95, ret., 1995. Mem. Tau Beta Pi, Pi Tau Sigma. Home: 920 Cranberry Hill Ct Houston TX 77079-5010

BONNEY, HAL JAMES, JR., federal judge; b. Norfolk, Va., Aug. 27, 1929; s. Hal J. and Mary (Shackelford) B.; m. Marie McBee, July 4, 1963 (div. 1979); children: David James, John Wesley. BA, U. Richmond, 1951, MA, 1953; JD, Coll. William and Mary, 1969. Bar: Va. 1969. Instr. Norfolk public schs., 1951-61; supt. Douglas MacArthur Acad., 1961-67; practiced law, 1969-71; law clk. U.S. Dist. Ct., 1969; prof. U. Va., 1964-71, Coll. William and Mary, 1969-71; U.S. bankruptcy judge Norfolk, 1971-95; ret., 1995; adj. prof. law Regent U. Sch. Law, 1987—. Tchr. Wesleymen Bible class Sta. WTAR-AM, 1962-98, tchr. emeritus, 1998; tchr. Good News TV Network, 1989—; treas. Wesleymen Found., Inc., Billy Graham Crusades, 1974-76; pres. adv. coun. CBN U., 1986-95; vice-chmn. Va. Meth. Bd. Edn., Inc., 1991—; bd. visitors Duke Div. Sch., 1991—; bd. dirs. Norfolk Union Mission, 1994—, The Tidewater Winds; mem. City of Norfolk Task Force on Pub. Housing, 1995-96; advisor Film Sch., Regent U., 1996—; mem. rules com. Va. United Meth. conf., 1996—; bd. ordained ministry United Meth. Ch., Va. Recipient S.A.R. Good Citizenship medal, Woodmen of the World History medal, U. Richmond Gold medal, George Washington honor medal Freedoms Found., Alli award Cultural Alliance Greater Hampton Rds., 1998; Judge Hal Bonney Day named in honor by City of Norfolk, Jan. 27, 1998. Mem. Nat. Conf. Bankruptcy Judges (pres. 1983, chmn. editl. bd. The Am. Bankruptcy Law Jour.), Va. State Bar, Norfolk and Portsmouth Bar Assn., Nat. Film Soc., Am. Film Inst., Brit. Film Inst., Am. Cinematheque, James Kent Inn of Ct. (pres. 1994-96, hon. mem.), Phi Alpha Theta, Pi Sigma Alpha, Phi Alpha Delta, Mason, Shriners, Elks. Methodist. Home: 1357 Windsor Point Rd Norfolk VA 23509-1311 Office: The Wesleymen 408 Boush St Norfolk VA 23510-1215

BONNEY, SAMUEL ROBERT, lawyer; b. Dallas, Mar. 10, 1943; s. Herbert Staats, Jr. and Anna Margaret (Hudnall) B.; m. Margaret Reynolds Palms, Nov. 3, 1984; 1 child, Anna Beth; children from previous marriage: Samuel Robert, II, Heather Noel, Sarah Emily. BA, Austin Coll., Sherman, Tex., 1965; JD, U. Tex., 1968. Bar: Tex. 1968. Ptnr. Bonney & Bonney, Dallas, 1968—. Served with AUS, 1969. Mem. Tex. Bar Assn., Dallas Bar Assn. Clubs: Dallas Country. Office: 3838 Oak Lawn Ave Ste 800 Dallas TX 75219-4509

BONNIE, RICHARD JEFFREY, legal educator, lawyer; b. Richmond, Va., Aug. 22, 1945; s. Herbert Herman and Helene Selma (Berz) B.; m. Kathleen Ford, June 15, 1967; children: Joshua Ford, Zachary Andrew, Jessica Katherine. BA, Johns Hopkins U., 1966; LLB, U. Va., 1969. Bar: Va. 1969, U.S. Dist. Ct. (ea. dist.) Va. 1969; U.S. Ct. Appeals (4th cir.) 1969, U.S. Supreme Ct. 1986. Asst. prof. law U. Va., Charlottesville, 1969-70, assoc. prof., 1973-77, prof., 1977-87; John S. Battle prof., 1987—, dir. Inst. Law, Psychiatry, and Pub. Policy, 1979—; vis. prof. Cornell Law Sch., 1993-94; assoc. dir. Nat. Commn. Marijuana and Drug Abuse, 1971-73; reporter Nat. Conf. Commrs. on Uniform State Laws, 1972-74; cons. Spl. Action Office for Drug Abuse Prevention Exec. Office of the Pres., 1973-75; spl. asst. to U.S. Atty. Gen., 1975; mem. and sec. Nat. Adv. Council on Drug Abuse, 1975-80; mem. Com. on Problem of Drug Dependence, Inc., 1979-84; charter fellow Coll. Problems of Drug Dependence, 1992—; cons. Am. Psychiat. Assn., Coun. Psychiatry and Law, 1979—; mem. U.S. State Dept. Del. to investigate psychiat. practices in the Soviet Union, 1989; mem. World Psychiat. Assn. rev. team to investigate Soviet psychiatry, 1991; mem. adv. bd. permanent coordination office Reforms in Psychiatry in Ctrl and Ea. Europe, former Soviet Union, 1993—; bd. dirs. Geneva Initiative on Psychiatry, 1996—; pres. Am. Friends of Geneva Initiatives on Pychiatry, 1997—, mem. MacArthur Found. Network on Mental Health and the Law, 1988-96; bd. dirs. Va. Capital Representation Resource Ctr 1994-97. Chmn. Va. Human Rights Com., Dept. Mental Health and Mental Retardation, 1979-85; bd. dirs. Coll. on Problem of Drug Dependence, 1996—. Served to capt. USAF, 1970-73. Inst. Criminology fellow Cambridge U., 1977. Fellow Va. Law Found.; mem. Inst. Medicine of NAS (mem. bd. neurosci. and behavioral health, 1992—, mem. com. on preventing nicotine dependence in children and youths, 1993-94, mem. membership com. 1995—, chair com. on opportunities in drug abuse rsch. 1995-96 chair com. injury prevention control, 1997-98), Nat. Resrch. Counc. (mem. comm. on data and resrch. for policy on illoicit drugs, 1998-2000), ABA (mem. criminal justice-mental health standards project adv. bd. 1981-87), NAS, Am. Psychiat. Assn. (Isaac Ray award 1998), Va. Bar Assn. (chmn. com. mentally disabled 1981-90, mem. criminal law sect. coun. 1992-96), World Psychiat. Assn. (rev. team to investigate Soviet Psychiatry 1991), Am. Acad. Psychiat. Law (Amicus award 1994), Inst. Medicine, Va. Law Found. (fellow). Author: The Marijuana Conviction: The History of Marijuana Prohibition in the United States, 1974, Legal Aspects of Drug Dependence, 1975, Psychiatrists and the Legal Process: Diagnosis and Debate, 1977, Marijuana Use and Criminal Sanctions: Essays in the Theory and Practice of Decriminalization, 1980, Criminal Law: Cases and Materials, 1982, 2nd edit., 1986, The Trial of John W. Hinckley, Jr.: A Case Study in the Insanity Defense, 1986, Criminal Law, 1997, Mental Disorder, Work Disability and the Law, 1997. Office: U Va Sch Law Charlottesville VA 22903

BONNIWELL, ANN GLENN, educational administrator; b. Nassawadox, Va., July 13, 1951; d. LeRoy Wilson and Kathryn Mae (Weaver) Glenn; m. Paul Reade Bonniwell, Oct. 15, 1977; 1 child, Andrew Ryan. BS, Longwood Coll., 1973; MEd, Salisbury (Md.) State U., 1979. Cert. elem. edn. K-7, and elem. adminstrn. and supervision, Va. Kindergarten tchr. Accomac (Va.) County Pub. Schs., 1973-77, tchr. 1st grade, 1977-86; prin. Northampton County Pub. Schs., Machipongo, Va., 1996—, adminstr. fed. programs and grant writing, 1996—. Mem. ASCD. Home: 33134 Hickman St Painter VA 23420-2642 Office: Northampton Co Pub Schs 7207 Young St Machipongo VA 23405-1725

BONO, MARY, congresswoman; b. Cleve., Oct. 24, 1961; d. Clay and Karen Whitaker; m. Sonny Bono, Feb. 1986 (dec.); children: Chesare Elan, Chianna Maria. BFA in Art History, U. So. Calif., 1984. Cert. personal fitness instr. Rep. Calif. 44th Congrl. Dist. U.S. House of Reps., 1998—; mem. com. nat. security, com. on the judiciary U.S. Congress. Past bd. dirs. Palm Springs Internat. Film Festival; active D.A.R.E program, Olive Crest Home for Abused Children, Tiempos de Los Ninos. Named Woman of Yr., San Gorgonio (Calif.) chpt. Girl Scouts Am., 1993. Avocations: outdoor activities, computer technology. Office: US House of Reps 516 Cannon HOB Washington DC 20515-0544*

BONOMETTI, ROBERT JOHN, technology management and strategy executive; b. N.Y.C., Sept. 29, 1953; s. Joseph Patrick and Fortunata Mary (Barba) B.; m. Virginia Anne Scyphers, Oct. 26, 1997; stepchildren: Jessica, Michael. BS summa cum laude, U.S. Mil. Acad., 1975; MS in Physics, MIT, 1981, PhD in Physics, 1985; MBA, L.I. U., 1987. Registered profl. engr., Va. Assoc. prof. physics U.S. Mil. Acad., West Point, N.Y., 1985-88; program mgr. Def. Advanced Rsch. Projects Agy., Arlington, Va., 1988-93; sr. policy analyst White House Sci. and Tech. Office, Washington, 1993-95; exec. dir. technology strategy Bell Atlantic Corp., Arlington, 1995-98; pres. MGB Enterprises, LLC, Winchester, Va., 1998—; prof. info. sys. and computer tech. Shenandoah U., Byrd Sch. Bus., 1999—; mem. industry adv. bd. Ctr. for Satellite and Hybrid Comm. Networks, U. Md., 1994—; chmn. rev. com. commercialization of space NASA, Washington, 1996; exec. dir. info. and comm. R&D com. Nat. Sci. and Tech. Coun., Washington, 1993-95; adj. prof. various univs., 1981—. *Dr. Bonometti is president of Strategic Technology Decisions, a consulting company of MGB Enterprises, LLC. He is a nationally recognized expert in strategic planning, technology management and advanced research and development. His areas of expertise include business development for advanced high-payoff rapid-time-to-market products, technology benchmarking and competitive analyses, executive decision support systems, computing and communications networking and interoperability, advanced telecommunications and radio technologies, and space systems. As Executive Director, Technology Strategy for a Fortune 100 company, he led corporate-level business strategy and planning for emerging and advanced technologies, including Internet and multimedia data networking technologies, broadband technologies, and network computing.* Contbr. articles to profl. jours. Active various animal rights and environ. orgns. Lt. col. U.S. Army, 1975-95. Recipient Laurel award Aviation Week and Space Tech., 1990; Sci. and Tech. fellow Dept. Commerce, 1993-94; Hertz Found. fellow, 1981-85. Mem. IEEE (sr.), AIAA (sr.), Am. Phys. Soc., Am. Astron. Soc. Avocations: music, weightlifting, tennis, running. Home: 260 Golds Hill Rd Winchester VA 22603-3129 Office: Majestik Global Bus Enterprises LLC 260 Golds Hill Rd Winchester VA 22603

BONOMI, FERNE GATER, public relations executive; b. Council Bluffs, Iowa, July 27, 1923; d. Roy Winfield and Leona Hazel (Bays) Gater; m. Robert Foch Bonomi, Sept. 3, 1949 (div. 1974); children: Robert Duff, David Scott; m. Wayne P. Davis, Apr. 20, 1991. BA magna cum laude, U. Iowa, 1948. Editor Silver City (Iowa) Times, 1940-41; reporter, photographer, Sunday editor Cedar Rapids (Iowa) Gazette, 1943-47; dir. pub. info. Iowa Devel. Commission, Des Moines, 1950-51; pub. info. officer Gov. William S. Beardsley, Des Moines, 1951-53; v.p. Bonomi Assocs. Inc., Des Moines, 1954-72; adminstr. Mid-Iowa Drug Abuse Council, Des Moines, 1972-74; cons. Plain Talk Pub. Co., Des Moines, 1974-75; communications dir. Iowa Assn. Sch. Bds., Des Moines, 1975-86; owner, operator Bonomi & Co., Des Moines, 1986—; chmn. pubs. evaluation Am. C. of C. Execs., Washington, 1977-81; workshop presenter various nat. and state confs., 1976—. Author: Show Me A Man, 1969, National Curriculum for Accreditation, 1998; editor Iowa Sch. Bd. Dialogue, 1975-86; assoc. editor Leader's Mag., 1964-72. Chmn. communications Des Moines Area Religious Council, 1980-82; mem. Gov.'s Com. on Employment Handicapped, 1968-74. Named Iowa Sch. Communicator of Yr., Iowa Sch. Pub. Rels. Assn., 1997. Fellow Pub. Rels. Soc. Am. (developer mentoring program 1994—, chmn. 1995, commendation for meaningful rsch. Bronze Anvil competition 1997, pres. Iowa chpt. 1980-82, chmn. accreditation 1982—, writer nat. curriculum for accreditation 1998, Outstanding Contbr. award 1983); mem. Nat. Sch. Pub. Rels. Assn. (cert., gold medallion award 1987), Am. Assn. Sch. Adminstrs., Phi Beta Kappa, Alpha Delta Pi (nat. editor 1959-62, Outstanding Alumna award 1977). Mem. United Ch. Christ. Avocations: canoeing, horseback riding, church choir, dancing, theater. E-mail: ferne@bonomi.com. Office: Bonomi & Co 1003 Kennedy St Ames IA 50010-4247

BONOMI, JOHN GURNEE, retired lawyer; b. N.Y.C., Aug. 13, 1923; s. Felix A. and Bessie (Gurnee) B.; m. Patricia Updegraff, Aug. 22, 1953; children: Kathryn, John. B.A., Columbia U., 1947; J.D., Cornell U., 1950; LL.M., N.Y.U., 1957. Bar: N.Y. 1952, U.S. Supreme Ct. 1966, U.S. Dist. Ct. (so. dist.) N.Y. 1975, U.S. Ct. Appeals (2d cir.) 1978. Asst. dist. atty. N.Y. County, 1953-60; spl. counsel subcom. antitrust and monopoly, for hearings on organized crime and monopoly in profl. boxing, Kefauver Com. U.S. Senate, 1960-61; spl. asst. atty. gen. investigating 1961 N.Y.C. mayor race N.Y. State, 1961-62; chief counsel com. grievances Assn. Bar City N.Y., 1963-76; vis. scholar Harvard U. Law Sch., 1976-77; counsel firm Anderson, Russell, Kill & Olick, N.Y.C., 1977-80; practice law N.Y.C., 1980-96; mem. com. grievances and admissions U.S. Ct. Appeals (2d cir.), 1983—; lectr. Fordham U. Law Sch., 1973; mem. N.Y. state judicial conf. com. on disciplinary enforcement, 1971-72. Columnist: N.Y. Law Jour. 1978-83; contbr. articles to legal jours. Trustee Village of Tarrytown, N.Y., 1965-67, 68-72; councilman, dep. supr. Town of Greenburgh, 1974; spl. counsel to Village of Irvington, N.Y., 1972. With USAAF, 1943-45, ETO. Mem. ABA (spl. com. on evaluation disciplinary enforcement Clark Com. 1967-70, cons. spl. com. on evaluation ethical stds. 1967-69), N.Y. State Bar Assn. (vice-chmn. com. grievances 1970-71, com. profl. discipline 1988-93), Am. Law Inst. (spl. com. peer rev. 1978-80), New York County Lawyers Assn. (com. profl. discipline 1993—), Assn. of Bar of City of N.Y. (cons. spl. com. on free press and fair trial, Medina com. 1966-67, com. profl. discipline 1983-88), Inst. Jud. Adminstrn., Nat. Orgn. Bar Counsel (pres. 1970-71, chmn. spl. com. on Watergate discipline 1974-76). Democrat. Club: Harvard (N.Y.C.). Home: 131 Deertrack Ln Irvington NY 10533-1013

BONOSARO, CAROL ALESSANDRA, professional association executive, former government official; b. New Brunswick, N.J., Feb. 16, 1940; d. Rudolph William and Elisabeth Ann (Betsko) B.; m. Donald D. Kummerfeld, Sept. 8, 1962 (div. Jan. 1970); m. Athanasios Chalkiopoulos, Nov. 21, 1976 (separated Dec. 1990); 1 dau., Melissa. B.A., Cornell U., 1961; postgrad., George Washington U., 1961-62. Analytical statistician Office Mgmt. and Budget, Exec. Office of Pres., Washington, 1961-66; asst. dir. fed. programs div. U.S. Commn. on Civil Rights, Washington, 1966-68; dir. Office Fed. Programs U.S. Commn. on Civil Rights, 1968-69, dir. tech. assistance div., 1969-71, spl. asst. to staff dir., 1972, dir. women's rights program, 1972-79, asst. staff dir. for program planning and evaluation, 1979-80, asst. staff dir. congressional and public affairs, 1980-86; pres. Sr. Execs. Assn., Washington, 1986—; mem. adv. com. Asian Am. Govt. Execs. Network, 1996—; mem. Nat. Partnership Coun., 1997—. Vice chmn. Nat. Com. on Asian Wives of U.S. Servicemen, 1975-85; pres. Catholics for a Free Choice, 1980-83. Mem. Exec. Women in Govt., Sr. Exec. Assn. (dir. 1981-86, chmn. bd. dirs. 1983-86). Democrat. Home: 5504 Jordan Rd Bethesda MD 20816-1366 Office: Sr Execs Assn PO Box 44808 Washington DC 20026-4808

BONOW, ROBERT OGDEN, medical educator; b. Camden, N.J., Mar. 11, 1947; m. Patricia Jeanne Hitchens, Sept. 12, 1982; children: Robert Hitchens, Samuel Crawford. BS in Chem. Engring. magna cum laude, Lehigh U., Bethelehem, Pa., 1969; MD, U. Pa., Phila., 1973. Diplomate Am. Bd. Internal Medicine, subspecialty bd. on cardiovascular disease. Intern in medicine Hosp. U. Pa., Phila., 1973-74, resident, 1974-76; clin. assoc. cardiology br. Nat. Heart, Lung and Blood Inst., Bethesda, Md., 1976-79, sr. investigator, attending physician cardiology br., 1979-92, chief nuclear cardiology sect., 1980-92, dep. chief, 1989-92; Goldberg Prof. Medicine, Chief Divsn. Cardiology Northwestern U. Med. Sch., Chgo., 1992—; attending physician dept. medicine VA Lakeside Med. Ctr., Chgo., 1993—, Evanston (Ill.) Hosp., 1994—; Pfizer vis. prof. cardiovascular medicine Yale U., 1992, U. Mass., 1998; AHA/ACC Task Force on Practice Guidelines Com. on Cardiac Radlonuclide Imaging, 1993-95; chair com. on mgmt. of patients with valvular heart disease, 1996—; vis. prof. various univs., 1982-99; ad hoc adv. panel on computer image tech. divsn. computer rsch. and tech. NIH, 1991, peer reviewer Clin. Practice Guideline on Unstable Angina, AHCPR, NHLBI, NIH, 1993-94, working group on methods/technologies Nat. Heart Attack Alert Program, 1994—; invited presenter at sci. sessions, symposia and acad. med. ctrs. Mem. editl. bd. Am. Jour. Cardiology, 1983—, Jour. Am. Coll. Cardiology, 1983-87, 91-95, Circulation, 1986—, Cardiovascular Imaging, 1988—, Am. Jour. Cardiac Imaging, 1990-95, Internat. Jour. Cardiac Imaging, 1990—, Jour. Heart Valve Disease, 1982—, Jour. Nuclear Cardiology, 1993—, Jour. Nuclear Medicine, 1994—, Cardiologia, 1995—, Am. Heart Jour., 1998—; contbr. over 290 publs. in med. jours. and textbooks. Recipient NIH Director's award, 1986, USPHS Commendation medal, 1990, USPHS outstanding svc. medal, 1991. Fellow ACP, Am. Coll. Cardiology (exhibits com. 1986-92, program com. 1991-92, chair extramural edn. com., 1998—, bd. trustees 1999—), Am. Heart Assn. Coun. on Clin. Cardiology (exec. com. 1989-91, 94—, chair long-range planning com., 1997—, chmn. program com. 1998—, sci. adv. coord. com. 1998—, bd. dirs. 1999—); mem. AAAS, Am. Bd. Internal Medicine (subspecialty bd. cardiovasc. disease 1996—), Am. Soc. Clin. Investigation, Assn. Am. Physicians, Am. Heart Assn. Met. Chgo. (bd. govs. 1992—, rsch. coun. 1992—), Am. Soc. Nuclear Cardiology (bd. dirs. 1994-98, chmn. edn. com. 1994—, nominating com. 1994—), Assn. Profs. Cardiology (nominating com. 1993—, councillor 1994—, sec., treas. 1996—), Chgo. Cardiology Group (pres. 1994-96), Soc. Nuclear Medicine (com. on coun. coordination 1991—, publs. com. 1994—), Am. Fedn. Clin. Rsch., Assn. Am. Physicians, Assn. Univ. Cardiologists, Ctrl. Soc. Clin. Rsch., Alpha Omega Alpha. Office: Northwestern U Med Sch Cardiology Divsn 250 E Superior St Ste 524 Chicago IL 60611-2958

BONSACK, ROSE MARY HATEM, state legislator, physician; b. Havre de Grace, Md., Oct. 24, 1933; d. Joseph Thomas and Nasma (Joseph) Hatem; m. James P. Bonsack, Aug. 24, 1957; children: Jeanette, Karen, Thomas, David, James J. BS in Chemistry cum laude, Washington Coll., 1955; MD, Med. Coll. Pa., 1960. Intern Easton (Pa.) Hosp., 1961; physician outpatient clinic Kirk Army Hosp., Aberdeen Proving Ground, Md., 1962-74; chief outpatient clinic Kirk Army Hosp., Aberdeen Proving Group, Md., 1968-72, chief dept. hosp. clinics, 1972-74; contract physician Harford County Dept. Health, Md., 1975-78; utilization rev. officer Harford Meml. Hosp., Havre de Grace, 1981-82; pvt. practice Aberdeen, Md., 1981—; mem. Md. Gen. Assembly, 1991-99, chmn. house rules and exec. nominations com., 1991-94, mem. house ways and means com., 1995-99; coord. clinics Hypertensive Coun. Md., 1977-81; reviewer quality assurance for nursing homes in Harford County, Md. Licensing Div., 1977-81; utilization rev. officer Harford Meml. Hosp., Havre de Grace, 1981-82; med. dir. Ashley Alcoholic Rehab., Havre de Grace, 1983-84; mem. Bd. Med. Examiners Md.; mem., exec. sec. Commn. on Med. Discipline, 1985-88. V.p. St. Joan of Arc Home-Sch. Assn., 1968, pres., 1969, mem., 1968-85; v.p. No. Md. Heart Assn., 1969, pres., 1970, bd. dirs., 1973; bd. dirs. Mann House, Bel Air, Md., 1973-82, Harford County Cancer Soc., 1973-86; mem. John Carroll Home-Sch. Assn., 1974—, 1st v.p., 1975, pres., 1975; bd. dirs. John Carroll H.S., 1975—, pres. bd. dirs., 1979-85; mem. Harford County Dem. Cen. Com., 1987-90; mem. chief exec.'s coun. Harford C.C., 1990. Recipient Outstanding Contbn. to Md. Traffic Safety citation State of Md., 1969, Cert. of Merit for svc. Md. Cancer Soc., 1977, Women Helping Women award Soroptomists Harford and Cecil Counties, 1983-84; named one of Top 100 Women in Md., Daily Record, 1996. Mem. Am. Acad. Family Physicians (bd. dirs. 1996, alt. del. 1990-94, del. from Md. 1994-96, chmn. chpt. affairs com. 1992—, commn. on regulations 1993-96), Med. Chirurgical Fac. Md., Hartford County Med. Soc. (sec. 1967, pres. 1968, v.p. 1978, Outstand Cmny. Svc. citation 1979), Md. Acad. Family Physicians (v.p. 1987, pres. 1988).

BONSELL, THOMAS ALLEN, journalist, publisher; b. Lusk, Wyo., Mar. 17, 1935; s. Dee V. and Neoma Vada (Bevens) B. BBA, Woodbury U., 1963; postgrad., Georgetown U., 1964-65. Journalist, reporter The Portland (Oreg.) Reporter, 1963-64; intelligence analyst Nat. Security Agy., Ft. Meade, Md., 1964-65; journalist, editor The Utica (N.Y.) Daily Press, 1965-67, The Denver Post, 1967-80; journalist, writer Port Orchard, Wash., 1980—; founder, editor Country Cottage Pub., Port Orchard, 1995—. Author: The Un-Americans, 1995. With USAF, 1956-60. Mem. Phi Gamma Kappa. Avocations: art (drawing, painting), gardening. Home and Office: Country Cottage Pub 285 SE Rim Rd Port Orchard WA 98367-7708

BONSIGNORE, MICHAEL ROBERT, electronics company executive; b. Plattsburg, N.Y., Apr. 3, 1941; s. Marco Romulo and Alice Marie (Enders) B.; m. Sheila Ani Gorman, June 7, 1963; children: Michelle, Michael Robert, Christopher. BS, U.S. Naval Acad., 1963; postgrad., Tex. A&M U. With Honeywell, Inc., 1969-71, 73—, v.p. mktg., 1977-80; v.p. ops. Honeywell Marine Sys., Seattle, 1981-83; pres. Honeywell Europe, Brussels, 1983-86, exec. v.p. internat., 1987, pres. internat., 1987-89, exec. v.p., COO, 1989-93, chmn., CEO, 1993—; bd. dirs. Donaldson Co., Honeywell Inc., St. Paul Cos.; mem. adv. coun. U.S. Trade Rep. (investment policy adv. com.), Office Tech. Assessment; mem. U.S.-USSR Trade and Econ. Coun. Mem. devel. bd. Global Leadership U. Mich.; bd. dirs. Minn. Orch., Met. Econ. Devel. Assn., Alliance to Save Energy, Hugh O'Brian Youth Found.; mem. adv. bd. Minn. Trade Office. Lt. USN, 1963-69. Mem. Sea-Space Symposium (pres. 1981), Am. C. of C. Brussels (v.p.), Nat. Assn. Underwater Instrs., U.S. Naval Acad. Alumni Assn. (past pres.), Met. Econ. Devel. Assn. Office: Honeywell Inc Honeywell Plz PO Box 524 Minneapolis MN 55440-0524*

BONSKY, JACK ALAN, chemical company executive, lawyer; b. Canton, Ohio, Mar. 12, 1938; s. Jack H. and Pearl E. Bonsky; m. Carol Ann Portmann, Sept. 2, 1960; children: Jack Raymond, Cynthia Lynn. AB, Ohio U., 1960; JD, Ohio State U., 1964. Bar: Ohio 1964, U.S. Dist. Ct. (so. dist.) Ohio 1969. With Metcalf, Thomas & Bonsky, Marietta, Ohio, 1964-69, Addison, Fisher & Bonsky, Marietta, 1969-70; asst. counsel GenCorp., Inc. (formerly Gen. Tire & Rubber Co.), Akron, Ohio, 1970-75, assoc. gen. counsel, 1975-86, asst. sec., 1977-86, v.p., sec., 1986; v.p., sec., gen. counsel DiversiTech Gen., Inc., 1986-87; v.p., gen. counsel GenCorp Polymer Products, 1988-94; asst. gen. counsel, dir. environ. affairs GenCorp, Inc., 1994-96; pvt. practice, 1996—; solicitor City of Marietta, 1966-67; legal advisor City of Marietta Bd. of Edn., 1966-67; police prosecutor, Belpre, Ohio, 1969-70; comml. law instr. Am. Inst. Banking, 1969; dir. Frontier Holdings, Inc., Denver, Frontier Airlines, Denver, 1985 (merged with People Express Airlines, 1985). Mem. Marietta Income Tax Bd. of Rev., 1966-67; mem. Traffic Commn., 1966-69, chmn., 1967; mem. Civil Svc. Commn., 1969; trustee Urban League, 1978-81, pres., 1980-81; trustee Akron Cmty. Svc. Ctr., 1978-81, United Way of Summit County, 1982-89; mem. Bath Twp. Merger Commn., 1995-96; v.p. Bath Twp. Homeowners' Assn., 1999—; bd. dirs. Washington County Soc. for Crippled Children, 1964-70, S.E. Ohio unit Arthritis Found., 1967-70, chmn., 1968-70; mem. Washington County Health Planning Com., 1968-70; ho. of dels. Ohio Easter Seal Soc., 1968-70. Recipient Akron Cmty. Svc. Ctr. and Urban League Leadership award, 1981. Mem. Ohio Bar Assn. Home: 4234 Idlebrook Dr Akron OH 44333-1726 Office: GenCorp Inc 4234 Idlebrook Dr Akron OH 44333-1726

BONTÁ, DIANA M., city manager; b. N.Y.C., Dec. 12, 1950. AAS in Nursing magna cum laude, Bronx C.C., 1972; BSN cum laude, SUNY, Buffalo, 1974; MPH, UCLA, 1975, D in Cmty. Health Scis., 1992. Adult, med.-surg. unit charge nurse Cross County Hosp., Yonkers, N.Y., 1972; acting charge nurse pediat., orthopedics unit Bellevue Hosp., N.Y.C., 1972; emergency rm., intensive care nursery charge nurse Children's Hosp. Buffalo, 1972-74; adult, med.-surg. unit clin. instr. Cedars-Sinai Med. Ctr., L.A., 1974-75; health rschr. Clinica Behrhorst, Chimaltenango, Guatemala, 1975; nursing cons. II divsn. licensing and cert. Calif. State Dept. Health, Santa Barbara, 1975-77; nursing cons. II rural health divsn. Calif. State Dept. Health, L.A., 1977-78, regional adminstr. rural health divsn., 1978-83; dir. dept. health and human svcs. City of Long Beach, Calif., 1988—. Mem. L.A. Adolescent Pregnancy Prevention Childwatch Project, Comision Fermenil Mexicana Nacional, Inc., Comision Fermenil de L.A.; mem. adv. com. to dir. Ctrs. for Disease Control; immediate past pres., bd. dirs. Calif. Women's Law Ctr., 1994-95; bd. dirs. New Econs. for Women; mem. dean's adv. bd. UCLA Sch. Pub. Health.; mem. adv. com. Ctr. for Health Care Innovation Calif. State U., Long Beach, AIDS Walk Long Beach, 1990-92, Coastal County Health Ctr., 1989—; trustee St. Mary Med. Ctr., Nat. AIDS Fund, 1992-96; mem. L.A. Managed Care Planning Coun., 1993-94; sec., bd. dirs. Pub. Health Found. Enterprises, 1992-95; mem. policy com. Latino Coaltion for a Health Calif., 1990-95; mem. com. Rebuild L.A. Health, among others. Recipient Pub. Svc. award Long Beach Cares, 1995, Woman of Distinction award Soroptimist Internat. Long Beach, 1994. Mem. APHA (vice chair exec. bd. dirs., immediate past pres. Latino caucus), Nat. Assn. County and City Health Ofcls., County Health Exec. Assn. Calif. (gov. coun. 1995-96). Office: City of Long Beach Dept Health and Human Svcs 2525 Grand Ave Long Beach CA 90815-1765*

BONTE, FREDERICK JAMES, radiology educator, physician; b. Bethlehem, Pa., Jan. 18, 1922; s. Frederick R. and Harriett (Stoudt) B.; m. Cecile Poetzel; children: Frederick W., Stephen J., John A., Therese A., Suzanne M., Ann E. BS, Western Res. U., 1942, MD, 1945. Diplomate: Am. Bd. Radiology (trustee 1969-75), Am. Bd. Nuclear Medicine. Intern Huntington Meml. Hosp., Pasadena, Cal., 1945-46; resident Univ. Hosp., Cleve., 1948-52; practice medicine, specializing in radiology and nuclear medicine Dallas, 1956—; mem. faculty Western Res. U. Sch. Medicine, 1952-56, asst. prof., 1952-56, chief radiotherapy and nuclear medicine, 1954-56; prof. U. Tex. Southwestern Med. Sch., Dallas, 1956—; chmn. dept. radiology U. Tex. Southwestern Med. Sch., 1956-73, dean, 1973-80; dir. Nuclear Medicine Research Center, 1980—, Effie and Wofford Cain disting. chair in diagnostic imaging; Dr. Jack Krohmer prof. in radiation physics; Mem. bd. Nat. Council Radiation Protection and Measurements, 1966-71; radiology tng. com. Nat. Insts. Gen. Med. Scis., USPHS, 1966-70, residency rev. com. radiology AMA, 1966-69, adv. and rev. coms. VA, 1972—; Founding trustee Am. Bd. Nuclear Medicine, 1971-73, chmn., 1977-80; internat. cons. on med. edn. Contbr. articles to profl. jours. Served to capt. USAAF, 1946-48. Fellow Am. Coll. Radiology, Am. Coll. Nuclear Physicians (Pres.'s award 1997); mem. AMA (del., chmn. grad. med. edn. com., Roentgen Centennial Hartman medal 1995), Soc. Nuclear Medicine (De Hevesy Nuclear Pioneer award 1995), Am. Roentgen Ray Soc. (exec. com.), Radiol. Soc. N.Am., Sigma Xi, Alpha Omega Alpha. Research on exptl. nuclear medicine and radiology. Home: 11138 Wonderland Trl Dallas TX 75229-3943 Office: 5323 Harry Hines Blvd Dallas TX 75235-9061

BONTEMPI, GAIL DIANE, small business owner; b. Buffalo, Jan. 22, 1939; d. Robert Lester and Stella Rose (Augustine) Baldauff; m. William R. Bontempi Sr., Aug. 2, 1958 (dec. Mar. 1993); children: William R. Jr., Mark E. Student, Bryan Stratton Bus. Sch., 1956, Niagara County C.C., 1992-95. Owner G.B. Bus Svcs., Lockport, N.Y., 1991—; corr. Lockport Union Sun & Jour., 1995. Author (poetry book) Misty Morning Musings, 1995, (short stories) Deadly Decision, 1996, (novel) Pearls in Time, 1999; co-author: 409 to LA, 1997; editor (anthology) Basic Black, 1999. Mem. Niagara County Coun. Girl Scouts, 1996—. Mem. The Write Touch (founder 1994, facilitator 1994-96, 99), Lockport Noon Toastmasters (treas. 1997-98, v.p. membership 1998-99, 99—, v.p. pub. rels. 1998-99, 99—), Ea. Niagara County C. of C. Republican. Avocations: reading, decorating, quilting. Office: GB Bus Svcs 5679 S Transit Rd # 130 Lockport NY 14094-5842

BONTING, SJOERD LIEUWE, biochemist, priest; b. Amsterdam, The Netherlands, Oct. 6, 1924; s. Sjoerd L. and Johanna H.M. (Hagedoorn) B.; m. Suzanne Maarsen, Jan. 10, 1951 (dec. Jan. 1986); children: Marion S., Paul S., Elizabeth J., Peter J.; m. Erica J.M. Schotman, Feb. 27, 1987. BSc in Chemistry, U. Amsterdam, 1944, MSc in Biochemistry cum laude, 1950, PhD in Biochemistry, 1952; lic. in theology (hon.), St. Mark's Inst. Theology, London, 1975. Ordained priest Episcopal Ch., 1964. Instr. U. Amsterdam, 1947-52; research assoc. State U. Iowa, Iowa City, 1952-55; asst. prof. biochemistry U. Minn., Mpls., 1955-56; asst. prof. U. Ill., Chgo., 1956-60; sect. chief NIH, Bethesda, Md., 1960-65; prof., chmn. dept. biochemistry U. Nymegen, The Netherlands, 1965-85; sci. cons. NASA Ames Research Ctr., Moffett Field, Calif., 1985-93. Author: Word and World, 1989, Creation and Evolution: Attempt at Synthesis, 1966, 2d edit., 1997, Humanity, Chaos, Reconciliation, 1998; editor: Transmitters in the Visual Process, 1981, Advances in Space Biology and Medicine, 1989-1999; contbr. over 370 articles to profl. jours. Bd. dirs. Multidisciplinary Ctr. for Ch. and Soc., Driebergen, Netherlands, 1981-85; curate St. Luke's Episcopal Ch., Bethesda, 1963-65; Anglican chaplain Ch. of Eng. in Netherlands, 1965-85, 93—; asst. priest St. Thomas' Episcopal Ch., Sunnyvale, Calif., 1985-90, St. Mark's Episcopal Ch., Palo Alto, Calif., 1990-93. Postdoctoral fellow USPHS, Iowa City, 1952-54; Rudolf Lehmann Fund scholar, Amsterdam, 1941-46; recipient Fight for Sight citation Nat. Council to Combat Blindness and Assn. for Research in Ophthalmology, N.Y., 1961, 62, Arthur S. Flemming award, Jaycees, Washington, 1964, 1st prize Competition on Enzymology of Leucocytes Karger Found., Basel, Switzerland, 1964. Fellow AAAS; mem. Am. Soc. Cell Biology, Am. Soc. Biol. Chemists, Netherlands Biochem. Soc. (officer 1973-76, v.p. 1976-79, pres. 1979-81), Soc. Ordained Scientists, Sigma Xi. Democrat. Home: 12 Specreyse, 7471 TH Goor The Netherlands

BONTOYAN, WARREN ROBERTS, chemist, state laboratories administrator; b. Balt., Aug. 2, 1932; s. Cesario Baron and Dorothy Bertha (Hunter) B.; m. Gladys Frances Daughaday, May 3, 1958; children: Warren Wendel, Suzanne Cheri. B.S., U. Md., 1956. Food and drug insp. FDA, Balt., 1956-58; rsch. chemist USDA, Beltsville, Md., 1958-60; head chemist methods devel., tng., standards and quality control lab. EPA, Beltsville, 1960-78; chief chem. and biol. investigation br. EPA, 1978-89, also dir. labs., 1978-89; state chemist, chief state chemistry sect. Md. Dept. Agriculture, Annapolis, 1990—; mem. vector and biol. control expert panel WHO.; U.S. rep. to Collaborative Internat. Pesticide Adv. Coun.; mem. expert panel pesticide chemistry FAO; cons. World Bank, 1987, Chesapeake Rsch. Consortium Inc.; chmn., organizer, participant numerous scientific symposiums. Editor: EPA Manual of Chem. Analysis of Pesticides and Devices, 1975; Contbr. articles to profl. jours. Fellow Assn. Ofcl. Analytical Chemists (pres. 1983, gen. referee pesticide formulation analysis, bd. dirs. 1978-84), Am. Inst. Chemists; mem. Am. Chem. Soc., Assn. Am. Control Ofcls., Alpha Chi Sigma. Office: 50 Harry S Truman Pkwy Annapolis MD 21401-8960

BONUCCELLI, DOMINIC ARIZONA, photographer; b. Spokane, Wash., Sept. 15, 1972; s. Robert Allen and Shirley May (Kleven) B. BA in Cinema Prodn. summa cum laude, Univ. So. Calif., 1993. Co-host, writer, dir. KHQ-TV, Spokane, Wash., 1989-91; production asst. Entertainment Ptnrs. Inc., Couer Dalene, Idaho, 1993; video editor Video Monitoring Svcs., L.A., 1994; custom printer Kodalux Profl. Lab, Seattle, 1994—; designer in field. Author: (screenplay) The Beginning Adventures of Montgomery Patpater and the Sea Stork of Paraguay, 1994; photographer Travel's Jour., Encino, Calif., 1994; photographer, designer album cover; composer, performer music for TV ad, 1994. Mem. Knights of the Leash, 1989-90. Pres. scholar Univ. So. Calif., 1990-93. Mem. Phi Kappa Phi. Avocations: cinema, piano, tennis, travel, louge. Home: 4828 N Northwood Dr Spokane WA 99212-1713

BONURA, LARRY SAMUEL, writer; b. Galveston, Tex., Jan. 4, 1950; s. Leo Bonura and Beatrice Sadie (Maiorka) Immel; m. Marilyn Esther Ward, Feb. 17, 1990; 1 child, Sean Joseph Sullins. BS in Journalism, U. Kans., 1977; MA in Am. History, Emporia (Kans.) State U., 1982. Asst. libr. U. Kans. Librs., Lawrence, 1975-77; instr. Butler County Community Coll., El Dorado, Kans., 1982-83; dir. Bike Libr., Emporia, 1977-84; mng. editor Agora Assocs., Balt., 1983-84; dir. Word Workers, Richardson, Tex., 1984—; mgr. editorial svcs. Convex Computer Corp., Richardson, 1987-94; sr. instr. No. Telecom Meridian Info. Products, Richardson, 1994-95; instr. Richland C.C., Dallas, 1988-91; leader seminar Solutions Inc., Boston, 1991-93; lectr. 2d World Congress on Sports Documentation, Vienna, Austria, 1982. Author: Fruit of a Fleeting Joy, 1975, Desktop Publisher's Dictionary, 1989, Desktop Publisher's Thesaurus, 1990, Indexing Technical Documents, 1991, The Art of Indexing, 1994. Mem. Richardson West Jr. High PTA, 1997—; coach Richardson Sports Inc., 1990-95. Mem. Am. Soc. Indexers (pres. D.C. chpt. 1985), Soc. for Tech. Comm. (sr. mem.), Dallas Sci. Mus., Dallas Hist. Soc., Dallas Geneal. Soc., Italian Club of Dallas, Nat. Trust for Hist. Preservation, N.Am. Soc. Sports History, Am. Assn. for State and Local History, Am. Hist. Assn., Assn. for History and Computing, Soc. foc. for Am. Baseball Rsch., So. History Assn., USS Forestal Assn., Learning Disbilities Assn. Richardson, U. Kans. Alumni Assn., Pi Gamma Mu. Avocations: walking, history, music, reading, computers. Home: 806 Clearwater Dr Richardson TX 75080-5032 Office: PO Box 831038 Richardson TX 75083-1038

BONUTTI, ALEXANDER CARL, architect, urban designer; b. Cleve., June 25, 1951; s. Karl Borromeo and Hermina (Rijavec) B. BArch, Ill. Inst. Tech., 1974; MSArch in Urban Design, Columbia U., 1978. Registered architect, Ohio, W.Va., Calif. With William B. Morris, AIA, Shaker Heights, Ohio, 1973; designer Stouffer's Hotels, Cleve., 1974, Ellerbe, Dalton, Dalton and Newport, Bethesda, Md., 1975-76; designer, asst. project mgr. Dalton, Dalton and Newport, Shaker Heights, 1976-79; prin. ACB Design, Cleve., 1980, Kaplan, McLaughlin and Diaz, San Francisco, 1981-91; sr. v.p., mng. prin. Hellmuth Obata Kassabaum, San Francisco, 1991—. Contbr. articles to profl. jours. Bd. dirs. Archtl. Found. San Francisco, 1997—, ARCPAC, 1996-99. Recipient Honor award Architects Soc. Ohio, Bay Village, 1979. Mem. AIA (steering com. 1989 Monterey Design Conf., Hon. awards U.S. Univ. Health Sci., Naval Facilities Command, Honor award for Pacific Presbyn. Profl. Bldg. 1987, Citation for Excellence, Urban Design Embarcadero Corridor Study, bd. dirs. Calif. coun. 1986-97, chmn. urban design com. San Francisco chpt. 1986-88, v.p., pres.-elect 1989, pres. 1990, chmn. Five Bay Area chpt. leaders forum 1991, Calif. Coun. Bldg. and Constrn. Legis. Commn. 1991), Urban Land Inst. (assoc.), Nat. Trust Hist. Preservation, Inst. Urban Design, Calif. Archtl. Polit. Action Com. (trustee 1997—), Archtl. Found. San Francisco (sec. 1998—), Phi Kappa Sigma (sec. 1970-71). Democrat. Avocations: jogging, cycling.

BONVILLIAN, WILLIAM BOONE, lawyer; b. Honolulu, Mar. 7, 1947; s. William Doughty and Florence Elizabeth (Boone) B.; m. Janis Ann Sposato, Apr. 12, 1980; children: Raphael William Boone, Marcus Doughty. AB, Columbia U., 1969; MA in Religion, Yale U., 1972; JD, Columbia U., 1974. Bar: Conn. 1975, D.C. 1976, U.S. Supreme Ct. 1983. Law clk. to Hon. Jack B. Weinstein U.S. Dist. Ct. (ea. dist.) N.Y., 1974-75; assoc. Steptoe & Johnson, Washington, 1975-77; dep. asst. sec., dir. congl. affairs U.S. Dept. Transp., Washington, 1977-81; ptnr. Brown, Roady, Bonvillian & Gold, Washington, 1981-85, Jenner & Block, Washington, 1985-89; chief counsel, legis. dir. to Sen. Joseph Lieberman U.S. Senate, Washington, 1989—; Editor Columbia Law Rev. 1973-74; contbr. articles to law jours. Recipient 2 outstanding Performance awards U.S. Sec. Transp., Washington, 1979, 80. Mem. Conn. Bar Assn., D.C. Bar Assn. Democrat. Episcopalian. Home: 930 Hickory Run Ln Great Falls VA 22066-1903 Office: Office Sen Lieberman 706 Hart Senate Office Bldg Washington DC 20510

BONVINCINI, JOAN M., university women's basketball coach; b. Bridgeport, Conn., Oct. 10, 1953. Grad., So. Conn. State U., 1975. Coach Calif. State U., Long Beach, 1980-91; head coach U. Ariz., Tucson, 1992—; spkr. basketball seminars and camps; mem. NCAA Rules com. Bd. dirs. Tucson Area Girl Scouts, Boys and Girls Club of Tucson. Named to Hall of Fame So. Conn. State U., 1989, Conn. Women's Basketball Hall of Fame, 1994, Hall of Fame Long Beach State U., 1996. Mem. Women's Basketball Coaches Assn. (pres. 1988). Office: U Ariz 236 McKale Ctr Tucson AZ 85721-0096*

BONYNGE, RICHARD, opera conductor; b. Sydney, Australia, Sept. 29, 1930; s. Carl Bonynge; m. Joan Sutherland, 1954; 1 child, Adam. Trained as pianist; specialist in bel canto and 19th century repertoire. Debut as condr. Santa Cecilia Orch., Rome, 1962, as opera condr. Faust, Vancouver, Can., 1963; condr. world opera houses Met. Opera, San Francisco Opera, Chgo. Opera, Teatro Liceo, Royal Opera House Covent Garden, Teatro Colon, Edinburgh Festival, Vienna Festival, Florence Festival; performed Tokyo, Seoul, Hong Kong, Warsaw, Lisbon, Paris, Rome, Stockholm, Copenhagen, Madrid, Hamburg, Munich, Dublin; prin. condr., artistic and mus. dir. various cos. including: Sutherland-Williamson Internat. Grand Opera Co., 1965, Vancouver Opera, 1974-78, Australian Opera, 1975-85; opera recs. include: Beatrice di Tenda, Norma, I Puritani, La Sonnambula, Lakmé, L'Elisir D'Amore, La Fille du Régiment, Lucia di Lammermoor, Lucrezia Borgia, Maria Stuarda, Faust, Alcina, Giulio Cesare, The Merry Widow, L'Oracolo, Esclarmonde, Le Roi de Lahore, Thérèse, Les Huguenots, Don Giovanni, Les Contes d'Hoffmann, Svor Angelica, Semiramide, Die Fledermaus, Hamlet, I Masnadieri, Rigoletto, La Traviata, Il Trovatore, Anna Bolena, Ernani, Adriana Lecouvreur, others; ballet recs. include: Le Diable a Quatre, Giselle, Marco Spada, La Péri, Coppelia, Sylvia, Le Carillon, La Cigale, Le Papillon, La Boutique Fantasque, Aschenbrödel, The Nutcracker, Sleeping Beauty, Swan Lake, La Source, Le Corsaire, La Flute Enchantée, Le Reveil de Flore, Manon, others; recital discs with Sutherland, Tebaldi, Tourangeau, Pavarotti. Decorated comdr. Order Brit. Empire; officer Order Australia; commdr. arts and letters French Govt. Office: care Colbert Artists Mgmt Inc 111 W 57th St New York NY 10019-2211

BONZAGNI, VINCENT FRANCIS, lawyer, program administrator, analyst, researcher; b. Boston, Dec. 10, 1952; s. Augustine Joseph and Augusta M. (Giarla) B.; m. Marie T. Rainville, Aug. 27, 1972 (div. Sept. 1982); 1 child, Gina Theresa; m. Donna J. Bachtell, May 14, 1988; stepchildren: Allison, Neil. BS in Math., Lowell (Mass.) Tech. Inst., 1974; JD, George Mason U., 1998. Bar: Va. 1998; notary pub. Claims adminstr. Social Security Adminstrn., 1976-79; quality assurance specialist Social Security Adminstrn., Boston, 1979-83; disability analyst Social Security Adminstrn., Arlington, Va., 1983-88; program adminstr. Corp. for Open Systems, McLean, Va., 1988-91; sr. hearings and appeals analyst Social Security Adminstrn., Falls Church, Va., 1991—; pvt. practice, 1998—; self-employed researcher and crossword puzzle cons., 1982—. Author: The Mensa Book of Lists, 1992, The Mensa Book of Lists II, 1997; co-author: A History of Mensa, 1990. Treas. Maplewood Village Condo. Assn., 1989-93, 1998—. Mem. ABA, NRA, Am. Fed. Gov. Employees, Mensa (local treas. 1986-90, local pres. 1990-91, nat. historian 1989—, nat. SIGs officer 1989-91, internat. archivist 1992—), Nat. Puzzlers League, Phi Alpa Delta. Democrat. Avocations: crossword puzzles, contests, games, trivia, genealogy. Home: 4737 Parkman Ct Annandale VA 22003-5046 Office: OHA 5107 Leesburg Pike Falls Church VA 22041-3234

BONZANI, RENÉE MARIE, anthropologist, researcher; b. Natrona Heights, Pa., May 20, 1962; d. James Stephen and Rogene Odelia (Remacle) B.; m. Augusto Oyuela-Caycedo, June 27, 1990; children: Isabel, Marcel. BS, Tufts U., 1984; MA, U. Pitts., 1990, PhD, 1995, Cert. Advanced Study Latin Am. Studies, 1995. Rsch. asst. III U. Pitts., 1985-88, editl. asst., 1988-90, grad. student rschr., 1990-91, tchg. fellow, 1992; vis. scholar U. Calgary, Alta., Can., 1994-95; rsch. assoc. U. Pa., Phila., 1995—; rsch. assoc. Nat. U. Colombia, Bogotá, 1991-92, Colombian Inst. Anthropology, Bogotá, 1997—. Author: (chpt.) Sardinia in the Mediterranean, 1992, Advances in the Archaeology of the Northern Andes, 1998; contbr. articles to profl. jours. Recipient Fulbright-Hays grant Inst. Internat. Edn., 1991-92, Rsch. Improvement grant NSF, 1993-94. Mem. Soc. Econ. Botany, Soc. Am. Archaeology (joint mem.), Sigma Xi (assoc., Grants-in-Aid of Rsch. 1994). Avocations: reading, music, horticulture, movies, walking. Home: 728 Campbell Ave New Kensington PA 15068-4606

BOOCHEVER, ROBERT, federal judge; b. N.Y.C., Oct. 2, 1917; s. Louis C. and Miriam (Cohen) B.; m. Lois Colleen Maddox, Apr. 22, 1943; children: Barbara K., Linda Lou, Ann Paula, Miriam Deon. AB, Cornell U., 1939, JD, 1941; HD (hon.), U. Alaska, 1981. Bar: N.Y. 1944, Alaska 1947. Law clk. Nordlinger, Riegel & Cooper, 1941; asst. U.S. atty. Juneau, 1946-47; partner firm Faulkner, Banfield, Boochever & Doogan, Juneau, 1947-72; assoc. justice Alaska Supreme Ct., 1972-75, 78-80, chief justice, 1975-78; judge U.S. Ct. Appeals (9th cir.), Pasadena, Calif., 1980-86; sr. judge U.S. Ct. Appeals, Pasadena, Calif., 1986—; mem. 9th cir. rules com. U.S. Ct. Appeals, 1983-85, chmn. 9th cir. libr. com., 1995—; chmn. Ala. Jud. Coun., 1975-78; mem. appellate judges seminar NYU Sch. Law, 1975; mem. Conf. Chief Justices, 1975-79, vice chmn., 1978-79; mem. adv. bd. Nat. Bank of Ala., 1968-72; guest spkr. Southwestern Law Sch. Disting. Lecture Series, 1992. Contbr. articles to profl. jours. Chmn. Juneau chpt. ARC, 1949-51, Juneau Planning Commn., 1956-61; mem. Alaska Devel. Bd., 1949-52, Alaska Jud. Qualification Commn., 1972-75; mem. adv. bd. Juneau-Douglas Community Coll. Served to Capt. U.S. Army, 1941-45. Named Juneau Man of Year, Rotary, 1974; recipient Disting. Alumnus award Cornell U., 1989. Fellow Am. Coll. Trial Attys.; mem. ABA, Alaska Bar Assn. (pres. 1961-62), Juneau Bar Assn. (pres. 1971-72), Am. Judicature Soc. (dir. 1970-74), Am. Law Inst., Juneau C. of C. (pres. 1952, 55), Alaskans United (chmn. 1972), Cornell Club L.A., Altadena Town and County. Office: US Ct Appeals PO Box 91510 125 S Grand Ave Pasadena CA 91105-1652

BOOCOCK, STEPHEN WILLIAM, lawyer; b. Wilkinsburg, Pa., Sept. 25, 1948; s. William Samuel and Zelda Elizabeth (Heginbotham) B.; m. Carol Ann Bennett, July 11, 1970; children: Eric Alan, Allison Anne, Megan Leigh. BS in Acctg., Pa. State U., 1970; JD, U. Pitts., 1973. Bar: Pa. 1974, U.S. Dist. Ct. (we. dist.) Pa. 1973. Supervising tax specialist Coopers & Lybrand, Pitts., 1973-76; tax counsel Incom Internat., Inc., Pitts., 1977-81; asst. treas., dir. tax Allegheny Ludlum Corp., Pitts., 1981-93, asst. v.p. taxes,

1994-96; asst. v.p. taxes, chief tax officer Allegheny Teledyne Inc., Pitts., 1996—. Treas. Meadow Wood Homeowner's Assn., 1990—. Served to capt. U.S. Army, 1970-79; with USAR. Mem. ABA, AICPA, Pa. Bar Assn., Allegheny County Bar Assn., Pa. Inst. CPAs, Pa. Chamber Bus. and Industry (tax subcom.), Pitts. C. of C. (tax subcom.), Com. on State Taxation, Splty. Steel Industry N.Am. (chmn. tax subcom. 1993—), Tax Execs. Inst. (treas. Pitts. chpt. 1985-86, sec. 1986-87, sr. v.p. 1987-88, pres. 1988-89, nat. inst. dir. 1989-91, v.p. region VI 1992-93, mem. IRS adminstrv. affairs com. 1993-95, vice chmn. 1995-97, chmn. 1997—, membership com. 1993-97, mem. alternative tax sys. com. 1995-97, tax info. sys. com. 1995-97, nominating com. 1994-95, 97-98, 50th ann. task force 1993-95). Republican. Avocations: golf, hunting, fishing. Home: 2625 Woodmont Ln Wexford PA 15090-7978 Office: Allegheny Teledyne Inc 1000 Six PPG Pl Pittsburgh PA 15222-5479

BOODEN, THEODORE, dean; b. Chgo., Sept. 17, 1936; s. Hyman and Gertrude (Rubenzik) B.; m. Betty B. Katz, June 28, 1959; children: Michael R., Stewart K., Rebecca E. BS, Roosevelt U., 1960; MS, Northwestern U., 1962; DPhil, Fla. State U., 1968. From instr. to assoc. prof. Chgo. Med. Sch. Flinch U., 1970-91, prof. Chgo. Med. Sch., 1991—; site sec. Liaison Com. Med. Edn., Chgo. and Washington. Office: FUHS/CMS 3333 Green Bay Rd North Chicago IL 60064-3037*

BOODEY, CECIL WEBSTER, JR., political science educator; b. Yonkers, N.Y., June 10, 1931; s. Cecil Webster and Dorothy (Mitchell) B.; m. Phyllis Ann Stensland, July 9, 1955; children: William Mitchell, John Barton, Pamela D. Ellen. BA, U. N.H., 1953; postgrad., Princeton U., 1953-54; MA, NYU, 1960. Tng. program Arabian-Am. Oil Co., Dhahran, Saudi Arabia, 1954; with N.Y. Telephone Co., Westchester, 1957-62; instr. polit. sci. Fashion Inst. Tech., N.Y.C., 1964-68, from asst. prof. to prof., 1968-95; ret. Fashion Inst. Tech., 1995; chmn. dept. social sci. Fashion Inst. Tech., N.Y.C., 1971-73; vis. prof. fgn. langs. Inner Mongolia U., Huhhot, People's Republic China, 1989-90, 96-97. Treas. Richards Boys Club, Yonkers, 1962-63; v.p. Manasquan-Brielle Little League, N.J., 1969; sec. Manasquan Babe Ruth League, 1972-96; Democratic municipal chmn., Manasquan, 1970-78; pres. 11th Ward Democratic Club, Yonkers, 1962; bd. dirs. Manasquan Area Human Rels. Coun., 1973—, Brookdale C.C., Lincroft, N.J., 1979-88; pres. Squan Soccer Club, 1980. With U.S. Army, 1954-56. Fellow Ford Found., 1953-54; Penfield scholar NYU, 1960. Mem. Am. Polit. Sci. Assn., Assn. Asian Studies, Internat. Studies Assn., Asia Soc., China Inst. in Am., Am. Profs. for Peace in the Middle East (nat. vice chmn. 1989-90), Phi Beta Kappa, Phi Kappa Phi, Pi Mu Epsilon, Pi Gamma Mu. Methodist. Home: 80 Allen Ave Manasquan NJ 08736-3426 Office: Fashion Inst Tech 7th Ave At 27th St New York NY 10001 *To assist young adults to develop their qualities for critical thinking and to encourage them to participate in extra-curricular activities—these are the goals of my life.*

BOOK, EDWARD R., consultant, retired association executive; b. Cleve., May 9, 1931; s. Raymond John and Grace Elizabeth (Bergstresser) B.; m. Inga M. Scheyer, Feb. 14, 1953; children: Sandra Book Liddick, Edward R. Jr., Frederick A. B.S. in Hotel Adminstrn, Pa. State U., 1954. Mgr. restaurant Howard D. Johnson Co., Harrisburg, 1950-54; mgr. food and beverage, asst. mgr. Hotel Harrisburger, Harrisburg, 1956-60; v.p., gen. mgr. Hotel Bethlehem, Pa., 1960-68; gen. mgr. Hospitality Motor Inn, Cleve., 1968-69, Hotel Hershey, Pa., 1969; mng. dir. Hotel Hershey and Country Club, 1970; dir. hostelry div. HERCO, Inc. (formerly Hershey Estates), 1971, v.p., 1973-74, exec. v.p., asst. to pres., 1974, chmn. bd., pres., CEO, 1974-80, chmn., CEO, 1980-87; vice chmn. bd. dirs. Hershey Trust Co., 1985-87; exec. v.p. Travel Industry Assn. Am., Washington, 1987-89, pres., 1989-94; interim pres. USA Nat. Tourism Orgn., 1996-97; mem. travel and tourism industry adv. com. U.S. Senate Commerce Com., 1989-94; mem. adv. com. travel and tourism caucus U.S. Ho. of Reps., 1989-94; charter mem. adv. bd. HRIM program U. Del., 1990—; mem. nat. adv. bd. Acad. Travel and Tourism, 1994-97. Bd. mgrs. Milton Hershey Sch., 1974-87; bd. mgrs. Milton S. Hershey Found., 1974-87, chmn., 1981-87; trustee Pa. State U., 1977-85, vice chmn. bd., 1982-85, chmn. adv. com. Milton S. Hershey Med. Ctr., 1977-82; trustee Harrisburg Area YMCA, 1978-87; campaign chmn. Tri-County United Way, 1980, pres., 1982-83; exec. bd. Keystone Area coun. Boy Scouts Am., 1975-87, Capital Area coun., 1988-89; mem. Ams. for Competitive Enterprise Sys., 1977-82; bd. dirs. Hwy. Users Fedn., 1993-95; mem. devel. coun. Pa. State U., 1982-89. With U.S. Army, 1954-56. Named Pa. Travel Man of Year, 1976, Disting. Alumnus, Pa. State U., 1986; recipient order of achievement Lambda Chi Alpha, 1976; elected to Travel Industry Hall of Leaders, 1986. Mem. VFW (life mem. post 8896), Pa. Travel Industry Adv. Coun. (chmn. 1972-76), Pa. State Hotel and Restaurant Soc. (pres. 1964), Harrisburg Area C. of C. (pres. 1975-76), Am. Hotel and Motel Assn. (industry adv. coun., long range planning com., trustee ednl. inst., resort com. 1975-87), Nat. Inst. for Food Svc. Industry (trustee 1979-82), Travel Industry Assn. Am. (chmn. 1981-82), Pa. State U. Alumni Assn. (pres. 1977-79), Pa. Soc. (life), Am. Legion, Dillsburg Lions Club. Presbyterian (elder). Home: 342 Lake Meade Dr East Berlin PA 17316-9370 Office: Travel Industry Assn Am 1100 New York Ave NW Ste 450W Washington DC 20005-6130

BOOK, JOHN KENNETH (KENNY BOOK), retail store owner; b. Hillsboro, Ill., June 26, 1950; s. Vern Ray Book and Pearl Iva (Foster) Book Alford Carrol; m. Betty L. Christy, Dec. 23, 1981; children: Elizabeth Marie Dunn Rose, Leslie Michelle Dunn. Assoc. in Acctg., Ky. Bus. Coll., 1974. Laborer, Lexington (Ky.) Army Depot, 1968-70; machine operator A.O. Smith, Mt. Sterling, Ky., 1971-72; laborer Irvin Industries, Lexington, 1973-75; owner Kenny's Signs & Bus. Svcs., Winchester, Ky., 1977-90, Book's Bookkeeping & Tax Svc., Winchester, 1990-97; rsch. bd. advisors ABI. Active Winchester Sch. Bd., 1976, 78; candidate for commr. City of Winchester, 1977, 79, 81, 83, 87, elected commr., 1989, re-elected, 1993, 96, 98, candidate for mayor, 1985. Named to Hon. Order Ky. Cols., 1973. Mem. Ky. Sheriff's Assn. (hon.). Democrat. Office: Book's Bookkeeping & Tax Svc PO Box 840 Winchester KY 40392-0840

BOOK, WILLIAM JOSEPH, manufacturing executive; b. Council Bluffs, Iowa, Feb. 20, 1942; s. Leo William and Marie Ann (Korth) B.; m. Phyllis Theresa Kurzak, Nov. 25, 1962 (div. 1983); children: Gregory, Gary, Carolyn, Janet; m. Marjorie Schuler, Sep. 21, 1985. BSEE, U. Minn., 1973. Registered profl. engr., Minn. Evaluation engr. Honeywell Inc., Mpls., 1966-74; dist. mgr. Bussmann Mfg. co., Mpls., 1974-77; sales mgr. Lakeland Engring. Equipment Co., Mpls., 1977-78; mktg. mgr. Onan Corp., Mpls., 1978-85; chief exec. officer Ainslie Co., Mpls., 1985—. Avocations: golf, boating, skiing, waterskiing. Home: 309 Westwood Dr S Minneapolis MN 55416-3362 Office: Ainslie Co 2909 Wayzata Blvd Minneapolis MN 55405-2187

BOOKBINDER, HYMAN H(ARRY), public affairs counselor; b. Bklyn., Mar. 9, 1916; s. Louis and Rose (Palger) B.; m. Bertha Losev, Dec. 25, 1938 (dec. 1976); children: Ellen, Amy. *Mr. Bookbinder's parents emigrated from Poland around 1900. Families of both were annihilated during the Holocaust. He was married to Boscha Losev from 1938 until her death in 1976. Since 1978, he was a companion to Ida Leivick, aretired teacher, who recognized authority on Yiddish language and history. His daughter Ellen Cohen, is a social therapist in New York, and is married to Bernard Cohen, a high school principal. His daughter Amy Bookbinder, is a social worker and video producer in Northampton, Massachusetts. His grandson Michael Cohen (PhD, Columbia), is a molecular biologist, and his granddaughter Rebecca Cohen is a school teacher in New Mexico. His second granddaughter Rose Bookbinder is a high school student. His brothers Sam and Selig are deceased.* B.S.S., CCNY, 1937; postgrad., NYU, New Sch. Social Research; LHD (hon.), Hebrew Union Coll., 1989. Economist Amalgamated Clothing Workers, 1938-43, 46-50; labor adv. Nat. Prodn. Authority, 1951-53; legis. rep. CIO, 1953-55, AFL-CIO, 1955-60; spl. asst. to sec. commerce, 1961-62; mem. President's Commn. on Status of Women, 1961-63; dir. Eleanor Roosevelt Meml. Found., 1963-64; exec. officer President's Task Force on Poverty, 1964; asst. dir. OEO, also spl. asst. to vice president U.S., 1964-67; Washington rep. Am. Jewish Com., 1967-86; rep. emeritus Am. Jewish Com., Washington, 1986—; mem. President's Commn. on Holocaust, 1979-80, U.S. Holocaust Meml. Council, 1980-87; mem. Com. on Conscience, 1996—; Washington chmn. Ad Hoc Coalition for Ratification of Genocide Treaty, 1970-87; chmn. public policy adv. com. Corp. Public Broadcasting, 1972-77; spl. advisor to Gov. Michael Dukakis, 1988; chmn. bd. advisers Nat. Jewish Dem. Coun., 1990—. Author: To Promote the General Welfare, 1950, Off the Wall, 1991; co-author: Through Different Eyes, 1987, also articles; editor: Washington Letter, 1970—; moderator: Washington Scene radio series, 1971-75. Bd. dirs. Ctr. for Nt. Policy, Friends of VISTA, Am. Jewish-Israeli Rels. Inst., Am. Jewish World Svcs., Multi-Issue Polit. Action Com., Found. for Mid. East Comm., Internat. Inst. for Study of Prejudice, Project Nishma (Let Us Listen), Washington Inst. for Jewish Leadership and Values, Mid. East Human Rights Watch, Jewish Fund for Justice, Israel Policy Forum, Operation Understanding. Recipient Nat. Brotherhood citation NCCJ, 1977, Lifetime Achievement award Thomas Jefferson H.S. Alumni Assn., 1982, Honored Am. award Americans by Choice, 1986, Franklin Roosevelt Four Freedoms medal Franklin and Eleanor Roosevelt Inst., 1990, Jewish Nat. Fund Sholom Peace award, 1992, Hubert Humphrey Humanitarian award Nat. Jewish Dem. Coun., 1994, Am. Jewish Com. Nat. Leadership award 1997. Mem. Am. Vets. Com., People for Am. Way, Common Cause, Coalition for Democratic Majority, Friends of Histadrut, Jewish Inst. Nat. Security Affairs, Americans for Dem. Action, Am. Com. on U.S.-Soviet Rels., Washington Hebrew Congregation Brotherhood Club. Democrat. Clubs: B'Nai B'rith, Workmen's Circle. Home: 6308 Bannockburn Dr Bethesda MD 20817-5404 Office: Am Jewish Com 1156 15th St NW Washington DC 20005-1704 *Born into a world that soon exposed me to depression, war, and the Holocaust, I fast acquired an almost compulsive interest in public affairs. It has been my good fortune to be able to combine career development with opportunities to help shape public policy. Government's principal purpose must indeed be to implement the great promise of America—the securing of life, liberty, and the pursuit of happiness. Above all, this has meant for me the lifting of discriminatory barriers to self-fulfillment—race, religion, gender, national origin. The Hebrew sage Rabbi Hillel, has provided the guideline for my life's work: "If I am not for myself, who will be for me? But if I am only for myself, what am I?".*

BOOKBINDER, ROBERT MAX, superintendent of schools; b. Newark, Apr. 28, 1923; s. Harry and Pearl (Barenberg) B.; m. Natalie Sonya Gelfand, Sept. 10, 1946 (dec. Feb. 1996); children: Howard, Susan Blauel, Pamela Spears. BA, U. Ky., 1947; MA, Columbia U., 1948, profl. diploma, 1952; EdD, East Coast U., 1971. Owner, dir. summer day camp Camp Gelfand, Mountaindale, N.Y., 1947-65; tchr. BOCES 3d Dist., Huntington, N.Y., 1948-50; tchr. Harborfields C. Sch. Dist., Greenlawn, N.Y., 1950-54, elem. prin., 1954-61, jr. h.s. prin., 1961-64, curriculum and adminstrv. coord., 1964-67, asst. supt., 1967-73; supt. East Stroudsburg (Pa.) Sch. Dist., 1973-87; prof. East Stroudsburg U., 1987-90; supr. student tchrs. Lynn U., Boca Raton, Fla., 1996—; ednl. cons. Careers/Cons. in Edn., Pompano Beach, Fla., 1977—; arbitrator Am. Arbitration Assn., N.Y.C., 1987—. Author: (textbook) Critical Issues in Education, 1972, The Principal, 1992; (books) Amusing Definitions, 1999, Witty Remarks, 1999, Noteworthy Proverbs, 1999, Concise Quotations, 1999, The Keys to the Classroom, 1999; (weekly article) Pocono Today, 1975-84. Pres. Monroe Arts Coun., 1980-81, United Way of Monroe County, 1983-84. 1st lt. U.S. Army, 1943-46, 51-52, ETO. Decorated Bronze Star. Mem. ASCD, Am. Assn. Sch. Adminstrs., B'nai B'rith (pres. 1996—), Phi Delta Kappa, Zeta Beta Tau. Democrat. Jewish. Avocations: golf, theater, public speaking, writing, swimming. E-mail: carconed@aol.com. Home: 3050 N Palm Aire Dr Apt 310 Pompano Beach FL 33069-3424

BOOKER, BETTY MAE, poet; b. Allentown, Pa., Nov. 26, 1948; d. Harold George and Bessie (Bealer-Miller) Bartholomew; m. Samuel Efford Booker III, June 27, 1970 (dec. May 1998); children: Liesel Tamarah, Dacey Justin, Jaeson Bartholomew. BA in English, Millersville (Pa.) State Coll., 1970. Contbr. poetry to jours. and lit. mags., including Plainsong, America, Christian Century, Poetry Now. Home: 27826 Island Dr Salisbury MD 21801-2350

BOOKER, JAMES DOUGLAS, retired lawyer, government official; b. Columbus, Ohio, June 27, 1933; s. Homer Newton and Grace Bernice (Hermann) B.; m. Onda Lee Minshall, Aug. 31, 1958; children: Christine E., Linda K. Booker Stanek, Molly A. Booker Lary, Andrew W. JD, Ohio State U., 1961. Bar: Ohio 1961, U.S. Dist. Ct. (so. dist.) Ohio 1962, U.S. Ct. Appeals (6th cir.) 1972, U.S. Supreme Ct. 1971. Asst. atty. gen. State of Ohio, Columbus, 1961-62; ptnr. Williams, Deeg, Ketcham, Booker & Obetz, Columbus, 1962-75; adminstrv. law judge SSA, Columbus, 1975-98. Past treas. PTA, Columbus; past deacon, Sunday sch. tchr. Presbyn. Ch., Columbus. With U.S. Army, 1953-55. Republican. Avocations: chess, music, history. Home: 1290 Smallwood Dr Columbus OH 43235-2503

BOOKER, LARRY FRANK, accountant; b. Mobile, Ala., May 22, 1950; s. Frank and Helen Louise Booker; m. Prudence E. Porter, Sept. 1, 1972; children: Jennifer Erin, Meggan Leah. BA, U. South Ala., 1972; student, U. N.C., 1976-77. Lic. pub. acct., Ala. Rsch. economist Rsch. Triangle Inst., Durham, N.C., 1974-76; with Providence Hosp., Mobile, 1978-80; pvt. practice acctg. Mobile, 1981—; enrolled IRS; lectr. in field. Author: Sales and Use Taxes in Alabama, 1999. Vol. Jr. Achievement. Mem. Nat. Assn. Accts., Nat. Assn. Tax Practitioners, Nat. Soc. Pub. Accts., Ala. Assn. Pub. Accts. (past dist. pres., bd. dirs.), Accreditation Coun. in Acctg. and Taxation (accredited in taxation and accountancy). Home: 6436 Brindlewood Ct Mobile AL 36608-3837 Office: 750 Downtowner Loop W Ste B Mobile AL 36609-5500

BOOKER, LEWIS THOMAS, lawyer; b. Richmond, Va., Sept. 22, 1929; s. Russell Eubank and Leslie Quarles (Sessoms) B.; m. Nancy Electa Brogden, Sept. 29, 1956; children: Lewis Thomas Jr., Virginia Frances, Claiborne Brogden, John Quarles. BA, U. Richmond, 1950, LLD, 1977; JD, Harvard U., 1953. Bar: Va. 1953, U.S. Ct. Mil. Appeals 1954, U.S. Supreme Ct. 1958, D.C. 1980, N.Y. 1985. Assoc. Hunton & Williams, Richmond, Va., 1956-63; ptnr. Hunton & Williams, 1963-95, sr. coun., 1995—; substitute Judge 13th Dist., Va., 1996—; lectr. in law Seinan Gakuin U., Fukuoka, Japan, 1985; vis. lectr. in law St. Thomas U., Miami, Fla., 1993; maj. gen., sr. mil. aide to Gov. of Va., 1997—. Mem. Va. Coun. on Human Rights, 1987; commr. chmn. Richmond Redevel. and Housing Authority, 1961-70; trustee U. Richmond, 1972—, rector, 1973-77, 81-85, 91-94, vice rector, 1985-87, chmn. exec. commn., 1977-81; trustee Va. Inst. Sci. Rsch., 1981-94, Richmond Symphony, 1987-92, Rouse-Bottom Found., 1989—; mem. Coun. Richmond Symphony, 1995, Westminster-Canterbury Found. Richmond, 1995—, pres., 1998—; mem. Robins Found., 1996—. With U.S. Army, 1953-56, USAR, 1956-83, col. ret. Fellow Am. Coll. Trial Lawyers, Am. Bar Found.; mem. ABA, Va. Bar Assn., Va. Law Found. (chmn. fellows coun.), Richmond Bar Assn., Westwood Racquet Club. Democrat. Baptist. Office: Hunton & Williams East Tower Riverfront Pla PO Box 1535 Richmond VA 23218-1535

BOOKER, MICHAEL JAMES, philosophy educator; b. Augsburg, Germany, Dec. 26, 1961; came to U.S., 1964; s. James Arthur and Elaine Marie (Glammeier) B.; m. Anne Marie Christiansen, Sept. 4, 1987; 1 child, Jonathan Andrew. BA, Mankato (Minn.) State U., 1982; MA, U. Tenn., 1987, PhD, 1990. Asst. prof. philosophy Mankato (Minn.) State U., 1991; adj. instr. Roane State C.C., Harriman, Tenn., 1993-99, Pelissippi State Tech. C.C., Knoxville, Tenn., 1993-99, Jefferson Coll., Hillsboro, Mo., 1999—. Mem. Am. Philos. Assn., Am. Soc. of Value Inquiry.

BOOKER, NANA LAUREL, public relations executive; b. Waco, Tex., Aug. 5, 1946; d. Karl and Helen Dorothy (Keene) B. BA, Baylor U., 1968; MA, U. Fla., 1970; MBA, Pepperdine U., 1980. Asst. prof. comm. U. New Orleans, 1970-74, 1977-78; pub. rels. cons. New Orleans, 1974-78; dir. pub. rels. Touro Infirmary, New Orleans, 1976-78; dir. comm. Lifemark Corp., Houston, 1978-81; pres. Comm. Alliance, Houston, 1981-82; dir. internat. rels., comm. Mayor's Office, City of Houston, 1982-84; pres. Nana Booker & Assocs. (now Booker/Hancock & Assocs.), Houston, 1984—. Co-author: Introduction to Theatrical Arts, 1972. Mem. South Tex. Dist. Export Coun., Houston, 1988-92; press aide campaign K. Whitmire for Mayor, Houston, 1982; mem. exec. adv. bd. coll. bus. adminstrn. U. Houston, 1990—; bd. dirs. Escape Ctr., 1990-93, YWCA, Houston, 1991-92. Recipient Internat. Assn. Bus. Communicators awards, Women in Comms. awards, Crystal award Am. Mktg. Assn., Outstanding Pub. Rels. Practitioner award Tex. Pub. Rels. Assn., 1996, Vol. of the Yr. award Houston Area Women's Ctr., 1998. Mem. Pub. Rels. Soc. Am. (accredited, chairperson internat. sect. 1993-95, Excalibur award 1988, Cert. of Appreciation 1993, 94, 95; mem. U.S. coun. 1994-96), Internat. Pub. Rels. Assn., Houston World Trade Assn. (bd. dirs. 1986—), Houston-Shenzhen Sister City Assn. (bd. dirs. 1987-94), Swiss-Am. C. of C. (bd. dirs. 1987-90), River Oaks Breakfast Club (bd. dirs. 1997), The Asia Soc. of Tex. (bd. dirs. 1995—). Avocations: hot air ballooning, photography, design. Fax: 713-782-7502. E-Mail: bookerhancock@hypercon.com.

BOOKER, RONALD JOSEPH, physician practice management; b. Houston, May 31, 1958; s. Roy Edward and Mildred Novelene (Thrower) B.; m. Lee Ann Ligon, Aug. 18, 1979; children: Melanie Lynn, Carl Joseph, John Michael. BBA, Abilene Christian U., 1980; JD, U. Houston Law Ctr., 1993. Bar: Tex. CPA. Acct., ptnr. Booker & Assocs., CPAs, Houston, 1980-89; controller, adminstr. MHA Anesthesiology, P.A., Houston, 1989-92; CEO, Preferred Healthcare Bus. Svcs., Houston, 1993—. Bd. dirs. Hydrocephalus Found. Houston, 1983. Mem. Nat. Health Lawyers Assn., Am. Soc. CPAs, Healthcare Fin. Mgmt. Assn., Anesthesia Adminstrs. Tex. (bd. dirs. 1990-92), Med. Group Mgmt. Assn. Republican. Mem. Ch. of Christ. Home: 4203 Austin Meadow Dr Sugar Land TX 77479-3037 Office: PHBS 5615 Kirby Dr Ste 850 Houston TX 77005-2458*

BOOKER, SHIRLEY RUTH, entertainment specialist; b. Center, Tex., Oct. 15, 1947; d. Preston and Elminer Brittian; m. Charles Seach, Jan. 3, 1967 (div.); 1 child, Charles Seach Jr.; m. Patrick Henry Booker, Dec. 31, 1975; 1 child, Roshon Booker. BS in Social Work, U. Ctrl. Tex., 1992. Recreation specialist Community Recreation Divsn., Ft. Hood, Tex., 1974-88; comml. entertainment specialist Community Recreation Divsn., Ft. Hood, 1988—; cons. in field; rest and recuperation coord. S.W. Asia Theatre during Operation Desert Storm. Author: (jour.) Desert Storm/A Time to Love, 1992. Recipient Desert shield, Desert Storm medal Dept. of Def., 1992, Dept. of Army Comdr.'s award, 1985, Cert. of achievement, 1991, Superior Civilian Svc. award, 1991. Democrat. Mem. Assembly of God Ch. Home: 1310 Hammond Dr Killeen TX 76543-5220 Office: Hdqs and III Corps Bldg 1001 Rm 217 W/DPCA Fort Hood TX 76544

BOOKHAMMER, EUGENE DONALD, state government official; b. Lewes, Del., June 14, 1918; s. William and Winifred (Jenkins) B.; m. Catherine Williams, Jan. 31, 1942; children: Joy, Jean. Student, Am. Tech. Soc., 1938. Owner-pres. Bookhammer Lumber Mill, Lewes, 1939-71, Joy Beach Devel. Co., Lewes, 1955; pres. Rehoboth Bay Dredging Co., Lewes, 1963; mem. Del. Senate, 1962-68; lt. gov. Del., 1969-76; mem. Del. Health Planning Council, 1976—; mem. Del. Coastal Zone Appeals Bd.; bd. dirs. Mellon Bank, Del. Life mem. Boy Scouts Am.; del. Rep. Nat. Conv., 1952, 56, 60, 80; chmn. Sussex County Rep. Com., 1964-66; Rep. nat. committeman from Del., 1977—; chmn. bd. dirs. Beebe Hosp., 1976—; trustee Wilmington Med. Ctr., 1971—, Wesley Coll., 1982—. Served with AUS, 1944-46, ETO. Decorated Purple Heart. Mem. Am. Inst. Banking, Am. Legion, Del. C. of C., VFW, DAV, 40 and 8, Masons (32 deg.), Shriners, Lions, Rehoboth Beach Country Club. Home: RR 24 Box 363 Lewes DE 19958 Office: Legislative Hall Dover DE 19901

BOOKHARDT, FRED BARRINGER, JR., architect; b. New Orleans, May 14, 1934; s. Fred B. and Leticia (Chevez) B. BArch, Tulane U., 1959; postgrad., U. Pa., 1960-61. Designer Freret and Wolf, Architects, 1959-60, Kenneth Ripnen, Architect, 1961-63, Francis X. Gina, Architects, 1963-64, Smith, Smith, Haines, Lundberg and Waehler, N.Y.C., 1965; ptnr., v.p. William F. Pedersen & Assocs., N.Y.C. and New Haven, 1965-77; prin. Fred B. Bookhardt, Architect, N.Y.C., 1977—; dir. 28 E. 4th St. Housing Corp.; cons. Engring. Cons. Group, Cairo, Heliopolis and Alexandria, Egypt, 1983—; dir. The Network of Bus. & Profl. Orgns. Contbg. editor Uptown mag., New Orleans; archtl. works include: Superior Cts. Bldg., New Haven, 1974, Hall Minerals and Gems of Am. Mus. Natural History, 1976, Fed. Office Bldg., New Haven, 1978, Restaurant Claire, Key West, Fla., 1978, Woodmere Kingdom of Minerals, 1980, exec. offices So. Container Corp., Hauppauge, N.Y., 1981, Mus. Shop Am. Mus. Natural History, N.Y.C., 1982, renovation of pub. spaces lower level, 1984, employees cafeteria, 1984, Children's Reception Ctr., 1986, Sadowsky residence, Northport, N.Y., 1987, Kaufman residence, N.Y.C., 1987, Grossman residence, Montauk, N.Y., 1983, St. Barts, W.I., 1990, Zweibel residences, N.Y.C., 1983, Ft. Lauderdale, Fla., 1984, exec. offices Bon Temps Employment Agy., N.Y.C., 1984, Dieckmann residence, Manhasset, N.Y., 1985, master plan Am. Mus. Natural History, N.Y.C., 1989, space analysis The Trotting Horse Mus., Goshen, N.Y., 1989, addition and renovation, 1990, De Roy residence, N.Y.C., 1991, Zweibel residence, Boca Raton, Fla., 1993, Kelley residence, St. James, N.Y., 1983, HIV Law Project, 1994, Hinlein residence, 1995, Price/Uribe Residence, East Northport, N.Y., 1996, Branford (Conn.) H.S. with David M. Chin, 1996-97, Mancini Residence, N.Y.C., with Charles Burke, 1998, Fitz Simons Residence, 1999. With U.S. Army, 1954-56. Recipient Lumen award Illuminating Engrs. Soc., 1977, 1st pl. award Home Mag. ceramic tile competition. Mem. AIA, N.Y. State Assn. Architects, Architects Coun. N.Y.C., N.Y. Soc. Architects, Am. Assn. Mus., N.E. Mus. Conf., Nat. Cert. Archtl. Rev. Bd. (cert.). Home and Office: 28 E 4th St New York NY 10003-7004

BOOKIN, DANIEL HENRY, lawyer; b. Ottumwa, Iowa, Oct. 16, 1951. BA, U. Iowa, 1973; JD, Yale U., 1976. Bar: Calif. 1978. Law clk. U.S. Dist. Ct. (no. dist.) Calif., 1976-77; asst. U.S. atty. U.S. Dist. Ct. (so. dist.) N.Y., 1978-82; ptnr. O'Melveny & Myers, San Francisco, 1982—. Mem. bd. editors Yale Law Jour., 1975-76. Fellow Am. Coll. Trial Lawyers, Phi Beta Kappa. Office: O'Melveny & Myers Embarcadero Ctr W Tower 275 Battery St San Francisco CA 94111-3305

BOOKOUT, JOHN G., insurance company executive. Pres. Woodmen of World Life Ins. Soc., Omaha. Office: Woodmen of the World Life 1700 Farnam St Ste 2200 Omaha NE 68102-2007*

BOOKSPAN, MICHAEL LLOYD, musician; b. Bklyn., Sept. 7, 1929; s. Harry and Sarah (Barban) B.; children: Jolie, Adam; m. Shirley Goldberg, 1991. Studied with, Fred Albright, Saul Goodman, Morris Goldenberg; BS, Juilliard, 1953. Xylophone soloist U.S.O. Camp Shows, 1943-46; percussionist N.Y.C. Ballet Orch., 1951-53, Little Orch. Soc., N.Y.C., 1951-53; snare drummer Goldman Band, 1953-55; percussionist and timpanist Phila. Orch., 1953—, prin. percussionist, assoc. timpanist, 1972—, commd. and premiered Robert Suderburg's Concerto for Solo Percussionist and Orch., 1979, marimba soloist, 1980, xylophone soloist, 1989, Suderburg Concerto for Solo Percussionist and Orch., 1993, 96; faculty Univ. of the Arts, Curtis Inst. Music.; participated in Marlboro, Casals, Aspen and Grand Teton festivals; Organizer Phila. Drummers for Peace, 1969. Past pres. Phila. Musicians for Nuclear Arms Control. Served with USAAF, 1946-48. Recipient C. Hartman Kuhn award, 1981. Mem. Percussive Arts Soc., SANE, ACLU, Vets. for Peace in Vietnam. Office: Acad Music Broad And Locust St Philadelphia PA 19102-5081

BOOKSTEIN, ABRAHAM, information science educator; b. N.Y.C., Mar. 22, 1940; s. Alex and Doris (Cohen) B.; m. Marguerite Vickers, June 20, 1968. BS, CCNY, 1961; MS, U. Calif., Berkeley, 1966; PhD, Yeshiva U., 1969; MA, U. Chgo., 1970. Asst. prof. U. Chgo., 1971-75, assoc. prof. info. sci., 1975-82, prof. info. sci., 1982—; vis. prof. Royal Inst. Tech., Stockholm, 1982, UCLA, 1985; vis. disting. scholar OCLC, Columbus, Ohio, 1988; bd. dirs. Religion Index, Evanston, Ill., 1984-96; adv. bd. Info. Sci. Rsch. Inst., U. Nev., 1995—. Bd. editors Info. Processing and Mgmt., Scientometrics, Information Retrieval, 1997—; editor Prospect for Change in Bibliographic Control, 1977, Operations Research: Implications for Librarians, 1970; contbr. articles to profl. jours. NSF grantee, 1981, 85, 93, U.S./Israel Binational Sci. Found. grantee, 1993-94; Fulbright fellow, India, 1992. Mem. IEEE Computer Soc., Am. Soc. Info. Scis. (Rsch. award 1991), Internat. Soc. Scientometrics and Informetrics (founding mem., chmn. conf. program com. 1995, keynote spkr., 1991, 97), Assn. Computing Machinery/SIGIR (gen. chmn. ann. internat. conf. 1991), Phi Beta Kappa. Avocations: personal computing, music, literature. Office: U Chgo/CILS 1010 E 59th St Chicago IL 60637-1512

BOOMER, JOHN D., artist, sculptor; b. Merced, Calif., Oct. 6, 1945. Work reviewed in Nat. Sculpture Rev., Artspace, Fine Woodworking, Masters of American Sculpture. Avocations: playing guitar and harmonica, movies, hiking, reading. Home and Studio: PO Box 696 Navajo NM 87328

BOOMER, WALTER EUGENE, marine officer; b. Rich Square, N.C., Sept. 22, 1938; s. Vigle Eugene and Helen Inez (Moore) B.; m. Sandra Lokey, Mar. 9, 1979; children from previous marriage: Susan, Helen, Steven. BA, Duke U., 1960; MS, Am. U., 1974; grad. (disting.), Naval War Coll., 1981. Commd. 2d lt. USMC, 1960, advanced through grades to gen., 1986, various assignments, 1960-66; co. comdr. 2d Bn., 4th Marines, Republic of Vietnam, 1966-67; marine inf. advisor Marine Corps, Republic of Vietnam, 1971-72; prof., dept. chmn. U.S. Naval Acad., Annapolis, Md., 1974-77; comdr. 2d Bn., 3d Marines, Kaneohe, Hawaii, 1978-79; dir. 4th USMC Dist., Phila., 1983-84; comdg. officer Marine Security Guard Bn., Quantico, Va., 1985-86; dir. pub. affairs Hdqrs. USMC, Washington, 1986-88; comdg. gen. 4th Marine Div., New Orleans, 1988-90, U.S. Marine Forces, U.S. Cen. Command, Saudi Arabia, 1990-91, U.S. Marine Corps. Combat Devel. Command, Quantico, Va., 1991-92; asst. commandant U.S. Marine Corp., Washington, 1992-94; retired USMC, 1994; pres., COO Babcock & Wilcox, Barberton, Ohio, 1994-96; pres., CEO Rogers (Conn.) Corp., 1997—. Contbr. articles to profl. jours. Decorated D.S.M., Silver Star (2), Legion of Merit, Bronze Star with combat V (2), Combat Action Ribbon, Nat. Def. Svc. medal; Cross of Gallantry (Republic of Vietnam). Office: Rogers Corp PO Box 188 Rogers CT 06263-0188*

BOOMERSHINE, DONALD EUGENE, bureau executive, development official; b. Brookville, Ohio, Oct. 5, 1931; s. Harold Everett and Elsie (Rhoads) B.; m. Marilyn Sullivan, Aug. 29, 1953 (dec.); children: Jeffrey, Alan; m. Patti Watson, May 29, 1985. BS, Bowling Green (Ohio) State U., 1953; grad., Northwestern U. Bank Mktg. Grad. Sch., 1965; M in Banking, Rutgers U. Stonier Sch. Banking, 1969-72; postgrad., U. Okla. Nat. Comml. Lending Sch., 1974. With jr. exec. program Frigidaire div. Gen. Motors Corp., Dayton, 1955-57; sr. sales rep. IBM, Dayton, 1957-61; bus. devel. rep., asst. cashier Exchange Security Bank, Birmingham, 1961-65; asst. v.p. charge nat. accounts divsn. Birmingham Trust Nat. Bank, 1965-78, v.p., 1968-71, v.p., sales mgr. Circle S div., 1978-80; dir. community devel. Met. Devel. Bd., 1980-82; pres. Better Bus. Bur. of Cen. Ala., Birmingham, 1982—; chmn. Bus. Tomorrow Conf., Auburn U., 1975; ednl. chmn. Assoc. Industries Ala., 1975-77; pres. Better Bus. Bur., Birmingham, 1982—; apptd. Atlanta-Birmingham br. Fed. Res. Bd., 1990-97, chmn., 1993, 96. Pres. North Central Ala. chpt. Muscular Dystrophy Found., 1964; trustee Birmingham YWCA, 1972—; gen. chmn. U.S. World Youth Game, 1973; charter mem. Downtown Action Com., 1966; bd. dirs. ARC, 1968—; mem. steering com. Mobile Coll., 1987—; mem. adv. bd. U. South Ala., 1975-78; chmn. Am. Cancer Crusade, 1976; bd. dirs. Birmingham Children's Theatre, 1974-78, Downtown YMCA, Met. YMCA, 1992—; mem. adv. bd. Ala. State Bd. Edn., 1976—; bd. dirs., 2d v.p. Birmingham Better Bus. Bur., 1980-82; bd. govs. Ala. Assn. Ind. Colls. and Univs.; v.p. Nat. Vet's Day; active Leadership Birmingham; mem. Blue and Gold Bd. U.S. Naval Acad., designated info. officer; mem. exec. com. Birmingham Cmty. Svc. award; mem. Ala. com. Employers Support of the Nat. Guard and Res. With USMCR, 1953-84; now col. Ret. Recipient Comdt. award U.S. Naval Acad., 1994, Outstanding Broadcasters Cooperation award Ala. Broadcasters Assn., 1998; Res. Day proclaimed in his honor, 1983. Mem. Bank Mktg. Assn. (nat. dir. 1971-75, nat. v.p. devel. 1971), Ala. Indsl. Devel. Council, So. Indsl. Council, World Trade Assn. Ala., Diplomats of Birmingham (founder, chmn. 1973), Marine Corps Res. Officers Assn. (nat. dir. 1974-76), Operation Native Sons and Daus. (chmn. 1972), Newcomen Soc. of U.S., Birmingham C. of C. (life), Vestavia Country Club, The Club, Touchdown Club (Birmingham, founder, dir., treas), Kiwanis (officer, dir., Birmingham 1971), Sigma Chi. Clubs: Vestavia Country, The Club, Touchdown (founder, dir., treas.) (Birmingham), Summit. Home: 3801 Cromwell Dr Birmingham AL 35243-5512 Office: Better Bus Bur PO Box 55268 Birmingham AL 35255-5268

BOON, KEVIN ALEXANDER, English educator, writer; b. Oct. 13, 1956; s. Robert Edwin and Robin Allaire (McCarthy) B.; m. Nancy Allyne Stephen, Nov. 2, 1984 (div. Jan. 1987). BA in Psychology, U. South Fla., 1983, MA in English, 1991, PhD in English, 1995. Instr. world and western lit. U. South Fla., Tampa, 1985-86; instr. Am. lit. U. Ala., Tuscaloosa, 1986-87; asst. prof. Am. studies SUNY Maritime, Bronx, 1987—. Author: Chaos Theory and the Interpretation of Literary Texts: The Case of Kurt Vonnegut, An Interpretive Reading of Virginia Woolf's The Waves, 1998, (novel) Absolute Zero, 1999; editor: At Millennium's End, 1999. Mem. N.Y. Coll. English Assn. (exec. com.). E-mail: kevin@boon.net. Office: SUNY Maritime Dept Humanities 6 Pennyfield Ave Bronx NY 10465

BOONE, BILLY WARREN, lawyer, judge; b. Perryton, Tex., Feb. 6, 1955; s. Kermit George and Verna Jean (Thomas) B.; m. Celia Trimble, 1990; children: Billy Warren II, Carol Ann. BA with honors, Tex. Tech U., 1977, JD cum laude, 1980. Bar: Tex. 1980, U.S. Dist. Ct. (no. dist.) Tex. 1982, U.S. Ct. Appeals (5th cir.) 1990, U.S. Supreme Ct. 1993. Assoc. David P. Hooper & Assocs., Abilene, Tex., 1980-82; prin. Billy W. Boone, Abilene, 1982—; part-time U.S. magistrate U.S. Dist. Ct. (no. dist.) Tex., Abilene, 1987—. Mem. ABA, Tex. Bar Assn., Abilene Bar Assn., Nat. Coun. U.S. Magistrates. Home: 49 Cypress Point St Abilene TX 79606-5130 Office: US Dist Ct 104 Pine St #705 PO Box 2797 Abilene TX 79604-2797

BOONE, BRET ROBERT, professional baseball player; b. El Cajon, Calif., Apr. 6, 1969; s. Bob Boone. Ed., U. So. Calif. With Seattle Mariners, 1992-93; second baseman Cin. Reds, 1994-98; infielder Atlanta Braves, 1999—. Office: Atlanta Braves PO Box 4064 Atlanta GA 30302*

BOONE, CELIA TRIMBLE, lawyer; b. Clovis, N.Mex., Mar. 3, 1953; d. George Harold and Barbara Ruth (Foster) T.; m. Billy W. Boone, Apr. 21, 1990. BS, Ea. N.Mex. U., 1976, MA, 1977; JD, St. Mary's U., San Antonio, 1982. Bar: Tex. 1982, U.S. Dist. Ct. (no. dist.) Tex. 1983, U.S. Ct. Appeals (5th cir.) 1985, U.S. Supreme Ct. 1986. Instr. English, Eastern N.Mex. U., Portales, 1977-78; editor Curry County Times, Clovis, 1978-79; assoc. Schulz & Robertson, Abilene, Tex., 1982-85, Scarborough, Black, Tarpley & Scarborough, 1985-87; ptnr. Scarborough, Black, Tarpley & Trimble, Abilene, Tex., 1988-90, Scarborough, Black, Tarpley & Boone, 1990-94, of counsel Scarborough, Tarpley, Boone & Fouts, 1994-96; prin. Law Office of Celia Trimble Boone, , Abilene, 1996—; instr. legal rsch. and writing St. Mary's Sch. Law, 1981-82. Legal adv. to bd. dirs. Abilene Kennel Club, 1983-85; mem. landmarks commn. City of Abilene, 1989-90. Recipient Outstanding Young Lawyer of Abilene, 1988. Mem. ABA, State Bar Tex. (mem. disciplinary rev. com. 1989-93), Am. Trial Lawyers Assn., Tex. Trial Lawyers Assn., Tex. Criminal Def. Lawyers Assn., Tex. Acad. Family Law Specialists, Tex. Bd. Legal Specialization (cert. 1987), Abilene Bar Assn. (bd. dirs. 1985-86, 87-88, sec./treas. 1985-86), Abilene Young Lawyers Assn. (bd. dirs. 1985-86, 87-89, treas. 1985-86, pres.-elect 1987-88, pres. 1988-89), NOW, ACLU, Phi Alpha Delta. Democrat. Avocations: needlework, gardening. Office: 104 Pine St Ste 705 Abilene TX 79601-5934

BOONE, FRANKLIN DELANOR ROOSEVELT, SR., cardiovascular perfusionist, realtor; b. Wake Forest, N.C., Aug. 19, 1942; s. John Henry and Beulah Bell (Massenburg) B.; m. Lois Mae Daye, July 20, 1962; children: Franklin Delanor Roosevelt Jr., Fredrick Louis (dec.). Student, N.C. Cen. U., 1960-62, U. N.C., 1968. Cert. cardiovascular perfusionist. Tech. trainee Dept. Cardiology Duke Med. Ctr., Durham, N.C., 1962-63, technician Hypobaric Surgery Dept., 1963-65; med. equipment specialist IV dept. cardiothoracic surgery N.C. Meml. Hosp., Chapel Hill, 1965-72, perfusionist, 1972—; chief cardiovascular perfusionist U. N.C. Hosps., Chapel Hill, 1991—; realtor Boone Realty Co., Durham, 1979—. Bd. dirs. Holy Cross Cath. Ch. Fellow Am. Soc. Extra-Corporeal Tech.; mem. Am. Acad. Cardiovasc. Perfusion, State Employees' Assn., Durham Bd. Realtors, Holy Cross Men's Soc. Democrat. Avocations: electronics, music, art, sports. Home: 6136 Yellowstone Dr Durham NC 27713-9708 Office: NC Meml Hosp Dept Cardiothoracic Su Chapel Hill NC 27514

BOONE, HAROLD THOMAS, retired lawyer; b. Oak Hill, W. Va., Dec. 14, 1921; s. Thomas Thumb and Cora Anna (McGlamery) B.; m. Ferne Miller, July 31, 1948; 1 dau., Cheryl Ann. B.S., W. Va., 1943; J.D., U. Va., 1948. With Md. Casualty Co., Balt., 1948-87, v.p., gen. counsel, corp. sec., 1979-87, dir., 1979-89; dir. N.C. Guaranty Fund, Calif. Def. Counsel; arbitrator Def. Research Inst., Inc., v.p. ins., 1986-87; part time freelance arbitrator. Served to 2d lt. USAAF, 1943-46. Mem. Internat. Assn. Ins. Counsel (v.p. 1979-81), Am. Arbitration Assn., Eliminate Hunt Valley Golf Club. Republican. Club: Hunt Valley Golf. Home: 551 Piccadilly Rd Baltimore MD 21204-3716

BOONE, JOHN LEWIS, religious organization administrator; b. Elkton, Ky., Oct. 5, 1927; s. Benjamin Edwards and Manie (Street) B.; m. Sally Hardcastle, Dec. 30, 1952; children: Sally Boone Wieland, John L. Jr., Martha Boone Bland. BA, Vanderbilt U., 1949. CLU. Bd. dirs. Inst. on Religion and Democracy, 1985—; chmn. Presbyn. Action, a caucus of IRD; bd. dirs. Presbyn. Lay Com., Presbyn. Coalition. mem. South Ctrl. Fin. Assocs. Recipient Faith and Freedom award Presbyns. for Democracy and Religious Freedom, Washington, 1990; named Man of the Yr., Tenn. Assn. of Life Underwriters, 1989. Mem. Nashville Chpt. CLUs (pres. 1957), Nashville Assn. of Life Underwriters (pres. 1955). Republican.

BOONE, KAREN, nutritionist, oriental medicine physician; b. L.A., Apr. 27, 1949; d. Elton Daniel Jr. and Barbara (Lombard) Boone; m. Paul Lester Doupe, Dec. 26, 1970 (div. Nov. 1989); children: Priscilla, Tyler. Student, Scripps Coll., Claremont, Calif., 1967-69; BA in Sociology, Willamette U., Salem, Oreg., 1971; OMD in Acupuncture, Herbs, Calif. Acupuncture Coll., L.A., 1986; PhD in Nutrition, Internat. U., Los Altos, Calif., 1990. Diplomate in acupuncture; lic. acupuncturist, Calif., Colo.; cert. hypnotherapist, nutritional cons., iridologist, Acu-Quit therapist for smoking termination, wellness counselor, reverse speech master analyst; qualified med. examiner State of Calif., 1990. Pvt. practice Crestone, Colo., 1986—; cons. Imbedded Comm. Rsch. Assn., 1998—; prof. Irvine U., Westminster, Calif., 1996—. Author: Taoist Book of Days, A Treatment Formulary, 1986, The Sacred Path of Pregnancy, 1993; contbr. articles to profl. jours. Mem. Am. Assn. Acupuncture and Oriental Medicine, Nat. Health Fedn., Calif. Assn. Acupuncture and Oriental Medicine. E-mail: karenb@fone.net.

BOONE, LOIS RUTH, legislator; b. Vancouver, B.C., Can., Apr. 26, 1947; d. George Charles Bearne and Ruth (Lindberg) Chudley; children: Sonia, Tanis. Tchr.'s cert., Simon Fraser U., 1969. Tchr. Sch. Dist. 57, Prince George, B.C., 1969-71, Sch. Dist. 27, Williams Lake, B.C., 1971-72; office mgr. Prince George YM-YWCA, 1972-73; case aide worker Vancouver YWCA, 1973-74; adminstrv. asst. Gov. B.C., Prince George, 1978-86; mem. legis. assembly Gov. B.C., Victoria, 1986—, min. govt. svcs., 1991-93, mem. bd. Ins. Corp. of B.C., 1994-96, min. mcpl. affairs, 1996; min. transp. and hwys. Gov. B.C., 1996-98, min. children and families, 1998—. Trustee Sch. Dist. 57, Prince George, 1981-85. Mem. New Democratic Party. Office: Rm 028, Parliament Bldgs, Victoria, BC Canada V8V 1X4

BOONE, MORELL DOUGLAS, academic administrator, information and instructional technology educator; b. Londonderry, Northern Ireland, Dec. 15, 1942; came to U.S., 1946; s. Paul J. and Margaret (Hill) B.; m. Carolyn June Gallagher, July 6, 1968; children—Ian Charles, Megan Elizabeth. B.S., Kutztown State Coll., Pa., 1964; M.S., Syracuse U., 1968, Ph.D., 1980. Librarian Pennridge Schs., Perkasie, Pa., 1964-66; reference librarian Hobart and William Smith Colls., Geneva, N.Y., 1968-70; lectr. Syracuse U., N.Y., 1970-72; dean learning resources U. Bridgeport, Conn., 1973-80; prof. interdisciplinary tech. Eastern Mich. U., Ypsilanti, 1980—, dean learning resources and techs., 1980—; cons. for internat. ednl. devel., Tehran, Iran, Swaziland, others. Presentations at profl. meetings; co-author: 1991 book; contbr. articles to profl. jours. Chmn. Community Cablecasting Commn., Ypsilanti, 1981-84, Ypsilanti Ednl. Found., 1988-94; bd. dirs. Meals on Wheels, Ypsilanti, 1998—. NSF rsch. grantee, 1972. Mem. ALA, EDUCAUSE, Assn. Coll. and Rsch. Libraries, Am. Assn. for Higher Edn. (mem. editl. bd. Library HiTech). Democrat. Presbyterian (elder). Avocations: travel, gardening, reading. Home: 5774 Pineview Dr Ypsilanti MI 48197-8983 Office: Eastern Mich U Bruce T Halle Library Ypsilanti MI 48197

BOONE, STEPHEN CHRISTOPHER, neurosurgeon; b. Navasota, Tex., Mar. 18, 1938; s. Berrill Harrison and Joyce (Taylor) B.; m. Elizabeth Thompson, Apr. 9, 1960 (div. June 1979); children: Stephen, Michael, Laura; m. Susan Pate, Nov. 3, 1979; children: Christopher, Emily. BS, Duke U., 1960, MD, 1965, PhD, 1965. Diplomate Am. Bd. Neurological Surgery. Surg. intern Duke Hosp., Durham, N.C., 1965, resident in neurosurgery, 1967-72; chief neurosurgeon Brooke Army Med. Ctr., 1973-75; asst. chief neurosurgery Walter Reed Army Med. Ctr., Washington, 1975-77; from assoc. prof. to prof. neurosurgery U. N.C., 1977-82; neurosurgeon Raleigh Neurosurgery Clinic, N.C., 1982—. Brig. gen. U.S. Army Res., 1962-87. Republican. Episcopal. Office: Raleigh Neurosurgery Clinic 3700 Barrett Dr Raleigh NC 27609-7213

BOONE, THEODORE SEBASTIAN, lawyer; b. Urbana, Ill., Jan. 7, 1961; s. William Werner and Eileen Georganna (Herweh) B. BA cum laude with highest deptl. distinction, U. Ill., 1983; JD, Columbia U., 1987. Bar: N.Y. 1988, D.C. 1989. Assoc. Arnold & Porter, Washington, 1991—; translator, speaker in field. Contbr. book revs., articles to profl. jours. Grantee Internat. Rsch. and Exchs. Bd., Budapest, 1987-88, Fulbright and Bavarian State, Munich, 1983-84; Fgn. Lang. Area Studies/U.S. Dept. Edn., 1986-87. Mem. ABA (vice chmn. com. internat. investment, devel. and privatization), Am. Soc. Internat. Law, Am. C. of C. in Hungary (bd. govs. 1989-93, pres. 1991-93), N.Y. Bar Assn., D.C. Bar Assn., Phi Beta Kappa. Avocations: German and Hungarian language. Office: Arnold and Porter 555 12th St NW Washington DC 20004-1206

BOONSHAFT, HOPE JUDITH, public relations executive; b. Phila., May 3, 1949; d. Barry and Lorelei Gail (R ienzi) B. BA, Pa. State U., 1972; postgrad. Del. Law Sch., Kellogg Inst. Mgmt. Tng. Program writer Youth Edn., N.Y.C., 1972; legal aide to judge, Phila., 1973; dir. spl. projects Guiffre Med. Center, Phila., 1975; Arlen Specter senatorial campaign fin. dir., Phila., 1975; fin. dir. Jimmy Carter Presdl. Campaign, Atlanta, 1976; nat. fin. dir. Dem. Nat. Com., 1977-78; dir. devel. World Jewish Congress, N.Y.C., 1978; dir. devel. Yeshiva U., L.A., 1979; dir. comm. Nat. Easter Seal Soc., Chgo., 1979-83; CEO Boonshaft-Lewis & Savitch Pub. Rels. and Govt. Affairs, L.A., 1983-93; sr. v.p. Edelman Worldwide, 1993-95; sr. v.p. external affairs Sony Pictures Entertainment, L.A., 1995—; spl. adv. cmty. rels. The White House, 1977-80; guest lectr. U. Ill., 1982, May Co.'s Calif. Women in Bus. Bd. dirs. L.A. Arts Coun., Hollywood Heritage Coun., Show Coalition, Jewish TV Network, NCCJ; mem. exec. com. Am. Jewish Com.; commr. Los Angeles County Citizens for Economy and Effiency in Govt., Calif. Film Commn. Home: 1967 Mandeville Canyon Rd Los Angeles CA 90049-2235 Office: Sony Pictures Entertainment 10202 Washington Blvd Culver City CA 90232-3119

BOOR, MYRON VERNON, psychologist, educator; b. Wadena, Minn., Dec. 21, 1942; s. Vernon LeRoy and Rosella Katharine (Eckhoff) B. BS, U. Iowa, 1965; MA, So. Ill. U., 1967, PhD, 1970; MS, U. Pitts., 1981. Lic. psychologist, Kans., Mo. Research psychologist Milw. County Mental Health Ctr., 1970-72; asst. prof. clin. psychologist Ft. Hays State U., Hays, Kans., 1972-76; assoc. prof. Ft. Hays State U., Hays, 1976-79; NIMH postdoctoral fellow in psychiat. epidemiology U. Pitts., Western Psychiat. Inst. and Clinic, 1979-81; research psychologist R.I. Hosp. and Butler Hosp., Providence, 1981-84; clin. psychologist Newman Meml. County Hosp., Emporia, Kans., 1985-93, Heartland Health Sys., St. Joseph, Mo., 1994—; clin. psychologist Ft. Hays State U., 1972-79; asst. prof. psychiatry and human behavior Brown U., Providence, 1981-84; adj. faculty Emporia State U., 1985-94. Contbr. articles to profl. jours. U.S. Pub. Health Service fellow, 1965-67, NIMH fellow 1979-81. Mem. Am. Psychol. Assn., Soc. for Psychol. Study of Social Issues, Internat. Soc. for Study of Multiple Personalities (charter). Office: Heartland Health Sys 801 Faraon St Saint Joseph MO 64501-1868

BOORMAN, HOWARD LYON, history educator; b. Chgo., Sept. 11, 1920; s. William Ryland and Verna (Lyon) B.; m. Mary Houghton, Jan. 20, 1972; 1 son by previous marriage—Scott A. B.A., U. Wis., Madison, 1941; postgrad., Yale U., 1946-47. Divisional asst., div. def. materials Dept. of State, Washington, 1942-43; fgn. service officer to Peking, Hong Kong, 1947-54; research asso. Sch. Internat. Affairs, Columbia U., N.Y.C., 1955-67; prof. history Vanderbilt U., Nashville, 1967-84; emeritus Vanderbilt U., 1984—; mem. Nat. Com. U.S.-China Relations, 1966—; vis. scholar Univ. Center of Va., 1963. Gen. editor: Biographical Dictionary of Republican China, 4 vols, 1967-71; contbr. articles to profl. jours. Served to lt. USNR, 1943-46. Recipient Rockefeller Public Service award, 1954-55. Mem. Am. Hist. Assn., Am. Polit. Sci. Assn., Assn. Asian Studies. Club: Univ. (Nashville). Home: 12 Redbud Dr Nashville TN 37215-2423 Office: Vanderbilt U Dept History Nashville TN 37235

BOORMAN, JOHN, film director, producer, screenwriter; b. Shepperton, Middlesex, Eng., Jan. 18, 1933; s. George and Ivy (Chapman) B.; m. Christel Kruse, 1957; 4 children. Broadcaster, critic BBC Radio; film editor ITN London, 1955-58; dir., producer So. TV, 1958-60. Contbr. articles to Manchester Guardian and mags.; 1950-54; head documentaries, Bristol, BBC-TV; dir. (documentary) The Citizens series The Newcomers, 1998: Lee Marvin: A Personal Portrait by John Boorman 1960-64, 1997; dir. films Catch Us If You Can, 1965, Point Blank, 1967, Hell in the Pacific, 1968, Leo the Last, 1969, Deliverance, 1970, Zardoz, 1973, Exorcist II: The Heretic, 1976, Excalibur, 1981, Emerald Forest, 1985, Hope and Glory, 1987 (Golden Globe award 1988 and Nat. Soc. Film Critics award), Where The Heart Is, 1989, I Dreamt I Woke Up, 1991, Beyond Rangoon, 1995, Two Nudes Bathing, 1995, Lumiere et Compagnie, 1995, The General, 1997; founder: TV mag. Day by Day; author: fiction The Legend of Zardoz, 1973, Money into the Light, 1985, Hope and Glory, 1987, Projections 1, 1992, Projections 2, 1993, Projections 3, 1994, Projections 4, 1995, Projections 4 1/2, 1995, Projections 5, 1996, Projections 6, 1997, Projections 7, 1997, Projections 8, 1998, Projections 9, 1999. Decorated Comdr. of Brit. Empire, 1994; recipient Best Dir. prize Cannes Festival, 1970, 98. Office: care Edgar Gross Internat Bus Mgmt 9696 Blvd # 203 Culver City CA 90232 also: Merlin Films, 16 Upper Pembroke St, Dublin 2, Ireland

BOORSTEIN, BEVERLY WEINGER, judge; b. Chgo., Apr. 25, 1941; d. Morris Aaron and Bess (Meisel) Weinger; m. Sidney L. Boorstein, July 3, 1962; children: Robin Anne, Michelle Loren. BA, Brandeis U., 1961; JD, Boston U., 1964. Bar: Mass. 1964, U.S. dist. Ct. Mass. 1967. Assoc. Siskind & Siskind, Boston, 1965-70; sole practice Boston, 1971-79; ptnr. Beverly Weinger Boorstein, P.C., Boston, 1980-92; assoc. justice Middlesex County Probate and Family Ct., 1992—; commr. Jud. Conduct Commn.; pres. Mental Health Legal Advisors Com. Contbr. articles to legal publs. Mem. Mass. Bar Assn., Middlesex County Bar Assn., Mass. Assn. Women Lawyers (adv. bd.), Boston Bar Assn. Office: The Trial Ct Probate & Family Dept Middlesex County Divsn 208 Cambridge St Cambridge MA 02141-1202

BOORSTEIN, LAURENCE, economist; b. Neuilly, France, Jan. 22, 1951; s. Edward and Regula (Simons) B. BA, Columbia U., 1972, MS, 1974; CE, 1978, MBA, 1988. Sys. analyst Frederic R. Harris, Inc. engring. divsn. Planning Rsch. Corp., N.Y.C., 1974-77, prin. sys. engr. Frederic R. Harris, Inc. divsn., 1977-79; sr. systems planner Frederic R. Harris Enging. Div., N.Y.C., 1979-83; sr. economist Frederic R. Harris, Inc. divsn. Planning Rsch. Corp., N.Y.C., 1983-86; sr. economist Soros Assocs., N.Y.C., 1988-94; prin. economist Frederic R. Harris, Inc divsn. AECOM Tech. Corp., N.Y.C., 1994—. Mem. Soc. Civil Engrs., Am. Mgmt. Assn. Home: 1 Ipswich Ave Apt 112 Great Neck NY 11021-3260 Office: Frederic R Harris Inc 300 E 42nd St New York NY 10017-5947

BOORSTIN, DANIEL JOSEPH, historian, lecturer, educator, author, editor; b. Atlanta, Oct. 1, 1914; s. Samuel and Dora (Olsan) B.; m. Ruth Carolyn Frankel, Apr. 9, 1941; children: Paul Terry, Jonathan, David West. AB summa cum laude, Harvard U., 1934; BA with honors, Balliol Coll., Oxford U., 1936, BCL with honors, 1937; postgrad., Inner Temple, London, 1934-37; JSD, Yale U., 1940; LittD (hon.), Cambridge U., 1967; LLD (hon.), Harvard U., 1993; other hon. degrees. Bar: Mass. 1942; barrister-at-law, Inner Temple, 1937. Instr., tutor history and lit. Harvard and Radcliffe Coll., 1938-42; lectr. legal history Harvard Law Sch., 1939-42; asst. prof. history Swarthmore Coll., 1942-44; from asst. prof. to prof. Am. history U. Chgo., 1944-64, Preston and Sterling Morton Disting. Service prof., 1964-69; Walgreen lectr. Am. instns., 1952; dir. Nat. Mus. History and Tech., Smithsonian Instn., Washington, 1969-73, sr. historian, 1973-75; libr. of Congress Libr. of Congress, 1975-87, libr. of congress emeritus, 1987—; Fulbright vis. lectr. Am. history U. Rome, Italy, 1950-51, Kyoto U., Japan, 1957; cons. Social Sci. Research Center, U. P.R., 1955; lectr. for U.S. Dept. State in, Turkey, Iran, Nepal, India, Ceylon, 1959-60, Indonesia, Australia, New Zealand, Fiji, 1968, India, Pakistan, Iceland, 1974, Philippines, Thailand, Malaysia, India, Egypt, 1975; 1st incumbent of chair Am. history U. Paris, 1961-62; Pitt prof. Am. history and instns. U. Cambridge, 1964-65, Shelby and Kathryn Cullom Davis lectr. Grad. Inst. Internat. Studies, Geneva, 1973-74; sr. fellow Huntington Library, 1969; mem. Commn. on Critical Choices for Ams., 1973-77, Dept. State Indo-Am. Joint Subcommn. Edn. and Culture, 1974-81, Japan-U.S. Friendship Commn., 1978-84; mem. Am. Revolution Bicentennial Commn.; sr. attorney Office Lend Lease Adminstr., Dept. Justice, Washington.; Fellow Trinity Coll., 1964-65; mem. task force on exploration NASA, 1989. Author: The Mysterious Science of the Law, 1941, new edit. 1996, Delaware Cases, 1792-1830, 3 vols., 1943, The Lost World of Thomas Jefferson, 1948, The Genius of American Politics, 1953, The Americans: The Colonial Experience, 1958 (Bancroft award 1959), America and the Image of Europe, 1960, The Image or What Happened to the American Dream, 1962, The Americans: The National Experience, 1965 (Francis Parkman prize 1966), The Landmark History of the American People, 2 vols., 1968, 70, 87, The Decline of Radicalism, 1969, The Sociology of the Absurd, 1970, The Americans: The Democratic Experience, 1973 (Pulitzer prize 1974, Dexter prize 1974), Democracy and Its Discontents, 1974, The Exploring Spirit, 1976, The Republic of Technology, 1978; (with Brooks M. Kelley) A History of the United States, 1981, 88, 91, The Discoverers, 1983 (Watson-Davis prize History of Sci. Soc. 1986), illus. edit., 1991, Hidden History, 1987, The Creators, 1992, Cleopatra's Nose, 1994, The Daniel J. Boorstin Reader, 1995, The Seekers, 1998; editor: An American Primer, 1966, American Civilization, 1972; editor Am. History; editor Ency. Britannica, 1951-55, mem. bd. editors, 1981—; contbr. articles and book revs. to various publs. Trustee Colonial Williamsburg, Kennedy Ctr., Cafritz Found., Woodrow Wilson Ctr., Thomas Gilcrease Mus.; mem. bd. visitors USAF Acad., 1968-70. Decorated Japanese Order of Sacred Treasure, 1st class; Grand Officer (Portugal); Legion of Honor (France); Order of Cultural Merit (Belgium); Rhodes scholar Balliol Coll., Oxford U., 1934-37; Sterling fellow Yale U., 1940; recipient Bowdoin prize Harvard Coll., 1934, Jenkins prize Balliol Coll., 1935, Younger prize, 1936, Charles Frankel prize NEH, 1989, Nat. Book award Nat. Book Award Com., 1989, numerous others. Fellow Am. Geog. Soc. (hon.), Royal Hist. Soc. (corr.); mem. Am. Acad. Arts and Scis., Am. Philos. Soc. (Thomas Jefferson medal 1999), Am. Antiquarian Soc., Am. Studies Assn. (pres. 1969-71), Orgn. Am. Historians, Colonial Soc. Mass., Internat. House Japan, Nat. Press Club, Cosmos Club, Elizabethan Club (Yale U. chpt.), Phi Beta Kappa (Disting. Svc. to Humanities award 1988). Jewish. Home: 3541 Ordway St NW Washington DC 20016-3173 Office: Libr Congress Libr Emeritus Washington DC 20540

BOOTE, ALFRED SHEPARD, marketing researcher, educator; b. N.Y.C., May 21, 1929; s. Alfred Denton and Katharine (Kerrison) B.; m. Joan Peterson, July 9, 1960 (div. Sept. 1963); m. Heath Drury, June 1, 1973. BA, Colgate U., 1951; MBA, Columbia U., 1953, MPhil, 1974, PhD, 1975; MA, Stanford U., 1957. Research mgr. design and market research labs., Container Corp. of Am., 1961-63; assoc. dir. mktg. research Pepsi-Cola Co., 1963-65; dir. mktg. research Far East area, PepsiCo Internat., 1965-67, dir. mktg. rsch. Worldwide, 1967-70; pvt. practice mktg. research cons. clients include Singer Co., McDonald's Corp., GTE, Gen. Elec. Co., Magic Chef Corp., and others. N.Y.C., 1970-75, 90—; cons. Arthur D. Little, Inc., Cambridge, Mass., 1975-76; gen. mgr., dir. research Decision Research Corp., Lexington, Mass., 1976-78; dir. mktg. research Singer Co., Stamford, Conn., 1978-81; mng. dir., founder Psychographics Research Corp., Inc., Bedford, N.Y., 1981-86; v.p. research Smith Stanley & Co., Inc., Darien, Conn., 1983-87; adj. assoc. prof. sociology Hunter Coll., 1983; adj. lectr. mktg. rsch. Nichols Coll., 1985; vis. prof. mktg. Clark U., 1985-89; presenter in field. Mem. editorial rev. bd. Jour. of Advt., 1982-87; mem. editorial bd. Psychology and Mktg., 1983-85; contbr. articles to bus. and profl. jours. Mem. Planning Commn., Woodstock, Conn., 1985-91; mem. Regional Planning Commn. N.E. Conn., 1987-91; founder, 1st chmn. Mktg. Rsch. Soc. of Hong Kong, 1967. Served to lt. (j.g.) U.S. Navy, 1953-56. Mem. Am. Sociol. Assn., Alpha Kappa Delta, Alpha Kappa Psi. Home: 73 Bull Hill Rd Woodstock CT 06281

BOOTH, ALAN RUNDLETT, history educator; b. Manchester, N.H., Mar. 20, 1934; s. Robert Plues and Lois (Rundlett) B.; m. Beatrice Edgcomb, June

23, 1956 (div. June 1978); children: Thomas E., Samuel R., Holly; m. Margaret Zoller, Aug. 6, 1988; 1 child, Grace Marie. AB, Dartmouth Coll., 1956; MA, Boston U., 1962, PhD, 1964. Asst. prof. history Ohio U., Athens, 1964-68, assoc. prof. history, 1968-73, prof. history, 1973—, Hamilton/Baker & Hostetler prof. humanities, 1994—; manuscript cons. Jour. of Devel. Areas, Kalamazoo, 1965-97, Internat. Jour. African Historical Studies, 1970-97, African Econ. History, Mpls., 1980-95; Fulbright lectr. Swaziland, 1980-81, 89-90. Author: The United States Experience in South Africa, 1976, Swaziland: Tradition and Change in a Southern African Kingdom, 1983, Historical Dictionary of Swaziland, 1999; contbr. articles to profl. jours. Lt. USNR, 1956-60. Fulbright lectr., Basutoland, 1965-66, Swaziland, 1980-81, 89-90. Mem. Ohio Acad. History (exec. com. 1994-95), African Studies Assn. Democrat. Roman Catholic. Avocations: tennis, hiking. Home: 1213 Bourgogne Ave Bowling Green OH 43402-1508 Office: Ohio U Dept History Bentley Hall 116 Athens OH 45701

BOOTH, ANNA BELLE, accountant; b. Homesville, Ohio, Jan. 15, 1912; d. John Wilson and M. Pearl (Toomey) B.; m. Guy DiAmbrosio, Apr. 29, 1930; 1 child, Guy Booth. BA, Taylor Coll., 1930. Office mgr. in charge of mfg. Jacobs Tailored Clothes, Inc., Phila., 1931-41; acct., corp. cashier Lehigh Coal and Navigation Co., Phila., 1941-55; acct. Bishop & Hedberg, Phila., 1955-57; acct., office mgr. The Camax Co., Phila., 1957-60; office mgr., cashier New Eng. Mutual Life Ins. Co., Phila., 1960-67; acct. Wall & Ochs, Inc., Phila., 1967-71; comptr. Bisler Packaging Div./Pet, Inc., Phila., 1971-82; ret. Mem. Am. Soc. Women Accts. (Phila. pres. 1956-58, dir. 1952-54, 62-64, 73-75), LWV (Phila.). Home: 2122 Sansom St Philadelphia PA 19103-4429

BOOTH, BONNIE NELSON, human resources consultant; b. Lynn, Mass., Aug. 28, 1942; d. Vincent Carl and Merchelle Romaine (Eastman) Nelson. Student, Mary Washington Coll., 1960-61, Columbia U., 1965, Carnegie-Mellon U., 1962, 78-80; EdM in Adminstrn., Planning and Social Policy, Harvard U., 1979. Exec. sec. Kenyon and Eckhardt, Inc., N.Y.C., 1964-65; exec. sec., asst. to assoc. dir. Am. Press. Inst., Columbia U., N.Y.C., 1965; prin. sec. to chief housing sect. UN Hdqrs., N.Y.C., N.Y.C., 1965-68; adminstrv. asst. sec. UN Mission, Magadiscio, Somalia, 1968, Tripoli, Libya, 1968-69; research asst. Stockholm Sch. Econs., 1970; adminstrv. sec. to dep. dir. UN Conf. Trade and Devel./GATT, Geneva, 1970; adminstrv. asst. Harvard U., 1970-74, personnel officer dept. psychology and social relations, 1974-75; adminstrv. asst. Dravo Corp., Pitts., 1975-76; assoc. dir. admissions Chatham Coll., Pitts., 1976-77, acting dir. admissions, 1977-78; mgmt. devel. trainer and adminstr. Westinghouse Credit Corp., Pitts., 1981-86, human resources adminstr., 1986-89, human resources cons., 1989-91, pension cons., 1991-95; human resources cons. in pvt. practice Pitts., 1995—. Dem. committeewoman 7th Ward, Pitts., 1980—, vice chmn., 1990-93, chmn., 1993-94; del. Shadyside Action Coalition, 1988—, sec., 1991-92, pres., 1992-96, 98—; mgmt. vol. cons. Pitts. Fund for Arts Edn.; mem. zoning adv. com. Pitts. Zoning Code Project, 1994—. Recipient Hon. diploma for outstanding performance Internat. Seminar on Rural Housing and Community Facilities, Venezuelan Govt., 1967, Outstanding Quality Circle Facilitator award Westinghouse Electric Corp., 1985. Mem. ASTD, Lions Internatl., bd. dirs., Bloomfield-Lawrenceville Lions Club, 1999—, Internat. Assn. Quality Cirs. (pres. Pitts. chpt. 1985-90), Am. Soc. Exec. Women, Rotary. Episcopalian. Avocations: literature, art, music, film, arranging silk flowers.

BOOTH, C(HESLEY) PETER WASHBURN, manufacturing company executive; b. Huntington, N.Y., Dec. 28, 1939; s. Francis A. and Jean Washburn (Chesley) B.; m. Simone Elaine Detweiler, June 21, 1969. BA, Harvard Coll., 1961, JD, 1965. V.p., sec. Corning (N.Y.) Glass Works, 1983-85; pres. Corning Japan, Tokyo, 1986-91; sr. v.p. Corning Inc., 1991—. Home: One Park Pl Corning NY 14830 Office: Corning Inc Riverfront Plaza Corning NY 14831

BOOTH, EDGAR HIRSCH, lawyer; b. Bklyn., June 8, 1926; s. Benjamin H. and Lee (Benzman) B.; m. Joan E. Blumberg, Oct. 7, 1956; children—Charles, Janet. Student, U. Va., 1944, 46-47; BA, Stanford, 1949; JD, Harvard, 1953. Bar: N.Y. State bar 1954. Since practiced in N.Y.C.; assoc. Booth, Lipton & Lipton, N.Y.C., 1954-65, ptnr., 1965-84; ptnr. Booth, Marcus & Pierce,, N.Y.C., 1984-87, Myerson & Kuhn, N.Y.C., 1988-89, Warshaw Burstein Cohen Schlesinger & Kuh, N.Y.C., 1989—; mem. nat. panel arbitrators Am. Arbitration Assn.; mem. mediators panel U.S. Bankrupty Ct. So. Dist. N.Y. Mem. Glen Rock Bd. Edn., 1971-77, pres., 1973-74; bd. dirs. S.M. Louis Fund, Inc., N.Y.C. Served with AUS, 1944-46. Mem. N.Y. State Bar Assn., Assn. Bar City N.Y. Home: 25 Belmont Rd Glen Rock NJ 07452-2305 Office: 555 5th Ave New York NY 10017-2416

BOOTH, FORREST, lawyer; b. Evanston, Ill., Oct. 31, 1946; s. Robert and Florence C. (Forrest) B.; m. Louise A. Hayes, June 14, 1980; 1 child, Kristin A. BA, Amherst Coll., 1968; JD, Harvard U., 1975. Bar: D.C. 1976, U.S. Ct. Appeals (D.C. cir.) 1976, Calif. 1977, U.S. Dist. Ct. (no. dist.) Calif. 1977, U.S. Ct. Appeals (9th cir.) 1977, U.S. Supreme Ct. 1979. Assoc. Graham & James, Washington, 1975-76, Mccutchen, Doyle, Brown & Emersen, San Francisco, 1976-78; ptnr. Hancock, Rothert & Bunshoft, San Francisco, 1978-89; sr. ptnr. Booth Banning LLP, San Francisco, 1990—; faculty mem. S.E. Admiralty Law Inst., Savannah, Ga., 1990; chmn. Pacific Admiralty Seminar, San Francisco, 1983-97; advisor U. San Francisco Maritime Law Jour., 1992—. Contbr. articles to profl. jours. Lt. USN, 1968-72, Vietnam. Mem. Maritime Law Assn. U.S. (proctor), World Trade Club of San Francisco, Marine Club London, Assn. Average Adjusters U.K., St. Francis Yacht Club. Avocations: sailing, photography, skiing. Office: Booth Banning LLP 275 Battery St Fl 27 San Francisco CA 94111-3305

BOOTH, GEORGE, cartoonist; b. Cainsville, Mo., June 28, 1926; s. William and Norene B.; m. Dione Babcock; 1 child, Sarah. Student, Chgo. Acad. Art, 1948-49, Corcoran Sch. Art, Washington, Adelphi U., Sch. Visual Arts, N.Y.C. Staff cartoonist Leatherneck Mag., USMC, 1946-52; art dir. Bill Communications, N.Y., 1958-64. Cartoons appearing regularly in The New Yorker mag., 1969—; author: Think Good Thoughts About a Pussycat, 1975, Rehearsal's Off, 1976, Pussycats Need Love, Too!, 1981, Omnibooth, 1984, Booth Again!, 1989; illustrator: Wacky Wednesday, 1974, Possum Come a' Knockin', 1990, Self-Editing for Fiction Writers, 1993, It's Not My Turn to Look for Grandma!, 1995, The Ballymara Flood, 1996. Recipient N.Y. Film Festival Animation award, 1994, Reuben Mag. Cartoon award Nat. Cartoonists Soc., 1994. Address: PO Box 1539 Stony Brook NY 11790-0830*

BOOTH, GEORGE GEOFFREY, finance educator; b. Athens, Ohio, Jan. 13, 1942; s. George Warren and Ellen (Cooley) B.; m. Elizabeth Brannigan, Aug. 30, 1986; children: Christopher, Timothy, James, Matthew, Michael. BBA, Ohio U., 1964, MBA, 1966; PhD, U. Mich., 1971. Fin. analyst Ford Co., Saline, Mich., 1966-67; systems analyst Dow Chem., Midland, Mich., 1967; prof., chmn., dir. research U. R.I., Kingston, 1970-81; prof., chmn. fin. dept. Syracuse (N.Y.) U., 1981-86; Union Nat. Life Ins. Coll. prof. La. State U., 1988-98, prof., 1986-98, chmn. fin. dept., 1986-94; docent U. Vaasa, Finland, 1995—; prof., chmn., Pasant chair Mich. State U., East Lansing, 1998—; dir. South Providence Credit Union, 1977-78. Editor Fin. Rev., 1973-76, assoc. editor, 1976-85, 94-97; editor New Eng. Jour. Bus. and Econs., 1974-81, assoc. editor, 1981-90; assoc. editor Multinat. Fin. Mgmt., 1989—, Internat. Jour. Fin., 1993—, European Jour. Fin., 1996—, Ekonomia, 1996—; co-editor: Multinat. Fin. Jour., 1995—; contbr. articles to profl. jours. Mem. Am. Econ. Assn., Am. Fin. Assn., Ea. Fin. Assn., European Fin. Assn., So. Fin. Assn., Fin. Mgmt. Assn., New Eng. Bus. and Econ. Assn., Multinat. Fin. Soc., Soc. Fin. Studies, Phi Kappa Phi, Beta Gamma Sigma, Alpha Iota Delta. *

BOOTH, GEORGE KEEFER, financial services executive; b. Rockville Center, N.Y., July 23, 1943; s. David Conover and Nan (Tracy) B.; m. Jeanne Marie Storey, May 12, 1979; 1 child, Sarah. B.A., C.W. Post Coll., 1970; M.B.A., Fordham U., 1973. Asst. cashier Franklin Nat. Bank, N.Y.C., 1970-74; mgr. facilities leverage leasing Gen. Electric Credit Co., Stamford, Conn., 1974-77; corp. mgr. sales fin. Harris Corp., Melbourne, Fla., 1977-83; exec. v.p. Internat. Capital Equipment Co., N.Y.C., 1983-85; exec. v.p., chief fin. officer, bd. dirs. Phoenixcor, South Norwalk, Conn., 1985-94; founder, mng. dir. Black Rock Capital Corp., 1994—. Contbr. articles to Leasing Digest, Monitor, ELA. With USN, 1967-69. Republican. Roman Catholic. Mem. Am. Assn. Equipment Lessors (industry future coun. 1982-84, captive com. 1981, acctg. com. 1988), KC, Eastern Assn. Equipment Lessors, Am. Mgmt. Assn., Black Rock Yacht Club (Bridgeport, Conn.; past commodore). Home: 41 Grist Mill Ln Southport CT 06490-1070 Office: Black Rock Capital Corp PO Box 416 Fairfield CT 06430-0416

BOOTH, GORDON DEAN, JR., lawyer; b. Columbus, Ga., June 25, 1939; s. Gordon Dean and Lois Mildred (Bray) B.; m. Katherine Morris Campbell, June 17, 1961; children: Mary Katherine Williams, Abigail Kilgore Curvino, Sarah Elizabeth, Margaret Campbell, Celecia. BA, Emory U., 1961, JD, 1964, LLM, 1973. Bar: Ga. 1964, D.C. 1977, U.S. Supreme Ct. 1973. Pvt. practice Atlanta, 1964-96; ptnr. Schreeder, Wheeler & Flint, Atlanta, 1995—; bd. dirs., v.p. Stallion Music Inc., Nashville, BAA USA, Inc.; chmn. CPS Systems, Inc., Dallas; trustee, sec. Inst. for Polit. Econ., Washington. Contbr. articles to profl. jours. Trustee Met. Atlanta Crime Commn., 1977-80, chmn., 1979-80; mem. assembly for arts and scis. Emory Coll., 1971-86, chmn., 1983. Mem. Internat. Bar Assn. (coun. sect. bus. law 1974-88, chmn. aero. law com. 1971-86), State Bar Ga., Capital City Club, Piedmont Driving Club, Univ. Club (N.Y.C.), Advocates Club, Sigma Chi. Home: 3226 Paces Mill Rd SE Atlanta GA 30339-3787

BOOTH, HAROLD WAVERLY, lawyer, finance and investment company executive; b. Rochester, N.Y., Aug. 8, 1934; s. Herbert Nixon and Mildred B. (Anderson) B.; m. Flo Rae Spelts, July 4, 1957; children: Rebecca, William, Eva, Harold, Richard. B.S., Cornell U., 1955; J.D., Duke U., 1961. Bar: Nebr. 1961, Ill. 1967, Iowa 1974; CLU; chartered fin. counselor; cert. fin. planner. Staff atty. Bankers Life Nebr., Lincoln, 1961-67; pres. First Nat. Bank, Council Bluffs, Iowa, 1970-74; exec. v.p., treas. Blue Cross-Blue Shield Ill., Chgo., 1974-77; pres., chief exec. officer, chmn. Bankers Life Nebr., Lincoln, 1977-84; exec. v.p. Colonial Penn Group, Phila., 1985-87; chmn., chief exec. officer VGVR Cos., 1985—. Served to 1st lt. USAF, 1955-58. Fellow Life Mgmt. Inst. (pres. 1981-84); mem. Ins. Fedn. Nebr. (past pres.). Home: 1000 Stony Ln Gladwyne PA 19035-1128

BOOTH, HILDA EARL FERGUSON, clinical psychologist, Spanish language educator; b. Pinehurst, N.C., Aug. 14, 1943; d. Arthur C. and Edna Estelle (Henry) Ferguson; m. Thomas Gilbert Booth, Oct. 25, 1966 (dec. Apr. 1990). AA, Montreat-Anderson Coll., 1963; BA, Pembroke State U., 1965; MS, Valdosta State U., 1985; postgrad., U. S.C., 1991. Lic. profl. counselor, S.C., cert. counselor, hypnotherapist. Spanish instr. C.C., Lake City, Fla., 1983-86; clin. counselor Columbia Counseling, Lake City, 1985-87; children's psychologist I Coastal Empire Mental Health Ctr., Allendale, S.C., 1987; psychologist II Coastal Empire Mental Health Ctr., Allendale, 1988, office mgr., 1987-91; pvt. practice Allendale, 1989-91; aquatics instr. Harbison Recreation Ctr., 1993; mem. mobile assessment team Richland Meml. Hosp., Rischland Springs, 1994, 1994; mem. assessment team, mutual health cons. Richland Meml. Hosp., Richland Springs; spl. svcs. coord., area coord. Allendale office, 1989; dir. women FORSPRO (Spain), Coral Gables, Fla., 1984-88; aquatics leader Nat. Arthritis Found., 1994; emergency svcs. staff Mental Health, Lake City, 1985-87; mem. Children at Risk team, Children's Advocacy team, 1987-91. Mem. extension cmty. planning com. City of Allendale, 1989-91, Shandon Presbyn. Ch.; pres. Protestant Women of Chapel, Nfld., Can., 1969, Ch. Women United, Lake City, 1976; deacon First Presbyn. Ch., Lake City, 1976-86, chmn. bd. deacons, 1982, elder 1985, elder Allendale Presbyn. Ch., 1988—, clk. of session, 1989—, tchr. Sunday sch., 1994; mem. mission com. to Nicaragua Shandon Presbyn. Ch., 1996, 98. Served to lt. (j.g.) USN, 1965-67. Fellow Internat. Biog. Assn.; mem. SEICUS, LWV, Inter-Am. Soc. of Psychology, Am. Legion (life), Nat. Beta Club, Robert Burns Soc. Republican. Avocations: painting, swimming, traveling, reading, Spanish. Home and Office: 3134 Prentice Ave Columbia SC 29205-3940

BOOTH, JANE SCHUELE, real estate broker, executive; b. Cleve.; d. Norman Andrew and Frances Ruth (Hankey) Schuele; m. George Warren Booth, Dec. 6, 1968. AA, Stephens Coll., 1946; student, U. Mo., 1946-47. Lic. real estate broker, Fla. Assoc. J.M. Mathes Inc., N.Y.C., 1947-48; dept. supr. Lord and Taylor, Scarsdale, N.Y., 1948-50; art coord. J. Walter Thompson, Inc., N.Y.C., 1953-58; art buyer SSC&B Inc. Advt., N.Y.C., 1959-80; pres. Jane Schuele Booth Realty, Ocala, Fla., 1982—. Mem. Fla. Thoroughbred Fillies, Ocala, 1980—; charter mem., trustee Royal Dames for Cancer Rsch., Inc., Ocala, 1986—; treas. Ladies Aux. Fla. H.C.H. Inc., Ocala, 1986-90; bd. visitors Fla. Horsemen's Children's Home, Inc., 1983-90. Mem. Ocala/Marion County Assn. Realtors, Ocala/Marion County C. of C. (agribus./equine com.), Nat. Assn. Realtors, Fla. Assn. Realtors, Estates Club. Home: 1771 SW 55th Street Rd Ocala FL 34474-5933 Office: PO Box 5538 Ocala FL 34478-5538

BOOTH, JOHN NICHOLLS, minister, magician, writer, photographer; b. Meadville, Pa., Aug. 7, 1912; s. Sydney Scott and Margaret (Nicholls) B.; m. Edith Kriger, Oct. 1, 1941 (dec. Sept. 1982); 1 child, Barbara Anne Booth Christie. BA, McMaster U., 1934; MDiv, Meadville/Lombard Theol. Sch., 1942; LittD, New Eng. Sch. Law, 1950. Ordained to ministry Unitarian Ch., 1942. Profl. magician, 1934-40; min. Unitarian Ch., Evanston, Ill., 1942-48, 1st Ch., Belmont, Mass., 1949-57, 2d Ch. (formerly Old North Ch.), Boston, 1958-64, Unitarian Ch., Long Beach, Calif., 1964-71; interim pastor N.Y.C., Gainesville, (Fla.), Detroit, 1971-73; celebrity platform lectr., performer on conjuring, 1942-58; ministerial adviser to liberal students MIT, 1958-63; mem. books selection com. Gen. Theol. Library, Boston, 1960-63. Author: Super Magical Miracles, 1930, Magical Mentalism, 1931, Forging Ahead in Magic, 1939, Marvels of Mystery, 1941, The Quest for Preaching Power, 1943, Fabulous Destinations, 1950, Story of the Second Church in Boston, 1959, The John Booth Classics, 1975, Booths in History, 1982, Psychic Paradoxes, 1984, Wonders of Magic, 1986, Dramatic Magic, 1988, Creative World of Conjuring, 1990, Conjurians' Discoveries, 1992, The Fine Art of Hocus Pocus, 1995, Keys to Magic's Inner World, 1999; contbr. articles to mags. and newspapers; photographer full length feature travel documentary films for TV, lecture platforms made in India, Africa, S.Am., Indonesia, South Seas, Himalayas; presented first color travelogue on TV in U.S. over NBC in N.Y.C., 1949; panel mem. radio program Churchmen Weigh The News, Boston, 1951-52; spl. corr. in Asia for Chgo. Sun-Times, 1948-49; byline writer Boston Globe, 1952-62; producer motion picture Heart of Africa, 1954; photographer films Golden Kingdoms of the Orient, 1957, Treasures of the Amazon, Ecuador and Peru, 1960, Adventurous Britain, 1962, South Seas Saga in Tahiti, Australia and New Guinea, summer 1966, The Amazing America of Will Rogers, 1970, Spotlight on Spain, 1975. Co-founder Japan Free Religious Assn., Tokyo, 1948; co-founder Mass. Meml. Soc., 1962, dir., 1962-64; organizer Meml. Soc. Alachua County (Fla.), 1972; pres. Long Beach Mental Health Assn., 1964-66; adv. coun. Fair Housing Found. Recipient John Nevil Maskelyne prize London Magic Cir., 1987; placed on former N.Y. Town Hall Cinematographers Wall of Fame, 1967; named Disting. Alumnae, Gallery of McMaster U.; lifetime achievement fellow Acad. Magical Arts, 1990. Mem. Unitarian-Universalist Mins. Assn. (past dir.), Am. Unitarian Assn. (past com. chmn.), Unitarian Mins. Pacific S.W. Assn. (v.p.), Clergy Counseling Svc. So. Calif., Soc. Am. Magicians (inducted into Hall of Fame 1983), Magic Castle Hollywood, Internat. Motion Picture and Lectrs. Assn., L.A. Adventurers Club (pres. 1983). First regularly scheduled TV broadcasts in U.S. by clergyperson, WBKB, Chgo., mid-1940s. Home and Office: 12032 Montecito Rd Los Alamitos CA 90720-4511 *Success often greets an imaginative, innovative approach to that which has been done in a settled way too long. An ability to time change properly and accept philosophically that which does not yield is to live maturely with one's own struggles and hopes. Bertrand Russell guides wisely in suggesting that a person living in a spirit that aims at creating rather than possessing has a certain fundamental happiness. Such a way of life is thereby freed from the tyranny of fear, since what one values most in one's existence is not at the mercy of outside power.*

BOOTH, JOHN THOMAS, investment banker; b. N.Y.C., Oct. 21, 1929; s. John E. and Katherine (Keeler) B.; m. Anne C. Mott, Feb. 26, 1960; children: Alison Booth Cramer, Miven Booth Trageser, Roxanna Booth Cistulli. Grad., Deerfield Acad., 1947; BA cum laude, Amherst Coll., 1951; LLB, Harvard U., 1957. Bar: N.Y. 1957. Assoc. firm Dewey Ballantine Bushby Palmer & Wood, N.Y.C., 1957-61; mem. buying dept. Eastman Dillon, Union Securities & Co., N.Y.C., 1961—; ptnr. Eastman Dillon, Union Securities & Co., 1963—; exec. v.p., dir. Blyth Eastman Dillon & Co., Inc., 1972-81; chmn. bd. Eastdil Realty, Inc., 1979-81, Am. Health Capital, Inc., 1982-86, Am. Health Capital Ventures, Inc., 1986-89; chmn. Franklin Venture Capital Inc., 1990-97, Greystone Communities, Inc., 1990—, Coleman, Swenson, Hoffman, Booth, Inc., 1997—; bd. dirs. Wells Hill Ptnrs. Ltd., Litchfield Bancorp; adv. bd. Saugatuck Capital, Inc.; mem. Eli Whitney investment adv. bd. Conn. Innovations, Inc.; asst. to dir. Harvard Def. Studies Program, 1956-57; counsel N.Y. State Assembly Com. on N.Y.C., 1960, Com. on Judiciary, 1961. Trustee Litchfield Hist. Soc., White Meml. Found.; mem. major gifts com. Capital Program for Amherst Coll. Lt. (j.g.) USNR, 1951-54. Mem. Newcomen Soc., Pilgrim Soc., Delta Kappa Epsilon, Delta Sigma Rho. Republican. Episcopalian. Clubs: Links, University (N.Y.C.); Litchfield (Conn.) Country. Office: PO Box 25 Litchfield CT 06759-0025

BOOTH, MARGARET A(NN), communications company executive; b. N.Y.C., Dec. 25, 1946; d. Herbert and Alice (Traum) B.; m. Marvin E. Schechter, Jan. 22, 1984. BS, U. Wis., 1968. Editl. asst. Bantam Books, N.Y.C., 1968-70; publicity asst. Ruder & Finn Inc., N.Y.C., 1970-71, dir. radio and TV, 1971-76, v.p., 1974-76; pres. Pub. Interest Pub. Rels., N.Y.C., 1976—, M. Booth & Assocs., Inc., N.Y.C., 1983—. Author: Promoting Issues and Ideas, 1987; contbr. articles to profl. jours. Bd. govs. Eugene Lang Coll. New Sch. for Social Rsch.; bd. dirs. N.Y. Found. Recipient YWCA Salute to Women Achievers, City of N.Y., 1985. Mem. Pub. Rels. Soc. Am., Women in Comm. (Matrix award for Pub. Rels. 1987), Women Execs. in Pub. Rels. Office: M Booth & Assocs Inc 470 Park Ave S # 10N New York NY 10016-6819*

BOOTH, MITCHELL B., lawyer; b. N.Y.C., June 26, 1927; s. Samuel and Rose (Waxman) B.; m. Barbara C. Ribman, July 13, 1952; 1 son, Brian S. A.B., Clark U., 1949; J.D., N.Y. U., 1952. Bar: N.Y. 1952. Assoc. I. Moldauer, N.Y.C., 1952-54, Sol A. Rosenblatt, N.Y.C., 1954-67; pvt. practice law N.Y.C., 1967—; minority counsel joint legis. com. unsatisfied judgments N.Y., 1958-59, joint legis. com. preservation restoration hist. sites N.Y., 1960-64; med. malpractice mediator First Jud. Dept. Supreme Ct. State N.Y., 1980-91; bd. dirs., treas. East Hampton Mews Tenants Corp., Burgos Art Galleries Ltd., Dorolyat Corp. Asst. to chmn. Dem. law com., N.Y. County, 1961-65; rep. admissions for states of N.Y., N.J. and Conn. Clark U., 1968-71. Served to lt. USNR, 1945-46, 49-53. Mem. ABA, N.Y. State Bar Assn., Assn. of Bar of City of N.Y. (mem. com. profl. discipline 1986-89), N.Y. Commandry, Mil. Order Fgn. Wars U.S. (life, judge advocate). Home: 75 E End Ave New York NY 10028-7909 Office: 156 W 56th St New York NY 10019-3800

BOOTH, RACHEL ZONELLE, nursing educator; b. Seneca, S.C., Feb. 10, 1936; m. Richard B. Booth, Feb. 13, 1957; 1 child, Kevin M. Student, Furman U., 1953-54; diploma in nursing, Greenville (S.C.) Gen. Hosp., 1956; student, U. Alaska, 1964-66; BS in Nursing, U. Md., Balt., 1968; MS in Nursing, U. Md., 1970, PhD in Adminstrn. Higher Edn., 1978. RN. Staff nurse VA Hosp., Murfreesboro, Tenn., 1956-57, U. Colo. Med. Ctr., Denver, 1957-58; nurse psychiatry dept. Patton State Hosp., Calif., 1958-59; staff nurse USAF Dispensary, Iraklion, Greece, 1959-60; charge nurse psychiatry Santa Rose Med. Ctr., San Antonio, 1961; staff nurse Shannon S.W. Tex. Meml. Hosp., San Angelo, 1962; supervisory clin. nurse, head nurse U.S. Dept. Health, Edn., and Welfare/USPHS/Indian Health Service, Anchorage, 1962-66; staff nurse U.S. Dept. Health, Edn., and Welfare/USPHS, Balt., 1966, 68; assoc. dir. dept. nursing U. Md. Hosp., 1970-76, dir. primary care nursing svc., 1976-81; asst. prof. Sch. Nursing U. Md., 1972-76, asst. prof. Sch. Pharmacy, 1972-80, acting assoc. dean Sch. Nursing, 1979-81, assoc. prof. Sch. Nursing, 1979, assoc. prof. clin. pharmacy, 1980-83, assoc. dean for undergrad. studies Sch. Nursing, 1981-83, co-dir. nurse practitioner program Sch. Nursing, 1972-76, chairperson grad. program dept. primary care, 1974-79; dean, Sch. of Nursing and asst. v.p. for health affairs Duke U., Durham, N.C., 1984-87; dean Sch. Nursing U. Ala. at Birmingham, University Station, 1987—; instr. Sch. Medicine U. Md., 1972-83, program dir. primary care nurse practitioner program continuing edn., 1976-82, project dir. Robert Wood Johnson Nurse Faculty Fellowship program, 1977-82; mem. joint practice com. Med. and Surg. Faculty Md., 1974-77, mem. tech. adv. com. for physician's assts. Bd. Med. Examiners Md., 1975-80; mem. adv. com. nursing program Community Coll. Balt., 1976-79; mem. Joint Commn. on Accreditation of Hosps., pres. Md. Council Dirs. of Assoc. Degree, Diploma, and Baccalaureate Programs, 1982-83; mem. adv. bd. nursing Essex Community Coll., 1983; mem. peer rev. panel advanced nurse edn. nursing div. U.S. Dept. Health and Human Services, 1987—. Editor (with others) Hospital Pharmacy, 1971-72; asst. editor Jour. Profl. Nursing, 1984-87; contbr. articles on nursing to prof. jours. Bd. dirs. Health and Welfare Coun. Ctrl. Md., Inc., 1974-78, v.p., 1975-78; mem. health adv. com. to Pres. of Pakistan, 1981—. Recipient numerous grants for nursing adminstrn., 1972—. Mem. ANA (mem. nat. rev. com. 1975-78, v.p. 1977, chair 1978), Internat. Coun. Nurses (observer conf. 1981), Nat. Acad. Practice for Nursing (vice chairperson 1984-89), Nat. Orgn. for Nurse Execs., Nat. League for Nursing, Coun. Nat. Acad. Practice, Am. Assn. Colls. in Nursing (dean's summer seminar com. 1984-85, edn. and credentialing com. 1985-86, nominating com. 1986-87, bd. dirs. 1989-96, pres.-elect 1992-94, pres. 1994-96), N.C. Orgn. Nurse Execs. (bd. dirs. 1986-87), So. Coun. Collegiate Edn. for Nursing (exec. com. 1986-91, v.p., bd. dirs. 1991-94, pres. 1997-99), Sigma Theta Tau (chairperson nominating com. 1974, mem. 1975, rec. sec. 1980-83). Avocations: genealogy, travel, swimming. Office: U Ala at Birmingham 1701 University Blvd Birmingham AL 35233-1815

BOOTH, ROBERT LEE, JR., banker; b. Nashville, Feb. 7, 1936; s. Robert Lee and Ruth (Allison) B.; children: Richard, Lee, Lindley; m. Melissa Blackwood. BA, Rhodes Coll., 1958; grad. advanced mgmt. program Bus Sch., Harvard U., 1972. Asst. v.p. 1st Tenn. Bank, Memphis, 1960-67, exec. v.p., 1980-82; asst. treas. CIT Fin. Corp., N.Y.C., 1967-73; v.p., treas. Leucadia Nat. Corp., N.Y.C., 1973-74; pres. Commerce Union Bank Memphis, 1974-79; exec. v.p. Commerce Union Corp., Nashville, 1979-80; pres. Boatmen's Bank Tenn., 1982-88; exec. v.p. Union Planters Corp., Memphis, 1988—. Vice chmn. Memphis Brooks Mus. Art, 1985. Mem. Fin. Execs. Inst. (chmn. 1978), Memphis C. of C. (chmn. 1985). Democrat. Episcopalian. Clubs: Economic (Memphis); Harvard (N.Y.C.). Office: Union Planters Bank 6200 Poplar Ave Memphis TN 38119-4713 also: PO Box 387 Memphis TN 38147-0002

BOOTH, THOMAS COLLINS, musician; b. Greensboro, N.C., Dec. 24, 1947; s. Roy Murphy and Marguerite (Collins) B.; m. Beth Johnson, Feb. 14, 1970; 1 child, Cheryl Alyce. MusB, U. N.C., 1970; postgrad., Julliard Sch., N.Y.C., 1971-74, Opera Sch. Chgo., 1975-76. Prin. baritone Lyric Opera Chgo., 1975-76, prin. tenor, 1985-86, 92; prin. baritone Met. Opera, N.Y.C., 1978-79, spring 1980, prin. tenor, 1984-85, 86-91; leading baritone Stadttheater Aachen, Fed. Republic of Germany, 1980-82; tenor soloist Italian Pavillion, Epcot Ctr., Orlando, Fla., 1983-84; leading tenor Städtische Bühnen, Frankfurt, Fed. Republic of Germany, 1987, New Orleans Opera Assn., 1988—, Seattle Opera Assn., 1988—, Spoleto Festival, U.S., 1988, Warsaw Philharm., Poland, 1988, Opera de Nice, 1989, San Diego Opera, 1989, Transvaal Opera, Pretoria, 1990, N.Y.C. Opera, 1991, Opera de Tenerife, Spain, 1991, Opera de Wallonie Liege, Belgium, 1992, Opera de Montepellier, 1992, Opera Monterrey, Mexico, 1993, Knoxville Opera, 1993, Opera de Nantes, France, 1993, Rome Opera, 1994, 95, Austin Lyric Opera, 1993, Wexford Opera Festival, 1992; prin. tenor The Netherlands Opera, Amsterdam, 1987; instr. in field. leading tenor John Cage's Europera II, Frankfurt, 1987; symphonic appearances Memphis Symphony, 1990, New World Symphony, 1990, Hartford Symphony, 1991, Knoxville Symphony, 1992, Dallas Symphony Orch., 1992, Akron Symphony, 1992, Jerusalem Symphony, 1993, Israel Philharm., 1993, Fort Wayne Philharm., 1995, Royal Philharm., Stockholm, 1995, Dubuque Symphony, 1997, Lawrence Symphony, 1997; additional appearances with Portland (Maine) Symphony, Boston Concert Opera, Brevard Music Festival; recordings (with Nat. Symphony) Boris Godunov, 1987, (with Welsh Nat. Opera) Vigil of Venus, 1990, (with Philharm. Orch.) John Socman, 1994. Recipient Montreal (Can.) Internat. Competition prize, 1977, Am. Wagner Assn. award for Wagnerian singers, 1985; Mario Lanza scholar, 1972-73, Liederkranz Found. Eugen Megerle Meml. scholar, 1985. Mem. Am. Guild Musical Artists, Am. Guild Variety Artists. Republican. Methodist. Avocations: biking, weight lifting, travel, writing. Home: 1043 E Broadway Ave Monmouth IL 61462-1948 Office: Chgo Concert Artists 431 S Dearborn St Apt 906 Chicago IL 60605-1151

BOOTH, WAYNE CLAYSON, English literature and rhetoric educator, author; b. American Fork, Utah, Feb. 22, 1921; s. Wayne Chipman and Lillian (Clayson) B.; m. Phyllis Barnes, June 19, 1946; children: Katherine, John Richard (dec.), Alison. AB, Brigham Young U., 1944; MA, U. Chgo., 1947, PhD, 1950; DLitt (hon.), Rockford Coll., 1965, St. Ambrose Coll., 1971, U. N.H., 1977; DHL (hon.), Butler U., 1984, Lycoming Coll., 1985, SUNY, 1987, Wabash Coll., 1990, Kalamazoo Coll., 1991, Ball State U., 1992, DePaul U., 1994, Earlham Coll., 1995, Carleton Coll., 1995. Instr. U. Chgo., 1947-50; asst. prof. Haverford Coll., 1950-53; prof. English, chmn. dept. Earlham Coll., 1953-62; George M. Pullman prof. English U. Chgo., 1962-91, dean Coll., 1964-69, prof. emeritus, 1992—, chmn. com. on ideas and methods, 1972-75; Beckman lectr. U. Calif., Berkeley, 1979, Sch. Criticism, Irvine, Calif., 1979; Whitney Oates vis. prof. Princeton U., 1984; vis. cons. (with wife) South African schs. and univs., 1963; lectr. English Coalition Conf., 1987; Amnesty Internat. lectr. Oxford U., 1992. Author: The Rhetoric of Fiction, 1961 (Christian Gauss prize Phi Beta Kappa 1962, David H. Russell award Nat. Coun. Tchrs. English 1966), Now Don't Try To Reason With Me: Essays and Ironies for a Credulous Age, 1970, A Rhetoric of Irony, 1974, Modern Dogma and the Rhetoric of Assent, 1974, Critical Understanding: The Powers and Limits of Pluralism, 1979 (Laing prize 1981), The Company We Keep: An Ethics of Fiction, 1988, Harper & Row Reader, 1984, Harper & Row Rhetoric, 1987, 90, (with M. Gregory) The Vocation of a Teacher: Rhetorical Occasions, 1967-88, 1988, The Craft of Research, 1997; editor: The Knowledge Most Worth Having, 1967, The Art of Growing Older, 1992, For The Love of It: Amateuring and Its Rivals, 1999; co-editor Critical Inquiry, 1974-85, Christian Gauss Seminars in Criticism, Princeton, 1974. Trustee Earlham Coll., 1965-75. Served with inf. AUS, 1944-46. Recipient Disting. Alumni award Brigham Young U., 1975, Lifetime Achievement award Assn. for Mormon Letters, 1995, Lifetime Achievement award Conf. on Christianity and Literature, 1995, Quantrell prize for undergrad. tchg. U. Chgo., 1971, lifetime tchg. award, 1997, award for contbns. to edn. Am. Assn. Higher Edn., 1986; Ford Faculty fellow, 1952-53, Guggenheim fellow, 1956-57, 69-70, NEH fellow, 1975-76, Rockefeller Found. fellow, 1981-82; Phi Beta Kappa vis. scholar, 1977-78. Fellow Am. Acad. Arts and Scis., Am. Philos. Soc.; mem. MLA (exec. coun. 1973-76, pres. 1981-92, Francis Andrew March award for Disting. Svc. of Profession of English 1991), AAUP, Nat. Coun. Tchrs. English (commn. on lit. 1967-70), Coll. Conf. on Composition and Comm., Nat. Commn. on Educating Undergrads. in Rsch. Univs. Democrat. Mem. LDS Ch. Home: 5411 S Greenwood Ave Chicago IL 60615-5103

BOOTH, WENDY CHRISTINA, nursing educator; b. Montreal, Que., Can., Aug. 28, 1944; d. Lester John and Josephine Louise (Tock) B. Diploma, Montreal Gen. Hosp., 1966; BSN, U. Ala., Birmingham, 1985, MSN, 1988. RN, Ala.; post Master cert. family nurse practitioner. Staff nurse orthopedic, trauma unit Montreal Gen. Hosp., 1966-67; staff nurse pediatric unit Foothills Provincial Hosp., Calgary, Alta., Can., 1967-68; staff nurse pediatrics The Queen's Med. Ctr., Honolulu, 1969-71, staff nurse surg. ICU, open heart surgery unit, 1971-75, asst. head nurse, 1975-78, head nurse, 1978-83; staff, relief charge nurse surg. ICU U. Ala. Hosp., Birmingham, 1983-88, supplemental staff nurse, 1987-89, nursing case mgr. aftercare, 1988; nursing dir. for 5 counties Ala. Dept. Pub. Health Area III, Pelham, 1989-95; cmty. health nurse instr. U. Ala., Birmingham, 1995—; instr. cmty. health nursing Clinic FNP, part-time, 1998—. Contbr. articles to profl. jours. Comdr. USNR, 1983—. Mem. ALPHA, AACN, ANA, Naval Res. Assn., U. Ala. Birmingham Alumnae Assn., Sigma Theta Tau (Nu chpt.). Home: 4109 Brookmont Dr Birmingham AL 35210-4102

BOOTHBY, WILLARD SANDS, III, bank executive; b. N.Y.C., Nov. 18, 1946; s. Willard Sands Jr. and Florence (Clifford) B.; m. Linda Kent, Sept. 8, 1973; children: Elizabeth, Willy. BA, Princeton U., 1969; MBA, Harvard U., 1972. Asst. treas. Morgan Guaranty Trust Co., N.Y.C., 1975-78, asst. v.p., 1978-80, v.p., 1980-86, sr. v.p., mng. dir., 1986—. Clubs: Links, River (N.Y.C.). Office: Morgan Guarnty Trust Co 60 Wall St Fl 25 New York NY 10005-2836

BOOTHBY, WILLIAM MUNGER, mathematics educator; b. Detroit, Apr. 1, 1918; s. Thomas Franklin and Florence (Munger) B.; m. Ruth Robin, June 8, 1947; children—Daniel, Thomas, Mark. A.B., U. Mich., 1941, M.A., 1942, Ph.D., 1949. Mem. faculty Northwestern U., Evanston, Ill., 1948-59; fellow Am.-Swiss Found. for Sci. Exchange, Swiss Fed. Inst. Tech., Zurich, 1950-51; assoc. prof. Washington U., St. Louis, 1959-62, prof. math., 1962-88; ret. Washington U., 1988—; NSF sr. postdoctoral fellow Inst. for Advanced Study, Princeton, N.J., 1961-62, U. Geneva, Switzerland, 1965-66; professeur associe U. Strasbourg, France, 1971, 77. Author: Introduction to Differentiable Manifolds and Riemannian Geometry; co-editor: Symmetric Spaces; contbr. articles to profl. jours. Served with USAAF, 1942-46. Mem. Am., London math. Socs., Math. Assn. Am., Soc. Indsl. and Applied Math., Sigma Xi. Home: 6954 Cornell Ave Saint Louis MO 63130-3128 Office: Washington U Dept Math Saint Louis MO 63130

BOOTHE, EDWARD MILTON, aeronautical engineer, pilot; b. Springfield, Va., July 8, 1935; s. Avis Reynolds and Mary Roseanna (Burch) B.; m. Inez Gregory, Dec. 6, 1958; children: Timothy Edward, Amy Dolores, Suzanne Frances. B in Mech. Engring., George Washington U., 1958; MS, Tex. A&M U., 1965. Rsch. engr., engring. pilot Calspan Corp., Buffalo, N.Y., 1969-74; aero. engr. & pilot U.S. FAA, Washington, 1974-78; aero. engr. U.S. FAA, Atlanta, 1978-80, test pilot, 1980-82, simulator evaluator, 1982-83, mgr. simulation, 1983-93; ind. cons. flight simulation and tng. Stone Mountain, Ga., 1993—; mem. SAE Simulation Tech. Com., Warren, Pa., 1989-94, AIAA Flight Simulation Tech. Com., Washington, 1990-94. Author (standards manuals) Airplane Simulator Qualifications, 1989, Airplane Flight Training Device Qualifications, 1990, Helicopter Simulator Qualifications, 1991; contbr. articles to profl. jours. Exec. Atlanta Area coun. Boy Scouts Am., 1984; pres. Clan Sutherland Soc. of N.Am., 1991-95. With USAF, 1958-69. Recipient Sec.'s award U.S. Dept. Transp., Washington, 1989, Disting. Career Svc. award FAA, 1993, Kitty Hawk award FAA, 1993, Pres.'s Citation Flight Safety Found., 1997. Fellow AIAA (assoc., DeFlorez Tng. award 1993), Royal Aero. Soc. (Silver medal flight simulation 1993). Republican. Home and Office: 927 John Alden Rd Stone Mountain GA 30083-4755

BOOTHE, LEON ESTEL, university president emeritus, consultant; b. Carthage, Mo., Feb. 1, 1938; s. Harold Estel and Merle Jane (Hood) B.; m. Nancy Janes, Aug. 20, 1960 (dec. Jan. 1997); children: Cynthia, Diana and Cheri (twins). BS (Curators' scholar), U. Mo., 1960, MA, 1962; PhD in History, U. Ill., 1966; LLD, Kyung Hee U., Korea, St. Thomas Inst. Advanced Study, 1985, Hebrew Union Coll., 1994. Tchr. history Valparaiso (Ind.) High Sch., 1960-61; asst. prof. history U. Miss., Oxford, 1965-68; assoc. prof. U. Miss., 1968-70; assoc. prof. history George Mason Coll., U. Va. (now George Mason U.), Fairfax, 1970-73, prof. history, 1973-80, assoc. dean, 1970-71, dean, 1971-72, dean coll. arts and scis., 1972-80; provost, v.p. acad. affairs Ill. State U., Normal, 1980-83; pres. No. Ky. U., Highland Heights, 1983-96, pres. emeritus, 1996—; sr. advisor Nat. Underground R.R. Freedom Ctr., 1997—; bd. dirs. Am. Assn. of State Colls. and Univs., 1990-93, chmn., 1993, Coun. Internat. Edn. Exchange, 1993, Jessie Stewart Found., 1990, Greater Cin. Consortium Colls. and Univs., 1988-91, Commn. on Internat. Edn. of Am. Coun. Edn., 1988—. Former mem. adv. bd. Cin. Coun. World Affairs; trustee Cin.-Kharkiv Project, hon. mem., 1995-96; bd. dirs. Met. YMCA, Met. Cin. chpt. ARC, McLean County Heart Assn., McLean County United Way, INROADS/Cin., Inc., NCCJ, 1983—, Cin.'s Enjoy the Arts, 1988-90; vice chmn. No. Ky. United Way, chmn., 1988; Greater Cin. YMCA; mem. steering com. Cin. Bicentennial; chmn. Multiple Sclerosis Soc. Gifts Campaign; mem. steering and exec. coms. Cin. Youth Collaborative; co-chair blue ribbon econ. devel. study No. Ky. Area Devel. Dist.; mem. Leukemia Soc.; bd. dirs. Greater Cin. Conv. and Visitor's Bur., 1989—, May Festival, 1998, Kids Helping Kids, 1998—, Merc. Libr., 1998—, Festival of Arts, 1998—; bd. dirs., mem. exec. com., vice-chair cmty. edn. svcs., 1989-90, Cin. chpt. ARC, Wood Hudson Cancer Rsch. Lab. Inc., 1987-92; chmn. Ky. Bicentnnial Com., 1990, chmn. steering com., 1992; chmn. Leadership Ky. Class; trustee Greater Cin. United Way and Cmty. Chest, 1991; steering com. greater Cin. summit on racism, 1994; sr. advisor Nat. Underground Railroad freedom Ctr., 1997. NEH postdoctoral fellow, 1967-68; scholar Diplomat Seminars Dept. State; recipient Coll. Liberal Arts and Scis. award U. Ill., 1988, Alumni Coun. Pres.'s Spl. Recognition award No. Ky. U., 1989, Alumni award U. Mo., 1989, Walter R. Dunlevey Frontiersman award, 1994, Disting. Citizens Citation award NCCJ, Disting. Pub. Svc. award No. Ky. U. Found., 1995, Character award YMCA, 1997, Kinsman award Urban Appalachian Coun., 1998. Mem. Soc. Historians for Am. Fgn. Rels., McLean County Assn. for Commerce and Industry, Am. Assn. State Colls. and Univs. (internat. programs com. 1986-94), No. Ky. C. of C. (Walter R. Dunlevey-Frontierman award 1994), Greater Cin. C. of C. (asst. sec.-treas. 1989), Rotary, Masons, Sigma Rho Sigma, Omicron Delta Kappa, Phi Alpha Theta, Phi Delta Kappa. Home: 3435 Golden Ave #901 Cincinnati OH 45226-2020 Office: No Ky U Office of Pres 800 Ken Lucas Ctr Highland Heights KY 41099-8002

BOOTHE, POWER, visual artist, filmmaker, set designer; b. Dallas, Mar. 12, 1945; s. Tom Wheeler and Shirlee (Barth) B.; m. Sarah Schoentgen, Mar. 22, 1969 (div. 1974); m. Elizabeth Rheem Rectanus, Aug. 17, 1980 (div. 1989); m. Lynne Steincamp, May 12, 1998. BA, Colo. Coll., Colorado Springs, 1969, D Arts (hon.), 1989. Fellow ind. study program Whitney Mus., 1967-68; educator, instr. painting Sch. Visual Arts, N.Y.C., 1979-88; assoc. prof. Princeton U., 1989-95; artist and critic-in-residence Md. Inst. Coll. Art, Balt., 1993—, acting dir. grad. Painting Sch., 1994-95; dir. Sch. Art, Ohio U., Athens, 1998—; guest artist SUNY, Buffalo, 1981, U. Iowa, Ames, 1979, Ohio Wesleyan U., 1986, N.Y. Studio Sch., 1987, San Francisco Art Inst., 1987; guest instr. N.Y. Studio Sch., 1987, Md. Art Inst., 1990, Bard Coll., 1990. Exhibited one-man shows A.M. Sachs Gallery, N.Y., 1973, 74, 77, 81, 82, 95, Inst. Contemporary Art, Boston, 1984, Lynne Mayhew Gallery, Ohio, 1984-86, Souyun Yi Gallery, N.Y., 1987, 89, Harrison Gallery, Boca Raton, Fla., 1989, Trenkmann Gallery, 1991, Robert Morrison Gallery, N.Y.C., 1992, Stephen Haller Gallery, 1995; group shows throughout U.S.; represented in permanent collections including Solomon R. Guggenheim Mus., Mus. Modern Art, N.Y.C., Hirschhorn Mus., and Sculpture Garden, Washington, Whitney Mus. Am. Art, Stanford (Calif.) U. Mus. Art, Chase Manhattan Bank, N.Y. Bank for Savs., Lehman Bros. Kuhn Loeb, Inc., Phillip Morris Corp., Sony Corp., Estee Lauder Corp.; set designer Bklyn. Acad. Opera House, 1986, Lynn Austin's Music Theater, 1982, Dance Theater Workshop, 1981-85, 87, 88, 91, Performing Garage, 1978, Guggenheim Mus., 1970, Loeb Theatre, Cambridge, Mass., 1986, San Francisco Opera House, 1987, Danny Kaye Theatre, N.Y., 1993, Paramount Theatre, Oakland, Calif., others; also prodr., dir., art dir. various short exptl. film; film showings: The Kitchen for Music, Film and Video, 1985, Collective for Living Cinema, 1987, San Francisco Cinema Theatre, 1987. Recipient Theodoron award Guggenheim Mus., 1971, Bessie award, 1984, Film Video, Angel award, 1989; Nat. Endowment Arts grantee, 1975, 83, 84, 87; N.Y. State Coun. grantee, 1982-86, 89, 91; Lila Wallace/Reader's Digest grantee, 1992; Pollack Krasner Found. grantee, 1989; Guggenheim Found. fellow, 1985. Address: Sch of Art Seigfred Hall Ohio U Sch Art Seigfred Hall Athens OH 45701

BOOTH GILLIAM, DIANE LORRAINE, yoga instructor, former philosophy educator; b. Ft. Benton, Mont., Sept. 4, 1957; d. Fred Van and Melba Laurel (Joslin) Booth; m. John Howard Gilliam, Aug. 9, 1991. BA in Philosophy, Mont. State U., 1988; MA in Philosophy, U. Mont., 1992. Sys. support technician United Software Tech., Billings, Mont., 1988; prof. philosophy U. Gt. Falls, Mont., 1992-98; yoga inst., yoga retreat facilitator, Missoula, Mont., 1998—. Freeman scholar Mont. State U., 1985-87, Erasmus scholar U. Mont., 1988-90. Avocations: yoga, oriental med. and philos. traditions, travel. Office: Coll of Gt Falls 1301 20th St S Great Falls MT 59405-4934

BOOTHROYD, GEOFFREY, industrial and manufacturing engineering educator; b. Radcliffe, Eng., Nov. 18, 1932; came to U.S., 1967; s. Arthur and Annie (Fletcher) B.; m. Shirley Lewis, Apr. 10, 1954; children: Janet Kaye, Lynda Jean. BS in Engring., U. London, 1956, PhD in Engring., 1962, DSc in Engring., 1974. Apprentice Mather & Platt Ltd., Manchester, Eng., 1948-56, designer, 1956-57; designer English Electric Co. Ltd., Leicester, Eng., 1957-58; lectr., reader Salford (Eng.) U., 1958-67; prof. U. Mass., Amherst, 1967-85; prof. U. R.I., Kingston, 1985-97, prof. emeritus; vis. prof. Ga. Inst. Tech., Atlanta, 1964-65; cons. mfg. industries, U.K. and U.S., also various pubs.; pres. Boothroyd Dewhurst, Inc. Author: Fundamentals of Metal Machining, 1965; (with A.H. Redford) Mechanized Assembly, 1968 (Japanese 1969), Fundamentals of Metal Machining and Machine Tools, 1975 (Spanish 1978, internat. student edit. 1979), (with others) Introduction to Engineering, 1975, (with C.R. Poli) Applied Engineering Mechanics, 1980, (with C.R. Poli, L.E. Murch) Automatic Assembly, 1980, Handbook of Feeding and Orienting Techniques for Small Parts, (with L. Alting) Manufacturing Engineering Prcesses, 1982, (with P. Dewhurst) Design for Assembly Handbook, Design for Robot Assembly, 1985, (with W.A. Knight) Metal Machining and Machine Tools, 1991, Assembly Automation and Product Design, 1992, (with P. Dewhurst and W.A. Knight) Product Design for Manufacture and Assembly, 1994. Recipient Teaching award Western Electric, 1969, Sr. Scholar award U. Mass., 1982, Sci. and Tech. award R.I. Gov., 1989, Nat. medal of Technology, U.S. Dept. Commerce Technology Admin., 1991, Providence Engring. Soc., 1991, UK Mensforth Internat. Gold medal Inst. Elec. Engrs., 1993; grantee NSF, 1967-87, GE, 1967, 69, 81, 83, AMP Inc., 1978, 81-84, IBM, 1983-85, AT&T, 1985, Ford Motor Co., 1984, 86, others. Fellow Soc. Mfg. Engrs.; mem. NAE. Avocations: squash, tennis, golf, painting. Office: Boothroyd Dewhurst Inc 138 Main St Ste 2 Wakefield RI 02879-3574

BOOTHROYD, HERBERT J., insurance company executive; b. Mason City, Iowa, Dec. 23, 1928; s. Herbert L. and Clara (Schmitt) B.; m. Barbara Elizabeth Dunne, Feb. 9, 1961; children: Diane Lea, John Herbert. AB, U. Mich., 1952, AM, 1953. Enrolled actuary, 1976. With Mass. Mut. Life Ins. Co., 1953-57; with New Eng. Mut. Life Ins. Co., Boston, 1957-87; v.p. New Eng. Mut. Life Ins. Co., 1967-77, sr. v.p. pension ops., 1977-82, exec. v.p. group ops., 1983-87; dir. New Eng. Pension and Annuity Co., 1980-87, pres., 1981-87; pres., dir. New Eng. Gen. Life, 1983-85; dir. New Eng. Mut. Life Ins. Co., 1984-87, New Eng. Variable Life Ins. Co., 1984-97. Contbg. author: Life and Health Insurance Handbook, 1973. Bd. dirs. New Eng. chpt. Am. Diabetes Assn., 1979-84; bd. govs. Handel and Haydn Soc., 1984-94, sec., 1986-94, overseer, 1994—; mem. nat. campaign com. U. Mich., 1983-90; bd. dirs. Better Bus. Bur. Ea. Mass., 1980-88, vice chmn., mem. exec. com., 1985-88. Fellow Soc. Actuaries; mem. SAR, Am. Acad. Actuaries, Internat. Congress Actuaries, New Eng. Hist. Geneal. Soc., U. Mich. Alumni Assn. (v.p. 1st dist. 1989-91, pres. 1991-93, nat. bd. dirs. and clubs coun. 1997—), Phi Beta Kappa, Theta Delta Chi. Fax: 781-894-5794. E-mail: herbbooth@aol.com. Home and Office: 51 Indian Hill Rd Weston MA 02493-2163

BOOTLE, WILLIAM AUGUSTUS, retired federal judge; b. Colleton County, S.C., Aug. 19, 1902; s. Philip Lorraine and Laura Lilla (Benton) B.; m. Virginia Childs, Nov. 24, 1928; children: William Augustus, Ann, James C. AB, Mercer U., 1924, LLB, 1925, LLD, 1982. Bar: Ga. 1925. Since practiced in Macon; U.S. dist. atty. Middle Ga. Dist., 1929-33; mem. firm Carlisle & Bootle, 1933-54; acting dean Law Sch., Mercer U., 1933-37, part-time prof. law, 1928-43; judge U.S. Dist. Ct. for Middle Dist. Ga., Macon, 1954-81; sr. judge U.S. Dist. Ct. for Middle Dist. Ga., 1972-81. Trustee Mercer U., 1933-79, chmn. exec. com., 1941-46, 48-53, life trustee, 1994—; trustee Walter F. George Sch. Law Found., 1961—, v.p., 1963-64, 83-86, pres., 1964-66, 86-88. Recipient Disting. Alumnus award Mercer U., 1971, Disting. Alumnus award Walter F. George Sch. Law, 1986. Mem. Phi Alpha Delta, Phi Delta Theta. Republican. Baptist. Clubs: Masons, Shriners, Civitan (pres. 1936).

BOOTY, JOHN EVERITT, historiographer; b. Detroit, May 2, 1925; s. George Thomas and Alma (Gamauf) B.; m. Catherine Louise Smith, June 10, 1950; children: Carol Holland, Geoffrey Rollen, Peter Thomas, Catherine Jane. B.A., Wayne State U., 1952; B.D., Va. Theol. Sem., 1953, DD, 1994; DD, U. of the South, 1997; M.A., Princeton U., 1957, Ph.D., 1960. Ordained to ministry Episcopal Ch., 1953. Curate Christ Episcopal Ch., Dearborn, Mich., 1953-55; asst. prof. ch. history Va. Theol. Sem., 1958-64, assoc. prof., 1964-67; prof. ch. history Episcopal Theol. Sch., Cambridge, Mass., 1967-82; acting dir. Inst. Theol. Rsch., 1974-76; dean Sch. Theology U. of South, Sewanee, Tenn., 1982-85, prof. Anglican studies, 1984-90, prof. emeritus, 1990—, historiographer Episc. Ch., 1988—; vis. prof., rsch. Yale Div. Sch., 1985-86; Disting. vis. prof. Episcopal Divinity Sch., 1990-91, prof. emeritus, 1991—; vis. prof. Anglican studies Gen. Theol. Seminary, 1992; Trotter vis. prof. Va. Theol. Sem., 1993, 98. Author: John Jewel as Apologist of the Church of England, 1963, Yearning to be Free, 1974, Three Anglican Divines on Prayer: Jewel, Andrewes, and Hooker, 1978, The Church in History, 1979, The Spirit of Anglicanism, 1979, The Godly Kingdom of Tudor England, 1981, The Servant Church, 1982, What Makes Us Episcopalians, 1982, Anglican Spirituality, 1982, Anglican Moral Choice, 1983, The Christ We Know, 1987, The Episcopal Church in Crisis, 1988, Mission and Ministry: A History of the Virginia Theological Seminary, 1996, An American Apostle: A Biography of Stephen F. Bayne, 1997, Reflections on the Theology of Richard Hooker: An Elizabethan Addresses Modern Anglicanism, 1999; editor: The Book of Common Prayer, 1559: The Elizabeth Prayer Book, 1976, John Jewel: The Apology of the Church of England, 1963, 74, John Donne: Divine Poems, Sermons, Meditations and Prayers, 1990, The Works of Richard Hooker, vol. 4, 1982; co-editor, contbr.: The Study of Anglicanism, 1988; contbr. articles to profl. jours. Chmn. Nat. Youth Commn., P.F. Ch., 1948-50; chmn. bd. St. Luke's Jour. Theology, 1987-91, Sewanee Theol. Rev., 1991—. Recipient Am. Philos. Soc. award, 1964; Folger Shakespeare Libr. fellow, 1964, NEH fellow, 1978-79. Mem. Soc. for Promoting Christian Knowlege (vice chmn. 1984-87). Home: 612 Mt Israel Rd Center Sandwich NH 03227-3710

BOOZ, GRETCHEN ARLENE, marketing executive; b. Boone, Iowa, Nov. 24, 1933; d. David Gerald and Katherine Bevridge (Hardie) Berg; m. Donald Rollett Booz, Sept. 3, 1960; children: Kendra Sue (dec.), Joseph David, Katherine Sue. AA, Graceland Coll., 1955. Med. asst. Robert A. Hayne M.D., Des Moines, 1955-61; mktg. dir. Herald Pub. House, Independence, Mo., 1975—. Author: (book) Kendra, 1979. Mem. Citizens Adv. Bd., Blue Springs, Mo., 1979-91, Independence Mayor's Christmas Concert Com., 1987-91; bd. dirs. Comprehensive Mental Health, 1981-83, Child Placement Svcs., Independence, 1987-94, Hope House, Inc., Independence, 1987-91, Ctr. for Profl. Devel. and Life-long Learning, Inc., 1995-96; trustee Graceland Coll., Lamoni, Iowa, 1984-96. Mem. Leadership Edn. Action Devel. (L.E.A.D.), Independence C. of C. (diplomat, Outstanding Mem. award 1981), Rotary. Republican. Mem. Reorganized Ch. Jesus Christ Latter Day Saints. Avocation: writing and presenting monologues of women in history. Home: 1200 Crestview Dr Blue Springs MO 64014-2312 Office: Herald Pub House 3225 S Noland Rd Independence MO 64055-1317

BOOZE, THOMAS FRANKLIN, toxicologist; b. Denver, Mar. 4, 1955; s. Ralph Walker and Ann (McNatt) B.; children: Heather N., Ian T. BS, U. Calif., Davis, 1978; MS, Kans. State U., 1981, PhD, 1985. Registered environ assessor, Calif. Asst. instr. Kans. State U., Manhattan, 1979-85; consulting toxicologist Chevron Corp., Sacramento, 1985-92; sr. toxicologist Radian Internat., Sacramento, 1992—; cons. in field, Manhattan, Kans., 1981-83. contbr. articles to profl. jours. Vol. Amigos de las Americas, Marin County, Calif., 1973, Hospice Care, Manhattan, 1985. Mem. N.Y. Acad. Sci., Soc. Toxicology, Soc. for Risk Analysis, Sigma Xi. Home: 8338 Titian Ridge Ct Antelope CA 95843-5627 Office: Radian Corp 10389 Old Placerville Rd Sacramento CA 95827-2506

BOOZELL, MARK ELDON, state official; b. Mason City, Iowa, Mar. 4, 1955; s. Eldon Dwayne Boozell and Betty Jean (Gordon) Kruger; m. Susan Elizabeth Abelt, Nov. 26, 1977; children: Kari Elizabeth, Lindsay Patricia. BA, Augustana Coll., 1977. Budget analyst rep. staff Ill. Ho. of Reps., Springfield, 1977-78, dep. dir. rep. staff, 1978-80; legis. liaison Ill. Dept. Transp., Springfield, 1980-83; dir. legis. affairs Ill. Sec. State, Springfield, 1983-95; chief of staff Office of Gov., State of Ill., Springfield, 1998—. Named one of Outstanding Young Men Am., 1980. Republican. Lutheran. Home: 78 Stony Creek Dr Chatham IL 62629-1551 Office: State of Ill Office of Gov Capitol Bldg Rm 207 Springfield IL 62706*

BOOZER, HOWARD RAI, retired state education official; b. Monterey, Ky., Aug. 14, 1923; s. Claud D. and Harriet Ruth (Foster) B.; m. Frances Aileen Kintner, Aug. 23, 1946; children: Claudia, Margaret, Catherine, Barbara. Diploma, Cumberland (Ky.) Coll., 1942; AB, Howard Coll., 1946; BS, Washington U., St. Louis, 1948, MEd, 1948, PhD, 1960; LLD (hon.), Baptist Coll. at Charleston, S.C., 1976; LittD (hon.), Lander Coll., 1986; LHD (hon.), Cumberland Coll., 1990. Asst. personnel dir. Mall Tool Co., Chgo., 1946-47; tchr. high sch. Webster Groves, Mo., 1949-51; staff assoc. Am. Council Edn., Washington, 1954-61; acting dir. Washington Internat. Center, 1957-58; asst. dir. N.C. Bd. Higher Edn., Raleigh, 1961-65, dir., 1965-68; v.p. Regional Edn. Lab., Durham, N.C., 1968-70; dir. Ednl. Devel. Adminstrn. RCA Corp., Cherry Hill, N.J., 1970-73; exec. dir. S.C. Commn. on Higher Edn., Columbia, 1973-86; adj. prof. edn. Duke U., 1968-70; mem. review panel for constrn. of nurse tng. facilities USPHS, 1965-69. Trustee Meredith Coll., 1963-66, Wingate Coll., 1967-70; bd. dirs. Learning Inst. N.C., 1965-68, Nat. League Nursing, 1973-77; S.C. del. Edn. Commn. of States, 1974-79; pres. N.C. League of Nursing, 1969-70; mem. So. Regional Edn. Bd., 1974-86. Lt. USNR, 1943-46, 51-54, ret. capt. Mem. Am. Assn. Higher Edn., Golden K Kiwanis. Democrat.

BOOZER, JAMES L., federal agency administrator. AA, Phoenix Coll., 1962; student, Ariz. State U., 1962-65, 75-78. Cmty. rels. specialist City of Phoenix, 1970-72, pub. housing asst., 1972-75, asst. pub. housing dir., 1975-77, project ops. adminstr., 1977, acting property conservation adminstr., 1977-78, asst. dir. neighborhood improvement housing dept., 1978-92, asst. dir. housing dept., 1992-96, acting housing dir., 1996—. Office: Housing Dept Calvin C Goode Bldg 251 W Washington St Fl 4 Phoenix AZ 85003-2201*

BOPP, THOMAS THEODORE, university administrator, chemistry educator; b. Glendale, Calif., Nov. 29, 1941; s. Clarence Hardecke and Mildred Lorine (Eggers) B.; m. Judith May Creamer, June 9, 1962 (div. 1972); children: William Richard, Christopher Paul; m. Georgia Ann Kinney, Apr. 22, 1973; children: Patricia Jayne, Jon Scott. BS, Calif. Inst. Tech., 1963; PhD, Harvard U., 1968. Asst. prof. chemistry U. Hawaii, Manoa, Honolulu, 1967-72, assoc. prof. chemistry, 1972-85, prof. chemistry, 1985—, asst. v.p., 1995—; chair chemistry dept., U. Hawaii, Manoa, 1992-95, chair faculty senate, 1991-92. Mem. Oahu Choral Soc. Avocation: choral music. Office: Univ Hawaii OSVP/EVC 2444 Dole St # 105 Honolulu HI 96822-2399

BOR, JONATHAN STEVEN, journalist; b. Washington, Sept. 22, 1953; s. Robert Myer and Judith Anne (Harkavy) B.; m. Sally Diane Mericle, June 3, 1984; 1 child, Benjamin Andrew. B.A. in History, Oberlin Coll., 1975; M.S. in Journalism, Columbia U., 1982. Editor Millbrook Round Table, N.Y., 1976-77; editor Rhinebeck Gazette-Advertiser, N.Y., 1977; reporter Poughkeepsie Jour., N.Y., 1977-81, Syracuse Post-Standard, N.Y., 1983-87, Balt. Sun, 1988—. Recipient Disting. Writing award Am. Soc. Newspaper Editors, 1985; 1st place award for spot news reporting UPI, 1985, 1st place for feature stories, 1986; 1st place for feature stories AP, 1986, Mark Twain award, 1990; 2d place in pub. svc. Md.-Del.-D.C. Press Assn., 1989, 2d place in features Md.-Del.-D.C. Press Assn., 1991, 1st place in med. reporting, 1998. Mem. Nat. Assn. Sci. Writers. Jewish. Home: 6214 Woodcrest Ave Baltimore MD 21209-3935 Office: Baltimore Sun Calvert St Baltimore MD 21225-1747

BORAH, KRIPANATH, pharmacist; b. Calcutta, India, Mar. 1, 1931; s. Ambicanath and Gunabati (Barooah) B.; married; children: Shambhunath, Arun. BS, Calcutta U., 1952, MS, 1956; PhD, U. Munich, 1961. Mgr. R&D Ciba-Geigy, Bombay, India, 1962-76; rsch. assoc. Boston Coll., Boston, 1976-77; group leader W.H. Rorer & Co., Ft. Washington, Pa., 1977-80; dir. pharm. devel. Organon Inc., W. Orange, N.J., 1980-91; assoc. dir. Enzon Inc., S. Plainfield, N.J., 1991-92; sci. dir. G & W Labs., S. Plainfield, N.J., 1992-96; sci. dir., head R&D Tomer Labs., 1997—; adj. prof. Temple U. Sch. Pharm., Phila., 1991—. Fellow Alexander von Humboldt Found., 1959-61. Mem. Am. Chem. Soc., Am. Assn. Pharm. Sci., Am. Assn. Indian Pharm. Scientists. Home: 34 Overlook Trl Morris Plains NJ 07950-1924 Office: Tomer Labs 4W Chimney Rock Rd Bound Brook NJ 08805-1148

BORAN, ROBERT PAUL, JR., orthopedic surgeon; b. Pottsville, Pa., May 21, 1952; s. Robert Paul Sr. and Ellen Elizabeth (Reisig) B.; m. Catherine Virginia Kling, Oct. 18, 1980; children: Catherine, Ellen, Mary. BS, St. Joseph U., 1974; MD, Jefferson Med. Coll., 1978. Diplomate Am. Bd. Orthop. Surgery. Lab. technician Pottsville Hosp., 1972-74; disc jockey WPPA-AM and WAVT-FM, Pottsville, 1972-75; intern Pa. Hosp., Phila., 1978-79; resident in orthop. surgery Thomas Jefferson U. Hosp., Phila., 1979-83; chief resident Alfred I. DuPont Inst. of Nemours Found. Crippled

Children, Wilmington, Del., 1981, U.S. VA Hosp., Wilmington; pvt. practice Pottsville, 1983—; mem. clin. adj. faculty dept. allied health sci. Kings Coll., Wilkes Barre, Pa. Bd. dirs. Schuylkill Rehab. Ctr., 1987—, chmn. bd. dirs, 1988—. Fellow ACS, Internat. Coll. Surgeons, Am. Acad. Orthopaedic Surgeons; mem. AMA, Pa. Med. Soc., Schuylkill County Med. Soc., Am. Assn. Hip and Knee Surgeons, Assn. Arthritic Hip and Knee Surgeons, Ea. Orthopaedic Assn., Pa. Orthopaedic Soc., N.Am. Faculty of Swiss Assn. for Study of Internal Fixation of Fractures, AO Alumni N.Am., Jefferson Orthopaedic Soc., Alfred I. DuPont Inst. Alumni Assn., Thomas Bond Soc. of Pa. Hosp., Union League of Phila., Schuylkill Country Club, Vesper Club, Pottsville Club, Skytop Club, Fountain Springs Country Club, Ancient Order of Hibernians, Elks, Alpha Sigma Nu. Republican. Roman Catholic. Avocations: golf, cards. Home: 146 Glenworth Rd Pottsville PA 17901-9595 Office: Bldg 100 101 Schuylkill Medical Plz Pottsville PA 17901-3661

BORAZ, ROBERT ALAN, dentist, surgery and pediatrics educator; b. St. Louis, Apr. 13, 1951; s. Herbert Sigmund and Pearl Yetta (Garber) B.; m. Janet Ruth Knie, Jan. 3, 1981; children: Jonathan Daniel, Katharine Elizabeth. Student, U. Mo., 1969-72, DDS, 1975, postgrad., 1975-77. Resident Children's Mercy Hosp., Kansas City, Mo., 1975-77; dir. dental svc. U. Kans. Med. Ctr., Kansas City, 1977-96, prof. surgery, 1984-96; assoc. prof. U. Mo. Dental Sch., Kansas City, 1977-96, chief dentistry Children's Rehab. Unit, Kansas City, 1977-96; assoc. dir. Sutherland Inst. Facial Rehab., Kansas City, 1984-96; specialty examiner Mo. Dental Bd., Jefferson City, Mo., 1987-96. Contbr. articles to profl. jours. Mem. Gov.'s Task Force on Hemophilia, Topeka, 1984-86; mem. prof. edn. com. Am. Cancer Soc., Topeka, 1987-96; mem. regional bd. Easter Seal Soc., Greater Kansas City, 1979-82; trustee Am. Soc. of Dentistry for Children, 1989-96. Fellow Am. Coll. Dentists, Internat. Coll. Dentists, Am. Acad. Pediatric Dentistry (component pres. 1984-96, trustee 1991-94, parliamentarian 1994-96, sec.-treas. 1996-97, v.p. 1997-98, pres.-elect 1998-99, pres. 1999—), Am. Soc. Dentistry for Children (Kans. pres. 1988-96, bd. trustees 1989-93, Cert. of Merit 1976), Am. Assn. Hosp. Dentists, Acad. Dentistry for the Handicapped; mem. ADA, S.W. Soc. Pediatric Dentistry (v.p. 1988-89, pres.-elect 1992, pres. 1992-93), Alpha Omega (local pres. 1973-75), Omicron Kappa Upsilon. Office: Ste 330 200 W County Line Rd Highlands Ranch CO 80126-2342

BORCH, RICHARD FREDERIC, pharmacology and chemistry educator; b. Cleve., May 22, 1941; s. Fred J. and Martha (Kananen) B.; m. Anne Wright Wilson, Sept. 8, 1962; children: Karen, Eric. BS, Stanford U., 1962; MA, PhD, Columbia U., 1965; MD, U. Minn., 1975. NIH postdoctoral fellow Harvard U., Cambridge, Mass., 1965-66; prof. chemistry U. Minn., Mpls., 1966-82, med. resident, 1975-76; dean's prof. pharmacology, prof. chemistry, dir. Cancer Ctr. U. Rochester, N.Y., 1982—; now dept. head medicinal chemistry & molecular pharmacology Perdue U., Lafayette, Ind.; dir. U. Rochester Cancer Ctr., 1993—; mem. cancer rsch. manpower com. Nat. Cancer Inst., 1982-86, chmn. cancer rsch. manpower rev. com. 1984-86; cons. 3M Pharms., St. Paul, 1972—. Contbr. over 70 articles to profl. jours.; patentee in field. Recipient Coll. Chemistry Tchr. award Minn. sect. Am. Chem. Soc., 1982, Louis P. Hammett award Columbia U., 1965, James P. Wilmot Disting. Professorship, U. Rochester, 1983-86; Alfred P. Sloan Found. fellow, 1970-72. Mem. Am. Chem. Soc., Am. Assn. Cancer Research, Am. Soc. Pharmacology Exptl. Therapeutics, AAAS. Office: Dept Medicinal Chemistry & Molecular Pharmacology Perdue U Lafayette IN 47907*

BORCHARDT, DONALD ARTHUR, visual and performing arts educator; b. St. Paul, June 4, 1931; s. Herbert Friedrich Gustav and Rosalie Bertha Hulda (Sahnow) B.; m. Audrey Anne Rayfield, June 15, 1957. BA, U. Minn., 1953, MA, 1958; PhD, U. Utah, 1960. Instr. U. Minn., St. Paul, 1953; asst. prof. U. Wis., River Falls, 1960-61, Macalester Coll., St. Paul, 1961-64, U. Fla., Gainesville, 1964-67; asst. prof. Rutgers U., Newark, 1967-73, assoc. prof., 1973-93, prof. emeritus, 1993—; pres. East Ctrl. Theatre Conf., 1982-84; adjudicator Am. Coll. Theatre Festival, 1972-86. Author: Think Tank Theatre, 1984; artist exhibit Forms in Space and Movement, 1991. With U.S. Army, 1953-55. Recipient AMOCO gold medallion award of excellence for svc. Am. Coll. Theatre Festival, Washington, 1977. Fellow Internat. Soc. for Exploring Tchg. Alternatives; mem. Internat. Soc. Individualized Instrn. (pres. 1985-86), Assn. Theatre in Higher Edn. (treas. 1987-89), Phi Kappa Phi, Phi Gamma Delta.

BORCHARDT, PAUL DOUGLAS, recreational executive; b. Osage, Iowa, Nov. 2, 1942; s. Raymond E. and Olive M. (Johnson) B.; m. Paula Ruth Roads, June 8, 1965; children: Rebecca, Kristen, Keira, Paige. BBA, U. Okla., 1965; MBA, West Tex. State U., 1973. Gen. mgr., pres. Wonderland Amusements Inc., Amarillo, Tex., 1969—; pres. Borchardt's Coin Machines Inc., Amarillo, 1969—; owner Buffalo Nickel Family Fun Inc., 1996—. Bd. dirs. Panhandle Hotel/Motel Assn., Amarillo, 1982-86, Tex. War on Drugs, 1993-96; mem. fin. adv. bd. Golden Spread coun. Boy Scouts Am., 1993-94; founding bd. dirs. Amarillo Drug Task Force, 1993. Mem. Internat. Assn. Amusement Parks and Attractions (bd. dirs. 1983-87, 88-91, chmn. pub. rels. com. 1986, fin. com. 1994-95, sustaining fin. com. 1994,, edn. com. 1996—), Amusement Music Operators Am., Amusement Music Operators Tex. (v.p. 1987-88, pres. 1988-90), Am. Mktg. Assn. (bd. dirs. Amarillo chpt. 1987-88), Tex. Family Amusement Assn. (v.p. 1997—), Amarillo C. of C. (chmn. conv. and tourism coun. 1988-90, exec. bd. 1989, Community Asset award 1989, Vol. of the Yr. award 1990, bus. com. of C. of C., 1994-96), Amarillo Exec. Assn. (pres. 1979-80, treas. 1977-78), Rotary (chmn. art show 1990, bd. dirs. 1992-95), Rotary Club Amarillo (pres. 1994-95, asst. dist. gov. 1998—). Democrat. Lutheran. Avocations: snow skiing, travel, fishing. Home: 3915 Kileen Dr Amarillo TX 79109-3921 Office: Wonderland Amusements Inc PO Box 2509 Amarillo TX 79105-2509

BORCHERDING, THOMAS EARL, economist; b. Cin., Feb. 18, 1939; s. Earl Schaff and Vivian Joan (Miller) B.; m. Rhoda Jean Larson, Nov. 23, 1968; children: Matthew James, Benjamin Adam. BA, U. Cin., 1961; PhD, Duke U., 1966. Asst. prof. U. Wash., Seattle, 1966-71; assoc. prof. Va. Polytech Inst., Blacksboro, 1971-73; prof. econs. Simon Fraser U., Burnaby, B.C., Can., 1973-83; prof. law and econs. U. Toronto (Ont., Can.), 1978-79; prof. econs. Claremont (Calif.) Grad. U., 1983—; editl. bd. CATO Jour., Washington; bd. of advisors Ind. Inst., Oakland, Calif., 1990—. Author: The Egg Board: The Social Cast of Monopoly, 1981; contbr. articles to profl. jours. NDEA fellow Duke U., 1961-64, postdoctoral fellow U. Va., 1965-66, Hoover Instn., Stanford U., 1974-75, Avery fellow Claremont U. Ctr., 1988-97. Mem. Am. Econ. Assn., Western Econ. Assn. (editor 1980-97), Can. Econ. Assn., Pub. Choice Soc., Mont Pelerin Soc., Phi Beta Kappa, Omicron Delta Epsilon, Phi Delta Theta. Republican. Home: 1374 Tulane Rd Claremont CA 91711-3420 Office: Claremont Grad U Sch Politics & Econs Claremont CA 91711

BORCHERS, KAREN LILY, museum administrator; b. Detroit, Apr. 4, 1940; d. Albert Oscar and Lily Louise (Denzler) B. BA in Psychology and Sociology, Mich. State U., 1961; AM in Social Svc. Adminstrn., U. Chgo., 1964; MS in Spl. Edn. Adminstrn., No. Ill. U., 1976; EdD in Early Childhood Edn./Adminstrn., Nova U., 1982. Cert. social worker. Child welfare worker Ill. Dept. Children & Family Svcs., Rockford, 1962-65; sch. social worker Komarek Schs., N. Riverside, Ill., 1965-67; exec. dir. Seguin Sch., Berwyn, Ill., 1967-72, Seguin Tng. Ctr., Cicero, Ill., 1967-72; adminstr. Orchard Hill, Madison, Wis., 1972-76; exec. dir. Children's Home Soc. Fla., West Palm Beach, 1976-96, Hist. Soc. Palm Beach County, 1997—; pres. Pathways to Growth, Inc., West Palm Beach, 1986—. Pres., founder Masterworks Chorus of the Palm Beaches, West Palm Beach, 1978—, Teen Musical Theatre, Inc., West Palm Beach, 1984—, Internat. Children's Chorus of the Palm Beaches, West Palm Beach, 1988-90; pres. Palm Beach Regional Achievement Ctr., West Palm Beach, 1979-84. Recipient Excellence in Health and Social Svcs. award Palm Beach County Commn., 1979. Mem. NASW, Civitan, Mensa. Avocations: travel, reading, choral music, instrumental music, bicycling. Home: 11984 Suellen Cir West Palm Beach FL 33414-6274 Office: Hist Soc Palm Beach County 400 N Dixie Hwy West Palm Beach FL 33401-4210

BORCHERS, RICHARD M., federal judge; b. 1945. AB, Ripon Coll., 1968; JD, U. Colo., 1970, MA, 1986. Bar: Colo. Assoc. Stitt, Wittenbrink and Roan, P.C., 1975-76; pvt. practice, Denver, 1976-84, dist. judge for 17th jud. dist., 1984-91; magistrate judge for Colo., U.S. Ct., Denver, 1991—; instr. U. Colo. Sch. Bus., Denver, 1976-80, U. Colo., 1989, Met. State Coll., Denver, 1989-90. Co-author: Colorado Juvenile Law: Case and Materials, 1991. With JAGC, U.S. Army, 1971-74. Mem. Colo. Bar Assn., D.C. Bar Assn. Office: US Courthouse 1929 Stout St Rm C-334 Denver CO 80294-0001

BORCHERT, DONALD MARVIN, philosopher, educator; b. Edmonton, Alta., Can., May 23, 1934; s. Leo Ferdinand and Lillian Violet (Bucholz) B.; m. Mary Ellen Cockrell, Dec. 27, 1960; children: Carol Ellen, John Witherspoon. AB, U. Alta., Edmonton, 1955; BD, Princeton Theol. Sem., 1958, PhD, 1966; ThM, Ea. Bapt. Theol. Sem., 1959. Teaching fellow Princeton (N.J.) Theol. Sem., 1960-61; asst. prof. Juniata Coll., Huntingdon, Pa., 1966-67; asst. prof. Ohio U., Athens, 1967-71, assoc. prof., 1971-75, prof. philosophy, 1975—, assoc. dean Coll. Arts and Scis., 1980-86, chmn. dept. philosophy, 1987—. Author: Being Human in a Technological Age, 1979, Introduction to Modern Philosophy, 1981, 6th edit., 1994, Exploring Ethics, 1986, Medical Ethics, 1992, Philosophy of Sex and Love, 1997; editor in chief: Encyclopedia of Philosophy Supplement, 1996, Compendium of Philosophy and Ethics, 1999; contbr. articles to profl. jours. Assoc. Danforth Found. Nat. Humanities Inst. fellow, 1976-77; NEH Implementation grantee, 1981. Mem. Ohio Philos. Assn. (v.p. 1983-85, pres. 1985-90), Ohio Humanities Council (vice chmn. 1981-83, chmn. 1983-85). Presbyterian. Home: 9 Coventry Ln Athens OH 45701-3717 Office: Ohio U Dept Philosophy Ellis Hall Athens OH 45701

BORCHERT, JOHN ROBERT, geography educator; b. Chgo., Oct. 24, 1918; s. Ernest J. and Maude (Gorndt) B.; m. Jane Anne Willson, June 10, 1942; children: Dianne, William, Robert, David. A.B., DePauw U., 1941; M.A., U. Wis., 1946, Ph.D., 1949. Instr. geography U. Wis., 1947-49; asst. prof. U. Minn., Mpls., 1949-51; assoc. prof. U. Minn., 1951-56, prof., 1956-81, Regent's prof., 1981-89, Regent's prof. emeritus, 1989—, chmn. dept. geography, 1956-61; urban research dir. Upper Midwest econ. study, 1961-64; dir. Center for Urban and Regional Affairs, 1968-77; chmn. earth scis. div. Nat. Acad. Scis.-NRC, 1967-69; mem. corp. Social Sci. Research Council, 1968—. Author: America's Northern Heartland, 1987, also publs. on urbanization and resource devel. in U.S., 1961—, frequency and distbn. of drought in Cen. N.Am., 1949-71. Served to major USAAF, World War II. Fellow Am. Acad. Arts and Scis.; mem. Nat. Acad. Scis., Assn. Am. Geographers (past pres., Honors award 1976), Am. Geog. Soc. (Van Cleef medal 1970), Nat. Council Geog. Edn. (Master Tchr. award 1985). Home: 23239 St Croix Trl N Scandia MN 55073-9725

BORCHERT, WARREN FRANK, elementary education educator; b. Faribault, Minn., Mar. 5, 1948; s. Harold C. and Beata J. (Hoffmann) B.; m. Mari L. Runquist, Aug. 7, 1971 (div. Oct. 1985); children: Nicholas, Kyle, Megan. BA, Gustavus Adolphus Coll., 1971; postgrad., Boise State U., 1975—, U. Idaho, 1979—; MEd, Coll. Idaho, 1983; cert. instr. leader level, Nat. Fedn. Interscholastic Coaches Edn. Program-Am. Coaching Effectiveness Program, 1991. Cert. advanced elem. and phys. edn. tchr. Phys. edn. tchr. Hopkins (Minn.) Sch. Dist., 1972-73; elem. tchr., phys. edn. tchr. Mountain Home (Idaho) Sch. Dist. 193, 1974-84, phys. edn. tchr., 1984—; coach boys basketball Mountain Home Jr. High Sch., 1986—; coach girls softball Mountain Home High Sch., 1993-97; instr. Intermountain Environ. Edn. Tng. Team, Salt Lake City, 1979—. Instr., mgr. ARC-pool, Mountain Home, 1975-83; pres. Men's Slo Pitch Softball Assn., Mountain Home, 1975-79; bd. dirs., coach Elmore County Youth Baseball Assn., Mountain Home, 1989-92; treas., bd. dirs. Grace Luth. Ch., Mountain Home, 1991-95. Mem. AAHPERD, Idaho Assn. Health, Phys. Edn, Recreation and Dance, Idaho ASCD, Idaho Soc. for Energy and Environ. Edn. (treas. 1985-87). Democrat. Avocations: reading, racquetball, fishing, hunting, horseback tour guide. Office: Base Primary Sch 100 Gunfighter Ave Mountain Home A F B ID 83648

BORCOVER, ALFRED SEYMOUR, journalist; b. Bellaire, Ohio, May 1, 1931; s. Joseph and Kate (Florman) B.; m. Doris E. Wellner, Sept. 13, 1958 (div. 1966); m. Linda A. Gredig, Oct. 11, 1989. B.Sc. in Journalism, Ohio State U., 1953; M.S.J., Northwestern U., 1957. Writer Northwestern U., Evanston, Ill., 1957-58; reporter, copy editor Chgo. Tribune, 1959-63, asst. travel editor, 1963-73, assoc. travel editor, 1973-79, editor travel sect., 1979-81, travel editor, columnist, 1982-93; ret., 1994; freelance travel columnist/writer, 1994—. Author: Dollarwise Guide to Chicago, 1967; contbg. editor Fodor's Chicago, 1985-88; contbr. to Around the World with the Experts, 1970. Served to 1st lt. USAF, 1953-55. Recipient spl. citation George Hedmon Awards, 1965, Outstanding Achievement in Travel Writing award N.Y. Travel Writers Assn., 1976, Econ. Impact Writing award Travel Industry Assn. Am., 1983, Lowell Thomas Writing award, 1986; Gold Medal Writing award Pacific Asia Travel Assn., 1987, Cen. States Consumerism Reporting award, 1987, Alumni Svc. award Northwestern U., 1991, Cen. States Best Fgn. Series award, Cen. States Henry E. Bradshaw Sweepstakes Writing award, 1991, Cen. States Fgn. Series and U.S. Article awards, 1992, Earl R. Lind Consumer Edn. award Better Bus. Bur. of Chgo., 1993. Mem. Soc. Am. Travel Writers (pres. 1973-74), Chgo. Headline Club (pres. 1983-84), Medill Sch. Journalism Alumni Assn. (bd. dirs. 1984-89, pres. 1989-91), Northwestern U. Alumni Assn. (bd. dirs. 1986-90), Soc. Profl. Journalists. Democrat. Jewish. Avocations: tennis, music, photography. Home and Office: 1022 Michigan Ave Evanston IL 60202-1436

BORDA, RICHARD JOSEPH, management consultant; b. San Francisco, Aug. 16, 1931; s. Joseph Clement and Ethel Cathleen (Donovan) B.; m. Judith Maxwell, Aug. 30, 1953; children: Michelle, Stephen Joseph. AB, Stanford U., 1953, MBA, 1957. With Wells Fargo Bank, San Francisco, 1957-70; mgr. Wells Fargo Bank, 1963-66, asst. v.p., 1966-67, v.p., 1967-70; exec. v.p. adminstrn. Wells Fargo Bank, San Francisco, 1973-85; asst. sec. Air Force Manpower Res. Affairs, Washington, 1970-73; vice chmn., chief fin. officer Nat. Life Ins. Co., Montpelier, Vt., 1985-90, also bd. dirs.; chmn., chief exec. officer Sentinal Group Funds, Inc., 1985-90, also bd. dirs.; mgmt. cons., 1990—. Former pres. Air Force Aid Soc., Washington; trustee Monterey Inst. Internat. Studies (chmn. bd. dirs.); govs. coun. Boys and Girls Club of Monterey Peninsula; bd. dirs. Sunset Ctr. for the Arts Found.; mem. internat. adv. bd. Ctr. for Nonproliferation Studies. Recipient Exceptional Civilian Svc. award, 1973, 95. Mem. USMC Res. Officers Assn., Air Force Assn., Bohemian Club, Monterey Peninsula Country Club, Old Capital Club, Air Force Aid Soc. (disting. counselor), Phi Gamma Delta. Republican. Episcopalian.

BORDALLO, MADELEINE MARY (MRS. RICARDO JEROME BORDALLO), lieutenant governor; b. Graceville, Minn., May 31, 1933; d. Christian Peter and Mary Evelyn (Roth) Zeien; m. Ricardo Jerome Bordallo, June 20, 1953; 1 dau., Deborah Josephine. Student, St Mary's Coll., South Bend, Ind., 1952; A.A., St. Katherines Coll., St. Paul, 1953; A.A. hon. degree for community service, U. Guam, 1968. Presented in voice recital Guam Acad. Music, Agana., 1951, 62; mem. Civic Opera Co., St. Paul, 1952-53; mem. staff KUAM Radio-TV sta., Agana, 1954-63; freelance writer local newspaper, fashion show commentator, coordinator, civic leader, 1963, nat. Dem. committeewoman for Guam, 1964-98, 1st lady of Guam, 1974-78, 81-85; senator 16th Guam Legislature, 1981-82, 19th Guam Legislature, 1987-88, 20th Guam Legislature, 1989-90, 21st Guam Legislature, 1991-92, 22nd Guam Legislature, 1993-94; Dem. Party candidate for Gov. of Guam, 1990, lt. gov. of Guam, 1994; lt. gov. of Guam, 1995—; del. Nat. Dem. Conv., 1964, 68, 72, 76, 80, 84, 88-92, 96, pres. Women's Dem. Party Guam, 1967-69; rep. Presdl. Inauguration, Washington, 1965, 77, 85; del. Dem. Western States Conf., Reno, 1965, L.A., 1967, Phoenix, 1968, conf. sec., 1967-69; del. Dem. Women's Campaign Conf., Wash., 1965, Dem. Inauguration, 1992. Pres. Guam Women's Club, 1958-59; del Gen. Fedn. Women's Clubs Convs., Miami Beach, Fla., 1961, New Orleans, 1965, Boston, 1968; v.p. Fedn. Asian Women's Assn., 1964-67, pres., 1967-69, pres. 1996-98; pres. Guam Symphony Soc., 1967-73, del. convs., Manila, Philippines, 1959, Taipei, Formosa, 1960, Hong Kong, 1963, Guam, 1964, Japan, 1968, Taipei, 1973; chmn. Guam Christmas Seal Drive, 1961; bd. dirs. Guam chpt. ARC, 1963, sec., 1963-67; pres. Marianas Assn. For Retarded Children, 1968-69, 73-74, 84—; bd. dirs. Guam Theatre Guild, Am. Cancer Soc.; mem. Guam Meml. Hosp. Vols. Assn., 1966—, v.p., 1966-67, pres., 1970-71; chmn. Hosp. Charity Ball, 1966; pres. Women for Service, 1974—, Beauty World Guam Ltd., 1981—, First Lady's Beautification Task Force of Guam, 1983-86; pres. Palace Restoration Assn., 1983—; nominee Dem. party for Gov. of Guam, 1990. Mem. Internat. Platform Assn., Guam Rehab. Assn. (assoc.), Guam Lytico and Bodig Assn. (pres. 1983-98), Spanish Club of Guam, Inetnon Famalaoan Club (pres. 1983-86), Guam Coun. of Women's Club (pres. 1993-95). Home: PO Box 1458 Agana GU 96932-1458 Office: PO Box 2950 Agana GU 96932-2950

BORDAO, RAFAEL, educator, writer, poet; b. Havana, Cuba, June 17, 1951; came to U.S., 1980; s. Mario and Marta (Herrera) B.; m. Miriam Parajon, Dec. 30, 1971 (div. Jan. 1980); 1 child, Aisné; m. Laura Garcia, Nov. 25, 1995. MA, Columbia U., 1988, MPh, 1999, PhD, 1999. Cert. tchr., N.Y. Founder, pub. La Nuez, N.Y.C., 1988-93, Editl. Arcas, N.Y.C., 1988-93; adj. prof. Mercy Coll., N.Y.C., 1988-89, Columbia U. Tchrs. Coll., N.Y.C., 1989-90; tchr. N.Y.C. Pub. Sch. Sys., 1991—; founder, pub. Editl. Palmar, 1993—. Author: La Revolution de Castro, 1999, (poetry): Proyectura, 1986, Acrobacia del Abandono, 1988, Escurriduras de la Soledad, 1995, El Libro de Las Interferencias, 1995, Propinas para la Libertad, 1998, El Lenguaje del Ausente, 1998; contbr. works to lit. mags. and poetry anthologies. Named Homme de Lettres, Acad. Francaise, Paris, 1998, Premio de Poesia Fernand Esquio, Galicia, Spain, 1998, others. Mem. PEN, Interam. Acad. Poetry (sec. N.Y. chpt.). Avocations: reading, tennis. Home: PO Box 023617 Brooklyn NY 11202

BORDELEAU, LISA MARIE, human services professional, consultant; b. Providence, Mar. 28, 1960; d. Roland John and Nancy Vivien (McIntosh) B.; m. John Theodore Endler, Sept. 8, 1991; children: Ian Endler Bordeleau, Meaghan Endler Bordeleau. BA cum laude, R.I. Coll., 1987; M in Liberal Arts, Harvard U., 1995. Devel. activities instr. Northern R.I. Assn. Retarded Citizens, Woonsocket, R.I., 1980-82; residential counselor Live In a Freer Environ., Mansfield, Mass., 1981-82; staff advocate, asst. program coord. Beta Hostel Corp., Attleboro, Mass., 1983-85; program mgr., residential dir. Alternatives Unlimited, Inc., Whitinsville, Mass., 1985-86; mental health worker Butler Hosp., Providence, 1986-87; program mgr. Work Inc., North Quincy, Mass., 1987-89; dir. residential svcs. Beta Cmty. Svcs., Attleboro, Mass., 1989-94, dir. devel., 1995—; facilitator cmty. membership project Eunice Kennedy Shriver Ctr., Waltham, Mass., 1993-95, cons., 1995-96; policy evaluator Eunice Kennedy Shriver Ctr., Waltham, 1997-98, tng. initiate coord. cmty. membership project, 1998—; cons. Cooperative for Human Svcs., Malden, Mass., 1989-91, Optima Cons., Inc., Cranston, R.I., 1991-96; cons. in field. Mem. North Attleborough Teen Ctr. Com., Mass., 1995. Mem. AAUW, NOW, The Feminist Majority. Avocations: weightlifting, body building, whale watching. Home: 11 Anthony E Greco Cir North Attleboro MA 02760-4745

BORDELON, CAROLYN THEW, elementary school educator; b. Shelby, Ohio, Dec. 28, 1942; d. Burton Carl and Opal Mae (Harris) VanAsdale; m. Clifford Charles Spohn, Aug. 28, 1965 (div. Feb. 1982); m. Al Ramon Bordelon, Oct. 26, 1985. BA in History and Polit. Sci., Otterbein Coll., 1966; MA in Edn., Bowling Green State U., 1972; postgrad., Ohio State U., 1986—. Cert. tchr. grades 1-8, Ohio. Elem. tchr. Allen East Schs., Harrod, Ohio, 1966-68; elem. tchr. Marion (Ohio) City Schs., 1968-78, chpt. I reading tchr., 1978-86, reading recovery tchr., 1986-88; reading recovery tchr. Dublin (Ohio) City Schs., 1988—; adj. instr. reading dept.grad. studies Ashland (Ohio) U., 1996. Author: The Parent Workshop, 1992, Octopus Goes to School, 1995. Vol. Am. Heart Assn., Worthington, Ohio, 1991; mem. Rep. Nat. Com., Washington, 1994-95; mem. Royal Scots Highlanders, Mansfield, Ohio, 1976—. Recipient Excellence in Edn. award Dublin City C. of C., 1991-93, 96, 97; Dublin City Schs./Ohio Dept. Edn. Tchr. Award grantee, 1993; Martha Holden Jennings Found. scholar, 1978. Mem. Archaeol. Inst. Am., Ohio Edn. Assn., Reading Recovery Coun. N.Am., Opera/Columbus, Mus. of Art, Columbus, Phi Delta Kappa, Phi Alpha Theta. Presbyterian. Avocations: bagpiping and Scottish activities, archaeology, interior design, harpsichord. Home: 3958 Fairlington Dr Columbus OH 43220-4531 Office: Griffith Thomas Elem Sch 4671 Tuttle Crossing Blvd Dublin OH 43017-3575

BORDELON, DENA COX YARBROUGH, retired special education educator; b. Gorman, Tex., June 20, 1933; d. William Thomas and Imogene (Dunlap) Cox; m. James Edgar Yarbrough, June 20, 1950. BA, Nicholls State U., 1964, MEd, 1971, postgrad., 1978. Supr. profl. pers., prin. schs., elem. tchr. Terrebonne Parish Sch. Bd., Houma, La., 1964-79, dir. spl. edn. svcs., 1980-91; ret., 1991. Bd. dirs. Terrebonne Literacy Coun., Dulac Community Ctr.; mem. adv. bd. Terrebonne Guidance Ctr. Mem. Terrebonne Retired Tchrs. Assn., Coun. for Exceptional Children, La. Mental Health Assn., La. Retired Tchrs. Assn., Alcohol and Drug Abuse Coun. for South La., Phi Delta Kappa. Democrat. Methodist. Avocations: golf, reading, theatre. Home: 202 White St Houma LA 70364-2934

BORDEN, AMANDA, gymnast, Olympic athlete; b. Cin., May 10, 1977. Student, U. Ga., 1998, Ariz. State Univ., 1998—. Mem. Nat. Team, 1990, 92-93, 93-94, 94-95, 95-96, 96—, Pan Am. Games Team, U.S. Olympic Gymnastics Team, Atlanta, 1996. Recipient Silver medal Team World Championships, 1994, Gold medal team competition Olympic Games, Atlanta, 1996; placed 1st in the floor exercise and 2d in the balance beam jr. divsn. Am. Classic, Salt Lake City, 1991, 1st in the floor exercise U.S. Classic, Knoxville, 1992, 2d for team Pacific Alliance Championships, Seoul, Korea, 1992, 3rd in all around and balance beam, 3rd for team in vault Am. Classic-World Championships Trials, Salt Lake City, 1993, 1st for team Hilton Challenge, L.A., 1993, 94, 3rd in uneven bars Tokyo Cup, 1993, 2d in all around Am. Classic-World Championships Trials, Orlando, 1994, 2d for team Team World Championships, Dortmund, Germany, 1994, 1st in the all around U.S. Classic, Palm Springs, Calif., 1994,, 3rd in all around, uneven bars and floor exercise Coca-Cola Nat. Championships, Nashville, 1994, 3rd in all around NationsBank World Team Trials, Richmond, Va., 1994, 2d for team in all around, 3rd for team in uneven bars, 2d in balance beam and floor exercise Am. Classic-Pan Am. Games Team Trials, Oakland, Calif., 1995, 1st in floor exercise, 2d in uneven bars Reese's Internat. Gymnastics Cup, Portland, 1995, 3rd in all around, 1st in balance beam and floor exercise McDonald's Am. Cup, 1995, 2d in all around Pan Am. Games, Mar del Plata, Argentina, 1995, 2d in all around and balance beam, 3rd for team in vault, 1st for team in uneven bars U.S. Classic, Colorado Springs, Colo., 1996, 1st for team and balance beam, 1st for team Budget Rent-a-Car Gymnastics Invitational USA vs. France, Miami, 1996. Avocations: bicycling, reading, shopping, playing on computer. Office: care USA Gymnastics Pan Am Plz 201 S Capitol Ave Ste 300 Indianapolis IN 46225-1058 also: Cin Gymnastics Acad 3536 Woodridge Blvd Fairfield OH 45014-6613*

BORDEN, DAVID M., state supreme court justice; b. Hartford, Conn., Aug. 4, 1937. BA magna cum laude, Amherst Coll., 1959; LLB cum laude, Harvard U., 1962. Bar: Conn. 1962, U.S. Dist. Ct. Conn. 1962, U.S. Ct. Appeals (2d cir.) 1965, U.S. Supreme Ct. 1969. Pvt. practice Hartford, Conn., 1962-77; judge Conn. Ct. Common Pleas, 1977-78, Conn. Superior Ct., 1978-83, Conn. Appellate Ct., 1983; assoc. justice Conn. Supreme Ct., 1990—; chief counsel joint com. on judiciary Conn. Gen. Assembly, 1975-76; lectr. Law U. Conn. Sch. Law, 1970-73; exec. dir. Conn. Commn. to Revise Criminal Statutes, 1963-71. Mem. Conn. Bar Assn., Hartford County Bar Assn., Phi Beta Kappa. Democrat. Jewish. Avocations: hiking, reading. Office: Conn Supreme Ct Drawer N Sta A Hartford CT 06106-1548*

BORDEN, DIANE LYNN, communications educator; b. Chgo., Jan. 25, 1947; d. H. Frederick and Vera L. Borden; m. Robert Easley (div. 1970). BA, Colo. State U., 1972; MA, Stanford U., 1989; PhD, U. Wash., 1993. Mng. editor Bellingham (Wash.) Herald, 1977-80; dep. mng. editor Tribune, Oakland, Calif., 1981-85; pres. Santa Fe (N.Mex.) New Mexican, 1986-87; assoc. prof. Temple U., Phila., 1993-95; project dir. Am. Soc. Newspaper Editors, Reston, Va., 1995-96; asst. prof. George Mason U., Fairfax, Va., 1996-98; assoc. prof. San Diego State U., 1998—; Gannett profl. in residence U. Kans., Lawrence, 1985-86; cons. and expert witness in communication law and ethics. Co-editor: The Electronic Grapevine, 1997; co-author: Creative Editing, 3d edit., 1999; contbr. articles to scholarly and profl. jours.; editor: (book) Women and Language, 1997—. Active Nat. Mus. for Women in Arts, Washington, Habitat for Humanity, World Wildlife Fund, Washington. Profl. journalism fellow Stanford U., 1980-81, fellow in telecomm. policy Annenberg Washington Program, 1995; rsch. grantee Temple U., 1994, San Diego State U., 1999. Mem. Assn. for Edn. in Journalism and Mass Communication, AAUW, Am. Journalism Historians

Assn. Avocations: hiking, tennis, reading mystery novels. Office: San Diego State U Sch of Comm 5500 Campanile Dr San Diego CA 92182-0002

BORDEN, ENID A., public relations executive; b. Bklyn., Feb. 15, 1950; d. Jack Harry and Eleanor (Miller) Borden. BA, Alfred U., N.Y., 1972; MA, Adelphi U., Garden City, N.Y., 1973. Editor/pubr. Wings Mag., Colorado Springs, Colo., 1975-76; press. sec. Guidera for Congress, Waterbury, Conn., 1977-78; press sec. Reagan for Pres., N.Y.C., N.Y., 1979-80; dir. pub. affairs U.S. Dept. HHS, N.Y.C., 1981-83; dir. pub. affairs/dir. policy and legis. Office Human Devel. Svcs. HHS, Washington, 1983-86; dep. commr. for policy and external affairs Social Security Adminstrn., Balt., 1986-88; pres. The Borden Group, Inc., Alexandria, Va., 1988—; cons. on pub. rels., govt. rels. assn. mgmt. primarily in human svcs.; mem. U.S. adv. bd. on child abuse and neglect, 1992-95; faculty Ctr. for Grad. and Continuing Studies, Goucher Coll., Balt. 1998—. Trustee Alfred U., 1985-88; exec. dir. Meals on Wheels Assn. Am., 1993—. Recipient Citation Alfred U. Alumni Assn. Office: The Borden Group Inc 1414 Prince St Alexandria VA 22314-2853

BORDEN, JOHN HARVEY, entomologist, educator; b. Berkeley, Calif., Feb. 6, 1938; s. Charles Edward Borden and Alice Victoria Witkin; m. Edna Rosalind McEachern, June 23, 1962; children: Patrick Carl, Ian McEachern. BS, Washington State U., 1963; MS, U. Calif., Berkeley, 1965, PhD, 1966. Bd. cert. entomologist Entomol. Soc. Am. Rsch. and tchg. asst. dept. entomology U. Calif., Berkeley, 1963-66; asst. prof. dept. biol. scis. Simon Fraser U., Burnaby, B.C., Can., 1966-69, assoc. prof., 1969-75, prof., 1975—, dir. chem. ecology rsch. group, 1981—, NSERC Indsl. Rsch. chair, 1991—; vis. scientist Forestry Commn. Rsch. Sta., Alice Holt Lodge, Wrecclesham, Farnham, Surrey, Eng., 1976-77; cons. to UN Devel. Program, 1989—. Contbr. chpts. to books and over 300 articles to profl. jours.; patentee in field. With USMC, 1957-61. Coop. Grad. fellow, NSF, 1964-66, Travelling fellow Nat. Rsch. Coun., 1976-77, Killam Rsch. fellow Can. Coun., 1990-91; recipient Gold medal Sci. Coun. B.C., 1985, Hewlett Packard Can. Forum award, 1997. Fellow Entomol. Soc. Can. (C.G. Hewitt award 1977, Gold medal 1988); mem. Entomol. Soc. Am. (cert., J.E. Bussart Meml. award 1984), Entomol. Soc. B.C., Nat. Assn. Advancement of Sci. (life), Can. Inst. Forestry (Sci. Achievement award 1986), Profl. Pest Mgmt. Assn. B.C. (Excellence award 1986), Internat. Soc. Chem. Ecology (life), Assn. B.C. Profl. Foresters, Assn. Profl. Biologists B.C. Office: Simon Fraser U, Dept Biol Scis, Burnaby, BC Canada V5A 1S6

BORDEN, ROBERT CHRISTIAN, editor; b. Fargo, N.D., Sept. 4, 1949; s. Jack Borden and Shirley Frances Borden. B Journalism, U. Tex., 1971. Edn. reporter Bryan (Tex.)-College Station Eagle, 1986-90, opinions editor, 1990—. Pres. Brazos Valley Symphony Soc., Bryan, 1987—; sec. Brazos Food Bank, Bryant, 1998—; coord. Cheer Fund holiday food dr., Bryan, 1990—. Democrat. Episcopalian. Avocations: reading, computer, needlework. Fax: (409) 776-8923. E-mail: rborden@theeagle.com. Home: 2109 Wayside Dr Bryan TX 77802-2447 Office: Bryan-College Station Eagle PO Box 3000 Bryan TX 77805-3000

BORDEN, WESTON THATCHER, chemistry educator; b. N.Y.C., Oct. 13, 1943; s. Martin L. and Doris (Weston) B.; m. Marcia E. Robbins, May 15, 1971 (div. 1987); children: Alice, Michael. BA, Harvard U., 1964, MA, 1966, PhD, 1968. Instr. Harvard U., Cambridge, Mass., 1968-69, asst. prof., 1969-73; assoc. prof. U. Wash., Seattle, 1973-77, prof., 1977—. Author: Modern Molecular Orbital Theory, 1975; editor: Diradicals, 1982; contbr. articles to profl. jours. Bd. dirs. Itteki Zendo Assn., 1995—. Fellow Fulbright Found., Sloan Found., Guggenheim Found., Japan Soc. for Promotion of Sci.; recipient Humboldt Scientist award. Mem. AAAS, Am. Chem. Soc. Buddhist. Avocation: traditional Japanese arts. Office: U Wash Dept Chemistry BG-10 Seattle WA 98195

BORDER, WILLIAM LAWSON, artist; b. Alton, Ill., May 31, 1933; s. Lawson Elwood and Cordelia Kelley B.; m. Laura Lea Baker, June 28, 1975; children: William Wesley, Alison Anne. Student, Pratt Inst., 1953; BFA, U. Colo., 1974. Freelance illustrator, graphic designer N.Y.C., 1955-69, Denver, 1969-74; biol. & scientific illustrator Biol. Scis. Curriculum Study, Louisville, Colo., 1974-82; freelance natural history illustrator Nederland, Colo., 1982-98. With U.S. Army, 1953-55. Mem. Guild Natural Sci. Illustrators, NAt. Assn. Interpretation, Rocky Mountain Nature Assn., Gupin County Artists Assn., Art Ctr. Estes Park. Avocations: horseback riding, dry fly fishing. Home: 285 Devon Pl Boulder CO 80302 Office: 463 Pineglade Rd Nederland CO 80466

BORDERS, WILLIAM ALEXANDER, journalist; b. St. Louis, Jan. 11, 1939; s. William Alexis and Kate (Thompson) B.; m. Barbara D. Burkham, June 17, 1967 (div. 1984); 1 son, William Borders. B.A., Yale U., 1960. Staff N.Y. Times, N.Y.C., 1960—; corr. N.Y. Times, Nigeria, 1970-72, Can., 1972-75, India, 1975-79, London, 1979-82; dep. fgn. editor N.Y. Times, 1982-83; editor Week in Rev. N.Y. Times, N.Y.C., 1983-89, sr. editor, 1989-90, news editor, 1990—. Home: 227 E 57th St New York NY 10022-2828 Office: NY Times Co 229 W 43rd St New York NY 10036-3959

BORDICK, MICHAEL TODD, professional baseball player; b. Marquette, Wis., July 21, 1965. Student, U. Maine. Shortstop Oakland (Calif.) Athletics, 1990-96, Balt. Orioles, 1996—. Mem. Am. League Champions, 1990, Am. League East Divsn. Champions, 1992. Office: Balt Orioles Oriole Park at Camden Yards 333 W Camden St Baltimore MD 21201-2435*

BORDIE, JOHN GEORGE, linguistics educator; b. Chgo., Apr. 3, 1931; s. John and Helena Jozefin (Kozubal) B.; m. Margaret Lyne Miller, July 22, 1950 (div. Dec. 1955); 1 child, Ruth Claire; m. Camilla May Berkley, Feb. 11, 1956; children: Helena Robin, Ralph Leon. B.A., U. Chgo., 1949; Ph.D., U. Tex., 1958. Asst. prof. linguistics and English Georgetown U., 1958-61; coord. linguistics and literacy Electronic Teaching Labs., Washington, 1961-63; dep. dir. tng. Peace Corps, North and East Africa, also South Asia, 1963-66; mem. faculty U. Tex.-Austin, 1966-95, prof. linguistics, curriculum and instrn., 1974-95, prof. emeritus, 1995—; prof. emeritus Fgn. Lang. Edn. Center, 1996—; vis. prof. Cornell U., 1965, Karachi U., 1980-81; mem. solar and wind energy adv. com. Tex. Energy and Natural Resources Coun., 1979; Fulbright sr. lectr., Pakistan, 1980-81, 82-83, Pakistan, 1991-92, Iraq, 1989-90. Author: The Teaching of African Languages, 1961, English Structure Drills, 1963, A Dari Course, 1968; editor: Jour. Linguistic Assn. S.W, 1976-82. Am. Coun. Learned Socs. fellow, 1954-55; Rockefeller Found. fellow, 1956-57. Mem. Linguistic Soc. Am., Tchrs. English to Speakers Others Langs., Am. Oriental Soc., AAAS. Home: PO Box 1217 Dripping Springs TX 78620-1217 Office: Linguistics U Tex Austin TX 78712

BORDIGA, BENNO, automotive parts manufacturing company executive; b. Vienna, Austria, July 25, 1920; came to U.S., 1940; s. Adolph and Grace V. (Blaustein) B.; m. Edna Bordiga, Feb. 5, 1944 (div. 1960); children: Robert S., Jeffrey S.; m. Melva E. Leftwich (div. 1986). B.S. in Mech. Engring., U. Vienna, 1938. v.p. mfg. Olympic Radio and TV, L.I., 1943-58; pres., chmn. bd. Allomatic Industries, Woodside, N.Y., 1958—, Allstar Automotive Co., Hyde Park, N.Y., 1962-80, All-O-Matic Instrument and Systems, New Hyde Park, N.Y., 1967-79; pres. William R. Davis Fine Arts Ltd., N.Y.C., 1967—; v.p., dir. Hotel Commander, N.Y.C., 1955-97; pres., dir. Fogel Mfg. Corp., Bklyn., 1959-64, W&B Industries, 1961-68; pres. Hotel Endicott, N.Y.C., Allomatic U.K. Ltd., Parzen Research Co. Contbr. articles to profl. jours. Pres., bd. dirs. 1050 Park Ave Tenants Corp., 1970-96. Served with U.S. Army, 1944-46. Home: 1050 Park Ave New York NY 10028-1031 Office: Allomatic Industries Inc 737 Park Ave New York NY 10021-4256

BORDLEY, JAMES, IV, surgeon; b. Balt., Nov. 24, 1942; s. James III and Julia (Ross) B.; m. Dianne Redmond; children: Jessica, James V. BA, Yale U., 1965; MD, Columbia U. Physicians/Surgeon, 1970. Surg. intern Bassett Hosp., Cooperstown, N.Y., 1970-71, surg. resident, 1971-75; att. surgeon Bassett Hosp., 1978—; staff surgeon Naval Regl. Med. Ctr., Newport, R.I., 1975-77; fellow biliary and pancreatic surgery U. Wash., Seattle, 1977; instr. surgery Columbia U., N.Y.C., 1978-80, asst. prof. clin. surg., 1980—. Contbr. articles to profl. jours./publs. Lt. cmdr. USN, 1975-77. Fellow Am. Coll. Surgeons; mem. Soc. Surgery of the Alimentary Tract, Soc. Am. Gastrointestinal Endoscopic Surgeons. Office: Bassett Hosp 1 Atwell Rd Cooperstown NY 13326-1301

BORDNER, GREGORY WILSON, chemical engineer; b. Buffalo, Aug. 16, 1959; s. Raymond Gordon and Nancy Lee (Immegart) B.; m. Margaret Patricia Toon, June 14, 1981; children: Eric Lawrence, Heather Rae. B-SChemE, Calif. State Poly. U., 1982; MS in Sys. Mgmt., U. So. Calif., 1987. Registered profl. engr., Calif., environ. assessor. Commd. 2nd lt. USAF, 1983, advanced through grades to capt., 1987; engr., mgr. various air launched missile, anti-satellite and strategic def. initiative projects Air Force Rocket Propulsion Lab., Edwards AFB, Calif., 1983-86; asst. mgr. space transp. Air Force Astronautics Lab., Edwards AFB, 1986-87; chief small intercontinental ballistic missiles ordnance firing system br. Hdqrs. Ballistic Missile Orgn., San Bernardino, Calif., 1987-90; sr. plant environ. engr. Filtrol Corp./Akzo Chems. Inc., L.A., 1991-92; water/soils project engr. TABC, Inc., Long Beach, Calif., 1992-98; prodn. engr. TABC, Inc., Long Beach, 1998—. Author: (manual) Pyrotechnic Transfer Line Evaluation, 1984, (with others) Rocket Motor Heat Transfer, 1984. Mem. AIChE, Am. Water Works Assn. Avocations: jogging, weight lifting, bowling. Home: 10841 Ring Ave Alta Loma CA 91737-4429

BORDOFF, JASON ERIC, consultant; b. Bklyn., Aug. 27, 1972; s. Fred and Ninette B. BA with honors, Brown U., 1994; MLitt, Oxford (Eng.) U., 1998. News dir. WBRU-FM, Providence, 1992, v.p., gen. mgr., 1993; legis. asst. Union Am. Hebrew Congregations, Washington, 1994-95; legal asst. Skadden, Arps, Slate, Meagher & Flom, Washington, 1995; assoc. McKinsey & Co., Inc., N.Y.C., 1997—. British Marshall scholar, Oxford, 1995-97. Avocations: tennis, opera. Office: 55 E 52nd St New York NY 10055-5907

BORDOGNA, JOSEPH, engineer, educator; b. Scranton, Pa., Mar. 22, 1933; s. Raymond and Rose (Yesu) B. BSEE, U. Pa., 1955, PhD, 1964; SM, MIT, 1960. With RCA Corp., 1958-64; asst. prof. U. Pa., Phila., 1964-68; assoc. prof. U. Pa., 1968-72, prof., 1972—, assoc. dean engring. and applied sci., 1973-80, acting dean, 1980-81, dean, 1981-90, dir. Moore Sch. Elec. Engring., 1976-90, Alfred Fitler Moore chair, 1979—; dir. engring. Nat. Sci. Foundation, Washington, 1991-96; COO, acting deputy dir. Nat. Sci. Found., Washington, 1996-99, dep. dir., COO, 1999—; bd. dirs. Indsl. Imaging Corp., Weston Inc. (chmn. 1996-97), Univ. City Sci. Ctr.; master Stoufer Coll. House, 1972-76; cons. industry, govt., founds.; mem. Nat. Medal of Sci. com., 1989-91; chair adv. com. for engring. NSF, 1989-91. Author: (with H. Ruston) Electric Networks, 1966, (with others) The Man-Made World, 1971; chmn. editorial bd. Engring. Edn., 1987-90. With USN, 1955-58. Recipient commendation for first spacecapsule recovery, 1957, Lindback award for disting. teaching U. Pa., 1967, Centennial medal Phila. Coll. Textiles and Sci., 1988, Am. Indsl. Modernization Leadership award Nat. Coalition for Advanced Mfg., 1993, Chmn.'s award Am. Assn. Engring. Socs., 1994, Engr. of Yr. award NSPE Phila., 1984, George Washington medal Engrs. Club. Phila., 1997; inducted into Engring. Educators Hall of Fame, 1993. Fellow AAAS (chair engring. sect. 1998-99), IEEE (chmn. Phila. sect. 1987-88, Centennial medal 1984, pres.-elect 1997, pres. 1998), Am. Soc. Engring. Edn. (George Westinghouse award 1974), Internat. Engring. Consortium; mem. Sigma Xi, Eta Kappa Nu, Tau Beta Pi, Phi Beta Delta. Office: Nat Sci Found Office Dir 4201 Wilson Blvd Ste 1205 Arlington VA 22203-1859

BORDONARO, SALVATORE, librarian; b. Montedero, Sicily, Italy, Apr. 29, 1952; s. Luigi and Anna B.; m. Julie A. Pierson, July 1, 1978; children: Teresa, Louis. BA, Canisius Coll., 1974; MLS, We. Mich. U., 1975. Cert. profl. pub. libr. Libr. I Buffalo and Erie County Pub. Librs., 1975-76; sr. libr. Attica (N.Y.) Correctional Facility, 1976-78; libr. II Amherst (N.Y.) Pub. Libr., 1978-87; libr. dir. Lackawanna (N.Y.) Pub. Libr., 1987—. Mem. ALA, Librs. Assn. B&ECPL (Scholarship award 1974, v.p. 1983-85, 93-97), Friends Lackawanna Pub. Libr. (pub. rels. 1988—, award 1997), Lackawanna C. of C. (sec. 1987—, Chamber Person of Yr. 1991). Democrat. Roman Catholic. Avocations: reading, home repairs, traveling. Office: Lackawanna Pub Libr 560 Ridge Rd Lackawanna NY 14218

BORDWELL, FREDERICK GEORGE, chemistry educator; b. Marmarth, N.D., Jan. 17, 1916; married, 1939; married 1972; 2 children. BS, U. Minn., 1937; PhD in Organic Chemistry, 1941; D (hon.), U. Göteborg, Sweden, 1991. Fellow Procter & Gamble, 1941-42; from instr. to prof., 1942-54; Emer Clare Hamilton Hall prof. chemistry Northwestern U., 1974—; Humble lectr., 1953, 57, NSF sr. fellow 1957, Guggenheim fellow, 1980; vis. prof. U. Ill., 1957, U. Wales, 1975, U. Western Ont., 1976, U. Calif., Irvine, 1979, 84, 85, 86, 87, 88. Recipient Correlation Analysis in Organic Chemistry medal, Paris, 1991, Weissberger-Williams lectr. award Eastman Kodak, 1993; HC Brown lectr. 1986, CK Ingold lectr. 1987. Mem. Am. Chem. Soc. (award petrol chem. 1986, Arthur C. Cope Scholar award 1991). Research in mechanisms of organic reactions; chemistry of organic sulfur compounds; acidities of weak acids; organic electrochemistry. Home: 609 Clinton Pl Evanston IL 60201

BORDY, BILL (WILLIAM JAMES BORDY), publisher; b. Pitts., Nov. 2, 1930; s. Samuel Alexander and Susan (Elischer) B. BA, Emerson Coll., 1958; cert., La Sorbonne, Paris, 1964. Dir. drama Suffolk U., Boston, 1955-58; pub., founder, pub. emeritus Drama-Logue, Hollywood, Calif., 1969-98; producer, writer, dir. Bill Bordy Prodns., Hollywood, 1980-99; ret., 1999. Producer, actor (TV comedy spl.) Une Soirée élegante, 1984 (Silver medal N.Y. Film and TV Festival 1985); producer, writer, dir., actor (TV movie) Twilight Blues, 1986, (motion picture) Side Roads, 1988; exec. prodr. (motion picture) Healer, 1994. With USMC, 1952-54. Recipient Alumni Recognition award Emerson Coll., 1985, 88, Cesar award Pan Am. Theatrical Assn., 1981, 90. Mem. AFTRA, Actors Equity Assn., Screen Actors Guild.

BORDY, MICHAEL JEFFREY, lawyer; b. Kansas City, Mo., July 24, 1952; s. Marvin Dean and Alice Mae (Rostov) B.; m. Marjorie Enid Kanof, Dec. 27, 1973 (div. Dec. 1983); m. Melissa Anne Held, May 24, 1987; children: Shayna Robyn, Jenna Alexis, Samantha Falyn. Bar: Calif., 1986, U.S. Dist. Ct. (cen. dist.) Calif., 1986, (so. dist.) Calif., 1987, U.S. Ct. Appeals (9th cir.), 1986. Tchg. asst. biology U. Kans., Lawrence, 1975-76, rsch. asst. biology, 1976-80; post-doctoral fellow Johns Hopkins U., Balt., 1980-83; tchg. asst. U. So. Calif., L.A., 1984-86; assoc. Thelen, Marrin, Johnson & Bridges, L.A., 1986-87, Wood, Lucksinger & Epstein, L.A., 1987-89, Cooper, Epstein & Hurewitz, Beverly Hills, Calif., 1989-93; ptnr. Jacobson, Runes & Bordy, Beverly Hills, 1994-96, Jacobson, Sanders & Bordy, LLP, Beverly Hills, 1996-97, Jacobson White Diamond & Bordy, LLP, Beverly Hills, 1997—. Bd. govs. Beverly Hills (Calif.) Bar Barristers, 1988-90, Cedars-Sinai Med. Ctr., L.A., 1994—; bd. dirs. Sinai Temple, 1998—; cabinet United Jewish Fund/Real Estate, L.A., 1995—; mem. planning com. Am. Cancer Soc., 1996—; mem. Guardians of the Jewish Home for the Aging, 1995—, Fraternity of Friends, 1997—; active Lawyers Against Hunger, 1995—. Pre-Doctoral fellow NIH, Lawrence, 1977-80; post-doctoral fellow Mellon Found., Balt., 1980-83. Mem. ABA, State Bar Calif., L.A. County Bar Assn., Beverly Hills Bar Assn. (gov., barrister 1988-92, chair real estate sect. 1998—), Profl. Network Group. Democrat. Jewish. Avocations: running, reading. Office: Jacobson White Diamond & Bordy LLP 9777 Wilshire Blvd Ste 918 Beverly Hills CA 90212-1907

BORECKI, KENNETH MICHAEL, real estate investment consultant; b. Rockville Ctr., N.Y., June 29, 1955; s. Theodore Buster and Florence (Konikowitch) B.; m. Yvette Angela Medici, Oct. 2, 1993. BS, L.I. U., 1976, MS, 1978. CPA, CFA. Sr. acct. Kenneth Leventhal & Co., N.Y.C., 1978-82; v.p. ltd. partnerships E.F. Hutton, N.Y.C., 1982-89; v.p. asset recovery Dime Bank, N.Y.C., 1989-92; cons. Greenwich, Conn., 1993-98; assoc. real estate investment banking Bankers Trust Co., N.Y.C., 1998—; lectr. NYU, 1993-95. Editor Undiscovered Values in Real Estate Securities, 1993-95. Mem. AICPA, Assn. Investment Mgmt. Rsch., N.Y. Soc. Securities Analysts. Republican. Avocations: tennis, golf, sailing. Office: Bankers Trust Co 130 Liberty St Mail Stop 2252 New York NY 10006

BORECKY, ISIDORE, bishop; b. Ostrowec, Ukraine, Oct. 1, 1911. Ed., Theol. Acad. Lwiw, 1932-36, Maximillian U., Munich, Germany, 1936-38. Ordained priest Ukrainian Greek Cath. Ch., 1938; missionary in Sask. and Man., Can., 1938-40; parish priest Niagara Peninsula, Ont., Can., 1940-48; titular bishop of Amathas, from 1948; 1st exarch Ukrainian Cath. Exarchate of Eastern Can., 1948-56; bishop of 1st Eparchy of Toronto, 1956. *

BOREEN, HENRY ISAAC, computer company executive; b. Warsaw, Poland, Mar. 7, 1927; came to U.S., 1949; s. Isaac and Grina (Goldstein) B.; m. Lois Adele Golwyn, June 22, 1958; children: Stuart Michael Boreen, Susan Tobey Hailman. *Wife Lois, BS 1957 Temple University; taught at junior high school, was therapeutic dietician at Germantown Hospital in Philadelphia, Pennsylvania. Son Stuart, BA 1981 University of Pennsylvania; MD 1986 Jefferson University; Anesthesia Residency 1990, currently employed as Anesthesiologist at St. Luke's Hospital, Bethlehem, Penna. Daughter-in-law Joan Lustig Boreen BS 1980 U. Pennsylvania; MBA 1985 Temple University. Daughter Susan Hailman, BA 1985 U. Pennsylvania; MA 1988 Harvard University, cum laude; MBA 1993 Pace University. Son-in-law Eric Peter Hailman, AB 1988 Harvard, Magna Cum Laude, PhD 1997 Rockefeller University, MD 1998 Cornell University, currently doing post doctorate at Washington University in St. Louis, Misso. Grandchildren: Kevin Andrew Boreen, Michael Alexander Boreen, Joshua Michael Hailman.* BSEE, Drexel U., 1956, MSEE, 1958. Asst. prof. Drexel Univ., Phila., 1958; v.p. engr. Vector Mfg. Co., Inc., Trevose, Pa., 1958-64; chmn., CEO Solid State Sci., Inc., Montgomeryville, Pa., 1964-86; chmn. US-Tech, Inc., Valley Forge, Pa., 1987—; chmn., CEO AM Comm., Inc., Quakertown, Pa., 1990—; chmn. Integrated Circuit Systems Inc., Valley Forge, Pa., 1993—; bd. trustees A. Roth Found., Meadowbrook, Pa., 1980—. Co-author: Aerospace Telemetry, 1961. Recipient Centennial medal Drexel Univ., 1991. Avocations: gardening, photography, car racing, hiking, bird watching. Office: Integrated Circuit Systems 2435 Blvd of the Generals Valley Forge PA 19482-0968

BOREI, SVEN HANS EMIL, translator; b. Stockholm, Dec. 21, 1941; s. Hans Georg and Maj Ellen (Österlin) B.; m. Gisela Wilms Möller; children: Bethany, Rolf, Emil. AA, Valley Forge Mil. Acad., 1961; BA in English, U. Pa., 1964; postgrad., Syracuse U. English and writing tchr. Meadowbrook Sch. for Boys, Phila., 1964-65; basic skills instr. adult edn. Syracuse (N.Y.) Pub. Schs., 1965-67; assoc. dir. Ednl. and Cultural Ctr. Onondaga and Oswego Counties, Syracuse, 1966-67; English instr. Maria Regina Jr. Coll., Syracuse, 1967-68; pres., founder, trustee, CEO Ctr. for Literacy, Inc., Phila., 1968-78; literacy project coord. Appalachia Ednl. Lab., Charleston, W.Va., 1980-81; founder, pres., CEO Literacy Inst., Inc., Syracuse, 1981-88; co-prop. H.E.S. Konsult AB, Transförlag, Lerum, Sweden, 1986—; English lang. coord. Språkverket AB, Göteborg, 1987-89; cons., presenter workshops, seminars in field. Author: Appalachian Adult Literacy Programs Survey, 2 vols., 1981, LLA Finance Handbook, 1982, A Measure of Freedom, 1995; editor: Quality Thinking, 1998; translator: Art at Astra, 1997, Jan Johnson, a Visionary Swedish Musician, 1998; contbr. articles to profl. jours. Supervisory tutor trainer Laubach Literacy Action, Syracuse, 1975, master tutor trainer, 1977, regional trainer cons., 1985, bd. dirs. 1972-80; co-founder, chair Tutors for Literacy in Pa., 1975-76, W.Va. Literacy Coalition, 1980-82, Tenn. Literacy Coalition, 1982-85; mem. Lerum Mcpl. Coun., 1991-98, mcpl. exec. com., 1995-98, mcpl. bldg. bd. 1999-02; bd. govs. Am.-Swedish Hist. Found., 1973-80, v.p., 1975-77, treas., 1977-78. Mem. Swedish Assn. Profl. Translators (bd. dirs. 1997—, vice chmn. 1998-99, chmn. 1999—). Avocations: music, local history, poetry, renovating furniture. Home: PL 3181, S-443 38 Lerum Sweden

BOREL, ARMAND, mathematics educator; b. Chaux-de-Fonds, Switzerland, May 21, 1923; m. Gabrielle Pittet, May 8, 1952; children: Dominique, Anne-Christine. Master Mathematics, Federal Inst. Tech., Zurich, Switzerland., 1947; Dr. Degree, U. Paris, 1952; Ph.D. (hon.), U. Geneva, 1972. Asst. Federal Inst. Tech., Zurich, 1947-49; prof. Federal Inst. Tech., 1955-57, 83-86; attaché de Recherches French Nat. Center Sci. Research, Paris, 1949-50; acting prof. algebra U. Geneva, Switzerland, 1950-52; mem. Inst. Advanced Study, Princeton, 1952-54, prof., 1957-93, prof. emeritus, 1993—; vis. prof. U. Chgo., 1954-55, 76, MIT, 1958, 69, Tata Inst. Fundamental Rsch. Bombay, 1961, 68, 83, 90, 92, 95, 99, U. Paris, 1964, U. Calif., Berkeley, 1975, Yale U., 1978. Recipient Brouwer medal Dutch Math. Soc., 1978, Balzan prize, 1992. Mem. NAS, Acad. Arts and Sci., Am. Philos. Soc. (fgn.), Finnish Acad. Scis. and Letters (fgn.), French Acad. Scis. (fgn.), Academia Europaea (fgn.), Am. Math. Soc. (Leroy P. Steele prize 1991), Swiss Math. Soc., French Math. Soc. Address: Inst for Advanced Study Sch Mathematics Olden Ln Princeton NJ 08540

BOREL, JAMES DAVID, anesthesiologist; b. Chgo., Nov. 15, 1951; s. James Albert and Nancy Ann (Sieverson) B. BS, U. Wis., 1973; MD, Med. Coll. of Wis., 1977. Diplomate Am. Bd. Anesthesiology, Nat. Bd. Med. Examiners, Am. Coll. Anesthesiologists. Research asst. McArdle Lab. for Cancer Research, Madison, Wis., 1972-73, Stanford U. and VA Hosp., Palo Alto, 1976-77; intern. The Cambridge (Mass.) Hosp., 1977-78; clin. fellow in medicine Harvard Med. Sch., Boston, 1977-78, clin. fellow in anesthesia, 1978-80, clin. instr. in anaesthesia, 1980; resident in anesthesiology Peter Bent Brigham Hosp., Boston, 1978-80; anesthesiologistt Mt. Auburn Hosp., Cambridge, 1980; fellow in anesthesiology Ariz. Health Scis. Ctr., Tucson, 1980-81; research assoc. U. Ariz. Coll. Medicine, Tucson, 1980-81, assoc. in anesthesiology, 1981—; active staff Mesa (Ariz.) Luth. Hosp., 1981—; courtesy staff Scottsdale (Ariz.) Meml. Hosp., 1982—; vis. anaesthetist St. Joseph's Hosp., Kingston, Jamaica, 1980. Contbr. numerous articles to profl. jours. Mem. AMA, AAAS, Ariz. Anesthesia Alumni Assn., Ariz. Soc. Anesthesiologists, Am. Soc. Regional Anesthesia, Can. Anesthetists' Soc., Internat. Anesthesia Rsch. Soc., Am. Soc. Anesthesiologists. Office: Valley Anesthesia Cons 2200 N Central Ave Ste 203 Phoenix AZ 85004-1431

BOREL, STEVEN JAMES, lawyer; b. Kansas City, Mo., Nov. 12, 1947; s. Mark and Margaret (Gibson) B.; m. Nancy Jean Dunaway, Aug. 31, 1967; children: Lindsay Kay, Emily Jean, Amy Lynn. BSBA, Pitts. State U., 1969; JD, U. Mo., Kansas City, 1972. Bar: Mo. 1972, Kans. 1989. Assoc. Stubbs, Epstein & Mann, Kansas City, 1972-79; pvt. practice Kansas City, 1979—. Rsch. editor U. Mo.-Kansas City Law Rev., 1971-72. Capt. U.S. Army, 1969-74. Mem. ATLA, Mo. Assn. Trial Attys., Kans. Trial Lawyers Assn., Kansas City Met. Bar Assn. (chmn. workers' compensation com. 1991-93). Office: 1101 Walnut St Ste 900 Kansas City MO 64106-2182

BORELLI, FRANCIS J(OSEPH) (FRANK BORELLI), insurance brokerage and consulting firm financial executive; b. Bklyn., Sept. 2, 1935; s. Anthony and Ida Borelli; m. Madlyn Quadrino, June 25, 1960; children: Frank, Richard. BBA, Baruch Coll. CUNY, 1956. CPA, N.Y. With Deloitte Haskins & Sells, 1956-79, ptnr., 1968-79, mng. ptnr. in charge Bergen County, N.J. office, 1976-79; sr. v.p. fin. and adminstr., dir. Airco, Inc., Montvale, N.J., 1980-84; sr. v.p., chief fin. officer, dir. Marsh & McLennan Cos., Inc., N.Y.C., 1984—; bd. dirs. The Interpub. Group, United Water Resources. qd. dirs., vice-chmn. Nat. Multiple Sclerosis Soc., Nyack Hosp., pvt. sector coun.; active numerous pub. service orgns. Mem. Fin. Execs. Inst. (bd. dirs., exec. com., chmn.), AICPAs, N.Y. State Soc. CPAs, Ridgewood Country Club, Columbus Found. Club. Office: Marsh & McLennan Cos Inc 1166 Avenue Of The Americas New York NY 10036-2708

BORELLI, JOHN, religious organization professional; b. Oklahoma City; s. John W. and Margaret (Eisenbeis) B.; m. Marianne Dulle, Jan. 30, 1971; children: Stephen, Marguerite, Eleanor. BA, St. Louis U., 1968; MA, Fordham U., 1972, PhD, 1976. Instr. dept. theology Fordham U., Bronx, N.Y., 1975-76; prof. religious studies Coll. of Mt. St. Vincent, Bronx, 1976-87; dir. interreligious rels. Nat. Conf. Cath. Bishops, Washington, 1987—; cons. Pontifical Coun. for Interreligious Dialogue, Vatican City, 1989—; advisor Monastic Interreligious Dialogue, 1990—, Inst. for Interreligious Study and Dialogue Cath. U. Am., 1998—. Editor: Handbook for Interreligious Dialogue, 1990; co-editor: The Quest for Unity, Orthodox and Catholics in Dialogue, 1996. With U.S. Army, 1969-71. Decorated Bronze Star, Vietnam, 1970; recipient Gustav Ohaus award NSF, 1986. Mem. Nat. Assn. Diocesan Ecumenical Officers (faiths in the world com. 1982—), Phi Beta Kappa. Roman Catholic. Office: Nat Conf Cath Bishops 3211 4th St NE Washington DC 20017-1194

BOREN, CLARK HENRY, JR., general and vascular surgeon; b. Marinette, Wis., Nov. 23, 1947; s. Clark Henry and Maryon Lillian (Peterson) B.; children: Jenna Marie, Matthew William, Nathan Clark. BMS, Northwestern U., 1971, MD with distinction, 1973. Diplomate Am. Bd. Surgery. Resident in gen. surgery U. Calif.-H.C. Moffitt Hosp., San Francisco, 1973-79; rsch. fellow in vascular surgery Ft. Miley VA Hosp., 1976-77; vascular fellow Med. Coll. Wis./Milwaukee County Med. Complex,

Milw., 1979-80; mem. staff Fox Valley Surg. Assocs., Ltd., Appleton, Wis., 1980—; chmn. bd. United Health of Wis., 1995-99. Contbr. articles to profl. jours. Mem. ACS, AMA, Wis. State Med. Soc., Peripheral Vascular Surgery Soc., Midwest Vascular Soc., Wis. Surg. Soc., Internat. Soc. for Cardiovascular Surgery, Alpha Omega Alpha, Phi Beta Pi, Phi Eta Sigma, Phi Kappa Psi. Democrat. Congregationalist. Home: 1106 S Ritger St Appleton WI 54915 Office: Fox Valley Surg Assocs 1818 N Meade St Appleton WI 54911-3454

BOREN, DAVID LYLE, academic administrator; b. Washington, DC, Apr. 21, 1941; s. Lyle H. and Christine (McKown) B.; m. Molly Shi, Dec. 1977; children: David Daniel, Carrie Christine. B.A. summa cum laude, Yale, 1963; M.A. (Rhodes scholar), Oxford (Eng.) U., 1965; J.D. (Bledsoe Meml. prize as outstanding law grad.), U. Okla., 1968. Bar: Okla. 1968. Asst. to dir. liaison Office Civil and Def. Moblzn., Washington, 1960-62; propaganda analyst Soviet affairs USIA, Washington, 1962-63; mem. Speakers Bur. Am. Embassy, London, Eng., 1963-65; mem. residential counseling staff U. Okla., 1965-66; practiced in Seminole, 1968-74; prof. polit. sci., chair divsn. social scis. Okla. Bapt. U., Shawnee, 1969-74; mem. Okla. Ho. of Reps., 1967-75; gov. Okla., 1975-79; mem. U.S. Senate from Okla., 1979-94; pres. U. Okla., Norman, 1994—; mem. Senate Fin. Com., Senate Agrl. Com.; chmn. Senate Select Com. on Intelligence, govt. dept. Okla. Bapt. U., 1969-74. Del. Dem. Nat. Conv., 1968, 76, 84, 88; trustee Yale U., 1989. Named One of 10 Outstanding Young Men in U.S., U.S. Jaycees, 1967. Mem. Assn. U.S. Rhodes Scholars, Phi Beta Kappa. Methodist. Office: U Okla 660 Parrington Oval Norman OK 73019-3070*

BOREN, ROBERT REED, communication educator; b. Burley, Idaho, Nov. 8, 1936; s. Gilbert Reed Boren and Olive Chambers McBride; m. Marjorie Jean Dixon, Sept. 9, 1958; children: David, Michael, Elisabeth, Stephen. BA, Brigham Young U., 1958, MA, 1964; PhD, Purdue U., 1965. Instr. Purdue U., Lafayette, Ind., 1959-61; asst. prof. Brigham Young U., Provo, Utah, 1961-67; assoc. prof. U. Mont., Missoula, 1967-71; prof. Boise (Idaho) State U., 1971—, chair, 1971-95; pres. Insight Cons., Boise, 1995—. Author: The Human Transaction, 1975, Communication Behavior, 1975, Communication Experiments, 1975, Conducting the Council's Business, 1976, Wildflowers of the Sawtooth Mountains, 1979, Facilitator's Guide for Public Meetings, 1981, Effective Business Writing, 1985, Effective Communication, 1985, Effective Business Communication, 1986, Mountain Wildflowers of Idaho, 1989. Mem. Nat. Comm. Assn., Western States Comm. Assn. (v.p., pres. 1971-73, Disting. Svc. award 1998), Western Forensics Assn. (v.p., pres. 1968-70), Phi Kappa Delta. Avocations: hiking, rafting, fishing, hunting. E-mail: rboren@cyberhighway.net. Home: HC67-Box 742 Clayton ID 83227 Office: Boise State U 1910 University Blvd Boise ID 83725

BOREN, WILLIAM MEREDITH, manufacturing executive; b. San Antonio, Oct. 23, 1924; s. Thomas Loyd and Verda (Locke) B.; m. Molly Brasfield Sarver, Dec. 3, 1976; children: Susan, Patricia, Janet, Jenny, Burton, Cliff. Student, Tex. A&M U., 1942-43, Rice U., 1943-44; B.S. in Mech. Engring., Tex. U., 1949. Vice pres., gen. mgr. Rolo Mfg. Co., Houston, 1949-54; mgr. sales engring. Black, Sivalls & Bryson, Houston, Oklahoma City, 1955-64; vice chmn., dir., mem. exec. com. Big Three Industries, Inc., Houston, 1965—; chmn. Bowen Tool Co., Houston.; bd. dirs. Engring. Adv. Coun., Tex. U.; dir. Air Liquide Am. Corp.; dir. Electric Reliability Coun. Tex. Inventor Classic Bridge game. Trustee S.W. Rsch. Inst., San Antonio; bd. dirs. Coun. Econ. Edn.; mem. chancellor's coun. U. Tex. Lt. (j.g.) USN, 1943-46. Named Disting. Grad. Engring. Dept., U. Tex., 1992. Mem. Internat. Oxygen Mfrs. Assn. (chmn.), French-Am. C. of C. (bd. dirs.), Tau Beta Pi, Pi Tau Sigma. Republican. Home: 2906 Midlane St Houston TX 77027-4912 Office: Air Liquide Am Corp 3535 W 12th St PO Box 3047 Houston TX 77253-3047

BORENSTEIN, DANIEL ASA, newspaper political editor; b. Berkeley, Calif., Sept. 23, 1955; s. Martin and Betty (Aron) B.; m. Susan Watkins, Jan. 3, 1982 (div. June 1996); 1 child, Crystal Fawn Knight; m. Marian Dabney Scott, Feb. 14, 1999. BA in Journalism, U. Calif., Berkeley, 1978, BA in Polit. Sci., 1978, Master of Journalism, 1985, Master of Pub. Policy, 1985. Reporter Antioch (Calif.) Daily Ledger, 1980-83; reporter, asst. city editor Valley Times, Pleasanton, Calif., 1983-85; reporter, asst. city editor Contra Costa Times, Walnut Creek, Calif., 1986-90, polit. editor, 1990—; free-lance commentator Sta. KRON-TV, San Francisco, 1995-97, Sta. KQED-TV, San Francisco, 1994—; free-lance writer Calif. Jour., Sacramento, 1986, 91. Mem. Better Govt. task force Contra Costa County, 1995-96. Recipient Pub. Svc. award Calif. Newspaper Pubs. Assn., 1993, Investigative Reporting award, 1994, Third place pub. svc. award Nat. Headliner Club, 1994, Golden Medallion award for legal reporting State Bar of Calif., 1985, 93, Third place investigative reporting award Nat. Newspaper Assn., 1987; numerous others. Mem. Soc. of Profl. Journalists (co-chair Freedom of Info. com. No. Calif. Chpt., 1996-99, invesigative reporting award 1992-93, James Madison Freedom of Info. award 1994). Office: Contra Costa Times 2640 Shadelands Dr Walnut Creek CA 94598-2578

BORENSTEIN, DANIEL BERNARD, physician, educator; b. Silver City, N.Mex., Mar. 31, 1935; s. Jack and Marjorie Elizabeth (Kerr) B.; m. Bonnie Denice Ulland, June 11, 1967; 1 child, Jay Brian. BSChemE, MIT, 1957; MD, U. Colo., 1962. Diplomate Am. Bd. Psychiatry and Neurology. Intern U. Hosp. U. Ky., 1962-63; resident in psychiatry U. Colo. Med. Ctr., 1963-66; chief resident, psychiatry instr. U. Colo. Sch. Medicine, 1965-66; psychiatry instr. U. So. Calif. Sch. Medicine, 1966-67; asst. clin. prof. psychiatry UCLA Sch. Medicine, 1972-84, assoc. clin. prof., 1984-96, clin. prof., 1996—; founder, dir. UCLA Mental Health Program for Physicians in Tng., 1980-84; clin. assoc. L.A. Psychoanalytic Soc. and Inst., 1967-71, pres. clin. assocs., 1970-71, faculty, 1973-83, sr. faculty, 1983—; pvt. practice medicine specializing in psychoanalysis and psychiatry, West L.A., 1966—; assoc. vis. psychiatrist UCLA Ctr. Health Scis., 1973-90; cons. Medicare Program, 1995—; examiner Am. Bd. Psychiatry and Neurology; reviewer Jour. Psychiat. Svcs., 1991—. Author: Manual of Psychiatric Peer Review: Prelude and Promise, 1985; contbr. articles to profl. jours. Bd. dirs. L.A. Child Devel. Ctr., 1981-85, mem. hon. adv. com., 1985—; founding mem., bd. dirs. Found. Advancement Psychiat. Edn. and Rsch., 1991—; bd. dirs. coop. Am. Physicians Mut. Protective Trust, 1994—. Lt. AUS, 1957-58. Fellow Am. Psychiat. Assn. (coun. area VI 1977-79, 81-82, dep. rep. assembly dist. brs. 1981-82, rep. 1982-89, com. to rev. psychiat. news 1979-81, work group on competition and legis. 1981-83, nominating com. 1982-83, assembly liaison to peer rev. com. 1982-86, assembly liaison to fni. and mktg. com. 1986-87, assembly corr. group on subspecialization 1986-89, assembly liaison to coun. on econ. affairs, 1987-89, med. student edn. com. 1987-90, bd. trustees 1989—, bd. liaison jud. action commn. 1989-91, com. managed care 1990-92, various coms., bd. liaison to managed care com. 1992-99, bd. liaison econ. affairs coun. 1992-99, chmn. bd. ethics appeals 1995-97, sec. 1995-97, v.p. 1997-99, pres.-elect 1999—); mem. So. Calif. Psychiat. Soc. (Outstanding Svc. citation 1975, chmn. peer rev. com. 1974-77, exec. coun. 1976-89, ethics com. 1977-85, pres. 1978-79, chmn. fellowship and awards com. 1979-85, chmn. Commn. on Psychiatry and the Law 1980-81, 1st recipient Disting. Svc. award 1984, Appreciation award 1979, Outstanding Achievment award 1993), AMA (alt. del. Ho. Dels. 1998—), L.A. County Med Assn. (exec. coun. 1988-91, com. on well-being 1986-89, com. on substance abuse 1981-86, Bay Dist. v.p. 1985-86, pres.-elect 1986, pres. 1987-88, bd. dirs. 1981—, chmn. mental health com. 1980-85), Calif. Med. Assn. (rep. for psychiat. specialty to Ho. Dels. 1979-87, com. on mental health and mental disabilities 1979-85, 1986-88, bd. trustees 1992—, chmn. physicians benevolence operating com. 1996—, chmn. bldg. com. 1999—, various coms.), Calif. Psychiat. Assn. (exec. coun. 1977-79, 81-95, chmn. jud. com. 1986-88, Spl. Recognition award 1995, bd. trustees 1989-95), Los Angeles Psychoanalytic Soc. and Inst. (co-chmn. extension divsn. 1973-74, chmn. peer rev. com. 1975-78, mem. curriculum com. 1980-84), Am. Psychoanalytic Assn. (com. on confidentiality 1983-96, com. on govt. relations and ins. 1983—), Internat. Psychoanalytic Assn. Office: 151 N Canyon View Dr Los Angeles CA 90049-2721

BORENSTEIN, DAVID GILBERT, physician, author; b. Bklyn.; s. Murray and Mollie (Koren) B.; m. Dorothy Regina Fait, Aug. 6, 1972; children: Sylvia, Elizabeth, Rebecca. AB, Columbia U., 1969; MD, Johns Hopkins U., 1973. Diplomate in internal medicine and rheumatology Am. Bd. Internal Medicine. Intern in medicine Johns Hopkins Hosp., 1973-74, resident in medicine, 1974-76; fellow in rheumatology Johns Hopkins U., 1976-78; asst. prof. medicine George Washington U., Washington, 1978-83, assoc. prof. medicine, 1983-89, prof. medicine, 1989-96, prof. neurosurgery, 1991-96, clin. prof. medicine and neurosurgery, 1996-98; cons. Vaccine Injury Compensation Program, Dept. HHS, Washington, 1993—, Sulzer Medica, Austin, Tex., 1997—, Searle, Skokie, Ill., 1997—, Merck-Medco, Rahway, N.J., 1997—, OSHA, Dept. Labor, 1998—. Author: Low Back Pain: Medical Diagnosis, 1995, Neck Pain: Medical Diagnosis, 1996; contbg. author: Low Back Pain in Rheumatology, 1997. Mem. Appellate Jud. Nominating Commn., State of Md., 1986-94; mem. med. adv. bd. Arthritis Found. D.C., 1986-88, bd. dirs., 1999—; mem. med. adv. bd. Lupus Found. Greater Washington, 1992—. Fellow Am. Coll. Medicine, Am. Coll. Rheumatology (govt. affairs com. 1998—); mem. Internat. Soc. Study Lumbar Spine, Rheumatism Soc. D.C. (pres. 1992-93), Cosmos Club. Jewish. Avocations: skiing, stereo equipment, squash. Office: Arthritis and Rheum Assocs 2021 K St NW Washington DC 20006-1003

BORENSTEIN, MARK A., lawyer; b. Bklyn., June 26, 1951. BA, SUNY, Buffalo, 1973; JD, George Washington U., 1976; LLM, Georgetown U., 1978. Bar: Va. 1976, D,C, 1977, Calif. 1978. Law clk. to Hon. Irving Hill U.S. Dist. Ct. (cen. dist.), Calif., 1976-77; mem. Tuttle & Taylor, L.A.; lectr. U. So. Calif., 1980-82, vis. prof. law, 1997. Exec. editor: George Washington Law Review, 1975-76. Inst. for Pub. Interest Representation Law fellow Georgetown U. Law Ctr., 1977-78. Mem. Phi Beta Kappa, Order of the Coif. Office: Tuttle & Taylor 355 S Grand Ave Ste 3900 Los Angeles CA 90071-3176

BORENSTEIN, MILTON CONRAD, lawyer, manufacturing company executive; b. Boston, Oct. 21, 1914; s. Isadore Sidney and Eva Beatrice B.; m. Anne Shapiro, June 20, 1937; children: Roberta, Jeffrey. AB cum laude, Boston Coll., 1935; JD, Harvard U., 1938. Bar: Mass. 1938, U.S. Dist. Ct. 1939, U.S. Ct. Appeals 1944, U.S. Supreme Ct. 1944. Pvt. practice law Boston, 1938—; officer, dir. Sweetheart Paper Products Co., Inc., Chelsea, Mass., 1944-61; pres. Sweetheart Paper Products Co., Inc., Chelsea, 1961-83, chmn. bd., 1984; with Sweetheart Plastics, Inc., Wilmington, Mass., 1958—; v.p. Sweetheart Plastics, Inc., Wilmington, 1958-84, also dir.; v.p. Md. Cup Corp., Owings Mills, 1960-77, exec. v.p., treas., 1977-84, also dir. Bd. dirs. Am. Assocs. Hebrew U., 1968—; trustee Combined Jewish Philanthropies, Boston, 1969—, N.E. Sinai Hosp., Stoughton, Mass., 1974—, Ben-Gurion U., 1975-85, 87—, Boston Coll., 1979-87, chmn. estate planning coun., 1981-83, mem. coun. exec. com. 1984—, assoc. trustee, 1987-96; mem. pres.'s coun. Sarah Lawrence Coll., 1970-79; bd. overseers Jewish Theol. Sem. Am., 1971—; mem. pres. Congregation Kehillath Israel, Brookline, Mass., 1977-79, hon. pres., 1979—; mem. pres's coun. Brandeis U., 1979-81, fellow, 1981—; v.p. Assoc. Synagogues of Mass., 1980-81; exec. com. New Eng. region Anti-Defamation League, 1980—; bd. dirs., nat. governing coun. Am. Jewish Congress, 1984—; assoc. chmn. scholarship com. Harvard Law Sch., 1964-66, mem. spl. gifts com., 1990, mem. Langdell com., 1991, 92, 93, 94, 95, 96, 97, 98, 99, Boston regional campaign com., 1992, chmn. class reunion gift, 1993, 98. Recipient Community Svc. award Jewish Theol. Sem. Am., 1970, Am. Jewish Congress, 1993, Bald Eagle Outstanding Alumnus award Boston Coll., 1991; named Rofeh Internat. Man of Yr., 1996. Fellow Mass. Bar Found.; mem. ABA, Mass. Bar Assn., Boston Bar Assn. (mem. bicentennial com. 1986-87), Harvard Club (Boston and N.Y.C.), Harvard Faculty Club. Home: 273 Eliot St Chestnut Hill MA 02467-1445 Office: Concorde Assocs 1 Devonshire Pl Ste 2912 Boston MA 02109-3533

BORENSTINE, ALVIN JEROME, search company executive; b. Kansas City, Mo., Dec. 14, 1933; s. Samuel and Ella C. (Berman) B.; m. Roula Alakiotou, Dec. 31, 1976; Ella Marie and Sami (twins). B.S. in Econs., U. Kans., 1956; M.B.A., U. Pa., 1960. Analyst, Johnson & Johnson, New Brunswick, N.J., 1961-62; systems mgr. Levitt & Sons, Levittown, N.J., 1962-66; dir. mgmt. info. svcs. Warren Brothers Co., Cambridge, Mass., 1966-71; mgr. fin. and adminstrv. systems Esmark, Inc., Chgo., 1971-72; pres. Synergistics Assocs. Ltd., Chgo., 1972—; mem. bus. adv. coun., Program Able, Hellenic Dimensions, transition team clk. Cook County. Mem. bus. adv. coun. St. Xavier U.; civic com. El Valor; mem. North Shore Cultural Ctr. Systems and Procedures Assn. rsch. fellow, 1959-60; Eddie Jacobson Found. scholar, 1958-60. Mem. Assn. Exec. Search Cons., Assn. for Systems Mgmt. (pres. Boston chpt. 1969, Disting. Svc. award 1970), Soc. Info. Mgmt., Assn. Exec. Search Cons., Carlton Club, B'nai B'rith. Home: 6033 N Sheridan Rd Chicago IL 60660-3003 Office: Synergistics Assocs Ltd 400 N State St Ste 400 Chicago IL 60610-4624

BORER, EDWARD TURNER, investment banker; b. Phila., Nov. 30, 1938; s. Robert Chamberlin and Helen Elizabeth (Clawges) B.; BS, U. Pa., 1960; m. Amy Hamilton Ryerson, Aug. 8, 1959; children: Edward Turner, Catherine Hamilton, Elizabeth Taft. Rep., Hopper Soliday & Co., Inc., Phila., 1960-67, v.p. research, 1967-73, sec., 1971-85, sr. v.p., 1973-82, exec. v.p., 1982-84, pres., 1984-88, also bd. dirs.; dir. Montech Internat., 1994-96, Manchester Gas Co. (N.H.), 1965-88, pres., 1970, chmn. bd., chmn. exec. com., 1970-82; chmn. bd. EnergyNorth, Inc., 1982—; pres., dir. Phila. Corp. for Investment Svcs., 1989-95, chmn. 1995—; dir., sec. Disaster Control, Inc., 1981-83, Omni Oil & Gas Mgmt. Co., 1981-84; dir. Hopper Soliday Corp., 1988-89; founder, treas., sec., dir. Creative Information Systems, Inc., Chadds Ford, Pa., 1967-77; v.p. Sovereign Investors, 1980-86 ; arbitrator N.Y. Stock Exch., 1992—, Phila. Stock Exch., 1992—; bd. dirs. Energy North Natural Gas, Inc., Energy North Propane, Inc., Chmn. West Met. Area-Wide Com. Pres. Swarthmore Home and Sch. Assn., 1973; bd. dirs. Freedom Valley council Girl Scouts U.S.A., 1974-75, also chmn. finance com.; bd. dirs., chmn. fin. com. Planned Parenthood Southeastern Pa., 1980-85, dir. 1988-90; treas., 1986-87 trustee George W. South Meml. Ch. of the Adv., Phila., 1978-88; dir. Nat. Kidney Found. Del. Valley, 1990-96, treas., 1990-93, chmn., 1993-95, mem. exec. com., 1990-97; mem. Nat. Kidney Found. N.Y.C., mem. fin. com., 1995—, bd. dirs. rsch. endowment, 1996-97. Served to 1st lt., Q.M.C., AUS, 1961-62. CFA. Mem. Fin. Analysts Fedn., Phila. Securities Assn. (dir. 1979-83, v.p. 1980-81, pres. 1981-82), Nat. Assn. Securities Dealers (arbitrator 1982—, chmn. dist. 11 and bus. conduct com. 1986), Fin. Analysts Phila. (treas. 1976-77), N.Y. Soc. Security Analysts, Am. Arbitration Assn. (arbitrator 1988-96), N.Y. Stock Exch. (arbitrator 1992—), Phila. Stock Exch. (arbitrator 1992—), Delta Upsilon. Episcopalian (vestryman 1970-73, 74-77, 85-88). Club: Union League (Phila.), Radley Run Country. Home: 1175 S Birmingham Rd West Chester PA 19382-8092 Office: One Liberty Pl Philadelphia PA 19103

BORER, JEFFREY STEPHEN, cardiologist; b. Deland, Fla., Feb. 22, 1945; s. Lee Norton and Rita Doris (Feldt) B.; m. Brondi Beth Topchik, Sept. 16, 1978; children: Justine Isolde, Jon Andrew. BA in Govt., Harvard U., 1965; MD, Cornell U., 1969. Diplomate Am. Bd. Internal Medicine, Am. Bd. Cardiovascular Disease; cert. Coun. Nuclear Cardiology. Intern, then resident in medicine Mass. Gen. Hosp., Boston, 1969-71; clin. fellow in medicine Harvard U. Sch. Medicine, Boston, 1969-71; clin. assoc. in cardiology Nat. Heart, Lung and Blood Inst., NIH, Bethesda, Md., 1971-74, chief resident physician, 1973-74, sr. investigator, cardiology br., 1975-79; sr. Fulbright-Hays scholar, Glorney-Raisbeck fellow med. scis Guy's Hosp., U. London, 1974-75; assoc. prof. medicine Cornell U. Med. Coll., N.Y.C., 1979-82, prof., 1982—, Gladys and Roland Harriman prof. cardiovascular medicine, 1983—; prof. cardiovascular med. in radiology Cornell Univ. Med. Coll., N.Y.C., 1990—, prof. cardiovascular medicine in cardiothoracic surgery, 1996—; chief divsn. cardiovascular pathophysiology N.Y. Hosp./Cornell Med. Ctr., 1996—; chmn. cardiac and renal adv. com., U.S. FDA, Washngton, 1981-82, 83-87, 99—, cons., 1989—; mem. life scis. adv. com. NASA, Washington, 1984-88, mem. aero. med. adv. com., 1988-93, microgravity and life scis. adv. com. NASA, 1993-96, chmn. NASA/Mir Peer Rev. adv. com. 1993-95; chmn. NASA-NIH Biomed. and Behavioral Rsch. adv. com. 1995—; mem. NASA adv. com., 1995—; vis. prof. Chinese Acad. Med. Scis., Beijing, 1993—; chief divsn. cardiovascular pathophysiology N.Y. Hosp.-Cornell Med. Ctr., 1996—. Mem. editl. bds. 11 med. jours.; contbr. more than 300 articles on cardiovascular disease to med. jours.; patentee in field. Trustee N.Y.C. Historic Properties Fund, 1984-90; mem. steering com. Assocs. of the Jewish Bd. of Family and Children Svcs., 1989-91; pres. Am. Friends of Israel Nat. Heart to Heart Assn., 1991—. Sr. surgeon USPHS, 1971-79. Recipient Investigator's award prize European Cardiol. Soc., 1978, spl. award for contbns. to cardiology, Assn. Thoracic and Cardiovascular Surgeons of India, 1985, William A. Johnston award, Internat. Soc. Heart Rsch., 1986, spl. citation Israel Nat. Heart to Heart Assn., 1992; travelling fellow Am. Physicians Fellowship, 1981. Fellow ACP, Am. Soc. Clin. Investigation, Am. Coll. Cardiology (steering com., bd. govs. 1998—, governing coun. N.Y. chpt. 1991-93, pres. N.Y. State chpt. 1997-98, gov. 1997—), chmn., ACC BOG Task Force on Cardiovasc. Econs., 1999—, Am. Heart Assn. (coun. clin. cardiology and circulation, established investigator 1979-84), Am. Coll. Chest Physicians (chmn. cardiology forum 1985-86, exec. com. clin. cardiology sect., 1991-95), Am. Coll. Clin. Pharm., N.Y. Cardiol. Soc. (pres. 1990-91), Argentine Heart Assn. (hon.); mem. Soc. Nuclear Medicine (trustee cardiovascular coun. 1991-94), Soc. Cardiac Angiography and Interventions (gov. 1995—), Am. Soc. Nuclear Cardiology (fin. com. 1993-95), Certification Bd. Nuclear Cardiology (trustee 1996—), adv. counc., New York Pub. Libr. for Performing Arts, Dance Divn., 1999—, Harvard Club N.Y.C. Avocations: athletics, theater, opera, Chinese and Japanese calligraphy, ancient Greek history. Office: NY Hosp 525 E 68th St New York NY 10021-4885

BORESI, ARTHUR PETER, author, educator; b. Toluca, Ill.; s. John Peter and Eva B.; m. Clara Jean Gordon, Dec. 28, 1946; children: Jennifer Ann Boresi Hill, Annette Boresi Pueschel, Nancy Jean Boresi Broderick. Student, Kenyon Coll., 1943-44; BSEE, U. Ill., 1948, MS in Mechanics, 1949, PhD in Mechanics, 1953. Research engr. N. Am. Aviation, 1950; materials engr. Nat. Bur. Standards, 1951; mem. faculty U. Ill., Urbana, 1953—, prof. theoretical and applied mechanics and nuclear engring., 1959-79; prof. emeritus U. Ill. at Urbana, Urbana, 1979; Disting. vis. prof. Clarkson Coll. Tech., Potsdam, N.Y., 1968-69; NAVSEA research prof. Naval Postgrad. Sch., Monterey, Calif., 1978-79; prof. civil engring. U. Wyo., Laramie, 1979-95, head, 1980-94, prof. emeritus, 1995—; vis. prof. Naval Postgrad. Sch., Monterey, Calif., 1986-87.; cons. in field. Author: Engineering Mechanics, 1959, Elasticity in Engineering Mechanics, 3d edit., 1987, Advanced Mechanics of Materials, 5th edit., 1993, Approximate Solution Methods in Engineering Mechanics, 1991; also articles. Served with USAAF, 1943-44; Served with AUS, 1944-46. Fellow ASME, ASCE, Am. Acad. Mechanics (founding, treas.); mem. Am. Soc. Engring. Edn. (Archie Higdon Disting. Educator award 1993), Soc. Exptl. Mechanics, Sigma Xi, Tau Beta Pi. Office: U Wyo Box 3295 Univ Station Laramie WY 82071

BORETZ, BENJAMIN AARON, composer, music educator; b. N.Y.C., Oct. 3, 1934; s. Abraham Jacob and Leah (Yullis) B.; children: Avron, Nina. BA, Bklyn. Coll., 1954; MFA, Brandeis U., 1957, Princeton U., 1960; PhD, Princeton U., 1970. Critic Nation Mag., N.Y.C., 1962-70; editor Perspectives of New Music, N.Y.C., 1962-83, 94-96; prof. music N.Y.U., N.Y.C., 1964-69, Columbia U., N.Y.C., 1969-72, Princeton (N.J.) U., 1972-74, Bald Coll., Annandale, N.Y., 1973—; editor Open Space Mag., Annandale, N.Y., 1998—; Fulbright prof. U. Southampton, U.K., 1971-72; vis. prof. U. Mich., Ann Arbor, 1973, UCLA, 1991, U. Calif., Santa Barbara, 1991. Author: Meta-Variations, 1970; composer: Group Variations for Orchestra/Computer, 1974, Language as a Music, 1977, My Chart Shines High, 1978, Passage, 1979, ONE, 1985, forMaMusic, 1987, Music/Consciousness/Gender, 1995, Echoic/Anechoic, 1997, Black/Noise I, 1998, Black/Noise II and III, 1998. Recipient composition award Fromm Found., 1956, grant Ingram Merrill Found., 1965; fellow Coun. Humanities, Princeton U., 1972-73. Mem. Am. Composers Alliance, Am. Soc. Univ. Composers (sec. 1966-68). Home: RR 2 Box 45E Red Hook NY 12571-9802 Office: Open Space RR 2 Box 45E Red Hook NY 12571-9802

BORETZ, NAOMI MESSINGER, artist, educator; b. Bklyn.; d. Joseph and Sarah (Lesser) Messinger; m. Benjamin A. Boretz; 1 child, Avron Albert. BA, Bklyn. Coll., 1957; MFA, CUNY, 1971; MA, Rutgers U., 1976; postgrad., Art Students League N.Y. Assoc. prof. fine arts, chair fine arts dept. Wilson Coll., Chambersburg, Pa., 1985—. Exhbns. include Westminster Arts Coun. Arts Ctr., London, 1971, Hudson River Mus., N.Y., 1975, Katonah Gallery, N.Y., 1976, Condeso-Lawler Gallery, N.Y.C., 1987, Carnegie-Mellon Art Gallery, Pitts., 1989, The Nelson Atkins Mus. of Art, St. Louis, 1994, Westbeth Gallery, N.Y., 1996, others; represented in pub. collections Met. Mus. Art, N.Y.C., Solomon R. Guggenheim Mus., N.Y.C., Brit. Mus., London, Nat. Mus. Am. Art, Washington, Yale U. Art Gallery, Joslyn Art Mus., Omaha, Walker Art Ctr., Mpls., Miami U. Art Mus., Oxford, Ohio, Fogg Art Mus. Harvard U., Cambridge, Mass., Glasgow (Scotland) Mus., San Jose (Calif.) Art Mus., Asheville (N.C.) Art Mus., others; contbr. to arts publs. Artist-fellow Va. Ctr. Creative Arts, 1973, 86, Ossabaw Found., 1975, Tyrone Guthrie Arts Ctr., Ireland, 1987, Writers-Artists Guild Can., 1988; grantee N.J. State Coun. on Arts, 1985-86. Office: Wilson Coll Art Dept Chambersburg PA 17201

BORG, DEAN JEREMY, real estate developer; b. White Plains, N.Y., Dec. 24, 1961; s. Robert F. and Ethel W. (Pench) B.; m. Lisa Eve Borg, Sept. 14, 1991; children: Cole Eric, Devin Amanda. BS in Bus. Adminstrn., U. Ariz., 1984; MS in Real Estate Devel., Columbia U., 1987. Lic. real estate salesman, Fla. Mktg. agt. Cienaga Properties Ltd., Tucson, Ariz., 1984-86; dir. bus. devel. Kreisler, Borg, Florman Constrn. Co., Scarsdale, N.Y., 1987-90; v.p., dir. comml. leasing Crocker & Co., Boca Raton, 1990-92; project exec. Kenco Communities/K & R Properties, So. Properties, 1992-94; sr. v.p., project dir., sales dir. Kenco Communities, Boca Raton, 1994—; adj. prof. Fla. Atlantic U., Boca Raton. Fundraiser Congregation B'nai Israel Bldg. Com., Boca Raton, Am. Diabetes Assn. South Fla. Mem. Goldcoast Builders Assn., Nat. Assn. Indsl. and Office Parks. Avocations: photography, music, wine collecting. Home: 2687 NW 39th St Boca Raton FL 33434-4443

BORG, HENRY FRANKLIN, retired manufacturing company executive; b. Springfield, Ill., Aug. 7, 1935; s. Gustav Adolph and Svea Caroline (Swanson) B.; m. Barbara A. Pulliam, Sept. 15, 1957; children: Eric A., Rebecca C. AB, Ripon Coll., 1957; MBA, U. Chgo., 1965. Sales exec. 3M Co., Chgo., 1959-64, sales mgr., 1964-66, br. mgr., 1966-69; mktg. mgr. 3M Co., St. Paul, 1969-72, internat. mgr., 1972-82; internat. dir., 1982-96; ret., 1996; internat. bus. cons., Mpls., 1996. Pres. St. Anthony Sports Boosters, St. Paul, 1976-80. 1st lt. U.S. Army, 1957-59. Recipient Salesman of Yr. award Chgo. Sales and Mktg., 1962, Gold Tee award Golf Course Supts. Am., 1992. Mem. PGA Europe Relais du Golf (bd. dirs. 1996). Avocations: golf, grandchildren, fishing, boating, travel. Home: 5021 Greenbriar Trail Mount Dora FL 32757

BORG, MALCOLM AUSTIN, communications company executive; b. N.Y.C., Jan. 28, 1938; s. Donald Gowen and Flora (Austin) B.; m. Sandra Jean Agemian, Sept. 9, 1961; children—John Austin, Jennifer Ann, Stephen Agemian. BS, Columbia U., 1965; postgrad., Harvard Bus. Sch., 1970; LHD (hon.), Ramapo (N.J.) Coll., 1985. Editl. trainee Bergen Record, Hackensack, N.J., 1959-60, gen. assignment reporter, 1960-62, adminstrv. asst. to pub., 1963-64, asst. pub., 1965-66, v.p., 1967-68, exec. v.p., 1968-70, pres., 1971-78, CEO, 1971—, chmn. bd., 1975—; chmn. bd. Gateway Comm., Inc. subs. Macromedia Inc., Hackensack, 1978—; chmn. bd., CEO Macromedia, Inc., Borg Family holding co., Hackensack, 1971—. Active numerous civic orgns., 1965—; bd. dirs. Wolfeboro (N.H.) Camp Sch., 1970—; mem. Palisades Interstate Park Commn., 1974—; chmn. Submarine Meml. Assn., Hackensack, 1974—; mem. adv. bd. Sch. Gen. Studies, Columbia U., 1981—, mem. nat. campaign com. Fund for Columbia, 1983-87, 92-98, mem. alumni adv. bd., 1987-95. Recipient 1st William H. Spurgeon III award Bergen council Boy Scouts Am., 1972, 1st Whitney M. Young award, 1986; Torch of Liberty award Anti-Defamation League, B'nai B'rith, 1973, ann. communications and leadership award Greater N.Y. dist. 46 Toastmasters Internat., 1976, Service to Others award N.J. div. Salvation Army, 1977, ann. community leadership award NO. N.J. Interprofl. Council, 1977, Man of Yr. award Holy Name Hosp., 1977, Editor of Yr. award Nat. Press Photographers Assn., 1985, Owl award Sch. Gen. Studies, Columbia U., 1986, Citizen's award Acad. Medicine N.J., 1986; Alumni Fedn. medal Columbia U., 1991. Mem. Newspaper Assn. Am., Am. Soc. Newspaper Editors, N.J. Press Assn., Bergen County C. of C. (bd. dirs. 1967-74), N.J. C. of C. (bd. dirs. 1977-79), Hill Sch. Alumni Assn. (pres. 1973-76), Advt. Coun. (bd. dirs. 1978-85), Harvard Bus. Sch. Alumni Assn. (pres. 1976-78), Arcola Country Club (Paramus, N.J.), Columbia Club (N.Y.C.), Englewood Field (N.J.) Club, Mid Ocean Club (Tucker's Town, Bermuda), Harvard Club (N.Y.C.), Bath and Tennis Club (Spring Lake, N.J.), Knickerbocker Country Club (Tenafly, N.J.), Manasquan River Golf Club (Brielle, N.J.), Moselem Springs Golf Club (Fleetwood, Pa.). Avocations: golf, travel. Office: Bergen Record Corp 150 River St Hackensack NJ 07601-7110

BORG, MARCUS JOEL, theologian, theology educator; b. Fergus Falls, Minn., Mar. 11, 1942; s. Glenn F. and Esther (Stortroen) B.; m. Marianne Wells, Aug. 24, 1985; children: Dane, Julie. BA, Concordia Coll., Moorhead, Minn., 1964; diploma in Theology, U. Oxford, Eng., 1966; D.Phil., U. Oxford, 1972; postgrad., Union Theol. Sem., U. Tübingen, Fed. Republic Germany. Prof. religion Carleton Coll., Northfield, Minn., 1976-79; prof. religion and culture Oreg. State U., Corvallis, 1979—; Disting. vis. prof. U. Puget Sound, Tacoma, Wash., 1986-87; vis. prof. N.T. Pacific Sch. Religion, Berkeley, Calif., 1989-91. Author: Year of Luke, 1976, Conflict and Social Change, 1971, Conflict, Holiness and Politics in the Teaching of Jesus, 1984, Jesus: A New Vision, 1987, Meeting Jesus Again for the First Time, 1994, Jesus in Contemporary Scholarship, 1994, Jesus at 2000, 1996, The God We Never Knew, 1997, Jesus and Buddha, 1997, The Meaning of Jesus: Two Visions, 1998; contbr. articles to religious jours. Recipient Burlington-No. Teaching award Oreg. State U., 1986, Faculty Excellence award Oreg. State Legislature, 1987. Fellow The Jesus Sem.; mem. Soc. Bibl. Lit., Cath. Bibl. Assn., Am. Acad. Religion. Office: Oreg State U Dept Philosophy Corvallis OR 97331

BORG, ROBERT FREDERIC, civil engineer; b. N.Y.C., Jan. 10, 1923; s. Herman Leo and Pauline (Leibman) F.; children: Christina Gordon, Lisa Borg-Broe, Eric (dec.), Kiri, Neil, Dean. B in Civil Engring., NYU, 1944, JD, 1949. Bar: N.Y. 1950; lic. profl. engr., N.Y., 1950, Ohio, 1950. Field engr. Turner Construction Co., Rome, N.Y., 1942, Spencer White & Prentis, N.Y.C., 1946-48; office engr. various gen. contractors, N.Y.C., 1948-55; co-founder, ptnr., chmn. Kreisler Borg Florman Gen. Construction Co. & affiliates, Scarsdale, N.Y., 1955--; co-founder Kensico Construction Co., Scarsdale, 1957--, pres., 1966--; structural engr. Chance Vought Aircraft, 1944; mem. bldg. rsch. adv. bd. Nat. Acad. Engring., Washington, 1963; adj. prof. NYU, 1971-79, Pratt Inst., Bklyn., 1983-86, Columbia U., N.Y.C., 1987-90; mem. US/USSR joint com. on coop. in housing and other forms construction U.S. Dept. Housing and Urban Devel., Washington, 1976-87; mem. Sino-US Trade Delegation to China, 1993. Contbg. author: (handbook) Building Design and Construction, 1999, Construction Project Management, (handbook) Temporary Structures in Construction, 1996, Technical and Business Practices; founder Photo Bulletin DeWitt Clinton H.S., N.Y.C.; photo editor Clinton News, 1940; editor-in-chief Quadrangle, NYU Coll. of Engring., 1943; one-man photography shows in various locations 1980-85, including Gallery Show in Soho, N.Y.C., 1985. Chmn., founder Garth Woods Conservancy, Scarsdale, N.Y., 1991— co-developer, ptnr. Bethune Tower Apts., N.Y.C., 1970, Heywood Tower Apts., 1972, Univ. Riverview Apts., 1973, Cooper Gramercy Apts., 1975, Marcus Garvey Park Village, 1976, Cove Club Apts., 1992; staff mem., docent Internat. Ctr. Photography, N.Y.C., 1994—. Served with USN, 1944-46. Recipient Outstanding Builder Developer award Associated Builders and Owners Greater N.Y., 1989-90, 91, Builder of Yr. award, 1996, Emma Lazarus award, 1997; finalist Entrepreneur of the Yr. award So. New Eng., 1996, 97, 98, Entrepreneur of the Yr. Inst. Fellow ASCE (mem. com. on contract administrn. 1952, 63-67, founder, 1st chmn. constrn. group met. sect. 1962, chmn. tech. activities met. sect. 1963, met. sect. bd. dirs. 1962-67, mem. exec. com. nat. constrn. div. 1971, chmn. exec. com. nat. constrn. div. 1973-74, founding chmn. com. on social and environ. concerns in constrn. 1971), Am. Arbitration Assn. (mem. nat. panel arbitrators 1957—, mem. nat. constrn. industry arbitration com. 1972—, chmn. 1974-76, bd. dirs. 1974-94, mem. de Jur Mediation Ctr. 1974—). Fax: 914-725-0346; E-mail: KBF General@Aol.com. Office: Kreisler Borg Florman Gen Constrn Co 97 Montgomery St Scarsdale NY 10583-5104

BORG, RUTH I., home nursing care provider; b. Chgo., Mar. 29, 1934; d. Axel Gunner and Charlotte (Benston) B. Diploma, West Suburban Sch. Nursing, 1956; tchr.'s degree, Chgo. Conservatory, 1958; BSN, Alverno Coll., 1981. Staff nurse Boath Meml. Hosp., Chgo.; head nurse psychiatry, head nurse long-term medicine VA North Chgo. Med. Ctr.; staff nurse, night supr. intermediate care VA Clement Zabiocki Med. Ctr., Milw.; pool nurse, in-home nursing care provider Milw. County Mental Health Complex; home nurse care provider Dr. Ghonsham Sooknandan, Kenosha, Wis., 1994—; in-home nursing care provider. Contbr. 2 articles to profl. jours. Recipient Mary D. Bradford Disting. Alumni award, 1998. Avocation: teaching and performing music.

BORGATTA, EDGAR F., social psychologist, educator; b. Milan, Italy, Sept. 1, 1924; came to U.S., 1929, naturalized, 1934; s. Edgar A. and Frances (Zinelli) B.; m. Marie Lentini, Oct. 5, 1946; children: Lynn, Kim, Lee. B.A., N.Y. U., 1947, M.A., 1949, Ph.D., 1952. Cert. psychologist, N.Y., Vt., Wis. Instr. N.Y. U., 1949-51, lectr., prof., 1954-59; lectr., research asso. Harvard, 1951-54; social psychologist, asst. sec. Russell Sage Found., 1954-59; prof. sociology Cornell U., Ithaca, N.Y., 1959-61; Brittingham Research prof. U. Wis., 1961-72, chmn. dept. sociology, 1962-65, chmn. div. social studies, 1965-68; Distinguished prof. sociology Queens Coll., City U. N.Y., 1972-77, prof Grad. Center, 1972-82; dir. Italian Social Sci. Center, Queens Coll., 1972-77; research dir. CUNY Case Center for Gerontol. Studies, 1978-81, dir. data service, 1981-82; prof. sociology U. Wash., Seattle, 1981—; chmn. dept. sociology U. Wash., 1992-93; dir Inst. on Aging U. Wash., Seattle, 1981-86; cons. to bus. and govt., 1953—, Russell Sage Found., 1970-72; lectr., prof., adj. prof. sociology NYU, 1954-59; cons. editor Rand McNally & Co., 1961-74; chmn. bd. F.E. Peacock Pubs., Inc.; Nat. Inst. Gen. Scis.; spl. research fellow, 1972. Editor: Research on Aging, Sociol. Methodology, Sociol. Methods and Research; co-editor: Handbook of Personality Theory and Research; editor-in-chief: Encyclopedia of Sociology, 2d edit.; contbr. articles to profl. jours. Fellow Am. Psychol. Assn., Am. Psychol. Soc.; mem. Psychometric Soc., Sociol. Research Assn., Am. Sociol. Assn. (v.p. 1983), Pacific Sociol. Assn. (pres. 1985), Internat. Inst. Sociology (pres. 1984-89). E-mail: bowgatta@u.washington.edu. Office: U Wash Dept Sociology PO Box 353340 Seattle WA 98195-3340

BORGDORFF, PETER, church administrator. Exec. dir. of ministries Christian Ref. Ch. in N. Am., 1990. Office: Christian Ref Ch in N Am 2850 Kalamazoo Ave SE Grand Rapids MI 49508-1433*

BORGE, VICTOR, entertainer, comedian, pianist; b. Copenhagen, Jan. 3, 1909; came to U.S., 1940, naturalized, 1948; s. Bernhard and Frederikke (Lichtinger) B.; m. Sarabel Sanna Scraper, Mar. 17, 1953; children—Sanna J., Victor Bernhardt, Frederikke; children by previous marriage—Ronald, Janet. Ed., Borgerdydskolen; D.Mus. (hon.), Butler U., 1970, Dana Coll., Blair, Nebr., 1977. Performed on concert stage, 1922-34; studied at Conservatory of Copenhagen, 1925; studied music in Vienna and Berlin (with Egon Petri and Frederic Lamond, 3 years; appeared in mus. rev., 1934; combined music ability and humor, creating new vogue of sophisticated mus. satire; wrote and directed own shows; entered motion pictures, 1937; became one of Denmark's foremost performers, writing script, composing mus. scores and playing the lead Scandinavian tour, 1938; came to U.S., 1940; guest 54 consecutive weeks on Kraft Music Hall; headed other radio programs incl. Victor Borge Radio and Victor Borge TV Series; soloist with many famed orchs.; guest condr. numerous symphony orchs. including: Amsterdam Concertgebouw, London Philharmonic, N.Y. Philharmonic, Phila. Orch., Nat. Symphony, Cleve. Orch.; one-man show at Golden Theatre, N.Y.C., 1953, 849 consecutive performances; numerous one-man TV spls. U.S., Gt. Britain incl. current PBS spl. Victor Borge Birthday Gala, 1993, Victor Borge Then and Now, Victor Borge Then and Now II, 1994; ltd. engagement Palace Theatre, London, 1957; appeared before U.S. Congress, UN, toured, Brit. Isles, 1958, N.Z., Australia, Europe, Far East; appeared in motion picture The King of Comedy, 1984. Author: (with Robert Sherman) My Favorite Intermissions; (home video) The Best of Victor Borge (platinum video award). Nat. chmn. pub. service com. CARE, 1959, chmn. internat. pub. service com.; nat. chmn. Multiple Sclerosis Soc.; a founder, nat. chmn. Thanks to Scandinavia scholarship fund; established Victor Borge Scholarship Funds at U. Conn. at Storrs, Dana Coll., Blair, Nebr. Awarded many honors; decorated knight 1st class Order St. Olav, Norway; Royal Order Daneborg, Absalom (Denmark); Order of Vasa, Sweden; recipient Brotherhood award, 1957; Wadsworth Internat. award, 1957; TV Father of Year award, 1958; Georg Jensen Silver award; CARE Pub. Service award, 1973; Gold award for best pub. service comml. Internat. Film and TV Festival N.Y., 1973; also honored U.S. Congress. Began study of music age 5. Address: care Gurtman & Murtha Assocs 450 7th Ave Ste 603 New York NY 10123-0699 *Being the recipient of physical and mental facilities assigned to me before my birth, I am convinced that, as custodian, my efforts toward accomplishments consist mainly of a reasonable amount of discipline and devotion to elementary decency. Perhaps part of my good fortune may be credited to my faults of which the greatest is modesty.**

BORGENS, RICHARD, biologist; b. Little Rock, May 7, 1946. BS, N. Tex. State U., 1970, MS, 1973; PhD in Biology, Purdue U., 1977. Rsch. assoc. biology Purdue U., 1977-78, Yale U., 1978-80; assoc. staff scientist Jackson Lab., Bar Harbor, Maine, 1980-81; staff scientist Inst. Med. Rsch., 1981-98; fellow Nat. Paraplegia Found., 1978-80; Dir., prof. devel. anatomy Purdue U. Ctr. Paralysis Rsch., 1998—. Mem. Am. Soc. Zoologists, Soc. Devel. Biology. Office: Purdue Univ Dept Anatomy 1244 Ctr for Paralysis Rsch West Lafayette IN 47907-1244*

BORGER, GLORIA, journalist, editor. Grad., Colgate U., 1974. Journalist Washington Star, 1975-78; chief congrl. corr. Newsweek, Washington, 1976-86; asst. mng. editor U.S. News and World Report, N.Y.C., 1986—, Washington. *

BORGER, JOHN PHILIP, lawyer; b. Wilmington, Del., Apr. 19, 1951; s. Philip E. and Jane (Smyth) B.; m. Judith Marie Yates, May 24, 1974; children: Jennifer, Christopher, Nicholas. BA in Journalism with high honors, Mich. State U., 1973; JD, Yale U., 1976. Bar: Minn. 1976, U.S. Dist. Ct. Minn. 1976, U.S. Ct. Appeals (8th cir.) 1979, U.S. Supreme Ct. 1982, N.D. 1988, U.S. Dist. Ct. N.D. 1988, Wis. 1993. Editor-in-chief Mich. State News, East Lansing, 1972-73; assoc. Faegre & Benson, LLP, Mpls., 1976-83, ptnr., 1984—; bd. dirs. Milkweed Edits.; adj. prof. U. Minn. Sch. Journalism and Mass Comm., 1999. Mem. ABA (chmn. media law and defamation torts com. torts and ins. practice sect. 1996-97), Minn. Bar Assn., State Bar Assn. N.D., Wis. Bar Assn., Hennepin County Bar Assn. Office: Faegre & Benson LLP 2200 Norwest Ctr 90 S 7th St Ste 2200 Minneapolis MN 55402-3901

BORGER, MICHAEL HINTON IVERS, osteopathic physician, educator; b. Kirksville, Mo., Nov. 10, 1951; s. Donald L. Borger and Dorothy M. Hinton. BA in Sociology, U. Akron, 1974; DO, Coll. Osteo. Medicine and Surgery, Des Moines, 1977. Diplomate Nat. Bd. Examiners in Osteo. Medicine and Surgery, Am. Coll. Osteopathic Family Physicians; ordained elder Presbyn. Ch., 1969. Rotating extern Youngstown (Ohio) Osteo. Hosp., 1976; extern in family medicine Dietz Diagnostic Clinic, Des Moines, 1977; rotating intern South Bend (Ind.) Osteo. Hosp. (now St. Mary's Cmty. Hosp), 1977-78; active staff South Bend (Ind.) Osteo. Hosp. (now St. Mary's Cmty. Hosp.), 1978-79, assoc. staff, 1979-82; pvt. practice Nappanee, Ind., 1978--; mem. staff Elkhart (Ind.) Gen. Hosp., 1978—, Goshen Gen. Hosp., 1981—; clin. asst. prof. gen. practice Kirksville (Mo.) Coll. Osteo. Medicine, 1990-93; apptd. clin. preceptor Kansas City U. of Health Scis. Coll. of Osteo. Medicine, 1993—; asst. clin. prof. family practice Kansas City U. of Health Scis. Coll. of Osteo. Medicine, Kansas City, 1995—; pres. Northwood Physicians, Inc., 1992—; assoc. manuscript reviewer Jour. Respiratory Diseases, 1986-88, Jour. Musculoskeletal Medicine, 1989—; pres. Northwood Profl. Assocs., Inc., 1995—; mem. quality improvement com. Ptnrs. Health Plan, 1996—; founder Circle of Care Healthcare Sys., 1996. Bd. dirs. Nappanee chpt. Families in Action, 1980-82; bd. dirs., chmn. Mission and Svcs. Commn., 1st Mennonite Ch., Nappanee, 1984-90, chmn. pastoral search com., 1989-90; mem. screening com. for elem. prin. Wa-Nee Sch. Dist., 1988; med. advisor United Presbyn. Ch. Nursery Sch., Nappanee, 1995—. Recipient Physician of Yr. award Ind. Assn. Emergency Med. Technicians, 1981, Good Citizens award Tower Savs., 1982, 1st degree black belt Tae Kwon Do, 1988, Tae Kwon Do Student of Yr. award, Hong's USA Tae Kwon Do, 1988; Burroughs-Wellcome Osteo rsch. fellow, 1980-81. Mem. Am. Osteo. Assn., Ind. Assn. Osteo. Physicians and Surgeons, Am. Acad. Applied Osteopathy, Nat. Honor Soc., Masons (3d degree), York Rite. Home: 353 N Hartman St Nappanee IN 46550-1417

BORGESE, ELISABETH MANN, political science educator, author; b. Munich, Apr. 24, 1918; arrived in U.S., 1938, naturalized, 1941, became Can. citizen, 1983; d. Thomas and Katia (Pringsheim) Mann; m. Giuseppe Antonio Borgese, Nov. 23, 1939; children: Angelica, Dominica. Diploma, Conservatory of Music, Zurich, 1937; multiple doctorates (hon.), Mt. St. Vincent U., 1986. Rsch. assoc., editor Common Cause, U. Chgo., 1945-51; editor Perspective USA; Diogenes (Intercultural Publs.), 1952-57; exec. sec. bd. editors Ency. Brit., Chgo., 1964-66; sr. fellow Ctr. for Study Dem. Instns., Santa Barbara, Calif., 1964-79; Killam sr. fellow Dalhousie U., Halifax, N.S., Can., 1979-80, prof. dept. polit. sci., 1980—, adj. prof. Sch. Law, 1996—; chmn. planning coun. Internat. Ocean Inst., 1972-92, hon. chmn. life, 1992; chmn. Internat. Ctr. for Ocean Devel., 1986-92; advisor Austrian del. 3d UN Conf. on Law of Sea, 1976-82, Prep. Commn., Jamaica, 1983-86. Author: To Whom It May Concern, 1962, Ascent of Woman, 1963, The Language Barrier, 1965, The Ocean Regime, 1968, The Drama of the Oceans, 1976, Seafarm: The Story of Aquaculture, 1980, The Mines of Neptune, 1985, The Future of the Oceans: A Report to the Club of Rome, 1986, (play) Only the Pyre, 1987, (juvenile) Chairworm and Supershark, 1992, Ocean Governance and the United Nations, 1995, The Oceanic Circle, 1998; editor: Pacem in Maribus, 1972, Ocean Yearbook, 13 vols., 1981—, Ocean Frontiers, 1992; contbr. short stories and essays to mags. Decorated medal of High Merit, Austria, Order of Merit, Govt. Columbia; recipient Sasakawa Internat. Environ. prize UN, 1987, Order of Can., 1987, Friendship award Govt. China, 1992, St. Francis of Assisi Internat. Environ. prize, 1993, Lifetime Achievement award Nuc. Age Peace Found., UN Honour medal Lt. Gov. N.S. Mem. AAAS, Acad. Polit. Sci., Am. Soc. Internat. Law, World Acad. Arts and Scis., Third-World Acad. Sci., Club of Rome. Office: Internat Ocean Inst, 1226 LeMarchant St, Halifax, NS Canada B3H 3P7

BORGMAN, JAMES MARK, editorial cartoonist; b. Cin., Feb. 24, 1954; s. James Robert and Florence Marian (Maly) B.; m. Lynn Goodwin, Aug. 20, 1977. B.A., Kenyon Coll., 1976. Editorial cartoonist Cin. Enquirer, 1976—, King Features Syndicate, 1980—; contbr. to Newsweek Broadcasting's Cartoon-A-Torial (animated editorial cartoon feature), 1978-81. Author: (collection of editorial cartoons) Smorgasborgman, 1982, The Great Communicator, 1985, The Mood of America, 1986, Jim Borgman's Cincinnati, 1992, Disturbing the Peace, 1995; co-creator comic strip Zits, 1997. Recipient Sigma Delta Chi award, 1978, 95, Thomas Nast prize, 1980, 2d prize for editorial cartooning Internat. Salon Cartoons of Montreal, 1981, Ohio's Gov.'s award, 1990, Pulitzer Prize for editorial cartooning, 1991, Nat. Headliner award, 1991, Reuben award for outstanding cartooning of yr., 1993. Mem. Am. Assn. Editorial Cartoonists, Nat. Cartoonists Soc. (Best Editorial Cartoonist award 1987, 88, 89, 94). Office: 312 Elm St Cincinnati OH 45202-2739*

BORGNINE, ERNEST, actor; b. Hamden, Conn., Jan. 24, 1917; s. Charles B. and Anna (Boselli) B.; m. Tova Newman, 1972. Student pub. schs., New Haven; student, Randall Sch. Dramatic Arts, Hartford, Conn. Actor N.Y. stage plays Mrs. McThing, Harvey, The Odd Couple, Hamlet, An Offer You Can't Refuse; actor Columbia Pictures Corp., Metro-Goldwyn Mayer, 20th Century-Fox; motion pictures include The Mob, From Here to Eternity, Bad Day at Black Rock, Demetrius and the Gladiators, Violent Saturday, Marty, Square Jungle, The Catered Affair, The Best Things in Life Are Free, Three Brave Men, Hell Below, Badlanders, Rabbit Trap, Man on a String, Barrabas, China Corsair, 1951, Johny Guitar, 1954, Vera Cruz, 1954, Run for Cover, 1955, Last Command, 1955, Jubal, 1956, Go Naked in the World, 1961, 10 Years a Counterspy, Summer of the Seventeenth Doll, Flight of the Phoenix, 1966, The Oscar, 1966, Chuka, 1967, The Dirty Dozen, 1968, Legend of Lylah Clare, 1968, The Wild Bunch, 1969, The Adventurers, 1970, Suppose They Gave a War and Nobody Came, 1970, A Bullet for Sandoval, 1970, Bunny, O'Hare, Hannie Caulder, 1971, Willard, 1971, The Poseidon Adventure, 1972, The Revengers, 1972, The Emperor of the North, 1973, Law and Disorder, 1974, Hustle, 1975, The Devil's Rain, 1975, Shoot, 1976, The Greatest, 1977, Convoy, 1978, Crossed Swords, 1978, The Day the World Ended, 1979, The Black Hole, 1979, The Double Mcguffin, 1979, When Time Ran Out, 1980, Escape from New York, 1981, Deadly Blessing, 1981, Codename: Wildgeese, 1986, Spike of Bensonhurst, 1988, Any Man's Death, 1990, Mortal Passions, 1990, Mistress, 1992, All Dogs go to Heaven 2, 1996, McHale's Navy, 1997, Gattaca, 1997; also appeared on TV series McHale's Navy, Future Cop, Airwolf, Sam Hill, The Single Guy; starred in TV films All Quiet on the Western Front, 1979, Blood Feud, 1983, Last Days of Pompeii, 1984, Dirty Dozen: The Next Mission, 1985; guest star TV series Little House on The Praire, Love Boat, Magnum, P.I., Matt Houston, Higway To Heaven, Murder She Wrote, The Boys. Active VA, across the country. With USNR, World War II. Recipient Oscar for best performance of year, 1956. Mem. Masons (33 degree). Lodge: Mason. Avocation: playing golf.

BORGSTAHL, KAYLENE DENISE, health facility administrator; b. Hampton, Iowa, May 21, 1951; d. Harry Dell and Berniece Irene (Muhlenbruck) Crabb; children: Elliot Michael, Brett Andrew. BS in Nursing, U. Iowa, 1973; MPA, Iowa State U., 1986. Asst. adminstr. Linn County Vis. Nurse Assn., Cedar Rapids, Iowa, 1975-85; v.p. program svcs. Voluntary Hosps. Iowa Home Health Care, Cedar Rapids, 1985-86; adminstr. Norell Home Health Svcs., Edina, Minn., 1986-87; case mgr. In Home Health Svcs., Mpls., 1987-88; adminstr. Sundance Med. Clinic Ltd., Shakopee, Minn., 1988-94, Apple Valley (Minn.) Med. Ctr., 1995-97, Resource Mgmt., Shakopee, Minn., 1997—. Mem. Sigma Theta Tau. Republican.

BORIE, BERNARD SIMON, JR., physicist, educator; b. New Orleans, June 21, 1924; s. Bernard Simon and Ruth (Lastrapes) B.; BS, U. S.W. La., 1944; MS, Tulane U., 1949; PhD, M.I.T., 1956; Fulbright fellow U. Paris, 1956-57; m. Martine Edith Descamps, May 2, 1957 (div. May 1964); children: Kathleen, Fabienne, Marianne. Research physicist metall. div. Oak Ridge Nat. Lab., 1949-53, group leader x-ray diffraction Metals and Ceramics Div., 1957-60, head fundamental research sect., 1960-69, sr. scientist, 1969-85 ; prof., U. Tenn., 1963—; vis. prof. Cornell U., 1971-72, U. Calif., Berkeley, 1980. Served to lt., USNR, 1944-45. Fellow AAAS; mem. AIME, Am. Soc. Metals, Am. Crystallographic Assn., Sci. Research Soc. Am. Research in diffraction effects of thermal motion, x-ray diffraction studies of imperfect solids; order-disorder effects in solid solutions. Home: 13 Brookside Dr Oak Ridge TN 37830-7616 Office: U Tenn Materials Sci & Engring Dept Dougherty Hall Knoxville TN 37996-2200

BORIGHT, JOHN PHILLIPS, science administrator; b. Barre, Vt., Mar. 1, 1943. BA, Cornell U., PhD. Counsellor sci. affairs U.S. Embassy, Paris, 1982-86; dir. internat. divsn. NSF, Washington, 1987-89; dep. asst. sec. state Office Oceans, Environment & Sci. Affairs, Washington, 1989-93; with Exec. Office Pres. Office Sci. & Tech. Policy, Washington, 1993-95; exec. dir. Office Internat. Affairs Nat. Acad. Scis., Washington, 1995—. Nat. scholar Cornell U.; NSF sr. fellow, Cornell U. Office: Nat Acad Scis 2101 Constitution Ave NW Washington DC 20418-0007

BORIN, GERALD W., zoological park administrator. CEO Columbus (Ohio) Zool. Park Assn., Inc., 1994—. Office: Columbus Zool Gardens PO Box 400 Powell OH 43065-0400*

BORIN, JEFFREY NATHAN, real estate developer; b. Detroit, Jan. 10, 1949; s. Ralph and Phyllis (Robinson) B.; m. Barbara Shapiro, Sept. 4, 1988; 1 child, Samuel. BS, U. Pa., 1971. Ptnr. Borin Investment Co., Livonia, Mich., 1971—; owner Jeffrey N. Borin Constrn. Co., Livonia, 1973—, Jeffrey N. Borin & Co. Real Estate Brokerage, Livonia, 1980—; pres. Borin Constrn. Mgmt., Inc., Livonia, 1987—, Turov Imports, Inc., Livonia, 1990—. Author: Turover Residences and Other Landmarks of Interest in Detroit, 1991, The Turover Aid Society of Detroit and the Turover Shul: Congregation B'nai Jacob, A Pictorial and Documentary History, 1993. Pres. jr. divsn. Jewish Welfare Fedn., Detroit, 1977-78; pres. Jewish Hist. Soc. of Mich., 1979-81. Mem. Western Wayne Oakland Assn. Realtors, Kiwanis, Skyline Club, Alpha Kappa Psi. Avocation: antiquing. Office: Borin Investment Co 11900 Globe St Ste 100 Livonia MI 48150-1141

BORIN, RALPH, real estate developer; b. Detroit, July 2, 1923; s. Samuel and Anna (Shifman) B.; m. Phyllis Robinson, Feb. 19, 1948; children: Jeffrey, Anne, Deborah. Grad., U.S. Maritime Svc. Tng. Sch., Gallups Island. Sec.-treas. Borin Builders Supply, Inc., Detroit, 1946-71; ptnr. Borin Investment Co., Livonia, Mich., 1971—; radio officer U.S. Merchant Marine, WWII; chmn. Borin Constrn. Mgmt., Inc., Livonia, 1987—. Office: Borin Investment Co 11900 Globe St Ste 100 Livonia MI 48150-1141

BORIS, JAMES R., investment company executive. Chmn. bd., CEO Everen Securities Inc., Chgo. Office: Everen Securities Inc 77 W Wacker Dr Chicago IL 60601-1651*

BORIS, RUTHANNA, dancer, choreographer, dance therapist, educator; b. Bklyn., Mar. 17, 1918; d. Joseph Jay and Frances (Weiss) B.; m. Frank W. Hobi (dec.). Student, Profl. Children's Sch., N.Y.C. dir. Boris-Hobi Concert Co., 1955-57. Prin. dancer Am. Ballet, N.Y.C., 1934, Ballet Caravan, N.Y.C., 1936; prima ballerina Met. Opera Co., N.Y.C., 1939-41, Ballet Russe de Monte Carlo, N.Y.C., 1942-49; prima ballerina, choreographer-in-residence Royal Winnipeg Ballet of Can., 1957-59, dir. 1957-58; choreographer Ballet Russe de Monte Carlo, 1947, N.Y.C. Ballet, 1951; prof. dance U. Wash., Seattle, 1965-83, prof. emeritus, 1983—; adj. prof. psychiatry U. Wash., 1982; pres. exec. dir. Ctr. for Dance Devel. & Research, Albany, Calif., 1986—; choreographer: Cirque de Deux, 1947, Quelques Fleurs, 1948, Cakewalk, 1951, Kaleidoscope, 1951, Will O' The Wisp, 1951, Pasticcio, 1955, Wanderling, 1957, Ragtime, 1975, Tape Suite, 1976, Four All, 1980. Mem. adv. bd. Seattle Psychoanalytic Inst., 1975-82. Mem. Am. Guild Mus. Artists (award 1964, gov. 1942-64), Am. Dance Therapy Assn. (pres. Calif. chpt. 1986-88, mem. dance therapy credentials com. 1990-92). Office: Ctr Dance Devel & Rsch 555 Pierce St Apt 1033 Albany CA 94706-1009 *I have always believed that each one of us has some specific mission to perform. My mission, to clarify my work and my human connections, keeps me very busy, active, curious and productive.*

BORISLOW, ALAN JEROME, hospital dental department chairman; b. Phila., Sept. 22, 1936; s. Nathan and Thelma (Kuperstein) B.; m. Susan Marcia Cohen, June 25, 1961; children: Lisa Anne Nadel, Steven Mark, Deborah Lynne. Student, Temple U., 1954-57, DDS, 1961; Cert. in Orthodontics, Albert Einstein Med. Ctr., 1967. Diplomate Am. Bd. Orthodontics. Gen. dentist U.S. Army Dental Corp, Fort Knox, Ky., 1961-63; dental practice assoc. Dr. Leonard Opack, Marcus Hook, Pa., 1963-64; resident in orthodontics Albert Einstein Med. Ctr., Phila., 1964-67; orthodontic practice assoc. Dr. Joseph Bernstein, Havertown, Pa., 1967-68; dir. dental externships Temple U., Phila., 1969-85; pvt. practice orthodontics Doylestown, Pa., 1969-87; orthodontic program dir. Albert Einstein Med. Ctr., Phila., 1978—, chmn. Maxwell S. Fogel Dept. of Dental Medicine, 1980—; clin. assoc. prof. Temple U. Sch. Dentistry, Phila., 1986—; adj. assoc. prof. U. Pa. Sch. Dental Medicine, Phila., 1989—. *Dr. Alan J. Borislow is recognized for a number of first accomplishments. In 1967, he was in the first graduating class of the first accredited hospital-based orthodontic residency program in the nation. He and a co-resident were the first dental residents to be awarded in the Einstein Medical Center's Outstanding Resident Prize. He also was the first board certified practicing orthodontist in Bucks County, Pennsylvania. In 1980, Dr. Borislow was selected to be the first full-time dental department chairman at Albert Einstein Medical Center. Through his leadership positions, he continues to advance the art and science of dentistry.* Co-author: (book) A Tradition of Excellence, 1993; contbr. to book The Combination Technique, 1972; referee, cons. Am. Jour. of Orthodontics and Dentofacial Orthopedics, 1995. Mem. B'nai Brith Svc. Orgn., Montgomery County, Pa., 1972—; exec. bd. Andorra Valley Civic Assn., Whitemarsh Twp., Pa., 1972-82; mem. Citizens Coun., Whitemarsh Twp., 1974—; bd. dirs. Greater Phila. Health Care Congress, 1991—. Recipient Outstanding Resident award Albert Einstein Med. Ctr., 1967, Disting. alumnus award Temple U. Dental Alumni Soc., 1994. Fellow Am. Assn. Hosp. Dentists, Am. Coll. Dentists, Internat. Coll. Dentists; mem. Am. Dental Assn., Am. Assn. Orthodontists, Temple U. Dental Alumni Soc. (bd. dirs. 1990—), Phila. Soc. Orthodontists, Am. Assn. Dental Schs. Democrat. Avocations: photography, architectural history, gardening. Office: Albert Einstein Med Ctr 5501 Old York Rd Philadelphia PA 19141-3001

BORISOFF, RICHARD STUART, lawyer; b. Rochester, N.Y., May 4, 1945; s. Samuel M. and Ida. B.; m. Risa W. Polgar, Aug. 17, 1967; children: Mindy, Dara. BA, U. Pa., 1967; JD, Columbia U., 1970. Bar: N.Y. 1971, D.C. 1981, U.S. Dist. Ct. (so. dist.) N.Y. 1973, U.S. Ct. Appeals (2nd cir.) 1973. Assoc. Paul, Weiss, Rifkind, Wharton & Garrison, N.Y.C., 1970-78, ptnr., 1978—. Office: Paul Weiss Rifkind Wharton & Garrison Ste 2330 1285 Ave of the Americas New York NY 10019-6065

BORJAS, GEORGE J(ESUS), economics educator; b. Havana, Cuba, Oct. 15, 1950; came to U.S., 1962; s. Juan V. Borjas and Edita F. Diaz; m. Jane Maureen Walsh, Nov. 11, 1989; children: Sarah Jane Irene, Timothy Jorge, Rebecca Kathryn. BS, St. Peter's Coll., Jersey City, 1971; MA, M in Philosophy, PhD, Columbia U., 1975. Asst. prof. Queens Coll., Flushing, N.Y., 1975-77; research assoc. Nat. Bur. Econ. Research, Cambridge, Mass., 1983—; prof. econs. U. Calif., Santa Barbara, 1978-90, San Diego, 1990-95; prof. pub. policy Kennedy Sch. Govt., Harvard U., Cambridge, Mass., 1995-97; Pferzheimer prof. pub. policy Kennedy Sch. Govt., Harvard U., Cambridge, 1998—; cons. Unicon Rsch. Corp., Santa Monica, Calif., 1982-94; econs. adv. panel NSF, 1988-90; mem. Gov.'s Coun. of Econ. Advisers, 1993—. Author: Wage Policy in the Federal Bureaucracy, 1980, International Differences in the Labor Market Performance of Immigrants, 1988, Friends or Strangers: The Impact of Immigrants on the U.S. Economy, 1990, Labor Economics, 1995, Heaven's Door: Immigration Policy and the American Economy, 1999; editor: Hispanics in the United States, 1985, Immigration and the Work Force: Economic Consequences for the United States and Source Areas, 1992, Issues in the Economics of Immigration, 2000, Rev. of Econs. and Statistics, 1998—; mem. editl. bd. Quar. Jour. Econs., 1992-98, Internat. Migration Rev., 1992—, Review of Economics and Statistics, 1997-98; contbr. articles to profl. jours. Fellow Columbia U. Alumni Fund, 1973, NIMH, U. Chgo., 1977; grantee Rockefeller Found., 1983-85, Sloan Found., 1986-93, NSF, 1986—, Russell Sage Found., 1991-93; vis. scholar Harvard U., 1988-89. Fellow Econometric Soc.; mem. NAS (panel 1984-85, 95—), Am. Econ. Assn., Soc. Labor Econs. Roman Catholic. Office: Kennedy Sch Govt Harvard U 79 Jfk St Cambridge MA 02138-5801

BORK, ROBERT HERON, lawyer, author, educator, former federal judge; b. Pitts., Mar. 1, 1927; s. Harry Philip and Elizabeth (Kunkle) B.; m. Claire Davidson, June 15, 1952 (dec. 1980); children: Robert Heron, Charles E., Ellen E.; m. Mary Ellen Pohl, Oct. 30, 1982. BA, U. Chgo., 1948, JD, 1953; LLD (hon.), Creighton U., 1975, Notre Dame Law Sch., 1982; LHD, Wilkes-Barre Coll., 1976; JD (hon.), Bklyn. Law Sch., 1984; ThD, DeSales Sch. Theology, 1990; LLD honoris causa, Adelphi U., 1990. Bar: Ill. 1953, D.C. 1977. Assoc., then ptnr. Kirkland, Ellis, Hodson, Chaffetz & Masters, Chgo., 1955-62; assoc. prof. Yale Law Sch., 1962-65, prof. law, 1965-75, on leave, 1973-75; solicitor gen. U.S. Dept. Justice, Washington, 1973-77, acting atty. gen., 1973-74; Chancellor Kent prof. law Yale Law Sch., 1977-79, Alexander M. Bickel prof. pub. law, 1979-81; ptnr. Kirkland & Ellis, Washington, 1981-82; judge U.S. Ct. Appeals for D.C. Cir., 1982-88, resigned, 1988; resident scholar Am. Enterprise Inst. for Pub. Policy Rsch., Washington, 1977, adj. scholar, 1977-82, John M. Olin scholar in legal studies, 1988—; mem. Presdl. Task Force on Antitrust, 1968; cons. Cabinet Com. on Edn., 1972; trustee Woodrow Wilson Internat. Ctr. for Scholars, 1973-78; nominated for position assoc. justice U.S. Supreme Ct., 1987, confirmation denied by U.S. Senate. Author: The Antitrust Paradox: A Policy at War with Itself, 1978, The Tempting of America: The Political Seduction of the Law, 1990, Slouching Towards Gomorrah: Modern Liberalism and American Decline, 1996. Mem. bd. govs. Smith Richardson Found., 1988; bd. dirs. Inst. for Ednl. Affairs, 1988; apptd. Permanent Com. for the Oliver Wendell Holmes Devise, 1989. With USMCR, 1945-46, 50-52. Recipient Francis Boyer award Am. Enterprise Inst., 1984, Henry Salvatori prize Intercollegiate Svcs. Inst., 1998. Fellow AAAS; mem. Federalist Soc. (co-chmn., bd. trustees).

BORKAN, WILLIAM NOAH, biomedical electronics company executive; b. Miami Beach, Fla., Apr. 29, 1956; s. Martin Solomon and Annabelle (Hoffman) B.; m. Vivienne Eliane; children: Martin and Kenneth. Student, Carnegie Mellon U., 1977; PhD, Sussex Coll. Tech., 1979; married. Tech., Dominicks' Radio & TV Co., Miami Beach, 1971-74; computer programmer Mt. Sinai Hosp., Miami Beach, 1973-74; chief studio engr. WGMA, Hollywood, Fla., 1973-74; disc. jockey WBUS-FM, Miami Beach, 1974; chief rec. engr. Dukoff Recording Studios', Miami, 1974-75; rec. studio design and constrn. TSI, Hollywood, Fla., 1975-77; chief design engr. Lumonics Co., Miami, 1974; svc. mgr. 21st Century Electronics Co., Miami, 1975; lab. tech. Carnegie-Mellon U.; mgr. Tech. Electronics Co., Pitts., 1976; pres. Borktronics Co. Miami, 1974-84; cons. specialist in neurobiometrics St. Barnabas Hosp., N.Y.C., 1978-83; rec. studio designer FXL Studios, Sunrise, Fla., 1978; pres., CEO Electronic Diagnostics, Inc., 1978-83, pres., CEO NeuroMed, Inc., 1980-95, Nice Tech., Inc., 1989-96, Electrovest, 1996—; pres. Master Angler, Inc., 1990-96; cons. specialist in home automation, home theater and audio; curricular coms. E.E. Dept. Grantee Carnegie Corp. and Carnegie Mellon U. Named Fla. Inc. Mag. Entrepreneur of Yr., 1992. Mem. Am. Soc. Heating, Refrigeration and Air Conditioning Engrs., Assn. Energy Engrs., Soc. Automotive Engrs., Assn. for Advancement Med. Instrumentation, AAAS, N.Y. Acad. Scis., Audio Engring. Soc. Author publs. in field; various U.S. and fgn. patents in energy and healthcare fields. Home: 3142 NE 166th St Miami FL 33160-3840 Office: Electrovest 12000 Biscayne Blvd Ste 502 Miami FL 33181-2725

BORKO, HAROLD, information scientist, psychologist, educator; b. N.Y.C., Feb. 4, 1922; s. George and Hilda (Karpel) B.; m. Hannah Levin, June 22, 1947; children: Hilda, Martin. Student, Coll. City N.Y., 1939-41; B.A., U. Calif. at Los Angeles, 1948; M.A., U. So. Calif., 1949, Ph.D. in Psychology, 1952. System tng. specialist Rand Corp., 1956-57; with System Devel. Corp., Santa Monica, Calif., 1957-68; assoc. staff head lang. processing and retrieval staff System Devel. Corp., 1965-68; instr. psychology U. So. Calif., 1957-65; instr. Sch. Library Service UCLA, 1965-68, prof. Grad. Sch. Library and Info. Sci., 1968-93; ret., 1993. Author: Computer Applications in the Behavioral Sciences, 1962, Automated Language Processing, 1967, Targets for Research in Library Education, 1973, (with H. Sackman) Computers and the Problems of Society, 1972, (with C. Bernier) Abstracting Concepts and Methods, 1975, (with C. Bernier) Indexing Concepts and Methods, 1978; Asso. U.S. editor: Information Processing and Management, 1963—; editorial bd.: Education for Information; editor: Academic Press Library and Information Science series, 1970—; book rev. editor: Jour. Ednl. Data Processing, 1963-75. Served with AUS, 1942-46; to capt., Med. Service Corps AUS, 1950-56. Mem. Am. Soc. for Info. Sci. (pres. 1966), Assn. Computing Machinery, Am. Psychol. Assn., Assn. Library and Info. Service Edn., Am. Soc. Indexers, Phi Beta Kappa, Sigma Xi, Phi Gamma Mu. Home: 11507 National Blvd Los Angeles CA 90064-3827 *It is unrealistic to expect a person to decide, at age twenty or thereabout, on a career to be followed for the rest of one's life. One should try to attain as good and as general an education as is possible and not be afraid to change professions. The world is changing, and we must be prepared to change with it; only then can we seize the opportunities presented.*

BORKON, DORIS, educational administrator, entrepreneur; b. Pitts., Nov. 23, 1936; d. Louis and Ruth (Ashinsky) B.; m. Joseph S. Tekula, June 6, 1957 (dec. 1980); children: Nadine, Juliana, Joan Michel. BA magna cum laude, Hunter Coll., 1954; MS, Bank St. Coll., 1973, EdM, 1982. Cert. ednl. adminstr. Tchr. N.Y.C. Bd. Edn., Spanish bilingual guidance counselor, 1968-77, bilingual ednl. evaluator, 1977-84, chair com. on spl. edn., 1984-85, ednl. adminstr., 1985—; pres. EduVal Ednl. Cons., N.Y.C., 1980—; charter mem. Adult Literacy Initiative, U.S. Dept. Edn.; cons. in field. Mem. youth com. Community Bd., N.Y.C., 1988—; mem. exec. bd. Ansonia Ind. Dems., N.Y.C., 1988—. Mem. Nat. Coun. on Assistance to Classroom Tchrs. (bd. dirs., founder), Chinese Lang. Study Inst., Am. Orthopsychiat. Assn., N.Y. C. of C., Orton Soc., Nat. Puzzlers' League, Women Entrepreneurs Bus. Assn. (co-founder, mem. exec. bd. 1994—), World Assn. for Psychosocial Rehab. Avocation: ballroom dancing. Office: EduVal PO Box 231139 New York NY 10023-1139

BORKOSKY, BRUCE GLENN, psychologist; b. Anchorage, Nov. 5, 1954; s. Glenn Edson and Gwendolyn (Copening) B. BA, Ohio Wesleyan U., 1978; MS, U. Dayton, 1984, Miami (Fla.) Inst. Psychology, 1990; D in Psychology, Miami (Fla.) Inst. Psychology, 1992. Cert. hypnotherapist, neuropsychology. Mgr. Domino's Pizza, Raleigh, N.C., 1978-81; computer programmer GMAC, Dayton, 1981-84; planner IBM Corp., Boca Raton, Fla., 1984-91; counseling intern Ctr. For Group Counseling, Delray Beach, Fla., 1991—; pvt. practice Fla., 1994—; bd. dirs. Ave. Creative Group, Delray Beach, Fla.; instr. Indian River C.C., 1993—. Landmark edn. therapist on-call, 1993—; psychologist Eckerd Youth Devel. Ctr., 1993-94, Okeechobee Counseling Ctr., 1994-95. Mem. APA, IEEE, Nat. Assn. Neuropsychology, Am. Assn. Individual Investors, Fla.Psychol. Assn., Mensa, Psi Chi. Avocation: singing. Office: 10 SE 1st Ave 2nd Fl Delray Beach FL 33444

BORKOVEC, VERA Z., Russian studies educator; b. Brno, Czechoslovakia, Aug. 13, 1926; came to U.S., 1952; d. Josef Zanda and Jarmila (Tuscher) Martinasek; m. Alexej B. Borkovec, Aug. 29, 1951. BA, Charles U., 1949; MA, Hollins Coll., 1961, The Am. U., 1966; PhD, Georgetown U., 1973. Secondary sch. tchr. English, French Montgomery County Pub. Schs., Md., 1961-64; from asst. prof. to assoc. prof. Russian studies The Am. Univ., Washington, 1966-91, prof. emerita. Mem. Czechoslovak Soc. of Arts and Scis. (v.p. 1994—). Avocations: theater, music, poetry. Home: 12013 Kemp Mill Rd Silver Spring MD 20902-1515

BORKOWSKI, FRANCIS THOMAS, university administrator; b. Weirton, W.Va., Mar. 16, 1936; s. Francis Thomas and Felicia Josephine (Pawlowski) B.; m. Kay Kaiser, Aug. 22, 1959; children: Stanley, Anne-Marie, Christian. B.S., Oberlin (Ohio) Coll., 1957; M.Mus., Ind. U., 1959; Ph.D., W.Va. U., 1967; LLD (hon.), St. Leo (Fla.) Coll., 1989. Clarinetist Indpls. Symphony Orch., 1957-59; music dir. Bishop Kenny High Sch., Jacksonville, Fla., 1959-61; dir. bands W.Va. U., 1961-67; assoc. prof. music edn. Ohio U., Athens, 1967-69; asst. dir. Sch. Music Ohio U., 1969-70, assoc. dean faculties, 1970-75; prof. music, vice chancellor, dean faculty Ind. U.-Purdue U., Ft. Wayne, 1975-78; v.p. Ft. Wayne Philharmonic Orch., 1976-78; provost U. S.C. System, 1978-83, exec. v.p., provost, 1983-88; pres. U. South Fla., Tampa, 1988-93; chancellor Appalachian St. Univ., Boone, NC, 1993—; bd. dirs. Citizens and Savs. State Bank, Nat. Bank. Author articles. Mem. nat. adv. coun. John F. Kennedy Ctr., 1978-80; pres. S.C. Orch. Assn., 1982; bd. dirs. United Way of Columbia, 1981; chmn. Moffitt Cancer Ctr. Bd., United Way Bd., Tampa; mem. urban affairs com. Nat. Assn. Land Grant Colls. Recipient Amicus Poloniae award Poland mag., 1971, award for research Sigma Xi; named Polonian of Yr., 1989, Gold medal with Diamond, INTERPROM, 1997. Mem. Am. Coun. Edn. (bd. dirs.), Am. Assn. Higher Edn., Music Educators Nat. Conf., Phi Beta Kappa, Mortar Bd., Omicron Delta Kappa, Eta Sigma Gamma, Golden Key, Phi Beta Delta. Roman Catholic. Office: Appalachian State Univ Office of Pres Boone NC 28608*

BORLAND, KATHRYN KILBY, author; b. Pullman, Mich., Aug. 14, 1916; d. Paul Melbourne and Vinnie (Bensinger) Kilby; m. James Barton Borland, May 16, 1942; children—James Barton, Susan Lee. B.S. in Journalism, Butler U., 1937. Editor North Side Topics, Indpls., 1938-42. Author: (all with Helen Ross Speicher) Southern Yankees, 1960, Allan Pinkerton, 1962, Miles and the Big Black Hat, 1963, Everybody Laughed, 1964, Eugene Field, 1964, Phillis Wheatley, 1968, Harry Houdini, 1969, Clocks from Shadow to Atom, 1969, Good-Bye to Stony Crick, 1975, The Third Tower, 1974, Stranger in the Mirror, 1974, Good-bye, Julie Scott, 1975, To Walk the Night, 1976, These Tigers' Hearts, 1978, Irena, 1979, Pseudonyms: Alice Abbott, Jane Land. Co-recipient award for most distinguished children's book pub. by Ind. author Ind. U., 1969. Mem. P.E.O., Theta Sigma Phi, Kappa Alpha Theta. Home: 1050 S Maish Rd Frankfort IN 46041-3213

BORLAUG, NORMAN ERNEST, agricultural scientist; b. Cresco, IA, Mar. 25, 1914; s. Henry O. and Clara (Vaala) B.; m. Margaret G. Gibson, Sept. 24, 1937; children: Norma Jean (Mrs. Richard H. Rhoda), William Gibson. BS in Forestry, U. Minnesota, Minneapolis, 1937, MS in Plant Pathology, 1940, PhD in Plant Pathology, 1941; ScD (honoris causa), Punjab (India) Agrl. U., 1969, Kanpur U., India, Royal Norwegian Agrl. Coll., Luther Coll., 1970, Michigan State U., U. de la Plata, Argentina, Uttar Pradesh Agrl. U., India, 1971; Sc.D. (honoris causa), U. Arizona, Phoenix, 1972, U. Florida, 1973, U. Católica de Chile, 1974, U. Hohenheim, Germany, 1976, U. Agr., Lyallpur, Faisalabad, Pakistan, 1978, Columbia U., N.Y.C., 1980, Ohio State U., Columbus, 1981, U. Minnesota, Minneapolis, 1982, U. Notre Dame, 1987, Oreg. State U., 1988, U. Tulsa, 1991; L.H.D., Gustavus Adolphus Coll., 1971, Iowa State U., 1992; LL.D. (hon.), New Mexico State U., 1973; D. of Agriculture (hon.), Tufts U., 1982; D. of Agricultural Sciences (hon.), U. Agricultural Sciences, Hungary, 1980, Tokyo U. Agriculture, 1981; D. Agricultural Sciences (hon.), U. Nacional Pedro Henriques Turena, Dominican Republic, U. Cen. del Estes, Dominican Republic, 1983; D. Honoris Causa, U. Mayor de San Simón, Bolivia, U. de Buenos Aires, 1983, U. de Cordoba, Spain, U. Politécnica de Catalunya, Barcelon, Spain, 1986, Colegio Postgraduadas, Mexico, 1990; Rector U. Dubuque, 1992-93; honoris causa, U. Studi de Bologna, Italy, 1991, Warsaw Agrl. U., Poland, 1993. With U.S. Forest Service, 1935-38; instr. U. Minn., 1941; microbiologist E.I. DuPont de Nemours, 1942-44; research scientist in charge wheat improvement Coop. Mexican Agrl. Program, Mexican Ministry Agr. Rockefeller Found., Mexico, 1944-60; assoc. dir. assigned to Inter-Am. Food Crop Program Rockefeller Found., 1960-63; dir. wheat research and prodn. program Internat. Maize and Wheat Improvement Ctr., Mexico City, 1964-79; cons. Internat. Maize and Wheat Improvement Ctr., 1980—; disting. prof. agricultural sciences TexasA & M Univ, College Station, Tex.; cons., collaborator Inst. Nacional de Investigaciones Agricolas, Mexican Ministry Agr., 1960-64; cons. FAO, North Africa and Asia, 1960; ex-officio cons. wheat research and prodn. problems to govts. in Latin Am., Africa, Asia, 1960—; mem. Citizen's Commn. on Sci., Law and Food Supply, 1973, Commn. Critical Choices for Am., 1973, Council Agr. Sci. and Tech., 1973—, Presdl. Commn. on World Hunger U.S.A., 1978-79, Presdl. Coun. Advisers Sci and Tech., 1990-93; dir. Population Crisis Com., 1971-92; asesor especial Fundacion para Estudios de la Poblacion A.C., Mexico, 1971-80; mem. adv. council Renewable Natural Resources Found., 1973; A.D. White Disting. prof.-at-large Cornell U., 1983-85; Disting. prof. Internat. Agr., Dept. Soil & Crop Scis., Tex. A&M U., Jan.-May, 1984—; adj. prof. dept. biology Emory U., Atlanta, 1991-92; advisor The Population Inst., U.S.A., 1978; bd. trustees Winrock Internat. U.S.A.; life fellow Rockefeller Found., 1983—. Recipient Disting. Service awards Wheat Producers Assns., and state govts. Mexican States of Guanajuato, Queretaro, Sonora, Tlaxcala and Zacatecas, 1954-60; Recognition award Agrl. Inst. Can., 1966; Recognition award Instituto Nacional de Tecnologia Agropecuaria de Marcos Juarez, Argentina, 1968; Sci. Service award El Colegio de Ingenieros Agronomos de Mexico, 1970; Outstanding Achievement award U. Minn., 1959; E.C. Stakman award, 1961; named Uncle of Paul Bunyan, 1969; recipient Disting. Citizen award Cresco Centennial Com., 1966; Nat. Disting. Service award Am. Agrl. Editors Assn., 1967; Genetics and Plant Breeding award Nat. Council Comml. Plant Breeders, 1968; Star of Distinction Govt. of Pakistan, 1968; citation and street named in honor Citizens of Sonora and Rotary Club, 1968; Internat. Agronomy award Am. Soc. Agronomy, 1968; Distinguished Service award Wheat Farmers of Punjab, Haryana and Himachal Pradesh, 1969; Nobel Peace prize, 1970; Diploma de Merito El Instituto Tecnologico y de Estudios Superiores de Monterrey, Mexico, 1971; medalla y Diploma de Merito Antonio Narro Escuela Superior de Agricultura de la U. de Coahuila, Mexico, 1971; Diploma de Merito Escuela Superior de Agricultura Hermanos Escobar, Mexico, 1973; award for service to agr. Am. Farm Bur. Fedn., 1971; Outstanding Agrl. Achievement award World Farm Found., 1971; Medal of Merit Italian Wheat Scientists, 1971; Service award for outstanding contbn. to alleviation of world hunger 8th Latin Am. Food Prodn. Conf., 1972; Nat. award for Agrl. Excellence in Sci. Nat. Agri-Mktg. Assn., 1982, Disting. Achievement award Council for Agrl. Scis. and Tech., 1982; inaugural lectr., medal recipient Dr. S.B. Hendrick's Meml. Lectureship., 1981, other honored lecturships; named to Halls of Fame Oreg. State U. Agrl., 1981, Agrl. Nat. Ctr., Bonner Springs, Kans., 1984, Scandinavian-Am., U.S.A., 1986, Nat. Wrestling, 1992; dedicated in his name Norman E. Borlaug Centro de Capitación y Formación de Agrs., Santa Cruz, Bolivia, 1983, Borlaug Hall U. Minn., 1985, Borlaug Bldg. Internat. Maize and Wheat Improvement Ctr., 1986; numerous other honors and awards from govts., ednl. instns., citizens groups. Hon. fellow Indian Soc. Genetics and Plant Breeding; mem. Nat. Acad. Sci., Am. Soc. Agronomy (1st Internat. Service award 1960, 1st hon. life mem.), Am. Assn. Cereal Chemists (hon. life mem., Meritorious Service award 1969), Crop Sci. Soc. Am. (hon. life mem.), Soil Sci. Soc. Am. (hon. life mem.), Sociedad de Agronomia do Rio Grande do Sul Brazil (hon.), India Nat. Sci. Acad. (fgn.), Royal Agrl. Soc. Eng. (hon.), Royal Soc. Edinburgh (hon.), Hungarian Acad. Sci. (hon.), Royal Swedish Acad. Agr. and Forestry (fgn.), Academia Nacional de Agronomia y Veterinaria (Argentina), Sasakaws African Assn. (pres. 1986—); hon. academician N.I. Vavilov Acad. Agrl. Scis. Lenin Order (USSR.), Am. Council on Sci. and Health (trustee 1978—), Internat. Food Policy Research Inst. (trustee 1976-82), Royal Soc. Eng., Chinese Acad. Agrl. Sci., 1994. Home: 15611 Ranchita Dr Dallas TX 75248-4982 Office: Tex A&M U Dept Soil & Crop Science College Station TX 77843-2474*

BORLEIS, MELVIN WILLIAM, management consultant; b. Balt., Jan. 13, 1943; s. Melvin Frederick and Louise (Pfeifer) B.; m. Sharon G. Gordon, Feb. 28, 1970. BS in Math., Va. Poly. Inst. and State U., 1964. V.p. Benefacts Inc., Balt., 1965-70, Kwasha Lipton, Inc., Englewood Cliffs, N.J., 1970-75; v.p. A.S. Hansen Inc., Lake Bluff, Ill., 1975-84, v.p., dir., 1984-87; mng. dir. William M. Mercer, Inc., Chgo., 1987-98; cons. Christiansburg, Va., 1998—; lectr. in field. Editorial bd. Benefits Quar., 1986-96; contbr. articles to profl. jours., chpts. to books. Mem. Internat. Found. of Employee Benefits, Internat. Soc. Cert. Employee Benefits Specialists (v.p. 1981-83, cert.). Avocations: tennis, golf, bridge, woodworking.

BORLING, JOHN LORIN, military officer; b. Chgo., Mar. 24, 1940; s. Edward Gustav and Vivian K. (Strietelmeir) B.; m. Myrna Lee Holmstedt, June 22, 1963; children: Lauren, Megan. BS, U.S. Airforce Acad., 1963; grad., Armed Forces Staff Coll., 1975, Nat. War Coll., 1980, Harvard U., 1991; White House fellow, Harvard U., 1998. Commd. 2d lt. USAF, 1963, advanced through grades to maj. gen., 1989; prisoner of war USAF, North Vietnam, 1966-73; fighter pilot, comdr. USAF, 1974-80; asst. dir. ops. HQ Pentagon USAF, Washington, 1981-82; comdr. 86th Combat Support Group USAF, Ramstein, Ger., 1982-83, comdr. 86th Fighter Group, 1983-84; exec. officer to COS NATO USAF, Mons, Belgium, 1984-86; dep. plans/analysis HQ/SAC Jt. Stategic Target Planning Staff USAF, Omaha, 1986-87; comdr. HQ 57th Air Divsn. USAF, Minot, N.D., 1987-88; dep. ops. HQ SAC USAF, Omaha, 1988-91; dir. operational reg(s) HQ Pentagon, 1991-92; dep. chief of staff NATO, Norway, 1992-94, chief of staff, sr. U.S. mil. officer in Scandinavia, 1994-96; pres., CEO United Way, Chgo., 1997-98; exec. v.p. BUM Comm. Inc., Chgo., 1999—; mem. Armed Forces Policy Coun., Chgo Coun. Fgn. Rels., Chgo. Com.; mem. adv. com. Ill. Fatherhood Initiative, Chgo. Founder, charter mem. Ramstein Coun. Internat. Rels., 1983; v.p., dir. Opera Omaha, 1988-91; treas., dir. White House Fellow Found., 1991—; mem. adv. com. Kellogg Sch., Northwestern U.; mem. fatherhood initiative Harris Sch., U. Chgo.; mem. exec. com. Internat. Eye Rsch. Decorated Def. Disting. Svc. medal with oak leaf cluster, Air Force Disting. Svc. medal, Silver Star, Def. Superior Svc. medal, Legion of Merit with oak leaf cluster, D.F.C. with oak leaf cluster, Bronze Star medal with V device and 2 oak leaf clusters, Air medal with 5 oak leaf clusters, Purple Heart with one cluster; White House fellow, 1974; recipient George Washington medal Freedom Found., Valley Forge, Va., 1975, Good Scout award Boy Scouts Am., Chgo., 1974. Mem. Assn. Grads. USAF Acad., VFW, Daedalians, Air Force Assn., Comml. Club Chgo., Execs. Club Chgo. Avocations: music, sports, reading. E-mail: jlbviking@yahoo.com. Home: 5000 S East End Ave Chicago IL 60615-3140 Office: 655 Rockland Rd Ste 209 Lake Bluff IL 60044

BORMAN, FRANK, former astronaut, laser patent company executive; b. Gary, Ind., Mar. 14, 1928; s. Edwin Borman; m. Susan Bugbee; children: Fredrick, Edwin. B.S., U.S. Mil. Acad., 1950; M. Aero. Engring., Calif. Inst. Tech., 1957; grad., USAF Aerospace Research Pilots Sch., 1960, Advanced Mgmt. Program, Harvard Bus. Sch., 1970. Commd. 2d lt. USAF, advanced through grades to col., 1965, ret., 1970; assigned various fighter squadrons U.S. and Philippines, 1951-56; instr. thermodynamics and fluid mechanics U.S. Mil. Acad., 1957-60; dir. Continental Airlines Holdings Inc. (formerly Tex. Air Corp.), Houston, 1992—; instr. USAF Aerospace Research Pilots Sch., 1960-62; astronaut Manned Spacecraft Ctr., NASA, until 1970; command pilot on 14 day orbital Gemini 7 flight, Dec. 1965, including rendezvous with Gemini 6; command pilot Apollo 8, 1st lunar orbital mission, Dec. 1968; sr. v.p. for ops. Eastern Air Lines, Inc., Miami, Fla., 1970-74, exec. v.p., gen. operations mgr., 1974-75, pres., chief exec. officer, 1975-85, chief exec. officer, 1975-86, chmn. bd., 1976-86; vice chmn., dir. Tex. Air Corp., Houston, 1986-92; chmn., CEO, dir. Patlex Corp., Las Cruces, N.Mex., 1992—; chmn. bd. Autofinance Group, Inc., Westmont, Ill.; Chm of Bd of Dir DBT OnLine Inc., Fort Lauderdale, FL, 1996-present; bd. dirs. Continental Airlines, Home Depot, Outboard Marine Corp. Recipient Disting. Svc. award NASA, 1965, Collier trophy Nat. Aeros. Assn., 1968, Congl. Space Medal of Honor, Harmon Internat. Aviation trophy. Office: Patlex Corp 745 Leonard Bryran Alley Las Cruces NM 88005 also: Autofinance Group Inc Ste 350 Oakmont Cir 1 601 Oakmont Ln Westmont IL 60559-5549*

BORMAN, LAURIE D., magazine editor-in-chief. BA in Journalism, Ind. U., Indpls., 1978. Editor-in-chief Endless Vacation Mag., Indpls. Office: Endless Vacation Mag 3502 Woodview Trace Indianapolis IN 46268*

BORMAN, PAUL DAVID, judge. BA, U. Mich., 1959, JD, 1962; LLM, Yale U., 1964. Staff atty. U.S. Commn. on Civil Rights, 1962-63; asst. U.S. atty. U.S. Atty. Office, 1964-65; spl. counsel Mayor's Devel. Team, 1967-68; asst. prosecuting atty. Wayne County Prosecutor's Office, 1974-75; dist. judge U.S. Dist. Ct. (ea. dist.) Mich., Detroit, 1994—. Mem. ABA, Fed. Bar Assn., State Bar Mich., Oakland County Bar Assn. Office: US Courthouse 740 240 W Lafayette Blvd Detroit MI 48226-2704*

BORMANN, FREDERICK HERBERT, forestry and environmental science educator; b. N.Y.C., Mar. 24, 1922; married 1952; four children. BS, Rutgers U., 1948; MA, Duke U., 1950, PhD in Plant Ecology, 1952. Instr., then asst. prof. botany Emory U., Atlanta, 1952-56; from asst. prof. to prof. Dartmouth Coll., 1956-66, prof. biology, 1969-80, prof. forestry and environ. studies, 1980-92, emeritus prof. forestry and environ. studies, 1992—; Oastler prof. emeritus forest ecology, dir. ecosys. rsch. Yale U. Sch. Forestry and Environ. Studies, New Haven, 1966—; ecologist Boston U. expedition to Alaska, 1953; vis. scientist Brookhaven Nat. Lab., 1963-64, Ctr. for Energy and Environ. Studies, Princeton U., 1984, Air Pollution Info. Exch., Rep. of China, 1985, E-W Environ. and Policy Inst., Honolulu, 1987, U. New Eng., Australia, 1990; mem. adv. com. Hubbard Brook, 1975—, Native Plants Inc., Salt Lake City, 1982-84, World Resources Inst., 1986-89, Wilderness Soc., 1987—; mem. nat. com. scope fire program, NRC, Nat. Acad. Sci., 1977-79, internat. environ. programs com., 1977-80; vis. prof. Ctr. for Advanced Studies, U. Va., 1980-81; Green prof. Tex. Christian U., Ft. Worth, 1987. Contbr. numerous articles to sci. and profl. jours. Recipient George Mercer award, 1954, Cert. of Merit Botanical Soc. Am. Fellow AAAS; mem. Ecol. Soc. Am. (pres. 1970-71), Am. Acad. Arts and Sci., Nat. Acad. Sci., Am. Inst. Biolog. Scis. *

BORN, BROOKSLEY ELIZABETH, agency administrator, lawyer; b. San Francisco, Aug. 27, 1940; d. Ronald Henry and Mary Ellen (Bortner) B.; m. Alexander Elliot Bennett, Oct. 9, 1982; children: Nicholas Jacob Landau, Ariel Elizabeth Landau, Andrew E. Bennett, Laura F. Bennett, Peter J. Bennett. AB, Stanford U., 1961, JD, 1964. Bar: D.C. 1966. Law clk. U.S. Ct. Appeals, Washington, 1964-65; legal rschr. Harvard Law Sch., 1967-68; assoc. Arnold and Porter, Washington, 1965-67, 68-73, ptnr., 1974-96; chair U.S. Commodity Futures Trading Commn., Washington, 1996—; lectr. law Columbus Sch. Law, Cath. U. Am., 1972-74; adj. prof. Georgetown U. Law Center, Washington, 1972-73. Pres. Stanford Law Rev, 1963-64. Chmn. bd. visitors Stanford Law Sch., 1987; bd. dirs. Nat. Legal Aid and Defenders Assn., 1972-79, Washington Legal Clinic for Homeless, 1993-96, Lawyers Com. for Civil Rights Under Law, 1993-96, Am. Bar Found., 1989—, Washington Lawyers Com. for Civil Rights and Urban Affairs, 1992-96, Nat. Women's Law Ctr., 1981—; trustee Ctr. for Law and Social Policy, Washington, 1977-96, Women's Bar Found., 1981-86. Mem. ABA (chair sect. ind. rights and responsibilities 1977-78, chair fed. judiciary com. 1980-83, chair consortium on legal svcs. and the pub. 1987-90, bd. govs. 1990-93, chair resource devel. coun. 1993-96; chair coun. Fund for Justice and Edn. 1995-96, state del. from D.C. 1994—), D.C. Bar (sec. 1975-76, mem. bd. govs. 1976-79), Am. Law Inst., Southwestern Legal Found. (trustee 1993-96), Order of Coif. Office: US Commodity Futures Trading Commn 1155 21st St NW Washington DC 20581

BORN, ROBERT HEYWOOD, consulting civil engineer; b. L.A., Nov. 7, 1925; s. Robert Bogle and Mignon Mary (Heywood) B.; m. Marilyn Alice Simpson, Aug. 15, 1947; 1 child, Stefanie Born. Student, Stanford U., 1943; BE, U. So. Calif., 1949, MSCE, 1956. Registered civil engineer Calif., Ariz., Nev., Utah, Tenn., Guam; registered agriculture engr. Calif. Assoc. hydraulic engr. Calif. Dept. of Water Resources, L.A., 1949-58; chief engr., county hydraulic engr. County Flood Control/Water Conservation Dist., San Luis Obispo, Calif., 1958-70; dir., exec. v.p., regional mgr. Camp, Dresser & McKee, Inc., Pasadena, Calif., 1970-78; v.p., regional mgr. Born, Barrett & Assoc./Barrett Cons. Group, Newport Beach, Calif., 1978-86, Memphis, 1978-86; prin. Robert H. Born Cons. Engrs., Memphis, 1986—, Irvine, Laguna Niguel, Calif., 1986—, Asheville, N.C., 1997—. Chmn. World Affairs Coun., San Luis Obispo, 1965. 1st lt. U.S. Army, 1943-47. Decorated Bronze star medal, 1944. Fellow ASCE (life, Engr. of Merit

1994); mem. Am. Water Works Assn. (com. chmn.), U.S. Com. on Large Dams, Am. Pub. Works Assn. (cert. outstanding pub. works achievement 1969, Floodplain Mgmt. Assn. Calif. Democrat. Presbyterian. Avocations: historical research, travel. Home: 15 Little Cedar Ct Asheville NC 28805-2487 Office: Robert H Born Cons Engrs 15 Little Cedar Ct Asheville NC 28805-2487

BORN, SAMUEL ROYDON, II, lawyer; b. Atwood, Ill., Apr. 19, 1945; s. Samuel Roydon and Mary Elizabeth (Derr) B.; m. Brenda Alice Anderson, June 18, 1988; children: Samuel R. III, Holly Jean; stepchildren: Jacob Corpenny Sipe III, Julie Chamberlain Sipe. Student, Northwestern U., 1963-64, Am. U., fall 1966; BA, Simpson Coll., 1967; JD, Ind. U., 1970. Bar: Ind. 1970, U.S. Dist. Ct. (so. dist.) Ind. 1970, U.S. Ct. Appeals (7th crct.) 1975, U.S. Dist. Ct. (no. dist.) Ind. 1990. Ptnr. Ice Miller Donadio & Ryan, Indpls., 1970—; mem. safety com. Associated Gen. Contractors Ind., 1988—. Co-author: Safety and Health Guide for Indiana Business, 1994, 3d edit., 1999; mem. bd. editors Ind. Law Jour., 1969-70; contbr. articles to profl. jours. Mem. bd. visitors Ind. U. Sch. Law, 1988-89, 95-98; chmn. ch. cmty. athletics First Bapt. Ch., Indpls., 1975-78, trustee, 1978-80. Mem. ABA (mem. nat. conf. bar pres. 1987—, ho. of dels. 1988-98, labor and employment law sect.), Am. Bar Found., Ind. State Bar Assn. (bd. govs. 1990-99, pres. 1997-98, labor law sect.), Ind. Bar Found., Indpls. Bar Assn. (bd. mgrs. 1987-95, pres. 1988), U.S. C. of C. (occupl. safety and health adminstrv. coun. 1981-86), Ind. C. of C. (past chmn. occupl. safety health com.), Ind. Mfrs. Assn. (pers. labor rels. com. 1982—), Highland Golf and Country Club, Crooked Stick Golf Club, Columbia Club, Univ. Club, Indpls. Lawyers Club, Masons, Shriners, Kiwanis, Phi Eta Sigma, Sigma Alpha Epsilon. Presbyterian. Avocations: downhill skiing, golf, fly fishing, public speaking. Home: 5202 Grandview Dr Indianapolis IN 46228-1938 Office: Ice Miller Donadio & Ryan 1 American Sq Indianapolis IN 46282-0001

BORNEMAN, JOHN PAUL JAY, pharmaceutical executive; b. Darby, Pa., Oct. 18, 1958; s. John A. III and Ann (Conway) B.; m. Anne Marie Albert, July 18, 1980; 1 child, Elizabeth Anne. BS in Chemistry, St. Joseph's U., Phila., 1980, MS in Chemistry, 1983, MBA in Fin., 1986. V.p. Boiron-Borneman Inc., Norwood, Pa., 1980-86; dir. mktg. Standard Homeopathic Co., L.A., 1986-89, v.p., 1989-96, exec. v.p., 1996—; pres. P&S Labs., L.A., 1996—; chmn. FDA liaison com. Am. Homeopathic Pharm. Assn., 1986—. Editor Homeopathic Pharmacopoeia U.S., 1983—; columnist Resonance mag., 1986-95; contbr. articles to homeopathic jours. Bd. dirs. Internat. Found. for Homeopathy, 1986-92, Nat. Ctr. for Homeopathy, 1987—. Mem. Am. Chem. Soc., Am. Pharm. Assn., Nat. Nutritional Foods Assn. (mem. legis. affairs com. 1996—), Sigma Xi. Avocation: photography. Office: Standard Homeopathic Co Box 61067 210 W 131st St Los Angeles CA 90061-1618

BORNET, VAUGHN DAVIS, former history and social science educator, research historian; b. Phila., Oct. 10, 1917; s. Vaughn Taylor and Florence Davis (Scull) B.; m. Mary Elizabeth Winchester, Dec. 28, 1944; children: Barbara Lee Stumph, Stephen Folwell. B.A. with honors, Emory U., 1939, M.A., 1940; postgrad. fellow, U. Ga., 1940-41; Ph.D., Stanford U., 1951. Staff Mercer U., 1946; instr. history U. Miami, 1946-48; research assoc. Inst. Am. History, Stanford U., 1951-53; dir. welfare research project Commonwealth Club of Calif., 1953-56; assoc. editor Ency. Britannica, 1958; rsch. assoc. med. econs. AMA, 1958-59; staff RAND Corp., Santa Monica, Calif., 1959-63; chmn. social scis. div. So. Oreg. U., Ashland, 1963-74, prof. history and social sci., 1963-80; vis. prof. history World Campus Afloat, winter-spring, 1969. Author: Struggle for Governmental Power in Georgia, 1754-1757, 1940, Labor and Politics in 1928, 1951, California Social Welfare, 1956, Welfare in America, 1960, Labor Politics in a Democratic Republic, 1964, Speaking Up for America, 1975; (with E.E. Robinson) Herbert Hoover: President of the United States, 1975, The Presidency of Lyndon B. Johnson, 1983; (juvenile) It's a Dog's Life and I Like It, 1991; (memoir) An Independent Scholar, 1995; co-author The Heart Future, 1961; article United States, Ency. Brit. Yearbooks, 1957, 58; contbr. Ideas in Conflict, 1958, Herbert Hoover Reassessed, 1981, The Quest for Security, 1982, Essays in Economics and Business History, 1988; pub. Bornet Books. Pres. So. Oreg. Symphony Assn., 1973-75; mem. U.S. Com. on Civil Rights, Oreg., 1985—. Served to lt. USNR, 1941-45, ret. comdr. Recipient Disting. Svc. awards Am., Oreg. Heart Assns., 1964, Disting. Svc. award Southern Oreg. State Coll. Alumni Assn., 1985, Freedoms Found. award 1986; also various fellowships. Mem. Rotary, Sigma Chi. Republican. E-mail: bornetvd@grrtech.com. Home: 365 Ridge Rd Ashland OR 97520-2830

BORNHEIMER, ALLEN MILLARD, lawyer; b. Brewer, Maine, June 10, 1942; s. Millard Genthner and Gertrude Evelyn (Kinney) B.; m. Deborah Russell Hill, June 17, 1967; children: Anneliese, Charles, Elizabeth. Student, Phillips Exeter Acad., 1961; AB, Harvard U., 1965, LLB, 1968. Bar: Mich. 1968, Mass. 1971. Assoc. Dickinson, Wright, McKean & Cudlip, Detroit, 1968-70; assoc. Choate, Hall & Stewart, Boston, 1970-76, ptnr., 1976—, mng. ptnr., 1988-95; bd. dirs. Cargex Properties, Inc. and affiliated cos., Portland, Maine. Town moderator, Duxbury, Mass., 1982—, chmn. fin. com., 1974-76, mem. capital budget com., 1977; bd. dirs. Jordan Hosp., Plymouth, Mass., 1974-81; trustee North Yarmouth (Maine) Acad., 1976-79. Mem. ABA, Mass. Bar Assn., Boston Bar Assn., Am. Coll. Investment Counsel, Mass. Moderators Assn., Duxbury Yacht Club (bd. dirs. 1982-84), Harvard Club (Boston). Republican. Avocations: golf, piano, sailing. Home: 76 Upland Rd Duxbury MA 02332-3930 Office: Choate Hall & Stewart Exchange Pl 53 State St Boston MA 02109-2804

BORNHOLDT, LAURA ANNA, university administrator; b. Peoria, Ill., Feb. 11, 1919; d. John and Barbara (Kohl) B. A.B., Smith Coll., 1940, M.A., 1942; Ph.D., Yale U., 1945. Asst. prof. history Smith Coll., Northampton, Mass., 1945-52; internat. relations asso. AAUW, Washington, 1952-57; dean Sarah Lawrence Coll., Bronxville, N.Y., 1957-59; dean women, adj. prof. history U. Pa., Phila., 1959-61; dean coll., prof. history Wellesley (Mass.) Coll., 1961-64; v.p. Danforth Found., St. Louis, 1964-73; sr. program officer Lilly Endowment Inc., Indpls., 1973-76; v.p. for edn. Lilly Endowment Inc., 1976-84; dir. office univ.-sch. rels. U. Chgo., 1984-94; Nat. adv. com. on black higher edn. and black colls. and univs. Dept. Edn., 1977-82; mem. Yale U. Council, 1977-82; emerita life trustee Coll. of Wooster, Ohio, 1967-77; trustee St. Louis U., 1971-75. Recipient Yale U. Wilbur Cross medal, 1976, Smith Coll. Alumnae medal, 1987. Mem. Am. Assn. Higher Edn., Phi Beta Kappa. Home: 5000 S East End Ave Apt A25 Chicago IL 60615-3171

BORNHORST, KENNETH FRANK, electromagnetics and systems engineer; b. Detroit, Feb. 5, 1929; s. Leo John and Alvina Anna (Laufersweiler) B.; m. Patricia Lucille Drayer, July 3, 1954; children: Kenneth Jr., David L., Patricia A. BEE, U. Dayton, 1951, PhD in Engring., 1985; MEE, Poly. Inst. N.Y., 1954. Project engr. monopulse radar receiver devel. Sperry Gyroscope Co., Great Neck, N.Y., 1951-54; project engr. autopilot, motor, timer, gyroscope devel. Globe Industries Inc., Dayton, Ohio, 1954-60; project engr. devel. of servo guided shoe machinery United Shoe Machinery Co., Xenia, Ohio, 1960; engring. sect. head mil. equipment divsn. locator and telemetry beacon and automatic direction finder devel. NCR, Dayton, 1960-74; br. chief, analyst electromagnetic threat analysis, radar, advanced weapon sys. Nat. Air Intelligence Ctr. USAF, Wright-Patterson AFB, Ohio, 1974-94; cons., 1995—. Radar Cross section measurement of troops and vehicles for U.S. Army, 1954-56. Mem. Tau Beta Pi. Achievements include patents for flight control system, UHF bypass capacitor, pulsed carrier radio beacon, UHF radio direction finder, low loss millimeter waveguide.

BORNHORST, MARILYN, Democrat party chariwoman; b. Dearborn, Mich.; m. Karl Bornhorst; 2 children. Student, L.A. City Coll., U. Calif., L.A. Tchr., pub. stenographer; owner Copy Right Duplicating; mem. Hawaii State Dem. Party, 1968—, precinct pres., dist. sec., 1997-98; mem. Honolulu City Coun., 1974-88, chair, 1977-78, 86-87, chair budget, transp., housing and govt. rels. coms. Del. Dem. State Conv., 1994, alt., 1996. Mem. NASW (Hawaii chpt. exec. dir.). Office: Hawaii State Dem Party Office 1525 Oneele Pl Honolulu HI 96822*

BORNMANN, CARL MALCOLM, lawyer; b. Somerville, N.J., Aug. 13, 1936; s. John Carl Bornmann and Dorothy Louise (Balliet) Capparelli; children: Carl, Gregory, Melissa. BS, Ohio U., 1958; JD with distinction, Ind. U., 1961; MA, Columbia U., 1989. Bar: Ind. 1961, N.Y. 1962, U.S. Dist. Ct. (so. and ea. dists.) N.Y. 1962, U.S. Ct. Appeals (2d cir.) 1962, U.S. Supreme Ct. 1965. Assoc. Cahill, Gordon, Reindel & Ohl, N.Y.C., 1961-69; ptnr. Cahill, Gordon & Reindel, N.Y.C., 1970—. dir. Residents for the Future of Briarcliff Manor, 1994-96; del. USSR People to People Internat., 1990. Mem. ABA (bus. law sect.), N.Y. State Bar Assn., Japan Soc. of N.Y.C., Collier County (Fla.) Bar Assn. (assoc.), Order of Coif. Home: 4419 Rosea Ct Naples FL 34104-4445

BORNS, HAROLD WILLIAM, JR., geologist, educator; b. Cambridge, Mass., Nov. 28, 1927; s. Harold William and Olive Blanche (Stevens) B.; m. Phyllis Clare Kuehl, May 23, 1954 (div. 1982); children—Harold William III, Donna Jean; m. Margaret Parker, Mar. 11, 1982. BS, Tufts U., 1951; MS, Boston U., 1955, PhD, 1959. Prof. geol. scis. U. Maine, Orono, 1971-74, chmn. dept. geol. scis., 1971-74, dir. inst. quaternary studies, 1974-88, prof. geological scis. inst. for quaternary studies, 1974—; program mgr. polar glaciology divsn. NSF, Washington, 1988-90. Contbr. articles to profl. jours. With USCG, 1946-48. Recipient Borns Glacier Antarctica award U.S. Bd. Geog. Names, 1962; Antarctic Service medal U.S. Antarctic Research Program, 1962; Research and Creative Achievement award U. Maine, 1984. Fellow Geol. Soc. Am., AAAS; mem. Explorers Club, Sigma Xi, Phi Kappa Phi. Office: U Maine Inst Quaternary Studies Orono ME 04469

BORNS, ROBERT AARON, real estate developer; b. Gary, Ind., Oct. 24, 1935; s. Irving Jonah and Sylvia (Mackoff) B.; m. Sandra Solotkin, Mar. 30, 1958; children: Stepahnie, Elizabeth, Emily. BS, Ind. U., 1957; hon. degree, U. indpls., 1987. Account exec. Reynolds & Co., Chgo., 1957-59, Francis I duPont co., Indpls., 1960; owner, operator Borns & Co., Indpls., 1960-63; chmn. Borns Mgmt. Corp., Indpls., 1963—, Correctional Mgmt. Co., L.L.C., 1996—; bd. dirs. Artistic Media Ptnrs. L.L.C., Indpls. Power and Light Co., Mid Am. Capital Resources Corp., Standard Mgmt. Corp., IPALCO Enterprises. Bd. dirs. Indpls. Mus. of Art, Indpls. Symphony Orch., Ind. U. Found.; mem. bd. visitors Borns Jewish Studies Program, Ind. U.; past bd. dirs. Indpls. Children's Mus., I.W.C. Resources Corp., Indpls. Water Co.; past trustee St. Vincent's Hosp., mem. adv. bd.; past trustee St. Vincent's Hosp. Found. Recipient Enterprise award Indpls. Bus. Jour., 1982, Peace award State of Israel, 1979. Mem. Confrerie des Chevaliers du Tastevin, Econ. Club (bd. dirs.), Thunderbird Country Club (Rancho Mirage, Calif.). Office: Borns Mgmt Corp 21 Beachway Dr Indianapolis IN 46224-8504

BORNSTEIN, DAVID NEIL, writer; b. Montreal, Mar. 8, 1963; s. Robert Edward and Barbara Francis (Cohen) B. B of Commerce, McGill U., 1985; MA, NYU, 1991. Author: The Price of a Dream: The Story of the Grameen Bank, 1996 (2d prize Harry Chapin Media award 1996).

BORNSTEIN, ELI, artist, sculptor; b. Milw., Dec. 28, 1922; dual citizen, U.S. and Can.; m. Christina Bornstein; children: Sarah, Thea. BS, U. Wis., 1945, MS, 1954; student, Art Inst. Chgo., U. Chgo., 1943, Academie Montmartre of Fernand Leger, Paris, 1951, Academie Julian, 1952; DLitt, U. Sask., Can., 1990. Tchr. drawing, painting and sculpture Milw. Art Inst., 1943-47; tchr. design U. Wis., 1949; tchr. drawing, painting, sculpture, design and graphics U. Sask., Can., 1950-90; prof. U. Sask., 1963-90, prof. emeritus, 1990—, head art dept., 1963-71. Painted in France, 1951-52, Italy, 1957, Holland, 1958; exhibited widely, 1943—; retrospective exhbn. (works 1943-64), Mendel Art Gallery, Saskatoon, 1965, one man shows, Kazimir Gallery, Chgo., 1965, 67, Saskatoon Pub. Library, 1975, Can. Cultural Center, Paris, 1976, Glenbow-Alta. Inst. Art, Calgary, 1976, Mendel Art Gallery, Saskatoon, 1982, York U. Gallery, Toronto, 1983, Confedn. Ctr. Art Gallery, Charlottetown, P.E.I., 1983, Owens Art Gallery, Mt. Allison U., Sackville, N.B., 1984, Fine Arts Gallery, U. Wis.-Milw., 1984, Mendel Art Gallery, Saskatoon, 1996; represented in numerous pvt. collections; executed marble sculpture now in permanent collection, Walker Art Center, Mpls., 1947, aluminum constrn. for Sask. Tchrs. Fedn. Bldg., 1956, structurist relief in painted wood and aluminum for, Arts and Scis. Bldg., U. Sask., 1958, structurist relief in enamelled steel for, Internat. Air Terminal, Winnipeg, Man., Can., 1962, four-part constructed relief for, Wascana Pl., Wascana Ctr. Authority, Regina, Sask., 1983; also structurist reliefs exhibited, Mus. Contemporary Art, Chgo., Herron Mus. Art, Indpls., Cranbrook Acad. Art Galleries, Mich., High Mus., Atlanta, Can. House, Cultural Centre Gallery, London, 1983, Can. Cultural Ctr., Paris, 1983, Brussels, 1983, Milw. Art Mus., 1984, Bonn, 1985; model of aluminium construction, 1956 and model version of structurist relief in 5 parts, 1962, now in collection, Nat. Gallery, Ottawa, Ont., others in numerous collections.; Co-editor: periodical Structure, 1958; founder, editor: The Structurist, ann. publ. 1960-72, biennial, 1972—; Contbr. articles, principally on Structurist art to various publs. Recipient Allied Arts medal Royal Archtl. Inst. Can., 1968; honorable mention for 3 structurist reliefs 2d Biennial Internat. Art Exhbn., Colombia, S.Am., 1970. Fax: (306) 966-8670. E-mail: eli.bornstein@usask.ca. Address: 3625 Saskatchewan Cres S, Corman Park, SK Canada S7T 1B7 Office: U Sask, Box 378 RPO U, Saskatoon, SK Canada S7N 4JB

BORNSTEIN, GEORGE JAY, literary educator; b. St. Louis, Aug. 25, 1941; s. Harry and Celia (Price) B.; m. Jane Elizabeth York, June 22, 1982; children—Benjamin, Rebecca, Joshua. A.B., Harvard U., 1963; Ph.D., Princeton U., 1966. Asst. prof. MIT, Cambridge, 1966-69, Rutgers U., 1969-70; assoc. prof. U. Mich., Ann Arbor, 1970-75, prof. English, 1975—, C.A. Patrides prof. lit., 1995—; cons. various univ presses, scholastic jours., funding agys., 1970—; mem. adv. bd. Yeats: An Annual, 1982—, South Atlantic Rev., 1985-88, Rev., 1991—, Text, 1993—. Author: Yeats and Shelley, 1970, Transformations of Romanticism, 1976, Postromantic Consciousness of Ezra Pound, 1977, Poetic Remaking, 1988; editor: Romantic and Modern, 1977, Ezra Pound Among the Poets, 1985, W.B. Yeats: The Early Poetry, vol. 1, 1987, vol. 2, 1994, W.B. Yeats: Letters to the New Island, 1990, Representing Modernist Texts, 1991, Palimpsest: Editorial Theory in the Humanities, 1993, W.B. Yeats: Under the Moon, the Unpublished Early Poetry, 1995, Contemporary German Editorial Theory, 1995, The Iconic Page in Manuscript, Print, and Digital Culture, 1998. Cubmaster Wolverine council Boy Scouts Am., 1977-79. Recipient good teaching award Amoco Found., 1983, Warner Rice prize for rsch. in humanities, 1988; fellow Am. Coun. Learned Soc., 1972-73, NEH fellow, 1982-83, fellow Old Dominion Found., 1968, fellow Guggenheim Found., 1986-87. Mem. MLA (exec. com. Anglo-Irish 1976-80, exec. com. 20th Century English 1980-85, exec. com. Poetry 1987-92, exec. com. bibliography and textual studies 1993-98, exec. com. methods of rsch. 1998—), Soc. for Textual Scholarship (program chair 1997), Am. Conf. on Irish Studies (book prize judge 1991), Racquet Club, Princeton Club (N.Y.C.), Phi Beta Kappa. Home: 2020 Vinewood Blvd Ann Arbor MI 48104-3614 Office: U Mich Dept English Ann Arbor MI 48109-1003

BORNSTEIN, LESTER MILTON, retired medical center executive; b. Boston, Feb. 19, 1925; s. Harry and Celia (Adlestein) B.; m. Marilyn Goldstein, Aug. 22, 1948; children: Aura Lynne, Michael Scott, Karen Jane. B.S., Boston U., 1948; M.P.H. in Hosp. Adminstrn, Yale U., 1955. Adminstrv. resident Charles S. Wilson Meml. Hosp., Johnson City, N.Y., 1953-54; asst. dir. Barnert Meml. Hosp., Paterson, N.J., 1954-57, Newark Beth Israel Hosp., 1957-68; pres. Newark Beth Israel Med. Center, Newark, 1968-96. Served with AUS, 1943-45, ETO; to maj., Korean War 1950-53. Decorated Bronze Stars. Fellow Am. Coll. Hosp. Adminstrs., N.J. Hosp. Assn. (chmn. bd. trustees 1978-79). Home: 6 Aherne Way West Orange NJ 07052-2102

BORNSTEIN, MORRIS, economist, educator; b. Detroit, Sept. 4, 1927; m. Reva Rice, Apr. 7, 1962; children—Susan, Jane. A.B., U. Mich., 1947, A.M., 1948, Ph.D., 1952. Economist U.S. Govt., 1951-52, 55-58; mem. faculty U. Mich., Ann Arbor, 1958—; prof. econs. U. Mich., 1964—, dir. Center Russian and E. European Studies, 1966-69; assoc. Harvard U. Russian Rsch. Ctr., 1962-63; vis. rsch. fellow Hoover Instn., Stanford, 1969-70; cons. in field, 1959—; mem. joint com. on Eastern Europe Am. Coun. Learned Socs.-Social Sci. Rsch. Coun., 1977-80. Author: Soviet National Accounts for 1955, 1961, The Soviet Economy, 1962, 4th edit., 1974, Comparative Economic Systems, 1965, 7th edit., 1994, Economia di Mercato ed Economia Pianificata, 1973, Sistemas economicos comparados, 1973, Plan and Market, 1975, Chinese transl., 1980, The Soviet Economy: Continuity and Change, 1981, East-West Relations and the Future of Eastern Europe, 1981, The Transfer of Western Technology to the USSR, 1985, French transl., 1985; mem. editorial bd. Jour. Comparative Econs., 1986-88, Problems of Economic Transition, 1987-97, Soviet Economy and Post Soviet Affairs, 1988—, Most: Economic Policy in Transitional Economies, 1994—, Communist Economies and Econ. Transformation, 1997-98, Post-Soviet Geography and Econs., 1997—, Post-Communist Economies, 1999—. With U.S. Army, 1953-55. Ford Found. faculty fellow, 1962-63, Sr. Fgn. Rsch. fellow French Ministry Rsch. and Tech., 1991. Mem. Am. Econ. Assn., Am. Assn. Advancement Slavic Studies, Assn. Comparative Econ. Studies (exec. com. 1965-67, 73-75). Office: U Mich Dept Econs Ann Arbor MI 48109-1220

BORNSTEIN, MYER SIDNEY, obstetrician, gynecologist; b. Boston, Sept. 7, 1938; s. Abram and Celia (Stein) B.; B.S., Northeastern U., 1961; M.D., U. Vt., 1965; Grad. N.Y. Inst. Photography, 1988; cert. advanced hysterectomy and laparascopy, obstetrical critical care; m. Janet L. Difonzo, July 15, 1977; 2 children; 3 children by previous marriage. Intern, Rochester (N.Y.) Gen. Hosp., 1965-66, resident, 1966-69; practice medicine specializing in gyn, laparoscopy and infertility, 1969—, drug and alcohol treatment, 1984-87; chief ob-gyn Kinchloe AFB, Mich., 1969-71; asst. chief Weisbaden (Germany) Regional Hosp., 1971-74; attending physician Charleton Meml. Hosp., Fall River Mass., 1974-83, New London (N.H.) Hosp., 1983-87, Morton Hosp., 1987—, dir. Assocs. in Women's Health, 1988—, chief ob-gyn., 1991—, chair by laws com., chmn. laparoendoscopy com.; med. dir. substance abuse treatment ctr. Seminole Point Hosp., N.E. Alcohol and Drug Svcs., 1984-87; med. dir. Greater Fall River Family Planning, 1981-83; owner SEMASS Photography , SEMASS Med. Cons.; cons. ob-gyn Fall River Cmty. Devel. Ctr., 1976-83, Taunton State Hosp., 1988—, Stanley Street Alcohol Rehab. Ctr., Fall River, Mass ; guest lectr. dept. social work Providence Coll., 1980; vis. prof. Facility CMH Physician Tng. Ctr., Nashville; freelance nature photographer; reviewer MassPro Blue Cross and Blue Shield; Mass. rep., chmn. sect. alternative to hysterectomy Ob-gyn. Net; bd. dirs. Morton Physician Assocs.; med. dir., COO Assocs. in Women's Health. Contbr. photographs to jours. and books. Bd. dirs. Kersang chpt. Am. Cancer Soc., Greater Fall River Children's Protective Services, Pilgrim Found. Med. Care; Bd. of Greater Berkley; bd. dirs., coach, pres. Wattupa Youth Hockey Assn., 1978-81. Lt. col. USAF, 1969-74. Diplomate Am. Bd. Ob-Gyn., Am. Bd. Utilization Rsch. and Quality Assurance Physicians, Am. Coll. Physician Execs. Mem. AMA, Fall River Med. Soc., Am. Coll. Healthcare Execs., Am. Soc. Gynecol. Laparascopy, Am. Soc. Colposcopy (asst. sec. treas.), Mass. Med. Soc. (tax support medicare com., managed care com., perinatal welfare com., vice chair nomination com. 1994-96, chair 1996-97, 98—, bd. trustees), Bristol North Med. Soc. (v.p., pres.), Am. Coll. Obstetricians and Gynecologists, Southeastern New Eng. Ob-Gyn Soc., Am. Inst. Ultrasound in Medicine, Am. Fertility Soc., N.H. Med. Soc., Am. Coll. Physcian Execs. (trainer Origin Medisys., trainer Ethicon Endosurgical), Merrimack County Med. Soc., N.H. Ob-Gyn Soc., Am. Legion. Lodge: Rotary (New London). Home: 13 Green St Berkley MA 02779-1510 Office: 72 Washington St Taunton MA 02780-2470

BORNSTEIN, PAUL, physician, biochemist; b. Antwerp, Belgium, July 10, 1934; came to U.S., 1947, naturalized, 1952; s. Abraham and Mina (Ginsburg) B. BA, Cornell U., 1954; MD, NYU, 1958. Intern in surgery Yale-New Haven Hosp., 1958-59, intern in medicine, 1959-60, asst. resident in medicine, 1960-62; sr. fellow Arthritis Found. Pasteur Inst., Paris, 1962-63; research asso. NIH, Bethesda, Md., 1963-65; research investigator NIH, 1965-67; asst. prof. biochemistry and medicine U. Wash., 1967-69, asso. prof., 1969-73, prof., 1973—, attending physician, 1968—. Mem. editl. bd. Jour. Biol. Chemistry, 1972-78, 80-85, Jour. Cell Biology, 1988-91, 94-97, Matrix Biology, 1993—; assoc. editor Arteriosclerosis, 1980-90, Collagen Related Rsch., 1981-88; contbr. articles to profl. jours. Served to sr. surgeon USPHS, 1963-67. Recipient Lederle Med. Faculty award USPHS, 1968; Rsch. Career Devel. award NIH, 1969; Macy Faculty Scholar award, 1975; Merit award NIH, 1989; Guggenheim fellow, 1985. Mem. Am. Soc. Clin. Investigation, Am. Soc. Biol. Chemistry, Western Soc. Clin. Rsch., Assn. Am. Physicians, Internat. Soc. Matrix Biology (v.p. 1999—). Home: 602 34th Ave E Seattle WA 98112-4306 Office: U Wash Sch Medicine Dept Biochemistry PO Box 357350 Seattle WA 98195-7350

BORNSTEIN, RITA, academic administrator; b. N.Y.C., Jan. 2, 1936; d. Carl and Florence (Gates) Kropf; children: Rachel, Mark, Per; m. Harland G. Bloland. BA in English, Fla. Atlantic U., 1970, MA in English, 1971; PhD in Ednl. Leadership and Instrn., U. Miami, 1975. Tchr., adminstr. Dade County Pub. Schs., Fla., 1971-75; adminstr. dept. edn. U. Miami, Coral Gables, 1975-81, adminstr. divsn. of devel., 1981-85, v.p., 1985-90; pres. Rollins Coll., Winter Park, Fla., 1990—; bd. dirs. Barnett Banks Ctrl. Fla., 1990-98, Barnett Banks, Inc., 1991-98, dir. emeritus, 1998—, Tupperware Corp., 1997—, NationsBank Corp., 1998. Author: Freedom or Order: Must We Choose?, 1976; Title IX Compliance and Sex Equity: Definitions, Distinctions, Costs and Benefits, 1981; contbr. articles to profl. jours. Mem. Am. Coun. on Edn. (com. leadership devel. 1991-93, bd. dirs. 1995-98), Nat. Assn. Ind. Colls. and Univs. (bd. dirs. 1992-95, chair govt. rels. com. 1994-95), Fla. Coun. of 100, Associated Colls. of the South (bd. dirs. 1992—, treas. 1993-95, sec. 1995-97, vice chair 1997-99, chair 1999—), Ind. Colls. and Univs. Fla. (coun. pres. 1990—, chair 1997-98), So. Assn. Colls. and Schs. (commn. colls. 1998—, exec. coun. 1999—). Office: Rollins Coll Office of Pres 1000 Holt Ave # 2711 Winter Park FL 32789-4499

BORNSTEIN, STEVEN M., broadcast executive; b. Fair Lawn, N.J., Apr. 20, 1952; m. Sharon Bornstein; children: Cori, Alanna, Carly. BS, U. Wis., 1974. Mgr. program coordination ESPN, Inc., Bristol, Conn., 1980-81, dir. program planning and qcauisitions, 1981, dir. programming, 1981-83, v.p. programming, 1983-85, sr. v.p. programming and prdn., 1985-88, exec. v.p. programming and prodn., 1988-90, pres., CEO, 1990-98, also bd. dirs.; pres. ABC Sports, N.Y.C., ABC Inc. Mem. Nat. Acad. Cable Programming (bd. govs.), European Sports Network (dir. Lafayette Beveer bd.), Cable TV Advt. Bur. Office: ABC Corp 77 W 66th St New York NY 10023-6298*

BORNTRAGER, JOHN SHERWOOD, principal; b. Oak Harbor, Wash., July 3, 1953; s. George H. and Norma E. Borntrager; m. Linda Diane, Aug. 30, 1975; children: Melissa, Shanna. BA, San Diego State U., 1975; MA, U. Ctrl. Ark., 1984. Cert. elem. educator, Ariz., Mo., Ark.; cert. prin., Mo., Ark. Tchr. Alhambra Pub. Schs., Phoenix, 1976-79; tchr., prin. Norfork (Ark.) Pub. Schs., 1979-87; prin. Cedarville (Ark) Pub. Schs., 1987—. Mem. ASCD, Ark. Edn. Assn., Ark. Christian Educators Assn., Ark. Assn. Elem. Sch. Prins., Phi Delta Kappa.

BOROCHOFF, IDA SLOAN, real estate executive, artist; b. July 29, 1922; d. Louis and Eva (Bistrick) Sloan; ed. U. Ga., 1939-40, Ga. State U., 1940, Chgo. Sch. Interior Decorating, 1966, Allegro Sch. Ballet, Chgo., Atlanta Ballet, 1948-54, Emory U., 1971-72; m. Charles Zachary Borochoff, Jan. 11, 1942 (dec. July, 1990); children: Lynn Borochoff Gould, Jean Sue Borochoff Shapiro, Toby Ann Borochoff Bernstein, Lance Mark. Investor and owner real estate, 1941—; v.p. Designs Unltd., Inc., Atlanta, 1964—; pres. Sloan Borochoff Gallery, Atlanta, 1970—; art lectr. Met. Ednl. Svc.; art tchr. Ga. Inst. Tech., 1991; producer live talk health show on cable TV, Atlanta, 1983-87; exhibited several one-woman shows include Lovett Sch., 1972, 75, Ga. Inst. Tech., 1972, 75, Atlanta Mdse. Mart, Saginaw Art Mus., 1998, 99; group shows include Ind. U., Purdue U., Gwinnett Art Mus., Duluth, Ga.; art rev. columnist Northside Neighbor Newspapers; columnist Around Ga. with Ida. Bd. dirs. Atlanta Ballet, 1950-57; bd. dirs. Atlanta Music Club, also co-editor Newsletter; hostess Atlanta Arts Festival; capt. Heart Fund, 1968-76, area chmn. dr.; elected to bd. dirs. Am. Cancer Rsch. Ctr. Atlanta Chpt.; active various multi-media groups; artistic dir. Atlanta Playhouse Theatre, Little Miss Ga. Pageant, Little Mr. Dogwood Festival Pageant; judge 17th Internat. Dogwood Festival Art Show, 1989; chmn., trustee Atlanta Playhouse Theatre; mem. U.S. Congl. adv. bd. Am. Security Coun., 1983—; archivist nat. oral history Nat. Coun. Jewish Women, 1990—; Ga. dir., chairperson Levi Hosp. Art Auction, Hot Springs, Ark., 1993-94; with Archives Exhibit Atlanta Jewish Fedn., 1994; donor Borochoff Libr. of A.A. Synagogue; com. mem., patron AJCC Book Festival, 1995-96. Recipient several art awards; Caber award, 1984; named hon. alumnus Atlanta Art Inst., 1968, One of Ten Leading Ladies of Atlanta, J.C. Singles, 1976, honored by Barbara Bush, White House, Washington, 1989, 90; City grantee, 1985. Mem. Atlanta Press Club, Atlanta Writers Club (membership com.), Atlanta Artists Club, Atlanta Women's C. of C. (chmn. fine arts 1977-78), LWV, High Mus. Art, Ga. Writers Assn., Arts High Mus. (patron),

Corcoran Gallery (patron), Nat. Mus. Women in Arts (charter mem.), Internat. Platform Assn., B'nai B'rith Women (pres. chpt. 1975, mem. S.E. regional bd.), Ga. Hist. Soc., AAUW, Women in the Arts, Jockey Club, Progressive Club, Capitol Hill Club (Washington). Home: 3450 Old Plantation Rd NW Atlanta GA 30327-2426 Office: 733 Glendale Rd Scottdale GA 30079-1409

BOROD, RICHARD MELVIN, lawyer; b. Providence, May 11, 1933; s. Esmond S. and Lena H. Borod; m. A. Gail Cohen, Aug. 22, 1959. AB, Brown U., 1954; LLB, Yale U., 1962. Bar: R.I. 1962, U.S. Dist. Ct. R.I. 1963, U.S. Ct. Appeals (1st cir.) 1966, U.S. Supreme Ct. 1979. Assoc. Edwards & Angell, Providence, 1962-70, ptnr., 1970-97, of counsel, 1997—; incorporator, 1st chmn. bd. R.I. Legal Svcs., Providence, 1969-72, bd. dirs., 1969-86. Vol. atty. R.I. Affiliate of ACLU, Providence, 1962—; trustee, officer Temple Beth El, Providence, 1986-93. With U.S. Army, 1956-59. Mem. ABA, fed. Bar Assn. (chmn. R.I. chpt. 1987-88), R.I. Bar Assn. Jewish. Avocations: tennis, biking, cross-country skiing, classical guitar, duplicate bridge (ACBL life master). Office: Edwards & Angell 2700 Hospital Trust Twr Providence RI 02903

BOROFF, HENRY JACK, federal judge, educator. JD, Boston U., 1975. Bar: Mass. Bankruptcy judge for Mass., U.S. Bankruptcy Ct., Worcester, 1993—; adj. prof. Western New Eng. Law Sch., 1996—. Office: US Bankruptcy Ct Donohue Fed Bldg 595 Main St Worcester MA 01608-2025

BORONICO, JESS STEPHEN, management science educator, academic dean; b. Bronx, N.Y., Oct. 23, 1956; s. Stelio and Helen (Michaels) B. BS in Math., Fairleigh Dickinson U., 1978, MS in Math., 1980; PhD in Ops. Rsch., U. Pa., 1992. Prof. mgmt. scis. Rutgers U., Camden, N.J., 1987-88, Phila. Coll. Textiles and Scis., 1988-92; prof. mgmt. scis. Monmouth U., West Long Branch, N.J., 1993—, assoc. dean Sch. Bus., 1998—; cons. United Postal Svc., 1990-92, Reality Techs., 1991, N.J. Hwy. Authority, 1991-92, Kennedy Western U., Calif., 1994-97; mem. adv. bd. to various jours., 1993—. Author: Computer Simulation in Operations Management, 1996; contbg. author: The Service Productivity and Quality Challenge, 1995; contbr. articles to profl. jours. Fellow U. Pa. Wharton Sch., 1983-87; recipient three Anbar citations of excellence for refereed publs., 1996-98. Mem. Inst. for Ops. Rsch. and Mgmt. Scis., Decision Scis. Inst., Am. Statis. Assn., Mensa. Avocations: softball, computer simulations. Home: 525 East St Long Branch NJ 07740-6815 Office: Monmouth U Sch Bus Adminstrn Bey Hall 213 West Long Branch NJ 07764

BORONOW, RICHARD C., gynecologist, educator; b. Appleton, Wis., Dec. 18, 1933; children: Robert, Thomas, Amy. BS in Medicine, Northwestern U., 1956, MD, 1959. Diplomate Am. Bd. Ob/Gyn. with cert. in gynecologic/oncology. Intern Cook County Hosp., Chgo., 1959-60; resident in ob/gyn Evanston Hosp., 1960-63; resident in surgery Meml. Hosp. Cancer, N.Y.C., 1963-64; fellow in gynecology Anderson Tumor Inst., Houston, 1964-65; mem. staff Miss. Baptist Med. Ctr., Jackson; clin. prof. gynecology U. Miss. Med. Ctr.; mem. med. alumni adv. bd. Northwestern U. Med. Sch. Author book; contbr. articles to profl. jours., chpts. to books. Fellow ACS, Am. Coll. Ob/Gyn; mem. Am. Radium Soc. (exec. com.), Soc. Gynecologic Oncologists (past pres.), Soc. Surg. Oncologists, Soc. Pelvic Surgeons (past pres.). Address: 1190 N State St Ste 402 Jackson MS 39202-2413

BOROS, JEROME S., lawyer; b. N.Y.C., Apr. 28, 1926; s. Edwin N. Boros and Margaret G. Guttman; m. Elayne N. Nossiter, Nov. 23, 1969; stepchildren: Richard, Ronald, Jill LeVine. AB, Syracuse U., 1947, MA, 1950, LLB, 1950; LLM, Yale U., 1951. Bar: N.Y. 1950, D.C. Bar 1966, U.S. Dist. Ct. (so. dist.) N.Y. 1950, U.S. Ct. Appeals (D.C. cir.) 1966. Atty. CAB, Washington, 1950-53, FCC, Washington, 1953-55; assoc. Fly, Shuebruk, Gaguine, Boros & Braun, N.Y.C., Washington, 1955-62, ptnr., 1962-88; ptnr. Rosenman & Colin, N.Y.C., 1988-96; coun. Robinson, Silverman, Pearce, Aaronsohn & Berman, N.Y.C., 1996—; faculty sch. speech Syracuse U., 1947; adj. prof. law NYU Sch. Law, 1971-95; chmn. Workshop on Broadcasting Practising Law Inst., 1969, also lectr., 1969-76; gen. counsel Internat. Radio and TV Soc., N.Y.C., 1973-93, sec., 1973-93, gov., 1973-93; co-trustee radio sta. WYRM, New Britain, Conn., 1987-96. Acting village justice Village of Sands Point, N.Y., 1988—; chmn. Sands Point Cable Com., 1993—. With U.S. Army, 1944-45. Mem. City Athletic Club (gov., chmn. legal legis. com.). Republican. Jewish. Office: Roberson & Silverman 1290 Ave of Americas New York NY 10104-0199*

BOROTSIK, RICK, member of Canadian parliament; b. Brandon, Man., Can.; m. Norma Green, 1972; children: Dustin, Marty. BA, Brandon U., 1971. Bramalea Ltd., Calgary, Alta., Can., 1985, Toronto, Ont., Can.; Mayor City of Brandon, 1989-97; M.P. from Brandon-Souris dist. Ho. of Commons, 1997—; mem. Progressive Conservative Party caucus; critic Agr. and Agri-Food issues, Can. Wheat Bd., Western Econ. Diversification; asst. critic govtl. affairs; chair western regional caucus; mem. Ho. Commons standing com. on agr. and agri-food; assoc. mem. standing com. transp. Nat. bd. dirs. Fedn. Can. Municipalities; past mem. exec. bd. Man. Assn. Urban Municipalities; past mem. Brandon & Area Dist. Planning Bd., Brandon Econ. Devel. Bd., several other bds. and commns. Fax: 613-992-1265. Office: House of Commons, Rm 668 Confederation Bldg, Ottawa, ON Canada K1A 0A6*

BOROVIK, ALEXEI PETER, ballet dancer, educator; b. Chelyabinsk, Russia, July 22, 1961; came to U.S., 1991; s. Peter Borovik and Valentina Borovik; m. Elena Levina, Dec. 4, 1981; children: Nikita, Alisa. Grad., Perm Ballet Acad. Sch., Russia, 1979. Prin. dancer Perm (Russia) Ballet Acad. Theatre, 1979-91, Pa. Ballet, Phila., 1992—; guest artist 7th St. Barts Music Festival, 1997. Choreographer ballet Romeo and Juliet, 1993; performed in world tour Stars of Russian Ballet, 1982-90; dancer XXV Internat. Festival of Ballet, Genoa, Italy, 1991, Stars of Bolshoi and Kirov Ballet, Stars of Russian Ballet. Bd. dirs. Friends of Russian Ballet, Phila., 1994-96. Recipient silver medal Internat. Balllet Competition, Moscow, 1984, gold medal Peru Internat. Competition, 1987; named Nat. Merited Artist of Russia, 1987. Avocations: fishing, tennis. Office: Pa Ballet 1101 S Broad St Philadelphia PA 19147-4410

BOROVOY, MARC ALLEN, podiatrist; b. Detroit, Oct. 22, 1960; s. Mathew and Joyce Francis (Weisman) B.; m. Michele Lynn Flusty, Oct. 23, 1983; children: Danielle, Brandon. Student, Wayne State U., 1978-81; D. Podiatric Medicine, Ohio Coll. Podiatric Medicine, 1985. Diplomate Am. Bd. Podiatric Sugery, Am. Bd. Quality Assurance and Utilization Rev. Resident Straith Hosp., Southfield, Mich., 1985-86; podiatrist Associated Podiatrists, Oak Park, Mich., 1986—; chief dept. podiatric surgery Providence Hosp., Southfield, Mich. Contbr. articles to profl. jours. Recipient Meritorious Svc. award Am. Podiat. Medicine Assn., 1997. Fellow Am. Coll. Foot Surgeons; mem. APHA, Am. Diabetes Assn., Am. Podiatric med. Assn. (meritorious svc. award 1997), Mich. Podiatric Med. Assn. (exec. sec. 1986-89, chmn. pub. rels. 1988—, v.p. 1990-91, pres.-elect 1992-93, pres. 1993-95). Avocations: swimming, photography. Office: Associated Podiatrists 25725 Coolidge Hwy Oak Park MI 48237-1392 also: 47601 Grand River Ave Ste B-230 Novi MI 48374-1257

BOROWIEC, ANDREW, art educator, photographer. BA in Russian, Haverford Coll., 1979; MFA in Photography, Yale U., 1982. Instr. Parsons Sch. Design, Paris, 1980-82, 83-84; tchr. photography and art Germantown Acad., Ft. Washington, Pa., 1982-83; instr. New Sch. Social Rsch., N.Y.C., 1982-84; instr. fashion photography Lab. Inst. Merchandising, N.Y.C., 1984; dir. Sch. Art U. Akron, Ohio, 1990-95, prof. art Mary Schiller Myers Sch. Art, 1995—; guest lectr. contemporary Am. photography U. d'Aix-Marseille, France; vis. assoc. prof. art history Oberlin (Ohio) Coll., 1990. One-man shows include Club House, UN, Geneva, 1978, Galerie Un Moment En Plus, Paris, 1981, Le Poisson Banane, Arles, France, 1981, Galerie Les Arcenaulx, Marseille, France, 1982, Radnor Gallery, Bryn Mawr Coll., Pa., 1983, Perkins Gallery, U. Akron, 1984, Midtown Y Photography Gallery, N.Y.C., 1984, Dishman Gallery, Lamar U., Beaumont, Tex., 1986, Vox Gallery, Akron, 1988, Rose Gallery, St. Edwards U., Austin, Tex., 1988, Dillingham Gallery, Ithaca (N.Y.) Coll., 1988, Exit Gallery, Reno, 1988, Canton (Ohio) Art Inst., 1989, Fla. Internat. U., North Miami, Fla., 1990, Coll. Wooster (Ohio) Art Mus., 1991, Blue Sky Gallery, Portland, Oreg., 1994, Soc. Contemporary Photography, Kansas City, Mo., 1995, 99, Regis U., Denver, 1996, O.K. Harris, N.Y.C., 1997, So. Light Gallery, Amarillo, Tex., 1999, numerous others; exhibited in group shows at Images Gallery, Cin., 1991, Ea. Mich. U., Ypsilanti, 1992, Photospiva 93, Joplin, Mo., 1993, Contemporary Artists Ctr., North Adams, Mass., 1994, U. Cin., 1995, Blue Sky Gallery, Portland, 1996, Open Space Gallery, Allentown, Pa., 1997, Cleve. Mus. Art, 1998, numerous others; represented in pub. collections Akron Art Mus., Can. Ctr. Arch., N.Y.C., Montreal, Can., Canton Art Inst., Midtown Y. Photography Gallery, N.Y.C., Yale U., New Haven, others; staff photographer Internat. Ctr. Photography, N.Y.C., 1979-80; freelance photography The Chronicle for Higher Edn., 1987-93; commn. by Nat. Trust Historic Preservation and Soc. Photographic Edn., 1987, Canton Art Inst., 1988-89; contbr. photography to numerous publs. Recipient Excellence award Kansas City Art Inst., 1987, Hon. Mention and Purchase award Cleve. Mus. Art, 1988, Third prize N.Mex. Photographer, 1994, Purchase prize Nat. Mus. Am. Art, 1996, Fellowship award Soc. Contemporary Photography, 1998; Nat. Endowment Arts/Arts Midwest Photography fellow, 1985; Summer Rsch. fellow U. Akron, 1988, 90, 97; Individual Artist fellow Ohio Arts Coun., 1988, 98; John Simon Guggenheim Meml. Found. fellow, 1998; Faculty Rsch. grantee U. Akron, 1986; Instl. Support grantee Ohio Arts Coun., 1988; Visual Artists Forums grantee Nat. Endowment Arts, 1988; Folk Endowment grantee U. Akron Sch. Art, 1993; Folk Endowment grantee U. Akrom Mary Schiller Myers Sch. Art, 1998. Fax: (330) 865-6629. E-mail: borowiec@uakron.edu. Address: 1062 West Market St Akron OH 44313

BOROWIK, ANN, writer; b. Providence, R.I., July 4, 1928; d. Albert de Russy and Edina (Davis) Baker; m. Val Coleman (div. 1965); m. Tom Borowik; children: Karen Borowik, Charles Coleman. Author: How Many Miles to Babylon, 1963, Lions 3: Christians, 1965, The Lottery Chronicles, 1996. Home: 310 Greenwich St Apt 3J New York NY 10013-2709

BOROWITZ, ALBERT IRA, lawyer, author; b. Chgo., June 27, 1930; s. David and Anne (Wolkenstein) B.; m. Helen Blanche Osterman, July 29, 1950; children: Peter Leonard, Joan, Andrew Seth. BA in Classics summa cum laude, Harvard U., 1951, MA in Chinese Regional Studies, 1953, JD magna cum laude, 1956. Bar: Ohio 1957. Assoc. firm Hahn, Loeser, Freedheim, Dean & Wellman, Cleve., 1956-62; ptnr. Hahn, Loeser, Freedheim, Dean & Wellman, 1962-83, Jones, Day, Reavis & Pogue, Cleve., 1983-90; of counsel Jones, Day, Reavis & Pogue, 1991-94. Author: Fiction in Communist China, 1955, Innocence and Arsenic: Studies in Crime and Literature, 1977, The Woman who Murdered Black Satin: The Bermondsey Horror, 1981, A Gallery of Sinister Perspectives: Ten Crimes and a Scandal, 1982, The Jack the Ripper Walking Tour Murder, 1986, The Thurtell-Hunt Murder Case: Dark Mirror to Regency England, 1987, This Club Frowns on Murder, 1990, (with H.O. Borowitz) Pawnshop and Palaces: The Fall and Rise of the Campana Art Museum, 1991, Jones, Day, Reavis & Pogue: The First Century, 1993; contr. articles to profl. jours. Hon. consul of France in Cleve., 1990-95; v.p. French-Am. C. of C. of No. Ohio, 1993-99; co-founder Borowitz True Crime Collection at Kent State U. Librs. Recipient Cleve. arts prize for lit., 1981. Mem. Am. Law Inst., Rowfant Club (Cleve.), Harvard Club (N.Y.C.).

BOROWITZ, JOSEPH LEO, pharmacologist; b. Columbus, Ohio, Dec. 19, 1932; s. Joseph Peter and Anna Louise (Grundei) B.; divorced, 1985; children: Jon Joseph, Peter Joseph, Lynn Anne. BS in Pharmacy, Ohio State U., 1955; MS in Pharmacology, Purdue U., 1957; PhD in Pharmacology (NIH fellow), Northwestern U., 1960. Postdoctoral fellow dept. pharmacology Harvard U. Med. Sch., Boston, 1963-64; instr., then asst. prof. pharmacology Bowman Gray Sch. Medicine, 1964-69; assoc. prof. pharmacology and toxicology Purdue U., 1969-74, prof., 1974—; sabbatical leave to Cambridge, Eng., 1976, to Basel, Switzerland, 1984. Contbr. articles to profl. jours. Treas. Tippecanoe County (Ind.) Comprehensive Health Planning Coun., 1971-76. Capt. USAR, 1960. Recipient award for excellence in teaching Bowman Gray Sch. Medicine, 1969, Henry Heine award for excellence in teaching Purdue U. Coll. Pharmacy, 1983; named NIH postdoctoral fellow, 1962-64; grantee NSF, 1965-68, NIH, 1971-74, 86-89, 89-94, 94-98, 99—, U.S. Army Med. Rsch., 1989-96, 97—. Mem. Am. Soc. Pharmacology and Exptl. Therapeutics, Rho Chi. Roman Catholic. Office: Purdue U Dept Medicinal Chemistry and Molecular Pharmacology West Lafayette IN 47907

BOROWITZ, SIDNEY, retired physics educator; b. N.Y.C., N.Y., June 12, 1918; s. Morris and Rose (Cohen) B.; m. Ruth Aaron Meyer, June 20, 1943; children: Michael, Elizabeth. BS, CCNY, 1937; MS, NYU, 1941, PhD, 1948. Physicist David Taylor Model Basin, 1942-43; indsl. engr. Western Electric Co., 1943-45; instr. NYU, N.Y.C., 1946-48, asst. prof., 1950-55, assoc. prof., 1955-59, prof. physics, 1959-84, prof. emeritus, 1984—, dean, 1969-71, chancellor, 1971-77; instr. Harvard U., Cambridge, Mass., 1948-50; chief exec. officer Cistron Biotech., Pine Brook, N.J., 1981-84; chmn. bd. dirs. Aesculapius Internat. Medicine, N.Y.C., 1987-90, Inst. for Sch. of the Future, N.Y.C., 1987—; cons. NYU, 1987-97; exec. dir. N.Y. Acad. Scis., N.Y.C., 1977-81; mem. investment adv. com. Am. Inst. Physics, 1992-97. Author: Fundamentals of Quantum Mechanics, 1967, Farewell Fossil Fuels, 1998; co-author: Essentials of Physics, 1966, A Contemporary View of Elementary Physics, 1968. Avocation: squash. Home: 70 E 10th St New York NY 10003-5102 Office: NYU Physics Dept Washington Sq N New York NY 10003

BOROWSKI, JENNIFER LUCILE, corporate administrator; b. Jersey City, Oct. 23, 1934; d. Peter Anthony and Ludwika (Zapolska) B. BS, St. Peter's Coll., 1968; postgrad., Pace Coll., 1976-77. Mgr. benefits Amerada Petroleum Corp., N.Y.C., 1951-66, Mt. Sinai Hosp., N.Y.C., 1966-67; mgr. payroll and payroll taxes Haskins & Sells, N.Y.C., 1967-74; mgr. payroll and payroll tax Cushman & Wakefield, Inc., N.Y.C., 1975-89. Mem. Am. Payroll Assn. (bd. dirs. 1979-81, cert.), Am. Mgmt. Assn., Am. Soc. Payroll Mgrs., Internat. Platform Assn. (hon.), Am. Soc. Profl. Exec. Women, NAFE. Avocations: golf, opera, boating. Home: 36 Front St North Arlington NJ 07031-5822

BOROWSKY, PHILIP, lawyer; b. Phila., Oct. 9, 1946; s. Joshua and Gertrude (Nicholson) B.; m. Judith Lee Goldwasser, Sept. 5, 1970 (div. 1996); children: Miriam Isadora, Manuel, Nora Jo. BA, UCLA, 1967; JD, U. San Francisco, 1973. Bar: Calif. Pres. and mng. ptnr. Cartwright, Slobodin, Bokelman, Borowsky, Wartnick, Moore & Harris, 1987-95; pres. Law Offices of Philip Borowsky, Inc., 1996—; mem. faculty Practicing Law Inst., N.Y.C., 1983-84; mem. adj. faculty Hastings Coll. Law, San Francisco, 1982-83; arbitrator Superior Ct., San Francisco, 1982—, Am. Arbitration Assn., 1982—, Nat. Assn. Securities Dealers, 1994—. Co-author: Unjust Dismissal and At-Will Employment, 1985; mem. bd. editorial cons. Bad Faith Law Update, 1986. Served with U.S. Army, 1968-70, Vietnam. Mem. Calif. Trial Lawyers Assn. Democrat. Office: Steuart St Twr Ste 2600 1 Market Pla San Francisco CA 94105-1417

BORRELL, PAUL NICHOLAS, sales executive; b. Hoboken, N.J., Apr. 17, 1949; s. Samuel Vincent and Dorothy Diane (Watt) B.; m. Linda Marie DiAnthony, Dec. 6, 1975; children: Vanessa Marie, Jessica Lin. AB in Econs., Muhlenberg Coll., 1971. Enforcement officer Pa. Liquor Control Bd., Pitts., 1971-73; sales rep. PVO Internat., St. Louis, 1973-80, Meer Corp., North Bergen, N.J., 1980-85, Fallek Chem., Ft. Lee, N.J., 1985-86; mgr. regional sales Takeda USA, Inc., Orangeburg, N.Y., 1986-98, Watson Foods, West Haven, Conn., 1998—. Mem. Amnesty Internat.; tutor Literacy Vols. Am. Mem. N.J. Pharm. Discussion Group, Inst. Food Technologists. Democrat. Roman Catholic. Avocations: gardening, jazz. Home: 16 Perera Ave Wayne NJ 07470-4330 Office: Watson Foods 301 Heffernon Dr West Haven CT 06516

BORRELLI, JOHN FRANCIS, architect; b. Buffalo, Nov. 6, 1955; s. Peter and Maria (Raimondo) B. BSCE, Columbia U., 1977; postgrad., Pratt Inst., 1977-81. Registered arch., N.Y., N.J., Conn., Vt., Ill., Va., Pa., Fla., Md., Mich. Project coord. C. Raimondo and Sons, Ft. Lee, N.J., 1971-78; project mgr. DAT Cons., N.Y.C., 1978-81, Litchfield Grosfeld Assocs., N.Y.C., 1981-83; project arch. Design Mgmt., Inc., N.Y.C., 1983-87; ptnr. Sys. Collaborative, Inc., N.Y.C., 1987-88, Davis Borrelli Assocs., N.Y.C., 1987-91; exec. v.p. Karco-Davis, Inc., N.Y.C., 1987-91; v.p. Rampart Constrn. Assocs., N.Y.C., 1987-91; prin. Meli Borrelli Assocs., N.Y.C., 1991-94; pres. John Francis Borrelli Arch., P.C., N.Y.C., 1991—; prin. MBA Mcpl., Inc., 1993, MBA Internat., Inc., 1991, SPGA MBA, Inc., 1993, Walter M. Ballard, Ltd., 1993, MBA&A, Inc., 1995, Vici Group, Ltd., N.Y.C., 1995. Prin. works include ING/Barings Securities, Inc. Hdqs., N.Y.C., Credit Suisse Hdqs., N.Y.C., Schonfeld Securities Inc. (various offices including N.Y.C., Chgo., N.J., Boca Raton, L.I. Hdqrs.), Netscape Comms. Corp. (various offices including N.Y., Chgo., Detroit, and Bethesda, Md.), H.S. for Environ. Scis., N.Y.C., Burlington Industries Hdqs., N.Y.C., Walt Disney Book and Product Licensing Offices, N.Y.C., Jefferson Ins. Corp. Hdqs., N.J., Western Union Corp. Hdqrs., N.J., Parade Publs. Corp. Hdqrs., N.Y.C., Covington Fabrics Corp. Hdqrs., N.Y.C., Otterbourg, Steindler, Houston and Rosen, P.C., N.Y.C., Lalique (N.Y.C. flagship boutiques and offices), Otterbourg, Steindler, Houston & Rosen, P.C., N.Y.C., Maesonedia, Inc., N.J. Recipient 1st prize Gabriel Industries, 1976; Columbia U. scholar, 1973-77. Mem. AIA, ASCE, Nat. Trust for Hist. Preservation, World Wildlife Fund, Greenpeace. Avocations: woodworking, antique collecting, book collecting, gardening, tennis. Office: John Francis Borrelli Architect PC 13 E 37th St New York NY 10016-2821

BORROFF, MARIE, English language educator; b. N.Y.C., Sept. 10, 1923; d. Albert Ramon and Marie (Bergersen) B. Ph.B., U. Chgo., 1943, M.A., 1946; Ph.D., Yale U., 1956. Teaching asst. U. Chgo., 1946-47; instr. dept. English Smith Coll., 1948-51, asst. prof., 1956-59, asso. prof., 1959; vis. asst. prof. English Yale U., 1957-58, vis. asso. prof., 1959-6O, asso. prof. English, 1960-65, prof., 1965-71, William Lampson prof., 1971-92, Sterling prof. English, 1992-94; Sterling prof. English emeritus, 1994—, Phi Beta Kappa vis. scholar, 1973-74; fellow Ezra Stiles Coll., Yale. Author: Sir Gawain and the Green Knight: A Stylistic and Metrical Study, 1962, (with J. B. Bessinger, Jr.); recorded dialogues read in Middle English, 1965, Sir Gawain and the Green Knight: A New Verse Translation, 1967, Pearl: A New Verse Translation, 1977, Language and the Poet: Verbal Artistry in Frost, Stevens, and Moore, 1979; editor: Wallace Stevens, A Collection of Critical Essays, 1963; videotaped lectures: To Hear Their Voices, Chaucer, Shakespeare and Frost, Assn. of Yale Alumni Great Tchrs. Series, Chapter Headings: Remarks Made at the Annual Initiation Ceremonies of Phi Beta Kappa, Alpha Chapter of Connecticut, 1989-1994, 1996. Bd. Govs. Yale U. Press, 1988-98. Recipient James Billings Fiske poetry prize U. Chgo., 1943; Eunice Tietjens Meml. prize Poetry mag., 1945; Margaret Lee Wiley fellow AAUW, 1955-56; Guggenheim fellow, 1969-70. Fellow Am. Acad. Arts and Scis.; mem. MLA, Acad. Am. Poets, Medieval Acad. Am., Phi Beta Kappa. Home: 311 St Ronan St New Haven CT 06511-2328

BORRONE, LILLIAN C., transportation executive. BA in Polit. Sci., Am. U.; MSCE, Manhattan Coll. Assoc. adminstr. Urban Mass Transp. Adminstrn.; dep. adminstr. U.S. Dept. Transp.; dir. mgmt. and budget dept., asst. dir. aviation dept. Port Authority N.Y. & N.J., dir. port commerce. Chmn. Transp. Rsch. Bd., 1995-96. Mem. Am. Assn. Port Authorities (bd. dirs.), N. Atlantic Ports Assn., Regional Bus. Partnership Newark. Office: Port Authority NY & NJ 1 World Trade Ctr Fl 68 New York NY 10048-0682*

BORROR, DONALD A., construction company executive; b. 1929. Grad., Ohio State Univ., Columbus, Ohio State Univ. Sch. of Law, Columbus. With Summer & Co. Inc., Columbus, Ohio, 1956-71; with The Borror Corp. (now Borror Realty Co.), Dublin, Ohio, 1971—, pres., 1976-82, chmn., 1977—; chmn. bd. dirs. The Borror Corp. (now Borror Realty Co.), Dublin, 1994-97, Dominion Homes Inc. (formerly The Borror Corp.), Dublin, 1997—. With USAF. Office: Dominion Homes Inc PO Box 7166 5501 Frantz Rd Dublin OH 43017-7502*

BORROR, DOUGLAS G., construction company executive; b. 1955. Grad., Ohio State U., 1977. With Huntington Nat. Bank, Columbus, 1977-79, Borror Corp. (now Borror Realty Co. Inc.), Dublin, Ohio, 1979—; pres., CEO, COO Borror Corp. (now Dominion Homes, Inc.), Dublin, Ohio, 1994—. Office: Dominion Homes Inc 5501 Frantz Rd Dublin OH 43017-7502*

BORSARI, GEORGE ROBERT, JR., lawyer, broadcaster; b. Washington, July 30, 1940; s. George Robert and Sara Totton (Dunning) B.; m. Regis Ann Herron, Oct. 23, 1964 (div. Jan. 1985); children: George Robert, III, William Grant. B.S., Va. Poly. Inst., 1962; LL.B., George Washington U., 1965. Bar: D.C. 1966. Since practiced in Washington; ptnr. Borsari & Paxson, 1969—; pres. Local TV Systems, Inc., 1981-89, Outdoor Inst., Inc., 1978—; chmn. Core Group Inc., 1991—. Councilman Town of Glen Echo, Md., 1969-74, mayor, 1977-81, 89-91; mem. Montgomery County (Md.) Muncipality Advisory Bd., 1972-74, Montgomery County CATV Task Force, 1973-74, 80-85, Cable TV Adv. Com., 1979-85; pres. Montgomery County chpt. Md. Mcpl. League. Served to lt. col. JAG USAR. Decorated Army Meritorious Service medal (2), Army Commendation medal with oak leaf clusters (3); recipient Presdl. commendation, 1970; St. George award Roman Catholic Archdiocese Washington, 1970; Silver Beaver award Nat. Capital Area council Boy Scouts Am., 1974. Mem. ABA (chmn. cable TV com. sect. sci. and tech. 1982-86, chmn. Broadcast Commn. 1986-90, chmn. Mass Media Com. 1990-92, mem. coun. sect. sci. and tech.), Am. D.C., Fed. Communications Bar Assns., Isaac Walton League, Phi Delta Phi. Democrat. Clubs: Kenwood Golf and Country. Home: 6107 Princeton Ave Glen Echo MD 20812-1125 Office: Borsari & Paxson 2033 M St NW Suite 630 Washington DC 20036

BORSCH, FREDERICK HOUK, bishop; b. Chgo., Sept. 13, 1935; s. Reuben A. and Pearl Irene (Houk) B.; m. Barbara Edgeley Sampson, June 25, 1960; children: Benjamin, Matthew, Stuart. AB, Princeton U., 1957; MA, Oxford U., 1959; STB, Gen. Theol. Sem., 1960; PhD, U. Birmingham, 1966; DD (hon.), Seabury Western Theol. Sem., 1978, Gen. Theol. Sem., 1988; STD (hon.), Ch. Div. Sch. of Pacific, 1981, Berk Div. Sch. Yale U., 1983. Ordained priest Episcopal Ch., 1960; curate Grace Episcopal Ch., Oak Park, Ill., 1960-63; tutor Queen's Coll., Birmingham, Eng., 1963-66; asst. prof. N.T. Seabury Western Theol. Sem., Evanston, Ill., 1966-69, assoc. prof. N.T., 1969-71; prof. N.T. Gen. Theol. Sem., N.Y.C., 1971-72; pres., dean Berk Div. Sch. Yale U., Berkeley, Calif., 1972-81; dean of chapel, prof. religion Princeton U., 1981-88; bishop Episc. Diocese, L.A., 1988—; rep. Faith and Order Commn., Nat. Coun. Chs., 1975-81; mem. exec. coun. Episc. Ch., 1981-88, Anglican Cons. Coun., 1984-88; chair bd. govs. Trinity Press Internat., 1989—; bd. adv. UCLA Sch. Pub. Policy & Social Rsch., 1998—; trustee Princeton U., 1998—. Author: The Son of Man in Myth and History, 1967, The Christian and Gnostic Son of Man, 1970, God's Parable, 1976, Introducing the Lessons of the Church Year, 1978, Coming Together in the Spirit, 1980, Power in Weakness, 1983, Jesus: The Human Life of God, 1987, Many Things in Parables, 1988, Christian Discipleship and Sexuality, 1993, Outrage and Hope, 1996; editor: Anglicanism and the Bible, 1984, The Bible's Authority in Today's Church, 1993. Trustee Princeton U., 1998—. Keasbey scholar, 1957-59. Fellow Soc. Arts, Religion and Contemporary Culture; mem. Am. Acad. Religion, Soc. Bibl. Lit., Studiorum Novi Testamenti Societas, Phi Beta Kappa. Home: 2930 Corda Ln Los Angeles CA 90049-1105 Office: Episcopal Diocese of LA PO Box 512164 Los Angeles CA 90051-0164

BORSCHEL, VALERIE LYNN, medical/surgical nurse; b. Kenmore, N.Y., Sept. 16, 1956; d. Richard N. and Patricia A. (Gowland) Graser; children: Scott Keven, Eric Dennis. BSN, D'Youville Coll., 1977. Staff nurse Roswell Park Meml. Hosp., Buffalo, 1977-84, St. Elizabeth's Hosp., Utica, N.Y., 1984-87; head nurse St. Luke's Meml. Hosp., Utica, 1987-89; staff nurse St. Francis Hosp., Poughkeepsie, N.Y., 1989—; project mgr. Nat. Surg. Breast and Bowel Project, 1992-94. Bd. dirs. Am. Cancer Soc., 1993—. Mem. Oncolog. Nurses Assn. (past pres., treas. Mohawk Valley chpt.). Home: 12 Schuyler Dr Poughkeepsie NY 12603-6109

BORSICK, MARLIN LESTER, data processing executive; b. Norwalk, Ohio, Feb. 16, 1953; s. Lester Charles and Delores Arlene (Yutzy) B.; m. Deborah Jean Taylor, May 6, 1988; 1 child, Tegan Marie. BA in Polit. Sci., Ohio State U., 1975; MBA, Ashland U. (formerly Ashland Coll.), 1987. Microsoft cert. profl. in networking, 3Com 3Wizard. Asst. mgr. F.W. Woolworth, Fremont, Ohio, 1978-81, K-Mart Enterprises, Marion, Ohio, 1982; v.p. MBA Systems Automation, Columbus, Ohio, 1982-83; v.p., dir., founder CBM Automated Systems (now Babbage-Simmel/And Assocs.), Columbus, 1983-88; dir., chmn. bd., pres. Coastalan, Inc. (formerly Coastal Marine Info. Svcs., Inc.), Huron, Ohio, 1988-96, Lodi, Ohio, 1996—; cons. Compu Bus Co. (acquired by CBM Systems), Norwalk 1986-87. Chmn.

Firelands coun. Boy Scouts Am., 1987-88. Lt. col. Ohio Mil. Res., 1991—. Mem. Local Area Network Dealers Assn. (pres. Ohio chpt. 1990-93, program chmn. and sec.-treas. 1987-89, contbg. editor The Network Report, chpt. adv. coun. 1991-93), State Def. Force Assn. U.S., Ohio Mil. Res. Assn., Assn. of U.S. Army (v.p. Firelands chpt.). Avocations: sailing, science fiction, reading, football official.

BORSKI, ROBERT ANTHONY, congressman; b. Philadelphia, Pa., Oct. 20, 1948; s. Robert Anthony and Rita (Savage) B.; children: Jill Michele, Dorothy Lynn, Jennifer Marie, Robert A. III, Margaret Rita. B.A., U. Balt., 1971. Floor mgr. Raymond James & Assoc., Phila., 1971-77; mem. Pa. Ho. of Reps., 1977-82, 98th-105th Congresses from 3rd Pa. dist., Washington, D.C., 1983—; mem. Trans. & Infrastructure com. ranking minority mem. Transp. & Infrastructure subcom. on Water Resources & Environ. Democrat. Roman Catholic. Office: Rm 2267 Rayburn House Office Bldg Washington DC 20515-3803

BORSODY, ROBERT PETER, lawyer; b. N.Y.C., Oct. 6, 1937; s. Benjamin F. and Edith Nora (Corcoran) B.; m. Paula Jane Bercutt, Oct. 14, 1973; children: Lisa M., Daniel B., Sarah E., Alexander S. B.E.E., U. Va., 1961, LL.B., 1964; diploma, U. Teheran, Iran, 1959. Bar: N.Y. 1965, D.C. 1978. Assoc. firm Sullivan & Cromwell, N.Y.C., 1964-69; founder, dir. Legal Services for Elderly Poor, 1969-71, Community Health Law Project, 1971-73; pvt. practice law N.Y.C., 1973-78; ptnr., founder Epstein Becker Borsody & Green, N.Y.C., 1978-87; of counsel Epstein, Becker & Green, N.Y.C., 1987-99, Fischbein, Badillo, Wagner & Harding, N.Y.C., 1999—; bd. dirs. numerous close bus. and pub. corps.; adj. prof. Manhattan Coll., 1978-82, Pace U. Sch. Law, 1986-90; mem. N.Y. State Coun. Health Care Financing, 1978—; sec. N.Y. Statewide Health Coordinating Coun., 1978-87; chmn. bd. dirs. N.Y. Bus. Group on Health. Bd. dirs. N.Y.C. Mental Health Assn. Mem. ABA, N.Y. State Bar Assn. (chmn. pub. health com.), Assn. of Bar of City of N.Y., Am. Assn. Hosp. Attys., Nat. Health Lawyers Assn., Hosp. Fin. Mgmt. Assn. (advanced), Yale Club. Home: 23 Winged Foot Dr Larchmont NY 10538-1124 Office: 250 Park Ave New York NY 10177-0001

BORST, JOHN NOBLE, television director, producer; b. N.Y.C., Jan. 5, 1961; s. Alan Wills and Frances Noble (Sackett) B.; m. Rita Marie Savino, Mar. 11, 1989; children: Kyle Noble Leonard, Daniel Peter Gray. BA, Cornell U., 1984. Distbn. coord. Electronic Arts Intermix, N.Y.C., 1985-87; quality and master control engr. Rainbow Networks, Woodbury, N.Y., 1988-89; prodr., dir. Discovery Comms., N.Y.C., 1989-95; pres., sr. prodr., dir. Grandvue Prodns., Upper Nyack, N.Y., 1995—; cons., sr. prodr. Discovery Comms., Bethesda, 1996-97. dir., prodr., writer (documentary) When Nature Rules, 1996, Disaster Proof?, 1996, Amusement Parks: The Pursuit of Fun, 1997, Great American Train Stations, 1997, Death Valley Chronicles, 1998, Fireworks, 1998. Methodist. Avocations: poetry, nature conservation, photography, video art, outdoor recreation. Office: Grandvue Prodns Inc 505 N Broadway Nyack NY 10960-1213

BORST, PHILIP CRAIG, veterinarian, councilman; b. Columbus, Ohio, May 19, 1950; s. Lawrence M. and Eldoris (Wood) B.; m. Jill Patrice Alexander, Sept. 12, 1980; children: Alex, Eric. BS, Purdue U., 1972, DVM, 1975. Vet. Shelby St. Animal Clinic, Indpls., 1975—; bd. dirs. Ind. Sports Corp., Indpls., Indpls. Econ. Devel. Corp. Councilman Indsl. City-County, 1980—; del. Ind. State Rep. Convention, 1982; bd. dirs. Indpls. Conv. and Visitors Assn.; mem. Marion County Capital Improvement Bd.; mem. exec. com. 2000 NCAA Final Four. Named Best City-County Councilman Indpls. Mag., 1986; recipient Svc. to Mankind award Southside Indpl. Sertoma Club, 1987. Mem. Cen. Ind. Vet. Med. Assn. (pres. 1990), Purdue Vet. Med. Alumni Assn. (pres. 1988). Republican. Methodist. Avocations: golf, basketball, Purdue athletics. Home: 6554 Robin Hood Dr Indianapolis IN 46227-7309 also: City-County Coun Office 200 E Washington St Ste 241 Indianapolis IN 46204-3310

BORST, PHILIP WEST, academic administrator; b. Fullerton, Calif., Feb. 11, 1928; s. Richard Warner and Beatrice Ione (West) B.; m. Marguerite A. Bruns, Mar. 21, 1959; children—David, Kristin, Pamela. A.A., Fullerton Coll., 1947; B.A., Stanford U., 1949, M.A., 1950; postgrad., U. Calif., 1950-54; Ph.D. (Sch. fellow), Claremont Grad. Sch., 1968. Tchr. history Carlmont High Sch., Belmont, Calif., 1954-57; asst. prof. polit. sci. and history Fullerton Coll., 1957-60, asso. prof., 1960-62, prof., 1962-67, asst. to pres., 1967-70, asst. dean instrn., 1970-72, asso. dean instrn., 1972-73, v.p. instrn., 1973-77, pres., 1977-94; retired, 1994. Mem. Assn. Calif. Community Coll. Adminstrs., Phi Delta Kappa. Democrat.

BORST, WILLIAM ADAM, educator, radio personality, writer; b. Greenwich Village, N.Y., Sept. 6, 1943; s. Adam Stiehl and Helen (Moyse) B.; m. Judith Carol O'Rourke, Aug. 27, 1966; children: Mark, Michelle, Matthew. BS, Holy Cross Coll., 1965; MA, St. John's U., 1969; PhD, St. Louis U., 1972. Talk show host Sta. WGNU-RAdio, 1984-97; appeared on NBC Radio Today Show, 1974; social sci. instr. Maryville U., 1991-97, continuing edn. instr., 1994-95. Author: Still Last in the American League: The St. Louis Browns, 1993, The Best of Seasons: The 1944 St. Louis Cardinals & St. Louis Browns, 1995, (with others) The Ball Players, 1990, The Biographical Dictionary of American Sports, 1987-96, The Baseball Chronology, 1991, The North American Encyclopedia, 1996, Liberalism: Fatal Consequences, 1999; contbr. Dugout Mag., 1994. Bd. dirs. Birthright, 1991-97 (James Hartnett award 1997), Found. for Spl. Edn., 1990-97, Chalfonte-Hannon Hall Co., 1973-76, YMCA, Brentwood, Mo., 1981-84; treas. Archdiocesan Pro Life Exec. Com., 1992-94. Named Man of Yr. Vatterott Found., 1995; recipient Staunder Grad. Sch. Alumni merit award St. Louis U., 1995. Roman Catholic. Home: 57 Portland Dr Saint Louis MO 63131-3317

BORSTELMANN, STEPHEN MATTHEW, radiologist; b. N.Y.C., Nov. 27, 1967; s. Walter Dietrich B. and Elselore Gaensslaen. BA in Chemistry, Columbia U., 1989; MD, N.Y. Med. Coll., 1996. Intern dept. medicine N.Y. Med. Coll./Westchester County Med. Ctr., Valhalla, 1996-97; resident dept. radiology Jackson Meml. Hosp., Miami, 1997—; presenter in field. Recipient award Pharmacia & Upjohn Corp., 1996, cor et manus N.Y. Med. Coll., 1996. Mem. AMA, Alpha Omega Alpha. Republican. Methodist. Avocations: gourmet cooking, electronic music, whitewater rafting. Home: 20 Island Ave Apt 1015 Miami Beach FL 33139-1311 Office: Jackson Meml Hosp Dept Radiology 1611 NW 12th Ave Dept Miami FL 33136-1096

BORSTING, JACK RAYMOND, business administration educator; b. Portland, Oreg., Jan. 31, 1929; s. John S. and Ruth (Nelson) B.; m. Peggy Anne Nygard, Mar. 22, 1953; children: Lynn Carol, Eric Jeffrey. B.A., Oreg. State U., 1951; M.A., U. Oreg., 1952, Ph.D., 1959. Instr. math. Western Wash. Coll., 1953-54; teaching fellow U. Oreg., 1956-59; mem. faculty Naval Postgrad. Sch., 1959-80, prof. ops. research, chmn. dept., 1964-73, provost, acad. dean, 1974-80; asst. sec. def. (comptroller) Washington, 1980-83; dean Sch. Bus. U. Miami, Fla., 1983-88; Robert Dockson prof. and dean bus. adminstrn. U. So. Calif., Los Angeles, 1988-94; E. Morgan Stanley prof. bus. adminstrn. and exec. dir. Ctr. for Telecomms. Mgmt./U. So. Calif. Marshall Sch. Bus., Los Angeles, 1994—; vis. prof. U. Colo. summers 1967, 69, 71; vis. disting. prof. Oreg. State U., summer 1968; bd. dirs. Northrop Grumman Corp., TRO Learning, Whitman Edn. Group, Bristol Retail Solutions; bd. visitors Def. Sys. Mgmt. Coll., 1985-91, chmn., 1988-91; mem. adv. bd. Naval Postgrad. Sch., 1982-86; bd. overseers Ctr. Naval Analysis, 1984-94; trustee Aerospace Corp., 1986-92, Inst. Def. Analysis, 1990—. Contbr. to profl. jours. Trustee Orthop. Hosp. Found., L.A., 1992—, chmn., 1996—; trustee Rio Hondo Found. 1996—; gov. Town Hall of Calif., 1988-94. Recipient Disting. Pub. Service medal Dept. Def., 1980, 82. Fellow AAAS, Mil. Ops. Rsch. Soc. (bd. dirs. 1965-72, pres. 1970-71); mem. Inst. Mgmt. Sci., Am. Statis. Soc., Ops. Rsch. Soc. Am. (mem. coun. 1969-79, sec. 1972-74, pres. 1975-76, Kimball medal 1982), Internat. Fedn. Ops. Rsch. Socs. (treas. 1980-88), Calif. Club, 100 Club L.A., Sigma Xi, Pi Mu Epsilon, Beta Theta Pi. Episcopalian. Home: PO Box 209 Los Angeles CA 90053-0209 Office: Marshall Sch Bus DCC 217 USC Los Angeles CA 90089-0871 also: Inst Def Analysis 1801 N Beauregard St Alexandria VA 22311-1772*

BORST-MANNING, DIANE GAIL, management consultant; b. Rochester, N.Y., Nov. 5, 1937; d. Howard Louis and Emily Kathleen (Crew) Borst; m. Steven Manning, Sept. 11, 1979 (dec. May 1991); m. Norman Edward Berg, Apr. 4, 1992. BA cum laude, Wagner Coll., 1959; MBA, NYU, 1966. Planner NYU Med. Ctr., N.Y.C., 1962-76, assoc. dir. planning, 1976-78, dir. mgmt. svcs., 1978-80; dir. human resources Mt. Sinai Med. Ctr., N.Y.C., 1980-85, dir. planning, 1985-86; sr. v.p. The Manning Orgn., Inc., 1986—; pres. Diane Borst Manning Assocs., Inc., 1986—; instr. dept. health care mgmt. CUNY, 1982-92; adj. faculty Orange County C.C., 1986-88, Sarah Lawrence Coll., New Sch. Social Rsch., 1986—, St. Joseph's Coll., 1992—. Author: (cassette) Managers and Secretaries--How to Achieve Teamwork, 1980; editor: Managing Non-Profit Organizations, 1979. Chair grants Port Jervis Coun. for Arts; mem. Health Sys. Agy. Bd., N.Y.C., 1976-79; trustee Helene Fuld Sch. Nursing, N.Y.C., 1989—; mem. planning com. of bd. Mercy Cmty. Hosp., Port Jervis, N.Y.; mem. adv. bd. Inst. Bus. Industry and Govt. Orange County C.C. Fulbright fellow, 1959, Outstanding Fac. Mem., 1999. Mem. Am. Assn. Hosp. Planners, Assn. Am. Med. Colls. Group on Instrnl. Planning, Am. Compensation Assn., Bur. Nat. Affairs (pers. policy forum 1983-84), N.Y. State Health Planning Soc., N.Y. Pers. Mgmt. Assn. (bd. dirs. 1974-76), Greater N.Y. Hosp. Assn., City Club. Avocations: gardening, auto mechanics, carpentry, real estate. Office: 40 W 55th St Ste 9D New York NY 10019-5320

BORTEN, WILLIAM H., research company executive; b. N.Y.C., Mar. 1, 1935; s. David and Susan B.; m. Judith Sue Becker, Feb. 13, 1957; children: Jeffry, Daniel, Matthew. BBA, Adelphi U., Garden City, N.Y., 1957. Contr. Avien, Inc., Woodside, N.Y., 1959-63; asst. gen. mgr. Fairchild Industries, Germantown, Md., 1963-71; exec. v.p., treas. Atlantic Rsch. Corp., Alexandria, Va., 1971-80; pres. Atlantic Rsch. Corp., 1980-89, chief exec. officer, 1986-89, also dir.; sr. v.p. Sequa Corp., 1987-89; bd. dirs. TransCen Inc., Rockville, Md. Trustee Adelphi U., Garden City, N.Y., 1982-90, chmn. fin. com., 1989-90; founder Montgomery Village Day Care Ctr., Gaithersburg, Md., 1972; bd. dirs. Geo-Ctrs., Inc., Newton, Mass., 1990—. Mem. Anxiety Disorders Assn. Am. (bd. dirs. 1990-95).

BORTKO, DANIEL JOHN, photographer, educator; b. Kansas City, Kans., Dec. 6, 1948; s. Stanley John Bortko and Anna Angelina Bartkoski. BFA, Kansas City Art Inst., 1972; MA, So. Ill. U., 1975; postgrad., U. N.Mex., 1976-80. Mem. staff photo dept. Kansas City (Mo.) Art Inst., 1973-74; grad. asst. So. Ill. U., Carbondale, 1974-75; asst. dir. Quivira Gallery, Albuquerque, 1976-79; grad. rsch. asst. U. N.Mex., Albuquerque, 1977; photomicrographer Weldon Labs., Kansas City, Mo., 1983; photographer Neal Ray's, Liberty, Mo., 1985—; adj. prof. William Jewell Coll., Liberty, 1986—. Rschr. for book: Photography in New Mexico, 1979. Mem. citizen's acad. Liberty Police Dept., 1998. Mem. Greater St. Louis Archaeol. Soc. Democrat. Roman Catholic. Avocations: collecting historic photographs, surface archaeology. Home: 207 Glendale Apt 202 Liberty MO 64068 Office: Neal Ray's 9 E Kansas Ave Liberty MO 64068

BORTKO, EDWARD JOSEPH, retired city official; b. Kansas City, Kans., May 15, 1929; s. Peter and Josephine (Siwicki) B.; m. Delores Ann Yonevich, Nov. 26, 1955; children: John Alexander, Mary Josephine. BSBA with honors, Rockhurst Coll., 1960; MBA, U. Mo., 1965. Investigator Retail Credit Co., Kansas City, Mo., 1947-51; elec. clk. GM, Kansas City, Kans., 1951-53; sr. methods analyst William Bros. Pipeline Co., Kansas City, Mo., 1955-66; systems mgr. Black, Sivalls & Bryson, Inc., Kansas City, Mo., 1966-67; dir. systems devel. Yellow Freight System, Kansas City, Mo., 1967-70; systems mgr. Certainteed Products Corp., Kansas City, Kans., 1970-75; banking analyst Commerce Bancshares, Kansas City, Mo., 1975; ret. Bd. Pub. Utilities, Kansas City, Kans., 1975-92, $, 1992; instr. mgmt. subjects U. Kans. Ext., 1960-67, Am. Inst. Banking, 1960-67, Rckhurst Coll., 1960-67; mem. Data and Analysis Task Force Mid-Am. Regional Coun., Kansas City, Mo., 1980-81; mem. comm. subcom. S.W. Power Pool, Little Rock, 1988-93. Trustee Polish Am. Citizens Club, Kansas City, Kans., 1977-81, fin. sec., 1982-87, v.p., 1988-93; mem. adv. bd YMCA, 1991-94, co-chair Invest-In-Youth Campaign, 1991-93, 96; mem. allocations com. United Way, 1988-92; mem. Assn. Systems Mgmt., 1965-92. Recipient Internat. Merit award Assn. Systems Mgmt., 1976, Achievement award, 1982, Disting. Svc. award, 1988, Diamond Merit award, 1989. Mem. Am. Pub. Power Assn. (vice chmn. info. system sect. 1988-89, chmn. 1989-90), Am. Assn. Ret. Persons (tax aide coord. 1993-98, tax instr. 1994—, tax instr. coord. 1995-98, dist. coord. 1998-99), Rockhurst Coll. Alumni Assn. (dir. 1961), Johnson County C.C. Brown and Gold Club, Am. Legion, Optimists (gov. Kans. dist. 1988-89, exec. bd. 1987-91, Kans. rep. to internat. found. 1992-93, 97-99), Serra Club (trustee Kansas City, Kans. chpt. 1993-94, v.p. 1994-95), Pub. Utilities Ret. Club (bd. dirs., v.p. 1995-96, pres. 1996-97), Kans. Acad. Decathlon Assn. (trustee 1994—, sec. 1999—), Serra Internat. (membership com. 1998—). Democrat. Roman Catholic. Avocations: golf, swimming, dancing, travel. Home: 10101 W 89th Ter Shawnee Mission KS 66212-4669

BORTMAN, DAVID, lawyer; b. Detroit, Sept. 17, 1938; s. Erwin Arne and Miriam Elaine (Shapiro) B. BA, U. Mich., 1962, JD, 1965. Bar: Mich. 1965, Ill. 1971. Asst. prosecutor Wayne County, Detroit, 1965-71; staff atty. Fed. Defender, Chgo., 1971-73; trial atty. SEC, Chgo., 1974-77; sole practice Chgo., 1977-79; ptnr. Bortman, Meyer & Barasa, Chgo., 1980-90; pvt. practice L.A., 1990—; mem. Fed. Ct. Jury Instructions Con., Chgo., 1984-85, adv. bd. Air Force Office of Public Affairs. Chmn. telethon com. Muscular Dystrophy Assn., Chgo., 1984; pres. Met. Chgo. Air Force Comty. Coun., 1985-88; mem. World Affairs Coun. Mem. ABA, ATLA, Acad. of TV Arts and Scis., State Bar Calif., Los Angeles County Bar Assn. (mem. lawyer referral com.), Fed. Bar Assn. (bd. dirs. Chgo. chpt. 1985-90), Century City C. of C., Rotary, U. Mich. Club of L.A., U. Mich. Club of Chgo. (bd. govs. 1987-89), Union League of Chgo. (bd. dirs. 1986-89), Variety Club Children's Charities, Jonathan Club, Thalians Charity, Brentwood C. of C. (bd. dirs.). Jewish. Home: 11908 Dorothy St Apt 102 Los Angeles CA 90049-5330

BORTON, GEORGE ROBERT, retired airline captain; b. Wichita Falls, Tex., Mar. 22, 1922; s. George Neat and Travis Lee (Jones) B.; m. Anne Louise Bowling, Feb. 5, 1944 (dec.); children: Trudie T., Robert B., Bruce M. AA, Hardin Coll., Wichita Falls, 1940. Cert. airline transport pilot, FAA flight examiner. Flight sch. operator Vallejo (Calif.) Sky Harbor, 1947-48; capt. S.W. Airways, San Francisco, 1948-55; check capt. Pacific Airlines, San Francisco, 1955-68, Hughes Air West, San Francisco, 1968-71; capt. N.W. Airlines, Mpls., 1971-82, ret., 1982. Col. USAF, 1943-73, ret. Decorated Air medal. Mem. Airline Pilots Assn., Res. Officers Assn., Air Force Assn., Horseless Carriage Club, Model T of Am. Club (San Jose, Calif.). Republican. Home: 325 Denio Ave Gilroy CA 95020-9203

BORTON, JOHN CARTER, JR. (TERRY BORTON), theatrical producer; b. Washington, Aug. 25, 1938; s. John Carter and Mary (Newlin) B.; m. Deborah H. Borton, June 18, 1960; children: Lynn, Mark. BA, Amherst Coll., 1960; MA, U. Calif., Berkeley, 1962; EdD, Harvard U., 1970. Cert. gen. tchr., Calif. Asst. dir. vol. program Berkeley Unified Schs., 1962-63; tchr. English, co-chmn. dept. Richmond (Calif.) Union H.S., 1963-66; cons. Phila. Bd. Edn., 1966-67, acting dir. Office Affective Devel., 1970-71, dir. dual audio TV project, 1971-77; editorial dir. Xerox Edn. Publs., Middletown, Conn., 1977-80, editor in chief, 1980-86; v.p., editor in chief Field Publs. (formerly Xerox Edn. Publs.), Middletown, 1986-91, Weekly Reader Corp. (formerly Field Publs.), Middletown, 1991-92; prodr., lead performer Am. Magic Lantern Theater, 1992; lectr. U. Pa., Phila., 1971-76, Phila. Coll. Art, 1976-77; cons. various sch. systems, univ./colls., founds., profl. orgns., govt. agys., 1975-77. Author: Reach, Touch and Teach: Student Concerns and Process Education, 1970, Emotionales und Soziales Lernen in der Schule, 1976; also numerous articles in profl. jours., including Weekly Reader; performer 2 records and tchr.'s manuals introducing poetry to high sch. students; author 20 scripts for The Storyphone, 1976, 80 scripts for Dual Audio, Sta. WUHY-FM, 1972-73, 10 prodns. for Am. Magic Lantern Theater. Bd. dirs. Oddfellow's Theater, Conn. River Tourism Coun. Mem. League Hist. Am. Theaters, N.E. Performing Arts Assn., Magic Lantern Soc. Avocations: carpentry, sculpture, writing, gardening. E-mail: www.magiclanternshows.com. Office: Am Magic Lantern Theater PO Box 44 East Haddam CT 06423-0044

BORTS, GEORGE HERBERT, economist, educator; b. N.Y.C., Aug. 29, 1927; s. Elias Alexander and Etta (Silberg) B.; m. Muriel Levenson, Dec. 26, 1948; children: David, Richard, Robert. AB, Columbia U., 1947; AM, U. Chgo., 1949, PhD, 1953; AM (hon.), Brown U., 1957. Prof. econs. Brown U., Providence, 1960—. Mng. editor Am. Econ. Rev., Nashville, 1968-80, World Bus. Adv., Providence, 1990-91; co-author: Economic Growth in a Free Market, 1964. Mem. Am. Econ. Assn., Phi Beta Kappa. Home: 220 Slater Ave Providence RI 02906-3440 Office: Brown U 64 Waterman St Providence RI 02912-9029

BORUCHOWITZ, STEPHEN ALAN, health policy analyst; b. Plainfield, N.J., Sept. 24, 1952; s. Robert and Earla Louise (Sloat) B.; m. Linda Susan Grant, Sept. 16, 1989; 1 child, Grant Stephen. BA in Internat. Affairs, George Washington U., Washington, 1974; MA in Sci., Tech. and Pub. Policy, George Washington U., 1981. Food prog. specialist U.S. Food & Nutrition Svc., Washington, 1978-81; internat. affairs specialist Office Internat. Cooperation & Devel., Washington, 1981-87; legis. analyst Wash. State Senate, Olympia, 1986-89; project dir. Wash. 2000 Project, Olympia, 1989-92; sr. health policy analyst Wash. Dept. Health, Olympia, 1992—; mem. Pew Commn. task force on regulation of health professions, 1994-95. Editor newsletter: Project Update, 1990-92. Study team mem. Gov.'s Efficiency Commn., 1990-91; com. mem. Coun. of State Govts. Strategic Planning Subcom., Lexington, Ky., 1990-92; chmn. Montclair Divsn. IV Neighborhood Assn., 1989-92, Shadywood Homeowner's Assn., 1992-94; bd. dirs. Classical Music Supporters, Seattle, 1987-89. Recipient Superior Performance award, U.S. Dept. Agr., 1986. Mem. World Future Soc., Internat. Health Futures Network, Internat. Soc. of Tech. Assessment in Health Care, Health Svcs. Rsch. Assn. Avocations: writing, travel, cooking, classical music. Office: Wash Dept Health PO Box 47851 Olympia WA 98504-7851

BORUM, BRADFORD R., policy analyst; b. Macon, Ga., Apr. 17, 1968; s. Richard E. Borum and Laverne S. Dooley. AB in Polit. Sci., U. Ga., 1990; MPA, Kennesaw State U., 1998. Loan adjuster C&S Nat. Bank, Macon, 1990-91; dispute analyst Equifax, Inc., Atlanta, 1991-95; dispute resolution specialist Ford Motor Co., Atlanta, 1995-98; dep. fin. mgr. Michael Coles for U.S. Senate, Atlanta, 1998; analyst Senate Rsch. Office Ga. State Senate, Atlanta, 1999—. Avocation: martial arts.

BORUM, OLIN HENRY, realtor, former government official; b. Spencer, N.C., Nov. 3, 1917; s. Oscar Henry and Marjorie Mae (Leigh) B.; m. Beatrice Star Comulada, Nov. 14, 1944; children: Pamela Leigh, Robin Olin, Denis Richard. BS, U. N.C., 1938, MA, 1947, PhD, 1949; postgrad., U. Md., 1940-41. Rsch. chemist E.I. duPont de Nemours & Co., Phila. Lab., 1949-50; interim rsch. asst. prof. Cancer Rsch. Lab., U. Fla., 1950; instr., asst. prof. chemistry U.S. Mil. Acad., 1952-55; rsch. adminstr. U.S. Army Chem. Corps R&D Command, Washington, 1956-60; rsch. adminstr. U.S. Army Material Command, Washington, 1964-76; realtor assoc. Unique Properties, Alexandria, Va., 1974-79; realtor, assoc. broker The J. Edwards Co., Inc., Alexandria, 1979-82; prin. broker Olin H. Borum Realty, 1982—; tchr. chemistry U. Va., Arlington, Va., 1966-68; tchg. fellow U. Md., 1940-41; grad. asst., tchg. fellow U. N.C., 1946-49. Adult scouter Nat. Capital Area council Boy Scouts Am., 1964-75, unit commr., 1968-75; sec. Mt. Vernon (Va.) Civic Assn., 1965-66; mem. Com. of 33 (nat. adv. group Nat. Sojourners, Inc.), 1962-71, chmn., 1969-71. Nat. trustee Nat. Sojourners, Inc., 1971-73. 2d lt. to maj. AUS, 1941-46; as maj. USAF, 1951-56, lt. col., 1960-64. Recipient cert. of Achievement Dept. Army, 1971. Fellow Am. Inst. Chemists; mem. Am. Chem. Soc., Masons, K.T. Shriners, Phi Beta Kappa, Sigma Xi. Presbyn. Contbr. articles to profl. jours. Home: 9002 Volunteer Dr Alexandria VA 22309-2921 Office: 6641 Backlick Rd Springfield VA 22150-2710

BORUM, RODNEY LEE, financial business executive; b. High Point, N.C., Sept. 30, 1929; s. Carl Macy and Etta (Sullivan) B.; m. Helen Marie Rigby, June 27, 1953; children: Richard Harlan, Sarah Elizabeth. Student, U. N.C., 1947-49; BS, U.S. Naval Acad., 1953. Design-devel. engr. GE, Syracuse, N.Y., 1956-58; design-devel. engr. GE, Cape Kennedy, Fla., 1956-58, missile test condr., 1958-60, mgr. ground equipment engr., 1960-61, mgr. ea. test range engring., 1961-65; adminstr. Bus. and Def. Svcs. Adminstrn.-Dept. Commerce, 1966-69; pres. Printing Industries Am., Arlington, Va., 1969-85, staff cons., 1985-86, mem. exec. com., 1969-85, dir.; pres. W.H. Rigby Cons., 1985-86; exec. v.p. Amasek Inc., Cocoa, Fla., 1986-87; assoc. Fin. Svcs. Orgn., Cocoa, Fla., 1987—; sec. Graphic Arts Show Corp.; dir. Inter-Comprint Ltd., Strangers Cay, Ltd.; mem. governing bd. Comprints Internat.; Rep. candidate 11th dist. U.S. congress, Fla., 1988-90; ops. mgr. COVIX Corp.; mgmt. cons. 1990—; exec. v.p. Pearl of Va., Inc. Mem. exec. coun. Cub Scouts Am., 1965; bd. dirs., v.p. Brevard County (Fla.) United Fund, 1964-65; bd. dirs. Brevard Beaches Concert Assn., 1965; mem. edn. coun. bd. dirs. Graphic Arts Tech. Found., Pitts., 1970-86; trustee, founder Graphic Arts Edn. and Rsch. Trust Fund, Arlington, Va., 1978-85; candidate for U.S. Ho. of Reps. from 11th dist. Fla., 1988. 1st lt. USAF, 1953-56. Named Boss of Yr., C. of C., 1965; recipient Bausch and Lomb Sci. award, 1947, Am. Legion award, 1952. Mem. U.S. Naval Inst., U.S. Naval Acad. Alumni Assn., Graphic Arts Coun. N.Am. (bd. dirs. 1977—), Phi Eta Sigma. Methodist.

BORUM, WILLIAM DONALD, engineer; b. St. Louis, Dec. 26, 1932; s. William Doris and Lura Mae (Jackson) B.; m. Mary Margaret Bullard, Nov. 29, 1952; children: Mary Bradley, Patricia Elaine, Kimberly Anne. BA in Bus. Adminstrn., U. Nebr., 1967; MS in Indsl. Mgmt., U.S. Army Command/Gen. Staff, Coll., Ft. Leavenworth, Kans., 1968; MS, NATO Def. Coll., Rome, 1975; MA in Internat. Rels., U. So. Calif., 1971; diploma, NATO Def. Coll., Rome, 1976. Commd. 2d lt. U.S. Army, 1954, advanced through grades to col., 1974; advisor to Imperial Iranian Army Chief of Engrs. Teheran, Iran, 1962-65; staff officer, Joint Chief of Staff Pentagon, Washington, 1965-66; ops. officer, 25th infantry divsn. Vietnam, 1966-67; with Office Chief of Engrs., Washington, 1967-68; asst. to Chief of Gen. Staff for operational requirements British Ministry of Def., White Hall, London, 1968-71; commdg. officer 36th combat engr. bn. Vietnam, 1971-72; Dept. of Army Staff and Inst. of Land Combat Pentagon, 1972-75; v.p. ICF Kaiser Internat., Oakland, 1984-98. Sustaining mem. Rep. Nat. Com., Washington, 1982-94. Decorated Bronze Star with oak leaf cluster, Purple Heart, Legion of Merit with oak leaf cluster, Air medal (4 awards), Dept. of Def. Superior Svc. medal, Meritorious Svc. medal with oak leaf cluster, Life Saving medal, Cross of Gallantry with gold palm, British Army Parachutist, Vietnam Campaign award (7 awards). Mem. NSPE, World Trade Club of San Francisco, Sovereign Mil. Order Temple Jerusalem (grand cross). Episcopalian. Home: 631 Keswick Ct Granite Bay CA 95746-7156

BORUSZAK, JAMES MARTIN, insurance company executive; b. Chgo., Dec. 9, 1930; s. Burton V. Boruszak and Priscilla H. (Zohn) Leshin; m. Joan D. Kohlenbrener, June 14, 1953; children: Allan N., Bruce L., Beth V. BS, U. Ill., 1953, PhD (hon.), 1994. CLU, 1962. Asst. mgr. Met. Life Ins. Co., Chgo., 1957-60, Acacia Life Ins. Co., Chgo., 1960-62; assoc. gen. agt. Pacific Mut. Life Ins., Chgo., 1962-70; pvt. practice Northfield, Ill., 1970-89; pres. BLU Benefits Group, 1989-94, chmn. of bd., 1994-98; retired, 1998. Lt. USAF, 1954-56. Mem. CLU (bd. dirs. 1967-69). Home: 88181 Overseas Hwy Apt C32 Islamorada FL 33036-3063

BORUT, DONALD J., professional society administrator; b. N.Y.C., July 12, 1941; s. Abraham and Helen (Silenski) B.; m. Carol A. Kirtley, July 12, 1965; children: Adam, Ezra. BA, Oberlin Coll., 1963; MPA, U. Mich., 1965. Adminstrv. asst. City of Ann Arbor, Mich., 1964-66; asst. to city adminstr. City of Ann Arbor, 1966-69, asst. city adminstr., 1969-71; instr. U. Mich., Ann Arbor, 1968-71; assoc. dir. Internat. City Mgmt. Assn., Washington, 1971-84, dep. exec. dir., 1984-90; exec. dir. Nat. League Cities, Washington, 1990—; dir. Program on Cmty. Problem Solving, Washington, 1987-92, Acad. for State and Local Govt., Washington, 1990—; bd. dirs. Pub. Tech., Inc., Washington, chair, 1991-93, 1997—; editl. adv. panel The Am. News Svc., 1995—; exec. com. nat. pub. svc. awards Nat. Acad. Pub. Adminstrn., 1995—; mem. pub. adv. group to D.C. Fin. Responsibility and Mgmt. Assistance Authority, 1996—; mem. directorate Am. Planning Assn. growing Smart Program, 1994—; mem. nat. adv. coun. on state and local budgeting Govt. Fin. Officers Assn., 1996—; mem. Task Force on D.C. Governance, 1996-97. Contbr. articles on local govt. mgmt. to profl. jours. Bd. dirs. Levine Sch. Music, Washington, 1985—, pres., 1989-91; bd. dirs. Downtown Bus. Improvement Dist. Corp., 1997—. Mem. Internat. City Mgmt. Assn., Nat. Acad. Pub. Adminstrn., Am. Soc. Pub. Adminstrn., Am. Soc. Assn. Execs., Nat. Press Club, City Club of Washington. Office: Nat League of Cities 1301 Pennsylvania Ave NW Washington DC 20004-1701

BORUT, JOSEPHINE, insurance executive; b. Bridgeport, Conn., Aug. 3, 1942; d. Frank and Catherine (Russo) Occhipinti; m. Arthur Lee Borut, Nov. 22, 1963; 1 child, Adam Seth. BS in Art, Hofstra U., 1964, MA in Humanities, 1971; cert. in mgmt., Adelphi U., 1984. Cert. art tchr., N.Y.; cert. mtgs. profl. Art tchr. Cen. Islip (N.Y.) Elem., 1964-65; coord. art dept. Mineola (N.Y.) Jr. High, 1965-70; art tchr., coord. Brandeis Sch., Lawrence, N.Y., 1979-81; mgr. community rels. Empire Blue Cross/Blue Shield, N.Y.C., 1984-85, mgr. conf. planning, 1985—; freelance artist, East Meadow, 1978-79; lectr. meeting planning. Contbr. articles to profl. jours. Recipient hon. mention L.I. Art Tchrs. Assn. Art Show,1966, 3d pl. art show Hofstra U., 1966, 2d pl. East Meadow Pub. Libr. Juried Art Show, 1979; Inst. II scholar, 1991, Profl. Edn. Conf. scholar, 1990, 97. Mem. NAFE, NOW, Am. Soc. Assn. Execs., Meeting Planners Internat. Greater N.Y. (bd. dirs., com. chmn., pres. 1992-93, Meeting Planner of Yr. 1991), Am. Soc. Profl. and Exec. Women, Ins. Conf. Planners. Home: 1823 Kent St Westbury NY 11590-5305 Office: Empire Blue Cross/Blue Shield 622 3rd Ave Fl 9 New York NY 10017-6707

BORWEIN, DAVID, mathematics educator; b. Kaunas, Lithuania, Mar. 24, 1924; s. Joseph Jacob and Rachel (Landau) B.; m. Bessie Flax, June 30, 1946; children—Jonathan, Peter, Sarah. B.Sc. in Engring, Witwatersrand (South Africa) U., 1945, B.Sc. Hons., 1948; Ph.D., University Coll. London, 1950, D.Sc., 1960. Lectr. St. Andrews U., Scotland, 1950-63; vis. prof. U. Western Ont., London, Can., 1963-64; prof. U. Western Ont., 1964-89, head math. dept., 1967-89, prof. emeritus, 1989—. Contbr. articles to profl. jours. Served with South African Forces, 1945. NSERC grantee, 1966—. Fellow Royal Soc. Edinburgh; mem. London Math. Soc., Am. Math. Soc., Math. Assn. Am., Canadian Math. Soc. (chmn. research com. 1970-73, v.p. 1973-75, pres. 1985-87). Home: 1032 Brough St, London, ON Canada N6A 3N4 Office: Dept Math, U Western Ont, London, ON Canada N6A 5B7

BORWEIN, JONATHAN MICHAEL, mathematics educator; b. St. Andrews, Scotland, May 20, 1951; arrived in Can., 1963; s. David and Bessie (Flax) B.; m. Judith Diedre Scott Roots, Sept. 17, 1973; children: Rachel, Naomi, Tova. BA in Math. with honors, U. Western Ont., 1971; MSc, Jesus Coll. Oxford, 1972, DPhil, 1974. dir. Ctr. for Exptl. and Constructive Math., Burnaby, B.C., Can., 1993-98. Postdoctoral fellow Dalhousie U., 1974-75, from asst. prof. to assoc. prof., 1976-82, lectr., rsch. assoc., 1975-76; from asst. prof. to assoc. prof. Carnegie-Mellon U., 1980-82; assoc. prof. Dalhousie U., 1982-84, prof., 1984; prof. math. Simon Fraser U., Burnaby, B.C., 1984—; French Nat. fellow Limoges, Prof. Invité, 1985; disting. vis. prof. Ctr. Math. Rsch., U. Montreal, 1986; Sr. Killam fellow Dalhousie U., 1987-88; visitor Technion, 1990; adj. prof. dept. math., stats. and computing sci. Dalhousie U., 1993-96; mem. math. grant selection com. Natural Scis. and Engring. Rsch. Coun., 1988-91, chmn., 1989-91, com. collaborative rsch. initiatives, 1992-95; mem. Simon Fraser Ctr. for Sys. Sci., 1992—, Simon Fraser U. Rsch. Coun., 1993; dir. Simon Fraser Ctr. Exptl. & Constructive Math., 1993—. Assoc. editor: Set-Valued Analysis, 1992, ZOR: Mathematical Methods of Operations Research, 1994—, Ramanujan Jour., 1996—, Experimental Mathematics, 1996—; mem. editl. bd. Jour. Convex Analysis, 1993—, Proc. Am. Math. Soc., 1999—; mem. editl. bd., hon. editor: Communications in Applied Nonlinear Analysis, 1993—; area editor: Dictionary of Theories, 1992—; editor: (with P. Borwein) CMS Series of Graduate Texts in Mathematics, 1990—; cons. editor for math. The Guinness Encyclopedia, 1989—. Mem. collaborative rsch. grants com. NATO, 1997-1999, chair, 1998, phys. engring. sci. tech. panel, 1999—; mem. Can. Inst. for Sci. and Tech. Info. Bd., 1998—; active New Dem. Party, 1967—. Recipient Atlantic Provinces Coun. on the Scis., Fraser medal for rsch. excellence, 1988, Merten Hasse prize Mathematical Assn. of Am., 1993; Ont. Rhodes scholar Jesus Coll., 1971-74, U.W.O. Faculty Assn. scholar, 1971, Albert O. Jeffrey scholar, 1969, Timkins Internat. Fund scholar, 1968; Australian Rsch. Grant Coun. fellow Australian Nat. U., Newcastle, 1988. Fellow Royal Soc. Can.; mem. AAAS (Coxeter-James lectr. 1987, bd. dirs., rsch. com. 1985-88, chmn. constn. revision com. 1987-88), Can. Math. Soc., Am. Math. Soc. (editl. bd. procs. 1999—), Math. Assn. Am. (Chauvenet prize 1993, Merten M. Hasse prize 1993), B.C. Confedn. Faculty Assn. (Faculty Mem. of Yr. 1996), Soc. Indsl. and Applied Math. Avocations: swimming, theater, politics.

BORWEIN, PETER BENJAMIN, mathematician; b. St. Andrews, Scotland, May 10, 1953; s. David and Bessie (Flax) B.; m. Jennifer Elaine Moore, Nov. 29, 1980; children: Alexandra, Sophie, Theresa. BSc, U. Western Ont., London, 1974; MA, U. B.C., Vancouver, 1976, PhD, 1979. Postdoctoral fellow Oxford (Eng.) U., 1979-80; asst. prof. Dalhousie U., Halifax, N.S., Can., 1980-85, assoc. prof., 1985-90, prof., 1990-93; prof. Simon Fraser U., Burnaby, B.C., Can., 1993—. Co-author: Pi and the AGM, 1987, A Dictionary of Real Numbers, 1990, Polynomials and Plynomical Inequalities, 1995, Pi: A Source Book, 1997; contbr. more than 100 articles to profl. jours. Recipient Merten Hasse prize Mathematical Assn. of Am., 1993, Faculty of Yr. BC/SCUFA, 1996. Mem. Am. Math. Soc., Can. Math. Soc., Math. Assn. Am. (Hasse prize 1993), Ctr. for Constructive and Exptl. Math. (assoc. dir. 1993). Office: Simon Fraser U, Dept Math and Statistics, Burnaby, BC Canada V5A 1S6

BORWICK, RICHARD, management consultant; b. Elmira, N.Y., Aug. 15, 1908; s. Abram and Phyllis (Gould) B.; m. Lillian Fine, June 22, 1938; 1 child: Anthony Stephen. AB in Classics and Philosophy with honors, Harvard U., 1929. Reporter Brockton Mass. Enterprise, 1928-30; researcher current history N.Y. Times, N.Y.C., 1932; analyst Fairchild Publs., N.Y.C., 1933; sales promotion Quality Group Mags., N.Y.C., 1933; fin. reporter Washington (D.C.) Herald, Washington Times Herald, 1934-42; pub. exec. Phila. Record, 1943; co-founder Newmyer Assocs. Inc., Washington, 1944—, v.p., 1959-83; cons. in oil industry, ins., electric mfg., telephone communications, industries., 1983—. Speech writer, policy adviser Presdl. Candidates Sen. Estes Kefauver, Washington, 1952, Sen. Henry Jackson, Washington, 1960-82. Mem. Nat. Press Club, Harvard Grad. Soc. (chmn. 1983-85). Clubs: International (Washington); Harvard (N.Y.C.). Home: 3301 O St NW Washington DC 20007-2814

BORYS, THEODOR JAMES, state agency data center administrator; b. Buffalo, N.Y., June 17, 1954; s. Svyatoslav and Lorenza Natalie (Bertolino) B.; m. Melissa Joy Ares, June 12, 1976; children: Tasha Rose, Leda Marie. BA in Math., SUNY, Albany, 1976, MS in Computer Sci., 1977. Computer programmer N.Y. State Dept. of Tax & Fin., Albany, 1976; programmer/analyst SUNY, Albany, 1976-78; data base adminstr. N.Y. State Dept. Mental Hygiene, Albany, 1978-81; software engr. Gen. Elec., Schenectady, N.Y., 1981; dir. tech. svcs. N.Y. State Office Mental Health, Albany, 1981-82, dir. systems devel., 1982-84, data adminstr., 1984-96, dir. tech. svcs. and ops., 1996—; lectr. SUNY, Albany, 1978—. Mem. Assn for Computing Machinery, IDMS User Assn. (guest speaker 1989 annual conf., N.Y.C., Seattle, 1990). Republican. Home: 125 E Poplar Dr Delmar NY 12054-2224 Office: State Office Mental Health 44 Holland Ave Albany NY 12208-3411

BORYSENKO, JOAN, psychologist, biologist; b. Boston, Oct. 25, 1945; d. Edward and Lillian Zakon; m. Miroslav Borysenko; children: Natalia, Justin, Andrei. BA in Biology, Bryn Mawr Coll., 1967; PhD, Harvard Med. Sch., 1972. Lic. psychologist. Asst. prof. anatomy and cellular biology Tufts U., 1973-78; former tchr. biol. scis. Harvard Med. Sch., Boston, 1981-88; pres., founder Mind/Body Health Scis., Boulder, Colo., 1988—; instr. yoga and meditation. Author: Minding the Body, Mending the Mind, 1987, Guilt is the Teacher, Love is the Lesson, 1990, Fire in the Soul, 1993, Mind/Body Health Sciences, 1998; others; mem. adv. bd. several jours. in field, including Yoga Jour., New Age Jour., others; pub. Circle of Healing newsletter. Achievements include pioneering work in the study of psychoneuroimmunology. Office: Mind/Body Health Scis 393 Dixon Rd Boulder CO 80302-9769*

BORYSEWICZ, MARY LOUISE, editor; b. Chgo.; d. Thomas J. and Mabel E. (Zeien) O'Farrell m. Daniel S. Borysewicz, June 11, 1955; children: Mary Adele, Stephen Francis (dec. 1997), Paul Barnabas. BA, Mundelein Coll., 1970; postgrad. in English lit., U. Ill, 1970-71; grad. exec. program, U. Chgo., 1981-82. Editor sci. publs. AMA, Chgo., 1971-73; exec. mng. editor Am. Jour. Ophthalmology, Chgo., 1973-95; asst. sec., treas Ophthalmic Pub. Co., 1985-95; guest lectr. U. Chgo. Med. Sch., 1979, Harvard U. Med. Sch., 1978, Northwestern U. Med. Sch., 1979, Am. Acad. Ophthalmology, 1976, 81. Editor: Opthalmology Principles and Concepts, 7th edit., 1992, 8th edit., 1996, Documenta Ophthalmologica History Issue, 1997, 98; contbr. articles to sci. publs. Active vol. svcs. Art Inst. Chgo. Mem. Coun. Biol. Editors (bd. dirs. 1988-91, mem. fin. com. 1985-88, mem. teller com. 1992-95), Internat. Fedn. Sci. Editors.

BOS, JOHN ARTHUR, retired aircraft manufacturing executive; b. Holland, Mich., Nov. 6, 1933; s. John Arthur and Annabelle (Castelli) B.; m. Eileen Tempest, Feb. 15, 1974; children: John, James, William, Tiffany. BS in Acctg., Calif. State Coll., Long Beach, 1971. Officer 1st Nat. Bank, Holland, Mich., 1954-61; dir. bus. mgmt. Boeing Airlift and Tanker Programs, Long Beach, 1962-99. Mem. Inst. Mgmt. Accts. (cert. mgmt. acct. 1979), Nat. Assn. Accts. Avocations: automobile marketing, golf, consulting. Office: Boeing Airlift and Tanker Programs 2401 E Wardlow Rd Long Beach CA 90807-5309

BOSCH, DONNA, home health nurse administrator; b. Emmons County, N.D., Sept. 26, 1945; d. Peter and Rose (Ternes) Silbernagel; m. Frank Bosch, June 5, 1965; children: Lynette, Darrin, Wade. BSN, Mary Coll., 1967; MSN, U. Mary, Bismarck, N.D., 1988. RN, N.D.; cert. in community health, 1986, 91. Instr. Mary Coll., Bismarck; EPS coord. Bismarck Burleigh Nursing Svc., home health nurse; home care coord., exec. dir. Home Med. Resources, Bismarck; task force Medicare. N.D. Nurses Assn. grantee. Mem. ANA, N.D. Pub. Health Assn., N.D. Home Health Assn. (pres.), Cath. Daus. Am., Sigma Theta Tau. Home: 4885 Wildrose Cres Bismarck ND 58501-8975

BOSCH, SAMUEL HENRY, electronics company executive; b. Waupun, Wis., Dec. 24, 1934; s. Henry Samuel and Emma (Elgersma) B.; m. Corinne Marilyn Aardema, June 21, 1958; children—Michelle, Jonathan, David, Sara. B.S. in Physics, San Diego State U., 1961; M.S. in Physics, UCLA, 1962. Sr. rsch. engr. Gen. Dynamics, San Diego, 1962-69; mgr. mktg. Digital Equipment Corp., Maynard, Mass., 1969-77; dir. mktg. System Engring. Lab., Ft. Lauderdale, Fla., 1977-79; mgr. mktg. Intel, Hillsboro, Oreg., 1979-81; dir. mktg. Metheus, Hillsboro, 1981-82; pres. ATM Techs., Beaverton, Oreg., 1982-86; pres., owner Peregrin Techs., Inc., Beaverton, 1986—, Peregrin Med. Rev. Inc., Beaverton, 1987—. Contbr. articles to profl. jours., invited speaker at bus. confs. Served with U.S. Army, 1955-57. Mem. Concord Coalition, NW Regional China Coun. Republican. Mem. Christian Ref. Ch. Home: 20055 NW Nestucca Dr Portland OR 97229-2821 Office: Peregrin Techs Inc 14179 NW Science Park Portland OR 97229

BOSCO, ANTHONY GERARD, bishop; b. New Castle, Pa., Aug. 1, 1927; s. Joseph M. and Theresa (Pezone) B. BA, St. Vincent Sem., Latrobe, Pa.; juris canonici licentiatus, Lateran U., Rome; LLD (hon.), Duquesne U., 1971; LHD (hon.), St.Vincent Coll., 1988. Ordained priest Roman Cath. Ch., 1952. Asst. chancellor Diocese of Pitts., 1955-65, vice chancellor, 1965-67, chancellor, 1967-85, aux. bishop, 1970-87; bishop Diocese of Greensburg, Pa., 1987—; chmn. Cath. Comms. Found., 1984—; hon. chmn., trustee Seton Hill Coll., Greensburg, 1987—; ex officio mem., chmn. bd. regents St. Vincent Sem., Latrobe, Pa., 1987—. Recipient Leonardo Da Vinci award for Religion Order of Italian Sons and Daughter, 1970; named Pitts.'s Man of Yr. in Religion Pitts. Jaycees, 1975. Mem. Nat. Conf. Cath. Bishops, Christian Assocs. S.W. Pa.

BOSCO, JAY WILLIAM, optometrist; b. Bay City, Mich., May 6, 1951; s. Frank Carl and Jeanette (Frontiera) B.; m. Mary Lou Roth, Jan. 22, 1972; children: Angela, Jason, Andrea. BS, Saginaw Valley State Coll., 1977; OD, Ill. Coll. Optometry, 1982. Pvt. practice optometry Bay City, Mich., 1982-83; dir. vision care services Blue Care Network of East Mich., Saginaw, 1983—. Served with USAF, 1969-73. Mem. Am. Optometric Assn., Mich. Optometric Assn., Beta Sigma Kappa. Roman Catholic. Lodge: Lions (chmn. Site-Mobile, Bay City, 1984—). Home: 1382 N Wagner Rd Essexville MI 48732-9532 Office: Blue Care Network East Mich 4200 Fashion Square Blvd Saginaw MI 48603-1291

BOSCO, PHILIP MICHAEL, actor; b. Jersey City, Sept. 26, 1930; s. Philip Lupo and Margaret Raymond (Thek) B.; m. Nancy Ann Dunkle, Jan. 2, 1957; children: Diane, Philip, Christopher, Jennifer, Lisa, Celia, John. B.A. in drama, Catholic U. Am., 1957. Roles include Brian O'Bannion in Auntie Mame, City Ctr., N.Y.C., 1958; Angelo in Measure for Measure, Belvedere Lake Amphitheatre, N.Y.C., 1960; Heracles in The Rape of the Belt, 1960; Will Danaher in Donnybrook, 1961; Hawkshaw in The Ticket-of-Leave Man, 1961; King Henry in Henry IV Part 1, Shakespeare Festival, Stratford, Conn., 1962; Kent in King Lear; Rufio in Antony and Cleopatra: Pistol in Henry V; Aegeon in Comedy of Errors, 1963; Benedick in Much Ado About Nothing: Claudius in Hamlet, 1964; title role in Coriolanus, 1965; Lovewit in Wind, 1967; appeared in Galileo, 1967, Saint Joan, 1968, Amphitryon in 3 Zones, Tiger at the Gates, 1968, Cyrano de Bergerac, 1968, Camino Real, 1970, Operation Sidewinder, 1970, The Playboy of the Western World, 1971, An Enemy of the People, 1971, Antigone, 1971, Mary Stuart, 1971, Narrow Road Into the Deep North, 1972, Twelfth Night, 1972, The Crucible, 1972, Enemies, 1972, The Plough and the Stars, 1973, The Merchant of Venice, 1973, A Streetcar Named Desire, 1973, Mrs. Warren's Profession, 1976, Man and Superman, 1978, Whose Life Is It Anyway?, 1979, A Month In The Country, 1979, Major Barbara, 1980, Inadmissable Evidence, 1981, Hedda Gabler, 1982, Ah! Wilderness, 1983, Misalliance, 1983, Come Back, Little Sheba, 1984, Eminent Domain, 1984, Caine Mutiny, 1984, Be Happy For Me, Masterclass, 1986, You Never Can Tell, 1986, A Man For All Seasons, 1986,The Devil's Disciple, 1988, (Broadway) Lend Me A Tenor, 1989, (Antoinette Perry award 1989), The Miser, 1990, Breaking Legs, 1991, (Broadway) An Inspector Calls, 1994, The Heiress, 1995, Moon Over Buffalo, 1995-96, Twelfth Night, 1998; films include: Requiem For a Heavyweight, A Lovely Way To Die, The Pope of Greenwich Village, Walls of Glass, Heaven Help Us, The Money Pit, Trading Places, 1983, Children of a Lesser God, 1986, Suspect, 1987, Three Men and a Baby, 1987, The Luckiest Man in the World, 1988, Working Girl, 1988, Dream Team, 1988, Another Woman, 1988, Blue Steel, Quick Change, FX-2, 1990, True Colors, 1990, Straight Talk, 1991, The Return of Eliot Ness, 1991, Shawdows and Fog, 1992, Attica: Line of Fire, 1993, Angie, 1993, Safe Passage, 1993, Milk Money, 1994, Nobody's Fool, 1994, It Takes Two, 1995, The First Wives Club, 1995, My Best Friend's Wedding, 1997, Critical Care, 1997, Deconstructing Harry, 1997; TV shows include: The Prisoner of Zenda, The Nurses, O'Brien, Hawk, The NET Play of the Month, Tribeca, Grandpa and the Globetrotters, 1987, Echoes in the Darkness, Internal Affairs, 1988, Murder in Black and White, 1989, Return of Eliot Ness, 1991, Law and Order, 1993, 96, 97, 98, Cosby, 1998, (TV movie) Carriers, 1997. Served with U.S. Army, 1951-54. Recipient Critic's Circle award N.Y. Drama Critics, 1960-61; recipient Clarence Derwent award, 1966-67, Tony award nominations, 1961, 84, 87, 96, OBIE award, 1987, Emmy award, 1988, Tony award, Drama Desk award, Outer Critic's Circle award all for best leading actor, 1988-89; inductee Theater Hall of Fame, 1998. Mem. Actor's Equity Assn., Screen Actor's Guild, AFTRA. Roman Catholic. Office: HWA/Harter Woo Assocs New York NY 10000

BOSCOV, ALBERT, retail executive. CEO, chmn. Boscov's Dept. Stores, Reading, Pa. Office: Boscov's Dept Stores 4500 Perkiomen Ave Reading PA 19606-3946*

BOSE, AMAR GOPAL, electrical engineering educator; b. Phila., Nov. 2, 1929; s. Noni Gopal and Charlotte (Mechlin) B.; children: Vanu Gopal, Maya. SB, SM, MIT, 1952, ScD, 1956. Mem. faculty MIT, Cambridge, 1956—, prof. elec. engring., 1966—; chmn., chief exec. officer Bose Corp., Framingham, Mass. Author: (with Kenneth N. Stevens) Introductory Network Theory, 1965; patentee in acoustics, nonlinear systems and communications. Fulbright fellow India, 1956-57; recipient Baker Teaching award MIT, 1964, Teaching award Am. Soc. Engring. Edn., 1965; named Inventor of Yr., Intellectual Property Owners, 1987. Fellow IEEE; mem. AAAS, Nat. Acad. Engring., Sigma Xi, Tau Beta Pi, Eta Kappa Nu. Office: Bose Corp The Mountain Framingham MA 01701-9168 also: Mass Inst Tech Dept Electrical Engring 77 Massachusetts Ave Cambridge MA 02139-4301

BOSE, ANJAN, electrical engineering educator, academic administrator; b. Calcutta, India, June 2, 1946; s. Amal Nath and Anima (Guha) B.; m. Frances Magdelen Pavlas, Oct. 30, 1976; children: Rajesh Paul, Shonali Marie, Jahar Robert. B Tech with honors, Indian Inst. Tech., Kharagpur, 1967; MS, U. Calif., Berkeley, 1968; PhD, Iowa State U., 1974. Systems planning engr. Con Edison Co., N.Y.C., 1968-70; instr., research assoc. Iowa State U., Ames, 1970-74; postdoctoral fellow IBM Sci. Ctr., Palo Alto, Calif., 1974-75; asst. prof. elec. engring. Clarkson U., Potsdam, N.Y., 1975-76; mgr. EMSD, Control Data Corp., Mpls., 1976-81; prof. elec. engring. Ariz. State U., Tempe, 1981-93; disting. prof. Wash. State U., Pullman, 1993—, dir. Sch. Elec. Engring. and Computer Sci., 1993-98, dean Coll. Engring. and Architecture, 1998—; v.p. Power Math Assocs., Tempe, 1981-84; program dir. power sys. NSF, Washington, 1988-89. Contbr. over 50 articles to engring. jours. Fellow IEEE.

BOSE, BIMAL KUMAR, electrical engineering educator; b. Calcutta, India, Sept. 1, 1932; came to U.S., 1971; s. Rajendra and Nirmala (Ghosh) B.; m. Arati Ghosh, June 26, 1961; children: Papia, Amit. BE, Calcutta U., 1956, PhD, 1966; MS, U. Wis., 1960. Asst. engr. Tata Hydro Power Co., Bombay, 1956-59; asst. prof. Bengal Engring. Coll., Calcutta, 1960-71; assoc. prof. Rensselaer Poly. Inst., Troy, N.Y., 1971-76; rsch. engr. GE R & D Ctr., Schenectady, N.Y., 1976-87; prof. Condra Chair of Exellence U. Tenn., Knoxville, 1987—; disting. scientist Power Electronics Appliance Ctr., Knoxville, 1987—; cons. PCI Ozone Corp., N.J., 1971-73, GE, 1971-76, Rsch. Triangle Inst., N.C., 1991-95, Bendix Corp., Electric Power Rsch. Inst., Lutron Electronics, UN for tech. devel. in People's Republic China and India; ; sr. advisor to Beijing Power Electronics R&D Ctr.; lectr. in field; hon. prof. Shanghai U. Tech., 1991, China U. of Mining and Technology, 1996, Xi'an Mining Inst., 1998. Author: Power Electronics and AC Drives, 1986; editor: Adjustable Speed AC Drive Systems, 1981, Micro Computer Control of Power Electronics and Drives, 1987, Modern Power Electronics, 1992, Power Electronics and Variable Frequency Drives, 1996; patentee in field; contbr. articles to profl. jours. Recipient Mouat Gold medal Calcutta U., 1967, Publ. award GE, 1982, Silver Patent medal GE, 1983. Fellow IEEE (life, chmn. power electronics, chmn. indsl. power converter com., Trans. Rev. chmn., static power converter com., assoc. editor Trans., neural network coun., Industry Applications Soc. outstanding achievement award 1993, Region 3 outstanding engr. award, 1994, Lamme Gold medal 1996); mem. IEEE Indsl. Electronics Soc. (Eugene Mittlemann Achievement award 1994, chmn. power electronics coun., Cont. Edn. award 1997). Hindu. Avocations: travel, gardening. Home: 404 Dixieview Rd Knoxville TN 37922-2609 Office: Univ of Tenn Dept Elec Engring 419 Ferris Hall Knoxville TN 37996

BOSE, NIRMAL KUMAR, electrical engineering, mathematics educator; b. Calcutta, West Bengal, India, Aug. 19, 1940; came to U.S., 1961; s. Dhruba Kumar and Roma (Guha) B.; m. Chandra Bose, June 8, 1969; children: Meenekshi, Enakshi. B.Tech., Indian Inst. Tech., Kharagpur, West Bengal, 1961; MS, Cornell U., 1963; PhD, Syracuse U., 1967. Asst. prof. U. Pitts., 1967-70, assoc. prof., 1970-76, prof., 1976-86; Singer prof. elec. engring. Pa. State U., University Park, 1986-91, HRB-Systems prof. elec. engring., 1992—; vis. assoc. prof. U. Calif., Berkeley, 1973-74; cons. RCA, Meadowland, Pa., 1968-69; spl. lectr. Coll. of Steubenville, Ohio, 1968-70; vis. assoc. prof. Am. U. Beirut, 1971, U. Md., College Park, 1972; vis. fellow Princeton U., 1996; apptd. vis. prof. Israel Inst. Tech., 1996; UN expert in neural networks to instns. and ctrs., India, 1994-95; rschr. Japan Soc. for Promotion of Sci., 1998. Author: Applied Multidimensional Systems Theory, 1982, Digital Filters: Theory and Applications, 1985, rev. edit., 1993; co-author: Neural Network Fundammentals, 1996; editor: Multidimensional Systems: Theory and Application, 1979, Multidimensional Systems; Progress, Directions and Open Problems, 1985; editor-in-chief Multidimensional Sys. and Signal Processing, 1990; co-editor: Handbook of Statistics vol. on Signal Processing and Its Applications, 1993; assoc. editor Cirs., Sys., and Signal Processing Jour., IEEE Trans. of Cirs. and Sys., Jour. Franklin Inst.; adv. com. Internat. Jour. Smart Engring. Sys. Design. Recipient invitational fellowship for rsch. in Japan, Japan Soc. for Promotion of Sci., 1998. Fellow IEEE (chmn. cirs. and systems tech. com. on edn. 1979-85); mem. AAAS, ASEE, Am. Math. Soc., N.Y. Acad. Scis., Am. Soc. Elec. Engrs. Sigma Xi. Hindu. Avocations: table-tennis, stamp collecting. Home: 1312 W Park Hills Ave State College PA 16803-3250 Office: Pa State U Dept Elec Engring University Park PA 16802 *Development and cultivation of spiritual and intellectual resources to the best of one's ability supported by parental blessings and encouragement provide the foundation on which the edifice of an individual's contributions to science and society is constructed.*

BOSEKER, BARBARA JEAN, education educator; b. Milw., Dec. 2, 1944; d. Edward Herbert and Alice Margaret (Maas) B.; m. Dale Leslie Sutcliff, Aug. 8, 1975. Student, U. Nigeria, Nsukka, 1966; BS (hon.) in secondary edn., U. Wis., Milw., 1968; MA in Anthropology, U. Wis., 1971, PhD in edn., 1978. cert. intermediante and secondary English tchr. Wis. Chemistry lab. technician Allen-Bradley Corp., Milw., 1963; coordinator Neighborhood Youth Corps., Madison, 1970; program devel. specialist Tchr. Corps., Madison, 1976-77; asst. prof. edn. Occidental Coll., 1978-80; asst. prof. edn. Mooehead State U., 1980-86, assoc. prof., 198690, prof., 1990-95; prof. Winona State U., 1995—; adv. bd.: Annual Editions: Teaching English as a Second Language, 1999—; cons. Inst. Latin Am. Studies U.Tex, Austin, 1980. Grant writer Fargo-Moorehead (N.D) Indian Center, 1980; evaluator Indian edn. grant Fargo Pub. Schs., 1985-90; contbr. articles to profl. jours. Elks Nat. and State Yough scholar U. Wis.; fellow Ford Found., 1968-69, NDEA, 1970-71, 78. Mem. NEA, Minn. Edn. Assn., Nat. Women's Studies Assn., Mortar Bd., Phi Kappa Phi, Pi Lamda Theta, Kappa Delta Pi, Sigma Tue Delta, Sigma Epsilon Sigma. Democrat. Christian Scientist. Home: 1317 Ridgewood Dr Winona MN 55987-5421 Office: Winona State U Winona MN 55987

BOSHART, EDGAR DAVID, editor, journalist, photographer; b. Carthage, N.Y., July 19, 1949; s. Eli Boshart and Edwina (Noftsier) Manchester. AAS, Rochester Inst Tech, 1969; BS, Rochester Inst. Tech., 1972; cert. in religious edn., Unification Theol. Sem., Kingston, N.Y., 1976. Tech. analyst Am. Cyanamid Corp., Bound Brook, N.J., 1970-71; chemist Xerox Corp., Rochester, N.Y., 1971-72; reporter News World, N.Y.C. & Washington, 1978-80; reporter, editor Oliphant Washington News Svc., 1981-83; reporter, writer, editor Foster Natural Gas Report, Washington, 1983—; owner, photographer PhotoSpeak Prodns., Arlington, Va., 1986—; v.p. Foster Assocs., Inc., Bethesda, Md. Mem. Nat. Press Club, Natural Gas Roundtable, No. Va. Photographic Soc. (bd. dirs., field trip coord.), Internat. Platform Assn., Wedding and Portrait Photographers Internat., Phi Kappa Phi Honor Soc. Avocations: photography, writing, skiing, travel. Home: 4628 Arlington Blvd Arlington VA 22204-1341 Office: Foster Assocs 4550 Montgomery Ave Ste 350N Bethesda MD 20814-3371

BOSHART, JEFFREY GLENN, sculptor, educator; b. Washington, Iowa, Dec. 16, 1955; s. William O. and Martha A. (Mace) B.; m. Karen L. Jurgens, May 12, 1978; children: Mace W., Will J. Student, Birney Inst. Tech., 1969-75; BA in art and sculpture, Mont. State U., 1978; MFA in sculpture, U. Mass., Amherst, 1981. Preparator Yellowstone Art Ctr., Billings, Mont., 1978; graphic designer Epcon Sign Co., Billings, 1979; tchg. assoc. U. Mass., Amherst, 1979-81, adj. prof., 1981-83, sceneographer, 1981-83; asst. prof. art U. Wis. Fox Valley, Menasha, 1983-88; assoc. prof. sculpture Ea. Ill. U., Charleston, 1988—; bd. dirs. Ill. Higher Edn. Art Assn., 1989—; mem. Coles County Arts Coun. (v.p. membership 1990-91). Sculptor: (site specific sculptures) RA's Crossing, 1987, Wingspread, 1988, Galleon Arc, 1988, Crossover, 1995, Prairie Chapel, 1995, Trilateral, 1997. Bd. dirs. Fine Arts Ctr., Amherst, 1981-83, Leverett (Mass.) Ctr. for Craftsmen and Artists, 1980-83; mem. local 1199 Health Care Workers, Amherst, 1981-82, AFT-UPI, Charleston, 1988—. Judged Best in Show Gallery 510, Decatur, Ill., 1997, New Eng. Arts Festival, 1981, 83; recipient individual project grants Wis. Arts Bd., 1981-88, aesthetic rsch. grants Ea. Ill. U., 1989-97. Mem. Founds. in Art: Theory and Edn. (v.p., sec.-treas., pres. 1983—), Internat. Sculpture Ctr., Mid-Am. Coll. Arts Assn. Roman Catholic. Avocations: furniture design and constrn., photography, Boy Scouts Am. Office: Eastern Ill U FAA 216 Charleston IL 61920

BOSHEARS, JAMES RAY, health system payroll administrator; b. Honolulu, June 25, 1945; s. Jesse Ray and Lillian A. Boshears; m. Carol A. Sumilas, Mar. 26, 1971; 1 child, Daryl J. AA, Merced Coll., 1965; BA in Dramatic Art, Fresno State Coll., 1968; BSBA, Robert Morris Coll., 1978; M of Pub. Mgmt., Carnegie Mellon U., 1986. Taxpayer assister IRS, Fresno, Calif., 1968; process control supr. Continental Can Corp., West Miflin, Pa., 1973; sales assoc. Edward Lupean Co., Pitts., 1974-77; payroll adminstr. I J & L Steel Corp., Pitts., 1978-81; mgr. payroll svcs. Carnegie Mellon U., Pitts., 1981-97; mgr. payroll dept. South Hills Health Sys., Homestead, Pa., 1997—; cons. CNA Ins., Pitts., 1985-86. Capt. USAF, 1968-73. Mem. Am. Payroll Assn. Avocations: collector and dealer of antiques, golf, photography. Home: 917 Hurl Dr Pittsburgh PA 15236-3636 Office: South Hills Health Sys 1800 West St Homestead PA 15120-2578

BOSHES, LOUIS D., physician, scientist, educator; b. Chgo., Oct. 15, 1908; s. Jacob and Ethel (London) B.; children: Arlene Phyllis Boshes Hirschfelder, Judi Myrl; m. Natalie A. Boshes. BS, Northwestern U., 1931, MD, 1936, postgrad., 1947-51; HHD (hon.), 1976. Diplomate neurology, psychiatry, and child neurology Am. Bd. Psychiatry and Neurology. Intern Michael Reese Hosp., Chgo., 1935-36, Cook County Hosp., 1936-37; fellow psychiatry Ill. Neuro-psychiat. Inst., Chgo., 1941-42, 46-47; sr. attending neurologist and psychiatrist, chief neurology clinic Michael Reese Med. Center, 1940—; sr. attending neurologist, psychiatrist emeritus Michael Reese Hosp. Med. Ctr.; prof. neurology and psychiatry Northwestern U., 1955-63; prof. neurology U. Ill. Coll. Medicine, Chgo., 1970-78, prof. emeritus, 1978—, historian and archivist in neurology; attending neurologist Ill. Research and Ednl. Hosps., 1963—, dir. consultation clinic for epilepsy, 1963-78; assoc. and attending neurologist, cons. neurology Cook County Hosp., 1947—; sr. cons. neurology Downey VA Hosp., 1952-60; prof. neurology Cook County Grad. Sch. Medicine, 1970—; practice medicine specializing in neurology and psychiatry, 1975—; mem. med. adv. com. Cook County chpt. Nat Found., 1947-55, March of Dimes, 1956—; mem. med. adv. com. Epilepsy Assn. Am., 1964—; bd. dirs., med. adv. com. Epilepsy Found. Am., 1964—; ambassador Internat. Bur. Epilepsy, 1969—; mem. profl. adv. com. Nat. Parkinson Found., 1960—, Nat. Myasthenia Gravis Found., 1972—, profl. adv. bd.; United Cerebral Palsy. Author, contbr. to books, med. jours.; assoc. editor Diseases of the Nervous System, 1962—; editor Chgo. Neurol. Soc. Bull., Behavioral Neuropsychiatry; mem. editorial bd. Excerpta Medica, Internat. Jour. Neurology and Neurosurgery. Historian, curator, archivist neurology U. Ill. Coll. Medicine at Chgo., 1990—, historian to Central Neuropsychiatric Assn, 1975—. Lt. comdr. M.C., USNR, 1941-46. Fellow ACP, Am. Acad. Neurology, Am. Psychiat. Assn. (life); mem. AMA (cons. AMA Jour., bd. govs. 1991—), Inst. Medicine Chgo., Pan Am. Med. Assn. (pres. sect. neurology, 1973—, hon. D. of Humanities 1976), Cen. Neuropsychiat. Assn. (pres. 1973-74, historian, curator), Ill. Psychiat. Soc. (life, sec.-treas. 1949-50, acting pres.), Chgo. Neurol. Soc. (pres. 1965-66, historian, curator), Michael Reese Hosp. and Med. Center Alumni Assn. (pres. 1961-62), Assn. for Research in Nervous and Mental Diseases, Internat. League Against Epilepsy, Am. League Against Epilepsy, Ill. League Against Epilepsy (med. adv. com.), Ill. Med. Soc. (chmn. sect. neurology and psychiatry 1961—), Chgo. Med. Soc., World Fedn. Neurology, AAAS, Am. Med. Soc. of Vienna (life), Central Assn. Electroence-Phalographers, Sigma Xi, Phi Delta Epsilon, Alpha Omega Alpha (A). Home: 3150 N Lake Shore Dr Chicago IL 60657-4829

BOSHIER, MAUREEN LOUISE, health facilities administrator; b. Elizabeth, N.J., Oct. 1, 1946; d. John Henry and Mary Hanora (McGarry) B.; m. Robert Hall Rea, May 23, 1987. BSN, Coll. Misericordia, Dallas, Pa., 1968; MS in Psychiat. Nursing, U. Colo., 1973; MBA, U. Phoenix, 1987. Cert. healthcare exec. Clin. specialist psychiat. nursing Denver Gen. Hosp., 1973-74; dir. rehab. svcs. N.Mex. Cancer Control, Albuquerque, 1976-80; exec. dir. N.Mex. State Bd. Nursing, Albuquerque, 1980-84; exec. v.p. N.Mex. Hosp. Assn., Albuquerque, 1984-88; adminstr. surg. svcs., sr. nursing adminstr. U. N.Mex. Hosp., Albuquerque, 1988-94; CEO, pres. N.Mex. Hosps. and Health Sys. Assn., Albuquerque, 1995—; dir. Profl. Seminar Cons., Inc., Albuquerque, 1982—; v.p. exec. bd. N.Mex. Health Resources, Albuquerque, 1981—, pres., 1989; vice chmn., bd. dirs. Hosp. Home Health Care, Albuquerque, 1978—; dir. Acad. Seminars, Inc., 1982—; mem. governing coun. for small and rural hosps. Am. Hosp. Assn., 1996—. Mem. adv. bd. N.Mex. Bus. Jour., 1995—; contbr. articles to profl. jours. Sec. N.Mex. Ballet Co., Albuquerque, 1982-87; vice chmn. Gov.'s Task Force on Nursing Issues, Albuquerque, 1982-88; adv. bd. Sub-area Coun. Health Sys., Albuquerque, 1980-84. Capt. U.S. Army, 1967-71. Recipient Woman on the Move award YWCA, 1992, Wharton Sch. of Bus. fellowship for health care execs., 1993, Gov.'s award for Outstanding N.Mex. Woman, 1997. Mem. Am. Orgn. Nurse Execs. (vice chmn. legis. advocacy com. 1992-94, chmn. 1993-94), Am. Coll. Healthcare Execs. (diplomate), N.Mex. Orgn. Nurse Execs. (treas. 1988-89, pres. 1990), N.Mex. League for Nursing, N.Mex. Nurses Assn. (Nurse Adminstr. award 1984), Rotary, Albuquerque C. of C. (mem. quality of life com. 1994—), Sigma Theta Tau (pres.-elect 1994, pres. 1995—, Mentor award Gamma Sigma chpt. 1994). Democrat. Avocations: music, dance, travel. Home: 9520 Kandace Dr NW Albuquerque NM 87114-4131 Office: N Mex Hosps and Health Sys Assn 2121 Osuna Rd NE Albuquerque NM 87113-1001

BOSKELLO, DENNIS JON, elementary education educator; b. Greenwich, Conn., June 10, 1953; s. Anthony Joseph and Irene Florence (Chiappetta) B.; m. Margo Lynn Godlewski, Dec. 18, 1976; 1 child, David Jon. BS in Elem. Edn., Western Conn. State U., 1975; MA in Edn. Media, Fairfield (Conn.) U., 1980, cert. of advanced study in adminstrn. and supervision, 1987. Cert. supervision and adminstrn., elem. and secondary tchr, mentor tchr., Conn. Ordained elder Presbyn. Ch., 1997. Elem. tchr. Fairfield (Conn.) Pub. Schs., 1975—, coord. bldg. computer edn., 1987-94; mem. Bldg. Tech. Com. Mill Hill Sch., 1994—; co-chair bldg. profl. devel. com. Fairfield (Conn.) Pub. Schs., 1989-93; mem. steering com. project SMARTNET, 1990-96; tchr. assessor, juror, mentor and cooperating tchr. State of Conn., 1990—; mem. project LEAD adminstrv. aspirant program, 1991-92. Mem. Barnum Festival com., Bridgeport, 1975, 82, Spirit of Discovery com., Discovery Mus., Bridgeport, 1992, 93; v.p. Calvin United Brotherhood, Fairfield, 1982-86, 88-90, sec., 1988; bldg. coord. 350th anniversary celebration for Stratfield Sch.; bd. dirs. nursery sch. 1st Presbyn. Ch., Fairfield. Grantee GE, 1984, 85. Mem. NEA, Conn. Edn. Assn. (dist. and bldg. profl. devel. com. 1989—), Fairfield Edn. Assn. (chmn. fin. com. 1981-85, exec. bd. 1981-85), Dist. Computer Edn. Com. Avocations: music, travel. Office: Fairfield Pub Schs Stillson Rd Fairfield CT 06430

BOSKELLO, MARGO LYNN, elementary education educator; b. Bridgeport, Conn., June 23, 1951; d. Charles Thomas and Margaret Helen (Szajko) Godlewski; m. Dennis Jon Boskello, Dec. 18, 1976; 1 child, David Jon. BS, Western Conn. State U., 1973; MA, Fairfield (Conn.) U., 1979. Cert. elem. tchr., English tchr., Conn. Tchr. Fairfield Pub. Schs., 1973—, lang. arts contact, 1990—; panelist conv. Nat. Coun. Tchrs. English, 1979, Gov.'s Symposium on Career Edn., Hartford, Conn., 1979; speaker Fairfield Sr. Ctr., 1990. Editor: Pencil Point, 1973-88. Edn. cons. nursery sch. Calvin United Ch. of Christ, Fairfield, 1988-91, Sunday Sch. tchr., 1965-76; tchr. vacation Bible sch. 1st Presbyn. Sch., Fairfield, 1991-93; active Barnum Festival Orgn., Bridgeport, 1975; mem. adv. com. Townwide Family Life, 1976; Spirit of Discovery Steering com. Discovery Mus., Bridgeport, 1992-93; elder First Presbyn. Ch. of Fairfield, 1994—, mission co-chairperson, 1994, 95; asst. clk. session First Presbyn. Ch. of Fairfield, 1995; sub. Sunday sch. tchr., 1994—; active Townwide Lang. Arts Program; clerk of session First Presbyn. Ch. Fairfield, 1995. Scholar Gould Found., 1969; named one of Outstanding Young Women of Am., 1989. Mem. Delta Kappa Gamma (chmn. publicity 1984, chmn. rsch. 1990, v.p. 1991-92, 93). Avocations: foreign doll collecting, travel, photography, gardening. Office: Roger Sherman Sch 250 Fern St Fairfield CT 06430-6825

BOSKEY, BENNETT, lawyer; b. N.Y.C., Aug. 14, 1916; s. Meyer and Janet (Lauterstein) B.; m. Shirley Ecker, July 3, 1940 (dec. 1998). A.B., Williams Coll., 1935; LL.B., Harvard U., 1939. Bar: N.Y. 1940, U.S. Supreme Ct. 1943, D.C. 1949. Spl. asst. to Atty. Gen. U.S. Dept. Justice, Washington, 1943; advisor on enemy property U.S. Dept. State, Washington, 1946-47; atty. U.S. Atomic Energy Commn., Washington, 1947-49; dep. gen. counsel U.S. Atomic Energy Commn., 1949-51; ptnr. firm Volpe, Boskey & Lyons (and predecessors), Washington, 1951-96; law clk. Judge Learned Hand, 1939-40, Justice Stanley Reed, 1940-41, Chief Justice Harlan F. Stone, 1941-43; trustee Analytic Svcs. Inc., Arlington, Va., 1962-91; adv. bd. internat. legal studies program Am. Univ., 1987—. Chmn. bd. trustees Primary Day Sch., Bethesda, Md., 1969—. Served with U.S. Army, 1943-46. Mem. ABA, Bar Assn. D.C., Fed. Bar Assn., Am. Law Inst. (treas. 1975—, mem. coun., Am. Law Inst.-ABA com. on continuing profl. edn. 1965—), Am. Soc. Internat. Law (bd. rev. and devel. 1973-88). Office: Ste 600 1800 Massachusetts Ave NW Washington DC 20036-1222

BOSKIN, MICHAEL JAY, economist, government official, university educator, consultant; b. N.Y.C., Sept. 23, 1945; s. Irving and Jean B.; m. Chris Dornin, Oct. 20, 1981. AB with highest honors, U. Calif., Berkeley, 1967, MA in Econs., 1968, PhD in Econs., 1971. Asst. prof. Stanford (Calif.) U., 1970-75, assoc. prof., 1976-78, prof., 1978—, dir. Ctr. for Econ. Policy Rsch., 1986-89, Wohlford prof. econs., 1987-89; chmn. Pres.'s Coun. Econ. Advisors, The White House, Washington, 1989-93; Friedman Prof. Econs. Stanford (Calif.) U., 1993—; pres. Boskin & Co., Menlo Park, Calif., 1993—; vis. prof. Harvard U., Cambridge, Mass., 1977-78; disting. faculty fellow Yale U., 1993, scholar Am. Enterprise Inst., 1993—; rsch. assoc. Nat. Bur. Econ. Rsch., 1976—; bd. dirs. Oracle Corp., Exxon Corp., First Health Group, Airtouch Comm., Inc.; chmn. Congl. Adv. Commn. on the Consumer Price Index; advisor, cons. numerous govt. agencies, pvt. businesses. Author: Too Many Promises: The Uncertain Future of Social Security, 1986, Reagan and the Economy: Successes, Failures Unfinished Agenda, 1987, Frontiers of Tax Reform, 1996; contbr. articles to profl. jours., popular media. Mem. several philanthropic bds. dirs. Faculty Rsch. fellow Mellon Found., 1973; recipient Outstanding Rsch. award Nat. Assn. Bus. Economists, 1987. Fellow Nat. Assn. Bus. Econs. (Presdl. medal Italian Republic, Adam Smith prie 1998). Avocations: tennis, skiing, reading, theater. Office: Stanford U 213 HHMB Stanford CA 94305-6010

BOSL, PHILLIP L., lawyer; b. Feb. 27, 1945. BA, U. Calif., Santa Barbara, 1968; JD, U. So. Calif., 1975. Bar: Calif. 1975. Ptnr. Gibson, Dunn & Crutcher, LLP, L.A., 1983—. Mem. U. So. Calif. Law Rev., 1973-75. Officer USCG, 1969-72. Mem. ABA, Los Angeles County Bar Assn., Fed. Bar Assn., Assn. Bus. Trial Lawyers Am., Securities Industry Assn. (compliance and legal divsn.), Nat. Assn. Securities Dealers (arbitrator), Order of Coif. Home: 6226 Napoli Ct Long Beach CA 90803-4800 Office: Gibson Dunn & Crutcher LLP 333 S Grand Ave Ste 4400 Los Angeles CA 90071-3197

BOSLAUGH, LESLIE, retired judge; b. Hastings, Nebr., Sept. 4, 1917; s. Paul E. and Ann (Herzog) B.; m. Elizabeth F. Meyer, Aug. 10, 1943; children: Marguerite Ann, Sarah Elizabeth, Paul Robert. B.B.A., U. Nebr., 1939, LL.B., 1941. Bar: Nebr. 1941. Mem. staff Nebr. Statute Revision Commn., 1941-43; pvt. practice law Hastings, 1946-47; asst. atty. gen. Nebr., 1947-48; mem. firm Stiner & Boslaugh, Hastings, 1949-60; judge Nebr. Supreme Ct., Lincoln, 1961-94. Served to lt. AUS, 1943-46. Mem. Nebr. Bar Assn., Order of Coif. *

BOSLEY, RONALD EDMUND, retired aircraft executive; b. Akron, Ohio, May 18, 1932; s. Osborne Walter and Donna Lenora (Davis) B.; m. Patricia Lou Kipp, Feb. 9, 1952; children: Patricia Lynn Bosley Brewer, Donna Esther Bosley Beers, Ronald Francis (dec.). Grad., Command & Gen. Staff Coll., Ft. Leavenworth, Kans., 1972; student, Army War Coll., Carlisle, Pa., 1975. Machinist wheel and brake divsn. GAC, Akron, 1951-66, supr. machine shop, 1966-73, shift foreman machine shop, 1973-74, gen. foreman, 1974-82, mgr. tech. and mfg., 1982-83, mgr. mfg. ops., 1983-88; ret., 1988. Author instnl. materials: (Communications, 1981, Commitment to Perfection, 1985 (Spirit award), Ideas for Managers, 1986 (Spirit award). Vol. survey ranger Nat. Park Svc., Cuyahoga Valley, 1997—. Lt. col. USAR, 1951-92, ret. Mem. NRA, Am. Legion, Clan Ramsay Assn. Am. (rep.), Country Music Assn., Hon. Order Ky. Cols., Ret. Officers Assn., Goodyear 25 Year Club. Roman Catholic. Avocations: molding and painting lead soldiers, hunting, fishing, model building, hiking. Home: 2840 Linwood Rd Akron OH 44312-3402

BOSLEY, TOM, actor; b. Chgo., Oct. 1, 1927; s. Benjamin and Dora (Heyman) B.; m. Jean Eliot, Mar. 8, 1962 (dec. Apr. 1978); 1 dau., Amy; m. Patricia Carr, Dec. 21, 1980. Ed. high sch., Chgo.; student, De Paul U., 1946, Radio Inst. Chgo., 1947-48; studied with, Lee Strasberg, 1952. Actor: various roles TV programs Alice in Wonderland, 1953, Arsenic and Old Lace, 1962, Focus, 1961, Naked City, The Right Man, The Nurses, Law and Mr. Jones, Route 66, The Perry Como Show, The Dean Martin Show, Joanie Loves Chachi, The Rebels, Death Trap, Castaways on Gilligan's Island, Return of Mod Squad, For the Love of It, Jessie Owens Story; TV film: Fatal Confession: A Father Dowling Mystery, 1987, The Love Boat, A Valentine Voyage, 1990; regular actor on TV shows Wait Til Your Father Gets Home, Murder She Wrote, 1984-87; star TV series Happy Days, 1974-83, Father Dowling Mysteries, 1989-92; also appeared on TV series Profiles in Courage, others; appeared in TV mini-series The Bastard, 1978; narrator TV series That's Hollywood; voice in animated cartoon The Stingiest Man in Town; actor numerous theatrical prodns. in stock companies, also off-Broadway prodns., 1952-56; Broadway debut as Fiorello LaGuardia in Fiorello, 1959 (Pulitzer Prize play); Broadway roles include: musical Nowhere to Go But Up, 1962, plays Natural Affection, 1963, A Murderer Among Us, 1964, The Education of H, Beauty and the Beast, 1994; film roles include Love with a Proper Stranger, 1963, The World of Henry Orient, 1964, Divorce American Style, 1967, Secret War of Harry Frigg, 1968, Yours, Mine and Ours, 1968, To Find A Man, 1972, Mixed Company, 1974, Gus, 1976, O'Hara's Wife, 1982 ; indsl. film Perfectly Normal Day. Served with USNR, World War II. Recipient Antoinette Perry award for 1959-60 season as best actor in featured role of musical; Newspaper Guild of Am. Page One award and ANTA award for distinguished contbn. to theatre, 1960; N.Y. Drama Critics award for performance in Fiorello, 1960; Festival of Leadership award Chgo.; Humanitarian award Performing Arts Theater of Handicapped, 1981; Tau award Sacred Heart Rehab. Hosp., Milw. Mem. Actors Equity Assn. (governing council 1961-69), AFTRA, Screen Actors Guild. Office: Shapiro-Lichtman-Stein 8827 Beverly Blvd Los Angeles CA 90048-2405 *I try to go through life by not hurting anyone's feelings, by respecting people for what they are and not what I think they should be: by honoring my heritage and the heritage of others; and by trying to smile at adversity, knowing that if I can, life can be softer and more comfortable than the realities really are.**

BOSMAJIAN, HAIG ARAM, speech communication educator; b. Fresno, Calif., Mar. 26, 1928; s. Aram and Aurora (Keosheyan) B.; m. Hamida Just, Feb. 27, 1957; 1 child, Harlan. BA, U. Calif., Berkeley, 1949; MA, U. of Pacific, 1951; PhD, Stanford U., 1960. Instr. U. Idaho, Moscow, 1959-61; asst. prof. U. Conn., Storrs, 1961-65; prof. speech comm. U. Wash., Seattle, 1965—. Author: Language of Oppression (Orwell award), 1983; editor: Censorship, Libraries and the Law, 1983; Justice Douglas, 1980, Freedom of Speech, 1983, First Amendment in the Classroom Series, 1987: vol. 1, The Freedom to Read, 1987, vol. II, The Freedom of Religion, 1987, vol. III, Freedom of Expression, 1988, vol. IV, Academic Freedom, 1989, vol. V, Freedom to Publish, 1989, Metaphor and Reason in Judicial Opinions, 1992, The Freedom Not to Speak, 1999. Recipient Bicentennial of the Bill of Rights award Western States Communication Assn., 1991. Mem. Nat. Coun. Tchrs. of English, Speech Comm. Assn.

BOSMAN, RICHARD, painter, printmaker; b. Madras, India, 1944. Student, Byam Sch Sch. Painting/Drawing, London, 1964-69, N.Y. Studio Sch., N.Y.C., 1969-71, Skowhegan Sch. Painting, Maine, 1970. Instr. N.Y. Studio Sch., 1972, Skowhegan Sch. Painting and Sculpture, 1982, Sch. Visual Arts, N.Y.C., 1982-84. Exhibited in one-man shows at Galerie La Maquina Espanola, Madrid, 1990, Galerie Biedermann, Munich, Germany, 1991, Brooke Alexander, 1991, 93, 94, Galleria Toselli, Milan, 1992, Fairfield (Conn.) U. Gallery, 1993, R.I. Sch. Design Print Gallery, 1993, Timmesch Gallery, Mpls., 1993; group shows include Am. Fedn. ARts, N.Y.C., 1989, Walker Art Ctr. from Mpls. to Balt., 1989, U. Maine Mus. Art, Orono, 1989, Galeria La Maquina Espanola, 1989, John Berggruen Gallery, San. Francisco, 1990; works included in collections at Albright-Knox Art Gallery, Buffalo, Australian Nat. Gallery, Canberra, Bklyn. Mus., Fogg Art Mus./Harvard U., Nat. Mus. Am. Art, Washington, Weatherspoon Art Gallery, Greensboro; co-author: Exit the Face, 1982; illustrator: Grasping at Emptiness, 1987, The Captivity Narrative of Hannah Duston, 1987, others. Address: c/o Brooke Alexander Edits 59 Wooster St New York NY 10012*

BOSOMWORTH, PETER PALLISER, university medical administrator; b. Akron, Ohio, May 2, 1930; s. George Palliser and Vera (Siddle) B.; m. Georgia Simester, July 20, 1956; children: Virginia Kay, David Palliser, Andrew Palliser, Jeffrey Palliser (dec.). BS, Kent State U., 1951; MD, U. Cin., 1955; M in Med. Sci., Ohio State U., 1958. Diplomate Am. Bd. Anesthesiology (assoc. examiner 1965-73). Intern Cin. Gen. Hosp., 1955-56; resident Ohio State U., Columbus, 1956-58, instr. anesthesiology, 1958, dir. anesthesia research, asst. dir. anesthesiology, 1960-62; chief anesthesia div. U.S. Naval Hosp., Great Lakes, Ill., 1958-60; prof., chmn. dept. anesthesiology Med. Ctr. U. Ky., Lexington, 1962-70, v.p. for Med. Ctr., 1970-82, chancellor for Med. Ctr., 1982-94, assoc. dean clin. affairs, 1968-70, also several coms., bds., 1962-94; prof. rsch. and health policy U. Ky., Lexington, 1994—, prof. anesthesiology Coll. Medicine, prof. health svc. mgmt., 1995—, chancellor emeritus, 1994—; dir. continuing med. edn. U. Ky. Coll. Medicine, 1999—; mem. Ky. Hill Burton Coun., 1970-73; mem. Ky. Comprehensive Health Planning Coun., 1971—; bd. dirs. Ea. Ky. Health Sys. Agy., Anthem Cmty. Health (dba Blue Cross/Blue Shield); vice chmn. Health Resources Devel. Corp. Ky., 1976-78; mem. Ky. Cancer Commn., 1978-82, Statewide Health Coordinating Coun., 1979-82; pres. Health Care Collection Agy., 1976-94; pres. steering com. State Ctr. Health Scis. Rsch. Prodr. movies, TV programs on med. topics, 1959—; contbr. articles to profl. jurs. Chmn. Commn. on Community Svcs. for Older Persons, 1980-87, chmn., 1982; trustee Hunter Found., 1971-74, St. Elizabeth Hosp., Covington, Ky., 1970-72; bd. dirs. Blue Grass coun. Boy Scouts Am., 1977-82, v.p., 1977-79; bd. dirs. E. McDowell Cancer Network, Lexington, 1975-94, Lexington Sister Cities Program, 1978, Frontier Nursing Svc., 1979—; chmn. found. bd. YMCA-Black Achievement, 1992-94. Recipient medal of honor Cheng Kung U., Republic of China, 1976, Daniel Drake award U. Cin. Coll. of Medicine, 1994. Fellow Am. Coll. Anesthesiologists (assoc. examiner 1967-73), Am. Coll. Clin. Pharmacology and Chemotherapy, Am. Coll. Chest Physicians, Royal Soc. Medicine; mem. Assn. Univ. Anesthetists, Ky. Med. Assn. (del. to Am. Soc. Anesthesiologists 1965-70, ho. of dels. 1985—, Faculty Sci. Achievement award 1969), Fayette County Med. Soc. (exec. com. 1965-86, v.p. 1970, 75, pres. 1980), Am. Assn. Inhalation Therapy (Ky. bd. dirs. 1968-70), Assn. Acad. Health Ctrs. (bd. dirs. 1975-82, chmn. 1981), Royal Soc. Medicine. Home: 2956 Four Pines Rd Unit 3 Lexington KY 40502-2944 Office: K117 Ky Clinic 740 S Limestone Lexington KY 40536-0284*

BOSS, AMELIA HELEN, law educator, lawyer; b. Balt., Apr. 3, 1949; d. Myron Theodore and Loretta (Oakjones) B.; m. Roger S. Clark, Mar. 3, 1979; children: Melissa, Seymour, Edward, Ashley. Student, St. Hilda's Coll., England, 1968; BA in Sociology, Bryn Mawr, 1970; JD, Rutgers U., 1975. Bar: N.J, Pa., U.S. Dist. Ct. (ea. dist.) N.J., U.S. Dist. Ct. (ea. dist.) Pa., U.S. Supreme Ct., U.S. Ct. Appeals (3d cir.). Law clk. Hon. Milton B. Cranford N.J. Supreme Ct., 1975-76; assoc. Pepper, Hamilton & Scheetz, Phila., 1976-78; assoc. prof. law Rutgers U. Sch. Law, Camden, N.J., 1983-87, Temple U., Phila., 1989-91; prof. law Temple U. Sch. Law, Phila., 1991—; vis. prof. law U. Miami Sch. Law, Coral Gables, Fla., 1985-86; Leo Goodwin disting. vis. prof. law Nova U., Sch. Law, 1998; mem. coms. Nat. Conf. Commrs. on Uniform State Laws; U.S. rep. to UN Commn. on Internat. Trade Law. Author: (books) Electronic Data Interchange Agreements: A Guide and Sourcebook, 1993, ABCs of the UCC: Article 2A, ABCs of the UCC: Article 5; editor-in-chief The Data Law Report, 1993-97, The Business Lawyer, 1998-99, ABCs of the UCC; mem. permanent editl. bd. Uniform Comml. Code; contbr. articles to profl. jours. Named among top 50 women lawyers in U.S. Nat. Law Jour., 1998. Fellow Am. Bar Found.; mem. ABA (chmn.-elect bus. law sect.), Am. Law Inst., Am. Bankruptcy Inst., Am. Coll. Comml. Fin. Lawyers, Nat. Assn. Women Lawyers. Home: 309 Westmont Ave Haddonfield NJ 08033-1714 Office: Temple U Sch Law 1719 N Broad St Philadelphia PA 19122-6002

BOSS, LENARD BARRETT, lawyer; b. Passaic, N.J., Mar. 6, 1960; s. Lawrence Steven and Laura (Ziegler) B. BA in Rhetoric, Bates Coll., 1982; JD with high honors, George Washington U., 1985. Bar: Pa. 1985, D.C. 1986, Md. 1995, U.S. Ct. Appeals (4th and 11th cirs.) 1986, U.S. Ct. Appeals (D.C. cir.) 1987, U.S. Dist. Ct. D.C. 1987, U.S. Ct. Appeals (3d cir.) 1988, U.S. Supreme Ct. 1989. Assoc. Asbill, Junkin, Myers & Buffone, Washington, 1986-91; ptnr. Asbill, Junkin & Myers, Washington, 1991-95; asst. fed. pub. defender Fed. Pub. Defender's Office, Washington, 1995—. Avocations: films, music, sports. Office: 625 Indiana Ave NW Ste 550 Washington DC 20004-2901

BOSSE, DENISE FRANCES, educational administrator, education educator; b. Syracuse, N.Y., Apr. 27, 1953; d. Rufus Elmer Nicholson and Vivian Margaret Herb; m. Philip Roger Bosse, Mar. 27, 1976; children: Matthew R., Jeannine M. BS in Elem. Edn., U. Maine, 1975, MEd, 1987. Cert. tchr./adminstr., Maine. Tchr. prin. Union #122 Stockholm (Maine) Elem. Sch., 1988; ind. ednl. cons. Caribou, Maine, 1988-93; human resource mgr., ednl. materials buyer Mementos Inc., Caribou, Maine, 1988-93; edn. coord., head tchr. Little Feathers Head Start, Presque Isle, Maine, 1995-96; local advisor Nat. Early Childhood Accreditation Assn., Washington, 1996—; adj. faculty U. Maine, Presque Isle, 1993-98; coord. Aroostook Coun. on Transition, Presque Isle, 1996-97; secondary resource rm. tchr. Caribou H.S., 1997—; bd. dirs. Youth Network, Caribou, 1996-97; mem. steering com. St. John Valley Sch.-to-Work Partnership, Frenchville, Maine, 1996-97, participant Com. on Transition, Augusta, Maine, 1996-97; mem. Coords. Alliance of Maine, Augusta, 1996-97. Grantee State of Maine and U.S. Dept. Edn., Ashland, Maine, 1987. Mem. Vol. Dirs. Assn. Northern Maine, Maine Support Network, KC Ladies Auxiliary, Alpha Delta Pi (permanent alumni sec. 1985—). Roman Catholic. Avocations: travel, reading, creative writing, music. Home: PO Box 594 Caribou ME 04736-0594 Office: Caribou HS Sweden St Caribou ME 04736

BOSSE, MALCOLM JOSEPH, JR., professional language educator, author; b. Detroit, May 6, 1926; s. Malcolm C. and Thelma (Malone) B.; m. Laura L. Mack; children: Mark Elliot, Malcolm-Scott. B.A., Yale U.; M.A., U. Mich.; Ph.D., NYU. Editorial writer Barron's Fin. Weekly, N.Y.C., 1950-51; freelance writer N.Y.C., 1957-66; mem. faculty CCNY, 1969-92, emeritus prof. English, 1992—; reviewer, writer N.Y. Times; Dept. State lectr., Asia. Author: The Incident at Naha (Edgar Allan Poe award nominee), 1972, The Man Who Loved Zoos (Edgar Allan Poe nominee), 1974, (film version entitled Agent Trouble, 1987, by French film maker J.P. Mocky and Catherine Deneuve, The 79 Squares (ALA Notable Book, named best children's book of the year by German TV, recipient Prix du Livre Pour La Jeunesse de la Fondation de France for exceptional lit., artistic, and moral qualities, 1986, Le Prix Lecture-Jeunesse 1987), 1980, Cave Beyond Time (Book Social Studies award, nominee Deutscher Jugendliteraturpreis), 1979, Ganesh (Omar award nominee; Austrian Ministry of Edn. and Arts Honor List of Books; Deutscher Jugendliteraturpreis, 1981, (film and paperback version Ordinary Magic, 1993), The Barracuda Gang, 1982, The Warlord (Book-of-the-Month Club main selection), 1983, The Journey of Tao Kim Nam (Saturday Rev. of Lit. one of best novels of yr.), 1960, Fire in Heaven, 1986 (Lit. Guild featured alt. selection), Captives of Time (Best Book for Young Adults ALA), 1987, (novel on Indonesian politics) Stranger at the Gate, 1989, Mister Touch, 1991, The Vast Memory of Love, 1992, Deep Dream of the Rainforest, 1993, The Examination, 1994 (Best Book for Young Adults award ALA), Tusk and Stone, 1995; co-editor: Flowering of the Novel, 1975, Foundations of the Novel, The Novel in England: 1700-1775, Major Critical Essay to Charles Johnstone's Chrysal, 1760-65; also short stories, poetry. Served with U.S. Army, U.S. Mcht. Marines, USN, 6 yrs., PTO, Korea. Decorated Bronze 3 Stars with oak leaf cluster; recipient spl. commendation ICA, 1980; Masefield award Yale U.; 2 Hopwood awards Mich. U.; Fulbright-Hays grantee, India; NYU fellow; Newberry Library fellow; Nat. Endowment Arts fellow; others. Mem. MLA, Fulbright-Hays Alumni Assn., Authors Guild, Soc. 18th Century Studies and Scholars, P.E.N., Henry James Assocs. (charter), Phi Beta Kappa, Phi Gamma Delta. Clubs: Yale, Andiron (N.Y.C.). Avocations: tai chi; archaeology; art; music; football.

BOSSE, MICHAEL JOSEPH, orthopedic trauma surgeon, retired medical officer; b. Balt., June 11, 1952; s. Vincent Leo and Patricia Ann (Toball) B.; m. Ellen Ann Farace, June 13, 1975; children: Shane, Kevin, Patrick, Colin. BS, U.S. Naval Acad., 1974; Md, U. Md., 1978. Diplomate Am. Bd. Orthopaedic Surgery. Comd. officer USN, 1974, advanced through grades to capt.; ret., 1997; orthopedic surgeon USN, Portsmouth, Va., 1983-91, Bethesda, Md., 1991-93; ortho trauma surgeon Shock Trauma Ctr., Balt., 1991-93, Carolinas Med. Ctr., Charlotte, N.C., 1993—. Rsch. grantee NIH, Bethesda, 1993. Fellow Am. Acad. Orthopaedic Surgery; mem. Orthopaedic Trauma Assn., Am. Assn. for Surgery of Trauma, Am. Orthopaedic Assn. Office: Carolinas Med Ctr 1001 Blythe Blvd Charlotte NC 28203-5866*

BOSSEN, WENDELL JOHN, insurance company executive; b. Vienna, S.D., Nov. 11, 1933; s. Hans Simonsen and Clara Patrina (Vorseth) B.; m. Jean Davidson, Jan. 6, 1956; children: Mark, Monica. Student, S.D. Sch. Mines, 1952. CLU. Agt. Northwestern Nat. Life Ins. Co., Mpls., 1957-61, dist. mgr., staff mgr., 1961-68, br. mgr., 1968-72, div. v.p., 1972-77; exec. v.p., chief operating officer Inter-Ocean Ins. Co., Cin., 1977-84; exec. v.p. corp. mktg. Mut. Benefit Life Ins. Co., Newark, 1984-92; pres. Internat. Corp. Mktg. Group ITT, Hartford, Conn., 1992—; cons. Newark Performing Arts Corp., 1986. Author: Businessmens Guide to Insurance, 1981; contbr. articles to profl. jours. Chmn. ARC, Waterstown, S.C., 1962, Northeast S.D. chpt. United Way, Waterstown, 1963, Waterstown County Reps., 1963-64; mem. exec. com. S.D. Reps., Pierre, 1964; bd. dirs. Am. Luth. Ch., Cin., 1979, Apostles' House, 1989. Recipient Danforth Found. award, 1952. Mem. Nat. Assn. Life Underwriters (pres. Watertown chpt. 1960-61, v.p. state chpt. 1961-62), Chartered Life Underwriters, Life Ins. Mktg. Research Assn. (com. chmn. 1975). Club: Golden Valley Country (Mpls). Lodges: Elks (pres. 1962-63), Lions (pres. 1961, 73), Kiwanis. Avocations: golf, tennis, photography. Home: 149 Wexford Way Basking Ridge NJ 07920-2433 Office: Internat Corp Mktg Group 100 Campus Dr Florham Park NJ 07932-1006

BOSSER, STEVEN JOHN, prosecutor; b. Yonkers, N.Y., Dec. 27, 1952; s. John Joseph and Margaret Frances (Flanagan) B.; m. Susan Virginia Coggins, Oct. 17, 1981; children: Timothy, Katharine. BA in Econ., SUNY, Albany, 1977; JD, St. John's U., Jamaica, N.Y., 1984. Bar: N.Y. 1985, N.J. 1985, U.S. Dist. Ct. N.J. 1985, Tex. 1986, U.S. Dist. Ct. (no. dist.) Tex. 1988, U.S. Supreme Ct. 1989, DC Ct. Appeals, 1989. Asst. city atty. City Atty's. Office, Ft. Worth, 1986-87; asst. criminal dist. atty. Tarrant County Dist. Atty's. Office, Ft. Worth, 1987—; lectr. Tex. Dept. Pub. Safety, Austin, 1993-97, Tarrant County Auto Theft Task Force, Ft. Worth, 1994-97. Com. chair Boy Scouts Am., 1994-96, various other positions, 1995—. With U.S. Army, 1973-76. Recipient Prosecutor Yr. award Tex. Assn. Vehicle Theft Investigators, 1994; named to Outstanding Young Men of Am., 1987. Mem. Tex. State Bar Assn., Tex. Dist. and County Attys. Assn., D.C. Bar Assn. Republican. Avocations: camping, hiking, computers. Office: Tarrant County Dist Atty 401 W Belknap St Fl 4 Fort Worth TX 76102-1913

BOSSERT, PHILIP JOSEPH, information systems executive; b. Indpls., Feb. 23, 1944; s. Alfred Joseph and Phyllis Jean (Cashen) B.; m. Jane Elisabeth Shade, June 29, 1968 (div. Dec. 1990); m. ChaoYing Deng, May 22, 1992; 1 child, Lian Brittni. BA in Econs., Rockhurst Coll., 1968; cert. in Philosophy, U. Freiburg, Fed. Republic Ger., 1970; MA in Philosophy, Washington U., St. Louis, 1972, PhD in Philosophy, 1973. Asst. prof. philosophy Hawaii Loa Coll., Honolulu, 1973-76, pres., 1978-86; dir. Hawaii com. for the humanities Nat. Endowment for the Humanities, Honolulu, 1976-77; dir. long range planning Chaminade U., Honolulu, 1977-78; pres. Strategic Info. Solutions, Honolulu, 1986—; mgr. strategic info. systems GTE Hawaiian Telephone, Honolulu, 1987-91; asst. supt. info. & telecom. svcs. Hawaii State Dept. Edn., 1991-94; project dir. Hawaii Edn. and Rsch. Network, 1994-97; chmn. bd. dirs., dir. Media Design & Devel., Inc., 1996-99; chmn. bd. dirs., CEO Baden Wines Internat., Ltd., 1997—; cons. Sangyong Bus. Group, Seoul, Korea, 1987-90, Nat. Assn. Colls. Univs. and Bus. Officers, Washington, 1980-90. Author: Strategic Planning and Budgeting, 1989; author, editor numerous books on philosophy; contbr. articles to profl. jours. Bd. dirs. Hawaii Childrens Mus., 1994-99, Friends of the East West Ctr., 1996-99, Hawaii Alliance for the Arts, 1996-99. Fulbright-Hays fellow, 1968-70, Woodrow Wilson fellow, 1972-73, Nat. Endowment for Humanities fellow, 1976. Mem. Pacific Telecom. Coun. (bd. dirs.). E-mail: pbossert@sis.net. Office: Strategic Info Solutions Inc 239 Merchant St Honolulu HI 96813-2923

BOSSES, STEVAN J., lawyer; b. Bronx, N.Y., July 29, 1937; s. Fred and Frieda (Picard) B.; m. Abbye Z. Bosses, May 24, 1964; children: Donna Lynne, David Keith, Gary Philip. BME, Cornell U., 1960; LLB, Columbia U., 1963. Bar: N.Y. 1963, U.S. Dist. Ct. (so. dist.) N.Y. 1964, U.S. Dist. Ct. (ea. dist.) N.Y. 1964, U.S. Patent Office 1964, U.S. Ct. Appeals (2d cir.) 1970, U.S. Ct. Appeals (3rd cir.) 1979, U.S. Ct. Appeals (fed. cir.) 1982, U.S. Supreme Ct. 1989. Assoc., Watson Leavenworth Kelton & Taggart, N.Y.C., 1963-71, ptnr., 1972-81; ptnr. Fitzpatrick, Cella, Harper & Scinto, N.Y.C., 1981—. Mem. ABA, ASME, N.Y. State Bar Assn., Am. Intellectual Property Law Assn., Fed. Bar Coun. (trustee 1989-94), Fed. Cir. Bar Assn., N.Y. Intellectual Property Law Assn. Home: 19 Springdale Rd Scarsdale NY 10583-7330 Office: 30 Rockefeller Plz New York NY 10112-0002

BOSSIDY, LAWRENCE ARTHUR, industrial manufacturing executive; b. Pittsfield, Mass., Mar. 5, 1935; m. Nancy, 1956; children: Lynn, Larry, Paul, Pam, Nancy, Mary Jane, Lucy, Michael, Kathleen. BA in Econs., Colgate U. With Gen. Electric, 1957-91; chmn., CEO AlliedSignal Inc., Morristown, N.J., 1991—; vice chmn., dir. GE Investment Corp., GE Indsl. and Power systems, GE Lighting, GE Motors, GE Elec. Distbn. and Control, GE Can. Inc., GE Communications and Svcs., Ladd Petroleum Corp., GE Fin. Svcs. Inc., Employers Reinsurance Corp., Kidder Peabody; bd. dirs. Merck & Co., Inc., J.P. Morgan & Co. Inc., Champion Internat. Corp. Mem. Bus. Roundtable, Bus. Coun., Elfun. Roman Catholic. Office: AlliedSignal Inc 101 Columbia Rd Morristown NJ 07962*

BOSSMAN, DAVID A., trade association administrator. Pres.-treas. Am. Feed Industry Assn., Arlington, Va., 1992—. Mem. Internat. Feed Industry Fedn. (v.p.), Latin Am. Balanced Feed Assn. (bd. dirs.), Animal Industry Found. (sec. treas.), Nat. Risk Retention Assn. (past chmn.). Office: Am. Feed Industry Assn 1501 Wilson Blvd Ste 1100 Arlington VA 22209-2403*

BOST, JOHN ROWAN, retired manufacturing executive, engineer; b. Spartanburg, S.C., May 9, 1922; s. John Rowan and May Netta (Swink) Bost-McDaniel; m. Martha Angela Simmons, June 8, 1963; children: John Rowan III, Warren Vincent. Aircraft fabrication grad., Anderson Airplane Sch., 1941-42; student spl. courses, USN, 1942-60. Assembler, leadman Goodyear Aircraft, Akron, Ohio, 1942; aviation chief metalsmith USN, 1942-46; v.p., sec., supt. Greenwood (S.C.) Meml. Gardens, 1950-56; owner, pres., engr. B & H Industries, Laurens, S.C., 1959-62; engr. The Torrington Co., Clinton, S.C., 1961-75; engr. and developer Byars Machine Co., Laurens, S.C., 1979-86; pres., engr. Downey Bost Corp., Fountain Inn, S.C., 1986-94; ret., 1994; owner, organizer NIFTI Industries Corp., Laurens, 1994-96; instr. Greenville (S.C.) Tech. Coll., 1962-82; instr. numerous cos., 1962—. Inventor and patentee in field. Baptist. Home: PO Box 902 Laurens SC 29360-0902 Office: NIFTI Industries Corp PO Box 902 Laurens SC 29360-0902

BOST, RAYMOND MORRIS, retired college president; b. Maiden, N.C., Aug. 18, 1925; s. Loy Robert and Virginia (Anderson) B.; m. Margaret Martha Vedder, Aug. 16, 1947; children: Timothy Lee, Penelope Ruth, Peter Raymond, Jonathan Otto. AB, Lenoir-Rhyne Coll., Hickory, N.C., 1949, D.D. (hon.), 1976; B.D., Luth. Theol. So. Sem., 1952; M.A., Yale U., 1959, Ph.D., 1963. Ordained to ministry Luth. Ch., 1952; pastor in Spartanburg, S.C., 1952-53, Raleigh, N.C., 1953-57; prof. ch. history, dir. field work Luth. Theol. So. Sem., 1960-66; acad. dean Lenoir-Rhyne Coll., Hickory, 1966-68, pres., 1968-76; pres. Luth. Theol. Sem., Phila., 1976-85; synod historian N.C. Synod, Luth. Ch. in Am., 1985-87; v.p. acad. affairs Newberry (S.C.) Coll., 1987, dean, 1988-89; dir. Ctr. Ethical Devel., Newberry Coll., 1990-92, pres., 1992-95; pres. emeritus, 1995—; contact min. Nat. Luth. Coun., N.C. State U., 1953-57, Yale U., 1957-59; part-time instr. sociology Columbia Coll., 1962-65; mem. Com. to Implement Refugee Act, 1953; mem. bd. theol. edn. Luth. Ch. Am., 1969-70, mem. standing com. on approaches to unity, 1971-72, del. convs., 1970-76, mem. bd. publs., 1976-84, v.p., 1983-84; pres. Ind. Coll. Fund N.C., 1974-75; v.p. commn. on future Luth. Ednl. Conf. N.Am., 1972-75; trustee Luth. Theol. So. Sem., 1969-76, 98—, sec. bd., 1975-76; sec. N.C. Found. Ch. Related Colls., 1969-71; adv. coun. Ctr. on Religion in the South, Luth. Theol. So. Sem., 1989—, mem. S.C. Tuition Grants Commn., 1993-95, chmn., 1994-95; vis. prof. Inst. Confucian Studies, Qufu (China) Tchrs. U., Shandong, 1993—; advisor Inst. Advanced Profl. Ethics, Jinan, Shandong, 1993—; chmn. archives com. region 9 Evang. Luth. Ch. in Am., 1991-95; interim pastor Christ's Luth. Ch., Stanley, N.C., 1998; bd. dirs. Ea. Cluster Luth. Theol. Seminaries, 1998—. Co-author: (with J.L. Norris) All One Body: The Story of the North Carolina Lutheran Synod, 1803-1993, 1994; contbg. author: A History of the Lutheran Church in South Carolina, 1971, Essays and Reports of Lutheran Historical Conference, Vol. 5, 1977, Vol. 9, 1980, editor vol. 16, 1994; contbr. A Truly Efficient School of Theology, 1981, Luth. Quar., 1988, 89. Pres. bd. dirs. James R. Crumley Jr. Archives, 1995-96. Luth. Brotherhood Sem. Grad. scholar, 1957-58; Martin Luther fellow Nat. Luth. Ednl. Conf., 1959; faculty fellow Am. Assn. Theol. Schs., 1959-60. Mem. So. Hist. Assn., Luth. Hist. Conf. (bd. dirs. 1994—, v.p. 1998—), Am. Soc. Ch. History, Rotary (bd. dirs. Newberry 1990-92, 95-96, treas. 1992, 95-96).

BOST, THOMAS GLEN, lawyer; b. Oklahoma City, July 13, 1942; s. Burl John and Lorene Bell (Croka) B.; m. Sheila K. Pettigrew, Aug. 27, 1966; children: Amy Elizabeth, Stephen Luke, Emily Anne, Paul Alexander. BS in Acctg. summa cum laude, Abilene Christian U., 1964; JD, Vanderbilt U., 1967. Bar: Tenn. 1967, Calif. 1969. Instr. David Lipscomb Coll., Nashville, 1967; asst. prof. law Vanderbilt U., Nashville, 1967-68; ptnr. Latham & Watkins, Los Angeles, 1968—; lectr. on taxation subjects. Chmn. bd. regents, law sch. bd. visitors Pepperdine U., Malibu, Calif., 1980—. Mem. ABA (chmn. standards of tax practice com., sec. taxation 1988-90), State Bar of Calif., Los Angeles County Bar Assn. (chmn. taxation sect. 1981-82). Republican. Mem. Ch. of Christ. Club: Calif. (Los Angeles).

BOSTED, DOROTHY STACK, public relations executive; b. Newark, Apr. 6, 1953; d. Richard Joseph and Dorothy Marie (Irvin) Stack; m. Kenneth James Bosted, Aug. 22, 1976; 1 child, Danielle Whitney. Student, Lyndon State Coll., 1971-73; BA, NYU, 1975. Reporter The Daily Advance, Succasunna, N.J., 1974-75; producer, tech. intern Manhattan Cable TV, N.Y.C., 1975; editorial asst. Calif. Sch. Employees Assn., San Jose, 1975-76; news dir., anchor UA-Columbia Cablevision, Oakland, N.J., 1977-79; dir. pub. relations Overlook Hosp., Summit, N.J., 1981-84; pres. Dorothy Bosted Pub. Relations, Harding Twp., N.J., 1984-86; dir. pub. relations, communications Middlesex County Coll., Edison, N.J., 1986-88; mgr. corp. communications Hoechst Celanese Corp., Bridgewater, N.J., 1988-89; ptnr. Bosted-Burton Assocs., Coral Springs, Fla., 1986—; cons. Coral Springs, 1986—. Co-author: Writing with Impact, 1986; contbr. articles to N.Y. Times, various mags. Seminar leader Kinnelon (N.J.) Enrichment Program, 1978; trustee Middlesex County Coll. Found., Edison, 1986-88; bd. dirs. Middlesex County Coll. Alumni Assn., 1986-88. Recipient News Program ACE award Nat. Cable TV Assn., 1979, Spectrum of Talent merit award Internat. Assn. Bus. Communicators, 1982, Percy award N.J. Hosp. Mktg. and Pub. Relations Assn., 1982, 84, Tribute to Women and Industry award YWCA, Ridgewood, N.J., 1979; Mennen Co. scholar, 1971, Neighborhood House scholar, 1971, KP scholar, 1971. Mem. Tribute to Women and Industry Mgmt. Forum (v.p. pub. rels. Ridgewood chpt. 1986-87, bd. dirs. cen. N.J. chpt. 1989-91), Pub. Rels. Soc. Am. (editor N.J. chpt. newsletter 1987-89, bd. dirs. N.J. chpt. 1989-91). Home: 8738 NW 19th Dr Coral Springs FL 33071-6155

BOSTER, DAVIS EUGENE, retired ambassador; b. Rio Grande, Ohio, Sept. 14, 1920; s. Ernest Gordon and Nelle (Davis) B.; m. Mary Elizabeth Shilts (div. 1942), m. Constanza Helena Gamero, 1978; children: Davis, Janis, James, Thomas, Barbara, Valerie. A.B., Mt. Union Coll., 1942, LLD, 1977. Newspaper reporter Canton Repository, 1939-42; polit. officer U.S. Embassy, Moscow, 1947-49; fgn. affairs specialist U.S. Dept. State, 1949-54; polit. officer U.S. Embassy, Bonn, Germany, 1954-58; staff asst. Sec. State, Washington, 1958-59; officer in charge Soviet Union Polit. Affairs State Dept., 1959-61; officer in charge of USSR bilateral affairs Sec. State, Washington, 1961-62; polit. officer U.S. Embassy, Mexico City, 1962-63; spl. asst. Asst. Sec. Inter-Am. Affairs U.S. Dept. State, 1964-65, spl. asst. to Under Sec. Econ. Affairs, 1965; polit. counselor U.S. Embassy, Moscow, 1965-67; dept. chief misson U.S. Embassy, Kathmandu, Nepal, 1967-70, Warsaw, Poland, 1970-73; head U.S. Del. European Security Conf., Geneva, Switzerland, 1973-74; U.S. amb. Bangladesh and India, 1974-76, Guatemala, 1976-78; dir. Radio Liberty, Munich, Germany, 1979-80; internat. rels. officer U.S. Dept. State, 1980-81; active in Japanese Peace Conf., San Francisco, 1951. With USN, 1942-47, ret. comdr. USNR. Home: 1600 N Oak St Apt 912 Arlington VA 22209-2755

BOSTIAN, HARRY EDWARD, chemical engineer; b. Lewisburg, Pa., Jan. 16, 1933; s. Harry Edward Sr. and Florence Anne (Musser) B.; m. Marion E. Maurer, July 30, 1955. BS, Bucknell U., 1954; M in Chem. Engring., Rensselaer Poly. Inst., 1956; PhD, Iowa State U., 1959. Asst. prof. U. N.H., Durham, 1959-61; engr. Exxon Research, Baton Rouge and Florham Park, N.J., 1961-65; assoc. prof. U. Miss., Oxford, 1965-70; sr. chem. engr., rsch. program mgr. U.S. EPA, Cin., 1970-94; chem. and environ. engring. cons., 1994—; cons., reviewer environ. topics, 1975—; mem. task forces, mem. work groups on environ. control and regulation U.S. EPA and Water Environ. Fedn., 1987-94. Mem. editl. bd. Process Safety and Environ. Protection, Transactions of Inst. Chem. Engrs., Eng., Part B, 1990-94; contbr. articles to profl. jours., meetings and symposia. NSF grantee, 1969-70, U.S. Dept. Agr. grantee, 1969-70. Mem. AAAS, Am. Inst. Chem. Engrs., Sigma Xi, Tau Beta Pi, Alpha Chi Sigma. Home and Office: 6001 Bagdad Dr Cincinnati OH 45230-1302

BOSTICK, BETTY JANE, retired elementary education educator; b. Groesbeck, Tex., Aug. 13, 1926; d. Guy Hamilton and Wilhelmina Irene (Odell) Bond; m. Raymond Harrison Bostick, July 24, 1954; children: Betsy Bond Hime, Becky Bolling Liljenwall, Barbara Brandon Walther. BA, So. Meth. U., 1946, MA, 1950. Permanent h.s. tchg. cert. Tchr. William Lipscomb Elem. Sch. Dallas Ind. Sch. Dist., 1946-50; tchr. Sul Ross Elem. Sch. Waco (Tex.) Ind. Sch. Dist., 1951-55; tchr. Pittsburg (Tex.) Elem. Sch. Pittsburg Ind. Sch. Dist., 1955-56; tchr. Robert Wilson Elem. Sch. Corpus Christi (Tex.) Ind. Sch. Dist., 1956-59; tchr. Howard Elem. Sch. Alamo Heights Ind. Sch. Dist., San Antonio, 1959-87. Author: (books) Bond Family History, 1958, Groesbeck High School Class of '43 Yearbook, 1993. Mem. Alamo City Rep. Women, San Antonio, 1996—. Recipient Yellow Rose of Tex. award Gov. William Clements, 1991, Servant Leadership award S.W. Tex. Conf., United Meth. Ch., 1997. Mem. DAR (geneal. records com. 1997-98), Soc. Descendants of Washington's Army at Valley Forge (10-Yr. Membership award 1995), Daus. of Colonial Dames 17th Century (rec. sec. pub. rels. com. 1997-99), Daus. of Republic of Tex. (membership com. 1997-98), Daus. Colonial Dames of Am., Jamestowne Soc. (chaplain 1997-99), Magna Charta (publicity com. 1998-2000), Meadowood Garden Club (former pres. 1989), Chi Omega (alumnae historian 1960—, Alumnae Svc. award 1995). Republican. Methodist. Avocations: bird watching, genealogy, bridge, Bible study, grandchildren. Fax: (210) 826-1805. E-mail: rbostick@swbell.net. Home: 6914 Scotsdale Dr San Antonio TX 78209-4275

BOSTICK, CHARLES DENT, lawyer, educator; b. Gainesville, Ga., Dec. 28, 1931; s. Jared Sullivan and Charlotte Catherine (Dent) B.; m. Susan Oliver, Sept. 8, 1956; children: Susan, Alan. Cert. spl. edn. tchr., Emory-at-Oxford U., 1948-49; BA, Mercer U., 1952, JD, 1958. Bar: Ga. 1957, Tenn. 1974, U.S. Dist. Ct. (no. dist.) Ga. 1958, U.S. Ct. Appeals (5th cir.) 1959. Individual practice law Gainesville, Ga., 1958-66; asst. prof. law U. Fla., Gainesville, 1966-68, assoc. prof., 1968; assoc. prof. Vanderbilt U., Nashville, 1968-71, prof., 1971—, assoc. dean, dir. admissions, 1975-79, acting dean, 1979-80, dean, 1980-85; retired, 1992; vis. prof. law U. Leeds, Eng., 1985-86, prof. law emeritus, dean emeritus Sch. Law, 1992. Served to lt. USNR, 1952-55. Mem. Tenn. Bar. Assn. Episcopalian. Office: Vanderbilt U Sch Law 21st Ave S Nashville TN 37240

BOSTICK, CURTIS VAN, history educator; b. Amarillo, Tex., Dec. 21, 1955; s. T Van Dyke and Francies Ann (Giles) B.; m. Debra Gwen Grove, Mar. 7, 1980; children: Andreah, Rebecca, Sean, Scot. BA, Wayland Bapt. U., 1978; MA, Auburn (Ala.) U., 1983; PhD, U. Ariz., 1993. Asst. prof. history Dept. Social Scis., So. Utah U., Cedar City. Author: The Antichrist and the Lollards: Apocalypticism in Late Medieval and Reformation England, 1998. Fulbright grant U.S. Ednl. Commn., 1990-91. Fax: 435-865-8193. E-mail: bostick@suu.edu. Office: Dept Social Scis Centrum Bldg So Utah Univ Cedar City UT 84720

BOSTIN, MARVIN JAY, hospital and health services consultant; b. Toronto, Ont., Can., July 3, 1933; s. Samuel and Rose (Mandel) B.; came to U.S., 1956; BS, U. Toronto, 1955; MS in Hosp. Adminstrn., Columbia U., 1958; PhD in Pub. Adminstrn. (Gottlieb Meml. scholar), N.Y.U., 1972; 1 child, Shepard Craig. Pharmacist, New Mount Sinai Hosp., Toronto, 1953-56; asst. adminstr. L.I. Jewish Hosp., New Hyde Park, N.Y., 1958-62; assoc. dir. Mt. Sinai Med. Ctr., Miami Beach, Fla., 1962-65; exec. v.p. E.D. Rosenfeld Assos. Inc., hosp. and health svcs. cons. White Plains, N.Y., 1965-78; pres. M. Bostin Assos., Inc., White Plains, N.Y., 1979—; guest scholar Brookings Instn., Washington, 1965; lectr. Sch. of Pub. Health and Adminstrv. Medicine, Columbia U., N.Y.C., 1965-78, Grad. Sch. of Pub. Adminstrn., N.Y.C., 1967; lectr. Grad. Sch. of Architecture and Planning, Columbia U., N.Y.C., 1975-78; cons. to Bur. of Hearings and Appeals, Social Security Adminstrn., HEW, 1967-68, task force on guidelines for constrn. and equipment hosp. and med. facilities USPHS, DHHS, 1987; mem. implementation work group on improving health, Nat. Commn. Children, 1992; spl. cons. to Office of Equal Health Opportunity, Office of Surgeon Gen., USPHS, 1966-67. Mem. Dade County (Fla.) Welfare Planning Coun., Miami, 1962-65; bd. dirs. South Fla. Hosp. Coun., Miami, 1963-65. Fellow Royal Soc. Health (London), Am. Pub. Health Assn., Am. Assn. Healthcare Consultants (chmn. monograph series com. 1970-71, exec. com. 1972-75, profl. standards com. 1974-76), mem. Am. Hosp. Assn., Forum for Health Care Planning (dir. 1982-95, treas. 1988-89, sec. 1989-90), Am. Coll. Healthcare Execs., AIA (mem. acad. on architecture for health 1974—), Can. Coll. Health Svc. Execs. (fgn. affiliate), Internat. Hosp. Fedn. Address: M Bostin Assoc Inc 106 Corporate Park Dr Ste 413 White Plains NY 10604-3818

BOSTLEY, JEAN REGINA, nun, library association administrator; b. Greenfield, Mass., Sept. 26, 1940. BA, Our Lady of the Elms Coll., 1970; MLS, SUNY, Albany, 1974. Joined Sisters of St. Joseph, Roman Cath. Ch., Springfield, Mass., 1958. Tchr. Sacred Heart Acad., Worcester, Mass., 1961-63; tchr., libr. St. Thomas the Apostle Sch., West Springfield, Mass., 1963-69; libr. St. Joseph Ctrl. H.S., Pittsfield, Mass., 1969-97; exec. dir. Cath. Libr. Assn., Pittsfield, 1995—. Editor, contbr. Cath. Libr. World, 1980—, chair editl. com., 1985-89; com. mem. Cath. Periodical and Lit. Index, 1991—. Vol. Bershire County Chpt. ARC, Pittsfield, Mass., 1970— (25 Yr. Svc. award 1995). Mem. ALA, Cath. Libr. Assn. (sec. New England chpt. 1977-81, v.p. 1987-89, pres. 1989-91, past pres. 1991-93, mem. nat. exec. bd. 1985-91, v.p. 1993-95, pres. 1995-97, mem. membership devel. com. 1981-85, vice chair h.s. libr. sect. 1978-81, chair sect. 1981-83). Fax: 413-442-2252. Office: Cath Libr Assn 100 North St Ste 224 Pittsfield MA 01201-5109

BOSTOCK, ROY JACKSON, advertising agency executive; b. Glen Ridge, N.J., Sept. 25, 1940; s. James Franklin Bostock and Jane (Ritter) Bostock Addis; m. Merilee Huser, 1962; children—Victoria, Matthew, Kate. A.B., Duke U., 1962; M.B.A., Harvard U., 1964. Asst. account exec. Benton & Bowles, N.Y.C., 1964-66, account exec., 1966-68, account supr., v.p., 1968-70, sr. v.p., from 1970, group exec., 1976-81, exec. v.p., gen. mgr., 1981-84; pres. Benton & Bowles, Inc., N.Y.C., 1984-85; pres. D'Arcy Masius Benton & Bowles, Inc., N.Y.C., 1985-88, pres., COO, 1988-89, pres., CEO, from 1989, chmn., CEO, 1990-96; chmn., CEO MacManus Group, N.Y.C., 1996—. Mem. Am. Assn. Advt. Agys., Phi Beta Kappa. Republican. Presbyterian. Clubs: Apawamis (Rye, N.Y.); Manursing Island (Rye) (pres. 1983-85); Racquet & Tennis (N.Y.C.). Home: S Manursing Island Rye NY 10580 Office: MacManus Group 1675 Broadway Fl 2R New York NY 10019-5820*

BOSTON, BETTY LEE, financial consultant, financial planner; b. Agana, Guam, Dec. 21, 1935; d. Homer Laurence and Bessie Margarete (Leech) Litzenberg; m. Filibert Roth Boston, Aug. 12, 1956; children: William Litzenberg, Beth Boston Tedesco, Brent Litzenberg. BA, U. Mich., 1958. CFP. Stockbroker I.M. Simon & Co., Murray, Ky., 1976-78, 1st of Mich. Corp., Murray, 1978-86; fin. cons. J.J.B. Hilliard, W.L. Lyons, Inc., Murray, 1986—; instr. adult edn. investment classes Murray State U., 1977—; investment commentator Sta. WKMS, Murray, 1987—. Investment columnist Purchase Area Bus. Jour., 1989-90. Chmn. Inter-Faith Coalition Congregations, Ann Arbor, 1971-73; pres. Need Line Ch. and Cmty. Ministry, Murray, 1981-83; mem. Murray regional bd. Ky. Coun. on Econ. Edn., 1987—. Recipient Woman of Yr. award Murray Bus. and Profl. Women, 1988. Mem. AAUW (treas. Murray br. 1982-87, pres. 1991-97), Rotary (sec. Murray club 1990-95, pres. 1998-99, Paul Harris fellow). United Methodist. Home: 917 N 16th St Murray KY 42071-1523 Office: JJB Hilliard WL Lyons Inc 414 Main St Murray KY 42071-2059

BOSTON, BILLIE, costume designer, costume history educator; b. Oklahoma City, Sept. 22, 1939; d. William Barrett and Margaret Emeline (Townsend) Long; m. William Clayton Boston, Jr., Jan. 20, 1962; children: Kathryn Gray, William Clayton III. BFA, U. Okla., 1961, MFA, 1962. Asst. to designer Karinski of N.Y., N.Y.C., 1966-67; prof. costume history Oklahoma City U., 1987—; rep. Arts Coun., Oklahoma City, 1987-90, Arts Festival, Oklahoma City, 1972-80; dir. ETC Theater, Oklahoma City SW Coll., 1979-83; actress Lyric Theatre, Oklahoma City, 1979-81; designer Casa Mahara Theatre, Ft. Worth, summer 1998. Exhibited in group shows at Taos, N.Mex., Santa Fe; represented in permanent collections in Dallas, Taos, Santa Fe, Tulsa, N.Y.C., La Jolla; costume designer Ballet Okla., Oklahoma City, 1979-84, Agnes DeMillie's Rodeo Ballet Okla., 1982, Royal Ballet Flanders, 1983, Pitts. Ballet, 1983, BBC's Childrens Prodn., 1984, 86, Lyric Theatre, Oklahoma City, 1987-95, Red Oak Music Theatre, Lakewood, N.J., 1988, Winter Olympics, 1988, Miss Am. Pageant, 1988, for JoAnne Worley in Hello Dolly, San Francisco Opera Circus, 1991, Jupiter (Fla.) Theatre, 1991-92, Mobile (Ala.) Light Opera, 1992, The Boy Friend, Temple U., Japan, 1995, The Sound of Music, Lyric Stage, Dallas, 1995, Annie Get Your Gun, Guys and Dolls with Vic Damone, 1995, Westbury Flash Valley Forge Music Fair, Oklahoma and Sound of Music, Casa Manana, Theatre, Ft. Worth, 1997, Singing in the Rain, Lone Star Theatre, Galveston, Tex., 1997, Most Happy Fellow, Lyric Stage Dallas, 1997, To Gillian on her 37th Birthday, Watertower Theatre, Dallas, 1998, Carousel, Annie Get Your Gun, Cinderella, Casa Manana, 1998. Rep. Speakers Bur. Oklahoma City for Ballet, 1979-85; judge State Hist. Speech Tournament, Oklahoma City, 1985-87; chmn. State of Okla. Conf. on Tchr./Student Relationships, Oklahoma City, 1981. Recipient Gov.'s Achievement award, 1988, Lady in the News award, 1987. Mem. Alpha Chi Omega (house corp. bd. 1986-90). Methodist. Avocation: watercolorist. Home: 1701 Camden Way Oklahoma City OK 73116-5121

BOSTON, GRETHA, mezzo-soprano, actress; b. Crossett, AK. B of Music, N Tex. State U., Denton; vocal study with vocal tech. and coaches, John Wustman, Neal Goren. Carnegie Hall debut, Mozart's Coronation Mass, 1991; concert performances include Beethoven's Ninth Symphony (Carnegie Hall), Handel's Messiah (Madison, WI & Arlington, TX), Bach's Magnificat & Vivaldi's Gloria (Dallas, TX), Durufle's Requiem (Champaign, IL) and appearances at the Cathedral of the Divine in Santa Barbara and the St. Louis Conservatory of Music; operatic roles include: Carmen in Bizet's Carmen, Lola in Mascagni's Cavalleria Rusticana (Westchester Lyric Fest), The Mother in Menotti's The Consul, Ciesca in Puccini's Gianni Schicchi, Delilah in Saint-Saens's Samson et Delilah, Maddalena in Verdi's Rigoletto (N.Y. Grand Opera), Amneris in Verdi's Aida (N.Y. Grand Opera), Azucena in Verdi's Il Trovatore, Queenie in Kern & Hammerstein's Show Boat (Tony award Best Supporting Actress in a Musical 1995), Maria & Strawberry Woman in Gershwin's Porgy and Bess, 1993. 3rd place D'Angelo Young Artist Internat. Competition. Address: care Von Reis Artists Mgmt 295 S Birdshill Loop Portland OR 97219*

BOSTON, HOLLIS BUFORD, JR., retired military officer; b. Athens, Ala., Sept. 29, 1930; s. Hollis Buford Sr. and Opie (Hargrove) B.; m. Nancy Thomas Delbridge, Dec. 27, 1955; children: Elizabeth Lynn Boston Chesnutt, James Warren, John David. BBA, Baylor U., 1958; M Polit. Sci., Auburn U., 1972. Commd. 2d lt. USAF, 1953, advanced through grades to col., 1972, ret., 1975; sr. assoc. Program Control Corp., Van Nuys, Calif., 1977-89. Author: Estate Papers of Jones Boston, 1995. Chmn. planning com. City of Montgomery, Ala., 1983; pres. Capital City Kiwanis Club, Montgomery, 1987. Mem. Natchez Trace Geneal. Soc., Smith County Tenn. Hist. Assn., Sons of the Republic of Tex., First Families Ala., Sigma Alpha Epsilon. Republican. Episcopalian. Avocations: historical research and writing. Home: 2341 Wentworth Dr Montgomery AL 36106-3253

BOSTON, WALLACE ELLSWORTH, JR., healthcare executive, financial consultant; b. Salisbury, Md., May 28, 1954; s. Wallace Ellsworth Sr. and Barbara Ellen (Widdowson) B.; m. Sharon K. Ochs, May 25, 1991. AB, Duke U., 1975; MBA, Tulane U., 1978. CPA, Md. Mktg. trainee John Deere Indsl. Equipment Co., Moline, Ill., 1978; acct. Price Waterhouse, Balt., 1978-80, sr. cons., 1980-83, mgr. cons., 1983; v.p. fin., chief fin. officer Nat. Realty Services, Inc., Vienna, Va., 1984-85, sr. v.p syndications, 1985-

86; v.p. fin. Meridian Healthcare, Towson, Md., 1986-90, v.p. bus. devel., 1991-92; also bd. dirs. Meridian Healthcare; v.p. fin. Manor HealthCare Corp., Silver Spring, Md., 1993-96; sr. v.p. acquisitions devel. ManorCare Health Svcs., Gaithersburg, Md., 1996-98; exec. v.p., COO NeighborCare, Inc., Balt., 1998—; bd. visitors Montebello Rehab. Hosp., Balt., 1988-96; bd. trustees McDonogh Sch., Balt., 1990—. Contbr. articles to profl. jours. Fellow Healthcare Fin. Mgmt. Assn.; mem. AICPA, Md. Assn. CPAs (mem. mgmt. adv. services com. 1980-84, mem. industry com. 1988-89), Inst. Mgmt. Acctg., Fin. Execs. Inst., McDonogh Sch. Alumni Assn. (pres. 1986), Duke Univ. Alumni Assn. (pres. Balt. chpt. 1983-84). Republican. Methodist. Clubs: Balt. Country, Ctr. (Balt.). Avocations: squash, golf, photography, bowling. Home: 3189 River Valley Chase West Friendship MD 21794 Office: NeighborCare Incare 7 E Lee St Baltimore MD 21202

BOSTON, WILLIAM CLAYTON, lawyer; b. Hobart, Okla., Nov. 29, 1934; s. William Clayton and Dollie Jane (Gibbs) B.; m. Billie Gail Long, Jan. 20, 1962; children: Kathryn Gray, William Clayton III. BS, Okla. State U., 1958; LLB, U. Okla., 1961; LLM, NYU, 1967. Bar: Okla. 1961. Assoc. Mosteller, Fellers, Andrews, Snider & Baggett, Oklahoma City, 1962-64; ptnr. Fellers, Snider, Baggett, Blankenship & Boston, Oklahoma City, 1968-69, Andrews, Davis, Legg, Bixler, Milsten & Murrah, Oklahoma City, 1972-86; pvt. practice, Oklahoma City, 1986—. Contbr. articles to profl. jours.; mem. adv. bd. The Jour. of Air Law and Commerce, 1995—. Past pres. and trustee Ballet Okla.; past v.p., bd. dirs. Oklahoma City Arts Coun.; past trustee Nichols Hills (Okla.) Methodist Ch.; past trustee, chmn. Okla. Found. for the Humanities; past trustee, vice-chmn., sec. Humanites in Okla., Inc., 1992-95. With U.S. Army, 1954-56. Mem. ABA (former chmn. subcom. on aircraft fin., former chmn. aircraft fin. and contract divsn. forum on air and space law), FBA, Internat. Bar Assn., Inter-Pacific Bar Assn., Okla. State Bar Assn., Oklahoma County Bar Assn. Home: 1701 Camden Way Oklahoma City OK 73116-5121 Office: 4005 NW Expressway St Oklahoma City OK 73116-1691

BOSTWICK, BARRY, actor; b. San Mateo, Calif., Feb. 24, 1945; s. Henry and Betty Bostwick. B.A., Calif. Western U. Made Broadway debut in Cock-a-Doodle Dandy; other theater appearances in Colette, Grease, The Robber Bridegroom (Tony award 1977), They Knew What They Wanted, Nick and Nora, 1991; TV movies include The Chadwick Family, 1974, The Quinns, 1977, Murder by Natural Causes, 1979, Once Upon a Family, 1980, Moviola: The Silent Lovers, 1980, Red Flag, 1981, Summer Girl, 1983, An Uncommon Love, 1983, Deceptions, 1985, Betrayed By Innocence, 1986, Body of Evidence, 1988, Addicted to His Love, 1988, Parent Trap III, 1989, Challenger, 1990, Captive, 1991, Between Love and Hate, 1993, Praying Mantis, 1993, Danielle Steele's Once in a Lifetime, 1994; TV miniseries include Scruples, 1980, George Washington, 1984, A Woman of Substance, 1984, George Washington: The Forging of a Nation, 1986, I'll Take Manhattan, 1987, War and Rememberance, 1989; TV series: Foul Play, 1981, Dads, 1986-87, Spin City, 1996; TV movies include The Return of Hunter: Everyone Walks in L.A., 1995; films include The Rocky Horror Picture Show, 1975, Movie Movie, 1979, Megaforce, 1982, Weekend at Bernie's II, 1993, The Secretary, 1995, Project Metalblast, 1995, The Secret Agent Club, 1996, Spy Hard, 1996, 919 Fifth Avenue, 1995, One Hot Summer Night, 1998, Men In White, 1998; TV guest appearances include Charlie's Angels, 1976, The Hitchhiker, 1983, The Golden Palace, 1992, High Society, 1995. Office: The Gersh Agy 232 N Canon Dr Beverly Hills CA 90210*

BOSTWICK, RANDELL A., retired retail food company executive; b. Niles, Ohio, Oct. 24, 1922; s. Clifton A. and May (Lloyd) B.; m. Jane Elizabeth Foster, Aug. 28, 1948; children: Suzanne Elizabeth, Anne, Randell A. Ed., U. Mich., Westminster Coll. Asst. traffic mgr. A&P, Youngstown, Ohio, 1948-50; asst. to div. traffic mgr. A&P, Pitts., 1952-58; div. traffic mgr. A&P, 1958-60, dir. ops., 1960-69, asst. to nat. dir. ops. N.Y. hdqrs., 1969-75; pres. subs. Super Market Service Corp., Montvale, N.J., 1975-88; corp. v.p. The Gt. A & P Tea Co., 1981-88; chmn. Supermarket Service Corp., 1988-91, ret., 1992. Served to capt. Med. Service Corps U.S. Army, 1943-46, 50-52. Presbyterian. Home: 39 Dale Dr Summit NJ 07901-3104

BOSTWICK, RICHARD RAYMOND, retired lawyer; b. Billings, Mont., Mar. 17, 1918; s. Leslie H. and Maude (Worthington) B.; m. Margaret Florence Brooks, Jan. 17, 1944; children: Michael, Patricia, Ed, Dick. Student, U. Colo., 1937-38; A.B., U. Wyo., 1943, J.D., 1947. Bar: Wyo. 1947. Claim atty. Hawkeye Casualty Co., Casper, Wyo., 1948-49; ptnr. Murane & Bostwick, Casper, 1949-91; ret., 1991; lectr. U. Wyo. Coll. Law. Contbr. articles profl. jours. Past trustee Casper YMCA; dep. dir. Civil Def., 1954-58; chmn. local SSS, 1952-70; mem. curriculum coordinating com. Natrona Co. Sch. Dist. 2, High Sch. Dist.; Wyom. rep. adv. com. U.S. Tenth Circuit Ct. Appeals, 1985-87; mem. U. Wyo. Coll. Law Adv. Com., 1987-91. Capt. AUS, 1943-46. Decorated Bronze Star medal; recipient Silver Merit awards Am. Legion. Mem. ABA (Harrison Tweed award 1968), Am. Coll. Trial Lawyers, Wyo. Bar Assn. (pres. 1964-65, 1st Pro Bono award 1987), Natrona County Bar Assn. (pres. 1956), Am. Judicature Soc. (exec. com. 1973-75, sec. 1975-77 Herbert Harley award), Internat. Assn. Def. Counsel, Fedn. Ins. and Corp. Counsel, Nat. Conf. Bar Pres. (exec. council 1970-72), Internat. Soc. of Barristers (dir. 1971-76, pres. 1975), Am. Legion (dir. 1951-58, post comdr. 1953-54), Wyo. Alumni Assn. (trustee 1955-57), Casper C. of C. (chmn. legis. com. 1955-57, dir. 1959-62, v.p.). Presbyterian. Lodges: Masons, Shriners, KT. Home: 1137 Granada Ave Casper WY 82601-5932 *I was fortunate enough to select a profession which I find I have liked from the beginning and with which I am still fascinated. This makes it easy to work hard and to maintain a high standard of pride in the profession and to donate and devote time to the upgrading of it over and above daily routine. To be able to work hard, to create a job well done, and to experience satisfaction over and above the mere elements of a livelihood is a goal worthy of effort.*

BOSTWICK, ROBERT O., municipal staff member; b. Mobile, Ala., Apr. 9, 1946. B, U. South Ala., 1967. Supr. Texaco Oil, Mobile, 1979-83; v.p. Midtown Restaurant Corp., Mobile, 1983-85; v.p., CEO, Signs Now, Mobile, 1985-87; v.p., dir. franchising CHECKERS Drive-In Restaurants, Mobile, 1987-89; exec. asst. to mayor Mobile, 1989—. Office: Office of the Mayor Govt Plaza 205 Government St Mobile AL 36633-1827

BOSTWICK, TODD WILLIAM, city archaeologist; b. Seattle, Dec. 18, 1952; s. Michael and Roxie Marilynn (Byers) B.; m. Heidi Bostwick. BA, U. Nev., Reno, 1979; MA, Ariz. State U., 1985. Rsch. asst. Nev. Archaeol. Survey, Reno, 1977; archaeol. technician U.S. Forest Svc., Plumas Nat. Forest, Calif., 1978; asst. crew chief Black Mesa project So. Ill. U., Carbondale, 1980-81; project dir. Northland Rsch., Inc., Flagstaff, Ariz., 1981-85; staff archaeologist, dept. anthropology Ariz. State U., Tempe, 1985-87; asst. city archaeologist City of Phoenix, 1987-90; city archaeologist City of Phoenix, Pueblo Grande Mus., 1990—; mem. adv. com. Deer Valley Rock Art Ctr., Phoenix, 1994—; mem. exec. com. Ariz. Archaeol. Coun., Phoenix, 1994-97, Ariz. Archeol. Council (pres., 1998-99). Co-author: First Street and Madison: Historical Archaeology of the Second and Phoenix Chinatown, 1992; co-editor, co-author 2 books; author articles. Bd. dirs. Ariz. Preservation Found., Phoenix, 1991-96, Pioneer Cemetery Assn., Phoenix, 1993—. With USAF, 1972-74. Recipient Gov.'s awards in hist. preservation State of Ariz., 1995, Spl. Recognition award State of Ariz., 1995, City Mgr.'s Excellence award City of Phoenix, 1996, others. Mem. Soc. for Am. Archaeology, Ariz. Archaeol. Soc., Ariz. Archaeol. and Hist. Soc., Sigma Xi. Democrat. Avocations: photography, hiking. Office: Pueblo Grande Mus 4619 E Washington St Phoenix AZ 85034-1909

BOSWELL, BILL REESER, religious organization executive; b. Cumby, Tex., Nov. 5, 1934; s. Thurman Festus and Nellie Gladys (Reeser) B.; m. Martha Raye Dawson, Feb. 23, 1958; children: Heather, Robin Boswell Music. BA, Barton Coll., Wilson, N.C., 1957; MDiv, Tex. Christian U., 1962, D Ministry, 1973. Ordained to ministry Christian Ch. (Disciples of Christ), 1957. Min. 1st Christian Ch., Brady, Tex., 1962-78; sr. min. 1st Christian Ch., Pampa, Tex., 1978-88; regional exec. min. Christian Ch. (Disciples of Christ) in La., Pineville, 1989—. Mem. Theta Phi. Avocations: music, blacksmithing, reading. Home: 6512 Melody Ln Pineville LA 71360-9713 Office: Christian Church (DOC) 3524 Holloway Prairie Rd Pineville LA 71360*

BOSWELL, DAN ALAN, health maintenance organization executive, health care consultant; b. Upland, Calif., July 25, 1947; s. Paul Leslie and Jana Delores (Thompson) B.; m. Lona Kathalene Bentley, Dec. 26, 1969; children: Bethanie Laurel, Daniel Alan II. Grad. in Mktg. and Sales Mgmt., UCLA. Mktg. dir. Maxicare Co., L.A., 1974-78; v.p. Gen. Med, Santa Ana, Calif., 1978-81; exec. v.p. IMC Health Maintenance Orgn., Miami, Fla., 1981-83, Protective Health Providers, San Diego, 1981-83; CEO U.S. Health Plan, San Diego, 1982-84; pres., CEO Serra Health Plan, Sun Valley, Calif., 1984-85, Amerimed (formerly Serra Health Plan), Burbank, Calif., 1985; pres. The Wellstarr Group, Inc., Upland, Calif., 1986-89, pres., CEO, 1990-93; pres., CEO Humantics Managed Care Corp., 1989-92; pres. The Garvey Group, Calif., Upland, 1993-97, Managed Care Specialists, Upland, 1993-97; nat. dir. corp. devel. Axiom Inc., Canoga Park, Calif., 1997-99; COO Internat. Dental Svc., Upland, 1999—; faculty fellow Nat. HMO George Washington U., 1982-83; tchg. asst. expert market devel., fed. rev. health maintenance qualification HHS, Rockville, Md., 1982-84. Mem. governing body Health-sys. Agy., San Diego and Imperial Counties, Calif., 1981-85, pres. trauma task force, San Diego, 1984; mem. adv. bd. Calif. Med. Asst. Commn., San Fernando Valley, 1986; dist. dir. Pony Baseball, Inc.; mgr. Upland Black Am. Legion Baseball, 1992-94. Mem. Am. Mgmt. Assn., Am. Mktg. Assn., Group Health Assn. Am., Marine Corps Assn. Am., El Prado Men's Club (Chino, Calif.; bd. dirs. 1985-86), Sierra Laverne Country Club, Towns Club (Pomona, Calif.). Republican. Avocations: golf, writing, cooking, camping, fishing, youth sports. Home: 851 Emerson St Upland CA 91784-1227 Office: Internat Dental Svc 188 N Central Ave Ste B Upland CA 91786

BOSWELL, GARY TAGGART, investor, former electronics company executive; b. Ft. Worth, Dec. 24, 1937; s. David W. and Marjory (Taggart) B.; m. Margaret Ruth Yelvington, Sept. 8, 1957 (dec. Jan. 1997); m. Tommie Jean Horn, Dec. 19, 1998; children: Michael David, Margaret McQuiston, Susannah Ruth. BA, Tex. Christian U., 1958, MS, 1965; postgrad., San Diego State Coll., 1960-61. Scientist U.S. Govt. White Sands (N.Mex.) Missile Range, 1958-59; rsch. engr. Gen. Dynamics, San Diego, 1959-60; programmer Bell Helicopter, Hurst, Tex., 1960-63; sect. head Collins Radio Co., Dallas, 1963-68; mgr. software devel. Tex. Instruments, Inc., Austin, 1968-72; mgr. ASC (Advanced Sci. Computer) Mktg., 1973-75, mgr. ASC divsn., 1975-76, mgr. computer sys., 1976-80, mgr. global positioning sys., 1980-81, mgr. TI engring. sys., 1981-83, v.p. equipment group, mr. intelligent sys. divsn., 1983-86; pres. Aydin Monitor Sys., Ft. Washington, Pa., 1987-88; pres. Aydin Computer and Monitor, Horsham, Pa., 1988-95, investor, 1995—; Mem. Am. Nat. Fortran Standards Com., 1970-74. Designer several Fortran Compliers. Winner Western Hemisphere Snipe championship, 1970, also other maj. regattas. Mem. Assn. Computing Machinery, Snipe Classs Internat. Racing Assn., White Rock Sailing Club. Home and Office: 107 Clubhouse Dr Lakeway TX 78734-4608

BOSWELL, G(EORGE) HARVEY, federal judge; b. 1947. BS, U. Tenn., 1969; JD, U. Memphis, 1979. Pvt. practice Milan, Tenn., 1980-83; atty. Kizer, Bonds, Boswell & Crocker, 1983-93; bankruptcy judge U.S. Bankruptcy Ct. (we. dist.), Tenn., 1993—. Fellow Tenn. Bar Found.; mem. Nat. Conf. Bankruptcy Judges, Am. Bankruptcy Inst., Tenn. Bar Assn. Office: US Bankruptcy Ct 111 S Highland Ste 324 Jackson TN 38301-6123

BOSWELL, GEORGE MARION, JR., orthopedist, health care facility administrator; b. Dallas, May 12, 1920; s. George Marion and Viola (Scarbrough) B.; m. Veta M. Fuller, Oct. 30, 1958; children: Brianna Boswell Brown, Kama Boswell Koudelka, Maia Boswell. BS, Tex. Tech U., 1940; MD, U. Tex., Southwestern Dallas, 1950. Diplomate Am. Acad. Orthopaedic Surgery. Intern Parkland Hosp., Dallas, 1950-51; resident gen. surgeryand orthopedic surgery Parkland, Baylor and Scottish Rite Hosps., Dallas, 1951-55; practice medicine specializing in orthopedics Dallas, 1955—; v.p. med. affairs Baylor Health Care System, Dallas, 1982-86; dir. orthopaedic clin. studies Baylor U. Med. Ctr., 1995—; owner Bee Aviation Inc., Dallas, 1968—, Boswell Realty Inc., Dallas, 1971—; lectr., cons. on health care delivery. Contbr. articles to profl. jours. Prof. George M. Boswell, Jr. chair in orthopaedic surgery named in his honor Baylor U. Med. Ctr. Fellow ACS; mem. AMA, Am. Acad. Orthopaedic Surgery (Key Man U.S. Congress 1980—), Am. Hosp. Assn., Tex. Hosp. Assn. (Key Man Tex. Legislature 1980—, council on hosp. staffs), Flying Physicians (pres. Tex. 1960-64). Republican. Methodist. Club: Cresent (Dallas). Avocations: flying, photography, fishing, saddle making. Home: 7249 Wabash Ave Dallas TX 75214-3535 Office: Baylor U Med Ctr Dept Orthopaedic Surgery 3500 Gaston Ave Dallas TX 75246-2017

BOSWELL, JAMES DOUGLAS, medical research executive; b. Tulsa, Feb. 12, 1942; m. Pamela Scott; children: Megan, Melanie. Student, U. Okla., 1960-61; B.A., U. Tulsa, 1964, M.A., 1966. Indsl. relations rep. Trans World Airlines, 1966-68; dir. placement Skelly Oil Co., 1968-72, mgr. employee and pub. relations, 1972-75, gen. mgr. adminstrn., 1975-77; corp. mgr. human resources Getty Oil Co., 1977-81; v.p. employee and pub. relations L.A. Times, 1981-91; CEO House Ear Inst., L.A., 1991—, trustee, 1995—; bd. dirs. Employers Group; pres. Skelly Oil Found., Tulsa, 1974-78, Getty Oil Co. Found., 1978-79. Bd. dirs. L.A. Boys and Girls Club, v.p., 1985; bd. dirs. L.A. Theatre Ctr., 1988-90, L.A. chpt. ARC; bd. dirs. L.A. Jr. Achievement, 1982-91, vice chmn. human resources, 1986; fellow Nat. Health Found., 1992, San Marino Cmty. Ch. Found., 1992-95; mem. Econ. Round Table, 1993, sec.-treas., 1995-96. Mem. Am. Soc. Personnel Adminstrn., Am. Psychol. Assn., Newspaper Personnel Relations Assn., Am. Newspaper Assn. (labor and personnel relations com. 1982-91). Avocations: tennis, skiing, golf. Home: 341 Palmetto Dr Pasadena CA 91105-1815 Office: House Ear Inst 2100 W 3rd St 5th Fl Los Angeles CA 90057-1922

BOSWELL, LARRY RAY, electronics company executive; b. Greencastle, Ind., Dec. 14, 1940; s. John Ernest and Thelma Ruth (Williams) B.; m. Sandra Jean Rains, Jan. 19, 1963; children: Tina Marie, Cynthia Kay, Brian Tad. BA, Ind. U., 1988; MBA, Marion Coll., 1990. Ordained to ministry Soc. of Friends, 1967. With R.R. Donnelly & Sons, Crawfordsville, Ind., 1962-65; analyst, researcher Delco Electronics, Kokomo, Ind., 1965—; minister Soc. of Friends Ch., West Middleton, Ind., 1967—. Contbr. articles to profl. jours. Bd. dirs. Love Haven Home, Jamestown, Tenn., 1972—, Pathway div. Ind. U., Kokomo, 1990—; mem. Pres.'s League of Underwriters Union Sem., Westfield, Ind., 1985—; internat. exchange coord. Education First, Boston, 1998—. Cooper fellow Earlham Sch. of Religion, 1994. Mem. Am. Philatelic Soc., Ind. Coun. Chs., Howard County Coun. Chs., No. Postal History Soc. (pres. 1976-84), Soc. Friends (mem. missionary bd. 1998—), Western Ind. Folklore Soc. (pres. 1980-84), Alpha Chi. Club: Quaker Men (pres. 1984—). Avocations: botanical research, study of war letters from 16th through 20th century. Home: 100 W 7971 S Fairmount IN 46928-1928 Office: Little Ridge Friends Church 1731 W 1050 S Fairmount IN 46928-9281

BOSWELL, LEONARD L., congressman; b. Harrison County, Mo., Jan. 10, 1934; s. Melvin and Margaret B.; m. Dody Boswell; 3 children. BA in Bus. Adminstrn., Graceland Coll. Commd. 2d lt. U.S. Army, 1957; advanced through grades to lt. col. U.S. Army, Vietnam, Germany, Portugal; mem. Iowa Senate, 1984-96, pres., 1993-97; mem. from 3d Iowa dist. 105th Congress, 1997—; grain and livestock farmer Decatur County, 1976—. Past pres., bd. dirs. local Coop. Elevator, Lamoni. Decorated DFC (2), Bronze Star (2). Mem. VFW, Am. Legion, Cattleman's Assn., Lamoni Lions Club. Home: RR 1 Box 130 Davis City IA 50065-9756 Office: US Ho of Reps 1029 Longworth HOB Washington DC 20515

BOSWELL, NATHALIE SPENCE, speech pathologist; b. Cleve., May 9, 1924; d. Harrison Morton and Nathalie Muriel (Clem) Spence; student Skidmore Coll, 1941-42; MusB in Edn., Northwestern U., 1945; MA, Western Res. U., 1961; m. June 15, 1946; children: Louis Keith, Donna Spence, Deborah Anne. Speech therapist Highland View Hosp., Cleve., 1961-64; speech pathologist Cleve. VA Hosp., 1964-87 ; chmn. Equal Employment Opportunity Counselors, 1969-74, Fed. Women Speakers Bur., 1968-87, Fed. Career Info. Program, 1970-72, Fed. Coll. Rels. Coun., 1970-74, Fed. Exec. Bd., 1972-73; adj. instr. Case Western Res. U., 1982-87; mem. adv. coun. sch. electromedicine scis., City U. Los Angeles, 1985; mem. adv. bd. Nat. Inst. Electromedicine Info., 1985; trustee, cons. Donna Spence Boswell Massther, 1992—. Mem. Cleve. Orch. Chorus, 1969-82; vol. Seamen's Svc., 1976—; patron Police Athletic League; mem. Citizen Adv. Com on Solid Waste, Cleveland Heights Ohio, 1989-94. Endowed Tuba Chair, Cleve. Orch., 1983. Recipient Performance award Equal Employment Opportunities, 1973; Quality Increase award, 1980; others; lic. speech pathologist, Ohio. Mem. Am. Speech and Hearing Assn. (cert. clin. competence), Ohio Speech and Hearing Assn., Aphasiology Assn. Ohio, Chi Omega Alumni Assn., Musical Arts Assn., Western Res. Hist. Soc., Cleve. Mus. Natural History (vol. 1988—), Cleve. Mus. Art, Smithsonian Assos., Nat. Wildlife Fedn., Audubon Soc., Nat. Trust Hist. Preservation, Am. Heritage Soc. Mem. Ch. Reorganized Latter-Day Saints. Author: Guidelines for EEO Counselors in their Training Program, 1973; prin. author: Laryngectomy-Orientation for Patients and Families, 1981; contbr., asst. editor: Am. Jour. Electromedicine, 1984. Home: 2946 Berkshire Rd Cleveland OH 44118-2444

BOSWELL, PHILIP JOHN, opera administrator; b. Paris, Apr. 28, 1949; s. William Osgood and Janine (Werner) B. BA, Harvard U., 1970. Asst. to bus. mgr. Santa Fe Opera, 1969-70; adminstrv. asst. Spoleto (Italy) Festival, 1971-73; subscription mgr. Opera Co. of Boston, 1971-73; co. coordinator Western Opera Theater, San Francisco, 1974-77; assoc. dir. ops. Can. Opera Co., Toronto, Ont., 1978-81, artistic adminstr., 1981-92, 94—. Home: 11 1/2 Saint Patrick Sq, Toronto, ON Canada M5T 1W8

BOSWELL, RUPERT DEAN, JR., retired academic administrator, math educator; b. Marshall County, Miss., Aug. 11, 1929; s. Rupert Dean and Mary Exyah (Ellis) B.; m. Grace Hadaway, Apr. 11, 1952; children: James Elton, Deanna Grace. BS, Miss. State U., 1950, MS, 1951; PhD, U. Ga., 1957. Grad. asst. Miss. State U., Mississippi State, 1950-51; instr. math. Reinhardt Coll., Waleska, Ga., 1951-53; grad. asst. U. Ga., Athens, 1953-56; assoc. prof. math. Miss. State U., 1957-61, prof., 1961-62; prof. math. Monmouth (Ill.) Coll., 1962-77; v.p. acad. affairs Rocky Mountain Coll., Billings, Mont., 1977-85; provost, prof. math. Upper Iowa U., Fayette, 1985-89; prof. math. Jacksonville (Ala.) State U., 1989-94. Mem. Am. Math. Soc., Math. Assn. Am. (chmn. com. on vis. lectrs. 1967-69, chmn. Ill. sect.), AAUP, Fayette C. of C. (sec. 1985-87). Presbyterian. Lodge: Rotary (pres. Monmouth club 1972-73). Home: PO Box 181 Jacksonville AL 36265-0181

BOSWELL, TOMMIE C., middle school educator; b. Gainesboro, Tenn., Nov. 8, 1942; d. Tommy and Ethel (Draper) Cassetty; m. Neal Stanley Boswell, Aug. 28, 1965; children: Brian Andrew, James Travis. AA, Cumberland U., Lebanon, Tenn., 1962; BS, Tenn. Technol. U., 1965; MAT, Rollins Coll., Winter Park, Fla., 1980, EdS, 1984. Cert. tchr. English, social studies; cert. adminstrv. supr. Tchr. English and social studies Beaumont Middle Sch., Kissimmee, Fla., 1965-72, tchr. social studies, 1978-89; tchr. social studies Neptune Middle sch., Kissimmee, 1989—; team leader 8th Grade Acad. Team "Challengers", Kissimmee, 1994—. Founding pres. Canterbury Lane Neighborhood Assn., Kissimmee, 1988; mem. N.M.S. Program Improvement Coun., Kissimmee, 1994—. Named Social Studies Tchr. of the Yr., Fla. Coun. for Social Studies, 1984, 86, 89, Outstanding Tchr. of Am. History, Joshua Stevens chpt. DAR, Kissimmee, 1982; Delta Kappa Gamma scholar, 1980. Mem. Upper Cumberland Geneal. Soc. Republican. Methodist. Avocations: geneology, reading, bottle and stamp collecting. Office: Neptune Middle Sch 2727 Neptune Rd Kissimmee FL 34744-6275

BOSWELL, WILLIAM DOUGLAS, lawyer; b. Harrisburg, Pa., June 7, 1918; s. Ralph Everett and Edna Stansberry (Heller) B.; m. Doris M. Lutz, June 9, 1945; children: William D. Jr., Jeffrey R., Nancy Jeanne, Joanne Elizabeth. PhB, Dickinson Coll., 1940, LLB, 1943. Bar: Pa. 1943, U.S. Dist. Ct. (mid. dist.) Pa. 1946, U.S. Dist. Ct. (ea. dist.) Pa. 1965, U.S. Ct. Appeals (3d cir.) 1966, U.S. Ct. Appeals (4th cir.) 1982, U.S. Supreme Ct. 1962. Ptnr. Compton, Handler, Berman & Boswell, Harrisburg, Pa., 1946-71, Berman, Boswell & Tintner, Harrisburg, 1971-86, Boswell, Tintner & Piccola, 1986-88, Boswell, Snyder, Tintner & Piccola, 1988-97, Boswell, Tintner, Piccola & Wickersham, 1997—; lectr. Pa. Bar Inst., Am. Soc. C.L.U.s, Pa. Banker's Assn.; bd. dirs. Byers Lumber Co., Inc.$d Doris M. Lutz, June 9, 1945; children: William D. Jr., Jeffrey R., Nancy Jeanne, Joanne Elizabeth. PhB, Dickinson Coll., 1940, LLB, 1943. Bar: Pa. 1943, U.S. Dist. Ct. (mid. dist.) Pa. 1946, U.S. Dist. Ct. (ea. dist.) Pa. 1965, U.S. Ct. Appeals (3d cir.) 1966, U.S. Ct. Appeals (4th cir.) 1982, U.S. Supreme Ct. 1962. Ptnr. Compton, Handler, Berman & Boswell, Harrisburg, Pa., 1946-71, Berman, Boswell & Tintner, Harrisburg, 1971-86, Boswell, Tintner & Piccola, 1986-88, Boswell, Snyder, Tintner & Piccola, 1988-97, Boswell, Tinther, Piccola & Wickersham, 1997—; lectr. Pa. Bar Inst., Am. Soc. C.L.U.s, Pa. Banker's Assn.; bd. dirs. Byers Lumber Co., Inc. Pres. Tri-County United Way, 1963-64, Tri-County Welfare Council, 1960-61, bd. dirs., Josiah W. and Bessie H. Kline Found., 1979—; v.p. Dauphin County unit Am. Cancer Soc., 1970-72; pres. Children's Home of Harrisburg, Inc., 1965-68, 75—, Estate Planning Council Central Pa., 1970, bd. dirs., solicitor, Harrisburg Symphony Assn., 1986—; solicitor County of Dauphin, 1990-92. Master sgt. AUS, 1942-46. Fellow Am. Coll. Trust and Estate Counsel, mem. ABA, Pa. Bar Assn., Dauphin County Bar Assn. (pres. 1962-63), Am. Judicature Soc., Woolsack Soc. Republican. Presbyterian. Clubs: Executive of Central Pa. (pres. 1978), Masons, K.T., Shriners, Tuesday, Country (pres. 1974-76) (Harrisburg). Pres. Tri-County United Way, 1963-64, Tri-County Welfare Coun., 1960-61; bd. dirs. Josia W. and Bessie H. Kline Found., 1979—; v.p. Dauphin County unit Am. Cancer Soc., 1970-72; pres. Children's Home of Harrisburg, Inc., 1965-68, 75—, Estate Planning Coun. Ctrl. Pa., 1970; bd. dirs., solicitor Harrisburg Symphony Assn., 1986—; solicitor County of Dauphin, 1990-92. Master sgt. AUS, 1942-46. Fellow Am. Coll. Trust and Estate Counsel, mem. ABA, Pa. Bar Assn., Dauphin County Bar Assn. (pres. 1962-63), Am. Judicature Soc., Woolsack Soc., Exec. Club of Ctrl. Pa. (pres. 1978), Masons, K.T., Shriners, Tuesday Club, Harrisburg Country Club (pres. 1974-76). Republican. Presbyterian. Office: Boswell Tintner Piccola & Wickersham PO Box 741 Harrisburg PA 17108-0741

BOSWELL, WILLIAM PARET, lawyer; b. Washington, Oct. 24, 1946; s. Yates Paret and Mary Frances (Hyland) B.; m. Barbara Stelle Schroeder, Sept. 6, 1969; children: Susan Anne, Sarah Mary, Christina Catherine. BA cum laude, Cath. U., 1968; JD, U. Va., 1971. Bar: Va. 1971, D.C. 1972, U.S. Ct. Mil. Appeals 1972, U.S. Supreme Ct. 1975, Pa. 1978. Atty. Peoples Natural Gas Co., Pitts., 1978-82, asst. sec., gen. atty., 1982-85, sec., gen. counsel, 1985-88, 1989—, also bd. dirs.; gen. counsel Hope Gas, Inc., 1998—; dep. gen. counsel Consol. Natural Gas Co., 1999—; bd. dirs., mem. exec. com. United Distbn. Cos.; mem. exec. com. Gas Industry Stds. Bd., 1994-97, bd. dirs., 1997—, vice chmn., 1998—. Pres. Borough Coun., Osborne, Pa., 1984-97, mayor, 1998—; bd. dirs. Mendelssohn Choir Pitts., 1996-98, pres. 1997-98; trustee Laughlin Found., 1995—. Capt. JAGC, USAF, 1971-78, col. USAFR, 1979-98. Decorated Legion of Merit. Mem. ABA (chair gas com. 1992—), Pa. Bar Assn., D.C. Bar Assn., Va. Bar Assn., Am. Gas Assn. (chair regulatory com. 1996-98), Pa. Gas Assn. (chmn. 1989-90), Am. Corp. Counsel Assn. (pres. Pa. chpt. 1991-92, Excellence in Corporate Practice award 1998), Am. Soc. Corp. Secs., Rivers Club, City Club Pitts., Army and Navy Club D.C. Republican. Roman Catholic. Avocations: reading, walking. Home: 405 Hare Ln Sewickley PA 15143-2050 Office: CNG Towers 625 Liberty Ave Pittsburgh PA 15222-3199

BOSWORTH, DOUGLAS LEROY, international company executive, educator; b. Goldfield, Iowa, Oct. 15, 1939; s. Clifford LeRoy and Clara (Lonning) B.; m. Patricia Lee Knock, May 28, 1961; children: Douglas, Dawn. BS in Agrl. Engring, Iowa State U., 1962; MS in Agrl. Engring, U. Ill., 1964. With Deere & Co., Moline, Ill., 1959-94; pres. WorkSpan, Inc., Mahomet, Ill., 1994—, Ill. Tech. Ctr., Savoy, Ill., 1995-97; div. engr. disk harrows Deere & Co., Moline, Ill., 1971-76, mgr. mfg. engring., 1976-80, works mgr., 1980-85, mgr. mfg., 1985-89, engring. test mgr., 1989-94; mem. Engring. Accreditation Commn., 1985-90; v.p. Skills Inc.; mem. Assoc. Employers Bd., 1989-91; adj. engring. prof. U. Ill., Champaign-Urbana, 1996—. Active Am. Cancer Soc., Rock Island Unit; bd. dirs. United Med. Ctr., 1984-95; exec. com. Quad-City United Way, 1984-89. Mem. Am. Soc. Agrl. Engrs. (chmn. Ill.-Wis. 1973-74, Engring. Achievement Young Designer award 1973, nat. bd. dirs. 1974-76, 79-82, v.p. 1979-82, pres. elect. 1991-92, pres. 1992-93), Sigma Xi, Alpha Epsilon, Gamma Sigma Delta. Lutheran. Lodge: Rotary. Home: 1111 Briarcliff Dr Mahomet IL 61853-9558 Office: WorkSpan Inc 1111 E Briarcliff Dr Mahomet IL 61853-9558

BOSWORTH, JEFFREY WILLSON, emerging technologies consultant, client/server specialist; b. Sayre, Pa., Dec. 5, 1948; s. Joseph Reinhart and Jean Margaret (Willson) B.; m. Marianne Bosworth. Student, Pa. State U.,

1966-68; AA in Communications, Harrisburg Area Community Coll., 1973; BS in Pub. Communications, Syracuse U., 1975. Comml. underwriter Nationwide Ins. Co., Syracuse, N.Y., 1975-78; mktg. rep. Ins. Co. N.Am., Lemoyne, Pa., 1978-80; systems analyst Nationwide Ins. Co., Columbus, Ohio, 1980-83; office mgr., fin. analyst Nationwide Ins. Co., Columbus, 1983-84, spl. projects analyst, 1984-85, systems programming mgr., 1985-97; owner Altair Four Software, Columbus, 1983—. Author: (software) PCSecure, 1986, FXFER, 1988, AREACALC, 1989, Ind. Tgn. Plan DB (ITP) Navy, 1991, NAVLOG, 1995. With USN, 1968-72 (Vietnam); with Res., 1980—. Mem. Am. Mgmt. Assn. Republican. Avocations: sailing, programming, computers, pvt. pilot. E-mail: jboswort@columbus.rr.com. Office: Compuware Corp 1103 Schrock Rd Ste 205 Columbus OH 43229

BOSWORTH, STEPHEN WARREN, ambassador; b. Grand Rapids, Mich., Dec. 4, 1939; s. Warren Charles and Mina (Phillips) B.; m. Christine Holmes, June 7, 1984; children—Andrew, Allison. A.B., Dartmouth Coll., 1961; LLD, Darmouth Coll., 1986. Joined U.S. Fgn. Service; service in Panama, Colon, Madrid and Paris; dep. asst. sec. state, 1976-79, ambassador to Tunisia, 1979-81, dep. asst. sec. Inter-Am. affairs, 1981-82; dir. policy planning staff coun. U.S. Fgn. Svc., 1983-84; ambassador Manila, Philippines, 1984-87; pres. U.S.-Japan Found., 1988-96; exec. dir. Korean Energy Devel. Orgn., 1995-97; amb. to Republic of Korea Seoul, 1997—; adj. prof. Columbia U., 1990—. Trustee Dartmouth Coll., 1992—, chmn. bd. trustees, 1996—. Recipient Dept. State Disting. Honor award, 1976, 86, Arthur S. Flemming award, 1976; named Diplomat of Yr., Am. Acad. Diplomacy, 1986. Office: Am Embassy Seoul South Korea Dept State Washington DC 20521-9600*

BOSWORTH, THOMAS LAWRENCE, architect, educator; b. Oberlin, Ohio, June 15, 1930; s. Edward Franklin and Imogene (Rose) B.; m. Abigail Lumbard, Nov. 6, 1954 (div. Nov. 1974); children: Thomas Edward, Nathaniel David; m. Elaine R. Pedigo, Nov. 23, 1974; stepchildren: Robert Haden Pedigo, Kevin Ian Pedigo. BA, Oberlin Coll., 1952, MA, 1954; postgrad., Princeton U., 1952-53, Harvard U., 1956-57; MArch, Yale U., 1960. Draftsman Gordon McMaster AIA, Cheshire, Conn., summer 1957-58; resident planner Tunnard & Harris Planning Cons., Newport, R.I., summer 1959; designer, field supr. Eero Saarinen & Assocs., Birmingham, Mich., 1960-61, Hamden, Conn., 1961-64; individual practice architecture Providence, 1964-68, Seattle, 1968—; asst. instr. architecture Yale U., 1962-65, vis. lectr., 1965-66; asst. prof. R.I. Sch. Design, 1964-66, asso. prof., head dept., 1966-68; prof. architecture U. Wash., Seattle, 1968-98; prof. emeritus U. Wash., 1998—; chmn. dept. U. Wash., Seattle, 1968-72; chief architecture Peace Corps Tng. Program, Tunisia, Brown U., summers 1965-66; archtl. cons., individual practice Seattle, 1972—; dir. multidisciplinary program U. Wash., Rome, Italy, 1984-86; vis. lectr. Kobe U., Japan, Oct., 1982, Nov., 1990, Apr., 1993, May, 1995, June, 1998; Pietro Belluschi Disting. Vis. Prof. U. Oreg., 1996; dir. arch. in Rome program U. Wash., Rome, 1996. Bd. dirs. N.W. Inst. Arch. and Urban Studies, Italy, 1983-90, pres., 1983-85; dir. Pilchuch Glass Sch., Seattle, 1977-80, trustee, 1980-91, adv. coun., 1993—; mem. Seattle Model Cities Land Use Rev. Bd., 1969-70, Tech. Com. Site Selection Wash. Multi-Purpose Stadium, 1970, Medina Planning Commn., 1972-74, steering adv. com. King County Stadium, 1972-74, others; chmn. King County (Wash.) Environ. Devel. Commn., 1972-74, King County Policy Devel. Commn., 1974-77; mem., bd. dirs. Arcade Mag., 1995—, pres. 1998—; bd. mgrs. YMCA Camping Sv cs., 1998—. With U.S. Army, 1954-56. Winchester Traveling fellow Greece, 1960; assoc. fellow Ezra Stiles Coll. Yale U.; mid-career fellow in arch. Am. Acad. in Rome, 1980-81, vis. scholar, Spring 1988. Fellow AIA; mem. Archtl. Inst. Japan, Soc. Archtl. Historians, Monday Club, Tau Sigma Delta. Home: 4532 E Laurel Dr NE Seattle WA 98105-3839 Office: U Wash Dept Architecture PO Box 355720 Seattle WA 98195-5720

BOTELHO, BRUCE MANUEL, state attorney general, mayor; b. Juneau, Alaska, Oct. 6, 1948; s. Emmett Manuel and Harriet Iowa (Tieszen) B.; m. Guadalupe Alvarez Breton, Sept. 23, 1988; children: Alejandro Manuel, Adriana Regina. Student, U. Heidelberg, Federal Republic of Germany, 1970; BA, Willamette U., 1971, JD, 1976. Bar: Alaska 1976, U.S. Ct. Appeals (9th cir.), U.S. Supreme Ct. Asst. atty. gen. State of Alaska, Juneau, 1976-83, 87-90, dep. commr., acting commr. Dept. of Revenue, 1983-86; mayor City, Borough of Juneau, 1988-91, dep. atty. gen., 1991-94; atty. gen. State of AK, 1994—. Editor: Willamette Law Jour., 1975-76; contbr. articles profl. jours. Assembly mem. City, Borough of Juneau, 1983-86; pres. Juneau Human Rights Commn., 1978-80, Alaska Coun. Am. Youth Hostels, 1979-81, Juneau Arts and Humanities Coun., 1981-83, SE Alaska Area Coun. Boy Scouts Am., 1991-93, coun. commr., 1993—; bd. dirs. Found. for Social Innovations, Alaska, 1990-93, Alaska Econ. Devel. Coun., 1985-87, Alaska Indsl. Devel. Corp., 1984-86, Juneau World Affairs Coun.; chair adminstrv. law sect. Alaska Bar Assn., 1981-82; chair Alaska Resources Corp., 1984-86, Gov.'s Conf. on Youth and Justice, 1995-96; trustee Alaska Children's Trust, 1996—; mem. exec. com. Conf. of Western Attys. Gen., 1997—; co-chair Alaska Justice Assessment Commn., 1997—, chair Gov. Task Force on Confidentiality of Chldns. Proceedings, 1998—. Mem. Nat. Assn. Attys. Gen. (exec. com. 1998—). Democrat. Methodist. Avocation: international folk dance. Home: 401 F St Douglas AK 99824-5353 Office: State Alaska Dept Law PO Box 110300 Juneau AK 99811-0300

BOTELLO, TROY JAMES, arts administrator, educator; b. Long Beach, Calif., Sept. 2, 1953; s. Arthur P. and Jayme Alta (McBride) B. AA in Spl. Edn., Cerritos Coll., 1979; BA in Music Therapy, Calif. State U., Long Beach, 1984; cert. in arts adminstrn., U. So. Calif., Orange County, 1988; MA in Adminstrn., Calif. Polytech. Inst., Pomona, 1992. Cert. tchr., Calif. Asst. music dir. St. John Bosco High Sch., Bellflower, Calif., 1969-72; music dir. Bellflower Unified Schs., 1971-74; tchr. severely handicapped L.A. County Office of Edn., 1974-88; vocat. rehab. counselor Tesseler Counseling Group, Anaheim, Calif., 1988-91; dir. edn. Orange County Performing Arts Ctr., Costa Mesa, Calif., 1991—; exec. dir., co-founder Project: Arts in Motion, Bellflower, 1983-92; ednl. cons. Edn. Div. Music Ctr., L.A., 1986—; vice chmn. La Mirada (Calif.) Community Concerts, 1976-79; v.p. grants Master Symphony Orch., Norwalk, Calif. Chairperson La Mirada Hist. Com., 1977-78; rep. Edn. Adv. Com., L.A., 1981; exec. prod., bd. dirs. Imagination Celebration of Orange County, 1991—; pres. Anaheim Cultural Arts Found., 1993-95; state pres., bd. dirs Very Special Arts Calif., 1992—. Mem. Assn. for Music Therapy Profls., So. Calif. Band and Field Judges, Profl. Arts Mgmt. Inst., Calif. Assn. Rehab. Profls., Am. Assn. Orff Schwelrk, Young Composers of Am., Alumni of Drum Corps Internat. Avocations: cultural events, gourmet cooking. E-mail: tbotello@olpac.org. Home: 14216 Neargrove Rd La Mirada CA 90638-3854 Office: Orange County Performing Arts Ctr 600 Town Center Dr Costa Mesa CA 92626-1997

BOTEZ, DAN, physicist; b. Bucharest, Romania, May 22, 1948; s. Emil and Ecaterina (Iacob) B.; m. Lynda Diane Arnold, Sept. 25, 1976; children: Anca, Adrian. BSEE with highest honors, U. Calif., Berkeley, 1971, MSEE, 1972, PhDEE, 1976; Dr. honoris causa, U. Politechnica, Bucharest, Romania, 1995. Postdoctoral fellow IBM Thomas J. Watson Rsch. Ctr., Yorktown Heights, N.Y., 1976-77; mem. tech. staff RCA David Sarnoff Rsch. Ctr., Princeton, N.J., 1977-82, rsch. leader, 1982-84; dir. device devel. Lytel Inc., Somerville, N.J., 1984-86; chief scientist TRW Electro-Optic Rsch. Ctr., Redondo Beach, Calif., 1986, lab dir., 1986-87; sr. staff scientist TRW Rsch. Ctr., Redondo Beach, Calif., 1987-93, TRW tech. fellow, 1990-93; Philip Dunham Reed prof. elec. engring. U. Wis., Madison, 1993—. Author: Electro-Optical Communications Dictionary, 1983, Diode-Laser Arrays, 1994; contbr. more than 200 articles to profl. jours.; patentee in field. Named Outstanding Young Engr., IEEE Lasers and Electro-Optics Soc., San Jose, 1984, recipient Key to Future award, 1984. Fellow IEEE (chmn. tech. com. on semiconductor lasers 1989-90), Optical Soc. Am.; mem. Phi Beta Kappa. Republican. Mem. Ea. Orthodox Ch. Avocations: racquetball, travel, photography, skiing. Home: 200 N Prospect Ave Madison WI 53705-4027 Office: U Wis Dept Elec Engring 1415 Engineering Dr Madison WI 53706-1607

BOTHA, FRANCOIS (FRANS), professional boxer; b. Sept. 28, 1968. Heavyweight champion Internat. Boxing Fedn.; N.Am. heavyweight champion World Boxing Assn., 1997—. Office: CCCT Local 21 Piso 2, Calle Petion Cruce Urdaneto, Turmero 2115 EA, Venezuela*

BOTHMER, DIETRICH FELIX VON, museum curator, archaeologist; b. Eisenach, Thuringia, Oct. 26, 1918; came to U.S., 1939, naturalized, 1944; s. Wilhelm Friedrich Franz Carl and Marie Julie Auguste Karoline (Freiin von und zu Egloffstein) von B.; m. Joyce de la Bégassière, May 28, 1966; children: Bernard Nicholas, Maria Elizabeth Villalba. Student, Friedrich Wilhelms U., Berlin, 1937-38, Wadham Coll., Oxford, 1938-39; diploma classical archaeology, Oxford U., 1939; Ph.D. in Classical Archaeology, U. Calif., Berkeley, 1944; DPhil (hon.), U. Trier, 1997. Asst. curator Greek and Roman art Met. Mus. Art, 1946-51, assoc. curator, 1951-59, curator, 1959-73, chmn., 1973-90, Disting. rsch. curator, 1990—; adj. prof. NYU, 1966—. Book rev. editor: Am. Jour. Archaeology, 1950-57; assoc. editor, 1970-76; author: Amazons in Greek Art, 1957, Ancient Art from New York Private Collections, 1961, An Inquiry into the Forgery of the Etruscan Terracotta Warriors, 1961, Corpus Vasorum Antiquorum, USA fasc. 12, 1963, Greek Vase Painting: An Introduction, 1972, Corpus Vasorum Antiquorum, USA fasc. 16, 1976, Greek Art of the Aegean Islands, 1979, A Greek and Roman Treasury, 1984, The Amasis Painter and His World, 1985, Greek Vase Painting, 1987, Glories of the Past, Ancient Art from the Shelby White and Leon Levy Collection, 1990, Euphronios, Peintre á Athènes au VI siècle avant Jesus Christ, 1990. Mem. Chancellor's Ct. of Benefactors, Oxford U. With AUS, 1943-45. Decorated Bronze Star, Purple Heart; Rhodes scholar Wadham Coll., 1938-39; Internat. House fellow U. Calif., Berkeley, 1940, Alfred B. Jordan fellow, 1940-41, Univ. fellow, 1941-42; Martin Ryerson fellow U. Chgo., 1942-43; Guggenheim Meml. Found. fellow, 1966, hon. fellow Wadham Coll.; Chevalier Légion d'Honneur, 1997. Mem. Archaeol. Inst. Am. (benefactor), Soc. Promotion Hellenic Studies (hon.), Deutsches Archaeol. Inst., Vereinigung der Freunde Antiker Kunst (Basle, Switzerland), Archaeologische Gesellschaft zu Berlin, Institut de France, Académie des Inscriptions et Belles-Lettres (associé), Piping Rock Club, Lyford Cay Club. Home: 401 Centre Island Oyster Bay NY 11771-5011 Office: Met Mus Art Fifth Ave at 82nd St New York NY 10028-0198

BOTHNER-BY, AKSEL ARNOLD, chemist, horseman; b. Mpls., Apr. 29, 1921; s. Aksel Conrad and Merle Marie (von Hagen) Bothner-B.; m. Christine Treuner, Oct. 15, 1949; children: Peter Ole, Anne Sigrun. Student, U. Nanking, China, 1939; B Chemistry, U. Minn., 1943; MS, NYU, 1947; PhD, Harvard U., 1949. Scientist Brookhaven Nat. Lab., 1949-53; fellow Am. Cancer Soc., Zurich, 1952-53; instr., lectr. Harvard U., 1953-58; cons. Retina Found., 1957-58; staff fellow Mellon Inst., 1958-71, dir., 1960-61, mem. adv. com., 1962-71; prof. chemistry Carnegie-Mellon U., 1967-77, chmn. dept., 1967-70; dean Mellon Inst. Sci., 1971-75, Univ. prof., 1977—, acting head, 1987-91, Univ. prof. emeritus, 1991—; Fulbright lectr. U. Munich, Germany, 1962-63; adj. prof. U. Pitts., 1964—; vis. prof. U. Calif. at San Diego, 1976-77; trustee MPC Corp., 1972-80; Bd. dirs. Pa. Jr. Acad. Scis., 1975-86. Author papers in field of theoretical organic chemistry. With AUS, 1943-45. Recipient Disting. Achievement award U. Minn., 1975, IR-100 award, 1978, Pitts. award, 1988. Mem. Am. Chem. Soc., Am. So. Biochemistry and Molecular Biology, U.S. Dressage Fedn. Home: 6317 Darlington Rd Pittsburgh PA 15217-1835 Office: Mellon Inst 4400 5th Ave Pittsburgh PA 15213-2683

BOTHWELL, DORR, artist; b. San Francisco, May 3, 1902; d. John Stuart and Florence Isabel (Hodgson) B. Student, Calif. Sch. Fine Arts, Rudolph Schaeffer Sch. Design, U. Oreg. Painter Tau, Manu'a, Am. Samoa, 1928-29, France, 1930-31, 49-51, 89, Eng., 1960-61, 89, West Africa and North Africa, 1966-67, Indonesia, 1974, People's Republic China, 1982, Japan, 1985, Mex., 1987; instr. Calif. Sch. Fine Arts, San Francisco, 1945-58, San Francisco Art Inst., 1959-60, Rudolph Schaeffer Sch. Design, 1960-61, Mendocino (Calif.) Art Ctr., 1962-93, San Francisco Art Inst., 1961; instr. Sonoma State Coll., summer 1964, U. Calif. Ext., Mendocino Art Ctr., 1965-71, 90; faculty Ansel Adams Yosemite Workshop, 1964-77, Victor (Colo.) Sch. Photography, 1979. Exhibitor, West Coast exhbns., 1927—, 3d biennial São Paulo, Brazil, Pitts. Internat., 1952, 55, Art: U.S.A., 1958, Bklyn. Mus., 1976, Mendocino (Calif.) Art Ctr., 1992; one-man shows include De Young Meml. Mus., San Francisco, 1957, 63; retrospective exhbn. Bay Window Gallery, Mendocino, 1985, Spl. Anniversary exhbn. 1986-87, Tobey Moss Gallery, L.A., 1989, 91, 93, Bothwell Studio, Mendocino, Calif., 1989, Mendocino Art Ctr., 1992, Gallery Mendocino, 1994-95; travelling exhbn. Oakland (Calif.) Mus., 1995, UCLA Mus., Westwood, 1995, Logan (Utah) Art Mus., 1995; works in permanent collection, San Diego Gallery Fine Art, Crocker Gallery, Sacramento, San Francisco Mus. Art, Whitney Mus. Am. Art, Bklyn. Mus., Mus. Modern Art, Fogg Mus., Met. Mus., Victoria and Albert Mus., London, Brit. Mus., London, Bibliothèque Nationale, Paris, France, Worcester (Mass.) Art Mus., Cleve. Mus. Art, Boston Mus. Art, Oakland (Calif.) Mus., DeYoung Mus, San Francisco, L.A. County Mus., 1994, Oakland Mus., 1995, Gene Autry Mus., L.A., 1995, Palms (Calif.) Art Guild, 1996; author: Notan: The Principle of Dark-Light Design, 1968, 2d edit., 1976, Danish edit., 1977, 3d edit., 1991, On The Edge of America: California Modernist Art, 1996. Recipient 1st prize, 4th ann. exhbn. San Francisco Soc. Women Artists, 1929; Pres.'s purchase prize, 1941; Leisser-Farnham award 7th ann. exhbn. San Diego Art Guild, 1932; hon. mention 7th ann. exhbn. So. Calif. Artists, 1933; spl. prize 9th ann. exhbn., 1937; Artists Fund prize ann. exhbn. drawings and prints San Francisco Art Assn., 1943; hon. mention 2d spring ann. Calif. Palace Legion of Honor, San Francisco, 1947; purchase prize 2d nat. print ann. Bklyn. Mus., 1948; 1st prize 9th ann. Nat. Serigraph Soc., N.Y.C., 1948; grantee Pollock-Krasner Found., 1998. Home: 925 N Plaza Dr # P93 Apache Junction AZ 85220-4135 Office: Tobey Moss Gallery 7321 Beverly Blvd Los Angeles CA 90036-2534

BOTHWELL, JOHN CHARLES, archbishop; b. Toronto, June 29, 1926; s. William Alexander and Anne (Campbell) B.; m. Joan Cowan, Dec. 29, 1951; children—Michael, Timothy, Nancy, Douglas, Ann. BA with honors in Modern History, U. Toronto, 1948; BD, Trinity Coll., Toronto, 1950, DD (hon.), 1972; DD (hon.), Huron Coll., U. Western Ont., Wycliffe Coll. U Toronto, 1989; hon. sr. fellow, Renison Coll., U. Waterloo, 1988. Ordained priest Anglican Ch., 1952; curate St. James Cathedral, Toronto, 1951-53, Christ Ch. Cathedral, Vancouver, B.C., 1953-56; rector St. Aidan's Ch., Oakville, Ont., 1956-60, St. James' Ch., Dundas, Ont., 1960-65; canon missioner Niagara Diocese, 1965-69; nat. exec. dir. Anglican Ch. Can., 1969-71; co-adjutor bishop Niagara, 1971-73; bishop Diocese of Niagara, 1973-92, archbishop, 1985-91; Met. of Ont., 1985-91, ret., 1991; chancellor Trinity Coll., U. Toronto, 1991—; hon. sr. fellow Renison Coll., U. Waterloo, 1988. Co-author: Theological Education for the 70's, 1969; author: Taking Risks and Keeping Faith, 1985, Living Faith Day By Day, 1990, Old-Time Religion or Risky Faith?, 1992; contbr. articles to various newspapers. Active numerous nat. and ecumenical coms.; Dir., com. chmn. Hamilton (Ont.) Social Planning Council, 1965-69, 71-75, v.p., 1975-77, pres., 1977-79; v.p. United Way, 1982, 83, pres., 1984-86; bd. dirs. Hamilton Found., 1982, v.p., 1983, pres., 1985. Inducted into City of Hamilton (Ont., Can.) Gallery of Distinction, 1993.

BOTIMER, ALLEN RAY, retired surgeon, retirement center owner; b. Columbus, Miss., Jan. 30, 1930; s. Clare E. and Christel J. (Kalar) B.; m. Dorris LaJean, Aug. 17, 1950; children: Larry Alan, Gary David. BS, Walla Walla Coll., 1951; MD, Loma Linda U., 1955. Diplomate Am. Bd. Surgery. Intern U.S. Naval Hosp., San Diego, 1955-56, surg. resident, 1955-60; asst. chief surgery U.S. Naval Hosp., Guam, 1960-62, Bremerton, Wash., 1962-64; chief surgery Ballard Community Hosp., Seattle, 1970, chief of staff, 1972, chief surgery, 1986-87; pvt. practice Seattle, 1964-87; ret., 1987; ptnr. Heritage Retirement Ctr., Nampa, Idaho, 1972-82, owner, 1982—. Lt. comdr. USN, 1955-64. Fellow ACS, Seattle Surg. Soc.; mem. Wash. State Med. Soc., King County Med. Soc. Avocations: golf, personal computers. Home and Office: 1319 Torrey Ln Nampa ID 83686-5665

BOTLEY, CALVIN, lawyer, magistrate judge; b. Pineville, La., Dec. 2, 1944; s. Clifford and Lee Esther (Fontenot) B.; m. Jean Carol Norman, Jan. 20, 1968; children: Nicola Lynnette, Reginald Anthony (dec.). BA, Grambling State U., 1966; JD, Tex. So. U., 1972; LLM, U. Houston Law Ctr., 1996. Bar: Tex. 1972, U.S. Dist. Ct. (so., no., we. dists.) Tex. 1973, U.S. Ct. Appeals (5th cir.) 1973, U.S. Dist. Ct. (ea. dist.) Tex. 1975, U.S. Supreme Ct. 1975, U.S. Ct. Customs and Patent Appeals 1976, U.S. Ct. Appeals (11th cir.) 1984, U.S. Ct. Internat. Trade 1984. Asst. dist. atty. Harris County (Tex.), Houston, 1972-73; asst. atty. gen. State of Tex., 1973-78, chief Houston Regional Office, 1974-78; asst. U.S. atty. So. Dist. Tex., Dept. Justice, 1978-79; magistrate judge U.S. Dist. Ct. (so. dist.) Tex., Houston, 1979—; chmn. criminal justice adv. council Tex. So. U., 1976-77. Bd. dirs., mem. exec. com. Houston Council on Human Relations; bd. dirs. Houston Child Guidance Ctr., bd. visitors Thurgood Marshall Sch. Law, Tex. So. U.; mem. fed. conf. com. on court security, 1988-92. Served with U.S. Army, 1966-69; Vietnam. Decorated Army Commendation medal with oak leaf cluster; recipient Pres. award Nat. Assn. Blacks in Higher Edn., 1984, Alumni of Yr. award Thurgood Marshall Sch. Law, 1994, Outstanding Achievement award Grambling State U. Polit. Sci. Honor Soc., 1981, Black and Gold Leadership award Grambling State U., 1996, Disting. Svc. award U. Houston Law Ctr., 1995, award for legal excellence NAACP, 1997, Disting. Alumni award Nat. Assn. for Equal Opportunity in Higher Edn., 1999; named to Grambling State U. Hall of Fame, 1996. Mem. ABA (Judge Edward R. Finch Law Day Speech award 1999), Tex. Bar Assn., Tex. Bar Found., Houston Bar Assn., Houston Lawyers' Assn., Fed. Magistrate Judges Assn., Houston Bar Found., Fed. Bar Assn., Nat. Geog. Soc., Coll. State Bar Tex., Phi Alpha Delta (justice Greener chpt. 1971-72, Acad. Achievement award 1972, Outstanding Mem. award 1972), Sigma Rho Sigma (pres. Grambling chpt. 1963, nat. v.p. 1964-65, nat. pres. 1965-66). Baptist. Club: Masons. Office: US District Court 7720 US Courthouse 515 Rusk St Houston TX 77002-2600

BOTSAI, ELMER EUGENE, architect, educator, former university dean; b. St. Louis, Feb. 1, 1928; s. Paul and Ita May (Cole) B.; m. Patricia L. Keegan, Aug. 28, 1955; children: Donald Rolf, Kurt Gregory.; m. Sharon K. Kaiser, Dec. 5, 1981; 1 dau., Kiana Michelle. AA, Sacramento Jr. Coll., 1950; AB, U. Calif.-Berkeley, 1954. Registered architect, Hawaii, Calif. Draftsman, then asst. to architect So. Pacific Co., San Francisco, 1953-57; designer J.H. Ferguson Co., San Francisco, 1955; project architect Anshen & Allen Architects, San Francisco, 1957-63; prin. Botsai, Overstreet & Rosenberg, Architects and Planners, San Francisco, 1963-79, Elmer E. Botsai FAIA, Honolulu, 1979—; of cousnel Groupe 70 Internat., 1998—; chmn. dept. architecture U. Hawaii, Manoa, 1976-80, dean Sch. Architecture, 1980-90, prof., 1990-98; lectr. U. Calif., Berkeley, 1976, dir. Nat. Archtl. Accrediting Bd., 1972-73, 79; adminstrv. and tech. cons. Wood Bldg. Rsch. Ctr., U. Calif., 1985-90, mem. profl. preparation project com. at U. Mich., Ann Arbor, 1986-87; co-author water infiltration seminar series for Bldg. Owners and Mgrs. Rsch. Ctr., 1986-87; chief investigator effects of Guatemalan earthquake for NSF and AIA, Washington, 1976; steering com. on structural failures Nat. Bur. Standards, 1982-84; chmn., dir. gen. svcs. Adv. Com. State of Calif. Co-author: Architects and Earthquake, Research Needs, 1976, ATC Seismic Standards for National Bur. of Standards, 1976, Architects and Earthquakes: A Primer, 1977, Seismic Design, 1978, Wood-Detailing for Performance, 1990, Wood as a Building Material, 2d edit., 1991; contbr. articles and reports to profl. jours.; prin. works include expansion of Nuclear Weapons Tng. Facility at Lemoore Naval Air Sta., Calif., LASH Terminal Port Facility Archtl. Phase, San Francisco, Incline Village (Nev.) Country Club, 1365 Columbus Ave. Bldg., San Francisco, modernization Stanford Ct. Hotel, San Francisco; monument area constrn. several Calif. ceneteries. With U.S. Army, 1946-48. Recipient Cert. Honor Fedn. Archtl. Colls. Mex. Republic, 1984; named to Wisdom Hall of Fame; NSF grantee for investigative workshop project, San Diego, 1974-80. Fellow AIA (bd. dirs., 1966-71, treas. No. Calif. chpt. 1968-69, pres. 1971, nat. v.p., 1975-76, nat. pres. 1978, pres. Hawaii 1985); hon. fellow Royal Can. Inst. Architects, N.Z. Inst. Architects, Royal Australian Inst. Architects, La Societed de Arquitectos Mexicano; mem. Archtl. Secs. Assn. (hon.), Soc. Wood Sci. and Tech., Internat. Conf. Bldg. Ofcls. Home: 321 Wailupe Cir Honolulu HI 96821-1524 Office: 925 Bethel St Fl 5 Honolulu HI 96813-4393

BOTSFORD, BETH, swimmer, Olympic athlete; b. Timonium, Md., May 21, 1981. Swimmer Pan Pacific Team, 1995, U.S. Olympic Team, Atlanta, 1996. Named Spring Nationals Rookie of the Meet, 1994; 1st place 200 meter backstroke, 1995, 200 meter backstroke Summer Nationals, 1995; recipient Gold medals 100 meter backstroke and 4x100 meter medley relay Olympic Games, Atlanta, 1996, 1st 200m on back, 1st 100m on back 1997 Spring Nats., 1st 400m MRP 1999 World Trials. Mem. North Balt. Aquatic Club. Office: US Swimming Inc 1 Olympic Plz Bldg 2A Colorado Springs CO 80909-5770*

BOTSTEIN, DAVID, geneticist, educator; b. Zurich, Switzerland, Sept. 8, 1942; naturalized, 1954; AB in Biochem. Scis. cum laude, Harvard U., 1963; PhD in Human Genetics, U. Mich., 1967. Woodrow Wilson fellow, 1963; instr. dept. biology MIT, Cambridge, 1967-69; asst. prof. genetics MIT, 1969-73, assoc. prof. genetics dept. biology, 1973-78, prof., 1978-88; Stanford W. Ascherman prof. Stanford U., Palo Alto, Calif., 1997—; sci. adv. bd. Collaborative Research, Inc., 1978-87. Editor in chief Molecular Biology of Cell, 1992—; mem. editorial bd. Virology, 1976-82, Jour. of Virology, 1976-85, Genetics, 1980—, NSF Study Sect. Genetic Biology, 1972-76, ACS Study Sect. Virology and Cell Biology, 1977-81; contbr. over 230 articles to profl. jours. Recipient Career Devel. award NIH, 1972-74; Eli Lilly and Co. award in microbiology and immunology, 1978, Rosenstiel award Brandeis U., 1992, Allen award Am. Soc. of Human Genetics, 1989, Inst. of Medicine, 1993. Mem. Genetics Soc. Am. (bd. dirs. 1984). Office: Stanford U 300 Pasteur Dr Dept Genetics Palo Alto CA 94304-2203

BOTSTEIN, LEON, college president, music historian, conductor; b. Zurich, Switzerland, Dec. 14, 1946; s. Charles and Anne (Wyszewianski) B.; m. Jill Lundquist, 1970; children: Sarah, Abigail (dec.); m. Barbara Haskell, 1982; children: Clara, Maxim. B.A. (Woodrow Wilson fellow, Danforth Found. fellow, Sloan Found. fellow), U. Chgo., 1967; A.M., Harvard U., 1968, Ph.D., 1985. Teaching fellow Harvard U., 1968-69; lectr. history Boston U., 1969; asst. to pres. N.Y.C. Bd. Edn.; pres. Franconia Coll., N.H., 1970-75, Bard Coll., Annandale-On-Hudson, N.Y., 1975—, Simon's Rock Coll. Bard, Great Barrington, Mass., 1979—; founder, artistic dir. Bard Music Festival, 1990—; music dir. Amer. Symphony Orchestra, N.Y.C., 1992—; editor The Musical Quarterly, 1992—; artistic dir. Am. Russian Young Artists Orch., 1995—; prin. condr. White Mountain Music and Art Festival, N.H., 1973-75; condr. Hudson Valley Philharm. Chamber Orch., 1989-92; guest condr. London Philharmonic, 1986, 88, 98, 99, Philharmonia Orch., 1986, Pro Arte Chamber Orch. of Boston, 1988, 89, other guest conducting appearances in Korea, Japan, Czech Republic, Philippines, Austria, Brazil, Lithuania, Romania, Scotland, Germany; past chmn. N.Y. Coun. Humanities, Assn. Episc. Colls.; cons. NEH; vis. faculty Manhattan Sch. Music, 1986; chmn. Salzburg Seminar, 1987; vis. prof. Hochschule für angewandte Kunst, Vienna, Austria, 1988. Author of several books; contbr. articles to publs. Mem. nat. adv. com. Yale-New Haven Tchrs. Inst. Fellow Am. Acad. Arts & Scis. Office: Bard Coll Office of Pres Annandale On Hudson NY 12504

BOTT, HAROLD SHELDON, accountant, management consultant; b. Chgo., Dec. 12, 1933; s. Harold S. and Mary (Moseley) B.; m. Audrey Anne Connor, May 15, 1964; children: Susan, Lynda. AB, Princeton U., 1955; MBA, Harvard U., 1959; postgrad., U. Chgo., 1960-62. Adminstrv. asst. to exec v.p. Champion Paper, Hamilton, Ohio, 1959-61; mgmt. cons. Arthur Andersen & Co., Chgo., 1961-65, mgr., 1965-71, ptnr., 1971-89; mng. dir. mgmt. info. cons., ptnr. Andersen Cons., 1988-91; ptnr. Strategic Tng. and Recruiting Svcs. Ctr.; vice chmn. The Assn. Mgmt. Cons.; bd. dirs. Harvard Bus. Sch. Assocs.; mem. faculty Grad. Sch. Bus., U. Chgo.; of counsel Omnitech Cons.; pres. H.S. Bott Co. Officer, pres., dir. Urban Gateways; treas., dir. sch. bd., pres. Kenilworth Caucus, Kenilworth United Fund; dir. Orch. of Ill. With USN, 1955-56. Mem. AICPA, Ill. Soc. CPA's, Harvard Bus. Sch. Club. Chgo. (officer, bd. dirs.), Am. Mktg. Assn., French-Am. C. of C. (bd. dirs.), Alliance Francaise (bd. dirs.), Kenilworth Sailing Club (commodore), Kenilworth Club (treas., bd. dirs.), Kenilworth Hist. Soc. (bd. dirs.), Indian Hill Club, Chgo. Club. Republican. Congregationalist. Home: 305 Kenilworth Ave Kenilworth IL 60043-1132 Office: U Chgo 6030 S Ellis Chicago IL 60637

BOTT, JOHN CRIST, artist, educator; b. Gassaway, W.Va., Sept. 12, 1936; s. Joseph Franklin and Blanche Hannah (Crist) B.; m. Glenda Morgan, May 25, 1960 (div. Aug. 1977), 1 child, Jason; m. Kathy Hicklin, Aug. 10, 1977. BS in Art, Troy State U., 1960; MFA, U. N.C., 1969. Tchr. Bratt (Fla.) Jr. H.S., 1961-62, Forest Park (Ga.) Sr. H.S., 1962-67; grad. asst. U. N.C., 1967-68; asst. prof. Greensboro (N.C.) Coll., 1969-72, U. Evansville, Ind., 1972-76, U. So. Ind., Evansville, 1976-77; from asst. to full prof. Colby-Sawyer Coll., New London, N.H., 1977—. One-man shows include Troy (Ala.) State Coll., 1960, Clark Coll.-Atlanta U., 1966, Union South Gallery, U. N.C., Chapel Hill, 1969, Alamance County Arts Ctr., Graham, N.C., 1969, Cullis Gallery, Greensboro Coll., 1970, Stone Galleries, Davidson

(N.C.) Coll., 1971, Ill. State U. Evansville, 1976; group exhibits include Amerika Haus, Nurnberg, Germany, 1959, Mobile (Ala.) Art Assn., 1962, Adair Art Gallery, Atlanta, 1966, N.C. State U., Raleigh, 1968, Greensboro Pub. Libr., 1969, Garden Gallery, Raleigh, N.C., 1969, 70, Meredith Coll., Raleigh, 1970, , N.C. Mus. Art, Raleigh, 1971, 72, N.C. Artists Traveling Exhbn., 1971, Old Gallery, Evansville, 1972, Evansville Mus., 1972, Krannert Gallery, Evansville, 1973, Anderson (Ind.) Fine Arts Ctr., 1974, State Ctr. Gallery, Evansville, 1975, Mugar Gallery, New London, 1978, 79, 81, 82, 83, 84, 85, Phenix Gallery, Concord, 1982, Thronja Gallery, Springfield, Mass., 1986, Dartmouth Faculty Club, Hanover, 1987, Libr. Arts Ctr., Newport, 1988, New Harmony Gallery Contemporary Art, 1988, Ctr. for the Arts, Nashua, 1990, McGowan Fine Art, Concord, 1990, Libr. Arts Ctr., Newport, 1996, Kimball-Jenkins Mansion, Concord, 1997, Millbrook Gallery, Concord, 1997, many others; represented in permanent collections Troy State U., Spring Mills, Inc., Lancaster, S.C., Burlington Industries, Greensboro, Witherspoon Gallery, U. N.C., Greensboro, Sheldon Swope Gallery, Terre Haute, Ind., Bank of N.H., Concord, Chrysler Mus., Norfolk, Va., others. With U.S. Army, 1956-59. Home: 426 Main St Springfield NH 03284 Office: Colby-Sawyer Coll New London NH 03257

BOTT, RAOUL, mathematician, educator; b. Budapest, Hungary, Sept. 24, 1923; s. Rudolf and Margit (Kovach) B.; m. Phyllis Aikman, Aug. 30, 1947; children: Anthony, Jocelyn, Renee, Candace. B Engring., McGill U., Montreal, 1945, M Engring., 1946, DSc (hon.), 1987; DSc, Carnegie Inst. Tech., 1949; DSc (hon.), Notre Dame U., 1979, Carnegie-Mellon U., 1989, U. Leicester, England. Fellow Inst. Advanced Studies, Princeton U., 1949-51, 55-57; instr. math. U. Mich., Ann Arbor, 1951-52, asst. prof., 1952-55, assoc. prof., 1957-59; prof. Harvard U., Cambridge, Mass., 1959—, W. Casper Graustein prof., 1969—. Author books and papers in various branches of math. and its relation to physics. Sloan fellow, 1956-60; hon. fellow St. Catharines Coll., 1985; recipient Nat. Sci. Medal, Pres. of U.S., 1987. Fellow Am. Acad. Arts & Scis., Am. Math. Soc. (Veblen prize 1964, Steele prize 1990); mem. NAS, London Math. Soc. (hon.), French Acad. Sci. Democrat. Roman Catholic. Avocations: music, nature. Home: 1 Richdale Ave Unit 9 Cambridge MA 02140-2610 Office: Harvard U Dept Math 1 Oxford St Cambridge MA 02138-2901*

BOTTEL, HELEN ALFEA, columnist, writer; b. Beaumont, Calif.; d. Alpheus Russell and Mary Ellen (Alexander) Brigden; m. Robert E. Bottel; children: Robert Dennis, Rodger M., R. Kathryn Bottel Bernhardt, Suzanne V. Bottel Peppers. AA, Riverside Coll. Calif.; student, Oreg. State U., 1958-59, So. Oreg. Coll., 1959. Writer, editor Illinois Valley News, Cave Junction, Oreg., 1950-56; writer Grants Pass (Oreg.) Courier, Portland Oregonian, Medford (Oreg.) Mail Tribune, 1952-58; daily columnist Helen Help Us and Generation Rap King Features Syndicate, N.Y.C., 1958-83, columnist (with Sue Bottel), 1969-83; adv. bd. Internat. Affairs Inst., N.Y.C., Tokyo, 1986—; freelance mag. writer, author, lectr., 1956—. Author: To Teens with Love, 1969, Helen Help Us, 1970, Parents Survival Kit, 1979; contbg. editor, columnist Real World mag., 1978-84; weekly columnist Yomiuri Shimbun, Tokyo, 1982-90; thrice weekly columnist Sacramento Union, 1986-88; newspaper and mag. columnist Look Who's Aging (with dau. Kathy Bernhardt), 1992-96; contbr. nonfiction to books and nat. mags. Staff mem. ACT Handicapped Children Games, Sacramento, 1986—; bd. dirs. Ill. Valley Med. Ctr., 1958-62, Childrens Ctr., Sacramento, 1969, Family Support Programs, Sacramento, 1991-95; active Grants Pass Br. Oreg. Juvenile Adv. Com., 1960-62, Nat. Spina Bifida Assn.; charter patron Cosumnes River Coll., Sacramento, 1972—; nat. adv. bd. Nat. Anorexic Aid Soc., 1977-83; scholarship com. judge Exec. Women Internat., 1985. Recipient Women's Svc. Cup Riverside Coll., citation for aid to U.S. servicemen in Vietnam Gov. Ga., 1967, Disting. Merit citation NCCJ, 1970, 1st place award for books Calif. Press Women, 1970, Sacramento Regional Arts Coun. Lit. Achievement award, 1974, Alumna of Yr. award Riverside Coll., 1987, Gold and Silver medals Calif. Sr. Games (tennis), 1990-91. Mem. Am. Soc. Journalists and Authors, Internat. Affairs Inst. Presbyterian. Clubs: Calif. Writers, Southgate Tennis. Home: 2060 56th Ave Sacramento CA 95822-4112 *"Leap before you look." That's for me. My best moments and finest achievements have resulted from spur-of-the-moment impulses on which I've acted before second thoughts or considered judgment could persuade me they were impossible.*

BOTTELLI, RICHARD, retired architect; b. Orange, N.J., Apr. 20, 1937; s. Romolo and Genevieve Bottelli; B.Arch., U. Va., 1962; m. Ann Erpenbeck, June 7, 1958; children: Richard, William, Suzanne, John. Designer. project mgr. Romolo Bottelli, Jr., Maplewood, N.J., 1963-67; prin. Becker & Becker Assos., N.Y.C. and London, 1967-73; propr. Bottelli Assos., Architects/Planners, Florham Park, N.J., 1973-95, ret., 1995; vis. lectr. U. Cin., 1974, So. Meth. U., 1974, Leicester (Eng.) Coll. Art, 1970; mem. adv. com. Sch. Architecture, N.J. Inst. Tech., 1982-83. Mem. Summit (N.J.) Planning Bd., 1971-82, chmn., 1973-82, mem. Zoning Bd., 1972-82, councilman-at-large, 1985-89 ; mem. N.J. Citizens Com. on Permit Coordination, 1981-85. Lic. architect, N.Y., N.J., Pa. Mem. AIA, N.J. Soc. Architects (pres. 1977), N.J. Soc. Profl. Planners, Nat. Trust Historic Preservation, Summit Tennis Club, Rotary (pres. 1987-88). Chmn. mag. editorial bd. Architecture N.J., 1974-78. Works include: Gregory Park Redevel., 1965, Bankers Trust Plaza Br. Bank, N.Y.C., 1973, Hackettstown Post Office, 1976, Norman Towers, 1980, New Brunswick Sr. Citizens Housing, 1982, East Orange Sr. Citizens Housing, 1983, Springfield Mcpl. Bldg., 1990. Home: 6 Primrose Pl Summit NJ 07901-4310

BOTT-GRAHAM, MICHELLE LYNN, behavior therapist; b. Spokane, Wash., Nov. 17, 1967; d. James Joseph Bott and Ann Marie (Harrington) McDowell; m. Preston Scott Graham, May 28; children: Justin Riley, William James. BA in Psychology, U. Idaho, 1989; MA in Psychology, Claremont U., 1992. Therapist, billing coord. Claremont Ctr. for the Rsch. and Treatment of Austin, 1989-90; rsch. asst. Kaiser Permanente, Pasadena, Calif., 1989-92; tchr. Tobinworld, Glendale, Calif., 1991-92; program coord. Grand Teton Svc. Group, Idaho Falls, Idaho, 1992-93; program dir. TBA, Inc., Pocatello, Idaho, 1993-94; psychologist extender, therapist The Ctr. for Human Rels., Pocatello, 1993-97; owner, founder, dir., behavior therapist The Advocacy and Learning Assocs., Pocatello, 1997—. Claremont Grad. U. rsch. grantee, 1990-91; U. Idaho scholar, 1988-89. Mem. ACA, Assn. for Behavior Analysis, Assn. for the Advancement of Behavior Therapy, Idaho Psychol. Assn., Autism Soc. of Am. Democrat. Methodist. Avocations: reading, traveling, family. Office: Advocacy and Learning Assocs 850 E Lander St Pocatello ID 83201-5763

BOTTIGLIA, FRANK ROBERT, bank executive; b. S.I., Jan. 12, 1946; s. Hugo and Rose (Renzi) B.; children: Christine Ann, Catherine Rose, Elizabeth Mary, Laura Michele. BBA, CCNY, 1968; MBA, Baruch Coll., 1976. Adv. profl. cert. pub. acctg. Fin. analyst corp. human resources Chase Manhattan Bank, N.Y.C., 1971-73, mgr. fin. controls corp. human resources, 1974-75, mgr. fin. and adminstrn. corp. human resources, 1976-77, sr. fin. mgmt. officer real estate fin., 1978-83, v.p., contr. U.S. regional comml. sector, 1984-89, v.p., budge dir. N.Am. sector, 1990-93, v.p., fin. mgr. global corp. fin., 1994-95; v.p., contr. Chase Manhattan Bank, Mex., 1995-96; v.p., contr. client access Chase Manhattan Bank, Bklyn., 1997-98, v.p., contr. global treasury mgmt., 1998—; dir. Chase Access Svcs. Inc. Bd. mgr. Town and Country Villas Home Owners Assn., S.I., 1991. Sgt. U.S. Army, 1968-70. Mem. Internat. Platform Assn. Roman Catholic. Avocations: tennis, travel. Home: 481 Mill Rd Staten Island NY 10306-4537 Office: Chase Manhattan Bank 4 Chase Metrotech Ctr Brooklyn NY 11245

BOTTIGLIA, WILLIAM FILBERT, humanities educator; b. Bernardsville, N.J., Nov. 23, 1912; s. Vincent Richard and Quintilia (Mastrobattista) B.; m. Mildred MacDonald, Dec. 21, 1943 (dec. Oct. 1966); children: Martha (Mrs. Milton Morris), Janet. AB, Princeton U., 1934, AM, 1935, PhD, 1948. Instr. modern langs. Princeton U., 1934-42; engaged in industry, 1942-47; gen. mgr. J & S Tool Co., East Orange, N.J., 1946-47; asst. prof. English, St. Lawrence U., 1948; prof. Romance langs. and lits., chmn. dept. Ripon Coll., 1948-56; faculty MIT, 1956—, prof. fgn. lit. and humanities, 1960-74, head dept. fgn. lit. and linguistics, 1964-73, prof. mgmt. and humanities, 1974-78, prof. emeritus and sr. lectr. mgmt. and humanities, 1978-91. Author: Voltaire's Candide: Analysis of a Classic, 2d edit., 1964, (with others) Voltaire (Twentieth Century Views), 1968, Toward Cosmic Meliorism: Memoirs of an Uncircumcised Jew, 1997; editor: Reports of N.E. Conf. on the Teaching of Fgn. Langs, 1957, 62, 63. Mem. Soc. Palmes Académiques, Dante Soc. Am., Phi Beta Kappa. Home: 34 Mary Chilton Rd Needham MA 02492-1138

BOTTITTA, JOSEPH ANTHONY, lawyer; b. Mar. 9, 1949; s. Anthony S. and Elizabeth (Bellisano) B.; m. Lynda Joan Kloss, Apr. 14, 1979; children: Michelle Emma, Gregory Joseph.; BSBA, Seton Hall U., 1971, JD, 1974. Bar: N.H. 1974, U.S. Dist. Ct. N.J. 1974, U.S. Supreme Ct. 1981. Ptnr. Rusignola & Pugliese, Newark, 1974-78; sr. ptnr. Joseph A. Bottitta, West Orange, N.J., 1979-88, Gilbert, Gilbert, Schlossberg and Bottitta, 1988-89; pvt. practice, 1989-95; with Bottitta and Bascelli, 1995—; chmn. Supreme Ct. Fee Arbitration Com. Dist. V-B., 1984-85; mem. N.J. Uniform Law Commn., 1987-91; mem. N.J. Commn. on Professionalism in Law, 1997—. Fellow Am. Bar Found.; mem. ABA, ATLA, N.J. State Bar Assn. (trustee 1988, sec. 1988-94, treas. 1994-95, v.p. 1995-97, pres.-elect 1997-98, pres. 1998-99), Essex County Bar Assn. (sec. 1983-84, treas. 1984-85, pres.-elect 1985-86, pres. 1986-87). Republican. Roman Catholic. Office: 80 Main St West Orange NJ 07052-5414

BOTTJER, DAVID JOHN, earth sciences educator; b. N.Y.C., Oct. 3, 1951; s. John Henry and Marilyn (Winter) B.; m. Sarah Ranney Wright, July 26, 1973. BS, Haverford Coll., 1973; MA, SUNY, Binghamton, 1976; PhD, Ind. U., 1978. NRC postdoctoral rsch. assoc. U.S. Geol. Survey, Washington, 1978-79; asst. prof. dept. geol. scis. U. So. Calif., L.A., 1979-85, assoc. prof. dept. geol. scis., 1985-91, prof. dept. earth scis., 1991—; rsch. assoc. L.A. County Mus. Natural History, 1979—, U. Calif., 1991—; vis. scientist Field Mus. Natural History, Chgo., 1986; guest prof. Swiss Fed. Inst. Tech., Zurich, 1993; Paleontol. Soc. Disting. lectr., 1992-93; mem. Nat. Sci. Found. panel on earth systems history, 1997—. Editor Palaios, 1989-96; assoc. editor Cretaceous Rsch., 1988-91; mem. editl. bd. Geology, 1984-89, 95—, Hist. Biology, 1988-93; co-editor Columbia U. Press Critical Moments in Paleobiology and Earth History (book series), 1990—; chmn. Columbia U. Press Adv. Com. for Paleontology, 1990—. Fellow Geol. Soc. Am., Geol. Soc. London; mem. AAAS, Paleontol. Soc., Soc. Sediment Geology, Internat. Paleontology Assn. Office: U So Calif Dept Earth Scis Los Angeles CA 90089-0740

BOTTOM, DALE COYLE, management consultant; b. Columbus, Ind., June 25, 1932; s. James Robert and Sarah Lou (Coyle) B.; m. Frances Audrey Wilson, June 6, 1954 (div.); children: Jane Ellen, Steven Dale, Sharon Lynn, Carol Ann; m. Elaine McAuliffe, Aug. 20, 1988. BS, Ball State U., Muncie, Ind., 1954. Admissions counselor Stephens Coll., Columbia, Mo., 1958-61; exec. asst., then staff v.p. Inst. Fin. Edn., Chgo., 1961-67, pres., 1967-92; exec. v.p., chief fin. officer U.S. League Savs. Instns., 1985-89; chmn., dir. SAF-Systems & Forms Co.; sec.-gen. Internat. Union Fin. Instns., Chgo., 1989-95; cons. Resource Strategies Internat., Hinsdale, Ill., 1995—; bd. dirs. Savs. Instn. Ins. Group, Ltd., v.p., chief fin. officer. Chmn. bd. Barrington (Ill.) United Meth. Ch., 1981. Served as officer USAF, 1955-58; comdr. USNR (ret.), 1967-78. Mem. Fin. Mgrs. Soc. (dir.), Savs. Instns. Mktg. Soc. Am., Navy League, Ind. Soc. Chgo., Tavern Club (v.p. 1993), Medinah. Republican. Home and Office: Resource Strategies 606 Burr Ridge Club Dr Burr Ridge IL 60521-5209

BOTTOMS, BARBARA ANN, nurse; b. Sept. 8, 1948; d. Homer Eugene and Etta (Simmons) B. Assoc. degree in Nursing, Wallace St. Cmty. Coll., Napierfield, Ala., 1974; BS in Nursing, Auburn U., Montgomery, Ala., 1981. RN, Tex., Fla.; cert. med.-surg., ANCC. Nurses aide Flowers Hosp., Dothan, Ala., 1969-74, charge nurse, 1974-76, evening supr., 1976; staff nurse, charge Enterprise Hosp., Dothan, Ala., 1976; charge nurse Baptist Med. Ctr., Montgomery, Ala., 1976-77, head nurse, 1977-78; staff nurse med. surg. unit U. Med. Ctr., Montgomery, Ala., 1978; staff nurse VA Adminstrn. Med. Ctr., Montgomery, Ala., 1978-86; staff nurse neurosurgery unit Tampa (Fla.) Gen. Hosp., 1986; SE Ala. Med. Ctr., Dothan, 1986-88, Flowers Hosp., Dothan, 1988-89; nurse level III neurosurgery Meth. Hosp., Houston, 1989—, coord. patient care, 1994-99; staff nurse Meml. Hermann Hosp., Houston, 1999—; mem. nursing standards com., 1993—, vice chair, 1994, mem. blood dr. com., 1993, 94, mem. nursing standards and procedures, 1995, Nursing Avenues Commn., 1995. Mem. Am. Assn. Neurosci. Nurses, Sigma Theta Tau (sec. Kappa Omega chpt. 1984-85, Zeta Pi chpt.). Avocations: reading, crocheting, knitting, watching sports, collecting mugs and models. Home and Office: 6239 Lymbar Dr Houston TX 77096-4620 Office: Meth Hosp 6565 Fannin St Houston TX 77030-2707

BOTTOMS, BRENDA PINCHBECK, elementary education educator; b. South Hill, Va., Sept. 30, 1958; d. Bernard Irving Jr. and Laura Etta (Rogers) Pinchbeck; m. Franklin Keith Bottoms, Apr. 20, 1984; children: David Keith, Heath Brennan. BS in Elem. Edn., Longwood Coll., Farmville, Va., 1979. Cert. 4-7 tchr., Va.; cert. talented and gifted tchr., 1997. Substitute tchr. Nottoway County Schs., Blackstone, Va., 1979-80; mid. sch. tchr. Greensville County Schs., Emporia, Va., 1981-83, elem. tchr., 1983—; 6th grade chmn. Belfield Elem. Sch., Emporia, 1990-93; Hugs tutorial tchr., 1987; cert. Spaulding tchr., 1989, reading in the content areas tchr. Participant Quality Schs. Com., 1993-94. Recipient Parent Vol. award Greensville County Schs., 1991, Women's Leadership award Greensville County, 1990, 91. A. Avocations: reading, crocheting, sports, children. Home: 2351 Zion Church Rd Emporia VA 23847-7347 Office: Belfield Elem Sch 515 Belfield Rd Emporia VA 23847-8065

BOTTOMS, ROBERT GARVIN, academic administrator; b. Birmingham, Ala., June 28, 1944; s. Dalton Garvin and Mary Inez (Cruce) B.; m. Gwendolynn Jean Vickers, June 14, 1968; children: David Timothy, Leslie Clair. BA, Birmingham So. U., 1966; BD, Emory U., 1969; D Ministry, Vanderbilt U., 1972. Chaplain Birmingham (Ala.) So. Coll., 1973-74, asst. to pres., 1974-75; asst. dean, asst. prof. church and ministry Vanderbilt U., Nashville, 1975-78; v.p. for univ. rels. DePauw U., Greencastle, Ind., 1978-79, exec. v.p. external rels., 1979-83, exec. v.p. of the univ., 1983-86, acting pres., 1985, pres., 1986—; cons. on theol. edn. The Lilly Endowment, Indpls., 1979-82; cons. Luth. So. Sem., Columbia, S.C., 1979-80, Fund for Theol. Edn., N.Y.C., 1981-82, Arthur Vining Davis Found., Jacksonville, Fla., 1978-79; Am. Ctr. for Internat. Leadership organizer Edn. Policy Commn. U.S.-USSR Emerging Leaders Summit, Phila., 1988; chmn. audit com. Centel Cable TV Co., Oak Brook, Ill, 1987-89, also bd. dirs.; bd. dirs. G.M. Constrn., Inc., Indpls. Author: Lessons in Financial Management, 1981-82. Chmn. com. on ch. and coll. Episcopal Diocese Ind., 1979-84; mem. bd. visitors Vanderbilt U., 1980—; bd. dirs. Joyce Found., 1994—, G.M. Constrn. Inc., Indpls., 1998—. Mem. NCAA (coun. 1989-95, subcom. eligibility appeals), Nat. Coun. Chs. (governing bd. 1985-91), Nat. Assn. Ind. Colls. and Univs. (task force on increasing the participation of minorities in ind. higher edn. 1989-95), Nat. Assn. Schs. and Colls. United Meth. Ch. (bd. dirs. 1987-90), Am. Coun. Edn. (commn. on women in higher edn. 1990—), Ind. Colls. of Ind. (bd. dirs. 1987—, exec. com. 1991—), Ind. Colls. of Ind. Found. (bd. dirs. 1987—, nominating com. 1990—), Great Lakes Colls. Assn. (bd. dirs. 1987—, chair 1994-96), Columbia Club (Indpls.), Univ. Club of N.Y.C., Cosmos Club (Washington), Chgo. Club. Avocation: boating. Home: 125 Wood St Greencastle IN 46135-1829 Office: DePauw Univ Office of Pres 313 S Locust St Greencastle IN 46135-1736

BOTTONE, FRANK MICHAEL, secondary education educator; b. Livingston, N.J., Jan. 8, 1931; s. Patsy and Carmela (Spagnola) B.; m. Doris Hollingsworth, 1953 (div. 1963); children: Lynda, Frank; m. Elizabeth Goodwin, June 27, 1976. BS, Panzer Coll., 1956; MEd, Seton Hall U., 1976. Permanent tchg. cert., N.J. Phys. edn. tchr., coach Madison (N.J.) H.S., 1956-63; tchr., coach New Providence (N.J.) H.S., 1963—; bd. dirs. Nat. Football Found., N.J. bd. dirs. La Barca Clinic, 1978, La Barca Coll. Day and Football Clinic Com. With U.S. Army, 1953-55. Recipient William Dioguardi N.J. Football Ofcls. Meml. award, 1997, Coach of Yr. NFICA, 1998, Duffy Daugherty Coach of the Yr. award, Coach of Yr., N.J. Football Coaches Assn., Coach of Yr., Ind. Press. Mem. Am. Football Coaches Assn., Nat. Football Found. (bd. mem. Essex County chpt., Nat. Fedn. H.S. Coaches, N.J. State Athletic Assn. Democrat. Roman Catholic. Avocations: golf, skiing. Home: 281 Beaufort Ave Livingston NJ 07039-1008

BOTTONE, JOANN, health services executive; b. Bklyn., June 20, 1943; d. Anthony and Claire (Bisesti) B.; m. William Recevuto, Feb. 12, 1989; children: Matthew, Sandra. RN, Kings County Hosp. Ctr., Bklyn., 1963; BS, St. Francis Coll., Bklyn., 1980; MPA, Russell Sage Coll., Albany, N.Y., 1986; PhD in Pub. Adminstrn. magna cum laude, Kensington U., 1995. Bd. cert. Health Care Mgmt. Am. Coll. Health Care Execs., 1997. From staff nurse, head nurse, quality assurance coord. Victory Meml. Hosp., Bklyn., 1961-81; instr. infection control Community Hosp. Bklyn., 1981-82; dir. quality assurance Profl. Stds. Rev. Orgn., Bklyn., 1982-85; devel. and coord. HIV post-test counseling program Greater N.Y. Blood Ctr., N.Y.C., 1985-88; dir. HIV/AIDS programs Health Sci. Ctr. SUNY, Bklyn., 1988—; tchr. SUNY Coll. Health Related Professions; mem. working group to develop statewide policies and procedures for health care workers involved in potential HIV exposures N.Y. State Health Commr., 1990; mem. tech. adv. group to develop guidelines for OSHA's bloodborne pathogen standard Greater N.Y. Hosp. Assn., 1992, N.Y.C. Mayor's HIV and Human Svcs. planning coun., 1999; lectr. in field. Contbr. articles to profl. jours. Mem. Am. Coll. Health Care Execs. (diplomate), Greater N.Y. Hosp. Assn. (tech. adv. group).

BOTTORFF, DENNIS C., banker; b. Clarksville, Ind., Sept. 19, 1944; s. Irvin H. and Lucille H. B.; m. Jean Brewington, Aug. 21, 1964; children: Todd, Chad. BE, Vanderbilt U., 1966; MBA, Northwestern U., Evanston, Ill., 1968. Pres. Commerce Union Bank, Nashville; also exec. v.p. Commerce Union Corp., Nashville; chmn., chief exec. officer Commerce Union Bank and Commerce Union Corp., Nashville, 1984-87; vice chmn., chief oper. officer Sovran Fin. Corp., Norfolk, Va., 1988-89, pres., chief oper. officer, 1989-90; pres., chief oper. officer C&S/Sovran Corp., Norfolk, Va., 1990—, C&S/Sovran Corp. (merger Citizens & So. Corp. and Sovran Fin. Corp. 1990), 1990—; chmn., CEO, dir. 1st Am. Corp., Nashville, 1991—; bd. advisors The Jack C. Massey Grad. Sch. Bus., Belmont, Coll., Nashville; bd. dirs. Ingram Industries, Dollar Gen. Corp. Bd. dirs. Tenn. Tomorrow; v.p., mem. exec. com., mem. investment com. Vanderbilt U., Nashville; chmn. Coun. Excellence in Higher Edn.; v.p., trustee Leadership Nashville. Mem. Am. Bankers Assn., Am. Bankers Coun. (bd. dirs.), Bankers Roundtable, Nashville Area C. of C. (bd. dirs.), Hundred Club, Belle Meade Country Club. Presbyterian. Home: 1314 Chickering Rd Nashville TN 37215-4522 Office: First Am Corp First Am Ctr 4th and Union St Nashville TN 37237-0615

BOTWAY, LLOYD FREDERICK, computer scientist, consultant; b. Flushing, N.Y., June 18, 1947; s. Albert Harold and Alice Rebecca (Halperin) B. BS, Tufts U., 1968; MS, U. Colo., 1970. Programmer Anaconda Co., Butte, Mont., 1970-72; systems analyst U. Mo., Columbia, 1972-77; tech. dir. Dataphase Systems, Inc., Kansas City, Mo., 1977-80; pres. Liberty Logic Corp., Pasadena, Md., 1980-84; computer scientist Computer Sci. Corp., Balt., 1984-86; dir. MIS Internat. Clin. Labs., Nashville, 1986-88; dir. info. systems Nat. Health Labs., Nashville, 1988-94; v.p., chief arch. Quest Diagnostics, San Juan Capistrano, Calif., 1994—; Cons. Internat. Clin. Labs., Nashville, 1981-85; grad. asst. Dale Carnegie. Contbr. articles to profl. jours., co-author: (reference pamphlet) Latex Command Summary, 1985. Libertarian candidate for U.S. Ho. of Reps. from 5th Tenn. Dist., 1994. Mem. Toastmasters. Avocations: composing music, flying, foreign languages, electronics, acting. Office: Quest Diagnostics/Nichols Inst 33608 Ortega Hwy San Juan Capistrano CA 92675-2042

BOTWINICK, MICHAEL, museum director; b. N.Y.C., Nov. 14, 1943; s. Joseph and Helen (Shlisky) B.; m. Harriet Maltzer, Aug. 14, 1965; children: Jonathan Seth, Daniel Judah. B.A., Rutgers Coll., 1964; M.A., Columbia U., 1967. Instr. Columbia U., N.Y.C., 1968-69, CCNY, CUNY, 1969; asst. curator medieval art Cloisters Met. Mus. Art, N.Y.C., 1969; asso. curator medieval art Cloisters Met. Mus. Art, 1970, asst. curator-in-chief, 1971—; asst. dir. art Phila. Mus. Art, 1971-74; dir. Bklyn. Mus., 1974-83, Corcoran Gallery Art, 1983-87; sr. v.p. Knoedler-Modarco, S.A., N.Y.C., 1987-88; pres. Fine Arts Group, Chgo., 1989-91; dir. Newport Harbor Art Mus., Newport Beach, Calif., 1991-97; dir. Ctr. Orange County Regional Studies U. Calif., Irvine, 1997-98; dir. Staten Island Inst. Arts & Scis., 1998—; pres. Cultural Instns. Group, 1975-76; mem. N.Y.C. Adv. Commn. Cultural Affairs, 1975-76, N.Y.C. Urban Design Coun., 1975; mem. adv. bd. WNET, N.Y.C., 1979-83; mem. Nat. Conservation Adv. Coun., 1979-80, exec. com. U.S. Com.-Internat. Coun. Mus., 1982-87, Yale U. Coun. Com. on the Art Gallery, 1983-88, Internat. Rsch. and Exch. Bd., fine arts com. German Dem. Republic, 1984-87, fine arts com. U.S. State Dept. Arts in Embassies Program, 1986-88; arts adminstrn. adv. com. U. Calif.-Irvine, 1993—. Mem. Assn. Art Mus. Dirs., Am. Assn. Museums, Coll. Art Assn., Steppenwolf Theater Co., Chgo. (bd. dirs. 1990-91). Office: Staten Island Inst Arts & Scis 75 Stuyvesant Pl Staten Island NY 10301 Office: U Calif PO Box 6050 Irvine CA 92616-6050*

BOTWINICK, MILTON EDWARD, genealogist, researcher; b. Phila., Feb. 25, 1942; s. Joseph J. and Beatrice R. (Miller) B. Cert. in Elec. Engring. Tech., Temple U., 1962; BA, Rowan U., 1970. Genealogist Phila., 1982. Columnist (newsletter) Chronicles. With USAF, 1966. Mem. Geneal. Soc. Pa. E-mail: botwinick@lycosmail.com. Home: PO Box 13464 Philadelphia PA 19101-3464

BOUBELIK, HENRY FREDRICK, JR., travel company executive; b. Chgo., Aug. 16, 1936; s. Henry Fredrick and Anna Mabel (Short) B.; m. Jane V. Boubelik, Oct. 27, 1978; children—Debra Ann, Henry Fredrick III, Steven W., Catherine Earle. Student, U. Ill., 1954-55, Trinity U., 1957-59. Asst. mgr. Avis Rent-A-Car, San Antonio, 1957-60; city mgr. Hertz Rent-a-Car, Corpus Christi, Tex., 1960-67; regional mgr. Nat. Car Rental System, Inc., Mpls., 1967-69; sr. v.p. Nat. Car Rental System, Inc., 1969-92; chmn. Meyer-Boubelik and Assocs., Mpls., 1992-95; pres. Leisure divsns. Northwestern Travel Svc., Minnetonka, Minn., 1995—. Mem. adv. bd. Corpus Christi Bayfront, 1963-66. Served with AUS, 1955-57. Mem. Car and Truck Rental and Leasing Assn. (v.p. 1973, dir. 1974-77), Am. Car Rental Assn. (pres. 1980-81). Club: Civitan (dir., pres.-elect 1963-66). Home: 6617 Cornelia Dr Minneapolis MN 55435-1654 Office: 14525 Highway 7 Ste 100 Minnetonka MN 55345-3734

BOUCHARD, JAMES PAUL, steel manufacturing and planning executive; b. Kansas City, Kans., May 2, 1961; s. Robert Clayton and Helen (Clancy) B.; m. Carolyn Keegan, July 19, 1986. BBA, Loyola U., Chgo., 1984. Asst. to dist. mgr. Inland Steel Co., Chgo., 1983-85; sales rep. Denver br. Westinghouse Electric, 1985-87, U.S. Steel (divsn. USX Corp.), Milw., 1987-91; Midwest area sr. rep. U.S. Steel (divsn. USX Corp.), Oak Brook, Ill., 1987-94, resident mgr., 1994-97; strategic planning and devel. mgr. U.S. Steel (divsn. USX Corp.), Pitts., 1997-98, mgr. mktg., 1998, nat. mgr. pipe, tube, and container group, 1999—; bd. dirs. Edgewood Valley C.C., U .S. Recovery, Hinsdale, Ill., Porcelain Enamel Inst., Nashville, AHAM, Chgo. Co-inventor patented light weight concrete, 1983. Mem. Evans Scholars Found., Japan Am. Soc. Chgo. Mem. Japan Am. Soc. Chgo., Loyola U. Alumni Assn., U. San Diego Alumni Assn. (scholar), Chgo. Dist. Golf Assn., Edgewood Valley Country Club, mem. Art Inst. of Chgo., Edgeworth Club (Pa.), Sewickley Heights Golf Club (Pa.). Republican. Roman Catholic. Avocations: golf, basketball, baseball, football. Home: 3 Beaver St Sewickley PA 15143-1217

BOUCHARD, LUCIEN, Canadian government official; b. St.-Coeur-de-Marie, Que., Can., Dec. 22, 1938; s. Philippe and Alice (Simard) B; m. Audrey Best; children: Alexandre, Simon. BA, Coll. de Jonquière, 1959; B in Soc. Sci., U. Laval, 1964, LL.L., 1964. Bar: Que. 1964. Pvt. practice Chicoutimi, Que., 1964-85; ambassador to France Can. govt., 1985-88; mem. Ho. of Commons Ottawa, Ont., Can., 1988-95; sec. of state of Can. House of Commons, Ottawa, 1988, minister for environment, 1989-90, ind. mem.; chmn., leader Bloc Québécois, 1991; leader official opposition, critic fgn. affairs Ho. Commons, 1993; prime min. Québécois Govt., 1996—; chmn. Arbitration Tribunals Edn. Sector, 1970-76; mem. Martin Bouchard Commn., 1974-75; coord., mem. various spl. teams , Govt. Québec; bd. dirs. Société générale de financement du Québec, Société Donohue Inc., Can. Investment Devel. Corp. Co-author: Martin-Bouchard Report, 1978; author: A visage découvert, 1992. Chmn. Que. Ednl. Arbitration Bd., 1970-76. Mem. Saquenay Bar (pres.), Québec Bar (mem. adminstrv. com., chmn. specialization com. Office: Office of PM, Bldg J, 885 Grande-Allia E 3d Fl, Quebec, PQ Canada G1A 1A2*

BOUCHARD, RONALD A., health care administrator; b. Kankakee, Ill., Jan. 15, 1942; s. Armand F. and Dorothy M. (Devine) B.; m. Judith Boyer; children: Breck, Michelle, Bryce. BS in Bus., Ea. Ill. U., 1964; MA in Mgmt., Ball State U., 1972. Asst. dir. pers. Ill. State U., Normal, 1964-67;

asst. to pres. Ball State U., Muncie, Ind., 1968-78; dir. pers. and employee rels. Calif. State U., Northridge, 1978-80; asst. v.p. for human resources U. Va., Charlottesville, 1980-84; dir. pers. and tng. Commonwealth of Va., Richmond, 1984-86; assoc. v.p. for adminstrn. U. Va., 1986-90; chief adminstrv. officer U. Va. Med. Ctr., Charlottesville, 1990—; v.p. Coll. and Univ. Pers. Assn., Washington, 1976-79, pres. 1980-81; mem. adv. bd. for retirement plan Met. Life Resources, N.Y.C., 1990-96. Author: (books) Personnel Practices for Small Colleges, 1980 (award 1980), Human Resource Practices for Small Colleges, 1992 (award 1993); co-author: (book) Interview Guide for Supervisors, 1988-89 (award 1989). V.p. Jaycees, Muncie, Ind., 1970; chmn. Commonwealth of Va. Decentralization Task Force for Higher Edn., Richmond, 1988. Recipient Donald Dickason award Coll. and Univ. Pers. Assn., Washington, 1983; named Outstanding First Yr. Mem., State of Ind. Jaycees, Indpls., 1969. Mem. Va. Hosp. Assn., Internat. Pers. Mgmt. Assn. Avocations: golf, tennis, reading. Home: 7 Beaverdam Ter Palmyra VA 22963-2515 Office: U Va Med Ctr PO Box 148 Charlottesville VA 22902-0148

BOUCHARD, THOMAS JOSEPH, JR., psychology educator, researcher; b. Manchester, N.H., Oct. 3, 1937; s. Thomas and Florence (Charest) B.; m. Pauline Marina Proulx, Aug. 13, 1960; children: Elizabeth, Mark. BA, U. Calif., Berkeley, 1963, PhD, 1966. Asst. prof. U. Calif., Santa Barbara, 1966-69; asst. prof. U. Minn., Mpls., 1969-70, assoc. prof., 1970-73, prof., 1973—, chmn. dept. psychology, 1985-91; dir. Minn. Ctr. Twin and Adoption Rsch., U. Minn., 1980—. Assoc. editor Jour. Applied Psychology, 1977-80, Behavior Genetics, 1982-86; contbr. over 145 articles to profl. jours. With USAF, 1955-58. Fellow AAAS, APA, Am. Psychol. Soc.; mem. Phi Beta Kappa, Sigma Xi. Home: 1860 Shoreline Dr Wayzata MN 55391-9771 Office: Univ of Minn Dept Psychology 75 E River Rd Minneapolis MN 55455-0280

BOUCHER, FREDERICK C., congressman, lawyer; b. Abingdon, Va., Aug. 1, 1946; s. Ralph E. and Dorothy (Buck) B. BA, Roanoke Coll., 1968; JD, U. Va., 1971. Bar: Va. 1971, N.Y. 1972. Assoc. Milbank, Tweed, Hadley, McCloy, N.Y.C., 1971-73; ptnr. Boucher & Boucher, Abingdon, Va.; state senator Va. Gen. Assembly, Richmond, 1975-79, 79-82; commerce judiciary com. 98th-105th Congresses from 9th Va. dist., Washington, D.C., 1983—; asst. whip; mem. House Com. on Judiciary, House Energy & Commerce Com; former chmn. subcom. on sci. Recipient Disting. Service award Va. Highlands Community Coll., Abingdon, 1984, Beamer award for Contributions to Vocational Edn., 1986, Legislator of Yr. award Vietnam Vets. Am., 1993. Mem. ABA, Assn. Bar of N.Y.C., Va. Bar Assn. Democrat. Methodist. Office: US Ho of Reps 2329 Rayburn HOB Washington DC 20515*

BOUCHER, HAROLD IRVING, retired lawyer; b. Chico, Calif., June 27, 1906; s. Charles Augustus and Nina Eugenia (Knickerbocker) B.; m. Beula Blair Davis, Apr. 11, 1931. LLB, JD, U. Calif., Berkeley, 1930. Bar: Calif. 1930. Assoc. to adv. ptnr. Pillsbury, Madison & Sutro, Attys. at Law, San Francisco, 1934-93, ret. ptnr., 1993. Named to Order of British Empire Queen Elizabeth II of England, 1972. Fellow Am. Bar, Am. Coll. Probate (regent 1966), Am. Coll. Counsel (pres. 1967-68); mem. ABA, State Bar Calif., Old Capital Club. Office: 114 Sansome St Ste 539 San Francisco CA 94104-3812*

BOUCHER, JOSEPH W(ILLIAM), lawyer, accountant, educator, writer; b. Menominee, Mich., Oct. 28, 1951; s. Joseph W. and Patricia (Coon) B.; m. Susan M. De Groot, June 4, 1977; children: Elizabeth, Bridget, Joseph William III. BA, St. Norbert Coll., 1973; JD, U. Wis., 1977, MBA in Fin., 1978. Bar: Wis. 1978, U.S. Dist. Ct. (we. dist.) Wis. 1978; CPA, Wis. Adminstrv. aide to Senator Wis. Senate, Madison, 1977; from assoc. to ptnr. Murphy, Stolper et al., Madison, 1977-84; ptnr. Stolper, Koritzinsky, Brewster & Neider, Madison, 1985-94; mng. ptnr. Stolper, Koritzinsky, Brewster, Neider, Madison, 1989-92, Neider & Boucher, S.C., 1995—; lectr. bus. U. Wis., Madison, 1980—; bd. dirs. St. Coletta's H.S., others, 1997—. Co-author: Organizing a Wisconsin Business Corporation, 1995, 99, Wisconsin LLCs and LLPs Handbook, 1996, 1999; contbr. articles to Wis. Bar Assn. Bd. dirs. Jackson Found., 1994-99, West Met. Bus. Assn., 1990-95, Dane County United Way, 1986-89, pres. 1994; bd. dirs. Wis. Chamber Orch., 1990-94, pres., 1993-94; mem. bd. advisors St. Mary's Med. Ctr., Madison, 1989-91; bd. dirs. St. Coletta's, 1997—, Edgewood H.S., 1997—. Named one of Outstanding Young Men of Am., 1979; named Wis. Lawyer Advocate of Yr., SBA, 1983. Mem. ABA, AICPA (mem. bd. examiners, mem. bus. law subcom. 1987-90), Wis. Bar Assn., Wis. State Bar Assn. (mem. corp. com. 1991—, co-chairperson interprofl. com. 1992-95, chair ltd. liability co. subcom.), Dane County Bar Assn., Wis. Inst. CPAs, U. Wis. Bus. Alumni Assn. (bd. dirs. 1980-87). Roman Catholic. Avocations: sports, reading. Office: Neider & Boucher SC 440 Science Dr Madison WI 53711

BOUCHER, LARRY GENE, sports association commissioner; b. Bowling Green, Ky., Jan. 23, 1947; s. Larry Gene and Virginia Elizabeth (Miller) B.; m. Paula Ann Feeback, Oct. 4, 1949 (div. Feb. 1996); children: Brooke Renee, Brenna Ann. BS in Bus. Edn., Ea. Ky. U., 1970. Unemployment ins. examiner Human Resource Cabinet Ky., Frankfort, 1972-73; budget/policy analyst Ky. Transp. Cabinet, Frankfort, 1973-87, br. mgr. mgmt. svcs., 1987-91; asst. commr. Ky. H.S. Athletic Assn., Lexington, 1991—; mem. Am. Govtl. Accts., Frankfort, 1984-87. Mem. allocation com. Frankfort/Franklin County United Way, 1987-91. Mem. Church of Christ. Home: 4030 Tates Creek Rd Apt 2911 Lexington KY 40517-3090 Office: Ky H S Athletic Assn 2280 Executive Dr Lexington KY 40505-4808*

BOUCHER, LOUIS JACK, retired dentist, educator; b. Ashland, Wis., May 24, 1922; s. Louis Napoleon and Clara (Rappatta) B.; m. Mary Lynn Phyllis Elsner, Nov. 5, 1949; children: Lynn Marie, Ellen Lou, Carol Joy, John Charles. Student, Northland Coll., 1945-48, U. Wis., 1948-49; D.D.S., Marquette U., 1953, Ph.D., 1961. Dir. grad. studies and research Marquette U. Sch. Dentistry, 1955-65, U. Ky. Coll. Dentistry, 1965-66; assoc. dean Med. Coll., Ga. Sch. Dentistry, 1966-71; dean Sch. Dentistry, Fairleigh Dickinson U., 1971-75; assoc. dean Coll. Medicine and Dentistry, N.J. Sch. Dentistry, Newark, 1976-77; dir. prosthodontics Sch. Dental Medicine, SUNY-Stony Brook, 1978-89, assoc. dean, 1978-82; cons. VA hosps., U.S. Army, Ft. Jackson, S.C., also Ft. Gordon, Ga.; cons. USAF Aerospace Medicine, Surgeon Gen. USAF, Nat. Inst. Dentistry, USPHS, Am. Dental Assn. Council on Dental Edn. Author: (with A.O. Rahn) Maxillofacial Prosthetics, 1970, A Comprehensive Review of Dentistry, 1979, Occlusal Articulation, 1979, (with T.W. Slaughter) Impacted Teeth and Occlusion, 1980, Treatment of Partially Endentulous Patients, 1982, (with R.P. Renner) Removable Partial Dentures, 1987. Served with AUS, 1942-45. Recipient Nat. Inst. Dental Research Spl. Research fellowship and Career Devel. award, 1961-65. Mem. Am., Internat. colls. dentists, Am. Bd. Prosthodontics, Am. Acad. Maxillofacial Prosthodontics (pres. 1965), Am. Acad. Plastics Research in Dentistry (pres. 1967), Am. Coll. Prosthodontists (pres. 1971), Fedn. Prosthodontics Orgns. (pres. 1967-68), Am. Equilibration Soc. (pres. 1976), Greater N.Y. Acad. Prothodontics (pres. 1988), Sigma Xi, Omicron Kappa Upsilon. Home: 4 Lyme Pl Avon CT 06001-4577 *I always tried to do my best.*

BOUCHER, PAMELA KAY, church consultant, editor; b. Ft. Worth, June 16, 1954; d. Billy Preston and Jean (Kay) B. BS, Dallas Bapt. U., 1976; MA in Religious Edn., Southwestern Bapt. Theol. Sem., 1982. Dir. presch./children's ministries Shearer Hills Bapt. Ch., San Antonio, 1982-85; min. childhood edn. Plymouth Park Bapt. Ch., Irving, Tex., 1985-87, First Bapt. Ch., Ellisville, Mo., 1987-92; dir. presch./children's ministies dept. Calif. So. Bapt. Conv., Fresno, 1992-95; presch./children's specialist Bapt. Sunday Sch. Bd., Nashville, 1995-96; ch. cons. for mins. of presch./children's edn. LifeWay Christian Resources of the So. Bapt. Conv., Nashville, 1996—; conf. leader Assn. Christian Schs. Internat., Anaheim, Calif., 1997 and many others. Author (curriculum) Preschool Bible Teach A, 1992-96, 1999; co-author: Children and Worship: An Administrative Guide, 1999; compilor: Teaching in Christian Weekday Early Education; contbr. articles to mags. and newsletters. Mem. ASCD, Nat. Assn. Edn. of Young Children, So. Bapt. Religious Edn. Assn. Republican. Avocation: reading. Office: LifeWay Christian Resources of the So Bapt Conv 127 9th Ave N Nashville TN 37234-0158

BOUCHER, RICHARD A., ambassador; b. Bethesda, Md., Dec. 13, 1951; s. Melville J. and Ellen (Kaufmann) B.; m. Carolyn L. Brehm, June 19, 1982; children: Madeleine Brehm, Peter Brehm. BA cum laude, Tufts U., 1973; postgrad., George Washington U., 1976-77. Vol. Peace Corps, Senegal, 1973-75; with Agy. Internat. Devel., Guinea, 1975-76; various positions Fgn. Svc., 1977-84; econ. officer U.S. Consulate Gen., Shanghai, 1984-86; sr. watch officer Dept. of State, 1986-87, dep. dir. polit. affairs office European security and polit. affairs, 1987-89, dep. spokesman, 1989-92, acting spokesman, 1992-93; U.S. amb. to Cyprus, 1993-96, U.S. consul gen. to Hong Kong, 1996—. Office: US Consulate Gen Hong Kong Psc 464 Box 30 FPO AP 96522-0030

BOUCHER, WAYNE IRVING, policy analyst; b. Bay City, Mich., Dec. 12, 1934; s. Harold Oscar and Mildred Christine (Born) B.; m. Donna Lou Collins, June 12, 1961 (div. 1972); children: Michèle Annette, Robert Alain. BA in English Lang. and Lit., U. Mich., 1956, MA in English Lang. and Lit., 1960; postgrad. in philosophy, U. Mo., 1959-61. Inst. English U. Mo., Columbia, 1958-63; asst. to pres. Rand Corp., Santa Monica, Calif., 1963-69; rsch. assoc. Inst. for the Future, Middletown, Conn., 1969-71; co-founder, v.p. The Futures Group, Glastonbury, Conn., 1971-76; dept. dir., dir. rsch. Nat. Commn. on Electronic Fund Transfers, Washington, 1976-78; sr. rsch. assoc. Ctr. for Futures Rsch., U. So. Calif., Los Angeles, 1978-84; exec. v.p. Benton Internat., Torrance, Calif., 1984-93; pres. The Ark. Inst., Little Rock, 1993-94; pres., chief ops. officer Electronic Funds Transfer Assn., Herndon, Va., 1994-95; mng. ptnr. Strategic Futures Internat., Washington, 1995—; adj. prof. U. Mo., St. Louis, 1962-63, UCLA, 1964, Grad. Sch. Bus. U. Conn., 1973, Sch. Pub. Adminstrn. U. So. Calif., 1979-80; mem. adv. panel on electronic funds transfer Office of Tech. Assessment U.S. Congress, 1979-81; mem. Task Force on Electronic Benefits Transfer, Electronic Funds Transfer Assn., 1990-92. Author: (with J.L. Morrison and W.L. Renfro) Futures Research and Strategic Planning, 1984; Spinoza in English, 1991, 2d edit., 1999, Spinoza: 18th and 19th Century Discussions, 6 vols., 1999; editor: (with J.L. Morrison and W.L. Renfro) Applying Methods and Techniques of Futures Research, 1983; author, editor: The Study of the Future, 1977; editor (with E.S. Quade) Systems Analysis and Policy Planning, 1968; mem. editorial bd. Technol. Forecasting and Social Change, 1978-82, Futures Rsch. Quar., 1984—; contbr. articles to profl. jours. Home: RR 2 Box 667 Harpers Ferry WV 25425-9414 Office: Strategic Futures Internat 1201 Pennsylvania Ave NW Washington DC 20004-2401

BOUCKAERT, CARL, manufacturing executive. CEO Beaulieu of Am. Group. Office: Beaulieu of Am Inc PO Box 1248 Dalton GA 30722-1248

BOUDART, MICHEL, chemical engineer, chemist, educator; b. Belgium, June 18, 1924; came to U.S., 1947, naturalized, 1957; s. Francois and Marguerite (Swolfs) B.; m. Marina D'Haese, Dec. 27, 1948; children: Mark, Baudouin, Iris, Philip. BS, U. Louvain, Belgium, 1944, MS, 1947; PhD, Princeton U., 1950; D honoris causa, U. Liège, U. Notre Dame, U. Nancy, U. Ghent. Research asso. James Forrestal Research Ctr., Princeton, 1950-54; mem. faculty Princeton U., 1954-61; prof. chem. engring. U. Calif., Berkeley, 1961-64, adj. prof. chem. engring., 1994—; prof. chem. engring. and chemistry Stanford U., 1964-80, Keck prof. engring., 1980-94, Keck prof. engring. emeritus, 1994—; adj. prof. chem. engring. U. Calif., Berkeley, 1996—; co-founder Catalytica, Inc.; mem. tech. adv. bd. Brit. Petroleum, 1992-98; mem. tech. adv. coun. Nova Chems., 1997—; Humble Oil Co. lectr., 1958; AIChE lectr., 1961; Sigma Xi nat. lectr., 1965; chmn. Gordon Rsch. Conf. Catalysis, 1962; bus. affairs com. Ann. Revs., 1982—. Author: Kinetics of Chemical Processes, 1968, (with G. Djéga-Mariadassou) Kinetics of Heterogenous Catalytic Reactions, 1983; editor: (with J.R. Anderson) Catalysis: Science and Technology, 11 vols., 1981-96, (with Marina Boudart and René Bryssinck) Modern Belgium, 1990; mem. adv. edit. bd. Catal. Letters, 1989—, Catalysis Rev., 1968—, Jour. Molecular Catalysis, 1995—, Cattech, 1996—. Recipient Curtis-McGraw rsch. award Am. Soc. Engring. Edn., 1962, R.H. Wilhelm award in chem. reaction engring., 1974, Chem. Pioneer award Am. Inst. Chemists, 1991; Belgium-Am. Ednl. Found. fellow, 1948, Procter fellow, 1949; Fairchild disting. scholar Calif. Tech. Inst., 1995. Fellow AAAS, Am. Acad. Arts. and Scis., Calif. Acad. Scis.; mem. NAS, NAE, Am. Chem. Soc. (Kendall award 1977, E.V. Murphee award in indsl. and engring. chemistry 1985), Catalysis Soc., Am. Inst. Chem. Engrs., Chem. Soc., Académie Royale de Belgique (fgn. assoc.). Home: 228 Oak Grove Ave Atherton CA 94027-2218 Office: Stanford U Dept Chem Engring Stanford CA 94305

BOUDEWYNS, TIMOTHY M., federal judge. Apptd. magistrate judge U.S. Dist. Ct. R.I. Office: 405 Federal Bldg US Courthouse Providence RI 02903-1720

BOUDIN, MICHAEL, federal judge; b. N.Y.C., Nov. 29, 1939; s. Leonard B. and Jean (Roisman) B.; m. Martha A. Field, Sept. 14, 1984. B.A., Harvard Coll., 1961, LL.B., 1964. Bar: N.Y. 1964, D.C. 1967. Law clk. U.S. Ct. Appeals, 2d cir., 1964-65, U.S. Sup. Ct., 1965-66; assoc. firm Covington & Burling, Washington, 1966-72, ptnr., 1972-87; dep. asst. atty. gen. Anti-trust div. Dept. Justice, Washington, 1987-90; judge U.S. Dist. Ct. of D.C., Washington, 1990-92, U.S. Ct. Appeals, Boston, 1992-98; vis. prof. Harvard Law Sch., 1982-83, lectr., 1983-98; lectr. U. Pa. Law Sch., 1984-85. Contbr. revs. to law jours. Mem. ABA, Am. Law Inst. Office: US Ct Appeals 1st Cir One Courthouse Way Ste 7710 Boston MA 02210

BOUDINOT, FRANK DOUGLAS, pharmaceutics educator; b. New Brunswick, N.J., Mar. 31, 1956; s. Frank Lins and Dorothy Jean (Libourel) B.; m. Sarah Garrett, Sept. 1992; 1 child, Frank Garrett. BS in Biology, Springfield Coll., 1978; PhD in Pharmaceutics, SUNY, Buffalo, 1986. Vet. technician Afton Animal Hosp., Williamsville, N.Y., 1978-79; rsch. technician SUNY-Millard Fillmore Hosp., Buffalo, 1979-80; grad. asst. SUNY, 1980-85; asst. prof. pharmaceutics U. Ga., Athens, 1986-90, assoc. prof., 1990-98, head dept. pharm., 1992-98, prof., head dept. pharm. & biomed. scis., 1998-99, prof. dept. pharm. and biomed. scis., 1998—, assoc. dean grad. sch., 1999—; cons. Assn. Minority Profl. Health Schs., Drug Devel. Group for AIDS, Tex. So. U. Coll. Pharmacy and Health Scis., Oneida Rsch. Svcs., Inc. Mem. editl. bd. Jour. Pharmacy Tchg., 1989—, Biopharm. and Drug Disposition, 1994—, Antimicrobiol. Agents and Chemotherapy, 1998—, Antimicrobial Agents and Chemotherapy, 1998—, Archives of Pharmacal Rsch.; referee Jour. Pharm. Scis., 1988—, Jour. Pharm. Rsch., 1989—; N.Am. editor Jour. Biopharmaceutics and Drug Disposition, 1998—; contbr. more than 100 articles to profl. jours. Bd. dirs. Oconee Animal Shelter, Watkinsville, Ga., 1986-88; vice chair govt. svcs. subcom. Oconee 2000, Watkinsville, 1986-87; del. Ga. State Rep. Conv., Atlanta, 1989, 91, 92; vol., event svcs. agent Summer Olympics, Athens, Ga., 1996. NIH grantee, 1987, 90, U.S. FDA grantee, 1989; named one of Outstanding Young Men of Am., 1987. Mem. AAAS, Am. Assn. Pharm. Scientists, Am. Assn. Colls. Pharmacy (del. 1989-90, mem. profl. affairs com. 1990-91), Am. Soc. Microbiology, Internat. Soc. Antiviral Rsch. (local organizing com. 10th conf. on antiviral rsch. 1997). Episcopalian. Achievements include research in pharmacokinetics of antiviral drugs, effects of age in drug disposition, veterinary pharmacokinetics, and drug pharmacodynamics. Office: U Ga Coll Pharmacy Brooks Dr Athens GA 30602

BOUDOULAS, HARISIOS, physician, educator, researcher; b. Velvendo-Kozani, Greece, Nov. 3, 1935; married; 2 children. *Wife Olga Boudoulas, M.D., is a dermatologist with a successful private practice. She also is clinical associate professor at the Ohio State University College of Medicine and Public Health. Daughter Sophia Boudoulas has a master's degree in Public Health. Presently she is a second year medical student at Midwestern University, Chicago, Illinois. Son Konstantinos Dean Boudoulas is a third year medical student at the Ohio State University College of Medicine and Public Health, Columbus, Ohio.* MD, U. Salonica, Greece, 1959. Resident in medicine Red Cross Hosp., Athens, Greece, 1960-61; resident in medicine U. Salonica First Med. Clinic, 1962-66, resident in internal medicine and cardiology, 1962-66, lectr., 1969-70; postgrad. fellow, instr. div. cardiology Ohio State U. Coll. Medicine, Columbus, 1970-73, asst. prof. medicine, 1975-78, assoc. prof., 1978-80, dir. cardiac non-invasive lab., 1978-80, prof. medicine div. cardiology, 1980—, prof. pharmacy, 1984—, dir. cardiovascular rsch. div., 1983-86, dir. cardiovascular teaching and rsch. lab., 1992—; prof. medicine div. cardiology Wayne State U., Detroit, 1980-82, chief clin. cardiovascular rsch., 1980-82, acting dir. div. cardiology, 1982; chief cardiovascular diagnostic and tng. center VA Med. Ctr., Allen Park, Mich., 1980-82; chief sect. cardiology Harper-Grace Hosps., Detroit, 1982; mem. antepistelon Athens Acad., 1998—. Editor in chief Hellenic Jour. Cardiology; mem. editl. rev. bd. jours. cardiology; contbr. numerous articles to med. jours. Named Disting. Research Investigator, Cen. Ohio chpt. Am. Heart Assn., Columbus, 1983. Fellow ACP, Am. Coll. Angiology, Am. Coll. Clin. Pharmacology, Am. Coll. Cardiology (trustee Ohio chpt. 1993-97), Am. Heart Assn. (coun. clin. cardiology 1989-93, coun. exec. com. 1991-93, sci. com. 1991-93), European Soc. Cardiology (sci. com. 1991-93, valvular heart disease working group 1993—), Greek Heart Assn., Am. Fedn. Clin. Rsch., Laeneck Soc. (chmn. 1991-93). Office: Ohio State U Div Cardiology 1655 Upham Dr Columbus OH 43210-1251

BOUDREAU, A. ALLAN, historian, writer, educator; b. Albany, N.Y., Aug. 1, 1936; s. Alexander and Lillian (Allan) B.; children: Kirstin Rosamund, Andrew Allan. Student, Albany Law Sch., 1955; BS, Russell Sage Coll., 1958; MS, Columbia U., 1972; MBA, NYU, 1964, PhD, 1973. Rockefeller intern N.Y. State Dept. Edn., 1958-59; adminstr. officer N.Y. State Libr., 1959-62; pub. acct. N.Y. State, 1961—; dep. dir. NYU Librs., 1962-73; sr. rsch. assoc. NYU, 1973-74; cons. to colls. and univs., govt., industry. Author: The Research Resources at Washington Square 1831-1970, 1972, 200 Years of Freemasonry in New York, 1981, George Washington in New York (state), 1987, George Washington and New York City, 1989; contbr. articles to profl. jours. Vol. fireman N.Y. State; sec. N.Y. State Libr. Trustee Found., 1973-93; trustee Allan Found., 1970—. With AUS, 1953-55, Korea. Recipient Founders Day award NYU, 1973. Mem. ALA (life), N.Y. Civil and Criminal Courts Bar Assn., Am. Philatelic Soc. (life), NRA (life), N.Y. State Ret. Tchrs. Assn. (life), Am. Orchid Soc., Am. Legion (life), DAV, N.Y. Athletic Club, Collectors Club (N.Y.C.), Masons (N.Y.C.). Home: 1 Washington Square Vlg New York NY 10012-1632

BOUDREAU, BEVERLY ANN, health care professional; b. Chgo., Mar. 1, 1940; d. Alvernon Holmberg and Mildred Catherine (Thomson) Hayes; m. Frederick Joseph Boudreau, Apr. 26, 1958 (div. Jan. 1971); children: Kenneth Joseph, Cynthia Lynn, Susan Marie. Student, Chgo. City Coll., 1967-72, Moraine Valley C.C., Palos Hills, Ill., 1974-77. Cert. med. asst., Chgo., 1974. Tech. sales rep. Diagnostic Tech., Inc., Hauppauge, N.Y., 1979-83; sec., technician Northwestern Meml. Hosp., Chgo., 1984-86; med. sec., asst. Howard Schachter, M.D., Chgo., 1986-95; med. billing staff Rush Presbyn. St. Lukes Medical Ctr., Chgo., 1995-96; med. sec. Rehab. Medicine Clinic, Wheaton, Ill., 1997—; developer/implementor Operation Beach Camp, USAR Drug Demand Reduction Edn. Program for Children, 1995-96; instr. USAR Family Program Activity Planning, 1994-96, Family Program Drug Demand Reduction, 1997. Mem. Chgo. Coun. Fgn. Rels., 1986-89; participant Ulster Project-DuPage/No. Ireland, Great Lakes, Ill., 1996-99, Logos After Sch. Program, Glen Ellyn, Ill., 1996-97; charter mem. USAR Family Program, Atlanta, 1991-96 (adv. council), Family Program Adv. Coun., Washington; deacon First Presbyn. Ch. of Glen Ellyn, 1996—, peacemaking/mission planning activities, 1999. Recipient Cert. of Achievement, USAR, 1995. Avocation: drug prevention programs for children. Office: Rehabilitation Med Clinic 26w171 Roosevelt Rd Wheaton IL 60187-6078

BOUDREAU, JAMES LAWTON, insurance company executive; b. Brockton, Mass., May 25, 1935; s. Lawton James and Mary Gladys (Doran) B.; m. Mary Margaret Henderson, Sept. 20, 1958; children: Caroline, David, James. BA in English, Bowdoin Coll., 1957; postgrad. in econs., Trinity Coll., Hartford, Conn., 1961-65. Supr. Conn. Gen. Life Ins. Co., Bloomfield, 1961-65; pension officer Shawmut Bank N.A., Boston, 1965-73; sr. v.p. fin. St. Paul Cos., Inc., 1973—. With U.S. Army, 1958-60. Mem. Nat. Investor Relations Inst., Nat. Assn. Corp. Treas., Fin. Execs. Inst. Roman Catholic. Avocations: reading, traveling. Office: St Paul Cos Inc 385 Washington St Saint Paul MN 55102-1309

BOUDREAU, RICHARD OWEN, retired English educator, freelance writer; b. Milroy, Minn., June 14, 1933; s. Louis Henry and Lena (Rykhus) B.; m. Joanne Margaret Kivlahan, Dec. 27, 1961; children: Anne Marie, Therese Marie, Mary Alice. BA in English, St. Mary's Coll., Winona, Minn., 1957; MEd in Adminstrn., Marquette U., 1964; MA in English, U. Wis., 1968; postgrad., U. Iowa, 1972-73. Cert. 7-12 tchr., secondary sch. prin., Wis. Tchr. Piux XI H.S., Milw., 1957-62, Lincoln H.S., Wisconsin Rapids, Wis., 1962-65; prin. Hillsboro (Wis.) H.S., 1965-68; prof. English, U. Wis., La Crosse, 1968-94, mem. faculty senate, 1987-90; ret., 1994. Editor: The Critical Receptions of Hamlin Garland, 1985, The Literary Heritage of Wisconsin, 1986, 95. Mem. adb. bd. St. Joseph's Nursing Home, La Crosse, 1976-83, pres. bd. govs., 1983-86; mem., chmn. bd. dirs. Western Wis. Chem. Dependency Svcs., La Crosse, 1975-77; bd. dirs., La Crosse Diocese Cath. Charities, 1974-77. With U.S. Army, 1955-57. Recipient Wis. Lit. Heritage award Wis. Humanities Com., 1983, 84, Taking Our lit. Heritage to Our People award, 1981. Mem. August Derleth Soc., Wis. Acad. Sci., Arts and Letters (v.p. letters 1986-89, chmn. publs. com. 1986-90), Coun. Wis. Writers (bd. dirs. 1982-85). Democrat. Roman Catholic. Avocations: reading, biking, fishing. Home: 2132 Winnebago St La Crosse WI 54601-5060

BOUDREAU, ROBERT JAMES, nuclear medicine physician, researcher; b. Lethbridge, Alta., Can., Dec. 27, 1950; came to U.S., 1983; s. George Joseph Boudreau and Eleanor Joyce (Dalzell) Hamilton; m. Francine Suzanne Archambault, Jan. 16, 1982. BSc with highest honors, U. Sask., Saskatoon, Can., 1972; PhD, U. B.C., Vancouver, Can., 1975; MD, U. Calgary (Alta.), 1978. Diplomate Am. Bd. Nuclear Medicine. Resident in diagnostic radiology and nuclear medicine McGill U., Montreal, Que., Can., 1978-82; asst. prof. U. Minn., Mpls., 1983-87, assoc. prof., 1987-93, prof., 1993—, dir. grad. studies dept. radiology, 1987-91, dir. nuclear medicine divsn., 1987—. Author book chpts.; contbr. articles to profl. jours. Recipient Gold Key award Soc. Chem. Industry, 1972, Soc. Clin. Investigation Young Investigator award, 1978; Can. Heart Found. Med. Scientist fellow, 1976-78. Fellow Royal Coll. Physicians; mem. Am. Heart Assn., Am. Coll. Nuclear Physicians, Assn. Univ. Radiologists, Soc. Chiefs of Acad. Nuclear Medicine Sects. (treas. 1989-93), Soc. Nuclear Medicine (edn. and tng. com. 1983-91, trustee 1994-95, bd. govs. ctrl. chpt. 1989—, treas. 1992-94, pres. 1994-95), Radiol. Soc. N.Am., Am. Coll. Radiology. Avocations: skiing, boating, travel, computers. Office: U Minn PO Box 292 FUMC 420 Delaware St SE Minneapolis MN 55455-0374

BOUDREAUX, BOB, broadcast journalist; b. Chicopee, Mass., Oct. 29, 1946; s. Rene and Veronica Patricia (Cook) Beaudreault; children: Carol Lynn, Rene William, Robert Jude. Student, U. Mass., 1964-68. News anchor, reporter Sta. KTVT-TV, Dallas, 1972-76; news anchor Sta. WTVR-TV, Richmond, Va., 1976-78; news anchor, reporter Sta. KTRK-TV, Disney, Houston, 1978—. Prodr., writer documentaries: Above the Finest, 1987, Open Door, 1995. Bd. dirs. Leadership Houston, 1983-90, chmn., 1990; bd. dirs. Houston Shakespeare Festival, 1990—, Worldfest Film Festival, Houston, 1987—, Alley Theatre, 1996—. Capt. U.S. Army, 1968-72, Vietnam. Decorated DFC with oak leaf cluster, Bronze Star, Purple Heart; recipient Citizen award for heroism Houston Police Chief, 1986, Man of Yr. award Cystic Fibrosis Found., 1995. Mem. Am. Legion, Chaine des Rotisseurs (chevalier), VFW, Houston City Club. Avocations: sports, running, acting. Office: KTRK-TV ABC TV 3310 Bissonnet St Houston TX 77005-2195*

BOUDREAUX, GLORIA MARIE, nurse, educator; b. Lafayette, La., May 2, 1935; d. Simon Zepherin and Orta Marie (Pierret) B. Diploma, Charity Hosp. Sch. Nursing, 1962; BA maxima cum laude, St. Edward's U., 1974; MS in Psychiatric-Mental Health Nursing, Tex. Women's U., 1976. Head surg., med. nurse Lafayette (La.) Charity Hosp., 1962-65; commd. 1st lt. U.S. Army, 1965; advanced through grades to col. Nurse Corps, U.S. Army, 1983; ret. U.S. Army, 1995; psychiat. staff nurse VA Hosp., New Orleans, 1968-72; psychiatric nurse U.S. Army Nurse Corp., San Francisco and Augusta, Ga., 1966-67; instr. Tex. Woman's Univ. Sch. of Nursing, Houston, 1976-80; clin. specialist VA Med. Ctr., Houston, 1980-87; psychiat. nursing coord. Spring Shadows Glen, Houston, 1987-88; instr. assoc. degree nursing program Houston Community Coll., 1988-91; asst. prof. nursing La. State U., Eunice, 1992-96; with Cmty. Rehab. Hosp. Counseling, 1997-99; clin. specialist, cons. in psychiat.-mental health nursing. Vol. ARC Disaster Health and Mental Health Svcs., bd. dirs. local chpt. Recipient Nat. Def. Svc. medal, 1968, Army Res. Component medal, 1972, Armed Forces Res. medal, 1977 (10-yr. device 1988), Army Commendation medal, 1978, Army Meritorious Svc. medal, 1990, Presdl. Sports award, 1989, 90, 91, Acadia

Red Cross Outstanding Vol. award for disaster svcs., 1998. Mem. Am. Psychiat. Nurses Assn., Res. Officers Assn. (chpt. pres. 1981-83), Assn. Mil. Surgeons of U.S., ANA (cert. in psychiat. mental health nursing), Vietnam Vets. Assn., Ret. Army Nurse Corps Assn., The Ret. Officers Assn., Sigma Theta Tau. Avocations: music, photography, jogging, bicycling, reading. Home: 307 Meadow Ln Lafayette LA 70506-6323

BOUDREAUX, JOHN, public relations/internet specialist; b. Franklin, La., July 28, 1946; s. Abel John and Dorothy (Bourgeois) B. BA, La. State U., 1969. Reporter, copy editor Morning Advocate, Baton Rouge, 1969-71; successively reporter, copy editor, asst. city editor Houston Post, 1971-76, city editor, 1976-84; pub. rels. cons., 1984-85; sr. communications specialist IBM, Dallas, 1985-87; comm. mgr. IBM, San Francisco, 1987-88; program mgr. IBM, Westchester County, N.Y., 1988—. Named Outstanding Journalism Grad., La. State U., 1969. Mem. Soc. Profl. Journalists, Sigma Delta Chi (bd. dirs. Houston chpt. 1975, 83). Office: PO Box 100 Somers NY 10589-0100

BOUDREAUX, KENNETH JUSTIN, economics and finance educator, consultant; b. New Orleans, Dec. 22, 1943; s. Aldwin John and Beverly Estelle (Swanton) B.; m. Carole Jean Barnette, May 28, 1966; 1 child, Beau Justin. A.B., Princeton U., 1965; M.B.A., Tulane U., 1967; Ph.D, U. Wash., 1970. Asst. prof. Sch. Bus., Tulane U., New Orleans, 1970-73; assoc. prof. Sch. Bus., Tulane U., 1973-78, prof., 1978—, assoc. dean faculty, 1981-83; cons. City of New Orleans. Author: Basic Theory of Corporate Fianance, 1977, Finance, 1990; editorial bd. Jour. Econs. and Bus., Jour. Fin. Rsch.; contbr. articles to scholarly jours. AACSB fellow, 1969-70; recipient Wissner award Tulane U., 1972, 75, Outstanding Prof., 1972, 75, Disting. Prof., 1973. Fellow Fin. Analysts Fedn.; mem. Am. Econ. Assn., Am. Fin. Assn., Western Fin. Assn., Western Econ. Assn. Club: Cannon (Princeton U.). Office: Sch Bus Tulane U New Orleans LA 70118

BOUDREAUX, MARGARET A., music educator; b. Elizabeth City, N.C., May 26, 1952; d. Charles Marion and Dalton Simms (Beville) Robertson; m. Rodney Charles Boudreaux, Nov. 27, 1979; 1 child, John Charles. BMus with high distinction, U. Ariz., 1974; postgrad. tng. in choral performance, with Helmuth Rilling, Stuttgart and Frankfurt, Germany, 1974-76; MMus, U. Oreg., 1980; D Musical Arts, U. Colo., 1989. Dir. choral activities Thunderbird High Sch., Phoenix, 1976-86; artistic dir. Vox Populi Chorale, Denver, 1987-89; bd. dirs. tchr., condr. Common Ground on the Hill Music Festival, 1994—; condr. Chamber Music on the Hill, Westminster, Md., 1991—; asst. condr. Opera Theater/U. Colo., Boulder, 1986-87; assoc. prof. music, dir. choral activities Western Md. Coll., Westminster, Md., 1989—; guest condr. numerous choruses; lectr. in field. Choral publs. include arrangements of renaissance and baroque era music and musical theater. Mem. Am. Choral Dirs. Assn. (life), Internat. Fedn. Choral Music, Am. Choral Found., Coll. Music Soc., Music Educator's Nat. Conf., Pi Kappa Lambda, Phi Kappa Phi. Avocations: hiking, sci. fiction. Home: 5792 Western View Pl Mount Airy MD 21771-5811 Office: Western Maryland Coll 2 College Hl Westminster MD 21157-4303

BOUDREAUX, MARJORY ANN, English language educator, consultant; b. Deweese, Nebr., Feb. 16, 1935; d. Roy James and Thelka Marie (Busboom) Ridgway; m. Sidney Alfred Boudreaux, Mar. 23, 1957; children: Roberta Lynn Pommert, Justin Scott, James Mark, Sharon Gay Martin, Carolyn Renee Pennick. BSL, Ozark Christian Coll., 1975; MA, Pittsburg (Kans.) State U., 1988; PhD, Indiana U. of Pa., 1998. Cert. ESL tchr. ESEC. Prof. Philippine Mission, Aparri, Cagayan, The Philippines, 1964-85, Pittsburg (Kans.) State U., 1988-96, Mo. So. State Coll., Joplin, 1988—; cons. U.S. Telecomm., Joplin, 1997, Coll. Press, Joplin, 1998; coord. Joplin NALA READ, 1994—; bd. dirs. ABE Adv. Bd., Joplin. Co-author: (video series) Contrast Philippine & Western Culture, 1992. Mem. Tchrs. of English as 2d Lang., Nat. Coun. Tchrs. English, Phi Kappa Phi. Avocations: writing, reading, music. Office: Joplin NALA READ 102 S Shiffer Decker Ave Joplin MO 64801-3315

BOUDRIA, DON, Canadian government official; b. Hull, Quebec, Can., Aug. 30, 1949; s. Roy and Jacqueline (Lavergne) B.; m. MaryAnn Morris, Aug. 28, 1971; children: Daniel, Julie. BA, U. Waterloo. With Fed. Govt., 1966, chief purchasing agent; mem. Legis. Assembly, Ont., 1981; M.P.P., 1981, opposition critic of govt. svcs., 1981-82, opposition critic of cmty. and social svcs., 1981-83, opposition critic of consumer and comml. rels., 1983-84; M.P. Ho. of Commons, 1984—; critic Fed. supply and svcs.; official opposition, mem. standing com. on Agriculture, 1984; dep. chmn. Ont. Liberal Caucus, 1984; Public Works critic, 1985; critic Can. Post. and Govt. Ops., 1988; dep. oppositon whip, 1989, asst. House leader for the Official Opposition; Min. Internat. Cooperation, Min. Responsible La Francophonie, 1996—; dep. govt. whip, 1993-94, chief govt. whip, 1994-96; min. of state, leader govt., House of Commons, 1997—. Mem. L'Assn. Internat. des Parlementaires de Langue Française (founding pres. Ont. sect.), Cumberland Twp. Housing Corp. (founding pres.), Sarsfield Optimist Club (founding pres.). Office: House of Commons, Confederation Bldg Rm 380, Ottawa, ON Canada K1A 0A6

BOUÉ, DANIEL ROBERT, pathologist; b. N.Y.C., June 22, 1958; s. Robert Charles and Dorothea Anna B.; m. Julie Marie Borgerding, Oct. 2; children: Rachel Hope, Jenna Elizabeth, AnnaMarie Monique, Sarah Jane. BA cum laude, Carleton Coll., 1980; PhD, U. Minn., 1988, MD, 1991. Diplomate AM. Bd. Pathology. Intern U. Calif., San Diego, 1991-92, resident in pathology, 1992-94, chief resident, 1994-95; attending physician U. Calif./San Diego Med. Ctr., 1994-95; clin. instr. U. Calif., San Diego, 1994-95; fellow pediat. pathology Columbus Childrens Hosp., 1995-96; clin. instr. Ohio State U., Columbus, 1995-96, clin. asst. prof. pediat. and pathology, 1997—; fellow pediat. neuropathology Columbus Childrens Hosp., 1996; staff pathologist, dir. Neuropathology program Childrens Hosp., Columbus, 1997—; interim dir perinatal pathology and autopsy svc. U. Calif., San Diego, 1994-95; rev. pathologist Biopathology Ctr., Children's Hosp. Rsch. Found.; presenter in field. Contbr. articles to profl. jours. Med. Scientist scholar U. Minn., 1982-91, G.T. Evan scholar Dept. Lab. Medicine and Pathology, 1982-85, Life & Health Ins. Med. Rsch. scholar, 1985-90; recipient J.T. Livermore award Minn. Med. Found., 1988, undergrad. med. student rsch. award 1991, Dr. Vernon D.E. Smith award, 1990. Fellow Am. Coll. Pathology, Am. Soc. Clin. Pathologists (Sheard-Sanford award 1988), Coll. Am. Pathologists; mem. Soc. Pediat. Pathology, Alpha Omega Alpha. Office: Columbus Childrens Hosp Dept Lab Med 700 Childrens Dr Columbus OH 43205-2664

BOUGALIS, KATHERINE G., medical surgical nurse, educator; b. Naupaktos, Greece, May 23, 1940; d. Dimitrios and Eleftheria (Mamalougas) Papadimitriou; m. George Bougalis, Feb. 19, 1961; children: Nickolas, Joanne, James, John. AD, Arrowhead Community Coll., Hibbing, Minn., 1971; BS in Community Svc., Bemidji (Minn.) State U., 1985; BA in Nursing, Coll. St. Scholastica, Duluth, Minn., 1986, MA in Nursing, 1987. Cert. in med.-surg. nursing, community health. Asst. head. nurse Mesabi Regional Med. Ctr., Hibbing, adminstr., supr., patient care facilitator; educator Hibbing Community Coll. Mem. ANA, AAUW, Minn. Nurses Assn., Sigma Theta Tau.

BOUGAS, JAMES ANDREW, physician, surgeon; b. Bismarck, N.D., Jan. 25, 1924; s. Andrew James and Mary (Psaltiras) B.; m. Tiina Parlin, June 27, 1953; children: Karen Louise, Tiina Maria. MD, Harvard U., 1948. Diplomate Am. Bd. Surgery, Am. Bd. Thoracic Surgery. Intern Columbia U. Svc., Bellevue Hosp., N.Y.C., 1948-50, chief resident in surgery, 1952-53; resident Presbyn. Hosp., N.Y.C., 1950-52, chief resident surgery, 1953; assoc. Overholt Clinic, Boston, 1955-65; chief thoracic surgery U. Hosp., Boston, 1965-70; assoc. prof. surgery Boston U. Sch. Medicine, 1965—; lectr. Tufts U. Sch. Medicine, Boston, 1965-70; chmn. Gordon Rsch. Confs., 1967-68. Contbr. articles to profl. jours. Pres. Heart Assn., Boston, 1967-69; chmn. Mass. Rehab. Commn. Adv. Com.; trustee Boston Tb Assn. With U.S. Army, 1942-44. Fellow AAAS; mem. ACS, Am. Coll. Cardiology, Am. Assn. Thoracic Surgeons, Soc. Thoracic Surgeons, Am. Coll. Cardiology, Mass. Med. Soc. (legis. com., coun.), Norfolk Dist. Med. Soc. (pres. 1989-90, Tri-State regional planning com.). Achievements include development of combined cardiac catheterization; porous metal fabrication and cardiopulmonary biology. E-mail jbougas@nebh.caregroup.harvard.edu. Office: NE Bapt Hosp 125 Parker Hill Ave Boston MA 02120-2847

BOUGHMAN, JOANN ASHLEY, dean; b. Kokomo, Ind., May 4, 1949; d. Robert George and Lydia Ann (Ashley) B. BS in Med. Tech., Ind. U., Indpls., 1972, PhD in Med. Genetics, 1978. Diplomate Am. Bd. Med. Genetics. Asst. prof. Med. Coll. Va., Richmond, 1979-82; assoc. prof. U. Md. Med. Sch., Balt., 1983-90, prof., 1990—; assoc. v.p. for rsch. U. Md. Balt. County, Balt., 1992-95, dean grad. sch., 1992—; v.p. for acad. affairs U. Md., Balt., 1995—; sec. Am. Bd. Med. Genetics, 1992-94, v.p., 1995-96; cons. NIH, Bethesda, Md., 1982—, Gallaudet U., Washington, 1977—. Contbr. articles to profl. jours., chpts. to 19 books; author ednl. materials. Bd. dirs., officer Har Sinai Congregation, Balt., 1987—; mem. exec. com. High Tech Coun., Balt., 1992—; com. chair Info. Tech. Bd., Balt., 1994—; mem. speaker bur. Jewish Family Svcs., Balt., 1987—. Grantee RP Genetics Registry Ctr., 1978-82, NIH, 1985-94, 90-94; Edwards fellow, 1976. Fellow Am. Coll. Med. Genetics; mem. Am. Soc. Human Genetics (cert., com. chair 1994), Am. Assn. Dental Rsch., Am. soc. Clin. Pathologists, Exec. Women's Network. Office: U Md Balt 520 W Lombard St Baltimore MD 21201-1603*

BOUGHTER, RONALD EDWARD, video specialist; b. Harrisburg, Pa., July 27, 1946; s. Edward A. and Helen O (Hines) B.; m. Linda E. Lighty, Oct. 19, 1968; children: Brian, Barbarella, Matthew. Grad. high sch., Harrisburg. Electrician ABC Electric, Harrisburg, 1970-72; salesman Coca-Cola Co., Harrisburg, 1972-80; mgr. video telecom. ops. NAVICP, Mechanicsburg, Pa., 1980—. With USN, 1966-69. Republican. Pentacostal. Avocations: camping, horseback riding, video taping, rock and roll music. Home: 575 Hogestown Rd Mechanicsburg PA 17055 Office: NAVICP-M Code MO855.1 5450 Carlisle Pike Mechanicsburg PA 17055-2411

BOUGHTON, JAMES MURRAY, economist; b. Chgo., Apr. 8, 1944; s. Stanley R. and Erminie (Bloyd) B.; m. Lesley Anne Simmons. BA, Duke U., 1966; MA, U. Mich., 1967; PhD, Duke U., 1969. Asst. prof. Ind. U., Bloomington, 1970-73, assoc.prof., 1973-81, prof., 1981-83; economist Orgn. Econ. Coop. and Devel., Paris, 1973-75, cons., 1976-79; economist IMF, Washington, 1981-86, advisor, 1986-92, historian, 1992—. Author: Monetary Policy and Federal Funds Market, 1971, Silent Revolution, 1999; co-author: Principles of Monetary Economics, 1975; co-editor: Fifty Years After Bretton Woods, Future of SDR; contbr. articles to profl. jours. V.p. Ind. Civil Liberties Union, Indpls., 1978-79; chmn. bd. dirs. Bretton Woods, Germantown, Md., 1990-93. Mem. Am. Econ. Assn., Royal Econ. Soc. Office: Internat Monetary Fund 700 19th St NW Washington DC 20431-0001

BOUGIE, JACQUES, aluminum company executive; b. Montreal, Que., Can., 1947. BABA, Ecole des Hautes Etudes Commerciales; JD, U. Montreal. Mgr. Beauharnois Works (a part of Alcan Smelters and Chems. Ltd.), Montreal, 1979-81; dir. devel. Aluminium Co. of Can., Manitoba, Que., 1981-82, asst. to v.p. planning and adminstrn. N.Am. and W.I., 1982-84; v.p. planning and adminstrn. Alcan Can. Products, 1985-88; pres. Alcan Extrusions, 1988-89; pres., COO Alcan Aluminium Ltd., Cleve., 1989-93, pres., CEO, 1993—; bd. dirs. Asia Pacific Found. Can.; vice chmn., bd. dirs. Bus. Coun. on Nat. Issues. Decorated officer Order of Can. Office: Alcan Aluminium Ltd, 1188 Sherbrooke St W, Montreal, PQ Canada H3A 3G2

BOUGIE, PETER JOHN, artist, educator; b. Manitowoc, Wis., Aug. 25, 1956; s. Jerome William and Joan Ellen Bougie. Apprentice, Atelier Lack, 1987. Dir. Bougie Studio, Mpls., 1988—; editor Classical Realism Jour., Mpls., 1996—. Grantee R.H. ives Grammell Studio Trust, 1994—, Rathmann Family Found., 1998. Mem. Am. Soc. Classical Realism Artist's Guild. Roman Catholic. Avocations: bicycling, running. E-mail: pbougie@pressenter.com. Office: Bougie Studio 2524 Nicollet Ave S Ste 201 Minneapolis MN 55404

BOUILLIANT-LINET, FRANCIS JACQUES, global management consultant; b. Garches, France, Aug. 20, 1932; came to U.S., 1977; s. Jacques Achille and Virginia Sutton (McKee) B.-L.; m. Carolyn Jeanine Taylor, Nov. 17, 1978. Diploma in sci., Admiral Farragut Acad., 1948; post., Hautes Etudes Commerciales, Paris, 1949, Duke U., 1949-50. Mgmt. trainee Harry Ferguson Cos., Europe, 1951-53; sales promotion mgr. Massey-Harris-Ferguson, Paris, 1957-59; gen. programs mgr. Massey Ferguson Ltd., Coventry, Eng., 1959-63; coord. office of pres. Massey Ferguson Ltd., Toronto, Ont., Can., 1963-65; group product mgr. Massey Ferguson Ltd., Toronto, 1966-68; dir. internat. logistics Allis Chalmers Corp., Milw., 1968-71; joint mng. dir. LePiol, s.a.r.l., Cannes, France, 1971-77; chmn. bd., chief exec. officer FBL, Inc., Hurtsboro, Ala., 1977—, also bd. dirs.; exec. dir. H.J. Crawley, Ltd., Leamington, Eng., 1961-66; bd. dirs. F.J.B., Inc., Thermal, Calif. Author: (manual) The New Product Process, 1963; trademark registrant for "Rent-a-Boss." Charter founder Ronald Reagan Rep. Ctr., Washington, 1987. With French Armed Forces, 1953-54, 56-57. Mem. Ala. Sheriff's Assn. (hon.), Capital City Club, Midland (Ga.) Fox Hounds. Office: FBL Inc PO Box 298 Hurtsboro AL 36860

BOULANGER, DONALD RICHARD, financial services executive; b. Berlin, N.H., May 28, 1944; s. Romeo James and Jeanette A. (Valliere) B.; m. Wendy Elwell, Nov. 26, 1990 (div. Sept. 1996). B.A., Harvard U., 1966, Ph.D., 1972. V.p. First Interstate Bank, L.A., 1972-76, Kaufman and Broad, L.A., 1976-80; sr. v.p. Kaufman and Broad, Los Angeles, 1983-89; v.p. Transam. Corp., San Francisco, 1981-83; exec. v.p. Far West Savs., Newport Beach, Calif., 1983; pres. Nat. Deposit Fin. Corp., Universal City, Calif., 1989—; bd. dirs. Nat. Deposit Life Ins. Co., Phoenix, Citadel Holding Corp, Am. Stock Exch., Glendale, Calif. Republican. Roman Catholic. Avocation: scuba diving. Office: Nat Deposit Fin Corp 10 Universal City Plz North Hollywood CA 91608-1009

BOULANGER, RODNEY EDMUND, energy company executive; b. Detroit, Apr. 4, 1940; m. Nancy Ann Ewigleben, Dec. 29, 1962; children: Brent, Karla, Melissa. BS, Ferris State Coll., Big Rapids, Mich., 1963; MBA, U. Detroit, 1967. Various fin. planning and econ. positions Am. Nat. Resources Co., 1963-78; v.p. system econs. and diversification Am. Natural Service Co., Detroit, 1978-80; v.p. fin. adminstrn ANG Coal Gasification Co., Detroit, 1980-82, v.p., fin. sec., 1983-84; treas., chief fin. officer Gt. Plains Gasification Assocs., Detroit, 1982-84; exec. v.p., chief fin. and adminstrv. officer ANR Pipeline Co., Detroit, 1984-86; pres., CEO ANG Coal Gasification Co., Bismarck, N.D., 1986-87, Midland Congeneration Venture, 1987-95; with CMS Generation Co., Dearborn, Mich., 1995—; bd. dirs. Chem. Bank. Mem. Tournament Players Club, Detroit Athletic Club, Duck Lake County Club (Albion, Mich.), Caloosa Country Club (Fla.), Beta Gamma Sigma. Office: CMS Generation Co 330 Town Center Dr Dearborn MI 48126-2712

BOULDEN, JUDITH ANN, bankruptcy judge; b. Salt Lake City, Dec. 28, 1948; d. Douglas Lester and Emma Ruth (Robertson) Boulden; m. Alan Walter Barnes, Nov. 7, 1982; 1 child, Dorian Lisa. BA, U. Utah, 1971, JD, 1974. Bar: Utah 1974, U.S. Dist. Ct. Utah 1974. Law clk. to A. Sherman Christianson U.S. Cts., Salt Lake City, 1974; assoc. Roe & Fowler, Salt Lake City, 1975-81, McKay Burton Thurman & Condie, Salt Lake City, 1982-83; trustee Chpt. 7, Salt Lake City, 1976-82, Standing Chpt. 12, Salt Lake City, 1987-88, Standing Chpt. 13, Salt Lake City, 1979-88; sr. ptnr. Boulden & Gillman, Salt Lake City, 1983-88; U.S. Bankruptcy judge U.S. Cts., Salt Lake City, 1988—. Mem. Utah Bar Assn. Avocations: gardening, golf. *

BOULDING, ELISE MARIE, sociologist, educator; b. Oslo, Norway, July 6, 1920; came to U.S., 1923, naturalized, 1929; d. Joseph and Birgit (Johnsen) Biorn-Hansen; m. Kenneth Boulding; Aug. 31, 1941; children: John Russell, Mark David, Christine Ann, Philip Daniel, William Frederic. BA, Douglass Coll., 1940; MS, Iowa State Coll., 1949; PhD, U. Mich., 1969. Research asso. Survey Research Inst., U. Mich., 1957-58, Mental Health Research Inst., 1959-60; research devel. sec. Center for Research on Conflict Resolution, 1960-63; prof. sociology, project dir. Inst. Behavioral Sci., U. Colo., Boulder, 1967-78; Montgomery vis. prof. Dartmouth Coll., 1978-79, chmn. dept. sociology, 1979-85; prof. emerita, 1985; sec. gen. Internat. Peace Rsch. Assoc., 1989-91; pres. IPRA Found., 1992-96; mem. program adv. council Human and Social Devel. Program, UN Univ., 1977-80; mem. governing council, 1980-86. Author: (with others) Handbook of International Data on Women, 1976, Bibliography on World Conflict and Peace, 1979, Social System of Planet Earth, 1980, Women and the Social Costs of Economic Development, 1981; author: The Underside of History: A View of Women Through Time, 1975, rev. edit., 1992, Women in Twentieth Century World, 1977, Children's Rights and the Wheel of Life, 1979, Building a Global Civic Culture: Education for an Interdependent World, 1988, 90, One Small Plot of Heaven, 1990, (with Kenneth Boulding) The Future: Images and Processes, 1994; editor: Peace Culture and Society: Transnational Research and Dialogue with Clovis Brigagao and Kevin Clements (eds.), 1990; New Agendas for Peace Research: Conflict and Security Reexamined (ed.), 1992; Building Peace in the Middle East: Challenges for States and Civil Society, (ed.), 1993. Internat. chair Womens Internat. League for Peace and Freedom, 1967-70; mem. Exploratory Project on Conditions for Peace, 1984-90; mem. U.S. Commn. for UNESCO, 1978-84; mem. UNESCO Peace Prize jury, 1980-87; chair bd. Boulder Cmty. Parenting Ctr., 1988-92; bd. dirs. Am. Friends Svc. Com., 1990-94; councillor Interfaith Peace Coun., 1995—; bd. dirs. Wayland MA Coun. on Aging, 1998—. Recipient Disting. Achievement award Douglass Coll., 1973, Ted. Lentz Peace award, 1976, Athena award, 1983, Nat. Women's Forum award, 1985, Inst. of Def., Disarmament, Peace and Democracy award, 1990, Jack Gore Meml. Peace award Denver Am. Friends Svc. Com., 1992, Global Citizen award Boston Rsch. Ctr., 1995, Peacemaker of Yr. award Rocky Mountain Peace and Justice Ctr., 1996, World Futures Studies Fedn. award, 1997; named to Rutgers Hall of Disting. Alumni, 1994; Danforth fellow, 1965-67. Mem. Am. Sociol. Assn. (Jessie Bernard award 1982, Peace and War sect. award 1994), Internat. Sociol. Assn., Internat. Peace Rsch. Assn. (newsletter editor 1983-87), World Future Studies Fedn., Colo. Women's Forum, U. Mich. Alumni Assn. (Athena award 1983). Quaker. Home: 44 E Plain St Wayland MA 01778-4934

BOULÉ, DENISE MARGUERITE, educational administrator; b. July 11, 1953. BA in Social Studies, U. R.I., 1975, MA in Ednl. Adminstrn., 1990. Tchr. social studies North Kingstown (R.I.) H.S., 1978-86, coord. at risk program, 1986-90; asst. prin. Coventry (R.I.) H.S., 1990-96; prin. Mt. Hope H.S., Bristol, R.I., 1996—. Office: Mt Hope HS 199 Chestnut St Bristol RI 02809

BOULEY, JOSEPH RICHARD, pilot; b. Fukuoka, Japan, Jan. 7, 1955; came to U.S., 1955; s. Wilfrid Arthur and Minori Cecelia (Naraki) B.; m. Sara Elizabeth Caldwell, July 6, 1991; children: Denise Marie, Janice Elizabeth, Eleanor Catherine. BA in English, U. Nebr., 1977; MAS, Embry Riddle Aeronautical U., 1988. Commd. 2d lt. USAF, 1977; advanced through grades to lt. col. USAFR, 1999; F-117A Stealth Fighter pilot USAF, Persian Gulf, 1991; pilot United Airlines, 1992—. Ct. apptd. spl. advocate Office of Guardian Ad Litem, Salt Lake City, 1996—. Decorated Disting. Flying Cross, 4 Air medals, 3 Meritorious Svc. medals, 2 Aerial Achievement medals, Joint Svc. commendation medal, 3 Air Force Commendation medals, Air Force Achievement medal; recipient Alumni Achievement award U. Nebr., 1998. Mem. VFW, Am. Legion, Disting. Flying Cross Soc., Airline Pilots Assn., Red River Valley Fighter Pilots Assn., Aircraft Owners & Pilots Assn. Republican. Roman Catholic. Avocations: flying, golf, running, photography. Home: 1544 Emerson Ave Salt Lake City UT 84105-2728

BOULEZ, PIERRE, composer, conductor; b. Montbrison, nr. Clermont-Ferrand, France, Mar. 26, 1925; s. Leon and Marcelle (Calabre) B. Student, recipient 1st prize, Olivier Messiaen at Paris Conservatory. Apptd. dir. music Jean-Louis Barrault's Theater Co., 1948; tchr., lectr., condr.; musical adviser, prin. guest condr. Cleve. Symphony Orch., 1970-71; chief condr. BBC Symphony Orch., 1970-75; musical dir. N.Y. Philharmonic Orch., 1971-77; prof. Coll. de France, 1976-95; dir. Inst. de Recherche et de Coord. Acoustique/Musique, 1976-91; apptd. prin. guest condr. Chgo. Symphony Orch., 1995; pres. The Ensemble Intercontemporain, 1976. Toured Orient, Europe, North and South Am., (with Barrault), conducting appearances include, Edinburgh Festival, 1965, Bayreuth Festival, 1966, 76-80; compositions include Sonatina for flute and piano, 1946, Three Piano Sonatas, 1946, 50, 57, Le Soleil des Eaux for voice and orchestra, 1947, Structures, 1952, Le Marteau sans maitre, 1955, Deux improvisations sur Mallarme, 1957, Doubles for orchestra, 1958, Tombeau (on text of Mallarmé), 1959, Pli selon pli, 1960, Structures II, 1962, Eclat, 1964, Domaines, 1968, Multiples, 1970, Cummings ist der Dichter, 1970, Explosante/Fixe, 1973, Rituel, 1975, Messagesquise, 1976, Notations, part I, 1980, Répons, 1981, Dialogue de l'Ombre double, 1986, Mémoriale, 1985, Visage Nuptial, 1989, Dérive I, 1985, Anthèmes pour violin solo, 1992, Explosante/Fixe for large ensemble and electronics, 1993, Anthèmes for Violin Solo and Electronics, 1997, Sur Incises, 1998; author: Relevé, 1966, Points de Repère, 1981, le pays fertile-Paul Klee, 1989, Jalon-10 ans d'enseignement au Collège de France, 1989; musical criticism and analysis, including Penser la Musique d'Aujourd'hui, 1963. Recipient Praemium Imperiale of Japan Art Assn., 1989, Grosses Verdienstkreuz RFA, 1990, Polar Music prize, Sweden, 1996. Office: Inst Recherche Coord Acoustique Musique, 1 place Igor Stravinsky, 75004 Paris France

BOULGER, FRANCIS WILLIAM, metallurgical engineer; b. Mpls., June 19, 1913; s. Francis J. and Mary (Armstrong) B. Metall. Engr., U. Minn., 1934; M.S. (Battelle fellow), Ohio State U., 1937. With A.P., 1929-34; engr. Minn. Dept. Hwys., 1935-36; metallurgist Republic Steel Corp., Cleve., 1937; research metallurgist Battelle Meml. Inst., Columbus, Ohio, 1938-45, div. chief, 1945-67, sr. tech. advisor, 1967-85, ret.; cons. USAF; Materials Adv. Bd. OECD. Author: (with others) Forging Materials and Practices, 1968, Tri-Lingual Dictionary of Production Engineering, 1969, Forging Equipment, Materials and Practices, 1973; also over 150 tech. articles. Named Man of Yr. Columbus Tech. Council, 1966, Disting. Alumnus, Ohio State U., 1984; Gold medalist Soc. Mfg. Engrs., 1967; recipient Am. Machinist award, 1975. Fellow Am. Soc. Metals, Soc. Mfg. Engrs., ASME; mem. AIME (Hunt medal 1955), Nat. Acad. Engring., Internat. Inst. for Prodn. Research (hon. mem., past pres.), N. Am. Mfg. Research Instn. (co-founder), Internat. Cold Forging Group (co-founder), Sigma Xi. Roman Catholic. Home: 1816 Harwitch Rd Columbus OH 43221-2811

BOULOS, EDWARD NASHED, transportation specialist; b. Damanhour, Egypt, May 19, 1941; came to U.S., 1979; s. Nashed Boulos and Lila (Habib) Georgy; m. Mervet Saleh, Aug. 31, 1967; children: Nermine E., Yasmine E. BS in Chemistry and Physics, Cairo U., 1963; MS in Solid State Sci., Am. U., Cairo, 1966; PhD in Ceramic Engring., U. Mo., 1970, profl. doctorate degree, 1997. Supr., cons. Ministry of Industry, Cairo, 1963-79; assoc. prof. Am. U., Cairo, 1972-79; vis. prof. Cath. U. Am., Washington, 1979-81; sr. scientist Anchor Hocking Co., Lancaster, Ohio, 1981-84; sr. staff tech. specialist Ford Motor Co./Visteon Glass Sys., Dearborn, Mich., 1984—; cons. USAF, Boston, 1984-89; liaison bd. mem. Alfred (N.Y.) U., 1985—, chmn.-elect, 1992. Co-editor: Advances in the Fusion of Glass, 1988, PAC RIM Glass and Optical Materials Issues, 2 vols., 1994; contbr. articles on glass tech. to profl. jours.; patentee in field. NSF rsch. grantee, 1967-71, 72-79. Fellow Am. Ceramic Soc. (chair Glass and Optical Materials Div., 1996-98); mem. ASTM, Materials Rsch. Soc., Deutsche Glastechnische Gesellschaft, Sigma Xi. Avocations: travel, sports. Office: Ford Motor Co Glass Divsn 15000 N Commerce Dr Dearborn MI 48120-1225

BOULOS, PAUL FARES, civil and environmental engineer; b. Beirut, June 28, 1963; came to U.S., 1983; s. Fares and Marie-Rose (Abou Hadid) B. BS, Beirut U., 1985; BSCE, U. Ky., 1985, MSCE, 1986, PhD, 1989. Asst. prof. U. Ky., Lexington, 1990-91; dir. water distbn. tech. Montgomery Watson, Pasadena, Calif., 1991-96; v.p. MW Soft Inc., Pasadena, 1996—; internat. hydraulic expert Consorcio Nitogui, Cali, Colombia, 1988-90; cons. in field; v.p. MW Soft, Inc., Pasadena, Calif., 1996—. Author: KYPIPED: Comprehensive Network Analyzer, 1990, H2ONET Water Distribution Modeling and Management, 1996; contbr. articles to profl. publs. Recipient Best Rsch. Paper award U.S. EPA, 1994, ASCE, 1996; grantee NSF, 1987, Am. Water Works Rsch. Found., 1992. Mem. ASCE (treas. 1992), Am. Water Works Assn., Sigma Xi, Tau Beta Pi, Chi Epsilon (U.S. delegation to NATO Advanced Study Inst. 1993). Achievements include work on computer-assisted water quality and hydraulic network modeling. Office: Montgomery Watson 301 N Lake Ave Ste 600 Pasadena CA 91101-4126

BOULOUKOS, THEODORE, II, writer, editor; b. Albany, N.Y., Jan. 2, 1962; s. Charles Theodore and Johanna Costas (Lecakes) B. BA, Columbia U., 1994. Editor-in-chief The Albany Rev., 1985-90; freelance writer, editor N.Y.C., 1990—. Collaborating author: Hiding My Candy, 1996; contbr. popular publs. Jr. com. N.Y.C. Ballet, Am. Assocs. Royal Acad. Art London, N.Y.C., English-Speaking Union, N.Y.C., Fedn. Protestant Welfare

Agys., N.Y.C.; mem. Young Friends of Save Venice, Inc., the Guild of the Princess Grace Found./U.S., St. James' Epis. Ch., others. Mem. Am. Soc. Journalists and Authors Inc., Albany Acad. Alumni Assn. (bd. dirs.), Williams Club, Authors Guild, Acad. Am. Poets, The Columbia Club of N.Y., Williams Club, others. Republican. Episcopalian. Home: 53 E 97th St Apt 1D New York NY 10029-7048

BOULTBEE, JOHN ARTHUR, publishing executive; b. Can., July 4, 1943; s. Thomas Edward and Helene Marion (Pattison) B.; m. Eleanor Rose Moore, Nov. 2, 1968 (div. 1985); children: Paul Keith, Leslie Elizabeth; m. Sharon Ann Whitby, Dec. 28, 1985; 1 child, Michael James Edward. B in Commerce, U. Toronto, Ont., Can., 1967, CA, 1970. Mgr. Coopers & Lybrand, Toronto, 1973-77, ptnr., 1977-85, ptnr. in charge of tax group, 1985-86; v.p., CFO Hollinger Inc., Toronto, 1986-98; exec. v.p., CFO Hollinger Inc. and Hollinger Internat. Inc., Chgo.; pub. Saturday Night Mag., Toronto, 1988-89; pres. Saturday Night Mag. Inc., Toronto, 1989-94; vice-chmn. Saturday Night Mag. Ltd., Toronto, 1994-96, vice-chmn., pres., 1996-98; bd. dirs. Hollinger Inc., Toronto, Argus Corp. Ltd., Toronto, Toronto, Consol. Enfield Corp., Toronto, Internat. African Mining Gold Corp., Toronto, Southam Inc., Toronto. Editor, contbr. Can. Tax Jour., 1980-86. Mem. Can. Inst. Chartered Accts., Boulevard Club, Mansfield Ski Club. Avocations: cycling, tennis, running, skiing, golf. Office: Hollinger Inc, 10 Toronto St, Toronto, ON Canada M5C 2B7

BOULTINGHOUSE, MARION CRAIG BETTINGER, editor; b. New Albany, Ind., Oct. 7, 1930; d. Losson Edward and Marion Craig (Klarer) Bettinger; m. Ray Allen Boultinghouse, Jan. 1, 1973. Student, Hanover Coll., 1948-50; BS, Fla. So. Coll., 1952; M.Ed., U. Louisville, 1960. Tchr. pub. schs. Lakeland, Fla., 1952, New Albany, 1953-55, 58-60, New Haven, 1955-58; editor Am. Edn. Publs., Middletown, Conn., 1960-63, Holt, Rinehart & Winston, N.Y.C., 1963-64, 69-72, Macmillan, Inc., N.Y.C., 1964-69, 72-75; editorial dir., v.p. sch. div. Macmillan, Inc., 1975-79; pres. Boultinghouse & Boultinghouse Inc.; pub. consultants Boultinghouse & Boultinghouse Inc., N.Y.C., 1976—. Author: Follow Me, Everybody, 1968. Office: 153 E 30th St New York NY 10016-7340

BOUMA, JOHN JACOB, lawyer; b. Ft. Dodge, Iowa, Jan. 13, 1937; s. Jacob and Gladys Glennie (Cooper) B.; m. Bonnie Jeanne Lane, Aug. 15, 1959; children: John Jeffrey, Wendy Sue, Laura Lynne, Jennifer Anne. BA, U. Iowa, 1958, JD, 1960. Bar: Iowa 1960, Wis. 1960, Ariz. 1962, U.S. Ct. Appeals (9th cir.) 1971, U.S. Ct. Appeals (D.C. cir.) 1971, U.S. Supreme Ct. 1975, U.S. Ct. Appeals (10th cir.) 1982, U.S. Tax Ct. 1983. Assoc. Foley, Sammond & Lardner, Milw., 1960; assoc. Snell & Wilmer, Phoenix, 1962-66, ptnr., 1967—, chmn. 1983—. Contbr. articles to profl. jours. Chmn. Phoenix Human Rels. Commn., 1973-75; mem. Phoenix Commn. on LEAP, 1971-72, Phoenix Community Alliance, 1991—; bd. dirs. Phoenix Legal Aid Soc., 1970-76, Ariz. Econ. Coun., 1989-93, Mountain States Legal Found., 1977-95; trustee Ariz. Opera Co. (pres. 1989-91), Phoenix Art Mus., 1994—, pres., 1996-98. Capt. JAGC, U.S. Army, 1960-62. Recipient Walter E. Craig Disting. Svc. award, 1998, Community Legal Svcs. Decade of Dedication award, 1998, Disting. Achievement medal Ariz. State U. Coll. of Law, 1998. Fellow Am. Coll. Trial Lawyers; mem. ABA (Ariz. house of dels. 1989-98, bd. govs. 1998—), Maricopa County Bar Assn. (pres. 1977-78), Nat. Conf. Bar Pres. (exec. coun. 1984-91, pres. 1989-90), Ariz. Bar Assn. (pres. 1983-84), Ariz. Bar Found. (pres. 1987-88), Iowa Bar Assn., Wis. Bar Assn., Phoenix Assn. Def. Counsel (pres. 1972), Attys. Liability Assurance Soc., Ltd. (bd. dirs. 1987—), Iowa Law Sch. Found. (bd. dirs. 1986—), Phoenix C. of C. (bd. dirs. 1988-94), Ariz. State Coll. Law Soc. (bd. dirs., pres. 1997—), Western States Bar Conf. (pres. 1988-89), Ariz Supreme Ct. Spl. Com. on Lawyer Discipline and Profl. Conduct, Order of Coif, Phi Beta Kappa, Phi Eta Signa, Omnicron Delta Kappa. Avocations: fishing, hunting, skiing, travel, golf, tennis. Home: 800 E Circle Rd Phoenix AZ 85020-4144 Office: Snell & Wilmer One Arizona Ctr Phoenix AZ 85004-0001*

BOUMIL, MARCIA MOBILIA, legal educator, mediator, writer; b. Boston, Apr. 1958; d. Nicholas J. and Eleanor A. (Fuschetti) M.; m. S. James Boumil, Jr., Aug. 10, 1986; children: S. James III, Gregory M. BS cum laude, Tufts U., 1979, MS in Pub. Health, 1982; JD with honors, U. Conn., 1983; LLM, Columbia U., 1984. Bar: Mass. 1983, U.S. Dist. Ct. Mass. 1985, U.S. Ct. Appeals (1st cir.) 1987. Assoc. clin. prof. family medicine and cmty. health Tufts U. Sch. Medicine, Boston, 1986—; assoc. Herrick & Smith, Boston, 1984-85, Parker, Coulter, Daley & White, Boston, 1985-89; guardian ad litem, ind. ct. investigator Commonwealth of Mass., 1995—; sr. mediator Commonwealth Mediation and Conciliation Inc., Brockton, Mass., 1995—; lectr. in psychology, Boston Coll., 1992—, lectr. in law, 1987-89; instr., grad. program in pub. health, Tufts U., 1984-92; vis. asst. prof. law, 1989-90, 90-91; presenter in field, various lectrs. and seminars. Author: (textbook) Law, Ethics and Reproductive Choice, 1994; co-author: (textbook) Medical Liability: Cases and Materials, 1990, (textbook) Medical Liability: Teachers Manual, 1990, (textbook) Women and the Law, 1992, Sexual Harassment, 1992, Date Rape: The Silent Epidemic, 1993, (textbook) Law and Gender Bias, 1994, (textbook) Medical Liability in a Nutshell, 1995, Betrayal of Trust: Sex and Power in Professional Relationships, 1995, Deadbeat Dads: A National Child Support Scandal, 1996; author (ednl. tng. videotape) Sexual Harassment, 1995; contbr. articles to profl. jours. Vol. Andover (Mass.) Sch. Com., 1993—. Avocation: child care. Home and Office: 243 River Rd Andover MA 01810-3217

BOUNDS, DONALD LEROY, landscape architect, educator; b. Springfield, Oreg., June 29, 1955; s. Robert W. and Patricia (Schrader) B. B.Landscape Arch., U. Oreg., 1978; M.Landscape Arch., Harvard U., 1983. Registered landscape architect, Tex., La., Oreg. Sr. assoc. The SWA Group, Sausauto, Calif., 1979-91; prin. Donald L. Bounds, Dallas, 1992—; prof. landscape architecture U. Tex., Arlington, 1997-98. Mem. Am. Soc. Landscape Architects. Lutheran. Avocations: snow skiing, water skiing, hiking, travel, photography. Home: 5927 Kenwood Ave Dallas TX 75206-5513 Office: PO Box 140368 Dallas TX 75214-0368

BOUNDS, NANCY, modeling and talent company executive; b. Rodney, Ark., 1928; d. William Thomas and Mary Jane (Fields) Southard; m. Robert S. Bounds, 1960 (div. 1965); 1 child, Ronnie Jean; m. Mark Curtis Sconce, Nov. 28, 1972. Exec. dir. Internat. Fashion/Modeling Assn., N.Y.C., 1978; founding pres. Internat. Talent and Model Schs. Assn., N.Y.C., 1979-80; pres. Nancy Bounds Internat., Omaha, 1959—. Contbr. articles to profl. jours.; prodr. TV Heart Fund Auction, 1965; dir., choreographer fashion show N.Y. fashion editors, 1989. Chairperson Douglas/Sarpy County Heart Assn., Omaha, 1966, 73-74; co-chmn. The Pushkin Project, 1997-99, v.p., 1997-99. Recipient Nat. Tchr.'s award MiLady Pub. Co., 1965, Outstanding Svc. award Mayor of Omaha, 1984, Uta Halee Girls Village, 1983-87, March of Dimes svc. award, 1977, 84, Toys for Tots service award, 1986, Muscular Dystrophy citation of merit, 1982; named Best of Omaha, 1988-92, Woman of Distinction YWCA, 1992, 93, 94, 95; Nancy Bounds Day proclaimed by City of Omaha, 1994. Avocations: reading, painting, traveling, golf, tournament bridge, The Pushkin Project. Home: 4803 Davenport St Omaha NE 68132-3108 Office: 11915 Pierce Plz Omaha NE 68144-1648

BOUNDS-SEEMANS, PAMELLA J., artist; b. Milton, Del., Nov. 5, 1948; d. James Wilson Bounds and Marguerite Edna (Rickards) Bounds Carey; m. Jeffrey Wayne Seemans, Mar. 20, 1984; children: Misty Autumn, Sterling Hunter, Jordan Windsor. BA, N.Mex. Highlands U., 1971, MA, 1972. Tchr. elem. art Indian River Sch. Dist., Frankford, Del., 1973-79; lectr. U. Md., 1981, U. Del., 1986, Del. Tech. and C.C., 1988, 75th Del. Womens Day Conf. at U. Del., U. Del. Coll. Arts and Mineralogy, 1999. Exhibited in group shows including Rehoboth (Del.) Art League, 1980, 89, 90, 92, 93, Tideline Gallery, Rehoboth Beach, Del., 1980—, Greenville, Del., 1993, Wicomico Art League, 1980, Del. Tech. and C.C., Georgetown, 1981, U. Md., 1981, Meth. Ch. Gallery, Milford, Del., 1981, Bluestreak Gallery, Wilmington, Del., 1989—, Blue Streak Art Gallery, Wilmington, 1993, Jamison Gallery, Santa Fe, 1993—, Del. Art Mus., 1996, Biennal 96 and 98 Del. Art Mus., U. Del., 1999, numerous others; represented in permanent collections including Wilmington (Del.) Trust Co., Del. Nat. Bank, Sussex County Courthouse, Del. Parks and Recreation Bldg., also numerous pvt. collections; poster for mayor's office Clifford Brown Jazz Festival, Wilmington, 1998; mem. cmty. adv. editl. bd. News Jour., Gannett Papers, Wilmington, 1997-98. Donated art work to oncology ctr. Beebe Hosp. Found., 1995, Multiple Sclerosis Found. Del., Ronald McDonald House Del.; mem. cmty. adv. bd. News Jour. editl. Staff, 1997—. Recipient award for outstanding body of work Torpedo Factory, Alexandria, Va., 1982; fellow State of Del. Divsn. of the Arts, 1995. Mem. Nat. Mus. of Women in the Arts, Del. Art Mus., Rehoboth Art League (2d prize 1981, Tunnel 2d place award for most outstanding work in exhibit 1990, Popular Vote award 1980, 93, 94, 95, 96, 1st place award 1993, hon.), Del. Ctr. for Contemporary Arts, Del. Ctr. for Creative Arts, Newark Arts Alliance, Del. Nature Soc., Mothers Multiple Births (v.p. 1987), Wicomo Art League (hon. mention 1981). Episcopalian. Avocations: criminology, fashion, study of primitive art, psychology, gourmet cooking. Home and Studio: 1203 Greenbank Rd Wilmington DE 19808-5842

BOUQUET, FRANCIS LESTER, physicist; b. Enterprise, Oreg., Feb. 1, 1926; s. Francis Lester and Esther (Johnson) B.; m. Betty Jane Davis, Sept. 26, 1979 (dec. Aug. 15, 1989); children: Tim, Jeffrey, Janet; stepchildren: John Perry, Peggy Korv. AA, U. Calif., Berkeley, 1948, BA, 1950; MA, UCLA, 1953. Physicist U.S. Radiol. Def. Lab., San Francisco, 1953-55; engr., mgr. Lockheed Aircraft Co., Burbank, Calif., 1955-74; physicist Jet Propulsion Lab., Pasadena, Calif., 1974-88; pres. Systems Co., Graham, Wash., 1988-93, FLB Assocs., Medford, Oreg., 1994—; cons. in field. Author: Solar Energy Simplified, 1984, 4th edit., 1994, Radiation Damage in Materials, 1985, 3d edit., 1990, Radiation Effects on Electronics, 1986, 5th edit., 1995, Introduction to Materials Engineering, 1986, 3d edit., 1990, Introduction to Seals, O-Rings and Gaskets, 1988, 2d edit., 1992, Great Chefs of the Southwest Cookbook, 1988, rev. edit., 1989 (new title Chefs of the Southwest Cookbook), Radiation Effects on Teflon, 1989, Engineering Properties of Teflon, 1989, 2d edit., 1994, Radiation Effects on Kapton, 1990, Engineering Properties of Kapton, 1990, Lake Havasu Cookbook, 1990, Spacecraft Design-Thermal and Radiation, 1991, Solar Energy Technology, 1991, Practical Guide to Autos, 1992, Starting Your Business, vols. 1 & 2, 1992, Nuclear Energy Simplified, 1992, Introduction to Biological Radiation Effects, 1992, 2d edit., 1994, Successful Decision-Making, 1993, True Life Stories, 1994, Exoatmospheric and Space Travel, 1994, Engineers' Guide to Autos, 1994, Radiation Effects on Nonelectronic Materials Handbook, 1994. Elder 1st Presbyn. Ch., Van Nuys, Calif. 1970-81. Served with U.S. Army, 1944-46, with Signal Corps U.S. Army, 1951-52, PTO. Recipient Eagle Scout award Boy Scouts Am., 1940, Performance commendations Lockheed Aircraft Co., 1964, 66, Mgmt. Achievement Program award, 1973, 20 NASA awards, 1980-92; named to Honor Roll of Inventors, 1966. Mem. N.Y. Acad. Sci., Calif. Soc. Profl. Engrs., Nat. Soc. Profl. Engrs., IEEE (chmn. Los Angeles chpt. Nuclear and Plasma Scis. Soc. 1973-74), Am. Inst. Physics, AIAA, Nat. Mgmt. Assn., Air Force Assn., Lockheed Mgmt. Club, Caltech Mgmt. Club. Republican. Office: FLB Assocs # 516 Office of the Pres 1200 Mira Mar Ave Medford OR 97504-8553*

BOURCIER, JOHN PAUL, state supreme court justice; b. Providence, Mar. 27, 1927; s. Louis J. and Lydia E. (Garceau) B.; m. Norma M. DiLuglio, Aug. 20, 1951; children: Carol Bourcier Fargnoli, Norma J. Bourcier Bucci. BA, Brown U., 1950; LLB, Vanderbilt U., 1953. Bar: U.S. Dist. Ct. R.I. 1955, U.S. Ct. Appeals 1956, U.S. Immigration Svc. 1956, U.S. Ct. Mil. Appeals 1958, U.S. Tax Ct. 1960, U.S. Army Bd. Rev. 1965, U.S. Dist. Ct. Fla. 1965, N.H. 1965, Va. 1965. Trial atty. Bourcier & Bordieri, Providence, 1953-74; assoc. justice R.I. Superior Ct., Providence, 1974-98; judtice R.I. Supreme Ct., Providence, 1998—; invited judiciary panelist Rev. of Supreme Ct. Cases, 1987-92; lectr. in field; instr. Roger Williams Coll., 1982-95; guest lectr. Brown U., 1979-95, Bryant Coll., 1990-93, R.I. C.C., 1989-90; lectr. R.I. Fire Marshalls Arson Seminars, 1989—, New Eng. Fire Marshalls Arson Seminars, 1990-95; chmn. Superior Ct. Jury Trial Instrn. Rev. Com., mem. Civil Rules Rev. Com., others. Asst. editor Vanderbilt Law Rev., 1951-53. With USN, 1944-46. Named for life Assoc. Justice R.I. Supreme Ct. by Gov. Lincoln Almond, 1995—. Home and Office: RI Supreme Court 250 Benefit St Providence RI 02903-2719

BOURCIER, RICHARD JOSEPH, French language and literature educator; b. New Bedford, Mass., Dec. 25, 1930; s. Adrien and Alida (Richard) B.; m. Florence Rita Michaud, June 17, 1961 (dec. Nov. 26, 1994); children: Michelle, Camille, Jeanine, Normand, Paul. AB, Assumption Coll., 1958; MA in French, Laval U., 1959; PhD in Comparative Lit., SUNY, Binghamton, 1983. Instr. New Bedford (Mass.) Pub. Sch. Sys., 1959-60, Coll. of the Holy Cross, Worcester, Mass., 1961-68; asst. then assoc. prof. U. Scranton (Pa.), 1968-84, prof., 1984—; dir. French house U. Scranton, 1989-94. *Organizer of the first International Colloquium on Georges Duhamel, renown 20th Century French writer and member of the Academie-francaise at Scranton, PA. Editor for the publication of the Proceedings of June 23-25, 1988 (the centennial year of the University of Scranton) under the Duhamel title: L'Humanisme de Georges Duhamel (1884-1966) - The Humanism of Georges Duhamel, Scranton, Les Presses Universitaires-The Scranton UP, 1992.* Cantor Ch. St. Gregory, Clarks Green, Pa., 1973—. Sgt. U.S. Army, 1953-55. Mem. MLA, AAUP, Am. Assn. Tchrs. French, Assn. des Amis de Georges Duhamel (chevalier Knights in the Order of the Academic Palms), U.S. Amateur Ballroom Dancers Assn. Avocations: woodworking, music, dancing. Home: 103 Belmont Ave Clarks Green PA 18411-1101 Office: U Scranton Dept Fgn Langs Scranton PA 18510

BOURDAIS DE CHARBONNIÈRE, ERIC, financial executive; b. Boulogne sur Seine, France, July 1, 1939; s. Roger and Edithe (Chesnot) BdeC.; m. Jill Hollister Adams, Aug. 30, 1968. BA, Lycée Michelet, Paris; MBA, Ecole des Hautes Etudes Commerciales, Jouy-en-Josas, France, 1963. With Morgan Guaranty Trust Co., Paris, 1965-73; with Morgan Guaranty Trust Co., N.Y.C., 1974-79; v.p., head treas. Morgan Guaranty Trust Co., Paris, 1979-81, v.p., mgr. gal, 1981-83, sr. v.p., area head, 1983-85, sr. v.p., Continental Europe, 1985-87, exec. v.p., head Europe, Mid. East and Africa, 1987-89, head pvt. banking, investment mgmt. and brokerage activities Europe, Mid. East and Africa, 1989—; CFO Compagnie Generale des Etablissements Michelin, Cedex, France, 1990—. Gov. Am. Hosp., Paris. Recipient Chevalier des Arts et Lettres award Ministry of Culture, Paris, 1985. Mem. Automobile Club (Paris). Avocations: cycling, swimming, music. Office: Michelin, Place des Carmes, 63040 Clermont Ferrand France

BOURDON, CATHLEEN JANE, executive director; b. Sparta, Wis., July 13, 1948; d. Cletus John and Josephine Marie (Bourdon) Scheurich; children: Jill Krzyminski, Jeff Krzyminski. BA in Polit. Sci., U. Wis., 1973, MLS, 1974. Tchr. Peace Corps, Arba Minch, Ethiopia, 1969-72; asst. prof., dir. Alverno Coll. Libr., Milw., 1974-83; dep. exec. dir. Assn. Coll. and Rsch. Librs., Chgo., 1983-93; exec. dir. Assn. Specialized and Coop. Libr. Agys., Chgo., 1993—. Mem. ALA (pres. Staff Assn. 1987-88). Avocations: reading mystery fiction, 1940s movies, building model doll house furniture. Office: Assn Specialized & Coop Libr Agys 50 E Huron St Chicago IL 60611-5295

BOURDON, ROGER JOSEPH, history educator; b. St. Paul, May 8, 1937; s. Napoleon Joseph and Isabel Marie (Lynch) B.; m. Elizabeth Jeanne Vavrek, Jan. 28, 1967 (dec. 1981); children: Lisa, Janine, Jean-Paul; m. Dorothy Fort Lasalle, May 21, 1983. BS, Loyola U. L.A., 1959; MA, U. Calif., L.A., 1961, PhD, 1965. Asst. prof. Wichita (Kans.) State U., 1965-67, Marquette U., Milw., 1967-68; from asst. to prof. Mary Washington Coll., Fredericksburg, Va., 1968—; dir. campus computer access ctr. for visually impaired Mary Washington Coll., 1988—. Chmn. patrons adv. coun. Va. State Libr., Richmond, 1985-95; mem., chair disability svc. bd. Va. Planning Dist. # 16, Fredericksburg, 1993—. Mem. AAUP, Am. Historians, Western History Assn., Am. Coun. of Blind. Roman Catholic. Avocations: swimming, piano playing, travel. Office: Mary Washington Coll Dept History 1301 College Ave Dept History Fredericksburg VA 22401-5300

BOURGAIZE, ROBERT G., economist. BA, U. Wash., 1949. Dir., sr. v.p. Peoples Nat. Bank, Seattle; pres. Central Bank, N.A., Tacoma, University Place Water Co., Central Capital Corp., Epsilon Econ. Inc. Mem. Nat. Assn. Bus. Economists, English-Speaking Union U.S.A. (nat. dir.), Royal Commonwealth Soc., Am. Waterworks Assn. (life), Internat. Platform Assn., Pacific Northwest Writers Conf., Adam Smith Econ. Found., Adam Smith Soc. (founder 1976). Office: 3502 Bridgeport Way W University Place WA 98466

BOURGEAULT, JEAN-JACQUES, air transportation executive; b. Montreal, Que., Can., Feb. 2, 1943; s. Henri M. and Jeanne C. (Cloutier) B.; m. Gilberte C. Tremblay, Sept. 26, 1964 (div. Jan. 1990); m. Manon C. Surprenant, Feb. 2, 1994; 1 child, Martin J. B in Commerce, U. Montreal, 1964. Mgr. pers. Dominion Textile, Montreal, 1964-67; dir. human resources Que. Air, Montreal, 1967-71; dir. labor rels. U. Montreal, 1972-73; from mgr. labor rels. to exec. v.p., COO Air Can., Montreal, Que., 1973—; apptd. sr. exec. v.p. Air Can., Montreal, 1996—; chmn. Can. Korea Bus. Coun.; bd. dirs. Centre Internat. de recherches et d'études en mgmt., Internat. Aviation Mgmt. Tng. Inst., Galileo Can. Bd. dirs. World Film Festival. Mem. Air Transport Assn. Can. (bd. dirs.), Club St. Denis. Avocations: jazz, cinema. Office: Air Canada, PO Box 14000 Air Can Ctr 272, Montreal, PQ Canada H4Y 1H4*

BOURGET, EDWIN ROBERT, marine ecologist, educator; b. Senneterre, Que., Can., July 6, 1946; s. Jean-Paul and Myrtle (O'Malley) B.; m. Paule Reny, June 16, 1969; children: Frédéric, Virginie. BSc, U. Laval, Que., 1969, MSc, 1971; PhD, U. Wales, 1974. Oceonology rschr. U. Que., Rimouski, 1974-76; adj. prof. U. Laval, 1976-80, assoc. prof., 1980-84, prof., 1984—, dir. biology dept., 1997—, vice dean rsch. faculty sci. engring., 1998. Author/co-author 6 books or book chpts.; contbr. numerous articles to profl. jours. Recipient Michel-Jurdant prize Can.-French Assn. Advancement Sci., 1996; grantee in field. Mem. Groupe Interuniversitaire de recherches oceanographiques du Que. (dir. 1993-96), Natural Sci. and Engring. Rsch. Coun. (adv. bds. 1987—), Fonds pour la Formation de Chercheurs et l'Aide a la Recherche. Office: U Laval Dept Biology, Pavillon Vachon, Quebec, PQ Canada G1K 7P4

BOURGOIGNIE, MARIE HELENE, educator; b. Louvain, Belgium, May 15, 1961; came to U.S., 1963; d. Jacques James B. and Chantal Marie Luyckx. BA, U. Miami, 1985; MFA, Ohio U., 1990, MA, 1992. Lab. supr. U. Miami, Coral Gables, Fla., 1985-87; grad. teaching assoc. Ohio U., Athens, 1988-90; asst. prof. U. Miami, 1992-97, assoc. prof., 1997—. Recipient Excellence in Teaching award U. Miami, 1998; Freedom Forum grantee, 1995, 98. Mem. Nat. Press Photographers Assn., Assn. Edn. Journalism & Mass Comm. Avocations: sailing, scuba diving. Office: U Miami 120 Merrick Bldg Coral Gables FL 33124

BOURGUIGNON, ERIKA EICHHORN, anthropologist, educator; b. Vienna, Austria, Feb. 18, 1924; d. Leopold H. and Charlotte (Rosenbaum) Eichhorn; m. Paul H. Bourguignon, Sept. 29, 1950. BA, Queens Coll., 1945; grad. study, U. Conn., 1945; PhD, Northwestern U., 1951. Field work Chippewa Indians, Wis., summer 1946; field work Haiti; anthropology Northwestern U., 1947-48; instr. Ohio State U., 1949-56, asst. prof., 1956-60, asso. prof., 1960-66, prof., 1966-90, acting chmn. dept. anthropology, 1971-72, chmn. dept., 1972-76, prof. emeritus, 1990—; dir. Cross-Cultural Study of Dissociational States, 1963-68; Bd. dirs. Human Relations Area Files, Inc., 1976-79. Author: Possession, 1976, rev. edit., 1991, Psychological Anthropology, 1979, Italian transl., 1983; editor, co-author: Religion, Altered States of Consciousness and Social Change, 1973, A World of Women, 1980; co-author: Diversity and Homogeneity in World Societies, 1973; adv. editor: Behavior Sci. Rsch., 1976-79; assoc. editor: Jour. Psychoanalytic Anthropology, 1977-87; editl. bd.: Ethos, 1979-89, 97—; editor: Margaret Mead: The Anthropologist in America—Occasional Papers in Anthropology, No. 2, Ohio State U. Dept. Anthropology, 1986; (with Barbara Riquey) Exile: A Memoir of 1939 by Bronka Schneider, 1998; contbr. articles to profl. jours. Fellow Am. Anthrop. Assn.; mem. Ctrl. State Anthrop. Soc. (treas. 1953-56, exec. com. 1995-98), Ohio Acad Sci., World Psychiat. Assn. (transcultural psychiatry sect.), Am. Ethnol. Soc., Current Anthropology (assoc.), Soc. for Psychol. Anthropology (nominations com. 1981-82, bd. dirs. 1991-93), Phi Beta Kappa, Sigma Xi. Office: Ohio State U Dept of Anthropology 124 W 17th Ave Columbus OH 43210-1316 *It is more important to enjoy doing what you do, and to be able to do what you want to do, than to be successful. Success, if it comes, is only a by-product, nothing more.*

BOURJAILY, VANCE, novelist; b. Cleve., Sept. 17, 1922; s. Monte Ferris and Barbara (Webb) B.; m. Bettina Yensen, 1946; children: Anna (dec.), Philip, Robin; m. Yasmin Mogul, 1985; 1 child, Omar. A.B., Bowdoin Coll., 1947, DLitt, 1993. Newspaperman, TV dramatist, playwright, lectr.; prof. U. Ariz., U. Iowa Writers Workshop. 1958-80; co-founder, editor Discovery, 1951-53; cultural mission to S.Am. auspices State Dept., 1959, 73; Boyd prof. La. State U., Baton Rouge, 1985—; Disting. vis. prof. Oreg. State U., summer 1968; vis. prof. U. Ariz., 1977-78. Author: The End of My Life, 1947, The Hound of Earth, 1953, The Violated, 1958, Confessions of a Spent Youth, 1960, (non-fiction) The Unnatural Enemy, 1963, The Man Who Knew Kennedy, 1967, Brill Among the Ruins, 1970 (nominated Nat. Book Award for fiction 1971),(non-fiction) Country Matters, 1973, Now Playing at Canterbury, 1976, A Game Men Play, 1980, The Great Fake Book, 1987, Old Soldier, 1990, (with Philip Bourjaily) Fishing By Mail: The Outdoor Life of a Father and Son, 1993. Mem. campaign staff Hughes for Senate, 1968. Served with Am. Field Service, 1942-44; Served with AUS, 1944-46. Recipient Academy Award in lit., American Academy of Arts and Letters, 1993. Office: Carlisle & Co 24 E 64th St New York NY 10021-7201

BOURKE, KEVIN, coach; b. Chgo.; m. Cindy Hendricks; children: Mackenzie, Mollie, Anna. BS, Iowa State Univ., 1983; M in athletic adminstrn., Univ. Ill. Head cross country coach Iowa State Univ., 1996—. Office: Iowa Stat Univ 1800 South 4th St Ames IA 50011

BOURKE, LYLE JAMES, electronics company executive, small business owner; b. San Diego, May 28, 1963; s. Robert Victor and Virginia (Blackburn) B. Cert. in electronics, Southwestern Coll., San Diego, 1984; cert. in microelectronics, Burr Brown, Miramar, Calif., 1985; student, NACS, Scranton, Pa., 1988; AA in Econs., Cuyamaca Coll., 1991, postgrad., 1991-92; student, Wendelstedt Umpire Sch., 1992-93. Counselor Dept. Parks and Recreation City of Imperial Beach, Calif., 1979-80; warehouse worker Seafood Cannery, Cordova, Alaska, 1981, Nat. Beef Packing, Liberal, Kans., 1983; night mgr. Southland Corp., San Diego, 1983-85; tech. developer Unisys Corp., San Diego, 1985-92; process technician Ben & Jerry's Homemade, Inc., Springfield, Vt., 1994-95; technician Laser Power Corp, San Diego, Calif., 1996-98; founder Sparrells Ltd., 1992; instr. Harmonium Enrichment Program, 1993. Editor (handbook) College Policies, 1991; contbr. Cleanrooms mag., 1992; inventor Jacuzzi pillow, no-sit snowboard bindings. Vol. United Way, San Diego, 1987—; donor Imperial Beach Boys and Girls Club, 1988-98, Cal Farley's Boys Ranch, 1985-93, Assn. Handicapped Artists, 1988—, San Diego Jr. Theatre, 1992, Cabrillo Elem. Sch. Found., 1992. Chulsa Vista Lit. Team, 1996-99. Named Most Valuable Player Mex. Amateur Baseball League, San Diego-Tijuana, 1990. Mem. Am. Assn. Ret. Persons, Am. Mgmt. Assn. (charter), Prognosticators Club. Democrat. Avocations: computer tech., writing, Olympics. Office: Unisys 8011 Fairview Ave La Mesa CA 91941-6416

BOURKE, THOMAS ANTHONY, librarian, writer; b. N.Y.C., Aug. 19, 1945; s. Anthony Francis and Nora Christina (Bulman) B.; m. Graciela Adelaida Rodriguez, Aug. 18, 1990; children: Isabella A., Nora R. BA, Fordham Coll., 1966; MA, Fordham U., 1967; MS, Columbia U., 1968. Clerical aide N.Y. Pub. Libr., 1963-68, rsch. libr., 1968-80, chief microforms divsn., 1980-95; spl. asst. Ctr. for Humanities, 1995—; reviewer Baseball History, Libr. Jour., Microform Rev., RQ, Reprint Bull., Spl. Librs. Editor-in-chief Microform Rev., 1985-90, mem. editl. bd., 1991—; asst. editor Libr. Resources and Tech. Svcs., 1991-93, cons., reviewer, 1990—; contbr. articles to profl. jours.; pub. translations from Spanish lang. to profl. libr. jours. Mem. ALA, Assn. for Info. and Image Mgmt., Libr. and Info. Tech. Assn., Assn. for Libr. Collections and Tech. Svcs. (preservation microfilming com. 1987-89, exec. com. reproduction of libr. materials sect. 1988-91), Soc. for Am. Baseball Rsch. Democrat. Roman Catholic. Avocations: writing, reading, sports. Office: NY Pub Libr Rm 117 Fifth Ave-42d St New York NY 10018

BOURKE, WILLIAM OLIVER, retired metal company executive; b. Chgo., Apr. 12, 1927; s. Robert Emmett and Mable Elizabeth (D'Arcy) B.; m. Elizabeth Philbey, Sept. 4, 1970; children: Judith A., Andrew E., Edward A. Student, U. Ill., 1944-45; B.S. in Commerce, DePaul U., 1951. With Ford Motor Co., Dearborn, Mich., 1956-60, nat. distbn. mgr., 1960-64; gen. sales mgr. Ford Can., Toronto, Ontario, 1964-67; asst. mng. dir. Ford Australia, Melbourne, 1967-70, mgr. dir., 1970-71; pres. Ford Asia-Pacific and South Africa, Inc., Melbourne, 1971-72, Ford Asia-Pacific, Inc., Melbourne, 1972-73; pres. Europe, Inc., 1973-75, chmn. bd., 1975-80; exec. v.p. Ford

N.Am. Automotive Ops., Dearborn, 1980-81, also bd. dirs.; exec. v.p. Reynolds Metals Co., Richmond, Va., 1981-83, pres., COO, 1983-86, pres., CEO, 1986-88, chmn. bd., CEO, 1988-92; ret. 1st lt. M.I., U.S. Army, 1944-48.

BOURLAND, D(ELPHUS) DAVID, JR., linguist; b. Wichita Falls, Tex., June 6, 1928; s. Delphus David and Margaret (Hawley) B.; m. Elizabeth Jagush, Oct. 16, 1981; children by previous marriages: David III, Meda, Ruskin, Ileana. AB, Harvard U., 1951, MBA, 1953; lic. in English linguistics, U. Costa Rica, 1973. Ops. analyst Ops. Evaluation Group MIT, Washington, 1955-61; with various corps., 1961-65; pres. IR Assocs., Inc., San Diego, 1965-69, Semantics Rsch. Corp., Washington, 1969-71; from instr. to assoc. prof. U. Costa Rica, San Jose, 1971-80; pres. Semantics Rsch. Corp., Wichita Falls, Tex., 1994—; trustee Inst. Gen. Semantics, 1964-89. Author: Introduccion a la Tagmemica, 1974; co-author: An Advanced Course in Squirrelly Semantics: A Coloring Book for Some Adults, 1993, Not So Great Moments in the Lives of Great Men and Women, 1994; editor Gen. Semantics Bull., 1964-70; co-editor: To Be or Not: An E-Prime Anthology, 1991, More E-Prime: To Be or Not II, 1994, E-Prime III!, 1997; contbr. numerous articles to profl. publs. Lt. USNR, 1953-65. Korzybski fellow Inst. Gen. Semantics, 1949-50. Mem. Inst. Gen. Semantics, Internat. Soc. Gen. Semantics (contbg. editor Et Cetera, bd. dirs. 1993—, v.p. devel. 1995-97, pres. 1998—), Am. Legion (comdr. dept. Panama Canal 1979-81, post comdr. Costa Rica 1980-84), Sons Am. Legion (nat. adjutant 1985, 86), Forty and Eight (nat. exec. com. 1983-86), Harvard Faculty Club, Harvard Club Boston, Univ. Club of Wichita Falls, Wichita Falls Country Club, Sons. Confederate Vets., Wichita Falls Yacht Club. Republican. Avocation: power lifting. Home: 1517 Celia Dr Wichita Falls TX 76302-3515

BOURNE, CHARLES PERCY, information scientist, educator; b. San Francisco, Sept. 2, 1931; s. Frank Percy and Edith (Dunlap) B.; m. Elizabeth A. Scheidtmann, Aug. 15, 1953; children—Glen Wade, Holly Ann. B.S. in Elec. Engring., U. Calif. at Berkeley, 1957; M.S. in Indsl. Engring., Stanford, 1963. Sr. research engr. Stanford Research Inst., Menlo Park, Calif., 1957-66; v.p. Information Gen. Corp., Palo Alto, Calif., 1966-70; pres. Charles Bourne & Assos., Menlo Park, 1970—; prof. in residence Sch. Library and Info. Studies; dir. Inst. Library Research U. Calif.-Berkeley, 1971-77; v.p. gen. info. div. Dialog Info. Svcs., Inc., Palo Alto, 1977-92; research in info. scis. for libraries, schs., acads., including Library of Congress, Nat. Agrl. Library, U.S. Patent Office, Nat. Acad. Sci.; Guest lectr. univs. including U. Calif. at Berkeley, 1963-66; Sarada Ranganathan lectr., Bangalore, India, 1978; cons. corr. Nat. Acad. Sci. com. on sci. and tech. information, 1968-70; mem. adv. bd. Chem. Abstracts, 1965-68, Ency. Library and Information Scis., 1967—, Documentation Abstracts, 1968-69, Ann. Rev. Information Sci. and Tech., 1966; mem. adv. bd. World Affairs Report, 1987-90; U.S. rep. to a com. of Internat. Fedn. for Documentation, 1966-76; UNESCO cons. to Indonesia and Tanzania; Nat. Acad. Scis. cons. to Ghana, 1976; mem. U.S.-Egyptian Task Force on Tech. Info. Problems, 1976, U.S. del. UNESCO Intergovtl. Conf. Sci. and Tech. Info. for Devel., 1979; mem. Network Adv. Com. Library of Congress, 1987-92; delegate -at-large White House Conf. Lib. and Info. Svcs., 1991. Author: Methods of Information Handling, 1963, Technology in Support of Library Science and Information Service, 1980; contbr. articles profl. jours. Served with USMCR, 1950-51. Recipient ann. award of merit Am. Documentation Inst., 1965. Mem. Am. Soc. Information Sci. (pres. 1970), ALA (dir. information scis. and automation div. 1966-67), Nat. Info. Standards Orgn. (bd. dirs. 1987-90). Home: 1619 Santa Cruz Ave Menlo Park CA 94025-5761

BOURNE, ELFREDA O., community health nurse; b. Lucky Lake, Sask., Can., Apr. 26, 1919; d. Robert Arthur and Catherine (Neely) Holley; children: Jo-anne, Nanette, Catherine. AA, Fullterton Coll., 1962; BS with honors, St. Joseph's Coll., Windham, Maine, 1979; cert. tchr., UCLA, 1980. Cert. hospice; cert. counselor. Head nurse Garden Park Hosp., Garden Grove, Calif.; clinic nurse Golden West Coll., Huntington Beach, Calif. Writer current health issues United Calif. Bank, Santa Ana, RN mag. Mem. Calif. Profl. Nurses, Calif. Womens Club (1st pl. award 1988), Ebell Club, Nat. Fedn. Women's Club. Home: 37 S Ocean Dr Gilbert AZ 85233-5612

BOURNE, HENRY CLARK, JR., electrical engineering educator, former academic official; b. Tarboro, N.C., Dec. 31, 1921; s. Henry Clark and Marion (Alston) B.; m. Margaret Barr Thomas, Aug. 15, 1953; children: Katherine Wimberley, Henry Clark III, Thomas Franklin, Margaret Alston. S.B., MIT, 1947, S.M., 1948, Sc.D., 1952. Registered profl. engr., Calif., Tex. Asst. prof. Mass. Inst. Tech., 1952-54; asst. prof., then assoc. prof. U. Calif. at, Berkeley, 1954-63; prof. elec. engring. Rice U., Houston, 1963-77; chmn. dept. Rice U., 1963-74; sect. head engring. div. NSF, Washington, 1974-75, div. dir. engring., 1977-79; dep. asst. dir. Directorate Engring. and Applied Sci., 1979-81; v.p. for acad. affairs Ga. Inst. Tech., Atlanta, 1981-86, 87-88, acting pres., 1986-87, prof. elec. engring., 1988-92, prof. elec. engring. emeritus, 1992—; cons. editor Harper & Row, N.Y.C., 1961-67; cons. elec. engring., 1952—. Author tech. papers in field of magnetics. Served to 1st lt. C.E. AUS, 1943-46. Sci. Faculty fellow NSF, 1960-61; hon. research asso. Univ. Coll. London; Eng., 1961. Fellow IEEE, AAAS; mem. Am. Phys. Soc., Am. Soc. Engring. Edn., Sigma Xi, Tau Beta Pi, Eta Kappa Nu, Phi Kappa Phi, Omicron Delta Kappa, Beta Gamma Sigma, Delta Tau Delta. Episcopalian. Home: 2877 Bainbridge Way NW Atlanta GA 30339-4250

BOURNE, HENRY R., biochemistry professor; b. Danville, Va., Mar. 1, 1940; m.; three children. MD, Johns Hopkins U., 1965. Prof. medicine and cellular and molecular pharmacology U. Calif., San Francisco, 1980—. Mem. Nat. Acad. Scis. Office: U Calif Med Ctr Dept Pharm S1210 Box 0450 S1212 Box 0450 San Francisco CA 94143*

BOURNE, JOHN DAVID, city finance executive; b. Barbados, West Indies, July 6, 1937; s. Daniel E. and Clarissa M. (Foster) B.; B.B.A., Baruch Coll., City U. N.Y., 1972; M.B.A., L.I. U., 1974. Mgr., Household Fin. Corp., N.Y.C., 1963-72, N.Y.C. Off-Track Betting Corp., 1972-92; notary pub., 1964—; prof. bus. adminstrn. St. Joseph's Coll., Bklyn., 1982—, Coll. of Adelphi U., 1986—. Served with USAF, 1959-63. Mem. Baruch Coll., L.I. U. alumni assns. Democrat. Home: 14436 182nd St Sprngfld Gdns NY 11413-3357

BOURNE, JOHN R., educator; b. Bryan, Tex., Aug. 31, 1944. BSEE, Vanderbilt U., 1966; MS in Engring., U. Fla., 1967, PhD, 1969. Prof. Vanderbilt U., Nashville, 1969—. Fellow IEEE. Office: Vanderbilt U Box 1570 Sta B Nashville TN 37202

BOURNE, KATHERINE DAY, journalist, educator; b. Lynn, Mass., Sept. 11, 1938; d. Schuyler Vandervort and Elsie Marie (Mayo) Day; m. William Nettleton Bourne; children: William Alexander, Katherine Loring. BS in Edn., Keene Tchrs. Coll., 1960; MEd, Harvard U., 1984. Tchr. Wachusett Regional High Sch., Holden, Mass., 1960-61; arts editor Bay State Banner, Boston, 1966—; dir. edn. Suffolk County House of Correction, Boston, 1979-84; edn. coord. Dept. Transitional Asst., Mass., 1984—. Contbr. music revs. to Christian Sci. Monitor. Dir. rels. Crime-out, Boston, 1983; mem. Gov.'s Commn. on Status of Women, 1970-74; co-founder, dir. Harvard-Radcliffe Forum Theatre, Cambridge, 1964-68; bd. dirs., mem. ARC Greater Boston, 1987-95, NAACP Boston, 1978-81. NEH journalism fellow, 1978; recipient Melnea A. Cass award Greater Boston YMCA, 1984. Mem. NAACP (life). Avocations: collecting African-American literature, aerobics, photography, stamps, art relating to black history and life. Home: 52 High St Brookline MA 02445-7707 Office: Bay State Banner The Fargo Bldg 68 Fargo St Boston MA 02210-2122

BOURNE, LYLE EUGENE, JR., psychology educator; b. Boston, Apr. 12, 1932; s. Lyle E. and Blanche (White) B. BA, Brown U., 1953; MS, U. Wis., 1955, PhD, 1956. Asst. prof. psychology U. Utah, 1956-61, assoc. prof., 1961-63; vis. assoc. prof. U. Calif.-Berkeley, 1961-62, vis. prof., 1968-69; assoc. prof. psychology U. Colo., Boulder, 1963-65, prof., 1965—, chmn. dept. psychology, 1983-91, dir. Inst. Cognitive Sci., 1979-83; clin. prof. psychiatry U. Kans. Med. Ctr., 1967-90; vis. prof. U. Wis., 1966, U. Mont., 1967, U. Hawaii, 1969; cons. in exptl. psychology, VA, 1965-93. Author: Human Conceptual Behavior, 1966, Psychology of Thinking, 1971, Psychology: Its Principles and Meanings, rev. edits., 1976, 79 82, 85, Cognitive Processes, 1979, rev. edit., 1986, Psychology: A Concise Introduction, 1988, Psychology: Behavior in Context, 1998; acad. editor: Basic Concept Series, Learning-Cognition Series, Scott, Foresman Pub. Co., 1970-76, Charles Merill Co., 1980-84, Advanced Psychological Texts Series, Sage Publications, 1992—; editor Jour. Exptl. Psychology: Human Learning and Memory, 1975-80; cons. editor Jour. Clin. Psychology 1975-97, Jour. Exptl. Psychology: Learning, Memory and Cognition, 1984-92, Memory and Cognition, 1984-89. Recipient Research Scientist award NIHM, 1969-74. Mem. APA (coun. editors 1975-80, bd. sci. affairs 1978-81, 89-92, chmn. early awards com. 1978-79, coun. reps. 1976-79, 86-89, pres. divsn. 3 1992, publ. and comm. bd. 1995—), Psychonomic Soc. (governing bd. 1976-81, chmn. 1980-81), Soc. Exptl. Psychologists (chmn. 1987-88), Fedn. Behavioral, Psychol. and Cognitive Scis. (v.p. 1994-95, pres. 1995-97), Rocky Mountain Psychol. Assn. (pres. 1987-88), Coun. Grad. Depts. Psychology (exec. bd. 1985-89), Sigma Xi. Home: 785 Northstar Ct Boulder CO 80304-1088

BOURNE, MATTHEW, performing company executive, artistic director. Degree in Dance/Theatre, Laban Centre, 1985. Dir., choreographer and artistic dir. Adventures in Motion Pictures, London, 1987—; founder mem. Lea Anderson's The Featherstonehaughs, 1988. Stage works include: Overlap Lovers, 1987, Spitfire, 1988, Buck and Wing, 1988, The Infernal Gallop, 1989, Town & Country, 1991, The Nutcracker, 1992, Deadly Serious, 1992, The Percys of Fitzrovia, 1992, Highland Fling, 1994, Swan Lake, 1996, Cinderella, 1997; TV work includes: Late Flowering Lust, 1993, Drip-A Narcissistic Love Story, 1993; other choreography includes: As You Like It, 1989, Children of Eden, 1990, A Midsummer Night's Dream, 1991-92, The Tempest, 1991, Show Boat, 1991, Peer Gynt, 1994, Watch With Mother, 1994, Oliver!, 1994, Watch Your Step, 1995, Boutique, 1995, Roald Dahl's Red Riding Hood, 1995. Winner Bonnie Bird award, A Place Portfolio commn. and a Barclays New Stages award for choreography. Office: Adventure in Motion Picture, 1400 Gloucester Mansions, London WC2, England*

BOURNE, PETER GEOFFREY, physician, educator, author; b. Oxford, Eng., Aug. 6, 1939; s. Geoffrey Howard and Gwen (Jones) B.; m. Mary Elizabeth King, Nov. 9, 1974. MD, Emory U., 1962; MA in Anthropology, Stanford U., 1969. Fellow dept. psychiatry Med. Sch.; co-dir. Alcoholism Project, Emory U., 1962-63; intern King County Hosp., Seattle, 1963-64; research psychiatrist Walter Reed Army Inst.; Research Washington, 1964-67; chief neuropsychiat. br. U.S. Army Med. Research Team, Vietnam, 1965-66; cons. S.E. Asia Health Br. (AID), Dept. State, 1966-67; resident dept. psychiatry, Stanford U. Med. Center, Palo Alto, Calif., 1967-69; dir. mental health unit Southside Comprehensive Health Center, Atlanta, 1969-71; founder, dir. Atlanta South Central Community Mental Health Center, 1970-71; dir. Ga. Office Drug Abuse, 1971-72; spl. adviser for health affairs to Gov. Jimmy Carter of Ga., 1971-73; asst. dir. White House Spl. Action Office for Drug Abuse Prevention, 1972-74; cons. Drug Abuse Council, Washington, 1974-76; pres. Found. for Internat. Resources, 1975-76; Mid-Atlantic coordinator, dep. campaign dir. Jimmy Carter Presdl. Campaign, 1975-76; spl. asst. for health issues to U.S. Pres., Washington, 1976-78; mem. U.S. del. to Exec. Council UNICEF, 1977; asst. sec. gen. UN, N.Y.C., 1979-81; pres. Global Water, 1981-98; exec. v.p., pub. Devel. Internat., 1986-90; mem. U.S. Pres. Commn. on White House Fellows; head U.S. delegation UN Devel. Program Governing Council, 1978; emergency room physician Casualty Hosp., Washington, 1966-67, Kaiser Permanente Hosp., Santa Clara, Calif., 1967-69; psychiat. cons. Santa Clara County Hosp., 1968-69, San Mateo County Hosp., 1969; cons. WHO, Geneva, 1972, UN Div. on Narcotic Drugs, 1976; asst. prof. dept. psychiatry Emory U. Med. Sch., 1969-72, asst. prof. dept. preventive medicine and community health, 1969-72; lectr. dept. psychiatry Harvard U. Med. Sch., 1974; v.p. Nat. Coordinating Council on Drug Abuse Edn., 1971-72; prof. psychiatry, chmn. dept. St. Georges Med. Sch., Grenada, 1979-98; pres. Peter Bourne Assocs., Washington, 1985-98; mem. of jury The Lasker Awards, 1978-79; vice chancellor St. Georges U., Grenada, 1998—. Author: Men, Stress and Viet Nam, 1970; editor: Psychology and Physiology of Stress, 1969, (with R. Fox) Alcoholism: Progress in Research and Treatment, 1973, Addiction, 1974, Acute Drug Abuse Emergencies, 1976, Water Resources: Social and Economic Aspects, 1983, Fidel, A Biography of Fidel Castro, 1986, Jimmy Carter: A Comprehensive Biography from Plains to the Post-Presidency, 1997; mem. editorial bd. Psychiatry, 1968—, Am. Jour. Drug Alcohol Abuse, 1973—; contbr. articles to med. jours. and chpts. to books. Bd. dirs. Save the Children Fedn., Inst. for So. Studies, Hunger Project; chmn., bd. trustees Council on Hemispheric Affairs, 1986—; chmn. bd. dirs. Am. Assn. World Health, 1982-98, Health and Devel. Internat., 1997—, Youth Advocate Program, 1998—, Med. Edn. Collaboration with Cuba, 1998—. Served to capt. U.S. Army, 1964-67. Decorated Bronze Star medal, Air medal, Combat Medics badge; recipient William C. Menninger award Central Neuropsychiat. Assn., 1967, Pub. Service award Nat. Assn. State Drug Abuse Program Coordinators, 1974, Pub. Service award Assn. Chinese Ams., 1978; named One of Five Outstanding Young Men, Atlanta Jaycees, 1971, One of Five Outstanding Young Men in Ga., Ga. Jaycees, 1972. Mem. AAAS, Am. Psychiat. Assn. (chmn. task force on drugs and drug abuse edn. 1969-73), Ga. Psychiat. Assn., Washington Psychiat. Soc., Royal Soc. Medicine, Med. Assn. Ga., Soc. for Internat. Health (pres. 1988-92), Am. Med. Soc. on Alcoholism, Am. Anthrop. Assn., World Fedn. for Mental Health. Democrat. Home and Office: 2119 Leroy Pl NW Washington DC 20008-1848 *I have always felt that my training as a physician was only a starting point in using my life to touch, for the better, the lives of as large a number of people as possible, whether formulating national health policy for the President of the United States, through the United Nations, through the private voluntary agencies or the academic world. I believe that ultimate gratification can only come from the sense that one has left the world a better place than when one arrived.*

BOURNE, RUSSELL, publisher, author; b. Boston, Oct. 10, 1928; s. Standish T. and Sylvia (Russell) B.; m. Miriam Anne Young, Aug. 22, 1953 (dec.); children: Sarah Perkins, Jonathan, Louise Taber, Andrew Russell; m. Dora Grabfield Flash, Oct. 31, 1992. A.B. magna cum laude, Williams Coll., 1950. Reporter Life mag., 1950-53, asst. to Henry R. Luce, 1953-56; assoc. editor Archtl. Forum, 1956-59; editor Am. Heritage Jr. Library, 1959-64, Time-Life Books, Great Ages of Man, 1964-69; assoc. chief Nat. Geog. Book Service, 1969-72; partner Bourne-Thompson & Assocs., Washington, 1972-77; sr. editor Smithsonian Exposition Books, Washington, 1977-80; pub. Hearst Gen. Books, N.Y.C., 1980-81; pub., editor Am. Heritage Books, N.Y.C., 1981-83; pub. cons., 1984—. Author: View From Front Street, 1989, Red King's Rebellion, 1990, Floating West, 1992, Best of the Best Sparkman and Stephens Designs, 1995, Americans on the Move, 1995, Invention in America, 1996, Rivers of America, 1998. Served with CIC, U.S. Army, Berlin, 1950-52. Home and Office: 2 Fairway Dr Ithaca NY 14850-2764

BOURNEUF, HENRI JOSEPH, JR., librarian; b. Beverly Farms, Mass.; s. Henri and Elizabeth (McKean) B.; m. Susan Peterson, June 19; 1 child, Anne Peterson. BA, Harvard U., 1969; MLS, Simmons Coll., Boston, 1980. Ref. libr. Widener Libr., Harvard U., Cambridge, Mass., 1980—, head ref. libr., 1995—. Democrat. Home: 119 Huron Ave Cambridge MA 02138-1366 Office: Widener Library Harvard Univ Cambridge MA 02138

BOURQUE, PIERRE, mayor; b. Montreal, Que., Can., May 29, 1942. Degree in hort. engring., Belgium. With City of Montreal, 1965—, coord. park maintenance and devel. for Expo 67, 1965-67, city adminstr., mayor, 1994—; coord. Biodome, Internat. Floralies; chmn. Regional Devel. Coun. of Montreal Island, Table des maires et des préfets du Grand Montreal. Named Officer of Order of Can., Chevalier de l'Ordre nat. du Que.; recipient Prix d'excellence de l'adminstrn. publique Assn. des diplomés d'adminstrn. publique, 1992. Office: Hôtel de Ville, Ville de Montreal, 275 rue Notre-Dame est, Montreal, PQ Canada H2Y 1C6*

BOURQUE, RAY, professional hockey player; b. Montreal, Que., Can., Dec. 28, 1960; m. Chris Bourque; children: Melissa, Christopher Ray. Hockey player Boston Bruins (NHL), 1979—; mem. QMJHL All-Star 1st team, 1977-78, 78-79, NHL All-Star 1st team, 1979-80, 81-82, 83-84, 84-85, 86-87, 89-90, 93-94, 2nd team, 80-81, 82-85, 85-86, 88-89; player NHL All-Star game, 1981-86, 88-94. Recipient Calder NHL Rookie of Yr. trophy, 1980, Norris Outstanding Defenseman trophy, 1987, Frank. J. Selke trophy, 1978-79, Emile (Butch) Bouchard trophy, 1978-79, James Norris Meml. trophy, 1986-87, 87-88, 89-90, 90-91, 93-94, King Clancy Meml. trophy, 1991-92; named to Sporting News All-Star 2nd team, 1980-81, 82-83, 85-86, 88-89, Sporting News All-Star 1st team, 1981-82, 83-84, 86-87, 87-88, 89-90, 93-94. Office: care Boston Bruins One Fleet Ctr Ste 250 Boston MA 02114-1303*

BOURQUE, RICHARD MICHAEL, foundation administrator; b. Omaha, Nebr., Mar. 9, 1967; s. Adrian Richard Bourque and Kathleen Marrie Van Ackeren; m. Kathy J. Green, June 26, 1993. BS in Agr., U. Mo., 1990. Mgr. Grandmother's, Omaha, 1990-91, Lute Ranch, Ogallala, Nebr., 1991—; owner, pres. Functional Agr. Resource Techs., Inc., Ogallala, 1993—; exec. dir. Lute Family Found., Inc., Ogallala, 1994—; pres. Packaging and Crating Svcs., Inc., North Platte, Nebr., 1996—; cons. Law Office of McGinley, O'Donnell, Ogallala, 1998—; pres. Keith County Housing Devel. Inc., Ogallala, 1997-98. Pres. Tech. Renovation Com., Ogallala, 1995-96; mem., bd. dirs. Comty. Redevel. Authority, Ogallala, 1996-98; bd. dirs. Nebr. Nat. Trails Mus., Keith County, 1996—, Western Nebr. Comty. Found. Inc., Keith County, 1996—. Recipient Outstanding Contbn. award Ogallala Sch. Bd., 1996. Mem. Nebr. Cattlemen's Assn., Elks (mem. ritual team, chaplain 1994-95, All State award 1995), Ogallala Yacht Club. Roman Catholic. Avocations: skiing, hunting, boating, off-road trail riding, fishing. E-mail: lffinc@megavision.com. Office: Lute Family Found Inc PO Box 187 Ogallala NE 69153

BOURRIE, SALLY RUTH, writer; b. Denver, Nov. 5, 1958; d. Lawrence John and Helen Leone (Atkins) B. AB, Vassar Coll., 1980; MA, U. So. Calif., 1983. Freelance writer Chgo., Denver and Portland, Oreg., Chgo. and Denver, 1987—. Author: (catalog) Art of Paul Landacre, 1983. V.p. Vassar Coll. Class of 1980, 1995—. Recipient 1st pl. award for individual writing Chgo. Women in Publishing, 1993, Hon. Mention award Writer's Digest, 1991. Mem. Haviland Collectors Club Internat. Avocations: art museums, running, pets, American china.

BOUSON, J. BROOKS, English educator; b. Washington, Pa.. BA, U. Ill., Chgo.; PhD, Loyola U. Chgo., 1979. Asst. prof. English, Mundelein Coll., Chgo., 1980-86, assoc. prof. English,, 1986-91; assoc. prof. English, Loyola U. Chgo., 1991—, dir. undergrad. programs in English,, 1998—. Author: The Empathic Reader: A Study of the Narcissistic Character and the Drama of the Self, 1989, Brutal Choreographies: Oppositional Strategies and Narrative Design in the Novels of Margaret Atwood, 1993; contbr. chpts. to books and articles to profl. jours. Mem. MLA, Midwest MLA, Toni Morrison Soc., Margaret Atwood Soc., Phi Kappa Phi, Alpha Sigma Nu. Office: Loyola Univ Chgo Lake Shore Campus 6525 N Sheridan Rd Chicago IL 60626

BOUTELLE, STEVEN W., army officer; b. Pasco, Wash., Feb. 24, 1948. BA in Bus. and Fin., U. Puget Sound, Tacoma; MBA, Marymount U., Arlington, Va. Commd. 2d lt. U.S. Army, 1970, advanced through grades to brig. gen.; program exec. officer Army Task Force XXI, 1996-97, Command, Control and Communications Systems, Ft. Monmouth, N.J., 1997—. Decorated Legion of Merit with oak leaf cluster, others. Office: Command Control and Comm Systems Fort Monmouth NJ 07703-5401

BOUTHILLIER, ANDRÉ, public relations executive, consultant; b. Montreal, Que., Can., July 8, 1952; s. Guy and Carmen (LeLiévre) B.; divorced; 1 child, Simon; m. Lise Cormier, Sept. 16, 1992. Degree in human scis. and comm., Coll. of Jonquiere, Que., 1972; degree in polit. scis. and journalism, Laval U., Que. City, 1975; degree in journalism (hon.), Ctr. Journalists in Europe, Paris, 1983. Journalist Montreal-Matin, 1973-78, Radio-Can. (TV), Montreal, 1978-80, Le DeVoir, Montreal, 1980-85; ptnr. Comms. Marsy, Montreal, 1985-87; sr. pntr. Nat. Pub. Rels., Montreal, 1987—. Pres. comms. com. C. of C. of Quebec, Montreal, 1992-95, World Kite Festival, Verdun, 1992-95. Recipient 1st prize investigative journalism award Fondation Pour La Liberté de Presse, Paris, 1984, 1st prize econ. journalism award Fondation d'Edn. and Econs., Montreal, 1983, 1st prize bus. writing award Toronto Press Club, 1984, 85, 2d prize Prix Judith-Jasmin award Cercle des Femmes Journalists, Montreal, 1984. Mem. Chambre de Commerce du Met. Montreal, Chambre de Commerce du Que., Can. Pub. Rels. Soc. Avocations: sailing, kite, ice hockey, golf, softball. E-mail: andre@pyramidcw.com. Office: Optimum Pub Rels, 2100 Drummond St, Montreal, PQ Canada H3G 1X1

BOUTIETTE, VICKIE LYNN, educator; b. Valley City, N.D., Mar. 13, 1950. BS in Elem. Edn., Valley City State U., 1972; MS in Reading, Moorhead State U., 1997; postgrad., U. S.D., 1998—. 4th-5th grade tchr. Pillsbury Pub. Sch., 1973-74; 3rd grade tchr. West Fargo Pub. Schs., 1984-90, remedial reading tchr., elem. tchr., 1993-98, tchr. leader Reading Recovery, 1998—. Sunday sch. tchr., 1975—, ch. newsletter editor, 1993—; vol. U. Minn. Hosps. and Clinics, 1991-93. Recipient Nat. Educator Award Milken Family Found., 1998, Courage award N.D. Edn. Assn., 1994; named N.D. Tchr. of Yr., 1998, West Fargo Tchr. of Yr. 1997-98. Mem. NEA, West Fargo Edn. Assn. (exec. bd. 1989-90, elem. chairperson 1988-89, pub. rels. chairperson 1988-90), N.D. Edn. Assn., Valley Reading Assn. (rec. sec. 1997—), N.D. Reading Assn., Phi Delta Kappa, Alpha Mu Gamma (pres. 1972). Fax: 701-282-8012. Home: 7103 64th Ave South West Fargo ND 58104-5715 Office: Westside Elem Sch 945 7th Ave W West Fargo ND 58078

BOUTIN, PETER RUCKER, lawyer; b. San Francisco, Oct. 6, 1950; s. Frank J. and Charlotte (Downey) B.; m. Suzanne Jones, Aug. 31, 1974; children: Jennifer, Lisa, Kevin. AB, Stanford U., 1972; JD magna cum laude, Santa Clara U., 1975. Bar: Calif. 1975, U.S. Dist. Ct. (no., ea., so. and ctrl. dists.) Calif. 1976, U.S. Ct. Appeals (9th cir.) 1977, U.S. Supreme Ct. 1982. Assoc. Keesal, Young & Logan, Long Beach, Calif., 1975-78, ptnr., 1978-84; mng. ptnr. San Francisco office Keesal, Young & Logan, San Francisco, 1984—; arbitrator San Francisco Superior Ct., 1989—, Nat. Assn. Securities Dealers, San Francisco, 1980—; mediator San Francisco Superior Ct., 1989—; early neutral evaluation panel U.S. Dist. Ct., 1993—. Co-author Am. Arbitration Assn. Arbitrator Tng. Materials, 1992. Mem. Bar Assn. San Francisco, Assn. Bus. Trial Lawyers, Securities Industry Assn. Compliance and Legal Divsn., San Francisco Bond Club, Stanford Buck/Cardinal Club. Office: Keesal Young & Logan 4 Embarcadero Ctr Ste 1500 San Francisco CA 94111-4122

BOUTIS, TOM, artist, painter, print maker; b. N.Y.C., Aug. 25, 1922; s. Athanasios and Olga (Toskos) B.; m. Bertha Peters, Nov. 15, 1953; 1 child, Athanasios. BFA, Cooper Union U. Artist: one-person exhibitions include Drawings, Cooper Union, N.Y.C., 1953, Paintings: Zabriesky Gallery, N.Y.C., 1955, Am. Embassy, Rome, Italy, 1957, Area Gallery, N.Y.C., 1959, 60, Art Ctr. No. N.J., Tenafly, N.J., 1968; Decade on Paper, Landmark Gallery, N.Y.C., 1976, Paper on Paper, 1978, Cylinders, Columns, Circles and Color, 1979, Shadow Drawings, 1989, Monoprints, 1981, Painting, 1972, 75, 77, 81, Paintings and Monoprints, Maurice M. Pine Libr., Fairlawn, N.J., 1985,Works on Paper, Greek Embassy, 1989; 2-man exhbn. (with Alex Katz) Tanager Gallery, N.Y.C., 1957; group exhibitions include Greek Am. artists Noemata, Bklyn. Mus., 1977, Art Callender, Cooper Union Alumni Exhibition, N.Y.C., 1978, Landmark Gallery, N.Y.C., 1972, 82, Contemporary Drawings, Louise Ross Gallery, N.Y.C., 1984, Xmas Invitation, A.I.R., N.Y.C., 1985, Works on Paper, Ann Weber Gallery, Georgetown, Maine, 1987, Gallery Artists and Friends, Am. Acad. Arts & Letters, N.Y.C., 1988, 89, Shapolsky Gallery, N.Y.C., 1988, Arsenal Invitational, Arsenal Gallery, N.Y.C., 1989, Out of the 50's Snyder Fine Art, N.Y.C., 1993, Nat. Acad. Design, N.Y.C., 1992, 93, 95, 97, 99, Monhegan Island Artists The Governor's Mansion, Augusta, Maine, 1996, Works on Paper, Bergen Mus., N.J., 1998; represented in public collections at NYU, Everson Mus., Syracuse, N.Y., Chem. Bank, N.Y.C., Prudential Bache, N.Y.C., Resource Mgmt., N.Y.C., St. Michel's Hosp., Newark, Calvin Klein Collection, N.Y.C., Calvin Klein Works on Paper, Weisbaden German, Nieully, France, N.Y. Hilton, Broad Nat. Bank of Newark and many others. Recipient scholarship to Skowhegan (Maine) School of Painting, 1951, Fulbright to Rome, 1955-57, Mark Rothko Found. award, 1974; grantee: N.Y. Coun. on Arts, 1975 (painting), 1979 (graphics), Nat. Endowment for the Arts, 1976, Adolf and Esther Gottleib Found., 1983, The Rockefeller Found. Residency, Bellagio, Italy, 1989. Mem. Nat. Acad. of Design. Home: 162 E 82nd St New York NY 10028-1826

BOUTON, MARSHALL MELVIN, academic administrator; b. N.Y.C., Aug. 8, 1942; s. Percy Marshall and Mary Fuller (Melvin) B.; m. Barbara Elizabeth Linn, Sept. 14, 1968; children: Christopher, Alexander. BA cum laude in History, Harvard Coll., 1964; MA in South Asian History, U. Pa., 1968; PhD in Polit. Sci., U. Chgo., 1980. Exec. sec., program dir. The Asia Soc., N.Y.C., 1975-77; spl. asst. to amb. U.S. Embassy, New Delhi, India, 1977-80; dir. policy analysis, internat. security affairs Dept. Def., Near East, South Asia,, Africa, 1980-81; dir. contemporary affairs The Asia Soc., N.Y.C., 1981-87, v.p. pres. program planning external affairs, 1987-90, exec. v.p., 1990—; tng. project dir. Peace Corps, Sacramento, summer 1967, tng. coord., Estes Park, Colo., summer 1968; tng. assoc. in internat. devel. The Ford Found., New Delhi, 1968-69; lectr. divsn. of social scis. U. Chgo., 1973-75; vis. scholar So. Asian Inst. Columbia U., 1975-77; cons. World Bank, 1980-81. Author: Agrarian Radicalism in South India, 1985, India's Problem is not Politics, 1998; co-author: Korea at the Crossroads: Implications for American Strategy, 1987; contbr., editor numerous articles to profl. jours. NSF Dissertation Rsch. fellow, 1972-74, U.S. Agy. on Internat. Devel. grantee, 1974-77, Rockefeller Found. travel grantee, 1977. Mem. Coun. on Fgn. Rels., Assn. for Asian Studies, Am. Polit. Sci. Assn., Harvard Club. Office: Asia Society 725 Park Ave New York NY 10021-5088

BOUTROS, LINDA NELENE WILEY, medical/surgical nurse; b. New Orleans, Aug. 31, 1951; d. Robert Vernon and Marye Dell (Adcock) Wiley; m. Eddy Boutros, Dec. 23, 1972; children: Scott, Mark, Natalie. BS in Nursing, U. S.W. La., 1973. Cert. health care risk mgr. RN, coord./supr. of nursing Kelsey Seybold Clinic, Missouri City, Tex., 1982-86; RN, head nurse S.W. Pediatric Ctr., Sugarland, Tex., 1986-87; RN, nursing supr. Westshore Hosp., Tampa, Fla., 1988-89; med.-surg. nurse Centurion Hosp., Carrollwood and Tampa, 1989-90, asst. head nurse med., 1990-91, relief supr., 1991, dir. surg. nursing svcs., 1992-93; nurse mgr. surg. floor, relief house supr. Univ. Cmty. Hosp. Carrollwood, Tampa, Fla., 1993-99, RN adminstrv. supr., 1999—. Mem. ANA, Fla. Nurses Assn. Home: 502 Brooktree Ct Lutz FL 33549-4427 Office: Univ Cmty Hosp Carrollwood 7171 N Dale Mabry Hwy Tampa FL 33614-2670

BOUTROS-GHALI, BOUTROS, former United Nations official; b. Cairo, Nov. 14, 1922. LLD, Cairo U., 1946; Diploma of Higher Studies in Pub. Law, Paris U., 1947, Diploma of Higher Studies in Econs., 1948, Diploma of Polit. Sci. Ins., 1949, PhD in Internat. Law, 1949; dr. h.c., René Descartes U., Paris, 1980, Uppsala (Sweden) U., 1986. Prof. internat. law, internat. rels., head dept. polit. scis. Cairo U., 1949-77; min. state Fgn. Affairs, Egypt, 1977-91, dep. prime min., 1991; sec.-gen. UN, N.Y.C., 1992-96, Francophonie, 1997—; assoc. dir. First Dag Hammarskjold Seminar, Netherland, 1963; dir. Ctr. Rsch. The Hague Acad. Internat. Law, 1963-64, mem. study group, 1965-66, mem. external program group, 1968-71, mem. curatorium adminstrv. coun., 1978—; vis. prof. faculty of law Paris U., 1967-68; co-dir. first session external program Acad. Internat. Law, Rabat, 1969; dir. first session of the sr. diplomats Union of the Abu Dhabi, 1973; lectr. internat. law, internat. rels. various univs. Author: (books) Contribution à l'Etude des Ententes Régionales, 1949, Cours de Diplomatie et de Droit Diplomatique et Consulaire, 1951, (with Youssef Chlala) Le Problème de Suez, 1957, Egypt and the United Nations: Carnegie Endowment for International Peace, 1957, Le Principe d'Egalité des Etats et les Organisations Internationales, 1961, Contribution à une Théorie Générale des Alliances, 1963, L'Organisation de l'Unité Africaine, 1969, Le Mouvement Afro-Asiatique, 1969, Les Difficultés Institutionelles du Panafricanisme, 1979, La Ligue des Etats Arabes, 1972, Les Conflits de Frontières en Afrique, 1973; co-author: Foreign Policies in a World of Change, 1983, Will We Survive?, 1989; founder, editor Al Ahram Al-Iktisadi, 1960-75, Al Siyassa Ad-Dawliya; mem. editl. bd. Egyptian Rev. Internat. Law, Yearbook of the Assn. of the Attenders, Alumni of the Hague Acad. of Internat. Law. Mem. Com. application of convs. and recommendations Internat. Labour Orgn., 1971-79; mem. cen. com. Polit. Bur. of the Arab Socialist Union, 1974-77; pres. Ctr. for Polit. and Strategic Studies, Al-Ahram, 1975—; mem. Internat. Commn. Jurist, Geneva, 1975-77; mem. Commn. Internat. Law of the UN, 1979—; mem. secretariat Nat. Dem. Party, 1980-91. Decorated Order of the Nile (Egypt), Grand Croix de l'Ordre de la Couronne (Belgium), Cavaliere di Gran Croce (Italy), Gran Cruz de la Orden de Boyaca (Colombia), Gran Cruz de la Orden de Antonio José de Irisarri (Guatemala), Grand Croix de la Légion d'Honneur (France), Gran Cruz de la Orden Nacional Al Merito (Ecuador), Gran Cruz de la Orden del Liberation San Martin (Argentina), Tishakti Patta (Nepal), Grand Croix de l'Ordre du Mérite du Niger, Grand Officer de l'Ordre du Mérite du Mali, La Condecoracion De Agulia Azteca (Mex.), Grand Croix de l'Ordre Pro Merito Melitensi de l'Ordre Souverain Militaire et Hospitalier de St. Jean de Jerusalem de Rhodes de Malte, Grand Cordon de l'Ordre du Phoenix de Grèce, Grand Cordon du Mérite du Chili, Order of the Crown of Brunei, Grand Cross of the Order of Merit (Germany), Gran Cruz del Sol del Peru, comdr. de l'Ordre du Mérite Nat. de la Côte d'Ivoire, Grand Croix de l'Ordre du Danebrog, Grand Officer Cross of the Order of the Polar Star (Sweden), The Order of Diplomatic Svc. Merit (Gwanghwa, Korea); Fulbright Rsch. scholar Columbia U., 1954-55. Mem. African Soc. Polit. Studies (pres. 1980—), Egyptian Soc. Internat. Law (v.p. 1965—), Inst. Pub. Internat. Law and Internat. Rels. Thessaloniki (curatorium 1976—), Acad. des Scis. morales et politiques (assoc. 1989—), Inst. Internat. Law (pres. 1985-87), Inst. Affari Internazionali (assoc. 1979—), Acad. Mondiale pour la Paix (sci. com. 1975—), Internat. Inst Human Rights (mem. coun., exec. com. 1975—), Assn. Colombiana de Estudios de Politica Internacional Y Diplomacia (hon. 1980—), Malgache Acad., Academia Mexicana de Dir. Internacional. Home: 2 Avenue El-Nil Giza, Cairo Egypt

BOUTWELL, ROSWELL KNIGHT, oncology educator; b. Madison, Wis., Nov. 24, 1917; s. Paul Winslow and Clara Gertrude (Brinkhoff) B.; m. Luella Mae Fairchild, Sept. 25, 1943; children—Paul F., Philip H., David K. B.S. in Chemistry, Beloit Coll., 1939; M.S. in Biochemistry, U. Wis., 1941, Ph.D., 1944; DSc, Beloit Coll., 1980. Instr. U. Wis., 1945-49, asst. prof., 1949-54, assoc. prof., 1954-67; prof. oncology med. ctr. U. Wis., Madison, 1967—; vis. lectr. Inst. for Environ. Medicine, NYU, summer 1966; mem. cancer study group Wis. Regional Med. Program, 1967-70; mem. adv. com. on inst. research grants Am. Cancer Soc., 1967-74, chmn., 1972-74; mem. food protection com. NRC, 1971-75; mem. lung cancer segment Nat. Cancer Inst., 1971-75; mem. adv. com. on pathogenesis of cancer Am. Cancer Soc., 1960-63; mem. Nat. Cancer Adv. Bd., 1983-90; chief research Radiation Effects Research Found., Hiroshima, Japan, 1984-86; prof. emeritus, 1988—. Mem. editorial adv. bd. Cancer Research, 1959-64, assoc. editor, 1973-83; mem. editorial bd. Jpn. J. Cancer Res., 1985—; assoc. editor: Nutrition and Cancer, 1988—; mem. sci. adv. bd. Internat. Coun. for Coordinating Cancer Rsch., 1989-92, Dermigen, 1990—. Mem. Monona Grove Sch. Bd., 1952-54; bd. dirs. Madison Gen. Hosp. Found. Fellow AAAS, Am. Assn. Cancer Research (dir.), Am. Soc. Biol. Chemists (Clowes award). Office: U Wis Dept Oncology McArdle Lab 1400 University Ave Rm 1125 Madison WI 53706-1526*

BOUVIER, LINDA FRITTS, publishing executive; b. Dover, N.J., Nov. 8, 1946; d. Fletcher Loomis and Dorothy Evelyn (Lukens) Fritts; m. Alan Moylan, May 30, 1971 (div.); m. John Emerson Ross, Dec. 28, 1985 (div.); m. Claude Edward Bouvier, Nov. 12, 1994. BFA in Advt. Design, Visual Comm., Pratt Inst., 1968. Designer MD Med. News Mag., N.Y.C., 1968-71; art dir. Miami (Fla.) Mag., 1973-74; ind. cons. Linda Moylan Design, Miami, 1974-84; prodn. mgr. U. Miami, 1984-85; product devel., sales The Mazer Corp., Dayton, Ohio, 1986-89; sales mgr. TSI Graphics, Cranford, N.J., 1989-92; product mgr., electronic svcs. RR Donnelley and Sons, N.Y.C., Waltham, Mass., 1992-94; v.p. emerging pub. technologies Simon & Schuster, N.Y.C., 1994-95; v.p. prodn., mfg., inventory sch. divsn. Houghton Mifflin Co., Boston, 1995-97; sr. acct. exec. Ames On-Demand, Woburn, Mass., 1998-99; dir., pub. rels. RoweCom, Inc., Cambridge, Mass., 1999—; adv. bd. The Heller Report: Internet Strategies for Education Markets, 1995—. Co-chair N.Y. Book Show, 1989. Enabling technologies com. Am. Assn. Publ., 1995. Recipient award Soc. Pub. Designers, 1970-82. Mem. Bookbuilders of Boston. Avocations: photography, gourmet cooking, artist, horticulture. E-mail: lbouvier@bicnet.net. Office: RoweCom Inc 60 Aberdeen Cambridge MA 02138

BOUVIER, VIRGINIA MARIE, foreign language educator, researcher, writer; b. New Haven, Conn., Nov. 9, 1958; d. Edouard Simon Pierre and Jane Marguerite (Mansfield) B.; m. James Nathaniel Lyons, Oct. 7, 1989; 1 child, Maya Alexandra Bouvier-Lyons. BA in Latin Am. Studies, Wellesley Coll., 1980; MA in Spanish, U. S.C., 1984; PhD in Latin Am. Studies, U. Calif., Berkeley, 1995. Sr. assoc. Washington Office on Latin Am., 1982-89; grad. student instr. depts. history, ethnic studies, devel. studies, Native Am. studies U. Calif., Berkeley, 1992-93; editor, intern The Emma Goldman Papers, Berkeley, 1994-95; asst. prof. dept. Spanish and Portuguese U. Md., College Pk., 1995—; cons. CS Fund, Freestone, Calif., 1986, Arca Found., Washington, 1986, Levi Strauss & Co., Levi Strauss Found., San Francisco, 1992-93, World Bank, Washington, 1997. Author: (book) Decline of the Dictator: Paraguay at a Crossroads, 1988, (monographs) Alliance or Compliance: Implications of the Chilean Experience, 1983, Conditions for Chile's Plebiscite on Pinochet, 1988. Mem., treas., pres. local chpt. Amnesty Internat., Wellesley, Mass., Columbia S.C. and Washington, 1978—; cons., mem. ednl. adv. bd. Culture for Peace Project, Mayor's Office, San Francisco, 1994; mem. Oxfam, 1996—; founder Ctr. for Young Children Fgn. Lang. Devel. Com., 1997. Fellow Nat. Hist. Publs. and Records Commn., 1994-95; Gen. Rsch. Bd. grantee U. Md., 1996, Dissertation grantee Cushwa Ctr., U. Notre Dame, 1994; recipient Grant-in-Aid award Recovering the U.S. Hispanic Literary Heritage Project, U. Houston, 1997. Mem. MLA, Am. Hist. Assn., Latin Am. Studies Assn., Conf. on Latin Am. History, Coordinating Coun. for Women in History, Assn. for Documentary Editing. Home: 11924 Crimson Ln Silver Spring MD 20904-1947 Office: U Md 2203 Jimenez Hall College Park MD 20742-4800

BOUYOUCOS, JOHN VINTON, research and development company executive; b. Lansing, Mich., Nov. 9, 1926; s. George John and Delia (Bemis) B.; m. Stella Wright, Sept. 29, 1953; children: Anne Stephanie, Peter Johnson, Hope Nicola; m. Kristine Thuesen Hordon, May 26, 1984. Student, U. Mich., 1944; A.B., Harvard U., 1949, S.M., 1951, Ph.D., 1953, Harvard Bus. Sch. Smaller Co. Mgmt. Program cert., 1976. Asst. dir. Harvard Acoustics Research Lab., Harvard U., 1955-59; mgr. hydroacoustics dept. Gen. Dynamics Electronics Div., Rochester, N.Y., 1959-71; pres., chief scientist Hydroacoustics Inc., Rochester, 1972—. Pres., chmn. bd. Soc. Chamber Music, Rochester, 1977-96, chmn. bd. 1996— ; bd. dirs., vice chmn. Rochester Philharm. Orch., 1978-89, hon. bd. dirs., 1990—. Served with U.S. Navy, 1944-46. Recipient Rochester Patent Law Assn.; Inventors award, 1973. Fellow Acoustical Soc. Am. (v.p. 1970-71), IEEE; mem. Soc. Exploration Geophysicists, Audio Engring. Soc., Inst. Noise Control Engrs. Club: Harvard Bus. Sch. Rochester (pres. 1984). Patentee in field. Home: 11 Elmwood Hill Ln Rochester NY 14610-3445 Office: Hydroacoustics Inc PO Box 23447 Rochester NY 14692-3447 Address (summer): 5475 Seneca Point Rd Canandaigua NY 14424-8955

BOVA, BENJAMIN WILLIAM, author, editor, educator; b. Phila., Nov. 8, 1932; s. Benjamin P. and Giove (Caporiccio) B.; m. Rosa Cucinotta, Nov. 28, 1953 (div. 1973); children: Michael Francis, Regina Marie; m. Barbara Ellen Berson, June 28, 1974. BS in Journalism, Temple U., 1954; MA in Communications, SUNY Albany, 1987; EdD, Calif. Coast U., 1996. Formerly newspaper reporter; mktg. mgr. Avco Everett Rsch. Lab.; formerly tchr. sci. fiction Harvard U.; formerly tchr. sci. fiction, dir. film courses Hayden Planetarium, N.Y.C.; editor Upper Darby (Pa.) News, 1954-56; tech. editor Project Vanguard, 1956-58; motion picture scriptwriter Phys. Sci. Study Com., Ednl. Svcs., Inc., Watertown, Mass., 1958-60; mgr. mktg. Avco Everett Rsch. Lab., Avco Corp., Everett, Mass., 1960-71; editor Analog Sci. Fiction-Sci. Fact mag. Conde Nast Pub. Co., N.Y.C., 1971-78; fiction editor Omni mag., N.Y.C., 1978-79, exec. editor, 1979-81, v.p., editorial dir., 1981-82; past mem. panel Office Tech. Assessment, U.S. Congress; lectr. Nat. Geog. Soc., major govt. and corp. exec. groups, univs.; adv. bd. Post Coll.; bd. contbrs. USA Today. Author: (fiction) The Star Conquers, 1959, Star Watchman, 1964, The Weathermakers, 1967, Out of the Sun, 1968, The Dueling Machine, 1969, Escape!, 1969, Exiled From Earth, 1971, (with George Lucas) THX 1138, 1971, Flight of Exiles, 1972, As On a Darkling Plain, 1972, When the Sky Burned, 1972, Forward in Time, 1973, (with Gordon R. Dickson) Gremlins, Go Home!, 1974, End of Exile, 1975, The Starcrossed, 1975, City of Darkness, 1976, Millennium, 1976, The Multiple Man, 1976, Colony, 1978, Maxwell's Demons, 1978, Kinsman, 1979, The Exiles Trilogy, 1981, Voyagers, 1981, Test of Fire, 1982, The Winds of Altair, 1983, Escape Plus, 1984, Orion, 1984, The Astral Mirror, 1985, Privateers, 1985, Promethians, 1986, Voyagers II: The Alien Within, 1986, Battle Station, 1987, The Kinsman Saga, 1987, Vengeance of Orion, 1988, Peacekeepers, 1988, Cyberbooks, 1989, Voyagers III, Star Brothers, 1990, Orion in the Dying Time, 1990, Future Crime, 1990; (with Bill Pogue) The Trikon Deception, 1992, Mars, 1992, (with A.J. Austin) To Save the Sun, 1992, Triumph, 1993, Empire Builders, 1993, Challenges, 1993, Sam Gunn, Unlimited, 1993, Orion and The Conqueror, 1994, Death Dream, 1994, (with A.J. Austin) To Fear the Light, 1995, Orion Among the Stars, 1995, Brothers, 1996, Moonrise, 1997, Moonwar, 1998, Sam Gunn Forever, 1998, Twice Seven, 1998, Return to Mars, 1999; (non-fiction) The Milky Way Galaxy, 1961, Giants of the Animal World, 1962, Reptiles Since the World Began, 1964, The Uses of Space, 1965, In Quest of Quasars, 1970, Planets, Life and LGM, 1970, The Fourth State of Matter, 1971 (Best Sci. Book award ALA 1971), The Amazing Laser, 1972, The New Astronomies, 1972, Starflight and Other Improbabilities, 1973, Man Changes the Weather, 1973, (with Barbara Berson) Survival Guide for the Suddenly Single, 1974, The Weather Changes Man, 1974, Workshops in Space, 1974, Through Eyes of Wonder, 1975, Science: Who Needs It?, 1975, Notes to a Science Fiction Writer, 1975, Closeup: New Worlds, 1977, Viewpoint, 1977, The Seeds of Tomorrow, 1977, The High Road, 1981, Vision of the Future: The Art of Robert McCall, 1982, Assured Survival, 1984, Star Peace, 1986, Welcome to Moonbase!, 1987 (Best Sci. Book award ALA 1988), (with Sheldon Glashow) Interactions, 1988, The Beauty of Light, 1988, (with Byron Preiss) First Contact, 1990, The Craft Of Writing Science Fiction That Sells, 1994, Space Travel, 1997, Immortality, 1998; appearances numerous radio and TV shows including Good Morning America, the Today show and as regular guest CBS Morning News; mem. editorial bds. World Future Soc., Tor Books pubs.; contbr. stories, revs., articles in all major sci. fiction mags., other mags., newspapers, periodicals; formerly tech. editor 1st satellite project Vanguard. Recipient 6 Sci. Fiction Achievement awards for best profl. editor (Hugo), E.E. Smith Meml. award for imaginative fiction New Eng. Sci. Fiction Soc., 1974, Balrog award, 1983, Inkpot award, 1985, Disting. Alumnus award Temple U., 1982, Isaac Asimov Meml. award, 1996. Fellow Brit. Interplanetary Soc.; mem. AIAA, AAAS, Nat. Space Soc. (pres. 1982-88, pres. emeritus, chmn. bd. 1988-92), N.Y. Acad. Scis., Sci. Fiction Writers Am. (charter, pres. 1990-92), Planetary Soc., Nature Conservancy, Nat. Space Club, Explorers Club, Amateur Fencer's League Am.

BOVA, VINCENT ARTHUR, JR., lawyer, consultant, photographer; b. Pitts., Apr. 25, 1946; s. Vincent A. and Janie (Pope) B.; m. Breda Murphy, Mar. 20, 1971; 1 child, Kate Murphy Bova. BA in Bus. Adminstrn., Alma (Mich.) Coll., 1968; MPA, Ohio State U., 1972; JD, Oklahoma City U., 1975. Bar: Okla. 1975, N.Mex. 1976, U.S. Dist. Ct. 1976, U.S. Tax Ct., 1976, U.S. Ct. Appeals (10th cir.) 1976, U.S. Supreme Ct. 1979. Mktg. and systems rep., computer systems div. RCA, 1968-70; research analyst Research Atlanta, 1972-73; assoc. Threet, Threet, Glass, King & Maxwell, 1976-78; ptnr. Lill & Bova, P.A., 1978-81; sole practice Albuquerque, 1981—; past pres. Bare Bulls Investment, 1982, Fumilan Investment, 1983, Toastmasters; rsch. analyst urban affairs Ohio Dept. Urban Affairs, Columbus, 1971; panel mem. N.Mex. Med. Rev. Commn., 1981—, N.Mex. Legal/Dental/Osteopathic Podiatry Com., 1981—. Contbr. articles on organizational behavior and mgmt. to profl. jours. Bd. dirs. Rio Grande Nature Ctr.; pres., v.p. spl. projects S.W. Arts and Crafts Festival, Albuquerque, 1986-89; pol. cons. Nov. Group; mem. N.Mex. Estate Planning Coun., 1978—; sec.-treas., vice-chmn. adv. bd. Salvation Army, 1987—; contbr. Ctr. for Home for Prevention of Domestic Violence, 1984-85, Ronald McDonald House, 1984; past chmn. N.Mex. Workers' Compensation Monthly; mem. advt. com. Supreme Ct. Panel; pres. Salvation Army Adv. Bd., Albuquerque; mem. Edn. Forum. With Air N.G., 1969-75. Recipient Pacesetters award Ohio State U., 1972; named one of Outstanding Young Men of Am., 1975, 76. Mem. ATLA (advanced grad. Nat. Coll. Advocacy), Ct. Practice Inst. (advanced diplomate), ABA, N.Mex. Bar Assn. (pres. small firm and solo sect.), State Bar N.Mex. (mem. med. legal panel, med.-dental podiatry legal panel, rep. probate, wills and trusts ann. report), Nat. Def. Lawyers, Assn. (staff chmn. 1986), N.Mex. Trial Lawyers Assn., Internat. Assn. Fin. Planners, Nat. Assn. Social Security Claimants Reps. (past state chmn.), Business Round Table, Albuquerque Bar Assn., N.Mex. Fin. Planning Assn., Sole Practitioners Assn., Internat. Credit Assn. (lectr.), Ohio State U. Alumni Assn. of N.Mex. (pres.), Image Profls. of the S.W. (bd. dirs.), Image Profls. S.W. (photography award), Profl. Photography Assn., Photog. Soc. Am. (pres. chpt.), Toastmasters (past pres., v.p., edn. chmn., Able Toastmaster award), Millionaires Tip Club, Enchanted Lens Camera Club (pres.), Profl. Photographers Am. (merit awards), Albuquerque Knife and Fork (pres., v.p., sec.-treas., bd. dirs.), Phi Alpha Delta, Sigma Tau Gamma. Democrat. Presbyterian. Avocations: flower gardening, photography - video and still, computers, investing, reading. Office: 5716 Osuna Rd NE Albuquerque NM 87109-2527

BOVAIRD, BRENDAN PETER, lawyer; b. N.Y.C., Mar. 9, 1948; s. John Francis and Margaret Mary (Endrizzi) B.; m. Carolyn Warren Boyle, Dec. 18, 1971; children: Anne Warren, Sarah Grant. BA, Fordham U., 1970; JD, U. Va., 1973. Bar: N.Y. 1974, D.C. 1980, Pa. 1983, U.S. Dist. Ct. (so. and ea. dists.) N.Y. 1974, U.S. Ct. Appeals (2d cir.) 1974. Atty., Dewey, Ballantine, Bushby, Palmer & Wood, N.Y.C., 1973-82; asst. gen. counsel Campbell Soup Co., Camden, N.J., 1982-90; sr. v.p., gen. counsel, sec. Orion Pictures Corp., N.Y.C., 1990-91; counsel, mem. exec. com. Wyeth-Ayerst Internat. Inc., St. Davids, Pa., 1992-95; pres. KDH Inc., 1994—; v.p., gen. counsel UGI Corp., Valley Forge, Pa., 1995—; v.p., gen. counsel AmeriGas Propane, Inc., Valley Forge, 1995—; bd. dirs. Motion Picture Export Assn. Am., Inc., 1990-91, United Valley Ins. Co. Mem. MPAA (legal com. 1990-91), ABA (corp., bus. law sect., internat. law sect.), Aircraft Owners and Pilots Assn., Phila. Country Club, Phi Delta Phi. Office: UGI Corp PO Box 858 Valley Forge PA 19482-0858

BOVAY, HARRY ELMO, JR., retired engineering company executive; b. Big Rapids, Mich., Sept. 4, 1914; s. Harry E. and Addibelle (Bentley) B.; m. Sue Goldston, Feb. 1, 1977; children—Mark Benson, Susan Stone. C.E., Cornell U., 1936. Jr. engring. aide U.S. C.E., 1936-37; jr. metal insp., project engr. Humble Oil & Refining Co., Baytown, Tex., 1937-45; cons. engr. Houston, 1946-62; pres. Bovay Engrs., Inc., Houston, 1962-73, chmn. bd., chief exec. officer, 1974-84; owner Bovista Farms, Somerville, Tenn., 1963—; pres. Mid-South Telecommunications Co., Inc., 1987—. Editor: Mechanical and Electrical Systems for Buildings. Pres., Sam Houston Area council Boy Scouts Am., 1963-64, exec. com. South Central region, 1973-76, bd. dirs., 1975-79, v.p., 1980-81, pres., 1981-82, mem. nat. exec. bd., 1981-84, chmn. camping/outdoor com., 1983-85, chmn. nat. audit com., 1982-87, mem. nat. adv. coun., 1985-98; chmn. Houston Commn. Zoning, 1959-60; bd. dirs. Vis. Nurse Assn., Houston, 1970-75, Retina Rsch. Found., 1998—; active United Fund Houston and Harris County; mem. Houston Adv. Council Naval Affairs, 1959; mem. Tex. Water Resources Adv. Com., 1968-71; mem. adv. com. Coastal Engring. Lab., Tex. A&M U., 1969, also mem. adv. council for Pres.; mem. engring. adv. com. Miss. State U., 1974-77; mem. Alumni Council Cornell U. Coll. Engring.; bd. visitors McDonald Obs., 1985—; mem. demand subpanel Energy Research Adv. Bd., 1985-86; mem. adv. com. rsch. programs Tex. Higher Edn. Coordinating Bd., 1992-95. Recipient Silver Beaver award Boy Scouts Am., 1965, Silver Antelope, 1976, Silver Buffalo, 1986, Disting. Svc. award SAR, 1998; named Disting. Engr., Tex. Engring. Found.; Baden-Powell fellow, World Scouting Orgn.; camping area Bovay Ranch Sam Houston Area Coun. Boy Scouts Am. Fellow ASCE, ASHRAE (ASHRAE-ALCO award); mem. Nat. Soc. Profl. Engrs. (pres. 1976, Achievement award 1987), Tex. Soc. Profl. Engrs. (pres. 1967-68), Am. Inst. Cons. Engrs. (past pres Tex. chpt.), Houston Engring. and Sci. Soc. (past 2d v.p.), Am. Rd. Builders Assn. (exec. com.), Am. Concrete Inst., Am. Wood Preservers Assn., ASTM (councilor 1960-64), Forest Products Research Soc., Tex. Forest Products Mfrs. Assn., SAME (Toulmin medal), Pres.' Assn., Newcomen Soc. N.Am., Nat. Acad. Engring. Episcopalian. Clubs: Houston, Kiwanis, Cosmos, Houston Country, Petroleum. Home: 2200 Willowick Rd Unit 12H Houston TX 77027-3925 Office: 3355 W Alabama St Ste 1140 Houston TX 77098-1799

BOVE, ALFRED ANTHONY, medical educator; b. Phila., Apr. 28, 1938; s. Alfred Anthony and Adeline Amelia (DeRose) B.; m. Sandra Ann Seltzer, June 25, 1966; children: Jacqueline, Christopher, Andrew. BSEE, Drexel U., 1962; MD, Temple U., 1966, PhD, 1970. Diplomate Am. Bd. Internal Medicine, Am. Bd. Cardiology. Med. intern Temple U. Hosp., Phila., 1966-67, med. resident, 1969-70, postdoctoral fellow, 1967-69, asst. prof. medicine, 1973-81, prof. medicine, 1986—; postdoctoral fellow Mayo Clinic, Rochester, Minn., 1970-71; prof. medicine Mayo Clinic, Rochester, 1981-86; chief of cardiology Temple U. Med. Sch., 1986-99, assoc. dean, practice plan affairs, 1999—; team cardiologist Phila. 76ers Basketball Team, Phila., 1987—. Author: Diving Medicine, 3d edit., 1997; co-author: Diving Medicine, 1990, Exercise Medicine, 1982; editor: (med. column) Skin Diver mag., 1981—; contbr. articles to profl. jours. Capt. USNR, 1971-73, 91, ret. Recipient Established Investigator award Am. Heart Assn., 1975. Fellow ACP, Am. Coll. Cardiology (state gov. 1989-92); mem. Am. Physiologic Soc., IEEE, Undersea and Hyperbaric Med. Soc. (pres. 1983, Craig Hoffman award 1988, Stover-Link award 1974). Roman Catholic. Avocations: scuba diving, marathon racing. Office: Temple Univ Hosp Cardiology Sect 3401 N Broad St Philadelphia PA 19140-5189

BOVE, JOHN LOUIS, chemistry and environmental engineering educator, researcher; b. N.Y.C., Apr. 15, 1928; s. Frank and Bridget (Randazzo) B.; m. June Althea Burns, Dec. 28, 1957; children: Adele, Catherine. B.A. in Chemistry, Bucknell U., 1949, M.S.A. in Chemistry, 1954; Ph.D. in Chemistry, Case Western Res. U., 1973. Asst. prof. chemistry Cooper Union, N.Y.C., 1958-67, prof. chemistry and environ. engring., chmn. dept. chemistry, 1970—, dir. environ. program, 1970—; v.p. Cooper Union Research Found., 1974-80; dep. dir. bur. tech. services N.Y.C. Air Resources, 1967-70; dir. Mid-Atlantic Consortium Air Pollution, 1970-76. Contbr. chpts., articles to profl. publs. Served with M.C. U.S. Army, 1950. Recipient Schweinburg Schweinburg Found., 1964; fellow Dow Chem. Co., 1953—; grantee NSF, 1960—;. Republican. Home: 125 Richards Rd Ridgewood NJ 07450-1115 Office: Cooper Union for Advancement Sci and Art 51 Astor Pl New York NY 10003-7132

BOVE, PATRICE MAGEE, elementary education educator; b. Fort Madison, Iowa, Apr. 29, 1946; d. Claude and Susie T. Magee; m. Roger E. Bove, Aug. 6, 1983; 1 child, Jonna. MusB, U. Iowa, 1968; M of Music Edn., Temple U., 1976. Tchr. elem. instrumental music Birmingham (Mich.) Sch. Dist., 1968-69; tchr. elem. music T-E Sch. Dist., Berwyn, Pa., 1969—. Co-author: Philadelphia Orchestra Student Concert Books, 1994—; contbr. MENC (Strategies for Teaching Elementary Music), 1996. Educator, writer edn. adv. com. Phila. Orch., 1994—; accompanist chorus, Wayne, Pa., 1995, Suzuki Concerts, Immaculata, Pa., 1994-97. Mem. AAUW, Nat. Assn. Music Therapy, Music Tchrs. Assn., Gordon Inst. Music Learning, Suzuki, Kodaly, Orff, Pa. Music Edn. Assn. (dist. 12 co-host elem. songfest 1995), Music Educators Nat. Conf. Avocations: reading, computers, cooking. Home: 325 Holly Rd West Chester PA 19380-4614

BOVEE, EUGENE CLEVELAND, protozoologist, emeritus educator; b. Sioux City, Iowa, Apr. 1, 1915; s. Earl Eugene and Martha Nora (Johnson) B.; m. Maezene B. Wamsley, May 18, 1942; m. Elizabeth A. Moss, May 9, 1968; children—Frances, Gregory, Matthew; stepchildren—Lynne, Lisa. BA, U. No. Iowa, 1939; MS, U. Iowa, 1948; PhD, UCLA, 1950. Instr. zoology Iowa U., 1940-41; biology tchr. Greene (Iowa) H.S., Iowa, 1941-42; instr. biology U. No. Iowa, 1946-48; instr. zoology UCLA, 1948-50, research zoologist, 1962-68; asst. prof. biology Calif. Poly. U., 1950-52; assoc. prof. zoology, dept. chmn. N.D. State U., 1952-53; asst. prof. biology U. Houston, 1953-55; assoc. prof. U. Fla., 1955-62; prof. physiology and cell biology U. Kans., Lawrence, 1968-85; prof. emeritus U. Kans., 1985—; cons. Am. Type Culture Collection, 1980-82, W.C. Brown, Pub., 1978-82. Editor Kans. Sci. Bull., 1974-79; co-editor, co-author: An Illustrated Guide to the Protozoa, 1985; co-author: How to Know the Protozoa, 2d edit., 1979; Microscop. Anat. Invert., Vol. 1, 1991; contbr. chpts. to books, articles to jours. 1st lt. U.S. Army, WWII. Research grantee NIH, 1957-62, NSF, 1970-74, NIH, NSF and ONR, 1962-68, Kans. Fed. Water Resources Inst. and U. Kans., 1968-81; recipient Disting. Alumni award U. No. Iowa, 1980. Fellow Iowa Acad. Sci.; mem. Soc. Protozoologists (hon., pres. 1979-80, v.p. 1970-71, treas. 1972-78, exec. com. 1970-81), Am. Microscop Soc. (mem.-at-large exec. com. 1959-62), Western Soc. Naturalists, Kans. Acad. Sci. (life mem., pres. 1979-80, exec. com. 1975-81), Acad. Am. Poets, Kans. State Poetry Soc., Kans. Authors Club (Writing Achievement award 1996), Nat. Woodcarvers Assn., Sigma Xi. Home: 808 Mississippi St Lawrence KS 66044-2659

BOVÉE, WARREN GILLES, retired journalism educator; b. Billings, Mont., Jan. 2, 1922; s. Claire L. and Ida (Gilles) B.; m. Gladys Helen Rose, Aug. 2, 1947; children: Priscilla, Christopher, David, John, Paul. BA cum laude, Marquette U., 1947, MA, 1949; postgrad., Columbia U., 1949-53. Instr. English and Journalism Coll. of New Rochelle, N.Y., 1948-53; asst. prof. Journalism Marquette U., Milw., 1953-59, assoc. prof., 1959-64, prof., 1964-90, prof. emeritus, 1991—; dir. grad. programs Marquette U. Coll. Journalism, Milw., 1970-77, asst. dean, 1975-77, acting dean, 1971-72, 77-78, chair dept. Journalism, 1988-89; bd. dirs. Cath. Renaissance Soc., Milw., 1950-53. Author: Research Materials, 1956, Magazine Editor-Writer Relationship, 1965, Discovering Journalism, 1999; editor The By-Lines Awards, 1995; contbr. articles to various publs. Dir. Wis. Freedom of Info. Ctr., Milw., 1979-86, Artist Series at the Pabst, 1978-87; bd. dirs. Sta. WUWM-FM, 1981-87, Bradley Inst. for Democracy, 1989-90. 1st lt. U.S. Army Air Corps, 1942-45, CBI. Mag. Pubs. Assn. fellow, 1963, Nat. Conf. Editorial Writers rsch. grantee, 1980, Atlantic Ctr. for the Arts assoc. grantee, 1987; recipient Andrew Hamilton award Marquette U., 1961. Mem. AAUP (pres. Marquette U. chpt. 1962-63), Quarter Century Club (pres. 1988-89), Nat. Conf. Editl. Writers (life, exec. bd. 1983-85, dir.), Milw. Press Club, Soc. Profl. Journalists. Democrat. Roman Catholic. Avocations: walking, reading, travel. Home: 527 N Story Pky Milwaukee WI 53208-3668 Office: Marquette U Brooks Hall Ste #200 Milwaukee WI 53233

BOVET, ERIC DAVID, economist, consultant; b. Frankfurt, Main, Germany, July 23, 1900; came to U.S., 1927; s. Paul Auguste and Clarisse (Lenoir) B.; m. Ethel Mae Lindsey, July 19, 1946; children: David Marc, Raymond Paul, Astrid Elaine, Marguerite Lynn. BA, Gymnase Littéraire, Neuchâtel, Switzerland, 1920; MDiv, Fac. Théologie Protestante, Lausanne, Switzerland, 1925; MBA, U. Geneva, Switzerland, 1927, PhD in Econs., 1953. Ordained to ministry, Unitarian Ch. Tutor to Franklin D. Roosevelt's sons, Hyde Park, N.Y., 1928; mgr. Mrs. E. Roosevelt's Val-Kill Furniture Shop, Hyde Park, 1929; acct. Dennison Mfg. Co., Framingham, Mass., 1928-29; economist, statistician Fairchild Publs., N.Y.C., 1931; rsch. economist Nat. Resources Com., Washington, 1935-37; statistician, economist Office of Sec. U.S. Dept. Navy, Washington, 1941-46; chief of budget R&D bd. U.S. Dept. Def., Washington, 1947-50; budget economist Air R&D Command, Balt., 1955-56; econ. advisor Devel. Coord. U.S. Navy, Washington, 1956-62; chief econs. divsn. Office of Saline Water Dept. Interior, Washington, 1962-70; cons. economist U.S. Govt. and freelance, Washington, 1970-90; prof. mktg. U. Md., 1967; prof. econs. U. Colo., Boulder, 1979-81. Author: Business Motivation, 1963, Stagflation, 1983; contbr. articles to profl. jours. Honored by creation of Eric D. Bovet Endowed Fellowship in Employment and Real Business Cycles, U. Colo. Found., 1994. Mem. Am. Econ. Assn., Flattop Mountain Landowners Assn. (treas. 1978-92). Unitarian. Avocation: composing classical music. Home and Office: 630 Mockingbird Way Charlottesville VA 22901-2800

BOW, STEPHEN TYLER, JR., insurance and computer industry consultant; b. Bow, Ky., Oct. 20, 1931; s. Stephen Tyler Sr. and Mary L. (King) B.; m. Kathy O'Connor, July, 1982; children: Jerry, Jon; children by previous marriage: Sandra Bow Morris, Deborah Bow Goodin, Carol, Clara. BA in Sociology, Berea (Ky.) Coll., 1953; grad. exec. program bus. adminstrn., Columbia U., 1976. CLU. With Met. Life Ins. Co., 1953-74, 76-89; agt. Lexington, Ky., 1953-55; sales mgr. Birmingham, Ala., 1955-58, field tng. cons., 1958-59; territorial field supr., 1959-60; dist. sales mgr. Frankfort, 1960-64, Lexington, 1964-66; exec. asst. field tng. N.Y.C., 1966-67; regional sales mgr. North Jersey, 1967-72; agy. v.p., officer-in-charge Can. hdqrs., 1972-74; exec. v.p., chmn., chief exec. officer Capital Holding Corp., Louisville, 1974-76; officer-in-charge Midwestern hdqrs. Met. Life Ins. Co., Dayton, 1976-83, sr. v.p., officer-in-charge Western Hdqrs., 1983-89; chmn., CEO Southeastern Group, Inc., Louisville, 1993-94; pres., CEO Anthem Life of Ind., Indpls., 1993-95; chmn., CEO Anthem Life Ins. Cos., 1995-96; exec. v.p. Assoc. Ins. Cos., Indpls., 1993-96; chmn. Acordia of San Francisco, 1993-96; pres., CEO Delta Dental Ky., Louisville, 1989-94, Blue Cross and Blue Shield Ky., Louisville, 1989-93; vice chmn. DeHayes Group, 1996—; pres. Steve Bow and Assocs., Inc., 1996—; chmn. Victory Tech., Inc., 1998—; past chmn. Dayton Power and Light Audit Com. Past bd. dirs. San Francisco Visitors and Conv. Bur., 1985-87, Ind. Coll. of No. Calif., Bay Area Coun., Lindsey Wilson Coll.; bd. dirs. Bay Area Boy Scouts Am., Bay Area Council, U. San Francisco; mem. adv. bd. Hugh O'Brian Youth Found.; bd. dirs. Calif. Legis. Adv. Commn. on Life and Health Ins., Metro United Way, Ky. Health Care Access Found., Greater Louisville Econ. Devel. Coun., Leadership Ky., Greater Louisville Fund for the Arts; mem. corp. council San Francisco UN Assn.; mem. bd. dirs. Ky. Home Mut., Ky. Forward, Asian Bus. League, McLaren Coll. of Bus.; past mem. San Francisco Pvt. Industry Council; past chmn. United Negro Coll. Fund of San Francisco, 1985-86; mem. exec. com. bd. dirs., v.p. county ops. United Way of San Francisco Bay Area, 1985-87; vol. chmn. U.S. Savs. Bond Campaign, Bay Area, 1987; trustee Ky. Ind. Coll. Fund, Berea Coll.; bd. dirs. Boy Scouts Am., My Old Ky. Home Coun. Recipient Outstanding Sales Mgmt. award N.Y. Sales Congress, 1972, Frederick D. Patterson award United Negro Coll. Fund San Francisco, 1986, Outstanding County Ops. Vol. award United Way of Bay Area, 1987, Bus. Appreciation award Jeffersontown, Ky. C. of C., 1993, Pres.'s award, 1993, Leadership award Internat. Women's Forum, Washington, 1993; named Citizen of Yr. Wright State U. Med. Sch., Dayton, 1982. Mem. Nat. Assn. Life Underwriters, Gen. Agts. and Mgrs. Assn., Calif. Bus. Roundtable, Nat. Assn. Corp. Dirs. (founder, former pres.), Calif. C. of C. (bd. dirs.), Ky. C. of C., Ky. Home Life Exec. Com., Am. Cancer Soc. Republican. Methodist. Club: Lincoln of Northern Calif.; San Francisco Bankers. Avocations: golf, oil painting, reading. Home: 20 Grand Miramar Dr Henderson NV 89011-2202 Office: 772 W Napa St Sonoma CA 95476-6452 *We achieve goals by thinking positively and focusing on objectives, not on problems. We achieve economic success by concentrating on serving our fellow man and finding new ways to satisfy his needs. We achieve personal satisfaction by doing more than is expected of us, and exceeding even our own expectations through determination and persistency. We achieve happiness by becoming so interested and absorbed in our work that we forget selfish, petty matters. We achieve a successful life by living each day as if our entire life is to be judged by that day alone.*

BOWDEN, BOBBY, university athletic coach; b. Birmingham, Ala., Nov. 8, 1929; m. Julia Ann Estock; children: Robyn Hines, Steve, Tommy, Terry, Ginger Madden, Jeff. BS, Howard Coll. (now Samford U.), 1953; grad. degree, Peabody Coll. Coach W.Va. U., 1965-75, head coach, 1969-75; head coach NCAA Divsn. 1A football Fla. State U. Seminoles, 1975—, nationally ranked #5, 1991, nationally ranked #2, 1992, nat. champions, 1993. Named So. Ind. Coach of Yr., 1977, 79, Nat. Coach of Yr., ABC-Chevrolet, 1979, Nat. Coack of Yr. (Bobby Dodd), 1980, Region II Coach of Yr., 1987, Walter Camp Coach of Yr., 1991; named to Fla. Sports Hall of Fame, 1983, Ala. Sports Hall of Fame, 1986; recipient Neyland Trophy. Office: Fla State Univ 307 Moore Athletic Ctr Tallahassee FL 32306-1096*

BOWDEN, DOUGLAS MCHOSE, neuropsychiatric scientist, educator, research center administrator; b. Durham, N.C., Apr. 7, 1937; s. Daniel Joseph and Charlotte (McHose) B.; m. Vivian Lee Bowden, 1966; children: Dana, Julie, Carlos, Luis. BA, Harvard U., 1959; MD, Stanford U., 1965. Staff assoc. NIMH, Bethesda, Md., 1966-69; asst. prof. psychiatry U. Wash., Seattle, 1969-73, assoc. prof. dept. psychiatry & behavioral scis., 1973-79, prof. psychiatry & behavioral scis., 1979—; core staff sci. Regional Primate Rsch. Ctr., U. Wash., 1969—, from asst. dir. to assoc. dir., 1977-88, dir., 1988-94; adj. assoc. prof. pharmacology U. Wash., 1975-79, adj. prof. pharmacology, 1979-88; rsch. fellow Japan Soc. Promotion of Sci., Japan Assn. Animal Sci., Tokyo, Tsukuba, Inuyama/Kyoto, Japan, 1989. Author: Neuronames (c) Neuroanatomical Nomenclature, 1992; editor: Aging in Nonhuman Primates, 1979; translator Traumatic Aphasia, its Syndromes, Psychology and Treatment, 1970, Primate Models of Human Neurogenic Disorders, 1976. Surgeon USPHS, 1966-69. Fellow Gerontol. Soc. Am.; mem. Am. Soc. Primatologists, Soc. Neurosci., Gerontol. Soc., Internat. Primatological Soc. Office: U Wash Regl Primate Rsch Ct Box 357330 1705 NE Pacific St Seattle WA 98195-7330

BOWDEN, HENRY LUMPKIN, JR., lawyer; b. Atlanta, Aug. 2, 1949; s. Henry Lumpkin and Ellen Marian (Fleming) B.; m. Roberta Jeanne Johnson, June 30, 1973; children: Caroline Bruton, Henry Lumpkin III. BA, U. Va., 1971; JD, Emory U., 1974. Bar: Ga. 1974. Law clk. for Hon. Griffin B. Bell U.S. Ct. Appeals (5th cir.), Atlanta, 1974-75; ptnr. King & Spalding, Atlanta, 1975-95; prin. Bowden Law Firm, P.C., Atlanta, 1995—. Trustee Atlanta Ballet, Inc., 1976-85, chmn., 1983-84; trustee Emory U., Atlanta, 1986—; trustee Hist. Oakland Found., Inc., Atlanta, 1987-95, chmn. 1992-95; trustee Westminster Schs., Atlanta, 1995—. Fellow Am. Coll. Trust and Estate Counsel (state chair 1991-96), Am. Bar Found.; mem. ABA, State Bar Ga. (chair fiduciary sect. 1990-91), Atlanta Bar Assn., Lawyers Club Atlanta, Piedmont Driving Club (dir. 1996—), Capital City Club, Nine O'Clocks (pres. 1977-78), Farmington Country Club, Gridiron Secret Soc., Homosassa Fishing Club, The Ten, Phi Beta Kappa, Omicron Delta Kappa, Phi Delta Theta. Methodist. Home: 2542 Habersham Rd Atlanta GA 30305-3519 Office: 191 Peachtree St NE Ste 849 Atlanta GA 30303-1741

BOWDEN, HENRY WARNER, religion educator; b. Memphis, Tenn., Apr. 1, 1939; s. Warner Hill and Jeannette Evelyn (Winn) B.; m. Karin Violet Svensson, June 9, 1962 (div. Aug. 1989); children: Robin Warner, Annika Hillery; m. Michele Clare Cairns, May 1997. AB magna cum laude, Baylor U., 1961; MA, Princeton U., 1964, PhD, 1966. Instr. faculty of arts and scis. Douglass Coll., Rutgers U., 1964-67, asst. prof., 1967-71, asst. dean acad. affairs, 1969-72, assoc. prof., 1971-79, prof., 1979—; editor religion books Greenwood Press, 1979—; cons. Funk & Wagnells Revised Ency., 1981-83; cons., author World Book Ency., 1984-94. Author: Church History in the Age of Science: Historiographic Patterns in the United States, 1876-1918, 1971, Church History in an Age of Uncertainty: Historiographical Patterns in the United States, 1906-1990, 1991, American Indians and Christian Missions: Studies in Cultural Conflict, 1981, Dictionary of American Religious Biography, 1977, 2d edit., 1993; author, consulting editor: American National Biography; editor: Religion in America, 1970, Indian Dialogues, 1980, A Century of Church History: The Legacy of Philip Schaff, 1988, Church History: A Centennial Collection of Landmark Studies, 1988; contbr. numerous articles to profl. jours.; assoc. editor Am. Nat. Bibliography, 1989-99. Honors fellowship Harvard U. summer session, 1960; religion fellow Princeton U., 1961-62, Roothbert fellow, 1962-64, Lilly Found. fellow, 1964-65, Rutgers Rsch. Coun. fellowship, 1969-70; Rutgers Rsch. Coun. summer grantee, 1967. Mem. Am. Soc. of Ch. History (pres. 1984), Am. Cath. Hist. Assn., Am. Soc. of Ch. History (sec.-treas. 1993-99, exec. sec. 1999—). Democrat. Episcopalian. Office: Religion Dept Rutgers Univ New Brunswick NJ 08903

BOWDEN, HOWARD KENT, accountant; b. New Bern, N.C., 1955; s. Paul Franklin and Virginia Belle Bowden; m. Laiad Jitrak; 1 child, Kirk Adam. BSS in Acctg. and Math. summa cum laude, Campbell U., 1976. CPA, Va., N.C. Staff acct. Arthur Andersen & Co., Greensboro, N.C., 1976-78; mgr. McGladrey & Pullen, Fayetteville, N.C., 1978-85; assoc. prin. Thompson, Greenspon & Co., P.C., Fairfax, Va., 1985-91; sr. audit mgr. U.S. Gen. Acctg. Office, Washington, 1991-94, asst. dir., 1994—. Treas. Vander Area Crime Watch, Fayetteville, 1980. Mem. AICPA, Va. Soc. CPAs (chmn. mems. in industry and govt. com. 1993-95, chmn. acctg. and auditing procedures com. 1990-92, Chpt. Pres.'s award 1989-90, Outstanding Mem. in Bus., Industry, and Govt. award 1995-96, chpt. pres. award, 1997-98), N.C. Assn. CPAs, Inst. Mgmt. Accts. (coord. tax symposium 1982, bd. dirs. 1978-84), Assn. Cert. Fraud Examiners (cert.), Assn. Govt. Accts. (cert. govt. fin. mgr.), Lions (bd. dirs. Fairfax club 1986-90, bd. dirs. Fayetteville club 1982-85), Phi Beta Lambda, Phi Kappa Phi. Presbyterian. Avocations: baseball, tennis, softball, other sports. Home: 4337 Farm House Ln Fairfax VA 22032-1613

BOWDEN, JAMES ALVIN, construction company financial executive; b. Vernal, Utah, Mar. 19, 1948; s. Alvin George and Erva (Kirk) B.; m. Jane Ruth Taylor, May 31, 1973; children: Scott James, Julie, Jeffrey Taylor, Camille, Timothy Kirk. BSCE, Brigham young U., 1972, MBA, 1974. Planning analyst Morrison Knudsen Corp., Boise, 1974, asst. mgr. corp. planning, 1974-75, mgr. fin. analysis, 1975-78, asst. treas., 1978-83, v.p. fin. real estate subs., 1983-84, treas., 1984-86, v.p., treas., 1986-89; sr. v.p., CFO J.A. Jones, Inc., 1990—; also bd. dirs.; bd. dirs. Palmer & Cay of the Carolinas, Hebel S.E.; spl. instr. Boise State U., 1977-78. Bd. dirs. Bouse chpt. ARC, 1982-89, treas., 1984-86, vice chmn., 1986-87, chmn., 1987-88, nat. nominating com., 1989-91; bd. dirs. Greater Carolinas chpt. ARC, 1991—, treas., 1982-93, chmn. elect, 1993, chmn., 1994-96; pres. Charlotte World Affairs Coun., 1991—, Charlotte N.C. North Stake, 1993—; dist. fin. chmn. Boy Scouts Am., 1997-99; pres. Idaho Edn. Project, 1990; mem. United Way, Boise, 1980-85; bd. dirs. Fundsy, 1989-91; mem. alumni bd. Brigham Young U. Sch. Mgmt., 1987-90. Mem. Beta Gamma Sigma. Republican. Mormon. Home: 2720 Flintgrove Rd Charlotte NC 28226-5621 Office: J A Jones Inc 6000 Fairview J A Jones Dr Charlotte NC 28287

BOWDEN, JESSE EARLE, newspaper editor, author, cartoonist, journalism educator; b. Altha, Fla., Sept. 12, 1928; s. Jesse Walden and Earlene (Rackley) B.; m. Mary Louise Clark, Feb. 4, 1951; children: Steven Earle, Randall Clark. B.S. in Journalism and Polit. Sci, Fla. State U., 1951; D.H.L., U. West Fla., 1985. Reporter, columnist Panama City (Fla.) News-Herald, 1950; sports editor Pensacola (Fla.) News-Jour., 1953-57, news editor, 1957-65, editorial page editor, 1965-66, editorial cartoonist, 1965—, editor in chief, 1966-97, v.p., editor, 1969-97, editor emeritus, 1998—; prof. journalist U. West Fla.; Charter mem., chmn. Pensacola Hist. Commn.; chmn. Gulf Islands Nat. Seashore Adv. Com., 1990-93; pres. U. West Fla. Found., 1977-79, Pensacola Hist. Soc., 1978-86. Author: Always the Rivers Flow, 1979, Iron Horse in the Pinelands, 1982, Pensacola: Florida's First Place City, 1989, The Write Way, 1990, When You Reach September, 1990, Gulf Islands: The Sands of All Time, 1994, Earle Bowden: Drawing from an Editor's Life, 1996; editor Emerald Coast Rev., 1993, 1997; editor Vol. v, 1993, Vol. VI, 1995, Vol. VII, 1997. Trustee Pensacola Jr. Coll.; bd. dirs. Fla. Hist. Soc. Served to capt. USAF, 1951-53. U. West Fla. Found. fellow, 1982; recipient Disting. Citizen award Pensacola Jr. Coll., 1966, Nat. Editl. Writing award Freedoms Found. at Valley Forge, 1967, 68, 69, 70, 72, 74, awards for editls. and cartoons, 1967, 68, 69, 72, 86, DeLuna award Pensacola Founders' Day, 1979, Pensacola Kiwanis Civic award, 1982, award Am. Assn. State and Local History, 1984, Founder's award Inspiring Pensacola Bus. awards, 1992, Bob Graham Hon. AIA Archtl. Awareness award Fla. Assn. Archs., 1992, Malcolm B. Johnson Fellowship award James Madison Inst., 1994, Spirit of Pensacola award, 1998; named Pensacola Profl. Bus. Leader of Yr., 1980, J. Earle Bowden Jr. Historian award named in honor Pensacola Jr. League, 1983, Preservationist of Yr., Fla. Trust Hist. Preservation, 1985, West Fla. Lit. Hall of Honor, 1989; Gulf Island Nat. Seashore Hwy. named J. Earle Bowden Way, 1997. Mem. Am. Soc. Newspaper Editors, Nat. Conf. Editorial Writers, Fla. Soc. Newspaper Editors (pres. 1970). Club: Rotary. Established J. Earle Bowden history endowment U. West Fla. Home: 2220 Mccutchen Pl Pensacola FL 32503-3422 Office: One NewsJour Pla Pensacola FL 32501

BOWDEN, JIM, professional sports team executive; b. May 18, 1961; m. Amy Bowden; children: J.B., Tyler, Chad. BBA, Rollins Coll., 1983. Asst. dir. player devel. and scouting Pitts. Pirates, 1985-88; asst. to sr. v.p. baseball ops. N.Y. Yankees, 1989-90; adminstrv. asst. scouting and player devel. Cin. Reds, 1982-92, gen. mgr., 1992—. Office: Cincinnati Reds 100 Cinergy Fld Cincinnati OH 45202-3543*

BOWDEN, NANCY BUTLER, school administrator; d. Rogers Davis and Lilla Ann (Yarbrough) B.; m. Robert C. Bowden, 1970 (div. 1981); 1 child, Linda Camille. BA in English, Spanish, Southwest Tex. U., 1964; MEd in Counseling, U. Houston, 1972, EdD in Curriculum Instrn., 1978, postgrad., 1979. Cert. profl. mid-mgmt. adminstrv., Tex., profl. supr., Tex., profl. reading specialist, Tex., profl. coun., Tex., elem. gen. English Spanish, Tex., high sch. English Spanish, Tex. Tchr., Spanish, English, reading Bowie Jr. High Sch., Odessa, Tex., 1964-65; tchr., reading Nimitz Jr. High Sch., San Antonio, 1965-66; tchr., Spanish Chofu High Sch., Tokyo, 1966-68; tchr., English, speech Carverdale High Sch., Houston, 1968-69; tchr., English Clear Creek High Sch., League City, Tex., 1969-71; instr., curriculum instrn. dept. U. Houston, University Park, 1974-75, 76-77; asst. prof. U. Houston at Clear Lake, Clear Lake, 1978-86; asst. prin. Travis Elem. Sch., Baytown, Tex., 1986-92; reading specialist Metcalf Elem. Sch., Houston, 1992-93; asst. prin. Holmsley Elem. Sch., Houston, 1993—; adj. faculty mem. U. Houston, 1989, 90, lectr., 1975-76, 77-78; presenter in field. Contbr. articles to profl. jours. Mem. Nat. Assn. Elem. Sch. Prins., Nat. Coun. Tchrs. English, Internat. Reading Assn., Tex. Elem. Sch. Prins. Suprs. Assn., Tex. State Reading Assn., Greater Houston Area Reading Coun., Bay Area Reading Coun. (past. pres.), Assn. Supervision Curriculum Devel., Kappa Delta Pi. Home: 14111 Queensbury Ln Houston TX 77079-3228 Office: Holmsley Elem Sch 7315 Hudson Oaks Dr Houston TX 77095-1149

BOWDEN, RANDALL GLEN, academic adminstrator; b. Council, Idaho, Sept. 26, 1959; s. Rocky Smith and Barbara (Chilcott) Loftis; children: Nikki, Sarah. BA, Colo. Christian Univ., 1987; MA, Univ. Colo., 1990; student, Univ. Denver, 1993—. Glazier All Glass Svc., Lakewood, Colo., 1983-87; sales rep. Kwik Temp Glass, Aurora, Colo., 1988-89; gen. mgr. United Glass Co., Aurora, 1989-90; acad. advisor Colo. Christian Univ., Colorado Springs, 1990-91, acad. coord., 1991-92, dir., 1992-96; exec. dir. Colo. Christian Univ., Lakewood, 1996-97; dean Colo. Christian U., 1997-98; project mgr. Denver Pub. Schs. Dist., 1998—; pres. Vintage Quest, Colorado Springs, 1995-97. Contbr. articles to profl. publs. Campaign media rels. rep. Mary Ellen Epps for State Rep., Colorado Springs, 1996. Mem. C. of C. Avocations: weightlifting, fly fishing. Office: Denver Pub Schs 1330 Fox St Denver CO 80204

BOWDEN, SALLY ANN, choreographer, teacher, dancer; b. Dallas, Feb. 27, 1943; d. Cloyd MacAnally and Sally Estelle. Student, Boston U., 1960-62. Mem. Paul Sanasardo Dance Co., N.Y.C., 1963-67; pvt. tchr., choreographer N.Y.C., 1968-70; faculty Merce Cunningham Dance Studio, N.Y.C., 1971-76; faculty, co-dir. Constrn. Co. Dance Studio, N.Y.C., 1972-77; choreographer Constrn. Co. Theater/Dance Assocs., N.Y.C., 1972—; artist-in-residence U. Wis., Madison, fall, 1975, N.C. Sch. of Arts, winter, 1978, U. Minn., Duluth, 1979, 1981-82, Kenyon (Ohio) Coll., fall 1980. Choreographer: Three Dances, 1969, Sally Bowden Dances and Talks at the New School, 1972, The Ice Palace, 1973, White River Junction, 1975, The Wonderful World of Modern Dance or The Amazing Story of the Plie, (1976) Wheat, 1976-77, Kite, 1978, Voyages, 1978, Morningdance, 1979, Crescent, 1980, Diverted Suite, 1983, Baby Dance, 1984. Recipient Creative Artists Public Service award for choreography, 1976-77; Nat. Endowment for the Arts Choreography fellow, 1975. Office: Theater/Dance Assocs 41 E 1st St New York NY 10003-9307

BOWDEN, TERRY WILSON, coach; b. Douglas, Ga., Y, Feb. 24, 1956; s. Robert Cleckler and Ann (Estock) B.; m. Shyrl A. Lambert; children: Tara Dawn, Jordan Leigh, Erin Renee, Cori Ann, Jamie Taylor, Terry Wilson Jr. BS, W.Va. U., 1978; postgrad., Oxford U., 1980; JD, Fla. State U., 1982. Grad. asst. W.Va. U., 1978, Fla. State U., 1979-82; coach football Salem (W.Va.) Coll., 1983-85; asst. coach Akron (Ohio) U., 1986; coach Samford U., Birmingham, Ala., 1987-92, Auburn (Ala.) U., 1993-98; head coach U. of Iowa, Iowa City, 1999-. Office: Univ. of Iowa Football Ofc Complex Iowa City IA 52242*

BOWDEN, WILLIAM DARSIE, retired interior designer; b. Palo Alto, Calif., Aug. 11, 1920; s. Edmund Robert and Elisabeth (Darsie) B.; m. Anne Minor Lile, July 29, 1948; children: Darsie Minor, Raleigh Anne, Elsiabeth Lile. B.A., Stanford U., 1942. Jr. exec. Frederick and Nelson Dept. Store, Seattle, 1946-48; v.p., co-owner William L. Davis Co., Seattle, 1948-84. Trustee Found. for Interior Design Edn. Rsch., Plestcheeff Inst. for Decorative Arts U. Wash. Served to 1st lt. AUS, 1943-46. Fellow Am. Soc. Interior Designers (pres. Wash. chpt. 1966-67, nat. v.p. 1969-71), Furniture History Soc. (London), Phi Beta Kappa, Alpha Delta Phi. Republican. Episcopalian. Clubs: University, Wash. Athletic. Home and Office: 2030 Beans Bight Rd NE Bainbridge Island WA 98110-2334

BOWDEN, WILLIAM P., JR., lawyer, banker; b. East Orange, N.J., Feb. 29, 1944; s. W. Paul and Catherine (Porter) B.; m. Margo Redman, June 8, 1968; children: Jennifer Porter, Peter Chandler. AB, Williams Coll., 1966; JD, Columbia U., 1969. Bar: N.Y. Atty. Davis Polk & Wardwell, N.Y.C., 1969-75, 77-80; gen. counsel, sec. Alaska Interstate Co., Houston, 1976-77; assoc. gen. counsel Citicorp, N.Y.C., 1980-85; dep. gen. counsel Marine Midland Banks, Inc., N.Y.C., 1985-91; chief counsel Office of Comptr. of Currency, U.S. Dept. Treasury, Washington, 1991-94; gen. counsel CS First Boston, Inc., N.Y.C., 1994-96, Société Générale Ams., N.Y.C., 1997—. Mem. ABA, Assn. of Bar of City of N.Y., Rockaway Hunting Club, Lawrence Beach Club, Univ. Club, Williams Club. Office: Société Générale 1221 Avenue Of The Americas New York NY 10020-1001

BOWDLER, ANTHONY JOHN, physician, educator; b. London, Eng., Oct. 16, 1928; came to U.S., 1967; s. Edward Thomas and Clara (Anthony) B.; m. Eleanor Madeleine Sladen, July 30, 1955; children: Noelle Clare, Jonathan Francis. BSc, U. Coll., London, 1949, MB, BS, 1952, MD (Bilton Pollard fellow), 1962, PhD, 1967; postgrad. (Buswell Sr. fellow), U. Rochester, 1962-64. Intern Univ. Coll. Hosp., London, 1952, Hammersmith Hosp., London, 1953, Brompton Hosp., London, 1956, Dorking Hosp., Surrey, Eng., 1957; registrar and research fellow U. Coll. Hosp., London, 1958-62; sr. instr. U. Rochester, N.Y., 1962-64; sr. lectr. U. Coll. Hosp. Med. Sch., London, 1964-67; assoc. prof. medicine Mich. State U., East Lansing, 1967-70; prof. medicine Mich. State U., 1971-80; prof. medicine Marshall U. Sch. Medicine, Huntington, W.Va., 1980-97, prof. medicine emeritus, 1997—; hon. cons. Univ. Coll. Hosp., 1967. Served as surgeon lt. Royal Navy, 1953-55. Fellow Royal Coll. Physicians, A.C.P., Royal Coll. Pathologists; mem. Am. Fedn. Clin. Research, Central Soc. Clin. Research (emeritus), Am. Soc. Hematology (emeritus), Am. Soc. Clin. Oncology (emeritus), Med. Research Soc. London, Brit. Med. Assn. Researcher in internal medicine. Home: 4609 Sawgrass Dr E Ann Arbor MI 48108-8644

BOWE, FRANK G., educator; b. Danville, Pa., Mar. 29, 1947; s. Francis and Catherine (Windsor) B.; m. Phyllis Barbara Schwartz, May 12, 1974; children: Doran Windsor, Whitney Paige. BA, Western Md. Coll., 1969; MA, Gallaudet Grad. Sch., 1971; PhD, NYU, 1976; LLD, Gallaudet U., 1981. Exec. dir. Am. Coalition Citizens Disabilities, Washington, 1976-81; pres. FBA, Inc., Woodmere, N.Y., 1981-84; dir. rsch. U.S. Access Bd., Washington, 1984-87; regional commr. U.S. Dept. Edn., N.Y.C., 1987-89; prof. Hofstra U., Hempstead, N.Y., 1989—; cons. in field. Mem. Coun. Exceptional Children. Office: Hofstra U 111 Mason Hall Hempstead NY 11549

BOWE, PETER ARMISTEAD, manufacturing executive; b. Balt., Apr. 13, 1956; s. Richard Eugene and Virginia Welbourn (Cooley) B.; m. Claudia DeSantis, May 31, 1980; children: Alexander Armistead, Clara Kathleen MacBain. BA with high honors, Yale U., 1978; MBA with distinction, Harvard U., 1982. Banker J. P. Morgan Co., N.Y.C., 1978-80; sec., treas. Ellicott Machine Corp. Internat., Balt., 1982-85; gen. mgr. dredge div. Ellicott Machine Corp. Internat., Balt., 1985-89, pres., 1989—; pres. Liquid Waste Tech., Inc., Balt., 1998—; apptd. by v.p. Al Gore to U.S.-Egypt Pres.'s Coun.; mem. regional adv. bd. Liberty Mut. Ins. Co. Contbr. articles to profl. jours. Pres. Harvard Bus. Sch. Club of Md., 1983-85; mem. Bretton Woods com. Recipient Pres.'s "E" award for exports, 1986, Venture award Greater Balt. Com., 1989; co-named Co. of Yr. Balt. Bus. Jour., 1989, Md. Gov.'s award for Internat. Bus. Leadership, 1997; named One of 40 Under 40 Balt. City Leaders, Balt. Bus. Jour., 1993. Mem. Young Pres.'s Orgn., World Trade Ctr. Inst. (bd. dirs.), Am. Bur. Shipping, Small Bus. Exporters Assn. Avocation: sailing. Office: Ellicott Machine Corp Internat 1611 Bush St Baltimore MD 21230-2093

BOWE, RIDDICK LAMONT, professional boxer; b. Bklyn., 1967; s. Dorothy Bowe; m. Judy Bowe, 1986; 3 children, Riddick Jr., Ridicia, Brenda. Amateur boxer, 1982-89, professional boxer, 1989—, defeated Evander Holyfield for WBA, WBC, IBF titles, 1992, defeated Evander Holyfield for WBA, IBF Titles, 1993, defeated Herbie Hide for WBO Title, 1995, defeated Jorge Luis Gonzalez to retain WBO title, 1995, defeated Evander Holyfield to retain WBO title, 1995. Silver medalist super heavyweight divsn. 1988 Olympics, Seoul, Korea. Ranked Undisputed Heaveyweight Champ, 1992-93, 95—. *

BOWE, ROGER LEE, small business owner; b. Pueblo, Colo., Aug. 30, 1954; s. William Roy and Ruth Ann (Penn) B.; 1 child, Patrick William; m. Wendy C. Kempf, June 5, 1981. Grad. high sch., Denver. Mechanic Crest Motors, Denver, 1970-74; svc. mgr. Grand Prix Imports, Denver, 1974-76; line tech. Kerlin & Son, Denver, 1976-80; owner, operator Wheels of Fortune, Inc., Littleton, Colo., 1981—. Past mem. Vat. Fedn. Ind. Bus., 1988. Mem. Z Car Club Colo. (tech. advisor), Better Bus. Bur. Avocations: boating, bicycling, collecting classic records, creating modern art from auto parts, scuba diving. Office: Wheels of Fortune Inc 2659 1/2 W Main St Littleton CO 80120-1914

BOWE, WILLIAM JOHN, lawyer; b. Chgo., June 23, 1942; s. William John Sr. and Mary (Gwinn) B.; m. Catherine Vanselow, Nov. 10, 1979; children: Andrew M., Patrick D. BA, Yale U., 1964; JD, U. Chgo., 1967. Bar: Ill. 1967, Tenn. 1984. Assoc. Ross, Hardies, O'Keefe, Babcock, McDougall & Parsons, Chgo., 1967-68; assoc., then ptnr. Roan & Grossman, Chgo., 1971-78; v.p., gen. counsel, sec. The Bradford Exchange Ltd., Niles, Ill., 1979-83; asst. gen. counsel, v.p., gen. counsel United Press Internat. Inc., Nashville, 1984-85; v.p. to exec. v.p., gen. counsel, sec. Ency. Britannica, Inc., Chgo., 1986—; sec. William Benton Found., Chgo., 1987-96; pres. Merriam-Webster, Inc., Springfield, Mass., 1995-96, Ency. Britannica Ednl. Corp., Chgo., 1995—; co-chmn. managing the smaller law dept. Corp. Legal Inst., 1995. Mem. bd. editors Intellectual Property Studies, Chinese Acad. Social Studies, Beijing; contbr. articles to legal jours. Gen. counsel Gov.'s Task Force on Sch. Fin., Chgo., 1975-76; trustee Hull House Assn., Chgo., 1977-79; pres., bd. dirs. Clarence Darrow Comty. Ctr., Chgo., 1975-84; mem. bd. overseers Ill. Inst. Tech.-Kent Coll. Law, 1982-86; mem. The Annenberg Washington Program Anti-Piracy Project, Washington, 1988-89; bd. dirs. Internat. Anticounterfeiting Coalition, Washington, 1993—, chmn., 1994-96; mem. Gov.'s Task Force on Workforce Preparation, 1991-93, Gov.'s Work Group on Early Childhood Care and Edn., 1994-95. Sgt. U.S. Army, 1968-71. Mem. ABA, Ill. Bar Assn., Chgo. Bar Assn., Ill. State C. of C. (mem. edn. com. 1989—, bd. dirs. 1989-96), Intellectual Property Assn. Chgo., Software Publs. Assn. (govt. affairs com. 1997-99), Software and Info. Industry Assn. (govt. affairs coun. 1999—). Office: Ency Britannica Inc 310 S Michigan Ave Ste 1100 Chicago IL 60604-4299

BOWEN, ALICE FRANCES, school system administrator; b. Worcester, Mass., Apr. 14, 1948; d. Vincent Francis and Alice Frances (Gray) B. BS in Edn., Worcester State Coll., 1971, MS in Math. Edn., 1973, MS in Computer Sci. Edn., 1985. Cert. prin., math. and social studies tchr., Mass. Tchr. math. Worcester Pub. Schs., 1971-83, tchr. computer sci., 1983-92, asst. prin., 1992—; instr. SAT prep. Ctrl. New Eng. Coll., Worcester, 1980-85; mem. Greater Worcester Urban Math. Collaborative Alliance for Edn., 1992-95. Leader Montachusetts coun. Girl Scouts U.S.A., 1968-85. Recipient St. Anne award Montachusetts coun. Girl Scouts U.S.A., 1978. Mem. ASCD, AAUW (bd. dirs. Worcester br. 1972-75, 90-96, Eleanor Roosevelt tchr. fellow 1991, Turtle award Worcester br.), Alliance for Edn., Delta Kappa Gamma, Phi Delta Kappa. Democrat. Roman Catholic. Avocations: travel, crafts, reading. Home: 43 Sheridan Dr Shrewsbury MA 01545-3865 Office: Burncoat Mid Sch 135 Burncoat St Worcester MA 01606-2405

BOWEN, CHRISTOPHER EDWARD, library director; b. Jamaica, N.Y., July 24, 1947; s. James Frederick Jr. and Roseanne Marie (McGrath) B.; m. Barbara Francine Heitman, Sept. 11, 1971; children: Melissa, Jason, Heather. BA in English, St. John's U., 1970; MLS, Queen's Coll., 1974; BS in Pharmacy, St. John's U., 1979. Head libr. L.I. Press, Jamaica, 1965-77; asst. head libr. N.Y. Post, N.Y.C., 1977-88; libr. dir. Star Mag., Tarrytown, N.Y., 1988—. Mem. Spl. Librs. Assn. Office: Star Mag 660 White Plains Rd Tarrytown NY 10591

BOWEN, CLOTILDE MARION DENT, retired army officer, psychiatrist; b. Chgo., Mar. 20, 1923; d. William Marion Dent and Clotilde (Tynes) D.; m. William N. Bowen, Dec. 29, 1945 (dec.). *Dr. Bowen's paternal grandfather, Thomas Marshall Dent, was born on a Georgia plantation, graduated from Atlanta University and Howard University Law, and was employed at U.S. Commerce Department for 50 years. His son, William Marion, graduated from Dartmouth College in 1913, on a Latin and Greek scholarship. He was the first accountant for the Supreme Liberty Life Insurance Company, Chicago. Uncle Francis M. graduated Amherst, with a law degree from Howard University. Uncle Thomas M. (Jr.) graduated Howard University, and during WWI, he received a battlefield promotion to Captain for bravery in 1918. Dr. Bowen's mother, Clotilde (Tynes), was a fashion designer and business owner in Chicago. Dr. Bowen was raised in Columbus by her aunt Maude (Tynes) and 1st Lt. Stephen Brady Barrows.* BA, Ohio State U., 1943, MD, 1947. Intern Harlem Hosp., N.Y.C., 1947-48; resident and fellow in pulmonary diseases Triboro Hosp., Jamaica, L.I., 1948-50; resident in psychiatry VA Hosp., Albany N.Y., 1959-62; asst. resident in psychiatry Albany Med. Ctr. Hosp., 1961-62; pvt. practice N.Y.C., 1950-55; chief pulmonary disease clinic N.Y.C., 1950-55; asst. chief pulmonary disease svc. Valley Forge Army Hosp., Pa., 1956-59; chief psychiatry VA Hosp., Roseburg, Oreg., 1962-66, acting chief of staff, 1964-66; ast. chief neurology and psychiatry Tripler Gen. Hosp., Hawaii, 1966-68; psychiatr. lcons. and dir. Rev. Br. Office Civil Health and Med. Program Uniform Svcs., 1968-70; commd. capt. U.S. Army, 1955, advanced through ranks to col., 1968; neuropsychiat. cons. U.S. Army, Vietnam, 1970-71; chief dept. psychiatry Fitzsimons Army Med. Ctr. U.S. Army, 1971-74, chief dept. psychiatry Tripler Army Med. Ctr., 1974-75; assoc. clin. prof. psychiatry U. Hawaii, 1974-75; comdr. Hawley Army Clin. U.S. Army, Ft. Benjamin, Harrison, Ind., 1977-78; chief dept. primary care and cmty. medicine U.S. Army, 1978-83, chief psychiat. consultation svc. Fitzsimons Army Med. Ctr., 1983-85; chief psychiatry svc. med./regional offfice ctr. VA, Chyenne, Wyo., 1987-90; staff psychiatrist Denver VA Satellite Clin., Colorado Springs, Colo., 1990-96; ret., 1996; Locum Tenens practice psychiatry, 1996—; surveyor Joint Commn. on Accreditation Healthcare Orgns., 1985-92; assoc. prof. psychiatary U. Colo. Med. Ctr., Denver, 1971—. Decorated Legion of Merit, several other medals; recipient Colo. Disabled Am. Vets. award, 1994-95, Pres.'s 300 Commencement award Ohio State U., 1987, Profl. Achievement award Ohio State U. Alumni Assn., 1998. Fellow Am. Psychiat. Assn. (life), Acad. Psychosomatic Medicine; mem. AMA, Nat. Med. Assn., Menninger Found (charter), Ctrl. Neuropsychiatric Assn. (councilor at-large). Home: 1020 Tari Dr Colorado Springs CO 80921-2257 *To be successful one must always aspire to a goal just beyond his or her immediate reach.*

BOWEN, DONNA DARLYN, educator; b. Frankfort, Germany, Mar. 17, 1958; d. Donald Herbert and Helen Lela (Ellis) McCreary; m. James Philip Bowen, Feb. 26, 1984; 1 child, James Patrick. BS in Secondary Edn., Ind. U. S.E., 1980, MS in Secondary Edn., 1984. Instr. Watterson Coll., Louisville, Ky., 1986-91; instr. adult edn. New Albany (Ind.) Sch. Corp., 1991-94. Author: (newsletter) Lincolnartions, 1997. Sec. troop 80 Boy Scouts Am., Charlestown, Ind., 1998, Charlestown Civil War Round Table, 1998; v.p. Jefferson County Civil War Round Table, Madison, Ind., 1994-96. Mem. Assn. Lincoln Presenters (bd. dirs. 1996—, Best Mary Todd Lincoln 1997), Charlestown C. of C. (pres. 1986-88). Presbyterian. Avocations: sewing, music, working with children, reading history, genealogy. Home: PO Box 493 Charlestown IN 47111-0493

BOWEN, DUDLEY HOLLINGSWORTH, JR., federal judge; b. Augusta, Ga., June 25, 1941. AB in Fgn. Lang., U. Ga., 1964, LLB, 1965; profesor invitado (hon.), Universidad Externada de Bogotá, 1987. Bar: Ga. 1965. Pvt. practice law Augusta, 1968-72; bankruptcy judge U.S. Dist. Ct. (so. dist.) Ga., Augusta, 1972-75, judge, 1979-97; chief judge U.S. Dist. Ct. (so. dist.) Ga., 1997—, Augusta, 1997—; ptnr. firm Dye, Miller, Bowen & Tucker, Augusta, 1975-79; bd. dirs. Southeastern Bankruptcy Law Inst., 1976-87; mem. Ct. Security Com. Jud. Conf. U.S., 1987-92. Mem. bd. visitors U. Ga. Sch. Law, 1987-90. Served to 1st lt. inf., U.S. Army, 1966-68. Decorated Commendation medal. Mem. State Bar Ga. (chmn. bankruptcy law sect. 1977), Fed. Judges Assn. (bd. dirs. 1985-90), 11th Cir. Dist. Judges Assn. (sec.-treas. 1988-89, pres. 1991-92, chief judge so. dist. Ga. 1997—). Presbyterian. Office: US Dist Ct PO Box 2106 Augusta GA 30903-2106

BOWEN, GARY ROGER, architect; b. Page, Nebr., Apr. 24, 1942; s. Roger David and Eugenia (Luben) B.; m. Elizabeth Ann Humphrey, Aug. 4, 1962; children—Ann, Leslie. Student Wayne State Coll., 1958-59; B.Arch., U. Nebr., 1964, M. Arch., 1974. Registered architect, Nebr., Iowa; cert. Nat. Council Archtl. Registration Bds. With Howell, Killick, Partridge, Amis, London, 1963, F.W. Horn Assocs., Quincy, Ill., 1964-66; design architect Leo A. Daly Co., Omaha, 1966-72; ptnr. Hartman Morford Bowen, Omaha, 1972-74, Bahr Vermeer Haecker, Omaha, 1974—, pres., 1996—; vis. critic Coll. Architecture, U. Nebr.; vis. lectr. Coll. Architecture, Kansas State U.; dir. Landmarks Inc., Omaha. Bd. dirs. Western Heritage Soc., Joslyn Castle Inst., Archtl. Found. Nebr., Omaha. Am. Collegiate Schs. of Architecture Fgn. Work Exchange scholar, 1963; recipient Housing Mag. Homes for Better Living Nat. Design award, 1981, 2 Ctrl. States Honor awards. Mem. AIA (nat. bd. dirs. 1994-96, Coll. of Fellows 1996, Richard Upjohn fellow 1996, S.D. award), Nebr. Soc. Architects (20 honor awards), Nebr. Coll. Architecture Alumni Assn. (bd. dirs.). Republican. Methodist. Club: Field of Omaha. Home: 6007 Lafayette Ct Omaha NE 68132-1200 Office: Bahr Vermeer & Haecker Arch LTD 1209 Harney St Ste 400 Omaha NE 68102-1801

BOWEN, GEORGE HAMILTON, JR., astrophysicist, educator; b. Tulsa, June 20, 1925; s. George H. and Dorothy (Huntington) B.; m. Marjorie Evelyn Brown, June 19, 1948; children—Paul Huntington, Margaret Irene, Carol Ann, Dorothy Elizabeth, Kevin Leigh. B.S. with honor, Calif. Inst. Tech., 1949, Ph.D., 1952. Asso. biologist Oak Ridge Nat. Lab., 1952-54; asst. prof. physics Ia. State Coll., 1954-57; asso. prof. physics Iowa State U., 1957-65, prof., 1965-92, emeritus prof. astrophysics, 1993—. Served with USNR, 1944-46. Recipient Iowa State U. Outstanding Tchr. award, 1970, Faculty citation Iowa State U. Alumni Assn., 1971. Mem. Am. Astron. Soc., Astron. Soc. Pacific, Am. Assn. Physics Tchrs. (chmn. Iowa sect. 1966-67), Internat. Astron. Union, Sigma Xi, Tau Beta Pi. Home: 1919 Burnett Ave Ames IA 50010-4970 Office: Iowa State U Dept Physics & Astronomy Ames IA 50011-3160

BOWEN, GILBERT WILLARD, minister; b. Muskegon, Mich., Dec. 30, 1931; s. Bruce Oliver and Beatrice Lillian (Sibley) B.; m. Marlene Mary Michell, July 31, 1954; children: Kathryn Leigh, Mark Kevin, Stephen James. BA, Wheaton Coll., 1955; MDiv, McCormick Theol. Sem., 1957, PhD in Ministry, 1976; cert., Ctr. for Religion and Psychotherapy, 1976; DLL (hon.), Nat. Coll. Edn., 1987. Ordained to ministry Presbyn. Ch., 1956. Minister 1st United Presbyn. Ch., Blue Earth, Minn., 1956-63, Faith United Presbyn. Ch., Tinley Park, Ill., 1963-65, Community Presbyn. Ch., Mt. Prospect, Ill., 1965-70, Kenilworth (Ill.) Union Ch., 1970—; exchange minister Johanneskirche, Neuwied, Fed. Republic Germany, 1961-62; pres. bd. Ctr. for Religion and Psychotherapy; bd. dirs. McCormick Theol. Sem., Chgo., Anatolia Coll., Thessaloniki, Greece, Presbyn. Home, Evanston. Mem. adv. com. North Shore Sr. Ctr., Winnetka, Ill.; bd. dirs. Hospice of North Shore, Wilmette, Ill., Shelter for Battered Women, Evanston; chmn. Instl. Rev. Bd., Evanston. Mem. Am. Assn. Pastoral Counselors, Acad. Parish Clergy, Am. Waldensian Aid Soc. Republican. Club: Indian Hill. Avocations: tennis, golf, vocal music. Home: 909 Westerfield Dr Wilmette IL 60091-1810 Office: Kenilworth Union Ch 211 Kenilworth Ave Kenilworth IL 60043-1299

BOWEN, H. KENT, engineering educator; b. Nov. 21, 1941; married; 5 children. BS, U. Utah, 1967; PhD, MIT, 1971. Staff MIT, 1970-76, prof., 1976-81, dir. Materials Processing Ctr., Ford prof. engring., 1981-93; faculty Harvard U., 1993—; dir. leaders for mfrs., MIT, 1988-93. Contbr. articles to profl. jours. Recipient R.M. Fulrath award, F. H. Norton award, Schwartzwalder-PACE award, Ross Coffin Purdy award, Robert Browning Sosman award, Gordon Y. Billard award, MIT, Henry B. Kane '24 award. Mem. NAE, AAAS,. Home: 178 Cross St Belmont MA 02478-3174*

BOWEN, HARRY ERNEST, management consultant; b. Elmira, N.Y., Jan. 31, 1941; s. Ernest William and Julia Cora (Forker) B.; m. Sandra Marie Fullerton, June 15, 1962; children: Harry Ernest Jr., Vicki Lynn Bowen Briggs, Nicholas Russel. AS in Gen. Studies, Mt. Wachusetts Coll., Gardner, Mass., 1975; BSBA, Ind. Inst. Tech., 1996. Enlisted U.S. Army, 1961; student Manual Morse Operator Sch. U.S. Army, Ft. Devens, Mass., 1961-62; sr. repairman U.S. Army, Sinope, Turkey, 1970-71; mem. maintenance officer Intelligence and Security Command U.S. Army, Arlington Hall, Va., 1961-83; ret., 1983; assoc. dir. Martin & Stern, Inc., Chantilly, Va., 1983-89; program mgr. Paragon Sys., Inc., Centreville, Va., 1989-91; program mgr., mem. mgmt. staff Telos Fed. Sys., Sierra Vista, Ariz., 1991-96; advisor Bowen Assocs., Sierra Vista, 1992-98; regional mgr., project mgr., mem. mgmt. staff FC Bus. Sys., Sierra Vista, 1996-97; mem. tech. staff, dep. program mgr. Telos Corp., Ashburn, Va., 1998; sr. program mgr. army programs FC Bus. Sys., Newington, Va., 1999—; sole owner T and L Sys., Sierra Vista, 1991—; advisor Bowen Assocs., Sierra Vista, 1992—. Mem. Soc. Logistics Engrs. (chmn. 1991-94, Sr. Membership award 1993), Kiwanis (pres. 1996-97)ú. Republican. Avocations: bowling, swimming, coaching, walking, golfing. Home: 10503 Montrose Way Manassas VA 20109-6464 Office: FC Bus Sys 8500 Cinder Bed Rd Ste 210N Newington VA 22020

BOWEN, JAMES RONALD, banker; b. Falls City, Nebr., July 3, 1941; s. Charles Addison and Vera Mae (White) B.; m. Jacquelyn Anne Westhoff, Mar. 3, 1962; children: Bryan Scott, Susan Lyn. B.S. in Bus. Adminstrn., Kans. State Tchrs. Coll., 1964; postgrad. cert., Rutgers U., 1973. Acctg. mgr. Fed. Res. Bank, Kansas City, Mo., 1968-69, asst. v.p., 1970-74, v.p., 1975-76, sr. v.p., 1977-87; exec. v.p. Fed. Res. Bank, St. Louis, 1987, first v.p., chief oper. officer, 1988-95; chmn. Fed. Res. System Automation Program Directorate, Kansas City, 1981-82; chmn. Conf. of First Vice Pres., 1990; exec. dir. Pricing Policy Com., 1991-94. Mem. exec. roundtable coun. U. Mo., Kansas City, 1984-87; mgmt. adv. com. U. Mo., Columbia, 1985-86; adv. coun. Sch. Bus., Emporia (Kans.) State U., 1990—. Mem. Ops. Mgmt. Assn. (bd. dirs. 1987-89).

BOWEN, JAMES THOMAS, military officer; b. Mason City, Iowa, May 4, 1948; s. Stanley Thomas and Marilyn Louise (Ott) B.; m. Joyce Anne Kermabon, Sept. 10, 1977; 1 child, Steven James. BBA, U. Iowa, 1969; MS, U. So. Calif., Los Angeles, 1974. Commd. 2nd lt. USAF, 1969, advance through grades to col., 1991; student pilot 3575th Pilot Tng. Wing, Vance AFB, Okla., 1969-70; co-pilot 773rd Tactical Airlift Squadron, Clark AFB, Phillipines, 1971; pilot 6594th Test Group, Hickam AFB, Hawaii, 1971-75; acquisition program mgr. Aeronautical Systems Div., Wright-Patterson AFB, Ohio, 1976-82; chief, standoff surveillance and attack systems HQ USAF, Rsch. Devel. and Acquistion, Pentagon, Va., 1984-87; chief, acquistion plans and programs br. Air Force Inspection and Safety Ctr., Norton AFB, Calif., 1988-90; dir. projects joint tactical autonomous weapons Aero. Systems Div., Wright-Patterson AFB, Ohio, 1990-91, dir. devel. and integration F-16, 1991-94; F-16 mgmt. dir. Ogden Air Logistics Ctr., Hill AFB, Utah, 1994-95; custom sys. program mgr. Hewlett-Packard, Co., Santa Rosa, Calif., 1996—. Active Rep. ctrl. com. Sonoma County. Decorated Air medal USAF, 1972. Mem. Air Force Assn., Def. Systems Mgmt. Coll. Alumni Assn., Nat. Def. U. Alumni Assn., Am. Mgmt. Assn., Assn. Old Crows, Ret. Officers Assn., Project Mgmt. Inst. Methodist. Avocations: skiing, deep sea fishing, golf. Office: Hewlett-Packard Co Santa Rosa Syss Divsn 1400 Fountain Grove Pkwy Santa Rosa CA 95403-1799

BOWEN, JEAN, librarian, consultant; b. Albany, N.Y., Mar. 23, 1927; d. John W. and Grace Lester (Quier) B.; m. Henry F. Bloch, June 26, 1962; 1 child, Pamela A. Bloch. AB, Smith Coll., 1948, AM, 1956; MS, Columbia U., 1957. Curator Rodgers & Hammerstein Archives of Recorded Sound, N.Y.C., 1962-67; asst. chief music divsn. N.Y. Pub. Libr., N.Y.C., 1967-85, chief music divsn., 1986-96, dir. Humanities and Social Scis. Libr., 1996—; cons. Rockefeller Bros. Found., N.Y.C., 1963, 67, N.Y. Philharm., N.Y.C., 1984, Schubert Archives, N.Y.C., 1982; mem. faculty Rare Book Sch. Columbia U., N.Y.C., 1984, 87, 91; bd. dirs. Composers Recs. Inc., N.Y.C., Amphion Found., N.Y.C. Contbr. articles to High Fidelity, Opera News, Am. Record Guide, Saturday Rev., MLA Notes, New Grove Dictionary of Am. Music. Mem. ALA. Office: Humanities and Social Scis Libr NY Pub Libr Fifth Ave and 42 St New York NY 10018-2788

BOWEN, JEWELL RAY, chemical engineering educator; b. Duck Hill, Miss., Jan. 9, 1934; s. Hugh and Myrtle Louise (Stevens) B.; m. Priscilla Joan Spooner, Feb. 4, 1956; children: Jewell Ray, Sandra L., Susan E. B.S., MIT, 1956, M.S., 1957; Ph.D., U. Calif., Berkeley, 1963. Asst. prof. U. Wis., Madison, 1963-67, assoc. prof., 1967-80, prof. chem. engring., 1970-81, chmn. chem engring. dept., 1971-73, 78-81, assoc. vice chancellor, 1972-76; prof. chem. engring. U. Wash., Seattle, 1981—, dean coll. engring., 1981-96; cons. in field; adviser NSF, Dept. Def. Contbr. articles to profl. jours.; editor: 7th-10th Internat. Colloquia on Dynamics of Explosions and Reactive Systems, 1979, 81, 83, 85. Bd. dirs. Wash. Tech. Ctr., 1983-97, interim exec. dir., 1989-91; mem. Wash. High Tech. Coordinating Bd., 1983-87. Recipient SWE Rodney Chipp award, 1995; NATO-NSF postdoctoral fellow, 1962-63, sr. postdoctoral fellow, 1968; Deutsche Forschungsgemeinschaft prof., 1976-77. Fellow AIAA, AAAS (com. on coun. affairs 1995-97, sect. chmn. 1996-97), Am. Soc. Engring. Edn. (deans coun. 1985-92, chmn. 1989-91, bd. dirs. 1989-94, 1st v.p. 1991, pres.-elect 1992, pres. 1993); mem. AIChE, Am. Phys. Soc., Combustion Inst., Sigma Xi, Taua Beta Pi, Beta Theta Pi. E-mail: bowen@engr.washington.edu. Home: 5324 NE 86th St Seattle WA 98115-3922 Office: U Wash Dept Chem Engring PO Box 351750 Seattle WA 98195-1750

BOWEN, JOHN PEARSON, video tape editor; b. Orange, Tex., Sept. 16, 1953; s. John Francis and Virginia H. Bowen. AA, Moorpark Coll., 1973; BA, Columbia Coll., 1974. Pres. J.B. Syndicuts, Westlake Village, Calif., 1989—, J.B. Prodn. & Consulting, Westlake Village, 1988—; sr. editor Modern Video Film Inc., Hollywood, Calif., 1976—. Editor Merv Griffin Show, 1978, Dance Fever, 1981, Jeopardy, 1981-85, Wheel of Fortune, 1981-85, Entertainment Tonight, 1985-87, Bob Hope Thanksgiving, 1984, Steve Allen Show, 1990, Mary Tyler Moore's 20th Anniversary Show, 1991, Evening Shade, 1992, Baywatch, 1995, 96, Sliders, 1995, Mighty Morphin Power Rangers, 1995, 96, Walker Texas Ranger, 1995-99, The Big Easy, 1996, Mr. and Mrs. Smith, 1996, Friends, 1997-99, Suddenly Susan, 1997-99, Fired Up, 1997, 98, Maximum Bob, 1998, Jesse, 1998, 99, Veronica's Closet, 1998, 99. Office: Modern Video Vilm Inc 4411 W Olive Ave Burbank CA 91505-4219

BOWEN, JOHN WESLEY EDWARD, IV, lawyer; b. Columbus, Ohio, July 11, 1954; s. John Wesley Edward III and Jeanne (Lehar) B. *Great grandfather John W.E. Bowen Sr., an African slave who was purchased out of slavery by his father, Edward Bowen, an ex-African slave, and was educated at Dillard University in New Orleans, Louisiana. He received the degree of Doctor of Philosophy from Boston University in 1887. Dr. Bowen was the first black President of Gammon Theological Seminary in Atlanta, Georgia.* BBA, So. Meth. U., 1976; JD, Columbia U., 1979. Bar: N.Y. 1980, U.S. Ct. Claims 1982, U.S. Supreme Ct. 1983, U.S. Dist. Ct. (so. and ea. dists.) N.Y. 1985, U.S. Ct. Appeals (fed. cir.) 1986. Trial atty. antitrust div. U.S. Dept. Justice, Washington, 1979-85; of counsel Howard & Rhone, N.Y.C., 1985-87; ptnr. Bowen & Bowen, 1989—; dir. N.Y. Bd. of Trade, 1987-89. Contbr. articles to profl. jours. Chmn. Manhattan Jr. Assn. Commerce and Industry, N.Y.C., 1985-87, pres., 1986-87; mem. housing com. N.Y.C. Cmty. Bd. #10. Named one of Outstanding Young Men in Am., U.S. Jaycees, 1981-87. Mem. ABA, Fed. Bar Assn., Nat. Bar Assn., N.Y. County Lawyers Assn., Internat. Platform Assn., Blue Key, Alpha Phi Alpha, French Inst./Alliance Francaise, Columbia U. Club. Methodist. Fax: (614) 418-1873. E-mail: bowenlaw@earthlink.net. Office: 2720 Airport Dr Columbus OH 43219

BOWEN, KIT HANSEL, JR., chemistry educator; b. Grenada, Miss., July 23, 1948; s. Kit Hansel and Virginia B.; m. Annette Beatrice Garofalo, May 18, 1976. BS, U. Miss., 1970; MS, Harvard U., 1972, PhD, 1977. Postdoctoral rsch. fellow Harvard U., Cambridge, Mass., 1977-80; prof. Johns Hopkins U., Balt., 1980—; vis. scientist U. Paris, 1990, 91, 93, Humboldt Sr. Fell., JSPS Fell. Contbr. articles to profl. jours.; mem. editl. adv. bd. Jour. Chem. Physics. With USNG, 1970-76. Ford fellow Harvard U., 1974. Fellow Am. Phys. Soc.; mem. Am. Chem. Soc., Materials Rsch. Soc. Methodist. Office: Johns Hopkins U Dept Chem Baltimore MD 21218

BOWEN, LINDA FLORENCE, pharmaceutical executive; b. Trenton, N.J., Apr. 21, 1960; d. Joseph John and Audrey (Würfel) Kish; m. Chris Bowen, Dec. 8, 1998. BA in English, BS in Microbiology, Rutgers Coll., 1982; MS in Pharmacy Adminstrn., L.I. Univ., 1996. Microbiologist Kalipharma-Purepac Pharm., Elizabeth, N.J., 1983-85; microbiologist Block Drug Co., Jersey City, 1985-88, sr. documentation specialist, 1988-93, internat. regulatory affairs mgr., 1993—. Bd. dirs. Theatre Guild of Old Bridge, 1993—. Mem. Regulatory Affairs Profl. Soc. (spkr. annual meetings), Drug Info. Assn., Rho Chi. Roman Catholic. Avocations: community theater, collecting antiques, traveling. Office: Block Drug Co Inc 257 Cornelison Ave Jersey City NJ 07302-3194

BOWEN, LOWELL REED, lawyer; b. Prince Frederick, Md., Jan. 29, 1931; s. Perry Gray and Melba (Hutchins) B.; m. Marilyn Sack, June 14, 1958; children: Mark Holdsworth, David Stockbridge. BA, U. Md., 1952; LLB, U. Md., Balt., 1957. Bar: Md. 1957, U.S. Dist. Ct. Md. 1958, U.S. Ct. Appeals (4th cir.) 1959, U.S. Supreme Ct. 1964. Law clk. to chief judge U.S. Dist. Ct. Md., Balt., 1957-58; assoc. Miles & Stockbridge, Balt., 1958-65, ptnr., 1966—, mng. ptnr., 1974-91; lectr. U. Md. Law Sch., 1958-63, U. Balt. Law Sch., 1965-70. Mem., chmn. various coms. Md. Commn. to Revise Annotated Code Md., Annapolis, 1973—; mem. Standing Com. on Rules of Practice and Procedure, Md. Ct. Appeals, Annapolis, 1980—; trustee, chmn. Balt. Opera Co., Inc., 1977-92; mem. Md. Humanities Coun., 1992-97; trustee, pres. Lyric Found., Inc., 1997—. 1st lt. USAF, 1952-54. Mem. ABA, Md. State Bar Assn., Maryland Club, Ctr. Club (bd. govs. 1984-93, sec. 1985-93). Office: Miles & Stockbridge 10 Light St Ste 1100 Baltimore MD 21202-1487

BOWEN, MARGARETA MARIA, interpretation and translation educator; b. Baden, Austria, June 28, 1928; d. Franz and Marie (Neumeyer) Brosch; m. Samuel R. Brooks, May 25, 1956 (div. 1958); m. David Bowen, Dec. 29, 1970 (dec. 1997). Diploma translator, U. Vienna, 1950, diploma interpreter, 1952, PhD, 1951; cert. conf. interpreter, translator, Georgetown U., 1957. Translator Ministry of Interior, Vienna, 1950-54; conf. interpreter Austria, Belgium, and U.S., 1956-68; chief interpreter UN Indsl. Devel. Orgn., Vienna, 1968-72; asst. prof. Georgetown U., Washington, 1972-78, assoc. prof., 1978—; spl. cons. in translation, Tangiers, Morocco, 1988; cons. to Can. Laval U., 1977, U. Ottawa, 1983, U. of York, 1993, U. W.I., 1989-91; mem. subcom. F15.34 of ASTM on Lang. Interpreting. Co-editor Jerome Quarterly, 1985—; ATA Scholary Monograph Series, vol. IV, 1990; contbr. to book Translators Through History (John Benjamin), 1995; contbr. numerous articles to profl. jours. Scholarship French Govt., 1948-49; fellowship AAUW, 1955-56; recipient Creditanstalt Bankverein award, 1987; grantee Nat. Resource Ctr. Transl. and Interpretation, 1981-91. Mem. Am. Assn. of Lang. Specialists (numerous coms.), Assn. Internat. des Interpretes de Conf. (statute revision com. 1967-68, liaison with World Bank 1972-73), European Soc. for Translation Studies. Roman Catholic. Home: Tower Villas #1206 3800 N Fairfax Dr Arlington VA 22203-1719 Office: Georgetown Univ Divsn Interpretation and Translation Box 571053 Washington DC 20057-1053

BOWEN, MARY LU, ecumenical developer, community organizer; b. Wheeling, W.Va., Feb. 14, 1930; d. Walter Philip and Helen Elizabeth (Luthy) Wagenheim; m. Robert Edward Bowen, June 13, 1953; children: Jeanne, Thomas, Robert, David. BS in Edn., Wittenberg U., 1952; MA in Social Scis., SUNY, Binghamton, 1989. Cert. tchr., Ohio, W.Va., Tex., N.Y. Various teaching positions, 1952-80; coord. ministry with the aging Coun. of Chs., Broome County, N.Y., 1979-82; adminstrv. asst. Coun. of Chs., Broome County, 1982-83, asst. dir., 1984-86; assoc. for ecumenical devel. N.Y. State Coun. of Chs., Albany, Syracuse, N.Y., 1990-94; regional dir. southern tier N.Y. State Coun. of Chs., Albany, 1995-96; dir. of pub. policy N.Y. State Cmty. of Churches, 1997—, exec. dir., 1998—; mem., sec. exec. cabinet N.Y. State Coun. Chs., Albany, Syracuse, 1986-88, 88-91; synodical lay rep. Evang. Luth. Ch. in Am. Region VII Coun., Phila., 1987-91, churchwide leadership team Social Min. Project, Chgo., 1990-91, sec. constituting conv. Upstate N.Y. Synod, Syracuse, 1987. Author: Reclaiming Christianity's Feminist Heritage: Reflections on Patriarchal Teachings and Women's Problems, 1989, Handbook for Clergy on Child Abuse and Neglect, 1995. Mem. Broome County Coordinating Coun. Child Abuse and Neglect, 1986-88, 96—, treas. 1997; mem. Luth. Statewide Advocacy, Albany, 1982-90, chmn. exec. com., 1991—; mem. regional adv. bd. Citizen Action N.Y., Binghamton, 1994—; co-chmn. Interreligious Health and Justice Coalition, N.Y. Ctrl. So. Tier Region; Evangelical Luth. Ch. in Am. Coalition for Mission in Appalachia, 1996—. Mem. Nat. Assn. Ecumenical Staff. Democrat. Lutheran. Avocations: travel, reading. Home: 14 Overbrook Dr Apalachin NY 13732-4234 Office: NY State Cmty Chs Main Office 362 State St Albany NY 12210-1202

BOWEN, MELANIE, state official; m. Ronald S. Bowen; children: Elysa, Lindsey. BS in Polit. Sci. and History, Brigham Young U. Intern to Senator Orrin Hatch Washington, 1977; dir. Ctrl. and Ea. Utah Office, dep. state dir., 1984, state dir.; mem. U.S. Delegation Am. Swiss Leadership Conf., Geneva; co-chair State Rep. Platform com.; mem. State of Utah's

Immunization Task Force, Utah Internat. Biomed. Conf. com., Utah State Vets. Nursing Home Oversight com.; chair Utah Women's and Srs. Confs. Office: Office of Senator Orrin Hatch 8402 Federal Bldg 123 South State St Salt Lake City UT 84138

BOWEN, MICHAEL ANTHONY, lawyer, writer; b. Ft. Monroe, Va., July 16, 1951; s. Harold James and Judith Ann (Carter-Waller) B.; m. Sara Armbruster, Aug. 30, 1975; children: Rebecca Elizabeth, Christopher Andrew, John Armbruster, Marguerite Judith, James Harold. AB summa cum laude, Rockhurst Coll., 1973; JD cum laude, Harvard U., 1976. Bar: Wis. 1976, U.S. Dist. Ct. (ea. and we. dists.) Wis., U.S. Ct. Appeals (4th, 5th, 7th, 8th and 10th cirs.), Wis. Supreme Ct. Assoc. Foley & Lardner, Milw., 1976-84, ptnr., 1984—. Author: Can't Miss, 1987, Badger Game, 1989, Washington Deceased, 1990, Fielder's Choice, 1991, Faithfully Executed, 1992, Act of Faith, 1993, Corruptly Procured, 1994, Worst Case Scenario, 1996, Collateral Damage, 1999; co-author: The Wisconsin Fair Dealership Law, 1988. Mem. ABA, Wis. Bar Assn., Milw. Bar Assn., St. Thomas More Lawyers' Soc. (pres. 1983), Milw. Young Lawyers' Assn. (pro bono legal services 1982). Democrat. Roman Catholic. Avocations: photography, running, cross-country skiing. Office: Foley & Lardner 777 E Wisconsin Ave Ste 3800 Milwaukee WI 53202-5367

BOWEN, PATRICK HARVEY, lawyer, consultant; b. Cin., July 7, 1939; s. Albert Vernon and Elsie Matilda (Harvey) B.; m. Karen A. Hunter; 1 child, Harvey Shaw. BA, Marietta Coll., 1961; JD, Duke U., 1964; MBA, Columbia U., 1975. Bar: N.Y. 1965, Conn. 1990. Assoc. Mudge, Rose, Guthrie & Alexander, N.Y.C., 1964-66; atty. Kennecott Copper Corp., N.Y.C., 1966-71, asst. counsel, 1971-79, asst. gen. counsel, 1979-83, asst. sec., 1980-83; sr. assoc. atty. Allied Stores Corp., N.Y.C., 1983-87, v.p., gen. counsel, sec., 1987-88, v.p., 1988-89; pvt. practice Stamford, Conn., 1990—. Mem. ABA, Conn. Bar Assn., N.Y. State Bar Assn., Assn. of Bar of City of N.Y., Am. Soc. Corp. Secs., Corp. Bar Assn. of Westchester and Fairfield. Avocation: traditional jazz musician. Office: 2001 W Main St Ste 140 Stamford CT 06902-4562

BOWEN, PETER GEOFFREY, arbitrator, investment advisor, business management lecturer; b. Iowa City, Iowa, July 10, 1939; s. Howard Rothmann and Lois Berntine (Schilling) B.; m. Shirley Johns Carlson, Sept. 14, 1968; children: Douglas Howard, Leslie Johns. BA in Govt. and Econs., Lawrence Coll., 1960; postgrad., U. Wis., 1960-61, U. Denver, 1963-64; cert. expert witness, Denver Dist. Ct., 1987. Dir. devel. Mobile Home Communities, Denver, 1969-71; v.p. Perry & Butler, Denver, 1972-73; exec. v.p., dir. Little & Co., Denver, 1973; pres. Builders Agy. Ltd., Denver, 1974-75, The Investment Mgmt. Group Ltd., Denver, 1975-87; independent investor, writer Vail, Colo., 1987—; arbitrator NASD Regulation, Inc., 1996—, Am. Arbitration Assn., 1996—; gen. ptnr. real estate ltd. ptnrships.; bus. faculty mem. Colo. Mt. Coll., 1994—; continuing legal edn. lectr. on real estate syndications, 1983. Contbr. articles to profl. publs. Mem. Colo. Coun. Econ. Devel., 1964-68; vice-chmn. Greenwood Village (Colo.) Planning and Zoning Comm., 1983-85; mem. Vail Planning and Environ. Commn., 1992-96; dir. Vail Partnership Environ. Edn. Programs, Inc., 1993—; elected mem. City Council Greenwood Village, 1985-86, also mayor pro tem, 1985-86; trustee Vail Mountain Sch. Found., 1987-88; bd. dirs. Colo. Plan for Apportionment, 1966; speaker Forward Metro Denver, 1966-67. Mem. Rotary Club (bd. dirs. Vail chpt., named Rotarian of Yr. 1992), Lawrence U. Alumni Assn. (bd. dirs. 1966-72, 82-86). Home: 4950 S Beeler St Greenwood Village CO 80111-1312

BOWEN, RAYMOND COBB, academic administrator; b. New Haven, Sept. 19, 1934; s. Ray Curtis Sr. and Lucille (Cobb) B.; m. Joan deMarro Massalena, July 21, 1959; children: Raymond III, Rebecca, Ruth, Rachel. BA, U. Conn., 1956, PhD, 1966; MS, U. N.Mex., 1962. Pres. LaGuardia Community Coll., N.Y.C., 1989—. With U.S. Army, 1956-59. Named Outstanding Educator, Shelby State Community Coll., Memphis Bd. Edn., 1982; recipient Govs. Staff award, Lamar Alexander, Gov. Tenn., 1982, Pres's. Acad. award AACJC, 1988. Office: CUNY LaGuardia Community Coll 31-10 Thomson Ave Long Island City NY 11101-3071

BOWEN, RICHARD LEE, academic administrator, political science educator; b. Avoca, Iowa, Aug. 31, 1933; s. Howard L. and Donna (Milburn) B.; m. Connie Smith Bowen, 1976; children: James, Robert, Elizabeth, Christopher; children by previous marriage—Catherine, David, Thomas. B.A., Augustana Coll., 1957; M.A., Harvard, 1959, Ph.D., 1967. Fgn. service officer State Dept., 1959-60; research asst. to U.S. Senator Francis Case, 1960-62; legis. asst. to U.S. Senator Karl Mundt, 1962-65; minority cons. sub-com. exec. reorgn. U.S. Senate, 1966-67; asst. to pres., assoc. prof. polit. sci. U. S.D., Vermillion, 1967-69, pres., 1969-76; pres. Dakota State Coll., Madison, 1973-76; commr. higher edn. Bd. Regents State S.D., Pierre, 1976-80; Disting prof. polit. sci. U. S.D., 1980-85; pres. Idaho State U., Pocatello, 1985—. Served with USN, 1951-54. Recipient Outstanding Alumnus award Augustana Coll., 1970; Woodrow Wilson fellow, 1957, Congl. Staff fellow, 1965; Fulbright scholar, 1957. Office: Idaho State U Office of Pres Campus Box 8310 Pocatello ID 83209-0009

BOWEN, RICHARD LEE, architect; b. Canton, Ohio, Nov. 1, 1935; s. Raymond Leed and Lillian E. (White) B.; m. Robin Herrington (div.); children: Richard Lee, David Herrington, Laurel Ann, Sean Andrew, Scott Edward; m. Gail Audrey; children: Tabitha Erin, Colin Leed. BA, Case Western Res. U., 1959. Registered architect 50 states, D.C., P.R., Eng., Can., Australia, Nat. Coun. Archtl. Registration Bds., Archtl. Registration Coun. U.K. Founder, pres. Richard L. Bowen & Assocs. Inc., archtl. engrs. and planners, Cleve., Richard L. Bowen & Assocs. Inc., Cleve., 1963—, Richard L. Bowen, Inc., Cleve., 1976—; pres. Enerwaste, Inc., 1992—; mng. ptnr. ComDel, 1970; pres. Richard L. Bowen & Assocs. of Fla., Pompano Beach, 1969—. Prin. works include Western Campus, Cuyahoga C.C., Akron State Office Bldg., West Jr. High Sch., Cleve. Cen. Police Hdqs., Cleve. Hopkins Internat. Airport, FAA Regional Office Bldg., classroom and libr. builds. Ashtabula Campus, Kent State U., Wade Park VA Hosp., Westerly Sewage Treatment Facility for Cuyahoga Regional Sewer Authority, Cuyahoa C.C. Manpower Skills Ctr. for Ohio; also others. Mem. Leadership Cleve.; mem. exec. com. Cuyahoga County Rep. Com., Cleve., 1963—; trustee St. Luke's Hosp. Assn., Cleve. Internat. Air Show; mem. adv. bd. Cleve. Inst. Art. Recipient energy conservation design award Fla. Power Winter Garden Shopping Ctr., 1986, merit award Cleve. Restoration Soc., 1992. Mem. AIA (design award of excellence 1976, award 1979), Architects Soc. Ohio (honor award 1988), Nat. Assn. Indsl. and Office Parks (awards 1985, 89), Royal Archtl. Inst. Can., Royal Inst. Brit. Architects, Am. Soc. Ch. Architecture, Soc. Archtl. Historians, Guild for Religious Architecture, Internat. Coun. Shopping Ctrs., Constrn. Specifications Inst., Bldg. Ofcls. Coun. Am., Am. Assn. Planners, Urban Land Inst., Am. Arbitration Assn., Rowfant Club, Cat Cay Club, Ft. Lauderdale Yacht Club, Useppa Island Club, Phi Gamma Delta, also others. Avocations: sailing, skiing, fly and deep sea fishing. Home: 15926 Hillbrook Dr Chagrin Falls OH 44126 Office: 13000 Shaker Blvd Cleveland OH 44120-2063

BOWEN, ROBERT WILLIAM, publishing executive; b. Wynnewood, Pa., Mar. 24, 1960; s. Thales Jr. and Sally Louise (Hale) B. BSBA, Drexel U., 1983. Program host Sta. WKDU-FM, Phila., 1980-83; announcer Sta. WZZD-AM, Phila., 1981-82; asst. to pres. Dash Communications, Inc., Phila., 1982; publicity and promotion mgr. Nat. Religious Broadcasters, Parsippany, N.J., 1983-85; program host Sta. WXMC-AM, Parsippany, Troy Hills, N.J., 1984-85; conv. coord. Nat. Religious Broadcasters, Morristown, N.J., 1985-87, dir. mem. svcs., 1987-92; pres. Optimum Mgmt. Corp. N.J., 1992—; pub. ReligionandMedia.com., 1992—. Contbg. editor: Religious Broadcasting mag. Charter mem. Rep. Presidl. Task Force (trustee, 1991—); mem. Rep. Nat. Com. Mem. Am. Mktg. Assn. (v.p. comm. N.J. chpt. 1998-99), Gospel Music Assn., Am. Soc. Assn. Execs., Am. Mktg. Assn., Fellowship Contemporary Christian Ministries, Nature Conservancy (life), Zool. Soc. Phila., Com. for an Affordable N.J. (adv. bd. 1991-94), Nat. Trust For Hist. Preservation, Western Reserve Hist. Soc. Republican. Avocation: photography. Home: 316 Hudson Ave Hopatcong NJ 07843-1710

BOWEN, ROBIN JANINE, non-profit agency executive; b. N.Y.C., Mar. 1, 1956; d. Sheldon and Dorothy (Kashdan) Reich; m. Richard William Bowen, July 27, 1975; children: Rigel Steven, Maxwell James, Hannah Robin. BS in Psychology, Sonoma State U., Rohnert Park, Calif., 1978; MS in Health Svcs. Adminstrn., St. Mary's Coll., Moraga, Calif., 1988. Cert. childbirth instr. Childbirth educator Santa Rosa, Calif., 1979-91; exec. dir. Calif. Parenting Inst., Santa Rosa, 1978—; tchr. Pacific Oaks Coll., Pasadena, 1990-91. Chmn. Children's Network of Sonoma County, Santa Rosa, 1988-91; adv. mem. Foster Parent Tng. Prog., Santa Rosa, 1987-92; mem. Early Intervention Area Planning Com., Santa Rosa, 1990-95; founder, chair Sonoma County Family Action, 1994—. Recipient Commendation for work in child abuse prevention, State Dept. Social Svcs. and Social Svcs. Adv. Bd., 1987, Maternal, Child Health award, 1998; named Pub. Health Champion Sonoma County, 1999. Office: California Parenting Inst 3650 Standish Ave Santa Rosa CA 95407-8113

BOWEN, THOMAS EDWIN, cardiothoracic surgeon, retired army officer; b. Lackawanna, N.y., Dec. 16, 1934; m. Margaret Marie Harrington, 1959; children: Matthew, Mark, James, John, Thaddeus, Mary Cristine. BS, St. Bonaventure U., 1961; MD, Marquette U., 1965; diploma, U.S. Army War Coll., 1985. Diplomate Am. Bd. Surgery, Am. Bd. Thoracic Surgery, Nat. Bd. Med. Examiners. Commd. 2d lt. U.S. Army, 1961, advanced through grades to brig. gen., 1988; intern Tripler Army Gen. Hosp., Honolulu, 1965-66, resident in gen. surgery, 1966-70; resident in gen. surgery Vietnam, 1970-71; resident in thoracic surgery Walter Reed Army Gen. Hosp., Washington, 1971-73; dep. dir. Profl. Svcs. Directorate Office of Surgeon Gen., Washington, 1985-87; comdr., surgeon 121st Evacuation Hosp., 1987-88; assoc. prof. dept. surgery Sch. Medicine Uniformed Svcs. U. of Health Scis., Bethesda, Md., 1981—; commanding gen. Fitzsimons Army Med. Ctr., Aurora, Colo., 1988-93; assoc. clin. prof. dept. surgery U. Colo. Sch. Medicine, Denver, 1989—; assoc. prof. surgery U. So. Fla. Sch. Med.; chief of staff James A. Haley VA Med. Ctr., Tampa, Fla., 1993—. Contbr. articles to profl. publs. Chmn. Combined Fed. Campaign, Denver, 1990. Decorated D.S.M., Legion of Merit with three oak leaf clusters, Bronze Star, Alfredo Lezcano Gomez medal for Svc. to Republic of Panama; recipient Raymond Franklin Metcalf award, 1971. Mem. Assn. Mil. Surgeons, Am. Coll. Surgeons, Soc. Thoracic Surgeons, Denver C. of C., Aurora C. of C., Rotary. Roman Catholic. Avocations: beekeeping, woodworking, reading, raising animals and crops. Office: James A Haley VA Med Ctr Tampa FL 33612

BOWEN, W. J., retired gas company executive; b. Sweetwater, Tex., Mar. 31, 1922; s. Berry and Annah (Robey) B.; m. Annis K. Hilty, June 6, 1945; children: Shelley Ann, Barbara Kay, Berry Dunbar, William Jackson. BS, U.S. Mil. Acad., 1945. Registered profl. engr., Tex. Petroleum engr. Delhi Oil Corp., Dallas, 1949-57; v.p. Fla. Gas Co., Houston, 1957-60; pres. Fla. Gas Co., Winter Park, Fla., 1960-74; pres., chief exec. officer Transco Cos., Inc., Houston, 1974-81; chmn. Transco Cos., Inc (name changed to Transco Energy Co.), Houston, 1976-92; chief exec. officer Transco Energy Co., Houston, 1981-87; ret., 1992; also bd. dirs. Transco Energy Co., Houston; ret., 1992; bd. dirs. J.P. Poindexter and Co., Inc., Houston; mem. adv. bd. Am. Indsl. Ptnrs., N.Y.; hon. vice-chmn. World Energy Coun. Bd. dirs. YMCA, Houston, Houston Soc. for Prevention Cruelty to Animals; trustee bd. Baylor Coll. Medicine, Jesse H. Jones Grad. Sch. Bus., Rice U. With AUS, 1945-49. Mem. U.S. Energy Assn. (past chmn.). Episcopalian. Office: Transco 2800 Post Oak Blvd Houston TX 77056-6100

BOWEN, WILLIAM AUGUSTUS, financial consultant; b. Greenville, N.C., Jan. 17, 1930; s. Joseph Francis and Dorothy Lee (Simmons) B.; m. Hilda Carolyn Rowlett, June 8, 1952; children: Carol Bowen Bernstein, Elizabeth Lee Bowen Jones, William Augustus Jr., Mary Jane Bowen Sullivan. B.S. in Bus. Adminstrn. U. N.C., 1951, grad. exec. program, 1965. With Wachovia Bank & Trust Co., Charlotte, N.C., 1955-79, regional v.p., mgr. So. region, 1970-79; pres., chief operating officer, dir. First Tulsa Bancorp., Tulsa, First Nat. Bank & Trust Co., Tulsa, 1980-84; chmn., CEO First Nat. Bank and Trust Co., Tulsa, 1984-87; pres. The Bowen Co., 1987—; dir., v.p., CFO AAON, Inc., Tulsa, 1988—. Pres. Met. Tulsa Econ. Devel. Found., 1987-88—; chmn. Tulsa Area United Way, , 1986, campaign chmn., 1985. Lt. USNR, 1951-55. Mem. DeBorieu Club Inc. (Georgetown, S.C.), Phi Beta Kappa, Beta Gamma Sigma (pres., 1950-51). Home: 1484 Wallace Pate Dr Georgetown SC 29440-7185

BOWEN, WILLIAM GORDON, economist, educator, foundation administrator; b. Cin., Oct. 6, 1933; s. Albert A. and Bernice (Pomert) B.; m. Mary Ellen Maxwell, Aug. 25, 1956; children: David Alan, Karen Lee. BA, Denison U., 1955; PhD, Princeton U., 1958. Mem. faculty Princeton (N.J.) U., 1958-88, prof. econs., 1965-88, dir. grad. studies Woodrow Wilson Sch. Pub. and Internat. Affairs, 1964-66, provost, 1967-72, pres., 1972-88; pres. Andrew W. Mellon Found., N.Y.C., 1988—; bd. dirs. Merck and Co., Inc., Am. Express Co., Univ. Corp. for Advanced Internet Devel. Internet2; bd. overseers Tchrs. Ins. and Annuity Assn.-Coll. Ret. Equities Fund.; chmn., bd. dirs. JSTOR. Author: The Wage-Price Issue: A Theoretical Analysis, 1960, Wage Behavior in the Postwar Period: An Empirical Analysis, 1960, Economic Aspects of Education: Three Essays, 1964, (with W. J. Baumol) Performing Arts: The Economic Dilemma, 1966, (with T. A. Finegan) The Economics of Labor Force Participation, 1969, Ever the Teacher, 1987, (with J. A. Sosa) Prospects for Faculty in the Arts and Sciences, 1989, (with Neil L. Rudenstine) In Pursuit of the PhD, 1992, Inside the Boardroom: Governance by Directors and Trustees, 1994, (with T. Nygren, S. Turner, E. Duffy) The Charitable Nonprofits, 1994, (with Derek Bok) The Shape of the River: Long-Term Consequences of Considering Race in College and University Admissions, 1998. Trustee Ctr. for Advanced Study in Behavioral Scis., 1978-84, 89-92, Denison U., 1992—; regent emeritus Smithsonian Instn. Recipient Joseph Henry medal Smithsonian Instn., 1996. Mem. Am. Econs. Assn., Indsl. Rels. Rsch. Assn., Coun. on Fgn. Rels., Phi Beta Kappa. Office: Andrew W Mellon Found 140 E 62nd St New York NY 10021-8142

BOWEN, WILLIAM HARVEY, banker, lawyer; b. Altheimer, Ark., May 6, 1923; s. Robert James and Lois Ruth Bowen; m. Mary Constance Wanasek, Aug. 31, 1947; children: Cynthia Ruth Bowen Blanchard, William Scott, Mary Patricia Bowen Barker. Student, Henderson State Tchrs. Coll., 1941-42; LL.B., U. Ark., 1949; LL.M. in Taxation, NYU, 1950; postgrad., Stonier Grad. Sch. Banking, Rutgers U., 1974. Bar: Ark. 1949, U.S. Supreme Ct. 1950. Atty. adviser U.S. Tax Ct., Washington, 1950-52; spl. asst. to atty. gen. trial sect., tax div. Dept. Justice, Washington, 1952-54; ptnr. Smith, Williams, Friday & Bowen, Little Rock, Ark., 1954-71; pres., dir. Comml. Nat. Bank, Little Rock, Ark., 1971-75, pres., dir., chief exec. officer, 1975-81, chmn., 1981-83; pres., chief exec. officer 1st Comml. Bank N.A., Little Rock, Ark., 1983-90; chmn., chief exec. officer 1st Comml. Bank N.A., 1984-87, First Comml. Corp., 1984-90; chief of staff Gov. Bill Clinton, 1991-92; pres., CEO Healthsource Ark. Ventures, Inc., 1993-95; dean Sch. of Law U. Ark., Little Rock, 1995-97; mem. staff Stonier Grad. Sch. Banking U. Del., Newark, 1985—, bd. regents, 1977-81; mem. fed. adv. coun. Fed. Res. Bank, St. Louis, 1984-86; lectr. assemblies for bank dirs., So. Meth. U. Author: (with M. Moore) Arkansas Estate Planners Handbook, 1967. Trustee Ben J. Altheimer Found., Altheimer, Ark., 1973, Philander Smith Coll., Little Rock, 1968-80, Hendrix Coll., 1986-98, Drs. Hosp., U. Ark, Little Rock; chmn. bd. visitors U. Ark., 1979-80; state chmn. com. for employer support of N.G. and Res., nat. chmn., 1994-98; chmn. bd. Ark. Sci. and Tech. Authority, 1986-91; adv. council LWV; past chmn. Radio Free Europe Fund, Pulaski County United Fund. Served with USN, 1943-46, to lt. comdr. Res., ret. Named Little Rock Man of Yr. Ark. Dem., 1963; recipient Sales and Mktg. Exec. Man of Yr. award, 1963, Citizen-Lawyer of Yr. award Ark. Bar Found., 1971, Disting. Alumni award U. Ark., 1976. Mem. ABA (adv. com. to Treasury), Ark. Bankers Assn. (pres. 1982, chmn. legis. com. 1978-79), Am. Bankers Assn. (govt. relations council 1984—), Assn. Res. City Bankers, Ark. Bar Assn., Pulaski County Bar Assn., Beta Gamma Sigma, Sigma Alpha Epsilon, Delta Theta Phi . Methodist. Club: Little Rock, Country of Little Rock. Lodge: Masons. Home: 2200 Beechwood St Little Rock AR 72207-2024 Office: care First Comml Bank PO Box 1471 Little Rock AR 72203-1471

BOWEN, WILLIAM HENRY, dental researcher, dental educator; b. Enniscorthy, Ireland, Dec. 11, 1933; came to U.S., 1956, naturalized,; s. William H. and Pauline (McGrath) B.; m. Carole Barnes, Aug. 9, 1958 children—William, Deirdre, Kevin, David, Katherine. BDS, Nat. U. Ireland, Dublin, 1955; MSc, U. Rochester, N.Y., 1959; PhD, U. London, 1965; DSc, U. Ireland, Dublin, 1974; D Odontologiae (hon.), U. Goteborg, Sweden, 1995, U. Oslo, Norway, 1991; D Odontologiae (honoris causa), U. Umeå, Sweden, 1993; MD (honoris causa), Nat. U. Irleland, 1995. Diplomate Am. Bd. Dentistry, Inst. Medicine-NAS. Assoc. pvt. dental practice private dental practice, London, 1955-56; Quinten Hogg fellow Royal Coll. Surgeons, London, 1956-59, Nuffield Found. fellow, 1962-65, sr. research fellow, 1965-69, Sir Wilfred Fish fellow, 1969-73; acting chief caries prevention br. Nat. Inst. Dental Research, NIH, Bethesda, Md., 1973-79; chief Nat. Inst. Dental Research, NIH, Bethesda, MD, 1979-82; chmn. dental research U. Rochester, N.Y., 1982-95; dir. Cariology Ctr., Rochester, 1984-95. Fellow AAAS (sect. R-Dentistry, chair elect 1989, chair 1990); mem. European Orgn. Caries Rsch., Internat. Assn. Dental Rsch. (treas. 1982-88, v.p. 1988, pres. elect 1989, pres. 1990), Fedn. Dentaire Internationale, Inst. Medicine, Lab. Animal Sci. Assn., Zool. Soc. Roman Catholic. Home: 315 Victor Egypt Rd Victor NY 14564-9710 Office: U Rochester Ctr for Oral Biology 601 Elmwood Ave Rochester NY 14642-0001

BOWEN, WILLIAM JOSEPH, management consultant; b. N.Y.C., May 13, 1934; s. Edward F. and Mary Alice (Drooney) B.; children: William J., Timothy M., Priscilla A., Robert B.; m. Betsy Bass, Oct. 31, 1983. BS, Fordham U., 1956; MBA, NYU, 1963. Trainee Smith, Barney, N.Y.C., 1959-61; asst. v.p. Citicorp, N.Y.C., 1961-67; v.p. Hayden, Stone, N.Y.C., 1967-69; 1st v.p. Shearson Hammill, N.Y.C., 1969-73; assoc. Heidrick & Struggles, 1973-77, ptnr., 1977—; mgr. Heidrick & Struggles, Chgo., 1978-81, pres., CEO, 1981-83; vice chmn. Heidrick & Struggles, N.Y.C., Chgo., 1983—. Capt. USAF, 1956-59. Mem. Chgo. Club, Onwentsia Club, N.Y. Club, Marco Polo, Union League (N.Y.C.). Republican. Office: Heidrick & Struggles Inc Sears Tower 233 S Wacker Dr Ste 7000 Chicago IL 60606-6350

BOWEN-FORBES, JORGE COURTNEY, artist, author, poet; b. Queenstown, Guyana, May 16, 1937; came to U.S., 1966; s. Walter and Margarita V. (Forbes) Bowen. BA, Queens Coll., Eve Leary, Guyana, 1969; MFA, Chelsea (Eng.) Sch. Design, 1972. Comml. artist Guyana Litographic, Georgetown; art dir. Corbin Advt. Agy., Bridgetown, Barbados; tech. advisor Ministry of Info. and Culture, Georgetown; nat. juror Nat. Arts Club, N.Y.C., 1985, Nat. Soc. Painters in Casein and Acrylic. Major exhbns. include Expo 67, Can., Nat. Acad. Design, N.Y., Frye Mus., El Paso (Tex.) Mus., Wichita (Kans.) Centennial, Caribbean Festival of the Arts, Newark Mus.; 10-one-man exhbns. worldwide; works in collections including Nat. and Colgrain Collections, Guyana, El Paso Mus. Art, Kindercare Internat., Leon Loards Gallery, The McCreery Cummings Fine Art Collection, Bomani Gallery, San Francisco; poetry and articles pub. various jours.; author: Best Watercolors, 1996, Creative Watercolor, 1996; published in Best in Watercolor, Best in Oil Painting, Best in Acrylic Painting, Creative Watercolor, Splash 11, Best Contemporary Watercolors, American Poetry Annual. Recipient Silver medal of honor Allied Artists of N.Y., 1978, Gold medal of honor, 1975. Mem. Nat. Watercolor Soc. (signature mem.), Nat. Soc. Painters in Casein and Acrylics, Audubon Artists, Knickerbocker Artists (Gold Medal of Honor 1977, 79), Am. Watercolor Soc. (signature mem., High Winds medal 1984).

BOWENS, EMMA MARIE, elementary education educator; b. East New Market, Md., July 20, 1927; d. Cornelius Henry and Emma Flossie Helena (Lee) McGrath; m. Edison Bowens, Apr. 3, 1953; children: Edison Alfred, Elva Marie. BS in Edn., State Tchrs. Coll., Bowie, Md., 1948. Cert. advanced profl. elem. edn. and middle sch. H.S. core/math. tchr. Caroline County Bd. Edn., Denton, Md., 1948-49, asst. H.S. libr., 1948-49; elem. tchr. Dorchester County Bd. Edn., Hurlock, Md., 1949, 61, Church Creek, Md., 1950-51; elem. tchr. Dorchester County Bd. Edn., Cambridge and Hurlock, Md., 1962-90, ret., 1990; adv. com. Hurlock Elem. Parent Involvement, 1988-89; mem. discipline com. Dorchester County Bd. Edn., Cambridge, 1962-89; mem. crisis team Hurlock Elem. Sch., 1989-90; curriculum developer Dorchester County Bd. Edn., Cambridge, 1962-90; pvt. tutor, 1990—; vol. resource person, 1990—. Pres. North Dorchester H.S. PTA and Parent-Tchr.-Student Assn., Hurlock, 1972; leader 4-H Club, Hurlock, 1971-75; past dir., supt. ch. sch. United Meth. Ch., Hurlock; surrogate parent North Dorchester H.S., 1997—. Recipient Silver Clover Leadership award Coop. Extension Svc., U. Md., 1972, Leadership award Extension svc. 4-H and Youth, Cambridge, Md., 1973, Spirit of Dorchester County award, 1991, Recognition award Lockerman H.S., 1997; grantee NDEA, Towson State Coll., 1965. Mem. ASCD, Nat. Coun. Tchrs. English, Am. Assn. Ret. Persons, Md. Coun. Tchrs. Math., Internat. Reading Assn., Mid-Shore Reading Coun. (life, bldg. rep. 1989-90, newspaper edn. com., exec. planning com. 1993—, publicity com. 1993—, midshore coun.), Md. Congress Parents and Tchrs. (life, mem. parent involvement orgn. Dorchester County 1962-90), Nat. Coun. Tchrs. Math., Md. State Reading Assn. Dorchester County Ret. Tchrs. Assn. (co-chair newsletter, chair archives, sunshine com.), Md. Ret. Tchrs. Assn., Md. Sheriff's Assn. (hon.). Methodist. Avocations: reading, writing, nature hikes, artifacts, crossword/word search puzzles. Home: 4463 Preston Rd Hurlock MD 21643-3709

BOWENS, THELLA, senior aviation director; b. Mount Enterprise, Tex.; 2 children. BA, Barnard Coll, 1970; post grad., Texas Christian U. Budget adminstr. Dallas/Ft. Worth Internat. airport; dep. dir. of aviation Kansas City Internat. airport; sr. dir. of aviation San Diego Unified Port Dist., 1996—. Bd. dirs. george Washington Carver Neighborhood Ctr. and Day Care; mem. Lejardin Sr. Citizens Home; bd. dirs. San Diego United Way; mentor for Welfare to Work Program. Mem. Am. Assn. of Airport Execs., Econ. Steering Com. for Airports Coun. Internat. North Am., Natl. Forum for Black Pub. Adminstr. Avocations: tennis, reading hist. novels, enjoying arts and theatre productions. Office: San Diego Unified Port Dist San Diego Internat Airport PO Box 120488 San Diego CA 92112-0488

BOWER, ALLAN MAXWELL, lawyer; b. Oak Park, Ill., May 21, 1936; s. David Robert and Frances Emily Bower; m. Deborah Ann Rottmayer, Dec. 28, 1959. BS, U. Iowa, 1962; JD, U. Miami, Fla., 1968. Bar: Calif. 1969, U.S. Supreme Ct. 1979. Internat. aviation law practice L.A., 1969—; ptnr. Kern & Wooley, L.A., 1980-85, Bronson, Bronson & McKinnon, L.A., 1985-90, Lane Powell Spears Lubersky, L.A., 1990-99, Bailey & Marzano, Santa Monica, Calif., 1999—. Contbr. articles to profl. publs. Mem. ABA, L.A. Bar Assn., Lawyer-Pilots Bar Assn., Am. Judicature Soc., Am. Arbitration Assn. (nat. panel arbitrators), Alpha Tau Omega. Republican. Presbyterian. Fax: 310-392-8091. Office: Bailey & Marzano 2nd Fl 2828 Donald Douglas Loop N Santa Monica CA 90405-2959

BOWER, BEVERLY LYNNE, education educator; b. Washington, Sept. 10, 1951; d. James Theodore and Bettylou Colleen Johnson; m. Jack Rupert Bower, Jr., July 3, 1978. BS in Edn., U. Kans., 1973; MLS, Emporia (Kans.) State U., 1980; PhD, Fla. State U., 1992. Reading tchr. Lansing (Kans.) Jr. H.S., 1973-74; tchr. French and English Chillocote (Mo.) H.S., 1974-75, U.S. Dept. Defense Dependent Schs., Ft. Campbell, Taegu, Ky., S. Korea, 1975-80; libr., libr. adminstr. Pensacola (Fla.) Jr. Coll., 1980-92; prof. higher edn. U. S.C., Columbia, 1993-96, Fla. State U., Tallahassee, 1997—; cons. Tchr. Oppty. Programmers, Capetown, S. Africa, 1993-94, Fla. State Bd. of Comty. Colls., 1999. Contbr. articles to profl. jours. Bd. dirs. YWCA, Pensacola, Fla., 1988-89; participant Nat. Inst. for Leadership Devel., 1989; bd. dirs. Hardee Ctr. for Women in Higher Edn., Tallahassee, Fla., 1997—. Recipient Nat. Merit scholarship, 1969, University fellowship Fla. State U., Tallahassee, 1990, Tchg. Excellence award Mortar Bd., U. S.C., Columbia, 1995. Mem. Am. Edni. Rsch. Assn., Assn. for Study Higher Edn. (program com. 1998), Coun. for Study Comty. Colls. (bd. dirs. 1994—). E-mail: bower@coe.fsu.edu. Office: Fla State U 113 Stone Bldg Tallahassee FL 32306-4452

BOWER, CATHERINE DOWNES, communications and public relations executive; b. Balt., Dec. 29, 1947; m. Réjean Pierre Proulx, Apr. 28, 1990. BA, Kent State U., 1969. Editor East Ohio Gas Co., Cleve., 1971-74; editor Personnel Administrator mag., Berea, Ohio, 1974-79, dir. communications, 1979-84; v.p. communications, pub. Am. Soc. Pers. Adminstrn. (name Soc. Human Resource Mgmt.), Alexandria, 1984-86; v.p. communications and pub. relations Am. Soc. Pers. Adminstrn. (name Soc. Human Resource Mgmt.), Alexandria, Va., 1986-91; sr. ptnr. Tecker Cons., Trenton, N.J., 1991-96, prin. ptnr., 1996—; pres. Cate Bower Communications, Alexandria and West River, Md., 1991—; project dir. Work in the 21st Century, 1984. Editor: Work Life Visions, 1987. Pres. Oak Cluster Community Council, Alexandria, 1985-89. Recipient Monument award Great Washington Soc. Assn. Execs., 1996. Fellow Am. Soc. Assn. Execs. (cert.; vice chmn. comms. sect. coun. 1986-87, chmn. 1987-88, planning com. 1989-91, bd. dirs. Found.

1989-93, chair rsch. com. 1995-96, Best Pub. Rels. Program award 1984); mem. Internat. Assn. Bus. Communicators (pres. Cleve. chpt. 1974), Greater Washington Soc. Assn. Execs. (chmn. visibility task force 1994-95, Monument award 1996), West River Sailing Club. Avocations: sailing, gardening. Home and Office: Cate Bower Comms 5109 Holly Dr West River MD 20778-9744

BOWER, DOUGLAS WILLIAM, pastoral counselor, psychotherapist, clergyman; b. Niagara Falls, N.Y., Jan. 6, 1948; s. Charles Henry Bower and Phyllis June (Rank) Ayres; m. Cheryl Stewart, May 25, 1980; children: Katherine Elizabeth, Erin Colleen. AA, Manatee Jr. Coll., Bradenton, Fla., 1969; BS, Oglethorpe U., 1972; PhD, U. Ga., 1989. RN, Ga.; ordained to ministry United Meth. Ch., 1981; cert. counselor, Ga. Nurse Northside Hosp., Atlanta, 1970-80; assoc. pastor 1st United Meth. Ch., Griffin, Ga., 1980-82; pastor, pastoral counselor Oconee Street United Meth. Ch., Athens, Ga., 1982-86; dir. Counseling Ministries, Athens, 1986—. Contbr. articles to profl. jours. Active Oglethorpe County Sr. Citizens Adv. Coun., United Way of N.E. Ga., Oglethorpe County Rep. Party, U. Ga. Nat. Alumni Assn. Mem. Ga. Sheriffs Assn. (hon.), Person-Centered Assn., Kiwanis (Athens chpt.). Avocations: music, walking, reading. Office: Counseling Ministries PO Box 209 Crawford GA 30630-0209 *While we may not make an impact on the world, we can and do make an impact on the immediate world around and within us. Persistence in maintaining faith, even in the face of adversity, makes a powerful impact on our immediate world.*

BOWER, FAY LOUISE, retired academic administrator, nursing educator; b. San Francisco, Sept. 10, 1929; d. James Joseph and Emily Clare (Andrews) Saitta; children: R. David, Carol Bower Tomei, Dennis James, Thomas John. BS with honors, San Jose State Coll., 1965; MSN, U. Calif., 1966, DNSc, 1978. Cert. pub. health nurse, sch. nurse, Calif. Office nurse Dr. William Grannis, Palo Alto, Calif., 1950-55; staff nurse Stanford Hosp., 1964-72; asst. prof. San Jose (Calif.) State U., 1966-70, assoc. prof., 1970-74, prof., 1974-82, coord. grad. program in nursing, 1977-78, chairperson dept. nursing, 1978-82; dean U. San Francisco, 1982-89, v.p. acad. affairs, 1988-89, dir. univ. planning and instl. rsch., 1989-91; pres. Clarkson Coll., 1991-97; spkr., cons. univs.; vis. prof. Harding Coll., 1977, U. Miss., 1976; lectr. U. Calif., San Francisco, 1975. Author: (with Em O. Bevis) Fundamentals of Nursing Practice: Concepts, Roles and Functions, 1978, (with Margaret Jacobson) Community Health Nursing, 1978, The Process of Planning Nursing Care, 3d edit., 1982, (with Mae Timmons) Medical Surgical Nursing, 1995, (with others) Concepts & Issues in Nursing, 3d edit., 1996, Creating Nursings' Features: Issues, Opportunities & Challenges, 1999; author: Approaches to Teaching Primary Care, 1981, The Newman Systems Model: Application to Nursing Education and Practice, 1982, Managing a Nursing Shortage: A Guide to Recruitment and Retention, 1989, Cracking the Wall: Women in Higher Education Administration, 1993, Nurses Taking the Lead..., 1999; contbr. articles to profl. jours. Fellow Am. Acad. Nursing; mem. Nurses Assn., APHA (Calif. chpt.), Nat. League for Nursing (pres. 1989-92), Western Gerontol. Assn., Sigma Theta Tau (internat. pres. 1993-95), Jesuit Deans in Nursing (chair 1982-85), Rotary (Omaha). Democrat. Roman Catholic. Home: 1457 Indianhead Cir Clayton CA 94517-1239

BOWER, GLEN LANDIS, lawyer; b. Highland, Ill., Jan. 16, 1949; s. Ray Landis and Evelyn Ferne (Ragland) B. BA, So. Ill. U., 1971; JD with honors, Ill. Inst. Tech., 1974. Bar: Ill. 1974, U.S. Ct. Mil. Appeals 1975, U.S. Ct. Appeals (7th cir.) 1976, U.S. Dist Ct. (so. dist.) Ill. 1977, U.S. Dist. Ct. (cen. dist.) Ill. 1992, U.S. Supreme Ct. 1978, U.S. Tax Ct. 1984, U.S. Ct. Claims 1986, U.S. Dist. Ct. (no. dist.) Ill. 1994, U.S. Ct. Veterans Appeals 1995. Sole practice Effingham, Ill., 1974-83; prosecutor Effingham County, Ill., 1976-79; mem. Ill. House of Reps., Springfield, 1979-83; asst. dir., gen. counsel Ill. Dept. Revenue, Springfield, Ill., 1983-90; Presdl. appointed chmn. U.S. Railroad Retirement Bd., Chgo., 1990-97; asst. to Ill. Sec. of State, Chgo., 1998-99; apptd. dir. revenue State of Ill., 1999—; mil. aide to Gov. of Ill.; liaison mem. Adminstrv. Conf. of U.S., 1991-95; mem. Nat. Adv. Com. for Juvenile Justice and Delinquency Prevention, Washington, 1976-80, U.S. Econ. Adv. Bd. of U.S. Dept. Commerce, Washington, 1981-85, Ill. Gen. Assembly State Adv. Com. on Cir. Ct. Fin., Springfield, 1984; mem. Revenue Bd. Appeals, Chgo., 1985-87, chmn., 1986-87; mem. Com. of 50 on Ill. Constn., 1987-88; active Am. Coun. Young Polit. Leaders to China, 1988. Co-editor: Handbook on State Taxation, 1991; contbr. articles to profl. jours. Alt. del. Rep. Nat. Conv., Miami Beach, Fla., 1972, Rep. Nat. Conv., New Orleans, 1988, Rep. Nat. Conv. Houston, 1992; vice chmn. Effingham County Rep. Ctrl. Com., Ill., 1976-90; bd. dirs. Dana-Thomas House Found., Springfield, Ill., 1989-90, So. Ill. U. at Carbondale Found., 1993—, pres.'s coun.; trustee McKendree Coll., Lebanon, Ill., 1978-81; chmn. State of Ill. Organ and Tissue Donors Adv. Bd., 1993-98. Lt. col. USAFR, 1974—. Recipient The Univ. Disting. Svc. award, 1971, Recognition citation Am. Legion, 1980, Outstanding Svc. cert. to tchg. profession Ill. Edn. Assn., 1981, Disting. Svc. award Am. Vets., 1980, 82, Presdl. citation Navy League U.S., 1981, Constitution award Mus. of Our Nat. Heritage, 1988, Silver Good Citizenship medal Ill. Soc. SAR, 1990, Profl. Achievement award Ill. Inst. Tech., 1993, Friend of History award Ill. State Hist. Soc., 1994, Alumni Achievement award So. Ill. U., 1994; named Outstanding Freshman Legislator, Ill. Edn. Assn., 1980, Legislator of Yr., Ill. Assn. Rehab. Socs., 1981, 82, One of 10 Dels. to China, Am. Coun. Young Polit. Leaders, 1988. Fellow Ill. Bar Found. (life), Am. Bar Found. (life); mem. ABA (adminstrv. practice com. of taxation sect., ct. procedure com., mem. exec. com. nat. assn. state tax bar sects., employment taxes com. 1990), Fed. Bar Assn., Fed. Cir. Bar Assn., Rep. Nat. Lawyers Assn., Ill. State Bar Assn. (sec. state taxation sect. coun. 1987-88, vice-chair 1988-89, chair 1989-90, labor law sect. coun. 1976-77, sect. coun. on employee benefits 1991-98), Effingham County Bar Assn. (sec. 1976-77, pres. 1983-84), Chgo. Bar Assn., Nat. Assn. Tax Adminstrs. (vice chmn. attys. sect. 1985-86, 88-89, chmn. 1986-88), Nat. Conf. Spl. Ct. Judges, Effingham County Old Settlers Assn. (pres., bd. dirs. 1983-86), Ill. State Hist. Soc., (v.p. 1979-81, bd. dirs. exec. com. 1983-86, Ralph C. Francis award 1967), Effingham Regional Hist. Soc., Small Bus. Adminstrn. Adv. Coun. (bd. dirs. 1973-77), Effingham County Mental Health Assn. (pub. affairs com. 1977-78), U.S. Capitol Hist. Soc. (charter), Abraham Lincoln Assn., Capitol Hill Club, Army and Navy Club Washington D.C., U.S. Supreme Ct. Hist. Soc., The Nat. Sojourners, Burgesses of Colonial Williamsburg (charter), Am. coun. of Young Political leaders, Art Institute of Chgo., Smithsonian Assocs., So. Ill. U. Carbondale Found. (bd. dirs. 1993—), Field Mus. of Natural History, So. Ill. Univ. Alumni Assn. (life), Am. Legion, Res. Officers Assn., Judge Advs. Assn., Air Force Assn., Shriners, Kiwanis (pres. 1977-78), Sons of Am. Revolution, Phi Alpha Delta (dist. justice Cen. Ill. and Ind. 1988-92). Methodist. Home: 1 E Scott St Apt 709 Chicago IL 60610-5244 Office: Ill Dept Revenue Dir's Office 100 W Randolph St Ste 7-375 Chicago IL 60601 also: Ill Dept Revenue Dir's Office 101 W Jefferson St Springfield IL 62702

BOWER, JEAN RAMSAY, lawyer, writer; b. N.Y.C., Nov. 25, 1935; d. Claude Barnett and Myrtle Marie (Scott) Ramsay; m. Ward Swift Just, Jan. 31, 1957 (div. 1966); children: Jennifer Ramsay, Julia Barnett; m. Robert Turrell Bower, June 12, 1971 (dec. June 1990). AB, Vassar Coll., 1957; JD, Georgetown U., 1970. Bar: D.C. 1970. Exec. dir. D.C. Dem. Ctrl. Com., Washington, 1969-71; pvt. practice Washington, 1971-78, 94—; dir. Counsel of Child Abuse and Neglect Office D.C. Superior Ct., 1978-94; Mem. Mayor's Com. on Child Abuse and Neglect, 1973-94, vice chmn., 1975-79; mem. Family Div. Rules Adv. Com., 1977-94; pres., bd. dirs. C.B. Ramsay Found., 1984—; cons. child welfare issues, writer. Active D.C. Child Fatality Rev. Com., 1992—; bd. dirs. Friends D.C. Superior Ct., 1994—, Family & Child Svcs., D.C., 1995—; mem. Folger poetry bd. Folger Shakespeare Libr., 1998—. Named Washingtonian of the Yr. Washington Mag., 1978. Mem. Women's Bar Assn. (bd. dirs. 1993-96, found. 1986-91, Woman Lawyer of Yr. 1986), D.C. Bar Assn. (election bd. 1994-96, Beatrice Rosenberg award 1994), Women's Bar Assn. Found. (bd. dirs. 1986-91).

BOWER, JOSEPH LYON, business administration educator; b. N.Y.C., Sept. 21, 1938; s. Morris L. and Florence (Turitz) B.; m. Nancy Milender, Feb. 16, 1958; children: Jonathan, Deborah. AB, Harvard U., 1959, MBA, 1961, D Bus. Adminstrn., 1963. Asst. prof. Grad. Sch. Bus. Adminstrn. Harvard U., Boston, 1963-68, assoc. prof. Grad. Sch. Bus. Adminstrn., 1968-71, Donald K. David prof. bus. adminstrn. Grad. Sch. Bus. Adminstrn., 1972—, sr. assoc. dean for external rels. Grad. Sch. Bus. Adminstrn., 1986-89, chmn. doctoral programs, dir. of rsch. Grad. Sch. Bus. Adminstrn., 1989-95; faculty mem. John F. Kennedy Sch. Govt. Harvard U., Cambridge, Mass., 1969—; bd. dirs. Anika Therapeutics Inc., Woburn, Mass., Brown Shoe Inc., St. Louis, Sonesta Internat. Hotels Corp., Boston, ML-Lee Acquisition Fund, L.P., Boston, New Am. High Income Fund, Boston; chair gen. mgr. program Grad. Sch. Bus. Adminstrn., 1996—. Author: Managing Resource Allocation Process, 1971 (McKinsey Found. award 1971), Two Faces of Management, 1983, When Markets Quake, 1986; co-author: Public Management: Text and Cases, 1978, Business Policy: Text and Cases, 7th edit., 1991, Business Policy: Managing Strategic Processes, 8th edit., 1995. Trustee Lincoln (Mass.) Found., 1968—, vice chair New Eng. Conservatory Music, Boston, 1984—; trustee DeCordova and Dana Mus. and Pk., Lincoln, 1987—. Co-recipient (with C.M. Christensen) McKinsey Found. award, 1995. Mem. Am. Econ. Assn., Coun. Fgn. Rels., St. Botolph Club (Boston), Harvard Club (N.Y.C.). Avocations: tennis, boating. Office: Harvard U Grad Sch Bus Adminstrn Morgan # 467 Boston MA 02163

BOWER, KATHLEEN ANNE, nurse consultant; b. Detroit, Oct. 9, 1946; d. Richard Edward and Edith M. (Enright) B. BSN, Georgetown U., 1968; MSN, Boston Coll., 1972; DNSc, Boston U., 1991. Staff nurse NYU Med. Ctr., N.Y.C., 1968-70; nurse leader, vice chair nursing New Eng. Med. Ctr., Boston, 1972-89; prin. The Ctr. for Nursing Case Mgmt., South Natick, Mass., 1989-91; co-owner, prin. The Ctr. for Case Mgmt., South Natick, Mass., 1991—. Author: Case Management by Nurses, 1991; contbr. articles to profl. jours. Mem. ANA, Am. Orgn. Nurse Execs., Mass. Orgn. Nurse Execs., Sigma Theta Tau. Office: Ctr for Case Mgmt 6 Pleasant St Natick MA 01760

BOWER, KENNETH FRANCIS, electrical engineer; b. Fostoria, Ohio, June 16, 1942; s. Carl Albert and Carmia June (Butzier) B.; m. Vicki Marie Lambert, Feb. 14, 1975; children: Candi Marie, Jillian June, Brett Kenneth, Michael Courtland, Daniel David. BSEE, Purdue U., 1965. Registered profl. engr., Ohio, Fla. Aerospace engr. NASA Manned Spacecraft Ops., Kennedy Space Center, Fla., 1965-67, NASA Unmanned Launch Ops., Kennedy Space Center, 1967-73; systems engr. Cin. Electronics, 1973-76; programmer AMF, Vandalia, Ohio, 1976-77, Access Corp., Cin., 1977-78; mgr. GTE Compact, Cin., Anaheim, Calif., 1978-81; cons. Telos Cons. Svcs., Hughes Aerospace, Irvine, Calif., 1982-83, Telos Fed. Systems, Jet Propulsion Lab., Pasadena, Calif., 1983-86; lead engr. GE Aircraft Engines, Cin., 1987-93; propr. software cons. bus. Quality Used Profls., Batavia, Ohio, 1993-96, pres., chmn. bd. dirs., 1996—; also chmn. bd. dirs. Quality Used Profls., Inc.; v.p., bd. dirs. Gedanken Systems, Inc., Cin. Patentee in field. Bd. trustees First Ch. of God, Rubidoux, Calif., 1982-83, 86. Named Father of Yr. First Ch. of God, Cin., 1978. Mem. Mensa (local sec. 1963-83), Purdue Alumnus. Democrat. Avocations: judo, designing computerized games. Home: 248 Seton Ct Batavia OH 45103-5233 Office: PO Box 97 Batavia OH 45103-0097

BOWER, MARILYN KAY, landscape artist; b. June 24, 1941. *Ms. Bower and her husband, Arlo Raymond, have a one daughter, Wendy Lynn Swearingen, who is currently a Nurse Practitioner in the Puget Sound area of Washington state. Her son, Taylor Austin Swearingen, completes the family. Her great grandparents on both sides of the family, the Beils, Swensons and Hensleys, were early settlers of Kansas. This plains heritage and the experience of having lived in four of the Great Plains states (Kansas, Nebraska, Oklahoma and Texas), makes the expanses of the prairie an important part of her work.* BS magna cum laude, Kans. State U., 1963. Group exhibits include Spiva Art Ctr., Joplin, Mo., 1985, Joslyn Art Mus., Omaha, 1986, Wichita (Kans.) Art Assn., 1988, 90, Am. Artist mag. landscape competition, 1990, Oil Painters Am., Long Grove, Ill., 1994; represented in permanent collections Enron Corp., Omaha, Peru (Nebr.) State Coll., Burlington No. R.R., Overland Park, Kans., Toyota Corp., L.A., Langworthy Collection, Seward, Nebr.; work represented in S.W. Art, Impact—The Art of Nebraska Women. Named to Top 200 paintings of nat. parks, Arts for Parks, 1990, 92, 96, 98, to Top 100, 1997.

BOWER, RICHARD JAMES, minister; b. Somerville, N.J., June 9, 1939; s. Oneil A. and Mildred R. (Goss) B.; m. Helen Ann Cheek, Dec. 29, 1962 (div. 1985); 1 child, Christopher Scott. Student, Sorbonne, Paris, 1959-60; B.A., Wesleyan U., 1961; M.Div., Drew U., Madison, N.J., 1965; student, Oxford U., Eng., 1983; DD, Piedmont Coll., 1999. Ordained to ministry, Congregational Christian Ch., 1965. Minister Community Congl. Ch., Kewaunee, Wis., 1965-67; sr. minister Congl. Ch., Bound Brook, N.J., 1967-78, Congl. Ch. of the Chimes, Sherman Oaks, Calif., 1978-95; preaching min. Congl. Ch. Messiah, L.A., 1995-96; mem. exec. com., dir. Nat. Assn. Congl. Christian Chs., 1973-77, chmn., 1976-77,asst. moderator, 1981-82, moderator, 1982-83, exec. search com., 1990-91, nominating com., 1991-93, chmn., 1992-93; mem. World Christian Rels. Commn., 1993-97. Appeared on TV programs; contbr. poetry and articles to periodicals. Organizer, pres. Am. Field Service, Kewaunee, 1966-67; dir. Children's Bur., Los Angeles, 1981-88; bd. fellows Hollywood Congl. Ctr., 1979-82; bd. dirs. Heritage Playhouse, 1986-96. Recipient Citation for Disting. Svc., Nat. Assn. Congl. Christian Chs., 1997. Mem. Cal-West Assn. (dir., moderator 1986-87). Republican. Lodge: Bound Brook Rotary (pres. 1975-76). Home: 365 W Alameda Ave Apt 302 Burbank CA 91506-3339

BOWER, RICHARD STUART, economist, educator; b. N.Y.C., Aug. 1, 1928; s. Jacob and Elsie (Vander Beugle) B.; m. Dorothy Ann Hagberg, June 23, 1953; children—Gari Ellen, Laura Jane, Nancy Lynne. A.B., Kenyon Coll., 1949; M.B.A., Columbia, 1955; Ph.D., Cornell U., 1962. Instr. econs. Kenyon Coll., 1949-50, Alfred U., 1955-57; asst. prof. econs. and bus. Vanderbilt U., 1959-62; prof. bus. econs. Dartmouth, 1972-95; ptnr. Bower Rohr and Assocs., Hanover, N.H., 1981—. Author: Investment and Liquidity: A Case Study of Clay Construction Products, 1965; Contbr. articles to profl. jours. Served with USNR, 1951-55. Mem. Am. Econ. Assn., Am. Finance Assn., Phi Beta Kappa, Beta Gamma Sigma, Phi Kappa Phi. Democrat. Jewish. Home: South Esker Hanover NH 03755 Office: Bower Rohr and Assocs Wheeler Professional Park West Lebanon NH 03784-3121

BOWER, ROY DONALD, minister, counselor; b. Pitts., June 20, 1939; s. Roy Clare and Evelyn June (Moorhead) B.; m. Sandra M. Daugherty, Mar. 16, 1963 (dec. 1976); children: Christine, Roy, Donald, Kathleen; m. Robin Jeanette Bird, Aug. 20, 1976; children: Daniel, Robin, William, Renée. Student, Indiana U. Pa., 1958, Geneva Coll., 1959-61; BS in Edn., Slippery Rock U., 1972; ThM, Am. Bible Coll., 1980; DD, Trinity Hall Sem., 1988; cert., Inst. Bibl. Studies, 1996. Ordained to ministry Ind. Christian Chs. Internat., 1970; cert. Christian counselor. Counselor La Casa Contenta, Colorado Springs, Colo., 1976-78; therapist Giles Inst., Colorado Springs, 1978-79; counselor Cheyenne Village, Manitou Springs, Colo., 1979-80, Tutoring and Counseling Svcs., Confluence, Pa., 1981—; therapist Laurel Springs Ctr. Human Svcs., Somerset, Pa., 1998—; resource counselor Family Rsch. Coun., Washington, 1985—; manuscript reviewer Nat. Coun. Social Studies, Washington, 1987; advisor Am. Pub. Welfare Assn., Chgo., 1970; rsch. theologian Ref. Faith Ctr., Confluence, Pa., 1986—, dir., 1986—; pres. Confluence Area Ministerium, 1986. Book reviewer Pastoral Counsel Newsletter, 1986—. Founder Yough Valley Symposium, Confluence, 1982—; mem. Western Pa. Conservancy, Pitts., 1980—; 1st lt. CAP, Scottdale, Pa., 1982—; state constable Somerset County Pa. Ct., 1988—; vol. talent bank Am. Assn. Ret. Persons, 1996. Recipient citation Dept. Social Svcs., El Paso County, Colo., 1975, Certs. of Merit ARC, Johnstown, Pa., 1987, Am. Cancer Soc., Somerset, Pa., 1990; Menninger Found. fellow, 1984—. Mem. United Assn. christian Counselors Internat., Am. Assn. Family Counselors, Nat. Christian Counselors Assn., Am. Assn. Christian Counselors, Guild of Clergy Counselors (Award of Excellence 1991), Am. Fedn. Police (state v.p. 1991—), Pa. State Constables Assn. Democrat. Avocations: philately, nature study, numismatics, tennis. Home and Office: Tutoring and Counseling Svc 609 Oden St Confluence PA 15424-1033 *Humanity's limited and created free will to think or to act pales miserably when compared to the completely free will of the sovereign Creator who foreordains all that comes to pass in the universe.*

BOWER, RUTH LAWTHER, retired mathematics educator; b. Bellaire, Ohio, Nov. 17, 1917; d. James Hood and Mary Blanche (Studebaker) Lawther; (widowed); 1 child, Bruce Alan. BA, Wooster (Ohio) Coll., 1939; EdS, Fla. Atlantic U., 1974, EdD, 1976. Cert. tchr., Fla. Cost acct. Peasley Constrn., New London, Conn., 1942-43; with Palm Beach County Sch. System, West Palm Beach, Fla., 1964-74, 74-85, chmn. math. dept., 1974-78, maths. cons., 1978-85; prof. maths. Palm Beach Atlantic Coll., West Palm Beach, 1985-94; adj. prof. math. Fla. Atlantic U., Boca Raton, 1965-85; prin. summer sch. Palm Beach County Schs., West Palm Beach, 1971, 72; speaker in field. Developer math. games Equivo, NOC, Add-In and others, 1971—; co-author: Individualizing Mathematics Series, 1970-71. Trustee Admiralty Bank, Juno Beach, Fla. Named Tchr. of the Yr., Fla. Math. Tchrs. Assn., 1977. Mem. Nat. Coun. Tchrs. of Maths., Math. Assn. Am., Phi Delta Kappa, Fibonacci Assn. Address: #532 11381 Prosperity Farms Rd Palm Beach Gardens FL 33410-3459

BOWER, SHELLEY ANN, business management consultant; b. Catskill, N.Y., Jan. 31, 1954; d. Edward Philip and Antoinette (Post) B.; m. Richard D. Connors, Aug. 28, 1976 (div. Mar. 1984). BA, Mich. Technol. U., 1977; JD, Detroit Coll., 1984. Bar: N.Y. Coord. Cadillac Motorcar, Detroit, 1980-84, employee in tng., 1984-85, supr. EEO, 1985-86; divsn. mgr. property profl. Saugerties, N.Y., 1986-88; engrng. tech., dir. corp. tng. and program adminstrn. Troy, Mich., 1988-92; cons. Electronic Data Syss., Southfield, Mich., 1992-95; dir. planning & devel., corp. counsel C.T. Male Assocs., PC, Latham, N.Y., 1995-96; prin. Oracle Corp., 1996-97; sr. cons. IBM Global Cons. Svcs. Mfg. Industries, White Plains, N.Y., 1997—. Mem. NAFE, N.Y. State Bar Assn. Avocations: skiing, hiking.

BOWER, WARD ALAN, management consultant, lawyer; b. Carlisle, Pa., Feb. 10, 1947; s. Dale Luther and Margaret Louise (Chapman) B.; m. Linda Elliott; children: Miles Robert, Chase Batchelor, Reid Alan, Seth Elliott. BA in Econs., Bucknell U., 1969; JD, Pa. State U., 1975. Bar: Pa. 1975. Group pension adminstr. Prudential ins. Co., Newark, 1969-70; methods analyst Liberty Mut. Ins. Co., Boston, 1972; prin. Altman Weil, Inc., Newton Square, Pa., 1977—; pres. Altman Weil, Inc., Newton Square, 1989—, also dir. Author: (with Frank Arentowicz, Jr.) Law Office Automation and Technology, 1980. Trustee Dickinson Sch. Law of Pa. State U., 1994—. With U.S. Army, 1970-71. Recipient Outstanding Alumni award Dickinson Sch. Law, 1997. Fellow Am. Bar Found., Coll. of Law Practice Mgmt.; mem. ABA (law practice mgmt. sect. divsn. chair 1986-92, coun. 1990-94), Internat. Bar Assn. (chair com. practice mgmt. and tech. 1992-96, standing com. on multidisciplinary practices 1996—, coun. sect. on legal practice 1996—), Pa. Bar Assn. Office: Altman Weil Inc PO Box 625 Two Campus Blvd Newtown Square PA 19073

BOWERFIND, EDGAR SIHLER, JR., physician, medical administrator; b. Cleve., May 7, 1924; s. Edgar Sihler and Edna (Strong) B.; m. Maria Washington Tucker, Apr. 28, 1956; children—Edgar Sihler III, Ellis Tucker, Jane Strong, William Minor Lile. Student, Creighton U. Med. Sch., 1945-47; M.D., Western Res. U., 1949. Diplomate Am. Bd. Internal Medicine. Intern Univ. Hosps. of Cleve., 1950-51, resident in medicine, 1954-56; practice medicine specializing in internal medicine Cleve., 1957-92; mem. faculty Case Western Res. U. Sch. Medicine, Cleve., 1956-92, asst. prof. medicine, 1965-92, dir. health clinics, utilization rev., 1965-92, asst. prof. emeritus, 1992—; chief med. services Horizon Ctr. Hosp., Cleve., 1981-83; sec. Citizens Commn. on Grad. Med. Edn., 1964-66. Sub-deacon Episcopal Diocese Ohio, 1970—; trustee The Sihler Mental Health Found. Served with AUS, 1943-46, to capt. USAF, 1951-53. Decorated Bronze Star; Ogelbay fellow in medicine U. Hosps. Cleve., 1955-56. Club: Farmington Country (Charlottesville, Va.). Home: 2373 Demington Dr Cleveland OH 44106-3617

BOWERING, GEORGE HARRY, writer, English literature educator; b. Penticton, B.C., Can., Dec. 1, 1936; s. Ewart Harry and Pearl Patricia (Brinson) B.; m. Angela May Luoma, Dec. 14, 1962; 1 dau., Thea Claire. Student, Victoria Coll., 1953-54; BA, U. B.C., 1960, MA, 1963; postgrad., U. Western Ont., 1966-67. Asst. prof. Am. lit. U. Calgary, 1963-66; writer in residence Sir George Williams U., Montreal, Que., 1967-68; asst. prof. Sir George Williams U., 1968-71; prof. Simon Fraser U., Burnaby, B.C., 1972—. Author: Mirror on the Floor, 1967, Autobiology, 1972, Flycatcher and Other Stories, 1974, Concentric Circles, 1977, A Short Sad Book, 1977, Protective Footwear, 1978, Another Mouth, 1979, Burning Water, 1980, A Place to Die, 1983, Caprice, 1987, Harry's Fragments, 1990, The Rain Barrel, 1994, Shoot!, 1994, Parents From Space, 1994, Piccolo Mondo, 1998, Diamondback Dog, 1998; poetry Points on the Grid, 1964, The Man in Yellow Boots, 1965, The Silver Wire, 1966, Rocky Mountain Foot, 1968, The Gangs of Kosmos, 1969, Touch, 1971, In the Flesh, 1973, The Catch, 1976, Particular Accidents: Selected Poems, 1981, Smoking Mirror, 1984, Kerrisdale Elegies, 1984, 71 Poems for People, 1985, Delayed Mercy, 1986, Sticks & Stones, 1989, Quarters, 1991, Urban Snow, 1992, George Bowering Selected, 1993, The Moustache, 1993, Blonds On Bikes, 1997; (essays) The Mask in Place, 1982, A Way with Words, 1982, Craft Slices, 1985, Errata, 1988, Imaginary Hand, 1988, Bowering's B.C., (history); editor Taking the Field: The Best of Baseball Fiction, 1990, 92, Likely Stories: A Postmodern Sampler, 1992. Served with RCAF, 1954-57. Mem. Assn. Can. TV and Radio Artists. Home: 2499 W 37th Ave, Vancouver, BC Canada V6M 1P4

BOWERMAN, ANN LOUISE, author, genealogist, educator; b. Branch County, Mich., June 4, 1933; d. George Allen and Mary (Thomas) Hubbard; m. Virgil Lee Bowerman, June 4, 1954 (div. 1977); children: William Lee, Sally Ann; m. Virgil Wayne Dunkel, Jr., May 23, 1987 (div. Dec. 1996). BA, Western Mich. U., 1966, MSLS, 1971, MA, 1976. Cert. tchr. K-8, Mich., libr. sci. Tchr. Bethel #6 Sch. Dist., Coldwater, Mich., 1951-53; tchr. kindergarten Union City (Mich.) Schs., 1963-64; children's libr. Sturgis (Mich.) Pub. Libr., 1971-72; libr./media specialist Coldwater H.S., 1972-91; mem. programming com., mem. ann. scholarships telethon com., camera staff, video editor Cable TV Channel 31, Coldwater, 1983-90. Author: The Bater Book, 1987, A Bowerman Family History, 1998, Historic Howe, Indiana Walking Tour, 1998, The William (6) Bowerman Family of Conneaut Township, 1998; co-author: Recommendations for High School Media Centers in Michigan, 1980 (booklet); contbr. articles to profl. jours. Mem., chair governing bd. Woodlands Libr. Coop., Albion, Mich., 1973-74, 83-86; adv. coun. Calhoun and Branch Counties Regional Ednl. Media Ctr., Marshall, Mich., 1972-91; com. mem. So. Mich. Region of Coop., Albion, 1989-91; leader All Around 4-H Club, Union City, 1954-74; mem. Sullivan Lady's Aid Soc., Union City, 1955-74, Twin Lakes Cmty. Assn., 1997—; chair winter program com. Tibbits Arts Found., Coldwater, 1980-90; mem. Coldwater Hist. Preservation Assn., 1978-86; del. Mich. Rep. State Conv., Detroit, 1986; candidate for Branch County Commr., Coldwater, 1988; mem. Mich. Assn. for Computer Users in Learning, 1975-91; mem. cultural arts com., mem. walking tour com. Howe (Ind.) Cmty. Assn., 1996—. Recipient Cert. of Appreciation, Mich. Assn. for Media in Edn., 1980, 91, Golden Apple Retirement award Coldwater H.S., 1991. Mem. U.S. Tennis Assn., Am. Assn. Ret. People, Soc. of Genealogists (London), New England Hist. Geneal. Soc., Descendants of Founders of Ancient Windsor, Ctrl. N.Y. Geneal. Soc., DAR (good citizen selection com., treas. Coldwater br. 1997-99), Mich. Assn. Ret. Sch. Pers., Schenectady County Hist. Soc., Old Brutus Hist. Soc., Union City Geneal. Soc., St. Joseph County Hist. Soc. (advisor to Land Office Mus. com. 1997-99), Crawford County Geneal. Soc., Coldwater Edn. Assn. (sec. 1980-90), Beta Phi Mu. Avocations: travel, coin collecting, tennis. Home: 1820 W 600 N Howe IN 46746-9406

BOWERMAN, RICHARD HENRY, utility company executive, lawyer; b. Apr. 29, 1917; s. Arthur Lewis and Constance Dorothea (Riehman) B.; m. Frances Annette Whitney, Mar. 7, 1942; children: Judith Condon, Richard Whitney Bowerman, Frances B. Gingrich. BA, Yale U., 1939, LLB, 1942; LLD, U. New Haven, 1982. Bar: Conn. 1946. Assoc. Gumbart, Corbin, Tyler & Cooper, New Haven, 1946-69; ptnr. Gumbart, Corbin, Tyler, Cooper and Tyler, Cooper, Grant, Bowerman & Keefe, New Haven, 1949-69; pres., chmn., CEO Conn. Energy Corp. & So. Conn. Gas Co., New Haven, 1969-80, chmn. bd., 1972-88, pres., 1988; chmn. sci. Park Devel. Corp., New Haven, 1981-94; bd. dirs. Conn. Agrl. Sta. Judge Mcpl. Ct. of Orange, Conn., 1951-55; 1st chmn. United Way of Greater New Haven; chmn. Yale New Haven Hosp., 1976-83. Capt. USNR, 1941-45, ATO, PTO. Decorated Bronze Star; recipient Disting. Pub. Svc. award New Haven C. of C., 1973, Disting. Pub. Svc. award YMCA, New Haven, 1982, Disting. Pub. Svc. award Lions Club of New Haven, 1981, others; named to Hall of Fame Jr. Achievement, 1984. Mem. New Eng. Gas Assn. (dir., chmn.), Assn. Gas. Distbrs. (nat. chmn.), Am. Gas Assn., Conn. Bar Assn. (pres.). Roman Catholic. Home and Office: 612 Thornhill Ln West Haven CT 06516-7914

BOWERS, BEGE K., English educator; b. Nashville, Tenn., Aug. 19, 1949; d. John and Yvonne (Howell) B. BA in English cum laude, Vanderbilt U.,

1971; student, U. Mich., 1985; MACT, U. Tenn., 1973, PhD, 1984. Asst. loan officer Ctr. for Fin. Aid and Placement, Baylor U., Waco, Tex., 1975-76; editorial asst. Wassily Leontief, NYU, N.Y.C., 1976-78; instr. bus. English Florence-Darlington Tech. Coll., Florence, S.C., 1979-80; tchr. English and French St. John's High Sch., Darlington, S.C., 1980-82; teaching asst. dept English U. Tenn., Knoxville, 1982-84; asst. prof. English Youngstown (Ohio) State U., 1984-88, assoc. prof., 1988-92, prof., 1992—, composition coord. dept. English, 1985-94, acting chmn. dept., 1989, asst. to dean Coll. Arts and Scis., 1992-93, dir. profl. writing and editing, 1996—; part-time freelance editor MLA, N.Y.C., 1978-80; cons. Project Arete, Youngstown and Mahoning County Pub. Schs., 1984-87, Youngstown Pub. Schs., 1986, 87-88, 90-91, Macmillan Pub. Co., 1986, Trumbull (Ohio) County Schs., 1988, Akron Beacon Jour., 1994-95, Ohio Dept. Edn., 1998, 99. Co-editor: CEA Critic, CEA Forum 1988—, (with Barbara Brothers) Reading and Writing Women's Lives: A Study of the Novel of Manners, 1991, (with Chuck Nelson) Internships in Technical Communication, 1991; editorial bd. South Atlantic Review, 1987-89; editor: of more than 40 pamphlets, 7 children's books, and 1 videoscript. Recipient John C. Hodges award U. Tenn., 1973, Disting. Professorship award for Tchg., 1987, Disting. Professorship award for Pub. Svc., 96, Youngstown State U.; Alumni Found. Rsch. fellow U. Tenn., 1978, Dissertation fellow U. Tenn., 1983, Davis Editl. fellow U. Tenn., 1984; Grad. Rsch. Coun. grantee Youngstown State U.; named Disting. Grad. Faculty Youngstown State U., 1988—. Mem. MLA, Coll. English Assn. (exec. bd., Disting. Svc. award 1996), Coun. Editors of Learned Jours., Coll. English Assn. Ohio, Coun. Editors of Learned Jours., Nat. Coun. Tchrs. English, Conf. on Coll. Composition and Comm., New Chaucer Soc. (asst. bibliographer 1986—), Assn. Tchrs. Tech. Writing, Soc. for Tech. Commn. (Jay R. Gould award for excellence in tchg. tech. comm. 1999), No. Ohio Soc. for Tech. Commn., Gould Soc. (faculty com. pres. 1991-93), Phi Beta Kappa, Phi Kappa Phi (pres. 1991-92, sec. 1994-98). Office: Youngstown State U Dept English Youngstown OH 44555

BOWERS, CURTIS RAY, JR., chaplain; b. Lancaster, Pa., Feb. 6, 1933; s. Curtis Ray and Oleita (Geisler) B.; m. Doris Jean, June 18, 1955; children: Sharon, William, Stephen. BA, Asbury Coll., 1958; MDiv, Asbury Theol. Sem., 1960. Pastor Methodist Ch., Cynthiana, Ky., 1956-60, Ch. of the Nazarene, Cape May, N.J., 1960-61; chaplain U.S. Army, 1961-84; dir. chaplaincy ministries Ch. of the Nazarene, Kansas City, Mo., 1984—. Author: Forward Edge of the Battle Area: A Chaplain's Story. Col. U.S. Army, 1961-84. Decorated Silver Star. Avocation: tennis,. Home: 12709 Oakmont Dr Kansas City MO 64145-1140 Office: Church of Nazarene 6401 Paseo Blvd Kansas City MO 64131-1213

BOWERS, ELLIOTT TOULMIN, university president; b. Oklahoma City, Aug. 22, 1919; s. Lloyd and Enah (McDonald) B.; m. Frances Marie Handley, May 29, 1940; children—Linda Lu Rushing, Cynthia Ann Bowers Kimmel. B.S., Sam Houston State U., 1941, M.A., 1942; Ed.D., U. Houston, 1959. Dir. music Huntsville High Sch., 1937-42; mem. faculty Sam Houston State U., 1946-89, v.p. univ. affairs and dean of students, 1964-70, acting pres., 1963-64, pres., 1970-89, pres. emeritus, 1990—; dir. First Nat. Bank, Huntsville, Tex. Mem. Tex. Criminal Justice Council; bd. dirs. Sam Houston Area council Boy Scouts Am., Salvation Army, Am. Cancer Soc.; pres. bd. Wesley Found., 1962-63. Served with USAAF, 1943-46. Mem. Assn. Higher Edn., Huntsville C. of C. (past pres.), Masons, K.T., SAR, Alpha Phi Omega, Kappa Delta Pi, Phi Mu Alpha. Home: 1802 16th St Huntsville TX 77340-4205

BOWERS, FRANCIS ROBERT, literature educator; b. N.Y.C., May 4, 1920; s. William Leo and Catherine (Callahan) B. B.A., Cath. U. Am., 1946, Ph.D., 1959; M.A., Fordham U., 1952. Tchr. Ascension Sch., N.Y.C., 1946-48, St. Augustine's High Sch., Bklyn., 1948-51, St. Peter's High Sch., Staten Island, 1951-53; instr. De La Salle Coll., Washington, 1953-59; assoc. prof. English and world lit. Manhattan Coll., 1959-70, 85-89, chmn. dept., 1967-70, chmn. grad. English dept., 1961-70, dean arts and scis., 1970-80, provost, 1980-85, acad. advisor to intercollegiate athletes, 1988—. Author: Characterization in Narrative Poetry of George Crabbe, 1959. Trustee scholarship Cath. U., 1953-58. Finn grantee, 1962; Manhattan Coll. grantee, 1966. Mem. Phi Beta Kappa (chpt. sec.-treas.). Office: Manhattan College Acad Support Svcs Dept Bronx NY 10471

BOWERS, GLENN LEE, retired professional society administrator; b. York, Pa., May 7, 1921; s. Elmer Frederick and Naomi Mae (Shellenberger) B.; m. Betty June Lehr, Apr. 21, 1943; children—Tina, Timothy. B.S., Pa. State U., 1946, M.S., 1948. Wildlife biologist Pa. Game Commn., various locations, 1948-57; chief div. research Pa. Game Commn., Harrisburg, 1957-59, dep. exec. dir., 1959-65, exec. dir., 1965-82; chmn. bd. dirs. Worldwide Furbearer Conf., Frostburg, Md., 1976-80. Contbr. articles to profl. jours. Served to capt. USMCR, 1942-45, PTO. Recipient John Pearce Meml. award N.E. sect. Wildlife Soc., 1982; Nat. Wildlife Conservationist award Nat. Wildlife Fedn., 1982. Mem. Wildlife Soc., Internat. Assn. Fish and Wildlife Agys. (exec. com. 1972-80, pres. 1978-79, gen. counsel 1983-95, Seth Gordon award 1982), N.E. Assn. Fish and Wildlife Agys. (various offices, v.p., pres. 1965-82). Republican. Methodist. Lodge: Masons. Avocations: fishing; hunting. Home: 221 Mountain Rd Dillsburg PA 17019-1514

BOWERS, JAMES W., retired lawyer. BSChemE, Ohio State U., 1961, MS, 1961, JD, 1966. Sr. counsel compliance programs Internat. Paper Co., 1992-95, sr. counsel imaging products and compliants programs, 1995—; ret. Office: 2 Manhattanville Rd Purchase NY 10577-2118*

BOWERS, JOHN CARL, minister; b. L.A., Oct. 7, 1943; s. John Gordon and Georgene (Kendle) B.; m. Dorothea Adeline Geffken, July 2, 1978 (div. May 1987). BA in Philosophy, Occidental Coll., 1965; MDiv, Union Theol. Sem., N.Y.C., 1972; DMin, Drew U, 1995; postgrad., Bklyn. Law Sch., 1997—. Ordained to ministry Presbyn. Ch. (U.S.A.), 1973. Interim supply pastor United Presbyn. Ch. of St. Andrew, Groton, Conn., 1972-73; asst. pastor Trinity Presbyn. Ch., East Brunswick, N.J., 1973-75; pastor Ft. Schuyler Presbyn. Ch., Bronx, N.Y., 1976-85, Presbyn. Ch. in Elmont (N.Y.), 1985-92, Homecrest Presbyn. Ch., Bklyn., 1992—; co-chair regional conf. Nat. Student Christian Fedn., Berkeley, Calif., 1965; commr. Synod of N.E., 1980-82; bd. dirs. Ft. Schuyler House, Bronx, 1981-84; mem. com. on ministry Presbytery of N.Y.C., 1980-85, 93-97. Mem. sch. bd. Elmont Union Free Sch. Dist., 1988-92; treas. Stanforth Action Com., Elmont, 1987-92; chair subcom. Citizens Adv. Com., Elmont, 1987; bd. dirs. Homecrest Cmty. Svcs., 1996—, v.p., 1997—; bd. mgrs. Bklyn. Coun. Chs., 1996—. Recipient Bausch and Lomb Sci. medal, 1961, cert. of appreciation Greater N.Y. coun. Girl Scouts U.S., 1985, appreciation plaque Elmont Union Free Sch. Dist., 1987, award for ecumenism Bklyn. Coun. Chs., 1998; Nat. Merit scholar, 1961-65; Sparer fellow in pub. intrest law, 1997—. Mem. ABA, N.Y. State Bar Assn., Assn. of Bar of City of N.Y., Nat. Lawyers Guild, Elmont Clergy Assn. (pres. 1987-91), Presbyn. Conf. Assn. (bd. dirs. 1990-92), So. Bklyn. Clergy, Phi Delta Phi (vice magister 1999—). Democrat. Home: 2048 E 14th St Brooklyn NY 11229-3314 Office: Homecrest Presbyn Ch 2048 E 14th St Brooklyn NY 11229-3314 *"Who knows? Who cares? What's the difference?"—that's what we hear, as we end the millenium. But that's wrong. We should know, because we can; we should care, because we are people of faith; and we can make a difference—the question is: will we? The truth of our faith, the depth of our love, will be judged on just that: whether our faith and love made any difference to anyone else.*

BOWERS, JOHN WAITE, communication educator; b. Alton, Iowa, Nov. 28, 1935; s. George E. and Clara Frances (Wathier) B.; m. Eleanore Frances Fyock, June 2, 1956 (div. 1975); children: John Steven, Jeanne Terese, Julie Michelle. BS, U. Kans., 1958, MA, 1959; Ph.D., U. Iowa, 1962. Faculty mem. U. Iowa, Iowa City, 1962-87, prof. communication, 1969-87, chmn. dept. communication and theatre arts, 1982-84; chmn. dept. comm. studies, 1984-85; prof., chmn. dept. communication U. Colo., Boulder, 1987-91; vol. Boulder (Colo.) Pub. Libr., 1992—; prof. emeritus U. Colo., Boulder, 1991—. Author: Designing the Communication Experiment, 1970, (with Ochs) Rhetoric of Agitation and Control, 1971, (with Courtright) Communication Research Methods, 1984; co-editor: Handbook of Rhetorical and Communication Theory, 1984. Recipient Alumni Honor citation U. Kans., 1985, Outstanding Vol. award Boulder Pub. Libr., 1992. Mem. AAUP, Internat. Comm. Assn., Nat. Comm. Assn. (editor Comm. Monographs 1978-80, 1st v.p. 1983, pres. 1984, Robert J. Kibler Meml. award 1979, Golden Anniversary Monograph award 1980, Samuel L. Becker Disting. Svc. award 1996), Cen. States Speech Assn. (Outstanding Young Tchr. award 1964), Iowa Comm. Assn. (award for outstanding contbns. to tch. 1984). Home: 2940 Shady Holw W Boulder CO 80304-2979

BOWERS, JOHN ZIMMERMAN, physician, scientist, educator; b. Catonsville, Md., Aug. 27, 1913; s. John Culler and Adelaide (Schuman) B.; children: John C., Mary I., David W.; m. Akiko Kobayashi, Apr. 17, 1970. B.S., Gettysburg Coll., 1933, Sc.D. (hon.), 1958; M.D., U. Md., 1938, Sc.D., 1959; L.H.D., Woman's Med. Coll., 1967; Docteur Honoris Causa, Universite d'Aix-Marseille, France, 1976; D.Sc., Morehouse Coll., 1985. Intern, resident Univ. Hosp., Balt., 1938-41; Harvard fellow in pathology New Eng. Deconess Hosp., Boston, 1943-44; fellow in tropical medicine U.S. Naval Med. Sch., Bethesda, Md., 1944; dep. dir. AEC, Washington, 1947-50; asst. prof. dept. medicine Johns Hopkins U., Balt., 1948-50; dir. radioactive isotope lab., rsch. fellow Crocker Radiation Lab., Balt., 1950; prof., dean Coll. Medicine radiobio. lab, med. cons. AEC U. Utah, 1950-55; dean, prof. medicine Med. Sch. U. Wis., 1955-62; pres. Macy Found., N.Y.C., 1965-80; cons. Ford Found., India, 1952-59, WHO, 1963-69, UNESCO, 1968, NAS, 1982, N.Y. Acad. Scis., 1967; mem. adv. com. The Pres.'s Health Resources, 1958-61; cons. to surgeon gen. USAF, 1959-64; mem. adv. com. for sci. publs. USPHS, 1962-66; vis. prof. Kyoto (Japan) U. Med. Sch., 1962-64, U. Philippines, 1962; mem. staff Rockefeller Found., 1964-65, cons., 1978-84; mem. adv. com. history of life scis. NIH, 1970-74; mem. exec. com. Nutrition Found., 1972, also trustee; adj. prof. N.Y. Med. Coll., 1980; bd. visitors Air U., Montgomery, Ala., 1959-62. Author: Medical Education in Japan, From Chinese Medicine to Western Medicine, 1965, Western Medical Pioneers in Feudal Japan, 1970, Doctor on Desima, 1970, Western Medicine in a Chinese Palace, 1972, An Introduction to American Medicine, 1975, When the Twain Meet: The Rise of Western Medicine in Japan, 1980, Hiroshima-It's Origin and Growth, 1985; editor, chmn. editl. bd. Jour. Med. Edn., 1956-62; mem. bd. assoc. editors Jour. History of Med. and Allied Scis., 1974; co-author, editor: Advances in American Medicine - Essyas at Bicentennial American Medicine, 1975; mem. editl. bd. Grants mag., 1978; contbr. articles to profl. jours. Mem. exec. com. Western Interstate Com. for Higher Edn., 1952-55; mem. adv. com. for med. and pub. health Kellogg Found., 1955-64; mem. bd. overseers Morehouse Coll. Med. Sch., 1976-79; mem. bd. med. acad. adv. com. Chinese U. Hong Kong, 1976—, mem. com. Am. Cancer Soc., 1977-80; trustee Gettysburg Coll., 1977-79, East Asian History Scis. Found., 1980—, Giovanni Lorenzini Found., Inc., 1980—; mem. Com. de Patronage Med. D'Afrique Noire, 1978—; mem. adv. coun. Am. Trust for Brit. Libr., 1980—. Served as comdr. USNR, 1941-45. Decorated Legion of Merit for Combat, Purple Heart; Order of the Legion of Honor (France); Order of the Rising Sun (Japan); Alan Gregg travel scholar China Med. Bd., 1962-63; Andrew Wellington Cordier fellow Columbia U. Sch. Internat. Affairs, 1977. Fellow ACP; mem. AMA (coun. on med. edn. in hosps. 1958-63), Assn. Am. Med. Colls. (v.p. 1952, exec. coun. 1953-59), Am. Osler Soc., Internat. Acad. History Medicine (sec.-treas. 1975), Japan Soc. for Med. Edn. (hon.), Indian Assn. Advancement Med. Edn. (hon.), Coun. Fgn. Rels., Century Assn., Asia Soc., Am. Soc. French Legion Honor, Med. Alumni Assn. U. Md., Union Club, Univ. Club, Cosmos, Alpha Omega Alpha (pres. 1968-78). Home: 400 Locust St B-2090 Lakewood NJ 08701

BOWERS, KLAUS D(IETER), retired electronics research development company executive; b. Stettin, Germany, Dec. 27, 1929; s. Franz A. and Elisabeth (Schneider) B.; m. Roswitha U. Rau, June 15, 1964; children: Pamela, Colin. B.A., Oxford (Eng.) U., 1950, M.A., Ph.D., 1953. Research lectr. in physics Christ Ch., Oxford U., 1952-56; with AT&T, 1956-90; researcher Bell Telephone Labs., Murray Hill, N.J., 1956-59, mgr. electronics devel., 1959-66; mgr. electronics devel. Bell Telephone Labs., Allentown, Pa., 1966-71; mng. dir., v.p. Sandia Nat. Labs., Albuquerque, 1971-75; exec. dir. Pa. Labs. Bell Telephone Labs., Allentown, 1975-79; v.p. Bell Telephone Labs., Murray Hill, 1979-90; bd. dirs. Semiconductor Research Corp., 1985-88, chmn., 1987-88;. Contbr. sci. articles to profl. jours. Trustee Cedar Crest Coll., 1983-87. Fellow IEEE (Frederik Philips award 1989); mem. Nat. Acad. Engring. Patentee in field. Home: 2890 Golf Cir Emmaus PA 18049-1735

BOWERS, MICHAEL JOSEPH, former state attorney general; b. Jackson County, Ga., Oct. 7, 1941; s. Carl Ernest and Janie Ruth (Bolton) B.; m. Bette Rose Corley, June 8, 1963; children: Carl Wayne, Bruce Edward, Michelle Lisa. BS, U.S. Mil. Acad., 1963; MS, Stanford U., 1965; MBA, U. Utah-Wiesbaden, Germany, 1970; JD, U. Ga., 1974. Bar: Ga. 1974. Sr. asst. atty. gen. State of Ga., Atlanta, 1975-81, atty. gen., 1981-97, candidate for gov., 1998—. Capt. USAF, 1963-70. Mem. Lawyers Club, Kiwanis. Republican. Methodist. Home: 817 Allgood Rd Stone Mountain GA 30083-4803*

BOWERS, PATRICIA ELEANOR FRITZ, economist; b. N.Y.C., Mar. 21, 1928; d. Eduard and Eleanor (Ring) Fritz. Student scholar, Goucher Coll., 1946-48; BA, Cornell U., 1950; MA, NYU, 1953, PhD, 1965. Statis. asst. Fed. Res. Bank N.Y., N.Y.C., 1950-53; lectr. Upsala Coll., East Orange, N.J., 1953-59; researcher Fortune mag., N.Y.C., 1959-60; teaching fellow NYU, N.Y.C., 1960-62, instr., 1962-64; mem. faculty Bklyn. Coll., CUNY, 1964—, prof. econs., 1974—, chair dept. econs., 1996—. Author: Private Choice and Public Welfare, 1974. Sec. Friends of the Johnson Mus., Cornell U., 1989-91. Mem. Am. Econ. Assn., Econometric Soc., Met. Econ. Assn. (sec. 1963-68, pres. 1974-75), Am. Statis. Assn. (univs. chmn. ann. forecasting confs. 1970-71, 71-72), Cornell Club N.Y., Kappa Alpha Theta. Home: 145 E 16th St New York NY 10003-3405 Office: CUNY Bklyn Coll Dept Econs Brooklyn NY 11210

BOWERS, PATRICIA NEWSOME, communications executive; b. Baton Rouge, June 21, 1944; d. Carl Allen and Sue Mayre (Powell) Newsome; m. Robert Lloyd Bowers Jr., Aug. 19, 1967 (div. Nov. 1979); children: Paige Ivy, Katherine Elizabeth. BJ, La. State U., 1967. Sr. writer, editor Litton Industries, Pascagoula, Miss., 1978-80; sr. presentations supr. Martin Marietta Aerospace, Orlando, Fla., 1980-81; mgr. presentations Martin Marietta Aerospace, Balt., 1981-85, mgr. pub. rels., 1985-90; dir. pub. rels. and corp. comm. Contraves USA, Pitts., 1990-92; sr. mgr. sector comms. Harris Electronic sys. sector Harris Corp., Melbourne, Fla., 1992-95; dir. mktg. and pub. rels. Intracoastal Health Systems, Inc., West Palm Beach, Fla., 1995-99; dir. mktg. and comms. Northside Hosp., Atlanta, 1999—. Coach Parkville Recreation Council, Balt., 1985-87; bd. dirs. Salvation Army, Human Resources Devel. Agy. Balt. County, Brevard Symphony Youth Orch.; adv. bd. Nat. Aquarium in Balt.; active Brevard Leadership; mem. corp. bd. Boys and Girls Club of Palm Beach County. Mem. Pub. Rels. Soc. Am. (bd. dirs. Chesapeake conf. 1987, Silver Anvil Judge, 1991, 92), Healthcare Forum for Strategic Planning and Mktg. Execs., Nat. Press Club, Navy League (bd. dirs. Balt. council 1986-87), Balt. County C. of C. (leadership program 1986-87), Pitts. Press Club, Forum Club of Palm Beach. Republican. Episcopalian. Avocations: golf, reading, photography. Office: Northside Hosp 1000 Johnson Ferry Rd NE Atlanta GA 30342-1611

BOWERS, PAUL D., transportation company executive; b. Rome, N.Y., Aug. 28, 1948. Dir. aviation Alaska Dept. Transp. and Pub. Facilities Statewide Aviation, Anchorage, 1995—. Office: Alaska Dept Transp and Pub Facilities Statewide Aviation 4111 Aviation Ave Anchorage AK 99502

BOWERS, RICHARD PHILIP, manufacturing executive; b. Reading, Pa., July 27, 1931; s. Clarence Philip and Lottie Rose (Linkowski) B.; married; children: Richard P., Karen M., Lisa Ann, Julie L. Student, St. Bonaventure Coll., Olean, N.Y., 1949-51. Sales engr. Bowers Battery and Spark Plug Corp., Reading, Pa., 1952-57; v.p. sales Gen. Battery Cord, Reading, Pa., 1957-64; v.p. sales and mktg. East Penn Mfg. Co., Lyon Station, Pa., 1964-67, exec. v.p., 1967-95; also bd. dirs. E. Penn Mfg. Co., Lyon Station, Pa.; pres. Fed. Battery and Cable Corp., Hialeah, Fla., 1987—; pres. TBS Systems of Ala., Birmingham, 1986—, Pioneer Auto Parts, Phila., 1980—, electro Battery Co., St. Louis; chmn. bd. Taylor Battery Co., Louisville, 1986—; chmn. bd. Power Battery Toronto, Can. Pres. Green Hills Lake Recreational Assn., Green Hills, Pa., 1984-87. Served with U.S. Army, 1962-64. Named Man of Yr., Automotive Merchandising, Chgo., 1984, 89. Mem. Battery Council Internat. (chmn. convention planning com. 1986-91), Ind. Battery Mfrs. Assn. (past pres., bd. dirs.). Democrat. Roman Catholic. Office: East Penn Mfg Co RDI PO 1794 Mohnton PA 19540

BOWERS, ROGER PAUL, radiologist; b. Rome, N.Y., May 5, 1951; s. Paul Roger and Cassie Ann (Evans) B.; m. Denise Rae Lyon, Aug. 2, 1976; children: Leslie Ann, Rebecca Jane, Matthew Paul. SB in Math., MIT, 1973; MD, SUNY, Buffalo, 1978. Diplomate Am. Bd. Radiology, Am. Bd. Nuclear Medicine. Internship U. Mich., 1978-79; resident in radiology U. Mich. Hosps., Ann Arbor, 1979-82, chief resident nuclear medicine dept., 1981-82; radiologist Guthrie Clinic, Sayre, Pa., 1982-89, St. Elizabeth Hosp., Utica, N.Y., 1989—; chief radiologist Little Falls (N.Y.) Hosp., 1995—. Contbr. articles to Guthrie Jour., Jour. Thoracic Cardiovascular Surgery, others, chpts. to book CRC Manual of Nuclear Medical Procedures, 1982. Trustee Athens (Pa.) Wesleyan Ch., 1986-88; chmn. fin. resource CNY Wesleyan Dist., Syracuse, N.Y., 1990—. Mem. Am. Coll. Radiology, Soc. Nuclear Medicine, Radiol. Soc. N.Am., Soc. Magnetic Resonance in Medicine, Sigma Xi. Republican. Home: 10 Hubbardton Rd New Hartford NY 13413-2743 Office: St Elizabeth Hosp 2209 Genesee St Utica NY 13501-5999

BOWERS, ZELLA ZANE, real estate broker; b. May 24, 1929. E-mail: zzb@juno.com and zaneb@clsp.uswest.net. Home: 128 W Rockrimmon Blvd Apt 104 Colorado Springs CO 80919-1876 Office: Haley Realty Inc 109 E Fontanero St Colorado Springs CO 80907-7494

BOWERS-BIENKOWSKI, EVELYN JOY, physical anthropologist, educator; b. Providence, Apr. 11, 1937; d. Thomas Albert and Dorothy Estelle (Tanner) Bowers; m. Howard Amandus Harner III, Aug. 24, 1957 (div. Sept. 1966); children: David (dec.), Janet, Nancy, Beverly (dec.); m. Joseph Vincent Bienkowski, Mar. 13, 1993. BA, U. Pa., 1959, MA, 1975, PhD, 1983. Rsch. asst. U. Medicine and Dentistry N.J., Camden, 1983-85; cons. rsch. analyst Statis. Ecology Group, U. Pa., Phila., 1975-87; cons. auxologist W.M. Krogman Ctr., U. Pa., Phila., 1983-87; auxologist Children's Hosp. of Pa., Phila., 1984-87; adj. asst. prof. Robert Wood Johnson Med. Sch./U. Medicine and Dentistry N.J., Camden, 1986-87; assoc. prof. anthropology Ball State U., Muncie, Ind., 1987—. Contbr. articles to profl. jours. Mem. AAAS, Am. Assn. Phys. Anthropologists (com. on profl. devel. 1987—), Phila. Anthrop. Assn. (treas. 1987, mem. coun. 1986-87), Human Biology Assn., Soc. for Study of Human biology, Sigma Xi, Lambda Alpha. Office: Ball State U Dept Anthropologie Muncie IN 47306

BOWERSOCK, GLEN WARREN, historian; b. Providence, Jan. 12, 1936; s. Donald Curtis and Josephine (Evans) B. AB, Harvard U., 1957; BA, Oxford U., Eng., 1959, MA, DPhil, 1962; Dr. h.c., U. Strasbourg, 1990. Lectr. ancient history Oxford U., 1960-62, vis. lectr., 1966; instr. Harvard U., 1962-64, asst. prof., 1964-67, assoc. prof. classics, 1967-69, prof. Greek and Latin, 1969-80, chmn. dept. classics, 1972-77, assoc. dean faculty arts and scis., 1977-80; prof. hist. studies Inst. Advanced Study, Princeton, N.J., 1980—; sr. fellow Dumbarton Oaks Ctr. for Byzantine Studies, Washington, 1984-93; cons. Ednl. Services, Inc., 1964, NEH, 1971—; sr. fellow Center for Hellenic Studies, Washington, 1976-90; sci. com. Scuola Normale Superiore di Pisa, Italy; chmn. sci. com. Maison de l'Orient Méditerranéen, Lyon, France; mem. Internat. Colloquium on the Cl. ssics in Edn., 1964-66; vis. prof. Australian Nat. U., 1972, Princeton U., 1986-87, Coll. France, 1997; Sather prof. U. Calif., Berkeley, 1991; Jerome lectr. U. Mich. and Am. Acad. in Rome, 1989; syndic Harvard U. Press, 1977-81; lect. Thompson Lectures, Pomona, 1993, Wiles Lectures, Queens U., Belfast, Ireland, 1993, Coll. de France, 1997. Author: Augustus and the Greek World, 1965, Pseudo-Xenophon, Constitution of the Athenians, 1968, Greek Sophists in the Roman Empire, 1969, Julian the Apostate, 1978, Roman Arabia, 1983, Hellenism in Late Antiquity, 1990, Fiction as History From Nero to Julian, 1994, Studies on the Eastern Roman Empire, 1994, Martyrdom and Rome, 1995; editor: Philostratus' Life of Apollonius, 1970, Approaches to the Second Sophistic, 1974, (with J. Clive and S. Graubard) Edward Gibbon and the Decline and Fall of the Roman Empire, 1977, (with C.P. Jones) L. Robert-Martyre de Pionios, 1994, (with T.J. Cornell) Momigliano-Studies on Modern Scholarship, 1994, (with P. Brown and O. Grabar) Late Antiquity-A Guide to the Postclassical World, 1999; mem. editl. bd. Arabian Archaeology and Epigraphy (Copenhagen), Ancient Civilizations from Scythia to Siberia (Russian Acad. Scis.), Berytus, Am. Jour. Philology, 1987-95, Am. Scholar, 1981-93; gen. editor: Revealing Antiquity. Trustee Am. Schs. Oriental Rsch., 1984-90; bd. dirs. Met. Opera Guild; adv. dir. Met. Opera Assn; mem. nat. coun. Glimmerglass Opera. Rhodes scholar, 1957-60; recipient James H. Breasted prize Am. Hist. Assn., 1992. Fellow Am. Acad. Arts and Scis., Am. Numis. Soc. (coun. 1983-96); mem. Am. Philos. Soc. (coun. 1992-98), Am. Philol. Assn., Leschetizky Assn. Am., Soc. Promotion Roman and Hellenic Studies (hon. Am. sec. of Roman Soc.), German Archaeol. Inst. (corr.), Acad. des Inscriptions et Belles-Lettres, Johnsonians, Knickerbocker Club (N.Y.C.), Century Club (N.Y.C.), Phi Beta Kappa. Office: Inst Advanced Study Sch Hist Studies Princeton NJ 08540

BOWERSOX, THOMAS H., lawyer; b. Beatrice, Nebr., May 1, 1941; s. William H. Bowersox and Fairy (Casey) Huff; m. Barbara Mathieson, Aug. 23, 1963; children: William T., Christopher T., Elizabeth A. BBA, U. Houston, 1965, JD, 1969. Bar: U.S. Dist. Ct. (so. and ea. dists.) Tex., U.S. Ct. Appeals (5th and 11th cirs.). Instr. South Tex. Jr. Coll., Houston, 1967-72; assoc. prof. Sam Houston State U., Huntsville, 1972-74; assoc. Baker & Botts, Houston, 1975-76; from assoc. gen counsel to pres. subs. co. Zapata Corp., Houston, 1976-93, exec. v.p., 1993-94; ptnr. Bowersox, Herron & Williamson, Houston, 1996—; adv. com. energy trade policy, U.S. trade rep. industry sector Dept. of Commerce, 1989-93. Bd. dirs. Offhore Energy Ctr., Houston, 1988-92, mem. adv. bd. 1992—; mem. adv. com. Sam Houston State U. Coll. Bus., 1985—. Mem. Internat. Assn. Drilling Contractors (vice chmn. contracts and risk mgmt. com. 1984-85, chmn. govt. affairs com. 1986-87, v.p. Tex. gulf coast 1989, v.p. offshore 1990-91, chmn., bd. dirs., 1992), Am. Bureau of Shipping. Avocations: golf, camping, reading. Fax: 281-820-2055. Office: Bowersox Herron and Williamson 16800 Imperial Valley Dr Houston TX 77060-3103

BOWES, FREDERICK, III, publishing executive; b. Norwalk, Conn., Dec. 20, 1941; s. Frederick Jr. and Mary Priscilla (Herron) B.; m. Margaret Anne Hathaway, Sept. 17, 1966; children: Heather Hathaway Ezzy, Catherine Herron. AB, Dartmouth Coll., 1963; MBA, Columbia U., 1965. Fin. staff Perkin-Elmer Corp., Norwalk, Conn., 1965-70; v.p. ops. and fin. South Shore Pub. Co., North Scituate, Mass., 1970-77; cons. Graphics Mgmt., Inc., Duxbury, Mass., 1977-79; pres. Info-Graphics Inc., Braintree, Mass., 1979-80; v.p. pub. New Eng. Jour. Medicine, Mass. Med. Soc., Waltham, Mass., 1981-90; pres. Macmillan New Media, Cambridge, Mass., 1990-94, Cadmus Digital Solutions, 1995-96; pres., CEO Bowes & Assocs., Inc., 1996—. Sr. warden Parish of St. John the Evangelist, Duxbury, 1981-84; trustee, treas. Soc. St. Margaret, Boston, 1984—; trustee Mass. Bible Soc., Boston, 1983-88. Mem. Soc. Scholarly Pub. (pres. 1998), Am. Assn. Pubs. Episcopalian. Avocations: Christian svc., ornithology. Office: 100 Ledgewood Rd #302 Rockland MA 02370

BOWIE, CALVERT S., architect; b. Washington, June 12, 1950; m. Christine Bjork Nicholson (div.); children: Alexandra, Blair. AB in Architecture with honors, Dartmouth Coll., 1973; MArch, Yale U., 1977. Registered architect, D.C., Md., Va., NCARB examiner 1989, 93, 94, 95, exam. writer 1995, 96, 97, 98. Architect Hartman Cox Architects, Washington, 1977-79, Keyes, Condon, Florance Architects, Washington, 1979-81; ptnr., prin. Bowie Gridley Architects, Washington, 1981—; chair D.C. Bd. Architects; speaker in field. Bd. dirs. St. Albans Sch.; trustee The Lab. Sch., Washington; mem. corp. campaign com. Washington Nat. Cathedral, 1990. Mem. AIA (chmn. design com. 1988, mem. govt. affairs commn. 1994-97), Nat. Trust Historic Preservation (mem. Decatur House property coun.), Sch. Architecture Yale U. Alumni Assn. (del. 1991-94), Yale Club (bd. dirs. 1990-93). Office: Bowie Gridley Archs 1010 Wisconsin Ave NW Washington DC 20007-3603

BOWIE, E(DWARD) J(OHN) WALTER, hematologist, researcher; b. Church Stretton, Shropshire, Eng., Mar. 10, 1925; came to U.S., 1958; s. Edgar Ormond and Ann Brown (Kirton) B.; m. Gertrud Susi Ulrich, Dec. 22, 1948; children—Katherine Ann, Christopher John, John Walter, James Ulrich. MA, Oxford (Eng.) U., 1950, BM, BCh, 1952, DM, 1981; MS, U. Minn., 1961. House physician Univ. Coll. Hosp., London, 1953; sr. house officer Bethlem Royal and Maudsley Hosps., London, 1953-54; pvt. practice medicine Treherne, Man., Can., 1954; fellow in medicine Mayo Clinic, Rochester, Minn., 1958-60, cons. in internal medicine and hematology, 1961-

90, head sect. hematology research, 1971-89; prof. medicine and lab. medicine Mayo Med. Sch., Rochester, Minn., 1974-90, prof. emeritus, 1990-96, ret., 1996; invited spkr. Gordon Confs., 1973, 76, 78, Royal Soc., London, 1980; chmn. thrombosis coun. Internat. Soc. and Fedn. Cardiology, 1991; internat. dir. Thrombosis Vascular Tng. Ctrs. Co-author 6 books; assoc. editor Jour. Lab. and Clin. Medicine, 1976-80; contbr. chpts. to books, numerous articles to profl. jours. Recipient Judson Daland travel award Mayo Found., 1963, named Disting. Investigator, 1988, Disting. Alumnus Mayo Found., 1996. Fellow ACP, AMA, Royal Coll. Pathology; mem. AAAS, Am. Heart Assn. Internat. Soc. on Thrombosis and Haemostasis (v.p. 1980-81, Disting. Career award 1991), Am. Soc. Hematology, Internat. Com. on Thrombosis and Haemostasis (chmn. 1989-90), Ctrl. Soc. for Clin. Rsch., Am. Fedn. for Clin. Rsch., World Fedn. Haemophilia.

BOWIE, NORMAN ERNEST, university official, educator; b. Biddeford, Maine, June 6, 1942; s. Lawrence Walker and Helen Elizabeth (Jacobsen) B.; m. Bonnie Jean Bankert, June 11, 1966 (div. 1980); children: Brian Paul, Peter Mark; m. Maureen Burns, Sept. 19, 1987. AB, Bates Coll., 1964; PhD, U. Rochester, 1968. Mem. faculty Lycoming Coll., Williamsport, Pa., 1968-69; asst. prof. philosophy Hamilton Coll., Clinton, N.Y., 1969-74; assoc. prof. Hamilton Coll., 1974-75; assoc. prof. U. Del., Newark, 1975-80, prof., 1980-89, dir. Ctr. for Study of Values, 1977-89; Elmer L. Andersen chairperson corp. responsibility U. Minn., Mpls., 1989-99, chairperson dept. strategic mgmt. and orgn., 1992-95; fellow in ethics and professions Harvard U., 1996-97; Dixons prof. bus. ethics and social responsibility London Bus. Sch., 1999—; Lynette S. Autrey vis. prof. bus. ethics Rice U., spring 1986; vis. prof. Sch. Mgmt. U. Scranton, 1986-87, Sch. Bus. Adminstrn., Georgetown U., 1988-89; exec. v.p. seminars The Aspen Inst., 1998—. Author: Towards a New Theory of Distributive Justice, 1971, Business Ethics, 1982, (with Ronald Duska) 2nd edit., 1990, University Business Partnerships: An Assessment, 1994, Business Ethics: A Kantian Perspective, 1999; co-author: The Individual and the Political Order, 1977, 2nd edit., 1986, 3d edit., 1998; editor: Ethical Issues in Government, 1981, Ethical Theory in the Last Quarter of the Twentieth Century, 1983, Equal Opportunity, 1988; co-editor: Ethical Theory and Business, 1979, 5th edit., 1996, Making Ethical Decisions, 1985, Ethics, Public Policy and Criminal Justice, 1982, The Tradition of Philosophy, 1986, Ethics and Agency Theory, 1992; co-editor Bus. and Profl. Ethics Jour., 1981-88. Mem. N.Y. Coun. for Humanities, 1974-75. NDEA fellow, 1965-68. Mem. AAUP, Acad. Mgmt., Am. Philos. Assn. (nat. exec. sec. 1972-77), Am. Soc. for Value Inquiry (pres. 1980-81), Am. Soc. Polit. and Legal Philosophy, Soc. Bus. Ethics (pres. 1988), Soc. for the Advancement Socio-Econs., Phi Beta Kappa. Home: PO Box 306 Queenstown MD 21658 Office: The Aspen Inst PO Box 222 Queenstown MD 21658

BOWIE, PETER WENTWORTH, judge, educator; b. Alexandria, Va., Sept. 27, 1942; s. Beverley Munford and Louise Wentworth (Boynton) B.; m. Sarah Virginia Haught, Mar. 25, 1967; children: Heather, Gavin. BA, Wake Forest Coll., 1964; JD magna cum laude, U. San Diego, 1971. Bar: Calif. 1972, D.C. 1972, U.S. Dist. Ct. D.C. 1972, U.S. Dist. Ct. Md. 1973, U.S. Dist. Ct. (so. dist.) Calif. 1974, U.S. Ct. Appeals (D.C. cir.) 1972, U.S. Ct. Appeals (9th cir.) 1974, U.S. Supreme Ct. 1980. Trial atty. honors program Dept. of Justice, Washington, 1971-74; asst. U.S. Atty. U.S. Atty.'s Office, San Diego, 1974, asst. chief civil div., 1974-82, chief asst. U.S. atty., 1982-88; lawyer rep. U.S. Ct. Appeals (9th cir.) Jud. Conf., 1977-78, 84-87; judge U.S. Bankruptcy Ct., San Diego, 1988—; lectr. at law Calif. Western Sch. Law, 1979-83; exec. com. mem. 9th Cir. Judicial Conf., 1991-94; mem. com. on codes of conduct Jud. Conf. of U.S., 1995—. Bd. dirs. Presidio Little League, San Diego, 1984, coach, 1983-84; mem. alumni adv. bd. Sch. Law U. San Diego, 1998—. Lt. USN, 1964-68, Vietnam. Mem. State Bar Calif. (hearing referee ct. 1982-86, mem. rev. dept. 1986-90), Fed. Bar Assn. (pres. San diego chpt. 1981-83), San Diego County Bar Assn. (chmn. fed. ct. com. 1978-80, 83-85), Assn. Bus. Trial Lawyers (bd. govs.), San Diego Bankruptcy Forum (bd. dirs.), Phi Delta Phi. Republican. Mem. Unitarian Ch. Office: US Bankruptcy Court 325 W F St San Diego CA 92101-6017

BOWIE, PHYLLIS, secondary education educator. Tchr. secondary geography S.A.V.E. High Sch., Anchorage. Recipient Disting. Tchr. K-12 award Nat. Coun. for Geog. Edn., 1992. Office: SAVE HS 410 E 56th Ave Anchorage AK 99518-1244*

BOWKER, ALBERT HOSMER, retired university chancellor; b. Winchendon, Mass., Sept. 8, 1919; s. Roy C. and Kathleen (Hosmer) B.; m. Elizabeth Rempfer, June 14, 1942; children: Paul Albert, Nancy Kathleen, Caroline Anne; m. Rosedith Sitgreaves, Sept. 26, 1964. B.S., Mass. Inst. Tech., 1941; Ph.D., Columbia U., 1949; D.H.L., City U. N.Y., 1971; LL.D., Brandeis U.; D.H.L., N.Y. Bd. Regents, 1972. Asst. statistician Mass. Inst. Tech., 1941-43; asst. dir. statis. research group Columbia, 1943-45; asst. prof. statistics Stanford, 1947-50, assoc. prof., 1950-53, exec. head statistics dept., 1948-59, dean grad. div., 1959-63, prof. math. and statistics, 1953-63, dir. applied math. and statistics labs., 1951-63; chancellor City U. N.Y., 1963-71; chancellor U. Calif., Berkeley, 1971-80, chancellor emeritus, 1980—; asst. sec. for postsecondary edn. Dept. Edn., Washington, 1980-81; dean Sch. Pub. Affairs U. Md., 1981-84, exec. v.p. univ., 1984-86; v.p. research found. CUNY, 1986—; mem. com. grad. edn. Am. Assn. Univs.; mem. Sloan Commn. on Govt. and Higher Edn.; mem. exec. com. div. math. Nat. Acad. Scis.-NRC, 1963-65. Author: (with Henry P. Goode) Sampling Inspection by Variables, 1952, (with Gerald J. Lieberman) Handbook of Industrial Statistics, 1955, Engineering Statistics, 1972; also articles profl. jours.; Asso. editor: Jour. Am. Statis. Assn, 1949-52. Mem. Corp. Mass. Inst. Tech., 1967-72; mem. Centennial Commn. Howard U., 1965; bd. dirs. San Francisco Bay Area Council, 1972-77; trustee Bennington Coll., U. Haifa. Fellow Am. Statis. Assn. (pres. 1964), Am. Soc. Quality Control, Inst. Math. Statistics (pres. 1961-62), AAAS; mem. Math. Assn. Am., Biometric Soc., Operations Research Soc. Am., Soc. for Indsl. and Applied Math., Am. Assn. Univs. (com. grad. edn.), Phi Beta Kappa (hon.), Sigma Xi (exec. com. 1963-66). Office: U Calif Dept Stats 367 Evans Hall Spc 3860 Berkeley CA 94720-3860

BOWKER, LEE HARRINGTON, academic administrator; b. Bethlehem, Pa., Dec. 19, 1940; s. Maurice H. Bowker and Blanche E. Heffner; m. Nancy Bachant, 1966 (div. 1973); 1 child, Kirsten Ruth; m. Dee C. Thomas, May 25, 1975; children: Jessica Lynn, Gwendolyn Alice. BA, Muhlenberg Coll., 1962; MA, U. Pa., 1965; PhD, Wash. State U., 1972. Instr. in Sociology Lebanon Valley Coll., Annville, Pa., 1965-66, Allbright Coll., Reading, Pa., 1966-67; assoc. prof. Whitman Coll., Walla Walla, Wash., 1967-77; prof., assoc. dean U. Wis., Milw., 1977-82; dean grad. sch. and research Ind. (Pa.) U. of Pa., 1982-85; provost, v.p. Augustana Coll., Sioux Falls, S.D., 1985-87; dean behavioral and social scis. Humboldt State U., Arcata, Calif., 1987-97, emeritus dean, prof. sociology, 1997—; cons. various pubs., colls., univs. and state agys; expert witness. Author: over 300 papers, articles and sci. revs. and 18 books including Prison Victimization, 1980, Humanizing Institutions for the Aged, 1982, Masculinities and Violence, 1997, The Role of the Department Chair, 3d edit., 1997, Ending the Violence, 3d edit., 1998; assoc. editor Pacific Sociol. Rev., 1975-78, Justice Quar., 1983-85, Criminal Justice Policy Rev., 1984-95. Pres. Blue Mountain Action Coun., OEO, Walla Walla, 1969-71; dir. social therapy program, Wash. State penitentiary, Walla Walla, 1971-73; bd. dirs. Milw. Bur. Community Corrections, 1979-81, Sioux Falls Symphony, 1985, United Way of Humboldt County, 1988-91; expert witness in criminal and civil cases involving wife battering, rape and child abuse. Grantee NIMH 1973, 79, 81, Washington Arts Commn. 1972, Washington Office Community Devel. 1974, Fulbright Found. 1985, Nat. Retired Tchrs. Assn./Am. Assn. Retired Persons Andrus Found. 1980; Law Enforcement Assistance Adminstrn. co-grantee, 1978. Mem. Am. Correctional Assn., Nat. Women's Studies Assn., Nat. Coun. Rsch. on Women, Pacific Sociol. Assn., Am. Sociol. Assn. (staff mem., chmn. for teaching and adminstrv. workshops). Home: 3513 H St Eureka CA 95503-5358 Office: Humboldt State U Sociology Faculty Arcata CA 95521

BOWKETT, GERALD EDSON, editorial consultant, writer; b. Sacramento, Sept. 6, 1926; s. Harry Stephen and Jessie (Fairbrother) B.; m. Norma Orel Swain, Jan. 1, 1953; children: Amanda Allyn, Laura Anne. B.A., San Francisco State Coll., 1952; postgrad., Georgetown U., 1954. Radio wire editor UP, Washington, 1956-57; reporter, columnist Anchorage Daily Times, 1957-64; spl. asst., press sec. to Gov. William A. Egan, 1964-66; pub. Alaska Newsletter, 1966-68; Juneau bur. chief Anchorage Daily News, 1967-68; editor S.E. Alaska Empire, Juneau, 1969-71; dir. info. svcs. U. Alaska, 1971-82; prof. English Shanghai Inst. of Tourism, 1992-93. Author: Reaching for a Star: The Final Campaign for Alaska Statehood, 1989. Served with USMC, 1944-46, PTO. Cited for outstanding news and feature writing, editorial works Alaska Press Club. Mem. Alpha Phi Gamma. Home and Office: 14604 W Horizon Dr Sun City West AZ 85375-2764

BOWLBY, RICHARD ERIC, retired computer systems analyst; b. Detroit, Aug. 17, 1939; s. Garner Milton and Florence Marie (Russell) B.; m. Gwendoline Joyce Coldwell, Apr. 29, 1967. BA, Wayne State U., 1962. With Ford Motor Co., Detroit, 1962-65, 66-94, now computer sys. analyst, ret. 1994; pres. 1300 Lafayette East-Coop., Inc., 1981-82. Mem. Antiquaries, Friends Detroit Pub. Libr., Detroit Symphony Orch. Vol. Coun., Founders Soc. Club (Detroit).

BOWLEN, PATRICK DENNIS, holding company executive, lawyer, professional sports team executive; b. Prairie du Chien, Wis., Feb. 18, 1944; s. Paul Dennis and Arvella (Woods) B. B.B.A., U. Okla., 1966, J.D., 1968. Bar: Alta. 1969. Read law Saucier, Jones, Calgary, Alta., Can., assoc., 1969-70; asst. to pres. Regent Drilling Ltd., 1970-71; pres. Batoni-Bowlen Enterprises Ltd., 1971-79, Bowlen Holdings Ltd., Edmonton, Alta., Can., 1979—; pres., chief exec. officer, owner Denver Broncos, 1984—. Mem. Law Soc. Alta., Can. Bar Assn., Young Presidents Orgn. Roman Catholic. Clubs: Mayfair Golf and Country; Edmonton Petroleum; Outrigger Canoe (Honolulu). Avocations: golf, skiing, surfing. Office: Denver Broncos 13655 Broncos Pkwy Englewood CO 80112-4150*

BOWLER, MARIANNE BIANCA, judge; b. Boston, Feb. 15, 1947; d. Richard A. and Ann C. (Daly) B. BA, Regis Coll., 1967; JD cum laude, Suffolk U., 1976, LLD (hon.), 1994. Bar: Mass. 1978. Rsch. asst. Harvard Med. Sch., Boston, 1967-69; med. editor Mass. Dept. of Pub. Health, Boston, 1969-76; law clk. Mass. Superior Ct., Boston, 1976-77, dep. chief law clk., 1977-78; asst. dist. atty. Middlesex Dist. Atty.'s Office, Cambridge, Mass., 1978; asst. U.S. atty. U.S. Dept. of Justice, Boston, 1978-90, exec. asst. U.S. atty., 1988-89, sr. litigation counsel, 1989-90; magistrate judge U.S. Dist. Ct. Mass., Boston, 1990—; chmn. bd. trustees New England Bapt. Hosp., Boston, 1990-95. Trustee Suffolk U., Boston, 1994—; bd. dirs. The Boston Found., 1995—; dir. South Cove Nursing Facilities Found., Inc., 1995—; co-pres. Boston Coll. Inn of Ct., 1998—. Mem. Jr. League Boston, Suffolk Law Sch. Alumni Assn. (pres. 1979-80), Vincent Club, Isabel O'Neil Found., Save Venice. Democrat. Roman Catholic. Avocations: faux finishing, trompe l'oeil painting. Office: US Dist Ct One Court House Way Ste 8420 Boston MA 02110

BOWLES, BARBARA LANDERS, investment company executive; b. Nashville, Sept. 17, 1947; d. Corris Raemone Landers and Rebecca Aima (Bonham) Jennings; m. Earl Stanley Bowles, Nov. 27, 1971; 1 son, Terrence Earl. BA, Fisk U., 1968; MBA, U. Chgo., 1971. Chartered fin. analyst. From bank official to v.p. First Nat. Bank of Chgo., 1968-81; asst. v.p. Beatrice Cos., Chgo., 1981-84; v.p. investor rels. Kraft Inc., Chgo., 1984-86; pres., founder The Kenwood Group Inc., Chgo., 1989—; bd. dirs. Black & Decker Corp., Hyde Pk. Bank. Bd. dirs. Children's Meml. Hosp., The Chgo. Urban League. Scholar United Negro College Fund, 1989. Mem. NAACP (life), Assn. for Investment Mgmt. and Rsch., Chgo. Fisk Alumni Assn. (pres. 1983-85), University (Chgo.). Mem. United Ch. of Christ. Avocations: tennis, bridge. *

BOWLES, DAVID STANLEY, engineering educator, consultant; b. Romford, Essex, Eng., June 30, 1949; m. Valerie Rosina Curd; children: Penny, Simon, Amy. BSc, City U., Eng., 1972; PhD, Utah State U., 1977. Registered profl. engr., Utah; cert. profl. hydrologist. Jr. civil engr. George Wimpey & Co., Hammersmith, London, 1967-72; rsch. asst. prof. Utah State U., Logan, 1976-80, rsch. assoc. prof., 1980-81, adj. rsch. assoc. prof., 1981-83, rsch. prof., 1983-85, prof., 1985—, assoc. dir., 1986-91, dir., 1992-96; vis. scientist Internat. Inst. Applied Systems Analysis, Laxenburg, Austria, 1979; br. mgr., engr. Law Engring., Denver, 1981-83; prin. Risk Assessment Cons. Engrs. and Economists (RAC), 1986—. Contbr. numerous articles to profl. jours. Mem. U.S. Com. on Large Dams. Fellow ASCE, Am. Water Resources Assn.; mem. Soc. Risk Analysis, Am. Geophys. Union, Am. Inst. Hydrology, European Geophys. Union, Assn. State Dam Safety Ofcls. Home: 1520 Canyon Rd Providence UT 84332-9431 Office: Utah Water Rsch Lab Utah State Univ Logan UT 84322-8200

BOWLES, ERSKINE, White House staff member; b. 1945; s. Hargrove "Skipper" Bowles; m. Crandall Bowles; 3 children. With Morgan Stanley & Co., N.Y.C., Bowles Hollowell Conner & Co., Charlotte, N.C., 1975-93; adminstr. Small Bus. Adminstrn., Washington, 1993-94; from dep. chief of staff to chief of staff The White House, Washington, 1994-98; ptnr. Forstmann Little & Co., N.Y.C., 1999—. pres. Juvenile Diabetes Found. Office: Forstmann Little & Co 767 Fifth Ave New York NY 10153*

BOWLES, L. THOMPSON, medical executive; b. Mineola, N.Y., Sept. 23, 1931; m. Judith E. Bowles, July 10, 1965; children: Julia, Amy, Lauren. AB, Duke U., 1953, MD, 1957; MS, NYU, 1964, PhD, 1971. Intern 4th surgery divsn. Bellevue Hosp., N.Y.C., 1957; acad. dean George Washington U. Med. Ctr., Washington, 1975-87, v.p., exec. dean, 1987-92; pres. Nat. Bd. Med. Examiners, Phila., 1992—; pres. Med. Licensing Bd., Washington, 1977-79. Founding editor: AAMC Curriculum Directory, 1973. Recipient Disting. Svc. award D.C. Med. Soc., 1981. Fellow ACS, Soc. Thoracic Surgeons, Am. Assn. for Thoracic Surgeons; mem. Alpha Omega Alpha. Office: Nat Bd Med Examiners 3750 Market St Philadelphia PA 19104-3190

BOWLES, LIZA K., construction executive. Pres. NAHB Rsch. Ctr., Upper Marlboro, Md. Office: NAHB Rsch Ctr 400 Prince Georges Blvd Upper Marlboro MD 20774-8759

BOWLES, PATRICIA MARY, secondary education educator; b. Reading, Pa., Jan. 15, 1950; d. Charles Worthington Doane and Mary Augusta (Kershner) B. BS, Kutztown (Pa.) U., 1971; MEd, Temple U., 1987. Cert. elem. tchr. and elem. prin., Pa. Tchr. visually impaired Reading (Pa.) Sch. Dist., 1972-75, adminstrv. intern, 1986-87; tchr. Berks County Intermediate Unit, Reading, 1973-93; tchr. visually impaired Reading Sch. Dist., 1993—. Account exec. United Way, Berks County, 1988—; bd. dirs. Leadership Berks, Reading, 1988—, Nat. Coun. on Alcoholism, Berks County, 1988—; pres. Leadership Berks Alumni Assn., Reading, 1987, bd. dirs., 1987—. Eleanor Long Tchr. of the Yr., Pa. Div. Visually Impaired, 1984. Mem. Assn. for Edn. and Rehab. Visually Impaired, Assn. for Supervision and Curriculum Devel., Flying Dutchmen Ski Club (trip dir. Reading chpt. 1975-76), Phi Delta Kappa, Delta Kappa Gamma. Republican. Lutheran. Avocations: snow and water skiing, dancing, theatre. Home: 5 Eagle Ct Reading PA 19605-3215 Office: Reading High Sch 801 N 13th St Reading PA 19604-2451

BOWLES, RICHARD ROBERT, retired investor, art appraiser; b. New Haven, July 15, 1962; s. Richard Roscoe and Eleanor Ann (Zebrowk) B.; m. Penelope Anne Keller-Smyth, Aug. 31, 1990 (div. Feb. 1997). Grad. with hons, U.S. Army Fgn. Lang. Sch., Monterrey, Calif., 1982; degree in liberal studies, U. N.C., Chapel Hill, 1985; degree in polit. sci., Yale U., 1996; degree in art history, So. Conn. State U., 1998. Industry analyst Abraham Co., N.Y.C., 1985-86; investment banker Goldman Saks, N.Y.C., 1986-91; fin. advisor Medicins Sans Frontieres, Brussels, 1991-92; med. vol. Medicins Sans Frontieres, Somalia, 1992-93; art historian, advisor Sotheby's, N.Y.C., 1993-94, 94-95; art appraiser Christie's, N.Y.C., 1995-97, ret., 1997—; advisor Am. Art Preservation Inst., N.Y.C., 1996—. Asst. Editor: Art in Pre-Revolutionary Russia, 1993; contbr. articles profl. jours. Bd. dirs. Yale-New Haven Hosp., 1994-95, St. Raphael's Hosp., New Haven, 1995-97, Yale Art Gallery, New Haven, 1997; with U.S. Army, 1980-85. Decorated Purple Heart; recipient Order King Leopold, Belgian Parliament, 1993, Humanitarian award Lions Club Internat., 1996; named Man of Yr. Kiwanis Club, 1995. Mem. VFW, Am. Assn. Ind. Investors, New Haven Lawn Club, Yale Club. Lutheran. Avocations: guitar, running, clock collecting, motorcycle riding, film preservation. Home and Office: 30 Thorpe St North Haven CT 06473-1823

BOWLES, SUZANNE GEISSLER, history educator; b. Somerville, N.J., Nov. 12, 1950; d. Alfred Henry and Suzanne Judith (Golembeski) Geissler; m. Arthur Graham Bowles, Oct. 15, 1994. BA, Syracuse U., 1971; MA, Rutgers U., 1972; PhD, Syracuse U., 1976; MTS, Drew U., 1979. Instr. history SUNY, Cortland, N.Y., 1975-77; lectr. history Drew U., Madison, N.J., 1977-79; adj. prof. history Upsala Coll., Sussex, N.J., 1979-95, William Paterson U., Wayne, N.J., 1995—; cons. in field. Author: Jonathan Edwards to Aaron Burr, 1981, Lutheranism and Anglicanism in Colonial New Jersey, 1988, A Widening Sphere of Usefulness: Newark Academy, 1993. Mem. Am. Soc. Ch. History, Am. Hist. Assn., U.S. Naval Inst., Orgn. Am. Historians, Hist. Soc. Episcopal Ch., Soc. Mil. History, Phi Beta Kappa. Office: William Paterson U History Dept Wayne NJ 07470

BOWLIN, EVE SALLEE, retired ob-gyn nurse practioner; b. San Jacinto, Calif., Nov. 16, 1913; d. Joseph and Theda (Bergman) Sallee; widow; children: Chad, Barbara, McKim, Jonathan (dec.). LVN, Mt. San Jacinto Coll., 1967; diploma in nursing, Loma Linda U., 1970; teaching credential, San Bernardino State Coll., 1976; RNP, U. Calif., San Francisco, 1977. Lic. vocat. nurse, Calif. Tchr. English to fgn.-born students Coachella Valley Sch. Dist., Thermal, Calif.; pub. health nurse Riverside County Health Dept., Indio, Calif., ob.-gyn. nurse; rural health clinic prenatal care provider El Progreso del Desierto, Coachella, Calif., 1981-90; gynecologic nurse Ribton Wade, M.D., 1990-94; ret., 1998. Vol. Liga Flying Drs. of Mercy; vol. counselor Peer Counseling Program. Mem. So. Calif. Pub. Health Assn. (charter), LaQuinta Soroptimist Internat. (recipient svc. awards), Toastmasters. Home: 25 Rustic Rock Ln Palm Desert CA 92260-6439

BOWLIN, GLORIA JEAN, artist; b. Middletown, Ohio, May 18, 1949; d. Leonard William and Margaret May (Hughes) Creager; m. Jerry Edward Bowlin, Mar. 3, 1969; children: Amy Beth, Jeremy Scott. Grad. h.s., Carlisle, Ohio. Owner, designer The Crow & the Weasel, New Carlisle, Ohio, 1994-99; artist Penny Lane Pub., New Carlisle, 1995-99. Author, creator (doll patterns/instrns.) Winter '95 Collection, Spring '96 Collection, Winter '96 Collection, Spring '97 Collection, Fall/Winter '97 Collection, Summer/Fall Collection, 98, Spring '98, 99, Collection; holder copyrights for various doll/soft sculpture designs. Vol. ABLE Literacy Program, Piqua, Ohio, 1993; student Am. Sign Lang., Cmty. Svcs. for Deaf, Dayton, Ohio, 1993-94. Avocations: herb gardening, antiques, writing simple verse, decorating. Home: 207 W Madison St New Carlisle OH 45344-1925

BOWLIN, MICHAEL RAY, oil company executive; b. Amarillo, Tex., Feb. 20, 1943; m. Martha Ann Rowland; 1 child, John Charles. BBA, North Tex. State U., 1965, MBA, 1967. Scheduler prodn. and transp. A. Brant Co., Ft. Worth, 1965-66; mktg. rep. R.J. Reynolds Tobacco Bo., 1967-68; personnel generalist Atlantic Richfield Co., Dallas, 1969-71; coll. relations rep. Atlantic Richfield Co., Los Angeles, 1971-72, mgr. internal profl. placement, 1973, mgr. corp. recruiting and placement, 1973-75, mgr. behavioral sci. services, 1975, sr. v.p. ARCO resources adminstrn., 1985, sr. v.p. ARCO internat. oil and gas acquisitions, 1987, sr. v.p., 1987—; employee relations mgr. Atlantic Richfield Co., Alaska, 1975-77; v.p. employee relations Anaconda Copper Co. (div. Atlantic Richfield Co.), Denver, 1977-81; v.p. employee relations ARCO Oil & Gas (div. Atlantic Richfield Co.), Dallas, 1981-82, v.p. fin. planning and control, 1982-84; sr. v.p. Atlantic Richfield Co., 1985-92; pres. ARCO Coal Co., 1985-87, ARCO Internat. Oil & Gas Co., 1987-92; CEO Atlantic Richfield Co., 1994—, chmn., CEO, 1998—; pres., COO ARCO Internat. Oil & Gas Co., 1993, 1993, pres., CEO, 1994-95, chmn., CEO, 1995—. Office: Atlantic Richfield Co 515 S Flower St Los Angeles CA 90071-2295

BOWLING, JOHN C., academic administrator. Pres. Olivet Nazarene U., 1991—. Office: Olivet Nazarene Univ Office of Pres PO Box 592 Kankakee IL 60901-0592*

BOWLING, JOYCE BLANKENCHIP, retired critical care nurse; b. White Deer, Tex., Nov. 17, 1932; d. Roy Lee and Myrtle Dove (Milhoan) Blankenchip; m. J.C. Bowling, July 24, 1952. Diploma, Northwest Tex. Sch. Nursing, 1953; AS, Amarillo Coll., 1953; BSN, West Tex. State U., 1983. RN, Tex.; cert. med.-surg. nursing. gerontology, nursing adminstrn. AACN; cert. emergency nurse. Staff nurse emergency rm. Parkland Hosp., Dallas, 1960-62; staff nurse Meth. Hosp., Dallas, 1962-68; staff nurse medicine, then head nurse CCU St. Paul Hosp., Dallas, 1969-73; charge nurse, supr. Southwestern Dialysis Ctr., Dallas, 1973-74; dir. nurses Caruth Rehab. Inst., Dallas, 1974-75; staff nurse VA Med. Ctr., Dallas, 1976-79; staff nurse VA Med. Ctr., Amarillo, Tex., 1979-85, head nurse surg. unit, 1985-88, clin. coord., 1988-96, ret., 1996. Mem. AACN (cert.), Emergency Nurses Assn. (cert.), Tex. Nurses Assn., Am. Heart Assn., Nat. Kidney Found., Am. Cancer Soc., Sigma Theta Tau. Avocations: reading, needlework, travel, fishing. Home: 8000 W 81st Ave # 10 Amarillo TX 79119-7431

BOWLSBY, BOB, athletic director; b. Jan. 10, 1952; m. Candice Bowlsby; children: Lisa, Matt, Rachel, Kyle. BS, Moorhead State U., 1975; MS, U. Iowa, 1978. Asst. athletic dir. Northern Iowa Univ.; athletic dir. Univ. Northern Iowa, 1984-91, Univ. Iowa, 1991—; chair NCAA Divsn. I Mgmt. Coun., 1997-99. Chmn. Big Ten Championships and awards com.; chair NCAA Olympic Sports Liaison Com., NCAA/USOC liaison com., Olympics com. mem; bd. dirs. Iowa Games. Mem. Nat. Assn. Collegiate Dir. of Athletics (exec. com.), 1997-99. Office: U Iowa Dir Athletics 338 Carver Hawkeye Arena Iowa City IA 52242-1020*

BOWMAN, ALISON FRANCES, writer; b. Pasadena, Calif., Feb. 15, 1968; d. Allen Paul and Frances Ann Bowman. BA in Politics, U. Calif., Santa Cruz, 1991; MA in Radio and TV, San Francisco State U., 1995. Radio news journalist KZSC-FM, Santa Cruz, 1986-87; radio news dir. KZSC, Santa Cruz, 1987-88; print journalist City on a Hill Press, Santa Cruz, 1988-89; city editor Cityona Hill Press, Santa Cruz, 1989-90; editor-in-chief Primer Mag., Santa Cruz, 1990; market rschr. Larry Wisch Assocs., San Francisco, 1992-96. Prodr. documentary film Green Dreams, 1994; contbr. articles to Santa Cruz Mag., Urban Tempo, S.F. Bay Guardian. Mem. Soc. Profl. Journalists, Media Alliance. Avocations: mountain climbing, writing essays. Home: 624 Brooklyn Ave Apt 204 Oakland CA 94606-1029 Office: 484 Lake Park Ave # 193 Oakland CA 94610

BOWMAN, BARBARA TAYLOR, institute president; b. Chgo., Oct. 30, 1928; d. Robert Rochon and Dorothy Vaugn (Jennings) Taylor; m. James E. Bowman, June 17, 1950, 1 child, Valerie Bowman Jarrett. BA, Sarah Lawrence Coll., 1950; MA, U. Chgo., 1952; DHL, Bankstreet Coll., 1988, Roosevelt U., 1998. Tchr. U. Chgo. Nursery Sch., 1950-52, Colo. Women's Coll. Nursery Sch., Denver, 1953-55; mem. sci. faculty Shiraz (Iran) U. Nemazee Sch. Nursing, 1955-61; spl. edn. tchr. Chgo. Child Care Soc., 1965-67; mem. faculty Erikson Inst., Chgo., 1967—, dir. grad. studies, 1978-94, pres., 1994—; mem. early childhood com. Nat. Bd. Profl. Tchg. Stds., 1992—; cons. early childhood edn., parent edn. Contbr. articles to profl. jours. Bd. dirs. Ill. Health Edn. Com., 1969-71, Inst. Psychoanalysis, 1970-73, Ill. Adv. Coun. Dept. Children and Family Svcs., 1974-79, Child Devel. Assoc. Consortium, 1979-81, Chgo. Bd. Edn. Desegregation Commn., 1981-84, Bus. People in Pub. Inst., 1980—, High Scope Ednl. Rsch. Found., 1986-93, Gt. Books Found., 1988—, Cmty.-Corp. Sch., 1988-90; with Family Resource Coalition, 1992-96, nat. bd. profl. tchr. stds., 1996—. Mem. Ill. Assn. Edn. Young Children, Nat. Assn. Edn. Young Children (pres. 1980-82), Chgo. Assns. Edn. Young Children (pres. 1973-77), Black Child Devel. Assn., Am. Ednl. Rsch. Assn. (chair Nat. Rsch. Coun. com. on early childhood pedagogy 1998-99). Research on math. teaching and school improvement. Office: Erikson Inst 420 N Wabash Ave Chicago IL 60611-3568

BOWMAN, BRUCE, art educator, writer, artist; b. Dayton, Ohio, Nov. 23, 1938; s. Murray Edgar Bowman and Mildred May (Moler) Elleman; m. Julie Ann Gosselin, 1970 (div. 1980); 1 child, Carrie Lynn. AA, San Diego City Coll., 1962; BA, Calif. State U.-Los Angeles, 1964, MA, 1968. Tchr. art North Hollywood Adult Sch., Calif., 1966-68; instr. art Cypress Coll., Calif., 1976-78, West Los Angeles Coll., 1969—; tchr. art Los Angeles City Schs., 1966—; seminar leader So. Calif., 1986—. Author: Shaped Canvas, 1976; Toothpick Sculpture and Ice Cream Stick Art, 1976; Ideas: How to Get Them, 1985, (cassette tape) Develop Winning Willpower, 1986, Waikiki, 1988. Contbr. articles to profl. jours. One-man shows include Calif. State U.-Los Angeles, 1968, Pepperdine U., Malibu, Calif., 1978; exhibited in group shows McKenzie Gallery, Los Angeles, 1968, Trebor Gallery, Los Angeles,

1970, Cypress Coll., Calif., 1977, Design Recycled Gallery, Fullerton, Calif., 1977, Pierce Coll., Woodland Hills, Calif., 1978, Leopold/Gold Gallery, Santa Monica, Calif., 1980. Served with USN, 1957-61. Avocation: karate (black belt Tang Soo Do). Home: 28322 Rey De Copas Ln Malibu CA 90265-4463

BOWMAN, C. MICHAEL, physician; married; two children. BS in Chemistry (with honors), U. Ill., 1968; PhD in Genetics, U. Wis., 1972, MD, 1975. Pediat. resident Vanderbilt U., 1975-78, chief resident, 1978-79; dir. comprehensive cystic fibrosis ctr. Childrens Hosp., L.A.; assoc. divsn. head Divsn. Pediat. Pulmonolgy. Fellow Am. Acad. of Pediat., mem. Am. Bd. of Pediat., Am. Thoracic Soc., Western Soc. for Pediat. Rsch. Achievements include research in lung disorders in children. Home: 3901 Ferntree Pl La Crescenta CA 91214-3247 Office: Childrens Hosp Los Angeles Box 83 4650 W Sunset Blvd Los Angeles CA 90027-6062

BOWMAN, CATHERINE MCKENZIE, lawyer; b. Tampa, Fla., Nov. 10, 1962; d. Herbert Alonzo and Joan Bates (Baggs) McKenzie; m. Donald Campbell Bowman, Jr., May 21, 1988; children: Hunter Hall, Sarah McKenzie. BA in Psychology and Sociology, Vanderbilt U., 1984; JD, U. Ga., 1987. Bar: Ga. 1987, U.S. Dist. Ct. (so. dist.) Ga. 1987. Assoc. Ranitz, Mahoney, Forbes & Coolidge, P.C., Savannah, Ga., 1987-91; ptnr. Forbes and Bowman, 1991—. Bd. dirs. Greenbriar Children's Ctr., exec. com. 1995, pres. 1996-98; active Jr. League Savannah; mem. Leadership Savannah, 1994-96. Mem. Am. Employment Law Coun., Ga. Def. Lawyers Assn., Savannah Young Lawyers Assn. (pres. 1996-97), 2000 Club (membership chair 1990-91, pres. 1992), South Atlantic Found. (bd. dirs. 1992). Home: 21 Jameswood Ave Savannah GA 31406-5219 Office: Forbes and Bowman PO Box 13929 7505 Waters Ave Ste D-14 Savannah GA 31406-3824

BOWMAN, CHARLES HAY, petroleum company executive; b. Pitts., Dec. 21, 1935; m. Lynn A. Holleran; 5 children. BS, Pa. State U., 1957; MS, Tex. A&M U., 1959, PhD, 1961. Rsch. engr. Gulf Oil Corp., Pitts., 1960-64; reservoir engr. Gulf Oil Corp., Venezuela, 1964-66; rsch. assoc. Gulf Oil Corp., Pitts., 1966-69; chief reservoir engr. Gulf Oil Corp., Venezuela, 1969-70, exploitation supt., 1970-73; spl. projects mgr. Gulf Oil Corp., Pitts., 1973-74; gen. mgr. crude oil sales Gulf Oil Trading Co., Pitts., 1974-76; v.p. energy and regulation and compliance Gulf Refining and Mktg. Co., 1976-80, sr. v.p., 1980-81, pres., 1981-83; pres. Gulf Oil Products Co., 1983-85; sr. v.p. petroleum products & refining Sohio Oil Co. (a subs. BP Am. Inc.), Cleve., 1985-86; pres. Old Ben Coal Co. (a subs. BP Am. Inc.), Lexington/Cleve., 1986-88; gen. mgr. Europe BP Oil Internat., London, 1988-90; mng. dir. BP Australia Ltd., Melbourne, 1990-94; chmn., CEO BP Am., Inc., Cleve., 1994-97; ret., 1997; prof., head of petroleum engring. dept. Tex. A&M U., College Station, 1997—; bd. dirs. Nat. City Corp. Bd. dirs. Case Western Res. U., Cleve. Initiative for Edn.; chmn. Cleve. Ballet. Avocations: antique collecting, model railroading, furniture restoration, woodworking, boating. *

BOWMAN, CYNTHIA D., library director; b. Decatur, Ill., July 31, 1950; d. Clyde Junior and Beverly June Beck; m. Delvan Gene Bowman, Dec. 6, 1969; children: Heath Eugene, Heather Michelle. Grad., Eisenhower H.S., Decatur, 1968. Sec., supr. Argenta (Ill.)-Oreana Pub. Libr. Dist., 1982-95, children's librarian, 1992-95, dir., 1995—. Office: Argenta-Oreana Pub Libr Dist 3 North Argenta IL 62501

BOWMAN, DAVID WESLEY, lawyer; b. Mpls., Dec. 14, 1940; s. Burton F. and Eldred (Frudenfeld) B.; m. Patricia L. Schlimme, Nov. 26, 1975; children: Christopher B., Sarah K., David W., Tulley B., Ashley B. B.A., U. Iowa, 1964, J.D., 1967. Bar: Iowa 1967. Asst. counsel Dept. Navy, Washington, 1968-72, Firestone Corp., Akron, Ohio, 1972-77; counsel Harris Corp., Melbourne, Fla., 1977-80, v.p., sec., gen. counsel documation, 1980-81, sector counsel, 1981-83; v.p., sec., gen. counsel Harris Graphics Corp., 1983-87; sr. v.p., gen. counsel, sec. MAPCO Inc., Tulsa, 1987—. Mem. ABA, Fed. Bar Assn., Iowa Bar Assn., Nat. Contract Mgmt. Assn., Nat. Security Indsl. Assn. Episcopalian. Home: 3104 S Columbia Cir Tulsa OK 74105-2329 Office: Mapco Inc 1800 S Baltimore Ave PO Box 645 Tulsa OK 74101-0645*

BOWMAN, DOROTHY LOUISE, artist; b. Hollywood, Calif., Jan. 20, 1927; d. Bruce L. and Dorothy L. (Kalkman) B; m. Howard Hugh Bradford, Dec. 30, 1949 (div. 1965); children: Brock, Cyndra, Tal Scott, Heather, Delia, Callia. Student, Chouinard Art Inst., Calif., 1945-48, Jepson Art Inst., L.A., 1948-49; BA, Webster U., 1979. One-woman show Ventana Gallery, Big Sur, 1998; serigrapher, printmaker, painter: represented in permanent collections: Immaculate Heart Coll., L.A. County Mus., Bklyn. Mus., Long Beach Mus., Crocker Art Gallery, Mus. Modern Art, Phila., Mus. Fine Arts, San Jose State Coll., De Cordova and Danna Mus., Boston Pub. Libr., Boston Mus. Fine Arts, N.Y. Pub. Libr., Rochester Meml. Gallery, U. Wis., U. Hawaii, U. Ill., U. Kans., Santa Barbara Mus., Achenbach Found. Legion of Honor, Mus. Modern Art, Monterey, Calif., Libr. Congress, Calif. State Libr. Archives, Arquivos Historicos De Arte Contemporanea Museu De Arte Moderna, San Paulo, Brazil, Ch. of Latter Day Saints History Mus., Salt Lake City, Nat. Mus. of Women in the Arts, Washington; twice juried internat. show 27 countries, 1987. Address: Nat Mus of Women in the Arts Archives 1250 New York Ave NW Washington DC 20005-3920

BOWMAN, ED, school administrator. Prin. Oakwood High Sch., Dayton, Ohio, 1988-95; dir. ednl. svcs. Oakwood Bd. Edn., Dayton, 1995—. Recipient Blue Ribbon Sch. award U.S. Dept. Edn., 1990-91. Office: Oakwood Bd of Edn 20 Rubicon Rd Dayton OH 45409-2298*

BOWMAN, FRANK LEE, admiral and director naval nuclear propulsion; b. Chattanooga, Tenn., Dec. 19, 1944; m. Linda Anne Rich, June 10, 1966; children: Greg, Christy. BS, Duke U., 1966; MS in Nuclear Engring., Naval Arch., MIT, 1973. Commd ensign USN, 1966, advanced through grades to admiral, 1996; naval officer at sea on USS Simon Bolivar, USS Pogy, USS Daniel Boone, 1966-77; exec. officer USS Bremerton USN, 1978-80, comdr. USS City of Corpus Christi, 1983-86, comdr. USS Holland, 1988-90; dep. dir. ops. joint staff USN, Washington, 1991-92, dir. polit.-mil. affairs, 1992-94, dep. chief naval ops., chief naval pers., 1994-96, dir. naval nuclear propulsion, 1996—. Decorated Disting. Svc. medal, Defense Disting. Svc. medal, Legion of Merit with 3 gold stars, Navy Expeditionary medal twice, Humanitarian Svc. medal twice. Office: Naval Sea Systems Commd (SEA-08) 2531 Jefferson Davis Hwy Arlington VA 22242-5160

BOWMAN, GEORGE ARTHUR, JR., judge; b. Milw., Dec. 1, 1917; s. George Arthur and Edna Oral (Hunter) B.; m. Rose Mary Thorpe, Aug. 8, 1947 (dec. 1980); children: George A. III, Daniel Andrew. Student, U. Wis., 1936-39; JD, Marquette U., 1943. Bar: Wis. 1943, U.S. Supreme Ct. 1943. Asst. dist. atty. Milw. County, 1947-48, children's ct. judge, 1967-72; asst. city atty. City of Milw., 1948-67; adminstrv. law judge Office of Hearing and Appeals Social Security Adminstrn. Dept. HHS, Chgo., 1973-97, adminstrv. law judge emeritus, 1997; pvt. practice, 1997—; appointed Pres.'s Task Force, Law Enforcement Assistance Adminstrn., 1972; former counsel Milw. Police Dept.; advisor Nat. Council of Juvenile Ct. Judges, Nat. Conv., Atlanta; chmn. conv. com. Nat. Council of Juvenile Ct. Judges, Milw., 1972; chmn. State Task Force on Juvenile Delinquency, 1970-71; legis. com. Wis. Bd. Juvenile Ct. Judges, 1970-71; former mem. numerous legis. coms., Milw.; pioneered Legal Defender System in Children's Ct.; lecturer, Marquette U. Co-author: LEAA Uniform Standards for Police Departments, 1973 (Pres.'s citation). Bd. dirs. Am. Indian Info. and Action Group, Inc. "Project Phoenix", Juneau Acad.; chmn. Milw. County Rep. Party, 1961-62; active supporter numerous community juvenile programs, including Milw. Boys' Club, St. Joseph's Home for Children, Mt. Mary Coll. Proglram for Truant and Delinquent Girls, Operation Outreach, others; Social Security judge. With USN, 1943-46. Recipient Continious Svc. award Office of Hearings and Appeals Soc. Security Adminstr., 1991. Mem. Fed. Assn. Adminstrv. Law Judges, Assn. Office of Hearing and Appeals Adminstrv. Law Judges, Wis. State Bar Assn., Milw. Bar. Assn., Nat. Council Juvenile Ct. Judges, Am. Judicature Soc., Nat. Council of Sr. Citizens, Inc., Internat. Juvenile Officers Assn., Am. Legion (former post comdr.), Nat. Probate Judges Assn., New Trier Rep. Orgn., Committeeman's Club, Hawthorne Turf Club, Sigma Alpha Epsilon. Roman Catholic. Home: 2824 Orchard Ln Wilmette IL 60091-2144

BOWMAN, GRAY, chemist, educator. Chemist Unipoint Industries, Inc., Thomasville, N.C.; prof. chemistry, chmn. dept. High Point U., 1976—. Office: High Point U Haworth Hall 219 833 Montlieu Ave High Point NC 27262-4221*

BOWMAN, HAZEL LOIS, retired English language educator; b. Plant City, Fla., Feb. 18, 1917; d. Joseph Monroe and Annie (Thoman) B.; AB, Fla. State Coll. for Women, 1937; MA, U. Fla., 1948; postgrad. U. Md., 1961-65. Tchr., Lakeview H.S., Winter Garden, Fla., 1939-40, Eagle Lake Sch., Fla., 1940-41; welfare visitor Fla. Welfare Bd., 1941-42; specialist U.S. Army Signal Corps, Arlington Hall, Va., 1942-43; recreation worker, asst. procurement officer ARC, CBI Theater, 1943-46; lab. technician Am. Cyanamid Corp., Brewster, Fla., 1946-47; instr., asst. prof. gen. extension div. U. Fla., Fla. State U., 1948-51; free-lance writer, editor, indexer, N.Y., Fla., 1951-55; staff writer Tampa (Fla.) Morning Tribune, 1956; staff writer, telegraph editor Winter Haven (Fla.) News-Chief, 1956-57; registrar/admissions officer U. Tampa, 1957-59; coll. counselor, Atlantic states, 1959-60; registrar/freshman adviser Towson State Tchrs. Coll., Balt., 1960-62; dir. student personnel, guidance, admissions Harford Jr. Coll., Bel Air, Md., 1962-64; instr. York (Pa.) Coll., 1965-66, asst. prof. English, journalism, 1966-69; tchr. S.W. Jr. H.S., Lakeland, Fla., 1969-70; tchr. learning disabled Vanguard Sch., Lake Wales, Fla., 1970-82; libr. asst. Polk County Hist. and Geneal. Libr., Bartow, Fla., 1986-91. Editor Tampa Altrusan, 1958-60, Polk County Hist. Calendar, 1986-90. Recipient Mayhall Music medal, 1933, Excellence in Cmty. Svc. award Nat. Soc. DAR, 1994. Mem. AAUW (hon. 50 year life), NOW, Nat. Geneal. Soc., Mortar Bd., Polk County Hist. Assn. (editor Newsletter, 1990-94), MidFla. PAF Users Group (editor newsletter 1994-96), Polk County Hist. Commn., 1992—, Alpha Chi Alpha, Chi Delta Phi. Home: 511 NE 9th Ave Mulberry FL 33860-2620

BOWMAN, JAMES EDWARD, physician, educator; b. Washington, Feb. 5, 1923; s. James Edward and Dorothy (Peterson) B.; m. Barbara Taylor, June 17, 1950; 1 child, Valerie June. BS, Howard U., 1943, MD, 1946. Intern Freedmen's Hosp., Washington, 1946-47; resident pathology St. Lukes Hosp., Chgo., 1947-50; chmn. dept. pathology Provident Hosp., 1950-53, Shiraz (Iran) Med. Ctr. Nemazee Hosp., 1955-61; vis. prof., chmn. dept. pathology faculty of medicine U. Shiraz, 1959-61; dir. labs. U. Chgo., 1971-80, prof. dept. pathology, medicine, com. on genetics, biol. scis., collegiate div., 1972-93, dir., 1973-93, prof. emeritus, 1993—; cons. pathology, div. hosp. and med. facilities HEW, USPHS, 1968; mem. Health and Hosps. Governing Commn., Cook County, 1969-72; mem. exec. com. hemalytic anemia study group NHLI, NIH, Bethesda, Md., 1973-75, Sabbatical fellow Ctr. for Advanced Study in Behavioral Scis., Stanford U., 1981-82, Ethical, Legal & Social Issues, Nat. Human Genome Program NIH/DOE. Contbr. to books and articles to profl. jours. Capt. M.C., AUS, 1953-55. Spl. rsch. fellow NIH Galton Lab., Univ. Coll., London, 1961-62. Mem. Coll. Am. Pathologists, Am. Soc. Clin. Pathologists, Am. Soc. Human Genetics, Cen. Soc. Clin. Rsch., Am. Soc. Hematology, Am. Assn. Phys. Anthropologists, Acad. Clin. Lab. Physicians and Scientists. Home: 4929 S Greenwood Ave Chicago IL 60615-2815 Office: U Chgo Dept Pathology 5841 S Maryland Ave Chicago IL 60637-1463

BOWMAN, JAMES KINSEY, publishing company executive, rare book specialist; b. Strongsville, Ohio, Nov. 1, 1933; s. Benjamin H. and Margaret A. (Kinsey) B.; m. Judith Ann Lofton, Mar. 29, 1957; children: J. Reed, Eustacia L., Todd K. BA, Denison U., Granville, Ohio, 1956. With McGraw-Hill Book Co., N.Y.C., 1956-90; gen. mgr., v.p. coll. div. McGraw-Hill Book Co., 1965-68, group v.p. higher edn., 1968-73, v.p. marketing, 1973-82, sr. v.p. adminstrn., 1982-84, sr. v.p. internat., 1984-87, v.p. gen. mgr. bookstores, 1987-90; chief exec. officer Judith Bowman Books, 1990—. Bd. dirs. Catskill Fly Fishing Ctr. and Mus., 1998—. Mem. Am. Assn. Pubs. (pres. coll. div. 1971-72), Slagle Trout Club (Mich.), Bedford Chowder and Marching Club (pres. 1976-77), Theodore Gordon Flyfishers Club (N.Y.C.), Campfire Club Am. (N.Y.), Anglers Club of N.Y., Phi Gamma Delta. Democrat. Presbyterian. Home and Office: 98 Pound Ridge Rd Bedford NY 10506-1241

BOWMAN, JEFFREY NEIL, podiatrist; b. Detroit, Apr. 25, 1957; s. Harry and Helen (London) B.; m. Carol Jane Bartlett, Apr. 12, 1986; 1 child, Dana. BS in Biology/Zoology, U. Mich., 1979; DPM, Ill. Coll. Podiatric Medicine, Chgo., 1983. Diplomate Am. Coun. Cert. Podiatric Physicians and Surgeons, Am. Acad. Pain Mgmt., Am. Bd. Podiatric Orthopedics. Resident Harris County Podiatric Surg. Found., Houston, 1983-84; physician Houston Foot Specialists, 1983-86, pres., CEO, 1986—; bd. dirs. West Houston Surgicare, 1994—, dept. chmn. surgery, 1995—; mem. residency selection com. Houston Podiatric Residency Found., 1990—. Mem. adv. bd. KTRH Radio Sta., Houston, 1994—; physician Houston Marathon, 1984—; health care advisor Houston Ind. Sch. Dist., 1992-94. Recipient Cert. of Excellence, Disting. Physicians Am., 1994, 95, 96, 97. Fellow Internat. Soc. Podiatric Laser Surgery, Acad. Ambulatory Foot Surgery; mem. Am. Podiatric Med. Assn., Tex. Podiatric Med. Assn., Harris county Podiatric Med. Assn. Republican. Jewish. Avocations: reading, golf, computers, investments. Office: 8945 Long Point Rd Ste 209 Houston TX 77055-3009

BOWMAN, JEFFREY R., protective services official; b. Akron, Ohio, Apr. 24, 1952; s. Roger Heath and Ruth Ann (Corrigan) B.; divorced; children: Katie, Andrew, Brian. BS in Orgnl. Behavior, U. San Francisco, 1986. Firefighter Anaheim (Calif.) Fire Dept., 1973-75, paramedic, 1975-79, capt., 1979-83, battalion chief, 1983-85, div. chief, 1985-86, fire chief, 1986—. Pres. bd. dirs. Anaheim Boys and Girls Club, 1988—; chmn. fundraising Boy Scouts Am., Anaheim, 1988. Mem. Internat. Assn. Fire Chiefs, Calif. Fire Chiefs Assn. Office: Anaheim Fire Dept 201 S Anaheim Blvd Ste 301 Anaheim CA 92805-3858

BOWMAN, JERRY WAYNE, artist, research scientist; b. Columbia City, Ind., Aug. 3, 1952; s. Wayne Austin and Patricia Ann Bowman; m. Susan Jolie Alexander, Feb. 12, 1988; children: Rachel, Lily. BA magna cum laude, Kalamazoo Coll., 1974. Rsch. scientist Pharmacia and Upjohn Inc., Kalamazoo, Mich., 1978—. Paintings published in book: Splash 5: Best of Watercolor, 1998, (mag.) Manhattan Arts Internat., 1995. Exhibited in group shows at San Diego Watercolor Soc., 1994, Northwest Watercolor Soc., 1994, Phila. Watercolor Soc., 1995, Grand Exhbn., 1993, 95, Watercolor USA, 1994-96. Mem. Watercolor West (signature, Nat. Watercolor Soc. prize 1997), Rocky Mountain Watermedia Soc. (signature, prize 1998, Daniel Smith award 1991), Kalamazoo Inst. Arts. Avocations: ornithology, travel, primitive art. E-mail: jabster1@ix.netcom.com. Home: 83626 Waldron Lawton MI 49065

BOWMAN, JOHN STEWART, writer, editor; b. Cambridge, Mass., May 30, 1931; s. John Russell and Anne Marie (Stewart) B.; m. Marion Palmedo, Dec. 17, 1957 (div. Sept. 1965); m. Francesca Maria DiPietro, Feb. 11, 1967; children: Michela Anne, Alexander Russell. BA, Harvard U., 1953; postgrad., Cambridge (Eng.) U., 1953-54, U. Munich, 1958-60. Assoc. editor Natural History Mag., N.Y.C., 1961, Book of Knowledge, N.Y.C., 1962-63; vis. lectr. continuing edn. U. Mass., Amherst, 1978-90. Author: Guide to Crete, 1963-92; co-author: Diamonds in the Rough, 1989; editor: Cambridge Dictionary of American Biography, 1995, Facts About American Wars, 1998, Columbia Chronologies of Asian History and Culture, 1999; librettist operas: The Face, 1978, Emperor Norton, 1981. With U.S. Army, 1954-56. Mem. Nat. Assn. Sci. Writers, Soc. for Am. Baseball Rsch., Phi Beta Kappa, Alpha Sigma Lambda. Avocations: reading, walking, music. Fax: (473) 584-0720; E-mail: jsbowman@crocker.com. Home and Office: 53 Massasoit St Northampton MA 01060-2015

BOWMAN, LAIRD PRICE, retired foundation administrator; b. Topeka, Jan. 28, 1927; s. Herbert Douglas and Marion Martha (Price) B.; m. Betty Lou Pote, Dec. 24, 1950; children: Bruce Pote, Susan Bowman Adams. BS, U. Kans., 1950, LLB, 1952. Bar: Kans. 1952, Mo. 1956. Law clk. chief judge U.S. Dist. Ct. Kans., 1952-53; assoc. firm McAnany, Van Cleave & Phillips, Kansas City, Kans., 1953-55; mem. firm Gage Hodges, Park & Kreamer, Kansas City, Mo., 1955-64; with Gas Service Co., Kansas City, Mo., 1964-83; asst. gen. counsel Gas Service Co., 1968-70, sec., asst. gen. counsel, 1970-83, v.p., 1978-83, dir., 1979-83; asst. to the pres. Kans. U. Endowment Assn., U. Kans., Lawrence, 1983-91, ret., 1991. With USMC, 1945-47. Mem. Kans. Bar Assn., Mo. Bar Assn., Sigma Chi, Phi Delta Phi. Congregationalist. Home: 1120 Jana Dr Lawrence KS 66049-4418

BOWMAN, LEAH, fashion designer, consultant, photographer, educator; b. Chgo., Apr. 21, 1935; d. John George and Alexandra (Colovos) Murges; m. Veron George Broe, Aug. 31, 1954; 1 child, Michelle; m. John Ronald Bowman, Feb. 28, 1959. Diploma, Sch. of Art Inst., Chgo., 1962. Designer Korach Bros. Inc., Chgo., 1962-65; costume designer Hull House South Theatre, Chgo., 1966-67, Wellington Theatre, Chgo., 1966-67; instr. Sch. of Art Inst., Chgo., 1967-70, asst. prof., 1970-73, assoc. prof., 1973-83, prof., 1983—, chmn. dept. fashion design, 1971-77, 81—, chmn. faculty senate, 1990-91; prodr. fashion performances and style exhbns.; vis. prof., cons. SNDT Women's U., Bombay, 1980, 85, 92, Ctrl. Acad. Arts and Design, Beijing, People's Republic of China, 1987; faculty sabbatical exhbn. Sch. of Art Inst., 1986, 93. Recipient Fulbright award Council for Internat. Exchange for Scholars, India, 1980. Office: Sch of Art Inst Chgo 37 S Wabash Ave Chicago IL 60603-3002

BOWMAN, LOUIS L., emergency physician; b. Toledo, Nov. 1, 1953; s. Louis J. and JAcquelyn (PErkins) B.; m. Deborah Lynn Hayden, Sept. 30, 1977; children: Heather, Kara, Jason, Benjamin, Michelle. BA in Chemistry, U. Toledo, 1976; DO, Kirksville Coll. Osteo. Med., 1980. Intern Doctor's Hosp., Columbus, Ohio; emergency physician Scioto Emergency Physicians, Columbus, Ohio, 1981—; med. dir. emergency medicine Columbis Cmty. Hosp., 1987-92; med. dir. Mid-Ohio Sports Car Course, Lexington, 1988—; med. dir., chmn. dept. medicine Med. Ctr. Hosp., Chillicothe, Ohio, 1995. Fellow Am. Coll. Emergency Physicians; Am. Osteo. Assn., Ohio Osteo. Assn., Columbus Acad. Osteo Medicine, Internat. Coun. Motor Sports Scis. Republican. Methodist. Avocations: golf, photography, travel, weight lifting. Office: Ambulatory Care Affiliates PO Box 292642 Columbus OH 43229-8642

BOWMAN, PASCO MIDDLETON, II, federal judge; b. Timberville, Va., Dec. 20, 1933; s. Pasco Middleton and Katherine (Lohr) B.; m. Ruth Elaine Bowman, July 12, 1958; children: Ann Katherine, Helen Middleton, Benjamin Garber. BA, Bridgewater Coll., 1955; JD, NYU, 1958; LLM, U. Va., 1986; LLD (hon.), Bridgewater Coll., 1988. Bar: N.Y. 1958, Ga. 1965, Mo. 1980. Assoc. firm Cravath, Swaine & Moore, N.Y.C., 1958-61, 62-64; asst. prof. law U. Ga., 1964-65, assoc. prof., 1965-69, prof., 1969-70; prof. Wake Forest U., 1970-78, dean, 1970-78; vis. prof. U. Va., 1978-79; prof., dean U. Mo., Kansas City, 1979-83; judge U.S. Ct. Appeals (8th cir.), Kansas City, Mo., 1983-98, chief judge, 1998-99. Mng. editor: NYU Law Rev, 1957-58; Reporter, chief draftsman: Georgia Corporation Code, 1965-68. Served to col. USAR, 1959-84. Fulbright scholar London Sch. Econs. and Polit. Sci., 1961-62, Root-Tilden scholar, 1955-58. Mem. N.Y. Bar, Mo. Bar. Office: US Ct Appeals 8th Circuit 10-50 US Courthouse 400 E 9th St Kansas City MO 64106

BOWMAN, PATRICIA LYNN, lawyer; b. Mpls., July 5, 1956; d. Robert Lee and Delores Helen (Roberts) B. BA in History with distinction, Stanford U., 1978; JD cum laude, Harvard U., 1981; MA, Grad. Theol. Union, 1999. Assoc. Perkins Coie, Seattle, 1981-84, Foster, Pepper & Shefelman, Seattle, 1984-89; v.p., assoc. counsel Washington Mut. Bank, Seattle, 1989-97. Bd. dirs., vice chair Common Ground, Seattle, 1987-93; bd. dirs. Elderhealth Northwest, Seattle, 1994-97. Mem. ABA, Wash. State Bar Assn., Seattle-King County Bar Assn., Seattle Mortgage Bankers Assn. (mem. legal com.), Phi Beta Kappa.

BOWMAN, RICHARD CARL, defense consultant, retired air force officer; b. Chgo., July 5, 1926; s. Carl Elias and Lucile (Rutan) B.; m. Lois Jean Hassenauer, June 10, 1950; children: Mary Bowman Millikin, Kristin Bowman Spencer, Margaret Bowman Flaherty, Victoria Bowman Smoke, Richard Carl. B.S., U.S. Mil. Acad., 1949; M.S., Okla. State U., 1954; M.P.A., Harvard U., 1958, Ph.D., 1964. Enlisted in U.S. Army, 1943; commd. 2d lt. USAF, 1949, advanced through grades to maj. gen., 1975; pilot, flight comdr. Korea, 1951; mem. initial staff Air Force Acad., 1955-57, assoc. prof. polit. sci., 1959-63; mem. staff Nat. Security Council, 1964-66, Office Sec. Air Force, 1967-73; dep. def. adviser to Am. ambassador to NATO, 1973-75; dir. European and NATO affairs Office Sec. Def., 1975-81, ret., 1981. Contbr. to mil. jours. Decorated Def. D.S.M. (2), Air Force D.S.M., Def. Superior Service medal, Legion of Merit (2), D.F.C., Air medal (3), Commendation medal (2); Grand Service Cross with Star W. Ger.; comdr. Order of St. Olaf (Norway). Mem. Coun. Fgn. Rels., West Point Assn. Grads., Harvard U. Alumni Assn., KC. Roman Catholic. Home: 7824 Midday Ln Alexandria VA 22306-2724

BOWMAN, ROGER MANWARING, real estate executive; b. Duluth, Minn., Dec. 3, 1916; s. Lawrence Fredrick and Gladys (Manwaring) B.; m. Judith Claypool, Apr. 10, 1942 (dec. 1993); Ann, David, Mary Bowman Johnson, Lawrence II. Attended, U. Mich., 1934-36; student, Wayne State U., 1937. Pres. N. Star Airways, Duluth, 1946-50, Lawrence F. Bowman Co., Duluth, 1950-70, Gen. Cleaning Corp., Duluth, 1954-92, Bowman Corp., Duluth, 1970-83, Bowman Properties, Duluth, 1983-92; chmn. Deltona Corp., Miami, Fla., 1985-89; cons. Topeka Group, Duluth, 1985-89; bd. dirs. Parish Corp., Minn. Power, Norwest Bank; chmn. Bowman Properties, 1988-96, Gen. Cleaning Corp., 1985—. Chmn. St. Louis County Welfare, Duluth, 1964-69, chmn. Govs. Real Estate Adv. Commn., 1968-70; pres. Duluth Devel. Corp., 1960-68; trustee Ordean Found., 1968-92; bd. dirs. Duluth Bd. Realtors, 1958-62; pres. Duluth Bldg. Owners and Mgrs. Assn. Internat., 1963-65. Lt. col. USMCR, 1940-45. Recipient Silver Beaver award Boy Scouts Am., 1959, Mayor's Commendation, City of Duluth, 1976. Mem. Duluth Steam Coop. (bd. dirs. 1970-86), Duluth Bldg. Owners and Mgrs. Internat., Duluth Bd. Realtors, Real Property Adminstrs. Republican. Episcopalian. Clubs: Kitchi Gammi (dir. 1974-78), Northland Country. Avocation: cooking. Office: 575 Norwest Center Duluth MN 55802

BOWMAN, SCOTT MCMAHAN, lawyer; b. Shaker Heights, Ohio, Mar. 16, 1962; s. George Henry and Patricia (McMahan) B.; children: Chad Marshall, David Chandler, Elizabeth Brooks; stepchildren: Garrett Richard Sevek, Grant Allen Sevek. AA in Bus., Fullerton Coll., 1987; BBA, Calif. State U., Fullerton, 1989; JD, U. Cin., 1992. Pvt. practice Salem, Ohio, 1992—; asst. city solicitor Salem, 1992-94; advisor YWCA Salem, 1994—; advisor Buler Inst. Art, Salem, 1994—; intermediary, counsel Unorganized Militia, 1996—. Author: The Turning Point, 1997. Mem. design review bd. City of Salem (Ohio), 1993-95, v.p., 1995; mem. Salem Planning and Zoning Commn., 1993-95, v.p., 1995; co-founder, trustee Salem Preservation Soc., 1993-95. Mem. ABA, Ohio Bar Assn., Columbiana County Bar Assn. Episcopal. Avocations: camping, hunting, surfing, coaching football, politics. Office: PO Box 558 Salem OH 44460-0558

BOWMAN, STEPHEN WAYNE, quality assurance engineer, consultant; b. Charlotte, N.C., Oct. 3, 1949; s. John Wayne and Dagmar Kathrine (Hege) B.; m. Patricia Faye Waldron, June 17, 1972 (div. 1988); 1 child, Jennifer Leigh. BS in Physics, Ga. Inst. Tech., 1972, MS in Nuclear Engring., 1974. Registered profl. engr., Tex.; cert. quality sys. lead auditor (RAB). Quality assurance engr. GE, Schenectady, N.Y., 1978-81; mgr. IEEE qualification program Stewart and Stevenson Svcs., Houston, 1981-86, mgr. nuclear projects, 1984-86; sr. engr. Pacific Engring. Corp., Portland, Oreg., 1988-89; pres. Bowman and Assocs., Kingwood, Tex., 1986—; project quality assurance mgr. M.W. Kellogg Co., Houston, 1990-96; sr. ptnr. Internat. Mgmt. Systems Co., Midvale, Utah, 1992—; quality assurance mgr. Intec Engring., Inc., Houston, 1997-99; chmn. curriculum adv. bd. dept. mfg. technology Houston C.C., 1984-87. Contbr. articles to profl. jours. 1st lt. U.S. Army, 1975-78. Mem. Am. Nuclear Soc., Am. Soc. Quality. Home and Office: Bowman & Assocs 1915 Crystal Springs Dr Kingwood TX 77339-3339

BOWMAN, TINA MARIE DAVIS, pediatric nurse; b. Chgo., Aug. 18, 1964; d. Albert Robert and Edith Lola (Richardson) D. BSN, Loyola U., Chgo., 1988. RN, Ill. Child care worker Northwestern Meml. Hosp., Chgo., 1985; nurse asst. St. Joseph's Hosp., Chgo., 1986-88; staff nurse Michael Reese Hosp., Chgo., 1988-90, Children's Meml. Hosp., Chgo., 1990-96, Maryville Clinic, 1996—, Hull House Pregnant/Parenting Teens, Chgo., 1999—. Office: Hull House 550 W Jackson Blvd Ste 450 Chicago IL 60661

BOWMAN, WILLARD NELSON, JR., architect; b. Lancaster, Pa., Apr. 8, 1933; s. Williard Nelson Bowman and Helen Ann (Myers) Decker; children: Tod, Mark, Andrew. BArch, U. Fla., 1961. Lic. architect, Fla. Carpenter

Trojan Boat Co., Lancaster; clk. U.S. Postal Svc., Pompano Beach, Fla.; architect S.W. Constrn., Ft. Myers; pvt. practice Punta Gorda, Fla., 1965—. Sec.-treas. Cedarwood Condominiums, Punta Gorda; past pres. SARA, Ft. Lauderdale, Fla., 1981-82. Cpl. USMC, 1982-85. Democrat. Roman Catholic. Avocations: computers, carpentry. Home: PO Box 511865 Punta Gorda FL 33951 Office: 232 W Henby St Punta Gorda FL 33950

BOWMAN, WILLIAM SCOTT "SCOTTY", professional hockey coach; b. Montreal, Sept. 18, 1933; s. John and Jane Thomson (Scott) B.; m. Suella Belle Chitty, Aug. 16, 1969; children—Alicia Jean, David Scott, Stanley Glen, Nancy Elizabeth and Robert Gordon (twins). Student, Sir George Williams Bus. Sch., 1954. Scout exec. Club de Hockey Canadien, Montreal, 1956-66; coach Club de Hockey Canadien, 1971-79; coach, gen. mgr. St. Louis Blues Hockey Club, 1966-71; coach, gen. mgr., dir. hockey ops. Buffalo Sabres Hockey Club, 1979-86; TV analyst Hockey Night in Can., 1987-90; dir. player devel. Pitts. Penguins Hockey Club, 1990-91, interim head coach, 1991-92, head coach, 1992-93; head coach Detroit Red Wings Hockey Club, 1993—, dir. player pers., 1993—. Recipient Jack Adams award, 1977, 96, Victor award for NHL Coach of Yr., 1993, 96, Stanley Cup Championship, 1997; named NHL Exec. of Yr. Sporting News, 1979-80, NHL Coach of the Yr. Sporting News, 1995-96, NHL Coach of the Yr. Hockey News, 1976, 77, 93-97, NHL Exec. of the Yr. Hockey News, 1996-97, NHL Coach of the Yr., 1967-68, Hockey News Coach of Yr., 1968, 76, 97, Exec. of Yr., 1997; inducted into Hockey Hall of Fame, 1991; holder NHL career regular season records for wins (1,083) and winning percentage (.658); holder NHL career playoffs records for wins (193) and games (305); recipient Stanley Cup as head coach Montreal Canadiens, 1973, 76, 77, 78, 79, Pitts. Penguins, 1992, Detroit Red Wings, 1997, 98; only coach in HHL history to win Stanley Cup with 3 different teams. Office: Detroit Red Wings Joe Louis Arena 600 Civic Center Dr Detroit MI 48226-4419

BOWMAN-DALTON, BURDENE KATHRYN, education testing coordinator, computer consultant; b. Magnolia, Ohio, July 13, 1937; d. Ernest Mowles and Mary Kathryn (Long) Bowman; BME, Capital U., 1959; MA in Edn., Akron U., 1967, postgrad. 1976-87; m. Louis W. Dalton, Mar. 13, 1979. Profl. vocalist, various clubs in the East, 1959-60; music tchr. East Liverpool (Ohio) City Schs., 1959-62; music tchr. Revere Local Schs., Akron, Ohio, 1962-75, elem. tchr., 1975-80, elem. team leader/computer cons., 1979-85, tchr. middle sch. math., gift-talented, computer literacy, 1981-92, dist. computer specialist, 1987-93, dist. statis. for standardize local testing, 1987-91, dist. tech. coord., 1993-97; local and regional dir., Olympics of Mind, also World Problem Captain for computer problem, 1984-86; cons., workshop presenter State of Ohio, 1987-91, dist. test coord., 1991-98; ret., 1998; coord. for Revere Schs., Ednl. Mgmt. Info. Sys., 1992-98. Mem. Citizen Com., Akron, 1975-76; profl. rep. Bath Assn. to Help, 1978-80; mem. Revere Levy Com. 1986, Revere Bond Issue Com., 1991; audit com. BATH, 1977-79; vol. chmn. Antique Car Show, Akron, 1972-81; dist. advisor MidWest Talent Search, 1987-93; dist. statistician of standardized rech. test results. Martha Holden Jennings Found. grantee, 1977-78; Title IV ESEA grantee, 1977-81. Mem. Assn. for Devel. Computer-Based Instrnl Sys. (dir. 1992-94), Ednl. Mgmt. Info. System (coord. for Revere Schs. 1992-98), Phi Beta. Republican. Lutheran. Home: 353 Retreat Dr Akron OH 44333-1623 Office: 3195 Spring Valley Rd Bath OH 44210-0339

BOWNE, JAMES DEHART, museum official; b. Phila., Mar. 5, 1940; s. Ira Ervin and Mary Bradway (Powell) B.; m. Cheryl Jean Thompson, June 15, 1974; 1 dau., Heather Leigh. Student, George Washington U. and Corcoran Sch. Art, 1962, 63, 66, 67; A.A., Sandhills Community Coll., Southern Pines, N.C., 1968; A.B. in Art History, E. Carolina U., Greenville, N.C., 1970; M.A. in Art History, U. N.C. at Chapel Hill, 1972. Profl. artist Channel Galleries, Washington, 1963-67; curatorial asst. Ackland Art Center, Chapel Hill, 1971; grad. asst. U. N.C., Chapel Hill, 1971; research fellow U. N.C., 1972; dir., curator, instr. art Lauren Rogers Library and Mus. Art, Laurel, Miss., 1973-75; dir. Sheldon Swope Art Gallery, Terre Haute, Ind., 1975-78, Everhart Mus. Natural History, Sci. and Art, Scranton, Pa., 1978-81; exec. dir. Greenville County Mus. Art, Greenville, S.C., 1981-82; pres. Laurel Arts Council, 1974-75. Contbr.: articles to A Medieval Treasury From Southeastern Collections, 1971; also to newspapers. Bd. dirs. Terre Haute Symphony Assn., 1976-78; mem. museums adv. panel Ind. Arts Commn., 1977-78. Served with U.S. Army, 1958-61. Recipient award Delta Phi Delta Alumni Scholarship Found., award E. Carolina U., 1970. Mem. Am. Assn. Museums, Coll. Art Assn., Smithsonian Instn. Nat. Assos., Asso. Councils of Arts, Midwest Art History Soc., Midwest Museums Conf., Northeastern Museums Conf., Assn. Ind. Museums, Nat. Soc. Lit. and Arts, Scranton C. of C., Visitors and Conv. Bur., Delta Phi Delta, Phi Sigma Pi. Republican. Clubs: Rotary Internat, Nat. Exchange. *Mistakes and advancing age seem to be two of the best teachers and are, perhaps, the most difficult to accept. It is not so difficult to reach a goal; rather it is more difficult to decide what the goal will be. If one sets a goal that is too high and is unable to attain it, more harm is done than if one had set no goal at all. Life is built on, and progresses from, one goal to the next. Each day of life is one day nearer death. Therefore, it is important that one choose wisely. To truly care about others is one goal that all men should strive to reach. By so doing, the problems that have faced us in the past, that face us in the present, and that will face us in the future, will be lessened. The decision is ours. One's character is one's soul; one's soul-one's philosophy.**

BOWNE, SHIRLEE PEARSON, finance and housing consultant; b. High Shoals Twp., N.C., Mar. 11, 1936; d. Lloyd E. Pearson and Parnell (James) Garland; divorced; 1 child, Gregory Charles. Grad. h.s., Gaffney, S.C. Various secretarial positions, 1955-64; sales repr., pres. Real Estate Marketers, Inc., Tallahassee, FL, 1964-80; chief exec. officer Shirlee Bowne Mktg. & Devel. Inc., Tallahassee, 1980-91; vice chmn. Nat. Credit Union Adminstrn., Washington, 1991-97; cons. in field. Treas. Rep. Party Fla., 1988-91. Episcopalian. Avocation: bridge.

BOWNES, HUGH HENRY, federal judge; b. N.Y.C., Mar. 10, 1920; s. Hugh Gray and Margaret (Henry) B.; m. Irja C. Martikainen, Dec. 30, 1944 (dec. Jan. 1991); children: Barbara Anne, David and Ernest (twins); m. Mary Davis, July 12, 1992. B.A., Columbia U., 1941, LL.B., 1948. Bar: N.H. bar 1948. Since practiced in Laconia; ptnr. firm Nighswander, Lord & Bownes, 1951-66; assoc. justice N.H. Superior Ct., 1966-68; judge U.S. Dist. Ct. N.H., Concord, 1968-77; judge U.S. Ct. Appeals (1st cir.), 1977-90, sr. judge, 1990—. Mem. Laconia City Council, 1953-57; chmn. Laconia Democratic Com., 1954-57; mayor, Laconia, 1963-65; mem. Dem. Nat. Com. from N.H., 1963-66; Chmn. Laconia chpt. A.R.C., 1951-52; pres. bd. Laconia Hosp. Assn., 1963-64. Served to maj. USMCR, 1941-46. Decorated Silver Star, Purple Heart. Mem. ABA, N.H. Bar Assn., Belknap County Bar Assn. (pres. 1965-67), Laconia C. of C. (past pres.), Lions Club (past pres. Laconia). Office: US Ct Appeals 1st Cir US Courthouse 1 Courthouse Way Ste 6730 Boston MA 02210

BOWRA, KENNETH R., career officer; b. Oct. 23, 1948. Commd. U.S. Army, advanced through grades to maj. gen.; maj. gen. John F. Kennedy Spl. Warfare Ctr. U.S. Army, Ft. Bragg, N.C., 1997—. Office: US Army John F Kennedy Spl Warfare Ctr Fort Bragg NC 28307

BOWRON, EDGAR PETERS, art museum curator, administrator; b. Birmingham, Ala., May 27, 1943; s. James Edgar Bowron and Dorothe Peters Lowles; children: James Edgar III, Clara Beatrice, St. John Grenfell. BA, Colgate U., 1965; MA, Inst. Fine Arts, NYU, 1969, PHD, 1979. Edn. lectr. Met. Mus. Art, N.Y.C., 1969-70; registrar Mpls. Inst. Arts, 1970-73; curator Renaissance and Baroque art Walters Art Gallery, Balt., 1973-78; adminstrv. asst. to dir. and curator Renaissance and Baroque art Nelson Gallery-Atkins Mus., Kansas City, Mo., 1978-81; dir. N.C. Mus. Art, Raleigh, 1981-85; Elizabeth and John Moors Cabot dir., prof. fine arts Art Mus. Harvard U., Cambridge, Mass., 1985-90; sr. curator paintings Nat. Gallery of Art, Washington, 1991-96; Audrey Jones Beck curator of European art Mus. Fine Arts, Houston, 1996—; mem. art adv. panel IRS, 1994—. Author: Pompeo Batoni and His British Patrons, 1982; European Paintings before 1900 in the Fogg Mus., 1990; editor: Selected Writings of Anthony M. Clark: Studies in Eighteenth Roman Painting, 1981, The North Carolina Museum of Art: Introduction to the Collections, 1983, Anthony M. Clark, Pompeo Batoni, A Complete Catalogue of his Works with an Introductory Text, 1985; contbr. articles to jours. in field and exhbns. Trustee Mus. Fine Arts, Boston, 1988-90. Mem. Assn. Art Mus. Dirs. (trustee 1987-90), Master Drawings Assn. (bd. dirs. 1987—). Office: Mus Fine Arts PO Box 6826 Houston TX 77265-6826

BOWRON, RICHARD ANDERSON, retired utilities executive; b. Birmingham, Ala., Jan. 18, 1924; s. James Edgar and Mary Elizabeth (Anderson) B.; m. Ruth Wolmesdorf Matthews, Dec. 29, 1961; children: Richard Anderson, Mary Anderson, Lee Matthews. BS, U. Ala., 1943; MBA, U. Pa., 1948. With Ala. Power Co., Birmingham, 1948-89, sec., 1963-89, ret., 1989. 1st lt. AUS, 1943-46, 50-52. Mem. Birmingham Exchange Club, Mountain Brook Club. Presbyterian. Home: 3629 Springhill Rd Birmingham AL 35223-2820

BOWSER, EDWIN LEONARD, academic counselor; b. Johnstown, Pa., July 2, 1958; s. James Irvin and Leona Francis (Nadonley) B.; m. Danna Lea Bevec, Aug. 4, 1986; children Zachary Andrew, Alaina Nicole. BS in Vocat. Edn., U. Pitts., 1987, M of Vocat. Edn., 1986; M Guidance Counseling summa cum laude, Frostburg State U., 1993; cert. in coop. edn., Ind. U. of Pa.; cert. secondary sch. principal, St. Francis Coll. Cert. elem. and secondary edn. guidance counselor. Body shop mgr. Marhefka Chevrolet, Windber, Pa., 1977-80; auto body instr. Greater Johnstown (Pa.) Area Vocat. and Tech. Sch., 1980-92; asst. wrestling coach Greater Johnstown (Pa.) Area Vocat. and Tech. Sch., 1981, 82, 87, 89; head wrestling coach Greater Johnstown (Pa.) Area Vocat. and Tech. Sch., 1983-86, football coach, 1986-92, track coach, 1991-87; secondary guidance counselor Greater Johnstown (Pa.) AVTS, 1993—; secondary prin., 1998—; secondary asst. prin. Forest Hills Sch. Dist., 1999—; mem. auto body adv. bd. Greater Johnstown Area Vocat. and Tech. Sch., 1981—. Advisor Vocat. Indsl. Club Am. Named Outstanding Vocat. Educator Pa., Pa. State U., 1992. Mem. NEA, GJAVTS Edn. Assn. (exec. com. mem. 1984-89, v.p. 1989—), Pa. Sch. Counselor Assn., Pa. State Edn. Assn., U. Pitts. Alumni Assn. Democrat. Roman Catholic. Avocations: hunting, fishing, coaching. Home: 3285 Elton Rd Johnstown PA 15904-2827 Office: Greater Johnstown AVTS 445 Schoolhouse Rd Johnstown PA 15904-2927

BOWSHER, CHARLES ARTHUR, retired government official, business executive; b. Elkhart, Ind., May 30, 1931; s. Matthew A. and Ella M. (West) B.; m. Mary C. Mahoney, Dec. 14, 1963; children: Kathryn M., Stephen C. BS, U. Ill., 1953; MBA, U. Chgo., 1956; DSc in Bus. Adminstrn. (hon.), Bryant Coll., 1984; D Pub. Svc. (hon.), George Washington U., 1993; DSc (hon.), U. Ill.-Chgo., 1994; Dr. Pub. Svc. (hon.), St. Joseph's U., 1994; DSc in Pub. Svc. (hon.), Am. U., 1996. C.P.A., Ill. Ptnr. Arthur Andersen & Co., Chgo., 1956-67, Washington, 1971-81; asst. sec. of Navy for fin. mgmt. Dept. Def., Washington, 1967-71; comptroller gen. U.S., 1981-96; mem. adv. coun. Fin. Acctg. Standards Bd.; mem. adv. coun. Govt. Acctg. Standards Bd., 1981; mem. adv. com. Gruss Program for Pub. Sector Mgrs., Wharton Sch., U. Pa.; bd. dirs. Am. Express Bank, Nat. Steel Corp., DeVry Inc.; trustee Ctr. Naval Analysis, Logistics Mgmt. Inst., U.S. Navy Meml. Found., Hitachi Found., Concord Coalition, Com. for a Responsible Fed. Budget; v.p. bd. trustees UN Found. Mem. editl. bd. Acctg. Horizons. Mem. adv. coun. dept. sociology Princeton U.; hon. bd. ctr. Excellence Govt.; adv. com. office for govtl. acctg. rsch. and edn. U. Ill. Coll. Bus. Adminstrn.; mem. bus. adv. coun. U. Ill.; pub. sector com. Internat. Fedn. of Accts; bd. of overseers Wharton Sch., U. Pa., Irving B. Harris Grad. Sch. of Policy Studies U. Chgo.; mem. vis. com. Sch. Bus., selection com. Roger W. Jones award for Exec. Leadership; trustee Ctr. for Naval Analysis, Logistics Mgmt. Inst., USN Meml. Found.; nat. adv. bd. Pvt. Sector Coun.; active Bus. Execs. for Nat. Security Commn. With U.S. Army, 1953-55. Recipient Enduring Lifetime Achievement award Am. Acctg. Assn., 1996, Integrity award Office of Insp. Gen., 1996; named to Acctg. Hall of Fame, 1996. Mem. AICPA, Nat. Acad. Pub. Adminstrn., Nat. Assn. Govt. Accts., Burning Tree Club (Washington), Met. Club (Washington), Beta Alpha Psi. Home: 4503 Boxwood Rd Bethesda MD 20816-1815

BOWYER, JOAN ELIZABETH, medical technologist, realtor; b. Ellensburg, Wash., July 11, 1944; d. Chester Joseph and Rita Geneva (Newell) Howarth; 1 child, Suzanne Elise. BA, Ft. Wright Coll. of Holy Names, 1966; grad., Real Estate Sch. Oreg., 1982. Lic. med. technologist. Med. technologist Lab. of Clin. Medicine, Seattle, 1967-69, Sacred Heart Gen. Hosp., Eugene, Oreg., 1969-73, 74-76. McKenzie Willamette Hosp., Springfield, Oreg., 1976-77, Mid-Columbia Hosp., The Dalles, Oreg., 1977-82; realtor Red Carpet/Rick Hall Realty, Hillsboro, Oreg., 1982-85, Century 21 Columbia Realty, Portland, 1985—; med. technologist ARC, Portland, 1982-89, Corning Nicholas Inst. formerly Physicians Med. Lab., 1989-95, East Moreland Hosp., 1995—. Co-editor: The Dalles Gen. Hosp. Newspaper, 1980-82. Pres. Wasco County Edn. Service Dist. Parents Group, The Dalles, 1978-82; founder, pres. Mid-Columbia Parents of Deaf, 1978-82; parental spokesperson Spl. Edn. Adv. Com., Salem, Oreg., 1980-82; activist parent for deaf/hearing impaired, 1977—. Mem. Med. Technologists of Am. Soc. Pathologists, Nat. Assn. Realtors, NAFE, Century 21 Investment Soc., Million Dollar Club. Democrat. Home: 704 SE 38th Ave Portland OR 97214-3206 Office: Century 21 Columbia 2208 SE 182nd Ave Portland OR 97233-5608

BOX, GEORGE EDWARD PELHAM, statistics educator; b. Gravesend, Eng., Oct. 18, 1919; s. Harry and Helen (Martin) B.; m. Claire Louise Box, Sept. 7, 1985; children by previous marriage: Helen Elizabeth, Harry Christopher. BSc, U. Coll., U. London, Eng., 1947; PhD, U. London, Eng., 1952, DSc, 1961; DSc (hon.), U. Rochester, 1975, Carnegie-Mellon U., 1989, U. Madrid, 1995. Statistician, head statis. techniques research sect. Imperial Chems. Industries, Blackley, Manchester, Eng., 1948-56; dir. statis. techniques research group Princeton U., 1957-59; prof. stats. U. Wis., Madison, 1960-91; prof. emeritus U. Wis., 1991—; William F. Vilas prof. U. Wis., Madison, 1980-91, dir. Ctr. for Quality and Productivity, 1986-92; dir. rsch. Ctr. for Quality and Productivity, 1992—; vis. research prof. U. N.C., 1952-53; Ford Found. vis. prof. Harvard Bus. Sch., 1965-66, U. Essex, Eng., 1970-71. Author: (with others) Statistical Methods in Research and Production, 1957, Design and Analysis of Industrial Experiments, 1959, Evolutionary Operation: A Statistical Method for Process Improvement, 1969, Time Series, Forecasting and Control, 1970, 3d edit., 1993, Bayesian Inference in Statistical Analysis, 1973, Statistics for Experimenters, 1978, The Collected Works of George E.P. Box, 1985, Empirical Modeling and Response Surfaces, 1986, Statistical Control by Monitoring and Feedback Adjustment, 1997; contbr. articles to profl. jours. Served with Brit. Army, 1939-45. Decorated Brit. Empire medal; recipient Profl. Progress award Am. Inst. Chem. Engrs., 1963, Benjamin Smith Reynolds teaching award 1972, Byron Bird rsch. award, U. Wis., 1990; Guggenheim fellow, 1990, Ctr. Advanced Study in the Behavioral Scis. fellow, Stanford U., 1990. Fellow AAAS (past v.p.), Am. Acad. Arts and Scis., Royal Soc., Royal Statis. Soc. (hon., Guy Silver medal 1964, Guy Gold medal 1993), Am. Statis. Assn. (pres. 1978, Wilks meml. medal 1972), Inst. Math. Stats. (pres. 1979), Am. Soc. Quality Control (hon., Shewhart medal 1968, Brumbaugh award 1988, 93, Deming medal 1989); mem. Internat. Stats. Inst., Biometrics Soc. *Theory and Practice are like man and wife in a happy marriage. Each complements and inspires the other and without interaction between them there can be no new life.**

BOX, JOHN HAROLD, architect, educator, academic dean; b. Commerce, Tex., Aug. 18, 1929; s. E.O. and Mary Emma (Haynes) B.; m. Dorothy Jean Baldwin, Jan. 19, 1952 (div. Jan. 1971); children: Richard B., Kenneth W., Gregory V.; m. Eden Van Zandt, Apr. 9, 1977; stepchildren: William D., Kate V.Z. BArch, U. Tex., 1950. Apprentice O'Neil Ford (architects), San Antonio, 1948; designer Broad & Nelson (architects), Dallas, 1954-56; assoc. Harrell & Hamilton (architects), Dallas, 1956-57; ptnr. Pratt, Box, Henderson & Ptnrs. (architects), Dallas, 1957-83, Box Architects, Austin, 1983—; prof., 1st dean Sch. Architecture and Environ. Design, U. Tex., Arlington, 1971-76; prof., dean Sch. Architecture, U. Tex., Austin, 1976-92, Moody prof., 1983—; Chmn. design of city task force Goals for Dallas, 1968-70; chmn. Goals Achievement Com., 1970—; chmn. design com. Greater Dallas Planning Council, 1969; v.p. Save Open Space, 1970. Prin. works include: St. Stephen's Meth. Ch., Dallas, 1962, Great Hall of Apparel Mart, Dallas, 1965, Quadrangle Shopping Ctr., Dallas, 1965, Garden Ctr., Dallas, 1970; master plan Griffin Sq., Dallas, 1971; Marsh House, Austin, 1982; Co-author: Prairies Yield, 1962, Goals for Dallas Proposals for Design of City, 1970. Bd. dirs. Dallas Chamber Music Soc., 1960-76, Austin Symphony, 1982-90, Laguna Gloria Art Mus., 1984-90, Austin History Ctr., 1984-88; regional dir. Assn. Collegiate Schs. Architecture, 1975-78. Served to lt. C.E. Corps, USNR, 1955. Co-recipient Enrico Fermi Meml. Archtl. Competition prize, 1957; recipient Grand prize Homes for Better Living Competition, 1959, Edward Rominec award, 1992, Llewelen W. Pitts award, 1998, others; Tex. Architecture Found. grantee, 1957. Fellow AIA (pres. Dallas 1967, nat. dir. 1975-78); mem. Tex. Soc. Architects (v.p., commr. edn. and research 1971, design awards 1964-66, 68, 70, 71, 82), Phi Kappa Phi, Alpha Rho Chi, Sigma Nu. Episcopalian. Avocation: flute. Office: U Tex Goldsmith Hall Austin TX 78712-1160 Studio: PO Box 50590 Austin TX 78763-0590 also: Callejon Blanco # 11, San Miguel Allende 37700, Mexico

BOXER, BARBARA, senator; b. Bklyn., Nov. 11, 1940; d. Ira and Sophie (Silvershein) Levy; m. Stewart Boxer, 1962; children: Doug, Nicole. BA in Econ., Bklyn. Coll., 1962. Stockbroker, econ. rschr. N.Y. Securities Firm, N.Y.C., 1962-65; journalist, assoc. editor Pacific Sun, 1972-74; congl. aide to rep. 5th Congl. Dist. San Francisco, 1974-76; mem. Marin County Bd. Suprs., San Rafael, Calif., 1976-82; mem. 98th-102d Congresses from 6th Calif. dist., mem. armed services com., select com. children, youth and families; majority whip at large, co-chair Mil. Reform Caucus, chair subcom. on govt. activities and transp. of house govt. ops. com., 1990-93, U.S. senator from Calif., 1993—, mem. banking, housing and urban affairs com., mem. budget com., mem. environ. and pub. works com. Pres. Marin County Bd. Suprs., 1980-81; mem. Bay Area Air Quality Mgmt. Bd., San Francisco, 1977-82, pres., 1979-81; bd. dirs. Golden Gate Bridge Hwy. and Transport Dist., San Francisco, 1978-82; founding mem. Marin Nat. Women's Polit. Caucus; pres. Dem. New Mems. Caucus, 1983. Recipient Open Govt. award Common Cause, 1980, Rep. of Yr. award Nat. Multiple Sclerosis Soc., 1990, Margaret Sanger award Planned Parenthood, 1990, Women of Achievement award Anti-defamation League, 1990. Jewish. Office: US Senate 112 Hart Senate Office Bldg Washington DC 20510-0505

BOXER, JEROME HARVEY, computer and management consultant, vintner, accountant; b. Chgo., Nov. 27, 1930; s. Ben Avrum and Edith (Lyman) B.; m. Sandra Schaffner, June 17, 1980; children by previous marriage: Michael, Jodi. AA magna cum laude, East L.A. Coll., 1952; AB with honors, Calif. State U., L.A., 1954. CPA, Calif.; cert. computing profl. Lab. instr. Calif. State U., L.A., 1953-54; staff acct. Dolman, Freeman & Buchalter, L.A., 1955-57; sr. acct. Neiman, Sanger, Miller & Beress, L.A., 1957-63; ptnr. Glynn and Boxer, CPAs, L.A., 1964-68; v.p., sec. Glynn, Boxer & Phillips Inc, CPAs, L.A. and Glendale, Calif., 1968-90; pvt. practice cons., 1990—; owner Oak Valley Vineyard; pres. Echo Data Svcs. Inc., 1978-90; instr. data processing L.A. City Adult Schs.; tchr., lectr., cons. wines and wine-tasting; instr. photography. Contbr. to Wine World Mag., 1974-82, also cons. Mem. ops. bd. evrywoman's Village; bd. dirs., v.p. So. Calif. Jewish Hist. soc., v.p. Jewish Hist. Soc. of ctrl. coast; founding pres. Congregation Ohr Tzafon; co-founder Open Space theatre; former officer Ethel Josephine Scantland Found.; past post adviser Explorer Scouts, Boy Scouts Am., also Eagle Scout. Recipient Youth Svc. award Mid-Valley YMCA, 1972-73. Mem. AICPAs, Calif. Soc. CPAs, Assn. for Systems Mgmt., Data Processing Mgmt. Assn., Am. Fedn. Musicians, Am. Jewish Hist. Soc., Friends of Photography, L.A. Photog. Ctr., Acad. Model Aeros., Nat. Model Railroad Assn., Maltese Falcons Home Brewing Soc., San Fernando Valley Silent Flyers, San Fernando Valley Radio Control Flyers, Associated Students Calif. State U. L.A. (hon. life), Acad. Magical Arts, Internal Brotherhood of Magicians, Soc. Preservation of Variety Arts, Am. Wine Soc., Knights of the Vine, Soc. Wine Educators, Napa Valley Wine Libr. Alumni Assn., L.A.-Bordeaux Sister City Affiliation, Soc. Bacchus Am., Paso Robles Dem. Club (pres. 1993), Ctrl. Coast Winegrowers Assn., Wines and Steins, Cellarmasters, Paso Robles Vintners and Growers Assn., German Shepherd Dog Club Am., German Shepherd Dog Club Los Angeles County, Blue Key, Alphi Phi Omega, Verdugo Club, Exch. Club, Kiwanis (pres. Sunset-Echo Park 1968), Braemar Country Club, Pacific Mariners Yacht Club, South Coast Corinthian Yacht Club (former dir., officer,) B'nai Brith, Paso Robles Masons. Home and Office: 1660 Circle B Rd Paso Robles CA 93446-9595

BOXER, LEONARD, lawyer; b. N.Y.C., Feb. 11, 1939; s. Max Boxer and Sally (Grill) Koffler; m. Enid Feuer, Nov. 24, 1965; children: Michael, Jason, Douglas. BS, NYU, 1960, LLB, 1963. Bar: N.Y. 1963, U.S. Dist. Ct. (so. and ea. dists.) N.Y. 1985, U.S. Supreme Ct. Assoc. Eisenberg & Weiss, Bklyn., 1964-65; ptnr. Olnick, Boxer, Blumberg, Lane & Troy, N.Y.C., 1965-86, Stroock & Stroock & Lavan, N.Y.C., 1987—; mem. adv. bd. Chgo. Title Ins. Co., N.Y.C., 1980—; gov. N.Y. Real Estate Bd. Trustee Nat. Jewish Ctr. Immunology and Respiratory Medicine, Jewish Assn. Svcs. for the Aged, Children's Hearing Inst., Manhattan Eye, Ear and Throat Hosp., NYU Law Sch., 1994—; mem. adv. bd. Real Estate Inst., NYU; bd. dirs. Patriot Hospitality, Inc./Wyndham Internat. Inc., 1995—. Sgt. USAR, 1963-69. Mem. N.Y. State Bar Assn., Bklyn. Bar Assn., Tax Certiorari Bar Assn. (bd. dirs. 1983-97), Beta Alpha Psi. Home: 245 E 58th St New York NY 10022-1201 Office: Stroock & Stroock & Lavan 180 Maiden Ln New York NY 10038-4925

BOXER, STANLEY ROBERT, artist, sculptor; b. N.Y.C., June 26, 1926; s. Max and Ida (Gordon) B.; m. Joyce Weinstein, Nov. 28, 1952. Student, Bklyn. Coll., Art Students League, 1946-49. Lectr. vis. artists' program Harvard Coll., Cambridge, Mass., 1984. Artist suite of etchings: vol. aquatint etchings Ringofdustinbloom, 1984, Monotypes, 1985-93, monotypes and prints, 1989-97; one-man exhbns.: Andre Emmerich Gallery, Zurich, Switzerland, 1975-91, N.Y.C., 1975-94, Galerie Wentzel, Cologne, Fed. Republic Germany, 1975, 78, 80, 82, 83, 85, 87, 88, 90, Tibor de Nagy Gallery, N.Y.C., 1971-75, 80, 82, 87, Galerie Winkelmann, Dusseldorf, Germany, 1993, Hokin Gallery, Bay Harbor Island, Fla., 1981, 90-93, Chgo., 1982, 84, 86, 88, Palm Beach, Fla., 1978, 81, 82, 85, 88, Galerie von Braunbehrens, Munich, Fed. Republic Germany, 1982, Am. House, Berlin, 1982, Gallery One, Toronto, Ont., Can., 1980, 81, 84, 86, 88, 90, 91, 93, 96, 99, Downstairs Gallery, Edmonton, Alta., Can., 1981, 83, Frances Aronson Gallery, Atlanta, 1983-88, Salander-O'Reily Gallery, N.Y.C., 1983, 96, 97, 99, Ivory Kimpton Gallery, San Francisco, 1983, 85, 86, Ruth Bachofner Gallery, Los Angeles, 1986, 87, 89, Pa. Acad. Fine Arts, Phila., 1976, Posner Gallery, Milw., 1990, Elka London Gallery, Montreal, Can., 1990, Dorsky Gallery, N.Y.C., 1991, Laca Gallery, L.A., 1991, Ruth Bochofner Gallery, L.A., 1992, Lewison Gallery, Boston, 1992, Rose Art Mus., Brandeis U., Waltham, Mass., 1992, Long Fine Art, N.Y.C., 1993, 97, Flanders Contemporary Art, Minn., 1996, 97, 98, Lyon Coll., Bottsville, Ark., 1996, U. Ctrl. Ark., Conway, 1996; sculpture exhbns: Boston Mus., 1977, Allrich Gallery, San Francisco, 1979, 81, Galerie Regard, Paris, 1979, 81, Meredith Long & Co., Houston, 1979-81, 83-93, Thomas Segal Gallery, Boston, 1980-82, 84, Richard Gray Gallery, Chgo., 1980, Woltjen/Udell Gallery, Edmonton, Alta., Can., 1984, and Vancouver, B.C., 1986, Art Mus. Santa Cruz County, 1987, Smith Anderson Gallery, Palo Alto, Calif., 1987, 90, Graystone Gallery, San Francisco, 1987, 90, Mixografia Workshop Gallery, L.A., 1987, 93, The Remba Gallery, L.A., 1998, Harvard U., Cambridge, Mass., 1988, Assoc. Am. Artists, N.Y.C., 1988, 90, Lafayette Coll., Williams Ctr. for Arts, Easton, Pa., 1988, Posner Gallery, Milw., 1990, Elca London Gallery, Montreal, Can., 1990, Galerie Wentzel, Cologne, Fed. Republic of Germany, 1990, Meredith Long & Co., Houston, 1990-93, Laca Gallery, L.A., 1991, Long Fine Art Gallery, NYC, 1993, 95, 97, Helander Gallery, Palm Beach, Fla., 1995, Jaffe Baker Blau Gallery, Boca Raton, Fla., 1996, Scarobb Gallery, Cleve., 1996, Robert Kid Gallery, Birmingham, Mich., 1997, Harmon-Meek Gallery, Naples, Fla., 1998, Tasende Gallery, L.A. and La Jolla, Calif., 1998, KL Fine Arts, Chgo., 1998, Dorothy Blau Gallery, Bay Harbor Islands, Fla., 1999, Butler Inst. Art Mus., Youngstown, Ohio, 1999; retrospectives: (paintings) Boston Mus. Fine Arts, 1977, (drawings) Mint Mus. Art, 1978, (paintings, sculpture, drawings) Rose Art Mus., Waltham, Mass., 1992; represented in permanent collections: Guggenheim Mus., N.Y.C., Whitney Mus., N.Y.C., Boston Mus. Fine Arts, Houston Mus. Fine Arts, Mus. Modern Art, N.Y.C., Corcoran Gallery Art, Washington, Albright-Knox Mus., Buffalo, Mint Mus. Art, Charlotte, N.C., Edmonton (Alta., Can.) Art Gallery Mus., San Francisco Mus. of Art, Hirshhorn Mus., D.C., Rose Art Mus., Brandeis U. Waltham, Mass., Houston Mus. of Art, Ark. Art Ctr., Little Rock, others; numerous group exhbns., numerous pvt. collections; designer, builder sculptural set Erick Howkins Dance Co., 1972. With USN, World War II. Guggenheim fellow, 1975, Visual Artists fellow Nat. Endowment for Arts, 1989. Mem. NAD (academician). *To become artist, to remain artist, is both idea and goal. All conduct is congruent to that purpose. The development of conscience to Art is the principle of the whole!.*

BOXLEITNER, WARREN JAMES, electrical engineer, researcher; b. Lewiston, Idaho, Jan. 8, 1948; s. Paul Henry and Lois Genelle (Samsel) B.; m. Linda Jane Schraufnagel, Aug. 23, 1969; 1 child, Kirk Lee. BSEE, U. Idaho, 1971. Design engr. Keytronic Corp., Spokane, Wash., 1975-79, project engr., 1981-83, sr. engr., 1983-86, tech. svcs. mgr., 1986-87; internat. sales mgr. Eurokey, Ravensberg, Fed. Republic Germany, 1979-81; dir. engring. Keytek Instrument Corp., Wilmington, Mass., 1987-89, v.p. engring., 1989-92, v.p. tech. and ventures, 1992-94; pres. The Boxleitner Group, Kirkland, Wash., 1994—; past U.S. del. to IEC Working Group for EMC Immunity; participant symposia in field. Author: ESD and Electronic Equipment, 1989; contbr. articles to profl. jours. 1st lt. USAF, 1971-75. Mem. IEEE (sr., chmn. working group 1989). Achievements include research on methods to improve immunity of electronic products to electromagnetic interference and to test for such immunity; developer first statistically accurate ESD test guidelines to be published in national or international test standards. Office: The Boxleitner Group PMB 332 218 Main St Kirkland WA 98033-6108

BOXWILL, HELEN ANN, primary and secondary education educator; b. Washington, Feb. 28, 1946; d. Melvin E. and Ann (Magnotta) Dorenbaum; children: Hope, David, Andre. BA, Dickinson Coll., Carlisle, Pa., 1967; MA, New Sch. Social Rsch., 1976; MS in Adminstrn. and Supervision, Coll. New Rochelle, 1995. Cert. in staff devel.; lic. reading specialist, elem. tchr., English tchr., sch. adminstr., N.Y. Caseworker City of N.Y., 1967-71; dir. Harriet Tubman Day Care Ctr., Bklyn., 1971-73; family counselor Family Inst. for More Effective Living, Westbury, N.Y., 1976-80; elem. tchr. Carousel Day Sch., Hicksville, N.Y., 1980-82, Pub. Sch. 160 Elem. Sch., Queens, N.Y., 1982-83; reading specialist Soterios Ellenos Parochial Sch., Bklyn., 1983-84, Hempstead (N.Y.) Pub. Schs., 1984-90; tchr. SAT The Sch. for Student Achievement, Jericho, N.Y., 1991-93; reading specialist L.I. U., Greenvale, N.Y., 1984-93; reading tchr. Robert Moses Mid. Sch., North Babylon, N.Y., 1990-93, North Babylon (N.Y.) High Sch., 1993—; advisor Sch. Improvement Planning Com., Hempstead, N.Y., 1987-89; mem. Dist. Planning Com., 1993—, Curriculum Adv. Com., 1993—; advisor/advisee com., staff devel. com., lang. arts com., site based mgmt. com. renaissance coord. North Babylon Sch. Dist., 1991—; tchr., trainer Nassau Tract Tchrs. Ctr., 1985-89, North Babylon Schs., 1991—, Hempstead Schs., 1985-90, insvc. courses Owl Tchrs. Ctr., 1991, 93—. Contbr. articles to profl. jours. Advisor Youth of Distinction, Huntington, N.Y., 1991-92; leader Girl Scouts Am., Westbury, 1978. Grantee City of N.Y. Children's Aid Soc., Tract Ctr., Owl Ctr.; recipient Commty. Svc. award, N.Y. State Tchrs., 1999. Mem. ASCD, Internat. Reading Assn., Nat. Coun. Tchrs. English, Orton Dyslexia Soc., Nassau Reading Coun. Avocations: swimming, reading, writing, coaching field hockey, guitar, public speaking on anti-racism. Home: 44 Foxwood Dr E Huntington Station NY 11746-2126

BOYAGIAN, LEVON, legislative administrator; b. Toronto, Dec. 5, 1968. BA, Hobart Coll., Geneva, N.Y., 1990. Legis. dir. to Rep. Don Young U.S. Ho. of Reps., Washington, 1997—. Office: US Ho of Reps 211 RHOB Washington DC 20515

BOYAJIAN, TIMOTHY EDWARD, public health officer, educator, consultant; b. Fresno, Calif., Feb. 22, 1949; s. Ernest Adam and Marge (Medzian) B.; m. Tassanee Bootdeesri, Apr. 23, 1987. BS in Biology, U. Calif., Irvine, 1975; M of Pub. Health, UCLA, 1978. Registered environ. health specialist, Calif. Rsch. asst. UCLA, 1978-81; lectr. Chapman U., 29 Palms, Calif., 1982-84, 88-89; refugee relief vol. Cath. Relief Svcs., Surin, Thailand, 1985-86; lectr. Nat. Univ., L.A., 1989-91; environ. health specialist Riverside County Health Svcs. Agy., Palm Springs, Calif., 1991-96; mem. adj. faculty U. Phoenix, 1998—; cons. parasitologist S. Pacific Commn., L.A., 1979; pub. health cons. several vets. groups, L.A., 1981-84, 97—; cons. Learning Link, Inc. 1999—, Assn. S.E. Asian Nations, Bangkok, Thailand, 1988. Veterans rights advocate, Vietnam Vet. Groups, L.A., 1981-84. With USMC, Vietnam, 1969-71. Recipient U.S. Pub. Health Traineeship, U.S. Govt., L.A., 1977-81. Mem. VFW, So. Calif. Pub. Health Assn., Calif. Environ. Health Assn. Avocation: writing. E-mail: Timothy 300@aol.com. Home: PO Box 740 Palm Springs CA 92263-0740

BOYAN, NORMAN J., retired education educator; b. N.Y.C., Apr. 11, 1922; s. Joseph J. and Emma M. (Pelezare) B.; m. Priscilla M. Simpson, July 10, 1943; children: Stephen J., Craig S., Corydon J. A.B., Bates Coll., Lewiston, Maine, 1943; A.M., Harvard U., 1947, Ed.D., 1951. Instr. U.S. history Dana Hall Sch., Wellesley, Mass., 1946-48; research assoc. Lab. Social Relations, Harvard U., 1950-52; asst. prin. Mineola (N.Y.) High Sch., 1952-54; prin. Wheatley Sch., East Williston, N.Y., 1954-59; assoc. prof. edn., dir. student teaching and internship U. Wis., 1959-61; assoc. prof. edn. Stanford U., 1961-67; dir. div. ednl. labs. U.S. Office Edn., 1967-68, assoc. commr. for research, 1968-69; prof. edn. Grad. Sch. Edn., U. Calif., Santa Barbara, 1969-90, prof. emeritus, 1990—, dean, 1969-80; assoc. in edn. Grad. Sch. Edn., Harvard U., 1980-81; dir. Ednl. Leadership Inst. U. Calif., 1989-91; vis. scholar Stanford U., 1974, 86; vis. prof. U. Ark. Program in Greece, 1977, Coll. Edn., Pa. State U., summer 1981, Faculty Edn. U. B.C., summer 1983, U. Alta., 1988, UCLA, 1991; cons. numerous U.S. sch. sys., U.S. govt. and Pacific Trust Ters. Co-author: Instructional Supervision Training Program, 1978; mem. editorial bd. Harvard Edn. Rev, 1948-50, Jour. Secondary Edn, 1963-68, Jour. Edn. Research, 1967-82, Urban Edn, 1967-90; cons. editor, contbr. 5th edit. Ency. Ednl. Research, 1982; editor, contbr. Handbook Research on Ednl. Adminstrn., 1988; contbr. articles to profl. jours. Served with USAAF, 1943-46. Recipient Shankland award for advanced grad. study in ednl. adminstrn., 1950, Roald F. Campbell Lifetime Achievement award U. Coun. for Ednl. Adminstrn., 1998. Mem. Am. Ednl. Rsch. Assn. (v.p. div. A 1978-80), Phi Beta Kappa, Phi Delta Kappa. Home: 742 Calle De Los Amigos Santa Barbara CA 93105-4439

BOYAR, JAY MITCHELL, film critic; b. Bklyn., Nov. 19, 1953; s. Samuel and Louise (Jay) B.; m. Deborah E. Beckman, Apr. 9, 1989; 1 child, Evan Paul. BA in English Lit. with honors, SUNY, Buffalo, 1975. Staff mem. New York Post, 1976-77; film critic and feature writer Buffalo Courier-Express, 1977-82; film educator SUNY and Medaille Coll., Buffalo, 1979; film critic E! Entertainment TV, 1992, WMFE-FM, Orlando, Fla., 1993—, MSNBC, 1996—, News channel 13, Orlando, 1997—, The Orlando Sentinel, 1982—; film faculty Rollins Coll., Orlando, 1994; panelist, program spkr. Ft. Lauderdale Internat. Film Festival, 1990, 96; filmaking contest judge Universal Studios, Orlando, 1997; journalism workshop leader Orlando Sentinel, 1989, 95, 97. Author: Be a Magician, 1981. Recipient Criticism award Buffalo Newspaper Guild, 1980, Feature Writing award AP, 1981, Criticism award Fla. Soc. Newspaper Editors, 1985, 86, Soc. Profl. Journalists, 1986; Pulitzer Prize nominee, 1981. Mem. Southeastern Film Critics Assn., Fla. Film Critics Cir. (chmn. 1996—), Phi Beta Kappa. Avocation: conjuring. Office: The Orlando Sentinel 633 N Orange Ave # Mp-6 Orlando FL 32801-1349

BOYARSKI, ADAM MICHAEL, physicist; b. North Bank, Alberta, Can., Apr. 14, 1935; came to U.S., 1963; s. Albert and Mary (Roskiewich) B.; m. Lorretta Sramek, June 1, 1968; children: Lisa A., Mike A. BA in Sci., U. Toronto, 1958; PhD, M.I.T., 1962. Rsch. assoc. M.I.T., Cambridge, 1962-63; staff physicist Stanford (Calif.) Linear Accelerator Ctr., 1963—; cons. in field; mem. team discovering psi family of elem. particles. Author: (software) HANDYPAK, A Histogram and Display Package, 1980; contbr. articles to scientific jours. Mem. Am. Phys. Soc. Avocations: woodworking, camping, computers, mechanics. Office: SLAC 2575 Sand Hill Rd Menlo Park CA 94025-7015

BOYARSKY, BENJAMIN WILLIAM, journalist; b. Berkeley, Calif., Oct. 21, 1934; s. Herman and Naomi (Heimy) B.; m. Nancy Elaine Belling, July 21, 1956; children: Robin Ann, Jennifer Lynn. AB, U. Calif., Berkeley, 1956. Copy boy, reporter Oakland (Calif.) Tribune, 1953-60; reporter, editor AP, San Francisco, 1960, Sacramento, 1961-65; polit. writer AP, 1965-70, L.A. Times, 1970-75; nat. polit. writer L.A. Times, Washington, 1975-76; writer met. staff L.A. Times, 1976-78, chief city-county bur., 1978-89, columnist, 1989-97, city editor, 1998—. Author: The Rise of Ronald Reagan, 1968, Backroom Politics, 1974, (with wife) Ronald Reagan: His Life and Rise to the Presidency, 1981. Recipient Profl. Journalist award Soc. Profl. Journalists, 1985, Pulizter prize, 1995. Office: LA Times Times Mirror Sq Los Angeles CA 90012-3816

BOYATT, THOMAS DAVID, former ambassador; b. Cin., Mar. 4, 1933; s. Lynn Craig Haven and Florine (Cloar) B.; m. Maxine Lorraine Shearwood, Dec. 30, 1971; children: Thomas Benton, Christopher Lynn, Jessica Allyn, Alexander Shearwood, Catherine Jordan. BA, Princeton U., 1955, MA, 1956. Vice consul Dept. State, Antofagasta, Chile, 1960-62; 2d sec. Am. Embassy, Luxembourg, 1964-66; 1st sec. Am. Embassy, Nicosia, Cyprus, 1967-70; dir. Cypriot affairs Near East Bur. Dept. State, Washington, 1970-74; assigned to Sr. Seminar Dept. State, 1974-75; dep. chief mission, minister counselor Am. Embassy, Santiago, Chile, 1976-78; U.S. ambassador to Upper Volta, Ouagadougou, 1978-80, Colombia, Bogota, 1980-84; v.p. market devel. Sears World Trade Inc., Washington, 1984-87; with Dept. Treasury, 1962-64; ptnr. IRC Group, 1988-96; pres. U.S. Def. Systems, 1990-96. Trustee Princeton U., 1984-89; bd. dirs. Patterson Sch./U. Ky., Inst. for Study of Diplomacy/Gerogetown U. Served to 1st lt. SAC, USAF, 1956-59. Decorated Legion d'Honneur (Upper Volta), Gran Cruz Order of San Carlos (Colombia); recipient Meritorious Honor award Dept. State, 1969, William R. Rivkin award Am. Fgn. Service, 1970, Christian A. Herter award, 1976. Mem. Am. Fgn. Svc. Assn. (pres. 1971-74), Acad. Diplomacy (bd. dirs.), Washington Inst. Fgn. Affairs (dir.), Diplomatic and Consular Officers Ret. (bd. dirs.), Cosmos Club.

BOYCE, ALFRED WARNE, analytical laboratory executive; b. Queenstown, South Africa, Aug. 26, 1929; s. Alfred Kingwell and Bertha (Berrington) B.; m. Doreen Vaughan, Aug. 11, 1956; children: Caroline, John Trevor Warne. BA, Rhodes U., Grahamstown, S. Africa, 1951; BA with Hons., Oxford U., Eng., 1954. Mem. faculty Wellington Coll., Crowthorne/Berks, N.Y., U.K., 1954-56; mgmt. trainee Brit. Oxygen Co., London, 1956-58; asst. mgr. Quasi-Arc Divsn. BOC, Wolverhampton, U.K., 1958-60; sales mgr. African Oxygen (BOC), Johannesburg, Republic S. Africa, 1960-62; exec. v.p. Megator Corp., Pitts., 1962-69; pres. Microbac Labs., Inc., Pitts., 1969-89; chmn. and CEO Orbeco Analytical Sys., Inc., N.Y., 1989—; bd. dirs. Mestek, Inc., Westfield, Mass.; pres. Am. Coun. Ind. Labs., Washington, 1994—. Pres. Smaller Mfrs. Coun., Pitts., 1973-74, Pressley Ridge Schs., Pitts., 1983-85; del. Pres. Ford's Conf. on Inflation, Washington, 1974; bd. dirs. Allegheny County Housing Authority, Pitts., 1976-78. Recipient Bursary to Rhodes U., Kingswood Coll., Grahamstown, S. Africa, 1950, to St. Edmund Hall, Oxford, Eng., 1953. Mem. Am. Chem Soc., Inst. of Food Technologists, The Duquesne Club (Pitts.), The Marylebone Cricket Club (London). Achievements include establishment and registration of Rhodes Charitable Trust. Avocations: rugby football (Oxford varsity 1952-53), refereeing 1965-74. Home: Fox Chapel Mews Apt 508 300 Fox Chapel Rd Pittsburgh PA 15238-2331*

BOYCE, BERT ROY, university dean, library and information science educator; b. Sharon, Pa., Jan. 10, 1938; s. Bert Roy and Julia (Loyd) B.; m. Judith Irene Warren, Aug. 25, 1968; children: Maria Natasha, Gabriel Augustus. BA in History, Marietta Coll., 1959; MS in Libr. Sci., Case Western Res. U., 1968; PhD, Cast Western Res. U., 1972. Asst. dir. Redevel. Authority, Sharon, 1966-67; rsch. analyst info. systems Libr. Congress, Washington, 1968-69; asst. prof. U. Mo., Columbia, 1972-78, chair dept. info. sci., 1976-83; assoc. prof. Sch. Libr. and Info. Sci. La. State U., Baton Rouge, 1983-85, prof. Sch. Libr. and Info. Sci., 1985—, dean Sch. Libr. and Info. Sci., 1990—. Author: Operations Research for Libraries and Information Agencies, 1991, Measurement in Information Science, 1994; contbr. articles to profl. jours. Lt. USN, 1960-66, Vietnam. Sr. Fulbright-Hays scholar (Brazil), 1974. Mem. ALA (Shera Rsch. award 1988), Am. Soc. for Info. Sci. (Outstanding Info. Sci. Teaching award 1989), La. Libr. Assn., Assn. for Libr. and Info. Sci. Edn. Democrat. Office: La State U Sch Libr and Info Sci 267 Coates Hall Baton Rouge LA 70803

BOYCE, DANIEL HOBBS, financial planning company executive; b. Flint, Mich., Oct. 19, 1953; s. James Edward and Alice Marilyn (Hobbs) B.; m. Suzanne Kay Williams; children: Kenneth C., Geoffrey A., Stephen J. BA, U. Mich., 1974, MA, 1979. Cert. fin. planner; cert. investment mgmt. cons. Rep. Mut. Svc. Corp., Detroit, 1982-87; br. mgr. Investment Mgmt. & Rsch. Inc., Atlanta, 1987—; treas., chief fin. officer Ctr. Fin. Planning Inc., Southfield, Mich., 1988-90; v.p. Southworth, Boyce & McFawn Planning Corp., Troy, Mich., 1982-85; owner, fin. planner Daniel H. Boyce Fin. Adv. Svcs., Birmingham, Mich., 1985-88; mem. adj. faculty Coll. Fin. Planning, Denver, 1985-90; mem. adv. coun. cert. program in personel fin. planning Oakland U., Rochester, Mich., 1987—; edn. cons. Nat. Ctr. for Fin. Edn., Denver, 1985—. *Boyce co-founded The Center for Financial Planning in 1985, and it has since been recognized as a leading Detroit-area financial planning firm. All three senior partners have served as chair of the state CFP professional organization, and the firm is the only one in Michigan to have two professionals named to Worth Magazine's annual listing of the nation's top 300 financial advisors. Mr. Boyce is actively involved in fundraising for several local and national non-profits, especially in the area of planned giving and endowment building. Of recent note was his role in a successful $1,100, 000 church building campaign.* Bi-weekly columnist Money Matters, Legal News newsletter, 1984-86; monthly columnist Personal Fin. for suburban Detroit newspaper chain, 1987-93. Bd. dirs. Great Lakes Chamber Music Festival, 1996—; choir dir. Birmingham Unitarian Ch., 1976—. Cited by Money Mag. and Worth Mag. as One of top 200 fin. planners in U.S., 1987, 96, 97, 98. Mem. Internat. Assn. Fin. Planning (bd. dirs. S.E. Mich. chpt. 1984-87, 89-91), Inst. for Investment Mgmt. Cons., Detroit Soc. Inst. CFPs (pres. 1986-87, chmn. 1987-88), Detroit Chamber Winds (bd. dirs., chmn. 1995-98). Office: Ctr Fin Planning Inc 26211 Central Park Blvd Ste 604 Southfield MI 48076-4164

BOYCE, DAVID EDWARD, transportation and regional science educator; b. Newark, Ohio, June 24, 1938; s. Francis Henry and Martha Ann (Neutzel) B.; m. Nani Kulish, 1992; children: Lynn, Susan, Michael, Anna, Gregory. BSCE, Northwestern U., 1961; M in City Planning, U. Pa., 1963, PhD in Regional Sci., 1965. Registered profl. engr., Ohio. Rsch. economist Battelle Meml. Inst., Columbus, Ohio, 1964-66; asst. prof. U. Pa., Phila., 1966-70, assoc. prof., 1970-74, prof., 1974-77; prof. transp. and regional sci. U. Ill., Urbana, 1977-88, Chgo., 1988—; sr. vis. fellow Brit. Sci. Rsch. Coun., Leeds, Eng., 1972-73; vis. prof. optimization U. Linkoping and Royal Inst. Tech., Sweden, 1983, 96. Co-author: Metropolitan Plan Making, 1970, Optimal Subset Selection, 1974, Regional Science, Retospect and Prospect, 1991, Modeling Dynamic Transportation Networks, 1996; co-editor Environment and Planning, 1979-88; assoc. editor Transp. Sci., 1978-94. Mem. Regional Sci. Assn. (sec. 1969-78, internat. conf. coord. 1978-86, pres. 1987), Informs (transp. sci. coun. 1978-80). Office: U Ill Civil Materials Engring Dep 842 W Taylor St Chicago IL 60607-7021

BOYCE, DOREEN ELIZABETH, lecturer, civic development foundation executive; b. Antofagasta, Chile, Apr. 20, 1934; d. George Edgar and Elsie Winifred Vaughan; m. Alfred Warne Boyce, Aug. 11, 1956; children: Caroline Elizabeth, John Trevor Warne. BA with hons., Oxford (Eng.) U., 1956, MA with hons., 1960; PhD, U. Pitts., 1983; B in Humane Lit., Westminister Coll., 1986; DHL, Washington & Jefferson Coll., 1993. Lectr. and tutor in econs. U. Witwatersrand, South Africa, 1960-62; provost and dean of faculty, prof. econs. Chatham Coll., Pitts., 1963-79; prof. econs., chmn. dept. econs. and mgmt. Hood Coll., Frederick, Md., 1979-82; pres. Buhl Found., Pitts., 1982—; dir. DQE Duquesne Light Co., Dollar Bank, FSB, Orbeco Analytical Svcs. Inc., Rsch. for Better Schs., Coun. Ind. Colls.; co-founder, dir. Microbac Labs., Inc.; Pa. Gov.'s Sports and Exposition Facilities Task Force, 1995; del. White House Conf. on Small Bus., 1980; mem. Gov.'s Conf. Small Bus., 1979-82, chmn. bd. dirs. Trustee Franklin and Marshall Coll., 1982—, Frick Edn. Commn., 1980-94, Carnegie Sci. Ctr., 1982—; mem. Fed.Jud. Nominating Commn., 1977-79, Pa. Gov.'s Commn. on Financing of Higher Edn., 1983-85; bd. dirs. World Affairs Coun., 1984-96; mem. appeal com. Somerville Coll., Oxford, Eng., 1986—. Named Disting. Dau. Pa., 1996, Hon. Fellow Somerville Coll., U. Oxford, Women Who Make A Difference award, Internat. Women's Forum, 1998. Mem. Am. Econs. Assn., Am. Assn. Higher Edn., Grantmakers of We. Pa. (pres. 1984), Internat. Women's Forum, Duquesne Club. Office: 4 Gateway Ctr Rm 1325 Pittsburgh PA 15222-1207

BOYCE, EMILY STEWART, retired library and information science educator; b. Raleigh, N.C., Aug. 18, 1933; d. Harry and May (Fallon) B. BS, East Carolina U., 1955, MA, 1961; MS in Library Sci., U. N.C., 1968; postgrad., Cath. U. Am., 1977. Librarian Tileston Jr. High Sch., Wilmington, N.C., 1955-57; children's librarian Wilmington Pub. Library, 1957-58; asst. librarian Joyner Library East Carolina U., Greenville, N.C., 1959-61, librarian III, 1962-63; ednl. supr. II ednl. media div. N.C. State Dept. Pub. Instrn., Raleigh, 1961-62; assoc. prof. dept. library and info. scis. East Carolina U., Raleigh, 1964-76, prof., 1976-92, chmn. dept., 1982-89; retired, 1992; cons. So. Assn. Colls. and Schs., Raleigh, 1975—. Active Asheville YWCA, Mediation Ctr., Botanical Gardens, Literacy Coun. Buncombe County. Mem. ALA, AAUW, N.C. Library Assn., Southeastern Library Assn., Assn. Library and Info. Sci. Educators, Spl. Libraries Assn. Democrat. Home: 30 Creekside Way Asheville NC 28804

BOYCE, GERALD G., artist, educator; b. Embarrass, Wis., Dec. 29, 1925; s. Charles William and Selma (Van Norman) B.; m. Kathryn Davis; 1 son, Charles William II. B.S., Wis. State U.; M.F.A., U. Iowa, 1950; postgrad., Americano Guatemaletco Instituto, Ind. U., U. Ill., Oxford (Eng.) U., 1979, Brit. Mus., Courtauld Inst., London. Prof. art history U. Indpls., 1950-88, prof. emeritus, 1988—, chmn. art dept., 1950-88; lectr. art history DePauw U., 1968-84; tchr. Fresno State Coll., Wabash Coll., DePauw U., Ind. U.; tchr. St. John's U., N.Y.C., 1989; cons. Ind. Bell Telephone Co., 1967-70, U.S. Post Office Dept., 1972, Smithsonian Instn.; mem. Gov.'s Commn. on the Arts. One-man retrospective show Swope Art Mus., Terre Haute, Ind., 1993; exhibited in group shows L.A. County Mus., San Francisco Mus. Art, Art Inst. Chgo., 1954, Mus. Modern Art, N.Y.C., 1956, Corcoran Gallery Art, Washington, 1971, Mus. Contemporary Crafts, N.Y.C.; represented in permanent collections Ball State U., DePauw U., Earlham Coll., Evansville Coll., St. John's U., Marquis Inc., Ind. State U., Minot Coll., S.D., Wabash Coll., U. Iowa, Swope Art Mus., Rose-Hulman Inst. Tech. Served with USAAF, World War II. Mem. Nat. Coll. Art Conf., Am. Crafts Council (sec. N. Central region 1962-66), Coll. Art Assn., Midwest Coll. Art Assn., Nat. Art Adminstrs. Conf., Ethnographic Arts Soc. (exec. com.), Assn. of Gravestone Studies. Methodist. Home: RR 1 8546 E Oakwood Ln Morgantown IN 46160-9565

BOYCE, JOSEPH NELSON, journalist; b. New Orleans, Apr. 18, 1937; s. John and Sadie (Nelson) B.; m. Carol Hill, Dec. 21, 1968; children: Leslie, Nelson, Joel, Beverly. Student, Roosevelt U., Chgo., 1955-65, John Marshall Law Sch., 1965-67. Mem. Chgo. Police Dept., 1961-66; reporter Chgo. Tribune, 1966-70; corr. Time mag., 1970-73, chief San Francisco bur., 1973-79, chief So. U.S. bur., 1979-85, dep. chief Eastern U.S. bur., 1985-87; sr. editor Wall St. Jour., 1987-98; ret., 1998; rotating faculty mem., summer program for minority journalists U. Calif., Berkeley, 1986, 87, 88, 89; bd. dirs. Jazzmobile, Inc., N.Y.C.; guest lectr. various colls. and univs.; vis. faculty summer progorm for minority journalists U. Ala.; vis. faculty Poynter Inst., 1993; William Randolph Hearst vis. prof.-in-residence, Howard U., 1996; mem. adv. bd. Lyndon B. Johnson Sch. of Public Affairs U. Tex., Austin, 1998—. Chmn. Marin County Black Leadership Forum, 1974-75; mem. Marine Justice Coun., 1977-78; bd. dirs. Jazzmobile, 1991-95. With USNR. Recipient Outstanding Black Achiever award Met. YMCA, N.Y.C., 1975; co-recipient Unity In Media award Lincoln U., 1975; Time Mag.-Duke U. fellow, 1981-82. Mem. NAACP, Nat. Assn. Black Journalist, Nat. Assn. Minority Media Execs. (bd. dirs. 1991-93). Episcopalian. Office: Wall Street Jour 200 Liberty St New York NY 10281-1003

BOYCE, RONALD N., federal judge; b. 1933. BS, U. Utah, JD, 1956. Magistrate judge U.S. Dist. Ct. Utah, Salt Lake City. Office: 403 US Courthouse 350 S Main St Salt Lake City UT 84101-2106

BOYCHUK, DALLAS, university head women's basketball coach; b. Orlando, Fla.. BS in Mktg., Stetson U., 1986; postgrad., U. Louisville. Asst. coach Stetson U., Deland, Fla., 1989-90, U. Louisville, 1990-92; coach Purdue U., 1992-95; head coach Long Beach State U., 1995—; profl. water skiing instr. Lake Buena Vista, Fla. Mem. Women's Basketball Assn. Office: Long Beach State U 1250 Bellflower Rd Long Beach CA 90801*

BOYD, ARTHUR BERNETTE, JR., surgeon, clergyman, beverage company executive; b. Durham, N.C., June 29, 1947; s. Arthur Bernette and Mammie Lee (Chalmers) B.; m. Delphine Victoria Huffman, Mar. 14, 1981; children: Arthur III, Vicki. BA, Fla. A&M Univ., 1969; postgrad., NYU, 1970; MD, Meharry Med. Coll., 1978; postgrad., U. N.C., Chapel Hill, 1998. Cert. ATLS instr., PALS. Intern in surgery Howard Univ. Hosp., Washington, 1978-80; resident and chief resident in surgery St. Luke's Hosp., Cleve., 1981-84; fellow in liver transplant U. Pitts., 1984-85; chief adminstrv. fellow trauma/surg. critical care R.A. Cowley Shock Trauma Ctr., U. Md. Med. Sys., Cali, Colombia, 1993-94; clin. instr. surgery, sr. fellow, traumatologist R.A. Cowley Shock Trauma Ctr., U. Md. Med. Sys., Baltimore County, 1994—; co-traumatologist Prince George Cmty. Hosp., Cheverly, Md., 1994-95; chief surgeon, pres. Phoenix Med. Surgical Svc., Inc., Cleve., Carribean, 1986—; clin. instr. surgery, sr. trauma fellow Shock Trauma Ctr. U. Md. Med. Ctr., Balt., 1995-96; pres., CEO Motown Beverage Co. of Ohio, Cleve., 1988—, Towne Club Internat. of Ohio, Inc., Cleve., 1988—; chief adminstrv. fellow in trauma/crit. care R.A. Cowley Shock Trauma Ctr./U. Md. Med. Systems, 1993-94, clin. instr., sr. trauma rsch. fellow, 1994-95; sr. trauma fellow, clin. instr. Shock Trauma Ctr./U. Md., 1995; CEO, pres. Nat. Fin. Group, Inc., Cleve., 1997—; adj. prof. Anatomy and Physiology Cuyhoga C.C., Cleve., 1988—; cons. surgeon other hosps. and physicians, Cleve., 1988—; continuing med. educator dept. surgery Case Western Res. U. Sch. Medicine, Cleve., 1997-98; faculty med. bd. profl. preparation course U. Mo., Kansas City, 1997. Inventor: wheelchair with mechanism to raise or lower left or right buttocks of person, hemostat that carries two sutures, synthetic covering with zipper to cover bowel when abdomen unable to be closed after surgery. Vol. Cleve. Community Action Against Addiction, 1987-88; mentor Case Western U. Inner City Program, Cleve., 1988—; judge honors sci. projects Shaker Heights Middle Sch., 1998. Fellow ACS (assoc.), Internat. Coll. Surgeons; mem. AAAS, AMA, N.Y. Acad. Scis., Nat. Med. Assn. (mentor 1990—), Ohio State Med. Soc., Cleve. Surg. Soc., Nat. Assn. Small Bus. Owners, Internat. Assn. Small Bus. Owners, Assn. Black Cardiologists, Greater Cleve. Ministers Alliance, Masons, Omega Psi Phi, Alpha Phi Omega. Democrat. Methodist. Avocations: reading, sports, golf. Fax: 216-283-6143. Home and Office: Motown Beverage Co 3466 Colton Rd Cleveland OH 44122-3829 also: Ste 107 20475 Farnsleigh Rd Shaker Heights OH 44122-3850

BOYD, BECKY M., secondary school educator; b. Springfield, Tenn., May 2, 1970; d. Charles Albert Jr. and Marsha Lynn (Wotring) McCloud; m. Ryan Stephen Boyd, Dec. 30, 1988. BS, U. So. Miss., 1992; MA, We. Ky. U., 1998. Cert. tchr. English grades 7-12, Tenn. Tchr. English Brookhaven (Miss.) H.S., 1992; tchr. English White House (Tenn.) H.S., 1992—, chair English dept. Team leader for speech Lads to Leaders, White House Ch. of christ, 1995—, speech coord. conv., Nashville, 1997—, bible tchr., 1992—; sponsor Nat. Beta Club, 1993—. Mem. Nat. Coun. Tchrs. English, Tenn. Coun. Tchrs. English, Kappa Delta Pi (v.p. 1991-92). Avocations: reading, softball. Office: White House High School 508 Tyree Springs Rd S White House TN 37188-5432

BOYD, BELVEL JAMES, newspaper editor; b. Winnemucca, Nev., May 15, 1946; s. James Connolly and Alice La Ferne (Elliott) B.; m. Carolyn Marie Friesen, Aug. 10, 1968 (div. July 1992); children: David, Christopher, Phillip. BS in Secondary Edn., Oreg. Coll. Edn., 1968; MA in Journalism, U. Mo., 1974; postgrad., Harvard U., 1979-80. Copy editor, reporter Idaho Statesman, Boise, 1974-76, state editor, 1976-77, editor editl. page, 1977-80; editl. writer Mpls. Tribune, 1980-82; dep. editor editl. page Star Tribune, Mpls., 1982—. Vestryman St. Mark's Cathedral, Mpls., 1983-90. Sgt. U.S. Army, 1968-72, Vietnam. Nieman fellow in journalism Harvard U., 1979-80. Mem. Nat. Conf. Editl. Writers. (chmn. for aff. com. 1997—). Home: 3305 46th Ave S Minneapolis MN 55406-2342 Office: Star Tribune 425 Portland Ave Minneapolis MN 55488-0002

BOYD, B(EVERLEY) RANDOLPH, lawyer; b. Richmond, Va., Mar. 8, 1947; s. Henry Armistead and Mary Archer (Randolph) B.; m. Julia Murray Williams, May 14, 1977; children: Peter Armistead Randolph, Alexander Page Monroe. BA, Williams Coll., 1969; JD, U. Va., 1972. Bar: Va. 1973, U.S. Dist. Ct. (ea. and we. dists.) Va. 1974, U.S. Ct. Appeals (4th cir.) 1986. Ptnr. Boyd & Boyd, Richmond, 1973-79, Randolph, Boyd, Cherry & Vaughan, Richmond, 1979—; Commonwealth's atty. Charles City County Va., 1976—. V.p., sec. James River Assn., Richmond, 1984-97, pres. 1998—. Capt. USAR. Mem. Va. Bar Assn., Va. Trial Lawyers Assn. Democrat. Episcopalian. Avocations: hunting, fishing, hiking. Fax: (804)

783-2765. Home: 4545 Kimages Wharf Rd Charles City VA 23030-3331 Office: Randolph Boyd Cherry & Vaughan 14 E Main St Richmond VA 23219-2110

BOYD, CAROLYN PATRICIA, history educator; b. San Diego, June 1, 1944; d. Peter James and Patricia Mae (de Soucy) B.; m. Frank Dawson Bean, Jan. 4, 1975; children: Peter Justin Bean, Michael Franklin Bean. AB with great distinction and with honors in History, Stanford U., 1966; MA, U. Wash., 1969, PhD, 1974. Tchg. asst. dept. history U. Wash., 1970-71; from instr. to prof. dept. history U. Tex., Austin, 1973-95, prof., 1995—, assoc. dean Office Grad. Studies, 1986-88, 90-92, chair dept. history, 1994—; dir. univ. honors program, assoc. prof. dept. history U. Md., College Park, 1989-90; lectr. in field. Author: Praetorian Politics in Liberal Spain, 1979, La política pretoriana en el reinado de Alfonso XIII, 1990, Historia Patria: Politics, History and National Identity in Spain, 1875-1975, 1997; mem. editl. bd. Essays, 1992-95; author chpts. to books; contbr. articles to profl. jours. Woodrow Wilson hon. fellow, 1966, Fulbright-Hays fellow, 1966-67, NDEA Title IV fellow, 1968-70, 71-72, AAUW fellow, 1972-73; ACLS Grant-in-Aid, 1977, Am. Philos. Soc. grantee, 1978, URI Rsch. grantee, 1985, ACLS fellow, 1985; recipient U. Tex. Rsch. Inst. Summer award, 1977. Mem. Am. Hist. Assn. (James Harvey Robinson prize com. 1992-94), Soc. Spanish and Portugese Hist. Studies (mem. exec. com. 1978-80, 83-85, 96—, chair local arrangements, program chmn. conf. 1987), So. Hist. Assn. (European history sect.), Coun. European Studies, Internat. Inst. in Spain, Ctrl. Tex. Fulbright Assn. Office: U Tex at Austin Dept History Austin TX 78712

BOYD, CLAUDE COLLINS, educational specialist, consultant; b. Kent, Tex., May 25, 1924; s. Edward Clarke and Nora (Morris) B.; m. Frances Arline Haley, Jan. 22, 1955; children: David Chand, Anese Nasim Boyd Forsyth, Mark Kevin, Kimberly Ann Boyd Surgeon. BA, Tex. A&M U., 1948; MEd, U. Tex., 1957, EdD, 1961. Cert. elem. tchr., prin., supt., Tex. Elem. sch. tchr. Culberson County Ind. Sch. Dist., Van Horn, Tex.; elem. sch. prin. The Austin (Tex.) Ind. Sch. Dist.; elem sch. bilingual tchr. Ector County Ind Sch. Dist., Odessa, Tex.; assoc. prof. Ind. U., Bloomington; curriculum specialist USAID, Guatemala City, Guatemala; project specialist in edn. The Ford Found., N.Y.C.; assoc. prof. edn. Pa. State U., Erie; edn. specialist Devel. Assocs., Inc., Washington; internat. edn. advisor/cons. U.S. Agy. for Internat. Devel., San Salvador; edn. adminstr., curriculum advisor U.S. Agy. for Internat. Devel., La Paz, Bolivia; Dominican Republic; edn. adminstr., curriculum advisor U.S. Agy. for Internat. Devel., Dominican Republic; free-lance edn. advisor, cons., worldwide svc. Odessa, Tex.; tchr. edn. specialist InterAm. Devel. Bank, Santo Domingo, Dominican Republic; ednl. supervision specialist InterAmerican Devel. Bank, Santo Domingo, Dominican Republic; substitute tchr. K-12, Ector County ISD, Odessa, Tex. Recipient Grand Order of Edn., Pres. of Rep. of Bolivia. Mem. ASCD, Phi Delta Kappa (past pres. Mu chpt.). Home: 2426 E 21st St Odessa TX 79761-1703

BOYD, DANNY DOUGLASS, financial counselor; b. Olustee, Okla., Oct. 18, 1933; s. Robert and Juanita Henrietta (Crawford) B.; B.A. magna cum laude, Abilene Christian U., 1954; M.A. in Linguistics, U. Tex., Arlington, 1976; CLU, chartered fin. cons.; cert. fin. planner; m. Mary Ann Thomas, Jan. 25, 1953; children: Robert Lee, Rebecca Dyann Boyd McCully, Scott Thomas, Douglas Dean. Min. Chs. of Christ, Ardmore, Okla., 1954-56, Velma, Okla., 1956-57, Cisco, Tex., 1958-60, Utrecht, Netherlands, 1960-65, Wilmington, Del., 1965-69, Dallas, 1969-71; v.p. Nat. Comp Assocs., Dallas, 1972-77; marriage and family counselor Adaptive Counseling Assocs., Dallas, 1977-94; fin. counselor CIGNA Ind. Fin. Svcs. Co., 1979-92, Dan Boyd & Assocs., 1992—; mng. dir. Fin. Edn. Assocs., Tex., 1994—; exec. v.p. WampumWare, Inc., 1996—; br. mgr. SunAmerica Securities, Inc., 1997—; founder Chair of Bible, Cisco Jr. Coll., 1959. Bd. dirs. Skyline High Sch. PTA, 1971; intervenor for integrated neighborhoods fed. dist. ct. desegregation suit, Dallas, 1977. Mem. Soc. Fin. Svc. Profls. (Dallas chpt.). Republican.

BOYD, DAVID PRESTON, business educator; b. N.Y.C., Oct. 19, 1943; s. David Preston and Mignon (Finch) B.; m. Sally Sparks, Sept. 9, 1989. BA in English Lit., Harvard U., 1965; DPhil in Behavioral Scis., Oxford U., 1973. Asst. headmaster Dedham (Mass.) Country Day Sch., 1965-69; co-owner the Old Cambridge (Mass.) Co., 1973-77; instr. coll. bus. adminstrn. Northeastern U., Boston, 1977-78, asst. prof., 1978-82, assoc. prof., 1982-87, Patrick F. and Helen C. Walsh rsch. prof., 1985-86, chmn. human resources mgmt. dept., 1986-87, prof., 1987—, acting dean, 1987, dean coll. and grad. sch. bus. adminstrn., 1987-94. Author: Elites and Their Education National Foundation for Educational Research, 1973; mem. editl. bd. Internat. Jour. Value-Based Mgmt., Cross-cultural Mgmt.; contbr. articles to profl. jours. Trustee Pine Mano rColl.; corporator Brooline Savs. Bank. Recipient Excellence in Teaching award Northeastern U., 1980; Northeastern U. grantee, 1982-84, Control Data Corp., 1983, NYU, 1985. Mem. Soc. Colonial Wars, S.R., Oxford Soc., Tennis and Racquet Club, Somerset Club, Mass Hort. Soc. (trustee), Comml. Club, Beta Gamma Sigma, Phi Kappa Phi. Home: 14 Bristol Rd Wellesley Hills MA 02481-2727 Office: Northeastern U 304 Hayden Hall Boston MA 02115-5000

BOYD, DAVID WILLIAM, mathematician, educator; b. Toronto, Ont., Can., Sept. 17, 1941; s. Glenn Kelvin and Rachael Cecilia (Garvock) B.; m. Mary Margaret Shields, Sept. 26, 1964; children: Deborah, Paul, Kathryn. B.S., Carleton U., 1963; M.A., Toronto U., 1964, Ph.D., 1966. Asst. prof. U. Alta., 1966-67; asst. prof. Calif. Inst. Tech., 1967-70, assoc. prof., 1970-71; assoc. prof. U. B.C., Vancouver, Can., 1971-74; prof. math. U. B.C., Vancouver, 1974—, dept. head, 1986-89. Recipient E.W.R. Steacie Prize, 1978; I.W. Killam sr. research fellow, 1976-77, 81-82. Fellow Royal Soc. Can.; mem. Am. Math. Soc., Can. Math. Soc. Office: Univ BC, Dept Math, Vancouver, BC Canada V6T 1Z2

BOYD, DAWN ANDREA WILLIAMS, airline employee, artist; b. Neptune, N.J., Mar. 9, 1952; d. John Arthur Williams and Narvie Denise (Hill) Puls; m. Joseph L. Boyd II, July 19, 1980 (div.); children: Dziko Ain Williams, Iyabo Kijakazi. BFA, Stephens Coll., 1974. Saleswoman Neusteters, Denver, 1976-77; instr. Opportunities Industrialization Ctr., Denver, 1977-78; reservations and sales agt. United Airlines, Inc., Denver, 1978—. Pres. ULOZI, African-Am. artists collective, Denver, 1995—. Recipient cmty. art award Colo. Black Women for Polit. Action, 1995, award of merit Colo. '96 Art Exhibit, 1996. Mem. Rocky Mountain Women's Inst. (assoc.), ULOZI Art Ctr. Office: ULOZI Art Ctr 2818 Welton St Denver CO 80205-3020

BOYD, DEAN WELDON, management consultant; b. Shreveport, La., July 15, 1941; s. Vernon Dean and Josie (Weldon) B.; m. Susan C. Wickizer; children: Jodie Boyd-Wickizer, Silas Boyd-Wickizer. BEE, MIT, 1963, MEE, 1965; PhD in Engring. Econ. systems, Stanford U., 1970. Rsch. engr. Jet Propulsion Lab., Pasadena, Calif., 1965-67; sr. decision analyst Stanford Rsch. Inst., Menlo Park, Calif., 1967-70; asst. prof. info. sci. U. Calif., Santa Cruz, 1970-75; mgr. cons. Cottage Grove, Oreg., 1975-77; founder Decision Focus, Inc., Mountain View, Calif., 1977-97, CEO, prin., pres., 1997; vice chmn. Talus Solutions (formerly Decision Focus Inc.), Mountain View, 1997—. Contbr. articles to profl. jours. Mem. Sch. Bd. South Ln. Sch. Dist., Cottage Grove, 1986—. Mem. Coun. Logistics Mgmt., Inst. Mgmt. Sci. Developer of methodologies for logical selection of portfolios of interrelated activities. Avocations: hiking, gardening, travel. Office: Talus Solutions 650 Castro St Ste 300 Mountain View CA 94041-2057

BOYD, EDWARD LEE, financial executive; b. Lenoir, N.C., Sept. 5, 1930; s. Frederick and Iva Boyd; AB, Lenoir Rhyne Coll., 1954; MBA U. N.C., 1960; m. Ellanor Fetner, July 10, 1954; children: Lawrence Fetner, Elizabeth Jane. With N.C. Nat. Bank, Charlotte, 1958-62; with Barclays Comml. Corp. and predecessors, Charlotte, 1962-94, pres., 1994; pres. Charlotte divsn. CIT Group/Comml. Svc., Charlotte, 1994, ret. 1994. Active United Cmty. Svcs. With U.S. Army, 1954-56. Mem. Charlotte C. of C. (life), Myers Park Country Club.

BOYD, F. ALLEN, JR., farmer, congressman; 3 children. BA, Fla. State U., 1969. Mem. Fla. Ho. of Reps., 1989-97; mem. 105th Congress from 2d Fla. dist., 1997—, mem. appropriations com. With U.S. Army, 1969-71. Office: 107 Cannon HOB Washington DC 20515

BOYD, FRANCIS R., geophysicists; b. Boston, Jan. 30, 1926; 2 children. AB, Harvard Coll., 1949, MS, 1951, PhD, 1958; MS, Stanford U., 1950. Fellow Harvard U., 1952-53; staff asst. geophysik lab Carnegie Inst., Washington, 1953-56, staff mem., 1956—. Fellow Geology Soc. Am., Am. Geophysic Union; mem. NAS, Geochemical Soc. (pres., sec.). Office: Carnegie Inst Geophysic Lab 5251 Broad Brance Rd NW Washington DC 20015-1305*

BOYD, FRANCIS VIRGIL, retired accounting educator; b. Livermore, Iowa, Feb. 1, 1922; s. Ernest and Gertrude (Marley) B.; m. Mary Celeste Cranny, Nov. 6, 1943 (dec. Sept. 11, 1981); children: Kevin, Therese.; m. Elizabeth Haynes Mauer, Oct. 8, 1983. B.A., Iowa State Tchrs. Coll., 1943; M.B.A., Northwestern U., 1948, Ph.D., 1956; LLD honoris causa, Loyola U., Chgo., 1990. C.P.A., Ill. Tchr. accounting Northwestern U., 1946-63; asso. dean Northwestern U. (Sch. Bus.), 1963-66; dean Sch. Bus., Loyola U., 1966-77, prof. acctg., 1977-87, ret., 1987; dir., acad. dean Ctr. Liberal Arts, Loyola U., Rome, 1988-89; cons., tchr. exec. programs, 1956—; cons.-evaluator North Central Assn. Colls. and Univs. Author: (with others) Quantitative Controls in Business. Past bd. dirs. Chgo. Crime Commn.; vice chmn. Bd. dirs. Lake Forest Sch. Mgmt.; past mem. faculty adv. bd. Pepsi Cola Mgmt. Inst. Served to lt. (j.g.) USNR, 1943-46. Mem. Am. Inst. C.P.A.'s (past), Econ. Club Chgo., Am. Accounting Assn. (past), Am. Econ. Assn. (past), Beta Gamma Sigma.

BOYD, GARY DELANE, electro-optical engineer, researcher; b. L.A., Sept. 14, 1932; s. Vroman O. and Bea L. (Crisp) B.; m. Diana Logan, June 13, 1964; children: Eric Logan, Cynthia Melinda. BSEE, Calif. Inst. Tech., 1954, MSEE, 1955, PhD in Elec. Engring. and Physics, 1959. Mem. tech. staff AT&T Bell Labs., Murray Hill, N.J., 1959-66; mem. tech. staff AT&T Bell Labs., Holmdel, N.J., 1967—, head electronic devel. rsch. dept., 1972-84; cons. Lucent Techs., 1994—; lectr. div. engring. and applied physics, Harvard U., Cambridge, Mass., 1966-67. Patentee laser and optical devices, liquid crystal displays, acoustics delay lines. Fellow IEEE (mem. awards bd. 1977-79); mem. Optical Soc. Am. Presbyterian. Home: 56 E River Rd Rumson NJ 07760-1549 Office: Lucent Technologies Crawfords Corner Rd Rm 4B 501 Holmdel NJ 07733

BOYD, HARRY DALTON, lawyer, former insurance company executive; b. Huntington Park, Calif., June 13, 1923; s. Randall and Thelma L. (Lewis) B.; m. Margaret Jeanine Gamewell, June 13, 1948; children: Leslie Boyd Cotton, Wayne, Lynn Boyd Denby, Evan, Lance. LLB, U. So. Calif., 1949, LLM, 1960; A degree in Mgmt., Ins. Inst. Am., 1972. Bar: Calif. 1950. Pvt. practice L.A.; assoc. Harvey & Viereck, L.A., 1952-55; assoc. gen. counsel, corp. sec. Farmers Ins. Group, L.A., 1955-77; group v.p., gen. counsel Swett & Crawford Group, L.A., 1977-83; gen. counsel, dir. Harbor Ins. Co., 1983-89; Calif. counsel Continental Ins. Co., 1987-89; of counsel Fidler & Bell, Burbank, Calif., 1990-93, Richard E. Garcia, Atty. at Law, L.A., 1994-96; bd. dirs. FIG Fed. Credit Union, 1958-61, pres., 1960-61; mem. Sherman Oaks Property Owners Assn., 1967—, pres., 1969, 72; mem. Western Ins. Info. Svc., Spkrs. Bur., 1971-77; bd. dirs. Buffalo Reins. Co., 1983-87; expert witness in ins. litigation, 1990—; arbitrator reins., 1990—. Mem. adv. coun. Chandler Elementary Sch., 1970-73, Milliken Jr. H.S., 1973-74. With USAAF, 1943-46. Mem. Calif. Ins. Guarantee Assn. (bd. govs. 1972-77), Los Angeles County Bar Assn. (chmn. exec. com. corp. law depts. sect. 1971-72), Reins. Assn. Am. (legal com. 1979-81), Nat. Assn. Ind. Insurers (chmn. surplus lines com. 1980-82), Calif. Assn. Ins. Cos. (exec. com. 1979-83), Wilshire C. of C. (bd. dirs. 1971-79, pres. 1975), Nat. Assn. Ins. Commrs. (industry adv. com. on reins. regulation 1983-90), Am. Arbitration Assn. (arbitrator). Republican. Lutheran (pres. coun. 1964-65). Home: 13711 Weddington St Van Nuys CA 91401-5825

BOYD, JAMES ROBERT, oil company executive; b. Nashville, July 29, 1946; s. James Clinton and Mary Avon (Motlow) B.; m. Elise White, June 27, 1970; children: Elizabeth, Mary Franklin. BSEE, U. Ky., 1969; MBA, NYU, 1972. Sales engr. Westinghouse Electric Co., N.Y.C. and St. Louis, 1970-75; mgr. generation sales Westinghouse Electric Co., St. Louis, 1975-77; cons. planning Westinghouse Electric Co., Pitts., 1977-79, mgr. div. planning, 1979-81; mgr. strategic planning Ashland (Ky.) Oil Co., 1982-84, dir. corp. planning, 1984-86, sr. v.p. , group oper. officer, 1989—; sr. v.p. adminstrn. Ashland Exploration, Houston, 1986-87, pres., 1987-89; pres. Foxcroft Sch., Middleburg, Va., 1996—; chmn. bd. dirs. Arch Coal Inc. Avocations: golf, hunting, swimming. Office: Ashland Inc PO Box 391 50 E RiverCenter Blvd Covington KY 41012-0391

BOYD, JOHN GARTH, manufacturing production and operations consultant; b. Greeley, Colo., Sept. 17, 1942; s. Jack Gardner and Madelyn Ilene (Bucher) B.; m. Cherie Kay Graves, Mar. 16, 1962 (div. June 1982); children: Jeffrey G., Daryl I., Peggy N.; m. Ellen Lea Meyers, Aug. 8, 1987; 1 child, Ian T. BA, U. No. Colo., 1963; MA, Colo. State U., 1965; MS, U. Colo., 1972. Teaching asst. Colo. State U., Ft. Collins, 1964-65; instr. No. Ariz. U., Flagstaff, 1965-67; teaching asst. U. Colo., Boulder, 1967-72; systems rep. Burroughs Corp., Englewood, Colo., 1972-76; mgr. Touche Ross & Co., Denver, 1977-84; chief fin. officer, chief operating officer Catalina Controls Corp., Longmont, Colo., 1984-86; ptnr. High Plains Ptnrship., Lakewood, Colo., 1987—; adminstr. Martin Marietta Astronautics Group, Denver, 1988-92, honorarium instr. Grad. Sch. Bus. Adminstrn., U. Colo.-Denver, 1991—; instr. U. Denver, U. Coll., 1992—, Coll. Engring. and Applied Sci., U. Colo.-Boulder, 1995. Scoutmaster Boy Scouts Am., Boulder, 1969-72, troop scoutmaster, Denver, 1972-75; loaned exec. Colo. Gov.'s Mgmt. and Efficiency Study, 1982; chair house dist. 26 Jefferson County Dem. Party, 1994-97. NASA fellow, 1968. Mem. Am. Soc. Quality, Am. Prodn. and Inventory Control Soc. (treas. Denver 1983-84, pres. 1984-85, Gold award 1985). Avocations: hiking, mountain climbing, fishing, cross-country skiing. Office: High Plains Ptnrship 9381 W Louisiana Ave Lakewood CO 80232-5178

BOYD, JOHN HAMILTON, osteopath; b. Wharton County, Tex., Sept. 20, 1924; s. John Hamilton and Grace Laura (Smith) B.; m. Myrtle Juanita Ferguson, Feb. 21, 1970. BA, Tex. Tech U., 1949; DO, Kirksville (Tex.) Coll. Osteo. Medicine, 1955. Diplomate Am. Bd. Quality Assurance and Utilization Rev. Physicians. Practice osteopathic medicine Louise, Tex., 1955-70, Silverton, Tex., 1971-74, Eden, Tex., 1974—; aviation med. examiner FAA, 1971—; clin. prof. Gen. and Family Practice Tex. Coll. Osteo Med.; clin. prof. health sci. ctr. U. North Tex., Ft. Worth, 1990—; mem. Tex. State Bd. Med. Examiners, 1987-93, sec., treas., 1989-93; health officer Wharton County, 1961-65, Briscoe County, 1971-74; health dir. City of Eden, 1974—; med. dir. Eden Detention Ctr., 1985-93; asst. adminstr. Concho County Hosp., 1987—; chmn. rev. com. Tex. Inst. Med. Assessment, 1979-81, pres., 1981-83. Mem. local SSS bd., 1967-70; bd. dirs. Concho County Hosp. Dist., 1975-84, Wharton County Jr. Coll., 1961-70, Tex. Med. Found., 1973-78, 82-91. Served with USAAF, 1942-46, ETO. Fellow Am. Coll. Utilization Rev. Physicians, Am. Med. Dir. Assn. (cert.), Am. Back Soc., Aerospace Med. Assn. (assoc.); mem. Am. Acad. Osteopathy, Tex. Osteo. Med. Assn. (pres. 1973-74, Disting. Svc. award 1994), Am. Osteo. Assn., Civil Aviation Med. Assn. (bd. dirs. 1978-80, v.p. 1980-84, 87—, pres. 1985-87), Am. Osteo. Coll. Preventive Medicine, Aerospace Med. Assn., Assn. Latinoam. de Aviación y del Espacio, Am. Med. Peer Rev. Assn. (chmn. by-laws com.), NRA, Am. Back Soc. Home and Office: Drawer W Eden TX 76837

BOYD, JOHN HOWARD, corporate location consultant; b. Trenton, N.J., Mar. 13, 1950; children: John A., Alison G. AB, Rutgers Coll., 1972; postgrad., Rutgers Grad. Sch., 1972-73. Location analyst div. mgmt. cons. Dun & Bradstreet, N.Y.C., 1973-75; pres. The Boyd Co., Inc., Princeton, N.J., 1975—; cons. U.S. and overseas corps. on facilities location. Bd. govs. Trenton Symphony Orch. Henry Rutgers scholar, 1971-72, Bevier fellow, 1973. Avocations: travel, music, swimming, golf, tennis. Office: The Boyd Co Inc 301 N Harrison St Ste 415 Princeton NJ 08540-3512

BOYD, JOSEPH ARTHUR, JR., lawyer; b. Hoschton, Ga., Nov. 16, 1916; s. Joseph Arthur and Esther Estelle (Puckett) B.; m. Ann Stripling, June 6, 1938; children: Joanne Louise Boyd Goldman, Betty Jean Boyd Jala, Joseph Robert, James Daniel, Jane N. Ohlin. Student, Piedmont Coll., Demorest, Ga., 1936-38, LLD, 1963; student, Mercer U., Macon, Ga., 1938-39; JD, U. Miami, Coral Gables, Fla., 1948; LLD, Western State U. Coll. Law, San Diego, 1981. Bar: Fla. 1948, U.S. Supreme Ct. 1959, D.C. 1973, N.Y. 1982. Practice law Hialeah, 1948-68, city atty., 1951-58; mem. Dade County Commn., Miami, Fla., 1958-68; chmn. Dade County Commn., 1963; vice mayor Dade County, 1967; justice Fla. Supreme Ct., Tallahassee, 1969-87, chief justice, 1984-86; assoc. Boyd Lindsey & Branch P.A., Tallahassee, 1987—; mem. Hialeah Zoning Bd., 1946-48; juror Freedoms Found., Valley Forge, Pa., 1971, 73. Bd. dirs. Bapt. Hosp., Miami, 1962-66, Miami Coun. Chs., 1960-64; emeritus trustee Piedmont Coll. Recipient Nat. Top Hat award Bus. and Profl. Women in U.S. for advancing status of employed women, 1967. Mem. ABA, Fla. Bar Assn., Hialeah-Miami Springs Bar Assn. (pres. 1955), Tallahassee Bar Assn., Hialeah-Miami Springs C. of C. (pres. 1956), Am. Legion (comdr. Fla. 1953-54), VFW, Shriners, Masons (33 deg.), Lions, Elks, Wig and Robe, Iron Arrow, Phi Alpha Delta, Alpha Kappa Psi. Democrat. Baptist (deacon). Office: Boyd Lindsey & Branch PA 1407 Piedmont Dr E Tallahassee FL 32312-2943

BOYD, JOSEPH AUBREY, communications company executive; b. Oscar, Ky., Mar. 25, 1921; s. Joseph Ray and Relda Jane (Myatt) B.; m. Edith A. Atkins, May 13, 1942; children: Joseph Barry, Joel Edd. S.B. in Elec. Engring., U. Ky., 1946, M.S., 1949; Ph.D., U. Mich., 1954. Instr., then asst. prof. elec. engring. U. Ky., 1947-49; mem. faculty U. Mich., 1949-62, prof. elec. engring., 1958-62; asso. dir., then dir. U. Mich. (Willow Run Labs.), 1958-60; dir. U. Mich. (Inst. Sci. and Tech.), 1960-62; exec. v.p. Radiation Inc., Melbourne, Fla., 1962-63, pres., 1963-72; exec. v.p. electronics Harris Corp., Melbourne, Fla., 1987-93; exec. v.p. ops. Harris Corp., Cleve., 1971-72, pres., 1972-85, dir., 1972-87; chmn. ex. com. Harris Corp., Cleve. (now in Melbourne, Fla.), 1987—; chmn., CEO Fairchild Space and Def. Corp., Germantown, Md., 1992-94, Fairchild Controls, Frederick, Md., 1994—; Cons. Inst. for Def. Analyses, 1956—, Nat. Security Agy., 1957-62; spl. cons. to (Army Combat Surveillance Agy.), 1958-62; mem., chmn. adv. group electronic warfare Office Dir. Def. Research, Engring., Def. Dept., 1959-61, cons., 1959—. Contbr. articles to profl. jours. Fellow IEEE; mem. Assn. U.S. Army, Armed Forces Communications and Electronics Assn. (pres. 1971, 72), AAAS, Sigma Xi, Eta Kappa Nu, Tau Beta Pi. Baptist. Home: 4650 Hamilton Ter Vero Beach FL 32967-7330 Office: Fairchild Controls 540 Highland St Frederick MD 21701-5716

BOYD, JOSEPH DON, financial services executive; b. Muncie, Ind., Jan. 22, 1926; s. Joseph Corneluis and Waneta May (Barrett) B.; m. Cynthia Reiley, Dec. 28, 1957; children—Jane Elizabeth, Craig A., Michael J. A.B. (Rector scholar), DePauw U., 1948; M.A., Northwestern U., 1950, Ed.D., 1955. Ednl. asst. First Meth. Ch., Anderson, Ind., 1948-49; residence hall counselor Northwestern U., Evanston, Ill., 1949-50, univ. examiner, instr. edn., guidance lab. asst., 1952-54, dean men, asst. prof. edn., 1955-61; exec. dir. Ill. Scholarship Commn., 1961-80; dir. instnl. relations and research Nat. Coll. Edn., Evanston, 1981-84; pres. Joseph D. Boyd & Assocs., Deerfield, Ill., 1984—; residence hall dir., head tennis coach, asst. basketball coach Albion Coll., 1950-52. Mem. Nat. Assn. Adminstrs. State Scholarship Programs, Phi Delta Kappa, Delta Tau Delta, Phi Eta Sigma. Methodist. Club: Rotarian. Home: 1232 Warrington Rd Deerfield IL 60015-3145 Office: 600 Deerfield Rd Deerfield IL 60015-3229

BOYD, JULIANNE MAMANA, theater director; b. Easton, Pa., Dec. 22, 1944; d. Joseph and Julia (Cericola) Mamana; m. Norman Wingate Boyd Jr., July 9, 1966; children: Sarah, Norman III, Emily. BA, Beaver Coll., 1966; MA, Adelphi U., 1968; PhD, CUNY, 1986. Lectr. NYU, 1987-91; artistic dir. Berkshire Theatre Festival, Stockbridge, Mass., 1992-94; artistic dir., founder Barrington Stage Co., Great Barrington, Mass., 1995—. Conceiver and dir. Broadway musical Eubie, 1978 (Audelco award Outstanding Dir 1978), off-Broadway play A...My Name is Alice, 1984 (Outer Critics award), A...Ny Name is Still Alice, 1992. Mem. adv. bd. Women's Project, Inc., N.Y., 1988-92. Recipient Golden Disc award Beaver Coll., 1981, Outstanding Young Entrepreneur award Citicorp, N.Y., 1980, Outstanding Alumni award CUNY, 1995. Mem. Soc. Stage Dirs. and Choreographers (pres. 1992-98).

BOYD, KENNETH WADE, publishing company executive, consultant; b. Jacksonville, Fla., Oct. 2. 1938; s. Wade Julius and Hariett Lucile (Rogers) B.; m. Linda Jean Adams, Dec. 29, 1962; 1 child, Lara Christine. BA in History, The Citadel, 1960; MS in LS, Drexel Inst. Tech., 1962. Extension librarian Flint River Regional Library, Griffin, Ga., 1962-64; acquisitions librarian Atlanta Pub. Library, 1964-65; v.p. sales Am. Library Line, Atlanta, 1965-68; mgr. Josten's Libr. Supplies, Atlanta, 1968-72; southeastern sales rep. Congl. Info. Svc., Washington, 1972-75; pub., pres. Cherokee Pub. Co.-Larlin Corp., Marietta, Ga., 1975—; mem. adv. bd. Coun. Authors and Journalists, Atlanta, 1987-90. Author, compiler: Vermont Historic Markers, 1989, Georgia Historical Markers, 3 Vols., 1990. Trustee Walker Sch., Marietta, 1982-94; bd. dirs. Reach of Song, Gainesville, Ga., 1988-94, Ga. Writers, 1993, Pubs. Assn. of the South, 1996. 2d lt. U.S. Army. Named Pub. of Yr., Ga. chpt. Nat. League Am. Pen Women, 1987. Mem. Ga. Book Pubs. Assn. (pres.), ALA, Southeastern Libr. Assn., Ga. Libr. Assn., Metro Atlanta Libr. Assn. (v.p., pres. 1967-68), Pubs. Assn. of the South (bd. dirs. 1996—). Republican. Avocations: Mustang restoration, historical research. Office: Atlanta Design Ctr 764 Miami Cir NE Atlanta GA 30324-3055

BOYD, LARRY CHESTER, recruitment manager; b. Newberry, S.C., Nov. 6, 1958; s. Andrew Larkin Sr. and Anna Lee (McMorris) B.; m. Paula Annette Harris, Aug. 19, 1989; 1 child, Larry Jr. BA in Polit. Sci. cum laude, S.C. State U., 1980; MBA in Adminstrn., Cen. Mich. U., 1990. Commd. 2d lt. U.S. Army, 1980, advanced through grades to lt. col., 1999—; adminstrv. officer 800th Materiel Mgmt. Ctr. U.S. Army, Nelligan, Fed. Rep. Germany, 1980-82; asst. sec. gen. staff, protocol officer Hdqrs. VII Corps U.S. Army, Stuttgart, Fed. Rep. Germany, 1982-83; chief reenlistment Hdrs. and Hdrs. Co. U.S. Army Garrison U.S. Army, Ft. Polk, La., 1984; comdr. 5th Adj. Gen. Replacement Co., Ft. Polk, La., 1984-85; chief, officer records 5th Adj. Gen. Co. U.S. Army, Ft. Polk, La., 1985, chief, pers. records 5th Pers. Svc. Co., 1985, chief, Co. Spt. Div., 1986, chief, G-1/Adj. Gen. Plans and Ops. Hdrs. and Hdqrs. Co. 5th Inf. Div., 1986; advisor Readiness Group Dix First U.S. Army, Ft. Dix, N.J., 1987-88; tng. mgmt. officer, asst. ops. officer U.S. Army, Ft. Dix, N.J., 1988-89, chief adminstrn. logistics assistance div., 1989-92; dep. chief mil. awards br. Dept. of The Army, Alexandria, Va., 1993-97; recruitment mgr. INROADS, Phila., 1992—; dir. mil. pers. directorate 1079th U.S. Army Garrison Support Unit, Fort Dix, N.J., 1997—. Intern State of S.C. Task Force on Structure of State and Local Govt., 1980; mem. Bush River Bapt. Ch., Newberry, S.C., 1973—; mem. Tabernacle Bapt. Ch., Burlington, N.J., 1988—. Decorated Army Commendation medal with oak leaf cluster, Meritorious Svc. medal with oak leaf cluster, Nat. Def. Svc. medal, Allen W. Reese Meml. scholar; named of Outstanding Men of Am., U.S. Jaycees, 1984, 86, 87, 88, 89, 92, 96, 97, 98. Mem. ASTD, NAACP, Assn. U.S. Army, Nat. Black MBA Assn., Nat. Mgmt. Assn., Am. Legion, S.C. State U. Alumni Assn., Adjutant Gen. Regimental Assn., Pi Gamma Mu, Omega Psi Phi (vice basileus 1978-79, basileus 1979-80, dean of edn. 1981-82, 85-86, area coord. 1982-83, keeper of records and seal 1984-86, 92-93, asst. keeper of records and seal 1990-92, basileus 1993-94, dir. pub. rels. 1994-95, 97-98, 98-99, Omega Man of yr. 1985, 86, 91), vice chmn., Omega Community Development, Inc., 1999—. Avocations: sports, music, reading. Office: 1601 Market St Ste 1010 Philadelphia PA 19103-2336 Home: 31 Tarnsfield Rd Westampton NJ 08060-2361

BOYD, LEONA POTTER, retired social worker; b. Creekside, Pa., Aug. 31, 1907; d. Joseph M. and Belle (McHenry) Johnston. Grad. Ind. (Pa.) State Normal Sch., 1927, student Las Vegas Normal U., N.Mex., 1933, Carnegie Inst. Tech. Sch. Social Work, 1945, U. Pitts. Sch. Social Work, 1956-57; m. Edgar D. Potter, July 16, 1932 (div.); m. Harold Lee Boyd, Oct. 1972. Tchr. Creekside (Pa.) Pub. Schs., 1927-30, Papago Indian Reservation, Sells, Ariz., 1931-33; caseworker, supr. Indiana County (Pa.) Bd. Assistance, 1934-54, exec. dir., 1954-68, ret. Bd. dirs. Indiana County Tourist Promotion, hon. life mem.; former bd. dirs. Indiana County United Fund, Salvation Army, Indiana County Guidance Ctr., Armstrong-Indiana Mental Health Bd.; cons. assoc. Community Rsch. Assocs., Inc.; mem. Counseling Ctr. Aux., Lake Havasu City, Ariz., 1978-80; former mem. Western Welcome Club, Lake Havasu City, Sierra Vista Hosp. Aux., Truth or Consequences, N.Mex. Recipient Jr. C. of C. Disting. Svc. award, Indiana, Pa., 1966, Bus. and Profl. Women's Club award, Indiana, 1965. Mem. Am. Assn. Ret. Persons, Daus. Am. Colonists. Lutheran. Home: 444 S Higley Rd Apt 219 Mesa AZ 85206-2186

BOYD, LIONA MARIA, musician; b. London; d. John Haig and Eileen (Hancock) B.; m. John B. Simon, Feb. 1992. BMusic, U. Toronto, 1972; hon. doctorate, 1981, 89, 91, 96. CBS and PolyGram rec. artist and composer; found. Moston Records. Classical guitarist appearing in concert tours in Can., China, England, U.S.A., Europe, Japan, C. Am., S.Am., N.Z., India, Russia, the Caribbean; appeared on numerous TV variety shows, The Life and Times of Liona Boyd (CBS), 1999; recs. include The Guitar, 1975, The Guitar Artistry of Liona Boyd, 1976, Miniatures for Guitar, 1977, The First Lady of the Guitar, 1978, Liona Boyd, Andrew Davis, English Chamber Orch, 1979, First Nashville Guitar Quartet, 1979, Spanish Fantasy, 1980, A Guitar for Christmas, 1981, The Best of Liona Boyd, 1982, Virtuoso Liona Boyd, 1983, Liona Live in Tokyo, 1984, The Romantic Guitar of Liona Boyd, 1985, Persona, 1986, Encore, 1988, Highlights, 1989, Christmas Dreams, 1989, Paddle to the Sea, 1990, Dancing On The Edge, 1991, Classically Yours, 1995, Baroque Favourites, 1998; The Spanish Album, 1998, Whispers of Love, 1999; author 5 music books, autobiog., In My Own Key-My Life in Love and Music, 1998. Decorated officer Order of Can., 1982, Order of Ont., 1991; recipient Juno award for instrumentalist of yr. Can. Music Industry, 1978, 81, 82, 84, 96, Vanier award Can., 1979; voted internat. poll Top Classical Guitarist in Guitar Player mag., 1985, 86, 87, 88, 93; inducted into Hall of Fame Gallery of Greats. Mem. Am. Fedn. Musicians, AFTRA, SOCAN. Website: www.lionaboyd.com.

BOYD, LYNNE KAPLAN, software company executive; b. Willimantic, Conn., June 17, 1951; d. Joseph and Rebecca Kaplan; m. William Randolph Boyd, Aug. 18, 1973; 1 child, Joel. Honors exch. student, U. Mich., 1970-71; BS with honors, Vassar Coll., 1973. Dist. mgr. Xerox Corp., Rosslyn, Va., 1973-85; dir. fed. sales Telic Corp., Rockville, Md., 1985-88; dir. sales Contel Fed. Sys., Fairfax, Va., 1988; sr. v.p. Uniplex Integration Sys., Inc., Dallas, 1988-93, pres., 1993-94; sr. v.p. Jetform Corp., Ottawa, Canada, 1994—. Mem. NAFE, Armed Forces Comms. and Elec. Assn., Business Forms Mgmt. Assn. Avocations: youth soccer, gardening, sailing. Home: 512 Janneys Ln Alexandria VA 22302-4004 Office: JetForm Corp 7600 Leesburg Pike Ste 430E Falls Church VA 22043-2004

BOYD, MALCOLM, minister, religious author; b. Buffalo, June 8, 1923; s. Melville and Beatrice (Lowrie) B.; life ptnr. Mark Thompson. B.A., U. Ariz., 1944; B.D., Ch. Div. Sch. Pacific, 1954; postgrad., Oxford (Eng.) U., 1955; S.T.M., Union Theol. Sem., N.Y.C., 1956; DD (hon.), Ch. Div. Sch. of Pacific, 1995. Ordained to ministry Episcopal Ch., 1955. V.p., gen. mgr. Pickford, Rogers & Boyd, 1949-51; rector in Indpls., 1957-59; chaplain Colo. State U., 1959-61, Wayne State U., 1961-65; nat. field rep. Episcopal Soc. Cultural and Racial Unity, 1965-68; resident fellow Calhoun Coll., Yale U., 1968-71, assoc. fellow, 1971—; writer-priest in residence St. Augustine-by-the Sea Episcopal Ch., 1982-95; chaplain to commn. on AIDS Ministries of Episcopal Diocese of L.A., 1993—; lectr. World Council Chs., Switzerland, 1955, 64; columnist Pitts. Courier, 1962-65; resident guest Mishkenot Sha'ananim, Jerusalem, 1974; chaplain AIDS Commn. Episcopal Diocese L.A., 1989—; poet-in-residence Cathedral Ctr. of St. Paul, L.A., 1996—. Host: TV spl. Sex in the Seventies, CBS-TV, Los Angeles, 1975; author: Crisis in Communication, 1957, Christ and Celebrity Gods, 1958, Focus, 1960, If I Go Down to Hell, 1962, The Hunger, The Thirst, 1964, Are You Running with Me, Jesus?, 1965, rev. 25th anniversary edit., 1990, Free to Live, Free to Die, 1967, Book of Days, 1968, As I Live and Breathe: Stages of an Autobiography, 1969, The Fantasy Worlds of Peter Stone, 1969, My Fellow Americans, 1970, Human Like Me, Jesus, 1971, The Lover, 1972, When in the Course of Human Events, 1973, The Runner, 1974, The Alleluia Affair, 1975, Christian, 1975, Am I Running with You, God?, 1977, Take Off the Masks, 1978, rev. edit. 1993, Look Back in Joy, 1981, rev. edit., 1990, Half Laughing, Half Crying, 1986, Gay Priest: An Inner Journey, 1986, Edges, Boundaries and Connections, 1992, Rich with Years, 1993, Go Gentle Into That Good Night, 1998; plays Boy, 1961, Study in Color, 1962, The Community, 1964, others; editor: On the Battle Lines, 1964, The Underground Church, 1968, Amazing Grace: Stories of Gay and Lesbian Faith, 1991; book reviewer: Los Angeles Times.; contbg. editor The Episcopal News; columnist Modern Maturity; contbr. articles to numerous mags. including Newsday, Parade, The Advocate, also newspapers. Active voter registration, Miss., Ala., 1963, 64; mem. Los Angeles City/County AIDS Task Force. Malcolm Boyd Collection and Archives established Boston U., 1973; Recipient Integrity Internat. award, 1978; Union Am. Hebrew Congregations award, 1980. Mem. Nat. Council Chs. (film awards com. 1965), P.E.N. (pres. PEN Ctr. U.S. West 1984-87), Am. Center, Authors Guild, Integrity, Nat. Gay Task Force, Clergy and Laity Concerned (nat. bd.), NAACP, Amnesty Internat., Episc. Peace Fellowship, Fellowship of Reconciliation (nat. com.). Office: PO Box 2164 Los Angeles CA 90051-0164 *The years have taught me the cost of getting involved in life. It is all a risk. One is on stage in an ever-new set without a script. The floor may give way without warning, the walls abruptly cave in. One may die at the hand of an assassin acting on blind impulse. Security, for which men sell their souls, is one of the few real jests in life. Yet the cost of not getting involved in life is higher; one has merely died prematurely. When one has stripped power of its mystique, its robes and artifices, it becomes vulnerable. When you stand up to power, you stand up to one or more individuals. Look an individual, then, in the eye, laugh, if you feel like it. This may be rightly received as a much-needed expression of human solidarity.*

BOYD, MORRIS J., military officer. BS in Bus., U. Nebr.; MBA, U. Puget Sound; student, U.S. Army Command/Gen. Staff, U.S. Army War Coll. Commd. 2d lt. U.S. Army, 1966, advanced through grades to maj. gen., 1996; comdr. C battery 2d Howitzer bn. 17th arty. U.S. Army, Vietnam, 1968, platoon comdr. 21st aviation co. 212th aviation bn., 1970; comdr. A battery, 1st bn., 14th arty., 2d armored divsn. Ft. Hood, Tex., 1971-72; ops. then exec. officer 1st bn., 79th field arty., exec. officer divsn. arty. Ft. Ord, Calif., 1980-82; comdr. 1st bn., 7th field arty. 7th infantry divsn. Ft. Ord, 1982-83, comdr. 6th bn. 8th field arty. 7th infantry divsn., 1983-84; staff officer Army legis. liason Office of Sec. of Army, 1985-88; dep. comdr. V corps arty. U.S. Army Europe and 7th Army, Germany, 1988-89, comdr. 42d field arty. brigade V corps arty., 1989-90, 91; comdr. 42 field arty. brigade VII corps arty. Operation Desert Shield/Desert Storm, Saudi Arabia, 1990-91; exec. officer to comdg. gen. U.S. Army Tng. and Doctrine Command, Ft. Monroe, Va., 1991-92; asst. divsn. comdr. 1st infantry divsn. Ft. Riley, 1992-93; dep. chief of staff for doctrine U.S. Army Tng. and Doctrine Command, Ft. Monroe, Va., 1993-95; chief legis. liaison Office of Sec. of the Army, Washington, 1995-97. Decorated Disting. Svc. medal, Legion of Merit with 3 oak leaf clusters, DFC, Bronze Star with oak leaf cluster, Meritorious Svc. medal with oak leaf cluster, 12 Air medals, Vietnam Cross of Galantry with silver star. Office: III Corps and Fort Hood Fort Hood TX 76544

BOYD, ROBERT COTTON, English language educator; b. Little Rock, Sept. 20, 1938; s. Robert Hampton and Jessie Leigh (Cotton) B.; m. Katherine Lenore Rock, Jan. 3, 1964; children: Robert Rock, Katherine Anne, Elizabeth Leigh. BA, U. Ark., 1965; postgrad., U. Hamburg, Fed. Republic of Germany, 1965-66; MA, U. Ark., 1967; PhD, Ind. U., 1989. Instr. English Ind. State U., Terre Haute, 1966-70; prof. English St. Louis Community Coll., 1970—, asst. chair english dept., 1993-96; editor Webster Review, 1992-96; theater critic Sta. KWMU-FM, St. Louis, 1980-94, Sta. KDHX, St. Louis, 1995—; v.p. bd. dirs. River Styx Arts Orgn., 1996—; Fulbright exch. tchr., Germany, 1997—; pres. bd. dirs. River Styx, 1999—. Mem. editl. bd. Gateway Heritage mag., 1996—; contbg. editor River Styx mag., 1996—. Mem. St. Louis-Lyon Sister Cities Com., 1988—, treas., 1993-96; pres. Kirkwood chpt. Am. Field Svc., 1986-87. Recipient Guy Owen Poetry prize So. Poetry Rev., 1991, Poetry award Mo. Writers' Week, 1995. Mem. Nat. Coun. Tchrs. English, Conf. on Coll. Composition and Comm. Democrat. Unitarian. Avocation: golf. Home: 804 Lisakay Dr Saint Louis MO 63122-3128 Office: Saint Louis Community Coll 11333 Big Bend Rd Saint Louis MO 63122-5720

BOYD, ROBERT FRIEND, lawyer; b. Richmond, Va., May 11, 1927; s. Oscar Linwood and Ruby (Friend) B.; m. Sara Grace Miller, Sept. 20, 1952; children: Robert Friend Jr., David M., Mary Boyd Horton, James M. AB, Coll. of William and Mary, 1950, JD, 1952. Bar: Va. 1952. Pvt. practice Norfolk, Va., 1955—; chmn. Boyd & Boyd, P.C., Norfolk, 1957—; commr. Chancery for Cir. Ct., Norfolk, 1967—, Cir. Ct. Chesapeake, Va., 1967—; bd. dirs. Holnam, Inc., Detroit; chmn. bd. dirs. Santee Portland Cement Corp., S.C., Holy Hill Lumber Co., S.C. Chmn. adv. com. Norfolk City Coun., 1966-71; trustee, vice chmn., mem. exec. com. Va. Wesleyan Coll.; trustee, v.p. Randolph-Macon Acad.; trustee William and Mary Endowment Assn., United Meth. Found. Va.; pres. bd. trustees Coll. of William and Mary Law Sch.; bd. dirs. Greater Norfolk Corp., Norfolk Mcpl. Hosp.; chmn. bd. Va. Cultural Found.; vice chmn., trustee Walk Thru The Bible Ministries, Atlanta; pres. Kiwanis, Norfolk, Am. Heart Assn. Named Great Citizen of Hampton Rds., 1996. Mem. ABA (com. on corp. counsel, bus. law sect.), Nat. Assn. Coll. and Univ. Attys., Va. Bar Assn. (chmn. judiciary com.), Va. Trial Lawyers Assn. (v.p.), Masons, Shriners, Order of Coif, Tau Kappa Alpha. Home: 3199 Adam Keeling Rd Virginia Beach VA 23454-1000 Office: 1 Commercial Pl Norfolk VA 23510-2103

BOYD, ROBERT GIDDINGS, JR., health facility administrator; b. San Juan, Mar. 16, 1940; s. Robert Giddings and Laura Jean (Stephenson) B.; m. Amanda Gail Rasmussen, July 28, 1967 (div. 1977); 1 child, Stephanie Gail; m. Denise Ann Ryll, Dec. 10, 1978; children: Robert Giddings III., Julianna Clare. B.A. in Sociology, Coll. William and Mary, 1962; MBA/MHA, Columbia State U., 1997. Lic. in real estate, Ariz.; lic. nursing home adminstr., Calif., N.C. Supr. staff services Bellcomm, Inc., Washington, 1964-67; budget mgr. Goodbody & Co., N.Y.C., 1968-70; bus. mgr. Westminster Sch., Simsbury, Conn., 1970-76; pres., gen. mgr. F & R Enterprises, Inc., Scottsdale, Ariz., 1976-78; mng. dir. San Diego Symphony Assn., 1981-84; exec. v.p. adminstrn. and fin. San Diego Ctr. for Children, 1985-95. Served to 1st lt. U.S. Army, 1962-64. Mem. Am. Coll. Health Care Adminstrs., Am. Coll. Health Care Execs. Republican. Office: Avante at Wilkesboro 1000 College St Wilkesboro NC 28697-2732

BOYD, ROBERT WRIGHT, III, lamp company executive; b. N.Y.C., July 21, 1945; s. Robert Wright and Ruth Simpson B.; m. Heather Riddle, June 7, 1968; children: Amy, Brook, Adam. Student, Universidad de Los Andes, Bogota, Columbia, 1965-66; BA cum laude, Princeton U., 1967; MA in Latin Am. studies, U. Fla., 1968. Sales rep. The Wilbur Ellis Co., N.Y.C., 1968-71; regional sales mgr. NPFC div. Nat. Can Corp., Phila., 1971-72; mktg. svcs. mgr. Lewis Foods div. Nat. Can Corp., Long Beach, Calif., 1972-73, western area sales mgr. Lewis Foods div., 1973-75; mgr. mktg. and sales Wells div. Nat. Can Corp., Monmouth, Ill., 1975-78; v.p. sales The Jim Dandy Co., Birmingham, Ala., 1978-80; owner R. W. Boyd & Assocs., Cherry Hill, N.J., 1980-81; mktg. dir. CBS spl. products div. CBS Records, CBS Inc., N.Y.C., 1982-85; v.p. mktg. and sales Action Internat. Ltd., div. Action Industries, Cheswick, Pa., 1985-90; pres., chief exec. officer Hi Lite Industries Inc., Wexford, Pa., 1990—. Pub.: His Father's Son, 1997. Deacon Trinity United Presbyn. Ch., Cherry Hill, N.J., 1982-84; trustee Ingomar (Pa.) United Meth. Ch., 1988-89, mem. adminstrv. coun., 1994-97. Mem. Colonial Club (Princeton, N.J.). Republican. Methodist. Avocation: physical fitness. Office: Hi Lite Industries Inc RD 6 Box 517 Woodward Drive Ext Greensburg PA 15601

BOYD, ROGER ALLEN, investment consultant; b. Meadville, Pa., May 30, 1954; s. Willis W. and Ida Elaine (Stewart) B.; m. Susan Janis Auwarter, July 24, 1982; children: Sara Janis, Emily Katherine. BS in Acctg., Gannon Coll., 1976. CFP. Acct. Arthur Andersen & Co., Pitts., 1976-77; investment real estate salesman Lloyd White Co., Realtors, Erie, Pa., 1977-80; fin. cons. Merrill Lynch, Erie, 1980-81; assoc. v.p. Dean Witter Reynolds, N.Y.C., 1981-88; sr. v.p. Morgan Stanley Dean Witter, Toms River, N.J., 1988—. Bd. dirs., v.p., chmn. artistic com. Garden State Philharm., Toms River, 1991—. Mem. Mensa, Kiwanis (bd. dirs. Toms River 1990-93). Republican. Office: Morgan Stanley Dean Witter 1433 Hooper Ave Toms River NJ 08753-2826

BOYD, ROZELLE, university administrator, educator; b. Indpls., Apr. 24, 1934; s. William Calvin Sr. and Ardelia Louise (Leavell) B. BA, Butler U., 1957; MA, Ind. U., 1965. Welfare dept. worker Marion County DPW, Indpls., 1956-57; tchr. Crispus Attucks High Sch., Indpls., 1957-68, adult edn. counselor, 1958-68; asst. dean U. Div., Ind. U., Bloomington, 1968-78, assoc. dean, 1978-82, dir., 1982—. Minority leader Indpls. City County Coun.; Dem. nat. committeeman, Dem. Party; mem. coms. Nat. League of Cities. Mem. Alpha Phi Alpha. Presbyterian. Office: Ind U Bloomington IN 47405 Office: Office City-County Council 241 City-County Bldg 200 E Washington St Indianapolis IN 46204-3307

BOYD, SHYLAH See WHYATT, FRANCES

BOYD, STEPHEN MATHER, arbitrator, mediator, lawyer; b. St. Louis, May 1, 1934; s. Ingram Fletcher and Adeline Ely (Smith) B.; m. Susan Brush Forney, May 9, 1964; children—Christopher Fletcher, Elizabeth Barrows, Charles Mather. A.B. in History with honors, Princeton U., 1955; LL.B., Harvard U., 1958. Bar: Mo. 1958, D.C. 1973. Assoc. Bryan, Cave, McPheeters & McRoberts, St. Louis, 1963-67; ptnr. Bryan, Cave, McPheeters & McRoberts, Washington, 1978-88; atty. adviser Dept. of State, Washington, 1967-69, asst. legal adviser Near East, South Asia, 1970-73; assoc. Surrey & Morse, Paris, 1973-74, ptnr., 1975-77; ptnr. Surrey & Morse, Washington, 1977-78; pres. Princeton Project 55, 1989-90, bd. dirs., 1989-92; pvt. practice arbitrator and mediator; mem. Washington Fgn. Law Soc., 1981-90, bd. govs., 1983-85; cons. in field. Contbr. articles to profl. jours. 1st lt. USAF, 1958-61; Taiwan, Japan. Mem. ABA (com. on internat. litigation chmn. 1978-81, mem. litigation sect.), Am. Soc. Internat. Law, D.C. Bar Assn., UN Assn. U.S.A. (bd. dirs. 1982-90), Character Edn. Partnership (bd. dirs. 1993-97), Am. Arbitration Assn. (arbitrator, mediator internat. and comml. disputes). Democrat. Unitarian. Avocations: hiking, sculling, skiing, tennis, classical music, reading history and biographies. Home: 4400 Cathedral Ave NW Washington DC 20016-3563

BOYD, THEOPHILUS BARTHOLOMEW, III, publishing company executive; b. Nashville, May 15, 1947; s. Theophilus B. Jr. and Mable (Landrum) B.; m. Yvette Jean Duke, May 5, 1984; children: Theophilus B. IV, LaDonna Yvette, Shalae Shantel, Justin Marriel. BS, Tenn. State U., 1969; DD, Shreveport Bible Coll., 1980; LittD (hon.), Easonian Bapt. Sem., 1983. Pers. dir. Nat. Bapt. Pub. Bd., Nashville, 1969-79, pres., chief exec. officer, 1979—; chmn. Citizens Bank, Nashville, 1982—. Vice chair Meharry Med. Coll. bd. trustees, Nashville, 1989—; trustee Fla. Meml. Coll., Miami, 1984-86; bd. dirs. Nashville Symphone Assn., 1986-87, Nashville chpt. March of Dimes, 1986—; past pres. 100 Black Men of Mid. Tenn.; v.p. fin., treas. 100 Black Men Am., 1992-94. Named Hon. Citizen, City of Dallas, 1980, Man of Yr., 1990; recipient Key to the City, Denver, 1985, New Orleans, 1986, Great Seal of U.S. award; named man of the yr. 1990 March of Dimes. Mem. Nashville Area C. of C. (exec. bd.), Kappa Alpha Psi, Sigma Pi Phi, Richland Country Club, Maryland Farms Country Club. Democrat. Baptist. Avocations: boating, marathon running. Office: Nat Bapt Pub Bd 6717 Centennial Blvd Nashville TN 37209-1017

BOYD, THOMAS MARSHALL, lawyer; b. Yorktown, Va., Sept. 10, 1946; s. Laurel Barnett and Mildred Warner Wellford (Marshall) B.; m. Torri Carol Tyler, Oct. 2, 1976; children: Brooke Warner, Tyler Randolph. BA in History, Va. Military Inst., 1968; JD, U. Va., 1971. Bar: Calif. 1973, D.C. 1974. Law clk. to fed. judge U.S. Dist. Ct. (cen. dist.) Calif., Los Angeles, 1973-74; trial atty., atty. advisor U.S. Dept. Justice, Washington, 1974-76; assoc. counsel com. on judiciary U.S. Ho. of Reps., Washington, 1976-86; dep. asst. atty. gen. Dept. Justice Office Legis. Affairs, Washington, 1986-88, asst. atty. gen., 1988-89, dir. office policy devel., 1989-91; dep. gen. counsel Kemper Corp., Washington, 1991-93, v.p. and legis. counsel, 1993-96; v.p. for legis. affairs Investment Co. Inst., Washington, 1996-98; ptnr. Ramsey, Cook, Looper & Kurlander LLP, Washington, 1998-99; sr. counsel Alston & Bird, LLP, Washington, 1999—; house counsel Presdl. Transition Com. on Criminal Justice, Washington, 1980-81; pub. mem. Adminstrv. Conf. U.S., 1992-95. Co-editor U.S. Atty.'s Criminal Trial Manual, 1971, Va. Bar Criminal Law Manual, 1971; contbr. articles to profl. jours. and pub. interest articles to newspapers. Served to capt. USAF, 1968-73. Recipient Nat. Media award Delta Soc., 1985, Edmund J. Randolph award, 1988. Mem. U.S. Supreme Ct. Bar Assn., Calif. Bar Assn., D.C. Bar Assn., Army-Navy Country Club, Leland Country Club. Republican. Episcopalian. Avocations: golf, jogging, writing.

BOYD, WILLARD LEE, academic administrator, museum administrator, lawyer; b. St. Paul, Mar. 29, 1927; s. Willard Lee and Frances L. (Collins) B.; m. Susan Kuehn, Aug. 28, 1954; children: Elizabeth Kuehn, Willard Lee, Thomas Henry. BS in Law, U. Minn., 1949, LLB, 1951; LLM, U. Mich., 1952, SJD, 1962. Bar: Minn. 1951, Iowa 1958. Assoc. Dorsey & Whitney, Mpls., 1952-54; from instr. to prof. law U. Iowa, Iowa City, 1954-64, assoc. dean Law Sch., 1964, v.p. acad. affairs, 1964-69, pres., 1969-81, pres. emeritus, 1981—; pres. The Field Mus., Chgo., 1981-96, pres. emeritus, 1996—; chmn. Nat. Mus. Scis. Bd., 1988-96. Bd. dirs. Nat. Arts Stabilization, Nat. Fedn. Humanities Couns., Women of the West Mus.; chair bd. dirs. Harry S. Truman Libr. Inst., 1997—, chair Ill. Arts Alliance; past mem. Nat. Coun. on Arts; adv. bd. mem. Met. Opera; past adv. com. Getty Ctr. for Edn. in Arts, Ill. Humanities Coun., Ill. Arts Coun., Chgo. Cultural Affairs Bd. Recipient Charles Frankel prize Nat. Endowment for Humanities, 1989. Mem. ABA (mem. sect. legal edn. and admission to bar chmn. 1980-81, coun. mem. 1975-82, com. social labor and indsl. legislations 1963-65, chmn. 1965-66, chmn. coun. of sect. on legal edn. and admission), Am. Assn. Univs. (chmn.), Nat. Commn. Accrediting (pres.), Iowa Bar Assn. Home: 620 River St Iowa City IA 52246-2433 Office: Univ Iowa Law Sch Iowa City IA 52242-1113

BOYD, WILLIAM, JR., business advisor, banker; b. Pitts., Mar. 14, 1915; s. William and Catherine (McCutcheon) B.; m. Ann Willets, Nov. 6, 1954; 1 child, Spencer. B.A., Yale U., 1937; postgrad., U. Pitts., 1946-50. With Gulf Oil Corp., Pitts., 1938-54; cons. to pres. Westinghouse Air Brake Co., Pitts., 1954-56; mgmt. cons. W. Boyd, Jr. & Assocs., Pitts., 1956-58; v.p. Pitts. Nat. Bank, 1958-68, sr. v.p., 1968-80, mgr. internat. div., 1962-71; pres. Wm. Boyd, Jr. & Co., 1980—, Table Point Co., 1975—; Mem. adv. bd. Export-Import Bank U.S., 1970-71. Chmn. trustees Laughlin Children's Ctr., 1971-98, bd. dirs., 1969—; bd. dirs. Found. for Calif. Univ. of Pa., Pitts. Symphony Soc.; vice chmn. devel. bd. Yale U., 1984-90; chmn. adv. com. Extra Mile Edn. Found., Pitts. With USNR, 1941-46. Decorated knight Order of Leopold II Belgium). Mem. Bankers Assn. for Fgn. Trade (pres. 1970-71), World Affairs Council Pitts. (past pres., dir.). Clubs: Allegheny Country (Pitts.), Duquesne (Pitts.); Royal Ocean Racing (London); Circolo dell'Unione (Florence, Italy). Home: Woodland Rd Sewickley PA 15143 Office: 1 Oliver Plz Ste 3475 Pittsburgh PA 15222-2600

BOYD, WILLIAM HARLAND, historian; b. Boise, Idaho, Jan. 7, 1912; s. Harland D. and Cordelia (Crumley) B.; m. Mary Kathryn Drake, June 25, 1939 (dec. Aug. 1997); children; Barbara A. Boyd Voltmer, William Harland, Kathryn L. Boyd Nemeyer. AB, U. Calif., Berkeley, 1935; MA, U. Calif., 1936, PhD, 1942. cert. Am. Assn. State and Local History, 1997. Tchr. Fall River H.S., McArthur, Calif., 1937-38, Watsonville (Calif.) H.S., 1941-42; prof. history Bakersfield (Calif.) Coll., 1946-73, chmn. social sci. dept., 1967-73. Author: Land of Havilah, 1952; co-author: (with G.J. Rogers) San Joaquin Vignettes, 1965, (with others) Spanish Trailblazers in the South San Joaquin, 1957, A Centennial Bibliography on the History of Kern County, California, 1966, A California Middle Border, 1972, A Climb Through history, 1973, Bakersfield's First Baptist church, 1975, Kern County Wayfarers, 1977, Kern County Tall Tales, 1980, The Shasta Route, 1981, Stagecoach Heyday in the San Joaquin Valley, 1983, Bakersfield's First Baptist Church A Centennial History, 1989, Lower River Country, 1997; contbr. articles to profl. jours. Pres. Kern County Hist. Soc., 1950-52; adv. com. Jern County Mus., 955-60; chmn. Ft. Tejon Restoration Com., Bakersfield, 1952-56, sec., 1955-60; mem. Kern County Hist. Records Commn., 1977—, Bakersfield Hist. Perservation Commn., 1984-87. Recipient Merit award Kern County Bd. Trade, 1960, Doctor Waddingham award Conf. Calif. Hist. Socs., 1996, commendation Kern County Bd. Suprs., 1982, 76, 78. Mem. Calif. Tchrs. Assn., Am. Hist. Assn., Phi Alpha Theta. Republican. Baptist. Home: 1301 New Stine Rd Apt 216 Bakersfield CA 93309-3501

BOYD, WILLIAM SPROTT, lawyer; b. San Francisco, Feb. 12, 1943; s. R. Mitchell S. and Mary (Mitchell) B.; children: Mitchell Sagar, Sterling McMicking. AB, Stanford U., 1964, JD, 1971. Bar: Calif. 1972, U.S. Dist. Ct. (no. dist.) 1972, U.S. Ct. Appeals (9th cir.) 1972, U.S. Dist. Ct. (cen. dist.) Calif. 1974, U.S. Dist. Ct. (ea. dist.) Calif. 1976. Assoc. Brobeck, Phleger & Harrison, San Francisco, 1971-77, ptnr., 1977—, of counsel. Mem. Lawyers Com for Urban Affairs, San Francisco, 1979—; bd. dirs. San Francisco Legal Aid Soc., 1980-85. Lt. USNR, 1965-68, Vietnam. Mem. ABA, Calif. Bar Assn., San Francisco Bar Assn. Office: Brobeck Phleger & Harrison 1 Market Pla Spear St Tower San Francisco CA 94105*

BOYDA, DEBORA, advertising executive. Sr. ptnr., acct. mgr. Tatham Euro RSCG, Chgo., mng. ptnr., 1997—. Office: Tatham Euro RSCG 980 N Michigan Ave Ste 500 Chicago IL 60611-4592*

BOYDEN, JOEL MICHAEL, lawyer; b. Muskegon, Mich., Apr. 18, 1937; s. Wilbur B. and Dorothy Elizabeth (Damm) B.; m. Jean Ann Zuiderveld, Apr. 18, 1964; children: Jacquelyn Kay, Kathryn Marie, Dorothy Elizabeth, Joel Michael. BA in Speech, U. Mich., 1959, JD, 1962. Bar: Mich. 1963, Fla. 1964, U.S. Ct. Appeals (6th cir.) 1963, U.S. Supreme Ct. 1968. Law clk. to judge U.S. Dist. Ct. (we. dist.) Mich., 1962-64; assoc. McCobb & Heaney, Grand Rapids, Mich., 1964-66; ptnr. Baxter & Hammond, Grand Rapids, 1966-84, Dykema Gossett, Grand Rapids, 1984-91, Boyden, Waddell, Timmons & Dilley, 1991—; mem. task force on gender bias, Mich. Supreme Ct., 1987-89. Bd. dirs. Kewano coun. Campfire Girls, 1969-73, v.p., 1972-73; bd. dirs. Western Mich. Alliance for Health, 1993—; mem. cen. bd. Grand Rapids YMCA, 1972-76, chmn., 1974-76, mem. met. bd. dirs., 1976-85, 89-92; mem. devel. bd., Porter Hills Found., 1993-96, bd. dirs. 1995—, Found. bd. 1996—; mem. com. visitors U. Mich. Law Sch., 1986-91; bd. deacons Eastminster Presbyn. Ch., 1977-79, elder, clk. session, 1987-90, founding pres. Christ Community Ch. of Grand Rapids, 1992. Named one of Mich.'s 20 Most Influential Pvt. Practitioners During 1989-90, 90-91, Mich. Lawyers Weekly. Fellow Am. Bar Found., Mich. State Bar Found. (chairperson fellows 1989-92, bd. drs. 1993—), Am. Coll. Trial Lawyers, Am. Bd. Trial Advocates, Internat. Acad. Trial Lawyers, Internat. Soc. Barristers (bd. govs. 1981-88, pres. 1986-87); mem. ABA (ho. of dels. 1974-75, 84-88, sec. litigation sect. 1976-77 coun. mem. 1973-77, legis. com. 1973-78), State Bar Mich. (pres. 1983-84, bd. commrs. 1973-84, dir. Bar Found. 1990—, chmn. Fellows MSB 1992-94), Grand Rapids Bar Assn. (trustee 1974-76), Am. Judicature Soc. (bd. dirs. 1979-83), Am. Counsel Assn. (bd. dirs. 1989-93), Inns of Ct., Torch Club, U. Mich. Pres.'s Club (exec. com. 1981-83), Cen. Mich. U. Pres.'s Club (nat. chairperson 1986—, Centennial award 1993), Rotary (pres. 1992-93 Grand Rapids). Office: Boyden Waddell Timmons & Dilly 5000 Riverfront Plz Bldg Grand Rapids MI 49503

BOYE, ROGER CARL, academic administrator, journalism educator, writer; b. Lincoln, Nebr., Feb. 8, 1948; s. Arthur J. and Matilda J. (Danca) B. BA with distinction, U. Nebr., 1970; MS in Journalism with highest distinction, Northwestern U., 1971. News editor The Quill, Chgo., 1971-73; instr. Medill sch. journalism Northwestern U., Evanston, Ill., 1973-76; vis. prof. journalism Niagara U., Niagara Falls, N.Y., 1976-78; gen. mgr. The Quill, 1980-84, bus. mgr., 1984-86; asst. dean, asst. prof. Medill sch. journalism Northwestern U., 1986-92, asst. dean, assoc. prof., 1992—. Weekly columnist Chgo. Tribune, 1974-93; contbr. Ency. Britannica Book of the Yr. and the Compton Yearbook, 1982—. Judge various journalism awards and contests, 1970s—; mem. editorial adv. com. Am. Numismatic Assn., Colorado Springs, 1989—; master comm. residential coll. Northwestern U., 1989-96. Recipient Maurice M. Gould award Numismatic Lit. Guild, 1981, 92. Mem. Phi Beta Kappa, Kappa Tau Alpha. Office: Northwestern Univ Medill Sch Journalism 1845 Sheridan Rd Evanston IL 60208-2101

BOYENGA, CINDY A., secondary education educator; b. Elgin, Ill., Aug. 5, 1957; d. Harley J. and Mary Ellen (Johnson) Carlson. BA, Augustana Coll., 1979; MSEd, No. Ill. U., 1989. Cert. tchr., Ill. Tchr. reading Laraway Sch., Joliet, Ill.; tchr. English Custer Park Sch., Braidwood, Ill., Streamwood High Sch., Elgin; tchr. reading and lang. arts Waldo Middle Sch., Aurora, Ill. Mem. NAt. Coun. Tchrs. English, Secondary Reading League, Internat. Reading Assn.

BOYER, ANDREW BEN, lawyer; b. Waukesha, Wis., Dec. 9, 1958; s. Selwyn L. and Gwen B. B. Spl. Studies, Cornell Coll., Mt. Vernon, Iowa, 1981; MA, No. Ill. U., 1982; JD, Valparaiso U., 1985. Bar: Ill. 1986, U.S. Dist. Ct. (no. dist.) Ill. 1985-86. Law clk. for presiding justice Ill. Ct. Appeals (3rd dist.), Pekin, Ill., 1985-86; sole practice Joliet, Ill., 1990—. Mem. ABA, Ill. Bar Assn., Chgo. Bar Assn., Will County Bar Assn. Office: 57 N Ottawa St Ste 502 Joliet IL 60432-4413

BOYER, CALVIN JAMES, librarian; b. Charleston, Ill., Mar. 4, 1939; s. Ernest Zimmerman and Velma Hazel (Childress) B.; m. Roberta Lorraine Davis, July 1, 1957; children—Carmellia Christine, Jeffrey Ernest; m. Ruth Nell Roden, Sept. 1, 1982. B.S. in Edn, Eastern Ill. U., 1961; M.L.S., U. Tex., 1964, Ph.D. (HEA Title II-B fellow 1969-72), 1972. Libr. Midwestern U., Wichita Falls, Tex., 1967-69; assoc. prof. Ind. U., Bloomington, 1972-75; libr. U. Miss., 1975-80, U. Calif., Irvine, 1980-93; libr. dir. Longwood Coll., 1993—; bd. dirs Southeastern Library Network, (SOLINET), Atlanta, 1977-80; treas. Southeastern Library Network, (SOLINET), 1979-80. Author: The Doctoral Dissertation, 1973; gen. editor: UMI Research Press, 1977-81. Mem. ALA. Methodist. Home: 1004 Hurd St Farmville VA 23901-2150 Office: Longwood Coll Library Farmville VA 23901-9999

BOYER, FORD SYLVESTER, relationship consultant, minister; b. Cadet, Mo., Jan. 12, 1934; s. Wilford Robert and Mary Elizabeth (DeClue) B.; m. Juelle-Ann Rupkalvis, May 2, 1970. BA in Psychology, USAF Inst., 1957; DD, Am. Bible Inst., Kansas City, Mo., 1977; MA, John F. Kennedy U., 1994. Cert. alcohol specialist. Adminstr. Getz Bros., San Francisco, 1969-73; supr. word processing U.S. Leasing Corp., San Francisco, 1977-82, dir. tng. and applications-word processing, 1982-84; computer cons Petaluma, Calif., 1984-87; massage therapist Petaluma, 1985-87; pvt. practice hypnotherapy Alameda, Calif., 1987—; cons. for chem. dependency Alameda, 1987—. Contbr. articles to profl. publs.; writer, pub.: (newsletter) Starfire, 1988—; participant (TV show) Right Human Relations, San Francisco. Vol. min. Pathways Hospice, Oakland, Calif. With USAF, 1953-57, Korea. Mem. Am Coun. Hypnotist Examiners, Nat. Assn. Alcohol and Drug Abuse Counselors, Calif. Assn. Alcohol and Drug Abuse Counselors, Calif. Assn. Alcohol Recovery Homes. Avocations: writing, volunteering, music, esotericism. Home and Office: Starfire Servers 3327 Cook Ln Alameda CA 94502-6939

BOYER, HEIDI HILD, public policy consultant; b. Denver, Dec. 25, 1961; d. Leonard Gene and Marilyn Ann (Handrock) Hild; m. Samuel Ralph Boyer, Dec. 27, 1992; children: Elliott Gene Boyer, Ryan Stuart Boyer. BA, Colo. State U., 1985. Sr. ptnr. H. Earhart & Assocs., Denver, 1987-90; dir. comm. Colo. Assn. Commerce and Industry, Denver, 1990; dir. legis. affairs Rocky Mountain Farmers Union, Denver, 1990-93; pres. Colo. Capitol Preservation Fund, Denver, 1995-98; state fin. dir. Norton for Gov., Denver, 1997-98; rsch. assoc. Gov.'s Unified Housing Task Force, Denver, 1987; cons. Planned Parenthood Rocky Mountains, 1988, Gov.'s Task Force on Homeless, 1989. Press sec. Sci. and Cultural Facilities Dist. Campaign, Denver, 1994; vol. Make-A-Wish Found., 1995—. Recipient Denver Post/ Am. Newspaper Publs. Assn. Scholastic Journalist award, 1980. Mem. LWV, Inst. Internat. Edn., CSU Devel. Coun., Kappa Alpha Theta. Avocations: gardening, skiing, reading, traveling.

BOYER, HELEN KING, artist; b. Pitts., Dec. 16, 1919; d. Ernest Wilson and Louise (Miller) B. Student, U. Pitts., Carnegie Tech. Advt. artist Pitts. Sun-Telegraph, 1943-45; mgr., designer Maison Andren Silk Painting, N.Y.C., 1948-49; bus. owner Boyer Originals, Leonia, N.J., 1952; wig designer Am. Character Doll, N.Y.C., 1952-54; needlework designer Reader Mail Co., N.Y.C., 1955; designer plush toys MyToy Co., Bklyn., 1955-57; designer plush and rag toy A&L Novelty Co., Queens, N.Y., 1957-59, Gund Toy Co., Flushing, N.Y., 1960, Columbia Toy Co., Kansas City, Mo., 1960-64, Gene Toys, St. Louis, 1964-68; mgr., curator Parkville (Mo.) Fine Arts Gallery, 1968-72; designer plush toys Beloved Toy Co., Kansas City, 1972-73; designer plush, rag toys Superior Toy & Novelty Co., Kansas City, 1973-81; ret., 1981. Executed Mural on World Religions, Pvt. Chapel, Clinton, Mo., 1996, Mural on Passion of Christ, Pvt. Chapel, Clinton, Mo., 1997; vol. painter on Murals for Kansas City Mus. Dinosaur Show, 1989, City Scapes, 1992; one-woman shows include Witte Mus., San Antonio, 1950, Arts & Crafts Ctr., Pitts., 1951, Parkville Fine Arts Assn., 1979; represented in permenant collections Carnegie Inst., Pitts., Libr. Congress, Nelson Atkins Mus., Kansas City, Mo., Lauenger Libr./Georgetown U., Met. Mus., N.Y.C., Smithsonian, Nat. Mus. Am. History. Donated and maintained garden on north side of Kansas City Mus., 1987-95. Recipient 100 Best Prints of Yr. award, 1938, Study grant Louis Comfort Tiffany, 1949, 1st prize Phila. Sketch Club, 1956, Mention for 1st Pl., Soc. Am. Graphic Artists, 1943, 3rd Pl., Libr. of Congress, 1943, 1st Pl. N.J. Fedn. Womens Clubs, 1952-54, Best of Show, 1954, 1st Purchase award N.J. Print Ann., 1985. Mem. Assn. Earth Sci. Clubs of Greater Kansas City. Avocations: donating paintings to fundraisers, earth sci. assn., homeopathic rsch. for beginning students adding homeopathy to their practices in other fields of medicine. Home: 3242 Norledge Ave Apt 2E Kansas City MO 64123-1192

BOYER, HERBERT WAYNE, biochemist; b. Pitts., July 10, 1936; m. Grace Boyer, 1959. BA, St. Vincent Coll., Latrobe, Pa., 1958, DSc (hon.), 1981; MS, U. Pitts., 1960, PhD, 1963. Mem. faculty U. Calif., San Francisco, 1966—; prof. biochemistry U. Calif., 1976—; prof. biochemistry U. Calif., San Francisco, 1976-91, prof. emeritus, 1991—; co-founder, dir. Genentech, Inc., South San Francisco, Calif. Recipient V.D. Mattai award Roche Inst., 1977; Golden Plate award Am. Acad. Achievement, 1981, Moet Hennessy-Louis Vuitton prize, 1988, Jerome H. Lemelson-MIT prize for excellence in invention and innovation, 1996; Albert and Mary Lasker award for basic med. research, 1980, Nat. Tech. medal, 1989, Nat. Sci. medal NSF, 1990. Fellow AAAS; mem. Am. Acad. Arts and Scis., Am. Soc. Biol. Chemists, Nat. Acad. Scis. Office: U Calif Dept Biochemistry and Biophysics PO Box 554 San Francisco CA 94104-0554*

BOYER, JAMES LORENZEN, physician, educator; b. N.Y.C., Aug. 28, 1936; s. Ralph R. and Alice M. B.; m. Phoebe Bennet, Feb. 23, 1963; children: Phoebe Christine, Anna Birch. A.B., Haverford (Pa.) Coll., 1958; M.D., Johns Hopkins U., 1962. Diplomate: Am. Bd. Internal Medicine. Med. intern N.Y. Hosp., N.Y.C., 1962-63, resident in medicine, 1963-64; resident in medicine Yale-New Haven Hosp., 1966; postdoctoral fellow liver study unit Yale U., 1966-68; mem. faculty U. Chgo. Pritzker Sch. Medicine, 1972-78, prof. medicine, 1976-78, dir. liver study unit, 1972-78; prof. medicine, dir. liver study unit, chief div. digestive diseases Yale U. Med. Sch., 1978-96; dir. Yale Liver Ctr., 1984—; treas., bd. dirs. Am. Liver Found., 1976-85; dep. chmn. Nat. Digestive Disease Adv. Bd., 1981-84; council mem. NIDDK, 1985-90. Author papers, abstracts in field. Chmn. bd. trustees Mt. Desert Island Biol. Lab., Salsbury Cove, Maine, 1995—. Lt. comdr. USPHS, 1964-66. Josiah Macey faculty scholar, 1976. Mem. Am. Assn. Study Liver Disease (pres. 1980), Am. Fedn. Clin. Rsch., A.C.P., Am. Gastroenterol. Assn. (councillor 1983-86), Internat. Assn. Study Liver Diseases (v.p. 1982-84, pres.-elect 1986-88, pres. 1988-90), Am. Soc. Clin. Investigation, Assn. Am. Physicians, Soc. Clin. Rsch., Am. Clin. and Climatologic Assn. Office: Yale U Sch of Medicine 333 Cedar St New Haven CT 06510-3289

BOYER, JOHN STRICKLAND, biochemist, biophysics; b. Cranford, N.J., May 1, 1937; m. Jean R. Matsunami; 2 children. MS, U. Wis., 1961; PhD in Botany, Duke U., 1964. Vis. asst. prof. botany Duke U., 1964-65; asst. physiologist Conn. Agrl. Expt. Station, 1965-66; asst. prof. to prof. botany and agronomy U. Ill., Urbana, 1966-78; plant physiologist USDA, 1978-84; prof. Tex. A&M U., 1984-87; dupont prof. marine biochemist and biophysics U. Del., 1987—; mem. vis. com. Carnegie Inst. Washington, Stanford U., Harvard U. Recipient von Humboldt Sr. Scientist award, Germany, 1983. Fellow Climate Lab (New Zealand), Am. Soc. Agronomy, Crop Sci. Soc. Am., Australian Nat. U., Japan Soc. Promotion Sci.; mem. NAS, Am. Soc. Plant Physiologists (pres. 1981-82, Shull award 1977), Sigma Xi. Office: U Del Col Marine Studies Rm 213 700 Pilottown Rd Lewes DE 19958-1242

BOYER, JOHN WILLIAM, history educator, dean; b. Chgo., Oct. 17, 1946; s. William Dana and Mary Frances (Corbley) B.; m. Barbara Alice Juskevich, Aug. 24, 1968; children: Dominic, Alexandra, Victoria. BA, Loyola U., 1968; MA, U. Chgo., 1969, PhD, 1975. From asst. prof. to assoc. prof. U. Chgo., 1975-85, prof., 1985—, Martin A. Ryerson Disting. Svc. prof., 1996—, acting dean divsn. social scis., 1992-93, dean of the coll., 1992—. Author: Political Radicalism in Late Imperial Vienna, 1981, Culture and Political Crisis in Vienna, 1995; editor: Jour. of Modern History. Capt. USAR, 1968-80. Recipient Theodor Kôrner prize Theodor Kôrner Found., 1978, John Gilmary Shea prize Am. Cath. Hist. Assn., 1982, Ludwig Jedlicka Meml. prize Kuratorium des Ludwig-Jedlicka-Gedächtnispreises, 1996; Alexander von Humboldt fellow, 1980-81. Mem. Am. Hist. Assn., Roman Catholic. Avocation: cooking. Home: 1428 E 57th St Chicago IL 60637-1838 Office: U Chgo 1126 E 59th St Chicago IL 60637-1580 also: U Chgo Press Jour Divsn 5720 S Woodlawn Ave Chicago IL 60637-1603

BOYER, LESTER LEROY, JR., architecture educator, consultant; b. Hanover, Pa., Apr. 6, 1937; s. Lester Leroy and Ruth Florence (Kessler) B.; m. Patricia Barbara Hayes, Dec. 28, 1958; children: Douglas Lester, Blane Edward, Darla Mae. B of Archtl. Engring., Pa. State U., 1960, MS in Archtl. Engring, 1964; PhD in Architecture, U. Calif., Berkeley, 1976. Instr. archtl. engring. Pa. State U., 1960-64; rsch. engr. Armstrong Cork Co., Lancaster, Pa., 1964-68; course dir. Nat. Soc. Profl. Engrs., 1964-74; sr. cons. acoustics and noise control Bolt Beranek and Newman Inc., Cambridge, Mass., 1968-70; faculty Okla. State U., Stillwater, 1970-84; dir. environ. control program Okla. State U., 1970-84, prof. architecture, 1979-84; prof. architecture Tex. A&M U., College Station, 1984—; chmn. div. design tech. Tex. A&M U. Coll. of Architecture, College Station, 1988-90; Fulbright scholar U. N.S.W. and U. Queensland, Australia, 1982, Tech. U., Delft, The Netherlands, 1992; dir. daylighting rsch. NSF, 1985-88; vis. researcher Solar Energy Rsch. Inst., Colo., summer 1985; cons. acoustics, environ. comfort and passive energy design, 1970—; dir. earth-sheltered bldg. rsch. Control Data Corp. and U.S. Dept. Energy, 1979-81; chair energy rsch. rev. panel on fenestration Office Energy Rsch., U.S. Dept. Energy, Washington, 1988; gen. chmn. Internat. Conf. Earth Sheltered Bldgs., Sydney, Australia, 1983; tech. chmn. Internat. Conf. Earth Sheltered Bldgs., Mpls., 1986; vis. prof., chair dept. arch. Kuwait U., 1997-98. Author: Earth Shelter Technology, 1987; editor: Building Design for Environmental Hazards, 1973, Earth Sheltered Building Design Innovations, 1980, Earth Shelter Performance and Evaluation, 1981, Earth Shelter Protection, 1983, Design in Geotecture, 1986, Proceedings of 5th Internat. Conf. on Underground Space and Earth Sheltered Structures, Tech. Univ. Delft, The Netherlands, 1992; contbg. author Simulating Daylight with Architectural Models, 1987. Mem. ASHRAE (nat. daylighting symposium organizer 1988), Am. Solar Energy Soc. (nat. coord. passive earth cooling program 1981), Am. Underground Space Assn. (bd. dirs. 1989-92), Illuminating Engring. Soc. Lutheran. Home: HC 68 Box 19 Fort Garland CO 81133-9702

BOYER, NICODEMUS ELIJAH, organic-polymer chemist, consultant; b. Daugavpils, Latgale, Latvia, June 1, 1925; came to U.S., 1949; s. Aloizs and Elvira Adele (Buchholtz) Bojars; married. BS in Natural Scis., U. Göttingen, Germany, 1949; PhD in Chemistry, U. Ill., 1955; postgrad., Princeton U., 1955-56. Rsch. chemist Hooker Chem. Corp., Niagara Falls, N.Y., 1956-61; project leader, lectr. Ill. Inst. Tech., Chgo., 1961-63; rsch. fellow Borg-Warner Chems., Washington, 1964-76; sr. staff mem. Raychem Corp., Menlo Park, Calif., 1976-78; asst. prof. Ind. State U., Terre Haute, 1978-80; sr. rsch. assoc. PPG Industries, Chgo., 1980-88; sr. cons. Delta Sci. Cons., Parkersburg, W.Va., 1988-92, Three Rivers, Mich., 1992—; lectr. evening sch. U. Buffalo, 1958-60; prof. Glen Oaks Coll., Centreville, Mich., 1995-97. Vol. abstractor Chem. Abstracts Svc., Columbus, Ohio, 1958-71; editor Cosmology Technikas Apskats, Montreal, Que., Can., 1987-93; author: Organophosphorus Chemistry, Vol. 1, 1957, Vol. 2, 1959, Radiation Chemistry: Monomers and Polymers, 1977, A New Theory of Cosmology, 1983, The Physics of Creation, 2 vols., 1990, Fire Retardants: A Review and Selected Patents, 1991, Cosmogony, 1992; contbr. over 70 articles to profl. jours.; 180 chemistry patents. Founding mem. Latvian Cath. Students' Assn., Germany, 1946-64; vice chmn. Latvian Acad. Soc. Valdemarija, Ill., Calif., Mich., 1964—; mem. Rep. Presdl. Task Force, 1989-93. With U.S. Army, 1945. Internat. Refugee Orgn. scholar U. Göttingen, 1946-49, Nat. Cath. Welfare Conf. scholar U. Ill., 1949-51; recipient Quality Control & Safety award PPG Industries Inc., 1987. Mem. AAAS, Am. Chem. Soc., N.Y. Acad. Scis. (life), Latvian Acad. Scis., U. Ill. Alumni Assn., Phi Lambda Upsilon, Sigma Xi. Republican. Roman Catholic. Achievements include discovery of extremely stable white coatings to heat and ultraviolet radiation for space applications; patent for the first large-scale fire retardant additive for ABS resins; invented a new theory of cosmology. Office: Delta Sci Cons PO Box 312 Three Rivers MI 49093-0312

BOYER, PAUL D., biochemist, educator; b. Provo, Utah, July 31, 1918; s. Dell Delos and Grace (Guymon) B.; m. Lyda Mae Whicker, Aug. 31, 1939; children: Gail Anne (Mrs. Denis Hayes), Marjorie Lynne, Douglas. B.S., Brigham Young U., 1939; M.S., U. Wis., 1941, Ph.D. in Biochemistry, 1943; D.Sc. (hon.), U. Stockholm, 1974. Asst. rschr. biochemistry U. Wis., 1939-43; Instr., research assoc. Stanford, 1943-45; from asst. prof. to prof. biochemistry U. Minn., 1945-56; Hill research prof. U. Minn. Med. Sch., 1956-63; prof. chemistry UCLA, 1963-89, dir. Molecular Biology Inst., 1965-83, dir. biotech. program, 1985-88, 1985-89, prof. emeritus, 1989—; chmn. biochemistry study sect. USPHS, 1962-67; mem. U.S. Nat. Com. for Biochemistry, 1965-71. Editor: Ann. Rev. of Biochemistry, 1965-71, assoc. editor, 1972-88; editor Biochemical and Biophysical Research Communications, 1969-79, The Enzymes, 1970—; Mem. editorial bd.: Biochemistry, 1969-76, Jour. Biol. Chemistry, 1978-83, 87—; Contbr. articles to profl. jours. Recipient McCoy award chem. rsch., 1976, Tolman award, 1984, Rose award Am. Soc. Biochem. and Molecular Biology, 1989; co-recipient Nobel prize for physics, 1997; Guggenheim fellow, 1955-56. Fellow AAAS (council, v.p. biol. scis. 1985-88); mem. Nat. Acad. Sci., Am. Soc. Biol. Chemists (past pres., council mem.), Am. Chem. Soc. (past div. chmn., enzyme chemistry award 1955), Biophys. Soc. Home: 1033 Somera Rd Los Angeles CA 90077-2625 Office: UCLA Molecular Biol Inst Dept Chem-Biochem Rm 200-A 607 Circle Dr S # Los Angeles CA 90095-8348*

BOYER, ROBERT ALLAN, business executive; b. Detroit, Mar. 2, 1934; s. Robert Allan and Elizabeth (Szabo) B.; children: Jennifer, Stephen, Lorna. MBA, Cornell U., 1959. Alfred P. Sloan fellow Cornell U. Grad. Sch., Ithaca, N.Y., 1958, 59; exec. asst. to pres. Merck & Co., Inc., Rahway, N.J., 1962-68; dir. fin. TWA Corp., N.Y.C., 1969-72; nat. dir. fin. Coopers & Lybrand, N.Y.C., 1972-79; exec. dir. Sullivan & Cromwell, N.Y.C., 1979-; chmn., founder Legal Execs. Group, Law Firm Tech. Group, 1979. Mem. congl. support com.; mem. Pres.'s Club Rep. Party, 1990. Fellow Coll. Law Practice Mgmt.; mem. ABA, Assn. Legal Adminstrs. (exec. com. 1986-87), Aircraft Owners and Pilots Assn., Yorktown Bicentennial Com. (bd. dirs., sec.), Echo Lake Country Club (Westfield, N.J.), Cornell Club (N.Y.), Cornell Club (N.J.), India House (N.Y.C.), N.Y. Acad. Sci. Republican. Presbyterian. Club: Echo Lake Country (Westfield, N.J.). Office: Sullivan & Cromwell 125 Broad St Fl 28 New York NY 10004-2489

BOYER, STEPHANIE ANN, music educator; b. Hughesville, Pa., Jan. 22, 1974; d. Jeremiah Stuart and Karen Louise (Binner) B. BS in Music Edn., Indiana U. of Pa., 1997. Waitress Spartan Sub Shop, Hughesville, 1989-92; crew mem. McDonalds, Hughesville, 1992-97; office mgr. to asst. dir. tng. and evaluation Indiana U. of Pa., 1993-97; gen. music tchr., choral dir. Eva Turner Elem. Sch., Waldorf, Md., 1997—. Vol. Williamsport (Pa.) Hosp., 1987-90. Mem. Residence Hall Assn. (pres. 1995-97), Nat. Residence Hall Hon. Roman Catholic. Avocations: cross stitching, reading, accompanying. Home: 2059 Red Spruce Ct Bryans Road MD 20616-3268

BOYER, TYRIE ALVIS, lawyer; b. Williston, Fla., Sept. 10, 1924; s. Alton Gordon and Mary Ethel (Strickland) B.; m. Elizabeth Everett Gale, June 9, 1945; children: Carol, Tyrie, Kennedy, Lee. BA, U. Fla., 1953, LLB, JD, 1954. Bar: Fla. Atty. Crawford, May & Boyer, Jacksonville, Fla., 1954-58, Boyer Law Offices, Jacksonville, 1958-60; judge Civil Ct. of Record, Jacksonville, 1960-63; cir. judge 4th Jud. Cir. of Fla., Jacksonville, 1963-67; atty. Dawson, Galant, Maddox, Boyer, Sulik & Nichols, Jacksonville, 1967-73; appellate judge 1st Dist. Ct. Appeal, Tallahassee, 1973-79; chief judge 1st Dist. Ct. Appeals, Tallahassee, 1975-76; atty. Boyer, Tanzler, Blackburn & Boyer, Jacksonville, 1979-84, Boyer, Tanzler & Boyer, Jacksonville, 1984—; adj. prof. Fla. Coastal Sch. Law, Jacksonville, 1996—, U. North Fla., 1998—; chmn. Supreme Ct. Com. on Standard Conduct Governing Judges, Tallahassee, 1976-79. Contbr. articles to profl. jours. Chmn. Duval County Hosp. Authority, Jacksonville, 1970-73, Jacksonville Bldg. Fin. Authority, 1980-81; pres. Jacksonville Legal Aid Assn., 1954-61; bd. dirs. Jones Coll., Jacksonville, 1978-85; bd. advs. Fla. Coastal Sch. Law, 1996—; adj. prof. U. North Fla., 1998—. With USN, 1942-45, PTO. Mem. ABA, Am. Judicature Soc., Fla. Bar, Amer. Bar Assn., Jacksonville Bar Assn., Fla. Acad. Trial Lawyers, Am. Bd. Trial Advs., SCV (comdr.), Mil. Order Stars and Bars (comdr.), Masons (bd. dirs.), dir., Safari Club Internat., Fla. Blue Key, Order of Coif, Phi Beta Kappa, Phi Kappa Phi. Methodist. Avocation: big game hunting. Home: 3966 Cordova Ave Jacksonville FL 32207-6019 Office: Boyer Tanzler & Boyer 210 E Forsyth St Jacksonville FL 32202-3320

BOYER, VINCENT SAULL, energy consultant; b. Phila., Apr. 5, 1918; s. Philip A. and Gertrude (Stone) B.; m. Ethel Wolf, June 6, 1942; children: Ruth Ann, Suzanne, Sandra Jean. B.S. in Mech. Engring., Swarthmore (Pa.) Coll., 1939; M.S., U. Pa., 1944; D.Engring. Tech. (hon.), Spring Garden Coll., 1979. With Phila. Electric Co., 1939-87, mgr. nuclear power, 1963-65, gen. supt. sta. operating, 1965-67, mgr. electric ops., 1967-68, v.p. engring. and research, 1968-80, sr. v.p. nuclear power, 1980-87; pres. Spring Garden Coll., Phila., 1992-95; mem. adv. com. Electric Power Rsch. Inst., 1978-80; cons., mem. nuclear safety rev. bd. TVA Browns Ferry Nuclear Plant; cons., mem. rsch. reactor rev. com. Oak Ridge Nat. Lab.; bd. dirs. ERIN Engring. and Rsch. Inc., Walnut Creek, Calif. Author papers in field. Bd. trustees Spring Garden Coll., 1979-95. With USNR, 1944-46. Named Engr. of Year of Delaware Valley, 1979. Fellow ASME (chmn. Phila. 1970-71, James M. Landis medal 1981), Am. Nuclear Soc. (pres. 1976-77, honors and award com.); mem. Nat. Acad. Engring., Franklin Inst., Engrs. Club Phila. (George Washington medalist 1982), Edison Electric Inst., Assn. Edison Illuminating Cos., Atomic Indsl. Forum (chmn. com. on Three Mile Island 2 recovery, mem. policy com. on nuclear regulation), Am. Nat. Standards Inst., Aronimink Golf Club (Phila.). Address: The Quadrangle 3300 Darby Rd Apt 3305 Haverford PA 19041-1070

BOYERS, JANETH MAUREE, interior designer; b. Wauseon, Ohio, Nov. 15, 1931; d. Ralph Harry Monroe and Fern Amanda (Nofziger) Slagle; m. Jerry Lee Boyers, Mar. 29, 1953; children: J.C., Nadine Magee, Matthew. Student, LaSalle U., Chgo., 1976-77. Sec. City Loan & Savings Co., Wauseon, Ohio, 1949-55; contr. Boyers Constrn. Co., Wauseon, Ohio, 1971-83; pvt. practice Wauseon, Ohio, 1983—; cons. Home Enterprises, Inc., 1982—, Interior Design firm. Dir. Community Choirs. Mem. Allied Am. Soc. of Interior Designers. Republican. Avocations: knitting, golfing. Office: Home Enterprises Inc PO Box 209 Wauseon OH 43567-0209

BOYERS, JOHN MARTIN, principal; b. San Antonio, Jan. 26, 1943; s. William Clyde and Mary Louis (Pulis) B.; divorced; children: John Jr., Jennifer D.; m. Patty Lynn, July 20, 1980; 1 child, Brett William. BS in Indsl. Arts Edn., S.W. Tex. U.; MEd, Our Lady of the Lake U. Cert. supr., mid mgmt. adminstr., spl. edn. educator. Vice prin. Anson Jones Middle Sch., Northside Ind. Sch. Dist., 1975-76, Holmes High Sch., 1976-84; prin. Health Careers High, Northside Ind. Sch. Dist., San Antonio, 1984—; cons. in field. Lt. USAR, 1968-79. Recipient award of Excellence Tex. Sch. Pub. Rels. Assn., 1989, Nat. Exemplary Blue Ribbon Sch. award U.S. Dept. Edn., 1991; sch. named One of Am.'s Best Sch./Best Sch. in Tex. Redbook mag., Apr. 1992. Mem. Nat. Assn. Secondary Sch. Prins., Tex. Assn. Secondary Sch. Prins. (Outstanding High Sch. Prin. 1991-92), Tex. Curriculum Assn., Tex. P.T.A. (life). Avocations: hunting, outdoor activities, woodworking. Office: Northside Health Careers High Sch 4646 Hamilton Wolfe Rd San Antonio TX 78229-3331*

BOYES, KARL W., state legislator; b. Erie, Pa., Mar. 1, 1936; s. Walter and Florence (Smith) B.; m. Barbara Jean Clark, June 27, 1964. BS, Edinboro State Coll., 1959; postgrad., Allegheny Coll., 1961. Govt. tchr. Millcreek Twp. Sch. Dist., Erie, 1959-66; town supr. Millcreek Twp., Erie, 1966-69; regional dir. Pa. Criminal Justice Commn., Northwestern, 1969-70; dep. dir. Pa. Criminal Justice Commn., Harrisburg, 1970-73; asst. prof. Mercyhurst Coll., Erie, 1973-74; county commr. Erie County, Erie, 1975-79; mem. Pa. Ho. of Reps., Harrisburg, 1981—, mem. house profl. lic. com., 1981—, mem. ho. appropriations com., 1987-92, majority chmn. ho. fin. com., 1995—. Recipient Guardian of Small Bus. award Nat. Fedn. Ind. Bus., 1989, Outstanding Citizen award Florence Crittenton Svcs., 1991. Mem. Coun. State Govts., Am. Legis. Exch. Coun. Presbyterian. Avocation: jogging. Office: Pa Ho of Reps 4602 Peach St Erie PA 16509-2045*

BOYES, PATRICE FLINCHBAUGH, lawyer, environmental executive; b. York, Pa., Aug. 1, 1957; d. Glenn Dale Flinchbaugh and Patricia Ann (Frey) Shultz; m. Stephen Richard Boyes, June 23, 1984. BA, Dickinson Coll., 1978; MA, U. Mich., 1980; JD, U. Fla., 1991. Bar: Fla. 1991, Fed. 1994. Law clk. Rakusin & Ivey, Gainesville, Fla., 1989; summer assoc. Hopping, Boyd, Green & Sams, Tallahassee, Fla., 1990; gen. counsel GeoSolutions, Inc., Gainesville/Tallahassee, Fla., 1986—; pres. Boyes & Assocs., P.A., Gainesville, Fla., 1991—, Wildcat Tech. Svc., Inc., 1995-99; pres. Wildcat Tech. Svcs., Inc., Gainesville, 1995—. Pres. Hist. Gainesville, Inc.; vice chair City's Hist. Preservation Adv. Bd.; vol. Kanapha Bot. Gardens; counsel Duckpond Neighborhood Assn., Inc. Recipient Keystone Press award Pa. Soc. Newspaper Editors and Pubs., 1981, City Beautification award, 1994, Hist. Preservation award, 1994, Fla. Trust for Hist. Preservation award, 1996; grad. fellow Modern Media Inst., St. Petersburg, Fla. Mem. Fla. Bar Assn. (pub. interest com. for environ. and land use sect.), 8th Jud. Cir. Bar Assn., Fla. Assn. Women Lawyers, Pi Delta Epsilon. Avocations: bodybuilding, hist. preservation, photography, gardening, reading. Office: GeoSolutions Inc 602 S Main St Gainesville FL 32601-6718

BOYES, STEPHEN RICHARD, hydrogeologic consultant; b. Evanston, Ill., May 17, 1950; s. Will W. and Beth (Henry) B.; m. Patrice Lynne Flinchbaugh, June 23, 1984. AA, U. South Fla., 1972, BA, 1974. Lic. profl. geologist, Fla. Geophys. engr. seismic process ctr. Geophys. Svcs., Inc., Midland, Tex., 1974; geophys. engr. field ops. Geophys. Svcs., Inc., Chickasha, Okla., 1975; geophys. engr. Geophys. Svcs., Inc., Saudi, Arabia, 1975-77; geologist Fla. Dept. Environ. Regulation, Tallahassee, 1978-82; hydrogeologist Fla. Dept. Environ. Regulation, Tampa, 1982-84; sr. hydrogeologist Groundwater Technology, Tampa, 1984-86, Handex Corp., Odenton, Md., 1986; pres. GeoSolutions, Inc., Gainesville, Fla., 1986—. Contbr. to profl. publs. Mem. Nat. Groundwater Assn., Heritage Club. Avocations: canoeing, computers, snorkeling, racquetball.

BOYETT, DOROTHY ELEANOR ANDERSON, dietitian, educator; b. Bear Lake Township, Mich., Oct. 17, 1915; d. Carl Emil and Julia (Johnson) Anderson; widowed; children: Marilyn Boyett Annan, John M. Jr., Carl E. BS, Mich. State U., 1937; Tchg. Cert., Fla. So. Coll., 1967; MA in Tchg., Rollins Coll., 1971. Cert. dietitian, Am. Dietetic Assn. Civil svc. dietitian Sta. Hosp., Ft. Bragg, N.C., 1939-43; chief dietitian, chief instr. Army Hosp., Ft. Bragg, N.C., 1943-45; kindergarten tchr. 1st Meth. Ch., Clermont, Fla., 1959-67; hosp. dietitian Southlake Meml. Hosp., Clermont, Fla., 1967-69, consulting dietitian, 1969-70; tchr. Clermont Elem. Sch., 1967-80. Charter mem. Nat. Mus. Women in Arts, Washington, 1986-87; gallery chmn. Southlake Art League, Clermont, 1985-86, corr. sec., 1986-97. Capt. U.S. Army Med. Corp, 1943-45. Mem. Clermont C. of C. (Gem of the Hills award, 1995). Avocation: poetry-prose writing, pastel artist.

BOYETT, JOAN REYNOLDS, arts administrator; b. L.A., May 2, 1936; d. Clifton Faris Reynolds and Jean Margaret (Howard) Hauck; m. Harry William Boyett, Oct. 5, 1956; children: Keven William, Suzanne Marie Boyett Liebherr. Student, Occidental Coll., 1954-55, Pasadena Playhouse, 1955-57. Mgr. youth activities L.A. Philharm. Orch., 1970-79; dir., founder edn. divsn. Music Ctr. Los Angeles County, 1979—, v.p. edn., 1988—; mem. supt.'s task force on arts edn. Calif. State Dept. Edn., 1997; cons. NEA, Washington; chmn. arts edn. task force Calif. Arts Coun., Sacramento, 1993-95; arts edn. mem. Nat. Working Group, Washington, 1992-95. Active various coms. and task forces, L.A., Sacramento. Named Woman of Yr. L.A. Times, 1976; recipient Labor's award of honor County Fedn. Labor, L.A., 1984, Susan B. Anthony award Bus. and Profl. Women, 1986, Gov.'s award Calif. Arts Coun. and Gov., 1989, R.O.S.E. Outstanding Svc. to Edn. award, U. So. Calif., 1999. Mem. Calif. Art Edn. Assn. (Behind the Scenes award 1985), Calif. Dance Educators Assn. (Svc. award 1985), Calif. Ednl. Theatre Assn. (Outstanding Contbn. award 1990, nominated for Nat. Medal Arts 1996, 97). Republican. Presbyterian. Avocations: reading, attending arts events, gardening, swimming. Home: PO Box 1805 Studio City CA 91614-0805 Office: The Music Ctr 717 W Temple St Ste 400 Los Angeles CA 90012-2632

BOYETTE, VAN ROY, lawyer, consultant; b. Alexandria, La., Dec. 20, 1952; s. Van Rex and Virginia (Cook) B. BA, Tulane U., 1974, JD, 1977; LLM, Cambridge (Eng.) U., 1978. Bar: D.C. 1979, La. Legal counsel Sen. Russell Long, Washington, 1978-81; gen. counsel Am. Petroleum Refinery Assn., Washington, 1981-83; ptnr. Nossman Gunther, Washington, 1983-85, Black, Manafort, Stone & Kelly, Washington, 1985-86, Bergner, Boyette, Bockorny & Clough, Washington, 1986-94, Smith, Martin & Boyette, Washington, 1994—. Mem. La. Bar Assn., D.C. Bar Assn., Univ. Club. Democrat. Presbyterian. Avocations: fly fishing, squash. Office: Smith

Martin & Boyette # 800 915 15th St NW Ste 800 Washington DC 20005-2311

BOYKAN, MARTIN, composer, music educator; b. N.Y.C., Apr. 12, 1931; m. Susan Schwalb, 1983. AB summa cum laude, Harvard U., 1951; student, U. Zurich, Switzerland, 1951-52; MusM, Yale, 1953. Asst. prof. music Brandeis U., Waltham, Mass., 1964-67; assoc. prof. music Brandeis U., 1967-76, prof., 1976—, Irving G. Fine prof., 1986—; composer-in-residence Composer's Conf., Wellesley, Mass., 1987; vis. prof. composition Columbia U., 1988-89, NYU, 1993; sr. Fulbright lectr. Bar Ilan U., Israel, 1994. Composer: String Quartets, 1949, 65, Flute Quintet, 1953, Psalm, 1958, Prelude for Organ, 1959, Chamber Concerto for 13 Instruments, 1971, String Quartet No. 2, 1973, Piano Trio, 1975, Elegy for soprano and 6 instruments, part I, 1979, part II, 1982, String Quartet No. 3, 1984, Epithalamion for baritone, violin and harp, 1985, Shalom Rav, 1985, Fantasy Sonata for Piano, 1987, Symphony for orch. with baritone solo, 1989, Piano Sonata # 2, 1990, Nocturne for Cello, Piano and Percussion, 1990, Eclogue for flute, violin, cello, horn and piano, 1991, Sonata for cello and piano, 1992, Echoes of Petrarch for flute, clarinet and piano, 1992, Voyages for Soprano and Piano, 1992, Sea-Gardens for Soprano and Piano, 1993, Impromptu for Solo Violin, 1993, Three Psalms for Soprano, 1993, Pastorale for Piano, 1993, Sonata for violin and piano, 1994, Ma'ariv Settings for chorus and organ, 1995, String Quartet No. 4, 1996, 3 Shakespeare Songs for Chorus, 1996, City of Gold for solo flute, 1996, 2d Trio for violin, cello and piano, 1997, Psalm 121 for soprano and string quartet, 1997, Usurpations for piano, 1997, Sonata for Solo Violin, 1998, Flume for Clarinet and Piano, 1998; mem. editl. bd. Perspectives of New Music.; contbr. articles to profl. jours. Nat. winner Jeunesses Musicales, 1967, League-ISCM, 1983; recipient Martha Baird Rockefeller award, 1974, Fromm Found. commn., 1975, award Internat. Soc. Contemporary Music, 1983, Koussevitzky commn., 1985, AAUL, 1986, 88, rec. award Am. Acad. and Nat. Inst. Arts and Letters, 1986, Walter Hinrichsen Publ. award Am. Acad. and Inst. Arts and Letters, 1988; Paine fellow, 1951, Fulbright fellow, 1953-55, Guggenheim fellow, 1984, Sr. Fulbright fellow, 1994; grantee Nat. Endowment for Arts, 1983, and numerous others. Mem. Am. Music Ctr., Phi Betta Kappa. Home: 10 Winsor Ave Watertown MA 02472-1460 Office: Music Dept Brandeis Univ Waltham MA 02454

BOYKIN, BETTY RUTH CARROLL, mortgage loan officer, bank executive; b. Mobile, Ala., Dec. 14, 1943; d. John Calvin Sr. and Zimmie Mae (Burdette) Carroll; m. William Henry Boykin Jr., Sept. 9, 1961; children: Helen Carroll Boykin Ferris, John William. Student, Auburn U., 1961-62, U. Fla., 1969-72, Santa Fe C.C., 1972-90; BSBA, U. Mo., St. Louis, 1992. Asst. v.p., loan officer Guaranty Fed. Savs. and Loan, Gainesville, Fla., 1973-80; mortgage loan officer Fortune Mortgage Corp., Gainesville, 1980-86; mgr. Svc. Title Corp., Gainesville, 1986-87; account exec. Fla. Fed. Savs. Bank, Gainesville, 1987-88; banking officer 1st Union Nat. Bank (merger Fla. Nat. Bank), Gainesville, 1988-90; br. mgr., mortgage loan officer 1st Fed. Bank Mortgage Lending, Huntsville, Ala., 1993—; dir. Sys. Dynamics, Inc., 1980-89, AMJ, Inc., 1980-83; instr. mortgage lending Inst. Fin. Edn., Gainesville, 1986. Amb. PBS, Gainesville, 1989-90; chmn. loan com. Neighborhood Housing Svcs., Inc., Gainesville, 1985-90; dir. Gainesville Homebuilder's Homeowners Warranty Coun., 1984-86. Recipient Outstanding Svc. award Neighborhood Housing Svcs., Inc., 1985-90. Mem. Am. Mgmt. Assn., Am. Mktg. Assn., Mortgage Bankers Assn. North Ctrl. Fla. (v.p., pres.-elect 1989-90), Mortgage Officers Soc. (pres. Dist. IV 1980-81), Mortgage Bankers Assn. Huntsville (co-chair program com. 1994—), Women's Coun. Realtors, Huntsville/Madison County Builders Assn. (assocs. coun. mem., mem. women's coun.), Huntsville Bd. Realtors (affiliate), Huntsville C. of C., Gainesville C. of C., Delta Sigma Pi. Avocations: tennis, gardening, walking, racquetball, bicycling. Home: 5044 Chancel Dr SE Huntsville AL 35802-1856 Office: First Fed Mortgage 2310 Market Pl SW Ste B Huntsville AL 35801-5250

BOYKIN, JOSEPH FLOYD, JR., librarian; b. Pensacola, Fla., Nov. 7, 1940; s. Joseph Floyd and Delree (Bailey) B.; m. Evelyn Louise Larson, Aug. 3, 1963; children: Suzanne Michelle, Pamela Denise. Student, Pensacola Jr. Coll., 1958-60; B.S., Fla. State U., 1962, M.S., 1965. Lic. pvt. pilot. Asst. to librarian U. N.C., Charlotte, 1965-68; acting head librarian U. N.C., 1968-70; dir. library, 1970-81; dean libraries Clemson (S.C.) U., 1981—; bd. dirs. Southeastern Libr. Network, Inc., 1975-78, 96-98, chmn., 1977-78. Trustee OCLC Online Computer Library Ctr., Inc., 1980-86; trustee OCLC Users Council, 1978-82, 89-92, pres., 1978-80. Democrat. Baptist. Democrat. Baptist. Home: 307 Bent Oak Ln Central SC 29630-9460 Office: Clemson Univ Robert Muldrow Cooper Clemson SC 29634

BOYKIN, ROBERT HEATH, banker; b. Carlsbad, N.Mex., Jan. 10, 1926; s. Calvin Clay and Ruby (Heath) B.; m. Camille Inkman, Nov. 26, 1948; 1 child, Robert Heath. B.B.A., U. Tex., 1950, LL.B., 1953; student, Park Coll., 1943-44; spl. courses, La. State U., Tex. A. and M. Coll., Am. Mgmt. Assn. Bar: Tex. bar 1952. Tabulating supr. Tex. Edn. Agy., 1948-52; with Fed. Res. Bank of Dallas, 1953-91, asst. counsel, 1959-61, asst. counsel, asst. sec. bd., 1961-65, asst. v.p., asst. sec. bd., 1965-67, asst. v.p., sec. bd., 1967-68, v.p., sec. bd., 1968-70, sr. v.p., sec. bd., 1971-75, sr. v.p., 1976, 1st v.p., 1976-80, pres., 1981-91; ret., 1991; sec. Conf. Pres.'s of Fed. Res. Banks, 1963-64, chmn., 1980; instr. negotiable instruments Dallas chpt. Am. Inst. Banking, 1959-61. Served as lt. (j.g.) USNR, 1943-47. Mem. Tex. Bar Assn., Tex. Bankers Assn., Delta Tau Delta, Phi Alpha Delta. Methodist.

BOYKIN, WILLIAM C., career officer; b. Wilson, N.C., Apr. 19, 1948. Commd. U.S. Army, advanced through grades to maj. gen.; comdg. gen. Spl. Forces Command U.S. Army, Ft. Bragg, N.C., 1998—. Office: US Army Spl Forces Command Airborne Fort Bragg NC 28307

BOYKIN, WILLIAM EDWARD, principal; b. Clarendon, Tex., June 27, 1932; s. Garland Lester and Lucy Edna (Matthews) B.; m. Bobby Jo Irving, July 26, 1958 (dec. Apr. 1992); children: Martha Anne, Douglas Irving, Kenneth Garland; m. Jane Ellen Larson, Mar. 1, 1996; stepchildren: Mike, Todd, Phillip Woods. BA in Journalism, N.Mex. State U., 1954, MA in English, 1964, ednl. adminstr., 1976. Tchr., coach, adminstr. Las Cruces (N.Mex.) H.S., 1958-70; asst. football coach N.Mex. State U., Las Cruces, 1970-73; agt., state dir. Fidelity Union Life Ins. Co., Albuquerque, 1973-76; vice-prin., prin. Farmington (N.Mex.) H.S., 1976-86; adminstr. Mesilla Valley Christian Sch., Las Cruces, 1996-98; ret., 1998. Author: The Principal of the Thing, The Journal of a High School Principal; edited: The End of the Pillow Slip, Emily Clair Watson, As Tolf To Edna Matthews Boykin; contbr. articles to profl. jours. Capt. USAF, 1954-58. Recipient Secondary Adminstr. of Yr. N.Mex. Adminstrs. Assn., 1986, Leadership award, 1986. Mem. NRA, Am. Legion, Aggie Scholarship Assn., N.Mex. State U. Alumni Assn. (life), People for the West, Phi Delta Kappa, Tau Kappa Epsilon. Republican. Methodist. Avocations: travel, fishing, reading, do-it-yourself, writing. Home: 3035 Hillrise Dr Las Cruces NM 88011-4703

BOYKO, CHRISTOPHER ALLAN, lawyer, judge; b. Cleve., Oct. 10, 1954; s. Andrew and Eva Dorothy (Zepko) B.; m. Roberta Ann Gentile, May 29, 1981; children: Philip, Ashley. B in Polit. Sci. cum laude, Mt. Union Coll., 1976; JD, Cleve. Marshall Coll. Law, 1979. Bar: Ohio 1979, U.S. Dist. Ct. (no. dist.) Ohio 1979, Fla. 1985, U.S. Tax Ct. 1986. Prin. Boyko & Boyko, Parma, Ohio, 1993, 94-95; asst. prosecutor City of Parma, 1981-87, dir. of law, 1987-93; exec. v.p., gen. counsel copy Am., Inc., 1993-94; judge Parma Mcpl. Court, 1993; ptnr. Boyko & Boyko, Attys., Parma, 1994—; judge Ct. Common Pleas, Cuyahoga County, Ohio, 1996—; guardian ad litem Juvenile Ct., 1979-93; legal advisor spl. weapons and tactics divsn. City of Parma Police Dept., 1984-93; chief counsel S.W. Enforcement Bur., 1991-93; mem. faculty Ohio Jud. Coll., Nat. Jud. Coll., lectr. FBI Nat. Acad. Active Citizens League of Greater Cleve., 1985—; trustee Cops & Kids, Inc.; mem. Parma Drug Task Force, 1987—; mem. adv. com. Paradale Children's Svcs., 1991—; mem. St. Anthony's Sch. Commn. Mem. ABA, Fla. Bar Assn., Ohio Bar Assn., Cleve. Bar Assn., Parma Bar Assn. (pres., trustee) Ukrainian Bar Assn., Cuyahoga County Police Chief Assn. (assoc.), Narcotics Law Officers Assn., Cleve. Am. Mid. Eastern Orgn., Mt. Union Coll. Alumni Assn., Cleve. Marshall Law Sch. Alumni Assn., Elks. Byzantine Catholic. Avocations: martial arts, running, weightlifting. Home: 5291 Huntington Reserve Dr Parma OH 44134-6172 Office: Justice Ctr 1200 Ontario St Cleveland OH 44113-1604

BOYKO, EDWARD JOHN, internist, medical researcher; b. Bethlehem, Pa., Feb. 19, 1953; s. Edward and Mary (Levan) B.; m. Beth Welcome Alderman, Sept. 27, 1980; children: Eva Jane, Bryan Martin. BA, Columbia U., 1975; MD, U. Pitts., 1979; MPH, U. Wash., 1984. Resident in internal medicine U. Chgo., 1979-82; fellow Robert Wood Johnson Found., Seattle, 1982-84; attending physician U. Colo., Denver, 1984—; asst. prof. medicine and preventive medicine U. Colo., 1984—; asst. prof. dept. medicine U. Wash, 1989-92, assoc. prof, 1992—; spl. mem. NIH study sect., Washington, 1988—; mem. Nat. Diabetes Data Group, Niddk, 1992—. Contbr. articles to med. jours. Recipient Career Devel. award, Nat. Found. Ileitis and Colitis, 1986, First award, NIH, 1988. Mem. Soc. Gen. Internal Medicine, Soc. Epidemiologic Rsch., Am. Fedn. clin. Rsch., Alpha Omega Alpha. Avocations: skiing, hiking. Home: 7141 NE Bay Hill Rd Bainbridge Is WA 98110-1220 Office: VA Med Ctr 111 M 1660 S Columbian Way Seattle WA 98108-1532

BOYLAN, BRIAN RICHARD, author, historian, director, photographer, literary agent; b. Chgo., Dec. 11, 1936; s. Francis Thomas and Mary Catherine (Kane) B.; children: Rebecca, Gregory, Ingrid. Student, Loyola U., 1954-58; DD, Universal Ch., 1969. CEO Otitis Media Lit. Agy.; prodr. OTM Prodns.; dir., prodr. Media Medica. Editor: Jour. AMA, Med. World News, Modern Medicine, 1956-77; author: The New Heart, 1969, Infidelity, 1971, The Legal Rights of Women, 1973, Benedict Arnold: The Dark Eagle, 1973, A Hack in a Hurry, 1980, Final Trace, 1983; works include 16 books, 3 plays, 3 screenplays; book reviewer, critic, 1952—; photographer, 1962—; theatre dir., 1970—; directed works include 31 plays, videotapes and films. Office: 1926 Dupont Ave S Minneapolis MN 55403-3035

BOYLAN, KEVIN BERNARD, neurologist; b. Arlington, Mass., Aug. 20, 1956; s. Charles Vincent and Edith Murial (Aho) B. BA in Social Sci. cum laude, U. Calif., Irvine, 1979, BS in Biology, 1979; MD, U. Calif., San Francisco, 1983. Diplomate Nat. Bd. Med. Examiners, Am. Bd. Med. Genetics, Am. Bd. Psychiatry and Neurology, also Sub.-Bd. Clin. Neurophysiology, Am. Bd. Electrodiagnostic Medicine. Intern Johns Hopkins Hosp., Balt., 1983-84; fellow neurology U. Calif., San Francisco, 1984-87, fellow med. genetics, 1985-87, resident, 1987-90; fellow neuromuscular diseas Johns Hopkins Hosp, 1990-91; instr. neurology Johns Hopkins U., 1991; asst. prof. Mayo Grad. Sch. Medicine, Jacksonville, Fla., 1992—; assoc. cons. Mayo Clinic, Jacksonville, Fla., 1992-94, cons., 1994—, 1994—; dir. EMG lab. Mayo Clinic, 1994—; dir. Muscular Dystrophy Assn. Clinic N.E. Fla., 1994—. Contbr. numerous articles to profl. jours. Multiple Sclerosis fellow Nat. Multiple Sclerosis Soc., 1984-87, Charles A. Dana fellow Charles A. Dana Found., 1990-91. Mem. AAAS, Am. Soc. Human Genetics, Am. Acad. Neurology, Fla. Med. Assn., Duval County Med. Assn. Office: Mayo Clinic Dept Neur 4500 San Pablo Rd S Dept Neur Jacksonville FL 32224-3899

BOYLAN, MERLE NELSON, librarian; b. Youngstown, Ohio, Feb. 24, 1925; s. Merle Nelson and Alma Joy (Kepple) B. B.A., Youngstown U., 1950; M.L.S., Carnegie-Mellon U., 1956; postgrad., U. Ariz., 1950-51, Ind. U., 1952. Librarian Pub. Health Library U. Calif., Berkeley, 1956-58; sci. librarian U. Ariz., Tucson, 1958-59; engring. librarian Gen. Dynamics/Convair, San Diego, 1959-61, Gen. Dynamics/Astronautics, 1961-62; assoc. librarian Lawrence Radiation Lab., U. Calif., Livermore, 1962-64; library mgr. Lawrence Radiation Lab., U. Calif., 1964-67; chief librarian NASA Ames Research Center, Moffett Field, Calif., 1968-69; asso. dir. libraries U. Mass., Amherst, 1969-70; dir. libraries, Univ. librarian U. Mass., 1970-72; dir. libraries U. Tex., Austin, 1973-77; dir. libraries U. Wash., Seattle, 1977-89, dir. emeritus, 1989—, prof. Sch. Librarianship, 1982-89; exec. bd. Amigos Bibliographic Council, 1974-77; mem. fin. com., governance com., user's council, computer service council Wash. Library Network, 1978—; del. Gov.'s Conf. Libraries and Info. Services, 1979; sec. Texas State Bd. Library Examiners, 1974-77; mem. bibliographic networking and resource sharing advisory group Southwestern Library Interstate Coop. Endeavor, 1975-77; sec., chmn. exec. bd. Pacific N.W. Bibliographic Center, 1977-83; mem. com. centralzed acquisitions of library materials for internat. studies Center for Research Libraries.; del. OCLC Users Council, 1981-86. Sec. bd. trustees Littlefield Fund for So. History, 1974-77, Fred Meyer Charitable Trust; mem. adv. bd. Library and Info. Resources for Northwest, 1984-87. Mem. ALA, Assn. Coll. and Research Libraries (legis. com. 1977-81), Assn. Research Libraries (bibliographic control com. 1979-83), Spl. Libraries Assn., Am. Soc. Info. Sci., Beta Phi Mu. Home: 1354 Bellefield Park Ln Bellevue WA 98004-6854 Office: Univ of Wash Libraries Suzzallo Library Seattle WA 98195

BOYLAN, MICHELLE MARIE OBIE, medical surgical nurse, hospital administrator; b. St. Louis, Jan. 22, 1962; d. James Martin and Yvonne Marie (DeLoof) Obie; m. Steven Arthur Boylan, June 5, 1962; children: Paige Brittany, Courtney Marie, Brandon James. BSN, Marquette U., 1984; MA, Webster U., 1996; DM(c), Colorado Tech. U., 1999. RN. Commd. 2d lt. U.S. Army, 1984, advanced through grades to maj., 1994; pediatrics charge nurse William Beaumont Army Med. Ctr., El Paso, 1984-86, neonatal ICU charge nurse, 1986-87; asst. head nurse pediatrics 98th Gen. Hosp., Neurenberg, Germany, 1987-88; head nurse 98th Gen.Hosp., Neurenberg, Germany, 1987-90, U.S. Army Ft. Huachuca, Sierra Vista, Ariz., 1990-92; head nurse Winn Army Cmty. Hosp., Ft. Stewart, Ga., 1992—, infection control/quality improvement nurse, 1994—, chief divsn. patient support, 1995-97, chief divsn. quality mgmt., 1996—; lectr. in field.; adj. mem. faculty Chapman U., U. Phoenix, Denver Tech. Coll., Nat. Am. U. Decorated Army Commendation medal with 5 oak leaf clusters, Meritorious Svc. medal with 2 oak leaf clusters, Army Achievement medal with 2 oak leaf clusters. Mem. Am. Profls. in Infection Control. Roman Catholic. Avocations: skiing, cooking, crafts. Home: 870 Piros Dr Colorado Springs CO 80922-1378 Office: University Hosp Denver CO 80913

BOYLAN, RICHARD JOHN, psychologist, hypnotherapist, researcher, behavioral scientist, educator; b. Hollywood, Calif., Oct. 15, 1939; s. John Alfred and Rowena Margaret (Devine) B.; m. Charnette Marie Blackburn, Oct. 26, 1968 (div. June 1984); children: Christopher J., Jennifer April, Stephanie August; m. Judith Lee Keast, Nov. 21, 1987; stepchildren: Darren Andrew, Matthew Grant. BA, St. John's Coll., 1961; MEd, Fordham U., 1966; MSW, U. Calif., Berkeley, 1971; PhD in Psychology, U. Calif., Davis, 1984. Cert. clin. hypnotherapist. Assoc. pastor Cath. Diocese of Fresno, 1965-68; asst. dir. Berkeley (Calif.) Free Ch., 1970-71; psychiat. social worker Marin Mental Health Dept., San Rafael, Calif., 1971-77; dir. Calaveras Mental Health Dept., San Andreas, Calif., 1977-85; prof., coord. Nat. U., Sacramento, 1985-86; lectr. Calif. State U., Sacramento, 1985-90, 98—; instr. U. Calif., Davis, 1984-88; assoc. prof. Chapman U., Sacramento, 1997-98; dir. U.S. Behavioral Health, Sacramento, 1988-89; pvt. practice psychotherapy, Sacramento, 1974-95; hypnotherapy practice, Sacramento, 1996—. Author: Extraterrestrial Contact and Human Responses, 1992, Close Extraterrestrial Encounters, 1994, Labored Journey to the Stars, 1996, Project Epiphany, 1997. Bd. dirs. Marin Mcpl. Water Dist., 1975-77; cons. Calif. State Legis., Sacramento, 1979-80; chmn. Calaveras County Bd. Edn., Angels Camp, Calif., 1981-84. Recipient Geriatric Medicine Acad. award NIH, 1984, Experiment Station grant USDA, Calif., 1983. Mem. APA, ACA, Am. Assn. for Spiritual/Ethical Values in Counseling, Nat. Bd. Hypnotherapy and Med. Anaesthesiology, Calif. Psychol. Assn., Sacramento Valley Psychol. Assn. (past pres.), Sacramento Soc. Profl. Psychologists (past pres.), Nat. Resources Def. Coun., Acad. Clin. Close-Encounter Therapists (founder, sec., treas.). Democrat. Avocations: hiking, jogging, UFO/ET research, camping. Office: 2826 O St Ste 2 Sacramento CA 95816-6400

BOYLAN, STEVEN ARTHUR, career officer; b. N.Y.C., June 5, 1962; s. Louis Kruegar and Barbara Elaine (Stein) B.; m. Michelle Marie Obie, July 23, 1992; children: Courtney, Brandon, Paige. BA in Comm., Mercer U., 1984; MA in Mgmt., Webster U., 1997. Commd. 2d lt. U.S. Army, 1984, advanced through grades to maj., 1995; spkr. in field. Media, disting. visitor rep. Pueblo (Colo.) Medal Honor Soc., 1995-96. Decorated Def. Meritorious Svc. medal with 2 oak leaf clusters, Army Commendation medal with 2 oak leaf clusters, Army Achievement medal with 2 oak leaf clusters, Multinational Forces and Observer medal with number 2; recipient Bronze medal Excellence in Competition, 1994, Army Avocation Order of St. Michael bronze medal, 1999. Mem. NRA (life), Assn. U.S. Army. Avocations: snow skiing, competition shooting, painting. Home: 870 Piros Dr Colorado Springs CO 80922-1378 Office: US Army Dir Pub Affairs Ops Officer HQ 9th Taarom (Japan) Fort Carson CO 80913

BOYLE, ANTONIA BARNES, audio producer, writer; b. Detroit, May 21, 1939; d. James Merriam and Florence (Maiullo) B.; 1 child, Caitlin Merriam. BS in Speech, Northwestern U., 1962. Staff announcer WEFM-FM, Chgo., 1975-78; pres. Boyle Communications, Chgo., 1978-85; exec. producer Nightingale-Conant Corp., Chgo., 1985-90, Cassette Prodns. Unltd., Irwindale, Calif., 1990-92; pres. Antonia Boyle & Co., 1992—; v.p. content Youachieve.com, Inc., 1997—. Author: The Optimal You, 1990, Taping Yourself Seriously, 1991; co-author: (with Jay Gordon) Good Food Today, Great Kids Tomorrow, 1994 (with Scott McKain) Just Say Yes, 1994, (with William McCurry) Guerrilla Managing for the Imaging Industry, 1997. Chmn., bd. dirs. Horizons for the Blind, Chgo., 1984. Mem. Am. Fedn. Radio, TV Artists, Com.100 Northwestern U., NU Club, San Francisco. Home: 2526 39th Ave San Francisco CA 94116-2751 Office: youachieve.com Inc 236 W Portal Ave San Francisco CA 94127-1423

BOYLE, BARBARA DORMAN, motion picture company executive; b. N.Y.C., Aug. 11, 1935; d. William and Edith (Kleiman) Dorman; m. Kevin Boyle, Nov. 26, 1960; children: David Eric, Paul Coleman. BA in English with honors, U. Calif., Berkeley, 1957; JD, UCLA, 1960. Bar: Calif. 1961, N.Y. 1964, U.S. Supreme Ct. 1964. Atty. bus. affairs dept, corp. asst. sec. Am. Internat. Pictures, L.A., 1960-65; ptnr. Cohen & Boyle, L.A., 1967-74; exec. v.p., gen. counsel, chief op. officer New World Pictures, L.A., 1974-82; sr. v.p. prodn. Orion Pictures Corp., L.A., 1982-85; exec. v.p. prodn. RKO Pictures, L.A., 1986-87; pres. Sovereign Pictures, Inc., L.A., 1988-92, Boyle and Taylor Prodns., 1993—; lectr. in field. Exec. prodr. (film) Eight Men Out, 1987, Bottle Rocket, 1995; prodr. (films) Mrs. Munck, 1995, Phenomenon, 1996, Instinct, 1999, The Hi Line, 1999; exec. prodr. The Hi Line, 1998. Bd. dirs. UCLA Law Fund Com., L.A. Women's Campaign Fund; pres. Ind. Feature Project/West; founding mem. entertainment adv. coun. sch. law UCLA, co-chmn. 1979-80; mem. adv. bd. Am. Film Inst., Womens Directing Workshop. Mem. Acad. Motion Picture Arts and Scis., Women in Film (pres. 1977-78), Hollywood Women's Polit. Com., Women Entertainment Lawyers Assn., Calif. Bar Assn., N.Y. State Bar Assn. Office: Boyle-Taylor Prodns 6320 Commodore Sloat Dr Los Angeles CA 90048-5406

BOYLE, BARBARA JANE, insurance company executive; b. Shenandoah, Iowa, Mar. 1, 1936; d. Thomas Henry and Hazel Ingred (Gell) Hill; m. Richard F. Smith, Jan. 6, 1990; children: Jill, Chris Richardson. BA, Iowa State Tchrs. Coll., Cedar Falls, 1960. Tchr. elem. United Community Schs., Boone, Iowa, 1975-79; mgr. dist. sales World Book Ency., St. Paul, 1980-83; ins. agt. Allstate Ins. Co., St. Paul, 1983-84; mgr. market sales Allstate Ins. Co., Eden Prairie, Minn., 1985-88, market mgr. ind. agts., 1989-94, mgr. agy., 1995—. Fellow Life Underwriting Tng. Coun.; mem. Nat. Assn. Life Underwriters, Minn. Ind. Agt. Assn. Methodist. Avocations: sewing, needlework, walking, photography. Address: Allstate Insurance 4530 W 77th St Ste 115 Edina MN 55435-5012

BOYLE, BRUCE JAMES, publisher; b. Mpls., Aug. 31, 1931; s. Lorille James and Norma Elizabeth (Blish) B.; m. Betty Jean Tucker, May 28, 1960; children: Katherine Ann, Julia Caroline, Amy Elizabeth. B.J., U. Mo., 1958. Copywriter Sta. KFRU, Columbia, Mo., 1958; continuity dir. KOMO-TV, Columbia, 1959; advt. salesman Better Homes & Gardens mag., 1960; advt. dir. Successful Farming mag., Des Moines, 1969-73; pub. Successful Farming mag., 1973-80, Meredith Pub. Svcs., 1976-80; pub. Meredith Video Pub., 1981-92, dir. mag. devel., 1984-92; mem. faculty Grandview Coll., 1993-95. Bd. dirs. Youth Homes Mid-Am., 1993-99. With USN, 1951-54. Mem. Nat. Agri-Mktg. Assn. (pres. 1973-74), Farm and Indsl. Equipment Inst., Farm Equipment Mfrs. Assn. (chmn. bd. govs. 1971-72), Agrl. Pubs. Assn. (bd. dirs. 1979-81), Alpha Delta Sigma. Clubs: Wakonda Country, Okoboji Yacht, Rio Verde Country Club. Home: 718 55th St Des Moines IA 50312-1827

BOYLE, CAROLYN MOORE, public relations executive, marketing communications manager; b. Los Angeles, Jan. 29, 1937; d. Cory Orlando Moore and Violet (Brennan) Baldock; m. Robert J. Ruppelt, Oct. 8, 1954 (div. Aug. 1964); children: Coy Robert, Traci Lynn; m. Jerry Ray Boyle, June 1, 1970 (div. 1975). AA, Orange Coast Coll., 1966; BA, Calif. State U., Fullerton, 1970; student, U. Calif., Irvine, 1970-71. Program coord. Newport Beach (Calif.) Cablevision, 1968-70; dir. pub. rels. Fish Communications Co., Newport Beach, 1970-74; mktg. rep. Dow Pharm. div. Dow Chem. Co., Orange County, Calif., 1974-77, Las Vegas, Nev., 1980-81; mgr. product publicity Dow Agrl. Products div. Dow Chem. Co., Midland, Mich., 1977-80; mgr. mktg. communications Dowell Fluid Services Region div. Dow Chem. Co. Houston, 1981-84; adminstr. mktg. communications Swedlow, Inc., Garden Grove, Calif., 1984-85; cons. mktg. communications, 1985-86; mgr. mktg. communications Am. Convertors div. Am. Hosp. Supply, 1986-87; mgr. sales support Surgidev Corp., Santa Barbara, Calif., 1987-88; owner Barrel House, Victorville, Calif., 1988-91, Saratoga Fences, Las Vegas, 1991; pub. info. officer Clark County Comprehensive Planning, Las Vegas, 1992-96; pub. info. officer, mgmt. analyst II Clark County, Las Vegas, 1996—; guest lectr. Calif. State U., Long Beach, 1970; seminar coordinator U. Calif., Irvine, 1972; mem. Western White House Press Corps, 1972; pub. relations cons. BASF Wyandotte, Phila., 1981-82. Author: Agricultural Public Relations/Publicity, 1981; editor Big Mean AG Machine (internal mag.), 1977; contbr. numerous articles to trade pubs.; contbg. editor Dowell Mktg. Newsletter, 1983; creator, designer Novahistine DMX Trial Size nat. mktg. program, 1977. Com. mem. Dow Employees for Polit. Action, Midland, 1978-80; bd. dirs. Dowell Employees for Polit. Action Com., Houston, 1983-84. World Campus Afloat scholar, U. Seven Seas, 1966-67; recipient PROTOS award, 1985. Mem. Pub. Relations Soc. Am. (cert.), Soc. Petroleum Engrs., Internat. Assn. Bus. Communicators. Episcopalian. Recipient first rights to televise President Nixon in Western White House. Office: 6340 Lanning Ln Las Vegas NV 89108-2605

BOYLE, DANNY, film director; b. Manchester, Eng., Oct. 20, 1956. Dir.: Shallow Grave, 1994 (Silver Seashell award San Sebastian Internat. Film Festival, best dir., 1994, Alexander Korda award, Brit. Acad. Awards, best Brit. film, 1994), Trainspotting, 1996 (Golden Space Needle award Seattle Internat. Film Festival, best dir., 1996, nominated Ind. Spirit award, Best Fgn. Film, 1997, nominated Alexander Korda award, Brit. Acad. Awards, best Brit. film, 1996, Bodil Festival award, best European film, 1996), A Life Less Ordinary, 1997, The Beach, 1999, Alien Love Triangle, 1999; dir. (TV series): Inspector Morse, 1987, Mr. Wroe's Virgins, 1993; exec. prodr.: Twin Town, 1997; prodr.: Elephant, 1989. Office: c/o DGA 7920 Sunset Blvd Los Angeles CA 90046*

BOYLE, DENNIS JOSEPH, III, computer company executive; b. San Diego, Aug. 31, 1955; s. Dennis Joseph, Jr. and Frances Helen (Zepp) B.; m. Paula Caro, Apr. 15, 1975 (div. May 1986); children: Jason, Ryan; m. Lisa Caron Blackstone, Oct. 28, 1989; 1 child, Joshua. Owner Frontier Log Homes, Waveland, Miss., 1973-85; aircraft engine repairer Corpus Christi (Tex.) Army Depot, 1985-96; owner, CEO Triad Svcs., Corpus Christi, 1996—, Triad Divers, Corpus Christi, 1996—; owner Third Coast Divers Outlet, Corpus Christi, 1997—; owner, CEO Triad Internet Svcs., Corpus Christi, 1997—; expedition leader Nat. Underwater Marine Agy., Austin, Tex., 1995—. Contbg. writer South Tex. Sports, Health and Fitness; inventor Tracher Coat device that enables people with trachea tubes to enjoy water sports. Mem. Corpus Christi Sister City Com., 1997—. With USN, 1972-73. Recipient Letter of Appreciation, Coastal Bend Vol. Ctr., 1991. Mem. Profl. Assn. Dive Instrs., Internat. Assn. Nitrox Tech. Divers, S.W. Underwater Archaeology Soc. (expedition leader 1995—), Triad Diver Adventure Team Dive Club (founding). Republican. Roman Catholic. Avocations: scuba diving, writing, reading, aerobics.

BOYLE, E. THOMAS, federal judge; b. 1939. BS in English, Holy Cross Coll., 1961; LLB, U. Va., 1964. Bar: N.Y. 1965, U.S. Ct Appeals (2d cir.) 1974, U.S. Dist. Ct. (ea. and so. dists.) N.Y. 1974. Assoc. Mendes & Mount, Bay Shore, N.Y., 1965-66; trial counsel Legal Aid Soc. Suffolk County, N.Y.C., 1966-72; appellate counsel Fed. Defender Svcs., Hauppauge, N.Y., 1972-75; pvt. practice, Hauppauge, N.Y., 1975-88; county atty. Suffolk County, Hauppauge, N.Y., 1988-92; ptnr. Boyle, Shea & Nornes, Hauppauge, N.Y., 1992-95; magistrate judge for ea. dist. N.Y., U.S. Magistrate

Ct., Uniondale, 1995—. Office: US Magistrate Ct US Courthouse 2 Uniondale Ave Uniondale NY 11553-1259

BOYLE, EDWARD ALLEN, oceanography educator; b. Aberdeen, Md., May 1, 1949. BA, U. Calif., San Diego, 1971; PhD, MIT, 1976. Postdoctoral fellow U. Edinburgh, Scotland, 1976-77; asst. prof. MIT, Cambridge, 1977-80, assoc. prof., 1980-90, prof., 1990—. NSF fellow MIT, 1971-75, Guggenheim Found. fellow, 1991-92; recipient Huntsman award Bedford Inst. of Oceanography, 1995. Fellow Am. Geophys. Union, Geochem. Soc. Office: MIT E34-258 77 Mass Ave Cambridge MA 02139-4307

BOYLE, FRANCIS JOSEPH, retired federal judge; b. 1927; m. M. Delores Roderick; children: Deborah, Carole, Christopher, Mathew, Susan, Patrick, Katherine. Postgrad., Providence Coll., 1949; JD, Boston Coll., 1952. Bar: bar 1952. Assoc. Cornelius C. Moore, 1953-61; ptnr. Moore, Virgadamo, Boyle & Lynch, 1961-77; judge U.S. Dist. Ct. for R.I., Providence, 1977-82, chief judge, 1982-92, now sr. judge, 1992-96. With USN, 1945-46. Mem. Am. Bar Assn., Fed. Bar. Assn., R.I. Bar Assn., Newport County Bar Assn.

BOYLE, GERTRUDE, sportswear company executive; b. Augsberg, Germany, 1924; came to U.S., 1938; d. Paul and Marie Lanfrom; m. Neil Boyle, 1948; children: Tim, Kathy, Sally. BA in Sociology, Univ. Ariz., 1947. Pres., CEO Columbia Sportswear Co., Portland, Oreg., 1970-88, CEO, 1988-94, chair, 1994—. Named one of Best Mgrs. Bus. Week Mag., 1994, Am.'s Top 50 Women Bus. Owners Working Woman mag., Woman of Yr. Oreg. chpt. Women's Forum, 1987. Office: Columbia Sportswear Co 6600 N Baltimore Ave Portland OR 97203-5403*

BOYLE, JANE J., federal judge; b. 1954. JD, So. Meth. U., 1981. Asst. dist. atty. Dist. Atty.'s Office, 1981-87; asst. U.S. Atty. U.S. Dist. Ct. (no. dist.) Tex., 1987-90; magistrate judge U.S. Dist. Ct. (no. dist.) Tex., Dallas, 1990—. Fax: (214) 767-3366. Office: US Dist Ct No Dist Tex 1100 Commerce St Rm 15C40 Dallas TX 75242

BOYLE, JOHN EDWARD WHITEFORD, cultural organization administrator; b. Milw., Mar. 8, 1915; s. Herman Edward and Margaret Lauretta (Casey) B.; m. Renée Colin Kent, Feb. 2, 1950; children: Vanessa Whiteford Wayne, Christopher Whiteford, Andrea Heller, Alexandra Whiteford. PhB, Marquette U., 1937; postgrad., Harvard U., 1946-47, Institut Franco-Iranien, 1959-60, U. Tehran, 1960-623, George Washington U., Georgetown U., UCLA; Doctorandus Lettres et Arts Persanes, Jungian Inst., Zurich, Switzerland, 1997. Journalist Hearst Mags., N.Y.c., 1937, WISN, Milw., 1937-38, Milw. Jour., 1938-40; exec. CIA, Washington, L.A., Frankfurt am Main, Germany, 1947-58, Washington, 1964-67; dir. Am. Friends of the Middle East, Tehran, 1958-62, Tunis, Algeria, Libya, 1962-64; dir. Whiteford Internat. Enterprise, Switzerland, 1967-72, France, 1972-74; fgn. corr. mag. Viewpoints, 1962-64, Middle East Mag., Beirut, Lebanon, 1963; pres. Fgn. Svcs. Rsch. Inst./Wheat Forders (press), Washington, 1974-99, pres. emeritus, 1999—; pres. emeritus Internat. Acad. Ind. Schs.; cons. to embassies on edn., 1974—; cons. on edn. Shah of Iran, 1958-62; prof. Nat. U. Iran, 1960-62; co-founder in cooperation with Ministry of Ct., Iran. Author: Primers for the Age of Inner Space: I-Beyond the Present Prospect, 1977, II-The Indra Web, 1983, III-Graffiti on the Wall of Time (poetry), 1983, IV-Of the Same Root: Heaven, Earth and I, 1990, V-The Way of the Essentialist: Contra Sartres Existentialism, 1993, VI-The Unperceived Revolution: Cracking the Code of the Ultimate Enigma, 1997. Campaign mgr. Roosevelt for Pres., No. Wis., 1940, John F. Kennedy for Pres., Iran, 1960; mem. Fulbright Commn., 1959-62; bd. dirs. Iran-Am. Soc., 1960-62, Pahlavi Found., Iran, 1959-62, Washington Humane Soc.; vol. Dem. Nat. Com., 1982. Served with USAAF, 1940-45. Recipient Priz Teilhard/Londres, 1982-83, Silver Poet award World of Poetry, 1990, Golden Poet award, 1992, Outstanding Alumni Scholar award Marquette U., 1991, 97, Editor's Choice award for Outstanding Achievemnt in Poetry Nat. Libr. Poetry, 1993. Mem. Acad. Ind. Scholars (pres.), N.Y. Acad. Sci., Expt. in Internat. Living (hon. life), Essentialist Philos. Soc. (pres. 1991—), Homer Hon. Soc. Internat. Poets. Quaker. Home: 2718 Unicorn Ln NW Washington DC 20015-2234 Office: PO Box 6317 Washington DC 20015-0317

BOYLE, KAMMER, management psychologist; b. New Orleans, June 17, 1946; d. Benjamin Franklin and Ethel Clair (Kammer) B.; m. Edward Turner Barfield, July 23, 1966 (div. 1975); children: Darren Barfield, Meloe Barfield. BS in Mgmt., magna cum laude, U. West Fla., 1976; PhD in Indsl./Organizational Psychology, U. Tenn., 1982. Lic. psychologist, Ohio, Tenn.; reg. securities rep. NASD. Pvt. practice mgmt. psychology, Knoxville, 1978-81; teaching and research asst. U. Tenn., Knoxville, 1977-81; mgmt. trainer U.S. State Dept., Washington, 1978; cons. PRADCO, Cleve., 1982-83; pres., cons. Mgmt. and Assessment Services, Inc., Cleve., 1983-90; pres. Kammer Investment Co., Cleve., 1989-96; fin. advisor O'Donnell Securities Corp., Cleve., 1997-98, Intersecurities Inc., Cleve., 1998—. Mem. editl. rev. bd. Jour. of Managerial Issues, 1987; author and presenter ann. Conf. APA, 1980, Southeastern Psychol. Conf., 1979, ann. Conf. Soc. Indsl./Orgnl. Psychologists, 1987, ann. conf. Am. Soc. Tng. & Devel., 1988. Mem. Jr. League Am., Pensacola, Fla., 1970-75; treas. Bar Aux., Pensacola, 1971. Recipient Capital Gifts Stipend, U. Tenn., 1976-80; Walter Bonham fellow, 1980-81. Mem. APA, Cleve. Psychol. Assn., Orgn. Devel. Inst., Acad. of Mgmt., Soc. Advancement Mgmt. (pres. 1974-75), Am. Soc. Tng. & Devel. (chpt. rep. career devel. 1984-86), Cleve. Psychol. Assn. (bd. dirs. 1987-88), Real Estate Investor's Assn. (Cleve., trustee/sec. 1992-94), Mensa. Office: Wealth Spring Bldg 4 Ste 600 23200 Chagrin Blvd Beachwood OH 44122

BOYLE, KATHLEEN MARIE, English educator, soccer coach; b. Boston, June 19, 1974; d. John Thomas and Mary Veronica (Ward) B. BA in English, St. Anselm Coll., Manchester, N.H., 1996; MEd in Secondary English, Emmanuel Coll., Boston, 1998. Cert. tchr., Mass. 6th grade tchr. St. Columkille Sch., Brighton, Mass., 1996-97; soccer coach Mt. St. Joseph Acad., Brighton, 1996-97; lit. tchr. North Cambridge (Mass.) Clinic, 1997—. Recipient Good Sportsmanship award Mass. Interscholastic Athletic Assn., 1996-97. Mem. Nat. Coun. Tchrs. English.

BOYLE, (CHARLES) KEITH, artist, educator; b. Defiance, Ohio., Feb. 15, 1930. Student, Ringling Sch. Art; B.F.A., U. Iowa. Prof. painting and drawing Stanford U., Calif., 1962-88. Group shows include Stanford U. Mus., 1964, San Francisco Mus. Art, 1965, Ann Arbor, Mich., 1965, Joslyn Art Mus., Omaha, 1970, San Jose Mus. Art, Calif., 1978; represented in permanent collections: San Francisco Mus. Art, Stanford U. Mus., Mead paper Corp., Atlanta, Nat. Fine Arts Collection, Washington, Oakland Mus., Continental Bank, Chgo., Seton Med. Ctr., Daily City, Calif., Schneider Mus., Ashland, Oreg. Grantee NEA, 1981-82, Pew Meml. Trust, 1986-87. Address: 6285 Thompson Creek Rd Applegate OR 97530-9639

BOYLE, KEVIN JOHN, economics educator, consultant; b. Montgomery, Ala., Sept. 15, 1955; s. John Farley and Eliane Ruth (Keaney) B.; m. Nancy Jean Becraft, June 12, 1983; children: Lindsey Jean, Grady John. BA in Econs., U. Maine, 1978; MS in Econs., Oreg. State U., 1981; PhD in Econs., U. Wis., 1985. Rsch. asst. Oreg. State U., Corvallis, 1979-80; economist U.S. Forest Svc., Corvallis, 198l; rsch. asst. U. Wis., Madison, 1982-85, rsch. assoc., 1985-86; asst. prof. econs. U. Maine, Orono, 1986-91, assoc. prof., 1991-97, Libra prof. environ. econ., 1997—; faculty assoc. Ctr. for Econs., Rsch. Triangle Inst., 1992-94; pres. regional project benefits and costs in natural resource planning USDA, 1988-89. Assoc. editor Jour. Environ. Econs. and Mgmt., 1995-99, Marine Rsch. Econs., 1996-98. Fish and Wildlife Svc. grantee, 1989—, Oak Ridge Nat. Labs. grantee, 1989-90, Exxon, USA grantee, 1989-92, Maine Dept. Inland Fisheries and Wildlife grantee, 1994—, Bangor Hydro-Electric Co. grantee, 1991-93, EPA, 1993-94, Econ. Rsch. Svc. grantee USDA, 1995—; recipient Merit cert. USDA, 1981, Outstanding Rsch. award Coll. Natural Scis. Forestry and Agr., U. Maine, 1999. Mem. Am. Econ. Assn., Am. Agrl. Econs. Assn., Assn. Environ. and Resource Economists, Northeastern Agrl. and Resource Econs. Assn. (bd. dirs. 1993-96, pres. 1998—). Avocations: running, biking, canoeing, reading. Home: 322 Main Rd S Hampden ME 04444-1103 Office: U Maine Econs Dept Winslow Hall Orono ME 04469

BOYLE, LARRY MONROE, federal judge; b. Seattle, June 23, 1943; s. Thomas L. and Winona (Green) B.; m. Beverly Rigby, Jan 31, 1969; children: Brian, Jeffery, Bradley, David, Melissa, Layne. BSc, Brigham Young U., 1968; JD, U. Idaho, 1972. Bar: Idaho 1973, U.S. Dist. Ct. Idaho 1973. Atty. Hansen, Boyle, Beard & Martin, P.A., Idaho Falls, Idaho, 1973-86; dist. judge 7th Jud. Dist., Idaho Falls, 1986-89; judge U.S. Supreme Ct. Idaho, Boise, 1989-92; magistrate judge U.S. Dist. Ct. Idaho, Boise, 1992—. Office: US Courthouse Box 040 550 W Fort St Boise ID 83724-0101*

BOYLE, LESTER JOSEPH, marketing and broadcast executive; b. Stamford, Conn., Sept. 1, 1933; s. Lester J. and Mary Katherine (Flanagan) B.; m. Mary Lou Abernethy, June 22, 1957; children: Lester Joseph, Katherine Margaret. BSBA, U. Conn., 1959. Mgr. of advt., mktg. rsch. Getty Oil Co., N.Y.C., Tulsa, 1959-84; mgr. advt., sales promotion Texaco, U.S.A., Houston, 1984-85; exec. v.p. J.L. Media, Inc., Tulsa and Union, N.J., 1985—; bd.dir. Dr.'s Med. Ctr., Tulsa, 1980—; guest lectr. in field. Bd. dirs. ARC, Tulsa, 1980—; pres. bd. dirs. Roy Clark Charity Golf, Tulsa, 1979-84. With U.S. Army, 1952-54. Mem. Am. Mktg. Assn., Am. Advt. Fedn. (v.p. 1981-83, recipient Silver Addy award 1984), Broadcast Execs. of Tulsa (hon. life), Okla. Assn. of Broadcasters. Republican. Home: 4923 E 75th St Tulsa OK 74136-8212 Office: JL Media Inc 401 S Boston Ave Tulsa OK 74103-4016

BOYLE, LISA C., marketing and communications executive; b. Newark, 1956; d. Melvin A. and Sally Pollack; m. Kenneth J. Boyle, Mar. 22, 1986 (dec. June 1996). BA in Social Studies magna cum laude, Montclair State Coll., 1978. Cert. K-12 tchr., N.J. Adminstrv. asst. Scholastic Inc., N.Y.C., 1978, ops. mgr., 1978-86; acct. exec. Mokrynski and Assocs. Inc., Creskill, N.J., 1986, Alvin Zeller, Inc., N.Y.C., 1986-87; sr. acct. exec. Am. List Counsel, Princeton, N.J., 1987-90; asst. mgr. Phillips Pub., Potomac, Md., 1990-91; sr. planner acquisitions divsn. Craver Mathews Smith & Co., Falls Church, Va., 1991-94; founder, pres., CEO Am. Mktg. and Comm. Corp., Rockville, Md., 1994—; cons. direct mail Lisa C. Boyle, Elmwood Park and Howell, N.J., 1986-90, Boyle Group, Germantown, Md., 1990-94; founder, pres., CEO Am. Mktg. d Comm. Corp., 1994—; spkr. in field. *Lisa C. Boyle has over 20 years direct mail experience. She is founder and president/CEO of American Marketing & Communications Corp., a direct mail agency providing consultation, strategic planning, list services, program development, creative services, and more. Lisa brings unique insight to her clients through her experience as a client, a list broker and manager, and consultant. Her many accomplishments include successful repositioning of a home office publication; the transformation of a low dollar winery (average purchace $15) to a high dollar ($75+ average purchase); building various clients to prospect on a profit basis; and turning $1.5MM revenue into $5.5MM.* Contbr. articles to profl. jours. Polit. campaign organizer Candidate Sch. Bd., Fair Lawn, N.J., 1976. Mem. Direct Mktg. Assn. Washington (founder, pres. FR coun. 1990-92, plaque 1994, super mem. 1998), Direct Mktg. Assn., Direct Mktg. Assn. N.J. (founder, pres. 1987-89). Office: Am Mktg Comm Corp 1688 E Gude Dr Ste 301303 Rockville MD 20850-5306

BOYLE, PATRICIA JEAN, state supreme court justice, retired; b. Detroit, Mar. 31, 1937. Student, U. Mich., 1955-57; B.A., Wayne State U., 1963, J.D., 1963. Bar: Mich. Practice law with Kenneth Davies, Detroit, 1963; law clk. to U.S. Dist. judge, 1963-64; asst. U.S. atty., Detroit, 1964-68; asst. pros. atty. Wayne County; dir. research, tng. and appeals Wayne County, Detroit, 1969-74; Recorders Ct. judge City of Detroit, 1976-78; U.S. dist. judge Eastern Dist. Mich., Detroit, 1978-83; assoc. justice Mich. Supreme Ct., Detroit, 1983-98, ret., 1999. Active Women's Rape Crisis Task Force, Vols. of Am. Named Feminist of Year Detroit chpt. NOW, 1978; recipient Outstanding Achievement award Pros. Attys. Assn. Mich., 1978, 98, Mich. Women's Hall of Fame award, 1986, Law Day award ABA, 1998, Champion of Justice award State Bar Mich., 1998. Mem. Women Lawyers Assn. Mich., Fed. Bar Assn., Mich. Bar Assn., Detroit Bar Assn., Wayne State U. Law Alumni Assn. (Disting. Alumni award 1979). Avocation: reading. Address: 15925 Warwick Detroit MI 48223

BOYLE, PATRICK KEVIN, journalist; b. Bklyn., July 14, 1959; s. Kenneth and Lola B. BA in Comm. Arts magna cum laude, U. Dayton, 1981. From reporter to mng. editor Bridgehampton (N.Y.) Sun, 1981-83; reporter Watertown (N.Y.) Daily Times, 1984; metro reporter N.Y.C. Tribune, 1984-86; metro reporter, desk editor Washington Times, 1986-92; freelance journalist, sr. editor Car & Travel Mag., 1994-98; editor Youth Today, 1998—; cons. for one Day One segment, ABC News, 1993; spokesman Am. Automobile Assn., 1994-98. Author: Scouts Honor, 1994. Recipient 3d Place award for Humerous Commentary, L.I. Press Club, 1998, 1st Place award for series Md.-Del.-D.C. Press Assn., 1991, 3d Place award Nat. Headliner Awards, 1991, 1st place award for spot news coverage Soc. Profl. Journalists, 1991, 3d Place award for investigative reporting Nat. Newspaper Assn., 1988, 3d place award for column writing N.Y. Press Assn., 1981, others. Office: Youth Today 1200 17th St NW Washington DC 20036-3006

BOYLE, PETER, actor; b. Phila., Oct. 18, 1935; m. Loraine Alterman, Oct. 1977. Ed., LaSalle Coll., Phila. Monk in Christian Bros. order, until early 1960's. Actor in Off-Broadway shows, N.Y.C., also Second City group, Chgo., and TV commls.; appeared in films including Medium Cool, 1969, Joe, 1970, Diary of a Mad Housewife, 1970, T.R. Baskin, 1972, The Candidate, 1972, Steelyard Blues, 1973, Slither, 1973, The Friends of Eddie Coyle, 1973, Kid Blue, 1973, Crazy Joe, 1974, Young Frankenstein, 1974, Taxi Driver, 1976, Swashbuckler, 1976, F.I.S.T, 1978, The Brink's Job, 1978, Hardcore, 1979, Beyond the Poseidon Adventure, 1979, In God We Trust, 1980, Where the Buffalo Roam, 1980, Hammett, 1980, Outland, 1981, Yellowbeard, 1983, Johnny Dangerously, 1984, Turk 182, 1985, Surrender, 1987, Walker, 1987, The In Crowd, 1988, Speedzone, 1989, Funny, 1989, The Dream Team, 1989, Men of Respect, 1991, Kickboxer 2, 1991, Honeymoon in Vegas, 1992, Malcolm X, 1992, The Shadow, 1994, The Killer, 1994, Exquisit Tenderness, 1994, The Santa Clause, 1994, Katie, 1995, While You Were Sleeping, 1995, Death and Compass, 1996, Final Vendetta, 1996, That Darn Cat, 1997, Milk and Money, 1997, Species II, 1998, Dr. Doolittle, 1998, Species 2, 1998; (TV movies) Tail Gunner Joe, 1977, From Here to Eternity, In the Lake of the Woods, 1996, A Deadly Vision, 1997, That Darn Cat, 1997; (TV series) Joe Bash, 1986, Comedy Tonight, 1970, Everybody Loves Raymond, 1996; TV guest appearances include NYPD Blue, Lois & Clark: The New Adventures of Superman, The X Files, The Single Guy, Cosby, The King of Queens, Tribeca, others. *

BOYLE, R. EMMETT, metal products executive; b. 1937. BS in Engring., MS in Engring. With Kaiser Aluminum Corp., Oakland, Calif., 1965-85; pres. Ravenswood (W.Va.) Aluminum Corp., 1989-92; chmn. Ormet Corp., Wheeling, W.Va., 1990—. *

BOYLE, RICHARD EDWARD, lawyer; b. Westville, Ill., Mar. 27, 1937; s. Kelley George and Florence (Weisert) B.; m. Janet E. Peskar, Nov. 22, 1968; children: Kevin, Douglas, Leslie. BA, U. Ill., 1959, LLB, 1961. Bar: Ill. 1962, Mo. 1985, U.S. Dist. Ct. (so. dist.) Ill. 1962, U.S. Dist. Ct. (cen. dist.) Ill. 1962, U.S. Dist. Ct. (ea. dist.) Mo. 1991, U.S. Ct. Appeals (7th cir.) 1975, U.S. Supreme Ct. 1985. Assoc. Costello, Wiechert, Roberts & Gundlach, 1962-68; ptnr. Gundlach, Lee, Eggmann, Boyle & Roessler, Belleville, Ill., 1968—. With USAFR. Fellow Am. Coll. Trial Lawyers, Am. Bar Found. (mem. Adv. Group Civil Justice Reform Act 1990—); mem. Nat. Assn. R.R. Trial Counsel (pres. 1991-92), St. Clair County Bar Assn. (pres. 1979-80). Home: 13 Oak Knoll Pl Belleville IL 62223-1817 Office: Gundlach Lee Eggmann Boyle & Roessler Box 23560 5000 W Main St Belleville IL 62226-4727

BOYLE, RICHARD JAMES, banker; b. Bklyn., Dec. 4, 1943; s. James F. and Marie E. (Rodden) B.; m. Denise T. Burke, Feb. 21, 1944; children: Ann Marie, Richard J. BA, Holy Cross Coll., 1965; MBA in Bus. Fin., NYU, 1969. V.p. Bank of Commonwealth, Detroit, 1971-72; vice pres. Chase Manhattan Bank, N.Y.C, 1971-75, sr. v.p., 1975-84, exec. v.p., 1984-87, vice-chmn. global banking, 1987-90; chief credit and investment officer Global Bank, 1990-96; ret., 1996; bd. dirs. Chase Preferred Capital Corp. Bd. dirs. Foundling Hosp., YMCA Greater N.Y., St. Vincents Hosps. Recipient Humanitarian award Nat. Jewish Hosp., Denver, 1978, Man of Yr., Cystic Fibrosis Found., N.Y., 1975. Republican. Roman Catholic. Clubs: Beacon Hill (Summit), Baltusrol Golf (Springfield).

BOYLE, ROBERT DANIEL, management consultant, program management and business process reengineering; b. Havre de Grace, Md., June 27, 1965; s. Vincent Michael Sr. and Margaret Kathleen (Helton) B. BS, U. Md., 1987; MBA, Loyola Coll., Balt., 1989, MS in Fin., 1990. CPA, cert. mgmt. acct., cert. fellow in prodn. and inventory mgmt., cert. integrated resource mgmt., cert. mgmt. cons. Pres. Sunquest of Md., Inc., Aberdeen, Md., 1985-88; adj. prof. Loyola Coll., Balt., 1989-90; rsch. fellow David D. Lattanze Ctr., Balt., 1989-92; prin. Sandlot Strategists, Balt., 1989-91; cons. Anderson Cons., Tampa, 1991-92; mgr. Deloitte & Touche Cons. Group, Atlanta, 1992-96; sr. prin. Diamond Technology Ptnrs., Inc., Chgo., 1996—; cons., speaker in field. Contbr. articles to profl. publs. David D. Lattanze Ctr. fellow, 1989-92. Mem. AICPA, Am. Prodn. and Inventory Control Soc., Inst. Cert. Mgmt. Accts., Inst. Cert. Mgmt. Cons., Mensa, Phi Theta Kappa, Alpha Sigma Lambda, Phi Kappa Phi, Alpha Sigma Nu, Beta Gamma Sigma. Avocations: reading, movies, fitness, travel. Home: 3222 Asbury Sq Atlanta GA 30346-2425

BOYLE, ROBERT JAMES, special education school director; b. Johnstown, Pa., June 20, 1967; s. Ralph James and Helen Elizabeth (Emerick) B.; m. Daun Michele Kuzma, Nov. 9, 1991; 1 child, Samantha Nicole. BS, Indiana U. Pa., 1989. Cert. secondary edn. math, Pa. Cmty. careworker Alternative Cmty. Resource Program, Johnstown, Pa., 1989-91; program coord. alternative spl. edn. program Alternative Cmty. Resource Program, Johnstown, 1990-93, asst. dir. St. Michael's Sch., 1993-96, dir. St. Michael's Sch., 1996—; med. courier Med-Chek Labs., Pitts., 1990-91; adv. bd. mem. Alternative Cmty. Resource Program, Johnstown, 1993—; Preparation for Adult Living mem. Appalachia Intermediate Unit 08, Ebensburg, Pa., 1996—. Active Ferndale Vol. Fire Co., 1984—. 1st lt. USAR, 1988-97. Mem. Western Pa. Firemen's Assn. Democrat. Roman Catholic. Avocations: wood working, softball, basketball. Office: ACRP/St Michaels Sch 188 Gilbert St Johnstown PA 15906-3238

BOYLE, ROBERT PATRICK, retired government agency consultant, lawyer; b. Kansas City, Mo., Nov. 21, 1913; s. Roscoe Virgil and Aletha (Pentecost) B.; m. Katherine Warren, Mar. 16, 1940; children: Elizabeth Ann, Carolyn Warren. B.A., Williams Coll., 1935; LL.B., Harvard U., 1938. Bar: Okla. 1938, D.C. 1940. With CAA, 1938-58, atty., asst. to gen. counsel, asst. gen. counsel, dep. gen. counsel, gen. counsel, 1953-58; sr. assoc. gen. counsel FAA, 1959-63; dep. asst. adminstr. Internat. Aviation Affairs, 1963-68, 70-72; cons. internat. aviation affairs Dept. Transp., 1972-76; chmn. U.S. del. legal com. Internat. Civil Aviation Orgn., 1957-60, 62, pres. legal commn. 14th assembly, 1962, U.S. rep. Coun., 1968-69, chmn. tech. com. extraordinary assembly, Montreal, 1970, cons., 1976-80; legal advisor on revision air law Govt. of Saudi Arabia, 1977-80; chmn. U.S. del. Diplomatic Conf. Pvt. Air Law, Guadalajara, Mex., 1961, Tokyo, 1963, Guatemala, 1971; mem. steering com., bd. dirs. Soc. Sr. Aerospace Execs., 1987-99, chmn. symposium on FAA, 1988, co-chmn. Symposium on Carry-on Luggage, 1995, treas., 1994-95. Contbr. articles to profl. publs. Chmn. legal div. Pres.'s Air Coordinating Com., 1953-60; chmn. working group on Warsaw Conv., Interagy. Group Internat. Aviation, 1971-75. Served to comdr. USNR, 1943-46. Mem. ABA (chmn. aviation criminal law 1953-67, mem. standing com. on aero. law 1974-79), Okla. Bar Assn., D.C. Bar Assn., Williams Coll. Alumni Assn. (pres. Washington chpt. 1960-61, co-class agt. 1986-99), Dacor Club (Washington), Kenwood Golf and Country Club (chmn. bd. govs. 1984, exec. com. 1984-91, sec. 1985, chmn. 1991), Vero Beach Golf and Country Club (Fla.), Theta Delta Chi. Home: 3929 36th St N Arlington VA 22207-5311

BOYLE, SUSAN JEAN HIGLE, elementary school educator; b. Tarrytown, N.Y., June 15, 1956; d. George Edward and Barbara Jean (Deverill) Higle. BA in Psychology, Elem. Edn., Ladycliff Coll., 1978; MS in Learning Disabilities, Fordham U., 1980; EdS in Ednl. Leadership, Stetson U., 1988. Cert. tchr., Fla. Tchr. St. Ursula Sch., Mt. Vernon, N.Y., 1978-81, Blue Lake Elem. Sch., DeLand, Fla., 1982-86, Deltona (Fla.) Lakes Elem., 1986-88, Discovery Elem. Sch., Deltona, 1988-89, Tomoka Elem. Sch., Ormond Beach, Fla., 1989-90, Ormond Beach Mid. Sch., 1990—; mem. discipline task force, Volusia County Schs., 1989, health task force, 1989. Eucharistic minister St. Brendan Ch. TOPS grantee, 1985, 86. Mem. Phi Delta Kappa, Daytona Beach Hummel Collectors Club. Avocations: reading, collecting hummels and baseball cards. Office: Ormond Beach Mid Sch 151 Domicilio Ave Ormond Beach FL 32174-3918

BOYLE, TERRENCE W., federal judge; b. 1945. BA, Brown U., 1967; JD, Am. U., 1970. Minority counsel housing subcom., banking and currence com. U.S. Ho. of Reps., 1970-73; legis. asst. U.S. senator J. Helms, 1973; judge U.S. Dist. Ct. Ea. Dist., N.C., 1984-97; chief judge 1997—. Office: US Dist Ct PO Box 306 306 E Main St Rm 217 Elizabeth City NC 27907-0429

BOYLE, WILLARD STERLING, physicist; b. Amherst, N.S., Can., Aug. 19, 1924; naturalized, 1969; s. Ernest Sterling and Bernice Teresa (Dewar) B.; m. Elizabeth Joyce, June 15, 1946; children—Robert, Cynthia, David, Pamela. B.Sc., McGill U., Montreal, Que., Can., 1947, M.Sc., 1948, Ph.D., 1950; LL.D. (hon.), Dalhousie U. Asst. prof. Royal Mil. Coll., Kingston, Ont., 1951-53; mem. staff Bell Labs., 1953-62, 64-79; exec. dir. semiconductor device devel. div. Bell Labs., Allentown, Pa., 1968-75; exec. dir. communications scis. div. Bell Labs., 1975-79; dir. space sci. Bellcommunications, 1962-64. Served with Canadian Navy, 1942-45. Recipient Ballantine medal Franklin Inst., Progress medal Photog. Soc. Am., 1986; Nat. Research Council Can. fellow, 1949. Fellow IEEE (Morris Liebman medal 1974), Am. Phys. Soc.; mem. Nat. Acad. Engring. Author, patentee in field; co-inventor charge coupled device and 1st continuously pumped ruby laser. Address: Wallace, NS Canada B0K 1Y0

BOYLE, WILLIAM CHARLES, civil engineering educator; b. Mpls., Apr. 9, 1936; s. Robert William and Daphne Jennette (Connell) B.; m. Nancy Lee Hahn, Apr. 11, 1959; children—Elizabeth Lynn, Michele Jenette, Jane Lynette, Robert William. CE, U. Cin., 1959, MS in Sanitary Engring., 1960; PhD in Environ. Engring., Calif. Inst. Tech., 1963. Registered profl. engr., Wis., Ohio. With Milw. Sewerage Commn., 1955-56; civil engr. O. G. Loomis & Sons, Covington, Ky., 1956-59; asst. engr. Ohio River Valley Water Sanitation Commn., summer 1959; asst. prof. dept. engring. U. Wis., Madison, 1963-66, assoc. prof., 1966-70, prof. dept. civil and environ. engring., 1970-96, chmn. dept. civil and environ. engring., 1984-86, assoc. chair, 1988-96, emeritus prof., 1996—; vis. prof. Rogaland Distriktshogskole, Stavanger, Norway, 1975-76; vis. prin. engr. Montgomery Engrs. Inc., Pasadena, Calif., 1988-89; cons. Procter & Gamble Co., Monsanto Co., S.B. Foot Tanning Co., Wis. Canners & Freezers Assn., Wis. Concrete Pipe Assn., Oscar Mayer & Co., Bartlett-Snow, Hide Service Corp., W.R. Grace & Co., Lake to Lake Dairies, Milw. Tallow, Wausau Paper Co., Packerland Packing Co., Ray-O-Vac, U.S. Army CERL, Owen Ayres & Assocs., Donohue Engrs., Davy Engrs., Carl C. Crane, Green Engring., RSE div. Ayres & Assocs., Schreiber Corp. Inc., Sanitaire, J.M. Montgomery, Engrs., Polkowski, Boyle, & Assocs., Rust E&I; mem. peer rev. panel on environ. engring. EPA; accreditation visitor Accreditation Bd. for Engring. and Tech., 1990—. Contbr. articles to profl. jours. Sr. warden St. Andrews Episcopal Ch., Madison, 1972-74, treas., 1979-85. Recipient Engring. Disting. Alumnus award U. Cin., 1986, Founders award U.S.A. nat. com. Internat. Assn. Water Pollution Rsch. & Control, 1988, commendation EPA, 1989; Mills Found. scholar U. Cin., 1954-59; USPHS trainee, U. Cin., 1959-60; fellow Ford Found., Calif. Inst. Tech., 1960-61, USPHS, Calif. Inst. Tech., 1961-63. Mem. ASCE (Wis. chpt., advisor U. Wis. student chpt. 1968-71, chmn. student affairs com. 1970-72, chmn. profl. activities com. 1972-74, nat., control mem. tech. council on codes and standards-environ. standards, chmn. environ. stds. devel. coun., mem. various coms., reviewer EED Jour., Rudolf Hering medal 1975, engring. achievement award from Wis. chpt. 1986, Engr. of Yr. award Wis. sect. 1998), Water Environment Fedn. (research com., joint task force-pretreatment of wastewater, tech. practice com.-energy in treatment plant design, author Manual of Practice Design Wastewater Treatment Plants, chmn. program com., mem. bd. control, 1996—, jour. reviewer, chmn. tech. practice com. task force on aeration, Radebaugh award 1978, mem. Eddy award com. 1992—, Harrison Prescot Eddy rsch. medal 1989, chmn. rsch. symposia, Gordon Maskew Fair medal for environ. engring. edn., 1992, Eddy award com.), Am. Water Works Assn. (chmn. task group on oxygen transfer, editorial bd.), Am. Acad. Environ. Engrs. (diplomate, accreditation vis. for Accreditation Bd. Engring and Tech., chmn. edn. com. 1993, trustee 1994-97, pres.-elect 1998, rep. bd. dirs. ABET, 1994—), Am. Foundrymen's Soc. (com. on waste disposal, Outstanding Rsch. Paper award environ. cen. div. 1989), Sigma Xi, Theta Tau, Phi Eta Sigma, Chi Epsilon, Tau Beta Pi. Episcopalian. Avocations:

photography, travel. Home: 105 Carillon Dr Madison WI 53705-4614 Office: Univ Wis 2205 Engineering Hall 1415 Engineering Dr Madison WI 53706-1607

BOYLE, WILLIAM LEO, JR., educational consultant, retired college president; b. Utica, N.Y., July 23, 1933; s. William Leo and Gladys (Kuney) B. AB, Colgate U., 1955; postgrad., Cornell U. Law Sch., 1960-61; MA, Columbia U., 1964, Profl. Diploma in Ednl. Adminstrn., 1967, EdD, 1969; LLD (hon.), Hawthorne Coll., 1979; postdoctoral, Harvard U., 1979-81; LHD (hon.), Mercy Coll., 1983; LittD (hon.), Curry Coll., 1992. Participant advanced mgmt. program, recruiter, ednl. adviser Procter & Gamble Co., Cin., 1958-60; legis. aide edn. com. N.Y. State Senate, Albany, 1961-62; account exec., ednl. cons. Batten, Barton, Durstine & Osborn, N.Y.C., 1962-64; assoc. dir. devel., presdl. asst. Wesleyan U., Middletown, Conn., 1964-65; program cons. Council for Fin. Aid to Edn., N.Y.C., 1965-70, asst. v.p., 1970-72, v.p., 1972-75; pres. Keuka Coll., Keuka Park, N.Y., 1975-78; pres. Curry Coll., Milton, Mass., 1978-92, pres. emeritus, 1992—; part-time pvt. practice as ednl. cons. to colls. and univs., Utica, 1992—. Author: The National Corporate Educational Support Movement, 1954-1966, 1969. Contbr. articles to ednl. and profl. jours. Vice chmn. nat. bus. and industry com. Colgate U. Hamilton, N.Y., 1974—, mem. nat. coun., 1975—, ann. fund exec. com., 1975—, Colgate '55 class agt., 1994—, mem. maj. gifts com.; ednl. cons. to Pres. Ford Com., Washington, 1976; bd. dirs. Slocum-Dickson Found., Utica, 1991—, Family Svcs. of the Mohawk Valley, Utica, 1992—, House of the Good Shepherd, Utica, 1992—, St. Luke's-Meml. Hosp. Ctr. Found., Utica, 1993—, Oneida County Hist. Soc., Utica, 1994—; mem. bd. devel. com. Utica Found., 1992—; established Boyle Scholarship at Colgate U., 1985, Boyle Fund, Utica Found., 1991, Boyle award in Polit. Sci. at Colgate U., 1997. Lt. USAF, 1955-58. Recipient Comdr.'s citation USAF. Mem. various ednl. and profl. orgns., also Colgate Univ. Club (N.Y.C.), Columbia Univ. Club (N.Y.C.), Ft. Schuyler Club (Utica) (bd. mgrs.), Sadaquada Golf Club (Utica), Yahnundasis Golf Club (Utica), Rotary. Home: 12 Rose Pl Utica NY 13502-5614

BOYLE, WILLIAM R., science administrator; b. Paterson, N.J., May 27, 1932; s. William J. and Mildred (Lynch) B.; m. D. Joanne Summers, Nov. 22, 1959; children—Deborah, Robert, Carol. B.S. in Chem. Engring., Newark Coll. Engring., 1954; M.S., W.Va. U., 1961, Ph.D., 1965. Registered profl. engr., Tenn. Dir. nuclear engring. project W.Va. U., Morgantown, 1967-68, acting chmn. dept. chem. engring., 1969, asst. dir. engring. exptl. sta., 1969-77, prof. chem. engring., 1972-77; chmn. MERT div. Oak Ridge Assoc. U., 1977-89, v.p., chmn. E/ES div., 1989-92; dir. energy environ. systems ORISE, 1992-95; mgr. Boyle & Assocs., 1995—; v.p. ORAU; cons. and lectr. in field. Contbr. articles to profl. jours. Commr. Engring. Manpower Commn. Served to capt. USAF, 1955-57. Mem. Nat. Soc. Profl. Engrs., Am. Soc. Engring. Edn., Am. Inst. Chem. Engrs., Am. Nuclear Soc., W.Va. Soc. Profl. Engrs. (pres. 1976-77), Tenn. Soc. Profl. Engrs. (chmn. edn. com. 1985-86), Tau Beta Pi, Sigma Xi, Sigma Pi Sigma. Methodist. Home: 110 Antioch Dr Oak Ridge TN 37830-7815 Office: Oak Ridge Inst for Sci Edn PO Box 117 Oak Ridge TN 37831-0117

BOYLES, FREDERICK HOLDREN, historian; b. Gainesville, Fla., Nov. 9, 1954; s. Eugene Harry and Frances Louise (Holdren) B.; m. Deborah Anne Beverly, Aug. 21, 1976; children: Cynthia Beverly, Joseph Holdren. A in Edn. and History, Abraham Baldwin Coll., 1974; BS in Edn. and History, U. Ga., 1976; M in Recreation and Parks Adminstrn., Clemson U., 1981. Dir. trail camp Goshen (Va.) Scout Camps, 1975-79; tchr. history and geography Waycross (Ga.) City Schs., 1976-78; instr. grad. students Clemson (S.C.) U., 1978-79; outdoor recreation planner Nat. Park Svc., Atlanta, 1979-81; historian Cumberland Gap Nat. Hist. Park, Middlesboro, Ky., 1981-85; supt. Moores Greek Nat. Battlefield, Currie, N.C., 1985-89, Andersonville (Ga.)-Jimmy Carter Nat. Hist. Sites, 1989—; adj. faculty Lincoln Meml. U., Harrogate, Tenn., 1983-84, U. N.C., Wilmington, 1987. Scout master troop 231 Boy Scouts Am., Americus, Ga., 1994; tchr. Sunday sch. 1st Presbyn. Ch., Americus, 1991—. Lt. comdr. USNR, 1987—. Grad. alumni scholar Clemson U., 1979; recipient Superior Achievement award U. S. Dept. Interior, 1980, Good Citizenship award SAR, 1989. Mem. Sumter C. of C. (bd. dirs. 1992—), Americus Rotary Club, Burgaw N.C. Rotary Club (bd. dirs. 1988, 90), Burgaw Area C. of C. (pres. 1989). Home: 200 Webber Rd Americus GA 31709-2136 Office: Nat Park Svc RR 1 Box 800 Andersonville GA 31711-9707

BOYLES, HARLAN EDWARD, state official; b. Lincoln County, N.C., May 6, 1929; s. Curtis E. and Kate S. B.; m. Frankie Wilder, May 17, 1952; children—Phyllis Godwin, Lynn Boyles Butler, Harlan Edward Jr. Student, U. Ga., 1947-48; B.B.A. in Acctg, U. N.C., 1951. C.P.A., N.C. Corp. tax auditor N.C. Dept. Revenue, 1951-56; exec. sec., local govt. com. N.C. Tax Rev. Bd., 1956-76, dep. treas., 1960-76; treas. State of N.C., 1977—; mem. Council of State; mem. mcpl. securities rulemaking bd. SEC, 1975-77. Mem. adv. bd. Raleigh Salvation Army; chmn. Local Govt. Commn.; chmn. State Banking Commn., Tax Rev. Bd.; mem. State Bd. Edn., State Bd. Community Colls., N.C. Capital Planning Commn., others. Mem. N.C. Assn. CPAs, Nat. Assn. State Auditors, Comptrs. and Treas. (past pres., exec. dir.), Raleigh C. of C. (past bd. dirs.), N.C. State Employees Assn., N.C. Young Dems. Club, Execs. of Raleigh Club (past pres.), Rotary (past pres.). Democrat. Presbyterian (deacon, elder, treas., clk.). Home: 1924 Fairfield Dr Raleigh NC 27608-2720 Office: Treasurer's Dept 325 N Salisbury St Raleigh NC 27603-1388

BOYLES, JAMES KENNETH, retired banker; b. Louisville, Jan. 27, 1916; s. Forrest Lee and Florence (Glenn) B.; m. Hilda Margaret Rose, Sept. 13, 1940; children: Margaret, James, Douglas, Kevin. Student, Columbia U., Am. Inst. Banking, Rutgers U. With Guaranty Trust Co., N.Y.C., 1933-37; loan officer Chem. Bank, N.Y.C., 1937-50; exec. v.p. The Nat. State Bank, Elizabeth, N.J., 1950-83; dir. The Nat. State Bank, Elizabeth, 1965-88. Trustee emeritus Union Coll., Cranford N.J. Served to 1st lt., inf., U.S. Army, 1942-46, ETO. Decorated 2 Bronze stars, Purple Heart. Mem. Robert Morris Assocs. (pres. 1963). Republican. Episcopalian.

BOYLL, DAVID LLOYD, broadcasting company executive; b. Terre Haute, Ind., Aug. 17, 1940; s. Lloyd A. and Stella Elizabeth (Ellinger) B.; m. Margie R. Coker, Apr. 14, 1962; children: Elizabeth Marie, Kelli Renae. BS in Edn., Abilene Christian U., 1964. Announcer Sta. KWKC, Abilene, Tex., 1959-64; program dir. Sta. KWKC-AM-FM, Abilene, 1964-68; sta. mgr. Sta. KFMN-FM, Abilene, 1968-74, owner, operator, 1974-80, ptnr., gen. mgr., 1980-82; ptnr., gen. mgr. Sta. KEYJ-AM-FM, Abilene, 1982-92; pres., mgr. Sta. KHXS/EZ106, Abilene, 1992-96; part-owner Sta. KYYD, Abilene, 1995—; owner KMPC-EZ 1560, 1997—. Pres. Abilene Downtown Assn., 1980-83; pres. Chisholm Trail coun. Boy Scouts Am., 1985-87; chmn. adv. com. Taylor County Juvenile Bd.; chmn. Abilene State Sch. Vols., 1987-90, named Vol. of Yr., 1990. Recipient Silver Beaver award Boy Scouts Am., 1987. Mem. Rotary (past pres., bd. dirs. Abilene club). Republican. Home: 3949 N 9th St Abilene TX 79603-5543 Office: KMPC/EZ 1560 Bank One Bldg 3444 N 1st St Abilene TX 79603-6920

BOYNE, WALTER JAMES, writer, former museum director; b. East St. Louis, Ill., Feb. 2, 1929; s. Walter William and Emily (Campbell) B.; m. Jeanne Quigley, Dec. 26, 1952; children: Mary Louise, Katherine Elizabeth, William James, Margaret Ann. BBA, U. Calif., Berkeley, 1958; MBA, U. Pitts., 1963; PhD (hon.), Salem Coll., 1985. Commd. 2d lt. USAF, 1952, advanced through grades to col., 1971, ret., 1974; asst. curator Nat. Air and Space Mus., Washington, 1974-75, curator, 1975-78, exec. officer, 1978-80, asst. dir., 1980-82; dep. dir. Nat. Air and Space Mus., 1982-83, dir., 1983-86; ret., 1986; chmn. bd. dirs. Wingspan TV Channel. Author: Boeing B-52, 1981, Messerschmitt Me-262, 1980, Treasures of Silver Hill, 1982, Flying, 1979, Jet Age, 1979, De Havilland DH-4, 1983, McDonnell Douglas F-4, 1983, Vertical Flight, 1983, Leading Edge, 1986, (novel) The Wild Blue, 1986, The Smithsonian Book of Flight, 1987, The Power Behind the Wheel, 1988, Trophy for Eagles, 1989, Weapons of Desert Shield, 1991, Gulf War, 1991, Eagles of War, 1991, Air Force Eagles, 1992, Classic Aircraft, 1992, Art in Flight, 1992, Silver Wings, 1993, Clash of Wings, 1994, Clash of Titans, 1995, Beyond the Wild Blue, 1997, Beyond the Horizons, 1998, Brassey Air Combat Reads, 1999; prodr., writer: (video) Beyond the Wild Blue; author, host, narrator: (video) Clash of Wings, 1998, The Sculptures of John Safer, 1998. Recipient Best Fgn. Book award Aero Club de France, 1982, Robert A. Brooks award Smithsonian Instn., 1980, Best Fiction and Non-Fiction awards Aviation Space Writers, 1987, Thomas McKean Meml. Cup, 1989, Cliff Henderson Trophy 1986, Gil Robb Wilson award AIA, 1997; named Elder Statesman of Aviatiion Nat. Aviation Assn., 1998. Mem. Daedalians, Am. Aviation Hist. Soc. (nat. advisor), Author's Guild, Sons of the Desert, Cosmos Club, Explorers Club. Club: Cosmos, Explorers. Home: 21028 Starflower Way Ashburn VA 20147-4700 *There is a pleasure in work; it is double if appreciated by a peer.*

BOYNTON, DONALD ARTHUR, title insurance company executive; b. Culver City, Calif., Sept. 6, 1940; s. A.A. and Margaret Lena (Slocum) B.; m. Jean Carolyn Ferrulli, Nov. 10, 1962; children: Donna Jean, Michael Arthur; m. Sharon C. Burns, Nov. 18, 1984; children: Cynthia, David, Sharie. Student, El Camino Jr. Coll., 1960-62, Antelope Valley Jr. Coll., 1963-64, Orange Coast Coll., 1969-72; BA, Bradford U., 1977. With Title Ins. & Trust Co., 1958-63; sales mgr. Title Ins. & Trust Co., Santa Ana, Calif., 1980-81; dep. sheriff County of Los Angeles, 1963-65; with Transamerica Title Ins. Co., L.A., 1965-69, state coord., 1981-82; sr. title officer Calif. Land Title Co., L.A. and Orange Counties, 1969-72; asst. sec., systems analyst Lawyers Title Ins. Corp., 39 states, 1972-77; county mgr. Am. Title Co., Santa Ana, Calif., 1977-79; v.p., mgr. Orange County ops. Chgo. Title Ins. Co., Tustin, Calif., 1979-80; pres. Stewart Title Co. of Fresno County, 1985-86; supr. builder svcs. Orange Coast Title Co., Santa Ana, San Diego, 1986-89; sr. title officer TSG dept. Orange Coast/Record Title, Whittier and La Mirada, Calif., 1990-94; sr. title officer, So. Calif. TSG Manager (5 County) State of Calif. for Orange Coast Title, 1993; sr. nat. coord. Chgo. Title and Ins., Irvine, Calif., 1993-96; title officer, claims officer N.Am. Title Ins., Orange, Calif., 1996-97; nat. underwriter/coord. 50 states and Canada LandAmerica/Lawyers Title Ins. Corp., L.A., 1997-98, LandAmerica/Elliptus Techs., Inc., Richmond, Va., 1998—. Mem. Calif. Trustees Assn., Orange County Escrow Assn., Optimists (sec.-treas.), Elks (life, chaplain), Rotary. E-mail: dboynton@elliptus.com. Home: 201 Arboreteum Pl Rucihmond VA 23236 Office: 888 W 6th St Fl 4 Los Angeles CA 90017-2703

BOYNTON, IRVIN PARKER, retired educational administrator; b. Chgo., Mar. 27, 1937; s. Ben Lynn and Elizabeth (Katterjohn) B.; m. Alyce Jane Coyle, Sept. 3, 1964; children: Gregory Allen, Cathy Lynn, Julie Marie, Michael Irvin, Jonathan David. BA, Ohio Wesleyan U., 1959; BS, U. Akron, 1964; MEd, Wayne State U., 1968; counseling endorsement, Siena Heights Coll., 1988. Cert. tchr., Ohio, Mich. Spl. edn. tchr., acting prin. Sagamore Hills Children's Psychiat. Hosp., Cleve., 1961-64; spl. edn. tchr. Fairlawn Ctr., Pontiac, Mich., 1964-68, Walled Lake (Mich.) High Sch., 1968-71; asst. prin. Oakland Tech. Ctr./Southwest Campus, Wixom, Mich., 1971-98; ret., 1998; mem. spl. needs guideline com. Mich. Dept. Edn., Lansing, 1973-78; keynote speaker Utah Secondary Conf., Salt Lake City, 1978; evaluator North Cen. Accreditation Assn., Waterford, Mich., 1971-73; adv. com. State Tech.Instn. and Rehab. Ctr., Plainwell, Mich., 1978-85. Pres. Roger Campbell Ministries, Waterford, 1987—. Cited as exemplary spl. needs program U. Wis. Mem. ASCD, Am. Vocat. Assn., Mich. Occupational Edn. Assn., Mich. Occupational Spl. Needs Assn. (Outstanding Spl. Needs Educator), Nat. Assn. Vocat. Spl. Needs Personnel (Outstanding Spl. Needs Program 1975), Phi Delta Kappa. Republican. Home: 4901 Juniper Dr Commerce Township MI 48382-1545

BOYNTON, JAMES ROBERT, educational institute professional; b. Salem, Mass., Nov. 20, 1941; s. Robert L. and Isabelle M. (Berube) B.; m. Linda Dewitt, Jan. 30, 1982; 1 child, Kimberly Anne. BS in Mgmt., BA in Acctg., Franklin Pierce Coll., Portsmouth, N.H., 1985; PhD in Bus. Adminstrn., Kennedy Western U., Idaho, 1999. Cost acctg. clk. EG&G Inc., Salem, Mass., 1967-68; unit mgr. Marshall's Dept. Stores, Mass., 1968-70; unit mgr., trainer Internat. Food Svc., Mass., 1970-73; materials mgmt. v.p. Gloucester (Mass.) Engring./Extrion, 1973-76; materials mgr. ITT Semiconductors, Mass., 1976-78; mfg. systems specialist D.G. O'Brien Inc., Seabrook, N.H., 1978-97; sales estimator Centorr/Vacuum Ind., Nashua, N.H., 1997—; chmn. bd. Focus N.H. Inst., 1993-97; CEO, mng. ptnr. Focus N.H. Inst. LLC, 1996—; cons., N.H., 1985-97; N.E. Region 1 edn. program mgr. Seminar 1, 1995-97; conf. chmn. Altschuller Inst. Trizcon 2000. Editor: APICS Region I Seminar One Compendium, 1994-97. Budget com., planning bd., chmn. econ. devel. com. Town of Epping, N.H., 1987-97, chmn. bd. selectman, 1996, econ. devel. dir., 1998—, econ. devel. dir., 1999—. With USN, 1959-67, USNR. Mem. Am. Legion, Fleet Res. Assn., Am. Prodn. and Inventory Control Soc. (chpt. bd. mem. 1985-97), Nat. Assn. Purchasing Mgrs., Am. Soc. Quality Control. Avocations: reading, educational, golf. Home and Office: 86 Meadowbrook Dr Epping NH 03042-1502

BOYNTON, PETER G., hotel executive; b. Torrance, Calif., May 2, 1943; m. Karia Boynton; children: Geoff, Randy. BA in Polit. Sci., Loyola U., L.A., 1965; postgrad., Calif. State U., Fullerton. Adminstrv. asst. Caesars World, Inc., 1975-77, asst. to pres., 1977-78, asst. v.p., pres., CEO, 1995—, chmn., CEO, 1998—; Caesars Atlantic City's exec. v.p., COO Caesar Atlantic City Hotel and Casino, 1981—, pres., COO, 1982—. Former mem. Partnership of N.J.; trustee Shore Meml. Hosp.; pres. Spl. Edn. Found. of Atlantic City; campaign chmn. United Way of Atlantic City, 1988, 93. Named Businessman of Yr. Greater Atlantic City C. of C., 1994. Mem. Atlantic City Casino Assn. (former pres.). Office: Caesars World Inc 3570 Las Vegas Blvd South Las Vegas NV 89109

BOYNTON, ROBERT GRANVILLE, computer systems analyst; b. North Bend, Oreg., Aug. 11, 1951; s. Granville Clarence Jr. and Leatrice Anne (Yoder) B.; m. Sandra Lynn Harrold, Aug. 17, 1991. Student, Ctrl. Oreg. C.C., 1969-70; BS, City U., 1999. cert. career data processing Heald Coll. Bus., 1972. Computer operator Coca-Cola Bottling Co. Calif., San Francisco, 1973-76, data processing mgr., 1977-78; computer operator Warn Industries, Milwaukie, Oreg., 1979-81, computer programmer, 1981-85, analyst, 1983-85, computer systems analyst, 1985-90, info. systems team leader, 1990—, sr. bus. analyst, 1993—. Vol. Oreg. Spl. Olympics, 1985-86. Democrat. Avocations: camping, hunting, fishing, reading. Home: 5712 SE 130th Pl Portland OR 97236-4175 Office: Warn Industries 13270 SE Pheasant Ct Portland OR 97222-1297

BOYNTON, ROBERT MERRILL, retired psychology educator; b. Evanston, Ill., Oct. 28, 1924; s. Merrill Holmes and Eleanor (Matthews) B.; m. Alice Neiley, Apr. 9, 1947 (dec. Oct. 1996); children: Sherry, Michael, Neiley, Geoffrey; m. Sheleah Maloney, Oct. 17, 1998. Student, Antioch Coll., 1942-43, U. Ill., 1943-45; AB, Amherst Coll., 1948; PhD, Brown U., 1952. Asst. prof. psychology and optics U. Rochester, N.Y., 1952-57; asso. prof. U. Rochester, 1957-61, prof., 1961-74, dir. Center for Visual Sci., 1963-71, chmn. dept. psychology, 1971-74; prof. psychology U. Calif., San Diego, 1974-91, assoc. dean grad. studies and research, 1987-91; ret., 1991; guest researcher Nat. Phys. Lab., Teddington, Eng., 1960-61; vis. prof. physiology U. Calif. Med. Center, San Francisco, 1969-70. Author: Human Color Vision, 1979, 2d edit., 1996; chmn. bd. editors Vision Research, 1982-86; contbr. articles to profl. jours. Served with USNR, 1943-45. Recipient Charles F. Prentice award Am. Acad. Optometry, 1997. Fellow AAAS, Optical Soc. Am. (dir.-at-large 1966-69, Frederick Ives medal 1995), APA, Assn. for Rsch. in Vision and Ophthalmology (trustee 1984-89); mem. NAS. Home: 376 Bellaire St Del Mar CA 92014-2207

BOYNTON, WILLIAM LEWIS, electronic manufacturing company official; b. Kalamazoo, May 31, 1928; s. James Woodbury and Cyretta (Gunther) B.; ed. pub. schs.; m. Kei Ouchi, Oct. 8, 1953. *In tracing his wife's and his genealogical history, found his wife's showed Samurais and Government officials served Japan. Examples are Supreme Court Justice Yokota (deceased) and Former Prime Minister Yasuhiro Nakasone (1981-87). Related by marriage to her Ouchi name. His relatives came from East Ridings, Yorkshire in England in 1638. Probably his most famous relative he knows was Dr. John F. Boynton who served U.S. Presidents Lincoln and Fillimore in many capacities documented in U.S. History. The other one was Commodore Louis R. Boynton who invented the Great Lakes Ice-Breaking system and later sold it to Russia. Came from a family of inventors and teachers.* Asst. mgr. Speigel J & R, Kalamazoo, 1947-48; with U.S. Army, 1948-74, ret., 1974; with Rockwell/Collins div., Newport Beach, Calif., 1974-78, supr. material, investment recovery coord., 1974-81, coord., 1981-88; investment recovery supr., coord. Rockwell/CDC, Santa Ana, Calif., 1981-88, coord. investment recovery, 1982-86, shipping supr., investment recovery, environ. coord., 1982-88, 1987-88, material coord., 1988, environ. coord. Rockwell/DCD, Newport Beach, 1988-89, ret.; mem. faculty Western Mich. U., 1955-58. Trustee Orange County Vector Control Dist., 1980—, bd. sec. 1991, bd. v.p. 1992—; pres., 1993. Trustee Corp. Bd., 1993, pres., 1993-94, mem. exec. bd. dirs., 1994, mem. bd.; mem. adv. panel for bus./econ.devel. Calif. State Legislature, 1979-86. *Professionally both in the military and industry took jobs others shunned and developed them into area that others would fight to get when he left. As examples, through review, work and coordination the Divisional and Corporate Policies on Investment recovery was re-written and provided greater returns more economically. The other area that was reviewed and setup was environmental control of hazardous waste in accordance with EPA rules and regulations. It helped make the division environmental friendly. In the military he led by example throughout his career.* Decorated Bronze Star. Mem. Assn. U.S. Army, Assn. U.S. Army, Non-Commd. Officers Assn., Mosquito and Vector Control Assn. Calif. (v.p. 1992, pres. 1993), Nat. Geog. Soc. Republican. Roman Catholic. Home and Office: 5314 W Lucky Way Santa Ana CA 92704-1048

BOYRER, ELAINE M., principal. Prin. North Shore High Sch., Glen Head, N.Y., 1988—. Recipient Blue Ribbon Sch. award U.S. Dept. Edn., 1990-91. Office: North Shore High Sch 450 Glen Cove Ave Glen Head NY 11545-1198*

BOYSE, EDWARD ARTHUR, research physician; b. Worthing, Sussex, Eng., Aug. 11, 1923; came to U.S., 1960; s. Arthur and Dorothy Vera (Mellersh) B. MB, BS, U. London, 1952, MD, 1957. Mem. med. staff various hosps. Eng., 1952-57; researcher Guy's Hosp., London, 1957-60; researcher Sch. Medicine, NYU, 1960-71, adj. prof., 1971—; prof. Cornell Grad. Sch. Med. Sci., N.Y.C., 1969-89; assoc. scientist Meml. Sloan-Kettering Inst., N.Y.C., 1962-64, assoc. mem., 1964-67, mem., 1967-89; Disting. prof. U. Ariz., Tucson, 1989-94; prof. emeritus, 1994—; affiliated scientist Monell Chem. Senses Ctr., Phila. Contbr. articles to profl. jours. Served with RAF, 1941-46. Recipient Tumor Immunology award Cancer Research Inst., N.Y.C., 1975, Isaac Adler award Rockefeller U., Harvard U., 1976. Fellow Royal Soc., Am. Acad. Arts and Sci., Nat. Acad. Sci. Office: Dept Microbiology Immunology U Ariz PO Box 24-5049 Tucson AZ 85724-5049

BOYSE, PETER DENT, academic administrator; b. Saginaw, Mich., Mar. 24, 1945; s. John Wesley and Ellen Elizabeth (Dent) B.; m. Barbra Ann Meehan, Sept. 2, 1972; children: Heather, Cassandra. BA, Albion Coll., 1967; MS, U. Mich., 1969, Oreg. State U., 1973; PhD, Oreg. State U., 1987. Nuclear scientist Westinghouse, Pitts., 1969-71; dir. student activities Calif. State U., Northridge, 1973-74, epic dir., 1974-76; dir. student devel. Linn-Benton Community Coll., Albany, Oreg., 1976-79, ctr. dir., 1979-82, asst. to pres., 1982-88; exec. v.p. Delta Coll., University Center, Mich., 1988—, pres., 1993—; facilitator Emerging Leaders Inst., Ann Arbor, Mich., 1990. Contbr. articles to profl. jours. Unit chmn. Bay County United Way, Bay City, Mich., 1990; com. mem. South Willamette Rsch. Corridor, Albany, 1988. Mem. Am. Assn. Community and Jr. Colls. (NCSPOD 1990, NCRD 1988, NCRP 1988, NCCR 1988), Partnerships in Edn., Midland C. of C. Leadership (com. mem. 1990), Bus., Union, Govt., Torch Club, Rotary, Phi Kappa Phi, Sigma Pi Sigma, Kappa Mu Epsilon. Avocations: fishing, golf, travel. Office: Delta Coll 1961 Delta Dr University Center MI 48710*

BOYSEN, LARS, financial consultant; b. Vejle, Denmark, Aug. 23, 1948; came to U.S., 1975; s. Svenn and Erna (Thomsen) B. BS in Bus. Adminstrn., The Aarhus Sch. Bus., Denmark, 1973, MS in Econs., 1975; postgrad., U. Wash., 1981-82. Mktg. research analyst Santa Fe Fed., San Bernardino, Calif., 1975-77, mktg. research mgr., 1977-79, v.p., mktg. dir., 1979-81; v.p., office adminstrn. mgr. Pacific Fed. Savs. & Loan Assn., Costa Mesa, Calif., 1981-82; v.p., human resources and corp. research dir. Pacific First Bank (formerly Pacific Savs. Bank), Costa Mesa, 1982-86, sr. v.p. corp. services, 1986-89, sr. v.p. adminstrn., 1989-90; v.p. client svcs. TSG Fin., Inc., L.A., 1991-95; franchise owner Jackson Hewitt Tax Svc., Upland, Calif., 1996—; fin. advisor Waddell & Reed, Rancho Cucamonga, Calif., 1997—. Recipient First award The Advt. Club, Los Angeles, 1979, Andy award of merit The Advt. Club, N.Y.C., 1980. Office: Jackson Hewitt Tax Svc 803 Frankfort Ave Huntington Beach CA 92648-4904

BOYSEN, MELICENT PEARL, finance company executive; b. Houston, Dec. 1, 1943; d. William Thomas and Mildred Pearl (Walker) Richardson; m. Stephen M. Boysen, Sept. 10, 1961 (dec. 1973); children: Marshella, Stephanie, Stephen. Student, Cen. Mo. State U., 1973-75. Owner, pres. Boysen Enterprises, Kansas City, Mo., 1973-93; fin. cons., underwriter New Eng. Life Ins. Co., Kansas City, 1978-81; owner, pres. Boysen Agri-Svcs., Kansas City, 1984-94; pres. Boysen & Assocs., Inc., Kansas City, 1987—; stockholder, pres. Am. Crumb Rubber, Inc., Kansas City, 1996—; cons. San Luis Rey (Calif.) Tribal Water Authority, Wind River (Wyo.) Reservation, Cheyenne River (S.D.) Sioux, Iroquois Nations (N.Y.), 1983—; founding bd. dirs. , pres. Am. Indian Youth Orgn., Visible Horizons, 1987—. Founding bd. dirs. Rose Brooks Ctr. Battered Women, Kansas City, 1979-87, treas., 1979-81; exec. dir. The Flame Spirit Run, 1992; citationist, 1993; pres. Vol. Action Awards Program. Recipient Women of Conscience award Panel Am. Women of Greater Kansas City. Mem. Internat. Fin. Planners Assn., Internat. Agri-Bus. Assn., DAR, Kans. C. of C. and Industry, Kansas City C. of C. Methodist. Avocations: stamp collecting, sports cars. Office: Boysen & Assocs 706 W 42nd St Ste 108 Kansas City MO 64111-4070

BOYSEN, THOMAS CYRIL, school system administrator; b. Sioux Falls, S.D., Nov. 16, 1940; s. Cyril Joseph and Dolores Margaret (Parry) B.; m. PoChan Mar, Aug. 25, 1964 (div. 1980); children: Thomas C., Anne-Marie Lee; m. Laurie Louise Shaffer, June 25, 1983. BA in History, Stanford U., 1962; Diploma in Grad. Edn., Makerere U., Kampala, Uganda, Africa, 1964; EdD in Edn. Adminstrn., Harvard U., 1969. Geography master Kabaa High Sch., Thika, Kenya, Africa, 1964-66; dir. adminstrn. Bellevue Pub. Schs., Wash., 1968-70; supt. schs. Pasco Sch. Dist. Wash., 1970-73, Pelham Pub. Schs., N.Y., 1973-77, Redlands United Sch. Dist., Calif., 1977-80, Conejo Valley Unified Sch. Dist., Thousand Oaks, Calif., 1980-87, San Diego County Schs., 1987-90, Ky. Commn. Edn., 1991-95, sr. v.p. edn., 1995—.*

BOYT, PATRICK ELMER, farmer, real estate executive; b. Liberty, Tex., Sept. 22, 1940; s. Elmer Vernon and Kathleen (Nelson) B.; B.S. in C.E., U. Tex., 1963; m. Elizabeth Ruth Jefferson, June 16, 1962; children: Jefferson Elmer, Mark Cecil. Owner, mng. ptnr. Boyt Properties; dir. First State Bank, Liberty, 1978-89, Beaumont State Bank, 1969-78, Farm Credit Banks of Tex., 1986-88; mem. Coun. on Small Bus. and Agr. of Fed. Reserve Bank of Dallas, 1989-94; mng. ptnr. Kathleen N. Boyt Family Ltd. Partnership, 1996-99, Ind. Executor, Estate of Kathleen Boyt, 1998—. Bd. dirs. Beaumont Art Mus., 1973—, Devers Ind. Sch. Dist., 1974-90; mem. Tex. Commn. for Arts, 1978-81; bd. dirs. Kersting Meml. Hosp., 1976-83; supr. Lower Trinity Soil and Water Conservation Dist., 1972-90. Democrat. Presbyterian. Home: 5672 Longwood St Beaumont TX 77707-1891 Office: PO Box 575 Devers TX 77538-0575

BOYUM, KEITH OREL, political scientist, consultant; b. Lakota, N.D., Aug. 20, 1945; s. Orel A. and Doris Marie (Craig) B.; m. Renae Ruth Pieri, June 19, 1971; children: Nicole, Andrew. BA, U. N.D., 1967; MA, U. Minn., 1971, PhD, 1974. Asst. prof. Calif. State U., Fullerton, 1972-76, assoc. prof., 1976-80, prof. polit. sci., 1980—, acting assoc. v.p., 1983-84, chair acad. senate, 1984-85, 95-96, chair divsn. polit. sci. and criminal justice, 1996—; study dir. Nat. Rsch. Coun./NAS, Washington, 1977-79; coord. edn. policy fellowship program Inst. for Ednl. Leadership, Washington, 1985-95; cons., evaluator Jud. Coun Calif., San Francisco, 1991-95; lectr. Young Pres.'s Orgn., Dallas, 1992, 96; mem. statewide adv. bd. Ctr. for Calif. Studies, Sacramento, 1992—. Editor-in-chief Justice Sys. Jour., 1989-94; co-editor: Empirical theories about Courts, 1983, California Government in National Perspective, 1998, Forecasting the Impact of Legislation on Courts, 1980. Pres. Good Shepherd Luth. Ch., Irvine, Calif., 1984; mem. policy bd. Luth. Office Pub. Policy, Sacramento, 1995-98; mem., chair govt. affairs Acad. Senate of Calif. State U., Long Beach, 1986-96; faculty, 1st nat. conf. on eliminating bias in the cts. Nat. Ctr. for State Cts., Williamsburg, Va., 1995. Recipient Warren E. Burger award for achievement in ct. adminstrn. Nat. Ctr. for State Cts., 1994. Mem. Am. Polit. Sci. Assn., Law and Soc. Assn., Western Polit. Sci. Assn., Phi Beta Kappa. Democrat. Avocation: youth sports coach. Office: Calif State U Divsn Polit Sci/Crim Just PO Box 6848 Fullerton CA 92834-6848

BOZALIS, JOHN RUSSELL, physician; b. St. Louis, Sept. 19, 1939; s. George Sauter and Ruth (Russell) B.; m. Sharon Louise Sabo, June 21, 1963; children: John Jr., David L., Diana. BA, U. Okla., 1961, MD, 1965; MS, U. Mich., 1971. Diplomate Am. Bd. Internal Medicine, Am. Bd. Allergy and Immunology. Intern Henry Ford Hosp., Detroit, 1965-66, resident, 1966-68, chief resident, 1968-69; fellow in allergy-immunology U. Mich., Ann Arbor, 1969-71, instr., 1969-71; clin. asst. prof. U. Tex., San Antonio, 1972-73; pvt. practice Okla. Allergy Clinic, Oklahoma City, 1973—; clin. instr. Coll. Medicine, U. Okla., 1973, clin. asst. prof., 1977-83, clin. assoc. prof., 1983-89, clin. prof., 1989—; mem. courtesy staff Mercy Hosp., Bapt. Hosp., Deaconess Hosp., St. Anthony Hosp., Presbyn. Hosp., Children's Hosp., Okla. Tchg. Hosp., S.W. Med. Ctr. Trustee Casady Sch., 1977-85, United Way Okla. City, chmn. profl. divsn. 1983, Okla. Health Scis. Found.; bd. dirs. Infant Ctr., 1983-86, Allied Arts Okla. City, 1984-86, 92, Hosp. Hospitality House, 1983-86; vice chmn. health scis. ctr. U. Okla. Centennial Commn.; bd. trustees McGee Eye Inst., mem. search com. for chmn. dept. ophthalmology and dir., 1991; active Com. of 100, 1991; bd. trustees Okla. City Pub. Schs. Found., 1989—, Okla. Orthopedic and Arthritis Found., Inc., Bone and Joint Hosp., 1993. Maj. USAF, 1971-73. Recipient Regents' Alumni award U. Okla., 1992; named Physician of Yr.-Pvt. Practice, U. Okla. Coll. of Medicine Alumni Assn., 1993, recipient dean's award, 1998. Fellow ACP, Am. Coll. Chest Physicians, Am. Acad. Allergy; mem. AMA, Am. Thoracic Soc., Okla. State Med. Assn. (del. 1993—, vice spkr. ho. dels. 1997, trustee 1993—), Okla. Lung Assn., Okla. Thoracic Soc. (pres. 1979), John M. Sheldon Soc., Okla. County Med. Soc. (editor Bull. 1978-83, chmn. orientation com. 1989—, pres. 1996, bd. trustees 1996—), Osler Soc. (pres. 1984), Okla. City Acad. Medicine, Robert M. Bird Soc., U. Okla. Coll. Medicine Alumni Assn. (chmn. rsch. com., pres. 1983-85), Okla. City C. of C. (bd. dirs. 1988-90). Republican. Episcopal. Avocations: bird hunting, golf, fly fishing, travel, gardening. Office: Okla Allergy Clin Inc PO Box 26827 Oklahoma City OK 73126-0827

BOZDECH, MAREK JIRI, physician; b. Wildflecken, Bavaria, Federal Republic Germany, Oct. 12, 1946; s. Jiri Josef and Zofia Jadwiga (Swiatecka) B.; m. Frances Barclay Craig, Dec. 22, 1967; children: Elizabeth, Andrew, Matthew. AB, U. Mich., 1967; MD, Wayne State U., 1972. Diplomate Am. Bd. Internal Medicine, Am. Bd. Med. Oncology, Am. Bd. Hematology. Intern and resident in internal medicine U. Wis. Hosps., Madison, 1972-75, dir. clin. hematology lab., 1978-82, dir. bone marrow transplantation, 1984-85; asst. prof. medicine U. Wis., Madison, 1978-84, assoc. prof. medicine, 1984-85; clin. fellow in hematology Moffitt Hosp. U. Calif., San Francisco, 1975-76, postdoctoral fellow in hematology Cancer Research Inst., 1976-78, research assoc. Cancer Research Inst., 1977-78, assoc. prof., 1985-89; dir. adult bone marrow transplantation U. Calif. Med. Ctr., San Francisco, 1985-89; chief oncology Kaiser Permanente Med. Ctr., Santa Rosa, Calif., 1989-91; pvt. practice specializing in oncology Hematology Redwood Regional Oncology Ct., Santa Rosa, 1991—. Contbr. articles to profl. jours. Scout leader Boy Scouts Am., Novato, Calif., 1985; bd. trustees Pacific Found. Med. Care, 1995—. Recipient Nat. Research Service award NIH, 1977-78; Wayne State U. scholar, 1971. Mem. ACP, Am. Soc. Hematology, Am. Soc. Clin. Oncology, Assn. No. Calif. Oncologists (bd. dirs. 1994-97), Sonoma County Med. Assn. (bd. dirs. 1994-96). Avocations: skiing, gardening, music, tennis, theatre. Home: 50 La Placita Ct Novato CA 94945-1244 Office: U Calif Med Ctr A502 M Redwood Regional Oncology 121 Sotoyome St Ste 203 Santa Rosa CA 95405-4822

BOZE, BETSY VOGEL, university dean, marketing educator; b. Shreveport, La., Sept. 18, 1953; d. Leroy Vogel and Betty Gray (Garrett) Vogel McDonald; children: Christopher Lee Boze, Broox Garrett Vogel Boze, Lee Gray Boze. BS in Psychology, So. Meth. U., 1974; postgrad., Am. Grad. Sch. Internat. Mgmt., 1975; MBA, So. Meth. U., 1975; PhD, U. Ark., 1984. Lectr. U. Md., 1975, 78-80; asst. prof. St. Bonaventure U., Olean, N.Y., 1977-78; instr. U. Ark., Fayetteville, 1979-83; asst. prof. Centenary Coll. of La., Shreveport, 1983-89; assoc. prof., chair U. Alaska, Anchorage, 1989-94; dean, prof. mktg. U. Tex., Brownsville, 1994—; pres. Boze & Assocs., Shreveport and Anchorage, 1983-94; dir. Women in Mgmt. Conf., Shreveport, 1983-89; mem. continuing edn. com. Hispanic Ednl. Telecomms. Sys., San Juan, P.R., 1995—; co-dir. Tex. Transp. Inst. Ctr. for Ports and Waterways, 1994—, HERS/Mid-Am. Summer Inst., 1996; vis. faculty Portland State U. in Khaborosk, Russia, 1994. Mem. editl. bd. Jour. for Not-for-Profit Mktg., 1990—; contbr. articles to profl. jours., chpts. to textbooks. V.p. Atlantic Mktg. Assn., Orlando, Fla., 1988-90; pres. Susitna coun. Girl Scouts U.S., Anchorage, 1992-94; pres. Wish Upon a Star, Shreveport, 1988-90; mem. program com. Commonwealth North, Anchorage, 1989-94; Tex. coord. Nat. Identification program Am. Coun. on Edn. U.S. Dept. Edn. Internat. fellow U. Hawaii, 1990. Mem. Leadership Tex., AAUP, AAUW, Petroleum Club of Anchorage, Delta Delta Delta (pres. alumnae chpt. 1989-92). Methodist. Avocations: reading, swimming, backgammon. Home: 1409 Avenida Santa Ana Rancho Viejo TX 78575 Office: U Tex Brownsville 80 Fort Brown St Brownsville TX 78520-4956

BOZEK, THOMAS, state legislator; b. Manchester, N.H.. VS, Ctrl. Conn. State U., 1969. Mem. Conn. State Senate, 1995—. Mem. Common Coun., New Britain, 1985-87, maj. leader, 1989—; commr., chmn. fin. bd.; pub. works commr.; chmn. Taxation and Assessment Commn. With U.S. Army and Air N.G., 1961-93. Office: 32 Ten Acre Rd New Britain CT 06052-1532*

BOZELL, L. BRENT, III, communications executive. Founder, chmn. bd. dirs. Media Rsch. Ctr., 1987—; founder, chmn. Parents TV Coun. Co-editor: And That's the Way It Isn't: A Reference Guide to Media Bias; contbr. articles to newspapers including The Wall St. Journal, The Washington Post, L.A. Times, Nat. Rev., others. Founder, pres. Conservative Victory Com.,1987—; nat. fin. chmn. Buchanan for President campaign; fin. dir., pres. Nat. Conservative Polit. Action Com. Office: Media Rsch Ctr 113 S West St Ste 200 Alexandria VA 22314-2851*

BOZEMAN, FRANK CARMACK, lawyer; b. Greenwood, Miss., Oct. 16, 1933; s. Frank Carmack and Mamie Hyatt (Pyle) B.; m. Mary Ireland Callcott, Dec. 29, 1961; children: Frank C. III, William Pyle, Thomas Anderson. BA, U. of South, 1955; MA, U. Va., 1956; JD, Washington and Lee U., 1960. Bar: Fla. 1960, Va. 1960. Assoc. Beggs and Lane, Pensacola, Fla., 1960-65; ptnr. Harrell, Wiltshire, Bozeman, Clark & Stone, Pensacola, 1965-75, Carlton, Fields, Ward, Emmanuel, Smith & Cutler, P.A., Pensacola, 1975-93, Bozeman, Jenkins & Matthews, Pensacola, 1993—. Editor Washington and Lee Law Rev., 1960. Chmn. Eagle Scout rev. com., Boy Scouts Am., Pensacola, 1961-63; trustee U. Of South, 1990-96. Capt. USAF, 1956-57. Mem. Am. Bd. Trial Advs. (pres. Pensacola chpt. 1989-90), Fla. Def. Lawyers Assn., Fedn. Ins. and Corp. Counsel, Register of Pre-Eminent Lawyers, Def. Rsch. Inst., Phi Delta Phi (Grad. of Yr. award 1960). Republican. Episcopalian. Avocations: sailing, gardening, Civil War history and research. Home: 122 W Lloyd St Pensacola FL 32501-2637 Office: Bozeman Jenkins & Matthews PO Box 13105 Pensacola FL 32591-3105

BOZEMAN, ROSS ELLIOT, engineering executive; b. New Orleans, Feb. 16, 1967; s. Robert Ray and Rita (Findley) B. BS cum laude, La. Tech. Inst., 1990. Registered profl. engr., Tex., 1998, La. 1999. Assoc. vessel engr. Litwin Engrs. and Constructors, Houston, 1990-94, vessel engr., 1994-96; engrng. mgr. Bergaila Engrng. Svcs., Inc., Houston, 1996-99; engrng. mgr., owner Bozeman Engrng., Houston, 1999—. Mem. ASME (assoc.), Tau Beta Pi. Avocations: country and western dancing, drag racing, study of vehicle dynamics, finite element analysis. Fax: 713-278-0405. E-mail: rossboz@aol.com. Home and Office: Ste 408 7979 Westheimer Ste 408 Houston TX 77063

BOZORTH, SQUIRE NEWLAND, lawyer; b. Portland, Oreg., Oct. 25, 1935; s. Squire Smith and Ethel Elizabeth (Newland) B.; m. Louise Crosby Mathews, Aug. 9, 1967; children: Squire Mathews, Caroline Rutgers. BS, U. Oreg., 1958; LLB, NYU, 1961. Bar: N.Y. 1961. Assoc. Milbank, Tweed, Hadley & McCloy, N.Y.C., 1961-70, ptnr., 1970-95, cons. ptnr., 1995—; assoc. counsel Rockefeller U., 1973-83. Bd. dirs., mem. exec. com., v.p. Fedn. Protestant Welfare Agys., 1970-89; bd. dirs. The Hess Found., 1988-99, The Hurricane Allen St. Lucia Rebuilding Fund, 1988-99; pres. bd. trustees Scarsdale Pub. Libr., 1991-93; trustee Marilyn M. Simpson Charitable Trusts; trustee, exec. com. The Parks Coun., 1991-94, Internat. House, 1991-94, Diocese of N.Y., Episcopal Ch., 1995-98. Mem. N.Y. State Bar Assn. (exec. com. internat. law sect., chmn. internat. estate and trust law com. 1990-93), N.Y. Law Inst. (exec. com.), Century Assn., Phi Beta Kappa. Episcopalian. Home: 25 E End Ave New York NY 10028-7052 Office: Milbank Tweed Hadley & McCoy 1 Chase Manhattan Plz Fl 47 New York NY 10005-1413

BOZZOLO, DONNA LOUISE, family nurse practitioner; b. Cambridge, N.Y., Dec. 12, 1961; d. John Charles and Donna Mae (Millington) Green; m. Alan M. Bozzolo, May 21, 1983. Diploma, St. Elizabeth Hosp., Utica, N.Y., 1982; BSN, SUNY, Utica, 1989; MS, Russell Sage Coll., 1991, cert. FNP program, 1996-98. CEN. Charge nurse med.-surg. dept. Meml. Hosp. Greene County, Catskill, N.Y., 1982-83; critical care nurse Meml. Hosp., Albany, N.Y., 1983-87; staff nurse N.Y. State Dept. Correctional Svcs., Coxsackie, 1987-89; nurse dir. emergency dept. Columbia Green Med. Ctr., Hudson, N.Y., 1994-95; nurse dir. emergency dept. Amsterdam (N.Y.) Meml. Hosp., 1995-96, FNP,, 1998—. Mem. ANA, N.Y. State Nurses Assn., Emergency Nurses Assn., N.Y. State Coalition Nurse Practitiones, Sigma Theta Tau.

BOZZUTO, MICHAEL ADAM, wholesale grocery company executive; b. Waterbury, Conn., 1956; s. Adam John and Lillian B. BBA, Stetson U., 1978. Pres., CEO, treas. Bozzuto's, Inc., Cheshire, Conn., 1978—; former mem. adv. bd. Bank of Boston-Conn.; bd. dirs. IGA USA. Trustee Cheshire Acad. Mem. Food Mktg. Inst., New Eng. Wholesale Food Distbrs. Assn. (former chmn.), Food Distbrs. Internat. (bd. govs.), Conn. Food Assn. (bd. dirs., Person of Yr. 1999), Lambda Chi. Roman Catholic. Office: Bozzuto's Inc 275 Schoolhouse Rd Cheshire CT 06410-1257

BRAATEN, LINDA MARIE SKURDELL, secondary education educator; b. Northwood, N.D., June 4, 1946; d. Theodore Arnold and Mildred Jeanette (Samnoen) Skurdell; m. Harvey Gordon Braaten, Sept. 3, 1966; children: Susan Marie Braaten Thorson, Jodee Miscielle Braaten Muus, Rachel Elizabeth, Jeffrey Michael. BS in Edn., N.D. State U., 1969. Lic. vocat. edn., N.D. Food technologist The Pillsbury Co., Mpls., 1970-73; salesperson Pierce Mobile Homes, West Fargo, N.D., 1974-76; tchr. Northwood (N.D.) Pub. Sch., 1976—. Sec.-treas. Northwood Tchr's. Assn., 1978, 85. Mem. NEA, Am. Vocat. Assn., N.D. Edn. Assn., Future Homemakers Am. (dist. advisor 1987, 88, 91-95, 96—, co-state advisor 1996—, Master Advisor award 1991, Advisor Mentor award 1996, hon. mem. N.D. 1997), Family and Consumer Scis. (N.D. assn., adv. bd. 1996—). Avocations: playing piano, traveling, flower gardening. Home: 4735 3d Ave NE Aneta ND 58212-9605 Office: Northwood Pub Sch 216 S Houghen St Northwood ND 58267-0250

BRAATEN, THOMAS A., career officer; b. Harvey, Ill., Apr. 15, 1946; m. Susan McCrory; 1 child, Kristin. Grad., Officer Candidates Sch., Quantico, Va., Basic Sch., Amphibious Warfare Sch., Marine Corps Command and Staff, Tex. Christian U., 1982, Dept. State Fgn. Svc. Inst., InterAm. Def. Coll. Enlisted USMC, 1965, advanced through grades to maj. gen., 1996, ground radar repairman, naval aviator, 1968; assigned to Marine Medium Helicopter Squadron 263 MCAS(H) USMC, Santa Ana, Calif.; instr. pilot HMT-302; officer-in-charge CH-46 Post Maintenance Inspection Pilot Sch.; joined HMM-263, aircraft maintenance officer; aircraft maintenance officer H&MS-36 Sub Unit 2, Atsugi, Japan; with British Royal Navy Royal Naval Air Sta., Yeovilton, 1975-77; with Marine Corps Amphibious Warfare Presentation Team, Quantico, 1977-78; aviation instr. Amphibious Warfare Sch.; asst. ops. officer for marine aircraft group 24 First Marine Brigade, Kaneohe Bay, Hawaii, 1982-84; exec. officer HMM-165, 1984-85; comdr. Marine Corps. Airt Bases, Eastern Area, Cherry Point, 1999—, General Marine Airstation, Eastern Area, Cherry Point, 1999—. Decorated Legion of Merit, D.F.C., Air medal with Strike Flight Numeral 52. Office: Marine Corp Air Station PSC Box 8003 Cherry Point NC 28533*

BRABANT, LORI ANN, nursing administrator; b. Lynn, Mass., Sept. 28, 1960; d. Richard Woodruff and Nancy Joan (Higgins) Amidon; m. Timothy Cecil Brabant, Sept. 1, 1984; children: Timothy Jr., Daniel, Jillian. AD in Secretarial Sci. cum laude, No. Essex C.C., 1980; diploma LPN, Whittier Regional Vocat., 1983; ADN cum laude, St. Clair County C.C., 1993; student, U. Mich., 1995—. Cert. BCLS instr., ACLS; RN, Mich. LPN staff nurse Whitter Rehab. Hosp., Haverhill, Mass., 1983-84; LPN charge nurse Amesbury (Mass.) Nursing and Retirement, 1984-85; LPN staff nurse River Dist. Hosp., East China, Mich., 1990-93, RN critical care, 1993-95, RN hosp. supr., 1994-97; RN relief staff nurse McKenzie Meml. Hosp., Sandusky, Mich., 1994-97; RN Personal Home Care, Marlette, Mich., 1997-98; continuous quality improvement mem. River Dist. Hosp., 1994-95. Mem. St. Mary Ch. Port Sanilac, 1988-94, PTA Orgn. Carsonville-Port Sanilac Sch., 1997-98; chairperson Port Sanilac Summer Festival com., 1990-94. Recipient Outstanding Achievement award Jerry Lewis Telethon, 1989. Mem. PTO, Carsonville Port Samilac Sch., 1997-98, United States Jaycees. Roman Catholic. Avocations: reading, camping, aerobics, travelling. Home: 7023 Palis Verdis Dr Port Sanilac MI 48469-9735 Office: Personal Home Care 3090 Main St Ste 4 Marlette MI 48453-1279

BRABEC, ROSEMARY JEAN, retail executive; b. St. Paul, Apr. 5, 1951; d. Peter Michael and Mary Jane (Nigro) Jacovitch; m. Loren W. Brabec, Sept. 16, 1972; children: Brenda Marie, Daniel Joseph. BS in Elem. Edn., St. Cloud State U., 1973. Tchr. Ind. Sch. Dist. 314, Braham, Minn., 1975-78; owner, mgr. Rosemary's Quilts and Baskets, Braham, 1988-97; dir. Community Edn. Adv. Coun., Braham, 1978-95, chmn., 1992-95. Designer quilt block representing Minn. div. AAUW for display at Internat. Fedn. Univ. Women conv., Calif. Chmn. P.I.C.K. Immunization Clinic, Braham, 1978-85; vol. driver coord. Home Delivered Meals, Braham, 1984—; vol. coord. Com. to Build Robert Leathers Playground, Braham, 1985. Mem. AAUW (Minn. sec. 1985-87, 98-99, v.p. 1987-88, historian 1997-98, pres. 1999—), Minn. Quilters.

BRACCO, LORRAINE, actress; b. Bklyn., 1955; m. Harvey Keitel (div.); m. Edward James Olmos, Jan. 28, 1994; children: Margaux, Stella. Studied, Actors Studio; studied with Stella Adler, Ernie Martin, John Strasberg. model in Europe. Films include The Pick-Up Artist, 1987, Someone to Watch Over Me, 1987, Sing, 1989, The Dream Team, 1989, Goodfellas, 1990 (Acad. award nominee for best supporting actress 1990), Talent for the Game, 1991, Switch, 1991, Medicine Man, 1992, Radio Flyer, 1992, Traces of Red, 1992, (Showtime movie) Scam, 1993, Being Human, 1994, Even Cowgirls Get the Blues, 1994, The Basketball Diaries, 1995, Hackers, 1995, Les Menteurs, 1996, Your Aura is Throbbing, 1999, Ladies Room, 1999; on TV in Getting Gotti, 1996, Lifeline, 1996, The Taking of Pelham One Two Three, 1998, The Sopranos, 1999; off-Broadway play Goose and Tom-Tom. *

BRACE, MARGARET DENISE, writer; b. Takoma Park, Md., Oct. 31, 1960; d. Kenneth Earl and Margaret (Moran) Lerch; m. Keith Allen Brace, Oct. 27, 1984; children: Kelin Moran, Devra Gwynn. Student, Oxford U., 1981; BA, St. Marys Coll., 1982; MA in Spl. Edn., Loyola Coll., Balt., 1986. Cert. tchr. spl. edn., Md. Clk. CIA, McLean, Va., 1978-79; tchr. St. Michaels Grammar Sch., Silver Spring, Md., 1982-83; tchr., adminstr. Chautauqua Acad., Balt., 1983-86; spl. edn. tchr. Balt. County Pub. Schs., Balt., 1986-91; pvt. practice Balt., 1991—; instr. Sylvan Learning Ctrs., Balt., 1986. Author: (poetry) The Voice Within, 1996, Best Poems of '97, 1997, of '98, 1998. Modeling instr. Barbizon, Bethesda, Md., 1982-84; founder Independence Day Parade, Bay Country, Md., 1996—; vol. Oliver Beach Elem. Sch., Balt., 1996—, Vacation Bible Sch., Balt., 1995—. Named to Athletic Hall of Fame, St. Marys Coll., 1991. Mem. Profl. Disc Golf Assn., Marian Garden Club (founder 1996). Roman Catholic. Avocations: gardening, basketball, tennis, disc golf, bonsai. Home and Office: 12850 Cunninghill Cove Rd Baltimore MD 21220-1177

BRACEWELL, RONALD NEWBOLD, electrical engineering educator; b. Sydney, Australia, July 22, 1921; s. Cecil Charles and Valerie Zilla (McGowan) B.; m. Helen Mary Lester Elliott; children: Catherine Wendy, Mark Cecil. BSc in Math. and Physics, U. Sydney, 1941, B in Engring., 1943, M. in Engring. with 1st class honors, 1948; PhD, Cambridge (Eng.) U., 1951. Sr. rsch. officer Radiophysics Lab., Commonwealth Sci. and Indsl. Rsch. Orgn., Sydney, 1949-54; vis. asst. prof. radio astronomy U. Calif., Berkeley, 1954-55; mem. elec. engring. faculty Stanford U., 1955—, Lewis M. Terman prof. and fellow in elec. engring., 1974-79, now Terman prof. emeritus elec. engring.; Pollock Meml. lectr. U. Sydney, 1978; Tektronix Disting. Visitor, summer 1981; Christensen fellow St. Catherine's Coll., Oxford, autumn 1987; sr. vis. fellow Inst. Astronomy, fellow commoner Churchill Coll., Cambridge U., autumn 1988; Bunyan lectr. Stanford U., 1996; mem. adv. panels NSF, Naval Rsch. Lab., Office Naval Rsch., NAS, Nat. Radio Astronomy Obs., Jet Propulsion Lab. Adv. Group on Radio Experiments in Space, Advanced Rsch. Projects Agy. Author: The Fourier Transform and Its Applications, 1965, 3rd edit., 1986, The Galactic Club: Intelligent Life in Outer Space, 1974, The Hartley Transform, 1986, Two-Dimensional Imaging, 1995; co-author: Radio Astronomy, 1955; translator: Radio Astronomy (J.L. Steinberg and J. Lequeux); editor: Paris Symposium on Radio Astronomy, 1959; former mem. editl. bd. Internat. Jour. Imaging Sys. and Tech., Planetary and Space Sci., Proceedings of the Astron. Soc. Pacific, Cosmic Search, Jour. Computer Assisted Tomography; mem. bd. ann. rev. Astronomy and Astrophysics, 1961-68; contbr. articles and revs. to jours., chpts. to books; patentee in field. Recipient Duddell Premium, Instn. Elec. Engrs., London, 1952, Inaugural Alumni award Sydney U., 1992; Fulbright travel grantee, 1954, William Gurling Watson traveling fellow, 1978, 86. Fellow IEEE (life, Heinrich Hertz Gold medal 1994), AAAS, Royal Astron. Soc., Astron. Soc. Australia; mem. Inst. Medicine of NAS (fgn. assoc.), Astron. Soc. Pacific (life), Am. Astron. Soc. (past councilor), Internat. Astron. Union, Internat. Sci. Radio Union, Order of Australia (officer). Home: 836 Santa Fe Ave Stanford CA 94305-1023 Office: Stanford U 329A Durand Bldg Stanford CA 94305-4055

BRACEY, COOKIE FRANCES LEE, minister; b. Phila., Mar. 14, 1945; d. John Daniels and Evelyn (Jarvis) Bracey. B in Social Work, Temple U., 1983; MDiv, Wesley Theol. Sem., 1990. Administrv. asst. United Meth. Ch., Phila., 1963-86, parish community devel., 1984-86; local pastor United Meth. Ch., Catonsville, Ellicott City, Md., 1986-90; chaplain Meth. Hosp., Phila., 1990—; pastor St. Luke Snyder Ave United Meth. Ch., Phila., 1990-92, St. Matthews United Meth. Ch., Trevose, Pa., 1992—; missionary El Salvador, 1998; missionary, Brazil, 1988, Costa Rica, 1989, Dominican Republic, 1992, Zim Babwe, Africa, 1998; pastor St. Matthews United Meth. Ch., Trevose, Pa., 1992; Meth. mission tour, London, 1992, Israel, 1994; adj. faculty Ea. Bapt. Theol. Sem., Wynnewood, Pa., 1994—, Henry George Sch., Phila., 1996—; mem. faculty Phila. Sch. Devel. Mins., 1997, fac. mem. Sch. of Devel. Ministries, 1997. Mem. Multi-Cultural Task Force, Phila. 1980, Victims & Crime Task Force, Phila. Ministers Law Enforcement Support Unit, Phila. Community Assistance Network; del. World Meth. Conf., Rio Janero, Brazil, 1996; chaplain CAP Auxiliary USAF, 1996—, Phila. Prison Sys., 1996—; mem. Phila. Mayor's Commn. on Literacy; missionary Zim Babwe, Africa, 1998; faculty Phila. Sch. of Developing Ministries, 1997; bd. dirs. Archives and History United Meth. Ch., 1997; del. Clergywoman Convocation, Atlanta, 1997; cert. mentor for supr. for ministry candidates. Recipient Outstanding Clergywoman award Nat. Assn. Clergywomen, 1990, Peace & Justice award Ch. Women United, 1992, Ministry award Harry Hosier United Meth. Ch., 1992, Preacher of Yr. award, 1998. Mem. Temple Univ. Soc. Adminstrn. Alumni Assn., Asian Am. Youth Assn., Nat. Fellowship Local, Black United Meth. Preachers (v.p.), Black Clergy Phila. & Vicinity (corr. sec.), Coalition Prison Evangelists, Chaplaincy Coalition of Greater Phila, Am. Univ. Women, Wesley Theological Sem. Alumni Assn. Democrat. Avocations: music, opera, historical researcher, board games, traveling. Home: 337 Christian St Apt 3 Philadelphia PA 19147-3219

BRACEY, EARNEST NORTON, political science educator; b. Jackson, Miss., June 8, 1953; s. Willard and Odessa Manola (Ford) B.; m. Atsuko Konuma, Apr. 2, 1995; children: Dominique, Princess, Omar. MPA, Golden Gate U., 1979; MA, Cath. U., Washington, 1983; D of Pub. Adminstrn., George Mason U., 1993. Commd. 2d lt. U.S. Army, 1975, advanced through grades to lt. col., 1992; ret., 1995; instr. polit. sci. C.C. of So. Nev., Las Vegas, 1996—; adj. prof. Ctrl. Tex. Coll., Camp Zama, Japan, 1993-95; mem. Nev. faculty alliance C.C. of So. Nev., Las Vegas, 1996—. Author: Choson, 1994. Mem. NAACP, Am. Soc. of Mil. Comptrs., Assn. of the U.S. Army, Retired Officer Assn. Avocations: jazz trumpeter, marathon runner, writing, poetry, American historian.

BRACH, PAUL HENRY, artist. BFA, U Iowa, 1948, MFA, 1950. Tchr. U. Mo., Columbia, 1950-51, New Sch. Social Rsch., N.Y.C., 1952-55, NYU, 1954-67, 86-90, Parsons Sch. Design, 1956-67, The Cooper Union, 1960-62, 79-82, Cornell U., 1965-67; chair dept. visual arts. U. Calif., San Diego, 1967-69; dean Sch. Art Calif. Inst. Arts, Valencia, 1969-75; chair divsn. arts Fordham U., N.Y.C., 1975-79, Empire State Coll., N.Y.C., 1979—; Milton Avery disting. prof. Bard Coll., N.Y.C., 1993; vis. artist U. N.Mex., Albuquerque, 1965; guest critic U. Minn., Mpls., Sarah Lawrence Coll., Bronxville, N.Y., Montclair (N.J.) State Coll., Art Forum Mag., 1976; vis. critic N.Y. studio program Empire State Coll., 1976—; cons. Rutgers U., New Brunswick, 1977; guest critic Bard Coll., Empire State Coll., N.Y.C., 1977; contbg. critic Art Forum Mag., 1977; vis. artist Banff (Can.) Art Ctr., 1979; contbg. critic Art in Am., 1979; guest lectr. Pratt Inst., N.Y.C., 1980, Tuscon Mus. Art, 1992; vis. artist Litho Workshop, Ariz. State U., Tempe, 1981, U. N.Mex., Albuquerque, 1981; guest lectr. Tuscon Mus. Art, 1992. One-man shows at Jean Millant Gallery, L.A., 1974, Benson Gallery, Bridgehampton, N.Y., 1975, Lerner Heller Gallery, N.Y.C., 1978, 80, Yares Gallery, L.A., 1979, Janus Gallery, L.A., 1980, Yares Gallery, Scottsdale, Ariz., 1981, Bernice Steinbaum Gallery Ltd., N.Y.C., 1983, 85, 87, 90, 91, Elaine Horwitch Galleries, Palm Springs, Calif., 1987, Benton Gallery, Southampton, N.Y., 1987, Vered Gallery, East Hampton, N.Y., 1989, Rancho Linda Vista Gallery, Oracle, Ariz., 1992, Steinbaum Krauss Gallery, N.Y.C., 1994, McAllen (Tex.) Internat. Mus., 1995, Tucson (Ariz.) Mus. Art, 1995, Guild Hall, East Hampton, 1995, others; exhibited in group shows at Wake Forest U. Art Gallery, Winston-Salem, N.C., 1988, Rose Art Mus., Brandeis U., Waltham, Mass., 1988, Anderson Gallery, Va. Commonwealth U., Richmond, 1988, Temple U., Phila., 1988, Alexandra Monet Fine Arts, New Orleans, 1989, Bernice Steinbaum Gallery, N.Y., 1990, Guild Hall Mus., East Hampton Ctr. Contemporary Art, 1990, Weatherspoon Art Gallery, Greensboro, N.Y.C., 1990, Tyler Art Gallery, Oswego, N.Y., 1990, Albright-Knox Art Gallery, Buffalo, 1990, LewAllen/Butler Gallery, Sante Fe, N.Mex., 1993, Vered Gallery, East Hampton, 1993, Steinbaum Krauss Gallery, N.Y.C., 1993, Kent (Conn.) Gallery, 1994, Andre Zarre Gallery, N.Y.C., 1995, others; represented in permanent collections at Mus. Modern Art, N.Y.C., Whitney Mus. Am. Art, N.Y.C., L.A. County Mus. Art, St. Louis Art Mus., Smith Coll. Mus., Nebr. Art Mus., Albuquerque Mus. Art, Mus. Fine Art, Santa Fe, Phoenix Art Mus., NYU, others; contbr. articles to profl. jours. Fellow Djerassi Found., Woodside, Calif., 1987, 90. Office: Steinbaum Krauss Gallery 132 Greene St New York NY 10012-3242*

BRACHMAN, MALCOLM K., oil company executive; b. Ft. Worth, Dec. 9, 1926; s. Solomon and Etta (Katzenstein) B.; m. Minda Fay Delugach, Sept. 4, 1951; children: Lynn, Malcolm K. Jr., Lisa. BA, Yale U., 1945; MA, Harvard U., 1947, PhD, 1949. CLU. Asst. prof. So. Meth. U., Dallas, 1949-50; assoc. physicist Argonne Nat. Lab., Chgo., 1950-53; rsch. staff Tex. Instruments, Inc., Dallas, 1953-54; v.p. Pioneer Am. Ins. Co., Ft. Worth, 1954-61, pres., 1961-73, chmn. bd., CEO, 1973-79; pres. N.W. Oil Co., Dallas, 1956—; chmn. adv. coun. Econ. Growth Ctr. Yale U. Capt. USAAF, 1950-57. Recipient Yale Presdl. medal. Fellow Am. Phys. Soc., Soc. Petroleum Engrs., Am. Math. Soc.; sr. mem. IEEE, Soc. Exploration Geophysics; mem. Dallas Petroleum Club, Century Assn. (N.Y.C.). Jewish. Avocation: bridge. Home: 3510 Turtle Creek Blvd Apt 16F Dallas TX 75219-5545 Office: NW Oil Co 3232 Mckinney Ave Ste 770 Dallas TX 75204-7416

BRACHMAN, RICHARD JOHN, II, financial services consultant, banking educator; b. Madison, Wis., Oct. 30, 1951; s. Richard John and Joan Katherine (Harrington) B.; m. Connie Beth Ten Haken, May 14, 1977; children: Samantha Joan, Richard John. BS, U. Wis., 1974. With The Rural Cos., Madison, 1975-83; v.p. CBI Ins. Svcs., Inc., Middleton, Wis., 1983-84; exec. v.p. CBI Ins. Svcs., Inc., 1984-85, pres., 1985-87; sr. v.p. Valley Bank Ins., Madison, 1987-94; pres. Community Life Ins. Co., div. Valley Bancorporation, Madison, 1987-94; owner, v.p., dir. Lexlawn, Inc., Lexington, Ky., 1993-98; pres., CEO, The Brachman Group, Ltd., Madison, 1994—; mem. faculty Iowa Sch. Banking, U. Iowa, 1998—; bd. dirs. Ins. Svcs. Inc., Cmty. Life Ins. Co., Madison, Career Mgmt. Group. Mem. parish coun. Our Lady Queen of Peace Ch., Madison, 1989—; bd. dirs. U. Wis. Meml. Union. Mem. U. Wis. Alumni Assn. (bd. dirs. 1988-94, Spark Plug award 1987), Mendota Gridiron Club (bd. dirs.), KC. Roman

Catholic. Avocations: photography, reading, golf. Home and Office: 1217 Tramore Trail Madison WI 53717-1054

BRACK, O. M., JR., English language educator; b. Houston, Nov. 30, 1938; s. O. M. and Olivia Mae (Rice) B.; m. Gay Wilson Stampler, Nov. 27, 1991; 1 child, Matthew Rice; stepchildren: Suzette Richardson, Christopher Luebkin. Student, U. Houston, 1956-57; B.A., Baylor U., 1960, M.A., 1961; Ph.D., U. Tex., Austin, 1965. Asst. prof. William Woods Coll., 1964-65; asst. prof. English lit. U. Iowa, Iowa City, 1965-68; assoc. prof. U. Iowa, 1968-73, dir. center textual studies, 1967-73; prof. English lit. Ariz. State U., Tempe, 1973—; chmn. 18th Century Short Title Catalogue Com., 1970-73; pres. Arete Publs., Ltd., 1976-81; Albert H. Smith Meml. lectr. bibliography Birmingham (Eng.) Bibliog. Soc., 1983 vis. fellow U. Oxford Wolfson Coll., 1986-87. Author: Bibliography and Textual Criticism, 1969, Samuel Johnson's Early Biographers, 1971, Hoole's Death of Johnson, 1972, Henry Fielding's Pasquin, 1973, A Catalogue of the Leigh Hunt Manuscripts, 1973, The Early Biographies of Samuel Johnson, 1974, American Humor, 1977, Twilight of Dawn, 1987, Writers, Books and Trade, 1994, Samuel Johnson in New Albion, 1997; textual editor: Works of Tobias Smollett, 1966—; gen. editor: Works of Tobias Smollett, 1973-86; editor: English Literature in Transition, 1981-82, mem. editl. com., 1982—; editor: Studies in Eighteenth Century Culture, 1981-86; mem. editl. com.: Yale edit. Works of Samuel Johnson, 1977—; editl. cons. The Literature of England, Scott, Foresman & Co., 1977-79, Works of David Hume, Princeton U. Press, 1990-91, Oxford U. Press, 1995—; asst. editor: Eighteenth-Century Bibliography, 1964-73, Books at Iowa, 1966-73; editor Eighteenth Century: A Current Bibliography, 1983-90 ; mem. editl. com.: Age of Johnson, 1985—, Rocky Mountain Rev. of Lang. and Lit., 1980-98, Clarissa Project, 1987—; mem. adv. bd. 18th-Century Brit. Periodical Subject Index, 1996—, Soc. for Textual Scholarship, 1998; bd. dirs. 18th-Century Short-Title Catalogue, Inc., 1993—. Mem. Salvation Army Coun., South Mountain Corps, 1996—, chair, 1999—. Recipient Grad. Coll. Disting. Rsch. award, 1981-82, Rocky Mountains MLA Huntington Libr. award, 1986, Humanities Rsch. award, 1989-90, Faculty Achievement award Ariz. State U. Alumni Assn., 1991; Am. Philos. Soc. grantee, 1967, NEH grantee, 1993-95, 95—; Phi Kappa Phi Disting. scholar, 1975; Huntington Libr. fellow, 1978, 96, 97, Am. Coun. Learned Soc. fellow, 1979-80, fellow Newberry Libr., 1982, Andrew W. Mellon Fund fellow, Huntington Libr., 1994. Mem. Am. Soc. 18th Century Studies, South Central 18th Century Soc. (pres. 1982-83), Western Soc. for 18th Century Studies, 1991-93, Rocky Mountain MLA, Bibliog. Soc. Am., Bibliog. Soc. U. Va., Bibliog. Soc. (London), Printing Hist. Soc., Am. Printing History Assn., Samuel Johnson Soc. So. Calif. (bd. dirs. 1989—, pres. 1994-95). Roman Catholic. Clubs: Grolier, The Johnsonians. Office: Ariz State U Dept English Tempe AZ 85287-0302

BRACKBILL, NANCY LAFFERTY, elementary education educator; b. Lancaster, Pa., Sept. 7, 1938; d. Jacob Martin and Erma Irene (Moser) Lafferty; m. Albert Landis Brackbill Jr., Aug. 6, 1960; children: Lynn Elizabeth, Lisa Ann. BS in Elem. Edn., Millersville U., 1960, cert. reading specialist, 1981. Tchr. kindergarten Hempfield Sch. Dist., Landisville, Pa., 1960-63; tchr. nursery sch. Zion U.C.C. Nursery Sch., Millersville, Pa., 1971-72; tchr. elem., reading Annville (Pa.)-Cleona Sch. Dist., 1978-79; tchr. reading Palmyra (Pa.) H.S., 1980-81; elem. tchr., reading specialist East Stroudsburg (Pa.) Area Sch. Dist., 1981—, chmn. elem. reading, 1991—. Mem. ASCD, Internat. Reading Assn., Colonial Area Reading Educators (legis. chair 1992—, rec. sec. 1994—), Pa. State Edn. Assn., Keystone State Reading Assn., Keystone State Leaders, East Stroudsburg Edn. Assn. Mem. Ch. of Christ. Avocations: tennis, reading, music, bike riding, yoga. Home: 188 Brookside Ln Nazareth PA 18064-9109 Office: East Stroudsburg Area Schs 321 N Courtland St East Stroudsburg PA 18301-2107

BRACKEN, BRUCE A., psychologist, educator; b. Flint, Mich., Nov. 5, 1949; s. Leo A. and Mildred R. Staffne B.; m. Mary Jo Byrne, Dec. 28, 1970; 1 child, Bruce A. Jr. BS, Coll. Charleston, 1975; MA, U. Ga., 1977, PhD, 1979. Diplomate Am. Bd. Assessment Psychology. Staff psychologist Rutland Ctr., Athens, Ga., 1977-79; asst., assoc. prof. U. Wis., Milw., 1979-86; prof. U. Memphis, 1986—. Editor: Handbook of Self-Concept, 1996; editor, co-founder Jour. Psychoednl. Assessment, 1982—. Fellow APA; mem. Nat. Assn. Sch. Psychologists, Tenn. Assn. Sch. Psychologists. Avocations: history, reading, travel, home renovation. Office: U Memphis Dept Psychology Memphis TN 38101

BRACKEN, CHARLES HERBERT, banker; b. Corry, Pa., June 5, 1921; s. Olin Williams and Vellah (Morgan) B.; m. Barbara E. Barton, June 19, 1948; children: Betsy Louise, Sally Anne, Charles Herbert, Barton William, Douglas Morgan. BS, U. Pa., 1948; student spl. banking courses. Successively asst. to pres., v.p., exec. v.p. and trust officer, pres., dir. Citizens Nat. Bank, Corry, 1948-64; pres., dir. Marine Bank, Erie, Pa., 1964-74, chmn. bd. dirs., chief exec. officer, 1974-87; dir. Country Fair Inc., 1965-85; vice chmn. PNC Bank, 1984-85. Bd. dirs. Erie Conf. Cmty. Devel.; trustee Hamot Med. Ctr., 1970-79, corporator, 1980—, pres., 1977-78; pres., trustee Erie Cmty. Found., 1970-96; treas. Erie Episc. Diocese, 1969-87; bd. govs., treas. Erie unit Shriners Hosp. Crippled Children, 1967-79; corporator St. Vincent Health Ctr., 1965—; adv. bd. Titusville campus U. Pitts., 1967-84, Gannon Coll., 1971-88, Mercyhurst Coll., 1968-97, trustee. Mem. Pa. Bankers Assn. (pres. 1966-67), Newcomen Soc. N.Am. (dir.), Masons, Shriners, Yacht Club, Rotary, Univ. Club, Erie Club, Kahkwa Club, Sigma Alpha Epsilon. Episcopalian. Home: 5060 Saybrook Pl Erie PA 16505-1324 Office: 901 State St Erie PA 16501-1414 also: PO Box 8480 Erie PA 16553-8480

BRACKEN, EDDIE (EDWARD VINCENT), actor, director, writer, singer, artist; b. N.Y.C., Feb. 7, 1920; s. Joseph L. and Catherine B.; m. Connie Nickerson, Sept. 25, 1939; 5 children. Student, Profl. Children's Sch. for Actors, N.Y.C.; doctorate (hon.), Hofstra U., 1997. lectr. U. Ga., 1998. Vaudeville, night club singer; stage debut in, Lottery, 1930; plays include Lady Refuses, Iron Men, So Proudly We Hail, Brother Rat, Too Many Girls, Seven Year Itch, What a Life, Shinbone Alley, Teahouse of the August Moon, You Know I Can't Hear You When the Water's Running, The Odd Couple, Never Too Late, Sunshine Boys, Hello Dolly!, 1978, Show Boat in Cairo Egypt, 1989 touring Australia in Sugar Babies, 1986-87, The Wizard of Oz, 1992, No, No, Nanette, 1997; appeared as toymaker in Houston Grand Opera's Babes in Toyland, also in Power of a Dream, and Home Alone II, 1991-92; motion picture debut in Life with Henry, 1940; others include Fleet's In, Sweater Girl, Young and Willing, Hail the Conquering Hero, Miracle of Morgan's Creek, Girl from Jones Beach, Two Tickets to Broadway, We're Not Married, About Face, Slight Case of Larceny, Caught in the Draft, National Lampoon's Vacation, Wind in the Willows, Happy Go Lucky, Star Spangled Rhythm, Summer Stock, Oscar, 1990, Little Shop of Horrors, 1990, Rookie of the Year, 1993, American Clock, 1993, Conduct Unbecoming, 1993, John Hughes Baby's Day Out; TV series Masquerade Party, Tales of the Darkside, Murder, She Wrote, Missing Persons; other TV programs including Great Performances, Show Boat, Golden Girls, Wise Guys, Winnetka Road, Bill Cosby Mysteries, It Runs in the Family; syndicated columnist Crackin' with Bracken, 1963—; actor, dir. (play) These Golden Years, Hofstra U., 1996, Follies, 1998. 14,000 performances on legitimate stage (more than any other actor in history). Office: 69 Douglas Rd Glen Ridge NJ 07028-1227*

BRACKEN, HARRY MCFARLAND, philosophy educator; b. Yonkers, N.Y., Mar. 12, 1926; s. Harry S. and Grace M. (McFarl) B.; m. Eva Maria Laufkotter, Dec. 24, 1949 (div.); children—Christopher, Timothy; m. Elisabeth van Gelderen, June 19, 1985. BA, Trinity Coll., Hartford, Conn., 1949; MA, Johns Hopkins, 1954; PhD, U. Iowa, 1956. Instr. U. Iowa, Iowa City, 1955-57; asst. prof. U. Iowa, 1957-61; asso. prof. U. Minn., Mpls., 1961-63; prof. Ariz. State U., Tempe, 1963-66; prof. philosophy McGill U., Montreal, Que., Can., 1966-91; prof. U. Calif., San Diego, 1970; vis. prof. Trinity Coll., U. Dublin, Ireland, 1972-73, 79-80; vis. prof. metaphysics U. Coll., Nat. U. Ireland, Dublin, 1972-73, 79-80; adj. faculty philosophy Erasmus U., Rotterdam, 1988—, Rijksuniversiteit Groningen, 1990-95; adj. prof. philosophy Ariz. State U., 1995—. Author: The Early Reception of Berkeley's Immaterialism: 1710-1733, 1959, 2d edit., 1965, Berkeley, 1974; Mind and Language: Essays on Descartes and Chomsky, 1984, Freedom of Speech: Words Are Not Deeds, 1994. Served with USNR, 1943-46, PTO. Recipient Acad. Freedom award Ariz. Civil Liberties Union, 1965; Edn. award J. I. Segal Found. for Jewish Culture, 1972. Mem. Am. Philos. Assn., Internat. Berkeley Soc., The Hume Soc., Brit. Soc. for History of Philosophy, USS Lauderdale Assn. E-mail: hbracken@imap2.asu.edu. Home: 9107 E Avenida Las Noches Apache Junction AZ 85219-4676

BRACKEN, KATHLEEN ANN, nurse; b. Chgo., Mar. 14, 1947; d. Thomas James and Catherine Anastasia (Cowal) B. Diploma, Little Company of Mary Hosp., Evergreen Park, Ill., 1968; BSN, Lewis U., 1984, MBA, 1989. RN, Ill. Mem. staff Little Company of Mary Hosp., Evergreen Park, Ill., 1968-69, 71-73, supr. ICUs, 1976-79, dir. ICU's, 1979-91; v.p. patient care svcs. South Chgo. Cmty. Hosp., 1991-93; staff nurse Chgo. Lying-In Clinic, U. Chgo., 1970-71; nurse mgr. VA Chgo. Healthcare Sys., 1994-98, assoc. chief nurse, 1998—; bd. dirs., chmn. nursing cardiovascular com. South Cook Heart Assn., 1977-83. Recipient Meritorious Svc. award, 1979, 81, 82, 83, 84, 85, 86. Mem. NAFE, NOVA, Beverly Area Planning Assn., Am. Orgn. Nurse Execs., Chgo. Heart Assn., Assn. Critical Care Nurses (pres. southside Chgo. Area chpt. 1983-84, rec. sec. 1984-85), Am. Heart Assn. (cardiovascular nursing coun.), Brain Injury Assn. Ill., Chgo. Healthcare Exec. Forum, Delta Epsilon Sigma, Sigma Theta Tau. Home: 10321 S Campbell Ave Chicago IL 60655-1016 Office: VA Chgo Health Care Sys Lakeside Divsn 333 E Huron St Chicago IL 60611

BRACKEN, PAUL, political science educator; b. Phila., Mar. 12, 1948; s. John Joseph and Gertrude (Logue) B.; m. Nanette Elizabeth Beattie, May 25, 1974; children: Kathleen, James, Margaret. BS, Columbia U., 1971, MS, 1976; PhD, Yale U., 1982. Rsch. asst. Fels Ctr. Govt., U. Pa., Phila., 1971-72; sr. staff Ketron, Inc., Arlington, Va., 1972-74; dir. rsch. Hudson Inst., Croton-on-Hudson, N.Y., 1974-83; asst. prof. Yale U., New Haven, 1983, assoc. prof., 1984-85, prof., 1986—; lectr. various univs. and colls.; cons. in field. Author: Command and Control of Nuclear Forces, 1983, Fire in the East, 1999; contbr. articles to profl. jours. Mem. Commn. of Conn.'s Future, 1981-85, Inst. Social and Policy Studies, Yale U. Mem. Internat. Inst. Strategic Studies, Yale Ctr. for Internat. Studies, Coun. Fgn. Rels. Avocations: skiing, golf, amateur radio. Home: 22 Green Ln Ridgefield CT 06877-3017 Office: Yale U PO Box 1A New Haven CT 06520

BRACKEN, PEG, author; b. Filer, Idaho, Feb. 25, 1918; d. John Lewis and Ruth (McQuesten) B.; m. John Hamilton Ohman, June 15, 1991; 1 child from previous marriage, Johanna Kathleen Edwards. A.B., Antioch Coll., 1940. Author: The I Hate to Cook Book, 1960, The I Hate to Housekeep Book, 1962, I Try to Behave Myself, 1963, Peg Bracken's Appendix to The I Hate to Cook Book, 1966, I Didn't Come Here to Argue, 1969, But I Wouldn't Have Missed It for the World, 1973, The I Hate to Cook Almanack - A Book of Days, 1976, A Window Over the Sink, 1981, The Compleat I Hate to Cookbook, 1986, On Getting Old for the First Time, 1996.

BRACKEN, THOMAS, bank executive. Pres., CEO N.J. Nat. Bank (named changed First Union Core States Bank), Pennington, 1993—; head govt. and comml. banking of N.J. First Union Core States Bank, Pennington, 1998—. Office: First Union Core States Bank 370 Scotch Rd Pennington NJ 08534*

BRACKEN, THOMAS ROBERT JAMES, real estate investment executive; b. Spokane, Wash., Jan. 1, 1950; s. James Lucas and Frances (Cadzow) B.; m. Linda Jacobson, Sept. 9, 1972; children: Karl Forest, David Erskine. BS, Yale U., 1971; MBA, Columbia U., 1972. Sr. appraiser Prudential Ins., N.Y.C., 1972-74; mgr. real estate Prudential Ins., N.Y.C. and Newark, 1974-76; assoc. gen. mgr. Prudential Ins., Seattle, 1977-78; v.p. First City Investments, Seattle, 1978-80; pres. Fenix, Inc., Seattle, 1980-86; v.p. Washington Mortgage Corp., Seattle, 1982-85; exec. v.p. Washington Mortgage Corp., 1986-88; sr. v.p. Pioneer Bank, Lynwood, Wash., 1985-86; pres.real estate financing USL Capital, San Francisco, 1988-97; sr. v.p. real estate fin. group Orix, USA, San Francisco, 1997-98; pres. Presidio Interfunding Corp., San Francisco, 1998—. Mem. Nat. Assn. Indsl./Office Parks (v.p. Seattle chpt. 1981-83), Yale Assn. Western Wash. (pres. 1984-86), Urban Land Inst., Mortgage Bankers Assn. Presbyterian. Avocations: running, sports. Office: Presidio Interfunding 25 Broadway San Francisco CA 94111

BRACKEN, WILLIAM EARL, JR., lawyer; b. Phila., Jan. 25, 1934; s. William Earl and Etholen Alabell (Terry) B.; m. Sarah Lou Graves, May 31, 1958; children: Elizabeth Louise, Terry Suzanne, Sarah Lynn. BBA, Baylor U., 1956, JD, 1958. Bar: Tex. 1958,. Assoc. Bryan-Maxwell, Waco, Tex., 1961-63; 1st asst. city atty. City of Waco, 1963-67, city atty., 1967-96; pvt. practice Waco, 1996—. Trustee Group Benefits Risk Pool Tex. Mcpl. League, Austin, 1979—, chmn., 1979-81; mem. adv. bd. S.W. Legal Found. Mcpl. Legal Ctr., Richardson, Tex., 1994—; bd. dirs. Evangelia Settlement, Waco; pres. Lake Air Meml. Little League, Waco, 1963-67; mem. Tejas Coun. Campfire Bd., 1997; active Bd. Ctrl. Tex. Sr. Ministry, 1997—. Lt. USAF, 1958-61, lt. col. USAFR, 1961-84. Recipient Disting. Svc. award Waco Jaycees. Fellow Tex. Bar Found.; mem. Baylor Law Sch. Alumni Assn. (bd. dirs.), Tex. City Atty. Assn. (hon. life, pres. 1969-71). Baptist. Avocations: family, travel, Texas Rangers baseball, Baylor University sports. Home: 5000 Ridgeview Dr Waco TX 76710-1727 Office: 5400 Bosque Blvd Ste 466 Waco TX 76710

BRACKENHOFF, LONNIE SUE, principal; b. Shaw AFB, S.C., Feb. 27, 1957; d. Marshall Alvin Jr. and Marcia Ann Sherrill; m. Charles Robert Brackenhoff, June 18, 1977; children: Christina, Justin. BS in Spl. Edn., East Carolina U., 1978, MA in Edn., 1983; student, Chapman U., 1997; ednl. specialist degree, U. Wyo., 1998; student, Chapman U., 1997. Cert. tchr. and adminstr., Wyo, Calif. Tchr. spl. edn. Edgecombe County Schs., Tarboro, N.C., 1978-84; tchr. spl. edn. Laramie County Sch Dist. 1, Cheyenne, Wyo., 1985-92, tchr. elem., 1992-93; prin. Lompoc (Calif.) Unified Sch. Dist., 1993—; instr. Ea. Wyo. C.C., 1993. Vol. Very Spl. Arts, Cheyenne, 1986, 90-92, coord., 1987-89. Mem. ASCD, Assn. Calif. Sch. Adminstrs., Assn. Lompoc Sch. Adminstrs., Learning Disabilities Assn., Phi Delta Kappa. Avocations: reading, family camping.

BRACKETT, COLQUITT PRATER, JR., judge, lawyer; b. Norfolk, Va., Feb. 24, 1946; s. Colquitt Prater Sr. and Antoinette Gladys (Cacace) B.; m. Pamela Susan Colwell, Oct. 11, 1969 (dec. Aug. 1978); 1 child, Susan Elizabeth; m. Frances Sybil Langford, Jan. 1, 1982. BS, U. Ga., 1966, MA, 1968, JD, 1973, LLM, 1976. Bar: Ga. 1973, U.S. Dist. Ct. (so. dist.) Ga. 1974, U.S. Dist. Ct. (mid. dist.) Ga. 1977, U.S. Supreme Ct. 1980, Tenn. 1987. Assoc. Surrett & CoCroft, Augusta, Ga., 1972-74; ptnr. Surrett & Brackett, Augusta, 1974-76; mem. faculty Sch. Law, U. Ga., Athens, 1977-82; mng. ptnr. Brackett, Prince & Neufeld, Athens, 1982-90; adminstrv. law judge Ga. Dept. Med. Assistance, Athens, 1990—; hearing officer Ga. State Bd. Edn., 1979-91; v.p. Mus. Dolls & Gifts, Inc., Pigeon Forge, Tenn., 1983—; pres. Bear County Lodge and Conf. Ctr., 1996—. Author: Court Administration, 1972. Pres. Athens Clarke Mental Health Assn., 1985; chmn. bd. dirs. N.E. Ga. Mental Health Assn., 1989-90; bd. dirs. Coalition for The Blue Ridge Pkwy., 1994—, Oconee Cultural Arts Found., 1995-97, Blue Ridge Pkwy. Assn., 1997—. Mem. ABA, Ga. State Bar Assn., Ga. Assn. Adminstrv. Law Judges (bd. dirs. 1990-91), Ga. Trial Lawyers Assn., Western Cir. Bar Assn., Internat. Platform Assn., S.E. Tourism Soc., Rotary Internat., Ea. Nat. Parks Assn., Sevier County Bar Assn., Soc. Am. Poets. Episcopalian. Avocations: reading, music, golf, cross-country skiing. Office: 636 Middle Creek Rd Ste 4 Sevierville TN 37862-5013

BRACKETT, EDWARD BOONE, III, orthopedic surgeon; b. Jan. 5, 1936; s. Edward Boone and Bessie Lee (Hudgins) B.; m. Jean Elliott, July 11, 1959; children: Bess E., Geoffrey, Elliott Mencken, Edward Boone IV, Anneke Gail; m. Andrea Inman, Jan. 30, 1992; children: Amelia, Louisa Jo. Student, Tex. Tech. Coll., 1957; MD, Baylor U., 1961; JD, Ill. Inst. Tech., 1993. Bar: Ill. 1993; diplomate Am. Bd. Orthopaedic Surgery, Am. Bd. Neurol. Orthopaedic Surgeons; cert. flight instr. single and multi-engine land, single engine sea and airline transport pilot, designated med. examiner FAA. Intern Cook County Hosp., Chgo., 1961-62; resident Northwestern U., Chgo., 1962-66; pvt. practice Oak Park, Ill., 1966—, Westgate Orthopaedics Ltd., Oak Park, 1969—; mem. staff Loyola U., Oak Park Hosp., Loretto Hosp., Hinsdale Hosp., Gottlieb Hosp., Westlake Hosp., Rush Med. Sch.; chmn. dept. orthopaedics West Suburban Hosp., pres. med. staff, 1982-84; clin. assoc. prof. orthopaedics Loyola U.; chmn. bd. Chgo. Loop Mediclinic, 1973-75; cons. orthopaedic surgery City Svc. Oil Co., 1970. Cons. orthopaedic editor: Jour. Indsl. Medicine, 1966-67; mem. editl. bd.: Jour. Clin. Orthopaedics. Guarantor Lyric Opera Chgo., 1971-84; guest condr. Chgo. Symphony Orch., 1979, gov. mem., 1992, Chgo. Chamber Orch., 1980; trustee Music of the Baroque; nat. patron Met. Opera Co., N.Y.C.; mem. humanities adv. coun. Triton Coll., 1983-84; charter mem. vis. com. Northwestern U. Sch. Music, 1982—; chmn. Friends of WFMT, Inc. Lt. comdr. USNR, 1967-69, Vietnam. Recipient Outstanding Tchr. award Dept. Orthopaedic Surgery, West Suburban Hosp., 1978, 79. Fellow ACS, Am. Acad. Orthopaedic Surgeons, Inst. of Medicine of Chgo., Am. Acad. Neurol. and Orthopaedic Surgeons, Am. Assn. for Hand Surgery, Internat. Coll. Surgeons; mem. AMA, Am. Trauma Soc. (founder), Royal Soc. Medicine, Ill. Orthopaedic Soc., Chgo. Orthopaedic Soc., Chgo. Med. Soc. (alt. councilor, chmn. ethical rels. com., mem. book rev. panel), Clin. Orthopaedic Soc. (chmn. membership com., libr. historian, 1994, 2d pres.-elect 1997), Internat. Platform Assn., Civil War Round Table, Friends Chgo. Symphony Orch. (governing mem.), Chgo. Chamber Orch. Assn. (dir., v.p.), Symphonia Musicale (dir.), Sigma Alpha Epsilon, Phi Eta Sigma, Phi Chi, Alpha Epsilon Delta, Phi Alpha Delta. Home: 25333 W Il Route 60 Grayslake IL 60030-9542 Office: 1125 Westgate St Oak Park IL 60301-1007

BRACKETT, MARTIN LUTHER, JR., lawyer; b. Charlotte, N.C., Feb. 23, 1947; s. Martin Luther and Helen Virginia (Smith) B.; m. Lisa Nichol; children—Martin Hunter, Alexander Jones, Amelia Kathleen, Lauren Hart. B.A., Davidson Coll., 1969; J.D., U. N.C., 1972. Bar: N.C. 1972, U.S. Dist. Ct. (we. dist.) N.C. 1973, U.S. Ct. Appeals (4th cir.) 1975. Ptnr. Bailey, Brackett & Brackett, P.A., Charlotte, N.C., 1973-83, Brackett & Sitton, Charlotte, 1983-85, Robinson, Bradshaw & Hinson, P.A., 1985—. Mem. Auditorium-Coliseum-Conv. Ctr. Authority, Charlotte, 1981-87, chmn., 1985-87. Served to capt. U.S. Army, 1972-73. Recipient Van Hecke-Wettach award U. N.C., 1972. Fellow Am. Coll. Trial Lawyers; mem. N.C. Acad. Trial Lawyers (bd. govs. 1980-86, 88-95, v.p. 1984-86). Democrat. Presbyterian. Office: 1900 Independence Ctr 101 N Tryon St Charlotte NC 28246-0100

BRACKETT, RONALD E., investment company executive, lawyer; b. Rockford, Ill., May 10, 1942; s. F. Earl Brackett and Anne (Christenberry) Townsend; m. Susan Catherine Stichnoth, May 31, 1975; 1 child, Charles William. BA, Trinity Coll., 1964; JD, U. Mich., 1967. Bar: N.Y. 1968. Assoc. Rogers & Wells, N.Y.C., 1968-74, ptnr., 1974-91, mng. ptnr., 1984-85, cons., 1992-94; founder, prin. Associated Growth Investors, L.P., Manhasset, N.Y., 1992—; bd. dirs. King Kullen Grocery Co., Inc., Westbury, N.Y., Heuer Time & Electronics Corp., Springfield, N.J. Mem. ABA, N.Y. State Bar Assn., Phi Beta Kappa. Office: Associated Growth Investors LP PO Box 1399 Manhasset NY 11030-6399

BRACKETT, SHARON (ELAINE), medical/surgical nurse; b. Worcester, Mass., June 4, 1964; d. George R. and Barbara L. (Phelps) Blakeney; m. William R. Brackett, Sept. 24, 1988. BSN, U. Rochester, 1986. RN, Mass.; cert. ACLS. Primary care staff nurse Mass. Gen. Hosp., Boston, staff nurse respiratory surgical ICU, 1994—; staff nurse rep. to nursing ethics com. Mass. Gen. Hosp. Finalist Clin. Excellence contest Am. Jour. Nursing, 1989. Office: Mass Gen Hosp-RIW 55 Fruit St Boston MA 02114-2621

BRACKETT, TRACY ANN, science journalist, consultant; b. Lynn, Mass., Mar. 24, 1970; d. William Anthony Brackett and Maureen Jude Mahar Woodell; m. Richard Degregorio, Oct. 17, 1998. BA, U. Lowell, Mass., 1992; MS in Neurosci., Brandeis U., 1995. Rschr. MIT, Cambridge, Mass., 1992-94; rsch. Harvard Med. Sch., Boston, 1996-97; sci. journalist, analyst Centerwatch, Boston, 1995-98; writer Decision Resources, Waltham, Mass., 1995—, pharm. cons., 1998—. Contbr. articles to profl. jours.; author poetry.

BRACKIN, PHYLLIS JEAN, recruiting professional; b. Aliquippa, Pa., Oct. 5, 1946; d. Matthew Edward and Trula Estelle (Venable) Plonka; children: Keith, Kevin. Student, Georgetown U., 1966, U. S. Fla., 1981. Librarian Def. Intelligence Agy., Washington, 1966-70, Aerospace Corp., Los Angeles, 1975-78; personnel mgr. Badger Engrs. Inc., Tampa, Fla., 1979-85; dir. career devel. PTC Inst., Tampa, 1985-86; dir. mktg. & pub. rels. DSI Staff RX, Inc., Clearwater, Fla., 1986—. Author: Personal Skills Development, How to Hire Eagles, 1988, Recruitment Services: A Viable Option, 1988, How to Get a Job and Keep It, 1990, Are We Having Fun Yet?, Celebrate Your Profession, 1992, Are You Hiring Ziggers or Zaggers?, Celebrate You!, 1994. Mem. NAFE, ASTD, Fla. Soc. Pers. Cons., Am. Healthcare Radiology Adminstrs. Republican. Roman Catholic. Avocations: reading, swimming. Home: 12915 Big Sur Dr Tampa FL 33625-4115

BRACKS, LEAN'TIN LAVERNE, African-American literature educator; b. Galveston, Tex., Sept. 27, 1952; d. Oscar Sr. and Vivian Mae Bracks; 1 child, Bobby-Joe. BA, Kenyon Coll., 1974; MA, U. Nebr., 1992, PhD, 1996. Commodity merchandiser Cargill Inc., Mpls., 1974-83, br. transp. mgr., 1983-91; grad. rsch. asst. U. Nebr., Lincoln, 1992-94, grad. instr., 1994-96; asst. prof. Fisk U., Nashville, 1996—. Author: Writings on Black Women of the Diaspora, 1997, Biographer Notable African-American Men, 1998. Mem. MLA. Office: Fisk U Dept English 1000 17th Ave N Nashville TN 37208-3051

BRADA, DONALD ROBERT, psychiatrist; b. Hutchinson, Kans., Oct. 11, 1939; s. Joseph Duane and Mary Elizabeth (Whitebread) B.; m. Carolyn Starr Cromb, Aug. 19, 1961; children: Donald Robert Jr., Stephen Andrew. AB, U. Kans., 1961, MD, 1965. Diplomate Am. Bd. Psychiatry and Neurology; Lic. Kans. State Bd. Healing Arts. Resident in psychiatry U. Kans., Kansas City, Kans., 1972; pvt. practice Hutchinson, 1976-77; med. dir., exec. dir. Horizons Mental Health Ctr., Hutchinson, 1977-87; med. dir. psychiatry St. Francis Regional Med. Ctr., Wichita, Kans., 1987-96; assoc. clinical prof. dept. psychiatry and behavior med. Sch. Med. U. Kans., Wichita, 1996—; bd. dirs. Kans. Found. Med. Care, Topeka, Wichita Preferred Providers Assn., Pschiat. Rsch. Inst., Wichita, 1989—; mem. Govs. Mental Health Svcs. Planning Coun., 1988-94. Contbr. articles to profl. jours. Elder First Presbyn. Ch., Hutchinson, 1984-86. Col. USAF, 1964-76. Fellow Am. Psychiat. Assn.; mem. Kans. Psychiat. Soc. (pres. 1988-90), Kans. Med. Soc. (treas. 1987-90, 2d v.p. 1991-92, 1st v.p. 1992-93, pres.-elect 1993-94, pres. 1994-95), Sedgwick County Psychiat. Assn. (chmn. 1990-92). Republican. Avocations: running, golf, tennis, aerobics, travel. Home: 52 Mission Rd Wichita KS 67207-1036 Office: 1010 N Kansas Wichita KS 67214-3124

BRADBEER, CLIVE, biochemistry and microbiology educator, research scientist; b. Tynemouth, Northumberland, Eng., Feb. 20, 1933; came to U.S., 1962, naturalized, 1994; s. Joseph Walter and Mary (Hall) B.; m. Wilma Jean Youngert, Sept. 1, 1960; children: Suzanne Mary, Thomas Clive. BSc with first class honors, Durham U., Newcastle Upon Tyne, Eng., 1954, PhD, 1957. Jr. rsch. biochemist U. Calif., Berkeley, 1957-59, Davis, 1959; postdoctoral fellow U. Wis., Madison, 1959-60; lectr. Queen Mary Coll., London U., 1960-62; asst. prof. Sch. Medicine, U. Va., Charlottesville, 1964-69, assoc. prof., 1969-79, prof., 1979—; vis. scientist NIH, Bethesda, Md., 1962-64, ad hoc mem. study sect., 1980-84; vis. prof. U. Otago, Dunedin, New Zealand, 1982-83, 93. Contbr. articles to profl. jours. Mem. Am. Soc. for Biochemistry and Molecular Biology. Episcopalian. Achievements include contbns. in elucidation of the molecular mechanisms involved in utilization of vitamin B12 in microbial and animal cells. Office: U Va Sch Medicine Charlottesville VA 22908

BRADBERRY, EDWARD, opera company executive; b. Augusta, Ga., June 6, 1941. BMus, U. Ga., 1961; postgrad., Ind. U. Pianist, tchr. Augusta, Ga., 1964-74; bd. dirs. Augusta Opera, 1972-74, gen. dir., 1975—. Recipient award in arts Gov.'s Office, 1978, Disting. Svc. award Opera Am., 1995. Office: Augusta Opera PO Box 3865 Augusta GA 30914-3865*

BRADBERRY, JAMES E., federal judge. Magistrate judge U.S. Dist. Ct. (ea. dist.) Va., Newport News. Fax: (804) 244-0398. Office: 218-A Post Office Bldg 101 25th St Newport News VA 23607-2449

BRADBERRY, KAREN LYNN, English educator; b. Little Rock, Oct. 26, 1970; d. Floyd Ervin and Judith Ann B. BS in Edn., U. Ark., 1993. Cert. tchr., Ark. Tchr. English Van Buren (Ark.) Pub. Schs., 1993—. Mem. Jr. League Ft. Smith, Ark., 1996—; bd. dirs. Western Ark. U. of Ark. Alumni Assn., Ft. Smith, 1996; chmn. Panhellenic Coun., Ft. Smith, 1997; ref. chmn.

Delta Delta Delta Alumnae, Ft. Smith, 1997—. Mem. Nat. Coun. Tchrs. English, Ark. Writers' Project (instr. 1993-94), Ark. Coun. Tchrs. English (bd. dirs. 1994-96, slate coord. 1996-98), Delta Kappa Gamma. Republican. Baptist. Avocations: travel, reading, drawing, golf. Office: Van Buren HS 2001 E Pointer Trl Van Buren AR 72956-2331

BRADBURN, DAVID DENISON, engineer, retired air force officer; b. Hollywood, Calif., May 27, 1925; s. Clarence Earl and Florence Lyle (Easton) B.; m. Bertha Evelyn Stout, Nov. 3, 1956; children: Carol (Mrs. Patrick V. Navagato), Susan (Mrs. Ronald G. Inloes), David Stout, Robert Easton. B.S., U.S. Mil. Acad., 1946; M.S.E., Purdue U., 1952; M.S. in Internat. Affairs, George Washington U., 1966. Commd. 2d lt. U.S. Army, 1946; advanced through grades to maj. gen. USAF, 1974; pilot, flight comdr. Korea, 1950-51; research and devel. staff officer Balt., 1952-57; mil. space research project officer Los Angeles, 1957-65; space program mgr., 1966-71; dir. space systems Washington, 1971-73; dir. spl. projects Office Sec. Air Force, Los Angeles, 1973-75; vice-comdr. Electronic Systems Div., Boston, 1975-76; ret., 1976. Mem. U.S. del. Joint Chiefs Staff rep. to U.S.-Soviet Anti-Satellite Negotiations, Helsinki, 1978, Bern, Vienna, 1979; sr. staff scientist TRW Def. Systems Group, 1980-84, dir. engring., 1984-87; chmn. bd. Beach Cities Symphony Assn., 1978-84, pres., 1984-87. Decorated D.S.M. (2), Legion of Merit (3), D.F.C., Meritorious Service medal, Air medal (4). Mem. Sigma Xi, Tau Beta Pi, Eta Kappa Nu. Mem. United Ch. of Christ. Pioneer mil. applications space vehicles. Home: 421 2nd St Manhattan Beach CA 90266-6513

BRADBURN, NORMAN M., behavioral science educator; b. Lincoln, Ill., July 21, 1933; s. Hubert Benjamin and Mary Celeste (Marshall) B.; m. Wendy McAneny, Dec. 15, 1956; children: Isabel Stuart, Andrew Marshall, Laura Humphreys. BA, U. Chgo., 1952, Oxford U., Eng., 1955; MA, Harvard U., 1958, PhD in Social Psychology, 1960. From asst. prof. to assoc. prof. behavioral sci. U. Chgo., 1960-67, prof., 1967—, chmn. dept. behavioral sci., 1973-79, Tiffany and Margaret Blake Disting. Service prof., 1977—, provost, 1984-89; sr. study dir. Nat. Opinion Research Center, Chgo., 1961—, dir., 1967-71, 79-84, 89-92, rsch. dir., 1992—. Author: (with D. Caplovitz) Reports on Happiness, 1967, The Structure of Psychological Well-Being, 1970, (with S. Sudman, G. Gockel) Side by Side: A Study of Integrated Neighborhoods, 1971, (with S. Sudman) Response Effects in Surveys, 1974, Asking Questions: A Practical Guide to Questionnaire Construction, 1982, Polls and Surveys: Understanding What They Tell Us, 1988, (with others) Improving Questionnaire Design and Interview Method, 1979, (with S. Sudman and N. Schwarz) Thinking About Answers, 1996. Alexander von Humboldt scholar U. Cologne (Germany), 1970-71. Fellow AAAS, Am. Statis. Assn.; mem. Internat. Statis. Inst., World Assn. Pub. Opinion Rsch., Am. Assn. Pub. Opinion Rsch. (pres. 1991-92), Am. Acad. Arts and Scis. Home: 5326 S University Ave Chicago IL 60615-5106

BRADBURY, DANIEL JOSEPH, library administrator; b. Kansas City, Kans., Dec. 7, 1945; m. Mary F. Callaghan, May 10, 1967 (div. 1987); children—Patricia, Tracy, Amanda, Anthony, Sean, m. Jobeth Baile Cannady, Nov. 23, 1988. B.A. in English, U. Mo., Kansas City, 1971; M.L.S., Emporia State U., 1972; LittD, Baker U., 1992. Assoc. dir. extension service Waco-McLennan Library, Tex., 1972-74; library dir. Rolling Hills Consol. Library, St. Joseph, Mo., 1974-77, Janesville Pub. Library, Wis., 1977-83; dir. leisure services City of Janesville, 1982-83; library dir. Kansas City Pub. Library, Mo., 1983—; interim exec. dir. Kansas City Sch. Dist., Mo., 1985; faculty Baylor U., Waco, 1973-74; participant Gov.'s Conf. on Library and Info. Sci., Wis., 1979; mem. council Kansas City Metro Library Network, 1984—, pres., 1987, mem. coordinating bd. for higher edn. library adv. com., 1984—, chmn., 1986-87, pres. 1991—; bd. dirs. Greater Kansas City Coun. Philantrophy. Bd. dirs. Arrowhead Library System, Janesville, 1978-83, Mid-Town Troost Assn., Kansas City, St. John's Sch., Janesville, 1980-83, Pub. Sch. Retirement Fund, Kansas City, 1995—, treas., 1996—. Named Libr. of Yr. Libr. Jour., N.Y.C., 1991; recipient Disting. Grad. award Emporia State U., 1985, Cornerstone award Kansas City Econ. Devel. Corp., 1988; Hon. Doctorate, Baker U., 1991. Mem. ALA (various offices 1972—), Am. Soc. Pub. Adminstrs. (bd. dirs. Kansas City chpt. 1994—), Mo. Libr. Assn. (legis. chmn. 1984-85), Libr. Adminstrn. and Mgmt. Assn. (sec. 1983-85), Wis. Libr. Assn. (pres. 1982). Roman Catholic. Lodge: Rotary. Home: 3318 Karnes Blvd Kansas City MO 64111-3628 Office: Kansas City Pub Libr 311 E 12th St Kansas City MO 64106-2412

BRADBURY, RAY DOUGLAS, author; b. Waukegan, Ill., Aug. 22, 1920; s. Leonard Spaulding and Esther Marie (Moberg) B.; m. Marguerite Susan McClure, Sept. 27, 1947; children: Susan Marguerite, Ramona, Bettina, Alexandra. Student pub. schs.; D. Litt., Whittier Coll., Calif., 1979. First pub. short story, 1941, stories pub. pulp mags., 1941-45. Author: (short story collections) Dark Carnival, 1947, The Illustrated Man, 1951, The Golden Apples of the Sun, 1953, Fahrenheit 451, 1953 (Commonwealth Club Calif. gold medal 1954), The October Country, 1955, A Medicine for Melancholy, 1959 (pub. in Eng. as The Day It Rained Forever, 1959), The Ghoul Keepers, 1961, The Small Assassin, 1962, The Machineries of Joy, 1964, The Vintage Bradbury, 1965, The Autumn People, 1965, Tomorrow Midnight, 1966, Twice Twenty-Two, 1966, I Sing The Body Electric!, 1969, (with Robert Bloch) Bloch and Bradbury: Ten Masterpieces of Science Fiction, 1969 (pub. in Eng. as Fever Dreams and Other Fantasies, 1970), (with Bloch) Whispers From Beyond, 1972, Harrap, 1975, Long After Midnight, 1976, The Best of Bradbury, 1976, To Sing Strange Songs, 1979, The Stories of Ray Bradbury, 1980, Dinosaur Tales, 1983, A Memory of Murder, 1984, The Toynbee Convector, 1988, Kaleidoscope, 1994; (poetry) Old Ahab's Friend, and Friend to Noah, Speaks His Piece: A Celebration, 1971, When Elephants Last in the Dooryard Bloomed: Celebrations for Almost Any Day in the Year, 1973, That Son of Richard III: A Birth Announcement, 1974, Where Robot Mice and Robot Men Run Round in Robot Towns, 1977, Twin Hieroglyphs That Swim the River Dust, 1978, The Bike Repairman, 1978, The Author Considers His Resources, 1979, The Aqueduct, 1979, The Attic Where The Meadow Greens, 1979, The Last Circus, 1980, The Ghosts of Forever, 1980, The Haunted Computer and the Android Pope, 1981, The Complete Poems of Ray Bradbury, 1982, The Love Affair, 1983, Forever and the Earth, 1984, Death has Lost Its Charm for Me, 1987; (novels) The Martian Chronicles, 1950 (pub. in Eng. as The Silver Locusts, 1951), Dandelion Wine, 1957, Something Wicked This Way Comes, 1962, Death is a Lonely Business, 1985, A Graveyard for Lunatics, 1990, Green Shadows, White Whale, 1992; (juvenile novels) Switch on the Night, 1955 (Boys Club Am. Jr. Book award 1956), R is for Rocket, 1962, S is for Space, 1966, The Halloween Tree, 1972, The April Witch, 1987, The Other Foot, 1987, The Foghorn, 1987, The Veldt, 1987, Fever Dream, 1987, The Smile, 1991; (non-fiction) Teacher's Guide: Science Fiction, 1968, Zen and the Art of Writing, 1973, Mars and the Mind of Man, 1973, The Mummies of Guanajuato, 1978, Beyond 1984: Remembrance of Things Future, 1979, Los Angeles, 1984, Orange County, 1985, The Art of Playboy, 1985, Yestermorrow: Obvious Answers to Impossible Futures, 1991, Ray Bradbury On Stage: A Chrestomathy of His Plays, 1991, Journey to Far Metaphor: Further Essays on Creativity, Writing, Literature, and the Arts, 1994, The First Book of Dichotomy, The Second Book of Symbiosis, 1995; (plays) The Meadow, 1960, Way in the Middle of the Air, 1962, The Anthem Sprinters, and Other Antics, 1963, The World of Ray Bradbury, 1964, Leviathan 99, 1966, The Day It Rained Forever, 1966, The Pedestrian, 1966, Dandelion Wine, 1967, Christus Apollo, 1969, The Wonderful Ice-Cream Suit and Other Plays, 1972, Madrigals for the Space Age, 1972, Pillar of Fire and Other Plays for Today, Tomorrow, and Beyond Tomorrow, 1975, That Ghost, That Bride of Time: Excerpts from a Play-in-Progress, 1976, The Martian Chronicles, 1977 (5 L.A. Drama Critics Circle awards), Farenheit 451, 1979, A Device Out of Time, 1986, Falling Upward, 1988; prodr. one-act plays, Royal Shakespeare Festival Theatre, The Pandemonium Theatre Co., 1963; screenwriter: (films) It Came from Outer Space, 1953, The Beast from 20,000 Fathoms, 1953, Moby Dick, 1956, Icarus Montgolfier Wright, 1962 (Academy award nomination best short film 1963), An American Journey, 1964, Picasso Summer, 1972, Something Wicked This Way Comes, 1983; (TV scripts for series) Alfred Hitchcock Presents, Jane Wyman's Fireside Theatre, steve Canyon, Trouble Shooters, Twilight Zone, Alcoa Premiere, Curiosity Shop, Ray Bradbury Television Theatre; editor: Timeless Stories for Today and Tomorrow, 1952, The Circus of Dr. Lao and Other Improbable Stories, 1956, A Day in the Life of Hollywood, 1992. Recipient O. Henry prize, 1947, 48, Benjamin Franklin award best story, 1954, Nat. Inst. Arts and Letters award, 1954, Golden Eagle award, 1957, Mrs. Ann Radcliffe award Count Dracula Soc., 1965, 71, Writers Guild award 1974, World Fantasy award for lifetime achievement, 1977, Balrog award best poet, 1979, Aviation and Space Writers award, 1979, Gandalf award, 1980, PEN Body of Work award, 1985. Mem. Screen Writers Guild, Sci. Fantasy Writers Am., Pacific Art Found. (v.p.), Writers Guild Am. (mem. screen writers bd.). Office: Bantam Doubleday Dell 1540 Broadway New York NY 10036-4039*

BRADDOCK, DAVID LAWRENCE, health science educator; b. Glendale, Calif., Mar. 10, 1945; s. Mark Perry and Christina Bain Braddock; m. Laura Stanlye Haffer, May 1, 1976; children: Gabriel, Autumn, Adam. BA, U. Tex., 1967, MA, 1970, PhD, 1973. Spl. asst. to dir. sec.'s com. on mental retardation HEW, Washington, 1972; prin. investigator Coun. for Exceptional Children, Reston, Va., 1973-77; cons. White House Conf. on the Handicapped, Washington, 1977-78; rsch. prof., program dir. Inst. Study Devel. Disabilities U. Ill., Chgo., 1979-88, prof. cmty. health scis. Sch. Pub. Health, 1985—, prof. human devel., head dept. Disability & Human Devel., 1988—, assoc. dean for rsch., 1997-98; cons. U.S. Dept. HHS, Washington, 1972—. Author: Federal Policy Toward Mental Retardation, 1987, Residential Services and Developmental Disabilities in U.S., 1992, The State of the States in Developmental Disabilities, 5th edit., 1997; contbr. numerous articles to profl. jours. Cons. Pres.'s Com. on Mental Retardation, Washington, 1973—, Joseph P. Kennedy Jr. Found.; active in promoting civil and human rights of people with mental retardation and other disabilities. Grantee U.S. Dept. Health and Human Svcs., U.S. Dept. Edn.; Nat. Inst. on Disability and Rehab. Rsch. fellow U.S. Dept. Edn., 1988-89; sr. univ. scholar U. Ill., 1998—. Fellow Am. Assn. on Mental Retardation (pres. 1993-94, editor books and monographs 1997—, Career Rsch. award 1998), Delta Omega; mem. AAAS, Assn. for Retarded Citizens of U.S. (mem. sci. adv. bd. 1987—, Disting. Rsch. awrd in Mental Retardation 1987), Am. Assn. Mental Retardation (Career Rsch. award 1998). Office: U Ill Chgo Dept Disability & Human Dev 1640 W Roosevelt Rd Chicago IL 60608-1316

BRADDOCK, JOSEPH VINCENT, physicist; b. Hoboken, N.J., Dec. 10, 1929; s. Ralph and Rose (Rago) Braddock; m. Teresa Marquez, June 24, 1961 (dec. Nov. 1961); m. Bertha Soto, Jan. 30, 1965; children: J. Anthony, Robert T. BS in Physics, St. Peter's Coll., 1951; MS in Physics, Fordham U., 1952, PhD in Physics, 1958. Asst. prof. Iona Coll., New Rochelle, N.Y., 1958-60; co-founder, exec. BDM Internat., McLean, Va., 1960-93; trustee Potomac Found., McLean, 1988—; cons. Dept. Def., Washington, 1975—, Dept. Army Sci. Bd., Washington, 1977-83, 93—; adv. bd. Nat. Security Agy., Ft. Meade, Md., 1977-85. Trustee Inova Hosp. Found., McLean, 1996—, Aztec Found., Alexandria, Va., 1988—, Alexandria Symphony Orch., 1990—; bd. dirs. Shrine of Immaculate Conception, Washington, 1995—. Mem. IEEE, Am. Phys. Soc. Roman Catholic. Avocations: travel, architecture, history of science and technology. Home: 1101 Saint Stephens Rd Alexandria VA 22304-1728 Office: Potomac Found 1311 Dolley Madison Blvd Ste 2A Mc Lean VA 22101-3925

BRADDOM, RANDALL L., physician, medical educator; b. Monarch, Va., Oct. 29, 1942; s. Audy Lee and Ruth Janet Braddom; m. Carolyn Lentz; children: Eric C., Steven R., Karen L. BA, DePauw U., 1964; MD, Ohio State U., 1968, MS, 1971. Diplomate Am. Bd. Electrodiagnostic Medicine, Am. Bd. Phys. Medicine and Rehab. Rotating intern Mt. Carmel Hosp., Columbus, Ohio, 1968-69; resident in phys. medicine and rehab. Ohio State Univ. Hosps., Columbus, 1969-72; physiatrist, electromyographer Rancocas Valley Hosp., Willingboro, N.J., 1972-74, Phila. Naval Med. Ctr., 1972-74; asst. prof. phys. medicine and rehab. U. Cin., 1974-75, assoc. prof., dir. phys. medicine and rehab., 1975-81; med. dir. phys. med. and rehab. St. Francis-St. George Hosp., Cin., 1987-89, Providence Hosp., Cin., 1982-89; assoc. prof., dep. chmn. rehab. medicine Temple U., Phila., 1989-91; chmn. rehab. medicine Albert Einstein Hosp., Phila., 1989-91; v.p. med. affairs Moss Rehab. Hosp., Phila., 1989-91; practitioner Rehab. Assocs., Indpls., 1991-96; med. dir. Hook Rehab. Ctr., Indpls., 1991-98; prof., chmn. phys. medicine and rehab. Ind. U. Sch. Medicine, Indpls., 1991-92; CEO, med. dir. Wishard Health Svcs, Indpls., 1998—; cons. physiatrist Albert Einstein Med. Ctr. N., Phila., 1973; clin. instr. rehab. medicine Thomas Jefferson Coll. Med., Phila., 1972-74; assoc. in medicine Jewish Hosp., Cin., 1974-89; cons. phys. medicine and rehab. VA Hosp., Cin., 1975-81; dir. phys. med. and rehab. U. Hosps., U. Cin., 1975-81; assoc. clin. prof. phys. med. Ohio State U., Columbus, 1984—; clin. assoc. prof. phys. medicine and rehab. U. Cin., Coll. Medicine, 1982-89; cons. St. Francis Hosp., Indpls., 1991-97; phys. med. and rehab. svc. chief Wishard Meml. Hosp., Indpls., 1991—; dir. phys. medicine and rehab. svc. Richard Roudebush VA Hosp., Indpls., 1991—; presenter Internat. Rehab. Fedn., Montreal, 1968, U. Wash., Seattle, 1972, Thomas Jefferson U. Med. Coll., Phila., 1974, 75, 76, Santa Clara Valley Med. Ctr., San Jose, Calif., 1976, Ohio State U., 1976, Nat. Paraplegia Found., 1977, Am. Acad. Orthopaedic Surgery, New Orleans, 1977, Jewish Hosp., Cin., 1977, Rehab. Inst. Chgo., 1982, 84, Am. Assn. Electromyography and Electrodiagnosis, Toronto, 1984, Las Vegas, 1985, Pitts., 1985, Ky. Family Practice Assn. Symposium, Covington, 1984, Am. Heart Assn., Cin., 1984, Ohio State U. Coll. Medicine, Salt Fork, 1985, Am. Acad. Phys. Medicine and Rehab., Kansas City, 1985, Nat. Spinal Cord Injury Assn., Cin., 1985, Am. Rehab. Edn. Network, Pitts., 1985; presenter in field; vis. prof. Dept. Phys. Medicine and Rehab. U. Ark., 1992, U. Ky. Dept Phys. Medicine and Rehab., 1992, Dept. Internal Medicine Dvsn. Phys. Medicine & Rehab. La. State U. Sch. Medicine, New Orleans, La., 1994, Baylor Coll. Medicine Dept. Physical Medicine & Rehab., 1994, N.J. Sch. Medicine and Dentistry Dept. P.M. & R., lectr. in field; Licht lectr. Dept. Phys. Medicine & Rehab. U. Minn., 1993. Author: (with others) Physical Medicine & Rehabilitation Review, 1980; editor: Sports Medicine and Rehabilitation: A Sport-Scientific Approach, 1994, Physical Medicine and rehabilitation, 1996; contbr. articles to profl. jours. Founder, med. dir. ECCO Family Health Ctr., Inc., Columbus, 1970-72; bd. dirs. Nat. Paraplegia Found., 1975-80; med. adviser Easter Seals Soc. Southwestern Ohio, 1980-82; asst. scoutmaster Troop 291, Boy Scouts Am., 1982-84; chmn. Citizens for Our Schs. Tax Levy Campaign, Forest Hills Sch. Dist., Cin., 1985; trustee Total Living Concepts, Inc., Cin., 1977-85, Disability Svcs. Group, Inc., Cin., 1985-89; bd. examiners The Henry B. Betts award, 1991-94. Lt. comdr. USNR, 1972-74. Recipient Kiwanis Club Citizenship award, Dayton, 1960, Rsch. award Am. Paralyzed Vets. Assn., 1968, Am. Therapeutic Soc., 1968, Landacre Soc. award Ohio State U., 1978, Sidney Licht Lectureship Ohio State U., 1985, Alumni Achievement award Ohio State U., 1993, Sidney Licht Lectureship U. Minn., 1993, Randy Braddom award U. Cin. Coll. Medicine, 1989; named Man of Yr. Columbus Citizen-Jour., 1970, Landerwerlen award Muscular Dystrophy Found. Ind., 1994. Mem. Indpls. Med. Soc., Ind. Soc. Phys. Med. and Rehab., Nat. Stroke Assn., Am. Kinesiotherapy Assn. (mem. adv. bd. 1993—), Am. Acad. Phys. Med. and Rehab. (med. edn. com. 1983-86, membership recruitment group 1987, career brochure devel. group 1987, joint annual meeting planning subcom. 1987-88, chairperson continuing med. edn. subcom. 1982-86, sci. program com. 1982-86, mktg. and comms. com. 1987-89, chairperson med. edn. com. 1986-88, sec. bd. govs. 1988-90, third-mem.-at-large 1990-91, 2nd mem.-at-large 1991-92, 1st mem.-at-large 1992-93, chair awards com. 1992-93, v.p. 1994-95, fin. com. 1994-95, chair annual meeting task force 1994-95, pres. elect 1994-95, pres. 1995-96, past pres. 1996-97, Disting. Clinician award 1997), Am. Assn. Electrodiagnostic Medicine (com. on edn. 1974-76, exam. com. 1975-76, liaision to assn. of acad. physiatrists 1988, chairperson courses com. 1986-89, pres.-elect 1989-90, bd. dirs. 1989-92, pres. 1990-91, immediate past pres.-chairperson long-range planning com. 1991-92, chmn. long range planning com. 1991-92, alt. del. AMA House of Dels. 1993-95, nominating com. 1993-94, chmn. 1994-95), Am. Assn. Electrodiagnostic Medicine, Assn. Acad. Physiatrists, Ohio State Med. Alumni Assn., AMA, Am. Bd. Electrodiagnostic Medicine (bd. dirs. 1994, long-range planning com. 1994, treas. 1995-98), Am. Kinesiotherapy Assn. (adv. bd. 1993—), Cin. Soc. of Phys. Medicine and Rehab. (pres., founder 1987-88), Internat. Med. Med. Assn. (U.S. counselor 1986-95). Office: Wishard Health Svcs 1001 W 10th St Indianapolis IN 46202-2859

BRADEMAS, JOHN, retired university president, former congressman; b. Mishawaka, Ind., Mar. 2, 1927; s. Stephen J. and Beatrice Cenci (Goble) B.; m. Mary Ellen Briggs, July 9, 1977. B.A. magna cum laude (Vets. nat. scholar), Harvard, 1949; D.Phil. (Rhodes scholar), Oxford (Eng.) U., 1954; LL.D. (hon.), U. Notre Dame, Middlebury Coll., Tufts U. (others); L.H.D., Brandeis U., CCNY (others). Legislative asst. to U.S. Senator Pat McNamara; adminstrv. asst. U.S. Rep. Thomas L. Ashley, 1955; exec. asst. to presdl. nominee Stevenson, 1955-56; asst. prof. polit. sci. St. Mary's Coll., Notre Dame, Ind., 1957-58; mem. 86th-96th Congresses from 3d Ind. Dist.; chief dep. majority whip 93d-94th Congresses; majority whip 95th-96th Congresses; mem. com. house adminstrn., com. on edn. and labor, joint com. on Library of Congress; pres. NYU, 1981-92, pres. emeritus, 1992—; chmn. bd. dirs. Fed. Res. Bank N.Y.; dir. RCA/NBC, Loew's Corp., Scholastic, Inc., N.Y. Stock Exchange, Rockefeller Found.; Past mem. bd. visitors John F. Kennedy Sch. Govt.; bd. overseers Harvard U.; mem. overseers' com. to visit Grad. Sch. Edn.; trustee, mem. adv. council Coll. Arts and Letters U. Notre Dame; bd. visitors dept. polit. sci. M.I.T.; bd. advs. Dumbarton Oaks Research Library and Collection, Woodrow Wilson Center Internat. Scholars; mem. Central Com. World Council Chs.; past mem. Nat. Hist. Publs. Commn., Nat. Commn. on Financing Post-Secondary Edn.; mem. Nat. Commn. Student Fin. Assistance, Study Nat. Needs Biomed. and Behavioral Research NRC, Nat. Acad. Sci. Com. Relations between Univs. and Govt.; bd. dirs. Am. Council Edn.; chmn. N.Y. State Coun. on Fiscal and Econ. Priorities; bd. dirs. Loews Corp., NYNEX, Scholastic Inc., Texaco Inc., Alexander S. Onassis Pub. Benefit Found., N.Y. Stock Exch., Rockefeller Found. Author: Anarcosindicalismo y revolucion en Espana, 1930-37, 1974, Washington, D.C. to Washington Square, 1986; co-author The Politics of Education: Conflict and Consensus on Capitol Hill, 1978. Bd. dirs. Aspen Inst., Berlitz Internat. Inc., Carnegie Endowment Nat. Commn. on Am. and the New World, Nat. Endowment for Democracy, Carnegie Commn. on Sci., Tech. and Govt., chmn. com. on Congress; mem. Nat. Adv. Coun. on the Pub. Svc.; bd. dirs Ctr. for Nat. Policy, chmn. exec. com.; chmn. Nat. Adv. Com. of Fighting Back; trustee U. Notre Dame, Spelman Coll.; bd. dirs. Am. Coun. for the Arts, Acad. for Ednl. Devel., Athens Coll. (Greece), Coun. to Aid Edn.; mem. Smithsonian Nat. Bd.; trustee Com. for Econ. Devel.; mem. Cons. Panel to Comptr. Gen of U.S., Bd. of Advisors of The Carter Ctr. Emory U., Carnegie Coun. on Ethics and Internat. Affairs, Trilateral Commn.; chmn.Internat. Adv. Coun. of Internat. Jewish Com. for Sepharad '92; co-chmn. Due Case Una Tradizione. Served with USNR, 1945-46. Decorated chevalier of Legion of Honor (France, High Knight Comdr. of Honor Order of the Phoenix (Greece); recipient Disting. Service award Inst. Internat. Edn., 1966, Disting. Service award NEA, 1968, Disting. Service award Tchrs. Coll., Columbia U., 1969; Merit award Nat. Council Sr. Citizens, 1972; Disting. Service award Council of State Adminstrs. of Vocat. Rehab., 1973; Disting. Service award Conservation Edn. Assn., 1974; Caritas Soc. award for outstanding contbns. in field of mental retardation, 1975; Gold Key award Am. Congress Rehab. Medicine, 1976; named Humanist of Year Nat. Assn. Humanities Edn., 1978; award for disting. service to arts AAAL, 1978; George Peabody award, 1980; Hubert H. Humphrey award Am. Polit. Sci. Assn., 1984, Ann. Gold medal The Spanish Inst., N.Y.C., 1985, Ellis Island Medal of Honor, 1986, Nat. Gov.s Assn. award, 1988, Athenagoras award for Human Rights, 1990, Gold Medal of Honor of City of Athens, 1991. Fellow Am. Acad. Arts and Scis. (coun.); mem. Am. Legion, Phi Beta Kappa (Senator). Methodist. Clubs: Masons, Ahepa. Office: NYU Office of President 53 Washington Sq S New York NY 10012-1098*

BRADEN, BERWYN BARTOW, lawyer; b. Pana, Ill., Jan. 10, 1928; s. George Clark and Florence Lucille (Bartow) B.; m. Betty J.; children—Scott, Mark, Mathew, Sue, Ralph, Ladd, Brad. Student, Carthage Coll., 1946-48, U. Wis., 1948-49; J.D., U. Wis., 1959. Bar: Wis. 1959, U.S. Supreme Ct. 1965. Ptnr. Genoar & Braden, Lake Geneva, Wis., 1959-63; individual practice law Lake Geneva, Wis., 1963-68, 72-74; ptnr. Braden & English, Lake Geneva, Wis., 1968-72, Braden & Olson, Lake Geneva, Wis., 1974—; city atty. City of Lake Geneva, 1962-64; tchr. Law Sch., U. Wis., 1977. Bd. dirs. Lake Geneva YMCA. Mem. ABA, Walworth County Bar Assn. (pres. 1962-63), State Bar Wis. (chmn. conv. and entertainment com. 1979-81, chmn. adminstrn. Justice and Judiciary com., 1986-87, bench bar rels. com., 1987-90, mem. exec. com. Wis. Bicentennial Com. on Constn.), Wis. Acad. Trial Lawyers (sec. 1975, treas. 1976, dir. 1977-79), Assn. Trial Lawyers Am. Home: 1031 W Main St Lake Geneva WI 53147-1700 Office: 716 Wisconsin St Lake Geneva WI 53147-1826 also: PO Box 940 Lake Geneva WI 53147-0940

BRADEN, CHARLES HOSEA, physicist, university administrator; b. Chgo., Mar. 21, 1926; s. Charles Eugene and Rachel Irene (Atchison) B.; m. Sara Caroline McKinley, Sept. 7, 1952; children—Patsy Irene, Jack David. BS in Engring, Columbia U., 1946; PhD in Physics, Washington U., St. Louis, 1951. Asst. prof. physics Ga. Inst. Tech., 1951-53, assoc. prof., 1953-59, prof., 1959-71, Regents prof. physics, 1971-91; assoc. dir. Sch. Physics, 1971-80, interim dir., 1980-82; assoc. program dir. for physics NSF, Washington, 1959-60; cons. Fernbank Mus. Natural History, 1989-96. Contbr. articles to Phys. Rev., Sys. Dynamics Rev. Served with USNR, 1943-47. Fellow Am. Phys. Soc. Episcopalian. Research in exptl. nuclear physics, modeling of socio-econ. systems.

BRADEN, GEORGE WALTER, II (BARRON OF CARRIGALINE), company executive; b. L.A., Sept. 1, 1936; s. Paul Sumner and Evelyn Widney (Traver) B.; m. Trina Rose Thomas, July 3, 1964; children: Barbara Diane, Beverly Eileen Braden Christensen. BS, Calif. State U., 1963; grad. cert., U. So. Calif., 1990, Harvard U., 1991; postgrad., UCLA, 1990—; MBA, Chadwick U.; JA, Blackstone Law Sch. Mgr. western region vet. div. Bristol-Myers, Syracuse, N.Y., 1970-79; pres. Braden Sales Assocs. Internat., Apple Valley, Calif., 1980—. Mem. Friends of Hoover Inst., Stanford, Calif.; charter mem. Rep. Presdl. Task Force, Washington, 1989—; commr. Rep. Presdl. Adv. Com., Washington, 1991—; active Nat. Rep. Senatorial Com. Capt. USMB, 1985-93, maj., 1993—. Recipient Presdl. order of Merit, Heritage Found., Rep. Presdl. award, 1994; numerous awards Boy Scouts of Am.; named Lord of North Bovey, Lord of Newton Bushel. Mem. Am. Mktg. Assn., Tex. A&M U. Internat. Assn. of Agri-Bus., Curia Baronis Guild for Barons, Lords of Manor, Pres.'s Club. Mem. LDS Ch.

BRADEN, JAMES DALE, former state legislator; b. Wakefield, Kans., Aug. 2, 1934; s. James Wesley and Olive (Reed) B.; m. Naomi Carlson, July 3, 1952 (div. Jan. 1982); children: Gregory, Michael, Ladd, Amy; m. Margie Clark Tidwell, Sept. 17, 1983; stepchildren: Richard, Lon, Dale. Grad. high sch., Wakefield. CLU, The Am. Coll. Meat cutter Wakefield, 1952-64; ins. agt., securities broker Braden Fin. Svcs., Clay Ctr., Kans., 1964—; state rep. Kans. Ho. of Reps., Topeka, 1974-91, house majority leader, 1985-87, speaker of the house, 1987-91; past chmn. econ. devel. com. Nat. Conf. State Legislatures, legis. coordinating council, calendar and printing com.; past chmn. assessment and taxation com.; mem. Council of State Govts. intergovtl. affairs com.; past chmn. taxation task force of Midwestern Conf. of Council State Govts.; chmn. Interstate Cooperation Commn.; former mem. State Fin. Council, Kans. Inc.; past chmn. Legis. Commn. on Kans. Econ. Devel.; past mem. Kans. Pub. Agenda Commn. Active St. Paul's Episcopal Ch., Clay Ctr.; mem. Rep. Party Exec. Com. Mem. NALU, Kans. Assn Life Underwriters (past pres.), Million Dollar Round Table (life), Rotary, Masons, Shriners, Elks. Episcopalian. Avocations: hunting, fishing, flying, sailing. Home: PO Box 58 Clay Center KS 67432-0058 Office: Braden Fin Svcs 1101 5th St # 58 Clay Center KS 67432-2021

BRADEN, JOHN ALAN, accountant; b. Houston, Feb. 9, 1945; s. John Earl and Marjorie (Wilson) B.; m. Leilani D. Fowler, Dec. 9, 1972; children: Meredith, Alana. BBA, U. Houston, 1967. CPA, Tex. Sr. acct. Haskins & Sells, Houston, 1967-71; pres. John A. Braden, Houston, 1971-86, Braden & Kikis, Houston, 1986-96, John A. Braden & Co., Houston, 1996—, Braden, Bennink, Goldstein, Gazaway & Co., PLLC, 1996—. Contbr. articles to profl. jours. Bd. dirs., treas. Northampton Mcpl. Utility Dist., Spring, Tex., 1986—; pres., commr. Harris County Rural Fire Protection Dist. # 1, 1989-92; officer parent orgn. Klein Oak H.S., 1986-94; chmn. audit com., mem. adminstrv. bd., fin. com., found. trustee, choir pres. Klein United Meth. Ch., Spring. Mem. AICPA, Tex. Soc. CPAs (bd. dirs., com. chmn. 1969—), Houston Chpt. CPAs (bd. dirs., com. chmn. 1969—, v.p. 1990-91), Houston Estate and Fin. Forum, Planned Giving Coun. Houston. Republican. Home: 6107 Knollview Dr Spring TX 77389-3748 Office: John A Braden & Co Ste 422 12941 North Fwy Houston TX 77060-1242

BRADEN, MARTHA BROOKE, concert pianist, educator; b. Sturgis, Mich., July 19, 1936; d. Frederick Richard and Laura Clemens (Brooke) B.; m. Edmund Sanford Jones, Mar. 14, 1959 (div. Aug. 1983); children: Carrie Brooke, David Sanford, Christopher Braden, Charles Clemens, Mary Evelyn Jones. Studied with Frances Oman Clark, Kalamazoo, 1942-60; student, Kalamazoo Coll., 1954-55; MusB, Westminster Choir Coll., Princeton, N.J., 1959; studied with Dr. Julius Hereford, N.Y.C., 1957-59; student, New Sch.

for Music Study, Princeton, 1960-61; studied with David Kraehenbuehl, Princeton, 1959-61, 84-97; studied with Erno Balogh, Washington, 1976-79; studied with Ross Lee Finney, N.Y.C., 1987-88, studied with Madame Ming Tcherepnin, 1979-91. Cert. directress Montessori primary edn. ages 2 1/2 to 6 Washington Montessori Inst.; cert. of attendance advanced course in Montessori edn. ages 6-12 State Ctr. for Montessori Studies, Bergamo, Italy; cert. of achievement Carl Orff Music Level I, Bloomingdale House of Music, N.Y.C. Piano tchr. Frances Clark Studios, Kalamazoo, 1951-54; piano faculty piano and prep. depts. Westminster Choir Coll., Princeton, 1956-60; founding faculty mem., co-dir. piano playshops, piano tchr. New Sch. for Music Study, Princeton, 1960-61; co-founder, kindergarten tchr., Montessori primary dir. Hope Montessori Sch., Annandale, Va., 1963-68; co-founder, lower elem. dir. New City Montessori Sch., Washington, 1969-74; piano faculty New Sch. for Music Study, Princeton, 1978-80; dir. of music upper elem. level St. Michael's Montessori Sch., N.Y.C., 1979-81; piano tchr./coach Braden Piano Studio, Washington, 1975-78, N.Y.C., 1979—; workshop leader on music and gen. edn. local and regional meetings, convs., N.Am. Montessori Tchrs. Assn., 1972-80. Featured artist (with Doris Jean Martin) Denver Symphony Orch., Red Rocks Ampitheater, 1951; pub. concerts at mus., schs., colls. and concert halls, 1948-60; featured artist Kalamazoo Symphony, Mich., South Bend (Ind.) Symphony, 1954; recitalist (with Doris Jean Martin) Frances Clark Piano Workshops for Piano Tchrs., nationwide, summers 1948-58; pianist (with Sanford Jones) Montessori schs., tchg. ctrs. and tchrs.' convs., N.Am., 1962-81; N.Y. debut solo recital Carnegie Recital Hall, 1977, Lincoln Ctr. debut solo recital Alice Tully Hall, 1980; solo recitals include Carnegie Recital Hall, N.Y.C., 1979, Abraham Goodman House, N.Y.C., 1981, Merkin Concert Hall, N.Y.C., 1984, 85; artist roster Circum-Arts Found., Inc., 1999—; recs. include Haydn Concerto in D Major, 1947, Music for Walking on the Line, 1977, (with Doris Jean Martin) Jig for a Concert, 1957; soloist, originator: (recs. and tchrs.' guide) Music Through History, 1974; soloist, project dir.: (recs.) David Kraehenbuehl, 1999, Alexander Tcherepnin, 1991, Ross Lee Finney, 1988; contbr. articles to profl. mags. and catalogs. Performer benefit concerts UN Internat. Sch., N.Y., St. Luke's Sch., N.Y., others, 1979—, Meadowlakes Retirement Home, Heightstown, N.J., 1980, 82, 83, Jewish Hosp. and Home for Aged, N.Y.C., 1996, 97; participant Concert Celebrating UN Day, Tex. Sch. for Boys and St. Alcuin's Montessori Sch., Dallas, 1984; mem. local 802 music union AFL-CIO, N.Y.C., 1984-89, 97—. 1st pl. winner (twice) Kalamazoo Symphony and the Battle Creek Symphony, 1953, 2d pl. winner Bartok-Kabalevsky Internat. Piano Competition, Radford Coll., 1992; recipient Tcherepnin award Ibla Internat. Piano Competition, Ragusa, Italy, 1993; grantee concert and tchg. tour of mainland China, Ministry of Culture and Conservatories of Music/The Tcherepnin Soc., 1982, Irving S. Gilmore Found., 1987; music scholar Kalamazoo Coll., 1954. Mem. Music Tchrs. Nat. Assn., N.Y. State Music Tchrs. Assn., NYU Interactive Performance Group. Avocations: family, friends, forests, cooking, traveling. Office: Martha Braden Studio # 7A 780 W End Ave Apt 7A New York NY 10025-5548

BRADEN, SAMUEL EDWARD, economics educator; b. Hoihow, Hainan, China, June 6, 1914; s. Samuel Ray and Mary (Altman) B.; m. Beth Black, 1937; children: Mary Beth, Stephen, John, David. A.B., U. Okla., 1932; M.A., U. Wis., 1935, Ph.D., 1941; LL.D. hon., Ill. State U., 1976, Ind. U., 1983. Instr. to prof. Ind. U., 1937-67; assoc. dean Coll. Arts and Sci., 1954-59, v.p., 1959-67; pres. Ill. State U., 1967-70; chmn. div. bus. and econs. Ind. U. S.E., 1970-80; mem. exec. com. Council Internat. Ednl. Exchange, N.Y., 1967-83; exec. dir. Ind. Conf. Higher Edn., 1963-67; sr. economist Combined Raw Materials Bd., Washington, 1942-43. Author: (with C.L. Christenson, others) Economics, Principles and Problems, 1946, (with G.A. Steiner, others) Economic Problems of the War; Contbr. articles to ednl. publs. Bd. overseers St. Meinrad Sem.; mem. bd. Hughes Group, Inc.; bus. economist Shaw Internat. Inc.; mem. bd. Christian edn. Presbyn. Ch. Fulbright sr. research fellow U.K., 1949-50. Mem. Am., Midwest econ. assns., Am. Finance Assn., Phi Beta Kappa. Home: 1056 Sassafras Cir Bloomington IN 47408-1279

BRADEN, THOMAS WARDELL, news commentator; b. Greene, Iowa, Feb. 22, 1918; s. Thomas Wardell and Louise (Garl) B.; m. Joan E. Ridley, Dec. 18, 1948; children: David, Mary, Joan, Susan, Nancy, Elizabeth, Thomas Wardell III (dec.), Nicholas R. AB, Dartmouth Coll., 1940, AM, 1964; LittD, Franklin Coll. Ind., 1979. Newspaperman; instr. English Dartmouth, 1946, asst. to pres. and asst. prof., 1947-48; exec. sec. Mus. Modern Art, N.Y.C., 1949; dir. Am. Com. on United Europe, 1950; editor, pub. Blade Tribune, Oceanside, Calif., 1954-68; columnist Los Angeles Times Syndicate, 1968-86; commentator CNN, CBS, NBC, 1978-89. Author: (with Stewart Alsop) Sub-Rosa, 1946, Eight is Enough, 1975. Mem. Calif. Bd. Edn., 1959-67; past. pres. Trustee Calif. State Coll., 1961-64, Dartmouth, 1964-74, Carnegie Endowment, 1970-82. Served with King's Royal Rifle Corps Brit. Army, Africa and Italy, 1941-44; trans. to inf. AUS, 1944.

BRADER, WILLIAM R., engineer, architectural firm executive; b. Phila., Dec. 9, 1947; s. Weldon Lee and Florence Mary Brader; m. Joyce DeLaurentis, July 10, 1971; children: Matthew D., Andrew D. BS in Mech. Engring., Drexel U., 1970, MS in Environ. Engring., 1974. Registered profl. engr., Pa., N.J., Md. Prin. Kling Lindquist, Phila., 1974—. Contbr. articles to profl. jours. Recipient Engr. of Yr. award Internat. Soc. for Pharm. Engrs., 1988, named Mem. of Yr., 1996. Mem. ASHRAE, Am. Soc. Agrl. Engrs., Soc. Am. Mil. Engrs. Avocations: travel, fishing, antiques. Email: wbrader@tklp.com. Home: 8 Boothby Ct Mount Laurel NJ 08054 Office: Kling Lindquist 2301 Chestnut St Philadelphia PA 19103

BRADFORD, BARBARA REED, lawyer; b. Cleve., June 13, 1948; d. William Cochran and Martha Lucile (Horn) B.; m. Warren Neil Davis, Oct. 9, 1976 (div. 1989); m. S. Jack Odell, Dec. 12, 1991. BA, Pitzer Coll., 1970; JD, Georgetown U., 1975, MBA, 1985. Bar: N.Y. 1976, D.C. 1976. Staff asst. Sen. Edward M. Kennedy, Washington, 1970-71; assoc. Breed, Abbott & Morgan, N.Y.C., 1975-76, Verner, Liipfert Law Firm, Washington, 1976-78; atty. AID, Washington, 1978-83; regional dir. U.S. Trade & Devel. Agy., Washington, 1986—; pres. Georgetown Export Trading, Inc., Washington, 1984-86. Bd. dirs. Jr. League, Washington, 1977-78. Democrat. Avocations: gardening, art, riding.

BRADFORD, BARBARA TAYLOR, writer, journalist, novelist; b. Leeds, Eng.; came to U.S., 1964; d. Winston and Freda (Walker) Taylor; m. Robert Bradford, Dec. 24, 1963. Student pvt. schs., Eng.; D of Letters (hon.), Leeds (Eng.) U., 1990, U. Bradford, West Yorkshire, Eng., 1995; D of Humane Letters (hon.), Teikyo Post U., Waterbury, Conn., 1996. Women's editor Yorkshire (Eng.) Evening Post, 1951-53, reporter, 1949-51; editor Woman's Own, 1953-54; columnist London Evening News, 1955-57; exec. editor London Am., 1959-62; editor Nat. Design Center Mag., 1965-69; syndicated columnist Newsday Spls., L.I., 1968-70; nat. syndicated columnist Chgo. Tribune-N.Y. (News Syndicate), N.Y.C., 1970-75, Los Angeles Times Syndicate, 1975-81. Author: Complete Encyclopedia of Homemaking Ideas, 1968, A Garland of Children's Verse, 1968, How to Be the Perfect Wife, 1969, Easy Steps to Successful Decorating, 1971, Decorating Ideas for Casual Living, 1977, How to Solve Your Decorating Problems, 1976, Making Space Grow, 1979, Luxury Designs for Apartment Living, 1981; (novels) A Woman of Substance, 1979, Voice of the Heart, 1983, Hold the Dream, 1985, screen adaptation, 1986, Act of Will, 1986, To Be the Best, 1988, The Women in His Life, 1990, Remember, 1991, Angel, 1993, Everything to Gain, 1994, Dangerous to Know, 1995, Love in Another Town, 1995, Her Own Rules, 1996, A Secret Affair, 1996, Power of a Woman, 1997, A Sudden Change of Heart, 1999. Recipient Dorothy Dawe award Am. Furniture Mart, 1970, 71, Matrix award N.Y. Women in Comms., 1985, Spl. Jury prize for body of lit. Deauville Festival of Am.Film, 1994. Mem. Coun. Authors Guild, Nat. Soc. Interior Designers (Disting. Editl. award 1969, Nat. Press award 1971), Authors Guild Am. (mem. coun. 1989—), Am. Soc. Interior Designers. Office: Bradford Enterprises 450 Park Ave New York NY 10022-2605

BRADFORD, CARL O., judge; b. Dallas, Nov. 16, 1932; s. Montie Leroy and Vivian Ila (Milam) B.; m. Claire Solange Chaloux, Jan. 15, 1955 (dec. 1972); children: Timothy, Kathleen, Elizabeth; m. Mary Ellen Sanborn, July 7, 1973; children: Bethany, Michael. Student, U. Detroit, 1956-59; JD, U. Maine, Portland, 1962. Bar: Maine 1963, U.S. Dist. Ct. Maine 1963, U.S. Ct. Appeals (1st cir.) 1963, U.S. Supreme Ct. 1978. Asst. atty. gen. State of Maine, Augusta, 1963-64, justice Superior Ct., 1981-98, active-ret. justice Superior Ct., 1998—; bd. dirs. Nat. Ctr. State Cts., 1996—; ptnr. Powers & Bradford, Freeport, Maine, 1964-81; commr. Uniform State Laws, 1972-76; mem. drafting com. Uniform Exemptions Act, 1974-76. Served with USN, 1951-55. Fellow Am. Bar Found., Maine Bar Found.; mem. Maine Bar Assn. (bd. govs. 1970-78, pres. 1977-78), Maine Trial Lawyers Assn. (bd. govs., sec. 1970-81), ABA (ho. of dels. 1978-81, 1990-95, state bar del. 1978-81, bd. govs. 1st dist. 1990-93, bd. liaison to Nat. Conf. Spl. Ct. Judges, 1990-91, liaison to Criminal Justice Sect. 1990-93, liaison to Nat. Conf. State Trial Judges 1991-93, chair subcom. nominations and awards com. 1991-93, bd. govs. program com. 1990-91, mem. oper. com. 1991-93, project 2000 subcom. 1991-93, bd. govs. chair compensation com. 1993, bd. govs. exec. com. 1993, bd. govs. exec. dir. search com. 1990), Nat. Conf. State Trial Judges (del. 1982-97, jud. immunity com. 1984-97, chair 1991—, conf. vice chair 1993, chair-elect 1994-95, chair 1995-96), Am. Judicature Soc. Home: 225 Sea Meadows Ln Yarmouth ME 04096-5523 Office: Superior Ct PO Box 287 Portland ME 04112-0287

BRADFORD, C.O., protective services officer; b. La., Aug. 25, 1955. BA, Grambling U.; JD, U. Houston; MBA, Tex. So. U. Patrolman Houston Police Dept., 1979-91, asst. chief police, 1991-97, chief of police, 1997—. Office: Houston Police Dept 1200 Travis St Houston TX 77002-6001*

BRADFORD, DANA GIBSON, II, lawyer; b. Coral Gables, Fla., Sept. 29, 1948; s. Dana Gibson and Jeanette (Ellis) B.; m. Mary E. Bradford, June 20, 1970 (div. Jan. 1982); 1 child, Jeffrey Dana; m. Donna P. Bradford, Apr. 14, 1984; 1 child, Shannon Claire. BA, U. Fla., 1970; JD, Duke U., 1973. Bar: Fla. 1973, U.S. Dist. Ct. Fla. 1973, U.S. Ct. Appeals (5th cir.) 1974, U.S. Ct. Appeals (11th cir.) 1982, U.S. Supreme Ct. 1977. Lawyer, ptnr. Mahoney, Hadlow & Adams, Jacksonville, Fla., 1973-82, Baumer, Bradford & Walters, Jacksonville, 1982—; mem. Fla. Bd. Bar Examiners, 1989-94, chmn. bd., 1992-93; mem. Fla. Supreme Ct. Commn. on Professionalism, 1996-98; seminar lectr. Contbr. chpt. to book, articles to profl. jours. Mem. Leadership Jacksonville, 1982; spl. counsel Jacksonville Sports Authority. Capt. U.S. Army Res., 1972-80. Mem. ABA, ATLA, Jacksonville Bar Assn. (bd. govs. young lawyers sect. 1976-78, chmn. trial sects. 1989-90), Jacksonville Assn. Def. Counsel (pres. 1978-79). Democrat. Methodist. Office: Baumer Bradford & Walters 50 N Laura St Ste 2200 Jacksonville FL 32202-3625

BRADFORD, DAVID FRANTZ, economist; b. Cambridge, Mass., Jan. 8, 1939; s. Mark Waldo and Matilda (Frantz) B.; m. Gunthild Klaerchen Huober, Feb. 20, 1964; children: Theodore Huober, Catherine Louise. BA magna cum laude (Nat. Merit scholar 1956-60), Amherst Coll., 1960, LHD (hon.), 1985; MS in Applied Math., Harvard U., 1962; Ford Found. dissertation fellow, Churchill Coll., Cambridge U., 1963-64; Ph.D. in Econs, Stanford U., 1966. Econ. cons. Office Asst. Sec. of Def., Germany, Eng. and; Washington, 1964-65; acting instr. econs. Stanford U., 1965-66; asst. prof. econs. Princeton U., 1966-71, assoc. prof. econs. and public affairs, 1971-75, prof. econs. and public affairs, 1975—; assoc. dean Woodrow Wilson Sch., 1974-75, 78-80, 85-88, 89-91, acting dean, 1980, 87; vis. prof. law Harvard U., 1991; adj. prof. Sch. Law NYU, 1993—; vis. scholar Am. Enterprise Inst., 1993; mem. Pres.'s Coun. Econ. Advisers, 1991-93; dep. asst. sec. for tax policy U.S. Treasury Dept., 1975-76; dir. rsch. in taxation Nat. Bur. Econ. Rsch., 1977-91, rsch. assoc., 1977—. Author: Blueprints for Basic Tax Reform, 1984; Untangling the Income Tax, 1986; contbr. articles to profl. jours. Vice chair N.J. State and Local Expenditure and Revenue Policy Commn., 1986-88; mem. Econ. Policy Coun. N.J., 1985-88, Nat. Commn. on R.R. Retirement Reform, 1989-90. Recipient Exceptional Svc. award U.S. Treasury Dept., 1976; Woodrow Wilson fellow Stanford U., 1960-61, Fulbright fellow Belgium, 1977, fellow Ctr. Advanced Study in Behavioral Scis., Stanford, 1988-89. Mem. Am. Econ. Assn., Econometric Soc., Nat. Tax Assn., Phi Beta Kappa. Office: Princeton U Woodrow Wilson Sch Princeton NJ 08544-1013

BRADFORD, DENNIS DOYLE, real estate broker, developer; b. Tulsa, Sept. 5, 1945; s. Doyle Earl and Elta (Price) B.; m. Richie Deloris Dawson. BSBA in Econs., U. Tulsa, 1969. Sales and mktg. rep. Xerox Corp., Oklahoma City, 1969-72; comml. loan officer Mager Mortgage Co., Oklahoma City, 1973-74; pvt. practice real estate Oklahoma City, 1973—; pres., owner Bradford Oil Co., Oklahoma City, 1977-80; pres. Blazer Oil Co., Oklahoma City, 1980—; v.p. Petro So., Inc., Tampa Fla., 1983-84; ptnr. Coachman Inns, Oklahoma City, 1981-86; chmn., CEO Coachman Inc., Oklahoma City, 1985-98; dir., CFO Coachman Inc, Oklahoma City, 1998—; pres., CEO Olympic Mills Corp., Guaynabo, P.R., 1995-97; pres. West Coast Ptnrs., Inc., Clearwater Beach, Fla., 1997—; mem. nat. adv. coun. to U.S. SBA, Washington, 1982-92, del. to White House Conf. on Small Bus., 1986. Bd. dirs. Okla. Med. Ctr. Found., 1989-94, Salvation Army of P.R., 1996-97; bd. dirs., sec. Okla. Air and Space Mus., 1989-95, v.p. 1991-92, pres. 1992-93; mem. Local Selective Svc. Bd., Oklahoma City, 1988-94, Rep. Eagles, 1979-92, Rep. Presdl. Round Table. Mem. Nat. Cowboy Hall of Fame, Okla. Heritage Assn., Okla. County Hist. Soc., Air Force Assn., Navy League, Young Pres.'s Orgn. (chmn. 1993-94, N.Am. spl. projects officer 1993-94), World Pres.'s Orgn., Oklahoma City C. of C., Balloon Fedn. Am., Oklahoma City Golf and Country Club, Summit Club (Tulsa). Republican. Methodist. Home: Pointe Tarpon 1574 Pointe Tarpon Blvd Tarpon Springs FL 34689-5887 Office: Coachman Inc 301 NW 63rd St Ste 500 Oklahoma City OK 73116-7989

BRADFORD, GAIL IDONA, minister; b. Mobile, Ala., Sept. 12, 1947; d. Estes Paul and Doris (Roe) B.; m. Benjamin C. Lann, Jr., May 28, 1971 (div. May 1986). AA, Clarke Meml. Coll., Newton, Miss., 1967; BS, Miss. Coll., 1969; MA, La. Tech U., 1973; postgrad., Western Ky. U., 1979-82, 88-92; MDiv, So. Bapt. theol. Sem., 1996. Cert. tchr., sch. adminstr., counselor, home economist; ordained minister United Meth. Ch. Vocat. counselor Mobile Rehab., 1970-71; tchr. kindergarten Lincoln Parish Schs., Ruston, La., 1971-73; state staff coord. Head Start, U. South Ala., Mobile, 1973-74; dep. dir. Jefferson County Com. for Econ. Opportunity, Birmingham, Ala., 1975-76; instr. vocat. edn. Lawson State C.C., Birmingham, 1977; mental health technician Commonwealth of Ky., Louisville, 1978-79; exec. dir. Tchr. Corps, Western Ky. U., Bowling Green, 1979-82; tchr. spl. edn. Jefferson County Pub. Schs., Louisville, 1982-88, tchr. vocat. home econs., 1988-92; chaplain various hosps., 1994—; dir. children's ministry PRP United Meth. Ch., Louisville, 1995-97; assoc. pastor St. Mark United Meth. Ch., 1997—; cons., condr. workshops various pub. programs, Ala., Ky., 1973—; tchr. workshops Ky. Tech., Jefferson State Campus, Louisville, 1989—; mem. com. practitioners Commonwealth of Ky. Workforce Cabinet, 1990-92. Bd. dirs. Ministries United South Ctrl., Louisville, 1989—; active various Rep. campaigns, La., Ky., 1971-86; mem. nat. adv. bd. Safe Places, 1991—; mem. campaign staff Rep. John Buchanan of Ala., 1975-77; dir. counselors Hugh O'Brian Youth Found., 1989-91, 97-98, state chmn., 1991-93, state bd. sec., 1993-95, dist. dir. 1994-95. Recipient Tchr. award Louisville Commmunity Found., 1986, Leadership Edn. award Bellarmine Coll., Louisville, 1987; named Ky. col. Commonwealth of Ky., 1988. Mem. Ky. Vocat. Home Econs. Tchrs. (pres. region 6, 1990-91), Ky. Home Econs. Assn. (chmn. adult, secondary and elem. edn. 1988-92), Am. Vocat. Assn., Coun. for Exceptional Children, Am. Insts. Parliamentarians, Thomas Jefferson Parliamentarians (treas. 1986), Toastmasters (area gov. dist. 11, 1986-87, Able Toastmaster award 1984), Golden Key, Kappa Delta Pi. Methodist. Avocation: youth leadership training and development. Home: PO Box 8134 Louisville KY 40257-8134

BRADFORD, J. MICHAEL, prosecutor; b. Sept. 10, 1952. BS summa cum laude, U. North Tex., 1975; JD, U. Tex., 1978. Bar: Tex. 1978, U.S. Dist. Ct. (ea. dist.) Tex. 1979, U.S. Ct. Appeals (5th cir.) 1980, U.S. Supreme Ct. 1982. Briefing atty. Tex. Ct. Criminal Appeals, 1978-79; ptnr. Mehaffy, Gardia and Bradford, 1979-87; exec. asst. U.S. Atty. for Eastern Dist. Tex., Beaumont, 1983-87; U.S. magistrate Eastern Dist. Tex., Beaumont, 1987-89; dist. judge Tex. 58th Dist. Ct., Jefferson County, 1989-94; U.S. atty. Eastern Dist. Tex., Beaumont, 1994—. Pres. Three Rivers coun. Boy Scouts Am. Recipient Disting. Leadership award Nat. Assn. Cmty. Leadership, 1994, Silver Beaver award Boy Scouts Am., 1994. Mem. Am. Law Inst., Tex. Bar Found., State Bar Tex., Jefferson County Bar Assn., Downtown Rotary Club of Beaumont (pres., Paul Harris fellow 1994). Presbyterian. Office: US Atty Eastern Dist Tex 350 Magnolia St Beaumont TX 77701-2248

BRADFORD, JAMES, city official. City coun. Indpls. Office: 200 E Washington St Rm 241 Indianapolis IN 46204*

BRADFORD, JAMES C., JR., brokerage house executive; b. Nashville, July 25, 1933; s. James C. and Eleanor (Avent) B.; m. Lillian Frances Robertson, Nov., 1967; children: Jay, Bryan. BA, Princeton U., 1955. Trainee Lehman Bros., N.Y.C., 1958; ptnr. J.C. Bradford & Co., Nashville, 1959—; chmn. dist. com. Nat. Assn. Securities Dealers, Atlanta, 1970-73; dir. Securities Industry Assn., N.Y.C., 1972-75; gov. Am. Stock Exch., 1986-87; bd. dirs. N.Y. Stock Exch., 1987-93, Nat. Assn. Securities Dealers Regulation. Trustee Mongomery Bell Acad., Nashville, 1968—; pres. Nashville Symphony Assn., 1969-70; pres. bd. trustees Ensworth Sch., Nashville, 1988-89. 1st lt. USAF, 1955-57. Mem. Belle Meade Country Club (bd. dirs. 1987-89), Nat. Assn. of Securities (gov. Washington 1996). Republican. Episcopalian. Office: J C Bradford & Co 330 Commerce St Nashville TN 37201-1899

BRADFORD, JAY TURNER, insurance executive, state legislator; b. Little Rock, Apr. 30, 1940; s. Turner and Chrystal (Jacobs) B.; m. Anne Taylor Coates, Dec. 6, 1986; 1 child, Chrystal. BA, Henderson Coll., 1963. Cert. ins. counselor. Ins. agent Metropolitan Life Co., Pine Bluff, Ark., 1963-65, McLellan Ins. Co., Pine Bluff, 1968-76; pres. Pine Bluff Ins. Exchange, 1976—. Alderman City of Pine Bluff, 1981-82; mem. Ark. State Senate, 1983—; mem. chmn. Health Labor Com., 1983—; chmn. Senate Efficiency Com.; pres. pro tem elect Ark. State Senate. Named Small bus. Man of Yr., 1988; recipient leadership award Leadership Pine Bluff, 1987. Mem. Soc. Ins. Agts. (cert. ins. counselor), Ind. Ins. Agts. Ark. (pres. 1981—), Subiaco Alumni Assn. (pres. 1977), Pine Bluff Civitan (pres. 1967). Democrat. Episcopalian. Office: Chmn First Ark Ins PO Box 8367 Pine Bluff AR 71611-8367*

BRADFORD, KARLEEN, writer; b. Toronto, Ont., Can., Dec. 16, 1936; d. Karl Heinecke and Myrtle Eileen (Ney) Scott; m. James Creighton Bradford, Aug. 22, 1959; children: Donald, Kathleen, Christopher. BA, U. Toronto, 1959. Author: Wrong Again, Robbie, 1983, The Other Elizabeth, 1982 (CommCept award 1979), I Wish There Were Unicorns, 1983, The Stone In the Meadow, 1984, The Haunting at Cliff House, 1985, The Nine Days Queen, 1986, Write Now!, 1988, Windward Island, 1989 (Max and Greta Ebel award 1990), There Will Be Wolves, 1992 (Young Adult Can. Book award Can. Libr. Assn. 1993, Animal Heroes, 1995, Thirteenth Child, 1994, Shadows on a Sword, 1996, More Animal Heroes, 1996, Dragonfire, 1997, A Different Kind of Champion, 1998, Lionheart's Scribe, 1999. Com. vice chair Pub. Lending Right Commn., 1996-98, chair, 1998-2000. Mem. Writers Union Can. (1st vice chair 1997-98), Can. Authors Assn. (v.p. 1994-96), Can. Childrens Authors, Illustrators and Performers, Internat. Bd. on Books for Young People, PEN Internat. Avocations: scuba diving, skiing, hiking. Home: RR #2, Owen Sound, ON Canada N4K 5N4

BRADFORD, LOUISE MATHILDE, social services administrator; b. Alexandria, La., Aug. 3, 1925; d. Henry Aaron and Ruby (Pearson) B. BS, La. Poly. Inst., 1945; cert. in social work, La. State U., 1949; MS, Columbia U., 1953; postgrad., Tulane U., 1962, 64, La. State U., 1967; cert., U. Pa., 1966. Diplomate NASW, Am. Bd. Clin. Social Work; cert. social worker Acad. Cert. Social Workers. With La. Dept. Pub. Welfare, Alexandria, 1945-78; welfare caseworker La. Dept. Pub. Welfare, Alexandria, La., 1950-53; children's caseworker La. Dept. Pub. Welfare, Alexandria, 1957-59, child welfare cons., 1959-73, social svcs. cons., 1973-78, state cons. day care, 1963-66; dir. social svcs. St. Mary's Tng. Sch., Alexandria, 1978—; del. Nat. Day Care Conf., Washington, 1964; mem. early childhood edn. com. So. States Work Conf., Daytona Beach, Fla., 1968; mem. La. adv. com. 1970 White House Conf. on Children, also del.; mem. So. region planning com. Child Welfare League Am., 1970-73; mem. profl. adv. com. Cenla chpt. Parents Without Partners, 1970-95; adj. asst. prof. sociology La. Coll. Pineville, 1969-85; lectr. Kindergarten Workshop, 1970-72; mem. La. 4-C Steering Com.; social svcs. cons. La. Spl. Edn. Ctr., Alexandria, 1980-86; del. Internat. Conf. on Social Welfare, Nairobi, 1974, Jerusalem, 1978, Hong Kong, 1980, Brighton, 1982, Montreal, 1984. Bd. dirs. Cenla Cmty. Action Com., Alexandria, 1966-68; mem. kindergarten bd. Meth. Ch., 1967-87, ofcl. bd., 1974-75, 77-81, 83-85, 96-98. Recipient Social Worker of Yr. award Alexandria br. NASW La. Conf. Social Welfare, 1984, Hilda C. Simon award, 1987, George Freeman award, 1987. Mem. NASW, Acad. Cert. Social Workers, La. Bd. Cert. Social Workers, So. La. Assn. Children Under Six, La. Conf. Social Welfare (George Freeman award 1987, Hilda C. Simon award 1987), Internat. Coun. on Social Welfare, Am. Pub. Welfare Assn. (S.W. region planning com. 1965), Am. Assn. on Mental Retardation (La. social work chair 1989-94), DAR, Ctrl. La. Pre-Sch. Assn. (dir. 1967-70), Rapides Golf and Country Club, Lions. Home: 5807 Joyce St Alexandria LA 71302-2510 Office: PO Box 7768 Alexandria LA 71306-0768

BRADFORD, MICHAEL LEE, religious organization administrator, clergyman; b. Johnson City, Tenn., May 4, 1942; s. Harry B. Bradford and Geneva Elizabeth (Lethco) Williams; m. Julia Ann Garrett, June 6, 1966; children: Stephen Allen, Rachel Leigh. BA, Milligan Coll., 1965; postgrad., Emmanuel Sch. of Religion, 1965-71, U. Louisville, 1985—. Ordained to ministry Christian Ch., 1965; accredited resident mgr. Inst. Real Estate Mgmt.; lic. nursing home adminstr., Ky., Tenn. Minister West Walnut St. Christian Ch., Johnson City, 1963-65, Poplar Ridge Christian Ch., Piney Flats, Tenn., 1966-71, East End Christian Ch., Bristol, Va., 1971-73; supt. East Tenn. Christian Home, Elizabethton, 1973-77; sr. minister Camden Ave. Christian Ch., Louisville, 1977-84; devel. officer, dir. communications Christian Ch. Homes of Ky. Inc., Louisville, 1984-86, mgr. Friendship House, 1986-90; dir. property mgmt., 1990-91; asst. adminstr. Appalachian Christian Village, Johnson City, Tenn., 1991-97; chief devel. officer Appalachian Christian Village, 1997—; chmn. emergency assistance South Louisville Community Ministry, 1979-82; bd. advisors Milligan Coll., Tenn., 1985—; mem. adv. coun. Lifespan. Bd. dirs. Neighborhood Devel. Corp. for Old Louisville. Named Hon. Col. Gov.'s Staff, State of Ky., 1981. Mem. Louisville Area Mins. Assn. (sec. 1979-80), N.Am. Christian Conv. (nat. com. 1981-84, 87-90, 91—, chmn. local arrangements 1981, 89), Ky. Assn. Homes for Aging, Tenn. Assn. Homes for Aging (state ednl. com.), Nat. Soc. Fund Raising Execs. (bd. dirs. Mountain Empire chpt., chmn. found. dr. 1995), So. Assn. HUD Mgmt. Agts., East Tenn. Christian Mins. Assn. (v.p. 1992), Johnson City C. of C. (amb. task force 1993-98, chmn. amb. task force 1994), Ruritan (sec. 1968-69), Lions (v.p. 1977). Republican. Avocations: salt water fishing. E-mail: bradml@aol.com. Home: 1019 Grace Dr Johnson City TN 37604-2903 Office: Appalachian Christian Village 309 Princeton Rd Johnson City TN 37601-3238

BRADFORD, PHILLIP GNASSI, financial analytics developer; b. Jersey City, N.J., May 8, 1964; s. Phillips Verner Bradford and Diane Gnassi. BA, Rutgers U., 1986; MS, U. Kans., 1989; PhD, Ind. U., 1995. Assoc. instr. Ind. U., Bloomington, 1991-94; postdoctoral fellow Max-Planck-Inst., Germany, 1994-96; fin. analytics developer Reuters Analytic Group, 1996—. Author/co-author works in field. Home: 1674 3rd Ave Apt 2B New York NY 10128-3713 Office: BlackRock Inc 345 Park Ave Fl 30 New York NY 10154-0004

BRADFORD, REAGAN HOWARD, JR., ophthalmology educator; b. Lawton, Okla., July 31, 1954; s. Reagan Howard Sr. and Conita Ann (Hargraves) B.; m. Cynthia Ann McGough, Apr. 22, 1988. BS, U. Okla., 1976; MD, U. Okla., Oklahoma City, 1980. Diplomate Am. Bd. Ophthalmology. Intern Bapt. Med. Ctr., Oklahoma City, 1980-81; resident Dean A. McGee Eye Inst. U. Okla., 1981-84; fellow in vitreo retina Bascom Palmer Eye Inst. U. Miami, Fla., 1984-85; assoc. clinical prof. Dean A. McGee Eye Inst., U. Okla., Oklahoma City, 1985—. Author: (with others) Basics of Neurophthalmology; contbr. articles to profl. jours. Fellow Am. Acad. Ophthalmology; mem. Okla. County Med. Soc., Okla. State Med. Assn., AMA, Okla. State Acad. Ophthalmology. Republican. Baptist. Avocations: tennis, softball. Office: Dean A McGee Eye Inst 608 Stanton L Young Blvd Oklahoma City OK 73104-5065

BRADFORD, RICHARD ROARK, writer; b. Chgo., May 1, 1932; s. Roark and Mary Rose (Sciarra) B.; m. Julie Dollard, Sept. 15, 1956 (div.); 1 son, Thomas Conway; m. Lee Head (dec.) June 25, 1977. BA, Tulane U., 1952; DLitt, N.Mex. State U., 1979. Staff writer, editor N.M. Tourist Bur., 1956-59, New Orleans C. of C., 1959-61, Zia Co., Los Alamos, 1963-65; research analyst N.M. Dept. Devel., 1967-68; screenwriter Universal Pictures, 1968-70. Author: Red Sky at Morning, 1968, So Far from Heaven, 1973. Served with USMC, 1953-56. Mem. Edouard Manet Soc., Sigma Chi. Club: Quien Sabe (Santa Fe). Home: PO Box 1395 Santa Fe NM 87504-1395 Office: care McIntosh and Otis Inc 310 Madison Ave New York NY 10017-6009

BRADFORD, SUSAN ANNE, political consultant, writer; b. Pasadena, Calif., Dec. 2, 1969; d. Wesley Gene and Nancy Cornelia (Dixon) B. Student, Coll. Cevenol, Le Chambon Sur Lignon, France, 1985, St. Andrews U., Scotland, 1989-90; BA in English, U. Calif., Irvine, 1992; MA in Internat. Rels., Essex U., Eng., 1996, postgrad. Editor-in-chief Gandalf's Gazette, Irvine, Calif., 1987-88; news editor New Univ., Irvine, Calif., 1987-88; intern Sta. CBS-TV News, L.A., 1989; host, exec. producer Witness the News TV show, Irvine, 1990-92; prodn. asst. PBS Red Car Film Project, L.A., 1992-93; intern in news writing Sta. KNX News, L.A., 1993; reporter City News Svc., L.A., 1994-95; founder/editor European Review, 1995-98; sr. rsch. fellow, polit. cons. Atlantic Coun., 1996-98; polit. cons. UK Shadow Fgn. Sec. Michael Howard, 1998. Author poems; contbr. articles to profl. jours.; founding editor: European Rev., 1995—; co-pub. European publs., 1999—. Bd. dirs. HWPC Scholarship Found., Hollywood, Calif., 1992-93; mem. NATO Univs. Adv. Com., 1996—; mem. com. European Movement, 1995—. Recipient Writing awards Palos Verdes Nat. Bank, 1987, AFL-CIO, 1987, 3d Pl. award Nat. Fedn. Press Women, 1992. Mem. Calif. Press Women (pub. rels. chair 1991-92), Hollywood Women's Press Club (bd. dirs. 1989-94), European Movement (committee member/London strategy group media coord.) 1995—, NATO Universities Advisory Committee, 1996—, Irvine Women's Crew (founder, pres.). Mem. United Ch. of Christ. Avocation: studying Japanese language, travel, skiing. Office: PO Box 7000-245 Rolling Hills Estates CA 90275

BRADFORD, WILLIAM ALLEN, JR., lawyer; b. Washington, Feb. 11, 1944; s. William Allen and May Astrid (Valentine) B. BA with honors, Swarthmore Coll., 1966; JD, Yale U., 1969. Bar: D.C. 1969, U.S. Supreme Ct. 1973. Assoc. Hogan & Hartson, Washington, 1969-79, ptnr., 1979—; assoc. spl. counsel D.C. Commn. on Jud. Disabilities and Tenure, Washington, 1971-72; chmn. civil subcom. D.C. Ct. System Study Com., 1978-83; mem. exec. com. Continuing Legal Edn. divsn. Georgetown U., Washington, 1984-94; bd. dirs. Mex. Am. legal Def. and Ednl. Fund, L.A., 1988-92; adj. faculty U. Va. Sch. Law, 1998—. Trustee D.C. Preservation League, 1988-94. Mem. ABA, Yale Club (N.Y.C.), Barristers Club, Phi Beta Kappa. Home: 1812 24th St NW Washington DC 20008-4024 Office: Hogan & Hartson Columbia Square 555 13th St NW Ste 800E Washington DC 20004-1161

BRADFORD, WILLIAM DALTON, pathologist, educator; b. Rochester, N.Y., Nov. 2, 1931; s. William Leslie and Lenora Dee (Dalton) B.; m. Anne Bevington Harden, July 8, 1961; children—Scott Harden, Lisa Graham. B.A., Amherst Coll., 1954; M.D., Western Res. U., 1958. Diplomate Am. Bd. Pediatrics, Am. Bd. Anatomic Pathology. Intern in pathology Boston Children's Med. Ctr., 1958-59, resident in pediatrics, 1959-61; teaching fellow in pathology Harvard Med. Sch., 1963-64; asst. prof. pathology Duke U., Durham, N.C., 1966-70, assoc. prof., 1970-81, prof., 1981—, assoc. dean, 1970-71, 74-78, 84-87, asst. to chancellor for health affairs, 1987-89, dir. pediatric pathology, 1966—, dir. pathology tng. program, 1974—. Pres. Durham YMCA, 1978, bd. dirs., 1976-83, 90—; faculty chmn. of athletics Duke U., 1979-85. Lt. comdr. USN, 1961-63. Recipient Golden Apple award Student Med. Assn., 1969, 93, 95, 98, Layman of Yr. award YMCA, 1974, 78, Disting. Tchr. award Duke Med. Alumni Assn., 1989; Mead Johnson fellow, 1963-64. Mem. Internat. Acad. Pathology, Am. Assn. Pathologists, Soc. Pediatric Research, Group for Research in Pathology Edn., Soc. for Pediatric Pathology (pres. 1987-88), Nat. Collegiate Athletic Assn. Council, Nat. Faculty Athletics Reps. Forum (chmn. 1985), Atlantic Coast Conf. (pres. 1982-83), Duke Med. Alumni Assn. (sec. 1997—). Office: Duke U Med Ctr Box 3712 Durham NC 27710

BRADFORD, WILLIAM EDWARD, oil field equipment manufacturing company executive; b. Dallas, Jan. 8, 1935; m. JoDeane Browning, Aug. 18, 1955; children: William B., A. Kathleen, Jon E. BS in Geology, Centenary Coll., 1958; grad., Tex. A&M U., 1975. Salesman Hycalog, Inc., 1958-61; v.p., gen. ptnr. Analytical Logging, Inc., 1961-70; with Dresser Industries, Inc., 1970—, dir., pres., 1979-80, group pres., 1980-83, v.p. ops., 1983-84, sr. v.p., 1984—; chmn., CEO Halliburton Energy Svcs. (formery Dresser Corp.), Dallas, N.Y., 1996—. Mem. Soc. Petroleum Engrs., Am. Assn. Petroleum Geologists, Petroleum Equipment Suppliers Assn., AAAS, Assn. Oilwell Drilling Contractors, Internat. Petroleum Assn., Nat. Ocean Industries Assn., Tex. Mid-Continentant Oil and Gas Assn. Republican. Presbyterian. Clubs: Petroleum, Raveneaux Country, Houston, University (Houston); Champions Golf, Heritage. Office: Halliburton Energy Svcs 3600 Lincoln Plz 500 N Akard Dallas TX 75201*

BRADFORD, WILLIAM HOLLIS, JR., lawyer; b. St. Petersburg, Fla., Feb. 11, 1937; s. William Hollis and Treva M. (Waymire) B.; m. Rebecca Mills, June 22, 1963 (div. 1969); children: Leslie, Stacey; m. Keith Ann McCausland, Jan. 23, 1999. AB, Duke U., 1959, JD, 1962; LLM, George Washington U., 1964. Bar: D.C. 1962, U.S. Supreme Ct. 1966, Md. 1972. Assoc. Hamel & Park, Washington, 1962-67, ptnr., 1967-88; ptnr. Hopkins & Sutter, Washington, 1988-95; shareholder/officer Sanders, Schnabel, Brandenburg & Zimmerman, P.C., Washington, 1995—; professorial lectr. George Washington U. Law Sch., 1991-97. Contbr. articles to Dem. View, 1983-93. Mem. Montgomery County Md. Dem. Cen. Com., Kensington, Md., 1974-86; vice-chair Md. State Dem. Cen. Com., Balt., 1982-83. Recipient Willis Smith prize Duke U., 1962. Mem. ABA, Md. State Bar Assn., D.C. Bar Assn., D.C. Estate Planning Council, Metropolitan Club, Order of Coif, Phi Beta Kappa. Unitarian. Avocations: photography, travel. Office: Sanders Schnabel Brandenburg & Zimmerman PC 900 17th St NW Washington DC 20006-2501

BRADHAM, TAMALA SELKE, audiologist; b. South Bend, Ind., Oct. 5, 1969; d. David Allan and Janice Marie (Hayden) Selke; m. William Simons, Jr., May 14, 1994. BA in Math., Columbia Coll., 1992; M in Audiology, U. S.C., 1994, PhD, 1998. Cert. audiologist, S.C. Bd. Examiners; cert. clin. competence Am. Speech Hearing Assn. Grad. rsch. asst. U. S.C., Columbia, 1992-94, clin. fellow, audiologist, 1994-95, instr., 1997-98, asst. prof., 1998—; aural rehab. cons. Dorn's Vet. Hosp., Columbia. Treas. Nat. Student Speech, Lang., Hearing Assn., Columbia; pres. Palmetto Columbia chpt. Self Help Hard of Hearing (SHHH), 1995-96, libr., 1993-95. Recipient Continuing Edn. award ASHA, 1998; sertoma scholar Carolina/West Region, 1993. Fellow Am. Acad. Audiology (Continuing Edn. award 1999); mem. Am. Speech, Lang., Hearing Assn., Am. Auditory Soc., Edni. Audiology Assn., Acad. Rehab. Audiology, Am. Auditory Soc., S.C. Speech and Hearing Assn., S.C. Acad. of Audiology (pres. 1998). Roman Catholic. Avocations: mathematics tutoring, backpacking, camping, canoeing. Home: 6450 Dare Cir Columbia SC 29206-1155 Office: U SC Speech & Hearing Ctr 1601 St Julian Pl Columbia SC 29204

BRADIE, PETER RICHARD, lawyer, engineer; b. Bklyn., Feb. 19, 1937; s. Alexander Robert and Blanche Isabelle Bradie; m. Anna Barbara Corcoran, Jan. 22, 1960; children: Suzanne J., Barbara L., Michell S. BSME, Fairleigh Dickinson U., 1960; JD, South Tex. Coll. Law, 1978. Bar: Tex. 1978, U.S. Dist. Ct. (so. dist.) Tex. 1981; registered profl. engr., Ala. Performance engr. Pratt & Whitney Aircraft, West Palm Beach, Fla., 1961-63; sr. engr. Hayes Internat. Corp., Huntsville, Ala., 1963-64, Lockheed Missiles and Space, Huntsville, 1964-68; fluidics engr. Double A Products Co., Manchester, Mich., 1968-69; cons. Spectrum Controls, Montvale, N.J., 1969-72; sr. project mgr. Materials Research Corp., Orangebury, N.Y., 1972-74; sr. contracts adminstr. Brown & Root Inc., Houston, 1974-85; sole practice Houston, 1985-91; ptnr. Bradie, Bradie & Bradie, Houston, 1991—; counsel Inverness Forest C.A, Houston., 1978-80; sr. counsel Raymond-Brown & Raymond-Molem, J.V., Houston, 1982-84. Contbr. articles on fluidic controls to mags.; patentee. Dem. committeeman Bergen County, Haworth, N.J., 1959; del. Harris County Reps., Houston, 1984; officer, bd. dirs. Inverness Forest Civic Assn., Houston, 1975-78. Served to 2d lt. USMCR, 1958-61. Mem. Tex. Bar Assn., Houston N.W. Bar Assn. (treas. 1986, bd. dirs. 1988, sec. 1988, pres.-elect 1988-89, pres. 1990-91), Assn. Trial Lawyers Am., Houston Trial Lawyers Assn., Comml. Law League Am., Rotary Club (Montvale bd. dirs. 1973-74), Am. Inn of Ct. Republican. Jewish. Avocations: classical music, history, computers. Home: 22007 Kenchester Dr Houston TX 77073-1315 Office: 3845 Fm 1960 Rd W Ste 330 Houston TX 77068-3519

BRADISH, WARREN ALLEN, internal auditor, operations analyst, management consultant; b. Adrian, Mich., June 9, 1937; s. Calvin Gamber and Florence Helen (Schulze) B.; m. Setsuko Arimatsui, May 18, 1959 (div.); children: Donna, John, Bradly, Jacqueline; m. Robert Mary Kalol, Sept. 26, 1969. BA in Bus. Adminstrn. summa cum laude, St. Leo Coll., 1977; MA in Bus. Mgmt., Ctrl. Mich. U., 1980. Commd. officer U.S. Army, 1956, advanced through grades to maj., 1976; retired, 1976; edn. & tng. officer State of Ga., 1977-80; dir. investigations Sec. of State, Ga., 1980-82, dir. surveillance, specialized investigative svcs., 1982-83; internal auditor, ops. analyst Ga. Dept. Revenue, 1983-84; govt. security specialist McPherson, Ga., 1984-88; intelligence ops. specialist MacDill AFB, Fla., 1988-99; adj. prof. St. Leo Coll. Decorated Bronze Star. Mem. Assn. Former Intelligence Officers, Spl. Forces Decade Assn., Disabled Vets. Am., Sigma Iota. Home: 4841 Foxshire Cir Tampa FL 33624-4309

BRADLEE, BENJAMIN CROWNINSHIELD, executive editor; b. Boston, Aug. 26, 1921; s. Frederick J. and Josephine (deGersdorff) B.; m. Jean Saltonstall, Aug. 8, 1942; 1 son, Benjamin Crowninshield; m. Antoinette Pinchot, July 6, 1956; children: Dominic, Marina; m. Sally Quinn, Oct. 20, 1978; 1 son, Josiah Quinn Crowninshield. A.B., Harvard U., 1943. Reporter N.H. Sunday News, Manchester, 1946- 48, Washington Post, 1948-51; press attaché embassy Paris, France, 1951-53; European corr. Newsweek mag., Paris, 1953-57; reporter Washington bur. Newsweek mag., 1957-61, sr. editor, chief bur., 1961-65; mng. editor Washington Post, 1965-68, v.p., exec. editor, 1968-91, v.p. at large, 1991—; chmn. Hist. St. Mary's City Commn., 1992—. Author: That Special Grace, 1964, Conversations with Kennedy, 1975, A Good Life--Newspapering and Other Adventures, 1995. Served to lt. USNR, 1942-45. Home: 3014 N St NW Washington DC 20007-3404 Office: care Washington Post 1150 15th St NW Washington DC 20071-0001

BRADLEY, AMELIA JANE, lawyer; b. Columbia, S.C., Apr. 18, 1947; d. Hugh Wilson and Amelia Jane (Wylie) B.; m. Richard Bancroft Hovey, Apr. 1, 1977. BA, U. Va., 1968; MA, George Washington U., 1971. Bar: Va. 1976, D.C. 1985. Budget and mgmt. analyst NLRB, Washington, 1968-71, 72; clk. Cohen and Vitt, PC, Alexandria, Va., 1972-76; assoc. Cohen, Vitt & Annand, PC, Alexandria, 1976-80; White House fellow USDA, Washington, 1980-81; White House fellow Office U.S. Trade Rep., Exec. Office of Pres., Washington, 1981, asst. gen. counsel, 1981-82, assoc. gen. counsel, 1982-84; legal advisor to U.S. GATT del. Office U.S. Trade Rep., Exec. Office of Pres., Geneva, 1984-87; prin. dep. gen. counsel Office U.S. Trade Rep., Exec. Office of Pres., Washington, 1989-92; asst. U.S. trade rep. for dispute resolution Office U.S. Trade Rep., Exec. Office of Pres., Washington, 1994; assoc. dir. for global environment White House Office on Environ. Policy, Washington, 1994-95; assoc. dir. internat. trade and devel. Coun. on Environ. Quality, Washington, 1995; asst. U.S. trade rep. for monitoring, enforcement Exec. Office of Pres., Washington, 1996—; counsel to U.S. Del. GATT Ministerial Conf., Punta del Este, Uruguay, 1986; chief negotiator U.S. GATT Uruguay Round Dispute Settlement Negotiating Group, 1986-87, 89-93; chmn. Interagy. Sect. 301 Com., Washington, 1988-92; vis. rsch. assoc. Fletcher Sch. Law and Diplomacy, Tufts U., Medford, Mass., 1987-88; vis. rschr. Harvard U. Law Sch., Cambridge, Mass., 1988. Mem., chmn. Alexandria Human Rights Commn., 1975-80; pres., trustee Alexandria Law Libr., 1978-80; founding mem. Lawyer Referral Svc., Alexandria, 1978. NEH fellow, 1978. Mem. ABA, Va. State Bar (mem., chmn. com. on legal edn. and admission to bar 1977-84), D.C. Bar (chmn. internat. trade com. 1989-90). Episcopalian. Office: Office of US Trade Rep 600 17th St NW Washington DC 20508

BRADLEY, ANN WALSH, state supreme court justice. Former judge Marathon County Circuit Ct., Wausau, Wis.; justice Wis. Supreme Ct., Madison, Wis. Office: PO Box 1688 Madison WI 53701-1688 also: 231 E State Capitol Madison WI 53702

BRADLEY, BILL, former senator; b. Crystal City, Mo., July 28, 1943; s. Warren W. and Susan (Crowe) B.; m. Ernestine Schlant, Jan. 14, 1974; 1 dau., Theresa Anne. BA, Princeton U., 1965; MA, Oxford (Eng.) U., 1968. Player N.Y. Knickerbockers Profl. Basketball Team, 1967-77; U.S. senator from N.J., 1979-96, mem. fin., energy coms., spl. com. on aging; Disting. leadership scholar, chair U. Md., College Park; Payne Disting. prof. Inst. for Internat. Studies, Stanford U., 1997-98; bd. advisors acad. leadership U. Md., College Park; chair advt. couns. adv. com. on pub. issues; essayist CBS TV Weekend Evening News; sr. advisor, vice chair internat. coun. J.P. Morgan and Co., Inc.; vis. prof. pub. affairs Univ. of Notre Dame, 1998; bd. trustee Princeton U.; mem. Coun. Fgn. Rels. Author: Life on the Run, 1976, The Fair Tax, 1984, Time Present, Time Past, 1996, Values of the Game, 1998. Chmn. Nat. Civic League, Ams. Promise (co-chmn. task force on safe spaces, structured activities). Served with USAFR, 1967-78. Rhodes scholar, 1965-67; named three-time basketball All-Am.; recipient Sullivan award as the country's outstanding amateur athlete. Democrat. Mem. NBA championship team, 1970, 73, gold medal team Tokyo Olympics. Office: The Legal Center 14th flr One Riverfront Plaza Newark NJ 07102 also: 395 Pleasant Valley Way West Orange NJ 07052*

BRADLEY, BOB, professional soccer coach; b. Montclair, N.J., Mar. 3, 1958. B.History, Princeton U.; M.Sports Adminstrn., Ohio U. Head coach soccer Ohio U., Athens, 1980-81; asst. coach U. Va., 1982-83; head coach Princeton U., 1984-95; asst. coach D.C. United, 1995-97; head coach Chgo. Fire, 1997—. Named Major League Soccer's 1998 All Sport Coach of the Yr., NCAA Divsn. I Men's Coach of the Yr., 1993. Office: Chicago Fire 311 W Superior Ste 444 Chicago IL 60610*

BRADLEY, CHARLES ERNEST, educational leadership consultant, music educator; b. Aurora, Colo., Oct. 20, 1962; s. Ernest Rayford and Mickey Marie (Cook) B. BS cum laude, Asbury Coll., 1985. Cert. facilitative leader. Music specialist Hillsborough County Schs., Tampa, Fla., 1985-94; profl. tng. specialist Fla. Dept. Edn., 1992—; leadership cons., ednl. cons./trainer, program coord. West Cen. Ednl. Leadership Network, Tampa, 1994-95; coord. instrnl. pers. Manatee County Schs., 1995—; chmn. Assemblies Com., Tampa, 1985—, ARea IX Music Coun., Tampa, 1986-87, Mid. Sch. Task Force, 1989-90; co-chmn. Site-Based Decision Making Com., graduation com. Very Spl. Arts Hillsborough County, 1989-90, chmn., 1991-92, coord., 1991—; cons. Music in Exceptional Edn., 1993—; Team Facilitation cons., 1993—. Composer: Sonata in G Minor, 1980, Sonata in B Minor, 1984, Five American Scenes, 1984, Two Anglican Office Anthems, 1989, Five Liurgical Alleluias, 1989-90, Who Am I, cantata, 1990, Three Early American Hymns for Choirs, 1991, Medieval Cortege (organ), 1994. Choirmaster, organist St. Anne of Grace Episcopal Ch., Seminole, Fla., 1986-91; organist/music dir. St. Andrews Presbyn. Ch., Dunedin, Fla., 1991-94, organist, 1994—. Recipient Mayor's Cert. merit, Mayor's Alliance for the Handicapped, 1988, Very Spl. Arts/Hillsborough County Schs. Achievement award, 1992; Tech. Retrofit grantee State of Fla., 1993, Competitive Tech. grantee, 1994. Mem. ASCD, Am. Guild Organists (governing body, 1989—, sub-dean, 1991—), Music Educators Nat. Conf., Fla. Music Educators Assn., Fla. Elem. Music Educators Assn., Stratford Shakespeare Soc., Gen. Music Nat. Assn., Royal Sch. Ch. Music, Internat. Interactive Comm. Soc. Republican. Avocations: scuba diving, swimming, drama, tennis, running. Home: 6565 Exeter Ct Seminole FL 33772-6509 Office: West Ctrl Ednl Leadership Network 12493 Telecom Dr Tampa FL 33637-0913

BRADLEY, CHARLES WILLIAM, podiatrist, educator; b. Fife, Tex., July 23, 1923; s. Tom and Mary Ada (Cheatham) B.; m. Marilyn A. Brown, Apr. 3, 1948 (dec. Mar. 1973); children: Steven, Gregory, Jeffrey, Elizabeth, Gerald. Student, Tex. Tech., 1940-42; D. Podiatric Medicine, Calif. Coll. Podiatric Medicine U. San Francisco, 1949, MPA, 1987, D.Sc. (hon.). Pvt. practice podiatry Beaumont, Tex., 1950-51, Brownwood, Tex., 1951-52, San Francisco, San Bruno, Calif., 1952—; assoc. clin. prof. Calif. Coll. Podiatric Medicine, 1992-98; chief of staff Calif. Podiatry Hosp., San Francisco; mem. surg. staff Sequoia Hosp., Redwood City, Calif.; mem. med. staff Peninsula Hosp., Burlingame, Calif.; chief podiatry staff St. Luke's Hosp., San Francisco; chmn. bd. Podiatry Ins. Co. Am.; cons. VA; assoc. prof. podiatric medicine Calif. Coll. Podiatric Medicine. Mem. San Francisco Symphony Found.; mem. adv. com. Health Policy Agenda for the Am. People, AMA; chmn. trustees Calif. Coll. Podiatric Medicine, Calif. Podiatry Coll., Calif. Podiatry Hosp.; mem. San Mateo Grand Jury, 1989. Served with USNR, 1942-45. Mem. Am. Podiatric Med. Assn. (trustee, pres. 1983-84), Calif. Podiatry Assn. (pres. No. div. 1964-66, state bd. dirs., pres. 1975-76, Podiatrist of Yr. award 1983), Nat. Coun. Edn. (vice-chmn.), Nat. Acads. Practice (chmn. podiatric med. sect. 1991-96, sec. 1996—), Am. Legion, San Bruno C. of C. (bd. dirs. 1978-91, v.p. 1992, bd. dir. grand jury assoc. 1990), Olympic Club, Commonwealth Club Calif., Elks, Lions. Home: 2965 Trousdale Dr Burlingame CA 94010-5708 Office: 560 Jenevein Ave San Bruno CA 94066-4408

BRADLEY, DONALD EDWARD, lawyer; b. Santa Rosa, Calif., Sept. 26, 1943; s. Edward Aloysius and Mildred Louise (Kelley) B.; m. Marianne Stark, Apr. 22, 1990; children: Evan Patrick, Matthew Jordan, Andrea Phelps. AB, Dartmouth Coll., 1965; JD, U. Calif., San Francisco, 1968; LLM, N.Y.U., 1972. Bar: Calif. 1968, U.S. Dist. Ct. (no. dist.) Calif. 1968, U.S. Ct. Appeals (9 cir.) 1968, U.S. Tax Ct. 1972, U.S. Ct. Claims 1973, U.S. Supreme Ct. 1981. Assoc. Pillsbury, Madison & Sutro, San Francisco, 1972-77, ptnr., 1978-84; with Wilson, Sonsini, Goodrich & Rosati, Palo Alto, Calif., 1984—; adj. prof. Golden State U., San Francisco, 1973-82; pres., chmn. bd. dirs. Atty.'s Ins. Mut. Risk Retention Group, Honolulu, 1986—. Capt. U.S. Army, 1969-70. Recipient Charles M. Ruddick award N.Y.U., 1972, award Bureau of Nat. Affairs, Washington, 1968. Mem. ABA, Internat. Bar Assn., Santa Clara Bar Assn., San Francisco Bar Assn., Internat. Tax Club, Peninsula Tax Club. Office: Wilson Sonsini Goodrich & Rosati 650 Page Mill Rd Palo Alto CA 94304-1050

BRADLEY, E. MICHAEL, lawyer; b. N.Y.C., Apr. 13, 1939; s. Otis Treat Bradley and Marian Booth (Alling) Ward; m. Judith Allen Thompson, June 29, 1962; children: Jennifer Treat, Michael Thompson, Thomas Alcott, Samuel Allen. BA, Yale U., 1961; LLB, U. Va., 1964. Bar: N.Y., 1965. Assoc. Davis, Polk & Wardwell, N.Y.C., 1964-72; assoc. Brown & Wood, N.Y.C., 1972-73, ptnr., 1974-95, mem. policy com., 1981-94, mem. exec. com., 1989-94; ptnr. Jones, Day, Reavis & Poque, N.Y.C., 1995—; lectr. Practicing Law Inst., N.Y.C., 1970-79; 86, Am. Law Inst.-ABA, Phila., 1977-78; arbitrator Am. Arbitration Assn., N.Y.C., 1975—. Contbg. editor: The Use of Experts in Corporate Litigation, 1978, Securites Law Techniques, 1985. Bd. dirs. Bennett Coll. Found., N.Y.C., 1984—; trustee Salisbury (Conn.) Sch., 1987—. Mem. ABA, N.Y. State Bar Assn., Fed. Bar Assn., Assn. of Bar of City of N.Y., River Club, Union Club, Coral Beach Club, Quogue Field Club, Shinnecock Yacht Club, Nat. Golf Links of Am., L.I. Wyandanch Club. Republican. Presbyterian. Home: 200 E 66 St New York NY 10021-4250 Office: Jones Day Reavis & Pogue 599 Lexington Ave Fl C1A New York NY 10022-6030

BRADLEY, EDWARD JAMES, state official, computer programmer and analyst; b. Syracuse, N.Y., Jan. 3, 1946; s. Robert Carroll and Hazel Irene (Malone) B.; m. Gwen Eileen Coats, Sept. 3, 1977 (div. 1984); 1 child, Edward James II. BA cum laude, SUNY, Albany, 1971, MPA, 1980; grad. Citizen's Police Acad., 1992. Specialist N.Y. State Dept. Social Services, 1973-78; pub. adminstr. N.Y. State Dept. Transp., Albany, 1978-81; pub. mgmt. intern N.Y. State Dept. Civil Service, 1981-82; personnel adminstr. N.Y. State Dept. Taxation and Fin., 1982-83; computer programmer, analyst N.Y. State Dept. Transp., 1983—; commr. City of Albany Municipal Civil Svc. Commn., 1992-93, chmn. 92-93. Author: Child and Family Genealogy Reporting System. Pres. Child and Family Enterprises, Inc., Albany, 1978-84, Traditional Am. Values, Albany, 1984—, Books Unbound, 1991—, V.O.T.E.S., 1992—; contbr. articles to profl. jours. Fundraiser United Way Am./Northeastern N.Y., Inc., 1976-78, Capital Area Council Chs., 1978, Birthright of Albany, Inc., 1984-88. Mem. Albany County Dem. Com., 1985-93; active Nat. Pro-life Dems., Inc., 1984-94, Nat. Right-to-Life Com., Inc., 1984—, N.Y. State Right-to-Life, 1984—, Human Life Internat., 1992—; mem. nat. nominating com. Outstanding Young Ams., 1997—. Served with USN, 1963-66. Named one of Outstanding Young Men of Am., 1982. Mem. DAV, ASPA, Am. Mgmt. Assn., Am. Pub. Welfare Assn., N.Y. State Forum for Info. Resources Mgmt., Vietnam Era Vets., Am. Legion, N.Y. Assn. Transp. Engrs., Capital Dist. Geneal. Soc (pres. 1982-84), Nat. Speakers Assn., Toastmasters, Elks. Roman Catholic. *From October, 1992 to April, 1996, Mr. Bradley wrote a series of seven published editorials and Op. Ed. articles on the topic of the marriage tax penalty imposed by the U.S. Income Tax Code on married working couples earning more than $22,500 each (i.e. $45,000 continued). This issue became a feature in 1994 with the Republican Party's Contract with America. As of 1999, no progress has been made to either eliminate or lessen this grossly unfair tax burden which was first placed on America's married working couples in 1970* Home: 7 Leonard Pl Albany NY 12202-1356 Office: Computer Svcs Bur State Office Campus Computer Svcs Bur Rm 218 Albany NY 12232

BRADLEY, EDWARD R., news correspondent; b. Phila., June 22, 1941; s. Ed. R. and Gladys Bradley; divorced. B.A. in Edn., Cheyney (Pa.) State Coll., 1964. Radio news reporter Sta. WDAS, Phila., 1963-67, Sta. WCBS, N.Y.C., 1967-71; with CBS Television News, 1971—, stringer, 1971-73, corr., 1973-78, prin. corr., 1978; prin. corr. CBS Television News, in Paris, 1971, Saigon, 1972-74, Washington, 1974—; prin. corr. CBS Reports, 1978-81, 60 Minutes, 1981—; anchorman CBS Sunday Night News, 1976-81. Anchorman: various documentaries including What's Happening to Cambodia, 1978, The Boat People, 1979, The Boston Goes to China, 1979. Recipient Du Pont award, 1978, 80, 97, George Foster Peabody Broadcasting award U. Ga., 1979, George Polk journalism award, 1980, Emmy award, 1979 (3), 1983 (2), 1985, 86, 92, 93. Office: CBS News 60 Minutes 555 W 57th St New York NY 10019-2925

BRADLEY, GILBERT FRANCIS, retired banker; b. Miami, Ariz., May 17, 1920; s. Ever and Martha (Piper) B.; m. Marion Bebb, June 21, 1941; children: Larry Paul, Richard Thomas, Steven Ever. Grad., LaSalle Extension U., 1942, U. Wash., 1953; Advanced Mgmt. Program, Harvard U. With Valley Nat. Bank, Ariz., Miami, Globe, Clifton, Nogales and Phoenix, 1937—; pres. Valley Nat. Bank, Phoenix, 1973-76; chmn. bd., chief exec. officer Valley Nat. Bank, 1976-82, ret., 1982, dir., vice chmn. exec. com., 1982—; dir., vice chmn. exec. com. Valley Nat. Corp., 1982—; mem. adv. council Fed. Res. Bd., Comptroller of the Currency, Denver; instr. Am. Inst. Banking. Mem. Tucson Airport Authority, 1960—; mem. adv. council Ariz. State U. Sch. Bus., pres. dean's adv. council; dean's adv. council U. Ariz., Tucson. Served to capt. USAAF, 1942-45. Decorated D.F.C., Air medal with three oak leaf clusters. Mem. Ariz. Bankers Assn. (pres.), Assn. Res. City Bankers, Ariz. C. of C. (v.p., dir.), Tucson C. of C. (dir.), Better Bus. Bur. (dir.), Tucson Clearing House Assn. (past pres.), Navy League, Air Force Assn., Beta Gamma Sigma. Clubs: Masons, Rotary, Phoenix Country, Ariz. Home: 5340 N La Plaza Cir Phoenix AZ 85012-1416 Office: 241 N Central Ave Phoenix AZ 85004-2225

BRADLEY, J. F., JR., retired manufacturing company executive; b. Wagoner, Okla., July 7, 1930; s. Jacob F. and Ilsa (Ellington) B.; m. Mary Joan Oberc, June 7, 1952 (div. 1978); children: Jeffrey F. (dec.), Michael B., Michelle J.; m. Angela C. Cutrone, Aug. 14, 1981; 1 child, Adam C.C. BBA, U. Mich., 1952; MBA, U. Detroit, 1959. Fin. analyst Ford Motor Co., Detroit, 1956-60; v.p. corp. fin. TRW Inc., Cleve., 1960-72; exec. v.p. adminstrn. and fin. Scott Fetzer Co., Lakewood, Ohio, 1972-83, dir., 1971-83; pres. Scott Fetzer Fin. Svcs. Group, Westlake, Ohio, 1983-86; chmn. Kadee Metalfab Inc., Bedford, Ohio, 1986-89, K.B.B. Enterprises Inc., Cleve., 1988-93. Trustee Ohio Coll. Podiatric Medicine, chmn., 1990-94; trustee Animal Protective League, Cleve. 1st lt. AUS, 1952-56. Mem. Masons, Shriners, Jesters, Elks, Knights Templar. Home: 13908 Edgewater Dr Lakewood OH 44107-1416

BRADLEY, JAMES ALEXANDER, software engineer, researcher; b. Van Nuys, Calif., May 16, 1965; m. Alyson Wait, July 11, 1992. BA in Math., Computer Sci., U. Colo., 1988, postgrad., 1991—. Software developer Sci. Computer Systems, Inc., Boulder, Colo., 1982-84; teaching asst. Boulder Valley Pub. Schs., Boulder, Colo., 1984-87; software engr. Martin Marietta Aerospace, Littleton, Colo., 1988-94; dir. software engring. Intelligent Energy Corp., Golden, Colo., 1994—. Recipient NASA New Tech. award, Martin Marietta Aerospace, 1990. mem. Am. Math. Soc., Math. Assn. Am., Golden Key Honor Soc. Achievements include design of LASER engraving system, high-speed target tracking and aquisition system. Office: Intelligent Energy Corp 607 10th St Ste 203 Golden CO 80401-5828

BRADLEY, JEFF(REY MARK), arts critic; b. Springfield, Mass., Jan. 9, 1944; s. Richard Gerald and Helen Virginia (Breglio) B. Student, Brown U. Reporter Springfield Union, 1965-69; western Mass. corr. AP, 1969-72; fgn. corr. AP, London, 1972-83; bur. chief AP, Beijing, 1983-86, Toronto, Ont., Can., 1986-88; arts critic-at-large Denver Post, 1989—; Knight journalism fellow Stanford U., 1988-89; lectr. on music and opera U. of Denver, Ctrl. City Opera, Colo. Symphony Orch., Denver, 1990-99. Co-author: Denver, Confluence of the Arts, 1995. Recipient Bell award Nat. Assn. Mental Health, 1969. Office: Denver Post 1560 Broadway Denver CO 80202-5177

BRADLEY, JOHN ANDREW, hospital management company executive; b. Hammond, Ind., Aug. 3, 1930; s. Andrew C. and Florence (Wolfe) B.; m. Judith E. Salmi, June 1, 1955; children: John Michael, Kerry Kathleen, Kelly Ann. BS, Loras Coll., 1952; MHA, St. Louis U., 1955, PhD, 1962. Asst. adminstr. Incarnate Word Hosp., St. Louis, 1958-61; from assoc. adminstr. to adminstr. Santa Rosa Med. Ctr., San Antonio, 1961-69; from v.p. to sr. v.p. Am. Medicorp, Inc., San Antonio, 1969-78; with Am. Healthcare Mgmt., Dallas, 1978-89, pres., 1978-84, chmn., chief exec. officer, 1985-89; chmn., chief exec. officer Chancellor Health Systems Inc., Dallas, 1989—. Capt. AUS, 1953-57. Home: 4228 Winding Way Ct Dallas TX 75287-2767

BRADLEY, JOHN M(ILLER), JR., forestry executive; b. Birmingham, Ala., Mar. 20, 1925; s. John Miller and Frances Watkins (Davis) B.; m. Isabella Elmore, Feb. 14, 1953; children: John M. III (dec.), I. Jocelyn. Student, U. Ala., Tuscaloosa, 1941-42, 46-47; BS in Math., Samford U., 1948; BS in Forestry, U. Calif., Berkeley, 1949; MF, Yale U., 1950. Lic. real estate broker, Ala. Laborer, smoke chaser U.S. Forest Svc., 1941, 47; foreman, project supt. U.S. Park Svc., Yellowstone and Glacier Nat. Parks, 1947-49; founder, pres. So. Timber Mgmt. Svc., Birmingham, 1950-63; chmn., pres. Resource Mgmt. Svc., Birmingham, 1963-90, chmn., 1991—; mem. adv. com. on state and pvt. forestry Sec. Agr., Washington, 1972-76; U.S. del. 8th World Forestry Congress, Jakarta, Indonesia, 1975; mem. univ. coun. com. on forestry and environ. studies Yale U., 1985-89. Contbr. articles on forestry to profl. jours. Pres., dir. Search Found., Washington, 1971—; bd. dirs. Red Mountain (Sci.) Mus. Soc., Birmingham, 1976-84, pres., 1976-78; bd. dirs. Birmingham Hist. Soc., 1975-84, pres., 1977-79; bd. dirs. Red Mountain Mus., Birmingham, 1976-84, chmn., 1978-83; past deacon Briarwood Presbyn. Ch., Birmingham; mem. adv. bd. Birmingham Area coun. Boy Scouts Am., 1992-98; dir. YMCA Camp Cosby, 1988-91. Mem. Soc. Am. Foresters (chmn. nat. conv. 1986), Assn. Cons. Foresters (sr. v.p. 1972-74, pres. 1974-76, pres. Profl. Forestry Inst. Trust 1986-89, dir. 1986-92), Ala. Forestry Assn. (bd. dirs. 1985-88, named to Hall of Fame 1984), Ala. Com. So. Timber Study, Newcomen Soc. U.S., Birmingham Country Club, Inverness Country Club, The Club, Rotary, Tau Beta Pi. Home: 5006 Applecross Rd Birmingham AL 35242-3916 Office: Resource Mgmt Svc Inc 100 Corporate Ridge PO Box 380757 Birmingham AL 35238-0757

BRADLEY, JUDY FAYE, elementary school educator; b. New Orleans, Aug. 26, 1950; d. Hunter L. and Virginia C. (Glaser) B. BA, McNeese Coll., 1978, MEd, 1981; diploma, Inst. Children's Lit., 1992. Cert. elem. sch. counselor, guidance and counseling, La. Tchr., counselor St. Margaret Elem. Cath. Sch., Lake Charles, La., 1978-84; dir. edn. Sylvan Learning Ctr., Lake Charles, 1984-88; tchr. Rosa Fondel Elem. Sch. (formerly Eastwood Elem. Sch.), Lake Charles, 1988-97; sch. counselor College Oaks Elem. Sch., Lake Charles, 1997—; coord. Rainbows for All Children program Eastwood Elem. Sch., 1990-92; Cayenne Crawfish mascot Sta. KPLC-TV, 1990-97; Discoveries facilitator, 1990-97. Named Outstanding Young Educator, Lake Charles Jaycees, 1983-84; Tchr. of Yr. nominee, 1992-93. Mem. La. Sch. Counselors, Calcasieu Sch. Counselors. Avocations: reading, gardening, handicrafts, pets. Office: College Oaks Elem Sch 3618 Ernest St Lake Charles LA 70605-2700

BRADLEY, KATHRYN, health facility administrator; b. Orlando, Fla., June 8, 1967; d. George William Jr. and Virginia Ann (Rich) Kessel; m. Kevin James Bradley, Dec. 5, 1987; children: Kara, Korryn, Kaley, Kevin James Jr. AA, Brevard C.C., 1986. Tour agt. Premier Cruise Lines, Cape Canaveral, Fla., 1985-87; libr. asst. Brevard County Pub. Libr., Cocoa, Fla., 1987-91; tchr., trainer Nat. Assn. Childbirth Assts., San Jose, 1991-93; childbirth asst. program facilitator Arnold Palmer Hosp., Orlando, Fla., 1996—; presenter in field. Vol. Space Coast Breastfeeding Coalition, Cocoa; chair Cmty. Adv. Bd., Orlando, 1998; breastfeeding peer counselor Women, Infants & Children Program, Brevard County, 1998; bd. dirs. Coalition of Childbirth Educators, Common Sense Childbirth. Mem. Nat. Assn. Childbirth Assts. (dir. pub. rels., bd. dirs.), Prenatal and Infant Health Care Coalition Brevard County, Childbirth Edn. Coalition, Fla. Nonprofit Resource Ctr. Avocations: reading, skiing. Fax: (407) 639-4163. E-mail: kbradley@digital.net.

BRADLEY, KEVIN J., publishing company executive; b. Phila., June 19, 1963. BA cum laude, U. Pa., 1988. Acct. U. Pa. Press, Phila., 1981-83; acct. Taylor & Francis Pubs. Inc., Bristol, Pa., 1984-86, contr., 1986-88, CFO, 1988-90, exec. v.p., 1990-96, CEO, 1996—. Fax: 215-625-2929. Office: Taylor & Francis Pubs Inc 325 Chestnut St Ste 1108 Philadelphia PA 19106-2675*

BRADLEY, LAWRENCE D., JR., lawyer; b. Santa Monica, Calif., Feb. 19, 1920; s. Lawrence D. Bradley and Virginia L. Edwards; m. Joan Worthington, Feb. 1, 1945; children—Gary W., Brooks, Eric Scott. B.S., U.S. Coast Guard Acad., 1942; LL.B., Stanford U., 1950. Bar: Calif. 1950, U.S. Dist. Ct. (cen. dist.) Calif. 1950, U.S. Dist. Ct. (so. dist.) Calif. 1967. Assoc. Pillsbury, Madison & Sutro, L.A., 1950-59, ptnr., 1959-90; of counsel Pillsbury, Madison & Sutro; lectr. admiralty and ins. law U. So. Calif., 1952-80. Pres. Stanford Law Rev., 1949-50; assoc. editor Am. Maritime Cases, 1990—. Mem. adv. bd. Tulane Admiralty Law Inst., 1990—. With USN, 1942-48; to lt. comdr. Res. Mem. ABA, Calif. Bar Assn., Maritime Law Assn. U.S. (mem. exec. com. 1974-78, chmn. cruise line com. 1991-94), Inst. Navigation, Order of Coif, Calif. Club, Chancery Club, Calif. Yacht Club, San Diego Yacht Club, Propeller Club, Transpacific Yacht Club, Tutukaka South Pacific Yacht Club. Office: Pillsbury Madison & Sutro 725 S Figueroa St Ste 1200 Los Angeles CA 90017-5443

BRADLEY, LEON CHARLES, musician, educator, consultant; b. Battle Creek, Mich., Sept. 8, 1938; s. Leon Harvey and Sigrid Pearl (Anderson) B.; m. Mary Elizabeth, Dec. 23, 1968; children: Kyle Newman, Shannon Sigrid, Karl Norman, Charles Nathan. BA, Mich. State U., 1961; MM Brass Splst., 1967; postgrad., U. Okla., summer 1974, U. Wis., summer 1975. Band dir. Owosso-St. Paul, Mich., 1958-61, Hopkins (Mich.) Pub. Schs., 1961-62, Cedar Springs (Mich.) Pub. Schs., 1962-65; grad. asst. music theory-aural harmaony Mich. State U., East Lansing, 1965-67; asst. prof., asst. dir. bands Minot (N.D.) State Coll., 1967-69; assoc. prof. instrumental music, music edn., dir. bands. Coll. of the Ozarks, Point Lookout, Mo., 1969-93; dept. chmn., 1987-89, ret., 1993; clinician low brass instruments Selmer, Inc., 1979—; founder instrumental ensembles including Am. Concert Band, Xian Conservatory of Music, China, fall 1995; vis. prof. S.W. Bapt. U., fall 1998. Performed with Springfield (Mo.) Symphony Orch., 1969-72, 81—, Springfield Regional Opera Orch., 1981-98, Branson Brass Quintet, 1982—, Coll. of the Ozarks, others; dir. Abou Ben Adhem Shrine Band, 1978-80; contbr. articles to profl. jours. Mem. Coll. Band Dir.'s Nat. Assn. (nat. chmn. Sacred Wind Music commn.), Music Educators Nat. Conf., Internat. Assn. Jazz Educators (state treas. 1980—), Nat. Assn. Wind and Percussion Instrs. (new musci reviewer, assn. jour. 1968-71), Mo. Music Edn. Assn., Mo. Bandmasters Assn., Am. Fedn. Musicians (local 150), Ducks Unltd. (mem. com. 1978-81, chmn. 1981), Masons (Scottish rite), Lions (pres. 1983-84), Phi Mu Alpha. Home: 119 South Dr Branson MO 65616-3708

BRADLEY, LISA M., artist; b. Columbus, Ohio, Dec. 15, 1951; d. Phillip Raymond Bradley and Jean Lichtenstein. BA, Boston U., 1973. Assoc. dir. Pace Primitive, N.Y.C., 1977-84, dir., 1984—. One-woman shows include Boston City Hall, 1973, Harvard U., Cambridge, Mass., 1976, Boston Ctr. for the Arts, 1977, Ludlow Hyland Gallery, N.Y.C., 1978, 79, Bette Stoler Gallery, N.Y.C., 1979, Major-Saxbe Gallery, Urbana, Ohio, 1986, Phillip Dash Gallery, N.Y.C., 1987, Donahue Gallery, N.Y.C., 1989, Ratner Gallery, Chgo., 1991, Donahue Gallery, 1993, Galerie Kaj ForsBlom, Helsinki, Finland, 1995, Donahue Gallery, N.Y.C., 1996, 98; exhibited in group shows Essex Inst., Salem, Mass., 1972, Cambridge Art Assn., 1972, 73, New Bertha Schaeffer Gallery, N.Y.C., 1975, Gallery 200, Columbus, 1975, Galeria Rosanna, Boston, 1976, Baak Gallery, Cambridge, 1977, 78, Betty Parsons Gallery, N.Y.C., 1978, 79, 80, 81, Bette Stoler Gallery, N.Y.C., 1979, 80, 81, 1st Women's Bank, N.Y.C., 1981, Fay Gold Gallery, Atlanta, 1982, Deicas Art, La Jolla, Calif., 1982, Elayne Marquis Gallery, San Francisco, 1982, Soker-Kaseman Gallery, San Francisco, 1983, Phillipe Guimiot Gallery, Brussels, 1983, Kouros Gallery, N.Y.C., Leonarda Di Mauro Gallery, N.Y.C., 1985, Chronocide Gallery, 1986, Mokotoff Gallery, 1986, Jan Baum Gallery, L.A., 1986, Phillip Dash Gallery, N.Y.C., 1986, Lavrov Gallery, Paris, 1987, Sensibilities Contemporaines, Cie Moderne & Contemporaine, Paris, 1991, Musee de Nationale de Dakar, Senegal, 1992, E.M. Donahue Gallery, N.Y.C., 1993, Solway Gallery, Cin., 1993, Face to Face Artists on Artists Gallery, 1995, Blue Broadway Gallery, N.Y.C., 1996, Women Artists in Vogel Collection, Brenau U. Mus., 1998; pub., The Art of Seeing, Fisher & Zelanski, "The Spiritual in Art", 1993. Jewish. Home: 356 W 20th St Apt 3B New York NY 10011-3385

BRADLEY, MARILYNNE GAIL, advertising executive, advertising educator; b. Rockford, Ill., Apr. 12, 1938; d. Sherwin S. and Lillian (Leopold) Gersten; m. Charles S. Bradley, 1959 (div. Feb., 1994); children: Suzanne, Scott. BFA, Washington U., 1960; MAT, Webster U., St. Louis, 1975; MFA, Syracuse U., 1981; postgrad., St. Louis Tchrs. Acad., 1990. With Essayons Studio, St. Louis, 1968-69; tchr. Webster Groves (Mo.) H.S., 1970-98; instr. Webster Univ., Webster Groves, 1973-82, 97-99, U. Mo., 1980—, St. Louis U., 1978—, Washington U., St. Louis, 1984-87; sec. Mo. Art Edn., State of Mo., 1986-87; mem. Tchrs. Acad. 1990-92. Author, illustrator: Arpens and Acres, 1976, Packets on Parade, 1980; illustrator: St. Louis Silhouettes, 1977; editor: (videos) 12 Water Color Lessons, 1987, Techniques of American Watercolor, 1990, The Santa Fe Trail Series, 1993, Over Gauguin's Shoulder, 1994, Aboriginal Art Techniques, 1994, City of Century Homes, 1995, Australian Dreamings, 1996, Aboriginal Art - Past, Present and Future, 1996, Drawing and Painting Techniques, 1997, Line, Shape, Value, 1998, Molas, Snip and Sew: The Kuna Indians. Bd. govs. Webster Groves Hist. Soc., 1965-72, 94—; mem. St. Louis Philharm. Soc., 1956-72; commr. City of Webster Groves, 1995—. Named Tchr. of Yr., 1987. Mem. So. Watercolor Soc. (sec. 1978-80), St. Louis Woman Artists, St. Louis Artist Guild (sec. 1985-86, pres. 1989-92, Disting. Woman 1987, v.p. pres.'s coun. 1995—), Monday Club (chmn. 1979-83). Avocations: music, art, travel.

BRADLEY, MELVIN LEROY, communications company executive; b. Texarkana, Tex., Jan. 6, 1938; s. S.T. and David Ella (Garth) B.; m. Ruth Ann Terry, Mar. 3, 1958; children: Cheryl, Eric, Jacqueline, Tracy. Student, Los Angeles City Coll., 1955, Compton Coll., 1965; B.S., Pepperdine U., 1973; LLD (hon.), Shaw U., 1982, Bishop Coll., 1984, Lane Coll., 1986. Real estate broker Los Angeles, 1960-63; dep. sheriff Los Angeles County, 1963-70; asst. to Gov. Ronald Reagan, 1970-75; dir. public relations Drew Med. Sch., Los Angeles, 1975-77; asst. v.p. United Airlines, 1977-81; sr. policy advisor to Pres. U.S., White House, 1981-82, asst. to Pres. U.S., 1982-89; pres. Garth & Bradley Assocs., Washington, 1989—; bd. dirs Essex Savs. Bank, Systems Mgmt. Am. Corp., Digit One, Inc. Republican. Baptist. Office: 1400 16th St NW Ste 210 Washington DC 20036-2217

BRADLEY, NOLEN EUGENE, JR., personnel executive, educator; b. Memphis, Nov. 29, 1925; s. Nolen Eugene and Anice Pearl (Luther) B.; m. Eloise Mullins, Jan. 7, 1947; children: Sharon (Mrs. Edward W. Vanderpool), Diana (Mrs. Wiley M. Rutledge), Nolen Eugene III, David Lee. BS, Memphis State U., 1951, MA, 1952; EdD, U. Tenn., 1966. Instr. polit. sci. Memphis State U., 1951-52; tchr. English Messick High Sch., Memphis, 1952-56; asst. dean admissions Memphis State U., 1956-64; dir. State Agy. for Title I, Higher Edn. Act, 1965, Div. Continuing Edn., U. Tenn., 1966-70; dean instrn. Vol. State Community Coll., Gallatin, Tenn., 1970-78; tutor, ednl. cons., 1978-79; pers. asst. Hoeganaes Corp., Gallatin, 1979-80; pers. mgr. Hoeganaes Corp., 1980-82; dir. pers. Music Village U.S.A., Hendersonville, Tenn., 1984—. Contbr. articles to profl. jours. Deacon Bapt. ch., 1966—. With AUS, 1944-46, ETO. Mem. Am. Assn. Sch. Adminstrs., Tenn. Adult Edn. Assn., Tenn. Edn. Assn., Omicron Delta Kappa, Pi Delta Epsilon, Phi Delta Kappa, Phi Kappa Phi. Democrat. Lion. Avocations: writing, travel, movies, reading. Home: 907 Harris Dr Gallatin TN 37066-3462

BRADLEY, PATRICIA ELLEN, professional golfer; b. Arlington, Mass., Mar. 24, 1951; d. Richard Joseph and Kathleen Maureen (O'Brien) B. Assoc. in Phys. Edn, Miami-Dade North Jr. Coll., 1971; B.S., Fla. Internat. U., 1974. Mem. Sun-Star Japan-U.S. Team Matches, 1975-76, All-Am. Collegiate Team, 1971, U.S.A. Com., 1974, 76, Golf Mag.'s All Am. Team, 1976, 77-78, 79-81; qualified for Colgate Triple Crown Tournament, 1975, 76, 77, 78; staff mem. Dunlop Golf Co.; under contract with Nabisco. Winner N.H. Womens Amateur Championship, 1967, 69, Fla. Collegiate Championship, 1970, Mass. Womens Amateur Championship, 1972, New Eng. Amateur Championship, 1972, 73, Colgate Far East Tournament, 1975, Girl Talk Classic Tournament, 1976, Bankers Trust Classic Tournament, 1977, Lady Keystone Open, Hoosier Classic, Rail Charity Classic, 1978, 91, J.C. Penny Classic, 1978, 89, Balt. Classic, Peter Jackson Classic, 1980, U.S. Womens Open, 1981, Du Maurier Classic, 1985, LPGA Pro-Am, 1985, Rochester Invitational, 1985, Turquoise Classic, 1990, Centel Classic, 1991, Safeco Classic, 1991, MBS Classic, 1991, HEALTHSOUTH Inaugural, 1995; recipient Most Improved Player award Golf Digest, 1976; named Player of Yr., 1986, Mazda Series, 1986, Vare Trophy, 1986; named to Ladies Profl. Golf Hall of Fame, 1991, mem. U.S. Solheim Cup Team, 1990, 92, 96. Mem. Ladies Profl. Golf Assn. Roman Catholic. Played exhbn. golf match with Pres. Ford, Vail, Colo., 1976; first woman golfer to win all four USGA Womens Open, LPGA Championship, Du Maurier Classic and Nabisco/Dinah Shore Tournaments; leading money winner PGA, 1986, 91. *

BRADLEY, PAULA E., retired state legislator; b. New Haven, Conn., Oct. 11, 1924; m. William L. Bradley, 1947; children: James R. Choukas-Bradley, Dwight C., Paul W. BA, Hiram Coll., 1945; postgrad., Middlebury Coll., 1946, Hartford Seminary, 1963-64. Ret. rsch. assoc. univ. devel. Yale U.; mem. N.H. Ho. of Reps., 1992-98. treas. Coos County Dem. Com., 1998—, N.H. State Dem. Com., 1992—; treas. Randolph Dem. Party, 1992—; bd. dirs. Coos County Family Health Svcs., Berlin, N.H., 1993—, Weeks Meml. Hosp., Lancaster, N.H., 1993-95; mem. Gorham (N.H.) Congregational Ch. Mem. AAUW (Androscoggin br. 1990—), Randolph Mountain Club (bd. dirs. 1986-91, 92-97, treas. 1989-91, pres. 1995-96). Avocations: music, hiking, gardening, singing. Office: RR 1 Box 1060 Randolph NH 03570-9714

BRADLEY, RAYMOND JOSEPH, lawyer; b. Phila., July 16, 1920; s. Michael Joseph and Emily Clotilda (Angiuli) B.; m. Sarah Ann Hill, Nov. 26, 1960; children: Michael J., Andrew W., David T. A.B., U. Pa., 1941, LL.B., 1947. Bar: Pa. 1948, U.S. Supreme Ct. 1957. Law clk. to justice Pa. Supreme Ct., 1948; assoc. Barnes, Dechert, Price, Smith & Clark, Phila., 1948-49; asst. prof. U. Pa. Law Sch., Phila., 1950-52; assoc. prof. U. Pa. Law Sch., 1952-55; ptnr. McBride, von Moschzisker & Bradley, Phila., 1955-62; ptnr. Wolf, Block, Schorr and Solis-Cohen, Phila., 1962-88, of counsel, 1988—; dep. controller City of Phila., 1950; trustee Community Legal Services, Phila., 1968; bd. dirs. Defender Assn., Phila., 1949-75. Served with USNR, 1942-46. Mem. Am. Coll. Trial Lawyers, Am. Judicature Soc., Am. Law Inst., ABA, Pa. Bar Assn., Phila. Bar Assn., ACLU (dir. 1951—, past pres. Greater Phila. br.), Order of Coif. Office: 12th Fl Packard Bldg Philadelphia PA 19102

BRADLEY, RICHARD EDWIN, retired college president; b. Omaha, Mar. 9, 1926; s. Louis J. and Betsy (Winterton) B.; m. Doris I. McGowan, June 8, 1946; children—Diane, Karen, David. Student, Creighton U., 1946-48; B.S.D., U. Nebr., 1950, D.D.S., 1952; M.S., State U. Iowa, 1958. Instr. State U. Iowa, 1957-58; asst. prof. Creighton U., 1958-59; asst. prof., chmn. dept. periodontics U. Nebr., 1959-62, assoc. prof., 1962-65, prof., 1965-67; assoc. dean Coll. Dentistry, 1967-68, dean, 1968-80; pres. Baylor Coll. Dentistry, 1980-90, pres., dean emeritus, 1990—; clin. prof. Coll. Dentistry U. Nebr. Med. Coll., Lincoln, 1990—; cons. dental edn., 199-93; mem. Commn. A, Coun. on Dental Edn., 1986-93; pres. Am. Assn. Dental Schs., 1977-78; mem. nat. adv. com. on health professions edn. Dept. Health and Human Resources, 1982-86; pres. Am. Fund for Dental Health, 1986-87. Editor: The New Dentist, 1992-94; contbg. editor Orban's Textbook of Periodontics, 1963; contbr. Clark's Clin., 1980. Served with USNR, 1944-46. Fellow AAAS, Internat. Coll. Dentists; mem. ADA, Am. Acad. Peridontology Found. (bd. dirs., pres. 1994-96), Am. Coll. Dentists (regent 1992-96, treas. 1996-98, v.p. 1998—), Sigma Xi, Omicron Kappa Upsilon. Home: 6424 Crooked Creek Dr Lincoln NE 68516-2955 Office: U Nebraska Coll Dentistry Lincoln NE 68583-0740

BRADLEY, RITAMARY, retired English educator; b. Stuart, Iowa, Jan. 30, 1916; d. James Francis Bradley and Mary Alice Muldoon. PhB, Marygrove Coll., 1938; MA, St. Louis U., 1942, PhD, 1953; LLD (hon.), Marquette U., 1960; DHL (hon.), Fordham U., 1960. Joined Sisters for Christian Cmty., Roman Cath. Ch. Prof. English Marycrest Coll., Davenport, Iowa, 1940-56, Ottumwa (Iowa) Heights Coll., 1956-61, St. Ambrose U., Davenport, 1965-97; adminstr., editor Nat. Cath. Edn. Assn., Washington, 1961-64; rsch. fellow U. Minn., St. Paul, 1964-65; ret., 1997; editor Sister Formation Bull., 1954-64, Mystics Quar., 1974-93; co-owner sister-1. Author: In the Jaws of the Bear, 1991, Julian's Way, 1993, Praying with Julian, 1995. Chair Davenport Civil Rights Commn., 1975-77; mem. Iowa Humanities Bd., Iowa City, 1980-85; chaplain County Jail, Davenport, 1986—. U. Minn. rsch. fellow, 1964-65; Mellon fellow, 1981. Mem. Medieval Acad. Am. Avocations: electronic discussion group. Home: 2317 Western Ave Davenport IA 52803

BRADLEY, RONALD JAMES, neuroscientist; b. Enniskillen, No. Ireland, Feb. 17, 1943; s. Samuel John and Mary Elizabeth (Irvine) B.; m. Doris Brown, Mar. 5, 1966; children—Nicola, Jason, Steven. B.Sc., Queens U., Belfast, No. Ireland, 1964; Ph.D., U. Edinburgh, Scotland, 1967. Mem. faculty Yale U., 1967-69, U. N.Mex., 1969-71, U. Ala., Birmingham, 1972-92; prof. psychiatry and neuroscis. U. Ala., 1976-92; prof. psychiatry and pharmacology La. State U. Med. Sch., Shreveport, La., 1992—; assoc. dean for instnl. devel., La. State U. Med. Sch.; guest prof. U. Saarlands, Fed. Republic of Germany, 1977-81. Editor: Internat. Rev. Neurobiology, 1974—. Recipient A. E. Bennett award Soc. Biol. Psychiatry, 1967. Mem. AAAS, Biophys. Soc., Neuroscis. Soc., Soc. Biol. Psychiatry. Home: 2407 Lakecrest Dr Shreveport LA 71109-3003 Office: LSU Med Ctr Dept Psychiatry PO Box 33932 Shreveport LA 71130-3932

BRADLEY, SANDRA LYNN GRANT, nursing administrator; b. Lubbock, Tex., Oct. 16, 1959; m. Clayton Allen Bradley, Feb. 11, 1994; children: Chelsea, Stephanie, Chance, Rachael. Cert. vocat. nursing, Frank Phillips Coll., 1980; BSN, Tex. Tech U., 1995. RN, Tex.; lic. vocat. nurse, Tex.; cert. CPR instr.; cert. vision and audiological and scoliosis screener. Nurse aide Dumas (Tex.) Meml. Home, 1978-79, lic. vocat. nurse, 1980-81; lic. vocat. nurse K.W. Pieratt, M.D., Dumas, 1981-82; LPN Pawnee (Okla.) Mcpl. Hosp., 1982-84; LPN, child birth educator Dr. James P. Riemer, Pawnee, 1984-88; lic. vocat. nurse (med.-surg.) Meth. Hosp., Lubbock, 1988-91, lic. vocat. nurse (cardiac telemetry), 1991-94; RN supr. home health divsn. South Plains Cmty. Action Assn., 1995; program dir./coord. Alternative Home Health Svcs., Lubbock, Tex., 1995-98; CBA/PHC/FC program dir. Essential Home Health, Lubbock, 1998—. Mem. Nurse Ambs. Avocations: guitar playing, sewing, camping, water-skiing.

BRADLEY, WALTER D., lieutenant governor, real estate broker; b. Clovis, N.M., Oct. 30, 1946; s. Ralph W. and M. Jo (Black) B.; m. Debbie Shelly, Sept. 17, 1977; children: Tige, Lance, Nicole, Kristin. Student Eastern N.M. U., 1964-1967. Supr. Tex. Instruments, Dallas, Tex. 1967-73; mgr., salesman Nat. Chemsearch, Irving, Tex., 1973-76; real estate broker Colonial Real Estate, Clovis, 1976; real estate broker Realtors Assn. N.Mex., Clovis, N.Mex., 1976—; state senator Curry County, State of N.Mex., 1989-93; Lt. Governor State of N.Mex., Santa Fe, N. Mex., 1995—. mem. N.Mex. Senate, 1989-92, 99—; lieutenant governor State N.Mex., 1995—. V.p., bd. dirs. Clovis Indsl. Commn., 1983-86, pres. econ. devel., 1987; bd. dirs. United Way, Clovis, 1984-86, Curry County Blood Adv. Bd., Clovis, 1980-85; chmn. Curry County Reps., Clovis, 1984-88; Cosmos Soccer, Clovis, 1984. Recipient Albuquerque NAACP Disting. Leadership award, 1997, Disting. Svc. award N.Mex. Farm and Livestock Bur., 1997; named Man of Yr., Progressive Farmer Mag., 1998. Mem. Realtors Assn. N.Mex. (v.p., bd. dirs. 1982-85, v.p. 1987-88), Clovis Bd. Realtors (pres. 1982, 93), Clovis C. of C., Curry County Jaycees, N.M. Jaycees. Baptist. Lodge: Lions. Office: Office of Lt Gov State Capitol Bldg Ste 417 Santa Fe NM 87503

BRADLEY, WALTER JAMES, emergency physician; b. Chgo., July 6, 1956; s. Walter James and Anna L. (Barbee) B. BS, Augsburg Coll., 1978; MD, U. Ill., 1984; MBA, U. South Fla., 1995. Diplomate Am. Bd. Emergency Medicine. Flight physician Flight for Life Milw. County Regional Med. Ctr., 1985-90; med. dir. PALS program Trinity Med. Ctr., Moline, Ill., 1990—; edn. dir. Sinai-Samaritan Med. Ctr., 1988-90, EMS dir., 1987-90; paramedic base sta. physician Milw. County Regional Med. Ctr., 1985-90; pres. Emergency Medicine Mgmt. & Diagnostics, Trinity Med. Ctr., 1990—, dir. EMS svcs., 1990—, asst. dir. regional trauma ctr., 1989—; state med. dir. Basic Traum Life Support, 1994—; pres., COO Trinity Ambulance, Inc. Fellow Am. Coll. Emergency Physicians; mem. AMA, Am. Coll. Emergency Physicians, Am. Coll. Physician Execs., Nat. Assn. Managed Care Physicians, Nat. Assn. Emergency Med. Svcs. Physicians. Office: Trinity Med Ctr 2701 17th St Rock Island IL 61201-5351*

BRADLEY, WESLEY HOLMES, physician; b. Chaumont, N.Y., Aug. 7, 1922; s. William Holmes and Margaret Jane (Bartrem) B.; m. Barbara Jean Sawyer, Sept. 23, 1945; children: James, Douglas, William, David. A.B., Syracuse U., 1944, M.D., 1946. Diplomate Am. Bd. Otolaryngology (exec. com. 1972, 74, 78). Intern Mass. Meml. Hosp., Boston, 1946-47; resident in otolaryngology U. Mich., 1949-53; practice medicine specializing in otolaryngology Syracuse, N.Y., 1953-75; mem. faculty SUNY Coll. Medicine, 1953-75, clin. prof., 1974-75; dir. communicative disorders program Nat. Inst. Neurol. and Communicative Disorders and Stroke, NIH, Bethesda, Md., 1975-78; med. dir. Commd. Corps UPSHS, 1975-78; prof. otolaryngology Albany (N.Y.) Med. Coll., 1978—; chief otolaryngology VA Med. Center, Albany, 1978—; mem. nat. adv. council Boys Town Nat. Inst. for Communicative Disorders in Children. Bd. editors: Rhinology and Laryngology, 1978—; contbr. articles to profl. jours. Served with USN, 1947-49. Mem. AMA, ACS, Am. Acad. Otolaryngology-Head and Neck Surgery (v.p. 1970, exec. v.p. 1979-81, exec. council 1972-76), Am. Laryngological Rhinological and Otological Soc. (v.p. 1982, exec. council 1983-85, pres. 1985-86), Otosclerosis Study Group (pres. 1976), Am. Otological Soc. (pres. 1974), Assn. Research in Otolaryngology, Deafness Research Found. (bd. dirs. 1967-75, 78—, exec. com. 1970-75, dir. med. affairs), Am. Council Otolaryngology (assoc. exec. dir. 1969-72, exec. com. 1972), Alpha Omega Alpha, Alpha Kappa Kappa, Lambda Chi Alpha. Republican. Methodist. Office: 113 Holland Ave Albany NY 12208-3410 *As I think about my life, these are a few of the feelings which seem to have a recurring consistency: maintaining a sense of awe and respect for the wonders of creation around us; keeping faith in oneself, in others, and in the ongoing pageant of life; and having fun each day while not taking oneself too seriously.*

BRADLEY, WILLIAM BRYAN, cable television regulator; b. Charleston, W.Va., Feb. 12, 1929; s. Floyd England and Florence Clara (O'Bryan) B.; m. Virginia Vanderhoof Logan, Oct. 27, 1951; children: Christopher, Thomas, Michael, John, Mary Clare (dec.), Mary Ellen, Ann. BA in Journalism cum laude, U. Notre Dame, 1950. Supr., indsl. engr. Martin Co., Denver, 1958-61, 62-65; cons. Reynolds, Ward & Carey, Denver, 1961-62; analyst Denver City Coun., 1965-69, staff dir., 1969-82; dir. Office of Telecommunications, Denver, 1982-94; sr. assoc. Media Mgmt. Svcs., Inc., 1994—; co-founder, dir., vice-chmn. Greater Metro Cable Consortium, 1992; initiated joint city-industry cable TV Tech. Stds., 1987, adopted by FCC, 1992. Participant Japanese-Am. conf. on Globalization and Cable TV, Suwa, Japan, 1991. Co-founder Nat. Assn. Telecomm. Officers and Advisors, Washington, 1980, bd. dirs., 1983-88, pres., 1985-87; chmn. telecomm. subcom. Colo. Mcpl. League, Denver, 1985-86; bd. dirs. Denver Cmty. TV, 1996-98. Line Officer USN, 1950-53. Roman Catholic. Avocations: chess, books.

BRADLEY, WILLIAM HAMPTON, lawyer; b. Chattanooga, May 22, 1944. BA, Emory U., 1965; LLB, Harvard U., 1968. Bar: Ga. 1969, D.C. 1971. Law clk. to Hon. Edward C. McLean U.S. Dist. Ct. (so. dist.) N.Y., 1968-69; ptnr. Sutherland, Asbill & Brennan LLP, Atlanta, 1969—, mng. ptnr., 1991-95; adj. prof. law Emory U., 1976-86. Bd. visitors Duke U. Sch. of Environment, Durham, N.C., 1988-93, Emory U., Atlanta, 1994—, bd. dirs., World Forestry Ctr., 1997—. Mem. Phi Beta Kappa. Office: Sutherland Asbill & Brennan 999 Peachtree St NE Ste 2300 Atlanta GA 30309-3996*

BRADLEY, WILLIAM LEE, retired foundation executive, educator; b. Oakland, Calif., Sept. 6, 1918; s. Dwight Jaques Bradley and Kathryn Lee (Culver) Bradley/Bovard; m. Paula Anne Elliott; children: James Richard, Dwight Culver, Paul William. BA, Oberlin Coll., 1941; PhD, Edinburgh (Scotland) U., 1949; BD, Andover Newton Theol. Sch., 1950. Instr. to prof. Hartford (Conn.) Theol. Sem., 1950-66; temporary field staff Rockefeller Found., N.Y.C., 1964-66; vis. prof. Thammasat U., Bangkok, Thailand, 1964-66; asst. to assoc. dir. Rockefeller Found., N.Y.C., 1966-70; pres. Edward W. Hazen Found., New Haven, 1970-84; ret., 1984. Author: (book) P.T. Forsyth-The Man and His Work, 1952, The Meaning of Christian Values Today, 1964, Siam Then, 1982. Mem. Gov.'s Commn. on Human Svcs., Hartford, 1962-64, Gov.'s Commn. on Libraries, Hartford, 1962, Gov.'s Commn. on Equity and Excellence in Edn., Hartford, 1984-85. Tech. sgt. USAF, 1942-45. Mem. Coun. on Fgn. Rels., Mountain View Publs. (editor 1990-99), Randolph Found. (pres. 1991-96), Obor Inc. (bd. dirs. 1984—). Democrat. United Ch. of Christ. Avocations: reading, writing, hiking, travel. Home and Office: RR 1 Box 1060 Randolph NH 03570-9714

BRADNA, JOANNE JUSTICE, manufacturer's representative; b. Evergreen Park, Ill., May 1, 1952; d. John George and Virginia Dorothy (Breault) Justice; m. William Charles Bradna, Aug. 20, 1972; children: Trevor William, Cameron Jon. Student, North Cen. Coll., Naperville, Ill., 1970-72; BS, Northwestern U., 1974; MS, U. Ill., Chgo., 1981. Med. technologist Northwestern U. Med. Sch., Chgo., 1974-76, Good Samaritan Hosp., Downers Grove, Ill., 1977-78; instr. med. lab. scis. U. Ill., Chgo., 1976-81, asst. prof., 1984-89, clin. coord., 1984-89, admissions coord., 1988-89; tech. sales rep. Analytab Products, Plainview, N.Y., 1981-84; owner, mgr. Rochelle Sci., mfr.'s reps. lab. equipment and supplies, Lisle, Ill., 1989—; ednl. cons. Hinsdale (Ill.) Hosp., 1979-80; mem. adv. com. Moraine Valley C.C., Palos Hills, Ill., 1982-92. Contbr. articles and abstracts to profl. jours. V.p. St. Isaac Jogues Home Sch. Assn., 1990-91, pres., 1991-92; mem. youth commn. St. Isaac Jogues Ch., Hinsdale, 1986-90, mem. edn. commn., 1988-92; bd. dirs. Care and Counseling Ctr., Downers Grove, Ill., 1993-95, treas., 1994-95; treas. Hinsdale Jr. Women's Clubs, 1983-85, 88-89, pres., 1985-86; 3d v.p. 5th dist. Ill. Fedn. Women's Clubs, 1986-88, treas., 1988-90; mem. alumni bd. U. Ill. Coll. Assoc. Health Professions, 1992-96, v.p. alumni bd., 1993-95. Recipient Outstanding Mem. award Hinsdale Jr. Woman's Club, 1981, 82, lifetime svc. award 5th-6th Dist. Jr. Orgn., 1990, Ill. Fedn. Women's Club, 1990, Heart of Gold citation United Way, 1994, Excaliber Tchg. award, 1989, Outstanding Sales awrads, 1990, 91, 93, 94, 97, 98. Mem. Am. Soc. Clin. Pathologists, Am. Soc. Med. Technologists (cert. of appreciation 1977), Chgo. Soc. Med. Technologists (bd. dirs. 1977-80, cert. of recognition 1978-80), Am. Soc. Microbiology, Ill. Soc. Microbiology (sec. 1981-83, bd. dirs. 1985-87, 92-94, nominations com. 1987-89, tellers com. 1994-95, pres.-elect 1995-96, pres. 1996-98, awards chmn. 1998—, Tanner Shaughnessy merit award 1992), Ill. Med. Technologists Assn. (cert. of recognition 1978, 79), South Ctrl. Assn. Clin. Microbiology. Roman Catholic. Avocations: children and family, sports. Office: Rochelle Sci PO Box 637 Lisle IL 60532-0637

BRADNER, DIANA JEAN, psychiatric and pediatric nurse; b. Nurenburg, Fed. Republic of Germany, Nov. 19, 1964; d. Henry Peter Steinmetz and Helen Marilyn (Popp) McKenzie; m. Joseph T. Bradner III, Nov. 2, 1984; children: Jaime Nicole, Joseph Thomas IV. BSN, Med. U. S.C., 1987. RN. Staff nurse Med. U. of S.C. Children's Hosp., Charleston, 1990-91, Waterman Med. Ctr., Eustis, Fla., 1991-92, Lawrence and Meml. Hosp., New London, Ct., 1992-95; elem. sch. nurse Pleaseant Valley Elem. Sch.-Groton Pub. Health Nursing, Groton, CT, 1993-95; nurse Kahi Mohala Behavioral Care Ctr., Ewa Beach, Hawaii, 1997-98. Mem. Sigma Theta Tau. Home: 8 New St Santa Rita GU 96915-1129

BRADSELL, KENNETH RAYMOND, minister; b. N.Y.C., Mar. 9, 1948; s. Robert Hosford and Doris Mildred (Pennie) B.; m. Marcia Ann Van Dyke, June 25, 1971; children: Adam, Mark, Rachel. BA, Hope Coll., 1970; MDiv, New Brunswick Sem., 1974; STM, Union Theol. Sem., N.Y.C., 1983. Cert min. edn. Ref. Ch. in Am., 1982. Assoc. pastor Community Ch. Douglaston, N.Y., 1974-76; pastor Blawenburg (N.J.) Ref. Ch., 1976-81; co-pastor 1st Ch. in Albany, N.Y., 1981-84; min. for edn. Ref. Ch. in Am., Grandville, Mich., 1984-85, dir. congl. svcs., 1992-95, dir. policy planning, adminstrv. svcs., 1995—; chmn. Ministries in Christian Edn., Nat. Coun. Chs. of Christ, U.S.A., N.Y.C., 199-95; chmn. Presbyn. and Ref. Edn. Ministry, Louisville, 1990-95; asst. sec. Reformed Ch. Am., 1997—. Editor: Designs for Teacher and Leader Education, 1990; also articles. Mem. Christian Educators Ref. Ch. in Am. (pres. 1981-84, Educator of Yr. award 1988), Assn. Presbyn. Educators, Religious Edn. Assn. Office: Ref Ch in Am 475 Riverside Dr New York NY 10015

BRADSHAW, BILLY DEAN, retail executive; b. Decatur, Ill., June 25, 1940; s. Lester H. and Gertrude (Davis) B.; children: Deborah, Amanda. Grad., Lakeview High Sch., Decatur, Ill., 1959. Retail div. supr. Schnepps Assocs., Decatur, 1964-74; store mgr. Firestone Tire & Rubber Co., Decatur, 1975—. Coach Decatur's Boys Baseball, 1965-69. With USAF, 1960-64. Mem. Am. Motorcyclist Assn., Tennesse-Squire, Am. Legion. Avocations: boating, golf. Home: 24 Lake Grove Clb Decatur IL 62521-2321 Office: Firestone Store 2605 N 22nd St Decatur IL 62526-4745

BRADSHAW, CARL JOHN, investor, lawyer, consultant; b. Oelwein, Iowa, Nov. 1, 1930; s. Carl John and Lorraine Lillian (Thiele) B.; m. Katsuko Anno, Nov. 5, 1954; children: Carla K., Arthur Herbert, Vincent Marcus. BS, U. Minn., 1952, JD, 1957; LLM, U. Mich., 1958; MJur, Keio U., Tokyo, 1962. Bar: Minn. 1960, U.S. Supreme Ct., 1981, Calif. 1985,. Assoc. Graham, James & Rolph, Tokyo, 1961-63; assoc. prof. law U. Wash., Seattle, 1963-64; sr. v.p. Oak Industries, Inc., Crystal Lake, Ill., 1964-84, dir. internat. ops., 1964-70, dir. corp. devel., 1970-72, pres. communications group, 1972-78, chief legal officer, 1979-84; counsel Seki & Jarvis, L.A., 1985-87, Bell, Boyd & Lloyd, L.A., 1987; prin. The Pacific Law Group, L.A., Tokyo and Palo Alto, Calif., 1987—, The Asian Mktg. Group, Torrance, Calif., 1992—; participant Japanese-Am. program for cooperation in legal studies, 1957-61. Contbr. articles to legal and bus. jours. Bd. dirs. Japan-Am. Soc., Chgo., 1966-72; bd. dirs., fin. dir. San Diego Symphony Orch. Assn., 1980-81. Served to lt. (j.g.) USN, 1952-55. Fulbright scholar, 1958-59, Ford Found. scholar, 1960-61. Fellow Radio Club Am.; mem. Minn. Bar Assn., Calif. Bar Assn., Am. Soc. Internat. Law, Internat. Fiscal Assn., Regency Club, Order of Coif. Avocation: reading, bible study. Home: 12958 Robleda Cv San Diego CA 92128-1126 Office: Pacific Law Group 12121 Wilshire Blvd Fl 2 Los Angeles CA 90025-1123

BRADSHAW, CONRAD ALLAN, lawyer; b. Campbell, Mo., Dec. 22, 1922; s. Clarence Andrew and Stella (Cashdollar) B.; m. Margaret Crassous Sanderson, Dec. 31, 1959; children—Dorothy A., Lucy E., Charlotte L. A.B., U. Mich., 1943, J.D., 1948. Bar: Mich. bar 1948. Since practiced in Grand Rapids with firm Warner, Norcross & Judd. Served to lt. USNR, 1943-46. Mem. Am. Bar Assn., State Bar Mich. (chmn. corp., fin. and bus. law sect. 1976), Grand Rapids Bar Assn. (pres. 1970). Home: 3261 Lake Dr SE Grand Rapids MI 49506-4320 Office: 900 Old Kent Bldg Grand Rapids MI 49503

BRADSHAW, CYNTHIA HELENE, educational administrator; b. S.I., N.Y., May 9, 1954; d. Frederick Thomas and Audrey Helene (Stetter) B. BS in Elem. Edn., Wagner Coll., 1975; MS in Edn., U. Miami, 1979. Cert. elem. tchr., adminstr., and supr. Tchr. Young Scholars Montessori Sch., S.I., 1975-76; tchr. Luth. Schs., Mo. Synod, S.I., 1976, Hialeah and North Miami, Fla., 1976-80; tchr. Dade County Pub. Schs., Miami, Fla., 1980-88, Rahway (N.J.) Pub. Schs., Bayonne (N.J.) Pub. Schs., 1988-91; tester, field worker, classroom surveyor Prospects-Chgo., Bklyn., 1991—; prin. Christ Luth. Sch., 1997-98, Calvary Luth. Sch., 1998-99; reliability study subject Fla. Dept. Edn., Tallahassee, 1984—; participated in 3 videos in cooperation with Wagner Coll., S.I., N.Y., Bayonne (N.J.) Bd. Edn.; co-produced videos with Wagner Coll. and S.I. Continuum, 1988—. Sch. chairperson United Way, Miami, 1983—. Recipient Cert. of Recognition Dade County Pub. Schs., 1984. Mem. United Tchrs. Dade, United Tchrs. Dade Polit. Orgn., Order Ea. Star, U. Miami Sch. Edn. Allied Professions Alumni Assn. (mem. alumni telephone funding campaign 1984), Wagner Coll. Alumni Assn. (alumni telephone funding campaign 1988—), Alpha Delta Kappa. Republican. Lutheran. Avocation: music. Office: 1 G Haspert Rd Baltimore MD 21236

BRADSHAW, DOVE, artist; b. N.Y.C., Sept. 24, 1949; d. David Nelson and Jean Katherine (Cormack) B. BFA, Boston Mus. Sch. Fine Arts, 1973. Artistic advisor The Merce Cunningham Dance Co., N.Y.C., 1984—. ne-man shows include Alan Stone Gallery, N.Y.C., 1979, 88, 89, 91, 93, 95, S. Gering Gallery, N.Y., 1989, PSI Mus., N.Y.C., 1991, Mattress Factory Mus., Pitts., 1990, 99, Pier Ctr., Orkney, Scotland, 1995, Stalke Gallery, Copenhagen, 1995, 96, 98, 99, Barbara Krakow Gallery, 1997, The MOCA, L.A., 1998, Mus. Comtemporary Art, L.A., 1998, many others; group shows include Mus. Modern Art, N.Y.C., 1989, Art Inst. Chgo., 1996, Met. Mus. N.Y., 1992, Carnegie Mus. Art, 1997, Whitney Mus. Am. Art, N.Y., 1997 Carnegie Internat., Pitts., 1990, Phila. Mus., 1992, Aldrich Mus., Ridgefield, Conn., 1993, Swiss Inst., N.Y.C., 1995, Baumgartner Gallery, Washington, 1996, Mus. Contemporary Art, L.A., 1996, Millennium Film Theatre, 1998, many others; represented in permanent collection at Met. Mus. Art, N.Y.C., Mus. Modern Art, N.Y.C., Bklyn. Mus. Art, Whitney Mus. Am. Art, N.Y., Art Inst. Chgo., Phila. Mus. Art, The Ark. Art Ctr., Little Rock, The Fogg Art Mus., Cambridge, Mass., Harvard U., The Getty Ctr., L.A., Mus. of Contemporary Art, L.A., Nat. Gallery, Washington, Internat. Le Pompidou Ctr., Paris, Pier Ctr., Orkney, Scotland, Mus. Art, Bilboa, Spain, Kunst Mus., Dusseldorf, Germany, Moderna Mus., Stockholm; outdoor sculptures affected by weather of marble, limestone, sandstone, and pyrite, 1995; paintings involved with humidity, 1984—; rock salt affected by water, 1998; prodr., dir., artist: (film) Indeterminacy, 1995; prodr.: Metropolitan Mus. postcard, 1992, Met. Mus. guerilla postcard; artist, prodr. handmade books, including Plain Air (installation with live birds 1969, 88, 91, documentation 1991), 1969-91, Indeterminacy Contingency, Equivalents, Removal, Riverstone. Recipient Pollock/Krasner award, 1985; grant Nat. Endowment of Arts, 1975. Mem. Sandra Gering Gallery (N.Y.), Stalke Gallerie (Copenhagen), Barbara Krakow Gallery (Boston), Linda Kirkland (N.Y.), Larry Becker (Phila.). Avocations: running, reading, gardening, yoga.

BRADSHAW, GLENN RAYMOND, art educator; b. Peoria, Ill., Mar. 3, 1922; s. Elza Raymond and Hilda Catherine (Johnson) B.; m. Inez Ellen Payne, June 5, 1947; children: Kristen, Todd, Lisa, Adam, Scott. BS, Ill. State U., 1947; MFA, U. Ill., 1950. Critic tchr. U. Ill., Urbana, 1947-50, prof. art, 1952-86; asst. prof. art Iowa State Tchrs. Coll., Cedar Falls, 1950-52. One-man shows include Ill. State Normal U., 1947, 50, 61, Cedar Falls Art Assn., 1951, Schermerhorn Gallery, Beloit, Wis., 1956, 57, 59, Millikin U., Decatur, Ill., 1955, Flint Art Ctr., Mich., 1957, Old Orchard Bank, Skokie, Ill., 1960, Gilman Gallery, Chgo., 1963, 65, Jane Haslem Gallery, Madison, Wis., 1966, 70, St. Louis Gallery, 1967, The Canal House, Indianapolis, 1969, Wustum Mus., Racine, Wis., 1969, Ill. State Mus., Springfield, 1972, Krannert Art Mus., Champaign, Ill., 1972, Tower Park Gallery, Peoria Hghts., Ill., 1973, 76, 78, 81, 85, Fanny Garver Gallery, Madison, Wis., 1976, 81, U. Wis., 1976, MacNider Mus., Mason City, Iowa, 1976, Prairie House, Springfield, Ill., 1980, Bicentennial Mus., Paris, Ill., 1980, Neville-Sargent Gallery, Evanston, Ill, 1980, 84, 87, 89, 91, U. San Diego, 1981, House of Art, Champaign, 1982, Humewood II Gallery, Toronto, Can., 1988, Ctr. for Vis. Arts, Wausau, Wis., 1997; group shows include Royal Watercolor Soc., London, Eng., 1962, Met. Mus. Art, N.Y.C., 1996-67, Clev. Inst. of Art, 1968, U. Colo., 1970, Am. Watercolor Soc. Invitational, Australia, 1975, Mexico City, 1989, Akron Art Inst., 1976, U. Ill. Faculty Exhibitions, Taiwan, 1981, Hong Kong, 1982, Tokyo, 1983, Albuquerque Mus. Art, 1985, June Kelly Gallery, N.Y.C., 1988, Galeri Hartl and Klier, Tubingen, Germany, 1988, L.A. County Century Gallery, 1993, Tex. Women's U., Denton, 1994, Nat. Taiwan Art Edn. Inst., 1994, Springfield Mus., 1997; represented in numerous permanent collections. With U.S. Army, 1942-45. Recipient John Young Hunter award Am. Watercolor Soc., N.Y.C., 1973, Ed Whitney Prize, 1974, Arches Paper Co. prize Long Beach Mus. Art, 1974, 1st prize Nat. Watercolor Soc., 1977, Dr. David Soletsky Memorial award Nat. Soc. of Painters in Caseinand Acrylic, N.Y.C., 1978, John J. Newman Medal and prize, 1996, William A. Paten prize Nat. Acad. Design, 1987, Schweitzer prize, 1993, Whitaker prize, 1996; numerous others. Mem. Nat. Acad., Nat. Watercolor Soc., Am. Watercolor Soc. Studio: 6403 Pine Point Dr McNaughton WI 54543

BRADSHAW, HOWARD HOLT, management consulting company executive; b. Phila., Feb. 28, 1937; s. Howard Holt and Imojean (Campbell) B.; m. Loretta Warren Sites, Aug. 13, 1982; children by previous marriage: Elaine Allen, Howard Holt. B.A., Yale U., 1958; postgrad., Duke U., 1958-60. Cert. mgmt. cons. Western Electric Co., various locations, 1960-67; personnel mgr., head behavioral scis. cons. Celanese Fibers Co., Charlotte, N.C., 1967-72; pres. Orgn. Cons., Inc., Charlotte, 1972—; adj. prof. Babcock Grad. Sch. Mgmt., Wake Forest U., 1997—; cons. in field. Author: Personal Power, Self Esteem and Performance, 1983; The Management of Self Esteem, 1981, Leadership and The Purpose of the Firm, 1998 ; mem. editorial rev. bd. Jour. Mgmt. Issues; contbr. articles to profl. jours. Regional chmn. Constl. Party of Pa., Harrisburg, 1964-66; pres. Coordinated Planning League, Inc., Charlotte, 1972-74; exec. com. Citizens for Effective Govt., Inc., Charlotte, 1987-93; mem. Mgmt. Review Com., Mecklenberg County, N.C., 1990—; bd. dirs. Chemi Metals, Inc., 1991-97. Recipient cert. of appreciation Charlotte Police Dept., 1969, Mecklenburg County Com., 1970. Mem. Inst. Mgmt. Cons., Am. Psychol. Assn., Soc. Indsl. and Organizational Psychology, Am. Soc. Tng. and Devel., Orgnl. Devel. Network. Republican. Presbyterian. Home: 488 Lakeview Loop Mooresville NC 28115 Office: Organization Consultants Inc 1909 Charlotte Dr Charlotte NC 28203-5768

BRADSHAW, JAMES EDWARD (JIM), consultant; b. Waco, Tex., Aug. 18, 1940; s. Leo Herman Sr. and Eleanor Rose (Cogdell) B.; m. Ouida P. Massey; children: Robin Louise, Dorenda and Dorette (twins), James E. Jr., Cogdell O'Neal. BBA in Mktg. and Fin., Baylor U., 1963. Ptnr. Cogdell's Westview, Waco, 1960-64, Kennedy-David & Assocs., Waco, 1966-68; sales rep. Fed.-Mogul Corp., Detroit, 1964-66; pres. Cogdell Auto Supply Co., Inc., Ft. Worth, 1968-77; chmn. bd. dirs. Auto Supply Co., Inc., Ft. Worth, 1979-91; mayor pro tem City of Ft. Worth, 1976-79; cons. pvt. practice, Fort Worth, Tex.; bd. dirs. Sr. Transp. Network, Geriatric Ctr. of Excellence; adv. bd. Betty Ford Ctr. Bd. dirs. Big Bros./Big Sisters Tarrant County, United Way, Jr. Achievement, Tarrant County Coun. Alcohol and Drug Abuse, Tex. Mcpl. League, Austin, 1976-78; mem. adv. bd. dirs. Betty Ford Ctr.; mem. cmty. devel. steering com. Nat. League Cities, 1978-79; chmn. Tarrant County March of Dimes, Ft. Worth, 1979, Future Pres. Orgn., Kansas City, Mo., 1974; councilman City of Ft. Worth, 1975-79, mayor pro tem 1976-79, mem. zoning commn., 1974-75; Republican. candidate 12th Congl. Dist., 1980. Named to Ten to Watch, D mag., 1977. Mem. Colonial Country Club, Masons. Methodist. Avocations: golf, reading, astronomy. Home: 4613 Briarhaven Rd Fort Worth TX 76109-4609 Office: PO Box 100338 Fort Worth TX 76185-0338

BRADSHAW, JEAN PAUL, II, lawyer; b. May 12, 1956; married; children: Andrew, Stephanie. BJ, JD, U. Mo., 1981. Bar: Mo. 1981, U.S. Dist. Ct. (we. dist.) Mo. 1982, U.S. Dist. Ct. (so. dist.) Ill. 1988, U.S. Ct. Appeals (8th cir.) 1986, U.S. Supreme Ct. 1987. Assoc. Neale, Newman, Bradshaw & Freeman, Springfield, Mo., 1981-87, ptnr., 1987-89; U.S. atty. we. dist. Mo. U.S. Dept. Justice, Kansas City, 1989-93; of counsel Lathrop & Gage, Kansas City, 1993—; named Spl. Asst. Atty. Gen. State of Mo., 1985-89; mem., chmn. elect U.S. Atty. Gen.'s adv. com., office mgmt. and budget subcom., sentencing guidelines subcom. Chmn. Greene County Rep. cen. com., 1988-89; pres. Mo. Assn. Reps., 1986-87; bd. dirs. Greene County TARGET, 1984-89; mem. com. on resolutions, family and community issues and del. 1988 Rep. Nat. Conv.; mem. platform com. Mo. Reps., 1988; chmn. Greene County campaign McNary for Gov., 1984, co-chmn. congl. dist. Dole for Pres., 1988, regional chmn. Danforth for Senate, 1988, co-chmn. 7th congl. dist. Webster for Atty. Gen., 1988; county chmn. U. Mo.-Columbia Alumni Assn., 1985-87; bd. dirs. Springfield Profl. Baseball Assn., Inc.; past mem. Mo. Adv. Coun. for Comprehensive Psychiat. Svcs., former bd. dirs. Ozarks Coun. Boy Scouts Am.; pres. bd. trustees St. Paul's Episcopal Day Sch., 1997—. Named Outstanding Recent Grad. U. Mo.-Columbia Sch. Law, 1991. Mem. ABA, Mo. Bar Assn., Kansas City Met. Bar Assn., U. Mo.-Columbia Law Sch. Alumni Assn. (v.p. 1988-89, pres. 1990-91), Law Soc. U. Mo.-Columbia Law Sch. Office: 2345 Grand Blvd Ste 2800 Kansas City MO 64108-2612

BRADSHAW, JOHN ROBERT, internet service company executive; b. Carthage, N.Y., Aug. 4, 1942; s. John Covington and Selma Pauline Bradshaw; 1 child, Sean. BS, U. Mo., 1966, MBA, 1968. Owner vending machine company, 1978, owner real estate and mortgage companies; pres. ATM Nat. Svcs., Clearwater, Fla., 1989—; pres./ceo Uniglobe Fin. Inc., Clearwater, 1998—. Mem. C. of C., BBB, Profl. Bus. Owners, Rotary, Score. Avocations: boating, travel, model trains.

BRADSHAW, LILLIAN MOORE, retired library director; b. Hagerstown, Md., Jan. 10, 1915; d. Harry M. and Mabel E. (Kretzer) Moore; m. William Theodore Bradshaw, May 19, 1946. BA, Western Md. Coll., 1937, DLitt (hon.), 1987; BLS, Drexel U., 1938, LittD (hon.), 1978; LHD (hon.), So. Meth. U., 1990—. Asst. adult circulation dept. Utica (N.Y.) Pub. Libr., 1938-41, asst. head, 1941-43; adult libr. Enoch Pratt Free Libr., Balt., 1943-44; asst. coord. work with young adults Enoch Pratt Free Libr., 1944-46; br. libr. Dallas Pub. Libr., 1946-47, readers adviser, 1947-52, head dept. circulation, 1952- 55, coord. work with adults, 1955-58, asst. dir., 1958-62, dir., 1962-84; asst. mgr. City of Dallas, 1984-85. Mem. bd. publs. So. Meth. U., 1970-78; mem. curriculum com. Leadership Dallas, 1978-79, mem. adv. com., 1978-82; mem. Tex. Gov.'s Commn. on Status of Women, 1970-72, Tex. Com. for Humanities, 1980-84, Nat. Reading Coun., Washington, 1970-73; pres. Tex. Humanities Alliance, 1986-88, bd. dirs., 1988-92; mem. Urban Design Adv. Coun., Dallas, 1987-92; conferee, asst. task force leader Goals for Dallas, 1966-69, vice chmn. achievement com. for continuing edn., 1971, chmn., 1972, chmn. citizen info. and participation com., 1976-77, trustee, 1977-78, sec., 1977, treas., 1979-83, exec. com., 1977-84; hon. chair Literacy Vols. Am., Dallas, 1987-90; mem. Com. to Plan the Future Goals for Dallas, 1973-74; mem. Dallas County Hist. Found., 1987-93, treas., 1990-93; adv. bd. Tex. Library Sys. Act, 1974-77; del. White House Conf. on Library and Info. Svcs.; ad hoc com. for planning and monitoring White House Conf. follow-up activities, 1980; bd. dirs. Hoblitzelle Found., 1971—, Univ. Med. Ctr., 1984-87, Friends of Fair Pk., 1989—; trustee Lamplighter Sch., 1974-81, Friends of Dallas Pub. Library, 1984—, pres., 1994-96, Dallas Ballet, 1986-88, Dallas Arboretum and Bot. Garden, 1986-88, Employees' Retirement Fund, City of Dallas, 1989-91, mcpl. adv. bd. Dallas Pub. Libr., 1991-93; bd. dirs. Sr. Citizens Greater Dallas, 1996—. Named Tex. Libr. of Yr., 1961; recipient Disting. Alumnus award Drexel U. Libr. Sch., 1970; Titche's Arete award for epitome of excellence in chosen field, 1970; Public Adminstr. of Yr. award, 1981; Excellence in Community Svc. award Dallas Hist. Soc., 1981; citation of honor Dallas chpt. AIA, 1982; Lillian Moore Bradshaw chair in libr. and info. studies established in her honor Tex. Woman's U. Mem. ALA (v.p. adult svcs. div. 1966-67, pres. adult svcs. div. 1967, 68, coun. 1968-69, pres. 1970-71, endowment trustee 1984-88, Honor Roll, Freedom to Read Found. 1993), Tex. Libr. Assn. (pres. 1964-65, chmn. pub. librs. div. 1955-56, chmn. awards com. 1973-74, 79-80, Disting. Svc. award 1975), Tex. Soc. Architects (hon. 1982), Dallas Hist. Soc. (trustee 1984-87), Zonta (pres. Dallas I 1976-77, Svc. award 1981, Dallas Humanitarian award 1991). Home: 6318 E Lovers Ln Dallas TX 75214-2016

BRADSHAW, MELISSA WEBB, librarian; b. Austin, Tex., Feb. 20, 1970; d. Benjamin Spencer and Mary Manry (Webb) B. BA in French, Austin Coll., 1992; M Libr. and Info. Sci., U. Tex., 1996. Sec. Audie Murphy Meml. Vets. Hosp., San Antonio, 1993-94; social sci. rsch. asst. U. Tex. Health Sci. Ctr., San Antonio, 1994; libr. asst. Perry-Castañeda Libr., Austin, Tex., 1994-96; electronic info. specialist U. Tex. Health Sci. Ctr., San Antonio, 1995; reference librarian Harris County Pub. Libr., Houston, 1997—; vol. librarian San Antonio Pub. Libr., 1994, McNay Art Mus., San Antonio, 1996-97, collections asst., Houston Mus. Nat. Sci., 1998—. Collections mgr. mus. exhibit Tex. Meml. Mus., 1996. Gallery guide San Antonio Mus. Art, 1995; collections vol. Houston Mus. Natural Sci., Houston, 1998—. Mem. Am. Assn. Museums, Alliance Française San Antonio (sec. 1993, cataloger 1994), U. Tex. Ex-Students' Assn. Democrat. Episcopalian. Avocations: ballroom dance, foreign languages, travel, arts and crafts. Office: Maud Marks Libr 1815 Westgreen Blvd Katy TX 77450-5370

BRADSHAW, MURRAY CHARLES, musicologist; b. Hinsdale, Ill., Sept. 25, 1930; s. Murray Andrew Bradshaw and Marie (Novak) Orth; m. Doris Hogg; children: Jean Marie, Murray Edward, Thomas Andrew; m. Sharon Ann Sitton, Apr. 19, 1997. MusM in Piano, Am. Conservatory Music, Chgo., 1955, MusM in Organ, 1958; PhD in Musicology, U. Chgo., 1969. Prof. UCLA, 1966—; organist and choirmaster various chs. in Illinois, Ind., Calif., 1948—; music critic Gary Post Tribune, Ind., 1962-64; chair dep. musicology, UCLA, 1993-95. Author: The Origin of the Toccata, 1972, The Falsobordone, 1978, Francesco Severi, 1981, Girolamo Diruta The Transylvanian, 1984, Giovanni Luca Conforti, 1985, Gabriele Fattorini, 1986, Emilio de' Cavalieri, 1990, Conforti, "Breve et facile", 1999; contbr. articles to profl. jours. Served with U.S. Army, 1954-56. Grantee: Am. Philos. Soc., 1987, NEH (travel), 1994. Mem. Internat. Musicol. Soc., Am. Musicol. Soc. (pres. local chpt. 1979-81), Am. Guild Organists, Ctr. for Medieval and Renaissance Studies. Avocations: reading, jogging, yoga, bridge. Home: 17046 Burbank Blvd Apt 3 Encino CA 91316-1830 Office: UCLA Dept Musicology 405 Hilgard Ave Los Angeles CA 90095-9000

BRADSHAW, OTABEL, retired primary school educator; b. Magnolia, Ark., Oct. 27, 1922; d. Grover Cleveland and Mae (Staggs) Peterson; AA, Magnolia A&M Coll., 1950; BS in Edn., So. State Coll., 1953; MS in Edn., Henderson State U., 1975; postgrad. U. Ark.; PhD, Kensington U., 1983; m. Charles Howard Bradshaw, Aug. 14, 1948; children: Susan Charla, Michael Howard. Tchr., English and drama Walkers Creek Schs., Taylor Ark., 1945-46, primary grades Locust Baypere Schs., Camden, Ark., 1946-52, 2d grade Fairview Sch., Camden, 1962-73; tchr. 1st grade Harmony Grove Sch., Camden, 1973-83, coordinator Title IX, gifted children and handicapped; tchr. East Camden Accelerated Sch., 1983-96, ret., 1996; cons. econ. edn. workshop U. Ark., Fayetteville. Life mem., sec., historian chmn. bicentennial com. PTA; active vol. fund-raising drives Am. Cancer Soc., Birth Defects Soc.; leader Missionary Soc., Camden 1st United Methodist Ch.; mem. Camden and Ouachita County Library bd., 1974-77; active Boys Club Aux. Recipient Disting. Alumni Award So. Ark. U., 1981, Valley Forge Tchr. medal and George Washington Honor medal Freedom Found., 1973; Achievement citation Kazanian Found., 1969, citation for ednl. leadership Pres. of U.S., 1976, 77; profl. achievement citation Internat. Paper Co. Found., 1981. Mem. Assn. Supervision and Curriculum Devel. (speaker San Francisco conf.), NEA, Ark. Edn. Assn. (speaker 1969), Harmony Grove Edn. Assn. (pres. 1978-79), Nat. Council for Social Studies (mem. sexism com.), Am. Assn. Adminstrs., Alpha Delta Kappa (outstanding mem.). Club: Tate Park Garden (sec.). Home: 3188 Roseman Rd Camden AR 71701-5533

BRADSHAW, PETER, engineering educator; b. Torquay, Devon, Eng., Dec. 26, 1935; came to U.S., 1988; s. Joseph Newbold and Frances Winifred (Finch) B.; m. Aline Mary Rose, July 18, 1959 (div. 1968); m. Sheila Dorothy Brown, July 20, 1968. BA, Cambridge U., Eng., 1957; DSc (hon.), Exeter U., Eng., 1990. Sci. officer Nat. Phys. Lab., Teddington, Eng., 1957-69; prof. Imperial Coll. Sci. and Tech., London, 1969-88; Thomas V. Jones prof. engrng. Stanford U., 1988-95, prof. emeritus, 1995—; cons. various engrng. cos. Author: Introduction to Turbulence, 1971, Momentum Transfer, 1977, Convective Heat Transfer, 1984; author nearly 200 journ. articles on aerodynamics. Recipient Bronze medal Royal Aero. Soc., London, 1971, Busk prize, 1972, Fluid Dynamics award AIAA, 1994. Fellow Royal Soc. London. Avocations: cycling, walking. Office: Stanford U Dept Mech Engring Stanford CA 94305

BRADSHAW, PHYLLIS BOWMAN, historian, historic site staff member; b. Cumberland, Ky., June 19, 1929; d. Lawrence David and Ann Rees Bowman; m. Glenn Lewis Bradshaw, June 30, 1949; children: Charles Lewis, David Bowman. Student, Ctr. Coll., Danville, Ky., 1947-50, N.Y Sch. Speed Writing, 1967. Sec. to dir. and asst. dir. Shakertown, Pleasant Hill, Ky., 1967-68, asst. food dir., 1968-70, mus. dir. dept. interpretation, 1970-72; mus. hist. interpreter Old Fort Harrod State Pk., Harrodsburg, Ky., 1993-98. Mem. Harrodsburg Hist. Soc., Ky. Hist. Soc., Girl Scouts Am., Nat. Trust, Libr. Congress, Washington; tchr. Sunday sch. Harrodsburg Presbyn. Ch.; life mem. Women's Soc., Burgin Meth. Ch., bd. dirs., tchr./leader H.S. group; pres., sec. Burgin PTA; den mother cub scouts Boy Scouts Am.; life mem. Ky. PTA, Shakertown at Pleasant Hill; founding mem. Harlan (Ky.) Musettes; active Mercer County Blood Bank; assisted in creation of The Ky.

Classic Sauces-Bluegrass Trade Assn. Mem. DAR (Jane McAfee chpt.), Lewis and Clark Assn., N.W. Territory Assn., Hite Family Assn., Ky. History Tchrs. Assn., Colonial Dames Ct. of Honor (Ky. chpt.), Ctr. Coll. Alumni Assn., Lions Club. Home: PO Box 304 350 Bradshaw Rd Burgin KY 40310

BRADSHAW, RALPH ALDEN, biochemistry educator; b. Boston, Feb. 14, 1941; s. Donald Bertram and Eleanor (Dodd) B.; m. Roberta Perry Wheeler, Dec. 29, 1961; children: Christopher Evan, Amy Dodd. BA in Chemistry, Colby Coll., 1962; PhD, Duke U., 1966. Asst. prof. Washington U., St. Louis, 1969-72, assoc. prof., 1972-74, prof., 1974-82; prof., chair dept. U. Calif., Irvine, 1982-93, prof., 1993—; study sect. chmn. NIH, 1979, mem., 1975-79, 80-85; mem. sci. adv. bd. Hereditary Disease Found., 1983-87, ICN Nucleic Acids Rsch. Inst., 1986-87; rsch. study com. physiol. chem. Am. Heart Assn., 1984-86, mem. Coun. on Thrombosis, 1976-90; fellowship screening com. Am. Cancer Soc. Calif., 1984-87; chmn. adv. com. Western Winter Workshops, 1984-88; dir., chmn., mem. organizing com. numerous symposia, confs. in field including Proteins in Biology and Medicine, Shanghai, Peoples Republic of China, 1981, Symposium Am. Protein Chemists, San Diego, 1985, mem. exec. com. Keystone Symp. Mol. Cell. Biol., 1991-97, chmn., 1991-94, bd. dirs., 1997—, treas., 1997—; trustee Keystone Ctr., 1991-97; mem. exec. com. Internat. Union Biochem. Mol. Biol., 1991-97, U.S. Nat. Commn. Biochem., 1987-96, chmn., 1992-96; bd. dirs. Fed. Am. Soc. Exptl. Biology, 1992-96, v.p., 1994-95, pres., 1995-96. Mem. editl. bd. Archives Biochemistry and Biophysics, 1972-88, Jour. Biological Chemistry, 1973-77, 78-79, 81-86, assoc. editor, 1989—, Jour. Supramolecular Structure/Cellular Biochemistry, 1980-91, Bioscience Reports, 1980-87, Peptide and Protein Reviews, 1980-86, Jour. Protein Chemistry, 1980-90, IN VITRO Rapid Communication in Cell Biology, 1984—; editor Trends in Biochemical Sciences, 1975-91, editor-in-chief, 1986-91, J. Neurochem, 1986-90, Proteins: Structure, Functions & Genetics, 1988-92; assoc. editor: Growth Factors, 1989—; assoc. editor: Protein Science, 1990-92, 97—, mem. editl. bd., 1992—; mem. editl. bd. Biotech. Appl. Biochem., 1995—; co-editor-in-chief Molecular Cell Biol.-Rsch. Comms., 1998—; contbr. numerous articles to scientific jours. Recipient Young Scientist award Passano Found., 1976. Fellow AAAS; mem. Am. Chem. Soc. (Sect. award 1979), Am. Soc. Biochem. Molecular Biologists (coun. 1987-90, treas. 1991-97), Am. Peptide Soc., N.Y. Acad. Scis., Protein Soc. (acting pres. 1986-87), Am. Soc. for Cell Biology, Soc. for Neuroscience, The Endocrine Soc., Am. Soc. Bone Mineral Rsch., Assn. Biomolecular Rsch. Facilities, Sigma Xi. Home: 25135 Rivendell Dr Lake Forest CA 92630-4134 Office: U Calif Irvine Coll Medicine Dept Physiol & Biophysics D238 Med Sci I Irvine CA 92697

BRADSHAW, RICHARD JAMES, conductor; b. Rugby, england, Apr. 26, 1944; s. Alfred James and Florence Mary B.; m. Diana Hepburne-Scott, June 30, 1977; children: Jenny Alexandra, James Edward Merton. BA with honors, U. London, 1965. Dir. Music at Higham, 1967-77, New London Ensamble, 1972-77; internat. freelance condr. symphonies & operas, 1972—; chorus dir. Glyndebourne Festival Opera, 1975-77; resident condr. San Francisco Opera, 1977-89; chief condr., head music Can Opera Co., Toronto, 1989—, artistic & music dir., 1994—, gen. dir., 1998—; disting. vis. faculty music U. Toronto, 1999. Conducting fellow Royal Liverpool (England) Philharmonic Orch., 1972; assoc. fellow Massey Coll., U. Toronto, 1995—, sr. fellow 1998—. Office: Can Opera Co, 227 Front St E, Toronto, ON Canada M5A 1E8

BRADSHAW, RICHARD ROTHERWOOD, engineering executive; b. Phila., Sept. 12, 1916; s. Joseph Rotherwood and Rosanna (Jones) B.; m. Audrey Grace Skinn, Oct. 3, 1940 (dec. Jan. 1981); children—Linda M., Barbara A., Vicki; m. Chanin Hale, Feb. 14, 1986. B.S., Calif. Inst. Tech., 1939; M.S., U. So. Calif., 1950. Pres. Richard R. Bradshaw, Inc., Van Nuys, Calif., 1946—; pres. br. office Richard R. Bradshaw, Inc., Honolulu. Contbr. articles to tech. jours.. Important works include, Disneyworld Hotels, Orlando, Fla., U.S. embassy, Warsaw, Poland, U.S. Exhbn. Bldg., Moscow USSR, Taraara Hotel, Tahiti, Gulf Life Bldg., Jacksonville, Fla., Los Angeles City Airport. Recipient Alfred Lindau award Am. Concrete Inst., 1968, many others for structural design. Mem. ASCE, Internat. Assn. Bridges and Structural Engring., Am. Seismol. Soc., Cons. Engrs. Assn., Internat. Assn. Thin Shells, Am. Concrete Inst., Am. Arbitration Assn. Office: Richard R Bradshaw Inc 17300 Ballinger St Northridge CA 91325-2005

BRADSHAW, ROD ERIC, personnel consultant; b. Washington, May 29, 1957; s. Howard Vernon and Ona A. (Joyce) B.; m. Rebecca Lynn Bell, Mar. 20, 1974 (div. 1981). BS, U. Md., 1973; M in Human Resource Mgmt. with honors, Pepperdine U., 1981. Pers. cons. Career Devel. Corp., Atlanta, 1977-79, regional office mgr., 1979-82, prin., mgr., 1982-93; pres. Bradshaw & Assocs., 1993—. Asst. to pres. Christopher's Corner Cmty. Assn., Marietta, Ga., 1978-79, chmn. planning com., 1979; rep. Gov.'s Environ. Symposium, Smithsonian Inst., 1971; fund raiser, charter mem. High Mus. Art, Atlanta, 1979—; mem. Envoy to 1996 Atlanta Olympic Games; sponsor Sch. Bd. Coop. Bus. Edn.; merit badge counselor Boy Scouts Am.; nominating com. bd. mem. Buckhead Bus. Assn., Young Bucks, Outstanding Ams.; dir. cmty. affairs Atlanta Games Legacy Orgn., 1998; pres. bd. dirs. Jefferson Twp., 1998—. Recipient J.P. Rice Scholarship, 1971; named one of Outstanding Young Men of Am., Atlanta C. of C., 1985. Mem. Nat. Assn. Pers. Cons. (cert.), Am. Mgmt. Assn., Internat. Platform Assn., Am. Legion, Atlanta Ski Club, Omicron Delta Kappa, Delta Tau Delta. Republican. Avocations: yachting, home improvement projects, sports, politics. Home: 4903 Township Overlook Marietta GA 30066-5001 Office: Bradshaw & Assocs 1850 Parkway Pl Ste 420 Marietta GA 30067-8222

BRADSHAW, TERRY, sports announcer, former professional football player; b. Shreveport, La., Sept. 2, 1948. Ed., La. Tech. U. With profl. football team Pitts. Steelers, 1970-84; color analyst CBS Sports Inc NFL Today, 1987-94, Fox Sports, 1995—. Country and western singer, entertainer, appears in numerous commls., pub. speaker. Named Most Valuable Player, Super Bowl XIII, 1978, Super Bowl XIV, 1979, Most Favorite TV Sportscaster TV Guide, 1999; named to Pro Bowl, 1978, 79; inducted into Hall of Fame, 1989. Quarterback in Super Bowl win, 1974, 75, 78, 79. Office: care Fox Network PO Box 900 Beverly Hills CA 90213-0900 Address: 3220 W Southlake Blvd Ste H Southlake TX 76092-6737

BRADSHAW, WILLIAM C., museum director. BA in Secondary Edn. Social Studies, U. Fla.; M in Liberal Studies Museum Emphasis, U. Okla. Program advisor La. State U. Union, Baton Rouge, 1965-68; curator jr. ctr. Valentine Mus., Richmond, Va., 1968-71; exec. dir. Peninsula Nature and Sci. Ctr., Newport News, Va., 1971-78, Cumberland Sci. Mus., Nashville, Tenn., 1978-93; v.p. for programs and exhibits The Franklin Mus., Phila., 1994; exec. dir. Mus. of Discovery, Little Rock, 1994—; co-founder regional Mus. Coun. of Va. Peninsula; co-founder, past pres. Va. History and Mus. Fedn.; past treas. Southeastern Mus. Coun.; co-founder and sec. Sci. Mus. Assn. Ea. Va.; past pres. Intermus. Coun. of Nashville. Mem. Am. Assn. for State and Local History, Nat. Sci. Tchrs. Assn., Am. Assn. of Mus., Assn. Sci. and Tech. Ctrs., Rotary Club of Little Rock. Office: Mus of Discovery 500 E Markham St Little Rock AR 72201*

BRADSHER, KEITH VINSON, journalist; b. Evanston, Ill., July 7, 1964; m. Robyn Meredith, June 19, 1993. BA in Econs. with highest honors, U. N.C., 1986; MPA in Econs., Princeton U., 1989. Bus. reporter The N.Y. Times, N.Y.C., 1989-91; Washington corr. The N.Y. Times, 1991-95, Detroit bur. chief, 1996—. Morehead scholar, 1986; recipient George Polk award for nat. reporting, 1998. Mem. Phi Beta Kappa. Office: The NY Times PO Box 2327 Ann Arbor MI 48106-2327

BRADSTOCK, JOHN, advertising executive. Pres., N.Am., Pacific Am. DDB Needham Worldwide, Inc., N.Y.C., 1994—. Office: DDB Needham Worldwide Inc 437 Madison Ave New York NY 10022-7001*

BRADT, HALE VAN DORN, physicist, x-ray astronomer, educator; b. Colfax, Wash., Dec. 7, 1930; s. Wilber Elmore and Norma (Sparlin) B.; m. Dorothy Ann Haughey, July 19, 1958; children—Elizabeth, Dorothy Ann. A.B., Princeton U., 1952; Ph.D. in Physics, M.I.T., 1961. Mem. dept. physics MIT, 1961—, prof., 1972—; sci. investigator Small Astronomy Satellite, NASA, 1975-79, High Energy Astronomy Obs., 1977-79; Rossi x-ray timing explorer, 1995—. Co-editor: X and Gamma Ray Astronomy, 1973; assoc. editor: Astrophys. Jour. Letters, 1974-77. Served with USNR, 1952-54. Recipient Exceptional Sci. achievement medal NASA, 1978. Mem. Am. Astron. Soc. (sec.-treas. high energy astrophysics div. 1973-75, chmn. 1981, co-editor The Active X-ray Sky 1998, Rossi prize HEAD div. 1999), Am. Phys. Soc., Internat. Astron. Union, Sigma Xi. Office: MIT 37 587th Cambridge MA 02139

BRADTKE, PHILIP JOSEPH, architect; b. Chgo., Aug. 13, 1934; s. Felix Anthony and Frances Agnes (Mach) B.; m. Diane Gloria Westol, Oct. 19, 1963 (div. July 1987); children: Michael, Christine; m. Catherine Adler, Nov. 25, 1989. BArch cum laude, U. Notre Dame, 1957. Registered architect, Ill. Project architect Belli & Belli, Chgo., 1957-64; project mgr., v.p. A.M. Kinney Assoc., Inc., Evanston, Ill., 1964-80, v.p., pres., 1987-96; v.p., sr. assoc. Kober/Belluschi Assoc., Chgo., 1980-87; archtl. divsn. mgr., v.p. Patrick Engring. Inc., Glen Ellyn, Ill., 1996—; lectr. U. Notre Dame, 1975. Commr. bldg. dept. Village of Glenview, Ill., 1980-83, commr. appearance commn., 1983—. Recipient Hon. Mention award Beaux Arts Inst. Design, 1955, 1st prize award Ch. Property and Adminstrn. Mag., 1956, 1st Mention award Indpls. Home Show Archtl. Competition, 1956, Hon. Mention award, 1959, Modernization Excellence award Bldgs. Mag., 1985. Mem. AIA (corp., housing com. 1968, chmn. honor awards com., 1973, treas., 1975-76), Notre Dame Club, Glenview Shoreline Tennis Team (capt. 1976—). Roman Catholic. Avocations: tennis, golf, basketball. Home: 1441 Canterbury Ln Glenview IL 60025-2252

BRADUNAS, JOHN JOSEPH, marine corps officer; b. Hartford, Conn., Dec. 28, 1955; s. Edward Anthony and Florence Eleanor Mae (Martel) B. BSEE, Cornell U., 1977; MS in Systems Mgmt., U. So. Calif., 1985; MA in Nat. Security Affairs, Georgetown U., 1988; MSEE, Naval Postgrad. Sch., Monterey, Calif., 1990. Cert. mil. acquisition specialist. Commd. 2nd lt. USMC, 1977, advanced through grades to maj., 1989; with Def. Intelligency Agy., Arlington, Va., 1986-88; assigned to Naval Postgrad. Sch., Monterey, Calif., 1988-90; with Marine Corps Systems Command, Quantico, Va., 1990-93, 22d Marine Expeditionary Unit, Camp Lejeune, N.C., 1993-95; participant UN Humanitarian Ops., Bosnia-Hercegovina, Somalia; combat devel. command USMC, Quantico, Va., 1995-97; ret. USMC, 1997; sys. engr. battlefield awareness and dissemination program Def. Advanced Rsch. Projects Agy.; sr. prin. software engr. The Boeing Co., Fairfax, Va., 1997—; systems engr., tech. advisor on battlefield awareness, data dissemination and moving target exploitation programs Def. Advanced Rsch. Projects Agy., 1997. Inventor laser diode power driver. Vol. genealogist Nat. Archives, Washington, 1990-93; reader for the blind Washington Ear, Rockville, Md., 1990. Decorated Joint Svc. Achievement medal. Mem. IEEE, Armed Forces Comms. and Electronics Assn., Soc. Young Intel Profls., Eta Kappa Nu. Avocations: alpine and nordic skiing, building plastic and wooden miniatures. Home: 4576 Fair Valley Dr Fairfax VA 22033-3815 Office: The Boeing Co Ste 300 11242 Waples Mill Rd Fairfax VA 22030-6079

BRADY, ANITA KELLEY, training and organizational development executive; b. Takoma Park, Md., June 2, 1961; d. Leonard B. and Elsie (Alvarez) Kelley; m. Mark C. Brady, Oct. 4, 1986; children: Kelley, Katelynn. BA, U. Md., 1982, MA, 1984; postgrad., George Washington U., 1988-90. Instr. tech. comm. and interpersonal comm. U. Md., College Park, 1983-84; pers. recruiter Children's Hosp. Nat. Med. Ctr., Washington, 1984-85, employee rels. specialist, 1985-86, edn. and tng. mgr., 1986-92; pres. Comm. Tng. Cons., Olney, Md., 1992—; adj. prof. Trinity Coll., Washington, 1992-93; nat. capital area chpt. sec. Am. Soc. Healthcare Edn. & Tng., Chgo., 1989-90, pres.-elect, 1990-91, pres., 1991-92, spkr. nat. conf., 1995; pres. tng. & edn. divsn. Greater Washington Met. Area Healthcare Coun., 1991-92; chair An. Inst. Mentoring Program & Kickoff program Fed. Govt. Tng. Officer's conf., 1993—, spl. event chair Ann. Inst., 1996. Campaign vol. Congressman Michael Barnes, 1982; coord. McKenney Hills/Homewood/Carroll Knolls Neighborhood Watch, 1987-88; mem. parish coun., adult & religious edn. vol. St. John Evangelist Ch., 1993-95; mem. spl. event com. St. Peter's Ch.; mem. adv. coun. Montgomery County Mid-County Citizens, 1997-98. Mem. ASTD (sec. internat. health industry group exec. com. 1990, lead coord. healthcare forum internat. conf. 1996, symposium coord. healthcare industry internat. conf. 1995, dir. healthcare spl. interest group 1994, bd. dirs. 1995-96, dir. spl. interest groups 1996, pres.-elect 1997, pres. 1998-99, past pres. 1999, nat. conf. program com.), Kappa Delta Alumnae Assn. (Panhellenic rep. 1996-97), Omicron Delta Kappa. Office: Comm Tng Cons 3358 Megans Way Olney MD 20832-2529

BRADY, CARL FRANKLIN, retired aircraft charter company executive; b. Chelsea, Okla., Oct. 29, 1919; s. Kirty A. and Pauline Ellen (Doty) B.; m. Carol Elizabeth Sprague, Mar. 29, 1941; children: Carl Franklin, Linda Kathryn, James Kenneth. Ed., U. Wash., 1940. Co-owner Aero Cafe, Yakima, Wash., 1946-47; pilot Central Aircraft, Yakima, 1947-48; partner Economy Helicopters, Inc., Yakima, 1948-60; pres. ERA Helicopters, Inc., Anchorage, 1960-85, ERA Aviation Center, Inc., 1977-85, Livingston Copters, Inc., 1977-85; exec. v.p. Rowan Companies, Inc., Houston, 1973-85, also bd. dirs.; owner, pres. Brady Investments Ltd. Mem. Alaska Ho. of Reps., 1965-66, Alaska Senate, 1967-68; pres. Alaska Crippled Childrens Assn., 1963; mem. Nat. Advisery com. Oceans and Atmosphere, 1981-86. Served with USAAF, 1943-46. Named Alaskan of Yr., 1989; named to Alaska Bus. Hall of Fame, 1990. Mem. Helicopter Assn. Am. (pres. 1953, 57, Larry D. Bell award 1976), Anchorage C. of C. (pres. 1963-64), Alaska Air Carriers Assn., Am. Helicopter Soc., Commonwealth North, Petroleum Alaska Club, Elks. Republican. Methodist. Home: 510 L St Anchorage AK 99501-1964 also (winter): 44-832 Santa Rosa Ct Indian Wells CA 92210-7622 Office: 1031 W 4th Ave Ste 502 Anchorage AK 99501-5906

BRADY, CATHERINE RAWSON, software company executive; b. Bloomington, Ill., Oct. 15, 1959; d. Norman Earl and Barbara (Stewart) Rawson; m. Patrick K. Brady, June 13, 1980; children: Ian A., Madeline K. BS in econs., Benedictine U., 1981; MS in fin., No. Ill. U., 1985. Futures trader Chgo., 1984-90; co-founder, dir. Apropos Techs. Inc., Oakbrook Terrace, Ill., 1990—; CEO Wasabi Software, Inc., Chgo., 1997—; adj. faculty Elmhurst (Ill.) Coll., 1989-92; faculty mem. Keller Grad. Sch., Schaumburg, Ill., 1989-91. Author: New York Institute of Finance Guide to Investing, 1991. Pres. Greater DuPage Meld's Young Moms, Glen Ellyn, Ill., 1992-93; bd. dirs. 1989-93. Mem. Chgo. Software Assn. Avocations: running, rowing, playing classical guitar. Office: Wasabi Inc 1101 E 58th St Walker 213 Chicago IL 60637

BRADY, CHRISTINE ELLEN, education coordinator; b. Manchester, N.H., Feb. 23, 1943; d. George Lewis and Lucy Eleanor (Broderick) B. BA in English, Manhattanville Coll., 1964; MA in English, U. Pa., 1966; EdD in Curriculum and Instrn., No. Ariz. U., 1987. Cert. tchr., N.Y., Ariz., Mass.; cert. adminstr., N.Y., Ariz. English instr. Bryn Mawr (Pa.) Coll., 1966-67; lang. arts tchr. Tuba City (Ariz.) H.S., 1978-82; asst. dir. Reading/Learning Ctr., Flagstaff, Ariz., 1982-83; supervisory home living specialist Apache Agy. Dept. Indian Affairs, Whiteriver, Ariz., 1983-85; English and edn. lectr. Cortland (N.Y.) State Coll., 1988-89; asst. dir. Tchr. Ctr. Broome County, Binghamton, N.Y., 1990-91; English instr. Broome Cmty. Coll., Binghamton, N.Y., 1989-91; labor svc. rep. N.Y. State Dept. Labor, Ithaca, 1992-94; Title I lang. arts tchr. N.Y. State Divsn. Youth N.Y. State Office of Children and Family Svcs., Highland, N.Y., 1994-98; edn. coord. S.I. Residential Ctr. N.Y. State Office Children and Family Svcs. Mem. AAUW, ASCD, Internat. Reading. Assn., Phi Delta Kappa (mem. exec. bd. 1998). Office: Office Children Family Svcs Staten Island Resdl Ctr 1133 Forest Hill Rd Staten Island NY 10314

BRADY, DON PAUL, school psychologist, therapist, consultant; b. Buffalo, Dec. 17, 1946; s. Leon J. and Katherine (Matthews) B.; m. Marilyn Grace Cook, Feb. 10, 1973; 1 child, S. Scott. BBA in Acctg., Siena Coll., 1968; MS in Rehab. Counseling, SUNY, Albany, 1972; MS in Psychology, Renssalaer Poly. Inst., 1979; D in Clin. Psychology, Newport U., Newport Beach, Calif., 1997; postgrad. clin. psychology, Union Inst., Cin. Cert. sch. psychologist, alcohol and substance abuse counselor; cert. addictions specialist Am. Acad. Health Providers. Psychiat. counselor N.Y. State Dept. Mental Hygiene, Delmar, 1972-74; counselor, coord. higher ednl. opportunity program Sage Colls., Jr. Coll. Albany, N.Y., 1974-76; lectr. in psychology Renssalaer Poly. Inst., Troy, N.Y., 1976-78; psychologist II Syracuse (N.Y.) Developmental Ctr., 1978-81; sch. psychologist Parkside Sch., Syracuse, 1982-83; pvt. practice Chittenango, N.Y., 1984—; sch. psychologist Utica (N.Y.) City Schs., 1983-84; rehab. psychologist Children's Hosp. and Rehab. Ctr., Utica, 1985-86; sch. psychologist Cazenovia (N.Y.) Ctrl. Sch. Dist., 1986—; instr. psychology Sage Colls./Jr. Coll. Albany, N.Y., 1973-78; mental health cons. Utica Head Start, 1984—, mem. health adv. bd., 1986—; presenter numerous confs. in field. Coord., coach 1st women's basketball team Sage Colls./Jr. Coll. Albany, 1975-77; v.p. Cazenovia Little League, 1995-97. Fellow HEW, 1969-71. Mem. Am. Psychol. Assn. (student affiliate), Nat. Psychology Adv. Assn., Nat. Assn. Sch. Psychologists, Am. Assn. Christian Counselors, Am. Assn. Marriage and Family Therapy, Pi Lambda Theta. Avocations: golf, basketball, gardening, baseball. Home: PO Box 313 Chittenango NY 13037-0313

BRADY, EDMUND MATTHEW, JR., lawyer; b. Apr. 24, 1941; s. Edmund Matthew and Thelma (McDonald) B.; m. Marie Pierre Wayne, May 14, 1966; children: Edmund Matthew III, Meghan, Timothy. BSS, John Carroll U., 1963; JD, U. Detroit, 1966; postgrad., Wayne State U., 1966-69; DHL (hon.), U. Detroit, 1998. Bar: Mich. 1966, U.S. Dist. Ct. (ea. dist.) Mich. 1966, U.S. Ct. Appeals (6th cir.) 1973, U.S. Supreme Ct. 1974. Sr. ptnr. Vandeveer & Garzia, 1973-90, Plunkett & Cooney, P.C., 1990—. Village clk. Grosse Pointe Shores, Mich., 1975-80; trustee St. John Hosp. and Med. Ctr., Detroit, 1992—, chmn., 1994—, Grosse Pointe Acad., Mich., 1977-83, adv. trustee, 1983-89; vice chmn. St. John Physicians Hosp. Orgn., 1994-95; supr. Grosse Pointe Twp., 1994—, trustee, 1989—; pres., dir. Grosse Pointe Hockey Assn., 1969-70; bd. dirs., chmn. maj. gifts divsn. 1st Fund, St. John Hosp. Guild; bd. dirs., pres. Friends of Bon Secours Hosp.; trustee, mem. exec. com., mem. fin. com. St. John Health Sys., 1998—. Recipient award of distinction U. Detroit Law Alumni, 1981, Michael Franck award State Bar of Mich. Rep. Assembly, 1998, Respected Advocate award Mich. Trial Lawyers Assn., 1998. Fellow Am. Bar Found, Mich. State Bar Found. (life); mem. ABA, Am. Coll. Trial Lawyers, Inter. Soc. Barristers, Am. Bd. Trial Advocates, Internat. Assn. Def. Counsel, Assn. Def. Trial Counsel (dir. 1975-80, pres. 1980-81), Mich. Def. Trial Counsel (dir. 1980-81), Def. Rsch. Inst.(Exceptional) Performance citation 1981), Cath. Lawyers Soc., Soc. Irish-Am. Lawyers (founding dir. 1979-81), Mich. Soc. Health Law Attys., Mediation Tribunal Assn. (mem. panel Wayne County, Macomb County mediator 1989-98), Detroit Bar Assn. (dir. 1986—, sec.-treas. 1988, pres.-elect 1989-90, pres. 1990-91), State Bar Mich. (commr. 1991-98, treas. 1994—, v.p. 1995, pres.-elect 1996, pres. 1997-98), Country Club of Detroit, Detroit Athletic Club, Delta Theta Phi. Republican. Roman Catholic. Office: Plunkett & Cooney 243 W Congress St Ste 910 Detroit MI 48226-3260

BRADY, FRANK BENTON, retired technical society executive; b. Pomeroy, Ohio, June 1, 1914; s. Charles Wesley and Julia Bessie (Cross) B.; m. Lucille Marie Svitzer, Feb. 3, 1950; children: Susan Erika, John Benton (dec.), Alan Gibson. Student, U. Cin., 1933-39. Registered profl. engr., D.C. Radio engring. asst. Crosley Radio Corp., Cin., 1933-39; radio engr. Aircraft Radio Lab., Dayton, Ohio, 1939-46; flight projects engr. Air Transport Assn., Washington, 1946-55, dir. nat. airspace systems engring., 1976-79; jr. ptnr. Mills Petticord & Mills Architects and Engrs., Washington, 1955-57; sr. staff cons. Singer Co.-Gen. Precision, Washington, 1957-74; aviation cons. Washington, 1974-76; exec. dir. The Inst. of Navigation, Washington, 1979-90; ret., 1990. Author: A Singular View-The Art of Seeing with One Eye, 1972, (with others) (textbook) Avionics Navigation Systems, 1968; patentee in field. Trustee Cosmos Club Found., 1970—, USN Sailing Found., Annapolis, Md., 1987—. Recipient Medal of Freedom War Dept., 1946, citation Radio Tech. Commn. Aeronautics, 1963, 92. Fellow IEEE (life; guest editor Proc. spl. issue Instrument Landing 1959, Global Navigation 1983); mem. Cosmos Club, New Providence Club, Naval Acad. Sailing Squadron Annapolis. Avocations: sailing, writing, restoration of nautical and scientific antiques. Home: 111 Severn Ave # C Annapolis MD 21403-2611 Office: PO Box 4653 Annapolis MD 21403-6653

BRADY, GEORGE MOORE, real estate executive, mortgage banker; b. Balt., Aug. 6, 1922; s. George Moore and Ellen Latimer (Atkinson) B.; BA, Johns Hopkins U., 1947; JD, U. Md., 1949; m. Maria Nomita von Barby, Dec. 3, 1971; children by previous marriage: Elizabeth Grant Brady Andrews, Frances Relyea Brady Siegler, Ellen Atkinson, George Moore III, Madeleine Vaughn Brady Cohen, Richard Grant; 1 stepchild, William L. Amoroso III. Sr. v.p. The Rouse Co., Columbia, Md., 1950-70; chmn. bd. Rouse-Wates, Columbia, 1970-72; pres., chmn. bd. Nat. Corp. for Housing Partnerships, Washington, 1972-88; ret. 1988, bd. dirs. The Rouse Co., First Am. Bank, NA, Washington, Enterprise Social Investment Corp.; former chair Ptrns. for Liveable Cmtys., mem. exec. com. Mem. Md. State Planning Commn., Md. Adv. Commn. on Industrialized Bldg. and Mobile Homes, 1989-95; exec. com. Nat. Housing Conf., life bd. dirs.; bd. overseers Corcoran Sch. Art; bd. dirs. Jubilee Enterprise Greater Washington, Washington Area Housing Partnership. With U.S. Army, POW. Decorated Purple Heart; named Man of Yr. Nat. Housing Conf., 1986. Mem. Sovereign Mil. Order of Malta So. Assn., Metropolitan Club (Washington), Chevy Chase Club (Md.).

BRADY, JAMES JOSEPH, economics educator; b. Jersey City, Mar. 2, 1936; s. James and Anna (Shine) B.; m. Sheila Hartney, July 24, 1965; children: Matthew, Michael, James. BA, U. Notre Dame, 1959, MA in Econs., 1963, PhD in Econs., 1969. Profl. baseball player Detroit Tigers, 1955-60; asst. prof. econs. Ind. U., South Bend, 1965-69; asst. prof., assoc. prof., prof. econs. Old Dominion U., Norfolk, Va., 1969-79; dean Coll. Arts and Scis. Jacksonville (Fla.) U., 1979-83, dean Coll. Bus., 1983-84, v.p. acad. affairs, 1984-88, pres.-elect, 1988-89, pres., 1989-95, prof. econs., 1995—; spl. master Fla. Pub. Employees Rels. Commn., Tallahassee, 1985—; pvt. labor cons., Jacksonville, 1978-88; mem. fed. Mediation and Conciliation Svc. Labor Panel, 1985—. Author: Arbitration Principles: Layoffs, 1989; co-author: Transportation Noise Pollution, 1970. With U.S. Army, 1959-61. NASA grantee, Norfolk, Va., 1970. Mem. Am. Arbitration Assn. (labor arbitrator 1965—, comml. arbitrator 1987-89), Soc. Profls. in Dispute Resolution, Jacksonville C. of C. (bd. dirs. 1989—), Rotary (bd. dirs. 1994—). Avocations: fishing, cooking, tennis. Home: 4454 Maywood Dr Jacksonville FL 32277-1036 Office: Jacksonville U Coll of Bus 2800 University Blvd N Jacksonville FL 32211-3394

BRADY, JEAN STEIN, retired librarian; b. Concord, Mass., Nov. 4, 1930; d. Walfred and Mary Selina (Jussila) Stein; m. Maurice Goodrich Klein, Feb. 22, 1957 (div. 1982); 1 child, Audrey Elaine; m. Lawrence Kevin Brady, Oct. 15, 1988. BS, Simmons Coll., 1952; cert. d'Etudes, U. Grenoble, France, 1954; MA, Northwestern U., 1957. Cert. pub. libr., N.Y. Sr. libr. N.Y. Pub. Libr., 1952-53, 57-60; cataloger Columbia U., N.Y.C., 1954-55; reference asst. Northwestern U., Evanston, Ill., 1955-57; cataloger U. W.Va., Morgantown, 1960-61; book reviewer ALA, Chgo., 1961-63; sr. cataloger Cleve. Pub. Libr., 1964-70; sr. catalog libr. Yale U. Libr., New Haven, Conn., 1970-92; cataloger Columbia U., N.Y.C., 1993-95; ret., 1995. Revision asst. Bibliographical Guide to Romance Langs. and Lits., 1956-57; reviewer: Booklist and Subscription Books Bulletin, 1961-63. Mem. AAUW, Simmons Coll. Club of Cape Cod. Democrat. Episcopalian. Avocations: reading, travel, walking, swimming.

BRADY, JEFFREY KEVIN, photographer; b. Reading, Pa., July 25, 1963; s. Jack Kenneth and Catherine May (Hartline) B. Cert., Lehigh County Vo-Tech., Schuecksville, Pa., 1981; BFA in Photography cum laude, Kurtztown U., 1997. Sole proprietor J. Brady Photography, Breinigsville, Pa., 1996—. With NCRC Ea. Region Cave Rescue, 1995-96. Recipient Cmty. Spirit award Allentown Morning Call, Pa., 1993, Karen L. Anderson Meml. award in fine arts, 1998. Mem. Nat. Speleol. Soc., Ilfopro Photographers Assn., Greater Allentown Grotto, New Arts Program, Chi Alpha Epsilon. Avocations: caving, hunting, fishing, camping, photography. Web-site: http://www.jbradyphotography.com. Office: J Brady Photography 1276 Little Creek Cir Breinigsville PA 18031

BRADY, JOHN PATRICK, JR., electronics educator, consultant; b. Newark, Mar. 20, 1929; s. John Patrick and Madeleine Mary (Atno) B.; m. Mary Coop, May 1, 1954; children: Peter, John P., Madeleine, Dennis, Mary G. BSEE, MIT, 1952, MSEE, 1953. Registered profl. engr., Mass. Sect. mgr. Hewlett-Packard Co., Waltham, Mass., 1956-67; v.p. engring. John Fluke Mfg. Co., Inc., Mountlake Terrace, Wash., 1967-73; v.p. engring. Dana Labs., Irvine, Calif., 1973-77; engring. mgr., tech. advisor to gen. mgr. Metron Corp., Upland, Calif., 1977-78; ptnr. Resource Assocs., Newport Beach, Calif., 1978-86; prof. electronics Orange Coast Coll., Costa Mesa, Calif., 1977-99, emeritus, 1999, faculty fellow, dean technology, 1983-84, chmn. electronics tech. dept., 1994-96, chmn. academic rank com., 1988-98; instr. computers and electrinc engring. Calif. State U., Long Beach, 1982-84. Mem. evaluation team Accrediting Commn. for Community and Jr. Colls., 1982-92; mem. blue ribbon adv. com. on oversees technology transfer U.S. Dept. of Commerce, 1974-76. With USN, 1946-48. Mem. Measurement Sci. Conf. (dir. 1982-83), MIT (L.A.). Contbr. articles in field to profl. jours.; mem. Eta Kappa Nu, Tau Beta Pi, Sigma Xi. Office: Orange Coast Coll Costa Mesa CA 92626

BRADY, JOHN PAUL, psychiatrist; b. Boston, June 23, 1928; s. James Henry and Evelyn Louise (Rice) B.; m. Christeen Nelson, Mar. 19, 1963; children—James Palmer, Pamela Eros, June Pamela, David Duncan. AB, Boston U., 1951, MD, 1955; MA (hon.), U. Pa., 1967. Intern Gorgas Hosp., Panama, 1955-56; resident in psychiatry Inst. of Living, Hartford, 1956-59; rsch. psychiatrist Ind. U. Med. Sch., Indpls., 1959-63; faculty U. Pa. Med. Sch., Phila., 1963—; prof. psychiatry U. Pa. Med. Sch., 1968—, Kenneth Appel prof., 1974—, chmn. dept., 1974-82; co-founder, asso. editor Behavior Therapy, 1970—. Author: An Introduction to the Science of Human Behavior, 1963, Classics of American Psychiatry, 1975, Psychiatry: Areas of Promise and Achievement, 1977, Voyage to Inishneefa, 1987; co-editor: Controversy in Psychiatry, 1978, Behavioral Medicine; Theory and Practice, 1979, Psychiatry at the Crossroads, 1980, also articles. Recipient Research Scientist award NIMH, 1963-74; Strecker award Inst. of Pa. Hosp., 1972. Fellow Am. Psychiat. Assn., Indian Psychiat. Soc.; mem. Assn. Advancement Behavior Therapy (past pres.), Soc. Biol. Psychiatry (pres. 1979-80), Psychiat. Research Soc. (program chmn. 1973), Soc. Behavioral Medicine (dir. 1980-81), Soc. Interam. de Psicologia, Am. Psychosomatic Soc. Office: 300 E Lancaster Ave Ste 207 Wynnewood PA 19096-2139

BRADY, JOSEPH VINCENT, behavioral biologist, educator; b. N.Y.C., Mar. 28, 1922; s. James J. and Mary F. (Michaelson) B.; m. Nancy Heaton; children: Barbara Ann, Michael Joseph, Kathleen Theresa, Nancy Marie, Joanne Cecelia, Jessica Lea, Margaret Mary. B.S., Fordham U., 1943; Ph.D., U. Chgo., 1951. Dep. dir. div. neuropsychiatry Walter Reed Inst. Research, 1951-71; prof. psychology U. Md., 1955-69; prof. behavioral biology Johns Hopkins Sch. Medicine, Balt., 1967—, prof. neurosci., 1982—; dir. Behavioral Biology Rsch. Ctr. Johns Hopkins U., Balt., 1992—; pres., chmn. bd. trustees Inst. for Behavior Resources, Balt., 1988—; cons. pres. sci. adv. com. Merck Inst. for Therapeutic Rsch., U.S. Army Med. Rsch. and Devel. Command, NASA; assoc. chmn. Nat. Commn. for Protection Human Subjects of Biomed. and Behavioral Rsch., 1974-79; chmn. sci. adv. com. New Eng. Regional Primate Rsch. Ctr., Harvard Med. Sch., Boston, com. on problems of drug dependence NRC, com. on space biology and medicine, com. on toxicology NAS. Contbr. articles to profl. jours. Col. M.C., U.S. Army. Fellow AAAS, APA (div. pres.), Am. Coll. Neuro-psychopharmacology, Coll. Problems Drug Dependence, Acad. Behavioral Med. Rsch.; mem. Eastern Psychol. Assn. (pres.), Soc. Behavioral Medicine (pres.), Pavlovian Soc. (pres.), Behavioral Pharmacology Soc. (pres.). Home: Unit 610 1000 Fell St Baltimore MD 21231-3554 Office: Johns Hopkins U Behavioral Biology Rsch Ctr 5510 Nathan Shock Dr Baltimore MD 21224-6823

BRADY, KEVIN, congressman; b. Vermillion, S.D., Apr. 11, 1955; m. Cathy Brady. BS, U. S.D. Mem. Tex. House of Reps., 1990-96; rep. 8th Dist. Tex. U.S. House of Reps., 1996—; mem. house internat. rels. com. U.S. Congress, internat. econ. policy and trade subcom., western hemisphere subcom., house sci. com., space and aeronautics subcom., tech. subcom., house resources com., energy and mineral resources subcom. Active Saints Simon and Jude Cath. Ch. Mem. Rotary. Fax: (202) 225-5524. Office: 1531 Longworth Bldg Washington DC 20515-4308*

BRADY, KIMBERLY ANN, editorial director; b. Omaha, Sept. 22, 1956; d. John Henry and Margaret Florence (Swatek) Robinson; 1 child, Jonathan Charles Brady. Student, Corcoran Sch. Art, Washington, 1974-75, George Mason U., 1974-76, Christopher Newport Coll., Newport News, Va., 1976-79. Editor-in-chief student newspaper Christopher Newport Coll., 1977-79; photojournalist Gloucester-Matthews Gazette-Jour., Gloucester, Va., 1979-80; mng. editor Journal of Analytical Toxicology Preston Publs., Niles, Ill., 1980-81; mng. editor Darkroom Techniques and Creative Camera Preston Publs., 1981-84; art dir., prodn. mgr. Profl. Photographers of Am., Des Plaines, Ill., 1984-86; sr. editor Profl. Photographer Profl. Photographers of Am., 1990-91; editor-in-chief PEI mag. Profl. Photographers of Am., Des Plaines, Atlanta, 1991-94; editl. dir. Atlanta, 1994—; editl. cons., photographer, graphic artist Chgo., 1986-90; instr. Winona Internat. Sch. Profl. Photography, Mt. Prospect, Ill., 1987; judge photography competitions, Chgo., 1981-84, electronic imaging competition, L.A., 1993-95. Exec. dir. Lake Shore Sr. Svc. Ctr., Chgo., 1988-93; vol. Adult Literacy Program, Chgo., 1988; coord. Mayor Harold Washington campaign, Chgo., 1983. Recipient Va. Press Assn. Journalism award, 1979, Christopher Newport Coll. Journalism award, 1977-78. Mem. Profl. Photographers of Am. Avocations: horseback riding, eventing. Office: Profl Photographers of Am Internat Tower 229 Peachtree St NE Ste 2200 Atlanta GA 30303-1608

BRADY, LAWRENCE PETER, lawyer; b. Jersey City, July 26, 1940; s. Lawrence Peter and Evelyn (Mauro) B.; div; children: Deegan, Tara, Kerry, Melissa, James; m. Mary Helen Reynolds, Mar. 28, 1984. BS in Acctg., St. Peters Coll., 1961; JD, Seton Hall U., 1964; LLM, Bklyn. Law Sch., 1966. Bar: N.J. 1964, U.S. Dist. Ct. N.J. 1964, U.S. Supreme Ct. 1969, U.S. Ct. Appeals (3rd cir.) 1972, N.Y. 1991; cert. civil trial atty. State of N.J. 1982; cert. Nat. Bd. Trial Advocacy 1989. Asst. prosecutor Hudson County, Jersey City, 1964-70; prosecutor Town of Kearny, N.J., 1971-74; sr. ptnr. Doyle & Brady, Kearny, 1974—; dir. and founding incorporator Growth Bank, New Vernon, N.J. Mem. ATLA, Nat. Bd. Trial Advocacy, N.J. State Bar Assn., Hudson County Bar Assn., West Hudson Bar Assn. (sec. 1980, treas. 1981, v.p. 1982, pres. 1983), Am. Trial Lawyers N.J. (bd. govs.), Roxiticus Golf Club (Mendham, N.J.), Sandalfoot Country Club (Boca Raton, Fla.), Ocean Reef Club (Key Largo, Fla.), Ocean Reef Yacht Club. Roman Catholic. Avocations: golf, tennis, travel, fishing, boating. Office: Doyle & Brady 377 Kearny Ave Kearny NJ 07032-2600

BRADY, LUTHER W., JR., physician, radiation oncology educator; b. Rocky Mount, N.C., Oct. 20, 1925; s. Luther W. and Gladys B. AA, George Washington U., 1944, AB, 1946, MD, 1948; DFA (hon.), Colgate U., 1988; DSc (hon.), Lehigh U., 1990; MD (hon), Toyama U., Japan, 1996; Dr. honoris causa, U. Heidelberg, Germany, 1997. Diplomate: Am. Bd. Radiology (treas. 1980-82, v.p. 1982-84, pres. 1984-86). Intern Jefferson Med. Coll. Hosp., Phila., 1948-50; resident in radiology Jefferson Med. Coll. Hosp., 1954-55; resident radiology Hosp. U. Pa., Phila., 1955-56; fellow Nat. Cancer Inst., 1953-57, 1957-59; practice medicine, specializing in radiation oncology Phila.; asst. instr. radiology Jefferson Med. Coll. Hosp., 1954-55, U. Pa., Phila., 1955, instr., 1956-57, assoc. radiology, 1957-59; asst. prof. radiology Coll. of Physicians and Surgeons, Columbia U., N.Y.C., summer, 1959; assoc. prof. radiology Hahnemann Med. Coll. and Hosp., Phila., 1959-62, prof., 1963—, chmn. dept. radiation oncology, 1970—; asst. prof. radiology Harvard Med. Sch., Boston, 1962-63; mem. med. radiation adv. com. Bur. Radiation Health, HEW, 1971-74; cons. radiation therapy various hosps.; mem. U.S. del. to Interam. Congress Radiology, 1975, Internat. Congress of Radiology, 1981; sec. gen. Internat. Congress Radiology, 1985; med. adv. radiation therapy, med. affairs com., 1984-97; dir. Pa. Blue Shield, Camp Hill; chair Pa. Cancer Control Bd., 1989-97. Author: Tumors of the Nervous System, 1975, Cancer of the Lung, Clinical Applications of the Electron Beam; editor Cancer Clin. Trials (Am. Jour. Clin. Oncology), (with C. Perez) Principles and Practice of Radiation Oncology; editorial bd. Cancer; assoc. editor: Gynecologic Oncology, Am. Jour. Roentgenology, Cancer Research; sr. editor: Internat. Jour. Radiol. Oncology; contbr. articles on radiation therapy to profl. jours. Bd. dirs. Assn. Artists Equity of Phila., Welcome House, 1974-94, Settlement Music Sch., 1973—, Phila. Art Alliance, 1977-84; trustee Phila. Mus. Art, also mem. oriental art com., 1974—, chmn. exec. com., 1968-72, mem. print, contemporary art and Indian art coms., 1974—. Served to lt. M.C. USN, 1950-54. Recipient Grubbe award Chgo. Radiol. Soc., 1977, Disting. Alumni award George Washington U., 1991; Gold medal Gilbert Fletcher Soc., 1984, Albert Soiland Gold medal U. So. Calif., 1985, del Regato Gold medal, 1986, Padro Pio medal, 1993. Fellow Am. Coll. Radiology (chmn. commn. radiation therapy 1975-81, bd. chancellors 1975-81, Gold medal 1983), Royal Coll. Radiology (hon.), Deutsches Roetngengesellschaft (hon.), Italian Radiology Soc. (hon.), German Soc. Radiol. Oncology (hon.); mem. Royal Soc. Med. Belgium (academician), Radiol. Soc. N.Am. (bd. dirs. 1977-84, chmn. bd. dirs. 1982-83, pres. 1984-85, chmn. refresher course com. 1971-75, Erksine lectr. 1979, Gold medal 1989), Pa. Radiol. Soc. (bd. dirs. 1970-77, councilor to Am. Coll. Radiology 1971-77), Am. Radium Soc. (pres. 1976-77, bd. dirs. Janeway medal 1979, Janeway lectr. 1980), Am. Cancer Soc. (pres. Phila. div. 1976-78, dir. 1968—, exec. com. 1976-78, mem. breast cancer task force 1974-90, nat. dir. 1970-76), Am. Soc. Therapeutic Radiologists (pres. 1971-72, Gold medal 1987), Assn. U. Radiologists, Am. Roentgen Ray Soc., Am. Assn. for Cancer Rsch., Radiation Rsch. Soc., Am. Soc. Clin. Oncology, Phila. Roentgen Ray Soc. (pres. 1976-77, mem. exec. com. 1976-78), Am. Fedn. Clin. Rsch., Coll. Physicians Phila. Coun., James Ewing Soc., Assn. Pendergrass Fellows, Phila. County Med. Soc., AMA (chair residency rev. com. for radiology 1982-84, mem. 1988-94, chair residency rev. com. radiation oncology 1992-94, Gold Medal for Dist. Svc. to Med., 1999), Med. Soc. State Pa., Internat. Skeletal Soc., Coun. Acad. Socs., Soc. Chmn. Acad. Radiation Oncology Programs (pres. 1977-79), Soc. Chmn. Acad. Radiology Depts. (pres. 1974-75), Gynecologic Oncology Group (exec. com. 1971-85, assoc. chmn. 1971-85), Radiation Therapy Oncology Group (chmn. 1980-87), Am. Coll. Radiation Oncology (pres. 1989-92, chmn. 1992-93, gold medal 1996), Pa. Cancer Adv. bd.,(1989-97, chm., 1990-97), Internat. Club Radiotherapists, Nat. Cancer Inst. (bd. sci. counselors, com. for radiation therapy studies 1971-84, chmn. cancer clin. trails com.), Smith-Reed-Russell Soc., Alpha Omega Alpha, Phi Lambda Kappa. Clubs: Merion Cricket; Racquet, Union League (Phila.), Phila., Peale. Office: 230 N Broad St Philadelphia PA 19102-1121

BRADY, M. JANE, state attorney general; b. Wilmington, Del., Jan. 11, 1951; m. Michael Neal. BA, U. Del., 1973; JD, Villanova U., 1976. Dep. atty. gen. Wilmington and Kent County, 1977-87; chief prosecutor Sussex County, 1987-90; solo law practice, 1990-94; atty. gen. State of Del., Wilmington, 1995—. Office: Office of Atty Gen Carvel State Office Bldg 820 N French St Wilmington DE 19801-3509

BRADY, MARY SUE, nutrition and dietetics educator; b. Sedalia, Mo., Mar. 29, 1945; d. H. Wesley and K. Virginia (McGaw) Steele; m. Paul L. Brady, Sept. 2, 1967; 1 child, Chad W. BA, Marian Coll., Indpls., 1968; MS, Ind. U., Indpls., 1970, DMSc, 1987. Registered dietitian; cert. specialist in pediatric nutrition Am. Dietetic Assn. Pediatric dietitian J.W. Riley Hosp. Children, Ind. U. Sch. Medicine, Indpls., 1970-75, acting dir. pediatric nutrition, 1975-78, 80-82, neonatal dietitian, 1978-80, dir. pediatric nutrition, 1982-96; asst. prof. Ind. U. Sch. Medicine, Indpls., 1975-88, assoc. prof., 1988-96, prof. 1996—. Contbr. articles to Jour. of Am. Dietetic Assn., Pediatric Pulmonology, Jour. of Pediatrics. Recipient Excellence in Svc. award Ind. U. Sch. Medicine, Sch. Allied Health Scis., 1994, Glenn W. Irwin Jr. Experience Excellence Recognition award IUPUI, 1994, Disting. Alumni award Marian Coll., 1998, Outstanding Educator's award Ind. Dietetic Assn., 1999. Fellow Am. Dietetic Assn. (charter mem., Excellence in Practice of Clin. Nutrition award 1991, Pediat. Nutrition Practice Group Outstanding Mem. of Yr. 1994, Outstanding Educators award Area 5, 1999); mem. Sigma Xi. Office: JW Riley Hosp for Children 702 Barnhill Dr Rm 3505 Indianapolis IN 46202-5200

BRADY, MICHAEL CAMERON, investment consultant; b. Michigan City, Ind., Jan. 28, 1957; s. Robert John and Patricia Ann (Moon) B.; m. Lisa Lee Blauvelt, June 25, 1983; children: Meagan Lee, Cameron Matthew, Collin Patrick. BSBA, Ohio State U., 1979; MBA, Cleve. State U., 1981. Cert. fin. planner; registered investment advisor. Vice pres. Nat. City Bank, Cleve., 1979-87; mng. dir. Brady, Foley & Co., Inc., Cleve., 1987-89, McCollum Fin. Svcs., Cleve., 1989-92; pres. Chapel Hill Advisors, Inc., Cleve., 1992-97; mng. dir. Brady & Co., Inc., Cleve., 1983-92; pres., registered prin. Chapel Hill Securities, Inc., Cleve., 1992-97; sr. v.p. Prim Capital Corp., Cleve., 1998—; pres. Prim Securities, Inc., Cleve., 1998—. Mem. exec. bd. Greater Cleve. coun. Boy Scouts Am., 1989—, Greater Cleve. chpt. ARC, 1988-89; v.p. Olmsted Falls Bd. Edn., 1992-97, pres. Recipient Silver Beaver award Nat. Coun. Boy Scouts Am., 1995. Mem. Inst. Cert. Fin. Planners, Estate Planning Coun. Cleve., Newcomen Soc. U.S., Edgewater Yacht Club, Cleve. Athletic Club, Columbia Hills Country Club. Roman Catholic. Avocations: sailing, skiing, mountaineering. Home: 8348 Old Post Rd Olmsted Falls OH 44138-1871 Office: Prim Capital Corp 4859 Dover Center Rd Ste 11 North Olmsted OH 44070-3191

BRADY, MICHAEL JOHN, chemical engineer, automotive engineer; b. Detroit, Dec. 6, 1946; s. Louis John and Catherine T. B.; m. Pamela Marion, May 23, 1970. BS in Chem. Engring., Wayne State U., 1969; MS in Chem. Engring., U. Detroit Mercy, 1978. Devel. engr. Celanese Corp., Detroit, 1969-71; product engr. Chrysler Corp., Detroit, 1971, rsch. scientist, 1979; engring. specialist Daimler Chrysler Corp. (formerly Chrysler Corp.), Detroit, 1990—; Chrysler rep. Am. Automotive Mfgs. Assn., 1995-97, Soc. Automotive Engrs., Part New Gen. Vehicle, Coop. Rsch. and Devel. Agreement, 1993—, Auto-Oil Com. of Coordinating Rsch. Coun., 1996—. Author papers in field. Assist. League of Women Voters. Recipient tech. accomplishment award Partnership for New Generation Vehicle, 1997. Mem. Soc. of Automotive Engrs. (reviewer 1986—), Oakland County Earth Sci. Club. Achievements include recognition in engring. circles as "Chrysler's catalyst expert"; helped reduce vehicle emissions 95% since 1975. Avocations: soccer, gardening, bridge, stamp collecting, golf. Office: Daimler Chrysler Corp 800 Chrysler Dr Auburn Hills MI 48326-2757

BRADY, PATRICIA MARIE, nurse; b. Taylor, Pa., Feb. 6, 1946; d. Herman John and Regina Theresa (Yonushka) Kovalan; m. Edward Joseph Brady, June 22, 1968 (dec. Mar. 1996); children: Maureen C., Edward M. RN, St. Joseph's Hosp., Carbondale, Pa., 1966. Cert. emergency nurse, ACLS; cert. diabetes educator. Staff nurse med.-surg. Wilkes-Barre (Pa.) Gen. Hosp., 1966; staff nurse med. Dept. VA Med Ctr., Wilkes-Barre, 1966-72, staff nurse ambulatory care and emergency rm., 1977—; mem. diabetes adv. com. Dept. VA Med. Ctr., 1993—. Assisted in formation diabetes edn. program VA, 1994; established and facilitated VA Med. Ctr. Pain Clinic, 1996—. Mem. Pittston (Pa.) Area Taxpayers Assn., 1995—; parishner Sacred Heart of Jesus Ch., Dupont, Pa., 1968—. Mem. Am. Assn. Diabetes Educators (by-laws com. 1995—), Wilkes-Barre C. of C. Golf League. Democrat. Roman Catholic. Avocations: wreath and flower crafts, country, ballroom, and swing dancing, golf. Home: 1289 Suscon Rd Pittston PA 18640-9596 Office: Dept VA Med Ctr 1111 E End Blvd Wilkes Barre PA 18711-0030

BRADY, PATRICK, French literature educator, novelist; b. Broken Hill, New South Wales, Australia, Oct. 27, 1933; came to U.S., 1969; naturalized, 1993; s. Patrick and Frances (Minahan) B.;. BA with first class honors, U. Sydney, Australia, 1953-56; D., Sorbonne, 1960. Asst. in English Poitiers (France) Tchr.'s Coll., 1957-58; lectr. in English U. Lille (France), 1959-60; lectr. in French U. Melbourne (Australia), 1961-64; sr. lectr. U. Queensland, Brisbane, Australia, 1964-68, reader in French, 1968; assoc. prof. Fla. State U., Tallahassee, 1969-72; prof. French Rice U., Houston, 1972-83, Favrot prof. French, 1983-88; Shumway chair of excellence U. Tenn., Knoxville, 1988—; vis. prof. comparative lit. Harvard U., Cambridge, Mass., 1978; Disting. Humanities lectr. S.W. Conf. Humanities Consortium, 1980-81; state rep. Australasian Univs. Lang. and Lit. Assn., 1967-68; founder New Paradigm Press, 1991, Studies on Lucette Desvignes jour., 1991, Synthesis jour., 1995. Author: L'Oeuvre d'Emile Zola, 1967, Structuralist Perspectives, 1978, Rococo Style, 1985, Chaos in the Humanities, 1995, Feminism, 1995, (novel) Guruwari, 1995, also others; contbr. over 100 articles to profl. jours. Decorated Ordre Palmes Académiques (France); travelling scholar U. Sydney, 1958-60; Mellon Found. rsch. grantee, 1982. Mem. Am. Comparative Lit. Assn., Internat. Soc. for Interdisciplinary Studies (founder), Tenn. Writers' Alliance. Office: Dept Modern Fgn Languages & Literatures U Tenn Knoxville TN 37996

BRADY, PATRICK, advertising executive. Pres., COO Cyrk, Inc., Gloucester, Mass., 1999—, CEO, 1999—. Office: Cyrk Inc 3 Pond Rd Gloucester MA 01930*

BRADY, PHILIP T., marketing professional. BA in Sociology, Merrimack Coll. Product mgr., sales promotion mgr., sales rep. Burroughs Wellcome Co., 1968-79; v.p., account supr. Fones & Mann, Inc., 1979-81; v.p., mgmt. supr. to pres., COO RWR Advt., Inc., 1981-91; sr. v.p., mgmt. supr. Thomas G. Ferguson Assocs., Inc., 1992-93, pres., CEO, 1993-95; vice-chmn. CommonHealth USA, Parsippany, N.J., 1995—. Office: CommonHealth 30 Lanidex Plz W Parsippany NJ 07054-2717*

BRADY, PHILLIP DONLEY, lawyer; b. Pasadena, Calif., May 20, 1951; s. Donley L. and Evelyn M. (Dorweiler) B.; m. Kathleen Ryan; children: Ryan Donley, Conor Phillip, Sean Patrick. BA cum laude, U. Notre Dame, 1973; JD cum laude, Loyola U., Los Angeles, 1976. Bar: Calif. 1976, U.S. Ct. Appeals (D.C. cir.) 1978, U.S. Supreme Ct. 1980, U.S. Ct. Mil. Appeals 1990. Assoc. atty. Spray, Gould & Bowers, L.A., 1976-78; dep. atty gen. State of Calif., L.A., 1978-79; legis. counsel U.S. Rep. Daniel E. Lungren, Washington, 1979-81; regional dir. ACTION Agy., San Francisco, 1981-82; dir., Congl. Affairs, Immigration and Naturalization Svc. Dept. of Justice, Washington, 1982-83, assoc. dep. atty. gen., 1983-84, acting asst. atty. gen., 1984-85; dep. asst. to V.P. The White House, Washington, 1985-88, dep. counsel to Pres., 1988-89; gen. counsel Dept. Transp., Washington, 1989-91; asst. to Pres. and staff sec. The White House, Washington, 1991-93; v.p, gen. counsel Am. Automobile Mfrs. Assn., Washington, 1993-96; COO ind. rels. Nat. Automobile Dealers Assn., McLean, Va., 1996—; mem. Coun. of the Administrv. Conv. of the U.S., 1988-93. Mem. ABA, Calif. State Bar Assn., FBA (chair gen. counsels sect. 1989-91, nat. coun. 1989—). Home: 5916 Colfax Ave Alexandria VA 22311-1024 Office: Nat Automobile Dealers Assn 8400 Westpark Dr McLean VA 22102*

BRADY, ROBERT, communications educator. Vice-chmn. dept. comms. U. Ark., Fayetteville, 1993—. Office: Dept Comms/Univ Ark 417 Kimpel Hall Fayetteville AR 72701*

BRADY, ROBERT A., congressman; b. Phila., Apr. 7, 1945; m. Debra; 2 children: Robert, Kimberly. Grad. H.S., Phila. Carpenter Phila., 1963-65; official Carpenter's Union, Phila., 1965-98; congressman 1st Congl. Dist., Pa., 1998—; mem. Pa. Dem. State Com., Dem. Nat. Com.; instr. Organizational Dynamics course, U. Pa. Voted in as mem. 34th Ward Dem. Exec. Com., 1967; elected 34th Ward leader, 1980, chmn. Phila. Dem. Party, 1986, congressman to finish unexpired term of Rep. Tom Foglietta, 1998; appointed asst. sgt.-at-arms for Phila. City Coun., 1975-83, Phila. dep. mayor for labor in the W. Wilson Goode adminstrn., cons. to the Pa. State Senate, Pa. Turnpike commr., mem. bd. dirs. Phila. City Redevel. Authority. Office: 216 Cannon Ho Office Bldg Washington DC 20515*

BRADY, RODNEY HOWARD, holding company executive, broadcast company executive, former college president, former government official; b. Sandy, Utah, Jan. 31, 1933; s. Kenneth A. and Jessie (Madsen) B.; m. Carolyn Ann Hansen, Oct. 25, 1960; children: Howard Riley, Bruce Ryan, Brooks Alan. BS in Acctg. with high honors, U. Utah, MBA with high honors, 1957; DBA, Harvard U., 1966; postgrad., UCLA, 1969-70; PhD (hon.), Weber State Coll., 1986, Snow Coll., 1991, Univ. Utah, 1997. Missionary Ch. Jesus Christ of Latter-day Saints, Great Britain, 1953-55; teaching assoc. Harvard U. Bus. Sch., Cambridge, Mass., 1957-59; v.p. Mgmt. Systems Corp., Cambridge, 1962-65, Center Exec. Devel., Cambridge, 1963-64; v.p., dir. Center Exec. Devel., Boston, 1964-65; v.p. Tamerand Reef Corp., Christiansted, St. Croix, V.I., 1963-65; v.p., dir. Am. Inst. Execs., N.Y.C., 1963-65; v.p., mem. exec. com. aircraft div. Hughes Tool Co., Culver City, Calif., 1966-70; asst. sec. adminstrn. and mgmt. Dept. HEW, Washington, 1970-72; chmn. subcabinet exec. officers group of exec. br., 1971-72; exec. v.p., chmn. exec. com., dir. Bergen Brunswig Corp., Los Angeles, 1972-78; chmn. bd. Uni-mgrs. Internat., Los Angeles, 1974-78; pres. Weber State Coll., Ogden, Utah, 1978-85; pres., CEO Bonneville Internat. Corp., Salt Lake City, 1985-96, also dir.; pres., CEO Deseret Mgmt. Corp., Salt Lake City, 1996—; bd. dirs. Bergen Brunswig Corp., 1st Security Bank Corp., Mgmt. and Tng. Corp., Deseret Mut. Benefit Assn., chmn.; bd. dirs. Maximum Svc. Television, Inc., Intermountain Health Care Found., Nat. Assn. Broadcasters TV Bd., Utah Opera Co.; bd. advisors Mountain Bell Telephone, 1983-87; chmn. Nat. Adv. Com. on Accreditation and Instl. Eligibility, 1984-86, mem., 1983-87; chmn. Utah Gov.'s Blue Ribbon Com. on Tax Recodification, 1984-90; cons. Dept. Def., Dept. State, Dept. Commerce, HEW, NASA, Govt. of Can., Govt. of India (and indsl. firms), 1962—. Author: An Approach to Equipment Replacement Analysis, 1957, Survey of Management Planning and Control Systems, 1962, The Impact of Computers on Top Management Decision Making in the Aerospace and Defense Industry, 1966, (with others) How To Structure Incentive Contracts—A Programmed Text, 1965, My Missionary Years in Great Britain, 1976, An Exciting Start Along an Upward Path, 1978; contbr. articles to profl. jours. Mem. exec. com. nat. exec. bd. Boy Scouts Am., 1977—; chmn. nat. Cub Scout commn., 1977-81, pres. Western region, 1981-83, chmn. nat. ct. of honor, 1984-88; mem. adv. com. program for health sys. mgmt. Harvard U., 1973-78, mem. nat. adv. coun. U. Utah, 1971—, chairperson, 1974-76, nat. adv. bd. Coll. Bus., 1985—, chmn., 1989-93, mem. adv. com. Brigham Young U. Bus. Sch., 1972—; mem. dean's round table UCLA Grad. Sch. Mgmt., 1973-78; trustee Ettie Lee Homes for Boys, 1973-79; mem. gov. bd. McKay Dee Hosp., Ogden, Utah, 1979-87; bd. dirs. Utah Endowment for Humanities, 1978-80, Nat. Legal Ctr. for the Pub. Interest, 1991—, vice chmn., 1994-95, chmn., 1995-97, Utah Shakespeare Festival, 1992—, Ogden C. of C., 1978-83; bd. dirs. Utah Opera Co., 1997—. 1st lt. USAF, 1959-62. Recipient Silver Antelope award Boy Scouts Am., 1976; recipient Silver Beaver award Boy Scouts Am., 1979, Silver Buffalo award Boy Scouts Am., 1982, Disting. Alumni award U. Utah, 1990. Mem. Nat. Assn. TV Broadcasters (bd. dirs.), Am. Mgmt. Assn. (award 1969), L.A. C. of C. (tax structure com. 1969-70), Salt Lake Area C. of C. (bd. dirs. 1985-88), SAR (pres. Utah chpt. 1986-87), Sons of Utah Pioneers, Freedoms Found. at Valley Forge (nat. bd. dirs. 1986—), L.A. Country Club, Alta Club, Rotary, Phi Kappa Phi, Tau Kappa Alpha, Beta Gamma Sigma. Mem. LDS Ch. (past pres. L.A. stake). Office: Deseret Mgmt Corp Eagle Gate Tower 60 E South Temple Ste 575 Salt Lake City UT 84111-1016

BRADY, ROGER A., brigadier general United States Air Force. BA in Fgn. Svc., U. Okla., 1968; MA in Polit. Sci., Colo. State U., 1969; grad., Squadron Officer Sch., Maxwell AFB, Ala., 1974; student, Air Command and Staff Coll., Maxwell AFB, Ala., 1982, Nat. War Coll., Ft. Lesley J. McNair, Washington, 1988; student exec. program in Bus. Adminstrn., Columbia U., 1994. Commd. 2d lt. USAF, 1968, advanced through grades to brigadier gen., 1995; air intelligence officer 20th Tactical Air Support Squadron USAF, Da Nang Air Base, S. Viet Nam, 1970-71; chief target processing br. 320th Bomb Wing USAF, Mather AFB, Calif., 1971-72; copilot aircraft and flight comdr. 301st Air Refueling Wing USAF, Rickenbacker AFB, Ohio, 1974-77; instr. pilot, flight comdr. and chief evaluation divsn. 64th Flying Tng. Wing USAF, Reese AFB, Tex., 1977-81; chief T-38 standardization, evaluation directorate ops. Hdqs. Air Tng. Command, Randolph AFB, Tex., 1982-84; staff office Airlift Spl. Ops. and Tng. Divsn. Hdqs. USAF Pentagon, Washington, 1984-85; spl. asst., exec. officer to dep. chief of staff rsch., devel. and acquisition USAF Hdqs. Pentagon, Washington, 1985-87; staff Policies and Studies Br. to chief long range plans br. AirSouth Arms Control then chief programs, requirement br., Allied Air So. Europe, Naples, Italy, 1988-91; comdr. 3415th support group USAF, Lowry AFB, Colo., 1991-92; dir. pers. Hdqs. Air Tng. Command, Randolph AFB, Tex., 1992-93; comdr. 54th flying tng. wing USAF, Reese AFB, Tex., 1993-95; dir. logistics Hdqs. USAF in Europe, Ramsten AFB, Germany, 1997-98, dir. plans and programs, 1998—. fecorated Defense Superior Svc. medal, Legion of Merit with oak leaf cluster, Bronze Star medal, Meritorious Svc. medal with 2 oak leaf clusters, Air Force commendation medal. Office: Hdqs USAF E/LG Unit 3030 Box 105 APO AE 09094-0105

BRADY, ROSCOE OWEN, neurogeneticist, educator; b. Phila., Oct. 11, 1923; s. Roscoe O. and Martha (Roberts) B.; m. Bennett Carden Manning, 1972; 2 sons. Student, Pa. State U., 1941-43; MD, Harvard U., 1947; postgrad., U. Pa., 1948-49. Intern Hosp. U. Pa., 1947-48; NRC fellow U. Pa., 1948-50, USPHS spl. fellow, 1950-52; sect. chief Nat. Inst. Neurol. Diseases and Blindness, NIH, 1954-67; asst. lab. chief neurochemistry Nat. Inst. Neurol. Diseases and Blindness, NIH, Bethesda, Md., 1967-72; chief developmental and metabolic neurology br. Nat. Inst. Neurol. Disorders and Stroke, 1972—; pres., CEO Targeted Techs., Inc., Rockville, Md.; professorial lectr. George Washington U. Sch. Medicine, 1963-73; mem. faculty

Georgetown U. Sch. Medicine, 1965—; mem. med. staff Children's Hosp. Washington, 1992—. Author: (with Donald B. Tower) Neurochemistry of Nucleotides and Amino Acids, 1960, Basic Neurosciences, 1975, (with John A. Barranger) Molecular Basis of Lysosomal Storage Disorders, 1984, also numerous articles. Recipient award Gairdner Found., 1973, Lasker Found., 1982, Passano Found., 1982, Warren Alpert Found. award, 1992, Myrtle Wreath award Hadassah, 1993, Exec. Excellence award Sr. Execs. Assn., 1993. Mem. NAS (J.S. Kovalenko medal 1991), Am. Soc. Biol. Chemists, Am. Acad. Neurology (Kotzias award 1980), Am. Acad. Mental Retardation, Am. Soc. Clin. Investigation, Am. Soc. Human Genetics, Inst. of Medicine. Achievements include first demonstration of enzyme system for fatty acid synthesis; biosynthesis of myelin sheath lipids, nature of metabolic defects in Gaucher's disease, Niemann-Pick disease, Fabry's diseases and Tay-Sachs disease; diagnostic and genetic counseling tests for Gaucher's, Niemann-Pick, Fabry's diseases; enzyme and gene replacement therapy of lipid storage diseases; metabolism of sphingolipids in neoplastic diseases, role of antigenic sphingolipids in neurological diseases. Home: 6026 Valerian Ln Rockville MD 20852-3410 Office: NIH 9000 Rockville Pike Bethesda MD 20892-0003

BRADY, SHEILA ANN, manufacturing company executive; b. Connersville, Ind., Dec. 11, 1935; d. Francis Elmer and Mary Eleanor (Underwood) B. BS, Ball State U., 1958; postgrad., Rutgers U., 1959-60. Art tchr. various N.J. schs., 1959-68; head dept. art Wardlaw Pvt. Boys Sch., Edison, N.J., 1968-72; asst. to pres. F.E. Brady Products, Inc., Clearwater, Fla., 1972-73; pres., treas. Brady Products, Inc., Clearwater, 1973—, chmn. bd., 1976—; pres., treas. Brady Air Controls, Inc., Muncie, Ind., 1975-84, Mountain Meadow Farms, Lake Toxaway, N.C., 1993—. Co-author: Water Systems Handbook, 5th edit. Recipient Art award City of Dunnellon, N.J., 1972; named Ky. Col., 1989. Mem. Water Systems Coun., Nat. Water Well Assn., RV Women, Carefree Club (Ft. Myers, Fla.). Avocations: composing, art, raising exotic animals. Office: Brady Products Inc 2151 Logan St Clearwater FL 33765-1312

BRADY, SHELAGH ANN, elementary education educator; b. Lowell, Mass., Aug. 4, 1943; d. Frank William and Margaret (Foye) B. BA in Tchr. Edn. and Social Studies, Emmanuel Coll., Boston, 1966; MEd, Fitchburg State Coll., 1983. Cert. tchr. elem. edn. Commonwealth of Mass. Dept. Edn. Tchr. grade 3 St. Joseph Elem. Sch., Somerville, 1965-69, tchr. grade 6, 1969-70; tchr. grade 5 St. Bridget Elem. Sch., Maynard, Mass., 1970-73, Norman E. Day Sch., Westford, Mass., 1973-76; lang. arts tchr. grade 6 Norman E. Day Sch., Westford, 1976-90, Abbott Middle Sch., Westford, 1990-92, Blanchard Middle Sch., Westford, 1992—. Mem. NEA, Westford Edn. Assn. Democrat. Roman Catholic. Avocations: genealogical research, reading, gardening, birding, hiking. Home: 302 Groton Rd Westford MA 01886-1346 Office: Blanchard Middle Sch 14 West St Westford MA 01886-1210

BRADY, STEPHEN R.P.K., physician; b. New London, Conn., Oct. 13, 1955; s. Richard Harris and Jeanne Margaret (Halpin) B.; m. Marsha Anne Erickson, June 18, 1978 (div. Jan. 1993); 1 child, Ericka Anuhea; m. Elizabeth Ada Rewick, Dec. 27, 1994. AB cum laude, Harvard U., 1977; MPH, U. Hawaii, 1978, postgrad., 1979; MD, U. Pa., 1982. Diplomate Am. Bd. Internal Medicine. Intern U. Hawaii, 1982-83, resident in internal medicine, 1983-85; physician Kaiser Clinics, Honolulu, 1985-86; physician, med. dir. Kokua Kalihi Valley, Honolulu, 1986-89; clin. instr. U. Hawaii Sch. Medicine, Honolulu, 1986—, co-chair dept. continuing med. edn., 1993—; physician Waianae (Hawaii) Coast Health Svcs., 1989-94; asst. med. dir., physician Am. Hawaii Cruises, Honolulu, 1989—; physician Straub Clinic & Hosp., Honolulu, 1984—; founding chair Hawaii Consortium for Continuing Med. Edn. U. Hawaii Sch. of Medicine, 1993—. Host weekly Ask the Dr. program KHON-Fox 2 News, Hawaii, 1996—. Cubmaster Boy Scouts Am., Kailua, Hawaii, 1995—. Comdr. U.S. Merchant Marine, 1989—. Recipient Po'okela awards, 1991, 93, 95; rsch. grantee Kuakini Med. Rsch. Inst., Honolulu, 1971, Pacific Health Rsch. Inst., Honolulu, 1972-78, Children's Hosp., Phila., 1979; Paul Harris fellow, 1995; named Scot of the Yr. State of Hawaii, 1999. Mem. AMA, Am. Coll. Physicians, Am. Soc. Internal Medicine, Am. Pub. Health Assn, Am. Statistical Assn., Hawaii Soc. Internal Medicine, Hawaii Med. Assn. (chair continuing med. edn. com. 1987—), Soc. Epidemiologic Rsch., Rotary, Soroptimist (pres.), Aumoana Cmty. Assn., (v.p. 1996—), Kaneohe Yacht Club, Plaza Club, Delta Omega. Congregationalist. Avocations: singing, running, sailing, scuba diving, music. Home: 758 Kapahulu Ave # 309 Honolulu HI 96816-1196 Office: Straub Clinic & Hosp 888 S King St Honolulu HI 96813-3083

BRADY, STEVEN MICHAEL, lawyer; b. Norwalk, Conn., June 17, 1962; s. Patrick E. and Gwendolyn (Caskey) B.; m. Jacqueline Nicole, Apr. 8, 1989; 1 child, Patrick Alexander. BS, Fla. State U., 1984; JD, U. Fla., 1987. Bar: Fla. 1988, U.S. Dist. Ct. (so. dist.) Fla. 1999, U.S. Dist. Ct. (mid. dist.) Fla. 1988. Corp. counsel The Travelers Cos., Orlando, Fla., 1987-89; diplomat U.S. Dept. of State, Washington, 1989-94; trial lawyer Floyd Pearson Richman & Greer, Miami, Fla., 1995-96, Richman, Greer, Weil, Brumbaugh, Mirabito & Christensen PA, Miami, Fla., 1994—. Master USCG, 1985—. Mem. Fla. Bar Assn., Phi Delta Phi. Avocation: sailing. Office: Richman Greer Weil Brumbaugh Mirabito & Christensen PA Miami Ctr 201 S Biscayne Blvd Miami FL 33131-4332

BRADY, TERRENCE JOSEPH, judge; b. Chgo., Dec. 24, 1940; s. Harry J. and Othele R. Brady; m. Debra René, Dec. 6, 1969; children: Tara René, Dana Rose. BA cum laude, Coll. St. Thomas, 1963; JD, U. Ill., 1968. Bar: Ill. 1969, U.S. Dist. Ct. (no. dist.) Ill. 1970, U.S. Ct. Appeals (7th cir.) 1971. Pvt. practice Crystal Lake, Ill., 1969-70, Waukegan, Ill., 1970-77; assoc. judge 19th Jud. Cir., Ill. Cir. Ct., Waukegan, 1977—; lectr. Ann. Ill. Assoc. Judge Seminars, Statewide Ill. Traffic Conf., 1982, Lake County Bar Assn. Seminar, 1983, 88, others; faculty Nat. Jud. Coll., Reno, Nev., 1997; presenter, lectr. in field. Contbr. articles to profl. jours. Served with U.S. Army, 1963-64, 68-69. Mem. ISBA (com. on jud. adv. polls 1994—, vice-chair adv. polls 1998, chair jud. adv. polls, 1999), Ill. Judges Assn. (bd. govs.), Ill. Bar Assn. (task force on domestic violence 1988—), Lake County Bar Assn., Libertyville Racquet Club, Am. Inns of Ct. Avocations: tennis, golf, writing, reading. Office: Lake County Courthouse 18 N County St Waukegan IL 60085-4304 *Notable cases include: Adams vs. Adams, 133 Ill. 2d 457 S. Ct., 1989, which involved the Ill. Appellate Ct., in a divided opinion, affirmed, Adams vs. Adams, 174 Ill. App. 3d 595 2d Dist., 1988. The Ill. Supreme Ct. reversed and remanded, holding the issues of paternity and consent must be determined under Fla. law; Agazim vs. Agazim, 176 Ill. App. 3d 225 2d Dist., 1988, which affirmed the trial ct.'s distbn. of marital property requiring the husband to pay off substantial marital debts which he had incurred of his own purposes; Chapman vs. Chapman, 162 Ill. app. 3d 308 2d Dist., 1987; which affirmed trial ct.'s denial of husband's motion to vacate a marital property settlement agreement, without an evidentiary hearing; Peppers vs. FNB of Lake Forest, 151 Ill. App 3d 909 2d Dist., 1987, which affirmed trial ct.'s enjoining the defendant bank, as trustee, from seeking forfeiture of a real estate purchase installment contract; People ex. rel. Foreman vs. Sojourner's Motorcycle Club Ltd.*

BRADY, THOMAS CARL, lawyer; b. Malone, N.Y., Sept. 5, 1947; s. Francis Robert and Rosamond Ethel (South) B.; m. Joan Marie Murray, Dec. 4, 1971; children: Erin Marie, Ryan Thomas, Trevor Michael. BA, Niagara U., 1969; JD, SUNY, Buffalo, 1972. Bar: N.Y. 1973, U.S. Dist. Ct. (we. dist.) N.Y. 1973, Fla. 1981. City ct. judge City of Salamanca, N.Y., 1973; atty. County of Cattaraugus, Little Valley, N.Y., 1973-76; ptnr. Eldredge, Brady, Peters & Brooks, Salamanca and Ellicottville, N.Y., 1976-82; sr. ptnr. Brady, Brooks & Smith, Salamanca, N.Y., 1982-96, Brady, Brooks & O'Connell, L.L.P., Salamanca, N.Y., 1996—. Trustee St. Patrick's Roman Cath. Ch., Salamanca, 1991—; mem. N.Y. State Office Parks, Recreation and Hist. Preservation Allegany Region Commn., 1998—, vice chair, 1999; mem. 8th Dist. Atty. Grievance Com., 1994—. Capt. USAR, 1969-76. Mem. ATLA, Nat. Lawyers Assn., Fla. Bar Assn., N.Y. State Trial Lawyers Assn., N.Y. State Bar Assn., Cattaraugus County Bar Assn. (pres. 1984), Kiwanis (pres. Salamanca club 1983-84). Republican. Roman Catholic. Avocations: skiing, golf, swimming, boating. E-Mail: BBOLAW@aol.com. Home: 6894 Woodland Dr Great Valley NY 14741-9752 Office: Brady Brooks & O'Connell LLP 41 Main St PO Box 227 Salamanca NY 14779-0227

BRADY, THOMAS GEOFFREY, artist; b. Melrose, Mass., Oct. 13, 1950; s. Thomas Bernard and Margaret (Mahoney) B.; m. Anne Weston, Jan. 26, 1974; children: Kate, Maggie, James. AB in Fine Arts, Amherst Coll., 1974; student, Heatherly Sch. of Art, London, Eng., 1971-72; MFA, Tyler Sch. of Art, Temple U., 1982. Painter: solo exhbns. include: Gallery 355, Boston, 1978, The Art Complex, Duxbury, Mass., 1978, Amherst (Mass.) Coll. Mead Art Mus., 1979, Anyart Art Ctr., Providence, R.I., 1979, Ocean Spray Cranberry Co. Hdqts., Plymouth, Mass., 1980, Da Vinci Art Ctr., Phila., 1984, St. Joseph's U., Phila., Spring Gallery, Elkins Park, Pa., 1990, Phila. Inquirer, 1990, Josephine Muller Gallery, Jenkintown, Pa., 1991, Harbs Gallery, Lexington, Va., 1992, Axis Gallery, Phila., 1993, 94, Lagerquist Gallery, Atlanta, 1994, DuPont Gallery, Washington and Lee U., Lexington, Va., 1995, Sch. of Commerce, Washington and Lee U., 1998; numerous group exhibits include Art at City Hall, Phila., 1986, Perkins Art Ctr., Moorestown, N.J., 1987, Del. Art Mus., Wilmington, 1993, Allentown Art Mus., Pa., 1996, Chinese Culture Inst., Boston, 1996, The Painting Ctr., N.Y.C., 1997; corp. collections include, Bell Atlantic, Sterling Winthrop, Woodmere Art Mus., First USA Bank, ICI Polyurethane and many more. Recipient Discipline winner award Pew Found., 1995, 97; painting fellowship Pitts. Coun. on the Arts. E-Mail: Brady@CFW.com. Home and Office: 6620 N 7th St Philadelphia PA 19126

BRADY, UPTON BIRNIE, editor, literary agent; b. Washington, Apr. 17, 1938; s. Francis Ignatius and Sue (Birnie) B.; m. Sally Ryder, Nov. 17, 1962; children—Sarah Schenck, Andrew Upton Birnie, Nathaniel Francis Ryder, Alexander Childs. AB, Harvard Coll., 1959. Coll. field editor Random House, N.Y.C., 1961-63; editor McGraw Hill, N.Y.C., 1963-65; mng. editor Atlantic Monthly Press, Boston, 1965-72, assoc. dir., 1972-79, dir., 1979-84, exec. editor, 1984-88; free-lance editor, cons., literary agt., 1988—. Served to lt. (j.g.) USNR, 1959-61. Roman Catholic. Club: PEN. Home and Office: Town Farm Hill PO Box 164 Hartland Four Corners VT 05049

BRADY, WRAY GRAYSON, mathematician, educator; b. Benton Harbor, Mich., July 20, 1918; s. Wray Grayson and Mildred (Sauters) B.; m. Emilie Peterson, Apr. 30, 1943; children—Susan, Wray Gordon. B.S., Washington and Jefferson Coll., 1940, M.A., 1942; Ph.D., U. Pitts., 1953. Prof., chmn. dept. math. Washington and Jefferson Coll., 1951-65, U. Bridgeport, Conn., 1965-69; dir. rsch., dean Slippery Rock U., 1969-72, prof. math., 1972-87, prof. emeritus, 1987—; cons. Bettis Plant, AEC, 1955-60; prof. math NSF U. Ariz., 1963-67. Co-author: Calculus, 1960, Analytic Geometry, 1961. Lt. USNR, 1943-46. Fellow AAAS; mem. Am. Math. Soc., Math. Assn. Am., Fibonacci Soc., AAUP. Democrat. Presbyterian. Home: 340 Bestwick Rd Mercer PA 16137

BRADY-BORLAND, KAREN, reporter; b. Buffalo, Mar. 13, 1940; d. Charles A. and Mary Eileen (Larson) B.; m. Gregg Robinson Borland, Sept. 6, 1969 (div. July 1985); children: Caitlin Luise, Kristin Robinson, Leila Nell. BA in English, Daemen Coll., 1961; MS in Journalism, Columbia U., 1962. Summer reporter Buffalo News, 1961, reporter, 1965-68, columnist, 1968-81; editor Prentice-Hall, Inc., Englewood, N.J., 1962-65; press officer for Rep. Max McCarthy U.S. Ho. Reps., Washington, 1967. Recipient numerous awards Buffalo Newspaper Guild, 1969-79, N.Y. State award for Major Dailies Mag. Writing AP, 1982, numerous community awards. Office: Buffalo News PO Box 100 Buffalo NY 14240-0100

BRAEN, BERNARD BENJAMIN, psychology educator; b. Boston, Oct. 11, 1928; s. Simon Peter and Ethel (Davis) B.; m. Judith Krom; children: Philip, Eric, Benson. BA, U. Maine, 1949; MA, Boston U., 1950; PhD, Syracuse U., 1955. Diplomate clin. psychology Am. Bd. Examiners Profl. Psychology, 1962-93; lic. psychologist, N.Y., 1957-93. Chief clin. psychologist Onondaga County Child Guidance Ctr., Syracuse, N.Y., 1956-60; pvt. practice clin. psychology Syracuse, 1960-64; assoc. prof. psychology SUNY Upstate Med. Ctr., Syracuse, 1964-69, prof., 1969; prof. Syracuse U., 1969-92; ret.; dir. grad. program in clin. psychology, dir. psychology clinic Syracuse U., 1969-83; exec. dir. Nat. Alliance Concerned with School Age Parents, Syracuse, 1971-74, dir. research and publs., 1974-76. Contbr. articles to profl. publs., 1959—; guest editor Jour. Sch. Health, 1977. Recipient Disting. Service award Nat. Alliance Concerned with Sch. Age Parents, 1976. Fellow Am. Orthopsychiat. Assn.

BRAENDEL, DOUGLAS ARTHUR, healthcare executive; b. Highland Park, Mich., Dec. 9, 1939; s. Helmuth Gunther and Constance Leah (Drysdale) B.; m. Cameron Lawry, Nov. 30, 1968; children: Jennifer Braendel Miller, Eric, Heike Braendel Batluck. BSBA, Lehigh U., 1961, MBA, 1971; Grad., Army Command and Gen. Staff, Coll., Army War Coll. Commd. U.S. Army, 1966, advanced through grades to col., 1989; bn. supply officer 24th Med. Bn., Fed. Republic of Germany, 1966-68; patient adminstr., detachment comdr. 3d Mobile Army Surg. Hosp., Vietnam, 1968-69; CFO Noble Army Community Hosp., Ft. McClellan, Ala., 1972-75; asst. prof. health adminstrn. Baylor U. Grad. Sch., San Antonio, 1975-79; exec. officer 45th Med. Battalion, Hanau, Fed. Republic Germany, 1980-82; adminstr. Army Regional Med. Lab., Landstuhl, Fed. Republic Germany, 1982-84; comdr. 10th Mobile Army Surg. Hosp., Ft. Meade, Md., 1984-86; dir. programs and evaluation Army Surgeon Gen., Washington, 1986-89; spl. asst. Office Managed Care, Health Care Fin. Adminstrn., Washington, 1989-90; CFO U.S. Army Health Svcs. Command, San Antonio, 1990-93; dir. capitation financing Office Asst. Sec. Def., Falls Church, Va., 1993-96; ret. U.S. Army, 1996; health care mgmt. cons., 1996—; adj. instr. Park Coll., San Antonio, 1976-79, Gadsdon (Ala.) State Jr. Coll., 1973-74, Allegany (Md.) Coll., 1997—. Vol. income tax asst. IRS, Falls Church, Va., 1986-90, 94—; unit commr. Boy Scouts Am., Kaiserslautern, Fed. Republic Germany, 1982-84, scoutmaster, Rochester, N.Y., and Augsberg, Fed. Republic Germany, 1965-68. Col. U.S. Army, 1966—. Decorated Def. Superior Svc. medal, Legion of Merit with oak leaf cluster, others; recipient Outstanding Author award Am. Soc. Mil. Comptrollers, 1994. Fellow Am. Coll. Healthcare Execs. (Regents award for leadership in health care 1994); mem. Assn. U.S. Army, Beta Gamma Sigma. Avocations: sailing, skiing. Office: Braendel Assocs PO Box 25 Buffalo Mills PA 15534-0025

BRAEUTIGAM, RONALD RAY, economics educator; b. Tulsa, Apr. 30, 1947; s. Raymond Louis Braeutigam and Loys Ann (Johnson) Henneberger; m. Janette Gail Carlyon, July 27, 1975; children: Eric Zachary, Justin Michael, Julie Ann. BS, U. Tulsa, 1969; MSc, Stanford U., 1971, PhD, 1976. Petroleum engr. Standard Oil Ind., Tulsa, 1966-70; staff economist Office of Telecom. Policy, Exec. Office of Pres., Washington, 1972-73; from asst. to prof. econs. Northwestern U., Evanston, Ill., 1975—; dir. bus. instns. program, 1995—; Harvey Kapnick prof. Bus. Instns. dept. econs. Northwestern U., Evanston, Ill., 1990—, Charles Deering McCormick prof. tchg. excellence, 1997—; vis. prof. Calif. Inst. Tech., Pasadena, 1978-79. Co-author: The Regulation Game, 1978, Price Level Regulation for Diversified Public Utilities, 1989; assoc. editor Jour. Indsl. Econs., Cambridge, Mass., 1987-90; mem. editorial bd. MIT Press Series on Regulation, Cambridge, 1980—, Jour. Econ. Lit., 1987-91, Rev. Indsl. Orgn., 1991—. Coach Skokie (Ill.) Indians Little League, 1985-91, Evanston Youth Baseball Assn., 1991-96. Grantee, Dept. Transp., NSF, Ameritech, Sloan Found., Mellon Found., others; sr. rsch. fellow Internat. Inst. Mgmt., Berlin, 1982-83, 91. Mem. Am. Econ. Assn., Econometric Soc., Internat. Telecommunications Soc. (bd. dirs. 1990—), European Econ. Assn., European Assn. for Rsch. in Indsl. Econs. (exec. com. 1992—, pres. 1997—), Soc. Petroleum Engrs. Avocations: travel, music, German lang., French lang. Home: 731 Monticello St Evanston IL 60201-1745 Office: Northwestern U Dept Econs Evanston IL 60208

BRAFF, HOWARD, brokerage house executive, financial analyst; b. Bklyn., July 18, 1952; s. Emanuel and Rose (Schlamberg) B.; m. Cindi Louise Sansone, Mar. 25, 1975; 1 child, Shana. BA in Math. and Psychology summa cum laude, Hofstra U., 1974, MBA in Fin., 1984. Fin. mgr. Save On Oil, Inc., Merrick, N.Y., 1974-83; acct. exec., portfolio mgr., high-tech. and health care ind. analyst Laidlaw, Adams & Peck, Inc., Westbury, N.Y., 1983-86; ind. investment adv. Merrick, 1977-83; account exec., portfolio mgr. high tech and health care industry analyst Investors Ctr. Inc., Farmingdale, N.Y., 1986-87; health care industry analyst, portfolio mgr. Strasbourger Pearson Tulcin Wolff Inc., N.Y.C., 1987-88; br. mgr. Olde Discount Corp., Hicksville, N.Y., 1988-91; pres., chmn., chief exec. officer Save on Discount Stockbrokers Corp., Bellmore, N.Y., 1991-93; br. mgr. Scottsdale Securities, Inc., Lake Grove, N.Y., 1993—. Mem. Phi Beta Kappa. Home: 4 Mews Ct Holtsville NY 11742-1900 Office: Scottsdale Securities Inc 2780 Middle Country Rd Ste 211 Lake Grove NY 11755-2121

BRAFFORD, WILLIAM CHARLES, lawyer; b. Pike County, Ky., Aug. 7, 1932; s. William Charles and Minnie (Tacket) B.; m. Katherine Jane Prather, Nov. 13, 1954; children—William Charles III, David A. JD, U. Ky., 1957; LLM (fellow), U. Ill., 1958. Bar: Ky. 1957, Ga. 1965, Tax Ct. U.S 1965, Ct. Claims 1965, Ohio 1966, U.S. Ct. Appeals 1966, U.S. Supreme Ct. 1970, Pa. 1973. Trial atty. NLRB, Washington and Cin., 1958-60; atty. Louisville & Nashville R.R. Co., Louisville, 1960-63, So. Bell Telephone Co., Atlanta, 1963-65; asst. gen. counsel NCR Corp., Dayton, Ohio, 1965-72; v.p., sec., gen. counsel Betz Dearborn, inc., Trevose, Pa., 1972-97, ret., 1997; former dir. Betz Process Chems., Inc., Betz, Ltd. U.K., Betz Paper Chem. Inc., Betz Energy Chems., Inc., Betz S.A. France, B.L. Chems., Inc., Betz GmbH, Germany, Betz Entec, Inc., Betz Ges. GmbH, Austria, Betz NV Belgium, Betz Sud S.p.A., Italy, Betz Internat. Inc., Betz Europe Inc., Primex Ltd., Barbados. Served as 1st lt. C.I.C. AUS, 1954-56. Mem. Am. Soc. Corp. Secs., Nat. Assn. Corp. Dirs., Atlantic Legal Found. Republican. Presbyterian.

BRAGDON, CLIFFORD RICHARDSON, city planner, educator; b. St. Louis, June 30, 1940; s. Dudley Acton and Ruth (Butler) B.; m. Sarah Vaughn, Aug. 21, 1965; children: Katherine, Rachel, Elizabeth. BA, Westminster Coll., 1962; MS, Mich. State U., 1965; PhD, U. Pa., 1970. Urban planner West Philadelphia Cmty. Mental Health Consortium, U. Pa., 1967-69; environ. specialist, acting chief bio-acoustics div. U.S. Environ. Hygiene Agy., Edgewood, Md., 1969-72; prof. dept. city planning Ga. Inst. Tech., Atlanta, 1972-93, asst. dean, dir. of extension, 1979-82, dir. continuing edn., 1982—, assoc. v.p., 1983-90, special asst. office of pres., 1990-93, head sensory spatial systems group, 1993; dean Sch. Aviation and Transp., v.p. Nat. Aviation and Transp. Ctr., Dowling Coll., 1993—, dir., 1999; clin. prof. Sch. of Pub. Health Emory U., Atlanta, 1979—; adj. prof. Auburn U., 1981—; pres. C.R. Bragdon & Assocs., environ. planning; bd. dirs. Transp. Rsch. Forum, U. Transp. Rsch. Ctr. Region II. Author: Noise Pollution: The Unquiet Crisis, 1972; Noise Pollution: A Guide to Information Sources, 1979; General Aviation Airport Noise and Land Use Planning, 1979; Municipal Noise Legislation: 1980, Installation Compatability Use Zone Planning: ICUZ Guide, 1987, Airport Land Use Planning and Noise Control, 1997; contbr. chpt. to Environ. Health, 1979, Politics of Neglect, 1974, Airport Noise Planning Transp. Noise Ctrl. Handbook; contbg. editor Sound and Vibration, 1974—; columnist Airport Press, 1994—; cable TV Host Transpo 2000, 1994—; adv. bd. Airport Noise Reporter; editl. bd. FAA Aviation Topics; chmn. STAR USA; patentee in field. Cons. to office noise abatement U.S. EPA, 1972—, also FAA; constrn. engr. rsch. lab. U.S. Army C.E., 1973—; pres. Friends of Redan, 1985-93; chmn. Specialized Tng. Transp. and Aeronautics Rsch., 1994—; bd. dirs. Opportunity Skyway, Inc., 1994—, mem. council advs. Nat. Sci. Ctr. for Communications and Electronics, 1984-89; bd. dirs. Network Instrnl. TV, 1983-86; mem. Lincoln Inst. for Land Policy, Harvard U., 1985-93; mem. Intermodal Transp. Task Force, Intelligent Transp. Soc. of Am., 1995—; chmn. Aviation Consortium for Edn. and Tng., 1992—; 1996 Summer Olympics Transp. Atlanta Regional Commn., 1993—. Served to capt. U.S. Army, 1969-72. Fellow Acoustical Soc. Am. (engr. achievement of yr. award 1998); mem. Nat. Acad. Sci. (mem. adv. bd. high speed rail and ITS coms.), Am. Indsl. Hygiene Assn. (pres. Ga. chpt. 1973-74), Am. Nat. Standards Inst. (com. chair 1979-81), Am. Planning Assn. (pres. Ga. chpt. 1979-81), Am. Inst. Cert. Planners, Assn. Energy Engrs. (dir.), ASCE, Transp. Research Bd. (adv. coms. transp. edn., simulation, airport compatibility, acoustics), Nat. Trust Hist. Preservation, Sigma Xi, Omicron Delta Kappa, Kappa Alpha Order. Home: PO Box 263 Remsenburg NY 11960-0263 Office: Nat Aviation and Transp Ctr Oakdale NY 11769-1999

BRAGDON, KATHERINE MCCOY, urban planner, civilian military employee; b. Phila., May 22, 1968; d. Clifford Richardson and Sarah Jane (Vaughn) B. BA, Vanderbilt U., 1990; M in City Planning, Ga. Inst. Tech., 1993. Noise technician CR Bragdon & Assocs., Remsenburg, N.Y., 1990—; planning intern Natchez, Miss., 1992, Ga. Dept. Cmty. Affairs, Atlanta, 1992-93; planner Birmingham (Ala.) Regional Planning Commn., 1993-95; policy analyst Army Environ. Policy Inst., Atlanta, 1995—. Mem. econ., develop.coms. South Atlantans for Neighborhood Develop., 1996—, mem. Atlanta Code Enforcement Task Force, 1997—. Mem. Am. Inst. Cert. Planners, Am. Planning Assn., Ga. Planning Assn., Generation Green/Ga. Conservancy. Avocations: tennis, swimming, horse-back riding, writing. Office: Army Environ Policy Inst Ga Inst Tech S-206 430 10th St NW Atlanta GA 30318-5768

BRAGDON, PAUL ERROL, educator; b. Portland, Maine, Apr. 19, 1927; s. Errol Freemont and Edith Lillian (Somerville) B.; m. Nancy Ellen Horton, Aug. 14, 1954; children: David Lincoln, Susan Horton, Peter Jefferson. BA magna cum laude, Amherst Coll., 1950, DHL (hon.), 1980; JD, Yale U., 1953; LLD (hon.), Whitman Coll., 1985; DLitt. (hon.), Pacific U., 1988; DHL (hon.), Reed Coll., 1989. Bar: N.Y. 1954. With firm Dewey, Ballantine, Bushby, Palmer & Wood, N.Y.C., 1953-58, Javits, Trubin, Sillcocks, Edelman & Purcell, N.Y.C., 1961-64; counsel Tchrs. Ins. and Annuity Assn. Coll. Retirement Equities Fund, N.Y.C., 1958-61; asst. to mayor City of N.Y., 1964-65, exec. sec. to mayor, 1965, exec. asst. to pres. City Council, 1966-67; v.p. NYU, 1967-71; pres. Reed Coll., Portland, Oreg., 1971-88; pres. emeritus, 1988—; asst. for edn. to gov. State of Oreg., 1988-91; dir. Office Edn. Policy and Planning Oreg., 1990-91; pres. Med. Rsch. Found. Oreg., Portland, 1991-94, Oreg. Grad. Inst. Sci. and Tech., Portland, 1994-98. Trustee Amherst Coll., 1972-78, Multnomah (Oreg.) County Libr. Bd., 1994—, The Oreg. Garden, 1994—; The Libr. Found., Multnomah County, 1995—. Mem. Phi Beta Kappa, Phi Beta Kappa Assocs., Beta Theta Pi, Arlington Club, Univ. Club.

BRAGE, CARL WILLIS, genealogist; b. Darien, Conn., Apr. 17, 1930; s. Carl Wilhelm and Nellie Frances (Youngs) B.; m. Barbara Ann West, May 28, 1955; children: Jon Michael, James Arthur. B.Gen.Studies, U. N.H., 1975. Commd. USAF, various locations, 1948; advanced through grades to lt. col. USAF, ret. 1980; prof. genealogist PATH-Analysis, Portsmouth, N.H., 1980—; chmn. bd. dirs. Great Bay Svcs., Inc., 1995-98. Editor Kinship Kronicle Quar., 1983—, Genie Quar., 1983-90. Bd. dirs. Seacoast United Way, Portsmouth, 1980-86, pres., 1984-85; bd. dirs. Great Bay Svcs. Inc., Newington, N.H., 1984-98, chmn., 1996-99; pres. Portsmouth Hist. Soc., 1987-93; pres. N.H. Soc. Genealogists, 1984-86; founder, bd. dirs., pres. Portsmouth Crimeline, 1981-85; incorporator Mark Wentworth Nursing Home, 1993—. Decorated Bronze Star, Air Force Commendation medal, Meritorious Svc. medal with one cluster, Air medal with two clusters. Mem. New Eng. Hist. Genealogy Soc., N.H. Hist. Soc., Rockingham Soc. Genealogists, Conn. Geneal. Soc., Rotary (asst. sec. 1985-88, sec. 1990—). Republican. Lutheran. Avocation: history. Home and Office: 495 Sagamore Ave Portsmouth NH 03801-5531

BRAGENZER, JUNE ANNA RUTH GRIMM, community health nurse; b. Detroit, July 21, 1923; d. Arthur John and Ruth Irene (Hamilton) Voss; m Ernest W. Grimm (dec. 1982); children: Betty Gondeck West, Cheryl Davis, Peggy Toth, Linda; m. Fred C. Bragenzer, June 30, 1985. Diploma, Evang. Deaconess Hosp., 1944; BSN, U. Mich., 1980; postgrad., Wayne State U., 1974, 75, 78-79, U. Mich., 1980-81. RN, Mich. Charge nurse Dana Corp., Riverview, Mich., 1969-70; supervisory care nurse Enrico Fermi II/Detroit Edison, Monroe, Mich., 1970-76; relief nurse McCords Stamping Plant, Wyandotte, Mich., 1983-86, ret., 1986. With N.C., U.S. Army, 1943-44. Mem. ANA, Am. Assn. Occupational Health Nurses (cert. specialist), Mich. Assn. Occupational Health Nurses, Sigma Theta Tau.

BRAGER, WALTER S., retired food products corporation executive; b. Kewaunee, Wis., Oct. 20, 1925; s. Walter and Rose (Dorner) B.; m. Lois Jean Park, May 31, 1952; children: Kimberly Ann Brager Erickson, James C., Todd J. BSMechE, U. Wis., 1950, MBA, 1951; cert. exec. devel., Cornell U., 1960. Indsl. engring. mgmt. Oscar Mayer & Co., Madison, Wis., 1951-66; corp. ops. mgr. Oscar Mayer & Co., Madison, 1966-71, v.p. East Cen. region, 1971-74, v.p. East Cen. and S.W. regions, 1974-77, v.p. regional mgmt., 1977-78, group v.p. regional mgmt. and ops., 1978, group v.p. regional mgmt., ops. and engring., 1978-80, group v.p. ops. and engring., 1980-85; exec. v.p. Oscar Mayer Foods Corp., Madison, 1985-88, also bd. dirs. Chmn. Edgewood High Sch. Adv. Bd., Madison, 1968-71; pres., bd. dirs.

Wis. AgriBus. Coun., Madison, 1971-75; mem. United Way Dane County, div. chmn., 1972-74; mem. United Madison Community Found., chmn., 1981, bd. dirs., 1974-81; mem. indsl. liaison coun. U. Wis. Coll. Engring., 1980-87. With USAF, 1943-46. Recipient Disting. Svc. award U. Wis. Coll. Engring., 1979. Mem. Wis. Mfrs. and Commerce Assn. (bd. dirs., exec. com. 1977-79), Madison C. of C. (bd. dirs., v.p. 1971-74), Bascom Hill Soc. Republican. Roman Catholic. Clubs: Madison, Nakoma Country (bd. dirs. 1969-72) (Madison); Maple Bluff Country, Lakeway Yacht and Country, The Hills of Lakeway. Home and Office: 31 Hedgebrook Way Austin TX 78738-1319 also: Oscar Mayer Foods Corp PO Box 7188 Madison WI 53707-7188

BRAGG, ALBERT FORSEY, retired airline captain; b. Providence, Oct. 25, 1932; s. Horatio Frederick Roy and Olive Lavinia (Bardsley) B.; m. Anne Dana Bernard, Mar. 22, 1955 (div. 1977); children: Steven Keith, Gail Marie; m. Anita Bürki, Aug. 6, 1983. Student, Duke U., 1950-53. Lic. air transport pilot, flight engr., FAA. First officer-capt. N.Y. Airways, Inc., N.Y.C., 1959-64; flight ops. instr. United Air Lines, Denver, 1964-65; flight engr. United Air Lines, Chgo., 1965-66; co-pilot United Air Lines, N.Y.C., Denver, 1967-83; capt. United Air Lines, 1983-92; check airman United Air Lines, Denver, 1984-85, 86-89, flight check mgr., 1985-86; internat. capt. United Air Lines, N.Y.C., 1991-92; aerospace edn. officer Civil Air Patrol, Boonton, N.J., 1972-74, Denver, 1974-79; ret. United Air Lines, N.Y.C., 1992. Designer, builder dome for astronomic obs., Sheep Hill Obs., Boonton, N.J., 1973. Mem. sch. bd. Town of Boonton, 1972-75; active Colo. Motor Sports Coun. Comdr. USN, 1954-59. Recipient Life Saving award Civil Air Patrol, Denver, 1977, First place short take off contest Nat. Stearman Fly-In, Galesburg, Ill., 1992-94, 96-97. Mem. Exptl. Aircraft Assn. (safety lectr., tech. counselor Rocky Mountain Builder Forum, instr. Young Eagles program; v.p. chpt. 301 1995-97), Tail Hook Assn., Am. Navion Soc., Antique Aircraft Assn., Stearman Restorers Assn., Mercedes Benz Club (bd. dirs. 1989—, treas. 1992-94, pres. 1994-97, Mem. of Yr. 1991, Otto Saborsky award 1994, Officer of Yr. 1996), Ret. United Pilots Assn., Colo. Mus. Natural History, U.S. Coast Guard Sea Vets., The East Wind Assn. Republican. Avocations: building, restoring and flying sport, classic and antique aircraft, autoshow judge, track steward. Home: 10695 W Rowland Ave Littleton CO 80127-2941

BRAGG, DAVID GORDON, physician, radiology educator; b. Portland, Oreg., May 1, 1933; s. George Tully and Edith (Lee) B.; m. Marcia Robertson, Aug. 19, 1955; children: Eric Allan, Daniel Robert, James Tully, Anne Elizabeth. AB in History, Stanford U., 1955; MD, U. Oreg., 1959. Intern Phila. Gen. Hosp., 1959-60; resident in radiology Columbia-Presbyn. Med. Ctr., Coll. Physicians and Surgeons, N.Y.C., 1962-64, chief resident, 1964-65, instr., 1965-66; asst. prof. Cornell U. Med. Coll., N.Y.C., 1966-70, assoc. prof., 1970; chmn. diagnostic radiology Meml. Sloan-Kettering Cancer Ctr., N.Y.C., 1967-70; prof., chmn. dept. radiology U. Utah Med. Ctr., Salt Lake City, 1970-96; spl. asst. to dir., interim dir. Diagnostic Imaging Program Nat. Cancer Inst., 1996-97; cons. Salt Lake City VA Hosp., Meml. Sloan-Kettering Cancer Soc., 1970—; mem. Nat. Cancer Adv. Bd., 1988-94; trustee Am. Bd. Radiology; mem. bd. sci. advisors Nat. Cancer Inst., 1996—. Editor: Oncologic Imaging ; mem. editorial bds. Internat. Jour. Radiation Oncology, Biol. Physics, Current Problems in Diagnostic Radiology, Cancer. Recipient RSNA Centennial Fellow award, 1996-97. Mem. AMA, Assn. Univ. Radiologists (pres. 1980-81, Gold medal 1995), Soc. Chmn. Acad. Radiology Depts. (pres. 1979-80), Am. Soc. Therapeutic Therapists Radiology and Oncology (hon.), Radiol. Soc. N.Am., Soc. for Cancer Imaging (founder), Am. Roentgen Ray Soc. (Gold Medal Achievement award 1997). Home: 10040 E Happy Valley Rd Scottsdale AZ 85255-2395

BRAGG, LYNN MUNROE, federal agency administrator; b. Ft. Leonard Wood, Mo., June 15, 1954; d. Irving William and Elaine Frances (Heath) Munroe; m. Raymond Frank Bragg, Jr., Aug. 12, 1989; children: Hudson, Rachael, Braxton. BA in English, Mary Washington Coll., 1976; MS in Pub. Rels., Boston U., 1978. Speech and fin. writer Potomac Electric Power Co., Washington, 1978-80; legis. dir., legis. asst. Office of U.S. Senator Malcolm Wallop, Washington, 1981-91; dir. govtl. affairs Edison Electric Inst., Washington, 1991-94; commr. U.S. Internat. Trade Commn., Washington, 1994—, vice chmn., 1996-98, chmn., 1998—. Republican. Episcopalian. Avocation: golf. Office: US Internat Trade Commn 500 E St SW Washington DC 20024-2760*

BRAGG, MICHAEL ELLIS, lawyer, insurance company executive; b. Holdrege, Nebr., Oct. 6, 1947; s. Lionel C. and Frances E. (Klinginsmith) B.; m. Nancy Jo Aabel, Jan. 19, 1980; children: Brian Michael, Kyle Christopher, Jeffrey Douglas. BA, U. Nebr., 1971, JD, 1975. Bar: Alaska 1976, Nebr. 1976. CLU, ChFC, CPCU. Assoc. White & Jones, Anchorage, 1976-77; field rep. State Farm Ins., Anchorage, 1977-79; atty. corp. law dept. State Farm Ins., Bloomington, Ill., 1979-81, sr. atty., 1981-84, asst. counsel, 1984-86, counsel, 1986-88; asst. v.p., counsel gen. claims dept. State Farm Fire and Casualty Co., Bloomington, 1988-94; v.p., counsel, gen. claims dept. State Farm Ins. Cos., Bloomington, Ill., 1994-97, assoc. gen. counsel corp. law dept., 1997—; lectr., contbr. legal seminars. Contbr. and editor of articles to legal and ins. jours. Pres. McLean County Crime Detection Network, 1988-95. With USNG, 1970-76. Recipient Disting. Legal Svc. award Corp. Legal Times, 1998. Mem. ABA (various offices tort and ins. practices sect. including chmn. ins. coverage litigation com. 1991-92, vice chmn. property ins. law com. 1986-91), Am. Corp. Counsel Assn., Def. Rsch. Inst., Fedn. Ins. and Corp. Counsel (chair industry coop. sect. 1995-97), Crestwicke Country Club. Republican. Avocations: golf, tennis. Office: State Farm Ins Cos Assoc Gen Counsel One State Farm Plz E-7 Bloomington IL 61710

BRAGG, ROBERT HENRY, physicist, educator; b. Jacksonville, Fla., Aug. 11, 1919; s. Robert Henry and Lilly Camille (McFarland) B.; m. Violette Mattie McDonald, June 14, 1947; children: Robert Henry, Pamela. BS, Ill. Inst. Tech., 1949, MS, 1951, PhD, 1960. Assoc. physicist rsch. lab. Portland Cement Assn., Skokie, Ill., 1951-56; sr. physicist physics div. Armour Rsch. Found. Ill. Inst. Tech., Chgo., 1956-61; sr. mem., mgr. phys. metallurgy dept. Lockheed Palo Alto Rsch. Lab., Palo Alto, Calif., 1961-69; prof. materials sci. U. Calif., Berkeley, 1969-87, chmn. dept. materials sci. and mineral engring., 1978-81, prof. emeritus, 1987—; faculty sr. scientist Lawrence Berkeley Lab., 1969-87, emeritus 1987—; mem. materials rsch. adv. com. NSF, 1982-86; program dir. div. materials rsch. U.S. Dept. Energy, 1981-82; cons. IBM, Siemens-Allis, NASA, NIH, NSF, NRC; vis. prof. Musashi Inst. of Tech., Tokyo, 1989; del. 2d Edward Bouchet Internat. Conf., Accra, Ghana, 1990. Contbr. articles to profl. jours. Pres. Palo Alto NAACP, 1967-68. With U.S. Army, 1943-46. Decorated Bronze star (2); recipient Disting. award No. Calif. sect. Am. Inst. Mining and Metall. Engrs., 1970; J. William Fulbright rsch. fellow, Nigeria, 1992-93. Fellow Nat. Soc. of Black Physicists; mem. AAUP, AAAS, Am. Phys. Soc., Am. Ceramics Soc. (chmn. No. Calif. sect. 1980), AIME (chmn. No. Calif. sect. 1970), Am. Carbon Soc., Am. Soc. Metals, No. Calif. Coun. Black Profl. Engrs., Nat. Tech. Assn., Sigma Xi, Tau Beta Pi, Sigma Pi Sigma., Am. Crystallographic Assn. Democrat. Home: 2 Admiral Dr Ste 373 Emeryville CA 94608-1502 Office: U Calif Dept Materials Sci Min Berkeley CA 94720

BRAGG, WILLIAM DAVID, film producer, screenwriter; b. Phila., Sept. 13, 1962; s. D. Gordon and Shirley Marie (Dutcher) B.; m. Kathleen Rose Dressler, Dec. 24, 1980; children: Amanda Lee, Holly Christine, William David, Joseph Edward, Jeff Allen. Student, Mastbaum Area Vocat. Tech. Sch, Phila., 1977-80, The Learning Annex, N.Y.C., 1987. Ind. agt. Mr. Bear Enterprises, North Brunswick, N.J., 1987-89; founder, adminstrv. consul Out House Prodns., Inc., North Brunswick, 1988-90, exec. producer spl. projects, 1989-90, pres., chief exec. officer, 1989—. Producer/screenwriter film Sugar Mountain, 1990; screenwriter films including Army/Navy Games, 1976, Witch Way to Salem, 1977, Skitso, 1986, Babywolf of Manville, 1986, Free, 1989; plays include The Christmas Dog, 1978, Mandi's Room, 1979; author children's series The Adventures of Fat One, 1970. Tng. specialist Raritan Valley workshop Easter Seals, North Brunswick, 1989-90. Recipient Multi-Svc. Rd. Vehicle Triple A award (Driver of Yr., 1995. Mem. SAG (signatory), Am. Film Inst., Internat. Soc. Dramatists. Methodist Christian. Avocations: soccer, softball, rock and roll music, family activities. Office: Jorgenson & Barnes 33 Wood Ave S Iselin NJ 08830-2719

BRAGGER, STACEY EILEEN, elementary education educator; b. Syracuse, N.y., Mar. 27, 1972; d. Robert Nolan and Barbara Elizabeth Bragger. BS, SUNY, Cortland, 1994, MS, 1997. Provisional cert. for tchg., N.Y. Substitute tchr. Skaneateles (N.Y.) CSD, 1994-97, Jordan (N.Y.) Elbridge (N.Y.) CSD, 1994-97, Marcellus (N.Y.) Ctrl. Sch. Dist., 1994-97; K-8 computer tchr. St. Joseph's Sch., Auburn, N.Y., 1996-97; tchr. grade 3 St. Joseph's Sch., Auburn, 1997—; mem. dean search com. SUNY, Cortland, 1997; policy bd. mem. Tchr. Ctr. in Cayuga County, Auburn, 1998—. Mem. ASCD, Coun. for Elem. Sci. Internat. Avocations: reading, writing, walking dog, hiking. E-mail: steile@aol.com. Home: Apt W 28 1/2 E Main St Marcellus NY 13108 Office: St Josephs Sch 101 E Genesee St Auburn NY 13021

BRAGMAN, MICHAEL J., state legislator; b. Cicero, N.Y., Aug. 11, 1940; m. Suzanne M. Collier; children: Michael J. Jr., (twins) Heather, Leslie. BA, Syracuse U., 1963. Mem. N.Y. State Assembly, Albany, 1980—, majority leader, also ex officio mem. standing coms., 1993—; mem. dist. 3 Onondaga County Legislature, 1969-81, minority leader, 1972-75, chmn., 1978-79; former chmn. transp., agr., vol. firefighters and wildlife mgmt. coms., former mem. environ. conservation, local govts., tourism, arts and sports devel., edn., and rules coms., chmn. Dem. campaign com., 1990-92. Chmn. Cicero Dem. Com., 1965-68; del. Dem. Nat. Conv., 1976, 84, 92, 96. Recipient Cmty. Team Spirit award Salvation Army, lifetime achievement award Empire Friends N.Y. Libr. Assn., Citizen of Yr. award Vietnam Vets. Am., legis. award NY. State Conf. Mayors; named to N.Y. State Outdoorsmen Hall of Fame. Mem. Marine Corps League, Vietnam Vets. Am. Office: 305 S Main St North Syracuse NY 13212

BRAHA, THOMAS I., business executive; b. Austin, Tex., Sept. 3, 1947; s. Jacob and Valentine (Capone) B.; m. Nancy Elizabeth Rowe, Mar. 31, 1973 (div.); children: Nancy Elizabeth, Jeanne Valentine, Travis Ian. BSME, U. Tex., 1969; MBA, Temple U., 1971; postgrad., NYU, 1971-73. Engr. Davis Electronics, Inc., Austin, 1967, Whirlpool Corp., Evansville, Ind., 1968; project engr. ITE Imperial Corp., Phila., 1969-71; sr. supply analyst Mobil Oil Corp., N.Y.C., 1971-74; pres. Western Hemisphere Bulk Oil (U.S.A.), Inc., N.Y.C., 1974-75; pres., CEO Braha Holding Corp., Braha Oil Corp. and Subs., Braha Estates, Inc., Braha Farms, Braha Profit and Pension Trusts; lectr. The Wharton Sch., U. Pa., 1997. Active Bryn Mawr Presbyn. Ch. Mem. ASME, Am. Mgmt. Assn., Am. Petroleum Inst., Inst. Petroleum (U.K.), Nat. Petroleum Refining Assn., Phila. Country Club. Office: Braha Holding Co PO Box 787 Bryn Mawr PA 19010-0787

BRAHAM, DELPHINE DORIS, government accountant; b. L'Anse, Mich., Mar. 16, 1946; d. Richard Andrew and Viola Mary Aho; m. John Emerson Braham, Sept. 23, 1967 j(div. Dec. 1987); children: Tammy, Debra, John Jr. BS summa cum laude, Drury Coll., 1983; M in Mgmt., Webster U., St. Louis, 1986. Bookkeeper Cmty. Mental Health Ctr., Marquette, Mich., 1966-68; acctg. technician St. Joseph Hosp., Parkersburg, W.Va., 1972-74; material mgr. U.S. Army, Ft. Leonard Wood, Mo., 1982-86; acct., 1986-92; supervisory acct. Dept. Def. Indpls., 1992—; instr., adj. faculty Columbia Coll., 1987-92, Park Coll., 1988-92. Leader Girl Scouts U.S., Williamstown, W.Va., 1972-74, Hanau, Germany, 1977-79. Mem. AAUW (treas. Waynesville br. 1986-90), Am. Soc. Mil. Comptrs., NAFE, Assn. Govt. Accts., Waynesville Bus. and Profl. Women's Orgn. Home: 2752 Pawnee Dr Indianapolis IN 46229-1418

BRAHAM, RANDOLPH LEWIS, political science educator; b. Bucharest, Romania, Dec. 20, 1922; came to U.S., 1948, naturalized, 1953; m. Elizabeth Sommer, Dec. 15, 1954; children: Steven, Robert. B.A., CCNY, 1948, M.S., 1949; Ph.D., New Sch. for Social Research, 1952. Research assoc. YIVO-Inst. for Jewish Research, N.Y.C., 1954-59; faculty CCNY, N.Y.C., 1959—; prof. polit. sci. CCNY, 1971—, disting. prof., 1987—, disting. prof. emeritus, 1992—, chmn. dept. polit. sci., 1971-81; dir. Inst. for Holocaust Studies, Grad. Ctr. CUNY, 1980—; faculty Fairleigh Dickinson U., Hofstra U., Hunter Coll., 1956-59. Author: The Politics of Genocide, 2 vols., 1981, 2d rev. edit., 1994, The Hungarian Labor Service System, 1977, Hungarian Jewish Studies, 3 vols., 1966-73, Soviet Government and Politics, 1965, Human Rights, 1979; writer, editor, contbr. to books in field. Democrat. Home: 11407 Union Tpke Flushing NY 11375-6850 Office: CUNY Graduate Ctr New York NY 10036

BRAHMBHATT, SUDHIRKUMAR, chemical company executive; b. Dabhoi, Gujarat, India, Apr. 4, 1951; came to U.S., 1973; s. Ramanlal Kalidas and Kamalaben Motilal Barot Brahmbhatt; m. Ashaben Amarsingh, May 22, 1977; children: Tejal Sudhirkumar, Nisha Sudhirkumar. B in Chem. Engring., Nadiad Inst. Tech., India, 1973; M in Chem. Engring., Steven Inst. Tech., 1975; MBA in Internat. Mgmt. and Mktg., Fairleigh Dickinson U., 1982; PhD in Chem. Engring., Kennedy Western U., 1991. Rsch. asst. Stevens Inst. Tech., Hoboken, N.J., 1975-77; chem. engr. Exxon Co. U.S.A., Linden, N.J., 1977-79; sr. process engr. Air Products and Chemicals, Inc., Allentown, Pa., 1979-84; applications engr. MG Industries div. of Hoechst, Valley Forge, Pa., 1984-87, sr. project engr., 1987-89, mgr. chems. group, 1989-92, head R&D dept., 1992-96; owner Ashutej Co., Trexlertown, Pa., 1982-84; mgr. chem. group MG Industries div. of Hoechst, Valley Forge, 1996-98, team leader global pulp and paper tech., 1996—, dir. techs. and global R&D, 1998—; owner Ashutej Co., Trexlertown, Pa., 1982-84; pres., founder Bal Vihar Sch. , St. Louis, 1992—. Patentee in environ. and chem. engring. fields; contbr. articles to profl. jours. Dir., host radio program Music of India, WMUH, Allentown, 1981-91, KDHX, St. Louis, 1992—; pres. Exxon Volleyball League, Linden, 1978-79; pres. Bal Vihar Assn., Hindu Temple Soc., Allentown, Pa., 1989-91; founder, pres. Bal Vihar (Children's Ethnic Sch.) of St. Louis, 1992—; pres.-elect Lafayette High Sch. Orch. Parents Assn., Ballwin, Mo. Recipient Merit cert. Poly-Olefins Industries Ltd., Bombay, India, 1972. Mem. AIChE, TAPPI, Am. Powder Metallurgy Inst. (chmn. Phila. sec. 1987-88), Am. Chem. Soc., Am. Ceramic Soc., Am. Soc. Metals. Avocations: cultural programs, radio, overseas travel. Home: 1700 Countrytop Ct Glencoe MO 63038-1446 Office: MG Industries 6 Research Park Dr Saint Charles MO 63304-5602

BRAHMS, THOMAS WALTER, engineering institute executive; b. Brookline, Mass., Mar. 12, 1945; s. Samuel David and Barbara Ann (Robinson) B.; m. Virginia Wahlen, Dec. 30, 1966; children—Theodore S., Anna Elisabeth. B.S. in Civil Engring, Northeastern U., 1971. Transp. planner Boston Redevel. Authority, 1965-69; sr. traffic engr. aide, traffic and parking dept. Town of Brookline, 1970-71; project engr. (traffic) Tippetts, Abbett, McCarthy & Stratton, Brookline, 1971-73; dir. tech. affairs Inst. Transp. Engrs., Arlington, Va., 1973-76; exec. dir. Inst. Transp. Engrs., 1976—; mini-bus officer Reston Commuter Bus, Inc., Va., 1973-76, 77; v.p. Reston Commuter Bus, Inc., 1976-77, 78-79, pres., 1979; v.p. Ward Six Civic Assn., West Somerville, Mass., 1972-73; bd. dirs. Reston Internal Bus System, 1977. Pres. Fairway Cluster Assn., Reston, 1973-75; coach Reston Soccer Assn., 1975-76; mem. Reston Homeowners Assn. Archtl. Bd. Rev., 1977; rep. Transp. Research Bd., 1976—; sec. Theodore M. Matson Meml. Award Com., 1974—; trustee Transp. Mus., Boston, 1981-84; mem. tech. edn. adv. coun. Fairfax County, 1990-93; sec. Intelligent Vehicle Hwy. Soc. Am., 1991-92, dir., 1991—; bd. regents Eno Ctr. for Transp. Leadership Devel., 1992—. Recipient Burton W. Marsh award for Disting. Svc. Inst. Transportation Engrs., 1988, Adminstr.'s award for outstanding svc. Urban Mass Transp. Adminstrn., U.S. Dept. Transp., 1988. Fellow Inst. Transp Engrs.; mem. ASCE, Coun. Engring. and Sci. Soc. Execs., Am. Soc. Assn. Execs., Rd. Gang, World Interchange Network (bd. dirs. 1995—), Roadway Safety Found. (rsch. subcom. 1995—), ITS World Congress (bd. dirs.), ITS Am. (bd. dirs. 1992-96). Office: 525 School St SW Washington DC 20024-2729*

BRAHNEY, THOMAS J., III, federal judge; b. 1936. LLB, Loyola U., New Orleans, 1963. Chief bankruptcy judge U.S. Dist. Ct. (ea. dist.) La., New Orleans, 1963—. Fax: (504) 589-7390. Office: US Dist Ct (ea dist) La 601 Hale Boggs Bldg 501 Magazine St New Orleans LA 70130

BRAIBANTI, RALPH JOHN, political scientist, educator; b. Danbury, Conn., June 29, 1920; s. Daniel Vincent and Jane Helena B.; m. Lucy Kauffman, Feb. 19, 1943; children—Claire, Ralph Lynn. B.S., Western Conn. State U., 1941, LHD (hon.), 1995; A.M., Syracuse U., 1947, Ph.D., 1949. Asst. prof. polit. sci. Kenyon Coll., 1949-52, assoc. prof., 1952-53; asst. dir. Am. Polit. Sci. Assn., Washington, 1950-51; cons. Govtl. Affairs Inst., 1950-51; assoc. prof. polit. sci. Duke U., Durham, N.C., 1953-58; prof. Duke U., 1958-68, James B. Duke prof. polit. sci., 1968-90, James B. Duke prof. emeritus, 1990—; dir. Islamic and Arabian devel. studies, 1977-89; scholar-in-residence Rockefeller Found., Bellagio Ctr., Italy, 1967; cons. AID, 1958-59, Ford Found., 1972, UN, 1974, Govt. Saudi Arabia, 1974—, UNESCO, 1977, Islamic Secretariat, 1980, World Bank, 1987; vis. prof. U. Kuwait, 1984; advisor on adminstrv. reform Pakistan, Malaysia, South Africa, Lebanon, Morocco, Saudi Arabia, Bangladesh; cons.; bd. advisors Nat. Coun. U.S.-Arab Rels., Moroccan-Am. Found., Mid East Policy Coun.; trustee Am. Inst. Pakistan Studies, Am. Inst. Yemeni Studies; bd. dirs. U.S. Mid-East Performing Arts Coun., 1995—; chmn. nat. selection com. Joseph J. Malone Postdoctoral Fellowships in Arabian Affairs; King Faisal Disting. Internat. lectr. Am.-Arab Affairs Coun., 1989—; mem. internat. adv. com. Global Forum of Spiritual and Parliamentary Leaders on Human Survival, 1996—. Author: Research on the Bureaucracy of Pakistan, 1966, The Nature and Structure of the Islamic World, 1995, Chief Justice Cornelius of Pakistan: Analysis, Letters, Speeches, 1999; co-author, editor: Political and Administrative Development, 1969, Pakistan: The Long View, 1976, Asian Bureaucratic Systems Emergent from the British Imperial Tradition, 1966, Tradition, Values and Socio-Economic Development, 1961, Administration and Economic Development in India, 1963, Evolution of Pakistan's Administrative System: The Collected Papers of Ralph Braibanti, 1987; gen. editor 7 vol. series on comparative adminstrn., 1968-73; bd. editors Arab Affairs, Jour. South Asian and Mid. Ea. Studies, Comparative Politics, Politikon, Asian Forum, Jour. Pakistan Studies, Internat. Jour. Islamic and Arabic Studies. Served to capt. U.S. Army, 1942-47. Recipient citation outstanding prof. Duke Student Assn., 1972, alumni award disting. undergrad. teaching, 1979; Maxwell fellow Syracuse U., 1949, Ford Found. fellow, 1955-56, Social Sci. Rsch. Coun. fellow, 1955-56; decorated commendation medal U.S. Army, 1947. Fellow Internat. Assn. Mid. Ea. Studies (mem. exec. com. 1991—); mem. Internat. Studies Assn.-South (pres.), Am. Inst. Pakistan Studies (founding pres. 1975-77, pres. 1986-90), Internat. Cultural Soc. Korea (hon.), Am. Council for Study Islamic Socs. (bd. dirs.). Home and Office: 3805 Darby Rd Durham NC 27707-5004 *The encouragement of a profound understanding of seemingly divergent cultural systems is of critical importance. This must embrace helping newly-developed political systems appreciate their own cultural values. Only the strength of such pride can withstand the dynamic interventionism which characterizes the relations of transitorily dominant superpowers and weak, newer political entities.*

BRAICO, CARMELLA ELIZABETH LOFRANO, clergy member; b. Chgo., Oct. 15, 1947; d. Anthony Alexander and Margarita A. (Cracco) Lofrano; 1 child, Kamie Lynn Plys. Student, Thornton C.C., 1972-76; BA magna cum laude, Elmhurst Coll., 1983; MDiv, Eden Theol. Sem., 1987. Ordained to ministry, United Ch. of Christ. Preacher Trinity United Ch. of Christ, Fayetteville, Ill., 1984; chaplain Good Samaritan Home for the Aged, St. Louis, 1983-84; youth minister Evangelical United Ch. of Christ, St. Louis, 1984-85; student minister Kirkwood (Mo.) United Ch. of Christ, 1985-87, Faith Presbyn. Ch., DesPeres, Mo., 1985-87; solo pastor First Congl. United Ch. of Christ, LaSalle, Ill., 1987-93, early ret., 1993; former pres. Clergy Coun. Ill. Valley. Contbr. poems to Dark Side of the Moon, 1994 (Editor's Choice award 1994), Best Poems of 1995 (Editor's Choice award 1995), Best Poems of 1996 (Editor's Choice award 1996), Best Poems of 1997. Former clergy coord. Hospice, St. Margaret's Hosp., Spring Valley, Ill.; past bd. dirs. Justice & Peace Network Ill.; former mem. missioner-in-residence com. No. Assn. United Ch. of Christ; mem. the church and higher edn. com. Elmhurst (Ill.) Coll.; founding mem., bd. dirs. SHARE Program, LaSalle County, Ill., The Excellence Found. LaSalle Sch. Dist.; bd. dirs. Cmty. Concert Series Ill. Valley; founder St. Paul Cmty. Players Theatrical Group, Homewood, Ill.; leader, preacher Heritage Manor Nursing Home, Peru, Ill.; leader Jr. Girl Scout Troop, Thornton, Ill.; founding bd. mem., sec. Thornridge Child Devel., Dolton, Ill. Lincoln scholar Elmhurst Coll., 1983. Mem. NAFE, Profl. Assn. Clergy, Internat. Soc. Poets (disting. mem. 1995), Acad. Am. Poets, Ill. Valley Newcomer's Club, LaSalle Federated Women's Club, Ill. Valley Christian Women's Club, The Women's Guild, Triple S Club, Evening Circle. Home: 314 Water St Thornton IL 60476-1165

BRAID, BERNICE, program director, dean; b. Oct. 18, 1933. BA with highest honors, UCLA, 1955, MA, 1957; PhD, Occidental Coll., 1965. Dir. univ. honors program Long Island U., Bklyn., 1967—, dean acad./instrnl. resourcces, 1988—. Mem. Nat. Collegiate Honors Coun. (mem. exec. com. 1976—, pres. 1979, chair honors semsters com. 1981—). E-mail: braid@liunet.edu.

BRAID, FREDERICK DONALD, lawyer; b. N.Y.C., Aug. 10, 1946; s. Donald Michael and Margaret Anna (Fluty) B.; m. Eleanor Mae Friedman, Oct. 23, 1980; children: Andrew Harris, Roy Leal, Josh Perry, David Barnett, Steven Gabriel. BS in Econs., St. John's U., Jamaica, N.Y., 1968; JD, St. John's U., Bklyn., 1971; LLM, NYU, 1979. Bar: N.Y. 1972, U.S. Dist. Ct. (so. and ea. dists.) N.Y. 1973, U.S. Ct. Appeals (2d cir.) 1973, (D.C. and 4th cirs.) 1997, U.S. Supreme Ct. 1975. Assoc. Rains & Pogrebin, Mineola and N.Y.C., N.Y., 1971-77, ptnr., 1978—; bd. dirs. Rains & Pogrebin, P.C., Mineola and N.Y.C., N.Y.; mem. adv. bd. NYU Sch. Law Ctr. for Labor and Employment Law, 1997—. Mng. editor St. John's Law Rev., 1970-71; contbr. articles to profl. jours. Served to capt. USAR, 1972-80. St. Thomas More scholar, St. John's U. Sch. Law, 1968-71. Mem. ABA, N.Y. Bar Assn., Assn. Trial Lawyers Am., Nassau County Bar Assn., Def. Rsch. Inst., Omicron Delta Epsilon, Delta Mu Delta. Home: 17 E 96th St New York NY 10128-0783 Office: Rains & Pogrebin PC 210 Old Country Rd Ste 12 Mineola NY 11501-4288

BRAIDE, ROBERT DAVID, broadcast executive; b. Montreal, Que., Can., Apr. 4, 1953; s. David and Janet Grace (Harbron) B.; children: Laura Victoria, Ian David. BA, U. Carleton, Ottawa, Ont., 1977. Music dir. CHOM-FM, Montreal, 1977-79; program dir. stas. CHOM & CKGM CHJM Ltd., Montreal, 1979-84, asst. mgr. sta. CHOM, 1984-87; v.p., gen. mgr. stas. CJAD & CJFM Standard Radio Inc., Montreal, 1987—. Dir. St. Mary's Hosp. Found., 1993, Saidye Bronfman Ctr. for Arts. Mem. Can. Assn. Rec. Arts and Scis. Avocations: downhill skiing, computers, formula auto racing. Office: Standard Radio Inc, 1411 Fort St, Montreal, PQ Canada H3H 2R1

BRAIDWOOD, ROBERT JOHN, archaeologist, educator; b. Detroit, July 29, 1907; s. Walter J. and Rhea (Nimmo) B.; m. Linda Schreiber, 1937; children: Gretel, Douglas. AB, U. Mich., 1932, AM, 1933; PhD, U. Chgo., 1942; ScD (hon.), U. Ind., 1971; Docteur (hon.), U. Sorbonne, Paris, 1975; LittD (hon.), U. Rome, 1984. Archeol. field work Iraq, Syria, Iran, Turkey, Ill., N.Mex., 1930—; faculty Oriental Inst., U. Chgo., 1933—, prof. Old World prehistory, 1954-76, prof. emeritus, 1976—; faculty U. Chgo., 1940—, prof. dept. anthropology, 1954-76, now emeritus.; vis. prof. Istanbul U., 1963-64. Recipient Frydell medal Soc. for Am. Archaeology, 1995. Fellow NAS, Am. Acad. Arts and Scis., Am. Philos. Soc., Soc. Antiquaries (London) (hon.); mem. Am. Anthrop. Assn. (exec. bd. 1962-64, disting. lectr. 1971), Internat. Union Pre-and-Protohistoric Scis. (former U.S. del. permanent council), Conf. Asian Archaeology-New Delhi (found. mem.); corr. mem. Deutsche Archaologische Institut, Académie des Inscriptions et Belles Lettres, Institut de France, Göteborgs Kungl. Vetenskaps och Vitterhets Samhalle, Istituto Italiano di Preistoria e Protostoria, Jysk Arkaeologist Selskab, Österreichsche Akademie der Wissenschaft. Office: U Chgo Oriental Institute Chicago IL 60637

BRAILEY, SUSAN LOUISE, quality analyst, educator; b. Omaha, Aug. 28, 1939; d. James Burt and Helen Frances (Skalak) B.; m. Hugh Pelham Whitt, Dec. 29, 1990. BS in Edn. with distinction, U. Nebr., Omaha, 1961; postgrad., U. Nebr., Lincoln, 1977-79; MA in Comm., U. Cin., 1970. Cert. quality analyst Quality Assurance Inst., Orlando, Fla. Instr., dir. debate Omaha Pub. Schs., 1965-67; tchr. Walnut Hills H.S., Cin., 1967-69, U. Cin., 1969-72, U. Nebr., Lincoln, 1978; dir. MIS Wayne (Nebr.) State Coll., 1979-80; sr. tech. writer, analyst 1st Data Resources, Omaha, 1981-82, supr. documentation, 1982-83, tng. specialist, 1983-85, sr. analyst quality assurance, 1988-92; tng. specialist Enron Corp., Omaha, 1985-86; sr. analyst quality assurance Enron Corp., Houston, 1986-88. Mem. Dem. Nat. Com., 1995—. Mem. AAUW, Nat. Coun. Tchrs. English, Planned Parenthood, Arthritis Found., Lupus Found. Am., Nat. Trust, Libr. of Congress, The Questers Internat., Pi Kappa Delta, Phi Delta Kappa, Phi Delta Gamma. Congregationalist. Avocations: reading, antiques, bridge, music, politics. Home: 9530 Davenport St Omaha NE 68114-3872

BRAIM, PAUL FRANCIS, history educator, writer; b. Phila., May 31, 1926; s. Paul Reed and Anna Kathryn (McAvoy) B.; m. Barbara Ann Redline, July 2, 1982 (div. Dec. 1990). AB, Shepherd Coll., 1949; MA, U. Del., 1956, PhD, 1983. Enlisted U.S. Army, 1943, advanced through grades to col., 1968, ret., 1977; pres. Mil. History and Strategy Inc., Daytona, Fla., 1980—; prof. history Embry-Riddle U., Daytona Beach, Fla., 1987-99; lectr. Army, Navy, and Air Force War Colls., 1966-99; strategic planner Offices of Joint Chiefs of Staff, Washington, 1970-74. Author: Revolutionary Warfare, 1966, The Test of Battle, 1998, The Will to Win, 1999, Fighting to Win, 1999; co-author: Military Heritage of America, 1992; editor: How to Defeat Saddam H., 1991. Decorated Silver Star with 2 oak leaf clusters, Bronze Star with 4 oak leaf clusters, Legion of Merit with 2 oak leaf clusters, D.F.C., Purple Heart with 2 oak leaf clusters. Mem. AAUP, The Strategic Inst., Assn. of U.S. Army, Ret. Officers Assn., Mil. Order World Wars. Republican. Avocation: hiking. Home: 121 Sweetwater Oaks Ln Daytona Beach FL 32114-1162 Office: Embry-Riddle Aero U Daytona Beach FL 32114

BRAIN, GEORGE BERNARD, university dean; b. Thorp, Wash., Apr. 25, 1920; s. George and Alice Pearl (Ellison) B.; m. Harriet Gardinier, Sept. 28, 1940; children—George Calvin, Marylou. B.A., Central Wash. State U., Ellensburg, 1946, M.A., 1949; Ed.D., Columbia Tchrs. Coll., 1957; postgrad., U. Wash., Wash. State U., Harvard U., U. Colo., Stanford U. Tchr. math. and sci. Yakima (Wash.) secondary schs., 1946-49; instr. Central Wash. State Coll., 1949-50; elementary sch. prin. Ellensburg, 1950-51; successively elementary sch. prin., asst. supt. schs., supt. schs. Bellevue, Wash., 1951-59; vis. prof. Central Wash. State Coll., 1953, Wash. State U., 1959, U. Md., 1964; supt. schs. Balt., 1959-66; dean Coll. Edn., also dir. summer schs. Wash. State U., Pullman, 1965-85; fellow Danforth Found., 1986—; lectr. Columbia, U. Conn., Harvard, U. Ga., U. Del., Johns Hopkins, Morgan U., U. Okla., Towson State U., Stanford, Wash. U.; chmn. Fulbright Group Western European Seminar Comparative Edn., 1959; chmn. ednl. policies commn. N.E.A.; ednl. cons. (Office Edn.), 1962—; cons. Ednl. Testing Service, Princeton, N.J., 1964-67; dir. Intext Pub. Inc., Scranton, Pa., Worldbook-Childcraft (Scott-Fetzer); bd. dirs. Md. Acad. Sci., 1960-65, Nat. Edn. Found., Field Enterprises Ednl. Corp., 1970—, Pacific Am. Inst., 1977—. Mem. editorial adv. bd.: Scholastics Publs, 1963—, Am. Sch. and Univ, 1960-64, Education, USA, 1964-71; mem. editorial bd.: World Book, 1966—, Jour. Tchr. Edn, 1966—. Served with USNR, 1941- 42; Served with USMCR, 1942-46; maj. lt. col. Res. Recipient Disting. Svc. award Wash. State Jr. Assn. Commerce, 1956, Disting. Svc. award in edn. NCCJ, 1963, Disting. Alumnus award Cen. Wash. U., 1989; named Man of Year Met. Civic Assn. Balt., 1962; Fulbright scholar, 1959; library named in his honor, Wash. State U., 1987. Life mem. Am. Assn. Sch. Adminstrs. (exec. com. 1964-66, pres. 1965), NEA; hon. life mem. Wash. State Assn. Sch. Adminstrs. (pres. 1959), Md. Assn. Sch. Adminstrs., Nat. Congress P.T.A.; mem. Wash. Edn. Assn. (pres. dept. adminstrn. and supervision 1957), AAAS (exec. com. commn. elementary and secondary sci. 1963-66), Assn. Supervision and Curriculum Devel., Univ. Council Ednl. Adminstrn., Nat. Joint Council Econ. Edn. (exec. com. 1963—), Nat. Conf. Profs. Ednl. Adminstrn., AAUP, Internat. Platform Assn., Nat. Council for Edn. in Health Professions, Nat. Acad. Sch. Execs., Nat. Council Fgn. Study League, Exec. Hall Fame, Phi Delta Kappa, Kappa Delta Pi. Presbyterian. Lodge: Rotary (dir. Balt. 1964-65).

BRAIN, JOSEPH DAVID, biomedical scientist; b. Paterson, N.J., Jan. 20, 1940; married, 1961; 3 children. SM, Harvard U., 1962, SMHyg, 1963, SDHyg, 1966. Rsch. assoc. in physiology Harvard U., Boston, 1966-68, from asst. prof. to assoc. prof., 1968-78; prof. physiology Harvard Sch. Pub. Health, Cambridge, Mass., 1978—, Cecil K. and Philip Drinker prof. environ. physiology, dir. Harvard Pulmonary Specialized Ctr. Rsch., 1977-96; dir. respirtory biol. program Harvard Sch. Pub. Health, Cambridge, 1981-93; dir. physiology program Harvard Sch. Pub. Health, Cambridge, Mass., 1993—, chair dept. environ. health, 1990—; mem. com. Cardiovasc. and Pulmonary Study Sect. NIH, 1975-79, program project rsch. rev. com. Nat. Heart, Lung and Blood Inst., 1980-83; bd. sci. counsellors Nat. Inst. Occupl. Safety and Health, 1992-96. Bd. trustees Taylor U., 1984—. Fellow AAAS, Am. Physiol. Soc., Am. Thoracic Soc., Reticuloendothelial Soc., Sigma Xi. Office: Harvard U Sch Pub Health 665 Huntington Ave Boston MA 02115-6021*

BRAINARD, PAUL HENRY, musicologist, retired music educator; b. Binghamton, N.Y., Apr. 18, 1928; s. George E. and Frances (Weinhauer) B. BA, U. Rochester, 1949, MA, 1951; postgrad., Heidelberg (Germany) U., 1954; PhD, Goettingen (Germany) U., 1960. Research asst. Deutsches Musikgeschichtliches Archiv, Kassel, Germany, 1960; instr. music Ohio State U., 1960-61; faculty Brandeis U., Waltham, Mass., 1961-81, prof. music, 1974-81, chmn. Sch. Creative Arts, 1965-68, chmn. dept. music, 1969-72, 75-77; prof. music Princeton (N.J.) U., 1981-87, Yale Inst. Sacred Music, 1987-93; ret., 1993; spl. research music history. Author: Le sonate per violino di Giuseppe Tartini, 1975; editor: Neue Bach-Ausgabe, Vols. II/7, 1977, II/8, 1979, I/16, 1981, Cantatas, Easter and Ascension Oratorios, Italienische Violinmusik der Barockzeit, Vols. I, 1987, II, 1988; contbr. articles to profl. jours. Served with AUS, 1951-53. Home: 7 Dover Dr Englewood FL 34223-4637

BRAINARD, WILLIAM CRITTENDEN, economist, educator, university official; b. Jersey City, July 2, 1935; s. William E. and Eleanor (Holston) B.; m. Ellen Rawlings, Oct. 18, 1958; children: David, Michael, Daniel. B.A., Oberlin Coll., 1957; M.A., Yale U., 1959, Ph.D., 1963. Asst. prof. econs. Yale U., 1962-66, assoc. prof., 1966-69, prof., 1969—, provost, 1981-86, chmn. econs. dept., 1992-97; research assoc. Brookings Instn., 1965-66; dir. Cowles Found., New Haven, 1971-73, 76-81, chmn. dept. econs., 1992-97; chmn. Fed. Reserve Bank, Boston, 1997—. Editor: Brookings Papers on Econ. Activity, 1980—; contbr. articles to profl. jours. Fellow Econometric Soc.; mem. Am. Econ. Assn. Home: 207 Everit St New Haven CT 06511-1335 Office: Yale U Dept Econs PO Box 208268 New Haven CT 06520-8268

BRAINERD, CHARLES J(ON), experimental psychologist, applied mathematician, educator; b. Lansing, Mich., July 30, 1944; emigrated to Can., 1971; s. Charles Donald and Geraldine Elaine (Leffler) B.; m. Susan Haske, Jan. 18, 1964 (div.); 1 dau., Tereasa Gail; m. Valerie Reyna, Oct. 5, 1985; 1 son, Bertrand. B.S., Mich. State U., 1966, M.A., 1968, Ph.D., 1970. Asst. prof. psychology U. Alta., Edmonton, Can., 1971-73, assoc. prof., 1973-76, H.M. Tory prof. social sci., 1983-86; prof. U. Western Ont., London, 1976-83, U. Ariz., Tucson, 1987—; vis. prof. U. Minn., Mpls., 1980-81, So. Meth. U., Dallas, 1986-87. Author: Piaget's Theory of Intelligence, 1978, Origins of the Number Concept, 1979; editor: Alternatives to Piaget, 1978, Recent Advances in Cognitive-Developmental Theory, 1983, Springer-Verlag Series in Cognitive Development, 1979—; assoc. editor: Behavioral and Brain Scis., 1980—. Fellow Am. Psychol. Assn., Can. Psychol. Assn. (pres. devel. psychology sect. 1986-87); mem. Psychonomic Soc., Soc. for Research in Child Devel. (assoc. editor Child Devel. 1977-80). Office: U Ariz Coll Edn Tucson AZ 85721

BRAINERD, MICHAEL CHARLES, international exchange organization executive; b. Gatesville, Tex., Apr. 15, 1943; s. Perley Charles and Muriel Eva (Hutchinson) B. AB, Hamilton Coll., 1965; PhD, Columbia U., 1976. Asst. prof. Middlebury (Vt.) Coll., 1974-78; cons. The College Bd., N.Y.C., 1978-79; exec. dir. Citizen Exch. Corps, N.Y.C., 1979-81; pres. CEC Internat. Ptnrs., Inc., N.Y.C., 1981—; host/narrator PBS documentary series: The Glasnost Film Festival, 1991. Editor: Spacebridges: Television and U.S.-Soviet Dialog, 1989. Mem. Alliance for Internat. Edn. and Cultural Exch. Office: CEC International Partners 12 W 31st St # 400 New York NY 10001-4415

BRAINERD, RICHARD CHARLES, human resources executive, consultant, educator; b. L.A., Dec. 22, 1944; s. Calvin Richard and Charlotte Louise (Roethe) B.; m. Phyllis Jean Cottingham Wentzel, July 14, 1966, (div. Dec. 1980); children: Bret, Staci; m. Mary Keith Knopp, Mar. 31, 1984; children: Andrew, Mary Angela. BS in Bus. and Econs., U. Wis., 1968; grad. leadership devel. program, Ctr. for Creative Leadership, Greensboro, N.C., 1985. Pers. analyst Wis. Bur. Personnel, Madison, 1968-74; dir. pers., asst. adminstr. for adminstrn. Wis. Dept. Justice, Madison, 1974-80; dep. commr. pers. Minn. Dept. Employee Rels., St. Paul, 1980-85; dir. pers. Ramsey County, St. Paul, Minn., 1985-97; human resources dir. Met. Coun., St. Paul, 1997—; instr. U. Minn. Carlson Sch. Mgmt. Employer Edn. Svc., Mpls., 1985—; co-chair, mem. exec. bd. Twin Cities Area Labor-Mgmt. Coun., Mpls., 1994—; advisor Inst. for Labor Mgmt. Studies, White Bear Lake, Minn., 1997; speaker on human rels., expert witness, 1985—,. Coach Mahtomedi (Minn.) Youth Baseball Assn., 1992-97; vice chair, mem. fin. com. City of Mahtomedi, 1994—; pres. Riverside Lions, St. Paul, Minn., 1995-98. Mem. Pub. Employer Labor Rels. Assn., Minn. Pub. Employer Labor Rels. Assn., Internat. Pers. Mgmt. Assn. (pres. 1990, bd. dirs.; hon. life), St. Paul Pers. Dirs. Assn. (pres., v.p., sec.-treas.). Lutheran. Avocations: skiing, hunting, swimming, reading, writing. Home: 1823 Park Ave Mahtomedi MN 55115-1932

BRAISTED, MADELINE CHARLOTTE, financial planner; b. Jamaica, N.Y., Nov. 23, 1936; d. Melvin Vincent and Charlotte Marie (Klos) B. AAS, Nassau C.C., 1968; BA, Hofstra U., 1973, MA, 1975, grad. Command and General Staff Coll., 1985. CFP Coll. for Fin. Planning, 1991. Enlisted, U.S. Marine Corps., Cherry Point, N.C., 1954-57; reservations agt. Airline Industry, N.Y.C., 1957-64; reservations controller Auto Lease Industry, N.Y.C., 1964-66; nuclear medicine technician Queens Gen. Hosp., Jamaica, N.Y., 1969-70; lab. mgr. CUNY, 1970-80; commd. capt. U.S. Army Res., 1977-80, advanced through grades to major, 1984; cons. Energy Etcetera, Flushing, N.Y., 1979-85; capt. USAR, Fort Totten, N.Y., 1975-80; ret. major, 1996; USA Health Profl. Support Agy., Office Surgeon Gen. Washington, 1980-92. Author, pub. Energy Etcetera catalog, 1981-85; artist On Shore painting (hon. mention 1974). Merit badge counselor Boy Scouts Am., Queens County, N.Y., 1980-83; active mem. PTA, Jamaica, 1980-84. Decorated Legion of Merit, Army Commendation medal with one oak leaf, Army Achievement medal with one oak leaf cluster; named Community Leader and Noteworthy Am., Hist. Preservation of Am., 1976. Mem. NAFE, APHA, Am. Acad. Med. Adminstrs., Internat. Assn. Fin. Planners, Am. Assn. Individual Investors, Assn. Mil. Surgeons of U.S., Res. Officers Assn., Ret. Officers Assn., Nat. Art League. Roman Catholic. Avocations: painting; sculpture.

BRAITERMAN, THEA GILDA, economics educator, state legislator, selectman; b. Balt., Sept. 11, 1927; d. Isaac E. and Clara (Fink) Bloom; m. Marvin Braiterman, Mar. 21, 1948; children: Kenneth, Marta, David. BS, Johns Hopkins U., 1949; MA, U. Md., 1966; PhD, Union Inst., 1977. Assoc. prof. econs. Balt. Coll. of Commerce, 1966-73; prof. econs. New England Coll., Henniker, N.H., 1973—; mem. N.H. Ho. of Reps., 1988-94; cons. on retirement, 1988—; selectman Town of Henniker, 1997—. Author: Workbook on Economic Theory, 1966; contbr. articles to profl. jours. Sec., bd. govs. United Way of Merrimack County, Concord, N.H., 1984-90; v.p., bd. govs. Cmty. Svcs. Coun., Concord, 1980-84. Jane Addams Peace Assn. grantee, 1976-77; Gilmore grantee New Eng. Coll., 1988-90. Mem. Am. Econ. Assn., Ea. Econ. Assn. Home: PO Box 686 Henniker NH 03242-0686 Office: New England Coll Henniker NH 03242

BRAITHWAITE, J(OSEPH) LORNE, real estate executive; b. Dewberry, Alta., Can., July 16, 1941; s. Joseph and Olga (Prill) B.; m. Josie Bey, Feb. 14, 1962; children: Todd, Jodi, Troy, Travis. B in Commerce, U. Alta., 1963; MBA, U. Western Ont., 1969; I.D.A., Investment Dealers' Assn., Calgary, 1970. With T. Eaton Co., Calgary, Alta., 1963-67, 71-74; group sales and mdse. mgr. T. Eaton Co., Edmonton, Alta., 1971-74; sales mgr., then v.p. and gen. mgr. South Park Industries Assoc. Cos.; project mgr., then sales mgr. ATCO Industries, Calgary, 1969-71; project mgr. Oxford Devel. Group, Edmonton, 1974-76; sr. v.p. devel. Oxford Devel. Group, Calgary, 1976-78; pres., chief exec. officer Cambridge Shopping Centres Ltd., Toronto, 1978—; bd. dirs. Cambridge Leaseholds Ltd., Jannock Ltd., Can. Inst. Pub. Real Estate Cos., OMERS Realty Corp., Interprovincial Pipe Line Inc., Coun. for Can. Unity. Gen. mgr., coach Thornhill Thunderbirds AAA Midget Hockey Team, 1983-85; mem. bd. govs. Jr. Achievement Met. Toronto and York Region; chmn. Can. Com. I.C.S.C., 1989-92, chmn. I.C.S.C., 1995-96; Real Estate divsn. of Corp. Capital Campaign for Hosp. for Sick Children, Toronto, 1986; pres. Can. Inst. of Pub. Real Estate Cos., 1995-97, Cirass Henry Singer award, 1996. Mem. Toronto Club, Goodwood Club, Bayview Golf and Country Club, Cambridge Club, World Pres.'s Orgn. Avocations: squash, hockey, golf, tennis. Office: Cambridge Shopping Ctrs Ltd, 95 Wellington St W Ste 300, Toronto, ON Canada M5J 2R2*

BRAITHWAITE, MARGARET CHRISTINE, elementary education educator; b. Toledo, Sept. 9, 1945; d. John William and Eleanor Margaret (Gedert) B. BS in Edn., U. Toledo, 1968. Cert. pvt. glider pilot, adv. ground instr. Tchr. 1-8th Toledo Pub. Schs. Mem. Women Soaring Pilots Assn., Aircraft Owners and Pilots Assn., Soaring Soc. Am., Adrian Soaring Club (past pres.), Delta Kappa Gamma. Avocation: soaring. E-mail: c.braithwaite@tps.org. Home: 1918 W Alexis Rd Apt K202 Toledo OH 43613-5471 Office: 3901 Shadylawn Dr Toledo OH 43614-3308

BRAITHWAITE, WILFRED JOHN, physics educator; b. Ferndale, Wash., Apr. 11, 1940; s. John Alfred and Joyce Elinor (Gunderson) B.; m. Wanda Pearl Chism, June 3, 1961 (div. 1974). BS in Physics with honors, Seattle Pacific U., 1962; MS in Physics, U. Wash., 1965, PhD in Physics, 1971; postgrad., U. Tex., 1988-89. Instr. physics Princeton (N.J.) U., 1970-72; asst. prof. physics U. Tex., Austin, 1972-79, rsch. scientist faculty, 1979-81; tech. and sci. cons. Austin, 1981-89; assoc. prof. physics U. Ark., Little Rock, 1989-95, prof. physics, 1995—; vis. staff mem. Los Alamos (N.Mex.) Nat. Lab., 1975-76, 78-79; vis. scientist Ind. U., Bloomington, 1990-96; affiliate prof. physics U. Wash., Seattle, 1991-96; sci. assoc. PPE divsn. CERN, Geneva, Switzerland, 1992—; guest scientist Brookhaven Nat. Lab., Upton, N.Y., 1992—; lectr. in field; grant referee Ark. Sci. and Tech. Authority, 1990—. Contbr. numerous articles to profl. jours., numerous unedited contbns.; jour. referee Phys. Rev. C and Phys. Rev. Letters, 1970—.
U.S. Dept. Energy rsch. grantee, 1992-95, 99—, Ark. Sci. and Tech. Authority rsch. grantee, 1993-94, 96-98; numerous grants from NSF, Dept. of Energy, Robert A Welch Found., U. Ark.-Little Rock, Ind. U., U. Tex., 1975—. Mem. IEEE, Am. Phys. Soc., Nat. Assn. for Rsch. in Sci. Teaching, N.Y. Acad. Sci., Tex. Acad. Sci., Ark. Acad. Sci., Am. Assn. Physics Tchrs., others. Achievements include research testing time reversal invariance; high excitation neutron particle-hole states in 140 Ce and 208 Pb; charge-dependence matrix elements in light nuclei; method for spin determinations using heavy ions; multiply-excited states in Z greater than or equal to 7 atoms; 3-alpha process in stellar helium burning; isospin mixing in nuclei from Pi+ versus Pi- scattering comparisons near the pion-nucleon resonance; measurement limits on source size formed in ultra-relativistic heavy ion collisions; distinguishing charged kaons and pions using their in-flight decays; experimental and instrumental design for HE nuclear physics. Avocations: astronomy, secondary science education, high-speed computing with 3-D visualizations. Home: 1 Broadmoor Dr Little Rock AR 72204-4818 Office: Univ of Ark Dept Physics and Astronomy Little Rock AR 72204-1000

BRAKAS, NORA JACHYM, education educator; b. Schenectady, N.Y., Aug. 9, 1952; d. Thaddeus Michael and Theresa Mary (Patnode) J.; m. Jurgis Brakas, June 15, 1996. BS in Elem. Edn., Plattsburg State U. Coll., 1974; MS in Reading, SUNY, Albany, 1977, Cert. Advanced Study in Reading, 1986, PhD in Reading, 1990. Cert. elem. sch. tchr., reading tchr. Elem. sch. and reading tchr. Lee (Mass.) Ctrl. Sch., 1976-82; reading specialist Guilderland (N.Y.) Sch. Dist., 1988-89; rsch. asst., tchg. asst. SUNY, Albany, 1985-88, instr. reading dept., 1989-90; asst. prof. tchr. edn., reading specialist Southeastern La. U., Hammond, 1990-91, Marist Coll., Poughkeepsie, N.Y., 1991—; presenter, spkr. in field. Contbr. articles to profl. jours. Student Literacy Corp. grantee U.S. Dept. Edn., 1991, IBM/Marist Joint Study Project grantee, 1992. Mem. Internat. Reading Assn., Soc. Children's Book Writers and Illustrators. Avocations: drawing, writing children's books, collecting antique children's books. Home: PO Box 176 Rhinecliff NY 12574-0176 Office: Marist Coll 341 Dyson Poughkeepsie NY 12601

BRAKE, CECIL CLIFFORD, retired diversified manufacturing executive; b. Ystrad, Mynach, Wales, Nov. 14, 1932; came to U.S., 1967; s. Leonard James and Ivy Gertrude (Berry) B.; m. Vera Morris, Aug. 14, 1954; children—Stephen John, Richard Colin, Vanessa Elaine. Chartered engr.; B.Sc. in Engring., U. Wales, 1954; M.Sc., Cranfield Inst., Bedford, Eng., 1957; grad. A.M.P., Harvard U. Sch. Bus., 1985. Mgr. research and devel. Schrader Fluid Power, Wake Forest, N.C., 1968-70, engring. mgr., 1970-75; mng. dir. Schrader U.K. Fluid Power, 1975-77; v.p., gen. mgr. Schrader Internat., 1977-78; group v.p. Schrader Bellows, Fluid Power, Akron, Ohio, 1978-82; exec. v.p. Scovill, Inc., Waterbury, Conn., 1982-86; pres. Yale Security, Inc. subs. Scovill, Inc.; group exec. Eagle Industries, Inc., Chgo., 1986—; retired, 1997; chief oper. officer Mansfield (Ohio) Plumbing Products Inc., Hart and Cooley Inc., Holland, Mich., Caron Internat., Inc., Rochelle, Ill., Caron Internat., Inc., Rochelle, Ill., Chemineer Inc., Dayton, Ohio, Pulsafeeder Inc., Rochester, N.Y., Clevaflex Inc., Cleve., Equality Specialties Inc., N.Y.C., De Vilbiss Co., Toledo, Hill Refrigeration, Trenton, N.J., Air-Maze Corp., Bedford Heights, Ohio, Burns Aerospace Corp., Winston Salem, N.C., Atlantic Industries, Inc., Nutley, N.J., Stimsonite Products, Niles, Ill.; ptnr., owner Prince of Wales Inc.; bd. dirs. CFI Industries. Avocations: sailing; golf. Office: Eagle Industries Inc 2 N Riverside Plz Chicago IL 60606-2600 Also: 17 Harborview Road Westport CT 06880

BRAKELEY, GEORGE ARCHIBALD, JR., fundraising consultant; b. Washington, Apr. 18, 1916; s. George Archibald and Lillian (Fay) B.; m. Roxana Byerly; children: George Archibald III, Deborah Fay, Joan Keller. BA, U. Pa., 1938. V.p., dir. John Price Jones Co., Inc. (fund-raising counsel), N.Y.C.; pres., treas. John Price Jones Co. (Can.), Ltd., 1950-52; chmn., CEO G.A. Brakeley & Co., Ltd., 1952-61, G.A. Brakeley & Co., Inc., L.A., 1956-69; chmn., chief exec. officer Brakeley, John Price Jones Inc., 1972-83; chmn. Brakeley, John Price Jones, Inc., 1983-87, sr. cons., 1987—. Author: Tested Ways to Successful Fund Raising. Trustee Ctr. for the Study of the Presidency. Capt. C.E. AUS, WWII. Mem. Mayflower Soc., Anglers Club (N.Y.C.), Montreal Racket Club (hon.), Wee Burn Golf Club (Darien, Conn.), Royal Poinciana Golf Club (Naples, Fla.). Episcopalian. Home: 185 South Ave # 26 New Canaan CT 06840-5729 Office: 2777 Summer St Stamford CT 06905-4310

BRAKEMAN, LOUIS FREEMAN, retired university administrator; b. Kalamazoo, Nov. 9, 1932; s. Louis Freeman and Ruth Adelaide (Parsons) B.; m. Lori Mallett, Aug. 16, 1953; children: David, Mark, Peter, Paul, Amy. BA, Kalamazoo Coll., 1954; MA, Fletcher Sch. Diplomacy, Tufts U., 1955, PhD, 1963; LHD, Denison U., 1985. Lectr. history Brown U., 1958-59; asst. prof. polit. sci. Carroll Coll., Waukesha, Wis., 1959-62; mem. faculty Denison U., Granville, Ohio, 1962-85; prof. polit. sci. Denison U., 1968-85, chmn. dept., 1965-70, dean Coll., 1970-73, provost, 1973-85, acting pres., 1974-75; dir. research project faculty devel. Gt. Lakes Colls. Assn., 1985-86; provost Stetson U., DeLand, Fla., 1987-93; vis. prof. polit. sci. Kalamazoo Coll., 1987; vis. scholar center for Study of Higher Edn. U. Mich., 1980; dir. Regional Council Center for Internat. Students, summers 1966-68; chmn. regional selection com. Danforth Found. Assocs. Program, 1971-73; mem. Common Cause, 1972—. Co-author: Research Problems in American Politics, 1969, What One Has Within, What the Context Provides, 1989; contbr. articles to profl. jours. Pres. Volusia County Arts Coun., 1994-96, West Volusia Habitat for Humanity, 1996-98. Fulbright scholar India, 1957-58; Danforth grad. fellow, 1954-57. Mem. Nature Conservancy, Phi Beta Kappa. Presbyterian (elder). Home: 522 Princewood Dr Deland FL 32724-8103

BRAKHAGE, JAMES STANLEY, filmmaker, educator; b. Kansas City, Mo., Jan. 14, 1933; s. Ludwig and Clara (Dubberstein) B.; m. Mary Jane Collom, Dec. 28, 1957 (div. 1987); children: Myrrena, Crystal, Neowyn, Bearthm, Rarc; m. Marilyn Jull, Mar. 30, 1989; children: Anton, Vaughn. Ph.D., San Francisco Art Inst., 1981; Doctorate (hon.), Calif. Arts, 1994. Lectr. Sch. Art Inst. Chgo., 1969-81; prof. U. Colo., Boulder, 1981; mem. Filmmakers Coop., N.Y.C., Canyon Cinema Coop., San Francisco, London Filmmakers Coop., Can. Filmmakers' Distbn. Ctr., Toronto, Lightcome, Paris, France; Faculty lectr. U. Colo., 1990-91. Films include Interim, 1952, Anticipation of the Night, 1958, The Dead, 1960, Blue Moses, 1962, Dog Star Man, 1964, Songs in 8mm, 1964-69, Scenes from Under Childhood, 1967-70, The Weir Falcon Saga, 1970, The Act of Seeing with One's Own Eyes, 1971, The Riddle of Lumen, 1972, Sincerity and Duplicity, 1973-80, The Text of Light, 1974, Desert, 1976, The Governor, 1977, Burial Path, 1978, Nightmare Series, 1978, Creation, 1979, Made Manifest, 1980, Salome, 1980, Murder Psalm, 1980, Roman Numeral Series, 1979-81, the Arabic series, 1980-82, Unconscious London Strata, 1982, Tortured Dust, 1984, The Egyptian Series, 1984, The Loom, 1986, Nightmusic, 1986, The Dante Quartet, 1987, Faust, parts I-IV, 1987-89, Marilyn's Window, 1988, Visions in Meditation, 1989-90, City Streaming, 1990, Glaze of Cathexis, 1990, Babylonian Series, 1989-90, Passage Through: A Ritual, 1990, A Child's Garden and the Serious Sea, 1991, Delicacies of Molten Horror Synapse, 1991, Christ Mass Sex Dance, 1991, Crack Glass Eulogy, 1992, Boulder Blues and Pearls and For Marilyn, Interpolations 1-5, 1992, Blossom Gift Favor, The Harrowing, Tryst Haunt, Study in Color and Black and White, Stellar, Atumnal, 1993, Three Homerics, 1993, Naghts, Chartres Series, Ephemeral Solidity, Elementary Phrases, Black Ice, First Hymn to the Night—Novalis, 1994, In Consideration of Pompeii, 1994, The Mammals of Victoria, 1994, Paranoia Corridor, 1994, Can Not Exist, 1994, Can Not Not Exist, 1994, I Take These Truths, 1994, We Hold These, 1994, I..., 1995, Earthen Aerie, 1995, Spring Cycle, 1995, The Lost Films, 1995, The B Series, 1995, Preludes 1-24, 1995, 96, The Fur of Home, 1996, Preludes 13-18, 1996, Preludes, 19-24, 1996, Beautiful Funerals, 1996, Polite Madness, 1996, Shockingly Hot, 1996, Sexual Saga, 1996, The Lost Films, 1996, Comingled Containers, 1996, Yggdrasill Whose Roots Are Stars in the Human Mind, 1997, Last Hymn to the Night - Novalis, 1997, I...Sleeping, 1989, Selfsong/Deathsong, 1998, "..." Reels #1,2,3, 1998; author: Metaphors on Vision, 1963, A Moving Picture Giving and Taking Book, 1971, The Brakhage Lectures, 1972, Seen, 1975, Film Biographies, 1977, Brakhage Scrapbook, 1982, Film at Wits End, 1989, Phillip Taffee: A Long Conversation with Stan Brakhage, 1998, "..." Reels # 1,2,3,4, 1998, The Birds of Paradise, 1999, The Lion and the Zebra Made God's Raw Jewels, 1999, The Earth Song of the Cricket, 1999. Recipient Brussels Worlds Fair Protest award, 1958, Brandeis citation, 1973, Colo. Gov.'s award for arts and humanities, 1974, Jimmy Ryan Morris Meml. Found. award, 1979, Telluride Film Festival medallion, 1981, Maya Deren award Am. Film Inst., 1986, medal U. Colo., 1988, Outstanding Achievement award Denver Internat. Film Festival, 1988, MacDowell medal, 1989, Libr. Congress Nat. Film Registry, 1992, Anthology Film Archives honor, 1993, The Colo. 100 Cert. of Recognition, 1993, Disting. Prof. award U. Colo., 1994; retrospective Mus. Modern Art, 1995; grantee Avon Found., 1965-69, NEA, 1974-75, 77, 80, 83, 88, U. Colo. Coun. Rsch. and Creative Work, 1983, Rocky Mountain Film Ctr., 1985; Rockefeller fellow, 1967-69, Guggenheim fellow, 1978. Democrat. Home: 2222 Walnut St #3 Boulder CO 80302-4517 Office: U Colo Film Studies Hunter 102 PO Box 316 Boulder CO 80309-0316

BRAKKE, MYRON KENDALL, retired research chemist, educator; b. Fillmore County, Minn., Oct. 23, 1921; s. John T. and Hulda Christina (Marburger) B.; m. Betty-Jean Einbecker, Aug. 16, 1947; children—Kenneth Allen, Thomas Warren, Joan Patricia, Karen Elizabeth. B.S., U. Minn., 1943, Ph.D., 1947; DSc (hon.), U. Nebr., 1996. Rsch. assoc. Bklyn. Bot. Garden, 1947-52; rsch assoc. U. Ill., 1952-55; rsch. chemist U.S. Dept. Agr., Lincoln, Nebr., 1955-86; prof. plant pathology U. Nebr., Lincoln, 1955-86. Editor: Virology, 1960-66; contbr. articles to profl. jours. Fellow AAAS, Am. Phytopath. Soc. (Award of Distinction 1988); mem. Am. Chem. Soc., Nat. Acad. Scis., Sigma Xi, Phi Lambda Upsilon, Gamma Sigma Delta, Alpha Zeta. Home: RR 1 Box 57 Crete NE 68333-9606

BRAM, LEON LEONARD, publishing company executive; b. Chgo., Sept. 20, 1931; s. Samuel and Rose Bram; m. Doris A. Hebel, Apr. 29, 1961 (div. 1972); children: Mark James, Alexander Anton; m. Joanne Frances Casino, Sept. 30, 1978 (div. 1990); 1 child, Victoria Lynn. B.Sc., DePaul U., 1967. Various positions Chgo. Pub. Library, 1949-55, F.E. Compton Co., Chgo., 1955-63; dir. editorial rsch. Standard Ednl. Corp., Chgo., 1963-69; exec. editor F.E. Compton Co., Chgo., 1969-74; v.p., editorial dir. Primedia Reference Corp., Mahwah, N.J., 1974-97; pub. cons., 1998—. Mem. ALA.

BRAMAN, HEATHER RUTH, technical writer, editor, consultant, antiques dealer; b. Wilmington, Ohio, Apr. 27, 1934; d. William Barnett and Violet Ruth (Davis) Hansford; m. Barr Oliver Braman, June 29, 1957 (div.); children: Sean Robert, Heather Paige. BA, Hiram Coll., 1956; postgrad., Sinclair Community Coll., Dayton, Ohio, 1977-85, Wright State U., Dayton, 1986. Pers. clk. USAF, Wright-Patterson AFB, Ohio, 1956, specifications editor, 1956-57, publs. editor, writer, 1957-63; vol. Children's Med. Ctr., 1963-67, Dayton Pubs. Schs., 1969-87; tchr. Gloria Dei Montessori Sch., Dayton, 1973-77; asst. mgr., acctg. mgr., mgr. tennis club USAF, Wright-Patterson AFB, Ohio, 1977-81; tech. writer Miclin, Inc., Alpha, Ohio, 1982, Indsl. Design Concepts, Dayton, 1982-83; tech. writer, cons. Belcan Corp.,

Cin., 1984—; owner Chimney Sweep Antiques Shoppe, Arcanum, Ohio, 1991—; real estate investor; editor Project Mercury Candidate Evaluation Program. Founder, bd. dirs. Trotwood (Ohio) Women's Open Tennis Tournament, 1976-81; mem. Harrison Twp. Parks Bd., 1980-82; ballpersons coord. Dayton Pro Tennis Classic, 1977-80; pres. Dayton Tennis Commn., 1978-80; mem. parents exec. com. Hiram (Ohio) Coll., 1985-91; ct.-appointed Spl. Advocate/Guardian Ad Litem (CASA GAL), 1988—; tutor English as a second lang. citizenship classes, 1991—. Mem. NOW, NAACP, Dayton Pub. Schs. Orgns., Dayton Tennis Umpires Assn., Mothers Against Drunk Drivers., AARP, WWF, HALT, Sigil of Phi Sigma. Democrat. Mem. Soc. Friends. Avocations: tennis, antiques, reading, property investment. Home: 320 Elm Hill Dr Dayton OH 45415-2943 Office: Belcan Corp 10200 Anderson Way Cincinnati OH 45242-4718

BRAMANTE, PIETRO OTTAVIO, physiology educator, retired pathology specialist; b. Rome, May 21, 1920; came to U.S., 1952; s. Michele Bramante and Amelia Ferriani; m. Aurora de Valle Medina, June 1, 1957. MD, U. Rome, 1944; MS in Biomed. Engring., Drexel U., 1965. Diplomate Am. Bd. Pathology. Intern to asst. dept. internal. medicine U. Rome, 1945-51; instr. to assoc. prof. St. Louis U. Sch. Medicine, 1952-65; assoc. prof. to prof. dept. physiology U. Ill., Chgo., 1965-75; resident pathology Loyola U., Chgo., 1975-78; pathologist William Beaumont Med. Ctr., El Paso, Tex., 1978-79, Sun Bay Hosp., St. Petersburg, Fla., 1981-82; cons. Italian Fedn. Sport Medicine, Rome, 1945-51; med. expert Ct. of Justice, Rome, 1948-49; vis. scientist Am. Physiol. Soc., Washington, 1964-67; glossary com. mem. Internat. Union Physiology, Washington, 1969; vis. prof. U. Westfalia, Münster, Germany, 1971-72. Contbr. articles, revs. to profl. publs., 1944-78; editl. reviewer Am. Physiol. Soc.; patentee in field. Pres. Chess Club, Pinellas Park, Fla., 1986-96; tchr. fgn. langs., sci. and math. in local schs. 2d lt. Air Force Italian, 1947-50. Postgrad. fellow Swedish Govt., Stockolm, 1951-52, fellow Nat. Heart Inst., Baylor U., Houston, 1957, spl. fellow Nat. Heart Inst., Drexel U., Phila., 1962-64. Republican. Roman Catholic. Avocation: chess. Home: 2022 Camelot Dr Apt 33 Clearwater FL 33763-4249

BRAMBLE, RONALD LEE, lawyer, business and legal consultant; b. Pauls Valley, Okla., Sept. 9, 1937; s. Homer Lee and Ethyle Juanita (Stephens) B.; m. Kathryn Louise Seiler, July 2, 1960; children: Julia Dawn, Kristin Lee. AA, San Antonio Coll., 1957; BS, Trinity U., 1959, MS, 1964; JD, St. Mary's U., 1975; DBA, Ind. No. U., 1973; cert. lay spkr. Meth. Ch. Mgr., buyer Fed-Mart, Inc., San Antonio, 1959-61; tchr. bus. San Antonio Ind. Sch. Dist., 1961-65, edn. coordinator, bus. tng. specialist, 1965-67; assoc. prof., chmn. dept. mgmt. San Antonio Coll., 1967-73; prin. Ron Bramble Assocs., San Antonio, 1967-77; pres. Adminstrv. Research Assocs., Inc., 1977-82; v.p. PIA, Inc., 1982-83; v.p. fin. Solar 21 Corp., 1983-84, sr. staff Ausburn, Astoria & Seale (formerly Ausburn, O'Neill & Assocs.), San Antonio, 1984-89; pvt. practice, 1990—; cons., comptr. TEL-STAR Systems, Inc., 1993-95; v.p. MegaTronics Internat. Corp., 1995—; lectr. bus., edn. and ch. groups, 1965—. Cons. editor: Prentice-Hall, Inc., Englewood Cliffs, N.J., 1969-71; contbr. articles to profl. jours. Mem. World Affairs Coun. of San Antonio, diplomat. Served with AUS, 1959. Recipient Wall Street Jour. award Trinity U., 1959, U.S. Law Week award St. Mary's Sch. of Law, 1975. Mem. ABA, San Antonio C. of C., Adminstrv. Mgmt. Soc. (pres. 1966-68, Merit award 1968), Bus. Edn. Tchrs. Assn. (pres. 1964), Sales and Mktg. Execs. San Antonio (bd. dirs. 1967-68, Disting. Salesman award 1967), Internat. Platform Assn., Internat. Assn. Cons. to Bus., Nat. Assn. Bus. Economists, Acad. Mgmt., Christian Legal Soc., Comml. Law League Am., Toastmasters, Phi Delta Phi, Lions. Republican. Home: 127 Palo Duro St San Antonio TX 78232-3026

BRAME, JOSEPH ROBERT, III, lawyer; b. Hopkinsville, Ky., Apr. 18, 1942; s. Joseph Robert and Atwood Ruth (Davenport) B.; m. Mary Jane Blake, June 11, 1966; children: Rob, Blake, Virginia, John, Thomas. BA with high honors, Vanderbilt U., 1964; LLB, Yale U., 1967. Bar: Ky. 1968, Va. 1968. Assoc. McGuire, Woods, Battle & Boothe, Richmond, Va., 1967-72; ptnr. McGuire, Woods, Battle & Boothe, Richmond, 1972-97; bd. dirs. NLRB, 1997—; lectr. in field. Contbr. articles to profl. jours. Mem. adv. bd. Salvation Army, Richmond, 1980-97, chmn., 1989-91; bd. dirs. Am. Vision, Atlanta, Horizons Expeditions Ltd.; troop com. chmn. Robert E. Lee coun. Boy Scouts Am., 1980-91; chair 10th Amendment Litig. com., Gov.'s Adv. Coun. on Federalism and Self Determination; gen. counsel Rep. Party Va., 1993-96. Mem. ABA, Am. Bar Found., Va. State Bar (chmn. sect. A 3d dist. com.), Va. Bar Assn., Phi Beta Kappa. Presbyterian. Office: NLRB 1099 14th St SE Washington DC 20570

BRAMHALL, PETER, artist, sculptor, designer, craftsman; b. Bridgewater, Vt., May 16, 1942. Student, Valparaiso U. Contemporary Art, 1962-65, Penland Sch. Crafts, 1967-68; BFA, Cleve. Inst. Art, 1970. Tchr. glass blowing, drawing and sculpture Earlham Coll. Vt. Studies Program. Exhibited in solo shows at village Gallery, Croton-on-Hudson, N.Y., 1970, Schenectady Mus., 1973, Gallery II, Woodstock, Vt., 1979, 83, Jackie Chalkey Gallery, Washington, 1980, Elements Gallery, Greenwich, Conn., 1982, Ree Schonlau Gallery, Omaha, 1984, Silvermine Guild of Artists, New Canaan, Conn., 1983, 94, others; group shows at DeCordova Mus., Lincoln, Mass., 1972, Contemporary Artisans, San Francisco, 1981, Smithsonian Instn., Washington, 1984, America House Gallery, Tenafly, N.J., 1986, Eileen Kremen Gallery, L.A., 1986, So. Vt. Arts Ctr., Manchester, Vt., 1993-95, Clifton (N.J.) Beautification Project, 1996, others; represented in collections at Saks Fifth Avenue, Bal Harbor, Fla., Ethan Allen Corp. Hdqrs., pvt. collections; commd. to produce Christa McAuliffe Planetarium Found. award, 1994, 95. Vol. fireman; founder Bridgewater Rescue Squad; trustee Vt. Coun. on the Arts. Address: PO Box 18 Bridgewater VT 05034

BRAMLETT, DAVID A., retired military officer. BS, U.S. Mil. Acad.; MA in English, Duke U.; student, U.S. Army Command/Gen. Staff, U.S. Army War Coll. Commd. 2d lt. U.S. Army, 1964, advanced through grades to gen., 1996, ret., 1998; exec. officer Co. C 1st bn. 14th infantry U.S. Army, Vietnam, 1966, comdr. Co. C 2d bn. 327th infantry 101st airborne divsn., 1968-69; ops. officer 2d bn. 503d infantry 101st airborne divsn. U.S. Army, Ft. Campbell, Ky., 1976-77, comdr. 1st bn. 503d infantry 3d brigade 101st airborne div., 1978-80; dep. dir. U.S. Nat. Security Studies U.S. Army War Coll., Carlisle Barracks, Pa., 1982; comdr. 1st brigade 92 airborne divsn. U.S. Army, Ft. Campbell, 1983, comdr. 3d brigade 101st airborne divsn., 1984-86; dep. dir. plans, policy and programs directorate U.S. Cen. Command, MacDill AFB, Fla., 1986-87; asst. divsn. comdr. 25th infantry divsn. U.S. Army, Schofield AFB, Hawaii, 1987-90; comdg. gen. 6th infantry divsn. U.S. Army, Ft. Wainwright, Alaska, 1992-94; dep. comdr. in chief, chief of staff U.S. Pacific Command, Camp H.M. Smith, Hawaii, 1994-96; comdg. gen. U.S. Army Forces Command, Ft. McPherson, Ga., 1996-98; instr. Fla. Ranger Camp, U.S. Army Infantry Sch., Ft. Benning, Ga., 1967-68. Decorated Def. Disting. Svc. medal, Disting. Svc. medal with oak leaf cluster, Silver Star, Legion of Merit, Bronze Star with 3 V device (with 5 oak leaf clusters), Def. Meritorious Svc. medal, Meritorious Svc. medal with 2 oak leaf clusters.

BRAMLETT, PAUL KENT, lawyer; b. Tupelo, Miss., May 31, 1944; s. Virgil Preston and McDuff (Goggans) B.; m. Shirley Marie Wilhelm, June 14, 1966; children: Paul Kent II (dec.), Robert Preston. AA with honors, Itawamba Jr. Coll., Fulton, Miss., 1962-64; BA, David Lipscomb Coll., 1966; postgrad., George Peabody Coll., 1966; JD, U. Miss., 1969. Bar: Miss. 1969, Tenn. 1980, U.S. Dist. Ct. (no. dist.) Miss. 1969, U.S. Dist. Ct. (we. dist.) Tenn. 1976, U.S. Dist. Ct. (mid. dist.) Tenn. 1980, U.S. Dist. Ct. (so. dist.) Miss. 1983, U.S. Dist. Ct. (we. dist.) Ky. 1988, U.S. Ct. Appeals (5th cir.) 1974, U.S. Ct. Appeals (6th cir.) 1980, U.S. Ct. Appeals (11th cir.) 1981, U.S. Supreme Ct. 1974. Pvt. practice Tupelo, Miss., 1969-80, Nashville, 1980—; mem. Million Dollar Advs. Forum, 1998. Mem. ABA, ATLA, Miss. Trial Lawyers Assn. (bd. govs. 1976-79), Tenn. Bar Assn., Miss. Bar Assn. (pub. info. com. 1979-81), Nashville Bar Assn. (fed. ct. com. 1980-81), Million Dollar Advocates Forum, Am. Arbitration Assn. (comml. panel), Civitan Club (past gov. and legal counsel no. dist. Miss.). Mem. Ch. of Christ. Avocation: music. Office: PO Box 150734 2828 Stouffer Tower Nashville TN 37215-0734

BRAMLETTE, DAVID C., III, federal judge; b. 1939. BA, Princeton U., 1962; JD, U. Miss., 1965. Assoc., then ptnr. Adams, Forman, Truly, Ward & Bramlette, Natchez, Miss., 1975-91; spl. cir. judge U.S. Cir. Ct. (6th dist.) Miss., 1977, 79; fed. judge U.S. Dist. Ct. (so. dist.) Miss., 1991—. Trustee Miss. Nature Conservancy, 1990—; pres. BBCHA, 1989-90; active Arcole Hunting Camp, Ducks Unlimited, Nat. Wild Turkey Fedn. Office: PO Box 928 Natchez MS 39121

BRAMMER, BARBARA RHUDENE, retired secondary education educator; b. Dawson, Tex., Aug. 20, 1936; d. William Alpheus and Eunice (Priddy) Hargis; m. Jerry Lane Brammer, Apr. 15, 1960; children: Cathy DeLane Brammer Francis, David Wayne Brammer, Karen Ann Brammer Shelfer. BS in Secondary Edn., U. North Tex., 1958. Cert. math tchr., Tex. Tchr., coach N.W. Ind. Sch. Dist., Justin, Tex., 1957-62; tchr. math. N.W. High Sch., Justin, Tex., 1970-93, dept. head, 1984-93; tchr., coach Decatur (Tex.) Ind. Sch. Dist., 1966-68; substitute tchr. math. dept. N.W. High Sch., Justin, Tex., 1993-95; coach Acad. Decathlon Team, World Book Ency., 1986-90; advisor Merrill Pub. Co., 1989-91. Recipient Tchr. award Tandy Computers and Tex. Christian U., 1989; named One of 300 Outstanding Tex. Tchrs., Ex Students Assn. U. Tex., Austin, 1989, One of 36 Outstanding Alumnus, Sch. Edn. U. North Tex., 1990; coach of State Champion Acad. Decathlon team, 1988. Mem. NEA, Tex. State Tchrs. Assn. (life), Tex. Ret. Tchrs. Assn., Tex. Math. Tchrs., Rhome Womens Club (pres. 1981-82). Mem. Ch. of Christ. Avocations: collecting math books, riding 4 wheeler, gardening, preserving foods, traveling. Home: 332 Private Rd # 4820 Rhome TX 76078-2217

BRAMMER, FOREST EVERT, electrical engineering educator; b. Mabscott, W.Va., July 21, 1913; s. Evert C. and V. Susan (Lilly) B.; m. Evelyn G. Klitzing, Mar. 7, 1942; children: Robert, Mary, William, Susan. A.B., Concord Coll., 1933; B.S., N.C. State U., 1933; postgrad., U. N.C., 1936-37, Johns Hopkins, 1947-48; Ph.D., Case Inst. Tech., 1951. High sch. tchr. Beaver, W.Va., 1933-36; geophys. engr. Schlumberger Well Surveying Corp., Tex., Ill., Mich., 1937-42; research Johns Hopkins Applied Physics Lab., 1946-48; faculty Case Inst. Tech., 1948-60; prof. elec. engring. Wayne State U., Detroit, 1960-82, prof. emeritus, 1982—; chmn. dept. Wayne State U., 1960-70; cons. Goodyear Aircraft Corp., 1954-58; Republic Steel Corp., 1958—. Served to capt. Signal Corps AUS, 1942-46. Mem. I.E.E.E., Am. Soc. Engring. Edn., Sigma Xi, Tau Beta Pi, Eta Kappa Nu. Home: 15101 Ford Rd Apt 223 Dearborn MI 48126-4611 Office: 5050 Anthony Wayne Dr Detroit MI 48202-3902*

BRAMMER, LAWRENCE MARTIN, psychology educator; b. Crookston, Minn., Aug. 20, 1922; s. Martin G. and Edna L. (Thiesen) B.; m. Marian S. Sjolin, Feb. 11, 1945; children: Karin Marie, Kristen Lenore. B.S., St. Cloud State U., 1943; M.A., Stanford U., 1948, Ph.D., 1950. Diplomate: Am. Bd. Prof. Psychology. Psychologist Stanford U. Counseling and Testing Ctr., 1948-50; assoc. dean students Sacramento State Coll., 1950-64; prof. ednl. psychology U. Wash., Seattle, 1964-88, prof. emeritus, 1988—. Author: Therapeutic Psuchology, 6th edit., 1993, Helping Relationships, 7th edit., 1999, Outplacement and Inplacement Counseling, 1984, How to Cope with Life Transitions, 1991, Caring for Yourself While Caring for Others: A Caregiver's Survival and Renewal Guide, 1999. Lt. M.S.C. AUS, 1944-46. Fulbright fellow, 1961-62. Fellow APA; mem. ACA, Queen City Yacht Club, Elks. Democrat. Lutheran. Home: 7714 56th Pl NE Seattle WA 98115-6329

BRAMNIK, ROBERT PAUL, lawyer; b. N.Y.C., Nov. 17, 1949; s. Abe and Ruth (Richman) B.; m. Sheryl Ann Kalus, Aug. 12, 1973; children: Michael Lawrence, Andrew Martin. BA, CCNY, 1970; JD, Bklyn. Law Sch., 1973. Bar: N.Y. 1974, Ill. 1980, U.S. Dist. Ct. (so. and ea. dists.) N.Y. 1974, U.S. Dist. Ct. (no. dist.) Ill. 1980, U.S. Dist. Ct. (ctrl. dist.) Ill. 1982, U.S. Ct. Appeals (2d cir.) 1974, U.S. Ct. Appeals (4th cir.) 1987, U.S. Ct. Appeals (3d and 7th cirs.) 1992, U.S. Ct. Fed. Claims 1994, U.S. Supreme Ct. 1977. Sr. trial atty. NYSE, Inc., N.Y.C., 1973-75; asst. gen. counsel E.F. Hutton & Co., Inc., N.Y.C., 1975-77, Nat. Securities Clearing Corp., N.Y.C., 1977-79; with Arvey, Hodes, Costello and Burman, Chgo., 1979-86, ptnr., 1982-86; ptnr. Wood, Lucksinger & Epstein, Chgo., 1987-88, Altheimer & Gray, Chgo., 1988-97, Wildman, Harrold, Allen & Dixon, Chgo., 1997—; lectr. Securities Industry Assn. Compliance and Legal div., N.Y.C., 1980-91, 95-97. Vice chmn. Ill. Adv. Com. on Commodity Regulation, Chgo., 1985-89, chmn., 1989—. Fellow Ill. Bar Found.; mem. ABA (coms. on futures and derivatives regulation, co-chmn. subcom. on futures commn. merchants 1992-97, membership subcom. 1997—, fed. regulation of securities, subcom. on market regulation), Chgo. Bar Assn., Assn. of Bar of City of N.Y., Nat. Assn. Sec. Dealers (arbitrator 1981—), Nat. Futures Assn. (arbitrator 1981—). Jewish. Office: Wildman Harrold Allen & Dixon 225 W Wacker Dr Ste 3000 Chicago IL 60606-1224

BRAMON, CHRISTOPHER JOHN, aerospace engineer; b. Marshalltown, Iowa, Oct. 15, 1960; s. Clayton Robert and Judith (Rolston) B.; m. Joy Frances Tomishima, May 4, 1985. BS in Indsl. Engring., Iowa State U., 1984. Mgr. tech. engring. ops. NASA Marshall Space Flight Ctr., Huntsville, Ala., 1985-87, tech. mgr. liquid propulsion sys., 1987-94, program mgr. tech. transfer office, 1994-98; program mgr. space sta. life support projects office NASA Marshall Space Flight Ctr., Huntsville, 1998—. Contbr. article to Aerospace Engring. Recipient Astronaut's Personal Achievement award NASA, 1989, dir.'s commendation NASA Marshall Space Flight Ctr., 1992. Mem. Inst. Indsl. Engrs. Office: NASA Marshall Space Flight Ctr JA21 Huntsville AL 35812

BRAMS, STEVEN JOHN, political scientist, educator, game theorist; b. Concord, N.H., Nov. 28, 1940; s. Nathan and Isabelle (Tryman) B.; m. Eva Floderer, Nov. 13, 1971; children: Julie Claire, Michael Jason. B.S., MIT, 1962; Ph.D., Northwestern U., 1966. Research assoc. Inst. Def. Analyses, Arlington, Va., 1965-67; asst. prof. polit. sci. Syracuse U., 1967-69; asst. prof. NYU, 1969-73, assoc. prof., 1973-76, prof., 1976—; vis. prof. U. Rochester, U. Pa., U. Mich., Yale U., U. Calif.-Irvine, U. Haifa, Inst. Advanced Studies, Vienna; cons. in field. Author: Game Theory and Politics, 1975, Paradoxes in Politics: An Introduction to the Nonobvious in Political Science, 1976, The Presidential Election Game, 1978, Biblical Games: A Strategic Analysis of Stories in the Old Testament, 1980 (with Peter C. Fishburn) Approval Voting, 1983, Superior Beings: If They Exist, How Would We Know?, 1983, Superpower Games: Applying Game Theory to Superpower Conflict, 1985, Rational Politics: Decisions, Games, and Strategy, 1985, (with D. Marc Kilgour) Game Theory and National Security, 1988, Negotiation Games: Applying Game Theory of Moves, 1994 (with A. D. Taylor) Fair Division: From Cake-Cutting to Dispute Resolution, 1996, The Win-Win Solution: Guaranteeing Fair Shares to Everybody, 1999; co-editor: Applied Gamed Theory, 1979, Modules in Applied Mathematics: Political and Related Models, 1983; mem. editl. bd. Pub. Choice, 1973-90, Am. Polic. Sci. Rev., 1978-82, Jour. Politics, 1968-73, 78-82, 91—, Math. Social Scis., 1980—, Theory and Decision, 1982—, Jour. Behavioral Decision Making, 1987-90, Jour. Theoretical Politics, 1988—, Group Decision and Negotiation, 1991—, Control and Cybernetics, 1993—; mem. manuscript rev. com. Behavioral Sci., 1972—. Social Sci. Rsch. Coun. fellow, 1964-65, Guggenheim fellow, 1986-87; Russell Sage Found. vis. scholar, 1998-99, grantee NSF, 1968-71, 73-75, 80-91, Social Sci. Rsch. Coun., 1968, Ford Found., 1984-85, Sloan Found., 1986-89, U.S. Inst. Peace, 1988-89. Fellow AAAS; mem. Am. Econ. Assn., Am. Polit. Sci. Assn., Internat. Studies Assn., Pub. Choice Soc., Policy Studies Orgn., Peace Sci. Soc. (pres. 1990-91). Democrat. Jewish. Home: 4 Washington Square Vlg Apt 17I New York NY 10012-1910

BRAMSON, LEON, social scientist, educator; b. Chgo., Dec. 6, 1930; s. William and Sophie (Dudowitz) B.; m. Mary Elizabeth Hamlin, Mar. 12, 1960 (div. 1982); children: Rachel, Ruth; m. Nathalie Hubbard Bonsal, 1984; 1 child, Samuel Appleton. A.B., U. Chgo., 1950, M.A., 1953; Ph.D., Harvard, 1959. Instr. social relations Harvard, 1959-61, asst. prof., 1961-65; assoc. prof., chmn. dept. sociology and anthropology Swarthmore Coll., 1965-77, prof. sociology, 1971-78; program officer Exxon Edn. Found., N.Y.C., 1978-80; coordinator social analysis, corp. planning dept. Exxon Corp., N.Y.C., 1980-82; asst. dir. div. gen. programs NEH, Washington, 1982-85, sr. program officer, 1985—; vis. prof. sociology U. Calif. at San Diego, 1972; cons. Peace Corps Agy., 1965; ednl. cons. Trustee Nat. Service Secretariat, 1967-74, Good Hope Sch., Frederiksted, St. Croix, U.S. V.I., 1972-78; policyholder-elected trustee Tchrs. Ins. and Annuity Assn., N.Y.C., 1973-78, Coll. Retirement Equities Fund, 1978-79. Author: The Political Context of Sociology, 1961; Asso. editor: Am. Sociol. Rev, 1967-69; editor: Robert MacIver: On Community, Society and Power, 1970, (with G. W. Goethals) War: Studies from Psychology, Sociology, Anthropology, 1964. Served with AUS, 1953-55. Fulbright scholar Netherlands, 1957-58. Fellow Am. Anthrop. Assn. Office: NEH Rm 318 1100 Pennsylvania Ave NW Washington DC 20004-2501

BRAMSON, ROBERT SHERMAN, lawyer; b. N.Y.C., Nov. 11, 1938; s. Oscar David and Gertrude (May) B.; m. Ruth Schaffer, June 27, 1942; children: Jonathan, Jennifer, James, Julia. B.M.E., Rensselaer Poly. Inst., 1959; J.D., Georgetown U., 1963; postgrad., U. Chgo. Sch. Bus., 1963-64. Bar: Ill. 1963, Pa. 1968, N.Y. 1984. Patent examiner U.S. Patent Office, Washington, 1959-60; patent agt. Stevens, Davis, Miller & Mosher, Washington, 1960-63; atty. Abbott Labs., North Chicago, Ill., 1963-66, Scott Paper Co., Phila., 1966-68; ptnr., head computer and tech. law group Schnader, Harrison, Segal & Lewis, Phila., 1968-89; v.p., gen. patent and tech. counsel Unisys Corp., Blue Bell, Pa., 1989-90; founder Bramson and Pressman, Conshohocken, Pa., 1991, 95—; pres., CEO InterDigital Tech. Corp., King of Prussia, Pa., 1992-95; pres. VAI Patent Mgmt. Corp., Conshohocken, Pa., 1995—; adj. prof. Temple U. Law Sch., Phila. Mem. ABA, Internat. Bar Assn., Am. Law Inst., Am. Patent Law Assn., Phila. Patent Law Assn., Phila. Bar Assn. Home: 112 Booth Ln Haverford PA 19041-1752 Office: VAI Patent Mgmt Corp 1100 E Hector St Ste 410 Conshohocken PA 19428-2378

BRAMUCCI, RAYMOND L., employment and training executive; b. Ludlow, Mass.. Sr. exec. Internat. Ladies' Garment Workers Union, 1957-79; dir. N.J. ops. Senator Bill Bradley, 1979-90; commr. N.J. Dept. Labor, 1990-94; asst. sec. labor Employment and Tng. Adminstrn., Dept. Labor, Washington, 1994—; exec. dir. Inst. on Work, Seton Hall U.; arbitrator N.J. Bd. Mediation; former spl. advisor to Pres. of Montclair State U.; adj. prof. polit. sci. Rutgers U. FAX: 202-219-6727. Office: Employment and Tng Adminstrn US Dept Labor 200 Constitution Ave NW Washington DC 20210-0001

BRAMWELL, HENRY, federal judge; b. Bklyn., Sept. 3, 1919; s. Henry Hall and Florence Elva (MacDonald) B.; m. Ishbel W. Brown, Jan. 29, 1966. LLB, Bklyn. Law Sch., 1948, LLD (hon.), 1979. Bar: N.Y. bar 1948. Asst. U.S. atty. Bklyn., 1953-61; assoc. counsel N.Y. State Rent Commn., 1961-63; judge Civil Ct., N.Y.C., Bklyn., 1966, 69—; asst. adminstrv. judge Kings County, Bklyn., 1974—; judge U.S. Dist. Ct., Bklyn., 1975—; U.S. Sr. Dist. judge, 1987—; Mem. Community Mayors N.Y. State; trustee Bklyn. Law Sch., 1978—. Active Bklyn. Old Times Found., Inc. Served with AUS, 1942-44. Profiled in Black Judges on Justice, 1994. Mem. ABA, Nat. Bar Assn. (life), N.Y. State Bar Assn., Bklyn. Bar Assn. (trustee), Fed. Judges Assn. (founding mem.). Home: 101 Clark St Brooklyn NY 11201-2746 Office: US Dist Ct 225 Cadman Plz E Brooklyn NY 11201-1818

BRAMWELL, MARVEL LYNNETTE, nurse, social worker; b. Durango, Colo., Aug. 13, 1947; d. Floyd Lewis and Virginia Jenny (Amyx) B. Diploma in lic. practical nursing, Durango Sch. Practical Nursing, 1968; AD in Nursing, Mt. Hood Community Coll., 1972; BS in Nursing, BS in Gen. Studies cum laude, So. Oreg. State Coll., 1980; cert. edn. grad. sch. social work, U. Utah, 1987, cert. counselor alcohol, drug abuse, 1988, MSW, 1992; M in Social Work, 1992. RN, Utah, Oreg., Ind., Nev.; cert. social worker, Utah, Ind., Nev.; cert. clin. social worker, Ind. Staff nurse Monument Valley (Utah) Seventh Day Adventist Mission Hosp., 1973-74, La Plata Cmty. Hosp., 1974-75; health coord. Tri County Head Start Program, 1974-75; nurse therapist, team leader Portland Adventist Med. Ctr., 1975-78; staff nurse Indian Health Service Hosp., 1980-81; coord. village health services North Slope Borough Health and Social Svc. Agy., Barrow, Alaska, 1981-83; nurse, supr. aides Bonneville Health Care Agy., 1984-85; staff nurse LDS Adolescent Psychiat. Unit, 1985-86; coord. adolescent nursing CPC Olympus View Hosp., 1986-87, 91; charge and staff nurse adult psychiatry U. Utah, 1987-88; nurse MSW Cmty. Nursing Svc., Salt Lake City, 1989-90, Willow Springs Ctr., Reno, Nev., 1996—; resident scvs. coord., dir. nursing Arden Cts., Reno, 1998—; med. social worker Meth. Home Health, Indpls., 1994-96; psychiat. nurse Willow Springs Ctr., 1996—; DON, resident svc. coord. Arden Cts., Reno, 1998—; per diem nurse Reno VA Med. Ctr.; assisted with design and constrn. 6 high tech. health clinics in Alaska Arctic, 1982-83; psychiat. nurse specialist Cmty. Nursing Svc. Contbr. articles to profl. jours. Active Mothers Against Drunk Driving, Program U. Alaska Rural Edn., 1981-83. Recipient cert. of appreciation Barrow Lion's Club, 1983, U.S. Census Bur., Colo., 1970, other awards and scholarships. Mem. NOW, Nat. Assn. Social Workers, Assn. Women Sci. Avocations: water color painting, photography, hiking, horseback riding. Home: Apt 150 6200 Meadow Wood Cir Reno NV 89502

BRANAGAN, JAMES JOSEPH, lawyer; b. Johnstown, Pa., Mar. 5, 1943; s. James Francis and Caroline Bertha (Schreier) B.; m. Barbara Jeanne Miller, June 19, 1965; children: Sean Patrick, Erin MacKay, David Michael. B.A. in English Lit. with honors magna cum laude (Woodrow Wilson fellow), Kenyon Coll., Gambier, Ohio, 1965; LL.B. cum laude, Columbia U., 1968. Bar: Ohio 1968. Assoc. Jones, Day, Reavis & Pogue, Cleve., 1968-72; with Leaseway Transp. Corp., Cleve., 1972-81; gen. counsel Leaseway Transp. Corp., 1975-80, sec., 1979-81, v.p. corp. affairs, 1980-81; also officer, dir. Leaseway Transp. Corp. (subsidiaries); v.p. Premier Indsl. Corp., Cleve., 1981-82; sr. counsel TRW Inc., 1982-88; pvt. practice Cleve., 1988—; treas., gen. counsel, sec. Biomec Inc., 1998—. Mem. ABA, Ohio Bar Assn., Cleve. Bar Assn., Phi Beta Kappa.

BRANAGH, KENNETH, actor, director; b. Belfast, Northern Ireland, Dec. 10, 1960; m. Emma Thompson, Aug. 1989 (div.). Grad., Royal Academy of Dramatic Art, 1981; LittD (hon.), Queens U., Belfast, 1990. Co-founder Renaissance Theater Co., England. For Renaissance Theater Co. authored play Public Enemy, dir. Twelfth Night, King Lear, A Midsummer Night's Dream, Uncle Vanya, acted in Romeo and Juliet, Hamlet, Much Ado About Nothing, As You Like It, Look Back in Anger, Midsummer Night's Dream, King Lear, Coriolanus, other roles; West End stage debut in Another Country, London; film appearances include High Season, 1987, A Month in the Country, 1987, Swing Kids, 1993, Othello, 1995, Gingerbread Man, 1997, Theory of Flight, 1997; actor, dir., script adaptation, producer: Henry V, 1989 (B.A.F.T.A. award Best Dir., 1990, Acad. award nominee Best Actor, Best Dir.), Much Ado About Nothing, 1993; actor, dir.: Dead Again, 1991, Peter's Friends, 1992, Hamlet, 1996 (Acad. award nominee Best Screenplay); dir., co-prodr., actor: Mary Shelley's Frankenstein, 1994; dir., writer In the Bleak Midwinter, 1995; TV work includes The Boy in the Bush, Billy, Maybury, To the Lighthouse, Coming Through, Ghosts, The Lady's Not for Burning, (mini-series) Fortunes of War, (series) Thompson; films include Looking For Richard, 1996, Hamlet, 1996, The Theory of Flight, 1998, The Gingerbread Man, 1998, The Dance of Shiva, 1998, Love's Labour's Lost, 1999, The Betty Schimmel Story, 1999, Alien Love Triangle, 1999, Wild Wild West, 1999, others; TV guest appearance Play for Tomorrow, 1982. Decorated French Order of Arts and Letters, 1994. Office: Creative Arts Agy 9830 Wilshire Blvd Beverly Hills CA 90212-1825*

BRANAN, BRADLEY THOMAS, journalist; b. Atlanta, Mar. 26, 1967; s. James Thomas and Karen (Williams) B. BA, Augsburg Coll., 1990. Freelance journalist, 1990-94; staff writer The Independent, Durham, N.C., 1994-95, The Times Leader, Wilkes-Barre, Pa., 1995-96, The Sun Herald, Biloxi, Miss., 1996—; organizer writers' group Sun Herald, 1997. Contbr. articles to various mags., profl. publs. Recipient Hon. Mention for continuing news coverage AP Mng. Editors Assn. La. and Miss., 1997, Best Gen. News and Best In-Depth Stories, Miss. Press Assn., 1998. Mem. Soc. Profl. Journalists, Investigative Reporters and Editors. Avocations: mountain biking, travel, tennis, history, politics. Home: 251 Eisenhower Dr Apt 144 Biloxi MS 39531-3604 Office: Sun Herald 205 Debuys Rd Gulfport MS 39507-2837

BRANCA, JOHN GREGORY, lawyer, consultant; b. Bronxville, N.Y., Dec. 11, 1950; s. John Ralph and Barbara (Werle) B. AB in Polit. Sci. cum laude, Occidental Coll., 1972; JD, UCLA, 1975. Bar: Calif. 1975. Assoc. Kindel & Anderson, Los Angeles, 1975-77, Hardee, Barovick, Konecky & Braun, Beverly Hills, Calif., 1977-81; ptnr. Ziffren, Brittenham, Branca & Fischer, L.A., 1981—; cons. N.Y. State Assembly, Mt. Vernon, 1978-82, various music industry orgns., L.A., 1981—. Editor-in-Chief UCLA-Alaska Law Rev., 1974-75; contbr. articles to profl. jours. Cons., bd. trustees UCLA Law Sch. Com., UCLA Athletic Dept., Occidental Coll., Musician's Assistance Program, 1995. Recipient Bancroft-Whitney award; named Entertainment Lawyer of Yr. Am. Lawyer mag., 1981. Mem. ABA (patent trademark and copyright law sect.), Calif. Bar Assn., Beverly Hills Bar Assn. (entertainment law sect.), Phi Alpha Delta, Sigma Tau Sigma. Avocations: art, antiques, music, real estate. Office: Ziffren Brittenham Branca & Fischer 1801 Century Park W Fl 9 Los Angeles CA 90067-6406

BRANCALEONE, SALVATORE JOSEPH, nutritionist, consultant; b. N.Y.C., Oct. 29, 1943; s. Joseph and Julia (Vitale) B.; m. Rebecca Diann Thornburg; children: Dina, Debra. AS, U. Fla., 1963; BS, Fla. Atlantic U., 1966, MEd, 1976. Cert. nutritionist Dept. Profl. Regulations Bd. Medicine Dept. of Health. Tchr. H.S. and Broward C.C., Hollywood & Coconut Creek, Fla., 1966-82; pres., clin. nutritionist Palm Lakes Natural Food Market, Margate, Fla., 1980-99; nutritional cons. Parkland, Fla., 1999—; radio talk show host WDJA-850, West Palm Beach, Fla., 1991-99; lectr. in field. Contbr. articles to profl. jours. Bd. dirs., v.p. Cypress Head Homeowners Assn. Mem. Nat. Nutritional Edn. Assn., Nat. Health Fedn., Nat. Counselors Assn. Democrat. Roman Catholic. Avocations: tennis, weight training, jogging, swimming. Home and Office: 7600 Marblehead Ln Parkland FL 33067-2336

BRANCALEONE KENNA, LAURIE ANN, social worker; b. Mineola, N.Y., Oct. 9, 1963; d. Peter and Kathleen (Marsala) B., m. June 20, 1997. B Social Worker, Adelphi U., 1985, MSW, 1986. Cert. clin. social worker. Caseworker III, Nassau County Dept. Social Svcs., Mineola, 1986-88; med. social worker Mercy Med. Ctr., Rockville Centre, N.Y., 1988—; pvt. practice in psychotherapy Garden City, N.Y., 1992—; cons. counselor St. Vincent De Paul Parish Outreach, Elmont, N.Y., 1985—. Bd. dirs. West Nassau Mental Health, Franklin Sq., N.Y., 1988. Mem. NASW, Acad. Cert. Social Workers. Roman Catholic. Avocations: music, poetry writing. Home: 296 Doherty Ave Elmont NY 11003-3019

BRANCATO, EMANUEL LEONARD, electrical engineering consultant; b. N.Y.C., Nov. 3, 1914; s. Settimo Emanuel and Filippa Maria (Di Gregorio) B.; m. Eloise Evelyn Fluharty, Aug. 23, 1958; children: Ann, Lori. BA, Columbia U., 1936, BSEE, 1937, MSEE, 1938; postgrad., U. Md., 1950-65. Registered profl. engr., N.Y. Jr. elec. engr. planning Boston Naval Shipyard, 1938-39; elec. engr., sci. sect. N.Y.C. Naval Shipyard, 1939-46; sect. head Naval Rsch. Lab., Washington, 1946-54, br. head, 1954-70, cons. to dir. rsch., 1970-74, head cons. staff, 1974-78, cons. to directed energy effects br., 1979—; cons. Electric Power Rsch. Inst., Palo Alto, Calif., 1979—; U.S. rep. Internat. Electrotechnical Commn., Geneva, 1960—. Author: Life Expectancy of Motors in Mild Nuclear Environment, 1985; patentee in field. Chmn. Fin. and Planning Com. City of New Carrollton, Md., 1974-76, councilman, 1976-79. Recipient Meritorious Civilian Svc. award USN, 1978, citation in Congl. Record, Ho. of Reps., 1979, Gov.'s citation State of Med., 1979, Thomas W. Dakin Disting. Tech. Achievement award Insulation Dielectrics & Elec. Insulation Soc., 1992. Fellow IEEE (Centennial medal 1984, Disting. Svc. award Insulation Soc. 1985), Washington Acad. Sci; mem. ASTM, Sigma Xi. Democrat. Lutheran. Avocation: research in sound reproduction to simulate concert hall reality. Home: 7370 Hallmark Rd Clarksville MD 21029-1809

BRANCATO, LEO JOHN, manufacturing company executive; b. N.Y.C., Oct. 27, 1922; s. Leo and Josephine (Abbruscato) B. B.S. in Mech. Engring, Cooper Union, 1950; M.S., Columbia U., 1952. Registered profl. engr., Conn. Design engr. Ermold Co., N.Y.C., 1946-51; with Heli-Coil Corp., Danbury, Conn., 1952-70; exec. v.p. Heli-Coil Corp., 1963-70, pres., 1970; v.p., dir. Mite-Corp., merger co. including Heli-Coil Co., Danbury, 1970-74; pres. Mite-Corp., 1974-88; incorporator Union Savs. Bank, Danbury, 1967-92. Trustee Danbury Hosp., 1961—, Union Savs. Bank Found. Inc., 1998; chmn. Housatonic Regional Mental Health Council, 1965-68; commr. conservation, Danbury, 1974-79; mem. bd. visitors U. Conn. Sch. Bus. Adminstrn., 1977-89. Lt. C.E., AUS, 1943-46. Fellow ASME; mem. N.Y. Acad. Scis., Tau Beta Pi. Clubs: Princeton (N.Y.C.); Ridgewood Country (Danbury). Patentee in field of fastener tech.

BRANCEL, BEN, state agency administrator; m. Gail Brancel; children: Micheleen, Tod, Brandon. Degree, U. Wis., Platteville. Mem. State Assembly, 1986-97, assembly spkr., 1997; sec. Wis. Dept. Agr., Trade and Consumer Protection, 1997—; mem. joint fin. com., gov.'s coun. on tourism, legis. coun., legis. audit com., joint com. on employment rels., state claims bd. Former mem. Portage Sch. Bd.; former chmn. Town of Douglas. Mem. Wis. Dairies Coop., Marquette County Farm Bur., Marquette Holstein Assn., World Dairy Authority. Office: PO Box 8911 Madison WI 53708-8911*

BRANCH, ANNE HEATHER, fund raiser; b. Fresno, Calif., Feb. 7, 1960; d. John Donald and Laurie Anne McFeeters; m. Kelly Christopher Branch, Dec. 23, 1987; children: Patrick Simpson, Spenser Morse. BA, U. So. Calif., L.A., 1982, cert. in bus. planning, 1989; M in Internat. Bus. Adminstrn., Monterey Inst. Internat. Study, 1984. Sales mgr. Hyatt Hotels, Inc., Washington, 1985-87; assoc. dir. devel. U. So. Calif., L.A., 1987-91; dir. devel. The Heart Inst., L.A., 1991-93, Northridge Hosp. Found., L.A., 1994-96; asst. dir. devel. Braille Inst. Am., Inc., L.A., 1994-96; with Hathaway Children's Svcs., 1996-97; prin. Interactive Auctions, 1995—; pro-bono cons. Jonathan Art Found., L.A., Cmty. Counseling Svc., L.A., World Children's Transplant Fund, L.A. Recipient scholarship to attend nat. conf. Assn. Hosp. Devel., 1993, commendation U. So. Calif. Annenberg Sch. Comm., L.A., 1995. Mem. Nat. Soc. Fund Raising Execs., Nat. Com. on Planned Giving, Planned Giving Roundtable So. Calif. (scholarship to nat. conf. 1985). Avocations: attending museums and concerts, foreign languages.

BRANCH, BRENDA SUE, library director; b. Buffalo, Apr. 27, 1947. BS in Edn., SUNY, Cortland, 1969; MLS, SUNY, Buffalo, 1972, postgrad., 1972; postgrad., S.W. Tex. State U., 1973-74, Stephen F. Austin State U., 1975-76; MPA, S.W. Tex. State U., 1985. Tchr. Kenmore Ind. Sch. Dist., 1969-70; asst. health scis. libr. SUNY, Buffalo, 1971-73; br. mgr. Austin Pub. Libr., 1973-75; acquisitions libr. Tex. Ea. U., 1975; humanities libr. Stephen F. Austin State U., 1975-76; dist. libr. coord. Longview Ind. Sch. Dist., 1976-77; program devel. coord. Austin Pub. Libr., 1977-80, supr. br. svcs., 1980-86, assoc. dir. pub. svcs., 1986-91, dir., 1991—; project mgr. reduction-in-force project City of Austin, 1988, co-chair customer svc. task force, coord. creativity program, 1990; mem. long range planning com. svcs. spl. populations Tex. State Libr., 1992. Mem. Austin Travis County Continuing Edn. Adv. Bd., Austin, 1981—, Tex. Mcpl. League, Mayor's Coalition Workplace Literacy, 1990, Literacy and Fundamental Edn. Speaker's Bur., 1991-93, Leadership Austin, 1991—, chair kids program, 1993; tutor, trainer Travis County Adult Literacy Coun., 1986-89; chair City of Austin Workplace Literacy Task Force, 1989—; mem. speaker's bur. United Way, 1990-92; mem. MPA adv. coun. S.W. Tex. State U., 1993; bd. dirs. Big Bros./Big Sisters, 1986-90, chair pub. rels. com., 1986-90, fundraiser, 1986-90, com. co-chair, 1986-90. Recipient Outstanding Achievement for Govt. Svc. award YWCA, 1991. Mem. ALA, Tex. Libr. Assn. (treas. dist. V 1976-77, mem. continuing edn. com. 1978-79, mem. membership com. 1986-89, mem. ann. conf. placement ctr. 1989, mem. literacy com. 1990, chair 1990-93, mem. resource sharing com. 1990—, mem. ad hoc property com. 1992, mem. minority recruitment com. 1992-93, co-chair legis. day 1992-93, chair-elect pub. libr. divsn. 1994-95, chair 1995-96), Austin Soc. Pub. Adminstrn. (chair membership com. 1984-89, newsletter editor 1984-89), Toastmasters (v.p., pres., newsletter editor). Office: Austin Public Library PO Box 2287 800 Guadalupe St Austin TX 78701-2314*

BRANCH, JOHN WELLS (JACK TWIG), lawyer; b. Rochester, N.Y., May 1, 1912; s. John W. and Luna H. (Howell) B.; m. Caroline Wilbur, May 29, 1937 (dec.); m. Margaret Zutterman, May 25, 1991. BA, Cornell U., 1934; J.S.D., 1937; MA in Econs., U. Rochester, 1937. Bar: N.Y. 1937, U.S. Ct. Appeals (2nd cir.) 1958. Assoc. Mann, Strang, Bodine & Wright, Rochester, N.Y., 1937-42; chief price atty. OPA, Rochester Dist., 1942-44; ptnr. and now of counsel Branch, Wise and Dewart, Rochester, 1945—; pres. Nat. Planning Data Corp., Ithaca, N.Y., 1970-76; co-founder, pres. The Branch-Wilbur Fund, Inc., 1967—, Eldergard Svcs., Inc., 1988-94; co-founder Genesee-Volkhov Connection, Inc., 1994—. Recipient Civic award Rochester, N.Y 1995. Mem. N.Y. State Bar Assn., Monroe County Bar Assn., Estate Planning Coun. Monroe County, Rotary, Phi Beta Kappa. Democrat. Christian Orthodox. Avocations: composing, helping foreign students, reciting light verse. Home and Office: 34A Larkspur Ct Asheville NC 28805-1368

BRANCH, MICHAEL PAUL, humanities educator; b. Wyandotte, Mich., Dec. 6, 1963; s. Stuart Elton and Sharon Eileen (Shuck) B. BA in English, Coll. William and Mary, 1985; MA in English, U. Va., 1987, PhD of English, 1993. Tchr. U. Va., Charlottesville, 1986-93; asst. prof. English Fla. Internat. U., Miami, 1993-95; asst. prof. lit. and environment U. Nev., Reno, 1995-96, assoc. prof. lit. and environment, 1997—; pres. Assn. for Study of Lit. and Environment, 1995-96. Book rev. editor Interdisciplinary Studies in Lit. and Environment, 1996—; assoc. editor Am. Nature Writing Newsletter, 1993-95; co-editor: The Height of Our Mountains, 1998, Reading the Earth, 1998; contbr. articles to profl. jours. Fellow State Coun. Higher Edn., 1988, 90; grantee Knapp Found., 1994. Mem. Modern Lang. Assn., Am. Lit. Assn., Am. Soc. Environ. History, Soc. Early Americanists, We. Lit. Assn., Sierra Club, Wilderness Soc., Wild Earth, Orion Soc., Phi Beta Kappa. Avocations: hiking, playing blues harp, writing poetry. Office: Univ Nevada Dept English/098 Reno NV 89557

BRANCH, PAULA JOHNSON, city councilwoman. Asst. dir. Kirk Multi-Purpose Ctr., Office of the Mayor, Balt., 1973-78, 81-84, dir. Berea Outreach Ctr.,, 1984-87, appointments sec., 1987; mem. Dem. State Ctrl. Com. Dist. 45 Balt. City Coun., 1982-94, city councilwoman, 1991—; co-owner, v.p. Bay Wood Prodns., Inc., Balt., 1978-90; CEO, v.p. Dee-Jay Bus. Svc., Inc., 1978-81; v.p., gen. mgr. Balt. Electronics Assn., Inc., 1988-90. Staff sgt. USAR, Balt., 1974-86. Democrat. Office: City Hall Rm 511 Baltimore MD 21202*

BRANCH, ROBERT HARDIN, radio and television educator, broadcast executive; b. L.A., Oct. 12, 1939; s. C.H. Hardin and Erma Mae (Smith) B.; m. Judy Nilsson, Mar. 1965 (div. June 1980); children: Kirsten Giard, Kelley R.H.; m. Carol Bussy, Mar. 1990. BA, Antioch U., 1990. Radio personality Sta. KSL, Salt Lake City, 1970-73; asst. news dir. Sta. KOGO, San Diego, 1973-80; reporter Sta. KSDO, San Diego, 1980-84; show host Sta. KTMS, Santa Barbara, Calif., 1984-86; news dir. Sta. KVSD, Vista, Calif., 1986-88; news anchor Sta. KSDO, San Diego, 1988-90; assoc. prof. radio and TV Palomar Coll., San Marcos, Calif., 1990—; gen. mgr. KKSM, San Marcos, 1990—. Staff sgt. U.S. Army, 1958-68. Recipient Golden Mike award So. Calif. Press Assn., L.A., 1974, Alumni of Yr. award Antioch U., Santa Barbara, 1995. Mem. MADD, Soc. Profl. Journalists, Radio and TV News Dirs. Assn., San Diego Press Club (bd. dirs. 1974-76, VIP award 1976, Spot News Feature award 1976). Amnesty Internat., Smithsonian Instn., Holocaust Mus. (charter mem.). Home: 7170 Rock Valley Ct San Diego CA 92122-2737 Office: Sta KKSM-AM 1140 W Mission Rd San Marcos CA 92069-1415

BRANCH, SONYA MEYER, library director; b. Cin., Jan. 25, 1933; m. Dan P. Branch, Dec. 10, 1960; children: Thomas, Martin. B in Music Edn., Fla. State U., 1954, MS in LS, 1959. K-8 tchr. music Redland Sch., Dade County, Fla., 1954-57; libr. Augusta Raa Jr. H.S., Tallahassee, 1959-61; asst. libr., instr. U. Fla. Librs., Tallahassee, 1966-73; libr. Shorecrest Sch., St. Petersburg, Fla., 1974-75, Blessed Sacrament Sch., Tallahassee, 1975-77; children's libr. Lafayette (La.) Pub. Libr., 1977-82, dir., 1982-98, ret., 1998; Bd. dirs. Southestern Libr. Network, 1986-89; mem. statewide steering com. for La. 1991 White House Conf. Bd. dirs. Friends of La. Pub. Broadcasting, 1984-94, Downtown Lafayette Unltd., 1990—, United Way Acadiana, 1988-93; mem. citizens adv. com. for long range facilities plan Lafayette Parish Schs. Mem. ALA, La. Libr. Assn. (chmn. literacy com., nominating com., Modisette award com., trustee, chmn. state conf. 1985, sec. trustees sect.), AAUW. Home: 211 Laurence Ave Lafayette LA 70503-3121 Office: Lafayette Pub Libr 211 Laurence Ave Lafayette LA 70503-3121

BRANCH, TAYLOR, writer; b. Atlanta, Jan. 14, 1947; s. Franklin T. and Jane (Worthington) B.; m. Christina Macy; 2 children. AB, U. N.C., 1968; postgrad., Princeton U., 1968-70. Staff member Washington Monthly mag., Washington, D.C., 1970-73, Harper's mag., N.Y.C., 1973-75, Esquire mag., N.Y.C., 1975-76. Author: (with Bill Russell) Second Wind: The Memoirs of an Opinionated Man, 1979, The Empire Blues, 1981, (with Eugene M. Propper) Labyrinth, 1982, Parting the Waters: America in the King Years, 1954-63, 1988 (Pulitzer Prize for history 1989, Nat. Book Critics Circle award for non-fiction 1988, Christopher award 1988, Nat. Book award nomination 1989); editor, contbr.: (with Charles Peters) Blowing the Whistle: Dissent in the Public Interest, 1972. Office: Larhansoff & Verrill 179 Franklin St New York NY 10013-2857

BRANCH, WILLIAM BLACKWELL, playwright, producer; b. New Haven, Sept. 11, 1927; s. James Matthew and Iola (Douglas) B.; m. Marie Louise Foster, Aug. 19, 1956 (div.); 1 dau., Rochelle Ellen. B.S., Northwestern U., 1949; M.F.A., Columbia U., 1958; ABC fellow, Yale U., 1965-66. Prof. Cornell U., 1985-94; vis. scholar, lectr. numerous univs.; vis. prof. U. Md., Baltimore County, 1979-82; U. Calif. Regents lectr., spring, 1985; vis. Luce fellow Williams Coll., fall, 1983; vis. disting. prof. William Paterson Coll. N.J., Wayne, 1994-96. Actor appearing in: Anna Lucasta, 1945, Detective Story, 1951; playwright for theatre, TV and motion pictures, 1951—; assoc. in film, Columbia Sch. of Arts, 1968-69; staff writer-producer, Channel 13, Ednl. TV, N.Y.C., 1962-64; dir. The Jackie Robinson Show, NBC, 1958-60; co-author: The Jackie Robinson Column N.Y. Post and syndication, 1959-61; screenwriter Universal Studios, 1968-69, producer, NBC News, 1972-73, pres., William Branch Assos., 1973—; works include (theatre) A Medal for Willie, 1951, In Splendid Error, 1954, A Wreath for Udomo, 1960, To Follow the Phoenix, 1960, Baccalaureate, 1975; (TV) Light in the Southern Sky, 1958 (Robert E. Sherwood TV award 1958), A Letter From Booker T., 1987; TV documentary Still a Brother: Inside the Negro Middle Class, 1968 (Emmy award nominee 1969, Blue Ribbon award Am. Film Festival 1969); documentary TV series Afro American Perspectives, 1974-83; screen Together for Days, 1971; exec. producer: Black Perspective on the News, Pub. Broadcasting System, 1978-79; author: Fifty Steps Toward Freedom, 1959; author, editor: Black Thunder: An Anthology of Contemporary African American Drama, 1992 (Am. Book award 1992), Crosswinds: An Anthology of Black Dramatists in the Diaspora, 1993. Bd. dirs. Am. Soc. African Culture, 1963-70; treas. Nat. Conf. African Am. Theatre, 1987-91; bd. dirs. Nat. Citizens Com. for Broadcasting, 1969-71; mem. nat. adv. bd. Ctr. for Book, Library of Congress, 1979-83, W.E.B. DuBois Found., 1987—. Served with AUS, 1951-53. John Guggenheim fellow, 1959-60; recipient Hannah B. Del Vecchio award Columbia, 1958. Address: 53 Cortlandt Ave New Rochelle NY 10801-2032

BRANCH, WILLIAM TERRELL, urologist, educator; b. Paragould, Ark., Dec. 7, 1937; s. William Owen and Mary Rose (Dempsey) B.; m. Mary Fletcher Cox, Dec. 11, 1965; children: Ashley Tucker, William T., Steven K. BS, Ark. State U., 1964, MD, 1971. Diplomate Am. Bd. Urology. Adminstrv. asst. mental retardation planning project State of Ark., Little Rock, 1964-66; intern U. South Fla. Sch. Medicine Affiliated Hosps., Tampa, 1971-72, resident in surgery, 1972-73, resident in urology, 1973-75, chief resident in urology, 1975-76, clin. prof. urology, chmn. dept. surgery, 1976—; practice medicine specializing in urology Tampa, 1976—; mem. staff, sec. urology Tampa Gen. Hosp., 1976-78, vice chief urology, 1978-80, chief urology, 1980-82; mem. staff, co-chief surgery Meml. Hosp., Tampa, 1978-80, vice chief med. staff, 1980-82, chief med. staff, 1982-84, trustee, 1983-88, bd. dirs.; mem. adv. bd. Suncoast Ednl. Telecommunications Systems, 1982; vice chmn., bd. dirs. Meml. Hosp., 1987-88; cons. in urology James A. Haley VA Hosp., Tampa, 1978—; mem. staff St. Joseph's Hosp., Tampa, 1976—, Tampa Gen. Hosp.; cons. staff Women's Hosp., Tampa; adv. bd. Glendale Fed. Savs., 1983-85, Beneficial Harbour Island Savs. Bank, 1985-87, South Trust Bank, 1988—, also bd. dirs., exec. com., chair audit com.; chmn. vol. faculty com. Dept. Surgery U. South Fla. Coll. Medicine. Author: (with others) Mental Retardation in Arkansas, 1964-66; A Demographic Study, 1966; cons. editor Jour. Fla. Med. Assn., 1978-93. Bd. dirs. Tampa Ballet, 1980, Tampa Charity Horse Show Bd. Dirs. Assn., 1985-87; United Way, Tampa, 1983-90, mem. exec. com., 1984-88; mem. med. adv. bd. Nat. Kidney Found. of Fla., Inc., 1983-90; mem. Tampa Bay Super Bowl Task Force; mem. adv. bd. dirs. Salvation Army; founding chmn. Kettle com., vice chmn. adv. bd. dirs., chmn., 1998—. Recipient Disting. Alumnus award Ark. State U., 1986. Fellow ACS (credit com. region IV, Fla. chpt. 1982—, exec. com. Fla. chpt. 1985—, sec., treas. 1987-88, pres.-elect 1989-90, pres. 1990-92, gov. 1990-96, bd. gov. chpt. activities com. 1991-96, alt. 1993, chmn. nomination com. 1995, chmn. applications com. region IV); mem. Am. Urol. Assn., Royal Soc. Medicine (affiliate), Fla. Med. Assn. (del. 1983, 88-96), Fla. Urol. Soc. (Milton Copeland award 1976, exec. com. 1978-82), Hillsborough County Med. Assn. (exec. com. 1978-81, treas. 1981-82, sec. 1983-84), Fla. Quality Med. Assurance, Inc. (bd. dirs., treas., chmn. exec. com. 1995, chmn. bd. govs.), Southeastern Surg. Congress, Greater Tampa C. of C. (dir. 1982-86, 87-90, chmn. med. meetings task force 1983-84, Super Star award 1983), Tampa Bay Surg. Soc. (founding mem., sec., bd. dirs. 1998, pres.-elect 1999), Tampa Hist. Soc., Hillsborough County Med. Soc. (pres. polit. action com. 1986-87, 88-89), Tampa Yacht and Country Club (gov. 1984-87), Centre of Tampa Club (founding mem. 1988-93, bd. dirs., chmn. mem. com.), Univ. Club (treas. 1998—, sec. 1999—, bd. dirs. 1998-99), Ye Mystic Krewe of Gasparilla (bd. dirs. 1991—, 1st lt. 1988-89, lord chamberlain 1994-95, chmn. exec. com. 1995-96, capt. 1996-98), King Gasparilla LXXXVI. Home: 909 S Golfview Ave Tampa FL 33629-5221 Office: 2919 W Swann Ave Ste 303 Tampa FL 33609-4051

BRANCO, JAMES JOSEPH, estate planner; b. Santa Maria, Azores, Portugal, Mar. 14, 1951; came to U.S., 1954; s. Leroy and Michele (Desroches) B.; married, Aug. 27, 1994; children: James II, Natalie. BA, Brandywine Coll., 1971. Chief exec. officer Profl. Fin. Mgrs., Inc., Spring Lake, N.J., 1974—; ptnr. Atlantic Drilling Co., Sea Girt, 1982—; pres. Profl. Condo Conversions, Belmar, N.J., 1977-93. Mem. Belman C. of C. (pres. 1995—), Pan Am. Club, Phi Epsilon. Republican. Roman Catholic. Avocations: racquetball, whitewater rafting, photography. Office: Profl Fin Mgrs Inc 1006 Main St Belmar NJ 07719

BRAND, CHARLES MACY, history educator; b. Stanford, Calif., Apr. 7, 1932; s. Carl F. and Nan (Surface) B.; m. Mary Joan Shorrock, Aug. 7, 1954; children: Catharine, Stephen. B.A., Stanford U., 1953; M.A., Harvard U., 1954, Ph.D., 1961. Asst. prof. history San Francisco State Coll., 1962-64; asst. prof. Bryn Mawr Coll., Pa., 1964-69, assoc. prof., 1969-75, prof. history, 1975-99, chmn. dept. history, 1978-81, 96-97; prof. emeritus Bryn Mawr Coll., 1999—. Author: Byzantium Confronts the West, 1180-1204, 1968, 2d edit., 1992; editor: Icon and Minaret, 1969; translator: Deeds of John and Manuel Comnenus (by J. Kinnamos), 1976. Served with U.S. Army, 1955-57. Dumbarton Oaks Center for Byzantine Studies fellow, 1961, 1988; Fulbright research fellow, 1968; Gennadius fellow, 1968; Guggenheim fellow, 1972. Mem. U.S. Nat. Com. for Byzantine Studies (1961), Medieval Acad. Am., Am. Hist. Assn., Byzantine Studies Conf. Home: 508 Montgomery Ave Haverford PA 19041-1409 Office: Bryn Mawr Coll Dept History Bryn Mawr PA 19010

BRAND, EDWARD CABELL, retail executive; b. Salem, Va., Apr. 11, 1923; s. William F. and Ruth (Cabell) B.; m. Shirley Hurt, June 20, 1964; children: Sylvia, Miriam, Liza, Richie, John, Edward, Marshall, Caroline. Grad., Va. Mil. Inst., 1944; HHD (hon.), Roanoke Coll., 1997, Washington and Lee U., 1999. Dept. of State econ. analyst, intelligence office Berlin Mil. Govt., 1947-49; v.p. Ortho-Vent Shoe Co., 1949-62; pres. Brand Edmonds Assocs. Advertising, 1962-66, chmn. bd., 1962-81; founder, pres. Stuart McGuire Co., Salem, Va., 1962-85; chmn. bd., chief exec. officer Stuart McGuire Co., 1973-85; chmn. emeritus, cons. Stuart McGuire Co. (merged with Home Shopping (TV) Network), 1985-86; pres. Recovery Systems, Inc., Salem, Va., 1986—; rsch. assoc., former instr. bus. adminstrn. and sales mgmt. Roanoke Coll. Chmn. Va. State Bd. Health, 1989-93; pres., founder Cabell Brand Ctr. for Internat. Poverty and Resource Studies of Roanoke Coll; former mem. Bus. Leadership Adv. Council.; past bd. dirs. Roanoke Council of Community Services; founder, pres. Total Action Against Poverty, Roanoke Valley, 1965-95; pres. Pvt. Sector Commn. Va. Community Action Agys., 1986-88; mem. Gov.'s Commn. on Fed. Funding of State Domestic Program, 1986-88; former trustee Council on Religion and Internat. Affairs, Ethics Resource Ctr.; past bd. dirs. Woodlands Conf. div. Woodlands Ctr. for Future Research and the Houston Area Research Ctr., Global Water, Washington; bd. dirs. Va. Health Care Found., Richmond, Va., 1993—, Va. Found. for the Humanities and Pub. Policy, Charlottesville, 1993—, Blue Ridge Pub. TV, Roanoke, Va., 1993—, Action Alliance for Va. Children and Youth, Richmond, 1994—, Va. Conservation Network, Richmond, 1996—; bd. trustees Western Va. Land Trust, Roanoke, Va., 1995—; assoc. World Resources Inst., Washington, 1985. Served from pvt. to capt. AUS, 1942-46, ETO. Decorated Bronze Star. Named Businessman in U.S. who has done most to help disadvantaged people, Vista, 1980; recipient LBJ Humanitarian nat. award, 1989, Outstanding Citizen Rotary Club, 1999. Mem. NAS (coun., pres. circle), Social Venture Network, Direct Selling Assn. (past dir., chmn. named to Hall of Fame), U.S. C. of C., Conf. Bd. (exec. coun.), Chief Execs. Orgn., World Resources Inst., World Pres. Assn (past dir., chmn. Argentina Conf. 1988), Newcomen Soc. N.Am., Roanoke Touchdown Club (past pres.), Valley Torch Club (past pres.), Roanoke Sales Execs. (past dir.), Rotary (past. pres. Salem). Home: 701 W Main St Salem VA 24153-3513 Office: Recovery Systems Inc PO Box 429 Salem VA 24153-0429 *In addition to trying to do the best job I could—whether in school, business, public service, or in my family—I have felt a continuing need to improve our system and society. This has led to extensive study, travels, and a variety of extra-curricular activities. Today I have great confidence in the future of the United States and the world, but see urgent need for dramatic changes in our value systems, and need for long range planning. Our New Center focuses on inter-relationship between poverty and resource limitation for sustainable development.*

BRAND, GEORGE EDWARD, JR., lawyer; b. Detroit, Oct. 25, 1918; s. George Edward and Elsie Bertie (Jones) B.; m. Patricia Jean Gould, June 7, 1947; children—Martha Christine, Carol Elsie, George Edward. B.A., Dartmouth Coll., 1941; postgrad., U. Minn., Harvard U., 1941; J.D., U. Mich., 1948. Bar: Mich. 1948, U.S. Supreme Ct. 1958. Mem. firm George E. Brand, Detroit, 1948-63, Butzel, Long, Gust, Klein & Van Zile, P.C., Detroit, 1963—; ptnr., dir., pres. Butzel, Long, Gust, Klein & Van Zile, 1974-89. Served with USNR, 1942-46. Fellow Am. Bar Found., Am. Coll. Trial Lawyers; mem. ABA, Am. Judicature Soc., Detroit Bar Assn., VFW. Club: N.S.S.C. Home: 1233 Kensington Ave Grosse Pointe MI 48230-1101 Office: 150 W Jefferson Ave Ste 900 Detroit MI 48226-4415

BRAND, GERHARD, retired English educator; b. Vienna, Austria, Aug. 18, 1927; came to U.S., 1939; s. Leo and Gertrude (Scharf) B.; m. Alice Mary Godfrey, Aug. 25, 1962 (div. May 1973); children: Madeleine, Rachel; m. Ann Kempe Lodwig, Nov. 26, 1983. BA, Trinity Coll., Hartford, Conn., 1949; MA, UCLA, 1953, PhD, 1969. Instr. Cornell U., Ithaca, N.Y., 1957-60; prof. Calif. State U., L.A., 1960-92. Contbr. articles to profl. jours. With U.S. Army, 1953-54. Democrat. Home: 2589 Magnolia Blvd W Seattle WA 98199-3631

BRAND, JOHN CHARLES, chemistry educator; b. Durban, South Africa, May 5, 1921; emigrated to Can., 1969, naturalized, 1975; s. Andrew Nevill and Helen Mabel B.; m. Evelyn Grace Meek, Sept. 8, 1943; 1 son, David Andrew. B.Sc., U. London, 1941, M.Sc., 1943, Ph.D., 1947, D.Sc., 1956. Lectr. chemistry U. Glasgow, Scotland, 1947-56; sr. lectr. U. Glasgow, 1957-64; prof. Vanderbilt U., 1964-69, U. Western Ont., 1969—. Author: Applications of Spectroscopy, 1965, Molecular Structure, 1976, Lines of Light, 1995; contbr. articles to profl. jours. Recipient Herzberg award Spectroscopy Soc. Can., 1982. Fellow Royal Soc. Can.; mem. Can. Inst. Chemistry (Chem. medal 1987), Can. Assn. Physicists, Chem. Soc.

BRAND, LEONARD, physician, educator; b. Bklyn., Dec. 21, 1923; s. Samuel and Sarah (Berrin) B.; m. Helen Frances Thomashow, Mar. 11, 1951; children: Dana Aron, Jennifer Susan, Stefanie Alice. Student, Bklyn. Coll., 1940-42, U. N.H., 1943-44; B.S., Yale U., 1946; M.D., Columbia U., 1949. Diplomate: Am. Bd. Anesthesiology. Intern L.I. Coll. Hosp., 1949-50; resident physician Leo N. Levi Meml. Hosp., Hot Springs, Ark., 1950-51; resident in anesthesiology Presbyterian Hosp., N.Y.C., 1953-55; asst. in anesthesiology Presbyterian Hosp., 1955-57, asst. attending in anesthesiology, 1957-66, assoc. attending in anesthesiology, 1966-72, attending anesthesiologist, 1972—; dir. Pain Treatment Service, Dept. Anesthesiology Columbia-Presbyn. Med. Ctr.; instr. anesthesiology Columbia U., 1955-57, assoc., 1957-59, asst. prof., 1959-66, assoc. prof. in clin. anesthesiology, 1966-72, prof., 1972-94; prof. emeritus, 1994—; vis. prof. Glostrup Hosp., Copenhagen, Denmark, 1966, Radcliffe Infirmary, Oxford, Eng., 1974; senator Columbia U. Senate, 1978—. Contbr. articles to profl. jours. Trustee Englewood Cliffs (N.J.) Sch. Bd., 1961-66, pres., 1964-66. Served with U.S. Army, 1942-46, 51-53. Recipient Carnegie Hero medal, 1952;

named Practitioner of the Yr., Soc. Practitioners, Columbia-Presbyn. Med. Ctr., 1991. Fellow Am. Coll. Anesthesiologists, Am. Scandinavian Found.; mem. N.Y. County Med. Soc., N.Y. State Med. Soc., N.Y. State Soc. Anesthesiologists, Am. Soc. Anesthesiologists, Am. Soc. for Regional Anesthesia, Am. Soc. Pharmacology and Exptl. Therapeutics, Found. Thanatology, Am. Pain Soc. Office: 622 W 168th St New York NY 10032-3720

BRAND, MYLES, academic administrator; b. N.Y.C., May 17, 1942; s. Irving Philip and Shirley (Berger) B.; m. Wendy Hoffman (div. 1976); 1 child: Joshua; m. Margaret Zeglin, 1978. BS, Rensselaer Poly. Inst., 1964, PhD (hon.), 1991; PhD, U. Rochester, 1967. Asst. prof. philosophy U. Pitts., 1967-72; from assoc. prof. to prof., dept. chmn. U. Ill., Chgo., 1972-81; prof., dept. head U. Ariz., Tucson, 1981-83; dir. cognitive sci. program U. Ariz., 1982-85; dean, social & behavioral scis. U. Ariz., Tucson, 1983-86; provost, v.p. acad. affairs Ohio State U., Columbus, 1986-89; pres. U. Oreg., Eugene, 1989-94, Ind. U., Bloomington, 1994—. Author: Intending and Acting, 1984; editor: The Nature of Human Action, 1970, The Nature of Causation, 1976, Action Theory, 1976. Bd. dirs. Ariz. Humanities Coun., 1984-85, Am. Coun. on Edn., Washington, 1992-97. Recipient research award NEH, 1974, 79. Mem. Clarion Hosps. Assn. of Am.a Phi. Office: Ind Univ Bryan Hall 200 Bloomington IN 47405

BRAND, OSCAR, folksinger, author, educator; b. Winnipeg, Man., Can., Feb. 7, 1920; s. Isidore and Beatrice (Shulman) B.; m. Rubyan Saber (div.); children: Jeannie, Eric, James; m. Karen Lynn Grossman, June 14, 1970; 1 child, Jordan. BA, Bklyn. Coll., 1942; Polit. Sci. Laureate, Fairfield U., 1972; PhD (hon.), U. Winnipeg, 1987. Host, performer Folksong Festival, Sta. WNYC-AM-FM, N.Y.C., 1945—; pres. Harlequin Prodns., Inc., Gypsy Hill Music, Inc.; trustee Newport Festival Found.; mem. faculty Hofstra U., New Sch., 1970-80; music adviser nat. bd. YWCA; mem. creative bd. Sesame Street, Pres.'s Com. on Nutrition; cons. Bill Moyers, PBS-TV, 1983; curator Songwriters Hall of Fame. Host: (TV show) World of Folkmusic, H.E.W., 1962-82, Oscar Brand's Am. Odyssey, 1970-72, Treasure Chest, The First Look, 1965-68, (radio show) Voices in the Wind, 1974-80, 13 of Segovia, First Person Am.; star: (TV series) Let's Sing Out, Can., 1962-68, Brand New Scene, Can., 1966; music dir. (TV series) Nat. Geog. Bicentennial, 1974, Sunday, Exploring; music advisor: (TV series) Nuclear Age, 1986-87, (PBS) Liberty, 1998; writer, dir.: (TV spl. and show) Sing, America, Sing, Kennedy Ctr. Bicentennial Celebration, 1975; composer, lyricist: (broadway show) Joyful Noise, 1966, HYMAN KAPLAN, 1967, (off-broadway show) In White America, 1965, How to Steal an Election, 1968, It's a Jungle, Bridge of Hope for lit. conf., 1969, Celebrate for N.Y. Presbytery, 1970, (off broadway show) Thunder Bay, Fun and Games, Protest, 1999, (songs for film) The Fox, Sybil, The Long Riders, Blue Chips, 1994; author: Singing Holidays, 1957, Bawdy Songs, 1960, Folksongs for Fun, 1961, The Ballad Mongers, 1964, Songs of '76, 1974, When I First Came to This Land, 1975, Party Songs, 1983; rec. artist 90 albums; performer (video) At Home, 1988, Campaigns for Smithsonian, 1999; editor: Words About Music, 1980—. Program coord. Nat. Hadassah, 1989-98; trustee BMI Found., 1995—; music dir. Rukeyser Guide, 1996. Served as sgt. M.C. AUS, 1942-45. Recipient Radio Pioneers of Am. award, 1986, Venice, Edinburgh, Valley Forge, Golden Reel and Cannes Film Festival awards for documentary and ednl. films, 1946, numerous other awards include Emmy, Peabody, Freedoms Found., Scholastic, Edison, Golden Lion for radio, TV and films, 1962-86, Lifetime Achievement award World Folk Music Assn., 1996, Peabody Personal award, 1996; honoree Coalition Against Domestic Violence (adv. bd. 1993—), United Cmty. Fund, 1997. Mem. Nat. Acad. Popular Music (bd. dirs. 1969—), N.Y. Folklore Soc., Sheet Music Soc. Avocations: sailing, carpentry. Office: Gypsy Hill Music Box 1362 Manhasset NY 11030 *I need more time.*

BRAND, STEVE AARON, lawyer; b. St. Paul, Sept. 5, 1948; s. Allen A. and Shirley Mae (Mintz) B.; m. Gail Idele Greenspoon, Oct. 9, 1977. BA, U. Minn., 1970; JD, U. Chgo., 1973. Bar: Minn. 1973, U.S. Dist. Ct. Minn. 1974, U.S. Supreme Ct. 1977. Assoc. Briggs & Morgan, St. Paul, 1973-78, ptnr. 1978-91; ptnr. Robins, Kaplan, Miller & Ciresi, L.L.P., 1991—. Pres. Jewish Vocat. Svc., 1981-84, Mt. Zion Hebrew Congregation, 1985-87, Sholom Found., 1996—; bd. dirs. Friends of the St. Paul Public Libr., 1997—. Mem. ABA, Minn. Bar Assn. (chmn. probate and trust law sect. 1984-85), Hebrew Union Coll.-Jewish Inst. Religion (bd. overseers 1987—, vice-chmn. 1996—), Am. Coll. Trust and Estate Counsel (Minn. chair 1991-96, regent 1998—), Ramsey County Bar Found. (pres. 1995—), Phi Beta Kappa, B'nai Brith. Democrat. Home: 1907 Hampshire Ave Saint Paul MN 55116-2401 Office: Robins Kaplan Miller & Ciresi LLP 2800 LaSalle Plz 800 Lasalle Ave Ste 2800 Minneapolis MN 55402-2015

BRAND, STEWART, editor, writer; b. Rockford, Ill., Dec. 14, 1938. BS in Biology, Stanford U., 1960. Formerly with Merry Pranksters; founder Am. Needs Indians; spl. cons. to Gov. Edmund G. Brown, Jr., Calif., 1976-78; rsch. scientist Media Lab, MIT, 1986; vis. scholar Royal Dutch/Shell, 1986. Author: Two Cybernetic Frontiers, 1974, The Media Lab, 1987, How Buildings Learn, 1994; editor/pub.: The Last Whole Earth Catalog, 1968-71 (Nat. Book award), Whole Earth Epilog, 1974, The Next Whole Earth Catalog, 1980-81, The Co-Evolution Quar., 1974-85; editor-in-chief: Whole Earth Software Catalog, 1983-85; writer, presenter: How Buildings Learn, 1997, The Clock of the Long Now, 1999. Founder The WELL teleconf. system, 1984—; co-founder Global Bus. Network, 1988—, The Long Now Found., 1996—; trustee Santa Fe Inst., 1989—. Address: 3E Gate 5 Rd Sausalito CA 94965-1401 *Life rides. Death drives.*

BRAND, VANCE DEVOE, astronaut, government official; b. Longmont, Colo., May 9, 1931; s. Rudolph William and Donna (DeVoe) B.; m. Joan Virginia Weninger, July 25, 1953; children: Susan Nancy, Stephanie, Patrick Richard, Kevin Stephen; m. Beverly Ann Whitnel, Nov. 3, 1979; children: Erik Ryan, Dane Vance. BS in Bus., U. Colo., 1953, BS in Aero. Engring., 1960; MBA, UCLA, 1964; grad., U.S. Naval Test Pilot Sch., Patuxent River, Md., 1963. With Lockheed-Calif. Co., Burbank, 1960-66; flight test engr. Lockheed-Calif. Co., 1961-62, traveling engr. rep., 1962-63, engring. test pilot, 1963-66; astronaut NASA Johnson Space Ctr., Houston, 1966-92; command module pilot Apollo-Soyuz mission NASA Johnson Space Ctr., 1975, comdr. STS-5 Mission, 1982, comdr. STS 41-B Mission, 1984, comdr. STS-35 Mission, 1990; chief plans Nat. Aero-Space Plane Joint Program Office, Wright-Patterson AFB, Ohio, 1992-94; asst. chief flight ops. directorate DFRC NASA, Edwards, Calif., 1994-98, dep. dir. aerospace projects, 1998—. With USMCR, 1953-57. Decorated 2 Disting. Svc. medals NASA, 2 Exceptional Svc. medals, 3 Space medals. Fellow AIAA, Am. Astron. Soc., Soc. Exptl. Test Pilots. Office: M/S D2084A DFRC PO Box 273 Edwards CA 93523-0273

BRANDAU, SUSAN CAROL, library director; b. Oct. 14, 1951. BA, U. Pitts., 1973. Libr. dir. Milton (Pa.) Pub. Libr., 1990—. E-mail: lbran@sunlink.net. Home: 201 Center St Milton PA 17847-1719

BRANDAUER, FREDERICK PAUL, Asian language educator; b. N.Y.C., Dec. 14, 1933; s. Frederick William and Grace Angeline (Martin) B.; children—Rebekah Susan, Frederick Jonathan. B.A., Lebanon Valley Coll., 1955; M.Div., United Theol. Sem., 1958; M.A., U. Pitts., 1965; Ph.D., Stanford U., 1973. Missionary United Meth. Ch., Hong Kong, 1959-69; acting dir. (Christian Study Center), Hong Kong, 1967-69; lectr. Chinese, Stanford (Calif.) U., 1972-73; asst. prof. Chinese U. Wash., Seattle, 1973-78, chmn. dept. Asian lang. and lit., 1978-82, assoc. prof., 1978-97, assoc. prof. emeritus, 1997—. Author: (with M. Berkowitz and J. Reed) Folk Religion in an Urban Setting, 1969, Tung Yueh, 1978; editor (with C.C. Huang) Imperial Rulership and Cultural Change in Traditional China, 1994; contbr. articles to profl. jours. NDEA Title IV fellow, 1969-71; NDFL Title VI fellow, 1971-72; ACLS Chinese Civilization grantee, 1976-77; Alexander von Humboldt fellow U. Munich, 1977-78. Mem. Assn. Asian Studies, Am. Oriental Soc., Soc. Study of Chinese Religions. Roman Catholic. Address: 1816 NE 55th St Seattle WA 98105*

BRANDAUER, KLAUS MARIA, actor; b. Altaussee, Austria, June 22, 1944; m. Karin Mueller. Educated, Acad. Music & Dramatic Arts, Stuttgart, Fed. Republic Germany. Actor German and Austrian theatre; motion pictures include The Salzburg Connection, 1972, Mephisto (Best Actor Cannes Film Festival 1981), Never Say Never Again, 1983, Colonel Redl, 1985, Out of Africa, 1985, The Lightship, 1985, Streets of Gold, 1986, The Death Ship, Burning Secret, 1988, Hanussen, 1988, Révolution franÇaise, 1989, Oskar Schindler-An Angel in Hell, Hitlerjunge Salomon, Das Spinnennetz, 1989, Georg Elser-Einer aus Deutschland, 1989, The Russia House, 1990, White Fang, 1991, The Resurrected, Becoming Colette, 1992, Felidae (voice), 1994, Rembrandt, 1999; actor, dir. (motion pictures) Seven Minutes, The Artisan, Georg Elser, 1989, Mario and the Magician, 1994; dir. Die Wand, 1995; appeared in TV program Quo Vadis?; TV guest appearance Derrick, 1974. *

BRANDENBERG, ALIKI LIACOURAS See ALIKI

BRANDENBURG, DAVID SAUL, gastroenterologist, educator; b. Linz, Austria, Apr. 12, 1948; came to U.S., 1948; s. Mayer and Syda Brandenburg; m. Bette Ellen Hirschberg, Aug. 8, 1971; children: Stacey, Mark, Marci. BA, Rutgers U., 1968; MD, Georgetown U., 1972. Bd. cert. internal medicine; bd. cert. GI. Med. intern, resident R.I. Hosp.-Brown U. Affiliated, Providence, 1972-75; gastroenterology fellow Emory U., Atlanta, 1975-77; pvt. practice Atlanta Digestive Diseases and Internal Medicine, 1977-82, Brandenburg and Kramer M.D., P.C., Atlanta, 1983-97; clin. asst. prof. medicine Emory U. Sch. Medicine, Atlanta, 1977—; with Atlanta Gastroenterology Assocs., 1998—; med. dir. North Atlanta Endoscopy Ctr., Atlanta, 1986—; sec., v.p., pres. Ga. Soc. GI Endoscopy, Atlanta, 1980-86; chmn., med. adv. com. Ga. chpt. Crohn's and Colitis Found., Atlanta, 1995-97. Bd. trustees Temple Emmanuel, Dunwoody, Ga., 1985-91, 95-96, treas., v.p., 1985-91. Fellow Am. Coll. Gastroenterology (gov. 1991-95); mem. Am. Gastroenterol. Assn., Am. Soc. Gastrointestinal Endoscopy. Office: 5671 Peachtree Dunwoody Rd NE Atlanta GA 30342-1725

BRANDENBURG, JAMIE ENRICO, elementary education educator; b. Gary, Ind.; d. James Anthony and Julia Kathryn (Wilk) Enrico; m. David George Brandenburg, Aug. 31, 1968; children: Julie, Sara. BE, Ind. U., 1970; MEd, Valparaiso U., 1981. Lic. tchr., Ind. Tchr. Lake Station (Ind.) Cmty. Schs., 1970-75, Sch. City of Hobart, Ind., 1977-99; instr. Purdue U. Calumet, Hammond, Ind., 1997-98; Purdue U. North Central, Westville, Ind., 1999. Named Tchr. of the Yr. Hobart Rotary, 1986; Gifted Edn. & Econs. grantee State of Ind., 1994. Mem. NEA, Ind. State Tchrs. Assn., Hobart Tchrs. Assn. (bldg. rep. 1977—), Delta Kappa Gamma. Home: 121 Fraser Ln Hobart IN 46342-3448 Office: Sch City of Hobart Joan Martin Sch 301 E 10th St Hobart IN 46342-5902

BRANDENBURG, RICHARD GEORGE, university dean, management educator; b. Oak Park, Ill., Feb. 21, 1935; s. George Arthur and Florence (Ream) B.; m. Maxine Toby Newman, Dec. 21, 1957; children: Suzanne Linda, Cynthia Anne. BME, Cornell U., 1958, MBA, 1960, PhD, 1964. Asst. to dean Grad. Sch. Indsl. Adminstrn., Carnegie Inst. Tech., Pitts., 1962-64; asst. dean, asst. prof. indsl. adminstrn. Grad. Sch. Indsl. Adminstrn., Carnegie Inst. Tech., 1964-67; acting dean, assoc. prof. indsl. adminstrn. Grad. Sch. Indsl. Adminstrn., Carnegie-Mellon U., Pitts., 1967-68; dean, prof. mgmt. Sch. Mgmt., SUNY, Buffalo, 1968-76, 80-87; adj. prof. mgmt.; v.p. mfg. and engring. The Carborundum Co., Niagara Falls, N.Y., 1976-80; chmn. Vt. Health Care Authority, 1992-94; dean, prof. mgmt. Coll. Bus. Adminstrn. Grad. Sch. Bus. and Pub. Mgmt., U. Denver, 1980-87; prof. bus. adminstrn. U. Vt., Burlington, 1987—, dean Sch. Bus. Adminstrn., 1987-92, dean divsn. engring., math. and bus. adminstrn., 1987-92; pres. Am. Assembly Collegiate Schs. Bus., 1984-85, Mid. Atlantic Assn. Colls. Bus. Adminstrn., 1974; mem. policy com. regents external degree in bus. adminstrn. N.Y. State Dept. Edn., 1975-80; mem. mfg. coun. Machinery and Allied Products Inst., Am. Mgmt. Assn., 1976-80; trustee arts devel. svcs., Buffalo, 1973-76; bd. dirs., mem. coun., mem. exec. seminar adv. com. Niagara Inst.; trustee N.Y. Coun. for Humanities, 1977-80; vice chmn. Advs. Com. on Mgmt. and Budget for Erie County; bd. regents Canisius Coll., Buffalo, 1974-80; past trustee Daemen Coll.; past dir. Assoc. Inns and Restaurants Co. Am.; past dir. HMO Colo., United Bank of Monaco, Denver, Mentor Corp., Denver; vis. prof. ctr. for the evaluative clin. scis. Dartmouth Med. Sch., 1994-95, adj. prof. cmty. and family medicine, 1995—; pres., bd. dirs. Vt. Inst. for Sci., Math. and Tech., 1998—. Author: (with H.I. Ansoff, Fred E. Portner, R. Radosevich) Acquisition Behavior of U.S. Manufacturing Firms, 1946-65, 1971, Japanese edit., 1972; mem. editorial bd.: Calif. Mgmt. Rev, 1967-76, Jour. Gen. Mgmt, 1970; editor mfg. sect.: AMA Mgmt. Handbook, 1983; mem. adv. bd.: Non Profit Mgmt. and Leadership; contbr. articles to profl. jours. Bd. dirs. Colo. Endowment of Humanities Program, 1981-84, Flynn Theatre, Burlington, 1987-92, trustee chmn., 1998—; bd. dirs. Vt. Inst. for Sci., Math. and Tech., 1995—, bd. dirs. and treas. Vt. Ethics Network, 1997—; mem. Gov.'s Commn. on Econ. Future of Vt.; bd. dirs., v.p. Child and Adolescent Psychiat. Clinic, Buffalo, 1974-80; bd. dirs., treas. Metro Denver Conv. and Visitors Bur., 1982-87, Denver Chamber Orch., 1984-87; chmn. trustee com. on acad. affairs and trustee exec. com., Champlain Coll., Burlington, 1991—. Recipient McKinsey award, 1969; named One of 10 Most Disting. citizens, Denver Bus. mag., 1984. Mem. Am. Mgmt. Assn. (president's coun. 1980-83, Rand D coun. 1983-86), Vt. Bus. Roundtable (pub. fin. and budgeting study com., econ. devel. study com.), Vt. C. of C. (bd. dirs. 1988-91), Denver C. of C. (small bus. steering com. 1986-87), Lake Champlain Regional C. of C. (bd. dirs. 1990-92, bd dirs. Leadership Champlain program 1988—), Phi Kappa Tau, Beta Gamma Sigma, Phi Kappa Phi, Pi Tau Sigma, Tau Beta Pi, Delta Sigma Pi, Mu Kappa Tau. Home: 131 Northshore Dr Burlington VT 05401-1273 Office: U Vt Sch Bus Adminstrn Kalkin Hall Burlington VT 05405

BRANDENSTEIN, DANIEL CHARLES, astronaut, retired naval officer; b. Watertown, Wis., Jan. 17, 1943; s. Walter C. and Agnes (Holzworth) B.; m. Jane A. Wade, Jan. 2, 1966; 1 dau., Adelle. B.S., U. Wis., River Falls, 1965; postgrad., U.S. Naval Test Pilot Sch., Patuxent River, Md., 1971. Commd. officer U.S. Navy, 1965, advanced through grades to capt., 1984, ret., 1993; student aviator U.S. Navy, Pensacola, Fla., 1965-67; aviator U.S. Navy, Whidbey Island, Wash., 1967-71; test pilot U.S. Navy, Patuxent River, Md., 1971-74; aviator U.S. Navy, Whidbey Island, Wash., 1974-78; astronaut NASA Johnson Space Ctr., Houston, 1978-93; chief astronaut office NASA Johnson Space Ctr., 1987-93; dir. program development Loral Space Info. Sys., Houston, 1993-96; exec. v.p. Kistler Aerospace Corp., Kirkland, Wash., 1996-99; v.p. Lockheed Martin Space Ops., 1999—. Decorated Legion of Honor (France); recipient 34 medals and awards USN, 1968-93; recipient Disting. Alumnus award U. Wis., 1982, Yuri Gagarin Gold medal Fedn. Aeronautique Internationale, 1990, Laurel Award, Space/Missiles, Aviation Week & Space Tech., 1993, Haley Space Flight award Am. Inst. of Aeronautics and Astronautics, 1993. Mem. AIAA (Haley Space Flight award 1993), Soc. Exptl. Text Pilots (Ivan C. Kinchloe award 1992), U.S. Naval Inst., Assn. Space Explorers. Office: Lockheed Martin Space Ops PO Box 58980 Houston TX 77058

BRANDES, RAYMOND STEWART, history educator; b. San Diego, Jan. 2, 1924; s. Raymond C. and María Rosario (Peters) B.; m. Irma Dolores Montijo, Jan. 28, 1961; children: Elena María, Elisa Anne, Laura Raquel, Claudia Reneé, Ramón Antonio, Marta Denise, Paula Nicole. BA, U. Ariz., 1961, PhD, 1965. Asst. prof. history U. San Diego, 1966-67, assoc. prof., 1967-71, prof., 1971-98, univ. archivist, 1992-98, chmn. dept., 1967-73, grad. dean, 1973-91; ret., 1998; dir. several grants related to hist. preservation and hist. site archaeology in San Diego area. Author: Diario of Miguel Costanso, 1969, Troopers West: Military and Indian Affairs on the American Frontier, 1970, Frontier Military Posts of Arizonia, 1960, San Diego: An Illustrated History, 1982; editor Brand Book 1, San Diego Corral of Westerners, 1970, Masterplanner for Old Town State Historical Park, 1973-74, Old Town San Diego, 1821-1974, 1976, History and Archaeology of New Town, San Diego, 1985, Coronado: The Enchanted Island, 1987, 3d edit., 1999, Coronado: We Remember, 1993, The Pacific Coast League San Diego Padres, 2 vols., 1936-1957, 1997. Mem. Gaslamp Quarter Project Area Com., 1977—, chmn., 1980; v.p. San Diego Sci. Found., 1978-87. With U.S. Army, 1943-46, USAR, 1950-53. Recipient medal of San Diego de Alcala, U. San Diego, 1997; NDEA grantee, 1961-64; CETA grantee, 1978, 79; named Outstanding Prof. Social Sci. U. San Diego, 1968, 69, Disting. Historian U. Ariz., 1989. Mem. Mex.-Am. Educators, Nat. Coun. Pub. History, Soc. Am. Baseball Rschrs., Pacific Coast League Baseball Hist. Soc., San Diego Baseball Hist. Soc. (1st pres.). Democrat. Roman Catholic. Home: 230 W Laurel St Apt 406 San Diego CA 92101-1464

BRANDES, STANLEY HOWARD, anthropology educator, writer; b. N.Y.C., Dec. 26, 1942; s. Emanuel Robert and Annette (Zalisch) B.; divorced; children: Nina Rachel, Naomi Clara. BA, U. Chgo., 1964; MA, U. Calif., Berkeley, 1969, PhD, 1971. Asst. prof. anthropology Mich. State U., East Lansing, 1971-75; asst. prof. anthropology U. Calif., Berkeley, 1975-78, assoc. prof., 1978-82, prof. anthropology, 1982—, chmn. dept., 1990-93, 97—; dir. Barcelona Study Ctr., U. Calif. and Ill., Spain, 1981-82, Mexico City Study Ctr., 1995—, U. Calif. Author: Migration, Kinship and Community, 1975, Metaphors of Masculinity, 1980, Forty: The Age and the Symbol, 1985, Power and Persuasion, 1988; co-editor: Symbol as Sense, 1980. NIH fellow, 1967-71; NICHD Rsch. fellow, 1975-77; fellow John Carter Brown Libr., 1994; Am. Council Learned Socs. grantee, 1977. Fellow Am. Anthrop. Assn.; mem. Am. Ethnological Soc., Soc. for Psychol. Anthropology. Office: U Calif Dept Anthropology Berkeley CA 94720

BRANDHORST, WESLEY THEODORE, information manager; b. Portland, Oreg., May 9, 1933; s. Wesley Theodore and Mary Margeurite (LaRouche) B.; m. Jane Smythe, Sept. 1, 1962; children—Tristan, Thea. B.A., U. Calif.-Berkeley, 1955, M.L.S., 1957. Spl. intern Library of Congress, Washington, 1957-59; librarian Documentation Inc., Washington, 1959-61; asst. dir. NASA Sci. and Tech. Info. Facility Washington, 1962-69; dir. ERIC Processing and Reference Facility, Washington, 1970—; chmn. Nat. Info. Standards Orgn. (NISO/Z39) 1985-87;. Contbr. articles to profl. jours. Mem. ALA, Spl. Libraries Assn., Am. Soc. Info. Sci., AAAS. Unitarian. Avocations: tennis; running; bicycling; chess; reading; travel. Home: 14504 Barkwood Dr Rockville MD 20853-2314 Office: ERIC Processing & Ref Facility 1100 West St Laurel MD 20707-3587

BRANDI, ANDY, tennis coach; m. Nancy Brandi; 1 child, Christopher Andres. BBA, Trinity U. Pvt. pro former N.Y. Gov. Nelson Rockefeller, 1972; camp dir., head pro and pvt. pro various clubs and acads., 1972-83; head coach U. Fla., Gainesville, 1985—; coach Wellington Aces, 1989, Wimbledon and U.S. Open jr. teams, 1987, Jr. Whitman Cup and Sisobault Cup teams; former exec. dir. Nick Bolletieri Tennis Acad. Contbr. articles to profl. jours.; guest columnist Stan Smith's syndicated col. Vol. Ronald McDonald House. Named Nat. Coach of the Yr., USPTA, 1988, Wilson/ITA, 1989, 96, South Region Coach of the Yr., 1988, 91, 92, 95, 96, Southeastern Conf. Coach of the Yr., 1987, 88, 93, 96, U.S. Profl. Tennis Registry Coach of the Yr., 1996. Avocations: Tae Kwon Do, Wado Kai, golf, read, W.C. Fields movies. Office: Univ of Florida Women's Athletics Dept PO Box 14485 Gainesville FL 32604-2485*

BRANDIMORE, WADIE MILLER, retired pediatrics nurse; b. Laconia, Tenn., Aug. 19, 1920; d. William and Lillie (Edwards) Miller; m. LeRoy Brandimore, Aug. 24, 1946; children: Geraldine F. Brandimore Anderson, LeRoy William. Student, Murray State Coll., 1939; diploma, Nazareth Sch. Nursing, Lexington, Ky., 1944. Oper. rm. circling nurse St. Joseph Hosp., Lexington, 1944; office nurse Dr. Adoplhus D. Butterworth, Murray, Ky., 1944-45;, 1945-46; office nurse Dr. Randall M. McLaughlin, Pasadena, Md., 1955-57; pvt. duty nurse USN Hosp., Annapolis, Md., 1958-67; staff nurse Anne Arundel Med. Ctr., Annapolis, Md., 1967-95; ret., 1995. Ensign, USN, 1945-46. Mem. ANA, Navy Nurse Corps Assn., Washington Metro Area Navy Nurse Corps Assn., Md. Nurses Assn. (bd. dirs. dist. 3). Home: 329 Clifton Ave Arnold MD 21012-1546

BRANDIN, ALF ELVIN, retired mining and shipping company executive; b. Newton, Kans., July 1, 1912; s. Oscar E. and Agnes (Larsen) B.; m. Marie Eck, June 15, 1936 (dec. 1980); children: Alf R., Jon, Erik, Mark.; m. Pamela J. Brandin, Jan. 28, 1983. A.B., Stanford U., 1936. With Standard Accident of Detroit, 1936-42; bus. mgr. Stanford U., Calif., 1946-52; bus. mgr., exec. officer for land devel. Stanford U., 1952-59, v.p. for bus. affairs, 1959-70; sr. v.p., dir., mem. exec. com. Utah Internat. Inc., San Francisco, from 1970; pres. Richardson-Brandin, 1964-86, also bd. dirs.; bd. dirs. Hershey Oil Co.; vice chmn. bd. dirs. Doric Devel. Inc. Bd. govs. San Francisco Bay Area Council; trustee Reclamation Dist. 2087, Alameda, Calif.; bd. overseers Hoover Instn. on War, Revolution and Peace, Stanford; mem. VIII Olympic Winter Games Organizing com., 1960. Served as comdr. USNR, 1942-46. Mem. Zeta Psi. Clubs: Elk, Stanford Golf, Bohemian, Pauma Valley Country, Silverado Country; Royal Lahaina. Home: 668 Salvatierra St Stanford CA 94305-8538 Office: 550 California St San Francisco CA 94104-1006

BRANDINGER, JAY JEROME, electronics executive; b. N.Y.C., Jan. 2, 1927; s. Abraham and Lillian (Newman) B.; m. Alice Levite, Dec. 23, 1949; children: Paul, Donna, Norman. BS in Elec. Engring., Cooper Union U., 1951; MS in Elec. Engring., Rutgers U., 1962, PhD in Elec. Engring., 1968. Group head display systems Research div. RCA Labs., Princeton, 1966-70, group head television systems, 1970-74, v.p. div. TV engring., 1974-79; div. v.p., gen. mgr. RCA SelectaVision VideoDisc Ops., Indpls., 1979-84; staff v.p. systems engring. RCA Electronics Products and Labs., Indpls., 1984-86; v.p. mfg. and materials div. David Sarnoff Rsch. Ctr., 1986-91; exec. dir. N.J. Commn. on Sci. and Tech., Trenton, 1991-95; pres., ceo Ja Brand Ass Inc., Pennington, N.J., 1995-98. Office: JA Brand Ass Inc 2 Queens Ln Pennington NJ 08534-2910

BRANDLER, JONATHAN M., lawyer; b. L.A., Jan. 8, 1946. AB, U. Calif., Berkeley, 1967; JD, U. So. Calif., 1970. Bar: Calif. 1971. Ptnr. Hill, Farrer & Burrill LLP, L.A.; lectr. Inst. Bus. Law, 1981-92. Mem. State Bar Calif. (labor law sect.), L.A. County Bar Assn. (labor law sect.). Office: Hill Farrer & Burrill LLP 1 California Plaza 300 S Grand Ave Ste 37 Los Angeles CA 90071-3110*

BRANDMEIR, CHRISTOPHER LEE, hospitality and food service consultant; b. Seattle, Mar. 6, 1950; s. Jack W. and Betty G. (Lyman) B. BA, U. San Francisco, 1972. Dir. coll. rels. Cogswell Coll., San Francisco, 1983-86; exec. dir. San Lorenzo (Calif.) Village, 1986-88; owner Inn Sight, Seattle, 1996—; pres., co-owner HBH Mgmt., Lopez Island, Wash., 1993-96, Inn at Swifts Bay, Lopez Island, Wash., 1988-96; instr., program mgr. hotel and tourism mgmt. Highline C.C., 1998—. Chair San Juan Islands Tourism Resource Coun.; bd. dirs., past chair San Juan Islands Visitor Info. Svc.; bd. dirs., fundraiser Lopez Island Cmty. Ctr.; pres. Lopez Island Chamber. Recipient Lyons Club Svc. award. Mem. Internat. Assn. Culinary Profls. Republican. Roman Catholic. Avocations: cooking, sailing, international studies, politics. E-mail: clb0563@aol.com. and cbrandme@hcc.ctc.edu. Home: 3543 Hampton Way Kent WA 98032 Office: 2400 240th St MS 18-1 Des Moines WA 98198

BRANDNER, CHRISTINE MARIE, curator, artist; b. Ocean City, N.J., Aug. 15, 1969; d. Roger Joseph and Judith Ann (Knueven) B. BA in Art Edn., U. Ky., 1991; MFA in Painting, Savannah Coll. Art & Design, 1997. Cert. art tchr. grades K-12, N.C. Art tchr. grades 7-9 Spring Lake (N.C.) Jr. High, 1992-94; exhibitions mgr. galleries dept. Savannah (Ga.) Coll. Art and Design, 1997—. One-person show, 1996, 97, 98, 99; works exhibited in group shows nationally, including Internat. Soc. Exptl. Artists, Longboat Key, Fla., 1997, Sarah Bain Gallery, Fullerton, Calif., 1997, Savannah Internat. Airport, 1997-98, Flight Safety Internat., Savannah, 1998, Galerie Lumière, Savannah, Tiverton and Four Corners, R.I., 1998, Roane State C.C., Harriman, Tenn., 1999, Soho Myriad, Inc., Atlanta, 1998-99; represented in corp. collections Am. Incontinental U., Vantosh, Savannah Coll. Art and Design, Omni/Chrysler; executed mural painter Lexington Children's Mus., Lexington, Ky., 1991. Supporter Epworth United Meth. Ch., Savannah, 1996-98. Acad. scholar U. Ky., Lexington, 1987. Mem. Internat. Soc. Exptl. Artists, Nat. Art Edn. Assn., Coll. Art Assn. Avocations: avid reader, painter, artist. Home: 1931 Hawthorne St Savannah GA 31404-1317

BRANDO, MARLON, JR., actor; b. Omaha, Apr. 3, 1924; s. Marlon and Dorothy Pennebaker (Myers) B.; m. Anna Kashfi, 1957 (div. 1959); 1 son, Christian; m. Movita Brando (div.); 1 child. Student, Shattuck Mil. Acad., 1939-41. Actor: N.Y. plays, including Streetcar Named Desire; motion pictures include The Men, 1950, Streetcar Named Desire, 1951, Viva Zapata, 1952 (Best Actor, Cannes Internat. Film Festival), Julius Caesar, 1953, The Wild One, 1953, Desirée, 1954, On the Waterfront, 1954 (Acad. award for best actor), Guys and Dolls, 1955,Teahouse of the August Moon, 1956, Sayonara, 1957, The Young Lions, 1958, The Fugitive Kind, 1960, One Eyed Jacks (also dir.) 1960, Mutiny on the Bounty, 1962, The Ugly American, 1963, Bedtime Story, 1964, The Saboteur, 1965, The Chase, 1966, The Appaloosa, 1966, A Countess from Hong Kong, Reflections in A Golden Eye,

1967, Candy, The Godfather, 1972 (Acad. award for best actor), Last Tango in Paris, 1972, Missouri Breaks, 1976, Superman, 1978, Apocalypse Now, 1979, The Formula, 1980, A Dry White Season, 1989, The Freshman, 1990, Jericho, Christopher Columbus: The Discovery, 1992, Don Juan DeMarco, 1995, The Island of Dr. Moreau, 1996, The Brave, 1997, Free Money, 1998, Autumn of the Patriarch, 1999; TV appearance in Roots: The Next Generations, 1979; author: (with Robert Lindsey) Brando: Songs My Mother Taught Me, 1994. *

BRANDON, EDWARD BERMETZ, retired banking executive; b. Davenport, Iowa, Sept. 15, 1931; s. William McKinley and Mary Elizabeth (Bermetz) B.; m. Phyllis Anne Probeck, Aug. 7, 1954; children: William M., Robert P., Beverly A., Beth A., E. Matthew. BS, Northwestern U., 1953; MBA, U. Pa., 1956. With Nat. City Bank, Cleve., 1956—, pres., 1984-87, chief exec. officer, 1985-89; pres., bd. dirs. Nat. City Corp., 1986-88, chmn., chief exec. officer, 1987-95, dir., 1986—; bd. dirs. Standard Products Co., RPM, Inc. Trustee Notre Dame Coll. of Ohio, John Carroll U., Cleve. Clinic Found. Lt. USSN, 1953-55. Mem. Bankers Roundtable, Union Club, Shaker Heights Country Club, Pepper Pike Club, Kirtland Country Club. Republican. Methodist. Address: Lakepoint Office Park 3201 Enterprise Pkwy Ste 470 Beachwood OH 44122-7320

BRANDON, ELVIS DENBY, III, financial planner; b. Memphis, Aug. 11, 1954; s. Elvis Denby Jr. and Helen (Deupree) B.; m. Sarah Buntin, Mar. 15, 1980; children: Elizabeth Holt, William Denby, Mary Buntin. BBA, So. Meth. U., 1976; MBA, Memphis State U., 1979. Cert. fin. planner; CLU; chartered fin. cons. Mgmt. candidate First Tenn. Bank, NA, Memphis, 1979-80; sr. credit analyst Banc Texas/Dallas NA, 1980-82; asst. v.p., comml. loan officer Banc Texas/Sherman NA, 1982; pres. Denby Brandon Orgn., Inc., Memphis, 1982—; v.p. Branco Planning Co., Inc., Memphis, 1982—; adj. faculty Coll. for Fin. Planning, Denver, 1984-85. Deacon Idlewild Presb. Ch. Mem. NASD (registered prin.), Am. Soc. CLUs and Chartered Fin. Cons., Inst. Cert. Fin. Planners. Presbyterian. Home: 5953 Brierdale Ave Memphis TN 38120-2345 Office: Branco Planning Co Inc 3100 Walnut Grove Rd Ste 404 Memphis TN 38111-3530

BRANDON, JEFFREY CAMPBELL, physician, interventional radiologist, educator; b. Reynoldsville, Pa., Dec. 5, 1953; s. Milton Boyd and Patricia Alfreda (Steele) B. BS, Allegheny Coll., 1975; MD, Jefferson Med. Coll., 1979. Diplomate Am. Bd. Radiology, Nat. Bd. Med. Examiners. Intern gen. surgery Bryn Mawr (Pa.) Hosp., 1979-80, resident gen. surgery, 1980-81; resident in diagnostic radiology Hahnemann U. Hosp., Phila., 1983-86; fellow interventional radiology, abdominal imaging Hahnemann U. Hosp., 1986-87; clin. instr. Hahnemann U. Hosp., Phila., 1987-88; asst. prof. U. Calif., Irvine, 1988-94, assoc. prof., chmn. radiol. scis., 1992-95; vice chmn. radiol. scis. U. South Ala., Mobile, 1995—, disting. prof. radiology, 1996—; mem. adv. bd. Baxter Health Care Tech. and Ventures Divsn., Irvine, 1990-92, Laparomed Corp., Irvine, 1991-94, Visioneering, Fullerton, Calif., 1993-95. Author: (chpt.) Common Problems in Gastrointestinal Radiology, 1989, Critical Care Imaging, 1990, Textbook of Gastrointestinal Radiology, 1991, Textbook of Diagnostic Imaging, 1994; contbr. articles to books and profl. jours. Recipient S. Macuen Smith Otolaryngology award Jefferson Med. Coll., 1979, Baxter Healthcare grant Baxter Corp., 1990, Faculty Rsch. grant U. Calif., Irvine Coll. of Medicine, 1990. Mem. Am. Bd. Radiology, Assn. Univ. Radiologists, Soc. Gastrointestinal Radiologists (lectr. 1989—), Am. Inst. Ultrasound in Medicine, Soc. Cardiovascular and Interventional Radiologists, Calif. Med. Assn. (bd. dirs., sci. adv. panel on radiology 1993-95), Phi Beta Kappa. Office: U South Ala Mastin 301 Radiology 2451 Fillingim St Mobile AL 36617-2238

BRANDON, JOHN MITCHELL, physician; b. Pitts., June 28, 1927; s. Albert Given and Adelaide Victoria (Mitchell) B.; m. Phyllis Katherine Wagner, June 22, 1966 (dec. 1976). BS, U. Pitts., 1952, MD, 1956. Diplomate in internal medicine and hematology Am. Bd. Internal Medicine; diplomate Am. Bd. Pathology. Intern Geisinger Meml. Hosp., Danville, Pa., 1956-57; resident in internal medicine Cleve. Clinic, 1957-60, renal fellow, 1960-61; pvt. practice internal medicine Allegheny Valley Hosp., Tarentum, Pa., 1961-66; resident in pathology VA Hosp. of Pitts., Oakland, Pa., 1966-70, resident in immunology, 1970-71; fellow in coagulation Ctrl. Blood Bank, Oakland, 1971-72; dir. lab. Monongahela Valley Hosp., Monongahela, Pa., 1972-94, part-time pathologist, 1994—; chmn. blood program Monessen (Pa.) Health Ctr., 1972-94; clin. asst. prof. pathology U. Pitts. Med. Sch., 1980—; prof. med. lab. tech. C.C. Allegheny County, Pitts., 1986—. Contbr. chpts. to books, articles to profl. jours. Cpl. USAAF, 1945-46. Recipient Sickman-Levin award for dimensions in medicine Monongahela Valley Hosp., 1993. Fellow ACP, Coll. Am. Pathologists, Am. Soc. Clin. Pathology, Internat. Pathology Soc.; mem. AMA, Pa. Med. Soc. Avocations: fishing, hunting, gardening. Office: Monongahela Valley Hosp Rte 88 Monongahela PA 15063

BRANDON, LIANE, filmmaker, educator. Student, St. Lawrence U., U. Edinburgh, Scotland; exchange student, U. Moscow; AB, Boston U., MEd. Ski instr. Mt. Tremblant, Que., Can.; actress Children's Theatre, Cambridge, Mass.; film project dir. English dept. Quincy pub. schs., Mass.; prof. film-TV prodn. and media studies Sch. Edn. U. Mass., Amherst, 1973—; co-founder, mem. New Day Films, 1971—; co-dir. UMass Ednl. TV, U. Mass., Amherst, 1994—; dir. Sch. Edn. Ednl. Tech. Program, U. Mass., 1998—; film cons. Mass. Gov.'s Commn. on Status of Women, 1974; cons. Mass. Artists Found., 1975, 82, Sta. WGBH-TV, 1992—; judge Regional Student Acad. Awards, 1991, New Eng. Regional Emmy Awards,1992; trustee Theaterworks, 1981-83; bd. dirs. Boston Film-Video Found., 1983-87, ACLU of Mass., 1988-97; mem. adv. bd. Children's Media Found. Boston, 1993-97; guest lectr. various confs. on edn. and film to colls. and art schs. in U.S. Exhibited film, Mus. Modern Art, Whitney Mus. Am. Art, Chgo. Art Inst., Nat. Film Theatre, London, Internat. Womens Film Festival, Paris, Mus. Fine Arts, Boston, John F. Kennedy Ctr. Performing Arts, Washington; dir., prodr. (film) Anything You Want to Be, 1971 (Blue Ribbon Am. Film Festival award), Betty Tells Her Story, 1972 (Internat. Festival of Womens Films award 1974), Once Upon a Choice, 1980 (Silver medal Houston Internat. Film Festival), How to Prevent a Nuclear War, 1987 (Blue Ribbon award Am. Film Festival 1988); prodr. (video) Goodnight Amherst, 1995, Fine Print, 1995, Try This At Home, 1998 (Judge's choice 1999), Fresh Ink, 1998. Mem. Mass. Media Literacy Coalition. Recipient Creative Artist award AAUW, 1975, Disting. Alumni award Boston U., 1985; Careth Found. grantee, 1988, Funding Exchange grantee, 1989, Mass. Found. for Humanities and Pub. Policy grantee, 1975, Film Fund grantee, 1985. Mem. New Eng. Screen Edn. Assn. (v.p. 1972-83), Assn. Ind. Video and Filmmakers, Women in Film and Video New Eng. Office: U Mass Sch Edn Furcolo Hall Amherst MA 01003

BRANDON, TABITHA A., health service administrator; b. Lubbock, Tex., Mar. 30, 1972; d. James E. and Shellie K. B. BS in Premed., Kans. State U., 1994; MPA, U. Mo., Kansas City, 1999. Front office coord. Rockhill Women's Care, Kansas City, 1994-96; adminstr. Clin. Assocs., P.A., Shawnee Mission, Kans., 1996—. Grantee grad. sch. PEO Chpt. Kansas City Mo., 1997. Mem. ASPA.

BRANDOW, THEO, architect; b. Phila., Nov. 18, 1925; s. Ralph and Minnie (Weinstock) B.; m. Selma Koss, July 22, 1945; children: Jonathan, Rinna, Shanna. BArch, U. Pa., 1949. Assoc. Oskar Stonorov, Phila., 1949-52; pvt. practice architecture Phila., 1952-78; project dir. Rochlin & Baran & Assocs., West Los Angeles, Calif., 1978-81; pres. Brandow Design Assocs., 1982-87; pvt. practice architecture Ambler, Pa., 1987—; cons. urban renewal; vis. speaker sch. system Wellspring Ecumenical Ctr., Phila., 1966—. Prin. works include houses, apt. and office buildings, churches; design architect Benjamin Franklin House; works pub. in various mags. including Life, House and Home, Am. Home; author: Closer to Saturday, 1971, Michla, A Trilogy; also articles and lectures on Israel's Day of Atonement War of 1973; group shows include Chestnut Hill Fine Arts Festival, Phila., 1995 (1st place prize 1995), New Hope Art Festival, Pa., 1995 (award of excellence 1995), Lansdale Festival of the Arts, Pa., 1995 (most unique craft award 1995). V.p. Erdenheim (Pa.) PTA, 1956; mem. Whitemarsh Valley Fair Housing Coun., 1966—; pack master local coun. Boy Scouts Am.; bd. dirs. local Jewish synagogue. With USNR, 1943-46. Recipient award World Traveling Exhibit Art in Arch., 1949, Homes for Better Living, 1957, 59, state citation Am. Home mag., 1957, nat. citation, 1958, spl. award Am. Builder mag., 1959, McCall's Congress for Better Living award, 1959, awards Nat. Assn. Home Builders, 1961. Mem. AIA (awards 1957, 61). Home: 1403 Seneca Run Ambler PA 19002-3615

BRANDRUP, DOUGLAS WARREN, lawyer; b. Mitchel, S.D., July 11, 1940; s. Clair L. and Ruth M. (Wolverton) B.; m. Patricia R. Tuck, Dec. 20, 1986; children: Kendra, Monika, Peter. AB in Econs., Middlebury Coll., 1963; JD, Boston U., 1966. Bar: N.Y. 1969, U.S. Dist. Ct. (so. dist.) N.Y. 1970, U.S. Ct. Appeals (2d cir.) 1970. Assoc. Donovan, Leisure, Newton & Irvine, N.Y.C., 1968-72; ptnr. Griggs, Baldwin & Baldwin, N.Y.C., 1972-80, sr. ptnr., 1980—; chmn. Equity Oil Co.; bd. dirs. Ardshiel, Inc. Mem. Govs. Security Adv. Com., State of N.J., 1975-90. Capt. U.S. Army, 1966-68. Recipient Ellis Island medal of Honor, 1999. Mem. ABA, N.Y. County Bar Assn., N.Y. State Bar Assn., Met. Club (N.Y.C., pres.), Mashomack Preserve Club. Republican. Episcopalian. Office: Griggs Baldwin & Baldwin 27 E 65th St Apt 7D New York NY 10021-6556

BRANDS, JAMES EDWIN, finance executive; b. Lebanon, Ind., July 5, 1937; s. Edwin Herman and Pearl Irene (Brown) B.; m. Gail Marian Knight, Sept. 12, 1959; children: Jeffrey, Scot, Alan, Susan. AB, Wesleyan U., Middletown, Conn., 1959; MBA, U. Chgo., 1961; JD, Kennedy-Western U., Boise, Idaho, 1992. CPA, Mo. Staff acct., mgr. Arthur Andersen & Co., Chgo., 1961-71; ptnr. Arthur Andersen & Co., St. Louis, 1971-82; sr. v.p. Scherer-Storz, Inc., St. Louis, 1982-86; vice chmn., CFO Scherer Healthcare Inc., Atlanta, 1982-95; exec. v.p. Scherer Sci. Ltd., Atlanta, 1986-95; chmn., CEO Marquest Med. Products, Inc., Denver, 1993-95; CFO Wilson Pest Control, Inc., Atlanta, 1997-99; sr. exec. v.p., bd. dirs. Able Tolcom Holding Corp., West Palm Beach, 1999—; chmn. bd. dirs. Ramco Acquisitions, Inc., Atlanta; bd. dirs., v.p. BodyCare Inc., Atlanta, Maximum Benefits, LLC, Atlanta, Throwleigh Technologies LLC, Atlanta; bd. dirs., pres. Ga. Am. Land Co., Atlanta; pres. Brands & Co., 1981—. Mem. AICPA, Mo. Soc. CPAs, Bellerive Country Club (St. Louis), Atlanta Nat. Golf Club. Republican. Presbyterian. Home: 4330 Bancroft Vly Alpharetta GA 30022-5175

BRANDS, ROBERT FRANCISCUS, marketing executive; b. Tilburg, Holland, June 18, 1957; came to U.S., 1982; s. Robert M. and Jetty Brands. BA, Inst. Tech., Eindhoven, Holland, 1981; student Small Bus. Mgmt. program NYU, 1984. Rsch. analyst French-Dutch C. of C., Paris, 1981-82; mgr., internat. trade advisor Netherlands C. of C., N.Y.C., 1982-84; v.p. mktg. Airspray Internat., Inc., N.Y.C., 1985-88; pres. Branco Internat., Inc., N.Y.C., 1985-88; mgr. new product, market mgr. consumer div. Philips Lighting, 1988-89; mktg. mgr., cons. divsn. U.S. Lighting, OSRAM Sylvania, Inc., 1989-93; v.p. mktg. Sterling Plumbing Group, Inc. a Kohler Co., 1993-94; v.p. mktg. Kohler Plumbing N.A., 1995-98, pres. Airspray Internat., Inc., Pompano Beach, fla., 1998—. Author trade surveys. Sgt. Royal Dutch Mil. Police, 1977-78; past pres. Erie # 4 Fire Assn., Georgetown, Mass.; supporter Netherlands-Am. Community Assn. Mem. Round Table USA (past nat. bd. dirs., internat. rels. officer), Gen. Mdse. Distbn. Coun. (past adv. bd.). Roman Catholic. Avocations: flying, sailing. Home: 1870 Merion Ln Coral Springs FL 33071-7825 Office: Airspray Internat Inc 4701 N Federal Hwy Ste 465 Pompano Beach FL 33064-6550

BRANDSTATER, MURRAY EVERETT, physiatrist; b. Hobart, Australia, Apr. 21, 1935. MB, BS, U. Melbourne, Australia, 1957. Cert. in Phys. Med. Rehab. Intern Box Hill Dist. Hosp., Melbourne, 1958; resident in internal medicine Alfred Hosp., Melbourne, 1959, 61-62; resident Royal Children's Hosp., Melbourne, 1960; rsch. in phys. med. rehab. Mayo Clinic, Rochester, Minn., 1964-68; prof. phys. med. rehab. McMaster U., Hamilton, Ont., Can., 1968-84; mem. staff Loma Linda (Calif.) U. Med. Ctr., 1984—; prof. phys. med. rehab. Loma Linda U., 1981—. Mem. AMA, AAEM, MRCP, RCPC. Office: Loma Linda Univ Med Ctr PO Box 2000 Dept Rehab Medicine Rm A237 Loma Linda CA 92354*

BRANDT, ALLAN M., medical history educator; b. Washington, Dec. 18, 1953. BA magna cum laude with honors in History, Brandeis U., 1974; MA, Columbia U., 1975, MPhil, 1978, PhD in American History, 1983. Rsch. assoc. project on value and ethics in health care Coll. Physicians and Surgeons, Columbia U., N.Y.C., 1977-82; teaching fellow humanities, faculty of medicine Coll. Physicians and Surgeons, Columbia U., 1979-82; instr. dept. history Smith Coll., 1982; instr. dept. social medicine and health policy, Harvard Med. Sch., and instr. dept. history of sci. Harvard U., 1982, asst. prof. history of medicine and sci. dept. social medicine and health policy, Harvard Med. Sch., and asst. prof. dept. history of sci., 1983-87, assoc. prof. history of medicine and sci., 1987-90; assoc. prof. dept. social medicine, dept. history U. N.C., Chapel Hill, 1990-92; prof. history of sci., dept. history of sci. Harvard U., Boston, 1992—, Amalie Moses Kass prof. history of medicine, dept. social medicine, 1992—; dir. program history of medicine Harvard Med. Sch., Boston, 1998—, dir. divsn. med. ethics, 1998—; cons. AIDS/HIV program WHO, Pan Am. Health Orgn., 1990; mem. Hastings Ctr. Study Group AIDS and Civil Liberties, 1985-87, fellow, 1993—; mem. com. monitoring social impact of AIDS, NAS, 1989-91; mem. sect. history of medicine Nat. Libr. Medicine Study NIH, 1989-91. Author: No Magic Bullet: A Social History of Venereal Disease in the United States Since 1880, 1985, paper, 1987; mem. edit. bds. Law, Medicine and Health Care, AIDS: Prevention and Education, Jour. of History of Sexuality, Human Nature, Jour. of Sex Rsch.; contbr. articles to profl. jours. Grad. Sch. Arts and Scis. fellow Columbia U., 1974-75, Pres. fellow Columbia U., 1975-79, Mrs. Giles Whiting Found. fellow, 1977-78, Rockefeller Found. fellow in Humanities, 1985-86, Pres. fellow Harvard U., 1989-90; Rockefeller Archives Grant-in-Aid, 1978, Clark Fund grantee Harvard U., 1983; Charles E. Culpeper scholar in Med. Humanities, 1992—; Pulitzer Prize nominee, 1985. Mem. Am. Studies Assn., History of Sci. Soc. (speakers bur. 1990-93), Soc. Health and Human Values, Am. Assn. History of Medicine (coun. 1990-92), Orgn. Am. Historians, Am. Hist. Assn. Office: Harvard U Med Sch Dept Social Medicine 641 Huntington Ave Boston MA 02115-6019*

BRANDT, CARL DAVID, research virologist; b. Bridgeport, Conn., Jan. 19, 1928; s. Carl August and Hildur (Wedberg) B.; m. Elsa Lund Erickson, Apr. 25, 1964; children—Karen, Erik. B.S., U. Conn., 1949; M.S., U. Mass., 1951; Ph.D., Harvard U., 1958. Research instr. dept. vet. sci. U. Mass., Amherst, 1949-52, 54; research virologist Charles Pfizer & Co., Inc., Ind. and Conn., 1958-62; assoc., dept. epidemiology Pub. Health Research Inst. N.Y.C., 1962-66; research assoc. virology research Children's Nat. Med. Ctr., Washington, 1966-79, sr. research assoc., 1979-86, sr. scientist, 1986—; instr. Georgetown U. Med. Sch., Washington, 1966-69; asst. prof. pediatrics George Washington U. Med. Sch., Washington, 1969-74, assoc. prof., 1974-94, emeritus prof., 1994. Contbr. articles to profl. jours. Served to 1st lt. USAF, 1952-54. Fellow Am. Acad. Microbiology, Infectious Diseases Soc. Am., Am. Coll. Epidemiology; mem. AAAS, Am. Soc. Microbiology, Soc. Epidemiologic Research, Pan Am. Group Rapid Viral Diagnosis, Sigma Xi. Clubs: N.Y Color Slide (bd. dirs. 1965-66); Silver Spring Camera (pres. 1970-71); Rock Creek Amateur Radio Assn (pres. 1985-89). Avocations: photography; amateur radio. Home: 819 E Franklin Ave Silver Spring MD 20901-4709 Office: Childrens Nat Med Ctr 111 Michigan Ave NW Rm 189A Washington DC 20010-2916

BRANDT, DAVID DEAN, accountant, financial planner, valuation analyst; b. Estherville, Iowa, Feb. 4, 1947; s. Floyd August and Evelyn Ruth (Littell) B.; m. Ruth Dorothea Adams, Aug. 25, 1968; children: Lesley Marie, Jonathan Dean. BA, U. No. Iowa, 1969. CPA, S.D., Iowa; CFP, S.D.; diplomate Am. Bd. Forensic Acctg., Am. Bd. Forensic Examiners; cert. valuation analyst. Staff acct. McGladrey, Hansen, Dunn & Co., Clinton, Iowa, 1969-73, supr., mgr., 1973-75; ptnr. Wohlenberg, Gage and Co., Sioux Falls, S.D., 1975-80; mng. ptnr. La Follette, Jansa, Brandt & Co., Sioux Falls, 1980—; mem. Internat. Bd. Stds. and Practices for CFP's. Mem. Sioux Falls Pub. Sch. Dist. Sch. Bd., 1977-82; treas. Asbury United Meth. Ch., Sioux Falls, 1982—; bd. dirs. Sioux Falls Vol. and Info. Ctr., 1982-88, Sioux Falls Area Jr. Achievement, 1984-88, Sioux Falls Literacy Coun., 1986-97; pres. bd. dirs. Vol. and Info. Ctr., 1987-88; chmn. S.D. affiliate Am. Diabetes Assn., 1993-97. Mem. AICPA (coun. 1987-88), S.D. Soc. CPAs (bd. dirs. 1982-84, pres.-elect 1986-87, pres. 1987-88), Nat. Assn. Cert. Valuation Analysts, Am. Coll. Forensic Examiners, Iowa Soc. CPAs, Nat. Assn. Accts. (pres. Sioux Falls chpt. 1981-82), Continental Assn. CPA Firms (acctg. and auditing com. 1978-80), Kiwanis (pres. Downtown Sioux Falls Club 1989-90). Republican. Methodist. Avocation: woodworking, antique Model A Ford's. Home: PO Box 945 Sioux Falls SD 57101-0945 Office: LaFollette Jansa Brandt & Co 622 S Minnesota Ave Sioux Falls SD 57104-4825

BRANDT, EDWARD NEWMAN, JR., physician, educator; b. Oklahoma City, July 3, 1933; s. Edward Newman and Myrtle (Brazil) B.; m. Patricia Ann Lawson, Aug. 29, 1953; children: Patrick James, Edward Newman III, Rex Carlin. BS, U. Okla., 1954, MD, 1960, PhD, 1963; MS, Okla. State U., 1955; LHD, Med. U. S.C., Rush U.; DSc, N.Y. Inst. Tech. Intern Oklahoma City VA Hosp., 1960-61; resident U. Okla. Hosps., 1961; from instr. to prof. preventive medicine and pub. health U. Okla. Med. Center, Oklahoma City, 1961-70; prof., chmn. dept. biostatistics U. Okla. Med. Center (Sch. Health), 1967-68; assoc. dean U. Okla. Med. Center (Sch. Medicine); assoc. dir. U. Okla. Med. Center (Med. Center), 1968-70; dean Grad. Sch., prof. preventive medicine and community health U. Tex. Med. Br., Galveston, 1970-72; acting dean U. Tex. Med. Br. (Grad. Sch.), 1972-74, assoc. dean clin. affairs, 1972-73, prof. preventive medicine and community health, 1970-84, acting dean medicine, 1973-74, prof. family medicine, 1973-84, dean medicine, 1974-76, exec. dean, 1976-77; vice chancellor health affairs U. Tex. System, Austin, 1977-81; asst. sec. health HHS, 1981-84; pres. U. Md.-Balt., 1985-89, also prof. epidemiology and preventive medicine, 1985-89; prof. internal medicine, exec. dean Coll. Medicine U. Okla., Oklahoma City, 1989-92; dir. Ctr. for Health Policy U. Okla., 1992—; prof. health adminstrn. Coll. Pub. Health, 1989—, Regents prof., 1996—; mem. primate ctr. rev. com. NIH, 1975-79, chmn., 1978-79, mem. rsch. career devel. award com., 1968-72, mem. adv. com. on rsch. in women's health, 1995-97; bd. regents Nat. Libr. Medicine, 1985-89, chmn., 1987-89; mem. exec. bd. WHO, 1982-84; chmn. adv. com. on injury control CDC, 1988-93; chmn. adv. coun. on food FDA, 1992—. Editor, contbr. Proc. of Conf. at U. Okla. Med. Ctr., 1968; editor Continuing Education for the Family Physician, 1974-77, AIDS and Pub. Policy Jour., 1988-91. Recipient Superior Performance award VA Hosp. Oklahoma City, 1961; Lloyd M. Southwick Meml. award for med. writing, 1974, 75; Spl. Appreciation award Tex. Acad. Family Physicians, 1974; Leone award for adminstrv. excellence, 1976; Outstanding Alumni Svc. award U. Okla. Coll. Medicine, 1977; Disting. Svc. award U. Tex. Med. Br., 1977; 19th Ann. Stoneburner lectr. Med. Coll. Va., 1966, Disting. Leadership award HHS, 1984, Disting. Pub. Svc. award Dept. Def., 1986, Pub. Health award Am. Acad. Family Physicians; Triennial Scholar, Phi Kappa Phi, 1998—. Fellow AAAS (chair med. scis. sect. 1992-93), Am. Coll. Cardiology (hon.); mem. AMA (chmn. sec. on med. schs. 1979-81, chmn. com. accreditation continuing med. edn. 1979-81), Assn. Am. Med. Colls. (exec. coun. 1986-89, Spl. Recognition award 1985), Okla. Med. Assn. (chmn. com. on family violence, 1993—, chmn. coun. on state legis. 1994—), Am. Acad. Family Physicians, Okla. Acad. Family Physicians, Philos. Soc. Tex., Inst. Medicine (governing coun. 1986-92), Sigma Xi, Alpha Omega Alpha, Phi Eta Sigma, Alpha Epsilon Delta, Phi Kappa Phi (nat. scholar), Phi Sigma Pi, Mu Epsilon. Office: U Okla Health Scis Ctr PO Box 26901 Oklahoma City OK 73126-0901

BRANDT, GENE STUART, fundraising consultant; b. N.Y.C., Aug. 29, 1950; s. Eugene Charles and Elsie Virginia (Williams) B.; m. Elizabeth Holland, July 20, 1991; children: Cameron Elizabeth, Christopher Holland. AB in Polit. Sci., Knox Coll., 1972. Asst. dir. admission Knox Coll., Galesburg, Ill., 1972-74; dir. alumni affairs Knox Coll., Galesburg, 1974-76; dir. univ. devel. U. Nev., Reno, 1976-79; dir. devel. Lake Forest (Ill.) Coll., 1979-81, v.p. devel., 1981-86; v.p. external affairs Mus. Sci. and Industry, Chgo., 1986-91; pres. sci. and tech. Mus. of Atlanta, 1991-97; prin., cons. TerMolen Bran, Atlanta, 1997—. Bd. dirs., vice-chmn. Pub. Broadcasting Atlanta; mem. Coun. for Advancement and Support of Edn. Named 1 of Outstanding Young Men of Am., 1981. Mem. Am. Assn. Mus., Nat. Soc. Fundraising Execs., Econ. Club Chgo. Office: TerMolen Brandt & Assocs 2854 Wesley Heath NW Atlanta GA 30327-1854

BRANDT, HARRY, mechanical engineering educator; b. Amsterdam, The Netherlands, Nov. 14, 1925; came to U.S., 1946, naturalized, 1962; s. Friedrich H. and Henny (Rous) B.; m. Muriel Ruth Harman, Jan. 24, 1953; children: Joyce Estelle, Marilyn Audrey, Robert Alan. B.S., U. Calif.-Berkeley, 1949, M.S., 1950, Ph.D., 1954. Supervising research engr. Chevron Research Co., La Habra, Calif., 1954-64; lectr. UCLA, 1962-64; prof. mech. engrng. U. Calif., Davis, 1964—, chmn. dept., 1969-74, 86-91; dir. Internat. Pipeline Techs. Inc., Beaverton, Oreg., 1985-91; chmn. bd. Clean Energy Systems, Inc., 1997—; cons. Lawrence Livermore Nat. Lab., 1969—, State of Calif., 1970-87, State of Alaska, 1972, Los Alamos Nat. Lab., 1988-93. Mem. ASME, Am. Welding Soc., AIAA, Sigma Xi, Tau Beta Pi. Presbyn. Home: 26934 Middle Golf Dr PO Box 3195 El Macero CA 95618-0795 Office: U Calif Dept Mech and Aero Engring Davis CA 95616

BRANDT, I. MARVIN, chemist, engineer; b. Shreveport, La., Nov. 26, 1942; s. David and Esta (Epstein) B. BS in Chemistry, Centenary Coll., 1965; postgrad., U. Tex., 1968-70. With Am. Pipe and Supply, Shreveport, 1970-73; rschr. Shell Oil, Houston, 1973-75; rsch. tech. svc. trainer NL Baroid, Houston, 1975-79; rschr., tech. svc. engr. drilling, tng. coord. Arco Oil & Gas Co., worldwide, 1979-86; specialist, project mgr. Petrolite Corp., St. Louis, 1986-90; sr. engr. drilling and completion tech., tng. mgr., environ. coord. Marathon Oil Co., Houston, 1990—; cons. for drilling ops. and environ. projects Dallas, S.Am., Cen. Am., Tex., Calif., Russia, N. Sea, Mid. East, Africa, Alaska, Australia, New Zealand, China, Indonesia, Mexico, Korea. Contbr. articles to profl. jours.; patentee in field. Active Am. Cancer Soc., Houston, Denver, St. Louis, Morris Animal Found., Denver, Am. Heart Assn., United Way. Recipient Grad. Tching. fellowship, U. Tex., Austin, 1968-70, Robert Welch Rsch. grant, U. Tex., Austin, 1969. Mem. Soc. Petroleum Engrs. (program chmn.), Internat. Assn. Drilling Contractors (drilling com.), Am. Chem. Soc., Am. Petroleum Inst. (subcoms. for drilling and environment), Am. Assn. Drilling Engrs. (co-chmn. drilling completion com., chmn. drilling fluids com., co-chmn. waste mgmt. com., planning com. for petro-safe offshore tech. conf. com.), N.Y. Acad. Scis., Internat. Platform Assn. Avocations: tennis, running, bicycling, music, fishing. Home: PO Box 571844 Houston TX 77257-1844 Office: 5555 San Felipe St Houston TX 77056-2723 *Life is much too serious to take so seriously.*

BRANDT, IRA KIVE, pediatrician, medical geneticist; b. N.Y.C., Nov. 9, 1923; s. Charles Zachary and Hilda Eleanor B.; m. Dorothy Godfrey, Nov. 26, 1947; children—Elizabeth, Laura, William, Rena. A.B., NYU, 1942; M.D., Columbia U., 1945. Diplomate Am. Bd. Pediatrics, Am. Bd. Med. Genetics. Intern Morrisania City Hosp., N.Y.C., 1945-46; resident Lincoln Hosp., N.Y.C., 1948-50; fellow pediatrics Yale U., New Haven, 1955-57, asst. prof., 1957-61, assoc. prof., 1961-68; chmn. dept. pediatrics Children's Hosp., San Francisco, 1968-70; clin. prof. pediatrics U. Calif., San Francisco, 1970; prof. pediatrics and med. genetics Ind. U. Sch. Medicine, Indpls., 1970-89, prof. emeritus, 1989—. Served to capt. U.S. Army, 1946-47, 52. Mem. Am. Pediatric Soc., Am. Acad. Pediatrics, Soc. Pediatric Rsch., Soc. Inherited Metabolic Disorders, Am. Soc. Human Genetics, Am. Coll. Med. Genetics. Office: Ind U Sch Medicine Dept Pediatrics 702 Barnhill Dr # 0907 Indianapolis IN 46202-5128

BRANDT, JOHN ASHWORTH, fuel company executive; b. Chgo., Oct. 3, 1950; s. William W. and Joan V. (Ashworth) B.; m. Debbie M. Fico, June 2, 1984; children: Briana Ashley, Bryan Ashworth. Student, U. Colo., 1969-72. Mgr. co. accounts Lincoln Wood Commodities, Chgo., 1972-74; pres. Lafayette Coal Co., Burr Ridge, Ill., 1974—, Hoosier King Coal Co., 1993—, Ind. Farms, Inc., 1996—; pres. Chgo. Coal Shippers, 1984—; pres. Hoosier King Coal Co.; dir. Muliganeers Non-Profit Orgn. Office: Lafayette Coal Co 200 S Frontage Rd Ste 310 Hinsdale IL 60521-6953

BRANDT, JOHN HENRY, physician; b. Cleve., July 30, 1940; s. Harold Paul and Dorothy Helen (Kern) B.; m. Jon Ellison, July 30, 1963 (div. 1971); children: Sylvia Ann, Laura Ann; m. Marilyn Ruth Brandt, July 25, 1980. BA, Yale U., 1962; postgrad., Cambridge (Eng.) U., 1962-64; MD, Harvard U., 1970. Asst. to dir. Harvard Ctr. for Community Health, Boston, 1968-69; clin. fellow Med. Sch. Harvard U., Boston, 1970-73, instr. in psychiatry Med. Sch., 1973-74, 74—; resident psychiatrist McLean Hosp., Belmont, Mass., 1970-73, dir. Waverley House, 1973-74, attending psychiatrist, 1974-90; attending psychiatrist Mass. Mental Health Ctr., 1991—; staff psychiatrist med. dept. MIT, Cambridge, 1979—. Mem. archives com. Trinity Ch., Boston, 1988—; active Mass. Hist. Soc., New Eng. Hist. Geneal. Soc. Mem. Am. Psychiat. Assn., Mass. Med. Soc., N.Y. Acad. Medicine, Internat. Inst., English Speaking Union, Boston Athenaeum, Yale Club of

Boston (sec. 1988-90, dir. 1990-93), Harvard Club of Boston (chmn. Ho. com. 1989-91, v.p. 1991-93), Harvard Musical Assn. (dir. 1990-93), St. Botolph Club, Cosmos Club, Yale Elizabethan Club, Yale Mory's Assn., Bostonian Soc., Colonial Soc., Phi Beta Kappa. Republican. Episcopalian. Avocation: music. Home: PO Box 530 Lincoln MA 01773-0530 Office: MIT Med Dept 77 Massachusetts Ave Cambridge MA 02139-4307

BRANDT, JOHN REYNOLD, editor, journalist; b. Amarillo, Tex., Aug. 25, 1959; s. Reynold Francis Jr. and Patricia Levonne (Wallace) B.; m. Svetlana Stevovich, May 28, 1989; children: Emma Evangeline Stevovich Brandt, Aidan Reynold Stevovich Brandt. BA, Case Western Reserve U., Cleve., 1981. Sales rep. Merrell Dow Pharmaceuticals, Cleve., 1982-84, Miles Pharmaceuticals, Cleve., 1984-88, Tokos Perinatal Nursing Svcs., Cleve., 1988-89; sr. assoc. M. Zunt Assocs., Cleve., 1989-90; dir. mgmt. devel. CSA Health System, Cleve., 1990-91; assoc. editor Corp. Cleve. Mag., 1991-94; exec. editor IndustryWeek Mag., Cleve., 1994-95, editor-in-chief, 1995—; v.p. Inst. Environ. Edn., Cleve., 1990-91. Bd. dirs. Work in N.E. Ohio Coun., 1997—; judge Workforce Excellence Awards of Nat. Assn. Mfrs., 1997—. Recipient numerous awards in field from Am. Bus. Press, Assn. of Area Bus. Publs., The Press Club of Cleve., March of Dimes, Am. Soc. Bus. Press Editors. Mem. Press Club of Cleve. (dir. 1994—, v.p. 1996-98, pres. 1998—). Office: IndustryWeek 1100 Superior Ave E Cleveland OH 44114-2518

BRANDT, KATHLEEN See WEIL-GARRIS BRANDT, KATHLEEN

BRANDT, KATHY A., public relations and events management executive, secondary school educator; b. Chgo., June 12, 1942; d. Leo J. and Helen J. (Briskin) Weisel; m. John M. Brandt, Nov. 28, 1967; children: Debra, Lee. BA, U. Iowa, 1963; MA, Fairfield U., 1975. Cert. secondary sch. tchr. Tchr. Golden Valley Jr. H.S., San Bernardino, Calif., 1963-64, Lake Forest (Ill.) H.S., 1964-68, Stamford (Conn.) H.S., 1968-72; pres. Brandt Assocs., Inc., Westport, Conn., 1984—. Vol. tchr., aide, mem. curriculum com. Westport Schs., 1976-83; editor newsletter Kings Hwy. Sch. PTA, Westport, 1984; mem. parent's com. Pine Manor Coll., Chestnut Hill, Mass., 1994—. Mem. LWV, N.Am. Ski Journalists Assn., Snow Sports Assn. Women (founding mem.). Home and Office: Brandt Assocs Inc 29 Washington Ave Westport CT 06880-2549

BRANDT, PHILIP H., federal judge; b. 1944. BA in Econs., Harvard U., 1966; JD, U. Wash., 1972. Atty. U.S. Dept. Justice and Fed. Maritime Commn., 1972-73; dep. prosecuting atty. Pierce County, Wash., 1973-75; dir. stds. project Wash. Gov.'s Com. on Law and Justice, 1975-76; with LeCocq, Simonarson, et al, 1976-86, Graham & Dunn, 1986-91; apptd. bankruptcy judge we. dist. U.S. Dist. Ct. Wash., 1991. Capt. USN, 1966-69, USNR, 1969-89; ret. Mem. ABA, Wash. State Bar, Nat. Conf. Bankruptcy Judges, Tacoma-Pierce County Bar. Office: 1717 Pacific Ave Rm 2100 Tacoma WA 98402-3234

BRANDT, REXFORD ELSON, artist; b. San Diego, Sept. 12, 1914; s. Alfred O. and Ellen D. (Woodward) B.; m. Joan Malloch Irving, June 22, 1938 (dec. Nov. 1995); children: Joan Dale, Shelley Nora. A.B., U. Calif., 1936; postgrad., Stanford, 1938. Dir. Riverside Jr. Coll. Art Center, 1937-41; chief designer South Coast Co. (shipbuilders), 1941-44; head Rex Brandt Assos., Corona del Mar, Calif., 1944-52, Brandt Painting Workshops, 1946-85. Author: Watercolor with Rex Brandt, 1949, Watercolor Technique in Fifteen Lessons, 1954, Watercolor Landscape in Fifteen Lessons, 1953, Composition of Landscape Painting, 1959, Watercolor Landscape, 1963, The Artists Sketchbook and Its Uses, 1966, San Diego, Land of the Sundown Sea, 1969, The Winning Ways of Watercolor, 1973, (with Jerome K. Muller) Rex Brandt, 1972, West Coast Portfolio, 1977, Seeing with a Painter's Eye, 1981, About Landscape, 1989; also articles.; numerous one man shows include, San Diego Fine Arts Gallery, Los Angeles County Mus., Faulkner Gallery Art, Crocker Gallery Art, Sacramento, Calif., Palace Legion of Honor, Santa Barbara Art Mus., numerous colls. and univs., numerous group exhbns. include, Am. Water Color Soc., N.Y.C., Phila. Acad. Fine Arts, Golden Gate Internat. Expn., N.Y. Water Color Soc., Calif. Centennial Exhbns., others, invitational exhibits include, Corcoran Biennial, Nat. Water Color Survey, Nat. Gallery Art, Riverside Mus., Calif. State Fair, John Herron Art Inst., Scripps Gallery, Pasadena Art Inst., others; represented in permanent collections, San Diego Fine Arts Gallery, Crocker Gallery Art, U.S. Treasury Dept., N.A.D., West Tex Mus., Los Angeles County Mus. Art, Walker Art Mus., San Francisco Mus. Art, Reading Mus., Grinnell Coll., Chico State Coll., Am. Airlines, Philco Corp., Ford Motor Co., U.S. Maritime Service, others. Recipient numerous awards, 1934—, including; Brugger award Calif. Watercolor Soc., 1952; 1st prize, 1970; prize Laguna Beach Festival Arts, 1952; 1st award; James D. Phelan awards de Young Mus., San Francisco, 1953; Adolph and Clara Obrig prize in watercolor N.A.D., 1961; Lena Newcastle Meml. award Am. Watercolor Soc.; Saportas award, 1968; Bronze medal, 1970; Morse medal N.A.D., 1968, 70; certificate of merit, 1977, 93. Fellow Royal Soc. Arts; mem. NAD (academician), Am. Watercolor Soc. (hon. life), Calif. Watercolor Soc. (past pres.). Home and Studio: 405 Goldenrod Ave Corona Del Mar CA 92625-2913 *It comes back to this peculiar sense of phenomena--to the smell of the earth and the splash of the sea. I hope these are never lost to us.*

BRANDT, RICHARD MARTIN, education educator; b. Cleve., Sept. 13, 1922; s. Arthur J. and Lucile (Martin) B.; m. Mattice Fritz, Feb. 14, 1947; children: Mattice Jensen, Richard Martin, William F., Mark A., Lucile (Mrs. Peter Hatch). B. Mech. Engring., U. Va., 1943; M.A., U. Mich., 1949; DEd, U. Md., 1954. Indsl. engr. Detroit, 1946-47; tchr. elem. sch. Willow Run, Mich., 1948-49; instr. edn. U. Del., Newark, 1950-52; instr. edn. U. Md., College Park, 1953-54, asst. prof., 1954-57, assoc. prof., 1957-65; assoc. prof. Sch. Edn., U. Va., Charlottesville, 1965-68, prof., 1968-90, Curry Meml. prof. edn., 1975-90, prof. emeritus, 1990—, chmn., 1968-74, dean, 1974-84; ret., 1990. Author: Studying Behavior in Natural Settings, 1972, 81, Public Education Under Scrutiny, 1981, Incentive Pay and Career Ladders for Today's Teachers, 1990; co-editor: Observational Methods in the Classroom; contbr. articles on edn. to profl. publs. Served to lt. (j.g.) USNR, 1943-46. Mem. Assn. Colls. and Schs. Edn. in State Univ. and Land Grant Colls. (pres. 1982-83), Va. Assn. Colls. for Tchr. Edn. (pres. 1980-82), Am. Ednl. Rsch. Assn., Phi Delta Kappa, Kappa Delta Pi. Home: Route 1 6403 Rivendell Ln Crozet VA 22932-3310 Office: Sch Edn Univ Va Charlottesville VA 22903

BRANDT, RICHARD PAUL, communications and entertainment company executive; b. N.Y.C., Dec. 6, 1927; s. Harry and Helen (Satenstein) B.; m. Helen H. Kogel, May 31, 1975; children: Claudia, David, Matthew, Thomas; 1 stepdau., Jennifer. BS with high honors, Yale U., 1948. With Trans-Lux Theatres Corp., 1950-54, v.p., 1952-54; with Trans-Lux Corp., Norwalk, Conn., 1954—, v.p., 1959-62, pres., 1962-80, chmn. bd., 1974—, chief exec. officer, 1974-92; dir. Am. Book-Stratford Press, Inc., 1962-87, Brandt Theatres, Presdl. Realty Corp.; founding gov. Ind. Film Importers & Distbrs. Am., 1959-63, bd. dirs., 1959-69; v.p., mem. exec. com. Theatre Owners Am., 1962-65; mem. bill of rights com. Council Motion Picture Orgns., 1963-65; bd. dirs. Film Soc. Lincoln Ctr., 1968-71; mem. N.Y. State Bus. Adv. Com. on Mgmt. Improvement, 1966-70; chmn. bd. Univ. Settlement Soc., 1964-66, hon. pres., bd. dirs., 1966-71; dir. Am. Theatre Wing, 1970—, United Neighborhood Houses, 1968-73; bd. dirs., treas. Settlement House Employment Devel., 1969-72; trustee, mem. exec. com. Am. Film Inst., 1971—, vice chmn., 1980-83, chmn. bd., 1983-86, chmn. emeritus 1986—; trustee Mus. Holography, 1979-82; mem. Tony awards mgmt. com., 1986—; founder live poets' soc., 1991—. Vice chmn. bd. Coll. of Santa Fe, 1987—; trustee Maritime Ctr., Norwalk, 1991-92. Named Exhibitor of Yr., ShoWest, 1984. Mem. Nat. Assn. Theatre Owners (dir. 1957-78, exec. com. 1965-78, Sherrill Corwin award 1983), Phi Beta Kappa, Sigma Xi. Office: Trans-Lux Corp 433 Paseo de Peralta Santa Fe NM 87501

BRANDT, ROBERT BARRY, lay worker; b. Lebanon, Pa., Nov. 13, 1948; s. Marlin Jay Brandt and Arlene Hilda (Bowman) Gable; m. Ruth Ann Peterson, June 6, 1970; 1 child, Matthew Scot. BA in Sociology, Lebanon Valley Coll., 1971; postgrad., United Theol. Sem., Dayton, Ohio, 1973. Lic. to ministry Meth. Ch., 1968. Min. Ea. Pa. United Meth. Ch., Harrisburg, Pa., 1968-72; deacon Ea. Pa. United Meth. Ch., Valley Forge, Pa., 1972-76; local ch. lay leader Ridgewood (N.J.) United Meth. Ch., 1985-87; dist. lay leader no. dist. North N.J. Conf. United Meth., Paramus, N.J., 1986-89; lay leader ann. conf. North N.J. Conf. United Meth., Madison, N.J., 1989-96; chair No. N.J. Bd. of Laity, Madison, 1989-96; chair coun. on ministries Ridgewood United Meth. Ch., 1988-89; mem. bishop's task force No. N.J. United Meth., Madison, 1989, 96-99; mem. Walk to Emmaus Community, 1987—, Disciplined Order of Christ, Nashville, 1988—; v.p. tech. and corp. svcs. Matrix Info. Consulting, Inc., Rochelle Park, N.J., 1987—; mem. gen. coun. on Ministries United Meth. Ch., 1992-96; lay dir. Skylands Walk to Emmaus Cmty., 1996-97. Mem., sec. gen. com. on gen. conf. United Meth. Ch., 1992-96, del. gen. conf., 1992, 96; mem. Episcopacy com., N.E. jurisdiction United Meth. Ch., 1991—; N.E. regional rep. for Internat. Walk to Emmaus, 1998—, internat. steering com., 1998—. Named Layperson of Yr. Northern N.J. Conf., United Meth. Ch., 1993, Man of Yr. Ripewood United Meth. Ch., 1996. Mem. Nat. Assn. Ann. Conf. Lay Leader. Democrat. Home: 250 Jefferson Ave River Edge NJ 07661-1308 Office: Matrix Info Cons Inc 365 W Passaic St Rochelle Park NJ 07662-3017 *We are each called to a life of service to others. It is in the losing of ourselves to others that we ultimately find who and what we were meant to be when God placed us on this earth.*

BRANDT, ROBERT FREDERIC, III, newspaper editor, journalist; b. Louisville, Sept. 17, 1946; s. Robert Frederic Jr. and Dorothea (Burton) B.; m. Annette Floyd, Aug., 1968 (div.); m. Walda Ruth DuPriest, Sept., 1980. Student, Ea. Ky. U., 1964-66; BA, U. Ky., 1968. Copy editor The Hartford (Conn.) Courant, 1968-69, The Tampa (Fla.) Tribune, 1971-72; news editor The Miami (Fla.) Herald, 1972-78; asst. mng. editor The Washington Star, 1978-81; asst. mng. editor Newsday, L.I., N.Y., 1981-87, mng. editor, 1987—. Bd. dirs. Guide Dog Found. for Blind, Inc., Smithtown, N.Y. Mem. AP Mng. Editors Assn., Am. Soc. Newspaper Editors. Presbyterian. Office: Newsday 235 Pinelawn Rd Melville NY 11747-4250*

BRANDT, RONALD STIRLING, writer; b. Neligh, Nebr., Aug. 14, 1932; s. Ferdinand B. and Ruth G. (Thornton) B.; m. Dorothy May Rice, May 13, 1951; children: Rhonda, Rebecca, Bonita. BS, U. Nebr., 1955; MA, Northwestern U., Evanston, Ill., 1960; EdD, U. Minn., 1970. Tchr. Racine (Wis.) Pub. Schs., 1957-62, prin., 1962-64; tchr., cons. No. Nigeria Tchr. Edn. Project, Maiduguri, 1965-66; program coord. Upper Midwest Regional Edn. Lab., Mpls., 1966-68; dir. staff devel. Mpls. Pub. Schs., 1968-70; assoc. supt. Lincoln (Nebr.) Pub. Schs., 1970-78; exec. editor Ednl. Leadership, Alexandria, Va., 1978-96; asst. exec. dir. ASCD, Alexandria, 1995-97; writer, cons. in field, 1997—. Co-author: Dimensions of Thinking, 1986, Dimensions of Learning, 1992, the Language of Learning, 1997; editor: Content of the Curriculum, 1988, Assessing Student Learning, 1998; author: Powerful Learning, 1998. 1st lt. U.S. Army, 1955-57. Inductee EdPress (Ednl. Press Assn.) Hall of Fame, Apr. 1996.

BRANDT, WERNER WILLIAM, federal agency official; b. N.Y.C., Aug. 29, 1938; s. Werner and Marie (Hittmeyer) B.; m. V. Martha Valuch, June 29, 1963; children: K. Alyssa, Nicholas C. BA, Hamilton Coll., 1960. Fgn. svc. officer Dept. State, Washington, 1962-72; exec. asst. to the speaker U.S. Ho. Reps., Washington, 1972-92, sgt. at arms, 1992-95; govt. affairs counselor Preston, Gates, Ellis & Rouvelas, Meeds, Washington, 1995—. Home: 4006 N Taylor St Arlington VA 22207-4657

BRANDT, WILLIAM ARTHUR, JR., consulting executive; b. Chgo., Sept. 5, 1949; s. William Arthur and Joan Virginia (Ashworth) B.; m. Patrice Bugelas, Jan. 19, 1980; children: Katherine Ashworth, William George, Joan Patrice, John Peter. BA with honors, St. Louis U., 1971; MA, U. Chgo., 1972, postgrad., 1972-74. Asst. to pres. Pyro Mining Co., Chgo., 1972-74; commentator Sta. WBBM-AM, Chgo., 1977; with Melaniphy & Assocs., Inc., Chgo., 1975-76; pres., cons. Devel. Specialists, Inc., Chgo., 1976—; mem. adv. bd. Sociol. Abstracts, Inc., San Diego, 1979-83. Contbr. articles to profl. jours. Trustee Fenwick H.S., 1991-99, Comml. Law League of Am., Internat. Coun. Shopping Ctrs., Nat. Assn. Bankruptcy Trustees, Ill. Sociol. Assn., Midwest Sociol. Soc., Urban Land Inst. LaVerne Noyes scholar, 1971-74. Mem. Am. Bankruptcy Inst., Am. Sociol. Assn., Amelia Island Plantation Club, Union League Club Chgo., City Club of Miami, sust. fellow of Art Inst. of Chicago, gov. mem. Chicago Symphony, Clinton/Gore '96 Natl. Finance Bd., mnging. trustee Democratic Natl. Comm., maj. trust mem. Democratic Senatorial Campaign Comm., life mem. Zoological Soc. of the Miami Metro Zoo. Democrat. Roman Catholic. Home: 2000 S Bayshore Dr Villa 39 Coconut Grove FL 33133-3251 also: Amelia Island Plantation 6518 Beachwood Rd Amelia Island FL 32034-6512 also: 1134 Sheridan Rd Winnetka IL 60093-1538 also: 23 Sea Colony Dr Santa Monica CA 90405-5321 Office: 3 First Nat Plz Ste 2300 Chicago IL 60602 also: 200 S Biscayne Blvd Ste 900 Miami FL 33131-2310 also: Devonshire House, 60 Goswell Rd, London EC1M 7AD, England also: Wells Fargo Ctr 333 S Grand Ave Ste 2010 Los Angeles CA 90071-1524 also: Two Oliver St 11th Fl Boston MA 02109-4901

BRANDT, WILLIAM NIELSEN, astronomer; b. Durham, NC, June 10, 1970; s. William Norman and Ardis Nielsen B. BS, Calif. Inst. Tech., 1992; PhD, U. Cambridge, Eng., 1996. Postdoctoral fellow Harvard U., Cambridge, Mass., 1996-97; prof. Pa. State U., University Park, 1997—. Contbr. articles to profl. jours. Recipient Sloan Fellowship, 1993—. Fellow Royal Astronomical Soc., mem. Am. Astronomical Soc. Achievements include discovery of x-ray spectral features and variability in many seyfert galaxies and quasars. Avocations: sailing, travel. E-mail: niel@astro.psu.edu. Office: Pa State Univ 525 Davey Lab University Park PA 16802-6305

BRANDT-RAUF, PAUL WESLEY, public health educator; b. Sept. 10, 1948. BS, Columbia U., 1970, MS, 1973, DSc, 1974, MD, 1979, MPH, 1980, D in Pub. Health, 1987. Prof. pub. health, dir. occupl. and environ. medicine Columbia U., N.Y.C., 1994—. Office: Columbia U 60 Haven Ave New York NY 10032-2604

BRANDWEIN, RUTH ANN, social welfare educator; b. Bklyn., Apr. 24, 1940; d. Charles and Kate (Berkowitz) Solin; divorced; children: Lorena Lisa Epstein, Garth Whitman. BA magna cum laude, Bklyn. Coll., 1960; MSW, U. Wash., 1970; PhD, Brandeis U., 1978. Libr. trainee Bklyn. Pub. Libr., 1960-61; substitute tchr. N.Y.C. Bd. Edn., 1961-63; recreation dir. Seattle Park Dept., 1964-66; exec. dir. Cen. Seattle Commn. Coun., 1967-69; rsch. assoc. Harvard U./Lab. Comm. Psychiatry, Boston, 1971-72; asst. prof., chair, comm. org. Boston U. Sch. Social Work, 1973-78; dir., assoc. prof. U. Iowa Sch. Social Work, Iowa City, 1978-81; dean SUNY, Stony Brook, 1981-89; prof. SUNY Sch. Social Welfare, Stony Brook, 1981—; commr. Suffolk County Dept. Social Svcs., Hauppauge, N.Y., 1989-93; holder Spafford Endowed chair U. Utah Sch. Social Work, 1994-96; co-founder Women's Rsch. Ctr. of Boston, 1971-78; co-dir. Women's Com. of 100, 1995-98; cons. U.S. Senate Subcom. on Vets.' Affairs, 1971; guardian ad litem Family Ct., Middlesex County, Mass.; expert witness Grevatt vs. U. Minn., Duluth; vis. assoc. Inst. Policy Studies, 1986-87; lead reviewer Nat. Inst. Justice, 1997—; spkr. in field. Contbr. articles to profl. jours. and chpts. to books; mem. editl. bds. Bd. dirs. United Way of L.I., Melville, N.Y., 1982-88, Suffolk Cmty. Coun., Islandia, N.Y., 1981-97; bd. dirs. exec. com. Am. Jewish Congress, Hauppauge, 1989; bd. dirs., v.p. Kehillath Shalom Synagogue, Cold Spring Harbor, N.Y., 1987-90; bd. dirs. N.Y. Civil Liberties Union, 1994-98, L.I. Cmty. Found., 1994-96; steering com. L.I. Fund for Women and Girls, 1993—; mem. N.Y. Gov.'s Mental Health Coun., 1990—, chair, 1992-95; chair Suffolk County Exec. Task Force on Family Violence, 1988-94, mem. Nat. Advisory Coun. Violence Against Women, 1997—. Recipient Disting. Alumnus award U. Wash. Sch. Social Work, Seattle, 1989, Congrl. award Congressman Mrazek, Suffolk County, N.Y., Hon. Supporter award Women on the Job. Mem. NASW (bd. dirs. 1991-96, 2nd v.p. 1994-96, pres.-elect N.Y. State chpt. 1997-98, pres. 1998—, Suffolk County Social Worker of Yr. 1989), N.Y. Pub. Welfare Assn. (bd. dirs. 1990-93), Women's Commn. Coun. Social Work Edn. (chair 1980-83), Internat. Commn. Coun. Social Work Edn. (bd. dirs. 1986-89), Huntington N.Y. NOW (bd. dirs. 1982-91, chair 1988-91), Phi Beta Kappa. Office: SUNY Stony Brook Sch Social Welfare Health Sci Ctr Level 2 Rm 093 Stony Brook NY 11794-8230

BRANEGAN, JAMES AUGUSTUS, III, journalist; b. Phila., June 6, 1950; s. James Augustus, Jr. and Emmeline Elizabeth (McBurney) B.; m. Stefania Pittaluga, Feb. 4, 1992. B.A., Cornell U., 1972; M.S. in Journalism, Northwestern U., 1973. Reporter Chgo. Today, 1973-74, Chgo. Tribune, 1974-81; with Time Mag., 1981—, chief econs. corr. Washington bur., 1986-87; corr. Time Mag., Hong Kong, 1987-93; European econ. corr. Time Mag., Brussels, Belgium, 1993-97; White House corr. Time Mag., Washington, 1997—. Co-recipient Pulitzer prize for spl. local reporting, 1976. Office: c/o Time 1050 Connecticut Ave NW Washington DC 20036-5303

BRANHAM, C. MICHAEL, lawyer; b. Columbia, S.C., Nov. 6, 1957; s. Mack C. and Jennie Louise (Jones) B.; m. Teresa Barrett; children: Anthony, Mark. BS, Auburn U., Montgomery, Ala., 1979; JD, U. S.C., 1983. Bar: S.C.; cert. tax law specialist; CPA. Acct. Wilson, Price, Barranco & Billingsley, CPAs, Montgomery, 1979-80; law clk. Atty. Gen.'s Office, State of S.C., Columbia, 1981-82; acct. Price, Waterhouse, Columbia, 1983-86; tax lawyer Young, Clement, Rivers & Tisdale, LLP, Charleston, S.C., 1986—, chmn. tax, estate planning and probate group, 1999—; chmn. taxation law specialization adv. bd. S.C. Supreme Ct., 1995-97; mem., pres. Charleston Tax. Coun., 1993-94; mem. dean's adv. bd. Med. U. S.C. Nursing Sch., Charleston, 1994-97; chmn. MUSC Planned Giving adv. coun., 1993-97; mem. exec. com. Roper Found. Planned Giving Coun., Charleston; S.C. case reporter ABA sect. real property, probate and trust law, 1997—; mem. Bishop Gadsden Estate Planning Adv. Coun., Charleston, 1998—. Soccer coach Hungryneck Internat. Soccer Assn., Mt. Pleasant, S.C., 1989—; mem. Charleston Estate Planning Coun. Recipient Am. Jurisprudence award, 1983. Mem. ABA, AICPA, S.C. Assn. CPAs, S.C. Bar Assn., Charleston Breakfast Rotary. Avocations: soccer coaching, weight lifting. Home: 829 Detyens Rd Mount Pleasant SC 29464-5181 Office: Young Clement Rivers & Tisdale LLP 28 Broad St Charleston SC 29401-3070

BRANHAM, ELIZABETH MULLEN, educational administrator; b. Greenville, Miss., Mar. 17, 1949; d. Graham and Billie (Turnley) Mullen; m. Rick. D. Branham, July 25, 1951; two children. BS, Ark. State U., 1971; MEd, Harding U., 1994. Kindergarten tchr. Des Arc (Ark.) Sch. Dist., 1979-91; early childhood adminstr. Wilbur Mills Edn. Svc. Coop., Beebe, Ark., 1991—. Mem. ASCD, Internat. Reading Assn., Ark. Early Childhood Assn., Delta Kappa Gamma. Home: 106 Erwin St Des Arc AR 72040

BRANHAM, GRADY EUGENE, principal; b. Birmingham, Ala., June 19, 1947; s. Grady B. and Pauline (Kelley) B.; m. Joy Canavan, Mar. 26, 1983; children: Joy Elizabeth, Gralynn. BS, Birmingham (Ala.) So. Coll., 1969; MEd, Montevallo (Ala.) U., 1976; PhD, U.N.A., St. Louis, 1988. Prin. Dallas Christian Sch., Selma, Ala., 1970-84, Briarwood Christian High Sch., Birmingham, Ala., 1984—. V.p. Community Concert Assn., Selma, 1980-84. Named Patriot of Yr., Patriotic Am. Youth, Jackson, Miss., 1982, Outstanding Alumnae of Yr., Jefferson State C.C., 1999. Mem. Am. Soc. Interior Design. Avocations: travel, design, music. Office: Briarwood Christian High 6255 Cahaba Valley Rd Birmingham AL 35242-4915

BRANHAM, PAMELA HELEN, special education educator; b. Knoxville, Tenn., July 24, 1960; d. John Author and Nancy Carolyn (Garth) Thomas. BS in Spl. Edn., U. Tenn., 1983, MS in Spl. Edn., 1986. Cert. tchr., Tenn., Fla., Ky., Ind. Interpreter, hearing specialist Knoxville County Schs., 1987-88; tchr. hearing impaired Pasco County Sch., Spring Hill, Fla., 1988-93; tchr. emotionally handicapped and hearing impaired Charlestown (Ind.) High Sch., 1993-95; tchr. educable mentally handicapped, deaf-hard of hearing Pine View Mid. Sch., Land O' Lakes, Fla., 1995—. Mem. Nat. Assn. of the Deaf, Fla. Registry of Interpreters for the Deaf, Alexander Graham Bell Assn. for Deaf. Presbyterian. Avocations: golf, bowling, needlework. Office: Pine View Mid Sch 5334 Parkway Blvd Land O'Lakes FL 34639-3801

BRANIGAN, HELEN MARIE, educational administrator; b. Albany, N.Y., Sept. 24, 1944; d. James J. and Helen (Weaver) B. BS in Bus. Edn., Coll. St. Rose, Albany, 1967, MA in English, 1972; postgrad., SUNY, Albany, 1973-81. Tchr., chair dept. bus. edn. S. Colonie Sch. Dist., Albany, 1968-81; assoc. Bur. Bus. Edn. N.Y. State Edn. Dept., Albany, 1981-87; assoc. Bur. Occupational Edn. Program Devel., Albany, 1987-91, Bur. Occupational Edn. Innovation and Quality, Albany, 1991-93, Cen./So. Regional Field Svcs., Albany, 1993-95, North Country/Regional Field Svcs., 1995-98; mem. regional sch. improvement team SUNY, Cobbleskill, 1998—; bd. trustees St. Catherine's Found., 1993-97; sr. cons. Internat. Cr. for Leadership in Edn., Schenectady, N.Y., 1991—. Editor McGraw-Hill Book Co., Glencoe Pub., 1986—; contbr. articles to profl. jours. Lay vol. Archdiocese of Anchorage, 1967-68; mem. N.Y. State Staff Devel. Coun. Mem. ASCD, Bus. Tchrs. Assn. N.Y. State, Delta Pi Epsilon. Roman Catholic. Avocations: skiing, mountaineering, golf, reading. Home: 540 New Scotland Ave Albany NY 12208-2318 Office: NY State Edn EBA Rm 467 Albany NY 12234

BRANIGIN, ROGER D., JR., lawyer; b. Louisville, Mar. 1, 1931; s. Roger D. and Josephine M. Branigin; m. Marilyn Bechdolt, 1961; children: Elizabeth H. Branigin Cayton, Roger D. III, John F. AB magna cum laude, Dartmouth Coll., 1952; LLB cum laude, Harvard U., 1955. Bar: Ind. 1955. Assoc. Stuart & Branigin, 1957-62, ptnr., 1962—. Trustee Lafayette Sch. Corp., 1963-64, 65-69, pres., 1968-69, United Community Svcs., 1967-68, Capital Funds Found., 1983-84, Tippecanoe County Boys Club, 1976-77; dir. Nat. Homes Corp., 1978-90; chmn. United Way Campaign, 1984; dir. Lafayette Home Hosp., 1978-84, Westminster Village West Lafayette, West Lafayette Econ. Devel. Commn.; dir., North Cen. Health Svcs., 1984—, vice chmn. 1994-96, chmn., 1996—; former trustee Cen. Presbyn. Ch. With U.S. Army, 1955-57, USAR, 1957-59. Fellow Am. Coll. Trust and Estate Counsel, Ind. Bar Found.; mem. ABA, Ind. State Bar Assn., Tippecanoe County Bar Assn. (pres. 1974-75). Office: PO Box 1010 Lafayette IN 47902-1010

BRANIN, JOAN JULIA, health services management educator; b. Newark, July 20, 1944; d. Alvin Edwin and Julia (White) B. BA, Newark State Coll., 1966; MA, Calif. State U., 1970; MBA, UCLA, 1979. CFP. Tchr. Los Alamitos (Calif.) Sch. Dist., 1966-70; sales mgr. Calif. Copy Products, 1970-73; with pharm. sales dept. Lederle Labs., L.A., 1973-75; med. mktg. analyst Am. Hosp. Supply, Glendale, Calif., 1975-78; corp. loan officer Security Pacific, L.A., 1978-80; v.p. First Interstate Bank, 1980-84; v.p., mgr. Std. Chartered Bank Pvt. Banking Group, L.A., 1989-91; fin. planner retirement and estate planning Mass. Mut. Ins. Co., 1991-93; asst. prof. U. LaVerne, Calif., 1993—; chmn. grad. programs in gerontology, 1997. Contbr. articles to profl. jours. Bd. dirs. Area Dance Alliance, Calif. Conf. Arts, Young Musicians Found., UCLA Internat. Student Ctr., 1983-93, Leadership Coun. United Way Med. div., 1989-93. Am. Diabetes Assn., 1989-93, Am. Heart Assn., 1990-93, Music Ctr. Unified Fund Cabinet and Spl. Gifts Com., CSULP Pres. Assocs. exec. bd., 1991-93, Chgo. chpt. Girl Scouts U.S.A., 1987-88, OxBox Summer Sch. Arts Inst., 1987-88. Recipient Disting. Alumni award Calif. State U. Long Beach, 1990. Mem. APA, Am. Coll. Healthcare Execs., Am. Evaln. Assn., Am. Soc. Aging, Women Health Adminstrn., Healthcare Fin. Mgmt. Assn. (local chpt.), Soc. Behavioral Medicine, Assn. Health Svcs. Rsch., Women Scholars, Internat. Assn. for Fin. Planning, Phi Kappa Phi, Pi Lambda Theta, Phi Delta Gamma, Kappa Delta Pi. Democrat. Home: 2043 Allen Ave Altadena CA 91001-3423

BRANKAMP, ROBERT GEORGE, biosystems specialist; b. Cin., Nov. 24, 1961; s. Robert James and Janice Darlene (Cupp) B. BS, Ky. Wesleyan, 1984. Rsch. asst. U. Cin., 1984-88; molecular biologist Hoechst Marion Roussel, Inc., Cin., 1988-96; field application specialist Applied Biosys., Foster City, Calif., 1996—; speaker in field. Contbr. articles to Jour. Biol. Chemistry, Jour. of Clin. and Lab. Medicine, Blood Coagulation and Fibrinolysis. Mem. ABRF. Office: Applied Biosys 850 Lincoln Centre Dr Foster City CA 94404-1128

BRANN, ALTON JOSEPH, manufacturing company executive; b. Portland, Maine, Dec. 23, 1941; s. Donald Edward and Marjorie Margaret (Curran) B. BA, U. Mass., 1969. Mgr. advanced programs Dynamics Research Corp., Wilmington, Mass., 1969-73; dir. engring. Litton Guidance & Control Systems, L.A., 1973-79, dir. program mgmt., 1979-81, v.p. engring., 1981-83, pres., 1983-86; group exec. Navigation Guidance and Control Systems Group, Beverly Hills, Calif., 1986-88; sr. v.p. Components and Indsl. Products Group Litton Industries, Beverly Hills, 1988-90, pres., COO, 1990-92, CEO, 1992-94, chmn., 1994-96; chmn., CEO Western Atlas Inc., Beverly Hills, 1994-97, UNOVA Inc., Beverly Hills, 1997—; trustee Mfrs. Alliance Productivity and Innovation, coun. fgn. diplomacy, U.S.-Russia bus. coun. Mem. IEEE (sr. mem.), Optical Soc. Am., L.A. World Affairs Coun., Town Hall of L.A. Avocations: skiing, sailing. Office: UNOVA 360 N Crescent Dr Beverly Hills CA 90210-4802

BRANN, DONALD TREASURER, manufacturing executive; b. Mt. Vernon, N.Y., Apr. 22, 1929; s. Mark Benjamin and Beatrice Elizabeth (Treasurer) B.; m. Joan Louise Stieb, June 23, 1951 (div. 1970); children: Duane, Joy, Daryl, Jan, Dale, Dennis; m. Margaret Peggy Ann Allen, Oct. 9, 1971. Grad. high sch., Carmel, N.Y. With Pontiac (Mich.) Motor Div., 1949-50; cabinet maker Rochester (Mich.) Cabinets, 1950-51, GEO F. Robertson Co., Romeo, Mich., 1951-53; draftsman Pontiac Millwork Co., Rubin Assocs., Pontiac, 1954; sales engr., v.p. Detroit Partition Co., 1954-67; owner, pres., chief exec. officer Don Brann Assocs., Inc., Oak Park, Mich., 1967—; owner, pres. Advance Mill & Cabinet, Oak Park, 1972-88. Inventor Modular Pole Supported Desk. Candidate Rochester Hills City Coun., 1987. Sgt. USAF, 1946-49. Mem. Constrn. Assn. Mich. (bd. dirs. 1996-00), Detroit Execs. Assn. (bd. dirs. 1985-89, 94-98, v.p. 1999), Constrn. Specifications Inst., Acad. MODEL Aeronautics, Detroit Athletic Club, Lake Shore Sail Club (commodore 1978-79), Optimists (pres. Birmingham 1978-79). Avocations: radio control aircraft, sailing, golf, bldg. homes. Office: Don Brann Assocs Inc 21840 Wyoming Pl Oak Park MI 48237-3112

BRANN, EDWARD R(OMMEL), editor; b. Rostock, Mecklenburg, Germany, May 20, 1920; s. Guenther O.R. and Lilli (Appel) B.; came to U.S., 1938, naturalized, 1966; BA, Berea Coll., 1945; MA, U. Chgo., 1946; postgrad. U. Wis., 1948-56; m. Helen Louise Sweet, Dec. 9, 1948; children: Johannes Weidler, Paul George. Asst. membership sec. central YMCA, Chgo., 1946-48; asst. editor Credit Union Mag., Madison, Wis., 1955-65; dir. hist. projects, asst. dir. publs. CUNA Internat., Inc., Madison, 1965-70, staff historian, 1958-65; asst. dir. publs. Credit Union Nat. Assn., Inc., Madison, 1970-72, 83-84, asst. dir. communications, 1973-83, sr. editor Credit Union mag., 1973-84, coordinator Innovative Ideas Center, 1980-84; contbg. editor Credit Union Exec. mag., 1982-84; dir. hist. projects World Council of Credit Unions, Inc., 1970-79, dir. European relations, 1972-83. Active ARC, various coms. Dane County chpt., vol. cons., 1984-96, vol. cons. Badger chpt., 1997—. Recipient Christo et Ecclesiae award Concordia Coll., Milw., 1968, Distinguished Alumnus award Berea Coll., 1977, Risser award Dane County chpt. ARC, 1983; named Ky. col. Mem. Am. Hist. Assn., NEA. Lutheran. Contbr. articles to profl. jours. Home: PO Box 383 Madison WI 53701-0383 Office: PO Box 5905 Madison WI 53705-0905 *Personal philosophy: We can do 10 times what we think we can do. Commitment makes the difference.*

BRANN, RICHARD ROLAND, lawyer; b. Olney, Ill., June 9, 1943; s. Roland John and Margaret (McVay) B.; m. Penny Sue Farrington, June 5, 1965; children: Wesley R., Patrick T. BA, Miss. State U., 1965; JD, U. Tex., 1968. Bar: Tex. 1968, U.S. Dist. Ct. (so., no., ea. and we. dists.) Tex. 1970, U.S. Ct. Appeals (5th and 11th cirs.) 1973, U.S. Supreme Ct. 1973; bd. cert. in labor and employment law Tex. Bd. Legal Specialization. Assoc. Baker & Botts, Houston, 1968-76, ptnr., 1976—; chmn. fed. judiciary rels. com. State Bar Tex., 1996—; chmn. Houston Mgmt. Lawyers Forum, Houston, 1981. Editor: Tex. Assn. of Bus. and C. of C. Labor Law Quarterly Rev., Tex. Labor Letter. With USMC, 1961-66. Mem. ABA, Tex. Bar Assn., Tex. Bar Coll., Houston Bar Assn. (chmn. labor and employment law sect. 1997—), Def. Rsch. Inst., Houston Club, Plaza Club, Phi Kappa Phi. Republican. Methodist. Avocations: running, fishing, hunting. Home: 13 Stonegate Dr Houston TX 77024-2703

BRANNAN, BEVERLY WOOD, curator of photography; b. Louisville, Aug. 19, 1946; d. Kenneth Wells and Ruth Marie (Bridges) Wood; m. Tod Allen Brannan, Oct. 10, 1969 (div. 1979); m. John Michael Vlach, Feb. 14, 1984; children: Kate Vlach, Molly Vlach. BA in History and Art History, U. Md., 1968, MLS, 1972; MA in Am. Studies, George Washington U., 1986. Archivist manuscript divsn. Libr. of Congress, Washington, 1970-74, curator of photography prints and photographs divsn., 1974—. Editor: A Kentucky Album: Farm Security Adminstration Photographs 1935-1943, 1986, Documenting American 1935-1943, 1988; contbr.: The African American Mosaic: A Library of Congress Resource Guide for the Study of Black History and Culture, 1993, Photography, 1933-67: Toni Frissell, 1994, Eyes of the Nation: A Visual History,. Democrat. Methodist. Office: Libr of Congress Prints & Photographs Divsn 10 1st Ave SW Washington DC 20540-4730*

BRANNAN, CLEO ESTELLA, retired elementary education educator; b. Turon, Kans., Feb. 22, 1924; d. Jesse Logan and Nancy Elma (Cox) Zink; m. Raymond Eugene Brannan, Aug. 4, 1946 (deceased); children: Raymond Eugene Jr., Nancy Estelle, Tricia Elaine. BS, Ft. Hays State U., 1964. Cert. elem. edn. educator, Kans. Elem. tchr. Pretty Prairie (Kans.) Schs., 1943-45, Meade (Kans.) Elem. Sch., 1945-48, 58-60, 61-87; substitute secondary sch. tchr. Meade (Kans.) Elem. Sch., 1987; ret., 1987. Contbr. articles to Meadowlark mag. Trustee Meade Pub. Libr., 1961-65, trustee, treas., 1990—; state bd. dirs. Friends of Kans. Librs., 1990-96; silver haired legislator, 1999—. Mem. AAUW (local pres. 1985-86), Kans. Ret. Tchr. Assn. (bd. dirs. 1991—, state pres. 1996-97), Silver Haired Legis., Delta Kappa Gamma. Avocations: collecting China, traveling, reading, arranging flowers. Home: PO Box 13 Meade KS 67864-0013

BRANNAN, EULIE ROSS, education consultant; b. Norwood, Ohio, Sept. 6, 1928; s. Olin Hiram and Bernice Cleo (Beall) B.; m. Ruby Merle Moore, Dec. 16, 1945 (dec.); children: Stephen Earl, Deborah Brannan Watkins, Rebecca Brannan, Julie Ross Brannan-Williams; m. Willie Metta Strong, Mar. 7, 1981. AA, Ala. Christian Coll., 1947; BA, Huntingdon Coll., 1949; MS, Auburn U., 1953, EdD, 1960; postgrad., Harding Grad. Sch., 1960-63, Oxford (Eng.) U., 1981. Tchr. high sch. Montgomery, Ala., 1949-51; guidance counselor Montgomery Bible High Sch., 1951-53; prin. Ala. Christian High Sch., Montgomery, 1953-55; prof. Ala. Christian Coll., Montgomery, 1953-55, asst. to pres., 1955-56, acad. dean, 1956-69, acad. v.p., 1969-73, pres., 1973-81; field dir. Nat. Edn. Program, Huntsville, Ala., 1981-82; pres. Jefferson Christian Acad., Birmingham, Ala., 1982-90; assoc. J. Robert Clark & Assocs., 1990-91; spl. counsel to pres. Faulkner U., Montgomery, Ala., 1991—. Chaplain Madison Police Dept., 1996—. Mem. Ala. Head Injury Found. (bd. mem.), Phi Delta Kappa. Mem. Ch. of Christ. Home: 117 Kensington Dr Madison AL 35758-7845 Office: Faulkner Univ 5345 Atlanta Hwy Montgomery AL 36189

BRANNEN, DANIEL JUDE, children's services administrator; b. Dayton, Ohio, Oct. 19, 1961; s. Michael Joseph and Martha Jayne (Tully) B.; m. Marilyn Jeanne Wukovich, Mar. 9, 1985; children: Dylan Jude, Jude Catherine, Jay Daniel. BS in Zoology, Miami U., Oxford, Ohio, 1984; MS in Urban Affairs, Hunter Coll., 1991. Program dir. Covenant House, N.Y.C., 1988-92; exec. dir. Ohio Boys Town, Inc., Cleve., 1992-99, The Altman Found. for Children, Boca Raton, Fla., 1999—. Capt. USMC, 1984-88. Mem. Alliance of Child Care Svc. Providers (sec., trustee 1996—, chmn. pub. policy advocacy com. 1996—), Ohio Assn. Child Caring Agys. (mem. legis. and pub. policy coms. 1996—), Cleve. Zool. Soc. Avocations: writing, family. Home: 31 Fillier St Berea OH 44017-1712

BRANNEN, GEORGE ELSDON, surgeon; b. Jan. 14, 1943. BA, Dartmouth Coll., 1965; MD, Northwestern U., Chgo., 1969; Bd. Cert. Urologist, Johns Hopkins Hosp., 1975. Diplomate Nat. Bd. Med. Examiners, Am. Bd. Urology. Surg. intern Duke U. Hosp. - Duke U. Med. Ctr., durham, N.C., 1969-70; surg. resident Duke U. Hosp., 1970-71; urology resident James Buchanan Brady Urol. Inst. - Johns Hopkins Hosp., Balt., 1971-75; rsch. fellow dept. urology and divsn. oncology Johns Hopkins Hosp., Balt., 1972-73, sr. asst. resident, 1973-74, chief resident, 1974-75, fellow American Cancer Soc., 1973-74; fellow kidney transplant U. Colo. Med. Ctr., Denver, 1977-78; staff urologist and dir. kidney transplantation Va. Mason Med. Ctr., Seattle, 1978-91, staff urologist, dir. kidney transplantation, 1978-91; urologist and gen. surgeon, physician Shisong Mission, Cameroon, W. Africa, 1991-94; prof. clin. urology, chmn. clin. faculty U. Wash., Seattle, 1994—, 98—; staff urologist, bd. dirs. MultiCare Health Svcs., Kent, Wash., 1994—; staff urologist Kent Med. Ctr. - MultiCare Health Systems, Valley Med. Ctr., 1994—; with Gen. Med. Missionary Svc., Cath. Med. Mission Hosp., Shisong, W. Africa, 1991-94;. Contbr. numerous articles to profl. jours. Bd. dirs., med. dir. YMCA Camp Orkila; bd. dirs. YMCA of Greater Seattle, 1998; trustee MultiCare Med. Group; mem. St. Brendan's Cath. Ch. Human Concerns Commn.; regional rep. United Network for Organ Sharing; first aid instr., vol. physician U.S. Forest Svc./ Nat. Ski Patrol; presenter slide lectr. series on personal wilderness experience in the Klondike to various civic and med. groups, others. With med. corps. U.S. Army, 1975-77. Grantee in field. Fellow Am. Coll. Surgeons, Seattle Surg. Soc.; mem. Am. Urol. Assn. (1st prize Joseph McCarthy contest 1979), Northwest Urol. Soc. (2nd prize scientific presentation 1978), Wash. State Med. Soc., Transplantation Soc., Am. Soc. Transplant Surgeons, Northwest Renal Soc., Northwest Transplant Soc., Nat. Renal Adminstr.s' Assn., Am. Fertility Soc. (Weck Urology Rsch. prize 1974), Am. Soc. Andrology, Am. Assn. Clin. Urologists, others. Office: Covington MultiCare Clinic Multi-Care Urology Svcs 17700 SE 272nd St Ste 260 Kent WA 98042-4951

BRANNEN, JOHN HOWARD, lawyer; b. Dover, Ohio, July 22, 1949; s. Howard G. and Margaret A. (Shoemaker) B. BA summa cum laude, Ohio U., 1972; JD cum laude, U. Mich., 1975. Bar: Ohio 1975, Fla. 1984, U.S. Dist. Ct. (no. dist.) Ohio 1975, U.S. Ct. Appeals (6th cir.) 1984. Ptnr. Day, Ketterer, Raley, Wright & Rybolt Ltd., Canton, Ohio, 1975—. Trustee Goodwill Industries Rehab. Ctr., Canton, 1979—, Stark County Law Libr., 1987—. Mem. ABA, Ohio Bar Assn., Fla. Bar, Stark County Bar Assn., Rotary Club of Canton, Phi Beta Kappa. Avocations: personal computers, reading, travel, swimming. Home: 911 Knollwood Dr NW Canton OH 44708-3424 Office: Day Ketterer Raley Wright & Rybolt Ltd 121 Cleveland Ave SW Ste 800 Canton OH 44702-1914

BRANNICK, ELLEN MARIE, management consultant; b. Rochester, Minn., Aug. 10, 1934; d. Daniel Ryther and Grace Ellen (Mills) Markham; m. Thomas L. Brannick,. BS in Health, Phys. Edn., MacMurray Coll., 1956, MS, 1959. Elem. phys. edn. Ritenour Consol. Sch. Dist., Overland, Mo., 1958-61; head tchr., summer dir. Civic League Day Nursery, Rochester, 1961-64; recreation therapist Rochester State Hosp., 1964-68; rehab. dir. Rochester State Hosp., 1968-70; rehab. therapist Napa State Hosp., Calif., 1971; indsl. therapy con. Napa State Hosp., 1971-73, community liaison rep., 1973-99; ret., 1999. Mem. Friends Napa County Library, 1977, Napa County Humane Soc., 1978. Mem. Napa County Hist. Soc. Democrat. Avocations:antique post cards, philately, bibliophily, military history, traveling.

BRANNON, LESTER TRAVIS, JR., lawyer; b. Atlanta, Feb. 10, 1926; s. Lester Travis and Esta Louise (Cherry) B.; m. Jean Mouchet, Sept. 8, 1950; children: Lester Travis III, Carole Brannon Blocker. BS in Indsl. Mgmt., Ga. Inst. Tech., 1949; JD, Emory U., 1952; LLD (hon.), Newberry Coll., 1987. Bar: Ga. 1952. Assoc. Crenshaw, Hansell, Ware & Brandon and successor firm Hansell & Post, Atlanta, 1952-55, ptnr., 1955-81; chief exec. ptnr. Hansell & Post, 1981-89; ptnr. Jones, Day, Reavis & Pogue, Atlanta, 1989-93, of counsel, 1994-96; chmn. bd. dirs. The Resource Ctr.; mem. large complex cases panel Am. Arbitration Assn., 1993—. Pub. cons. to commns. Nat. Assn. Schs. Music, Reston, Va., 1975-80; chmn. Mayor's Task Force on Ethics in City Govt., Atlanta, 1981-82; pres. Ga. Tech. Found., Inc., 1985-87; vice. chmn. bd. trustees Newberry Coll., S.C., 1980-83; mem. Emory Law Sch. Coun., Emory U.; bd. dirs., mem. exec. com. Atlanta Arts Alliance, Inc., 1982-89. 2d lt. USAAF, 1944-52. Recipient Alumni Disting. Service award Ga. Inst. Tech., 1987, Gregory A. Robertson Meml. award Atlanta Bar Assn., 1990-91, Ivan Allen award Atlanta Rotary Club, 1994, George A. Pindar award State of Ga., 1997. Mem. Am. Coll. Real Estate Lawyers, Am. Land Title Assn. (assoc.), Anglo-Am. Real Property Inst., Ga. Tech. Alumni Assn. (pres. 1974-75). Republican. Lutheran. Clubs: Piedmont Driving. Lodge: Rotary. Office: Jones Day Reavis & Pogue 3500 One Peachtree Ctr 303 Peachtree St NE Ste 3500 Atlanta GA 30308-3242

BRANNON, RONALD ROY, minister; b. Aberdeen, S.D., Apr. 16, 1928; s. Walter Carlos and Mary Erma (Snyder) B.; m. Rosalee Vernela Carry, July 20, 1949; children: Rhonda Lee Storer, Rodney Vaughn, Randall Roy. BA, Bartlesville Wesleyan Coll., Okla., 1950; DD, Southern Wesleyan U., 1987. Ordained to ministry Wesleyan Ch., 1951. Pastor Heber Wesleyan Ch., Miltonvale, Kans., 1949-52, First Wesleyan Ch., Wichita, Kans., 1952-68; dist. supt. Kans. Dist. of the Wesleyan Ch., Miltonvale, 1968-83; gen. sec. Internat. Ctr.-The Wesleyan Ch. Hdqtrs., Indpls., 1982—; co-founder, coord. police chaplaincy, Wichita. Trustee/sec. bd. dirs. Miltonvale Wesleyan Coll., 1967-72, Bartlesville Wesleyan Coll., 1968-84, So. Wesleyan U., 1984-92; mem., sec. Hephzibah Children's Home, 1983-92, chair bd. dirs., 1992—; bd. dirs. Wesleyan Investment Found., 1983—. Mem. Nat. Assn. Evangelicals (bd. dirs. 1970-72), Christian Holiness Assn. (treas. 1984-88). Republican. Home: 1412 N Marlin Dr Marion IN 46952-1536 Office: The Internat Ctr TWC 6060 Castleway West Dr Indianapolis IN 46250-1930

BRANNON, TREVA LEE (WOOD), insurance company executive; b. Burleson, Tex., Oct. 6, 1932; d. William Albert and Virginia May (Garner) Wood; m. Lone J. Brannon, Aug. 3, 1951 (dec. Apr. 1989); 1 child, Ralph Eugene. Grad. high sch., Godley, Tex. Acctg. clk. Internat. Svcs. Life Ins. Co., Ft. Worth, 1950-63; sec. John Hancock Life Ins. Co., Ft. Worth, 1963-64; asst. v.p. Olympic Life Ins. Co., Ft. Worth, 1964-70; v.p. Transport Life Ins. Co., Ft. Worth, 1970-97; with TLC Nat. Mktg. Co., Dallas, 1997. Avocations: reading, travel. Home: 349 Heirloom Dr Fort Worth TX 76134-3950

BRANNON, WINONA EILEEN, electrical contractor; b. Austell, Ga., Jan. 3, 1948; d. John Milton and Vera Inez (Banks) McDaniel; m. Harold Wallace Smith, May 9, 1966 (div. June 1967); m. Jerry Edward Weddington, Feb. 24, 1968 (div. Feb. 1984); children: Michael Richard, Paula Daniell; m. David Lee Brannon, Dec. 9, 1985; 1 step-child, Kimberly Lorraine. Cert. in data processing, DeKalb Tech., Chamblee, Ga., 1968; cert. in keypunch, Ga. State, 1969; cert. in elec. codes, Cobb Voc. Tech., Marietta, Ga., 1983. Lic. hair stylist, Ga.; lic. low voltage elec. contractor, Ga. Hair stylist Casa Di Bella and Modella, Atlanta and Mableton, Ga., 1965-68; sec. and keypunch operator Ga. Sec. of State, Atlanta, 1968-70; data transcriber IRS, Chamblee, Ga., 1969-73, data processor, 1978-79, IDRS operation, 1980-82; sch. bus driver Cobb County Bd. Edn., Marietta, 1974-77; meat packer Cudahy (Bar-s Meats), Atlanta, 1979-80; electrician J&J Electric, Mableton, 1982-85; owner, elec. contractor Watts New Electric, Mableton, 1985—; network rep. Internat. Heritage Inc., 1998—; cons. lighting design, home remodeling, 1995—. Trustee Trinity United Meth. Ch., Austell, 1992—; sponsor South Cobb Athletic Assn. T-Ball Team, 1994—, baseball team, 1998—; organizer, sponsor contractor's bowling league, Austell, Ga., 1994—. Recipient First Pl. Hair Styling award, Mableton, 1965, 66. Mem. Adams Rainbow (worthy advisor 1965), Ea. Star (Assn. matron 1983). Republican. Home and Office: 5923 Ridge Dr SE Mableton GA 30126-3524

BRANNON-PEPPAS, LISA, chemical engineer, researcher; b. Houston, Sept. 19, 1962; d. James Graham and Patricia Ann (Hightower) Brannon; m. Nicholas A. Peppas, Aug. 10, 1988. BS, Rice U., 1984; MS, Purdue U., 1986, PhD, 1988. Sr. formulations chemist Eli Lilly & Co., Indpls., 1988-91; pres., founder Biogel Tech., Indpls., 1991—. Author, editor: Absorbent Polymer Technology, 1990; editl. bd. Jour. Applied Polymer Sci., 1995—, Jour. Controlled Release, 1997—, Jour. Nanoparticle Rsch., 1998—, Med. Plastics & Biomaterials, 1998—. Vol. Indpls. Mus. Art, 1990—, Humane Soc. Indpls., 1990—, Indpls. Zoo, 1994—. Recipient Harold B. Lamport award Biomed. Engring. Soc., 1989; named Outstanding Young Alumna, Kinkaid Sch., 1998. Fellow Am. Inst. of Med. and Biol. Engring.; mem. AIChE (dir. 1998—, exec. bd. programming coun., dir. materials divsn., chmn. subcom. biomaterials divsn. 1990-93, dir.-at-large food, pharm. and bioengring. divsn. 1992-94, 2d vice chair materials divsn. 1994-95, 1st vice chmn. materials divsn. 1995-96, chmn. 1996-97, bd. dirs. 1998—), Am. Chem. Soc. (membership com. 1990—), Controlled Release Soc. (treas. 1995-98, internat. planning com. 1991, bd. govs. 1992-95), Jr. League Indpls. (bd. dirs. 1992-94). Avocations: fine art, dance, travel. Office: Biogel Tech PO Box 681513 Indianapolis IN 46268-7513

BRANSCOMB, HARVIE, JR., lawyer; b. Dallas, Mar. 24, 1922; s. Bennett Harvie and Margaret (Vaughan) B.; m. Mary Josephine Goodearle, Dec. 28, 1951; children: Mary Margaret, Bennett Hill, Richard Lee. A.B., Duke U., 1943; LL.B., Yale U., 1948. Bar: Tex. 1948, D.C. 1980, CPA, Tex. Shareholder Matthews & Branscomb, Attys.-at-Law, Corpus Christi, Tex., 1948—. Contbr. articles to profl. jours. Trustee Art Mus. Endowment Fund, Corpus Christi, Found. Scis. and Arts, Corpus Christi, Tex. A&M U. Corpus Christi Found.; trustee emeritus Southwestern Legal Found.; trustee, pres. Una Chapman Cox Found.; bd. dirs. Corpus Christi Indsl. Found. Served with USNR, 1943-46. Fellow Am. Coll. Tax Counsel; mem. ABA, (chmn. tax sect. 1979-80), State Bar Tex. (chmn. sect. taxation 1961-62), Am. Law Inst., Am. Inst. CPA's, Phi Beta Kappa, Phi Delta Phi. Episcopalian. Home: 4500 Ocean Dr Apt 8B Corpus Christi TX 78412-2500 Office: 802 N Carancahua St Ste 1900 Corpus Christi TX 78470-0102

BRANSCOMB, LEWIS CAPERS, JR., librarian, educator; b. Birmingham, Ala., Aug. 5, 1911; s. Lewis Capers and Minnie Vaughn (McGehee) B.; m. Marjorie Berry Stafford, Jan. 15, 1938; children: Lewis Capers III, Ralph Stafford, Carol Jean, Lawrence McGehee. Student, Birmingham-So. Coll., 1929-30; AB, Duke U., 1933; AB in Libr. Sci., U. Mich., 1939, AM in Libr. Sci., 1941; postgrad., U. Ga., 1940; PhD, U. Chgo., 1954. Clk. Young & Vann Supply Co., Birmingham, 1933-38; order libr. U. Ga., 1939-41; libr. Mercer U., 1941-42; libr., prof. libr. sci. U. S.C., 1942-44; asst. dir. pub. svc. depts., assoc. prof. libr. sci. U. Ill., 1944-48; assoc. dir. librs., prof., 1948-52; dir. librs., prof. Ohio State U., Columbus, 1952-71, prof. Thurber studies, 1971-81, prof. emeritus, 1981—; mem. faculty compensation and benefits com. Ohio State U., 1981-90; chmn. Adv. Coun. on Libr. Svcs. and Constrn. Act, Ohio, 1967-70; cons. Punjab Agrl. U., India, 1967, Mansfield (Ohio) Pub. Libr., 1977; mem. adv. coun. Hitachi Found., 1985-88. Author: Ernest Cushing Richardson Research Librarian, Scholar, Theologian, 1993; editor: The Case for Faculty Status for Academic Librarians, 1970; contbr. articles to profl. jours. mem. Ohio Commn. to Abolish Capital Punishment, 1960-69; bd. dirs. Ctr. for Rsch. Librs., 1953-64, mem. exec. com., 1954-56, chmn. bd. dirs., 1961-62, mem. coun., 1965-71; chmn. bd. trustees Ohio Coll. Libr. Ctr., 1968-70, vice chmn., 1970-72. Mem. AAUP (sec.-treas. U. Ill. chpt. 1947-48; sec.-treas. Ohio State U. chpt. 1948-52, pres. 1953-54; nat. council 1952-55, co-author History of the Ohio Conf. 1949-74, chmn. com. E 1979-91, mem. exec. com. 1981-91), ALA (chmn. nominating com. 1954-55), Assn. Coll. and Research Libraries (dir. 1953-55, v.p. 1957-58, pres. 1958-59), Ohio Library Assn. (chmn. coll. and univ. sect. 1952-53, chmn. library adminstrn. sect. 1969-70, chmn. local conf. com. 1970, chmn. awards and honors com. 1974-75, chmn. notable Ohio librarians com. 1978-79, award of merit 1971, Hall of Fame 1982), Franklin County Library Assn., Acad. Library Assn. Ohio, ACLU (exec. com. Central Ohio chpt. 1958-60, 64-66), Common Cause, Thurber Circle, Thurber House (bd. trustees 1985—), Friends of Ohio State U. Libraries, Ohio State U. Retirees Assn. (exec. bd. 1983-92), Beta Phi Mu (exec. council 1955-58), Sigma Alpha Epsilon. Democrat. Home: 3790 Overdale Dr Columbus OH 43220-4749 Office: Ohio State Univ Main Libr Columbus OH 43210

BRANSCOMB, LEWIS MCADORY, physicist; b. Asheville, N.C., Aug. 17, 1926; s. Bennett Harvie and Margaret (Vaughan) B.; m. Margaret Anne Wells, Oct. 13, 1951; children—Harvie Hammond, Katharine C. Branscomb Kelley. AB summa cum laude, Duke U., 1945, DSc (hon.); MS, Harvard U., 1947, PhD, 1949; DSc (hon.), Poly. Inst. N.Y., Clarkson Coll., Rochester U., U. Colo., Western Mich. U., Lycoming Coll., U. Ala., Pratt Inst., Rutgers U., Lehigh U., U. Notre Dame; DEng (hon.), Colo. Sch. Mines, 1999; DSc (hon.), SUNY, Binghamton; LHD (hon.), Pace U. Instr. physics Harvard U., 1950-51; lectr. physics U. Md., 1952-54; vis. staff mem. Univ. Coll., London, 1957-58; chief atomic physics sect. Nat. Bur. Standards, Washington, 1954-60; chief atomic physics div. Nat. Bur. Standards, 1960-62; chmn. Joint Inst. Lab. Astrophysics, U. Colo., 1962-65, 68-69; chief lab. astrophysics div. Nat. Bur. Standards, Boulder, Colo., 1962-69; prof. physics U. Colo., 1962-69; dir. Nat. Bur. Standards, 1969-72; chief scientist, v.p. IBM, Armonk, N.Y., 1972-86; mem. corporate mgmt. bd. IBM, Armonk, 1983-86; dir. sci. and tech. policy program Kennedy Sch. Govt., Harvard U., Cambridge, Mass., 1986-96, Albert Pratt pub. service prof., 1988-94; Aetna prof. pub. policy and corp. mgmt. Harvard U., Cambridge, Mass., 1994-96, prof. emeritus, 1996—; mem.-at-large Def. Sci. Bd., 1969-72; mem. high level policy group sci. and tech. info. Orgn. Econ. Coop. and Devel., 1968-70; mem. Pres.'s Sci. Adv. Com., 1965-68, chmn. panel space sci. and tech., 1967-68; mem. Nat. Sci. Bd., 1978-84, chmn., 1980-84; mem. Pres.'s Nat. Productivity Adv. Com., 1981-82; mem. standing com. controlled thermonuclear research AEC, 1966-68; mem. adv. com. on sci. and fgn. affairs Dept. State, 1973-74; mem. U.S.-USSR Joint Commn. on Sci. and Tech., 1977-80; chmn. Com. on Scholarly Communications with the People's Republic of China, 1977-80; mem. tech. assessment adv. coun. Office of Tech. Assessment, U.S. Congress, 1990-95; chmn. Carnegie Forum Task Force on Teaching as a Profession, 1985-86; dir. Lord Corp., Mitre Corp.; mem. pres.'s bd. visitors U. Okla., 1968-70; mem. astronomy and applied physics vis. coms. Harvard U. 1969-83, bd. overseers, 1984-86; mem. physics vis. com. M.I.T., 1974-79; mem. Pres.'s Com. Nat. Medal Scis., 1970-72; bd. dirs. Am. Nat. Standards Inst., 1969-72; trustee Carnegie Instn., 1973-90, mem. Carnegie Commn. on Sci., Tech. and Govt., 1988-93; trustee Poly. Inst. N.Y., 1974-78, Vanderbilt U., 1980—, Nat. Geog. Soc., 1984—, Woods Hole Oceanographic Instn., 1985-92, 93-98; chmn. Nat. Info. Infrastructure-2000 steering com. NRC, 1994-95. Author: Empowering Technology, 1993, Confessions of a Technophile, 1995, Korea at the Turning Point, 1996, Investing in Innovation, 1998; editor Rev. Modern Physics, 1968-73. Trustee Telluride Inst., 1996-97; mem. Commn. on Global Info. Infrastructure, 1995—. USPHS fellow, 1948-49; Jr. fellow Harvard Soc. Fellows, 1949-51; recipient Rockefeller Pub. Service award, 1957-58, Gold medal exceptional service Dept. Commerce, 1961, Arthur Flemming award D.C. Jr. C. of C., 1962, Samuel Wesley Stratton award Dept. Commerce, 1966, Career Service award Nat. Civil Service League, 1968, Proctor prize Research Soc. Am., 1972, Okawa prize in Info. and Telecomm., 1998, prize for Info. and Telecomms. Ohtawa Found., 1998. Fellow Am. Phys. Soc. (chmn. divsn. electron physics 1961-68, pres. 1979), AAAS (dir. 1969-73, 99—), Am. Acad. Arts and Scis.; mem. NAS (coun. 1972-75, 98—), Nat. Acad. Engring. (Arthur Bueche award), Engring. Acad. Japan (fgn. assoc.), Washington Acad. Scis. (Outstanding Sci. Achievement award 1959), Nat. Acad. Pub. Adminstrn., Am. Philos. Soc., Phi Beta Kappa, Sigma Xi (pres. 1985-86). Office: Harvard U Kennedy Sch Govt 79 J F Kennedy St Cambridge MA 02138-5801 *No achievement is entirely one's own nor is there satisfaction without sharing. Taking pride in my late wife's professional achievements, my colleagues ideas and my students promise keeps me creative.*

BRANSDORFER, STEPHEN CHRISTIE, lawyer; b. Lansing, Mich., Sept. 18, 1929; s. Henry and Sadie (Kohane) B.; m. Peggy Ruth Deisig, May 24, 1952; children: Mark, David, Amy, Jill. AB with honors, Mich. State U., 1951; JD with distinction, U. Mich., 1956; LLM, Georgetown U., 1958. Bar: Mich. 1956, U.S. Supreme Ct. 1959. Trial atty. Dept. Justice, Washington, 1956-58; atty., editor Office of Public Info., Office of Atty. Gen., 1958-59; spl. asst. U.S. Atty. for D.C., 1958-59; assoc. firm Miller, Johnson, Snell & Cummiskey, Grand Rapids, Mich., 1959-63; ptnr. Miller, Johnson, Snell & Cummiskey, 1963-89; dep. asst. atty. gen. civil div. U.S. Dept. Justice, Washington, 1989-92; pres. Bransdorfer & Bransdorfer, P.C., Grand Rapids, Mich., 1993—; pres. State Bar of Mich., 1974-75, commr., 1968-75, chmn. sr. lawyers sect., 1994-95; pres. Grand Rapids chpt. Am. Inns of Ct., 1995—; trustee Am. Inns of Ct. Found., 1997—; chmn. Mich. Civil Svc. Commn., 1977-78, mem., 1975-78; adv. com. 6th Cir. Jud. Conf., 1984-89; co-chair Mich. polit. leadership program Mich. State U., 1992-94; mem. comml. panel Am. Arbitration Assn. Asst. editor: U. Mich. Law Rev, 1956. Pres. Grand Rapids Child Guidance Clinic, 1969-71; chmn. Kent County Coms., Griffin for Senator, 1972, Lenore Romney for Senator, 1966; mem. council legal advisers Rep. Nat. Com., 1981-89; Rep. candidate for atty. gen., Mich., 1978; trustee, v.p., Mich. State Bar Found., 1985-87, chmn., fellows, 1987-89; chmn. Mich. State Bd. Canvassers, 1985-87, Commn. on Future Directions in Health Care, West Mich., 1987-89. With U.S. Army, 1951-53. Recipient Spl. award for Superior Performance Civil Divsn. U.S. Dept. Justice, 1990. Fellow Am. Bar Found.; mem. ABA, 6th Cir. Jud. Conf. (life), Grand Rapids Bar Assn., FBA (pres. West Mich. chpt. 1984, Disting. Life Svc. award 1989), Rep. Nat. Lawyers Assn. (bd. govs. 1985-89), Mich. Rep. Party (Svc. award 1989), Rotary, Cascade Hills Country Club, Phi Kappa Phi. Presbyterian. Fax: 616-458-4422. Home: 7250 Bradfield Ave SE Ada MI 49301-9130 Office: Bransdorfer & Bransdorfer PC Ledyard Bldg 125 Ottawa Ave NW Ste 305 Grand Rapids MI 49503-2898 *Life is a series of challenges. Do your best and you need not worry about the results.*

BRANSFIELD, JAMES JOSEPH, surgeon; b. Chgo., Nov. 8, 1932; s. James Joseph and Beatrice Catherine (Greene) B.; m. Virginia Kaye Paully, Dec. 17, 1967; 1 child, Helena Theresa. BS, Loyola U., 1955, MD, 1957. Diplomate Am. Bd. Emergency Medicine, Am. Bd. Surgery. Pvt. practice specializing in surgery Chgo., 1968—. Chief of police Chgo. Police Dept., 1983-94. Lt. comdr. USNR, 1960-63. Avocations: swimming, sailing. Home: 6200 N Knox Ave Chicago IL 60646-5030

BRANSFIELD, JOAN, principal. Prin. Sch. St. Mary, Lake Forest, Ill. Recipient Elem. Sch. Recognition award U.S. Dept. Edn., 1989-90, Nat.

Disting. Prin. award, 1998. Office: Sch of St Mary 185 E Illinois Rd Lake Forest IL 60045-1915

BRANSFORD, HELEN M., writer, jewelry designer; b. Nashville, Mar. 28, 1948; d. John Sterling Bransford and Helen (Trenholm) Dickinson; m. Jay McInerney; children: John Barrett III, Maisie Bransford. cons. in field. Author: Welcome to Your Facelift, 1997; contbr. to Vogue Mag. Episcopalian. Address: 1572 Old Hillsboro Rd Franklin TN 37069

BRANSON, ALBERT HAROLD (HARRY BRANSON), magistrate judge, educator; b. Chgo., May 20, 1935; s. Fred Brooks and Marie (Vowell) B.; m. Siri-Anne Gudrun Lindberg, Nov. 2, 1963; children: Gunnar John, Gulliver Dean, Hannah Marie, Siri Elizabeth. BA, Northwestern U., 1957; JD, U. Chgo., 1963. Bar: Pa. 1965, Alaska 1972. Atty. Richard McVeigh law offices, Anchorage, 1972-73; ptnr. Jacobs, Branson & Guetschow, Anchorage, 1973-76, Branson & Guetschow, Anchorage, 1976-82; pvt. practice Law Offices of Harry Branson, Anchorage, 1982-84, 85-89; atty. Branson, Bazeley & Chisolm, Anchorage, 1984-85; U.S. magistrate judge U.S. Dist. Ct., Anchorage, 1989—; instr., adj. prof. U. Alaska Justice Ctr., 1980-93; U.S. magistrate, Anchorage, 1975-76. Mem. steering com. Access to Civil Justice Task Force, 1997-98. With U.S. Army, 1957-59. Mem. Alaska Bar Assn. (bd. dirs., v.p. bd. govs. 1977-80, 83-86, pres. bd. govs. 1986, Disting. Svc. award 1992, Spl. Svc. award 1988, editor-in-chief Alaska Bar Rag 1978-86), Anchorage Bar Assn. (bd. dirs., bd. govs. 1982-86), Anchorage Inn of Ct. (pres. 1995). Democrat. Avocations: book collecting, cooking, poetry. Office: US Dist Ct 222 W 7th Ave Unit 33 Anchorage AK 99513-7504

BRANSON, BRANLEY ALLAN, biology educator; b. San Angelo, Tex., Feb. 11, 1929; s. Branley Allan and Era Elizabeth (Rogers) B.; m. Mary Louise Lewis, June 3, 1964; 1 son, Rogers McGowan. A.A., Northeastern Okla. A. and M. Coll., 1954; B.S., Okla. State U., 1956, M.S., 1957, Ph.D., 1960. Asst. prof. biology Kan. State Coll., Pittsburg, 1960-64; prof. biology Eastern Ky. U., Richmond, 1964—, found. prof., 1989-90. Contbr. articles to mags. Recipient Sci. award Okla. A. and M. Coll., 1953; named Disting. Scientist of Ky., 1984. Fellow Okla. Acad. Sci., AAAS; mem. Southwestern Assn. Naturalists (bd. govs. 1965—), Am. Malacological Union, Soc. for Study Evolution, Kan. Acad. Sci., Ky. Acad. Sci. (editor transactions), Soc. Systematic Zoologists, Am. Soc. Zoologists, Am. Soc. Ichthyologists and Herpetologists, Sigma Xi, Phi Theta Kappa, Phi Kappa Phi. Research and numerous publs. on description several species unknown animals; described structural workings lateral-line system in various fishes; olfactory system, geog. distbn. fishes and mollusks. Home: 100 Walnut Hill Dr Richmond KY 40475-3620 Office: Eastern Ky U Richmond KY 40475 *I've had a long-term love affair with the nature of things, and the fervor doesn't seem to be lessening any with the passage of time. And strongly supported by the very real love affair with my wife and son, I've simply had the best of conditions for being creative.*

BRANSON, HARLEY KENNETH, finance executive; b. Ukiah, Calif., June 10, 1942; s. Harley Edward and Clara Lucile Branson; 1 child, Erik Jordan. BS in Acctg. and Fin., San Jose State U., 1965; JD, Santa Clara U., 1968. Bar: Calif. 1969-98. Law clk. to judge U.S. Ct. Appeals (9th cir.), San Diego, 1968-69; pvt. practice San Diego, 1969-78; div. counsel Ralston Purina Co., San Diego, 1978-83; group gen. counsel Castle & Cooke, Inc., San Diego, 1983-85; exec. v.p., gen. counsel, corp. sec. Bumble Bee Seafoods, Inc., San Diego, 1985-89; pres., CEO Flying Palms LLC, San Diego, 1995—; bd. dirs. Picazo Comm., Inc., San Jose, Calif., Wind and Weather, Inc.; gen. ptnr. Hankins Ptnrs., LLC, 1997—. Exec. prodr. (feature motion picture) Love Always, 1997. Bd. dirs. U. C. Univ. Art Gallery, 1995—. Avocations: reading, collecting contemporary art, travel. Office: PO Box 500308 San Diego CA 92150-0308

BRANSON-BERRY, KAREN MARIE, nurse; b. Phila., Aug. 22, 1956; d. Floyd Ralph and Regina (Marter) Banbury; m. John Joseph Branson III, Oct. 23, 1977 (div. 1991); children: John Joseph IV, Katherine Marie; m. Steven Wayne Berry, July 4, 1992. BSN, San Diego State U., 1991; MSN, U. San Diego, 1998. RN, Calif.; EMT, Japan, BCLS EMT; cert. ACLS provider, BLS instr., Post Anesthesia Care Unit; cert. FNP, PNP. Unit asst. Cooper Med. Ctr., Camden, N.J., 1975-76; pvt. duty nurse aide Nursing Staff, Annapolis, Md., 1977; ward clerk Community Hosp., Chula Vista, Calif., 1979-80; unit asst. Bay Gen. Hosp. ICA, Chulavista, 1985-86; med. asst. Dr. D. Burrows, ob.-gyn., San Diego, 1988-89; nurse Scripps, Chula Vista, 1990; ensign nurse corp. Naval Hosp. Camp Pendleton, Oceanside, Calif., 1990-91, Naval Hosp. Camp. Pendleton, Oceanside, 1991-93; clin. cons. 21 Area Br. Med. Clinic, 1993—, lt. jr. grade, 1993, promoted to lt., 1994; edn. and tng. com. Camp Pendleton, 1991—, mem. ward rm. social com., nurse corp. social com., 1991-92, chmn. social com., 1993-94, nurse corp. strategic task force, 1993-94; nurse Adult Girl Scout Troop, 1991—; mem. command infection control com Naval Hosp. Camp Pendleton, 1994; interium clinic supr. 21 Area Br. Med. Clinic, 1994, Naval Med. Clinic Long Beach, 1995-98, Naval Hosp. Twentynine Palms, 1998—. Interviewer Navy Relief Soc., Pensacola, Fla. 1977-79; pres., sec. Helicopter Sq. 8/HS-10, San Diego, 1979-86; fundraiser Atsugi Wives Club, Japan, 1986-88; vol. ARC, Japan, 1986-88. Lt. USN, 1993-95. Decorated Meritorious Svc. medal USN, Achievement medal, 1995-96; recipient Cert. Appreciation award Dept. Def. Schs., 1987, ARC, Japan, 1987, Alfred award Navy League U.S. Newport County Coun., 1991; U. San Diego scholar, 1996; named Jr. Navy Nurse of Yr. Naval Hosp. Camp Pendleton, 1991-92, 93-94. Mem. Am. Acad. Ambulatory Care Nurses (vice-chair 1995-96), Calif. Nurses Assn., Navy Nurse Corps Social Com, Wardroom Com., Sigma Theta Tau Internat. Republican. Home: 523 Chantel Ct Chula Vista CA 91910-7438 Office: Naval Hosp Twenty-Nine Palms Camp Pendleton Twenty Nine Palms CA 92055

BRANSTAD, TERRY EDWARD, former governor, lawyer; b. Leland, Iowa, Nov. 17, 1946; s. Edward Arnold and Rita (Garl) B.; m. Christine Ann Johnson, June 17, 1972; children: Eric, Allison, Marcus. BA, U. Iowa, 1969; JD, Drake U., 1974. Bar: Iowa. Sr. ptnr. firm Branstad-Schwarm, Lake Mills, Iowa, until 1982; farmer Lake Mills; mem. Iowa Ho. of Reps., 1973-78; lt. gov. State of Iowa, 1979-82, gov., 1983-98; Bd. dirs. Am. Legion of Iowa Found. With U.S. Army, 1969. Mem. Nat. Govs. Assn. (past chmn.), Midwestern Govs. Assn., Am. Legion, Farm Bur. Republican. Roman Catholic. Lodges: Lions, KC. Office: Regency West 2 Ste 325 401 50th St West Des Moines IA 50266*

BRANSTETTER, RUSSELL WAYNE, minister; b. Barnsdall, Okla., Dec. 28, 1946; s. Marvin Martin and Beulah Belle (Chambers) B.; m. Helen Gail Moody; children: Christopher Jon, Jennifer (Jenna) Beth. Student, Tulsa U., 1965-68; BA, So. Nazarene U., 1969, postgrad., 1969-71. Ordained to ministry Ch. of the Nazarene, 1973. Pastor Forest Home Ch. of the Nazarene, Jonesboro, Ark., 1971-74, Sun Valley Ch. of the Nazarene, Houston, 1974-80; sr. pastor First Ch. of the Nazarene, Bartlesville, Okla., 1980-84, Clovis, N.Mex., 1984-87; sr. pastor Pineville Ch. of the Nazarene, Charlotte, N.C., 1987-92; dist. supt., south Ark. dist. Ch. of the Nazarene, Little Rock, 1992—; Christian life chmn. Houston dist. Ch. of the Nazarene, 1979-80, mem. adv. bd. N.E. Okla. dist., 1987-88, N.M. dist., 1986, N.C. dist., 1990-92. Vol. chaplain High Plains Hosp., Clovis, 1984-87; trustee So. Nazarene U., 1992—. Recipient Disting. Alumni award So. Nazarene U., 1995. Mem. Kiwanis (bd. dirs. Clovis chpt. 1984-87). Republican. Avocations: golf, fishing, reading, computers. Office: PO Box 55005 Little Rock AR 72215-5005 Home: Ch of the Nazarene 38 9th Fairway Loop Maumelle AR 72113

BRANT, DONNA MARIE, journalist; b. N.Y.C., Oct. 17, 1955; d. Earl Evans and Catherine Marie (Schatz) B. BA in Philosophy, George Washington U., 1977; MS in Broadcast Journalism, Boston U., 1979. Desk asst. nat. news desk NBC News, N.Y.C., 1979, news and feature asst. presdl. campaign, 1979-80; bur. coord. nat. news bur. NBC News, Pitts., 1980-82; futures editor nat. news desk NBC News, Washington, 1982-83, polit. assignment editor presdl. campaign, 1983-84, assignment editor nat. news desk, 1984-89; West Coast reporter, prodr. Am.'s Most Wanted, Fox Broadcasting Co., Washington, 1989-95, N.Y. reporter, prodr., 1995-96, mng. editor, 1996-99, sr. prodr. spl. projects, 1999—. Sr. rschr.: Barter, 1978. Resident assoc. Smithsonian Instn., Washington, 1982. Recipient citation Internat. Assn. Asian Crime Investigators, citation Davis (Calif.) Police Dept., citation Multnomah County (Oreg.) Sheriff's Office, citation Riverside County (Calif.) Sheriff's Office, citation U.S. Marshals Svc. Mem. Washington Hist. Soc., Internat. Platform Assn., Sigma Delta Chi. Avocations: photography, travel, history, swimming, designing and building furniture. Office: America's Most Wanted 5151 Wisconsin Ave NW Washington DC 20016-4124

BRANT, HENRY, composer; b. Montreal, Que., Can., Sept. 15, 1913; s. Saul and Bertha (Dreyfuss) B.; children: Piri, Joquin, Linus; m. Katu Wilkovska, 1989. Student, Juilliard Sch. Music, N.Y.C., 1930-34; DFA (hon.), Wesleyan U., 1998. Mem. faculty Juilliard Sch. Music, 1947-55; dept. music Columbia U., 1943-53; mem. faculty Bennington (Vt.) Coll., 1957-80. Composer, condr. documentary films, U.S. Govt. OWI, State Dept., Dept. Agr. 1940-47; composer, condr. various radio network program series for NBC, CBS, ABC, 1942-46; large ensemble works include Angels and Devils, 1931, Origins: Percussion Symphony, 1952, Signs and Alarms, 1953, Antiphony 1, 1953, Millenium 2, 1954, Encephalograms 2, 1954, Ceremony, 1954, Galaxy 2, 1954, December, 1954, spatial opera Grand Universal Circus, 1956, Hieroglyphics, 1957, The Children's Hour, 1958, Mythical Beasts, 1958, Atlantis, 1960, Concerto with Lights, 1961, Barricades, 1961, Headhunt, 1962, Voyage 4; Total Antiphony, in 83 Parts, 1963, Odyssey-Why Not?, 1965, Kingdom Come, 1970, Crossroads, 1971, Immortal Combat, 1972, American Requiem, 1973, Prevailing Winds, 1974, Solomon's Gardens, 1974, Homage to Ives, 1975, A Plan of the Air, 1975, Spatial Piano Concerto, 1976, Antiphonal Responses, 1977, Trinity of Spheres, 1978, Orbits: 80 Trombones, 1979, The Secret Calendar, 1980, The Glass Pyramid, 1980, Meteor Farm, 1982, Western Springs, 1984, Fire in the Amstel, 1984, Desert Forests, 1985, Northern Lights Over the Twin Cities, 1986, Ghost Nets, 1988, Rainforest, 1989, 500: Pathways to Security, 1990, Prisons of the Mind, 1990, Hidden Hemisphere, 1992, Fourscore, 1993, Homeless People, 1993, Trajectory, 1994, Plowshares and Swords, 1996, Mergers, 1998, others; recs: Columbia, Desto, CRI, New World, Nonesuch, Sonic Arts, AmCam, Newport Classic. Recipient Prix Italia, 1955, Alice M. Ditson award, 1962, 64, ASCAP/Nissim award 1985, Mcpl. citations: Boston, 1983, N.Y.C., 1992; Guggenheim fellow 1946, 55, Thorne fellow, 1972; grantee: Inst. Arts and Letters, 1955, Copley, 1960, Huber, 1960, Dollard 1966, N.Y. State Coun. for Arts, 1974, NEA, 1976, ASCAP/Nissim 1984, Fromm, 1992, Koussevitzky Found., 1996. Mem. Am. Acad. Arts and Letters (life). Pioneer in development of spatial-antiphonal music. Office: 1607 Chino St Santa Barbara CA 93101-4757 *Undoubtedly, the answer to the riddle of existence must be: perpetual discovery.*

BRANT, SANDRA J., magazine publisher. Pub., pres. Brant Publs., N.Y.C. Publisher, Art in America, The Magazine Antiques, Interview. Office: Brant Publs 575 Broadway New York NY 10012-3230*

BRANTIGAN, CHARLES OTTO, surgeon; b. Balt., Jan. 24, 1943; s. Otto Charles and Edith May (Reinhart) B.; m. Linda Anne Reynolds, 1972 (dec. 1978); m. Kathleen Sharon Aylsworth, July 16, 1983; 1 child, Charles Aylsworth. BA in Chemistry, Cornell U., 1964; MD, Johns Hopkins U., 1968. Intern U. Colo., 1968-69, resident, 1969-70, 72-73; fellow in cardiovascular surgery U. Colo., Denver, 1973-74; resident in thoracic surgery Denver Gen. Hosp., 1974-75; sr. resident U. Colo. Med. Ctr., 1975-76; pvt. practice Denver, 1976—; assoc. clin. prof. surgery U. Colo., 1976—; chief of surgery Presbyn. St. Lukes Med. Ctr., Denver, 1994—; dir. Denver Vascular Diagnostic Ctr., 1984—; med. dir. Denver Wound Care Ctr., 1991—; chief thoracic surgery Denver Gen. Hosp., 1976; asst. dir. surg. tng. program St. Joseph Hosp., Denver, 1984-86; chmn. nutritional support com. Presbyn. Med. Ctr., 1983-87; many others. Contbr. articles to profl. jours.; author 3 books. Chmn. Hosp. Dist. Urban Design Forum, Denver, 1993—; participated in creation of Lafayette St. Historic Dist., Denver, 1987. Lt. comdr. USN, 1970-72. Recipient Spl. Citizen award Planning Office City of Denver, 1995, Historic Preservation award Historic Denver, 1988, Stephen H. Hart award Colo. State Hist. Soc., 1988, People's Choice award Capitol Hill United Neighborhoods, 1997. Mem. AMA, ACS, Denver Med. Soc., Rocky Mountain Traumatologic Soc., Colo. Med. Soc., Am. Heart Assn., Western Thoracic Surgery Soc., Internat. Soc. for Cardiovasc. Surgery, Am. Coll. Chest Physicians, Soc. Critical Care Medicine, Denver Brass Inc. (chmn. bd. dirs.). Lutheran. Avocations: urban land use planning, architectural historical research. Home: 2105 Lafayette St Denver CO 80205-5337 Office: Vascular Inst Rockies 2253 Downing St Denver CO 80205-5234

BRANTINGHAM, BARNEY, journalist, writer; b. Chgo., Feb. 26, 1932; s. Carl Brantingham and Frances Bell; m. Angela Mendez, Oct. 30, 1957 (div.); children: Barclay Carl, Frances, Wendy, Kenneth. Grad., U. Ill., 1954. Reporter Star Newspapers, Chicago Heights, Ill., 1957-59; editor San Clemente (Calif.) Sun-Post, 1959-60; reporter Santa Barbara (Calif.) News-Press, 1960—, columnist, 1977—; commentator Sta. KTMS, Santa Barbara, 1989-91, Sta. KIST, Santa Barbara, 1991, SAM, 1990, 92; radio sta. feature and travel commentator KQSB, 1994-97; co-host Around the World with Arthur and Barney, Sta. KTMS, 1998, KEYT-AM, 1998—. Prodr. TV program Santa Barbara Traveler; author: The Pro Football Hall of Fame, 1988, Barney's Santa Barbara, 1989, Around Santa Barbara County with Barney, 1992; co-dir. The Opinionated Traveler Internet Site. With U.S. Army, 1955-57. Mem. Internat. Food, Wine and Travel Writers Assn. (dir. 1991-95), Am. Travel Media Assn. (founding dir.). Avocation: traveling. Office: Santa Barbara News-Press PO Box 1359 Santa Barbara CA 93102-1359

BRANTINGHAM, PATRICIA LOUISE, criminology educator; b. St. Louis, June 28, 1943; d. Frederic Lawrence and Mary Louise (Kelley) Matthews; m. Paul J. Brantingham, Aug. 26, 1967; 1 child, Paul Jeffrey Jr. AB in Math., Barnard Coll., 1965; MA in Math., Fordham U., 1966; MSP in Planning, Fla. State U., 1974, PhD in Planning, 1977. System analyst Johnson & Johnson, New Brunswick, N.J., 1966-67, Technicon Corp., Terrytown, N.Y., 1967-68, Hunt-Wesson Foods, Fullerton, Calif., 1968-69, Census Processing Ctr., Tallahassee, Fla., 1971-74; asst. prof. Simon Fraser U., Burnaby, B.C., Can., 1977-80, assoc. prof., 1980-89, prof., 1989—; dir. program evaluation Dept. Justice Can., Ottawa, Ont., 1985-89; cons. crime prevention Tumbler Ridge New Town, B.C., 1980-82; cons. Dept. Justice, Can., 1978-81. Editor: Courts and Diversion, 1981, Enviromental Criminology, 1981, 2d edit. 1991; author: Patterns in Crime, 1984. Mem. Am. Planning Assn., Am. Soc. Criminology (program com. 1978, 85, 94), Can. Criminal Justice Assn. Office: Simon Fraser U Sch Criminol, 8888 University Dr WMC-2630, Burnaby BC Canada V5A 1S6*

BRANTINGHAM, PAUL JEFFREY, criminology educator; b. Long Beach, Calif., June 29, 1943; s. Charles Ross and Lila Carolyn (Price) B.; m. Patricia Louise Matthews, Aug. 26, 1967; 1 child, Paul Jeffrey Jr. BA, Columbia U., 1965, JD, 1968; Diploma in Criminology, Cambridge U., 1970. Bar: Calif. 1969. Asst. prof. Fla. State U., Tallahassee, 1971-76, assoc. prof., 1976-77; assoc. prof. Simon Fraser U., Burnaby, B.C., Can., 1977-85, assoc. dean faculty interdisciplinary studies, 1980-82, prof., 1985—; dir. spl. revs. Pub. Svc. Commn. Can., Ottawa, Ont., 1985-87. Editor: Juvenile Justice Philosophy, 1974, 2d edit. 1978, Environmental Criminology, 1981, 2d edit. 1991; author: Patterns in Crime. Recipient Eisenhower Watch award Columbia U., 1966; Ford Found. fellow, 1969-70, Western Soc. Criminology fellow, 1996. Mem. ABA, AAAS, Calif. Bar Assn., Am. Soc. Criminology (chmn. nat. program 1978), Acad. Criminal Justice Scis., Canadian Criminal Justice Assn., Soc. for Reform of Criminal Law. Home: 4680 Eastridge Rd, North Vancouver, BC Canada V7G 1K4 Office: Simon Fraser U Sch Criminol, 8888 University Dr WMC 2630, Burnaby BC Canada V5A 1S6*

BRANTLEY, JEFFREY HOKE, professional baseball player; b. Florence, Ala., Sept. 5, 1963. Student, Miss. State U. With San Francisco Giants, 1988-93; pitcher Cin. Reds, 1994-97, St. Louis Cardinals, 1997-98, Phila. Phillies, 1999—. Selected to Nat. League All-Star Team, 1990. Achievements include member of Nat. League Championship Team, 1989. Office: Phila Phillies Vets Stadium 3501 S Broad St Philadelphia PA 19101*

BRANTLEY, JOHN RANDOLPH, lawyer; b. Freeport, Tex., Oct. 1, 1951; m. Joan Lawlor, May 17, 1975; children: Brian C., David R., Caroline E. BBA magna cum laude, St. Mary's U., 1974, JD, 1977. Bar: Tex. 1977. Assoc. Bracewell & Patterson LLP, Houston, 1977-83, ptnr., 1983—. Fellow Tex. Bar Foun., Houston Bar Found.; mem. ABA, Tex. Bar Assn., Houston Bar Assn. (coun. antitrust sect. 1989-96, vice chmn. 1993-94, chmn. 1994-95), Phi Delta Phi. Office: Bracewell & Patterson LLP 2900 S Tower Pennzoil Pl Houston TX 77002

BRANTON, DANIEL, biology educator; b. Antwerp, Belgium, Jan. 13, 1932; came to U.S., 1941; (parents Am. citizens). AB in Math., Cornell U., 1954; MS in Pomology, U. Calif., Davis, 1957; PhD in Plant Physiology, U. Calif., Berkeley, 1961. Postdoctoral fellow ETH, Zurich, Switzerland, 1961-63; asst., assoc., full prof. botany U. Calif., Berkeley, 1963-73; Higgins prof. biology Harvard U., Cambridge, Mass., 1973—; vis. scientist La. Molecular Biology, Cambridge, Eng., 1970-71; mem. Molecular Biology Study Sect. NIH, 1974-78. Mem. editl. bd. Jour. Molecular Biology, 1970-73, Jour. Cell Biology, 1970-73, Jour. Membrane Biology, 1973—, Protoplasma, 1973-95. Recipient N.Y. Bot. Garden prize, 1972; NIH fellow, 1959-61, NSF postdoctoral fellow, 1961-62, Miller Found. Rsch. Prof., Berkeley, 1968-69, J.S. Guggenheim fellow, 1970-71; Storer lectr. U. Calif., Davis, 1984, Disting. lectr. Roswell Park Meml. Inst., 1988. Mem. AAAS, NAS (chmn. sect. on cellular and devel. biology), Am. Acad. Arts and Scis., Biophys. Soc., Am. Soc. for Cell Biology (coun. 1972-75, pres. 1984-85), Sigma Xi. Research in cell biology, protein interactions and molecular organization of erythrocyte and other membranes, cell shape, freeze-etching techniques for electron microscopy. Office: Harvard U Molecular & Cellular Biol 16 Divinity Ave Cambridge MA 02138-2020*

BRANTZ, GEORGE MURRAY, retired lawyer; b. Phila., Oct. 19, 1930; s. Louis Paul and Jeannette (Vinitz) B.; m. Joan Nadler, Mar. 29, 1953; children: Nancy Brantz Ginsberg, Amy L. Brantz Bedrick. AB, Princeton U., 1952; LLB magna cum laude, Harvard U., 1957. Bar: Pa. 1957, U.S. Dist. Ct. (ea. dist.) Pa., U.S. Ct. Appeals (3rd cir.). Ptnr. Wolf, Block, Schorr and Solis-Cohen, Phila., 1966-93; ret., 1993. Pres. Council Migration Service, Phila., 1971-73; bd. dirs. Phila. Port Corp., 1982-84. With U.S. Army, 1952-54. Mem. Am. Law Inst., Jane Austen Soc. (treas. 1993-98), Locust Club. Jewish. Avocation: sailing.

BRANYAN, ROBERT LESTER, retired university administrator; b. Phila., Jan. 15, 1930; s. Lester Spencer and Martha Augusta (Border) B.; m. Helen Louise Baird, June 9, 1956; children: Jane Baird, George Robert. B.A., Wis. State U., 1955; M.A., U. Iowa, 1957; Ph.D., Okla. U., 1961. Grad. teaching asst. U. Okla., 1957-59; from instr. to prof. history U. Mo., Kansas City, 1959-75; chmn. dept. U. Mo., 1964-73; dean Sch. Grad. Studies, Central Mich. U., Mt. Pleasant, 1976-83; dir. acad. affairs Pa. State U., Schuylkill, 1983-90; ret.; mem. region 6 Archives Adv. Council, 1970-74; cons. in field. Author: Taming the Mighty Missouri, 1974; co-author: The Eisenhower Administration, 1953-61, A Documentary History, 1971, (play, with Helen B. Branyan) Camden County: Our Heritage our Hope, 1993; Co-editor: Urban Crisis in Modern America, 1971. Bd. mem. Camden County Hist. Soc.; bd. mem., sec. Citizens Against Domestic Violence, Camden County; treas., vestry St. George Epis. Ch. Served with AUS, 1951-53. Danforth Assoc. Mem. Soc. for Historians of Am. Fgn. Relations, Phi Alpha Theta, Sigma Iota Epsilon. Democrat. Episcopalian.

BRANYAN, W. DAVID, novelist; b. Orleans, France, May 16, 1965; born U.S. citizen; s. William Henry and Bessie May Day Branyan. Student, Yale U., 1984, Columbia U., 1988. Legal permissions editor Random House, N.Y.C., 1989-91; mem. editl. staff Paris Rev., N.Y.C., 1991-94; sec. Lloyd Richards, N.Y.C., 1994-95; editor Mark Sullivan Literacy Agy., N.Y.C., 1998—; evaluator Eugene O'Neil Theater Ctr., N.Y.C., 1992—. Author: The Vile Beginners, 1993, Finessing Meadowhampton, 1998; co-author, editor: All the President's Lawyers, 1999; contbr. articles to Newman Jour. Bd. dirs. L.I. Opera, Oyster Bay, N.Y., 1998—. Mem. Civitas. Avocation: guitar. E-mail: wdbranyan@aol.com.

BRANZEI-VELASQUEZ, SYLVIA CAROL, secondary education educator; b. Royal Oak, Mich., Aug. 20, 1958; d. Alexander and Sylvia Jean (Anderson) Branzei; m. Brian Pascal Dunstan, Sept. 18, 1982 (div. Mar. 1989); m. Byron William Velasquez, July 14, 1990; stepchildren: Ian Mantha, Alison Mantha, Aaron Montgomery, Jon Robin Montgomery. BS, U. Mich., 1980, tchg. cert., 1982; MEd, Calif. State Poly., 1986. Cert. tchr., Calif. Sci. tchr. The Buckley Sch., Sherman Oaks, Calif., 1983-85, Marin Acad., San Rafael, Calif., 1986-87; sci. tchr. and coord. Corden Redwood Sch., Alameda, Calif., 1987-88; chemistry outreach coord. Lawrence Hall of Sci., Berkeley, Calif., 1988-91; editor, writer Addison-Wesley, Menlo Park, Calif., 1992-94; project co-mgr. Project CREATE, Oakland, Calif., 1993-95; sci. tchr. Whale Gulch Sch., Whitethorn, Calif., 1995-97; ednl. cons. Hughes Galaxy Classroom, L.A., 1990; curriculum cons. NASA-SETI, Mountain View, Calif., 1991-92, Alameda County Office Edn., Hayward, 1995; mus. cons. Davis St. Transfer Sta., San Leandro, Calif., 1995, Sci. World, Vancouver, B.C., Can., 1999. Author: Environmental Science, 1995, Grossology, 1995 (Pub. Weekly Best Seller 1996), Animal Grossology, 1996 (Pub. Weekly Best Seller 1997), Grossology Begins at Home, 1997, Hands on Grossology, 1999; editor: Science Insights—Exploring Earth and Space, 1994, Science Insights—Exploring Matter and Energy, 1994; co-author (play) A Soap Opera, 1991; contbr. articles to profl. jours. Active Green Party, Oakland, 1989—; sec. Clover Gardens Neighborhood Assn., Oakland, 1993-95; trustee Leggett Valley Unified Sch. Dist., 1997—. Norse Civic Assn. scholar, Detroit, 1976, Minority Edn. scholar Calif. State Poly., Pomona, 1985. Mem. Nat. Sci. Tchrs. Assn. Avocations: walking, traveling, reading, singing. Home: PO Box 216 Redway CA 95560-0216

BRAR, GURDARSHAN SINGH, soil scientist, researcher; b. Fazilka, Punjab, India, Dec. 25, 1946; came to U.S., 1983; s. Mall Singh and Gurnam Kaur (Aulakh) B.; m. Kuldeep Kaur Sran; children: Ramandeep, Samrita, Yashmeen. BS, Punjab Agrl. U., Ludhiana, 1969, MS, 1972; PhD, Indian Inst. Tech., Kharagpur, West Bengal, 1986. Soil sci. extension specialist dept. soils Punajb Agrl. U., Ludhiana, India, 1973-77; soil physicist dept. soil sci. Punabj Agrl. U., 1977-83; soil scientist environ. firm, Va., 1985-88; rsch. assoc. Tex. Tech. U., Lubbock, 1988-89; soil scientist agrl. rsch. svc. USDA, Bushland, Tex., 1989-92; rsch. phys. scientist U.S. Army C.E., Hanover, N.H., 1992-96; pres. EarthCare, Dallas, Tex., 1995—. Contbr. articles to profl. jours. Mem. Agronomy Soc. Am., Crop Sci. Soc. Am., Soil Sci. Soc. Am. Office: Earthcare Inc 7515 Danfield Ct Denison TX 75021-1922

BRAS, RAFAEL LUIS, engineering educator; b. San Juan, P.R., Oct. 28, 1950; s. Rafael and Amalia Antonia (Muniz) B.; m. Patricia Ann Brown, June 29, 1974; children—Rafael Edmundo, Alejandro Luis. BSCE, MIT, 1972, MSCE, 1974, ScD in Water Resources and Hydrology, 1975; Laurea honoris causa, U. Perugia, Italy, 1991. Registered profl. engr., Mass., P.R. 1992. Asst. prof. U. P.R., Mayaguez, 1975-76; from asst. prof. hydrology to assoc. prof. MIT, Cambridge, 1976-82, prof., 1982—; head water resources and environ. engring. divsn. MIT, 1983-91, dir. Ralph M. Parsons Lab., 1983-91, dir. Minority Intro. to Eng. and Sci., 1987, William E. Leonhard prof. engring., 1988-95; Bacardi & Stockholm Water Founds. prof. MIT, Cambridge, 1995—; assoc. dir. Ctr. for Global Change Sci., 1990—; head dept. civil and environ. engring., 1992—; cons. to govt. and industry; vis. assoc. prof. Universidad Simon Bolivar, Caracas, Venezuela, 1982-83; vis. scholar Internat. Inst. Applied Systems Analysis, Vienna, 1983; vis. prof. Iowa Inst. Hydraulic Rsch., U. Iowa, 1989-90; adv. bd. engring. divsn. NSF, 1988-91; bd. atmospheric scis. and climate NRC, 1989-93; earth scis. and applications divsn. adv. subcom. NASA, 1990, sci. team TRMM mission, 1991-94, mem. earth sys. sci. and applications adv. com., 1998—; sci. steering group GCIP-Global Energy and Water Cycle Experiment, 1991-95; adv. coun. for com. Nat. Insts. for Environ.; ASCE task com. on edn. initiatives, 1996—. Author: (with I. Rodriguez-Iturbe) Random Functions and Hydrology, 1985, 94, Hydrology: An Introduction to Hydrologic Science, 1990; editor: The World at Risk: Natural Hazards and Climate Change, 1993; editor Nonlinear Processes in Geophysics, 1996—; contbr. articles to profl. jours.; assoc. editor Water Resources Rsch., 1980-88, Jour. Geophys. Rsch.-Atmospheres, 1996—; mem. editl. bd. Jour. Hydrology, Internat. Jour. Environ. Tech.; mem. editl. adv. bd. Serra, 1998—. Recipient Walter L. Huber Civil Engring. prize, 1993, A.R.I. Clarke prize, 1998; Guggenheim fellow, 1982; P.R. Econ. Devel. Adminstrn. fellow; Gilbert Winslow Career Devel. chair MIT; Horton lectr. AMS, 1997. Fellow ASCE (task com. 1996—, Huber prize 1993), Am. Geophys. Union (Horton award 1981, James B. Macelwane award 1982, chmn. bd. jours. editors 1984-88, chair budget and fin. 1990—, assoc. editor), Am. Meteorol. Soc. (Robert E. Horton lectr. 1999); mem. AAAS, AMS, Boston Soc. Civil Engrs., Sigma Xi,

Tau Beta Pi, Chi Epsilon. Roman Catholic. Email: rlBras@mit.edu. Office: MIT Rm 1-290 Dept Civil Environ Engring Cambridge MA 02139

BRASEL, JO ANNE, physician; b. Salem, Ill., Feb. 15, 1934; d. Gerald Nolan and Ruby Rachel (Rich) B. BA, U. Colo., 1956; MD, U. Colo., 1959. Diplomate Am. Bd. Pediatrics, Am. Bd. Pediatric-Endocrinology. Pediatric intern, resident Cornell U. Med. Coll.-N.Y. Hosp., N.Y.C., 1959-62; pediatric endocrine fellow Johns Hopkins U. Sch. Medicine, Balt., 1962-65, asst. prof. pediatrics, 1965-68; asst. prof. then assoc. prof. pediatrics Cornell U. Med. Coll., N.Y.C., 1969-72; assoc. prof. then prof. pediatrics Columbia U. Coll. Physicians and Surgeons, N.Y.C., 1972-79, asst. dir. Inst. Human Nutrition, 1972-79; prof. pediatrics Harbor-UCLA Med. Ctr., UCLA Sch. Medicine, 1979—, program dir. Gen. Clin. Research Ctr., 1979-93, prof. medicine, 1980—; mem. adv. com. FDA, Rockville, Md., 1971-75; mem. nutrition study sect. NIH, Bethesda, Md., 1974-78; mem. select panel for promotion of child health HEW, Washington, 1979-80; mem. life scis. D adv. screening com. Fulbright-Hays program, Washington, 1981-84, digestive disease and nutrition grant review group NIADDK, 1985-89, U.S. Govt. Task Force on Women, Minorities and the Handicapped in Sci. and Tech., 1987-89. Recipient Rsch. Career Devel. award NIH, 1973-77, Irma T. Hirschl Trust Career Sci. award, 1974-79, Sr. Fulbright Sabbatical Rsch. award, 1980. Mem. Soc. Pediatric Rsch. (sec.-treas. 1973-77, pres.-elect 1977-78, pres. 1978-79), Am. Fed. Clin. Rsch., Endocrine Soc., Am. Soc. Clin. Nutrition, Am. Inst. Nutrition, Western Assn. Physicians, Lawson Wilkins Pediatric Endocrine Soc. (bd. dirs., mem. bd. 1972-74, pres.-elect 1991-92, pres. 1992-93), Am. Pediatric Soc., Assn. Program Dirs. for Gen. Clin. Rsch. Ctrs. (pres. 1982-83), Western Soc. Pediatric Research, Phi Beta Kappa, Alpha Omega Alpha. Office: Harbor-UCLA Med Ctr Box 446 1000 W Carson St Torrance CA 90502-2004

BRASFIELD, EVANS BOOKER, lawyer; b. Richmond, Va., Sept. 21, 1932; s. George Frederick and Minna (Booker) B.; children: Evans Booker, John McDonald, Elizabeth Lee; m. Anne Dobbins Heilig, June 28, 1980; stepchildren: J. Randall Heilig, Mollie P. Heilig. BA, U. Va., 1954, LLB, 1959. Bar: Va. 1959. Pvt. practice Richmond; ptnr. Hunton & Williams, Richmond, 1965—; gen. counsel Va. Electric & Power Co., Richmond, 1976-94, Dominion Resources, 1983-91. Pres. Children's Home Soc. Va., 1972-73, bd. dirs., 1965-91; chmn. Cen. Va. Ednl. TV Corp., 1978-84, bd. dirs., 1965—; bd. dirs. Richmond Community Action Program, 1974-76, Richmond Area Community Coun., 1973-75, Big Bros. Richmond, 1970-75. With USNR, 1954-56. Fellow Am. Bar Found., Va. Law Found.; mem. ABA (chmn. sect. pub. utility law 1996-97), Va. Bar Assn. (exec. com. 1981-86, pres. 1985), Richmond Bar Assn., Fed. Energy Bar Assn., Va. State Bar, Phi Beta Kappa (pres. Richmond chpt. 1982-83). Presbyterian. Clubs: Country of Va., Commonwealth, (Richmond). Home: 9 Maxwell Rd Richmond VA 23226-1627 Office: Hunton & Williams Riverfront Pla East Tower PO Box 1535 Richmond VA 23218-1535

BRASHEARS, SUMNER, funeral director; b. Paris, Ark., Dec. 11, 1949; s. Felix Sumner and Mary Jo (Boomer) B.; m. Jackie Sue Taylor, Feb. 11, 1988; children: Stacy K. Easterling, Gara M. Mosier. Diploma, Dallas Inst. Mortuary Sci., 1971; AS, N.Ark. C.C., 1976; BS, U. of the State of N.Y., Albany, 1980. Lic. funeral dir. and embalmer, Ark.; cert. funeral svc. practitioneer Acad. Profl. Funeral Svc. Practice. Exec. v.p. Brashears Funeral Home, Inc., Huntsville, Ark., 1971-91, pres., CEO, 1991—; bd. dirs. Madison Bank and Trust, Kingston, Ark.; bd. dirs. Selected Funeral and Life Ins. Co., Hot Springs, Ark., chmn. bd. dirs., 1996—; vice chmn. bd. Selected Fin. Svc. Corp., Hot Springs, 1982—. Alderman Huntsville City Coun., 1974-88; pres. Ark. State Bd. Embalmers and Funeral Dirs., 1986-94; commr. Huntsville Water and Sewer Commn., 1976—. Named Funeral Dir. of Yr., Morticians of the S.W., 1987. Mem. Nat. Funeral Dirs. Assn. (pres. 1995), Ark. Funeral Dirs. Assn. (pres. 1987), Masons (life, master), Kiwanis Club of Huntsville (life, pres. 1981), Western Ark. Scottish Rite Bodies (comdr. 1994, 33d degree), York Rite (grand high priest 1985, grand master 1994). Democrat. Presbyterian.

BRASHER, GEORGE WALTER, physician; b. Jackson, Tenn., Dec. 7, 1936; s. George W. and Verla S. Brasher; m. Martha S. Brasher, Dec. 23, 1960; children: Suzanne Cheshier, George Brasher, John Brasher, David Brasher. BA, Lambuth U., 1959; MD, U. Tenn., 1961. Diplomate Am. Bd. Allergy and Immunology, Am. Bd. Pediatrics. Cons. Scott & White Clinic & Hosp., Temple, Tex., 1966—; dir. Allergy and Immunology Scott & White Clinic and Hosp., Temple, Tex., 1975—; prof. Medicine and Pediatrics Tex. A&M U. Coll. of Medicine, Temple, Tex., 1977—. Contbr. articles to profl. jours. Fellow Am. Acad. Allergy and Immunology, Am. Acad. Pediatrics, Am. Coll. Allergy and Immunology; mem. AMA, Tex. Med. Assn., Bell County Med. Soc., Tex. Allergy Soc. Avocations: civil war history, amateur radio. Office: Scott & White Clinic & Hosp 2401 S 31st St Temple TX 76508-0001

BRASIER, ALLAN R., medical educator. BA in Biomed. Engring., U. Calif., San Diego, 1979; MD, U. Calif., San Francisco, 1983. Diplomate Am. Bd. Internal Medicine. Intern, med. resident Brigham & Women's Hosp., Boston, 1983-86; endocrinology/ metabolism fellow Mass. Gen. Hosp., Boston, 1986-87, clin. & rsch. fellow dept. molecular endocrinology, 1987-89, rsch. assoc. Howard Hughes Med. Inst., 1988-91; assoc. prof. medicine Sealy Ctr. Molecular Sci. U. Tex. Med. Br., Galveston, 1991-98, prof., 1998—, sr. scientist, 1996; instr. medicine Harvard Med. Sch., Boston, 1989-90, asst. prof., 1990-91; lectr. Nat. Coun. High Blood Pressure Rsch. Contbr. articles to profl. jours. Recipient Acad. Excellence award U. Calif. San Francisco Alumni Faculty Assn., 1983, Established Investigator award Am. Heart Assn., 1995. Mem. Phi Beta Kappa, Alpha Omega Alpha. Office: U Tex Med Br MRB 8.138 Divsn Endocrinol 301 University Blvd Galveston TX 77555-1060*

BRASKET, CURT JUSTIN, systems analyst, chess player; b. Tracy, Minn., Dec. 7, 1932; s. Curt John and Mary Ann (Jenniges) B.; m. Rita Ann Bronk, July 20, 1963; children: Monica, Barbara, Rebecca. Student, U. Minn., 1950-51; B.A. in Math, St. John's U., Collegeville, Minn., 1954. Systems analyst Unisys (Sperry, Univac), St. Paul, 1957-88. Served with AUS, 1955-57. Mem. U.S. Chess Fedn. (life master, life mem.), Internat. Chess Fedn. (master 1983—). U.S. Chess master, 1953—; U.S. jr. champion, 1952; 16 times Minn. champion, 4 times North Central champion. Home: 220 Spring Valley Dr Minneapolis MN 55420-5540

BRASOVEANU, DAN, systems analyst; b. Bucharest, Romania, Aug. 11, 1954; came to U.S., 1986; s. Gheorghe and Steliana Cornelia (Popescu) B. MS in Aero. Engring., Poly. Inst., Bucharest, 1979; MS in Chem. Physics, U. Md., 1991, PhD in Chem. Physics, 1997. Staff engr. Turbomecanica, Bucharest, 1979-82, sr. engr., 1982-86; mem. tech. staff Computer Scis. Corp., Lanham-Seabrook, Md., 1988-91, sr. mem. tech. staff, 1997—. Patentee in field. Mem. AIAA. Avocation: photography. Home: 4603 Virginia Ave Baltimore MD 21225-2514 Office: Computer Scis Corp 7700 Hubble Dr Lanham Seabrook MD 20706

BRASS, ALAN W., healthcare executive. MS in Hosp. and Health Svc. Adminstrn., Ohio State U., 1973. Pres., CEO Pro Medica Health Sys., 1998—. Recipient Pub. Health Svc. Traineeship award, 1973. Office: 2121 Hughes Dr Toledo OH 43606

BRASSWEL, KERRY, tax accountant, horsewoman; d. J.D. Jr. and Kathryn Elizabeth (Rimmer) Braswell. Student, Occidental Coll., L.A., 1964-66. Cert. tax profl. Am. Inst. Tax Studies; qualified Ariz. and Calif. Superior Cts. and Fed. Ct. Bus. mgr. to entertainers Segal, Skaff and Co., L.A., 1968, Cary Harwin and Assocs., Beverly Hills, Calif., 1968-72, Bisgeier, Breslauer and Co., L.A., 1972-74, M. Klaiman Accountancy Corp., Beverly Hills, 1974-75, Michael L. Laney, CPA, Beverly Hills, 1975-77; pvt. practice Tucson, Ariz., 1977—; owner Brasswel Arabians, L.A. 1966-76, KaBeAraby, Tucson, 1977—; appraiser St. Paul's Ins. Co., St. Paul, Minn.; equine, also accounting expert witness; lectr. herbal horse care. Author: Herbal Horse Handbook, 1989. Judge, leader 4-H Club, Tucson, 1981-84; travel del. Calif. Horsemans People to People Goodwill Tour, 1970. Mem. Nat. Soc. Tax Profls., Arabian Horse Registry Am., Internat. Arabian Horse Assn. (judge 1976-83), Am. Horse Show Assn. (judge 1976-83), Desert Show Horse Assn. (bd. dirs. 1980-83), So. Ariz. Arabian Horse Assn. (cert. appreciation 1978). Republican. Avocations: sidereal astrology, holistic herbalogy, organic gardening. Home and Office: 10151 W Picture Rocks Rd Tucson AZ 85743-9386

BRASUNAS, ANTON DE SALES, metallurgical engineering educator; b. Elizabeth, N.J., Mar. 11, 1919; s. Anthony J. and Stefana (Zekus) B.; m. Ellen Lydia Wirth, Nov. 16, 1946; children—James Anton, Kay Ellen, Anne Elizabeth. B.S., Antioch Coll., Yellow Springs, Ohio, 1943; M.S., Ohio State U., 1946; Sc.D., M.I.T., 1950. Cert. advanced metric specialist. Research engr. Battelle Meml. Inst., Columbus, Ohio, 1943-46; research metallurgist Oak Ridge Nat. Lab., 1950-53; asso. prof. metallurgy U. Tenn., Knoxville, 1953-55; dir. edn. ASM Internat. (formerly Am. Soc. Metals), Metals Park, Ohio, 1955-64; mem. faculty U. Mo., Rolla, St. Louis, 1964-84, assoc. dean engr., prof. metall. engring., 1964-84, prof. emeritus, 84—; cons. in field; guest lectr. U. Antioquia, Colombia, 1986. Author, editor in field. Recipient Alumni award U. Mo., Rolla, 1971, Fullbright award, 1986. Fellow Am. Soc. Metals, U.S. Metric Assn. (nat. sec. 1988-92, chmn. Cert. Metrication Specialist Bd. 1992-96); mem. Alpha Sigma Mu (pres. 1968-69). Home: 8030 Daytona Dr Saint Louis MO 63105-2510 Office: U Mo 8001 Natural Bridge Rd Saint Louis MO 63121

BRASWELL, CRUSE C., JR., public relations executive. Exec. dir. pub. rels. Bellsouth Corp., Atlanta, asst. v.p. strategic comm., 1998—. Office: Bellsouth Corp 1155 Peachtree St NE Rm 2001 Atlanta GA 30309-3610*

BRASWELL, GARY JOSEPH, secondary school educator, military officer; b. New London, Conn., Dec. 23, 1946; s. Upshaw J., Honora A. (McAvoy) B.; m. Nancy Lou Steiger, June 26, 1976; children: Robert, Michael. BA in History, Va. Mil. Inst., 1969; MA in History, George Mason U., 1991; postgrad., Air Candidate Sch., 1982-83. Commd. 2d. lt. USAF, 1969; served at Scott AFB and Germany, 1969-74; with Air Intelligence Svc., Pentagon, 1974-78, HQ TAC, Langley AFB, Va., 1978-82; served in Korea, 1983-84; with USECOM, Stuttgart, Germany, 1984-87; with J-6 joint chief of staff Pentagon, Washington, 1987-89; advanced through grades to lt. col. USAF, 1985, retired, 1989; tchrs. aide Fairfax (Va.) County Pub. Schs., 1990-91; tchr. Winchester (Va.) Pub. Schs., 1991—. Bd. dirs. Winchester Frederick County Hist. Soc., 1997—. Mem. Moose, Lions (pres. Winchester-Shawnee chpt. 1997-98), Phi Delta Kappa, Phi Alpha Theta. Home: 129 Omps Dr Winchester VA 22601-2834 Office: John Handley HS PO Box 910 Winchester VA 22604-0910

BRASWELL, JACKIE BOYD, state agency administrator; b. Leon County, Fla., Feb. 15, 1938; d. Chalmer Parks and Kathryn Iris (Johnson) Boyd; m. Fletcher Braswell, Nov. 28, 1957; children: Flecia Lori, Carmen Ethelee. BS, Fla. State U., 1964; M in Ednl. Adminstrn., 1976. edn. cert. Valdosta State Coll., 1968. Lic. tchr., adminstr. Fla. single mgr., ammunition, base clothing fund, security clearance USAF, Moody AFB, 1958-61; tchr. bus. edn. Berrien H.S., Nashville, Ga., 1966-69, Rickards H.S., Tallahassee, 1970-75; bus.-vocat. tchr. Lincoln H.S., Tallahassee, 1975-99; dir. ednl. affairs and policy Fla. Lottery, Tallahassee, 1999—; co-owner, fin. mgr. Rundown Farms, Tallahassee, 1969—. Editor: In Touch, 1979-80; contbr. articles to profl. jours. Apptd. to Fla. State Bd. Pub. Schs., 1987-90, vice chmn., 1990—, acting chmn., 1991, Fla. Commn. Edn. Reform and Accountability, 1991-93; invited del. Citizens Amb. Program People Internat., Beijing, Hangzhou, Shanghai, China, 1995; fundraising chmn. Dist. Sch. Supts. Campaign, 1996; sponsorship chair Capital Cultural Ctr., Chukker Challenge, 1997-98. Recipient Merit award Future Farmers Am., 1974; selectee Harvard Inst., 1991. Mem. Nat. Mus. Women in the Arts (charter), Nat. Bus. Edn. Assn., Fla. Vocat. Assn., Fla. Bus. Edn. Addn., Leon Vocat. Assn. (pres. elect 1987-88, pres. 1988-89), Leon Classroom Tchrs. Assn. (sec.-treas. 1987-88, chair pub. rels., parliamentarian 1988-89, govtl. rels. 1991), Dance Arts Guild, Leon County Farm Bur., Quill and Scroll, Phi Kappa Phi. Republican. Home: 7006 N Meridian Rd Tallahassee FL 32312-8017 Office: Fla Lottery 250 Marriot Dr Tallahassee FL 32399

BRASWELL, LAURA DAY, periodontist; b. Bowling Green, Ky., July 22, 1958; d. Lawson Moyers and Bettye (Wall) B.; m. DeFord Smith III; children: DeFord Lawson Smith, Ashley Smith, Alison Smith, Jeanette Smith. DDS, U. N.C., 1982; cert., Emory U., 1988. Diplomate Am. Acad. Periodontology. Staff dentist Sam Rudd DDS, Raleigh, N.C., 1982-83; mem. faculty Emory U., Atlanta, 1983-93; assoc. scientist Yerkes Regional Primate Ctr., Atlanta, 1984-98; zoo dentist Zoo Atlanta, 1986—; pvt. practice Atlanta, 1988—. Vol. Healing for the Poor, Kingston, Jamaica, 1986, Ctrl. Presbyn. Health Ctr., Atlanta, 1986-91, Grant Park Family Health Ctr., 1989-93, dentist Ga. Part for Caring; 1st vice chmn. Arthritis Found., Ga., 1997; dental coord. Face-to-Face. Master Acad. Laser Dentistry (charter); mem. ADA, Internat. Assn. Dental Rsch., Am. Assn. Dental Rsch., Ga. Dental Assn., No. Dist. Dental Soc. (mem. exec. coun.), Psi Omega. Methodist. Avocations: aerobics, windsurfing, hang gliding, kayaking, camping. Home: 5064 Fields Pond Cv Marietta GA 30068-1572 also: 3312 Piedmont Rd NE Ste 270 Atlanta GA 30305-1781

BRASWELL, LOUIS ERSKINE, lawyer; b. Selma, Ala., Mar. 11, 1937; s. Erskine McKinley and Leota (Grubb) B.; m. Anne, June 1, 1985 (dec. Feb. 20, 1996); children by previous marriage: Margaret, Anne, Helen. AB, Birmingham So. Coll., 1959; JD, Harvard U., 1962. Bar: Ala. bar 1962. Assoc. firm Hand, Arendall, Bedsole, Greaves & Johnston, Mobile, Ala., 1963-68; partner Hand & Arendall, 1968—; participant Nat. Conf. on Discovery Reform, U. Tex. Law Sch., 1982; program participant 11th Cir. Jud. Conf., 1984, others. Bd. dirs. Children's Dental Clinic, Mobile, 1965-75; past pres. Friends of Mobile Public Library; bd. dirs. Jr. Achievement of Mobile; past pres. YMCA Rockies Alumni Assn.; bd. dirs. Kidney Found. South Ala., 1978-85. Served with U.S. Army, 1962-63. Mem. ABA, Am. Law Inst., Ala. Law Inst., Ala. Bar Assn., Ala. Def. Lawyers Assn., Athelstan Club, Rotary Internat., Point Clear Rotary Club (bd. dirs. 1997—, pres. 1998-99). Presbyterian. Home: PO Box 236 Point Clear AL 36564-0236 Office: PO Box 123 Mobile AL 36601-0123

BRASWELL, PAULA ANN, artist; b. Decatur, Ala., May 6, 1955; d. Andrew Leon and Dorothy Faye (Fretwell) B.; m. Roger Armand Robichaud, June 22, 1990. BA, Jacksonville State U., 1978; postgrad., New Orleans Acad. Fine Arts, 1987, U. New Orleans, 1987-88; MFA, Fla. State U., 1990. Instr. art Butler Sch., Marrero, La., 1984, Fla. Keys Coll., Tavernier, 1985; grad. instr. Fla. State U., Tallahassee, 1989-90; adj. prof. Calhoun Coll., Decatur, Ala., 1990, Chattanooga State Coll., 1991, Cleveland (Tenn.) State Coll., 1991; studio artist Knoxville, Tenn., 1991-96, Toronto, Ont., Can., 1996—. Artist (video sculpture) Museum of Fine Arts, 1998, Fla. State U., Museum of the Ams., Washington, 1997, ARC Gallery, 1997, New American Talent, 1996, Transforming Tradition, 1996, Combined Talents Fla. Nat., 1995, Knoxville (Tenn.) Mus. Art, 1994-95, Contemporary Arts Ctr., New Orleans, 1992, Mus. of the Ams., Washington, 1997, Points of Compass show FSU Mus., 1998; represent Can. in OAS exhibit at The Mus. of the Ams., Washington, 1997. Nat. Endowment Arts grantee, 1991, Ontario Arts Coun. grantee, 1997. Mem. AAUW, NOW, Women's Caucus for Arts (exhibitor), Knoxville Mus. Art (exhibitor), Knoxville Arts Coun. (exhibitor), Coll. Art Assn., Contemporary Arts Ctr. (exhibitor), People for Protection of Animals, Humane Soc. U.S. Democrat. Mem. Ch. of Christ. Avocations: gardening, environmental concerns, animal care, skiing, camping. Address: 326 Carlaw Ave Ste 230, Toronto, ON Canada M4M 3N8

BRASWELL, WALTER E., prosecutor; b. Shreveport, La., Apr. 2, 1954. BA, U. Ala., 1976, JD, 1979. Bar: Ala. 1979. Pvt. practice Tuscaloosa, Ala., 1979-86, 93; adminstrv. asst. to Rep. Claude Harris (Dem., Ala.), 1987-93; sr. litigation officer U.S. Dist. Ct. (no. dist.) Ala., Birmingham, 1995—; U.S. atty. Active Birmingham Com. Fgn. Rels. William Randolph Hearst scholar. Mem. Ala. Bar Assn. Methodist. Office: US Attorney for No Dist Alabama Rm 200 Federal Bldg 1800 5th Ave N Ste 200 Birmingham AL 35203-2189*

BRATCHER, JUANITA, journalist; b. Columbus, Ga.; d. Benjamin Pickens and Tommie (English) Forte; m. Neal Archie Bratcher; children: Pamela, Angela, Sonya, Neal Jr. AA, Olive Harvey Coll.; BA in Journalism, Columbia Coll., 1976. News reporter South End Rev., Chgo., Roseland Rev., Chgo., Chgo. Defender; editor, publ. Southeast Alliance, Chgo., Copyline Mag., Chgo. Author: Harold: The Making of a Big City Mayor, 1993, I Cry for a People: In Their Struggle for Justice, 1996; recordings include Too Many Memories, 1996, Everything But Love, 1996, I'm Here for You, 1997, You've Been Gone Too Long, 1997. Recipient everyday hero award Ill. Sec. State George Ryan, 1993, Kizzy award The Kizzy Found., 1983; named black bus. woman of yr. Parkway Cmty. House, Chgo., 1993. Mem. Internat. Soc. Poets. Baptist. Home: 9026 S Cregier Ave Chicago IL 60617-3533

BRATHWAITE, HARRIET LOUISA, nursing educator; b. Rye, N.Y., Aug. 28, 1931; d. James Pierce and Mattie (Collins) Bowling; m. Leroy L. Brathwaite, Feb. 18, 1950; 1 child, Helene Ann Brathwaite Ward. AAS in Nursing, CUNY, 1959; BSN, L.I. U., 1965; postgrad., Columbia U., 1965-68; MSN, Adelphia U., 1973. Staff nurse Kings County Hosp., Bklyn., 1959; head nurse City Hosp. at Elmhurst, Queens, N.Y., 1959-62; instr. Kings County Hosp. Sch. Nursing, 1963-65, Downstate Med. Ctr. Sch. Nursing, 1965-69; nurse community mental health South Beach Psychiat. Ctr., 1969-73; cons. psychiat. nursing sect. HEW and N.Y. State Health Dept., Albany, 1973-74; chief of service Creedmoor Psychiat. Ctr., Queens Village, N.Y., 1974-87; asst. prof. nursing L.I. U., 1987-92. Co-leader Allied Dems., Jamaica, N.Y., 1959-62; bd. dirs. South Queens Dems., Howard Beach, N.Y.; mem. adv. bd. Transitional Services, Queens, 1983-85; appointed Senatorial dist. coord. for Senator Charles Schumer, 1999. Mem. AAUW, NAACP, Nat. Black Nurses Assn. (chmn. legis. com. Queens chpt. 1981—, Cert. of Appreciation 1989), N.Y. State Nurses Assn. (coun. on legislation 1990—, trustee Polit. Action Com. 1991—, 25 Yr. Membership award 1986, Legis. award 1988, Ruth W. Harper award for Disting. Svc. 1991, inducted into Leadership Inst. 1998, inducted into Leadership Inst. 1998, Maggie Jacobs award 1999), 100 Black Women of L.I., Bklyn. Coll. Alumni Assn. (bd. dirs. 1995), Knickerbocker Club (chmn. fin. and scholarship com.), Chi Eta Phi, Kappa Eta, Sigma Theta Tau. Home: PO Box 1841 10 Cuffee Dr Sag Harbor NY 11963-0064

BRATHWAITE, ORMOND DENNIS, chemistry educator; b. Parish Land, Barbados, W.I., Jan. 19, 1956; s. Dennis Berisford and Erin Eulene (Forde) B.; m. Maria Roslyn Alleyne, May 28, 1983; children: Marcus, Shayna. BS in Med. Tech., York Coll., 1982; MA in Biochemistry, CCNY, 1985; PhD in Biochemistry, CUNY, 1991. Phlebotomy technician, med. technologist intern Brookdale Hosp. Med. Ctr., Bklyn., 1981-84; adj. instr. CCNY, N.Y.C., 1985-91; asst. rsch. scientist Borough Manhattan C.C., N.Y.C., 1991-94; asst. prof. chemistry and biology Cuyahoga C.C., Highalnd Hills, Ohio, 1994—; adj. instr. Bklyn. Coll., 1982-83; adj. prof. biology Kean Coll. N.J., Union, 1988-89; vis. scientist dept. cancer biology Cleve. Clinic Found., 1994-95. Avocations: table tennis, running, swimming, gardening, reading. Office: Cuyahoga CC 4250 Richmond Rd Highland Hills OH 44122

BRATRUD, LINDA KAY, secondary education educator; b. Salt Lake City, May 14, 1944; d. Milton Niels and Marian Lucy (Criswell) Peterson; m. Richard L. Settle, Sept. 10, 1965 (div. Sept. 1982); children: Courtney Settle Dodson, Dana R.; m. Jeffrey C. Bratrud, Aug. 27, 1990; children: Jennifer Bratrud Stauffacher, Jeff, John. 1st diploma, U. Grenoble, France, 1964; 2d diploma, U. Paris, 1965; BA, U. Wash., 1966; MBA, U. Puget Sound, 1987. Tchr. French, South H.S., Bakersfield, Calif., 1967-68, Peninsula H.S., Gig Harbor, Wash., 1984-93; instr. French, Tacoma C.C., 1970-71; owner bookstore Smith, Settle, Bingham & Wagner, Tacoma, 1980-82; client exec. asst. Frank Russell Co., Tacoma, 1981-84. Avocations: freelance writing, gardening, golf, tennis, cooking. Home: 5230 W Old Stump Dr NW Gig Harbor WA 98332

BRATSCH, STEVEN GARY, chemistry educator; b. Torrance, Calif., Nov. 26, 1951; s. Paul James and Marjorie Ruth (Hagen) B. BS, U. Tex., 1977, PhD, 1985. Lab. coord. U. Tex., Austin, 1985-86, instr., 1986-87; asst. prof. U. Conn., Storrs, 1987-88, S.W. Tex. State U., San Marcos, Tex., 1988-90; instr. Honolulu C.C., 1991-92; cons. Fetzer Inst., Kalamazoo, Mich., 1990—; lectr. U. Tex., Austin., 1998—. Reviewer Jour. of Chem. Edn., 1984—; contbr. articles to profl. jours. Asst. dir. Inner Light Ministries, Honolulu and Austin, 1990—. Sgt. USAF, 1972-76. Mem. Internat. Union of Pure and Applied Chemistry (affiliate), Am. Chem. Soc., Sigma Xi. Avocations: popular music history, fitness and nutrition.

BRATT, BENJAMIN, actor; b. San Francisco, Dec. 16, 1963. Actor: (film) Bright Angel, 1991, One Good Cop, 1991, Bound by Honor, 1993, Demolition Man, 1993, The River Wild, 1994, Clear and Present Danter, 1994, Follow Me Home, 1997, The Next Best Thing, 1999, (TV) Police Story: Gladiator School, 1988, Nasty Boys, 1989, Chains of Gold, 1991, Shadowhunter, 1993, Texas, 1994, Woman Undone, 1996, Exiled, 1998, (tv series) Knightwatch, 1988, Nasty Boys, 1990, Law & Order, 1995-99; prodr.: Follow Me Home, 1997; TV guest appearances include: Homicide: Life on the Street, 1993. Winner ALMA award as best lead actor in a TV series for Law & Order, 1998. Office: Wolf Films Inc c/o Universal TV 100 Universal City Plz #69 Universal City CA 91608-1085*

BRATT, NICHOLAS, investment management and research company executive; b. Gerrards Cross, Eng., June 6, 1948; came to U.S., 1976; s. Guy Maurice and Francoise Nelly (Girardet) B.; m. Kuniko Matsui, Aug. 10, 1976; 1 child, Emi Margaret Matsui. Degree in Politics and Econs., Oxford U., 1970; MIA, Columbia U., 1972. Rsch. analyst Morgan Grenfell & Co. Ltd., London, 1972-75; portfolio mgr. Morgan Grenfell S.A., Geneva, 1976; portfolio mgr. Scudder, Stevens & Clark, N.Y.C., 1976—, mng. dir., 1984—; pres. Scudder Internat. Fund, N.Y.C., 1982, Korea Fund, N.Y.C., 1984—, Scudder New Asia Fund, N.Y.C., 1987—, Brazil Fund, N.Y.C., 1988—, Scudder New Europe Fund, N.Y.C., 1990, Argentina Fund, N.Y.C., 1991—, First Iberian Fund, N.Y.C., 1992—, Scudder Greater Europe Fund, 1994—. Mem. N.Y. Assn. for Fgn. Investment (chmn. 1978-80), Japan Soc., Korea Soc. (bd. dris.). Avocations: mountain climbing, skiing, tennis, paddle tennis, sailing, golf.

BRATTON, HOWARD CALVIN, federal judge; b. Clovis, N.Mex., Feb. 4, 1922; s. Sam Gilbert and Vivian (Rogers) B. BA, U. N.Mex., 1941, LLB, 1971; LLB, Yale U., 1947. Bar: N.Mex. 1948. Law clk. U.S. Cir. Ct. Appeals, 1948; ptnr. Grantham & Bratton, Albuquerque, 1949-52; spl. asst. U.S. atty. charge litigation OPS, 1951-52; assoc., then ptnr. Hervy, Dow & Hinkle, Roswell, N.Mex., 1952-64; judge U.S. Dist. Ct. N.Mex., Albuquerque, 1964-87, chief judge, 1978-87; sr. judge U.S. Dist. Ct. N.Mex., Las Cruces, 1987—; chmn. N.Mex. Jr. Bar Assn., 1952; pres. Chaves County (N.Mex.) Bar Assn., 1962; chmn. pub. lands com. N.Mex. Oil and Gas Assn., 1961-64, Interstate Oil Compact Commn., 1963-64; mem. N.Mex. Commn. Higher Edn., 1962-64, Jud. Conf. of U.S. Com. on Operation of Jury Sys., 1966-72, 79-85, Jud. Conf. U.S. Com. on Ethics, 1987-92; mem. Ad Hoc Com. on Internat. Jud. Rels., 1992-94; 10th cir. rep. Jud. Conf. U.S., 1984-86. Bd. regents U. N.Mex., 1958-68, pres., 1963-64; bd. dirs. Fed. Jud. Ctr., 1983-87. Served to capt. AUS, 1942-45. Mem. Trial Judges Assn. 10th Circuit (pres. 1976-78), Nat. Conf. Fed. Trial Judges (exec. com. 1977-79), Sigma Chi. Office: US Dist Ct 200 E Griggs Ave Las Cruces NM 88001-3523

BRATTON, IDA FRANK, secondary school educator; b. Glasgow, Ky., Aug. 31, 1933; d. Edmund Bates and Robbie Davis (Hume) Button; m. Robert Franklin Bratton, June 20, 1954; 1 son, Timothy Andrew. B.A., Western Ky. U., 1959, M.A., 1962. Cert. secondary tchr., Ky. Tchr. math. and sci. Gottschalk Jr. High Sch., Louisville, 1959-65; tchr. math. Iroquois High Sch., Louisville, 1965-79; tchr. Waggener High Sch., Louisville, 1979—, chair math. dept. co-chair sch. based decision making coun. Waggener High Sch. Mem. NEA, Ky. Edn. Assn., Jefferson County Tchrs. Assn., AAUW. Democrat. Methodist. Avocations: travel, needle crafts. Home: 304 Paddington Ct Louisville KY 40222-5541 Office: Waggener High Sch 330 S Hubbards Ln Louisville KY 40207-4099

BRATTON, JAMES HENRY, JR., lawyer; b. Pulaski, Tenn., Oct. 9, 1931; s. James Henry and Mabel (Shelley) B.; m. Alleen Sharp Davis, Oct. 15, 1960; children: Susan Shelley McGonigle, James Henry III, Margaret Alleen. B.A. optime merens, U. South, 1952; B.A., Oxford (Eng.) U., 1954, M.A., 1978; LL.B., Yale U., 1956. Bar: Tenn. 1956, Ga. 1957. With antitrust div. Dept. Justice, summer 1955; since practiced in Atlanta; partner firm Smith, Gambrell & Russell; vis. lectr. U. Ga. Law Sch., 1967; adj. prof. law Emory U., 1984—. Editor Yale Law Jour.; contbr. articles to profl. jours. Mem. Gov.'s Citizens Adv. Council on Environ. Affairs, 1970-74; trustee Trust Fund for Sibley Park, Ga. chpt. Multiple Sclerosis Soc., U. of the South, 1984-87, 95—, Pembroke Coll. Found., Peachtree Rd. United

Meth. Ch., chmn.-elect bd. trustees; bd. dirs. Soccer in the Streets, Buckhead Christian Community Ministry, pres., 1996; pres. Peachtree Heights West Civic Assn., 1984—; co-chmn. Sewanee Parents Council, 1987-88; v.p. Pembroke Coll. Soc. of N.Am.; mem. Williams Parents' Fund, 1984-86; mem. parents adv. coun. Hamilton Coll., 1988-91. Named Alumnus of Yr., Sewanee Club Atlanta, 1990. Fellow Ga. Bar Found., Am. Law Inst.; mem. ABA (standing com. on aero. law 1962-84, chmn. 1977-80), Ga. Bar Assn. (founding chmn. environ. law sect. 1970-73), Fed. Bar Assn., Atlanta Bar Assn., Lawyers Club Atlanta, Old Warhorse Lawyers Club, Am. Acad. Polit. and Social Scis., Am. Judicature Soc., Associated Alumni U. of South (v.p. admissions 1993-95, pres. 1995-97), Yale Law Alumni Assn. (exec. com. 1976-79), Phi Beta Kappa, Phi Delta Phi, Pi Gamma Mu, Gridiron. Democrat. Methodist. E-Mail: jbratton@sgrlau.com. Home: 63 N Muscogee Ave NW Atlanta GA 30309-3592 Office: 1230 Peachtree St NE Atlanta GA 30309-3574

BRATTON, WILLIAM EDWARD, electronics executive, management consultant; b. Dallas, Oct. 25, 1919; s. William E. and Edna (Walker) B.; m. Betty Thume, May 30, 1942; children: Dale, Janet, Donna. AB in Econs., Stanford U., 1940; MBA, Harvard U., 1945. From v.p. to pres. Librascope, Glendale, Calif., 1947-63; v.p., gen. mgr. Ampex, Culver City, Calif., 1963-66; pres. Guidance Tech., Santa Monica, Calif., 1967-68; v.p. electronics div. Gen. Dynamics, San Diego, 1969-72; pres. Theta Cable T.V., Santa Monica, 1974-82; pres., chief exec. officer Stagecoach Properties, Salado, Tex., 1959—. Served to lt. (j.g.) USNR, 1944-46. Republican. Episcopalian. Club: El Niguel Country (Laguna, Calif.) (pres. 1978-79). Avocations: golf, skindiving.

BRATTSTROM, BAYARD HOLMES, biology educator; b. Chgo., July 3, 1929; s. Wilber LeRoy and Violet (Holmes) B.; m. Cecile D. Funk, June 15, 1952 (div. May 1975); children: Theodore Allen, David Arthur.; m. Martha Isaacs Marsh, July 8, 1982. B.S., San Diego State Coll., 1951; M.A., UCLA, 1953, Ph.D., 1959. Dir. edn. Natural History Mus., San Diego, 1949-51; asst. curator herpetology Natural History Mus., 1949-51; assoc. zoology UCLA, 1954-56; research fellow paleoecology Calif. Inst. Tech., Pasadena, 1955; instr. biology Adelphi U., Garden City, N.Y., 1956-60; asst. prof. Calif. State U., Fullerton, 1960-61; assoc. prof. Calif. State U., 1961-66, prof., 1966-94, prof. emeritus, 1994—; co-owner Horned Lizard Ranch, Horned Lizard Press; rschr., author publs. in osteology, ecology, conservation, zoogeography of vertebrates, social behavior; hon. rsch. assoc. herpetology, vertebrate paleontology Los Angeles County Mus., 1961—; pres. Fullerton Youth Mus. and Natural Sci. Ctr., 1962-64, dir., 1962-66; assoc. prof. zoology UCLA, summers 1962-63; vis. prof. zoology Sydney U., Australia, 1978, U. Queensland, Brisbane, Australia, 1984; vis. rschr. James Cook U., Townsville, Australia, 1993-94; ecol. cons. to numerous govtl. agys. and pvt. corps. Author: poetry The Talon Digs Deeply into My Heart, 1974; Contbr. chpts. to books. Recipient Disting. Teaching award Calif. State U., Fullerton, 1968, Dean's award for Outstanding Teaching and Rsch., 1992; Am. Philos. Soc. grantee to Mex., 1958, to Panama, 1959; NSF grantee, 1964-66; NSF fellow Monash U., Australia, 1966-67. Fellow AAAS (mem. coun. 1965-90), Herpetological League; mem. Am. Soc. Ichthyologists and Herpetologists (bd. govs. 1962-66, v.p. western div. 1965), Orange County Zool. Soc. (mem. bd. 1962-65, pres. 1962-64), So. Calif. Acad. Sci. (dir. 1964-67), Ecol. Soc. Am., Soc. for Study Evolution, Soc. Systematic Zoology, San Diego Soc. Natural History, Soc. Vertebrate Paleontology, Am. Soc. Mammalogists, Cooper Ornithol. Soc., Am. Ornithol. Soc., Am. Soc. Zoologists, Sigma Xi. Office: Calif State U Dept Biology Fullerton CA 92834 *My life and research have been based on an insatiable curiosity about the natural world, especially as seen in the evolutionary adaptations of animals to their environment and their interactions with each other.*

BRATZLER, MARY KATHRYN, desktop publisher; b. Albuquerque, Sept. 16, 1960; d. William James and Nancy Jane (Hobbs) Colby; m. Zim Emig, May 30, 1987 (div. Nov. 1990); 1 child, Aeriel Kaylee Emig; m. Steven James Bratzler, Mar. 16, 1996, 1 child, Cody Benjamin. B of Univ. Studies, U. N.Mex., 1995. Comml. artist Modern Press, Albuquerque, 1978-80; asst. composition supr. Graphic Arts Pub., Albuquerque, 1980-84, composition supr., 1984-85, asst. plant mgr., 1985-86; typesetter Universal Printing and Graphics, Albuquerque, 1986-87, Bus. Graphics, Albuquerque, 1988-90; office asst. UNM Gen. Honors, Albuquerque, 1992-93; desktop pub., 1990—; computer specialist NEDA Bus. Cons., Inc., 1996-98; cons. Mary Kay Cosmetics, 1991-96. Participant N.Mex. Pub. Utilities Commn., Santa Fe, 1993; coord. clothing bank PTA, Zia Elem. Sch., 1995-96; parent rep. Unified Student Centered Classroom, 1996-98. Mem. Golden Key, Phi Beta Kappa. Avocations: piano playing, bicycling, hiking, camping.

BRAUCH, WILLIAM LELAND, lawyer. Bachelor's degree, U. Wis., Milw., 1980; JD, U. Iowa, 1987. Asst. atty. gen. Consumer Protection Divsn., Des Moines, 1987-95, spl. asst. atty. gen., dir., 1995—. Pres. Beaver Dale Neighborhood Assn. Recipient Consumer Advocate award Nat. Assn. Consumer Advocates. Mem. ABA (vice-chmn. consumer protection commn.), Polk County Bar Assn. Office: Consumer Protection Divsn 2d Fl Hoover State Office Bldg Des Moines IA 50319

BRAUCHLI, MARCUS WALKER, foreign correspondent; b. Boulder, Colo., June 19, 1961; s. Christopher R. and Margot L. Brauchli; m. Maggie Farley. AB, Columbia U., 1983. Foreign corr. Wall St. Jour., Shanghai.

BRAUDE, EDWIN SIMON, manufacturing company executive; b. Chgo.; s. Simon Arthur and Marie (Selz) B.; m. Olga Bergstad, May 4, 1951 (dec. Dec. 1992); children: Mitchell, Edwin S. Jr., Bradford, Timothy, Tammy, Teena; m. Dorothy Herzberg, Sept. 10, 1998. BSCE, U. Colo., 1949; postgrad., Chgo. Tech., 1959; MBA, Rockford (Ill.) Coll., 1967. From pipefitter to sr. plant layout engr. Fisher Body Div. Gen. Motors, Willow Springs, Ill., 1954-61; materials mgr., mgr. mfg. Ingersoll Milling Machine Co., Rockford, 1961-71; factory mgr., v.p. mfg. NATCO, Richmond, Ind., 1972-73; plant mgr. Graphic Systems div. Rockwell Internat., Chgo. and Cedar Rapids, Iowa, 1973-76; pres. Barth Industries subs. NESCO, Cleve., 1976-82; chmn. bd. Lester Engrng. subs. NESCO, Cleve., 1976-82; pres. Hiram & E.S.D. subs. NESCO, Mich., N.C. and Calif., 1976-82, Lexington Switch, Flex Cable & Kirkhof, Mich. and Ohio, 1982-84, Nat. Acme, Cleve., 1984—; v.p. ops. Acme Cleve., 1984—; pres. A.A. Gage, Ferndale, Mich., 1990—; work with cos. Magdeburg, East Germany, 1992, Novosibirsk, Siberia, 1994; cons. Wolverine Diecast, 1998. Chmn. City of Roscoe (Ill.) Zoning Commn.; mem. Roscoe Planning Bd. With USCG, 1944-46, PTO; with USAF, 1950. Republican. Lutheran. Clubs: Univ., Cleve. Athletic. Avocations: racquetball, scuba diving. Home: 178 Crystal Ln Aurora OH 44202-7523

BRAUDE, MICHAEL, commodity exchange executive; b. Chgo., Mar. 6, 1936; s. Sheldon and Nan B.; m. Linda Rae Miller, Aug. 20, 1961; children—Peter, Adam. B.S., U. Mo., 1957; M.S., Columbia U., 1958. Vice pres. Commerce Bank, Kansas City, Mo., 1960-73; vice pres. Mercantile Bank, Kansas City, Mo., 1966-73; exec. v.p. Am. Bank, Kansas City, Mo., 1973-84; pres., CEO Kansas City Bd. Trade, Mo., 1984—; bd. dirs. Country Club Bank, Kansas City, Mo., Midwest Grain Products, Inc., Atchison, Kans. Author: Managing Your Money, 1975, also 12 childrens books. Pres. Metr. Community Coll. Found., Kansas City, Mo., 1982-84; mayor City of Mission Woods, Kans., 1982-84. Mem. Futures Industry Assn., Nat. Futures Assn. (bd. dirs.), Nat. Grain Trade Coun. (bd. dirs., immediate past chmn.), U. Mo. Alumni Assn. (bd. dirs. 1985-87). Jewish. Avocations: running; public speaking. Home: 5319 Mission Woods Ter Shawnee Mission KS 66205-2013 Office: Kansas City Board of Trade 4800 Main St Ste 303 Kansas City MO 64112-2519

BRAUDE, ROBERT MICHAEL, medical library administrator; b. L.A., Sept. 27, 1939; s. Aaron and Dorothy (Lishner) B.; m. Sharon Helene Katz, Dec. 16, 1961; children—Michael, Daniel, Julianne. BA, UCLA, 1962, MLS, MA, 1964; PhD, U. Nebr., 1987. Reference librarian Biomed Library Ctr. for Health Scis., UCLA, Los Angeles, 1964-65, head Medlars search sta., 1965-68; assoc. dir. U. Colo. Med. Library, Denver, 1968-75, dir., 1975-77; dir. U. Nebr. Med. Library, Omaha, 1978-86; asst. dean for info. resources, Frances and John Loeb librarian Cornell U. Med. Coll., 1986—; adj. faculty U. Denver, 1972-78; vis. assoc. prof. Sch. Libr. Sci., Pratt Inst., 1988—; del. White House Conf. on Libraries and Info. Services, 1979; mem. biomed. library rev. com. Nat. Library Medicine, Bethesda, Md., 1980-84, mem. panel on med. informatics long range planning project, 1985-86, mem. planning panel on outreach programs, 1988-89. Author: (continuing edn. syllabus) Planning: Strategic and Tactical, 1983, also articles and book chpts.; mem. editorial adv. bd. Bibliography of Bioethics; mem. editorial bd. ann. Statis. of Med. Sch. Librs. and U.S. and Can., 19887-93; mem. editorial bd. Jour. Am. Med. Informatics Assn. Sec.-treas. Children's Chorale, Denver, 1974-75, trustee, 1975-77. Fellow N.Y. Acad. Medicine, Med. Libr. Assn. (sec., bd. dirs. 1972-75, Janet Doe lectr. 1996chmn. numerous coms. N.Y.-N.J. chpts., Outstanding Achievement award Midcontinental chpt. 1986), Am. Coll. Med. Informatics; mem. ALA, Acad. Health Info. Profls. (disting.), Health Scis. Libr. Dirs. (stds. and practices com. 1980-83),Assn. Western Hosps. (chmn. hosp. librs. sect. 1976-77, membership com. 1976-77), Am. Med. Informatics Assn. (mem. editl. bd.). Home: 1320 York Ave Apt 34G New York NY 10021-4878 Office: Weill Med Coll Cornell Univ 1300 York Ave New York NY 10021-4805

BRAUDY, SUSAN ORR, author; b. Phila.; d. Bernard and Blanche (Malin) Orr. BA cum laude, Bryn Mawr Coll.; postgrad., U. Pa. Editor, writer The New Jour. Yale U., New Haven; assoc. editor Newsweek Mag., N.Y.C.; editor, writer Ms. Mag., N.Y.C.; freelance writer The N.Y. Times, N.Y.C.; v.p. Warner Bros., N.Y.C. and L.A., Michael Douglas Prodns., N.Y.C. and L.A. Author: Between Marriage and Divorce, 1975, Who Killed Sal Mineo, 1981, What the Movies Made Me Do, 1984, This Crazy Thing Called Love, 1991; screenwriter Scorsese Co., Am. Zoetrope, Ixtlan, Disney. Mem. NOW, PEN Club Internat., Nat. Bd. Rev., Vet. Feminists of Am., Writers Guild Am. Home: 240 Central Park S Apt 16B New York NY 10019-1413

BRAUER, HARROL ANDREW, JR., broadcasting executive; b. Richmond, Va., Oct. 17, 1920; s. Harrol Andrew and Bertie (Gregory) B.; m. Elizabeth Anne Hill, May 18, 1946; children: Harrol Andrew III, William Lanier, Gregory Hill. BA, U. Richmond, 1942; LLD, Christopher Newport U. Chief announcer, program dir., account exec. various radio stas. in Va., 1939-42, 45-49; v.p. Sta. WVEC radio, Hampton, Va., 1949-80; v.p., dir. sales Sta. WVEC-TV, Hampton, 1953-82; v.p. Peninsula Cable Corp., 1966-82; chmn. Wyatt Bros., 1983-90; bd. dirs. Peninsula Broadcasting Corp. Pres. Hampton Community Chest, 1951-52; crusade chmn. Peninsula unit Am. Cancer Soc., 1960—. Mem. Hampton Sch. Bd., 1963—, vice chmn., 1964-68, chmn., 1968-70; pres. Hampton Parking Authority, chmn. 1988—; bd. dirs. YMCA, Va. USO; bd. dirs., vice chmn. Va. Pub. Telecommunications Bd., chmn. 1985—; chmn. Soc. Founders of Mace Christopher Newport U., 1989—; chmn. bd. trustees Hampton Roads Ednl. TV Assn., 1965-70; rector Christopher Newport U., 1976-82; co-chmn. for 375th Anniversary Celebration City of Hampton, 1985. Served as lt. USNR, 1942-45. Recipient Thomas P. Chisman award Va. Air and Space Ctr., Disting. Service medallion Christopher Newport U., NCCJ award, Disting. Citizen award City of Hampton, Outstanding Man of Yr. award Peninsula Ad Club, 1993. Mem. Hampton Retail Mchts. Assn. (past pres., bd. dirs.), Chesapeake Acad. Found. (vice-chmn. 1988—), Jamestowne Soc., Peninsula C. of C. (past bd. dirs.), Broadcast Pioneers, Sigma Alpha Epsilon. Clubs: James River Country, Hampton Yacht, Peninsula Exec.'s (past pres., bd. dirs.); Town Point. Lodge: Kiwanis (past bd. dirs., pres., lt. gov.). Home: 35 N Boxwood St Hampton VA 23669-2401

BRAUER, RHONDA LYN, lawyer; b. Gary, Ind., Nov. 23, 1959; d. Hugh Donald and Charlotte Gloria (Danzig) B.; m. Gregory John Holch, Sept. 7, 1989; children: Jillian Brauer Holch, Justin Brauer Holch. BA magna cum laude, Cornell U., 1981; JD magna cum laude, Ind. U., 1984. Bar: N.Y. 1985, U.S. Dist. Ct. (so. and ea. dist.) N.Y. 1991, U.S. Supreme Ct. 1992. Assoc. Cleary, Gottlieb, Steen & Hamilton, N.Y.C., 1984-86, 89-92, Brussels, 1986-88; asst. sec. and sr. counsel The New York Times Co., N.Y.C., 1992—. Contbr. articles to profl. jours. Pro bono work Lawyers Com. for Human Rights, N.Y.C., 1984-86, ACLU, 1989-90, Vol. Lawyers for the Arts, N.Y.C., 1989-92, N.Y. Lawyers for the Pub. Interest, 1992-95. Recipient Anne MacIntyre Litchfield prize of history Cornell U. Coll. Arts and Scis., 1981; Salzburg (Austria) Seminar fellow, 1988. Mem. Assn. Bar City N.Y., N.Y. Women's Bar Assn. Avocations: swimming, hiking, film.

BRAUER, RIMA LOIS, psychiatrist; b. Bklyn., Feb. 5, 1938; d. Gerald and Freeda (Rubin) Rubenstein; m. Lee David Brauer, Dec. 29, 1959; children: Samuel, Jennifer, Nathan. BA, Goucher Coll., 1959; MD, U. Md., 1964. Biochemistry researcher Sinai Hosp., Balt., 1958-60; med. intern Montefiore Hosp., Bronx, N.Y., 1964-65; psychiatry resident Yale Sch. Medicine, New Haven, Conn., 1966-69, child fellow, 1969-72; psychoanalyst Western New England Inst. for Psychoanalysis, New Haven, 1977-84; pvt. practice Hartford, Conn., 1984—; clin. faculty Yale Sch. Medicine, New Haven, 1973-84, U. Conn. Sch. Medicine, Hartford, 1984—. Mem. Am. Psychoanalytic Assn. (com. on analytic practice 1991—), Western New Eng. Inst. Psychoanalysis (pres. 1998—), N.Y. Acad. Sci. Office: 2 Hartford Sq W Hartford CT 06106-5105

BRAUER, STEPHEN FRANKLIN, manufacturing company executive; b. St. Louis, Sept. 3, 1945; s. Arthur John, Jr. and Jane (Franklin) B.; m. Camilla Cary Thompson, June 12, 1971; children: Blackford Fitzhugh, Rebecca Randolph, Stephen Franklin. Student Washington and Lee U., 1963-64; BA, Westminster Coll., 1967; LLD (hon.), 1997. Sales and mktg. ofcl. Hunter Engrng. Co., St. Louis, 1971-78, exec. v.p., 1978-81, pres., 1981—; bd. dirs. Boatmen's Trust Co., St. Louis, 1986-96; ptnr. St. Louis Cardinals baseball club, 1996—; pvt. client bd. Nation's Bank, 1996—. Civilian aide Sec. Army, 1991-95; trustee Mo. Bot. Garden, Washington U., St. Louis; mem. Mo. 21st Jud. Dist. Commn., 1992-96; hon. consul Govt. Belgium, 1987—; mem. St. Louis Consular Corps.; mem. nat. bd. Smithsonian Inst., Washington. Served to 1st lt. C.E., AUS, 1968-70. Recipient St. Louis Regional Commerce Growth Assn. Tech. award, 1993, Recognition of Outstanding Bus. Leadership award U.S. Ho. of Reps., 1993, Dean's award Washington U. Sch. Engrng., 1998. Republican. Episcopalian. Clubs: St. Louis Country, St. Louis, Log Cabin. Home: 13501 Ladue Rd Saint Louis MO 63141-7212 Office: 11250 Hunter Dr Bridgeton MO 63044-2306

BRAUGHER, ANDRE, actor; b. Chgo., July 1, 1962; m. Amy Brabson; 1 son, Michael. MA, Julliard Coll. TV series include: Kojak (ABC Saturday Mystery), 1989-90, Homicide: Life on the Street, 1993—; TV movies include: The Court-Martial of Jackie Robinson, 1990, Murder in Mississippi, 1990, Somebody Has to Shoot the Picture, 1990, Without Warning: Terror in the Towers, 1993, Simple Justice, 1993, Class of '61, 1993; film appearances include: Glory, 1989, Striking Distance, 1993, The Tuskegee Airmen, 1995, Primal Fear, 1996, Get on the Bus, 1996, City of Angels, 1998, Thick as Thieves, 1998; stage appearances include: Twelfth Night, 1989, Othello, 1990, The Way of the World, 1991, Richard II, 1994, Shakespeare in the Park, Festival in New York, Henry V. *

BRAUHN, RICHARD DANIEL, university administrator; b. Dubuque, Iowa, June 14, 1944; s. Leon Henry and Emma Henrietta (Holtmeyer) B.; m. Mary Ann Elizabeth Ceman, June 21, 1969; children: Richard Daniel II, David Michael, Caroline Ann, Sharon Marie. BA, U. No. Iowa, 1968, MA, 1970; PhD, U. N.D., 1979. Cert. secondary sch. social scis. tchr., life, Iowa. Social sci. instr. Clinton (Iowa) H.S., 1970-72, Clinton C.C., 1972-77; dean of instr. Wabash Valley Coll., Mt. Carmel, Ill., 1979-82; v.p. acad. affairs Mount Marty Coll., Yankton, S.D., 1982-86; Dean of West Plains campus S.W. Mo. State U., Springfield, Mo., 1986-91; dean Coll. Arts and Scis. Dickinson (N.D.) State U., 1991-94, v.p. for acad. affairs, 1995—; interim pres. Dickinson State U., 1998-99; asst. coach Clinton H.S. Baseball State Champs, 1972; mem. Blue Ribbon Task Force on Higher Edn., S.D., 1984-86, Bur. Land Mgmt., Adv. Com. Dickinson Region W., N.E. Mont., 1993—. Author: (book) The Prarie du Chien, Dubuque, Galena Region, 1979; also book chpt. Ethical Management of Human Resources, 1994, articles to Ducks Unlimited Mag., 1974, 76. Pres. St. Joseph Roman Cath. Ch. Parish Coun., Dickinson, 1992-96; mem. N.D. State Humanities Coun., Bismarck, 1992-98, chmn. 1996-98; pres. Sch. Bd. Trinity H.S., Dickinson, N.D., 1995-98; Chmn. Democratic Orgn., Dist. 36, Dickinson, 1994. With U.S. Army, 1962-64, Viet Nam. Decorated First Class medal for gallantry with palm, Republic of S. Viet Nam, 1964, Meritorious unit citation and Purple Heart, U.S. Army, 1964; recipient 3 higher Edn. scholarships, N.D. State Bd. Higher Edn., 1977, 78, 79, 20 Yr. Svc. award Fedn. of State Humanities Couns., 1997. Mem. K.C. (4th degree Grand Knight 1995), VFW, Am. Legion, Am. Assn. U. Adminstrs., Rotary Club, Dickinson. Democrat. Avocations: hunting, fishing, athletic sports, gardening, photography. Home: 3261 Lakeview Dr Dickinson ND 58601-7213 Office: Dickinson State U Office Acad Affairs Dickinson ND 58601-4896

BRAULT, G(AYLE) LORAIN, healthcare executive; b. Chgo., Jan. 3, 1944; d. Theodore Frank and Victoria Jean (Pribyl) Hahn; m. Donald R. Brault, Apr. 29, 1971; 1 child, Kevin David. AA, Long Beach City Coll., 1963; BS, Calif. State U.-Long Beach, 1973, MS, 1977. RN, Calif; cert. nurse practitioner. Dir. nursing Canyon Gen. Hosp., Anaheim, Calif., 1973-76; dir. faculty critical care masters degree program Calif. State U., Long Beach, 1976-79; regional dir.. nursing and support svcs. Western region Am. Med. Internat., Anaheim, Calif., 1979-83; v.p. Hosp. Home Care Corp. Am., Santa Ana, Calif., 1983-85; pres. Hosp. Home Health Care Agy. Calif., Torrance, 1986-92; v.p. Healthcare Assn. So. Calif., L.A., 1993—; invited lectr. China Nurses Assn., 1983; cons. AMI, Inc., Saudi Arabia, 1983; advisor dept. grad. nursing Calif. State U., L.A., 1988, advisor Nursing Inst., 1990-91; guest lectr. dept. pub. health UCLA, 1986-87; assoc. clin. prof. U. So. Calif., 1988—; lectr. Calif. State U., L.A., 1996-97; editl. advisor RN Times, Nurseweek, 1988—, chmn. editl. adv. bd.; bd. dirs. Health and Human Svcs., City of Long Beach, Calif., 1997—. Contbr. articles to profl. jours., chpts. to books. Commr. HHS, Washington, 1988; bd. of Health & Humas Svcs. City of Long Beach, Calif., 1997—. HEW advanced nurse tng. grantee, 1978. Mem. Women in Health Adminstrn. (sec. 1989, v.p. 1990), Nat. Assn. Home Care, Am. Orgn. Nursing Execs., Calif. Assn. Health Svcs. at Home (task force chmn. 1988, bd. dirs. 1988-93, chmn. bd. dirs. 1990-93), Calif. League Nursing (bd. sec. 1983, program chmn. 1981-82), Am. Coll. Health Care Execs., ASAE, AONE, Phi Kappa Phi, Sigma Theta Tau. Republican. Methodist. Home: 1032 E Andrews Dr Long Beach CA 90807-2406

BRAULT, GERARD JOSEPH, French language educator; b. Chicopee Falls, Mass., Nov. 7, 1929; s. Philias J. and Aline E. (Rémillard) B.; m. Jeanne Lambert Pepin, Jan. 23, 1954; children: Francis Gerard, Anne-Marie, Suzanne Eveline. A.B., Assumption Coll., Worcester, Mass., 1950, D. Litt., 1976; A.M. cum laude, Laval U., 1952; Ph.D., U. Pa., 1958. Teaching fellow U. Pa., 1954-56, assoc. prof. Romance langs., 1961-65, vice dean Grad. Sch., 1962-65; instr. French Bowdoin Coll., Brunswick, Maine, 1957-59, asst. prof. French, 1959-61; prof. French Pa. State U., University Park, 1965-90, Disting. prof. French and medieval studies, 1990, Edwin Erle Sparks prof. French and medieval studies, 1990-97, head dept. French, 1965-70, Edwin Erle Sparks prof. emeritus French and medieval studies, 1998—; fellow Inst. Arts and Humanistic Studies, 1976—; dir. NDEA Summer Insts., Bowdoin Coll., 1961, 62, Assumption Coll., 1964; Fulbright fellow, Strasbourg, France, 1956-57, Fulbright rsch. scholar and Guggenheim fellow, Strasbourg, 1968-69; sr. fellow in Can. studies, Quebec City, 1984, Camargo Found. fellow, Cassis, France, 1987, 94. Author: Celestine: A Critical Edition of the First French Translation (1527) of the Spanish Classic La Celestina, 1963, Cours de langue française destiné aux jeunes Franco-Américains, 1963, rev. edits., 1965, 69, Early Blazon, 1972, rev. edit., 1997, Eight Thirteenth-Century Rolls of Arms in French and Anglo-Norman Blazon, 1973 (prix Paul Adam-Even), The Song of Roland: An Analytical Edition (named outstanding book Choice 1979), 2 vols., 1978, La Chanson de Roland: Student Edition, 1984; The French-Canadian Heritage in New England, 1986, Rolls of Arms of Edward I (1272-1307) (Aspilogia III), 2 vols., 1997 (Bickersteth medal, Riquer prize); mem. editl. bd. French Forum, 1975—, Purdue U. Monographs, 1978—; contbr. articles to profl. jours. Mem. Cath. Commn. on Intellectual and Cultural Affairs, also, Comité de Vie Franco-Américaine, Société Historique Franco-Américaine. Served with CIC, U.S. Army, 1951-53. Decorated Palmes Académiques French Ministry Edn., 1965, officer, 1975; officer, Ordre National du Mérite, 1980, Ordre des Francophones d'Amérique, 1980; recipient Faculty Scholar medal Pa. State U., 1981, Class of 1933 Humanities award, Pa. State U., 1987. Fellow Soc. Antiquaries of London, Heraldry Soc. London, Medieval Acad. Am. (adv. bd. Speculum 1972-75), Académie Internationale d'Héraldique; mem. MLA, Société Rencesvals pour l'étude des épopées romanes (pres. 1985-88, pres. Am.-Canadian br. 1970-73, editorial bd. Olifant 1975—), Am. Assn. Tchrs. French, Assn. for Can. Studies in U.S., Middle Atlantic Conf. Canadian Studies (pres. 1981-83), Internat. Arthurian Soc., Harleian Soc. (council 1987-98). Home: 705 Westerly Pky State College PA 16801-4227 Office: Pa State U Burrowes Bldg Rm 325 University Park PA 16802

BRAULT, JAMES WILLIAM, physicist; b. New London, Wis., Feb. 10, 1932; s. Lucian Joseph and Alvina Lucy (Boville) B.; m. Margueritte Elaine Bryan, June 29, 1952 (div. May 1986); children: Stephen Michael, Lisa Lynn, Jennifer Elaine; m. Lynda Margaret Harris Faires, July 5, 1992. BS in Physics, U. Wis., 1953; student, Cornell U., 1953-55; PhD in Physics, Princeton U., 1962. Research staff member project Matterhorn Princeton U., N.J., 1955-57, instr., 1961-64; asst. physicist Kitt Peak Nat. Obs., Tucson, 1964-68, assoc. physicist, 1969-70; physicist Nat. Solar Obs., Tucson, 1971-94; rsch. assoc. U. Colo., Boulder, Colo., 1994—. Contbr. articles to profl. jours. Recipient Alexander von Humboldt award (Rep. of Germany), 1986-87. Fellow Optical Soc. Am.; mem. Am. Phys. Soc., Am. Geophysical Union. Democrat. Address: 1006 Honeysuckle Ln Louisville CO 80027-1096*

BRAUMAN, JOHN I., chemist, educator; b. Pitts., Sept. 7, 1937; s. Milton and Freda E. (Schlitt) B.; m. Sharon Lea Kruse, Aug. 22, 1964; 1 dau., Kate Andrea. BS, MIT, 1959; PhD (NSF fellow), U. Calif., Berkeley, 1963. NSF postdoctoral fellow UCLA, 1962-63; asst. prof. chemistry Stanford (Calif.) U., 1963-69, asso. prof., 1969-72, prof., 1972-80, J.G. Jackson-C.J. Wood prof. chemistry, 1980—, chmn. dept., 1979-83, 95-96; cons. in phys. organic chemistry; adv. panel chemistry divsn. NSF, 1974-78; adv. panel NASA, AEC, ERDA, Rsch. Corp., Office Chemistry and Chem. Tech., NRC; coun. Gordon Rsch. Confs., 1989-95, trustee, 1991-95. Mem. editl. adv. bd. Jour. Am. Chem. Soc., 1976-83, Jour. Organic Chemistry, 1974-78, Nouveau Jour. de Chimie, 1977-85, Chem. Revs., 1978-80, Chem. Kinetics, 1987-89, Accts. Chem. Rsch., 1995-97, 98—, Ann. Revs., 1995—; dep. editor for phys. scis. Sci., 1985—. Fellow Alfred P. Sloan, 1968-70, Guggenheim, 1978-79; Christensen, Oxford U., 1983-84. Fellow AAAS (chmn. sect. 1996-97, mem.-at-large sect. 1997—), Calif. Acad. Scis. (hon.); mem. NAS, Am. Acad. Arts and Scis., Am. Chem. Soc. (award in pure chemistry 1973, Harrison Howe award, 1976, R.C. Fuson award, 1986, James Flack Norris award 1986, Arthur C. Cope scholar, 1986, exec. com. phys. chemistry divsn., com. on sci. 1992-97), Brit. Chem. Soc., Sigma Xi, Phi Lambda Upsilon. Home: 849 Tolman Dr Palo Alto CA 94305-1025 Office: Stanford U Dept Chemistry Stanford CA 94305-5080

BRAUMILLER, ALLEN SPOONER, oil and gas exploration company executive, geologist; b. Texarkana, Tex., Feb. 1, 1934; s. Jack and Jennie (Spooner) B.; m. Patsy Lois McCoy, Dec. 23, 1955; children: Allen Spooner Jr., Dana Ruth Braumiller Nance, Adrienne Brevard, Colin McCoy. Student Tulane U., 1952-53; BS, U. Miss., 1955; MS, U. Ill., 1957. Sr. exploration geologist Carter Oil Co. (merged into Humble Oil & Refining Co. 1961), 1957-69; v.p., exploration geologist Helmerich & Payne, Inc., Tulsa, 1969-96, ret., 1996; pres. Braumiller & Braumiller, Inc., Tulsa, 1995—; mgr. East Tex. Seismic Data, LLC, Tulsa, 1996—; geol. cons. No. Ill. Natural Gas, Urbana, 1956-57. Elder area Presbyn. ch. Mem. Internat. Assn. Energy Advs., Internat. Platform Assn., Philbrook Mus. of Art, Tulsa, Thomas Gilcrease Mus., Tulsa. Mem. Am. Assn. Petroleum Geologists, Geol. Soc. Am., Am. Assn. Profl. Landmen, Ill. Geol. Soc., Okla. City Geol. Soc., Tulsa Geol. Soc. (del. to AAPG 1989—), Soc. Petroleum Engrs., Internat. Wine and Foods Soc., Tulsa C. of C., U.S. C. of C., Nat. Trust for Hist. Preservation, Knife and Fork Club, Petroleum Club (bd. dirs. 1989-92). Republican. Avocations: reef diving, cycling, swimming, gardening, music. Home: 4979 E 113th St Tulsa OK 74137-7607 also: Braumiller & Braumiller Inc Philtower Bldg 427 S Boston Ave Ste 1308 Tulsa OK 74103-4118

BRAUN, BENJAMIN, basketball coach; b. Chgo., 1953. BA in English, U. Wis., 1975; MA in Guidance & Counseling, Siena Heights Coll., 1980. Asst. coach Park H.S., Racine, Wis.; head basketball coach Siena Heights Coll., 1977-1984, tchr. English, phys. edn.; assoc. head coach Ea. Mich. U., 1985, interim head coach, 1986-96; head coach U. Calif., Berkeley, 1996—; head coach U.S. men's basketball team Maccabiah Games, 1989. Named Pac-10 Coach Yr., 1997; finalist Nat. Coach Yr., 1997. Office: U Calif 210 Memorial Stadium Berkeley CA 94720-4426*

BRAUN, BENNETT GEORGE, psychiatrist; b. Chgo., Aug. 7, 1940; s. Milton L. and Thelma H. (Gimbel) B.; m. Renate E. Deutsch, Sept. 1, 1963 (div. April 1984); children: Eric, Tamara; m. Jane E. Epstein, June 22, 1986; children: Robyn, Alex, Megan. BS, Tulane U., 1963, MS in psychology, 1964; MD, U. Ill., 1968. Diplomate Am. Coll. Forensic Examiners, Am. Bd. Psychiatry and Neurology, Am. Bd. Med. Hypnosis. Rotating med. intern Michael Reese Hosp., Chgo., 1968-69; resident in psychiatry U. Chgo. Hosp., 1969-71, Rush-Presbyterian-St. Lukes Med. Ctr., Chgo., 1982-84; psychiatrist, administrator Assoc. Psychotherapists of Chgo., 1973-75; med. dir. Assn. Mental Health Svcs., Chgo., 1975-95; practice dir. Apogee, Inc., Chgo., 1995-97; med. dir. Assocs. in Behavioral Medicine Ltd., Skokie, Ill., 1997—; dir. Dissociative Disorders Program sect. on psychiat. trauma Rush-Presbyn. St. Luke's Med. Ctr., 1994-98; med. dir. dissociative disorders program inpatient unit Rush North Shore Med. Ctr., 1989-98; cons. in hypnosis Am. Soc. for Clin. Hypnosis. Editor: Treatment of Multiple Personality, 1986, Society for the Study of Dissociation (newsletter) 1984-97, Dissociation (annual abstract book) 1984-95; assoc. editor Dissociation (jour.) 1988—; asst. editor American Journal Clinical Hypnosis, 1987—; contbr. over 100 articles and book chpts. Asst. scoutmaster Boy Scouts Am. 505, Chgo., 1964-66. Major, US Army, 1971-73. Recipient Army Commendation medal U.S. Army, 1973, Elena D. Benedetto de Sabelli award for achievement in biol. psychiatry, 1984, Cornelia B. Wilbur award, 1987, Pres.' award, 1989, Disting. Svc. award, 1996, Morton Prince award for scientific achievement, Internat. Soc. Study of Dissociation, 1991, Best Doctors in Am. areas of post traumatic stress disorder and dissociative disorder (2 categories), 1992, 93, 94, 95, Best Doctors MidWest, 1996-97, in post traumatic stress disorder, dissociative disorders and affective disorders (3 categories). Fellow Am. Soc. Clin. Hypnosis (1st v.p. 1975-91), Internat. Soc. for Study Dissociation (pres. 1984-96), Am. Orthopsychiatric Assn., Soc. for Clin. and Experimental Hypnosis; mem. Am. Psychiatry Assn., Internat. Soc. Traumatic Stress Studies. Avocations: scubadiving, skiing, horseback riding, skydiving. Office: Assocs in Behavioral Medicine 9701 Knox Ave Ste 103 Skokie IL 60076-1230

BRAUN, CHARLES LOUIS, chemistry educator, researcher; b. Webster, S.D., June 4, 1937; s. Louis Fred and Myrene Clarise (Strand) B.; m. Kathleen Louise Brickel, Aug. 10, 1958; children: Sarah Kathryn, David Charles. B.S., S.D. Sch. Mines and Tech., Rapid City, 1959; Ph.D., U. Minn., 1963; M.A. (hon.), Dartmouth Coll., 1978. Instr. chemistry Dartmouth Coll., 1965-66, asst. prof., 1966-71, assoc. prof., 1971-77, prof., 1977—, chmn. dept., 1982-85; vis. prof. U. Stuttgart, 1969-70, Cornell U., 1980-81, U. Calif. San Diego, 1993, U. Rochester, 1993; cons. Eastman Kodak Co., Rochester, N.Y., 1979-93, Exxon Rsch. and Engring. Lab., 1984-90; co-chmn. Gordon Rsch. Conf. on Photoconductivity, 1982, Dartmouth Presdl. Search Com., 1986-87; chmn. Gordon Rsch. Conf. on Radiation Chemistry, 1992; vis. scientist Nat. Renewable Energy Lab., 1998. Contbr. articles to profl. jours. Served to 1st lt. U.S. Army, 1963-65. Recipient Centennial award S.D. Sch. Mines and Tech., 1985, Dartmouth Disting. Teaching award 1987, Catalyst award Chem. Mfrs. Assn., 1991; grantee NSF, 1966-79; grantee Petroleum Research Found., 1981-85, Dept. Energy, 1983—; named N.H. Prof. of Yr., 1992. Mem. Am. Chem. Soc., Am. Phys. Soc. Home: 28 Hawk Pine Rd Norwich VT 05055-9634 Office: Dartmouth Coll Dept Chemistry 6128 Burke Lab Hanover NH 03755

BRAUN, DAVID A(DLAI), lawyer; b. N.Y.C., Apr. 23, 1931; s. Morris and Betty Braunstein; m. Merna Feldman, Dec. 18, 1955; children: Lloyd Jeffrey, Kenneth Franklin, Evan Albert. AB, Columbia U., 1952, LLB, 1954. Bar: N.Y. 1955, Calif. 1974. Assoc. Ellis, Ellis and Ellis, N.Y.C., 1954-56, Davis and Gilbert, 1956-57; ptnr. Pryor, Cashman, Sherman and Flynn, 1957-73; ptnr. Hardee, Barovick, Konecky & Braun, N.Y.C., 1973, L.A., 1974-81; pres., CEO Polygram Records, Inc., N.Y.C., 1980-81; counsel Wyman, Bautzer, Rothman, Kuchel & Silbert, L.A., 1982-85; ptnr. Braun, Margolis, Burrill & Besser, L.A., 1985-87; counsel Silverberg, Rosen, Leon & Behr, 1987-89, Silverberg, Katz, Thompson & Braun, 1989-91; spl. counsel Proskauer, Rose, Goetz & Mendelsohn, 1991-93; ptnr. Monasch Plotkin & Braun, 1993-94; pvt. practice, 1994-98; sr. counsel Akin, Gump, Strauss, Hauer & Feld, L.L.P., 1998—. Bd. visitors Columbia Coll., Columbian Law Sch.; bd. dirs. Reprise! Broadway's Best in Concert, Musician's Assistance Program. Mem. Assn. of City of N.Y., L.A. County Bar Assn., Beverly Hills Bar Assn., NATAS, Am. Arbitration Assn., Sigma Chi, Phi Alpha Delta. Jewish. Home: 211 S Spalding Dr Apt 401S Beverly Hills CA 90212-3664 Office: Akin Gump Strauss Hauer & Feld LLP Ste 2600 2029 Century Park St Los Angeles CA 90067

BRAUN, DAVID JOSEPH, financial executive; b. Perryville, Mo., Apr. 17, 1957; s. Robert Joseph and Mildred Ann Braun; m. Karen Denise Wilson, Mar. 30, 1992; children: Jessica Renee, Jayme Rachel. BSBA, Columbia Coll., 1979. Asst. contr. RC Cement Co., Inc., St. Louis, 1980-92; CFO Risk Analysis & Mgmt. Corp., St. Louis, 1992-93, Am. Pulverizer Co., St. Louis, 1993—. Soccer coach Holy Infant Parish, St. Louis, 1994—; t-ball coach Ellisville Athletic Assn., St. Louis, 1998—. Republican. Avocations: soccer, golf. E-mail: wilbra4@aol.com. Home: 1604 Stone Hollow Wildwood MO 63038

BRAUN, EUNICE HOCKSPEIER, author, religious order executive, lecturer; b. Alta Vista, Iowa; d. George Phillip and Lydia (Reinhart) Hockspeier; student Gates Coll., 1932-34, Coe Coll., 1941-43, Northwestern U., 1944-47; m. Leonard James Braun, May 29, 1937. Freelance writer for mags., newspapers, 1947-52; bus. mgr. Baha'i Publishing Trust, Wilmette, Ill., 1952-55, mng. dir., 1955-71; internat. news editor Baha'i News, 1952-70; tchr. Baha'i schs., Alaska, Can., Europe and U.S., 1958—; lectr. Baha'i Faith in U.S., Central Am., Europe, Africa, Asia, 1953—; cons. Baha'i Pub. Trust, New Delhi, India, 1972; mem. aux. bd. Continental Bd. Counselors, Baha'i Faith in the Ams., 1972-86. Mem. Nat. League Am. Pen Women, Baha'i Faith, Iota Sigma Epsilon. Author: Know Your Baha'i Literature, 1959; The Dawn of World Peace, 1963; Baha'u'llah: His Call to the Nations, 1967; From Strength to Strength, Half Century of the Formative Age of the Baha'i Faith, 1978; A Crown of Beauty, 1982; The March of the Institutions, 1984; A Reader's Guide: The Development of Baha'i Literature in English, 1986; From Vision to Victory, 1993; contbr. essays to Baha'i World, Internat. Record. Home: 1025 Forestview Ln Glenview IL 60025-4433

BRAUN, JEFFREY LOUIS, lawyer; b. N.Y.C., Oct. 2, 1946; s. Arthur and Berta (Freimark) B.; m. Beth Essig, June 6, 1982; children: Arthur Paul, Emily Claire. BA, Rutgers U., 1968; JD, Yale U., 1971. Bar: N.Y. 1974, U.S. Dist. Ct. (so. and ea. dists.) N.Y., U.S. Tax Ct., U.S. Ct. Appeals (2d cir.), U.S. Supreme Ct. Law clk. to Judge Harry Pregerson U.S. Dist. Ct. (cen. dist.) Calif., L.A., 1971-72; assoc. Paul, Weiss, Rifkind, Wharton & Garrison, N.Y.C., 1972-74; assoc. Rosenman & Colin LLP, N.Y.C., 1974-80, ptnr., 1980—. Mem. Assn. of the Bar of the City of N.Y. (com. on internat. human rights 1985-88, com. on mcpl. affairs 1988-91, com. on recruitment and retention of lawyers 1992-94, long-range planning com. 1994-97), Fed. Bar Coun. (com. on cts. of the second cir. 1995—). Home: 1 Gracie Sq # 2E New York NY 10028-8001 Office: Rosenman & Colin LLP 575 Madison Ave New York NY 10022-2585

BRAUN, JEROME IRWIN, lawyer; b. St. Joseph, Mo., Dec. 16, 1929; s. Martin H. and Bess (Donsker) B.; children: Aaron, Susan, Daniel; m. Dolores Ferriter, Aug. 16, 1987. AB with distinction, Stanford U., 1951, LLB, 1953. Bar: Mo. 1953, Calif. 1953, U.S. Dist. Ct. (no. dist.) Calif., U.S. Tax Ct., U.S. Ct. Mil. Appeals, U.S. Supreme Ct., U.S. Ct. Appeals (9th cir.). Assoc. Long & Levit, San Francisco, 1957-58, Law Offices of Jefferson Peyser, San Francisco, 1958-62; founding ptnr. Farella, Braun & Martel (formerly Elke, Farella & Braun), San Francisco, 1962—; instr. San Francisco Law Sch., 1958-69; mem. U.S. Dist. Ct. Civil Justice Reform Act Adv. Com., 1991—; spkr. various state bar convs. in Calif., Ill., Nev., Mont.; request moderator/participant continuing edn. of bar pgorams; past chmn. 9th Cir. Sr. Adv. Bd., past chmn. lawyer reps. to 9th Cir. Jud. Conf.; mem. appellate lawyers liaison com. Calif. Ct. Appeals 1st dist.; jud.conf. U.S. Com. Long Range Planning; founder Jon Samuel Abramson Scholarship Endowment Stanford U. Law. Revising editor: Stanford U. Law Rev.; contbr. articles to profl. jours. Mem. Jewish Community Fedn. San Francisco, The Peninsula, Marin and Sonoma Counties, pres., 1979-80; past pres. United Jewish Community Ctrs. 1st lt. JAGC, U.S. Army, 1954-57, U.S. Army Res., 1957-64. Recipient Lloyd W. Dinkelspiel Outstanding Young Leader award Jewish Welfare Fedn., 1967, Professionalism award 9th cir. Am. Inns of Ct., 1999. Fellow Am. Acad. Appellate Lawyers; mem. ABA, Am. Bar Found., Calif. Bar Assn. (chmn. adminstrn. justice com. 1977), Bar Assn. San Francisco (spl. com. on lawyers malpractice and malpractice ins.), San Francisco Bar Found. (past trustee), Calif. Acad. Appellate Lawyers (past pres., mem. U.S. Dist. Ct. Civil Justice Refomr Act adv. com., Calif. Ct. of Appeals 1st Dist. Appellate Lawyers liaison com., jud. conf. of the U.S., com. on long-range planning, panelist 1994), Am. Judicature Soc. (past dir.), Stanford Law Sch. Bd. of Visitors, Am. Coll. Trial Lawyers (teaching trial and appellate advocacy com.), U.S. Dist. Ct. of No. Dist. Calif. Hist. Soc. (past pres., bd. dirs.), 9th Cir. Ct. of Appeals Hist. Soc. (past. pres.), Mex.-Am. Legal Def. Fund (honoree), Order of Coif.

BRAUN, KAZIMIERZ PAWEL, theatrical director, writer, educator; b. Mokrsko Dolne, Kielce, Poland, June 29, 1936; came to U.S., 1985; s. Juliusz and Elzbieta (Szymanowska) B.; m. Zofia M. Reklewska, July 15, 1962; children: Monika Braun Beres, Grzegorz, Justyna. M in Letters, Poznan U., Poland, 1958, PhD, 1971; MFA in Directing, Sch. Drama, Warsaw, Poland, 1962; PhD in Theatre, Wroclaw (Poland) U., 1975. Prof., dir. Teatr Polski, Warsaw, 1962-64, Teatr Horzycy, Torun, Poland, 1965-67; artistic dir., gen. mgr. Teatr Osterwy, Lublin, Poland, 1967-74, Contemporary Theatre, Wroclaw, 1975-84; head of acting program SUNY, Buffalo, 1987-90, prof. dept theater and dance, 1989—; prof. Wroclaw U., 1974-85, Sch. Drama, Wroclaw, 1978-85; vis. prof. NYU, 1985, Swarthmore Coll., Pa., 1985-86; regents prof. U. Calif., Santa Cruz, 1986. Dir. plays U.S., Poland, Germany, Ireland. Recipient Japanese Found. award, Tokyo, 1981, Guggenheim Found. award, 1990; Best Dir. award, Critics Com., Wroclaw, 1976, 80, 84, 85; named Prof. in Poland by Pres. Lech Walesa, 1992. Mem. Internat. Theatre Inst. (Young Dir. award 1961), Actors Union Poland, Writers Union Poland, PEN Club. Roman Catholic. Avocation: travel. Office: SUNY Dept Theater and Dance 278 Alumni Arena Amherst NY 14260-6030

BRAUN, LUDWIG, educational technology consultant; b. Bklyn., May 14, 1926; s. Ludwig and Wetie (Schmidt) B.; m. Eva Margaret Taylor, Sept. 7, 1947; children: Barbara Ann, Edith Elizabeth, Anne Catherine, John Ludwig. BEE, Poly. Inst. Bklyn., 1950, MEE, 1955, DEE, 1959. Elec. engr. Allied Control Co., N.Y.C., 1950-51; head electronics dept. Anton Electronics Labs., Inc., Bklyn., 1951-55; from instr. elec. engring. to prof. sys. and elec. engring. Poly. Inst. Bklyn., 1955-72; prof. engring. SUNY, Stony Brook, 1972-82, dir. bioengring. program, 1976-79, dir. personal computers in edn. lab., 1979-82; prof. computer sci., dir. acad. computing lab. N.Y. Inst. Tech., Central Islip, 1982-87; rsch. prof. NYU, N.Y.C., 1987-89; ret., 1989; adj. prof. C.W. Post Campus, L.I.U., 1998—; dir. Nat. Inst. Microcomputer Based Learning, 1981-87, Intercounty Tchr. Resource Ctr., 1985-87, Mecklenburger Group, 1993-96; lectr., med. scientist Downstate Med. Ctr., 1970-82; cons. ednl. tech., 1990—, Vertol divsn. Boeing Co., GE, Ford Found., NSF, Nat. Inst. Edn., IBM, NET Schs., Inc.; tech. advisor Orton Soc., Suffolk. Author: (with E. Mishkin) Adaptive Control Systems, 1961; contbg. author: Signals and Systems in Electrical Engineering, 1962, Perry's Chemical Engineering Handbook, 1961, System Engineering Handbook, 1965, Computer Techniques in Biomedicine and Medicine, 1973, Vision Test Recommendations for American Education Decision Makers, 1990, Celebrating Success, 1995. Mem. Women's Action Alliance, 1985-88; bd. dirs. Playing To Win, Inc., 1983-90, Internat. Coun. for Computers in Edn., 1987-89. With AUS, 1944-46. First recipient Paul Pair award for contbns. to edn. through tech.; fellow Global Village Schs. Inst., 1996—. Mem. IEEE (sr. 1990), Internat. Soc. for Tech. in Edn. (bd. dirs. 1989-90), Sigma Xi, Tau Beta Pi, Eta Kappa Nu. Home: 11 Parsons Dr Dix Hills NY 11746-5217

BRAUN, NEIL S., communications executive. BA, U. Pa., 1974; JD, U. Chgo., 1977. Corp. atty. Paul, Weiss, Rifkind, Wharton & Garrison, 1977-78; sr. v.p., gen. counsel Internat. Film Investors, N.Y., 1978-82; dir. motion picture planning HBO, 1982, v.p. motion picture planning, 1983, sr. v.p. film programming; exec. v.p. HBO Video; pres., COO Image Films Entertainment, Inc.; sr. v.p. corp. devel. & planning Viacom Entertainment, 1988-92, chmn., CEO, mem. ops. com., 1992-94; pres. NBC TV Network, N.Y.C., 1994-98; pres., CEO iCast Corp., N.Y.C., 1998—; bd. dirs. Advt. Coun., Inc. Mem. adv. bd. Children's Health Fund; bd. trustees Rheedlen Ctrs. Children & Families. Office: iCast Corp 304 Park Ave S 11th Fl New York NY 10010*

BRAUN, RETO, computer systems company executive; b. 1941. With Memorex Internat., 1967-83; group pres. Memorex, 1983-84; exec. v.p. Unisys Corp., 1984-91, pres., COO, 1991-93; chmn. bd., pres., CEO Moore Corp. Ltd., Toronto, Ont., Can., 1993-97; CEO Swiss Post, Bern, Switzerland, 1998—. Office: Swiss Post, CH-3030 Bern Switzerland

BRAUN, STEPHEN HUGHES, psychologist; b. St. Louis, Nov. 20, 1942; s. William Lafon and Jane Louise Braun; 1 son, Damian Hughes. BA, Washington U., 1964, MA, 1965; PhD, U. Mo., Columbia, 1970. Fellow in clin. psychology USPHS, U. Mo., Columbia, 1970; asst. prof. psychology Calif. State U., Chico, 1970-71; dir. social learning divsn. Ariz. State Hosp., Phoenix, 1971-74; chief bur. planning and evaluation State of Ariz., Dept. Health Svcs., Phoenix, 1974-79; pres. Braun and Assocs., Scottsdale, 1979-95; v.p. Ariz. Healthcare, 1991-95; dir. clin. svcs. Cmty. Partnership So. Ariz., 1995-97; asst. prof. psychology Ariz. State U., 1971-79; v.p. ValueOptions, Phoenix, 1997—; vis. asst. prof. Ctr. of Criminal Justice, 1974-79, Ctr. for Pub. Affairs, 1979-81; cons. Law Enforcement Assistance Adminstrn., NIMH, Alcohol, Drug Abuse and Mental Health Adminstrn., State of Ariz. Dept. Health Svcs., Dept. Corrections, Dept. Econ. Security, and local and regional human svc. agys. Editl. cons.; contbr. articles to sci. and profl. publs. Grantee NIMH, 1971-74, State of Calif., 1971. Mem. APA, Sigma Xi. Home: 9724 E San Salvador Scottsdale AZ 85258

BRAUN, WILHELM, retired educator; b. June 29, 1921. PhD, U. Toronto, 1953. Prof. U. Rochester, N.Y., 1956-91, emeritus prof., 1991—. Author articles in fields of German lit. and criticism. Home: 415 Hillside Ave Rochester NY 14610

BRAUN, WILLIAM JOSEPH, life insurance underwriter; b. Belleville, Ill., May 21, 1925; s. Walter Charles and Florence (Lauer) B.; m. Elizabeth Ann Braun, July 7, 1951; children: Brian William (dec.), Roger Edward, Christopher Burnes, Thomas Barrett, Maura Tracey. B.S. in Mktg, U. Ill., 1949; grad., Inst. Life Ins. Mktg., So. Methodist U., 1950. CLU; chartered fin. cons.; accredited estate planner Nat. Assn. Estate Planners. Life underwriter Mass. Mut. Life Ins. Co., Decatur, Ill., 1949—; pres. Am. Soc. C.L.U.s, 1976-77; bd. dirs. Am. Coll. C.L.U.s, Bryn Mawr, Pa., 1975-78. Served with USNR, 1943-46. Decorated Navy Air medal. Life mem. Million Dollar Round Table; mem. Assn. Advanced Life Underwriters, Nat. Assn. Life Underwriters, Nat. Editl. Bd. Leaders Mag., Nat. Assn. Estate Planning Couns. (pres. 1985-86), KC, Decatur Club, Country Club Decatur, Decatur Athletic Club. Roman Catholic. Home: 4606 E Powers Blvd Decatur IL 62521-2549 Office: Mass Mutual Decatur Club Bldg 158 W Prairie Decatur IL 62523-1230

BRAUN, ZEV, motion picture and television producer; b. Chgo.; s. Julius and Charlotte (Brandau) B.; children: Benjamin, Jonathan, Jeremy; m. MayLing Cheng, Mar. 22, 1972; 1 child, Sue-Ling. Student, Roosevelt U., Chgo., Marquette U., U. Chgo. Producer: Goldstein, 1964 (U.S. rep. Cannes Film Festival, recipient Prix de la Nouvelle Critique), Wanted: Babysitter, 1974-75, The Little Girl Who Lives Down the Lane, 1976 (Best Horror Film, Acad. Sci-Fi, Fantasy and Horror Films), Freedom Road, 1978, The Fiendish Plot of Dr. Fu Manchu, 1979-80, Marlene, 1984 (Acad. award nomination, N.Y. Film Critics award Nat. Bd. Rev. award, Nat. Soc. Film Critics award), Where Are the Children, 1985, (TV mini-series) Menendez: A Killing in Beverly Hills, 1994; exec. prodr.: Madron, 1970, Angela, 1977, Murphy's Law, 1987, Stillwatch, 1987, Murder Ordained, 1987, Tour of Duty, 1987, 88, 89, Father Clements, 1987, (TV movie) Abducted: A Father's Love, 1996; co-prodr.: The Pedestrian, 1973 (Acad. award nomination, Nat. Bd. Rev. award, Golden Globe award), Bagdad Cafe, 1990, Seduction in Travis County, 1991, Split Images, 1992. Bd. dirs. Little City Found., Palatine, Ill., 1962-63; v.p., dir. Gastro-Intestinal Research Found., U. Chgo., 1964-65; v.p. City of Hope, 1970—; gen. chmn. Ann. Salute to Med. Research, 1969; chmn. bd. dirs. Internat. Kidney Inst., UCLA, 1981-83; bd. dirs. Am. Found. AIDS Rsch., 1995, Albert B. Sabin Inst. at Georgetown U., 1996. Jewish. Office: Braun Entertainment Group 280 S Beverly Dr Ste 500 Beverly Hills CA 90212-3908

BRAUNER, RONALD ALLAN, religion educator; b. Phila., Aug. 5, 1939; s. Samuel Joseph Brauner and Ann Ruth (Soloner) Levin; m. Marcia Faith Silver, Sept. 9, 1962; children: Yaakov Baruch, Miriam Aliza. Cert. in teaching, Greenberg Inst., Jerusalem, 1960; BS in Edn., Temple U., 1962; PhD, Dropsie Coll., 1974. Cert. tchr., Pa. Assoc. prof. Gratz Coll., Phila., 1967-78; acad. dean Reconstructionist Rabbinical Coll., Phila., 1972-83; dir. Brandeis-Bardin Inst., L.A., 1983-85; exec. dir. Hebrew Inst. Pitts., 1985-91; pres. Found. for Jewish Studies, Inc., Pitts., 1991—; prof. Jewish studies Cleve. Coll. Jewish Studies, 1994—. Editor Jewish Civilization: Essays and Studies, 1979-85, Straightalk, 1991—; author: Being Jewish in a Gentile World: A Survival Guide, 1995. Mem. Coun. for Jewish Edn. (v.p. 1990—), Coalition Alternatives in Jewish Edn., Am. Oriental Soc., Soc. Biblical Lit. Democrat. Office: Found for Jewish Studies 1531 S Negley Ave Pittsburgh PA 15217-1419

BRAUNGART, MARGARET MITCHELL, psychology educator; b. Washington, Jan. 1, 1942; d. Nelson Paul and Isabel (Carney) Mitchell; m. Richard G. Braungart, Aug. 29, 1964; children: Julia, Katherine, Elizabeth. BS in Elem. Edn., U. Md., 1964, MA in Human Devel., 1972; PhD in Psychology, Syracuse U., 1980. Instr. Syracuse (N.Y.) U., 1978-79; instr. SUNY Upstate Med. Ctr., Syracuse, 1976-79, asst. prof. psychology, 1979-84; assoc. prof. psychology SUNY Health Sci. Ctr., Syracuse, 1984-90, prof. psychology, 1990—, chair dept. health scis. and human studies, 1991-97; pres. gen. faculty assembly, SUNY Health Scis. Ctr., 1984-86; mem. exec. adv. com. for geriat., SUNY Health Scis. Ctr., 1982-95, mem. adv. bd. geriat. patients, 1987-89; co-dir. Life Course Rsch. Ctr., Syracuse U., 1985—; cons. WETA-TV, Washington, 1989, 91; lectr., cons. UN, N.Y.C., 1995—; lectr. SUNY Health Scis. Ctr. Coll. Medicine, 1996—. Editor: Political Sociology of the State, 1990; editor, author: Life Course and Generational Politics, 1993; editor, author (rsch. series) Research in Political Sociology, 1985-89; contbr. over 80 articles to profl. jours., chpts. to books; assoc. editor Jour. Polit. and Mil. Sociology, 1984—; mem. editl. bd. Rsch. in Polit. Sociology, 1990—. Citizen rep. Town of Manlius (N.Y.) Environ. Com., 1982-85. Rsch. grantee U.S. Dept. HEW, 1977-78, Ctr. Study Vietnam Generation, Washington, 1987. Mem. Internat. Soc. Polit. Psychology. Democrat. Roman Catholic. Avocations: walking, travel, reading. Home: 4783 Armstrong Rd Manlius NY 13104 Office: SUNY Health Sci Ctr 750 E Adams St Syracuse NY 13210-2399

BRAUNGART, RICHARD GOTTFRIED, sociology and international relations educator; b. Balt., Apr. 21, 1935; s. Paul Peter and Jean Mary (Stanton) B.; m. Margaret Lombard Mitchell, Aug. 29, 1964; children—Julia, Katherine, Elizabeth. BA, U. Md., College Park, 1961, MA, 1963; PhD, Pa. State U., State College, 1969. Research asst. Bur. Social Sci. Research, Washington, 1964; instr. sociology Pa. State U., State College, 1966-69; asst. prof. sociology U. Md., College Park, 1969-72; assoc. prof. sociology Syracuse U., N.Y., 1972-76, prof. sociology, 1976—, prof. internat. rels., 1993—; prof. polit. sci. Syracuse U., 1998—; rsch. dir. President's Commn. on Campus Unrest, 1970; vis. lectr. USIA, 1971; prof. assoc. East-West Ctr., Honolulu, 1978; lectr., cons. Nat. U. Mex., 1980, USSR Acad. Scis., Moscow, 1989; German Marshall Fund U.S., Berlin and Fed. Republic Germany, 1990, China Youth Coll. for Politics, Beijing Acad. Social Scis., Shanghai Ctr. Youth Rsch., Shanghai Acad. Social Scis., Ewha U., Seoul, Han Nam U., Taejon, Republic of Korea, 1991, Vista U., U, Pretoria, Potchefstroom U., U. Orange Free State, U. Port Elizabeth, Witwatersrand U., South Africa, 1992, UN, N.Y.C., 1995, 98. Author: Family Status, Socialization and Student Politics, 1979; editor: Society and Politics, 1976, Jour. Polit. and Mil. Sociology, 1983, Life Course and Generational Politics, 1984, 93, The Political Sociology of the State, 1990, Critical Issues in the U.S., 1997; series editor: Research in Political Sociology, 1985-89; assoc. editor Western Sociol. Rev., 1976-82, Sociol. Spectrum, 1980-83; book rev. editor Jour. Polit. and Mil. Sociology, 1977-84; mem. editl. bd. Sociol. Symposium, 1972-77, Polit. Behavior, 1978-84; Micropolitics, 1980-84; Quar. Jour. Ideology, 1983-90; mem. adv. bd. Internat. Jour. Comparative Sociology, 1992—. Served with U.S. Army, 1954-56. Mem. Am. Sociol. Assn. (polit. sociology sect. co-founder, treas. 1982-84, sect. coun. 1985-88, collective behavior sect. coun. 1984-86), Internat. Soc. Polit. Psychology (nominating com. 1983-84, chmn. nominating com. 1989-90. governing coun. 1989-91; chmn. search com. 1990-91), Internat. Sociol. Assn. (v.p. rsch. com. 1982-90, 98—, pres. com. polit. sociology 1994-98), Soc. Study Social Problems (chmn. internat. conflict and coop. divsn. 1984-86, chmn. com. stds, rsch., tchg. 1996-98), Internat. Polit. Sci. Assn. (pres. com. on polit. sociology 1994-98, v.p. rsch. com. 1998—). Democrat. Roman Catholic. Avocations: Gardening; jogging; travel. Home: 4783 Armstrong Rd Manlius NY 13104-1422 Office: Syracuse U Dept Sociology Syracuse NY 13244-1090

BRAUNSDORF, JAMES ALLEN, physics educator; b. South Bend, Ind., Apr. 13, 1938; s. Walter Louis and Ruth Harriet (Tuttle) B.; m. Donna Lou Munson, June 10, 1960; children: Kevin Scott, Allen Keith, Walter James. AB in Physics, De Pauw U., 1960; MS in Math., Purdue U., 1965. Cert. secondary tchr., Ind. Tchr. physics Greencastle Schs., 1960-62, Mishawaka (Ind.) Sch., 1962—; tax preparer, Mishawaka, 1967—; adj. lectr. Ind. U., South Bend, 1981-89. Pres. Beiger Heritage Corp., Mishawaka, 1981-86; active Youth for Understanding, 1990—. Mem. NEA, Ind. State Tchrs. Assn., Am. Assn. Physics Tchrs. (Ind. Disting. Physics Tchr. 1984), Nat. Sci. Tchrs. Assn., Mishawaka Edn. Assn. (pres. 1970-74), Phi Beta Kappa. Methodist. Avocations: computing, plate collecting. Home: 449 Edgewater Dr Mishawaka IN 46545-6909

BRAUNSDORF, PAUL RAYMOND, lawyer; b. South Bend, Ind., June 18, 1943; s. Robert Louis and Marjorie (Breitenstein) B.; m. Margaret Buckley, June 18, 1966; children: Christopher, Mark, Douglas, Amy. BA magna cum laude, U. Notre Dame, 1965; LLB, U. Va., 1968. Bar: N.Y. 1968; U.S. Dist. Ct. (we. dist.) N.Y. 1969, U.S. Dist. Ct. (no. dist.) N.Y. 1980; U.S. Ct. Appeals (2d cir.) 1975; U.S. Supreme Ct. 1980. Assoc. Harris, Beach & Wilcox, Rochester, N.Y., 1968-75; ptnr., 1976—; instr. Nat. Inst. for Trial Advocacy, Rochester, 1988. Contbg. author: Antitrust Health Care Handbook II, 1993, Antitrust Law in New York, 1995. Bd. dirs. Mercy Parents' Club, 1989-90, McQuaid Parents' Club, 1984-90, pres. 1986-87, Brighton Baseball, 1987-90. Republican. Roman Catholic. Avocations: tennis, photography, music. Office: Harris Beach & Wilcox 130 Main St E Rochester NY 14604-1687

BRAUNSTEIN, ETHAN MALCOLM, skeletal radiologist, paleopathologist, educator; b. Chgo., June 16, 1945. BA, Dartmouth Coll., 1967; MD, Northwestern U., Chgo., 1970. Instr. radiology U. Mich., Ann Arbor, 1976-81, assoc. prof., 1983-87; asst. prof. radiology Harvard U., Cambridge, Mass., 1981-83; prof. Ind. U., Indpls., 1987—; adj. prof. anthropology Ind. U., Indpsl., 1990—. Contbr. numerous articles to profl. jours. and chpts. to books. Bd. dirs. Kelsey Mus. of Archeology, Ann Arbor, 1983-87. Mem. Internat. Skeletal Soc., Am. Assn. Physical Anthropologists, Radiologic Soc. N.Am., Assn. Univ. Radiologists. Office: Ind U Hosps Dept Radiology Indianapolis IN 46202

BRAUNSTEIN, GLENN DAVID, physician, educator; b. Greenville, Tex., Feb. 29, 1944; s. Mervin and Helen (Friedman) B.; m. Jacquelyn D. Moose, July 5, 1965; children: Scott M. Braunstein, Jeffrey T. Braunstein. BS summa cum laude, U. Calif. San Francisco, 1965, MD, 1968. Diplomate Am. Bd. Internal Medicine, subspecialty endocrinology, diabetes, metabolism. Intern, resident Peter Bent Brigham Hosp., Boston, 1968-70; clin. fellow in medicine Harvard U. Med. Sch., Boston, 1969-70; clin. assoc., reproduction rsch. br. NIH, Bethesda, Md., 1970-72; chief resident in endocrinology Harbor Gen. Hosp. UCLA, 1972-73; dir. endocrinology Cedars-Sinai Med. Ctr., L.A., 1973-86, chmn., dept. medicine, 1986—; asst. prof. medicine UCLA Sch. Medicine, 1973-77, assoc. prof., 1977-81, prof., 1981—, vice chair dept. medicine, 1986—; cons. for AMA drug evaluations, 1990—; mem. internat. adv. com. Second World Conf. on Implantation and Early Pregnancy in Human, 1994; mem. endocrinologic and metabolic drugs adv. com. FDA, 1991-95, chmn., 1994-95, spl. advisor, 1995—; bd. mem. Am. Bd. Internal Medicine Endocrinology, Diabetes, Metabolism Subspecialty, 1991—, chmn., 1995—, bd. dirs., 1995—; bd. dirs. Cedars-Sinai Med. Ctr., 1997—. Mem. editl. bd. Mt. Sinai Jour. Medicine, 1984-88, Early Pregnancy: Biology and Medicine, 1994—, Am. Family Physician, 1995—, The Am. Jour. Medicine, 1996—, Clin. Endocrinology & Metabolism, 1978-80; assoc. editor Integrative Medicine: Integrating Allopathic, Alternative and Complementary Medicine, 1997—. Bd. dirs. Israel Cancer Rsch. Fund,

1991-94, Cedars-Sinai Med. Ctr., 1997—; mem. Jonsson Comprehensive Cancer Ctr., 1991—. Recipient Gold Headed Cane Soc. award U. Calif. San Francisco Med. Ctr., 1968, Merck scholarship, 1968, Mosby scholarship, 1968, Soc. of Hacham award Cedars-Sinai Med. Ctr., 1976, Morris Press Humanism award Cedars-Sinai Med. Ctr., 1984, outstanding achievement and cmty. svc. award Anti-Defamation League, 1997. Fellow ACP (mem. adv. com. to gov., So. Calif. region 1989—, credentials com. So. Calif. region 1993); mem. AAAS, Am. Diabetes Assn., Cross Town Endocrine Club (chmn. 1982-83), Endocrine Soc. (publs. com. 1983-89, long range planning com. 1986-87, recent progress hormone rsch. com. 1993—, ann. meeting steering com. 1993—), Pacific Coast Fertility Soc. (pres. 1988), Western Soc. for Clin. Rsch., Am. Fedn. for Clin. Rsch., Am. Fertility Soc., Western Assn. Physicians (pres. 1998), Assn. Am. Physicians, Am. Soc. Clin. Investigations (mem. nominating com. 1989), USCF Sch. Medicine Alumni Faculty Assn. (regional v.p. so. Calif., mem. bd. dirs. Israel Cancer Rsch. Fund 1991-94, mem. Jonsson Comprehensive Cancer Ctr. 1991—), Phi Delta Epsilon, Alpha Omega Alpha. Office: Cedars Sinai Med Ctr Dept Med Pla Level B118 8700 Beverly Blvd Los Angeles CA 90048-1865

BRAUNWALD, EUGENE, physician, educator; b. Aug. 15, 1929; m. Nina H. Starr, 1952 (dec.); m. Elaine R. Smith, 1993; children: Karen G., Allison Jill. AB, NYU, 1949, MD, 1952; AM (hon.), Harvard U., 1972; MD (hon.), U. Lisbon, 1984, U. Lisbon, 1985; ScD (hon.), Mt. Sinai Med. Ctr., 1991; MD (hon.), U. Rome, 1991, U. Portg, 1992, U. Vienna, 1995, U. La Plata (Argentina), 1995. Diplomate Am. Bd. Internal Medicine, Am. Bd. Cardiovascular Disease. Intern, fellow Mt. Sinai Hosp., N.Y.C., 1952-54; research fellow Columbia U. Coll. Physicians and Surgeons, N.Y.C., 1954-55; clin. assoc. cardiovascular physiology lab. Nat. Heart Inst., Bethesda, Md., 1955-57; asst. resident Osler Med. Service, Johns Hopkins Hosp., Balt., 1957-58; chief cardiology sect., chief cardiology br., clin. dir. Nat. Heart and Lung Inst., Bethesda, 1958-68; prof., chmn. dept. medicine U. Calif.-San Diego, 1968-72; Hersey prof. of theory and practice of medicine Harvard U. Med. Sch., Boston, 1972-96, Herrman Blumgart prof. Medicine, 1980-89, Disting. Hersey prof. theory and practice of medicine, 1996—, faculty dean for acad. programs, 1996—; sr. cons. in medicine Mass. Gen. Hosp., 1994—; v.p. acad. programs Ptnrs. HealthCare Sys., 1996—; chmn. dept. medicine Brigham and Women's Hosp., 1972-96, Beth Israel Hosp., 1980-89; lectr. physiology George Washington U., 1959-62; from asst. clin. prof. to clin. prof. Georgetown U. Sch. Medicine, 1960-68; lectr. medicine Johns Hopkins U., 1960-68; trustee Brigham and Women's and Mass. Gen. Hosps. Health Sys., 1993—; vis. prof. numerous U.S. and fgn. univs.; lectr. in field; v.p. acad. programs, ptnrs. health care system, faculty dean for acad. programs Harvard Med. Sch., 1996—. Co-editor: Year Book of Cardiovascular and Renal Diseases, 1965-72, Year Book of Medicine, 1973-93, Harrison's Principles of Internal Medicine, 1967—; editor Heart Disease, 1980—; mem. editorial bds. Circulation, Jour. Clin. Investigation, 164-71, Jour. Cardiovascular Pharmacology, Am. Jour. Medicine, Am. Jour. Cardiology, New Eng. Jour. Medicine, numerous others. Bd. visitors Rockefeller U., 1978-82; mem. vis. com. MIT, 1979-85, Technion U., 1979. Recipient Arthur S. Fleming award, 1965, Superior Svc. award HEW, 1967, Disting. Achievement award Modern Medicine, 1968, Gustav Nylin award Swedish Med. Soc., 1970, Williams award Outstanding Chmn. and Medicine, 1987, Bristol Myers Squibb Excellence in Cardiovascular Rsch. award, 1993, J. Allyn Taylor Internat. prize Robarts Rsch. Inst., 1993. Fellow ACP (Phillips award 1991), Am. Acad. Arts and Scis., Am. Coll. Cardiology (v.p. 1967, trustee 1967, 70-75, Disting. Scientist award 1987); mem. Nat. Acad. Scis., Johns Hopkins Soc. Scholars, Assn. Profs. Medicine (pres. 1974-75), Assn. Am. Physicians (Kober medal 1998), Western Assn. Physicians, Am. Soc. Clin. Investigation (pres. 1974-75), Am. Fedn. Clin. Research (pres. 1969-70), Western Soc. for Clin. Research (pres. 1971-72), Assn. Univ. Cardiologists, New England Cardiovascular Soc. (pres. 1987-88), Am. Physiol. Soc., Am. Soc. Pharmacology and Exptl. Therapeutics (John Jacob Abel award 1965), Am. Heart Assn. (bd. dirs. 1966-75, v.p. 1966-70, Research Achievement award 1972, Herrick award 1981), Harvey Soc., Royal Soc. Medicine, Internat. Soc. Cardiology, Alpha Omega Alpha. Office: Partners Healthcare 800 Boylston St Boston MA 02199-8001

BRAUNWORTH, BRENT TAYLOR, firefighter, paramedic, police officer; b. Orange, N.J., May 29, 1961; s. Robert Taylor and Ginevra Garside Braunworth; m. Mary Ann Jackson, Sept. 3, 1983; children: Cory, Christina. Degree in pub. affairs, Fla. Atlantic U., 1986; EMS mgmt., Palm Beach C.C., 1997. Cert. SWAT medic. Paramedic Palm Beach C.C., Lake Worth, Fla., 1983—; firefighter South Tech. Sch., Boynton Beach, Fla., 1984—; police officer Palm Beach C.C., Lake Worth, 1991—; pub. rels. coord. West Palm Fire Dept., West Palm Beach, 1996-98; ACLS instr. Am. Heart Assn., Palm Beach County, 1987—, CPR instr., 1985—, PALS instr., 1994—; pension trustee West Palm Firefighter's Pension Fund, West Palm Beach, 1996. Author: (books) Street Scenes from the EMT and Paramedic, 1994, Blood, Guts, and Tears at 3 am, 1999; editor, owner: (newspaper) Native Sun, 1988-92. Campaign mgr. John Udell for County Commr., Palm Beach County, 1990. Avocations: working out in gym, coaching football and baseball.

BRAUTH, MARVIN JEFFREY, lawyer; b. Far Rockaway, N.Y., Feb. 3, 1950; s. Paul A. and Rosalie (Hauser) B.; divorced; children: Jason, Brian, Laura. BA, Colgate U., 1971; JD, U. Pa., 1974. Bar: N.J. 1974, U.S. Ct. Appeals (3rd cir.) 1978, U.S. Supreme Ct. 1981, N.Y. 1988. Assoc. Wilentz, Goldman & Spitzer, P.A., Woodbridge, N.J., 1974-81, shareholder, 1981—; lectr. Profl. Ins. Agt. Am., Trenton, N.J., 1993, N.J. Automobile Dealers Assn., 1994, 96, 98, CPCU Soc., 1995. Bd. dirs. Jewish Cmty. Ctr. Middlesex County, Edison, N.J., 1988—, treas., 1989-92, v.p., 1994-96. Mem. ABA (nat. resources and environ. com.), N.Y. State Bar Assn., N.J. Bar Assn., Middlesex County Bar Assn., Middlesex County Regional C. of C. (bd. dirs. 1996—). Democrat. Home: 502 Westgate Dr Edison NJ 08820-1174 Office: Wilentz Goldman & Spitzer PA 90 Woodbridge Ctr Dr Ste 900 Woodbridge NJ 07095-1142

BRAVERMAN, ALAN N., lawyer. BA, Brandeis U., 1969; JD, Duquesne U., 1975. Bar: D.C. 1976. Assoc. Wilmer, Cutler & Pickering, 1976-82, ptnr., 1983-93; sr. v.p., gen. counsel ABC, Inc., N.Y.C., 1993—. Office: ABC Inc 77 W 66th St New York NY 10023-6298*

BRAVERMAN, HERBERT LESLIE, lawyer; b. Buffalo, Apr. 24, 1947; s. David and Miriam P. (Cohen) B.; m. Janet Marx, June 11, 1972; children: Becca Danielle, Benjamin Howard. BS in Econs., U. Pa., 1969; JD, Harvard U., 1972. Bar: Ohio 1972, U.S. Dist. Ct. Ohio 1972, U.S. Supreme Ct. 1975, U.S. Ct. Appeals (6th cir.) 1980, U.S. Ct. Claims 1980. Assoc. Hahn, Loeser, Freedheim, Dean & Wellman, Cleve., 1972-75; sole practice Cleve., 1975-87; ptnr. Porter, Wright, Morris & Arthur, Cleve., 1987-95, Walter & Haverfield, Cleve., 1996—. Councilman Orange Village, Ohio, 1988—, pres., 1998—. Capt. USAR, 1970-82. Fellow Am. Coll. Trust and Estate Counsel; mem. ABA, Ohio Bar Assn., Bar Assn. Greater Cleve. (former chmn. estate planning trust and probate sect.), Suburban East Bar Assn. (pres. 1978-80), Rotary (Cleveland Heights pres. 1980), B'nai Brith (local pres. 1978-84), Wharton Club Cleve. (pres. 1991—), Am. Jewish Congress (Ohio pres. 1992—). Avocations: golf, symphony, reading. Home: 3950 Orangewood Dr Cleveland OH 44122-7406 Office: Walter & Haverfield 1300 Terminal Tower 50 Public Sq Ste 1300 Cleveland OH 44113-2253 also: 23200 Chagrin Blvd Ste 600 Beachwood OH 44122-5402

BRAVERMAN, IRWIN MERTON, dermatologist, educator; b. Boston, Apr. 17, 1929; s. Morris and Molly (Singer) B.; m. Muriel S. Freedman, June 5, 1955; children: Paula, David, Michael. A.B., Harvard U., 1951; M.D., Yale U., 1955. Diplomate: Am. Bd. Med. Examiners, Am. Bd. Dermatology, Am. Bd. Pathology. Practice medicine specializing in dermatology New Haven; asst. prof. dermatology Yale U., New Haven, 1962-68, assoc. prof., 1968-73, prof., 1973—. Author: Skin Signs of Systemic Disease, 1970, 3d edit., 1997; contbr. articles to profl. jours. Served to capt. U.S. Army, 1956-58. Recipient Mr. and Mrs. J.N. Taub Internat. Meml. award for research in psoriasis Baylor Med. Coll., 1980. Mem. AMA, New Eng. Dermatol. Soc. (v.p. 1990-91, pres. 1991-92), Am. Dermatol. Assn., Am. Acad. Dermatology (dir. 1980-83, Sulzberger Internat. lectr. 1989, Master of Dermatology 1993), Soc. Investigative Dermatology (bd. dirs. 1982-87, pres. elect 1991-92, pres. 1992-93), Am. Fedn. Clin. Rsch., Am. Assn. Physicians. Office: Yale U Med Sch 333 Cedar St New Haven CT 06510-3289

BRAVERMAN, RAY HOWARD, secondary school educator; b. Bklyn., Feb. 28, 1947; s. Irving Leonard and Josephine (Segan) B.; divorced; 1 child, Christopher Marc; m. Barbara Diane Braverman, July 30, 1994. BA in History, U. Del., 1969; MA in History, Wash. Coll., 1979; postgrad., Wash. Coll., U. Del., 1979-85. Cert. tchr., Del. History tchr. Dover (Del.) H.S., 1970—. Recipient Certs. of Appreciation U. Del., 1987, Nat. Coun. History Edn., 1991. Mem. NEA, Nat. Coun. for the Social Studies, Del. Coun. for Social Studies, Nat. Coun. for History Edn., World History Assn., Del. Edn. Assn., Capital Educators Assn., Orgn. of Am. Historians, Am. Hist. Assn. Home: 33 Elizabeth Ave Dover DE 19901-5803 Office: Dover HS One Pat Lynn Dr Dover DE 19904-2853

BRAVERMAN, ROBERT JAY, international consultant, public policy educator; b. N.Y.C., Mar. 4, 1933; s. Arthur and Ruth Edith (Beck) B.; m. Alice Glantz, Dec. 24, 1954; 1 son, John Nachem; m. Claire Hurney, Dec. 31, 1964; children: Sam, Amy. AB with honors and distinction, Columbia U., 1954; postgrad., Harvard U. Sch. Law, 1956-57, Sch. Bus., 1963. With Harbridge House, Inc. (Mgmt. Cons.), Cambridge, Mass., 1957-66; with ITT, N.Y.C., 1966-86; sr. v.p., CEO ITT Coins Inc., 1986—; chief exec. officer Braverman Adv. Svcs., 1986-91; prof. of practice of pub. policy studies Duke U. Served with U.S. Army, 1954-56. Mem. Phi Beta Kappa. Home and Office: 235 W 76th St New York NY 10023-8210

BRAVO, KENNETH ALLAN, lawyer; b. Cleve., July 27, 1942. BS, Rutgers U., 1964; JD cum laude, Ohio State U., 1967. Bar: Ohio 1967, D.C. 1967. Trial atty. Criminal Divsn., U.S. Dept. Justice, 1967-69, spl. atty., 1969-79; ptnr. Benesch, Friedlander, Coplan & Aronoff, Cleve., 1979-94; of counsel Ulmer & Berne LLP, Cleve., 1994-96, ptnr., 1997—. Mem. ABA, Cleve. Bar Assn. (chmn. fed. ct. com. 1984-85), Cuyahoga County Bar Assn. (chmn. fed. ct. com. 1980-82, chmn. cert. grievance com. 1986-88), Nat. Assn. Criminal Def. Lawyers, Lawyer-Pilots Bar Assn., Jud. Conf. 8th Dist. Ohio (life). Office: Ulmer & Berne LLP Bond Ct Bldg 1300 E 9th St Ste 900 Cleveland OH 44114-1583

BRAVO, PAUL, professional soccer player; b. San Jose, Calif., July 19, 1968. Student, Santa Clara U. Midfielder San Francisco Bay Blackhawks, 1991, San Francisco Greek-Ams.; U.S. Open Cup champions, 1994; midfielder Monterey Bay Jaguars, 1995, San Jose Clash, 1996; advanced to play-offs, 1996; midfielder Colo. Rapids, Denver, 1997—; advanced to play-offs, 1997, 98. Office: c/o Colo Rapids 55517th St Ste 3350 Denver CO 80202*

BRAVO, ROSE MARIE, retail executive; b. N.Y.C., Jan. 13, 1951; d. Biagio and Anna (Bazzano) LaPila; m. William Selkirk Jackey, Oct. 9, 1983. B.A. in English, Fordham U., 1971. Exec. trainee, dept. mgr. A&S, Bklyn., 1971-74; assoc. buyer Macy's, N.Y.C., 1974-75, buyer, 1975-79, councilor, 1979-80, adminstr., 1980-84, group v.p., 1984-85, sr. v.p. 1985-88; chmn., CEO, I. Magnin, San Francisco, 1988-92; pres., Saks Fifth Ave., Inc., N.Y.C., 1992-97; CEO Burberrys Ltd., London, 1997—; bd. dirs. Tiffany & Co.

BRAWER, CATHERINE COLEMAN, foundation executive, curator; b. N.Y.C., Feb. 19, 1943; d. Joseph A. and Beatrice R. Coleman; m. Robert A. Brawer, Sept. 7, 1962; children: Christopher Paul, Nicholas Andrew. BA, Sarah Lawrence Coll., 1964; MA in Art History, NYU, 1966. Publicity coord. Evehjem Mus. Art, Madison, Wis., 1970-75, curator Liebman Collection, 1974-75; mktg. mgr. Maidenform, Inc., N.Y.C., 1975-78; ind. curator N.Y.C., 1978; v.p. Ida and William Rosenthal Found., N.Y.C., 1981-90, pres., 1990—; dir. pub. affairs Maidenform Inc., N.Y.C., 1990-97, bd. dirs., 1970-97; curator Maidenform Mus., 1992-97; trustee Katonah (N.Y.) Mus. Art, 1982—, Ind. Curators, Internat., N.Y.C., 1989—, Inst. Fine Arts, NYU, 1993—, Musica Viva, 1995—. Author: (catalogues) The Auspicious Dragon in Chinese Decorative Arts, 1978, Many Trails: Indians of the Lower Hudson Valley, 1983, Trade Winds: The Lure of the China Trade, 1985; (book) Making Their Mark: Women Artist Move into the Mainstream 1970-85, 1989, Chinese Export Porcelain from the Liebman Porcelain Collection, 1992. Mem. Am. Ceramic Circle, N.Y. Regional Assn. Grantmakers (mem. com. 1990-91), Art Table N.Y.

BRAWER, MARC HARRIS, lawyer; b. N.Y.C., June 11, 1946; s. Leonard and Diana R. Brawer; m. Susan L. Brunswick, Nov. 23, 1975; 3 children. BA, Queens Coll., 1967; JD, Bklyn. Law Sch., 1969. Bar: N.Y. 1970, Fla. 1978, U.S. Dist. Ct. (ea. and so. dists.) N.Y. 1974, U.S. Ct. Appeals (2nd cir.) 1974, U.S. Supreme Ct. 1975, U.S. Dist. Ct. (so. dist.) Fla. 1981, U.S. Ct. Appeals (5th cir.) 1980; cert. marital and family lawyer, family mediator. Staff atty. Legal Aid Soc., N.Y.C., 1972-78; ptnr. Meyerson Resnicoff & Brawer, N.Y.C., 1978-83, Meyerson & Brawer, Tamarac, Fla., 1983-84; head firm Marc H. Brawer, Sunrise, Fla., 1984—; of counsel Resnicoff, Samanowitz & Brawer, Great Neck, N.Y., 1985-91; adj. prof. family law St. Thomas Law Sch., 1992; spkr. various orgns. and colls., 1980-96. Contbr. articles to profl. jours., 1970-84. Fellow Am. Acad. Matrimonial Lawyers; mem. Broward County Bar Assn., Queens County Bar Assn. (cert. of svc. 1982-83), Fla. Bar (sec. Family Law Commentator). Avocations: scuba diving, photography, ornamental horticulture. Office: 7771 W Oakland Park Blvd Fort Lauderdale FL 33351-6749

BRAWLEY, MARGARET WACKER, communications executive; b. Washington, Dec. 12, 1951; d. Warren Ernest Clyde and Ann Romeyn (MacMillan) W.; m. Richard Warren Brawley, Feb. 26, 1994. BA, Carnegie Mellon U., 1974. Promotion specialist Millipore Corp., Bedford, Mass., 1974-77, dir. comm. Lab. Products div., 1981-82, corporate comm. mgr., 1982-88, human resources project mgr., 1989-93, sr. acct. mgr. bioscience divsn., 1993-94, mgr. tech. pubs. and life sci. promotion, lab. & health care products divsn., 1994-95, mgr. mktg. comm. analytical divsn., 1995—; dir. advt. IVAC div. Eli Lilly Co., San Diego, 1977-79, dist. sales mgr., L.A., 1979-80; bus. unit mgr. Sage divsn. Orion Rsch., Cambridge, Mass., 1980-81; counselor to handicapped individuals in bus. Democrat. Episcopalian. Avocations: painting, sewing. Home: The Brook House 77 Pond Ave Apt 701C Brookline MA 02445-7114 Office: Millipore Corp 80 Ashby Rd Bedford MA 01730-2271

BRAWNER, LEE BASIL, librarian; b. Seguin, Tex., May 1, 1935; s. Lee Basil and Thelma (Davenport) B.; m. Nancy Jayne Wallis, Dec. 6, 1958; children: Betsy Lynn, Allen Lee. Student, Tex. A. and M. U., 1953-55; B.A., North Tex. State U., 1957; M.A., George Peabody Coll. Tchrs., 1960. Head popular libr. and circulation dept. Dallas Pub. Libr., 1958-60, head Lakewood br., 1961-62, chief br. svcs., 1964-67; dir. Waco (Tex.) Pub. Libr., 1962-64; asst. state libr. Tex. State Libr., 1967-71; dir. Met. Libr. System, Oklahoma City, 1971—; libr. cons.; trustee AMIGOS Bibliog. Coun., 1987-90; panelist libr. bldg. awards AIA-ALA, 1990-92; mem. state adv. bd. U. Okla. Sch. Librs. and Info. Studies, 1994—. Co-author: (with Donald K. Beck, Jr.) Determining Your Public Library's Future Size: A Needs Assessment and Planning Model, 1996, Disaster Response and Planning for Libraries, 1998, In Celebration of Intellectual Freedom, 1999. Trustee, v.p. Okla. Ctr. for the Book, 1987-93; trustee Okla. Humanities Com., 1977-78; mem. Leadership Oklahoma City, 1994-95; chmn. Okla. Found. for Humanities; trustee Freedom to Read Found., 1982-85, pres., 1985-86; mem. Murrah Fed. Bldg. Meml. Com., 1995—. Recipient Alumni award U. North Tex., 1989, First Amendment award Okla. Soc. Profl. Journalists, 1997-98, Downtown Now Pioneer award, 1997, Hugh M. Hefner 1st Amendment award, 1998; named to 30th Anniversary Honor Roll, ALA Intellectual Freedom to Read Found., 1999. Mem. ACLU, ALA (coun. 1978-81, intellectual freedom com. 1979-82), Libr. Adminstrn. and Mgmt. Assn. (libr. bldg. awards com. 1987-90, 92-93, chmn. 1990, chmn. libr. bldgs. and equipment sect. 1992), Pub. Libr. assn. (effectiveness com. 1992), Okla. Libr. Assn. (chmn. libr. devel. 1982-83, pres. 1984-85, chmn. legis. com. 1990, Disting. Svc. award 1983, chmn. awards com. 1992-93, SIRS Intellectual Freedom award 1997), Okla. Acad. for State goals, Urban Librs. Coun., Okla. C. of C., Rotary Club of Oklahoma City, Sigma Phi Epsilon. Office: Met Libr Sys Okla County 131 Dean A McGee Ave Oklahoma City OK 73102-6438

BRAWNER, PATRICIA ANN, English educator; b. Rolla, Mo., Mar. 14, 1939; d. Charles and Dorothy (Flett) Trotter; m. Gary L. Bagwill, Jan. 21, 1968 (div. 1993); children: Bryce, Brooke; m. Charles E. Brawner, May 31, 1997. BA, Ctrl. Meth. Coll., 1961; MA, Murray State U., 1966; postgrad., St. Louis U., 1996. Tchr. Fayette (Mo.) Pub. Schs., 1957-59, Mehlville (Mo.) H.S., 1959-61, Paducah (Ky.) Jr. Coll., 1966-68; English tchr. Northside H.S., Memphis, 1968-69, Mehlville H.S., 1972-77, Coll. DuPage, Glen Ellen, Ill., 1977-82, Fontbonne Coll., Clayton, Mo., 1983-89; English instr. Mo. Bapt. Coll., St. Louis, 1988—. Mem. Nat. Coun. Tchrs. English, Phi Delta Kappa, Sigma Tau Delta. Methodist. Avocations: travel, painting, reading, writing. Home: 1631 Strecker Ridge Ct Wildwood MO 63011-1992

BRAWNER, SHARON LEE, bilingual education educator, researcher; b. Marietta, Ga.; d. Robert Felton and Ruby Lee B.; div.; 1 child, Marion Eugene Sealy III. BA, Clemson U., 1975; MEd, U. S.C., 1987; EdD, U. Ga., 1994. ESL cert., gifted and talented tchg. cert. English tchr. grades 7-12 Columbia, S.C., 1981-88; English instr. U. Ga., Athens, 1990, grad. asst., 1990-94; asst. prof. No. Ariz. U., Yuma, 1994-96; adj. sr. faculty English U. Ariz., 1997—; presenter Ga. Children's Lit. Conf., Athens, 1991, Ga. Coun. Tchrs. English Conf., 1991, TESOL Nat. Conf., Balt., 1994; dir. Connections Tutoring Program, 1997-99. Author: New Ways in Teaching Listening, 1995. Pres., governing bd. Yuma County Juvenile Ct. Sys. Charter Sch., 1995-96; mem. San Luis, Ariz./San Luis, Sonora, Mex. Edn. Commn., 1994-96; essay judge Ga. Acad. Decathlon, Athens, 1991; vol. tutor Athens Regional Libr., 1993-94. Mem. Internat. Reading Assn. (rsch. com. No. Ariz. U. 1994-96), Nat. Council for Tchrs. of English, mem., Tchrs. of English to Speakers of Other Languages. Avocations: foreign languages, computers, baseball cards, travel, piano.

BRAXTON, TONI, popular musician; b. Severn, Md., Oct. 7, 1967. Albums include Toni Braxton, 1993; contbr. Boomerang soundtrack, 1992, Secrets, 1997. Recipient Grammy award Best Female R&B Vocal, 1994, 95. Office: Arista Records care LaFace 6 W 57th St New York NY 10019-3901*

BRAY, ABSALOM FRANCIS, JR., lawyer; b. San Francisco, Nov. 24, 1918; s. Absalom Francis and Leila Elizabeth (Veale) B.; m. Lorraine Cerena Paule, June 25, 1949; children: Oliver, Brian, Margot. BA, Stanford U., 1940; JD, U. So. Calif., 1949. Bar: Calif. 1949, U.S. Supreme Ct. 1960. Sr. ptnr. Bray & Baldwin and successive firms to Bray & Bray, Martinez, Calif., 1949—, now pres.; founder, bd. dirs. John Muir Nat. Bank, Martinez. Chmn. Martinez Recreation Commn., 1949-54; chmn. nat. bd. dirs. Camp Fire Girls, 1959-61, 1969-71; pres. Contra Costa County (Calif.) Devel. Assn., 1959-60; pres. Contra Costa County Hist. Soc., 1995-97. Lt. USNR, 1942-46. Mem. State Bar Calif. (chmn. adoption com. 1955-56), Martinez Hist. Soc. (pres. 1984), John Muir Meml. Assn. (pres. 1989-92), Navy League U.S. (pres. Contra Costa Coun. 1981-83), Martinez High Twelve Club (pres. 1987). Republican. Episcopalian. Lodges: Masons, Rotary (pres. Martinez chpt. 1970-71). Home: 600 Flora St Martinez CA 94553-3268 Office: Ward and Ferry Sts Martinez CA 94553-1697

BRAY, CAROLYN SCOTT, educational administrator; b. May 19, 1938; d. Alonzo Lee and Frankie Lucile (Wood) Scott; m. John Graham Bray Jr., Aug. 24, 1957 (div. May 1980); children: Caron Lynn, Kimberly Anne, David William. BS, Baylor U., 1960; MEd, Hardin-Simmons U., 1981; PhD, U. North Tex., 1985. Registered med. technologist. Dir. career placement Hardin-Simmons U., 1979-82, adj. prof. bus. comm., 1981-84, assoc. dean students, 1982-85; assoc. dir. career planning and placement U. North Tex., Denton, 1985-95, adj. prof. higher edn. adminstrn., mem. Mentor program; dir. career ctr. U. Tex. at Dallas, Richardson, 1995—. Bd. dirs. Irving Christian Counseling, Inc., 1993-95. Mem. Am. Assn. for Employment in Edn. (bd. dirs. 1989-94, treas. 1994-95, nat. conf. com. 1999, conf. com. local arrangements 1999), S.W. Assn. Colls. and Employers (4-yr. coll. dir. 1998-99, co-chmn. Tech. Com., vice chair ops. 1992-93, chair ann. conf. registration 1991-92, pres.-elect 1999—), Tex. Am. Assn. for Employer of Edn., SStaffing (v.p. 1986-87, pres. 1987-88), Nat. Assn. Colls. and Employers (co-chair nat. conf. planning com. 1996-98), Internat. Assn. Career Mgmt. Profls., North Ctrl. Tex. Assn. Sch. Pers. Adminstrs. and Univ. Placement Pers. (pres. 1987-88, sec. 1988-95), Denton C. of C. (pub. rels. com. 1988-95), Dallas Human Resources Mgmt. Assn., Leadership Denton (co-dir. curriculum 1988-89, chair membership selection com., steering com. 1990, 93-94), Richardson C. of C., Kappa Kappa Gamma (chpt. advisor, chair adv. bd. Zeta Sigma chpt. 1987-93). Republican. Avocations: skiing, tennis, golf, reading. Office: U Tex at Dallas PO Box 830688 Richardson TX 75083-0688

BRAY, CHARLES WILLIAM, III, foundation executive; b. N.Y.C., Oct. 24, 1933; s. Charles William and Katherine (Owsley) B.; children: Charles W., David C., Katherine M. AB, Princeton U., 1955; postgrad., Univ. de Bordeaux, France, 1955-56, U. Md., 1966-67. With Dept. State, 1958-77, 81-88, dep. asst. sec. for inter-Am. affairs, 1976-77, dir. Fgn. Svc. Inst., 1987-88; dep. dir. Internat. Communication Agy., Washington, 1977-81; Am. ambassador to Senegal, 1981-85; pres. The Johnson Found., Racine, Wis., 1988—; adj. lectr. U. Georgetown. With U.S. Army, 1956-58. Recipient Disting. Svc. award Pres. of U.S., 1984; Fulbright fellow, 1955-56; Presdl. fellow, 1966-67. Office: Johnson Found Racine WI 53401-0547

BRAY, DONALD LAWRENCE, religious organization executive, minister; b. Olwein, Iowa, Oct. 14, 1942; s. Arthur L. and Rachel C. (Archer) B.; m. Joy F. Failing, Aug. 15, 1964; children: Juli, Steven, Jeffrey. BA in Religion, Ind. Wesleyan U., 1964, DD (hon.), 1993; MA in Religion, Olivet Nazarene U., 1965. Ordained to ministry Wesleyan Ch., 1967. Pastor Mich. Dist. Wesleyan Ch., Grand Rapids, Mich., 1965-68; missionary Wesleyan World Missions, Indpls., 1968-77, dir. personnel, 1977-84, asst. gen. sec., 1984-88; dist. supt. Delta dist. Wesleyan Ch., Jackson, Miss., 1988-92; gen. dir. Wesleyan World Missions, Indpls., 1992—; adj. prof. Wesley Bibl. Sem., Jackson, 1989-92. Author: (tng. manual) Christian Witness, 1985; contbr. articles to profl. jours. Trustee So. Wesleyan U., Central, S.C., 1989—. Mem. Evang. Fellowship of Mission Agys. (bd. dirs. 1994—), U.S.-World Evang. Fellowship, Ind. Wesleyan U. Alumni Assn. (bd. dirs. 1984-86). Office: PO Box 50434 Indianapolis IN 46250-0434

BRAY, GEORGE AUGUST, physician, scientist, educator; b. Evanston, Ill., July 25, 1931; s. George A. and Mary H. B.; m. Martha, Aug. 8, 1959 (div. July 1983); children: George, Thomas, Susan, Nancy; m. Marilyn Rice, Jan. 1, 1984. BA summa cum laude, Brown U., 1953; MD magna cum laude, Harvard U., 1957. Diplomate Am. Bd. Internal Medicine; cert. Nat. Bd. Med. Examiners, Mass. Bd. Registration Medicine, Calif. Bd. Med. Examiners, La. Bd. Med. Examiners. Intern Johns Hopkins Hosp., Baltimore, Md., 1957-58; rsch. assoc. NIH, Bethesda, Md., 1958-60; resident U. Rochester, N.Y., 1960-61; rsch. assoc. Mill Hill Nat. Inst. Med. Rsch., London, 1961-62; asst. prof. medicine Tufts U., Boston, 1964-69, assoc. prof., 1969-70; assoc. prof. UCLA, 1970-72, prof., 1972-81; prof. U. So. Calif., Los Angeles, 1981-89, prof. medicine and physiology, 1983-89, chief of Diabetes and Nutrition Los Angeles County USC Med. Ctr., 1981-89; prof. medicine, vice chancellor Med. Ctr. La. State U., Baton Rouge, 1989—; exec. dir. Pennington Biomed. Rsch. Ctr., Baton Rouge, 1989—; vis. prof. U. Ill., 1981; cons. FDA, 1971, 95, Can. Dept. Health and Welfare, Ottawa, Ont., 1974, Nat. Inst. on Aging; mem. adv. coun. Nat. Inst. Diabetes, Digestive and Kidney Diseases, 1985-90. Author: Obese Patient, 1976; editor: Obesity in America, 1979, Obesity in Perspective, 1976, Treatment of Obesity, 1985, 89, Obesity: Basic Aspects and Clinical Applications, 1989; contbr. articles to profl. jours. Recipient Travel award Am. Thyroid Assn., 1970, Sam E. Roberts award Kans. Nutrition Soc., 1977, Wellcome Vis. Prof. award Mich. State U., 1978, U. Chgo., 1985, Alumni Day spkr. Harvard Med. Sch., Boston, 1982, Osborne and Mendel award Am. Inst. Nutrition, 1989, E.V. McCollum award Am. Soc. Clin. Nutrition, 1989, Joseph Goldberger award in Clin. Nutrition AMA, 1994; grantee NIH, 1965—, Weight Watchers Found., 1979-81, Kroc Found., 1980-81; fellow NSF, 1961-62, NIH, 1962-64. Master ACP (chmn.-elect coun. med. spltys. 1987-88, chmn. 1988-91, bd. regents 1987-91), Am. Coll. Endocrinology (pres. 1993-95, editor Endocrine Practice 1993-95); fellow AAAS (coun. del. for med. scis. 1985-88), Am. Soc. Nutrition Sci.; mem. Am. Assn. Clin. Endocrinology (bd. dirs. 1990-96), Am. Soc. for Clin. Nutrition (councilor 1982-84, v.p. 1985-86, pres.-elect 1986-87, pres. 1987-88, McCollum award 1989), Assn. Am. Physicians (hon.), Endocrine Soc., Am. Diabetes Assn. (bd. dirs. So. Calif. 1984-87, 88-89), Am. Fedn. for Clin. Rsch., Peripatetic Club (hon.), Am. Soc. Clin. Investigation (hon.), Am. Inst. Nutrition (Osborne-Mendal award 1988), N.Am. Assn. for Study Obesity (chmn. organizing com. 1980-82, councilor 1984-88, pres.-elect 1988-89, pres. 1989-90, editor Internat. Jour.

Obesity 1974-91, Obesity Rsch. 1991—), Internat. Assn. Study Obesity (pres.-elect 1990-94, pres. 1994-98, Willendorf award 1980), Johns Hopkins U. Soc. Scholars, 1999, Phi Beta Kappa, Sigma Xi, Alpha Omega Alpha. Avocations: medical history, travel. Office: Pennington Ctr 6400 Perkins Rd Baton Rouge LA 70808-4124

BRAY, JOAN, state legislator; b. Sept. 16, 1945; m. Carl Hoagland; 2 children. BA, Southwestern U.; MEd, U. Mass. Former tchr., journalist, former dist. dir. for Congresswoman Joan Kelly Horn; mem. Mo. Ho. of Reps. Bd. dirs. Citizens for Modern Transit. Flemming fellow, 1995. Mem. PTO, Nat. Womens Polit. Caucus. Democrat. Home: 7120 Washington Ave Saint Louis MO 63130-4312 Office: Mo Ho of Reps Rm 412 State Capitol Building Jefferson City MO 65101-1556*

BRAY, LAURACK DOYLE, lawyer; b. New Orleans, Nov. 13, 1949; s. Laudrack Doyle Bray and Helen Davis. AA, L.A. City Coll., 1969; BA, Long Beach State U., 1972, MS, 1977, MPA, 1981; JD, Howard U., 1984. Bar: Pa. 1986, D.C. 1986, U.S. Ct. Appeals (D.C. and fed. cirs.) 1987, U.S. Dist. Ct. D.C. 1987, U.S. Ct. Appeals (4th cir.) 1991, Md. 1991, U.S. Supreme Ct. 1992. Cmty. rsch. worker Crenshaw Consortium, L.A., 1977-79; adminstrv. intern City of Lawndale, Calif., 1981; legis. intern U.S. Congress, Washington, 1982; law clk. FDIC, Washington, 1983-84; pvt. practice, Washington, 1987—; mem. moot ct. team Howard U., Washington. Contbr. articles to law jours. Recipient Am. Jurisprudence award, 1982, Best Brief award ABA, 1984. Mem. D.C. Bar Assn., Pi Alpha Alpha, Phi Kappa Phi. Democrat. Avocations: sports, dancing, travel. Home and Office: 1019 E Sauta Clara St Ventura CA 93001

BRAY, PHILIP JAMES, physicist; b. Kansas City, Mo., Aug. 25, 1925; s. Harry James and Ruth (Moerdyke) B.; children—Carolyn, Philip James, Katherine. Sc.B. in Physics, Brown U., 1948; A.M., Harvard U., 1949, Ph.D., 1953. Asst. prof. physics Rensselaer Poly. Inst., 1952-55; asso. prof. physics Brown U., Providence, 1955-58; prof. Brown U., 1958—, chmn. dept., 1963-68, Hazard prof. physics, 1985-90, prof. emeritus, 1990—; vis. prof. dept. glass tech. U. Sheffield, Eng., 1961-62, 68-69; vis. prof. dept. chemistry U. Exeter, Eng., 1975-76; mem. Internat. Com. on Nuclear Quadrupole Interactions, 1991-97. Assoc. editor: Revs. Modern Physics, 1963-65; editorial bd. Jour. Non-Crystalline Solids, 1968-71, Jour. Non-metals, 1971-77, Jour. Biol. Physics, 1973-77, Magnetic Resonance in Chemistry, 1985-90. NSF fellow, 1961-62; Guggenheim fellow, 1968-69. Fellow Am. Phys. Soc. (chmn. New Eng. sect. 1965-67), Soc. Glass Tech. (Sir Nevill Mott award for outstanding contbns. to field of glass sci. 1991), Korean Phys. Soc., Am. Acad. Arts and Scis., AAAS, Sigma Xi (nat. lectr. 1969-70), Am. Ceramic Soc. (George W. Morey award for outstanding contributions to glass sci. and tech. 1970); mem. Internat. Soc. Magnetic Resonance, Groupement Ampere, Assn. Koreans of R.I. (hon.). Unitarian. Home: 133 Power St Providence RI 02906-1060 Office: Brown U Dept Physics PO Box 1843 Providence RI 02912-1843

BRAY, PIERCE, business consultant; b. Chgo., Jan. 16, 1924; s. Harold A. and Margaret (Maclennan) B.; m. Maud Dorothy Minto, May 14, 1955; children—Margaret Dorothy, William Harold, Andrew Pierce. BA, U. Chgo., 1948, MBA, 1949. Fin. analyst Ford Motor Co., Dearborn, Mich., 1949-55; cons. Booz, Allen & Hamilton, Chgo. and Manila, Philippines, 1955-58; mgr. pricing, then corp. controller Cummins Engine Co., Columbus, Ind., 1958-66; v.p. fin. Weatherhead Co., Cleve., 1966-67; v.p. Mid-Continent Telephone Corp. (now ALLTEL Corp.), Hudson, Ohio, 1967-70, treas., 1967-77, v.p. fin., 1970-81, exec. v.p., chief fin. officer, 1981-85, dir., 1976-85, chmn. various subs.; instr. fin. and econs. U. Detroit, 1952-54; chmn. investor relations com. U.S. Telephone Assn., 1974-85; chmn. exec. com. Inst. Public Utilities, 1981-83. Trustee Beech Brook, Cleve., Ohio, 1972-96, life trustee, 1996—, treas., 1976-79, pres., 1979-81; bd. dirs. Breckenridge Village Retirement Cmty., 1991—, chmn. fin. com. 1995—; bd. trustees Ohio Presbyn. Retirement Svcs., 1996—; chmn. fin. com., 1999—. With AUS, 1943-46. Mem. Fin. Execs. Inst. (bd. dirs. 1993-96), Cleve. Treasurers Club, Union Club Cleve., Hillbrook Club (Chagrin Falls, Ohio), Walloon (Mich.) Yacht Club (chmn. bd. 1980-81, 85-86, 93—, commodore 1981-82, 87-88, bd. dirs., sec. 1988—), Ohio Masters Swim Club (trustee 1985-92, 96—, sec. 1989-93), Lake Erie Local Masters Swim Com. (chmn. 1992-96), Delta Upsilon. Presbyterian. Avocations: competitive swimming, sailing, volunteer and church activities. Home and Office: 31173 Northwood Dr Pepper Pike OH 44124-5411

BRAY, RICK, curator; b. Dana, Ind., June 30, 1965. BS, Franklin Coll., 1989. Curator Ernie Pyle State Hist. Site, Dana, Ind., 1997—. Office: Ernie Pyle State Hist Site PO Box 338 Dana IN 47847-0338*

BRAY, R(OBERT) BRUCE, music educator; b. La Grande, Oreg., July 24, 1924; s. Ernest C. and Leta M. (Haight) B.; m. Donna Marie Siegman, July 2, 1949 (div. 1980); children: Stephen Louis, Ruth Elizabeth, Katherine Ernestine, Anne-Marie. BA, U. Oreg., 1949, MMus, 1955; postgrad., U. Strasbourg, France, 1949-50, U. Wash., 1960-61. Music tchr. Helen McCune Jr. High Sch., Pendleton, Oreg., 1951-54; dir. choral music Albany (Oreg.) Union High Sch., 1954-56; elem. music supr. Ashland (Oreg.) Public Schs., 1956-57; asst. prof. music Cen. Wash. U., Ellensburg, 1957-60; from asst. to prof. U. Idaho, Moscow, 1961-89, prof. emeritus, 1989—; sec. faculty U. Idaho, Moscow, 1968-88, sec. emeritus, 1988—. Editor: Oreg. Music Educator, 1954-57, Wash. Music Educator, 1957-60, U. Idaho Music, 1961-68, Idaho Music Notes, 1963-68, U. Idaho Register, 1974-88 ; editorial bd. Music Educators Jour., 1964-68. With USNR, 1942-46. Mem. Music Educators Nat. Conf. (bd. dirs., pres. N.W. divsn. 1963-65, nat. exec. com. 1964-66), Phi Mu Alpha Sinfonia. Democrat. Episcopalian. Home and Office: 2614 E Everett Ave Spokane WA 99207-6210

BRAY, SHARON ANN, management company executive; b. Long Beach, Calif., June 12, 1944; d. George Knight and Oweta Izeda (Little) B.; m. Larry Dwane Collins, Jan. 29, 1967 (dec. July 1981); children: Elinor F., Claire J.; m. John C. Renner, May 20, 1989. BA in Sociology, San Jose (Calif.) State U., 1967; MEd, Mt. St. Vincent U., Halifax, Nova Scotia, 1981; EdD in Applied Psychology, U. Toronto, Can., 1986. Cert. tchr., Calif. Tchr. San Jose, Ottawa and Halifax Schs., 1967-80; psychologist Halifax County Sch. Bd., 1980-83; instr. St. Mary's U., Halifax, 1981-83; pvt. cons. Toronto, 1985-86; sr. cons. Stevenson, Kellogg, Ernst & Whinney, Toronto, 1985-86; dir. profl. svcs. Right Assocs., Toronto and Cupertino, Calif., 1988-90; v.p., dir. profl. svcs. Lee Hecht Harrison, San Jose, Calif., 1990-91, sr. v.p., gen. mgr., 1991-93, regional sr. v.p., 1993-94; sr. v.p. corporate dir. profl. svcs. and devel. Lee Hecht Harrison, N.Y.C., 1994—; disting. vis. lectr. Calif. Polytech. U., San Luis Obispo, 1987; keynote speaker Calif. Career Devel. Conf., Calif., 1992. Author: This Way to Canada, 1978; contbr. articles to profl. jours. Bd. dirs. Young Peoples' Theatre, Toronto, Ont., 1988-90, TheatreWorks, Palo Alto, Calif., 1990-92, Project Hired, Sunnyvale, Calif., 1992-95, Plays for Living, N.Y., 1996-97. Mem. Internat. Assn. Career Mgmt. Profls., Am. Assn. Counseling and Devel., Am. Mgmt. Assn., Calif. Career Devel. Assn., Soc. for Human Resources Mgmt. Democrat. Methodist. Avocations: jazz dancing, theatre, writing.

BRAY, WILLIAM SCOTT, retired school system administrator; b. Northampton, Mass., Dec. 29, 1939; s. William Howard Bray and Catherine (Scott) Bray Hatch; m. Beverly M. Chapman, July 1, 1967; children: Scott Hutchison, Robert Christian. BS in Edn., Westfield (Mass.) State Coll., 1962; MA, U. Conn., 1968, diploma in edn., 1979. Tchr. Norwalk (Conn.) Pub. Schs. Nathan Hale Mid. Sch., 1962-85; prin. Wolfpit Elem. Sch., Norwalk, 1987-89; asst. prin. Nathan Hale Mid. Sch., Norwalk, 1985-87, 89-97, ret., 1997. Asst. scoutmaster Boy Scouts Am., Norwalk 1987—; active Nat. Geneal. Soc., New England Hist. Geneal. Soc., Vt. Geneal. Soc. Mem. NEA (life), Phi Delta Kappa. Republican. Home: 315 Flax Hill Rd Norwalk CT 06854-2507

BRAYE, RUBYE HOWARD, army officer; b. Montgomery, Ala., July 7, 1953; d. Prince Albert Braye and Bertha M. Davis. Howard-Bray. BA, Hollins Coll., Roanoke, Va., 1975; MSBA, Boston U., 1982. Commd. 2d lt. U.S. Army, 1977, advanced through grades to lt. col., 1993; dir. software dept. U.S. Army Computer Sci. Sch., Indpls., 1984-86; instr., ops. officer Dept. Def. Computer Inst., Washington, 1987-89; commdr. Mil. Traffic Mgmt. Command Terminal, San Juan, P.R., 1989-91; automation officer U.S. Transp. Command, Scott AFB, Ill., 1991-94; dep. commdr. 20th Support Group, Taegu, 1995-96; transp. officer 9th TAACOM, Taegu, Korea, 1986-87; transp. fellow Office Asst. Dep. under Sec. of Def. for Transp. Policy, Washington, 1994-95; transp. ops. analyst U.S. Army Concepts Analysis Agy., Bethesda, 1996-97; project mgr. Exec. Security and Engring. Techs., Inc., 1997—. Mem. exec. bd., edn. com. Mental Health Assn., Alexandria, Va., 1996. Recipient Broadcast award Atlanta Interfaith Broadcast Assn., 1970. Mem. Soc. Computer Simulation Internat., Nat. Def. Transp. Assn. (treas. Scott/St. Louis chpt. 1978-97), 9th & 10th U.S. Cavalry Assn.-Buffalo Soldiers (chmn. scholarship com. D.C. chpt., sec. 1997), Phi Delta Kappa. Methodist. Avocations: travel, SCUBA diving, snow skiing, reading.

BRAYSON, ALBERT ALOYSIUS, II, educational association administrator; b. Port Jefferson, N.Y., June 28, 1953; s. Albert Aloysius and Julie Elizabeth (Krantz) B.; m. Barbara Norris Skretch, June 18, 1977; children: Albert III, Caroline Elizabeth. BA, Elmira (N.Y.) Coll., 1975; MS in Edn., Adelphi U., 1979. Tchr. Lake Grove (N.Y.) Sch., 1975-77, asst. headmaster, 1977-79, exec. dir., 1979—; pres., CEO Lake Grove Schs. and Treatment Ctrs., Durham, Conn., 1985—; cons. Valleyhead Sch., Lenox, Mass., 1985—; grant reviewer U.S. Govt., 1985-87; pres. BABSCorp., Sayville, N.Y., 1984—; sec. Safeway, Inc., Simsbury, Conn., 1989—; ptnr. Second Realty, Durham, Conn., 1985, Housatonic Everfloat Shelton, Conn., 1987. Treas. Lake Grove Village Ind. Party, 1980; co-chmn. com. to re-elect Sen. LaValle, 1990; co-chmn. fin. com. Rep. A Conn. Party, 1991; mem. dept. stewardship Episcopal Diocese of L.I.; trustee Stonybrook Sch., 1999. Mem. Nat. Assn. Pvt. Schs. for Exceptional Children, Coun. for Exceptional Children, Orgn. to Assure Svcs. to Exceptional Students, Mental Health Assn of N.Y. (bd. dirs. 1990-99, exec. com. 1991), Lions (pres. 1986), Stony Brook Yacht Club, Hartford Club. Republican. Avocations: sailing, skiing, equestrianism. Office: Lake Grove Experience PO Box 1306 Lake Grove NY 11755-0606

BRAYTON, ROBERT K., computer science educator; b. Des Moines; married; children: Jane, Jim, Mike. BS, Iowa State U., 1956; PhD in Math., MIT, 1961. Elec. engr. Remington Rand Univac, 1956-57; rsch. assoc. artificial intelligence MIT, 1957-61, mgr. differential equations and numerical analysis, 1963-81, vis. assoc. prof., 1966-67; asst. dir. IBM Rsch., 1971-72; vis. prof. Imperial Coll., London, 1975-76; mgr. Logic Design, 1981-85, 2d level mgr. differential equations & computer algebra, 1981-84, 2d level mgr. math algorithms, 1984-87; prof. elec. engring. and computer sci. U. Calif., Berkeley, 1987—; vis. McKay prof. U. Calif., Berkeley, 1985-86; vis. prof. elec. engring. TU Delft, 1992-93; rsch. staff mem. IBM Thomas J. Watson Rsch. Ctr., 1961-67. Contbr. articles to profl. jours. Fellow AAAS, IEEE; mem. NAE. Office: Univ Calif Dept-EECS 231 Cory Hall Berkeley CA 94720*

BRAZ, EVANDRO FREITAS, management consultant; b. Jan. 20, 1943; came to U.S., 1966; s. Jose Nunes and Edir (Freitas) B.; m. Darline Kristina Ryther, Dec. 28, 1968; children: Erica Denise, Daniel Williams, Max Elliot. BSME, Rio de Janeiro U., 1965; MS in Indsl. Engring., Columbia U., 1967, MBA, 1968. Registered profl. engr., Brazil. Assoc. engr. Mass Transit Authority, Rio de Janeiro, 1964; prodn. engr. GE Corp., Rio de Janeiro, 1965-66; cons. mgmt. cons. svcs. Coopers & Lybrand, N.Y.C., 1968-72, mgr. mgmt. cons. svcs., 1972-76, prin., ptnr. mgmt. cons. svcs., 1976-98; ptnr. mgmt. cons. svcs. Price Waterhouse Coopers, 1998—. OAS fellow Columbia U., 1968. Mem. Inst. Mgmt. Cons. (cert.), Nat. Assn. Accts., Am. Prodn. and Inventory Control Soc., Am. Arbitration Assn., Mt. Kisco (N.Y.) Country Club. Roman Catholic. Home: 14 Whitlaw Close Chappaqua NY 10514-1008 Office: Price Waterhouse Coopers 1301 Avenue Of The Americas New York NY 10019-6013

BRAZAITIS, THOMAS JOSEPH, journalist; b. Cleve., Aug. 8, 1940; s. Joseph R. and Regina G. (Greicius) B.; m. Eleanor Clift, Sept. 30, 1989; children: Mark Thomas, Sarah Jean. BS, John Carroll U., Cleve., 1962. Mng. editor newspapers Collinwood Pub. Corp., Cleve., 1964-71; reporter, then Washington corr. Cleve. Plain Dealer, 1971-79, Washington bur. chief, 1979-98, Washington sr. editor, 1998—. Co-author: (with Eleanor Clift) War Without Bloodshed: The Art of Politics, 1996. Served to 1st lt. USAR, 1962-64. Mem. Regional Reporters Assn. (founder), Nat. Press Club, Washington Press Club Found. (bd. dirs. 1994—, pres.), Gridiron Club. Office: 930 National Press Building Washington DC 20045-1901

BRAZEAL, AURELIA ERSKINE, former ambassador; b. Chgo., Nov. 24, 1943. BS, Spelman Coll., 1965; M of Internat. Affairs, Columbia U., 1967; postgrad., Harvard U., 1972. With Foreign Svc., 1968; consular and econ. officer U.S. Embassy, Buenos Aires, 1969-71; econ. reports officer Econ. Bureau U.S. State Dept., 1971-72, watch and line officer Office of Secretariat, 1973-74, desk officer Uraguay, Paraguay, 1974-77; review officer Office of Secretariat U.S. Dept. Treasury, 1977-79; econ. officer Tokyo, 1979-82; officer ECON Bur. U.S. Dept. State, 1982-84; dep. dir. Econ. Office Japan, 1984-86; dir. econs. Office Japan Affairs, 1984-86; mem. sr. seminar, 1986-87; min. counselor econ. affairs U.S. Embassy, Tokyo, 1987-90; U.S amb. to Micronesia, 1990-93, U.S. amb. to Kenya, 1993-96; deputy asst. sec. East Asian & Pacific Affairs, 1996-98; dean sr. seminar Fgn. Svc. Inst.fairs, Arlington, Va., 1998—. Office: State Dept/Fgn Svc Inst 4000 Arlington Blvd Arlington VA 22204-1586

BRAZEAL, EARL HENRY, JR., electrical engineer; b. Springfield, Vt., Aug. 24, 1949; s. Earl Henry and Nellie Mary (Krasofski) B.; m. Jennifer Pease Clark, 1962 (div. 1980); children: Tracy, Suzanne, Jeremy; m. Beverly May Green, Apr. 24, 1982; 1 stepchild, Dulcie. Cert., Ward Tech. Inst., Hartford, Conn., 1959; BSEE, U. Conn., 1964, MSEE, 1966. Engr. electronics United Technologies, East Hartford, Conn., 1965-69; sr. engr. Scan-Optics, East Hartford, 1969-76, mgr. electronic engring., 1976-78; sr. engr. electronics Mediscan/Smith-Kline Instruments, South Windsor, Conn., 1978-81; mgr. surface receiver devel. program Teleco Oilfield Svcs., Meriden, Conn., 1981-82; adv. engr. electronics Scan-Optics, East Hartford, Conn., 1982-85, mgr. imaging electronics, 1985-90, mgr. electronic imaging and hardware support, 1990-94; mgr. mech. and elec. sys. devel. Scan-Optics, East Hartford, 1994-96, mgr. elec. engring., 1996—; instr. Sch. Engring., U. Conn., Storrs, 1974-80. Inventor various systems, 1970—. Mem. stewardship com. United Ch. of Christ, 2d Congl., Coventry, Conn., 1983-86, 89-92, 95-96, 98, treas. deacon's, 1984, 85, asst. fin. sec., 1995-96, chmn. property bd., 1999—. Mem. IEEE (first prize N.E. sect. 1964), Internat. Soc. for Optical Engring., Sigma Xi, Eta Kappa Nu. Democrat. Avocations: amateur radio, antique radio collecting and restoring, skiing, reading. Home: 134 Ash Brook Dr Coventry CT 06238-1401 Office: Scan-Optics Inc 169 Progress Dr Manchester CT 06040-2294

BRAZELL, IDA HERNANDEZ, judge; b. Mercedes, Tex., Jan. 28, 1951; d. Guadalupe C. and Juanita (Gamez) Hernandez; children: Patrick Bryan, Andrew Owen. BA, U. Tex., 1973, JD, 1971. Bar: Tex. 1978, U.S. Dist. Ct. (ea. dist.) Tex. 1981, U.S. Dist. Ct. (so. dist.) Tex. 1986. Instr. legal rsch. Lamar U., Beaumont, Tex., 1979-80; briefing clk. Ct. Appeals, 9th Supreme Jud. Dist., Beaumont, Tex., 1978-80; mng. atty. Continental Ins. Cos., Beaumont, Tex., 1980-82; atty. Brazell & Brazell, Corpus Christi, Tex., 1982-85; dir. immigration svcs. Diocese of Corpus Christi, 1984-86; assoc. Calame, Linebarger & Graham, Corpus Christi, 1985-86; atty. pvt. practice, Corpus Christi, 1986-93; mem. commrs. ct. Nueces County Commr., Precinct 3, 1994; judge State of Tex., Office Ct. Adminstrn., 1994—. Mem. Nueces County Cmty. Action Agy., Robstown Econ. Devel. Corp., Vol. Lawyers Project; mem. exec. com. Workforce Devel. Corp. Nueces County; bd. dirs. Vol. Ctr. Fellow, Tex. Bar Found. Mem. Am. Immigration Lawyers Assn. (program chair 1988, sect. co-chair San Antonio sect. 1988-90), Coastal Bend Criminal Defense Lawyers Assn., Coastal Bend Women Lawyers Assn. (v.p. 1993-94, pres. 1994-95), Family Law Assn., Hispanic Women's Network, Latin Am. Coun. Labor Assns., Leadership Western Nueces County, Mexican-Am. Bar Assn. Coastal Bend, Coll. State Bar Tex. Avocations: bicycling, tennis, racquetball. Office: IV-D Ct Master 901 Leopard St Rm 404 Corpus Christi TX 78401-3602

BRAZELL, JAMES ERVIN, oil company executive, lawyer; b. Cromwell, Okla., Sept. 11, 1926; s. John Edward and Eva May (Black) B.; m. Peggy Lee Carson, Feb. 9, 1951; children: James, Mary Margaret, April Kay. B-SMechE, Okla. State U., 1950; JD, U. Tulsa, 1959. Bar: Okla. 1959, U.S. Supreme Ct. 1976. With Texaco, Inc., various locations, 1950—; exec. v.p. Texaco Can. Inc., Toronto, Ont., Can., 1978-80; staff dir. exploration and producing exec. com. Texaco Inc., White Plains, N.Y., 1980—, also bd. dirs. With USAF, 1945. Mem. Am. Petroleum Inst., Soc. Petroleum Engrs., Okla. Bar Assn., Can. Geographic Soc., Granite Club (Toronto), Country Club of Asheville. Home: 2202 Timber Pl Asheville NC 28804-3952 Office: Texaco Inc 2000 Westchester Ave White Plains NY 10650-0002

BRAZELTON, THOMAS BERRY, pediatrician, educator; b. Waco, Tex., May 10, 1918; s. Thomas Berry and Pauline (Battle) B.; m. Christina Lowell, Dec. 3, 1949; children: Catherine Bowles, Pauline Battle, Christina Lowell, Thomas Berry. AB, Princeton U., 1940; MD, Columbia U., 1943; DSc (hon.), Russell Sage Coll., 1987, Wheaton Coll., 1991, Tufts U., 1994, Loyola U., Chgo., 1994; honoris causa, U. Lisbon, Portugal, 1992; LHD (hon.), Northeastern U., 1990; EdD (hon.), Wheelock Coll., 1991; D in Pub. Svc. (hon.), Cedar Crest Coll., 1992. pres. Nat. Ctr. Clin. Infancy Programs, 1988-1990. Intern Roosevelt Hosp., N.Y.C., 1944; resident Mass. Gen. Hosp., Boston, 1945-47, Children's Hosp., Boston, 1947; resident in child psychiatry Putnam Children's Ctr., Roxbury, Mass., 1947-50; practice medicine specializing in pediatrics Cambridge, Mass., 1950—; clin. prof. emeritus pediatrics Children's Hosp., Boston, 1999—; instr. pediatrics Harvard U. Med. Sch., 1951-72, assoc. prof., 1972—, clin. prof. pediatrics, 1986; dir. child devel. unit Children's Hosp. Med. Ctr., Boston, 1972-92; researcher in child devel. Putnam Children's Ctr. and Harvard Ctr. Cognitive Studies, 1968-88; sch. physician Shady Hill Sch., 1966-76, Cambridge Nursery Sch., 1967-70; pres. Nat. Ctr. for Clin. Infant Programs, 1988-91; mem. Nat. Commn. on Children, 1989-92. Author: Infants and Mothers: Individual Differences in Development (Child Study Assn. Ann. award 1970), 1969; Toddlers and Parents, 1974; Neonatal Behavioral Assessment Scale, 1974; The Family— Can It Be Saved?, 1975; Doctor and Child, 1976; The Family: Setting Priorities, 1979; On Becoming a Family, 1981, To Listen to a Child, 1984, Working and Caring, 1984; Affective Development in Infancy, 1986, What Every Baby Knows, 1988, Families Crises and Caring, 1989, The Earliest Relationship, 1990, Touchpoints: Your Child's Emotional and Behaviorial Development, 1992, Going to the Doctor, 1997; contbr. articles to Family Circle mag., profl. jours.; appears Lifetime Cable TV show What Every Baby Knows (Emmy award for Daytime Host, 1994); author nationally syndicated column on parenting, N.Y. Times. Served with USNR, 1944-45. Mem. Am. Acad. Pediatrics (chmn. child devel. sect. 1970), Soc. Rsch. in Child Devel. (pres. 1987-90), Mass. Med. Soc., New England Pediatric Soc., Am. Assn. Child Care in Hosps., Nat. Assn. Edn. of Young Children, Zero to Three (Washington) (pres. 1989-91), Barnstable (Mass.) Yacht Club. Office: Children's Hosp Ste 320 1295 Boylston St Boston MA 02215-3407*

BRAZELTON, WILLIAM THOMAS, chemical engineering educator; b. Danville, Ill., Jan. 22, 1921; s. Edwin Thomas and Gertrude Ann (Carson) B.; m. Marilyn Dorothy Brown, Sept. 23, 1943; children—William Thomas, Nancy Ann. Student, Ill. Inst. Tech., 1939-41; B.S. in Chem. Engring, Northwestern U., 1943, M.S., 1948, Ph.D., 1952. Chem. engr. Central Process Corp., 1942-43; instr. chem. engring. Northwestern U., 1947-51, asst. prof., 1951-53, asso. prof., 1953-63, prof., 1963-91, prof. emeritus, 1991—, chmn. dept., 1955-56, asst. dean Technol. Inst., 1960-61, assoc. dean, 1961-94, acting asst. dean, 1994-96, ret., 1996; engring. and ednl. cons., 1949—. Mem. Prospect Heights (Ill.) Bd. Edn., 1957-61; bd. dirs., exec. com. Chgo. Area Pre-Coll. Program. Recipient Vincent Bendix Minorities in Engring. award ASEE, 1986. Mem. Am. Inst. Chem. Engrs. (chmn. Chgo. sect. 1966-67), Am. Chem. Soc., Am. Soc. Engring. Edn. (chmn. Ill.-Ind. sect. 1963-64, 73-74, Vincent Bendix Minorities in Engring. award, 1986), Soc. for History of Tech., Soc. for Indsl. Archeology, Sigma Xi, Tau Beta Pi, Phi Lambda Epsilon, Alpha Chi Sigma, Triangle. Home: 10 E Willow Rd Prospect Heights IL 60070-1332 Office: Northwestern U Technol Institute Evanston IL 60208

BRAZIER, DON ROLAND, retired railroad executive; b. Pittsburg, Kans., Mar. 30, 1921; s. Hosie O. and Lola Frances (Tow) B.; m. June Darla Harr, Nov. 8, 1941. B.C.S., Benjamin Franklin U., Washington, 1950, M.C.S., 1951. Civilian budget officer Ordnance Corps, Dept. Army, 1940-43, 46-53; OFC asst. sec. def., 1953-67; comptroller Def. Supply Agt., 1967; dep. asst. sec. army, 1967-68; prin. dep. asst. sec. def.-comptroller, 1968-74; treas. AMTRAK, 1974-75, v.p. fin., treas., 1975-82, exec. v.p. fin. and adminstrn., 1982-86; dir. Washington Union Terminal; pres., dir. Chgo. Union Sta. With USAAF, 1943-46; maj. AUS ret. Decorated Meritorious Service medal; recipient Def. Disting. Civilian Service award, 1971, 73, 74.

BRAZIL, HAROLD EDMUND, political science educator; b. Bearden, Ark., Aug. 24, 1920; s. Paul Brazil and Lavenia (Govenor) Pullen; children: Leslie, Christopher, Susan, Paul, Ernest, Harold, Michael. BS, Tuskegee U., 1942; MA, Ohio State U., 1957; PhD, Ohio State U., Columbus, 1961. Placement officer VA, Columbus, 1946-49; dir. civil personnel Internat. Refugee Orgn., Fed. Republic of Germany, 1949-50; personnel officer USAF, Philippines, 1955-57, dir. research and community relations, 1957-59; command historian USAF, Philippines and S.E. Asia, 1959-62; attaché Am. Embassy, Cairo and Monrovia, Liberia, 1962-66; prof., chmn. dept. polit. sci. Sienna Coll., Loudonville, N.Y., 1966-70; co-dean sch. humanities and social sci. Rensselaer Poly. Inst., Troy, N.Y., 1970-72, prof., chmn. dept. history and polit. sci., 1972-75, prof. polit. sci., 1975-90, prof. emeritus, 1990—; instr. Indsl. Coll. of Armed Forces, Washington, 1964, Fgn. Service Inst. of Dept. of State, Washington, 1965. Author: The Taiwan Straits Crisis of 1958, 1959, The Politics of Philippine Economic Development, 1962, A World Apart: America Military Diplomacy in S.E. Asia, 1976, The Law of the Oceans: Pursuing Order in the Twenty-First Century, 1988, The Third World, Multinationals, and the Law of the Sea Treaty, in Papers in Public Law and Comparative Political Science, 1989. Served as capt. USAF, 1942-46. Mem. Am. Internat. Polit. Sci. Assn., African Studies Assn., Inter-Univ. Seminar on Armed Forces and Soc. Home: PO Box 1560 Troy NY 12181-1560 Office: Rensselaer Poly Inst Dept Sci & Tech Studies Sage Hall Troy NY 12181

BRAZIL, JOHN RUSSELL, academic administrator; b. Los Angeles, Mar. 5, 1946; s. Burton R. and Helen Frances (Douglas) B.; m. Janice Hosking; children: Adrian, Morgan;. AB, Stanford U., 1968; MPhil, Yale U., 1971, PhD, 1975. Coordinator Am. studies program San Jose (Calif.) State U., 1976-79, assoc. prof., prof., 1979-84, spl. asst. to acad. v.p., 1979-81, exec. asst. to pres., 1981-83, assoc. acad. v.p., 1983, acad. v.p., 1983-84; pres. Southeastern Mass. U., North Dartmouth, 1984-92, Bradley U., 1992-99, Trinity U., San Antonio, 1999—; chmn. S.E. Mass. Partnership, 1988-92; exec. dir. Sourisseau Acad. State and Local History, San Jose, 1977-79; cons. Calif. Coun. for Humanities in Pub. Policy, 1976-78, NEH; chmn. Coun. of Pub. Pres.'s and Chancellors, Mass., 1986-87; hon. adv. bd. SHARE, Inc., 1986-92; mem. Am. Coun. Edn., 1984—; bd. dirs. Cilcorp, Inc., Caterpillar Inc., Meth. Med. Ctr., NAICU; exec. com. FIICU, 1992—. Contbr. articles on Twain, London, Sterling, Bierce, the 1920's, numerous book revs. Bd. dirs. Mass. Ctr. for Excellence in Marine Sci., 1986-92; mem. Fall River Regional Task Force, 1984-92; com. mem. SEMTECH, Mass., 1984-92; trustee Greater New Bedford Indsl. Found., 1984-92; mem. Charlton Meml. Hosp., 1985-92; pres. S.E. Mass. U. Found., 1985-92; bd. govs. Forest Pk. Found., 1995-99. Fulbright Sr. scholar, U. Sydney, 1980; Phi Kappa Phi Disting. Faculty Achievement award, San Jose State U., 1984; S&H Found. lectureship grant. Mem. NCAA (Pres.'s Commn. 1987-92, chair Walter Byers scholarship com. 1991-96), Am. Assn. State Colls. and Univs., Am. Studies Assn., Am. Assn. Higher Edn., New Bedford C. of C. (bd. dirs. 1984-88), No. Calif. Am. Studies Assn. (exec. bd. 1978-80), Soc. Advancement of Mgmt. (adv. rev. bd. 1991-92), Fall River C. of C. (bd. dirs. 1984-87), Phi Beta Kappa, Phi Kappa Phi, Omicron Delta Kappa. Democrat. Office: Trinity U Office of President San Antonio TX 78212-7200

BRAZIL, WAYNE D., federal judge. BA, Stanford U., 1966; MA, Harvard U., 1967, PhD, 1975; JD, U. Calif., Berkeley, 1975. Extern clk. to Hon. John J. Purchivo Calif. Superior Ct., 1973-74; extern clk. to Hon. Donald R. Wright Calif. Supreme Ct., 1975-78; with Farella, Braun & Martel, San Francisco; apptd. magistrate judge no. dist. U.S. Dist. Ct. Calif., 1984; tchr. Vols. in Asia, 1966; tchr., counselor Upward Bound, U. Mass., 1968-69; vis. prof. law U. Ky., 1978; assoc. prof. law U. Mo., 1978-80; prof. law Hastings Coll., 1980-84. Contbr. articles to law jours. Capt. USAR, 1974. Mem. ABA, Am. Law Inst., Calif. Bar Assn., Phi Beta Kappa, Order of Coif. Fax: (510) 637-3327. Office: Oakland Federal Courthouse 1301 Clay St Oakland CA 94612-5217

BRAZINSKY, IRV(ING), chemical engineering educator; b. N.Y.C., Oct. 27, 1936; s. Israel and Rebecca (Singer) B.; m. Rosalie Seligson, June 14, 1959; children: Howard, Michael. BSChemE, Cooper Union, 1958; MS, Lehigh U., 1960; ScD, MIT, 1967. Chemist Freeport Sulfur Co., Port Sulfur, La., 1957; rsch. engr. NASA, Cleve., 1958, 59-61, Polaroid Corp., Waltham, Mass., 1966-69; sr. rsch. engr. Celanese Corp., Summit, N.J., 1969-76; sr. engr. R & D Halcon Internat., N.Y.C., 1976-81; process devel. mgr. Foster Wheeler Energy Corp., Livingston, N.J., 1981-85, cons., 1985-88; adj. prof. N.J. Inst. Tech., Newark, 1971-81; assoc. prof. chem. engring. Cooper Union, N.Y.C., 1985-91, prof., 1991—, chmn. dept., 1989—; cons. Gen. Foods Inc., Philip Morris Inc., N.Y.C. Dept. of Pers., 1985-91. Pioneer, patentee processes for heat stabilizing microporous plastic film, improving melt strength of polyester and nylon melts, and rapid chilling of beverages; contbr. articles to profl. jours. Mgr., coach Matawan Little League, 1975-81; active YMCA Indian Guides Program, 1972-80; coach Aberdeen-Matawan Basketball League, 1979-85; v.p. Matawan High Sch. Parents Athletic Assn., 1986-90. Recipient Schweinburg award, 1954; Petroleum Rsch. Fund fellow, 1958-59, A.D. Little fellow, 1963-64, Proctor & Gamble fellow, 1964-66; N.Y. State Regents scholar, 1954-58, Campbell, Reilly, Schiff and O'Rourke scholar, 1955-58. Mem. Am. Soc. Engring. Edn., Am. Inst. Chem. Engrs., Am. Chem. Soc., Soc. Plastics Engrs., Soc. Rheology, N.Y. Acad. Scis., Sigma Xi. Home: 6 Rustic Ln Matawan NJ 07747-2865 Office: Cooper Union 51 Astor Pl New York NY 10003-7132

BREAKSTONE, ROBERT ALBERT, consumer products, information technology and consulting executive; b. N.Y.C., Feb. 20, 1938; s. Morris and Minnie E. (Guon) B.; m. Eileen Fogel, Nov. 5, 1966; children: Warren, Ron, David. BS in Math., CCNY, 1960, MBA in Mgmt., 1964. Systems engring. mgr. IBM, N.Y.C., 1960-64; dir. mgmt. systems Continental Copper & Steel Industries, Inc., N.Y.C., 1964-68; v.p., CFO, Sys. Audits, Inc., N.Y.C., 1968-70; v.p., group exec. Chase Manhattan Bank, N.Y.C., 1970-74; group v.p., bd. dirs. Chesebrough-Pond's, Inc., Greenwich, Conn., 1974-85; chmn. bd., pres., CEO Health-Tex Inc., N.Y.C., 1985-88; exec. v.p., COO GTech Corp., West Greenwich, R.I., 1988-95; pres., CEO Landmark Internat. Group, Stamford, Conn., 1995—; adj. asst. prof. Pace U. and NYU, 1964-71; adj. prof. Mercy Coll. Grad. Sch. of Bus., 1997—; apptd. to bd. dirs. State of Conn. Conix Program; spkr. in field; bd. dirs. OSF, Inc., Hoffinger Industries. Bd. dirs. Stamford (Conn.) Mus. and Nature Ctr., Bi-Cultural Sch.; pres. United Jewish Fedn. of Stamford, 1996-98. Mem. N.Am. Soc. Corp. Planning, Am. Apparel Mfrs. Assn. (dir.), Mu Gamma Tau (pres.). Home: 95 Lynam Rd Stamford CT 06903-4527 Office: Landmark International Group Inc 4 Landmark Sq Ste 300 Stamford CT 06901-2502

BREAM, JULIAN, classical guitarist and lutanist; b. London, Eng., July 15, 1933; s. Henry G. B. Ed., Royal Coll. Music; hon. degree, U. Surrey, Eng., 1968. First recital, 1947, London debut, 1950, U.S. debut, 1958; formed Julian Bream Consort, 1960; since performed tours in all 5 continents, regular tours to Europe and U.S.A.; performed concerts, recitals, including with Sir Peter Pears, also chamber music, string quartets, duo with John Williams, Julian Bream Consort world tour with Robert Tear, 1988; appeared in festivals and recitals: Aldeburgh , Berlin, Edinburgh, Bath, Paris, Vienna, Tokyo, New York, recital series at Concertgebouw, Amsterdam, 1992-93, 60th birthday concert at the Wigmore Hall, London, 1993; transcriber Romantic and Baroque works; commd. new works from Benjamin Britten, William Walton, Hans Werner Henze, Malcolm Arnold, others; frequent radio and TV appearances including TV biog. film, A Life in the Country, 1976, series of master classes, film of Elizabethan music and poetry with the late Dame Peggy Ashcroft, 1987, all for BBC; producer, performer 8 films on location in Spain on devel. Spanish music for lute and guitar; numerous recs. for RCA; now under exclusive contract with EMI Classics; recordings include Julian Bream Edition Vol. 1-28, Highlights From the Julian Bream Edition, The Baroque Guitar, A Celebration of Andrés Segovia, Guitar Greatest Hits, La Guitarra Romantica, Impressions for Guitar, Popular Classics for Spanish Guitar, The Romantic Guitar, Julian & John/2; subject of book pub. by Macdonald, 1982. Served with Brit. Army, 1952-55. Decorated Comdr. Brit. Empire, 1985; recipient Grammy award for Classical Performance: An Evening of Elizabethan Music, 1963, Villa-Lobos Gold medal, 1976, 6 awards Nat. Acad. Recording Arts and Scis., 2 Edison awards, various awards from Gramophone mag., Gold Silver and Platinum discs. Research in Elizabethan lute music. Office: care Hazard Chase Ltd, Richmond Hs 16-20 Regent St, Cambridge CB2 1DB, England

BREATHED, BERKELEY, cartoonist; b. Encino, Calif., June 21, 1957; s. John William Breathed and Martha Jane (Martin) de Varennes; m. Jody Elizabeth Boyman, May 10, 1986. BA, U. Tex., 1980. Syndicated cartoonist Washington Post Writer's Group, Washington, 1980-95. Cartoonist: Bloom County, 1980-89, Outland, 1989-95; author: (compilations) Loose Trails, 1983, Toons for Our Times,1984, Penguin Dreams and Stranger Things, 1985, Bloom County Babylon: Five Years of Basic Naughtiness, 1986, Billy and the Boingers Bootleg, 1987, Tales Too Ticklish To Tell, 1988, Night of the Mary Kay Commandos, 1989, Classics of Western Literature, 1990, Politically, Fashionably and Aerodynamically Incorrect, 1992, His Kisses Are Dreamy But Those Hairballs Down My Cleavage..., 1994, One Last Peek: The Final Hits, The Special Hits, The Inside Tips, 1995, (children's books) A Wish for Wings that Work (also TV spl., home video), 1991, The Last Basselope, 1992, Goodnight Opus, 1993, Red Ranger Came Calling, 1994. Recipient Pulitzer prize for editorial cartooning Columbia U., 1987. Avocations: power boating, travel, animal rights, motorcycling.

BREATHITT, EDWARD THOMPSON, JR., lawyer, railroad executive, former governor; b. Hopkinsville, Ky., Nov. 26, 1924; s. Edward Thompson Sr. and Mary Josephine (Wallace) B.; m. Lucy Alexander Breathitt; children: Mary Frances, Linda Key, Susan Holleman, Edward Thompson III. BS in Commerce, U. Ky., 1947, LLB, 1950, JD, 1970, LLD (hon.), 1965; LLD (hon.), U. Marshall, 1966, U. Ky., 1967. Bar: Ky. 1950, U.S. Supreme Ct. 1974. Ptnr. Trimble, Soyars & Breathitt, Hopkinsville, 1960-62; gov. State of Ky., Frankfort, 1963-67; ptnr. Trimble, Soyars & Breathitt, Hopkinsville, 1968-72; v.p. Southern Ry. Co., Washington, 1972-82; v.p. Norfolk Southern Corp., Washington, 1982-86, sr. v.p., 1986-92; with Wyatt Tarrent & Combs Law firm, Lexington, Ky., 1992—; mem. adv. bd. Am. Security Bank, Washington, 1987-90; mem. Ky. Econ. Devel. Corp., 1979—; chmn. bd. trustees U. Ky., 1992—. Mem. legis. State of Ky., Frankfort, 1952-56; chmn. and pres. Commn. on Rural Property, Washington, 1965-67; pres. Commn. to Fulfill These Rights, Washington, 1965-67. With USAAF, 1942-45. Named Conservationist of Yr. Nat. Wildlife Fedn. and Outdoor Life Mag., 1966; recipient Conservationist award U.S. Dept. of Interior, 1967, Lincoln Key award for Civil Rights, 1966. Fellow U. Ky.; mem. Ky. Bar Assn., D.C. Bar Assn., Chevy Chase Club, Pendenis Club. Democrat. Methodist. Avocations: fishing, hunting, golf, tennis, hiking. Home: 1703 Fairway Dr Lexington KY 40502-1648 Office: Wyatt Tarrant and Combs Lexington Fin Ctr 250 W Main St Ste 1700 Lexington KY 40507-1746

BREAULT, JEAN WINSOR, nursing consultant; b. Providence, June 8, 1932; d. William R. and Margery (Rueckert) Winsor; m. Murnie L. Breault, Dec. 17, 1955; children: Thomas L., Edward W. RN, Mass. Gen. Hosp. Sch. Nursing, Boston, 1952. Cert. gerontol. nurse. Nursing cons. Mill Pond Rest Home, Ashland, Mass., 1987—, Rehab. Assocs., Inc., Canton, Mass., 1991—, Golden View Health Care Ctr., Meredith, N.H., 1995. Mem. ANA, Mass. Nurses Assn., Mass. Extended Care Fedn. Office: 36 Mellen St Hopedale MA 01747-1524

BREAULT, THEODORE EDWARD, lawyer; b. N.Y.C., Mar. 7, 1938; m. Gretchen S. Clements, Dec. 10, 1966; children: Victoria Ann, Theodore Edmund, Heidi Sherwin, Edmund Clements. BS, Manhattan Coll., 1960; JD, Cath. U. Am., 1963. Bar: D.C. 1964, Va. 1964, Pa. 1970, U.S. Ct. Appeals (D.C. cir.) 1964, (4th cir.) 1969, U.S. Supreme Ct. 1967. Assoc. Seltzer & Suskind, Washington, 1964-69, Egler & Reinstadtler, Pitts., 1969-77; pvt. practice Fairfax, Va., 1967-69, Pitts., 1977—; lectr. Cath. U. Am. Sch. Nursing, Robert Morris Coll.; mem. Pa. Workmen's Compensation Sect.; spl. master Allegheny County Ct. of Common Pleas; arbitrator U.S. Dist. Ct. Pres. Sewickley (Pa.) Symphony Orch., 1974-75. Fellow Pa. Bar Found. (life); mem. Pa. Bar Assn. (civil litigation sect.), Va. State Bar Assn., D.C. Bar Assn., Allegheny County Bar Assn. (health law sect., workmen's compensation sect.), Am. Soc. Law and Medicine, Pa. Def. Inst., Am. Arbitration Assn. (arbitrator accident and comml. claims), Am. Coll. Legal Medicine (assoc. in law). Home: 108 Claridge Dr Moon Township PA 15108-3204 Office: Breault & Assocs PC 428 Forbes Ave 2200 Lawyers Bldg Pittsburgh PA 15219

BREAUX, CINDY ADDISON, accountant; b. Hammond, La., Apr. 16, 1971; d. William Huey and Peggy Mashon (Farmer) Addison; m. Ricky Paul Breaux; children: Michael, Mark, Lee, Sara. BS in Actg., Southeastern La. U., Hammond, 1993. CPA, La. Asst. contracts fiscal coord. La. Systemic Initiatives Program, Baton Rouge, 1994—. Mem. soc. La. CPAs. Avocations: camping, hunting, fishing, boating, bike riding. Email: cbreaux@regents.state.la.us. Office: La Systemic Initiatives Program 1885 Wooddale Blvd 11th Fl Baton Rouge LA 70806

BREAUX, JOHN B., senator, former congressman; b. Crowley, La., Mar. 1, 1944; s. Ezra H., Jr. and Katherine (Berlinger) B.; m. Lois Gail Daigle, Aug. 1, 1964; children: John B., William Lloyd, Elizabeth Andre, Julia Agnes. B.A. in Polit. Sci, U. Southwestern La., 1964; J.D., La. State U., 1967. Bar: La. 1967. Ptnr. Brown, McKernan, Ingram & Breaux, 1967-68; legis. asst. to Congressman Edwin W. Edwards, 1968-69, dist. asst., 1969-72; mem. 92d-99th Congresses from 7th Dist. La., 1972-86; U.S. Senator from La. Washington, 1987—; mem. Fin. com., 1990—, chief dep. whip, 1993—; mem. commerce, sci. and transp. com., aviation subcom., comm. subcom., consumer affairs subcom., oceans and fisheries subcom., surfact transp. and merchant marine subcom., fgn. commerce and tourism, fin. com., internat. trade subcom., taxation and IRS oversight com.; ranking mem. subcom. on Social Security and Fgn. Policy; mem. Senate Dem. steering coord. com., senate dem. tech. comm. com.; ranking mem. spl. com. on aging, fgn. commerce and tourism subcom., social security and family policy subcom.; chmn. Nat. Water Alliance, 1987-88, Nat. Dem. Senatorial Campaign Com., 1989-90, Dem. Leadership Coun., 1991-93; co-chmn. Nat. Bipartisan Commn. on Future of Medicare, 1998-99; co-chmn. Nat. Commn. on Retirement Policy, 1997-98. Leader Centrist Coalition of Senate Dems. and Reps. Recipient Am. Legion award; Moot Ct. finalist La. State U., 1966; Neptune award Am. Oceanic Orgn., 1980. Mem. La. Bar Assn., Crowley Jr. C. of C., La. Jr. C. of C., Pi Lambda Beta, Phi Alpha Delta, Lambda Chi Alpha. Office: US Senate 503 Hart Senate Bldg Washington DC 20510-1803

BREAUX, MARION MARY, secondary education educator; b. Raceland, La., June 16, 1950; d. Irby Joseph Breaux and Alvina Doretha (Comardelle) Baudouin, Edwin Joseph Baudouin (stepfather). BA, Nicholls State U., 1972. Cert. tchr. social studies and English edn., La. Tchr. Destrehan (La.) High Sch., 1972-76, Hahnville High Sch., Boutte, La., 1976—; cons. St. Charles Parish and La. State U. Writing Projects, 1991-98. Author: (poetry) The Red Popsicle, 1991; (prose) I Do, I Do, 1991, Old Wine in New Bottles, 1991. Named Tchr. of Month, Hahnville H.S., 1991, 97, Tchr. of Yr., 1995. Mem. La. Fedn. of Tchrs., St. Charles Parish Fedn. of Tchrs., Nat. Coun. of Social Studies. Avocations: writing, reading. Home: PO Box 279 Boutte LA 70039-0279 Office: Hahnville High Sch 200 Tiger Dr Boutte LA 70039-3520

BREAUX, PAUL JOSEPH, lawyer, pharmacist; b. Franklin, La., Mar. 11, 1942; s. Sidney J. and Irene (Bodin) B.; m. Marilyn Anne Jones, Aug. 21, 1965; children: Jason E., James P. BS in Pharmacy, Northeast La. U., 1965; JD, La. State U., 1972. Bar: La. 1972, U.S. Supreme Ct. 1975. Pharmacist Belanger's Pharmacy, Morgan City, La., 1965-66, Clinic Pharmacy, Morgan City, La., 1966-69; pvt. practice of law Lafayette, La., 1972-73, 93—; assoc. Allen, Gooch, Bourgeois, Breaux, Robison, Theunissen Attys., Lafayette, 1973-75; ptnr. Allen, Gooch, Bourgeois, Breaux, Robison & Theunissen, Lafayette, 1975-93; sec., bd. dirs. Bank of Lafayette. Bd. dirs. Lafayette Community Health Care Clinic, 1992—, Hvice chmn., 1996—; bd. dirs. Hospice of Acadiana, Inc., 1996—, The Hospice Found., pres. 1998—; mem. Gov.'s Universal Health Care Law Reform Commn., 1992—; active Boy Scouts Am., 1984-92. Mem. ABA, La. Bar Assn., Lafayette Parish Bar Assn., La. Bankers Assn. (mem. bank counsel com. 1983-85, 88-90, La. banking code legislation revision com. 1983), Am. Land Title Assn., Am. Pharm. Assn., La. Pharmacists Assn. (bd. dirs. 1991-99, Pharmacist of Yr. award 1992), Am. Compliane Inst., Nat. Assn. Retail Druggists, Am. Soc. Law and Medicine, Am. Soc. Pharmacy Law, Nat. Health Lawyers Assn., Acad. Hosp. Attys. of Am. Hosp. Assn., Soc. Hosp. Attys. of La. Hosp. Assn., Lafayette C. of C., Kappa Psi, Phi Eta Sigma. Republican. Roman Catholic. Office: 600 Jefferson St Ste 503 Lafayette LA 70501-6998

BREBBIA, JOHN HENRY, lawyer; b. Boston, Feb. 16, 1932; s. Joseph Dante and Gertrude (Hogan) B.; m. Patricia Mary Burke, Jan. 9, 1965. A.B., Stonehill Coll., 1953; LL.B., Boston Coll., 1956. Bar: Mass. 1957, D.C. 1965, Nev. 1988. Pvt. practice Boston, 1960-61; trial atty. Bur. Restraint of Trade, FTC, 1961-64; assoc. firm Davies, Richberg. Tydings, Landa & Duff, Washington, 1965-67; partner firm Alston & Bird, Washington and Atlanta, 1967-83; mng. partner Washington office Alston & Bird, 1971-76; v.p., gen. counsel First Western Fin. Corp., Las Vegas, 1966-67, 69-83, pres., 1967-69, 83-87, dir., 1966-87; dir. First Western Bank, Las Vegas, 1966-87, vice chmn., 1983-87; mem. atomic safety and licensing bd. panel Nuc. Regulatory Commn., 1972-82; pres. Savs. and Loan League Nev., 1987-88; counsel Edwards & Kolesar, Las Vegas, 1988-92, Foley & Jones, Las Vegas, 1992-93; chmn. Composite Power Corp., Las Vegas, 1992-95; v.p., gen. counsel RSCECAT, USA, INC., Las Vegas, 1995-96, exec. v.p., gen. counsel, 1996-98, pres., 1998—, dir., 1995—; exec. v.p., gen. counsel, dir. RSCECAT Internat. Ltd., V.I., 1996—; sec., treas., dir. Semper Resources Corp., 1996-99; sec., treas. Utility Comm., Inc., 1996—; pres. Titanic Devel. Corp., Las Vegas, 1998—; pres. Lab. of Electrotech. USA, Ltd., Las Vegas, 1998—. Mem. campaign staff Senator Robert F. Kennedy, 1964, Humphrey-Muskie, 1968, Muskie Election Com., 1971-72, Carter-Mondale, 1976; counsel for Inaugural Com., 1976; nat. chmn. Lawyers for Carter-Mondale, 1979-80; mem. Pres.'s Commn. on White House Fellowships, 1977-81; mem. Nev. Humanities Com., Inc., 1987-95, vice chmn., 1991-93, chmn., 1993-94; bd. dirs. So. Nev. Clean Communities, Inc., 1985-87, Downtown Progress Assn., 1984-87, Nev. Devel. Authority, 1985-87, Fedn. State Humanities Coun., 1991-95; mem. citizens adv. com. on Downtown Redevel., Las Vegas, 1986-91; chmn. honors program adv. com. Univ. Nev.-Las Vegas, 1986-90; vice chmn. Gov.'s Adv. Coun. on Edn. Relating to the Holocaust, 1990—; mem. Nev. Commn. Cultural Affairs, 1993-94. Served to capt. AUS, 1957-60. Mem. ABA, FBA, Bar Assn. D.C. (chmn. antitrust law com. 1972-74, 80-82). Home: 2832 Via Terra St Henderson NV 89014-1446 Office: 340 E Warm Springs Rd Ste 1A Las Vegas NV 89119-4202

BRECHBILL, SUSAN REYNOLDS, lawyer, educator; b. Washington, Aug. 22, 1943; d. Irving and Isabell Doyle (Reynolds) Levine; children: Jennifer Rae, Heather Lea. BA, Coll. William and Mary, 1965; JD, Marshall-Wythe Sch. Law, 1968. Bar: Va. 1969, Fed. Bar, 1970. Atty. AEC, Berkeley, Calif., 1968-73; indsl. rels. specialist AEC, Las Vegas, 1974-75; atty. ERDA, Oakland, Calif., 1976-77; atty. Dept. Energy, Oakland, 1977-78, dir. procurement divsn. San Francisco Ops. Office, 1978-85, asst. chief counsel for gen. law, 1985-93, acting asst. mgr. environ. mgmt. and support, 1992, acting asst. mgr. def. programs, 1993; chief counsel Dept. Energy Richland Ops. Office, 1994-99; mgr. Ohio field office Dept. of Energy, 1999—; mem. faculty U. Calif. Extension; speaker Nat. Contract Mgmt. Assn. Ann. Symposiums, 1980, 81, 83, 84, 88. Contbr. articles to profl. jours. Spkr. on doing bus. with govt. leader Girl Scouts U.S.A., San Francisco area; bd. dirs. Am. Heart Assn. Eastern Wash., 1997—, Sexual Assault Response Ctr., Tri Cities, Wash., 1997—; vol. tchr. Jr. Achievement, 1999. Named Outstanding Young Woman Nev., 1974; recipient Meritorious Svc. award Dept. Energy, 1992. Mem. NAFE, Va. State Bar Assn., Fed. Bar Assn., Nat. Contract Mgmt. Assn. (pres. Golden Gate chpt. 1983-84, N.W. regional v.p. 1984-86). Republican.

BRECHER, ARMIN G., lawyer; b. Prague, Czechoslovakia, July 7, 1942; s. Gerhard Otto and Eleanor (Baker) B.; m. Elizabeth Pardue Rountree, July 2, 1966; children: Lindsay Brecher Cobb, Stefan Ryan, Alden Kelsey. BA summa cum laude, Emory U., Atlanta, 1966; LLB, U. Va., 1969. Ptnr., chair exec. com. Powell, Goldstein, Frazer & Murphy, Atlanta, 1969—. Mem. The ESOP Assn. Presbyterian. Office: Powell Goldstein Frazer & Murphy LLP 191 Peachtree St NE Fl 16 Atlanta GA 30303-1740

BRECHER, ARTHUR SEYMOUR, biochemistry educator; b. N.Y.C., Mar. 30, 1928; s. Harry and Mollie (Rudich) B.; m. Laura Alma Lyman, June 19, 1966; children—Benjamin, Sharon. B.S., CCNY, 1948; Ph.D., UCLA, 1956. Postdoctoral appointee Purdue U., Lafayette, Ind., 1956-58; biochemist FDA, Washington, 1958-60; assoc. research scientist Bklyn. State Hosp., 1960-63; asst. prof. biochemistry George Washington U., Washington, 1963-69; assoc. prof. chemistry Bowling Green State U., Ohio, 1969-75, prof. chemistry, 1975—. Contbr. articles to profl. jours. Bd. dirs. Wood County Cancer unit Wood County Heart br. N.W. Ohio Heart Assn., chmn. heart health in young com. Recipient research and devel. award Bowling Green State U., 1974, spl. achievement award, 1975. Fellow AAAS; mem. Am. Soc. Biochemistry and Molecular Biology, Internat. Soc. Neurochemistry, Am. Soc. Neurochemistry, Soc. Exptl. Biology and Medicine, Am. Chem. Soc., Sigma Xi, Phi Lambda Upsilon. Jewish. Home: 3317 Brantford Rd Toledo OH 43606-2435 Office: Bowling Green State U Bowling Green OH 43403*

BRECHER, BERND, management consultant; b. Germany, Oct. 2, 1932; came to U.S. 1940; s. Jacob and Betty (Lewinsohn) B.; m. Helen Edith Casel, Feb. 1, 1959; children: Jacalyn Naomi, Alison Fay, Daniel Evan. BA, Columbia U., 1954, MS in Journalism, 1955. Dir. devel., pub. rels. and alumni affairs Coll. Physicians and Surgeons, Sch. Dentistry, Columbia U., N.Y.C., 1954-57; campaing dir., supr. John Price Jones Co., Inc., N.Y.C., 1958-67; v.p. Hamilton Coll. and Kirkland Coll., Clinton, N.Y., 1967-69; exec. v.p. John Price Jones Internat., Inc., N.Y.C., 1969-71; sr. v.p. Brakeley, John Price Jones, Inc., N.Y.C., 1971-73; pres. Bernd Brecher & Assocs., Inc., N.Y.C. and Scarsdale, 1973-93, Instl. Advancement Programs, Inc., N.Y.C. and Tuckahoe, N.Y., 1979—; cons., strategic planner for arts, health, edn., youth, religious, cmty., environ., and other not-for-profit instns.; exec. dir. The Grad. Ctr. Found., N.Y.C., 1994-97; cons. Lilly Endowment, Indpls., 1994—. Pres. Bd. Edn., Greenburgh, N.Y., 1977-78, Woodlands Scholarship Fund, Hartsdale, N.Y., 1965-66, Soc. of Columbia Graduates, 1980-85; mem. exec. com. Columbia Journalism Sch. Alumni, 1981-89; trustee Berkshire Children's Mus., 1998—. With U.S. Army, 1957-58. Recipient alumni medal for svc. Columbia U., 1983, Pres.'s Cup, 1981, Lion Awards, 1979, 80, 94. Mem. Coun. for Advancment and Support of Edn. (Quarter Century Svc. award 1981), Nat. Soc. Fund Raising Execs. (v.p. N.Y. chpt. 1987-89), Am. Assn. Community and Jr. Colls., Am. Hosp. Assn., Am. Assn. Mus., Princeton Univ. Club, Univ. Club of Chgo. Avocations: theatre, tennis, travel, fine dining. Home: 35 Parkview Ave Bronxville NY 10708-2953 Office: Instl Advancement Programs Inc 65 Main St Tuckahoe NY 10707-2908

BRECHER, HOWARD ARTHUR, lawyer; b. N.Y.C., Oct. 18, 1953; s. Milton and Dorothy (Zahler) B. AB magna cum laude, Harvard U., 1975, MBA, 1979, JD cum laude, 1979; LLM, NYU, 1984. Bar: N.Y. 1980, U.S. Dist. Ct. (so. dist.) N.Y. 1983, U.S. Tax Ct. 1981. Assoc. Roberts & Holland, N.Y.C., 1979-82, Chadbourne, Parke, Whiteside & Wolff, N.Y.C., 1982-84; atty. legal dept. N.Y. Telephone Co., N.Y.C., 1984-91, counsel, 1991-96; v.p. law Value Line, Inc., 1996—; mem. tax com. N.Y.C. C. of C., 1985-88, 94—. Mem. ABA (tax sect.), N.Y. State Bar Assn. (tax sect., com. taxation of affiliated corps., trusts and estates sect.), Assn. of Bar of City of N.Y., Harvard Bus. Sch. Club of Greater N.Y., N.Y.C. C. of C. (mem. tax com. 1994—). Democrat. Jewish. Clubs: Harvard (N.Y.C. and Boston). Office: 220 E 42nd St Ste 6000 New York NY 10017-5806

BRECHER, IRVING, economics educator; b. Montreal, Que., Can., Feb. 1, 1923; m. Toba Brecher, May 11, 1944; children: Richard, Thomas, Ronald, Teresa. BA, McGill U., 1943; MA, Harvard U., 1947, PhD, 1951; JD, Yale U., 1953. Asst. prof. econs., lectr. law Northwestern U., Evanston, Ill., 1953-55; asst. prof. econs. McGill U., Montreal, 1948-50; assoc. prof. McGill U., 1955-61; prof., 1962-84; chmn. dept. McGill U., 1981-84, prof. emeritus, 1985—, dir. Centre for Developing-Area Studies, 1963-71; joint dir. Pakistan Inst. Devel. Econs., Karachi, 1960-61; bd. govs. Internat. Devel. Research Centre, Ottawa, 1970-73; vice chmn. Econ. Council Can., Ottawa, 1972-74. Author: Monetary and Fiscal Thought and Policy in Canada, 1919-1939, 1957, Capital Flows between Canada and The United States, 1965, Canada's Competition Policy Revisited, 1982; co-author: Canada-United States Economic Relations, 1957, Foreign Aid and Industrial Development in Pakistan, 1972; editor: Human Rights, Development and Foreign Policy: Canadian Perspectives, 1989; co-editor: Development Planning and Policy in Pakistan, 1950-70, 1973, Equity and Efficiency in Economic Development, 1992; contbr. numerous articles on pub. policy and internat. affairs to profl. publs., magazines and newspapers. Bd. dirs. Can. Human Rights Found., Montreal, 1988-91, Internat. Ctr. for Human Rights and Dem. Devel., Montreal, 1990-94. Recipient Queen's Silver Jubilee medal, 1978; Leave fellow Can. Council, 1971-72. Mem. Am. Econ. Assn., Can. Econs. Assn., Can. Inst. Internat. Affairs. Office: McGill U-Dept of Econs, 855 Sherbrooke St W, Montreal, PQ Canada H3A 2T7

BRECHER, KENNETH, astrophysicist; b. N.Y.C., Dec. 7, 1943; s. Irving and Edythe (Grossman) B.; m. Aviva Schwartz, Aug. 18, 1965; children: Karen, Daniel. B.S., MIT, 1964, Ph.D., 1969. Research physicist U. Calif., San Diego, 1969-72; asst. prof. physics MIT, Cambridge, 1972-77; assoc. prof. MIT, 1977-79; assoc. prof. astronomy and physics Boston U., 1979-81, prof., 1981—, dir. Sci. and Math. Edn. Ctr., 1990—. Author, editor: (with G. Setti) High Energy Astrophysics and Its Relation to Elementary Particle Physics, 1974, (with M. Feirtag) Astronomy of the Ancients, 1979; contbr. numerous articles to profl. jours. Mem. Mass. Cultural Coun., 1989-91. Guggenheim fellow, 1979-80; W.K. Kellogg fellow, 1985-88; NRC sr. research assoc., 1983-84. Fellow Am. Phys. Soc. (chmn. astrophysics div. 1990-91); mem. Am. Astron. Soc., Internat. Astron. Union, Am. Assn. Physics Tchrs., N.Y. Acad. Scis., Sigma Xi. Home: 35 Madison St Belmont MA 02478-3535 Office: Boston U Dept Astronomy 725 Commonwealth Ave Boston MA 02215-1401

BRECHER, MICHAEL, political science educator; b. Montreal, Mar. 14, 1925; s. Nathan and Gisela (Hopmeyer) B.; m. Eva Danon, Dec. 7, 1950; children: Leora, Diana, Seegla. BA, McGill U., 1946; MA, Yale U., 1948, PhD, 1953. Mem. faculty McGill U., Montreal, 1952—; prof. polit. sci. McGill U., 1963—, R.B. Angus prof. polit. sci., 1993—; founder Shastri Indo-Can. Inst., 1968, pres., 1969, 70; vis. prof. U. Chgo., 1963; vis. prof. internat. rels. Hebrew U., Jerusalem, 1970-75, U. Calif., Berkeley, 1979, Stanford U., 1980. Author: The Struggle for Kashmir, 1953, Nehru: A Political Biography, 1959, The New States of Asia, 1963, Succession in India, 1966, India and World Politics, 1968, Political Leadership in India, 1969, The Foreign Policy System of Israel, 1972, Israel: The Korean War and China, 1974, Decisions in Israel's Foreign Policy, 1975, Studies in Crisis Behavior, 1979, Decisions in Crisis, 1980, Crisis and Change in World Politics, 1986, Crises in the 20th Century: Vol. 1, Handbook of International Crises, Vol. 2, Handbook of Foreign Policy Crises, 1988, Crisis, Conflict and Instability, 1989, Crises in World Politics, 1993, A Study of Crisis, 1997; contbr. over 80 articles in field to profl. jours. Recipient Watumull prize Am. Hist. Assn., 1960, Killam awards Can. Coun., 1970-74, 76-79, Woodrow Wilson Found. award Am. Polit. Sci. Assn., 1973, Fieldhouse teaching award McGill U., 1986, Disting. Scholar award Internat. Studies Assn., 1995; Nuffield fellow, 1955-56, Rockefeller fellow, 1964-65, Guggenheim fellow, 1965-66, Can. Coun. and Soc. Sci. and Humanities Rsch. Coun. of Can. rsch. grantee, 1960, 65, 68, 69-70, 75-76, 80-87, 90-92, 93-96. Fellow Royal Soc. Can.; mem. Internat. Studies Assn. (pres. 1999-2000), Brit. Internat. Studies Assn., World Assn. Internat. Relations, Internat., Am., Can., Israeli polit. sci. assns. Jewish. Home: 5 Dubnov St, Jerusalem 91043, Israel Office: McGill U, 855 Sherbrooke St W, Montreal, PQ Canada H3A 2T7

BRECHNER, STANLEY, artistic director; b. N.Y.C., Apr. 11, 1944; s. Irving and Jane (Rabinowitz) B.; m. Adele Avramoff, Apr. 20, 1970 (div. July 1992); 1 child, Gabrielle. BA, Hunter Coll., 1964, MA in Theatre, 1972. Artistic dir. Am. Jewish Theatre, N.Y.C., 1974—, Nat. Jewish Theatre, Chgo., 1986-87. Co-author plays: The Jewish Woman, 1976, The White Room, 1977. Avocations: golf, puppet collecting. Office: Am Jewish Theatre 307 W 26th St New York NY 10001-5812

BRECHT, ALBERT ODELL, library and information technology administrator; b. Dallas, n, Nov. 19, 1946. BA in Govt. and Sociology, North Tex. State U., 1969; JD, U. Houston, 1972; LLM, U. Wash., 1973. Bar: Tex. 1972. Asst. law libr. U. So. Calif., L.A., 1973-74, asst. law libr. in-charge Law Libr., 1975, lab libr., asst. prof. law, 1975-77, dir. Law Libr., 1977—, assoc. prof., 1977-79, prof., 1979—, interim dep. univ. libr. for ctrl. libr. sys., 1984-85, assoc. dean Law Libr. and Info. Tech., 1995—; pres. Libraria Sodalitas, 1980; mem. Westlaw Acad. Adv. Bd., 1988-92. Author: (with A.

Holoch and K. Pecarovich) Medical Malpractice Insurance and Its Alternatives: The Legal, Medical, and Insurance Literature—A Bibliography, 1975; contbr. articles and book revs. to profl. jours. Mem. Am. Assn. Law Librs. (audio-visual com. 1975, chmn. nominations com. 1978, recruitment com. 1975-76, placement com. 1979-81, cons. law librs. of correctional instns., chmn. program com. ann. meeting 1983, v.p. 1986-87, pres. 1987-88, moderator program on law librs. 1991), Spl. Librs. Assn., So. Calif. Assn. Law Librs. (v.p. 1974-75, pres. 1975-76, bd. dirs. 1978, chmn. com. on cons. for non-law librs. 1981). Office: U So Calif Law Libr University Park Los Angeles CA 90089-0072*

BRECHT, BLAINE RICHARD, manufacturing company executive; b. Plainfield, N.J., Feb. 6, 1958; s. Joseph Thomas and Gloria Maria (Calabrese) B. BSBA, The Citadel, 1980; cert., The Quality Coll., Orlando, Fla., 1987. Cert. lead assessor Registrar Accreditation Bd. Mgmt. trainee Milliken & Co., Bostic, N.C., 1980-81; texturing shift mgr. Milliken & Co., Saluda, S.C., 1981-83, knit, dye and packing shift mgr., 1983-84, quality control supr., 1984-85; asst. quality control mgr. Collins & Aikman, Graham, N.C., 1985-87, div. mgr. quality services, 1987; div. mgr. planning and customer service Burlington Industries, Madison, N.C., 1987-88, engr. process improvement, tech. service, 1988-89; dir. quality assurance Dixie Yarns, Inc., Threads USA div., Gastonia, N.C., 1989-94; quality assurance mgr. U.S. Label, Greensboro, N.C., 1994—; team mem. Small Bus. Adminstrn., 1979-80. Sunday sch. tchr. Glen Hope Bapt. Ch., Burlington, N.C., 1985-87, dir. brotherhood, 1987—, mem. bd. deacons, 1996—; examiner N.C. Quality Leadership award, 1994—. Named one of Outstanding Young Men in Am., 1984. Mem. Am. Soc. Quality Control (sr.; cert. quality auditor, cert. quality mgr.). Republican. Home: 2604 Regents Park Ln Greensboro NC 27455-2237

BRECHT, SALLY ANN, quality assurance executive; b. Trenton, N.J., Aug. 5, 1951; d. Charles L. and Helen (Orfeo) B. BBA, Coll. William & Mary in Va., 1973; MBA, Rider Coll., 1981. Cert. quality engr., quality auditor, quality mgr., software quality engr. Electronic data processing auditor McGraw Hill, Inc., Hightstown, N.J., 1976-79, State of N.J., Mercerville, 1979-80, NL Industries, Hightstown, 1980-84; systems tech. planning specialist Ednl. Testing Svc., Princeton, N.J., 1984-85, acting div. dir. application devel., 1985-87, mgr. computer standards and security, 1987-88, asst. dir. office corp. quality assurance, 1988-98; dir. softward quality assurance Y2K Renovalion, 1998—. Contbr. articles to popular publs. Mem. Am. Soc. for Quality Control (cert. quality engr., mgr., auditor and software quality engr.). Avocation: riding show hunters.

BRECHT, WARREN FREDERICK, business executive; b. Detroit, May 21, 1932; s. August F. and Margaret (Roos) B.; m. Barbara Boone, July 31, 1983; children: Amy E., Stephen F., David C., Peter J. BA, DePauw U., 1954; postgrad., U. Mich., 1955; MBA, Harvard U., 1959. Systems analyst W.R. Grace & Co., Cambridge, Mass., 1959-61; v.p., treas. Mgmt. Systems Corp., Cambridge, 1961-65; partner in charge adminstrn. Peat, Marwick, Livingston & Co., Boston, 1965-69; prin. in charge profl. practice, mgmt. cons. dept. Peat, Marwick, Mitchell & Co., N.Y.C., 1969-71; dep. asst. sec. for mgmt. and budget U.S. Dept. Interior, Washington, 1971-72; asst. sec. for adminstrn. U.S. Dept. Treasury, 1972-77; v.p. acctg. and mgmt. info. systems Northeast Utilities, Hartford, Conn., 1977-85; sr. v.p. N. Am. Holding Corp. and Subs., East Hartford, Conn., 1985-89; sr. v.p., sec. Butler Internat. (formerly N.Am. Ventures Inc.), Montvale, N.J., 1985—; sr. v.p. adminstrn. and sec. Butler Svc. Group., Inc., Montvale, 1990—; mem. panel deregulation govt. mgmt. Nat. Acad. Pub. Adminstrn., 1982-83. Trustee Conn. Pub. Expenditure Coun., 1978-84; vice-chmn. ch. coun., treas., trustee Riverside Ch., N.Y.C., 1993—; exec. bd. Bergen County N.J. coun. Boy Scouts Am., 1997-98. With USAF, 1955-57. Recipient Outstanding Young Man award Lexington (Mass.) Jaycees, 1968; Exceptional Service award Dept. Treasury, 1976; Alumni citation DePauw U., 1976; Rector Scholar 25th Anniversary Achievement award DePauw U., 1979. Mem. Phi Beta Kappa. Home: 23 Tallman Ave Nyack NY 10960-1605 Office: Butler Internat 110 Summit Ave Montvale NJ 07645-1762

BRECHTEL, TERRY M., San Antonio budget and analysis director; m. Dennis Martinez; children: Colleen, Brian. BS in Polit. Sci., N. Tex. State U.; MPA in Pub. Adminstrn., So. Meth. U. Mem. budget staff City of San Antonio, budget mgr., dir. employee svcs., 1994—. Mem. Leadership S.W., Dallas, 1989-90, steering com. City of San Antonio leadership devel. com.; catechism instr. Our Lady of Grace Cath. Sch., San Antonio. Mem. Govt. Fin. Officers Assn., Govt. Fin. Officers Assn. of Tex., Internat. City-County Mgmt. Assn., Performance Measurement Consortium Policy Bd: Pub. Tech. Inst (urban consortium rep.). UMAST. Office: City of San Antonio PO Box 839966 San Antonio TX 78283-3966*

BRECHTEL, UNDA JURKA, library director; b. Riga, Latvia, Mar. 3, 1935; came to U.S., 1951; d. Aleksanders and Irene (Stesingers) Jurka; m. Philipp Jack Brechtel Jr., Sept. 3, 1960 (div. Aug. 1986); children: Philipp Jack III, Peter Kevin. BS in Psychology, St. Thomas Aquinas, 1981; MLS, L.I. U., 1982. Reference librarian Haverstraw (N.Y.) Pub. Libr., 1982-83; libr. dir. Sloatsburg (N.Y.) Pub. Libr., 1983-85, Wanaque (N.J.) Pub. Libr., 1985-88, Oakland (N.J.) Pub. Libr., 1988—. Mem. N.J. Libr. Assn., N.Y. Libr. Assn. Lutheran. Avocations: ballroom dancing, travel, gardening. E-mail: brechtel@bccls.org. Home: 5 Skahen Dr South Tomkins Cove NY 10986 Office: Oakland Pub Libr 2 Municipal Plaza Oakland NJ 07436

BRECKE, BARRY JOHN, weed scientist, researcher, educator; b. Milw., Jan. 16, 1947; s. Melvin Albert and Marie Catherine (Goerg) B.; m. Gayle Linda Naggatz, June 14, 1969; children: Darren John, Suzanne Marie. PhD, Cornell U., 1976. Asst. prof. U. Fla., Gainesville, 1976-81, assoc. prof., 1981-97, prof., 1997—. Author: (chpt) Model Crop Systems: Sorghum, Napiergrass, 1988, Weed Management in Peanuts, 1990, Management of Weeds, 1995; assoc. editor Weed Tech., 1993-96; contbr. articles, referee to Weed Tech., Peanut Sci., Weed Sci., 1980—. With U.S. Army, 1970-72. Grantee USDA, 1987-89, Cotton Inc., 1992-99, Ctr. for Integrated Pest Mgmt., 1995-96, GCSAA, 1998-99. Mem. Am. Soc. Agronomy, So. Weed Sci. Soc., Am. Peanut Rsch. and Edn. Soc., Weed Sci. Soc. Am., Internat. Weed Sci. Soc., Fla. Weed Sci. Soc. (pres. 1979). Roman Catholic. Achievements include research in weed biology and weed crop interactions. Office: West Fla Rsch and Edn Ctr 4253 Experiment Rd # Hwy182 Jay FL 32565-7332

BRECKENFELDER, LYNN E., health and physical education educator; b. Milw., Dec. 2, 1964; d. Roy Arthur and Nancy Lee (Sobocinski) B. BS, Winona State U., 1987; MPH, Ill. Benedictine Coll., Lisle, 1992; postgrad., No. Ill. U. Tchr. health and phys. edn. Newark (N.Y.) Cen. Sch. Dist., 1987-88, Wheaton (Ill.) Warrenville Dist. 200, 1988—; coach track and volleyball Wheaton Warrenville South High Sch., 1989-94; coach track West Chicago H.S., 1997-98, Hubble Mid. Sch., 1999—; coach volleyball, Hubble Mid. Sch., 1995—. Vol. Wheaton Recycling Ctr., 1990-94. Named Acad. All Am. U.S. Achievement Acad., 1987, outstanding student major, Nat. Assn. Sport and Phys. Edn., 1987; recipient traineeship USPHS, 1989. Mem. IEA, Am. Assn. Health, Phys. Edn., Recreation and Dance, Ill. Edn. Assn., Ill. Assn. Health, Phys. Edn., Recreation and Dance. Democrat. Roman Catholic. Avocations: softball, volleyball, crafts, floral arranging, golf. Home: 4732 Sailboat Bay # 2A Lisle IL 60532-1475 Office: Hubble Mid Sch 603 S Main St Wheaton IL 60187-5240

BRECKENRIDGE, BETTY GAYLE, management development consultant; b. Austin, Tex., Dec. 8, 1945. BA, Baylor U., 1966; MA, So. Meth. U, 1984. Cons. leadership continuity program AT&T, 1993—; cons. Leadership Devel. Ctr. Bellsouth Corp., 1990—; cons. Devel. Dimensions Internat., Pitts., Pa., 1984—. Office: 2615 Dekalb Pike # 503 Norristown PA 19401-1831

BRECKENRIDGE, KLINDT DUNCAN, architect; b. Iowa City, Apr. 24, 1957; s. Jack Duncan and Florence (Kmiecik) B.; m. Nancy Ann Dernier, Apr. 19, 1986; children: Wilson Reid, Lauren Alessandra. BArch, U. Ariz., 1981. Registered architect, Ariz., Calif., Nev.; cert. NCARB. Architect Finical & Dombrowski, Tucson, 1981-84; pres. The IEF Group, Inc., Tucson, 1984—; assoc. faculty Pima Community Coll. Bd. dirs., pres. Miracal Sq. Mem. AIA (past pres., past treas. So. Ariz. chpt., com. on architecture for edn., pres.-elect), Leadership Tucson Alumni (bd. dirs.). Democrat. Episcopalian. Avocation: running. Home: 5535 N Waterfield Dr Tucson AZ 85750-6473 Office: The IEF Group 705 N 7th Ave Tucson AZ 85705-8306

BRECKER, JEFFREY ROSS, lawyer, educator; b. N.Y.C., June 9, 1953; s. Milton S. and Charlotte (Alpert) B.; m. Phyllis L. Gordon, Oct. 30, 1983. BA in Polit. Sci., NYU, 1975; JD, New Eng. Sch. Law, Boston, 1978. Bar: N.Y. 1979, U.S. Dist. Ct. (so. and ea. dists.) N.Y. 1979, U.S. Supreme Ct. 1982. Atty. Nassau (N.Y.) County Legal Svcs. Commn., 1978-80, Dist. Coun. 37 Legal Svcs., N.Y.C., 1980-82, Wingate & Shamis, N.Y.C., 1982-85; sr. trial atty., unit supr. Jacobowitz & Lysaght, N.Y.C., 1985-89; mng. atty. Damashak Godosky & Gentile, N.Y.C., 1989-95, Godosky & Gentile, N.Y.C., 1995—; adj. prof. New Coll., Hofstra U., 1981. Office: Godosky & Gentile 61 Broadway 20th Fl New York NY 10006-2701

BRECKER, MICHAEL, saxophonist. Recipient Best Jazz Instrumental Performance Grammy award, 1996, 97, Best Jazz Instrumental Solo Grammy award, 1996-97. Office: Dept Field Mgmt 1501 Broadway Ste 1304 New York NY 10036-5601

BRECKER, RANDAL EDWARD, musician, arranger; b. Phila., Nov. 27, 1945; s. Robert John and Sylvia (Tecosky) B.; m. Eliane Elias; 1 child, Amanda Elias. Student, Ind. U., 1963-66. Profl. trumpeter, 1966—, bandleader, arranger, 1975—. Composer numerous pub. songs including Some Skunk Funk, 1975, Squids, 1976, Sponge, 1975, Inside Out, 1978, Guaruja, 1983, Toe to Toe, 1985, Songs of Rhyme Reason Romance & Raunch, 1999; leader Brecker Bros. and Randy Brecker Band; arranger music for numerous artists including Diana Ross, George Benson, Chaka Khan; albums include In The Idiom, 1992, Live at Sweet Basil, 1994, Into the Sun, 1998. Inducted to Walk of Fame, Phila., 1997; nominated Best Jazz Solo Grammy award, 1998; recipient Grammy award Best Contemporary Jazz Performance, 1997. Mem. Nat. Acad. Rec. Arts and Scis. (7 Grammy award nominations 1976-78, Most Valuable Player award N.Y. chpt. 1979, 86, 87, 88, 89, 90), Nat. Assn. Jazz Educators (3 Grammy award nominations 1992—, clinician), Am. Fedn. Musicians.

BRECKINRIDGE, JAMES BERNARD, optical science engineer, program manager; b. Cleve., May 27, 1939; s. Albert Coles and Catherine Rose (Wengler) B.; m. Ann Marie Yoder, July 24, 1965; children: Douglass E., John Brian. B.S. in Physics, Case Inst. Tech., 1961; M.S. in Optical Sci., U. Ariz., 1970, Ph.D. in Optical Sci., 1976. Research asst. Lick Obs., Mt. Hamilton, Calif., 1961-64; electron tube engr. Rauland Corp., Chgo., 1967; rsch. asst. Kitt Peak Nat. Obs., Tucson, full time, 1964-66, 68, 75-76, part time, 1969-74; mem. tech. staff Jet Propulsion Lab., Calif. Inst. Tech., 1976—, part-time faculty in applied physics, 1981—, mgr. optics sect., 1981-94; program mgr. for innovative imaging tech. and sys. Flight Projects Office, 1994-98; leader NASA Team to Assess Optics Tech. in Former Soviet Union, 1992-97; mgmt. & tech. cons., 1994—; mgr. Innovative Imaging Sys., 1998—; co-investigator NASA Spacelab 3; mem. adv. com. NASA, NSF, Dept. Def.; staff mem. Hubble Space Telescope Failure Bd., 1990, tech. mgr. Hubble Space Telescope Camera Optics Repair. Contbr. articles to jours. in field; 5 patents in field. Scoutmaster Boy Scouts Am.; bd. trustees United Ch. of Christ. Fellow Optical Soc. Am. (bd. dirs.), Royal Astron. Soc., Internat. Soc. Optical Engring. (bd. govs., pres. 1994); mem. IEEE, Am. Astron. Soc., Coun. of Scientific Soc. Pres.'s (bd. dirs. 1996), Internat. Astron. Union (U.S. com. rep. to the internat. congress on optics), Astron. Soc. of Pacific. Research in remote optical and infrared sensing instrumentation, interferometry, spectroscopy, image intensifiers and image analysis. Home: 4565 Viro Rd La Canada Flintridge CA 91011-3763 Office: JPL Caltech MS 126-244 4800 Oak Grove Dr Pasadena CA 91109-8099

BRECKINRIDGE, SCOTT DUDLEY, JR., author, government executive; b. Washington, Apr. 17, 1917; s. Scott Dudley and Gertrude Ashby (Bayne) B.; m. Helen Virden Babbitt, Aug. 29, 1942. BA, U. Ky., 1940, LLB, 1941. Atty. Breckinridge & Breckinridge, Lexington, Ky., 1947-53; employee Ctrl. Intelligence Agy., Washington, 1953-79, deputy inspector gen., 1972-79; lectr. U. Ky., Lexington, 1980-86. Co-author: Sword Play, 1941; author: CIA and U.S. Intelligence System, 1986, CIA and The Cold War, 1993. Asst. sec. gen. Soc. Cin., Washington, 1971-76; exec. com. U. Ky. Libr. Assoc., Lexington, 1981-85, Ky. Hist. Soc., Frankfort, Ky., 1988-92; bd. dirs. The Filson Club, Louisville, Ky., 1991-93. Recipient two Disting. Intelligence medal Ctrl. Intellegence Agy., Washington, 1977, 79; Disting. Svc. award Ky. Hist. Soc., 1990. Mem. Ky. Bar Assn., Del. State Soc. of Cin., U.S. Fencing Assn. (v.p. 1949-52). Avocations: history, current affairs. Home: 395 Redding Rd Apt 13 Lexington KY 40517-2369

BRECKNER, WILLIAM JOHN, JR., retired air force officer, corporate executive, consultant; b. Alliance, Ohio, May 25, 1933; s. William John and Frances P. (Bertchey) B.; m. Cheryl V. Carmell, Aug. 30, 1963; children: William R., Kristen C. B.A., SUNY, 1976; postgrad., Harvard U., 1980. Commd. 2d lt. USAF, 1955, advanced through grades to maj. gen., 1983; various pilot and command positions USAF, worldwide, 1955-72; POW Hanoi, Vietnam, 1972-73; comdr. USAF Interceptor Weapons Sch., 1973-75; vice commandant cadets USAF Acad., Colo., 1976-79; comdr. 82d Flying Tng. Wing Williams AFB, Ariz., 1979-80; dep. chief staff logistics Hdqrs. Air Tng. Commd., Tex., 1980-83; chief staff Hdqrs. USAF Europe, 1983-84; commdr. 17th Air Force, Sembach AFB, Germany, 1984-86; ret., 1986. Decorated D.S.M., 1986, Silver Star, 1972, Legion of Merit, 1973, Bronze Star medal, 1973, Air medal, 1968, 72, Purple Heart, 1972, 73, Republic of Vietnam Cross of Gallantry with palm, 1973. Mem. Nat. War Coll. Alumni Assn., Order Daedalians, Air Force Assn., Nam Prisoners of War Inc., Red River Valley Fighter Pilots Assn., C. of C. (chmn. mil. affairs coun. 1994-95). Lutheran. Prisoner of war, Vietnam, 1972-73. Avocations: golf; skiing; tennis. Home: 17865 Fairplay Way Monument CO 80132-8581

BREDDAN, JOE, systems engineering consultant; b. N.Y.C., Sept. 18, 1950; s. Hyman and Sylvia (Hauser) B. BA in Math. and Psychology, SUNY, Binghamton, 1972; MS in Ops. Research, U. Calif., Berkeley, 1975; PhD in Systems Engring., U. Ariz., 1978. Teaching and research assoc. Dept. Systems and Indsl. Engring. U. Ariz., Tucson, 1975-79; project engr. B.D.M. Services Co., Tucson, 1979-80; mem. tech. staff Bell Labs., Am. Bell, AT&T Info. Systems, Denver, 1980-86; staff mgr. AT&T, Denver, 1986-91; pvt. practice cons. Boulder, Colo., 1991—. Patentee in field. Bd. dirs. Colo. Environ. Coalition, 1996—. bd. dirs. Colo. Environ. Coalition, 1996—. Home and Office: 2120 Goddard Pl Boulder CO 80303-5616

BREDE, ANDREW DOUGLAS, research director, plant breeder; b. Pitts., Feb. 4, 1953; s. James Faris and Adele Katherine (Konefal) B.; m. Linda Davis Rudd, Jan. 11, 1992; children from previous marriage: Loralee Elizabeth, Michael Douglas. BS, Pa. State U., 1975, MS, 1978, PhD, 1982. Asst. golf course supt. Valley Brook Country Club, McMurray, Pa., 1975-76; grad. rsch. asst. Pa. State U., University Park, 1976-82; assoc. prof. Okla. State U., Stillwater, 1982-86; dir. rsch. Jacklin Seed Co., Post Falls, Idaho, 1986—; v.p. Turfgrass Breeders Assn., Tangent, Oreg., 1989-91; chmn. variety rev. Lawn Inst., Marietta, Ga., 1990—; bd. dirs. Nat. Turfgrass Evaluation Program; golf course supr. Assn. Am. Rsch. Com., 1996—. Assoc. editor Agronomy Jour., 1993—; contbr. articles to Agronomy Jour., 150 articles to mags.; prodr. 15 ednl. videos. Rsch. grantee, 1983-86. Mem. Am. Soc. Agronomy. Republican. Achievements include organization of 1st turfgrass conf. in People's Republic of China; developer, patentee 40 plant varieties. Avocation: amateur radio operating. Office: Jacklin Seed Co 5300 W Riverbend Rd Post Falls ID 83854-9499

BREDEHOFT, ELAINE CHARLSON, lawyer; b. Fergus Falls, Minn., Nov. 22, 1958; d. Curtis Lyle and Marilyn Anne (Nesbitt) Charlson; children: Alexandra Charlson, Michelle Charlson. BA, U. Ariz., 1981; JD, Cath. U. Am., 1984. Bar: Va. 1984, U.S. Ct. Appeals (4th cir.) 1984, U.S. Bankruptcy Ct. (ea. dist.) Va. 1987, D.C. 1994, U.S. Ct. Appeals (D.C. cir.) 1994. Assoc. Walton and Adams, McLean, Va., 1984-88, ptnr., 1988-91; ptnr. Charlson Bredehoft, P.C., Reston, Va., 1991—; spkr. Fairfax Bar Assn., CLE, 1992—, VB Assn., CLE, 1993—, 12th Ann. Multistate Labor and Employment Law Seminar, 1994, Va. CLE Ann. Employment Law Update, 1993-96, Va. Women's Trial Lawyers Assn. Ann. Conf., 1998, Va. Bar Assn. Labor and Employment Conf., 1994-97, Va. Trial Lawyers Assn., 1995, 97, Va. Law Found., 1995—, Va. Assn. Def. Attys., 1996; mem. faculty Va. State Bar Professionalism Courses, 1997—; invitee 4th Circuit Judicial Conf., 1997—; invitee, Boyd Groves Conference, 1999; substitute judge 19th Judicial Dist., 1998—; faculty Va. State Bar Professionalism Courses, 1997—, chair Fairfax Bar Assn. Diversity Taskforce, 1998— (Pres. Vol. award 1998). Bd. dirs. Va. Commn. on Women and Minorities in the Legal System, 1987-90, sec., 1988-90. Mem. Va. Bar Assn. (mem. exec. com. young lawyers sect., mem. litigation com., mem. nominating com., chmn. model jud. com., spkr. CLE 1993—, spkr. labor and employment conf. 1994-97), Va. Trial Lawyers Assn. (vice chmn. ann. conv. 1996-98, mem. com. on long-range planning 1996-97, spkr. 1995, 97), Minn. State Soc., Fairfax Bar Assn. co-chair subcom. on minorities, diversity task force 1997-98, Pres.'s Vol. award 1998, George Mason Inns of Ct. (master 1996—). Office: Charlson Bredehoft PC 11260 Roger Bacon Dr Ste 201 Reston VA 20190-5203

BREDEHOFT, THOMAS EVAN, newspaper publisher; b. Sterling, Colo., Oct. 4, 1961; s. Ralph Lauren and Betty Jean B.; m. Jean Ann, Nov. 25, 1995; 1 child, Taylor Jean Knolton; 3 stepchildren. BA in Journalism, U. No. Colo., 1984. Owner, pub. Mile Saver Shopper, Flagler, Colo., 1985—, The Flagler News, 1993—. Coach Arriba-Flagler Sch. Dist., 1986-91; bd. dirs. Kit Carson County Meml. Hosp., Burlington, Colo., 1994-96; mem. Flagler Town Coun., 1986-98. Mem. Am. Legion, Lions. Republican. Lutheran. Avocations: writing, golf, family. Home: 220 E 5th Flagler CO 80815 Office: Mile Saver Shopper/The Flagler News 321 Main Ave Flagler CO 80815

BREDELL, FRANK FULSTON, public relations company executive; b. Lockport, N.Y., May 29, 1930; s. Frank F. and Florence J. (Cramp) B.; m. Elisabeth Shannon, Oct. 18, 1953 (div. Jan. 1994); children: Paul, John, Marie. BA, Alfred U., 1952; MS in Journalism, Columbia U., 1953. Editor Courier-Express, Buffalo, 1953-57, Detroit News, 1958-65; v.p. Kenneth Drake Assocs., Detroit, 1965-74; dir. pub. rels. Harper-Grace Hosps., Detroit, 1974-87; pres. Frank Bredell Pub. Rels., Inc., Lincoln Park, Mich., 1987—. Contbr. articles on travel, pub. rels. and bus. to various mags. Trustee St. Peter's Home for Boys, Detroit, 1966-72; sr. warden St. Luke's Ch., Allen Park, Mich., 1969; head Sch. Millage Com., Lincoln Park, 1972; mem. parish com. Christ Good Shepherd Ch., Lincoln Park, 1989-92. Mem. Greater Detroit Pub. Rels. Counselors (pres. 1995, v.p. 1997). Democrat. Roman Catholic. Avocations: travel, writing, photography, reading. Home and Office: PO Box 484 Lincoln Park MI 48146-0484

BREDESEN, PHILIP NORMAN, mayor; b. Oceanport, N.J., Nov. 21, 1943; s. Philip Norman and Norma (Walborn) B.; m. Andrea Conte, Nov. 22, 1974; 1 child, Benjamin. AB in Physics, Harvard U., 1967. Computer programmer Itek Corp., Lexington, Mass., 1967-70; dir. systems devel. Searle Medidata, Lexington, 1970-73; div. mgr. Searle Medidata, London, 1973-75; dir. spl. project Hosp. Affiliates Internat., Nashville, 1975-78; v.p. internat. div. INA Health Care Group, Nashville, 1978-80; chmn. and chief exec. officer HealthAmerica Corp., Nashville, 1980-86; chmn., co-founder Coventry Corp., Nashville, 1986-90; chmn. Clin. Pharms., Nashville, 1986-93; mayor Met. Nashville and Davidson County, 1991—. Bd. dirs. Nashville Symphony, 1985-91, Univ. Sch. Nashville, 1986-95, United Cerebral Palsy, 1988-92, United Way of Middle Tenn., 1985-90, Tenn. State U. Found.; founder Nashville's Table, 1989, bd. dirs., 1989-91; candidate for mayor Nashville, 1987, 91, 95, Dem. nominee for gov., 1994. Democrat. Presbyterian. Avocations: skiing, reading, computers. Home: 1724 Chickering Rd Nashville TN 37215-4908 Office: Office of the Mayor Public Sq 107 Metro Courthouse Nashville TN 37201-5099

BREDFELDT, JOHN CREIGHTON, economist, financial analyst, retired air force officer; b. Great Bend, Kans., Oct. 31, 1947; s. Willis John and Geraldine Elizabeth (Creighton) B.; m. Barbara Elaine Gutow, June 6, 1984; children: Jason Caulter, Bryan Thomas. BBA, Wichita State U., 1969, MA in Econs., 1971; PhD in Pub. Adminstrn. La Salle U., 1995; grad., Air Command and Staff Coll., 1984, Nat. Def. U., 1987. Dir. Brennan Halls, Wichita State U., 1969-71; commd. 2d lt. U.S. Air Force, 1971, advanced through grades to lt. col. 1987, ret., 1993; budget/cost ananlyst Aero. System div., Dayton, Ohio, 1971-76; insp. Air Force IG, Andrews AFB, Md., 1976-79; chief economist Dir. Programs AF/PRP, Pentagon, Va., 1979-83; chief cost analyst div. U.S. Air Force Europe, 1985-87; dep. dir. program control, engine program office, Dayton, 1987-89; dir. program control spl. ops. forces, 1989-93; prin. econs./fin. analyst Modern Techs. Corp. Warner Robins, Ga., 1993—; instr. econs. Wichita State U., 1969-71; bus. prof. Bowie State Coll., 1980-83; econs. instr. European divsn. U. Md., Germany, 1985-87, Sinclair C.C., Dayton, 1988-93, Macon (Ga.) State Coll., 1994—; adj. prof. Mercer U., 1996—, Wesleyan Coll., 1998—. Contbr. articles to profl. jours. Rep., Sunday sch. tchr. Ramstein Protestant Parish Council Germany, 1984-86; asst. scout master Ramstein council Boy Scouts Am., 1984-87, den leader Weblos, 1998; v.p. St. Timothy Lutheran Ch., Dayton, 1989-91. Mem. Assn. Govt. Accts., Soc. Cost Estimating and Analysis, Am. Soc. Mil. Comptrollers, Nat. Eagle Scout Assn.

BREDWELL, JO, advertising executive. Sr. v.p. corp. mktg. comm. dir. Bernard Hodes Group, N.Y.C., 1990—. Office: Bernard Hodes Group 555 Madison Ave Fl 15 New York NY 10022-3479*

BREE, MARLIN DUANE, publisher, author; b. Norfolk, Nebr., May 16, 1933; s. George F. and Luile Bree; m. Loris Bree; 1 child, William Marlin. BA, cert. in journalism, U. Nebr., 1955. Mng. editor Davidson Pub. Co., 1958-61; editor Greater Mpls. mag., 1962-63; pub. rels. specialist Blue Shield, 1964-67; editor Sunday Mag., Star and Tribune, Mpls., 1968-72; columnist Corp. Report, Mpls., 1973-77; publs. cons., 1978-83; co-founder, ptnr., editorial dir. Marlor Press, Inc., St. Paul, 1983-91, co-owner, pub., 1992—; chmn. Midwest Book Awards, St. Paul, 1992. Author: In the Teeth of the Northeaster: A Solo Voyage on Lake Superior, 1988, Call of the North Wind: Voyages and Adventures on Lake Superior, 1996; co-author: Alone Against the Atlantic, 1981. Dir. comm. Mpls. Bicentennial Celebration, 1976. With U.S. Army, 1955-57. Named Pub. of Yr., Midwest Ind. Pubs. Assn., 1994; honored as one of Best Ind. Pubs. in U.S., Top 101 Ind. Book Pubs., 1997. Avocation: sailing. Office: Marlor Press Inc 4304 Brigadoon Dr Saint Paul MN 55126-3100

BREECE, ROBERT WILLIAM, JR., lawyer; b. Blackwell, Okla., Feb. 5, 1942; s. Robert William Breece Sr. and Helen Elaine (Maddox) Breece Robinson; m. Elaine Marie Keller, Sept. 7, 1968; children: Bryan, Justin, Lauren. BSBA, Northwestern U., 1964; JD, U. Okla., 1967; LLM, Washington U., St. Louis, 1970. Bar: Oklahoma 1967, Mo. 1970. Pvt. practice St. Louis, 1968—; pres., chmn. bd. dirs. Crown Capital Corp., St. Louis. Mem. ABA, Internat. Bar Assn., Mo. Bar Assn., Okla. Bar Assn., Phi Alpha Delta, Beta Theta Pi, Melrose Club, Univ. Club, Forest Hills Country Club (pres. 1978). Home: 35 Crown Manor Dr Chesterfield MO 63005-6805 Office: 540 Maryville Centre Dr Ste 12 Saint Louis MO 63141-5828

BREED, ALLEN FORBES, correctional administrator; b. Wisconsin Rapids, Wis., Oct. 1, 1920; s. Noel Jerub and May Belle (Forbes) B.; m. Virginia Mae Plaskett, June 24, 1945; children: Marla, Eleanor, Carol. B.A. cum laude, U. Pacific, 1942. With Dept. Youth Authority, State of Calif., 1945-76; supt. correctional schs. Dept. Youth Authority, 1947-65, chief div. instns., 1965-67; chmn. Youth Authority Bd., State of Calif., 1967-76; dir. Dept. Youth Authority, State of Calif., 1967-76; vis. fellow Dept. Justice, 1976-77; spl. master U.S. Dist. Ct., R.I., 1977-78; dir. Nat. Inst. Corrections, Dept. Justice, Washington, 1978-83; chmn. bd. Nat. Council Crime and Delinquency, Washington, 1983-91, 98—; spl. master to fed. and state cts. on prison litigation issues, 1983—; chmn. Task Force on Corrections and mem. Joint Commn. on Juvenile Justice Standards, ABA and Inst. Judicial Adminstrn.; mem. nat. adv. com. on Juvenile Justice and Delinquency Prevention; mem. U.S. del. UN Congress on Prevention of Crime and Treatment of Offenders, Caracas, Venezuela, 1980; mem. UN Congress on Prevention Crime and Treatment of Offenders, Milan, Italy, 1985; del. Internat. Conf. on Criminology, Hamburg, Federal Republic of Germany, 1988, Internat. Conf. on Future of Corrections, Ottawa, Can., 1991—; leader del. on juvenile justice to Russia, 1989—; lectr. 1st Sino-Am. Criminal Justice Inst., People's Republic China, 1986; criminal and juvenile justice del. People's Republic China, 1992; del. Internat. Conf. Corrections, Warsaw, 1993. Contbr. articles to profl. jours., newspapers, mags. Mem. justice programs adv. com. Edna McConnel Clark Found., 1983-89. Served to maj. USMC, 1942-45. Decorated Purple Heart. Mem. Nat. Assn. State Correctional Adminstrs. (state and nat. awards), Nat. Assn. State Juvenile Delinquency Program Adminstrs. (past pres.), Interstate Compact on Probation and Parole (past pres.), Am. Correctional Assn. (v.p. 1984-86, bd. govs. 1986-91), Am. Arbitration Assn., Nat. Coun. Crime and Delinquency (chmn. emeritus bd. dirs.), Calif. Probation, Parole and Correctional Assn. Episcopalian. Home: PO Box 698 San Andreas CA 95249-0698

BREED, EILEEN JUDITH, small business owner; b. Chgo., Sept. 18, 1945; d. John Joseph and Helen Agatha (Hoy) Kennedy; m. Harvey Breed, Feb. 3, 1973; 1 child, Diana Marie Parks. BA, Northea. Ill. U., 1966, MA, 1976, postgrad., 1980-81; postgrad., Nat. Coll. Edn., 1981, 83, No. Ill. U., 1987—. Tchr. Canty Elem. Sch., Chgo., 1967-76, St. Raymond's Sch., Mt. Prospect, Ill., 1976-78; pvt. practice diagnosis, remediation learning disabilities; cons. spl. edn. Des Plaines, Ill., 1976-78; prin. Angel Town Pvt. Sch., Des Plaines, 1978-79; tutoring, coop. work tng. coord. Nipper Sch., Des Plaines, 1979-86; tchr. acad. resources Oak Terr. Sch., Highwood, Ill., 1986-87; vocat. coord. North and West regions Sch. Assn. Spl. Edn. Du Page County, Roselle, Ill., 1987-89; prin. Sch. Assns. Spl. Edn./Du Page N. Alternative Sch., 1989-91, Aura Extended Day Sch., 1990-91; asst. prin. Stratford Jr. H.S., Bloomingdale, Ill., 1991-94; founder, pres. Handy Ma'ams, Inc., Allegan, Mich., 1994—, Heartfelt Creations, Saugatuck and Allegan, Mich., 1996; tchr. parent-edn. classes; cons. in field to pvt. schs., various groups and agys. Past chmn. Smiles Campaign; active Glen Lakes Beautification Com. Mem. NAFE, TRADE Industries (parent group), Alabama Coast Area C. of C. Home & Office: 9462 Lakeview Dr Foley AL 36535

BREED, JOSEPH ILLICK, financial economist; b. Troy, N.Y., Nov. 1, 1962; s. Henry Eltinge and Helen (Illick) B. BS in Materials Sci., Cornell U., 1984; MS in Scientific Computing, Stanford U., 1990; MS in Finance, George Washington U., 1997. Microwave engr. Varian SSMD, Santa Clara, Calif., 1984-87; computer scientist Lord Corp., Erie, Pa., 1988; numerical analyst Stanford (Calif.) Linear Accelerator, 1988-90; computer scientist Dalkin Industries, Osaka, Japan, 1989, Nat. Inst. Stds. and Tech., Gaithersburg, Md., 1990; info. systems analyst Fed. Res. Bd., Washington, 1990-98; fin. economist Office of Comptroller of the Currency, Washington, 1999—. Vol. Internat. Student Ho., Washington, 1995—. Avocations: piano, volleyball, bicycling. Home: 532 20th St NW Apt 407 Washington DC 20006-5037 Office: Office of the Comptroller of the Currency 250 E Street SW Washington DC 20219

BREED, MICHAEL DALLAM, environmental, population, organismic biology educator; b. Kansas City, Mo., Sept. 2, 1951; s. Laurence W. and Loree (Dallam) B.; m. Cheryl A. Ristig, Aug. 9, 1975. BA, Grinnell Coll., 1973; MA, U. Kans., 1975, PhD, 1977. Asst. prof. environ., population, organismic biology U. Colo., Boulder, 1977-83, assoc. prof., 1983-89, prof., 1989—, chmn. dept., 1986-90, 97-99, acting chmn. dept. anthropology, 1991-93, acting assoc. dean, 1991-93. Contbr. articles to sci. jours. Mem. Internat. Union for Study of Social Insects (pres. N.Am. sect. 1984, sec. gen. 1994—), Animal Behavior Soc., Internat. Bee Rsch. Assn., Entomol. Soc. Am. (officer sect. C 1992-95), Sigma Xi. Home: 700 Dahlia St Denver CO 80220-5112 Office: U Colo Dept Biology #102 Boulder CO 80309-0334

BREED, RIA, anthropologist; b. Helden, The Netherlands, Feb. 5, 1944; d. Jan Mathys and Maria Arnoldina (Gommans) Trienekens; m. David Scranton Breed, Sept. 5, 1976; children: Christian, Genevieve. Med. technologist Profl. Sch. Venlo (Netherlands), 1962; BA in Social Anthropology, U. Amsterdam, 1972; MA in Phys. Anthropology, NYU, 1977, PhD, 1984. Clin. technologist St. Lambertus Hosp., Helmond, 1962-65, DePaul Hosp., Norfolk, Va., 1965-66; research technician U. Amsterdam, 1968-70; research technician cardiovascular research NYU Med. Ctr., N.Y.C., 1966-68, 72-77; research assoc. NYU, N.Y.C., 1984; head biomechanics dept. Breed Corp., 1984-88; with Automotive Tech. Internat., Denville, N.J. Home: 48 Hillcrest Rd Boonton NJ 07005-9433 Office: Automotive Tech Internat PO Box 8 Denville NJ 07834-0008

BREEDEN, DAVID, clarinetist; b. Ft. Worth; m. Barbara Bernhard; children: Anne, Mark, Christopher. Pvt. study with his father, also Leo Gibson, Harold Wright, Loren Kitt, Rosario Mazzeo; grad., North Tex. State U.; MusM, Cath. U. With USN Band, until 1972; with San Francisco Symphony, 1972—, now prin. clarinet, 1974—; former mem. Caselli Wind Ensemble, San Francisco Opera Orch. Office: San Francisco Symphony Orch Davies Symphony Hall 201 Van Ness Ave Ste 107 San Francisco CA 94102-4585*

BREEDEN, MICHAEL EDWARD, defender; b. Manassas, Va., July 30, 1963; s. Elvin Burl and Nancy Lee Breeden. BA, Am. U., 1984; JD, U. Oreg., 1993. Bar: Oreg. 1993, U.S. Ct. Appeals (9th cir.) 1994, Calif. 1997. Asst. pub. defender Intermountain Pub. Defender's Office, Pendleton, Oreg., 1994-98, Yolo County Pub. Defender's Office, Woodland, Calif., 1998—. Democrat. Address: PO Box 817 Woodland CA 95776

BREEDIN, BERRYMAN BRENT, journalist, public relations, historian, consultan; b. Beaufort, S.C., Nov. 3, 1925; s. Berryman Brent Breedin and Jane Cunningham Dixon; m. Allain Crenshaw, Sept. 1959 (div. Jan. 1978); children: David Singleton, Sarah Chase, Amelia Twarogowski. BA, Washington and Lee U., 1947. Reporter Caller-Times, Corpus Christi, Tex., 1947-48; sports editor, columnist Daily Mail, Anderson, S.C., 1949-52; publicist, editor Clemson (S.C.) U., 1952-55, 64-66; resident mgr. Hunt Internat. Oil Co., Pakistan, 1955-58, Australia, 1996-97; press sec. U.S. Senator Strom Thurmond, Washington, 1958-59; info. specialist DuPont Co., Wilmington, Del., 1960-63; editor Am. Coll. Pub. Rels. Assn., Washington, 1966-71, Coun. Libran Resources, Washington, 1972-75; dir. pub. rels. Georgetown U., Washington, 1977-79, Rice U., Houston, 1981-87; pvt. practice Columbia, S.C., 1988—; historian White House Weekly, Washington, 1998—; adv. Washington D.C. Libr., 1972-76, Houston Zoo, 1981-87. Founding mem. Capital Hill Montessori, Washington, 1964, Field Sch., Washington, 1972. With USN, 1944-45. Mem. Nat. Press Club, Sigma Delta Chi. Episcopalian. Avocations: family history, sports history, movie history. E-mail: brent@compuzone.net. Home and Office: 1829 Senate St 4C Columbia SC 29201

BREEDLOVE, JIMMIE DALE, JR., elementary education educator; b. Pekin, Ill., Jan. 18, 1958; s. Jimmie Dale Sr. and Kay Maria (Goodin) B. BA in Elem. Edn. magna cum laude, Eureka (Ill.) Coll., 1980; postgrad., No. Ill. U., Pekin. Cert. elem. tchr. K-9, high sch. tchr. 6-12. Homebound instr., learning resource room aide Lewistown (Ill.) Community High Sch., 1980-81; elem. tchr. San Jose (Ill.) Community Unit Sch. Dist. 122, 1981-89, Illini Cen. Community Unit Sch. Dist. 189, 1989—; geography curriculum, developer; sch. librarian, gifted/talented instr. San Jose Grade Sch. Dir. choir, mem. worship com. San Jose United Meth. Ch. Mem. NEA, Internat. Reading Assn., Ill. Edn. Assn., Illini Cen. Edn. Assn., Alpha Chi. Office: Illini Central Grade Sch Mason City IL 62664

BREEN, DAVID HART, lawyer; b. Ottawa, Ont., Can., Mar. 27, 1960; came to U.S., Aug. 19, 1978; naturalized, 1993; s. Harold John and Margaret Rae (Hart) B.; m. Pamela Annette Mitchell, Sept. 17, 1988; 1 child, Matthew Mitchell. BA cum laude, U. S.C., 1982, JD, 1986. Bar: S.C., U.S. Dist. Ct. S.C., U.S. Ct. Appeals (4th cir.), U.S. Bankruptcy Ct. S.C. 1987. Law clk. to Hon. Don S. Rushing Cir. Ct. (6th cir.), S.C., 1986-87; sr. ptnr. David H. Breen, P.A., Myrtle Beach, 1988—; C.J.A. panel atty. U.S. Dist. Ct. S.C., 1991-97; mem. family ct. adv. com. 15th Jud. Ct., 1998—. Campaign asst. Joe Clark for Prime Minister, Ottawa, 1975-76. Mem. ABA, S.C. Trial Lawyers Assn., Assn. Trial Lawyers Am., S.C. Bar Assn., Horry County Bar Assn., Am. Bankruptcy Inst., Oshawa Gun Club, Phi Delta Phi. Methodist. Avocations: swimming, computers. Home: Prestwick Country Club 2187 N Berwick Dr Myrtle Beach SC 29575-5835 Office: 4603 Oleander Dr Ste 6 Myrtle Beach SC 29577-5738

BREEN, J. DANIEL, federal judge; b. 1950. BA summa cum laude, Spring Hill Coll., 1972; JD, U. Tenn., 1975. Atty. Waldrop and Hall, Jackson, Tenn., 1975-91; magistrate judge U.S. Dist. Ct. (we. dist.), Tenn., 1991—. Mem. exec. com. West Tenn. Boy Scouts of Am.; lifetime bd. dirs. West Tenn. Cerebral Palsy Ctr. Mem. ABA, Am. Bar Found., Fed. Magistrate Judges Assn., Am. Judicature Soc., Tenn. Bar Found., Tenn. Bar Assn. (pres. 1996-97), Jackson-Madison County Bar Assn. (pres. 1983-84). Fax: 901-421-9255. Office: US Dist Ct 345 US Courthouse 111 S Highland Ave Jackson TN 38301-6123

BREEN, JANICE DEYOUNG, health services executive, community health nurse; b. Paterson, N.J., Apr. 15, 1947; d. Cornelius and Catherine (Van Ostenbridge) DeYoung; m. Robert Neal Breen, Aug. 1, 1969; children: Gregory Neal, Karen Elizabeth. BSN, William Paterson Coll., Wayne, N.J., 1970; MEd, Rutgers U., 1976, postgrad.; MSN, U. Pa., 1988. Cert. clin. specialist in community health nursing. Insvc. edn. instr. Community Meml. Hosp., Toms River, N.J., 1972-75; instr. nursing Ocean County Coll., Toms River, 1977-82, program. coord. for allied health, 1980-82; dir. cmty. svcs. St. Francis Med. Ctr., Trenton, N.J., 1988-94; pres., CEO Advanced Cmty. Health Sys., Verona, N.J., 1994-97; bus. devel. v.p. Sr. Care Ctrs. of Am., 1997—; vis. asst. prof. William Paterson Coll., Wayne, N.J.; healthcare cons. Care & Consulting, Middletown, N.J. Mem. ANA, N.J. State Nurses Assn., Vis. Nurses Assn. N.J. (treas., chmn., CEO, cons.), Home Health Assembly of N.J. (bd. dirs.), Sigma Theta Tau.

BREEN, JOHN EDWARD, civil engineer, educator; b. Buffalo, May 1, 1932; s. Timothy J. and Alice C. (Keenan) B.; m. Marian T. Killian, June 20, 1953; children: Mary L., Michael T., Dennis P., Sheila A., Sean E., Kerry T., Christopher D. B.C.E., Marquette U., Milw., 1953; M.S. in Civil Engring., U. Mo., 1957; Ph.D., U. Tex., Austin, 1962. Registered profl. engr., Tex., Mo. Structural designer Harnischfeger Corp., Milw., 1952-53; asst. prof. U. Mo., Columbia, 1957-59; mem. faculty U. Tex., Austin, 1959—, prof. civil engring., 1969—, J.J. McKetta prof. engring., 1977-81, Carol Cockrell Curran chair engring., 1981-84, Nasser I. Al-Rashid chair civil engring., 1984—; dir. P.M. Ferguson Structural Engring. Lab., Balcones Research Center, 1967-85; cons. in field. Contbr. articles to profl. jours. Served to lt. USNR, 1953-56. Recipient Teaching Excellence award Gen. Dynamics Corp., 1971, Teaching Excellence award U. Tex. Student Assn., 1963, Teaching Excellence award Std. Oil Found. Ind., 1968, Fedn. Internat. Precontrainte medal, 1990. Mem. Am. Concrete Inst. (hon., bd. dirs. 1974-77, Wason medal 1972, 83, Raymond C. Reese Rsch. medal 1972, 79, Kelly medal 1981, Anderson medal 1987, Raymond Davis lectr. 1978, Bloem award 1989, Alfred E. Lindau award 1994), ASCE (T.Y. Lin medal 1985, 89, 91, A.J. Boase Reinforced Concrete Rsch. Coun. award 1987), Nat. Acad. Engring., Swiss Acad. Engring. Scis., Austin Yacht Club (commodore 1977), Sigma Xi. Democrat. Roman Catholic. Home: 8603 Azalea Trl Austin TX 78759-7501 Office: Univ Tex Ferguson Lab 10100 Burnet Rd Austin TX 78758-4445

BREEN, JOHN GERALD, manufacturing company executive; b. Cleve., July 21, 1934; s. Hugh Gerald and Margaret Cecelia (Bonner) B.; m. Mary Jane Brubach, Apr. 12, 1958; children: Kathleen Anne, John Patrick, James Phillip, David Hugh, Anne Margaret. B.S., John Carroll U., 1956; M.B.A., Case Western Res. U., 1961. With Clevite Corp., Cleve., 1957-73, gen. mgr. foil div., 1969-73, gen. mgr. engine parts div., 1973-74; group v.p. indsl. group Gould Inc., Rolling Meadows, Ill., 1974-77, exec. v.p., 1977-79; pres. Sherwin Williams Co., Cleve., 1979-86, CEO, 1979—, chmn., 1980—, also dir.; dir. Parker Hannifin Corp., Cleve., Nat. City Bank, Cleve., Mead Corp., Dayton, Ohio. With U.S. Army, 1956-57. Clubs: Pepper Pike, Union, Cleve. Skating. Home: 18800 N Park Blvd Cleveland OH 44122-1809 Office: Sherwin-Williams Co 101 Prospect Ave NW Cleveland OH 44115-1075*

BREEN, KATHERINE ANNE, speech and language pathologist; b. Chgo., Oct. 31, 1948; d. Robert Stephen and Gertrude Catherine (Bader) Breen; B.S., Northwestern U., 1970; M.A. (U.S. Rehab. Services trainee), U. Mo., Columbia, 1971. Speech/lang. pathologist Fulton (Mo.) pub. schs., 1971-73; co-dir. Easter Seal Speech Clinic, Jefferson City, Mo., summers 1972, 73; speech/lang. pathologist Shawnee Mission (Kans.) pub. schs., 1973-96; staff St. Joseph's Hosp., Kansas City, Mo., 1978-81, Midwest Rehab. Ctr., Kansas City, 1985; pvt. practice speech therapy; cons. East Central Mo. Mental Health Center; guest lectr. Fontbonne Coll., St. Louis. Clin. certification in speech pathology. Mem. Am., Kans. speech and hearing assns., NEA, Mo. State Tchrs. Assn., Kansas City Alumni Assn. of Northwestern U. (dir. alumni admissions council, Outstanding Leadership award for work on alumni admissions council 1981, Svc. award, 1991), Friends of Art Nelson/Atkins Art Gallery and Museum (vol.), Nat. Trust Hist. Preservation, Kansas City Hist. Found., Zeta Phi Eta. Methodist. Home: 6865 W 51st Ter Apt 1C Shawnee Mission KS 66202-1576

BREEN, RICHARD F., JR., law librarian, lawyer, educator; b. Providence, Aug. 1, 1940; s. Richard F. and Elizabeth (Hurlin) B.; children: Stephanie, Jonathan. AB in Econs., Dartmouth Coll., 1962; LLB, U. Maine, Portland, 1967; MLS, U. Oreg., 1973. Bar: Maine, N.H. Asst dean U. Maine Sch. Law, Portland, ., 1967-70; with firm Tesreau and Gardner, Lebanon, N.H., 1970-72; assoc. law libr., assoc. prof. law U. Maine Sch. Law, Portland, 1974-76; law libr., assoc. prof. law Willamette U. Coll. Law, Salem, Oreg., 1976-80, law libr., prof. law, 1980—, interim adminstrv. dean., law libr., 1986-87. Mem. U.S. Olympic Biathlon Tng. Team, 1963. Capt. USAR, 1962-64. Mem. Am. Assn. Law Librs., Oreg. Libr. Assn., Casque and Gauntlet Honor Soc. Democrat. Congregationalist. Avocations: cross-country skiing, hiking. Office: Willamette U Law Libr 245 Winter St SE Salem OR 97301-3916

BREEN, STEPHEN P., editorial cartoonist. Grad., U. Calif., Riverside, 1992. Editl. cartoonist Asbury Park Press, Neptune, N.J., Home News Tribune; adj. prof. Rutgers U., Drew U. Artist caricatures Sunday "Celebs" page; work featured in hundreds of newspapers and nat. mags. Copley News Svc. Recipient John Locher Meml. award Assn. Am. Editl. Cartoonists, Charles M. Schulz award Scripps Howard, Pulitzer Prize, 1999. Office: c/o Asbury Park Press The Gannett Co 3601 Hwy 66 PO Box 1550 Neptune NJ 07754-1551*

BREEN, VINCENT DE PAUL, bishop; b. Bklyn., Dec. 24, 1936. BA, Cathedral Coll., 1959; Licentiate in Sacred Theology, Gregorian U., 1963. Ordained priest, 1962. Asst. pastor St. Genevieve, Rockaway Point, summer 1963, St. Edmund, Bklyn., 1963-66; asst. supt. schs. Diocese of Bklyn., N.Y., 1966-73, assoc. supt. of schs., 1973-76, supt. of schs., 1976-78, supt. of edn., 1978-94, vicar for edn., 1994-97; bishop Diocese of Metuchen, N.J., 1997—; chmn. Com. of Nonpublic Sch. Ofcls. of the City of N.Y., 1978-97; mem. adv. com., pub. policy and cath. schs. U.S. Cath. Conf., 1978-97; past pres. N.Y. State Coun. Cath. Schs. Supts., 1979-80; bd. dirs. Nat. Cath. Ednl. Assn., 1985-88; pres. Nat. Chief Adminstrs. of Cath. Edn., 1985-88; mem. coord. com. N.Y.C. Regional Edn. Ctr. for Econ. Devel.; mem. adv. com. on social policy Diocese of Bklyn., N.Y.; active Interdiocesan Com. on Social Policy, Borough Pres.'s Adv. Panel, Cath. Edn. Leadership Devel., Diocesan Cmmn. on the Elderly, St. John's Univ. Consortium; mem. NCCB Com. on Edn., 1998-2001. Mem. Commn. of Elem. Schs. Officers of the Middle States Assn., N.Y. State Gov.'s Ednl. Adv. Com., N.Y. State Com. for Pub. Higher Edn., Commr.'s Adv. Coun. for Pub. Schs., N.Y. State Cath. Conf. Pub. Policy Com., Gov.'s Task Force on Equal Opportunity Edn., N.Y. Alliance for Pub. Schs. Roman Catholic. Office: Roman Cath Diocese Metuchen PO Box 191 Metuchen NJ 08840-0191

BREEZE, WILLIAM HANCOCK, college administrator; b. Cin., Nov. 25, 1923; s. William T. and Nancy (Hancock) B.; m. JoAnne Robertson Watson, Oct. 8, 1949 (dec. Jan. 1983); 1 child, Nancy Louise Breeze Beal; m. Barbara L. Hall, Dec. 15, 1990. Student, Berea Coll., 1943-44; A.B., Centre Coll., Danville, Ky., 1945; M.A., U. Ky., 1948. Various actuarial positions Ohio Nat. Life Ins. Co., Cin., 1948-56, actuary, 1956-65, asst. to pres., 1965-67, sr. v.p., 1967-72, exec. v.p., 1972-86; v.p., gen. sec. Centre Coll., Danville, Ky., 1987-88, 89-91, acting pres., 1988-89; spl. asst. to pres. for endowment Centre Coll., Danville, 1991—; bd. dirs. Ohio Nat. Life Ins. Co., 1966-88. Bd. dirs. Jr. Achievement Greater Cin., 1974-84; trustee Centre Coll., 1980-86. Served to lt. (j.g.) USNR, 1943-46, PTO. Fellow Soc. Actuaries. Republican. Presbyterian. Avocations: reading; classical music. Home: 468 W Broadway St Danville KY 40422-1420 Office: Centre Coll Danville KY 40422

BREGA, CHARLES FRANKLIN, lawyer; b. Callaway, Nebr., Feb. 5, 1933; s. Richard E. and Bessie (King) B.; m. Betty Jean Witherspoon, Sept. 17, 1960; children: Kerry E., Charles D., Angie G. B.A., The Citadel, 1954; LLB, U. Colo., 1960. Bar: Colo. 1960. Assoc. firm Hindry & Meyer, Denver, 1960-62; partner Hindry & Meyer, 1962-75, dir., 1975; dir. firm Roath & Brega, Denver, 1975-89, Brega & Winters, Denver, 1989—; lectr. in field; guest prof. U. Colo., U. Denver, U. Nev. (numerous states and), Can. Trustee Pres.'s Leadership Class, U. Colo., 1977—. Served with USAF, 1954-57. Mem. Colo. Trial Lawyers Assn. (pres. 1972-73), Assn. Trial Lawyers Am. (gov. 1972-79), ABA, Am. Law Inst., Am. Bd. Trial Advs., Internat. Acad. Trial Lawyers, Internat. Soc. Barristers, Cherry Hills Country Club, Denver Athletic Club. Episcopalian. Home: 4501 S Vine Way Englewood CO 80110-6027 Office: Brega & Winters PC 1700 Lincoln St Ste 2222 Denver CO 80203-4522

BREGEN, LOUIS, music professional; b. Nov. 9, 1915. Grad. high sch., Phila. Free-lance writer, 1956—; vocalist, mgr. Wilkinsen Dance Band, Northridge, 11979—; prodr. Cafe Rosse Cabaret, Northridge, Calif., 1992—; sec., treas. Club Comedy (formerly Hollywood Comedy Club), 1985—. Author: Grasshopper's Journey, Golden Legacy. Home: 19933 Acre St Northridge CA 91324

BREGER, WILLIAM N., architect, educator; b. N.Y.C., Aug. 1, 1922; s. S.A. and B. (Kalvar) B. BArch., Harvard, 1945, MArch., 1945. Asst. to Walter Gropius, Cambridge, Mass., 1944-46; tchr. N.Y. Sch. Interior Design, 1945—; chmn. dept. archtl. design Pratt Inst., 1946-69; lectr. Columbia Sch. Pub. Health and Hosp. Adminstrn., 1964-78; practice architecture with S. Salzman, 1947-55; architect Breger Terjesen Assoc., 1955—; vis. Disting. prof. architecture Pratt Inst., 1983-84, dir. mechs. inst., 1998—. Exhibited, Mus. Modern Art, 1952, 79, 80, Chgo. Art Inst., 1954, Gold Medal Exhbn. Archtl. League, 1960, Bklyn. Mus., 1955; author: (with William Pomeranz) Nursing Home Development, 1985; Mem. editorial bd.: Ency. Philosophy, 1967. Trustee, dir. N.Y. Sch. Interior Design, 1960—. Served with AUS, 1942-43. Recipient Langford Warren prize, 1944, 3d prize Jefferson Nat. Meml. Competition, St. Louis, 1947; Prix de Rome Alternate, 1947; 3d prize N.Y. Pub. Housing Award (with S. Salzman) 1950; Good Design award Mus. Modern Art, 1952; 1st prize House and Garden mag., 1950; 1st prize Carson Pirie Scott Chicago Loop design, 1954; hon. mention hosp. design Rubberoid Competition, 1958; 1st prize Allegheny Sq. competition (with J. Terjesen and W. Winter) Pitts., 1964; hon. mention Fremont Civic Center Master Plan, 1966; AIA award, 1968; Queens C. of C. award; Bard award City Club of N.Y., 1977; N.Y. State Assn. Architects award, 1978, 80; Archi design award L.I. chpt. AIA, 1979. Fellow AIA. Office: 33 Rector St Rm 601 New York NY 10006-2213 Office: Breger Terjesen Assocs 21 West St New York NY 10006-2904

BREGG, PETER, photojournalist; married; 2 children. Student, Algonquin Coll., Ottawa, Ont., Can., Ryerson U., Toronto, Ont. Photographer Can. Press Ottawa, 1967-74, chief photographer, 1978-84; photographer AP, Boston and Washington, 1974-78; dep. European photo editor AP, London and N.Y., 1985-89; ofcl. photographer Office of Prime Min., 1984-85; photo editor Maclean's Mag., 1989—. Recipient Nat. Newspaper award, World Press Photo award, The Hague, The Netherlands, ONPA awards, numerous nat. and internat. photography awards; named NPPA Photographer of Yr. Office: Maclean's, 777 Bay St/Maclean Hunter Bldg, Toronto, ON Canada M5W 1A7*

BREGLIO, JOHN F., lawyer; b. N.Y.C., June 5, 1946; s. John N. and Sylvia V. (Calucci) B.; m. Nan K. Proctor, May 22, 1976; children: Eliza Mason, Nola Keene. BA, Yale U., 1968; JD, Harvard U., 1971. Bar: N.Y. 1972, U.S. Dist. Ct. (ea. and so. dists.) 1974, U.S. Ct. Appeals (2d cir.) 1975, U.S. Ct. Appeals (D.C. cir.) 1982. Ptnr. Paul, Weiss, Rifkind, Wharton & Garrison, N.Y.C., 1971—; chmn., lectr. on entertainment industry N.Y. Law Jour. Seminars, N.Y.C., 1984-88, Practising Law Inst. Bd. dirs. The Acting Co., N.Y.C., 1982-92, The Golden Fund, N.Y.C., 1989—, The Alliance for the Arts, Inc., 1989—, Am. Found. for AIDS Rsch., N.Y.C., 1994—, Young Playwrights Inc., 1995—; chmn. bd. Theater Devel. Fund, N.Y.C., 1982—; mem. adv. com. Theatre Collection Coun., Mus. of City of N.Y. Mem. ABA, N.Y. State Bar Assn., Assn. of Bar of City of N.Y., Am. Arbitration Assn. (panel arbitrators), The Century Assn. (N.Y.C.), Yale Club (N.Y.C.), Waccabuc Country Club (Westchester, N.Y), Phelps Assn. (New Haven). Home: 1120 5th Ave New York NY 10128-0144 also: 103 Bouton Rd South Salem NY 10590-1431 also: 52 W Miacomet Rd Nantucket MA 02554-4369 Office: Paul Weiss Rifkind Wharton & Garrison 1285 Avenue of the Americas New York NY 10019-6064

BREGMAN, ARTHUR RANDOLPH, lawyer, educator; b. Phila., Dec. 9, 1946; s. Nathan and Stella (Husock) B.; m. Patrice Rosalie Gancie, May 30, 1980. BA, Columbia U., 1968; MA, Yale U., 1969; JD, Georgetown U., 1985. Bar: D.C. 1985, U.S. Ct. Appeals (D.C. cir.) 1985, U.S. Dist. Ct. D.C. 1985, U.S. Claims Ct. 1985. Treas. Nat. Coun. for Soviet and E. European Rsch., Washington, 1981-83; law clk. Washington Lawyers' Com. for Civil Rights, 1983-84; assoc. Klores, Feldesman and Tucker, Washington, 1985-86; dir. Soviet and E. European Svcs. APCO, Washington, 1988-91; of counsel Steptoe & Johnson, Washington, Moscow, USSR, 1991-92; ptnr. Steptoe & Johnson, Washington D.C. and Moscow, 1992—; adj. prof. Georgetown U. Law Ctr., Washington, 1986-89; program dir. Internat. Law Inst., Washington, 1986-91; chmn. bd. adv. U.S.-Russia Bus. Law Report, 1990—. Editor: U.S.-Soviet Contract Law, 1987. Recipient Civil Procedure prize Lawyers Coop. Pub. Co., Balt., 1982. Mem. ABA (internat. bar sect.), D.C. Bar. Home: 3059 Porter St NW Washington DC 20008-3272 Office: 1330 Connecticut Ave NW Washington DC 20036-1704

BREGMAN, JACOB ISRAEL, environmental consulting company executive; b. Hartford, Conn., Sept. 17, 1923; s. Aaron and Jennie (Katzoff) B.; m. Mona Madan, June 27, 1948; children: Janet, Marcia, Barbara. BS, Providence Coll., 1943; MS, Poly. Inst. Bklyn., 1948, PhD, 1951. Research chemist Fels & Co., 1947-48; head phys. chem. labs. Nalco Chem. Co., Chgo., 1950-59; supr. phys. chemistry research sect. Armour Research Found., Chgo., 1959-63; asst. dir. chemistry research Ill. Inst. Tech. Research Inst., Chgo., 1963-65; dir. chem. scis. Ill. Inst. Tech. Research Inst., 1965-67; dep. asst. sec. U.S. Dept. Interior, 1967-69; pres. Wapora Inc., 1969-82; v.p. Dynamac Corp., 1983-84; pres. Bregman and Co., 1984—; Chmn. N.E. Ill. Met. Area Air Pollution Control Bd., 1962-63; chmn. Ill. Air Pollution Control Bd., 1963-67; chmn. adv. bd. on saline water conversion NATO Parliamentarians Conf., 1963; chmn. Water Resources Research Council, 1964-67. Author: Corrosion Inhibitors, 1963, Surface Effects in Detection, 1965, The Pollution Paradox, 1966, Handbook of Water Resources and Pollution Control, 1976, Environmental Regulations Handbook, 1991, Environmental Impact Statements, 1992, Environmental Compliance Handbok, 1996; patentee in field; contbr. 63 articles to profl. jours. Mem. plan commn., Park Forest, Ill., 1956-58, trustee, 1958-62; mem. Md. Democratic State Cen. Com., 1974-78; treas. Montgomery Dem. Cen. Com., 1974-76; del. Dem. Conv., 1976; chmn. Montgomery County (Md.) Citizens Task Force on Georgetown Br. Right of Way, 1986-90. With AUS, 1943-46, ETO. Decorated two Battle Stars, AUS. Fellow Am. Inst. Chemists; mem. Am. Legion, VFW, Am. Chem. Soc., Rotary (pres. Friendship Heights, Md. 1994-95, profl. lectr. George Washington U., 1980-98), Sigma Xi, Phi Lambda Upsilon. Home: 5630 Old Chester Rd Bethesda MD 20814-1025 Office: 4827 Rugby Ave Bethesda MD 20814-3034

BREGMAN, MARTIN, film producer; b. N.Y.C., May 18, 1936; s. Leon and Ida (Granowski) B.; children: Michael Scott, Christopher Neill, Marissa Cornelia. Student, Ind. U., NYU. Owner Martin Bregman Prodns., Inc., 1978—; chmn. Office Motion Pictures and TV, Mayor of N.Y.C., 1976-91. Prodr. films, including The Secret of Bear Mountain, 1955, Serpico, 1974, Dog Day Afternoon, 1975, The Next Man, 1976, The Seduction of Joe Tynan, 1979, S*H*E, 1980, Simon, 1980, The Four Seasons, 1981, Venom, 1982, Eddie Macon's Run, 1983, Scarface, 1984, Sweet Liberty, 1985, Real Men, 1987, A New Life, 1988, Listen to Me, 1989, Sea of Love, 1989, Betsy's Wedding, 1990, Whispers in the Dark, 1992, The Real McCoy, 1993, Carlito's Way, 1993, The Shadow, 1994, Gold Diggers, The Secret of Bear Mountain, 1995, Nothing to Lose, 1997, One Tough Cop, 1997. Office: Martin Bregman Prodns Inc 641 Lexington Ave New York NY 10022-4503*

BREGMAN, STEVEN HOWARD, library director; b. N.Y.C., Feb. 1, 1951; s. Harry and Sylvia Bregman. BA, Queens Coll., Flushing, N.Y., 1972, MLS, 1973. Cert. pub. libr. N.Y. State Edn. Dept. Asst. dir. Nassau Libr. Sys., Uniondale, N.Y., 1986-90; dir. Bellmore (N.Y.) Meml. Libr., 1990—. Pres. Nassau County Libr. Assn., 1999. Mem. ALA, N.Y. Libr. Assn., Nassau County Libr. Assn., Libr. Dirs. Nassau County (chair 1998-

99). Democrat. Jewish. Avocations: music, travel. E-mail: steve.bregman@mailcity.com. Fax: 516-785-2798. Office: Bellmore Meml Libr 2288 Bedford Ave Bellmore NY 11710-3615

BREGOLI-RUSSO, MAUDA RITA, language educator; b. Iesi-Aneona, Italy; came to U.S., 1965; d. Antonio Bregoli and Libe Maria Scipioni; m. Franco Gino Russo, June 27, 1964; 1 child, Antonella. Laurea, Bologna (Italy) U., 1963; PhD in Romance Langs., U. Chgo., 1978. Vis. asst. prof. Northwestern U., Chgo., 1981-83; asst. prof. U. Ill., Chgo., 1984-90, assoc. prof., 1990—. Author: Boiardo Lirico, 1979, Renaissance Italian Plays, 1984, Impresa Come Ritratto, 1990, Teatro D'Isabella D'Este, 1997. NEH grantee, 1981. Mem. MLA, Renaissance Soc. Am., Associazione Italiana per Gli Studi Di Langua E Letteratura Italiana. E-mail: mabrer@uic.edu. Home: 345 N Canal St Apt 1608 Chicago IL 60606 Office: U Ill Chgo 601 S Morgan St Chicago IL 60612

BREHL, JAMES WILLIAM, lawyer. BS engring., U. Notre Dame, 1956; JD, U. Mich., 1959. Bar: Wis. 1989; Minn. and various fed. cts. Lawyer Maun & Simon, St. Paul. Contbr. articles to law jours. Chmn. Minn. builder's adv. coun. Minn. Dept. Commerce, 1991-95; mem. planning commn. City of Afton, 1975-93; dir. Granville House Inc., 1985-95. Recipient Good Neighbor award WCCO, 1968. Mem. ABA, Minn. Bar Assn. (exec. com. 1996-97), Ramsey County Bar Assn. (exec. coun. 1977-80, 87-90, pres. 1993-94), Washington County Bar Assn., St. Paul C. of C. Fax: 612-904-7424. Office: Maun & Simon PLC 2000 Midwest Plaza W 801 Nicollet Mall Minneapolis MN 55402

BREHM, LORETTA PERSOHN, secondary art educator, librarian, consultant; b. New Orleans, Jan. 31, 1954; d. Edwin Joseph and Loretta (Persohn) B. BA, Nicholls State U., Thibodaux, La., 1975, MEd, 1979, postgrad., 1980. Cert. tchr., La. Substitute tchr. Jefferson Parish Sch. Bd., Gretna, La., 1971-74; tchr. art John Ehret Sch., John Ehret High Sch., Marrero, La., 1974-95; art tchr., libr. Westbank Cathedral Acad., 1995-98; cons. Ventures Edn. Sys., 1998—; trustee mem., chmn. bd. Jefferson Parish Coun. on Aging. Mem. ladies aux. Westwego Vol. Fire Co.; historian Westwego Bicentennial; vol. Westwego Com. on Aging, Gumbo Festival, Bridge City, La., ARC, Operation Mainstream, others; founding mem. Jefferson Parish Cmty. Arts Commn.; alumni pres., former sch. advisor Jefferson Parish 4-H Clubs; art dir. Knights of King Arthur Mardi Gras Orgn.; libr. asst. Westbank Cathedral Acad.; mem. choir, set designer Holy Guardian Angels Ch.; trustee Jefferson Parish Coun. on Aging, 1993—; bd. dirs. Westwego Hist. Soc., Jefferson Parish Hist. Soc.; commnr. Westwego Law Enforcement Commn., Westwego Zoning Commn. Recipient awards from Jefferson Parish Sch. Bd., 1978, Westwego Vol. Fire Co., 1982, 4-H Club, 1983, Am. Automobile Assn. Nat. Sch. Traffic Safety Program, 1987-92, others. Mem. Nat. Art Edn. Assn., La. Art Edn. Assn., Internat. Reading Assn. (chmn. Jefferson Parish coun.), Jefferson Parish Hist. Soc. (charter), New Orleans Mus. Art, La. Children's Mus., Nicholls State U. Alumni Assn., Delta Kappa Gamma, Kappa Kappa Iota, Phi Delta Kappa. Democrat. Christian. Avocations: travel, gardening, social work, freelance art work. Home: 250 Louisiana St Westwego LA 70094-4114

BREHM, SHARON STEPHENS, psychology educator, university administrator; b. Roanoke, Va., Apr. 18, 1945; d. John Wallis and Jane Chappel (Phenix) Stephens; m. Jack W. Brehm, Oct. 25, 1968 (div. Dec. 1979). B.A., Duke U., 1967, Ph.D., 1973; M.A., Harvard U., 1968. Clin. psychology intern U. Wash. Med. Ctr., Seattle, 1973-74; asst. prof. Va. Poly. Inst. and State U., Blacksburg, 1974-75; asst. prof. U. Kans., Lawrence, 1975-78, assoc. prof., 1978-83, prof. psychology, 1983-90, assoc. dean Coll. Liberal Arts and Scis., 1987-90; prof. psychology, dean Harpur Coll. of Arts and Scis. SUNY, Binghamton, 1990-96; prof. psychology and interpersonal comm., provost Ohio U., Athens, 1996—; vis. prof. U. Mannheim, 1978, Istituto di Psicologia, Rome, 1989; Fulbright sr. rsch. scholar Ecole des Hautes Etudes en Sciences Sociales, Paris, 1981-82; Soc. for Personality and Social Psychology rep. APA's Coun. of Reps., 1995—; chair governing bd. Ohio Link, 1998-99. Author: The Application of Social Psychology to Clinical Practice, 1976, (with others) Psychological Reactance: A Theory of Freedom and Control, 1981, Intimate Relationships, 1985, 2d edit., 1992, (with others) Social Psychology, 1990, 2d edit., 1993, 3d edit., 1996, others, also numerous articles, and chpts. Mem. APA (fin. com. 1999—). Office: Ohio U Office of Provost Cutler Hall Athens OH 45701-2979

BREHM, WILLIAM ALLEN, JR., urban planner; b. Jan. 18, 1945; s. Silliam Allen and Katharine (Gilbert) B.; m. Patricia Lee Kelley, Dec. 30, 1967; children: Laura Kelley, William Hunt, Katharine Ann. BA, Lawrence U., 1967; M Urban Planning, Mich. State U., 1973. Lic. real estate broker, Wis. Dir. planning Charter Twp. of Meridian, Mich., 1969-72; v.p., treas. Planning Cons. Svcs., Inc., Lansing, Mich., 1972-76; dir. planning Manson, Jackson, Kane, Architects, Inc., Lansing, 1974-76; dir. planning and devel. City of Appleton, Wis., 1976-90, exec. dir. Redevel. Authority, 1979-90; owner Brehm Real Estate, 1991—; gen. mgr. CDS divsn. Martenson & Eisele, Inc., Neenah, Wis., 1996—; mem. Wis. State Hist. Soc., 1978—, Outagamie Hist. Soc., 1980—, bd. dirs. 1993, v.p., 1995, 99—. Trustee Charter Twp. of Meridan, 1972-74, supr., 1974-76; dist. chmn. Boy Scouts Am., 1979-81; bd. dirs. Pub. Art Found., 1985-91, Houdini Hist. Ctr., 1995—; bd. supr. Outagamie County, 1988—. Richard King Mellon fellow, 1967-68; awarded Cert. Nat. Recognition Cmty. Devel. Excellence HUD, 1986. Mem. Am. Inst. Cert. Planners, Am. Planning Assn., Nat. Assn. Realtors, Nat. Trust Hist. Preservation, Assn. Wis. Planners (treas. 1977-79, pres. 1981-82), Soc. Am. Magicians, Internat. Brotherhood Magicians, Realtors Assn., N.E. Wis., Houdini Club Wis., Rotary (pres. 1991-92), Delta Tau Delta. Mem. United Ch. of Christ. Home: 716 S Fidelis St Appleton WI 54915-3559 Office: PO Box 1502 Appleton WI 54913-1502

BREHM, WILLIAM KEITH, information systems company executive; b. Dearborn, Mich., Mar. 29, 1929; s. Walter E. and Lucille (Hankinson) B.; m. Delores Soderquist, June 28, 1952; children: Eric William, Lisa Karen. B.S. with honors in Math, U. Mich., 1950, M.S., 1952. Asst. sec. army Dept. Army, Washington, 1968-70; v.p. corporate devel. Dart Industries, Inc., Los Angeles, 1970-73; asst. sec. def. Dept. Def., Washington, 1973-77; exec. v.p. Computer Network Corp., Washington, 1977-80; chmn. bd. SRA Internat., Inc., Arlington, Va., 1980—. trustee, former chmn. bd. Fuller Theol. Sem.; dir. Herman Miller, Inc.; trustee Ctr. for Naval Analyses, Guideposts. Recipient Disting. Civilian Service award Dept. Army; recipient Disting. Pub. Service award Dept. Def. Mem. Ops. Research Soc. Am. Home: 1167 Orlo Dr Mc Lean VA 22102-1748 Office: SRA Internat Inc 4350 Fair Lakes Ct Fairfax VA 22033-4233

BREIDEGAM, DELIGHT EDGAR, JR., battery company executive; b. Fleetwood, Pa., Oct. 3, 1926; s. DeLight Daniel and Helen Mamie (Fenstermacher) B.; m. Helen Merkel, Feb. 28, 1948; children: Daniel, Sally. LLD (hon.), Kurtztown U., 1997; attended, Gettysburg Coll., 1944-45, LLD (hon.), 1995; LLD (hon.), Moravian Coll., 1995. Chmn., CEO East Penn Mfg. Co., Inc., Lyon Sta., Pa.; dir. Battery Council Internat.; dir. Battery Coun. Internat. Trustee Moravian Coll.; bd. dirs. Kutztown U. Served with USAF. Recipient Grow with Berks award Reading Assn. Realtors, 1994, Richard J. Caron award of excellence, 1997; named Entrepreneur of Yr., Ea. Pa./Delaware Valley, 1990; named to Jr. Achievement Hall of Fame, 1994, Moravian Coll. Hall of Fame. Mem. Kutztown Jaycees, Ind. Battery Mfrs.' Assn., Reading-Berks C. of C. (Bus. Person of Yr. 1984), Lead Industries Assn. (bd. dirs.), Moselem Springs Golf Club, Bonita Bay Country Club, Fox Fire Golf and Country Club, Saucon Valley Country Club, Huguenot Lodge, Shriners. Lutheran. Office: East Penn Mfg Co Inc Deka Rd Lyon Station PA 19536

BREIDENBACH, CHERIE ELIZABETH, lawyer, accountant; b. Aberdeen, S.D., Aug. 20, 1952; d. Neil Allen and Portia Elizabeth (Bradner) Johnson; m. Steven Theodore Breidenbach, Aug. 9, 1975. BS, U. S.D., 1975, JD, 1979. Bar: S.D. 1979, Calif. 1981; CPA, Calif. Sole practice La Jolla, Calif., 1982-84; assoc., acct. Sussman & Siegel, San Diego, 1984-86; ptnr. Fout, Breidenbach & Chin, San Diego, 1986-88, Rose, Munns & Fout, Coronado, Calif., 1988-90, Rose, Munns, Breidenbach & Fout, Coronado, 1990-91, Rose, Munns, Fout, Breidenbach & Chin, 1992-96; bus. planner Hewlett-Packard Corp., San Diego, 1997—. Mem. Calif. Bar Assn., Phi Delta Phi. Republican. Methodist. Avocations: antique restoration, interior decoration, piano, horses.

BREIDENBACH, FRANCIS ANTHONY, lawyer; b. Oakes, N.D., May 12, 1930; s. Theodore Michael and Elizabeth Ann (Ackerman) B.; m. Carol Ann Erenfeld, June 15, 1955; children: Francis Anthony, Kelly Ann, Andrew T. PhB, U. N.D., 1952, JD, 1957. Bar: N.D. 1957, Calif. 1965; diplomate: Am. Bd. Trial Advocates. Asst. atty. gen. State of N.D., 1957-60; pvt. practice Bismarck, N.D., 1960-63; assoc. firm Welsh & Cummins, L.A., 1963-65, Breidenbach, Buckley, Hutching, Halm & Hamblet, 1965—. Served with AUS, 1948-49, 52-53. Mem. ABA, N.D. Bar Assn., Los Angeles County Bar Assn., State Bar Calif., Assn. So. Calif. Def. Counsel (pres. 1976-77), Am. Bd. Trial Advocates (diplomate, pres. L.A. chpt. 1996), Nat. Assn. Def. Counsel in Criminal Cases (dir. 1962-64). Office: 611 W 6th St Los Angeles CA 90017-3101

BREIDENBACH, MONICA EILEEN, educator, career counselor; b. Dayton, July 2, 1932; d. Clement and Mary (Deschler) B. BS in Music Edn., Mt. St. Joseph Coll., 1969. Music educator St. Bernard Sch., Springfield, Ohio, 1952-54; elem. sch. educator grade schs., Ohio, Mich., 1954-63; music educator St. Mary's H.S., Jackson, Mich., 1963-67, DeKalb (Ill.) Pub. Schs., 1967-68; dir. edn. Diocese of Columbus, Ohio, 1968-75; exec. dir. The Liturgical Conf., Washington, 1975-76; dir. counseling Pierson Assocs., Washington, 1976-78; owner, counselor Career Mgmt. Svcs., Prairie Village, Kans., 1978—; sr. prof. DeVry Inst. Tech., Kansas City, Mo., 1983—. Author: Career Development, 1988, 2d edit., 1992; 3d edit., 1998; contbr. articles to profl. jours. E-mail: mbreidenbach@kc.devry.edu. Home: 5401 W 80th St Prairie Vlg KS 66208-4912

BREIHAN, ERWIN ROBERT, civil engineer, consultant; b. St. Louis, Oct. 31, 1918; s. Arthur George and Genevieve Louise (Wolz) B.; m. Antoinette V. Corcoran, Nov. 24, 1945; children: John Robert, Patricia Anne, Steve Michael. BSCE, Washington U., St. Louis, 1940, postgrad., 1940-41. Registered profl. engr., Mo., Ill., Ark., Ohio, W. Va. Structural engr. St. Louis Ordnance Plant, 1941-42; with Horner & Shifrin, Inc., St. Louis, 1940-88, exec. v.p., 1971-73, pres., chief exec. officer, 1973-88, sr. cons., 1988-91; ret.; bd. dirs. BSI Constructors Inc., Mark Twain Banks. Chmn. Tomahawk dist. Boy Scouts Am., 1978; v.p., bd. dirs. Transp. and Devel. Coun. of Mo., 1979-89. Served to capt. USNR, 1942-71. Recipient Washington U. Engring. Alumnus Achievement award, 1979; named Engr. of Yr., St. Louis Mo. Soc. Profl. Engrs., 1980. Fellow ASCE (chmn. profl. activities com. 1983), Cons. Engrs. Coun. Mo. (pres. 1977, 81-83); mem. NSPE (life), ASTM, Am. Assn. Airport Execs., Am. Def. Preparedness Assn., Am. Soc. Mil. Engrs., Am. Water Works Assn. (life), Am. Road and Transp. Builders Am., Am. Pub. Works Assn., Mo. Soc. Profl. Engrs. (pres. 1982-83), Mil. Order World Wars, Navy League (life), St. Louis, Washington U. Engring. Alumni Assn. (pres. 1970), Century Club Engring. (pres. 1969), Engrs. Club. St. Louis (hon., pres. 1975-76, award of merit 1971, Achievement Award medal 1982), Eliot Soc., Washington U. Club, Mo. Athletic Club, Whittmore House, St. Louis Engrs. Cir. Club. Home: 12945 Star Hill Dr Saint Louis MO 63128-3241

BREILLATT, JULIAN PAUL, JR., biochemist, biomedical engineer; b. Pensacola, Fla., Mar. 2, 1938; s. Julian Paul and Ruth (Walser) B.; m. Gaye Sorensen, Apr. 9, 1962; children: Elise, Adrienne, Alain, Andre. BA in Biochem., U. Calif., Berkeley, 1959; PhD in Biochem., U. Utah, 1967. Rsch. assoc. Oak Ridge (Tenn.) Nat. Lab., 1967-69, rsch. scientist, 1967-74, acting dir. molecular anatomy program, 1974-77; rsch. supr. E I DuPont, Wilmington, Del., 1977-78, sr. rsch. chemist, 1978-85; Baxter rsch. scientist Baxter Healthcare Corp., Round Lake, Ill., 1986-90, rsch. dir., 1990-94, sr. rsch. dir., 1994—. Contbr. articles to scientific jours.; patentee in field. Active Boy Scouts Am., 1949-99. Recipient IR-100 Indsl. Rsch. award, 1977. Mem. LDS Ch. Office: Baxter Healthcare Corp Baxter Tech Pk Round Lake IL 60073-0490

BREIMAYER, JOSEPH FREDERICK, patent lawyer; b. Belding, Mich., May 4, 1942; s. Ronald and Crystal Helen (Reeves) B.; m. Margaret Anne Murphy, Aug. 26, 1967; children: Kathleen A., Deborah L., Elizabeth L. BEE, U. Detroit, 1965; JD, George Washington U., 1969. Bar: D.C. 1970, N.Y. 1973, Minn. 1975. Cooperative engr. Honeywell Inc, Mpls., 1962-65; patent examiner U.S. Patent and Trademark Office, Washington, 1965-70; patent atty. Eastman Kodak Co., Rochester, N.Y., 1970-73; sr. patent counsel Medtronic Inc., Mpls., 1973-90; assoc. Fredrikson & Byron, Mpls., 1990-93. pres. Good Shepherd Home and Sch. Assn., 1984; precinct chmn. Dem. Farmer Labor Party, 1980-82. Mem. Minn. Intellectual Property Law Assn. (treas. 1986). Avocations: boating, skiing, travel. Home: 4700 Circle Down Minneapolis MN 55416-1101 Office: Breimayer Law Office 1221 Nicollet Mall Ste 206 Minneapolis MN 55403-2472

BREIMYER, HAROLD FREDERICK, agricultural economist; b. Ft. Recovery, Ohio, Apr. 13, 1914; s. Fred Christian and Ella Anna Margaret (Schulz) B.; m. Rachel Eudora Styles, Dec. 13, 1941; 1 child, Frederick Styles. B.S., Ohio State U., 1934, M.S., 1935; Ph.D., Am. U., 1960. Staff economist Agrl. Adjustment Adminstrn., 1936-39, Bur. Agrl. Econs., 1939-53, Agrl. Mktg. Service, 1954-59, 61-66, Council Econ. Advisers, 1959-61; mem. faculty U. Mo., Columbia, 1966-84; prof. agrl. econs. U. Mo., 1966-84, extension economist, 1968-84; vis. Anderson scholar Ohio State U., 1985; teaching assoc. U. Mo., 1986—. Author: Individual Freedom and the Economic Organization of Agriculture, 1965, Economics of the Product Markets of Agriculture, 1976, Farm Policy: 13 Essays, 1977, Over-fulfilled Expectations: A Life and an Era in Rural America, 1991. Mem. Montgomery County (Md.) Bd. Edn., 1959-62, pres., 1961; pres. Columbia Council Chs., 1974-76. Served with USNR, 1942-45. Recipient Superior Service award Dept. Agr., 1954, 59, Centennial award Coll. Agr. and Home Econs., Ohio State U., 1970, Faculty-Alumni award U. Mo., 1975, Thomas Jefferson award U. Mo., 1983. Fellow Am. Agrl. Econs. Assn. (pres. 1969); mem. Internat. Assn. Agrl. Economists. Democrat. Methodist. Club: Lions. Home: 78 1408 Business Loop 70W Columbia MO 65202-1364 Office: U Mo 214 Mumford Hall Columbia MO 65211 *A farm boy reared on Horatio Alger who later adopted Santayana (Last Puritan) and Henry Adams (Education) finds himself molded. Whether success as the world views it is thereby accounted for is moot; that outlook and character are influenced is beyond doubt.*

BREINER, SHELDON, geophysics educator, business executive; b. Milw., Oct. 23, 1936; s. James and Fannie Breiner; m. Phyllis Farrington, Feb. 4, 1962; children—David, Michelle. BS, Stanford U., 1959, MS, 1962, PhD in Geophysics, 1967. Registered geophysicist. Geologist, Calif. product mgr. Varian Assocs., 1961-68; founder, pres. Geometrics, Sunnyvale, Calif., 1969-83, Syntelligence Inc., 1984-87; pres., founder, dir. Wireless Note Systems, Inc., 1995—; dir. Sherpa Corp., Optical Spltys. Inc., Solis Therapeudics Inc.; pres., CEO, chmn., founder Para Magnetic Logging Inc.; pres. Foothill Assocs.; cons., prof., lectr. geophysics Stanford U. and Grad. Sch. Bus.; cons. archaeol. exploration problems and search for buried objects; adv. coun. Sch. of Earth Scis., Stanford U. Author: Applications Manual for Portable Magnetometers, 1973; contbr. articles to profl. jours.; patentee in oil exploration; inventor gun detector for airports. Founder, trustee Peninsula Open State Trust; bd. dirs. Resource Ctr. for Women; maj. gifts com. Stanford U. With U.S. Army, 1960. Honors scholar, 1955-56; NSF grantee for earthquake research, 1965. Fellow Explorers Club; mem. Soc. Exploration Geophysicists (Best presentation award 1985), Soc. Petroleum Engrs., Am. Geophys. Union, European Assn. Exploration Geophysicists, Stanford Assocs. Achievements include discovery of oldest monuments in Western Hemisphere (colossal Olmec heads) using magnetometers. Avocation: running Boston Marathon. E-mail: sheldon@breiner.com. Office: New Ventures West 706 Comper St 3rd Fl Palo Alto CA 94301-2128

BREINES, SIMON, architect; b. Bklyn., Apr. 4, 1906; s. Louis and Anna (Backrack) B.; m. Nettie Weissman, 1935; children: Paul, Joseph. B.Arch., Pratt Inst., 1941. Partner Pomerance & Breines, N.Y.C.; adviser Gen. Services Adminstrn.; bd. dirs. Fine Arts Fedn. of N.Y., N.Y. Landmarks Conservancy.; Mem. Citizens Union, Community Service Soc., Parks Assn., all N.Y.C.; architect mem. Art Commn. City N.Y., 1971-74. Architect for: pub. bldgs. including Grand Concourse Pub. Library, Bronx, N.Y.C., Lexington Sch. for Deaf, Rose F. Kennedy Research Center, Albert Einstein Coll. of Medicine, New Campus, State U. N.Y. at Brockport, New Coll. Dentistry, N.Y. U. Cons. Housing Assistance Adminstrn; Author: Architecture and Furniture of Alvar Aalto, 1942, (with John Dean) The Book of Houses, 1946, (with William Dean) The Pedestrian Revolution: Streets Without Cars, 1976; Contbr.: chpt. to USSR: A Concise Handbook, 1947, Small Urban Spaces, 1969. Arnold W. Brunner scholar N.Y. chpt. AIA, 1947, 66; Recipient Bard award City Club N.Y., 1967. Fellow AIA (honor award 1967). Home: 8 Horseguard Ln Scarsdale NY 10583-2311 Office: Pomerance & Breines Architects 30 E 42nd St New York NY 10017-6908 *When I was an architectural student, I was taught "Make no little plans; they have no magic to stir men's souls." Actually, this persuasive dictum has served society poorly. The combination of vast, over-weening projects and the technology to carry them out quickly hastened the pollution of our environment and the disintegration of our central cities. I have learned that large-scale, "instant" projects leave little room for adjustment for errors or experience. What architecture and planning need, in the future, are a more deliberate pace and a more human scale.*

BREININ, GOODWIN M., physician; b. N.Y.C., Dec. 10, 1918; s. Louis and Mary (Mirsky) B.; m. Rose-Helen Kopelman, June 22, 1947; children: Bartley James, Constance. B.S., U. Fla., 1939; A.M., Emory U., 1940, M.D., 1943. Diplomate Am. Bd. Ophthalmology (dir., vice chmn., cons.). Intern U.S. Marine Hosp., Stapleton, N.Y., 1944; resident ophthalmology N.Y. U.-Bellevue Med. Center, 1947-51, sr. Heed fellow ophthalmology, 1954, Daniel B. Kirby prof. research ophthalmology, 1957, Daniel B. Kirby prof., chmn. dept. ophthalmology, 1959—, chmn. med. bd., 1975-77; dir. eye service Bellevue and U. Hosps., N.Y.C., 1959—; mem. vision commn. NRC, 1960-65; hon. assoc. U. Coll., London, 1966-67; chmn. vision research tng. com. Nat. Insts. Neurol. Diseases and Blindness, 1963-64; chief cons. Manhattan VA Hosp.; cons. Manhattan Eye, Ear and Throat, St. Vincent's, Beth Israel hosps., Lenox Hills Hosp.; surg. gen. USPHS; chmn. Nat. Res. Rev. Com., 1976-77; vis. prof., cons. Hailie Selassie I Univ. Found., Ethiopia, 1972; lectr. Mem. various adv. coms. relating to field, mem. med. adv. bd. Nat. Council to Combat Blindness; pres. Council for U.S./USSR Health Exchange, 1977; mem. Am. com. Internat. Agy. for Prevention of Blindness, 1980—; pres. 2d Internat. Symposium in Visual Optics, Tucson, 1982. Author: The Electrophysiology of Extraocular Muscle, 1962; editor: Advances in Diagnostic Visual Optics, 1983; mem. editorial bd. Investigative Ophthalmology, Archives of Ophthalmology; Contbr. articles to profl. jours. Mem. nat. coun. for medicine Emory U., Atlanta; mem. coun. visitors Marine Biol. Labs., Woods Hole, Mass. Recipient Knapp medal for contbn. ophthalmology A.M.A., 1957, Edward Lorenzo Holmes lectr. citation and award for contbns. to med. sci. Inst. Medicine Chgo., 1959, Gifford lectr. and award Chgo. Ophthal. Soc., 1970, Heed Ophthalmic Found. award, 1968, Emory U. medal, 1993; Wright lectr. U. Toronto, 1972; Lloyd lectr. Bklyn. Opthal. Soc., 1971; May lectr. N.Y. Acad. Medicine, 1974; guest of honor Australian Coll. Ophthalmologists, 1974, Japanese Cong. Neuro-ophthalmalogy, 1979; Scobee lectr., 1977. Fellow Am. Acad. Ophthalmology and Otolaryngology (v.p. 1979, Sr. Honor award 1984), ACS, N.Y. Acad. Medicine (sec. sect. ophthalmology 1962-63, chmn. sect. 1967-68); mem. AMA (sec. sect. on ophthalmology 1966-69, chmn. 1970-71), Rsch. Ophthalmology, Am. Ophthal. Soc., N.Y. Ophthal. Soc. (pres. 1980), Harvey Soc., AAAS, Am. Commn. for Optics and Visual Physiology (chmn. 1970—), Am. Orthoptic Coun., Assn. Univ. Profs. Ophthalmology, Pan. Am. Assn. Ophthalmology, Sigma Xi, Alpha Omega Alpha. Clubs: Century Assn., Practitioners, Charaka (N.Y.C.). Home: 912 Fifth Ave New York NY 10021-4159 Office: NYU Med Ctr 550 1st Ave New York NY 10016-6497

BREIPOHL, WALTER EUGENE, real estate broker; b. Ottawa, Ill., Mar. 24, 1953; s. Eugene E. and Margaret L. (Hughes) B. Student, Ill. Valley C.C.; BS, Loyola U., Chgo., 1974. Real estate broker and devel. Breipohl Co., Ottawa, 1975—; bd. dirs. No. Ill. Devel. Corp., Union Banc Corp., Ottawa, Union Bank, Ea. Divsn., Ottawa. Bd. dirs. Greater Ottawa, Inc., 1984—, pres., 1997; bd. dirs. Main Street U.S.A. Program, Ottawa, 1991-93, Cmty. Hosp. of Ottawa Found., 1994-97; chmn. Indsl. Devel. Commn., Ottawa, 1985-88; gov. Cmty. Hosp. Ottawa, 1986-89. Mem. Illini Valley Assn. Realtors (sec.-treas. 1983-85, President's award 1985), No. Ill. Comml. Assn. Realtors, Ill. Assn. Realtors, Nat. Assn. Realtors, Nat. Assn. Real Estate Appraisers, Ottawa Area C. of C. and Industry (chmn. bd. dirs. 1988), Ill. C. of C. (bd. dirs. 1997, Polit. Action Com. dir. 1998), Ill.-Mich. Canal Corridor Assn. (dir. 1997), Internat. Club (Chgo.), Boat Club, Union League Club (Chgo.), Elks, KC. Republican. Roman Catholic. Home and Office: PO Box 1039 Ottawa IL 61350-6039

BREISACH, ERNST A., historian, educator; b. Schwanberg, Austria, Oct. 8, 1923; came to U.S., 1953; s. Otto and Maria (Eder) B.; m. Herma E. Pirker, Aug. 2, 1945; children: Nora Sylvia, Eric Ernst. PhD in History, U. Vienna, Austria, 1946; D in Econs., Wirtschafts U., 1950. Prof. Realgymnasium Vienna XIV, Austria, 1946-52; assoc. prof. Olivet (Mich.) Coll., 1953-57; prof. Western Mich. U., Kalamazoo, 1957-96. Author: Introduction to Modern Existentialism, 1962, Caterina Sforza: A Renaissance Virago, 1967, Renaissance Europe, 1300-1517, 1973, Historiography: Ancient, Medieval, and Modern, 1983, 2d edit., 1994, American Progressive History, 1993; editor: Classical Rhetoric and Medieval Historiography, 1985. Recipient fellowship, Nat. Found. for the Humanities, Washington, 1989-90. Mem. Am. Hist. Assn., German Studies Assn. Home: 228 W Ridge Cir Kalamazoo MI 49009-9108 Office: Western Mich U Dept Of History Kalamazoo MI 49008

BREIT, JEFFREY ARNOLD, lawyer; b. Norfolk, Va., Apr. 14, 1955; s. Calvin W. and Mildred J. (Jacobs) B.; m. Suzanne Reigel, Aug. 23, 1980. BA, Tulane U., 1977, JD, 1979. Bar: Va. 1979, La. 1979, D.C. 1988, N.Y. 1991, N.C. 1991, U.S. Ct. Appeals (4th, 5th adn 11th cirs.), U.S. Supreme Ct. Ptnr. Breit, Rutter & Montagna, Norfolk, 1979-87, Breit, Drescher & Breit, Norfolk, 1987—. Contbr. articles to profl. jours. Chmn. Virginia Beach. Dem. Party, 1992—, vice chmn., 1995-97; pres. Operation Smile, Norfolk, 1987-90. Mem. ABA, ATLA (bd. govs. 1988—), Va. Trial Lawyers Assn. (pres. elect 1997-98, pres. 1998-99), La. Trial Lawyers Assn., N.C. Trial Lawyers Assn., Maritime Law Assn. U.S., Va. Trial Lawyers Assn. (pres. 1998-99). Jewish. Avocations: tennis, surfing. Home: 608 Linkhorn Dr Virginia Beach VA 23451-2440 Office: Breit Drescher & Breit 1000 Dominion Tower 999 Waterside Dr Ste 1000 Norfolk VA 23510-3304

BREITENECKER, RUDIGER, pathologist; b. Vienna, Austria, 1929; came to U.S., 1954, naturalized, 1969; s. Leopold and Irma B.; m. Robin Jacques, 1963; children: Rudiger, Richard C., Roland. M.D., U. Vienna, 1954. Intern E.W. Sparrow Hosp., Lansing, Mich., 1955-56; resident in pathology Clevel. Met. Gen. Hosp., 1957-59; mem. teaching staff Western Res. U., 1958-59; mem. tchg. staff Duke U., 1960-61; asst. med. examiner State of Md., Balt., 1962-67; asst. prof. forensic pathology U. Md., 1962-98; prof. justice adminstrn. U. Louisville, 1978—; lectr. Johns Hopkins Sch. Medicine, 1979-84; pathologist Greater Balt. Med. Ctr., 1967-98, assoc. dir. pathology lab., 1970-98; cons. legal medicine to fed. govt. Contbr. research publs. on forensic pathology. Fellow Am. Soc. Clin. Pathologists; mem. AMA, Am. Acad. Forensic Sci., Nat. Assn. Med. Examiners, Coll. Am. Pathologists, Am. Med. Soc., Md. Soc. Pathologists (pres. 1988, 89). Address: 2000 Western Run Rd Cockeysville MD 21030-1125

BREITENFELD, FREDERICK, JR., educational consultant, former public broadcasting executive; b. N.Y.C., Sept. 26, 1931; s. Frederick and Dorothy (Falk) B.; m. Mary Ellen Fitzgerald, Dec. 27, 1954; children: Ann Clark, Kathleen Ellen. BS in Engring., Tufts U., 1953, MEd, 1954; MS in TV-Radio, Syracuse U., 1960, PhD, 1963; LHD (hon.), U. Md., 1976, Salisbury State Coll., 1982, Phila. Coll. Textiles and Sci., 1987, Wesley Coll., 1992. Tchr. physics and chemistry pub. H.S. North Creek, N.Y., 1958-59; program adminstr. U. Coll., Syracuse U., 1960-61; asst. dean Syracuse U., 1961-63; resident cons. in comm. U.S. Air Force, Cape Canaveral, Fla., 1963-64; rsch. project dir. Nat. Assn. Ednl. Broadcasters, Washington, 1964-65; assoc. dir. ednl. TV stas. divsn. Nat. Assn. Ednl. Broadcasters, 1965-66; exec. dir. Md. Center for Pub. Broadcasting, Owings Mills, Md., 1966-83; CEO, pres. WHYY Inc., 1983-97; chmn. Ea. Ednl. TV Network, 1974-76; founding chmn. Am. Program Svc., 1991, vice-chmn., 1993; vice-chmn. bd. mgrs. PBS, 1973; cons., lectr. in field; adj. prof. Cath. U. Am., 1967-72, Am. U., 1972-74; vis. prof. Syracuse U., 1976, Johns Hopkins U., 1978-83; charter mem., chmn. Nat. Univ. Consortium for Telecomms. in Tchg. Trustee Thomas Jefferson U., 1988—, Valley Forge Mil. Acad. and Coll., 1992—, Bucks County C.C., 1994—; bd. dirs. Nat. Bd. Med. Examiners, 1995—; active Lower Makefield Zoning Hearing Bd., Bucks County, Pa., 1998—, Pennsbury Bd. Sch. Dirs., 1998—. With USNR, 1954-58. Recipient Disting.

Alumnus award Radio TV dept. U. Syracuse, 1967; Andrew White medal Loyola Coll., Balt., 1979; Lord Baltimore medal St. Mary's Coll., 1980; Man of Yr. award Boys and Girls Club of Phila., 1987; Globe and Anchor award USMC Scholarship Found., 1991; Williamson award for excellence in cmty. svc. Williamson Free Sch., 1993. Mem. Screen Actors Guild, AFTRA. Home: 1525 Harvest Dr Yardley PA 19067-4234 *To live is both to care and to laugh.*

BREITENSTEIN, DAVID E., newswriter; b. Belleville, Ill., Jan. 17, 1975; s. Eugene R. and Linda J. B. BS in Journalism, U. Kans., 1997. Writer, editor Univ. Daily Kansan, Lawrence, Kans., 1996-97; writer Anderson (S.C.) Ind.-Mail, 1997-99, Naples (Fla.) Daily News, 1999—. Vol. Kans. Spl. Olympics, Lawrence, 1997, Anderson Literacy Festival, 1998. Recipient Cert. Spl. Merit, William Randolph Hearst Found., 1997, 2d Pl. award S.C. Press Assn., 1998. Mem. Soc. Profl. Journalists (Mark of Excellence in In-depth Reporting 1997). Avocations: writing, athletics, reading, vacationing. Home: Apt 110 22220 Fountain Lakes Blvd Estero FL 33928 Office: Naples Daily News 1075 Central Ave Naples FL 34102

BREITKREUZ, GARRY, member of parliament; b. Springside, Sask., Can., Oct. 21, 1945. BA, U. Saskatchewan. Mem. of parliament, agr. critic House of Commons. Office: House of Commons, Wellington Bldg/RM 252, Ottawa, ON Canada K1A 0A6

BREITMAN, JOSEPH B., prosthodontist, dental educator; b. Phila., Aug. 4, 1952; s. Abraham A. and Natalie (Ketchurin) B.; m. Barbara Susan Beitman, May 13, 1990; children: Ilana Michelle, Ariel Judah, Leela Sivie. BA, LaSalle Coll., 1974; DMD, U. Pa., 1977; Cert. of Tng. in Prosthodontics, Temple U., 1979; Cert. of Tng. in Biomaterials, VA Hosp., Elsmere, Del., 1979. Gen. practice dentistry, Lafayette Hill, Pa., 1978-79; prosthodontist, Marlton, N.J., 1979-80; pvt. practice, Phila., 1980—; asst. prof. dental materials Temple U., Phila., 1978-84; assoc. in restorative dentistry U. Pa., Phila., 1985—; asst. prof. post-doctoral prosthodontics Temple U., 1990. Oral biology fellow Temple U., Phila., 1978. Fellow Internat. Congress of Oral Implantologists (elected 1994); mem. ADA, Am. Coll. Prosthodontics, N.E. Dental Soc. (pres. 1988-89), Ea. Dental Soc., Pa. Assn. Dental Surgeons (pres. 1984-85). Jewish. Lodge: Masons. Avocations: play bagpipes, tae kwon do. Office: 8021B Castor Ave Philadelphia PA 19152-2733

BREITMAN, RICHARD DAVID, historian, educator, writer; b. Hartford, Conn., Mar. 27, 1947; s. Saul Harold and Gloria Pearl Breitman; m. Carol Rose Wax, Sept. 12, 1982; children: David Russell, Marc Eduard. BA, Yale U., 1969; MA, Harvard U., 1971, PhD, 1975; DHL honoris causa, Hebrew Union Coll., 1999. From asst. prof. history to assoc. prof. history Am. U., Washington, 1976-86, prof. history, 1987—, chair history dept., 1995-97; cons. Office of Spl. Investigations, U.S. Dept. Justice, Washington, 1995-98. Author: (books) German Socialism and Weimar Democracy, 1981, The Architect of Genocide, 1991 (Fraenkel prize 1991), Official Secrets, 1998; co-author: (with Walter Laqueur) Breaking the Silence, 1986; editor: (jour.) Holocaust and Genocide Studies, 1996—; mem. editl. bd.: Jour. Contemporary History, 1994—. Mem. Am. Hist. Assn., German Studies Assn., World War II Studies Assn., Conf. Group for Cen. European History. Democrat. Jewish. Avocations: tennis, chess. E-mail: rbreit@american.edu. Office: Am U Dept History 4400 Massachusetts Ave NW Washington DC 20016-8003

BREITROSE, HENRY S., communications educator; b. Bklyn., July 22, 1936; s. Charles and Ruth (Leib) B.; m. Prudence Elaine Martin, Oct. 11, 1968; children—Charles Daniel, Rebecca Marjorie. B.S., U. Wis., 1958; M.A., Northwestern U., 1959; Ph.D., Stanford U., 1966. Writer Internat. Film Bur., 1958; mgr. Midwest office Contemporary Films Co., 1959; mem. faculty Stanford (Calif.) U., 1959—, prof. communication, 1975—, chmn. dept. communication, 1976-82; vis. prof. London Sch. Econs., 1976-77; mem. public media panel NEA, 1974—; ednl. adv. com. Am. Film Inst., 1974; vice chmn. tng. for developing countries, v.p. for rsch pub. Ctr. Internat. des Liasions des Ecoles du Cinema et du TV, 1989—; Christensen vis. rsch. fellow St. Catherine's Coll., Oxford, 1996; v.p. for publs. and rsch. Ctr. Internat. des Liasons des Ecoles du Cinema et de TV. Gen. editor: Cambridge Studies in Film; mem. editorial bd. Calif. Lawyer, 1980-86; author articles, chpts. in books. Bd. dirs. Sta. KQED, San Francisco, 1985-90, vice chmn. 1988; mem. adv. bd. Sta. KCSM. Grantee Rockefeller Found., 1965-66; Lilly Endowment, 1976-77; Stanford U. fellow, 1972-74, Christensen fellow Oxford U., 1996. Mem. Univ. Film Assn. (exec. v.p. 1987-89), Broadcast Educators Assn., Internat. Documentary Assn., Internat. Communication Assn., Internat. Inst. Communications. Home: 897 Tolman Dr Stanford CA 94305-1017 Office: Stanford U Dept Communication Stanford CA 94305-2050

BREKKE, GAIL LOUISE, broadcasting administrator; b. Fargo, N.D., Dec. 9, 1949; d. Curtis Eugene Sr. and Geraldine Ann (Hughes) B.; m. Harold E. Protter (div. 1991). BS in Edn., U. N.D., 1971; AA in Retailing, Lucerne, Switzerland, 1972; MA, Webster Coll., 1981. News reporter WXIX-TV, Cin., 1973-74; news reporter KPLR-TV, St. Louis, 1974-75, in sales, 1975-77, sales mgr., 1977-80; gen. mgr. KRBK-TV, Sacramento, 1980-83, WNOL-TV, New Orleans, 1983-86, WGBO-TV, Chgo., 1986-87, KITN-TV, Mpls., 1987-93, WBNE, New Haven, 1996—; dir. new sta. devel. LIN TV, 1997—; owner, pres. Black Diamond Communications Inc., 1994—. mem. Nat. Alumni Leadership Coun., U. N.D., 1992—. Mem. Minn. Broadcasters Assn. (pres. 1991—), Women in Cable & Telecom. Midwest (bd. dirs. 1993-96). Avocations: sailing, aerobics.

BREKKE, JUDY LYNN, state agency administrator; b. Mpls., Mar. 9, 1948; d. Raymond Luverne and Evelyn (Sigafoos) B.; m. Stephen Spaulding Morse, June 22, 1976; children: Raymond Thomas. BA in Early Childhood Edn., Mills Coll., 1981. Exec. dir., tchr. Mills Coll. Infant and Toddler Ctr., Oakland, Calif., 1978-82; exec. dir. Shoreline Early Childhood Devel. Ctr., Navarre, Minn., 1982-84; sr. tchr. North Netro Devel. Achievement Ctr., Golden Valley, Minn., 1984-85; exec. dir. Daybridge Learning Ctr., Eagan, Minn., 1985-90, Minnetonka, Minn., 1985-90; human svcs. licensor State of Minn., St. Paul, 1990—; freelance organizer Get It Together, Oakland, 1974-73. Flr. dir., camera Cable Ch. 6, 1974-75; editor Juice, 1974-82; author numerous poems (Ina Coolbrith Meml. poetry award 1979). Child caregiver Children's Hosp., Oakland, 1977; vol. Minn. Aids Project, 1988—, St. Stephens Homeless Shelter, Mpls., 1990—; treas. Steve Morse Campaign, Excelsior, Minn., 1994—. Mem. Minn. Assn. Edn. Young Children, Phi Beta Kappa. Avocations: reading, sewing, weaving, hiking, films. Home: 640 3rd Ave Excelsior MN 55331-3227

BRELIS, MATTHEW DEAN BURNS, journalist; b. Boston, Aug. 30, 1957; s. C. Dean Brelis and Nancy Emerson (Burns) Jay; m. Mary Morgan Baker, Sept. 10, 1988; children: Mary Margaret, Elinor Baker. AB, Vassar Coll., 1980. Reporter trainee/clk. The Washington Star, 1980-81; reporter The Pitts. Press, 1981-89, Boston Globe, 1989—. Recipient Pulitzer Prize, Columbia U., 1987, Keystone award Pa. Newspaper Pubs. Assn., 1987, Roy Howard award Scripps-Howard, 1987. Club: Boston Vassar, Mt. Auburn, Cambridge Skating. Office: Boston Globe Globe Newspaper Co 135 Morrissey Blvd Dorchester MA 02125-3338*

BREMAN, JOEL GORDON, epidemiologist, science administrator; b. Chgo., Dec. 1, 1936; s. Herman Iman and Irene (Grant) B.; m. Vicki Ann Vaughan, June 26, 1966; children: Matthew Grant, Johanna Vaughan. AB, UCLA, 1958; MD, U. So. Calif., L.A., 1965; diploma in tropical pub. health, U. London, 1971. Cert. physician, surgeon Calif. Bd. Med. Examinations; diplomate Am. Coll. Preventive Medicine. Chief Smallpox Eradication/Measles Control, Conakry, Guinea, 1967-69; chief epidemiology sect. Orgn. de Coordination et de Coopération pour la lutte contre les Grandes Endémies, Bobo-Dioulasso, Burkina Faso, 1972-76; epidemic intelligence svc. officer Ctrs. for Disease Control, Lansing, Mich., 1976-77; med. officer Smallpox Eradication Unit WHO, Geneva, 1977-80; chief Malaria Control Activity Nat. Ctr. for Infectious Disease, Ctr. Disease Ctrl., Atlanta, 1982-89, dep. chief Malaria Br., 1989-93; assoc. dir. Nat. Vaccine Program Office Office of Asst. Sec. for Health, DHHS, Washington, 1993-95; dep. dir. divsn. internat. tng. and rsch. Fogarty Internat. Ctr., NIH, Bethesda, Md., 1995—; adj. instr. Harvard Sch. Pub. Health, Boston, 1988-97; adj. prof. Emory U. Sch. Pub. Health, Atlanta, 1990-93; adj. assoc. prof. Johns Hopkins Sch. Hygiene and Health, Balt., 1995-97. Contbr. chpts. to books and articles to profl. jours. Founder cmty. policing group Police Svc. Area 108 Orange Hat Patrol, Washington, 1995—. Named Officer of the Leopard, Govt. Zaire, Kinshasa, 1981. Fellow Am. Coll. Epidemiology, Am. Coll. Preventive Medicine, Infectious Diseases Soc. Am., Royal Soc. Tropical Medicine and Hygiene; mem. WHO Internat. Commn. for the Cert. of Dracunculiasis Eradication. Achievements include involvement of smallpox eradication in Guinea, West Africa and Geneva; original investigation and control of Ebola virus in Dem. Rep. Congo; defined epidemiology and control of malaria in Africa; research on the epidemiology and control of infectious diseases. Avocations: mountain climbing, bicycling, photography. Home: 317 A St SE Washington DC 20003-3812 Office: Nat Inst Health Fogarty Internat Ctr Bldg 31 Room B2C39 31 Center Dr Bethesda MD 20892

BREMEL, THOMAS JOHN, biochemist, researcher; b. Eau Claire, Wis., Apr. 19, 1959; s. Herbert Gerald and Gail Beverly (Erdman) B.; m. Tracy Ann Faber, Oct. 7, 1989. BS in Biochemistry, U. Minn., Mpls., 1991. Prodn. technician Cargill, Inc., Wayzata, Minn., 1991-94, lab. technician, 1994-95, application technician, 1995-96, physical testing technician, 1996-97, environmental affairs, 1997—; area coord. Cargill Rsch. Safety Com., Wayzata, 1995—. Mem. Lake Sarah Improvement Assn., Greenfield, Minn., 1994—. Avocations: golf, fly tying. Home: 6355 Lake Sarah Heights Dr Rockford MN 55373-9729 Office: Cargill Inc 2301 Crosby Rd Wayzata MN 55391-2313

BREMER, CELESTE F., judge; b. 1953. BA, St. Ambrose Coll., 1974; JD, Univ. of Iowa Coll. of Law, 1977. Asst. county atty. Scott County, 1977-79; asst. atty. gen. Area Prosecutors Div., Iowa, 1979; with Carlin, Liebbe, Pitton & Bremer, 1979-81, Rabin, Liebbe, Shinkle & Bremer, 1981-82; with legal dept. Deere and Co., 1982-84; corp. counsel Economy Forms Corp., 1985-89; magistrate judge U.S. Dist. Ct. (Iowa so. dist.), 8th cir., Des Moines, 1984—; instr. Drake Univ. Coll. of Law, 1985-96. Mem. ABA, Fed. Magistrate Judge Assn., Nat. Assn. Women Judges, Am. Judicature Soc., Iowa State Bar Assn. (bd. govs., 1987-90), Iowa Judges Assn., Iowa Supreme Ct. Coun. on Jud. Selection (chmn. 1986-90), Iowa Orgn Women Attys., Polk County Bar Assn., Polk County Women Attys. Office: US Courthouse Ste 435 123 E Walnut St Des Moines IA 50309-2036

BREMER, HOWARD WALTER, consulting patenting and licensing lawyer; b. Milw., July 18, 1923; s. Walter Hugo and Lydia Martha (Schmidt) B.; m. Caryl Marie Faust, May 28, 1948; children: Katharine, William (dec.), Thomas, Timothy, Margaret. BSChemE, U. Wis., 1944, LLB, 1949. Bar: Wis. 1949, U.S. Patent and Trademark Office 1954, U.S. Supreme Ct. 1957, U.S. Ct. Appeals (fed. cir.) 1959, U.S. Dist. Ct. (so. dist.) Ohio 1960. Patent atty. Procter & Gamble Co., Cin., 1949-60; patent counsel Wis. Alumni Rsch. Found., Madison, 1960-88; cons., Madison, 1988—; mem. adv. com. Coun. on Govtl. Rels., Washington, 1975-93; panel mem. Office Tech. Assessment, Washington, 1981-83; mem. Adv. Commn. on Patent Law Reform, Washington, 1991-92. Mem. internat. adv. bd. Industry and Higher Edn. Jour., 1996—; contbr. articles to profl. jours. Pres. Edgewood Campus Sch. PTA, Madison, 1967-69; mem. adv. bd. Edgewood H.S., 1971-80, chmn. adv. bd., 1973-74. With USN, 1944-46. Recipient alumni appreciation award Edgewood H.S., 1990. Mem. ABA (chmn. com. 1993—), Am. Intellectual Property Law Assn. (chmn. com. 1996—), State Bar Wis. (chmn. intellectual property sect. 1967-68, 79-80), Wis. Intellectual Property Law Assn. (pres. 1989-90), Assn. Univ. Tech. Mgrs. (trustee 1977-78, 80-82, pres. 1978-80, com. chmn. 1985-93, mem. editl. bd. jour. 1990—, Birch award 1980). Avocations: building furniture, home maintenance, model railroading, travel, reading. Home: 1106 Brookwood Rd Madison WI 53711-3116

BREMER, JOHN M., lawyer; b. 1947. BA, Fordham U., 1969; JD, Duke U., 1974. Bar: Wis. 1974. Atty. law dept. Northwestern Mutual Life Ins., Milw., 1974-78, asst. gen. counsel, 1978-90, v.p., gen. counsel and sec., 1990-94, sr. v.p., gen. counsel, sec., 1995-98, exec. v.p., gen. counsel, sec., 1998—. Office: Northwestern Mutual Life Ins Co 720 E Wisconsin Ave Milwaukee WI 53202-4703

BREMER, MICHAEL STEWART, management consultant; b. St. Louis, Nov. 24, 1948; s. Walter S. and Mary L. (Chadwell) B.; m. Lynn M. Sieben, Nov. 25, 1978; children: Kate S., Andrew S. BS in Bus., U. Mo., 1971. CPA, Ill.; cert. mgmt. cons. Auditor Gale, Takahashi & Channon, Chgo.; sr. auditor Seidman & Seidman, Chgo., 1973-75; sr. acct. Beatrice Foods Co., Chgo., 1975-76, mgr. corp. planning, 1977-79; mgr. quality Beatrice Cos., Inc., Chgo., 1980-83, dir. mgmt. info. systems, 1983-86; prin. Bremer & Assocs., Chgo., 1987-89; pres. Cumberland Group Chgo., 1990—; spkr. White House Conf. on Productivity, Washington, 1984. Contbr. article to profl. jours. Pres., bd. dirs. Old Town Sch. Folk Music, Chgo., 1978-88; vol. Ind. Labor Mgmt. Coun., Indpls. Mem. Strategic Leadership Forum (bd. dirs., v.p. 1996-97), Assn. Mfg. Excellence (bd. dirs., v.p. 1994—), Assn. Quality and Participation (pres., bd. dirs. 1981-82). Avocations: family, backpacking, running, reading, tennis. Office: The Cumberland Group 40 Shuman Blvd Ste 160 Naperville IL 60563-8464

BREMER, RONALD ALLAN, genealogist, editor; b. South Gate, Calif., May 2, 1937; s. Carl Leonard and Lena Evelyn (Jury) B.; m. Trudy Graham; children: Blindy, Ron, Trina, Rebecca, Melinda, Aaron, Serena, Lorrie, Jennie, Elizabeth, Hans, Adam, Rachel. Student Los Angeles Trade Tech., Cerritos Coll., Am. U., Brigham Young U., grad. Nat. Inst. Geneal. Rsch., 1961. Profl. Genealogist, 1959—; Research specialist Fam. Hist. Libr., Salt Lake City, 1969-72; profl. lectr. on genealogy, Salt Lake City, 1973—; editor Genealogy Digest mag., Salt Lake City, 1983-84, Roots Digest, 1984-85; lectr. in field. Author: World's Funniest Epitaphs, 1983; Compendium of Historical Sources, 1983. Office: PO Box 345 Paradise UT 84328 *Money and things don't matter. Position and education mean little. Genius and slow-normal have the same opportunity. Happiness is achieving your greatest potential. Go for the goose-bumps!.*

BREMER, VICTOR JOHN, broadcasting executive; b. L.A., Jan. 22, 1943; s. John Victor B. and Mary Ellen (Kelley) Gerwig; m. Marilyn Smith, Feb. 20, 1962 (div. 1966); 1 child, Alicia Anne Taylor; m. Sheila Anne Goldstein, Sept. 9, 1969; children: Joel Victor, Noah David. BA in Polit. Sci., Pepperdine U., 1965. News dir. Sta. KVEC-Radio, San Luis Obispo, Calif., 1970-72; news and program dir. Sta. KXRX-Radio, San Jose, Calif., 1972-78; v.p. news and programming Sta. KIRO Newsradio, Seattle, 1978-87; ops. dir. Sta. WCCO Radio, Mpls., 1987-89; dir. news and programming Sta. WBBM Newsradio, Chgo., 1989-90; v.p. broadcasting Minn. Pub. Radio, St. Paul, 1990-95; real estate agt. Burnet Realty, Mpls./St. Paul, 1995-97; with Metro Networks, Seattle, Wash., 1997-98, Greyhound Lines Inc., Seattle, 1998—.

BREMNER, JOHN MCCOLL, agronomy and biochemistry educator; b. Dumbarton, Scotland, Jan. 18, 1922; came to U.S., 1959; s. Archibald Donaldson and Sarah Kennedy (McColl) B.; m. Eleanor Mary Williams, Sept. 30, 1950; children: Stuart, Carol. BS, Glasgow U., 1944, DSc, 1987; PhD, U. London, 1948, DSc, 1959. With chemistry dept. Rothamsted Exptl. Sta., Harpenden, Eng., 1945-59; assoc. prof. Iowa State U., Ames, 1959-61, prof. agronomy and biochemistry, 1961-75, C.F. Curtiss disting. prof. agriculture, prof. agronomy, biochemistry, 1975-93; disting. prof. emeritus, 1993—; tech. expert IAEA, Austria, 1964-65, Yugoslavia, 1964-65. Author or co-author over 300 publs. including 30 chpts in sci. monographs. Recipient Outstanding Research award First Miss. Corp., 1979, Alexander Von Humboldt medal Alexander Von Humboldt Found., Fed. Republic of Germany, 1982, Gov.'s Sci. medal State of Iowa, 1983, Harvey Wiley award U.S. Assn. Ofcl. Analytical Chemists, 1984, Spencer medal Am. Chem. Soc., 1987, Burlington No. Found. Faculty Achievement award for Research, Gamma Sigma Delta award of merit for disting. service to agriculture, Regents award for faculty excellence, 1992, Award for Advancement of Agrl. & Food Chemistry, Am. Chem. Soc.; fellow Rockefeller Found., 1957, Guggenheim Found., 1968. Fellow AAAS, Am. Acad. Microbiology, Am. Soc. Agronomy (Agronomic Rsch. award 1985, Environ. Quality Rsch. award 1990), Soil Sci. Soc. Am. (Achievement award 1967, Bouyoucos Disting. Career award 1982, Disting. Svc. award 1993), Iowa Acad. Sci. (disting.); mem. NAS, Am. Soc. Microbiology, Brit. Soc. Soil Sci., Internat. Soil Sci. Soc., Phi Kappa Phi (centennial medalist 1997), Sigma Xi, Gamma Sigma Delta. Achievements include patent for nitrification inhibitor; development and evaluation of nitrification and urease inhibitors for control of adverse transformations of fertilizer nitrogen in soils; development of methodology for research on the nitrogen cycle and environmental problems related to agriculture; research on microbial, enzymatic, and chemical processes responsible for nitrogen transformations in soils, such as nitrification, denitrification, chemodenitrification, and urease activity.

BREMS, DAVID PAUL, architect; b. Lehi, Utah, Aug. 10, 1950; s. D. Orlo and Geraldine (Hitchcock) B.; m. Johna Devey Brems; children: Stefan Tomas Brems, Beret Alla Brems. B.S., U. Utah, 1973, M.Arch., 1975. Registered arch., Utah, Calif., Colo., Ariz., Wyo., N.Mex., Idaho, Mont., Wash. Draftsman, Environ. Assoc., Salt Lake City, 1971-73; draftsman/architect intern Environ. Design Group, Salt Lake City, 1973-76; architect/intern Frank Fuller AIA, Salt Lake City, 1976-77; prin. Edwards & Daniels, Salt Lake City, 1978-83; pres. David Brems & Assocs., Salt Lake City, 1983-86; prin. Gillies, Stransky, Brems, Smith P.C., Salt Lake City, 1986—; adj. prof. U. Utah Grad. Sch. Architecture, 1990-93; mem. urban design com. Assist, Inc., Salt Lake City, 1982-85, Salt Lake County Planning Commn., 1991-97, chmn., 1992-96; mem., chmn. Emigration Township Planning Commn., 1997—; mem. Emigration Masterplan Adv. Com., 1997; invited lectr. Wyo Soc. Archs., 1992, sch. engrng. U. Utah, 1993, 95, VA, 1993, Utah Soc. Archs., 1994, Utah Power and Light, 1994, Utah Soc. Archts., 1994; juror U. Utah Grad. Sch. Architecture, 1975—, Utah Soc. Am. Planning Assn., 1994—, Sunstone Symposium, 1995, Contemporary Arts Group, 1995—. Pub. Firm Profile Intermountain Architecture, 1996, Web Mag., 1997; prin. works include solar twin homes Utah Holiday, (Best Solar Design award), Sun Builder, Daily Jour., Salt Lake Tribune, Brian Head Day Lodge, Easton Aluminum, Four Seasons Hotel, Gore Coll. Bus., CMF Tooele, Utah Regional Corrections Facility, St. Vincents De Paul Ctr., Steiner Aquatic Ctr., U. Utah Football Support Facility, Sports Medicine West, West Jordan Community Water Park, Utah Nat. Guard Apache Helicopter Hangar & Armory, Kashmitter I Residences, St. Thomas More Cath. Ch., Spanish Fork Cmty. Water Park, Natures Herbs, ABC Office Bldg. Divsn. of Natural Resources Bldg., Kashmitter II Residence, Litton Residence, Elliott Residence, and others; ALTA Club mem., Great Salt Lake Yacht Club mem., mem. Leadership Utah; mem. 2002 Olympic Energy and Water subcom., 1996—; mem. State of Utah Divsn. of Facilities Mgmt. Com. on Energy Efficient Architecture. Recipient 3 awards Am. Concrete Inst., 1993, Chief Engrs. Honor award U.S. Army Corps Engrs., 1994; Bronze medalist Utah Summer Games, 1991, Silver medalist, 1992, Gold medalist, 1994, Design award Dept. Def., 1995, Blue Seal award, 1995, Outstanding Project award U.S. Dept. Defense, 1995, Salt Lake County Citizen Vol. of Yr. award, 1995, Western Mountain Region Honorable Mention St. Thomas More, 1996, Solar Today award, Sun award, Energy Uses News award Dept. Natural Resources, 1996; named Best Pvt. Project by Intermountain Architecture, 1994, Salt Lake County Vol. of Yr. Salt Lake County Planning Commn., 1995, Best Recreation Progect Intermountain Arch., 1995. Mem. AIA (pres. Salt Lake chpt. 1983-84, pres. Utah Soc. 1987, chmn. Western Mountain Region conf., 1986, com. on design 1990—, chmn. com. on environment AIA Utah 1993, chmn. Design for Life Workshop at Sundance, 1993, Honor awards 1983, 88, Merit awards 1983, 85, 88, 93, chmn. Western Mountain Region honor awards 1983, 88, PCI award 1988, IFRAA award 1988, 94, Juror Colo. West awards 1992, award Utah sect. IES for St. Thomas More), Am. Planning Assn. (juror awards 1994), Acorn Hills Water assn. (pres.), Utah Soc. Architects, Am. Solar Energy Soc., Hobie Fleet 67 (commodore 1985-86), Salt Lake Olympic Com. (environ. adv. com.), Great Salt Lake Yacht Club, Alta Club, Boulder Mountain Res. club (v.p.), Illuminating Engring. Soc. (assoc.). Home: 3497 Little Tree Rd Salt Lake City UT 84108

BREMS, HANS JULIUS, economist, educator; b. Viborg, Denmark, Oct. 16, 1915; s. H. and Andrea (Golditz) B.; m. Ulla Constance Simoni, May 20, 1944; children: Lisa, Marianne, Karen Joyce. Cand. polit., U. Copenhagen, 1941, Dr. polit., 1950; Hedersdoktor (hon.), Helsinki, Finland, 1970; Dr. merc. (hon.), Copenhagen Sch. Bus., Copenhagen, Denmark, 1992. Asst. prof. U. Copenhagen, 1943-51; lectr. U. Calif., Berkeley, 1951-54; mem. faculty U. Ill., Champaign-Urbana, 1954-86; prof. U. Ill., 1955-86, prof. emeritus, 1986—; vis. prof. U. Calif., Berkeley, 1959, Harvard U., 1960, U. Kiel (Fed. Republic of Germany), 1961, U. Colo., 1963, U. Göttingen (Fed. Republic of Germany), 1964, U. Hamburg (Fed. Republic of Germany), 1967, U. Uppsala (Sweden), 1968, U. Stockholm, 1980, U. Zurich, 1983, others. Author: Product Equilibrium under Monopolistic Competition, 1951, Output, Employment, Capital, and Growth, 1959, 2d edit., 1973, Quantitative Economic Theory, 1968, Labor, Capital and Growth, 1973, Inflation, Interest, and Growth-A Synthesis, 1980, Dynamische Makrotheorie-Inflation, Zins und Wachstum, 1980, Fiscal Theory--Government, Inflation and Growth, 1983, Pioneering Economic Theory, 1630-1980, A Mathematical Restatement, 1986, Japanese translation, 1996; contbr. articles to profl. jours. and Ency. Americana. Rockefeller fellow, 1946-47; Fulbright prof., 1961, 64. Mem. Am. Econ. Assn., Danish Acad. Scis. and Letters, Finnish Acad. Scis. and Letters. Home: Clark-Lindsey Village #3201 101 W Windsor Rd Urbana IL 61802-6663

BREMSER, GEORGE, JR., electronics company executive; b. Newark, May 26, 1928; s. George and Virginia (Christian) B.; m. Marie Sundman, June 21, 1952 (div. July 1979); children: Christian Fredrick II, Priscilla Suzanne, Martha Anne, Sarah Elizabeth; m. Nancy Kay Woods, Oct. 27, 1983 (div. Feb. 1989); m. Betty Glover Lohse, Oct. 8, 1997. BA, Yale U., 1949; postgrad., U. Miami, 1959; MBA, NYU, 1962. With McCann-Erickson Inc., N.Y.C., 1952-61; asst. gen. mgr. McCann-Erickson Inc., Bogota, Columbia, 1955, gen. mgr., 1955-57; account supr. McCann-Erickson Inc., N.Y.C., 1958; v.p., mgr. McCann-Erickson Inc., Miami, Fla., 1959-61; with Gen. Foods Corp., White Plains, N.Y., 1961-71; v.p., gen. mgr. internat. div. Gen. Foods Europe, White Plains, N.Y., 1967; pres. Gen. Foods Internat., White Plains, 1967-71; group v.p. Gen. Foods Corp., White Plains, 1970-71; chmn., pres., chief exec. officer Texstar Corp., Grand Prairie, Tex., 1971-81; exec. v.p. Shaklee Corp., San Francisco, 1981-82; chmn., pres., chief exec. officer Etak Inc., Menlo Park, Calif., 1983-88, 96, chmn., 1989-96, 97—; chmn., pres., CEO Etak, Inc., Menlo Park, Calif., 1996-97, chmn., 1997—; bd. dirs. PBI Industries Inc. Trustee Union Ch., Bogota, 1956-57; Dem. county committeeman, Ridgewood, N.J., 1962-63; mem. New Canaan (Conn.) Town Council, 1969-73; founder, past pres. Citizens Com. for Conservation, New Canaan; mem. coun. Save the Redwoods League, 1987—. Served to 2d lt. USMC 1950-52, capt. Res. Mem. New Canaan Country Club, Brook Club, Yale Club (N.Y.C.), Block Island Club, Casino Club (Nantucket, Mass.), Explorers Club, Phi Beta Kappa, Beta Gamma Sigma, Beta Theta Pi. Home: 5575 Hilltop Cres Oakland CA 94618-2605 also: 535 Everett Ave Palo Alto CA 94301-1547 also: Mansion Beach Rd Block Island RI 02807 Office: care Etak Inc 1605 Adams Dr Menlo Park CA 94025-1432

BREN, DONALD L., real estate company executive; b. 1932. BA in Bus., U. Wash., MBA. With Calif. Pacific Homes, Inc., Newport Beach, Calif., 1956—; chmn. bd. Calif. Pacific Homes, Inc., Newport Beach; founder Mission Viejo (Calif.) Co.; CEO Irvine Co., Newport Beach, chmn. bd., 1998—. With USMC, 1954-57. Office: The Irvine Co 550 Newport Center Dr Newport Beach CA 92660-7011*

BRENCHLEY, JEAN ELNORA, microbiologist, researcher; b. Towanda, Pa., Mar. 6, 1944; d. John Edward and Elizabeth (Jefferson) B.; m. Bernard Asbell, July 21, 1990. BS, Mansfield U., 1965; MS, U. Calif., San Diego, 1967; PhD, U. Calif., Davis, 1970; hon. degree, Lycoming Coll., 1992. Rsch. assoc. biology dept. MIT, Cambridge, 1970-71; from asst. prof. to assoc. prof. microbiology Pa. State U., Univ. Pk., 1971-77; head. dept. molecular and cell biology, dir. Biotech. Inst. Pa. State U., University Park, 1984-87, prof. microbiology, dir. Biotech. Inst., 1984-90, prof. microbiology and biotech., 1990—; assoc. prof., then prof. biology Purdue U., West Lafayette, Ind., 1977-81; research dir. Genex Corp., Gaithersburg, Md., 1981-84; mem. Nat. Biotech. Policy Bd., 1990-93; trustee Biosis, 1983-88; vis. scholar NIH, 1991. Editor Applied and Environ. Microbiology, 1981-85; mem. editorial bd. Jour. Bacteriology, 1974-84, Butterworth Biotech. Series, 1988-92; editor Microbiol. Revs., 1992-97. Recipient Outstanding Alumni award Manfield U., 1983; Waksman award Theobald Smith Soc., 1985; named to Pa. Hall of Fame, 1988. Fellow AAAS (nominating com. 1990-92), Am. Acad. Microbiology; mem. NAS (bioprocess com.), Am. Soc. Microbiology (pres. 1986-87, ASM Found. lectr. 1975, Alice Evans award 1996), Assn. Women in Sci., Am. Soc. Biol. Chemists, Am. Chem. Soc., Found. for Microbiology (trustee 1988-95), Sigma Delta Epsilon (hon.). Office: Pa State Univ Frear Lab University Park PA 16802*

BRENDEL, ALFRED, concert pianist; b. Wiesenberg, Austria, Jan. 5, 1931; s. Albert and Ida (Wieltschnig) B.; m. Iris Heymann-Gonzala, 1960 (div. 1972); m. Irene Semler, 1975; 1 son, 3 daus. Studied piano under, Sofija Dezelic, Zagreb, Yugoslavia, Ludovika V. Kaan, Graz, Austria, Edwin Fischer, Lucerne, Switzerland, Paul Baumgartner, Basel, Switzerland, Edward Steuermann, Salzburg, Austria; studied harmony under Franjo Dugan, Zagreb; studied composition under A. Michl, Graz, Austria; DMus (hon.), U. London, 1978; DLitt (hon.), Sussex U., 1981; DMus (hon.), Oxford U., 1983, Warwick U., 1991, Yale U., 1992; fellow, Royal No. Coll., Manchester, 1988; Bayer, Akademie der Wissenschaften. First piano recital Graz, 1940, concert tours through Europe, Latin Am. and N.Am., 1963—, Australia, 1963, 66, 69, 76, appeared at many music festivals including Salzburg, 1960—, Vienna, Berlin, Montreux, Lucerne, Edinburg, Aldeburgh, Athens, Granada, P.R.; has performed with most maj. orchs. in Europe and U.S. and others; performed all Beethoven piano sonatas in concert cycle Paris, London, Berlin, Amsterdam, Vienna, Hamburg, Basel, Dusseldorf, Freiburg, Vevey, N.Y.C., 1983, 92—; recording The Alfred Brendel Collection. Recipient Premio Citta de Bolzano Concorso Busoni, 1949; recipient Grand Prix du Disque, 1965, 84, Edison prize, 1973, 81, 84, 87, Brit. Music Trade Assn. award 1973, 78, 81, Grand Prix des Disquaires de France, 1975, Deutscher Schallplattenpreis, 1976, 77, 81, 82, 84, Wiender Flotenuhr, 1976, 77, 79, 82, 84, 87, Gramophone award, 1978, 80, 82, 84, Japanese Grand Prix award, 1977, 78, 80, 82, 84, 87, Franz Liszt prize, 1979, 80, 82, 83, 87, Frankfurt Music award 1984, Busoni Found. award, 1990, Diapason D'Or award, 1992, Preis der deutschen Schallplatten-Kritik, 1992, Orden pour le Merite fur Wissenschaften und Kunste, 1991; decorated knight British Empire, 1989. Fellow Exeter Coll., 1987—; mem. Am. Acad. Arts and Scis. (hon.), Royal Acad. Music (hon.), Comdr. des Arts et Letters. Office: care Colbert Artists Mgmt Inc 111 W 57th St New York NY 10019-2211*

BRENDER, ART, lawyer; b. Chgo., Feb. 21, 1946; s. Arthur John Sr. and Elenore (McGauley) B.; m. Lynda Gayle Tankersley, Dec. 14, 1968; children: Sarah Blankenship, Erin, John. BA, U. Tex., 1968, JD, 1973. Bar: Tex. 1973, U.S. Dist. Ct. (no. dist.) Tex. 1973, U.S. Dist. Ct. (so. dist.) Tex. 1987, U.S. Dist. Ct. (we. dist.) Tex. 1988, U.S. Dist. Ct. (ea. dist.) Tex. 1989, U.S. Ct. Appeals (5th cir.) 1974, U.S. Ct. Appeals (9th cir.) 1980, U.S. Supreme Ct. 1977; cert. Tex. Bd. Legal Specialization, Criminal Law, Personal Injury Trial Law. Assoc. Law Offices of Don Gladden, Ft. Worth, 1973-77; adj. prof. Tex. Christian U., Ft. Worth, 1976-84; pvt. practice Ft. Worth, 1977—; assoc. Brender, Casey and Colosi, Ft. Worth, 1984-90; advocate Am. Bd. Trial Advocates, 1985—. Contbr. articles to profl. jours. Pres. Humane Soc. North Tex., 1986—; bd. dirs. Tarrant Youth Svcs. Bur., 1973-76; bd. dirs., legal counsel Tarrant County Harvest, Inc., 1991—; parrish coun. St. Ritas Cath. Ch., 1992-93; inner city sch. com. Diocese of Ft. Worth, 1992-95; bd. dirs. S.E. Area Chs., 1978—; basketball coach 6th, 7th, 8th grades St. Rita's Sch., 1985-92; del. state and dist. conv. Tex. Dem. Party, 1974-92; alt. del. Dem. Nat. Conv., Senate Dist. 12, 1988. Lt. USN, 1969-71. Recipient Good Guy award Women's Polit. Caucus, 1985, Fair Employment Practices award Ft. Worth Human Rels. Commn., 1987, award for outstanding svc. in field of civil rights NAACP Tex. br., 1988, Pro Bono award for outstanding contbns. of legal svcs. to low income Texans, 1994. Fellow Tex. Bar Found.; mem. Am. Bd. Trial Advocates, Assn. Trial Lawyers Am., State Bar Tex. (co-chairperson individual ABA rights sect. 1983-84), Tex. Trial Lawyers Assn. (assoc. dir. 1988—), Tarrant County Bar Assn. (dir. 1987-89, law libr. com. 1980-91), Tarrant Count Trial Lawyers Assn. (treas. 1984), Tarrant County Criminal Def. Lawyers Assn. (pres. 1980-81), T Assn. U. Tex., Ex Student Assn. U. Tex. Austin, ACLU (bd. mem. Ft. Worth chpt. 1975-87). Democrat. Roman Catholic. Avocations: organic farming, ranching, gardening, mountain hiking and climbing, fishing, camping. Home: 4121 Hampshire Blvd Fort Worth TX 76103-3920 Office: 600 8th Ave Fort Worth TX 76104-2020

BRENDER, JEAN DIANE, epidemiologist, nurse; b. Bellingham, Wash., Nov. 23, 1951; d. Otto and Jennie Wilma Tolsma; m. Dennis Ray Brender, Aug. 30, 1975; 1 child, Valerie. BSN summa cum laude, Whitworth Coll., 1974; M of Nursing, U. Wash., 1979, PhD of Epidemiology, 1983. RN, Tex. Staff nurse, infection control Sacred Heart Med. Ctr., Spokane, Wash., 1974-80; instr. nursing Intercollegiate Ctr. for Nursing Edn., Spokane, 1979-80, asst. prof. nursing, 1982-84; teaching asst. epidemiology U. Wash., Seattle, 1981-82; rsch. health scientist Audie L. Murphy Vets. Hosp., San Antonio, 1984-85; staff epidemiologist bur. epidemiology Tex. Dept. Health, Austin, 1986-87, acting program dir. environ. epidemiology program, 1987, dir. environ. epidemiology program, 1987-93, dir. noncommunicable disease epidemiology and toxicology, 1993-97; infectious disease epidemiologist Bur. Disease Control, 1997—; also state environ. epidemiologist Tex. Dept. Health, Austin, 1993-97; bd. dirs. Agriculture Resources Protection Authority; adj. instr. allied health scis. and health adminstrn. S.W. Tex. State U., 1988-90; adj. asst. prof. epidemiology U. Tex. Health Sci. Ctr.-Houston Sch. Pub. Health, 1985-93, adj. assoc. prof., 1993—. Contbr. articles to profl. jours. Tchr., mem. adult choir St. Martin's Luth. Ch., Austin, 1991—. Recipient H.E.A.L.T.H. award, 1994; grantee in field. Mem. Soc. Epidemiologic Rsch., Coun. State and Territorial Epidemiologists. Avocations: reading, computers, church activities, snow skiing. Home: 6902 Alder Cv Austin TX 78750-8161 Office: Tex Dept Health 1100 W 49th St Austin TX 78756-3160

BRENDER, WILLIAM CHARLES, plastic and reconstructive surgeon, artist; b. N.Y.C., Sept. 29, 1951; s. Edward and Ruth Brender; m. Francine Shelley Doran, Nov. 25, 1977 (div. 1995); children: Jessica, Jared, Matthew. BS summa cum laude, Union Coll., 1973; MD, NYU, 1976. Diplomate Am. Bd. Surgery, Am. Bd. Plastic Surgery, added qualification in surgery of the hand. Assoc. Glens Falls (N.Y.) Plastic Surgeons, 1984-85; pres. Adirondack Plastic Surgery, Glens Falls, 1985—, Brender's Gallery, Glens Falls, 1991—. Fellow ACS; mem. Am. Soc. for Aesthetic Plastic Surgery, Am. Soc. Plastic and Reconstructive Surgery, Am. Assn. for Surgery of the Hand, Am. Assn. Physician Arts, Soc. Plastic Surgeons of Upstate N.Y. (pres. 1998-99), Niagara Falls Watercolor Soc., Upper Hudson Valley Watercolor Soc., Phi Beta Kappa. Avocations: drawing, painting, photography, computers. E-mail: artistmd@pol.net. Office: Adirondack Plastic Surgery/Brender's Gallery 115 Maple St Glens Falls NY 12801

BRENDLE, STEVEN MICHAEL, municipal official, accountant; b. St. Louis, Mo., Jan. 27, 1956; s. Lawrence William and Velma Jean (McCauley) B.; m. Jean, Oct. 27, 1984; 1 child, Molly. BS, BA in Acctg., St. Louis U., 1979, MBA, 1993. Internal auditor St. Louis Police Dept., 1982-85, acctg. supr., 1985-88, dir. purchasing, 1988-97; supply commr. City of St. Louis, 1997—. Mem. Mo. Assn. Pub. Purchasing, Clifton Heights Neighborhood Assn. (v.p. 1988-91, treas. 1995—), Gateway Pub. Purchasing Assn. Office: City of Saint Louis 1200 Market St Rm 324 Saint Louis MO 63103-2806

BRENDLER, CHARLES BURGESS, urologist; b. Charlottesville, Va., June 20, 1944; s. Herbert and Virginia Burgess B.; m. Lucretia Cattley Rock, June 18, 1966; children: Christopher, Amy, Emily, Peter. AB, Harvard Coll., 1966; MD, U. Va., 1974. Instr. urology Johns Hopkins U., Balt., 1980-81, asst. prof. urology, 1981-85; assoc. prof. urology Johns Hopkins U., 1985-93; chief urology Balt. City Hosps., 1981-84; prof., chief urology U. Chgo., 1994—; mem. surg. exec. com. U. Chgo. Med. Ctr., 1994—, mem. surgery edn. com., 1994—. Assoc. editor: Urologic Surgery, 5th edit., 1998; mem. editl. bd. Jour. Urology, 1988-93; co-author: Campbell's Urology, Urologic Surgery, Urology; contbr. articles to profl. jours. Capt. USAF, 1967-71. Mem. Am. Urol. Assn. (2d prize clin. rsch. 1983, 1st prize clin. rsch. Mid-Atlantic sect. 1991, 92), Am. Assn. Genito-Urinary Surgeons, Nat. Urol. Forum, Soc. Basic Urol. Rsch., Soc. Urol. Oncology, Chgo. Urol. Soc. (mem. exec. com. 1997—), Am. Joint Commn. on Cancer (advisor task force on urol. cancer 1997), Alpha Omega Alpha. Democrat. Unitarian. Avocations: skiing, hiking, jogging, travelling. E-mail: jswanson@surgery.bsd.uchicago.edu. Home: 6301 S County Line Rd Burr Ridge IL 60521 Office: U Chgo Sect Urology 5841 S Maryland Ave MC 6038 Chicago IL 60637

BRENDLINGER, LEROY R., college president; b. Frederick, Pa., Dec. 14, 1918; s. Claude R. and Elsie May B.; m. Virginia Steltz, Dec. 28, 1941; children: Dawn, Brian, Craig. B.S., West Chester State Coll., 1946; M.S., U. Pa., 1949; Ed.D., Temple U., 1959. Former tchr. East Greenville, Pa.; Ordnance Officer Candidate Sch., Aberdeen, Md.; former prin. Pottsgrove (Pa.) Schs.; former asst. supt. Montgomery (Pa.) Schs.; pres. Montgomery County Community Coll., now pres. emeritus; chmn. SCORE, chpt. 594 Tri County area. Author: The Brendlinger Family History 1660-1994, 1995. Past pres. Montgomery County (Pa.) Health and Welfare Coun.; bd. dirs. Montgomery Hosp., Lutheran Children and Family Svc.; pres. Tri-County Area local chpt. Score 594, Pottstown, Pa. With U.S. Army, 1942-46, ETO. Recipient Outstanding Alumnus award West Chester U., 1984. Mem. Am. Assn. Jr. and C.Cs. (past pres. Pa. Commn. C.Cs.). Club: Brookside Country (treas. bd. govs.). Office: 340 Dekalb Pike Blue Bell PA 19422-1412

BRENDSEL, LELAND C., federal mortgage company executive; b. Sioux Falls, S.D.; married. BA, U. Colo.; D in Fin., Northwestern U. Prof. U. Utah; economist Farm Credit Banks, Fed. Home Loan Bank, Des Moines; exec. v.p., CFO Fed. Home Loan Mortgage Corp., McLean, Va., 1982-85, acting pres., CEO, 1985-87, pres., CEO, 1987-89, chmn., CEO, 1989—; mem. adv. bd. J. L. Kellogg Grad. Sch. Northwestern U.; bd. dirs. Local Initiatives Support Corp.; chmn. bd. Freddie Mac Found. Named Washingtonian of the Yr., 1991, Children's Champion UNICEF Coun., 1992, Corp. Citizen of the Yr. Nat. Black Child Devel. Inst., 1993, Corp. Advocate of the Yr. Child Welfare League Am., 1995; recipient N.Y. Coun. Adoptable Children's award, 1993, Give Your Heart to Child award Vo. Emergency Families for Children, 1997. Office: Fed Home Loan Mortgage Corp 8200 Jones Branch Dr Mc Lean VA 22102-3107*

BRENDTRO, LARRY KAY, psychologist, organization administrator; b. Sioux Falls, S.D., July 26, 1940; s. A. Kenneth and Bernice (Matz) B.; m. Janna Agena, July 14, 1973; children: Daniel Kenneth, Steven Lincoln, Nola Kristine. BA, Augustana Coll., 1961; MS, S.D. State U., 1962; PhD, U. Mich., 1965. Prin. Crippled Children's Hosp. and Sch., Sioux Falls, 1962-63; psychology intern Hawthorn Ctr., Northville, Mich., 1964-65; instr. U. Mich., 1965; asst. prof. U. Ill., Urbana, 1966-67; pres., CEO Starr Commonwealth, Albion, Mich., 1967-81; prof. Augustana Coll., Sioux Falls, S.D., 1981-99; pres. Reclaiming Youth Internat., Lennox, S.D., 1997—; mem. U.S. Coordinating Coun. on Juvenile Justice and Delinquency Prevention, 1997—. Co-author: The Other 23 Hours, 1969, translated in German, Dutch, Danish, Japanese, Positive Peer Culture, 1974, 1985, Japanese edit., 1988, Re-educating Troubled Youth, 1983, Reclaiming Youth at Risk, 1990; co-editor: Reclaiming Children and Youth, 1992—. Lutheran. Home: PO Box 57 Lennox SD 57039-0057 Office: Reclaiming Youth Internat PO Box 57 Lennox SD 57039

BRENEMAN, DAVID WORTHY, dean, educator; b. Albuquerque, Oct. 24, 1940; s. Clement Daniel and Muriel Ruth Breneman; m. Judith Dodge, June 10, 1962 (div. 1992); children: Erica, Carleton; m. Donna J. Plasket, Sept. 11, 1993. BA, U. Colo., 1963; PhD, U. Calif.-Berkeley, 1970. Asst. prof. econs. Amherst Coll., 1970-72; staff dir. Nat. Acad. Sci., 1972-75; sr. fellow Brookings Instn., 1975-83; pres. Kalamazoo Coll., 1983-89; prof. Harvard U., Cambridge, Mass., 1990-95; Univ. prof., dean Curry Sch. Edn., U. Va., Charlottesville, 1995—; professorial lectr. econs. George Washington U., 1979-82; vis. fellow The Brookings Instn., 1989-91; cons. NAS, 1991—. Author: Public Policy and Private Higher Education, 1978, Financing Community Colleges, 1981, Academic Labor Markets and Careers, 1988, Liberal Arts Colleges: Thriving, Surviving or Endangered?, 1994; exec. editor Change Mag., 1980-84. Trustee Woodrow Wilson Nat. Fellowship Found., 1980-90, W.E. Upjohn Inst., 1983-90, Goucher Coll., 1997—; bd. dirs. Am. Coun. on Edn., 1985-89; chair steering com. on direct loans U.S. Dept. Edn.; mem. Brown Ctr. on Ednl. Policy, The Brookings Inst., 1993—; mem. adv. com. Office of Sci. Pers., NAS, 1992-98; chair Task Force on Fair Share Funding, Higher Edn. Coord. Coun., Mass., 1994; chair com. spl. edn. NAS, 1997-98; mem. adv. com. on tech. in higher edn. Andrew W. Mellon Found., 1997—. Woodrow Wilson fellow, 1963; Danforth fellow, 1963; NDEA fellow, 1967; recipient Buchanan prize U. Calif.-Berkeley, 1970; recipient Disting. Svc. award Coun. Ind. Colls., 1999. Mem. Am. Econ. Assn., Am. Assn. Higher Edn. (bd. dirs. 1982-85), Assn. Pub. Policy and Mgmt., Phi Beta Kappa. Democrat. E-mail: dwb8n@Virginia.edu. Home: PaviLion I West Lawn Charlottesville VA 22903 Office: U Va Office of Dean Curry Sch Edn Ruffner Hall Charlottesville VA 22903-2495

BRENMAN, STEPHEN MORRIS, lawyer; b. San Francisco, Mar. 25, 1945; s. Irving I. and Vivian H. (Weiss) B.; m. Laura R. Yocum, Aug. 14, 1968; children: Jeremy S., Sara N. BS, Miami U., Oxford, Ohio, 1967; JD with distinction, Valparaiso (Ind.) U., 1970. Bar: Ind. 1970, U.S. Dist. Ct. (no. and so. dist.) Ind. 1970, U.S. Ct. Appeals (7th cir.) 1970, U.S. Supreme Ct. 1973, U.S. Tax Ct. 1973, U.S. Ct. Claims 1973. Assoc. Saul I. Ruman & Assocs., Hammond, Ind., 1970-73; ptnr. Katz & Brenman, Gary and Merrillville, Ind., 1973-78; mng. ptnr. Katz & Brenman, Merrillville, 1978—; lectr. Valparaiso U. Sch. Law, 1970; chief pub. defender Gary City Ct., 1973-78, staff atty. 1973-78; dir. and officer Dunes Volkswagen, Inc., Gary, 1977-80, Len Pollak Buick, Inc., Gary, 1977-83, Merrillville Volkswagen, Porshe-Audi, Inc., Merrillville, 1980-83; lectr. alcoholic beverage laws in Ind., miscellaneous trade orgns., 1980—; temp. probate commr., pro-tem and temp. judge Superior Ct. Lake County, Civil Divsn., East Chicago, Ind., 1980—; lectr. estate planning and right to die Congregation Beth Israel, Inc., Hammond, 1989—, Jewish Fedn., Inc., Highland, Ind., 1989—. Note editor Valparaiso U. Law Rev., 1969-70; contbr. articles to profl. jours. Co-chmn. Ind. Alcoholic Beverage Commn. Study Com., Rules, Regulations and Forms Rev., 1990; election judge and commr. Lake County Election Bd., Crown Point, Ind., 1973-78; dir. Munster (Ind.) Little League, 1980-84, umpire and coach, 1980-84; bd. dirs. Munster Youth Athletic Assn., 1980-84; bd. dirs. Jewish Fedn., Inc., Highland, 1980-85, Congregation Beth Israel, Inc., Hammond, 1980-85; dir. Hoosier Boys Town, Inc., Schererville, Ind., 1990-94, dir. and officer Hoosier Boys Town Found., 1990-94; mem. Munster H.S. Booster Club, 1987—; mem., dir., officer Alpha Epsilon Pi Parents Club, Inc., Bloomington, Ind., 1990-94./. Recipient Disting. Svc. award Jewish Fedn., 1980, 83, 84, Red and White Club, Munster H.S. Booster Club, 1989, Mustang Club, 1989; Valparaiso U. scholar, 1968-70. Mem. ABA (sect. bus. law, adminstrv. law and regulatory practice, real property, probate, trust law sects.), Nat. Assn. Estate Planners and Couns., Nat. Assn. Criminal Def. Attys., Ind. State Bar Assn., Fed. Bar Assn., Assn. Trial Lawyers Am., Ind. Trial Lawyers Assn., Lake County Bar Assn. (chmn. legal forms com.), Am. Judicature Soc. (corp. counsel inst. mem.), Phi Alpha Delta, B'nai B'rith, Miami U. Alumni Assn., Valparaiso U. Sch. Law Alumni Assn., Zeta Beta Tau. Democrat. Avocations: racquetball, tennis, boating, motor vehicle racing. Office: Katz & Brenman 7895 Broadway Merrillville IN 46410-5529

BRENNAN, CAREY M., lawyer; b. Meadville, Pa., June 22, 1948. BA, U. Ark., 1972, JD with honors, 1976; LLM in Taxation, NYU, 1977. Bar: Ark. 1976, Tex. 1978, Pa. 1993. Ptnr. Jones, Day, Reavis & Pogue, Pitts. Office: Jones Day Reavis & Pogue One Mellon Bank Ctr 500 Grant St Pittsburgh PA 15219-2502*

BRENNAN, CHARLES MARTIN, III, construction company executive; b. New Haven, Jan. 30, 1942; s. Charles Martin Jr. and Margaret Mary (Gleeson) B.; m. Mary Day Ely, June 22, 1966; children: Elizabeth Brennan Lekberg, Cynthia Brennan Annibali. BA, Yale U., 1964; MBA, Columbia U., 1969. Gen. mgr. New Haven Malleable Iron co., 1966-68; fin. analyst Scovill Mfg. co., 1969-71; treas. Cerro Corp., N.Y.C., 1971-74, Gould Inc., Chgo., 1974-76; mng. dir. Imperial Trans Europe N.V. (46 percent subs. of Gould Inc.), London, 1976-79; v.p. Latin Am. Gould, Inc., Sao Paulo, Brazil, 1979-80; sr. v.p., chief. fin. officer Gould, Inc., Chgo., 1980-88, also bd. dirs.; chmn., chief exec. officer MYR Group Inc., Rolling Meadows, Ill., 1988—; bd. dirs. ROHN Industries, Inc., Control Devices Inc., Northwestern Meml. Hosp., Mettawa Open Lands Assn., Lake County Rep. Fedn.; trustee Village of Mettawa, Ill. Mem. Chgo. Club, Comml. Club Chgo., Econ. Club Chgo. Republican. Episcopalian. Avocations: skiing, golf, fly fishing, shooting. Office: The MYR Group Inc 1701 Golf Rd Ste 1012 Rolling Meadows IL 60008-4227

BRENNAN, DONALD P., merchant banker; b. 1941. BA, SUNY, 1961; MBA, CCNY, 1966. Vice chmn. Internat. Paper Co. Inc., N.Y.C., 1967-82; chmn. Morgan Stanley Capital Ptnrs., N.Y.C., 1982-96; adv. dir. Morgan Stanley Dean Witter, N.Y.C., 1996-98; bd. dirs. ICT Group, Inc. With USN, 1961-65. Home: 1620 S Ocean Blvd Manalapan FL 33462

BRENNAN, DONNA LESLEY, public relations company executive; b. Washington, Mar. 13, 1945; d. Don Arthur and Louise (Tucker) B.; m. James L Bergey, Mar. 6, 1999. BA, Denison U., 1967. Tchr. Souderton Area H.S., Pa., 1967-69; mgr. media rels. Ins. Co. N.Am., Phila., 1969-72; dir. press rels. Colonial Penn Group, Phila., 1972-75, 1975-81, dir. comm., 1981-83; v.p. corp. comm. Norstar Bancorp, Albany, N.Y., 1983-85; v.p. comm. Meritor Fin. Group, Phila., 1986-87; prin. Donna Brennan Assocs., 1988—. Mem. Pub. Rels. Soc. Am. (pres. Phila. chpt. 1988), Phila. Women's Network (founder, bd. dirs.), Women's Assn. for Women's Alternatives (vice-chmn., bd. dirs.), Forum of Exec. Women (pres. 1992-93, bd. dirs. 1989-97).

BRENNAN, EILEEN REGINA, actress; b. Los Angeles, Sept. 3, 1935; d. John Gerald and Jeanne (Menehan) B.; m. David John Lampson, Dec. 28, 1969 (div. 1975); children: Samuel John, Patrick Oliver. Student, Am. Acad. Dramatic Arts, 1955-56. Appeared off-Broadway in Little Mary Sunshine (Theatre World award 1960, Obie award 1960, Newspaper Guild award 1960); appeared on Broadway in Hello, Dolly, 1964-66, appeared in nat. co. The Miracle Worker, 1961-62; films include Divorce American Style, 1967, The Last Picture Show, 1971, The Sting, 1974, Murder By Death, 1976, The Cheap Detective, 1978, FM, 1978, Private Benjamin, 1980 (Acad. award nomination for best supporting actress 1981, Golden Globe award 1981), Clue, 1985, Texasville, 1990, White Palace, 1990, Reckless, 1995, Pants on Fire, 1997, Nunzio's Second Cousin, 1997, Changing Habits, 1997, Boy's Life 2, 1997, Pants on Fire, 1998, The Last Great Ride, 1999; in TV series Private Benjamin, 1980-81 (Emmy award as best supporting actress 1981), 7th Heaven, 1996; TV movies include In Search of Dr. Seuss, 1994, My Name is Kate, 1994, Take Me Home Again, 1994, Trail of Tears, 1995, Freaky Friday, 1995, If These Walls Could Talk, 1996; TV appearance in Off the Rack, Toothless, 1997; TV guest appearances include Tales From the Crypt, McMillan and Wife, All in the Family, Taxi, Magnum P.I., Murder, She Wrote, Newhart, Blossom, The Ray Bradbury Theatre, Home Improvement, Walker, Texas Ranger, ER, Veronica's Closet, Mad About You. Mem. Actors Equity, Screen Actors Guild, AFTRA. Roman Catholic. Office: David Shapira & Associates 15301 Ventura Blvd Ste 345 Sherman Oaks CA 91403-3129*

BRENNAN, FRANCIS PATRICK, banker; b. Somerville, Mass., Jan. 9, 1917; s. John Joseph and Bridget (Sullivan) B.; m. Mary J. Gilhooly, July 23, 1949; children: Mary Ann, Eileen, John, Thomas. A.B. cum laude, Boston Coll., 1939; postgrad., Bentley Coll. Accounting and Finance, 1941. Loan officer Reconstrn. Finance Corp., Boston, 1941-42, 46-53; exec. v.p. Mass. Bus. Devel. Corp., Boston, 1954-61; chmn., chief exec. officer Union Warren Savs. Bank, Boston, 1961-87; vice chmn. Home Owners Savs. Bank (merger Union Warren Savs. Bank), Boston, 1987-90; bd. dirs., trustee, chmn. audit com. Boston Co. Funds, Inc.; chmn., pres., treas. Laurel Mut. Funds, 1993—; bd. dirs., exec. and fin. coms., chmn. audit and salary com. Boston Mut. Life Ins. Co., chmn. Dreyfus/Laurel Mutual Funds. Former trustee vice chmn. exec. com., chmn. fin. com. Stonehill Coll.; chmn. Mass. Bus. Devel. Corp.; mem. Sidney Farber Cancer Inst., Boston; mem. Mass. Hist. Soc.; past bd. dirs. Boston Mcpl. Research Bur., Greater Boston Real Estate Bd., Boston met. chpt. ARC. 2d lt. AUS, 1942-45, ETO. Decorated Bronze Star. Mem. Savs. Banks Assn. Mass. (pres. 1972-73), Mass. Bankers Assn. (dir.-at-large), Greater Boston C. of C. (v.p., admitted to Acad. of Disting. Bostonians 1992), Algonquin Club (Boston), Clover Club (Boston), Winchester Country Club, Madison Sq. Garden Club, Knights of Malta, Knights of Holy Sepulchre. Roman Catholic. Home: 36 Central St Winchester MA 01890-2630

BRENNAN, HENRY HIGGINSON, architect; b. Chgo., Nov. 25, 1932; s. Henry D. and Ann (Higginson) B.; m. Margaret Butler, 1960; children—Jennifer Margaret, Henry Higginson Jr., Kathryn Ann Brennan Smith, Martin Timothy. B.Arch., U. Ill., 1958. Registered architect in 12 states. Draftsman, Westchester Constrn., White Plains, N.Y., 1958-59; job capt. Ketchum & Sharp, N.Y.C., 1959-61, project architect, dir. prodn., 1961-73; sr. v.p., dir. N.Y. office Welton Becket, 1973-84; ptnr. Brennan Beer Gorman/Architects, 1984—. Prin. works include master plan and design of maj. office bldgs., hotels, retail and mixed-use complexes. Mem. AIA. Club: Apawamis (Rye, N.Y.). Office: Brennan Beer Gorman Architects 515 Madison Ave New York NY 10022-5403

BRENNAN, JAMES JOSEPH, lawyer, banking and financial services; b. Chgo., July 14, 1950; s. John Michael and Rosemary (Rickard) B.; m. Donna Jean Blessing, June 2, 1973; children: Michael James, Laura Jessica. BS, Purdue U., 1972; JD, Indiana U., 1975. Bar: Ind. 1975, Ill. 1978, U.S. Dist. Ct. (so. dist.) Ind. 1975, U.S. Dist. Ct. (no. dist.) Ill. 1978, U.S. Tax Ct. 1975, U.S. Ct. Appeals (6th cir.) 1976, U.S. Ct. Appeals (4th cir.) 1977, U.S. Ct. Appeals (7th cir.) 1978, U.S. Supreme Ct. 1981. Law clk. to judge U.S. Dist. Ct. (ea. dist.), Tenn., 1975-77; from assoc. to ptnr. Pope, Ballard, Shepard & Fowle, Ltd., Chgo., 1977-87; ptnr. Hopkins & Sutter, Chgo., 1987-91; ptnr., co-chmn. fin. svcs. group Barack, Ferrazzano, Kirschbaum & Perlman, Chgo., 1991—; chmn. legal affairs com. Ill. Bankers Assn., Chgo., 1986, chmn. bank counsel sect., 1987, mem., 1988—; lectr. programs for bankers, bank examiners, accts. and bank counsel; participant drafting of various Ill. banking laws; adj. prof. grad. sch. bank law Ill. Inst. Tech. Kent Coll. Law, 1992—. Articles editor Ind. Law Rev., 1974-75; editor: Ill. Bankers Assn. Law Watch, 1988-94; contbr. articles to profl. jours. 1st recipient Disting. Bank Counsel award Ill. Bankers Assn., 1989. Mem. ABA (subcom. bank regulation YLD bus. com.), Ill. Bar Assn., Chgo. Bar Assn. (com. fin. instns.), Riverside Golf Club (bd. dirs. 1994—, sec.-treas. 1995-98), Western Golf Assn. (bd. dirs. 1998—, Evans Scholars (Purdue chpt. 1968-72, pres. 1970-71). Office: Barack Ferrazzano 333 W Wacker Dr Ste 2700 Chicago IL 60606-1227

BRENNAN, JERRY MICHAEL, economics educator, statistician, reseacher, clinical psychologist; b. Grosse Pointe, Mich., July 17, 1944; s. Walter X. and Aretta May (Gempler) B. Student Kalamazoo (Mich.) Coll., 1962-64, Pasadena (Calif.) City Coll., 1966-67; B.A., UCLA, 1969; M.A., U. Hawaii, 1973, Ph.D., 1978. Researcher, UCLA, 1968-69; researcher U. Hawaii, 1972, 74-78, cons., 1975, 77, 78, data analyst and statis. cons., 1979-80, lectr., 1976-80, asst. prof. econs., 1980-83; pres. Sugar Mill Software, 1986-97; cons. WHO; v.p. Forest Inst. Profl. Psychology. Light scholar, 1964-66. Mem. Am. Psychol. Assn., Soc. Multivariate Exptl. Psychology, Psychometric Soc., Western Psychol. Assn., AAUP, Hawaii Ednl. Research Assn. Contbr. psychol. articles to profl. jours. Address: 651 Kaumakani St Honolulu HI 96825-1827

BRENNAN, JOAN STEVENSON, federal judge; b. Detroit, Feb. 21, 1933; d. James and Betty (Holland) Stevenson; m. Lane P. Brennan, June 26, 1954 (div. 1970); children: Suzanne, Steven, Clayton, Elizabeth, Catherine. BA, Skidmore Coll., 1954; JD, Santa Clara U., 1973. Bar: Calif. Dep. dist. atty. Dist. Attys. Office, Santa Clara, Calif., 1974-78; legal counsel U.S. Leasing Internat., San Francisco, 1978-79; asst. U.S. atty. U.S. Dist. Ct. (no. dist.) Calif., San Francisco, 1980-82, U.S. Magistrate judge, 1982—. Mem. Nat. Assn. Women Judges, Nat. Assn. Magistrate Judges. Democrat. Office: US Dist Ct PO Box 36054 450 Golden Gate Ave Ste 36052 San Francisco CA 94102-3482

BRENNAN, JOHN JOSEPH, lawyer, legal administrator; b. Troy, N.Y., Nov. 1, 1958; s. James Patrick and Grace Marie (Bartolomeo) B. AAS, Schenectady (N.Y) Community Coll., 1978; BA cum laude, Siena Coll., 1981; JD cum laude, Union U., 1985. Bar: N.Y. 1986, U.S. Dist. Ct. (no. dist.) N.Y. 1986, U.S. Supreme Ct. 1999. Law clk. to Appellate Divsn. Justice 4th Dept., Herkimer, N.Y., 1985-86; assoc. law ck. to justice State Supreme Ct., Herkimer, 1986-90; law clk. to U.S. Magistrate-Judge, Utica, N.Y., 1991-92; assoc. law clk. to justice N.Y. Supreme Ct., Utica, 1992—. Mem. ABA, N.Y. State Bar Assn., Oneida County Bar Assn., Herkimer County Bar Assn. (treas. 1990), KC, Pi Gamma Mu. Roman Catholic. Avocations: running, skiing. Home: 119 Court St Herkimer NY 13350-1923 Office: Oneida County Ct House Utica NY 13501

BRENNAN, JOSEPH GERARD, philosophy educator; b. Boston, Nov. 2, 1910; s. Joseph and Nora (Sheridan) B.; m. Mary Jean McLeod, June 7, 1938; children—Peter, Colin, Mario, Ainslie, Nicholas, Patrick. AB, Boston Coll., 1933; AM, Harvard U., 1935; PhD, Columbia U., 1942; LHD (hon.), Salve Regina U., 1984. Instr., then assoc. prof. philosophy Coll. New

Rochelle, N.Y., 1937-47; faculty Barnard Coll., Columbia U., 1947—, prof. philosophy, 1962-76, emeritus, 1976, chmn. dept., 1953-65; lectr. Hofstra U., 1949—; vis. lectr. Sarah Lawrence Coll., 1965-66; prof. Naval War Coll., Newport, R.I., 1978—; prof. emeritus, 1992—. Author: Thomas Mann's World, 1942, The Meaning of Philosophy, 1953, A Handbook of Logic, 1957, Three Philosophical Novelists, 1964, Ethics and Morals, 1973, The Education of a Prejudiced Man, 1977, Foundations of Moral Obligation, 1992; creator exhibits Thomas Mann Revisited, Emma Clark Libr., Setauket, N.Y., 1996, 97, Boston Coll., Burns Libr. Rare Books, Chestnut Hill, Mass., 1997. Founding trustee Levittown Pub. Library, N.Y., 1950-54; dir., trustee Boston Coll., 1969-73; trustee Bethpage Pub. Library, N.Y., 1956-80. Served to lt. USNR, 1943-46; comdr. Res. ret. Recipient Medal of Distinction, Barnard Coll., 1984, Centennial medal, 1988, Boston Coll. Presdl. Bicentennial award, 1978, Superior Civilian Svc. award USN, 1992. Mem. Am. Philos. Assn., Am. Comparative Lit. Soc., Phi Beta Kappa. Home: 8 Stratton Ln Stony Brook NY 11790-3214 Office: US Naval War Coll Newport RI 02841

BRENNAN, LAWRENCE EDWARD, electronics engineer; b. Oak Park, Ill., Jan. 29, 1927; s. Lawrence John and Lillian Irene (Day) B.; m. Mary Ellen Green, Aug. 9, 1947; children: Kathleen, Marianne, Teresa, James. B.S. in Elec. Engring., U. Ill., 1948; Ph.D. Elec. Engring., U. Ill., 1951. Mem. tech. staff Rand Corp., Santa Monica, Calif., 1957-67; chief scientist Tech. Service Corp., Santa Monica, 1967-80; v.p. Adaptive Sensors, Inc., Santa Monica, 1980-93; cons. pvt. practice, Orange Beach, Ala., 1993—. Served with USN, 1944-46. Fellow IEEE. Home: 9196 Neumann Dr Elberta AL 36530-5521 Office: Larry Brennan and Assoc 9196 Neumann Dr Elberta AL 36530-5521

BRENNAN, LEONARD ALFRED, research scientist, administrator; b. Westerly, R.I., Aug. 2, 1957; s. Leonard Alfred Brennan Jr. and Louise (Gagne) Ladd; m. Teresa Leigh Pruden, Jan. 1, 1980; adopted children: Jessica, Michelle. BS, Evergreen State Coll., 1981; MS, Humboldt State U., 1984; PhD, U. Calif., Berkeley, 1989. Technician USDA Forest Svc., Arcata, Calif., 1984-85; biologist Calif. Dept. Food & Agr., Ukiah, 1985; rsch. asst. U. Calif., Berkeley, 1986-89; lectr. Humboldt State U., Arcata, 1989-90; rsch. scientist dept. wildlife and fisheries Miss. State U., Mississippi State, 1990-93; dir. rsch. Tall Timbers Rsch. Station, Tallahassee, Fla., 1993—; Habitat ecology cons. The Chukar Found., Boise, 1989—. Author: (chpt.) The Use of Multivariate Statistics for Developing Habitat Suitability Index Models, 1986, The Use of Guilds and Guild-Indicator Species for Assessing Habitat Suitability, 1986, Arthropod Sampling Methods in Ornithology: Goals and Pitfalls, 1989, Influence of Sample Size on Interpretation of Foraging Patterns by Chestnut-backed Chickadee, The Habitat Concept in Ornithology: Theory and Applications; editor (with T.L. Pruden) Fire in Ecosystem Management Proceedings 20th Tall Timbers Fire Ecology Conference, 1998; contbr. articles to profl. jours. U. Calif. fellow, 1987; grantee Calif. Dept. Forestry, Internat. Quail Found., USDA Forest Svc.; San Francisco Bay Area chpt. Wildlife Soc. scholar, 1984; judge Mendocino County Pub. Schs. Sci. Fair, Laytonville, Calif., 1988, Miss. Sci. and Engring. Fair, Miss., 1990-91. Mem. AAAS, Am. Ornithologists' Union, Assn. Field Ornithologists, Cooper Ornithological Soc., Ecol. Soc. Am., Wildlife Soc. (faculty advisor Miss. chpt.), Miss. Wildlife Fedn., Pacific N.W. Bird and Mammal Soc., Wilson Ornithological Soc., Ottawa Field Naturalists' Club. Achievements include design of mathematical sex determination model for the Dunlin, of first data-based habitat suitability index models using multivariate statistics; research on contaminant levels in Dunlins in western Washington state, on factors responsible for long-term Northern Bobwhite population decline, on impact of habitat management for the endangered Red-cockaded Woodpecker on terrestrial vertebrates. Office: Tall Timbers Rsch Sta RR 1 Box 678 Tallahassee FL 32312-9712

BRENNAN, MARYANN, business consulting executive; b. Passaic, N.J., Aug. 3, 1946. BA in Psychology, Columbia U., 1971; MBA in Fin., St. John's U., 1990. Cert. quality analyst. V.p. Chase Manhattan Bank, N.Y.C., 1984-97; pres. Brennan Worldwide Inc., Cons. for Bus. Excellence, S.I., N.Y., 1997—. Contbr. articles to profl. publs. Sr. examiner, trainer, case writer Malcolm Baldridge Nat. Quality Award, 1995—; judge, sr. examiner, trainer N.Y. State Gov.'s Quality Award, 1993-99; judge Aruba Nat. Quality Award; AQP v.p. Strategic Partnerships. Recipient Best-of-Best award Quality Assurance Inst., 1990; scholar Columbia U., 1970-71. Mem. Fin. Svcs. Quality Coun. (chair conf. bd. FSQC Coun. 1995), Am. Soc. for Quality (sr.), Banking Adminstrn. Inst. (cash mgmt. quality forum 1991-95), Quality Productivity and Mgmt. Assn. (editor newsletter 1991-92, bd. dirs. 1996—), Coalition Quality Orgns. Greater N.Y. (founder, chmn. 1993-96), Assn. for Quality and Participation (v.p., bd. dirs. 1996—).

BRENNAN, MATTHEW CANNON, English literature educator, poet; b. Richmond Heights, Mo., Jan. 18, 1955; s. William Joseph and Suzanne (Simon) B.; m. Laura Lee Fredendall, Aug. 13, 1977 (div. June 1987); 1 child, Daniel William; m. Beverley Simms, May 21, 1994. AB, Grinnell Coll., 1977; MA, U. Minn., Mpls., 1980, PhD, 1984. Editor Golle and Holmes Fin. Learning, Minnetonka, Minn., 1982-84; vis. asst. prof. U. Minn., Mpls., 1984-85; asst. prof. Ind. State U., Terre Haute, 1985-88, assoc. prof., 1988-92, prof. English, 1992—. Author: (poetry) Seeing in the Dark: Poems, 1993, The Music of Exile: Poems, 1994, (monograph) Wordsworth, Turner and Romantic Landscape, 1987, The Gothic Psyche, 1997; (exhbn. catalog) Is Poetry a Visual Art?, 1993. Ind. Arts Commn. fellow, 1994; Thomas Merton Ctr. Poetry Prize, 1999; Univ. Rsch. grantee Ind. State U., Terre Haute, 1991, 96, Univ. Arts grantee, 1993, 98; named to Acad. Am. Poets, U. Minn., Mpls., 1979, 80, 84. Mem. Wordsworth-Coleridge Assn., Inst. Evolutionary Psychology, Phi Beta Kappa, Phi Kappa Phi. Avocations: travel, film. Home: 1013 Maple Ave Terre Haute IN 47804-2936 Office: Ind State U Dept English Terre Haute IN 47809

BRENNAN, MAUREEN, lawyer; b. Morristown, N.J., Aug. 7, 1949. BA magna cum laude, Bryn Mawr Coll., 1971; JD, Boston Coll., 1977. Bar: Pa. 1977, U.S. Dist. Ct. (ea. dist.) Pa. 1978, Ohio 1989. Atty. U.S. EPA, Washington, 1977-80; asst. dist. atty. Phila. Trial and Appellate Divs., 1980-84; in-house environ. counsel TRW, Inc., 1985-87; assoc. Baker & Hostetler, Cleve., 1987-91, ptnr., 1991—; adj. prof. Case Western Res. U., Cleve., 1990-92. Active Cleve. Tree Commn., 1991-96, co-chair, 1993-95; trustee Clean-Land Ohio, 1990—. Recipient Bronze Medal for Achievement, U.S. EPA, 1980. Mem. ABA (natural resources and environ. sect.), Pa. Bar Assn. (environ. law com., standing com. on environ. law 1996-98), Ohio State Bar Assn. (environ. law com.), Cleve. Bar Assn. (environ. law sect., chair wetlands com. 1991-92, sect. chair 1996-97, mem. steering com. adv. OEPA on Brownfield regulations 1995-97). Office: Baker & Hostetler 3200 Nat City Center 1900 E 9th St Ste 3200 Cleveland OH 44114-3475

BRENNAN, MURRAY FREDERICK, surgeon, oncologist; b. Auckland, New Zealand, Apr. 2, 1940; came to U.S., 1970; m. Susan Chambers, May 26, 1973; children: Sean, Ryan, Meghan, Patrick. BSc, U. New Zealand, 1961; MD, U. Otago, New Zealand, 1964, ChM, 1983; MD (hon.), U. Goteborg, Sweden, 1991; DSc (hon.), U. Otago, 1997. Surg. intern and resident U. Otago, 1965-69; clin. rsch. fellow Harvard Med. Sch., Boston, 1970-72; sr. resident, clin., rsch. fellow Peter Bent Brigham Hosp., Boston, 1973-75; sr. investigator, vis. scientist Nat. Cancer Inst., Bethesda, Md., 1975-81; prof. surgery, attending surgeon N.Y. Hosp./Cornell Med. Ctr., N.Y.C., 1981—; vis. physician Rockefeller U., N.Y.C., 1981—; attending surgeon Meml. Sloan-Kettering Cancer Ctr., N.Y.C., 1981—, chmn. dept. surgery, 1985—. Fellow ACS, Royal Australian Coll. Surgeons, Brazilian Coll. Surgeons (hon.), Royal Coll. Surgeons in Ireland (hon.); mem. Inst. Medicine NAS, Royal Coll. Surgeons Edinburgh (hon.), Royal Coll. Physicians and Surgeons Glasgow (hon.), Asian Surg. Soc. (hon.), Assn. Surgeons of Gt. Britain and Ireland (hon.), Royal Coll. Surgeons Eng. (hon.), Royal Australasian Coll. Surgeons (hon.), Royal Coll. Physicians and Surgeons in Can. (hon). Office: Meml Sloan-Kettering Cancer Ctr 1275 York Ave New York NY 10021-6007

BRENNAN, NOEL-ANNE GERSON, anthropology educator, writer; b. N.Y.C., Apr. 12, 1948; d. Noel Bertram Gerson and Nancy (Hasenwinkle) Hendriks; m. James Beach Brennan, July 27, 1968; 1 child, Anne Wendy. B.A. in Anthropology, Brown U., 1970; M.A. in Sociology and Anthropology, U. R.I., 1982. Writer and researcher, 1973-78, 80—; teaching asst. anthropology U. R.I., Kingston, 1978-80; ptnr. Ocean Wind Electric Co., Peace Dale, R.I., 1980-86; mem. women's studies adv. bd. U. R.I., 1980—, women's ctr. governing bd., 1981-83; instr. anthropology YWCA of R.I., Saunderstown, 1983; instr. sociology U. R.I., 1985—, adj. asst. prof. women's studies, 1986—. Author: The Goodspeed Opera House, 1974, Winter Reckoning, 1986. Contbr. poetry anthology Nine Apples, 1979 (poetry competition winner Northeast Jour. 11986). Contbr. articles and poems to various profl. jours. and mags. Sponsor, Ctr. Environ. Edn., 1981—. Mem. Internat. Snow Leopard Trust, World Wildlife Fund. Mem. Nat. Women's Anthropology Caucus, New England Women's Studies Assn., Nature Conservancy, Planetary Soc., R.I. Animal Rescue League. Home: 231 Curtis Corner Rd Peace Dale RI 02879-2129

BRENNAN, NORMA JEAN, professional society publications director; b. Helena, Mont., Apr. 16, 1939; d. Harland Sanford Herrin and Elizabeth (Wardlaw) Brumfield; m. Anthony E. Brennan, Dec. 4, 1964 (div. Mar. 1986); children: Christopher E., Kimberly A. BA, U. Pacific, 1960. Editorial asst. Am. Rocket Soc., N.Y.C., 1961-62, asst. mng. editor, 1962-65; mng. editor AIAA, N.Y.C., 1978-80; publs. divsn. dir. AIAA, N.Y.C., Washington,Reston, Va., 1980—. Mem. Young Republicans, Stockton, Calif., 1958-60; vol. Mt. Sinai Hosp., N.Y.C., 1962-64. Mem. AIAA (sr., Space Shuttle Flag award), Soc. for Scholarly Pub. (chair edn. com.), Coun. Biology Editors, Assn. Am. Pubs., Coun. Engring. and Sci. Soc. Execs., N.Am. Serials Interest Group, Washington Women's Info. Network. Avocations: reading, travel, gardening. Home: 11551 Links Dr Reston VA 20190-4820 Office: AIAA 1801 Alexander Bell Dr Reston VA 20191-4344

BRENNAN, PATRICK JEREMIAH, software developer; b. Price, Utah, Nov. 9, 1940; s. Jeremiah Patrick and Orabelle Agnes (Broe) B.; 1 child, Kelly Matthews. BS in Psychology, Weber State Coll., 1975. Programmer Continental Bank, Salt Lake City, 1964-68, Idaho 1st Nat. Bank, Boise, 1968-69; data processing mgr. John Wiley & Sons. Pub. Co., Salt Lake City, 1969-70; programmer self-employed Salt Lake City, 1970-71; programmer, data base architect Evans & Sutherland Computer Corp., Salt Lake City, 1971-72; project mgr. Radix Corp., Salt Lake City, 1972-73; programmer Kenway Engring., Salt Lake City, 1973-74; architecture specialist Unisys Corp., Eagan, Minn., 1974-96; chief tech. officer PSC, Houston, 1996—. Mem. Ocean Park Civic League, Virginia Beach, Va., 1993-95. Staff sgt. USAF, 1959-63. Mem. IEEE, Assn. for Computing Machinery. Avocations: motorcycling, hiking, beach activities. Home: 3805 Surry Rd Virginia Beach VA 23455-1623 :

BRENNAN, ROBERT LAWRENCE, educational director, psychometrician; b. Hartford, Conn., May 31, 1944; s. Robert and Irene Veronica (Connors) B. BA, Salme State Coll., 1967; M of Art in Tchg., Harvard U., 1968, EdD, 1970. Rsch. assoc., lectr. Grad. Sch. Edn., Harvard U., Cambridge, Mass., 1970-71; asst. prof. edn. SUNY, Stony Brook, 1971-76; sr. rsch. psychologist Am. Coll. Testing Program, Iowa City, 1976-79, dir. measurement rsch. dept., 1979-84, asst. v.p. for measurement rsch., 1984-92, disting. rsch. scientist, 1990-94; adj. faculty Sch. Edn. U. Iowa, 1979-94, E.F. Lindquist prof. edn. measurement, dir. Iowa testing programs, 1994—. Author: Elements of Generalizability Theory, 1983, Test Equating Methods and Practices, 1995; editor: Methodology Used in Scaling the Act Assessment and P-ACT, 1989, Cognitively Diagnostic Assessment, 1995; assoc. editor Applied Psychological Measurement, 1982—, Jour. Ednl. Measurement, 1978-83, 96—; contbr. articles to profl. jours. Harvard U. prize fellow, 1967. Fellow APA; mem. Am. Ednl. Rsch. Assn. (v.p. 1994-96, Divsn. D award 1980), Midwestern Ednl. Rsch. Assn. (pres. 1987-88), Am. Statis. Assn., Nat. Coun. Measurement Edn. (bd. dirs. 1987-90, v.p. 1995, pres. 1997-98, Tech. Contbn. award 1997), Psychometric Soc., Iowa Acad. Edn. (pres. 1996-99). Home: 1925 Liberty Ln Coralville IA 52241-1071 Office: U Iowa 334 Lindquist Ctr S Iowa City IA 52242-1533

BRENNAN, ROBIN LYNN, producer; b. Logan, W. Va., Oct. 17, 1960; d. William Arnold and Elaine (Salyers) B. BA in Journalism, W. Va. U., 1982; MA in Journalism, Marshall U., 1989. News anchor, prodr. WCHS-TV, Chas, W. Va., 1988-90; comms. instr. St. Pete Jr. Coll., Clearwater, Fla., 1990-91; prodr., writer Winchester (Va.) Regional Health Sys., 1991-92; station mgr. City of Norfolk's (Va.) TV Station, 1992-93; freelance WCTV, Coastal Video, Norfolk, Va., Washington, 1994; contractor Dept. Vets. Affairs, Washington, 1994-95; freelance Fox TV Network, Washington, 1996; prodr. Office of Personnel Mgmt., Washington, 1996-97; news anchor, assignment editor WOAY-TV, Beckley, W. Va., 1983-84; news anchor WKPT-TV, Kingsport, Tenn., 1984-86, WSAZ-TV, Hunt, W. Va., 1986-88; instr., grad. asst. Marshall U., Hunt, 1988-89. Fellow to Russia Nat. Forum Found., Washington. Democrat. Avocations: guitar, reading, white water rafting. Home: 140 F St SE Washington DC 20003-2603 Office: Air Can Terminal C Washington DC 22222

BRENNAN, RONALD WESLEY, retired secondary school educator; b. Cin., July 8, 1933; s. Charles Daniel and Leona (White) B.; m. Ruth Esther Fornash, Apr. 21, 1956; 1 child, Rhonda Faye (Mrs. Jeffrey Arthur Raible). BA in Edn., Villa Madonna Coll., 1959. Cert. tchr., Ky. Tchr. Bellevue (Ky.) H.S., 1960-96, ret., 1996; chairperson dept. social studies, mem. prin.'s adv. coun. Bellevue H.S., 1985-94. Active Campbell County Hist. and Geneal. Soc., Soc. Ky. Pioneers, Md. Geneal. Soc., Ohio Geneal. Soc.; life mem. Ky. Hist. Soc. Cpl. U.S. Army, 1954-56. Recipient Knight Grand Cross, l'Etoile de la Paix, Mil. Order Crusades, Order of Crown of Charlemagne in U.S.A.; named to Niadh Nask, 1995; named Lordship of Downyne, MacCarthy Mór, Prince of Desmond, Clonmel, Ireland, 1995. Fellow Augustan Soc. (life); mem. NEA (ret., life), Ky. Edn. Assn., No. Ky. Ednl. Assn., Bellevue Edn. Assn., Am. Legion, Soc. Am. Mil. Engrs., Fedn. Combattants Alliés en Europe, SAR, Sons of Revolution, Baronial Order of Magna Carta (Somerset chpt.), Gen. Soc. of War of 1812, Mil. Soc. of War of 1812, Sons of Union Vets. of Civil War, Colonial Order of the Crown, Plantagenet Soc., Soc. Colonial Wars, First Families Ohio, First Families Hamilton County (Ohio), Sons and Daus. of Pilgrims, Washington Family Descendants, Nat. Hugenot Soc., Descendants of Washington's Army at valley Forge, Internat. Soc. Descendants of Charlemagne, Descendants of Knights of the Bath (charter), Order of 1st World War, Clan Dunbar Soc., Sons of Am. Colonists, Order of Crown of Charlemagne in U.S.A., Octavian Soc. (life), Hereditary Order of Armigerous Augustans, Noble Co. of the Rose, Internat. Churchill Soc., Chivalric Order of Temple, Knights of Order of Polonia Restituta (Officers cross 1990), Order of St. Stanislaus (Comdr.'s Cross with star 1990), Supreme Mil. Order of Knights Templar of Jerusalem. Methodist. Avocation: genealogy. Home: 209 Ridge Hill Dr Highland Heights KY 41076

BRENNAN, STEPHEN JAMES, physical education educator, consultant. BA in Broadcast Journalism and English, U. Nebr., 1973, MEd in Ednl. Adminstrn., 1978, M in Phys. Edn. and Sport Psychology, 1986. Tchr., basketball coach Archbishop Ryan H.S., Omaha, 1974-75; tchr., coach Ralston (Nebr.) H.S., 1975-80, Valley (Nebr.) H.S., 1980-84, U. Nebr., Lincoln, 1984-86; founder, pres. Peak Performance Cons., Omaha, 1986—; performance cons. Kansas City Royals, 1989-94; head basketball coach East All Star Team, Fremont, Nebr., 1981; founder, exec. dir. Midwest Youth Coaches Assn., 1990—; exec. dir. The Recruiters Inst., 1993—. Author: The Mental Edge: Basketball's Peak Performance Workbook, 1987, 2nd edit., 1993, The Sport Performance Report, 1990, Competitive Excellence: The Psychology and Strategy of Successful Team Building, 1990, Competitive Excellence: The Psychology and Strategy of Successful Team Building, 2nd edit., 1995, (with others) Basketball Resource Guide, 1989, 2nd edit., 1995; editor: Inside Recruiting: The Master Guide to Successful College Athletic Recruiting, Vol. I, 1998, Vol. II, 1999; contbr. numerous articles to profl. jours. Mem. AAHPERD, Assn. for Advancement of Applied Sport Psychology, Nat. Assn. Sport and Phys. Edn., Nat. Assn. Basketball Coaches, Nat. Fedn. State H.S. Assns., Nat. Assn. Sports Ofcls., Nat. Fedn. Interscholastic Ofcls. Assn., Nat. H.S. Athletic Coaches Assn., Nebr. Coaches Assn., Midwest Officials Assn., Omaha Met. Area Basketball Coaches Assn. Home and Office: 14728 Shirley St Omaha NE 68144-2144

BRENNAN, TERESA MARY ISABEL, social theory educator, writer; b. Melbourne, Australia, Jan. 5, 1952; came to U.S., 1994; d. Columb Henry Brennan and Joan Marie (Hollingshead) Crosland. BA with honors, Sydney (Australia) U., 1976; MA, Melbourne U., 1986; PhD, Cambridge (Eng.) U., 1989. Affiliated lectr. social sci. Cambridge U., 1990-94; vis. prof. New Sch. for Social Rsch., N.Y.C., 1994-97, Brandeis U., Boston, 1997-98, Harvard U., Cambridge, Mass., 1998; fellow social and polit. sci. U. Melbourne, 1994; vis. disting. prof. U. Alta., Can., 1993; spkr. UN World Health Orgn. Working Group in Genetic Engring., 1994, UNESCO, Nat. Inst. Sci., Tech. and Devel. Studies, India, 1994, 96. Author: The Interpretation of the Flesh, 1992, History after Lacan, 1993, Jenseits der Hybris, 1997; co-editor: (with Martin Jay) Vision in Context, 1996. Advisor U.S. Congress, 3d dist. Md., 1981. Mem. MLA, Am. Sociol. Assn., Am. Philos. Assn. Avocations: Egyptology, archaeology. Office: Fla Atlantic U Schmidt Chair in Humanities 777 Glades Rd Boca Raton FL 33431-6424

BRENNAN, TERRENCE MICHAEL, publisher; b. Phila., Jan. 6, 1947; s. Bernard J. and Ruth (Cantwell) B.; m. Andrea C. Loscalzo; children: Michael, Patrick, Meghan, Matthew. BA in Secondary Edn., Pa. State U., 1968. Sports editor Today's Spirit, Hatboro, Pa., 1970-75; Sunday sports editor The Bull., Phila., 1975-82; asst. sports editor The Daily Times, Primos, Pa., 1982-85; editor The Mercury, Pottstown, Pa., 1985-88; pub., pres. The Telegraph, Alton, Ill., 1988-89; exec. editor Ingersoll Publs., Princeton, N.J., 1989-90; editor, pub. The Record, Troy, N.Y., 1990-91, pub., 1991-92; pres. The Christian Herald, Valatie, N.Y., 1992-96; nat. sales mgr. S/N Precision Enterprises, Inc., Troy, N.Y., 1993-96; v.p. ops. The Christian Herald Assn., New York, N.Y., 1996—. Found. mem. Samaritan Hosp., Troy, N.Y., 1991-93; bd. dirs. Troy Area YMCA, 1991-93; trustee LaSalle Inst., Troy, 1991-96; chmn. sch. bd. Loudonville Christian Sch., 1994-96. Recipient Sports Writing award Keystone Press Assn., 1985, 86, Pulitzer prize for edit. writing, 1987. Mem. Rensselaer County C. of C. (bd. dirs. Troy chpt. 1990-93). Avocations: tennis, hiking, gardening. Office: Christian Herald Assn 132 Madison Ave New York NY 10016

BRENNAN, THOMAS EMMETT, law school president; b. Detroit, May 27, 1929; s. Joseph Terence and Jeannette Frances (Sullivan) B.; m. Pauline Mary Weinberger, Apr. 28, 1951; children: Thomas Emmett, Margaret Ann and John Seamus (twins), William Joseph, Marybeth, Ellen Mary. LL.B., U. Detroit, 1952; LL.D., Thomas M. Cooley Law Sch., 1976. Bar: Mich. 1953. Assoc. Kenny, Radom, Rockwell & Mountain, Detroit, 1952-53; ptnr. Waldron, Brennan & Maher, Detroit, 1953-61; judge Detroit Ct. Common Pleas, 1962-63, Wayne County Circuit Ct., 1963-66; justice Mich. Supreme Ct., 1967-73, chief justice, 1969-70; adj. prof. polit. sci. U. Detroit, 1970-72; founder, pres., acting dean Thomas M. Cooley Law Sch., Lansing, 1972-73; dean Thomas M. Cooley Law Sch., 1974-78, pres., 1978—, chmn. bd., 1980-81, 90—, also dir.; mem. Mich. Commn. Law Enforcement and Criminal Justice, 1969-70; bd. dirs. Motor Wheel Corp., 1987-89. Bd. dirs. Cath. League for Religious and Civil Rights, 1993—. Fellow Am. Bar Found., Mich Bar Found.; mem. ABA, Ingham County Bar Assn., State Bar Mich. (bd. commrs. 1979-83), Mich. Assn. of Professions (Disting. Citizens award 1982), Assn. of Ind. Colls. and Univs. Mich. (bd. dirs., exec. com., sec. 1990, chmn. 1991), Cath. Lawyers Soc. (Thomas More award 1987), Am. Jurisprudence Soc., Inc. Soc., Irish Am. Lawyers, Cooley Legal Author's Soc. (charter), Lansing City Club (bd. dirs. 1989-91), Mich. Supreme Ct. Hist. Soc. (bd. dirs. 1988—, v.p.-treas. 1990—), Mich. State C. of C. (bd. dirs. 1988-94), Walnut Hills Country Club (bd. dirs. 1992-95), Mich. State U. Club, Detroit Athletic Club, Lansing City Club, KC, Delta Theta Phi. Roman Catholic. Home: 6151 Park Lake Rd East Lansing MI 48823-9721 Office: Thomas M Cooley Law Sch 217 S Capitol Ave Lansing MI 48933-1503

BRENNAN, THOMAS JOHN, city and state official, consultant, educator; b. Bklyn., Mar. 23, 1923; s. Thomas Joseph and Violet Emma (Jurgens) B.; m. Margaret Karen Jensen, Sept. 18, 1948; children: Debra Gail, Mark Kevin, Laurie Kathleen. AB, Wittenberg Coll., 1949; MGA, Fels Inst. of Local and State Govt., Wharton Grad. Sch., 1950. Dep. sec. for adminstrn. Dept. Welfare, Commonwealth Pa., Harrisburg, 1957-59, dep. sec. for state properties Pa. Dept. Property and Supplies, 1959-64; exec. officer Del. Dept. Mental Health, Dover, 1965-67; v.p. Exec. Mgmt. Svc., Arlington, Va., 1967-76; exec. dir. Gov.'s Justice Commn. and Pa. Commn. on Crime and Juvenile Delinquency, 1976-79; dir. water utility City of New Brunswick, N.J., 1983-91; chief labor negotiator City of New Brunswick, N.J., 1988-91; pers. mgr., 1988-91, exec. officer police dept., 1989-91; pub. mgmt. cons., 1991—; adj. instr. U. Del., 1965-67; adj. assoc. prof. Rider Coll., Lawrenceville, N.J., 1983-84, 84-85; hearing officer N.J. Dept. Civil Svc., Trenton, 1976—, cons. exam. constrn., 1985; cons. to staff com. UN, 1982-84; cons. various municipalities and agys.; presenter papers to profl. orgns. Bd. dirs. Bucks County Opera, Pa., 1975-80, Bucks County Play House, New Hope, Pa., 1970s; active mem. Bucks County Hist. Soc., Doylestown, Pa., 1983—; elected mem. alumni coun. Wittenberg U., 1989—; mem. Merrill's Mauraders, World War II. Decorated Silver Star, Bronze Star with 2 oak leaf clusters, Combat Infantry badge; recipient various plaques; Fels scholar U. Pa., 1948. Mem. VFW (Post #6393), Internat. Personnel Mgmt. Assn., Am. Pub. Works Assn. (dist. rep. Eastern Pa. bldg. and grounds com.), Am. Water Works Assn., Internat. Chiefs of Police Assn., Nat. Conf. State Justice Planning Adminstrn. (regional chmn., mem. exec. com.), Criminal Justice Tng. Inst. (chmn. planning com. 1978, 79). Club: Huntington Valley Hunt (Bucks County) (bd. dirs. 1975-80), Am. Legion (Post #79), Upper Makefield Hist. Soc. (dir.), Wharton Alumni (Phila.), U. Pa. Faculty. Lodge: Fraternal Order of Police. Avocations: fox hunting, pleasure riding. Home: 327 Pineville Rd Newtown PA 18940-3111

BRENNAN, WILLIAM JOSEPH, manufacturing company executive; b. Buffalo, Feb. 11, 1928; s. Laurence J. and Mary Julia (Scherer) B.; m. Rita Jeanne Brooks, Dec. 27, 1947; 1 dau., Susan. B.A., Bryant and Stratton Coll., 1949. With Fedders Corp., 1949—, asst. controller corp., 1962-64, dir. distbn. brs., 1965-67, v.p., dir. sales, 1967-74, v.p., dir. adminstrn., 1974-77; pres. Fedders Fin. Corp., 1977-78, group v.p. diversified products, 1978-80, v.p. fin., chief fin. officer, 1980; exec. v.p., chief fin. officer, dir. Fedders Corp., Peapack, N.J., 1986-87; pres. NYCOR Inc., Peapack, 1987-88; fin. cons. Fedders Corp., NYCOR Inc., 1988—; bd. dirs. Fedders Corp.; chmn. bd. dirs. CSM Environ.; arbitrator NYSE. Served with AUS, 1946-47. Republican. Roman Catholic. Home and Office: 4 Pompano Dr Rumson NJ 07760-1217

BRENNAN, WILLIAM JOSEPH, III, lawyer; b. Newark, Apr. 29, 1933; s. William J. Jr. and Marjory (Leonard) B.; m. Georgianna V. Franklin, Sept. 10, 1960; children: William J. IV, Alexandra V. BA, Colgate U., 1955; LLB, Yale U., 1962. Bar: N.Y. 1963, N.J. 1967, U.S. Dist. Ct. (so. and ea. dists.) N.Y. 1964, U.S. Dist. Ct. N.J. 1967, U.S. Ct. Appeals (1st cir.) 1987, U.S. Ct. Appeals (2nd cir.) 1968, U.S. Ct. Appeals (3rd cir.) 1968, U.S. Ct. Appeals (Fed. cir.) 1991, U.S. Supreme Ct. 1967. Assoc. Breed, Abbott & Morgan, N.Y.C., 1962-67; asst. atty. gen in charge of litigation Office of Atty. Gen. of N.J., Trenton, 1967-68; spl. counsel to gov. Office of the Gov. of the State of N.J., Trenton, 1969; ptnr., mng. ptnr. Smith, Stratton, Wise, Heher & Brennan, Princeton, N.J., 1970—. Assoc. editor N.J. Law Jour., 1979—. Trustee St. Peter's Coll., Jersey City, 1988-94. Served to 1st lt. USMC, 1956-59. Recipient Award of Distinction, N.J. State Grand Jurors' Assn., 1969, Alumni Achievement award Newark Acad., 1986, Trial Bar award Trial Attys. N.J., 1994. Fellow Am. Coll. Trial Lawyers (chmn. com. on legal ethics 1987-93, chmn. com. on professionalism 1993-97), Internat. Acad. Trial Lawyers, Am. Acad. Appellate Lawyers, Am. Bar Found. (lic, state chmn. 1990); mem. ABA (mem. com. on legal ethics 1989, 3d cir. mem., com. on fed. judiciary 1989-93, ho. of dels. 1986-95), N.J. State Bar Assn. (pres. 1984-85), Assn. of Fed. Bar of State of N.J. (pres. 1992-94), Assn. of Bar of City of N.Y., Yale Law Sch. Assn. N.J., Am. Law Inst. Avocations: scuba diving, flying. Office: Smith Stratton Wise Heher & Brennan 600 College Rd E Princeton NJ 08540-6636

BRENNECKE, ALLEN EUGENE, lawyer; b. Marshalltown, Iowa, Jan. 8, 1937; s. Arthur Lynn and Julia Alice (Allen) B; m. Billie Jean Johnstone, June 12, 1958; children: Scott, Stephen, Beth, Gregory, Kristen. BBA, U. Iowa, 1959, JD, 1961. Bar: Iowa 1961. Law clk. U.S. Dist. Judge, Des Moines, 1961-62; assoc. Mote, Wilson & Welp, Marshalltown, Iowa, 1962-66; ptnr. Harrison, Brennecke, Moore, Smaha & McKibben, Marshalltown, 1966—. Contr. articles to profl. jours. Bd. dirs. Marshalltown YMCA, 1966-71; mem. bd. trustees Iowa Law Sch. Found., 1973-86, United Meth. Ch., Marshalltown, 1978-81, 87-89; fin. chmn. Rep. party 4th Congl. Dist., Iowa, 1970-73, Marshall County Rep. Party, Iowa, 1967-70. Fellow ABA (chmn. ho. of dels. 1984-86, bd. govs. 1982-86), Nat. Jud. Coll. (bd. dirs. 1982-88), Am. Coll. Trusts and Estates Counsel, Am. Coll. Tax Counsel, Am. Bar Found., Iowa Bar Assn. (pres. 1990-91, award of merit 1987); mem.

Masons, Shriners, Promise Keepers. Republican. Methodist. Avocations: golf; travel; sports. Home: 703 Circle Dr Marshalltown IA 50158-3809 Office: Harrison Brennecke Moore Smaha & McKibben 302 Masonic Temple Marshalltown IA 50158

BRENNEMAN, DELBERT JAY, lawyer; b. Albany, Oreg., Feb. 4, 1950; s. Calvin M. and Velma Barbara (Whitaker) B.; m. Caroline Yorke Allen, May 29, 1976; children: Mark Stuart, Thomas Allen. BS magna cum laude, Oreg. State U., 1972; JD, U. Oreg., 1976. Bar: Oreg. 1976, U.S. Dist. Ct. Oreg. 1977, U.S. Ct. Appeals (9th cir.) 1977. Assoc. Schwabe, Williamson, and Wyatt, Portland, Oreg., 1976-83, ptnr., 1984-92; ptnr. Hoffman, Hart & Wagner, Portland, Oreg., 1993—; speaker Oreg. Self-Ins., 1978, 90; seminar instr. U. Oreg. Law Sch., Eugene, 1980. Mem. ABA, Oreg. State Bar Assn., Multnomah County Bar Assn. (speaker 1983-84), Order of Coif, Multnomah Athletic Club, Propeller Club of U.S. (bd. dirs. 1983-85), Phi Kappa Phi, Beta Gamma Sigma. Office: Hoffman Hart & Wagner 1000 SW Broadway Fl 20 Portland OR 97205-3035

BRENNEN, CAROLE J., researcher in human services; b. Pitts., Sept. 3, 1942; d. James J. and Gaynell (Farwell) B.; children: Eric L. Slaney, Erin C. Slaney-Miller. Diploma, Presbyn. U. Hosp. Sch. Nursing, 1963; BSN, U. Pitts., 1969; MSN, Duquesne U., 1977; postgrad., NYU, 1980. Pub. health nurse Bklyn. Vis. Nurses Assn.; vis. nurse Vis. Nurse Assn. Allegheny County, Pitts.; instr. Duquesne U. Sch. Nursing, Pitts.; infection control nurse VA Hosp.-Univ. Dr., Pitts., 1982—. Contbr. articles to profl. jours. With Army Nurse Corps Res., 1990. Mem. VA Soc. Practitioners in Infectious Disease, Assn. for Practitioners in Infection Control, Sigma Theta Tau. Office: Va Med Ctr Infectious Dis (111E) University Dr Pittsburgh PA 15240

BRENNEN, STEPHEN ALFRED, international business consultant; b. N.Y.C., July 7; s. Theodore and Margaret (Pembroke) B.; m. Yolanda Alicia Romero, Sept. 28, 1957; children: Stephen Robert, Richard Patrick. AB cum laude, U. Americas, Mexico City, 1956; MBA, U. Chgo., 1959. Supr. Montgomery Ward, Chgo., 1956; credit mgr. Aldens, Chgo., 1956-59; gen. mgr. Purina de Guatemala, 1964-66; pres. Purina Colombiana, Bogotá, 1967-69; founding pres. Living Marine Resources, Inc., San Diego, 1969-70; mng. dir. Central and S. Am. Ralston Purina, Caracas, Venezuela, Coral Gabels, Fla., 1970-74; pres. Van Camp Seafood Co., San Diego, 1974-79; chmn. P.S.C. Corp., Buena Park, Calif., 1979-81; pres. Inter-Am. Cons. Group, San Diego, 1981-85; chmn. Beta Enterprises Inc., 1986-91; advisor Nat. Productivity Exch.; spl. asst. C.A.O., County of San Diego, Calif., 1987-95; mng. ptnr. Interam. Cons. Group, 1983-95; ptnr. Acad. Interpreting & Translations, Internat., 1995; assoc., owner the Montgomery Group, Inc., La Jolla. Author: Successfully Yours. Past mem. adv. bd. Mexican-Am. Found. Served with USAF. Mem. Am. Soc. Profl. Cons. Roman Catholic. Club: U. Chgo. in San Diego (past pres.).

BRENNEN, WILLIAM ELBERT, management consultant; b. Mo., Sept. 30, 1930; s. William E. and Frances (Andrew) B.; m. Natalia Summers, Nov. 14, 1958 (div. 1979); children: William, Natalia Jane, Elizabeth; m. Sharon Russell, Aug. 8, 1987 (dec. Feb. 1991); m. Nancy Wiese, Apr. 6, 1997. BS, U.S. Mcht. Marine Acad., 1952; MBA, U. Chgo., 1964. Ship's officer, traffic and ops. mgr. States Marine Lines Inc., Korea and Japan, 1952-61; with Case & Co./Stevenson Jordan & Harrison, Inc. Mgmt. Cons., Chgo. and N.Y.C., 1961-68; dir. internat. materials mgmt. Internat. Minerals & Chems., Skokie, Ill., 1968-71, Abbott Labs., North Chicago, Ill., 1971-73; pres. W.E. Brennen Cons., Inc. (name changed to Brennen Cons., Inc. 1987), 1987-88; mgmt. cons. Evanston, Ill., 1973-88, South Bend, Ind., 1988—; v.p. mng. prin. Fry Cons., 1982-88; adj. assoc. prof. mktg. U. Notre Dame, 1991-92. Bd. dirs., v.p. Corvilla, Inc., 1991-94, pres. 1993-94. Lt. (j.g.) USNR, 1953-55. Mem. Am. Mktg. Assn. (pres. Chgo. chpt. 1982-83, bus. mktg. coun. 1987-90, ethics com. 1990-92), Inst. Mgmt. Cons. (dir. Chgo. chpt. 1987-91, 98—, vice chmn. cons. round table South Bend 1998—), St. Joseph County Friends of the Library (dir. 1997), Rotary Internat., Elkhart C. of C. Episcopalian. Office: 300 N Michigan St South Bend IN 46601-1295

BRENNER, ALFRED EPHRAIM, physicist; b. Bklyn., Sept. 11, 1931; s. Hyman and Ricky (Levine) B.; m. Rosamond Deborah Drooker, June 30, 1958 (div. 1987); children: Tamara Jean, Kendra Susan, Lyle Abraham. BS, MIT, 1953, PhD, 1958. Fellow Ctr. for European Nuclear Rsch., Geneva, Switzerland, 1958-59; instr. Harvard U., Cambridge, Mass., 1959-62, asst. prof., 1962-66, sr. rsch. assoc., 1966-70; sr. physicist, head computing dept. Fermilab, Batavia, Ill., 1970-85; pres. Consortium for Scientific Computing, Princeton, N.J., 1985-86; dir. applications rsch. Supercomputing Rsch. Ctr., Bowie, Md., 1986-93; dep. dir. computer software engring. div. Inst. for Defense Analyses, Alexandria, Va., 1993—; chmn. Nat. Inst. Standards and Tech. Rev. Panel for Computing and Applied Math., Gaithersburg, Md., 1985-91; sci. computer cons. U.S. Dept. Energy, Germantown, Md., 1980-85, tech. cons., 1972-86. Editor Jour. of Supercomputing, Internat. Jour. High Speed Computing; contbr. 90 articles to profl. jours. Fellow Am. Phys. Soc.; mem. AAAS, IEEE (sci. supercomputer com. 1983—, computer soc., chmn. tech. com. on supercomputing applications 1990-94), Assn. for Computing Machinery, Am. Math. Soc., N.Y. Acad. Scis., Soc. for Indsl. and Applied Math. Achievements include 2 patents in field. Office: Inst for Defense Analyses 1801 N Beauregard St Alexandria VA 22311-1733

BRENNER, BARRY MORTON, physician; b. Bklyn., Oct. 4, 1937; s. Louis and Sally (Lamm) B.; m. Jane P. Deutsch, June 12, 1960; children: Robert, Jennifer. B.S., L.I. U.; M.D., U. Pitts.; MA (hon.), Harvard U.; DSc (hon.), Long Island U.; D.M.Sc. (hon.), U. Paris, (Pierre et Marie Curie); diploma (hon.), Charles U., Prague; fellow (hon.), Royal Coll. of Physicians, London. Asst. prof. medicine U. Calif.-San Francisco, 1969-72, asso. prof. medicine and physiology, 1972-75; prof. medicine and physiology U. Calif., San Francisco, 1975-76; Samuel A. Levine prof. medicine Harvard Med. Sch., Boston; with Peter Bent Brigham Hosp., Boston, 1976—; dir. renal div. Brigham and Women's Hosp., Boston, 1979—; dir. physician-scientist program, Harvard Med. Sch., 1984-90, Harvard Ctr. for Study of Kidney Diseases, 1987—; cons. NIH. Editor: The Kidney, 2 vols., 1976, 6th edit., 2000, Renal Pathology, 2 vols., 1989, 2d edit., 1994, Textbook of Hypertension, 2 vols., 1990, 2d edit., 1995; Acute Renal Failure, 1985, 3d edit., 1994; co-editor Contemporary Issues in Nephrology, 1978-90; founding editor Current Opinion in Nephrology and Hypertension, 1992—; contbr. numerous articles to profl. jours. Recipient Homer W. Smith award N.Y. Heart Assn., 1984, George E. Brown award Am. Heart Assn., 1983, Merit award NIH, 1984, SKF Disting. Scientist award 1985, Donald W. Seldin award NKF, 1995, Philip S. Hench Disting. Alumnus award, U. Pitt., 1995; rsch. grantee NIH, 1969—. Fellow AAAS, Molecular Med. Soc.; mem. Am. Soc. Cell Biology, Am. Physiol. Soc., Assn. Am. Physicians (councillor), Am. Soc. Clin. Investigation (councillor, v.p., Am. Soc. Hypertension (exec. com., pres., Richard Bright award), Internat. Soc. Nephrology (councillor, Jean Hamburger award), Western Assn. Physicians, Salt and Water Club, Interurban Clin. Club, Alpha Omega Alpha, Phi Sigma. Office: 75 Francis St Boston MA 02115-6110

BRENNER, BETH FUCHS, publishing executive. Grad., U. Vt., 1980. Sales promotion coordinator Chanel, Inc., 1980-83; promotion mgr. M mag., 1983-86; adv. sales rep. New York mag., 1986-91, adv. dir., 1991-93; adv. dir. SELF mag., 1993-94, pub., 1994—. Office: SELF Magazine 350 Madison Ave New York NY 10017-3704*

BRENNER, DANIEL LESLIE, lawyer; b. L.A., May 25, 1951; s. John and Dorothy (Cohen) B. BA, Stanford U., 1973, MA, 1973, JD, 1976. Law clk. to Judge William Matthew Byrne, Sr. U.S. Dist. Ct., L.A., 1976-77; assoc. Wilmer, Cutler & Pickering, Washington, 1977-79; sr. advisor to chmn. FCC, Washington, 1979-86; prof., dir. comms. law program UCLA Law Sch., 1986-92; v.p. law and policy Nat. Cable TV Assn., Washington, 1992—; bd. dirs. Tekelec, Calabasas, Calif.; bd. advisors Falcon Cable TV, L.A., 1986-96; cons. Rand Corp., L.A., 1990-92; of counsel LeBoeuf, Lamb, Green & MacRae, L.A., 1990-92. Author: Law and Regulation of Common Carriers, 1992, 2d edit., 1996; co-author: Cable TV and Other Non Broadcast Video, 1986, rev. edit., 1997, Free But Regulated, 1992. Bd. dirs. Cable Positive, N.Y., 1996—, Corp for Pub. Broadcasting, Washington, 1986-92; trustee Stanford U., 1987-92, Fed. Comms. Bar Found., Washington, 1996—. Democrat. Jewish. Avocation: stand-up comedy. Office: Nat Cable TV Assn Ste 500 1724 Massachusetts Ave NW Washington DC 20036-1969

BRENNER, DAVID H., marketing executive; m. Denise Brenner; 3 children. BBA in Mktg. summa cum laude, U. Notre Dame, 1973. With dept. gen. advt. Procter & Gamble, Cinn., 1973-76; sales promotion mgr. divsn. health care Johnson & Johnson, 1976-78, brand mgr. first aid products, 1978-80; new product devel. mgr. Kellogg's, 1980-82; past new product devel mgr. Kellogg's, Europe; past mng. dir. bus. ops. Kellogg's, England, Ireland, Belgium and The Netherlands; pres. U.S. subs. Kellogg's, 1988-91; sr. v.p. new bus. ventures Amway, Ada, Mich., 1991—; regent Edison New Products Yr.; guest lectr. Yale U., Notre Dame U., Aquinas Coll., Grand Valley State U. Bd. trustees Grand Rapids Art Mus., Cath. Soc. Svcs., Grand Rapids, Killgoar Found. Immaculate Heart Mary Sch.; chmn. ann. fund GRAM, 1995-97. Mem. Am. Mktg. Assn., Cascade Hills Country Club, Beta Gamma Sigma. Office: Amway Corp 4760 East Fulton St Ada MI 49301

BRENNER, DONALD JOHN, journalism educator; b. Lorain, Ohio, Apr. 12, 1932; s. John and Gertrude Emily (Bohm) B.; m. Kathleen Shuler, Aug. 7, 1955 (dec. June 2, 1996); children: Jay Allan, John Martin, Jerrell Don. BS, Bowling Green State U., 1954; MS, Ohio U., 1957; PhD, U. Mo., 1965. Instr. in journalism Bowling Green (Ohio) State U., 1959-61; asst. prof. journalism No. Ill. U., DeKalb, 1964-66; from asst. to assoc. prof. journalism U. Mo., Columbia, 1966-72; prof., chair of health comm. Tex. Tech Sch. of Medicine, Lubbock, 1972-77; assoc. dir. health care tech. ctr. U. Mo., Columbia, 1977-81, prof., assoc. dean journalism, 1981-86, prof., dir. Stephenson Rsch. Ctr., 1986-92, prof. emeritus journalism, 1992—; cons. in devel., 1966—; mem. editl. bd. Am. Diabetes Assn., 1975-80. Co-editor: (book) Science, Psychology & Communication, 1972; contbr. numerous articles to profl. jours. Pvt. first class U.S. Army, 1954-56. Named Disting. Gregory fellow U. Mo., 1961-63. Mem. Internat. Soc. for Sci. Study of Subjectivity (first head 1985-86), Internat. Comm. Assn. (two Top 3 Papers awards 1980, 86), Assn. for Edn. in Journalism and Mass Comm., Phi Kappa Tau, Kappa Tau Alpha, Sigma Delta Chi. Avocations: music, photography. Home: 4004 Defoe Dr Columbia MO 65203-0254

BRENNER, EDGAR H., legal administrator; b. N.Y.C., Jan. 4, 1930; s. Louis and Bertha B. (Guttman) B.; m. Janet Maybin, Aug. 4, 1979; children from previous marriage—Charles S., David M., Paul R. B.A., Carleton Coll., 1951; J.D., Yale U., 1954. Bar: D.C. 1954, U.S. Ct. Claims 1957, U.S. Supreme Ct. 1957. Mem. 2d Hoover Commn. Legal Task Force Staff, Washington, 1954; trial atty. U.S. Dept. Justice, Washington, 1954-57; assoc. Arnold & Porter, Washington, 1957-62, ptnr., 1962-89; nat. dir. The Behavioral Law Ctr., Washington, 1989—; vis. rsch. prof. law Nat. Law Ctr.; sr. counsel terrorism studies program George Washington U., 1993-99; chmn. conf. com. Alternative Dispute Resolution, 1990-91; dir. Insts. for Behavior Resources, Inc.; co-dir. Inter Univ. Ctr. for Legal Studies, 1999—. Contbr. articles to profl. jours. Commr. Fairfax County Econ. Devel. Corp., Va., 1963-78; pres., bd. dirs. Stella and Charles Guttman Found., N.Y.C., Ams. for Med. Progress, Arlington, Va. Fellow Coll. Problems of Drug Dependency. Mem. ABA (chmn. arbitration com. litigation sect. 1984-87), D.C. Bar Assn., Yale Club, Explorers Club (N.Y.C.). Democrat. Home: 340 Persimmon Ln Washington VA 22747-1845 Office: 4620 Lee Hwy Ste 216 Arlington VA 22207-3400

BRENNER, EGON, university official, education consultant; b. Vienna, Austria, July 1, 1925; s. Aaron and Margarethe (Adler) B.; m. Rhoda Greenberg, Dec. 24, 1950; children: Dorothy, Claudia. B.E.E., CCNY, 1944; M.E.E., Poly. Inst. Bklyn., 1949, D.E.E., 1955. Mem. faculty CCNY, 1946-81, prof. elec. engring., 1966-81, dean engring., 1971-73, acting provost, 1973-74, provost, v.p. acad. affairs, 1974-76; acting vice chancellor for acad. affairs CUNY, 1976-77, dep. chancellor, 1978-81; exec. v.p. Yeshiva U., 1981-93, prof. emeritus; vis. prof. Tex. Tech. U., summer 1965, U. Okla., 1966. Author: (with M. Javid) Analysis of Electric Circuits, 1959, 2d rev. edit., 1967, Analysis, Transmission and Filtering of Signals, 1963. Served with AUS, 1944-46. Decorated Bronze Star. Fellow IEEE, AAAS; mem. Am. Soc. Engring. Edn., Sigma Xi, Eta Kappa Nu, Tau Beta Pi. Address: 61 W 62nd St New York NY 10023-7015

BRENNER, ERMA, author; b. N.Y.C., Dec. 1, 1911; d. Robert and Amy (Schoenbrunn) Brandt; m. Charles Brenner, Sept. 8, 1935; children: Elsa Brenner Cohen, Lucy (Mrs. Barrie Biven). Student, Harvard, 1931-34; studied with, Eduard Steuermann, 1954-61. Dir., owner Camp Sherbo, Bridgeton, Maine, 1933-40; tchr. nursery sch. Children's Ctr., Roxbury, Mass., 1942-44, Colonial Heights Nursery Sch., Yonkers, N.Y., 1946-48; owner, developer Scenichrome, 1946-48; mem. staff White Plains (N.Y.) Day Care Ctr., 1976-77; coordinator play ctr. dept. child psychiatry, mem. staff therapeutic nursery Albert Einstein Med. Coll., 1977—; cons. to staff children's day hosp. N.Y. Hosp. Westchester Div., 1980-81; creator, dir. Small House Program for Children N.Y. Hosp., Cornell Med. Ctr., Westchester divsn., Rockland State Children's Psychiat. Hosp., Queens Children's Psychiat. Hosp., Newtown (Pa.) Elem. Sch.; cons. Parent Child Ctr., N.Y. Psychoanalytic Inst., N.Y.C., 1993—. Author: A New Baby! A New Life!, 1973, repub. as When Baby Comes Home, (with others) The Vulnerable Child, vol. 2, 1994. Recipient Christophers award, 1973. Home and Office: 35 East 85th St New York NY 10028-0954

BRENNER, FRANK, lawyer; b. N.Y.C., Oct. 26, 1927; s. Jack and Betty (Teifer) B.; children: Jay Marlow, Matthew Adam, Amy Rebecca, Diane Rachel. B.A. cum laude, Lehigh U., 1948; J.D., Harvard U., 1951. Bar: N.Y. 1951, U.S. Supreme Ct. 1955, U.S. Tax Ct. 1975. Asst. dist. atty. N.Y. County, 1951-55; pvt. practice, N.Y.C., 1955-83, 85—; judge N.Y.C. Criminal Ct., 1983-84; mng. dir. InterEquity Capital Corp., 1991-98; adminstrv. judge Waterfront Commn. N.Y. Harbor, 1994—. Mem. mediation and arbitration panel JAMS/Endispute, 1993-99. With USNR, 1945-46. Recipient commendation Brit. Royal Commn. on Capital Punishment, 1950. Fellow Am. Acad. Matrimonial Lawyers ; mem. ABA (litigation sect. com. on trial complex crimes 1977—, criminal justice sect. com. on def. function 1979—, RICO subcom. on white collar crime 1982-84), N.Y. State Bar Assn. (ho. dels. 1978-83, 85-90, 92-96, fellow, bar found. 1992—, com. on unlawful practice law 1984-89, criminal justice sect. com. on criminal discovery 1985—), Assn. Bar City N.Y. (spl. com. on legal aid inquiry 1971-2, com. on penology 1972-77, com. profl. discipline 1982-85), N.Y. County Lawyers Assn. (dir. 1977-83, pres. coun. of assn. 1992—, jud. com. 1991—, chmn. Pres. adv. com. criminal law, 1990—, chmn. com. criminal law 1968-70, 80-83, com. matrimonial law 1975-80, spl. com. on selection and tenure of judges 1975-77, spl. com. to review jud. discipline 1979-80), Fund for Modern Cts. (com. on ct. facilities 1985—), N.Y. State Dist. Attys. Assn. Club: Harvard (N.Y.C.). Home: 470 Park Ave New York NY 10022-1903 Office: 460 Park Ave New York NY 10022-1906

BRENNER, GERRY, English educator; b. Seattle, Oct. 7, 1937; s. Eugene Nansen and Gladys Marie (Western) Brenner; m. Teresa Joan Mays, June 11, 1960; children: Patrick Mays, Kyle Frederick, John Keegan. BA, U. Wash., 1961, MA, 1962, PhD, 1965. Asst. prof. U. Idaho, Moscow, 1965-67; assoc. prof. Boise (Idaho) State U., 1967-68; asst. prof. U. Mont., Missoula, 1968-71, assoc. prof., 1971-78, prof. English, 1978—; Fulbright sr. lectr. U. Cyril & Methodius, Skopje, Macedonia, 1980-81; exch. prof. lit. LaTrobe U., Bendigo, Vic., Australia, 1994-95. Author: Concealments in Hemingway's Works, 1983, The Old Man and the Sea: Story of a Common Man, 1991; co-author: Ernest Hemingway, 1986; contbr. articles to profl. jours. Mem. adv. bd. Inst. Medicine and Humanities, Missoula, Mont., 1989-93, exec. bd., 1995-99; trustee, sec. Hemingway Found./Soc., 1996-99; exec. com. U.S. Healthcare-Reform Symposium, Missoula, 1990-91; mem. air-pollution adv coun. Missoula City-County Health Dept., 1988-92. With U.S. Army, 1955-57. Mem. MLA, Hemingway Soc., Rocky Mountain MLA, Soc. for Study of Narrative Lit., Phi Kappa Phi (treas. 1997-98, pub. affairs officer 1998-99). Democrat. Avocations: camping, hiking, fly-fishing. E-mail: koala2@selway.umt.edu. Home: 670 East North Ave Missoula MT 59801-6002 Office: Univ of Montana Dept of English Missoula MT 59812

BRENNER, HOWARD, chemical engineering educator; b. N.Y.C., Mar. 16, 1929; s. Max and Margaret (Wechsler) B.,; children: Leslie, Joyce, Suzanne; m. Lisa Glucksman, Sept. 8, 1995. BChemE, Pratt Inst., 1950; MChemE, NYU, 1954, D in Engring. Sci., 1957. Instr. chem. engring. NYU, 1955-57, asst. prof. chem. engring., 1957-61, assoc. prof., 1961-65, prof., 1965-66; prof. Carnegie-Mellon U., 1966-77; prof., chmn. dept. chem. engring U. Rochester, N.Y., 1977-81; W.H. Dow prof. chem. engring. MIT, Cambridge, Mass., 1981—; sr. vis. fellow Sci. Rsch. Coun. Gt. Britain, 1974; Fairchild Disting. scholar Calif. Inst. Tech., 1975-76, Chevron vis. prof., 1988-89; Gulf vis. prof. Carnegie-Mellon U., Pitts., 1991; Lady Davis fellow, Israel, 1995-96; vis. prof. U. Calif., Berkeley, 1996. Author: (with J. Happel) Low Reynolds Number Hydrodynamics, 1965, 2d edit., 1973, Russian edit., 1976; (with D.A. Edwards and D.T. Wasan) Interfacial Transport Processes and Rheology, 1991; (with D. A. Edwards) Macrotransport Processes, 1993; contbr. articles to profl. jours.; co-editor in chief Physico-Chem. Hydrodynamics, 1988-89; chmn. editorial adv. bd. Butterworth-Heinemann Series on Chem. Engring. Guggenheim fellow, 1988. Fellow AAAS, Am. Acad. Mechanics, Am. Inst. Chem. Engrs. (Alpha Chi Sigma award 1976, Walker award 1985); mem. NAE, Soc. Rheology (Bingham medal 1980), Soc. Nat. Philosophy, Am. Chem. Soc. (Kendall award 1988, 11th ann. Honor Scroll Indsl. Engring. Chemistry Divsn. 1961), Am. Soc. Eng. Edn. (gen. electric sr. rsch. award 1996). Office: MIT Dept Of Chem Engring Cambridge MA 02139-4307

BRENNER, HOWARD MARTIN, banker; b. New Brunswick, N.J., May 5, 1933; s. Philip and Rita Brenner; children: Andrew, Pamela. BA, Yale U., 1954. With Ira Haupt & Co., N.Y.C., 1956-63; account exec. Burnham & Co., N.Y.C., 1963, mgr. retail sales, 1971-72; with Drexel Burnham Lambert Inc., N.Y.C., 1963-90, dir. equity sales, 1985-86, dir. systems, human resources, ops., 1986-89; pres. Drexel Burnham Lambert Specialists, N.Y.C., 1987-90, pres., bd. dirs., N.Y.C., 1990; founder, pres. Brenner Securities Corp., N.Y.C., 1990—; vice-chmn. Southcoast Capital Corp., N.Y.C.; pres. Lowenbaum Co., N.Y.C., 1998—; chmn., CEO HCFP Brenner Securities, N.Y.C., 1999; former bd. mem. Securities Industry Assn., Options Clearing Corp. (vice-chmn.); gov. Am. Stock Exchange, 1985-90;. Mem. Securities Industry Assn. (chmn. coms.). Avocations: tennis, jogging. Office: HCFP Brenner Securities 277 Park Ave New York NY 10172-0003

BRENNER, JANE SEGREST, city council member; b. Tuskegee, Ala., Aug. 18, 1930; d. Benjamin Howell Segrest and Doris Spradley Segrest Serrett; m. Edward John Brenner, June 1, 1951 (dec. June 1992); children: Beverly, Douglas, Carolyn, Mary. Student, La. State U., 1948-50. City coun. mem. City of Punta Gorda, Fla., 1996-99. Trustee, past pres. Charlotte County Mental Health Ctr., Punta Gorda, Fla., 1986-96; chair bd. dirs. Ctr. for Abuse and Rape Emergencies, Punta Gorda, 1984-89; co-chair United Way Campaign, Charlotte County, Fla., 1992-94; pres. Southwest Fla. League Cities, 1996-98. Mem. DAR, Nat. Capital Lawyers Aux., Special Tng. and Rehab. Found., Kentucky Colonels, Burnt Shore Country Club, Isles Yacht Club. Republican. Avocations: genealogy, golf. Office: City of Punta Gorda 4 Ocean Dr Punta Gorda FL 33950

BRENNER, JANET MAYBIN WALKER, lawyer; b. Arkansas City, Kans.; d. D. Arthur and Maybin (Gardner) Walker; children: Margaret Maybin Burns, Theodore Kimball Jonas, Amanda Nash Freeman; m. Edgar H. Brenner, Aug. 4, 1979. AB, U. So. Calif.; JD, George Washington U., 1978. Bar: D.C. 1978; U.S. Dist. Ct. (D.C.). Mem. Brenner Women's Leadership com.; mem. women's com. Corcoran Gallery Art, Washington, 1969—, Pres.'s Cir., Planned Parenthood D.C., 1990—, Found. for Preservation of Historic Georgetown; mem. com. restoration Salon Doré. Mem. D.C. Bar Assn., Sulgrave Club (Washington). Home: 3325 R St NW Washington DC 20007-2310 also: Shadow Ridge Farm Washington VA 22747

BRENNER, LYNNETTE MARY, reading specialist, educator; b. Woodbury, N.J., July 20, 1959; d. Bernhard A. and Anna Rose (Rickert) B. BS in Bible and Elem. Edn., Lancaster (Pa.) Bible Coll., 1981; MEd in Reading, Beaver Coll., 1991. Cert. elem. and reading tchr., N.J., Pa. Elem. tchr. Killian Hill Christian Sch., Lilburn, Ga., 1981-83, Bethel Bapt. Ch. Sch., Cherry Hill, N.J., 1984-92; reading specialist Cherry Hill Bd. Edn., 1992—; adj. faculty Ea. Coll., St. Davids, Pa., 1994-96; mem. steering com. Cherry Hill Tchrs. applying Whole Lang., 1993-95. Sec. missions com. Columbus Bapt. Ch., 1992-97, discipleship ministry, 1993—, Sun. sch. tchr., 1992-94, chmn. missions com., 1992; leader precepts Bible study. Recipient recognition for geography awareness N.J. Senate, 1990, recognition Gov.'s Tchr. Recognition Program award, 1995, Celebrate Literacy award Internat. Reading Assn., 1999; named Tchr. of Yr., Kilmer Sch. Mem. NEA, N.J. Edn. Assn., West Jersey Reading Coun. (bd. dirs. 1995-98, Celebrate Literacy award 1999), N.J. Reading Assn., Internat. Reading Assn. Republican. Baptist. Avocations: reading, travel, Bible study, crafts, cross-stitch. Office: Joyce Kilmer Elem Sch Chapel Ave Cherry Hill NJ 08002

BRENNER, MARCELLA SIEGEL, retired education educator; b. Balt., Dec. 5, 1912; d. Moses and Annie (Affachiner) Siegel; m. Morris Bernstein, July 1947 (dec. 1962); m. Abner Brenner, Oct. 1964. BS, Johns Hopkins U., 1934; MA, Am. U., 1949; EdD, George Washington U., 1962. Tchr. Balt. Pub. Schs., 1930-43; writer, editor USPHS, Washington, 1945-52; tchr. Lone Oak Elem. Sch., Md., 1952-54, prin., 1954-64; lectr. in edn. George Washington U., 1961, assoc. prof. Sch. Edn., 1965-83, assoc. dir. MA Tchg. Program, 1966-83, ret., 1983; mem. staff Washington Sch. Psychiatry, 1962—; cons. U. Calif. Sch. Sys. of Washington, Tchr. Edn. and Profl. Standards Commn.; founder, dir. Mus. Edn. Program George Washington U., 1974-83; dir. Ctr. for Mus. Edn. George Washington U., 1976-79. Co-author: Interview Art and Skill, 1980; contbr. articles to profl. jours. Bd. dirs. Boston Mus. Fine Arts, 1985—, Balt. Mus. Art, 1985—, B'nai Brith Klutznick Nat. Jewish Mus., 1985—, Project Interchange Dept. Am. Jewish Com., 1985—, George Washington U., 1985—; bd. Palestine Endorsement Fund, Israel Endowment Funds, Inc., 1985—. Brenner award established in her honor George Washington U., 1983; recipient Yakir Bezalel award Bezalel Acad. Arts and Design and Culture, 1988, award of appreciation State of Israel Min. Edn., 1991. Fellow Am. Orthopsychiatric Assn., Israel Mus. (hon.). Avocations: teaching people preparing for U.S. citizenship, reading for visually impaired. Home: 7204 Pomander Ln Chevy Chase MD 20815-3135

BRENNER, RAYMOND ANTHONY, priest; b. Evansville, Ind., Feb. 12, 1943; s. George Frederick and Marie Catherine (Gries) B. BA, St. Meinrad (Ind.) Coll., 1965; MDiv, St. Meinrad Sch. Theology, 1969. Ordained priest Roman Cath. Ch., 1969. Deacon Nativity Ch., Indpls., 1968; assoc. pastor St. John's Ch., Loogootee, Ind., 1969-74, Sts. Peter and Paul Ch., Haubstadt, Ind., 1974-78; pastor St. Mary's Ch., Sullivan, Ind., 1978-86, St. Joan of Arc Ch., Jasonville, Ind., 1982-86, Resurrection Ch., Evansville, 1986—; mem. Cath. Charities Bd., Evansville, 1972-75; v.p. Ministerial Assn., Sullivan, 1985-86; pres. Coun. of Priests, Evansville, 1989; diocesan chaplain St. Vincent de Paul Soc., Evansville, 1990-94. Mem. Wabash Valley Human Svcs., Vincennes, Ind., 1982-86, Sullivan Housing Authority, 1983-85, Fed. Emergency Mgmt. Agy., Sullivan, 1984-86, Emergency Food Bank, Sullivan, 1984-86; spiritual advisor Evansville Cath. Cursillo, 1994—; chaplain German Twp. Vol. Fire Dept., 1998—. Mem. Optimists (chaplain Evansville Westside club 1990—), Elks. Democrat. Home and Office: Resurrection Cath Ch 5301 New Harmony Rd Evansville IN 47720-1740 *It takes so little time to offer a smile, and the rewards are beyond imagining. Somehow they know you care and that God cares too.*

BRENNER, ROBERT DAVID, federal agency administrator; b. Washington, July 26, 1953; s. Norbert and Ruth (Sternheim) B.; m. Barbara Friling, Feb. 18, 1988. AB, Princeton U., 1975, MPA, 1977. Mem. rsch. faculty Ctr. Internat. Studies, Princeton, N.J., 1977-80; energy policy analyst EPA, Washington, 1980-87, dir. Air Policy Office, 1987-99; dep. asst. adminstr. Office of Air and Radiation, EPA, Washington, 1999—. Recipient Gold medal EPA, 1989. Avocations: golf, tennis, hiking. Office: EPA Policy Analysis & Review 401 M St SW Washington DC 20460-0002*

BRENNER, THEODORE ENGELBERT, retired trade association executive; b. N.Y.C., Apr. 18, 1930; s. Engelbert F.J. and Julie M. (Kierschner) B.; m. Maria T. Finn, Sept. 12, 1953; children—John Finn, Elisabeth Ann, Christopher. BCE, Manhattan Coll., 1951; MS, Johns Hopkins, 1954. Registered profl. engr., Pa., NJ. Diplomate Am. Acad. Environ. Engrs. Mgr. waste treatment dept. Permutit div. Sybron Corp., Paramus, N.J., 1959-62; prin. Hydroscience, Inc., Ft. Lee, N.J., 1963; with Soap and Detergent Assn., N.Y.C., 1963-93, v.p., tech. dir., 1970, v.p., dir. govt. affairs, 1971, pres., 1972-93; ret., 1993; Exec. dir. Joint Industry Govt. Task Force Eutrophication, 1968-70; mem. Dept. Interior Water Resources Sci., Info. Center Adv. Group, 1969-70; mem. spl. adv. com. N.Y. Temp. State Commn. on Water Resources Planning, 1964-67. Contbr.: chpt. to Advances in Environmental

Sciences, Vol. II, 1969; articles to profl. jours. Mem. Rumson Bd. Edn., 1968-74, 1st v.p., 1973-74; mem. Rumson-Fair Haven Regional Bd. Edn., 1974-77, v.p., 1976-77. Served to capt. USAF, 1952-59; lt. col. ret. Mem. ASCE, AIChE, Am. Soc. Assn. Execs., Am. Oil Chemists Soc., Union League (N.Y.C.), Seabright (N.J.) Beach Club. Home: 5 Tyson Ln Rumson NJ 07760-1912

BRENT, HELEN TERESSA, school nurse; b. Grand Rapids, Mich., Oct. 4, 1946; d. William Henry and Anita Broyles Burress; m. Robert Lee Brent, June 10, 1967. AS, Grand Rapids C.C., 1966; diploma, Butterworth Hosp. Sch. Nursing, 1968; BSN summa cum laude, U. Mich., 1981; MPA, Western Mich. U., 1992. RN, Mich. Staff nurse Butterworth Hosp., Grand Rapids, Mich., 1968-69, head nurse psychiat. unit, 1969-72; DON Forest View Psychiat. Hosp., Grand Rapids, Mich., 1972-75; asst. DON, staff devel. coord. Kent Oaks Psychiat. Unit Kent Community Hosp., Grand Rapids, Mich., 1975-80; DON Kent Community Hosp. Complex, Grand Rapids, Mich., 1980-94; psychiat. nurse Pine Rest Christian Mental Health Svcs., Grand Rapids, 1994—, Kent County Pub. Health Dept., Grand Rapids, 1996-97; sch. nurse Grand Rapids Pub. Schs., 1997—. Mem. adv. coun. Mich. Family Planning Mich. Dept. Cmty. Health, 1991—, Family Outreach Ctr., Grand Rapids, 1980-95; mem. hospice care study panel United Way Kent County, 1984; vol. nursing health svcs. Kent County chpt. ARC, Grand Rapids, 1974—; vol. mediator West Mich. Dispute Resolution Ctr., 1995—. Recipient Outstanding Svc. award Family Outreach Ctr. Kent County Cmty. Mental Health, 1988, Helen Barnes award for outstanding vol. contbns. in nursing svcs. Kent County chpt. ARC, 1994, Eugene Browning Med. Svc. award Giants Orgn., Grand Rapids, 1995. Mem. Vis. Nurses Assn. (bd. dirs. local chpt. 1991—), Harambe Black Nurses Assn. Grand Rapids, Alpha Kappa Mu (Mu Omicron chpt.). Democrat. Avocations: reading, traveling, volunteer and various ch. related activities. Home: 3834 Old Elm Dr SE Kentwood MI 49512 Office: Grand Rapids Pub Schs KEC Mayfield 225 Mayfield NE Grand Rapids MI 49503

BRENT, ROBERT LEONARD, radiology and pediatrics educator; b. Rochester, N.Y., Oct. 6, 1927; s. Charles and Rose (Katz) B.; m. Lillian H. Hoffman, Aug. 21, 1949; children: David A., James R., Lawrence H., Deborah A. AB, U. Rochester, 1948, MD with honors, 1953, PhD, 1955, DSc (hon.), 1988. Fellow Nat. Found., Strong Meml. Hosp., 1953-54; intern pediatrics Mass. Gen. Hosp., Boston, 1954-55; chief radiation biology Walter Reed Army Inst. Rsch., 1955-57; mem. faculty Jefferson Med. Coll., 1955—, prof. radiology, 1962—, also prof. pediatrics, Louis and Bess Stein prof. pediatrics, 1985—; apptd. Disting. prof. Thomas Jefferson U., 1989; hon. prof. Norman Bethume U. Med. Sci., People's Republic of China, 1992, West China U. Med. Scis., Chengdu, People's Republic of China, 1992; chmn. med. adv. bd. Nat. Found.; mem. fertility and maternal health com. FDA; mem. human embryology study sect. NIH, 1970-74; bd. trustees Health and Environ. Sci. Inst., 1991-94; pres. First Internat. Congress on Birth Defects, People's Republic of China, 1994. Editor in chief Teratology, 1976-93. Pres. Teratology Soc., 1968. Served with U.S. Army, 1955-57. Recipient Richie Meml. prize U. Rochester Med. Sch., 1953, Lindback Found. award for disting. tchg., 1968, Med. Sch. award Alpha Omega Alpha, 1952, Burlington Internat. award, 1990, Landauer award Health Physics Soc., 1995; travelling fellow Royal Soc. Medicine, 1971-72, vis. fellow FitzWilliam Coll., Cambridge, 1971-72; Lady Davis scholar Hadassah Med. Ctr., Jerusalem, 1983-84. Mem. AAAS, NAS Inst. Medicine, Teratology Soc. (pres. 1967-68), Internat. Life Sci. Inst., Radiation Rsch. Soc., Am. Soc. Exptl. Pathology, Soc. Pediat. Rsch., Am. Pediats. Soc., Am. Acad. Pediats., Soc. Exptl. Biology and Medicine, Phila. Coll. Physicians, Phila. Pediat. Soc., Am. Assn. Immunology (emeritus), Soc. Developmental Biology, Nat. Coun. Radiation Protection, Nat. Acad. Sci. (elected Inst. Medicine 1996), Japan Teratology Soc., European Teratology Soc., Ambulatory Pediat. Assn., Sigma Xi.

BRENT, RUTH STUMPE, design educator, researcher, educator; b. Washington, Mo., Sept. 11, 1951; d. Clarence Frank and Dorothy May (Horstick) Stumpe; m. Edward Everett Brent, Jr., May 14, 1972 (div. Mar. 1999); children: Jessica Elizabeth, Jonathan Edward. BS cum laude, U. Mo., 1972; MA, U. Minn., 1974, PhD, 1978. Cert. of qualification Nat. Coun. Interior Design Qualification. Postdoctoral fellow in socio-clin. geriatrics NIMH, 1978-79; asst. prof. U. Mo., Columbia, 1981-86, assoc. prof. design, 1986-92, prof., 1992—, acting dept. chair, 1984-85, chair environ. design dept., 1985—; project dir. Adminstrn. on Aging Grant, 1979-81; v.p. Idea Works, Inc., Columbia, 1981-99; chair campus planning com. for facilities and grounds, U. Mo., Columbia, 1993—. Co-author: (computer software) Home-Safe-Home, 1989; co-editor: Popular American Housing, 1995, Aging, Autonomy and Architecture: Advances in Assisted Living, 1999; contbr. articles to profl. jours. Active Mayor's Task Force, Columbia Low-Income Housing, 1984-85; mem. Main St. adv. coun. dept. econ. devel. State of Mo., 1989-90; regional chairperson dists. 84 and 85 United Way, Columbia, 1989, 90, 98, 99; mem. adv. bd. Pub. Housing Authority, Columbia, 1984-85; chairperson North Cen. Region-54 Agrl. Expt. Sta. Rsch., 1989-91; mem. Columbia Regional Home Health and Hospice Adv. Bd., Columbia Regional Hosp., 1993—; bd. trustees The Mo. 4-H Found., 1997—; chair campus planning com. for facilities and grounds U. Mo., 1993—. Grantee Adminstrn. on Aging, 1979-81, VA, 1981, Am. Home Econs. Assn., 1981-82, 2 Joel Polsky Found. Interior Design Rsch. grantee, 1986, 87; recipient Fulbright award Chinese History and Culture, 1988, exch. faculty award Prince of Sonkla U., Thailand, 1990, Chonnam U., Korea, 1992; Fulbright fellow to Morocco and Tunisia, 1993. Mem. Am. Home Econs. Assn. (chmn. art/design sect. 1984-87, New Achievers award 1987), Am. Assn. Housing Educators, Am. Soc. Interior Designers (allied mem., chmn. position papers com. 1988-90, Presdl. citation 1990), Interior Design Educators Coun., Nat. Coun. for Interior Design (cert.), Environ. Design Rsch. Assn., Illuminating Engring. Soc. (participant workshop for tchrs.), Gerontol. Assn., Mo. Fulbright Alumni Assn. (membership chmn. 1989-90, v.p. 1990-92, pres. 1992-94), Univ. Club Inc. (pres. 1991-92, bd. dirs., sec. 1993-95, U. Mo. faculty alumni award 1992), Gamma Sigma Delta (pres. 1993-94, Disting. Adminstrn. award 1997), Omicron Nu, Phi Upsilon Omicron. Home: 108 E Burnam Rd Columbia MO 65203 Office: U Mo Dept Environ Design 137 Stanley Hall Dept Environ Columbia MO 65211-7700

BRENTLINGER, PAUL SMITH, venture capital executive; b. Dayton, Ohio, Apr. 3, 1927; s. Arthur and Welthy Otello (Smith) B.; m. Marilyn E. Hunt, June 23, 1951; children: Paula, David, Sara. BA, U. Mich., 1950, MBA, 1951. With Harris Corp., Melbourne, Fla., 1951-84, v.p. corp. devel., 1969-75, v.p. fin., 1975-82, sr. v.p. fin., 1982-84; ptnr. Morgenthaler Ventures, Cleve., 1984—; bd. dirs. Allegheny-Teledyne Corp., Pitts., chmn. bd. Hypres, Inc., Elmsford, N.Y., Wastequip, Inc., Cleve.; mem. adv. bd. Wolverine Venture Fund. Trustee Cleve. Inst. Art. Mem. Union Club, Phi Beta Kappa. Home: 2755 Eaton Rd Cleveland OH 44122-1800 Office: Morgenthaler Ventures 629 Euclid Ave Ste 700 Cleveland OH 44114-3054

BRENTLINGER, WILLIAM BROCK, college dean; b. Flora, Ill., Aug. 21, 1926; s. Arthur Kenneth and Frances (Maxwell) B.; m. Barbara Jean Weir, Dec. 29, 1946; children: Gregory, Gary, Rebecca Anne, Garth, Barbara Sue. Student, Washington U., 1946-47; A.B., Greenville Coll., 1950; M.A., Ind. State U., 1951; Ph.D., U. Ill., 1959. Instr. speech Greenville Coll., 1951-59, chmn. dept., 1959-62, dean of coll., 1962-69, dean coll. fine arts and comm., 1969-92; interim pres. Lamar U., Beaumont, Tex., 1992-93; asst. to pres. Lamar U., Beaumont, 1993—; cons. higher edn. Served with USNR, 1944-46. Recipient tchr. study award Danforth Found., 1957. Mem. Internat. Council Fine Arts Deans, Speech Communication Assn. Am., Tex. Speech Assn., Tex. Assn. Coll. Tchrs., Tex. Council Arts in Edn. (pres.), Phi Kappa Phi. Baptist. Club: Rotary (Beaumont). Home: 6530 Salem Cir Beaumont TX 77706-5552 Office: Lamar U PO Box 10001 Beaumont TX 77710-0001 *I have always attempted to treat people as subjects, not objects, as fellow creatures of God, and thus to be worked with not worked upon.*

BRENTS, DANIEL RUGEL, architectural firm executive; b. Detroit, Dec. 25, 1938. BArch, Tex. A&M U., 1962; M in Architecture and Urban Design, Washington U., St. Louis, 1969. Registered arch., Md., Tex.; cert. Nat. Coun. Archtl. Registration Bds. Designer John S. Bolles Assoc., San Francisco, 1965-68; assoc. RTKL Assocs., Inc., Balt., 1969-72; v.p. EDI Archs., Dallas, 1972-76; sr. v.p. 3D/Internat., Houston, 1976-89; v.p. Euro Disney, S.A., Paris, 1989-92; prin. Daniel R. Brents, Inc., Houston, 1992-96; v.p. Gensler, Houston, 1996—; mem. ULI Internat. Commn. Prin. works include Ballpark at Union Station, Houston, Tex. Med. Ctr., Houston, U. Houston Univ. Park, Yerba Buena Ctr., San Francisco, SpringPark, Dallas, Wintergreen Resort, Nelson County, Va., South Shore Harbor, League City, Tex., Heartland Village, Ohio, Medina (Saudi Arabia) Satellite Cmty., Asian Devel. Bank, Manila, The Philippines, IBM Corp. Hdqrs. Facilities, Southeast Asia, Spl. Econ. Zone, Shen Zhen, China, Euro Disney, Paris, Sony Center, Berlin, Philippines Centennial Expo. Mem. energy task force Goals for Dallas, 1975; mem. task force City of Dallas Urban Design, 1976-77, Hong Kong Am. C. of C. Community Affairs Com., 1985-87. Fellow AIA; mem. Am. Planning Assn., Am. Inst. Cert. Planners, Urban Land Inst., Tex. Soc. Archs. (internat. commn. co-chair). Home: 11902 Laurie Ln Houston TX 77024-5032 Office: Gensler 700 Milam St Ste 400 Houston TX 77002-2815*

BRENTS, MAGGIE M., city official. City coun. Indpls. Office: 200 E Washington St Ste 241 Indianapolis IN 46204-3310

BRENZ, GARY JAY, publishing executive; b. Belvidere, Ill., Dec. 21, 1945; s. Gerald J. and Shirley W. (Berg) B.; m. Elaine E. Swanson, Jan. 9, 1969; 1 child, Graham Jofrei. BS in Art, U. Wis., Platteville, 1969; MA in Teaching, Beloit Coll., 1979. Asst. to city mgr. City of Beloit, Wis., 1970-71; adminstrv. asst. Wis. Dept. Justice, Madison, 1971-76; graphic designer The Design Group, Madison, 1976-78; mgr. Sand End Inc., Madison, 1980-85; owner Arclight/Midwest Books, Stoughton, Wis., 1985—; cons. Arlington Nat. Cemetery, Vietnam War Meml. Bd. Hist. Rsch. Unit, Washington, 1989—. Author: (reference book) Military Insignia of the Republic of South Vietnam, 1979; designer, author: (promotional program book) U.N. Public Promotion, 1971. Mem. local spiritual assembly Baha'i Cmty., Beloit, 1970-72; mem. local spiritual assembly Baha'i Cmty., Stoughton, 1973-79, 90-92, dist. tchg. com., 1973-76; exec. dir. Stoughton Housing Authority, 1975-79; asst. scoutmaster Troop 164, Boy Scouts Am., Stoughton, 1988-98; sec. Bus. Improvement Dist., Stoughton, 1992-93. With USNR, 1969-70, Vietnam. Recipient Amos Alonzo Stagg medal, 1964, Chgo. Tribune Achievement medal, Res. Officers Assn. medal. Mem. Rotary Club Stoughton (bd. dirs. 1991-93, sec. 1993—, Paul Harris fellow 1998), Great Northern Railway Hist. Soc., Spl. Forces Assn., VFW, Mac-V Alumni Assn., Wis. Mil. Insignia Collectors Assn., Badger Mil. Assn. Office: Arclight/Midwest Books 111 E Main St Stoughton WI 53589-1720

BRESANI, FEDERICO FERNANDO, business executive; b. Lima, Peru, Apr. 27, 1945; came to U.S., 1964; s. Federico L. and Beatriz (Ferrer) B.; m. Patricia Anne Grannis, Aug. 26, 1972; children: Christina Anne, Vianna Clarissa. BS in Elect. Engring., Milw. Sch. of Engring., 1970; MBA, Fairleigh Dickinson U., 1980. Engr. Cerro Corp., Lima, Peru, 1973-76; supr. Cerro Corp./CMP, N.Y.C., 1976-77, mgr., 1978, purchasing mgr., 1979-80; product mgr. Schumag, Inc., Norwood, N.J., 1980-82, v.p., 1982; sales, mktg. mgr. EVG, Inc., N.Y.C., 1983-85; v.p. EVG, N.Y.C., 1986-92, pres., 1992—. Mem. Wire Assn. Internat., Wire Reinforcement Inst., Latin Am. Iron and Steel Inst., Am. Concrete Inst., Concrete Reinforcing Steel Inst., Rowayton Yacht Club, Omicron Delta Epsilon. Avocations: sailing, amateur radio. Home: 77 Chuckanutt Dr Oakland NJ 07436-3728 Office: EVG 220 E 42nd St New York NY 10017-5806

BRESCHER, JOHN B., JR., lawyer; b. Elizabeth, N.J., July 8, 1947. BS, Lehigh U., 1969; JD, Georgetown U., 1972, LLM, 1976. Bar: N.J. 1973, D.C. 1975. Atty. McCarter & English, Newark; adj. prof. law Seton Hall U., 1980-84. Mem. ABA, N.J. State Bar Assn., Essex County Bar Assn. Office: McCarter & English PO Box 652 Four Gateway Ctr 100 Mulberry St Newark NJ 07102-4004

BRESEE, JAMES COLLINS, federal agency scientist; b. N.Y.C., Oct. 25, 1925; s. John James and Mabel Elizabeth (Collins) B.; m. Mary Kathryn Duncan, July 5, 1952 (dec. Mar. 1973); children: Kathryn Ann Bresee Brooke, Stuart James; m. Susan Lynn Austermiller, Aug. 3, 1974; children: James Michael, Benjamin Carter, Nathan John, Joanna Meghan, Andrew Paul. BSChemE, U. Ill., 1945, MSChemE, 1947; ScDChemE, MIT, 1953; JD, U. Tenn., 1971. Bar: Tenn. 1972, D.C. 1979. Asst. prof. chem. and nuclear engring. MIT, Cambridge, Mass., 1951-54; br. chief and asst. dir. chem. tech. div. Oak Ridge Nat. Lab., Oak Ridge, Tenn., 1954-64; dir. civil def. rsch. project Oak Ridge Nat. Lab., 1964-72; asst. dir. for gen. energy devel. div. applied tech. AEC, Washington, 1972-75; dir. div. geothermal energy ERDA, Washington, 1976-77; dir. N.C. Energy Inst., N.C. State Dept. Commerce, Raleigh, 1978-81; supervisory engr. and mgr. geosci. rsch. Geothermal Tech. Div., U.S. Dept. Energy, Washington, 1982-86; mem. sr. tech. svc. Office Civilian Radioactive Waste Mgmt., U.S. Dept. Energy, Washington, 1986—, dir. repository coordination div., 1986-88; dep. assoc. dir. for program and resources mgmt. Office Civilian Radioactive Waste Mgmt. U.S. Dept. Energy, 1988-94, acting dir. Office Human Resources and Adminstrn., Office Civilian Radioactive Waste Mgmt., 1994-96, dep. dir. Office of Program Mgmt. and Adminstrn., 1996-98, sr. tech. specialist, 1998—; adj. prof. chem. engring. N.C. State U., 1978-81. Editor-in-chief Geothermal Sci. and Tech., 1987—; contbr. numerous papers to profl pubs. Mem. Oak Ridge Planning Commn., 1963-67. Lt. USNR, 1944-46, CBI. Mem. Tenn. Bar Assn., D.C. Bar Assn., Beta Theta Pi, Sigma Xi, Kappa Kappa Lambda, Phi Kappa Phi. Presbyterian. Avocation: music. Home: 3213 Birchtree Ln Silver Spring MD 20906-3041 Office: US Dept Energy 1000 Independence Ave SW Washington DC 20585-0001

BRESLAUER, CHARLES S., chemical company executive; b. N.Y.C., Mar. 13, 1925; s. Lewis R. and Anna (Helen) B.; m. Carol Sweet; children: Ann Louise, Robert Ardon, Kenneth Charles. BA, U. Mich., 1948. V.p. Seaboard Vermiculite Corp., West Palm Beach, Fla., 1952-56; product mgr. Zonolite Co., Chgo., 1956-60; regional mgr. Zonolite Co., Boca Raton, Fla., 1960-67; gen. mgr. Concrete Products Div. W.R. Grace & Co., Brunswick, Ga., 1967-71; regional mgr. Concrete Products Group, W.R. Grace & Co., Pompano Beach, Fla., 1971-92; v.p. Darex Puerto Rico, Inc. subs. W.R. Grace & Co., San Juan, P.R., 1980-92; pres. Bermuda Roof Co., Inc., Fort Lauderdale, Fla. 1983—. Patentee Portland cement wood flake structural panels, ultra lightweight mortar for roof and floor tiles. Liaison officer USAF Acad., South Fla., 1960-70. Lt. col. USAF ret. Mem. Jaycees (pres. Delray Beach, Fla. 1956), Air Force Assn. (charter mem.), Reserve Officers Assn. (life mem.). Avocations: boating, fishing, aviation. Home: 10709 SE Flotilla Ct Hobe Sound FL 33455-3220 Office: Bermuda Roof Co Inc 1499 W Palmetto Park Rd Boca Raton FL 33486-3328

BRESLAUER, GEORGE WILLIAM, political science educator; b. N.Y.C., Mar. 4, 1946; s. Henry Edward and Marianne (Schaeffer) B.; m. Yvette Assia, June 5, 1976; children: Michele, David. BA, U. Mich., 1966, MA, 1968, PhD, 1973. Asst. prof. polit. sci. U. Calif., Berkeley, 1971-79, assoc. prof., 1979-90, prof., 1990—, Chancellor's prof., 1998—, chmn. dept., 1993-96, chmn. Ctr. for Slavic and East European Studies, 1982-94; prof. polit. sci U. Calif., 1994—; vice chmn. bd. trustees Nat. Coun. for Soviet and East European Rsch., Washington, 1988-91. Author: Khrushchev and Brezhnev as Leaders, 1982, Soviet Strategy in the Middle East, 1989; editor: Can Gorbachev's Reforms Succeed?, 1990, Learning in U.S. and Soviet Foreign Policy, 1991. Grantee Ford Found., 1982-84, Carnegie Corp., 1985-94. Mem. Am. Assn. for Advancement Slavic Studies (bd. dirs., exec. com. 1990-93). Office: U Calif Dept Polit Sci 210 Barrows Hall Berkeley CA 94720-1950*

BRESLAW, CATHY LEE, artist, educator; b. Coral Gables, Fla.; d. William Howard and Miriam Roberts (Lasker) B.; m. Paul K. Cohen, Nov. 24, 1986; children: Adam, Micah. BA, George Washington U., 1973; MSW, Howard U., 1978. Educator, artist Lee Press, Encinitas, Calif., 1992—; instr. fine art in painting and creativity. Exhbns. include Nat. Watercolor Ann. Exhbn. and Travel Show, 1996-97, Gallery Contemporary Art U. Colo., 1997, Tubac Ctr. Arts, 1997, Downey (Calif.) Mus. Art, 1997, Calif. Watercolor Assn., Hilton Corp. Hdqrs., Art Inst., San Francisco, 1997, Nat. Oil and Acrylic Painting Soc., 1998, San Diego Art Inst., 1998, Internat. Soc. Exptl. Painters, 1999; one-woman shows include Curbside Cafe, Vista, Calif., 1996, Emerald Plaza, San Diego, 1996, Off Track Gallery, 1997, 1st Nat. Bank, San Diego, 1998, Acme Restaurants, Del Mar, Calif., 1998; represented in numerous corp. and pvt. collections. Bd. dirs., sec. United Cerebral Palsy Bay Area, San Francisco, 1978-82. Mem. Nat. Watercolor Soc. (signature mem.), San Diego Mus. Fine Arts Guild. Avocations: reading, golf, travel, cooking, skiing. E-mail: swxd05c@prodigy.com. Office: PO Box 231122 Encinitas CA 92023-1122

BRESLER, BORIS, consulting engineer; b. Harbin, Republic of China, Oct. 18, 1918; came to U.S., 1937, naturalized, 1943; s. Samuel and Hena (Gonopolsky) B.; m. Joy Bloom, July 5, 1946; 1 child, Deborah. BS, U. Calif., Berkeley, 1941; MS, Calif. Inst. Tech., 1946. Structural designer Kaiser Shipyards, 1941-43; stress analyst Convair Co., 1943-45; mem. faculty U. Calif., Berkeley, 1946-77, prof. civil engring., 1958-77, prof. emeritus, 1977—, asst. dean Coll. Engring., 1956-59, chmn. div. structural engring. and structural mechanics, 1963-64, dir. structural materials lab., 1963-65; prin. Wiss, Janney, Elstner Assocs., Inc. Cons. Engrs., Emeryville, Calif., 1977-87; pub. Benmir Books, 1983—. Author: (with T.Y. Lin) Design of Steel Structures, 1959, 2d edit., 1968; also articles; editor: Reinforced Concrete Engineering, Vol. 1, 1974. NSF postdoctoral fellow, 1961, Guggenheim fellow, 1962; recipient State of the Art of Civil Engring. award, 1968, Engring. News Record citation, 1982. Fellow ASCE (hon.; chmn. structural div. exec. com. 1975), Am. Concrete Inst. (hon.; dir. 1970-73, Wason medal for research 1959, J.W. Kelly Award 1978, Raymond Davis lectr. 1982, Arthur R. Anderson award 1986); mem. NAE (hon.), Structural Engring. Assn. No. Calif., Reinforced Concrete Rsch. Coun. (Arthur J. Boase award 1989). Office: Wiss Janney Elstner & Assocs 2200 Powell St Emeryville CA 94608-1809

BRESLIN, ELIZABETH WALKER, biological scientist, biomedical consultant; b. Phila., Jan. 10, 1940; d. Edwin Olin and Delphine Jane (Durkin) Walker; m. Michael Joseph Breslin, June 5, 1965; children: Anne Marie B. Sullivan, Michael Joseph Jr., Thomas Edwin. AS, Gwynedd Mercy Coll., 1959; BS, Hahnemann Med. Coll. and Hosp., 1961; postgrad., Bryn Mawr Coll., 1988-94. Lic. med. technologist, CAlif., Fla. Staff technologist Meml. Hosp. of Jacksonville, Fla., 1974-78; supr. hematology lab. Daroff Divsn. Albert Einstein Med. Ctr., Phila., 1979-81; rsch. med. technologist Geometric Data Corp., A SmithKline Co., Wayne, Pa., 1981-86; scientist Smith Kline & French R&D, Swedeland, Pa., 1986-88; biol. scientist Zynaxis, Inc., Malvern, Pa., 1988-92, quality assurance/quality control specialist, 1993-94, quality control supr., 1994-95; quality control supr. Intracel Corp., West Chester, Pa., 1995-96, biomed. cons., 1996—. Contbr. articles to profl. jours. Mem. Am. Soc. Clin. Pathologists (assoc., cert. med. technologist). Avocations: reading, gardening, wood finishing.

BRESLIN, ELVIRA MADDEN, tax lawyer, educator; b. Phila., Oct. 28, 1943; d. Daniel Joseph and Elvira Rose (Leichner) Madden; m. John Anthony Breslin, June 19, 1971; children: Kristen, John A.V. AB in English, Secondary Edn., Chestnut Hill Coll., Phila., 1961-65; MA in High Sch. Adminstrn., Villanova (Pa.) U., 1968; JD, Cath. U. Am., Washington, 1990; LLM in Taxation, Villanova U., 1996. Bar: Pa. 1991, D.C. 1992, U.S. Dist. Ct. D.C. 1992, U.S. Dist. Ct. Pa. 1994, U.S. Ct. Appeals (3rd cir.) 1994, U.S. Tax Ct. 1996. Tchr. Baldwin-Whitehall Pub. Schs./Cheltenham Pub. Schs., Pa., 1965-75; educator counsel duties, prin. cert., legal intern Fairfax County (Va.) Pub. Schs., 1979-94; of counsel, bd. treas., computer and career specialist, guidance and curriculum specialist, tchr. Thomas Jefferson H.S. for Sci. and Tech, Gov.s Sch. for Gifted, Alexandria, Va., 1987-94; computer/paralegal specialist Personnel Pool, Washington, 1987; rsch. assoc. Meade & Assocs., Fairfax, 1988, Akin, Gump, Strauss, Hauer & Feld, Washington, 1988; law clk. Fedn. of Tax Adminstrs., Washington, 1989, Beins, Axelrod, Osborne & Mooney, Washington, 1989-90; pvt. practice Washington and Pa., 1991—; rsch. assoc. Villanova U., 1994-96; legal/computer specialist Nat. Acad. Scis., Smithsonian Instn., Steptoe & Johnson, Akin, Gump, Strauss, Hauer & Feld, Office of Ind. Counsel; legal resource/rsch. specialist Dir. Testing and Evaluation, Walnut Hill Ctr., dir. grad. tax. program. Contbr. articles to profl. jours. Mem. Oakton Glen Homeowners Assn., 1978-97, Neighborhood Watch, 1978-97; mem., religious instr., usher Our Lady of Good Counsel Roman Cath. Ch., Vienna; judge moot ct. competitions Cath. U. Columbus Sch. Law, Washington, 1993-95; exec. treas. Thomas Jefferson H.S. for Sci. and Tech., also investment advisor and counsel computer tchr.; coord. VITA Tax Ctr, Phila., 1997—. Mem. ABA (tax sect. and legal edn. sect.), Fed. Bar Assn. (tax sect.), D.C. Bar Assn. (tax sects.), Pa. Bar Assn. (tax sects., taxation coms., chair edn. com. 1997). Avocations: reading, biking, swimming, gardening, genealogy/family history. Fax: (724) 942-3741. E-mail: taxlaw.sgi.net. Office: 306 Doubletree Dr Venetia PA 15367-1434

BRESLIN, EVALYNNE LOUISE WOOD-ROBERTSON, retired psychiatric nurse; b. Richmond, Ohio, July 7, 1931; d. Evan P. and Ada Augusta (Huscroft) Wood-Robertson; m. Donald Joseph Breslin, Jan. 30, 1954; children: Lisa Karen, Mark Nathaniel, Paul Andrew Scott. Diploma, Cleve. Met. Gen. Hosp., 1952; student, Case Western Res. U., 1953-55, Akron U.; HHD (hon.), London Inst. of Applied Rsch., 1973. Lic. RN, Ohio, Mass; RN, Ohio, Mass. Head nurse Cleve. Met. Gen. Hosp., 1952-55, Cleve. State Receiving Hosp., 1952-55; cons. mental illness and addictions Mass.; ret. *Founder of Triple Trouble at Westborough Massachusetts State Psychiatric Facility. Became member of the board, then volunteer to monitor care and physical facilities through the Alliance for the mentally ill. Taught English as Second Language first to Spanish speaking children, then to Vietnamese children in inner city Boston. For 20 years, took abandoned adolescents into her home, one at a time, both in Greater Boston and in London, England. They were given what they lacked, be it caring, food, clothing, discipline, shelter or all of these.* Bd. dirs. Triple Trouble; ret. vol. monitor state hosp. facilities Alliance for Mentally Ill; vol. nursing/psychiat. work with abandoned adolescents, 1968-89; vol. tour guide Barefoot Beach Preserve, Inc.; tchr. ESL, 1999—.

BRESLIN, JIMMY, columnist, author; b. Jamaica, N.Y., Oct. 17, 1929; s. James Earl and Frances (Curtin) B.; m. Rosemary Dattolico, Dec. 26, 1954 (dec. June 1981); children: James and Kevin (twins), Rosemary, Patrick, Kelly, Christopher.; m. Ronnie Myers Eldridge, Sept. 12, 1982; stepchildren: Daniel, Emily, Lucy Eldridge. Student, L.I. U., 1947-50. Syndicated columnist N.Y. Herald-Tribune, Paris Tribune, N.Y. Daily News, Newsday, L.I., N.Y., 1984—. Commentator Sta. WNBC-TV; host: (TV series) Jimmy Breslin's People, 1986; author: Can't Anybody Here Play This Game?, 1963, The Gang That Couldn't Shoot Straight, 1969, World Without End, Amen, 1973, How The Good Guys Finally Won, 1975, (with others) Forty-Four Caliber, 1978, Forsaking All Others, 1982, The World According to Breslin, 1984, Table Money, 1986, He Got Hungry and Forgot His Manners, 1988, Damon Runyon, 1991; drama: The Queen of the Leaky-Roof Circuit, 1988. N.Y.C. Candidate for pres. City Council, N.Y.C., 1969; del. Democratic Nat. Conv., 1972, 76. Recipient award for nat. reporting Sigma Delta Chi, 1964, Meyer Berger award for local reporting, 1964, N.Y. Reporters Assn. award reporting, 1964, Pulitzer Prize for commentary, 1986, George K. Polk award, 1986. Mem. Screen Actors Guild, AFTRA, Writers Guild Am. Office: Newsday 80-02 Kew Gardens Rd Kew Gardens NY 11415*

BRESLIN, MICHAEL JOSEPH, III, social services administrator, educator; b. Fountain Springs, Pa., Feb. 5, 1949; s. Michael Joseph Jr. and Barbara Ellin (Mellet) B. BS in Sociology, U. Scranton, 1971; MS in Adminstrn., Shippensburg (Pa.) U., 1984. Tchr. aide Selinsgrove (Pa.) Ctr., 1968, 69, 70; caseworker Northumberland County Children and Youth Agy., Sunbury, Pa., 1971-73; juvenile probation officer Northumberland County Juvenile Ct., 1973-74, supr., 1974-75, dir., 1976-87; dir. human svcs. Northumberland County Human Svcs., 1987-91; exec. dep. sec. Dept. Pub. Welfare, Harrisburg, Pa., 1992-95; v.p. Northwestern Corp., Harrisburg, Pa., 1995-97; sr. v.p. Northwestern Human Svcs., Harrisburg, 1997—; adminstr. Northumberland County Mental Health and Mental Retardation Program, 1984-87; mem. adj. faculty Susquehanna U., Selinsgrove, 1989-91; cons. Tng. & Mgmt. Systems, Gibsonia, Pa., 1983-85; mem. Youth Svcs. Tng. Ctr., 1986-90. Mem. adv. bd. White Deer Run Treatment Ctr., Allenwood, Pa., 1975-77; advisor Explorer Pres. Assn., Netami dist. Boy Scouts Am., 1980-81, tng. coord. Explorer program, 1982-86, scouting coord. Explorer Post 2312, 1986-91; coord. high sch. youth program St. Michael's Ch., Sunbury, 1981-91, pres. parish coun., 1989-91; vice chmn. SSS, Sunbury, 1982-89; chmn. Sunbury Govt. Study Commn., 1989-90; bd. dirs. Hemlock coun. Girls Scouts U.S.A., 1990-95; bd. dirs. Pa. Partnerships for Children, 1996—; mem. parish coun. St. Patrick Cathedral, Harrisburg, 1997—; chairperson Citizen Review Panel United Way Capitol Region, 1998—. Named Chief Probation Officer of Yr., Juvenile Ct. Judges Commn., Harrisburg, Pa., 1985; recipient Liberty Bell award Northumberland County Bar Assn., 1986, Meritorious Svc. award Pa. Foster Parents, 1988, affiliate award Pa. Assn. County Commrs., 1990, Citizen of Yr., City of Sunbury, 1992, Pres.'s award Pa. Assn. County Human Svc. Dirs., 1994, Disting. Svc. award Juvenile Detention Ctr. Adminstrs. Pa., 1994. Mem. Nat. Juvenile Ct. Svcs. Assn.

(regional rep. 1989-93), Nat. Coun. Juvenile and Family Ct. Judges (awards com.), Nat. Juvenile Detention Assn., Nat. Juvenile Ct. Svcs. Assn., Mental Health and Mental Retardation Program Adminstrs. Assn., Mental Health and Mental Retardation Adminstrs. Assn. Pa. (chmn. 1989-91). Republican. Home: 3838 Laraby Dr Harrisburg PA 17110-3641 Office: Northwestern Human Svcs 2205 Forest Hills Dr Ste 10 Harrisburg PA 17112-1005

BRESLOW, ESTHER MAY GREENBERG, biochemistry educator, researcher; b. N.Y.C., Dec. 23, 1931; d. Harry Daniel and Lillian (Solomon) Greenberg; m. Ronald Charles David Breslow, Sept. 4, 1955; children: Stephanie Ruth, Karen Ann. BS with distinction, Cornell U., 1953; MS in Biochemistry, NYU, 1955, PhD in Biochemistry, 1959; postgrad., Radcliffe Coll., 1954-55. Postdoctoral fellow Cornell U. Med. Coll., N.Y.C., 1959-61, rsch. assoc., 1961-64, asst. prof., 1964-72, assoc. prof., 1972-78, prof. biochemistry, 1978—, acting chmn. dept. biochemistry, 1992-95; mem. rev. panels NIH, Bethesda, Md., 1973-77, 94—, NSF, Bethesda, 1981-84. Mem. editorial bd. Jour. Biol. Chemistry, 1982-87, Internat. Jour. Peptide and Protein Rsch., 1981-97; contbr. articles to profl. jours. Mem. Englewood (N.J.) Bd. Health, 1986-94; mem. Dem. Mcpl. Com., Englewood, 1985-91. Eli Lilly fellow, 1954-55; USPHS fellow, 1959-61; NIH grantee, 1961—. Fellow AAAS; mem. Am. Soc. for Biochemistry and Molecular Biology, Am. Chem. Soc. (sec. div. biol. chemistry 1972-76), Harvey Soc., Sigma Xi. Home: 275 Broad Ave Englewood NJ 07631-4350 Office: Joan and Sanford I Will Med Coll Cornell U 1300 York Ave New York NY 10021-4805

BRESLOW, JAN LESLIE, scientist, educator, physician; b. N.Y.C., Feb. 28, 1943; s. Frank and Pearl (Feit) B.; m. Marilyn Ganon, June 25, 1965; children: Noah, Nicholas. AB, Columbia U., 1963, MA, 1964; MD, Harvard Med. Sch., 1968. Diplomate Am. Bd. Pediatrics. Intern in pediatrics, then jr. asst. resident Children's Hosp., Boston, 1968-70; staff assoc. Nat. Heart Lung and Blood Inst., Bethesda, Md., 1970-73; from instr. to assoc. prof. pediatrics Harvard Med. Sch., Boston, 1973-83; prof. Rockefeller U., N.Y.C., 1984-86, Frederick Henry Leonhardt prof., 1986—; dir. Lab. of Biochem. Genetics and Metabolism, Rockefeller U., N.Y.C., 1984—; sr. physician Rockefeller U. Hosp., N.Y.C., 1984—; mem. arteriosclerosis, hypertension and lipid metabolism adv. com. Nat. Heart, Lung and Blood Inst., 1986-90. Mem. editorial bd. Jour. Lipid Rsch., 1983-85, Arteriosclerosis and Thrombosis, 1984—, Genomics, 1987—; cons. editor Jour. Clin. Investigation, 1988-92, Jour. Biol. Chemistry, 1989-91. Served as surgeon USPHS, 1970-73. Eugene Higgins fellow Columbia U., 1963-64; recipient MERIT award Nat. Heart, Lung and Blood Inst., 1986-95, Heinrich Wieland prize, 1991, Pasarow Found. award for cardiovascular rsch., 1995. Mem. AAAS, Inst. Medicine (elected), NAS (elected), Am. Acad. Pediatr. (E. Mead Johnson award 1984), Am. Heart Assn. (coun. on arteriosclerosis 1974—, credentials com. 1984-86, award coms. 1984-87, chmn. award com. 1987-89, program com. 1986-89, exec. com. 1988—, N.Y.C. affiliate rsch. coun. 1985-87, chmn. 1987-89, chmn. policy com. 1989-91, chmn. nominating com. 1992-94, bd. dirs. 1987-90, 92—, Nat. Ctr. v.p. for rsch. 1994, bd. dirs. 1994-98, pres.-elect 1995, pres. 1996, past pres. 1997, Estab. Investigator award 1981-86, Basic Rsch. prize 1994 Nat. Ctr. Rsch. Com. (vice chmn. 1989-90, chmn. 1990-92), Rsch. program and Evaluation Com. (vice chmn. 1992-94, chmn. 1994—), Am. Soc. Clin. Nutrition, Soc. Pediat. Rsch., N.Y. Acad. Scis., Am. Fedn. Clin. Rsch., Am. Soc. Clin. Investigation (v.p. 1987-88), Internat. Arteriosclerosis Soc., Am. Soc. Biol. Chemists, Assn. Am. Physicians, Inst. of Medicine. Avocations: reading, skiing, hiking. Achievements include research in lipid and lipoprotein metabolism, genetic and environ. causes of arteriosclerosis, inborn errors of metabolism. Office: Rockefeller U Hosp 1230 York Ave New York NY 10021-6307

BRESLOW, LESTER, physician, educator; b. Bismarck, N.D., Mar. 17, 1915; s. Joseph and Mayme (Danziger) B.; children: Norman, Jack, Stephen; m. Devra J.R. Miller, 1967. BA, U. Minn., 1935, MD, 1938, MPH, 1941, DSc (hon.), 1988. Diplomate Am. Bd. Preventive Medicine and Public Health. Intern USPHS Hosp., Stapleton, N.Y., 1938-40; dist. health officer Minn. Dept. Health, 1941-43; preventive medicine officer U.S. Army, 1943-45; chief bur. chronic diseases Calif. Dept. Public Health, Berkeley, 1946-60; chief divsn. preventive medicine Calif. Dept. Public Health, 1960-65, dir. dept., 1965-68; lectr. U. Calif. Sch. Pub. Health, Berkeley, 1950-68; prof. pub. health UCLA Sch. Pub. Health, 1968—, chmn. dept. preventive medicine and social medicine, 1969-72, dean, 1972-80, mem. divsn. cancer control, 1980—, dir. health promotion ctr., 1988-91, dean, prof. emeritus, 1991—; dir. study Pres.'s Commn. Health Needs of Nation, 1952; cons. Nat. Cancer Inst., 1981—, chmn. bd. sci. counsellors div. cancer prevention and control, 1982-84; cons. Office of Technology Assessment, Nat. Heart, Lung, Blood Inst., 1977; chmn. Nat. Com. on Vital and Health Stats., 1979-81; mem. U.S.-China Health Scis. Com., Dept. HHS, 1982. Author med. publs.; editor: Ann. Rev. Pub. Health, 1979-90; editorial cons. Preventive Medicine, other med. and pub. health jours. Capt. U.S. Army, 1943-45. Decorated Bronze Star; recipient Lasker award Lasker Found., 1960, Dana award Dana Found., 1988, Healthtrac prize Healthtrac Found., 1995, Lienhard award Inst. Medicine, 1997. Fellow ACP, AAAS, Am. Coll. Preventive Medicine (Disting. service award 1976); mem. APHA (past pres., Sedgwick medal 1977), Am. Heart Assn. (fellow epidemiology sect.), Public Health Cancer Assn. (past pres.), Am. Epidemiol. Soc., Internat. Epidemiol. Assn. (past pres.), Am. Cancer Soc. (nat. dir., Calif. dir., chmn. adv. com. on research etiology), Assn. Schs. Public Health (pres. 1973-74), Inst. Medicine, Nat. Acad. Scis. (council 1978-80, chmn. bd. health promotion and disease prevention 1980-82). Home: 10926 Verano Rd Los Angeles CA 90077-2224

BRESLOW, MARILYN GANON, portfolio manager; b. Cleve., Apr. 23, 1944; d. Joseph M. and Edith (Rubin) Ganon; m. Jan L. Breslow, June 27, 1965; children: Noah J., Nicholas M. BA, Barnard Coll., 1965; MBA, Harvard U., 1970. Market rsch. analyst Polaroid Corp., Cambridge, Mass., 1965-68, project cons., 1973-78, bldg. W-4 mgr., 1978-80, dir. mktg. svcs., 1980-83; cons. Peat, Marwick, Mitchell & Co., Washington, 1970-71; assoc. ICF, Inc., Washington, 1971-73; cons. Brookline, Mass., 1983-84; v.p. Dillon, Read & Co., Inc., N.Y.C., 1984-90; gen. ptnr. Concord Ptnrs., 1984-90; portfolio mgr., analyst, pres. W.P. Stewart & Co. Ltd., Inc., N.Y.C., 1990—; also pres. and bd. dirs. W.P. Stewart & Co. Growth Fund, Inc., N.Y.C.; bd. dirs. Alteon, Inc., Ramsey, N.J. Mem. N.Y. Soc. Security Analysts, IEEE. Avocations: piano, skiing, gardening. Home: 10 Horseguard Ln Scarsdale NY 10583-2311

BRESLOW, NORMAN EDWARD, biostatistics educator, researcher; b. Mpls., Feb. 21, 1941; s. Lester and Alice Jane (Philp) B.; m. Gayle Marguerite Bramwell, Sept. 7, 1963; children: Lauren Louise, Sara Jo. BA, Reed Coll., 1962; PhD, Stanford U., 1967. Trainee Stanford U., 1965-67; vis. research worker London Sch. Hygiene, 1967-68; instr. U. Wash., Seattle, 1968-69, asst. prof., 1969-72, assoc. prof., 1972-76, prof., 1976—, chmn. dept. biostats., 1983-93; statistician Internat. Agy. Research Cancer, Lyon, France, 1972-74; mem. Hutchinson Cancer Ctr., Seattle, 1982—; statistician Nat. Wilms' Tumor Study, 1969—; cons. Internat. Agy. Research Cancer, Lyon, 1978-79, Stats. and Epidemiology Research Corp., Seattle, 1980—; assoc. prof. U. Geneva, 1994—. Recipient Spiegelman Gold medal APHA, 1978, Preventive Oncology Acad.award, NIH, 1978-83, Snedecor award Com. of Pres.'s on Statis. Socs., 1995, R.A. Fisher lectr. and award, 1995; rsch. grantee NIH, 1984—; sr. U.S. Scientist, Alexander Humboldt Found., Fed. Republic of Germany, 1982; sr. Internat. fellowship Fogarty Ctr., 1990. Fellow AAAS, Am. Statis Assn. (com. on fellows 1996—), Royal Statis. Soc.; mem. Internat. Statis. Inst., Inst. Medicine-Nat. Acad. Scis., Internat. Biometric Soc. (regional com. 1975-78, coun. 1994—). Avocations: ski mountaineering, hiking, bicycling. Office: Univ of Wash Dept Biostatistics Seattle WA 98195-7232

BRESLOW, RONALD CHARLES, chemist, educator; b. Rahway, N.J., Mar. 14, 1931; s. Alexander E. and Gladys (Fellows) B.; m. Esther Greenberg, Sept. 7, 1955; children: Stephanie, Karen. A.B. summa cum laude, Harvard, 1952, M.A., 1953, Ph.D., 1955. NRC fellow Cambridge (Eng.) U., 1955-56; mem. faculty Columbia, 1956—, prof. chemistry, 1962-66, S.L. Mitchell prof., 1966—; univ. prof., 1992—; cons. to industry, 1958—; mem. medicinal chemistry panel NIH, 1964—; mem. adv. panel on chemistry NSF, 1971—; mem. sci. adv. com. Gen. Motors Corp., 1982—; A.R. Todd vis. prof. Cambridge U., 1982. Editor: Benjamin, Inc., 1962—; author: Organic Reaction Mechanisms, 1965, 2d edit., 1969; also articles.; mem. editl. bd. Organic Syntheses, 1964—, Jour. Organic Chemistry, 1969—, Jour. Bioorganic Chemistry, 1972—, Tetrahedron, 1975—, Tetrahedron Letters, 1975—, Proc. of Nat. Acad. Scis., 1984—. Trustee Rockefeller U., 1981—; bd. sci. advisers Alfred P. Sloan Found., 1978-85. Recipient Fresenius award Phi Lambda Upsilon, 1966, Mark Van Doren award Columbia, 1969, Roussel prize, 1978, Gt. Tchr. award Columbia U., 1981, T.W. Richards medal, 1984, A.C. Cope award, 1987, G.W. Kenner award U. Liverpool, Eng., 1988, Paracelsus prize Swiss Chem. Soc., 1990, Arthur Day award, 1990, Nat. Medal of Sci. NSF, 1991, U.S. Nat. medal of sci., 1991, Paraselsus Awd., 1990, New Swiss Chem. Soc.; Centenary lectr. London Chem. Soc., 1972. Fellow Am. Acad. Arts and Scis., Indian Acad. Scis.; mem. Am. Philos. Soc. (coun. 1987—), NAS (chmn. chemistry divsn. 1974-77, award in chemistry 1989), Am. Chem. Soc. (Pure Chemistry award 1966, Baekeland medal 1969, chmn. divsn. organic chemistry 1970, Harrison Howe award 1974, Remsen award 1977, J.F. Norris award 1980, N.Y. sect. Nichols medal 1989, pres.-elect 1995-96, pres. 1996, Priestley medal 1999), New Swiss Chem. Soc. (Paracelsus award 1990), Royal Soc. Chemistry (London)(hon.), Phi Beta Kappa (first marshall 1952). Home: 275 Broad Ave Englewood NJ 07631-4350 Office: Columbia U Dept Chemistry 116th St & Broadway New York NY 10027

BRESNAHAN, JAMES FRANCIS, medical ethics educator; b. Springfield, Mass., Dec. 28, 1926; s. James Francis and Margaret Anna (Riley) B. AB, Coll. Holy Cross, 1947; MA, Weston Coll, 1953, STL, 1960; JD, Harvard U., 1954, LLM, 1955; PhD, Yale U., 1972. Bar: Mass. 1955, U.S. Dist. Ct. Mass. 1975; joined S.J., Roman Cath. Ch., 1949. Tchr. Cheverus H.S., Portland, Maine, 1955-56; asst. prof. religious studies Fairfield U., 1962-66, 69-70; vis. prof. ethics Weston Coll., 1971-72; assoc. prof. religious studies and philosophy Regis U., 1972-74; prof. ethics Jesuit Sch. Theology in Chgo., 1975-81; vis. lectr. in med. ethics Northwestern U. Med. Sch., Chgo., 1978-80; vis. lectr. in legal ethics Northwestern U. Law Sch., Chgo., 1979; co-dir. ethics program Northwestern U. Med. Sch., Chgo., 1980-96, prof. med. ethics and humanities, clin. medicine, 1989-97, prof. emeritus, 1997—; ethics cons. Northwestern Meml. Hosp., 1982—; treas. Chgo. Clin. Ethics Programs, 1989-90, pres.-elect, 1990-91, pres. 1991-92. Mem. adv. com. Jour. of Law and Religion; mem. editl. bd. Cambridge Quar. for Health Care Ethics, Annals of Health Law; contbr. articles to profl. jours. Mem. com. to draft code for profl. conduct Canon Law Soc. Am., 1978-79. Fellow Soc. Values in Higher Edn.; mem. AAUP (v.p. chpt. 1973-74), Soc. Christian Ethics (convenor ethics and law task force 1979-80, dir. 1981-85), Coun. on Religion and Law, Ill. Coalition Against Death Penalty, Am. Soc. Law, Medicine and Ethics, Am. Soc. for Bioethics and Humanities, Inst. Medicine Chgo. Home: Jesuit Residence 2058 N Clark St Chicago IL 60614-4713 Office: Northwestern U Med Sch Ward Bldg 3-130 303 E Chicago Ave Chicago IL 60611-3072

BRESNAHAN, THOMAS J., radio station executive; m. Sandy Bresnahan; 4 children. Student, Prince Georges Coll., Md. Account exec. Sta. WWDC-AM/FM, 1974-76; account exec. Sta. WLTT-FM, 1976-78, local sales mgr., 1978-82, gen. sales mgr., 1982-83; v.p., gen. mgr. Sta. KFKF-AM/FM, Kansas City, Kans., 1983-88; pres., gen. mgr. Sta. WMAL, Washington, 1988—. Past mem. USMC. Office: WMAL 4400 Jenifer St NW Ste 400 Washington DC 20015-2183*

BRESS, MICHAEL E., retired lawyer; b. Mpls., Aug. 23, 1933; s. Michael J. and Anna (Tema) B.; m. Grace Billings, June 3, 1966; 1 child, Anne Ruth. BA, U. Minn., 1954, LLB, 1957. Bar: N.Y. 1958, Minn. 1959. Assoc. Donovan Leisure Newton & Irvine, N.Y.C., 1957-59, Dorsey & Whitney LLP, Mpls., 1959-64; ptnr. Dorsey & Whitney LPP, Mpls., 1964-91, of counsel, 1992-97, ret., 1998. Mem. ABA, Minn. Bar Assn., Hennepin County Bar Assn., Phi Beta Kappa. Home: 2007 W Franklin Ave Minneapolis MN 55405-2422

BRESSAN, PAUL LOUIS, lawyer; b. Rockville Centre, N.Y., June 15, 1947; s. Louis Charles Bressan and Nance Elizabeth Batteley. BA cum laude, Fordham Coll., 1969; JD, Columbia U., 1975. Bar: N.Y. 1976, Calif. 1987, U.S. Dist. Ct. (so., ea. and no. dists.) N.Y. 1976, U.S. Dist. Ct. (no. and ctrl. dists.) Calif. 1987, U.S. Ct. Appeals (2d cir.) 1980, U.S. Supreme Ct. 1980, U.S. Ct. Appeals (1st and 4th cirs.) 1981, U.S. Ct. Appeals (11th cir.) 1982, U.S. Ct. Appeals (9th cir.) 1987, U.S Ct. Appeals (7th cir.) 1991, U.S. Dist. Ct. (ea. dist.) Calif. 1995; U.S. Dist. Ct. (so. dist.) Calif. 1997. Assoc. Kelley, Drye & Warren, N.Y.C., 1975-84; ptnr. Kelley, Drye & Warren, N.Y.C. and Los Angeles, 1984—. Served to lt. USNR, 1971-72. Named One of Outstanding Coll. Athletes of Am., 1969; Harlan Fiske Stone scholar Columbia Law Sch. Mem. ABA, Calif. Bar Assn., Phi Beta Kappa. Republican. Roman Catholic. Office: Kelley Drye & Warren LLP 777 S Figueroa St Ste 2700 Los Angeles CA 90017-5825

BRESSAN, ROBERT RALPH, accountant; b. Yonkers, N.Y., Feb. 8, 1945; s. Alfred D. and Antionette (Desivo) B.; m. Florence L. Vigna, June 9, 1968 (dec.); children: Anne Marie, Robert A., Tiffany L. BBA in Acctg., Iona Coll., 1967. CPA, Colo.; cert. tax profl. Am. Inst. Tax Studies. Staff to sr. Coopers & Lybrand, N.Y.C., 1967-70; sr. to audit mgr. Fox & Co., Colorado Springs, 1970-80; ptnr., owner Robert R. Bressan, Colorado Springs, 1980-98, Farmer, Bressan & Co, CPA, LLC (formerly Robert R. Bressan), 1998—; mem. exec. com. GAO Intergovtl. Audit Forum. Mem. charity rev. com. BBB. Mem. AICPA, Sertoma, Inst. Mgmt. Accts., Govtl. Fin. Officers Assn., Colo. Govtl. Fin. Officers, Nat. Assn. Counties. Avocations: coins, golf, dancing. Office: 829 N Circle Dr Ste 214 Colorado Springs CO 80909-5008

BRESSLER, BARRY E., lawyer; b. Phila., Apr. 7, 1947; s. Joseph and Shirley M. (Eiseman) B.; m. Risé Sharon Cohen, June 14, 1970 (dec.); children: Allison Ivy, Michelle Amy. AB, Franklin and Marshall Coll., Lancaster, Pa., 1968; JD, U. Pa., 1971. Bar: Pa. 1971, U.S. Dist. Ct. (ea. dist.) Pa. 1973, U.S. Ct. Appeals (3d cir.) 1977, U.S. Supreme Ct. 1988, U.S. Dist. Ct. (mid. dist.) Pa. 1990. Law clk. to judge Superior Ct. Pa., Phila., 1971-73; assoc. Meltzer & Schiffrin, Phila., 1973-79, ptnr., 1979-86; ptnr. Fox, Rothschild, O'Brien & Frankel, Phila., 1987-88; mem., sr. lawyer real estate litigation & creditors' rights Pelino & Lentz, P.C., Phila., 1988—; coadj. instr. landlord-tenant law Delaware County C.C., Media, Pa., 1985-96, Montgomery County C.C., Blue Bell, Pa., 1987—. V.p. English Ceramic Study Group, Phila.; v.p., sec. Temple Sinai, Dresher, Pa., 1991-97; mem. Leadership, Inc., Phila. Mem. ABA (litigation sect.), Pa. Bar Assn. (corp. banking and bus. sect.), Phila. Bar Assn. (real property sect.), Bankruptcy Conf. Ea. Dist. Pa. (treas.), Am. Arbitration Assn. Republican. Jewish. Avocations: tennis, ceramics, bridge. Office: Pelino & Lentz PC One Liberty Pl 32d Fl 1650 Market St Fl 32 Philadelphia PA 19103-7393

BRESSLER, BERNARD, lawyer; b. N.Y.C., Jan. 2, 1928; s. Morris and Masha (Roitman) B.; m. Teresa Stern, June 25, 1950; children: Lisa, Jeanette. BA, Rutgers U., 1949; LLB summa cum laude, Harvard U., 1952. Bar: N.Y. 1953, N.J. 1977. Atty. firm Greenman, Shea, Sandomire & Zimet, N.Y.C., 1952-60; ptnr. Bressler, Amery & Ross, N.Y.C., 1960—, Florham Park, N.J., 1981—; sec., bd. dirs. Gradco Systems Inc.; dir., chmn. bd. N.J. Pub. Interest Law Ctr., 1996—. Author: (with others) Tax Annotations Nichols Ency. Forms, 1954-59; Editor: (with B. Meislin) New York Lawyers Manual, 1954, Harvard Law Rev., vol. 65. Campaign dir. Summit (N.J.) United Jewish Appeal, 1957-60; chmn. Summit Democrat Club, 1957; trustee Summit Civic Found., 1958-65; chmn. Summit Area United Negro Coll. Fund, 1979-92. With USNR, 1945-46. Club: Lotos (N.Y.C.), Park Ave. Club (N.J.). Home: 3 Kimberwick Ct Morristown NJ 07960-6993 Office: 17 State St New York NY 10004-1501 also: 325 Columbia Tpke Florham Park NJ 07932-1212

BRESSLER, MARCUS N., consulting engineer; b. Havana, Cuba, July 31, 1929; came to U.S., 1942; s. Isaac and Augustine (Draiman) B.; m. Sondra Kipnes, Nov. 7, 1954; children: Eric L., Lisa A., Karen J. Lee. B of Mech. Engring., Cornell U., 1952; MSME, Case Inst. Tech., 1960. Registered profl. engr., Ohio, Tenn. Stress analysis engr. The Babcock & Wilcox Co., Barberton, Ohio, 1955-66; design engr. Lenape Forge, West Chester, Pa., 1966-70; mgr., product design and devel. engr. Taylor Forge, Cicero, Ill., 1970-71; supr. codes, standards and materials TVA, Knoxville, 1971-79; sr. engring. specialist TVA, 1979-88; pres. M.N. Bressler, PE, Inc., Knoxville, 1988—. Served to 1st lt. U.S. Army, 1952-54, capt. USAR, 1957. Fellow ASME (mem. boiler and pressure vessel main com., bd. conformity assessment, bd. nuc. codes and stds., Century Medallion 1980, Bernard F. Langer Nuc. Codes and Stds. award 1992, J. Hall Taylor medal for pressure tech. codes and stds. outstanding contbns. 1996). Home and Office: M N Bressler PE Inc 829 Chateaugay Rd Knoxville TN 37923-2017

BRESSLER, RICHARD J., communications company executive; married; two children. Grad. summa cum laude, Adelphi Coll., 1979. CPA. Ptnr. Ernst & Young, Inc., 1979-88; from asst. controller to exec. v.p., CFO Time Warner, Inc., N.Y.C., 1988—. bd. dirs. Prep for Prep, Outward Bound; mem. Chase Nat. Adv. Bd., CFO Adv. Coun.; trustee Citizen's Budget Commn. Mem. Am. Inst. CPAs, N.Y. State Soc. Cert. CPAs. Office: Time Warner Bldg 75 Rockefeller Plz New York NY 10019-6990*

BREST, MARTIN, film director; b. Bronx, N.Y., 1951. Ed., NYU Film Sch. Dir. films Hot Tomorrows, 1977, Going in Style, 1979, Beverly Hills Cop, 1984; producer, dir. Midnight Run, 1988, Scent of a Woman, 1992; prodr. Josh and S.A.M., 1993. Mem. Dirs. Guild Am. Office: care Creative Artists Agy 1888 Century Park E Ste 1400 Los Angeles CA 90067-1718 Office: Creative Artist Agy 9830 Wilshire Blvd Beverly Hills CA 90212-1804*

BREST, PAUL A., law educator; b. Jacksonville, Fla., Aug. 9, 1940; s. Alexander and Mia (Deutsch) B.; m. Iris Lang, June 17, 1962; children: Hilary, Jeremy. AB, Swarthmore Coll., 1962; JD, Harvard U., 1965; LLD (hon.), Northeastern U., 1980, Swarthmore Coll., 1991. Bar: N.Y. 1966. Law clk. to Hon. Bailey Aldrich U.S. Ct. Appeals (1st cir.), Boston, 1965-66; atty. NAACP Legal Def. Fund, Jackson, Miss., 1966-68; law clk. Justice John Harlan, U.S. Supreme Ct., 1968-69; prof. law Stanford U., 1969—, Kenneth and Harle Montgomery Prof. pub. interest law, Richard E. Lang prof. and dean, 1987-99. Author: Processes of Constitutional Decisionmaking, 1992. Mem. Am. Acad. Arts and Scis. Home: 814 Tolman Dr Palo Alto CA 94305-1026 Office: Stanford U Sch Law 559 Nathan Abbott Way Stanford CA 94305-8610

BRESTEL, MARY BETH, librarian; b. Cin., Feb. 5, 1952; d. John Wesley and Laura Alice (Knoop) Seay; m. Michael Charles Brestel, Aug. 3, 1974; 1 child, Rebecca Michelle. BS, U. Cin., 1974; MLS, U. Ky., 1984. Libr. asst. history and lit. dept. Pub. Libr. Cin. and Hamilton County, 1974-78, children's asst. Pleasant Ridge br., 1978-81, children's asst. Westwood br., 1981-84, reference libr. sci. and tech. dept., 1984-90, 1st asst. sci. and tech. dept., 1990-92, dept. head, 1992—. Mem. United Methodist Ch. Office: Pub Libr Cin and Hamilton County Sci and Tech Dept 800 Vine St Cincinnati OH 45202-2009

BRET, DONNA LEE, elementary education educator; b. Pottsville, Pa., Dec. 18, 1950; d. S. Allen and Georgene Katherine (Heiser) Zimmerman; m. Donald Louis Bret, Oct. 11, 1969; 1 child, Thomas Donald. AA, Glendale C.C., 1988; BEd, Ariz. State U., 1990, MEd, 1995. Cert. elem., ESL tchr., Ariz. Kindergarten tchr. Glendale (Ariz.) Elem. Dist., 1991-92, 1st grade ESL tchr., 1992-93, multi-age ESL tchr., 1993—; rep. Glendale Elem. Assn., 1998-99. Mem. NEA, Ariz. State U. Alumni Assn., Bilingual Club. Office: Glendale Elem Sch Dist 7301 N 58th Ave Glendale AZ 85301-1893

BRETHAUER, WILLIAM RUSSELL, JR., claim investigator; b. Pitts., Apr. 5, 1953; s. William Russell and Cecelia Helen Brethauer; m. Barbara L. Summers, Mar. 8, 1980; children: Laura Diane, Stacey Lynn. BA magna cum laude, Thiel Coll., 1975; grad., Inst. Paralegal Tng., Phila., 1976. Cert. paralegal, casualty-property claim law assoc. Claim rep. St. Paul Cos. Inc., Ft. Washington, Pa., 1977-80; claim supr. St. Paul Cos. Inc., San Jose, 1980-82, St. Paul, 1982-84; spl. claim investigator St. Paul Cos. Inc., Orlando, Fla., 1984—; intern WQED-TV, Pitts., 1974; mem. Fla. adv. com. arson prevention, Maitland, 1984—. Author: (novel) Boardwalk, 1991, (book) If I Were A Horse, They'd Shoot Me, 1993, My Enemies, Small Devils, 1993, Insurance Fraud: Deceit & Ingenuity, 1992; asst. prodr.: (multi-media program) When to Say When, 1974. Libertarian. Avocations: whitewater rafting, windsurfing, rollerblading, skiing, travel. Home and Office: PO Box 621329 Oviedo FL 32762-1329

BRETHERTON, FRANCIS P., atmospheric and oceanic sciences educator. Prof. atmospheric and oceanic scis., dir. Space Sci. and Engring. Ctr., U. Wis., Madison, Wis., 1988—. Recipient Cleveland Abbe Award for Distinguished Service to Atmospheric Sciences, Am. Meteorological Assn., 1994. Office: U Wis Space Sci & Engring Ctr 1225 W Dayton St Madison WI 53706-1612*

BRETT, ARTHUR CUSHMAN, JR., banker; b. Bronxville, N.Y., Mar. 23, 1928; s. Arthur Cushman and Mary Kathryn (Clark) B.; m. Mary Elizabeth Cunliffe, Aug. 21, 1954; children: Margaret Brett Uzarski, Catherine Brett Main, John, Patricia, Matthew. B.S., Fordham U., 1953; M.B.A., NYU, 1959. Asst. v.p. Bowery Savs. Bank, N.Y.C., 1950-68; instl. registered rep. Salomon Bros., N.Y.C., 1968-71, 73-75, Blyth Eastman Dillon, Boston, 1971-73; v.p. Mut. Am. Life Ins. Co., N.Y.C., 1975-78; v.p. investments, sec. East River Savs. Bank, N.Y.C., 1978-80; sr. v.p., treas., chief investment officer Apple Bank for Savs., N.Y.C., 1980-92. Mem. investment com. Social Sci. Rsch. Coun., 1976-86, NYU Fed. Credit Union, 1983-89. Mem. N.Y. Soc. Security Analysts, Nat. Assn. Bus. Economists. Roman Catholic. Home: 2514 Redding Rd Fairfield CT 06430-1745 also: 441 Ocean Ave Stratford CT 06615-7829

BRETT, GEORGE HOWARD, baseball executive, former professional baseball player; b. Glen Dale, W.Va., May 15, 1953; s. Jack Francis and Ethel (Hansen) B. Student, Longview C.C., Mo., El Camino Coll., Torrance, Calif. Former third baseman Kansas City (Mo.) Royals Profl. Baseball Team, v.p. baseball ops. Named Am. League batting champion, 1976, 80, 90, Am. League Most Valuable Player, 1980; player Am. League All-Star Game, 1976-88; Inductee Baseball Hall of Fame, Cooperstown, N.Y., 1999. Address: care Kansas City Royals PO Box 419969 Kansas City MO 64141-6969*

BRETT, GEORGE WENDELL, retired geologist, philatelist; b. Spirit Lake, Iowa, May 30, 1912; s. John Franklin and Jessie Cary (Cummings) B.; m. Louise Schindler, 1941 (div. 1942). BA, U. Chgo., 1953, MS, 1961. Statistician U.S. Dept. Agr., Spirit Lake, Iowa, 1933; clk. Dickinson County Corn-Hog Control Assn., Spirit Lake, 1934-36; ry. postal clk. U.S. P.O. Dept., on trains Iowa, Ill., Wis., Chgo. terminal, 1936-42; fiscal acctg. clk. U.S. Dept. of Navy, Coco Solo, Canal Zone, Republic of Panama, 1942-45, 46-49; geologist U.S. Geol. Survey, Washington, 1953-72, geologist, cons., 1976-79, ret., 1979—. Author: The Giori Press, 1961, Printing Methods and Techniques, 1985; contbr. several hundred published articles to jours. in field, 1930—. With USN, 1945-46. Recipient Nat. Merit award Assoc. Stamp Clubs of Southeastern Pa. and Del., 1964, Phoenix award Ariz. Fed. of Stamp Clubs, Phoenix, 1964, Scroll of Honor, U.S. Geol. Survey, Washington, 1972, Luff award Am. Philatelic Soc., 1978, Writers Hall of Fame, Unit 30, Am. Philatelic Soc., 1979, Meritorious Svc. award The Philatelic Found., N.Y.C., 1981, U.S. Philatelic Rsch. award The Cryer Found., 1983, Lichtenstein Meml. award Collector's Club of N.Y., 1982, McCoy award Am. Philatelic Congress, 1989, Dist. Philatelist award U.S. Philatelic Classics Soc., 1991, Dorothy Colby Meml. award Am. Philatelic Congress, 1993. Mem. Bur. Issues Assn. (Hopkinson Meml. award 1954, 58, 92, spl. award for 20 yrs. svc. as officer 1974, Southgate Disting. Philatelist award, 1980). Republican. Avocations: studying postage stamp prodn., travel, photography, mountain climbing. Home: 2412 Lincoln Ave Spirit Lake IA 51360-7032

BRETT, JAMES CLARENCE, retired journalism educator; b. Watertown, N.Y., July 28, 1931; s. Clarence Richard and Justina Leone (Cleland) B. BA, Notre Dame U., 1953. With Watertown Daily Times, 1955-71, author series on Frederick Exley, 1968; adj. assoc. prof. Oswego (N.Y.) State U. Coll., 1970-71, asst. prof., 1971-96; ret., 1996; mem. organizing com. SUNY Colls. in the North Country, Fort Drum, Watertown, N.Y., 1985; organizer, dir. student internship program New York Times, 1972. Pvt. first class U.S. Army, 1953-55. Mem. Royal Hort. Soc., Am. Hort. Soc., Jefferson County Hist. Soc., Master Gardeners Am., Am. Legion. Republican. Roman Catholic. Avocations: gardening, traveling, reading. Home and Office: 146 Ward St Watertown NY 13601-4616

BRETT, JAN CHURCHILL, illustrator, author; b. Hingham, Mass., Dec. 1, 1949; d. George and Jean (Thaxter) B.; m. Daniel Bowler, Feb. 27, 1970 (div. 1979); 1 child, Lia; m. Joseph Hearne, Aug. 18, 1980. Student, Colby Jr. Coll., 1968-69, Boston Mus. Fine Arts Sch., 1970; DHL (hon.), Fitchburg State Coll., 1996. Author, illustrator: Fritz and the Beautiful Horses, 1981 (Parent's Choice award Parents' Choice Found., 1981), Good Luck Sneakers, 1981, Annie and the Wild Animals, 1985, The First Dog, 1988, Beauty and the Beast, 1989, The Wild Christmas Reindeer, 1990, The Twelve Days of Christmas, 1990, The Mitten, 1990, Goldilocks and the Three Bears, 1990, The Owl and the Pussycat, 1991, Berlioz the Bear, 1991, The Trouble with Trolls, 1992, Christmas Trolls, 1993, Town Mouse, Country Mouse, 1994, Armadillo Rodeo, 1995, Comet's Nine Lives, 1996, The Hat, 1997 (Am. Booksellers Abby award 1998), The Night Before Christmas, 1998, The Gingerbread Baby, 1999; illustrator: Woodland Crossings, 1978, Inside A Sand Castle and Other Secrets, 1979, The Secret Clocks Time Senses of Living Things, 1979, St. Patrick's Day in the Morning, 1980 (Parent's Choice award Parents' Choice Found. 1981), Young Melvin and Bulger, 1981, In the Castle of the Cats, 1981, Some Birds Have Funny Names, 1981 (Amb. Honor award English Speaking Union U.S. 1983), I Can Fly, 1981, Prayer, 1983, The Valentine Bears, 1983, Some Plants Have Funny Names, 1983, Where Are All the Kittens, 1984, Old Devil Is Waiting, 1985, The Mother's Day Mice, 1985, Scary, Scary Halloween, 1986, Noelle of the Nutcracker, 1986, The Enchanted Book, 1987, Happy Birthday, Dear Duck, 1988. Overseer Boston Symphony Orchestra; trustee Thayer Acad., Braintree, Mass. Mem. Nat. Soc. Colonial Dames Am., Chilbin Club. Office: 132 Pleasant St Norwell MA 02061-2523

BRETT, JOHN BRENDAN, JR., corporate advertising and public relations executive; b. Jacksonville, Fla., Mar. 28, 1944; s. John Brendan and Vera Mae (Locke) B.; m. Alyene Maybeth Wales, Apr. 30, 1966; children: Heather Allyson, Sean Timothy. Student, U. Md., 1964-65, U. So. Miss., 1965-66; BS in Advt., U. Fla., 1969. Advt. supr. Armstrong Cork Co. Lancaster, Pa., 1969-72; mgr. advt. K-D Mfg. Co., Lancaster, 1972-75; dir. mktg. communications Brodart Inc., Williamsport, Pa., 1975-78; mktg. communications supr. E.I. duPont de Nemours & Co., Wilmington, Del., 1978-80, group mgr. mktg. communications, carpet fibers, 1980-85, mgr. corp. advt., 1985-87, group mgr. mktg. com. electronics, 1987-91, sr. cons., external affairs, 1991-92, mgr., mkt. comm. and pub. affairs Sontara Tech./Dupont Nonwovens, 1992—; mem. Idea98 & Idea2001 com. INDA Nonwovens Assn., 1997—; mem. advt. adv. council U. Fla., 1984-87; chmn. Country Hills Archtl. com., 1994—. Vice chmn. Del. all-star football game com. Del. Found. for Retarded Children, 1982-83, chmn., 1984, trustee, 1989-92; bd. govs. Automotive Advertisers Council, 1975; mem. editl. sounding bd. Advertising Age mag., 1985-87. Mem. vestry St. Thomas Episc. Ch., 1974-75, St. David's Episc. Ch., Wilmington, 1989-92, sr. warden, 1991-92; treas. N.E. Missionary Convocation, Diocese of Middle Tenn., Diocesesan Conv. delegate, 1995; chmn. bldg. com. Country Hills Homeowners Assn., 1994—; mem. INDA IDEA '98 & IDEA2000 expn. coms., 1996-99; chmn. bldg. com. Country Hills Homeowners Assn., 1994—; judge Effie awards, 1986. Served with USAF, 1963-66, honorable discharge. Recipient outstanding advt. campaign award Am. Bus. Press/Bus.-Profl. Advt. Assn., 1974. Mem. Assn. Nat. Advertisers (corp. advt. com. 1985-86). Avocations: outdoor photography, gardening, antique autos. Home: 119 Spy Glass Way Hendersonville TN 37075-8550 Office: DuPont Co 1002 Industrial Rd Old Hickory TN 37138-3696

BRETT, MAUVICE WINSLOW, retired educational administrator, consultant; b. Xenia, Ohio, May 24, 1924; d. Perle Alonzo and Lurena Belle (Hamilton) W.; m. John Woodrow Brett, Sept. 20, 1943; children: Diane, John, Anthony, Loretta. BS in Psychology, Howard U., 1944, MS in Psychology, 1946; PhD in English, Union Grad. Sch., Cin., 1978. Tchr. English, Hertford County Schs., Winton, N.C., 1959-76, ednl. supr., 1977-80, dir. personnel, 1981-87, asst. supt., 1988-89; ret., 1989; cons. N.C. Coun. English Tchrs., Charlotte, 1979; com. mem. quality assurance program N.C. State Dept. Pub. Instn., Raleigh, 1980-81; bd. visitors Chowan Coll., 1991-97; mem. found. bd. Roanoke-Chowan C.C., 1991-97; adj. prof. psychology Roanoke-Chowan C.C., 1992-97, Chowan Coll., 1993-97, East Carolina U., 1994-97. Sec. Hertford County Arts Coun., 1977; mem. Hertford County 400th Anniversary Com., 1982-83; trustee Elizabeth City State U., 1983-91. Mem. N.C. Assn. Sch. Adminstrs. (dist. rep.), Am. Assn. Sch. Adminstrs., N.C. ASCD, Bus. and Profl. Women's Club, Rotary, Delta Sigma Theta. Home: RR 2 Box 260A Ahoskie NC 27910-9563 Office: Chowan Coll PO Box 1848 Murfreesboro NC 27855

BRETT, NANCY HELÉNE, artist. BFA, Wayne State U., 1969; MFA, Cranbrook Acad. of Art, 1972. One-woman shows include Gallery Seven, Detroit, 1976, Ericson Gallery, N.Y.C., 1980, Harm Bouckaert Gallery, N.Y.C., 1982, Hillwood Art Mus., C.W.Post, Long Island U., N.Y., 1987, L'Ecole Gallery, N.Y.C., Victoria Munroe Gallery, N.Y.C., 1989, 91, 93, Victoria Munroe Fine Art, N.Y.C, 1993, Lake George Arts Project, N.Y., 1996, The Painting Ctr., N.Y.C., 1997, Cranbrook Art Mus., 1998, Hyde Collection Art Mus., Glen Falls, N.Y., 1999; group shows include Mich. Focus, Detroit Inst. of Art and Grand Rapids Mus. of Art (Catalog), 1974, Mus. of Modern Art, Touchstone Gallery, N.Y.C., 1979, Susan Caldwell, N.Y.C., 1979, Landscape Anthology, Grace Borgenicht Gallery, N.Y.C., 1988, Lines of Vision: Drawings by Contemporary Women, Blum Helman Warehouse and Hillwood Art Mus., Long Island U. Catalog, N.Y., 1989, Notions of Place: Paintings and Drawings, Victoria Munroe Gallery, N.Y.C., 1990, The Painters, 1991, Summer Salon, 1992, Celebrating Nature, Champion Internat. Corp. Collection Exhibit., Stamford, Conn., 1991, Landscape Not Landscape, Gallery Camino Real, Boca Raton, Fla. Catalog, 1994, Bklyn. Mus. Art, Gasworks Gallery, London, Cornerstone Gallery, Manchester; represented in pub. collections: J.P. Morgan, Morgan Guaranty Trust Co., N.Y., Champion Internat., Stamford, Conn., Amerada Hess Corp., GE, Manhattan Savings Bank, Milbank, Tweed, Hadley and McCloy, N.Y.C., Herbert F. Johnson Mus. of Art, Cornell U., Prudential Ins., Best Products, IBM, Morgan Stanley, N.Y.C., Cranbrook Acad of Art Mus., Kidder Peabody, Inc., Hosp. Corp. Am., Power Inst. of Fine Arts, Sydney, Australia, IBM, GE, Princess Cruise Lines, Marsh and McClennan Cos. Inc. Studio: 457 Broome St New York NY 10013-2681

BRETT, STEPHEN M., lawyer, entertainment company executive. BS, U. Pa., 1962, JD, 1966. Bar: N.Y. 1966, Colo. 1971. Assoc. Dewey, Ballantine, Bushby, Palmer & Wood, 1966-71; ptnr. Sherman & Howard, 1971-88; exec. v.p. legal, gen. counsel, sec. United Artists Entertainment Co., Denver, 1988-91; gen. counsel, v.p., sec. Tele-Comm., Inc., Englewood, Colo., 1991—, exec. v.p., gen. counsel. Office: Tele-Comm Inc 5619 Dtc Pky Englewood CO 80111-3017*

BRETT, THOMAS RUTHERFORD, federal judge; b. Oklahoma City, Oct. 2, 1931; s. John A. and Norma (Dougherty) B.; m. Mary Jean James, Aug. 26, 1952; children: Laura Elizabeth Brett Tribble, James Ford, Susan Marie Brett Crump, Maricarolyn Swab. B.B.A., U. Okla., 1953, LL.B., 1957, J.D., 1971. Bar: Okla. 1957. Asst. county atty. Tulsa, 1957; mem. firm Hudson, Hudson, Wheaton, Kyle & Brett, Tulsa, 1958-69, Jones, Givens, Brett, Gotcher, Doyle & Bogan, 1969-79; judge U.S. Dist. Ct. (no. dist.) Okla., Tulsa, 1979—. Bd. regents U. Okla., 1971-78; mem. adv. bd. Salvation Army; trustee Okla. Bar Found. Col. JAG, USAR, 1953-83. Fellow Am. Coll. Trial Lawyers, Am. Bar Found.; mem. Okla. Bar Assn. (pres. 1970), Tulsa County Bar Assn. (pres. 1965), Am. Judicature Soc., U. Okla. Coll. Law Alumni Assn. (bd. dirs.), Order of Coif (hon.), Phi Alpha Delta. Democrat. Office: US Dist Ct US Courthouse 224 S Boulder Ave Rm 210 Tulsa OK 74103-3026

BRETTELL, RICHARD ROBSON, art historian, museum consultant, educator; b. Rochester, N.Y., Jan. 17, 1949; s. Herbert Robson and Ellen (Sackett) B.; m. Zoe Caroline Bieler, June 9, 1973. BA, Yale U., 1971, MA/PhD, 1977. Acad. program dir., asst. prof. history of art U. Tex., Austin, 1976-80; Searle curator European painting Art Inst. of Chgo., 1980-88; dir. The Dallas Mus. of Art, 1988-92; founding dir. McKinney Ave. Contemporary, 1992-93; prof. visual aesthetic studies U. Tex., Dallas, 1998—; adj. prof. Northwestern U., Evanston, Ill., 1984-88; vis. prof. Yale U., 1994, Harvard U., 1995; prin. organizer exhbns. The Art of the Edge: European Frames, Art Inst. Chgo., 1986, The Art of Paul Gauguin, Nat. Gallery, Washington, 1988-89, Art Inst. Chgo., Grand Palais, Paris, Pissaro: Urban Series, 1992-93, Dallas Mus. of Art, Royal Acad., Camille Pissarro in the Caribbean 1850-55, St. Thomas and the Jewish us., 1997; mem. organizing com. Camille Pissarro, The Hayward Gallery, London, 1980-81, Grand Palais, Mus. Fine Arts, Boston. Author: Pisarro and Pontoise, 1990, Modern Art: Capitalism and Representation, 1999; co-author: The Art of Paul Gauguin, 1988, Painters and Peasants in the 19th Century, 1983, A Day in the Country: Impressionism and the French Landscape, 1984, Degas in the Art Inst. of Chgo., 1984, (exhbn. catalogues) Gauguin, 1988. Bd. dirs. Mus. African-Am. Life, Dallas, 1988, DARE, 1991—; mem. Dallas Com. for Internt. Cultural Affairs, 1988. Decorated Chevalier Order of Arts and Letters (France); vis. fellow J. Paul Getty Mus., spring 1985; fellow Nat. Endowment for Humanities, summer 1980, U. Rsch. Inst. U. Tex., Austin, summer 1978, The Whiting Found, 1975-76, Samuel Kress fellow, Yale U., 1974-75. Mem. Coll. Art Assn. Am. (bd. dirs. 1986-89), Midwest Art History Assn., Soc. Archtl. Historians, Am. Assn. Museums, The Getty Grant Program (publs. com. 1987-91), Elizabethan Club. Avocation: piano playing.

BRETTHAUER, ERICH WALTER, chemist, educator; b. Denver, Sept. 12, 1937; s. Walter V. and Lucy E. (Feeley) B.; m. Sharlene Marie Stimpson, Oct. 10, 1966; children: Terrance Magee, Anthony Magee, Heidi, Erich Walter II. BS, U. Nev., 1960, MS, 1962. Various sci. rsch. and mgmt. positions Pub. Health Svc. and EPA, 1962-68; dir. monitoring ops. div. EPA, Las Vegas, 1978-79, dir. nuclear radiation assessment div., 1979-80; detail to U.S. radiation policy coun. EPA, Washington, 1980-81; lab. dir. Office Rsch. Devel. Environ. Monitoring Systems Lab. EPA, Las Vegas, 1985-89; asst. administr. Office Rsch. & Devel. EPA, Washington, 1990-93; rsch. prof. U. Nev., Las Vegas, 1993-95; pres. Bryce Meadows Devel. Corp., Las Vegas, 1996—. Congl. fellow U.S. Senate Com. on Environ. and Pub. Works, 1982—; recipient Gold medal for directing and monitoring outreach program at Three Mile Island EPA, 1979. Mem. Am. Chem. Soc., Am. Water Works Assn., Sigma Xi.

BRETTSCHNEIDER, RITA ROBERTA FISCHMAN, lawyer; b. Bklyn., Nov. 12, 1931; d. Isidore M. and Augusta T. (Singer) Fischman; m. Bertram D. Brettschneider, June 25, 1950 (dec. Nov. 17, 1986); children: Jane King, Joseph Brettschneider; m. Bertram D. Cohn, June 30, 1991. BA, CUNY, 1953; JD, Bklyn. Law Sch., 1956; postgrad., NYU, 1968-69, Nat. Inst. Trial Advocacy, 1976. Bar: N.Y. 1961, U.S. Dist. Ct. N.Y. 1971. Pvt. practice Huntington, N.Y., 1961—; instr. women and the law C.W. Post Coll., Brookville, N.Y., 1969-70; arbitrator med. malpractice arbitration com. Suffolk County (N.Y.), 1974-76; spl. assoc. prof. philosophy and law New Coll. Hofstra U., Hempstead, N.Y., 1974-76; faculty N.Y. Law Jour. Conf. Changing Concepts in Matrimonial Law, 1976; legal advisor Am. Arbitration Assn., 1977-84; arbitrator night small claims ct. Nassau County, 1978-83; of counsel Nassau County Psychol. Assn., 1987—, Suffolk County Psychol. Assn., 1990-95. Contbr. numerous articles to profl. jours. Pres., bd. dirs. For Our Children and Us, 1992—. Mem. Nassau-Suffolk Women's Bar Assn. (chair judiciary com. 1974-80), Nassau County Bar Assn. (demonstrating atty. mock trial contested matrimonial action 1975), Suffolk County Bar Assn. (demonstrating atty. mock trial contested matrimonial action 1976), Am. Arbitration Assn. (legal advisor 1977-84), Nassau-Suffolk Women's Bar Assn. (pres. 1980-81). Home: 2 Crosby Pl Cold Spring Harbor NY 11724-2403 Office: Brettschneider & Brettschneider 83 Prospect St Huntington NY 11743-3306

BRETZ, CONNIE, poet, storyteller; b. Oak Park, Ill, Nov. 11, 1927; d. Clarence Edward Frybarger and Elsie Meissner; m. Robert Earl Bretz, June 22, 1951 (dec. Aug. 19, 1994); children: Fred, Patricia and Paula (twins), Benjamin. BA, Ind. U., 1949; postgrad., Temple U., 1966, Westchester U., 1967-69. Cert. elem. tchr., Pa. Tchr. kindergarten O.J. Roberts Sch. Dist., Pottstown, Pa., 1964-66, Pottstown Sch. Dist., 1966-76; freelance storyteller Phoenixville, Pa., 1975—; reader, critic The Writing Acad., dir. Nancy James, New Wilmington, Pa., 1996-97; pres., mem. Magnolia (N.J.) Sch. Bd., 1962-63. Author: Geronimo!, 1985 (award Am. Family Inst. 1990), Pepperoni Poetry, 1993, poems; prodr., host (radio show) Connychat WYIS, 1986-88 (award Am. Family Inst. 1989); contbr. articles to profl. jours. Chairwoman Pa. Dutch Day Lincoln Elem. Sch., Pottstown, Pa., 1976. Mem. Nat. League Am. PEN Women (editor humor 1982, award 1986), St. David's Christian Writers Assn. (bd. dirs. Beaver Falls, Pa. 1977-97, AMY award 1992, Fritz Kemper award 1992, Adult and Young Adult Fiction award 1994, Wendell August award 1997, Heart award 1997), Friends of Phoenixville Libr., Phoenixville Iron Canal and Trails Assn. Avocations: books, biking, babysitting, bells, hedgehogs. Home: 352 Nutt Rd Phoenixville PA 19460-3910

BRETZ, RONALD JAMES, law educator; b. Detroit, Nov. 11, 1951; s. James Louis and Nancy Kathleen (Murphy) B.; m. Leslie Jane Lucas, June 13, 1973; children: Jeffrey, Elissa, Sarah. BA, Mich. State U., 1973; JD, Wayne (Mich.) State U., 1976. Bar: Mich. 1976, U.S. Supreme Ct 1985. Asst. defender Appellate Defender Office State of Mich., Lansing, 1977-96; assoc. prof. Thomas M. Cooley Law Sch., Lansing, 1997—; lectr. Mich. Appellate Assigned Counsel System, Lansing, 1985, 88; lectr. Cooley Law Sch., Lansing, 1985-90, adj. prof., 1991-96; bd. dirs. Legal Aid Ctrl. Mich., 1987-93, pres. bd., 1991-93. Mem. adv. com. Community Alternatives Program, Lansing, 1984-85; bd. dirs. Legal Aid Cen. Mich., 1987—, sec., 1988, v.p., 1990. Mem. Nat. Lawyers Guild (pres. Lansing chpt. 1985-86, sec. 1986-87), U.S. Supreme Ct. Bar Assn., State Bar Assn. Mich. (com. standard criminal jury instrns. 1988-96), Criminal Def. Attys. Mich. (lectr. 1982, Outstanding Criminal Def. Work award 1986). Avocations: reading, playing guitar, cycling, movies, sports. Office: Thomas M Cooley Law Sch 217 S Capitol Ave Lansing MI 48933-1503

BRETZFELDER, DEBORAH MAY, museum exhibit designer, photographer; b. Hazelton, Pa., Sept. 21, 1932; d. Joseph and Rose (Smulyan) Hirsh; m. Robert Bretzfelder, Dec. 24, 1955; children: Karl, Marc. Student, Syracuse U., 1950-53. Textile colorist, designer Cohn-Hall-Marx, N.Y.C., 1954-55; fashion coordinator Hecht's Dept. Store, Washington, 1956; free lance artist Washington, 1956-58; exhibits technician Smithsonian Instn., Washington, 1958-59, supr. exhibits prodn., 1959-63, exhibits specialist Nat. Mus. Am. History, 1963-75, visual info. specialist, project mgmt. officer, 1975-83, acting chief of design, 1983; chief of design Smithsonian Instn., 1983-87, assoc. asst. dir. exhibits and pub. spaces, 1987-88, ret., 1988; cons. various firms, orgns., mus. personnel, instr. mus. programs; free-lance photographer and exhibit designer D & R Bretzfelder; project dir.; ind. cons. Mus. Svcs. Internat., Washington. Contbr. works to various publs. Mem. violin sect. George Washington U. Orch. Mem. Am. Assn. Mus., Nat. Soc. Hist. Preservation, Internat. Com. on Mus., Tau Sigma Delta. Jewish. Club: Potomac Appalachian Trail. Home: 2748 Woodley Pl NW Washington DC 20008-1517

BREU, GEORGE, accountant; b. Milw., May 8, 1954; s. George and Grace (Rossmaier) B.; m. Nancy Lee Roblee, June 6, 1987; children: Michael G., Lisa A. BBA in Acctg. cum laude, U. Wis., Milw., 1976. CPA, Wis. Audit staff Reilly, Penner & Benton, Milw., 1976-78; tax mgr. Radke, Schlesner & Wernecke, S.C., Milw., 1978-88; contr. Megal Devel. and Constrn. Corp., Milw., 1988—. Treas. Elmbrook Hist. Soc., Brookfield, Wis., 1981-83. Mem. Am. Inst. CPA's (tax div.), Wis. Inst. CPA's, U. Wis. Milw. Tax Assn., Germany Philatelic Soc. (treas. Milw. chpt. 1978—), U. Wis. Milw. Philatelic Soc. (founder, treas. 1972-81), Milw. Philatelic Soc. Inc. (corp. registered agt. 1986—), U. Wis. Milw. Alumni Assn., Beta Gamma Sigma, Phi Eta Sigma. Republican. Roman Catholic. Avocations: stamp collecting, reading history, traveling. Home: 15840 Fieldbrook Dr Brookfield WI 53005-1419 Office: Megal Devel Corp 12650 W Lisbon Rd Brookfield WI 53005-1891

BREUER, MELVIN ALLEN, electrical engineering educator; b. L.A., Feb. 1, 1938; s. Arthur and Bertha Helen (Friedman) B.; m. Sandra Joyce Scalir, Apr. 7, 1967; children: Teri Lynn, Jeffrey Steven. BS in Engring., UCLA, 1959, MS in Engring., 1961; PhD in Elec. Engring., U. Calif., Berkeley, 1965. Asst. prof. U. So. Calif., L.A., 1965-71, assoc. prof., 1971-80, prof., 1980—, chmn. elec. engring. systems dept., 1991-94, chair of the faculty, Sch. Engring., 1997-98, Charles Lee Powell prof., 1995—. Co-author: Diagnosis and Reliable Design, 1976, Digital Systems Testing and Testable Design, 1990; editor, co-author: Design Automation, 1972; editor: Digital Systems Design Automation, 1975; editor-in-chief Jour. Design Automation, 1980-82; co-editor: Knowledge Based Systems for Test and Diagnosis, 1990; contbr. articles to profl. jours. Recipient Assocs. award U. So. Calif., 1991; Fulbright-Hays scholar, 1972. Fellow IEEE (Taylor Booth award for edn. 1993); mem. Sigma Xi, Tau Beta Pi, Eta Kappa Nu. Democrat. Office: U So Calif University Park Los Angeles CA 90089-2562

BREUER, STEPHEN ERNEST, temple administrator; b. Vienna, Austria, July 14, 1936; s. John Hans Howard and Olga Marion (Haar) B.; came to U.S., 1938, naturalized, 1945; BA cum laude, UCLA, 1959, gen. secondary credential, 1960; m. Gail Fern Breitbart, Sept. 4, 1960 (div. 1986); children: Jared Noah, Rachel Elise; m. Nadine Bendit, Sept. 25, 1988. *Stephen Breuer's grandparents, Felix and Marie Breuer, perished with dozens of family members in the Holocaust. Stephen's parents, Hans and Olga Breuer, fled Vienna, with him at the age of two, along with his Uncle Fred and Aunt Gisela Ehrlich, on the eve of "kristalnacht," the nazi pogram against German and Austrian Jews in November 1938. The family settled in Los Angeles, where Stephen's grandparents Helen and Henry Haar joined them in 1941. Stephen's brother, Robert, born in 1944, is a college administrator living in Berkeley, California with his wife Fredericka and their son Noah. Stephen's cousins Bill Ehrlich and Shirley Ehrlich Kouffman are Los Angeles natives and residents.* Tchr. L.A. City Schs., 1960-62; dir. Wilshire Blvd. Temple Camps, L.A., 1962-86; exec. dir. Wilshire Blvd. Temple, 1980—; dir. Edgar F. Magnin Religious Sch., Los Angeles, 1970-80. Instr. Hebrew Union Coll., Los Angeles, 1965-76, 92—, U. Judaism, 1991; field instr. San Francisco State U., 1970-80, Calif. State U., San Diego, Hebrew Union Coll., 1977-81, U. of Judaism UCLA extension. Vice pres. L.A. Youth Programs Inc., 1967-77; youth adviser L.A. County Commn. Human Rels., 1969-72. Bd. dirs. Cmty. Rels. Conf. So. Calif., 1965-85; bd. dirs. Alzheimer's Disease and Related Disorders Assn., 1984-95, v.p. L.A. County chpt., 1984-86, pres., 1986-88, nat. exec. com., 1987-95, nat. devel. chair, 1992-95, Calif. state coun. pres. 1987-92, chmn. of Calif. gov.'s adv. com. on Alzheimer's disease, 1988-97; mem. goals program City of Beverly Hills, Calif., 1985-91; bd. dirs. Pacific SW regional Union Am. Hebrew Congregations, 1985-88, mem. nat. bd. , exec. com., 1993-97; bd. dirs. Echo Found., 1986-88, Mazon-Jewish Response to Hunger, 1993-97, Wilshire Stakeholders, exec. com., 1987-94; west coast adv. bd. Internat. Rescue Com. 1999—; treas. Wilshire Community Prayer Alliance, 1986-88; active United Way. Recipient Service awards Los Angeles YWCA, 1974, Los Angeles County Bd. Suprs., 1982, 87, Ventura County Bd. Suprs., 1982, 87, Weinberg Chai Lifetime Achievement award Jewish Fed. Council Los Angeles, 1986, Nat. Philanthropy Day L.A. Medallion, 1993, L.A. County Redevel. Agy. recognition, 1994, L.A. Bus. Coun. award, 1997; Steve Breuer Conference Ctr. in Malibu named in his honor at Wilshire Blvd. Temple Camps, 1990. Mem. So. Calif. Camping Assn. (dir. 1964-82), Nat. Assn. Temple Adminstrs. (nat. bd. dirs. 1987—, v.p. 1991-93, pres. 1993-97, Svc. to Judaism award 1989, Svc. to the Community award 1990, Svc. award), Nat. Assn. Temple Educators (Kaminker award 1973), Los Angeles Assn. Jewish Edn. (dir.), Profl. Assn. Temple Adminstrs. (pres. 1985-88), Jewish Communal Profls. So. Calif., Assn. Supervision and Curriculum Devel., Am. Mgmt. Assn., So. Calif. Conf. Jewish Communal Workers, Jewish Profl. Network, Amnesty Internat., Jewish Resident Camping Assn. (pres. 1976-82), World Union for Progressive Judaism, UCLA Alumni Assn., Wilderness Soc., Center for Environ. Edn., Wildlife Fedn., Living Desert, Maple Mental Health Ctr. of Beverly Hills, Los Angeles County Mus. Contemporary Art, People for the Am. Way, Assn Reform Zionists Am. (bd. dirs. 1993—). Office: Wilshire Blvd Temple 3663 Wilshire Blvd Los Angeles CA 90010-2798

BREUER, WERNER ALFRED, retired plastics company executive; b. Sinn, Hessia, Germany, Jan. 30, 1930; came to U.S., 1959; s. Christian and Hedwig (Cunz) B.; m. Gertrud Ackermann, June 21, 1950 (dec. 1998); children: Patricia, Julia, Eva-Maria. BS in Human Rels. and Orgnl. Behavior, U. San Francisco, 1983; MS in Bus. Mgmt., U. La Verne, 1985, DPA, 1988. Lab. technician Firma E. Leitz GMBH, Wetzlar, Germany, 1954-59; lab. supr. Dayco Corp. (Am. latex divsn.), Hawthorne, Calif., 1959-65; tech. ops. mgr. Olin Corp., Stamford and New Haven, Conn., 1965-69; gen. mgr., exec. v.p. Expanded Rubber and Plastics Corp., Gardena, Calif., 1969-96; ret., 1996; gen. mgr. Schlobohm Co. Inc., Dominguez Hills, Calif., 1989-96; ret.; cons. human resources Stabond Corp., Gardena, 1988-95. Author/composer various popular and sacred recordings, 1970s; contbr. articles to jours. Recipient Portfolio award U. San Francisco, 1983-84. Mem. ASTM, ASCAP, Am. Soc. for Metals, Soc. for Plastics Engrs., N.Y. Acad. Scis., U. La Verne Alumni Assn. Republican. Avocations: play music, writing, horseback riding, composing, sketching. Achievements include pioneering use of plastics especially polyurethanes in defense missiles and space and communication aviation industry; defense projects for DEW Line N.A. radar defense to Stealth Fighter B-2 Project. Home: 564 Sage Cir Highlands Ranch CO 80126-2118

BREUER, WILLIAM BENTLEY, writer. Frequent keynote spkr.; guest numerous radio shows and TV programs; former guest lectr. salesmanship, publicity and promotion seminars. Author: An American Saga, 1982, Bloody Clash at Sadzot, 1982 (transl. into Belgian), Captain Cool, 1983, They Jumped at Midnight, 1983, Drop Zone Sicily, 1984 (transl. into Japanese and French), Hitler's Fortress Cherbourg, 1984, Agony at Anzio, 1985 (transl. into Czechoslovakian), Storming Hitler's Rhine, 1985 (transl. into Serbo-Croatian), Death of a Nazi Army, 1985, Operation Torch, 1986, Retaking the Philippines, 1987, Devil Boats, 1987 (transl. into Japanese), Operation Dragoon, 1988 (transl. into French), The Secret War with Germany, 1988, Sea Wolf, 1989, Nazi Spies in America, 1989, Geronimo!, 1990, Hoodwinking Hitler, 1993, Race to the Moon, 1993 (transl. into Burmese, Choice award ALA 1995), The Great Raid on Cabanatuan, 1994, J. Edgar Hoover and His G-Men, 1995, MacArthur's Undercover War, 1994, Feuding Allies, 1995 (trans. into Polish), Shadow Warriors, 1996, War and American Women, 1997, Unexplained Mysteries of World War II, 1997 (transl. into Polish and Czech), Vendetta: Castro and the Kennedy Brothers, 1997 (transl. into Polish), Undercover Tales of World War II, 1998. Sgt. U.S. Army, WWII. Recipient numerous awards. Hon. mem. numerous vets. assns. Home: 3815 Westview Dr NE Cleveland TN 37312-5057

BREUL, JONATHAN DUTRO, government official; b. Bridgeport, Conn., Aug. 18, 1947; s. Alvin C. and Helena (Plumb) B.; m. Nancy Mathers, May 4, 1974; children: Hannah P., Sarah M. BA, Colby Coll., 1969; MPA, Northeastern U., 1972. With U.S. Gen. Svcs. Adminstrn., 1973-75, U.S. Dept. of Health and Human Svcs., 1976-82; sr. policy analyst for fin. mgmt. U.S. Office Mgmt. and Budget, Washington, 1983-93, chief evaluation and planning, 1990-93, sr. advisor to dep. dir., 1993—. Mem. editl. bd. New Directions for Evaluation. With USAF, 1969-72. Recipient Mydral Pub. Svc. award Am. Evaluation Assn., 1996. Fellow Nat. Acad. Pub. Adminstrn.; mem. ASAP. Avocation: fly fishing. Home: 3809 Jenifer St NW Washington DC 20015-1917

BREUNIG, ROBERT G., botanical facility administrator; b. Indpls., Nov. 16, 1945; s. Henry Latham and Nancy (Tyree) B.; m. Karen Enyedy Breunig, Feb. 16, 1979; 1 child, Lydia Ann. BA, Ind. U., 1968; PhD, U. Kans., 1973. Asst. prof. anthropology No. Ariz. U., Flagstaff, 1972-74; educator Mus. No. Ariz., Flagstaff, 1975-77, curator, 1977-81, curator, head dept. anthropology, 1981-82; chief curator, dep. dir. The Heard Mus., Phoenix, 1982-85; exec. dir. Desert Botanical Garden, Phoenix, 1985-94; dir. Santa Barbara (Calif.) Mus. Natural History, Lady Bird Johnson Wildflower Ctr., Austin; vis. asst. prof. anthropology U. Conn., 1974, Denison U., Granville, 1975; trustee Ctr. for Plant Conservation, St. Louis, 1991-94, 99—; mem. bd. dirs. (presdl. appointment) Nat. Mus. Svcs. Bd., Washington, 1992—. Mem. Am. Assn. Mus. Office: Lady Bird Johnson Wildflower Ctr 4801 LaCrosse Ave Austin TX 78739

BREVE, FRANKLIN STEPHEN, pharmacist; b. Phila., Jan. 25, 1955; s. Albert Francis and Lillian Marie (Di Biase) B.; m. Linda Ruth Maedel, Mar. 16, 1985; children: Christina Lynn, Rebecca Anne, Allison Marie. BA in Psychology, Temple U., 1977, BS in Pharmacy, 1981; MBA in Pharm. Mktg., St. Joseph's U., 1998. Registered Pharmacist. Oncology pharmacist Thomas Jefferson U., Phila., 1981-86, nuclear pharmacist, 1986-87; oncology pharmacist Rancocas Valley Hosp., Willingboro, N.J., 1987-88; night phramacy coord. West Jersey Hosp., Camden, N.J., 1988-97; pres., CEO Pharmatech Cons. Group, Blackwood, N.J., 1992—; cons. and instr. in field. Mem. Am. Soc. Hosp. Pharmacists, Am. Pharm. Assn., N.J. Soc. Hosp. Pharmacists, N.Y. Acad. Scis., Am. Soc. Cons. Pharmacists, N.J. Pharm. Assn., N.J. Acad. Cons. Pharmacists. Republican. Roman Catholic. Avocations: woodworking, science fiction, white-water rafting. Fax: (609) 627-5297. E-mail: fbreve@erols.com. Home and Office: 6 Briarwood Dr Blackwood NJ 08012-5387

BREVER, MICHAEL STEPHEN, non-profit executive director, alderman; b. Milw., Apr. 21, 1955; s. Robert Thomas and Dorothy Helen (Schoofs) B.; m. Mary Beth Burns, Aug. 29, 1987; children: Megan Lanie, Timothy Michael, Patrick Burns, Daniel Fredrick. BA in History, U. Wis., Milw., 1979; MS in Mgmt., Cardinal Stritch Coll., 1990. VISTA vol. South Cmty. Orgn., Milw., 1981, exec. dir., 1982—; panelist and lectr. confs. Bd. pres. Southside Housing Coop., Milw., 1987—; alderman City of Oak Creek, Wis., 1993—, common coun. pres., 1996-97, temporary acting mayor, 1996; bd. govs. Wis. Ins. Plan, Milw., 1994—; adv. bd. mem. Lincoln Neighborhood Redevel. Corp., Milw., 1994—; commr. Cmty. Devel. Authority, Oak Creek, 1995—; mem. Affordable Housing Task Force, Milw., 1997. Recipient Bronze award United Way Greater Milw., 1991, Disting. Svc. award Southside Civic Assn., Milw., 1994, Am. Hometown Leadership award Nat. Assn. Towns & Twps., 1996, Proclamation of Distinction, Oak Creek Common Coun., 1996. Mem. Southside Bus. Assn., Southside Civic Assn. (Disting. Svc. award 1994), U. Wis. Milw. Alumni Assn., St. Josephs Found. (bd. dirs. 1995—), Oak Creek Tax Incremental Fin. Dist. II (chmn. 1997), KC. Avocations: golf, reading, basketball, spectator sports. Home: 615 E Parkway Estates Dr Oak Creek WI 53154-4528 Office: South Cmty Orgn Inc 1635 S 8th St Milwaukee WI 53204-3455

BREVERMAN, HARVEY, artist; b. Pitts., Jan. 7, 1934; s. Theodore and Sarah (Haffner) B.; m. Deborah Dobkin, June 26, 1960. BFA, Carnegie Inst. Tech., 1956; MFA, Ohio U., 1960. Tchr. Carnegie Inst. Tech., summer 1959; tchr. drawing Ohio U., Athens, 1960-61, Ill. State U., Normal, summer 1969, Falmouth (Eng.) Art Sch., 1969; prof. art SUNY, Buffalo, 1961-99, disting. prof., 1999—. Resident painter, State Acad. Fine Arts, Amsterdam, 1965-66, vis. painter, Kalamazoo Inst. Art, summer 1972, 73, vis. artist, Oxford U., 1974, 77, U. Mich., 1978, Md. Inst. Coll. Art, 1984, 92d St. Y, N.Y.C., 1989, Coll. William & Mary, 1990, Skidmore Coll., 1990, Pont Aven Sch. Art, France, 1995, Jagiellonian U., Poland, 1997; one man shows include Albright-Knox Art Gallery, Buffalo, 1967, 89, U. Oreg., U. Ill., 1970, Canton (Ohio) Art Inst., 1971, 87, Middlebury Coll., 1973, FAR Gallery, N.Y.C., 1974, 79, Gadatsy Gallery, Toronto, 1975, 76, 79, 80, Kalamazoo Inst. Art, 1976, Hackley Art Mus., Muskegon, Mich., 1977, 97, Grand Rapids (Mich.) Art Mus., 1977, Gadatsy Gallery, Toronto, 1978, 81, 84, U. Mich., 1978, Nardin Galleries, N.Y.C., 1980, U. N.H., 1981, Art Gallery of Hamilton (Ont., Can.), 1981, Hollins Coll., 1982, Niagara U., 1984, Miami (Ohio) U. Art Mus., 1987, Gadatsy Gallery, Toronto, 1987, Meml. Art Gallery, Rochester, N.Y., 1988, Wenniger Gallery, Boston, 1988, St. Lawrence U., 1989, Taller Galeria Ft., Cadaqués, Spain, 1990, Babcock Galleries, N.Y.C., 1990, 91, Brigham Young U., 1993, Nina Freudenheim Gallery, Buffalo, 1994, Butler Inst. Am. Art, 1997, Yeshiva U. Mus., N.Y.C., 1997, Milton Weill Gallery, N.Y.C., 1997; exhibited in group show at Corcoran Biennial, Washington, 1963, Bklyn. Mus., 1964, Assn. Am. Artists, N.Y.C., 1965, Rijksakademie, Amsterdam, 1968, Boston Mus. Fine Arts, 1968, NAD, 1968, Pa. Acad. Fine Arts Biennial, 1969, 2d and 3d Brit. Internat. Biennial, Bradford, Eng., 1970 72, FAR Gallery, 1972-74, Whitechapel Gallery, London, 1973, Pushkin Mus., Moscow, 1972, 2d Norwegian Internat. Biennial, 1974, Mus. Modern Art, Oxford, Eng., 1974, Honolulu Acad. Fine Arts, 1975, 8th Internat. Art Fair, Basel, Switzerland, 1977, Auslands Institut, Dortmund, W. Ger., 1977, Arte Fiere '78, Bologna, 1978, Art Gallery Ont., Toronto, 1979, Am. Acad. and Inst. Arts and Letters, N.Y.C., 1980, 81, NYU, N.Y.C., 1980, Jewish Mus., N.Y.C., 1982, Queens Mus., N.Y.C., 1983, Rose Art Mus., Brandeis U., 1985, Minn. Mus. Art, St. Paul, 1985, Roger Ramsay Gallery, Chgo., 1986, Va. Mus. Fine Arts, Richmond, 1986, Lever House Gallery, N.Y.C., 1986, Albright-Knox Art Gallery, 1987, Harvard U., Carpenter Ctr., 1987, Mus. Art, San Juan, P.R., 1987, Contemporary Arts Ctr., Cin., 1988, Mus. of Fine Arts, Houston, 1988, Oakland (Calif.) Mus., 1988, 8th Print Internat., Barcelona, 1988, 4th Internat. Print Biennal, Taipei Fine Arts Mus., Taiwan, 1989, Inst. of Contemporary Art, Boston, 1990, La Jolla Mus. of Contemporary Art, 1990, Grand Palais, Paris, 1990, Yurakucho Art Forum, Tokyo, 1991, Denver Art Mus., 1991, Scottsdale Ctr. for the Arts, 1991, Nat. Acad. Design, N.Y.C., 1992, Internat. Print Triennal, Krakow, Nüremberg, 1994, 97, Mus. Applied Arts. Belgrade, 1995, XIII Premio Internat. Per L' Incisione, Biella, Torino, 1997, Bermuda Nat. Gallery, 1997, 9th Internat. Print Biennale, Varna, Bulgaria, 1997, Beijing Internat. Ex-Libris Exhbn., China, 1998, Embassy of France, La Maison Française, Washington, 1998, Florean Mus., Carbunari, Romania, 1999, Mus. Civico Di Grafica, Brlonico, Italy, 1999, Chateau du Puget, Alzonne, France, 1999, 12th Deutsche Internat. Grafik Triennale, Frechen, Germany, 1999; also traveling exhibits in U.S., Europe, Central Am., Japan, paintings for, U.S. embassies, 1976; represented in permanent collections Mus. Modern Art, N.Y.C., Whitney Mus., Albright-Knox Art Gallery, Phila. Mus., Butler Inst. Art, Youngstown, Ohio, Nat. Mus. Am. Art, Washington, Library of Congress, Israel Mus., Jerusalem, Bradford City Art Mus., St. Catharines Dist. Arts Council, Ont., Can., Victoria and Albert Mus., London, Cleve. Mus., Balt. Mus. Art, Nat. Portrait Gallery, Washington, British Mus., London, Met. Mus. Art, N.Y.C., Smithsonian Inst., Washington. Served with AUS, 1956-58, Korea. Grantee Louis Comfort Tiffany Found., 1962, Netherlands Govt., 1965, N.Y. Coun. Arts, 1972; named fellow NEA, 1974-75, 80-81, Va. Ctr. for the Creative Arts, 1992; elected mem. Nat. Acad. Design, N.Y.C., 1992; recipient Nat. Alumni Assn. medal of merit Ohio U., 1992. Address: 76 Smallwood Dr Snyder NY 14226-4027

BREVETTI, FRANCINE CLELIA, journalist; b. San Francisco, July 20, 1943; d. Frank Albert and Tecla Puccetti Brevetti. BA in French, U. Calif., Berkeley, 1966; MA in Theater, UCLA, 1969. Staff writer Jour. Commerce, N.Y.C., 1977-85; pvt. practice Hong Kong, 1985-97; bus. writer The Oakland (Calif.) Tribune, 1998—; dir. Francine Brevetti Prodns., 1984—; West Coast corr., past Hong Kong corr. Seatrade Rev., Seatrade Orgn., 1994—; Hong Kong corr. Pensions & Investments, Crain Comm., 1995—; cons. Renwick-McCormick, Hong Kong, 1995-97, Harris Mgmt., Hong Kong, 1997. Editor ECA China News, 1995—; contbr. Hobson's Publs., 1996—, The Securities Jour., 1996—. Mem. Soc. Profl. Journalists, PR Roundtable San Francisco, Women in Pub. (pres. 1994-96), Hong Kong Journalists' Assn., Fgn. Corr. Club (com. mem. 1987—), N.Y. Fin. Writers Assn. E-mail: francineb@earthlink.net. Fax: 415-421-6225. Office: The Oakland Tribune Oakland CA 94607

BREVIK, J. ALBERT, communications consultant; b. Seattle, Aug. 1, 1920; s. Anton Christian and Olga Elise (Setter) B.; m. Norma Jacquelin Ringman, June 26, 1953 (dec. 1987); children: Jay Christian, Jon Henry; m. Joann Bradford, Jan. 20, 1990. B.A., U. Wash., 1947, M.A., 1951. Guidance counselor music dept. U. Wash., Seattle, 1947-52; entertainment dir. athletic dept. U. Wash., 1947-52; vocal music educator Clover Park High Sch., Tacoma, Wash., 1952-54; television coordinator Pierce County Schs., Tacoma, 1954-59; dir. television edn., gen. mgr. KPEC-TV, Clover Park Schs., Tacoma, 1959-72; dir. communications KPEC-TV, Clover Park Schs., 1972-80; mgr. KPEC-TV, KPEC-FM, 1960-76; also in charge publs. and pub. relations dept., film prodn. unit, new media prodn. and services; gen. mgr. Sta. KCPQ-TV, Tacoma, 1976-80; communications cons., 1980—; pres. Avcom Pacific, Communications Cons., 1981—; assoc. faculty dept. edn. U. Puget Sound, 1955-69; dir. Intermarket Corp., Norwegian Male Chorus, Seattle, 1946-48, Clarion Chorus, Seattle, 1947-52; free-lance radio musician, Seattle, 1938-52; entertainment dir. BC Lions (profl. football club), Vancouver, Can., 1954-55; ednl. TV cons., B.C., Can., 1960-61; v.p. Wash. Ednl. Network, 1978. Mem. Fir Tree, Fircrest Golf Club (Tacoma), Kiwanis (pres. Tacoma club 1963, bd. dirs. 1955-71), Phi Mu Alpha Synfonia, Phi Delta Kappa. Lutheran (v.p., dir. 1959-69). Home and Office: 1920 Day Island Blvd W Tacoma WA 98466

BREVOORT, RICHARD WILLIAM, public relations executive; b. Bklyn., Nov. 7, 1937; s. Patricia Gallivan. Student, Hunter Coll.; CUNY. Supervising adjustor The Home Ins. Co., 1960-66; dir. weight and measures City of N.Y., 1966, deputy commr. markets, 1966-68, 1st deputy commr. commerce, 1968-69, asst. adminstr. econ. devel., 1969-70, commr. tax collection, 1970-75; dir. program-minority N.Y. State Senate, Albany, 1975-77, sec. to minority, 1977-83; v.p. The Whitney Leadership Group, Inc., 1991—; pres. The Hudson Agy., Inc., Cape Coral, Fla., 1984—; bd. dirs. N.Y.C. Convention Ctr. Corp., 1982-84; mem. N.Y. State Task Force on Cigarette Bootlegging, 1976, N.Y. State Econ. Stblzn. Bd., 1970; mem. adv. coun. to N.Y.C. supt. schs., 1968-69. With U.S. Army, 1957-60. Mem. Am. Mgmt. Assn., Am. Soc. Pub. Adminstrn., Soc. Advancement Mgmt., Adminstrv. Mgmt. Soc. Office: Hudson Agy 4818 Coronado Pky Cape Coral FL 33904-9526

BREWER, BARBARA BAGDASARIAN, nursing administrator; b. Providence, Apr. 18, 1950; d. Bagdasar and Grace (Sarkisian) Bagdasarian; m. Timothy F. Brewer III, May 28, 1983. BSN, U. R.I., 1972; MA in Liberal Studies, Conn. Wesleyan U., 1986; MSN, Yale U., 1988; MBA, Columbia U., 1992; postgrad., Sch. Nursing U. Ariz., 1998—. RN, Ariz., Conn., R.I. Staff nurse Miriam Hosp., Providence, R.I., 1972; head nurse orthopeds. unit Frisbie Meml. Hosp., Rochester, N.H., 1973-76; staff nurse St. Francis Hosp. and Med. Ctr., Hartford, Conn., 1976; clin. coord. continuing care unit Middlesex Meml. Hosp., Middletown, Conn., 1976-86; dir. cardiology svcs. Lawrence and Meml. Hosp., New London, Conn., 1988-92, v.p. ambulatory svcs., 1992-95; adminstrv. leader emergency svcs. Tucson Med. Ctr., 1996-97; rsch. assoc. U. Ariz., Coll. of Nursing, 1998—; rschr. in field. Co-author: Improving Your Skills in 12-Lead ECG Interpretation, 1990. Mem. Sigma Theta Tau. Home: 4575 E Blue Mountain Dr Tucson AZ 85718-3560

BREWER, BRETT, lawyer; b. Oklahoma City, Sept. 1, 1966; s. David Louis and Marjorie Joy Brewer; m. Shauna Renee Nowell, Apr. 12, 1997. BA, Baylor U., Waco, Tex., 1989; JD, U. Okla., 1992. Bar: Tex. 1992. Assoc. David Line & Assocs., Dallas, 1993; senate aide U.S. Senator Phil Gramm, Dallas, 1993-97; assoc. Norman, Thrall, Angle, Guy & Day, LLP, Jacksonville, Tex., 1997—. Dist. com. chmn. Boy Scouts Am. Mem. Christian Legal Soc. (v.p. 1991-92), State Bar Tex., Cherokee County Bar Assn. (v.p. 1998-99, pres. 1999—), C. of C. (amb. com. 1997—), Rotary (sec. Jacksonville 1999—). Republican. Avocations: literature, music. Office: Norman Thrall Angle Guy & Day 215 E Commerce St Fl 2 Jacksonville TX 75766-4955

BREWER, CAREY, retired academic administrator; b. Lynchburg, Va., July 8, 1927; s. James Allen and Esther Goode (Leftwich) B.; m. Betty Ann Brighton, Sept. 3, 1949; children—Mary Elizabeth, Robert Allen, Ruth Ann, Catherine Lee. B.A., Lynchburg Coll., 1949; student, Am. U., 1951; M.P.A., Harvard U., 1952, Ph.D., 1956. Analyst with legislative reference service Library of Congress, 1949-56; sr. def. specialist mil. ops. subcom. Ho. of Reps., 1956-60; mem. staff joint com. atomic energy U.S. Congress, 1960-61; various positions Office Emergency Planning, Exec. Office of Pres., 1961-64; pres. Lynchburg Coll., 1964-83; lectr. Am. U., 1954-56; Mem. bd. higher edn., also mem. gen. bd., ch. fin. council Christian Ch. (Disciples of Christ); mem. Pres.'s Civil Def. Adv. Council, 1970-72; Bd. dirs. Nat. Lab. for Higher Edn.; pres. Va. Found. Ind. Colls., 1978-80. Author: Civil Defense in the United States, 1951, Implications of a National Service Program, 1952, Science and Defense, 1956, also numerous articles. Served with USNR, 1945-46. Littauer fellow Harvard, 1951-53. Mem. Council Ind. Colls. Va. (pres. 1972-74), Greater Lynchburg C. of C. (past pres.). Mem. Christian Ch. Clubs: Sphex, Waterfront Golf.

BREWER, DAVID MADISON, lawyer; b. Bordeaux, Gironde, France, July 8, 1953; s. Herbert L. and Paulyne B. (Ver Benec) B.; m. Andrea M. Bordiga, May 20, 1978; children: James David Madison, Caroline Elizabeth, Geoffrey Andrew. AB summa cum laude, Yale U., 1975, JD, 1978. Bar: N.Y. 1979. Assoc. atty. Cravath Swaine & Moore, N.Y.C., 1978-84; assoc. gen. tax counsel Union Pacific Corp., N.Y.C. and Bethlehem, Pa., 1984-89; pres. Madison Co., Inc., N.Y.C., 1990—; pres. Madison Oil Co., Madison Oil Co. Europe, 1993—. Editor Yale Law Jour., 1977-78. Vice-chmn. Bush/Quayle '92 Fin. Com.; policy asst. Office of the Campaign Mgr., Bush-Quayle campaign, 1988; bd. dirs. Yale U. Law Sch. fund, 1989-93, Yale Alumni Fund, 1989-95; spl. gifts chmn. Yale U. Class of 1975 and Law Sch. Class of 1978, 1985—; nat. vice-chmn. Smithsonian Friends of First Ladies, 1989-92; mem. world bd. USO, 1995—; trustee Pine Ridge Sch. (Vt.), 1998—. Nominated to Bd. Fed. Agrl. Mortgage Corp. by Pres. Bush, 1992. Mem. N.Y. Bar Assn., Phi Beta Kappa. Republican. Episcopalian. Office: Ste 1209 9400 N Central Expressway Dallas TX 75231-5044

BREWER, EDWARD CAGE, III, law educator; b. Clarksdale, Miss., Jan. 20, 1953; s. Edward Cage Brewer Jr. and Elizabeth Blair (Alford) Little; m. Nancy Corr Martin, Dec. 27, 1975 (div. Sept. 1985); children: Katherine Martin, Julia Blair; m. Laurie Carol Alley, June 27, 1993 (div. 1999); 1 child, Caroline Elizabeth McCarty. BA, U. of the South, 1975; JD, Vanderbilt U., 1979. Bar: Ala. 1980, U.S. Ct. Appeals (11th and 5th cirs.) 1981, U.S. Dist. Ct. (so. dist.) Ala. 1981, Ga. 1982, U.S. Dist. Ct. (no. dist.) Ga. 1982, U.S. Ct. Appeals (3d and 8th cirs.) 1983, U.S. Dist. Ct. (mid. dist.) Ga. 1992, U.S. Supreme Ct. 1996. Law clk. to Hon. Virgil Pittman U.S. Dist. Ct. (so. dist.) Ala., Mobile, 1979-81; law clk. to Hon. Albert J. Henderson U.S. Ct. Appeals (11th and 5th cirs.), Atlanta, 1981-82; pvt. practice Atlanta, 1982-96; instr. Coll. of Law Ga. State U., Atlanta, 1992, 94; adj. prof. law Emory U., Atlanta, 1994-96; asst. prof. law No. Ky. U., Highland Heights, 1996—. Co-author: Railway Labor Act of 1926: Legislative History, 1988, Georgia Appellate Practice, 1996; contbr. articles to profl. jours. Mem. Phi Beta Kappa, Omicron Delta Kappa. Episcopalian. Avocations: choral music, guitar, motorcycles, hiking, canoeing. Office: No Ky U Salmon P Chase Coll Law Nunn Dr Highland Heights KY 41099

BREWER, ELIZABETH, family therapist; b. Chambersburg, Pa., Sept. 14, 1936; d. Ellsworth Franklin and Katharine Jane (Kriechbaum) B.; m. Donald Gordon Rose, June 20, 1959 (div. 1976); children: Dawn Rose, Martha Ann Rose; m. Glenn Louis Strong, Jan. 25, 1980; children: Donald Strong, Janet Lee Strong Gray. BS, Washington U., 1969; MA, Webster U., 1975; PhD, St. Louis U., 1991. Lic. marriage and family therapist. Office nurse Bertalan Bolgar, M.D., Festus, Mo., 1957-60; ednl. asst. 1st Meth. Ch., Festus, 1966-68; sci. tchr. R-6 Sch. Dist., Festus, 1968-72, Fox Sch. Dist., Arnold, Mo., 1972-78, Mo. Sch. Blind, St. Louis, 1978-80; dir. Marriage & Family Life Educators, St. Louis, 1982—; exec. dir. Circle of Concern, Valley Park, Mo., 1992-93; dir. caring ministries Centenary Ch., St. Louis, 1995-98. Author: Perceptions of Family 1930-1988, 1991. Mem. Am. Assn. Family Counselors & Mediators (cert. supervisor 1986-88), Mo. Assn. Marriage & Family Therapy (pres. 1998—, bd. dirs.), Mo. Counselors Assn., Mo. Assn. Religious Values. Avocations: singing, drawing. Home and Office: 2228 Rutger St Saint Louis MO 63104-2436

BREWER, FLOYD I., history consultant; m. A. Coleen Hamilton, 1944; children: Jeffrey H., Mark A. Diploma in Elem. Edn., U. No. Maine, Presque Isle, 1942; BS in History and Elem. Edn., U. So. Maine, Gorham, 1944; MA in Vocat. Guidance, Columbia U., 1947, profl. diploma, 1952, EdD, 1956. Asst. prof., coll. adminstr. U. Bridgeport, Conn., 1947-56; coll. adminstr. U. Cin., 1956-66; assoc. prof. edn. SUNY, Albany, 1966-83; history cons. Delmar, N.Y., 1983—; archaeology apprentice, 1972-80; instr. archaeology Hudson Valley C.C., Troy, N.Y., 1980-83, continuing edn. program Bethlehem (N.Y.) Ctrl. Schs., 1981-85; field dir., editor publs. Bethelhem Archaeology Group, 1981-96. Sr. editor: Bethlehem Revisited, A Bicentennial Story 1793-1993, 1993; sr. author: Bethlehem Diary, Stories and Reflections 1983-1993, 1994; author: A Dutch-English Odyssey: Stories of Brewer and Estey Families in North America 1636-1996, 1997. With USAF, 1943-46. Mem. N.Y. Archaeol. Assn., Towne Family Assn., Holland Soc. N.Y., New Netherland Connections. Office: 18 Willow Dr Delmar NY 12054-2639

BREWER, GAIL LEE, pre-cast concrete company executive, banker; b. Arlington, Mass., Nov. 15, 1964; d. Robert James and Joan Williams (Lepper) B.; m. Glen Petrosso, Aug. 30, 1997. BSBA, Bryant Coll., Smithfield, R.I., 1986; MBA, Northeastern U., Boston, 1991. Sr. credit analyst Bank of Boston, Providence, 1992-94; underwriter Fleet Bank, Providence, 1994-97, reporting analyst, 1997—; pres. Castcrete Inc., Warwick, R.I., 1997—; dir. Pawtucket (R.I.) Day Nursery, 1995—. Ward com. person, Pawtucket, 1995—.

BREWER, GARRY DWIGHT, social scientist, educator; b. San Francisco, Oct. 2, 1941; s. Dwight Cleland and Querida Mae (Colson) B.; m. Saundra Neville Tonsager, Dec. 3, 1962 (div. 1976); children: Gabrielle Anne, Gregory David; m. Shelley Lane Marshall, May 11, 1976; 1 child, Matthew Douglas. Student, U.S. Naval Acad., 1959-61; AB in Econs, U. Calif., Berkeley, 1963; MS in Pub. Adminstrn, Calif. State U., San Diego, 1966; MPhil in Polit. Sci., Yale U., 1968, PhD, 1970. Rsch. fellow Advanced Rsch. Projects Agy., Dept. Def., Washington, 1967; cons. social sci. dept. Rand Corp., Santa Monica, Calif., 1969-70, mem. staff social sci. dept., 1970-72, mem. sr. staff, 1972-74; asst. prof. dept. polit. sci. U. Calif., Berkeley, 1970-71; lectr. pub. adminstrn. U. So. Calif., L.A., 1972-74; fellow Ctr. Advanced Studies in Behavior Scis., Palo Alto, Calif., 1974-75; assoc. prof. Yale U., New Haven, 1974-78, prof. orgn. and mgmt., polit. sci., forestry and environ. studies, 1978-84, Fredrick K. Weyerhaeuser prof. resource policy and mgmt., 1984-90; fellow Pearson Coll., New Haven, 1989-92; Edwin Weyerhaeuser Davis prof. resource policy and mgmt. Yale U., New Haven, 1990-91, acting dir. Instn. Social and Policy Studies, 1991; prof. resource policy and mgmt. U. Mich., Ann Arbor, 1991-98, dean Sch. Natural Resources and Environ., 1991-95, prof. bus. adminstrn., 1992-98, prof. pub. policy studies, 1992-98, dir. Frederick A. Erb Environ. Mgmt. Inst., 199-98; dean U. Calif. Berkeley Ext.; prof. environ. pol. and mgmt. Energy Resources Grp., U. Cal. Berkeley, 1998—; cons. NSF, 1972—, Ford Found., 1972-80, DATUM, Bonn, Germany, 1972-80, infas GmbH, Bonn, 1976-90, Russell Sage Found., 1975-76, MEDIPLAN GmbH, Germany, 1977-80, UN Food and Agr. Orgn., 1978-80, Resources for the Future, 1978-90, Solar Energy Rsch. Inst., 1979-81, Sci. Applications, Inc., 1979-84, Rockfeller Bros. Fund, 1990—; counselor The Policy Scis. Ctr., 1973-84, trustee, 1984-89; trustee Children's Rsch. Inst. Calif., 1974-80; chmn. Nat. Adv. Com. on Children, 1975-80; mem. rsch. adv. bd. Com. Econ. Devel., 1979-84; screener Coun. Internat. Exch. Scholars Pub. Adminstrn., 1986-89, chair, 1988-89; mem. sr. adv. com. Woods Hole Oceanog. Instn. Marine Policy Ctr., 1981-88; mem. sr. adv. bd. The Ocean and Coastal Policy Ctr., U. Calif., Santa Barbara, 1987-92; mem. faculty European Inst. Bus. Adminstrn., France, 1990-91; dir. Yosemite Nat. Insts., 1990-95, mem. exec. com., 1990-92; mem. nat. adv. bd. Duke U., Ctr. Tropical Conservation, 1991-96; mem. bd. Orgn. Tropical Studies, 1989-94, 97—, mem. exec. com., 1990-93; mem. pres. adv. com. U. B.C., Can., 1992-94; active U.S. Sec. Energy's Bd. on Environ., Safety and Health, 1992, U.S. Nuc. Waste Tech. Rev. Bd., 1992-96, U.S. Com. of IIASA, 1993—; King Carl XVI Gustaf prof. environ. scis. Royal Inst. Tech., Stockholm, 1998-99; lectr. in field. Author: Organized Complexity, 1971, Politicians, Bureaucrats and the Consultant, 1983, Political Development and Change, 1975, Handicapped Children, 1979, The War Game, 1979, The Foundations of Policy Analysis, 1983, Caught Unaware, 1983, Redirecting the Resources Planning Act, 1988; author chpts. to books; editor Policy Studies, 1974-76, 90-91, Simulation and Games, 1977-79; mem. editl. bd. Pub. Policy, 1973-81, Policy & Politics, 1977-79, TRANSFER, 1975-85, Policy Studies Rev. Ann., 1977-81, Jour. Acctg. & Pub. Policy, 1981-85, Jour. Conflict Resolution, 1981—, Pub. Adminstrn. Rev., 1985-88; contbr. numerous articles to profl. jours. Lt. USNR, 1963-66, Vietnam. Kent fellow Danforth Found., 1966-67; grantee NSF, 1969-70, Fleischman Found., 1973-75, Sloan Found., 1978-79, Gen. Svc. Found., 1982-84, Mellon Found., 1986, Pew Meml. Trust, 1987, Hewlett Found., 1990-91; recipient Silver medal Am. Fisheries Soc., 1989, Silver medal Fusion do Dos Culturas, Govt. Mex., 1991. Fellow Soc. for Values in Higher Edn.; mem. NAS (bd. ocean sci. and policy 1983-85, mem. ocean studies bd. 1985-87, NOAA panel 1985-86, and other coms.), AAAS, ASPA (editl. bd. PAR, Mosher award com. 1986-88, Dimock award com. 1986, Karl Bosworth award 1991), Oceangraphic Soc. (life), Royal Swedish Acad. Agr. and Forestry (life), Conn. Acad. Arts and Scis., Sigma Xi. Office: Univ Calif Berkley Sch Natural Resources and Environ 1995 University Ave Ste 300 Berkley MI 48109-1115

BREWER, JOHN CHARLES, journalist; b. Cin., Oct. 24, 1947; s. Harry Marion and Barbara Ann (Burrier) B.; m. Adeline Laude, Dec. 22, 1973 (div. 1994); children: Andrew John, Jeffrey Joseph; m. Ann Hagen Kellett, 1997. B.S., Calif. State Poly. U., Pomona, 1970. Newsman, photographer Daily Report, Ontario, Calif., 1967-69; newsman AP, L.A., 1969-74; news editor AP, 1974-75; asst. chief bur. AP, Seattle, 1975-76, chief of bur., 1976-82; chief of bur. AP, L.A., 1982-86; gen. exec. membership dept. AP, N.Y.C., 1986-88; exec. editor news svc. The N.Y. Times, 1988-90, editor in chief news svc., 1990—; pres. N.Y. Times Syndication Sales Corp., 1990-97; publisher Peninsula Daily News, Port Angeles, Wash., 1997—. Bd. dirs. Peekskill Bus. Improvement Dist. Mem. Fedn. of Fly Fishers, World Editors Forum. Republican. Roman Catholic. Clubs: Northwest Steelheaders-Trout Unlimited, Nat. Steelhead Trout Assn. Office: Peninsula Daily News 305 W 1st St Port Angeles WA 98362-2205 *I enjoy very much being a journalist and newspaper executive. Nothing can compare with it. As for finding time for everything—the news and photo reports, relations with advertisers and subscribers, my family, my personnel, problems—always the problems—I am reminded of a woman who had eleven children. She was asked how she had time to take care of all of them. She replied that when she had one child it took 100 percent of her time, and eleven could not take more. I think there's an analogy in this.*

BREWER, JUDITH ANNE, special education educator; b. Pontiac, Mich., Jan. 25, 1952; d. Lorenz Robert and Jane Francis (Behen) Einheuser; m. Randall Edward Brewer, May 17, 1974; children: Michael E., Julie M. BS in Spl. Edn. summa cum laude, Western Mich. U., 1974; MA in Teaching, Oakland U., 1977. Cert. spl. edn. tchr. for emotionally impaired and learning disabled; cert. Project Adventure; cert. advanced stds. Project Adventure. Spl. edn. resource tchr. Mayfield-Woodside Elem. Sch., Lapeer, Mich., 1974-75; learning disabled tchr. Pine Tree Elem. Sch., Lake Orion, Mich., 1976, elem. self-contained learning disabled tchr., 1977-79; spl. edn. resource tchr. Carpenter-Blanche Sims Elem. Sch., Lake Orion, 1977; spl. edn. tchr. Lake Orion Middle Sch., 1983-85; spl. edn. tchr., cons. Lake Orion High Sch., 1985—, spl. edn. dept. chair, 1992—; interim asst. prin. Lake Orion H.S., 1994; MATRIX interdisciplinary block program co-chair, tchr. Lake Orion High Sch., 1994-98; jr. class advisor Lake Orion H.S., 1985-87, sophomore class advisor, 1987-88, ski club sponsor, 1990-97, sch. improvement com. mem., 1990-94, mem. bldg. coun., 1992—, mem. new bldg. com., 1994-96, mem. block scheduling com., 1995—, mem. insvc. subcom., 1995—; exec. bd. rep. Lake Orion Edn. Assn., 1987-89, 94-95, 98—; student activities chair, sch. improvement team, 1990; high sch. level steering com. North Ctrl. Accreditation, 1989-90, evaluator, 1991; mem. Cmty. Svc. Com., 1993, mem. portfolio com., 1991; lectr. in field Cath. Social Svcs., Oakland County, Mich., 1985—. Social chmn. Sylvan Manor Homeowners Assn., West Bloomfield, Mich., 1982-84, pres. 1985; sec. Marina Pk. Estates, Subdiv., Lake Orion, 1987-89, soc. chmn., 1991-92. Grantee Lake Orion Bd. Edn., 1990. Mem. Mich. Assn. Learning Disability Educators, Oakland County Educators Learning Disabled, Coun. for Exceptional Children. Roman Catholic. Avocations: reading, sewing, cross-country skiing, swimming, boating. Home: 365 Bay Pointe Rd Lake Orion MI 48362-2572 Office: Lake Orion High Sch 495 E Scripps Rd Lake Orion MI 48360-2249

BREWER, KAREN, librarian; b. Janesville, Wis., Apr. 29, 1943; d. Gordon A. and Charlotte (Warren) Schultz; m. Eugene N. Brewer, June 22, 1963. BA, U. Wis., 1965, MA, 1966; PhD, Case Western Res. U., 1983. Libr. Middleton Med. Libr. U. Wis., Madison, 1966-67; libr. Med. Libr. U. Tenn., Memphis, 1968-69; libr. Cleve. Health Sci. Libr. Case Western Res. U., Cleve., 1970-76; dir. libr. Coll. Medicine Northeastern Ohio U., Rootstown, 1976-88; dir. libr. Med. Ctr. NYU, 1988—. Mem. editorial bd. Ann. Stats. Acad. Health Sci. Libr., 1986-91. Fellow N.Y. Acad. Medicine; mem. Assn. Acad. Health Sci. Librs. (sec.-treas. 1986-89, pres.-elect 1994, pres. 1995), Med. Libr. Assn. (bd. dirs. 1991-94), Acad. Health Info. Profls. (disting. mem.), Am. Med. Informatics Assn. Office: NYU Med Ctr Libr 550 1st Ave New York NY 10016-6481

BREWER, KEITH F., plastic surgeon; b. Sept. 16, 1952. BA, Ind. U., 1974; MD, Washington U., 1978. Ptnr. Woodland (Calif.) Clinic, 1985-91; pvt. practice plastic surgery Davis, Calif., 1992—.

BREWER, LEO, physical chemist, educator; b. St. Louis, June 13, 1919; s. Abraham and Hanna (Resnik) B.; m. Rose Strugo, Aug. 22, 1945; children: Beth A., Roger M., Gail L. BS, Calif. Inst. Tech., 1940; PhD, U. Calif., Berkeley, 1943. Faculty U. Calif., Berkeley, 1946-55, prof. phys. chemistry, 1955—; research assoc. Lawrence Berkeley Lab. (formerly Radiation Lab.), 1943-61, head inorganic materials div., 1961-75, prin. investigator, 1961-94, assoc. dir. lab., 1967-75; Huffman Meml. lectr. Calorimetry Conf., 1966; Coover lectr. Am. Chem. Soc., 1967; Robert W. Williams lectr. MIT, 1963; Henry Werner lectr. U. Kans., 1963; O.M. Smith lectr. Okla State U., 1964; G.N. Lewis lectr. U. Calif., 1964, Faculty lectr., 1966; Corn Products lectr. Pa. State U., 1970; W.D. Harkins lectr. U. Chgo., 1974; Oak Ridge Nat. Lab. lectr., 1979; Frontiers in Chem. Rsch. lectr. Texas A & M U., 1981; rsch. scholar lectr., Drew U., 1983; 10th Louis J. Bircher lectr., Vanderbilt

U., 1986; Frontiers in chemistry Eyring lectr., Ariz. State U., 1989, Leo Brewer retirement symposium on high temperature and materials chemistry Lawrence Berkely Lab., 1989; mem. rev. com. reactor chem. div. Oak Ridge Nat. Lab.; rsch. assoc. Manhattan Dist. U. Calif., Berkeley, 1943-45; sec. gas subcom. high temperature commn. Internat. Union Pure and Applied Chemistry, 1957-60; assoc. mem. commn. on thermodynamics and thermochemistry, 1973—; chmn. materials adv. bd. Com. Investigation Application Plasma Phenomena, 1959-60. Author: (with others) Thermodynamics, 1961; assoc. editor: Jour. Chem. Physics, 1959-63; mem. editorial adv. bd.: Jour. Physics and Chemistry Solids, Progress Inorganic Chemistry, Jour. Chem. Thermodynamics, 1968-77, Jour. High Temperature Sci., Leo Brewer Special Festschrift Volume, 1984, Jour. Solid State Chemistry, Jour. Chem. Engring. Data, 1977-83, Jour. Phys. Chemistry Reference Data, 1978-81, 89—; divisional editor high temperature sci and tech. div.: Jour. Electrochem. Soc., 1977-84. Recipient Ernest Orlando Lawrence Meml. award, 1961, Disting. Alumni award Calif. Inst. Tech., 1974; Berkeley citation U. Calif., 1989, Berkeley fellow, 1992; Gt. Western Dow fellow, 1942, Guggenheim fellow, 1950. Fellow AAAS, Am. Phys. Soc., Am. Soc. for Metals Internat.; mem. AAUP, Am. Ceramic Soc. (hon.), Nat. Acad. Scis. (exec. com. Office Critical Tables 1961-66, com. on Data Needs, 1975-78, com. on High Temperatures1975-85), Am. Acad. Arts and Scis., Am. Chem. Soc. (Leo H. Baekeland award 1953), Electrochem. Soc. (lectr. 1970, Palladium Medalist 1971, Linford award for disting. teaching 1988), Am. Plant Life Soc., ACLU, Cobletz Soc., Combustion Inst., Royal Soc. Chemistry, Fedn. Am. Scientists, Calif. Assn. Chemistry Tchrs., Internat. Plansee Soc. Powder Metallurgy, Am. Optical Soc., Materials Rsch. Soc., Metall. Soc. (William Hume-Rothery award 1983, Extractive Metallurgy Sci. award 1991), Coun. on Alloy Phase Diagrams, Calif. Acad. Sci., Calif. Native Plant Soc., Calif. Botanic Soc., Lawrence Hall of Sci., Nature Conservancy, Save Redwoods League, Sierra Club, Sigma Xi, Alpha Chi Sigma, Tau Beta Pi. Home: 15 Vista Del Orinda Rd Orinda CA 94563-2044 Office: U Calif Dept Chemistry Berkeley CA 94720

BREWER, MARK COURTLAND, lawyer; b. Hammond, Ind., Apr. 1, 1955; s. Harold Russell and Carol Joan (Odell) B. BA, Harvard U., 1977; JD, Stanford U., 1981. Bar: U.S. Dist. Ct. (ea. and we. dist.) Mich. 1983, U.S. Ct. Appeals (6th cir.) 1983. Law clk. U.S. Ct. Appeals (5th cir.), Austin, 1981-82; law clk. to justice Mich. Supreme Ct., Lansing, 1982-83; assoc. Sachs, Waldman, O'Hare, P.C., Detroit, 1983-89; mem. Sachs, Waldman & O'Hare, Detroit, 1989-95; Chm. Mich Dem Party; pres. Stanford Pub. Interest Law Found. Palo Alto, Calif., 1980-81; bd. dirs. Interfaith Ctr. for Racial Justice, Warren, Mich. Contbr. articles on AIDS discrimination, drug testing, and employee privacy to profl. publs. Mem. Macomb County Dem. Com., Mich., 1982—, 12th Congl. Dist. Dem. Com. Macomb County, 1983-93, 10th Congl. Dist. Dem. Com. Macomb County, 1993—. Mem. ABA, State Bar Mich. (Outstanding Young Lawyer 1988), Detroit Fed. Bar Assn. (bd. dirs. 1989—), Sierra Club (Detroit chpt. 1987—). Democrat. Lutheran. Office: Mich Democratic Party 606 Townsend St Lansing MI 48933-2313

BREWER, NATHAN RONALD, veterinarian, consultant; b. Albany, N.Y., June 28, 1904; s. William and Rose (Johnson) B.; m. Jean Lees, Apr. 1, 1936; children: Maureen Pasik, Sandra Ginsberg, Jacquelyn Fechter. BS, Mich. State U., 1930, DVM, 1937; PhD in Physiology, U. Chgo., 1936; DSc (hon.), Chgo. Coll. Osteo. Medicine, 1977. Diplomate Am. Coll. Lab. Animal Medicine. Instr. pharmacology U. Ill., Chgo., 1935-36; veterinarian Detroit Bd. Health, 1937-38; prof. physiology Middlesex Vet. Sch., Waltham, Mass., 1938-39; pvt. practice Irvington (now Fremont), Calif., 1940-45; assoc. prof. physiology, dir. lab. animal facilities U. Chgo., 1945-69; pvt. cons. Chgo., 1969—. Contbr. articles to profl. jours. Named Man of Yr., Nat. Soc. Med. Rsch., 1956; recipient Arthur Brown award Delaware Valley Coll., 1983, Disting. Vet. Alumni award Mich. State U., 1997. Mem. Am. Vet. Med. Assn. (chmn. various coms., Charles River award 1992), Nat. Acad. Sci. (chmn. parasitism com. 1953-58), Ill. State Vet. Med. Assn. (life), Chgo. Vet. Med. Assn. (life), Am. Physiol. Soc. Conf. Rsch. Workers in Animal Diseases, Ill. State Acad. Sci. (chmn. animals in rsch. com. 1968), Am. Assn. Lab. Animal Sci. (editor 1950-62, pres. 1950-55. editor emeritus, chmn. arrangements com. 1950-53, 59, 62, 66, Griffin award 1960, Ann. Nathan R. Brewer award established in his name 1994—), Inst. Lab. Animal Resources, Am. Coll. Lab. Animal Medicine (pres. 1957-59), Am. Soc. Vet. Physiologists and Pharmacologists, Am. Soc. Lab. Animal Practitioners (chmn. mgmt. practice com.), Ill. Acad. Vet. Practice. Avocation: chess. Home and Office: 10800 Tara Rd Potomac MD 20854-1340

BREWER, NEVADA NANCY, elementary education educator; b. Balt., Jan. 21, 1949; d. Leo and Rebecca (Johnson) B. BS, Coppin State Coll., 1973, MEd, 1974; MEd, Coppin State Coll., 1981; postgrad., C.C. Balt., 1985. Cert. elem. tchr., spl. edn. tchr. Tchr. Balt. County Adult Edn., Towson, Md., 1973-88; coord. just say no to drugs program Balt. City Sch. Sys., tchr.; coord. Heads Up Program, 1980, math-a-thon program for St. Jude Rsch. Ctr., 1993—, 24 Challenge Math. Tournament, 1996—; supr. tchr. for student tchrs. Towson State U., Coll. Notre Dame, Coppin State Coll., 1989—; leadership tchr. STARS sci. program, 1995. Coord. Echo Hill Outdoor Sch., 1988—. Recipient Freedom Found. award 1974. Home: 1616 Wentworth Ave Baltimore MD 21234-6125

BREWER, PETER GEORGE, ocean geochemist; b. Ulverston, Eng., Dec. 30, 1940; came to U.S., 1967, naturalized, 1982; s. Frederick and Irene (Clarkson) B.; m. Hilary Williams, Mar. 29, 1966; children: Jillian Anne, Alastair Michael, Erica Christine. BSc, Liverpool (Eng.) U., 1962, PhD, 1967. Asst. scientist Woods Hole (Mass.) Oceanographic Inst., 1967-71, assoc. scientist, 1971-78, sr. scientist, 1978-91; program dir. marine chemistry NSF, 1981-83; exec. dir. Monterey Bay Aquarium Rsch. Inst., Pacific Grove, Calif., 1991-96, sr. scientist, 1996—; leader of ocean sci. expeditions. Contbr. articles to profl. publs. Grantee NSF, NASA, Office Naval Rsch., Dept. Energy. Fellow AAAS, Am. Geophys. Union. Office: Monterey Bay Aquarium Rsch Inst PO Box 628 Moss Landing CA 95039-0628

BREWER, PHILIP WARREN, civil engineer; b. Hagerstown, Md., Dec. 18, 1923; s. J. Chester and Ruth (Emmert) B.; m. Elizabeth Marvel Wynn, Aug. 29, 1947; children—Dorothy Wynn, Bruce Douglas. B.S., U. Md., 1945. Hydraulic engr. Water Resources Br., U.S. Geol. Survey, College Park, Md., 1945-47; designing engr. Wash. Suburban San. Commn., Hyattsville, Md., 1947-53; san. engr., civil engr. Bur. Yards and Docks, Dept. Navy, Washington, 1953-68, head spl. design Naval Facilities Engring. Command, 1968-73, chief civil engr., 1973-80. Bd. dirs. Madison County Wildlife Assn. Clubs: Monument River Sportmen's Assn. (Houlton, Maine); Ruritan (Wolftown, Va.). Lutheran. Home: Rural Route 1 Box 66-C Madison VA 22727

BREWER, RICKY LEE, investment broker, estate planner; b. Amarillo, Tex., June 20, 1948; s. Murry Lee and Carmelia (Grantham) B.; m. Kathy Jean Hall, Apr. 5, 1974; children: Ricky Lee II, Robert Neil. Student, Hardin-Simmons U., 1967-68, Tex. Tex. U., 1968-70. Account rep. CIT Fin., Lubbock, Tex., 1970-71; collection officer Cleburne (Tex.) Nat. Bank, 1971-73; salesman Baldwin Piano and Organ, Lubbock, 1973-75; owner Averitt Music Co., Lubbock, 1975-80, Piano Warehouse, Lubbock, 1980-84; agy. mgr. La. Farm Bur., Gonzales, 1984-88, Tex. Farm Bur., Bonham, 1988-92; investment broker A.G. Edwards & Sons, Inc., McKinney, Tex., 1992—. Mem. Bonham C. of C. (bd. dirs. 1991—), Bonham Rotary Club (pres. elect 1990, pres. 1991). Republican. Baptist. Avocations: cooking, golf. Home: 2024 Fleming Dr Mc Kinney TX 75070-3986 Office: A G Edwards & Sons Inc VP Investments 1836 W Virginia St Ste 102 Mc Kinney TX 75069-7868

BREWER, ROBERT ALLEN, physician; b. Inpls., Jan. 29, 1927; s. Robert Dewayne and Viola Mae (Grant) B.; m. Mildred Noreen Barnett, Jan. 1, 1950 (dec. May 1997); children: Robert A. Jr., Raymond, Richard, Brian, Andrew. AA, St. Petersburg Jr. Coll., Fla., 1949; AB, Ind. U., 1952; MD, Ind U., Inpls., 1955. Emergency dept. staff physician Mound Park Hosp., St. Petersburg, Fla., 1960; staff physician Pinellas Hosp., Largo, Fla., 1961-68; pvt. practice Logansport, Ind., 1969—. Mem. Cass County Republican Com., Logansport, Ind., candidate for city coun., 1995. Capt. U.S. Army, 1957-59. Mem. AMA, Am. Acad. Family Practitioner (bd. cert. diplomate), Ind. Med. Assn., Cass County Med. Assn. Republican. Avocations: stamp collecting, coin collecting. Office: PO Box 119 831 E Broadway Logansport IN 46947-3161*

BREWER, STANLEY R., wholesale grocery executive; b. Preston, Idaho, Nov. 5, 1937; s. G. Stanley and Emily (Wallentine) B.; m. Diane Rose, Aug. 1, 1960; children: Dee S., Douglas R., John-David, Jennifer. AS, Weber State Coll., 1957; student, U. Utah, 1960-63. Various positions from clk. to dir. store devel. Associated Food Stores, Inc., Salt Lake City, 1960-78, gen. dir., 1978-81, treas., 1981-85, v.p., treas., 1985-91, v.p., sec.-treas., 1991-97; sr. v.p., 1994-97; pres. S. Brewer & Co., 1997—; pres., gen. ptnr. EMC Land Group Ltd., Salt Lake City, 1982—; bd. dirs. Wesco Explosives, Inc., Pinacle Respond, Inc. Chmn. Salt Lake City chpt. March of Dimes, 1998—; nat. trustee March of Dimes Birth Defects Found., White Plains, N.Y., 1987—; chmn. Salt Lake County Voting Dist., 1965-66, 76-78. Republican. Mem. LDS Ch. Avocations: alpine and cross country skiing, hiking, boating, jogging.

BREWER, THOMAS BOWMAN, retired university president; b. Fort Worth, July 22, 1932; s. Earl Johnson and Maurine (Bowman) B.; m. Betty Jean Walling, Aug. 4, 1951; children: Diane, Thomas Bowman Jr. B.A., U. Tex., 1954, M.A., 1957; Ph.D., U. Pa., 1962. Instr. St. Stephens Episcopal Sch., Austin, Tex., 1955-56, S.W. Tex. State Coll., San Marcos, 1956-57; from instr. to asso. prof. N. Tex. State U., Denton, 1959-66; asst. prof. U. Ky., 1966-67; asso. prof. Iowa State U., 1967-68; prof. history, chmn. dept. U. Toledo, 1968-71; dean Tex. Christian U., Fort Worth, 1971-72, vice chancellor, dean univ., 1972-78; chancellor E. Carolina U., Greenville, N.C., 1978-82; v.p. acad. affairs Ga. State U., Atlanta, 1982-88; pres. Met. State Coll. of Denver, 1988-93; interim provost U. Alaska, Anchorage, 1995-97. Editor: Views of American Economic Growth, 2 vols, 1966, The Robber Barons, 1969; gen. editor: Railroads of America Series. Home: 104 Javelin Dr Austin TX 78734-5016

BREWERTON, TIMOTHY DAVID, psychiatrist; b. Baton Rouge, Mar. 26, 1953; s. John Lee and Helen (Bouy) B.; m. Therese Kathleen Killeen, June 16, 1990. BS, La. State U., 1974; MD, Tulane U., 1978. Diplomate Am. Bd. Psychiatry and Neurology, Am. Bd. Child and Adolescent Psychiatry. Intern, resident in psychiatry U. Calif., San Francisco, 1978-82; staff psychiatrist Hawaii State Hosp., Kaneohe, 1982-84; med. staff fellow NIMH, Bethesda, Md., 1984-87, guest rschr., 1987-95; asst. prof. psychiatry and behavioral scis. Med. U. S.C., Charleston, 1987-90, assoc. prof. psychiatry and behavioral scis., 1990-97, prof. psychiatry and behavioral scis., 1997—, fellow in child and adolescent psychiatry, 1994-96, tenure, 1999—; dir. Eating Disorders Program, Inst. Psychiatry, Charleston, 1987—; med. cons. Nat. Crime Victims Rsch. and Treatment Ctr., 1996—. Contbr. articles to profl. jours. Recipient Award for Creative Achievement Dept. Psychiatry U. Calif. San Francisco, 1982. Mem. Am. Psychiat. Assn., Soc. Biol. Psychiatry, Am. Acad. Clin. Psychiatrists (Clin. Rsch. award 1989, bd. dirs. 1993-97), N.Y. Acad. Sci., Eating Disorders Rsch. Soc., Acad. Eating Disorders, Am. Acad. Child and Adolescent Psychiatry, Soc. Light Treatment and Biol. Rhythms, Am. Profl. Soc. on Abuse of Children, Internat. Soc. for Traumatic Stress Studies. Office: Med U SC Inst Psychiatry PO Box 250861 67 President St Charleston SC 29425-0001

BREWINGTON, ARTHUR WILLIAM, retired English language educator; b. Bklyn., Nov. 10, 1906; s. Oscar and Julia (Wenisch) B.; m. Thelma Sherman, Aug. 18, 1955. AB, Asbury Coll., 1928; MA, Cornell U., 1931; PhD, Vanderbilt U., 1941. Head English dept. Tenn. Wesleyan Coll., Athens, 1929-31; instr. English Pa. State U., State College, 1932-33; prof. English and speech Memphis State U., 1940-43; inspector quality control Glenn Martin Co., Balt., 1943-45; head English and speech dept. Towson State U., Balt., 1945-71; dir. drama and theater Towson State U., 1946-69. *Sent to India by the Fulbright Committee of the State Department and engaged by the Indian Ministry of Education at the time of developing Indian independence following the separation from England. At the time some Indian political leaders were set to remove the English language from India and replace it with Hindu. Helped to save the English language for India. Sent to lecture at colleges and universities in many Indian states, and to work with many leaders of Indian public education. First speech educator employed by Towson State University in 1945. Introduced and developed a program of speech education, theater and dramatics, speech and hearing.* Contbr. rsch. to profl. publs. Fund-raiser, bd. dirs. Am. Heart Assn., Green Valley, 1995-96. Fulbright grantee U.S. State Dept., 1955-56, Danforth grantee, 1963. Mem. Kiwanis (com. chmn. 1971-95), Masons (chaplain lodge 171 1972-75), Cornell Club., Green Valley Shrine Club (pres. 1974). Democrat. Episcopalian. Avocations: theater, movies, TV, opera, symphony. Home: 69 W Cedro Dr Green Valley AZ 85614-4203

BREWSTER, ANDREA B., artist; b. Boston, Aug. 31, 1962; d. C. Stuart and Renate (Falkenheim) B. Student, U. Heidelberg, Germany, 1982; BA in Sculpture cum laude, Pomona Coll., 1984; MFA in New Genre, San Francisco Art Inst., 1991. resident Djerassi Found., Woodside, Calif., 1992; guest artist Art Thing Wing Ding, Palo Alto, 1978, 79, 80, Pacific Art League, Palo Alto, 1984, Pacific Art League, Palo Alto, 1986, Hands on the Arts, Santa Clara, Calif., 1986, San Jose (Calif.) Unified Sch. Dist., 1986, Hands on the Arts, Sunnyvale, Calif., 1987, Berryessa, Cupertino and Alum Rock Sch. Dists., San Jose, 1987; art instr. Parents and Profls. for Art, Palo Alto, 1985, Rainbow Montessori, Santa Clara, 1985-86; outreach facilitator Triton Mus., 1986-87, Children's Discovery Mus., San Jose, 1987. One-woman shows include Montgomery Gallery, Claremont, Calif., 1984, Monadnock Bldg., San Francisco, 1988, Berkeley (Calif.) Arts Commn., 1989, Hayward (Calif.) State U., 1992, The Lab, San Francisco, 1993, San Francisco Art Commn., 1993, Fairfield (Calif.) Ctr. for Arts, 1995; exhibited in group shows Montgomery Gallery, 1984, Lang Gallery, Claremont, 1985, 90, Sunnyvale (Calif.) Civic Art Gallery, 1986, San Mateo Arts Coun., Belmont, Calif., 1986, Gallery Sanchez, San Francisco, 1987, Triton Mus. Art, Santa Clara, Calif., 1988, Weir Gallery, Berkeley, 1989, Art Space Annex, San Francisco, 1990, Immanuel Walter McBean Gallery, San Francisco, 1990, Bayfront Gallery, San Francisco, 1990, Diego Rivera Gallery, San Francisco, 1990, New Langton Arts, San Francisco, 1991, Zen Ctr. Hospice, San Francisco, 1992, Bechtel Internat. Ctr., Stanford U., Palo Alto, Calif., 1992, Acme Art Gallery, San Francisco, 1993, San Francisco State Union Gallery, 1993, San Francisco Camerawork, 1994, SOMAR Gallery, San Francisco, 1995, Trojanowska Gallery, San Francisco, 1995, San Francisco Art Commn., 1996, 97, Arts Benecia, Calif., 1996, Benecia Pub. Libr., 1989, Berkeley Pub. Libr., 1989; works included in publs. Bay Arts Catalog, 1986, San Francisco Bay Guardian, 1990, San Francisco Art Inst. Viewbook, 1991, San Francisco Chronicle, 1991, San Francisco Examiner, 1991, Hayward Pioneer, 1992, West Coast Weekend Radio Show, 1992, Art Week, 1993, Fairfield Daily Republic, 1995. Recipient Susan Watkins award, 1991, Best of Show award for mixed media Sunnyvale Civic Art Gallery, 1986; William and Ester B. Davidowitz fellow, 1993; Nat. Endowment for Arts Fellowship grantee, 1993. Home: 698 56th St Oakland CA 94609-1606

BREWSTER, BILL K., business executive, former congressman; b. Ardmore, Okla., Nov. 8, 1941; m. Mary Sue Nelson, 1963; children: Balynda Karel, Betsy Kecia (dec.), Bradley Kent (dec.). BS in pharmacy, Southwestern Okla. State U., 1964. Cattleman and farm co-owner; owner, pharmacist, operator Colleyville Drug. Inc. Colleyville, Okla., 1964-77; cattleman Brewster Angus Farms, 1968—; state rep. Okla., 1982-89; mem. 102nd-104th Congresses from 3rd Okla. dist., Washington, 1991-96; pres. R. Duffy Wall and Assoc., Washington, 1996—; mem. South/West Energy Coun., 1982-90; del. Nat. Conf. of State Legislatures, 1983-90. With USAR, 1968-71. named Disting. alumnus, Southwestern Okla. State U. Office: R Duffy Wall and Assoc 601 13th St NW Washington DC 20005-3807*

BREWSTER, CARROLL WORCESTER, former academic adminstrator; b. N.Y.C., Mar. 26, 1936; s. Carroll Harwood and Blandina (Worcester) B.; m. Ursula Mary Orange, Mar. 9, 1968 (dec. Apr. 1996); children—Abraham Carroll, Ursula Constant, Blandina Worcester. B.A., Yale, 1957, LL.B., 1961; L.H.D. (hon.), Hollins Coll., 1981, Hobart and William Smith Coll., 1991; postgrad., Kings Coll., Cambridge U., 1957-58. Bar: Conn. 1962. Law clk. to chief judge U.S. Dist. Ct., Conn., 1961-62; legal asst. to Hon. Mohamed Ahmed Abu Rannat, Chief Justice of the Sudan, Khartoum, 1962-64; assoc. Tyler, Cooper, Grant, Bowerman & Keefe, New Haven, 1965-69, also U.S. commr., 1966-69; lectr. Yale Law Sch., 1967-69; coll. dean Dartmouth Coll., 1969-75; pres. Hollins Coll., Va., 1975-81, Hobart and William Smith Colls., N.Y., 1982-91; exec. dir. Hole in the Wall Gang Fund, New Haven, 1991-98; trustee Phillips Exeter Acad., 1970-80, Anatolia Coll, 1990—, U. New Haven, 1995—; chmn., bd. dirs. Presiding Bishop's Fund for Wold Relief, 1986-91, The Episcopal Ch. Found., 1985-93. Editor: Sudan Law Jour. and Reports, 1961-65. Senior Fulbright scholar, U. Khartoum, Sudan, 1981-82. Home: 126 Lounsbury Rd Ridgefield CT 06877-4730

BREWSTER, CLARK OTTO, lawyer; b. Marlette, Mich., Nov. 5, 1956; s. Charles W. and June V. (Hoff) B.; m. Deborah K. Trowhill, Aug. 3, 1974; m. Cassie Mae, Corbin Clark. BA cum laude, Cen. Mich. U., 1977; JD with honor, Tulsa U., 1980. Bar: Okla. 1981, U.S. Dist. Ct. (no. and ea. dists.) Okla. 1982, Tex. 1993. Assoc. Riddle and Assocs., Tulsa, 1981, Braly and McEachin, Tulsa, 1981-82; ptnr. Brewster & Shallcross, Tulsa, 1982—; bd. dirs. Redy Corp., Tulsa, Cottontail Oil Corp., Tulsa; trustee Travis Kerr Magana Trust, Tulsa, 1985—. Mem. ABA, ATLA, Okla. Bar Assn., Okla. Trial Lawyers Assn. (pres. 1998), Tulsa County Bar Assn., Order of Curule chair, Order of Barristers. Avocations: golf, hunting, horseback riding. Home: 2109 E 30th St Tulsa OK 74114-5425 Office: Brewster Shallcross & DeAngelis 2021 S Lewis Ave Ste 675 Tulsa OK 74104-5725

BREWSTER, DANIEL FERGERSON, minister, religious organization executive; b. Newnan, Ga., Dec. 23, 1916; s. Daniel Fergerson and Sara Josephine (Stevens) B.; m. Helen Howe Glawson, June 7, 1943. AB, Emory U., 1945; MDiv, Candler Sch. Theology, 1948; DD (hon.), LaGrange Coll., 1966. Ordained to ministry, United Meth. Ch., 1948. Pastor various chs., Ga., 1943-64; exec. dir. Ga. Meth. Commn. on Higher Edn., Atlanta, 1964-84; trustee LaGrange Coll., Ga., 1965—; mem. exec. com., sec. Southeastern Jurisdiction Commn. on Higher Edn., Atlanta, 1980-84; dean Ga. Meth. Pastors Sch., 1960-64; sec. Conf. Bd. of Edn., 1956-60. Editor: Higher Education in Southeastern Jurisdiction 1787-1984 (United Methodist Church), 1984, North Ga. Conf. Handbook, 1963-70. Chmn. history-writing com. Newnan-Coweta County Hist. Soc., 1983. Recipient Spl. Achievement award 9 Meth. Colls., 1983, Brewster Endowment in Liberal Arts, Ga. Meth. Commn. on Higher Edn.; fellow LaGrange Coll., Ga., 1981. Mem. Nat. Coun. Boy Scouts Am. (recipient Silver Beaver award 1986), Nat. Eagle Scout Assn. Democrat. Home: 20 W Broad St Newnan GA 30263-2045

BREWSTER, ELIZABETH WINIFRED, English language educator, poet, novelist; b. Chipman, N.B., Can., Aug. 26, 1922; d. Frederick John and Ethel May (Day) Brewster. BA, U. N.B., 1946; MA, Radcliffe U., 1947; BLS, U. Toronto, 1953; PhD, Ind. U., 1962; DLitt, U. N.B., 1982. Cataloger Carleton U., Ottawa, Ont., 1953-57; cataloger Ind. U. Library, Bloomington, 1957-58, N.B. Legis. Library, 1965-68, U. Alta. Library, Edmonton, Can., 1968-70; mem. English dept. Victoria U., B.C., 1960-61; reference libr. Mt. Allison U. Libr., Sackville, N.B., 1961-65; vis. asst. prof. English U. Alta., 1970-71; mem. faculty U. Sask., Saskatoon, Can., 1972—, asst. prof. English, 1972-75, assoc. prof., 1975-80, prof., 1980-90, prof. emeritus, 1990—. Author: East Coast, 1951, Lilloot, 1954, Roads, 1957, Passage of Summer, 1969, Sunrise North, 1972, In Search of Eros, 1974, Sometimes I Think of Moving, 1977, The Way Home, 1982, The Sisters, 1974, It's Easy to Fall on the ice, 1977, Digging In, 1982, Junction, 1982, A House Full of Women, 1983, Selected Poems 1944-84, 2 vols., 1985, Visitations, 1987, Entertaining Angels, 1988, Spring Again, 1990, The Invention of Truth, 1991, Wheel of Change, 1993, Away from Home, 1995, Footnotes to the Book of Job, 1995, Garden of Sculpture, 1998. Recipient E.J. Pratt award for poetry U. Toronto, 1953, Pres. medal for poetry U. Western Ont., 1980, Lit. award Can. Broadcasting Corp., 1991, Lifetime award for excellence in the arts Sask. Arts Bd., 1995, Short List award Gov. Gen., 1996. Mem. League Can. Poets (life), Writers' Union Can., Assn. Can. Univ. Tchrs. English.

BREWSTER, GERRY LEIPER, educator, lawyer; b. Balt., Sept. 6, 1957; s. Daniel Baugh and Carole Helme (Leiper) B. AB cum laude, Princeton (N.J.) U., 1979; JD, U. Balt., 1984. Bar: Md. 1985, D.C. 1988. Law clk. to judge State of Md., Towson, 1984-85; asst. state's atty. Baltimore County, Towson, Md., 1985-88, asst. to county exec., 1988-90; legislator Md. State Legislature, Annapolis, Md., 1991-95; tchr. Balt. County Pub. Schs., 1995—; bd. dirs. Md. State Fair, Timonium. Exec. dir. Young Dems. of Md., 1987-88; del. Dem. Nat. Conv., Atlanta; bd. dirs. Franklin Sq. Hosp., Citizens Outreach of Baltimore County; mem. adv. bd. Sexual Assault and Domestic Violence Ctr., Inc.; Dem. nominee for Congress, Md. 2d Congl. Dist., 1994. Named 1 of 10 Outstanding Young Marylanders, Towson Jaycees, 1989, Merit award Common Cause Md., 1993, Gold Star award League Conservation Voters, 1993, Humanitarian award Gov. of Md., 1993, Md. Law Enforcement Officers Inc. honoree, 1993, Co-Legis. of Yr. award Md. State Fraternal Order of Police, 1994. Mem. ABA, Md. Bar Assn., D.C. Bar Assn., Baltimore County Bar Assn., Nat. Dist. Attys. Assn., Md. State's Atty. Assn., Gilman Alumni Assn. (bd. dirs. 1986—, pres. 1991-92), W. Towson Neighborhood Assn. Episcopalian. Avocations: steeplechase riding, sailing, golf. Home: 527 Allegheny Ave Baltimore MD 21204-4233

BREWSTER, GREGORY BUSH, telecommunications educator; b. Richmond, Ind., Sept. 6, 1959; s. Robert Riggs and Nancy Huff (Terrell) B.; m. Gerianne Smith, Aug. 1, 1981. BA in Math. magna cum laude, Carleton Coll., 1981; MS in Computer Sci., U. Wis., 1983, PhD in Computer Sci., 1994. Mem. tech. staff AT&T Bell Labs., Naperville, Ill., 1987-90; assoc. dir. grad. telecomm. DePaul U., Chgo., 1990-94, dir. grad. telecommunications, asst. prof., 1995—. Mem. IEEE, ACM, Spl. Interest Group on Comm. and Performance, Sigma Xi, Phi Beta Kappa. Avocations: music, piano, dogs. Office: DePaul Univ Sch of Computer Sci 243 S Wabash Ave Chicago IL 60604-2302

BREWSTER, JAMES HENRY, retired chemistry educator; b. Ft. Collins, Colo., Aug. 21, 1922; s. Oswald Cammann and Elizabeth (Booraem) B.; m. Christine Barbara Germain, Jan. 23, 1954; children—Christine Carolyn, Mary Elizabeth, Barbara Anne. A.B., Cornell U., 1942; Ph.D., U. Ill., 1948. Chemist Atlantic Refining Co., Phila., 1942-43; postdoctoral fellow U. Chgo., 1948-49; instr. Purdue U., 1949-50, asst. prof., 1950-55, assoc. prof., 1955-60, prof., 1960-91, prof. emeritus, 1991—. With Am. Field Service, 1943-45. Fellow AAAS; mem. Am. Chem. Soc., Chem. Soc. (London), Phi Beta Kappa, Sigma Xi, Phi Lambda Upsilon. Research in bond molecular orbitals, relation optical rotation and constitution, and origins of life. Home: 334 Hollowood Dr West Lafayette IN 47906-2146 Office: Purdue U Dept Chemistry Lafayette IN 47907

BREWSTER, LINDA JEAN, family nurse practitioner; b. Portland, Maine, Nov. 6, 1956; d. Thomas Stuart and Patricia Noreen (Dixon) Warden; m. James Ernest Brewster, Aug. 20, 1977; children: Ryan James, Seth Thomas. BS summa cum laude, U. So. Maine, 1987, MS, 1992; FNP, U. N.H., 1995. Cert. nurse clinician, cert. family nurse prctitioner; cert. ACLS. Staff nurse II Maine Med. Ctr., Portland, 1987-89, clin. level nurse III, 1989-91, case mgr., 1990-91, asst. head nurse, 1991-94; ICU and emergency rm. nurse So. Maine Med. Ctr., 1994-95; intravenous nurse clinician Homedco, Lewiston, Maine, 1994-95; instr. nursing So. Maine Tech. Coll., South Portland, 1994-95; FNP Family Care Assocs., PA, Cumberland, Maine, 1995—; site investigator Multisite Study Harvard Med. Sch., 1993-94; co-investigator Maine Med. Ctr., 1993. Author: Section Review Book for RNC Certification Examination, 1994; developer in field. Bd. dirs. Am. Heart Assn., 1989-93, programs chair, 1991-93. Mem. Am. Acad. Nurse Practitioners, Maine Nurse Practitioner Assn., Sigma Theta Tau (Kappa Zeta chpt.). Methodist. Avocation: women's health, adolescent health, patient education, wellness and preventive care. Home: 27 Old Gray Rd Cumberland Center ME 04021-9778

BREWSTER, ROBERT CHARLES, diplomat, consultant; b. Beatrice, Nebr., May 31, 1921; s. Charles Lee and Lillian Asenath (French) B.; m. Mary Virginia Blackman, Feb. 22, 1951. Student, Grinnell Coll., 1939-41; AB, U. Wash., 1943; postgrad., U. Mex., 1946, George Washington U., 1947, Columbia U., 1946-48. Fgn. affairs analyst State Dept., Washington, 1948-49, fgn. service officer, 1949-81; 3d sec. Am. Embassy, Managua, Nicaragua, 1949-51; 2d sec. Am. Embassy, 1951-52; vice consul Am. consulate gen. Stuttgart, Germany, 1952-55; policy briefing officer ICA, staff asst. to under sec. of state for econ. affairs, 1958, spl. asst. to under sec. of state, 1959-60; assigned Nat. War Coll., 1960-61; fgn. service insp., 1961-63; counselor Am. Embassy, Asuncion, Paraguay, 1964-66; dep. exec. dir. Bur. of European Affairs, 1966-67, exec. dir., 1967-69; dep. exec. sec. Dept. State, 1969-71, dir. personnel, 1971-73; amb. Ecuador, 1973-76; coord. for Law of Sea Dept. State, 1976, dep. asst. sec. for oceans and internat. environmental and sci. affairs, 1977-78, insp. gen., 1979-81, cons., 1981-89; Mem. D.C. Commn. on Aging, 1984-85; bd. dirs. Nat. Defense Univ. Found., 1984-87; mem. Com. on Research for Security of Future U.S. Embassy Bldgs. Nat. Acad. Scis., 1985-86. With USNR, 1943-46. Mem. Nat. War Coll. Alumni Assn. (pres. 1981-83), Foggy Bottom Assn. (v.p. 1984-85, pres. 1985-87), Diplomatic and Consular Officers Ret. Club: Cosmos (Washington). Home: 2528 Queen Annes Ln NW Washington DC 20037-2148

BREWSTER, ROBERT GENE, concert singer, educator; b. Pinson, Ala., July 7, 1938; s. Hubert and Chrisella (Ayers) B.; m. Premala Edwards (div.); 1 child, Ravindra Robert. MusB in Piano Performance with honors, Wheaton Coll., 1958; MusM in Voice with distinction, Ind. U., 1961; PhD in Vocal Performances Practices and Musicology, Washington U., St. Louis, 1967; Konzertreife Diploma, Staatliche Hochschule fuer Musik und Darstellender Kunst, Stuttgart, Fed. Republic Germany, 1970; diploma in Lieder and Opera, Mozarteum, Salzburg, Austria, 1969. Tchr. music and French Westfield (Ala.) High Sch., 1959-60; chmn. dept. music Miles Coll., Birmingham, Ala., 1960-62; chmn. area fine arts Jackson (Miss.) Coll., 1962-63; asst. tchr. voice Washington Univ., 1963-66; touring tenor throughout Europe, 1966-73; chmn. dept. music Dillard Univ., New Orleans, 1974; chmn. dept. voice Univ. Miami, Coral Gables, Fla., 1974-82; past pres. Breff Agy., Inc., N.Y.C.; pres. European Fashion Imports, N.Y.C., 1984-88, Fashion Suite, Inc., 1988—; guest lectr. Stanford U. in, Germany, Beutelsbach, 1968-70; dozent fur gesang Berliner Kirchenmusikschule, 1970-72. Concert tours throughout, Europe, Asia and, The Ams.; Recs. include I See the Stars, 1961; rec. artist (album) I See the Stars, 1960. Seely Mudd fellow, 1964-66; Fulbright fellow, 1966-68; Deutsche Akademische Austausch Dienst award, 1968-70. Mem. Nat. Assn. Tchrs. Singing, Coll. Music Soc., AAUP, Am. Musicol. Soc., Fla. Vocal Tchrs. Assn., Nat. Assn. Schs. Music, Nat. Arts Club, Phi Mu Alpha. Democrat. Episcopalian. Home and Office: 475 W 57th St Apt 18A New York NY 10019-1778

BREWSTER, RUDI MILTON, state judge; b. Sioux Falls, S.D., May 18, 1932; s. Charles Edwin and Wilhemina Therese (Rud) B.; m. Gloria Jane Nanson, June 27, 1954; children: Scot Alan, Lauri Diane (Alan Lee), Julie Lynn Yahnke. AB in Pub. Affairs, Princeton U., 1954; JD, Stanford U., 1960. Bar: Calif. 1960. From assoc. to ptnr. Gray, Cary, Ames & Frye, San Diego, 1960-84; judge U.S. Dist. Ct. (so. dist.) Calif., San Diego, 1984—. Served to capt. USNR, 1954-82 Ret. Fellow Am. Coll. Trial Lawyers; mem. Am. Bd. Trial Advs., Internat. Assn. Ins. Counsel, Am. Inns of Ct. Republican. Lutheran. Avocations: skiing, hunting, gardening. Fax: (619) 702-9927. Office: US Dist Ct Ste 4165 940 Front St San Diego CA 92101-8902

BREYER, JAMES WILLIAM, venture capitalist; b. New Haven, July 26, 1961; s. John Paul and Eva Breyer; m. Susan Zaroff, June 20, 1987. BS, Stanford U., 1983; MBA, Harvard U., 1987. Sr. bus. analyst McKinsey & Co., N.Y.C., 1983-85; assoc. Accel Ptnrs., San Francisco, 1987-90, gen. ptnr., 1990-95, mng. gen. ptnr., 1995—; bd dirs. TechNet, Silicon Valley Cmty. Ventures, Harvard Bus. Sch. Calif. Rsch. Ctr. Baker scholar Harvard U., 1987. Mem. Nat. Assn. Venture Capitalists (bd. dirs.), Western Assn. Venture Capitalists (bd. dirs.), Harvard Bus. Sch. Club of No. Calif. Office: Accel Ptnrs 428 University Ave Palo Alto CA 94301-1812

BREYER, NORMAN NATHAN, metallurgical engineering educator, consultant; b. Detroit, June 21, 1921; s. Max and Fannie (Landesman) B.; m. Dorothy Atlas, Feb. 10, 1952 (dec. Sept. 1987); children: Matthew, Richard, Marjorie; m. Claire Shore, Mar. 16, 1989. B.S., Mich. Tech. U., Houghton, 1943; M.S., U. Mich., 1948; Ph.D., Ill. Inst. Tech., 1963. Aero. research scientist NACA, Cleve., 1948; chief armor sect. Detroit Tank Arsenal, Warren, Mich., 1948-52; dir. research cast steels and irons Nat. Roll & Foundry, Avonmore, Pa., 1952-54; metallurgist-in-charge armor Continental Foundry & Machine div. Blaw-Knox Co., East Chicago, Ind., 1955-57; mgr. tech. projects LaSalle Steel Co., Hammond, Ind., 1957-64; assoc. prof. metall. engring. Ill. Inst. Tech., Chgo., 1964-69, prof., 1969-91, prof. emeritus, 1991—, chmn. dept., 1976-85. Capt. U.S. Army, 1943-46, ETO. Mem. AIME, Am. Soc. Metals. Home: 858 Timber Hill Rd Highland Park IL 60035-5121 Office: Ill Inst Tech Dept Metall & Materials Engring 10 W 33rd St Chicago IL 60616-3730

BREYER, STEPHEN GERALD, United States supreme court justice; b. San Francisco, Aug. 15, 1938; s. Irving G. and Anne R. B.; m. Joanna Hare, Sept. 4, 1967; children: Chloe, Nell, Michael. A.B., Stanford U., 1959; B.A. (Marshall scholar), Oxford U., 1961; LL.B., Harvard U., 1964; LL.D. (hon.), U. Rochester, 1983. Bar: Calif. 1966, D.C. 1966, Mass. 1971. Law clk. Justice Goldberg, U.S. Supreme Ct., 1964-65; spl. asst. to asst. atty. gen. U.S. Dept. Justice, 1965-67; asst. prof. law Harvard U., 1967-70, prof., 1970-81, lectr., 1981—, prof. govt. J.F. Kennedy Sch., 1978-81; asst. spl. prosecutor Watergate Spl. Prosecution Force, 1973; spl. counsel U.S. Senate Judiciary Com., 1974-75, chief counsel, 1979-81; judge U.S. Ct. Appeals (1st cir.), Boston, 1981-90, chief judge, 1990-94; Oliver Wendell Holmes lectr. Harvard Law Sch., 1992; assoc. justice U.S. Supreme Ct., Washington, 1994—; mem. Jud. Conf. of U.S., 1990-94, U.S. Sentencing commn., 1985-89; vis. lectr. Coll. Law, Sydney, Australia, 1975, Salzburg (Austria) Seminar, 1978, 93; Jud. Conf. rep. to Adminstrv. Conf. U.S., 1981-94; vis. prof. U. Rome, 1993. Author: (with Paul MacAvoy) The Federal Power Commission and the Regulation of Energy, 1974, (with Richard Stewart) Adminstrative Law and Regulatory Policy, 1979, 3rd edit., 1992, Regulation and its Reform, 1982, Breaking the Vicious Circle, 1993; contbr. articles to profl. jours. Trustee U. Mass., 1974-81; bd. overseers Dana Farber Cancer Inst., Boston, 1977—. Mem. ABA, Am. Bar Found., Am. Law Inst., Am. Acad. Arts and Scis., Coun. Fgn. Rels. Office: US Supreme Ct Supreme Ct Bldg 1 1st St NE Washington DC 20543

BREYMAN, STEVE, political science educator; b. Milw., May 6, 1960; s. James M. and Patricia A. (Pasch) B.; m. Sheryl A. Evans, May 2, 1981; children: Karl, Natasha, Vanessa. BA, U. Calif., Santa Barbara, 1983, MA, 1985, PhD, 1992. Vis. asst. prof. Marquette U., Milw., 1991-93; asst. prof. Rensselaer Poly. Inst., Troy, N.Y., 1993—; dir. ecol., econs., values and policy program Rensselaer Poly. Inst., Troy; bd. dirs. Environ. Advocates, Albany, N.Y.; mem. adv. coun. Jacques Ellul Inst., Riverside, Calif., 1995—. Author: Movement Genesis, 1997, Why Movements Matter, 1999; host On the Barricades, WRPI-FM. Meml. legis. com. Green Party of N.Y. State, 1997—. With U.S. Army, 1978-80. Mem. Soc. for Social Studies of Sci., Conf. Group on German Politics, Ctr. for Campus Organizing, German Studies Assn., Am. Polit. Sci. Assn., Am. Sociol. Assn. Office: Rensselaer Poly Inst Dept Sci and Tech Studies Troy NY 12180-3590

BREZZO, STEVEN LOUIS, museum director; b. Woodbury, N.J., June 18, 1949; s. Louis and Ella Marie (Savage) B.; m. Dagmar Grimm, Aug. 10, 1975. B.A., Clarion State Coll., 1969; M.F.A., U. Conn., 1973. Chief curator La Jolla Mus. Contemporary Art, Calif., 1974-76; asst. dir. San Diego Mus. Art, 1976-78, dir., 1978—. Mem. Am. Assn. Mus. (del. to China 1981, to Italian mus. study trip 1982), Calif. Assn. Mus. (pres. 1992—), La Jolla Library Assn. (pres. 1980). Club: University (San Diego). Lodge: Rotary.

BRIACH, GEORGE GARY, lawyer, consultant; b. Youngstown, Ohio, Apr. 11, 1954; s. George William and Donna Jean (Phillips) B.; m. Loretta Ann Lepore, May 17, 1985; 1 child, Rachel Renee. BS magna cum laude, Youngstown State U., 1976; JD, U. Akron, Ohio, 1982. Bar: Ohio 1983, Mahoning County, 1983. Assoc. Flask & Policy, Youngstown, 1983-91; asst. atty. gen. State Atty. Gen.'s Office, Youngstown, 1984-90; solicitor Poland (Ohio) Village, 1988-89; cons., dir. Mahoning County (Ohio) Auditor, 1990—; ptnr. White & Briach, Youngstown, 1991—. Fundraiser United Way, Youngstown, 1989-92; bd. dirs., treas. D&E Counseling Ctr., Youngstown, 1992-98; trustee, treas. Children' Challenge Found., Inc., 1998—; bd. dirs. Interfaith Home Maintenance. Mem. Ohio Bar Assn., Mahoning County Bar Assn., Youngstown State U. Alumni Assn., Allegheny Club, Fonderlac Country Club, Tippecanoe Country Club. Avocations: aerobic and weight training, golf, reading, travel. Home: 45 Russo Dr Canfield OH 44406-9666 Office: White & Briach 755 Boardman Canfield Rd Youngstown OH 44512-4300

BRIAN, JACKSON, artistic director. Music dir. Victoria Choral Soc., Kingston Choral Soc.; asst. condr. to resident to prin. pops condr. Orch. London, prin. guest condr., artistic advisor, 1998—; guest condr. Internat. Symphony, Kingston Symphony. Organ scholar Oxford. Fellow Royal Coll. of Organists. Office: London Orchestra Can, 520 Wellington St, London, ON Canada NGA 3R1

BRIAN, LAURA ANNA, freelance writer; b. Quincy, Ill., Sept. 18, 1968; d. Dennis Roger and Sharon Lynn (Winder) B. BA in English, U. Colo., Boulder, 1990; MS in Journalism, Columbia U., 1997. City reporter Brighton (Colo.) Std. Blade, 1991; reporter, editor Vail (Colo.) Daily, 1991; real estate editor The Denver Post, 1991-95; spl. projects editor The McKinley Group, San Francisco, 1995-96; freelance writer Colo. Expression, Denver, 1995—, The Resident, N.Y.C., 1995—; Web site prodr., field prodr. Sta. NBC4-TV, N.Y.C., 1997—. Mentor Columbia Journalism Sch. Alumni, N.Y.C.; ski coach Spl. Olympics, Denver, 1992-93; vol. mentor For Children Only, Denver, 1993; mem., student rep. Columbia Journalism Sch. Libr. Com., N.Y.C., 1996-97. Scholar Columbia U. Alumni Assn., 1997. Mem. Soc. Profl. Journalists, U. Colo.-Boulder Alumni Assn. (alumni contact 1996—). Republican. Evangelical. Avocations: running, skiing, traveling, architecture and interior design studies, music. Office: NBC 7th Fl 30 Rockefeller Plz Fl 7 New York NY 10112-0002

BRIAN, PATRICIA ANN, social services administrator; b. Sioux Falls, S.D.; d. Lawrence Alexander and Ethelyn Lucille (Milaney) Dumas; children: Robert Milling III, Courtney Dumas. BS, Northwestern U., 1959; postgrad., So. Ill. U., 1982. Cert. instr. human potential, parent effectiveness tng., rational behavior theory. Tchr. Belleville (Ill.) Pub. Schs., 1963-76; instr., project dir., dir. spl. svcs. ctr. Belleville Area Coll., 1977—; cons. Ill. Bd. Edn., 1978—, Ill. C.C. Bd., 1985—; presenter seminars. Author, editor: (resource books) Help for Addictive Diseases, 1988, Out of the Darkness: Arresting Rape, 1988, Survival Study Skills, 1989, Values Clarification, 1979, Attitudes and Communications, 1986. Bd. dirs. So. Ill. Network for Women, Parents in Action, Living Independently Now Ctr., Care and Counseling Social Svcs., Metro East, Ill., Pregnant Teen Svcs., Job Track, 1991—; mem. mayoral steering com. Belleville's 175th Birthday, 1989, co-chmn. Celebration Ball, 1989. Recipient Bright Idea award Ill. Coun. C.C. Adminstrs., 1994. Mem. Nat. Assn. Vocat. Edn. Spl. Needs Pers., Ill. Assn. Vocat. Edn. Spl. Needs Pers. (pres. 1994, Person of Yr. 1990), Ill. Vocat. Assn. (bd. dirs. 1993-94, ho. of dels. mem. 1997-98, Outstanding Programming in Cmty. and Coll. Alcohol Awareness award 1988). Avocations: water sports, travel. Office: Belleville Area Coll 2500 Carlyle Ave Belleville IL 62221-5859

BRIANT, CLYDE LEONARD, metallurgist, educator; b. Texarkana, Ark., May 31, 1948; s. Clyde Leonard and Bonnie Barbara (Green) B.; m. Jacqueline Louise Duffy, July 16, 1977; children—Paul, Judith, Bonnie. B.A., Hendrix Coll., Conway, Ark., 1971; B.S., Columbia U., 1971, M.S., 1973, Eng. Sc.D., 1974. Postdoctoral fellow U. Pa., Phila., 1974-76; staff metallurgist Gen. Electric Co., Schenectady, 1976-94; prof. of engring. Brown U., Providence, Rhode Island, 1994—; vis. scientist Rsch. Inst. for Tech. Physics, Hungarian Acad. Scis., Budapest, 1991. Author monograph; editor: Embrittlement of Engineering Alloys, 1983; contbr. numerous articles to tech. jours. Recipient Alfred Noble prize, 1980; named one of 100 Most Outstanding Young Scientists in U.S.A., Sci. Digest, 1984; overseas fellow Churchill Coll., Cambridge, Eng., 1987-88. Fellow Am. Soc. Metals; mem. AIME (Robert Lansing Hardy gold medal Metall. Soc. 1977, Rossiter W. Raymond 1979). Democrat. Methodist. Home: 9 Wedgewood Ln Barrington RI 02806-3218 Office: Brown Univ Divsn of Engring Box D Providence RI 02912

BRIANT, MARYJANE, newspaper editor; b. Cape May Court House, N.J., Dec. 29, 1951; d. William Lincoln and Jane Hutchison (Bicking) B.; 1 child, Erica Nicole. BS in Journalism, Boston U., 1974. Reporter The Cape May County Times, North Wildwood, N.J., 1975; reporter The Gazette-Leader, North Wildwood, 1976, city editor, 1977, mng. editor, 1978-79; copy editor The Press of Atlantic City, Pleasantville, N.J., 1979; asst. city editor The Press, Pleasantville, 1984-87; news editor The Press of Atlantic City, Pleasantville, 1987-90; asst. mng. editor The Gazette-Leader, North Wildwood, 1990-91; mng. editor The Press of Atlantic City, Pleasantville, N.J., 1992—. Bd. dirs. Boys and Girls Club Atlantic City, 1992—. Mem. N.J. Press Assn., Atlantic City Press Club (presenter Headliners Awards 1993-94). Office: The Press of Atlantic City 11 Devins Ln Pleasantville NJ 08232-4107*

BRIARE, JOHN M., business official; b. Bklyn., July 13, 1965; s. Robert and Carol Ann (Rizzoto) B.; m. Karen Ann Soja, June 6, 1987. BA in Criminal Justice, SUNY, Albany, 1986. Dist. sales mgr. Am. Express, Englewood, Colo., 1988-93; pres. PC-Buyer Inc., Dudley, Mass., 1993-98, bd. dirs., 1993—; govt. accounts mgr. Nextel, Lexington, Mass., 1997—. Chmn. Webster Rep. Town Com., 1994-99; candidate for U.S. Ho. of Reps. from 2d congl. dist. Mass., 1994; candidate for Mass. Senate, 1996; mem. Dudley Master Planning Bd., 1999—. Republican. Roman Catholic. E-mail: john@pc-buyer.com.

BRICCETTI, JOAN THERESE, theater manager, arts management consultant; b. Mt. Kisco, N.Y., Sept. 29, 1948; d. Thomas Bernard and Joan (Filardi) B. AB in Am. History, Bryn Mawr Coll., 1970. Adminstrv. asst., program guide editor Sta. WIAN-FM, Indpls., 1970-72; adminstrv. asst. T. Briccetti, condr., Indpls., 1970-72; dir. pub. rels. The Richmond (Va.) Symphony, 1972-73, mgr., 1973-80; mgr. St. Louis Symphony Orch., 1980-84, gen. mgr., 1984-86, chief oper. officer, 1986-92; ind. cons. for arts & Edn., 1993—; mng. dir. Metro Theater Co., St. Louis, 1996—; cons., panelist Arts Couns. Ohio, Va., Ky. Active orch. and planning sects., music programs Nat. Endowment fot the Arts, 1974-78, chmn. orch. panel, 1975-78, cons., evaluator, panelist, 1974—, mem. first challenge grant rev. panel, 1977, co-chmn. recording panel, 1983-84; mem. grant rev. panel Va. Commn. for the Arts, 1976-78; adv. bd. Eastern Music Festival, 1977-83, Richmond Friends Opera, 1979-80; adv. coun. Va. Alliance for Arts Edn., 1978, Federated Arts Coun. Richmond, 1979-80; steering com. BRAVO Arts, 1978-79 (gov.'s award); cons. Tenn. Arts Commn., 1979-80; bd. dirs. Theatre IV, Richmond, 1974-80, Am. Music Ctr, N.Y.C., 1980-84, St. Louis Forum, 1983—, New City Sch., St. Louis, 1987—, Metro Theatre Co., 1994—; mem. challenge grant evaluation panel Ky. Arts Commn., 1983; participant Leadership St. Louis, 1983-84, bd. dirs., 1987-89; commr. subdistrict Mo. History Mus., 1987—, sec., 1993; speaker, panelist, cons. numerous arts orgns. Mem. Am. Symphony Orch. League (chmn. orch. library info. svc. adv. com., recruiter, mem. final interview com., advisor mgmt. fellowship program), Regional Orch. Mgrs. Assn. (v.p. 1976, policy com. 1977-79), Women's Forum Mo. Office: Metro Theatre Co 8308 Olive Blvd Saint Louis MO 63132-2814*

BRICE, ROGER THOMAS, lawyer; b. Chgo., May 7, 1948; s. William H. and Mary Loretta (Ryan) B.; m. Carol Coleman, Aug. 15, 1970; children: Caitlin, Coleman, Emily. AB, DePaul U., 1970; JD, U. Chgo., 1973. Bar: Ill. 1973, Iowa 1973, U.S. Ct. Appeals (10th, 4th and 7th cirs.) 1975, U.S. Dist. Ct. (no. and ctrl. dists.) Ill. 1977, 1995, U.S. Trial Bar (no. dist.) 1982, U.S. Supreme Ct. 1978. Staff atty. Office of Gen. Counsel NLRB, Washington, 1974-76; assoc. Kirkland & Ellis, Chgo., 1976-79; assoc. Reuben & Proctor, Chgo., 1979-80, ptnr., 1980-86; ptnr. Isham, Lincoln & Beale, Chgo., 1986-88; ptnr. Sonnenschein, Nath & Rosenthal, Chgo., 1988—, legal counsel. Legal counsel, bd. dirs. Boys and Girls Clubs Chgo., 1991—. Roman Catholic. Home: 3727 N Harding Ave Chicago IL 60618-4026 Office: Sonnenschein Nath & Rosenthal 233 S Wacker Dr Ste 8000 Chicago IL 60606-6342

BRICHFORD, MAYNARD JAY, archivist; b. Madison, Ohio, Aug. 6, 1926; s. Merton Jay and Evelyn Louise (Graves) B.; m. Jane Adair Hamilton, Sept. 15, 1951; children—Charles Hamilton, Ann Adair Brichford Martin, Matthew Jay, Sarah Lourena. B.A., Hiram Coll., 1950; M.S., U. Wis., 1951. Asst. archivist State Hist. Soc. Wis., 1952-56; methods and procedures analyst Ill. State Archives, 1956-59; records and space mgmt. supr. Dept. Adminstrn. State of Wis., Madison, 1959-63; archivist U. Ill., Urbana, 1963-95; asso. prof. U. Ill., 1963-70, prof., 1970—. Contbr. articles in field. Mem. gen. commn. on archives and history United Meth. Ch., 1988-96; bd. chmn. U. Ill. YMCA, 1987-89. With U.S. Navy, 1944-46. Council on Library Resources grantee, 1966-69, 70-71; Nat. Endowment for the Humanities grantee, 1976-79; Fulbright grantee, 1985; Am. Phil. Soc. grantee, 1992. Fellow Soc. Am. Archivists (pres. 1979-80); mem. Ill. Archives Adv. Bd. (chmn. 1979-84). Republican. Methodist. Home: 409 Eliot Dr Urbana IL 61801-6725 Office: 19 Library 1408 W Gregory Dr Urbana IL 61801-3607

BRICK, BARRETT LEE, lawyer; b. Middletown, N.Y., Jan. 12, 1954; s. Michael and Barbara Lilian (Rosen) B. BA, Columbia U., 1976, JD, 1979. Bar: N.Y. 1980, U.S. Ct. Appeals (D.C. cir.) 1981, U.S. Supreme Ct. 1984. Atty.-adviser FCC, Washington, 1980—. Contbr. to book, Positively Gay, 1979; book review columnist Washington Blade newspaper, 1982-83; editor National Gay Task Force Action Report, 1975-76. Active Community Bd. Nine, N.Y.C., 1978-80; mem. Gay Men's Chorus, Washington, 1984—; bd. dirs. Congregation Bet Mishpachah, Washington, 1980-84, pres., 1984-85; exec. dir. World Congress Gay and Lesbian Jewish Orgns., Washington, 1987-93. Recipient Advocate 400 award, The Advocate, San Francisco, 1984; named one of Outstanding Young Men of Am. U.S. Jaycees, 1983, 84. Mem. ABA, N.Y. State Bar Assn., Nat. Lesbian and Gay Law Assn. Republican. Jewish. Club: Capital (Washington). Home: 1901 Wyoming Ave NW Washington DC 20009-5079 Office: FCC 445 12th St SW Washington DC 20554-0001

BRICK, DONALD BERNARD, consulting company executive; b. Bklyn., Oct. 1, 1927; s. Maxwell B. and Edna (Newman) B.; m. Phyllis Madeline Hahn, Oct. 19, 1952; children: James Laurence, Susan Carol Weinbaum, Howard Andrew. Student, Newark Coll. Engring., 1945-46; A.B. cum laude, Harvard U., 1950, S.M., 1951, Ph.D., 1954. Registered profl. engr., Mass.; registered real estate broker, Mass. Teaching fellow, research asst., fellow Harvard U., 1950-55; sr. scientist, sci. dir. GTE Sylvania, Waltham, Mass., 1955-65; tech. mgmt. cons. Lexington, Mass., 1954-55, 65-75; founder, pres., chmn., tech. dir. Info. Research Assoc.-Infoton Inc., Burlington, Mass., 1965-71; v.p. Addressograph-Multigraph Corp., 1972-73; tech. dir., dep. for devel. plans Elec. Systems div. U.S. Air Force, Bedford, Mass., 1975-83; pres. D.B. Brick and Co., Inc. (now 10 Vehicle Com, Inc.), Lexington, 1983—; v.p. Aetna Telecommunications Cons., Centerville, Mass., 1983; cons. in field. Contbr. articles to profl. jours.; patentee in field. V.p., bd. dirs. Temple Emunah, Lexington, 1970; assoc. campaign chmn. Combined Jewish Philanthropies of Greater Boston, 1974-78, life trustee, 1985—, mem. exec. bd., 1980-89, chmn. cash collections, 1982-84, chmn. high tech. team, 1984-87; chmn. fundraising Am. Technion Soc., N.E. Region, 1989-93. With U.S. Army, 1946-47. Fellow IEEE (life, chmn. 1969-70); mem. Armed Forces Comms. and Electronics Assn., N.E. Israel C. of C. (exec. bd. 1993—). Home: 39 Solomon Pierce Rd Lexington MA 02420-2536 Office: 10 Vehicle Com Inc Lexington MA 02173 *Not compromising ideals or moral standards for easy gain. Striving to produce quality work that I am proud of.*

BRICKA, EVELYN CHANTEL, educator; b. Strasbourg, France, Mar. 24, 1954; came to U.S., 1956; d. Ivan and Frieda Elisabeth Gera; m. Gerard Bricka, Sept. 25, 1976; 1 child, Christopher Andre. AD, Suffolk County C.C., 1994. Tchr. asst. Ea. Suffolk BOCES, Patchogue, N.Y., 1988—; cons. Mary Kay Cosmetics, Dallas, 1997—. Democrat. Lutheran. Avocations: travel, art films, reading, creative handwork. Hme: 531 A Canal Rd PO Box 78 Mount Sinai NY 11766

BRICKELL, CHARLES HENNESSEY, JR., marine engineer, retired military officer; b. Memphis, Apr. 13, 1935; s. Charles Hennessey and Mary Ellen (Viau) B.; m. Barbara Virginia Davis, Jan. 4, 1958; children: David Brian, Patricia Ellen, Susan Elizabeth, Timothy Paul, Joel Howard. BS in Marine Engring., U.S. Merchant Marine Acad., 1957; MA in Bus. Mgmt., Cen. Mich. U., 1980. Enlisted USN, 1953, commd. ensign, 1957, advanced through grades to rear adm., 1984; dir. research and devel. Undersea and Strategic Warfare, and Nuclear Energy, 1984-87; dir. USN Strategic Def. Initiative Program, 1984-88; dep. dir. Navy Rsch. Devel., Test and Evaluation, 1987-88; ret. USN, 1988; gen. mgr. advanced technologies Stone & Webster Engring. Corp., Boston, 1988-91; dir. Ops. ea. region N.Am. Energy Svcs., Issaquah, Wash., 1991-93; assoc. lab. dir. Applied Rsch. Lab. Pa. State U., State Coll., 1993—; mem. bd. advisors Applied Rsch. Lab Pa. State U., 1988-93; cons. NAS. Decorated Def. Superior Service Medal, Legion of Merit with three Gold Stars, Meritorious Service Medal with two Gold Stars. Mem. Sigma Iota Epsilon. Roman Catholic. Avocations: baseball, basketball sports officiating.

BRICKER, DONALD LEE, surgeon; b. Denver, Jan. 7, 1935; s. J.F. and Marjorie Ellen (Mahon) B.; m. Evelyn Lucy Borst, Aug. 31, 1958 (div.); children—Donald Lee, II, Alex, Adam.; m. Sammie Lou Mavar, June 5, 1981. B.S., Colo. State U., 1956; M.D., Cornell U., 1959. Diplomate: Am. Bd. Surgery (spl. qualifications in gen. vascular surgery 1984), Am. Bd. Thoracic Surgery. Intern, then resident in surgery N.Y. Hosp., N.Y.C., 1959-61; resident in surgery, then resident in thoracic surgery Baylor U. Affiliated Hosp., Houston, 1961-68; practice medicine specializing in thoracic and cardiovascular surgery Houston, 1968-70, Lubbock, Tex., 1970—; chief of staff St. Mary of Plains Hosp., 1979-80, now dir. hemodynamics lab.; mem. staff St. Luke's Hosp., Tex. Inst. Rehab. and Research, Bellaire Gen., Methodist, Ben Taub Gen. and W. Tex. hosps.; from instr. to asst. prof. surgery Baylor U. Coll. Medicine, Houston, 1961-70; active chief surgery Ben Taub Gen. Hosp., 1968-70; clin. prof. surgery, dir. div. cardiovascular surgery Tex. Tech. U. Med. Sch., Lubbock, 1972-79; pres. Heart Inst. Southwest, 1971; dir. vascular labs. Meth. Hosp., Lubbock, chief cardiovasc. surg. sect., acting past chief staff; mem. med. staff Meth. Hosp., Lubbock, St. Mary of the Plains Hosp., Lubbock. Contbr. numerous articles in field to med. jours. Served to capt. MC USAF, 1965-67; maj. Res. 1968-70. Fellow ACS, Am. Coll. Chest Physicians, Am. Coll. Cardiology (regional dir. 1992—), Am. Assn. Thoracic Surgery, Am. Assn. Surgery Trauma, Tex. Surg. Soc.; mem. So. Thoracic Surg. Assn. (President's award for best sci. paper 1973), Soc. Thoracic Surgeons, Tex. Med. Assn., Soc. Vascular Surgery, Houston Surg. Soc., Lubbock County Med Soc., Internat. Cardiovascular Surg. Soc., Denton A. Cooley Cardiovascular Soc. (pres.), Michael E. DeBakey Internat. Cardiovascular Surg. Soc. (bd. dirs.). Republican. Methodist. Home: Lake Ransom Canyon 19 Sunrise Ln Ransom Canyon TX 79366-2522 Office: 3420 22nd Pl Lubbock TX 79410-1314 *America remains the land of opportunity, a land where those of humble origin canstill, through hard work, diligence and the willingness to accept responsibility, gain great rewards, the most important of these being the privilege to serve.*

BRICKER, GERALD WAYNE, marketing executive; b. York, Pa., Dec. 21, 1947; s. Wayne Gilbert Bricker and Grace Fern (Quickel) Geisler; m. Linda Lee Desenberg, June 21, 1969; children: Kristin Lorraine, Scott Michael. BSME, Drexel U., 1970; MBA, No. Ill. U., 1976. Jr. product engr. Borg-Warner Corp., Ithaca, N.Y., 1970-71; product engr. Borg-Warner Corp., Aurora, Ill., 1971-72; with Maremont Corp., Chgo., 1972-86, dir. sales divsn., 1981-84, V.P. sales divsn., 1984-86; dir. mtkg. Intelligent Controls, Inc., Novi, Mich., 1986-90, v.p. mktg., 1990-93; v.p. products group Intelligent Controls, Inc., Novi, 1993-95; mktg. mgr. Pierburg Instruments, Inc., Clinton Twp., Mich., 1995-96; gen. sales mgr. Omron Automotive Electronics, inc., Farmington Hills, Mich., 1996—. Pres. Gethsemane Luth. Ch., Berkley, Mich., 1979-80, Cana Luth. Ch., Berkley, 1980-81, chmn. audit com., 1991-95, treas. endowment com., 1998—. Mem. Soc. Automotive Engrs. (assoc.), U.S. Golf Assn., Drexel U. Alumni of Mich. (b. dirs. 1990—), Lambda Chi Alpha, Pi Tau Sigma, Beta Gamma Sigma. Avocations: golf, tennis, reading, cross-country skiing. Home: 47765 Lake View Ct Northville MI 48167-8503 Office: Omron Automotive Electronics Inc 30600 Northwestern Hwy Ste 250 Farmington Hills MI 48334

BRICKER, HARVEY MILLER, anthropology educator; b. Johnstown, Pa., June 29, 1940; s. George Harry and Florence Helen (Miller) B.; m. Victoria Evelyne Reifler, Dec. 27, 1964. BA, Hamilton Coll., 1962; MA, Harvard U., 1963, PhD, 1973. Successively instr., asst. prof., assoc. prof. to prof. anthropology Tulane U., New Orleans, 1969—. Co-author: The Analysis of Certain Major Classes of Upper Palaeolithic Tools, 1969, Excavation of the Abri Pataud: The Perigordian VI Assemblage, 1984; co-editor: Hunting and Animal Exploitation in the Later Palaeolithic and Mesolithic of Eurasia, 1993; editor: La Paléolithique Supérieur de l'abri Pataud (Dordogne), 1995; contbr. articles on French prehistory and Maya archaeoastronomy to profl. jours. Decorated Order Palmes Académiques (France). Fellow AAAS;

mem. Am. Anthrop. Assn., Soc. Am. Archaeology, Soc. French Prehistory. Office: Tulane U Dept Anthropology 1021 Audubon St New Orleans LA 70118

BRICKER, NEAL S., physician, educator; b. Denver, Apr. 18, 1927; s. Eli D. and Rose (Quiat) B.; m. Miriam Thalenberg, June 24, 1951 (dec. 1974); children: Dusty, Cary, Susan, Dan Baker; m. Ruth T. Baker, Dec. 28, 1980. B.A., U. Colo., 1946, M.D., 1949. Diplomate Am. Bd. Internal Medicine (bd. govs. 1972-79, chmn. nephrology test com. 1973-76). Intern, resident Bellevue Hosp., N.Y.C., 1949-52; sr. asst. resident Peter Bent Brigham Hosp., Boston, 1954-55; asso. dir. cardio-renal lab. Peter Bent Brigham Hosp., 1955-56; instr. Harvard, 1955-56; fellow Howard Hughes Med. Inst., 1955-56; from asst. prof. to prof. Washington U., 1956-72, dir. renal div., 1956-72; Mem. sci. adv. bd. Nat. Kidney Found., 1962-69, chmn. research and fellowship grants com., 1964-65, mem. exec. com., 1968-71; prof. medicine, chmn. dept. Albert Einstein Coll. Medicine, 1972-76; prof. medicine U. Miami, Fla., 1976-78; vice chmn. dept. U. Miami, 1976-78; Disting. prof. medicine UCLA, 1978-86; disting. prof. medicine, dir. sci. and tech. planning Loma Linda (Calif.) U., 1986-92; exec. v.p. Naturon Pharm., Riverside, Calif., 1992—; cons. NIH, 1964-68, chmn. gen. medicine study sect., 1966-68, chmn. renal disease and urology tng. grants com., 1969-71; vis. investigator Inst. Biol. Chemistry, Copenhagen, 1960-61; investigator Mt. Desert Island Biol. Labs.; advisor on behalf Inst. Medicine to Sen. Lowell Weicker; clin. prof. medicine U. Calif. Riverside/UCLA program in biomed. scis., 1997—. Assoc. editor: Jour. Lab. and Clin. Medicine, 1961-67, Kidney Internat, 1972; editorial com.: Jour. Clin. Investigation, 1964-68, Physiol. Revs, 1970-76, Am. Heart Assn. Publs. Com., 1974-79, Calcified Tissue Internat., 1978-86, Proc. Soc. Exptl. Biology and Medicine, 1978-86; editor: Supplements, Circulation and Circulation Research, 1974-79; contbr. articles to profl. jours., chpts. to books. Served with USNR, 1944-45; Served with U.S. Army, 1952-54. Recipient Gold-Headed Cane award U. Colo., 1949, Silver and Gold Alumni award, 1975; USPHS Research Career award, 1964-72; Skylab Achievement award NASA, 1974; Pub. Service award, 1975; George Norlin Silver medal award U. Colo. 1982; citation Kidney Found. So. Calif., 1984. Fellow A.C.P.; mem. Am. Fedn. for Clin. Research, Central Soc. Clin. Research (council 1970-73), Assn. Am. Physicians, Am. Soc. for Clin. Investigation (pres. 1972-73, chmn. com. nat. med. policy 1973-77, Disting. Service award 1969), Internat. Soc. Nephrology (exec. com. 1966-81, v.p. 1966-69, treas. 1969-81), Internat. Congress Nephrology (pres. 1981-84), Am. Soc. Nephrology (1st pres., John Peters medal 1991), Am. Physiol. Soc., Soc. for Exptl. Biology and Medicine, Western Soc. Clin. Research, So. Soc. Clin. Investigation, Nat. Acad. Scis. (com. on space biology and medicine, ad hoc panel on renal and metabolic effects space flight 1971-72, mem. drug efficacy com. 1966-68, com. space biology, chmn. medicine in space sci. bd. 1972-81, com. chmn. 1978-81, chmn. com. renal and metaboloic effects space flight 1972-74, chmn. study com. on life scis. 1976-81, mem. space sci. bd. 1977-81), Inst. Medicine of NAS, Sigma Xi, Alpha Omega Alpha. Home: 1820 Oxford Ave Claremont CA 91711-2613 Office: UCR/UCLA Riverside CA 92521-0121

BRICKER, VICTORIA REIFLER, anthropology educator; b. Hong Kong, June 15, 1940; came to U.S., 1947, naturalized, 1953; d. Erwin and Henrietta (Brown) Reifler; m. Harvey Miller Bricker, Dec. 27, 1964. A.B., Stanford U., 1962; A.M., Harvard U., 1963, Ph.D., 1968. Vis. lectr. anthropology Tulane U., 1969-70, asst. prof., 1970-73, assoc. prof., 1973-78, prof., 1978—, chmn. dept. anthropology, 1988-91. Author: Ritual Humor in Highland Chiapas, 1973, The Indian Christ, The Indian King: The Historical Substrate of Maya Myth and Ritual, 1981 (Howard Francis Cline meml. prize Conf. Latin Am. History), A Grammar of Mayan Hieroglyphs, 1986, (with Gabrielle Vail) Papers on the Madrid Codex, 1997, (with Eleuterio Po'ot Yah and Ofelia Dzul de Po'ot) A Dictionary of the Maya Language as Spoken in Hocaba, Yucatan, 1998; book rev. editor: Am. Anthropologist, 1971-73; editor: Am. Ethnologist, 1973-76; gen. editor: Supplement to Handbook of Middle American Indians, 1977—. Guggenheim fellow, 1982; Wenner-Gren Found. Anthropol. Rsch. grantee, 1971; Social Sci. Rsch. Coun.l grantee, 1972; NEH grantee, 1990. Fellow Am. Anthrop. Assn. (exec. bd. 1980-83); mem. NAS, Am. Soc. Ethnohistory (exec. bd. 1977-79), Linguistic Soc. Am., Seminario de Cultura Maya, Societe des Americanistes. Office: Tulane Univ Dept Anthropology New Orleans LA 70118

BRICKER, WILLIAM RUDOLPH, organization executive; b. Reading, Pa., May 5, 1923; s. William Theodore and Elsie Elizabeth (Weber) B.; m. Eleanor Schubert, June 9, 1945; children: Cynthia Anne (Mrs. Mark Hilgendorf), William Randall, Suzanne Lee (Mrs. William Sullivan). B.S., Millersville (Pa.) U., 1947; M.A. (Hayden grad. fellow), NYU, 1948; D.H.L., George Williams Coll., 1980. Exec. dir. Boys' Clubs Am., 1948-72, nat. dir., ceo, 1972-89; chmn. Nat. Collaboration for Youth, 1975; mem. U.S. Pres.'s Commn. for Juvenile Justice and Delinquency Prevention, 1975; mem. adv. bd. Nat. Inst. Justice, 1975, U.S. Pres. Commn. Employment, 1978; bd. dirs. U.S. Congl. Award, 1979; trustee Nat. Commn. for Coop. Edn., 1980. Mem. U.S. Pres. Commn. on Pvt. Sector Initiatives, 1982, U.S. Pres. UNESCO Commn, 1984; vice chmn. U.S. Presdl. Commn. on Child Safety, 1986; trustee Freedoms Found., 1986; chmn. U.S. Nat. Panel for Teen Pregnancy, 1987; U.S. Presdl. envoy to UNESCO, 1985, Micronesia, 1987; adv. bd. Cummings Meml. Fund, 1988; vice chmn. Jamestown Philomenian Libr., 1989. Air comdr. USN, 1942-45, 50-70. Mem. Soc. Mil. Horologists, (pres. 1995). Avocations: aviation, horology, management.

BRICKEY, KATHLEEN FITZGERALD, law educator; b. Austin, Tex., Sept. 16, 1944; d. Robert Bernard and Ina Marie (Daw) Fitzgerald; m. James Nelson Brickey, Aug. 22, 1969. BA, U. Ky., 1965, JD, 1968. Criminal law specialist/cons. Ky. Crime Commn., Frankfort, Cin., 1968-71; exec. dir. Ky. Judicial Conf. and Coun., Frankfort, 1971-72; adj. prof. law U. Ky., Lexington, 1972; asst. to assoc. prof. law U. Louisville, 1972-76; assoc. prof. to prof. law Washington U., St. Louis, 1976-89, George Alexander Madill prof. law, 1989-93, James Carr prof. of criminal jurisprudence, 1993—; cons. U.S. Sentencing Commn., 1988, 91; witness U.S. Senate Com. on Judiciary, Washington, 1986. Author: Kentucky Criminal Law, 1974, Corporate Criminal Liability, 1984, 2d edit., 1992-94, Corporate and White Collar Crime, 1990, 2d edit., 1995; contbr. articles to profl. jours. Mem. Am. Law Inst., Soc. for Reform of Criminal Law, Assn. Am. Law Schs. (sect. on criminal justice chair 1989, exec. com. 1985-91, 94-95). Office: Washington U Sch Law PO Box 1120 Saint Louis MO 63130

BRICKHILL, WILLIAM LEE, international finance consultant; b. Rahway, N.J., Oct. 13, 1937; s. William Welch and Wilma Eloise (Gay) Mumford; m. Margaret A. Stempel, June 16, 1961 (div. 1971); children: William L., Barbara A., Cynthia A., Robert L.; m. Joan Marie Ward, May 19, 1988. Student, U. Ga., 1957, Sophia U., Tokyo, 1958-60; BBA, George Washington U., 1970. Lic. comml. and instrument rated pilot. Internat. specialist Am. Security & Trust Co., Washington, 1960-62; loan officer Export-Import Bank of U.S., Washington, 1962-90, dep. mgr. contract adminstrn., 1990-91, dep. v.p. contract adminstrn., 1991-94, ret., 1994; cons. internat. fin., 1994—. Contbr. articles to profl. jours. With U.S. Army, 1956-58, Germany. Mem. Nat. Capital Bromeliad Soc. (1st v.p. 1991—), Nat. Capital Orchid Soc., Gem, Mineral and Lapidary Soc. (bd. dirs., v.p. 1965-75). Roman Catholic. Avocations: aviation, botany, horticulture, woodworking. Home and Office: 6338 Phyllis Ln Alexandria VA 22312-6402

BRICKHOUSE, EUGENE A., federal agency administrator; b. Exmore, Va., Feb. 13, 1940; m. Phyllis A. Fluellyn, Apr. 3, 1969. BS, Va. State U., 1962; MS in Human Resources Mgmt., U. Tex., San Antonio, 1976. Commd. 2nd lt. U.S. Army, 1962, advanced through grades to col., 1983, various assignments in Europe and Pacific; formerly assigned to Office Asst. Sec. Def. for Health Affairs, Washington; ret., 1992; staff mem. com. on vets. affairs U.S. Ho. of Reps., Washington, 1992-93; asst. sec. for human resources and adminstrn. VA, Washington, 1993—, also agy. safety and health ofcl. Decorated Def. Superior Svc. medal, Legion of Merit. Office: Human Resources & Administrn 810 Vermont Ave NW Washington DC 20420-0001

BRICKLER, JOHN WEISE, lawyer; b. Dayton, Ohio, Dec. 29, 1944; s. John Benjamin and Shirley Hilda (Weise) B.; m. Marilyn Louise Kuhlmann, July 2, 1966; children: John, James, Peter, Andrew, Matthew. AB, Washington U., St. Louis, 1966; JD, Washington U., 1968. Bar: Mo. 1968, U.S. Supreme Ct. 1972, U.S. Dist. Ct. (ea. dist.) Mo. 1974, U.S. Ct. Appeals (8th cir.) 1974. Assoc. Peper, Martin, Jensen, Maichel and Hetlage, St. Louis, 1973-77, ptnr., 1978-98; ptnr. Blackwell Sanders Peper Martin LLP, St. Louis, 1998—; chmn. bd. dirs. Concordia Pub. House, St. Louis, 1998—. Bd. dirs. Luth. Family and Children's Svcs. Mo., St. Louis, 1988-93, vice chmn., 1988-89. Capt. JAGC, U.S. Army, 1969-73. Mem. ABA, Nat. Assn. Bond Lawyers, Bar Assn. Met. St. Louis. Office: Blackwell Sanders Peper Martin LLP 720 Olive St Fl 24 Saint Louis MO 63101-2338

BRICKLEY, JAMES H., state supreme court justice; b. Flint, Mich., Nov. 15, 1928; s. J. Harry and Marie E. (Fischer) B.; 6 children. B.A., U. Detroit, 1951, LL.B., 1954, Ph.D. (hon.), 1977; LL.M., NYU, 1957; Ph.D. (hon.), Spring Arbor Coll., 1975, Detroit Coll. Bus., 1975, Ferris State Coll., Big Rapids, Mich., 1980, Saginaw Valley State Coll., University Center, Mich., 1980, Detroit Coll. Law, 1981. Bar: Mich. 1954. Spl. agent FBI, Washington, 1954-58; sole practice law Detroit, 1959-62; mem. Detroit City Council, 1962-67, pres. pro tem, 1966-67; chief asst. prosecutor Wayne County, Detroit, 1967-69; U.S. atty. U.S. Dist. Ct. (ea. dist.), Detroit, 1969-70; lt. gov. State of Mich., Lansing, 1971-74, 79-82; justice Supreme Ct. of Mich., Lansing, 1982—; chief justice, 1995-96; pres. Eastern Mich. U., Ypsilanti, 1975-78; lectr., adj. prof. U. Detroit, Wayne State U., U. Mich., Ann Arbor, Cooley Law Sch., 1958-73. Mem. Mich. Bar Assn., ABA, Inst. Jud. Adminstrn. Republican. Roman Catholic. Office: Supreme Ct Mich PO Box 30052 Traverse City MI 48909*

BRICKLEY, RICHARD AGAR, retired surgeon; b. Bluffton, Ind., Aug. 15, 1925; s. Harry Dwight and Ina (Agar) B.; m. Suzanne Slusser, Nov. 28, 1964; children: Dinah B. Olson, Sarah Jane, Richard Agar II, Laura Brickley Whitman, Andrew John. Student, Ind. U., 1943-44; B.S., B.M., Northwestern U., 1947, M.D., 1948. Diplomate: Am. Bd. Surgery. Intern Cook County Hosp., Chgo., 1947-49; surg. resident Cook County Hosp., 1955-56; gen. practice Bluffton, 1949-50; surg. preceptorship with Drs. Gatch and Owen, Indpls., 1950-51, 54; pvt. practice medicine, specializing in surgery Indpls., 1957-86; chmn. gen. surgery div. Meth. Hosp., Indpls., 1962-66, Winona Meml. Hosp., Indpls., 1971-73; chief of med. staff Winona Meml. Hosp., 1974-75, bd. dirs., 1977-84. Served with M.C. USAF, 1951-53. Fellow ACS; mem. AMA, Ind. Med. Assn., Aerospace Med. Assn., Marion County Med. Soc. (chmn. bd. dirs. 1976-77), Seven-Up Club (Hillman, Mich.) (owner), Beta Theta Pi, Nu Sigma Nu. Home: 4530 Crooked Creek Ridge Dr Indianapolis IN 46228-2859

BRICKLIN, MARK HARRIS, magazine editor, publisher; b. Phila., Apr. 13, 1939; s. Arthur Benjamin and Rose (Gaurd) B.; m. Alice Goddard Terry, Apr. 26, 1963 (div.); children: Deirdre, Brendon. B.A., Temple U., 1960, postgrad., 1961-62; postgrad., Boston U., 1960-61. Teaching fellow English Boston U., 1960-61; city editor Phila. Tribune, 1962-71; freelance writer, photographer, 1962-71; with Rodale Press, Emmaus, Pa., 1971—; v.p. Rodale Press, 1975—; exec. editor Prevention mag., 1974-97; founding editor, editorial dir. Spring mag., 1982-84; edit. dir. Men's Health mag., Emmaus, 1980—, Heart & Soul mag., Emmaus, 1994—; editor-in-chief Pets: Part of the Family, 1997—, founding editor, 1998; journalism preceptor Pwky. Exptl. program Phila. Sch. Dist.; cons. book pub. Author: The Practical Encyclopedia of Natural Healing, 1976, Lose Weight Naturally, 1979, Natural Healing Cookbook, 1981, Rodale's Encyclopedia of Natural Home Remedies, 1982; co-author: Positive Living and Health, 1990, Secrets of Executive Success, 1991. Founder Prevention Walking Club, 1986. Home: 2803 W Chew St Allentown PA 18104-5351 Office: Prevention 33 E Minor St Emmaus PA 18098-0001

BRICKMAN, KENNETH ALAN, state lottery executive; b. Hannibal, Mo., Sept. 10, 1940; s. Roy Frederick and Nita Wilma (Swearingen) B.; m. Mildred Darlene Myers, Aug. 10, 1963; children: Heather Katherine, Erik Alan. BS in Bus. and Econs., Culver-Stockton Coll., Canton, Mo., 1963; JD, U. Mo., 1970. Bar: Ill. 1970, Mo. 1970. Ptnr. firm Scholz, Staff & Brickman, Quincy, Ill., 1970-78; pres. real estate brokerage Landmark of Quincy, Inc./Better Homes & Gardens, 1978-79; counsel, chief counsel Ill. Dept. Commerce and Community Affairs, Springfield, 1980-85; gen. counsel, dep. dir. Ill. State Lottery, Springfield, 1986-91; sec.-treas., exec. v.p. La. Lottery Corp., Baton Rouge, 1991-95; exec. v.p. Iowa Lottery, Des Moines, 1995—. Served as capt. USAF, 1963-67. Mem. Mo. Bar, Ill. State Bar Assn., Culver Stockton Coll. Alumni Assn. (pres. 1979). Office: Iowa Lottery 2015 Grand Ave Des Moines IA 50312-4999

BRICKNER, ALICE, painter, illustrator; b. N.Y.C., Feb. 12, 1931; d. Warren Rinenberg and Lillian Smolin; m. Philip Walter Brickner, June 17, 1950; children: Jed Walter, Nell Cecilie Brickner Eakin, Maude Lillian. BA, Sarah Lawrence Coll., 1952; studied with, Kurt Roesch, Ezio Martinelli, Lux Feininger, Theodore Roszak, Seong Moy, Arnold Singer, Erich Monch, Ansei Uchima. One-person shows include Howell Ctr., Beacon, N.Y., 1998; exhibited in group shows Poulsen Gallery, Pasadena, Calif., 1988-89, Elaine Benson Gallery, Bridgehampton, N.Y., 1988, 91, 92, 96, Goat Alley Gallery, Sag Harbor, N.Y., 1991, Hammerquist/FACS Gallery, N.Y.C., 1993, River Gallery, Irvington, N.Y., 1994, 95, 96, 97, Millenium Gallery, Easthampton, N.Y., 1995, Sch. House Gallery, Croton Falls, N.Y., 1997, Chrysalis Gallery, Southampton, N.Y., 1998—, Donnell Libr., N.Y.C., 1999; represented in pub. collections Johnson & Johnson, Pratt Graphic Art Ctr., Stuttgart U., also pvt. collections; works featured in Soc. Illustrators Annuals, Comm. Arts Mag., others. Mem. N.Y. Artists Equity Assn., Artist's Space. Avocations: grandchildren, theater, reading, traveling. E-mail: alicebric@aol.com. Home and Studio: 4720 Grosvenor Ave Bronx NY 10471-3307

BRICKNER, ROGER KENNETH, secondary school educator; b. N.Y.C., Aug. 27, 1930; s. Charles Erwin and Gertrude Martha (Duerr) B. BA in History cum laude, CUNY, 1952, MA in Edn., 1953. Cert. tchr., N.Y. Tchr. Richmond Hill H.S., N.Y.C., 1954-67, Brooklands Tech. Coll., Weybridge, Eng., 1964-65; prof. Queens Coll., CUNY, N.Y.C., 1967, 71; chmn. social studies Cardozo H.S., N.Y.C., 1967-70, tchr., 1971-85. Author: The Long Island Express, 1988. Candidate for U.S. Congress, 1962. Sgt. U.S. Army, 1952-54, Korea. Recipient 2000 Mile Cert., Appalachian Trail, 1987. Mem. Mus. Am. Weather (bd. dirs. 1992—), L.I. Weather Observers (pres. 1986-87), Appalachian Trail Conf., Internat. Weather Watchers (v.p. 1993-95, co-founder). Republican. Congregationalist. Avocations: weather, political analysis, travel, writing, hiking. E-mail: nhnypr@aol.com. Home: South Common Haverhill NH 03765

BRICKSON, RICHARD ALAN, lawyer; b. Madison, Wis., Feb. 10, 1948; s. William Louis and Nancy May (Gay) B.; m. Marilyn Joan Serenco, June 20, 1971; children: Jennifer Lynne, Katherine Anne, Evan Leigh. BA, Wabash Coll., 1970; JD, Georgetown U., 1973. Bar: Mo. 1973. Staff atty. The May Dept. Stores Co., St. Louis, 1973-77, assoc. gen. counsel, 1977-79, asst. gen. counsel, 1979-81, counsel, 1981-82, counsel, sec., 1982-88, sr. counsel, sec., 1988—. Office: May Dept Stores Co 611 Olive St Saint Louis MO 63101-1721

BRICKWOOD, SUSAN CALLAGHAN, lawyer; b. Sydney, NSW, Australia, Dec. 6, 1946; d. Graham Callaghan Brickwood and Nan (Cahaley) Nichols). BA, Swarthmore Coll., 1969; postgrad., Harvard U., 1969-71; JD, U. So. Calif., 1980. Bar: Calif. 1980, U.S. Tax Ct. 1981. Controller Howard Smith, Ltd., Sydney, 1972-74; assoc. Rifkind & Sterling, Beverly Hills, Calif., 1980-81, Armstrong, Hendler & Hirsch, Century City, Calif., 1981-82; pvt. practice L.A., 1982—. Author: Start Over!, 1990. Office: 6500 Wilshire Blvd Los Angeles CA 90048-4920

BRIDE, JOHN W(ILLIAM), communications executive, entrepreneur; b. Boston, Sept. 12, 1937; s. William T. and Elsie Francis (Duffy) B.; m. Marjorie McHenry, May 13, 1966 (div. 1984); children: John Hambleton, Christopher McHenry; m. Mary Eileen Kiniry, Feb. 15, 1985. BA in Econs., Norwich U., 1960; LLB, U. Maine, 1964; OMP, Harvard U., 1980. Staff atty. FCC, Washington, 1964-66; account exec. Sta. KDKA-TV, Pitts., 1966-70; pres. Bride Broadcasting, Inc., Pitts., 1970-86, Chandler Broadcasting, Inc., Portland, Maine, 1970-86, Greater Portland Radio, Inc., Portland, Maine, 1972-86, B-T Satellite, Portland, Maine, 1980-96, Triangle Properties, Portland, Maine, 1980-85, Bride Communications, Inc., Portland, Maine, 1980-96, Portland Broadcast, Inc., Portland, Maine, 1987-96; trustee John W. Duffy Trusts, Boston, 1978—; mem. com. fgn. rels., Portland, 1976-96; mem. adv. com. Back Cove Improvement Project, Portland, 1984-86; mem. adv. bd. Lifeline U. So. Maine, Portland, 1983-95; chair comm. adv. bd. Norwich U., 1988—; pres. Bride Charitable Found., Portland, 1980; instr. Jr. Achievement, Portland, 1980-96, bd. dirs. 1993; treas. bd. dirs. ABC Talkradio Affiliates, N.Y.C., 1983-88; mng. ptnr. Airwave Investments, LLC, 1997—. Mem. bd. visitors U. Maine Sch. Law, 1991—. Served with U.S. Army, 1960-61. Mem. Maine Bar Assn. Harvard Bus. Club (v.p. 1984—), Pitts. Golf Club. Unitarian. Avocation: triathlons. Home: 83 West St Portland ME 04102-3415 Office: Airwave Investments LLL 2320 Congress St Portland ME 04102-1908

BRIDEAU, LEO PAUL, healthcare executive; b. Leominster, Mass., Mar. 1, 1947; s. Alfred Joseph and Marie Yvonne (Poulin) B.; m. Kathleen Margaret Quinlan, Oct. 5, 1968; children: Alexander, Elizabeth, Neil, Katherine, William. BS, Georgetown U., 1968; MHA, Med. Coll. of Va., 1980. Counselor vets. benefits VA, Togus, Maine, 1971-73; asst. dist. coord. VA, Richmond, Va., 1975-80; mgmt. analyst VA Med. Ctr., Togus, 1973-75; dep. dir. patient care services Strong Meml. Hosp., Rochester, N.Y., 1980-84; acting exec. dir. Strong Meml. Hosp., Rochester, 1984, dir. hosp. ops., 1984-89, exec. dir., 1990-94, gen. dir., CEO, 1995-97; pres., CEO Strong Ptnrs. Health Sys. Inc., Rochester, 1997—; preceptor dept. health svcs. Va. Commonwealth U., Richmond, 1985—; preceptor Washington U. Sch. Medicine, St. Louis; instr. health svcs. U. Rochester, 1985—; mem. N.Y. State Pub. Health Coun., 1996—. Author: chpt. Cost Containment in a University Hosp., 1987. Chmn. adv. bd. Lifeline, Rochester, 1982-85; bd. dirs. Monroe County Medicap Inc., Rochester, 1984-87, Finger Lakes Health Systems Agy., Rochester, 1985-92; bd. dirs. Rochester Regional Joint Ventures Corp., 1985—, chmn., 1987-89, bd. dirs. Rochester Area Health Maintenance Orgn., Inc., 1985-88. Fellow Am. Coll. Healthcare Execs.; mem. Healthcare Assn. N.Y. State (chmn. bd. dirs. 1996, chair govt. rels. com. 1985-86, trustee 1989—, chair strategic planning com. 1991—), Rochester Regional Hosp. Assn. (bd. dirs. 1985-96, chmn. 1987-8 Assn. Univ. Programs in Health Adminstrn., Pi Sigma Alpha. Avocation: music. Office: Strong Meml Hosp 601 Elmwood Ave # 612 Rochester NY 14642-0002

BRIDEGAM, WILLIS EDWARD, JR., librarian; b. Pottstown, Pa., Oct. 15, 1935; s. Willis Edward and M. Emma (Eberhart) B.; 1 child, Martha Ann. BMus, Eastman Sch. Music, 1957; MS, Syracuse U., N.Y., 1963; MA (hon.), Amherst Coll., 1985. Med. librarian U. Rochester (N.Y.) Sch. Medicine, 1966-69, asso. dir. univ. libraries, 1969-72; dir. libraries State U. N.Y., Binghamton, 1972-75; librarian Amherst (Mass.) Coll., 1975—. Served with AUS, 1957. Mem. ALA, Assn. Coll. and Rsch. Libraries (chair coll. libr. sect. stds. com.). Club: Grolier (N.Y.C.). Home: 15 Woodside Ave Amherst MA 01002-2524 Office: Amherst Coll Robert Frost Libr Amherst MA 01002

BRIDENBAUGH, PETER REESE, industrial research executive; b. Franklin, Pa., July 28, 1940; s. Charles Sumner and Helen Catherine (Reese) B.; m. Mary Ann Ellis, Apr. 17, 1965; children: Matthew B., Gabrielle L. BSME, Lehigh U., 1962, MS in Metallurgy, 1966; PhD in Materials Sci., MIT, 1968. With Alcoa Labs., Alcoa Ctr., Pa., R & D group leader, sect. head, spl. program engr. Warrick Ops., 1968-75, mgr., 1975-78; mgr. quality assurance Alcoa, Tenn., 1978-80; dir. ops. Alcoa Labs., 1980-83, dir., 1983-84, v.p. R & D, 1984-91, exec. v.p., chief tech. officer, 1991-95, exec. v.p.-automotive, 1995—; mem. adv. bd. Carnegie-Bosch; chmn. Fedn. Materials Socs. 10th Biennial Conf., 1988; bd. dirs. Precision Castparts Corp., 1995—. Patentee in field. Mem. Pa. State Rsch. Found.; mem. vis. com. Carnegie-Mellon U., 1984—, Pa. State U., 1984—, Stanford U., 1987—, Lehigh U., 1989—, Northwestern U., 1991—. Fellow Am. Soc. Metals; mem. AIME, NAE, Indsl. Rsch. Inst., Dirs. Indsl. Rsch., Sigma Xi. Clubs: Duquesne (Pitts.), Fox Chapel Golf (Pitts.).

BRIDENBAUGH, PHILLIP OWEN, anesthesiologist, physician; b. Sioux City, Iowa, Dec. 17, 1932; s. Lloyd Donald and Harriet (Anderson) B.; m. Kathleen Conway, June 22, 1957 (div. Apr. 1980); children: Sue, Tom, Dan; m. Diann Hurd, Mar. 7, 1981; children: Rob, Jeff. BA, U. Nebr., 1954; MD, U. Nebr., Omaha, 1960. Diplomate Am. Bd. Anesthesiology. Staff anesthesiologist Mason Clinic, Seattle, 1965-70, dir. dept. anesthesia, 1970-77; prof., chmn. dept. anesthesiology U. Cin. Med. Ctr., 1977—; pres. UAA, Inc., Cin., 1977—. Co-editor: Neural Blockade, 1980, 2d edit., 1988, 3d edit., 1997; sect. editor Anesthesia and Analgesia, 1989-95; sr. editor Regional Anesthesia, 1989-97. Trustee Wood Libr. Mus. Anesthesiology, 1992-94. 1st lt. U.S. Army, 1954-56. Mem. Assn. Univ. Anesthetists, Soc. Acad. Anesthesia Chmn. (pres. 1988-90), Am. Soc. Anesthesiology (bd. dirs., v.p. sci. affairs 1992-94, 1st v.p. 1994-95, pres. elect 1995-96, pres. 1996-97, immediate past pres. 1997-98), Am. Soc. Regional Anesthesia (pres. 1990-91), Ohio Soc. Anesthesiologists (pres. 1991-92). Office: U Cin Dept Anesthesia 231 Bethesda Ave Cincinnati OH 45229-2827

BRIDENSTINE, LOUIS HENRY, JR., lawyer; b. Detroit, Nov. 13, 1940; s. Louis and Mary Ellen (O'Keefe) B.; m. Lucia Elizabeth Pucci, June 18, 1966; 1 child, Lucia McMullin. BS, John Carroll U., 1962; MA, U. Detroit, 1966, JD, 1965. Bar: Mich. 1966, U.S. Dist. Ct. (ea. dist.) Mich. 1966. Trial atty., atty.-advisor FTC, Washington, 1966-72; sr. legal counsel, v.p. dir. comms. Motor Vehicle Mfrs. Assn. U.S., Inc., Detroit, 1972-81; sr. v.p., gen. counsel, sec. Campbell-Ewald Co., Warren, Mich., 1981—; exec. dir. Motorists Info., Inc., Detroit, 1977; legal affairs com. Am. Assn. Advt. Agys., N.Y.C., 1990—. Youth allocations panelist United Way Cmty Svcs., Detroit, 1991-98, chair, 1993-98, fund distbn. panelist, 1994-98; trustee, bd. dirs. Catholic Youth Orgn., Detroit, 1981-97, 99—, chair bd. dirs., 1990-92. Fellow Mich. State Bar Found. (life); mem. Mich. Bar Assn., Am. Corp. Counsel Assn., Alpha Sigma Nu, Blue Key, Detroit Athletic Club. Avocations: travel, reading. Office: Campbell Ewald Co 30400 Van Dyke Ave Warren MI 48093-2368

BRIDESTOWE, LORD See MOORE, THOMAS RONALD

BRIDEWELL, DAVID ALEXANDER, lawyer; b. Forrest City, Ark., Dec. 8, 1909; s. Alexander Carver and Martha Elizabeth (Hatcher) B.; m. Mary Frances Badger, May 21, 1949; children: Jonathan Lee (dec.), Alexander Hunt. AB, U. South, 1931; MA, Princeton U., 1932; JD, George Washington U., 1938. Bar: Ark. 1933, D.C. 1938, Ill. 1940, U.S. Supreme Ct. 1940. Assoc. Mann & Mann, Forrest City, Ark., 1932; dist. atty. Home Owners Loan Corp., Jonesboro, Ark., 1933-34; atty. and asst. to gen. counsel Fed. Home Loan Bank Bd., Washington, 1935-40; ptnr. Russell & Bridewell, Chgo., 1940-85, Righeimer, Martin, Bridewell & Ciquino, Chgo., 1985-88; counsel Spindell & Kemp, Chgo., 1988-90, Lewis, Overbeck & Furman, Chgo., 1990-93, DeWolfe, Poynton & Stevens, Chgo., 1993-95; pvt. practice Chgo., 1995—; bd. dirs. First Bank & Trust Co., Palatine, Ill., Kankakee (Ill.) Fed. Savs. Bank, No. Ark. Tel. Co., Flippin; rev. atty. Fed. Savings and Loans Ins. Corp., 1936; lectr. John Marshall Law Sch., Northwestern U., 1946-70; arbitrator Cir. Ct. Cook County, 1990—; counsel 1st Fed. Savs and Loan Assn. Chgo., 1960-85, 2d Fed. Savs. and Loan Assn. Chgo., 1945—; sec. Ctrl. Housing Com. Law and Legis. Author: The Legislative History of Federal Home Loan Bank Board and Its Agencies, 1935, Bridewell on Credit Unions, 3d edit., 1945, Bridewell on Bailments, Liens and Pledges, 1945, Credit Unions; editor: Selected Illinois Statutes, 1947; A Lawyer's Guide to Retirement, 3d edit., 1998, Housing Legal Digest; co-editor: Reverse Mortgages and Other Senior Income and Housing Options, 1997. Chancellor Christ Episcopal Ch., Winnetka, Ill., 1960-75. Capt. JAGD, U.S. claims commr. U.S. Army, 1943-46, ETO. Mem. ABA (bus. law sect. 1965—, chmn. savs. and loan comm. 1965-70, coun. 1970-75, sr. lawyer divsn. coun. 1985-93, chmn. bd. editors Experience Mag. 1995), Ill. Bar Assn. (chmn. savs. and loan com. 1980-85), Chgo. Bar Assn. (chmn. sr. lawyer com. 1985-87), Univ. Club Chgo. (chmn. lit. and arts com. 1980-85), Kappa Sigma. Republican. Episcopalian. Avocations: tennis, golf, swimming. Home: 789 Burr Ave Winnetka IL 60093-1802 Office: 135 S La Salle St Chicago IL 60603-4105

BRIDGE, ANDREW, theatrical lighting designer. Formerly lighting designer to Shirley Bassey; now lighting cons. Imagination design co., London. Lighting designer (prodns.) Torvill and Dean-The World Tour, Oliver!, An Evening With Tommy Steele, (West End prodns.) The Phantom of the Opera, Little Me, Billy Bishop Goes to War, Canterbury Tales, The Boyfriend, Tomfoolery, Carte Blanche, Blondel, Abbracadabra, Time, Aspects of Love, (Broadway prodn.) The Phantom of the Opera (Tony award

1988, Drama Desk and Outer Critics' Circle awards 1988), Sunset Boulevard (Tony award 1995); also designer floodlighting Lloyd's of London hdqrs. Won Tony award, Lighting Design-Musical, Fosse, 1999.

BRIDGE, HERBERT MARVIN, jewelry executive; b. Seattle, Mar. 14, 1925; s. Ben and Sally (Silverman) B.; m. Shirley Selesnick, Jan. 25, 1948; children: Jonathan J., Daniel E. BA in Polit. Sci., U. Wash., 1947. Pres. Ben Bridge Jeweler Inc., Seattle, 1955-76, chmn., 1977—. Past pres. Downtown Seattle Assn., 1980-81, Am. Jewish Com.; bd. dirs. Naval Acad. Found., Naval Undersea Mus., Alliance for Edn.; chair Puget Sound USO; chmn. sr. adv. bd. Goodwill Games of 1990; co-chair King County chpt. United Way, 2000. Rear adm. USNR, 1942-85. Decorated Legion of Merit with Gold Star in lieu of 2d award; recipient Israel Bonds Masada award, 1974, Am. Jewish Com. Human Rels award, 1978, Navy League scrool hon., 1980, 96, U. Wash. Alumni Legend award, 1987, Vol. of Yr. award Jewish Fedn., 1991, Privacy Fund Humanitarian award, 1991, Heritage award Mus. History and Industry, 1993, A.K. Guy Cmty. Svc. award YMCA, 1995, Sea 1st Cmty. Svc. award, 1998; named to Nat. Jewelers Hall of Fame, 1998. Mem. Am. Gem. Soc. (cert.; trustee 1993—, chair trustees 1994—), Pacific N.W. Jewelers (past pres.), Greater Seattle C. of C. (past chmn. 1986-87, pres. club, past pres. 1974-75), Naval Res. Assn. (past pres.), Wash. Athletic Club (pres. 1992-93), City Club (founder), Rotary (dir. found., Seattle Rotary bd.), Shriners. Democrat. Office: PO Box 1908 Seattle WA 98111-1908

BRIDGELAND, JAMES RALPH, JR., lawyer; b. Cleve., Feb. 16, 1929; s. James Ralph and Alice Laura (Huth) B.; m. Margaret Louise Bates, March 24, 1950; children: Deborah, Cynthia, Rebekah, Alicia, John. BA magna cum laude, U. Akron, 1951; MA, Harvard U., 1955, JD, 1957. Bar: Ohio 1957. Mem. internat. staff Goodyear Tire & Rubber Co., Akron, Ohio, 1953-56; ptnr. Taft, Stettinius & Hollister, Cin., 1957—; dir., mem. exec. com. Firstar Corp. and Star Bank Cin.; dir. SHV N.Am., Inc., The David J. Joseph Co., Robert A. Cline Co., Art Stamping, Inc., Seinau-Fisher Studios, Inc.; instr., lectr. in lit. U. Cin.. Pres., trustee Cin. Symphony Orch.; sec., trustee Louise Taft Semple Found.; trustee Cin. Opera Co., Hillside Trust, Jobs for Cin. Grads., Cin. Inst. Fine Arts; past bd. dirs. Legal Aid Soc.; mayor, mem. coun. City of Indian Hill, Ohio, 1985-91; pres. Indian Hill Sch. Bd., 1971-77. 1st lt. USAF, 1951-53, Korea. Mem. ABA, Ohio Bar Assn., Cin. Bar Assn., Am. Arbitration Assn., Harvard Law Sch. Assn. (past pres. Cin. chpt.), Harvard Alumni Assn. (nat. v.p. 1978-85). Harvard Club (pres. 1983-84), Queen City Club, Commonwealth Club (treas. 1984-86), Assn. Liberary Scholars and Critics, Cin. Literary Club. Republican. Episcopalian. Home: 8175 Brill Rd Cincinnati OH 45243-3937

BRIDGER, BALDWIN, JR., electrical engineer; b. Savannah, Ga., Sept. 18, 1928; s. Baldwin and Helen Bush (Stubbs) B.; m. Wilma Grace Martz, Mar. 21, 1953; children: Ruth Carson, John Wesley, Mary Gere. BS in Engring., Emory U., 1948; postgrad., U. Iowa, 1966-68. Registered profl. engr., Tex., Pa. Test engr. GE, Lynn, Mass., Trenton, N.J., Ft. Wayne, Ind., Schenectady, N.Y., 1948-50; design engr. GE, Phila., 1953-65; engring. mgr. GE, Burlington, Iowa, 1965-68; engring. mgr. GE, Phila., 1968-71, product planner, 1972-73; chief engr. Powell Elec. Mfg. Co., Houston, 1973-83, mgr. engring., 1983-85, mgr. application and new products engring., 1985-90, tech. dir., 1990-96; pres. Bridger Engring. Co., 1996—. Contbr. articles to tech. jours. With USN, 1951-52. Fellow IEEE (dept. chmn. 1987-88, soc. treas. 1989-90, soc. sec. 1991, soc. v.p. 1992, pres. 1993, editor, tech. jour. 1997—); mem. Phi Beta Kappa. Republican. Methodist.

BRIDGER, CAROLYN ANN, pianist, music educator; b. Memphis, Tenn., June 20, 1943; d. Grover Leon and Elizabeth Lou (Everett) B.; m. Waldie Alfred Anderson, Dec. 30, 1983. Student, Mozarteum Akademie, Salzburg, Austria, 1963-64; MusB, Oberlin (Ohio) Coll., 1965; MusM, Ind. U., 1967; postgrad., Boston U., 1970-72; D Mus. Arts, U. Iowa, 1977. Adj. lectr. music Emory U., Atlanta, 1967-70; vis. asst. prof. music U. N.C., Chapel Hill, 1974-75; asst. prof. music Delta State U., Cleveland, Tenn., 1975-76; prof. piano and chamber music, coord. accompanying Fla. State U., Tallahassee, 1976—; artistic advisor The Artist Series, Tallahassee; keyboardist Tallahassee Symphony; violist Big Band Cmty. Orch., Tallahassee. Piano soloist Atlanta Symphony, Balt. Symphony and other orchs.; concert tours solo and chamber music in Europe, S.Am., S.E. Asia, U.S.A. Rsch. grantee Fla. State U. Mem. Music Tchrs. Nat. Assn., Fla. State Music Tchrs. Assn. (chamber music chair 1988—), P.E.O. Sisterhood, Pi Kappa Lambda. Avocations: travel, birding. Office: Fla State U Sch Music Tallahassee FL 32306-1180

BRIDGER, WAGNER H., psychiatrist, educator; b. N.Y.C., Jan. 9, 1928. BA, NYU, 1946, MD, 1950. Diplomate Am. Bd. Psychiatry and Neurology. Intern U. Chgo., 1950-51; asst. resident psychiatry Bellevue Hosp., 1951-52; research fellow Pavlovian lab. Johns Hopkins Med. Sch., Balt., 1952-53; staff psychiatrist William Beaumont Army Hosp., 1953-54; resident psychiatrist River Crest Sanitarium, N.Y.C., 1954-55, Bronx Mcpl. Hosp. Ctr. and Yeshiva U., 1955-56; research fellow dept. psychiatry, Yeshiva U., N.Y.C., 1956-57, research instr., 1957-58, instr., 1958-60, asst. prof., 1960-65, assoc. prof., 1965-70, dir. research, 1965-82, prof., 1970-82, prof. neurosci., 1974-82, acting chmn., 1976-81; jr. psychiatrist Bronx Mcpl. Hosp. Ctr., 1956-57, asst. attending psychiatrist, 1958-65, assoc. attending psychiatrist, 1965-70, attending psychiatrist, 1970-82; chmn. dept. psychiatry, prof. psychiatry and pharmacology Med. Coll. Pa. at Ea. Pa. Psychiat. Inst., 1982-93, prof. psychiatry, 1993—; vis. scientist Istituto Superiore di Sanita, Rome, 1969-70; vis. scholar psychology Harvard U., Cambridge, Mass., 1994-95, U. Calif., Berkeley, 1995; cons. Hastings Ctr.-Inst. of Soc., Ethics, and Life Scis.; investigator mental health career USPHS, 1958-63. Editor Biol. Psychiatry Jour., 1992. Recipient USPHS Research Sci. award, 1968-73. Fellow Am Psychiat. Assn., Am. Coll. Neuropsychopharmacology, Am. Coll. Psychiatrists; mem. Am. Psychopathological Assn. (council 1960), Group for Advancement of Psychiatry (com. pn psychopathology 1968-72), Pavlovian Soc. Am. (pres. 1968-69), Soc. Psychiat. Research (pres. 1970-71), Biol. Psychiatry (chmn. program com. IV World Congress 1984-85), Soc. Biol. Psychiatry (pres.-elect 1987-88, pres. 1988-89). Office: Med Coll Pa Dept Psychiatry 3200 Henry Ave Philadelphia PA 19129-1137

BRIDGERS, WILLIAM FRANK, physician, educator; b. Asheville, N.C., July 26, 1932; s. John Dixon and Ruth (Norberg) B.; m. Judith Ann Ware, Nov. 27, 1974; 1 child, Jana; children from previous marriage: Jeffrey, David, Daniel. BA, U. of the South, 1954; MD, Washington U., St. Louis, 1959, fellow in preventive medicine, 1963-65. Intern Barnes Hosp., Washington U., St. Louis, 1959-60, resident, 1962-63; assoc. prof. medicine U. Miami, Fla., 1968; prof., dir. neurosci. program U. Ala. - Birmingham, 1970-72, spl. asst. v.p. health affairs, 1976, chmn., prof. dept. pub. health, 1976-93; former dean U. Ala., Birmingham, 1981-89, prof., 1981-93, univ. scholar emeritus, 1993—; head Eutaw Health Policy Group, Birmingham, 1993—; staff mem. NAS, Washington, 1974; mem. governing bd. Nat. Coun. Internat. Health, Washington, 1979-87; dir. Lister Hill Ctr. for Health Policy, 1987-90; mem. com. on vital and health stats. HHS, USPHS, 1990-94. Co-editor (monthly feature) Policy Watch Am. Jour. Medicine and Am. Jour. Surgery, 1990-97; contbr. articles to profl. jours. Mem. APHA, Assn. Schs. Pub. Health (pres., mem. exec. com.), Am. Men and Women of Sci., Am. Inst. Nutrition, Am. Soc. Biol. Chemistry, Phi Beta Kappa. Democrat. Home: 2221 English Village Ln Birmingham AL 35223-1730

BRIDGES, ALAN LYNN, physicist, computer scientist, systems software engineer. BS in Physics, Ga. Inst. Tech., 1972, MS in Physics, 1974, postgrad., 1975-78. Cert. C-130J R&M HUD & BIU FMECA. Asst. research scientist Ga. Tech. Research Inst., Atlanta, 1975-78; asst. product mgr. Humphrey Instruments Inc., San Leandro, Calif., 1978; pres., cons. ETC West Ltd., 1979—; with Lockheed Aero Systems Co., 1983-88; sr. prin. engr. new bus. devel. Lockheed Electronics Co., Atlanta, 1988-90; sr. engr., program mgr. Flat Panel & Graphics Display Systems SCI Tech., Inc., Hunstville, Ala., 1990-92; software engr. specialist life cycle software support and C130JRM & S sys. engring. Lockheed Martin Aeronautical Systems Co., Marietta, Ga., 1992-98, sr. S.W. software specialist, 1998—; mem. Lockheed Software Process Std. ISO 9000/SEI CMM software and sys. engring. CMM process action team, ACM stds. com. tech. adv. group ISO 9241. Contbg. editor Computer Tech. Rev., PC Graphics & Video Mag.; bi-monthly columnist Hardcopy; contbr. articles to profl. jours. Mem. IEEE (sr., dir. Atlanta sect., 1987-88, sec. 1988-89, treas. 1989-90, chmn. student activities com. 1985-87, sec.-treas. computer soc. chpt. 1985-86, chmn. computer soc. chpt. 1986-87, 88-89, vice chmn. 1987-88, gen. chmn. Atlanta software tech. conf. 1987, mem P1226 ABBET com., mem. P1498/12207 stds. com.), Assn. for Computing Machinery, Optical Soc. Am., Soc. Photo-Optical Instrumentation Engrs., Nat. Security Indsl. Assn. (mem. integrated diagnostic working group, co-chair integrated avionics task group), Soc. for Tech. Communications, Computer Press Assn., Soc. for Info. Display, Nat. Telesystems Conf., Control and Displays Session Orgn., Am. Nat. Standards Inst./Internat. Standards Orgn., Sigma Pi Sigma. Home: 8523 Colony Club Dr Alpharetta GA 30022-5407 Office: Lockheed Martin Aero Sys Co Bldg B-18 Zone 0307 86 S Cobb Dr Marietta GA 30063-1000

BRIDGES, B. RIED, lawyer; b. Kansas City, Mo., Oct. 20, 1927; s. Brady R. and Mary H. (Nieuwenhuis) B.; m. Lou George, Feb. 9, 1955; 1 son, Ried George. B.A., U. So. Calif., 1951, LL.B., 1954. Bar: Calif. 1954. Assoc. Overton, Lyman & Prince, L.A., 1956-58, ptnr., 1958-63; ptnr. Bonne, Jones & Bridges, L.A., 1963-74, Bonne, Bridges, Mueller & O'Keefe, L.A., Santa Ana, Santa Barbara, Ventura, San Luis Obispo and Riverside, Calif., 1974—. Served with U.S. Army, 1954-56. Fellow Am. Coll. Trial Lawyers, Internat. Acad. Trial Lawyers; mem. ABA, Calif. Bar Assn., Assn. So. Calif. Def. Counsel, L.A. County Bar Assn., Wilshire Bar Assn., Santa Barbara County Bar Assn., Am. Bd. Trial Advs. (diplomate), Pacific Corinthian Yacht Club, Balboa of Mazatlan (Sinaloa, Mex.). Republican. Avocation: boating. Home: 3608 Ocean Dr Channel Islands CA 93035-4141 Office: Bonne Bridges Mueller O'Keefe & Nichols 801 Garden St Ste 300 Santa Barbara CA 93101-1597

BRIDGES, BEAU (LLOYD VERNET BRIDGES, III), actor; b. L.A., Dec. 9, 1941; s. Lloyd Vernet and Dorothy (Simpson) B.; m. Wendy Bridges; children: Casey, Jordan, Dylan, Emily. Attended, U. Calif. at Los Angeles. Film appearances include The Incident, For Love of Ivy, 1968, Gaily, Gaily, 1969, The Landlord, 1970, Adam's Woman, The Christian Licorice Store, 1971, Hammersmith is Out, 1972, Child's Play, 1972, Your Three Minutes Are Up, 1973, Lovin' Molly, The Other Side of the Mountain, 1975, Swashbuckler, 1976, Two-Minute Warning, 1976, Dragon Fly, 1976, Greased Lightning, 1977, Norma Rae, 1979, The Fifth Musketeer, 1979, The Runner Stumbles, 1979, Honky Tonk Freeway, 1980, Night Crossing, 1982, Love Child, 1982, Heart Like a Wheel, 1983, The Hotel New Hampshire, 1984, Iron Triangle, 1987, The Fabulous Baker Boys, 1989, (also dir.) Seven Hours to Judgment, 1988, The Wizard, 1989, Daddy's Dying...Who's Got the Will?, 1990, Married to It, 1993, Sidekicks, 1993, Nightjohn, 1996, Losing Chase, 1996, Jerry Maguire, 1996, Rocket Man, 1997, Meeting Daddy, 1998, White River Kid, 1999; TV appearances include The Man Without a Country, 1973, The Stranger Who Looks like Me, 1974, The Whirlwind, 1974, Medical Story, The President's Mistress, 1978, The Four Feathers, 1978, The Child Stealer, 1979, United States, 1980, The Kid from Nowhere, 1982, Dangerous Company, 1982, Witness for the Prosecution, 1982, The Red-Light Sting, 1984, A Fighting Choice, Outrage, 1989, Wildflower, 1991; TV film Wildflower, 1991, Kissenger and Nixon, 1995, Hidden In America, 1996, The Second Civil War, 1997; TV mini-series Space, 1985, Without Warning: The James Brady Story, HBO, 1992 (Emmy award leading actor, 1992), The Positively True Adventures of the Alleged Texas Cheerleader-Murdering Mom, HBO, 1993 (Emmy award, Outstanding Supporting Actor in a Miniseries or Special, 1993, Golden Globe Award, Best actor in a miniseries or movie made for television, 1994), Million Dollar Babies, 1994; T.V.(also Prod.), The Denders: payback, 1997; The Defenders: Choice of Evils, 1998; T.V. Series, Maximum Bob, 1998. Office: Creative Artists care Steve Tellez 9830 Wilshire Blvd Beverly Hills CA 90212-1825*

BRIDGES, CLAYTON GARY, retired career officer. BS in Acctg., U. Tenn., 1972; MS in Mgmt., Troy State U., 1976; student, Squadron Officer Sch., 1976, Air Command and Staff Coll., 1978, Armed Forces Staff Coll., 1982, Indsl. Coll. Armed Forces, 1988. Cert. level III in fin. mgmt. cell of acquisition profl. devel. program. Commd. 2d lt. USAF, 1972, advanced through grades to brig. gen., 1996; acctg. and fin. officer Air Force Spl. Weapons Ctr., Kirtland AFB, N.Mex., 1972-74; stationed at 81st Tactical Fighter Wing, RAF Bentwaters, U.K., 1974-78; various positions Hdqs. USAF, Washington, 1978-81; stationed at Hdqs. USAF Europe, Ramstein Air Base, W. Germany, 1982-84; chief investment funds div., dep. chief staff plans/programs Hdqs. Air Force Logistics Command, Wright-Patterson AFB, Ohio, 1984-87; dep. comptroller Arnold Engring. Devel. Ctr., Arnold AFB, Tenn., 1988-89; asst. budget programs and dir. budget mgmt. and execution Air Force secretariat, Washington, 1989-91; asst. dep. chief staff fin. mgmt., comptr. Hdqs. Air Force Sys. Command, Andrews AFB, Md., 1991-92, chmn. program rev. com., 1991-92; from asst. dep. chief staff to dir. fin. mgmt., comptr. Hdqs. Air Force Materiel Command, Wright-Patterson AFB, 1992-95, dir. fin. mgmt., comptroller, 1994-95; dir. fin. mgmt., comptroller Hdqs. Pacific Air Forces, Hickam AFB, Hawaii, 1993-94; comptroller Hdqs. Air Mobility Command, Scott AFB, Ill., 1995-99; ret. Hdqs. Air Mobility Command, Scott AFB, 1999. Decorated Silver Star, Legion of Merit, D.F.C., Air medal with two oak leaf clusters, Rep. Vietnam Gallantry Cross with Palm, Rep. Vietnam Campaign medal, Svc. medal with four oak leaf clusters. Named USAF Assn. Outstanding Logistics Comptroller, 1986. Office: HQ AMC/FM 402 Scott Dr Unit 1K1 Scott AFB IL 62225-5311

BRIDGES, DAVID MANNING, lawyer; b. Berkeley, Calif., May 22, 1936; s. Robert Lysle and Alice Marion (Rodenberger) B.; m. Carmen Galante de Bridges, Aug. 16, 1973; children: David, Stuart. AB, U. Calif., Berkeley, 1957, JD, 1962. Assoc. Thelen, Marrin, Johnson & Bridges, San Francisco, 1962-70, ptnr., 1970-94; mng. ptnr. Thelen, Marrin, Johnson & Bridges, Houston, 1981-91. Served as lt. (j.g.) USN, 1957-59. Mem. ABA, State Bar of Tex., Tex. Bar Assn., Houston Bar Assn., Internat. Bar Assn., Houston Club, Coronado Club, Pacific-Union Club. Office: 1111 Bagby St Ste 2450 Houston TX 77002-2555

BRIDGES, DOUGLAS M., musician, small business owner; b. Belleville, Ill., Jan. 22, 1958; s. Donald Miles and Geneva (Verduce) B.; m. Laura L. Missey, Oct. 21, 1978. Ordained to ministry Universal Life Ch., 1993. Musician Easy St., Belleville, 1981, Cimmaron, Las Vegas, Nev., 1981-85; co-owner Cimarron Music Works, Estes Park, Colo., 1990-94; composer, music adv. Horizon Video Prodn., Denver, 1995—. Author: Banjo Owners Notebook, 1989; composer; patentee in field. Park watcher nat. Parks Conservation Assn., 1994—. Avocations: camping, hiking, reading, music, environmental work. Office: DM Bridges PO Box 2186 Estes Park CO 80517-2186

BRIDGES, ELIZABETH ANN, marketing consultant; b. New Orleans, Sept. 13, 1950; d. Johnnie and Augustine Elmira (Calice) B.; 1 child, Elizabeth Alexis. BS, So. U., 1975, MS, 1977; MBA, Atlanta U., 1982; cert. of achievement, U. Oslo, 1983. Lic. broadcaster. Resident dir. So. U., Baton Rouge, 1976-77, Spelman Coll., Atlanta, 1981-84; material analyst Xerox Corp., Webster, N.Y., 1977-80; edn. asst. Atlanta U., 1980-84; account exec. Inter-Urban Broadcasting, New Orleans, 1984-87; meml. counselor Stewart Enterprises, Metairie, La., 1987-89; mgr. pub. health City of New Orleans, 1989-92; dep. dir. Mayor's Office for Drug Affairs, New Orleans, 1992-94; dir. human resources, cons. Housing Authority New Orleans, 1994-95; mktg. cons. New Orleans, 1995—; health educator chmn. Teen Screen Drug Awareness Summit, 1989; chmn. Inst. Pub. Leadership, 1990; mentor, career day spkr. Gregory Jr. H.S., 1992; adj. prof. U. Phoenix. Del. Dem. Nat. Conv., Atlanta, 1988; mem. Orleans Parish Exec. Com., New Orleans, 1991, La. Dem. Ctrl. Com., Baton Rouge, 1991; bd. dirs., com. chmn. YWCA, 1992-96; bd. dirs., vice chmn. New Orleans Job Corps, 1992-96; bd. dirs., past chmn. New Orleans Mental Health, 1993-95. Recipient award for outstanding profl. achievement New Orleans Health Dept., 1989; fellow Loyola U. Inst. Politics, New Orleans, 1989, Met. Area Com. Leadership Forum, 1989, Leadership La., 1990, Leadership Am., 1991; named one of Outstanding Young Women of Am, Role Model, YWCA, 1998. Mem. Kappa Delta Epsilon. Avocations: travel, creative writing, public speaking, singing, community service. Home and Office: 2119 Sumpter St New Orleans LA 70122-3941

BRIDGES, GERALD DEAN, religious organization executive; b. Tyler, Tex., Dec. 4, 1929; s. Rufus Emmett and Lillian Ruth (Reeves) B.; m. Eleanor Louise Miller, Oct. 19, 1963 (dec. Nov. 1988); children: Kathleen Louise, Daniel Mark; m. Jane Bertha Mollet, Nov. 24, 1989. BS in Gen. Engr., U. Okla., 1951. Dept. supr. The Navigators, Colorado Springs, Colo., 1955-59, asst. to overseas dir., 1963-64, office mgr., 1965-69, sec., treas., 1969-79, v.p. for corp. affairs, 1979-94; adminstrv. asst. to Europe dir. The Navigators, Hague, The Netherlands, 1960-63; Bible tchr. The Navigators Collegiate Ministry, 1995—; bd. dirs. Evang. Coun. for Fin. Accountability, Washington, chmn. bd., 1991-92; ruling elder Grace Presbyn. Ch., Colorado Springs, 1972—. Author: (books) The Pursuit of Holiness, 1978, The Practice of Godliness, 1983, The Crisis of Caring, 1985, Trusting God, 1988, Transforming Grace, 1991, The Discipline of Grace, 1994, The Joy of Fearing God, 1998. Chaplain Sertoma, Colorado Springs, 1979-80. Ensign USN, 1951-53. Republican. Office: The Navigators PO Box 6000 Colorado Springs CO 80934-6000

BRIDGES, JACK EDGAR, electronics engineer; b. Denver, Jan. 6, 1925; s. Byron Edgar and Edith Katherine (Kimmel) B.; m. Martha Jane Ernest, Dec. 22, 1951; children: Victoria Ann, Amelia Joan, Cynthia Sue. BSEE, U. Colo., 1945, MSEE, 1947. Instr. of elec. engr. Iowa State Coll., Ames, 1947-48; antenna engr. Andrew Corp., Chgo., 1948-49; rsch. engr. Zenith Radio Corp., Chgo., 1949-55; head of color TV rsch. Magnavox, Ft. Wayne, Ind., 1955-56; chief electronics engr. Warwick Mfg., Niles, Ill., 1956-61; sr. sci. adv. IIT Rsch. Inst., Chgo., 1961-92; pres. Interstitial, Park Ridge, Ill., 1993—. Patentee in field; contbr. articles to profl. jours. With USN, 1943-46. Recipient Browder J. Thompson prize Inst. Radio Engrs., 1956, Disting. Engring. Alumnus award U. Colo., 1983. Fellow IEEE (life, cert. of achievement Group on EMC, 1976, Prize Paper award Power Engring. Soc., 1980); mem. Eta Kappa Nu, Tau Beta Pi, Sigma Xi. Home and Office: 1937 Fenton Ln Park Ridge IL 60068-1503

BRIDGES, JAMES A., vocational school educator. Pres. Valdosta (Ga.) Tech. Inst. Named Outstanding Vocat. Educator, 1993. Office: Valdosta Tech Inst PO Box 928 Valdosta GA 31603-0928*

BRIDGES, JAMES D., SR., quality manager, former military officer; b. Durham, N.C., Sept. 13, 1950; s. George Nathaniel and Alice Louise (Allen) B.; m. Portia Felicia Matthews, Aug. 18, 1984; children: Keino, Tomeka, James Jr., Portia F. BS in French, N.C. A&T State U., 1971; MS in Human Resources Mgmt., Golden Gate U.; MS in Tng. and Devel., Lesley Coll. Commd. 2d lt. U.S. Army, 1972, advanced through grades to major; equal opportunity staff officer 18th Combat Intelligence Group U.S. Army, Ft. Bragg, N.C., mobile tng. team instr., trainer 18th Combat Intelligence Group; officers advanced course instr. 6222d USAR sch. U.S. Army, Pasadena, Calif.; assoc. prof. ROTC instr. group Old Dominion U., Norfolk, Va.; ops. officer, course mgr. First U.S. Army Intelligence Tng. Area Sch., Fort Devens, Mass.; exec. officer 338th Mil. Intelligence Bn., Ft. Meade, Md.; ret. U.S. Army, 1994. Mem. ASTD, ASCD, Am. Soc. Indsl. Security, Nat. Assn. Sports Ofcls., Am. Mgmt. Assn., Internat. Soc. Performance Improvement, Soc. Human Resource Mgmt., Internat. Pers. Mgmt. Assn., Nat. Fedn. Interscholastic Ofcls. Assn., IAABO. Home: 2027 Brigadier Blvd Odenton MD 21113-1040

BRIDGES, JAMES EDWARD, JR., dean; b. Selma, Ala., Dec. 17, 1946; s. James Edward Sr. and Ethel Mae (Dees) B. BS, U. Ala., 1970; MS, Troy State U., 1973; M Adminstrv. Sci., U. Ala., Huntsville, 1979; D Pub. Adminstrn., U. Ala., Tuscaloosa, 1991. Quality control lab. technician Ala. Metallurg. Corp., Selma, 1966-69; statistician State of Ala. Dept. Pensions and Security, Montgomery, 1970-72; employment counselor Ala. State Employment Svc., Birmingham, 1972-73; counselor supr. Ala. State Employment Svc., Huntsville, 1973-79; asst. mgr. Ala. State Employment Svc., Birmingham, 1979-82, mgr., 1982-98; dean Sch. Civil Scis. Andrew Jackson U., Birmingham, 1995—; adj. faculty The Univ. Ala., Birmingham; cons. in field, 1998—. Co-leader career transition ministry Briarwood Presbyn. Ch., Birmingham, 1993—; chair job opportunities com. Ctrl. Ala. Task Force, Birmingham, 1997-98, Jefferson County JOBS, Birmingham, 1995-98; mem. steering com. Sch. to Work, Birmingham, 1996-98, One-Stop Career Ctr., Birmingham, 1996-98; pres. family self sufficiency Housing Authority, Birmingham, 1996-97. Mem. ASPA (pres., mem. coun. Greater Birmingham chpt., Adminstr. of Yr. award 1997), Birmingham Soc. Human Resource Mgmt. (pres., sec., treas.), Human Resource Cert. Inst. (cert.), Internat. Assn. Pers. in Employment Security, Commerce Exec. Soc. U. of Ala. Presbyterian. Avocation: travel. E-mail: jbrid95805@aol.com. Home: 4935 Caldwell Mill Ln Birmingham AL 35242

BRIDGES, JEFF, actor; b. Los Angeles, Dec. 4, 1949; s. Lloyd Vernet and Dorothy (Simpson) B.; m. Susan Bridges; 2 children. Made acting debut at age 8 in Sea Hunt TV series; appeared in films Halls of Anger, 1970, The Last Picture Show, 1971, Fat City, 1972, Bad Company, 1972, The Iceman Cometh, 1973, The Last American Hero, 1973, Thunderbolt and Lightfoot, 1974, Hearts of the West, 1975, Rancho Deluxe, 1975, King Kong, 1976, Stay Hungry, 1976, Somebody Killed Her Husband, 1978, Winter Kills, 1979, The American Success Company, 1979, Heaven's Gate, 1980, Cutter's Way, 1981, Tron, 1982, Kiss Me Goodbye, 1982, Starman, 1984, Against All Odds, 1984, Jagged Edge, 1985, The Morning After, 1986, 8 Million Ways To Die, 1986, Nadine, 1987, Tucker, 1988, See You In The Morning, 1989, The Fabulous Baker Boys, 1989, Texasville, 1990, The Fisher King, 1991, American Heart, 1992, The Vanishing, 1993, Fearless, 1993, Blown Away, 1994, Wild Bill, 1995, White Squall, 1996, The Mirror Has Two Faces, 1996, The Big Lebowski, 1998, Arlington Road, 1999; produced Hidden in America. Office: Creative Artists Agency care Rick Nicita 9830 Wilshire Blvd Beverly Hills CA 90212-1825*

BRIDGES, JULIAN CURTIS, sociologist educator, department head; b. Miami, Apr. 3, 1931; s. Clyde Clifton and Bessie Myrtle (Williams) B.; m. Charlotte Annelle Martin, Aug. 24, 1954; children: Rebecca Ann, Deborah Lea Gil, Esther Marelyn Shedd. AB, U. Fla., 1952; BD, ThD, Southwestern Bapt. Theol. Sem., Ft. Worth, 1956, 61; MA, U. Fla., 1968, PhD, 1973. Cert. family life educator; lic. marriage and family therapist. Pastor So. Bapt. Conv., Dallas, Rhome, Tex., 1953-59; rep. in Mexico Fgn. Mission Bd., Mexico City, 1959-73; prof., dept. head sociology Hardin-Simmons U., Abilene, Tex., 1973—; cons. William Jewel Coll., Liberty, Mo., 1984; prof. sociology and ethics Bapt. Theol. Sem., Madrid, Spain, 1981, Arusha, Tanzania, 1987, Hong Kong Bapt. U., 1991. Editor, sr. author: Sociology: A Pragmatic Approach, 1986; author: Celulas de Companerismo Cristiano, 1965, Expansion Evangelica en Mexico, 1973, Into Aztec Land, 1968; contbr. articles to profl. jours. and encys. Mem. city coun. City of Abilene, 1982-85, mayor pro tem, 1984-85, mem. human rels. com., 1988-96, pres. 1995-96; chair election com. Atty. Gen., State of Tex., Taylor County, 1984; v.p., bd. dirs. Mental Health Mental Retardation, Abilene, 1985-88; pres. bd. Harmony Family Svcs., Abilene, 1992-93, Harmony Family Svcs. Holding Co., 1998—, City Light Cmty. Ministries, 1997—. Recipient Faculty Rsch. award Hardin-Simmons U., 1985, Amigo award Hispanic Heritage Commn., 1996; Lily Found. Teaching fellow, Southwestern Bapt. Theol. Sem., Ft. Worth, 1957-58; named Nat. Def. Edn. Act Title VI fellow U. Fla., 1969-70. Mem. Tex. Coun. on Family Rels. (pres. 1983-84), Southwestern Sociol. Assn., Am. Assn. Marriage & Family Therapists, Southwest Rotary Club (co-chair program com. 1999—). Baptist. Avocation: community svc. Home: 1526 N Pioneer Dr Abilene TX 79603-4035 Office: HSU PO Box 16216 Abilene TX 79698

BRIDGES, LINDA KAY, journalist; b. L.A., Apr. 25, 1949; d. Roy Gordon and Beulah Lorene (Stromsmoe) B. BA, U. So. Calif., L.A., 1970. Editl. asst. Nat. Rev., N.Y.C., 1970-74, asst. mng. editor, 1974-88, mng. editor, 1988-98, sr. editor, 1998—. Co-author: (book) The Art of Persuasion, 1991. Trustee Ch. of St. Mary the Virgin, N.Y.C., 1996—; bd. dirs. Anglican Soc., 1997—. Mem. Phila. Soc. (trustee 1990-92), N.Y. C.S. Lewis Soc. Republican. Episcopalian. Avocations: music, skiing, cooking. Office: National Review 215 Lexington Ave New York NY 10016-6023

BRIDGES, ROBERT LYSLE, retired lawyer; b. Altus, Ark., May 12, 1909; s. Joseph Manning and Jeffa Alice (Morrison) B.; m. Alice Marian Rodenberger, June 10, 1930; children: David Manning, James Robert, Linda Lee. AB, U. Calif., 1930, LLB, 1933. Bar: Calif. 1933, U.S. Supreme Ct 1938. Pvt. practice San Francisco, 1933-92; assoc. firm Thelen & Marrin, 1933-39, ptnr., 1938-92. Trustee, former chmn. U. Calif. Berkeley Found. Mem. Am., Calif., San Francisco bar assns. Republican. Clubs: Commonwealth of Calif. (San Francisco), World Trade (San Francisco), Pacific Union (San Francisco); Claremont Country (Oakland). Home: 3972 Happy Valley Rd Lafayette CA 94549-2426 Office: Thelen Reid & Priest 2 Embarcadero Ctr San Francisco CA 94111-3823

BRIDGES, ROBERT MCSTEEN, mechanical engineer; b. Oakland, Calif., Apr. 17, 1914; s. Robert and Josephine (Hite) B.; BS cum laude in Mech. Engring., U. So. Calif., 1940; postgrad. UCLA; m. Edith Brownwood, Oct. 26, 1945; children: Ann, Lawrence, Robert. Registered profl. engr., Calif. Engr. Nat. Supply Co., Torrance, Calif., 1940-41; design engr. landing gear and hydraulics Lockheed Aircraft Corp., Burbank, Calif., 1941-46; missile hydraulic controls design engr. Convair, San Diego, 1946-48; sr. staff engr. oceanic systems mech. design Bendix Corp., Sylmar, Calif., 1948—; adv. ocean engring. U.S. Congress. Com. chmn. Boy Scouts Am., 1961. Recipient award of Service Am. Inst. Aero. Engrs., 1965. Mem. Marine Tech. Soc. (charter; com. cables, connectors 1969), Tau Beta Pi. Republican. Patentee in field of undersea devices (54 internat., 14 U.S.), including deep ocean rubber band moor; inventor U.S. Navy sonobuoy rotochute; contbr. articles to profl. jours. and confs. Home: 10314 Vanalden Ave Northridge CA 91326-3326 Office: L-3 Communications Ocean Sys 15825 Roxford St San Fernando CA 91342-3537

BRIDGES, ROGER DEAN, historical agency administrator; b. Marshalltown, Iowa, Feb. 10, 1937; s. Floyd F. and Beatrice Andrea (Pipher) B.; m. Karen Maureen Buckley, June 4, 1960; children: Patrick Sean, Kristin Joy, Jennifer Lynn. BA, Iowa State Tchrs. Coll., 1959; MA, State Coll. of Iowa, 1962; PhD, U. Ill., 1970; LHD, Lincoln (Ill.) Coll., 1987, Tiffin U., 1994. Tchr., libr. Keokuk (Iowa) Pub. Schs., 1959-62; instr. in history Bradley U., Peoria, Ill., 1967; asst. prof. history U. S.D., Vermillion, 1968-69; asst. editor Papers of Ulysses Grant, Carbondale, Ill., 1969-70; dir. rsch. Ill. State Hist. Libr., Springfield, 1970-76, head libr., 1976-85; dir. Ill. State Hist. Libr./Ill. Hist. Press Agy., Springfield, 1985-87; dir., editor Lincoln legal papers project Ill. Hist. Preservation Agy, Springfield, 1987-88; dir. Rutherford B. Hayes Presdl. Ctr., Fremont, Ohio, 1988—; part-time instr. Ill. State U., Normal, Ill., 1974-84; prof. Sangamon State U., Springfield, 1985-88, Bowling Green (Ohio) State U., 1989—. Author, editor: Illinois: It's History and Legacy, 1984; asst. editor: Papers of Ulysses S. Grant, vol. 4, 1972. Bd. dirs. Springfield Urban League, 1976-82, Gt. Am. People Show, New Salem, Ill., 1978-85; bd. dirs., sec., v.p. Birchard Pub. Libr. Sandusky County, Fremont, 1988-96, pres., 1996-99; bd. dirs., pres. Conv. and Visitors Bur. Sandusky County, Fremont, 1988-93. Nat. Hist. Publs. Commn. fellow, 1969-70; recipient Disting. Svc. awrd Springfield Urban League, 1977. Mem. Am. Hist. Assn., So. Hist. Assn., Abraham Lincoln Assn. bd. dirs. 1985—), Orgn. Am. Historians, Soc. for Historians of Gilded Age and Progressive Era (sec., treas. 1989—), Ill. State Hist. Soc. (Disting. Svc. award 1988), Ohio Acad. History (exec. coun. 1996-98), bd. trustees Ohioana Library Assn., 1998—, C. of C. of Sandusky County (bd. dirs. 1999—), Rotary Internat. Democrat. Baptist. Home: 1500 Buckland Ave Fremont OH 43420-3205 Office: Rutherford B Hayes Presdl Ctr Libr Fremont OH 43420-2796

BRIDGES, ROY DUBARD, JR., federal agency administrator; b. Atlanta; m. Benita Louise Allbaugh; children: 2. BS in Engring. Sci., USAF Acad., 1965; MS in Astronautics, Purdue U., 1966. Commd. 2d lt. USAF, advanced through grades to maj. gen.; comdr. 6510th Test Wing USAF, Edwards AFB, Calif., 1986-89; comdr. Ea. Space and Missile Ctr. USAF, Patrick AFB, Fla., 1989-90; comdr. Air Force Flight Test Ctr. USAF, Edwards AFB, 1991-93; dir. requirements Air Force Materiel Command USAF, Wright-Patterson AFB, Ohio, 1993-96; ret. USAF, 1996; dir. John F. Kennedy Space Ctr. NASA, 1997—. As a NASA astronaut, piloted Space Shuttle Challenger July and August, 1985. Office: Mail Code AA John F Kennedy Space Ctr Kennedy Space Center FL 32899

BRIDGES, WILLIAM BRUCE, electrical engineer, researcher, educator; b. Inglewood, Calif., Nov. 29, 1934; s. Newman K. and Doris L. (Brown) B.; m. Carol Ann French, Aug. 24, 1957 (div. 1986); children: Ann Marjorie, Bruce Kendall, Michael Alan; m. Linda Josephine McManus, Nov. 15, 1986. B.E.E., U. Calif. at Berkeley, 1956, M.E.E. (Gen. Electric Rice fellow), 1957, Ph.D. in Elec. Engring. (NSF fellow), 1962. Assoc. elec. engring. U. Calif., Berkeley, 1957-59, grad. research engr., 1959-61; mem. tech. staff Hughes Research Labs. div. Hughes Aircraft Co., Malibu, Calif., 1960-77, sr. scientist, 1968-77, mgr. laser dept., 1969-70; prof. elec. engring. and applied physics Calif. Inst. Tech., Pasadena, 1977—, Carl F Braun prof. engring., 1983—, exec. officer elec. engring., 1978-81; lectr. elec. engring. U. So. Calif., L.A., 1962-64; Sherman Fairchild Disting. scholar Calif. Inst. Tech., 1974-75; chmn. Conf. on Laser Engring. and Applications, Washington, 1971. Author: (with C.K. Birdsall) Electron Dynamics of Diode Regions, 1966; contbr. articles on gas lasers, optical systems and microwave tubes to profl. jours.; assoc. editor: IEEE Jour. Quantum Electronics, 1977-82, Jour. Optical Soc. Am., 1978-83; inventor noble gas ion laser; patentee in field. Active Boy Scouts Am., 1968-82; bd. dirs. Ventura County Campfire Girls, 1973-76; mem. Air Force Sci. Adv. Bd., 1985-89. Recipient L.A. Hyland Patent award, 1969, Arthur L. Schawlow award Laser Inst. Am., 1986. Fellow IEEE (chmn. Los Angeles chpt. Quantum Electronics and Applications Soc. 1979-81, Quantum Electronics award 1988), Optical Soc. Am. (chmn. lasers and electro-optics tech. group 1974-75, objectives and policies com. 1981-86, 89-91, bd. dirs. 1982-84, v.p. 1986, pres.-elect 1987, pres. 1988, past pres. 1989), Laser Inst. Am.; mem. Nat. Acad. Engring., Nat. Acad. Scis., Am. Radio Relay League, Phi Beta Kappa, Sigma Xi, Tau Beta Pi, Eta Kappa Nu (One of Outstanding Young Elec. Engrs. for 1966). Lutheran. Achievements include invention of noble gas ion laser. E-mail: w6fa@caltech.edu. Office: Calif Inst Tech Watson Bldg 136-93 Pasadena CA 91125

BRIDGETT, NOEL WILLIAM, convalescent center administrator; b. Jamaica, Nov. 21, 1933; s. George and Mary (Bowen) B.; m. Thelma Bridgett, (dec.); m. Rachel R. Reid, July 15, 1967. BS, Atlantic Union Coll., 1976. Acct. Jamaica Broadcasting Corp., W.I., 1959-67, Knickerbocker Hosp., N.Y.C., 1968-69, Beth Israel Hosp., N.Y.C., 1970-71, Arthur G. Logan Meml. Hosp., N.Y.C., 1972-78; adminstr. Guardian Care Convalescent Ctr., Orlando, Fla., 1978—; treas., sec. Fla. Health Care Assn., Dist. 2, Orlando. Treas. Christian Svc. Ctr., Orlando, 1985. Recipient Community Svc. award Orlando C. of C., 1985. Mem. Am. Coll. of Nursing Home Adminstrs., Health Care Fin. Mgmt. Assn., Am. Coll. of Health Care Adminstrs. Mem. Seventh-day Adventist. Avocations: walking, cricket, swimming, reading. Office: Guardian Care Inc 2500 W Church St Orlando FL 32805-2399

BRIDGEWATER, ALBERT LOUIS, science foundation administrator; b. Houston, Nov. 22, 1941; s. Albert Louis and Rita (Narcisse) B.; children: Ramesi, Akin. B.A. in Physics, U. Calif.-Berkeley, 1963; Ph.D. in Physics, Columbia U., 1972. Postdoctoral fellow Lawrence Berkeley Lab., Berkeley, Calif., 1970-73; staff asst. physics NSF, Washington, 1973-76, spl. exec. asst., 1976-81, dep. asst. dir., 1981-86, sr. staff assoc., 1986-88, sr. sci. assoc., 1988—, acting asst. dir., 1983-85; adj. asst. prof. Howard U., Washington, 1975-76. Mem. Am. Geophys. Union, Am. Physical Soc. Avocations: reading; outdoor sports. Office: NSF 4201 Wilson Blvd Arlington VA 22230-0001

BRIDGEWATER, BERNARD ADOLPHUS, JR., footwear company executive; b. Tulsa, Mar. 13, 1934; s. Bernard Adolphus and Mary Alethea (Burton) B.; m. Barbara Paton, July 2, 1960; children: Barrie, Elizabeth, Bonnie. AB, Westminster Coll., Fulton, Mo., 1955; LLB, U. Okla., 1958; MBA, Harvard, 1964. Bar: Okla. 1958, U.S. Supreme Ct. 1958, U.S. Ct. of Claims 1958. Asst. county atty. Tulsa, 1962; assoc. McKinsey & Co.; mgmt. cons. McKinsey & Co., Chgo., 1964-68, prin., 1968-72, dir., 1972-73, 75; assoc. dir. nat. security and internat. affairs Office Mgmt. and Budget, Exec. Office Pres., Washington, 1973-74; exec. v.p. Baxter Travenol Labs., Inc., Chgo. and Deerfield, Ill., 1975-79, dir., 1975-85; pres. Brown Group, Inc., Clayton, Mo., 1979-87, 90—, CEO, 1982—, chmn., 1985—, also dir.; bd. dirs. FMC Corp., Chgo., NationsBank Corp., Charlotte, N.C., EEX Corp., Houston; cons. Office Mgmt. and Budget, 1973, 75. Author: (with others) Better Management of Business Giving, 1965. Trustee Rush-Presbyn. St. Luke's Med. Ctr., 1974-84, Washington U., St. Louis, 1983-94, 95—, Barnes Hosp., St. Louis, 1987-90; bd. visitors Harvard U. Bus. Sch., 1987-93. Served to lt. USNR, 1958-62. Recipient Rayonier Found. award Harvard U., 1963; George F. Baker scholar, 1964. Mem. Beta Theta Pi, Omicron Delta Kappa, Phi Alpha Delta. Clubs: River (N.Y.C.); St. Louis Country, Log Cabin (St. Louis); Indian Hill Country (Winnetka, Ill.). Office: Brown Group Inc 8300 Maryland Ave Saint Louis MO 63105-3645*

BRIDGEWATER, BRAD, Olympic athlete; b. Dallas, Tex., Mar. 29, 1973. Student, U. So. Calif. Winner 1st pl. 100 meter backstroke SPG Nats., 1994, gold medal 200 meter backstroke Pan Am. Games, 1995, Gold medal 200 meter backstroke Atlanta Olympics, 1996, silver medal 200m backstroke, 6th fastest man ever in 200m backstroke, 2d fastest in Am., 1998 Goodwill Games; named U.S. Nat. Champion 3 times. *

BRIDGEWATER, HERBERT JEREMIAH, JR., radio host; b. Atlanta, July 3, 1942; s. Herbert Bridgewater and Mary Sallie (Clark) Bridgewater-Hughes. B.A., Clark Coll., Atlanta, 1968; postgrad., Atlanta U.; L.H.D., Faith Coll., 1978; LL.D., Heed U., 1978. Tchr. bus. edn. and English Atlanta Pub. Sch. System, 1964-67; relocation and family svcs. cons. Atlanta Housing Authority, 1967-70; columnist, writer Atlanta Daily World, 1968—, Lovely Atlanta; consumer protection specialist FTC, Atlanta, 1970-83; pres. Bridgewater's Personnel Service, 1971—; assoc. prof. bus. edn. and mass communication Clark Coll., instr., 1983-86; instr. Atlanta Jr. Coll., 1986—, The Univ. System of Ga., 1986—; with reservations sales Delta Airline Inc., Atlanta, 1984—; host radio program Enlightenment (WGKA-AM), 1975-79; host pub. affairs program Confrontation WZGC FM and WIGO AM, 1975-79, WYZE AM, 1979—; TV talk show host Bridging the Gap. Mem. Epilepsy Found. Am., Nat. Urban League, Big Bros. Council of Atlanta, Met. Boys Clubs of Atlanta, YMCA, NAACP; active So. Christian Leadership Conf., Ga. and nationwide civil rights movements; bd. dirs. Atlanta Dance Theater, Ralph C. Robinson Atlanta Boys Club, Proposition Theater Co., Am. Cancer Soc., Just-Us Theatre Task Force. Recipient Pres.'s award Clark Coll. United Negro Coll. Fund, 1960, 61, Best Citizens award Delta Sigma Theta, 1962, Humanitarian award Future Soc. Orgn., 1975, award Atlanta Dance Theatre, 1978-79, also; Met. Atlanta Boys Club; FTC Superior service medal, 1978; Bronner Bros. Nat. Beauticians Conv. Excellence in Communication award, 1978; named One of Most Outstanding Young Men in Am., Nat. Jr. C. of C., 1969, One of Most Eligible Bachelors in Am., 1970, One of 1,000 Successful Black Americans, 1973; both Ebony Mag.; One of 10 Outstanding Young People of Atlanta, 1977-78; One of 20 Most Progressive Young People in Atlanta, 1977; Herbert Bridgewater Day proclaimed in his honor Atlanta. Mem. Atlanta Jr. C. of C., Young Men on the Go, Clark Coll. Alumni Assn., Clark Coll. Assn., Heritage Valley Community Civic Orgn., Hungry Club Forum, Internat. Assn. for African Heritage and Black Identity (founding). Baptist (founder, chmn. bd. jr. deacons). Home: 2963 Duke Of Windsor East Point GA 30344-5606 Office: Delta Airlines Inc Bldg A-2 Reservations Sales PO Box 45007 Hartsfield Internat Airport Atlanta GA 30320 *Any success which I may have achieved is attributed to my deeply rooted religious rearing which impels me to put God first in all my undertaking. Applying myself to the task with diligence, being prayerful in all my endeavors, and having a mother who is not only my backbone, but who has also stood steadfastly by my side, are the essential factors which I deem vital in my life's achievement.*

BRIDGMAN, G(EORGE) ROSS, lawyer; b. New Haven, Dec. 27, 1947; s. George Ross Bridgman and Betty Jean (Soderquist) Burrows; m. Patricia Hess; children: Taylor Wilson, Katharine June, Elizabeth Honey. BA cum laude, Yale U., 1970; JD, Northwestern U., 1におけ1973. Bar: Ohio 1973, U.S. Dist. Ct. (so. dist.) Ohio 1974, U.S. Dist. Ct. (no. dist.) Ohio 1976, U.S. Ct. Appeals (6th cir.) 1984, U.S. Supreme Ct. 1990. Assoc. Vorys, Sater, Seymour & Pease, Columbus, Ohio, 1973-80, ptnr., 1980—. Mem. editorial bd. Northwestern U. Law Rev., Chgo., 1972-73. Trustee Columbus Jr. Theatre of the Arts, 1976-80, pres., 1978-80; trustee, v.p. London (Ohio) Pub. Libr., 1979-84; bd. dirs. Ctrl. Ohio Regional Coun. on Alcoholism, Columbus, 1987-89; trustee Kidscope, Columbus, 1988-89, Recovery Alliance, Columbus, 1989-97, Ohio Parents for Drug-Free Youth, 1991—; mem. exec. bd. Simon Kenton Coun., Boy Scouts Am., 1996—. Mem. ABA, Columbus Bar Assn., Ohio Bar Assn., Nat. Assn. Coll. and Univ. Attys., Capital Club, Columbus Country Club. Republican. Episcopalian. Office: Vorys Sater Seymour & Pease PO Box 1008 52 E Gay St Columbus OH 43215-3161

BRIDGMAN, RICHARD DARRELL, lawyer; b. Madison, S.D., Mar. 1, 1929; s. Lloyd Alton and Fay Catherine (Turner) B.; m. Marilyn Elizabeth Smith, May 25, 1952 (div. June 1987); 1 child: Richard Darrell. AB, U. Calif., 1951; JD, Golden Gate U., 1958. Bar: Calif. 1958, U.S. Dist. Ct. (no. dist.) Calif. 1958, U.S. Dist. Ct. (ea. dist.) Calif. 1982, U.S. Dist Ct. (cen. dist.) Calif. 1985, U.S. Ct. Appeals (9th cir.) 1958. Ptnr. Ericksen, Ericksen, Kincaid & Bridgman, Oakland, Calif., 1959-69; ptnr. O'Neill & Bridgman, Oakland, Calif., 1969-86, San Francisco, 1986-88; pvt. practice Richard D. Bridgman, San Francisco, 1988-92; ptnr. Bridgman & Bridgman, San Francisco, 1992—; mem., bd. dirs. Lawyer's Mutual Ins. Co., Burbank, Calif., 1978-88; faculty Golden Gate U., San Francisco, 1963-69, Hastings Coll. Trial & Appellate Advocacy, San Francisco, 1978-91. Co-author: Legal Malpractice-Suing & Defending Lawyers, 1984; contbr. articles to profl. jours. Lt. U.S. Navy, 1951-54, Korea. Named Lawyer of Yr. Lawyers Club of Alameda Co., 1980. Mem. Inner Cir. Advocates, Am. Bd Trial Advocates, Am. Bd. Profl. Liability Attys. (diplomate), Calif. Trial Lawyers Assn. (bd. govs. 1976-83, sec. 1978-81), Alameda Conta Costa Trial Lawyers Assn. (pres. 1982). Office: Bridgman & Bridgman 5 Marietta Dr San Francisco CA 94127-1839

BRIDGMAN, THOMAS FRANCIS, lawyer; b. Chgo., Dec. 30, 1933; s. Thomas Joseph and Angeline (Gorman) B.; m. Patricia A. McCormick, May 16, 1959; children: Thomas, Kathleen Ann, Ann Marie, Jane T., Molly. B.S. cum laude, John Carroll U., 1955; J.D. cum laude, Loyola U., Chgo., 1958. Bar: Ill. 1958, U.S. Dist. Ct. 1959. Assoc. McCarthy & Levin, Chgo., 1958; assoc. Baker & McKenzie, Chgo., 1958-62, ptnr., 1962—. Trustee John Carroll U., 1982-88. Fellow Am. Coll. Trial Lawyers, Am. Bd. Trial Advs. (adv.), Internat. Acad. Trial Lawyers (past pres.), Union Club, Beverly Country Club (Chgo., pres. 1983). Democrat. Roman Catholic. Home: 9400 S Pleasant Ave Chicago IL 60620-5646 Office: Baker & McKenzie 1 Prudential Plaza 130 E Randolph St Ste 3700 Chicago IL 60601-6342

BRIDSTON, PAUL JOSEPH, strategic consultant; b. Grand Forks, N.D., May 28, 1928; s. Joseph and Anna (Pederson) B.; m. Peggy C. Cullen, Aug. 26, 1955; children—Peter, Rebecca, Sarah. BA magna cum laude, Yale U., 1950; MBA, Stanford U., 1952. Sec.-treas. First Fed. Savs. & Loan Assn., Grand Forks, N.D., 1955-61, pres., 1962-81, chmn. bd., 1961-82; pres. J.B. Bridston Ins. Co., 1963-80; chief Housing Guaranties Program Latin Am., AID, Washington, 1964-65; cons. U.S. Dept. State, 1968-70; asst. insp. gen. fgn. assistance, 1970; mem. N.D. Ho. Reps., 1972-74; cons. Bridston Co., 1990—; chmn. Pioneer Mortgage Co., 1980-84; vis. prof. mgmt. U. Okla., 1988-92. Pres. Grand Forks YMCA, 1959-60, GrandForks United Fund, 1961-62; bd. dirs. Tyrone Guthrie Theatre, Mpls., 1963-69, Boys Club Am., 1963-69; chmn. Martin County Atlantic-Pacific Housing, Inc., Fla., 1984-86. With USNR, 1952-55. Mem. Nat. Savs. and Loan League (bd. dirs. 1981), U.S. Savs. League (chmn. internat. devel. com. 1968-69), Yale U. Alumni Assn., Stanford Alumni Assn., Augusta Nat. Club. Lutheran. Home: 6843 Tall Pines Rd NE Bemidji MN 56601-7095

BRIDWELL, G. PORTER, retired aerospace engineer; b. Linton, Ind., Oct. 4, 1935; s. Searle Alton and Madge (Porter) B.; children: Michael Gene, Kendra Lou. BS, Purdue U., 1958. Engr. Rocketdyne, Huntsville, Ala., 1958-62; engr., mgr. NASA, Marshall Space Flight Ctr, Ala., 1962-94; dir. NASA, Marshall Space Flight Ctr, 1994—. Named Engr. of Yr. AIAA Ala.-Miss. Sect., 1995. Mem. North Ala. Radio Control Assn., Huntsville Quarterback Club, Valley Hill Country Club. Baptist. Home: 8712 Edgehill Dr SE Huntsville AL 35802-3642 Office: NASA DA01 Marshall Space Flight Ctr Huntsville AL 35812*

BRIEANT, CHARLES LA MONTE, federal judge; b. Ossining, N.Y., Mar. 13, 1923; s. Charles La Monte and Marjorie (Hall) B.; m. Virginia Elizabeth Warfield, Sept. 10, 1948; children: Cynthia W. Brieant Hendricks, Charles La Monte III, Victoria E. Misuraca, Julia W. Brieant Clavette. B.A., Columbia U., 1947, LL.B., 1949. Bar: N.Y. 1949. Mem. firm Bleakley, Platt, Schmidt & Fritz, White Plains, 1949-71; water commr. Village of Ossining, 1948-51; town justice, 1952-58, town supr., 1960-63; village atty. Briarcliff Manor, N.Y.; also spl. asst. dist. atty. Westchester County, 1958-59; asst. counsel N.Y. State Joint Legis. Com. Fire Ins., 1968; judge U.S. Dist. Ct. (so. dist.) N.Y., N.Y.C., 1971-86, chief judge, 1986-93; judge U.S. Dist Ct. So. Dist. N.Y., White Plains, 1993—; adj. prof. Bklyn. Law Sch.; mem. Jud. Conf. U.S., 1989-95, mem. exec. com., 1991-95. Mem. Westchester County Republican Com., 1957-71; mem. Westchester County Legislature from 2d Dist., 1970-71. Served with AUS, World War II. Mem. ABA, N.Y. State Bar Assn., Westchester County Bar Assn., Ossining Bar Assn. Episcopalian (vestryman). Club: SAR. Office: US Dist Ct US Courthouse 300 Quarropas St White Plains NY 10601-4140*

BRIEGER, GERT HENRY, medical historian, educator; b. Hamburg, Germany, Jan. 5, 1932; came to U.S., 1938, naturalized, 1943; s. Carl Helmuth and Ylse (Fuchs) B.; m. Katharine Crenshaw, July 2, 1955; children: Heidi E., William N., Benjamin C. A.B., U. Calif., Berkeley, 1953; M.D., UCLA, 1957; M.P.H., Harvard U., 1962; Ph.D., Johns Hopkins U., 1968. Intern UCLA Med. Center, 1957-58; asst. prof. history of medicine Johns Hopkins U. Sch. Medicine, Balt., 1966-70; assoc. prof. community health scis., assoc. prof. history Duke U., Durham, N.C., 1970-75; prof. history of health scis., chmn. dept. U. Calif., San Francisco, 1975-84; William H. Welch prof., dir. Inst. History of Medicine Johns Hopkins U., Balt., 1984—, chair dept. hist. sci. med. and tech., 1993—. Author: (with A.M. Harvey, S.L. Abrams and V.A. McKusick) A Model of Its Kind, A Centennial History of Johns Hopkins Medicine, 2 vols., 1989; editor: Medical America in the Nineteenth Century, 1972, Theory and Practice in American Medicine, 1976; co-editor Bull. of the History of Medicine, 1990—. Served to capt. U.S. Army, 1958-61. Mem. Am. Assn. History of Medicine (pres. 1980-82), History of Sci. Home: 10 E Lee St Baltimore MD 21202-6003 Office: Johns Hopkins U Inst History Medicine 1900 E Monument St Baltimore MD 21205-2113*

BRIEGER, STEPHEN GUSTAVE, management consultant; b. Marburg, Germany, Sept. 7, 1935; came to the U.S., naturalized, 1945; s. Heinrich and Kate L. (Steitz) B.; m. Karen L. Jentes, Nov. 27, 1968; children: Jennifer B., Benjamin A. BSc, Springfield (Mass.) Coll., 1955; MS, Fla. State U., 1970, PhD, 1972. Tchr. Calif. schs., 1954-69; indsl. cons. mgmt. tng., 1960-70; mgmt. cons. Nebr. Criminal Justice Sys., 1972; rsch. criminologist Stanford Rsch. Inst., 1972-74; evaluation cons. Office Gov. Calif., 1974-76; mgmt. devel. assoc. Am. Electronics Assn., 1976-80; mgr. employee and mgmt. devel. ISS Sperry Univac, Santa Clara, Calif., 1980-83; mgr. tng. recruiting and devel. Lawrence Livermore Nat. Lab., U. Calif., 1983-95; human resources cons. ETAK, Inc., Menlo Park, Calif., 1995-98; cons. Aradigm, Hayward, Calif., 1998—; mem. faculty U.S. Internat. U., St. Mary's Coll., U. San Francisco. Author studies, reports in field. Mem. ASSTD, Am. Mgmt. Assn., Am. Electronics Assn. Home: 1158 Meredith Ave San Jose CA 95125-3242 Office: PO Box 5508 Livermore CA 94551-5508

BRIERLEY, GERALD P., physiological chemistry educator; b. Ogallala, Nebr., Aug. 14, 1931; s. Phillip and Myrtle (Shireman) B.; m. Miriam Grove, Apr. 17, 1971; children: David, Steven, Glenn, Lynn. B.S., U. Med.-Coll. Park, 1953, Ph.D., 1961. Asst. prof. U. Wis., Madison, 1962-64; faculty mem. Ohio State U., Columbus, 1964—; prof. physiol. chemistry Ohio State U., 1969—, chmn. dept., 1981-95, prof. emeritus, chmn. emeritus of dept. med. biochemistry, 1996—. Capt. USAF, 1953-56. USPHS grantee to study ion transport by heart mitochondra, 1965—; USPHS grantee to study pathology mitchondria in ischemia, 1977—. Mem. Am. Soc. Biol. Chemistry, Biophys. Soc., Am. Heart Assn. Office: Dept of Medical Biochemistry 333 Hamilton Hall 1645 Neil Ave Columbus OH 43210-1218*

BRIERLEY, JAMES ALAN, research administrator; b. Denver, Dec. 22, 1938; s. Everette and Carrie (Berg) B.; m. Corale Louise Beer, Dec. 21, 1965. BS in Bacteriology, Colo. State U., 1961; MS in Microbiology, Mont. State U., 1963, PhD, 1966. Research scientist Martin Marietta Corp., Denver, 1966-69; asst. prof. biology N.Mex. Inst. Mining and Tech., Socorro, 1966-68, from asst. prof. to prof. biology, chmn. dept. biology, 1969-83; research dir. Advanced Mineral Techs., Golden, Colo., 1983-88; chief microbiologist Newmont Metall. Svcs., Englewood, Colo., 1988—; vis. fellow U. Warwick, Coventry, Eng., 1976, vis. prof. Catholic U., Santiago, Chile, 1983; adj. prof. dept. metallurgy U. Utah, 1994-96; cons. Mountain State Mineral Enterprises, Tucson, 1980, Sandia Nat. Lab., Albuquerque, 1976, Bechtel Civil and Minerals, Scottsdale, Ariz., 1984. Contbr. numerous articles to profl. jours.; patentee in field. Served to staff sgt. Air N.G., 1956-61. Recipient 32 research grants. Fellow AAAS; mem. Am. Soc. Microbiology, Soc. Gen. Microbiology, Mining and Metall. Soc. Am., Sigma Xi. Avocations: travel, model railroading, gardening. Home: 2074 East Terrace Dr Highlands Ranch CO 80126-2692 Office: Newmont Tech Facility 10101 E Dry Creek Rd Englewood CO 80112-1556

BRIERLEY, JOHN E. C., legal educator, former university dean; b. Montreal, Que., Can., Mar. 5, 1936. B.A., Bishop's U., Lennoxville, Que., 1956; B.C.L., McGill U., 1959; Docteur de l'Universite de Paris, 1964; LL.D., Dickinson U., 1985. Teaching fellow Faculty of Law, McGill U., Montreal, 1960-61; asst. prof. Faculty of Law, McGill U., 1964-68, asso. prof., 1968-73, prof., 1973—, Sir William Macdonald prof. law, 1980-94; Wainwright prof. civil law, 1994—; dean faculty law Faculty of Law, McGill U., 1974-84; vis. prof. U. Montreal, 1967-68, U. Toronto, 1971-72, U. Paris II; occasional lectr. McGill Mental Hygiene Inst., McGill Sch. Social Work, 1969-73; vis. occasional lectr. Dalhousie U., 1970-73; cons. Royal Commn. on Status of Women in Can., 1970; mem. Canadian Delegation of Experts, UNIDROIT, Rome, 1971, Conseil des affairs sociales et de la famille, Ministerial Coun. to min. Social Affairs, Que., 1971-73; pres. Sous-comite sur les Politiques et programmes familiaux, 1971-73; mem. Commn. des Biens culturels de Que., ministerial coun. to min. Cultural Affairs, Que., 1972; cons., secretaire-rapporteur various coms. Civil Code Revision Office, Que., 1967—; chmn. Com. Can. Law Deans, 1981—. Felllow Royal Soc. Can., 1995; mem. Canadian, Que., bar assns.; Assn. des professeurs de droit de Que., Assn. Canadian Law Tchrs., John Howard Soc. Que. (dir. 1965-67), Canadian Soc. for Legal History (exec. com. 1972—), Inter-Am. Comml. Arbitration Commn. (exec. com. 1972—), Internat. Acad. Comparative Law, Internat. Acad. Estate & Trust Law (exec. com.). Office: 3644 Peel St, Montreal, PQ Canada H3A 1W9*

BRIGANCE, MARCELENA, critical care nurse; b. Mobile, Ala., Sept. 16, 1941; d. Maurice Jr. and Dorothy (Bell) B.; children: Monica Renee Burch, Alana Jeanne Burch. Student, Samford U., 1959-60, 61-62; BSN, U. Wash., 1975. RN, Ala.; CEN; cert. ACLS instr. Staff nurse surg. ICU, med. ICU, CCU Harborview Med. Ctr., Seattle, 1975-77; staff nurse, supr. oral surg. U. Wash., Seattle, 1979-81; staff nurse emergency room, mobile intensive care nurse Sequoia Hosp., Redwood City, Calif., 1983-87; staff nurse emergency dept. Springhill Meml. Hosp., Mobile, Ala., 1987-91; staff nurse emergency rm. Thomas Hosp., Mobile, 1992-93; PRN emergency nurse Providence and Knollwood Emergency Rm., Mobile, 1992—; emergency rm. nurse Springhill Hosp., 1992-95, Knollwood Park Hosp., 1995—.

BRIGEOIS, EVELYNE BRIGITTE, artist, publisher; b. Troyes, Aube, France, Feb. 18, 1946; came to U.S., 1984.; Student, B.E.P.C., Aix-en-Othe, France, 1951. Trilingual exec. sec. Eng., France, Germany, Spain, 1965-79; owner, mgr. Brigeois Pub., Vallejo, Calif., 1987—; spkr. in field. One-woman shows include Lawrence Gallery, Portland, Oreg., 1984, Scott Gallery, Orinda, Calif., 1985, Leslie Levy Gallery, Scottsdale, Ariz., 1986, 89, Charleston Heights Art Ctr., Las Vegas, Nev., 1987, Horvath Gallery, Sacramento, 1993 ; exhibited in group shows at Transco Gallery, Houston, 1988; represented by Leslie Levy Fine Art, Scottsdale; contbr. articles to profl. jours. Recipient numerous awards, including Robert Wiegand Meml. award La. Watercolor Soc., 1985, award Detroit Inst. Arts Drawing and Print Club, 1985, award of honor Birmingham Mus. Art, 1986, lst place award Assoc. Artists Southport, N.C., 1986. Mem. Nat. Watercolor Soc. (Helen Wurdeman award 1985), Ala. Watercolor Soc.

BRIGGAMAN, ROBERT ALAN, dermatologist, medical educator; b. Hartford, Aug. 14, 1934; m. Irene Taluskie, Sept. 17, 1960; children: Kimberly Ann, John Scott. BS, Trinity Coll., Hartford, 1956; MD, NYU, 1960. Diplomate Am. Bd. Dermatology; cert. spl. competence in dermatopathology, Am. Bd. Pathology and Am. Bd. Dermatology, 1974. Med. intern U. Va. Hosp., Charlottesville, 1960-61, med. resident, 1961-62; resident in dermatology N.C. Meml. Hosp., Chapel Hill, 1964-65, dermatology fellow, 1965-67; instr. medicine and dermatology U. N.C. Sch. Medicine, Chapel Hill, 1967-68, asst. prof. medicine and dermatology, 1968-71, assoc. prof. medicine and dermatology, 1971-74, prof. medicine and dermatology, 1974—, chmn. dept. dermatology, 1987—. Contbr. numerous articles to med. and dermatology jours., chpts. to dermatology textbooks;

dep. editor Jour. Investigative Dermatology, 1992-97. N.C. State chmn. Leaders Soc., Dermatology Found., 1996—. Recipient J.N. Taub Internat. Meml. award for psoriasis rsch., 1983, Marion B. Sulzberger Meml. award, Am. Acad. Dermatology, 1985, MERIT award NIH, 1990, Clayton E. Wheeler Jr. Disting. professorship, 1992. Mem. AMA, Am. Acad. Dermatology, Am. Dermatologic Assn., Assn. Profs. Dermatology, Dermatology Found., Soc. for Investigative Dermatology, Assn. of Am. Physicians. Office: UNC Sch Medicine Dept Derm CB #7287 3100 Thurston-Bowles Bldg Chapel Hill NC 27599-7287

BRIGGLE, GARY LEE, singer, actor, director; b. Moorhead, Minn., Oct. 31, 1953; s. Leland Wilson and Harriet Maxine (Dickerson) B.; m. Christine Helen Maloney, Dec. 10, 1977 (div. Apr. 1982); life ptnr. Wendy Lehr, Feb. 14, 1983. MusB, St. Olaf Coll., Northfield, Minn., 1975. Resident artist Minn. Opera Co., Mpls., 1979-82, Children's Theater Co. & Sch., Mpls., 1979-82; artistic assoc. Seaside Music Theater, Daytona Beach, Fla., 1983—; artistic dir. Ariz. Theater Co., Tuscon, Phoenix, 1991-94, LYRIC Opera Cleve., 1995-98. Recipient Carbonal award S. Fla. Critics Assn., 1983; Irene Ryan scholar Am. Coll. Theater Festival, 1975. Avocations: aquatics, painting, drawing, hiking, camping.

BRIGGMAN, JESSIE B., secondary education educator; b. Branchville, S.C., May 7, 1945; d. Jesse and Louise (McCormick) Bowman; m. Lemuel D. Briggman, Aug. 21, 1970; children: Wydreda JaVonne, Lemetrius Deon. BA, Claflin Coll., Orangeburg, S.C., 1970; MEd, S.C. State Coll., Orangeburg, 1985, postgrad., 1987. Cert. in social studies, learning disabilities, educable mentally retarded, trainable mentally retarded. Tchr. social studies Orangeburg Dist. 7, Elloree, S.C.; 9th grade world geography Orangeburg Dist. 5, Orangeburg-Wilkinson H.S. Acitve Orangeburg-Wilkinson H.S. PTSA. Tchr. grantee State of S.C., 1987-88. Mem. NEA, S.C. Edn. Assn., Orangeburg Edn. Assn., Zeta Phi Beta. Home: 1275 Cherokee St SW Orangeburg SC 29115-7634

BRIGGS, ALAN LEONARD, lawyer; b. Dayton, Ohio, Oct. 1, 1942; s. Donald M. and Helen (Barker) B.; m. Linda Ann Dobie, Sept. 10, 1966 (div. 1991); children: Jason, Aimee, Anna; m. Christine M. McCormick, 1991; 1 child, Caitlin. AB, Miami U., Oxford, Ohio, 1964; JD, Ohio State U., 1967; LLM in Patent/Intellectual Property Law, George Washington U., 1998. Bar: Ohio 1967, Calif. 1970, Fla. 1989, D.C. 1995, Va. 1995, Md. 1995. Ptnr. Murphey, Young & Smith, Columbus, Ohio, 1970-88; ptnr. Squire, Sanders & Dempsey, Columbus, 1988-91, Miami, Fla., 1991-94, Washington, 1994—. Trustee Legal Aid Soc. Fellow Am. Coll. Trial Lawyers; mem. ABA, Ohio State Bar Assn. (coun. of dels. 1980-86, chmn. screening com. coun. dels. 1983-84, sect. litigation bd. govs. 1986-90), Columbus Bar Assn. (pres. 1985, chmn. litigation practice inst. 1987-90), Am. Arbitration Assn. Office: Squire Sanders & Dempsey 1201 Pennsylvania Ave NW Washington DC 20004-2491

BRIGGS, ARLEEN FRANCES, mental health nurse, educator; b. Bklyn., Sept. 4, 1939; d. Thomas Frances and Margaret Elizabeth (McCann) Whelan; (div.); children: Lisa J., Jon M., Kara J., Lora M. Diploma in Nursing, Helene Fuld Sch. Nursing, 1960; BSN, Coll. Santa Fe, 1987; MSN in Nursing Adminstrn., U. N.Mex., 1993. RN; ANA cert. adult psychiat. and mental health nurse. Staff Helene Fuld Hosp., Trenton, N.J., 1960-61; supr. psychiatry Trenton (N.J.) State Hosp., 1960-61; 1st lt. USAF, 1961-63; supr. med. surg. Coeur de Alene (Idaho) Hosp., 1966-67, Centinella Hosp., Hawthorne, Calif., 1967-68, Laguna Meml. Hosp., Laguna Beach, Calif., 1968-70; staff operating rm. Mission Cmty. Hosp., Mission Viejo, Calif., 1970-77; supr., educator Las Vegas Med. Ctr., 1977-94; asst. prof. McNeese State U., Lake Charles, La., 1994—; mem. Recovering Nurse Program Adv. Com., Bon, La., 1995—; part-time psychol. nursing cmty. cons. Director, author: (program) Research Cooperative Care of PT with Two Psychiatric Diagnoses, 1993. Chairperson Regional Bd. Nursing-Diversion Program, Las Vegas, 1989-94; intervention nurse alcoholism Alcoholics Anonymous-McNeese, Lake Charles, 1990—, Las Vegas, N. Mex.; counsellor Reach to Recovery, Lake Charles, 1994—; psychiatric counselor HIV patient, 1989—. Recipient award Bd. of Nursing, 1994. Mem. Nat. Soc. Addictions Nursing, Nat. Soc. Medicine, Law and Ethics, Sigma Theta Tau. Office: McNeese State U PO Box 90415 Lake Charles LA 70609

BRIGGS, BONNIE JEAN, secondary school educator; b. North Bend, Oreg., Sept. 28, 1952; d. Glenn and Mary V. (Crnkovich) B. AA, Southwest Oreg. Community Coll, 1972; BS, So. Oreg. State Coll., 1974, MS, 1978. Cert. tchr. math. Tchr. Camas Valley (Oreg.) H.S., 1974-84, Lane C.C., Eugene, Oreg., 1986-91, Creswell (Oreg.) H.S., 1984-97, Willamette (Oreg.) H.S., 1997—; mem. Onward to Excellence Leadership Team; coord., trainer Tchr. Expectations and Student Achievement; computer equity expert trainer; collatorator, editor SMITE math./logo teaching materials; mem. steering com. Creswell H.S. assessment and standardization, mem. 21st century site com.; Oreg. math. leader, 1985—; presenter to nat. and Oreg. profl. confs. and workshops. Recipient Presdl. award NSF, 1988; named U.S. West Outstanding Tchr. for Oreg., 1993; Women's Action Alliance Group grantee, 1991-93, Math. Tchr. of Yr. Am. Electronics Assn., 1995, Award for Excellence in Math. Tchg. Tektronix, 1995. Mem. NEA, Nat. Coun. Tchrs. Math., Coun. Presdl. Awardees Math., Oreg. Edn. Assn., Oreg. Coun. Tchrs. Math. (area rep. 1989-91), Oreg. Math. Leaders Conf. (registration chair), Oreg. Math. Edn. Coun. (secondary edn. rep. 1989-93, pres. 1991-92), Eugene Edni. Assn., Lane County Secondary Tchrs. Math., Creswell Edn. Assn. (treas. 1994-95), Delta Kappa Gamma. Avocations: photography, travel, fishing, camping, computers. E-mail: bbriggs@pond.net. Home: PO Box 476 Creswell OR 97426-0476

BRIGGS, CYNTHIA ANNE, educational administrator, clinical psychologist; b. Berea, Ohio, Nov. 9, 1950; d. William Benajah and Lorraine (Hood) B.; m. Thomas Joseph O'Brien, Nov. 28, 1986; children: Julia Maureen, William Thomas. B Music Edn., U. Kans., 1973; MusM, U. Miami, 1976; D. Psychology, Hahnemann U., 1988. Lic. psychology, Mo.; bd. cert. music therapist. Music therapist Parsons (Kans.) State Hosp., 1973-74; grad. asst. U. Miami, Coral Gables, Fla., 1974-76; asst. prof., dir. Hahnemann U., Phila., 1976-85, asst. prof., 1985-91; psychology resident Assocs. in Psychol. and Human Resources, Phila., 1988-91; clin. dir. Child Ctr. of Our Lady, St. Louis, 1991—. Author chpts. to books; editl. bd. Jour. Music Therapy, 1997—; contbr. articles to profl. jours. Mem. Am. Assn. Music Therapy (pres. 1987-89), Nat. Coalition Arts Therapies Assns. (chair 1991-93). Democrat. Avocations: cooking, piano, music, theatre. Office: Child Ctr of Our Lady 7900 Natural Bridge Rd Saint Louis MO 63121-4628

BRIGGS, DAVID MELVIN, information systems executive; b. Peru, Ind., May 31, 1944; s. Melvin Arthur and Helen Louise (Landis) B.; m. Linda Fields, Feb. 10, 1967 (div. June 1976); children: Brian, Elizabeth; m. Bettie Lee Hale, Aug. 12, 1981; children: Robyn Reid, Richard Reid, Shannon Reid. BS, Ball State U., 1966; MBA, Loyola Coll., Balt., 1975. Commd. 2d lt. USAF, 1967, advanced through grades to maj., 1977, resigned, 1979; project mgr. McCormick & Co., Inc., Balt., 1971-76; cons. D.M. Briggs & Assocs., Balt., 1976-79; sys. mgr. W.R. Grace/Constrn. Products, Cambridge, Mass., 1979-81, dir. info. sys., 1981-99; chief information ofcr., 1999—. Bd. dirs. N.E. Youth Ballet, Boston, 1996—. Mem. Soc. Info. Mgmt. (chmn. 1991-92, bd. dirs. 1992—). Republican. Methodist. Avocations: antiques, genealogy, racquetball, gardening. Office: Brockway-Smith 146 Dascomb Rd North Andover MA 01810

BRIGGS, DOUGLAS D., communications executive. Pres. QVC, West Chester, Pa., 1995—. Office: QVC 1200 Wilson Dr West Chester PA 19380-4262*

BRIGGS, EDWARD SAMUEL, naval officer; b. St. Paul, Oct. 4, 1926; s. Charles William and Lois Ione (Johnson) B.; m. Nanette Parks, June 7, 1949; 1 child, Jeffrey Charles. BS, U.S. Naval Acad., 1949. Commd. ensign U.S. Navy, 1949, advanced through grades to vice adm., 1980; commanding officer USS Turner Joy, USS Jouett; asst. chief of staff plans, chief of staff U.S. 7th Fleet, 1972-73; fleet ops. officer, asst. chief staff ops. U.S. Pacific Fleet, Makalapa, Hawaii, 1973-75; comdr. Crusier-Destroyer Group 3, San Diego, 1975-77, Navy Recruiting Command, Arlington, Va., 1977-79, Naval Logistics Command, U.S. Pacific Fleet, Naval Base, Pearl Harbor, Hawaii, 1979-80; dep. comdr.-in-chief U.S. Pacific Fleet, Pearl Harbor, 1980-82; comdr. Naval Surface Force U.S. Atlantic Fleet, 1982-84; ret., 1984. Mem. com. on K-12 curricula and instrn. San Diego Unified Sch. Dist.; mem. curriculum coun. Escondido Union H.S. Dist., Escondido Union Elem. Sch. Dist. Decorated Bronze Star with combat device and one star, Air medals (2), Navy Commendation medal with combat device and two stars, Legion of Merit with combat device and four stars, D.S.M.; Vietnamese Navy Gallantry medal. Mem. Surface Navy Assn., U.S. Naval Acad. Alumni Assn., Naval Inst., Navy League, Rancho Bernardo Veterans Meml. Assn. Home: 3648 Lago Sereno Escondido CA 92029-7902 *Dedication to our nation and devotion to its ideals are the duties of all.*

BRIGGS, ETHEL D., federal agency administrator. BA, N.C. Ctrl. U.; M in Counseling, U. N.C. Dir. adult svcs. Nat. Coun. on Disability, Washington, dep. dir., acting exec. dir., exec. dir. Named One of Top 100 African-Am. Bus. and Profl. Women, Dollars and Sense Mag., 1989. Office: Nat Coun on Disability 1331 F St NW Ste 1050 Washington DC 20004-1107

BRIGGS, GEOFFREY HUGH, retired librarian; b. Leeds, Eng., Apr. 14, 1926; came to Can., 1967; s. Harry and Charlotte Irene (Black) B.; m. Judith Mary de la Mare, Dec. 6, 1950; children: Nicholas, Peter. BA, Cambridge (Eng.) U., 1947, MA, 1949; diplomas in archives and librarianship, Univ. Coll. London, 1949. Asst. librarian London U., 1949-54; dep. librarian Victoria U., Wellington, N.Z., 1954-67, U. Calgary, Alta., Can., 1967-69; univ. librarian Carleton U., Ottawa, Ont., Can., 1969-91. Mem. Can. Assn. Research Libraries (pres. 1979-80). Avocations: music; fishing. Home: 10 Caroline Ave, Belair SA 5052, Australia

BRIGGS, HENRY PAYSON, JR., headmaster; b. Boston, Apr. 14, 1932; s. Henry Payson Sr. and Eleanor Temple (Smith) B.; m. Charlin Shoenberger Devanney, Nov. 28, 1987; children from previous marriage: Payson Stewart, Heather Whittaker. BA, Harvard U., 1954, MAT, 1959. Dir. admissions and fin. aid Harvard U., Cambridge, Mass., 1956-66; headmaster Western Res. Acad., Hudson, Ohio, 1966-76, The Seven Hills Sch., Cin., 1976-95; interim head The St. James' Sch., L.A., 1995-96; dir. major gifts Cin. Opera, 1996-99; interim head The Potomac Sch., McLean, Va., 1999—. Mem. steering com. Leadership Cin., 1990—; mem. 2012 Amateur Olympic Com., 1996—; bd. dirs. Queen City Found., Commn. of Greater Cin. Found.; vestryman, warden, mem. com. Christ Episcopal Ch. Cathedral, Cin., 1977—. 1st lt. U.S. Army, 1954-56. Mem. Headmasters Assn. Country Day Sch. Headmasters Assn., Literary Club, Univ. Club, Tennis Club Cin. (pres.), St. Botolph Club (Boston). Avocations: tennis, theater, outdoors, politics. Home: 7937 Bar Harbor Dr Cincinnati OH 45255-4430

BRIGGS, JAMES HENRY, II, engineering administrator; b. San Francisco, Dec. 25, 1953; s. James Henry and Barbara (Cordes) B.; m. Niwana Alice Page, Sept. 1, 1979; children: Melanie Shannon, James Henry III. AA in Bus. Adminstrn., Albany (Ga.) Jr. Coll., 1976; BS in Computer Sci., U. N.C., Wilmington, 1979; BSEE, So. Tech., Marietta, Ga., 1985. Lic. 1st class radio telephone; registered profl. engr., Calif. Asst. chief engr. WECT-TV, Wilmington, 1978-82; maintenance supr. Cable News Network, Atlanta, 1982-85; mgr. engring. ops. KCOP-TV, L.A., 1985-87; sr. product support engr. Abekas Video Systems, Redwood City, Calif., 1987-92; dir. engring. D.T.S., Union City, Calif., 1991-97; chief engr. Sta. CSUH-TV Calif. State U., Hayward, 1997—; v.p. Charis Constrn., 1997—. Editor: Video Prodn. in the 90's. Mem. Soc. Motion Picture and TV Engrs., Soc. Broadcast Engrs., Greenpeace, Toastmasters Club, Lions. Avocations: biking, model trains, music, camping, sailing.

BRIGGS, JAMES T., marketing executive; b. Princeton, N.J., June 22, 1954; s. Joseph Curtis and Nancy (Pierce) B.; m. Paula Drain, Sept. 16, 1978; children: Peter, Andrew, Julia. BA, Conn. Coll., New London, 1976; postgrad., Harvard Bus. Sch., 1985. Regional sales mgr. Twyman Films Inc., Dayton, Ohio, 1976-77; sales rep. Lawyers Coop. Pub., Rochester, N.Y., 1977-81, sales adminstrn. supr., 1981-85, v.p. mktg., 1989-91, v.p. nat. products, 1991-96, pres., 1996-97; v.p. bus. devel. West Group (formerly Lawyers Coop. Pub.), Rochester, 1997—; gen. mgr. VERAEX Inc., subs. Lawyers Coop. Pub., Rochester, 1985-89. Dir., treas. Planned Parenthood of Genesee Valley, Rochester, 1985—. Mem. Country Club Rochester, Oenessa Valley Club. Republican. Avocations: golf, skiing, tennis, sailing. Home: 111 Old Mill Rd Rochester NY 14618-3217 Office: West Group Aqueduct Bldg Rochester NY 14694*

BRIGGS, JANET MARIE LOUISE, nurse practitioner; b. Pitts., June 11, 1951. RN, Ohio; cert. adult nurse practitioner. Staff nurse neonatal ICU Univ. Hosps. Cleve., 1972-73; staff nurse gen pediatrics Mt. Sinai Hosp. Cleve., 1973-76; head nurse health svc. Mt. Sinai Med. Ctr., Cleve., 1976-82; grad. rsch. asst. Case Western Res. U., Cleve., 1983-84; dir. nursing Ashtabula County Health Dept., Jefferson, Ohio, 1984-85; staff nurse, dir. nursing insvc., coord., clin. nurse specialist, coord. infection control Meml. Hosp. Geneva, Ohio, 1985-87; nurse practitioner, unit mgr. Parkside Health Mgmt. Corp., Toledo, 1986-87; nurse practitioner ambulatory surgery. Met. Gen. Hosp., Cleve., 1987; nurse practitioner domiciliary homeless program VA Med. Ctr., Cleve., 1987-91, clin. nurse specialist, nurse practioner AIDS team, 1991—; project dir., chmn. Child and Family Health Svc. Grant, Ashtabula County, Ohio, 1984-85; cons. case mgmt. head injuries subcom. Gov.'s Task Force, Ohio, 1988; nurse practitioner Free Clinic, Cleve., 1988—; mem. ethics com. VA Med. Ctr., 1989—; adj. clin. faculty Kent. State U., 1993—; clin. faculty Frances Payne Bolton Sch. Nursing Case Western Reserve U.; investigator multiple clinically based AIDS rsch. projects. Contbr. chpts. to books and articles to profl. jours.; cons. on-line nursing jour. Kent State U. Lectr., group leader Hitchcock House, Cleve., 1981-83. Recipient Fed. Exec. Bd. award, 1995, Hearts and Hands award, Sec. Vet. Affairs, 1995, Most Treasured Vol. award for 1996 Fedn. for Cmty. Planning of Greater Cleve., 1997; grantee Fed. Facility Based HIV/AIDS Edn. Demonstration, 1991, Fed. Facility HIV/AIDS Edn. Rsch., 1992, 93, Dept. Vet. Affairs. Mem. Frances Payne Bolton Sch. Nursing Alumni Assn. (bd. dirs.), Sigma Theta Tau. Roman Catholic. Avocations: bicycling, reading, photography, classical music, motorcycling.

BRIGGS, JOHN MANCEL, III, lawyer; b. Muskegon, Mich., May 24, 1942; s. John M. II and Margaret Jane (Wren) B.; m. Janice R. Dykema, May 20, 1967; children: Jennifer Anne, Jill Margaret. BS, U. Mich., 1964, JD, 1967. Bar: Mich. 1968, U.S. Dist. Ct. (we. dist.) Mich. 1968, U.S. Ct. Appeals (6th cir.) 1974. Assoc. Parmenter, Forsythe, Rude, Van Epps, Briggs & Fauri and predecessors, Muskegon, 1967-70; ptnr. Parmenter, Forsythe, Rude, Van Epps, Briggs & Fauri and predecessors, 1970-92; shareholder Parmenter O'Toole, Muskegon, Mich., 1992—. Active Muskegon United Appeal, 1968-73; bd. dirs. Big Bros., Muskegon, 1969-74; bd. dirs. Y Family Christian Assn., 1970-80, 81-83, 1st v.p., 1973-76, pres., 1977-78; bd. dirs. Muskegon-Oceana Legal Aid Soc., 1970-73, pres., 1972-73; bd. dirs. Berean Ch., 1985-86, 99, sec., 1988-90, v.p., 1993, pres., 1994, 99. With USAR, 1967-73. Recipient Disting. Svc. award Muskegon Jaycees, 1977. Fellow Mich. State Bar Assn.; mem. ABA, Muskegon County Bar Assn. (sec. 1970-71, v.p. 1974-75, pres. 1975-76), Rotary (bd. dirs. 1981-85, pres.-elect 1982-83, pres. 1983-84, Presdl. Citation). Republican. Office: Parmenter O'Toole PO Box 786 175 W Apple Ave Muskegon MI 49443-0786

BRIGGS, LAURA, humanities; b. N.Y.C., July 15, 1964; d. Adam Briggs and Karen Chase Williams. BA, Mt. Holyoke Coll., 1986; MTS, Harvard U., 1989; PhD, Brown U., 1998. Cert. secondary edn., social studies, Mass. Organizer Svc. Employees Internat. Union, Boston, 1986-87; staff writer Gay Cmty. News, Boston, 1989-91; asst. editor Sojourner: The Women's Forum, Boston, 1991-92; asst. prof. women's studies U. Ariz., Tucson, 1997—. Mem. editl. bd. Sojourner: The Women's Forum, 1993—. Dissertation grantee in women's health Woodrow Wilson Found./Johnson and Johnson, 1996; Charles Warren Ctr. fellow Harvard U., 1999. Mem. Orgn. Am. Historians, Am. Studies Assn., Am. Hist. Assn. Democrat. E-mail: lbriggs@u.arizona.edu. Fax: 520-621-7338. Office: Womens Studies Dept Univ Ariz Tucson AZ 85721

BRIGGS, PHILIP, insurance company executive; b. Paris, Feb. 28, 1928; s. Robert E. and Madeleine (Boell) B. (parents Am. citizens); m. Jean M. Sloan, July 9, 1949; children: Karen, Heather, Peter. AB, Middlebury Coll., 1948. With Met. Life Inst. Co., N.Y.C., 1948-93; v.p., gen. mgr. Met. Life Ins. Co., 1971-73, sr. v.p., 1973-77, exec. v.p., 1977-86; vice chmn. bd. dirs., CFO Met. Life Ins. Co., N.Y.C., 1986-93; chmn. Empire Blue Cross and Blue Shield, N.Y.C., 1993—. Fellow Soc. Actuaries, Am. Acad. Actuaries, Health Ins. Am. (past chmn.), Life Ins. Coun. N.Y. (past chmn. bd. dirs.); mem. desert Forest Golf Club, Sky Club, Mid Ocean Club (Bermuda). Home: 40947 N 107th Pl Scottsdale AZ 85262-4905 Office: Empire Blue Cross & Blue Shield One World Trade Ctr New York NY 10048

BRIGGS, PHILIP TERRY, biologist; b. Boston, Dec. 4, 1934; s. Clifford E. and Leah (Handy) B.; BS, U. Mass., 1956. Conservation biologist N.Y. Dept. Environ. Conservation, 1960-71, sr. aquatic biologist, 1971-77, assoc. aquatic biologist, 1977-81, marine resources specialist III, 1981-96. Served with U.S. Army, 1957-59. Cert. fisheries scientist. Contbr. articles in field. Mem. Am. Fisheries Soc. (pres. N.Y. chpt. 1979), Atlantic Fishery Biologists (pres. 1981), Am. Soc. Ichthyologists and Herpetologists, Am. Inst. Biol. Sci., Am. Inst. Fishery Research Biologists, Crustacean Soc. Unitarian. Office: NY State Dept Environ Conservation 205 Belle Mead Rd East Setauket NY 11733-3456

BRIGGS, ROBERT HENRY, infosystems specialist; b. Elk River, Minn., Apr. 25, 1937; s. Archie Elwin and Charlotte Lorette (Rand) B.; m. Jacqueline Hascoet, Apr. 20, 1963; children: Thomas Henry, Terence Gregory. BA in Bus., U. Wash., 1960. Indsl. engr. Boeing Co., Seattle, 1962-66; with 3M, St. Paul, 1966-97, catalog analyst, 1966-68, sr. file control coordinator, 1968-74, advanced analyst, 1974-80, sr. analyst, 1980-85, lead analyst, 1985-96; supr. 3M, 1996-97; pres. Data Consulting Svcs., Cottage Grove, Minn., 1997—. Mem. cmty. edn. adv. coun. South Washington County (Minn.) Schs., 1977-94, chmn., 1981-83, 88-89; with Cottage Grove (Minn.) Parks and Recreation Commn., 1974-80, chmn., 1978; mem. Internat. Inst. Minn., St. Paul, 1982—; treas. Twin Cities Area Camera Club Coun., 1993-96; pres. 3M Camera Club, 1995-97; v.p. South Washington County Schs. Edn. Found., 1995—. Mem. Data Adminstrn. Mgmt. Assn., Cottage Grove Jaycees (bd. dirs. 1972-73). Lutheran. Avocations: coaching, photography, golf. Home: 8369 80th St S Cottage Grove MN 55016-2019

BRIGGS, SUE, academic administrator; b. Hoboken, N.J., Apr. 27, 1956; d. William Anthony and Dorothy Jeanette (Seip) B.; m. Todd Alan Scott, Aug. 7, 1982. BA, Washington Coll., 1978; MA, Va. Tech., 1980; MBA, U. Balt., 1986; PhD, U. Md., 1995. Resident dir. St. Mary's Coll. Md., St. Mary's Coll., 1980-81; asst. dir. resident life Fairleigh Dickinson U., Madison, N.J., 1981-82, U. Md., Catonsville, 1982-85; asst. dean U. Balt., 1986-95, assoc. dean, 1995-96, assoc. dean Sch. Pharmacy, 1996-98; dir. civicus U. Md., College Pk., 1999—. Mem. Am. Coun. Edn.-Nat. Identification Program (co-chair planning bd. 1994-96), Md. Assn. Higher Edn. Democrat. Home: 8557 Dark Hawk Cir Columbia MD 21045-5613 Office: U Md 2141 Tydings Hall College Park MD 20742

BRIGGS, SUSAN SHADINGER, lawyer; b. Norfolk, Va., Oct. 25, 1941; d. Gail Jenner Shadinger and Betty Marx Hirshfield; m. Ronald F. Briggs, June 27, 1964. AB, U. Calif., Berkeley, 1963; JD, U. Calif., Hastings, 1967. Bar: Calif. 1967, U.S. Tax Ct. 1976, U.S. Dist. Ct. (no. dist.) Calif. 1967, U.S. Ct. Appeals (9th cir.) 1967. Assoc. McCutchen, Doyle, Brown & Enersen LLP, San Francisco, 1967-68, 69-75, ptnr., 1975—; panelist CEB and Rutter Group programs on will drafting, probate and estate planning, 1970-86. Author: (with others) Executors and Their Powers, 1981, supplement, 1984; contbr. to Calf. Continuing Edn.of Bar, 1979-83; assoc. editor Hastings Law Jour., 1966-67. Trustee, sec. of bd. San Francisco Ballet Assn., 1983—; trustee San Francisco Ballet Endowment Found., 1983—. Fellow Am. Coll. Trust and Estate Counsel; mem. ABA (real property and trust law sect.), Bar Assn. San Francisco (chmn. probate and trust law sect. 1983, vice chmn. 1982, sec. 1981), St. Francis Yacht Club (San Francisco). Avocations: golf, ballet, boating. Office: McCutchen Doyle Brown & Enersen LLP 3 Embarcadero Ctr San Francisco CA 94111-4003*

BRIGGS, TAYLOR RASTRICK, lawyer; b. Buffalo, June 5, 1933; s. Ernest Rastrick and Althea (Taylor) B.; m. Jane Genske, Sept. 15, 1956; children: Cynthia B. Kittredge, Jennifer B. Braswell, Pamela B. Besnard, Taylor Rastrick. AB, Williams Coll., 1954; LLB, Columbia U., 1957. Bar: N.Y., U.S. Supreme Ct. Assoc. Simpson Thacher & Bartlett, N.Y.C., 1957-59; counsel N.Y. Com. on Govtl. Ops. of City of N.Y., 1959-60; asst. chief counsel N.Y. State Com. of Investigation, Special Unit, 1960-61; ptnr. LeBoeuf, Lamb, Greene & MacRae, N.Y.C., 1961-95, counsel, 1995—; bd. dirs. Nova NET Learning, Inc.; mng. dir. The Berkshires Capital Investors LLP, 1997—. Chmn. Tuxedo Park (N.Y.) Zoning Bd. Appeals, 1972-88; pres. Tuxedo Park Libr., 1971-79; chmn., trustee N.Y. Law Sch., N.Y.C., 1984—; trustee Citizens Budget Commn., 1990-95, Marlboro Sch. Music, Inc., 1992—; trustee Williamstown Art Conservation Ctr., 1997—; mem. adv. coun. Trinity Ctr. for Ethics and Corp. Policy, N.Y.C., 1982-93. Fellow Am. Bar Found., Am. Coll. Trial Lawyers; mem. ABA (ho. of del. 1985-88), Assn. of Bar of City of N.Y., Royal Tennis Club, Mid-Ocean Club, Royal Bermuda Yacht Club, Masons, Phi Delta Phi, Delta Upsilon. Republican. Episcopalian. Home: 1425 Main St Williamstown MA 01267-2623 Office: LeBoeuf Lamb Greene MacRae 125 W 55th St New York NY 10019-5369

BRIGGS, WILLIAM BENAJAH, aeronautical engineer; b. Okmulgee, Okla., Dec. 13, 1922; s. Eugene Stephen and Mary Bettie (Gentry) B.; m. Lorraine Hood, June 6, 1944; children—Eugene Stephen II, Cynthia Anne, Julia Louise, Spencer Gentry. BA in Physics, Phillips U., 1943, DSc (hon.), 1977; MSME, Ga. Inst. Tech., 1947. Aero. scientist NACA, Cleve., 1948-52; propulsion engr. Chance Vought Aircraft/LTV, Dallas, 1952-64; mgr. advanced planning McDonnell Douglas Co., St. Louis, 1964-80, dir. program devel. fusion energy, 1980-87; mem. planetary quarantine adv. panel NASA. Contbr. articles on aero. engring. and energy to profl. jours.; patentee in field. Chmn. Disciples Coun. Greater St. Louis, 1969-73; chmn. bd. Christian Bd. Publs., St. Louis, 1974-91; bd. dirs. Joint Cmty. Ministries, 1987-92, Emergency Childrens Home, 1994—; chmn. arrangements gen. assembly/synod Disciples of Christ/United Ch. of Christ, 1993; trustee Phillips U., Enid, Okla., 1996—. With USN, 1943-46. Assoc. fellow AIAA (dir. region 5 1974-77, v.p. mem. svcs. 1978-79); mem. VFW, Am. Nuclear Soc., Navy League. Mem. Disciples of Christ Ch. Lodge: Masons. Home: 1819 Bradburn Dr Saint Louis MO 63131-1517 *Facing a problem, size up the factors involved, determine what needs to be done, then take action. Steadfastly working the plan does produce results; just give serendipity a chance to happen.*

BRIGGS, WINSLOW RUSSELL, plant biologist, educator; b. St. Paul, Apr. 29, 1928; s. John DeQuedville and Marjorie (Winslow) B.; m. Ann Morrill, June 30, 1955; children: Caroline, Lucia, Marion. BA, Harvard U., 1951, MA, 1952, PhD, 1956. Instr. biol. scis. Stanford (Calif.) U., 1955-57, asst. prof., 1957-62, asso. prof., 1962-66, prof., 1966-67; prof. biology Harvard U., 1967-73, Stanford U., 1973—; dir. dept. plant biology Carnegie Instn. of Washington, Stanford, 1973-93. Author: (with others) Life on Earth, 1973; mem. editl. bd. Ann. Rev. Plant Physiology, 1961-72; contbr. articles on plant growth and devel. and photobiology to profl. jours. Recipient Alexander von Humboldt U.S. Sr. Scientist award, 1984-85; John Simon Guggenheim fellow, 1973-74, Deutsche Akademie der Naturforscher Leopoldina, 1986, Sterling Hendricks award USDA Agrl. Rsch. Svc., 1995. Fellow AAAS; mem. NAS, Am. Soc. Plant Physiologists (pres. 1975-76, Stephen Hales award 1994), Calif. Bot. Soc. (pres. 1976-77), Am. Acad. Arts and Scis., Am. Inst. Biol. Scis. (pres. 1980-81), Am. Soc. Photobiology, Bot. Soc. Am., Nature Conservancy, Sigma Xi. Home: 480 Hale St Palo Alto CA 94301-2207 Office: Carnegie Inst Washington Dept Plant Biology 260 Panama St Palo Alto CA 94305-4101 *With gifted students, remarkable things are possible.*

BRIGHAM, CHRISTOPHER ROY, occupational medicine physician; b. Guelph, Ontario, Can., Dec. 27, 1950; s. Kenneth Roy and Jean McCrea B.; m. Cathy Violet White, July 1, 1989; children: Melinda, Alison, Gina. BA, Rutgers Coll., 1972; MMS, Rutgers U., Piscataway, N.J., 1974; MD, Washington U., 1976. Diplomate Nat. Bd. Med. Examiners, Am. Bd. Preventive Medicine (occupational medicine), Am. Bd. Family Practice; lic. Maine, Mass; cert. ind. med. examiner Am.Bd. Ind. Med. Examiners. Resident in family practice Eastern Maine Med. Ctr., Bangor, 1976-79; ptnr. and family physician Med. Assocs. of Bar Harbor, Maine, 1979-85; pres. Marine Health Svcs., Bar Harbor, 1980-86; cons. med. dir. Emergency and Safety Programs, Inc., Media, Pa., 1983-86, 86-90; med. dir. St. Joseph Ambulatory Care, Inc., Bangor, Maine, 1985-86; occupational health cons. Envirologic Data, Portland, Maine, 1986-88; pres. and founder Occupational Health Excellence, Inc., Falmouth, Maine, 1988-94; exec. v.p. SEAK, Inc., Falmouth, Mass., 1996—; sr. cons. Occupational Health Excellence of Maine, South Portland,

1992-97; v.p. med. affairs Occupational Health Resources, Inc., Phila., 1993-94; pres. Brigham and Assocs., Inc., Portland, Maine, 1994—; CEO Audio Traveler, Inc., Portland, Maine, 1998—; dir. divsn. occupational health, Depts. Medicine and Family Practice, Maine Med. Contbr. articles to profl. jours., presenter at numerous confs., workshops and sci. meetings in field. Mem. Am. Coll. Occupational and Environ. Medicine (vice chmn. sect. on computers in occupational medicine, 1986-87, mem. 1986—, chmn. com. on occupational mental health, 1988-92, coun. on social issues 1988-92, com. on confs., 1995—, dir. 1996-99, others), Am. Acad. Disability Evaluating Physicians, Am. Bd. Ind. Med. Examiners (founding dir., sr. cons.), Humanities, Inc. (bd. dirs.), New Eng. Occupational Med. Assn. (bd. dirs. 1988-90). Avocations: travel, sailing, running, biking, singing. Home and Office: 31 Summer Pl Portland ME 04103-4707

BRIGHAM, JOHN ALLEN, JR., financial executive, environmentalist, polititian; b. San Francisco, June 17, 1942; s. John Allen, Sr. and Susan (Endberg) B.; m. Patricia Katherine Carney, Feb. 4, 1968; 1 child, Jennifer. BS in Acctg., San Jose State U., 1967. Acct. Shell Oil Co. Data Ctr., Palo Alto, Calif., 1963-66; asst. plant controller Brown Co., Santa Clara, Calif., 1966-68; budget mgr. Varian Assocs., Palo Alto, 1968-80; cost acctg. mgr. Adac Labs., San Jose, Calif., 1980-86; contr. Crystal Tech., Palo Alto, 1986-90; contr., v.p. fin., CFO GV Custom Modular Constrn., Inc., Healdsburg, Calif.; controller GV Contractors, Heraldsburg, Calif., 1994—; part-time sci. tchr. Insects and Dinosaurs, 1994-96. Del. League Calif. Cities, 1974-78; mem. Saratoga (Calif.) City Council, 1974-78; vice-chmn. Santa Clara County Polity Planning Use Commn., 1975-78; chmn. Santa Clara Com. on Mass Transit, 1976-78; chmn. Open Space Bond Issure, 1976; treas. Calif. State Solar Bond Issue, 1976; mem. Castle Rock State Pk. Com., 1972-74; vice-chmn. Saratoga Hillside Com. 1978-79. Recipient 10 and 25 Yr. Sierra Club Activist awards, 1989, Chpt. Svc. award, 1990, Spl. Achievement award, 1990; Local Outstanding Young Man of Am. award, 1974, Siemens USA Personality of the Month award, Jan. 1990. Mem. Am. Entomol. Soc., Archeol. Inst. Am., Nat. Acctg. Assn., Sierra Club (vice chmn., treas. Loma chpt. 1985-94, treas. Redwood chpt. 1994-97, internat. chmn. 1989-97, Centennial chmn. 1990-92, liaison to USSR and Mex., co-chair Earth Day 1990, taskforce 1989, chmn. fin. commn. 1985-90), Am. Diabetes Soc. (treas., bd. dirs. Santa Clara County chpt.), Nat. Wildlife Fedn., Cousteau Soc., Planetary Soc., Napoleonic Soc., Bromiliad Soc., Am. Diabetes Assn., Sierra Club. Independent. Roman Catholic. E-mail: johnb@gucm.com.

BRIGHAM, KENNETH LARRY, medical educator; b. Tenn., Oct. 29, 1939; m. Betty Brigham; 1 child, Heather. BA, David Lipscomb Coll., 1962; MD, Vanderbilt U., 1966. Intern Osler Med. Service, Johns Hopkins Hosp., Balt., 1966-67, asst. resident in medicine, 1967-68; with cholera research unit Johns Hopkins Ctr. for Med. Research and Tng., Calcutta, India, 1968; med. epidemiologist Ecol. Investigations program USPHS Nat. Communicable Disease Ctr., Phoenix, 1968-70; instr. in medicine, fellow in pulmonary diseases Vanderbilt U. Sch. Medicine, Nashville, 1970-71, dir. pulmonary research, 1973-76, asst. prof. medicine, 1973-74, assoc. prof., 1974-78, dir. Ctr. for Lung Research, 1976—, assoc. prof. biomed. engring., 1977-86, prof. of medicine, 1978—, dir. div. pulmonary medicine, 1978—, asst. prof. physiology, 1983-85, assoc. prof. molecular physiology and biophysics, 1985—, Joe and Morris Wethan prof. investigative medicine, 1984—, prof. biomed. engring., 1986—, now dir. divsn. allergy, pulmonary, & crit. care med., 1998—; research fellow Cardiovascular Research Inst., U. Calif. Med. Ctr., San Francisco, 1971-73; dir. of Div. Allergy, Pulmonary & Critical Care Med.; mem. council on cardiopulmonary disease Am. Heart Assn., investigator, 1975-80; mem. cardiovascular and pulmonary study sect. USPHS, Nat. Heart Lung Inst., 1975-79, mem. pulmonary nat. research service award group, 1975; mem. lung research rev. com. VA, 1976; mem. A program project rev. com. Nat. Heart Lung and Blood Inst., 1982-85, chmn., 1984-85, mem. pulmonary disease adv. com., 1986—; prin. investigator Specialized Ctr. Research in Pulmonary Vascular Disease, 1976—, Parker B. Francis Found. Fellowships in Pulmonary Research, 1977-83, Multidisciplinary Lung Research Tng. Grant, 1975—; mem. Am. Lung Assn./Am. Thoracic Soc. steering com., 1988-89; chmn. pulmonary diseases adv. com. NIH, 1988-90. Mem. editorial bd. Jour. Applied Physiology, 1978-84, Respiratory, Environ. and Exercise Physiology, 1978-84, Circulation Research, 1982—, Exptl. Lung Research, 1982—, Am. Jour. Med. Scis., 1983—, Am. Rev. Respiratory Diseases, 1984—. Jour. Clin. Investigation, 1985—, Intensive Care Medicine, 1985—; contbr. articles to profl. jours. Mem. planning com. Am. Lung Assn., 1983—; rep. Vanderbilt Univ. Senate, Nashville, 1986—. Grantee NIH, 1985—. Mem. Am. Physiol. Soc. (circulation and respiration groups), Am. Fedn. for Clin. Research (pres. So. sect. 1980-81), Am. Thoracic Soc. (pres.-elect pulmonary circulation sect. assembly on structure and function 1979-80, pres. pulmonary circulation sect. 1980-81, chmn.-elect assembly on respiratory structure function and metabolism 1981-82, chmn. assembly 1982-83, fed. lung program com. 1987—, pres.-elect 1988-89, bd. dirs. 1988-89, budget com. 1988-89), AAAS, Johns Hopkins Med. and Surg. Assn., Microcirculatory Soc., So. Soc. for Clin. Investigation (councilor 1988-89), Am. Soc. for Clin. Investigation, N.Y. Acad. Scis., Assn. Am. Physicians, ACP, Am. Soc. for Cell Biology, Nashville Soc. for Internal Medicine (v.p. 1985-86), Am. Lung Assn. (exec. com. 1988-89, planning com. 1988-89, program coordinating/program and budget com. 1988-89)). Home: 211 Printers Aly Nashville TN 37201-1414 Office: Vanderbilt U Pulmonary Med T-1217 Medical Center N 1161 21st Ave S Nashville TN 37212-2708*

BRIGHAM, SAMUEL TOWNSEND JACK, III, lawyer; b. Honolulu, Oct. 8, 1939; s. Samuel Townsend Jack, Jr. and Betty Elizabeth (McNeil) B.; m. Judith Catherine Johnson, Sept. 3, 1960; children: Robert Jack, Bradley Lund, Lori Ann, Lisa Katherine. B.S. in Bus. magna cum laude, Menlo Coll., 1963; J.D., U. Utah, 1966. Bar: Calif. 1967. Asso. firm Petty, Andrews, Olsen & Tufts, San Francisco, 1966-67; accounting mgr. Western sales region Hewlett-Packard Co., North Hollywood, Calif., 1967-68; atty. Hewlett-Packard Co., Palo Alto, Calif., 1968-70; asst. gen. counsel Hewlett-Packard Co., 1971-73, gen. atty., asst. sec., 1974-75, sec., gen. counsel, 1977-82, v.p., gen. counsel, 1982-85, v.p. corp. affairs, gen. counsel, mgr./dir. law dept., 1985—, sr. v.p. corp. affairs, gen. counsel, mgr./dir. law dept., 1994—; lectr. law Menlo Coll.; speaker profl. assn. seminars. Bd. dirs. Palo Alto Area YMCA, 1974-81, pres., 1978; bd. govs. Santa Clara County region NCCJ; trustee Menlo Sch. and Coll.; bd. dirs. Just Say No. Served with USMC, 1957-59. Mem. ABA, Calif. Bar Assn., Peninsula Assn. Gen. Counsel, MAPI Law Council, Am. Corp. Counsel Assn. (chmn. 1985, bd. dirs. 1983—), Am. Soc. Corp. Secs. (pres. No. Calif. Chpt. 1983—), Assn. Gen. Counsel (sec.-treas. 1991—). Home: 920 Oxford Dr Los Altos CA 94024-7032 Office: Hewlett-Packard Co 3000 Hanover St Palo Alto CA 94304-1181

BRIGHT, CRAIG BARTLEY, lawyer; b. Mineola, N.Y., May 23, 1931; s. Herbert Lester and Gertrude Lillian (Smith) B.; m. Judith Alice Pollard, July 31, 1955 (dec. Aug. 1956); m. Ann Sharpe, July 18, 1959. B.A. summa cum laude Colgate U., 1952; J.D. magna cum laude Harvard U., 1955. Bar: N.Y. 1956, U.S. Dist. Ct. (so. and ea. dists.) N.Y. 1961, U.S. Dist. Ct. Conn. 1961, U.S. Ct. Appeals (2d cir.) 1961. Staff judge advocate Judge Adv. Gen.'s Group, 1955-57; assoc. Patterson, Belknap, Webb & Tyler, N.Y.C., 1957-64, ptnr., 1965-92. Co-author: The Law and the Lore of Endowment Funds, 1969; The Developing Law of Endowment Funds, 1974; also law rev. articles. Served to capt. USAF, 1955-57. Mem. N.Y. State Bar Assn. (chmn. com. on profl. ethics 1981-84), Assn. of Bar of City of N.Y., ABA. Republican. Presbyterian. Club: Hermitage (Goochland, Va.). Home and Office: 21 Hunting Ridge Rd Manakin Sabot VA 23103-2614

BRIGHT, DAVID FORBES, academic administrator, classics and comparative literature educator; b. Winnipeg, Man., Can., Apr. 13, 1942; s. John Hamilton and Pauline Murray (Forbes) B.; m. Marlene Joanne Mayercik, Feb. 20, 1965; children: Jennifer, Sarah. BA (hons.), U. Man., 1962; AM, U. Cin., 1963, PhD, 1967. Asst. prof. classics Williams Coll., Williamstown, Mass., 1967-70; asst. then assoc. prof. classics U. Ill., Urbana-Champaign, 1970-85, prof. classics and comparative lit., 1985-89, chmn. dept. classics, 1977-81, 85-88, dir. comparative lit. dept., 1986-88, acting dean Coll. Liberal Arts and Scis., 1988-89; dean Coll. Liberal Arts and Scis. Iowa State U., Ames, 1989-91; dean, v.p. for arts and scis. Emory U., Atlanta, 1991-97, prof. classics and comparative lit., 1991—. Author: Haec mihi fingebam. Tibullus in his World, 1978, Elaborate Disarray, 1980, Miniature Epic in Vandal Africa, 1987; editor: Classical Texts and Their Traditions, 1984. Bd. dirs. Atlanta Ballet Co., Savoyards Light Opera, Coun. of Arts and Scis., pres. 1996-97. Woodrow Wilson Found. fellow, 1962, U. Cin. travel fellow Am. Acad. in Rome, 1965-66, Am. Council Learned Socs. fellow, 1981-82; research scholar Delmas Found., 1987. Mem. Am. Philol. Assn., Archeol. Inst. Am., Classical Assn. Middle West and South (exec. com. 1985-89, pres. 1989), Vergilian Soc. (trustee 1983-86), Soc. of Fellows Am. Acad. Rome. Episcopalian. Home: 2646 Rangewood Dr NE Atlanta GA 30345-1516 Office: Emory U Dept Classics N404 Callaway Ctr Atlanta GA 30322

BRIGHT, JOSEPH CONVERSE, lawyer; b. Richmond, Va., July 28, 1940; s. Joseph Elliott and Marion (Converse) B.; m. Jill Giddens, May 5, 1989; children: Thomas Converse, Elizabeth Chase. BA, U. Va., 1962; LLB, U. Ga., 1965. Bar: Ga. 1964, U.S. Dist. Ct. (so. dist.) Ga. 1965, U.S. Dist. Ct. (mid. dist.) Ga. 1967, U.S. Dist. Ct. (no. dist.) Ga. 1983, U.S. Ct. Appeals (5th cir.) 1965, Fla. 1976, U.S. Dist. Ct. (mid. and no. dist.) Fla. 1982, U.S. Supreme Ct. 1976, U.S. Ct. Appeals (11th cir.) 1981, U.S. Dist. Ct. (no. dist.) Fla. 1998. Assoc. Joseph B. Bergen, Savannah, Ga., 1965-67; sole practice Valdosta, Ga., 1967-69; ptnr. Blackburn & Bright, Valdosta, 1969-91; pvt. practice Valdosta, 1991—; instr. part time Valdosta State U., 1967-81; mem. Ga. Bd. Bar Examiners. Fellow Am. Bd. Criminal Lawyers, Am. Coll. Trial Lawyers; mem. ATLA, Am. Bd. Trial Advocates (advocate), Nat. Assn. Criminal Def. Lawyers, Ga. Trial Lawyers Assn. (v.p.). Avocations: riding, English history, skeet shooting. Office: PO Box 5889 Valdosta GA 31603-5889

BRIGHT, KEVIN S., producer; b. 1955. With Bright-Kauffman-Crane Prodns., Burbank, Calif. Creator, exec. prodr. Dream On, 1990—, Friends, 1994— (Emmy nominee 1995, 96), Veronica's Closet, 1997—, Jesse, 1998. Office: Bright Kauffman Crane Prodns Bldg 160 Ste 750 4000 Warner Blvd Burbank CA 91522*

BRIGHT, M. W. A., physical science administrator. Supt. quality engring. test establishment, Ottawa, ON, Canada. Office: Quality Engring Test Establishment, Ottawa, ON Canada K1A 0K2*

BRIGHT, MARGARET, sociologist; b. Bentonville, Ark., Nov. 19, 1918; d. William Ray and Edna May (Woolwine) B.; m. Herman Binder, 1983. AB, U. Calif., Berkeley, 1941; MA, U. Mo., 1944; PhD, U. Wis., 1950. Lectr. rural sociology U. Mo., 1944-47; asst. project dir. U. P.R., 1950-51; acting assoc. prof. Cornell U., 1951-52; social affairs officer population br. UN, N.Y.C., 1952-54; research assoc. Bur. Applied Social Research Columbia U., 1954-57; sociologist-demographer UN Tech. Assistance, Bombay, India, 1957-59; asst. prof. chronic diseases Johns Hopkins U., Balt., 1959-63; assoc. prof. Johns Hopkins U., 1963-68; dir. research Center for Urban Affairs, 1968-72, assoc. prof. behavioral scis., 1968-70, prof., 1970-83, prof. emerita, 1983—; mem. U.S. Mission Coop. Health and Sanitation to, Brazil, 1960. Author: Cooperativas de Consumo de Puerto Rico: Análisis Socio-Económicó, 1957; co-author: Graduates of American Schools of Public Health, 1976; contbr. articles to profl. jours. Mem. Balt. Mayor's Task Force on Polit. Redistricting, 1971; mem. Rockefeller Commn. on Population and the Am. Future, 1970-72. Mem. Am. Pub. Health Assn. Democrat. Home: 3900 N Charles St Apt 1314 Baltimore MD 21218-1738 Office: 624 N Broadway Baltimore MD 21205-1900

BRIGHT, MYRON H., federal judge, educator; b. Eveleth, Minn., Mar. 5, 1919; s. Morris and Lena A. (Levine) B.; m. Frances Louise Reisler, Dec. 26, 1947; children: Dinah Ann, Joshua Robert. BSL, U. Minn., 1941, JD, 1947. Bar: N.D. 1947, Minn. 1947. Assoc. Wattam, Vogel, Vogel & Bright, Fargo, N.D., 1947, ptnr., 1949-68; judge 8th U.S. Cir. Ct. Appeals, Fargo, 1968-85, sr. judge, 1985—; disting. prof. law St. Louis U., 1985-88, emeritus prof. of law, 1989-95. Capt. AUS, 1942-46, CBI. Recipient Francis Rawle award ALI-ABA, 1996, Lifetime Achievement award U. N.D. Law Sch., 1998. Mem. ABA, N.D. Bar Assn., Met. St. Louis Bar Assn., U.S. Jud. Conf. (com. on adminstrn. of probation sys. 1977-83, adv. com. on appellate rules 1987-90, com. on internat. jud. rels. 1996—). Office: US Ct Appeals 8th Cir 655 1st Ave N Ste 340 Fargo ND 58102-4952*

BRIGHT, WILLARD MEAD, manufacturing company executive; b. N.Y.C., Mar. 26, 1914; s. William Van Horn and Bernice Hartwell (Reynolds) B.; m. Martha Norris Land, May 15, 1944 (dec.); 1 child, Willard Mead; m. Virginia L. Jones, Mar. 14, 1981 (div. Aug. 1996). B.S., U. Toledo, 1936, M.S., 1937; postgrad., U. Pitts., 1937-38; A.M., Harvard U., 1941, Ph.D., 1942. Research chemist Kendall Co., Boston, Chgo., 1942-52; asst. lab. dir. Kendall Co. (Bauer & Black div.), 1944-48; lab. dir. (Theodore Clark Lab. div.), Cambridge, Mass., 1948-52; asst. research dir. Lever Bros. Co., 1952-54, research dir., 1954-60, v.p. research and devel., 1960-64; chmn. bd. W. H. Norris Lumber Co., Houston, 1957-64; treas. Border Lumber Co., Weslaco, Tex., 1957-64; v.p. R.J. Reynolds Tobacco Co., 1964-68; sr. v.p., pres. profl. products group Warner-Lambert Pharm. Co., 1968-70; pres., chief exec. officer Kendall Co., Boston, 1970-73; pres. Curtiss-Wright Corp., 1973-74, Boehringer Mannheim Corp., 1974-81; chmn. Zoll Med. Corp, 1982-96; bd. dirs. CSS Industries, Furman Lumber Co., Macrochem Corp., Zoll Med. Corp.; mem. adv. com. on patents U.S. Dept. Commerce, 1966-69; bd. visitors dept. chemistry Boston U. Recipient Gold T award U. Toledo, 1960. Mem. N.A.M. (chmn. sci. tech. com. dir. 1970-73), Am. Chem. Soc., N.Y. Acad. Scis., Assn. Rsch. Dirs., Indsl. Rsch. Inst. (dir. 1963-69, pres. 1967-68), Dirs. Indsl. Rsch., Sigma Xi, Phi Kappa Phi, Univ. Club (N.Y.C.), Somerset Club (Boston), Harvard Club (Boston), Comml. Club (Boston), The Country Club (Brookline, Mass.), Bent Pine Golf Club (Vero Beach, Fla.). Home: 112 Prestwick Cir Vero Beach FL 32967-7514 Office: Zoll Med Corp 32 2nd Ave Burlington MA 01803-4408

BRIGHTBILL, DAVID JOHN, state senator, lawyer; b. Lebanon, Pa., Nov. 3, 1942 s. Jonathan McMichael and Verda (McGill) B.; m. Donna Long Brighthill; children: David, Jonathan, Andrew, Christian. B.S., Pa. State U., 1964; J.D., Duquesne U., 1970. Bar: Pa. 1970 Sch. dir. Lebanon Sch. Dist. (Pa.); 1965-67 dist. atty. Lebanon, 1977-81; mem. Pa. Senate, Harrisburg, 1982—. Office: 307 Municipal Bldg 400 S 8th St Lebanon PA 17042-6794 also: Pa State Senate State Capitol Harrisburg PA 17120

BRIGHTMAN, ROBERT LLOYD, importer, textile company executive, consultant; b. Rockville Center, N.Y., July 17, 1920; s. Harold Warren and Florence (Pennington) B.; m. Marion Altreuter, Oct. 31, 1942 (dec. Nov. 1989); children: Richard Warren, Shelley Anne, Susan Boyd; m. Vera Elisabet Holmsten, Dec. 5, 1990. Grad. cum laude, Montclair Acad., 1936, Phillips Exeter Acad., 1937; B.A., Princeton, 1941. With A. Johnson & Co., Inc., N.Y.C., 1946-48; with Johaneson, Wales & Sparre, Inc., N.Y.C., 1948-67; v.p. Johaneson, Wales & Sparre, Inc., 1952-64, pres., 1964-67; v.p. Grangesberg Am. Corp., N.Y.C., 1967-68; pres. R.L. Brightman Co., Verona, N.J., 1967—; dir. purchases West Point-Pepperell, N.Y.C., 1968-76; corporate v.p. West Point-Pepperell, 1976-88; Mem. Nat. Council Am. Importers, Inc., 1954-69, dir., 1956-69, v.p., 1959-61, pres., 1961-63, sr. councillor, 1963-69; mem. nat. panel arbitrators Am. Arbitration Assn., 1958—. Served with USNR, 1942-46. Home and Office: Claridge House One Apt 318 Verona NJ 07044

BRIGHTMIRE, PAUL WILLIAM, retired judge; b. Washington, Mo., June 12, 1924; s. Quinton Claude and Alvena Matilda (Wehr) B.; m. Lorene E. Edwards, Nov. 7, 1952; children: Deborah Sue, William Paul, Jon Edward, Christina Ann, Thomas Christopher. BA, U. Tulsa, 1949, JD, 1951. Bar: Okla. 1951, U.S. Supreme Ct. 1973. With Rogers & Brightmire, 1954-57, Brightmire & Assoc., Tulsa, 1957-70; judge Okla. Ct. Appeals, Divsn. 2, Tulsa, 1971-94, presiding judge, 1971-75; spl. justice Supreme Ct. Okla.; vice- chief judge Okla. Ct. Appeals, 1989, chief judge, 1990-94; vis. prof. med. jurisprudence Okla. Coll. Osteo. Medicine and Surgery, 1975-82. Founding editor: Tulsa Lawyer, 1962-64; editor in chief: Advocate, 1967-70. Served to 2d lt. USNR, USAR, 1943-46, 51. Recipient Outstanding Svc. award Okla. Ct. Appeals, 1990. Fellow Internat. Acad. Law and Sci.; mem. Am. Trial Lawyers Assn., Okla. Trial Lawyers Assn. (pres. 1967, Outstanding Service award 1968, Appellate Judge of Yr. award 1991), Okla. Bar Assn. (Outstanding Service award 1969), Tulsa County Bar Assn. (Outstanding Service award 1965, exec. com. 1962-64), Am. Inns of Ct. (master emeritus), Tulsa Press Club, Kappa Sigma, Phi Beta Gamma, Pi Kappa Delta. Lodge: Masons (32 deg., Shriner). Home: 4041 S Birmingham Ave Tulsa OK 74105-8230

BRIGHTON, CARL THEODORE, orthopedic surgery educator; b. Pana, Ill., Aug. 20, 1931; s. Louis Frederick and Helen (Frinke) B.; m. Ruth Louise Krentz, July 27, 1954; children: David Carl, Susan Ruth, Andrew Paul, Joel Theodore. BA, Valparaiso U., 1953; MD, U. Pa., 1957; PhD, U. Ill., 1969; DSc (hon.), Valpraiso U., 1998. Diplomate: Am. Bd. Orthopedic Surgery. Intern U.S. Naval Hosp., Phila., 1957-58; resident orthopedics U.S. Naval Hosp., 1958-61; resident in orthopedics U. Pa., Phila., 1961-62; staff orthopedist U.S. Naval Hosp., Phila., 1962-63, Naval Hosp., Great Lakes, Ill., 1963-66, USS Sanctuary, South China Sea, 1966-67; asst. prof. orthopedic surgery U. Pa. Med. Sch., Phila., 1968-70, dir. orthopedic rsch., 1968-93, assoc. prof., 1970-73, prof., 1973—, chmn. dept. orthopedic surgery, 1977-93, Paul B. Magnuson prof. bone and joint surgery, 1977-96, Paul B. Magnuson prof. emeritus bone and joint surgery, 1996—; cons. orthopedic surgery U.S. Naval Hosp., Phila., 1968-78; attending staff VA Hosp., Phila., 1968-84. Editor-in-Chief: Clinical Orthopaedics and Related Research, 1993—. Lt. comdr. (j.g.) USN, 1957-62. Recipient Kappa Delta award for outstanding research, 1974; spl. postdoctoral fellow NIH, 1967-68; Career devel. research award, 1971-76; Shands lectr. award, 1985, Merit award NIH, 1987, Bristol-Myers Squibb/Zimmer award for Disting. Achievement in Orthopaedic Rsch., 1992. Fellow ACS, Am. Acad. Orthopedic Surgeons; mem. Am. Orthopedic Assn., Orthopedic Rsch. Soc. (pres. 1977), Orthopedic Forum, Can. Orthopedic Rsch. Soc. (hon.), Bioelectric Repair and Growth Soc. (co-founder, pres. 1981, 82), Acad. Orthopaedic Soc., Assn. of Bone and Joint Surgeons. Lutheran. Pioneered use of electricity in treating nonunion fractures. Home: 14 Flintshire Rd Malvern PA 19355-1108 Office: Univ City Sci Ctr Clinical Opthopaedics 3550 Market St Ste 220 Philadelphia PA 19104-3329

BRIGHTON, GERALD DAVID, accounting educator; b. Weldon, Ill., May 14, 1920; s. William Henry and Geneva (Ennis) B.; m. Lois Helen Robbins, June 7, 1949; children: Anne, William, Joan, John, Jeffrey. B.S., U. Ill., 1941, M.S., 1947, Ph.D., 1953. C.P.A., Ill. Instr. accountancy U. Ill., Urbana, 1947-53, prof., 1954-83, Ernst & Whinney Disting. prof., 1983-88, prof. emeritus, 1988—, dir. undergrad. acctg. program, 1978-86; staff acct. Touche, Niven, Bailey & Smart, Chgo., 1953-54; cons. G.D. Brighton, C.P.A., Urbana, 1954—; vis. prof. U. Tex.-Austin, 1973; program specialist Dept. HUD, Washington, 1979; vice chmn. U. Ill. Athletic Assn., Urbana, 1982-86. Contbr. articles to profl. jours. Alderman City of Urbana, 1967-69; officer, bd. dirs. U. Ill. YMCA, Champaign, 1959-81, 89-95, Wesley Found., U. Ill., 1986—; treas. John Gwinn for Congress, Urbana, 1982-83, Green Meadows coun. Girl Scouts U.S., 1981-83. Served to maj. U.S. Army, 1941-46. AACSB Faculty fellow, 1978-79; recipient Bronze Tablet for high honors U. Ill., 1941. Mem. AICPA (hon.), Ill. Soc. CPAs (disting.), Am. Acctg. Assn., Assn. Govt. Accts., Govtl. Fin. Officers Assn., Nat. Tax Assn., Tax Inst. Am. Democrat. Methodist. Home: 609 W Green St Urbana IL 61801-3944 Office: U Ill 1206 S 6th St Champaign IL 61820-6915 *Happiness comes very indirectly. "Seek and ye shall find." That is at best a half truth. If we rely on direct rewards for our happiness we are in trouble. At best, the string of treats will be irregular. The key is to widen one's circle. Try to rejoice in the good fortunes of your colleagues. Sometimes, jealousy gets in the way. What is the greatest satisfaction I have had from teaching? It is the occasional glimpses that I see that former students are doing well.*

BRIGHTON, JOHN, academic administrator; b. Gosport, Ind.. BS, MS, PhD in Mech. Engring., Purdue U. Prof. mech. engring. Carnegie-Mellon U.; chmn. dept. mech. engring. Mich. State U., 1977-82; dir. Sch. Mech. Engring. Ga. Inst. Tech., 1982-88; dean Coll. Engring. Pa. State U., 1988-91, exec. v.p., provost, 1991—. Office: Pa State U 201 Old Main University Park PA 16802-1589

BRIGHTON, RUTH LOUISE, lay worker, educator; b. Harrisburg, Pa., Apr. 18, 1931; d. Paul Gerhard and Ruth Genevieve (Lee) Krentz; m. Carl T. Brighton, July 27, 1954; children: David, Susan, Andrew, Joel. BA, Valparaiso U., 1953; MS in Math., U. Wis., 1955. Cert. tchr. Tchr. Sunday sch., adult Bible class Christ Meml. Luth. Ch., Malvern, Penn., 1969—; coord. adult edn., Ea. dist. Luth. Ch.-Mo. Synod, Buffalo, 1986-89, bd. dirs., 1988-90; bd. dirs. Concordia Pub. House, St. Louis. Teaching fellow in math. U. Wis., 1953. Home: 14 Flintshire Rd Malvern PA 19355-1108

BRIGHTUP, CRAIG STEVEN, lobbyist; b. Aurora, Ill., Jan. 10, 1954; s. James Roscoe and Neoma Arlene (Thomas) B. BA in Polit. Sci., Pa. State U., 1976; postgrad., Am. U., 1980. Info. specialist Fed. Election Commn., Washington, 1976-78, chief of pub. records, 1978-81; dir. legis. and polit. issues U.S. C. of C., Washington, 1981-83; mgr. polit. affairs and state rels. S&A Restaurant Corp., Dallas, 1983-86; polit. affairs mgr. Southwestern Region, U.S. C. of C., Dallas, 1986-87; dir. congrl. rels. Fed. Trade Commn., Washington, 1987-90; dir. govt. rels., assoc. exec. dir. Nat. Roofing Contractors Assn., Washington, 1990—; mem. labor rels. com. U.S. C. of C., 1991—, mem. regulatory affairs com., U.S. C. of C., 1994—. Dep. voter registrar Dallas County, 1984; participant GOP Conv., Houston, 1992, New Orleans, 1988, Dallas, 1984, San Diego, 1996; del. Va. State GOP Conv., 1993. Republican. Avocation: running. Home: 1317 Prince St Alexandria VA 22314-2913 Office: Nat Roofing Contractors Assn 324 4th St NE Washington DC 20002-5821

BRIGNANO, RUSSELL CARL, English educator, research specialist; b. Hartford, Conn., June 26, 1935; s. Joseph Frank Brignano and Adelina Alda Accomasso; m. Mary Louise Germann, Jan. 24, 1969. BA, Dartmouth Coll., 1957; MS, U. Wis., 1963, PhD, 1966. Tchg. asst. English U. Wis., Madison, 1961-66; asst. prof., then assoc. prof. English Carnegie Mellon U., Pitts., 1966-75; assoc. prof. English Pa. State U., Monaca, 1975-96; emeritus prof. Pa. State U., University Park, 1997—; owner I/D Rsch., Pitts., 1999—; vis. assoc. prof. U. Pitts., 1970. Author: Richard Wright, 1970, Black Americans in Autobiography, 1974, rev. edit., 1984; contbr. articles to profl. jours. Local election judge, Pitts., 1992-96. With U.S. Army, 1957-59. Recipient Younger Humanist award NEH, 1970-71; Brigano Collection of African american autobiography at Pa. State U. Libr. dedicated in his honor. Mem. MLA. Avocations: travel, gardening, baseball. Home: 150 Hartwood Dr Pittsburgh PA 15208-2702

BRILEY, JOHN RICHARD, writer; b. Kalamazoo, June 25, 1925; s. William Treve and Mary Stella (Daly) B.; m. Dorothy Louise Reichart, Aug. 23, 1950; children: Dennis Patrick, Paul Christian, Mary Sydney, Shaun William. BA, U. Mich., 1951, MA, 1952; PhD, U. Birmingham, Eng., 1961. Lectr. Gen. Motors Detroit, 1947-50; dir. orientation USAF, London, 1955-60; writer MGM, Elstree, Eng., 1960-64; freelance writer Trevone Prodns. Inc., L.A. and Amersham, Eng., 1970—; Bob Shaye artist is residence U. Mich., 1995; vis. lectr. Univ. Mich., 1969. Author: (criticism) Shakespeare Survey, 1964, (novels) The Traitors, 1968, The Last Dance, 1978, Cry Freedom, 1988, The First Stone, 1997, (plays) Seven Bob a Buck, 1964, So Who Needs Men!, 1976; screenwriter: (films) (with Jack Trevor Story) Invasion Quartet, 1961, (with Story) Postman's Knock, 1962, Children of the Damned, 1964, Pope Joan, 1972, That Lucky Touch, 1975, The Medusa Touch, 1978, Eagle's Wing, 1979, Gandhi, 1982 (Academy award best original screenplay 1982), Enigma, 1983, Marie, 1985, (with Stanley Mann) Tai-Pan, 1986, Cry Freedom, 1987, (with Cary Bates and Mario Puzo) Christopher Columbus: The Discovery, 1992, , Molokai--The Story of Father Damien, 1999, (TV series) Hits & Misses, 1962, The Airbase, 1965. Served to capt. USAF, 1943-46. Recipient Golden Globe award Fgn. Press Assn., Los Angeles, 1983, Acad. award Acad. Motion Picture Arts and Scis., Los Angeles, 1983, Christopher award St. Christopher Soc., N.Y., 1983, 85, 88. Mem. Writers Guild Great Britain (exec. com. 1975-85), Writers Guild Am., Authors Guild, Dramatists Guild. Avocations: swimming, tennis, skiing. Home: PO Box 2365 Sun Valley ID 83353-2365

BRILL, AARON BERTRAND, nuclear medicine educator; b. N.Y.C., Dec. 19, 1928; s. Louis And Cecile (Sroge) B.; m. Joan Booth Morrison, Sept. 1, 1950; children: Paul, David, Laurie. AB, Grinnell Coll., 1949; MD, U. Utah, 1956; PhD in Biophysics, U. Calif., Berkeley, 1961. Statistician Contra Costa County Health Dept., Martinez, Calif., 1949-51; biophysicist U. Utah Pediatrics Dept., Salt Lake City, 1952-56; intern Salt Lake City Gen. Hosp., 1956-57; USPHS officer Div. of Radiol. Health, Rockville, Md., 1957-64; asst. prof. radiology dept. radiology scis. Johns Hopkins Hosp. and Sch. of Hygiene, 1961-64; assoc. prof. radiol. Vanderbilt U. Sch. Medicine, Nashville, 1964-72; assoc. prof. medicine, biomed. engring. and physics, 1964-79; prof. radiology Vanderbilt U. Sch. Medicine, Nashville, 1972-79,

SUNY, Stony Brook, 1979-87; sr. scientist, nuc. medicine coord. Brookhaven (N.Y.) Nat. Lab., 1979-87; prof. nuclear medicine U. Mass. Sch. Medicine, Worcester, 1987—; rsch. affiliate MIT, Cambridge, 1993—; affil. prof. Worcester Polytechnic Inst., Worcester, 1995-97; rsch. prof. radiol. sci. Vanderbilt U. Sch. Medicine, Nashville, 1997—, rsch. prof. physics, adj. prof. biomed. engring., 1998—. Editor: Low Level Radiation Fact Book, 1st edit. 1982, 2d edit., 1985; editor: IEEE Trans Med. Imaging, 1986-92. Med. dir. USPHS, 1957-64,. U. Calif. at Berkeley fellow, 1959-61. Fellow Inst. for elec. and electronic engring., Am. Coll. Nuclear Physicians, Am. Inst. Med. and Biol. Engring.; mem. NAS (com. on atomic casualties 1964-70, com. on biol. effects of ionizing radiation 1978-80; nat. coun. on radiation protection and measurement 1972-82, 92-97). Democrat. Unitarian. Avocations: tennis, sailing, skiing. Office: Vanderbilt U Med Sch Dept Radiol Sci MCN R-1302 Nashville TN 37232-2675

BRILL, ALAN RICHARD, entrepreneur; b. Evansville, Ind., July 5, 1942; s. Gregory and Bernice Lucille (Froman) B.; m. Valerie Hermes, 1998; AB, DePauw U., 1964; MBA, Harvard U., 1968; children: Jennifer Leigh, Katherine Anne, Alison Elizabeth. Mgmt. cons. Peace Corps, Ecuador, 1964-66; sr. acct., cons. Arthur Young & Co., N.Y.C., 1968-71; v.p. ops. Charter Med. Mgmt. Co., Inc. and v.p.-controller Hosp. Investors, Atlanta, 1972-73; v.p., treas., dir. Worrell Newspapers, Inc., and Worrell Broadcasting Inc., Charlottesville, Va., 1973-79; pres. Brill Assos., Evansville, Ind., 1979—, Brill Media Co., Inc., Evansville, 1980—; bd. visitors U. So. Ind. Sch. Bus. Mem. AICPA, N.Y. State Soc. CPAs, Evansville C. of C. (bd. dirs.), Jobs for S.W. Ind. (bd. dirs.), The Alliance: A Forum of Chairman and Presidents, Beacon Group. Republican. Methodist. Clubs: Farmington Country (Charlottesville), Safari Internat. Home: PO Box 3517 Evansville IN 47734-3517 Office: Brill Media Co Inc PO Box 3353 Evansville IN 47732-3353

BRILL, ARTHUR SYLVAN, biophysics educator; b. Phila., June 11, 1927; s. Edward Abram and Lillian (Milner) B.; m. Patricia Anne Hartig, Feb. 10, 1957; children: Julie Anne, Claire Bernice. AB in Physics with highest honors, U. Calif., Berkeley, 1949; PhD, U. Pa., 1956. Postdoctoral fellow in med. physics U. Pa., Phila., 1956-58; rsch. assoc. dept. engring. physics Cornell U., Ithaca, N.Y., 1959-60; asst. prof. biophysics Yale U., New Haven, Conn., 1961-64, assoc. prof. molecular biophysics, 1964-68; prof. materials sci. U. Va., Charlottesville, 1968-73, mem. Ctr. for Advanced Studies, 1968-71, prof. physics, 1973-97, program dir. interdisciplinary biophysics program, 1989-93, prof. emeritus, rsch. prof. physics, 1997—. Author: Transition Metals in Biochemistry, 1977; assoc. editor Biophys. Jour., 1978-81, publ. com., 1981-84; contbr. numerous articles to profl. jours., books. Cpl. U.S. Army, 1945-46. Predoctoral rsch. fellow NIH, U. Pa., 1950-55, Donner fellow in med. sci. NRC-Nat. Acad. Sci., Oxford U., Eng., 1958-59. Fellow Am. Phys. Soc. (chmn. div. biol. physics 1975-76, 90-91); mem. Biophys. Soc. (charter), Am. Chem. Soc., Microscopy Soc. Am. Office: Univ Va Dept Physics JW Beams Lab Physics Charlottesville VA 22903

BRILL, DONALD MAXIM, educator, writer, researcher; b. Elk Mound, Wis., Sept. 8, 1922; s. John James and Grace Darling (Mayo) B.; m. Meredith Joy Wright, June 25, 1955; children: John Richard, Rebecca Jean, Linda Marie, Susan Elizabeth. BS, Stout State U., 1947; MA, U. Minn., 1949; PhD, U. Wis., 1972. Tchr. Mpls. Pub. Schs., 1949-50, Eau Claire (Wis.) Pub. Schs., 1950, Chippewa Valley Tech. Coll., 1951-58; supr. Wis. Tech. Colls., Madison, 1958-65; coord. Great Cities Program for Sch. Improvement Rsch. Coun., Chgo., 1965-67; supr. rsch. Wis. Tech. Colls., Madison, 1967-70, asst. state dir., 1970-83; adj. prof. U. Wis., Stout, 1983-86. Mem. state com. for employment support of Guard and Res., 1983-86; mem. Eau Claire Dist. Sch. Bd., 1989-92; bd. dirs. Fourth Dimension, Inc., WHEM-FM, 1994-98, ret. 1998; primary candidate 3d Congl. Dist., Wis., 1994. With U.S. Army, 1942-45, ETO. Mem. DAV, VFW, SAR, Am. Vocat. Assn. (life). Republican. Baptist. Avocations: writing, genealogy, poetry, travel, restoring Victorian home. Home: 316 Hudson St Eau Claire WI 54703-5447

BRILL, EDWARD N., hotel executive; b. Mpls., Dec. 29, 1951. BS in Mktg., U. Minn., 1951. With Marriott Hotels and Resorts; v.p. sales and mktg. Continental Cos., J.C. Penney Travel Svcs., 1985-87; pres., prin. Four Winds Travel Inc., 1987-90; sr. v.p. the Americas SRS-Worldhotels, 1990—. Office: SRS Hotels 152 West 57th St 33nd Fl New York NY 10019

BRILL, GERRILYN G., federal judge; b. 1951. JD, Emory U., 1975. Bar: Ga. Assoc. Harmon and Smith, 1975-76; with Office of U.S. Atty. (no. dist.) Ga., 1978-94; magistrate judge U.S. Dist. Ct. (no. dist.) Ga., Atlanta, 1995—. Mem. Fed. Bar Assn., State Bar Ga., Atlanta Bar Assn. Office: 1690 US Courthouse 75 Spring St SW Atlanta GA 30303-3309

BRILL, JAMES P., petroleum engineer, educator; b. Mpls., July 18, 1938. BS, U. Minn., 1962; PhD in Engring., U. Tex., Austin, 1966. Rsch. engr. Chevron Oil Co., 1965-66; prof. engring. U. Tulsa, 1966-87, Floyd M. Stevenson presdl. chair petroleum engring., 1987—. Recipient Prodn. Engring. award Soc. Petroleum Engrs., 1994, John Franklin Carll award, 1997. Mem. Nat. Acad. Engring. Home: 6914 E 64th Pl Tulsa OK 74133-4001 Office: Tulsa U Dept Engring 600 S College Ave Dept Engring Tulsa OK 74104-3189*

BRILL, LESLEY, literature and film studies educator; b. Chgo., Sept. 3, 1943; s. Walter Henry and Fay (Trolander) B.; m. Megan Parry, Jan. 18, 1970; children: Benjamin, Calista. BA, U. Chgo., 1965; MA, SUNY, Binghamton, 1967; Ph.D., Rutgers U., 1971. Asst. prof. English U. Colo., Boulder, 1970-80, assoc. prof., 1981-89, chmn. dept. English, 1981-85, grad. dir., 1985-87; prof. and chmn. dept. English Wayne State U., Detroit, 1989-94; vis. lectr. U. Kent, Canterbury, Eng., 1978-79; vis. prof. U. Paul Valery, Montpellier, France, 1984, U. de Nantes, France, 1995. Author: The Hitchcock Romance: Love and Irony in Hitchcock's Films, 1988, John Huston's Filmmaking, 1997; contbr. articles on lit. and film to profl. jours. Rockefeller Found. fellow, 1977-78. Mem. Soc. Cinema Studies. Office: Wayne State U Dept English Detroit MI 48202

BRILL, MARLENE TARG, writer; b. Chgo., Sept. 27, 1945; d. Irving and Genevieve (Worshill) Targ; m. Richard Benjamin Brill, Feb. 4, 1973; 1 child, Alison. BS in Spl. Edn., U. Ill., 1967; MS, Roosevelt U., 1973. Spl. edn. tchr. Dept. Mental Health, Chgo., 1967-70, Chgo. Bd. Edn., 1970-73; spl. educator Wayne County Intermediate Sch., Detroit, 1973-75; curriculum specialist Cook County Office of Pub. Instrn., Chgo., 1975-78; media coord. South Metropolitan Assn., South Holland, Ill., 1979-80; writer, author MTB Comms., Wilmette, Ill., 1980—. Author: Hide-and-Seek Safety, 1985, John Adams, 1986, I Can Be a Lawyer, 1987, James Buchanan, 1988, Rainy Days and Rainbows, 1989, Why Do We Have To?, 1991, Keys to Parenting a Child with Down Syndrome, 1993, Guatemala, 1993, Allen Jay & The Underground Railroad, 1993, Trail of Tears: A Journey from Home, 1994, Keys to Parenting a Child with Autism, 1994, Guyana, 1994, Extraordinary Young People, 1996, Building the Capital City, 1996, Illinois, 1996, Honduras, 1996, Journey for Peace: The Story of Rigoberta Menchu, 1996, Let Women Vote, 1996, Women for Peace, 1997, Indiana, 1997, Short Mort and the Big Bully, 1997, Tooth Tales From Around the World, 1998, Michigan, 1998, The Diary of a Drummer Boy, 1998, The AMA Book of Asthma, 1998, Sport Success: Winning Women in Ice Hockey, 1999, Sport Success: Winning Women in Soccer, 1999. Mem. Soc. Midland Authors, Soc. Children's Book Writers and Illustrators, Children's Reading Round Table. Avocations: reading, music, drawing, crafts, walking. Office: MTB Comms 314 Lawndale St Wilmette IL 60091-3215

BRILL, RALPH DAVID, architect, real estate developer, venture capitalist; b. Nov. 24, 1944; came to U.S., 1949; naturalized, 1955; s. Walter and Irmgard (Levy) B.; m. Gail J. Koff, Oct. 8, 1978; children: Micah Levy, Loren Koff, Wade Sydney. Student, U. Ill., 1962-66; student urban design, Kunstskolen, Copenhagen, 1967. Registered architect; lic. real estate broker, N.Y. V.p., founder Node 4 Assocs., Inc., Bklyn., 1968-70; dir. devel. Townland Mktg. and Devel. Corp., Cherry Hill, N.J., 1970-72; pres. Ralph Brill Assocs., Garrison, N.Y., 1973—; ptnr. Brill Kawakami Wilbourne, Architects, Cold Spring, N.Y., N.Y.C. and Telluride, Colo., 1973-93, Deer Hollow Ptnrs., 1984—, Manhattan Strategic Venture Fund, 1988—, Cara Ventures, 1988-93, Woodbury Tech. Ventures, 1992—; pres. Finsky Group Inc., 1974-88, White Column Farms, Pawlet, Vt., 1988—, Southmont Devel. Group, Inc., Montrose, Colo., 1993—; founder Manitou Realty, Cold Spring, 1976—, Swallow Comm., Cold Spring, 1982—; archtl. critic Columbia U., 1969; adj. asst. prof. urban sys. Fairleigh Dickinson U., 1974-76; chmn. Dutchess Ptnrs., Inc., N.Y.C., 1989; bd. dirs. Brill GmbH, Herzebrock. Author: The Hudson River Catalogue, 1978. Bd. dirs. Garrison Art Ctr., 1976-83, Spectra Arts, 1983-88, Chapel of Our Lady Restoration, 1977; co-chmn. Prism Applicance Sys., Inc., 1992-96, Ster-L-Tech, Inc., 1996. Grantee N.Y. State Hist. Preservation, 1977, Pure Water Technologies, Inc., 1988—; recipient First Honors award Mid-Hudson AIA, 1988, 89. Mem. Soc. Indsl. Archeology, Ctr. for Hudson River Valley. Jewish. Home: PO Box 200 Garrison NY 10524-0200 Office: 77 Main St Cold Spring NY 10516-0248 also: PO Box 3559 Montrose CO 81402-3559

BRILL, WINSTON JONAS, microbiologist, educator, research director, publisher and management consultant; b. London, June 16, 1939; came to U.S., 1949; s. Walter and Irmgard (Levy) B.; m. Nancy Carol Weisburd, June 11, 1964; 1 child, Eric David. B.A., Rutgers U., 1961; Ph.D. in Microbiology, U. Ill., 1965. Postdoctoral fellow MIT, Cambridge, 1965-67; asst. prof. dept. bacteriology U. Wis., Madison, 1967-70, assoc. prof., 1970-74, prof., 1974-79, Vilas research prof., 1979-83, adj. prof., 1983—; v.p., dir. research Agracetus, 1981-89; pres. Winston J. Brill & Assocs., Madison, 1989—; panel mem. NSF, USDA, Pontifical Acad. Scis.; mem. recombinant DNA adv. com. NIH, 1979-83; mem. policy adv. com. USDA, 1985—; mem. genetic engring. adv. panel to U.S. sec. state, 1981; mem. exec. bd. Nat. Inst. Emerging Tech. Pub., editor: Innovative Leader, 1992—; mem. editl. bd. Jour. Biotech., Trends in Biotech., Critical Revs. in Biotech.; contbr. articles to profl. jours. Recipient Eli Lilly award in microbiology and immunology, 1979, Alexander von Humboldt Found. award, 1979, Award of Distinction U. Wis., 1990; Henry Rutgers fellow Rutgers U., 1961. Fellow AAAS, Am. Acad. Microbiology; mem. NAS, Am. Soc. Microbiology, Am. Soc. Plant Physiologists, Am. Soc. Biochemistry and Molecular Biology, Internat. Soc. Plant Molecular Biology.

BRILL, YVONNE CLAEYS, engineer, consultant; b. St. Norbert, Manitoba, Canada, Dec. 30, 1924; d. August and Julienne (Carette) Claeys; m. William Franklin Brill, Dec. 15, 1951; children: Naomi, Matthew, Joseph. BS, U. Manitoba, Canada, 1945; MS, U. So. Calif., 1951. Mathematician Douglas Aircraft, Santa Monica, Calif., 1945-46; research analyst Rand Corp., Santa Monica, 1946-49; group leader Marquardt Corp., Van Nuys, Calif., 1949-52; staff engr. UTC Research, East Hartford, Conn., 1952-55; project engr. Wright Aeronautical, Wood Ridge, N.J., 1955-58; mgr. propulsion systems RCA AstroElectronics, Princeton, N.J., 1966-81, staff engr., 1983-86; mgr. solid rocket motor NASA Hdqrs., Washington, 1981-83; with space engring segment Internat. Maritime Satellite Orgn., London, 1986-91; cons. Brill Assocs., Skillman, N.J., 1991—; mem. USAF Sci. Adv. Bd., Washington, 1982-83, Nat. Acad. Engring.; Com. on Internat. Orgns. and Programs, 1992-96; apptd. mem. aerospace safety adv. panel NASA, 1994—. Contbr. articles to sci. jours.; patentee in field. Bd. dirs. Princeton YWCA, 1981-82. Recipient Engr. of Yr. award Cen. Jersey Engring. Councils, 1979, Diamond Superwoman award Harpers Bazaar/DeBeers Corp., 1980, Marvin C. Demlar award AIAA, 1983; inductee Women in Tech. Internat. Hall of Fame, 1999. Fellow AIAA, Soc. Women Engrs. (dir. student affairs 1979-80, 83-84, treas. 1980-81, Engring. Achievement award 1986, Resnik Challenger medal 1993); mem. NAE, Internat. Astronautical Acad. (academician, edn. com. 1983-85), Sigma Xi, Tau Beta Pi. Republican. Avocations: needlework, sewing, dress designing. Home and Office: 914 Route 518 Skillman NJ 08558-2616

BRILL DE RAMÍREZ, SUSAN BERRY, English educator; b. N.Y.C., Apr. 25, 1955; d. Robert M. and Dorothy Ann (Retallack) B. Student, St. Johns Coll., 1974-75; BA in English, U. Wis., 1977; MA in English, U. Chgo., 1978; MBA in Mgmt., U. Wis., 1982; PhD in English, U. N.Mex., 1991. Asst. prof. English Bradley U., Peoria, Ill., 1991-97, assoc. prof. English, 1997—. Author: Wittgenstein and Critical Theory, 1995, Contemporary American Indian Literatures and the Oral Tradition, 1999; mem. editl. adv. bd. Jour. Baha'i Studies; mem. editl. bd. Jour. Comm. and Rels. Mem. MLA, Nat. Women's Studies Assn., Nat. Coun. Tchrs. of English, Semiotic Soc. Am., Internat. Assn. Philosophy and Lit., Assn. Study Am. Indian Lit., Assn. Baha'i Studies, Phi Kappa Phi. Avocations: weight lifting, running. Office: Bradley U English Dept Peoria IL 61625

BRILLIANT, BARBARA, television host, producer, columnist, consultant, journalist, communications and media consultant; b. Montreal, Que., Canada, Sept. 24, 1935; d. Saul and Esther (Saltzman) Lecker; m. Erwin Brilliant, June 29, 1958; children: Bradley, Todd, Michelle. Student, McGill Tchrs. Coll., 1953, McGill Conservatory of Music; AA, Sir George Williams U., Montreal, 1955; BA in Psychology summa cum laude, Boston Coll., 1975. Tchr. Protestant Sch. Bd., Montreal, 1953-58, dir. drama sch., 1957-58; artist-in-residence City of Boston, 1978-83; TV host, producer Sta. WBZ-TV, Boston, 1979-90; freelance news producer AARP News Network, 1989—; freelance writer, composer, lyricist; columnist A&E Picks, "Dear Barbara," advice for people 40 plus; advisor Radcliff Coll., Cambridge, Mass., 1985—; pres. SpeechWorks; media and pub. speaking coach and trainer; TV location host New England Cable News "Time For Living" program; free-lance journalist Boston Herald, Boston Bus. Jour., Banker and Tradesman, Cape Cod Times, Wedding Day; aerobics instr. various workout ctrs. Actress Montreal area, 1957-58, Boston area, 1985—; artistic dir. City of Boston, 1985—; vocalist, mus. dir. Two on the Aisle, Newton, Mass., 1985—; contbg. writer Vitality Mag., Wedding Day Mag., Boston Woman Mag., Boston Herald, N.H. Senior Times, Cape Cod Times, among others; composer songs (with Charles Segal) You're Not Alone, Time to Care, Talk to Me, many others; columnist: "Tell It to Barbara" in the Jewish Advocate, 1992—, Senior Times, Arts & Entertainment, A&E Picks; prodr., co-host (nat. cabl TV show) Barbara & Bill, Conversations with the Conducotr (Best Program award 1997); special corr. arts and entertainment editor Time for Living, New England Cable News, 1996; journalist Opportunity Mag., Boston Herald, Boston Bus. Jour., Banker & Tradesman; composer, lyricist, prodr. (CD) Brilliant!. Advisor Cultural Affairs Commn., Newton, Mass., 1980-82, Nat. Com. to Study and Resolve Problems of Older Ams., Boston, 1984—; mem. adv. bd. Radcliffe Coll. Women; spokesperson Alzheimers Disease and Related Disorders aslsn., Boston, 1985—; mem. White House Conf. on Aging, Washington, 1981; mem. Time Capsule Harvard Schlessinger Libr., Cambridge, Mass., 1980; advisor to Mass. Sec. Elder Affairs, 1992-93. Recipient Cert. of Recognition City of Boston, 1979, Media award Am. Assn.Retired Persons, 1980, Lifestyle Achievement award WW Group Internat., Boston, 1987, Sandoz Gerentol. Found. awards, 1989, 91; Nat. Press Found., fellow Washington, 1987; named to Hon. Order Ky. Cols., 1987, One of Boston's 100 Most Interesting Women, Boston Woman Mag., 1988, Gov. Michael Dukakis proclamation service in media to elderly, 1989; Mayor Raymond Flynn declared Barbara Brilliant Day, Sept. 24, 1989; Awareness of Aging tree planted in her honor Newton City Hall, Bronze/Nat. Mature Media award for "Barbara Bill" 6 part TV series exec. producer, co-host Barbara Brilliant. Mem. Screen Actors Guild, Am. Fedn. TV and Radio Artists. Avocations: singing, tennis, piano, reading, aerobics. Office: Brilliant Communications PO Box 610310 Newton MA 02461-0310

BRILLIANT, RICHARD, art history educator; b. Boston, Nov. 20, 1929; s. Frank and Pauline (Apt) B.; m. Eleanor Luria, June 24, 1951; children: Stephanie, Livia, Franca, Myron. BA magna cum laude, Yale U., 1951, MA, 1957, PhD, 1960; LLB, Harvard U., 1954. Bar: Mass. 1954. From asst. prof. to prof., chmn. dept. art history U. Pa., Phila., 1962-70; prof. art history and archaeology Columbia U., N.Y.C., 1970—, Anna S. Garbedian prof. in the Humanities, 1990—; vis. Mellon prof. fine arts U. Pitts., 1971; vis. prof. Princeton U., 1986; vis. prof. Scuola Normale Superiore, Pisa, Italy, 1974, 80, 88; chmn. governing bd. Soc. Fellows Columbia U., 1981-84; cons. Sta. WNET-TV, N.Y., 1984-89; dir. Italian Acad. for Advanced Studies in Am., Columbia U., 1996—. Author: Gesture and Rank in Roman Art, 1966, Arch of Septimius Severus in the Roman Forum, 1967, The Arts of the Ancient Greeks, 1973, Roman Art, 1974, Pompeii: A.D. 79, 1979, Visual Narratives, 1984, Portraiture, 1991, Commentaries on Roman Art, 1994, Facing the New World, 1997; co-author: (film) The Fayum Portraits, 1988, editor Art Bull., 1990-94; co-curator exhbn. Ctr. for African Art, N.Y.C., 1990; guest curator, exhibitor Jewish Mus., N.Y.C., 1997. Fulbright grantee Rome, Italy, 1957-59; fellow Am. Acad. in Rome, 1960-62; Guggenheim fellow, 1967-68; NEH sr. fellow, 1972-73. Mem. Mass. Bar Assn., Coll. Art Assn., Am. Numis. Soc. (Roman/Byzantine com. 1976—), German Archaeol. Inst. (corr.), Am. Sch. Classical Studies (mng. com. 1974—), Conn. Acad. Arts and Scis., N.Y. Acad. Sci., Phi Beta Kappa. Democrat. Avocations: reading, travel, wine. Home: 10 Wayside Ln Scarsdale NY 10583-2908 Office: Columbia U Dept Art History New York NY 10027

BRILLIANT, ROBERT LEE, advertising agency executive; b. Boston, May 16, 1948; s. Harold and Charlotte (Prince) B.; m. Karen Kaufteil, July 1, 1973; children: Jamie, Ashley. BA, U. Va., 1970; cert. in acctg., Bentley Coll., 1973; MBA, NYU, 1976. CPA, N.Y. Asst. mgr. Coopers & Lybrand, Boston, 1973-75; mgr. Citibank, N.Y.C., 1975-78; asst. corp. contr. Pepsico, Purchase, N.Y., 1978-82; mgr. Tonche Ross, N.Y.C., 1982; sr. v.p., contr. Benton & Bowles (now Darcy Masins Benton & Bowles), N.Y.C., 1983-85; exec. v.p. fin. and adminstrn. Klemtner Advt., N.Y.C., 1985—. Treas. Blind Brook Sch. Dist., Rye Brook, N.Y., 1988—. With USAR, 1970-76. Home: 9 Parkridge Ct Rye Brook NY 10573-1944 Office: Klemtner Advt 375 Hudson St New York NY 10014-3658*

BRILLSTEIN, BERNIE J., producer, talent manager; b. N.Y.C., Apr. 26, 1932; s. Moe and Tillie Brillstein; m. Deborah Ellen Koskoff, 1975; children: Leigh, David Koskoff, Nick Koskoff, Michael, Kate. BS in Advt., NYU. Mailroom/talent rep. William Morris Agy., N.Y.C., 1955-64; talent rep. Mgmt. III, N.Y.C., 1964-69; packager, owner, producer The Brillstein Co., L.A., 1969—; CEO Lorimar Film Entertainment, L.A., 1996—; co-chair Brillstein-Grey Entertainment, Beverly Hills, Calif., 1991-96. Exec. producer (TV) Alf, It's The Garry Shandling Show, The Days and Nights of Molly Dodd; exec. producer (films) Dangerous Liaisons, Blues Brothers, Ghostbusters I and II, Larry Sanders Show, Neighbors, Continental Divide, Spies Like Us, Celluloid Closet, Cat and Mouse, Happy Gilmore. Served with U.S. Army, 1953-55. Recipient Peabody awards, Emmy nominations, Cable Ace award; honoree L.A. Free Clinic, 1987. Mem. N.Y. Friars Club, Beverly Hills C. of C. (bd. dirs.), Acad. Motion Picture Arts and Scis., TV Acad. Office: care Lorimar Film Entertainment Warner Bros Inc 4000 Warner Blvd Burbank CA 91522*

BRIM, ORVILLE GILBERT, JR., former foundation administrator, author; b. Elmira, N.Y., Apr. 7, 1923; s. Orville G(ilbert) and Helen (Whittier) B.; m. Kathleen J. Vigneron, May 30, 1944; children: John G., Scott W., Margaret L., Sarah M. B.A., Yale U., 1947, M.A., 1949, Ph.D. in Sociology, 1951. Instr. sociology U. Wis., 1952-53, asst. prof., 1953-55; sociologist Russell Sage Found., N.Y.C., 1955-64; asst. sec. Russell Sage Found., 1959-64, pres., 1964-72, trustee, 1964-72, cons., 1972-74; pres. Found. for Child Devel., 1974-85; mem. core study group MacArthur Found. Rsch. Program Successful Aging, 1985-89; dir. MacArthur Found. Rsch. Network on Successful Mid Life Devel., 1989—; pres. Life Trends, Inc., 1991—; vis. scholar Russell Sage Found., 1985-86; interim pres. Social Sci. Rsch. Coun., 1998—; vice chmn. Am. Inst. for Research, 1971-88, chmn. 1988-91; chmn. bd. dirs. Automation Engring. Lab., 1959-67; dir. Consumer Behavior, Inc., 1957-61; chmn. environ. panel U.S. Office Edn., 1962-64; mem. drug research bd. Nat. Acad. Scis., 1964-66, adv. com. on child devel., 1971-76; mem. mental health tng. com. NIMH, 1959-62; chmn. commn. social scis. NSF, 1968-69; nat. adv. food and drug council HEW, 1967-69; chmn. com. on work and personality in middle years Social Sci. Research Council, 1972-79; trustee Found. for Child Devel., 1972-85, Center for Creative Leadership, 1972-78, Mental Health Law Project, 1973-77, William T. Grant Found., 1975-84, Greenwich Hosp., 1972-77. Author: Sociology and the Field of Education, 1958, Education for Child Rearing, 1959, Personality and Decision Processes, 1962, Intelligence: Perspectives 1965, 1966, Socialization after Childhood: Two Essays, 1966, American Beliefs and Attitudes Toward Intelligence, 1969, The Dying Patient, 1970, Learning to Be Parents, 1980, Ambition: How We Manage Success and Failure Throughout Our Lives, 1992; editor: Lifespan Development and Behavior, Vol. 2-6, 1979-83, Constancy and Change in Human Development, 1980; cons. editor: Child Devel., 1958-61, Sociology of Edn., 1963-69, Sociometry, 1959-62; mem. publ. com.: The Public Interest, 1967-75. Served as 1st lt. USAAF, 1943-46. Recipient Wilbur Lucius Cross medal Yale Grad. Sch. Assn., 1975; Kurt Lewin Meml. award Soc. Psychol. Study Social Issues, 1979. Fellow Am. Sociol. Assn., Am. Psychol. Assn., Am. Acad. Arts and Scis., AAAS, Am. Orthopsychiat. Assn. (pres. 1974-75), Eastern Sociol. Soc. (pres. 1971-72); mem. Inst. Medicine of Nat. Acad. Scis., Soc. Research Child Devel. (Disting. Sci. Contbns.award, 1985).

BRIM, SUE, community health nurse; b. North Chgo., Ill., Aug. 28, 1956; d. Norman and Janet (Nibur) Zeldis; m. Jim Brim, May 9, 1987. BSN, Syracuse U., 1978. RN, Calif. Nursing asst. instr. Cabrillo Sch. Nursing, San Diego; nursing supr. San Diego Home Patient Care; nursing supr. Spl. Care, San Diego, home care RN. Mem. APHA, Nat. Nurses Assn., NAFE. Home: 11413 Matinal Cir San Diego CA 92127-1235

BRIMBLE, ALAN, business executive; b. Langwith, Eng., June 5, 1930; came to U.S., 1967; s. Arthur George and May (Emery) B. BA with honors, St. Edmund Hall, Oxford (Eng.) U., 1952, MA, 1958; fellow, Chartered Inst. Secs. Asst. sec. Crompton Parkinson Ltd., London, 1960-62; music and arts programmes organizer BBC-TV, 1962-67; sec., controller St. Louis Art Mus., 1969-79; dir. adminstrn. Conv. and Visitors Bur. Greater Kansas City, Mo., 1979-87; fin. cons., plan adminstr., 1987—. Mem. citizens com. Met. St. Louis Zoo-Mus. Dist., 1970-71; bd. dirs. Internat. Inst., St. Louis, 1970-73, Kansas City Arts Coun., 1980-84; v.p., CFO Meridian Residential Assn., 1995-99. With RAF, 1948-49. Mem. Meridian Master Assn. (pres. 1997—). Home: 700 Front St Ste 2304 San Diego CA 92101

BRIMELOW, PETER, journalist; b. Warrington, Eng., Oct. 13, 1947; s. Frank Sanderson and Bessie (Knox) B.; m. Margaret Alice Laws, 1980; children: Alexander James Frank, Hannah Claire Catherine. BA in history and econs. with honors, U. Sussex, Eng., 1970; MBA, Stanford U., 1972. Security analyst Richardson Securities of Can., Winnipeg, Man., 1972-73; asst. editor Fin. Post, Toronto, Ont., Can., 1973-76, columnist, contbg. editor, 1978-80, 88-90; bus. editor Maclean's mag., Toronto, 1976-78; guest writer editorial page Wall St. Jour., N.Y.C., summer 1978; econ. counsel to U.S. Senator Orrin G. Hatch of Utah, Washington, 1979-81; columnist Toronto Sun Syndicate, 1980-82; assoc. editor Barron's, N.Y.C., 1981-83, contbg. editor, 1984-86; assoc. editor Fortune, N.Y.C., 1983-84; sr. editor Forbes, N.Y.C., 1986—, Nat. Rev. Mag., 1993-98; contbg. editor Chief Exec. mag., N.Y.C., 1984-86, Influence mag., Toronto, 1984-86; columnist The Times, London, 1986-90. Author: The Wall Street Gurus: How You Can Profit from the Investment Newsletters, 1986, The Patriot Game: Canada and the Canadian Question Revisited, 1987, Alien Nation: Common Sense About America's Immigration Disaster, 1995; contbr. articles to profl. jours. Recipient Fulbright award, 1970, Nat. Bus. Writing award Royal Bank Can./Toronto Press Club, 1976, Nat. Bus. Writing citation, 1977, Gerald Loeb award, 1990; Stanford U. scholarship, 1970. Episcopalian. E-mail: pbrimelow@forbes.com. Office: Forbes Mag Forbes Bldg 60 5th Ave New York NY 10011-8802

BRIMEYER, JAMES LEON, English educator; b. Dubuque, Iowa, July 19, 1947; s. Leon Joseph and Grace Carolyn (Link) B.; m. Kay Ann Frye, Aug. 8, 1970; children: Joseph, Ellen. BA, Lora Coll., Dubuque, 1969, MA, 1977. Tchr. Beckman H.S., Dyersville, Iowa, 1969-70, Wahlert H.S., Dubuque, 1970-95; instr. English N.E. Iowa C.C., Peosta, 1995—; cons. tchg. English, Advanced Placement, Evanston, Ill., 1995—; edn. presenter numerous confs. Named State of Iowa Outstanding Tchr. Iowa Dept. Instrn., 1987-88, Educator of the Yr., U. Notre Dame, 1996; recipient Outstanding Tchr. award U. Chgo., 1989, Tchg. Excellence award NISOD, U. Tex., Austin, 1997. Avocations: reading, walking, golf. Home: 2630 Marywood Dr Dubuque IA 52001-0707

BRIMIJOIN, WILLIAM STEPHEN, pharmacology educator, neuroscience researcher; b. Passaic, N.J., July 1, 1942; s. William Owen and Georgiana (Macklin) B.; m. Margaret Murray Ross, June 22, 1964; children: Megan Rebekkah Brimijoin Vaules, William Owen, Alexander. AB in Psychology, Harvard Coll., 1964; PhD in Pharmacology, Harvard U., 1969. Asst. prof Mayo Med. Sch., Rochester, Minn., 1972-76, assoc. prof., 1976-80, prof. pharmacology, 1980—, Winston and Iris Clement prof., 1989—; chair dept. pharmacology Mayo Clinic, Rochester, Minn., 1993—; assoc. cons. Mayo Clinic Rochester Minn., 1971-72, cons. 1972—; vis. scientist Karolinska Inst. Stockholm, Sweden, 1978-79, U. Würzburg, Germany, 1987-88; assoc. dir. dean Mayo Grad. Sch., Rochester, 1983-87; mem. behavioral and neuroscience study sect. NIH, 1989-93, scientific adv. panel

U.S. EPA, 1993—; mem. Gulf War Grants Rev. Bd. Dept. Def., 1997. Mem. editorial bd. Muscle and Nerve Journal, 1980-88, Diabetes Journal, 1985-93; contbr. to numerous profl. jour. With USPHS, 1969-71. Recipient Career Devel. award NIH, 1975, Javits Neuroscience Investigator award NINDS, 1987, Sr. Disting. U.S. Scientist award Humboldt Found., 1987-88, Mayo Disting. Investigator award Mayo Clinic, 1993. Mem. Soc. Neuroscience (social issues com. 1987), Internat. Soc. Neurochemistry, Am. Soc. Neurochemistry (program com. 1993-94), Am. Soc. Pharmacology and Exptl. Therapeutics. Office: Mayo Clinic Dept of Pharmacology 200 1st St SW Dept Of Rochester MN 55905-0002*

BRIMLEY, WILFORD, actor; b. Salt Lake City, Sept. 27, 1934; m. Lynne Brimley; children: Jim, John, Bill. Appeared in films, True Grit, 1969, including The Lawman, 1971, The China Syndrome, 1979, The Electric Horseman, 1979, Brubaker, 1980, Borderline, 1980, Absence of Malice, 1981, Death Valley, 1982, The Thing, 1982, Tender Mercies, 1983, Tough Enough, 1983, 10 to Midnight, 1983, High Road to China, 1983, The Natural, 1984, Harry and Son, 1984, Country, 1984, The Hotel New Hampshire, 1984, The Stone Boy, 1984, The Natural, 1984, Cocoon, 1985, American Justice, 1985, Remo Williams, The Adventure Begins, 1985, End of the Line, 1988, Cocoon II: The Return, 1988, Eternity, 1990, The Firm, 1993, Hard Target, 1994, Mutant Species, 1995, Last of the Dogmen, 1995, My Fellow Americans, 1996, In and Out, 1997, The Apostle, 1997, A Place to Grow, 1996, Chapter Perfect, 1996, Lunker LAke, 1997, Summer of the Monkeys, 1998; star of TV series Our House, 1986-88, Boys of Twilight; TV films include The Wild West Revisited, 1979, Rodeo Girl, 1980, Amber Waves, 1980, Roughnecks, 1980, Murder in Space, 1985, Ewoks: The Battle for Endor, 1985, Thompson's Last Run, 1986, The Good Old Boys, 1995, OP Center, 1995.

BRIMMER, ANDREW FELTON, economic and financial consultant; b. Newellton, La., Sept. 13, 1926; s. Andrew and Vellar (Davis) B.; m. Doris Millicent Scott, July 18, 1953; 1 dau., Esther Diane. B.A., U. Wash., 1950, M.A., 1951; postgrad. (Fulbright fellow), U. Bombay, India, 1951-52; Ph.D., Harvard U., 1957; LL.D., Nebr. Wesleyan U., 1968, Marquette U., 1968, L.I. U., 1969, Oberlin Coll., 1969, Tufts U., 1970, Colgate U., 1970, Atlanta U., 1970, Middlebury Coll., 1971, U. Notre Dame, 1971, Bishop Coll., 1971, Upsala Coll., 1972, U. Md., 1976, U. Mich., 1979, U. So. Calif., 1980, Washington U., 1982; D.Soc.Sc., Boston Coll., 1971, Temple U., 1974; D.C.L., U. Miami, 1971, U. of the South, 1984; D.H.L., DePaul U., 1975. Economist Fed. Res. Bank, N.Y.C., 1955-58; asst. prof. Mich. State U., 1958-61, Wharton Sch. Finance and Commerce, U. Pa., 1961-66; dep. asst. sec. Dept. Commerce, Washington, 1963-65; asst. sec. for econ. affairs Dept. Commerce, 1965-66; mem. Fed. Res. Bd., 1966-74; Thomas Henry Carroll Ford Found. vis. prof. Grad. Sch. Bus. Adminstrn. Harvard, 1974-76; pres. Brimmer & Co., Inc., Washington, 1976—; Wilmer D. Barrett prof. econs. U. Mass.-Amherst; bd. govs., vice chmn. Commodity Exchange, Inc.; bd. dirs. Bank of Am., Am. Security Bank, MNC Fin., Inc., Du Pont Co., Gannett Co., Inc., BellSouth Corp., Conn. Mut., Navistar Internat. Corp., Blackstone Investment Income Trust; mem. Fed. Res. Central Banking Mission to Sudan, 1957; cons. SEC, 1962-63; mem. Trilateral Commn.; trustee Coll. Retirement Equities Fund. Author: Survey of Mutual Funds Investors, 1963, Life Insurance Companies in Capital Market, 1962, Economic Development: International and African Perspectives, 1976, The World Banking System: Outlook in a Context of Crisis, 1985, International Banking and Domestic Economic Policies, 1986; Contbr. articles to profl. jours. Chmn. bd. trustees Tuskegee U., Com. for Econ. Devel.; bd. dirs. Interracial Council for Bus. Opportunity; mem. internat. panel UN Mgmt. and Decision Making Project, 1986-88; panel on fgn. trade stats. NAS. With AUS, 1945-46. Named Govt. Man of Year Nat. Bus. League, 1963; recipient Arthur S. Flemming award, 1966, Russworm award, 1966, Capital Press Club award, 1966, Golden Plate award Am. Acad. Achievement, 1967, Alumnus Summa Laude Dignatus U. Wash. Alumni Assn., 1972, Nat. Honoree Beta Gamma Sigma, 1971, Horatio Alger award, 1974, Equal Opportunity award Nat. Urban League, 1974, One Hundred Black Men and N.Y. Urban Coalition award, 1975, Disting. Svc. award Interracial Coun. Bus. Opportunity, 1986, Pub. Svc. award North Adams State Coll., 1987. Fellow Am. Acad. Arts and Scis., Nat. Assn. Bus. Economists; mem. Am. Econ. Assn. (Richard T. Ely lectr. 1982, v.p. 1989), Am. Fin. Assn., Assn. for Study Afro-Am. Life and History (pres. 1970-73, 89—), Coun. Fgn. Rels., Nat. Economists Club, Am. Statis. Assn., Soc. Govt. Economists (Disting. lectr. on econs. in govt. 1988), Ea. Econ. Assn. (v.p. 1989). Office: Brimmer & Co Inc 4400 Macarthur Blvd NW Washington DC 20007-2521*

BRIMMER, CLARENCE ADDISON, federal judge; b. Rawlins, Wyo., July 11, 1922; s. Clarence Addison and Geraldine (Zingsheim) B.; m. Emily O. Docken, Aug. 2, 1953; children: Geraldine Ann, Philip Andrew, Andrew Howard, Elizabeth Ann. BA, U. Mich., 1944, JD, 1947. Bar: Wyo. 1948. Pvt. practice law Rawlins, 1948-71, mcpl. judge, 1948-54; U.S. commr., magistrate, 1963-71; atty. gen. Wyo. Cheyenne, 1971-74; U.S. atty., 1975; chief judge U.S. Dist. Ct. Wyo., Cheyenne, 1975-92, dist. judge, 1975—; mem. panel multi-dist. litigation, 1992—; mem. Jud. Conf. U.S., 1994-97, exec., 1995-97. Sec. Rawlins Bd. Pub. Utilities, 1954-66; Rep. gubernatorial candidate, 1974; trustee Rocky Mountain Mineral Law Found., 1963-75. With USAAF, 1945-46. Mem. ABA, Wyo. Bar Assn., Laramie County Bar Assn., Carbon County Bar Assn., Am. Judicature Soc., Masons, Shriners, Rotary. Episcopalian. Office: US Dist Ct PO Box 985 Cheyenne WY 82003-0985

BRIN, ROYAL HENRY, JR., lawyer; b. Dallas, Oct. 9, 1919. B.A., U. Tex., 1941, J.D., 1941; postgrad. fellow, Harvard U., 1941-42. Bar: Tex. 1941. Atty. OPA, Washington, 1942; asso. firm Strasburger & Price, Dallas, 1946-56; ptnr. Strasburger & Price, 1956—. Editor-in-chief Tex. Law Rev., 1940-41; contbr. articles to profl. jours. Fellow Am. Bar Found. (life); mem. ABA, Am. Acad. of Appellate Attorneys, State Bar Tex., Tex. Assn. Def. Counsel (pres. 1981-82), Dallas Bar Assn., Dallas Assn. Def. Counsel, Def. Rsch. Inst., Am. Acad. Appellate Lawyers, Internat. Brotherhood Magicians (pres. 1969-70), The Chancellors (grand chancellor), Order of Coif, Phi Beta Kappa, Phi Eta Sigma. Home: 6506 Lupton Dr Dallas TX 75225-2323 Office: 4300 Nations Bank Plz 901 Main St Dallas TX 75202-3714

BRINBERG, HERBERT RAPHAEL, information management, publishing company executive; b. N.Y.C., Jan. 27, 1926; s. Henry and Anna (Stambler) B.; m. Blanche Leiman, July 15, 1945; children: Amy Lynn, Todd Michael. AB, Cornell U., 1947; MS, Columbia U., 1948; PhD, NYU, 1955; DSc (hon.), Syracuse U., 1989. Research economist Conf. Bd., 1948-50; cons. economist Boni Watkins, 1951-54; asst. dir. research Licensed Beverage Industries, 1954-55; mgr. econ. research and planning Canco div. Am. Can Co., 1956-61, dir. comml. research, 1961-66, v.p. planning, 1966-71, v.p. info. tech., 1971-78; pres., chief exec. officer Aspen Systems, Rockville, Md., 1978-85, Panel Pubs., Inc., Greenvale, NY, 1982-85; mng. dir. Wolters Kluwer U.S. Corp., N.Y.C., 1978-85, pres., chief exec. officer, dir., 1986-89; pres., CEO Parnassus Assocs. Internat., Inc., 1990—; chmn. Assoc. Info. Mgrs., 1988-90; bd. dirs. K&F Industries, Best Software Inc., Brill Academic Publishers, The Associated Blind; adj. prof. Baruch Coll., 1988—, chmn. bus. adv. coun. Bernard L. Schwartz Comm. Inst., 1998—; chmn. bd. visitors Sch. Info. Studies, Syracuse U., 1996—. Served with USAAF, 1944-45. Mem. Info. Industry Assn. (past chmn., vice chmn. 1994-98), Software and Info. Industry Assn.(bd. dirs. 1999—), Cornell Club N.Y.C.

BRINCKERHOFF, RICHARD CHARLES, retired manufacturing company executive; b. Middletown, N.Y., Apr. 4, 1931; s. Gilbert Stryker and Audrey Martina (Kniffin) B.; m. Barbara Wainwright Freir, Nov. 13, 1954; children: Mark Harrison, Scott Eric. AAS in Aircraft Ops., SUNY, Farmingdale, 1950; BS in Aeronautical Engring., Ind. Inst. Tech., 1956; M in Automotive Engring., Chrysler Inst., Detroit, 1958. Installation mgr. Chrysler Missile Div., Taronto, Italy, 1958-60; dir. ops. Chrysler Missile Div., Izmir, Turkey, 1961-62; chief Bendix test conductor Kennedy Space Ctr., Fla., 1963-68; export mgr. Bendix Internat., N.Y.C., 1969-73; dir. internat. licensing Bendix Corp., Southfield, Mich., 1974-75; dir. licensing Facet Enterprises Inc., Tulsa, 1976-77, group dir. engring., 1978-79, v.p. filter group, 1980-84, exec. v.p. ops., 1985-88. Photographer: A Mobile Family's Corporate Odyssey, 1975. With USAF, 1950-54. Mem. Exptl. Aircraft Assn., Rotary Internat., Internat. Exec. Svc. Corps, Brevard Hist. Soc., The Holland Soc. of N.Y., Nat. Silver-Haired Legislature. Republican. Episcopalian. Avocations: gardening, history, sailing, tennis, traveling.

BRIND'AMOUR, ROD JEAN, professional hockey player; b. Ottawa, Ont., Can., Aug. 9, 1970. Grad., Mich. State U. With St. Louis Blues, 1988-91; left wing/center Phila. Flyers, 1991—; mem. CCHA All-Rookie team, 1988-89; player NHL All-Star game. Recipient CCHA Rookie of the Year award, 1988-89. Office: Phila Flyers CoreStates Ctr 1 Corestates Complex Philadelphia PA 19148-5250*

BRINDLE, DAVID LOWELL, minister; b. Richmond, Ind., Sept. 16, 1948; s. Richard Lowell and Barbara Ann (Myers) B.; m. Linda Jean Pickard, Aug. 15, 1976; 1 child, Ruth Marie. BA, St. Meinrad (Ind.) Coll., 1972; MDiv, Earlham Sch. Religion, 1980; postgrad., United Theol. Sem., Dayton, Ohio. Ordained to ministry United Meth. Ch., 1991. Pastor Fountain City (Ind.) Friends Meeting, 1981-84; grad. asst. U. Dayton, 1984-85; dir. religious edn. St. Christopher Cath. Ch., Vandalia, Ohio, 1985-86, St. Joan of Arc Cath. Ch., Hershey, Pa., 1989-90; dir. admissions Earlham Coll. Sch. Religion, Richmond, 1986-88; interim pastor Wilmington (Ohio) Friends Meeting, 1988-89; jud. assessor Tribunal, Diocese of Harrisburg, Pa., 1990-91; pastor St. Paul United Meth. Ch., Harrisburg, 1991-92, Shermans Dale United Meth. Charge, 1992-96, Mt. Olivet United Meth. Ch., Mechanicsburg, Pa., 1996-98, Wilmington (Ohio) Friends Meeting, 1998—; mem. Edn. Commn., Ind. Yearly Meetings of Friends, Muncie, 1981-84; chmn. Yokefellow Inst., Richmond, 1986-89. Contbr. to religious publs. Mem. Yokefellow Internat., Oblates of St. Benedict. Democrat. Home: 330 N Lincoln St Wilmington OH 45177 Office: 66 N Mulberry Sr Wilmington OH 45177 *Many of our creeds and personal beliefs begin as descriptions of our experience. We must guard against our tendency to turn descriptions into prescriptions which seek to regulate the experiences of others.*

BRINEGAR, CLAUDE STOUT, retired oil company executive; b. Rockport, Calif., Dec. 16, 1926; s. Claude Leroy Stout and Lyle (Rawles) B.; m. Elva Jackson, 1950 (div.); children: Claudia, Meredith, Thomas; m. Mary Katharine Potter, 1983 (dec. 1993); m. Karen Bartholomew, 1995. BA, Stanford U., 1950, MS, 1951, PhD, 1954; LLD (hon.), Elmira Coll., 1997. V.p. econs. and planning Union Oil (now Unocal), L.A., 1965; pres. Pure Oil divsn. Union Oil (now Unocal), Palatine, Ill., 1965-69; sr. v.p., pres. refining and mktg. Union Oil (now Unocal), L.A., 1969-73; U.S. Sec. of Transp. Washington, 1973-75; sr. v.p. adminstr. Unocal Corp., L.A., 1975-85, mem. exec. com., 1968-73, 75-92, exec. v.p., CFO, 1985-91, also bd. dirs., 1968-73, 75-95, vice chmn. bd., 1990-95; founding dir. Conrail, Inc., 1974-75, 90-98; bd. dirs. Maxicare Health Plans, Inc., CSX Corp.; vis. scholar Stanford U., 1992-97. Author: monograph on econs. and price behavior, 1970; contbr. articles to profl. jours. on statistics and econs. Chmn. Calif. Citizens Compensation Commn., 1990—; mem. regional selection panel White House Fellows Program, 1976-83, chmn., 1983. Mem. Am. Petroleum Inst. (bd. dirs. 1976-85, 88-91, hon. life dir. 1992), Georgetown Club, Boothbay Harbor Yacht Club, Southport Yacht Club, Phi Beta Kappa, Sigma Xi. Avocation: collecting first editions of Mark Twain. Home and Office: PO Box 4346 Stanford CA 94309-4346

BRINEGAR, ELIZABETH ANNE, critical care nurse, educator; b. Ottumwa, Iowa, Apr. 26, 1949; d. H.M. and Dorothy Jean (Fitzgerald) Thompson; children: Holly, Adam. ADN, Indian Hills Community Coll., Ottumwa, 1971, AA, 1982; BSN cum laude, N.E. Mo. State U., 1983; MS in Nursing, U. Mo., Columbia, 1994. Cert. critical care nurse; cert. ACLS. CCU and emergency room nurse St. Joseph's Hosp., Ottumwa, 1971-87; pub. health nurse Wapello County, Ottumwa, 1981-88; nursing resource pool Ottumwa Regional Health Ctr., 1988-91; instr. nursing Indian Hills Community Coll., 1987-91; clin. supr. med. ICU, U. Mo., Columbia, 1991-97; FNP/GNP Clarence (Mo.) Med. Clinic, 1994—; tchg. asst. MS RN clin. specialist/family nurse practitioner U. Mo. Sch. Nursing; geriatric nurse practitioner, 1995. Mem. AACN. Home: 5620 Waterfront Dr N Columbia MO 65202-9056

BRINEY, ALLAN KING, retired radiologist; b. Wilkinsburg, Pa., Nov. 17, 1921; s. Alonzo Tripp and Helen Marie (Hardman) B.; m. Gayle Diane Briney, July 4, 1986; children: Ronald A., Nancy E., Barbara A., Douglas C. BS summa cum laude, U. Pitts., 1943, MD, 1945; fellow for Radiology, Hosp. U. for Pa., 1948-51. Diplomate Am. Bd. Radiology. Intern Pitts. Hosp., 1945-46; fellow in radiology Hosp. U. Pa., Phila., 1948-51; radiologist Topeka Med. Ctr., 1951-53, Murphy Meml. Hosp., Whittier, Calif., 1953-62, Whittier Radiology Med. Group, 1953-94, Memrad Med. Group, Whittier, 1995-97; chief staff Presbyn. Intercommunity Hosp., Whittier, 1979, chmn. risk mgmt., 1981-91, radiologist, 1959-97; ret., 1997; bd. dirs. So. Calif. Physicians Ins. Exch., Beverly Hills. Capt. USAF, 1946-48. Fellow Am. Coll. Radiology, 1969. Libertarian. Mem. Deist Ch. Avocations: skiing, biking, hiking, swimming, sailing. Home: 14084 Bronte Dr Whittier CA 90602-2608

BRINEY, WALTER GEORGE, rheumatologist; b. Benton Harbor, Mich., July 30, 1934; s. Walter Lee and Coral Inez (Rogers) B; m. Martha Lydia George, June 29, 1957 (div. 1980); children: David, Daniel, Andrew; m. Mary Jane Davis, May 31, 1980; children: Jeffrey, Jerri Lu. MD, U. Mich., 1959. Diplomate Am. Bd. Internal Medicine. Intern, resident, chief resident internal medicine U. Colo. Health Scis. Ctr., Denver, 1959-65, fellow in rheumatology, 1965-66; pvt. practice rheumatology Gilpin Med. Clinic, Denver, 1966-73; rehab. dir. Spalding Rehab. Hosp., Denver, 1973-76; pvt. practice rheumatology Denver Arthritis Clinic, Denver, 1976—; from asst. clin. prof. to clin. prof. U. Colo. Health Scis. Ctr., Denver, 1968—. Deacon, elder Wellshire Presbyn. Ch., Denver, 1967-80; dir., v.p. Colo. Health Careers Coun., Denver, 1968-70. Capt. USAF, 1961-63. Recipient commendation medal USAF, 1963, disting. svc. award Rocky Mtn. chpt. Arthritis Found., Denver, 1984. Fellow Am. Coll. Rheumatology, Am. Coll. Physicians; mem. Rocky Mtn. Rheumatism Soc., Am. Soc. Internal Medicine, Colo. Soc. Internal Medicine, AMA, Colo. Med. Soc., Denver Med. Soc. Republican. Avocations: scuba diving, woodworking, photography. Office: Denver Arthritis Clinic 4545 E 9th Ave Ste 510 Denver CO 80220-3981

BRING, MURRAY H., lawyer; b. Denver, Jan. 19, 1935; s. Alfred Alexander and Ida (Molinsky) B.; m. Constance Brooks Evert, Dec. 30, 1963 (div. June 1989); children: Beth, Catherine, Peter; m. Kathleen Delaney, May 19, 1990. BA, U. So. Calif., 1956; LLB, NYU, 1959. Bar: N.Y. 1960, D.C. 1963, U.S. Supreme Ct. 1966. Law clk. to Chief Justice Earl Warren U.S. Supreme Ct., Washington, 1959-61; spl. asst. to asst. atty. gen. civil div. Dept. Justice, Washington, 1961-62; spl. asst to dep. undersec. state Dept. State, Washington, 1962-63; dir. policy planning anti-trust divsn., 1963-65; ptnr. Arnold & Porter, Washington, 1965-87; sr. v.p., gen. counsel Philip Morris Cos., Inc., N.Y.C., 1988-94, exec. v.p. external affairs and gen. counsel, 1994-97, vice chmn., gen. counsel, 1997—. Editor-in-chief N.Y. Law Rev., 1958-59. Bd. dirs. N.Y.C. Opera, NYU Law Sch. Found.; trustee Whitney Mus. Am. Art. Mem. ABA, Assn. Bar City N.Y., D.C. Bar Assn., Order of Coif, Phi Beta Kappa, Phi Kappa Phi. Avocations: photography; art. Office: Philip Morris Cos Inc 120 Park Ave New York NY 10017-5592

BRINGARDNER, JOHN MICHAEL, lawyer, clergyman; b. Columbus, Ohio, Nov. 7, 1957; s. John Krepps and Elizabeth (Evans) B.; m. Emily Presley, June 19, 1982; children: John Taylor, Michael Steven, Malee Elizabeth. BA, U. Central Fla., Orlando, 1979; postgrad., Mercer U., 1979; JD, Fla. State U., 1981. Bar: Fla. 1982, Calif. 1994, U.S. Dist. Ct. (mid. dist.) Fla., U.S. Dist. Ct. (no. dist.) Fla., U.S. Ct. Appeals (11th cir.). Assoc. McFarlain, Bobo, Sternstein, Wiley & Cassidy, Tallahassee, Fla., 1982-87, Finley, Kumble Wagner, Tallahassee, 1987; minister Boston Ch. of Christ, 1987-90; evangelist Bankok Christian Ch., 1990-92, Metro Manila Christian Ch., 1992-93; gen. counsel Internat. Chs. of Christ, L.A., 1993—; bd. dirs. Eye Care Corp., Orlando, Fla., Quality Coffee Corp., Tallahassee. Mem. ABA, Fla. Bar Assn. Avocations: football, baseball, triathalons, hiking, music. Office: International Churches of Christ 3530 Wilshire Blvd Ste 1750 Los Angeles CA 90010-2238

BRINGMAN, JOSEPH EDWARD, lawyer; b. Elmhurst, N.Y., Jan. 31, 1958; s. Joseph Herman and Eileen Marie (Sheehy) B.; m. Laurie Lynn Cunningham, July 11, 1992; children: Joseph Edward Jr., Elizabeth Grace. BA, Yale U., 1980; JD, Stanford U., 1983. Bar: N.Y. 1984, Wash. 1985, U.S. Dist. Ct. (we. dist.) Wash. 1986, U.S. Ct. Appeals (9th cir.) 1986, U.S. Ct. Appeals (fed. cir.) 1988. Acting asst. prof. U. Wash. Law Sch., Seattle, 1983-85; assoc. Perkins Coie, Seattle, 1985-91, of counsel, 1992—; dir. Perkins Coie Cmty. Fellowship, Seattle, 1990-96, chair assoc. tng. com., 1997—. Editor: Stanford Jour. Internat. Law, 1980-83. Mem. Yale Alumni Schs. Com., Seattle, 1983—, Palo Alto, Calif., 1980-83. Nat. Merit scholar, 1976; recipient Pro Bono Publico award Trumbull Coll. (Yale U.), 1980. Mem. ABA, Wash. State Bar Assn., King County Bar Assn. (mem. judicial screening com. 1993-96, chair fair campaign practices com. 1997—). Democrat. Roman Catholic. Office: Perkins Coie LLP 1201 3rd Ave Fl 48 Seattle WA 98101-3099

BRINK, ARTHUR M., hospital administrator; b. Madison, Wis., Sept. 20, 1943; s. Arthur M. and Shirlee (Quinn) B.; children: Damon J., Justin K., Sunny A.; m. Katharin R. Brink; children: Sean K. Riehl, Caroline M. Riehl, Katie K. Davis. BS in Edn., U. Vt., 1966, MAT in History, 1969. Cert. fin. planner. Alumni dir. U. Vt., Burlington, 1966-77, dir. ann. fund, 1977-78; dir. devel. U. Vt. and Med. Ctr. Hosp., Burlington, 1978-95; v.p. Vt. Health Found., Burlington, 1983-95; v.p. devel. and pub. affairs Fletcher Allen Health Care, 1995-98; exec. dir. Presbyn. Hosp. Found., Charlotte, N.C., 1998—; bd. dirs. Stratevest Group, Bank North Group, Inc., 1996-98; chmn. dist. 1 Council for Advancement and Support Higher Edn., New Eng., 1982-83; chmn. Assn. Am. Med. Colls./Group on Pub. Affairs, Washington, 1986-87. Contbr. articles to profl. jours. Pres. Burlington Boys Club, 1986-88; bd. dirs. United Way, Burlington. Served to capt. F.A. U.S. Army, 1969-71, Vietnam. Decorated Bronze Star with Oak Leaf cluster, Air Medal with Oak Leaf cluster. Fellow Nat. Assn. Hosp. Devel.; mem. Rotary (pres. 1985-86). Avocations: handball, sailing, skiing, reading. Home: 3607 Mountain Cove Dr Charlotte NC 28216 Office: Presbyn Hosp Found The Belk House Presbyn PO Box 33549 Charlotte NC 28233-3549

BRINK, DAVID RYRIE, lawyer; b. Mpls., July 28, 1919; s. Raymond Woodard and Carol Sybil (Ryrie) B.; m. Irma Lorentz Brink; children: Anne Carol, Mary Claire, David Owen, Sarah Jane. BA with honors, U. Minn., 1940, BSL with honors, 1941, JD with honors, 1947; LLD, Capital U., 1981, Suffolk U., 1981, Mitchell Coll. Law, 1982. Bar: Minn. 1947, U.S. Dist. Ct. Minn. 1947, U.S. Tax Ct. 1967, U.S. Supreme Ct. 1980, U.S. Ct. Appeals (D.C. Cir.) 1982. Assoc. firm Dorsey & Whitney, Mpls., 1947-53; ptnr. Dorsey & Whitney, 1953-89, head Washington office, 1982-84, ret. ptnr.; trustee Lawyers Com. Civil Rights Under Law, 1978—; bd. dirs. Nat. Legal Aid and Defender Assn., 1978-80; U.S. panelist for Dispute Resolution under Free Trade Agreement with Can.; bd. visitors U. Minn. Law Sch., 1978-81; chmn. trust and estates dept. Dorsey & Whitney, 1956-82; qualified neutral for mediation and arbitration Supreme Ct. of Minn., 1996—. Bd. editors: U. Minn. Law Rev, 1941-42; contbr. numerous articles to law jours. Bd. govs. Am. Coll. Trust and Estate Counsel Found., 1987-95. Served to lt. comdr. USNR, 1943-46. Recipient Outstanding Achievement award U. Minn., 1982. Fellow Coll. Law Practice Mgmt. (hon.), Am. Coll. Trust and Estate Counsel (regent, exec. com.); mem. ABA (gov. 1974-77, 80-83, pres. 1981-82), Ctrl. and Ea. European Legal Initiative, Com. on Law and Nat. Security, Fund for Pub. Edn. of ABA (pres. 1981-82), Am. Bar Found. (state chmn. 1977-80, gov. 1980-83), Am. Bar Retirement Assn. (pres. 1976-77), Am. Judicature Soc. (bd. dirs. 1988—), Nat. Conf. Bar Pres., Inst. Jud. Adminstrn., Am. Arbitration Assn. (trustee 1981—), Can.-U.S. Law Inst. (adv. bd. 1987—), Minn. Bar Assn. (pres. 1978-79), Internat. Mgmt. and Devel. Inst., Hennepin County Bar Assn. (pres. 1967-68), Nat. Inst. Citizen Edn. in Law (nat. adv. bd. 1983—, chmn. 1985-88), N.W. Racquet Club, Sr. Tennis Players Club, Inc. Office: Dorsey & Whitney Pillsbury Ctr South 220 S 6th St Ste 2200 Minneapolis MN 55402-1498

BRINK, FRANK, JR., biophysicst, former educator; b. Easton, Pa., Nov. 4, 1910; s. Frank and Lydia (Wilhelm) B.; m. Marjory Gaylord, May 1, 1939; children—Patricia Brink Mayer, David Warner. B.S., Pa. State Coll., 1934; M.S., Calif. Inst. Tech., 1935; Ph.D., U. Pa., 1939; D.Sc. (hon.), Rockefeller U., 1983. Instr. physiology Cornell U. Med. Coll., N.Y.C., 1940-41; instr. biophysics Johnson Research Found., U. Pa., Phila., 1941-49; assoc. prof. biophysics Johns Hopkins U., Balt., 1949-53; prof. biophysics Rockefeller U., N.Y.C., 1953-81, dean grad. studies, 1958-72, Detlev W. Bronk prof., 1974-81, prof. emeritus, 1981—; cons. to sec. of war Dept. Army, Washington, 1941-44; mem. com. for biology and medicine NSF, Washington, 1953-59; chmn. Pres.'s Com. for Nat. Med. Sci., Washington, 1963-64. Editor Biophysics Jour., 1960-64; mem. editorial bd. various jours., 1955-71; contbr. articles on phys. chemistry of nerve cells to profl. jours. Johnson scholar U. Pa., 1935-38; Lalor Found. fellow U. Pa., 1939-40. Fellow AAAS (life); mem. AAAS, NAS, Biophys. Soc. (charter), Am. Physiol. Soc., Soc. Gen. Physiologists, Am. Acad. Arts and Scis. Avocations: reading; cycling; traveling. Home: Pine Run Community Apt E-1 Ferry and Iron Hills Rds Doylestown PA 18901

BRINK, JOHN WILLIAM, finance corporation executive; b. Chgo., July 14, 1945; s. M.W. and Alice L. (Nelson) B.; m. Cynthia Hollowell, Jan. 2, 1982; children: Bethany, Peter, Gwendolyn, Courtney. BBA, U. Wis., 1967; MBA, West Tex. State U., 1970. Comml. lending officer Huntington Nat. Bank of Columbus, Ohio, 1970-72; asst. treas. Peabody Internat., Galion, Ohio, 1972-75; v.p., treas. Avis, Inc., Garden City, N.Y., 1975-82, Savin Corp., Valhalla, N.Y., 1983; A.G. Becker Paribas, N.Y.C., 1983-84, U.S. Surg. Corp., Norwalk, Conn., 1984; pres. Treasury Adv. Corp., Pound Ridge, N.Y., 1985-86; exec. v.p., treas., CFO, Green Tree Fin. Corp., Inc., St. Paul, 1986-97; mem. faculty Franklin U. Gen. Evening Coll., Columbus, 1971-75. Served with AUS, 1968-70. Mem. Fin. Execs. Inst. (pres. twin cities chpt.), Hazeltine Nat. Golf Club. Address: 895 Ponte Vedra Blvd Ponte Vedra Beach FL 32082-3404

BRINK, MARION ALICE, employee assistance professional; b. Boston, Feb. 15, 1928; d. Martin Bernhard and Astrid Marie (Bjaastad) Windedal; m. A. Rudie Shobaken, Feb. 5, 1947 (div. 1963); children: Richard Michael, Ron Eric; m. James A Brink, Jan. 29, 1977. Student, Cambridge Jr. Coll., 1945-47, Framingham State Coll., 1967, Boston U., 1967-69; BA, U. N.H., 1983; M in Theol. Studies, Harvard U., 1987; postgrad., U. N.H. From lab tech. to chemist Liberty Mut. Rsch., Hopkinton, Mass., 1963-77; asst. to mgr. Rec. Sec. Office Harvard U., 1977-79; sec. Sloan Sch. MIT, 1980-82; owner tech. typing svc. New Castle, N.H., 1982-84; counseling intern Green Pastures Counseling Ctr., Dover, N.H., 1984-85; alcohol educator Freedom From Chem. Dependency Found., Inc., Needham, Mass., 1985-87; dir. devel., editor News Bulletin Freedom From Chem. Dependency Found., Inc., Needham, 1987-88; ptnr. Palmerbrink, Charlestown, Mass., 1989-90; founder MB Assocs., Charlestown, 1991-96. Counselor Women's Resource Ctr., Portsmouth, 1980; bd. dirs. Friends of Metro Boston, Inc.; mem. Harvard Inst. for Learning in Ret., U. N.H. Marine Docent Program. Mem. Am. Acad. of Health Care Providers in the Addictive Disorders. Democrat. Unitarian. Avocations: sailing, women's studies, reading, spiritual development. Home: 86 Wentworth Rd New Castle NH 03854

BRINK, MARION FRANCIS, trade association administrator; b. Golden Eagle, Ill., Nov. 20, 1932; s. Anton Frank and Agnes Gertrude B. BS, U. Ill., 1955, MS, 1958; PhD, U. Mo., 1961. Rsch. biologist U.S. Naval Radiol. Def. Lab., San Francisco, 1961-62; assoc. dir. div. nutrition rsch. Nat. Dairy Council, Chgo., 1962-65, dir. div. nutrition rsch., 1965-70; pres. Nat. Dairy Council, Rosemont, Ill., 1970-85; exec. v.p. ops. United Dairy Industry Assn., Rosemont, 1985-88, chief exec. officer, 1988-91; vice chmn. human nutrition adv. com. USDA, 1980-81. Contbr. articles to prof. jours. Recipient citation of merit U. Mo. Alumni Assn. Mem. Am. Soc. for Nutritional Scis., Am. Soc. Clin. Nutrition, Am. Dietetic Assn., Dairy Shrine Club, Soc. for Nutrition Edn., Chgo. Nutrition Assn., Alpha Tau Alpha, Gamma Sigma Delta. Home: 444 Highcrest Dr Wilmette IL 60091-2358

BRINK, RICHARD EDWARD, lawyer; b. Renwick, Iowa, Apr. 27, 1923; s. John Allyn and Sylvia Lonella (Warman) B.; m. Helen M. Ladwig, Nov. 2, 1946 (dec. Feb. 1987); children: Thomas W., Gretchen K., Sara Jane (dec.), Paul E. (dec.); m. Ruth Brady Cousins, Apr. 22, 1989. BSChemE with distinction, State U. Iowa, 1944, BA in Chemistry with high distinction, 1944; JD cum laude, William Mitchell Coll., 1952. Bar: Minn. 1952, U.S. Dist. Ct. Minn. 1962, U.S. Dist. Ct. Mich. 1971, U.S. Ct. Appeals (Fed. cir.) 1982, U.S. Ct. Appeals (6th cir.) 1973. With Minn. Mining and Mfg. Co., St. Paul, 1946-59; mgr. Minn. Mining and Mfg. Co., 1955-59; mem. firm Carpenter, Abbott, Kinney & Coulter, St. Paul, 1959-70; ptnr. Alexander, Sell, Steldt & DeLaHunt, St. Paul, 1970-76; sr. patent atty. 3M Co., St. Paul, 1976-78; assoc. patent counsel 3M Co., 1978-84, sr. assoc. patent counsel,

1986, sr. patent counsel, 1986-90, ret., 1990. Author: (with others) An Outline of U.S. Patent Law, 1959. Pres. Minn. Interprofl. Assn., 1993-94; bd. dirs. Walker Meth., Inc., 1993-96; mem. White Bear Lake United Meth. Ch. (charter), White Bear Lake Sch. Bd., 1960-75, chmn., 1969-75; leader People to People tour, China and Russia, 1985. Served with USNR, 1944-46. Mem. ABA (chmn. pub. info. com. patent, trademark and copyright sect. 1983-84, chmn. sub-com. cooperation with fgn. patent offices com. 1988-89), SAR, Minn. Bar Assn., Minn. Intellectual Property Law Assn. (chmn. pub. info. com., bd. dirs. 1983-90, rep. to Nat. Council of Intellectual Property Law Assns., pres. 1985), Am. Intellectual Property Law Assn., Holland Soc. N.Y., Am. Contract Bridge League, Sons of Norway, Phi Beta Kappa, Tau Beta Pi, Phi Lambda Upsilon, Phi Beta Gamma. United Methodist.

BRINK, ROBERT ROSS, plastic surgeon; b. Cleve., Dec. 1, 1943; s. Ross Allan Brink and Aileen Elizabeth Waters; m. Heather Ann Brink, July 11, 1987; children: Natalie, Daniel. BA, Harvard U., 1966; MD, U. Mich., 1970. Diplomate Am. Bd. Plastic Surgery. Intern William Beaumont, Royal Oak, Mich., 1970-71; resident gen. surgery U. Calif., Davis, 1973-77; resident plastic surgery U. Calif., San Francisco, 1977-79; pvt. practice plastic surgery San Francisco, 1979-96, San Mateo, Calif., 1996—. Capt. USAF, 1971-73, Vietnam. Mem. Am. Soc. Plastic and Reconstructive Surgeons, Calif. Soc. Plastic and Reconstructive Surgeons, Internat. Soc. Clin. Plastic Surgeons, Lipoplasty Soc. Office: 66 Bovet Rd Ste 101 San Mateo CA 94402-3126

BRINKEMA, LEONIE MILHOMME, federal judge; b. N.J., June 26, 1944; d. Alexander Juste and Modeste Leonie Milhomme; m. John Robert Brinkema, Dec. 22, 1966; children: Robert Aaron, Eugenie Alexandra. BA with honors, Douglass Coll., 1966; MLS, Rutgers U., 1970; JD with honors, Cornell U., 1976. Bar: D.C. 1976, Va. 1978. Trial atty. U.S. Dept. Justice, Washington, 1976-77, 1983-84; asst. U.S. atty. U.S. Atty's Office Ea. Va., Alexandria, 1977-83; prin. Leonie M. Brinkema Atty., Alexandria, 1984-85; U.S. magistrate judge U.S. Dist. Ct. (ea. dist.) Va., Alexandria, 1985-93, U.S. dist. judge, 1993—; legal lectr. Va. State Bar Professionalism Faculty, 1990-92, No. Va. Criminal Justice Acad., 1984-85; guest lectr. Alexandria Bar Assn., Alexandria Women Attys. Assn., Va. Women Attys. Assn., U.S. Dept. Justice Advocacy Inst., Va. Law Found. Active Fairfax Choral Soc., Alban Chorale. Woodrow Wilson grad. fellow, 1966, Danforth Found. grad. fellow, 1966. Mem. ABA, Va. State Bar, D.C. Bar, Nat. Assn. Women Judges, Va. Women Attys. Assn., George Mason Inn of Ct. (master), Phi Beta Kappa. Avocation: singing. Office: US Dist Ct 401 Courthouse Sq Alexandria VA 22314-5704*

BRINKER, THOMAS MICHAEL, finance executive; b. Phila., Sept. 8, 1933; s. William Joseph and Elizabeth C. (Feeley) B.; m. Doris Marie Carlin, Oct. 11, 1958; children: Thomas Michael, James E., Joseph F., Diane M. Student, St. Joseph's U., U. Pa.; MS in Fin. Svcs., Am. Coll., 1980; DBA, Heed U., 1990; BA in Orgnl. Mgmt., Ea. Coll., 1991. Registered investment advisor; CLU, ChFC, CFP, AEP. With Ice Capades, 1951-52, 56; with Casa Carioca, Garmisch, Fed. Rep. Germany, 1954-56; profl. ice skating tchr. and mfrs. rep. Ridley Park, Pa., 1956-60; agt., div. mgr. Prudential Ins. Co., Phila., 1960-65; gen. agt. Mut. Trust Life Ins. Co., 1965-70; pres., founder Fringe Benefits Inc., Havertown, Pa., 1970—, Fin. Foresight Ltd., Havertown, Pa., 1983—; adj. prof. Pa. State U., 1984—, St. Joseph's U., 1985—. Host weekly radio show: Financial Forum, Sta. WWDB-FM, 1982-90, Sta. WCZN-AM, 1990-91, daily report on fin. foresight Sta. WFLN-FM, 1992—, WCZN-AM, 1994—, children's fin. reports on Dr. Tom on Money Matters, WPWA-AM, 1994—, weekly radio program WWCN, Estero, Fla., 1997, others; co-host weekly radio program Fin. Foresight, Sta. WFIL-AM, Phila., 1998—; author: HI, I'm Tom Brinker, You're on WWDB, 1987; columnist: Financially Yours, 1983—, Dollars and $ense, 1999—; ghostwriter: Nat. Assn. Life Underwriter's Fin. Fitness campaign, 1985; columnist Dollars and $ense, 1999—; contbr., author, condr. of seminars on fin. planning; contbr. articles to profl. jours. Pres., Delaware County Estate Planning Coun., 1979-80, Pipeline Inc., Springfield, Pa., 1970-71; dir. nat. coun. Invest-in-Am., 1986; bd. dirs. Pacific Advisors Fund, Inc., 1992—, Cypress Benefit Svcs., Inc., 1997—. Recipient Nat. Quality awards Nat. Assn. Life Underwriters, 1966—, Nat. Sales Achievement awards, 1970—. Mem. CLU (ChFC), Delaware County Life Underwriters (pres. 1975-76, 82-83), Am. Coll. Life Underwriters, Nat. Assn. Life Underwriters, Internat. Platform Assn., Internat. Assn. Fin. Planners (CFP practitioner, v.p. Delaware Valley chpt. 1986-88, pres. 1989—, chmn. 1990—), Million Dollar Round Table (mem. Ct. of the Table 1986—, Top of the Table 1991, 93, 94, 95, Twenty-Five Million Dollar Internat. forum 1992-93), Lake Naomi Club (v.p., mem. bd. govs. 1982, pres. 1986), KC, Manor Club, Tom Brinker's Op. Christmas Baskets (pres.), Kingsport Club, Inc. (bd. dirs., treas. 1997—). Roman Catholic. Home: 115 Locust Ave Springfield PA 19064-1619 Office: 1 N Ormond Ave Havertown PA 19083-5010

BRINKHAUS, ARMAND J., lawyer, state senator; b. Nov. 7, 1935; BA U. Southwestern La., Springhill Coll., 1958, Mobile, Ala.; LL.B., Loyola U., New Orleans, 1960; m. Margaret Bellemin. Pvt. practice Sunset, La.; mem. La. Ho. of Reps., 1968-76, La. Senate, 1976-96 . Mem. Am. Bar Assn., La. Bar Assn., La. Trial Lawyers Assn., Am. Judicature Soc., St. Landry Cattlemen's Assn., La. Farm Bur., KC. Democrat. Roman Catholic. Address: PO Drawer E Sunset LA 70584

BRINKHOUS, KENNETH MERLE, retired pathologist, educator; b. Clayton County, Iowa, May 29, 1908; s. William and Ida (Voss) B.; m. Frances E. Benton, Sept. 5, 1936; children: William Kenneth, John Robert. Student, U.S. Mil. Acad., 1925; AB, U. Iowa, 1929, MD, 1932; DSc, U. Chgo., 1967, U. N.C., 1995. Asst. in pathology U. Iowa, 1932-33, instr., 1933-35, assoc. in pathology, 1935-37, asst. prof., 1937-45, assoc. prof., 1945-46; prof. pathology U. N.C., Chapel Hill, 1946-61; alumni distinguished prof. U. N.C., 1961-80, emeritus, 1980—; Mem. Nat. Adv. Heart and Lung Council, 1969-74; chmn. med. adv. council Nat. Hemophilia Found., 1954-73; sec. gen. Internat. Com. Hemostasis and Thrombosis, 1966-78. Bd. editors Perspectives in Biol. Medicine, 1968—; editor Archives Pathology and Lab. Medicine, 1974-83, Yearbook Pathology Clin. Pathology, 1980-91. Served from capt. to lt. col. M.C. U.S. Army, 1941-46; col. Med. Res. Corps 1946—. Co-recipient Ward Burdick award Am. Soc. Clin. Pathologists, 1941, 63, O. Max Gardner award, 1961, N.C. award, 1969, Internat. Heart Rsch. award, 1969, Murray Thelin award Nat. Hemophilia Found., 1972, Disting. Achievement award Modern Medicine, 1973, Maude Abbott award Internat. Acad. Pathology, 1985, Disting. Svc. award AMA, 1986, 50th Yr. Rsch. award NIH, 1992, Landsteiner award Am. Assn. Blood Banks, 1994; named H.P. Smith lectr., 1974. Mem. Nat. Acad. Scis. Inst. of Medicine, Am. Acad. Arts and Scis., Assn. Am. Physicians, Internat. Soc. Thrombosis and Haemostasis (pres. 1971, Robert P. Grant award 1985), Am. Assn. Pathologists and Bacteriologists (sec., treas. 1968-71, pres. 1973, Gold-headed Cane award 1981), Am. Soc. Exptl. Pathology (pres. 1965-66), Fedn. Am. Socs. Exptl. Biology (pres. 1966-67), Univs. Assoc. Research and Edn. Pathology (pres. 1964-68), Assn. Pathology Chmn. (Disting. Svc. award 1989), Acad. Clin. Lab. Physicians and Scientists (Cotlove award 1991). Home: 524 Dogwood Dr Chapel Hill NC 27516-2884*

BRINKLEY, CHARLES ALEXANDER, geologist; b. Moody, Tex., Oct. 3, 1929; s. Jess Daniel and Vera Allene (Anderson) B.; m. Jeraldine Athalene Skeeter, June 18, 1952 (dec. 1992); m. Patricia Ann McCluney, Jan. 13, 1996. Student Temple Jr. Coll., 1947-48; BS in Geology, Midwestern State U., 1957; MS in Geology, Pa. State U., 1960. Registered profl. geologist, Ark., Fla. Checker, stock mgr. A & P Tea Co., Temple and Waco, Tex., 1947-50; office asst. John M. Mouser, ind. oil operator, Wichita Falls, Tex., 1957; grad. asst. Pa. State U., 1957-59; geologist Texaco, Inc., New Orleans and Jackson, Miss., 1959-70, dist. geologist, 1970-72, dist. stratigrapher, 1972-75; regional geologist Gen. Crude Oil Co., Houston, 1975-77, exploration mgr. West Gulf dist. 1977-79; exploration mgr. (West Gulf) Mobil-GC Corp., 1979; exploration mgr./chief geologist Maralo, Inc., Houston, 1979-85; ind. petroleum geologist, Kingwood, Tex., and Houston, 1985; petroleum geologist, co-owner High Star Oil and Gas Exploration Co., Houston, Kingwood, Humble, Tex., 1986—. With USN, 1950-54. Fellow AAAS; mem. Am. Assn. Petroleum Geologists (cert., v.p. div. profl. affairs 1980-82), Soc. Econ. Paleontologists and Mineralogists (nat. gulf coast sect. and permian basin sect.), Am. Inst. Profl. Geologists (cert., sec.-treas. Tex. sect. 1985-87), Soc. Ind. Profl. Earth Scientists (cert., treas. Houston chpt. 1990), New Orleans Geol. Soc., Houston Geol. Soc., Miss. Geol. Soc., West Tex. Geol. Soc., Internat. Airline Passengers Assn., Houston Club, Midland Petroleum Club. Baptist. Home and Office: High Star Oil & Gas Exploration 8007 Hurst Forest Ln Humble TX 77346-1704

BRINKLEY, CHRISTIE, model, spokesperson, designer; b. L.A., Feb. 2, 1954; d. Don and Marge B.; m. Jean François Allaux, 1974 (div. 1981); m. Billy Joel, 1985 (div. 1994); 1 child, Alexa Ray; m. Ricky Taubman, 1995 (div. 1995); m. Peter Cook, 1996; children: Jack Paris, Sailor Lee. Attended, U. Calif., Northridge, La Grande Chaumiere. Model Elite Model Mgmt., Ford Models Inc., 1982—; co-owner Christie Brand Cosmetics, 1995—; spokeswoman Nuskin Internat. Modeled for over 500 mag. covers incl. Sports Illustrated's annual swimsuit issue, 1979, 80, 81; product promotions incl. longest cosmetic contract with Cover Girl, Prell, Chanel No. 19 perfume; pub. Christie Brinkley's Outdoor Beauty and Fitness Book, 1983; appearance (film) National Lampoon's Vacation, 1983, Vegas Vacation, 1997, (video) Billy Joel's "Uptown Girl", River of Dreams, Keepin the Faith, Matter of Trust, (TV) Mad About You, 1994; designed album cover Billy Joel's "River of Dreams"; active infomercials Total Gym; past host Living in the 90's with Christie Brinkley CNN, others. Office: Ford Models Inc 142 Green St New York NY 10012 also: William Morris Agy 1325 Avenue Of The Americas New York NY 10019-6026*

BRINKLEY, GLENDA WILLIS, medical/surgical nurse, women's health nurse; b. Gore Springs, Miss., Dec. 23, 1961; d. Stark Willis and Loree Conley; m. Timothy L. Brinkley, Sept. 15, 1984; children: Victoria Celeste, Tia Danielle. BSN, Miss. U. for Women, 1987; BS in Biology, Miss. Valley U., 1984. RN, Miss.; cert. perinatal nurse. Edn. coord. Clay County Med. Ctr. Named to Outstanding Young Women of Am., 1987. Mem. Miss. Nurses Assn. (mentor), Assn. Women's Health, Obstetrics, and Neonatal Nursing.

BRINKLEY, JACK THOMAS, lawyer, former congressman; b. Faceville, Ga., Dec. 22, 1930; s. Lonnie Elester and Pauline (Spearman) B.; m. Alma Lois Kite, May 29, 1955; children: Jack Thomas Jr., Fred Alen II. Student, Young Harris Coll., 1947-49, Okla. A. and M. Coll., 1952; LL.B. cum laude, U. Ga., 1959. Bar: Ga. 1958, D.C. 1973. Sch. tchr. Ga., 1949-51; assoc. firm Young, Hollis & Moseley, Columbus, Ga., 1959-61; partner firm Coffin & Brinkley, Columbus, 1961-66; mem. Ga. Ho. Reps., 1965-66; sr. ptnr. Brinkley and Brinkley, 1983-95, of counsel, 1996—; mem. 90th-97th Congresses from 3d Ga. dist.; chmn. mil. facilities and installations subcom. 97th Congress; mem. Ga. Ho. Rep., 1965-66. Trustee Young Harris Coll. Mem. Ga. Bar Assn., Columbus Bar Assn., Young Lawyers Club of Columbus (pres. 1963-64), Blue Key, Civitan Club, Masons. Democrat. Baptist. Office: Corporate Ctr Ste 901 Columbus GA 31902

BRINKLEY, JACK THOMAS, JR., lawyer; b. Ft. Bragg, N.C., Apr. 27, 1956; s. Jack Thomas and Alma Lois (Kite) B.; m. Stacy Patricia Smith, Jan. 2, 1988; children: Jack Thomas III, Matthew, Victoria, Maryelle, Abbigail, Fredrick. BA summa cum laude, Columbus (Ga.) Coll., 1978; JD cum laude, Mercer U., 1981. Bar: Ga. 1981, U.S. Dist. Ct. (mid. dist.) Ga. 1981, U.S. Ct. Appeals (5th and 11th cirs.) 1981, U.S. Dist. Ct. (no. dist.) Ga. 1986, U.S. Dist. Ct. (ea. dist.) Tenn. 1997. Assoc. Law Offices of Billy E. Moore, Columbus, 1981-83; ptnr. Brinkley, Brinkley & Dugan, Columbus, 1983-85, Brinkley & Brinkley, Columbus, 1986-96; pvt. practice Columbus, 1997—; spkr. in field. Contbr. articles to law jours. Former mem. bd. dirs. March of Dimes, Columbus; campaign chmn. Com. To Elect Rosa Barker, Columbus; leader Cub Scouts Am., Columbus; coach Little League, Columbus. Mem. ATLA, Ga. Trial Lawyers Assn., Columbus Lawyers Club. Avocations: family, gardening, travel, collecting antique furniture and stained glass, attending auctions. Office: PO Box 2016 Columbus GA 31902-2016

BRINKLEY, JAMES WELLONS, investment company executive; b. Suffolk, Va., Jan. 30, 1937; s. Lee and Gertrude Rachel (Wright) B.; m. Dana Lynn Brenner, June 12, 1959; children: Robert, Douglas, Susan. Student, U. Richmond, 1955-56; BA in Econs., Coll. William & Mary, 1959. Exec. v.p. Mason & Co., Investment Bankers & Brokers, Newport News, Va., 1962-70; exec. v.p. Legg, Mason, Wood & Walker, Inc., Balt., 1970-84, pres., 1984—, also bd. dirs.; sr. exec. v.p., bd. dirs. Legg Mason, Inc., Balt., 1982—; dir. regional firms com. N.Y. Stock Exch. Chmn. Leadership Greater Balt. Com.; bd. dirs. United Way Ctrl. Md.; chmn. investment com., trustee endowment com., former rector, mem. bd. visitors Coll. William and Mary, Williamsburg, Va.; chmn. investment com. Episcopal Ministries, Balt. Capt. U.S. Army, 1960-62. Mem. Balt. Soc. Security Analysts, Nat. Fedn. Fin. Analysts, Securities Industry Assn. (trustee, vice chmn., chmn. elect), Md. Acad. Scis. (dir., vice chmn.), Md. Chamber Commerce and Industry (dir.), Bond Club Balt., Rotary. Avocation: tennis. Office: Legg Mason Wood Walker Inc 100 Light St Baltimore MD 21202-1036

BRINKLEY, WILLIAM JOHN, secondary education educator; b. Shawneetown, Ill., Dec. 8, 1925; s. William Henry and Frances (Leath) B.; m. Venita J. Schwarm, Aug. 7, 1988; BS, U. Ill., 1945. Tchr. high sch., Mc Leansboro, Ill., 1945—, high sch. coord. vocations, 1968—; owner Brinkley Interiors and Galleries, antique porcelain, Mc Leansboro. Mem. editorial bd. Schroeders Antique Guide, 1979—; adv. bd. Ill. Edn. Coun., 1967—; mem. Pres.'s Com. 100, 1968; mem. Hamilton County Bicentennial Com.; chmn. rehab. com. McCoy Meml. Libr. and Hamilton County Hist. Soc. Bldg.; mem. Friends of Mus., Mitchell Mus., Mt. Vernon, Ill., 1978-84; mem. adv. coun. Hamilton-Jefferson County Comprehensive Svcs., Ill., 1991—; mem. Hamilton County Rep. Com., 1950-68; bd. trustees Trade Industries, 1994—; deacon Presbyn. Ch., 1995. Recipient Tchr. of Year award U. Ill. Edn. Dept., 1963; Disting. Svc. award Vocat. Edn., 1981; Merit award Gov. Ill. 1964; Disting. Svc. award Future Farmers Am., 1967, Thor Agr. award outstanding svc., 1972, FAA disting. svc. award, 1968; George Washington medal honor Freedoms Found. Am., 1966, 69; Outstanding Vocat. Edn. award Ill. State Vocat. Edn. Svc., 1981; Presbyn. Svc. award, 1984. Mem. NEA, Ill. Edn. Assn., Hamilton County (pres. 1970), Gallatin County Hist. Socs., Nat., Ill. Assn. Vocat. Agr. Tchrs. (Tchr. of Tchrs.), Rend Lake Symphony Soc., Arts and Humanities Soc., SAR (bd. govs. Ill., state chmn. constructive citizenship com.), Hamilton County Hist. Soc. (pres. 1994—), Cedarhurst Dinner Theater Club, Hereditary Register of U.S., Phi Beta Kappa, Delta Sigma Phi. Lodges: Masons, Kiwanis, Elks, Lions, Rotary (charter mem., bd. dirs. 1986). Home: 401 S Washington St Mc Leansboro IL 62859-1235 Office: 200 S Pearl St Mc Leansboro IL 62859-1157

BRINKMAN, DALE THOMAS, lawyer; b. Columbus, Ohio, Dec. 10, 1952; s. Harry H. and Jean May (Sandel) B.; m. Martha Louise Johnson, Aug. 3, 1974; children: Marin Veronica, Lauren Elizabeth, Kelsey Renee. BA, U. Notre Dame, 1974; JD, Ohio State U., 1977. Bar: Ohio 1977, U.S. Dist. Ct. (so. dist.) Ohio 1979. Assoc. Schwartz, Shapiro, Kelm & Warren, Columbus, 1977-82; asst. tax counsel Am. Elect. Power, Columbus, 1982; gen. counsel Worthington Industries, Inc., Columbus, 1982-99, v.p. adminstrn., gen. counsel, 1999—. Author: Ohio State U. Law Jour.,1975-76, editor, 1976-77. Trustee, officer Friends of Dahlberg Ctr., Columbus, 1980-86; dir., officer Assn. for Developmentally Disabled, Columbus, 1986-94. Mem. ABA, Ohio Bar Assn., Columbus Bar Assn. Republican. Roman Catholic. Office: Worthington Industries Inc 1205 Dearborn Dr Columbus OH 43085-4769

BRINKMAN, JOHN ANTHONY, historian, educator; b. Chgo., July 4, 1934; s. Adam John and Alice (Davies) B.; m. Monique E. Geschier, Mar. 24, 1970; 1 son, Charles E. A.B., Loyola U., Chgo., 1956, M.A., 1958; Ph.D., U. Chgo., 1962. Research asso. Oriental Inst., U. Chgo., 1963, dir. inst., 1972-81, asst. prof. Assyriology and ancient history, 1964-66, asso. prof., 1966-70, prof., 1970-84, Charles H. Swift Disting. Service prof., 1984—, chmn. dept., 1969-72; ann. prof. Am. Schs. Oriental Rsch., Baghdad, 1968-69; chmn. Baghdad Schs. Com., 1970-85, chmn. exec. com., 1973-75, trustee, 1975-90; chmn. vis. com. dept. Near Ea. Langs. and Civilizations, Harvard U., 1995—. Author: Political History of Post-Kassite Babylonia, 1968, Materials and Studies for Kassite History, Vol. I, 1976; Prelude to Empire, 1984; editorial bd. Chgo. Assyrian Dictionary, 1977—, State Archives Assyria, 1985—; editor in charge Babylonian sect. Royal Inscriptions of Mesopotamia, 1979-91; contbr. numerous articles to profl. jours. Fellow Am. Research Inst., in Turkey, 1971; sr. fellow Nat. Endowment Humanities, 1973-74; Guggenheim fellow, 1984-85. Fellow Am. Acad. Arts and Scis.; mem. Am. Oriental Soc. (pres. Middle West chpt. 1971-72), Am. Schs. of Oriental Rsch., Brit. Inst. Persian Studies, Brit. Sch. Archaeology in Iraq, Deutsche Orient Gesellschaft, Brit. Inst. Archaeology at Ankara, Am. Coun. Learned Socs. Roman Catholic. Home: 1321 E 56th St Apt 4 Chicago IL 60637-1762 Office: U Chgo 1155 E 58th St Chicago IL 60637-1540

BRINKMAN, JOSEPH N., umpire; b. Little Falls, Minn., Apr. 9, 1944; married; 1 child. Student, Al Somers Sch., Umpire Specialization Program, St. Cloud (Minn.) State Coll. Former umpire Midwest League, So. League, Am. Assn.; umpire maj. league baseball Am. League, N.Y.C., 1973—; with Umpires Union, Phila.; co-operator Brinkman-Froemming Umpire Sch. Avocation: golfing. Office: Am League 350 Park Ave New York NY 10022 also: Umpires Union 1735 Market St Philadelphia PA 19103

BRINKMAN, MICHAEL OWEN, health care consultant, educator; b. Chgo., May 15, 1936; s. Adam John and Alice Corrine (Davies) B.; m. Mary Judith Zeitz, Jan. 18, 1958; children: Stephen, Daniel, Julie, Amy, Carl, Mary Alice. BEE magna cum laude, Marquette U., 1958. Instr. Marquette U., Milw., 1957-59; engr. Wis. Electric Power, Milw., 1958-59, A.C. Electronics, Oak Creek, Wis., 1959-62; svc. engr. Nuclear-Chgo. Corp., Des Plaines, Ill., 1962-63, dir. of svc., 1963-66, plant mgr., 1966-67; gen. mgr. Electrovac, Melrose Park, Ill., 1968; mktg. analyst A.C. Electronics, Oak Creek, Wis., 1969-70; pres. On-Call Nat., Barrington, Ill., 1970-72, Hosp. Maintenance Cons., Columbus, Wis., 1972—. Co-author: (books) Clinical Engineering, 1975, Managing Your Medical Equipment, 1978, 82; contbr. numerous articles to profl. jours. Dep. committeeman Schaumburg Twp. Rep., Hoffman Estates, Ill., 1964-67; supt. Country Christian Schs., Nashotah, Wis., 1978-90, bd. dirs., 1990-95; bd. dirs. Victory Christian H.S., Neosho, Wis., 1991—, vol. tchr., 1991—; mem. Oconomowoc Bible Fellowship, elder, 1996—. Mem. Med. Equipment Repair Assocs. (exec. dir. 1973—), Eta Kappa Nu, Pi Mu Epsilon, Tau Beta Pi, Alpha Sigma Nu. Avocations: Bible teacher, golf, stamp collecting, basketball, antique glassware. Home: 443 W Prairie St Columbus WI 53925 Office: Hosp Maintenance Cons Inc PO Box 309 Columbus WI 53925-0309

BRINKMAN, PAUL DEL(BERT), foundation executive; b. Olpe, Kans., Feb. 10, 1937; s. Paul Theodore and Delphine Barbara (Brown) B.; m. Evelyn Marie Lange, Aug. 5, 1961 (dec. June 1988); m. Carolyn L. Backer, July 27, 1990; children: Scott Michael, Susan Lynn. BS, Emporia State Coll., 1958; MA in Journalism (Newspaper Fund fellow), Ind. U., 1963, Ph.D. in Mass Communications (Scripps-Howard fellow), 1971. Editor, reporter Emporia (Kans.) Gazette, 1954-59; instr. journalism Leavenworth (Kans.) High Sch., 1959-62; lectr. Ind. U., Bloomington, 1962-65, 68-70; asst. prof. Kans. State U., Manhattan, 1965-68; prof., dean Sch. Journalism U. Kans., Lawrence, 1970-86, vice chancellor for acad. affairs, 1986-93; dir. journalism programs John S. and James L. Knight Found., Miami, 1993—; Balt. Sun disting. lectr. Coll. Journalism, U. Md., 1993. Bd. dirs. William Allen White Found., 1974; chmn. Big Eight Athletic Conf., 1980-81, 87-88; faculty rep. Nat. Collegiate Athletic Assn., 1978-93. Named Trayes Prof. of Yr. Mass Communications Soc. div. Assn. Edn. Journalism, 1990; recipient Disting Alumni award Emporia State Coll., 1978, Ind. U., 1986. Mem. Am. Assn. Schs. and Depts. Journalism (pres. 1977-78), Inland Daily Press Assn. (chmn. edn. com. 1980-83), Assn. Edn. Journalism (chmn. publs. com. 1974-75, pres. 1980-81), Soc. Profl. Journalists, Lawrence C. of C. (v.p. 1987-88), Rotary (pres. Lawrence chpt. 1987-88), Sigma Delta Chi, Kappa Tau Alpha. Home: 161 Crandon Blvd Apt 212 Key Biscayne FL 33149-1553 Office: John S and James L Knight Found One Biscayne Tower 2 S Biscayne Blvd Ste 3800 Miami FL 33131-1808

BRINKMAN, WILLIAM FRANK, physicist, research executive; b. Washington, Mo., July 20, 1938; s. William F. Sr. and Mildred A. (Bocklege) B.; m. B. Carol, Aug. 27, 1960; children: David, Curtis. BS, U. Mo., 1960, PhD, 1965. Postdoctoral fellow Oxford U., 1966; mem. staff Bell Labs., Murray Hill, N.J., 1966-72, dept. head, 1972-74, dir., 1974-84; v.p. research Sandia Nat. Lab., Albuquerque, 1984-87; v.p. phys. scis. rsch. Lucent Techs./Bell Labs., Murray Hill, N.J., 1987—. Contbr. numerous articles on theoretical physics to sci. jours. Fellow AAAS, Am. Phys. Soc. (George E. Pake prize 1994); mem. Am. Acad. Arts and Scis., Nat. Acad. Sci. (chmn. 8-vol. report Physics Through the 1990's). Home: 45 Jeffrey Ct Basking Ridge NJ 07920-1967 Office: Lucent Technologies Bell Labs 600 Mountain Ave New Providence NJ 07974-2008

BRINKMANN, ROBERT JOSEPH, lawyer; b. Cin., Dec. 25, 1950; s. Robert Harry and Helen R. (Streuwing) B.; children: Christopher, Julia. BA, U. Notre Dame, 1972; postgrad., Alliance Française, 1974-75; AM, Brown U., 1977; JD, Loyola U., Los Angeles, 1980. Bar: Calif. 1980, D.C. 1981, U.S. Ct. Appeals (D.C. and 9th cirs.) 1981, U.S. Supreme Ct. 1984, U.S. Ct. Appeals (6th cir.) 1987. Tchr. secondary schs., Los Angeles and Paris, 1974-77; assoc. Hedrick & Lane, Washington, 1980-82; gen. counsel Nat. Newspaper Assn., Washington, 1982-92; exec. dir. Red Tag News Publs. Assn., 1990-92; v.p., postal and regulatory affairs Newspaper Assn. Am., Reston, Va., 1992—; mem. faculty Am. Press. Inst., Reston, Va., 1982-92; adj. faculty U. Md., 1997—. Mem. ABA, Fed. Communications Bar Assn. (former vice chmn. postal affairs com.). Roman Catholic. Home: 9815 Bristol Square Ln #204 Bethesda MD 20814-5440 Office: Newspaper Assn Am National Press Bldg 529 14th St NW Ste 440 Washington DC 20045-1407

BRINKMEYER, DOTTY STEWART, maternal/child nurse; b. Denver, Sept. 12, 1945; d. Dan and May Irene (Davis) Clark; m. LeRoy Brinkmeyer, Jan. 8, 1977; children: Gail Herin, Brian Stewart, Bruce, Amy. BS in Nursing, U. Colo., Boulder and Denver, 1967, MS in Nursing, 1969. Staff nurse U. Colo. Health Scis. Ctr., Denver, 1967-76, 78-88, flex staff nurse, 1991-96; dir. nursing Plateau Valley Hosp.-Nursing Home, Collbran, Colo., 1976-78; coord., acting clin. supr. Physicians' Home Care, Denver, 1986, 87; nurse cons. HHS, Denver Regional Office Health Care Financing Adminstrn., 1988-90, survey and certification program rev. specialist, 1991—. Mem. Am. Nurses Assn., Colo. Nurses Assn., Sigma Theta Tau (Nightingale award 1999). Home: 1224 Fraser St Aurora CO 80011-7051

BRINSMADE, LYON LOUIS, lawyer; b. Mexico City, Feb. 24, 1924; s. Robert Bruce and Helen (Steenbock) B. (Am. citizens); m. Susannah Tucker, June 9, 1956 (div. 1978); children: Christine Fairchild, Louisa Calvert; m. Carolyn Hartman Lister, Sept. 22, 1979. Student, U. Wis., 1940-43; B.S., Mich. Technol. U., 1944; J.D., Harvard U., 1950. Bar: Tex. 1951. Assoc. Butler, Binion, Rice, Cook & Knapp, Houston, 1950-58, ptnr. in charge internat. dept., 1958-83; ptnr. in charge internat. dept. Porter & Clements, Houston, 1983-91; sr. counsel Porter & Hedges (formerly Porter & Clements), Houston, 1991—. Bd. dirs. Houston br. English-Speaking Union of U.S., 1972-75. Served with AUS, 1944-47. Mem. ABA (chmn. com. internat. investment and devel. of sect. internat. law and practice 1970-76, council 1972-76, 81-82, vice chmn. 1976-79, chmn.-elect 1979-80, chmn. 1980-81, co-chmn. com. Mex. 1982-85), Internat. Bar Assn., Inter-Am. Bar Assn. (co-chmn. sect. oil and gas laws, com. natural resources 1973-76, council 1984-87), Houston Bar Assn., State Bar Tex. (chmn. internat. law com. 1970-74, mem. council sect. internat. law 1975-78), Am. Soc. Internat. Law (exec. council 1984-86), Houston World Trade Assn. (sec., dir. 1967-70), Houston World Trade Assn. (chmn. legis. com. 1967-72), Houston C. of C. (chmn. legis. subcom. internat. bus. com. 1970-72), Houston Com. on Fgn. Relations, SAR, Allegro of Houston, Houston Club, Petroleum Club, Harvard Club (Houston), Sigma Alpha Epsilon. Episcopalian. Home: The Beaconsfield 1700 Main St Houston TX 77002-8119 Office: 700 Louisiana St Fl 35 Houston TX 77002-2700

BRINSON, BARBARA ANN, music educator; b. Columbus, Ga., Dec. 11, 1948; d. Carey Owen and Carolyn Ann (Cox) B. MusB in Music Edn., Wesleyan Coll., Macon, Ga., 1971; MEd in Music Edn., Columbus Coll., 1976; MusM in Choral Conducting, U. Tenn., 1983; PhD in Music Edn., Fla. State U., 1986. Tchr. music Muscogee County Schs., Columbus, 1971-72, 74-81; tchr. music, elem. music specialist Fulton County Schs., Atlanta, 1972-74; asst. prof. music S.W. Tex. State U., San Marcos, 1986-87; asst. prof. choral music edn. So. Meth. U., Dallas, 1987-93, assoc. prof., 1993—, dir. Meadows Chamber Singers, 1987-93, dir. women's vocal ensemble, 1993-96; choral dir. Rothschild Jr. H.S., Columbus, 1974-78, Shaw High Sch., Columbus, 1978-81; grad. asst. U. Tenn., Knoxville, 1981-83, Fla. State U.,

Tallahassee, 1983-86; participant Western Wind Vocal Ensemble Workship, U. Mass., Amherst, 1990, Dalcroze Eurhythmics Workshop, Carnegie Mellon U., Pitts., 1988; asst. dir., dir. numerous choirs at univs. and chs., 1981—; participant convs. in field, 1989—; condr. choral clinics, 1990—; adjudicator, 1989—; guest condr. various sch. choirs and choruses, 1986—. Author: Choral Music Methods and Materials, 1996; contbr. articles to profl. jours. Dir. New Braunfels (Tex.) Cmty. Chorale, 1986-87; ordained elder North Park Presbyn. Ch., Dallas, 1995—. Faculty devel. grantee So. Meth. U., 1988-90, 92, 94, 96, svc. learning grantee, 1997. Mem. Music Educators Nat. Conf., Phi Kappa Phi, Pi Kappa Lambda (pres. Alpha Eta chpt. 1993-95), Sigma Alpha Iota, Kappa Delta Epsilon. Avocations: swimming, reading, gardening, movies. Office: So Meth U Meadows Sch Arts Divsn Music PO Box 750356 Dallas TX 75275-0356

BRINSON, CORA KATHERINE, principal; b. Palatka, Fla., Mar. 18, 1951; d. Walter Horne Jr. and Katherine Blossom; m. Milton Adams, Dec. 20, 1986 (div. June 1989); m. Rupert Glenn Brinson, May 11, 1991; 1 child, William Milton. BS in Edn., Ga. So. U., 1974, MEd, 1978; EdD, Nova Southeastern U., 1995. Coord. Liberty County Bd. Edn., Hinesville, Ga., 1974-86; coord. project success Fulton County Bd. Edn., Atlanta, 1986-88, Rockdale County Bd. Edn., Conyers, Ga., 1988-89, Lee County Bd. Edn., Leesburg, Ga., 1989-91, Bulloch County Bd. Edn., Statesboro, Ga., 1991-96; prin. Glynn County Bd. Edn., Brunswick, Ga., 1996—; com. mem. Ga. Dept. Edn., Atlanta, 1997-98, Govs. Com. Drop Outs Ga., Atlanta, 1986. Bd. dirs. Boys & Girls Club Glynn, 1997. Mem. Ga. Vocat. Assn., Ga. Assn. Spl. Needs Personnel (pres. 1992-96), Ga. Assn. Mid. Sch. Prins., Ga. Assn. Secondary Sch. Prins., Ga. Assn. Ednl. Leaders, Profl. Assn. Ga. Educators. Methodist. Avocations: golf, fishing, reading, needlepoint. Home: 5011 Riverside Dr Brunswick GA 31520 Office: Noedwood Mid Sch 2560 Altamaha Blvd Brunswick GA 31525

BRINSON, GAY CRESWELL, JR., lawyer; b. Kingsville, Tex., June 13, 1925; s. Gay Creswell and Lelia (Wendelkin) B.; m. Bette Lee Butter, June 17, 1979; children from former marriage: Thomas Wade, Mary Kaye. Student, U. Ill.-Chgo., 1947-48; B.S., U. Houston, 1953, J.D., 1957. Bar: Tex. 1957, U.S. Dist. Ct. (so. dist.) Tex. 1959, U.S. Dist. Ct. (ea. dist.) Tex. 1965, U.S. Dist. Ct. (no. dist.) Tex. 1990, U.S. Ct. Appeals (5th cir.) 1962, U.S. Supreme Ct. 1974; diplomate Am. Bd. Trial Advocates, Am. Bd. Profl. Liability Attys. Spl. agt. FBI, Washington and Salt Lake City, 1957-59; trial atty. Liberty Mut. Ins. Co., Houston, 1959-62; assoc. Horace Brown, Houston, 1962-64; assoc. Vinson & Elkins, Houston, 1964-67, ptnr., 1967-91; of counsel McFall, Sherwood & Sheehy, Houston, 1992—; lectr. U. Houston Coll. Law, 1964-65; mem. staff Tex. Coll. Trial Advocacy, Houston, 1978-86; prosecutor Harris County Grievance Com.-State Bar Tex., Houston, 1965-70. Served with AUS, 1943-46, ETO. Fellow Tex. Bar Found. (life); mem. Tex. Acad. Family Law Specialists (cert.), Tex. Assn. Def. Counsel, Tex. Bd. Legal Specialization (cert.), Fedn. Ins. Counsel, Nat. Bd. Trial Advocacy (cert.), Houston Ctr. Club, Phi Delta Phi. Home: 3740 Del Monte Dr Houston TX 77019-3018 Office: McFall Sherwood & Sheehy 2500 2 Houston Ctr 909 Fannin St Houston TX 77010

BRINSON, HAROLD THOMAS, retired university president emeritus; b. Harper Springs, Ark., Jan. 22, 1930; s. Emmitte Melton and Hazel Eula (Harris) B.; m. Nelda Gene Lee, Dec. 29, 1951; children: Kathryn Ann, Max Harold, Paul Thomas. AA, State A&M Coll., Ark., 1949; BEd, Tulane U., 1951; MEd, U. Tex., 1954, PhD, 1970. Asst. prin. Abilene H.S., Tex., 1965-68; tng. cons. U. Tex.-Austin, 1969-70; asst. supt. Abilene Ind. Sch. Dist., 1970-74, supt., 1974-76; pres. So. Ark. U., Magnolia, 1976-91, pres. emeritus, disting. prof. edn. and bus. adminstrn., 1992-95. Bd. dirs. United Way, Magnolia, 1979. Mem. Am. Assn. Sch. Adminstrs., Magnolia C. of C. (bd. dirs. 1978-81), Rotary (bd. dirs. 1980-84, pres. 1984-85, gov. dist. 617 1987-88, Paul Harris fellow 1985), Phi Delta Kappa. Baptist. Avocations: snow skiing, fishing, walking, travelling. Home: PO Box 880 114 Arjona Way Hot Springs AR 71909*

BRINSTER, RALPH LAWRENCE, biologist; b. Montclair, N.J., Mar. 10, 1932. BS, Rutgers U., 1953; VMD, U. Pa., 1960, PhD in Physiology, 1964. Teaching fellow U. Pa., Phila., 1961-64, instr. Sch. of Medicine, 1964-65, asst. prof., then assoc. prof. Sch. Vet. Medicine, 1965-70, prof. physiology Sch. Vet. Medicine, 1970—, Rich King Mellon prof. reproductive physiology, 1975—; lectr. Harvey Soc., 1984. Recipient Charles-Leopold Mayer prize French Acad. Scis., 1994, March of Dimes prize Devel. Biology, 1996, Bower award and prize Sci., 1997. Fellow Am. Acad. Arts and Scis.; mem. NAS, AVMA, Inst. Medicine. Office: Univ Pa Sch Vet Medicine Philadelphia PA 19104

BRINT, STEVEN GREGORY, sociologist, educator; b. Albuquerque, May 22, 1951; s. Harold Louis Brint and Shirl F. Grayson; m. Michele Renee Salzman, Aug. 4, 1985; children: Juliana Rose, Benjamin Piero. BA, U. Calif., Berkeley, 1973; PhD, Harvard U., 1982. Asst. dir. rsch. inst. NYU, 1984-85; from asst. to assoc. prof. Yale U., New Haven, Conn., 1985-92; prof. U. Calif., Riverside, 1992—; cons. Carnegie Found. for Advancement of Tchg., Menlo Park, Calif., 1998-99. Author: The Diverted Dream, 1998 (AREA Outstanding award 1991), In an Age of Experts, 1994, Schools and Societies, 1998. Mem. bd. admissions and rels. with schs. U. Calif., 1997-98; v.p. acad. senate U. Calif., Riverside, 1995-96; mem. program adv. com. Spencer Found., Chgo., 1997-99. Recipient AERA Outstanding Book award. E-mail: brint@mail.ucr.edu. Office: U Calif Riverside Dept Sociology Dept Sociology Claremont CA 92521-0419

BRINTNALL, MICHAEL ARTHUR, association executive, political scientist; b. Milw., Apr. 1, 1946; s. Arthur Kelly and Gladys (Merchant) B.; m. Isabel Victor, June 22, 1968; 1 child, Rachel Isabel. BA, Amherst (Mass.) Coll., 1968; PhD, MIT, 1976. Asst. prof. Brown U., Providence, R.I., 1976-80; rsch. analyst U.S. HUD, Washington, 1981-85; v.p., assoc. prof. Mt. Vernon Coll., Washington, 1985-90; dir. profl. affairs Am. Polit. Sci. Assn., Washington, 1990-96; exec. dir. Nat. Assn. Schs. Pub. Affairs & Adminstrn., Washington, 1996—. Mem. coun. Town of Glen Echo, Md., 1991—. With U.S. Army, 1969-71, Vietnam. Home: 44 Wellesley Cir Glen Echo MD 20812-1017 Office: Nat Assn Schs Pub Affairs & Adminstrn 1120 G St NW Washington DC 20005-3801

BRINTON, RICHARD KIRK, marketing executive; b. Hanover, Pa., Apr. 21, 1946; s. James Henry and Mabel (Adelung) B.; m. Joan Marita Ayo, Mar. 21, 1970; children: Katherine, Mark, Michael. BA in Liberal Arts, BS in Indsl. Engring., Pa. State U., 1968. Registered profl. engr., Ohio. From systems engr. to dir. mktg. AccuRay/ABB, Columbus, Ohio, 1968-82; group mktg. dir. AccuRay/ABB, London, 1982-84; internat. sales mgr. Flow Systems, Seattle, 1984, v.p. sales and mktg., 1985-87; dir. mktg. and bus. devel. UTILX Corp., Seattle, 1987-90, v.p. mktg. and bus. devel., 1990-93, v.p. internat. ops., 1993-96; chmn. Nippon FlowMole, Tokyo, 1991-93; dir. worldwide mktg. and sales Lamb-Grays Harbor, Hoquiam, Wash., 1996-97; pres. BBD Internat., Edmonds, Wash., 1997—; sr. mgmt. advisor, dir. mktg. Pacific N.W. Advisors, Seattle, 1997—. Mem. World Trade Club Seattle (bd. dirs. 1993-95). Home: 541 Pine St Edmonds WA 98020-4028 Office: 541 Pine St Edmonds WA 98020-4028

BRIONES, DAVID, judge; b. 1943. BA, U. Tex., El Paso, 1969; JD, U. Tex., Austin, 1971. Ptnr. Moreno & Briones, 1971-91; judge El Paso County Ct. No. 1, El Paso, 1991-94; dist. judge U.S. DIst. Ct. (we. dist.) Tex., El Paso, 1994—. With U.S. Army, 1964-66. Fellow Tex. Bar Found.; mem. State Bar of Tex., El Paso Bar Assn., Mexican-Am. Bar Assn. Office: US Courthouse Courtroom 2 511 E San Antonio Ave El Paso TX 79901-2401

BRISBANE, ARTHUR SEWARD, newspaper publisher; b. N.Y.C., Sept. 30, 1950; s. Seward Scatcherd and Doris Mae (Fauser) B.; m. Jo Ellen Hull, Oct. 16, 1982; children: Allison Faith, Madeline Mariah, Laura Calista. AB, Harvard Coll., 1973. Child care worker McLean Hosp., Belmont, Mass., 1973-74; pvt. practice musician, 1974-76; reporter Glen Cove (N.Y.) Guardian, 1976-77; reporter Kansas City (Mo.) Star & Times, 1977-79, columnist, 1979-84; reporter Washington Post, 1984-87, asst. city editor, 1987-89; columnist Kansas City Star, 1990-92, editor, v.p., 1992-97, pub., pres., 1997—. Author: Arthur Brisbane's Kansas City, 1982. Mem. Am. Soc. Newspaper Editors. Avocations: tennis, reading. Office: The Kansas City Star 1729 Grand Blvd Kansas City MO 64108-1458

BRISBIN, RICHARD A., JR., political scientist, educator; b. Bellevue, Pa., Jan. 10, 1948; s. Richard A. and Frances M. (Kornman) B. BA, W.Va. Wesleyan Coll., 1969; MA, Johns Hopkins U., 1973, PhD, 1975. Prof. Ctrl. Mich. U., Mt. Pleasant, Mich., 1974-75, Denison U., Granville, Ohio, 1975-79, St. Mary's Coll., Notre Dame, Ind., 1979-85, SUNY, Potsdam, 1985-86, W.Va. U., Morgantown, 1986—. Author: West Virginia Politics and Government, 1996, Justice Antonin Scalia & The Conservative Revival, 1997. Pvt. U.S. Army, 1970. Mem. Am. Polit. Sci. Assn., W.Va. Polit. Sci. Assn. (pres. 1997-98). Meth. Office: WVa U Dept Polit Sci PO Box 6317 Morgantown WV 26506-6317

BRISBIN, ROBERT EDWARD, insurance agency executive; b. Bklyn., Feb. 13, 1946; m. Sally Ann Tobler-Norton. BSBA, San Fancisco State U., 1968. Cert. safety exec. Field rep. Index Research, San Mateo, Calif., 1969-82; mgr. loss control Homeland Ins. Co., San Jose, Calif., 1982-87; ins. exec. Morris and Dee Ins. Agy., San Luis Obispo, Calif., 1987—; prin., cons. Robert E. Brisbin & Assocs., Pismo Beach, Calif., 1972—; mgt. cons.; pres. Profl. Formulas Amino Acid Food Supplements, 1987-90. Author: Amino Acids, Vitamins and Fitness, 1986, Loss Control for the Small- to Medium-Sized Business, 1989, (with Carol Bayly Grant) Workplace Wellness, 1992; composer: Country Songs and Broken Dreams, 1978, America the Land of Liberty, 1980. Mem. Am. Soc. Safety Engrs., World Safety Orgn. (cert. safety exec.), UN Roster Safety Cons. Republican. Avocations: photography, flying, scuba diving, musical composition. Office: PO Box 341 Pismo Beach CA 93448-0341

BRISBIN, STERLING G., engineering executive, consultant; b. Gloversville, N.Y., Apr. 8, 1929; s. Sterling L. and Eleanor (Holly) B.; m. Joan Cooke, Feb. 28, 1954; children: Sterling G. Jr., James C., Elizabeth. SB, MIT, 1950, SM, 1951. Registered profl. engr., N.Y., N.H., Conn., W.Va. Sanitary engr. Chase T. Main, Boston, 1953-55; rsch. & sales engr. Dorr Oliver Inc., Stamford, Conn., 1955-62; mng. ptnr. Stearns & Wheler Engrs., Cazenovia, N.Y., 1962-85; cons. S.G. Brisbin, Nokomis, Fla., 1985—; adj. prof. Cornell U., Ithaca, N.Y., 1980. Contbr. articles to profl. jours. 1st lt. U.S. Army Corps Engrs., 1951-53. Recipient Engring. Project award Consulting Engrs. Coun. Mem. Am. Water Works Assn. (life), Water Environment Fedn. (life), Masons. Avocations: golfing, woodworking. Home: 420 Picasso Dr Nokomis FL 34275-1497

BRISCOE, JOHN, lawyer; b. Stockton, Calif., July 1, 1948; s. John Lloyd and Doris (Olsen) B.; divorced; children: John Paul, Katherine. JD, U. San Francisco, 1972. Bar: Calif. 1972, U.S. Dist. Ct. (no., ea. and ctrl. dists.) Calif. 1972, U.S. Supreme Ct. 1978, U.S. Ct. Appeals (9th cir.) 1981. Dep. atty. gen. State of Calif., San Francisco, 1972-80; ptnr. Washburn and Kemp, San Francisco, 1980-88, Washburn, Briscoe & McCarthy, San Francisco, 1988—; bd. dirs. San Francisco Bay Planning coalition, chmn., 1990-93; vis. scholar U. Calif., Berkeley, 1990—; spl. adviser UN Compensation Commn., Geneva, Switzerland, 1998—. Author: Surveying the Courtroom, 1984, Falsework, 1997; editor: Reports of Special Masters, 1991; contbr. articles to profl. and lit. jours. Mem. ABA, San Francisco Bar Assn., Law of the Sea Inst. Roman Catholic. Office: Washburn Briscoe & McCarthy 55 Francisco St San Francisco CA 94133-2122

BRISCOE, MARY BECK, federal judge; b. 1947. BA, U. Kans., 1969, JD, 1973; LLM, U. Va., 1990. Rsch. asst. Harold L. Haun, Esq., 1973; atty.-examiner fin. divsn. ICC, 1973-74; asst. U.S. atty. for Wichita and Topeka, Kans. Dept. Justice, 1974-84; judge Kans. Ct. Appeals, 1984-95, chief judge, 1990-95; judge U.S. Ct. Appeals (10th cir.), Topeka, 1995—. Fellow Am. Bar Found., Kans. Bar Found.; mem. ABA, Am. Judicature Soc., Nat. Assn. Women Judges, Topeka Bar Assn., Kans. Bar Assn. (Outstanding Svc. award 1992), Women Attys. Assn. Topeka, Kans. Hist. Soc., Washburn Law Sch. Assn. (hon.), U. Kans. Law Soc. Office: US Ct Appeals 10th Cir 645 Massachusetts Ste 400 Lawrence KS 66044-2235

BRISEBOIS, MARCEL, museum director; b. Valleyfield, Que., Can., Oct. 25, 1933; s. Marc and Rose-Alma (Emond) B. BA, Coll. Valleyfield, 1954; PhD, La Sorbonne U., Paris, 1967; Lic. in Theology, Grand Seminar, Montreal (Que), 1968. Prof. French, philosophy Coll. Valleyfield, 1958-61, prof. philosophy, head dept., 1968-71, asst. dir., 1971-79, sec. gen., 1979-85; animator, interviewer Radio-Can., Montreal, 1960—; dir. gen. Mus. of Contemporary Art, Montreal, 1985—. Decorated Legion d'Honneur, Ordre du Canada, Ordre de Malte, Ordre de la Pleiade. Office: Musee d'Art Contemp/Montreal, 185 Rue Ste Catherine Quest, Montreal, PQ Canada H2X 3X5

BRISKIN, MAE, writer; b. Bklyn., Oct. 20, 1924; d. Sam Seidman and Yetta Rubin; m. Herbert Briskin, Dec. 1, 1946 (deceased); children: Jonathan, Lauren, Allen. BA, Bklyn. Coll., 1944; MA, Columbia U., 1946; grad. writing program, Stanford U., 1980. Author: A Boy Like Astrid's Mother, 1988 (Pen/West award for short fiction 1989), (novel) The Tree Still Stands, 1991; contbr. stories to various mags., 1975-92. Home: 3604 Arbutus Dr Palo Alto CA 94303

BRISKMAN, ARTHUR B., federal judge; b. 1947. BA, U. Ala., 1969; JD, Samford U., 1972. Asst. state ct. adminstr. State Ala., 1972-73; ptnr. Perloff, Reid & Briskman, Mobile, Ala., 1973-79; assoc. mcpl. judge City of Mobile, 1977-79; mcpl. judge City of Chicksaw, Ala., 1978-79; chief counsel, staff dir. subcom. on jurisprudence & govt. U.S. Senate, 1979-81, chief minority counsel subcom. on cts., com. on judiciary, 1981-85; bankruptcy judge U.S. Bankruptcy Ct. (so. dist.) Ala., 1985-93. Mem. Nat. Conf. Bankruptcy Judges, Am. Bankruptcy Inst., Ctrl. Fla. Bankruptcy Law Assn., Jud. Conf. U.S. (com. on the adminstrn. bankruptcy sys.), Ala. Bar Assn., Mobile County Bar Assn. Office: Ste 950 135 W Central Blvd Orlando FL 32801

BRISKMAN, LOUIS J., lawyer. BA, U. Pitts., 1970; JD, Georgetown U., 1973. Bar: Pa. 1973. Chief counsel Westinghouse Electric Corp., 1978-81; v.p., sec., gen. counsel Group W Cable, Inc. divsn. Westinghouse, 1981-83; v.p., sec. Westinghouse Broadcasting Co., 1983-86; assoc. gen. counsel energy and advanced tech. & broadcasting divsn. Westinghouse, 1986-87; dep. gen. counsel Westinghouse Electric, 1987-92, counsel, 1992-94; sr. v.p., gen. counsel Westinghouse Electric Corp., 1993-98; exec. v.p., gen. counsel CBS Corp., Pitts., 1998—. Office: CBS Corp Westinghouse Bldg 51 West 52nd St New York NY 10019

BRISKMAN, ROBERT DAVID, engineering executive; b. N.Y.C., Oct. 15, 1932; s. Nathan S. and Rose L. (Fishman) B.; m. Lenore Heffner, Mar. 30, 1957; children: Laura G., Sharon L., Robert D. Jr., Douglas E. BSE, Princeton U., 1954; MSEE, U. Md., 1961. Registered profl. engr., D.C. Devel. engr. IBM, Poughkeepsie, N.Y., 1954-55; analyst Army Security Agy., Washington, 1956-58; chief of program support tracking and data acquisition NASA, Washington, 1959-63; asst. v.p. domestic systems Communication Satellite Corp., Washington, 1964-72; asst. v.p. space and info. systems Comsat Gen. Corp., Washington, 1973-76; dir. pre-operational program Satellite Bus. Systems, McLean, Va., 1977-79; v.p. systems implementation Comsat Gen. Corp., Washington, 1980-85; sr. v.p. engring. and ops. Geostar Corp., Washington, 1986-91; exec. v.p. engring. and ops. CD Radio Inc., N.Y.C., 1992—. Contbr. articles on satellite systems and applications, 1956—; telecommunications editor: McGraw-Hill Ency. Sci. and Tech., 1985—; patentee in field. Capt. U.S. Army, 1955-57. Recipient Founders award Electronics and Aerospace Systems Conf., 1980. Fellow AIAA, IEEE (v.p. tech. activities, sec.-treas., 1976-78, Centennial medal, 1984), Washington Acad. Sci., Washington Soc. Engrs. (pres. 1988-89); mem. Old Crows, Internat. Acad. Astronautics, Armed Forces Comm. and Electronics Assn., Cosmos Club. Republican. Office: CD Radio Inc Ste 700 3 Bethesda Metro Ctr Bethesda MD 20814-4000

BRISSETTE, MARTHA BLEVINS, lawyer; b. Salisbury, Md., Apr. 30, 1959; d. Reuben Wesley and Miriam Rebecca (Walters) Blevins; m. Henry Joseph Brissette III, May 24, 1980. BA, U. Richmond, 1981, JD, 1983. Bar: Va. 1983, U.S. Supreme Ct. 1987, Ill. 1997. Law clk. Supreme Ct. Va., Richmond, 1983-84; atty. Dept. Justice, Washington, 1984-88; staff atty. Office of the Exec. Sec., Supreme Ct. Va., Richmond, 1988; asst. atty. gen. Office of the Atty. Gen. of Va., Richmond, 1989-92; atty., v.p. counsel Lawyers Title Ins. Corp., Richmond, 1992-97; asst. counsel State Farm Ins. Cos., 1997-99; asst. atty. gen. Office of Atty. Gen. of Va., Richmond, 1999—. Mem. ABA, Va. Bar Assn., Phi Beta Kappa. Catholic. Avocation: cake decorating. Home: 8307 Forge Rd Richmond VA 23228-3127 Office: 900 E Main St Richmond VA 23219

BRISSIE, EUGENE FIELD, JR., publisher; b. N.Y.C., Nov. 28, 1949; s. Eugene Field Brissie and Sara Louise (Phillips) Brissie Beckwith. B.A., Princeton U., 1972. Dir. fgn. rights Farrar, Straus & Giroux, N.Y.C., 1973-77; v.p. Simon & Schuster, N.Y.C., 1977-84, 95-98, G. P. Putnam's Sons, N.Y.C., 1984-92, Contemporary Books, Chgo., 1992-95, Prentice Hall, N.J., 1998—. Club: Princeton of N.Y. Office: Simon & Schuster Bus & Self Improvement 240 Frisch Ct Paramus NJ 07652-5240

BRISSMAN, BERNARD GUSTAVE, insurance company executive; b. St. Paul, May 10, 1919; s. Gustave Erie and Emma Barbara (Beetsch) B.; m. Frances Irene Shackleton, May 30, 1942; children—Gerald, Jonathan, Joan, Roland, William. Student, U. Minn., 1937-52, Butler U., Indpls., 1962-64. CPCU. Spl. agt. Gen. Accident, Mpls., 1945-49; casualty mgr. Fireman's Fund Ins. Co., Mpls., 1949-54; sr. v.p., dir. Am. States Cos., Indpls., 1954-84. Capt. U.S. Army, 1941-45. Mem. Minn. CPCU Assn. (pres. 1951-52, Ind. CPCU Assn. (pres. 1958-59). Republican. Roman Catholic. Avocations: sailing; computers, acting, dancing. Home: 3373 S Calle Del Acle Green Valley AZ 85614-4809

BRISTAH, PAMELA JEAN, librarian; b. Highland Park, Mich., May 13, 1956; d. James Werner and Emily Ann (Josif) B.; m. David Dukehart Wright, July 20, 1984. MusB, Westminster Choir Coll., 1978; MLS, Columbia U., 1985. Cataloger Manhattan Sch. Music, N.Y.C., 1985-88, head libr., 1988—. Author: A Basic Music Library, 3d edit., 1997. Mem. Music Libr. Assn. Avocation: photography. Office: Manhattan Sch Music 120 Claremont Ave New York NY 10027-4698

BRISTO, MARCA, healthcare executive; b. Albany, N.Y., June 23, 1953; d. Earl C. and Dorothy (Moore) B.; m. J. robert Kettlewell, Oct. 15, 1988; children: Samuel Clayton Kettlewell, Madeline Elizabeth Kettlewell. BA in Sociology, Beloit Coll., 1974; BSN, Rush Coll. Nursing, Chgo., 1976. Cert. nursing. RN Rush Presbyn. St. Luke's Med. Ctr., Chgo., 1976-77; RN Northwestern Meml. Hosp., Chgo., 1977, family planning nurse specialist, 1978-79; exec. dir. Access Living Met. Chgo., 1979-84; chmn. Nat. Coun. Disability, Washington. Mem. nat. adv. bd. Access Am., Austin, Tex.; bd. dirs. Donors Forum of Chgo.; bd. dirs., chairperson Ill. Pub. Action Coun.; co-founder, pres. Nat. Coun. on Ind. Living. Named Outstanding Young Citizen, Chgo. Jr. C. of C., 1984; recipient Commr.'s Disting. Svc. award U.S. Dept. Edn. Rehab. Svcs. Adminstrn., 1987, Cert. of Esteem & Recognition, Stte of Ill. Office of Sec. of State, 1987. Mem. Nat. Coun. on Ind. Living. Avocations: cooking, traveling. Office: Nat Coun Disability 1331 F St NW Ste 1050 Washington DC 20004-1138*

BRISTOL, NORMAN, lawyer, arbitrator, former food company executive; b. Bronx, N.Y., June 14, 1924; s. Lawrence and Bell (Allchin) B.; m. Doreen Kingan, Mar. 28, 1952; children: Charles L., Norman, Alexander, Barnaby. Grad., Phillips Exeter Acad., 1939-41; A.B., Yale, 1944; LLB, Columbia Law Sch., 1947-49. Bar: N.Y. bar 1950, Mich. bar 1954. Atty. Root, Ballantine, Harlan, Bushby & Palmer, N.Y.C., 1949-53; with Kellogg Co., Battle Creek, Mich., 1954-78, asst. gen. counsel, 1958-64, sec., 1960-78, gen. counsel, 1964-78, sr. v.p., 1968-75, dir., 1972-78, exec. v.p., 1975-78; atty. Howard & Howard, Kalamazoo, 1979-93. Mem. Gull Lake Comty. Schs. Bd. Edn., 1963-70, pres., 1965-67; trustee Kalamazoo Symphony Soc., Inc., 1983-94, pres., 1990-91; bd. dirs. Southwest Mich. Land Conservancy, Inc., 1996— . Lt. (j.g.) USNR, 1943-46. Mem. Am. Bar Assn., State Bar Mich., Kalamazoo Bar Assn., Am. Soc. Corp. Secs., SCORE (counsellor). Home and Office: 2962 Sylvan Dr Hickory Corners MI 49060-9319

BRISTOL, STANLEY DAVID, mathematics educator; b. Mankato, Minn., Dec. 30, 1948; s. Robert Frederick Bristol and Ruth Charlotte (Buckeye) Bristol Bond; m. Elaine Metzer, Jan. 30, 1970; children: Thomas Alan, Jennifer Elise. BS, Ariz. State U., 1969, MA, 1970. Cert. secondary tchr. with gifted endorsement. Math. tchr. Saguaro H.S., Scottsdale, Ariz., 1973-74, Poston Jr. H.S., Mesa, Ariz., 1974-77, Corona del Sol H.S., Tempe, Ariz., 1977—; math. tchr. Ariz. State U., Tempe, 1989—, chair math. dept., 1990—. Sunday sch. tchr. 1st United Meth. Ch., Tempe, 1983-93. With U.S. Army, 1970-73. Named Tchr. of Yr., Tempe Diablos (C. of C.), 1987, 98, Tribune Educator of Yr., 1995, honored educator The Flinn Found., 1997; recipient Presdl. award for Excellence in Math. Teaching, 1990; tchr. of yr. Tempe Diablos, 1998. Mem. Nat. Coun. Tchrs. Math., Ariz. Assn. Tchrs. Math., Nat. Edn. Assn., Ind. Order of Foresters, Math. Assn. Am. Avocations: photography, reading, bowling, computers. Office: Corona del Sol High Sch 1001 E Knox Rd Tempe AZ 85284-3204

BRISTOW, CLINTON, JR., academic administrator; b. Montgomery, Ala., Mar. 15, 1949; s. T.C. and Betty Bristow; 1 child, Maya. JD, Northwestern U., 1974, PhD, 1977; postgrad., U. Minn., 1983; MBA, Governor's State U., 1984. V.p. adminstrn. Olive-Harvey Coll., Chgo., 1980-81; dean Coll. Bus. Chgo. State U., 1985-93; pres. Chgo. Bd. Edn., 1990-92, Alcorn State U., Lorman, Miss., 1995—; cons. in field. Contbr. articles to profl. publs. Chmn. Miss. Rhodes Scholarship Com., 1996; bd. dirs. Miss. Agr./Forestry Mus., Jackson, Chgo., Congl. Award Bd., HBCU Capital Fin. Bd.; mem. exec. com. 1890 Coun. Pres. Fellow Northwestern U. Ctr. for Urban Affairs, 1973-74; recipient Role Model award Top Ladies of Distinction, Inc., 1987, Greater Roseland Area Planning, 1990. Mem. Am. Assn. State Colls. and Univs. (state rep.), Miss. Instns. of Higher Learning (coun. of pres.), Southwestern Athletic Conf. (treas. 1996). Baptist. Avocations: reading, golf, jogging. Home: 1000 ASU Dr # 719 Lorman MS 39096 Office: Alcorn State U 1000 ASU DR # 359 Lorman MS 39096

BRISTOW, DAVID IAN, lawyer; b. Toronto, May 19, 1931; s. Horace George and Elizabeth (Bourne) B.; m. Suzanne Snow, Sept. 9, 1959; children: Timothy Charles, Julie Anne, Lori Anne. BA, U. Toronto, 1953; LLB, Osgoode Hall, Toronto, 1957. Bar: Ont. 1957, apptd. Queen's counsel 1969. Since practiced in Toronto; mem. firm Shibley Righton McCutcheon, 1969-74, Bristow, Gilgan & Glaholt, 1974-88, Fraser Milner, 1988—; tchr. Osgoode Hall Law Sch., 1967-74; mem. Pacific Rim adv. coun. repsecting preparation internat. arbitration; chartered mediator accreditation com. Arbitration and Mediation Inst. Ont. Co-author: Construction and Mechanics Liens in Canada, 1962, 85; mem. edit. bd. Constrn. Law Letter, Constrn. Law Reports. Bd. dirs. McInnis Undersea Found. Mem. ATLA, Can. Bar Assn. (founding chmn. constrn. law sect. Ont., Disting. Svc. award 1996), Advs. Soc., Country of York Bar Assn., Internat. Bar Assn., Inter-Pacific Bar Assn., Am. Arbitration Assn., Am. Nuclear Soc., Lawyes Club Toronto, Cambridge Club, Granite Club, Phi Delta Phi. Home: 88 Blythwood Rd, Toronto, ON Canada M4N 1A4 Office: 1st Canadian Pl, PO Box 100, Toronto, ON Canada M5X 1B2

BRISTOW, LONNIE ROBERT, physician; b. N.Y.C., Apr. 6, 1930; s. Lonnie Harlis and Vivian (Wines) B.; m. Margaret Jeter, June 1, 1957 (div. Aug. 1961); children: Mary, Mark; m. Marilyn Hingslage, Oct. 18, 1961; children: Robert, Elizabeth. B.S., CCNY, 1953; M.D., NYU, 1957. Diplomate: Am. Bd. Internal Medicine. Intern San Francisco City and County Hosp., 1957-58; resident VA Hosp., San Francisco, 1959-60, Francis Delafield Hosp., N.Y.C., 1960, VA Hosp., Bronx, N.Y., 1961; practice medicine specializing in internal medicine San Pablo, Calif., 1964—; mem. staff Brookside Hosp., San Pablo, 1998; cons. Calif. Dept. Health Care in Prisons, Sacramento, 1976-77, chmn. sickle cell com., 1976-79; mem. admissions com. U. Calif.-Berkeley, 1972-75; mem. Nat. Council Health Care Tech., Washington, 1980; mem. physician discussion group on physician payment Health Care Financing Adminstrn., Washington, 1983-86; chmn. bd. regents Uniformed Svcs. U. Health Scis., Bethesda, Md., 1996—. Recipient ann. award of excellence Calif. Med. Polit. Action Com., 1977. Fellow ACP (master); mem. Inst. of Medicine of Nat. Acad. Scis., Am. Soc. Internal Medicine (trustee 1976-83, pres. 1981-82), AMA (coun. med. svc. 1976-85, trustee 1985-94, pres.-elect 1994-95, pres. 1995). Home: 3324 Ptarmigan Dr 3B Walnut Creek CA 94595-3157 Address: 1966 Tice Valley Blvd # 411 Walnut Creek CA 94595-2203

BRISTOW, ROBERT O'NEIL, writer, educator; b. St. Louis, Nov. 17, 1926; s. Jesse Reuben and Helen Marjorie (Utley) B.; children by previous marriage—Cynthia Lynn, Margery Jan Wu, Gregory Scott, Kelly Robert. B.A. in Journalism, U. Okla., 1951, M.A. in Journalism, 1965. Asst. advt. mgr. Altus (Okla.) Times Democrat, 1951-53; free-lance writer Altus, 1951-60; prof. English Winthrop Coll., Rock Hill, S.C., 1960-87, prof. emeritus, 1987—. Author: Time for Glory, 1968, Night Season, 1970, A Faraway Drummer, 1973, Laughter in Darkness, 1974. Served with USNR, 1944-45. Recipient award for lit. excellence U. Okla., 1969, award for novel Friends of Am. Writers, 1974. Mem. Alpha Tau Omega. Home: 613 1/2 Charlotte Ave Rock Hill SC 29730-3648

BRISTOW, WALTER JAMES, JR., retired judge; b. Columbia, S.C., Oct. 14, 1924; s. Walter James and Caroline Belser (Melton) B.; m. Katherine Stewart Mullins, Sept. 12, 1952; children: Walter James III, Katherine Mullins (dec.). *Father was a medical doctor specializing in eye, ear, nose and throat, practicing in Columbia. Son Walter III is a medical doctor specializing in gastroenterology, practicing in Columbia. On August 1, 1981, he married Anne Land Jackson of Manning. They have four children: Abbot Land (Abby), Katherine Stewart (Katy), Walter James IV (James), and William Melton II (Melton).* Student, Va. Mil. Inst., 1941-43; AB, U. N.C., 1947; LLB cum laude, U. S.C., 1947-49. Mem. Marchant, Bristow & Bates, 1953-76, S.C. Ho. of Reps., 1956-58; resident judge 5th Cir. Ct. S.C., 1978-88; ret., 1988; nat. pres. Conf. Ins. Legislators, 1974-75. *Mr. Bristow enlisted in the U.S. Army Reserve on December 1, 1942, and was called to active duty on June 19, 1943. He served as an enlisted man during World War II, serving overseas in the European Theater of Operations as a platoon sergeant of Battery B, 292nd Field Artillery Observation Batallion, receiving battle stars for the battles of Central Europe and Rhineland.* Trustee Elvira Wright Fund for Crippled Children, 1963-76; mem. bd. visitors ex officio The Citadel, Charleston, S.C., 1967-76. Served with AUS, 1943-45; ETO, brig. gen. S.C. Army N.G. Decorated Meritorious Svc. medal. Mem. ABA, Wig and Robe, S.C. Law Inst., S.C. Coun. on Holocaust, Capital City Club, Cotillion Club, Forest Lake Club, Palmetto Club, Columbia Ball Club, Sertoma, Alpha Tau Omega. Democrat. Office: PO Box 1147 Columbia SC 29202-1147

BRITES, JOSÉ BAPTISTA, secondary education educator, writer, artist; b. Alcorochel, Torres Novas, Portugal, June 7, 1945; came to U.S., 1970; s. José and Ludovina (Guia) B.; m. Olga M. Boyd; children: David Joseph, Kevin Daniel. BA in Art, Brown U., 1981, BA in Lang., 1981, MEd, 1982. Cert. secondary tchr., R.I. Interpreter Davies Vocat. High Sch., Lincoln, R.I., 1983-86; bilingual tchr. Davies Vocat. High Sch., 1986-87, LEP tchr., coord., 1987-96, guidance counselor, 1997—; LEP state adv. bd., Providence, 1990-92; vice dir. Immigrants Cultural Found., Lisbon, Portugal, 1988-91; co-founder Peregrinação-Arts/Letters, Lisbon, 1983-91, Sol XXI Arts/Letters, 1992—; founder, pres. Peregrinação Publs., 1995; apptd. Gov. Bruce Sundlum to bd. R.I. State Coun. Arts, 1993-97; guest poet II and III Internat. Symposium on Poetry, U. Coimbra, Portugal, 1995, 98; mem. Portuguese-Am. Leadership Coun. of U.S., Washington. Author: (poetry) Poemas Sem Poesia, 1975, Imigramar, 1981, (short stories) Imigramantes, 1984, Estórias Para A História de Alcorochel, 1994, Twenty Five Years of Poetry, 1995, Coisas e Loisas das nossas terras, 1996, Coisas do Coiso e da Coisa, 1996, Do Ribatejo ao Além-Tejo, 1998, (novel) Por Terras de Cristo e do Diabo, 1999; singer Portuguese Heritage Choral, Pawtucket, R.I.; staff writer Portuguese Times, New Bedford, Mass., Portuguese Tribune, San Jose, Calif., O Emigrante, Lisbon, O ALMONDA, Torres Novas, O Mirante, Chamusca, O Ribatejo, Santarèm LUSO-AMERICANO, The Portuguese Post, Newark, Correio dos Açores, Azores, Português na Austrália, Voice, Can. Recipient Community award Portuguese Am. Citizens, 1984, 1st prize in several poetry contests, citations from Sen. Claiborne Pell, 1984, Gov. Joseph Garrahy, 1984, Mayor Henry S. Kinch, 1979, New Bedford Mayor Rosemary Tierney; honored by CASA DA SAUDADE Libr., 1995. Mem. Portuguese Writers Assn. Avocations: painting, sculpting (metal), book reviews, travel. Home: 36 Brayton Ave Rumford RI 02916-2513 Office: Davies Jr HS Jenckes Hill Rd Lincoln RI 02865

BRITNER, PRESTON ARTHUR, IV, developmental psychologist, educator; b. Washington, Sept. 14, 1968; s. Preston Arthur III and Connie Lou (Holloway) B.; m. Suzanne Jean LaFleur, May 28, 1994. BA in Developmental Psychology, U. Miami, 1990; MA in Developmental Psychology, U. Va., 1993, PhD in Developmental Psychology, 1996. Asst. prof. psychology Smith Coll., Northampton, 1996-97; asst. prof. Sch. Family Studies U. Conn., Storrs, 1997—, dormitory faculty advisor, 1997—; cons. Child-Parent Attachment Clinic, Charlottesville, Va., 1994—, Inst. for Psychiatry, U. London, 1996—. Author: Preventing Child Abuse and Neglect through Parent Education, 1997; mem. editl. bd. Jour. Sch. Psychology, 1997—; contbr. more than 30 articles to profl. jours. including Child Welfare, Jour. Child and Family Studies. Mem. Comm. on Children, Hartford, Conn., 1997—; pres., bd. dirs. Barrett Day Care Ctr., Charlottesville, Va., 1996, bd. dirs., 1994-96. Grantee U. Conn. Rsch. Found., 1997-98. Mem. APA, Am. Psychol. Soc., Soc. for Rsch. in Child Devel., Raven Soc., Iron Arrow Soc., Sigma Xi. Avocations: soccer, community service, running. Office: U Conn Sch Family Studies 348 Mansfield Rd Unit U2058 Storrs Mansfield CT 06269-2058

BRITO, DAGOBERT LLANOS, economics educator; b. Mex., Apr. 6, 1941; came to U.S., 1945, naturalized, 1958; s. John L. and Guadalupe G. (Llanos) B.; m. Patricia Ann Kendrick, June 29, 1968. B.A., Rice U., 1967, M.A., 1970, Ph.D., 1970. Asst. prof. econs. U. Wis., Madison, 1970-72; asso. prof. econs. and polit. sci. Ohio State U., Columbus, 1972-75; prof. Ohio State U., 1976-79; dir. Murphy Inst. Polit. Economy; chmn., prof. econs. Tulane U., New Orleans, 1979-84; Peterkin prof. polit. econs. Rice U., Houston, 1984—; cons. Dept. State, Dept. Def. Author: A Dynamic Model of the Armaments Race, 1972, Strategic Nuclear Weapons and the Allocation of International Rights, 1977, Conflicts and Outbreak of War, 1985, Stock Externalities, Pigovian Taxation and Dynamic Stability, 1987, Richardsonian Arms Race Models, 1989, On the Limits of Economic Control, 1990, Externalities and Compulsory Vaccinations, 1991, The Economic and Political Incentives to Acquire Nuclear Weapons, 1993; (with M.D. Intriligator) The Economics of Disarmament, Arms Races and Arms Control, 1993, Minimizing the Risks for Accidental Nuclear War: An Agenda for Action, 1993; (with P.R. Hartley) Consumer Rationality and Credit Cards, 1995, Proliferation and the Probability of War: A Cardinality Theorem, 1996; editor: Strategies for Managing Nuclear Proliferation, 1983; assoc. editor Jour. Optimization Theory and Applications. Served with U.S. Army, 1963-66. NSF grantee, 1972, 74, 77, 78, 81; Mershon Center grantee, 1973, 78. Mem. Am. Econ. Assn., Econometric Soc., Public Choice Soc., Internat. Inst. of Strategic Studies, Houston Philo. Soc. Club: Houston Yacht. Office: Rice U PO Box 1892 Houston TX 77251-1892

BRITO, MARIA CRISTINA, sculptor, educator; b. Havana, Cuba, Oct. 10, 1947; came to U.S., 1961; d. Rafael and Maria Cristina B.; children: Otto Zequeira, Alexis Zequeira. BE, U. Miami, 1969; MS, Fla. Internat. U., 1976, MFA, 1977; MFA, U. Miami, 1979. Instr. U. Miami, Fla., 1977, grad. asst., 1978-79; art instr. Miami Sr. High Sch. Adult Edn. Ctr., 1979—; ceramics instr. Ceramic League Miami, 1979-80, Metro. Mus. and Art Ctr., Coral Gables, Fla., 1980-81; juror Coconut Grove (Fla.) Arts Festival, 1981, Santa Fe C.C., Gainesville, Fla., 1988, Nat. Endowment for Arts Sculpture Panel, Washington, 1990, WESTAF/Nat. Endowment for Arts Regional Fellowships for Visual Artists, 1993; juror Miami-Dade C.C., 1981, 86, 91-93, off-campus art instr., 1980-86; speaker in field. One-woman shows include The Gallery at 24, Miami, Fla., 1980, 82, 85, Kennesaw Coll., Marietta, Ga., 1987, Anne Jaffe Gallery, Bay Harbour, Fla., 1988, 91, Inter-Am. Art Gallery, Miami, 1989, Mus. Contemporary Hispanic Art, N.Y.C., 1989, Spirit Sq. Ctr. for Arts, Charlotte, N.C., 1990, Middleton-McMillan Gallery, 1990, Barry Univ., Miami Shores, 1991, M. Gutierrez Fine Art, Miami Beach, 1994, Mus. Art, Fort Lauderdale, Fla., 1998; exhibited in group shows at Frances Wolfson Art Gallery, Miami, 1981, Ralph Wilson Gallery, Bethlehem, Pa., 1982, 90, Aaron Berman Gallery, N.Y.C., Cuban Mus. Art and Culture, 1983, Fisher Gallery, U. So. Calif., L.A., 1984, Fla. Ctr. Contemporary Art, 1985, Fla. State U., 1985, 89, Mus. Comtemporary Hispanic Art, N.Y., 1985, S.E. Ctr. Contemporary Art, Winston-Salem, N.C., 1985, Thomas Center Gallery, Gainesville, Fla., 1986, The Tampa (Fla.) Mus., 1986, Real Art Ways, Hartford, Conn., 1987, North Miami Mus., 1987, Zimmerli Art Mus., Rutgers U., New Brunswick, N.J., 1987, University Gallery, U. Fla., Gainesville, 1987, L.A. Mcpl. Art Gallery, 1988, Olympic Park, Seoul, Korea, 1988, Lannan Mus., Fort Worth, 1989, North Miami Ctr. Contemporary Art, 1989, New Mus. Contemporary Art, Mus. Contemporary Hispanic Art, Studio Mus. Harlem, N.Y., 1990, Mus. Contemporary Art Chgo., 1991, High Mus. Art, Atlanta, 1991, Mus. Art, Ft. Lauderdale, 1991, 92, 93, Galaria de la Raza, San Francisco, 1992, Dowd Fine Arts Gallery, SUNY Cortland, 1993, Women and Their Work traveling exhbn., Austin, Tex., 1993, Herbert F. Johnson Mus. Art Cornell U., Ithaca, N.Y., 1993, Norton Gallery Art, West Palm Beach, Fla., 1994, Moreau Galleries, St. Mary's Coll. Notre Dame, Ind., 1994, Altlantic Ctr. Modern art, Las Palmas de Gran Canaria, Spain, La Caixa Found., Palma de Mallorca, Spain. Santa Monica Art Ctr., Barcelona, Spain, 1996, 2d IberoAm. Art Biennial of Lima, Peru, 1999. U. Miami scholar, 1977-78; Fla. Arts Coun. fellow, 1979, Cintas fellow Inst. Internat. Edn., 1981, 85, Artist-in-Residence fellow Djerassi Found., 1983, Visual Arts fellowship grantee Nat. Endowment for Arts, 1984, 88, Ind. Artist fellow Fla. Dept. State, 1988, South Fla. Consortium fellow, 1990, 92, Pollock-Krasner Found. grant, 1990, Virginia A. Groot Found. grantee, 1994. Home: 8995 SW 75th St Miami FL 33173-3438

BRITT, DAVID VAN BUREN, educational communications executive; b. Needham, Mass., July 30, 1937; s. Paul Merwyn and Ellen Sibront (Bent) B.; m. Marjorie Joan Hoag, Feb. 15, 1958 (div. 1984); children: Pamela B. Barr, Barbara B. Schaefer, Paul David; m. Sue Britt Cushman, July 22, 1989. AB, Wesleyan U., 1959; MPA, Harvard U., 1967. Ops. mgmt. staff No. Trust Co., Chgo., 1959-62; legis. chief U.S. AID, Washington, 1962-68; chief programs and plans U.S. EEOC, Washington, 1968-69; dep. dir. policy planning U.S. Overseas Pvt. Investment Corp., Washington, 1969-70; ind. cons. Washington, 1970-71; from v.p. to COO Children's TV Workshop, N.Y.C., 1971-90, CEO, 1990—. Trustee New World Found., N.Y.C., 1978-86, Wesleyan U., Middletown, Conn., 1989-92, CTW, 1990—; chmn. Am. Ctr. for Children's TV, 1993—; bd. dirs. Kids Voting, USA; mem. Coun. on Fgn. Rels. Recipient Disting. Alumnus award Wesleyan U., 1994. Episcopalian. Home: 14 Sylvester Ct Norwalk CT 06855-2615

BRITT, DONNA MARIE, school nurse; b. Phila., Oct. 27, 1950; d. Joseph D. and Margaret M. (Cullen) Finn; divorced; children: Colleen Marie, Patricia Ann, Joseph James. BA in Biology, Holy Family Coll., 1972, BSN, 1974. cert. sch. nurse, N.J. Staff nurse Jeannes Hosp., Phila., 1975; tchr. Archdiocese of Phila., 1985-91; sch. nurse Camden City Bd. of Edn., N.J., 1991-93; sch. nurse, health tchr. Riverside (N.J.) Bd. edn., 1994-95; sch. nurse City of Burlington, N.J., 1995—; chairperson Mid. States Com. Our Lady Help of Christians, Phila., 1988-91, co-chairperson Mid. States Com. Camden City Sch., 1991-93. Cons.: (book) Tough Love for Teachers, 1989. Merit badge counselor Boy Scouts Am., Frontier Dist., Phila., 1990—. Mem. Nat. Sch. Nurses Assn., N.J. State Sch. Nurses Assn., Burlington County Sch. Nurses Assn., NEA, N.J. Edn. Assn., Burlington County Edn. Assn. Roman Catholic. Avocations: needlework, gardening, art. Home: 9 Primrose Pl Delran NJ 08075-2817 Office: Capt James Lawrence Sch 315 Barclay St Burlington NJ 08016-1737

BRITT, EARL THOMAS, lawyer; b. Phila., July 14, 1940; s. Earl Francis and Marie Rita (Lawless) B.; m. Maureen Wong, Dec. 26, 1964; children: Denise, Karen, Eileen, Mary, Kevin, Stephen. AB, St. Joseph's U., Phila., 1961; JD, U. Pa., 1964. Bar: Pa. 1964, U.S. Dist. Ct. (ea. dist.) Pa. 1964, U.S. Ct. Appeals (3rd cir.) 1964, U.S. Dist. Ct. Appeals (D.C. cir.) 1981, U.S. Supreme Ct. 1982. Atty. Pa. Mfrs. Assn. Ins. Co., Phila., 1964-67; assoc. Swartz Campbell & Detweiler, Phila., 1967-68; assoc., then ptnr. Duane Morris & Heckscher, Phila., 1968-92; founder, ptnr., chmn. Britt, Hankins, Schaible & Moughan, Phila., 1992—; judge pro tem Ct. Common Pleas, Phila., 1991—; lectr. Comey Inst. Indsl. Rels. St. Joseph's U., 1961-92; adj. faculty Temple U. Sch. Law-Acad. Advocacy, 1994—. Mem. adv. bd. Norwood-Fontbonne Acad., 1997—. Mem. ABA, Pa. Bar Assn., Phila. Bar Assn. (trustee campaign for qualified judges 1989, hon. trustee 1990-91), Phila. Assn. Def. Counsel (bd. dirs. 1983-89, 93-94, pres. 1988-89), Pa. Def. Inst. (lectr. Trial Acad. 1990—), Internat. Assn. Def. Counsel, Def. Rsch. Inst., Lawyer's Club Phila. (bd. dirs. 1988-90). Republican. Roman Catholic. Home: 106 Sparango Ln Plymouth Meeting PA 19462-1115 Office: Britt Hankins Schaible & Moughan Ste 202 633 W Germantown Pike Plymouth Meeting PA 19462

BRITT, GLENN ALAN, media company executive; b. Hackensack, N.J., Mar. 6, 1949; s. Walter E. Britt and Helen Crupi; m. Barbara Jane Little, Oct. 25, 1975. AB, Dartmouth Coll., 1971, MBA, 1972. Contr.'s asst. Time, Inc., N.Y.C., 1972-74; fin. dir. Iran project, Time-Life Books Time, Inc., Alexandria, Va., 1976-78; dir. video group new bus. devel. Time, Inc., N.Y.C., 1980-81, sr. v.p. fin. video group, 1984, v.p., treas., 1986-88, v.p., CFO, 1988-90; sr. v.p., treas. Time Warner Inc., N.Y.C., 1990; exec. v.p. Time Warner Cable Group, Stamford, Conn., 1990-92; pres. Time Warner Cable Ventures, Stamford, Conn., 1999—; v.p., treas. Manhattan Cable TV, N.Y.C., 1974-76; v.p. network and studio ops. HBO Inc., N.Y.C., 1978-80, sr. v.p., CFO, 1984-86; sr. v.p. fin. Am. TV and Comm. Corp., Stamford, Conn., 1981-84. Mem. Fin. Exec. Inst., Woodway Country Club, Eastward Ho, Cape Cod National Golf Club and Country Club. Avocations: skiing, gardening, golf. Office: Time Warner Cable Group 290 Harbor Dr Stamford CT 06902-7475

BRITT, JOHN ROY, banker; b. Los Angeles, Oct. 9, 1937; s. Roy Arthur and Virginia Alice (Vaughn) B.; children: Jeffrey John, Belinda Lynn, Gregory Scott. B.A., Claremont Men's Coll., 1959; grad., Pacific Coast Banking Sch., U. Wash., 1973, Managerial Policy Inst., U. So. Calif., 1978. Diplomate Am. Bd. Forensic Examiners (bd. cert. forensic examiner). With Security Pacific Nat. Bank, 1959-83; regional v.p. Security Pacific Nat. Bank, Los Angeles, 1972-74, sr. v.p., 1974-83; adminstr. Mid City-Eastern div. Security Pacific Nat. Bank, 1978-83; instr. Essentials of Banking Sch., U. Notre Dame, 1979; sr. v.p. Coast Savs. and Loan, Los Angeles, 1983-85; exec. v.p., chief operating officer Pacific Inland Bank, Anaheim, Calif., 1985-86; pres., chief exec. officer Pacific Inland Bank, 1986-89; pres. JRB Assocs., 1990—; pres., chief exec. officer United Citizens Nat. Bank, L.A., 1992. Mem. pres.'s adv. coun. Claremont McKenna Coll., 1993; past chmn. bd. dirs., mem. exec. com. Commuter Transp. Svcs., Inc., L.A. Capt. USAR, 1959-67. Mem. The Nat. Forensic Ctr., Newcomen Soc., Robert Morris Assocs. (pres. So. Calif. chpt. 1988-89), Claremont McKenna Coll. Alumni Assn. (pres. 1968-69). Republican. Methodist.

BRITT, LOIS G., farming executive; b. Duplin County, N.C., Sept. 30, 1935. BS in Home Econs., East Carolina U., 1956; MEd in Adult Edn., N.C. State U., 1969. Mgr. family farm; pub. affairs dir. Murphy Farms Inc., Rose Hill, N.C.; bd. govs. U. N.C., 1989, 93, 97, sec. bd., standing com. svc., chmn. 1993-98, vice chmn. 1992, sec. 1991, ad hoc comm. svc., presdl. search com. 1996-97, co-chmn. com. on tchg. excellence, 1994, com. on inclusion, 1994; chmn. com. on tchg. awards, 1997, issues com. 1996, bd. assessment com., 1995, others; exec. bd. N.C. Agribusiness, pres.-elect 1997, pres. 1998. Sunday sch. tchr., adminstrv. bd. Bethel Meth. Ch., Mount Olive, N.C.; life mem. Women of the Ch., N.C. Meth. Conf.; past chmn. Duplin Outdoor Drama Soc.; extension com. on personnel and program devel. USDA. Named Woman of Yr. Bus. and Profl. Womens Club, Tarheel of Week News and Observer; recipient Disting. Svc. awards N.C. Grange 1996, Nat. Assn. of Extension Home Economists, Nat. Assn. of Extension 4-H Agts., Reynolds Extension Agt. award of excellence, Melvin Cording Leadership award Duplin Agri-Bus. Coun., 1998, Order of the Long Leaf Pine, 1991. Mem. Epsilon Sigma Phi, Alpha Zeta.

BRITT, MAISHA DORRAH, protective services official; b. S.C.; d. Charles Joseph Britt and Versena (Kennedy) Dorrah; m. W. Benjamin Williams, Dec. 14, 1963 (div. June 1976); children: Terri Rochelle, Trina Michelle. AS, BS, Phila Coll. Textiles and Sci.; MA, Antioch U., Phila., 1986; postgrad., Del. State U., 1999. Cert. in electronic surveillance. Police officer Phila. Police Dept., 1976-79; sgt., county detective Phila. Dist. Atty's Office, 1979-90; orgn. devel. cons., pres. M. Dorrah-Britt and Assocs., 1991—; family devel. specialist Norristown Family Ctr., 1994—; founder, dir. Creative Awareness Workshop, Phila., 1978—. Poet: (contbr. anthologies) Famous Poems of the Twentieth Century, 1996, Nat. Libr. of Poetry, 1998 (Editor's award). Sec. bd. Horizon House, Phila., 1988—; vol. Women Against Abuse, Phila., 1983—, mem. women's ministry Calvary Bapt. Ch., Phila.; mem. bd. trustees Ctr. for Literacy, 1990—, vice chmn.; vol. security team program mem. Atlanta Com. Olympic Games, 1996. Inducted into Murrell Dobbins H.S. Hall of Fame, 1988; named Woman of Yr., Fedn.Bus. and Profl. Women's Clubs Inc., 1991. Mem. AAUW, Am. Soc. for Indsl. Security, County and State Detectives Assn. Pa. (exec. bd. 1990—, Leadership award 1989), Fraternal Order of Police, Internat. Police Assn., Internat. Assn. Women Police (Officer of Yr. 1989), Nat. Women's Hall of Fame, Bus. and Profl. Women's Club, Internat. Platform Assn. Republican. Avocations: music, creative writing, creative dance, walking. Address: PO Box 1381 Dover DE 19903-1381

BRITT, RONALD LEROY, manufacturing company executive; b. Abilene, Kans., Mar. 1, 1935; s. Elvin Elbert and Lona Helen (Conn) B.; B.S.M.E., Wichita State U., 1963; m. Judith Ann Salter, June 29, 1957; children—Brett Gavin, Mark Damon, Melissa Ann. Product engr. to product planner Hotpoint div. Gen. Electric Co., Chgo., 1963-68; product planner Norge Co., Chgo., 1968; product mgr., asst. dir. engring. Leigh Products Inc., Coopersville, Mich., 1968-74; mgr. rsch. and devel. Miami Carey div. Jim Walter Corp., Monroe, Ohio, 1974-84; sr. v.p. mfg. and engring. Belvedere (Ill.) USA Corp., 1984—; industry rep. for electric fans Underwriters Labs. Active, Boy Scouts Am., 1970-73, PTA, 1973-78; exec. adviser Jr. Achievement, 1984-85, Boone County chmn., 1986-88; bd. dirs. YMCA, Belvidere, 1990-96, vice chmn., chmn. fin. com., 1991, v.p., 1992; dir. on adv. bd. St. Joseph Hosp., 1990-95, 97—, chmn. long range planning com., 1991; bd. dirs. Boone County Dist. # 100 Edn. Found., 1991-95. Served with U.S. Army, 1958-60. Recipient Inventor's award Gen. Electric Co., 1967. Mem. ASME, Home Ventilation Inst. (engring. com. 1975-84), Belvidere C. of C. (bd. dirs. 1986-89). Republican. Congregationalist. Clubs: Free Blown Glassblowing, No. Ill. Corvette Club, Carnival and Art Glass Collectors. Lodge: Rotary. Patentee in field. Home: 1628 Riverside Rd Belvidere IL 61008-8655 Office: 1 Belvedere Blvd Belvidere IL 61008-8594

BRITT, W. EARL, federal judge; b. McDonald, N.C., Dec. 7, 1932; s. Dudley H. and Martha Mae (Hall) B.; m. Judith Moore, Apr. 17, 1976. Student, Campbell Jr. Coll., 1952; BS, Wake Forest U., 1956, JD, 1958. Bar: N.C. 1958. Pvt. practice law Fairmont, N.C., 1959-72, Lumberton, N.C., 1972-80; judge U.S. Dist. Ct. (ea. dist.) N.C., from 1980, chief judge, 1983-90, sr. judge, 1997—; mem. Jud. Conf. Com. on Automation and Tech., 1990-95; 4th cir. dist. judge rep. to Jud. Conf. U.S., 1991-97. Trustee Southeastern Community Coll., 1965-70, Southeastern Gen. Hosp., Lumberton, 1965-69, Pembroke State U., 1967-72; bd. govs. U. N.C. Served with U.S. Army, 1953-55. Mem. N.C. Bar Assn., Fed. Judges Assn. (bd. dirs., v.p., 1993-95, pres. 1995-97). Baptist. Office: US Dist Ct PO Box 27504 Raleigh NC 27611-7504

BRITTAIN, JAMES EDWARD, science and technology educator, researcher; b. Mills River, N.C., May 20, 1931; s. Randall Francis and Velma Hassie (Gillespie) B.; m. Louise Mary Lambert, March 29, 1969 (dec. Mar. 27, 1972); m. Jo Ann Layne, Apr. 14, 1973. BS, Clemson U., 1957; MS, U. Tenn., 1959; MA, Case Western Res. U., 1969, PhD, 1970. Jr. rsch. engr. U. Tenn., Knoxville, 1958-59; asst. prof. elec. engring. Clemson (S.C.) U., 1959-66; asst. prof. history of sci. and tech. Ga. Inst. Tech., Atlanta, 1969-71, assoc. prof., 1972-91, prof., 1992-94; prof. emeritus, 1994—. Author: Engineering the New South, 1985, Alexanderson: Pioneer in American Electrical Engineering, 1992; editor: Turning Points in American Electrical History, 1977. With USAF, 1950-54. Smithsonian Instn. rsch. fellow, 1972-73; recipient rsch. contract Nat. Park Svc., 1974-75; grantee NSF, 1979. Fellow IEEE (chmn. history com. 1978-79, 88-89, assoc. editor proceedings 1990—, Centennial medal 1984), Royal Soc. Arts, Radio Club Am. (Batcher Meml. prize 1989); mem. Soc. History of Tech. (mem. exec. coun. 1978-80, 89-91, Usher prize 1971), History of Sci. Soc., Soc. Indsl. Archeology. Baptist. Avocations: trout fishing, hiking, photography of historical industrial sites. Home: 189 Mountain Valley Dr Hendersonville NC 28739-9723

BRITTAIN, WILLARD W., JR. (WOODY BRITTAIN), diversified financial services company executive. BA in Econs., Yale U.; MBA, Harvard U. With Price Waterhouse L.L.P. - U.S., 1974, prin., 1983, head Chesapeak Area Consulting Group, 1985, head Office Govt. Svcs., 1990; head Price Waterhouse L.L.P. - U.S., Washington, 1993; vice chmn. Price Waterhouse L.L.P. - U.S., N.Y.C., 1995; mem. policy bd. Price Waterhouse L.L.P. - U.S., 1992. Bd. dirs. Washington Ballet, No. Va. Urban League, Inroads Greater Washington, Greater Washington Bd. Trade, Fed. City Coun., Nat. Assn. Black Accountants (Metro-Washington chpt., Pres.'s Spl. Achievment award), Com. Econ. Devel. Office: Price Waterhouse Coopers LLP US 1301 Avenue Of The Americas New York NY 10019*

BRITTELL-WHITEHEAD, DIANE PEEPLES, secondary education educator, addiction counselor; b. Binghamton, N.Y., Feb. 2, 1950; d. Berbie Winfred and Vera (Bufano) Peeples; m. Edward James Brittell, June 14, 1975 (div. 1991); children: Jesse, Aimeé, Jeneé; m. Paul Whitehead, July 20, 1996. BS in Mental Health, Hahnemann U., 1974; MEd, cert. reading specialist, Widener U., 1987, MEd. Cert. in spl. edn., allied addictions practitioner, Pa.; cert. criminal justice specialist. Cashier Pantry Pride Markets, Norristown, Pa., 1964-74; tchr. Parkway Day Sch., Phila., 1973-77; diagnostic tchr. Sleighton Farms, Wawa, Pa., 1984-85; tchr., reading specialist Ridley Sch. Dist., Ridley Park, Pa., 1987—; mental health worker, tchr. Hahnemann Hosp., Phila., summers 1988-94; addictions counselor Crozer Chester (Pa.) Med. Ctr., 1991—, Keystone Rehab. Ctr., Chester, 1993—; tutor, Chester, 1985-87; lectr. state tchrs. convs., Pa., N.J., 1986-88, various rehab. workshops, 1986—. Contbr. articles to various publs. Vol. St. Mary's Orphanage, Ambler, Pa., 1967-69. Mem. NEA, ASCD, AAUW, Nat. Assn. Drug Abuse Counselors, Pa. Edn. Assn., Pa. Assn. Drug Abuse Counselors. Republican. Avocations: shark research, scuba diving, writing, reading, music. Home: 400 E Hinckley Ave Ridley Park PA 19078-2518 Office: Ridley Mid Sch Ridley Park PA 19078

BRITTEN, ROY JOHN, biophysicist; b. Washington, Oct. 1, 1919; s. Rollo Herbert and Marion (Hale) B.; m. Jacqueline Reid, 1986; children: Gregory, Kenneth. BS, U. Va., 1941; PhD, Princeton U., 1951. Staff mem. dept. terrestrial magnetism Carnegie Instn., Washington, 1951-89; sr. research assoc. Calif. Inst. Tech., Corona del Mar, 1973-81, disting. Carnegie sr. rsch. assoc. biology, 1981-99, emeritus, 1999—; adj. prof. U. Calif., Irvine, 1991—; discoverer repeated DNA sequences in genomes of higher organisms. Inventor in field. Named Disting. Carnegie Sr. Research Assoc. in Biology, 1981-99. Fellow Am. Acad. Arts and Scis., AAAS; mem. Nat. Acad. Scis. Office: Calif Inst Tech Kerchkhoff Marine Lab 101 Dahlia Ave Corona Del Mar CA 92625-2814

BRITTENHAM, RAYMOND LEE, investment company executive; b. Moscow, Russia, Feb. 8, 1916; s. Edward Arthur and Marietta (Wemple) B.; m. Mary Ann Stanard, Nov. 3, 1956; children: Edward C., Carol. AB, Principia Coll., Elsah, Ill., 1936; postgrad., Kaiser Wilhelm U., Berlin, Germany, 1937; LLB, Harvard U., 1940. Bar: Ill. 1940, N.Y. 1946. Assoc. Pope & Ballard, Chgo., 1940-42, Mitchell Carroll, N.Y.C., 1947-56; v.p., gen. counsel ITT and subs., 1962-68, sr. v.p. law, counsel, 1968-80, dir., 1965-80; with Lazard Freres & Co., N.Y.C., 1980-89; pres. Spanish Inst., 1980-82, vice chmn., 1982-90. Maj. AUS, 1942-46. Decorated Bronze Star medal; Croix de Guerre France and Belgium; chevalier Ordre de Leopold Belgium). Mem. ABA, Coun. Fgn. Rels., University Club (N.Y.C.). Home: 925 Park Ave New York NY 10028-0210 also: Skyline Ridge Rd # 184 Bridgewater CT 06752-1729

BRITTENHAM, SKIP, lawyer; b. Port Huron, Mich.. BS, USAF Acad., 1963; JD, UCLA, 1970. Bar: Calif. 1971. Sr. ptnr. Ziffren, Brittenahm, Branca & Fischer, L.A., 1978—. Office: Ziffren Brittenham Branca Fischer 1801 Century Park W Los Angeles CA 90067-6406*

BRITTINGHAM, JAMES CALVIN, nuclear engineer; b. Hamlet, N.C., Apr. 6, 1942; s. James Calvin and Elizabeth (McCanless) B.; m. Margaret Kitchen, Feb. 12, 1978; 1 child, James Robert. BS in Nuc. Engring., N.C. State U., 1964, MS in Nuc. Engring., 1966; PhD in Nuc. Engring., U. Calif., Berkeley, 1975. Registered nuc. engr., Calif. Engr. Rockwell Internat., Canoga Park, Calif., 1975-80; engr. Pacific Gas and Electric, San Francisco, 1981-85; sr. cons. engr. Ariz. Pub. Svc., Phoenix, 1986—; assoc. faculty Ariz. State U., 1991-93. Contbr. articles to profl. jours. Recipient Talent for Svc. scholarship N.C. State U., 1960-63, AEC fellowship, 1964-66, NSF traineeship, 1967-69. Mem. Am. Nuc. Soc. Republican. Achievements include development of new, improved methodology for ranking new and partially burned fuel assemblies as candidates for reinsertion into a reload core; devel. original rod cluster control assembly inventory model for Diablo Canyon power plant. Home: 3367 W Grandview Rd Phoenix AZ 85053-2953 Office: Palo Verde Nuclear Generation Sta Mail Sta 7693 5801 S Wintersburg Rd Tonopah AZ 85354-7529

BRITTINGHAM, KIMBERLY ANNE, magazine publisher; b. Pa., Dec. 5, 1970; d. Anthony Wozniak and Ada (Satterthwaite) B. Editor-in-chief Cafe Eighties Mag., N.O.C., 1993—. Mem. Internat. Women's Writing Guild, Acad. Am. Poets, Associated Writing Programs, Poetry Soc. Am. Office: Cafe Eighties Mag 1562 1st Ave Ste 180 New York NY 10028-4004

BRITTON, CLAROLD LAWRENCE, lawyer, consultant; b. Soldier, Iowa, Nov. 1, 1932; s. Arnold Olaf and Florence Ruth (Gardner) B.; m. Joyce Helene Hamlett, Feb. 1, 1958; children: Laura, Eric, Val, Martha. BS in Engring., U. Mich., Ann Arbor, 1958, JD, 1961, postgrad. U. Mich Artificial Intelligence Lab., Elec. Engring. and Computer Sci., 1988-91. Bar: Ill. 1961, U.S. Dist. Ct. (no. dist.) Ill. 1962, U.S. Ct. Appeals (7th cir.) 1963, U.S. Supreme Ct. 1970, Mich. 1989. Assoc., Jenner & Block, Chgo., 1961-70, ptnr., 1970-88; pres. Clarold L. Britton & Assoc., Inc., 1991—. Lectr. DePaul U., 1988. Comdr. USNR, 1952-57. Fellow Am. Coll. Trial Lawyers; mem. Chgo. Bar Assn. (past chmn. fed. civil procedure com., mem. judiciary and computer law coms., civil practice com.), Ill. State Bar Assn. (chmn. Allerton House Conf. 1984, 86, 88, chmn. rule 23 com. 1985-87, chmn. civil practice and procedure coun. 1987-88, antitrust com.), ABA (litigation sect., antitrust com., past regional chmn. discovery com. 1961), 7th Cir. Bar Assn., Def. Rsch. Inst. (com. on aerospace 1984), Mich. Bar Assn., Ill. Soc. Trial Lawyers, Order of Coif, Alpha Phi Mu, Tau Beta Pi, Law Club (Chgo.), Racine Yacht Club (Wis.), Macatawa Yacht Club (Mich), Masons. Republican. Lutheran. Author: Computerized Trial Notebook, 1991; asst. editor Mich. Law Rev., 1960. Office: 411 E Washington St Ann Arbor MI 48104-2015

BRITTON, DENNIS A., newspaper editor, newspaper executive; b. Santa Barbara, 1940; m. Theresa Romero Britton; children: Robert, Patrick, Anne. Attended, San Jose State U. Joined L.A. Times, 1966, various positions, including copy editor, reporter, news editor, asst. nat. editor, nat. editor, 1977-83, then dep. mng. editor; editor Chgo. Sun-Times, 1989-96, also exec. v.p., until 1996; now editor-in-chief Denver Post, 1996—. Mem. Nat. Assn. Hispanic Journalists. Office: Denver Post 1560 Broadway Denver CO 80202-5177

BRITTON, KATHERINE LELA QUAINTON, lawyer; b. Sydney, N.S.W., Australia, Mar. 21, 1960; d. Anthony Cecil Eden and Susan (Long) Quainton; m. Edward Charles Britton, Aug. 23, 1986; children: Peter Edward Quainton, Gillian Amanda Oates, Matthew Joseph McDonald. AB cum laude, Princeton U., 1982; JD magna cum laude, Harvard U., 1986. Bar: D.C. 1986. Assoc. Arnold & Porter, Washington, 1986-96. Knox fellow Harvard U., 1985. Mem. D.C. Bar Assn., Phi Beta Kappa. Home: 5000 Glenbrook Rd NW Washington DC 20016-3225

BRITTON, LAURENCE GEORGE, research scientist; b. Hampton Court, Eng., Sept. 26, 1951; came to U.S., 1981; s. George and Barbara Mavis (Card) B.; m. Helen Lynn Grass, Apr. 16, 1983 (dec. 1989); 1 child, Robert; m. Carol-Ann Kirby, Jan. 6, 1995. BS with 1st class honors, U. Leeds, Eng., 1974; PhD in Fuel and Combustion Sci., U. Leeds, 1977. Chartered engr., Eng. Rsch. fellow dept. elec. engring. U. Southhampton, Eng., 1978-81; sr. combustion scientist Union Carbide Corp. Tech. Ctr., South Charleston, W.Va., 1981-84; project scientist process fire and explosion hazards Union Carbide Corp. Tech. Ctr., South Charleston, 1984-89, rsch. scientist, 1990-97, prin. engr., 1998—; guest lectr. Coll. Grad. Studies, Sch. Engring. and Sci., U. W.Va., 1991-94; mem. fueling systems com. U. K. Ministry Def., 1978-81; speaker at profl. metings and symposia; mem. U.S. Coast Guard/U.S. Dept. Transp. Static Electricity Adv. Group, 1993—. Author: Avoiding Static Ignition Hazards in Chemical Operations, 1999, Avoiding Static Ignition Hazards in Chemical Operations, 1999; contbr. articles to sci. jours. Fellow Inst. Energy; mem. AIChE (mem. editl. rev. bd. Process Safety Progress 1993—, William H. Doyle award 1986, 89), ASTM (mem. E.27 com. on hazard potential of chemicals 1997—), Combustion Inst., Ctr. for Chem. Process Safety (engring. practices com. 1988—, reactive materials storage and handling com. 1990—), Nat. Fire Protection Assn. (explosion protection sys. com., classification and properties of hazardous chems. com., static electricity com.), Chem. Mfrs. Assn. (flame resistant clothing issues group 1995), Chem. Mfrs. Assn./Am. Petroleum Inst. (reactive hazards tech. task force 1995). Office: Union Carbide Corp Tech Ctr PO Box 8361 S Charleston WV 25303-0361

BRITTON, LEANN G., federal official. BA in Econs., Hamline U. Various position to bank examiner Office Comptroller of the Currency, various, 1975-1989; dir. Mpls. field office Office Comptroller of the Currency, 1989-95, dep. comptroller Cen. Dist., 1996, sr. dep. comptroller for Bank Supervision Ops., 1996—. Office: Dept of Treasury/Bank Supr 250 E St SW Washington DC 20024-3208*

BRITTON, M(ELVIN) C(REED), JR., physician, rheumatologist; b. San Francisco, Apr. 11, 1935; s. Melvin Creed and Mathilda Carolyn (Epeneter) B.; m. Mary Elizabeth Phillips, Nov. 2, 1957; children: Elizabeth Carolynne, Lisa Marie. AB, Dartmouth Coll., 1957, MS, 1958; MD, Harvard U., 1960. Diplomate Am. Bd. Internal Medicine, Am. Bd. Rheumatology, Am. Bd. Quality Assurance. Resident Dartmouth Coll. Sch. Medicine, Hanover, N.H., 1964-67; fellow Harvard U. Sch. Medicine, Boston, 1967-69; ptnr. Palo Alto (Calif.) Med. Clinic, 1969—, chmn. dept. medicine, 1990-97; pres. med. staff Stanford (Calif.) U. Med. Ctr., 1985-87, mem. med. staff bd., 1969-87; bd. dirs. Hosp. Conf. No. Calif., 1988-92, Inst. for Med. Quality, 1998—; mem. Relative Value Update Commn., 1996—;. Contbr. articles to med. jours. Pres. Found. for Med. care Santa Clara county, Campbell, 1983-89; mem. Bay Area Lupus Found., 1978—, chmn., 1987-88, 94-95; v.p. Calif. Founds. for Med. Care, 1996, pres., CEO, 1996—. Fellow ACP, Am. Coll. Rheumatology (bd. dirs. 1986-89, Paulding Phelps medal 1994), Calif. Acad. Medicine (exec. com. 1996—); mem. AMA (alternate del. 1988—), Calif. Med. Assn., Santa Clara County Med. Soc. (pres. 1980-81, Bd. Svc. award 1988), Arthritis Found. No. Calif. (chmn. bd. dirs. 1984-87, Disting Svc. award 1985), Vintners Club (San Francisco, v.p. 1975-78), Commonwealth Club (San Francisco). Republican. Episcopalian. Avocations: skiing, traveling, enology. Office: Palo Alto Med Clinic 300 Homer Ave Palo Alto CA 94301-2726

BRITTON, ROBERT AUSTIN, manufacturing company executive; b. Valley Stream, N.Y., Sept. 26, 1946; s. Austin and Kathryn Nora (Jones) B.; m. Arlette Wahba, July 22, 1972; children: Robert Austin, Rebecca. BS, Siena Coll., 1968; MBA in Mktg., NYU, 1969, MBA in Fin., 1978. Rsch. analyst Morgan Guaranty Trust Co., N.Y.C., 1969-74; asst. to treas. ASARCO, Inc., N.Y.c., 1974-77; mgr. fin. svcs. Am. Maize Products Co., Stamford, Conn., 1977-80, treas., 1980-89, v.p., treas., 1989-95; treas. Am. Fructose Corp., 1986-89, v.p., treas., 1989-93; v.p., CFO Swisher Internat., Inc., 1995, exec. v.p., CFO, dir., 1995—; manufacturing company executive; b. Valley Stream, N.Y., Sept. 26, 1946; s. Austin and Kathryn Nora (Jones) B.; BS, Siena Coll., 1968; MBA in Mktg., NYU, 1969, MBA in Finance, 1978; m. Arlette Wahba, July 22, 1972; children: Robert Austin, Rebecca. Rsch. analyst Morgan Guaranty Trust Co., N.Y.C., 1969-74; asst. to treas. ASARCO, Inc., N.Y.C., 1974-77; mgr. fin. svcs. Am. Maize Products Co., Stamford, Conn., 1977-80, treas., 1980-89, v.p., treas., 1989-95; treas. Am. Fructose Corp., 1986-89, v.p., treas., 1989-93; v.p., CFO Swisher Internat., Inc., 1995; exec. v.p., CFO, dir. Swisher Internat., Inc., 1995—;. Home: 630 Ponus Rdg Rd New Canaan CT 06840-3407 Office: Swisher Internat Inc 20 Thorndal Cir Darien CT 06820-5421*

BRITTON, THOMAS WARREN, JR., management consultant; b. Pawhuska, Okla., June 16, 1944; s. Thomas Warren and Helen Viola (Haynes) B.; BS in Mech. Engring., Okla. State U., 1966, MS in Indsl. Engring. and Mgmt., 1968; m. Jerlyn Kay Davis, 1964 (div. 1970); 1 child, Natalie Dawn; m. Deborah Ann Mansour, Oct. 20, 1973; 1 child, Kimberly Ann. Cons., Arthur Young & Co., Los Angeles, mgr., 1972-76, prin., 1976-79, ptnr., 1979-87, office dir. mgmt. svcs. dept., Orange County, Calif., 1979-88; ptnr. Price Waterhouse; ptnr.-in-charge west coast mfg. cons. practice, Nat. Aero space and Def. Industry, 1988-95; part-in-charge west coast products and logistics practice, 1995—, Price Waterhouse Coopers mng. ptnr. west region MCS Products Practice, chmn. US MCS Tech. Industry Practice, chmn. Global MCS Tech. Industry Practice; lectr. in field. Mem. City of San Dimas Creative Growth Bd., 1976-77, chmn. planning commn., 1977-83; trustee World Affairs Council of Orange County, 1980; benefactor, founders com., v.p. ann. fund, pres., chair long range planning, trustee South Coast Repertory Theater, 1982-92; trustee Providence Speech and Hearing Ctr., 1985-90, Spl. Olympics of So. Calif., 1995-97; mem. devel. com. U. Calif.-Irvine Med. Sch.; chmn. Costa Mesa Arts Council. Served to capt. USAR, 1971-86. Cert. mgmt. cons. Mem. Los Angeles Inst. CPAs, Mgmt. Adv. Svcs. Com., Am. Prodn. and Inventory Control Soc., Am. Inst. Indsl. Engrs., Greater Irvine Indsl. League, Okla. State Alumni Assn., Kappa Sigma Alumni Assn. Clubs: Jonathan, Ridgeline Country, Santa Ana Country. Home: 18982 Wildwood Cir Villa Park CA 92861-3137

BRITTON, WESLEY ALAN, English language educator; b. Munich, Sept. 29, 1953; came to the U.S., 1955; s. Royce J. and Betty Ruth (Somers) B. BA in English, Calif. U. Pa., 1977; MA in English, U. North Tex., 1986, PhD, 1990. News dir. Calif. U. Pa., 1975-77; prin. Wes Britton Advt. Agy., Dallas, 1977-79; pub. rels. dir. VISTA, Dallas, 1982-83; teaching fellow U. North Tex., Denton, 1983-90, prof. English, 1990-92; instr. Paul Quinn Coll., Dallas, 1991-93; prof. Bacone C.C., Muskoqee, Okla., Southeast Okla. Coll., Durant Cooke C.C., 1993-94, Grayson C.C., Sherman, Tex., 1994-98; cons. Wentwork Films, Washington, 1991; instr. Cedar Valley C.C., Dallas, 1992, Harrisburg (Pa.) Area C.C., 1998—; bd. dirs. KNON, Dallas, 1992. Contbr. poetry, plays, articles to profl. jours., ency. entries and indices. Trustee Assn. Individuals with Disabilities, Dallas, 1981-83; adv. bd. North Tex. Radio for Blind, Dallas, 1983; writer, producer Sta. KERA-Fm Radio, Dallas, 1978-79. Mem. MLA, North Tex. Interdisciplinary Forum (pres. 1990-91), Grad. Students in English (v.p. 1988-89), Rsch. Soc. Am. Periodicals, Texoma Area Poetry Soc. (program dirs. 1995-98), Mark Twain Circle Am., Friends Mark Twain Ctr., We. Lit. Assn., Sigma Tau Delta. Democrat. Avocations: collecting '60s music, drums, travel. Home: 2439 Penn St Harrisburg PA 17110-1120

BRITZ LOTTI, DIANE EDWARD, investment company executive; b. York, Pa., June 15, 1952; d. Everett Frank and Billie Jacqueline (Sherrill) B.; m. Marcello Lotti, Sept. 9, 1978 (dec. Apr. 1990); children: Ariane Elizabeth, Samantha Alexis. BA, Duke U., 1974; MBA, Columbia U., 1982. Asst. mgr. Columbia Artists, N.Y.C., 1974-76; gen. mgr. Ea. Music Festival, Greensboro, N.C., 1977-78; v.p. Britz Cobin, N.Y.C., 1979-82; pres. Pan Oceanic Mgmt., Inc., N.Y.C., 1983-90, Pan Oceanic Advisors, Ltd., N.Y.C., 1988-94; chmn. Pan Oceanic Mgmt. Ltd., N.Y.C., 1994—; also bd. dirs Pan Oceanic Advisors, Ltd., N.Y.C.; mnging. dir. Am. Capital Ptnrs., Ltd., N.Y.C., 1996—; bd. dirs. Pan Oceanic Mgmt., Inc.; undergrad. bd. Duke U. Bd. advisors Turtle Bay Music Sch.; mem. Nat. Com. on Am. Fgn. Policy; bd. dirs. N.Y.C. Opera, chair corp. com.; pres. The Marcello Lotti Found. Mem. Fin. Women's Assn., Columbia Bus. Sch. Club of N.Y., Doubles Club. Mem. Soc. of Friends. Office: 45 Rockefeller Plz Ste 2000 New York NY 10111-2099

BRIUER, ELKE MOERSCH, editor; b. Darmstadt, Germany, Feb. 20, 1943; came to U.S., 1962; d. Karl Wilhelm and Ilse (Hohorst) Moersch; divorced; children: Patricia Mae Monroe, Kenneth Frank Gaston; m. Frederick L. Briuer, Oct. 9, 1986. BA in German cum laude, U. Md., 1977, postgrad., 1984; postgrad., U.T., 1980; MS in Comm., Miss. Coll., 1992. Accredited pub. rels. profl. Pub. affairs officer Med. Ctr. 97th Gen. Hosp., Frankfurt, Germany, 1982-84; supr. pub. affairs officer USMCA, Aschaffenburg, Germany, 1984-86; pub. affairs specialist 5th rctg. brigade U.S. Army, San Antonio, 1986-88; writer, editor (Technology Transfer Specialist) U.S. Army Engr. Waterways Expt. Sta., Vicksburg, 1988—. Author: (recruitment pamphlet) The Quick Answer Book of U.S. Army Recruiting Support Command Exhibits, 1989, (booklet) The Young Scientist's Introduction to Wetlands, 1993; dir. (video) The Black Swamp, 1995; editor: Caduceus, 1982-84, Ad Libs, 1986-88, Wetlands Rsch. Program Bull., 1991-96; writer, editor: (multi-media CD-ROM) Wetlands Rsch. Program Summary, 1991-94; contbr. numerous articles to newspapers and mags. Sec. Vicksburg Art Assn., 1990-91, newsletter editor, 1990-93; mem. Soc. Wetland Sci., 1991—, Miss. Heritage Trust, 1991—, Heritage Herald editor, 1994-96; 2d v.p. Vicksburg Cmty. Concert Assn., 1994-97. Mem. So. Pub. Rels. Fedn., Pub. Rels. Assn. Miss. Office: US Army Engr Waterways Expt Sta CEWES-IM-VP 3909 Halls Ferry Rd Vicksburg MS 39180-6133

BRIXEY, SHAWN ALAN, digital media artist, media educator, director; b. Springfield, Mo., Jan. 23, 1961; s. Alan M. and Mary Lou (Peters) B.; m. Sonja Max, 1998. BFA in New Media, Kansas City Art Inst., 1985; MS in Advanced Visual Studies, MIT, 1988. Grad. tchg. asst. dept. arch. MIT, Cambridge, 1985-87; Leonardo fellow, inaugural vis. fellow Leonardo Project U. Mich., Ann Arbor, 1988; adj. faculty, lectr. CAVS dept. arch. MIT, Cambridge, 1989; asst. prof., dir. media arts program art U. Ky., Lexington, 1990, grad. faculty, assoc. mem. Coll. Fine Arts, 1991; asst. prof., chair cross-disciplinary arts program Sch. Art U. Wash., Seattle, 1994, grad. faculty Coll. Arts and Scis., 1995-98; disting. fellow Inst. for New Media San Francisco State U., 1997-98; asst. prof. digital media/new genre U. Calif., Berkeley, 1998—, dir. Ctr. Digital Art and New Media Rsch., 1998—; dir. exptl. media lab. dept. art U. Ky., Lexington, 1992; dir. studio for media arts rsch. and techs. lab U. Wash., Seattle, 1994-98, co-dir. lab animation for arts, 1995-98, acting dir. Ctr. Advanced Rsch. Tech. in the Arts and Humanities, 1996-97; Disting. mentor in multimedia San Francisco State U., 1997; keynote spkr. Mayor's Internat. Tech. Summit, San Francisco, 1998; mem. U. Calif., Pres.'s Planning Group on Digital Art, 1998. Exhbns. include Documenta 8, Kassel, Germany, 1987, 85th Anniversary of the German Art Union, Badischer, Kunstverein, Karlsruhe, Germany, 1988, Cranbrook Acad. Art Mus., Bloomhill Hills, Mich., 1990, Contemporary Art Ctr., Cin., 1991, State Mus., Columbia, S.C., 1992, MIT Mus., Cambridge, Mass., 1995, Del. Ctr. Contemporary Art, Wilmington, 1996, Internat. Symposium Electronic Art ISEA 97, Chgo., Cultural Olympiad, 1998, Winter Olympics Nagano, Japan, 1999. Mentor advanced placement new media and digital video/audio courses Fayette County H.S. Sys., Lexington, Ky., 1990-93; bd. dirs. Ctr. for Contemporary Art, Seattle, 1996-98; keynote spkr. Seattle-Northshore Sch. Dist. Leadership Conf., 1998. Recipient Major Equip. award Silicon Graphics Industries, 1994, Apple Computer Inc., 1994, Newport/Klinger, 1996, Intel Corp., 1997. Democrat. Episcopalian. Avocations: scuba diving, tennis, collecting old film, media electronics, electric toys. Office: Univ Calif Digital Media/New Genre 345 Kroeber Hall Berkeley CA 94720

BRIZENDINE, ROBERT E., federal judge; b. 1946. BA, Ga. Inst. Tech., 1968; JD, Vanderbilt U., 1971. Atty. Scroggins & Brizendine, 1971-93; bankruptcy judge U.S. Dist. Ct. (no. dist.) Ga., Atlanta, 1993—. Office: 1234 US Courthouse 75 Spring St SW Atlanta GA 30303-3309

BRIZZOLARA, CHARLES ANTHONY, lawyer; b. Chgo., Nov. 20, 1929; s. Ralph D. and Florence H. (Hurley) B.; m. Audree Doyle, Aug. 24, 1968. B.A., Lake Forest (Ill.) Coll., 1951; J.D., Ill. Inst. Tech., 1957. Bar: Ill. 1959. Practiced law Chgo., 1959-67; with Walter E. Heller & Co., also Walter E. Heller Internat. Corp. (later Amerifin Corp.), Chgo., 1967-85; v.p., sec., gen. counsel Walter E. Heller & Co., also Walter E. Heller Internat. Corp., 1974-85, sr. v.p., 1980-85; v.p. Chgo. Bears Football Club, Inc., 1975-88; mem. firm Chadwell & Kayser Ltd., 1985-90; ptnr. Michael Best & Friedrich, Chgo., 1990—; bd. dirs. Abacus Real Estate Fin. Co., Walter E. Heller & Co. S.E., Heller Factoring (Hong Kong) Ltd., Factoring Serfin, S.A., Chandler Leasing Corp., 1975-80; lectr. seminars Am. Mgmt. Assn. Editor: Chgo.-Kent Law Rev, 1956. Bd. dirs. Cath. Charities Archdiocese of Chgo., 1978—, sec., 1991-94; bd. dirs. Ill. Inst. Tech. Chgo. Kent Alumni Assn., 1980-89. Served with AUS, 1952-54. Mem. Internat. Bar Assn., ABA, Ill. Bar Assn. Roman Catholic. Home: 253 E Delaware Pl Chicago IL 60611-1758

BRO, KENNETH ARTHUR, plastic manufacturing company executive; b. Tsingdao, Shandung, China, Aug. 28, 1921 (parents Am. citizens); s. Albin Carl and Marguerite (Harmon) B.; m. Patricia Welch, May 6, 1944; children: William, Peter, Kenneth M., Patricia, Elizabeth, A. Charles. BS, Northwestern U., 1949, D. Pub. Svc. (hon.) Northland Coll., 1994. Purchasing agent Welch Mfg. Co., Chgo., 1950-56; v.p. Welch Sci. Co., Chgo., 1957-64; v.p., co-owner Webb Plastic Co., Northbrook, Ill., 1965-87, ret. 1987. Pres. bd. dirs. Chgo. Commons Assn., 1962, 70-74; dist. chmn. bd. dirs. Jr. Achievement, Chgo., 1970, 72-74; pres. Found. for Sci. Relaxation, 1965-94; dir. Presbyn. Home, Evanston, Ill., 1976—; chmn. bd. trustees Northland Coll., 1971-75, mem. bd. trustees, 1957-94. Served to pvt. 1st class U.S. Army, 1944-46, ETO. Decorated Bronze Star, Purple Heart. Mem. Am. Vaccum Soc., Am. Assn. Physics Tchrs. Republican. Congregationalist. Clubs: Indian Hill (Winnetka, Ill.); University, Chgo. Ya[illegible], Economic, Executive (Chgo.). Avocations: sailing, flying, travel. Home: 375 Sheridan Rd Winnetka IL 60093-2626 Office: PO Box 583 Wilmette IL 60091-0583

BRO, WILLIAM PRICE, communications executive; b. Evanston, Ill., Apr. 7, 1946; s. Kenneth Arthur and Patricia (Welch) B.; m. Johanna Ellen Hintze, Apr. 9, 1986; children: Ellen Price, John Kenneth. BS in Bus. Mgmt. with honors, U. Phoenix, 1998. Licensed 1st class radiotelephone, FCC. Meteorologist WISN-TV, Milw., 1968-69; ops. mgr. WXCL Radio, Peoria, Ill., 1969-80; pres. Broadcast Assoc., Inc., Springfield, Ill., 1980-82, PSR Corp., Peoria, 1982-94; news anchor WHOI-TV, Peoria, 1984; pres. High Point Group, Inc., Peoria, 1994—; advisor minority-owned radio, Peoria, 1993-96. Co-author (radio play) Peoria's War of the Worlds, 1972; author (text) How to Become an Announcer, 1973. Mem. Rep. Nat. Com., 1995-96; treas. Pack Four Cub Scouts, Peoria, 1996; mem. bd. Peoria Civic Opera, 1983-84; chair, CEO Nat. Kidney Cancer Assn., 1998—; exec. com. Ill. Valley Power Squadron, 1998—. Recipient Past Pres.'s award Peoria Heights C. of C., 1991. Mem. Kidney Cancer Assn. (chmn. 1998—), Peoria Radio Orgn. (founding mem.), Exptl. Aircraft Assn., Aircraft Owners and Pilots Assn., Cherokee Pilots' Assn., Rotary Club Peoria-North (sec. 1991-92), Willow Knolls Country Club (bd. dirs. 1998), Phi Theta Kappa. Republican. Unitarian. Avocations: flying, camping, boating. Home: 335 E High Point Rd Peoria IL 61614-3011 Office: HPG Inc 4541 N Prospect Rd Peoria Hts IL 61614-6529

BROAD, BARBARA PRENTICE, real estate agent; b. Easton, Pa., Mar. 3, 1920; d. Donald Bishop and Mary Louise (Farnham) Prentice; m. Henry Sawyer Broad, Aug. 16, 1942 (dec. Mar. 1997); children: Louise Broad Lavine, Richard G., William G. BA, Wellesley Coll., 1941; postgrad., Northeastern U., 1951-52. Legal sec. Hutchins & Wheeler, Boston, 1946-48; sec. to Judge Charles Wyzanski U.S. Dist. Ct., Boston, 1948-52; real estate agt., 1975—. chmn. Princeton (N.J.) Nursery Sch.; pres. Wellesley Club Ctrl. N.J., Class of 1941 Wellesley; bd. dirs., pres. Young Audiences of N.J., 1975-93. Lt. USN-WAVES, 1943-45. Democrat. Presbyterian. Avocations: singing in church choir, tennis, bridge. Home: 33 Hedge Row Rd Princeton NJ 08540-4111 Office: Stockton Real Estate 32 Chambers St Princeton NJ 08542-3708

BROAD, CYNTHIA ANN MORGAN, special education educator, consultant; b. Toledo, Ohio, Apr. 19, 1947; d. James Glenn and Elaine Louise (Morris) Morgan; m. Alan Hugh Broad, Aug. 2, 1975; children: Travis Alan, Trevor Morgan. BS in Edn., Bowling Green State U., 1969, MEd, 1970, Accomplished Grad. (hon.), 1993. Cert. spl. edn. tchr., elem. tchr. Tchr. remedial reading ednl. therapy unit Toledo (Ohio) State Hosp., 1970; spl. edn. tchr. Green Elem. Sch. L'Anse Creuse (Mich.) pub. schs., 1970-81, spl. edn. tchr. Lobbestael Elem. Sch., 1982-95, spl. edn. cons., 1989-95, spl. edn. tchr. Higging Elem. Sch., 1995—. Contbr. articles to profl. jours.; developer talking animal idea telephone teachng tool, 1978. Fellow Masters Level Bowling Green State U., 1969-70; recipient Tchr. of Yr. State of Mich. Dept. Edn., 1989-90, Nat. Educator award Milken Family Found., 1990, Burger King Disting. Svc. to Edn. award, 1990. Mem. NEA, Mich. Edn. Assn., Mich. Reading Assn., Mich. Assn. Children with Learning Disabilities, Coun. Exceptional Children (Golden Nugget award 1989), Delta Kappa Gamma, Kappa Delta Pi. Avocations: technology, golf, biking, telecommunications, reading. Home: 71 S Deeplands Rd Grosse Pointe MI 48236-2643 Office: L'Anse Creuse Higgins Elem Sch 29901 24 Mile Rd Chesterfield MI 48051-1760

BROAD, ELI, financial services executive; b. N.Y.C., June 6, 1933; s. Leon and Rebecca (Jacobson) B.; m. Edythe Lois Lawson, Dec. 19, 1954; children: Jeffrey Alan, Gary Stephen. BA in Acctg. cum laude, Mich. State U., 1954. CPA, Mich. 1956. Co-founder, chmn., pres., CEO SunAmerica Life Ins. Co. (formerly Kaufman & Broad, Inc.), L.A., 1957; chmn. SunAmerica Life Ins. Co., Anchor Nat. Life Ins. Co., First SunAmerica Life Ins. Co.; chmn. Kaufman and Broad Home Corp., L.A., 1986-93, chmn. exec. com., 1993-95, founder, chmn., 1993—; chmn. Stanford Ranch Co.; mem. exec. com. adv. bd. Fed. Nat. Mortgage Assn., 1972-73; active Calif. Bus. Roundtable, 1986—; co-owner Sacramento Kings and Arco Arena, 1992—; trustee Com. for Econ. Devel., 1993-95; mem. real estate adv. bd. Citibank, N.Y.C., 1976-81; bd. dirs. Am. Internat. Group, Inc., L.A. Bus. Advisors, Sacramento Kings and ARCO Arena. Mem. bd. dirs. L.A. World Affairs Coun., 1988—, chmn., 1994—, DARE Am., 1989-95, hon. mem. bd. dirs. 1995—; founding trustee Windward Sch., Santa Monica, Calif., 1972-77; bd. trustees Pitzer Coll., Claremont, Calif., 1970-82, chmn. bd. trustees, 1973-79, life trustee, 1982—, Haifa U., Israel, 1972-80, Calif. State U., 1978-82, vice chmn. bd. trustees, 1979-80, trustee emeritus, 1982—, Mus. Contemporary Art, L.A., 1980-93, founding chmn., 1980, Archives Am. Art, Smithsonian Instn., Washington, 1985—, Am. Fedn. Arts, 1988-91, Leland Stanford Mansion Found., 1992—, Calif. Inst. Tech., 1993—, Armand Hammer Mus. Art and Cultural Ctr. UCLA, 1994—; pres. Calif. Non-Partisan Vote Registration Found., 1971-72; chancellor's assoc. UCLA, 1971—, mem. vis. com. Grad. Sch. Mgmt., 1972-90, trustee UCLA Found., 1986—, exec. com. bd. visitors Sch. of the Arts & Architecture, 1997—; assoc. chmn. United Crusade, L.A., 1973-76; chmn. Mayor's Housing Policy Com., L.A., 1974-75; del., spkr. Fed. Econ. Summit Conf., 1974, State Econ. Summit Conf., 1974; mem. contemporary coun. L.A. County Mus. Art, 1973-79, bd. trustees acquisitions com., 1978-81, trustee, 1995—; bd. fellows, mem. exec. com. The Claremont (Calif.) Colls., 1974-79; nat. trustee Balt. Mus. Art, 1985-91; mem. adv. bd. Boy Scouts Am., 1982-85, L.A. Bus. Jour., 1986-88; mem. adv. coun. Town Hall of Calif., 1985-87; trustee Dem. Nat. Com. Victory Fund, 1988, 92, 96; mem. painting and sculpture com. Whitney Mus., N.Y.C., 1987-89; chmn. adv. bd. ART/LA, 1989; bd. overseers The Music Ctr. of L.A. County, 1991-92, mem. bd. govs., 1996—; mem. contemporary art com. Harvard U. Art Mus., Cambridge, Mass., 1992—; mem. internat. dirs. coun. Guggenheim Mus., N.Y.C., 1993—; active Nat. Indsl. Pollution Control Coun., 1970-73, Maeght Found., St. Paul de Vence, France, 1975-80, Mayor's Spl. Adv. Com. on Fiscal Adminstrn., L.A., 1993-94; bd. dirs. UCLA/Armand Hammer Mus. Art And Cultural Ctr., 1994—. Recipient Man of Yr. award City of Hope, 1965, Golden Plate award Am. Acad. Achievement, 1971, Housing Man of Yr. award Nat. Housing Coun., 1979, Humanitarian award NCCJ, 1977, Am. Heritage award Anti Defamation League, 1984, Pub. Affairs award Coro Found., 1987, Honors award visual arts L.A. Arts Coun., 1989; Eli Broad Coll. Bus. and Eli Broad Grad. Sch. Bus. named in his honor Mich. State U., 1991; knighted Chevalier in Nat. Order Legion of Honor, France, 1994. Mem. Beta Alpha Psi, Regency Club and Hillcrest Country Club (L.A.). Home: 75 Oakmont St Los Angeles CA 90049-1901 Office: SunAmerica Inc 1 Sun America Ctr Los Angeles CA 90067-6022

BROAD, MARGARET (MOLLY) CORBETT, university executive; b. Wilkes-Barre, Pa., Feb. 22, 1941; d. Stanley A. and Margaret (Kelly) Corbett; m. Robert William Broad, Aug. 25, 1962; children: Robert W. Jr., Matthew David. BA in Econs., Syracuse U., 1962, postgrad., 1971; MA in Econs., Ohio State U., 1965. Rsch. assoc. to comptr., v.p. finance Ohio State U., Columbus, 1963-65; budget and planning officer Syracuse (N.Y.) U., 1971-76; dep. dir. State Commn. Future of Postsecondary Edn. in N.Y., Albany, 1976-77; v.p. govt. and corp. rels. Syracuse (N.Y.) U., 1977-85; exec. dir., chief exec. officer Ariz. Bd. Regents, Phoenix, 1985-92; sr. vice chancellor adminstrn. and fin. Calif. State U., 1992-93, exec. vice chancellor, COO, 1993-97; chair bd., CEO Calif. State U. Inst., 1994-97; pres. U. N.C., Chapel Hill, 1997—. Mem. Phi Beta Kappa, Beta Gamma Sigma. Roman Catholic. Avocations: tennis, bicycling, gardening. Home: 400 E Franklin St Chapel Hill NC 27514-3707 Office: U NC Gen Adminstrn Bldg 910 Raleigh Rd Chapel Hill NC 27514

BROAD, PETER G., Spanish educator. AB, Dartmouth U., 1966, MA, 1969; PhD, Johns Hopkins U., 1977. Prof. Spanish Indiana U. of Pa., 1990-96, chair dept. of Spanish and Classical Langs., 1990-96; assoc. editor Hispanic jour. Indiana U. of Pa. Co-dir. Am. Friends Svc. Com. Work Project, Mex. Home: 215 North Fourth St Indiana PA 15701

BROADBENT, AMALIA SAYO CASTILLO, graphic arts designer; b. Manila, May 28, 1956; came to U.S., 1980, naturalized, 1985; d. Conrado Camilo and Eugenia de Guzman (Sayo) Castillo; m. Barrie Noel Broadbent, Mar. 14, 1981 (div. 1998); children: Charles Noel Castillo, Chandra Noel Castillo. BFA, U. Santo Tomas, 1978; postgrad. Acad. Art Coll., San Francisco, Alliance Francaise, Manila, Karilagan Finishing Sch., Manila, Manila Computer Ctr.; BA, Maryknoll Coll., 1972. Designer market research Unicorp Export Inc., Makati, Manila, 1975-77; asst. advt. mgr. Dale Trading Corp., Makati, 1977-78; artist, designer, pub. relations Resort Hotels Corp., Makati, 1978-81; prodn. artist CYB/Young & Rubicam, San Francisco, 1981-82; freelance art dir. Ogilvy & Mather Direct, San Francisco, 1986; artist, designer, owner A.C. Broadbent Graphics, San Francisco, 1982—; faculty graphic design & advt. depts. Acad. Art Coll., San Francisco. Works include: Daing na Isda, 1975, (Christmas coloring) Pepsi-Cola, 1964 (Distinctive Merit cert.), (children's books) UNESCO, 1973 (cert.). Pres. Pax Romana, Coll. of Architecture and Fine Arts, U. Santo Tomas, 1976-78, chmn. cultural sect., 1975; v.p. Atelier Cultural Soc., U. Santo Tomas, 1975-76; mem. Makati Dance Troupe, 1973-74. Recipient Merit cert., Inst. Religion, 1977. Mem. Alliance Francaise de San Francisco. Roman Catholic.

BROADBENT, J. STREETT, engineering executive; b. Balt., Nov. 15, 1942; s. Walter Scott and Mabel Naomi (House) B.; m. Barbara Bea Petschke, Aug. 14, 1965; children: Kenneth Streett, Sandra Lynn. AB in Physics, Western Md. Coll., Westminster, 1964; postgrad., Johns Hopkins U., 1969-75. Applied research engr. Black & Decker, Towson, Md., 1964-67; instrumentation engr. Black & Decker, 1967-68, test supr., test mgr., 1969-76; resident engring. mgr. Black & Decker, Hampstead, Md., 1976-79; engring. mgr. Black & Decker, 1979-84; real estate sales rep. Broadbent Realty, Reisterstown, Md., 1972-76; engring. mgr. Black & Decker, Towson, Md., 1985-94, sr. tech. mgr., 1994-96, sr. support sys. mgr., 1996-97; dir. Engring. Tech., 1997—. Treas. Greenbrier Improvement Assn., 1967-69, pres., 1969-70; fund raising com. Western Md. Coll., 1968-72; sec. Reisterstown Jaycees, 1976; com. Reisterstown Revitalization, 1976-77; treas. Md. Jr. Miss Scholarship Program, 1979-83, state chmn., 1983-92, chmn. of bd., 1992—; advancement chmn. Boy Scouts Am., Reisterstown, Md., 1985-87; mem. adv. bd. Essex C.C., 1988-89. With U.S. Army N.G., 1964-70. Mem. NSPE, Instrumentation Soc. Am. (sr.), Am. Soc. for Metals, Computer and Automated Sys. Assn., Soc. Exptl. Mechanics, Soc. Plastic Engrs., U.S. Power Squadrons (Dunalk instr. 1990—), Bull/Bear Investment Club (treas. 1985-91). Avocations: boating, skiing, hunting, skeet and trap shooting, tennis. Home: 3 Meadow Mist Ct Reisterstown MD 21136-1324 Office: Black & Decker Corp 701 E Joppa Rd Baltimore MD 21286-5559

BROADDUS, JOHN ALFRED, JR., bank executive, economist; b. Richmond, Va., July 8, 1939; s. John Alfred Sr. and Norma (Coleman) B.; m. Margaret C. Lemley, Apr. 16, 1966; children: John Alfred III, Christopher McRae. BA, Washington & Lee U., 1961; diplome, U. Strasbourg, France, 1962; MA, Ind. U., 1970, PhD, 1972; LLD (hon.), Washington and Lee U., 1993. Intelligence rsch. specialist Def. Intelligence Agy., Washington, 1964-66; economist Fed. Res. Bank Richmond, 1970-72, asst. v.p., 1972-75, v.p., 1975-85, sr. v.p., dir. rsch., 1985-92, pres., 1993—; mem. adv. coun. U. Richmond Sch. Bus. Author: A Primer on the Fed, 1988; contbr. articles to publs. Chmn. bd. trustees United Way of Greater Richmond, 1990; vice chmn. bd. trustees Health Corp. of Va., 1980s; pres. Richmond Meml. Hosp. Found., 1980-85; chmn. bd. govs. St. Christopher's Sch., 1992-96; mem. Gov.'s Adv. Coun. on Revenue Estimates, Va., 1993—; trustee Va. Coun. Econ. Edn., 1994—, Confed. Meml. Lit. Soc., 1995—, E. Angus Powell Endowment Econ. Edn., 1995—, Bon Secours Richmond Health, 1995-98, Richmond Meml. Found., 1998—; exec. com. Metro Richmond Coalition Against Drugs, 1994-95, Richmond Renaissance, 1998—. 1st lt. U.S. Army, 1962-64. Named Fulbright scholar, 1961. Mem. Am. Econ. Assn., Nat. Assn. Bus. Economists, So. Econ. Assn., Phi Beta Kappa, Omicron Delta Kappa. Avocations: running, tennis. Office: Fed Res Bank Richmond 701 E Byrd St PO Box 27622 Richmond VA 23261-7622

BROADFOOT, ALBERT LYLE, physicist; b. Milestone, Sask., Can., Jan. 8, 1930; came to U.S., 1963; s. Morris Alexander and Lydia Georgina (Jacklin) B.; m. Katherine Eileen Deacon, Sept. 26, 1964; children: Alexander Lyle, Marilyn Louise. BE in Engring., Physics, U. Sask., Saskatoon, 1956, M.Sc. in Physics, 1960, Ph.D. in Physics, 1963. Engr. Def. Rsch. Bd., Ottawa, Ont., Can., 1956-58; jr. physicist space div. Kitt Peak Nat. Obs., Tucson, 1963-64, asst. physicist, 1964-68, assoc. physicist, 1968-70, physicist, 1971-79; rsch. scientist, assoc. physicist Earth and Space Scis. Inst., U. So. Calif., 1979-82; sr. rsch. scientist Lunar and Planetary Lab., U. Ariz., Tucson, 1982—. Home: 5231 E 17th St Tucson AZ 85711-4429 Office: U Ariz Lunar and Planetary Lab 901 Gould-Simpson Blvd Tucson AZ 85721

BROADHEAD, JAMES LOWELL, electrical power industry executive; b. New Rochelle, N.Y., Nov. 28, 1935; s. Clarence James and Mabel Roseader (Bowser) B.; m. Sharon Ann Rulon, May 6, 1967; children: Jeffrey Thornton, Kristen Ann, Carolyn Mary, Catherine Lee. B.M.E., Cornell U., 1958; LL.B., Columbia U., 1963. Bar: N.Y. 1963. Mech. engr. sales dept. Ingersoll-Rand Co., 1958-59; assoc. Debevoise, Plimpton, Lyons & Gates, N.Y.C., 1963-68; asst. sec. St. Joe Minerals Corp., N.Y.C., 1968-70, sec., 1970-77, gen. counsel, 1973-74, v.p. devel., 1976-77, exec. v.p., 1980-81, pres., 1981-82, also dir.; sr. vp. GTE Corp., Stamford, Conn., 1984-88; also pres. GTE Corp. telephone ops., Stamford, Conn., 1984-88; pres., CEO, chmn. bd. Fla. Power & Light Co./FPL Group, Inc., West Palm Beach, Fla., 1989—; chmn., CEO Energy Rsch. Corp., Danbury, Conn., 1973-74; v.p. St. Joe Petroleum Co., N.Y.C., 1974-76; pres. St. Joe Zinc Co., Pitts., 1977-80; exec. v.p., dir. U.S. Industries, 1983; dir. Pittston Co., Delta Air Lines, Inc., N.Y. Life Ins. Co. Editor: Columbia Law Rev., 1963. Served with U.S. Army, 1960-61. Office: FPL Group Inc 700 Universe Blvd Juno Beach FL 33408-2657

BROADHEAD, RONALD FRIGON, petroleum geologist, geology educator; b. Racine, Wis., July 22, 1955; s. Ronald Leslie and Thereise (Frigon) B. BS, N.Mex. Tech. U., 1977; MS, U. Cin., 1979. Geologist, Cities Svc. Oil Co., Oklahoma City and Tulsa, 1979-81; prin. sr. petroleum geologist N.Mex. Bur. Mines, Socorro, 1981—, asst. dir., 1994-98; mem. adj. faculty N.Mex. Tech. Coll., 1983—; mem. potential gas com. Potential Gas Agy. Union Oil Co. summer fellow Duke U. Marine Lab., 1977. Mem. Am. Assn. Petroleum Geologists (Ho. of Dels.), Soc. Econ. Paleontologists and Mineralogists, N.Mex. Geol. Soc. (past pres.) , Roswell Geol. Soc., Four Corners Geol. Soc., West Tex. Geol. Soc., Sigma Xi. Office: NMex Bur Mines Campus Sta Socorro NM 87801

BROADHURST, AUSTIN, JR., executive recruiter; b. Boston, Aug. 9, 1947; s. Austin and Deborah (Lowell) B.; m. Janine Boyajian, June 15, 1974; children: Robert James, Lauren Cox. BA, Williams Coll., 1969; MBA, Harvard U., 1972. With sec.'s office HEW, Washington, 1972-76; asst. to corp. exec. v.p. Baxter Labs., Deerfield, Ill., 1976-78; group product mgr. Baxter Labs., Deerfield, 1978-79; dir. corp. planning Nat. Med. Care, Boston, 1979-80, corp. v.p., 1980-83; sr. v.p. UHA Enterprises, N.Y.C., 1983-84; pres., CEO, dir. OcuSys., Inc., 1985-86; exec. dir. Russell Reynolds Assocs., 1986-88, mng. dir., 1988-96, office mgr., 1990-91, health care practice head, 1991-95; ptnr. LAI Ward Howell, 1996-98; v.p. Korn/Ferry International., 1998—. Incorporator Greenwich Hosp., 1990-96, trustee, 1996—; dir. Norwalk Cmty. Tech. Coll. Found., 1996—. Mem. Harvard Club N.Y., Stanwich Club, Indian Harbor Y.C., Milbrook Club. Episcopalian. Home: 1 North St Greenwich CT 06830-4720 Office: One Landmark Square Stamford CT 06901

BROADHURST, JEROME ANTHONY, lawyer; b. Cleve., Feb. 4, 1945; s. William and Estelle M. (Bozak) B.; m. Annette Lou Wilt, Sept. 3, 1966; children: Stephanie Ann, Jerome A., Elizabeth Marie. BS in Bus., U. Akron, 1967, JD, 1971. Bar: Ohio 1973, Tenn. 1987. Acctg. supr., fin. analyst B.F. Goodrich Co., Akron, Ohio, 1971-73, corp. counsel, 1973-76; counsel, asst. sec. The Weatherhead Co., Cleve., 1976-77; asst. counsel Gen. Tire and Rubber Co., Akron, 1977-80; sr. corp. atty. Holiday Inns, Inc. (subs. Holiday Corp.), Memphis, 1980-81, sec., sr. corp. atty., 1981-84; sec., assoc. gen. counsel Holiday Corp., Memphis, 1984-87, v.p., sec., assoc. gen. counsel, 1987-88; v.p., gen. counsel, sec. Perkins Family Restaurants, L.P., Memphis, 1989-91; pvt. practice law, 1991—; mediator Tenn. Mediation/Arbitration Svc., 1994-95; adj. prof. Christian Brothers U. Sch. Bus., Memphis, 1997—, asst. prof. MBA program. Bd. dirs. Memphis Urban League, 1987-94; trustee Memphis Urban League Endowment Fund, 1987—. Mem. ABA (mem. bus. law sect. subcoms. on corp. litigation and environ. control 1995—, intellectual property law sect. com. on unfair comp.-trade identity 1996—), Tenn. Bar Assn., Ohio Bar Assn., Memphis Bar Assn., Shelby County Bar Assn., Am. Soc. Corp. Secs. (corp. practices com. 1981-97), Memphis Intellectual Property Roundtable (founding mem.). Republican. Roman Catholic. Avocations: photography, jogging, fishing, racquetball. Office: Peabody Office Tower 100 Peabody Pl Ste 1300 Memphis TN 38103-3649

BROADHURST, NORMAN NEIL, foods company executive; b. Chico, Calif., Dec. 17, 1946; s. Frank Spencer and Dorothy Mae (Conrad) B.; BS, Calif. State U., 1969; MBA, Golden Gate U., 1975; m. Victoria Rose Thomson, Aug. 7, 1976; 1 child, Scott Andrew. With Del Monte Corp., San Francisco, 1969-76, product mgr., 1973-76; product mgr. Riviana Foods, Inc., div. Colgate Palmolive, Houston, 1976-78; new products brand devel. mgr. foods div. Coca Cola Co., Houston, 1978-79, brand mgr., 1979-82, mktg. dir., 1982-89, v.p. mktg. Beatrice Foods Co., Chgo., 1983-86; pres., COO Famous Amos Chocolate Chip Cookie Co., Torrance, Calif., 1986-88; corp. sr. v.p., gen. mgr. Kerr Group Inc., L.A., 1988-92, corp. sr. v.p., pres. Kerr Group Consumer Products, 1992-95; chmn. dir. Double Eagle Holdings, Inc., 1995—; chmn., pres. and CEO Trusted Brands, Inc., 1995-98. Chmn. youth soccer program Cystic Fibrosis Found., Houston, 1982-83; chmn., pres. South Coast Symphony, 1985-88; mem. nat. bd. Literacy Vols. Am., 1988—, vice chmn. 1993-95, chmn. 1997—); bd. dirs. Human Options, 1997—. Mem. Assoc. Sales and Mktg. Co., Am. Mktg. Assn., Am. Mgmt. Assn.

BROADIE, THOMAS ALLEN, surgeon, educator; b. St. Paul, June 26, 1941; s. Thomas Edward and Laura Marjorie (Allen) B.; m. Victoria Taylor, July 20, 1968; children: Frances, Thomas. AB, Princeton U., 1963; MD, Northwestern U., 1967; PhD, U. Minn., 1977. Diplomate Am. Bd. Surgery. Intern, resident Johns Hopkins Hosp., 1967-69; resident U. Minn., 1969-75; from asst. prof. to prof. surgery Ind. U., Indpls., 1978-92, prof., 1992—; mem. at large Com. on Trauma, Chgo., 1990-97; chmn. Ind. State Com. on Trauma, Indpls., 1991-97. Fellow ACS (pres. Ind. chpt. 1989-90, gov. at large 1992-97); mem. Soc. Univ. Surgeons, Midwest Surg. Assn. (pres. 1995-96), Ctrl. Surg. Assn., Am. Assn. Surgery Trauma, Western Surg. Assn., Am. Assn. Endocrine Surgeons, Am. Thyroid Assn. Office: Wishard Meml Hosp Dept Surgery 1001 W 10th St Indianapolis IN 46202-2859*

BROADNAX, WALTER D., public policy educator; b. Starcity, Ark., Oct. 21, 1944; s. Walter and Mary Lee (Cotton) B.; m. Angel LaVerne Wheelock; 1 child, Andrea Alyce. BA, Washburn U., 1967; MPA, Kans. U., 1969; PhD, Syracuse U., 1975; Hon. Degree, Washburn U., Topeka, Ctrl. State U. Ohio. Dir. Svcs. Children, Youth and Adults, Kans., 1979-80; prin. dep. asst. sec. HHS, 1980-81; lectr. pub. mgmt. and pub. policy John F. Kennedy sch. govt. Harvard U., 1981-87, dir. innovations state and local govt., 1985-87; pres. N.Y. State Civil Svc. Commn., 1987-90; commr. N.Y. State Dept. Civil Svc., 1987-90; pres. Ctr. Govtl. Rsch., Inc., Rochester, N.Y., 1990-93; dep. sec. HHS, Washington, 1993-96; prof. school of pub affairs Univ of Md, College Park, MD, 1996; dean Coll. Pub. Affairs Am. U., 1999; bd. dirs. Medecision. Contbr. articles to profl. jours. Bd. Trustees Syracuse U. Whiting scholar Washburn U. Fellow Nat. Acad. Pub. Adminstrn.; mem. Am. Soc. Pub. Adminstrn. (Outstanding Pub. Svc. award Nat. Capital Area chpt.), Am. Polit. Sci. Assn. Avocations: reading, jogging, music. Home: 1612 Beekman Pl NW Apt B Washington DC 20009-4023 Office: Univ of Maryland School of Public Affairs College Park MD 20742

BROADWATER, DOUGLAS DWIGHT, lawyer; b. Preston, Minn., May 31, 1944; s. George and Marion Elaine (Gleason) B.; m. Beatrice Kinney, July 8, 1978; children: Ian Dwight, George Francis, Mark Fowler. BA, Harvard Coll., 1966; JD, Columbia U., 1969. Bar: N.Y. 1969. Staff atty. Employment Project of Ctr. Social Welfare Policy and Law, N.Y.C., 1969-71; assoc. Cravath, Swaine & Moore, 1971—, ptnr., 1978—. Office: Cravath Swaine & Moore Worldwide Plz 825 8th Ave Fl 41 New York NY 10019-7475

BROADWATER, JAMES E., publisher; b. Tacoma, Nov. 5, 1945; s. Robert L. and June J. B.; m. Diane K. Plummer, Apr. 22, 1967; children: James Tegan, Kelly Diane, Robert Charles, Krista Dawn. BS in Journalism, U. Fla., 1967. Acct. mgr. Young & Rubicam, Inc., Detroit, Kansas City, Kans., N.Y.C. and Houston, 1968-73; assoc. pub. Tex. Monthly Mag., Austin, 1973-78; pres., pub. Saturday Rev. Mag., N.Y.C., 1978-80; regional pub. dir. Baker Publs., Houston, 1980-87; pres. HBC, Inc., Houston, 1982-84; assoc. pub. Tex. Sportsworld Mag., 1985-86; pub. Washington Journalism Rev., 1987-92; pres. The Broadwater Co., Houston, 1993—. Mem. Mag. Pub. Assn., Nat. Press Club, Am. Mgmt. Assn., Direct Mail Mktg. Assn., Lambda Chi Alpha. Baptist. *All things are possible through Christ. Success requires that one deal in results and not succumb to the desire to rationalize excuses.*

BROADWAY, NANCY RUTH, landscape design and construction company executive, consultant, model and actress; b. Memphis, Dec. 20, 1946; d. Charlie Sidney and Patsy Ruth (Meadows) Adkins. BS in Biology and Sociology cum laude, Memphis State U., 1969; postgrad., Tulane U., 1969-70; MS in Horticulture, U. Calif.-Davis, 1976. Lic. landscape contractor, Calif. Claims adjuster Mass. Mut. Ins., San Francisco, 1972-73; community garden coord. City of Davis, Calif., 1976; seed propagation supr. Bordier's Wholesale Nursery, Santa Ana, Calif., 1976-78; owner, founder Calif. Landscape Co., 1978-88, Design & Mgmt. Consultare, 1988—; prs. Calif. Landscape & Maintenance, Inc., 1998&. Actress: Visions of Murder, 1993, Eyes of Terror, 1994. NDEA fellow Tulane U., 1969-70. Fellow Am. Hort. Soc.; mem. Nat. Assn. Gen. Contractors, Calif. Native Plant Soc., Stockton C. of C. Democrat. Home and Office: 80 Terra Vista Ave Apt 8 San Francisco CA 94115-3878

BROAS, DONALD SANFORD, hospital executive; b. Poughkeepsie, N.Y., July 30, 1940; s. Smith Wilton and Ethel Mae (Sanford) B.; m. Betty Jane Langer; children: Nancy Beth, Donald S. Jr., Kimberley Ann, Gregory Michael. BS cum laude, Springfield Coll., 1963; MHA, Med. Coll. Va., 1965. Resident Newton (Mass.) Wellesley Hosp., 1964-65; asst. dir. Malden (Mass.) Hosp., 1966, Norwood (Mass.) Hosp., 1966-69; asst. dir. Robert B. Brigham Hosp., Boston, 1969-72, dir., 1972-77; exec. dir. Hosp. for Spl. Surgery, N.Y.C., 1977-88, pres., 1988-93; pres. Health Care Devel. Internat. Inc., Tarrytown, N.Y., 1993-95; exec. v.p. InterFaith Med. Ctr., Bklyn., 1995-96; pres., CEO Excelcare System Inc., Elmsford, N.Y., 1996—. Bd. dirs. Hosp. Chaplaincy, Inc., N.Y.C., 1978-93; mem. exec. com., bd. dirs., sec. Medic Alert U.S., 1991-97. Capt. USAR, 1965-73. Fellow Am. Coll. Health Care Execs.; mem. Greater N.Y. Hosp. Assn. (bd. dirs. 1978-82, 87-93), Hosp. Pres. Assn. (charter mem.), Hosp. Adminstrs. Club N.Y. (sec. 1979-81, pres. 1981-83). Avocations: skiing, swimming, travel. Home: 1 Larboard Dr Southampton NY 11968-1005 Home: 360 E 65th St New York NY 10021-6712 Office: Excelcare System Inc 33 Palmer Ave Bronxville NY 10708

BROBECK, DAVID GEORGE, middle school administrator; b. Rochester, Pa., Nov. 7, 1953; s. Stanley Clark and Jane Kirk (McBurney) B.; m. Gretchen Ann Bricker, June 18, 1977; children: Melissa Ann, Emily Elizabeth, Lauren Rebecca, Sarah Jane. BA, Calif. Luth. U., 1975; MEd, Kent State U., 1978, PhD, 1998. Cert. reading and English tchr., Ohio; cert. elem. and secondary prin., Ohio; cert. supt., Ohio. Tchr. Kent (Ohio) City Schs., 1975-92; asst. football coach Roosevelt High Sch., Kent, 1975-92, summer prin., 1987-92, head track coach, 1990-92; track coach Davey Middle Sch., Kent, 1978-89, asst. prin., 1992-96; prin. Woodridge Mid. Sch., Peninsula, Ohio, 1996—; guest lectr. Kent State U., 1985-98, Akron U., 1997, Ursuline Coll., 1996-98; presenter in field. Bd. dirs. Kent Credit Union, 1981-90; coun. pres. Trinity Luth. Ch., Kent, 1986-87; dir. Kent Youth Ctr., 1986. Named Metro League Coach of Yr., Record Pub., 1990, 91, 92, Akron Dist. Coach of Yr., Akron Area Track Coaches Assn., 1991; recipient Bowman fellow Kent State Univ., 1993-94. Mem. ASCD, Ohio Middle Sch. Assn. (exec. bd. 1998—), Nat. Middle Sch. Assn., Ohio Assn. Secondary Sch. Prins., Nat. Assn. Secondary Sch. Prins., Ohio Assn. Elem. Sch. Prins., Phi Delta Kappa (IDEA fellow). Democratic. Avocations: jogging, woodworking, playing guitar, singing, reading. Home: 7485 Skyview Dr Kent OH 44240-6322 Office: Woodridge Mid Sch 4451 Quick Rd Peninsula OH 44264-9706

BROBECK, JOHN RAYMOND, physiology educator; b. Steamboat Springs, Colo., Apr. 12, 1914; s. James Alexander and Ella (Johnson) B.; m. Dorothy Winifred Kellogg, Aug. 24, 1940; children: Stephen James, Priscilla Kimball, Elizabeth Martha, John Thomas. B.S., Wheaton Coll., 1936, LL.D., 1960; M.S., Northwestern U., 1937, Ph.D., 1939; M.D., Yale U., 1943. Instr. physiology Yale, 1943-45, asst. prof., 1945-48, asso. prof. physiology, 1948-52; prof. physiology, chmn. dept. U. Pa., Phila., 1952-70; Herbert C. Rorer prof. med. scis. U. Pa., 1970-82, prof. emeritus, 1982—. Editor: Yale Jour. Biology and Medicine, 1949-52; chmn. editorial bd.: Physiol. Revs, 1963-72. Fellow Am. Acad. Arts and Scis.; mem. Am. Physiol. Soc. (pres. 1971-72), Am. Inst. Nutrition, Nat. Acad. Scis., Am. Soc. Clin. Investigation, Halsted Soc., Phila. Coll. Physicians, Sigma Xi, Alpha Omega Alpha. Home: 1343 W Baltimore Pike #C118 Media PA 19063 Office: U Pa Dept Physiology Philadelphia PA 19104-6085

BROBECK, STEPHEN JAMES, consumer advocate; b. New Haven, Sept. 15, 1944; s. John Raymond and Dorothy Winifred (Kellogg) B.; m. Susan Cheney Williams, May 9, 1971. BA, Wheaton Coll., 1966; PhD, U. Pa., 1972. Asst. prof. Case Western Res. U., 1970-79; exec. dir. Consumer Fedn. Am., Washington, 1980—; vis. assoc. prof. Cornell U., 1989; adj. assoc. prof. U. Md., 1990-92. Author: The Product Safety Book, 1983, The Bank Book, 1986, The Modern Consumer Movement, 1990, Encyclopedia of the Consumer Movement, 1997; contbr. articles to profl. jours. Bd. dirs. Consumer Fedn. Am., 1976-79, Cleve. Consumer Action, 1976-80, Citizens for Tax Justice, 1980—, Citizens for a More Responsive Philanthropy, 1980-95, Nat. Coalition for Consumer Edn., 1981—, Joint Coun. Econ. Edn., 1981-88, Pub. Voice for Food and Health Policy, 1983—, Inst. Civil Justice, 1984-90, 93—, Nat. Ctr. Fin. Svcs., 1984-90, Tele-Consumer Hotline, 1984-98, Advocates for Hwy. and Automobile Safety, 1989—, Fed. Res. Bank Richmond, 1990-96, Coalition Against Ins. Fraud, 1993—, Alliance to Save Energy, 1994—, Ctr. for Study of Svcs., 1995—. Mem. Am. Council Consumer Interests. Home: 4700 Connecticut Ave NW Washington DC 20008-5629 Office: Consumer Fed Am 1424 16th St NW Ste 604 Washington DC 20036-2239

BROBERG, MERLE, retired social worker; b. Eagle Bend, Minn., Sept. 7, 1929; s. Herbit and Goldie (Johnson) B.; m. Hazel Irene Holst, Dec. 16, 1949 (div. Dec. 1979); children: Richard, Robert, Christopher, Rebecca; m. Dolores Elizabeth Melching, Feb. 8, 1980. BA, U. Minn., 1949; M in Social Svc., Bryn Mawr Coll., 1957; PhD, Am. U., 1969. Relocation advisor U.S. Urban Renewal Adminstrn., Phila., 1962-65; vis. asst. prof. Lehigh U., Bethlehem, Pa., 1965-66; from asst. prof. to assoc. prof., assoc. dean Bryn Mawr (Pa.) Coll., 1966-85, assoc. prof. emeritus, 1985—; acting dir. Green Tree Sch., Phila., 1988-89. Author: Barbados, 1989; contbr. articles to profl. publs. Bd. dirs. YMCA Germantown, Phila., 1968-79; v.p. Cmty. Svcs. Planning Coun., Phila., 1978-85; pres. Cmty. Renewal Germantown, 1981-86. Mem. NASW.

BROCA, LAURENT ANTOINE, aerospace scientist; b. Nov. 30, 1928; came to U.S., 1957; naturalized, 1963; s. Paul L. and Paule Jeanne (Ferrand) B.; m. Leticia Garcia Guerra, Dec. 18, 1972; 1 child, Marie-There Yvonne. BS in Math., U. Bordeaux, France, 1949; lic. es Scis. in Math. and Physics, U. Toulouse, France, 1957; grad., Inst. Technique Professionnel, France, 1960; PhD in Elec. Engring., Calif. Western U., 1979; postgrad., Boston U., 1958, MIT, 1961, Harvard U., 1961. Tchg. fellow physics dept. boston U., 1957-58; spl. instr. dept. physics N.J. Inst. Tech., Newark, 1959-60; sr. staff engr. advanced rsch. group ITT, Nutley, N.J., 1959-60; examiner math. and phys. scis. univ. Paris and Caen (France) Exam Ctr., N.Y.C., 1959-69; sr. engr. surface radar divsn. Raytheon Co., Waltham, Mass., 1960-62, Hughes Aircraft Co., Culver City, Calif., 1962-64; asst. prof. math. Calif. State U., Northridge, 1963-64; prin. engr. astrionics lab. NASA, Huntsville, Ala., 1964-65; fellow engr. Def. and Space Ctr. Westinghouse Electric Corp., Balt., 1965-69; cons. and sci. adv. electronics, phys. scis. and math. to indsl. firms and broadcasting sats., 1969-80; head engring. dept. Videocraft Mfg. Co., Laredo, Tex., 1974-75; asst. prof. math. Laredo State U., summer 1975; engring. specialist dept. sys. performance analysis ITT Fed. Electric Corp., Vandenberg AFB, Calif., 1980-82; engring. mgr. Ford Aerospace and Comms. Corp., Nellis AFB, Nev., 1982-84, Arcata Assocs., Inc., North Las Vegas, Nev., 1984-85; sr. scientific specialist engring. and devel. EG&G Spl. Projects, Inc., Las Vegas, 1985—. With French Army, 1951-52. Recipient Published Paper award Hughes Aircraft Co., 1966; Fulbright scholar, 1957. Mem. IEEE, Am. Nuclear Soc. (vice chmn. Nev. sect. 1982-83, chmn. 1983-84), Am. Def. Preparedness Assn., Armed Forces Comms. and Electronics Assn., Air Force Assn. Home: 5040 Lancaster Dr Las Vegas NV 89120-1445 Office: EG&G Spl Projects Inc PO Box 93747 Las Vegas NV 89193-3747

BROCCHINI, RONALD GENE, architect; b. Oakland, Calif., Nov. 6, 1929; s. Gino Mario and Yoli Louise (Lucchesi) B.; m. Myra Mossman, Feb. 3, 1957; 1 child, Christopher Ronald. B.A. in Architecture with honors, U. Calif., Berkeley, 1953, M.A. in Architecture with honors, 1957. Registered architect, Calif., Nev. Architect, designer SMP, Inc., San Francisco, 1948-53, designer, assoc., 1956-60; assoc. architect Campbell & Wong, San Francisco, 1961-63; prin. architect Ronald G. Brocchini, Berkeley, Calif., 1964-67, Worley K Wong & Ronald G Brocchini Assocs., San Francisco, 1968-87, Brocchini Architects, Berkeley, 1987—; lectr. Calif. Coll. Arts and Crafts, Oakland, 1981-83; commr. Calif. Bd. Archtl. Examiners, 1961-89; mem. exam. com. Nat. Coun. Archtl. Registration Bds., 1983-85. Author: Long Range Master Plan for Bodega Marine Biology, U. Calif., 1982; prin. works include San Simeon Visitor Ctr., Hearst Castle, Calif., Mare Island Med.-Dental Facillity, IBM Ednl. and Data Processing Hdqrs., San Jose, Calif., Simpson Fine Arts Gallery, Calif. Coll. Arts, Ceramics and Metal Crafts, Emery Bay Pub. Market Complex, Analytical Measurement Facility, U. Calif., Berkeley, Bodega Marine Biology Campus, U. Calif., Berkeley, Fromm & Sichell (Christian Bros.) Hdqrs., The Nature Co., Corp. Offices, Berkeley, Merrill Coll., Athletic Facilities, U. Calif., Santa Cruz, Coll. III Housing, U. Calif., San Diego, Ctr. Pacific Rim Studies, U. San Francisco, married student housing Escondido II, III, IV, Stanford (Calif.) U. With U.S. Army, 1953-55. Recipient Bear of Yr. award U. Calif., Berkeley, 1987, Alumni Citation, 1988; recipient 18 Design Honor awards for architecture, Design award State of Calif. Dept. Rehab., 1995. Fellow AIA (bd. dirs. Calif. coun., pres. San Francisco chpt. 1982); mem. Bear Backers Club (bd. dirs. U. Calif.-Berkeley athletic coun.), Berkeley Breakfast Club (bd. govs.), Order of the Golden Bear, Chi Alpha Kappa. Republican. Roman Catholic. Avocations: auto restoration; photography; sports; art. Office: Brocchini Architects Inc 2748 Adeline St Berkeley CA 94703-2251

BROCHES, PAUL ELIAS, architect; b. N.Y.C., July 10, 1945; s. Aron and Catharina (Pothast) B.; m. Julie Spain, Sept. 2, 1984; children: Rebecca, Emma. BA, Columbia Coll., 1967; MArch, Columbia U., 1970. Registered architect, N.Y., D.C., Pa., Calif., Conn., Mass., N.J., Iowa, Tex., Fla., Nat. Coun. Archtl. Registration Bds. Staff designer Henry Dreyfus Assocs., N.Y.C., 1970-71; staff arch. Mitchell/Giurgola Archs., N.Y.C., 1971-75, assoc., 1976-79, ptnr., 1980—; vis. critic and juror Columbia U., 1973—, N.J. Coll. Arch., 1981, 82, Tulane U., 1976, Va. Polytechnic Inst., 1974; juror design awards program Ark. chpt. AIA, 1990, Internat. Assn. Lighting Design, 1985, N.Y. State Assn. Arch., 1982; advisor Nat. Endowment for the Arts' Pub. Art Policy Project, 1987; symposium panelist Am. Soc. Landscape Archs. Ann. Conv., 1987, Site Specific Art and Collaboration Among Artists, Archs. and Landscape Archs., U. Mass., 1985. Author: (with others) Going Public: A Field Guide to Developments in Art in Public Places; contbr. articles to profl. jours.; prin. works include East Campus Devel. Plan, Health Svcs. Bldg. Whitaker Coll. of Health Scis., MIT, Tilles Ctr. for the Performing Arts Renovation and Interiors, L.I. U., Burke Libr. Renovation and Interiors, Union Theol. Sem., L.I. U. Health Sci. Ctr., Ctr. West Office Bldg., NYU Med. Ctr., IBM Advanced Bus. Inst., Solana IBM Office Complex, N.Y.C. Pub. Schs. PS88 and PS56, CUNY Coll. of Staten Island Lab. Sci. Bldg. and Hostos Cmty. Coll. Adminstrn. Bldg., Comprehensive Devel. Plan Tchrs. Coll., Columbia U., New Acad. Ctr. Southampton Coll., L.I. U., Powdermaker Hall Renovation Queens Coll., CUNY. Alumni trustee nominating com. Columbia U., 1983-92. William Kinne Fellows Meml. fellow Columbia U., 1969. Mem. Fellow AIA (assoc. editor N.Y. Architecture 1988, N.Y.C. sch. constrn. authority task force

1994); mem. Am. Planning Assn. (urban design task force 1989—, N.Y.C./ AIA urban design com., bd. advisors 1996—), Architects, Designers, Planners for Social Responsibility (chmn. design awards jury 1993). Office: Mitchell/Giurgola Archs 170 W 97th St New York NY 10025-6492*

BROCHU, CLAUDE RENAUD, professional baseball team executive; b. Quebec City, Quebec, Can.; m. Michelle Dénommée. BA, U. Ottawa, Ont., Can., 1966; MBA, McMaster U., Hamilton, Ont., 1971. Worked in cosmetics industry, 1971-76; exec. v.p. mktg. Joseph E. Seagram & Sons, Ltd., Montreal, Can., 1976-86; pres., operating officer Montreal Expos, 1986—, pres., gen. ptnr. Capt. Can. armed forces. Office: Montreal Expos, Montreal Expos, 4549 Pierre-de-Coubertin Ave, Montreal, PQ Canada H1V 3N7*

BROCK, CHARLES LAWRENCE, lawyer, business executive; b. Ottumwa, Iowa, Mar. 7, 1943; s. Charles Harlan and Betty Arlene (Ream) B.; m. Mary Jane Hipp, June 17, 1978; children: William Walker, Susanna Lawrence. BA with highest distinction, Northwestern U., 1964; JD, Harvard U., 1967; postgrad. (Rotary Found. fellow), U. Delhi (India) and India Law Inst., 1967-68; grad., Advanced Mgmt. Program, Harvard Bus. Sch., 1979. Bar: N.Y. 1968. Asso. firm Sullivan & Cromwell, N.Y.C., 1969-74; v.p., corp. sec., gen. counsel Scholastic Mags., Inc. (now Scholastic, Inc.), N.Y.C., 1974-80; interim CFO and COO Scholastic Mags., Inc., 1975-76, pub. internat. div., 1976-80; pres. Scholastic Tab Publs. Ltd., Can., 1976-80, Ashton-Scholastic Pty. Ltd., Australia, 1976-80, Ashton-Scholastic Ltd., New Zealand, 1976-80; chmn. Scholastic Publs. Ltd., U.K., 1976-80; sr. v.p., mgmt. dir. Compton Communications, 1980-82; mgr. subsidiaries Compton Advertising, 1980-82; counsel Drinker, Biddle & Reath, N.Y.C., Phila., Washington, 1982-84; ptnr. Carter, Ledyard & Milburn, 1984-95, Brock Silverstein McAuliffe LLC (now Brock Silverstein), 1995—; bd. dirs., chmn. audit coms. B&H Bulk Carriers Ltd., B&H Ocean Carriers Ltd., B&H Maritime Carriers Ltd.; bd. dirs. Harvard Alumni Assn., 1990— (two terms), chmn. grad. schs. com. 1992-95; mem. Harvard Coll. Bd. Overseers Com. on Univ. Resources, 1992—, chmn. Harvard Bd. Overseers Nominating Com. 1996—, coun. Harvard Law Sch. Assn., 1983-85, sec., 1988-90, treas., 1990—, exec. com., 1986—, chmn. membership com., 1987—, internat. sect., 1991—, pres. 1996—; mem. vis. com. Coll. Arts and Scis., Northwestern U., 1989—, Campaign for Gt. Tchrs. Com., 1989-90, John Evans Club, Northwestern U. 1989—; guild hall trustee Acad. of the Arts, 1990—, mem. exec. com., chmn. nominating com., 1986-90, chmn. bd., 1990-92; trustee, treas. Family Dynamics, 1981-88. Editorial adv. bd. Minority Law Jour. Anniversary gift chmn. Harvard Law Sch. Fund, 1967-68, vice chmn., 1975-77; trustee Harvard Law Sch. Assn. N.Y.C., 1982-85, chmn. placement com., 1983-86, v.p., 1985-96, originator, chmn. summer reception, 1982; chmn. Harvard Community Ptnrs., 1984-86; co-chmn. ann. giving St. Barnard's Ch., 1989-95; mem. adv. bd. Minority Atty. Reporter; deacon Brick Presbyn. Ch., N.Y.C., 1973-76, regent Cathedral St. John The Divine. Recipient Mentor award for pioneering efforts creating opportunities for minorities and women. Mem. ABA, N.Y. State Bar Assn., N.Y. County Lawyers Assn., Assn. Bar City of N.Y., Assn. Am. Pubs., Harvard Bus. Club of N.Y. (v.p. 1984-86), Union Club, N.Y. Yacht Club, Down Town Assn., The Pilgrims, Piping Rock (Locust Valley, N.Y.), Maidstone (East Hampton, N.Y.), Phi Beta Kappa, Kappa Sigma. Home: 765 Park Ave New York NY 10021-4254 Office: Brock Silverstein One Citicorp Ctr 56th Fl New York NY 10022-4611*

BROCK, DAVID ALLEN, state supreme court chief justice; b. Stoneham, Mass., July 6, 1936; s. Herbert and Margaret B.; m. Sandra Ford, 1960; 6 children. AB, Dartmouth Coll., 1958; LLB, U. Mich., 1963; postgrad., Nat. Jud. Coll., 1977. Bar: N.H. 1963. Assoc. Devine, Millimet, McDonough, Stahl & Branch, Manchester, N.H., 1963-69; U.S. atty. State of N.H., 1969-72; ptnr. Perkins, Douglas & Brock, Concord, N.H., 1972-74, Perkins & Brock, 1974-76; spl. counsel to gov. and exec. coun. N.H., 1974-76, legal counsel to gov. N.H., 1976; assoc. justice N.H. Superior Ct., 1976-78; assoc. justice N.H. Supreme Ct., 1978-86, chief justice, 1986—; chmn. State of N.H. Legal Svcs. Adv. Commn., 1977-79; chmn. dist. ct. reform subcom. Gov.'s Commn. for Ct. System Improvement, 1974-75; chmn. N.H. Commn. Ct. Accreditation, 1986—; mem. Select Commn. on Unified Ct. System, 1980-84, chmn. N.H. Supreme Ct. Com. on Jud. Conduct, 1981-89, rules adv. com., 1985-97; mem. State N.H. Jud. Coun., 1979-87; mem. nat. adv. bd. Leadership Inst. for Jud. Edn., 1989-96, Nat. Jud. Coll. long range planning com., 1990-91; mem. Jud. Edn. and Tech. Assistance Consortium, 1989-97; chmn. Interbranch Coun. on Substance Abuse and the Criminal Justice System, 1991-95; bd. dirs. State Justice Inst., 1992-98, vice-chmn., 1994-95, co-chmn., 1995-98; bd. dirs. Conf. Chief Justices, 1993-94, v.p., 1996-97, pres-elect 1997-98, pres., 1998-99; bd. dirs. Nat. Ctr. for State Cts., 1996—, chmn.-elect, 1997-98, chmn., 1998-99. Bd. dirs. Manchester Cmty. Guidance Ctr., 1966-72, pres., 1969-72; chmn. Manchester Rep. Com., 1967-69; vice chmn. N.H. Rep. State Com., 1968-69; Rep. candidate U.S. Senate, 1972; del. N.H. Constl. Conv., 1974: mem. Gov.'s Commn. for Handicapped, 1978-79. Fellow ABA (mem. edn. com. of appellate judges conf. 1981-97, appellate advocacy com. 1982-84, faculty appellate judges' seminar program 1984-89, del. ho. of dels. 1994-96), N.H. Bar Assn. (chmn. constl. revision com. 1976-77), N.H. Bar Found. (hon.). Office: NH Supreme Ct Noble Dr Concord NH 03301

BROCK, DAVID GEORGE, lawyer; b. Buffalo, Oct. 13, 1945; s. Joseph Louis and Julia Strauss (Amram) B.; m. Marilyn Sandra Katz, May 25, 1969; children: Lauren, Joel. BA in English, Union Coll., 1967; JD, SUNY, Buffalo, 1972. Bar: N.Y. 1973, U.S. Dist. Ct. (we. dist.) N.Y. 1973; cert. civil trial specialist Nat. Bd. Trial Advocacy. Atty. Liberty Mut. Ins. Co., Buffalo, 1973-77; assoc. Jaeckle, Fleischmann & Mugel, Buffalo, 1977-79, ptnr., 1980—; vice-chair N.Y. State Atty. Grievance Com. (8th judicial dist.), 1994—. Mem. cmty. schs. adv. bd., bd. trustees Temple Beth Zion Buffalo, N.Y., 1988-98, pres., 1994-96; bd. dirs. Planned Parenthood Buffalo and Erie County, 1999—. Mem. ABA, N.Y. State Bar Assn., Erie County Bar Assn. (chmn. profl. ethics com. 1991-95, bd. dirs. 1996-99), Western N.Y. Trial Lawyers Assn. (bd. dirs. 1993-95), Def. Rsch. Inst., Inc., Am. Arbitration Assn., Internat. Assn. Def. Counsel (bd. editors Def. Counsel Jour. 1992—), Nat. Inst. Trial Adv. Jewish. Avocations: reading, photography, traveling. Home: 49 Northington Dr East Amherst NY 14051-1721 Office: Jaeckle Fleischmann & Mugel LLP 12 Fountain Plz Buffalo NY 14202-2222

BROCK, DAVID LAWRENCE, periodontist; b. N.Y.C., Sept. 27, 1956; s. Charles Henry and Mary (Campisi) B.; m. Paige McMichael, Feb. 2, 1980 (div. Oct. 1987); m. Sharon Margaret Meldrum, Dec. 16, 1989; children: Allison Bloking, Leslie Bloking, Kelly. BS, U. South Fla., 1978; DMD, U. Fla., 1982, cert. in periodontics, 1985. Staff dentist Sunland Ctr., Gainesville, Fla., 1982, dental dir., 1982-83; pvt. practice, Hackettstown, N.J., 1985—; periodontal dir. Bergen Pines Hosp., Paramus, N.J., 1987-92; chief dental dept. Hackettstown Cmty. Hosp., 1994-97. Newspaper columnist Dental Health Topics, 1986; contbr. articles to dental jours.; inventor periodontal probe. Asst. scoutmaster Boy Scouts Am., Mansfield Twp., N.J., 1987-89; pres. bd. Warren County chpt. am. Cancer Soc., Oxford, N.J., 1995-97. Recipient best presentation award Fla. Periodontal Soc., 1985. Mem. ADA, Am. Acad. Periodontology, N.J. Soc. Periodontics, N.J. Dental Assn., Tri-County Dental Assn., Kiwanis. Republican. Avocations: music, hunting, fixing things, nature, antique autos. Office: 117 Grand Ave Hackettstown NJ 07840-2128

BROCK, DEE SALA, television executive, educator, writer, consultant; b. Covington, Okla., June 7, 1930; d. Lester Edward and Vera Mae (Bowers) Sala; m. Robert Wesley Brock, June 8, 1952 (div. 1979); children: Baron Sala, Bishop Chapman, Bevin Bowers. BA, U. North Tex., 1950, MA, 1956, PhD, 1985. Tchr. high sch. Dallas Ind. Sch. Dist., 1952-66; dir. Dallas Cowboy Cheerleaders, 1960-75; mem. faculty, adminstr. Dallas County Community Coll. Dist., 1966-74, telecourse writer, producer, adminstr., 1974-75, dir. mktg. info., 1975-80; dir., v.p. PBS, Washington, 1980-89; sr. v.p. edn. PBS, Alexandria, Va., 1989-90; pres. Dee Brock & Assocs., Plano, Tex., 1991—; bd. dirs. Pub. Svc. Satellite Consortium, U.S. Basics; mem. adv. bd. Learning Link, 1987-90, Telcon Industry, 1990-91; chair exec. coun. U. of the World, 1989-91; mem. adv. coun. Triangle Coalition, 1989-91. Author: Writing for a Reason: Study Guide, 1974 (with Jeriel Howard) Writing for a Reason, 1978, (with Laura Derr) The World of F. Scott Fitzgerald, 1980; mem. editorial bd. Am. Jour. Distance Edn., 1987-90; producer (internat. teleconf.) Out of the Red, 1991; producer, writer (TV series and workbook) Communicating in English in the Healthcare Workplace, 1994; speaker in field; contbr. articles in field; co-patentee video indexing system. Trustee Coun. for Adult and Experiential Learning, 1989—; bd. dirs. Coalition for the Advancement of Citizenship, 1988-90, active Met. Police Chief's Boys and Girls Club, Washington, PTA, Dallas; chair spl. task force Mcpl. Libr. Friends of Libr., 1996, pres., 1997—; lay rep. N.E. Tex. Libr. Sys., 1996—, chair planning to plan com., 1997-98, mem. adv. coun., 1998—, vice chair, 1998—; co-chair Komen Tyler Race for the Cure, 1999. Reynolds Econ. fellow U. N.C., 1966; Literacy award N. Tex. Reading Coun., 1980, Nat. Person of Yr. award Nat. Coun. on Community and Continuing Edn., 1985, Award for Excellence in TV Programming NEA, 1986; recipient Outstanding Career Achievement award ITC Am. Assn. Community and Jr. Colls., 1990. Mem. NEH (nat. bd. cons. 1980-85), U.S. Distance Learning Assn. (bd. dirs. 1989-91, mem. adv. bd. 1989), So. Assn. Colls. and Schs. (mem. Project 1990 task force 1984-86), Nat. Assn. Ednl. Broadcasters (steering com. 1979-81), Assn. Ednl. Communications Technology, Nat. Coun. Tchrs. English (pres. S.W. regional coun. 1972-74), Tex. Libr. Assn. (legis. com. 1999—, spl. taskforce for friends and trustees roundtable 1999—). Methodist. Home and Office: 1708 Wendover Pl Tyler TX 75703-2428

BROCK, ERIC JOHN, urban planner, historian, consultant; b. Berkeley, Calif., Sept. 24, 1966; s. Robert Donald and Victoria Claire (Berg) B.; m. Pamela Grace Viviano, Nov. 14, 1988 (div. Feb. 1996). BA in English and History, Centenary Coll., 1988. Editl. page writer Shreveport Jour., 1992—; pvt. practice consulting historian and planner Shreveport, 1993—; adv. bd. Shreveport Regional Arts Coun., 1990-93; cons. City of Shreveport, 1993—, Parish of Caddo, Shreveport, 1995—, State of La. Hist. Preservation Office, Baton Rouge, 1996—. Author: The Old Oakland Cemetery, 1988, The Jewish Cemeteries of Shreveport, 1995, Holiday-In-Dixie: 50 Years, 1998, Images of America, 1998, Shreveport in the 20th Century, 1998, Cities of the Dead, 1999, Steamboats on the Red River, 1999 (newspaper column) Shreveport Forum News, 1992—, (mag. column) Shreveport Forum News, 1996—. Vol. Holiday-in-Dixie Festival, Shreveport, 1996—; v.p. ACLU of N.W. La., Shreveport, 1993. Recipient Commendation La. State Senate, Baton Rouge, 1991, Key to the City of Shreveport, 1990, 94, 97. Fellow The Tarshar Soc.; mem. SAR, SCV, Holiday-in-Dixie Ambs. (bd. mem. 1996—), La. Preservation Alliance (bd. mem. 1990-94), Hist. Preservation of Shreveport (bd. mem., v.p. 1991-96, pres. 1996—), Shreveport Beautification Found. (bd. mem. 1990-92), Highland Area Partnership (bd. mem. 1991-95). Jewish. Avocations: photography, writing. Office: EJ Brock Planning and Preservation Cons PO Box 5877 Shreveport LA 71135-5877

BROCK, GERALD WAYNE, telecommunications educator; b. Hanford, Calif., Mar. 31, 1948; s. Aston A. and Leila L. (McAtee) B.; m. Ruth Carol Reisner, June 27, 1971; children: Jane, Sara, David, James. BA, Harvard U., 1970, PhD, 1973. Asst. prof. U. Ariz., Tucson, 1973-78; assoc. prof. Bethel Coll., St. Paul, 1978-79; econ. cons. Brock Econ. Rsch., St. Paul, 1979-83; economist FCC, Washington, 1983-86, chief acctg. and audits divsn., 1986-87, chief common carrier bur., 1987-89; prof. telecom. George Washington U., Washington, 1990—. Author: The U.S. Computer Industry, 1975, The Telecommunications Industry, 1981, Telecommunication Policy for the Information Age, 1994. Office: George Washington U Telecommunications Program 812 20th St NW Washington DC 20006-4307

BROCK, HELEN RACHEL MCCOY, retired mental health and community health nurse; b. Cromwell, Okla., Dec. 10, 1924; d. Samuel Robert Lee and Ire Etta (Pounds) McCoy; m. Clois Lee Brock, Sept. 29, 1963; children: Dwayne, Joyce, Peggy, Ricki, Stacey. AS, Southwestern Union Coll., Keene, Tex., 1968; BS in Nursing, Union Coll., Lincoln, Nebr., 1970; postgrad., Vernon Regional Jr. Coll., Tex., 1972, 76; MPH, Loma Linda (Calif.) U., 1983. Cert. ARC nurse. Dir. nursing Chillicothe (Tex.) Clinic-Hosp., 1970-77, Pike County Hosp., Waverly, Ohio, 1977-79, Marion County Hosp., Jefferson, Tex., 1979-81; nurse III, nursing unit supr. patient health educator Vernon State Hosp., Maximum Security for Criminally Insane, 1981-96; retired, 1996; nurse, admissions and assessments Texhoma Community Health Svcs., 1987-94. Mem. Am. Nurses Assn., Tex. Nurses Assn. Home: PO Box 238 Chillicothe TX 79225-0238

BROCK, HORACE RHEA, accounting educator; b. Leggett, Tex., Aug. 26, 1927; s. Hobby B. and Winona (Epperson) B.; m. Frances Euline Williams, May 24, 1955; children: Alan Howard, Mary Ann, Charles. B.S., Sam Houston State U., 1946, B.B.A., 1951, M.A., 1951; Ph.D., U. Tex., 1954. Prof. U. Ark., 1954-55; disting. prof. North Tex. State U., Denton, 1965-93, chmn. dept. accounting, 1966-74, dean Coll. Bus. Adminstrn., 1983-85; dir. Chief Execs. Round Table U. North Tex., Denton, 1993—; adviser AID, Istanbul, Turkey, 1967-69; cons. taxation and financial reporting. Author: Introduction to Taxation, 1972, 17th edit., 1988, Cost Accounting, 1970, 6th edit., 1998, College Accounting, 1974, 9th edit., 1998, Intermediate and Advanced Accounting, 1966, Accounting for Oil and Gas Producers, 1960, Accounting for Oil and Gas Producing Companies, 1982, 4th edit., 1996. Served with USAF, 1946-49. Mem. Am. Inst. CPA's, Tex. Soc. CPA's, Beta Gamma Sigma. Home: 1900 Westridge St Denton TX 76205-6925 Office: U North Tex 302 Marquis Hall Denton TX 76203

BROCK, JAMES RUSH, chemical engineering educator; b. Mission, Tex., Dec. 31, 1930; s. Jerome Dalton and Elizabeth (Beeler) B.; m. Mary Lou Waghorn, July 4, 1964; children: Ianthe, Alison. BA, Rice U., 1952, BS, 1953; MS, U. Wis., 1954, PhD, 1960. Registered profl. engr., Tex. Rsch. engr. Humble Oil & Refining Co., Houston, 1954-55; asst. prof. chem. engring. dept. U. Tex., Austin, 1959-62; postdoctoral fellow at Svc. de Chimie Physique II Université Libre de Belgique, Brussels, 1962-63; asst. prof. chem. engring. dept. U. Tex., Austin, 1963-65, assoc. prof., 1965-69, prof., 1969-73, 73-80, K.A. Kobe prof., 1980—; vis. prof. U. Paris VI Faculty Scis., Paris, 1973, Tokyo Inst. Tech., 1988; mem. rsch. grants adv. com. EPA, Washington, 1970—; v.p. ONG Producing Inc., Austin, 1986—; cons. to govt. agys. Co-author: The Dynamics of Aerocolloidal Systems, 1970; co-editor Internat. Revs. in Aerosol Physics and Chemistry, 1971-73; assoc. editor Jour. Environ. Sci. and Health, 1978—, Jour. Aerosol Sci., 1986-88; mem. editorial bd. Jour. Colloid Sci., 1965-66, Aerosol Sci. and Tech., 1984-88; contbr. more than 150 articles to profl. jours.; holder 20 patents in field. Recipient Disting. Svc. award U.S. Army Rsch. Devel. Engring. Ctr., 1987; grantee NSF. Mem. Am. Chem. Soc., Am. Assn. Aerosol Rsch. (Sinclair award 1992), Gesellschaft fur Aerosol Forschung, Tau Beta Pi, Alpha Chi Omega, Phi Lambda Upsilon. Office: U Tex Coll Engring Dept Chem Engring Austin TX 78712-1062*

BROCK, JAMES SIDNEY, lawyer; b. Newbury, Vt., Sept. 2, 1913; s. Frank Nelson and Louise (Johnson) B.; m. Gladys H. Linton, Sept. 14, 1940; children: Linda L. Brock Scoggins, Richard L., Elizabeth A. Brock Duncan. B.S., Middlebury Coll., 1935; LL.B., Bklyn. Law Sch., 1942. Bar: N.Y. 1942, Vt. 1947. Practiced in N.Y.C., 1942-46, Montpelier, Vt., 1947—; claims adjuster Liberty Mut. Ins. Co., 1935-42; assoc. LeBoeuf & Lamb, 1942-46; pvt. practice Montpelier, 1947-50; judge Montpelier Mcpl. Ct., 1948-50; atty. Nat. Life Ins. Co., 1950-56, asst. counsel, 1956-63, gen. counsel, 1963-73, v.p., 1968-70, sr. v.p., 1970-73, exec. v.p. corp. relations, 1973-74, exec. v.p., 1974-78; ptnr. Cheney Brock Saudek & Mullett, Montpelier, 1979-92; of counsel Cheney Brock Saudek & Mullett, 1992—; chmn., pres. Sentinel Group Funds, Inc., 1976-78; dir. emeritus Nat. Life Ins. Co. Bd. dirs. Champlain Coll., chmn., 1989-92; bd. dirs. Ctrl. Vt. Med. Ctr., Inc., chair, 1993-95; sec. Wash. County R.R., 1989-93; trustee emeritus Wood Art Gallery; chmn. Vt. Human Svcs. Bd., 1979-85; mem. Jud. Responsibility Bd., 1977-81, East Montpelier bd. adjustment, 1989-92. Mem. Assn. Life Ins. Counsel, ABA, Vt. Bar Assn. (pres. 1975). Republican. Congregationalist. Home: 234 Cutler Heights Rd Montpelier VT 05602-9609 Office: Cheney Brock & Saudek 159 State St Montpelier VT 05602-3301

BROCK, JOHN MORGAN, JR., composer, synthesist; b. San Angelo, Tex., June 15, 1956. Pres. Alternative Music Prodns., Inc., L.A., 1981—; spl. music instr. City of North Las Vegas, 1995-97. Composer, performer, engr. producer records Ahead Of Your Time, 1981, In Tune With Tomorrow, 1982, Android/A 21st Century Band, 1989, (CDs) Christina-Reminiscence, 1991, Mr. Ectomy, 1992, Entoptic Whores, 1994, Making Waves in the Desert - The New Age Symphony, 1998; (films) Doin' Time on Planet Earth, Martians Go Home, Repossessed, Mother Goose-Rock and Rhyme; also performed on NBC-TV, 1990; comml. music aired on CNN, 1994; commd. by N.W. Youth Ballet, 1995. Choir dir. Showmens League Am., 1997-98; music dir. Westminster Presbyn. Ch., 1997—. Nev. State Coun. on Arts/Commn. on Tourism grant, 1996. Mem. ASCAP (writer, pub.), NARAS, Internat. Electronic Music Assn. Avocations: graphic design, choreography, video production.

BROCK, LINDA M., educator; d. Thomas William Jr. and Margaret Ann Cobb; m. Christopher Lee Brock, Aug. 8, 1986; 1 child, Haley Lynn. BS in Edn., Ctrl. Mo. State U., 1986, M, 1993. Tchr. Blue Springs (Mo.) H.S., 1986—. Mem. ASCD, Nat. Coun. Tchrs. English. Office: Blue Springs High Sch 2000 W Ashton Blue Springs MO 64015

BROCK, MITCHELL, lawyer; b. Wyncote, Pa., Nov. 10, 1927; s. John W. and Mildred A. (Mitchell) B.; m. Gioia Connell, June 21, 1952; children: Felicity, Marina, Mitchell Hovey, Laura. AB, Princeton U., 1950; LLB, U. Pa., 1953. Bar: N.Y. 1954. Assoc. firm Sullivan & Cromwell, N.Y.C., 1953-59, ptnr., 1960-92; ptnr. Sullivan & Cromwell, Paris, 1965-68; ptnr. in charge Sullivan & Cromwell, Tokyo, 1987-90. Bd. dirs. Frost Valley YMCA, Oliverea, N.Y., 1980-87, 90—, Am. Found. Blind, 1967-87; pres., trustee Helen Keller Internat., N.Y.C., 1970-87, 90-94, chmn., trustee, 1994-96, sec., 1996—. Served with USN, 1945-46. Mem. ABA, Anglers Club, Princeton Club, Ivy Club, Boca Grande Pass Club. Republican. Episcopalian. Home: PO Box 452 Boca Grande FL 33921-0452

BROCK, PHILLIP LESLIE, talent agent; b. Santa Monica, Calif., Dec. 25, 1953; s. Elrie Louis and Beverly Rose B.; m. Kesmat Kereim, Sept. 15, 1979 (div. June 1982). AA, Santa Monica Coll., 1976; BA, UCLA, 1978; MEd, Loyola Marymount Coll., 1981. Tchr., coach L.A. Unified Schs., 1979-84; CEO Royal Scandinavian Industries, L.A., 1984-90, Studio Talent Group, Santa Monica, Calif., 1994—. Numerous TV and film appearances. Chancellors assoc. UCLA, L.A., 1998—; mem. athletic adv. com. Santa Monica Unified Schs., 1996—. Mem. SAG, AFTRA, AEA, Acad. Television Arts & Scis., Bruin Athletic Club (sustaining). Democrat. Office: Studio Talent Group 1328 12th St #3 Santa Monica CA 90401

BROCK, RANDALL J., poet; b. Colfax, Wash., Nov. 24, 1943; s. Homer Clarence and Roberta Mildred (Keith) B. Student, Wash. State U., 1962-68; BA in History, BA in Edn., Ea. Wash. U., 1970; MFA, U. Oreg., 1973. Tchr. Christian Action Ministry, Chgo., 1967; mailman Yellowstone (Wyo.) Park Co., 1968; janitor Spokesman-Rev., Spokane, Wash., 1978-79. Author of 18 chapbooks; over 1600 poems published in over 500 periodicals; author of four cassette tapes; photographer: Pockets of Origin, 1983. Poetry scholar Centrum, Port Townsend, Wash., 1977. Mem. Spokane Open Poetry Assn., Poets and Writers, PEN West U.S.A. Avocations: mysteries, history, anthropology. Home: PO Box 1673 Spokane WA 99210

BROCK, RUSSELL ERNEST, educational administrator; b. Wichita, Kans., Aug. 2, 1959; s. Ira Jay and Dottie Faye (Russell) B.; m. Sheree Denise Horner, Jan. 6, 1979; children: Matthew, Shian. BS in Edn., Mo. So. State Coll., 1981; MA in Comm., S.W. Mo. State U., 1988. Disc jockey Sta. KPCG Radio, Joplin, Mo., 1979-81; dir. speech and debate Washington H.S., Kansas City, Kans., 1981-83; retail salesman Gen. Tire, Springfield, Mo., 1983-84; shipping clk. Gospel Publ. House, Springfield, 1984; dir. speech and debate Webb City (Mo.) H.S., 1984-86, Monett (Mo.) H.S., 1986-97; dir. curriculum and instrn. Monett R-1 Sch. Dist., 1997—. Recipient Diamond Coaching award Nat. Forensic League, Ripon, Wis., 1988, 93, 98. Mem. Nat Forensic League, Nat. Fedn. Interscholastic Speech and Debate Assn., Speech and Theatre Assn. Mo. (bd. govs. 1987-97), S.W. Mo. Speech Assn. (pres., v.p., sec. 1986-97), Mo. State Tchrs. Assn., Monett Cmty. Tchrs. Assn. (pres. 1986—). Avocations: golf, fishing, woodworking, landscaping, hunting.

BROCK, THOMAS DALE, microbiology educator; b. Cleve., Sept. 10, 1926; s. Thomas Carter and Helen Sophia (Ringwald) B.; m. Mary Louise Louden, Sept. 13, 1952 (div. Feb. 1971); m. Katherine Serat Middleton, Feb. 20, 1971; children: Emily Katherine, Brian Thomas. B.S., Ohio State U., 1949, M.S., 1950, Ph.D., 1952. Research microbiologist Upjohn Co., Kalamazoo, 1952-57; asst. prof. Western Res. U., Cleve., 1957-59; asst. prof. Ind. U., Bloomington, 1960-61, assoc. prof., 1962-64, prof., 1964-71; E.B. Fred prof. natural scis. U. Wis., Madison, 1971-90, prof. emeritus, 1990—, chmn. dept. bacteriology, 1979-82; pres. Sci. Tech. Pubs., Madison, 1990-94; Found. for Microbiology lectr., 1971-72, 78-79. Author: Milestones in Microbiology, 1961, Principles of Microbial Ecology, 1966, Thermophilic Microorganisms, 1978, Biology of Microorganism, 7th edit., 1994, Basic Microbiology with Applications, 3d edit., 1986, A Eutrophic Lake, 1985, Thermophiles: General, Molecular and Applied Microbiology, 1986, Robert Koch: A Life in Medicine and Bacteriology, 1988, The Emergence of Bacterial Genetics, 1990. Recipient Research Career Devel. NIH, 1962-68. Fellow AAAS; mem. Am. Soc. for Microbiology (hon. mem., chmn. gen. div. 1970-71, Fisher award 1984, Carski award 1988). Home and Office: 1227 Dartmouth Rd Madison WI 53705-2213

BROCK, WILLIAM ALLEN, III, economics educator, consultant; b. Phila., Oct. 23, 1941; s. William Allen and Margaret Elizabeth (Holcroft) B.; m. Joan Elaine Loutenshlager, Aug. 31, 1962; 1 child, Caroline Christine. AB with honors in Math., U. Mo., 1965; PhD, U. Calif., Berkeley, 1969. Asst. prof. econs. U. Rochester, N.Y., 1969-71; assoc. prof. econs. U. Chgo., 1972-75; vis. assoc. prof. econs. U. Rochester, 1973; assoc., full prof. econs. Cornell U., 1974-77; prof. econs. U. Chgo., 1975-81; Romnes prof. econs. U. Wis., Madison, 1981—, F.P. Ramsey prof. econs., 1984—, W.F. Vilas rsch. prof., 1990—; cons. U.S. Dept. Justice, SBA, EPA, FTC. Assoc. editor Jour. Econ. Theory, Internat. Econ. Rev., 1972—; contbr. articles to profl. jours.; co-author: (with A. Malliaris) Differential Equations, Stability and Chaos in Dynamic Economics, 1989, (with D. Hsieh, B. LeBaron) Nonlinear Dynamics, Chaos and Instability: Statistical Theory and Economic Evidence, 1991. NSF grantee, 1970—, Sherman Fairchild disting. scholar Calif. Inst. Tech., 1978, Guggenheim fellow, 1987-88; recipient Roger F. Murray 3rd pl. prize Inst. Quantitative Rsch. in Fin., 1989. Fellow Econometric Soc.; mem. Am. Acad. Arts and Scis., NAS (elected). Office: U Wis Dept Econs 1180 Observatory Dr Madison WI 53706-1320

BROCKA, BRUCE, editor, educator, software engineer; b. Davenport, Iowa, Nov. 1, 1959; s. Donald H. and Daisy Ann (Robertson) B.; m. M. Suzanne St. Ledger, Mar. 17, 1984; children: Melinda Athena, Bennett Paul. BS, St. Ambrose U., 1981; MS, U. Iowa, 1984. Instr. Army Mgmt. Engring. Coll., Rock Island, Ill., 1984-90; exec. editor, assoc. pub. Exec. Scis. Inst., Davenport, 1986—. Editor: Quality Control and Applied Statistics, 1987—, Operations Research/Management Science, 1987—, Automation in Quality Assurance, 1988, Biostatistica, 1990—, Quality Management, 1992; contbr. articles on sci. tech. to profl. jours. Ptnr. Preservation Group Partnership, Davenport, 1985—. Republican. Avocation: hist. preservation. Home and Office: 1005 Mississippi Ave Davenport IA 52803-3938

BROCKA, M. SUZANNE, controller; b. Moline, Ill., May 25, 1960; d. Paul Edmund and Therese Clemence (Fleischman) St. Ledger; m. Bruce Brocka, Mar. 17, 1984; children: Melinda Athena, Bennett Paul. BA in Acctg., St. Ambrose U., Davenport, Iowa, 1981; postgrad., Teikyo-Marycrest U., Davenport, Iowa, 1984-86. CPA, Ill. Acct. Iowa-Ill. Gas and Elec. Co., Davenport, 1981-86; acctg. supr. Frank E. Basil/Gen. Dynamics, Rock Island, Ill., 1986-87, mgr. fin., 1988-90, mgr. fin./contracts, 1990-91; controller City of Davenport, 1991—; cons. Frank E. Basil Inc., Washington, 1990-91, Rocky Mountain Metals, Inc., Raton, N.Mex., 1994-97, Exec. Scis. Inst., Davenport, Iowa, 1987—; bd. dirs., sec.-treas. AMEC Multimedia Inc., 1997-99. Author: Quality Management, 1992. Bd. dirs. Scott County Historic Preservation Soc., Davenport, 1985-88. Mem. Am. Mgmt. Assn., Fin. Mgmt. Assn., Am. Econ. Assn., Govt. Fin. Officers Assn., Alpha Chi. Avocations: historic preservation, antiques, stained glass, interior design. Home: 1005 Mississippi Ave Davenport IA 52803-3938 Office: City of Davenport 226 W 4th St Davenport IA 52801-1308

BROCKENBROUGH, EDWIN CHAMBERLAYNE, surgeon; b. Balt., July 24, 1930; s. Edwin Chamberlayne Sr. and Martha Davis (Coale) B.; m. Jean McClure, May 4, 1968; children: John, Martha, Andrew, Ann, Susan. BA, Coll. William & Mary, 1952; MD, Johns Hopkins U., 1956. Intern Johns Hopkins Hosp., Balt., 1956-57, resident, 1957-59; sr. asst.

surgeon Nat. Heart Inst., Bethesda, Md., 1959-61; chief resident surgery U. Wash., Seattle, 1961-64, faculty mem. dept. surgery, 1964-75; pvt. practice Seattle, 1975—; clin. prof. surgery U. Wash., 1984—; pres. King County Med. Soc., Seattle, 1992; trustee Health Resources N.W., Seattle; med. dir. Pacific Vasc. Inst., 1996—. Contbr. chpt. to book and articles to profl. jours. Sr. asst. surgeon USPHS, 1959-61. Fellow ACS (pres. Wash. State chpt. 1985), Seattle Surg. Soc. (sec. 1972); mem. North Pacific Surg. Assn. (pres. 1995-96), Pacific Coast Surg. Assn., Am. Rhododendron Soc. (pres. 1977-79, Silver medal 1985). Republican. Episcopalian. Avocations: gardening, hybridizing rhododendrons, photography, culinary arts, fishing. Home: 3630 Hunts Point Rd Bellevue WA 98004-1114 Office: 1560 N 115th St Seattle WA 98133-8414

BROCKENBROUGH, HENRY WATKINS, lawyer; b. Richmond, Va., Aug. 28, 1923; s. Benjamin Willard and Kathleen Reading (Watkins) B.; m. Mary Lane Williams, Oct. 30, 1948; children: Henry Watkins, Rebecca Lane, John Reading, Willson Williams. BA cum laude, Hampden-Sydney Coll., 1944; LLB, U. Va., 1948; grad. degree, Rutgers U., 1957. Bar: Va. 1949. With Crestar Bank, Richmond, 1948-88, v.p., trust officer, 1963-67, sr. v.p., trust officer, 1967-88, spl.counsel and trust cons. to Crestar Bank, 1988-91; ptnr.unsel Taylor, Hazen, Kauffman & Pinchbeck, Richmond, 1991—; chmn. trust com. Va. Bankers Assn., 1970-71. Past pres. Estate Planning Coun., Richmond; chmn. bd. dirs. Tuckahoe YMCA, 1975; bd. dirs. Good Neighbor Village, Varina, Va. Lt. (j.g.) USNR, 1943-46. Mem. Va. State Bar Assn., Va. Bar Assn., The Cohoke Club (West Point, Va.), Lambda Chi Alpha, Delta Theta Phi. Presbyterian. Home: 802 Horsepen Rd Richmond VA 23229-6725 Office: PO Box 2465 Richmond VA 23218-2465

BROCKERT, JOSEPH PAUL, government executive, writer, editor, designer; b. Tipp City, Ohio, Sept. 17, 1954; s. Paul Edwin and Mary (Aten) B.; m. Deborah Sue Schaefer, Apr. 10, 1976; children: Jonathan Andre, Jason Anthony. BS in Journalism with honors, Ohio U., 1975. Sr. editor Linn's Stamp News, Sidney, Ohio, 1976-84; sr. stamp program specialist U.S. Postal Svc., Washington, 1984-87, program mgr. stamp design, 1987-93, coord. Citizen's Stamp Adv. Com., 1985, art dir. U.S. stamps and stationary, 1986—, designer, 1988—, mgr. Stamps OnLine website; agy. rep. Commn. Bicentennial of U.S. Constn., 1986-91. Author: Basic Knowledge for the Stamp Collector, 1978, 4th rev. edit., 1983 (Silver medal Am. Philatelic Soc. 1979, Internat. Bronze medal 1986), (with Elaine Durnin Boughner) Stamp Collecting Made Easy, 1984, 3d rev. edit., 1986; editor: The Postal Service Guide to U.S. Stamps, 20th-22d edits., 1993-95, Stamps etc., 1993—, USA Philatelic, 1996—; contbr. articles to profl. and hobby jours. Chmn. publicity Gunston (Va.) Elem. PTA, 1985, pres., 1986-87; bidget chmn. Fairfax County (Va.) Coun. PTA's, 1988-92, sec., 1992; pres. Hewington Forest (Va.) Elem. PTA, 1989-91; coach Lorton Little League, 1987-88. Mem. Mensa. Roman Catholic. Avocations: music, collecting stamps, photography, composing, bowling. Home: 34652 Crew Rd Pomeroy OH 45769-8907

BROCKET, JUDITH ANN, elementary education mathematics educator; b. Muscatine, Iowa, Feb. 3, 1942; d. Kenneth McKay and Dorothy Pearl (Stewart) Uebe; m. Raymond Gene Brocket, July 28, 1963; 1 son, Jamie. AA, Muscatine Jr. Coll., 1962; BA, Parsons Coll., 1965; grad., Children's Inst. of Lit., 1987. Cert. tchr., Iowa. Swim instr. for handicapped ARC, Burlington, IA, 1965; 3d grade tchr. Burlington Community Sch. Dist., 1965-68, 5th grade tchr., 1970-80, chpt. I math. tchr., 1980—; 4th grade tchr. West Burlington (Iowa) Community Sch. Dist., 1968-70; presenter in field; mem. North Cen. Accreditation Com., 1984-87; mem. Lit. Mag. Com., 1988—. Contbr. articles to profl. publs.; author math. workbooks, curriculum guide. Pres. Burlington PTA, 1981-82, treas., 1988-89; mem., spokesperson Burlington Sch. Dist. Adv. Com., 1980—; mem. Burlington Parent Adv. Com., 1980—; nom. coun. Messiah Lutheran Ch. Recipient cert. of merit U.S. Dept. Edn., 1987; Fed. Govt. grantee, 1983, 84. Mem. NEA, Iowa State Edn. Assn., Burlington Edn. Assn., Burlington Art Guild, Alpha Delta Kappa. Democrat. Lutheran. Avocations: reading, oil painting, bridge, golf, sewing. Home: 13084 115th St Burlington IA 52601-8705

BROCKETT, OSCAR GROSS, theatre educator; b. Hartsville, Tenn., Mar. 18, 1923; s. Oscar Hill and Minnie Dee (Gross) B.; m. Lenyth Spenker, Sept. 4, 1951; 1 dau., Francesca Lane. B.A., Peabody Coll., 1947; M.A., Stanford U., 1949, Ph.D., 1953. Instr. English U. Ky., 1949-50; asst. instr. drama Stanford U., 1950-52; asst. prof. drama Stetson U., DeLand, Fla., 1952-56; asst., then asso. prof. U. Iowa, 1956-63; prof., then distinguished prof. Ind. U., 1963-78; Ashbel Smith prof. drama U. Tex., Austin, 1978-80; dean U. Tex. (Coll. Fine Arts), 1978-80; DeMille prof. drama U. So. Calif., Los Angeles, 1980-81; Waggener prof. fine arts U. Tex., Austin, 1981-87, Virginia L. Murchison Regents prof., 1987-88, holder Z.T. Scott Family Chair in Drama, 1988—. Author 10 books; contbr. numerous articles to profl. jours. Served with USNR, 1943-46. Recipient Fulbright award, 1963-64, Medallion of Honor Theta Alpha Phi, 1977, Am. Coll. Theatre Festival Gold Medallion, 1978, Career Achievement award Assn. for Theatre in Higher Edn., 1991; Guggenheim fellow, 1970-71. Fellow Am. Theatre Assn. (past pres., Merit award 1979); mem. Am. Soc. Theatre Rsch., Internat. Fedn. Theatre Rsch., Nat. Theatre Conf., Nat. Comm. Assn., Shakespeare Assn. Am., Lit. Mgrs. and Dramaturgs of the Americas. Democrat. Episcopalian. Home: 1800 Lavaca St Apt 208 Austin TX 78701-1326 Office: U Tex Theater and Dance Dept Austin TX 78712

BROCKETT, ROGER WARE, engineering and computer science educator; b. Seville, Ohio, Oct. 22, 1938; s. Roger Lawrence and Grace Ester (Patch) B.; m. Carolann Christina Riske, Aug. 20, 1960; children: Mark William, Douglas Matthew, Erik Roger. BS in Engring. Sci., Case Western Res. U., 1960, MS in Instrumentation Engring., 1962, PhD, 1964; MS (hon.), Harvard U., 1969. Asst. prof. MIT, Cambridge, Mass., 1963-67, assoc. prof., 1967-69; Gordon McKay Prof. Applied Math. Harvard U., Cambridge, Mass., 1969-90, Wang prof., 1990—; cons. Lincoln Lab., Lexington, Mass., 1965-78, GE, Schenectady, N.Y., 1989-90, ORNL, 1990—. Author: Finite Dimensional Linear Systems, 1970. Recipient Donald P. Eckman award Am. Automatic Control Coun., 1974, Richard Bellman award, 1989; John Simon Guggenheim fellow, 1976-77. Fellow IEEE (Control Systems Sci. and Engring. award 1991); mem. NAE, Am. Math. Soc., Soc. Indsl. and Applied Math, Sigma Xi. Office: Harvard U Pierce Hall 29 Oxford St Cambridge MA 02138-2901*

BROCKHOUSE, BERTRAM NEVILLE, physicist, retired educator; b. Lethbridge, Alta., Can., July 15, 1918; s. Israel Bertram and Mable Emily (Neville) B.; m. Doris Isobel Mary Miller, May 22, 1948; children: Ann, Gordon, Ian, James, Alice Elizabeth, Charles. BA, U. B.C., 1947; MA, U. Toronto, 1948, PhD, 1950; DSc, U. Waterloo, 1969, McMaster U., 1984, U. Toronto, 1995, U. B.C., Can., 1996; Doctor of Laws, Dalhousie U., 1996; D Arts and Scis, U Lethbridge, 1997. Research officer Atomic Energy of Can., Ltd., Chalk River, Ont., 1950-60; br. head, neutron physics Atomic Energy of Can., Ltd., 1960-62; prof. physics McMaster U., Hamilton, Ont., 1962-84; chmn. dept. physics McMaster U., 1967-70. Contbr. sci. articles on neutron physics and condensed matter physics to profl. jours. Served with Royal Canadian Navy Vol. Res., 1939-45. Recipient Centennial medal of Can., 1967, Queen's Jubilee medal, 1977, Order of Can., 1982, Companion, 1995, Duddell medal and prize Inst. Physics and Phys. Soc., 1963, Nobel Prize in Physics, 1994; Guggenheim fellow, 1970-71; NRC of Can. grantee, 1962-78. Mem. Royal Soc. Can. (Tory medal), Royal Soc. London, Can. Assn. Physicists (medal), Am. Phys. Soc. (Buckley prize), Am. Acad. Arts and Scis. (hon. fgn. mem.), Royal Swedish Acad. Scis. (fgn. mem.). Roman Catholic. Home: PO Box 7338, Ancaster, ON Canada L9G 3N6

BROCKINGTON, DONALD LESLIE, anthropologist, archaeologist, educator; b. Weslaco, Tex., Apr. 28, 1929; s. Buford Maurice and M. Juanita (Young) B.; m. Lolita Gutierrez, Dec. 19, 1955; children: Laura Alicia, John Carlos, Peter Daniel. B.A., U. N.Mex., 1954; student, U. Calif.-Berkeley, 1953; M.A., Mexico City Coll., 1956-57; Ph.D., U. Wis., 1965. Instr., adminstrv. asst. Mexico City Coll., 1956-57; asst. prof. San Diego State Coll., 1963-67; assoc. prof. anthropology to prof. U. N.C., Chapel Hill, 1967-96, chmn. dept. anthropology, 1980-85, prof. emeritus, 1996—; dir. hwy. archaeology Wis. State Hist. Soc., Madison, 1960-62; manuscript evaluator various pub. cos., 1969—; cons. Museum Archaeology, Cochambamba, Bolivia, 1982—. Served with U.S. Army, 1951-53. Mexico City Coll. fellow, 1956-57, U. Wis. fellow, 1959-63, 65, Bobbs-Merrill fellow, NSF fellow, 1963, 68, 70, U. N.C. fellow, 1968, 71, 74, 76, 84, 86-89; Nat. Geog. Soc. grantee, 1984—. Fellow Soc. Am. Archaeology. Home: 808 Tinkerbell Rd Chapel Hill NC 27514-3016

BROCKLES, ARGE JAMES, pastor, educator; b. Dallas, July 13, 1930; s. Andrew Arge and Ola Lillian (Feltnor) B.; m. Pauline Menos, July 13, 1952; children: Linda, James. Student, Tex. A&M U., 1948-51; M, Dallas Theol. Sem., 1968. Ordained minister, 1968. Pres. Brockles Restaurants, Inc., Dallas, 1958-64; v.p. Brockles Foods Co., Dallas, 1958-64; pastor, tchr. Mesquite (Tex.) Bible Ch., 1968-72, Northlake Bible Ch., Garland, Tex., 1972—. Author: Doctrines of the Sovreignty and Grace of God, 1975; contbr. articles to jours. in field. Mem. adv. bd. Dallas Evang. Assn., 1970-72; bd. dirs. So. Bible Sch., Dallas, 1969-72. Avocations: golf, fishing, travel. Office: Northlake Bible Ch 505 Mayfield Ave Garland TX 75041-5431

BROCKLEY, JOHN P., state agency executive, airport executive. Dir. aviation Port of Portland, Oreg. Office: Dir Aviation Port of Portland PO Box 3529 Portland OR 97208-3529*

BROCKMAN, LESLIE RICHARD, social worker; b. St. Paul, Aug. 10, 1940; s. Leslie Blair Brockman and Mary Emma (Miller) Hemenway; m. Rosemarie Lemus, Aug. 18, 1962; 1 child, Christopher Scott. BA, Loyola U. of L.A., 1963; MS, Troy (Ala.) State U., 1977; MS in Social Work, U. Tex., Arlington, 1984. Lic. profl. counselor; lic. chem. dependency counselor, marriage and family therapist, master social worker; advanced clin. practitioner ACSW; diplomate clin. social work; cert. cognitive-behavioral therapist; cert. compulsive gambling counselor, criminal justice specialist; diplomate Am. Acad. Forensic Counseling. Exec. dir. Family Assessment Consultation Therapy Svc., Ft. Worth, 1984—; commd. 2d lt. USAF, 1963, advanced through grades to maj., retired, 1983. Fellow NASW (diplomate), Am. Bd. Med. Psychotherapists (diplomate); mem. ACA, Am. Assn. Marriage and Family Therapists, Am. Mental Health Counselors Assn., Am. Assn. Behavioral Therapists, Internat. Assn. Marriage and Family Therapists, Nat. Assn. Forensic Counseling. Home: 6400 Trail Lake Dr Fort Worth TX 76133-4810 Office: FACTS Inc 5801 Curzon Ave Ste 2B Fort Worth TX 76107-5896

BROCKMANN, WILLIAM FRANK, medical facility administrator; b. South Bend, Ind., Nov. 14, 1942; s. Ervin William and Elizabeth Marie (Kassidy) B.; m. Ellen Meier, June 10, 1967; children: William Edward, Rebecca Jayne. BS in Mgmt., Ind. U., 1966; MHA, St. Louis U., 1968. Administrv. asst. St. Anthony Hosp., Okla. City, 1968; asst. hosp. adminstr. Caylor-Nickel Med. Ctr., Bluffton, Ind., 1972-77, hosp. adminstr., 1977-86, pres., 1986-89, chief exec. officer, 1989—, also mem. exec. com., 1985—; bd. dirs. Old First Nat. Bank. Gen. campaign mgr. Wells County United Way, 1973; past pres. Bluffton United Meth. Ch., Wells County Found.; pres., bd. dirs. Wells County Coun. on Aging; spkr. in field. Capt. M.S.C., U.S. Army, 1969-71. Fellow Am. Coll. Healthcare Execs.; mem. Ind. Hosp. Assn. (chmn. bd. 1990-91, PRO negotiating team), Am. Hosp. Assn. (ho. dels. 1991-93). Republican. Methodist. Avocations: scuba diving, pool, reading, jogging. Home: 1127 Ridgewood Ln Bluffton IN 46714-3827 Office: Caylor Nickel Med Cntr 1 Caylor Nickel Sq Bluffton IN 46714-2529

BROCKS, ERIC RANDY, ophthalmologist, surgeon; b. N.Y.C., Apr. 24, 1946; s. William Benjamin and Muriel (Welk) B.; m. Irene Loretta Kraut, Dec. 19, 1970; children: Jason Matthew, Daniel Charles. BA with high honors, U. Rochester, 1968, MD, 1972. Diplomate Am. Bd. Ophthalmology, Nat. Bd. Med. Examiners. Intern medicine NYU Sch. Medicine, N.Y.C., 1973, resident, chief resident ophthalmology, 1973-76; chief resident ophthalmology Bellevue Hosp., NYU Hosp., Manhattan VA Hosp., N.Y.C., 1975-76; attending physician St. Francis Hosp., Beacon, N.Y., 1976-89; asst./assoc. attending physician Vassar Bros. Hosp., Poughkeepsie, N.Y., 1976-80, attending physician, 1980—; clin. asst. ophthalmology Tisch (NYU) Hosp., N.Y.C., 1976—; clin. asst. attending physician Bellevue Hosp. Ctr., N.Y.C., 1976—; eye physician and surgeon Hudson Valley Eye Surgeons, P.C., Fishkill, N.Y., 1976—; med. dir. laser vision correction LCA Vision Laser Assocs., Mt. Kisco, N.Y., 1996-98; cons. ophthalmology Julia Butterfield Hosp., Cold Spring, N.Y., 1981-94, West Point (N.Y.) Mil. Acad., Keller Army Hosp., 1989-96; chief surgery St. Francis Hosp., Beacon, 1988-89, dir. ophthalmology sect., 1981-88, chief of staff, 1979-81; dir. dept. ophthalmology Vassar Bros. Hosp., 1992—, mem. peer rev. com., 1994—; clin. asst. prof. ophthalmology NYU Sch. Medicine, N.Y.C., 1983—, course dir. ophthalmology elective, 1976-91; so. N.Y. coord. Nat. Eye Care Project, San Francisco, 1985—; adj. clin. asst. prof. ophthalmology Mt. Sinai Sch. Medicine, N.Y.C., 1993—. Contbr. articles to profl. jours. Vol. admissions network U. Rochester, 1986—, co-chmn. 25th reunion com., 1993. Fellow ACS, Am. Acad. Ophthalmology (media coord. N.Y. state Nat. Eye Care projects 1978—, mem. pub. info. coun. 1985—); mem. AMA, Am. Soc. Cataract and Refractive Surgery, Med. Soc. State N.Y. (mem. ho. dels. 1984-89, 93-96, mem. subcom. officers and adminstrv. matters 1994, mem. govt. affairs subcom. 1987, mem. fed. legis. com. 1993—), Dutchess County Med. Soc. (mem. exec. com. 1992-96, chmn. legis. liaison com. 1990-92, pres. 1990-91), Boca West Club. Avocations: tennis, golf, reading, family travel. Office: Hudson Valley Eye Surgeons So Dutchess Profl Park 335 State Route 52 Fishkill NY 12524

BROCKWAY, DAVID HUNT, lawyer; b. Paterson, N.J., Dec. 18, 1943; s. George Pond and Lucille (Hunt) B.; m. Marilyn Bofshever, July 29, 1979. A.B., Cornell U., 1968; J.D., Harvard U., 1971. Bar: N.Y. 1972, Washington 1990. Assoc. firm Donovan Leisure Newton & Irvine, N.Y.C., 1971-76; legis. atty. Joint Com. on Taxation, U.S. Congress, Washington, 1976, internat. tax counsel, 1978, deputy chief of staff, 1981, chief of staff, 1983-87; ptnr. Dewey Ballantine, Washington, N.Y.C., 1987—, co-chmn. tax dept., 1997—; mem. Am. Law Inst. Project on Sub-chpt. C, 1988—; mem. adv. bd. European Am. Tax Inst., 1989—; cons. Am. Law Inst. Project on Tax Treaties, 1989—; bd. dirs. Nat. Fgn. Trade Coun., 1993—; GE (Bermuda) Ltd., 1993—. With U.S. Army, 1963-66. Recipient Outstanding Achievement award NYU Tax. Soc., 1998—. Mem. N.Y. State Bar Assn. (exec. com. tax sect. 1988-89, 94—). Home: 2829 Woodland Dr NW Washington DC 20008-2743 Office: Dewey Ballantine LLP 1301 Avenue Of The Americas New York NY 10019-6022

BROCKWAY, LAURIE SUE, editor, journalist, author, minister; b. N.Y.C., Dec. 18, 1956; d. Lee L. and Shirley Ruth Brockway; 1 child, Alexander Kent Garrett. AA, Laguardia C.C., 1978; student, Hunter Coll. CUNY, 1978-81; MSC, The New Seminary, 1999. Features editor, crime reporter The Bklyn. Paper, 1978-81; editor-in-chief The Iniator, N.Y.C., 1982-83; pub., editor The Transformer, N.Y.C., 1983-84; co-prodr., writer The Brockway Good News Report, N.Y.C., 1984-85; N.Y. bur. chief Women's News, N.Y.C., 1983-85, Manhattan corr., 1985—, mng. editor, 1990; account supr. Brockway Assocs., Inc., N.Y.C., 1985-88; tchr. women's sexuality, spirituality, 1990—. Free lance editor, writer, 1988—; editor/owner, syndicated writer Star Reporter News Svc., 1989-94; editor in chief Playgirl Mag., N.Y.C., 1994-95, editor at large, 1996-97; editor-in-chief Single Living Mag., 1997; co-prodr., writer, host, news anchor/writer, moderator This Is the New Age, The One Show, Whole Life Expo., The Learning Annex Interview Series, N.Y.C., 1995-97; author: Network Your Way to Endless Romance, 1997, The Couples Guide to Great Sex Over 40, 1997, How to Seduce a Man and Keep Him Seduced, 1998; med. corr. Life in Medicine mag., 1992-94; editor: Playgirl's Favorite 50 Fantasies, 1996; contbr. articles to mags., newspapers. Recipient LaGuardia Meml. award, 1978, LaGuardia Student Coun. scholar, 1978, Expository Writing award, LaGuardia English Dept., 1978, Woman of Achievement award Women's News, 1997.

BROCKWAY, LEE J., architect; b. Mecosta, Mich., Aug. 13, 1932; s. Byron Maxwell and Mildred Loro (Wolfe) B.; m. Mary Haglind, Aug. 4, 1956; children: David, Michael, Anne McDonough, Bill. BArch, U. Notre Dame, 1955. Archtl. intern Haughey, Black and Williams, Architects, Battle Creek, Mich., 1959-61; chief architect Charles W. Cole & Son, Engrs. and Architects, South Bend, Ind., 1961-65; ptnr. The Shaver Partnership, Architects and Engrs., Michigan City, Ind., 1965-73; owner, architect Brockway Assocs., Architects, Michigan City, 1974-76; prin., corp. dir. Fanning/Howey Assoc., Inc., Michigan City, Ind., 1976-98, prin. emeritus, 1998—. Pres. Ind. Soc. Architects, 1990. Recipient Outstanding Svc. award Ind. soc. Architects, 1987, 89, Mich. City C. of C., 1978. Mem. AIA (corp. mem., mem. nat. com. on architecture for edn. 1978—, chmn. 1988), Coun. for Archtl. Rsch., Nat. Coalition Edn. Facilities (chmn. 1991-92), Coun. Edn. Facility Planners (bd. dirs. 1986-92, pres. 1990-91). Home: 2922 Belle Plaine Trl Michigan City IN 46360-1777 Office: Fanning Howey Assoc Inc 114 York St Michigan City IN 46360-3654

BROCKWAY-HENSON, AMIE, producing artistic director; b. Warren, Ohio, Oct. 13, 1938; d. Raymond Horatio and Amabelle Virginia (Willard) Woodworth; m. Ronald F. Brockway, June 3, 1956 (div. 1980); children: Adrienne J., Ginny A.; m. Richard G. Henson, June 30, 1984. BFA, SUNY, Purchase, 1975; MFA, Rutgers U., 1978. Adminstrv. asst. Ashtabula (Ohio) Arts Ctr., 1967-69; exec. asst. McCarter Theatre, Princeton, N.J., 1969-72; artistic dir. St. Theatre, Princeton, 1970-72, Creative Theatre Unlimited, Princeton, 1975-78; dir. audience devel., resident dir. The Open Eye: New Stagings, N.Y.C., 1980-82, assoc. artistic dir., 1982-84, artistic dir., 1984-94, producing artistic dir., 1994—. Editor TYA Today, 1991-94; author: stage adaptation of The Odyssey by Homer; co-author stage adaptation The Nightingale (Hans Christian Anderson), 1999. Trustee U.S. chpt. Internat. Assn. Theatres for Children and Young People (ASSITEJ/USA), 1991-94, U.S. rep. 22nd Danish Children's Theatre Festival, Denmark, 1992. Recipient Paul Green Found. award, 1991, Performers at Work Artistic Visionary award, 1994. Mem. League Profl. Theatre Women (co-pres. 1992-94), Soc. Stage Dirs. and Choreographers, Dramatists Guild. Home and Office: The Open Eye Theater PO Box 959 Margaretville NY 12455-0959

BROD, CATHERINE MARIE, foundation administrator; b. Aurora, Ill., Sept. 16, 1959; d. Harold Keith and Arlene Ruth (Peterson) Feltz; divorced; children: Ryan Michael, Kelsey Taylor. BA in Comm., Ea. Ill. U., 1981, MA in Comm., 1986. Grad. asst. Ea. Ill. U., Charleston, 1982-83; acct. exec. B&G Enterprises, Inc., Champaign, Ill., 1984-85; program coord., program dir. U. Ill., Chgo., 1985-91, exec. dir. Ill. Eye Found., 1991-95; assoc. exec. dir. Cancer Treatment Rsch. Found., Arlington Heights, Ill., 1995-97; exec. dir. Internat. Soc. Refractive Keratoplasty, Chgo., 1989-93, mng. editor newsletter, 1989-93. Vol. Ill. Crossroads coun. Girl Scouts, chair silver trefoil; exec. dir. William Rainey Harper Coll. Ednl. Found., Palentine, Ill., 1997—. Mem. Coun. for Advancement and Support of Edn. (2 Silver medals 1993, 2 Bronze medals 1994), Jaycees (v.p. 1987), Nat. Soc. Fund Raising Execs., Nat. Assn. Planned Giving Profls. (mem. Chgo. coun.), Barrington Exec. Breakfast Club (program com.). Avocations: golf, roller blading, creative writing, theatre, dance aerobics. Home: 1223 Montego Ct Elk Grove Village IL 60007-7132 Office: William Rainey Harper Coll Palatine IL 60067

BROD, EVELYN FAY, foreign language educator; b. Cin., Apr. 23, 1942; d. Joseph Theodore and Freda Edith (Mandell) B. BA in Spanish magna cum laude, U. Cin., 1964, BS in Secondary Edn., 1964, MA in Spanish, 1966, MEd, 1975, postgrad. Cert. secondary tchr., Ohio, cert. guidance counselor, Ohio. Teaching asst. U. Cin., 1964-67, 69-70, instr. in Spanish, 1970-75, asst. prof., 1975-80, assoc. prof., 1980-89, prof., 1989—; instr. in Spanish Mount Union Coll., Alliance, Ohio, 1967-69; vice chair faculty and faculty senate U. Cin., 1989-90, 93-94, 96-98, 98—, mem. faculty devel. coun., 1996—, mem. provostal search com., 1999; faculty rep. to U. Cin. Bd. Trustees, 1999-2001. Author: (poetry) Mirage, 1978, (book) Viajemos 2001: Repaso y Progreso text, workbook and tchr.'s manual, 1990; contbr. articles to profl. jours. Mem. alumni adv. coun. Walnut Hills High Sch., Cin., 1997—. Mem. AAUP, Am. Assn. Tchrs. Spanish and Portuguese (editor Enlace 1986-90), OhioFgn. Lang. Assn., Am. Coun. on Teaching of Fgn. Langs., Phi Beta Kappa, Alpha Lambda Delta, Sigma Delta Pi, Kappa Delta Pi. Avocations: reading, travel, drawing, painting. Office: U Cin Raymond Walters Coll 9555 Plainfield Rd Cincinnati OH 45236-1007

BROD, MORTON SHLEVIN, oral surgeon; b. Bklyn., Apr. 19, 1926; s. Joseph and Celina (Fromberg) B.; m. Anne Turville Bigelow, June 3, 1955; children: Brian Seth, Timothy Andrew, Abbe Rena. Student, U.S. Mil. Acad., 1947-48; BA, Adelphi Coll., 1951; DDS, Columbia U., 1955. Diplomate Am. Bd. Oral Surgery, Am. Bd. Forensic Dentistry. Intern oral surgery Columbia Presbyn. Med. Ctr., N.Y.C., 1955-56; resident oral surgery Bronx VA Hosp., N.Y.C., 1956-58; pvt. practice oral surgery Norwalk, Conn., 1958-98; attending oral surgeon chief dental service Norwalk Hosp.; attending oral surgeon Bellevue Hosp.; attending surgeon Seaview Hosp.; cons. Manhattan State Hosp., Bronx State Hosp., Psychiat. Inst. N.Y.; instr. dentistry div. clin. oral physiology Columbia Sch. Dental and Oral Surgery, N.Y.C., 1957-69, asst. prof. dentistry, 1969-72, assoc. prof., 1972-84, research assoc. dept. stomatology, 1968-84; mem. dental mission to Govt. Anguilla, West Indies, 1969, 70, 71; assoc. prof. dentistry NYU; dir. clin. rev.-oral surgery Physicians Health Svcs.; lectr., Eng., Russia, China, Japan. Contbr. articles to profl. jours., textbooks. Sec. Westport Flood and Erosion Control Bd.; capt. CAP Flying Sharks Search and Rescu Squadron, Conn., 1968—; exec. com. Boy Scouts Am., Westport; mem. Westport Rep. Town Meeting, chmn. pub. works com.; trustee Westport-Weston br. Am. Cancer Soc.; bd. dirs. Norwalk Bd. Dental Health Clinic; dir. Westport Transit Dist., Precision Closure Corp., Auto-Grip Corp.; v.p., treas. Riverview E. Assocs. Real Estate, Inc.; mem. Southwestern Regional Planning Agy., Fairfield County adv. bd. Bridgeport Hydraulic Co. With USAF, 1943-47. Fellow Am. Coll. Oral Surgeons, Am. Soc. Oral Surgeons, Internat. Soc. Oral Surgeons, N.Y. Acad. Dentistry, Am. Coll. Forensic Examiners; mem. ADA, New Eng. Soc. Oral Surgeons, Conn. Soc. Oral Surgeons, Am. Soc. Dentistry for Children (pres. Fairfield County sect. 1962-63), Am. Acad. History Dentistry, Fedn. Dentaire Internat., N.Y. Acad. Scis., N.Y. State Dental Soc. (exec. com. 1966-67, pres. 1967-68), Norwalk Dental Soc., Christian Dental Soc., Flying Dentists Assn., Airplane Owners and Pilots Assn., Pilots Internat. Assn. Home: 10 Rosewood Dr Lakewood NJ 08701-5709 Office: 10 Rosewood Dr Lakewood NJ 08701-5709 Home after 8/1/: 10 Rosewood Dr Lakewood NJ 08701-5709

BROD, ROY DAVID, ophthalmologist, educator; b. Phila., Oct. 8, 1957; s. Kenneth Lester and Carlene Marcy (Chalick) B.; m. Janice Hope Prossack, May 7, 1983; children: Jamie, Rebecca. BS in Biochemistry magna cum laude, Tulane U., 1979; MD with honors, Temple U., 1983. Diplomate Am. Bd. Ophthalmology. Intern Presbyn. U. Pa. Med. Ctr., Phila., 1983-84; resident in ophtholmology La. State U. Eye Ctr., New Orleans, 1984-87; fellow in vitreoretinal Bascom Palmer Eye Inst., Miami, Fla., 1987-88; assoc. vitreoretinal surgeon Geisinger Med. Ctr., Danville, Pa., 1988-91; pvt. practice Lancaster, Pa., 1991—; asst. prof. Thomas Jefferson U. Sch. Medicine, Phila., 1991-92; clin. asst. prof. Pa. State U. Sch. Medicine-Hershey Med. Ctr., 1992-95, clin. assoc. prof., 1995—; presenter in field. Contbr. articles to med. jours., chpts. to books. Recipient Outstanding Tchr. award Geisinger Med. Ctr., 1990, 91; Tulane scholar, 1976, E.J. and Sarah Evans scholar, 1979, scholar Measy Found., 1982. Fellow Am. Acad. Ophthlmology (Honor award 1998); mem. AMA, Assn. for Rsch. in Vision and Ophthalmology, Vitreous Soc. (exec. com.), Retina Soc., Rsch. To Prevent Blindness, Soc. for Contemplation Fascinating Fluorescein Angiograms, Atlantic Coast Vitreoretinal Study Group, Atlantic Coast Fluorescein Angiography Club, Pa. Med. Soc., Pa. Acad. Ophthalmology, Phi Beta Kappa, Alpha Omega Alpha, Phi Eta Sigma, Alpha Epsilon Delta, Omicron Delta Kappa. Avocations: sailing, tennis, bicycling. Office: 2100 Harrisburg Pike Lancaster PA 17601-2644

BROD, STANFORD, graphic designer, educator; b. Cin., Sept. 29, 1932; s. Morris and Rebecca (Mitman) B.; m. McCrystle Wood; children: Deborah, Daniel, Michael. B.S in Design, U. Cin., 1955. Graphic designer Rhoades Studio, Cin., 1955-62; tchr. exptl. typography Art Acad. Cin., 1960-75; graphic designer Lipson, Alport & Glass Assocs., Inc. and predecessor firm Lipson Assos. Inc., Cin., 1962-94, Wood/Brod Design, Cin., 1994—; prof. graphic design U. Cin., 1962—; tchr. illustration and packaging Art Acad. Cin., 1991-92, 94, 96-98, tchr. corp. identity, 1992-93, 94-96, 97, tchr. illustration, packaging, 1997, 98, tchr. adv. design, corp. design, 1994-97, tchr. visual comms., 1997, 98. Exhbns. include Mus. Modern Art, N.Y.C., 1966, Urban Walls, Cin., 1972, City Banners, Sao Paulo, Brazil, 1975, ITC Ctr., N.Y.C., 1981, Tel Aviv Mus., 1982, Internat. Art Exhbn., Dusseldorf, Germany, 1982, Calligraphia U.S.A./USSR, 1990-96, UN, 1994; one man shows include Skirball Mus. Hebrew Union Coll., Cin., 1989. Recipient Communications Arts awards, 1959, 64, 66, 70, 73, 76, Creativity on Paper awards, 1960-67, Internat. Typographic awards, 1965, 70, N.Y. Type Dirs.

Club award, 1968, Typographic Composition Assn. awards, 1970-76. Office: 2401 Ingleside Ave Cincinnati OH 45206-2118 *The more I design and paint the more I am sensitive to the movement of my pen and brush, and am able to transmit the image of the subject in my head by way of my arm into my hand, and so to my work. I have become aware that pressure demands counter-pressure, and the difference between order and chaos. This points out the importance of the smallest detail, and that order is the basis of all creative work.*

BRODALE, LOUISE LADO, medical, post surgery and geriatrics nurse; b. Cleve., Dec. 2, 1924; d. Louis G. and Velma Susan (Palady) Lado; m. Roger M. Brodale, Sept. 18, 1953; 4 children. Diploma, Maumee Valley Hosp., Toledo, 1947; AA, Tarrant County Jr. Coll., Ft. Worth, 1974, AAS, 1976; BSN, Tex. Christian U., 1980, MA in Liberal Arts, 1984; diploma fashion merchandising, Internat. Corr. Schs., 1991, diploma dressmaking and design, 1993. RN, Tex., Ohio; cert. tchr., Tex. Head nurse med. ward San Antonio Tuberculoses Hosp., 1962-69; supr. Campbell-White Co., Forest Hill, Tex., 1986, Forest Hill Nursing Home, Ft. Worth, 1986; with Home Care Svc. Am., 1986-89, geriatrics nurse, 1990-93. With Nurse Corps U.S. Army, 1947-51; capt. USAF, 1951-54. Avocations: sewing, tailoring, reading. Home: 3805 Kimberly Ln Fort Worth TX 76133-2020

BRODBECK, WILLIAM JAN, marketing consultant, speaker; b. Platteville, Wis., Feb. 14, 1944; s. Richard William and Helen (Stoneman) B.; m. Janet Piwonka, Feb. 4, 1967; children: Allison S., Courtney K., Stephanie L. BA in Econs., Hillsdale (Mich.) Coll., 1966. Asst. to v.p. Hillsdale Coll., 1966-68; mgr. advt. Brodbeck Enterprises, Inc., Platteville, 1968-72, v.p., 1972-79, pres., CEO, 1980-96; pres. Relationship Mktg., Sanibel, Fla., 1996—; gov. Uniform Product Code Coun., Dayton, Ohio, 1977-86; chmn. First Nat. Bank, Platteville, 1986-92. Contbr. articles to profl. jours. Chmn. Third Congl. Dist. Reagan Campaign, 1976; pres. Platteville Area Indsl. Devel., 1976-79; bd. dirs. Thursday's Child, Madison, Wis., 1983-96, Wis. Shakespeare Festival, Platteville, 1986-96, Barrier Island Group for Arts, 1999—; trustee Hillsdale Coll., 1991—; bd. dirs. Neenah Springs, Inc., Oxford, Wis., 1997—, Noodles and Co., Boulder, Colo., 1998—. Mem. Nat. Grocers Assn. (bd. dirs. 1977-85), Food Mktg. Inst. (bd. dirs. 1982-96, mem. efficient consumer response exec. com. 1993-96), U. Wis. Platteville Found. (pres. 1980-81), Hillsdale Coll. Assocs., Hillsdale Coll. Alumni Forum, Platteville C. of C. (pres. 1972-73), Omicron Delta Kappa (chpt. v.p. 1966). Office: Relationship Mktg 2964 Wulfert Rd Sanibel FL 33957-2213

BRODELL, ROBERT THOMAS, internal medicine educator; b. Rochester, N.Y., Nov. 24, 1953; s. Harold Louis and Alma Jean (Moreland) B.; m. Linda P. Brodell, July 2, 1977; children: Lindsey Ann, Julie Lynn, David William, Erin Elizabeth, Nathan Thomas. BA, Washington and Jefferson Coll., 1975; MD, U. Rochester, 1979. Bd. cert. in dermatology and dermatopathology. Asst. prof. dermatology Washington U., St. Louis, 1984-85; asst. prof. internal medicine Northeastern Ohio U. Coll. Medicine, Rootstown, Ohio, 1986-90, 1990-94, prof. internal medicine, 1994—, master tchr., 1997—; assoc. clin. prof. dermatology Case Western Res. U., Cleve., 1986-94, asst. clin. prof., 1994—; chmn. Midwest Congress Derm. Socs., Dayton, Ohio, 1995—. Trustee Ohio divsn. Am. Cancer Soc., Columbus, 1992—; bd. dirs. Warren (Ohio) Sports Hall of Fame, 1996. Named Cleve. Cavaliers Profl. Basketball Team Fan of Year, 1997. Fellow Am. Acad. Dermatology, Am. Soc. Dermatopathology; mem. AMA, Ohio State Med. Assn., Wilderness Med. Assn., Ohio Dermatol. Assn. (trustee 1994—), Masons (Master Old Erie # 3), Phi Beta Kappa, Alpha Omega Alpha. Home: 2660 E Market St Warren OH 44483-6204 Office: Northeastern Ohio Univ Coll Med PO box 95 4209 State Route 44 Rootstown OH 44272-9698

BRODER, DAVID SALZER, reporter; b. Chicago Heights, Ill., Sept. 11, 1929; s. Albert I. and Nina M. (Salzer) B.; m. Ann Creighton Collar, June 8, 1951; children: George, Joshua, Matthew, Michael. BA, U. Chgo., 1947, MA, 1951; LittD, Denison U., 1975; LLD (hon.), Wabash Coll., 1977, Kenyon Coll., 1980, Cleve. State U., 1981, Wittenberg Coll., 1982, Yale U., 1984, Ind. U., 1985, Kalamazoo Coll., 1988, Rider Coll., 1989, Dartmouth Coll., 1990, Colby Coll., 1990, Lawrence U., 1991; Bates Coll., 1992; LLD (hon.), Stetson U., 1993, U. Mich., 1994, Coll. of William & Mary, 1995, Am. U., 1997; DLitt, Gov.'s State U., 1994. Reporter Pantagraph, Bloomington, Ill., 1953-55, Congressional Quar., Washington, 1955-60, Washington Star, 1960-65, N.Y. Times, Washington bur., 1965-66; reporter Washington Post, 1966-75, assoc. editor, 1975—; syndicated columnist. Author: (with Stephen Hess) The Republican Establishment, 1967, The Party's Over: The Failure of Politics in America, 1972, Changing of the Guard: Power and Leadership in America, 1980, Behind the Front Page: A Candid Look at How the News is Made, 1987, (with Bob Woodward) The Man Who Would be President: Dan Quayle, 1992, (with Haynes Johnson) The System: The American Way of Politics at the Breaking Point, 1996; contbr. articles on pub. affairs to mags. and books. Former mem. U. Chgo. Alumni cabinet. Served with AUS, 1951-53. Recipient Pulitzer prize in journalism, 1973, Common Wealth award, Elijah Parrish Lovejoy award, 1990, William Allen White medal U. Kans., 1997, Lifetime Achievement award Nat. Soc. Newspaper Columnists, 1997; fellow Inst. Politics, John F. Kennedy Sch. of Govt., Harvard U., 1969-70; Poynter fellow Yale and Ind. univs., 1973. Fellow Inst. Policy Scis. and Pub. Affairs of Duke, Am. Acad. Arts and Scis., Sigma Delta Chi; mem. Am. Polit. Sci. Assn. (adv. bd. Congrl. Fellows Program 1964—, Carey McWilliams award 1983), Am. Soc. Pub. Adminstrn., Nat. Press Club (4th Estate award 1988), Gridiron Club. Home: 4024 27th St N Arlington VA 22207-5207 Office: Washington Post 1150 15th St NW Washington DC 20071-0002

BRODER, DOUGLAS FISHER, lawyer; b. Cleve., Sept. 30, 1948; s. Harry M. and Peggy (Fisher) B.; m. Rebecca Northey, Jan. 24, 1976; 1 child, Julia N. BA, Vassar Coll., 1970; JD cum laude, Boston U., 1977. Bar: N.Y. 1978, U.S. Dist. Ct. (so. and ea. dists.) N.Y. 1978, U.S. Ct. Appeals (2d cir.) 1983, U.S. Ct. Appeals (6th cir.) 1986, U.S. Ct. Appeals (4th cir.) 1987, U.S. Dist. Ct. (ea. dist.) Mich. 1987, U.S. Supreme Ct. 1993, U.S. Ct. Appeals (9th cir.) 1997. Assoc. Lord, Day & Lord, N.Y.C., 1977-86; ptnr. Coudert Bros., N.Y.C., 1986—. Lead editor: "International Joint Ventures" Professional Information Publishing Ltd., 1996; mem. editl. bd. European Competition Law Rev.; contbr. articles to profl. publs. Mem. ABA, Fed. Bar Coun., Assn. of Bar of City of N.Y. Home: 300 Central Park W New York NY 10024-1513 Office: Coudert Bros 1114 Avenue Of The Americas New York NY 10036-7703

BRODERICK, ANTHONY JAMES, air transportation executive; b. N.Y.C., Feb. 23, 1943; s. Anthony James and Geraldine (Cummings) B.; m. Sylvia Fantasia, May 30, 1967; children: Sean, Pia. BS in Physics, St. Bonaventure U., 1964. Project mgr. pvt. industry, various locations, 1964-71; physicist U.S. Dept. Transp., Cambridge, Mass., 1971-76; staff chief environment and energy FAA, Washington, 1976-79, tech. advisor aviation standards dept., 1979-82, dep. assoc. adminstr. aviation standards dept., 1982-85, assoc. adminstr. aviation standards dept., 1985-88, assoc. adminstr. regulation and cert., 1988-96; ind. aviation safety cons., 1996—. Author numerous sci. and tech. articles; patentee in field. Recipient Arthur S. Fleming award Jaycees, 1979, Presdl. Meritorious Exec. Rank award, 1982, Sr. Exec. Svc. awards U.S. Govt., 1983-87, 89-90, 92-95, Presdl. Disting. Exec. Rank award, 1991, Aviation Week Laurel award, 1992, Flight Internat. Aerospace Personality of Yr. award, 1995, Disting. Career Svc. award Aviation Week/Flight Safety Found., 1996, RTCA achievement award, 1999. Roman Catholic. Home: 4711 Dumfries Rd PO Box 119 Catlett VA 20119-0119

BRODERICK, DENNIS JOHN, lawyer, retail company executive. BA, U. Notre Dame, 1970; JD, Georgetown U., 1976. Bar: Ohio 1976. Assoc. Hahn Loeser Freidheim Dean & Wellman, 1976-81; from staff atty. to asst. gen. counsel Firestone Tire & Rubber Co., 1982-87; counsel for regions, v.p. Federated Dept. Stores, Inc. (formerly Allied Stores Corp.), Cin., 1987-88, v.p., gen. counsel, 1988-90, sr. v.p., gen. counsel, sec., 1990—. Mem. Am. Corp. Counsel Assn. (dir. NE Ohio chpt. 1986). Office: Federated Dept Stores Inc 7 W 7th St Cincinnati OH 45202-2424*

BRODERICK, DONALD LELAND, electronics engineer; b. Chico, Calif., Jan. 5, 1928; s. Leland Louis and Vera Marguerite (Carey) B.; m. Constance Margaret Lattin, Sept. 29, 1957; children: Craig, Eileen, Lynn. BSEE, U. Calif., Berkeley, 1950; postgrad., Stanford U., 1953-54. Jr. engr. Boeing Co., Seattle, 1950-52; design engr. Hewlett-Packard Co., Palo Alto, Calif., 1952-59; sr. staff engr. Ampex Computer Products, Culver City, Calif., 1959-60; dir. engring. Kauke & Co., Santa Monica, Calif., 1960-61; program mgr. Space Gen. Corp., El Monte, Calif., 1961-68, Aerojet Electronics Div., Azusa, Calif., 1968-89; prin. D.L. Broderick, Arcadia, Calif., 1989—. Contbr. articles to profl. jours. Mem. Jr. C. of C., Woodland Hills, Calif., 1963-64. With USN, 1945-46. Fellow Inst. for Advancement of Engring.; mem IEEE (chmn. profl. group on audio 1955-59, mem. exec. com. San Francisco sect. 1957-59, chmn. San Gabriel Valley sect. 1964-71, chmn. sects. com. L.A. coun. 1971-72, chmn. L.A. coun. 1972-76, chmn. bd. WESCON conv. 1976-80, bd. dirs. IEEE Electronics Conv. Inc. 1981-84, 1995-98, Centennial medal 1984), AIAA (sec. L.A. sect. 1986-88, sec. nat. tech. com. on command control comm. and intelligence, Washington, 1985-89, chmn. devel. com. L.A. coun. 1986-94). Achievements include 2 patents on high frequency communications technology; design of USAF 487-L low frequency communications system; first successful aircraft-ground station communications via satellite; design of first INTELSAT communications station in Africa; design and development of Ground Station computer software program for the USAF Satellite System, which achieved first successful detection and reporting of missile launches. Home: 519 E La Sierra Dr Arcadia CA 91006-4321

BRODERICK, HAROLD CHRISTIAN, interior designer; b. Oakland, Calif., Apr. 8, 1925; s. Harold Christian and Laura Jane (Lloyd) B. BA, U. Tex., 1947. Founder Arthur Elrod Assocs., Inc., Palm Springs, Calif., 1954; pres.; designer Calvin R. Vander Woode, inc., Sonoma, Calif. Bd. dirs. The Living Desert; mem. planning commn. City of Palm Springs, 1972-74; trustee Palm Springs Desert Mus.; mem. devel. com. Barbara Sinatra Children's Ctr. Mem. Am. Soc. Interior Designers. Republican. Office: Calvin Vanderwood Inc PO Box 350 Sonoma CA 95476

BRODERICK, JAMES ALLEN, art educator; b. Chgo., July 25, 1939; s. James and Catherine (Cahill) B.; m. Alice Moehelenhof, Aug. 24, 1963 (div. June 1977); children: Brian, Mark; m. Cindy Gambell, Dec. 21, 1978; children: Victoria, Catherine, Maureen. BA, St. Ambrose Coll., Davenport, Iowa, 1962; MA, U. Iowa, 1966. Asst. prof. N.W. Mo. U., Maryville, 1966-76, dir. art gallery, 1967-76, chmn. art dept., 1970-76; prof. art Tex. Tech U., Lubbock, 1976-83, chair art dept., 1976-83; prof. art U. Tex., San Antonio, 1983—, dir. visual arts divsn., 1983—. Photographer, painter, etcher; exhibited works throughout U.S., 1960s—. Mem. Nat. Assn. Schs. Art and Design (v.p. 1996-99, pres. 1999-02, accreditation reviewer 1977—), Nat. Coun. Art Adminstrs. (bd. dirs. 1994—). Democrat. Home: 2511 Old Gate San Antonio TX 78230-5230 Office: U Tex San Antonio 6900 N Loop 1604 W San Antonio TX 78249-1130

BRODERICK, JOHN CARUTHERS, retired librarian, educator; b. Memphis, Tenn., Sept. 6, 1926; s. John Patrick and Myrtle Vaughn (Newson) B.; m. Kathryn Price Lynch, Sept. 10, 1949; children: Kathryn Price, John Caruthers, Jr. A.B., Rhodes Coll., Memphis, 1948; M.A., U. N.C., 1949, Ph.D., 1953. Instr. English U. Tex., Austin, 1952-57; asst. prof. Wake Forest (N.C.) U., 1957-58, assoc. prof., 1958-63, prof., 1963-65; with Library of Congress, Washington, 1964-88; specialist Library of Congress, 1964-65, asst. chief, 1965-74, chief, manuscript div., 1975-79, asst. librarian for research services, 1979-88; adj. prof. English George Washington U., 1964-84; vis. prof. U. Va., 1959, U. N.C., 1968, Cath. U. Am., 1990-91. Compiler: Whitman The Poet, 1961; editor: The Journal of Henry David Thoreau, 1981-90; contbr. to profl. jours. Adv. com. U.S. Senate Hist. Office, 1974-78; mem. Nat. Hist. Publs. and Records Commn., 1978-82, Christopher Columbus Quincentennial Jubilee Commn., 1986-88. Served with U.S. Army, 1945-46. Danforth Found. grantee, 1960; Am. Coun. Learned Socs. grantee, 1962-63; Coun. on Library Resources fellow, 1971. Mem. Acad. Am. Poets, Am. Antiquarian Soc., Cosmos Club, Lit. Soc. Washington, Sigma Alpha Epsilon, Omicron Delta Kappa. Home: 8005 Inspection House Rd Potomac MD 20854-3426

BRODERICK, JOHN T., JR., state supreme court justice. BA magna cum laude, Coll. Holy Cross, 1969; JD, U. Va., 1972. Atty. Devine, Millimet, Stahl & Branch, Manchester, N.H., 1972-89; shareholder Broderick & Dean (formerly Merrill & Broderick), Manchester, 1989-95; assoc. justice N.H. Supreme Ct., Concord, N.H., 1995—; bd. dirs. Legal Svcs. Corp. Fellow Am. Coll. Trial Lawyers, N.H. Bar Found. (bd. dirs. 1985-91); mem. ABA, Mass. Bar Assn., N.H. Bar Assn. (bd. govs. 1985-91, pres. 1990-91), N.H. Trial Lawyers Assn. (bd. govs. 1977-82, pres. 1982-83). Office: NH Supreme Ct One Noble Dr Concord NH 03301*

BRODERICK, MATTHEW, actor; b. N.Y.C., Mar. 21, 1962; s. James and Patricia (Biow) B.; m. Sarah Jessica Parker May, 1997. Student high sch., N.Y.C. Actor: (stage prodns.) Valentine's Day, 1980, Torch Song Trilogy, 1982 (Villager award 1982, Outer Critics Circle award 1982), Brighton Beach Memoirs, 1983 (Los Angeles Critics award 1983, Drama League award 1983, Theatre World award 1983, Antoinette Perry award 1983), Biloxi Blues, 1985, The Widow Claire, 1986-87, How to Succeed in Business Without Really Trying, 1995 (Tony award Lead Actor in a Musical, Outer Critics Cir. award, Drama Desk award); (feature films) Max Dugan Returns, 1983, WarGames, 1983, Ladyhawke, 1984, Ferris Bueller's Day Off, 1986, On Valentine's Day, 1986, Project X, 1987, Biloxi Blues, 1988, Torch Song Trilogy, 1988, Glory, 1989, Family Business, 1989, The Freshman, 1990, Out on a Limb, 1992, The Night We Never Met, 1993, The Lion King (voice), 1994, The Road to Wellville, 1994, Mrs. Parker and the Vicious Circle, 1994, The Cable Guy, 1996, Addicted to Love, 1997, Inspector Gadget, 1999; prodr., dir., actor (film) Infinity, 1996; voice-over (film) Arabian Knight, 1995, Godzilla, 1998, Election, 1998; teleplays: Master Harold...and the Boys, PBS, 1984, A Life in the Theatre, TNT, 1993 (Emmy nomination, Supporting Actor - Special, 1994). Mem. Actors' Equity Assn., SAG. Address: care CAA 9830 Wilshire Blvd Beverly Hills CA 90212-1804*

BRODERICK, RAYMOND JOSEPH, federal judge; b. Phila, May 29, 1914; s. Patrick Joseph and Catharine (Haines) B.; m. Marjorie Beacom, Oct. 2, 1945; children—Patrick J., Timothy B., Tara M., Deidre C., Brian X. A.B. magna cum laude, U. Notre Dame, 1935; J.D., U. Pa., 1938; L.H.D., Pa. Coll. Podiatric Medicine, 1968; LL.D. (hon.), Phila. Coll. Osteo. Medicine, 1969, Allentown Coll. St. Frances De Sales, 1977. Bar: Pa. bar. Civilian agt. U.S. Naval Intelligence, 1941-42; practiced in Phila., 1945-62; sr. partner firm Broderick, Schubert & FitzPatrick, Phila., 1962-71; lt. gov. State of Pa., 1966-71; judge U.S. Dist. Ct. for Eastern Dist. Pa., Phila., 1971-84, sr. judge, 1984—; chmn. Adminstrv. Task Force for Constl. Revision, 1966; mem. Prep. Com. Pa. Constl. Conv., 1967, pres., 1967-68. Chmn. lawyers div. Cath. Charities, Phila.; mem. Phila. Republican Policy Com. Served with USNR, 1942-45. Mem. Am., Pa., Phila. bar assns., Notre Dame Law Assn. Clubs: Constl, Overbrook Farms. Home: 6408 Church Rd Philadelphia PA 19151-2411 Office: US Dist Ct 10613 US Courthouse 601 Market St Philadelphia PA 19106-1510*

BRODERSEN, ARTHUR JAMES, electrical engineer; b. Fresno, Calif., Aug. 31, 1939; s. Arthur James and Edith Elizabeth (McAllister) B.; m. Rebecca Ray Turton, Feb. 6, 1965; children—Arthur James, Kristina. B.S., U. Calif., Berkeley, 1961, M.S., 1963, Ph.D., 1966. Asst. prof. elec. engring. U. Fla., 1966-69, asso. prof., 1969-74, prof., 1974; prof. elec. and computer engring. Vanderbilt U., Nashville, 1974—; chmn. dept. elec. and biomed. engring. Vanderbilt U., 1974-81; asso. dean Vanderbilt U. (Sch. Engring.), 1979-86; chmn. dept. elec. and computer engring. Vanderbilt U., 1998—. Contbr. articles to profl. jours. Mem. IEEE (sr.; chmn. Nashville 1978-79), Eta Kappa Nu, Tau Beta Pi. Democrat. Home: 6722 Duquaine Ct Nashville TN 37205-3003 Office: Vanderbilt U PO Box 1628 Station B Nashville TN 37235

BRODERSEN, ROBERT W., engineering educator. BSEE, BS in Math., Calif. State Polytechnic U., 1966; MS in Engring., MIT, 1968, PhD in Engring., 1972. Mem. technical staff Ctrl. Rsch. Lab. Texas Instruments, 1972-76; prof. dept. elec. engring. and computer scis. U. Calif., Berkeley, 1976—, John R. Whinnery chair, 1995—; nat. chair Info. Sci. and Tech. Study Group, 1992-94. Contbr. articles to profl. jours., chpts. to books including Anatomy of a Silicon Compiler, 1992, Low Power Digital CMOS Design, 1995; patentee in field. Recipient Best Paper award Eascon, 1973, Internat. Solid States Circuits Conf., 1975, European Solid-States Circuits Conf., 1978. Fellow IEEE (editl. bd. various jours., Morris Libermann award 1983, Solid-States Circuits award 1997); mem. Nat. Acad. Engring. Achievements include research in application of integrated circuits as applied to personal communication systems. Office: U Calif Dept EECS 402 Cory Hall Berkeley CA 94720-1771*

BRODERSON, THELMA SYLVIA, marketing professional; b. St. Louis, Feb. 6, 1932; d. Harry and Lillian (Fishman) B. BA, U. Denver, 1953. Lic. ins. broker, Mo. Marketer Marsh & McLennan, Inc., St. Louis, 1966-85; account exec. Daniel & Henry Co., St. Louis, 1985-87; marketer G. Steven DeMaster, Inc. at Crane Agy., St. Louis, 1987—. Prodr. Harry Fender Program Sta. KMOX-CBS, St. Louis, 1968-74; columnist The Oil Can, 1972-75. Tchr. religious sch. United Hebrew Temple, St. Louis, 1956-63. Donor Harry Fender Memorabilia to St. Louis Pub. Libr. Media Archives and Rare Books Collection, 1997. Mem. Phi Beta Kappa. Avocations: theater, arts.

BRODEUR, ARMAND EDWARD, pediatric radiologist; b. Penacook, N.H., Jan. 8, 1922; s. Felix and Patronyne Antoinette (Lavoie) B.; m. Gloria Marie Thompson, June 4, 1947; children: Armand Paul, Garrett Michael, Mark Stephen, Mariette Therese, Michelle Bernadette, Paul Francis. AB, St. Anselm Coll., 1945; MD, St. Louis U., 1947, M.Rd., 1952; LLD (hon.), St Anselm Coll., 1974. Intern St. Louis U. Hosps., 1947-48, resident in pediat., 1948-49; resident in radiology St. Louis U. Hosps. and St. Louis U. Grad. Sch., 1949-52; instr. St. Louis U. Sch. Medicine, 1952-60, sr. instr., 1960-62, asst. prof., 1962-65, assoc. prof., 1965-70, prof. radiology, 1970—, chmn. dept. radiology, 1975-78, vice chmn. dept., 1978-88, prof. pediat., 1979—, prof. juvenile law, 1979—; pvt. practice specializing in pediat. radiology St. Louis, 1954-56; radiologist-in-chief Cardinal Glennon Meml. Hosp. for Children, St. Louis, 1956-88, Shriners Hosp. for Children, 1988—; assoc. v.p., bd. govs. Cardinal Glennon Children's Hosp., St. Louis; lectr. and cons. in field; med. dir. radiography Sanford Brown Coll., 1996—. Radio show host Doctor to Doctor, Sta. KMOX-CBS, St. Louis; host daily To Your Health; health reporter Sta. KMOV-TV, also Sta. WFUN-FM, Sta. KSIV-AM; TV host Sta. WCVB Channel 5, Boston; author: Radiologic Diagnosis in Infants and Children, 1965, Radiology of the Pediatric Elbow, 1980, Radiologic Pathology for Allied Health Professions, 1980, Child Maltreatment, 1993, also monographs; contbr. articles to profl. jours., numerous tchg. tapes. Bd. dirs. ARC, TB Soc., March of Dimes, 15 others. With U.S. Army, 1942-46, with USPHS, 1952-54. Decorated Knight Equestrian Order Holy Sepulchre Jerusalem; recipient Mo. Health Care Communicator of Yr. award, 1991, Welby award Nat. Acad. Radio and TV Health Communicators, Healthcare Leadership award Met. Hosp. St. Louis, 1994, Lifetime Achievement award Nat. Assn. Physician Broadcasters, numerous civic awards; Armand Brodeur Day proclaimed by City of St. Louis; named St. Paul Man of Yr., 1991; ann. lecture named in his honor dept. radiology St. Louis U. Sch. Medicine, 1998. Fellow Am. Coll. Radiology, Am. Acad. Pediat.; mem. AMA (Bronze medal, Golden Apple), Soc. Pediat. Radiology, Radio. Soc. N.Am., Nat. Assn. Physician Broadcasters (charter, co-founder, pres. 1987-88), Sigma Xi, Alpha Omega Alpha, Alpha Sigma Nu, Rho Kappa Sigma. Roman Catholic. Home: 6 Huntleigh Trails Ln Huntleigh MO 63131-4801 Office: 2001 S Lindbergh Blvd Saint Louis MO 63131-3504 *Success is being pleased with what you see in the mirror—every day. It should not be measured by the size of your home or bank account. What you see in the mirror is all that you can take with you. It is measured by what you do for people!.*

BRODEUR, MARTIN, professional hockey player; b. Montreal, Que., Can., May 6, 1972. Selected 1st round NHL entry draft N.J. Devils, 1994, goalie, 1991—; named to QMJ Hockey League All-Star 2d team, 1991-92, NHL All-Rookie team, 1993-94; played in NHL All-Star Game, 1996; mem. Stanley Cup Championship team, 1995. Recipient Calder Meml. Trophy, 1993-94. Office: c/o New Jersey Devils PO Box 504 East Rutherford NJ 07073-0504*

BRODEUR, MICHAEL STEPHEN, dean; b. Jacksonville, Fla., Oct. 15, 1949; s. Victor Edward Jr. and Amy (Ropke) B.; m. Crystal Cazalas, Aug. 9, 1975 (div. Oct. 1979); m. Cheri Anne Winton, Apr. 10, 1982; children: Trey, Aaron, Dana, Margaret, Deborah. BA in Econs., U. South Fla., 1972, BA in Fin., 1972; MPA, U. North Fla., 1989. Acctg. mgr. Raymond James Fin., St. Petersburg, Fla., 1974-78; asst. OMB dir. Pinellas County, Fla., Clearwater, 1978-79; dir. OMB Alachua County, Clearwater, Fla., 1979-83; treas. City of Orlando, Fla., 1983-84; dir. OMB Orange County, Fla., Orlando, 1984-86; dir. of fin. State of Fla., Gainesville, 1986-91; chief of staff U. Fla. Coll. of Pharmacy, Gainesville, 1994-98, asst. dean fin. and adminstrv. affairs, 1999—. Exec. v.p. COP Faculty Practice Assn., Inc., Gainesville. Recipient David Productivity award Davis Found. Fla. Taxwatch, Inc., 1993, 98, Disting. Svc. Alachua County Bd. Commrs., 1983. Mem. Heritage Club Inc., Heritage Links Country Club. Democrat. Presbyterian. Avocations: watch collecting, golf, target shooting. Fax: 352-392-7826. E-mail: brodeur@ufl.edu. Home: 4818 NW 37th Way Gainesville FL 32605-1034 Office: U Fla Coll of Pharmacy PO Box 100484 1600 SW Archer Rd Gainesville FL 32610-0484

BRODHEAD, DAVID CRAWMER, lawyer; b. Madison, Wis., Sept. 16, 1934; s. Richard Jacob and Irma (Crawmer) B.; m. Nancie Christensen, Aug. 17, 1963; children: Compton, Peter, Christoffer. B.S., U. Wis., 1956, LL.B., 1959. Bar: N.Y. 1960, Wis. 1959, D.C. 1979. Assoc. firm Paul, Weiss, Rifkind, Wharton & Garrison, N.Y.C., 1959-68, ptnr., 1969—; dir. Centennial Industries, Inc., N.Y.C. Editor-in-chief: Wis. Law Rev, 1958-59. Trustee Collegiate Sch., N.Y.C., 1978-85; vestryman Christ and St. Stephen's Episcopal Ch., 1972-82. Mem. N.Y. State Bar, Assn. of Bar of City of N.Y., Wis. Bar. Assn., D.C. Bar Assn., ABA, Westside C. of C. of City of N.Y. (dir. 1970-83), Order of Coif, Delta Theta Phi. Clubs: Washington (Conn.); Holland Soc. of N.Y. *Take life one day at a time. Yesterday is gone forever and tomorrow is not here. That leaves only today to deal with.*

BRODHEAD, JAMES E(ASTON), actor, writer; b. St. Louis, Jan. 30, 1932; s. James Easton II and Martha Pusey (Mithoefer) B.; m. Sue Hawes, June 21, 1963; children: William James Pusey, Daniel Alexander Hawes. BA in Speech, U. Mich., 1954. Announcer/news editor Sta. WNOP, Newport, Ky., 1954-55; actor stage and TV N.Y.C., 1955-62; copywriter/reporter Time Mag., N.Y.C. and Calif., 1963-69; pub. rels. account exec. Laurie & Assocs. and Mahoney & Assocs., L.A., 1971-74; actor Querencia Prodns., L.A. and Santa Barbara, 1974—; bd. dirs. Western Adv. Bd., Actor's Equity, L.A., 1978-83, ANTA West, L.A., 1978-80, Western Coun. Actor's Fund Am., 1993-95, Santa Barbara Symphony, 1998—. Author: Inside Laugh-In, 1969; appeared in 15 films including Leadbelly, First Monday in October, Frances, Hammett, Mame; TV films include War & Remembrance, Helter Skelter, Gideon's Trumpet; TV series include The Judge, General Hospital, Here's Lucy, Kraft TV Theatre; more than 100 stage prodns. including Inherit the Wind, First Monday in October. Mem. Ensemble Theatre Co., Pacific Pioneer Broadcasters, Actors' Fund (life), Edwin Forrest Soc. (founding) Am. Atheists, Freedom from Religion Found., Santa Barbara Club. Democrat. Avocations: reading, cooking, travel, languages. Home and Office: Querencia Prodns 506 Yankee Farm Rd Santa Barbara CA 93109-1060

BRODHEAD, THOMAS MCCOURTNEY, music engraver, computer programmer; b. St. Louis, Mar. 31, 1968; s. William Pierson and Marcia Mallory (Williams) B. BA in History, Oberlin Coll., 1989. Freelance music typesetter, editor, programmer Lebanon, Tenn., 1993—; cons. Dancing Dots, Inc., 1997—; ofcl. Charles Ives program-note writer Cleve. Orch., 1992—; author Beam and Editscor, aux. programs to use with Score music typography sys. Author Ives's Celestial Railroad and his Fourth Symphony. Charles Ives scholar. Avocation: classical music composition. Home: 2174 Wyandotte Ave Lakewood OH 44107-6147

BRODHEAD, WILLIAM MCNULTY, lawyer, former congressman; b. Cleve., Sept. 12, 1941; s. William McNulty and Agnes Marie (Franz) B.; m. Kathleen Garlock, Jan. 16, 1965; children: Michael, Paul. A.B., Wayne State U., 1965; J.D., U. Mich., 1967. Bar: Mich. 1968, D.C. 1983. Tchr. Detroit, 1964-66; atty. City of Detroit, 1969-70; mem. Mich. Ho. Reps., 1971-74; mem. 94th-97th Congresses from 17th Dist., mem. com. on ways and means, 1977-82, mem. budget com., 1979-80; chmn. Democratic Study Group, 1981-82; ptnr. firm Plunkett & Cooney P.C., Washington and Detroit, 1982—. Trustee The Skillman Found., Mich.'s Children. Home: 5096

Mirror Lake Ct West Bloomfield MI 48323-1534 Office: Plunkett & Cooney 505 N Woodward Ave Ste 3000 Bloomfield Hills MI 48304-2967

BRODIE, ALICE VELMA, health and ethics advocate; b. Akron, Ohio, June 20, 1924; d. Charles Alvin and Lillian Snowden (Twentyman) Keller; m. Milton John Brodie, Dec. 8, 1980 (dec. 1983). Student, U.S. Nurse Cadet Corps, 1944-47; grad., Mt. Sinai Sch. Nursing, Cleve., 1947; BSN in Pub. Health Nursing, Western Res. U., 1952; postgrad., U. Wash., 1963-64, U. Calif., Berkeley, 1969-70, 81, 86, U. San Francisco, 1987-89, Calif. State U., Dominguez Hills, 1997—. RN, Ohio, Calif.; cert. pub. health nurse. Nursing supr. Mt. Sinai Hosp., Cleve., 1952-54; sch. nurse Renton (Wash.) Sch. Dist., 1958-60; pub. health nurse, vis. nurse, sch. nurse King County Health Dept., Seattle; people to people citizen amb. to UN Internat. Red Cross, 1967; with Ministry of Health, England, Ireland, Germany, France, Italy, Switzerland, Netherlands, 1967; cmty. health advocate, 1952—. Vol. BSF Internat., 1968-74, 93-99, ARC, Seattle, 1958-67, Buck Ctr. for Rsch. in Aging, Marin County, Calif., 1989, 90, Family Radio Tours to China, Hong Kong, Taiwan, 1985, Siberia, Mongolia, 1990s, Argentina, Brazil; mem. Vision for Progress, Vallejo, Calif., 1996—, Calif. Lawyers for Arts, San Francisco, 1996—; amb. People-to People citizen amb. UN Internat. Red Cross Ministry of Health, U.K., Eng., Germany, Italy, Switzerland, Ireland, Holland, Netherlands, France; family radio tours to China, Siberia, Hong Kong, Argentina, Brazil, 1985-94. Mem. APHA, ANA (founding mem. Calif. chpt. 1996), AAUW, Calif. Nurses Assn. (former del. to ANA conv. Detroit), Nat. Coun. for Aging, Calif. Lawyers for Arts. Avocations: health policy analysis, world travel, education, health legislation.

BRODIE, HARLOW KEITH HAMMOND, psychiatrist, educator, past university president; b. Stamford, Conn., Aug. 24, 1939; s. Lawrence Sheldon and Elizabeth White (Hammond) B.; m. Brenda Ann Barrowclough, Jan. 26, 1967; children: Melissa Verduin, Cameron Keith, Tyler Hammond, Bryson Barrowclough. AB, Princeton U., 1961; MD, Columbia U., 1965; LLD hon., U. Richmond, 1987; LHD (hon.), High Point U., 1992. Diplomate Am. Bd. Psychiatry and Neurology. Intern Ochsner Found. Hosp., New Orleans, 1965-66; resident in psychiatry Columbia-Presbyn. Med. Center, N.Y.C., 1966-68; clin. assoc. intramural research program NIMH, 1968-70; asst. prof. psychiatry, dir. gen. clin. research center Stanford U. Med. Sch., 1970-74; prof. psychiatry, chmn. dept. Duke U. Med. Sch., 1974-82, James B. Duke prof. psychiatry and behavioral scis., 1981—, prof. dept. psychology, prof. law, 1980—; psychiatrist-in-chief Duke U. Med. Center, 1974-82; chancellor Duke U., 1982-85, pres., 1985-93, pres. emeritus, 1993—; mem. Pres. Biomed. Rsch. Panel, 1975; mem. Carnegie Coun. on Adolescent Devel., 1986-97; trustee Com. for Econ. Devel., 1986-93, mem. subcom. on edn. and child devel., 1990; trustee Nat. Humanities Ctr., 1988-93; mem. nat. rev. and adv. panel for improving campus race rels. Ford Found., 1990-94; mem. subcom. on Edn. on Child Devel. Com., 1990; bd. dirs. Inst. of Medicine, Mental Health and Behavioral Medicine, 1981-83, chmn., 1981-82; mem. Com. on Leadership Devel., Am. Coun. on Edn., 1990-93; chmn. Com. on Substance Abuse and Mental Health Issues in AIDS Rsch., 1992-95. Co-author: The Importance of Mental Health Services to General Health Care, 1979, Modern Clinical Psychiatry, 1982; co-editor: American Handbook of Psychiatry, vols. 6, 7 and 8, 1975, 81, 86, Controversy in Psychiatry, 1978, Psychiatry at the Crossroads, 1980, Critical Problems in Psychiatry, 1982, Signs and Symptoms in Psychiatry, 1983, Consultation-Liaison Psychiatry and Behavioral Medicine, 1986, AIDS and Behavior: An Integrated Approach, 1994, Keeping an Open Door: Passages in a University Presidency, 1996; assoc. editor Am. Jour. Psychiatry, 1973-81. Recipient Disting. Med. Alumni award Columbia U., 1985, Disting. Alumnus award Ochsner Found. Hosp., 1984, Strecker award Inst. of Pa. Hosp., 1980, N.C. award for sci., 1990, William C. Menninger Meml. award ACP, 1994. Fellow Royal Soc. Medicine; mem. NAS, Am. Psychiat. Assn. (sec. 1977-81, pres. 1982-83), Inst. Medicine, Royal Coll. Psychiatrists, Soc. Biol. Psychiatry (A.E. Bennet rsch. award 1970). Home: 63 Beverly Dr Durham NC 27707-2223 Office: Duke U Office of Pres Emeritus 205 E Duke Bldg Durham NC 27708

BRODIE, M. J. (JAY BRODIE), architect, city planner, government executive; b. Balt., Sept. 25, 1936; s. Meyer and Sarah (Rachliss) B.; m. Georgene Ann Gonzales, May 30, 1958; children: Kimberly Brodie-Hopkins, Ellen Maria Jarrett. B.Arch., U. Va., 1958; M.Arch, Rice U., 1960. Registered architect, Md. Architect, prin. city planner, chief planner Balt. Urban Renewal and Housing Agy., 1967-69; dep. commr. Dept. Housing and Community Devel., Balt., 1969-77, commr., 1977-84; exec. dir. Pennsylvania Avenue Devel. Corp., Washington, 1984-93; sr. v.p. RTKL Assocs., Inc., Washington, 1993-95; pres. Balt. Devel. Corp., 1996—; com. mem. Urban Land Inst., Washington, 1980—; mem. Gov.'s Task Force on Housing, Annapolis, Md., 1981-83; guest speaker numerous univs., confs., orgns.; bd. dirs. Empower Baltimore Mtmg. Corp., Md. Bioprocessing Ctr., Technology Devel. Corp. Past trustee Balt. City Life Mus's.; past mem. Presidio Coun., San Francisco; chair adv. bd. U. Va. sch. of architecture. Recipient Thomas Jefferson award Am. Inst. of Architects, 1994. Fellow AIA (bd. dirs. Balt. chpt. 1977-78, Thomas Jefferson award 1994): mem. Am. Inst. Cert. Planners, Citizens Planning and Housing Assn. (bd. dirs. 1976-77), Lambda Alpha. Unitarian. Avocations: ice dancing; writing; music. Home: 2217 Foxbane Sq Baltimore MD 21209-4607 Office: Balt Devel Corp 36 S Charles St Fl 16 Baltimore MD 21201-3020

BRODIE, SHELDON J., physician; b. N.Y.C., Apr. 10, 1926; s. Barnet and Mildred (Maidman) B.; m. Charlotte Kaplan, Dec. 18, 1954; children: Martha Jane, Barnett. BS, L.I. U., 1946; MD, U. Lausanne, Switzerland, 1952; postgrad. med. degree, NYU, 1959. Diplomate Am. Bd. Dermatology, 1961. Intern Kings County Hosp., N.Y.C., 1953-54, resident specializing in Dermatology, 1954; base dermatologist Camp Lejeune, N.C., 1955-56; chief dermatology St. Albans Naval Hosp., N.Y.C., 1956; attending dermatologist NYU Hosp., N.Y.C., 1960—; prof. clin. dermatology NYU Med. Sch., 1961—; dermatologist Bellevue Med. Ctr., Vets. Adminstrn. Hosp., N.Y.C., Mid Island Hosp., Beth Page N.Y. Author: (with others) Archives of Dermatology, Yearbook of Dermatology. Served to lt. M.C., U.S. Navy, 1954-56. Fellow Am. Acad. Dermatology. Home: 12 Donald Dr Syosset NY 11791-5208 Office: Bethpage Med Ctr 4277 Hempstead Tpke Bethpage NY 11714-5706

BRODINE, CHARLES EDWARD, physician; b. Sioux City, Iowa, May 10, 1925; s. Ivar and Dorothy B.; m. Lois Bliss, June 26, 1949; children: Stephanie Kay, Jennifer Leah, Charles Edward. B.S., Iowa State U., Ames, 1948, research fellow malaria project, 1948-49; M.D., Washington U., St. Louis, 1953. Intern St. Louis County Hosp., 1953-54, resident in internal medicine, 1954-55; resident in internal medicine U.S. Naval Hosp., Oakland, Calif., 1957-59; fellow in hematology, clin. instr. medicine U. Cin. and Cin. Gen. Hosp., 1955-57; head hematology svc. U.S. Naval Hosp., Oakland, 1959-61, Bethesda, Md., 1961-62; cons. in hematology U.S. Naval Hosp., 1962-73; head divsn. rsch. hematology Naval Med. Rsch. Inst., Bethesda, 1962-66; chmn. dept. clin. investigation Naval Med. Rsch. Inst., 1966-70, exec. officer, 1970-73; program mgr. Navy frozen blood and trauma rsch. program research div. Bur. Medicine and Surgery U.S. Dept. Navy, Washington, 1962-71; dir. rsch. divsn. Bur. Medicine and Surgery U.S. Dept. Navy, 1973-74; spl. asst. med. rsch. and devel. to Surgeon Gen. U.S. Navy, 1974-77; comdg. officer Naval Med. Rsch. and Devel. Command, Nat. Naval Med. Center, Bethesda, 1974-77; asst. med. dir. environ. health and preventive medicine Office Med. Svcs. Dept. State, Washington, 1977-90; mem. Agt. Orange Working Group, 1982-90; exec. com. Nat. Council Internat. Health, 1982-90; Bd. dirs. Gorgas Meml. Inst. Tropical and Preventive Medicine, 1973-89; mem. Bur. Medicine and Surgery Policy Council, 1974-77; med. adviser ARC, 1975-79; adv. com. Nat. Sickle Cell Disease, NIH, 1974-77; mem. com. on biomed. rsch. U.S.-Egypt Joint Working Group, 1975-77; mem. White House Working Group on Internat. Health, 1977; clin. asso. prof. dept. medicine Georgetown U., Washington, 1971—; Dept. State mem. Nat. Council for Internat. Health, 1978-89. Contbr. articles in field to med. jours. Exec. com. Gorgas Meml. Inst., 1978-88. Decorated Legion of Merit for blood rsch. project, 1968; recipient Meritorious Service medal for work at Naval Med. Rsch. Inst. U.S. Dept. Navy, 1973; Robert Dexter Conrad award for outstanding sci. achievement Sec. of Navy, 1977. Mem. AMA, Assn. Mil. Surgeons (sustaining membership award 1967), Acad. Medicine of Washington (bd. dirs. 1992—), Soc. for Cryobiology (editorial bd. 1964-66), Soc. Fed. Med. Agys., Western Soc. Clin. Investigation, Soc. Med. Cons. Armed Forces. Home: 9213 Friars Rd Bethesda MD 20817-2313

BRODING, MARILYN A., librarian; b. St. Cloud, Minn., Dec. 4, 1940; d. Leslie James and Della Emma (Parkins) Keehr; m. Rodney Charles Broding, July 21, 1962; children: Dana Charles, Loni Renèe, Blake James. BS, St. Cloud State U., 1961; MLS, Rosary U., 1977. Cert. tchr., Minn. Tchr., speech coach Grand Rapids Sch. Dist., Bigford, Minn., 1983-86; substitute tchr., speech coach Pine River (Minn.) Sch. Dist., 1988-90; libr. coord. Land O' Lakes, Arden Hills, Minn., 1992—; mem. comty. edn. bd. Grand Rapids Sch. Dist., 1983-85. Reviewer: (book) Luth. Librs., 1992. Mem. Spl. Librs. Assn. (officer Minn. chpt. 1971—), Toastmasters (sec. 1994, sgt.-at-arms 1995). Avocations: dance, music, Ta Chi Chih, book clubs, gourmet cooking. Home: 404 113th Ave NW Coon Rapids MN 55448-3378 Office: Land O' Lakes Inc 4001 Lexington Ave N Saint Paul MN 55126-2998

BRODKEY, ROBERT STANLEY, chemical engineering educator; b. L.A., Sept. 14, 1928; s. Harold R. and Clara (Goldman) B.; m. Martha Mahr, Dec. 22, 1958 (div. Nov. 1971); 1 son, Philip Arthur; m. Carolyn Patch, Dec. 6, 1975. A.A., San Francisco City Coll., 1948; B.Chemistry with highest honors, U. Calif.-Berkeley, 1950, M.S. in Chem. Engring, 1950; Ph.D. in Chem. Engring. (Gulf Oil fellow), U. Wis., 1952. Research chem. engr. Esso Research & Engring. Co., Linden, N.J., 1952-56; research chem. engr. Esso Standard Oil Co., Bayway, N.J., 1956-57; asst. prof. chem. engring. Ohio State U., Columbus, 1957-60; assoc. prof. Ohio State U., 1960-64, prof., 1964-92, prof. emeritus, 1992—; cons. on turbulent motion, mixing kinetics, rheology, 2-phase flow, fluid dynamics, image processing and analysis; expository lectr. GAMM Conf., 1975; vis. prof. Japan Soc. Promotion Sci., 1978; Clyde chair engring. U. Utah, fall 1994. Author: Transport Phemomena, A Unified Approach, 1988, The Phenomena of Fluid Motions, 1967, reprint edit., 1995; editor: Turbulence in Mixing Operations, 1975; contbr. articles to profl. jours.; patentee in field. Recipient Outstanding Paper of Yr. award Can. Jour. Chem. Engring., 1970; NATO sr. fellow in sci. Max Planck Institut für Strömungsforschung, Göttingen, Fed. Republic Germany, 1972; Alexander Von Humboldt Found. sr. U.S. scientist award, 1975, 83; sr. rsch. award Coll. Engring. Ohio State U., 1983, 86; Disting. Sr. Rsch. award Am. Soc. Engring. Edn., 1985; Chem. Engr. lectureship award Am. Soc. Engring. Edn., 1986; North Am. Mixing Forum award, 1994. Fellow AAAS, AIChE, Am. Phys. Soc., Am. Inst. Chemists; mem. Am. Chem. Soc., Am. Acad. Mech., Soc. Engring. Sci., Soc. Rheology, Sigma Xi, Phi Lambda Upsilon, Alpha Gamma Sigma, Phi Beta Delta. Achievements include patents in field. Office: Ohio St Univ 140 W 19th Ave Columbus OH 43210-1110

BRODKIN, ADELE RUTH MEYER, psychologist; b. N.Y.C., July 8, 1934; d. Abraham J. and Helen (Honig) Meyer; m. Roger Harrison Brodkin, Jan. 26, 1957; children: Elizabeth Anne Brodkin Brauer, Edward Stuart. BA, Sarah Lawrence Coll., 1956; MA, Columbia U., 1959; PhD, Rutgers U., 1977. Lic. psychologist, N.J. Sch. psychologist pub. schs., River Edge, Norwood, 1961-66, Morristown, Chatham, N.J., 1967-73; cons. psychologist United Hosp. Newark, 1973; assoc. dir. Infant Child Devel. Ctr. St. Barnabas Med. Ctr., Livingston, N.J., 1977-79; clin. asst. prof. dept. psychiatry U. Medicine and Dentistry N.J., Newark, 1979-90, clin. assoc. prof., 1990—; vis. scholar Hasting (N.Y.) Ctr. for Life Scis., 1979; mem. Essex County Mental Health Adv. Bd., Essex County, N.J., 1985-87; sr. child devel. cons.; cons. Scholastic, Inc., 1988—; clin. assoc. prof. psychiatry UMDNJ-N.J. Med. Sch., 1990—. Author: The Lonely Only Dog, 1998, Between Teacher and Parent, Supporting Young Children As They Grow, 1994, (with A.T. Jersild and E. Alina Lazar) The Meaning of Psychotherapy in the Teacher's Life and Work, 1962; author, prodr. (video documentary) Competing Commitments, 1984 (Best Ednl. Videotape award N.J. Cable); co-author, prodr. ednl. videotapes: Passage to Physicianhood, 1985, The Insidious Epidemic, 1986; columnist Between Tchr. and Parent, Pre-K Today mag., 1988-93, Early Childhood Today, 1993—, Scholastic Parent and Child mag., 1994—; child devel. columnist, 1991-92; columnist You and Today's Child, Instr. mag., 1992-93, Kids in Crisis, Instr. mag., 1993-96; columnist Adolescent Devel., Mid. Yrs. mag., 1990-95; columnist Scholastic.com "Ask Dr. Brodkin" 1997—; columnist Scholastic Network, 1995— contbr. articles to profl. jours. Grantee Gannett Found., Cmty. Fund for N.J., Carter-Wallace, Inc., Schering Corp.; Adelaide M. Ayer fellow Columbia U., 1962-63, NIMH fellow, 1962, Louis Bevier fellow Rutgers U., 1976-77. Fellow Am. Orthopsychiat. Assn.; mem. APA, N.J. Psychol. Assn. (Psychol. Recognition award 1982, 86, 90), Am. Sociol. Assn. Avocations: cairn terrier, photography, bicycling. Home and Office: 2 Trevino Ct Florham Park NJ 07932-2724

BRODL, RAYMOND FRANK, lawyer, former lumber company executive; b. Cicero, Ill., June 1, 1924; s. Edward C. and Lillian (Cerny) B.; m. Ethel Jean Johnson, Aug. 15, 1953; children: Mark Raymond, Pamela Jean, Susan Marie. Student, Norwich U., Northfield, Vt., 1943, Ill. Coll., 1946-48; J.D., Loyola U., Chgo., 1951. Bar: Ill. 1951. Atty. law office Joseph A. Ricker, Chgo., 1951-58, Brunswick Corp., Chgo., 1958-62; sec., gen. atty. Edward Hines Lumber Co., Chgo., 1962-84; atty., cons., 1985—. Democratic candidate for local jud. office, 1953, 57. Served with AUS, 1943-46. Mem. Ill. Bar Assn., Chgo. Bar Assn.,. Home and Office: 366 Lance Dr Des Plaines IL 60016-2628

BRODMAN, ESTELLE, librarian, retired educator; b. N.Y.C., June 1, 1914; d. Henry and Nettie (Sameth) B. A.B., Cornell U., 1935; B.S., Columbia U., 1936, M.S., 1943, Ph.D., 1954; post-doctoral study, UCLA, 1959, U. N.Mex., 1960; D.Sc. (hon.), U. Ill., 1975. Asst. librarian Cornell U. Sch. Nursing Library, N.Y.C., 1936-37; asst. med. librarian Columbia Libraries, N.Y.C., 1937-49; asst. librarian for reference services Nat. Library Medicine, Washington, 1949-61; librarian, assoc. prof. med. history Washington U. Sch. Medicine, St. Louis, 1961-64; librarian, prof. med. history Washington U. Sch. Medicine, 1964-81, librarian, prof. med history emerita, 1981—; documentation expert UN Tech. Assistance program UN, Central Family Planning Inst., New Delhi, 1967-68; documentation expert WHO, New Delhi, 1970, Manila, 1983; documentation expert ECAFE, Bangkok, 1973, AID, 1975, UNFPA, 1976; Mem. Pres.'s Commn. Libraries, 1968-70, Mo. Gov.'s Adv. Commn. Libraries, 1977-78; study sect. NIH, 1971-75, chmn., 1973-75; instr. Columbia U., 1946-52, 84, Cath. U. Am., 1957; vis. prof. Keio U., Tokyo, 1962, U. Mo., 1971, 73, Washington U. Med. Sch., 1964-81. Author: Development of Medical Bibliography, 1954, Japanese translation, 1994; author: Bibliographical Lists for Medical Libraries, 1950; editor: Bull. Med. Libr. Assn., 1947-57; guest editor N.J. Medicine, 1988. Recipient Holloway award Archivists and Librs. in History of Health Sci., 1993. Mem. Med. Libr. Assn. (pres. 1964-65, spl. award 1957, Noyes award 1971, Gottlieb award 1977, Frank B. Rogers info. advancement award 1985, centennial award 1998), Spl. Librs. Assn. (bd. dirs. 1949-52, John Cotton Dana award 1981), Am. Assn. History Medicine, N.J. Med. History Soc. (treas. 1985-88, v.p. 1988-92). Home: 19 Meadow Lks Apt 9 Hightstown NJ 08520-3325 *The transmission of scientific, especially medical, information from research worker to research worker, and from them to the deliverer of medical care and to the laymen who make decisions about these matters, in the past few decades has been an exciting and mind-expanding enterprise. The development of such tools as the computer, and the social diversity of those needing the information for daily use have completely changed scientific librarianship from a passive to an active operation. Transfer versus storage are the keywords. I have just been lucky to be involved in this field at so interesting and purposeful a time.*

BRODSKY, BEVERLY, artist. Postgrad., The Bklyn. Mus., 1954; BA in Art, Bklyn. Coll., 1965, postgrad., 1966; postgrad., Sch. Visual Arts, N.Y., 1969-70, The New Sch., 1969-70, The Bklyn. Mus., 1969-70. tchr. Parsons Sch. Design, 1979—, Adelphi U., 1980-85, Vt. Grad. Sch., Vt. Coll., others; lectr. in field. Author, illustrator: The Crystal Apple, 1974, Sedna, An Eskimo Myth, 1975, The Golem, 1976 (Caldecott honor medal 1977, Notable Book award 1977), Jonah, 1977, Secret Places, 1979, The Story of Job, 1986; illustrator Forest of the Night, 1975), Gooseberries to Oranges, 1982 (Notable Book award 1983); illustrator: The Purim Players, 1984; one woman shows include B.E.L. Gallery, Westport, Conn., 1979, Washington (Conn.) Art Assn., 1979, SUNY Plattsburgh, 1980, The Wilson Arts Ctr., Rochester, N.Y., 1982, The Open Gallery Parsons Sch. Design, N.Y.C., 1986, The Kimberly Gallery, N.Y.C., 1990, The Elizabeth Stone Gallery, Birmingham, Mich., 1991, West Beth Gallery, N.Y.C., 1998; group shows include 92nd St. YMCA, N.Y.C., 1982, The N.Y. Pub. Libr., N.Y.C., 1982, Ruth S. Harley U. Ctr. Gallery Adelphi U., 1983, Yeshiva U. Mus., N.Y.C., 1983, City Gallery, N.Y.C., 1984, The Houghton Gallery Cooper Union, N.Y.C., 1985, The Internat. Gallery, San Diego, 1987, The Triangle Artists' Workshop, Pine Plains, N.Y., 1988, The Jewish Mus., N.Y.C., 1988, Parsons Sch. Design, N.Y.C., 1989, LÖrhl Gallery, MÖnchengladbach, Germany, 1990, M-13 Gallery, N.Y.C., 1992, Galerie Berhard Steinmetz, Bonn, Germany, 1992-93, Blondies' Contemporary Art, High, N.Y.C., 1992, Janice Scharry Epstein Mus., West Bloomfield, Mich., 1992, Art Ctr. Battle Creek, Mich., 1992, The Painting Ctr., Soho, N.Y.C., 1994, 1996, ALJIRA Found., Newark, 1994, Elsa Mott Ives Gallery, N.Y.C., 1994, The Painting Ctr., 1996, Heller Archives Gallery, Hebrew Union Coll., N.Y.C., 1996, Abney Gallery Internat., Soho, N.Y.C., 1997, Broome Street Gallery, Soho, N.Y.C., 1997-98, Westbeth Gallery, 1997-98; reviewed in Print Mag., Art Direction Mag., The N.Y. Art Review, 1988, N.Y. Times, The Villlage Voice, Publisher's Weekly, The Booklist, Juni Magazin Fur Kultur and Politik, 1991; curator: Westbeth Gallery, 1999. Conn. Commn. on the Arts fellow; Triangle Artists Workshop resident. Home: 55 Bethune St New York NY 10014-2010

BRODSKY, DAVID M., lawyer; b. Providence, Oct. 16, 1943; s. Irving and Naomi (Richman) B.; m. Stacey J. Moritz; children: Peter, Isabel, Nell. AB cum laude, Brown U., 1964; LLB, Harvard U., 1967. Bar: N.Y. 1968, U.S. Dist. Ct. (so. dist.) N.Y. 1969, U.S. Ct. Appeals (2d cir.) 1974, U.S. Dist. Ct. (ea. dist.) N.Y. 1977, U.S. Supreme Ct. 1977, U.S. Ct. Appeals (D.C. cir.) 1981, U.S. Ct. Appeals (3d cir.) 1984, U.S. Tax Ct. 1984, U.S. Dist. Ct. (no. dist.) Tex. 1986. Law clk. to U.S. Dist. judge U.S. Dist. Ct. (so. dist.) N.Y., 1967-69; asst. U.S. atty. So. Dist. N.Y., 1969-73; assoc. Guggenheimer & Untermyer, N.Y.C., 1973-75, ptnr., 1976-80; ptnr., chmn. litig. dept. Schulte Roth & Zabel, N.Y.C., 1980—; lawyer; b. Providence, Oct. 16, 1943; s. Irving and Naomi (Richman) B.; m. Stacey J. Moritz; children: Peter, Isabel, Nell. AB cum laude, Brown U., 1964; LLB, Harvard U., 1967. Bar: N.Y. 1968, U.S. Dist. Ct. (so. dist.) N.Y. 1969, U.S. Dist. Ct. (ea. dist.) N.Y. 1977, U.S. Dist. Ct. (no. dist.) Tex. 1986, U.S. Ct. Appeals (2d cir.) 1974, U.S. Ct. Appeals (3d cir.) 1984, U.S. Ct. Appeals (D.C. cir.) 1981, U.S. Supreme Ct. 1977, U.S. Tax Ct. 1984. Law clk. to U.S. Dist. judge U.S. Dist. Ct. (so. dist.) N.Y., 1967-69; asst. U.S. atty. So. Dist. N.Y., 1969-73; assoc. Guggenheimer & Untermyer, N.Y.C., 1973-75, ptnr., 1976-80; ptnr., chrmn. litigation dept., Schulte Roth & Zabel, N.Y.C., 1980—, chmn. litig. dept.; lectr. in field. Co-author: Federal Securities Litigation: A Deskbook for the Practitioner, 1997. Chmn., bd. dirs. N.Y. Lawyers for Pub. Interest, Inc., 1991-94, vice chair, 1994-96. Recipient Pathways to Justice award. Fellow Am. Coll. Trial Lawyers; mem. ABA (co-chmn. ann. mtg. 1998, co-chmn. trial practice com. 1990-94, litigation sect. task force on jury sys. 1995—), Assn. of Bar of City of N.Y., Anti-Defamation League (exec. com., legal com. 1994—), Am. Law Inst., N.Y. County Lawyers Assn., Fed. Bar Coun., Harvard Club, Scarsdale Golf Club. Jewish. Co-author: Federal Securities Litigation: A Deskbook for the Practitioner, 1997. Chmn., bd. dirs. N.Y. Lawyers for Pub. Interest, Inc., 1991-94, vice chair, 1994-96. Recipient Pathways to Justice award. Fellow Am. Coll. Trial Lawyers; mem. ABA, (litig. sect., co-chmn. ann. meeting 1998, co-chmn. trial practice com. 1990-94, task force on jury sys. 1995—), Assn. of Bar of City of N.Y., Anti-Defamation League (exec. com., legal com. 1994—), Am. Law Inst., N.Y. County Lawyers Assn., Fed. Bar Coun., Harvard Club, Scarsdale Golf Club. Jewish. *

BRODSKY, JULIAN A., broadcasting services, telecommunications company executive; b. 1933. Student, U. Pa.; Wharton Sch. CPA. With Adler Faunce & Leonard Phila., Pa., 1955-60; with Internat. Equity Corp. Phila., from 1960; v.p., contr.; with Comcast Corp., 1969—, vice chmn., dir. Office: Comcast Corp 1500 Market St Fl 35 Philadelphia PA 19102-4782*

BRODSKY, MARC HERBERT, physicist, research and publishing executive; b. Phila., Aug. 9, 1938; m. Vivian Harriet Simon, Nov. 24, 1966; children: Alexander, Emily. BA in Physics, U. Pa., 1960, MA in Physics, 1961, PhD in Physics, 1965. Rsch. staff mem. IBM T.J. Watson Rsch. Ctr., Yorktown Heights, N.Y., 1968-80, mgr. semicondr. physics and devices, 1980-87, program dir. Advanced Gallium Arsenide Tech. Lab., 1987-89, dir. tech. planning, 1989-91; mgr. consumer electronics, 1992-93; IEEE Tech. Adminstrn., Fellow U.S. Dept. Commerce, 1991-92; exec. dir., CEO Am. Inst. Physics, College Park, Md., 1993—; mem. adv. coms. U. Pa. Engring. Schs., 1985—, U.S. Dept. Energy, 1986-89; mem. liaison com. to Internat. Union of Pure and Applied Physics, 1994—; mem. exec. coun. Am. Assn. Pubs. Profl. and Scholarly Pub. Divsn., 1998—. Editor: Amorphous Semiconductors, 1979, 2d edit., 1985; co-editor: Tetrahedrally Bonded Amorphous Semiconductors, 1974; contbr. numerous articles to profl. jours. Patentee in field. Trustee Mt. Kisco (N.Y.) Pub. Libr., 1986-91. Capt. U.S. Army, 1966-68. Fellow IEEE (mem. competitiveness com. 1993-94), Am. Phys. Soc. (exec. com. condensed matter div. 1981-84, edn. com. 1985-88, undergrad. prize com. 1987-88, advisor to coun. 1994—); mem. AAAS (physics nomination com. 1989-91). Avocations: photography, stamp collecting, biking. Office: Am Inst Physics One Physics Ellipse College Park MD 20740-3843*

BRODSKY, MICHAEL CARROLL, ophthalmologist, educator; b. San Francisco, Mar. 4, 1955; s. Carroll M. and Herma Hill (Kay) B. BA in Biology, U. Calif., San Diego, 1977; MD, U. Tex., San Antonio, 1981. Diplomate Am. Bd. Ophthalmology. Intern internal medicine Meth. Hosp., Dallas, 1981-82; resident in ophthalmology Wayne State U., Detroit, 1983-86; fellow in neuro-ophthalmology U. Calif., San Francisco, 1987; fellow pediat. ophthalmology Duke U., Durham, N.C., 1988; asst. prof. ophthalmology U. Ark. for Med. Sci., Little Rock, 1988-92, assoc. prof. ophthalmology and pediat., 1992-97, prof., 1997—, prin. investigator optic neuritis treatment trial, 1989-91, prin. investigator longitudinal optic neuritis study, 1992-97; chief pediat. ophthalmology Ark. Children's Hosp., Little Rock, 1988—. Co-author: Pediatric Neuro-Ophthalmology, 1996; prin. investigator Optic Neuritis Treatment Trial and Longitudinal Optic Neuritis study. Mem. AMA, Am. Assn. Pediat. Ophthalmology and Strabismus, N.Am. Neuro-Ophthalmology Socs. Democrat. Avocations: running, swimming, musical composition. Home: 11901 Pleasant Ridge Rd Little Rock AR 72223-2399 Office: Ark Childrens Hosp 800 Marshall St # 111 Little Rock AR 72202-3591*

BRODSKY, PHILIP HYMAN, chemical executive, research director; b. Phila., Pa., July 7, 1942; s. Herbert and Gladys (Ettenger) B.; m. Rita Kissen, Sept. 13, 1964 (div. 1974); children: Michelle, Andrew; m. Sunny Jo Kurn, Feb. 18, 1977; 1 child: Noah. BSChemE, Cornell U., 1965, PhD, 1969; postgrad., MIT, 1988. Sr. research engr. Monsanto Co., Springfield, Mass., 1968-1973; Research specialist Monsanto Co., Springfield, 1973-77, research group leader, 1977-80; mgr. results mgmt. Monsanto Co., St. Louis, 1980-82; mgr. Lustran New Products Monsanto Co., Springfield, dir. Plastics Tech., 1984-87; dir. cen. rsch. labs. Monsanto Co., St. Louis, 1987-90, dir. corp. rsch. and environ. tech., 1991-95, corp. v.p., corp. rsch. and environ. tech., 1996—; mem. bd. chem. scis. and tech. NRC, 1992-98, mem. critical techs. com., 1992; mem. remediation techs. devel. forum EPA, 1992—; mem. groundwater remediation tech. rsch. and analytical ctr. guide com., 1993—; bd. dirs. Metaphore Pharms.; chair rsch. on rsch. com. Ind. Rsch. Inst., 1991, chair fin. com., 1996; mem. adv. bd. dept. chem. and environ. engring. U. Ariz., 1994—; mem. adv. bd. dept. chem. engring. Cornell U., 1995—, Wash. U., 1999—; mem. bd. visitors Idaho Nat. Engring. and Environ. Lab., 1998—; mem. com. on chem. and pub. affairs Am. Chem. Soc., 1996—. Patentee in field; contbr. articles to profl. publs. including Environ Sci. and Tech., Rsch. Tech. Mgmt., Chem. Engring., SPE Jour., Am. Inst. Chem. Engring. Reprints, Chem. Health and Safety. Pres. Cmty. Day Alternative Sch., Springfield, 1974-77, St. Louis Rsch. Coun., 1987—; mem. sci. and engring. com. St. Louis Regional Commerce and Growth Assn., 1987—; bd. dirs. Inroads Inc., St. Louis, 1988—. Mem. MIT Soc. Sr. Execs. (bd. dirs. 1988-95), Sigma Xi. Avocations: skiing, backpacking, tennis, golf. Office: Monsanto Co (02A) 800 N Lindbergh Blvd Saint Louis MO 63141-7843

BRODSKY, ROBERT FOX, aerospace engineer; b. Phila., May 16, 1925; s. Samuel H. and Sylvia (Fox) B.; m. Patricia Wess, Jan. 24, 1959; children: Bette W., Robert D., David V., Jeffrey M. BME, Cornell U., 1947; MAero. Engring., NYU, 1948, DSc in Engring, 1950; MS in Math., U. N.Mex., 1957. Registered profl. engr., Calif., Iowa. Instr. NYU, 1948-50; supr. theoretical aerodynamics Sandia Corp., Albuquerque, 1950-56; chief aerodynamics Convair/Pomona, 1956-59; with Aerojet-Gen. Corp., 1959-71; chief engr. Space-Gen., El Monte, Calif., 1963-67; corp. mgr. European ops. AeroJet-Gen., Paris, 1969-70; mgr. systems test Aerojet ElectroSystems Co., 1970-71; prof., head dept. aerospace engring. Iowa State U., Ames, 1971-80; on faculty improvement leave with space and communications group Hughes Aircraft Co., 1978-79; sr. systems engr. TRW Space and Tech. Group, Redondo Beach, Calif., 1980-83, dir. technol. planning, 1982-86, program mgr., 1986-88; chief engr. Microcosm, Inc., Torrance, Calif., 1988-98; adj. prof. aerospace engring. U. So. Calif., 1982-96, Nat. Technol. U., 1994-96; vis. prof. The Technion, Haifa, Israel, 1989-90, 94; seminar lectrs. on remote sensing from space, Turin, Italy, 1988, Paris, London, Munich, 1991, Washington, 1992, 93, 94, 96, Albuquerque, 1995, L.A. & Cocoa Beach, 1996-98, Israel, 1999; cons. in field. Assoc. editor: Handbook of Astronautics, 1991—; author chpt. on space payloads: Space Mission Analysis and Design, 1991, 2d edit., 1992; contbr. articles to profl. jours. Served with USN, 1944-46. Recipient Ednl. Achievement award AIAA/Am. Soc. Engring. Edn. Aerospace Div., 1978; NSF/NATO sr. fellow in sci., 1973. Fellow AIAA (deceleration tech. com. 1963-65, ednl. activities com. 1972-97, spacecraft sys. tech. com. 1978-82, space transp. tech. com. 1985-88, editl. adv. bd. A&A 1977-81, chmn. L.A. sect. 1986-87), Inst. Advancement Engring; mem. NSPE, Internat. Coun. Sys. Engring., Am. Astronautical Soc., Am. Soc. Engring. Edn. (Centennial Citation 1993), Am. Soc. Aerospace Edn. (v.p. 1979-80, Educator of Yr. 1979), Rotary, Sigma Xi. Inventor space lifeboat (Time mag., Feb. 1, 1963). E-mail: rfoxbro@aol.com. Home: 110 The Vlg Unit 410 Redondo Beach CA 90277-2546

BRODSKY, SAMUEL, lawyer; b. Kansas City, Mo., June 12, 1912; s. Abraham and Anne (Brodsky) B.; m. Margery J. Bach, Oct. 17, 1944; children: Joan E., Alice E. B.A., U. Tulsa, 1933; LL.B., Harvard U., 1936. Bar: N.Y. 1937. Since practiced in N.Y.C.; law clk. to Fed. Circuit Ct. Judge Julian W. Mack, 1936-37; asst. U.S. atty. So. Dist. N.Y., 1937-43, 46, charge civil div., 1942-43, 46; partner firm Aranow, Brodsky, Bohlinger, Einhorn & Alter, 1947-79, Botein, Hays & Sklar, 1979-89; counsel Robinson, Brog, Leinwand, Greene, Genovese & Gluck, N.Y.C., 1989-97; lectr. taxation NYU Law Sch., 1953, 56-64, also; Inst. on Fed. Taxation, NYU, Practicing Law Inst. Contbr. articles to profl. jours. Served to lt. USNR, 1943-46. Mem. ABA, N.Y. State Bar Assn. (past chmn. tax sect.), Harvard Law Sch. Assn. N.Y. Jewish (past pres., trustee synagogue). Home: 120 E 81st St New York NY 10028-1428 Office: care Robinson Brog Leinwand Greene Genovese & Gluck 1345 Avenue Of The Americas New York NY 10105-0302

BRODSKY, WILLIAM J., options exchange executive; b. N.Y.C., 1944. Student, Syracuse U., 1965, JD, 1968. Bar: N.Y. 1969, Ill. 1985. Atty. Model, Roland & Co., 1968-74; with Am. Stock Exch., 1974-82, exec. v.p. ops., 1979-82; exec. v.p., COO Chgo. Merc. Exch., 1982-85, pres., CEO, 1985-97; chmn., CEO Chgo. Bd. Options Exch., 1997—; adv. mem. internat. capital mktgs. adv. com. Fed. Res. Bank N.Y.; mem. adv. coun. J.L. Kellogg Grad. Sch. Mgmt.; bd. dirs. Peoples Energy Corp. Mem. bd. visitors Northwestern U. Law Sch.; bd. dirs. Northwestern Meml. Corp.; trustee Syracuse U.; mem. Midwest regional adv. bd. Inst. Internat. Edn. Mem. N.Y. State Bar Assn., Ill. Bar Assn., Swiss Futures and Options Assn. (bd. dirs.), Futures Industry Assn. (bd. dirs.), Econ. Club Chgo., Comml. Club Chgo. Office: Chgo Bd Options Exch LaSalle at Van Buren Chicago IL 60605-7413

BRODY, ALAN JEFFREY, investment company executive; b. Newark, Apr. 19, 1952; s. Robert and Marcia (Ostroff) B.; m. Miriam Kahan, May 22, 1977. B.A., Northwestern U., 1974; J.D., Rutgers U., 1977. Bar: N.Y. 1978, N.J. 1978. Assoc. Baer Marks & Upham, N.Y.C., 1977-80; v.p. counsel Commodity Exchange Inc., N.Y.C., 1980-81, pres., chief exec. officer, 1981-89, chmn., 1987-88; v.p. Commodities Exchange Ctr. Inc., 1981-84, alternate dir., 1984-89; sr. v.p. futures div. Lehman Bros., N.Y.C., 1990-96; mng. dir. Lehman Bros. Futures Asset Mgmt. Corp., N.Y.C., 1991-96; sr. v.p. internat. divsn. Prudential Securities, Inc., N.Y.C., 1997—; mem. commodity policy adv. com. to U.S. trade rep.; past mem. coun. Found. Internat. Futures and Commodities Inst., Geneva. Mem. ABA, N.J. Bar Assn., Assn. of Bar of City of N.Y. (commodities regulation com.), New York County Lawyers Assn., Nat. Futures Assn. (bd. dirs., exec. com. 1986-89), Futures Industry Assn. (past mem. exec. com. law and compliance div.), Am. Copper Council (past bd. dirs.), Copper Club (past bd. dirs.), Swiss Commodities & Futures Assn. (bd. dirs.). Office: Prudential Securities Inc One New York Plaza New York NY 10292

BRODY, ANITA BLUMSTEIN, judge; b. N.Y.C., May 25, 1935; d. David Theodore and Rita (Sondheim) Blumstein; m. Jerome I. Brody, Oct. 25, 1959; children: Lisa, Marion, Timothy. AB, Wellesley Coll., 1955; JD, Columbia U., 1958. Bar: N.Y. 1959, Fla. 1960, Pa. 1972. With Office of Atty. Gen., State N.Y., 1958-59; dep. asst. atty. gen. State N.Y., 1959; sole practice Ardmore, Pa., 1972-79; ptnr. Brody, Brown & Hepburn, Ardmore, 1979-81; judge Pa. Ct. Common Pleas 38th Jud. Dist., Norristown, 1981-82, U.S. Dist. Ct. (ea. dist.) Pa., Phila., 1992—; lectr. in law U. Pa., Phila., 1978-79. Mem. ABA, Am. Judicature Soc., Nat. Assn. Women Judges, Pa. Bar Assn., Montgomery Bar Assn. (bd. dirs. 1979-81), Temple Am. Inn of Ct. (pres. 1994-95). Republican. Jewish. Office: US Courthouse Philadelphia PA 19106

BRODY, ARNOLD RALPH, research scientist, educator; b. Boston, Mar. 24, 1943; s. Sumner H. and Charlotte S. (Shuldiner) B.; m. Toby Pellman, Aug. 30, 1967; children: Janna Beth, Leah Meredith. BS, Colo. State U., 1965, PhD, 1969; MS, U. Ill., 1967. Postdoctoral fellow Ohio State U., Columbus, 1969-72; asst. prof. pathology U. Vt., Burlington, 1972-78; lab. dir. Nat. Inst. Environ. Health Scis., Research Triangle Park, N.C., 1978-93; prof. pathology Med. Ctr. Tulane U., New Orleans, 1993—, dir. lung biology Ctr. for Environ. Rsch., 1993—, prof. environ. health sci. Sch. Pub. Health, 1993—; Wellcome vis. prof. in basic med. scis. Burroughs Wellcome Fund, 1995; mem. adv. bd. Aspen (Colo.) Lung Conf., 1990—. Author more than 40 chpts. to books; assoc. editor Am. Jour. Respiratory Cell Molecular Biology, 1992—, Exptl. Lung Rsch., 1988—; mem. editl. bd. Jour. Environ. Pathology and Toxicology, 1990—; sect. editor pathology Jour. Lipid Mediators & Cell Signal, 1994—; contbr. more than 115 articles to profl. jours. Travel fellowship to Paris, 1986; grantee NIH, 1994, 97. Mem. AAAS, Am. Thoracic Soc., Internat. Wildlife Fedn., Nature Conservancy, Defenders of Wildlife, Wilderness Soc. Democrat. Jewish. Avocations: basketball, tennis, European travel, French food and wine, horses. Office: Tulane U Med Ctr Dept Pathology 1430 Tulane Ave New Orleans LA 70112-2699

BRODY, ARTHUR, industrial executive; b. Newark, June 30, 1920; s. Samuel A. and Ruth (Marder) B.; m. Sophie Mark, Mar. 5, 1944; children: Janice, Donald. Student, Columbia U., 1939-42. Organizer, operator Library Service, 1940-42; exec. buyer L. Bamberger & Co., Newark, 1942-43; chmn. Brodart Co., Williamsport, Pa., 1946—, BDI Investment Corp., San Diego, Tura Inc., Lake Success, N.Y.; past mem. adv. panel study on librs. and industry Nat. Adv. Com. on Librs.; past pres. Friends of N.J. Librs. Past trustee Newark Symphony Hall., Ctr. for Book, Libr. of Congress, L.A. County Libr. Found., Friends of Libr. USA, San Diego Community Found.; past commr. San Diego Pub. Libr. With AUS, 1943-46. Mem. ALA, NEA, San Diego Yacht Club, Rancho Sante Fe Golf Club, Masons, Shriners. Patentee in field. Office: Brodart Co 990 Highland Dr Ste 100 Solana Beach CA 92075-2409

BRODY, BERNARD B., physician, educator; b. N.Y.C., June 24, 1922; s. Abraham and Sarah (Berman) B.; m. Ruth M. Miller, Jan. 15, 1954; children: Sarah, Rachel. BS, U. Wis., 1943; MD, U. Rochester, 1951. Diplomate Am. Bd. Internal Medicine, Nat. Bd. Med. Examiners. Rsch. chemist U. Chgo. and Monsanto, Dayton, Ohio, 1943-47; resident U. Rochester, N.Y., 1951-53, clin. prof. pathology and medicine, 1981-90, prof. emeritus, 1990—; resident Genesee Hosp., Rochester, 1955-56, dir. clin. labs., 1967-81, sr. v.p. med. affairs, 1975-87; pvt. practice internal medicine Rochester, 1956-67; cons. Eastman Kodak Co., 1971-92, Robert Wood Johnson Found., 1975-80, EDMAC Assocs., Inc., 1976-83; trustee Freedom Forum, 1980-98; mem. adv. bd. Freedom Forum Media Studies Ctr., N.Y.C., 1985-98, adv. trustee Freedom Forum, 1998—. Bd. dirs. Rochester Mus. and Sci. Ctr., 1994—, Genesee Valley Med. Care, Rochester, 1962-68, Crestwood Children's Ctr., 1985-97; chmn. med. adv. bd. St. Ann's Home, 1964-67; corp. mem. United Way, Rochester, 1980-87; mem. Citizens Com. Human Rels., 1980-85; v.p., mem. exec. bd. Otetiana coun. Boy Scouts Am., 1981-91. 1st lt. U.S. Army, 1953-55. Mem. AMA, ACP, Am. Soc. Internal Medicine, Acad. Clin. Lab. Physicians and Scientists, Am. Assn. Clin. Chemistry, Sigma Xi, Alpha Omega Alpha. E-Mail: BBBrody@Frontiernet.net. Home and Office: 12 Huntington Brk Rochester NY 14625-1811 *Stay open-minded and flexible in thinking. It helps to recognize and take advantage of opportunities for adjuncts to or career enhancements or changes. It also makes for an interesting and exciting journey through life.*

BRODY, BONNIE, clinical social worker; b. N.Y.C., Dec. 1, 1947; d. Richard and Edith (Tranes) Mechlowe; m. A. William Brody, June 22, 1969; children: Laura, Davya, Sol. BA, Ripon (Wis.) Coll., 1973; MEd, U. Alaska, 1983; MSW, Washington U., St. Louis, 1992. Lic. clin. social worker; lic. marriage and family therapist. Dir. Alaska Tchr. Placement, Fairbanks, 1987-90; sr. clinician Human Affairs Alaska, Fairbanks, 1992-95; pvt. practice Fairbanks, 1992—; mem. adj. faculty U. Alaska, Fairbanks, 1996—. Mem. Alaska Mental Health Bd., 1996—; mem. sch. bd. Fairbanks North Star Borough Sch. Dist., 1984-90. Mem. NASW (state Com. On Gay and Lesbian Issues 1995—). Home and Office: PO Box 82533 Fairbanks AK 99708-2533

BRODY, EUGENE B., psychiatrist, educator; b. Columbia, Mo., June 17, 1921; s. Samuel and Sophie B.; m. Marian Holen, Sept. 23, 1944; children: Julie Anne, James Clarke, John Holen. AB, MA, U. Mo., 1941, DSc (hon.), 1991; MD, Harvard, 1944; grad., N.Y. Psychoanalytic Inst., 1957. Resident Yale Med. Sch., 1944-46, 48-49, from instr. to assoc. prof., 1949-57; prof. psychiatry U. Md. Sch. Medicine, Balt., 1957-76; chmn. dept., also dir. Inst. Psychiatry and Human Behavior, 1959-76, prof. psychiatry and human behavior, 1976-87, prof. emeritus, 1987—; sr. assoc. sch. of hygiene and pub. health Johns Hopkins U., 1986—; vis. prof. U. Brazil, 1968, U. W.I., Kingston, Jamaica, 1972, 73, James Cook U., No. Queensland, Australia, 1992; vis. prof. psychiatry Harvard Med. Sch., 1997—; fellow Center for Advanced Studies in Behavioral Scis., Stanford, 1975-76, U. Otago (N.Z.), 1981, Inst. for Advanced Studies, Tel Aviv U., 1986; mem. adv. bd. Inst. Social Psychiatry, U. San Marcos, 1968-70; mem. nat. profl. adv. bd. psychiatry, psychology and neurology service VA, 1963-67; cons. WHO (Pan Am. Health Orgn. and Geneva, Switzerland), 1965—; program dir. Interam. Mental Health Studies Program, 1967-69; mem. exec. bd. World Fedn. Mental Health, 1969-83, adminstrv. mem., 1972-74, mem.-at-large, 1979-81, pres., 1981-83, sec. gen., 1983—; mem. epidemiol. studies rev. com. NIMH, 1975-79, cons. clin. infant devel. program, 1979-81, hosp. rev. com., 1979-86, AIDS grant rev. com. 1987-92; mem. internat. adv. bd. Peruvian Nat. Inst. Mental Health, 1984—, mem. editl. bd. jours., 1985—; mem. adv. coun. Hogg Found., 1986-89; mem. sci. com. Internat. Social Sci. Coun., 1989, exec. com. 1989-91, 92-95; cons. UNESCO, 1986—; sr. advisor in Refugee Trauma, Harvard Program, 1989—. Author: The Lost Ones, Social Forces and Mental Illness in Rio de Janeiro, 1973, Sex, Contraception and Motherhood in Jamaica, 1981, Psychoanalytic Knowledge, 1990, Biomedical Technology and Human Rights, 1993, The Search for Mental Health: A History and Memoir of WFMH, 1948-1997, 1998; editor: (with F.C. Redlich) Psychotherapy with Schizophrenics, 1952, (with R. Monroe and G. Klee) Psychiatric Epidemiology and Mental Health Planning, 1967, Minority Group Adolescents in the United States, 1968, Behavior in New Environments, 1970; cons. editor Jour. Nervous and Mental Disease, 1959-67, editor in chief, 1967—; adv. editor: Tice Med. Ency., 1967-80, Harper & Row Med. Ency., 1980-86; mem. editorial bd. Psychiatry Digest, 1967-71, Mental Hygiene, 1968-70, Social Psychiatry, 1970-81, Internat. Jour. Psychosomatic Obstetrics and Gynecology, 1984-92, Population and Environment, 1987-92; contbr. numerous articles to profl. jours. Chmn. adv. bd. Balt. chpt. Internat. Students Council, ARC, 1964-67; bd. dirs. Md. Partners of Alliance for Progress, 1965-66, Nat. Assn. Mental Health, 1964-66, mem. profl. adv. bd., 1967-71; mem. adv. bd. Inst. for Victims of Trauma, 1988-97. Served to capt. M.C. AUS, 1946-48. Fellow Am. Psychiat. Assn. (life; chmn. com. transcultural psychiatry 1966-68, rep. internat. council 1965-71, trustee 1968-71, chmn. task force family planning 1973-75), Am. Coll. Psychiatrists (charter), Am. Coll. Psychoanalysts (charter); mem. Assn. Behavioral Sci. and Med. Edn. (pres. 1981), Am. Psychoanalytic Assn. (life), Internat. psychoanalytic assns., Internat. Coll. Pediatrics (senate 1978-86), Internat. Assn. Psychosomatic Ob-Gyn (exec. bd. 1977-86), Peruvian Psychiat. Assn. (hon.), Peruvian Assn. Psychiatry, Neurology and Neurosurgery (hon.). Club: Cosmos (Washington), West River Sailing Assn., 14 W. Hamilton St. Club (Balt.). Home: 70 Olmstead Green Ct Baltimore MD 21210-1508 Office: Jour Nervous/Mental Disease care Sheppard & Enoch Hosp PO Box 6815 Baltimore MD 21285-6815

BRODY, EUGENE DAVID, investment company executive; b. Bklyn., Feb. 6, 1931; s. Leon K. and Ruth (Parkoff) B.; m. Jacqueline Galloway, Apr. 5, 1959; children: Jessica, Leslie. BS, U. Pa., 1952; MBA, NYU, 1963. Gen. ptnr. A.W. Jones Assocs., N.Y.C., 1965-70; v.p., bd. dirs. Downe Communications, N.Y.C., 1970-74; chief exec. officer Founders Mut. Depositor Corp., Denver, 1970-74; pres. Beekman Capital, Inc., N.Y.C., 1974-75; sr. v.p., ptnr. Oppenheimer & Co. Inc., N.Y.C., 1975-86; mng. dir. Oppenheimer Capital, 1986-96; pres. Picanet, Inc., N.Y.C., 1997—; pub. Print Collectors Newsletter, 1971-96; bd. dirs. Quest for Value Dual Purpose Fund, 1987-97, Alara, Inc.; trustee Manhattan Inst. for Policy Rsch. Author: Odds-On Investing, 1978. Lt. USNR, 1952-55. Mem. N.Y. Futures & Options Soc. (founding dir., pres. 1978-79), City Athletic Club N.Y.C., Stamford Yacht Club, Regency Whist Club (bd. govs. 1985-94). Home and Office: Picanet Inc 119 E 79th St New York NY 10021-0339

BRODY, HAROLD, neuroanatomist, gerontologist; b. Cleve., May 15, 1923; s. Julius and Esther (Barowitz) B.; m. Anne Pertz, Mar. 24, 1951; children: David Andrew, Evan Barrett. Student, L.I. U., 1941-43; BS, Western Res. U., 1947; PhD, U. Minn., 1953; MD, U. Buffalo, 1961. Instr. anatomy U. Minn., Mpls., 1949-50; asst. prof. U. N.D., Grand Forks, 1950-54, U. Buffalo, 1954-59; assoc. prof. SUNY (merger with U. Buffalo 1961), 1959-63; prof. SUNY (merger with U. Buffalo 1961), Buffalo, 1963-95, disting. tchg. prof., 1995—; asst. dean SUNY, Buffalo, 1968-69; assoc. dean SUNY (merger with U. Buffalo 1961), 1969-70, Buswell rsch. fellow, 1970—, chmn. dept. anat. scis., 1971-92; acting dir. Ctr. for Study of Aging, SUNY, Buffalo, 1977-80, organizer, curator Mus. Neuroanatomy, 1994—; vis. prof. neurophthalmology St. Mary's Hosp., Rochester, N.Y., 1965-75, U. Copenhagen, 1987, 90, 91, 92, 93, 95; Anthes Wilson Abernathy disting. lectr. U. Toronto, Ont., Can., 1987; mem. com. on rsch. and demonstration White House Conf. on Aging, 1971; mem. biology coun. Canisius Coll., Buffalo, 1969; mem. sci. bd. Buffalo Otol. Found., 1968; mem. nat. adv. coun. Nat. Inst. on Aging, NIH, 1975-79. Abstractor, Excerpta Medica Sect. Gerontology and Geriat., 1959—; sci. referee Science, 1956—, Jour. Morphology, 1958—; sci. referee Jour. Gerontology, 1957-73, assoc. editor, 1973-75, editor-in-chief, 1975-80; editor Neurobiology of Aging, 1981—; mem. editl. bd. Gerontology and Geriat. Edn., 1980—, Exptl. Gerontology, 1984—. Trustee Erie County Meals on Wheels, Legal Svcs. for Elderly; pres. Friends of Health Scis. Med. Libr. SUNY, Buffalo, 1999. With M.C., AUS, 1943-46. Recipient NSF travel award, 1957, Robert W. Kleemeier Rsch. award in gerontology Gerontol. Soc. Am., 1978; co-recipient Lyn Millane Cmty. Svc. award Amherst (N.Y.) Sr. Citizens' Found., 1998-99; Fulbright sr. rsch. scholar, Copenhagen, 1963. Mem. AAAS, Roswell Park Med. Club (pres. 1978-79), Am. Assn. Anatomists, Am. Assn. Anatomy Chmn., Am. Geriat. Soc., Am. Aging Assn. (trustee 1970-77), Gerontol. Soc. Am. (mem. exec. com. 1961-63, 68-71, pres. 1974-75), Buffalo Neuropsychiat. Soc. (pres. 1967-68), Alpha Omega Alpha. Achievements include research on effects of aging on human central nervous system. Home: 144 Capen Blvd Amherst NY 14226-3053 Office: SUNY Buffalo Main St Campus Dept Anatomy & Cell Biology Rm 315 Farber Hall Buffalo NY 14214

BRODY, JACOB JEROME, art history educator; b. Bklyn., Apr. 24, 1929; s. Aladar and Esther (Kraiman) B.; m. Jean Lindsey, Feb. 13, 1956; children: Jefferson, Jonathan, Allison. Cert. fine arts, Cooper Union, 1950; BA, U. N.Mex., 1956, MA, 1964, PhD, 1970. Curator of art Everhart Mus., Scranton, Pa., 1957-58; curator collections Isaac Delgado Mus. Art, New Orleans, 1958-60; Mus. Internat. Folk Art, Santa Fe, 1960-61; prof. anthropology U. N.Mex., 1965-85, prof. art history, 1972-89; prof. emeritus, 1989—; curator Maxwell Mus., U. N.Mex., Albuquerque, 1962-72; dir. Maxwell Mus., U. N.Mex., 1972-85; mem. adv. bd. Ghost Ranch Mus., N.Mex. Mus. Natural History, 1981-84, Wheelwright Mus. of the Am. Indian, 1989-92, Zuni Pueblo Mus., 1992—; rsch. curator Maxwell Mus., Sch. of Am. Rsch., Lab. of Anthropology; mem. fine arts bd. City of Albuquerque, vice chmn., 1970-74; mem. Gov. N.Mex. Task Force Paleontol. Resources, 1978-79. Author: Indian Painters and White Patrons, 1971, Mimbres Painted Pottery, 1977, Between Traditions, 1977, Yazz: Navajo Painter, 1982, The Chaco Phenomenon, 1983, The Anasazi, 1990, Beauty From the Earth, 1990, Anasazi and Pueblo Painting, 1991, Pueblo Indian Painting: Tradition and Modernism in New Mexico 1900-1930, 1997; co-author: Mimbres Pottery: Ancient Art of the American Southwest, 1983, To Touch the Past: The Painted Pottery of the Mimbres People, 1996. Recipient Tom L. Popejoy Dissertation award U. N.Mex., 1970, Gov.'s award of honor N.Mex. Hist. Com., 1978; Non-Fiction award Border-Regional Libr. Assn., 1972; Art Book award, 1979; Conservation and Preservatin award Am. Rock Art Rsch. Assn., 1998; resident scholar Sch. Am. Rsch., 1980-81; honoree Archeol. Soc. N.Mex., 1990, Native Am. Art Rsch. Assn., 1997. Mem. Am. Assn. Museums, Soc. Am. Archaeology, Coun. Mus. Anthropology, N.Mex. Mus. Assn., Native Am. Art Studies Assn., Am. Rock Art Rsch. Assn.

BRODY, JACQUELINE, editor; b. Utica, N.Y., Jan. 23, 1932; d. Jack and Mary (Childress) Galloway; m. Eugene D. Brody, Apr. 5, 1959; children: Jessica, Leslie. AB, Vassar Coll., 1953; postgrad., London Sch. Econs., 1953-56. Assoc. editor Crowell Collier Macmillan, N.Y.C., 1963-67; writer Coun. Fgn. Rels., N.Y.C., 1968-69; mng. editor Print Collector's Newsletter, N.Y.C., 1971-72, editor, 1972-96, art writer, 1996—; dir., v.p. Picanet, Inc., N.Y.C., 1996—. Office: 119 E 79th St New York NY 10021-0339

BRODY, JANE ELLEN, journalist; b. Bklyn., May 19, 1941; d. Sidney and Lillian (Kellner) B.; m. Richard Engquist, Oct. 2, 1966; children: Lee Erik and Lorin Michael Engquist (twins). B.S., N.Y. State Coll. Agr., Cornell U., 1962; M.S. in Journalism, U. Wis., 1963; HHD (hon.), Princeton U., 1987; LHD (hon.), Hamline U., 1993, SUNY Hlth. Sci. Ctr., 1999. Reporter Mpls. Tribune, 1963-65; sci. writer, personal health columnist N.Y. Times, N.Y.C., 1965—; mem. adv. council N.Y. State Coll. Agr., Cornell U., 1971-77. Author: (with Richard Engquist) Secrets of Good Health, 1970, (with Arthur Holleb) You Can Fight Cancer and Win, 1977, Jane Brody's Nutrition Book, 1981, Jane Brody's The New York Times Guide to Personal Health, 1982, Jane Brody's Good Food Book, 1985, Jane Brody's Good Food Gourmet, 1990, (with Richard Flaste) Jane Brody's Good Seafood Book, 1994, Jane Brody's Cold and Flu Fighter, 1995, Jane Brody's Allergy Fighter, 1997, The New York Times Book of Health, 1997. Recipient numerous writing awards, including; Howard Blakeslee award Am. Heart Assn., 1971; Sci. Writers' award ADA, 1978; J.C. Penney-U. Mo. Journalism award, 1978; Lifeline award Am. Health Found., 1978. Jewish. Office: NY Times 229 W 43d St New York NY 10036-3913

BRODY, KENNETH DAVID, investment banker; b. Phila., June 30, 1943; s. Herbert Brody and Esther (Forman) Brody Shimberg; m. Judy E. Donahue, Feb. 5, 1964 (div. Feb. 1974); m. Helen M. Tandler, Apr. 6, 1974 (div. Oct. 1978); m. Carolyn J. Schwenker, June 26, 1987. B.S.E.E. with high honors, U. Md., 1964; M.B.A. with high distinction, Harvard U., 1971. Foreman and staff asst. Chesapeake & Potomac Telephone Co., Washington, 1964-66; with Goldman, Sachs & Co., N.Y.C., 1971-91, ptnr., 1978-91; chmn., pres. Export-Import Bank of U.S., Washington, 1993-96; founding ptnr. Winslow Ptnrs., LLC, Washington, 1996—; chmn., founder Chartwell Health Mgmt., Inc., 1997—; Bd. dirs. Alex. Brown Inc., Fed. Realty Investment Trust, Quest Diagnostics, Inc. Bd. dirs. Alvin Ailey Am. Dance Theater, N.Y.C., 1981-93, ARC, 1994—, St. John's Coll., 1996—, Yurie Systems, Inc., 1996—, Washington Tennis Found., 1996—; chmn. Presdl. Commn. U.S.-Pacific Trade and Investment Policy, 1996-97. Capt. U.S. Army, 1966-69. Baker scholar, 1970; Loeb Rhoades fellow, 1971. Mem. Coun. Fgn. Rels., Urban Land Inst. (comml. and retail devel. council 1987), Tau Beta Pi, Eta Kappa Nu, Omicron Delta Kappa, Alpha Tau Omega. Democrat. Unitarian. Club: Harvard (bd. mgrs. N.Y.C.). Office: Winslow Ptnrs LLC 1300 Connecticut Ave NW Washington DC 20036-1703 Address: 2991 Woodland Dr NW Washington DC 20008-3542*

BRODY, LAWRENCE, lawyer, educator; b. St. Louis, Aug. 12, 1942; s. Max and Jeannette (Cohen) B.; m. Janice Dobinsky, Dec. 25, 1967; 1 child, Michael Allen. BS in Econs., U. Pa., 1964; JD, Washington U., St. Louis, 1967; LLM in Tax, NYU, 1968. Bar: Mo. Assoc. atty. Husch, Eppenberger, Donohue, Elson & Cornfeld, St. Louis, 1968-74, ptnr., 1974-86; ptnr. Bryan Cave, LLP, St. Louis, 1986—; adj. prof. Washington U. Sch. Law, 1968—. Author: Missouri Estate Planning, 1988; author, editor Life Insurance Counsellor Series, 1990, 91. Fellow Am. Coll. of Trust and Estate Counsel, Am. Coll. Tax Counsel; mem. Adv. Bd. of Tax Mgmt. Office: Bryan Cave LLP 1 Metropolitan Sq Saint Louis MO 63102-2733

BRODY, LESLIE GARY, social worker, sociologist; b. Albany, N.Y., Aug. 30, 1944; s. Sanford and Cyrille L. (Kosatsky) B.; m. Marjorie A. Rubin, Feb. 1, 1970; children: Jennifer, Jonathan, David. AA, Corning Community Coll., 1966; BA, U. Maine, 1970; MSW, Ind. U., Indpls., 1972; PhD, Boston U., 1984. Lic. ind. clin. social worker, Mass. Dir. regional- statewide planning &devel. drug abuse div. Indpls., 1972-74; dep. dir. Iowa Drub Abuse Authority, Des Moines, 1974-76, dir., 1976-77; exec. dir. Eliot Community Mental Health Ctr., Concord, Mass., 1977-83; pres. Les Brody Assocs., Acton, Mass., 1983—. Author: Effective Fund Raising, 1994; contbr. chpt. to book and articles to profl. jours. Vice pres. Congregation Beth Elohim, Acton, 1979-81, pres., 1982-84; v.p. campaign Acton-Boxborough Cmty. Chest, 1986-87; pres. Acton-Boxborough United Way, 1990-93. With U.S. Army, 1964-67. Jewish. Avocations: landscaping, running, karate, tennis. Office: PO Box 1121 Acton MA 01720-0121

BRODY, MARTIN, food service company executive; b. Newark, Aug. 8, 1921; s. Leo and Renee (Kransdorf) B.; m. Florence Gropper, Nov. 22, 1946; children: Marc, Renee. B.A., Mich. State U., 1943. Pres. Indsl. Feeding Co., Newark, 1951-61; pres., dir. A.M. Capital Corp., N.Y.C., 1961-71; chmn. bd., dir. Waldorf System Inc., Boston, 1963-66, Restaurant Assocs., Inc., N.Y.C., 1964-66; chmn. bd., CEO Restaurant Assocs. Industries Inc., 1966-99; chmn. bd. St. Barnabas Corp.; dir. Jaclyn Inc., several Smith Barney mut. funds, Washington Nat. Life Ins. Co. of N.Y. Trustee St. Barnabas Med. Ctr.; bd. dirs. N.J. Transit Corp. Served to capt. AUS, 1943-45. Mem. Orange Lawn Tennis, Greenbrook Country (North Caldwell, N.J.).

BRODY, MORTON AARON, federal judge; b. Lewiston, Maine, June 12, 1933; s. Henry S. and Pearl (Meltzer) B.; m. Judith Levine, July 3, 1960; children: Ronald, Elizabeth Brody Gluck, John. BA, Bates Coll., Lewiston, 1955; JD, U. Chgo., 1958. Bar: Maine 1959, U.S. Dist. Ct. D.C. 1959, U.S. Ct. Appeals (D.C. cir.) 1959, U.S. Dist. Ct. Maine 1961. Lawyer Washington, 1958-61, Waterville, Maine, 1961-80; justice Superior Ct. of Maine, 1980-85, chief justice, 1985-90; assoc. justice Supreme Judicial Ct. of Maine, Augusta, 1990-91; judge U.S. Dist. Ct., Bangor, Maine, 1991—; city solicitor City of Waterville, 1961-66, 68-70; adj. prof. Colby Coll., 1987-96. Bates Coll. scholar, 1951-55; U. Chgo. Law Sch. scholar, 1955-58; recipient Disting. Citizen of Yr. award, 1981, Elks Citizen of Yr. award, 1984. Mem. Maine Bar Assn., Kennebec County Bar Assn., Waterville Bar Assn., Phi Delta Phi. Jewish. Office: US Dist Ct PO Box 756 Bangor ME 04402-0756

BRODY, RICHARD ALAN, political science educator, researcher; b. N.Y.C., Mar. 2, 1930; s. Lee and Felice Auslander; m. Marjorie Jean Brody, Aug. 23, 1964; children: Gordon Christopher, David Eric, Aaron Jed. BA, San Francisco State U., 1956, MA, 1959; PhD, Northwestern U., 1963. Asst. prof. Stanford (Calif.) U., 1962-66, assoc. prof., 1966-70, prof., 1970-95, chmn. dept., 1972-73, 74-77, prof. emeritus, 1995—; Fulbright prof. U. Leiden, The Netherlands, 1970-71; bd. overseers Am. Nat. Election Study, 1980-87. Author: Simulation Internat., 1963, Assessing the President, 1991; co-author: Reasoning and Choice, 1991 (Woodrow Wilson prize 1992); coeditor: Political Persuasion and Attitude, 1996; editor Polit. Behavior jour., 1990-97. Fellow, Ctr. Advanced Study in Behavioral Sci., 1967-68, Am. Acad. Arts and Scis., 1992; Parthemos fellow U. Ga., 1998. Mem. Am. Polit. Sci. Assn. (coun. 1977-79), Western Polit. Sci. Assn. (pres. 1987-88), Midwest Polit. Sci. Assn. Democrat. Avocations: wines, food, travel, birding. E-mail: Brody@leland.Stanford.edu. Home: 1636 Edgewood Dr Palo Alto CA 94303-2820 Office: Stanford Univ Dept Polit Sci Bldg 160 Stanford CA 94305-2004

BRODY, RICHARD ERIC, lawyer; b. N.Y.C., Sept. 9, 1947; s. Harold I. and Lillian C. (Albert) B.; m. V. Jane Cohen, May 25, 1974; children: Lauren, Erica. BA, Washington and Jefferson Coll., 1969; JD, Boston U., 1975. Bar: Mass. 1975, U.S. Dist. Ct. Mass. 1975, U.S. Ct. Appeals (1st cir.) 1975, U.S. Supreme Ct. 1987. Law clk. Mass. Superior Ct., Boston, 1975-76, chief law clk., 1976-77; assoc. Sisson, Lee & Bloomenthal, Boston, 1977-78; asst. dist. atty. Atty.'s Office Middlesex County Dist., Cambridge, Mass., 1978-82; assoc. Morrison, Mahoney & Miller, Boston, 1982-85, ptnr., 1985-95; ptnr. Brody, Hardoon, Perkins & Kesten, Boston, 1995—; lectr. Nat. Inst. Trial Advocacy, trial practice series Harvard U., Mass. Continuing Legal Edn., Def. Rsch. Inst.; evaluator Middlesex Multi-Door Courthouse, Cambridge, 1989—; mediator Arbitration Forums, Inc., Tarrytown, N.Y., 1989—, cons. Liability Cons., Inc., Sudbury, 1988—; mem. nat. adv. bd. Govtl. Liability Ins., Richmond, 1985—. Trustee Mass. Civil Liability Ins., Boston, 1983-89. Mem. Mass. Bar Assn. (civil litigation sect. coun.), Mass. Assn. Trial Lawyers, Boston Bar Assn., Def. Rsch. Inst., City Solicitors and Town Counsel Assn. Office: Brody Hardoon Perkins & Kesten 1 Exeter Plz Fl 12 Boston MA 02116-2848

BRODY, SAUL NATHANIEL, English literature educator; b. N.Y.C., Mar. 6, 1938; s. Irving Bernard and Ethel (Spiegel) B.; m. Frohma-Esther Besner, Jan. 24, 1960; children: Audrey Rachel (dec.), Ruth Elizabeth. BA, Columbia U., 1959, MA, 1960, PhD, 1968. Lectr. Hunter Coll., N.Y.C., 1962-65, City Coll., N.Y.C., 1965-68; asst. prof. City Coll., 1968-73, assoc. prof., 1974-78, prof. English, 1979-98, dept. chmn., 1979-85; co-prin. investigator Mellon Found. grant, 1978; project dir. NEH Summer Inst. for Tchrs., 1984, 86, 88; project dir. Ford Found. grant, 1987-89, 91-95, Dept. Edn. grant, 1991, Mellon Found. grant, 1989-95. Author: The Disease of the Soul: Leprosy in Medieval Literature, 1974; editor: Readings in Asian Literatures, 1992; contbr. articles to scholarly publs. Mem. Medieval Acad. Am., Univ. Seminar in Medieval Studies (Columbia U.). Home: 20 Glenwood Ave Demarest NJ 07627-2625

BRODY, THEODORE MEYER, pharmacologist, educator; b. Newark, May 10, 1920; s. Samuel and Lena (Hammer) B.; m. Ethel Vivian Drelich, Sept. 7, 1947; children—Steven Lewis, Debra Jane, Laura Kate, Elizabeth. B.S., Rutgers U., 1943; M.S., U. Ill., 1949, Ph.D., 1952. Mem. faculty U. Mich. Med. Sch., Ann Arbor, 1952-66; prof. pharmacology Coll. Medicine, Mich. State U., East Lansing, 1966-90, prof. emeritus, 1990—, chmn. dept., 1966-86; cons. NIH, 1969-73, NIDA, 1975-79, Internat. Soc. Heart Rsch., 1973—; mem. sci. adv. com. Pharm. Mfrs. Assn. Found., 1973—; U.S. rep. Internat. Union Pharmacology, 1973-76; mem. bd. Fedn. Am. Socs. for Exptl. Biology, 1973-76; mem. Com. Sci. Soc. Presidents; NSF Disting. scholar lectr. U. Hawaii, 1974. Mem. editl. bd. Jour. Pharmacology and Exptl. Therapeutics, 1965-80, specific field editor, 1981-92; mem. editl. bd. Rsch. Comm. in Chem. Pathology and Pharmacology, Molecular Pharmacology, 1972-90; editor: Human Pharmacology Molecular to Clinical, 1991, 94, 97; cons. Random House Dictionary of English Lang., 1964—; contbr. 300 articles to profl. jours. Served with AUS, 1943-46. Recipient Disting. Faculty award Mich. State U., 1984. Mem. Soc. Pharmacology and Exptl. Therapeutics (John Jacob Abel award 1955, chmn. Abel award com. 1966, mem. council 1969-72, sec.-treas. 1970, pres. elect 1973, pres. 1974, Torald Sollmann award in pharmacology 1995), Internat. Soc. Biochem. Pharmacology, Am. Coll. Clin. Pharmacology, Assn. Med. Sch. Pharmacologists (sec. 1984-86), Soc. Toxicology, Soc. Neurosci., Japanese Pharmacology Soc., AAUP, Sigma Xi, Rho Chi, Phi Kappa Phi. Home: 842 Longfellow Dr East Lansing MI 48823-2444 Office: Mich State U Dept Pharmacology East Lansing MI 48824

BRODY, WILLIAM RALPH, radiologist, educator; b. Stockton, Calif., Jan. 4, 1944. BSEE, MIT, 1965, MSEE, 1966; MD, Stanford U., 1970, PhDEE, 1972. With Nat. Heart, Lung, and Blood Inst., USPHS, Balt., 1973-75; intern, then resident and fellow dept. cardiovasc. surgery Sch. Medicine Stanford (Calif.) U., 1970-73, tng. med. fellow cardiovasc. surgery, resident diag. radiol., 1975-77, from assoc. prof. to prof. dept. radiology, dir. rsch. labs., 1977-82; prof. Stanford (Calif.) U., 1982-84; founder, pres., CEO Resonex, Inc., 1984-87, chmn. bd. dirs., 1987-89; radiologist-in-chief Johns Hopkins Hosp., Balt., 1987-94; prof. radiology, provost U. Minn. Acad. Health Ctr., 1994-96, spl. asst. to pres., 1996; mem. staff depts. elec., computer engring., biomed. engring. Sch. Medicine Johns Hopkins U., Balt., 1987-94, Martin Donner prof., dir. dept. radiology, 1987-94; pres. Johns Hopkins U., Balt., 1996—. Contbr. articles to profl. publs.; patentee in field. Fellow coun. on cardiovasc. radiology Am. Heart Assn.; mem. internat. adv. bd. Inst. Sys. Sci., Nat. U. Singapore, 1994-97; mem. internat. acad. adv. panel, 1997; mem. sci. adv. com. Whitaker Found., 1992-97, governing com. Whitaker Found., 1997—; bd. dirs. Greater Balt. Com., 1997; trustee Goldseker Found., 1996, Balt. Mus. Art, 1997. Recipient Established Investigator award Am. Heart Assn., 1980-84. Fellow IEEE, NAS (Inst. Medicine), Am. Coll. Radiology, Am. Coll. Cardiology, Am. Inst. Med. and Biomed. Engring. (founding). Office: Johns Hopkins Univ 242 Garland Hall 3400 N Charles St Baltimore MD 21218-2680*

BROECKER, WALLACE S., geophysics educator; b. Chicago, IL, Nov. 29, 1931. Attended Wheaton Coll., Wheaton, IL; A.B., Columbia, N.Y.C., 1953, Ph.D., 1958. Asst. prof. Columbia U., N.Y.C., 1959-61, Assoc. prof., 1961-64, prof., 1964—, Newberry prof. of earth and environ. scis., 1977—. Author 6 books, articles in scholarly jours. Recipient Arthur L. Day Medal, Geol. Soc. Am., 1984, Harold Urey Award, European Geochemical Soc., 1986, Vetlesen Prize, Columbia U., 1987, Goldschmidt award, 1986, Priestley award Dickinson Coll., 1990, Roger Revelle medal Am. Geophysical Union, 1995, Nat. Med. Sci., 1996, blue planet prize Asahi Glass Found., Tokyo, 1996, Vetlesen award G. Unger Vetlesen Found., 1987, Alexander Agassiz medal NAS, 1986. Mem. Am. Acad. Arts Scis., Nat. Acad. Scis. (Agassiz Medal, 1986), Geochem. Soc.; fellow European Geophys. Union (Urey medal 1986), Am. Geophys. Union (Ewing Medal, 1979, Roger Revelle Medal, 1995), Geol. Soc. London (Wollaston medal 1990), Geol. Soc. Am. (Arthur L. Day medal 1984). Office: Columbia U Lamont-Doherty Earth Obs PO Box 1000 61 Rt 9W Palisades NY 10964-8000*

BROEDLING, LAURIE ADELE, human resources consultant, psychologist, educator; b. Plainfield, N.J., Aug. 1, 1945; d. Dana Adams and Olga (Goerke) Griffin; m. Timothy John Broedling, Sept. 9, 1967; children: Abigail, Emily. BA, Brown U., 1967; MA, George Washington U., 1969, PhD, 1973. Grad. teaching fellow George Washington U., Washington, 1967, prof., 1992—; social svc. worker Kern County Welfare Dept., Bakersfield, Calif., 1968-69; rsch. psychologist Naval Pers. R&D Lab., Washington, 1970-73; rsch. psychologist Naval Pers. R&D Lab., San Diego, 1973-74, supervisory pers. rsch. psychologist, 1975-84, head div., 1985-87, dir. dept., 1988-89; dep. undersec. def. Office Sec. Def., Washington, 1990-92; prof. San Diego State U., 1975-77; assoc. adminstr. for continual improvement Nat. Aeronautics and Space Adminstrn., Washington, 1992-95; sr. v.p. human resources and quality McDonnell Douglas Corp., 1995-97; v.p. people, sys. and employee involvement Boeing Co., 1997; pres.orgnl. cons. LB Orgnl. Consulting, 1998—. Editor: Perspective on Attitude Assessment, 1976, Military Productivity and Work Motivation, 1978; contbr. numerous articles to profl. jours. Recipient Rev. award Air U., 1977. Mem. Acad. Mgmt., Am. Soc. Quality, Deming Users Group San Diego (pres. 1985-86), Coun. for Excellence in Govt.

BROEG, BOB (ROBERT WILLIAM BROEG), writer; b. St. Louis, Mar. 18, 1918; s. Robert Michael and Alice (Wiley) B.; m. Dorothy Carr, June 19, 1943 (dec.); m. Lynette A. Emmenegger, July 23, 1977. BJ, U. Mo., 1941. With A.P., Columbia, Mo., 1939-40, Jefferson City, Mo., 1941, Boston, 1941-42; reporter St. Louis Star-Times, 1942; staff sports dept. St. Louis Post-Dispatch, 1945-85, sports editor, 1958-85, asst. to pub., 1977-85. Author: Don't Bring That Up, 1946, Stan Musial: The Man's Own Story, 1964, Super Stars of Baseball, 1971, Ol' Missou, a Story of Missouri Football, 1974, We Saw Stars, 1976, The Man Stan...Musial, Now and Then, 1977, Football Greats, 1977, The Pilot Light and the Gas House Gang, 1980, Bob Broeg's Redbirds, 1981, My Baseball Scrapbook, 1983, Baseball From a Different Angle, 1988, Baseball's Barnum, 1989, Ol' Mizzou, A Century of Tiger Football, 1990, Bob Broeg's Redbirds, A Century of Cardinals Baseball, 1992, Super Stars of Baseball No. 2, 1993, Autobiography, Bob Broeg, Memories of Hall of Fame Sportswriter, 1995; co-author: That's a Winner, Jack Buck Autobiography, 1997; co-author, St. Louis Cardinals' Encyclopedia, 1998, contbr. articles. Bd. dirs. Vets. com. Baseball Hall of Fame, 1972—, bd. dirs. 1975; bd. dirs. Honors Ct., Nat. Football Found., 1975. Served with USMCR, 1942-45. Recipient Nat. Sportscasters, Sportswriters awards Mo., 1962-65, 67; Journalism medal U. Mo., 1971; Faculty-Alumni award U. Mo., 1969, Hall of Fame Writing award, 1980; elected to Mo. Sports Hall of Fame, 1978, Nat. Sportscasters/Sportswriters Hall of Fame, 1997, Nat. Baseball Congress Hall of Fame, 1998. Mem. Baseball Writers Assn. Am. (pres. 1958), Kappa Tau Alpha, Sigma Delta Chi, Sigma Phi Epsilon, Omicron Delta Kappa. Home: 60 Frontenac Estates Dr Saint Louis MO 63131-2602 Office: Pulitzer Pub Co 900 N Tucker Saint Louis MO 63101 *As a newspaperman, I seek as an epitaph only: "He was fair." Hopefully "fair" as in "just," not as in "mediocre".*

BROENING, WALTER STEPHENS, JR., journalist, history educator; b. Balt., Aug. 15, 1935; s. Walter Stephens and Evelyne (Powers) B.; m. Christine Zucker, Feb. 3, 1962; children: Alexander (dec.), John, Benjamin, Thomas. BA in Polit. Sci., Johns Hopkins U., 1959. Reporter AP, Balt., 1963-65; corr. AP, Paris, 1965-70, Moscow, 1970-74, Lisbon, Portugal, 1974-76; asst. city editor Balt. Sun, 1976-77, op-ed page editor, 1977-85, diplomatic corr., 1985-90; news editor Internat. Herald-Tribune, Paris, 1990-96; vis. scholar in history Johns Hopkins U., Balt., 1996—. With U.S. Army, 1954-56. Mem. Johns Hopkins Club. Home: 5701 Greenleaf Rd Baltimore MD 21210-1319 Office: Johns Hopkins U Dept History 3400 N Charles St Baltimore MD 21218-2608

BROERS, SIR ALEC NIGEL, engineering educator; b. Calcutta, India, Sept. 17, 1938; s. Alec William and Constance Amy (Cox) B.; m. Mary Therese Phelan, Dec. 27, 1965; children: Mark, Christopher. BSc, Melbourne U., 1958, 59; BA in Mech. Scis., Cambridge U., 1962, PhD in Elec. Engring., 1965, ScD, 1990; DEng (hon.), Glasgow U., 1996; DSc (hon.), Warwick U., 1997. Mem. rsch. staff IBM Thomas J. Watson Rsch. Ctr., Yorktown Heights, N.Y., 1965-81, mgr. electron beam tech., 1967-72, mgr. photo and electron optics, 1972-81; mgr. advanced tech. IBM East Fishkill Devel. Lab., Hopewell Junction, N.Y., 1981-84; mem. corp. tech. com. IBM Hdqrs., Armonk, N.Y., 1984; prof. elec. engring., head elec. div. dept. engring. Cambridge U., 1984-92, head dept. engring., 1992-96, vice chancellor, 1996—; mem. rsch. staff IBM Thomas J. Watson Rsch. Ctr., Yorktown Heights, N.Y., 1965-81; fellow Trinity Coll., Cambridge, 1985-90; master Churchill Coll., Cambridge, 1990-96; mem. Royal Acad. of Engring. Coun., 1994-96, Engring. and Phys. Scis. Coun. U.K., 1992—; non-exec. dir. gen. bd. Lucas Industries, 1995-96; non-exec. dir. Vodafone Group; mem. Coun. for Sci. and Tech. Contbr. numerous articles to profl. jours., chpts. to books; patentee in field. Recipient Am. Inst. of Physics prize for indsl. applications of physics, 1982, Cledo Brunetti award IEEE, 1985; hon. fellow Gonville and C. Coll., Trinity Coll. Fellow Instn. Elec. Engrs. (hon.), Inst. of Physics, Royal Acad. Engring. (coun. 1992-96), Royal Soc.; mem. U.S. Nat. Acad. Engring. (fgn. assoc.). Avocations: music, small-boat sailing, skiing, tennis. Home: Vice-Chancellor's Lodge, 5 Latham Rd, Cambridge CB2 2EG, England also: 32 Mount Hope Ave Jamestown RI 02835-1466 Office: The Old Schools, Trinity Ln, Cambridge CB2 1TN, England

BROFFITT, JAMES DRAKE, professor statistics and actuarial science; b. Indpls., Apr. 8, 1941; s. Wilgus Stanley and Virginia Elizabeth (Drake) B.; m. Barbara Helen Alford, Dec. 20, 1975; children: Daniel James, Virginia Lea. BA in Mathematics, DePauw U., 1963; MS in Statistics, Colo. State U., 1965, PhD in Statistics, 1969. Statis. analyst Computer Technology, Inc., Dallas, 1969-70; asst. prof. stats. and actuarial sci. U. Iowa, Iowa City, 1970-75, assoc. prof., 1975-85, 86-88, prof., 1988—, chmn. stats. and actuarial sci., 1993—; vis. prof. U. Western Ontario, Can., 1985-86; cons. Soc. Actuaries Part 2 Actuarial Exam, Am. Coll. Testing, 1984-85, Iowa Med. Svcs., 1988. Conducted presentations in field at various univs. and confs. in the U.S. and Can.; Contbr. numerous articles to profl. jours. Mem. Am. Statistical Assn., Inst. Mathematical Statistics, Internat. Actuarial Assn., Soc. of Acutaries (assoc. mem. 1980, academic cons. to com. which constructs compound interest examination 1993-95), Sigma Xi, Phi Kappa Phi. Baptist. Home: 3029 E Court St Iowa City IA 52245-4907

BROFSKY, HOWARD, musician, music educator; b. N.Y.C., May 2, 1927; s. Barney L. and Frances (Reich) B.; m. Robin Westen; children: Alexander, Natasha, Gabriel. PhD, NYU, N.Y.C., 1963. Asst. prof. U. Chgo., Chicago, IL, 60-67; prof. Queens Coll., CUNY, N.Y.C., 1967-92, prof. emeritus, 1992—; prof. U. B.C., Vancouver, Can., summers 1974, 75, Boston U., summer 1978, U. Oslo, Norway, fall 1993; spl. editor music Harper & Row, Pubs., N.Y.C., 1969-71. Co-author: (with J. Bamberger) The Art of Listening, 5th edit., 1988; contbr. articles to profl. jours.; several jazz recs. Pres. Vt. Jazz Ctr., 1998—. Mem. Am. Musicol. Soc., Internat. Musicol. Soc., Internat. Assn. Jazz Educators. Home: 684 Bonnyvale Rd Brattleboro VT 05301-2573

BROG, DAVID, consultant, former air force officer; b. Manchester, Conn., Aug. 11, 1933; s. Israel and Pesha (Blonstein) B.; m. Verda Anna Raney, Nov. 9, 1959; children: Kai Ling, Tov Binyamin. BA, U. Pitts., 1955; MS, U. So. Calif., 1967. Commd. 2d lt. USAF, 1956, advanced through grades to col., 1978; dir. readiness and electronic combat, Hdqrs. USAF, Europe, from 1981; dep. chief staff ops. for command control and communications countermeasures USAF, until 1982, ret., 1982; pres. IRD, Inc. (internat. R & D), domestic and internat. cons. on def. issues, Silver Spring, Md., 1982—. Contbr. articles to profl. jours. Decorated D.F.C., Legion of Merit, Air medal with 12 oak leaf clusters; named Disting. Grad. USAF Air War Coll. Mem. Red River Valley Fighter Pilots Assn., Assn. Old Crows, Air Force Assn. Jewish. Home: 9200 Three Oaks Dr Silver Spring MD 20901-3362 Office: PO Box 877 Silver Spring MD 20918-0877*

BROGAN, FRANK T., lieutenant governor. BA magna cum laude, U. Cin.; M in Ednl. Leadership, Fla. Atlantic U. m. Mary Brogan. Supt. schs. Martin County Sch. Dist., Fla., 1988-94; commr. edn. Fla. Dept. Edn., Tallahassee, 1994-99; lt. gov. State of Fla., Tallahassee, 1999—; former tchr., dean of students, asst. prin., prin. Martin County Sch. Dist.; chair task force Fla. Classrooms First; mem. development team Tech Prep program. Named Supt. of yr., Fla. Legislature, 1992. Republican. *

BROGAN-WERNTZ, BONNIE BAILEY, retired police officer, photographer; b. Pine Grove Mills, Pa., Mar. 28, 1941; d. Gilbert Chester and Rosalie Evelyn (Reed) Bailey; m. Donald M. Brogan, Aug. 12, 1960 (div. Oct. 1971); children: Donna Lynn Gregory, Rodney Marshall Brogan; m. Robert R. Werntz, Aug. 28, 1982 (dec. June 7, 1992). A in Criminal Justice, Ind. U., 1976, BS, 1981. Cert. instr. law enforcement tng., Ind. Stenographer South Bend (Ind.) Police Dept., 1970-73, police officer, 1973—, cpl. accident investigation, 1975-80, detective sgt., investigator sex crimes, 1980-85, lt., 1985-97, field tng. officer adminstr., shift comdr., 1985-88, dir. tng., 1988-92, investigative supr., 1992-96, juvenile supr. sex crimes, chld abuse supr., 1996-97; self-employed Golden Age Images Photography, South Bend, 1997—; bd. dirs. Women's Com. on Sex Offenses, South Bend; vol., trainer rape crisis Sex Offense Svcs., South Bend, 1980-87; recorder, treas. Child Sexual Abuse Consortium, South Bend, 1982-85; mem. Giarretto Task Force/Family and Children Ctr., Mishawaka, Inc., 1985. Iniator ordinance St. Joseph County Funds for Examinations and Victims of Sex Crimes, 1983. Bd. dirs. Parents Anonymous, South Bend, 1982, Women's Shelter for Battered Women, South Bend, 1985, South Bend Credit Union Supervisory Commn., 1983; mem. Children and Adolescent Adv. Council, South Bend, 1984. Recipient Joseph J. Newman award Protective Bd./Council for Retarded St. Joseph County, 1982, Child Abuse Investigator award The Breakfast Exchange Club, 1982, award for Exceptional Quality in Investigative Child Abuse/Neglect, Child Protective Services of St. Joseph County Dept. Pub. Welfare, 1983, Outstanding Service award Women's Com. on Sex Offenses, 1983, Outstanding Officer of Yr. award, St. Joseph County Council of Clubs, 1985, Police Officer of Yr. award, Ind. Council Fraternal Vets. and Social Scis., 1985, Outstanding Achievement award YWCA Tribute to Women, 1986. Mem. Internat. Assn. of Women Police (Hon. Mention Officer of Yr. 1985), Fraternal Order of Police. Democrat. Avocations: camping, photography. Home and Office: Golden Age Images Photography 5776-51 Grape Rd #258 Mishawaka IN 46545-8460 Mailing: 5776-51 Grape Rd #258 Mishawaka IN 46545

BROGDON, BYRON GILLIAM, physician, radiology educator; b. Fort Smith, Ark., Jan. 22, 1929; s. Paul Preston and Lela Florence (Gilliam) B.; m. Barbara Walkow Schreiber, June 23, 1978; 1 child, David Pope; stepchildren: William and Diane Schreiber. BS, U. Ark., 1951, BS in Medicine, 1951, MD, 1952. Intern Univ. Hosp., Little Rock, 1952-53, resident, 1953-55; resident in radiology N.C. Bapt. Hosp., Winston-Salem, 1955-56; asst. prof. radiology U. Fla., 1960-63; assoc. prof. radiology and radiol. scis., radiologist-in-charge diagnostic radiology div. Johns Hopkins U. and Hosp., 1963-67; prof., chmn. dept. radiology U. N.Mex., 1967-77; prof. radiology U. South Ala., Mobile, 1978-89, chmn. dept., 1985-92, univ. disting. prof. of radiology, 1989-96, emeritus univ. disting. prof., 1996—, asst. dean continuing med. edn., 1981-88; sabbatical leave Univ. Coll., Galway, Ireland, 1988. Author: Opinions, Comments and Reflections on Radiology, 1983, Forensic Radiology, 1998; contbr. articles to med. jours. Maj. USAF, 1953-60. Recipient Disting. Alumnus award U. Ark., 1978, Ark. Travelers Commn. award Gov. of Ark., 1985, Disting. Achievement award Wake Forest U. Med. Alumni Assn., 1990, medal from city of Brescia, Italy, 1991, Joint Resolution of Commendation for outstanding profl. achievement Ala. Legis., 1994. Fellow Am. Coll. Radiology (pres. 1978-79, gold medal 1987), Am. Acad. Forensic Scis. (John B. Hunt award 1995); mem. AMA (ho. of dels. 1988-95, Physician-Spkr. award 1979), Am. Roentgen Ray Soc. (life, exec. coun. 1974-75, 77-80, 84-90, 2d v.p. 1979-80, gold medal 1996), So. Radiol. Conf. (life hon., pres. 1967-68, sec. 1984-86, Eskridge lectr. 1994), Radiol. Soc. N.Am., Am. Assn. Acad. Chief Residents in Radiology (faculty advisor 1979—, nat. sponsor 1983-93, Malcolm Jones orator 1996), Soc. Pediat. Radiology, Assn. Univ. Radiologists (pres. 1973-74, gold medal 1985), Soc. Chmn. Acad. Radiol. Depts. (sec.-treas. 1969-70), Swiss Soc. Med. Radiology (hon., coord. internat. diagnostic course in Davos 1984-96, Schinz medal 1992, Medal of Honor Leopold-Franzens U., Innsbruck Austria 1997), Internat. Skeletal Soc., Country Club Mobile, Sigma Xi, Alpha Omega Alpha, Sigma Chi (Significant Sig 1999). Office: U South Ala Med Ctr Dept Radiology 2451 Fillingim St Mobile AL 36617-2238 *For the physician-scientist-educator, the mere transference of knowledge or the acquisition of new data is not enough. He must participate fully in the affairs of the larger community and has a duty to help others to think about, or form an opinion on, issues they otherwise might not have considered.*

BROGGINI, CAROLYN, orthopedics and neuroscience nurse; b. Barre, Vt., Apr. 10, 1957; d. Leslie John and Cassie (Tucker) MacLeod; m. Martin James Broggini, Feb. 20, 1982; children: Anthony James, John Mathew. AS, Vt. Coll., 1978. Nurses aide Cen. Vt. Hosp., Berlin, Vt., 1974-79, grad. nurse, 1979-80; staff nurse St. Vincent's Med. Ctr., Jacksonville, Fla., 1980—; staff nurse RN III Fletcher Allen Health Care Med. Ctr. Hosp. Campus, Burlington. Recipient Nursing Excellence award, 1990.

BROGLIATTI, BARBARA SPENCER, television and motion picture executive; b. L.A., Jan. 8, 1946; d. Robert and Lottie Spencer; m. Raymond Haley Brogliatti, Sept. 19, 1970. BA in Social Scis. and English, UCLA, 1968. Asst. press. info. dept. CBS TV, L.A., 1968-69, sr. publicist, 1969-74; dir. publicity Tandem Prodns. and T.A.T. Comm. (Embassy Comm.), L.A., 1974-77, corp. v.p., 1977-82; sr. v.p. worldwide publicity, promotion and advt. Embassy Comm., L.A., 1982-85; sr. v.p. worldwide corp. comm. Lorimar Telepictures Corp., Culver City, Calif., 1985-89; pres., chmn. Brogliatti Co., Burbank, Calif., 1989-90; sr. v.p. worldwide TV publicity, promotion and advt. Lorimar TV, 1991-92; sr. v.p. worldwide TV publicity, promotion and pub. rels. Warner Bros., Burbank, 1992-97; sr. v.p. corp. comm. Warner Bros., Inc., 1997—. Mem. bd. govs. TV Acad., L.A., 1984-86; bd. dirs. KIDSNET, Washington, 1987—, Nat. Acad. Cable Programming, 1992-94; mem. Hollywood Women's Polit. Com., 1992-93; mem. steering com. L.A. Free Clinic, 1997-98. Recipient Gold medallion Broadcast Promotion and Mktg. Execs., 1984. Mem. Am. Diabetes Assn. (bd. dirs. L.A. chpt. 1992-93), Am. Cinema Found. (bd. dirs. 1994-98), Dirs. Guild Am., Publicists Guild, Acad. TV Arts and Scis. (vice chmn. awards com.). Office: Warner Bros Studios 4000 Warner Blvd Burbank CA 91522-0002

BROHAMMER, RICHARD FREDERIC, psychiatrist; b. Rockford, Ill., Nov. 9, 1934; s. Joseph C. and Marthe Marie (Ringuette) B.; m. Shirley Ruth Noble, June 22, 1956; children: Richard Frederic II, Renee Marie, Rory Christopher. PhB, U. Detroit, 1960; MD, U. Fla., 1964; postgrad. basic tng. diving medicine, Internat. Underwater Explorers Soc., 1973, advanced tng. diving medicine, 1974. Diplomate Am. Bd. Psychiatry and Neurology, Am. Bd. Forensic Medicine. Rsch. fellow tropical medicine La. State U., Costa Rica, 1963, Ctrl. Am., 1968; intern Duval Med. Ctr., Jacksonville, Fla., 1964-65; resident psychiatry U. Fla., 1965-68; practice medicine specializing in psychiatry, Ft. Lauderdale, Fla., 1968-97; mem. staff Broward Gen. Med. Ctr., 1968—, Imperial Point Med. Ctr., 1974—, Holy Cross Hosp., 1968—; chmn. dept. psychiatry Imperial Point Hosp., 1975-80, Holy Cross Hosp., 1981-83. Served with USAF, 1954-58, Korea. Mem. AMA (pres. student chpt. 1961-64), Broward County (Fla.) Med. Assn., Broward County Psychiat. Soc., Undersea Adventurers, Internat. Soc. Diving Medicine. Republican. Roman Catholic.

BROHN, WILLIAM DAVID, conductor, orchestrator; b. Flint, Mich.. BA in Music, Mich. State U., 1955; MMus, New Eng. Conservatory Music. played with local ensembles and performed on double bass Boston Pops orch.; played string bass and piano with numerous mus. orgns. incl. classical, theatrical and jazz groups; condr. nat. tours Robert Joffrey Ballet, Royal Ballet; commd. to adapt and arrange program pice for ann. Christmas concer Cleve. Orch., 1961; recreated sound track for 1938 Russian classic film Alexander Nevsky, 1987; vis. lectr. Oxford U., Eng. Scores orchestrated include Miss Saigon, The Secret Garden, Crazy for You, Carousel, Show Boat; ballet orchestrations include those for Agnes de Mille, Twyla Tharp, Lar Lubovich, Am. Ballet Theatre; scores for the big screen include: Blue Thunder, Endless Love, War Games, Whose Life is it Anyway?; recordings for artists include James Galway (RCA CD Wind Beneath My Wings), Placido Domingo (Atlantic CD The Broadway I Love), Jerry Hadley (BMG CD Golden Days), Marilyn Horne (RCA CD The Men in My Life); recreated sound track for Russian Classic, Alexander Nevsky, MSU hosted first university presentation, April 30, 1995, Great Hall, Wharton Ctr., current projects include the West End revival of Lionel Barts "Oliver!". Winner 1998 Tony Award for orchestrations for Raytime, N.Y. Drama Desk awards (2) for Miss Saigon and The Secret Garden. Office: c/o American Guild of Musical Artists 1727 Broadway New York NY 10019-5284*

BROIDE, MACE IRWIN, public affairs consultant; b. Burlington, Vt., May 21, 1924; s. Abraham A. and Ida (Rosenberg) B.; m. Gloria Leah Goldsholl, Dec. 24, 1943; children: Cheryl Ruth Broide Light, Beverly Elaine Broide Frye, Sandra Pat Broide Banas. A.B. (Ernie Pyle scholar 1946), Ind. U., 1947. Polit. editor Evansville (Ind.) Press, 1947-58; senatorial adminstrv. asst., 1959-68; co-owner DeHart and Broide, Inc.; public affairs cons. Washington, 1968-78; exec. dir. com. on budget U.S. Ho. of Reps., 1978-86; pub. affairs cons., 1986—; adj. prof. George Washington U., 1986, 87; lectr. in field. Co-author: Inside the New Frontier, 1963; contbr. articles to newspapers, mags. Sec. Nat. Dem. Senatorial Campaign Com., 1961-62; past bd. dirs. Jewish Community Coun. Evansville; past bd. govs. Nat. Dem. Club. With AUS, 1943-46. Decorated Silver Star, Bronze Star. Mem. Assn. Adminstrv. Assts. U.S. Senate (past pres.), B'nai B'rith (past pres.). Home: 4450 S Park Ave Apt 1111 Chevy Chase MD 20815-3641

BROIDO, ARNOLD PEACE, music publishing company executive; b. N.Y.C., Apr. 8, 1920; s. Samuel S. and Ruth (Lewis) B.; m. Lucille Janet Tarshes, Mar. 5, 1944; children: Jeffrey, Laurence, Thomas. BS magna cum laude, Ithaca Coll., 1941; MA, Columbia U., 1954; DMus (hon.), Ithaca Coll., 1990. Tchr. instrumental music East Jr. High Sch., Binghamton, N.Y., 1941-42; editor, prodn. mgr. Boosey & Hawkes Inc. (music pub.), 1945-55; v.p., gen. mgr. Century Music & Mercury Music Corp., 1955-57; edn. dir. Edward B. Marks Music Corp., 1957-62; dir. publs. and sales Frank Music Corp., 1962-69; v.p. Boston Music Co., 1968-69; pres. Theodore Presser Co., 1969-95, chmn., 1995; also dir.; chmn. Elkan-Vogel Inc., 1970—; pres. Music Industry Coun., 1966-68, v.p., 1969-70; sec. Harry Fox Agy., 1989—. Co-author: Music Dictionary, 1956, Invitation to the Piano, 1959; Asso. editor: Univ. Soc. Ency. of Piano Music; Contbr. articles to profl. jours. Mem. Nassau County (N.Y.) Dem. Com., 1952-63; bd. dirs. N.Y. Citizens Com. for Pub. Schs., 1963-68, Am. Music Ctr., 1968-72, 78-83, 85-91, Am. Music Conf., 1979-80, Nat. Music Coun., 1979-85, 93—, Music Educators Nat. Conf., 1966-68; trustee ASCAP Found., 1976—, treas., 1990—; trustee Union Free Sch. Dist. 21 Bd. Edn., Rockville Centre, N.Y., 1963-69, sec., dist. clk., 1966-67, v.p., dist. clk., 1967-69. With USCGR, 1942-45. Mem. ASCAP (bd. dirs. 1972—, bd. rev. 1980-82, asst. treas. 1989-90, treas. 1990—), Music Pubs. Assn. U.S. (pres. 1972-74, 80-82, bd. dirs. 1980-82, 83-92, 96—), Nat. Music Pubs. Assn. (bd. dirs. 1980—, sec. 1989—), Internat. Pubs. Assn. (v.p. sect. music 1972-73), Internat. Confedn. Music Pubs. (v.p.

1978-88, bd. dirs. 1992—, pres. 1993-94, 96—, chmn. 1994-96, pres. 1996-98, chmn. 1998—), Internat. Fedn. Serious Music Pubs. (v.p. 1978-93, pres. 1993—), Music Industry Mfrs. Assn. (dir. 1980-82), Charles Ives Soc. (bd. dirs. 1985—), Phi Mu Alpha Sinfonia. Home: 908 Wootton Rd Bryn Mawr PA 19010-2228 Office: 1 Presser Pl Bryn Mawr PA 19010-3416

BROILI, ROBERT HOWARD, lawyer; b. Reno, Sept. 2, 1942; s. Julius and Verna June (Bradbury) B.; m. Sally Sue M. Atkinson, Jan. 24, 1965; children: Eric Anthony, Susan Heather. AA, Menlo Coll., 1962; BA, U. Nev., 1964; JD, Nev. Sch. Law, 1986. Bar: Nev. 1989, U.S. Dist. Ct. (no. dist.) Nev., 1991. Sales rep. Nev. Machinery & Electric, Reno, 1964-70, ptnr., gen. mgr., 1970-83; paralegal Washoe Legal Svcs., Reno, 1984-86; legal asst. White Law Chartered, Reno, 1986-89; law clk. Douglas County Dist. Ct., Minden, Nev., 1989; chief prosecutor Lander County Office of the Dist. Atty., Battle Mountain, Nev., 1989-91; prin. Robert Broili Law Offices, Reno, 1991—. Mem. State Bar Assn. Nev. (atty. discipline com. 1993-96, fee dispute com. 1991-95), Masons, Lions. Avocations: fishing, hunting, shooting, skiing, biking. Office: 335 W 1st St Reno NV 89503-5301

BROKAW, CLIFFORD VAIL, III, investment banker, business executive; b. N.Y.C., Sept. 17, 1928; s. Clifford Vail and Audrey (Stransom Joel) B.; m. Elizabeth Stokes Rogers, June 29, 1960; children: Clifford Vail, George Rogers. B.A., Yale U., 1950; JD, U. Va., 1956. Bar: N.Y. 1957. Assoc. White & Case, N.Y.C., 1956-59; assoc. Blyth & Co., Inc., N.Y.C., 1959-61; assoc., then gen. ptnr. W.E. Hutton & Co., N.Y.C., 1961-67; gen. ptnr., sr. v.p. Eastman Dillon Union Securities & Co. and successor firm Blyth, Eastman, Dillon & Co., Inc., N.Y.C., 1967-77; chmn., CEO Invail Capital, Inc., N.Y.C., 1977-95; CEO IRT Corp., San Diego, 1977-95, chmn. bd., 1986-94; bd. dirs., chmn. fin. com. Brazos River Gas Co., Mineral Wells, Tex., 1962-91; chmn. bd. Cayman Resources Corp., Tulsa, 1977-88, bd. dirs., 1992-95. Bd. advisors Marine Mil. Acad., Harlingen, Tex., 1985-91; mem. alumni assn. coun. U. Va. Sch. Law, 1976-79; founder Brokaw chair corp. law U. Va. Sch. Law, 1985, mem. dean's coun., 1990—, bus. adv. coun., 1995—; mem. indsl. adv. com. Sch. Engring and Applied Sch. U. Va., 1987-94; vestryman French Ch. du St. Espirit, 1986-88, treas., 1988-92, warden, 1989-93. Lt. col. USMCR, 1950-73. Decorated Purple Heart. Mem. ABA, Suffolk County Bar assn., Pilgrims U.S., Mil. Order Carabao, Mil. Order World Wars (vice comdr. N.Y. chpt.), Mil. Order Fgn. Wars U.S., Nat. Inst. Social Scis. (bd. dirs. 1991-94, pres. 1992-94), Nat. Gavel Soc., Ends of Earth, Huguenot Soc. Am. (coun. 1974-80, v.p. 1986-89, pres. 1989-92), Nat. Gavel Soc., Am. Soc. Order of St. John, U. Va. Lawn Soc., Burning Tree Club, Lyford Cay Club, The Meadow Club, Bathing Corp. of Southampton, Union Club, Masons, Shriners, Yale Club N.Y.C. Republican. Episcopalian. Avocations: tennis; golf; scuba; photography. Office: PO Box 5002 Southampton NY 11969-5002

BROKAW, NORMAN ROBERT, talent agency executive; b. N.Y.C., Apr. 21, 1927; s. Isadore David and Marie (Hyde) B.; children—David M., Sanford Jay, Joel S., Barbara M., Wendy E., Lauren Quincy. Student pvt. schs., Los Angeles. With William Morris Agy., Inc., Beverly Hills, Calif., 1943—, sr. agt. and co. exec., 1951-74, v.p. world-wide ops., 1974-80, exec. v.p., dir., 1980—, co-chmn. bd., 1986-91, pres., CEO, 1989-91, chmn. bd., CEO, 1991-97, chmn. bd. worldide, 1997—. Pres. Betty Ford Cancer Center, Cedars-Sinai Med. Center, Los Angeles, 1978—; bd. dirs. Cedars-Sinai Med. Center; industry chmn. United Jewish Welfare Fund, 1975. With U.S. Army, World War II. Mem. Acad. Motion Picture Arts and Scis. Clubs: Hillcrest Country (Los Angeles). Clients include former Pres. and Mrs. Gerald R. Ford, Bill Cosby, Gen. Alexander Haig Jr., Tony Randall, Donald Regan, C. Everett Koop, Priscilla Presley, Andy Griffith, Brooke Shields, Juliette Lewis, Marcia Clarke, Christopher Darden. Office: William Morris Agy 151 S El Camino Dr Beverly Hills CA 90212-2775 also: William Morris Agy Inc 1325 Avenue Of The Americas New York NY 10019-6026

BROKAW, THOMAS JOHN, television broadcast executive, correspondent; b. Webster, S.D., Feb. 6, 1940; s. Anthony Orville and Eugenia (Conley) B.; m. Meredith Lynn Auld, Aug. 17, 1962; children—Jennifer Jean, Andrea Brooks, Sarah Auld. BA in Polit. Sci, U. S.D., 1962, hon. degree; hon. degree, Washington U., St. Louis, Syracuse U., Hofstra U., Boston Coll., Emerson Coll., Simpson Coll., Duke U., 1991, Notre Dame U., 1993. Morning news editor Sta. KMTV, Omaha, 1962-65; news editor, anchorman Sta. WSB-TV, Atlanta, 1965-66; reporter, corr., anchorman Sta. KNBC-TV, Los Angeles, 1966-73; White House corr. NBC, Washington, 1973-76; anchorman Sat. Night News, N.Y.C., 1973-76; host Today show, N.Y.C., 1976-82; anchorman, editor NBC Nightly News, 1982—; corr. Exposé NBC, 1991—; corr. NBC coverage U.S. Presdl. elections, 1976, 80, anchor, 1984, 88; mem. adv. com. Reporters Com. for Freedom of Press. Corr. numerous NBC News specials, including To Be A Teacher, 1987, Wall Street: Money Greed and Power, 1987, A Conversation with Mikhail S. Gorbachev (Alfred I. DuPont award), 1987, Home Street Home, 1988, To Be An American (George Foster Peabody award). Trustee Norton Simon Mus. Art, Pasadena, Calif., U. S.D. Found.; adviser Asia Soc. Mem. AFTRA (dir. 1968-72), Sigma Delta Chi. Office: NBC News 30 Rockefeller Plz Fl 2 New York NY 10112-0036*

BROKER, JEFFREY JOHN, accountant; b. Penn, Pa., Aug. 25, 1949; s. John F. and Leonilla G. (Laudadio) B.; m. Linda Pugliano, Sept. 25, 1971; 1 child, Jennifer Nicole. BS in Acctg., Pa. State U., 1971; MBA, U. Pitts., 1984. CPA, Pa. Staff acct. Bernard Haberman, CPA, Monroeville, Pa., 1971-75; contr. Mgmt. Problem Solvers, Inc., Monroeville, 1976-81; treas. Your Fathers Mustache Enterprise, Monroeville, 1981-84; pvt. practice Pitts., 1984—. Mem. Pa. Inst. CPAs, Pa. Assn. Notaries, Monroeville C. of C. (treas. 1987-89, Merit award 1989). Democrat. Roman Catholic. Avocation: racquetball, sailing, biking. Office: 7641 Saltsburg Rd Pittsburgh PA 15239-1755

BROLICK, HENRY JOHN, energy company executive; b. Chgo., July 15, 1944; s. Henry Harry and Helen (Andrich) B.; m. Sharon Ann Carlisle, Sept. 23, 1965; children: Kelly, Peter, Jennifer, Heather. BSCE, Mich. State U., 1966, MBA, 1968. Engr. Shell Oil Co., Indpls., 1968-70, project engr., 1970-71; sr. analyst Shell Oil Co., Houston, 1972-73; project engr. Williams Bros. Engring. Co., Tulsa and Houston, 1974-78; engr. mgr. Williams Bros. Engring. Co., Sydney, Australia, 1979-81; v.p. Spectral Entreprises, Holland, Mich., 1981-82; v.p. ops. Tamny Inc., Tulsa, 1983-84; v.p. Williams Techs., Inc., Tulsa, 1984-88, exec. v.p., 1988-97, pres., 1997—; v.p. Black Mesa Pipeline Inc., 1988-92, pres., 1992—; chmn. Coal & Slurry Tech. Assn., Washington, 1989-97; bd. dirs. Williams Techs., Inc., Black Mesa Pipeline, Inc. Bd. dirs. Big Brothers and Sisters, Tulsa, 1992. Mem. Okla. Pvt. Entreprise Forum, Tulsa C. of C. Roman Catholic. Avocations: tennis, golf, water sports. Office: Williams Technologies Inc 320 S Boston Ave Ste 831 Tulsa OK 74103-3728

BROLIN, JAMES (JAMES BRUNDERLIN), actor; b. Los Angeles, July 18, 1940; m. Jan Smithers, 1986; m. Barbra Streisand. Student, UCLA. Regular in TV series The Monroes, 1964-65, Marcus Welby M.D. 1969-76, Hotel, 1983-88, Extreme, 1995—, (also exec. prodr.) Pensacola: Wings of Gold, 1997, Beyond Belief: Fact of Fiction, 1998; host Body Human 2000: Love, Sex and the Miracle of Birth, 1999; TV movie appearances include Marcus Welby M.D, 1969, Short Walk to Daylight, 1972, Class of '63, 1973, Trapped, 1973, Steel Cowboys, 1978, The Ambush Murders, 1982, Mae West, 1982, White Water Rebels, 1983, Cowboy, 1983, Beverly Hills Cowgirl Blues, 1985, Hold the Dream, 1986, Intimate Encounters, 1986, Deep Dark Secrets, 1987, Finish Line, 1989, Voice of the Heart, 1990, Nightmare on the 13th Floor, 1990, And the Sea Will Tell, 1991, Visions of Murder, 1993, Gunsmoke: The Last Ride, 1993, Parallel Lives, 1994, Hijacked: Flight 285, 1996, Marriage of Convenience, 1998; film appearances include Take Her, She's Mine, 1963, Goodbye, Charlie, 1964, Von Ryan's Express, 1965, Morituri, 1965, Our Man Flint, 1966, The Boston Strangler, 1968, Skyjacked, 1972, Westworld, 1973, Gable and Lombard, 1976, The Car, 1977, Capricorn I, 1978, Night of the Juggler, 1978, Amityville Horror, 1978, The Gringos, 1980, Pee Wee's Big Adventure, 1985, Indecent Behavior II, The Expert, 1994, Tracks of a Killer, 1995, Terminal Virus, 1995, Last Chance, 1995, Blood Money, 1996, (also dir.) My Brother's Way, 1997, Haunted Sea, 1997, Goodbye America, 1997. Named Most Promising Actor of 1970 Fame mag., Photoplay mag.; recipient Emmy award. Office: care Met Talent Agy 4526 Wilshire Blvd Los Angeles CA 90010-3801*

BROM, ROBERT H., bishop; b. Arcadia, Wis., Sept. 18, 1938. Ed., St. Mary's Coll., Winona, Minn., Gregorian U., Rome. Ordained priest Roman Catholic Ch., 1963, consecrated bishop, 1983. Bishop of Duluth Minn., 1983-89; coadjutor bishop Diocese of San Diego, 1989-90, bishop, 1990—. Office: Diocese of San Diego Pastoral Ctr PO Box 85728 San Diego CA 92186-5728

BROMBERG, JOHN E., lawyer; b. Dallas, May 9, 1946; s. Edward S. and Mildred J. (Rosenberg) B.; children from previous marriage: Spencer Harkness, Whitney Payne, Kemp Howitt, Campbell Wynne; m. Beth Jenkins; children: Susan Elizabeth, Melissa Anne. B.A., Columbia U., 1968; J.D., U. Tex., 1972. Bar: Tex. 1972. Pres., mem., dir. Stutzman & Bromberg, P.C., Dallas, 1984; bd. dirs. T-Land Corp. and T-Investment Properties Corp. subs. Tchrs. Ins. Annuity Assn. Am. Past pres. Preston Hollow Park Assn., pre-sch. playground, Dallas. Mem. Am. Contract Bridge League (past pres. Dallas unit). Home: 6214 Desco Dr Dallas TX 75225-2101 Office: 2323 Bryan St Ste 2200 Dallas TX 75201-2655*

BROMBERG, MYRON JAMES, lawyer; b. Paterson, N.J., Nov. 5, 1934; s. Abraham and Elsie (Baker) B.; m. Lisa Murtha, Nov. 28, 1987; children—Kenneth Karl, Eric Edward, Bruce Abraham. BA, Yale U., 1956; LLB, Columbia U., 1959. Bar: N.J. bar 1960, N.Y. bar 1981. Law asst. to dist. atty. N.Y. County, 1958; law asst. U.S. atty. So. Dist. N.Y., 1958-59; asso. mem. firm Ralph Porzio, Morristown, N.J., 1960-61; ptnr. Porzio, Bromberg & Newman, Morristown, 1962-77, mng. prin., 1980-96; atty. Morris County Bd. Elections, 1963-64; town atty., Town of Morristown, 1965-67; lectr. trial practice Rutgers Inst. CLE, 1965-94. Chmn. fund and membership Morristown chpt. ARC, 1965; chmn. retail div. Community Chest Morris County, 1963; chmn. Keep Morristown Beautiful Com., 1963; mem. Morris Twp. Com., 1970-72; committeeman Morris County Democratic Com., 1962-63, 72-77; lay trustee Delbarton Sch., Morristown, 1972-75; trustee Morris Mus., 1973-79. Fellow Am. Coll. Trial Lawyers (chmn. com. on admission to fellowship 1986-91, com. on complex litigation 1992-98, com. on tchg. of trial and appellate advocacy 1998—), Am. Law Inst. (cons. group product libility), Am. Bar Found. (life); mem. ABA, Internat. Acad. Trial Lawyers (chair N.J. 1997-99, regional chair 3d jud. cir. 1997—), N.J. Bar Assn. (named outstanding young lawyer 1970, chmn. joint conf. com. with N.J. Med. Soc. 1970-72), Morris County Bar Assn., Am. Judicature Soc., Trial Attys. N.J. (pres. 1976-77, Trial Bar award 1989), Internat. Soc. Barristers (N.J. State chmn., bd. govs., sec.-treas. 1996-97, v.p. 1998—), Internat. Assn. Def. Counsel (chair com. on toxic and hazardous substances 1994-96, dir. Def. Counsel Trial Acad. 1996), Andover Alumni Assn. N.Y.C., Columbia U. Law Sch. Assn. of N.J. (bd. dirs. 1986-95), Yale Club (N.Y.C. and ctrl. N.J.), Park Ave. (N.J.) Club, Merchants Club (N.Y.C.), Chi Phi, Phi Delta Phi. Home: 9 Thompson Ct Morristown NJ 07960-6326 Office: 163 Madison Ave Morristown NJ 07962-1997

BROMBERG, PHILIP ALLAN, internist, educator; b. N.Y.C., Apr. 27, 1930; s. Jacob Abramovitch and Frieda (Kijner) B.; m. Françoise Vergnes, Nov. 28, 1959; children: Jacqueline F., Marc D., David A. BS, Queens Coll., 1949; MD, Harvard U., 1953. Diplomate Am. Bd. Internal Medicine (mem. pulmonary diseases com. 1986-92). Intern in medicine Peter Bent Brigham Hosp., Boston, 1953-54, jr. resident in medicine, 1957-58, rsch. fellow, 1958-59, sr. resident in medicine, 1959-60; rsch. fellow Mt. Sinai Med. Ctr., N.Y.C., 1954-55; from instr. to assoc. prof. U. Pitts. Sch. Medicine, 1960-68; from assoc. prof. to prof. Ohio State U. Coll. Medicine, Columbus, 1968-75; prof. medicine U. N.C. Sch. Medicine, Chapel Hill, 1975—, dir. Ctr. for Environ. Medicine and Lung Biology, 1979—; chmn. rsch. manpower rev. com. Nat. Heart Lung Blood Inst. NIH, Bethesda, Md., 1989-90. Contbr. numerous articles, revs., book chpts. to profl. jours. Capt. M.C., U.S. Army, 1955-57. Queens Coll. scholar 1949; grantee NIH, EPA, others. Fellow ACP; mem. Am. Thoracic Soc. (bd. dirs. 1983-85), Am. Physiol. Soc. (edtl. bd. Physiolic Revs., Jour. Applied Physiology, 1985-89), So. Soc. Clin. Investigation, Phi Beta Kappa, Alpha Omega Alpha. Democrat. Avocation: chamber music performance. Office: U NC Sch Medicine Ctr Environ Medicine & Lung Bio CB 7310 Chapel Hill NC 27599-7310

BROMBERG, ROBERT SHELDON, lawyer; b. Bklyn., May 3, 1935; s. Jack and Bertha (Toskey) B.; m. Barbara W. Schwartz, Apr. 1, 1978; children: Jason, David. AB, Columbia U., 1956, LLB, 1959; LLM in Taxation, NYU, 1966. Bar: N.Y. 1960, D.C. 1972, Ohio 1972, U.S. Ct. Claims 1976, U.S. Supreme Ct 1975. Practiced law N.Y.C., 1960-66; atty. exempt orgns. br. IRS, Washington, 1966-70, Office Chief Counsel, 1970-72; partner firm Baker, Hostetler & Patterson, Cleve., 1972-79; prin. Robert S. Bromberg, L.P.A., Cleve., 1979-81, Paxton & Seasongood, Cin., 1981-85; sole practice Cin., 1985—; lectr. tax and health law confs. Author: Tax Planning for Hospitals and Health Care Organizations, 2 vols., 1979; cons. editor: Prentice Hall Tax Exempt Organizations Service, 1973-84; nat. adv. bd. Integrated Healthcare Report; adv. bd. The Exempt Organization Tax Review; contbr. articles to profl. jours. Recipient award (5) Dept. Treasury, 1966-72, citation Am. Assn. Homes for Aged, 1973. Mem. Am. Health Lawyers Assn. (pres. 1986-87, program chmn. Ann. Tax Inst. 1975-95). Home: 1144 E Rookwood Dr Cincinnati OH 45208-3334 Office: 36 E 4th St Ste 1119 Cincinnati OH 45202-3726

BROMBERG, STEPHEN AARON, lawyer; b. Detroit, Aug. 28, 1930; s. Paul D. and Suzanne (Beerbohm) B.; m. Carol Altman, Sept. 1, 1953; children: David J., Nancy S. Wolfe, Daniel H. BA with distinction, U. Mich., 1952, JD, 1954. Bar: Mich. 1954, U.S. Supreme Ct. 1964. Ptnr. Bromberg, Robinson, Shapero, Cohn & Burgoyne, Southfield, Mich., 1957-85; stockholder, dir. Butzel Long, Birmingham, Mich., 1985—, pres., 1994—; lectr. State Bar Conf., 1984, Inst. Continuing Legal Edn., 1981, 82, 83, 85, 87, 89, 90. Pres. Jewish Vocat. Svc. and Cmty. Workshop, Southfield, Mich., 1983-85; bd. dirs. Detroit Symphony Orch., 1992—. Named Best Lawyers in Am., Woodward/White, Inc., 1992—. Mem. ABA, Am. Judicature Soc., Am. Coll. Real Estate Lawyers, Am. Coll. Mortgage Attys., State Bar Mich., Detroit Bar Assn., Oakland County Bar Assn., Franklin Hills Country Club, Phi Beta Kappa. Avocations: 16th and 17th century cartography maps and atlases. Home: 3287 Bradway Blvd Bloomfield Hills MI 48301-2507 Office: Butzel Long 32270 Telegraph Rd Ste 200 Birmingham MI 48025-2457

BROMBERT, VICTOR HENRI, literature educator, author; b. France, Nov. 11, 1923; came to U.S., 1941, naturalized, 1943; s. Jacques and Vera B.; m. Beth Anne Archer, June 18, 1950; children: Lauren Nora, Marc Alexis. BA, Yale U., 1948, MA, 1949, PhD, 1953; postgrad., U. Rome, 1950-51; HHD (hon.), U. Chgo., 1981, U. Toronto, 1997. Faculty Yale U., New Haven, 1951-75; from assoc. prof. to prof. Yale U., 1958-75, Benjamin F. Barge prof. Romance lits., 1969-75, chmn. dept. Romance langs. and lit., 1964-73; Henry Putnam univ. prof. romance and comparative lit. Princeton (N.J.) U., 1975—, dir. Christian Gauss seminars in criticism, 1984-94, chmn. Coun. Humanities, 1989-94; summer prof. Middlebury Coll., 1951-53, Institut d'Etudes Françaises, Avignon, 1962, 64, 73, U. Colo., 1965; Christian Gauss Seminar in criticism Princeton U., 1964; vis. prof. Scuola Normale Superiore, Pisa, Italy, 1972, U. Calif., 1978, Johns Hopkins U., 1979, Columbia U., 1980, NYU, 1980, 81, U. P.R., 1983, 84, U. Bologna, Italy, 1984, Yale U., 1985; Phi Beta Kappa vis. scholar, 1986-87, 89-90; lectr. Alliance Française, humanities U. Kans., 1966; lectr. Collège de France, 1991; mem. Fulbright screening com., 1965; dir. fellowships in residence NEH, Princeton U., 1975-76, dir. summer seminar, 1979, 82, 84, 86, 88; mem. adv. com. for humanities Libr. of Congress, 1976; mem. Yale U. Coun., 1977-83; mem. ednl. adv. bd. Guggenheim Found., 1982—. Author: The Criticism of T.S. Eliot, 1949, Stendhal et la Voie Oblique, 1954, The Intellectual Hero, 1961, The Novels of Flaubert, 1966, Stendhal: Fiction and the Themes of Freedom, 1968, Flaubert par lui-même, 1971, La Prison romantique, 1976, The Romantic Prison: The French Tradition, 1978, Victor Hugo and the Visionary Novel, 1984, The Hidden Reader, 1988, In Praise of Antiheroes, 1999; editor: Stendhal: A Collection of Critical Essays, 1962, Balzac's La Peau de Chagrin, 1962, The Hero in Literature, 1969, Flaubert's Madame Bovary, 1986; co-author: The World of Lawrence Durrell, 1962, Ideas in the Drama, 1964, Malraux, 1964, Instants Premiers, 1973, Romanticism, 1973, Literary Criticism, 1974, Die Romanische Novelle, 1977, The Author in His Work, 1978, Essais sur Flaubert, 1979, Writers and Politics, 1983, Flaubert and Postmodernism, 1984, Writing in a Modern Temper, 1984, Literary Theory and Criticism, 1984, Hugo le Fabuleux, 1985, 19th Century Literary Criticism, 1985, Charles Baudelaire, 1987, Albert Camus, 1989, André Malraux, 1989, Gustave Flaubert, 1989, Dilemmes du Roman, 1989, Nineteenth Century French Poetry, 1990, Literature, Culture and Society in the Modern Age, 1991, Literary Generations, 1992, Dix Etudes sur Baudelaire, 1993, George Sand et son temps, 1994, Pratiques d'écriture, 1996Stendhal et le comique, 1999; contbr. articles to profl. jours. Served with M.I. AUS, 1943-45. Decorated officer Ordre des Palmes Academiques; recipient Harry Levin prize in comparative lit., 1978, Howard T. Behrman award for disting. achievement in humanities, 1979, Wilbur Lucius Cross medal for outstanding achievement Yale U., 1985, Medaille Vermeil de la Ville de Paris, 1985; Am. Coun. Learned Socs. grantee, 1966; Fulbright fellow, 1950-51, Guggenheim fellow, 1954-55, 70, NEH sr. fellow, 1973-74, Rockefeller Found. resident fellow, Bellagio, Italy, 1975, 90. Fellow Am. Acad. Arts and Scis.; mem. MLA (edtl. adv. comm. 1979-83, pres. 1989), Am. Assn. Tchrs. French, Am. Comparative Lit. Assn., Am. Philos. Soc., Soc. des Etudes Françaises, Soc. des Etudes Romantiques, Acad. Lit. Studies (pres. 1983), Soc. d'Histoire Littéraire de la France, Soc. U. per gli Studi di Lingua e Letteratura Francese, Inst. Romance Studies, Elizabethan Club (pres. 1968-70), Yale Club, Phi Beta Kappa. Home: 187 Library Pl Princeton NJ 08540-3072 Office: Princeton U 245 E Pyne Princeton NJ 08544

BROME, THOMAS REED, lawyer; b. N.Y.C., Aug. 24, 1942; s. Robert Harrison and Mary Elizabeth (Reed) B.; m. Marie Olszewski, June 5, 1971; children: Clinton Reed, Bethan, Heather. AB, Harvard Coll., 1964; LLB, NYU, 1967. Bar: D.C. 1967, N.Y. 1968. Law clk. to hon. Warren E. Burger U.S. Ct. Appeals, Washington, 1967-68; assoc. Cravath, Swaine & Moore, N.Y.C., 1968-75; ptnr. Cravath, Swaine & Moore, 1975—; dir. Legal Aid Soc., N.Y.C., 1989-98, pres., 1994-96. V.p. sch. bd., Ridgewood, N.J., 1989-90, pres., 1991-92; trustee NYU Law Ctr. Found., 1992—; pres. Ridgewood Pub. Edn. Found., 1993-96. Mem. ABA, N.Y. State Bar Assn., Assn. Bar of City of N.Y. Republican. Episcopalian. Home: 500 Knollwood Rd Ridgewood NJ 07450-4700 Office: Cravath Swaine & Moore 825 8th Ave Fl 38 New York NY 10019-7475

BROMELKAMP, DAVID JOHN, investment officer; b. Poughkeepsie, N.Y., Aug. 2, 1960; s. Henry James and Elaine Teresa (Kuhl) B. BS, St. Johns U., Collegeville, Minn., 1982; Masters in intl. mgmt., U. St. Thomas, St. Paul, Minn., 1989. CPA, Minn., 1985-88, cert. invest. mgmt. cons. (CIMC), 1996. Corp. acct., 1982-85; mgr. Durafin Radiator Corp., St. Paul, 1984-85; acct. Mork, Harvey and Co., St. Paul, 1985-86, Stirtz, Bernards and Co., Mpls., 1986-88; v.p., investment officer Dain Rausher, Inc., Mpls., 1988—. Mem. AICPA, Am. Mgmt. Assn., Minn. World Trade Assn., Minn. Soc. CPAs., Inst. for Investment Mgmt. Cons., Minn. Athletic Club. Republican. Roman Catholic. Home: 4705 Fremont Ave S Minneapolis MN 55409

BROMKE, CINDY ROSE, geriatrics nurse, rehabilitation nurse; b. Mt. Pleasant, Pa., Aug. 18, 1960; d. Clark Raymond and Sara Ann (Fisher) Hancock; m. Craig Eugene Bromke, Oct. 6, 1979 (div. Mar. 1989); children: Crystal, Craig Jr., Casey. ASN, Westmoreland County C.C., 1992. RN, Pa. Charge nurse Integrated Health Svcs. of Greater Pitts., Greensburg, Pa., 1992-93, supr., 1993-94, RN assessment coord., 1994-95, staff nurse rehab. unit, 1995-96; skilled unit mgr. Integrated Health Svcs. Mt. View, Greensburg, Pa., 1996; RNAC Briarcliff Pavilion, North Huntington, Pa., 1996-97; staff nurse Barclay Inpatient Rehab. Unit Westmoreland Regional Hosp., Greensburg, 1997—. Sunday sch. supt. St. John's United Ch. of Christ, Mt. Pleasant, Pa., 1991-97, 98, sec., 1992-97, treas., 1997—; mem. program com. Westmoreland Assn. of the Penn West conf. United Ch. of Christ, 1994—, chairperson, 1997-98, registrar Westmoreland Assn. Penn West Conf., 1997—. Home: RR 1 Box 352 Hunker PA 15639-9726

BROMLEY, DAVID ALLAN, physicist, engineer, educator; b. Westmeath, Ont., Can., May 4, 1926; s. Milton Escort and Susan Anne (Anderson) B.; m. Patricia Jane Brassor, Aug. 30, 1949 (dec. Oct. 1990); children: David John, Karen Lynn. BS in Engring. Physics, Queen's U., Kingston, Ont., 1948, MS in Physics, 1950; PhD in Nuclear Physics, U. Rochester, 1952; MA (hon.), Yale U., 1961; D of Natural Philosophy (hon.), U. Frankfurt, 1978; Docteur (Physique) (hon.), U. Strasbourg, 1980; DSc (hon.), Queen's U., 1981, U. Notre Dame, 1982, U. Witwatersrand, 1982, Trinity Coll., 1988; LittD (hon.), U. Bridgeport, 1981; Dott. (hon.), U. Padua, 1983; LHD (hon.), U. New Haven, 1987; DSc (hon.), Rensselaer Polytechnic Inst., 1990; LHD (hon.), Ill. Inst. Tech., 1990; DSc (hon.), Lehigh U., 1991, Bklyn. Polytechnic Inst., 1991, U. Guelph, 1991, Fordham U., 1991, Northwestern U., 1991, Coll. of William and Mary, 1991; D Engring. Tech. (hon.), Wentworth Inst., 1991; DSc (hon.), SUNY, U. Mass., Adelphi U., 1993; DHL (hon.), Mt. Sinai Med. Ctr., 1993; D. Eng. (hon.), Colo. Sch. Mines, 1992; DSc (hon.), Fla. State U., 1993, Mich. State U., 1994, Mt. Sinai Med., 1996, U. Pitts., 1997, U. Toronto, 1998. Oper. engr. Hydro Electric Power Commn. Ont., 1947-48; rsch. officer Nat. Rsch. Coun. Can., 1948; instr., then asst. prof. physics U. Rochester, 1952-55; sr. rsch. officer, sect. head Atomic Energy Can. Ltd., 1955-60; assoc. prof. physics, asso. dir. heavy ion accelerator lab. Yale U., 1960-61, prof. physics, dir. A. W. Wright Nuclear Structure Lab., 1961-89, chmn. physics dept., 1970-77, Henry Ford II prof. physics, 1972-93; Sterling prof. scis., dean engring. Yale U., New Haven, 1994—; asst. to Pres. for sci. and tech. Washington, 1989-93; dir. Office of Sci. and Tech. Policy, Washington, 1989-93; chmn. Pres.'s Coun. Advisers on Sci. and Tech., Washington, 1989-93, Fed. Coordinating Coun. Sci., Engring. and Tech., Washington, 1989-93, Nat. Critical Materials Coun., Washington, 1990-92; cons. Brookhaven, Argonne, Berkley and Oak Ridge Nat. Labs., Bell Telephone Labs., IBM, GTE; mem. panel nuclear physics Nat. Acad. Scis., 1964, chmn. com. on nuclear sci., 1966-74, chmn. physics survey, 1969-74; mem.-at-large, mem. exec. com. divsn. phys. scis. NRC, 1970-74, mem. exec. com., assembly phys. and math. scis., 1974-78, mem. naval sci. bd., 1974-78; mem. high energy physics adv. panel ERDA, 1974-78; mem. nuclear sci. adv. panel NSF and Dept. Energy, 1980-89; mem. White House Sci. Coun., 1981-89, Nat. Sci. Bd., 1988-89; bd. dirs. MBARI, Monterey, Calif., Echlin Inc., New Haven, Thermo Vision, Cambridge, Mass., Sci. Applications Internat., Paris; founding ptnr. Washington Adv. Group, 1997. Editor: Physics in Perspective, 5 vols, 1972, Large Electrostatic Accelerators, 1974, Nuclear Detectors, 1978, Heavy Ion Science, 8 vols, 1981-84; co-editor: Procs. Kingston Internat. Conf. on Nuclear Structure, 1960, Facets of Physics, 1970, Nuclear Science in China, 1979, The President's Scientists: Reminiscences of a Presidential Science Advisor, 1993; assoc. editor: Annals of Physics, 1968-89, Am. Scientist, 1969-81, Il Nuovo Cimento, 1970-89, Nuclear Instruments and Methods, 1974-89, Science, Technology and the Humanities, 1978-89, Jour. Physics, 1978-89, Nuclear Science Applications, 1978-89, Technology in Soc, 1981-89; cons. editor: McGraw Hill Series in Fundamentals of Physics, 1967-89, McGraw Hill Ency. Sci. and Tech. Bd. dirs. Oak Ridge Assoc. Univs., 1977-80, U. Bridgeport, 1981-86, Sheffield Scientific Sch., 1995—. Recipient medal Gov. Gen. Can., 1948, Disting. Alumnus award U. Rochester, 1986, U.S. Nat. medal of sci., 1988, Presdl. medal N.Y. Acad. Scis., 1989, Yale medal in sci. and engring., 1991, Disting. Svc. award IEEE, 1991, Louis Pasteur medal of sci. U. Strasbourg, 1991, Harvey medal Pierce Found., 1991, Disting. Svc. medal NSF, 1992, Pub. Svc. medal Ctr. Study of Presidency, 1992, Exec. Yr. award R&D Mag., 1992, Disting. Scholar medal U. Rochester, 1993; decorated Commander's Cross Order of Merit, Fed. Rep. Germany, 1993; NRC fellow, 1952; fellow Timothy Dwight Coll., 1961—; Guggenheim fellow, 1977-78; Humboldt fellow, 1978, 85, 96; Benjamin Franklin fellow Royal Soc. Arts, London, 1979—. Fellow Am. Phys. Soc. (v.p. 1995, pres.-elect 1996, mem. coun. 1967-71, pres. 1997), Am. Acad. Arts and Scis., AAAS (chmn. physics sect. 1977-78, pres.-elect 1980, pres. 1981—, chmn. bd. 1982—, William Carey medal 1993, Philip Abelson prize 1997), Washington Adv. Group (sr.); mem. NAS, Can. Assn. Physicists, European Phys. Soc., Conn. Acad. Arts. and Scis., N.Y. Acad. Arts and Scis. (gov. 1994—), Conn. Acad. Sci. and Engring. (coun. 1976-78), Internat. Union Pure and Applied Physics (U.S. nat. com. 1969—, chmn. 1975-76, v.p. 1975-81, pres. 1984-87), Southeastern U. Rsch. Assn. (bd. dirs. 1984-89), Coun. on Fgn. Rels., N.Y. Acad. Scis. (bd. govs. 1994—), Coun. Engring. Deans (bd. dirs. 1994—), Am. Soc. for Engring. Edn. (bd. dirs. 1995—), Am. Assn. Engring. Edn. (bd. dirs. 1995—), Sigma Xi (pres. Yale 1962-63). Home: 35 Tokeneke Dr North Haven CT 06473-4348 Office: Yale Univ Physics Dept 272 Whitney Ave PO Box 208124 New Haven CT 06520-8124 also: Dunham Lab 10 Hillhouse Ave New Haven CT 06511-6814

BROMLEY, DENNIS KARL, lawyer; b. Berkeley, Calif., Nov. 8, 1940; s. Karl S. and Fae R. (Christensen) B.; m. Lynne Harris, Apr. 10, 1960;

children: Karl S., Alexander H., Eric H. BS, Brigham Young U., 1962; LLB, Yale U., 1965. Bar: Calif. 1966, U.S. Dist. Ct. (no., ea., cen. dists.) Calif., U.S. Ct. Appeals (9th, 10th cirs.), U.S. Tax Ct., U.S. Ct. Fed. Claims, U.S. Supreme Ct. Assoc. Pillsbury, Madison & Sutro, San Francisco, 1965-72, ptnr., 1973-94; prin. Law Offices of Dennis K. Bromley, San Francisco, 1994—. Mem. Olympic Club, Yale Club (N.Y.C.). Office: Law Office Dennis K Bromley 44 Montgomery St Ste 3585 San Francisco CA 94104-4808*

BROMLEY, HANK J., sociologist, educator; b. Stamford, Conn., Aug. 1, 1960; s. Irwin and Adele (Tates) B. BS in Math., BS in Computer Sci., MIT, 1983; MA in Ednl. Policy Studies, U. Wis., 1989, PhD in Ednl. Policy Studies, 1995. Rsch. asst. Umeå (Sweden) U., 1983-84; sr. tech. assoc. AT&T Bell Labs., Murray Hill, N.J., 1984-86; asst. prof. Sociology Edn., assoc. dir. ednl. resource tech. SUNY, Buffalo, 1994—; mem. steering com. Inst. for Rsch. and Edn. on Women and Gender, 1997—. Author: Lisp Lore: A Guide to Programming the Lisp Machine, 1986, Education/Technology/Power: Educational computing as a Social Practice, 1998. Vol. coord. Tech. Assistance to Nicaragua, N.Y.C., 1985-86; mem. spkrs. bur. Dane County Rape Crisis Ctr., Madison, 1990-93; bd. dirs. Computer Profls. for Social Responsibility, 1987-90; mem. edn. working group Erie County Commn. on the Status of Women, 1997-98. Recipient J. Austin Kelly prize MIT, 1983; WARF prize fellow U. Wis., Madison, 1986-88, Assigned State fellow, 1990-91, Arvil S. Barr Grad. fellow, 1993-94. Mem. Am. Ednl. Rsch. Assn., Soc. for Social Studies of Sci., Tau Beta Pi, Eta Kappa Nu. Home: 246 Norwood Ave Buffalo NY 14222-1710 Office: Univ at Buffalo 222 Baldy Hall Buffalo NY 14260-0104

BROMSEN, MAURY AUSTIN, historian, bibliographer, antiquarian bookseller; b. N.Y.C., Apr. 25, 1919; s. Herman and Rose (Eisenberg) B. BSS cum laude with spl. honors, CCNY, 1939; MA, U. Calif., Berkeley, 1941, Harvard U., 1945; doctoral postgrad. in history, Harvard U., 1945-50; LHD (hon.), Northeastern U., 1987. Vis. lectr. Am. history Cath. U., Santiago, Chile, 1942; instr. history CCNY, 1943-44; founding editor Inter-Am. Rev. Bibliography, 1950-53; editor, sect. chief dept. cultural affairs Pan Am. Union, Washington, 1950-54; on leave, 1953-54; adv. editor, U.S. rep. Inter-Am. Rev. Bibliography, 1956—; founder, dir. Maury A. Bromsen Assocs. (rare book, manuscript and fine art dealers), Boston, 1954—; pres., treas. Maury A. Bromsen Assocs., Inc. (rare book, manuscript and fine art dealers), 1963-89; proprietor, dir. The Maury A. Bromsen Co. (antiquarian booksellers and appraisers), 1990—; hon. curator Latin Am. collections Boston Pub. Library, 1977—; hon. curator, bibliographer Latin Americana John Carter Brown Libr., Brown U., Providence, 1996—; vis. prof. U. Chile, Santiago, 1947; exec. sec. Medina Centennial Celebration, Washington, 1952; mem. adv. council univ. libraries U. Notre Dame, 1981-84, emeritus adviser, 1984—; bd. govs. Am. Jewish Hist. Soc., 1987-92; est. Maury A. Bromsen-Simon Bolivar Room John Carter Brown Libr., Providence, R.I., 1999. Author: Simón Bolívar: A Bicentennial Tribute, 1983; editor: José Toribio Medina, Humanist of the Americas: an Appraisal, 1960, Spanish transl., 1969; research and publs. in history and bibliography of Ams. Established Medina and Harrisse rare book collections, U. Fla. Library, 1958, 63. Endowed Archibald Bromsen Meml. scholarship, CCNY, 1964; endowed Bromsen lectureship in Humanistic Bibliography, Boston Pub. Library, 1970, Maury A. Bromsen Latin Am. Acquisitions Fund, 1976, Bromsen Fund, Mass. Gen. Hosp. (Health Scis. Lib.), 1983. Decorated Orden al Mérito Bernardo O'Higgins, Knight Comdr. (Chile), 1952, Orden de Francisco de Miranda, First Class (Venezuela), 1985; elected Colonial Soc. Mass., 1985; Carnegie Endowment for Internat. Peace and U.S. Govt. Exch. fellow U. Chile, 1942; Harvard Woodbury Lowery Travelling fellow, 1946-47, Social Sci. Rsch. Coun. fellow, 1946-48. Mem. Antiquarian Booksellers Assn. Am., Am. Hist. Assn., ALA, Bibliog. Soc. Am., Manuscript Soc. (charter), Conf. on Latin Am. History, Academia Nacional de la Historia, Buenos Aires (corr.), Latin Am. Studies Assn., Bibliog. Soc. (London), Bibliog. Soc. U. Va., Boston Athenaeum, Harvard Coll. Library Friends, Boston Pub. Library Assocs. (hon.), Boston U. Library Assocs. (life), Iowa Library Assocs. (patron), Bell (Minn.) Library Assocs., Clements (Mich.) Library Assocs., Yale Library Assocs., Am. Hist. Soc., Am. Jewish Hist. Soc., Va. Hist. Soc. (life), N.Y. Hist. Soc., Sociedad Chilena de Historia y Geografía, Filson Club (life), Phi Beta Kappa. Clubs: Harvard (Boston), Boston Athenaeum (Boston). Address: 770 Boylston St Boston MA 02199-7700 *The true bibliographer should be more than an inventory maker and describer of the physical qualities of books and other printed material. This is but a minimal qualification of the craftsman. He ought rather to know something about the ideas to which a work relates and in what manner it supplements the known history of its field. Thereby he will make a contribution to humanism, and this should be the prime motivator of the scholarly bookman worthy of the name bibliographer.*

BROMWICH, MICHAEL RAY, federal official; b. L.A., Dec. 19, 1953; s. Leo and Rose (Meyer) B.; m. Felice B. Friedman, Dec. 27, 1980; children: Daniel R., Jonah E., Kira A. AB summa cum laude, Harvard Coll., 1976; MPP, Harvard U., 1980, JD, 1980. Assoc. Foley & Lardner, Washington, 1980-83; asst. U.S. atty. U.S. Attys. Office, (so. dist.) N.Y., N.Y.C., 1983-87; assoc. counsel Office of Ind. Counsel, Iran-Contra, Washington, 1987-89; spl. counsel Office Ind. Counsel, Iran-Contra, Washington, 1990, 91; ptnr. Mayer, Brown & Platt, Washington, 1989-93; inspector gen. Dept. Justice, Washington, 1994—; mem. Pres. Coun. on Integrity and Efficiency, 1994—. Mem. Phi Beta Kappa. Jewish. Office: Inspector Gen Dept Justice 950 Pennsylvania Ave NW Washington DC 20530-0001

BRON, WALTER ERNEST, physics educator; b. Berlin, Jan. 17, 1930; came to U.S., 1939, naturalized, 1946; s. Arthur and Edith (Seidel) B.; m. Ann Elisabeth Berend, June 1, 1952; children: Karen Susanne, Michelle Elise. B.M.E., N.Y. U., 1952; M.S., Columbia, 1953, Ph.D., 1958. Research assoc. IBM Watson Lab., Yorktown Heights, N.Y., 1957-58; research physicist IBM Watson Lab., 1958-66; assoc. prof. physics Ind. U., Bloomington, 1966-69; prof. Ind. U., 1969-86; prof. dept. physics U. Calif., Irvine, 1986—, chmn., 1989-92; lectr. George Washington U., 1955-56, Columbia, 1957, adj. lectr., 1964; vis. prof. Physikalisches Institut der Technischen Hochschule, Stuttgart, Germany, 1966-67; vis. scientist Max Planck Inst. for Solid State Research, Stuttgart, Germany, 1973-74, 81-82, 83. Contbr. articles sci. jours.; mem. editl. bd., divisional assoc. editor Physics Rev. Letters. Mem. Bloomington Environ. Quality and Conservation Commn., 1972-81, chmn., 1974-76. Served with AUS, 1954-56. Gen. Electric fellow, 1952-53; W. Campbell fellow, 1953-54, 56-57; Guggenheim fellow, 1966-67; sr. Scientist award Alexander von Humboldt Found., 1973. Fellow Am. Phys. Soc.; mem. Optical Soc. Am., Sassafras Audubon Soc. (pres. 1976-78), Sigma Xi, Tau Beta Pi, Pi Tau Sigma. Patentee in field. Office: Dept Physics and Astronomy Univ Calif Irvine Irvine CA 92697

BRONAUGH, DEANNE RAE, home health care administrator, consultant; b. Cameron, Mo., Feb. 3, 1952; d. Myron McMillin and Kathryn Marie (Ogden) Bell; m. Richard N. Bronaugh, July 18, 1987; 1 child, Elisabeth Catherine. BSN magna cum laude, Avila Coll., 1974. Cert. nursing adminstr., ANA. Staff nurse Bapt. Meml. Hosp., Kansas City, Mo., 1974-77; nurse clinician North Kansas City (Mo.) Meml. Hosp., 1977-78; asst. dir. Bethany Med. Ctr., Kansas City, 1978-79, spl. projects dir., 1979-80, dir. critical care, 1980-81; DON Lee's Summit (Mo.) Community Hosp., 1981-84; asst. adminstr. Muskogee (Okla.) Regional Med. Ctr., 1984-86; cons. Creative Nursing Mgmt., Mpls., 1986-87; pres. Liberty Cons., Muskogee, 1992-93; state liaison for accreditation affairs ABC Home Health, 1993-94; regional adminstr. 1st Am. Home Care (formerly ABC Home Health), 1994-96; regional dir. clin. svcs. Integrated Health Svcs., Overland Park, Kans., 1996-97; assoc. Corridor Group, Inc., Overland Park, Kans., 1997; sr. assoc. Curran Care, North Riverside, Ill., 1997-98; gen. mgr. VNA Plus, Lenexa, Kans., 1998-99; design cons. Norwork Furniture, Lenixa, 1999—; mem. adv. bd. Am. Heart Assn., Kansas City, Kans., 1979-81. Mem. Rep. Women's Club, Muskogee, 1988, P.E.O., Muskogee, 1992. Mem. Sigma Theta Tau. Home: 11502 W 127th Ter Overland Park KS 66213-3534

BRONAUGH, EDWIN LEE, electromagnetic compatibility engineer, consultant; b. Salina, Kans., July 22, 1932; s. Edwin and Violet Mary (Dryden) B.; m. Geraldine Kelley, Dec. 10, 1955: children: Cecilia Ann Bronaugh Snodgrass, Dana Lea Bronaugh Weinberg. BA in Physics and Math., East Tex. State U., Commerce, 1955. Commd. USAF, 1955, advanced through grades to capt., 1961, various comm. and ops. assignments, 1955-68; major USAFR, 1968; rsch. scientist Southwest Rsch. Inst., San Antonio, 1968-70, sr. rsch. scientist, 1970-76, rsch. dir., 1976-82; dir. R & D, tech. dir. Electro-Metrics Divsn. Penril, Amsterdam, N.Y., 1982-89; prin. electromagnetic compatibility scientist Electro-Mechanics Co., Austin, Tex., 1989-92; v.p. engrng., 1992-94; prin. EdB EMC Cons., Austin, 1994—; lead engr. comm. devices divsn. Siemens Info. and Comm. Products, LLC, Austin, 1997—. Author: Electromagnetic Interference Test Methodology and Procedures, 1988; contbr. over 150 articles to profl. jours.; patentee in field. Decorated Bronze Star, Air Force Commendation medal. Fellow IEEE; mem. Electromagnetic Compatibility Soc. of IEEE (stds. com. 1980—, dir. tech. svcs. 1981-87, v.p. 1988-90, pres. 1990-92, Cert. of Appreciation 1979, Cert. of Achievement 1983, Cert. of Acknowledgement 1985, Richard R. Stoddart award 1985, Stds. Medallion 1992, Lawrence G. Cumming award 1992), Am. Nat. Stds. Inst. (vice chmn. accredited stds. com. C63 on electromagnetic compatibility 1986—), Nat. Assn. Radio and Telecom. Engrs. (sr., cert.), Electromagnetic Compatibility Soc. (hon. life.). Avocations: music, camping, model railroads, learning additional languages. Home and Office: 10210 Prism Dr Austin TX 78726-1364 also: Siemens 2205 Grand Ave Pkwy Austin TX 78728

BRONDELLO, SANDY, professional basketball player; b. Australia, Aug. 20, 1968. B.Elem.Tchg., 1990. Guard Blazers, Australia, 1995-96, BTV Wuppertal, Germany, 1996-98, Detroit Shock, 1998—; participant World Championships, 1990, 94; mem. Australian Olympic team, 1988; guard Australian Nat. Team, Women's World Championship, Germany, 1998. Named Australian Internat. Baksetball Player of the Yr., 1992, WNBL's Most Valuable Player, 1995, European Cup Most Valuable Player, 1996. Office: Detroit Shock 2 Championship Dr Auburn Hills MI 48326*

BRONDIZIO, EDUARDO SONNEWEND, ecological researcher, consultant; b. Sao Joas dos Campos, Brazil, Aug. 30, 1963; came to U.S., 1991; s. Joel Vieira and Maria Apparecida (Sonnewend) B.; m. Andrea Balledone Siqueira; 1 child, Maira Siqueira Brondizio. Degree in Agronomy, UNITAU, Taubate, Brazil, 1987; PhD, Ind. U., 1996. Project coord. Fundacao Sosmato Atlantic, Sao Paulo, 1988-91; asst. rschr. ACT-Ind. U., Bloomington, 1991-96, asst. dir., 1998—; rsch. assoc. ACT-U. Ariz., Tucson, 1997-98. Coord. Atlas Atlantic Forest Remnants, 1990; contbr. articles to profl. jours. NASA Global change fellow, 1994-95; McArthur scholar, 1993. Roman Catholic.

BRONES, LISA ANN MARI, news anchorperson, reporter; b. Albert Lea, Minn., May 12, 1967; d. Max Beene and Marge Leene (Thrond) B. BA in Journalism, English, U. Iowa, 1989, JD, 1992. Bar: Calif. TV news anchorperson, reporter Sta. KIMT, Mason City, Iowa, 1992-94; TV news reporter Sta. WOI-TV, Des Moines, 1994-95; TV news anchorperson, reporter Sta. WHO-TV, Des Moines, 1995-99; TV news reporter WHAS-TV, Louisville, KY, 1999—. Bd. dirs. Crimestoppers of Mason City, 1993; mem. Flood Relief Com., Mason City, 1993. Mem. ABA, Calif. State Bar Assn., Soc. Profl. Journalists, Iowa Broadcasters Assn., Phi Delta Phi, Phi Beta Kappa. Lutheran. Avocations: boating, swimming, baseball, volleyball, piano. Office: Sta WHAS-TV 520 W Chestnut Ave Louisville KY 40202

BRONFIN, FRED, lawyer; b. New Orleans, Nov. 30, 1918; m. Carolyn Pick; children by previous marriage: Daniel R., Kenneth A. BA, Tulane U., 1938, JD, 1941. Bar: La. 1941, U.S. Dist. Ct. (ea. dist.) La. 1941, U.S. Ct. Appeals (5th cir.) 1951, U.S. Supreme Ct. 1973. Assoc. Rittenberg & Rittenberg, New Orleans, 1946-48; ptnr. Rittenberg, Weinstein & Bronfin, New Orleans, 1948-56, Weinstein & Bronfin, New Orleans, 1956-62, Bronfin, Heller, Steinberg & Berins and precessor firms, New Orleans, 1962-91; of counsel Bronfin & Heller, 1991-98, Heller, Draper, Hayden & Horn, 1998—. With USN, 1942-46. Mem. ABA, La. Bar Assn., New Orleans Bar Assn., Order of Coif, Phi Beta Kappa. Office: Heller Draper Hayden Et Al 650 Poydras St Ste 2500 New Orleans LA 70130-6103

BRONFMAN, EDGAR MILES, beverage company executive; b. Montreal, June 20, 1929; s. Samuel and Saidye (Rosner) B.; married. Student, Williams Coll., 1946-49; B.A., McGill U., 1951; LHD (hon.), Pace U., 1982; LLD (hon.), Williams Coll., 1986. Chmn. adminstrv. com. Joseph E. Seagram & Sons, Inc., 1955-57, pres., 1957-71; chmn., CEO, pres. Distillers Corp.-Seagram Ltd., Montreal, 1971-75; now chmn. The Seagram Co. Ltd. and Joseph E. Seagram & Sons Inc.; bd. dirs. Am. Technion Soc. Mem. citizens com. for N.Y.C., U.S.-USSR Trade and Econ. Coun.; chmn. Samuel Bronfman Found.; pres. N. Am. Consortium for Free Market Study, World Jewish Congress; mem. internat. adv. bd. Sch. Internat. and Pub. Affairs, Columbia U.; mem. exec. com. Am. Jewish Congress, Am. Jewish Com.; chmn. Anti-Defamation League N.Y.; bd. dirs. Am. Com. Weizmann Inst. Sci., Israel; mem. Bus. Com. for Arts, United Jewish Appeals; hon. chmn. Fedn. Jewish Philanthropies; bd. dels. Union Am. Hebrew Congregation. Named Chevalier de la Légion d'Honneur French Govt. Mem. Coun. Fgn. Rels., Ctr. Inter-Am. Rels., Hundred Year Assn. N.Y., Com. for Econ. Devel., Fgn. Policy Assn., B'nai B'rith (bd. overseers). Office: Joseph E Seagram & Sons Inc 375 Park Ave New York NY 10152-0006 also: The Seagram Co Ltd, 1430 Peel St, Montreal, PQ Canada H3A 1S9*

BRONIS, STEPHEN J., lawyer; b. Miami, Fla., Feb. 23, 1947; s. Larry and Thelma (Berger) B.; children: Jason Michael, Tyler Adam, Kenneth Lawrence. BSBA, U. Fla., 1969; JD, Duke U., 1972. Bar: Fla. 1972, D.C. 1973, U.S. Dist. Ct. (so. dist.) Fla. 1973, U.S. Ct. Appeals (5th cir.) 1977, U.S. Supreme Ct. 1978, U.S. Ct. Appeals (11th cir.) 1981, U.S. Dist. Ct. (mid. dist.) Fla. 1989, Colo. 1994, U.S. Dist. Ct. Colo. 1996, U.S. Ct. Appeals (10th cir.) 1996, U.S. Tax Ct. 1998. Asst. pub. defender 11th Jud. Cir. Fla., Miami, 1972-75; ptnr. Rosen & Bronis, P.A., Miami, 1975-77, Rosen, Portela, Bronis, et al, Miami, 1977-82, Bronis & Potela, P.A., Miami, 1982-90; pvt. practice Miami, 1990-93; ptnr. Davis, Scott, Weber & Edwards, Miami, 1993-95, Zuckerman, Spaeder, Taylor & Evans, Miami, 1996—; mem. faculty Nat. Inst. of Trial Adv., U. N.C., Yeshiva U, Nova Sch. Law; nominated Fla. Supreme Ct. 1999. Contbr. articles to profl. jours. Recipient Am. Jurisprudence award Bancroft-Whitney Co., 1972, cert. of appreciation Fla. Shorthand Reporters Assn., 1984. Mem. ATLA, Nat. Criminal Def. Attys. Assn., Am. Bd. Criminal Lawyers (v.p. 1981-82), Fla. Criminal Def. Attys. Assn. (Outstanding Svc. award 1981), Calif. Attys. Criminal Justice, Acad. Fla. Trial Lawyers (criminal law sect. dir.). Democrat. Home: 3 Grove Isle Dr Apt 1506 Miami FL 33133-4103 Office: 201 S Biscayne Blvd Ste 900 Miami FL 33131-4326

BRONK, WILLIAM, writer, retail businessman; b. Fort Edward, N.Y., Feb. 17, 1918; s. William M. and Ethel Elizabeth (Funston) B. A.B., Dartmouth Coll., 1938. Author: (collected poems) Life Supports, 1981, Careless Love and Its Apostrophes, 1985, Manifest: And Furthermore, 1987, Death Is the Place, 1989, Living Instead, 1991, Some Words, 1992, The Mild Day, 1993, (collected essays) Vectors and Smoothable Curves, 1983, Our Selves, 1994, Selected Poems, 1995, The Cage of Age, 1996. Served to 1st lt. AUS, 1941-45. Home: 57 Pearl St Hudson Falls NY 12839-2438

BRONKAR, EUNICE DUNALEE, artist, art educator; b. New Lebanon, Ohio, Aug. 8, 1934; d. William Dunham and Helen Kate (Hypes) Connor; m. Charles William Bronkar, Jan. 26, 1957; 1 child, Ramona. BFA, Wright State U., 1971, M in Art Edn., 1983, postgrad. art studies, 1989; postgrad. art studies, Dayton Art Inst., 1972. Cert. art tchr., Ohio. Part time tchr. Springfield (Ohio) Mus. of Art, 1967-77; adjunct instr. Clark State C.C., Springfield, 1974-84, lead tchr., 1984-94, adj. asst. prof., 1998, asst. prof., 1989-94; ret., 1994; artist private practice, Urbana, Ohio, 1995—; edn. chmn. Springfield Mus. Art, 1973-74; image banks participant, Ohio Arts Coun., Columbus, Visual Arts Network, Dayton, Ohio, 1994—; affiliated with The Art Ctr. of St. Augustine, Fla. Art Scene, Little Gallery, Springfield, Ohio. Artist: One woman shows include in Springfield, Ohio: Polo Club, Upper Valley Mall Cinema, Security Nat. Bank, Mr. C's Beauty Salon, Lakewood Beach, Springfield Mus. of Art, Clark State C.C.; Dayton, Ohio: Miami Valley Hosp., High St. Gallery, Stoeffer's Restaurant, Wegerzyn Garden Ctr., Meml. Hall, Wright State Univ., Urbana, Ohio: Champaign County Arts Coun., Urbana Cinema; South Charleston, Ohio: Cmty. Park Dedication, Philip Caldwell spl. guest speaker, Chmn. of the Bd. and CEO Ford Motor Co; accepted in over 90 area, state, regional, and nat. juried exhibitions including: Ohio Water Color Soc.'s Annual Traveling shows 1983-84, 86-87, Western Ohio Watercolor Soc., Hon. Mention 1983, Chase Patterson award, 1985, Spl. Merit award, 1990, 1st, 1995, Merit award 1997, 98; Springfield Mus. of Art: awards 1965, 68; 2d pastel 1972, 2d pastel and 1st drawing 1976, Jurors award pastel 1979, 1st drawing 1986, 3d drawing 1987, 2d drawing 1989, 1st drawing 1990, 1st drawing and 2d painting 1991, 1st drawing 1992, 2d, 1998, 2d pastel 1998; Dayton Soc. Painters and Sculptors: Best of Show 1974, 1st painting, 2d painting 3d drawing 1978, Hon. Mention 1979, 3d Graphic 1980, Best of Show drawing and 1st pastel 1981, 1st drawing 1991, 3d painting 1993; Champaign County Fair: Best of show drawing and 1st pastel 1968; drawings and paintings in Am. Artist Renown, 1981, Shades of Gray, 1983, 84, 86, 87, 90, 91, 93, 94, 97; represented in six public and numerous private collections. Cleaned and restored art collections at Springfield Pub. Schs., Hist. Soc. in Springfield, Warder Pub. Libr., Foos Manor Bed & Breakfast and the Masonic Temple, Penn House and Mus. of Art in Springfield, Ohio, 1970-97, other groups and numerous pvt. collections, 1970—; mem. adv. com. comml. art, Clark County JVS Sch., Springfield, 1991-97; judge more than 10 pub. h.s. art shows, 1970s-90s; judge Logan County (Ohio) Fair Fine Art Show profl. and amateur, 1998. Recipient medal Bicentennial Com. and 4H Found. of Ohio, Springfield, 1976, Outstanding Tchr. award Clark State C.C., 1992, commd. to paint 2 past pres. Generals of the Natl. Soc. Daughters of the Amer. Revolution, will hang in Wash. D.C. Mem. Western Ohio Water Color Soc, Springfield (Ohio) Mus. of Art, Dayton Soc. Painters and Sculptors, Cin. Art Club, Ohio Water Color Soc., Nat. Mus. Women in Arts, Audubon Artists Soc., Pastel Soc., St. Agugstine (Fla.) Art Assn., others. Avocations: swimming, walking, sewing, flower arranging, travel to Europe, Caribbean, Russia, Israel and Ireland. Studio and Home: 5516 S US Highway 68 Urbana OH 43078-9420

BRONKEMA, FREDERICK HOLLANDER, retired minister and church official; b. Albany, N.Y., Feb. 1, 1934; s. Frederick and Sadie (Hollander) B.; m. Marguerite Cobble, June 5, 1959; children: Frederick David, Timothy Dunning, John Hollander, Robert Kelton. BA magna cum laude, Whitworth Coll., 1956; MDiv, Princeton Theol. Sem., 1959, ThM, 1965; postgrad., New Coll., U. Edinburgh, Scotland, 1959-60, Union Theol. Sem., 1971-72, Ctr. for Intercultural Documentation, Cuernavaca, Mex., 1972. Ordained to ministry United Presbyn. Ch. in U.S.A., 1960. Asst. min. Craigsbank Ch. of Scotland, Edinburgh, 1959-60; min. Atlantic Highlands (N.J.) Presbyn. Ch., 1960-63; assoc. min. Red Clay Creek Presbyn. Ch., Wilmington, Del., 1963-65; fraternal worker United Presbyn. Ch., Lisbon and Figueira de Foz, Portugal, 1966-71; dir. Reconciliation Ecumenical Ctr., Figueira de Foz, 1966-71; prof. Evang. Theol. Sem., Carcavelos, Portugal, 1967-70; missionary Christian Ch. (Disciples of Christ) and Commn.; assoc., fraternal worker United Presbyn. Ch., Rome, 1972-76; dir., mng. editor The Future of Missionary Enterprise, documentation/publs. project Internat. Documentation and Communication Ctr., Rome, 1972-76, assoc. gen. sec., 1974-76; U.S.A. rep. Ecumenical Devel. Coop. Soc., N.Y.C., 1977-86; fraternal worker, missionary Presbyn. Ch. (U.S.A.) and Christian Ch. (Disciples of Christ); coord. Program and Ctr. Reconciliation, Honduran Christian Commn. for Devel., Tegucigalpa, 1986-88; dir. Human Rights Office, Nat. Coun. Chs. of Christ in U.S.A., N.Y.C., 1989-93; ret., 1994; pres. Ecumenical Group of Portugal, 1967-69; cons. Commn. on World Mission and Evangelism, World Coun. Chs., 1973-75, advisor cen. com. meeting, Geneva, 1984; advisor 7th Assembly of Luth. World Fedn., Budapest, Hungary, 1984. Contbr. articles to ch. jours. Mem. Ecumenical Assn. of Acads. and Laity Ctrs. in Europe. Democrat. Home: PO Box 483 Penney Farms FL 32079-0483 *The greatest gift we have is our common humanity. Our basic problem is our lack of humanity—our inhumanity. Life is a struggle daily to become more human.*

BRONKESH, ANNETTE CYLIA, public relations executive; b. Vineland, N.J., Dec. 18, 1956; d. Manasha and Miriam (Kutlan) B.; m. Steven Silver Schwartz, Aug. 18, 1985; children: Sarah, Emily, Julie. BA, NYU, 1979. Sr. editor Instnl. Investor, N.Y.C., 1979; chief editor McGraw-Hill, N.Y.C., 1980-85; dir. Am. Stock Exchange, N.Y.C., 1985-87; v.p. pub. rels. Nikko Securities, N.Y.C., 1987-90; pres. Bronkesh Assocs., Clifton, N.J., 1990—. Mem. Securities Industry Assn. (pub. rels. roundtable), Fin. Women's Assn. N.Y., Phi Beta Kappa. Avocation: playing piano. Office: Bronkesh Assocs 23 Virginia Ave Clifton NJ 07012-1003 also: 23 Virginia Ave Clifton NJ 07012-1222

BRONNER, FELIX, physiologist, biophysicist, educator, painter; b. Vienna, Austria, Nov. 7, 1921; came to U.S., 1937, naturalized, 1943; s. Maurice and Lotte (Vogler) B.; m. Leah Horowitz, Oct. 12, 1947; children: Deborah Rachel, Ethan Samuel. BS, U. Calif., Berkeley and Davis, 1941; PhD (Quaker Oats fellow 1950-52), MIT, 1952; student, Kans. State Coll., 1938; postgrad., U. Minn., 1943, U. Va., 1946; D (hon.), Ecole Pratique des Hautes Etud, Paris, 1996. Rsch. assoc. MIT, 1952-54; Helen Hay Whitney fellow, Arthritis and Rheumatism fellow Rockefeller Inst. Med. Rsch., N.Y.C., 1954-56, asst., 1956; dir. lab. mineral metabolism Hosp. for Spl. Surgery, N.Y.C., 1957-63; asst. prof. Cornell U. Med. Coll., 1961-63; assoc. prof. physiology U. Louisville Sch. Medicine, 1963-69; prof. oral biology U. Conn., 1969-86, prof. nutritional scis., 1976-89, prof. biostructure and function, 1986-89, prof. emeritus, 1989—; vis. scientist Weizmann Inst., Israel, 1965, 76, Varon vis. prof., 1988; vis. scientist Pasteur Inst., Paris, 1977; vis. scientist U. Cape Town Med. Sch., 1984, 88, MRC disting. vis. scientist, 1991; guest scientist INSERM, Paris, 1972, Lyon, France, 1988; cons. USPHS, 1965-68, 70-71, USDA, 1978-79; vis. prof. Tel Aviv U. Sch. Medicine, 1976. Editor: (with C. L. Comar) Mineral Metabolism: An Advanced Treatise, 1960-69; (with A. Kleinzeller) Current Topics in Membranes and Transport, 1970-90; (with J. Coburn) Disorders of Mineral Metabolism, 1981-82; (with M. Peterlik) Calcium and Phosphate Transport Across Biomembranes, 1981; Epithelial Calcium and Phosphate Transport: Molecular and Cellular Aspects, 1984; Cellular Calcium and Phosphate Transport in Health and Disease, 1988; (with W. D. Stein) Cell Shape Defect Determinants, Regulation, and Regulatory Role, 1989; (with D. Pansu) Calcium Transport and Intracellular Calcium Homeostasis, 1990; Intracellular Calcium Regulation, 1991; (with R. V. Worrell) A Basic Science Primer in Orthopaedics, 1991; Etra- and Intracellular Calcium and Phosphate Regulation: From Basic Research to Clinical Medicine, 1992, Nutrition and Health-Topics and Controversies, 1996, Nutrition Policy in Public Health, 1997, Orthopaedics: Principles of Basic and Clinical Science, 1999; mem. editl. bd. Am. Jour. Clin. Nutrition, 1968-76, Am. Jour. Physiol., 1985-96, Jour. Nutrition, 1986-95; contbr. articles to profl. jours.; exhibited in one-man shows, numerous juried shows. Pres. Bur. Jewish Edn., Louisville, 1968-69. Served with AUS, 1942-46. Recipient André Lichwitz prize, 1974. Fellow AAAS, Am. Soc. Nutritional Sci.; mem. Am. Physiol. Soc., Biophys. Soc., Harvey Soc., Soc. Exptl. Biology and Medicine, Orthopedic Rsch. Soc., Am. Fedn. Clin. Rsch., N.Y. Acad. Scis., Am. Soc. Clin. Nutrition, Am. Soc. Bone and Mineral Rsch., Am. Soc. Gravity Space Biology. Home: 33 Ferncliff Dr West Hartford CT 06117-1013 Office: U Conn Health Ctr Dept BioStructure and Function Farmington CT 06030-3705 *This has been a bloody century, one where entire peoples were murdered. But it has also been a period of great intellectual and artistic advances. I feel privileged to have survived and to have participated in the science and art of our time.*

BRONNER, MICHAEL, advertising executive. CEO, new bus. contact Bronner Slosberg Humphrey, Boston, 1980-96, chmn., 1996—. Office: Bronner Slosberg Humphrey The Prudential Tower 800 Boylston St Boston MA 02199-8001*

BRONNER, WILLIAM ROCHE, lawyer; b. N.Y.C., Mar. 13, 1946; s. Leonard and Gloria (Roche) Bronner; m. Nancy L. Bloomgarden, Oct. 14, 1973; children: Gregory R.B., Caitlin L.B. BA, Dartmouth Coll., 1967; JD, Columbia U., 1970. Bar: N.Y. 1970, U.S. Dist. Ct. (so. and ea. dists.) N.Y. 1972, U.S. Ct. Appeals (2d cir.) 1973, U.S. Ct. Claims 1977, U.S. Ct. Appeals (9th cir.) 1986, U.S. Dist. Ct. (no. dist.) N.Y. 1990, U.S. Ct. Appeals (fed. cir.) 1992, U.S. Internat. Trade, 1995. Law clk. to presiding judge U.S. Dist. Ct. (so. dist.) N.Y., N.Y.C., 1970-72; asst. U.S. atty. State of N.Y., N.Y.C., 1972-76; assoc. Burns & Jacoby, N.Y.C., 1977; counsel div. NL Industries, N.Y.C., 1978-80, counsel govt. affairs, 1980-82, group counsel, 1982-84, assoc. gen. counsel, 1984-87; gen. counsel NL Chems., Inc., N.Y.C., 1987-90; v.p., sec., gen. counsel Kronos, Inc., Hightstown, N.J., 1990—. Office: Kronos Inc PO Box 700 Hightstown NJ 08520-1007

BRONSDON, ROBERT LAWRENCE, acoustical engineer, artist; b. Balt., Jan. 5, 1949; s. William Prentise and Mary E. Bronsdon; m. Kathleen L. Bronsdon, 1975. B Eng., Pa. State U., 1971, M Eng., 1978. Cons. Bolt

Beranek and Newman Inc., Cambridge, Mass., 1978-83, Harris Miller Miller and Hanson, Burlington, Mass., 1987; prin. engr. Wang Computer Co., Lowell, Mass., 1983-87; mgr. Bruel and Kjaer Am., Marlborough, Mass., 1987-89; prin. engr. Walt. Disney Imagineering, Glendale, Calif., 1990—. Contbr. articles to profl. jour. Petty officer USNR, 1971-77. Mem. Inst. Noise Control engring. (assoc.), Acoustical Soc. Am. (assoc.), Nat. Watercolor Soc. (assoc.). Fax: 818-544-7750. E-mail: robert.L.bronsdon@Disney.com.

BRONSON, CAROLE, publishing executive. Coo Greenwood Pub. Group Inc., Westport, Conn. Office: Greenwood Publishing Group Inc PO Box 5007 88 Post Rd W Westport CT 06880-4208*

BRONSON, CHARLES (CHARLES BUCHINSKY), actor; b. Ehrenfeld, Pa., Nov. 3, 1921; m. Harriet Tendler (div.); 2 children; m. Jill Ireland, 1969 (dec.); 1 child, Zuleika; 2 stepchildren. Appeared in films You're in the Navy Now, 1951, Red Skies of Montana, 1952, Pat and Mike, 1952, House of Wax, 1953, Drumbeat, 1954, Vera Cruz, 1954, Jubal, 1956, Machine Gun Kelly, 1958, Never So Few, 1959, The Magnificent Seven, 1960, A Thunder of Drums, 1961, Lonely Are the Brave, 1962, The Great Escape, 1963, The Battle of the Bulge, 1965, The Sandpiper, 1965, This Property is Condemned, 1966, The Dirty Dozen, 1967, Adieu, L'Ami, Once Upon a Time in the West, 1969, Rider in the Rain, 1970, You Can't Win Them All, 1970, Someone Behind the Door, 1971, Chato's Land, 1971, Red Sun, 1972, The Valachi Papers, 1972, The Mechanic, 1972, Pancho Villa, The Stone Killer, 1973, Death Wish, 1974, Breakout, 1975, Mr. Majestyk, Hard Times, Breakheart Pass, 1976, St. Ives, 1976, Chino, 1976, From Noon Till Three, 1976, Telefon, 1977, Love and Bullets, 1979, Cabo Blanco, 1979, Borderline, 1980, The White Buffalo, Death Hunt, 1981, Death Wish II, 1982, The Evil that Men Do, 1984, Death Wish III, 1985, Murphy's Law, 1986, Assassination, 1987, Messenger of Death, 1988, Kinjite, 1989, The Indian Runner, 1991, Death Wish, V, 1993, Dead to Rights, 1995; TV appearances include Redigo, Man With a Camera, The Travels of Jamie McPheeters, Twilight Zone, The Big Valley, The FBI, Raid on Entebbe, The Line-Up, The Legend of Jesse James, Act of Vengeance, 1986, Yes Virgina, There is a Santa Claus, 1991, The Sea Wolf, 1993; (TV movie) Family of Cops, 1995, Breach of Faith: Family of Cops II, 1997. Served with AUS, 1943-46. Office: William Morris Agy care Lee Rosenberg 151 S El Camino Dr Beverly Hills CA 90212-2775*

BRONSON, DAVID LEIGH, physician, educator; b. Bath, Maine, Mar. 24, 1947; s. Frank Edgar Bronson and Edna Louise (Sullivan) Belanger; m. Susan Kylei McEvoy, May 27, 1973 (div. Dec. 1988); children: Chad Devin, Carly Anne, Jaclyn Ruth, Jonathan David; m. Kathleen Susan Franco, Jan. 30, 1993; children: Roberto Anthony Franco, John Carlos Franco. BA, U. Maine, 1969; MD, U. Vt., 1973. Diplomate Am. Bd. Internal Medicine, Am. Bd. Geriatrics. Med. resident U. Wis., Madison, 1973-74; med. resident U. Vt., Burlington, 1974-76, asst. prof. medicine, 1977-83, assoc. prof. medicine, 1983-92, vice chmn. dept. medicine, 1990-92; chmn. dept. internal medicine Cleve. Clinic Found., 1992-96, chmn. regional med. practice, 1995—; assoc. prof. internal medicine Ohio State U., Columbus, 1992—; clin. prof. medicine Pa. State U., Hershey, 1995—; pres. med. staff, trustee Med. Ctr. Hosp. Vt., Burlington, 1989-90; trustee Univ. Health Ctr., Burlington, 1987-92. Contbr. numerous articles to profl. jours. Fellow ACP; mem. Am. Coll. Physician Execs., Am. Mgmt. Assn., Med. Group Mgmt. Assn., Am. Fedn. for Clin. Rsch., Soc. Gen. Internal Medicine. Office: Cleve Clinic Found 9500 Euclid Ave # S13 Cleveland OH 44195-0001*

BRONSON, FRANKLIN H., zoology educator; b. Pawnee City, Nebr., Apr. 6, 1932; s. Harry and Vida (Shanklin) B.; m. Virginia Rowe, Nov. 14, 1951 (div. 1975); children—Barbara Ann, Steven Michael; m. Rebecca Barnett, Nov. 16, 1978. B.S., Kans. State U., 1956, M.S., 1957; Ph.D., Pa. State U., 1961. Assoc. staff scientist Jackson Lab., Bar Harbor, Maine, 1961-65, staff scientist, 1965-68; assoc. prof. U. Tex., Austin, 1968-72, prof., 1972—, dir. Inst. Reproductive Biology, 1978—; cons. NIH, NSF. Author: Mammalian Reproductive Biology, 1989; contbr. articles to profl. jours. Avocation: fly fishing. Home: 2725 Trail Of The Madrones Austin TX 78746-2344

BRONSON, JOHN ORVILLE, JR., librarian; b. Memphis, Apr. 6, 1937; s. John Orville and Elinor (Sutherland) B.; student N.E. Miss. Jr. Coll., 1957-59; B.S., Miss. State U., 1961; M.L.S., U. Miss., 1965; m. Patricia Ann Packer, June 11, 1963; 1 stepson, Richard Wayne McCoy; children—Victoria Patricia Elizabeth, Glenn Charles. Field sec. Miss. Library Commn., 1961-63; field sec. Acacia Nat. Frat., 1963-65; instr. U. Miss., 1965-66; head librarian Calhoun Jr. Coll., Decatur, Ala., 1965-67, Chesapeake Coll., Wye Mills, Md., 1967-82; telecommunications specialist, 1982-91; coord. Media Technology, 1991—; pres. Wye Milling Co., Inc. Historiographer, Easton Diocese, Episcopal Ch., 1980-83; pres. Talbot County Democratic Club, 1984-85, 99, Congregatl. Counc., St. Marks Lutheran Church; delegate to DE-MD Synod, ELCA, 1998-99; bd. dirs., Integrity, Cathedral of the Annunciation, Episcopal Diocese of Maryld., Baltimore, 1999. Served with USAF Res., 1955-63. Mem. ALA, Md., Ala., Ala. Jr. Coll. (founder, pres. 1966-67) library assns., Md. Assn. Jr. Colls., Congress Acad. Librarians, Old Wye Mill Soc. (treas.), Soc. for Preservation Md. Antiquities (dir.), Upper Shore Geneal. Soc. (founder), Acacia. Mason (Shriner). Editor: Ala. Jr. Coll. Librarian, 1966-67. Home: 7288 Shirley Dr Easton MD 21601-4804

BRONSON, MARTHA ANN, secondary education educator; b. Hubbard, Ohio, Jan. 18, 1944; d. Frank Ellsworth and Eleanor Mildred (Wardell) McClain; m. Allan James Bronson, June 25, 1966 (dec. Aug. 1995); children: Christopher James, Jeffrey Allen. BS in Edn., Kent (Ohio) State U., 1965; M in Ednl. Profl. Devel., U. Wis., Whitewater, 1986; MA in Edn., Marian Coll., Fond Du Lac, Wis., 1997. Tchr. Big Foot H.S., Walworth, Wis., 1966, Delavan (Wis.)-Darien H.S., 1966-67, Harvard (Ill.) Jr. High, 1967-68, Fontana (Wis.) Elem., 1968-71; tchr., dir. instrn. Cambria (Wis.)-Friesland Schs., 1971—. Mem. Cambria Pk. Bd., 1974-78; chair, moderator book discussion group Cambria-Jane Morgan Libr., 1996—. Mem. Phi Kappa Delta, Delta Kappa Gamma (past pres., parliamentarian). Avocations: reading, crocheting, computers. Office: Cambria-Friesland Sch Dist 410 E Edgewater Cambria WI 53923

BRONSON, OSWALD PERRY, religious organization administrator, clergyman; b. Sanford, Fla., July 19, 1927; s. Uriah Perry and Flora (Hollingshed) B.; m. Helen Carolyn Williams, June 8, 1952; children—Josephine Suzette, Flora Helen, Oswald Perry. B.S., Bethune-Cookman Coll., 1950; B.D., Gammon Theol. Sem., 1959; Ph.D., Northwestern U., 1965. Ordained to ministry Meth. Ch., 1957; pastor in Fla., Ga. and Rock River Conf., Chgo., 1950-66; v.p. Interdenominational Theol. Center, Atlanta, 1966-68; pres. Interdenominational Theol. Center, 1968-75, Bethune-Cookman Coll., 1975—; dir. Fla. Bank and Trust Co.; Past trustee Carrie Steel Pitts Home, Atlanta; past pres. and chmn. bd. edn. Ga. Conf., Central Jurisdiction, United Meth. Ch.; now mem. bd. ministry DeLand dist., also Fla. Ann. Conf., mem., univ. senate, past chmn. div. ministry, mem.-at-large bd. global ministries; mem. Pres.'s Bd. Advisors HBCU, USAF Bd. Advisors HBCU. Bd. dirs. United Meth. Com. on Relief; past mem. Volusia County (Fla.) Sch. Bd., Fla. Gov.'s Adv. Council on Productivity; past mem. exec. com. So. Regional Edn. Bd.; mem. adv. com. Fla. Sickle Cell Found., Inc.; past mem. council presidents Atlanta U. Center; mem. Fla. Bd. Ind. Colls. and Univs.; past trustee Hinton Rural Life Center; past bd. dirs. Inst. of Black World, Wesley Community Center, Atlanta, Martin Luther King Center Social Change, Work Oriented Rehab. Center, Inc., Fund Theol. Edn.; mem. nat. selection com. Rockefeller Doctoral Fellowships in Religion; bd. dirs. Am. Nat. Red Cross, United Way, Nat. Assn. Equal Opportunity in Higher Edn., United Negro Coll. Fund; also mem. fund raising strategy adv. com. Ga. Pastors' Sch. Crusade scholar, 1957-64. Mem. Am. Assn. Theol. Schs. (v.p. 1968-70), Ministerial Assn. of Halifax Area, Religious Edn. Assn. (past pres., past chmn. bd. dirs.), Mid-Atlantic Assn. Profs. Religious Edn., Fla. Assn. Colls. and Univs. (pres. 1997—), Atlanta Theol. Assn. (past vice chmn.), AAUP, Daytona Beach area C. of C., NAACP, Theta Phi (past dir. internat. soc.), Alpha Kappa Mu, Phi Delta Kappa, Sigma Pi Phi, Alpha Phi Alpha. Clubs: Rotary, Daytona Beach area Execs, Daytona Beach Quarterback. Office: Bethune-Cookman Coll 640 Dr Mary Mcleod Bethune Blv Daytona Beach FL 32114-3012*

BRONSTEIN, ALVIN J., lawyer; b. Bklyn., June 8, 1928. LLD, N.Y. Law Sch., 1951, LLD (hon.), 1990. Bar: N.Y. 1952, Miss. 1967, La. 1971, U.S. Ct. Appeals (D.C., 1st, 2d, 3d, 4th, 5th, 9th, 10th and 11th cirs.), U.S. Supreme Ct. 1961. Ptnr. Bronstein & Bronstein, Bklyn., 1952-63; pvt. practice Elizabethtown, N.Y., 1963-64; chief staff counsel Lawyers Constl. Def. Com., Jackson, Miss., 1964-68; fellow Inst. Politics, Kennedy Sch. Govt. Harvard U., Cambridge, Mass., 1968-69, assoc. dir. Inst. Politics, Kennedy Sch. Govt., 1969-71; ptnr. Elie, Bronstein, Strickler & Dennis, New Orleans, 1971-72; exec. dir. Nat. Prison Project, Nat. Jail Project ACLU Found., Washington, 1972-96; cons. nat. legal dept. ACLU Found., 1996—; cons., trial counsel CORE, NAACP, NAACP Legal Def. Fund, SCLC, SNCC, Miss. Freedom Dem. Party, Black Panther Party, Nat. Inst. for Edn. in Law and Poverty, and others; guest lectr. various law schs., 1964—; cons. various state corrections depts., 1972—; adj. prof. Am. U. Law Sch., 1973; expert witness in various prison litigations, 1978—; appointed mem. Fed. Jud. Ctr. Adv. Com. on Experimentation in the Law, 1978-81. Contbg. author: The Evolution of Criminal Justice, 1978, Prisoners' Rights Sourcebook, Vol. II, 1980, Confinement in Maximum Custody, 1980, Sage Criminal Justice Annual, Vol. 14, 1980, Readings in the Justice Model, 1980, Our Endangered Rights, 1984, Prisoners and the Courts: The American Experience, 1985; author: (with Rudovsky and Koren) The Rights of Prisoners, 1988; author, editor: Representing Prisoners, 1981; editor: Prisoners' Self-Help Litigation Manual, 1977; contbr. articles to profl. jours. MacArthur Found. fellow, 1989; named one of the 100 most influential lawyers in Am., Nat. Law Jour., 1985, 88, 91, 94; recipient Roscoe Pound award Nat. Coun. on Crime and Delinquency, 1981, Karl Menninger award Fortune Soc., 1982, Pa. Prison Soc. award, 1991. Office: Nat Prison Project ACLU Found 1875 Connecticut Ave NW Washington DC 20009-5728*

BRONSTEIN, ARTHUR J., linguistics educator; b. Balt., Mar. 15, 1914; s. Gershon and Bessie B.; m. Elsa Meltzer, May 15, 1941; children: Nancy Ellen, Abbot Alan. B.A., CCNY, 1934; M.A., Columbia U., 1936; Ph.D., NYU, 1949. Vis. scholar and rsch. assoc. in linguistics U. Calif., Berkeley, 1987—; prof. Queens Coll., N.Y.C., 1938-67; Fulbright prof. U. Tel Aviv, (Israel), 1967-68, U. Trondheim, (Norway), 1979; prof. linguistics Lehman Coll. and Grad. Sch., CUNY, 1968-83, prof. emeritus, 1983—; exec. officer PhD program in speech and hearing scis. CUNY, 1969-72; exec. officer Ph.D. program in linguistics Grad. Sch., CUNY, 1981-83; cons. in field; with dept. linguistics U. Calif., Berkeley. Author: Pronunciation of American English, 1960, Essays in Honor of C.M. Wise, 1970, Biographical Dictionary of the Phonetic Sciences, 1977; project dir.: Dictionary of American English Pronunciation. Served with Signal Corps and AGD USAAF, 1942-46. Fellow Am. Speech and Hearing Assn., Internat. Soc. Phonetic Scis., N.Y. Acad. Sci.; mem. MLA, Linguistics Soc. Am., Am. Dialect Soc., Internat. Phonetic Assn., Am. Assn. Phonetic Scis., Dictionary Soc. N.Am., Phi Beta Kappa. Office: U Calif Dept Linguistics Berkeley CA 94720

BRONSTEIN, LYNNE, writer; b. Dec. 30, 1950. Staff writer Showtime Mag., Santa Monica, Calif., 1998—; freelance journalist, 1972—. Author: Astray from Normalcy, 1974, Roughage, 1977, Thirsty in the Ocean, 1980. Mem. PEN West.

BRONSTEIN, PHIL, executive editor. Reporter Sta. KQED-TV, San Francisco; reporter, fgn. corr. San Francisco Examiner, 1980—, exec. editor, 1991—. Recipient awards Overseas Press Club, AP, World Affairs Coun., Media Alliance, Pulitzer Prize finalist. Office: San Francisco Examiner 110 5th St San Francisco CA 94103

BRONSTEIN, RICHARD J., lawyer; b. Chgo., May 11, 1949; s. Jack and Elaine (Abrams) B.; children: Andrew, Grace; m. Eileen S. Silvers, Aug. 24, 1995. AB, U. Pa., 1970; JD, U. Chgo., 1974. Bar: Ill. 1974, N.Y. 1977, U.S. Tax Ct., D.C. 1984. Law clk. to Hon. Spottswood W. Robinson III U.S. Ct. Appeals, Washington, 1974-75; law clk. to Hon. William J. Brennan, Jr. U.S. Supreme Ct., Washington, 1975-76; assoc. Paul, Weiss, Rifkind, Wharton & Garrison, N.Y.C., 1976-82, ptnr., 1982—; lectr. Practising Law Inst., N.Y.C., 1981—, NYU, N.Y.C., 1985. Mem. ABA, N.Y. State Bar Assn. (com. on depreciation), Assn. of Bar of City of N.Y. (com. on taxation). Office: Paul Weiss Rifkind Wharton & Garrison Ste 506 1285 Avenue Of The Americas Fl 21 New York NY 10019-6065*

BRONSTER, MARGERY S, state attorney general; b. N.Y., Dec. 12, 1957; married; 1 child. BA in Chinese Lang., Lit. and History, Brown U., 1979; JD, Columbia U., 1982. Assoc. Sherman & Sterling, N.Y., 1982-87; ptnr. Carlsmith, Ball, Wichman, Murray, Case & Ichiki, Honolulu, 1988-94; atty. gen. State of Hawaii, 1994—; co-chair planning com. Citizens Conf. Judicial Selection, 1993. Mem. Am. Judicature Soc. (bd. dirs.; chair gov. com. on crime, VAWA planning com.). Office: Office Attorney General 425 Queen St Honolulu HI 96813-2903*

BRONTOLI, MARGRETH J., ophthalmologist; b. N.Y.C., Dec. 7, 1957; d. John and Helene Brontoli; m. Robert J. Klein. BA, SUNY, New Paltz, 1979; MD, SUNY, Bklyn., 1985. Pvt. practice Bklyn., 1990, Long Beach, N.Y., 1991—. Contbr. sci. articles to profl. jours. Fellow ACS, Am. Acad. Ophthalmology; mem. N.Y. State Ophthalmol. Soc., Bklyn. Ophthalmol. Soc. Office: 202 W Park Ave Long Beach NY 11561

BRONWELL, NANCY BROOKER, writer; b. Columbia, S.C., Oct. 11, 1921; d. Norton Wardlaw and Lucile Duty (Michaux) Brooker; m. Alvin Wayne Bronwell, June 21, 1943 (div. Mar. 1975); children: Betsy Randolph Bronwell Jones, Cynthia Alison. BS, Mary Washington Coll., 1942; post-grad., U. Ky., 1942-43, Tex. Tech. U., 1965, 87. Tchr. English, phys. edn. Louisville Pub. Schs., 1943-46; sec. edn. dept. Jos. S. Seagram & Sons Inc., Louisville, 1945-46; sec. to sales mgr. Marshall Field Corp., Chgo., 1946; sec. to dir. purchases Jos. E. Seagram & Sons., Inc., 1946-48; freelance writer Lubbock, Tex., 1978—. Author: Lubbock: A Pictorial History, 1980. Co-founder, bd. dirs. Young Women's Christian Assn., Lubbock, 1953; vol. Lubbock Jr. League, Lubbock Symphony Orch., Palsy Ctr., ARC, Tech. Mus., St. Paul's Ch. Mem. South Plains Writers Guild, Lubbock Heritage Assn. (Excellence award 1981), DAR, Huguenot Soc., Friends of Libr. (life). Republican. Episcopalian. Avocations: reading, word games, tennis, needlework. Home and Office: 4108 18th St # A Lubbock TX 79416-6009

BRONZINO, JOSEPH DANIEL, electrical engineer; b. Bklyn., Sept. 29, 1937; s. Joseph Rocco and Antoinette (Saporito) B.; m. Barbara Louise McGrath, Dec. 2, 1961; children: Michael J., Melissa J., Marcella J. BSEE, Worcester Poly. Inst., 1959, PhD in Elec. Engring, 1968; MSEE, U.S. Naval Postgrad. Sch., 1961. Registered profl. engr., Conn. Instr. elec. engring. U. N.H., 1964-66, asst. prof. elec. engring., 1966-67; NSF faculty fellow Worcester Found. for Exptl. Biology, Shrewsbury, Mass., 1967-68; mem. cooperating staff Worcester Found. for Exptl. Biology, 1968-94; assoc. prof. engring. Trinity Coll., 1968-75, prof., 1975—, Vernon Roosa prof. applied sci., 1977—, chmn. dept. engring., 1981-91; adj. faculty Boston U. Med. Sch., 1987—; dir. and chmn. biomed. engring. program Hartford (Conn.) Grad. Ctr., 1969-97; clin. assoc. dept. surgery U. Conn. Health Ctr., Farmington, 1971-77; rsch. assoc. Inst. for Living, Hartford, 1968-97; reviewer NSF; panelist NSF Rsch. Initiation Grants; dir. Biomed. Engring. Alliance for Conn., 1997—; lectr., spkr. in field. Author: Technology for Patient Care, 1977, Computer Application in Patient Care, 1982, Biomedical Engineering Basic Concepts and Instrumentation, 1986, Medical Technology: Economic and Ethical Issues, 1990, Expert Systems: Basic Concepts, 1990, Management of Medical Technology: A Primer for Clinical Engineers, 1992, Biomedical Engineering Handbook, 1995, Introduction to Biomedical Engineering, 1999; contbr. articles to profl. publs. Mem. Simsbury (Conn.) Planning Commn., 1977-82. Served to 1st lt. Signal Corps U.S. Army, 1961-63. Fellow IEEE (sr., regional dir. group engring. in medicine and biology 1973-78, v.p. tech. activities 1982-85, pres. 1985-86, chmn. health care engring. policy com. 1986-90, vice chmn. tech. policy coun. 1990-91, chmn. tech. policy coun.), Am. Inst. Med. and Biol. Engrs., Am. Soc. Engring. Edn. (exec. com. divsn. biomed. engring. 1973-82, vice chmn. career devel. 1974-76, vice chmn. profl. devel. 1976-77, divisional newsletter editor 1977-79, chmn.-elect divsn. 1979-80, exec. com. 1990-91, chmn. tech. policy coun. 1992-94, editor in chief Acad. Press Biomedical Engineering Book Series), AAAS, Biol. Psychiatry, Neurosci. Soc., Rotary (pres. Simsbury club 1971-89, 91-93, Hartford club 1989-91), Cosmos Club. Republican. Roman Catholic. Achievements include rsch. in signal analysis concepts and applications, basic neurophysiol. concepts involved in identifying specific neural circuits associated with specific functions of the brain. Home: 12 Brenthaven Avon CT 06001-3941 Office: Trinity Coll Dept Engring Hartford CT 06106

BROOK, ADRIAN GIBBS, chemistry educator; b. Toronto, May 21, 1924; s. Frank Adrian and Beatrice Maud (Wellington) B.; m. Margaret Ellen Dunn, Dec. 18, 1954; children—Michael A., Katherine M., David L. BA, U. Toronto, 1947, PhD, 1950. Lectr. chemistry U. Sask., 1950-51; research fellow Imperial Coll., London, 1951-52, Iowa State Coll., 1952-53; lectr. chemistry U. Toronto, 1953-56, asst. prof., 1956-60, assoc. prof., 1960-62, prof., 1962-87, univ. prof., 1987-89, univ. prof. emeritus, 1989—, chmn. dept. chemistry, 1969-74; vis. prof. U. Sussex, 1974-75, Cambridge (Eng.) U., 1982, Ind. U., 1988. Contbr. articles to profl. jours. Nuffield Overseas fellow, 1951; recipient Izaak Walton Killam Meml. prize for Sci., 1994. Fellow Royal Soc. Can., Chem. Inst. Can. (CIC medal 1985); mem. Am. Chem. Soc. (Frederic Stanley Kipping award 1973). Home: Apt 202, 7 Thornwood Rd, Toronto, ON Canada M4W 2R8 Office: U Toronto Dept Chemistry, 80 St George St, Toronto, ON Canada M5S 3H6

BROOK, DAVID WILLIAM, psychiatrist, researcher; b. N.Y.C., Sept. 19, 1936; s. Michael Marysson and Hilda Jeanette (Ascher) B.; m. Judith Suzanne Muser, Dec. 15, 1962; children: Adam Michael, Jonathan Edward. BA, U. Rochester, 1958; MD, Yale U., 1961. Diplomate Am. Bd. Psychiatry and Neurology; cert. gen. psychiatry; cert. addiction psychiatry. Intern U. Chgo. Hosps., 1961-62; resident Mt. Sinai Hosp., 1962-65, asst. attending psychiatrist, 1973-80, assoc. attending psychiatrist, 1980-90, attending psychiatrist (cmty. medicine), 1994—; practice medicine specializing in psychiatry N.Y.C., 1965—; clin. asst. in psychiatry Hillside Hosp., 1965-67; sch. psychiatrist N.Y.C. Bur. Child Guidance, 1967-69; asst. clin. prof. psychiatry Mt. Sinai Sch. Medicine, 1977-88, assoc. clin. prof., 1988-90, adj. assoc. prof., 1990-92; prof. cmty. medicine, 1994—; assoc. prof. psychiatry N.Y. Med. Coll., Valhalla, 1990-94, 1990-92, prof. clin. psychiatry, 1992-94; adj. asst. prof. psychiatry Fordham U. Sch. Social Work, 1970-73; med. dir. Washington Sq. Inst. Psychotherapy and Mental Health, 1977-82; assoc. attending psychiatrist, dir. dept. psychiatry Mt. Sinai Svcs., Elmhurst Hosp. Ctr., 1989-90; attending psychiatrist Westchester County Med. Ctr., 1990-94; dir. divsn. drug abuse rsch., prevention and treatment N.Y. Med. Coll., Valhalla, 1990-94, adj. prof. psychiatry, 1994—; prin. investigarot, co-prin. investigator rsch. grants Nat. Inst. Drug Abuse. Co-author, co-editor 5 books including Psychology of Adolescence, 1978; contbr. over 75 articles to profl. jours., chpts. to books on group psychotherapy, adolescence, alcoholism, drug abuse and behavioral medicine; mem. editl. bd. Internat. Jour. Group Psychotherapy, 1995—. Fellow Am. Group Psychotherapy Assn. (bd. dirs. 1992-95, 98—), Am. Psychiat. Assn. (exec. coun. N.Y. County dist. br. 1988-91), N.Y. Acad. Medicine; mem. AAAS, Group Psychotherapy Found. (bd. dirs. 1992-98), Am. Acad. Addiction Psychiatry. Fax: (212) 423-0548. Office: Mt Sinai Sch Medicine Box 1044A One Gustave L-Levy Place New York NY 10029

BROOK, JUDITH SUZANNE, psychiatry and psychology researcher and educator; b. N.Y.C., Dec. 31, 1939; d. Robert and Helen E. (Zimmerman) Muser; m. David W. Brook, Dec. 15, 1962; children: Adam, Jonathan. BA, Hunter Coll., 1961; MA in Psychology, Columbia U., 1962, EdD in Devel. and Ednl. Psychology, 1967. Lic. psychologist, N.Y. Asst. prof. psychology Queens Coll., CUNY, Flushing, 1967-69; rsch. assoc. Columbia U., N.Y.C., 1969-77, sr. rsch. assoc., 1977-80; assoc. prof. psychiatry Mt. Sinai Sch. Medicine, N.Y.C., 1980-90, adj. prof., 1990-94; prof. N.Y. Med. Coll., Valhalla, N.Y., 1990-94; prof. cmty. medicine Mt. Sinai Sch. Medicine, 1994—; rsch. scientist devel. award Nat. Inst. on Drug Abuse, 1982-90, sr. rsch. scientist, 1992—, ad hoc reviewer, 1989—, chair study sect. epidemiology, prevention & rsch; ad hoc reviewer NIMH, NSF, 1992—. Author: The Psychology of Adolescence, 1978, others; contbr. numerous articles to profl. jours. Recipient 1st ann. Dean's Disting. Rsch. award N.Y. Med. Coll., 1992; grantee Nat. Inst. on Drug Abuse, 1979—. Fellow Am. Psychopathol. Assn.; mem. APA, Am. Psychol. Soc. (liaison officer 1989—), Assn. for Med. Edn. and Rsch. in Substance Abuse, N.Y. State Psychol. Assn., Coll. on Problems of Drug Dependence. Office: Mt Sinai Sch Medicine Dept Cmty Med Box 1044A One Gustave Levy Pl New York NY 10029

BROOK, ROBERT HENRY, physician, educator, health services researcher; b. N.Y.C., July 3, 1943; s. Benjamin and Elizabeth (Berg) B.; m. Susan Jean Weiss, June 26, 1966 (div. 1980); children: Rebecca, Daniel; m. Jacqueline Barbara Kosecoff Pliant, Jan. 17, 1982; children—Rachel, Davida. BS, U. Ariz., 1964; MD, Johns Hopkins U., 1968, ScD, 1972. Diplomate: Am. Bd. Internal Medicine. Intern Balt. City Hosp., 1968-69, resident in medicine, 1969-72; project officer Nat. Ctr. Health Svcs. Rsch., HEW, Washington, 1972-74; vice chmn. medicine UCLA, 1990-92, dir. clin. scholar program, 1974—, prof. of medicine and pub. health, 1974—; dir. health program RAND Corp., Santa Monica, Calif., 1990—, v.p., 1998—. Mem. editorial bd. Health Adminstrn. Press., 1986-92, Jour. Gen. Internal Medicine, 1987-89, Health Policy, 1986—; contbr. articles to profl. jours. Served as asst. surgeon USPHS, 1972-74. Lita Annenberg Biomed. fellow Inst. Humanistic Studies, Aspen, Colo., 1981; recipient Rsch. prize Baxter Found. Health Svcs., 1988, Glazer award Soc. Gen. Internal Medicine; selected as one of 75 pub. health heroes of Johns Hopkins, 1991. Fellow ACP (Rosenthal award); mem. Inst. Medicine, Am. Soc. Clin. Investigation, Assn. Health Svcs. Rsch. (bd. dirs. 1982-89, Disting. Health Svc. Researcher award), Assn. Am. Physicians, Johns Hopkins Soc. Scholars. Democrat. Jewish. Home: 1474 Bienveneda Ave Pacific Palisades CA 90272-2346 Office: Rand Corp 1700 Main St Santa Monica CA 90401-3297

BROOK, SUSAN G., state agency administrator, horse farmer; b. N.Y.C., Dec. 7, 1949; d. Alvin Ira and Sally (Behar) Greenberg. BA, Northwestern U., 1971; MA in Child Devel. and Pub. Adminstrn., Mich. State U., 1975. Community rep. Office Child Devel. HEW, Chgo., 1971-72; program asst. office of pres. OEO, Chgo., 1972-73; exec. coord. Mich. 4-C Coun. Mich. Dept. Mgmt. and Budget, Lansing, 1973-80; adminstr. office interagy. transp. coordination Mich. Dept. Transp., Lansing, 1980-83; adminstr. freight svcs. and safety Bur. Urban and Pub. Transp., Mich. Dept. Transp., Lansing, 1983—; chairperson legis. com. Mich. Coun. Family Rels., Lansing, 1976-77; mem. coalition on children and youth, Lansing, 1976-80; co-chairperson Mich. White House Conf. on Families, Lansing, 1979-80, gov's liaison Internat. Yr of the Child, Lansing, 1978-79; guest lectr. Mich. State U., East Lansing, 1976, Davenport Coll., 1985; inst. Lansing Community Coll., 1978; mem. curriculum devel. adv. com. Lansing community coll., 1979-80. Advisor neighborhood health clinic, Chgo., 1969; youth group advisor Shaare Tikvah Congregation, Chgo., 1967-71; campaign treas. city council candidate, East Lansing, Mich., 1981. Mem. ASPCA, Am. Morgan Horse Assn., Am. Donkey and Mule Soc., Nat. Assn. Edn. Young Children, Nat. Assn. State Dirs. Child Devel., Nat. Conf. State Ry. Ofcls., Am. Horse Shows Assn., Mich. Horse Show Assn., Mich. Justin Morgan Horse Assn., Mich. Morgan Horse Breeders Futurity, Mich. Assn. Edn. Young Children (hon.), Mich. Farm Bur., Capital Area Humane Soc., Calif. Marine Mammal Ctr., Gt. Lakes Miniature Horse Club, Am. Miniature Horse Club, Ingham County Farm Bur., Soc. Women in Transp., Women in State Govt., Animal Protection Inst., Am. Miniature Horse Assn., Australian Shepherd Club Am., Hadassah. Avocations: horseback riding, breeding, training and showing Miniature and Morgan horses, miniature donkeys and Australian Shepherds, cross-country skiing. Office: Mich Dept Transp 425 W Ottawa St Lansing MI 48933-1532

BROOK, WINSTON ROLLINS, retired audio-video design consultant; b. Cameron, Tex., Aug. 20, 1931; s. Winston Marshall and Maude Katherine (Woody) B. BA, U. Denver, 1955. Lic. radiotelephone operator, FCC. Engr. Sta. WKNO-TV, Memphis, 1965-67; instr. Memphis State U., 1967-69; audio-visual dir. So. Coll. Optometry, Memphis, 1968-73; sr. cons. Bolt Beranek and Newman, Chgo. and L.A., 1973-87; prin. RB Sys., L.A., 1987-97; ret., 1997; assoc. editor Theater Design & Tech. mag., N.Y.C., 1981-87; tech. cons. Sound & Video Contractor mag., Overland, Kans., 1987—; lectr. in field. Co-author: Handbook for Sound Engineers, 1987; contbr. articles to profl. jours. Mem. Audio Engring. Soc., Acoustical Soc. Am., U.S. Inst. for Theater Tech. Democrat. Mormon. Home: 5715 Calvin Ave Tarzana CA 91356-1108

BROOKBANK, JOHN W(ARREN), retired microbiology educator; b. Seattle, Apr. 3, 1927; s. Earl Bruce and Louise Sophia (Stoecker) B.; m.

Marcia Ireland, Sept. 16, 1950 (div. 1978); children: Ursula Ireland, John W. Jr., Phoebe Bruce; m. Sally Satterberg Cahill, Aug. 6, 1983. BA, U. Wash., 1950, MS, 1953; PhD, Calif. Inst. Tech., 1955. Asst. prof. biology U. Fla., Gainesville, 1955-58, assoc. prof., 1958-68, prof. microbiology and cell sci., 1968-85, prof. emeritus, 1985—; vis. assoc. prof. U. Fla. Coll. Medicine, Gainesville, 1961-63, U. Wash., Seattle, 1965; cons. in field, Friday Harbor, Wash. 1986—. Author: Developmental Biology, 1978, (with W. Cunningham) Gerontology, 1988; editor: Improving Quality of Health Care of the Elderly, 1977, Biology of Aging, 1990; contbr. articles to profl. jours. Pres. Griffin Bay Preservation Com., Friday Harbor, 1985—, Bridge Council on Narcotics Addiction, Gainesville, 1974, Marine Environ. Consortium, 1986-89, San Juan Nature Inst., 1997-98; founding pres. Gainesville Regional Council on Alcoholism, 1976; mem devel. adv. bd. U. Wash. Friday Harbor Lab., 1995-98. Research grantee NIH, 1957-80, NSF, 1972-73. Mem. Gerontol. Soc. Am., Seattle Tennis Club. Republican. Episcopalian. Avocations: fishing, boating, tennis, skiing. Home: PO Box 2688 Friday Harbor WA 98250-2688

BROOKE, AVERY ROGERS, publisher, writer; b. Providence, May 28, 1923; d. Morgan Witter and Lucy Avery (Benjamin) Rogers; m. Joel Ijams Brooke, Sept. 14, 1946; children—Witter, Lucy, Sarah. Student, R.I. Sch. Design, 1942-45; B.F.A., Union Theol. Sem., 1970. Founder Vineyard Books, Inc., Noroton, Conn., 1971-88; pub., v.p. Seabury Press, N.Y.C., 1980-83; mentor Annand Program Spiritual Growth, Yale/Berkeley Divinity. Author: Youth Talks with God, 1959, Doorway to Meditation, 1973, How To Meditate without Leaving the World, 1975, Plain Prayers for a Complicated World, 1975, 93, Roots of Spring, 1975, As Never Before, 1976, Hidden in Plain Sight, 1978, Cooking with Conscience (under pseudonym Alice Benjamin), 1975, The Vineyard Bible, 1980, Celtic Prayers, 1981, Trailing Clouds of Glory, 1985, Finding God in the World, 1989, 2d edit., 1994, Plain Prayers in a Complicated World, 1993, Healing in the Landscape of Prayer, 1996. Mem. The Author's Guild, Oblate Order of the Holy Cross, Spiritual Dirs. Internat. Democrat. Episcopalian. Home: 27 Pasture Ln Darien CT 06820-5618

BROOKE, EDWARD WILLIAM, lawyer, former senator; b. Washington, Oct. 26, 1919; s. Edward W. and Helen (Seldon) B. B.S., Howard U., 1940, LL.D., 1967; LL.B. (editor Law Rev.), Boston U., 1948, LL.M., 1949, LL.D., 1968; LL.D., George Washington U., 1967, Skidmore Coll., 1969, U. Mass., 1971, Amherst Coll., 1972; D.Sc., Lowell Tech. Inst., 1967; D.Sc. numerous other hon. degrees. Bar: Mass. 1948, D.C. Ct. Appeals 1979, D.C. Dist. Ct. 1982, U.S. Supreme Ct. 1962. Chmn. Boston Fin. Com., 1961-62; atty. gen. State of Mass., Boston, 1963-66; mem. U.S. Senate from Mass., 1967-79; chmn. Nat. Low-Income Housing Coalition; former ptnr. O'Connor & Hannan, Washington; formrly of counsel Csaplar & Bok, Boston; former pub. mem. Adminstrv. Conf. U.S.; chmn. bd. dirs. Boston Bank Commerce; bd. dirs. Meditrust, Inc., Wellesley, Mass., Grumman Corp., Bethpage, N.Y. Chmn. Boston Opera Co.; former commr. Pres.'s Commns. on Housing and of Wartime Relocation and Internment of Civilians; bd. dirs. Washington Performing Arts Soc. Served as capt. inf. AUS, World War II, ETO. Decorated Bronze Star; recipient Disting. Svc. award Amvets, 1952, Charles Evans Hughes award NCCJ, 1967, Spingarn medal, NAACP, 1967. Fellow Am. Bar Assn., Am. Acad. Arts and Scis. Office: Hanied Brooke Ste 301-S 2500 Virginia Ave NW Washington DC 20037*

BROOKE, FRANCIS JOHN, III, foundation administrator; b. Charleston, W.Va., Mar. 4, 1929; s. Francis John Jr. and Elizabeth (Baird) B.; m. Helen Holmes Morgan, Dec. 20, 1958; children: Francis John, Haynes Morgan, David Tucker. BA, Hampden-Sydney Coll., 1949; MA, U. Chgo., 1951; PhD, U. N.C., 1954. Instr. German Roanoke Coll., Salem, Va., summers 1950-52; teaching fellow, part-time instr. U. N.C., Chapel Hill, 1951-54; mem. faculty, to assoc. prof. German U. Va., Charlottesville, 1956-65, asst. dean. Coll. Arts & Scis., 1959-62, acting chmn. dept. modern langs., 1962-63; exec. dean, prof. German Centre Coll., Danville, Ky., 1965-68; v.p. acad. affairs Va. Commonwealth U., Richmond, 1968-74, provost, acad. campus, 1973-79, spl. asst. to pres., 1979-80, prof. German, 1968-80; pres. Columbus (Ga.) Coll., 1980-87; spl. asst. to chancellor Univ. System of Ga., Atlanta, 1988; Pacific N.W. regional rep. Presbyn. Ch. Found., Seattle, 1989—; vice chmn. So. Humanities Conf., 1965; pres. South Atlantic region Am. Assn. Tchrs. German, 1965-67; exec. com. South Atlantic chpt. MLA, 1963-66. Mem. gen. assembly com. on theol. edn. Presbyn. Ch., 1988-90. With AUS, 1954-56. Old Dominion Found. grantee, 1960; intern acad. adminstrn. Ellis L. Phillips Found., Cornell U., 1963-64. Mem. Assn. State Colls. and Univs. (com. on humanities 1984-86, com. on urban affairs 1986-87), Omicron Delta Kappa. Office: Presbyn Ch Found Regional Office 217 6th Ave N Seattle WA 98109-5005

BROOKE, GEORGE MERCER, JR., historian, educator; b. Tokyo, Oct. 21, 1914; (parents Am. citizens); s. George Mercer and Isabel Elsie (Tilton) B.; m. Frances Fleming Bailey, June 13, 1942; children: George Mercer III, Marion Bailey Brooke Philpott. BA in Liberal Arts, Va. Mil. Inst., 1936; MA in History, Washington and Lee U., 1942; PhD in History, U. N.C., 1955. Spl. agent Md. Casualty Co., Balt., 1936-41; history instr. Va. Mil. Inst., Lexington, 1942-43, from asst. prof. to prof., 1948-80, prof. emeritus, 1980—; history instr. Washington & Lee U., Lexington, 1946-47. Author: John M. Brooke, Naval Scientist, 1980, General Lee's Church, 1984, John M. Brooke's Pacific Cruise, 1986; contbr. numerous articles to profl. publs. Chmn. Citizen-Soldier Meml. Va. Mil. Inst., 1983-84, Sesquicentennial celebration, 1986-89; unit pres. Am. Cancer Soc., 1980-82; pres. Stonewall Jackson area coun. Boy Scouts Am., 1964-67. 1st lt. U.S. Army, 1943-46, PTO. Fulbright rsch. scholar Keio U., 1962-63; Fulbright teaching grantee Nat. Taiwan U., 1963; recipient Silver Beaver award Boy Scouts Am., 1967, Citizen-Scouter of Yr. award, 1989. Mem. SAR, So. Hist. Assn., Assn. for Preservation Va. Antiquities (br. pres. 1975-77), Soc. of the Cin. (standing com. 1984-87), Rockbridge Hist. Soc. (pres. 1960-62, editor procs. 1989), English Speaking Union (br. pres. 1980-82), Internat. House of Japan, Am. Legion, Phi Beta Kappa, Kappa Alpha Order. Republican. Episcopalian. Avocations: travel, reading, walking. Home: 405 Jackson Ave Lexington VA 24450-1905

BROOKE, JAMES BETTNER, news correspondent; b. N.Y.C., Feb. 21, 1955; s. John Louis Barde and Louisa (Ludlow) B..; m. Elizabeth Heilman Brooke, Sept. 7, 1985; children: James, Alexander, William. BA in Latin Am. Studies, Yale U., 1977. Reporter S.Am. region The Miami Herald, Rio de Janeiro, 1982-84; metro reporter The N.Y. Times, N.Y.C., 1984-86, West Africa bur. chief, 1986-89; Brazil bur. chief The N.Y. Times, Rio de Janeiro, 1989-95; Rocky Mountain bur. chief The N.Y. Times, Denver, 1995—. Office: The New York Times 1624 Market St Ste #304 Denver CO 80202-1518

BROOKE, JOHN L., history educator; b. Mass., May 19, 1953; m. Sara C. Balderston, July 31, 1979. BA in History and Anthropology, Cornell U., 1976; MA in History, U. Pa., 1977, PhD in History, 1982. Vis. asst. prof. Amherst (Mass.) Coll., 1982-83; asst. prof. to prof. Tufts U., Medford, Mass., 1983—; dept. chair, 1996-97. Author: The Heart of the Commonwealth: Society and Political Culture in Worcester County, Massachusetts, 1713-1861, 1989, The Refiner's Fire: The Making of Mormon Cosmology, 1644-1844, 1994; contbr. articles to scholarly jours. Recipient award Nat. Soc. Daus. Colonial Wars, 1989, E. Harold Hugo Meml. Book prize Old Sturbridge Village Rsch. Libr. Soc., 1989, Merle Curti award for intellectual history, 1991, book prize for Am. history Nat. Hist. Soc., 1991, Bancroft prize Columbia U., 1995, ann. book prize Soc. for Historians of Early Am. Republic, 1995, ann. book award New Eng. Hist. Assn., 1995; S.F. Haven fellow Am. Antiquarian Soc., 1982, faculty rsch. fellow Tufts U., 1983, 88, Charles Warren fellow Harvard U., 1986-87, jr. fellow NEH, 1986-87, sr. fellow Commonwealth Ctr., 1990-91, fellow Am. Coun. Learned Socs., 1990-91, NEH fellow 1997-98, Guggenheim fellow, 1997-98. Mem. AAUP, Am. Antiq. Soc., Am. Hist. Assn., Orgn. Am. Historians, Mass. Hist. Soc. Democrat. Office: Tufts U History Dept Medford MA 02155*

BROOKE, PAUL ALAN, finance company executive; b. N.Y.C., Nov. 12, 1945; s. Paul Peter and Anna Mary (Babey) B.; m. Sarah Lyman Nicholson, Nov. 27, 1975 (div.); children: Anna Crosby, Joseph Wistar; m. Kathleen McCarragher, Apr. 29, 1995; 1 child, Maxwell Alan. AB, Columbia U., 1967, MA, 1982. Dir. devel. coun. on econ. priority City of N.Y, 1973-75; assoc. dir. rsch. C.J. Lawrence, N.Y.C., 1975-82; v.p. Wertheim Co., N.Y.C., 1982-83; v.p. Morgan Stanley, N.Y.C., 1983-85, prin., 1986-89, mng. dir., 1990-99; mgmt. dir. Tiger Mgmt. LLC, N.Y.C., 1999—; gen. ptnr. PMSV Ptnrs., N.Y.C., 1993—; bd. dirs. Inform, Morgan Stanley Venture Group. Author: Resistant Prices, 1975. Mem., chmn. Planning Bd., 1978-85, Tuxedo Park, N.Y.; mem bd. Archtl. Devel., Tuxedo Park, 1978-85; bd. dirs. Madeira Sch., Buxton Sch. William Mitchell fellow Columbia U., 1967. Mem. Health Care Analysts Group (chmn. 1979-83), Tuxedo Club, N.Y. Racquet and Tennis Club. Office: Tiger Mgmt LLC 101 Park Ave 48th Fl New York NY 10178*

BROOKE, PEGAN STRUTHERS, artist, art educator; b. Santa Ana, Calif., July 19, 1950; d. Lee Edwin and Maxine (Jones) Struthers; children: Marshall Payne, Clara Payne. BA in Lit., U. Calif., San Diego, 1972; BFA in Painting, Drake U., 1976; MA in Painting, U. Iowa, 1977; MFA in Painting, Stanford U., 1980. Instr. Sonoma (Calif.) State U., 1983; vis. artist U. Calif., Berkeley, 1982, Davis, 1984; prof. art, grad. dir. San Francisco Art Inst., 1985—; guest artist Calif. Coll. Arts and Crafts, Oakland, 1983. One-woman shows include Hansen Fuller Gallery, San Francisco, 1981, 83, Fuller Goldeen Gallery, San Francisco, 1985, 87, Parnas Gallery, Santa Monica, Calif., 1994, U. Calif., Davis, 1994, Terrain Gallery, San Franciso, 1995, Joan Roebuck Gallery, Lafayette, Calif., 1996, 97, R.B. Stevenson Gallery, La Jolla, Calif., 1996, R. B. Stevenson Gallery, La Jolla, Calif, 1998, Winfield Gallery,Carmel, Calif., 1998; exhibited in group shows Guggenheim Mus., N.Y.C., 1987, Documenta, Sao Paulo, Brazil, 1994, Washburn Gallery, N.Y.C., 1995, R.B. Stevenson Gallery, 1996, U. Calif., San Diego, 1997. Grantee Tiffany Found., 1983-84, Marin Arts Coun., 1992, 1998, U.S. Govt., 1995—. Home: PO Box 857 Bolinas CA 94924-0857 Office: San Francisco Art Inst 800 Chestnut St San Francisco CA 94133-2206

BROOKE, RALPH IAN, dental educator; b. Leeds, Eng., Apr. 25, 1934; s. Michael and Jeanette (Cohen) B.; m. Lorna Ruth Shields; children: Michael Jeremy Richard, Andrew Timothy. Baccalaureus Chirurgiae Dentium, Licentiate in Dental Surgery, Leeds U., England, 1957. Licentiate Royal Coll. Physicians, 1963. Sr. lectr. Leeds U., 1970-72; prof., chmn. dept. oral medicine U. Western Ont., London, Can., 1972-82, dean dentistry faculty, 1982-97, vice provost health scis., 1987-97; chief dentistry Univ. Hosp., London, 1973-92. Contbr. articles to profl. jours. Fellow Acad. Dentistry Internat. (hon.), Royal Coll. Dentists Can., Royal Coll. Surgeons; mem. Nat. Dental Exam Bd. (past chmn. Can. commn. on dental accreditation), Can. Faculties Dentistry (past pres.), Can. Acad. Oral Medicine (past pres.), Can. Dental Assn. (hon.). Avocations: music, cycling.

BROOKER, RICHARD I., architect; b. Boston, June 9, 1927; s. Bernard and Esther (Friedman) B.; m. Maria Rivalta, Sept. 3, 1966; 1 child, Niccolo. BArch, Ill. Inst. Tech., 1953. Registered arch. Mass., Colo., Maine, Mo., Ill., N.Y., N.J., Pa., Vt., Md., N.H.; cert. Nat. Coun. of Archtl. Registration Bds. Prin., arch. The Archs. Collaborative, Cambridge, Mass., 1953-95, Boston Design Assocs., Waltham, Mass., 1995—. Prin. works include Schneider Childrens Hosp., Long Is. Jewish Hillside Med. Ctr., New Hyde Park, N.Y., new constrn. and replacement project Temple U. Hosp., Phila., U.S. Postal Svc. gen. mail and bulk mail and vehicle maint. facilities, Springfield, Mass., Ctrl. Mass. Mail Processing Ctr., Shrewsbury, Mass., U.S. Postal Svc. Westchester Mail Processing/Distbn. Ctr., vehicle maint. facility, Harrison, N.Y., new facilities and renovations Cabot Corp., Billerica, Mass., hqrs. facilities, Waltham, Mass., electron microscope lab., Billerica, Mass., Al-Hasa campus King Faisal U., Saudi Arabia, clin. labs., med. office bldg., maternity ctr. New Eng. Meml. Hosp., Stoneham, Mass., Essex County House of Correction, Middleton, Mass., Kuwait Postal Svcs. complex, Kuwait City, Mass. Correctional Instn., Shirley, exec. meeting, dining rooms, urology operating rooms, outpatient recovery area, patient ste. renovations, dialysis, cardiology, cardia operating ste., med. office conversion, fit-up, new emergency generator plant St. Vincent Hosp., Worcester, Mass., Weehawken (N.J.) Waterfront Consultancy, Roc Harbour Master Plan and Condominium Devel., N. Bergen, N.J., numerous others. With U.S. Army, 1945-46. Mem. AIA, Boston Soc. Archs., Mass. State Assn. Archs. Home: 265 The Valley Rd Concord MA 01742-4924 Office: Boston Design Assocs Inc 393 Totten Pond Rd Waltham MA 02451-2013

BROOKER, ROBERT ELTON, JR., retired manufacturing company executive; b. L.A., Apr. 12, 1937; s. Robert Elton and Sarah (Smith) B.; m. Katherine Jones, Mar. 21, 1964; children: Robert III, Carolyn, Christopher, Alison. BS, MIT, 1959; MBA, Harvard U., 1965. With Cummings Engine Co., 1965-81; gen. mgr. Great Lakes Foundry divsn. Cummings Engine Co., South Bend, Ind., 1966-69; pres. fleetguard Cummings Engine Co., Dallas, 1970-77; v.p. Latin Am. Cummings Engine Co., Miami, Fla., 1977-80; v.p. components group Cummings Engine Co., Columbus, Ind., 1981; pres. info. svcs. group N.L. Industries, Houston, 1981-86; pres., COO Lord Corp., Erie, Pa., 1987-90, CEO, 1990-91; pres., COO Connell Ltd. Partnership, Boston, 1993-95; dir. Dura Automotive Sys., 1995-98; ret., 1998; dir. FCI, 1991—, Innovative Components Inc., 1998—, Dura Automotive Sys., 1995—. Author: British Military Pistols, 1603-1887, 1978, Parole Sachen, 1990; contbr. articles to profl. jours. Mem. Sea Space Symposium. Capt. USMC, 1959-63.

BROOKER, SUSAN GAY, employment consulting firm executive; b. Washington, Sept. 4, 1949; d. Robert Morris and Mildred Ruby (Parler) B. BA, St. Mary's Coll., St. Mary's City, Md., 1971. News editor WPGC Radio, Lanham, Md., 1971; mgr. trainee Household Fin. Corp., Silver Spring, Md., 1972; career counselor Place-All, Bethesda, Md., 1972-73; exec. v.p. New Places, Inc./ Get-A-Job, Washington, 1973-89; employment cons., owner, pres. SGB Consultants, Reston, Va., 1989—; mem. Emploibank, Washington, 1978-79; guest condr. LGCW 15th Aniv. Concert, 1999. Outreach vestry chair Grace Episcopal Ch., 1992-94; conservation chairperson Silver Spring Woman's Club, 1993-94. Recipient Cert. Appreciation U.S. Fish and Wildlife Assn., 1985, Cert. of Recognition Chaplaincy Assocs., Howard Gen. Hosp, Letter of Appreciation Pres. Bill Clinton, 1996. Mem. Pell-Capital Pers. Svc. Asssn. (cert.), St. Mary's Coll. (Md.) Alumni Assn. (bd. dirs. 1987-91). Democrat. Avocations: swimming, travel, gardening, golf, snorkling. Home and Office: 2209 Coppersmith Sq Reston VA 20191-2305

BROOKER, THOMAS KIMBALL, oil company executive; b. L.A., Oct. 1, 1939; s.Robert Elton and Sally Burton Harrison (Smith) B.; m. Nancy Belle Neumann, 1966; children: Thomas Kimball Jr., Isobel, Vanessa. BA in French Lit., Yale U., 1961; MBA, Harvard U., 1968; MA in Art History, U. Chgo., 1989, PhD in Art History, 1996. Assoc. in corp. fin. Morgan Stanley & Co., Inc., N.Y.C., 1968-73, v.p., 1973-75, mng. dir., 1976-88; head Chgo. office Morgan Stanley & Co., Inc., 1978-88; pres. Barbara Oil Co., Chgo., 1989—, also bd. dirs.; bd. dirs. Arthur J. Gallagher & Co., Zenith Electronics Corp., Miami Corp., Cutler Oil & Gas Corp.; bd. govs. Midwest Stock Exch., 1980-88, vice chmn., 1986-88. Contbr. articles to profl. jours. Chmn. vis. com. libr. U. Chgo., mem. vis. com. music dept.; mem., chmn. com. on libr. Yale U. President's Coun., 1980-84; bd. dirs. Lyric Opera Chgo., Alliance Francaise Chgo., Bibliog. Soc. Am. Recipient Sir Thomas More medal U. San Francisco, 1992; assoc. fellow Saybrook Coll., Yale U. Mem. Adminstrv. Coun. (v.p.), Assn. Internat. de Bibliophilie, Coun. Am. Bibliog. Soc., Bandar-Log, Caxton Club, Chgo. Club, Comml. Club, Econ. Club, River Club (N.Y.C.), Knickerbocker Club (N.Y.C.), Grolier Club (N.Y.C.), The Casino, Saddle and Cycle Club, Edgartown (Mass.) Yacht Club, The Reading Room (Edgartown), Quadrangle Club, Racquet Club, Rockaway Hunt Club, Wayfarers Club. Home: 1500 N Lake Shore Dr Chicago IL 60610-6657 Office: Barbara Oil Co 1 First Natl Plz Ste 5030 Chicago IL 60603-2003

BROOKES, CAROLYN JESSEN, early childhood education educator; b. Orlando, Fla., June 16, 1946; d. Thomas M. and Hilda Marie (Hanson) Jessen: m. Edward N. Brookes, Aug. 8, 1970 (dec. Oct. 1990); 1 child, Donna Marie. BA, U. So. Fla., 1969; MS, Nova U., 1990. Asst. dir., dir. lower schs. Gables Acad., Winter Park, Fla., 1973-83; tchr. Orange County Pub. Schs., Orlando, 1983-98, early childhood resource tchr., high-scope trainer, 1983-92, coord. edn. homeless children and youth program, 1992-95; coord. mentor tchr. program U. Ctrl. Fla. and Orange County Pub. Schs., 1993-96; regional specialist State Dept. of Edn., 1997-98; parent educator, adj. instr. U. Ctrl. Fla.; ednl. cons.; literacy first trainer distance educator Ednl. Mgmt. Group, Phoenix, 1994-96; pres. People to People, Inc., non-profit computer-based svc.; lit. coach U. North Fla. Contbr. article to profl. publ. Mem. ASCD, Assn. for Childhood Edn. Internat., Nat. Assn. for Edn. Young Children, So. Early Childhood Assn. (trainer), Orange County Assn. for Edn. Young Children, Delta Kappa Gamma Soc. Internat. for Key Women Educators, Phi Delta Kappa. Home: 6064 Raleigh St Apt 2510 Orlando FL 32835-2242 Office: Carolyn Jessen Brookes Ednl Cons PO Box 682901 Orlando FL 32868-2901

BROOKHART, MAURICE S., chemist; b. Cumberland, Md., Nov. 28, 1942; married, 1965; 2 children. BA, Johns Hopkins U., 1964; PhD in Organic Chemistry, U. Calif., L.A., 1968. NATO fellow U. Southampton, 1968-69; assoc. prof., 1969-76; prof. organic chemistry U. N.C., Chapel Hill, 1976—; vis. prof. Oxford U., 1982-83. Fellow Am. Acad. Arts and Scis.; mem. Am. Chem. Soc. (award in Organometallic Chemistry 1992, Arthur C. Cope Scholar award 1994). Research in mechanistic and synthetic organometallic chemistry; applications of transition metal complexes in organic synthesis and catalysis. Office: U North Carolina Dept Chemistry Chapel Hill NC 27514

BROOKINS, WAYNE, municipal official; b. Tampa, Fla., July 10, 1944. BS, Fla. Meml. Coll., 1967. Tchr. Middleton H.S., Tampa, Fla., 1967-68, Marsha H.S., Plant City, Fla., 1968-69; advisor, speaker comty. rels. dept. City of Tampa, 1969-79, from pers. mgr. to dir. solid waste dept., 1979-92, dir. solid waste dept., 1992—. Chmn. bd. trustees First Union Missionary Bapt. Ch.. Exec. fellow U. So. Fla. Sch. of Govt., Omega Psi (pres. 1965—). Office: City of Tampa Dept Solid Waste 4010 W Spruce St Tampa FL 33607-2329*

BROOKMAN, ADAM L., lawyer; b. Summit, N.J., July 26, 1961; s. Robert S. and Ellen R. (Zelnick) B.; m. Susan M. Vlies, May 15, 1988; children: Anne, Steven, David. B of Indsl. Engring., Ga. Inst. Tech., 1983; JD, George Washington U., 1987. Bar: N.Y., Wis., U.S. Patent and Trademark Office. Engr./cons. Frito Lay Inc., Beloit, Wis., 1983-85; assoc., ptnr. Curtis, Morris & Safford, N.Y.C., 1987-95; ptnr. Godfrey & Kahn, Milw., 1995—; adj. prof. law Marquette U., Milw., 1997—. Mem. ABA, Milw. Bar Assn., N.Y. State Bar Assn., State Bar Wis., Internat. Trademark assn., Licensing Execs. Soc., Nat. Inst. for Trial Advocacy. Avocations: biking, volleyball, golf, tennis, photography. Office: Godfrey & Kahn SC 780 N Water St Ste 1500 Milwaukee WI 53202-3590

BROOKMAN, ANTHONY RAYMOND, lawyer; b. Chgo., Mar. 23, 1922; s. Raymond Charles and Marie Clara (Alberg) B.; m. Marilyn Joyce Brookman, June 5, 1982; children: Meribeth Brookman Farmer, Anthony Raymond, Lindsay Logan Christensen. Student, Ripon Coll., 1940-41; BS, Northwestern U., 1947; JD, U. Calif., San Francisco, 1953. Bar: Calif. 1954. Law clk. to presiding justice Calif. Supreme Ct., 1953-54; ptnr. Nichols, Williams, Morgan, Digardi & Brookman, 1954-68; sr. ptnr. Brookman & Talbot, Inc. (formerly Brookman & Hoffman, Inc.), Walnut Creek, Calif., 1969-92, Brookman & Talbot Inc., Sacramento, 1992—. Pres. Young Reps. Calif., San Mateo County, 1953-54. 1st lt. USAF. Mem. ABA, Alameda County Bar Assn., State Bar Calif., Lawyers Club Alameda County, Alameda-Contra Costa County Trial Lawyers Assn., Assn. Trial Lawyers Am., Calif. Trial Lawyers Assn., Athenian Nile Club, Masons, Shriners. Republican. Office: 901 H St Ste 200 Sacramento CA 95814-1808 also: 1990 N California Blvd Walnut Creek CA 94596-3742 also: 1746 Grand Canal Blvd Ste 11 Stockton CA 95207-8111

BROOKMAN, CAROL JOYCE, writer; b. Lansing, Mich., Apr. 24, 1934; d. Abraham Summerbell Reedy and Alice Regina (Mooney) Reedy; m. Stanley Ross Brookman, Dec. 29, 1931; children: Karen Lee Conolly, Paul Stanley. Grad. with honors, Grand Rapids Sch. Bible & Mus., 1954. Writer, prodr. Radio Sta. ELWA, Monrovia, Liberia, 1956-64; writer club curriculum Christian Edn Publ., Calif.; profile writer CCI, Kalamazoo, Mich.; writer children's scripts Two Talk Publs., Sebring, Fla., 1998—. Contbg. author: Book of Family Devotions, 1989, Book of Devotions for Kids, 1993, 2d edit., 1997; contbr. 9 short stories; contbr. articles to mags. and local newspaper. Avocations: reading, playing piano, walking.

BROOKNER, ANITA, writer, educator; d. Newson and Maude B. Ed., King's Coll., 1946-49, U. London, Courtauld Inst., Paris, 1949-53. vis. lectr. U. Reading, 1959-64; Slade prof. U. Cambridge, 1967-68; lectr. Courtauld Inst. of Art, 1964. Author: Watteau, 1968, The Genius of the Future, 1971, Greuze: The Rise and Fall of an Eighteenth Century Phenomenon, 1972, Jacques-Louis David, 1980, (novels) A Start in Life, 1981, Providence, 1982, Look At Me, 1983, Hotel du Lac, 1984 (Booker McConnell prize), Family and Friends, 1985, A Misalliance, 1986, A Friend From England, 1987, Latecomers, 1988, Lewis Percy, 1989, Brief Lives, 1991, Fraud, 1992, A Family Romance, 1993, A Private View, 1995, Altered States, 1996, Visitors, 1997; contbr. articles to mags.

BROOKNER, ELI, electrical engineer; b. N.Y.C., Apr. 2, 1931; s. Angel and Fanny Brookner; m. Ethel Bobick, Nov. 20, 1955; children: Lawrence, Richard. BEE, CCNY, 1953; MEE, Columbia U., 1955, DSc, 1962. Jr. engr. radar div. Rome (N.Y.) Air Devel. Ctr., summer 1952; rsch. engr. Columbia U. Electronics Rsch. Lab., N.Y.C., 1953-57, sr. rsch. engr., 1960-62; project engr. Fed. Sci. Corp. (name now Nicolet), N.Y.C., 1957-60; cons. scientist Raytheon Co., Sudbury, Mass., 1962—; internat. lectr. in radar tech.; served on coms. for Nat. Acad. Sci., DARPA, Air Force Sci. Adv. Bd., Air Force Mil. Space Systems Tech. Workshops. Author, editor: Radar Technology, 1977, Aspects of Modern Radar, 1988, Practical Phased-Array Antenna Systems, 1991, Tracking and Kalman Filtering Made Easy, 1998; achievements include conception and lead technical engr. for the wake measurements radar, first pulse doppler travelling wave tube radar put into space, system engring. for active phase array RADARSAT II-Plus. Recipient Jour. Premium award Franklin Inst., 1966. Fellow AIAA, IEEE (Centennial medal 1984, IEEE Region I award for continuing edn. course devel. 1986, Meritorious Achievement award edn. activities bd. 1990); mem. IEEE Aerospace and Electronics Systems Soc. (chmn. Boston chpt. 1972—, Outstanding Chpts. award 1977-78, 83-84, Disting. lectr. 1988—), IEEE Antennas and Propagation Soc. (Disting. lectr. 1983-85), Internat. Union Radio Sci. (commns. B and C, invited session chmn. 1973), Tau Beta Pi, Eta Kappa Nu. Avocations: swimming, dancing, classical music, comedy, photography. E-mail: EliüBrookner@Notes.res.ray.com. Home: 282 Marrett Rd Lexington MA 02421-7009

BROOKS, ALBERT (ALBERT EINSTEIN), actor, writer, director; b. Los Angeles, July 22, 1947; s. Harry and Thelma (Leeds) Einstein. Appeared in films Taxi Driver, 1976, Private Benjamin, 1980, Twilight Zone-The Movie, 1983, Unfaithfully Yours, 1983, Terms of Endearment, 1983, Broadcast News, 1987 (Acad. award nominee Best Supporting Actor), I'll Do Anything, 1994, The Scout, 1994, Critical Care, 1997, Out of Sight, 1998, Dr. Dolittle (voice only), 1998; dir., writer, actor films Real Life, 1979, Modern Romance, 1982, Lost in America, 1985, Defending Your Life, 1991, Mother, 1996, Out of Sight, 1998, The Muse, 1999; writer, actor The Scout, 1994, Critical Care, 1997; TV appearances include The Tonight Show, Merv Griffin Show, Steven Allen Show, Gold Diggers, The Simpsons (voice only) 1993; dir., writer short films Saturday Night Live, 1975-76; recs. include Comedy Minus One, A Star is Bought (Grammy nomination).

BROOKS, ANDRÉE AELION, journalist, educator, author; b. London, Feb. 2, 1937; d. Leon Luis and Lillian (Abrahamson) Aelion; m. Ronald J. Brooks, Aug. 16, 1959 (div. Aug. 1986); children: Allyson, James. Journalism cert., N.W. London Poly., 1958. Reporter Hampstead News, London, 1954-58; story editor Photoplay mag., N.Y.C., 1958-60; N.Y. corr. Australian Broadcasting Co., N.Y.C., 1961-68; elected rep. Elstree, Eng., 1973-74; columnist N.Y. Times, N.Y.C., 1978-95; free-lance journalist, 1978—; adj. prof. journalism Fairfield U., Conn., 1983-87; assoc. fellow Yale U., 1989—; founder, pres. Women's Campaign Sch. Yale U., 1993-96; v.p. Minuteman Media, 1995-96; coord.-dir. "After Spain" hist. curriculum, 1997; presently writing biography of Dona Gracia Nasi, 16th century Jewish woman leader, 1998—. Author: Children of Fast Track Parents, 1989 (Best Non-fiction Book award 1990). Exec. bd. Am. Jewish Com., 1987-91; trustee Temple Israel, Westport, Conn., 1991-97. Recipient 1st place for news writing Conn. Press Women, 1980, 83, 85-86, 87, 94, Outstanding Achievement award Nat. Fedn. Press Women, 1981, 1st place award Fairfield County chpt. Women in Comms., 1982-83, 86-87, 92, 93, 97, 2d place award in mag. writing Nat. Assn. Home Bldrs., 1983, Spl. Svc. award Conn. chpt. Am. Planning Assn., 1983, 1st place award for mag. writing

Nat. Fedn. Press Women, 1983; named one of Am. Women of Achievement Am. Jewish Com., 1989. Mem. Conn. Press Women (chmn. nominating com. 1983-86), Women in Communications (contest co-chmn. 1983-84). Home: 15 Hitchcock Rd Westport CT 06880-2630 *Keep true to what you believe and don't become cynical or full of hate - for hate only breeds more hate.*

BROOKS, ANITA HELEN, public relations executive; b. N.Y.C.; d. Arthur and Bertha (Stewart) Sayle; m. Arnold Brooks, July 1, 1954 (div.). BA, Hunter Coll., 1950; MA, Columbia U., 1952, MLS, 1954. Tchr. Latin Hunter Coll. H.S., N.Y.C., 1955; publicity rep. WOR Radio, N.Y.C., 1955; writer King Features Syndicate, N.Y.C., 1955-59; pub. rels. exec. NBC-TV, N.Y.C., 1956; dir. pub. rels. N.Y. State Mental Health Fund Campaign, 1956, WMCA Radio, N.Y.C., 1957; account exec. various pub. rels. agys., N.Y.C., 1957-65; pres. Anita Helen Brooks Assocs., Pub. Rels., N.Y.C., 1965—; lit. agt. Anita Brooks Lit. Agt., N.Y.C., 1956—. Writer radio-TV shows. Vice chmn. Sinatra for Meml. Sloan-Kettering Cancdr Hosp. Benefit; mem. patroness com. Harkness Ballet Found.; mem. benefit com. Mannes Coll. Music, N.Y.C.; mem. legis. adv. com. of Senator Roy M. Goodman, N.Y. State Senate. Decorated dame comdr. Knights of Malta; named hon. citizen Venezuela. Mem. Am. Women in Radio and TV, Pub. Rels. Soc. Am., Internat. Radio and TV Soc., Publs. Publicity Assn., Assn. Motion Picture Advertisers, Mystery Writers Am., Columbia U. Alumni Assn., Sisters in Crime Soc., Smithsonian Assocs., N.Y. Press Club, Eta Sigma Phi, Latin/Greek Honor Soc. Office: 155 E 55th St New York NY 10022-4038

BROOKS, BABERT VINCENT, publisher; b. N.Y.C., Sept. 2, 1926; s. Babert Vincent and Florence (Goodwin) B.; m. Audrey Stephenson, Dec. 6, 1952 (div.); children—Torrey, Scott, Wendy; m. Kathryn Frazer, May 23, 1987. A.B. magna cum laude, Dartmouth Coll., 1947, M.B.A. with distinction, 1949. Security analyst Arnold Bernhard & Co., N.Y.C., 1952-56; cons. Booz, Allen & Hamilton, N.Y.C., 1956-58; v.p. finance Schine Enterprises, N.Y.C., 1958-61; v.p., treas. Murray Corp. Am., N.Y.C., 1961-62; pres. Brooks, Torrey & Scott, Inc., Westport, Conn., 1962—; pres. Westport Travel Svc., Inc., 1963, chmn., 1988-92; pres. Brooks Community Newspapers, 1974-82, chmn., 1982-99; pub. Westport (Conn.) News, 1964-99, Darien (Conn.) News-Rev., 1973-99, Fairfield (Conn.) Citizen-News, 1973-99, Norwalk Citzen News, 1997-99, Greenwich (Conn.) News, 1983-96, Inside Fairfield County, Westport, 1993-99; sec.-treas. Airspur Corp., N.Y.C., 1969-70; trustee King Indsl. Properties, Boston, 1965-82; dir. Westfair, Inc., Westport, CFS Corp., County Fed. Savs. & Loan Assn., Westport, 1969-85, United Printing & Litho Corp., Bridgeport, Conn., 1984-89, Warner Investing Corp., Westport; trustee Am. Inst. Econ. Rsch., Great Barrington, Mass., 1997—. Bd. dirs., treas. Dartmouth in Greenwich, 1972-81; trustee Conn. Policy and Econ. Coun. Inc., Norwalk Hosp., 1988-93, 95—, Norwalk Health Svcs., Inc., 1994—, U. Bridgeport, 1991—. With USNR, 1945-47. Mem. Riverside Yacht Club, Phi Beta Kappa.

BROOKS, CHARLES LEE, III, computational biophysicist, educator; b. Detroit, May 14, 1956; married; 2 children. BS in Chemistry and Physics, Alma (Mich.) Coll., 1978; PhD in Physical Chemistry, Purdue U., 1982. Postdoc. fellow Harvard U., Boston, 1982-85, NIH, 1983-85; from asst. prof. to prof. Carnegie Mellon U., 1985-92, prof., 1992-94; prof. molecular biology Scripps Rsch. Inst., 1994—; mem. spl. rev. panels, site visit coms., mem. reviewers reserve Cell Biology & Biophysics Divsn. A study section, NIH; reviewer, mem. cellular and molecular biophysics panel, NSF; mem. adv. bd. Nat. Biomed. Computation Resource Inst., San Diego Supercomputing Ctr., sr. fellow; presenter in field. Contbr. over 100 articles to profl. jours.; author 1 book, several book chpts. A.P. Sloan fellow, 1990-93; grantee Swedish Rsch. Coun., 1992. Office: Dept Molecular Biology TPC6 The Scripps Rsch Inst 10550 N Torrey Pines Rd La Jolla CA 92037-1000

BROOKS, CHARLOTTE MARIE, educator, counselor; b. Olmsted, Ill., Jan. 19, 1951; d. Charles and Minnie (Cheney) Williams; m. Donald E. Brooks, May 26, 1973; chldren: Lattefah, Omari. BA in English and Speech comm., Albion (Mich.) Coll., 1972; MEd in Spl. Edn., Wayne State U., 1974, MA in Guidance, 1981, EdS in Adminstrn., 1997. Upward Bound tutor, supr., counselor Wayne State U., Detroit, 1988-93; tchr. lang. arts Detroit Bd. Edn., 1972-93, counselor, 1993-97, spl. edn. tchr., 1997—. Mem. minority alumni bd. Albion Coll., 1992-95. Mem. ASCD, Detroit Urban League, Mich. Driver and Traffic Safety Edn. Assn. Democrat. Avocations: consumer advocacy, modeling, gardening, coaching. Home: 18316 Trinity Detroit MI 48129

BROOKS, DANA D., dean; b. Hagerstown, Md., Aug. 1, 1951; s. Fred and Helen (Brooks) Miles. AA, Hagerstown Jr. Coll., 1971; BS, Towson State Coll., 1973; MS, W.Va. U., 1976, EdD, 1979. Asst. prof. W.Va. U., Morgantown, 1979-83, assoc. prof., 1983-88, prof., 1988—, acting asst. dean, 1986-87, acting dean, 1988, assoc. dean, 1987-92, interim dean, 1992-93, dean, 1993—. Recipient Rev. Dr. Martin Luther King, Jr. Achievement award W.Va. U., 1997, Social Justice award W.Va. U., 1992, Cheikh Anata DIOP award for outstanding African-Centered Rsch. and Scholarship W.Va. U., 1999; grantee in field. Mem. AAHPERD (Young Profl. award 1982), Midwest APPHERD (v.p. 1988-89, pres.-elect 1993, pres. 1994-95), W.Va. Assn. Health, Phys. Edn. and Recreation (pres. 1983-84, Ray O. Duncan award 1991), Golden Key (hon.), Phi Delta Kappa. Avocations: tennis, softball, fencing, white water rafting. Home: 811 Timberline Morgantown WV 26505-1120 Office: W Va U 257 Coliseum Morgantown WV 26506

BROOKS, DANIEL TOWNLEY, lawyer, electrical engineer; b. N.Y.C., Apr. 15, 1941; s. Robert Daniel and Mary (Lee) B.; m. Barbara Ann Badertscher, June 16, 1973; children: Daniel Townley, Jr., Andrei Matthew. BS in Engring. cum laude, Princeton U., 1963; LLB, Stanford U., 1967, MS in Engring., 1968. Bar: Calif. 1968, U.S. Dist. Ct. (no. dist.) Calif. 1968, U.S. Ct. Appeals (9th cir.) 1968, N.Y. 1970, U.S. Ct. Appeals (2d cir.) 1972, Va. 1982, D.C. 1998. Assoc., Cadwalader, Wickersham & Taft, N.Y.C., 1968-79, ptnr., Washington, 1985—; atty., fellow U.S. SEC, Washington, 1979-81; with Computer Law Advisers, Springfield, Va., 1981-85; cons. and lectr. in computer law. Mem. ABA, Calif. Bar Assn. (inactive), N.Y. State Bar Assn., Va. Bar Assn., D.C. Bar Assn., Computer Law Assn. Inc. (bd. advisors), Assn. Computing Machinery, D.C. Computer Law Forum, IEEE. Club: Princeton (Washington). Home: 6106 Lorcom Ct Springfield VA 22152-1320 Office: Cadwalader Wickersham Ste 700 1333 New Hampshire Ave NW Washington DC 20036-1574

BROOKS, DAVID BARRY, resource economist; b. Easton, Mass., Feb. 15, 1934; s. Abraham and Mae (Fox) B.; m. Toby Judith Haftka, Sept. 11, 1955; children: Michael Jan, Naomi Sara. S.B. in Geology, MIT, 1955; M.S. in Geology, Calif. Inst. Tech., 1956; Ph.D. in Econs., U. Colo., 1963. Geologist U.S. Geol. Survey, 1956-59; research assoc. Resources for the Future, Washington, 1961-66; asst. prof. econs. Berea Coll., 1966-67; chief div. mineral econs. Bur. Mines, Dept. Interior, 1967-70; chief Mineral Econs. Research div. Can. Dept. Energy, Mines and Resources, 1970-73; dir. Office Energy Conservation, 1974-77; dir. Ottawa office Energy Probe, 1977-82; bd. dirs. Can. Friends of the Earth, pres., 1977-81, 85-88; prin. Marbek Resource Cons. Ltd., Ottawa, Ont., Canada, 1983-88; rsch. mgr. Internat. Devel. Rsch. Ctr., Ottawa; cons. Can. Internat. Devel. Agy., 1983, 85, 86, 88, UN Conf. on Human Environ., 1971-72, Labrador Resources Adv. Coun., 1979, Dept. Indian and No. Affairs, Ottawa, 1979; mem. study team on nonrenewable materials, environ. studies bd. Nat. Acad. Scis., 1972-73; mem. study team on environ. Fed. Task Force and Program Rev.; mem. energy options adv. com. Office of Ministry of Energy, Ottawa, 1986-88; cons. Highlander Rsch. and Edn. Ctr., New Market, Tenn., 1979; exec. dir. Beaufort Sea Rsch. Coalition; bd. dirs. Ont. Hydro; keynote spkr. First Israeli-Palestinian Internat. Academic Conf. on Water in Zurich, 1992. Author: Supply and Competition in Minor Metals, 1965, Peaceful Use of Nuclear Explosives: Some Economic Aspects, 1969, Minerals: an Expanding or a Dwindling Resource?, 1973, Zero Energy Growth for Canada, 1981; coauthor: Life After Oil: A Renewable Energy Policy for Canada, 1983, Watershed: The Role of Fresh Water in the Israeli-Palestian Conflict, 1994; also monographs on environ. problems of mining and energy conservation, energy and internat. devel.; also articles. Chmn. No. Va. chpt. Congress Racial Equality, 1963-65; sec. Fed. Employees for a Democratic Soc. Served with AUS, 1957. Ashley fellow Trent U., Can., 1992. Home: 1-202 Flora St, Ottawa, ON Canada K1R 5R7 Office: Internat Devel Rsch Ctr, PO Box 8500, Ottawa, ON Canada K1G 3H9

BROOKS, DAVID WILLIAM, farmer cooperative executive; b. Royston, Ga., Sept. 11, 1901; s. David William and Letty Jane (Tabor) B.; m. Ruth McMurray, Aug. 7, 1930; children: David William, Nancy Ruth. B.S. in Agr. U. Ga., 1922, M.S., 1923; LL.D., Emory U., 1964; D.H.L., Morris Brown Coll., 1978. Tchr. agronomy div. U. Ga., 1922-25; field supr. Ga. Cotton Growers Coop. Assn., 1925-33; gen. mgr. Gold Kist Inc. (formerly named Cotton Producers Assn.), Atlanta, 1933-68; chmn. bd. dirs. Gold Kist Inc. (formerly named Cotton Producers Assn.), 1968-77, chmn. bd. emeritus, chmn. policy com., 1977—; pres. Cotton States Life & Health Ins. Co., 1955-59, chmn. bd., 1959-83, chmn. bd. emeritus, 1983—; pres. Cotton States Mut. Ins. Co., 1947-59, chmn. bd., 1959-83, chmn. bd. emeritus, 1983—; dir. Ga. So. & Fla. Ry. Co., 1963—; Dir. Am. Cotton Coop. Assn., Atlanta, 1940-70; dir. Nat. Council Farmer Coops., Washington, 1938-68, mem. exec. com., 1944-63, pres., 1951-52; mem. cotton adv. com. Dept. Agr., 1947-50; mem. Textiles Industry Adv. Com. of Army-Navy Munitions Bd., 1947-51; industry adv. Internat. Cotton Adv. Com., Washington, 1950; mem. nat. adv. bd. Moblzn. Policy, 1951-52; mem. Nat. Agrl. Adv. Commn., 1953-56, Benson's Cotton Export Adv. Com., 1953-56, chmn., 1953; mem. nat. cotton adv. com. USDA, 1961-63; dir. Found. for Am. Agr., 1960—; mem. Nat. Agrl. Adv. Commn., 1964-65; dir. Agrl. Mission, 1959-67, Coop. Fertilizers Internat., Chgo., 1968-71; mem. Agribus. Industry Adv. Com., Washington, 1968-70, Nat. Adv. Com. Trade Negotiations, 1975—, Presdl. Commn. on World Hunger, 1978—. Trustee Am. Inst. Cooperation, Washington, 1944-69; pres. Ga. Coop. Council, Athens, 1940-47; trustee Reinhardt Coll., Waleska, Ga., Emory U., Atlanta, Wesleyan Coll., Macon, Ga.; chmn. Emory U. Com. of One Hundred, 1958—; bd. govs. Agrl. Hall of Fame, 1958—. Selected Man of Year in Agr. for Ga. Progressive Farmer, 1950, Southwide Man of Year in Agr., 1966; named to Agrl. Hall of Fame U. Ga., 1972; recipient Nat. Coop. Statesmanship award, 1973; Man of Yr. in Ga. award Morris Brown Coll., Atlanta, 1978; named United Meth. Man of Achievement S.E. Jurisdictional Council, United Meth. Ch., 1979; named to Coop. League U.S.A. Hall of Fame, 1979. Mem. N.Y. Cotton Exchange (adv. com. 1948-68), New Orleans Cotton Exchange (adv. com.), Nat. Cotton Council (adv. com., v.p. 1958-69), Farmers Chem. Assn. (chmn. bd. 1960-69, dir. 1969-73), Nat. Council Chs. (governing bd. 1960-72), Nat. Planning Assn. (agrl. com. 1946-63), Alpha Zeta, Phi Kappa Phi. Methodist (steward, bd. mgrs., exec. com. bd. missions). Clubs: Mason, Kiwanian. Home: 2374 Dellwood Dr PO Box 2210 Atlanta GA 30301-2210 *You must have absolute confidence that your goal in life will improve the condition of mankind. You must give complete dedication to the accomplishment of this goal, believing that no personal sacrifice can be considered too great.*

BROOKS, DEBRA LYNN, neuromuscular therapist, educator; b. Cedar Rapids, Iowa, Dec. 10, 1950; d. Rex L. and Phyllis M. (Harman) B.; divorced; children: Brei, Benjamin, Bryan. BA, Coe Coll., 1973. Cert. in neuromuscular therapy, Fla.; cert. natural therapeutics specialist. Tchr. Cedar Rapids Cmty. Sch. Dist., 1973-92; owner, neuromuscular therapist Neuro Muscular Therapy Ctr., Walford, Iowa, 1994—; educator Helping Hands Seminars, Cedar Rapids, 1992—, Debra Brooks' Seminars, Walford, 1993—; bus. and edn. cons. Brooks Cons., Cedar Rapids, 1990-96. Contbr. articles to profl. jours. and newsletters. Fundraiser, performer in musicals St. Luke's Hosp., Cedar Rapids, 1978-91, in Follies Cedar Rapids Symphony, 1981—, in telethons Variety Clubs Am., Cedar Rapids, 1989-91; mem. Walford Cmty. Devel., 1994—. Recipient First in the Nation in Edn. award State of Iowa, 1991. Mem. Am. Massage Therapy Assn. (cert., state v.p., editor, edn. dir. 1992-94, nat. bd. dirs. 1994—, nat. trustee Found. 1994-98). Avocations: singing, painting, pianist, power walking, having friends over. Office: NeuroMuscular Therapy Ctr PO Box 277 Walford IA 52351-0277

BROOKS, DENNIS MARK, secondary education educator; b. Beaver Dam, Wis., Feb. 11, 1951; s. Robert William and Helen Barbara B.; m. Sharon Marie Traczyk, June 26, 1976; 1 child, Eric Michael. B in Music Edn., U. Wis., Eau Claire, 1974; M in Sci. of Edn., U. Wis., Whitewater, 1991. Tchr. Hartland (Wis.) Elem., 1975-78, Hartland Arrowhead H.S., 1978-83; salesman Henco, Inc., Waukesha, Wis., 1983—; tchr. Pewaukee (Wis.) H.S., 1985—. Name Person of Yr., Pewaukee C. of C., 1989; recipient Disting. Educator award Ptnrs. for Edn. Inc. Avocations: baseball, swimming, skiing, weight lifting.

BROOKS, DIANA B., auction house executive; b. 1950; m. Michael C. Brooks; two children. Grad., Miss Porter's Sch., Farmington, Conn., 1968, Yale U., 1973. Lending officer Nat. Banking Group, Citibank, N.Y.C., 1973-79; sr. v.p. to pres., CEO Sotheby's North Am., 1979-90; pres., CEO Sotheby's Holdings, Inc., N.Y.C., 1994—, Sotheby's North and South Am., 1990—. Trustee Yale U., Deerfield Acad., The Allen-Stevenson Sch.; pres. coun. assocs. Frick Art Reference Libr.; adv. bd. dirs. Old Westbury Gardens; bd. dirs. N.Y.C. Partnership. Office: Sotheby's 1334 York Ave New York NY 10021-4806*

BROOKS, DONALD LEE, civil engineering and scientific consulting firm executive; b. Boston, 1956; s. Douglas Lee and Elizabeth Brooks; m. Terry O'Sullivan, 1987 (div. 1989); m. Jill Blondin, 1991; children: Nathan Donald, Kylie Elizabeth. BA in Environ. Biology, Earlham Coll., Richmond, Ind., 1979; postgrad., U.Ariz., 1984. Registered profl. engr., Ariz.; diplomate Am. Coll. Forensic Examiners. Field biologist/vegetation mgr. Colo. River Projects Ariz. State U. Ctr. for Environ. Studies, 1980-81; rsch. asst. dept. watershed mgmt. U. Ariz., Tucson, 1982-84; subdivsn. engr., devel. divsn. mgr. Pima County Dept. Transp. & Flood Control Dist., Tucson, 1984-89; mgr. water resources Anderson-Passarelli, Tucson, 1989; v.p. URBAN Engring., Tucson, 1989-92; project mgr. Johnson-Brittain Assocs., Tucson, 1992; client mgr. David Evans & Assocs., Tucson, 1992-93; pres., prin. engr. ICON Cons. USA, Inc., Tucson, 1993—; prin. engr., environ. scientist Total Infrastructure Solutions LLC, Tucson, 1998—; hydraulic engr., cons. Devel. Alternatives Inc./U.S. Agy. Internat. Devel., Cochabamba, Bolivia, 1993. Contbr. articles to profl. jours. Bd. dirs. Saguaro Credit Union, 1998,. Mem. ASCE, Am. Inst. Hydrology (profl. hydrologist), Ariz. Floodplain Mgmt. Assn. (Outstanding Svc. award 1990-91), Assn. State Floodplain Mgrs., Am. Water Resources Assn., So. Ariz. Home Builders Assn., Adventure Club N.Am., Rocks & Ropes Tucson, Cliffhanger Soc. (v.p.). Mem. Soc. Friends. Avocations: rock climbing, skiing, electronic music, motorcycling. E-mail: dbrooks@iconusainc.com. Home: 1514 N Plaza De Lirios Tucson AZ 85745-1600 Office: ICON Cons USA Inc 1931 W Grant Rd Ste 350 Tucson AZ 85745-1104

BROOKS, E. R. (DICK BROOKS), utility company executive; b. Slaton, Tex., 1937; m. Martha Garrett; 2 children. BSEE, Tex. Tech U., 1961; postgrad., Harvard U., 1985, U. Mich. Engr. West Tex. Utilities Co., Abilene, 1961-82; v.p. customer svcs. West Tex. Utilities Co., 1980-82; v.p. engring. Ctrl. Power & Light Co., 1982-83; chief engring. officer, sr. v.p. Cen. Power & Light Co., 1983-86, pres., CEO, 1986-87; exec. v.p. elec. ops. Cen. & S.W. Corp., Dallas, 1987, exec. v.p., 1988-89, chmn., CEO, 1990—; also past pres., CEO Cen. & S.W. Svcs., Inc.; also pres., CEO Transok, Inc.; various positions West Tex. U. Engring. Dept. Trustee Dallas Theater Ctr.; chmn. exec. bd. Cir. Ten Coun. Boy Scouts Am.; exec. bd. United Way of Met. Dallas; deacon Park Cities Bapt. Ch., Dallas; trustee Dallas Symphony; past chair Tex. Coun. Econ. Edn.; chmn. N.Am. Elec. Reliability Coun., Edison Electric Inst., 1997-98. Named Disting. Engr. award Tex. Tech U., 1988, Disting. Alumni, 1993. Mem. Assn. Elec. Cos. Tex. (mem. exec. bd.), Tex. Rsch. League, Tex. C. of C. Office: Cen and SW Corp PO Box 660164 Dallas TX 75266-0164 Also: Central & SW Corp 1616 Woodall Rodgers Fwy Dallas TX 75202-1234*

BROOKS, EDWARD HOWARD, college administrator; b. Salt Lake City, Mar. 2, 1921; s. Charles Campbell and Margery (Howard) B.; m. Courtaney June Perren, May 18, 1946; children: Merrillee Brooks Runyan, Robin Anne (Mrs. R. Bruce Pollock). B.A., Stanford U., 1942, M.A., 1947, Ph.D., 1950. Mem. faculty, adminstrn. Stanford U., 1949-71; provost Claremont (Calif.) Colls., 1971-81; v.p. Claremont U. Center, 1979-81; sr. v.p. Claremont McKenna Coll., 1981-84; provost Scripps Coll., 1987-89, pres., 1989-90; ret., 1990. Trustee EDUCOM, 1978-80, Webb Sch. of Calif., 1979-90, Menlo Sch. and Coll., 1985-88; bd. overseers Hoover Instn., 1972-78; bd. dirs. Student Loan Mktg. Assn., 1973-77; mem. Calif. Student Aid Commn., 1984-88, chmn., 1986-88. Served with AUS, 1942-45. Mem. U. Club Pasadena. Home: 356 S Orange Grove Blvd Pasadena CA 91105-1746 *Looking back since retirement, I have concluded that the most useful and, perhaps, enduring contribution an institutional leader can make is clearly committed efforts to make the institution better and the individuals within it better; holding everyone to even higher standards.*

BROOKS, FREDERICK PHILLIPS, JR., computer scientist; b. Durham, N.C., Apr. 19, 1931; s. Frederick Phillips and Octavia Hooker (Broome) B.; m. Nancy Lee Greenwood, June 16, 1956; children: Kenneth Phillips, Roger Greenwood, Barbara Brooks LaDine. AB summa cum laude in Physics, Duke U., 1953; SM, Harvard U., 1955, PhD, 1956; D. Tech. Sci. (hon.), ETH-Zurich, 1991. Engr. IBM, Poughkeepsie, N.Y., 1956-59, Yorktown Heights, N.Y., 1959-60; mgr. devel. computer System/360 IBM, Poughkeepsie, 1960-64, mgr. devel. Operating System/360, 1964-65; founder computer sci. dept. U. N.C., Chapel Hill, 1964, prof., 1964-75, chmn. dept. computer sci., 1964-84, Kenan prof., 1975—; bd. dirs. Triangle U. Computation Ctr., 1966-84, chmn., 1975-77, N.C. Ednl. Computing Svc., 1965—; active Def. Sci. Bd., 1982-86, Nat. Sci. Bd., 1987-92. Author: The Mythical Man-Month-Essays on Software Engineering, 1975, 95; (with K.E. Iverson) Automatic Data Processing, 1963, Automatic Data Processing System/360 Edition, 1969; (with G.A. Blaauw) Computer Architecture: Concepts and Evolution, 1997; contbr. articles to profl. jours.; inventor (with D. W. Sweeney) program interruption system, alphabetical read-out device. Chmn. exec. com. Cen. Carolina Billy Graham Crusade, 1972-73; trustee Durham Acad., pres., 1977-80; mem. corp. Inter-Varsity Christian Fellowship, 1968-77. Recipient McDowell award IEEE Computer Soc., 1970, Man of Yr. award Data Processing Mgmt. Assn., 1970, Nat. Medal of Tech., 1985, Harry Goode Meml. award Am. Fedn. Info. Proc. Socs., 1989; grantee NSF, AEC, NIH, NASA, Def. Advanced Projects Rsch. Agy.; Guggenheim fellow, 1975, Bower Award and Prize for Acheivement in Science, Franklin Institute, 1995. Fellow IEEE (John von Neumann medal 1993), Am. Acad. Arts and Scis., Assn. Computing Machinery (coun. mem.-at-large 1966-70, Disting. Svc. award 1987, Allen Newell award 1994), Brit. Computer Soc. (disting.); mem. NAE, Royal Netherland Acad. Arts and Scis., Royal Acad. Engring. (U.K.). Methodist. Home: 413 Granville Rd Chapel Hill NC 27514-2723 Office: Univ NC Dept Computer Sci Chapel Hill NC 27599-3175

BROOKS, GARTH (TROYAL GARTH BROOKS), country music singer; b. Tulsa, Okla., Feb. 7, 1962; s. Troyal Raymond and Colleen Carroll Brooks; m Sandy Mahl, 1986; children: Taylor Mayne Pearl, August Anna. BS in Avtg. and Journalism, Okla. St. Univ., 1984. Recording artist (albums) Garth Brooks, No Fences (Album of Yr. Acad. Country Music, 1991), Ropin' The Wind, 1991, Beyond the Season, 1992, The Chase, 1992, In Pieces, 1993 (Grammy nomination, Best Country Male Vocal for "Ain't Goin' Down (Til the Sun Comes Up)"), The Hits, 1994, Fresh Horses, 1995, Sevens, 1997, The Limited Series, 1998, Double Live, 1998; songs include The Dance (Video of Yr. award Country Music Assn. 1991, Song of Yr. and Video of Yr. awards Acad. Country Music 1991), Friends in Low Places (Single Record of Yr. Acad. Country Music 1991, Grammy award nomination), If Tomorrow Never Comes (Am. Music award for Country Song of Yr. 1991), The Thunder Rolls, We Shall Be Free (Video of Yr., Acad. Country Music 1 4), Somewhere Other Than The Night, Learning to Live Again; TV: This is Garth Brooks, 1992, This is Garth Brooks, Too, 1994, Garth Brooks: The Hits, 1995, Garth Brooks Live in Central Park, 1997. Recipient Entertainer of Yr. award Acad. Country Music, 1991, 92, 93, 94, Male Vocalist of Yr. award, 1991, Horizon award, Entertainer of Yr. award Country Music Assn., 1991, 92, Grammy award for Best Male Country Vocalist, 1992, Grammy award for Best County Collaboration with Vocals, 1998; named Best Male Country Music Performer, 1992, 93, Best Male Musical Performer, People's Choice Awards, 1992, 93, 94, 95, Artist of Decade, Acad. Country Music Awards, 1999; inducted into Grand Ole Opry. *

BROOKS, GARY, management consultant. BS in Biochem. Engring. and Ind. Mgmt., MIT, 1955; MSChemE and Ops. Rsch., U. Rochester, 1959. With GE Co., 1955-56, Eastman Kodak Co., 1956-64; mgr. Technomic Cons. Inc., 1968-71; divsn. exec. Scott Paper Co., 1971-76; founder, strategic planning and tech. forecasting firm N.Y.; mng. prin. turnaround cons. firm New Eng., 1976-85; chmn., CEO Allomet Ptnrs., Inc., N.Y.C., 1985—; lectr. in field. Contbr. articles to profl. jours. Mem. Turnaround Mgmt. Assn. (founding mem., former bd. dirs., chair certification com., 1st pres.), Assn. Cert. Turnaround Profls., Inst. Mgmt. Cons. (nat. chair, cert. mgmt. cons., turnaround profl.). Office: Allomet Ptnrs Ltd 370 Lexington Ave Ste 210 New York NY 10017

BROOKS, (LESLIE) GENE, cultural association administrator; b. Fletcher, Okla., June 15, 1936; s. Frank and Ethel E. (Spears) B.; m. Nancy E. Carman, Aug. 17, 1970; 1 child, Steven Frank. B of Music Edn., Okla. Bapt. U., 1959; M of Music Edn., U. Okla., 1962, D of Music Edn., 1968; postgrad., U. Colo. Chmn. music dept. Cameron U., Lawton, Okla., 1962-69, Midwestern State U., Wichita Falls, Tex., 1969-75, U. Ark., Little Rock, 1975-77; exec. dir. Am. Choral Dirs. Assn., Lawton, 1977—; sec.-gen. Internat. Fedn. Choral Music, 1982-85. Recipient Disting. Alumni award Okla. Bapt. U., 1985, in music, 1996, U. Okla., 1997. Mem. Music Tchrs. Nat. Assn. (chmn. music in higher edn. 1975-77, nat. choral chmn. 1972-75), Music Educators Nat. Conf. (life), Coll. Music Soc. (life), Am. Choral Dirs. Assn. (life). Southern Baptist. Avocations: traveling, snow skiing. Home: 18816 Woody Creek Dr Edmond OK 73003-4108 Office: Am Choral Dir Assn PO Box 6310 Lawton OK 73506-0310

BROOKS, GLADYS SINCLAIR, public affairs consultant; b. Mpls.; d. John Franklin and Gladys (Phillips) Sinclair; m. Wright W. Brooks, Apr. 17, 1941; children: Diane Brooks Montgomery, John, Pamela (Mrs. Jean Marc Perraud). Student U. Geneva, Switzerland, 1935; BA, U. Minn., 1936; LLD, Hamline U., 1966. Dir. Farmer's and Mechanics Bank, 1973-82; mem. Met. Council, 1975-83; lectr. world affairs, 1939—; mem. Mpls. City Council, 1967-73; mem. Met. Airports Commn., 1971-74; pres. World Affairs Ctr. U. Minn., 1976-83; instr. continuing edn. for women U. Minn.; lectr. on world tour as Am. specialist U.S. Dept. State, 1959-60; pres. Brooks/Ridder & Assocs., 1983-94. Mem. Mpls. Charter Commn., 1948-51; pres. YWCA, Mpls., 1953-57, 62-65, mem. nat. bd., 1959-71, del. world meeting, Denmark; pres. Minn. Internat. Ctr., 1953-63; chmn. Minn. Women's Com. for Civil Rights, 1961-64; mem. U.S. Com. for UNICEF, 1959-68; mem. Gov.'s Adv. Com. Children and Youth, 1953-58, Minn. Adv. Com. Employment and Security, 1948-50; Midwest adv. com. Inst. Internat. Edn.; mem. nat. com. White House Conf. Children and Youth, 1960; chmn. Gov.'s Human Rights Commn., 1961-65; dir. Citizens Com. Delinquency and Crime, 1969-93; chmn. Mpls. Adv. Com. on Tourism, 1976-82, Ctr. Women in Govt., 1987-92; chmn. adv. com. Office World Trade, 1988-92; vice chmn. Nat. Community Partnerships Seminars, 1977-82; mem. Midwest Selection Panel, White House Fellows, 1981. Del. Rep. Nat. Conv., 1952; state chmn. Citizens for Eisenhower, 1956; founder, pres. Rep. Workshop; co-chmn. Mpls. Bicentennial Commn., 1974-76; pres. Internat. Center for Fgn. Students; dir. Minn. Alumni Assn.; trustee United Theol. Sem., YWCA, Met. State U.; bd. dirs. Hamline U., Midwest China Ctr., Walker Health Services; mem. pres.'s adv. council St. Catherine's Coll.; trustee Hamline U., Met. State U. Recipient Centennial Women of Minn. award Hamline U., 1954, Woman of Distinction award AAUW, Mpls. 1956, Outstanding Achievement award U. Minn., 1962, Woman of Yr. award YWCA, 1973, Brotherhood award NCCJ, 1975, State Bar award for community leadership, 1976, Service to Freedom award Minn. State Bar Assn., 1976, Community Leadership award YWCA, 1981, Svc. Beyond Self award Rotary, 1990. Mem. World Affairs Council (pres. 1942-44), Minn. LWV (dir. 1940-45), Mpls. Council Ch. Women (pres. 1946-48), Nat. Council of Chs. (mem. gen. bd., v.p. 1961-69), Minn. Council of Chs. (1st woman pres. 1961-64, Christian service award 1967), Mpls. Council of Chs. (v.p. 1946-48), United Ch. Women (bd. mgrs.), Minn. UN Assn. (dir.), Nat. League Cities (human resources steering com. 1972-73, coun. fgn. rels.), Am. Acad. Polit. Sci., Minn. Women's Polit. Caucus, Minn. Women's Econ. Roundtable, AAUW, Delta Kappa Gamma (hon.). Presbyn. Clubs: Horizon 100, Women's. Home: 5056 Garfield Ave Minneapolis MN 55419-1253

BROOKS, GLENN ELLIS, political science educator, educational administrator; b. Kerrville, Tex., Aug. 6, 1931; s. Glenn Ellis and Ellen (Mason) B.; m. Ann Rankin, May 31, 1953 (div. Apr. 1992); children—Elizabeth Lee Brooks, Amy Mason, Celia Brooks Brown. B.A. magna cum laude, U. Tex., Austin, 1953, M.A., 1956; Ph.D. with distinction, Johns Hopkins U., 1960. Sales mgr. Univ. Tex. Press, Austin, 1953-55; research assoc. Com. on Govt.

and Higher Edn., Balt., 1957-59; instr. to prof. polit. sci. Colo. Coll., Colorado Springs, 1960-96, prof. emeritus, faculty asst. to pres., 1968-70, chmn. dept. polit. sci., 1973-76, dean of coll. and faculty, 1979-87, dir. strategic planning, 1991-93; Rockefeller vis. lectr. U. Nairobi, Kenya, 1967-68; acad. visitor London Sch. Econs., 1972; NEH faculty fellow-in-residence Princeton (N.J.) U., 1978-79; bd. dirs. Am. Conf. Acad. Deans, 1982-85; cons. Nat. U. Lesotho, 1990, Am. Coun. Edn., 1992—; chief of party Fenix project Autonomous U. Puebla, Mex., 1994—. Author: When Governors Convene: The Governors' Conference and National Politics, 1961; (with Frances E. Rourke) The Managerial Revolution in Higher Education, 1966. Contbr. chpts. to books, articles, essays to profl. publs. Bd. dirs. Colo. Humanities Program, Boulder, 1975-78, Citizens Goals for Colorado Springs, 1977—; mem. Chmn.'s Nat. Adv. Com. on Humanities in Primary and Secondary Schs. NEH, 1987—. Mem. Am. Conf. Acad. Deans (bd. dirs. 1982-86), Phi Beta Kappa, Phi Eta Sigma. Democrat. Home: 526 Observatory Dr Colorado Springs CO 80904-3970

BROOKS, GWENDOLYN, writer, poet; b. Topeka, June 7, 1917; d. David Anderson and Keziah Corinne (Wims) B.; m. Henry L. Blakely, Sept. 17, 1939; children: Henry L., Nora. Grad., Wilson Jr. Coll., Chgo., 1936; L.H.D., Columbia Coll., 1964. Instr. poetry Columbia Coll., Chgo., Northeastern Ill. State Coll., Chgo.; mem. Ill. Arts Council; cons. in poetry Library of Congress, 1985-86; Jefferson lectr., 1994. Author: (poetry) A Street in Bronzeville, 1945, Annie Allen, 1949 (Pulitzer prize 1950), Maud Martha: (novel) Bronzeville Boys and Girls, 1953; (for children) The Bean Eaters, 1956; poetry, 1960, Selected Poems, 1963, In the Mecca, 1968, Riot, 1969, Family Pictures, 1970, Aloneness, 1971, To Disembark, 1981; (autobiography) Report From Part One, 1972, The Tiger Who Wore White Gloves, 1974, Beckonings, 1975, Primer for Blacks, 1980, Young Poets' Primer, 1981, Very Young Poets, 1983, The Near-Johannesburg Boy, 1986, Blacks, 1987, Gottschalk and the Grande Tarantelle, 1988, Winnie, 1988, Children Coming Home, 1991, Report From Part Two, 1995. Named one of 10 Women of Yr. Mademoiselle mag., 1945; recipient Creative Writing award Am. Acad. Arts and Letters, 1946, Aninsfield-Wolf award, 1969, Essence award, 1988, Frost medal Poetry Soc. Am., 1989, Lifetime Achievement award Nat. Endowment for the Arts, 1989, Soc. for Lit. award U. Thessaloniki, Athens, Greece, 1990, Aiken-Taylor award, 1992, Jefferson lectr. award NEH, 1994, Nat. Book Found. medal for lifetime achievement, 1994, Am. Book award Gwendolyn Brooks Jr. H.S., 1995, Nat. medal of arts, 1995; Guggenheim fellow, 1946, 47; named poet laureate of Ill., 1968; inducted into Nat. Women's Hall of Fame, 1988; Gwendolyn Brooks chair in Black Lit. and Creative Writing established in her honor Chgo. State U., 1990; The Gwendolyn Brooks Ctr. established, 1992; Gwendolyn Brooks Elem. Sch. named in her honor, Aurora, Ill., 1995. Mem. Soc. Midland Authors. Home: 5530 S South Shore Dr Apt 2A Chicago IL 60637-1921
Personal philosophy: To be clean of heart, clear of mind, and claiming of what is right and just.

BROOKS, H. ALLEN, architectural educator, author, lecturer; b. New Haven, Nov. 6, 1925; s. Harold Allen and Mildred (McNeill) B. BA, Dartmouth Coll., 1950; MA, Yale U., 1955; PhD, Northwestern U., 1957; DEng. (hon.), Dalhousie U., 1984. Asst. prof. U. Ill., 1957-58; lectr. U. Toronto, 1958-61, asst. prof., 1961-64, assoc. prof., 1964-71, prof., 1971-86; vis. prof. Dartmouth Coll., 1969; Mellon chair Vassar Coll., 1970-71; vis. prof. Archtl. Assn., London, 1977-82. Author: The Prairie School: Frank Lloyd Wright and His Midwest Contemporaries, 1972 (recipient Alice Davis Hitchcock Book award 1973), Frank Lloyd Wright and the Prairie School, 1984, Le Corbusier's Formative Years: Charles-Edouard Jeanneret et La Chaux-de-Fonds, 1997 (Assn. Am. Pubs./Scholarly Pub. Divsn. Ann. award 1997); editor: Prairie School Architecture, 1975, Writings on Wright, 1981, The Le Corbusier Archive, 32 vols, 1982-85, Le Corbusier, 1987; editl. cons. Le Corbusier Sketchbooks, 1981-82; contbr. to numerous books and jours. With U.S. Army, 1946-47. Guggenheim Found. fellow, 1973-74; Can. Coun. fellow, 1975-76; Social Scis. and Humanities Rsch. Coun. Can. fellow, 1977-79, 83-85; Victoria U. fellow. Fellow Soc. Archtl. Historians; mem. Internat. Com. Monuments and Sites, Soc. Archtl. Historians U.S. (past pres., dir.), Soc. Archtl. Historians Gt. Britain, Soc. Study Architecture Can., Frank Lloyd Wright Bldg. Conservancy. Address: 9 River Ridge Rd Hanover NH 03755-1910

BROOKS, HARVEY, physics educator; b. Cleve., Aug. 5, 1915; married, 1945; 4 children. AB, Yale U., 1937; PhD, Harvard U., 1940; DSc (hon.), Yale U., 1962, Union Coll., 1962, Harvard U., 1963, Kenyon Coll., 1963, Brown U., 1964. Mem. staff underwater sound lab. Harvard U., 1942-45; asst. dir. ord rsch. lab. Pa. State U., 1945; rsch. assoc. rsch. lab., assoc. lab. head. Knolls Atomic Power Lab. Gen. Electric Co., 1946-50; prof. applied physics Harvard U., Cambridge, Mass., 1950-86, prof. tech. and pub. policy, 1975-86, dean divsn. engring. and applied physics, 1957-75, Benjamin Peirce emeritus prof. tech. and pub. policy, 1986—, Gordon McKay emeritus prof. applied physics, 1986—; chmn. com. undersea warfare NRC, 1957-63, chmn. comm. soc. tech. sys., 1975-78; mem. adv. com. reactor safeguards, programs and policies AEC, 1958; chmn. solid state adv. panel Office Naval Rsch.; mem. Pres.'s Sci. Adv. Com., 1959-64, Nat. Sci. Bd., 1962-74; mem. adv. com. sci. and technol. devel. UN, 1987-91. Author one book and numerous tech. publs.; editor-in-chief Jour. Physics and Chem. Solids, 1956-80. Recipient E.O. Lawrence award Am. Engring. Soc., 1960; Guggenheim fellow, 1956-57. Fellow AAAS (Philip Hauge Abelson award 1993), Am. Phys. Soc. (Forum award 1993); mem. NAS (sr. mem. inst. medicine, chmn. com. sci. and pub. policy 1966-72), Nat. Acad. Engring., Am. Philos. Soc., Am. Acad. Arts and Sci. (pres. 1970-75). Achievements include research on solid state physics, underwater sound, nuclear reactors, and science policy. Office: Harvard U JFK Sch Govt 79 Jfk St Cambridge MA 02138-5801*

BROOKS, IRIS, writer, editor, musician; b. N.Y.C., Oct. 24, 1954; d. Lee Cedar and Sondra (Aronoff) B. Student, Wesleyan U., Middletown, Conn., 1973-74; BA, Bowdoin Coll., 1975. Freelance writer, 1980—; editor EAR Mag., N.Y.C., 1988-90, N.Y. Philharmonic, N.Y.C., 1995, Lincoln Ctr. Festival, N.Y.C., 1997. Author: (liner notes) CRI, 1992, Triloka/Worldly Music, 1993, Ellipsis, 1996; author, editor: New Music Across America, 1992; editor: (book and CD) Jali Kunda: Griot Music of West Africa and Beyond, 1996 (Naird nominee 1997); contbr. articles to profl. jours.; performed in concerts Carnegie Hall, N.Y.C., Whitney Mus. Am. Art, N.Y.C., Smithsonian Instn., Washington, Am. Mus. Natural History, N.Y.C. Bd. dirs. New Music Am. Fellow Watson Found., 1975-76. Avocation: travel. Home and Office: PO Box 460 Pomona NY 10970-0460

BROOKS, ISRAEL, JR., protective services official; b. Newberry, S.C.. Grad., Palmer Coll. Patrol officer Beaufort County S.C. Highway Patrol, 1967-76; instr. S.C. Criminal Justice Acad., 1976-82; lt. S.C. Highway Patrol, 1982-87, capt. Internal Affairs Unit, 1987-90, maj., Patrol Adminstrv. Officer, 1990-94; U.S. Marshall Dist. S.C., Columbia, 1994—. Deacon St. Johns Bapt. Ch., choir mem. Recipient Nat. Pub. Svc. award Am. Soc. Pub. Adminstrn. and Nat. Acad. Pub. Adminstrn., 1995, Disting. Dist. of Yr. award, 1996. Mem. U.S. Marshals Svc. Dir.'s Assn. (adv. com.), S.C. Correctional Assn. (award). Fax: 803 765-5824. Office: US Marshals Svc 1845 Assembly St Columbia SC 29201-2455*

BROOKS, JACK BASCOM, congressman; b. Crowley, La., Dec. 18, 1922; s. Edward Chachere and Grace Marie (Pipes) B.; m. Charlotte Collins, Dec. 15, 1960; children: Jack Edward, Katherine Inez, Kimberly Grace. AA, Lamar Jr. Coll., Beaumont, Tex., 1939-41; BJ, U. Tex., 1943, JD, 1949. Bar: Tex. 1949. Mem. Tex. Legislature, 1946-50, 83rd-89th Congresses from 2nd Tex. dist., 90th-103rd Congresses from 9th Tex. dist., Washington, 1967-94. Author, Lamar Coll. bill, 1949. lst lt. USMCR, 1942-46; col. Res. ret. Mem. ABA, State Bar Tex., Am. Legion, VFW, Sigma Delta Chi. Home: 1029 East Dr Beaumont TX 77706-4738 Office: 3535 Calder Ave Beaumont TX 77706-5036

BROOKS, JAMES ELWOOD, geologist, educator; b. Salem, Ind., May 31, 1925; s. Elwood Edwin and Helen Mary (May) B.; m. Eleanore June Nystrom, June 18, 1949; children: Helen and Nancy, Kathryn, Carolyn. AB, DePauw U., 1948; MS, Northwestern U., 1950; PhD, U. Wash., 1954. Research assoc. Ill. Geol. Survey, 1950; geologist Gulf Oil Corp., Salt Lake City, summers 1951-53; instr. geol. scis. So. Meth. U., Dallas, 1952-55, asst. prof., 1955-59, assoc. prof., 1959-62, prof., 1962-95, chmn. dept., 1961-70, dean, assoc. provost univ., 1969-72, provost, v.p., 1972-80, interim pres., 1980-81; prof. emeritus So. Meth. U., 1995—; provost emeritus So. Meth. U., Dallas, 1995—; pres., trustee Inst. for Study Earth and Man, Dallas, 1981-97, vice chmn., trustee, 1997—; cons. geologist firm DeGolyer & MacNaughton, Dallas, 1954-59. Contbr. articles to profl. jours. Trustee Hockaday Sch., 1982-88, Dallas Mus. Natural History Assn., 1984—, v.p., 1986-88, pres., 1988-90, hon. life trustee, 1990—; mem. exec. bd., internat. rep. Circle Ten coun. Boy Scouts Am., 1982—, internat. com., chmn. 1984—; bd. vis. DePauw U., 1979-83, chmn., 1983; mem. Mayor's Task Force on Fair Park, 1992; chmn. Coun. Fair Park Instns., 1992-94. Fellow AAAS, Geol. Soc. Am., Tex. Acad. Sci., Explorers Club; mem. Am. Assn. Petroleum Geologists, Dallas Geol. Soc., Sigma Xi, Sigma Gamma Epsilon, Sigma Phi. Home: 7055 Arboreal Dr Dallas TX 75231-7315 Office: Inst Study Earth and Man PO Box 750274 Dallas TX 75275-0274

BROOKS, JAMES JOE, III, accountant; b. Augusta, Ga., July 15, 1948; s. James J. Jr. and Pattie (D.) B. AA, Mid. Ga. Coll., Cochran, 1968; BBA in Acctg., Ga. So. Coll., Statesboro, 1970. CPA, Ga. Internal auditor Ga. Dept. Transp., Atlanta, 1972-77; staff acct. Webb, Dreher & Clark, Atlanta, 1977-78, Gaddis & Eidson, Atlanta, 1978-80; contr. Food Svcs., Inc., Atlanta, 1980-81; pvt. practice Atlanta, 1981—; cons. in field. Coach First Bapt. Ch. of Atlanta softball team, 1985-86, 90—. Mem. Personal Computers Users Group, Ga. Soc. CPA's, Ga. Real Estate Investor Assn., Northcrest Swim & Tennis Club (bd. dirs. 1989—). Republican. Avocations: fishing, hunting, basketball, tennis, softball. Home: 3532 Bowling Green Way Atlanta GA 30340-4187

BROOKS, JAMES L., writer, director, producer; b. Bklyn., May 9, 1940; s. Edward M. and Dorothy Helen (Sheinheit) B.; m. Marianne Catherine Morrissey, July 7, 1964 (div.); 1 dau., Amy Lorraine; m. Holly Beth Holmberg, July 23, 1978; children: Chloe, Cooper. Student, N.Y. U., 1958-60. Writer CBS News, N.Y.C., 1964-66; writer-producer documentaries Wolper Prodns., L.A., 1966-67; founder & owner Gracie Films, 1984; guest lectr. Stanford Grad. Sch. Communications. Creator TV series Room 222, 1968-69 (Emmy award for outstanding new series 1969); co-creator, producer TV series Lou Grant (Peabody award 1978); exec. producer, co-creator TV series Mary Tyler Moore Show, 1970-77 (Emmy award for comedy writing 1971, 74-77, Outstanding Comedy Series 1975-77, Peabody award, 1977, Writers Guild Am. winner best teleplay The Last Show, nominated best teleplay in episodic comedy, 1972, 77, TV Critics Achievement in Comedy award 1977, Achievement in Series award 1977, Humanitas 1977); writer, producer TV series Paul Sand in Friends and Lovers, 1974; co-creator, co-exec. producer TV series Rhoda show, 1974-75 (Emmy awards for outstanding writing in drama 1978-80, outstanding drama 1979, 80, 2 Humanitas for 1977, 82); writer TV show The New Lorenzo Music Show, 1976; co-writer, co-producer TV film Thursday Game, from 1971; co-creator, exec. producer TV series Taxi, 1978-80 (Emmy award for best show, best writing, 1978-79, 79-80, 80-81, TV Film Critics Circle award for achievement in comedy and in a series, 1976-77, Golden Globe awards for best comedy series, 1978, 79, 80, Humanitas prize for episode entitled Blind Date, 1979); co-exec. producer, co-writer TV series Cindy, 1978 (Writers Guild nomination for outstanding script 1978); co-creator, exec. producer TV series The Associates, 1979; exec. producer, co-exec. producer, co-creator The Tracey Ullman Show, 1986-90 (Emmy awards Outstanding Variety or Comedy series 1987, 88, 90, winner Emmy awards Outstanding Writing Variety or Music Show 1988-89), The Simpsons, 1990— (winner Emmy awards Outstanding Animated Spl., Outstanding Animated Program, winner Outstanding Animated Program); writer, co-producer film Starting Over (Writers Guild nomination for Best Screen Comedy Adaption 1979); actor film Modern Romance, 1981; producer, writer, dir. film Terms of Endearment, 1983 (Gloden Globe Best Screenplay award 1983, Acad. awards for best film, best dir., best screenplay 1984, Best Dir. award Dirs. Guild Am. 1983, winner comedy based on material from another medium, 1983, Nat. Bd. Rev. Best Picture, 1983, Golden Globe award Best Picture 1983, N.Y. Film Critics Best Picture; writer, dir., producer film Broadcast News, 1987 (winner best picture, best. dir., best screenplay N.Y. Film Critics Awards, Dirs. Guild nomination for best dir., Acad. award nomination for Best Picture and Best Screenplay); exec. producer film Big, 1988 (Peoples Choice award for favorite comedy motion picture), The War of the Roses, 1989; exec. producer Say Anything, 1989, (TV series) The Critic, 1994, writer, co-prodr. I'll Do Anything, 1994; dir. (play) Bklyn. Laundry; prodr. Bottle Rocket, 1996, Jerry Maguire, 1996, As Good As It Gets, 1997. Mem. Dirs. Guild Am., Writers Guild Am., TV Acad. Arts and Scis., Screen Actors Guild, Acad. Motion Picture Arts and Scis. Office: Gracie Films/Columbia Pictures/Sony Pictures Ent Poitier Bldg 10202 Washington Blvd Culver City CA 90232-3119*

BROOKS, JANICE WILLENA, educator; b. Warrenton, Ga., Nov. 6, 1946; d. Willie and Rebie Virginia (Wellington) B. Student, NYU, 1974, U. Phoenix, 1988, Northern Ariz. U., 1999. Mem. WESTOP (bd. dirs. 1991-92, mem. Ariz. chpt.). Home: 604 Sir Charles Dr Fairburn GA 30213

BROOKS, JEFFREY MARTIN, marketing and sales executive; b. Charlotte, N.C., Oct. 14, 1958; s. Jack M. and Margaret Anne (Reap) B.; m. Kim Marie Whitaker, Sept. 26, 1981; 2 children: Justin Jeffrey Whitaker, Evan Martin Whitaker. BSBA in Acctg., East Carolina U.; MS in Econs., N.C. State U. Staff acct. Ernst & Whinney, Raleigh, N.C., 1980-82; account rep. Data Gen. Corp., Charlotte, 1982-85; mgr. systems mktg. AT&T Charlotte, 1985-86; pres. Fastfly Corp., 1985-89; v.p. sales and distbn. Vanguard Cellular Systems, Inc., Greensboro, N.C., 1989-94; v.p. mktg. and sales So. Comm. (subs. The So. Co.), Atlanta, 1994-97; asst. v.p. corp. mktg. BellSouth, Atlanta, 1997—; cons. Charlotte Hornets, GTE. Vol. Jr. Achievement, Habitat for Humanity, YMCA Youth Sports; mem. Mt. Pisgah United Meth. Ch., Alpharetta, Ga. Mem. AICPA, Aircraft Owners and Pilots Assn., Nat. Bus. Aircraft Assn., U.S.A. Soccer, Nat. Youth Coaches Assn. Home: 10635 Oxford Mill Cir Alpharetta GA 30022-6369 Office: BellSouth 2400 Century Center Pky Atlanta GA 30345

BROOKS, JEROME BERNARD, English and Afro-American literature educator; b. Houston, Mar. 20, 1932; s. Osburn Bernard and Agnes (Harrison) B. BA, Holy Cross Sem., Chgo., 1956, MA, 1960; MA, Notre Dame U., 1962; PhD, U. Chgo., 1972. Instr. English Holy Cross Sem., 1962-66; lectr. English CCNY, 1968-72, asst. prof., 1972-75, assoc. prof., 1985-90, prof., 1991-95, chmn. dept. English, 1985-88, acting dean U. Affairs, 1988-89, dep. to the pres., 1991-95, prof. emeritus, 1996—; cons. NEH, Washington, 1985, U. Mo. Press, Columbia, 1986; bd. dirs. N.Y. Alliance for Pub. Schs., Transp. Rsch. Consortium, Rice H.S.; vis. prof. English, Bard. Coll., Annandale-on-Hudson, N.Y. Author: Black Women Writers 1950-80, 1984; contbr. World Authors Encyclopedia, 1986, The Paris Review, 1994; co-editor Continuities mag., 1973-76. NEH grantee, 1979; named Fulbright Sr. Lectr. at U. Madagascar, USIA, 1976-78. Mem. The Williams Club, The Penn Club. Democrat. Roman Catholic. Avocation: play classical piano. Office: CUNY Dept English 138th St and Convent Ave New York NY 10031

BROOKS, JOAE GRAHAM, psychiatrist; b. Boston, June 14, 1926; d. Collins and Hannah Slade (Benton) Graham; RN, Mass. Gen. Hosp. Sch. Nursing, 1947; AB with distinction, U. Rochester, 1950, MD, 1954; m. Bernard Charles Brooks, Jan. 11, 1976; children by previous marriage, Anne Benton Millman, Jane Graham Selzer. Intern in medicine Duke Hosp., Durham, N.C., 1954-55; resident in psychiatry Mass. Mental Health Center, Boston, 1955-57; resident in child psychiatry Beth Israel Hosp., Boston, 1957-59, mem. staff, 1959-97; pvt. practice, Brookline, Mass., 1959-97; cons. New Eng. Home for Little Wanderers, Boston, 1959-75, Kimberly Clark Corp., 1983-97; asst. clin. prof. psychiatry Harvard U. Med. Sch., Boston, 1978-97; vol. psychiatrist Sr. Friendship Ctr. Health Clinic, Naples, Fla., 1998—; mem. Bd. Registration in Medicine of Mass., 1991-95. Diplomate Am. Bd. Psychiatry and Neurology. Fellow Am. Psychiat. Assn. (life), Acad. Child and Adolescent Psychiatry (life); mem. Mass. Psychiat. Soc., New Eng. Council Child Psychiatry (bd. dirs. 1979-82, pres. 1987-89). Author: No More Diapers! A Guide to Toilet Training, 1971, 2d edit., 1991, When Children Ask about Sex—A Guide for Parents, 1975, I'm a Big Kid Now! A Guide to Toilet Training for Children and Parents, 1989. Home: 5950 Almaden Dr Naples FL 34119-4627

BROOKS, JOHN C., federal judge; b. 1950. Magistrate judge U.S. Dist. Ct. Wyo., Cheyenne, 1986—. Office: 2120 Capitol Ave Cheyenne WY 82001-3633

BROOKS, JOHN EDWARD, college president emeritus; b. Boston, July 13, 1923; s. John Edward and Mildred (McCoy) B. B.S. in Physics, Coll. Holy Cross, 1949; postgrad. in geophysics, Pa. State U., 1949-50; M.A. in Philosophy, Boston Coll., 1954, M.S. in Geophysics, 1959; S.T.D. in Dogmatic Theology, Gregorian U., Rome, Italy, 1963; H.H.D. (hon.), St. Ambrose Coll., 1976; D.Sc. (hon.), Worcester Poly. Inst., 1980; D Humanities, Assumption Coll., 1990; HHD (hon.), St. Anselm Coll., 1993; D Humanities (hon.), U. New England, 1994, Anna Maria Coll., 1994, Coll. of the Holy Cross, 1994. Joined Soc. of Jesus, 1950; ordained priest Roman Catholic Ch., 1959; instr. math. and physics Coll. of Holy Cross, Worcester, Mass., 1954-56, instr. theology, 1963-64, asst. prof., 1964-67, assoc. prof. religious studies, 1967-93, chmn. dept. theology, 1964-69, Loyola prof. humanities, 1993—, v.p., dean coll., 1968-70, pres., trustee, 1970-94, pres. emeritus, 1994—, sec. com. ednl. policy, 1968-70; chmn. Coll. of Holy Cross, 1970-94; participant bibl. and archeol. consortium Jewish Inst. on Religion, Hebrew Union Coll., 1968; inst. acad. deans Am. Coun. Edn., St. Louis U., 1968; trustee St. Peter's Coll., Jersey City, 1969-75, Canisius Coll., Buffalo, 1974-80, Spring Hill Coll., 1981-94, Anna Maria Coll., Worcester, 1998—; mem. Mass. Postsecondary Edn. Commn., Mass. 1202 Commn., 1974-77; mem. exec. com. New Eng. Colls. Fund, 1974, 78; mem. Mass. Pub./Pvt. Forum; mem. Worcester Downtown Devel. Corp., Mass. Biotech. Rsch. Inst., 1985—; bd. visitors Air U., 1978-86; bd. dirs. Worcester Mcpl. Rsch. Bur., Inc. Community trustee United Way Cen. Mass.; consortium dir. Social Svcs. Corp., Worcester; bd. dirs. Worcester Mechanics Hall Assn.; mem. commn. govtl. rels. Am. Coun. on Edn., 1989-92. With U.S. Army, 1942-46. Mem. Assn. Jesuit Colls. and Univs. (bd. dirs. 1970-94), Assn. Ind. Colls. and Univs. in Mass. (v.p. 1972-73, chmn. coms., exec. com.), New Eng. Assn. Schs. and Colls. (sec.-treas. 1985-92, pres.-elect 1993, pres. 1994), Econ. Club (pres. Worchester chpt. 1977-78, exec. com. 1978-86), Delta Epsilon Sigma, Alpha Sigma Nu. Office: Coll of Holy Cross Ciampi Hall Worcester MA 01610

BROOKS, JOHN SAMUEL JOSEPH, pathologist, researcher; b. Phila., Feb. 2, 1948. BS in Biology, St. Joseph's Coll., Phila., 1970; MD, Thomas Jefferson U., 1974. Diplomate Am. Bd. Pathology. Resident in pathology U. Pa., Phila., 1974-78, chief resident, 1978, asst. prof., 1979-84, assoc. prof., 1984-88, prof., 1988-93; chmn. dept. pathology Roswell Pk. Cancer Inst., Buffalo, 1993—, chmn. dept. lab. medicine, 1997—, pres. med. staff, 1997-98; prof., vice chmn. pathology Med. Sch. SUNY, Buffalo, 1993—; vis. prof. Royal Marsden Hosp./Inst. Cancer Rsch., London, 1987; expert in immunohistochemistry. Author: Pathology, 1989; contbr. articles to New Eng. Jour. Medicine, Jour. of AMA, Jour. Urology, Internat. Jour. Ob.-Gyn. Pathology, Am. Jour. Pathology; editor Internat. Jour. Surg. Pathology, 1993—; mem. bd. editors: Jour. Modern Pathology, Jour. Surg. Pathology, and reviewer; contbr. over 140 articles to profl. jours. Fellow Royal Coll. Pathology; mem. AAAS, Am. Assn. Cancer Rsch., Pathology Soc. Phila. (pres. 1988-90), Ea. Coop. Oncology Group (chmn. sarcoma pathology com. Madison chpt. 1988-95), Internat. Acad. Pathology (edn. com. Atlanta chpt. 1989—), U.S.-Can. Acad. Pathology (coun. mem. 1993-96), Am. Soc. Clin. Pathologists (chair anatomical pathology coun. 1995-97, dep. commr. 1997—), Arthur Purdy Stout Soc. for Surg. Pathologists (coun. mem. 1994), Am. Assn. Clin. Rsch., Fedn. Am. Soc. for Exptl. Biology (mem. medicine coverage adv. com. lab. diagnostics panel, 1999—, Nat. Internat. Reputation in Diagnostic Surg. Pathology. Democrat. Roman Catholic. Achievements include research in significance of double phenotypes in sarcomas, growth factors in sarcomas, in immunohistochemistry; posthumous diagnosis of Pres. Cleveland's tumor. Home: 34 Deer Run Orchard Park NY 14127-3454 Office: Roswell Pk Cancer Inst Dept Pathology Elm & Carlton Sts Buffalo NY 14263

BROOKS, JOHN W., military officer. BA, Roanoke Coll., 1970; disting. grad., Squadron Officer Sch., 1977; MA, Cen. Mich. U., 1979; grad., Armed Forces Staff Coll., 1983, Nat. War Coll., 1989; advanced mgmt. program, U. Ill., 1995; nat. security program, Harvard U., 1998. Commd. 2d lt. USAF, 1972, advanced through grades to maj. gen., 1998; flight examiner 62d Mil. Airlift Wing, McChord AFB, Wash., 1978-79; air staff tng. program officer Office of Vice Chief of Staff Hdqs. USAF, Washington, 1978-79; airlift dir. current ops. Hdqs. Mil. Airlift Command, Scott AFB, Ill., 1979-80, exec. officer to dep. chief of staff for ops., 1980-81, chief of protocal, 1981-83; chief of plans UN Truce Supervision Orgn., Lebanon, 1983; chief combat ops., C-141 pilot 438th Mil. Airlift Wing, McGuire AFB, N.J., 1984-86; comdr. 345th Tactical Airlift Squadron, Yokota Air Base, Japan, 1986-88; chief Sec. of Air Force Staff Group, Washington, 1989-91; comdr. 438th Ops. Group, McGuire AFB, N.J., 1991-92; commandant Air Command and Staff Coll., Maxwell AFB, Ala., 1995-96; comdr. 86th Airlift Wing and Kaiserslautern Mil. Comty., Ramstein Air Base, Germany, 1996-98; vice dir. for logistics Joint Staff, The Pentagon, Washington, 1998—. Decorated Legion of Merit, Def. Meritorious Svc. medal with oak leaf cluster, Meritorious Svc. medal with 2 oak leaf clusters. Office: VJ4 4000 Joint Staff Pentagon Washington DC 20318-4000

BROOKS, JOHN WHITE, lawyer; b. Long Beach, Calif., Sept. 3, 1936; s. John White and Florence Belle (O'Grady) B.; m. Elizabeth Ann Bellmore, June 21, 1958; children: Stephen Sanford, John Tinley. AB, Stanford U., 1958, LLB, 1966. Assoc. Luce, Forward, Hamilton and Scripps, San Diego, 1966-71, ptnr., 1971-81, sr. ptnr., 1981—; chmn. Internat. Svcs. Group, 1989—; mem. Internat. Coun. Inst. Ams., Pacific Coun. Internat. Policy. 1996-98; panelist Ctr. for Internat. Comml. Arbitration, 1987—; bd. dirs. Union of Pan-Asian Communities, , 1989-98, Ctr. for Dispute Resolution, 1986—; chmn. Pacific Rim Adv. Coun., 1984-91. Author: Passport Pal, The Pacific Rim, 1996—, The Heads Up Report; contbr. articles to profl. jours. Dir. corp. fin. council of San Diego, 1977-82, chmn., 1980-81; bd. visitors Stanford Law Sch., 1978-80; mem. Commn. of the Californias, 1977-79; chair San Diego Regional Yr. 2000 Working Group, 1998—. With USN, 1958-63. Named Alfred P. Sloan scholar Stanford U., 1958, Rocky Mountain Mineral Law Found. Research scholar, 1966. Mem. ABA (bus. law sect., com. on internat. bus. law, subcom. on Asia-Pacific law and internat. bus. structures and agreements, internat. law sect., subcom. on multinat. corps., com. on internat. comml. transactions), Calif. Bar Assn. (bus. law sect. com. on corps. 1977, vice chmn. com. on internat. practice 1986-87, exec. com. internat. law sect. 1987), San Diego County Bar Assn., Internat. Bar Assn. (com. on issues and trading in securities 1980-89, com. on procedures for settling disputes 1980—, com. on bus. orgns. 1989—), Inter-Pacific Bar Assn. (com. on internat. trade), Am. Arbitration Assn. (panel of arbitrators 1975-96), State Bar Calif. Avocations: greenhouse gardening, horse competitions, wine, food. Office: Luce Forward Hamilton & Scripps 600 W Broadway Ste 2600 San Diego CA 92101-3391

BROOKS, JOYCE JULIANNA, gerontological nurse; b. WaKeeney, Kans., Oct. 13, 1931; d. Mark R. and Flora E. Hammond; m. Marion G. Brooks, Oct. 15, 1950; children: Gale E., Charles L., Mark F., Rita J. Avila. Student, Cen. Mo. State U., 1949-50; AS, Colby Community Coll., 1988; student, 1990—. LPN, RN, Kans. Staff nurse Gove County Hosp., Quinter, Kans. Mem. Phi Theta Kappa. Home: RR 1 Box 1C Quinter KS 67752-9801

BROOKS, KATHLEEN, journalist; b. Atlanta, Jan. 25, 1957; d. William Chesley and Sara (Brooks) Howton. BA, Stephens Coll., Columbia, Mo., 1978. Mktg. asst. The Laitram Corp., New Orleans, 1978-79; reporter Daily Home, Talladega, Ala., 1979-80, copy editor, 1980-81; asst. wire editor, reporter Gastonia (N.C.) Gazette, 1981, wire editor, 1981-84; asst. wire editor Comml. Appeal, Memphis, 1984-88, Washington editor, 1988-91, nat. editor, 1991—. Methodist. Office: The Comml Appeal 495 Union Ave Memphis TN 38103-3221

BROOKS, KEITH, retired speech communication educator; b. Tigerton, Wis., May 14, 1923; s. Oscar Derby and Henrietta (Mierswa) B.; m. Laquata Sue Walters, Dec. 29, 1951; children: Todd Randall, Craig William. BS, U. Wis., 1949, MS, 1949; PhD, Ohio State U., 1955. Mem. faculty Eastern Ky. State U., Richmond, 1949-53, Ohio State U., Columbus, 1953-87; prof. communication Ohio State U., 1968-87, prof. emeritus, 1987—, chmn. dept., 1968-75; comms. cons. Procter & Gamble, Ohio Bd. Regents, Mead World Hdqs., U.S. Dept. Agr., Ohio Bell Telephone, Ea. R.R. Assn., Shaw U., Raleigh, N.C. Author: (with Bahn and Okey) Literature for Listening, 1968, The Communicative Act of Oral Interpretation, 1967, 2d edit., 1975, The Communicative Arts and Sciences of Speech, 1967, (with Dietrich) Practical

Speaking, 1969. With USNR, 1945-46. Mem. Speech Communication Assn. (chmn. interpretation div., vice chmn., sec.), Internat. Communication Assn. (co-editor Newsletter 1979-80), Cen. States Speech Assn. (editor Jour. 1958-61), Am. Ednl. Theatre Assn. (bd. dir. 1958-60). Home: 364 Stonewall Ct Dublin OH 43017-1333 *The most important attribute of all is taking the time to care.*

BROOKS, KENNETH N., forestry educator; m. Pamela Naylor; children: Marianne, Robin, Cherie, Nicole. BS in Range Sci., Utah State U., 1966; MS in Watershed Mgmt., U. Ariz., 1969, PhD in Watershed Mgmt., 1970. Hydrologist North Pacific Divsn. Corps of Engrs., Portland, Oreg., 1971-73, Tng. and Methods br. Hydrologic Engring. Ctr., Davis, Calif., 1973-75; asst. prof. dept. forest resources U. Minn., St. Paul, 1975-79, assoc. prof., 1979-85, prof., 1985—, dir. grad. studies in forestry Coll. Natural Resources, 1987—; fellow Environment and Policy Inst. East-West Ctr., Honolulu, 1983-84; cons. nat. and internat. agencies and firms including Food and Agrl. Orgn. of UN, U.S. Agy. for Internat. Devel., World Bank; condr. workshops in field; Fulbright lectr., Taiwan, 1997-98. Co-author: Guidelines for Economic Appraisal of Watershed Management Projects, 1987, Watershed Management Project Planning, Monitoring and Evaluation: A Manual for the ASEAN Region, 1989, Hydrology and the Management of Watersheds, 1991, 2d edit. 1997, Challenges in Upland Conservation: Asia and the Pacific, 1993, Dryland Forestry, 1995; contbr. articles to profl. jours. Am. Inst. Hydrology (chmn. bd. registration 1995—, sec. 1992), Soc. Am. Foresters (chmn. water resources working group 1991-93), Am. Water Resources Assn. (dir. West North Ctrl. dist. 1987-90, assoc. editor Water Resources Bull. 1982-88), Western Snow Conf., Internat. Soc. Tropical Foresters, Xi Sigma Pi, Sigma Xi, Phi Kappa Phi.

BROOKS, LILLIAN DRILLING ASHTON, adult education educator; b. Grand Rapids, Mich., May 27, 1921; d. Walter Brian and Lillian Church; m. Frederick Morris Drilling, 1942 (div. Apr. 1972); children: Frederick Walter, Stephen Charles, Lawrence Alan, Lynn Anne; m. Richard Moreton Ashton, Aug. 25, 1973 (dec.); m. Ralph J. Brooks, May 21, 1994. Student, Grand Rapids Jr. Coll., 1939-41, Wayne State U., 1941-42, Grand Rapids Art Inst., 1945-49, UCLA, 1964-69, Loyola Marymount Coll., Westchester, Calif., 1970-73. Life teaching credential, Calif. Decorator John Widdicomb Furniture Co., 1945-49; tchr. art Inglewood (Calif.) Sch. Dist., 1965-73; tchr. adult edn. art Downey (Calif.) Unified Sch. Dist., 1973-95; lectr. Downey Art League, 1990-92, Whittier (Calif.) Art Assn., 1991, h.s. and mid. sch. lectr., 1994-95; judge Children's Art Exhibit, Downey, 1992; participant Getty Found. at San Francisco, 1993, Getty Found. seminar at Cranbrook, 1994, Getty Conf. on Aesthetics, 1995, Cin. U., 1992, El SEgundo, 1994; mem. state accreditation com. Inglewood and Downey United Sch. Dists., 1966-70, 75-80, 85—; owner A & B Furniture Svc. Ctr., 1995—. One woman shows include El Segundo Mcpl. Libr., 1965, Pico Rivera Art Gallery, 1978, Downey Art Mus., 1999; exhibited in group shows at Fairlane Show, Dearborn, Mich., 1959, Jane Lessing Art Gallery, 1966, Westchester Mcpl. Libr., 1971, Inglewood City Hall, 1973, Aegina Sch., Greece, 1973, Downey Art Mus., 1992; retrospective at Downey Mus. Art; represented in permanent collection at U. Mich. Pres. bd. dirs. Downey Art Mus., 1998-99, dir. Mus., 1998, vol. dir., 1999; former mem. Mich. Cultural Com.; art commr. City of Dearborn, Mich., 1954-59; former pres. Dearborn Art Inst., Pacific Art Guild; pres. bd. dirs. Downey Art Mus., 1997-98; pres. Downey Art League, 1991-92, 93-94, Exhbn. Ch., 1995, v.p. 1996-98; vol. dir. Art Mus., 1998-99; lectr. on art as a career local Downey high and mid. schs. Recipient Certs. of Appreciation for contbn. of leadership Coord. Coun. Downey, Downey Governing Bd., Downey Bd. Edn., 1997, Cmty. Svc. award for Outstanding Svc. Downey Rotary, 1994; named Tchr. of Yr., Masons, Downey, 1986. Mem. Calif. Coun. on Art Edn. (parliamentarian Downey 1990-92, Calco Excellence in Tchg. award 1991, various certs.). Avocations: reading, hiking, internat. travel, photography, painting. Home: 9318 Fostoria St Downey CA 90241-4020

BROOKS, LORIMER PAGE, patent lawyer; b. Swampscott, Mass., May 11, 1917; s. William Lorimer and Maude (Page) B.; m. Arlene M. Cook, Nov. 9, 1941; children: Lorriane E. Brooks Phillips, Jr., Rosalind P. Brooks O'Malley. B.S. in elec. engring. with honors, Northeastern U., 1939; J.D., Fordham U., 1948; postgrad., NYU Law Sch., 1951. Bar: N.Y. 1948, U.S. Dist. Ct. (so. dist.) N.Y. 1952, U.S. Dist. Ct. (ea. dist.) N.Y. 1957, U.S. Ct. Appeals (2d cir.) 1964, U.S. Dist. Ct. (we. dist.) N.Y. 1971, U.S. Supreme Ct. 1971, U.S. Ct. Appeals (fed. cir.) 1982. Patent agt. ITT, 1939-41, patent atty., 1945-50; patent atty. Ward, Crosby, & Neal, N.Y.C., 1950-54; ptnr. firm Ward, McElhannon, Brooks & Fitzpartrick, N.Y.C., 1954-71, Brooks, Haidt, Haffner & Delahunty, N.Y.C., 1971-98; ptnr. Norris McLaughlin & Marcus, PA, N.Y.C., 1998—; rep. Nat. Council Patent Law Assns., 1976-77. Patentee in field. Sec. Westchester Park Citizens Assn., 1950-52, pres., 1952-54; dir. Westchester County Cerebral Palsy Assn., 1962-64; mem. Young Men's Republican Club Eastchester, N.Y., 1952-56. Served with AUS, 1941-45. Mem. Westchester County Bar Assn. (ethics com. 1978-86), N.Y. Patent Law Assn. (bd. govs. 1961-64, 74-78, chmn. subcom. practice and procedure in cts. 1961-62, chmn. com. ethics and grievances 1973-74, 1st v.p. 1974-75, pres. 1975-76, past pres. com. 1976—), IEEE, Aircraft Owners and Pilots Assn., Tau Beta Pi. Home: 6 Hyatt Rd Briarcliff Manor NY 10510-2610 Office: Norris McLaughlin and Marcus 805 3d Ave New York NY 10022

BROOKS, LORRAINE ELIZABETH, music educator; b. Port Chester, N.Y., Mar. 10, 1936; d. William Henry Sr. and Marion Elizabeth (Harrell) B. BS in Music Edn., SUNY, Potsdam, 1958; M of Performance, Manhattan Sch. Music, 1970. Dir. Camp Spruce-Mountain Lakes, North Salem, N.Y., 1964-73; youth adviser St. Peter's Episcopal Ch., Port Chester, N.Y., 1964-65, St. Andrew's-St. Peter's Ch., Yonkers, N.Y., 1970-73; v.p. South Yonkers Youth Council, 1970-76; assoc. Sisters Charity of N.Y., Scarsdale, 1978—; eucharistic minister, lector Our Lady of Victory Ch., Mt. Vernon, N.Y., 1981-93, eucharistic ministry lector, youth dir., 1988—; Roman Cath. asst. chaplain White Plains (N.Y.) Hosp. Ctr., 1981—; cons. Quincy Tenants Assn., Mt. Vernon, 1986—. Soloist Greenhave Correctional Facility retreat, N.Y., 1994; recital St. Mary's Ch. Outreach Program, 1994. Vestrywoman St. Andrew's Episc. Ch., Yonkers, 1971-75; contralto soloist St. Peter's Episc. Ch., Port Chester, 1959-69, Cape Cod Roman Cath. Charismatic Conf., 1993; mem. Collegiate Chorale, N.Y.C., 1958-68; svc. team mem. Charismatic Cmty., Scarsdale, 1975-91; v.p. Willwood Tenant Assn., Mt. Vernon, 1981-82, pres., 1982-84; vol. speaker N.Y. Regional Transplant Program, 1992—; active Montefiore Med. Ctr. TRIO, 1991—, presenter kidney transplant program, 1995; active Teen/Twenty Encounter Christ, 1990—; soloist concert Holy Spirit Episcopal Ch., Orleans, Mass.; facilitator Our Lady of the Cape, Brewster, Mass.; lector, eucharistic min. St. Mary's Roman Cath. Ch., 1993—, facilitator RENEW program, 1994—, CORE team mem., 1996, coord. prayer group Day of Reflection, elected leader prayer group, 1998—, adviser young adult ministry, 1998—; asst. coord. RENEW, St. Mary's Ch., Mt. Vernon, N.Y., 1995—, coord. sponsor's program, leader Charismatic Prayer Group, 1998—; coord. Life in the Spirit Program, 1997; active Edn. Parish Svc. Program, N.Y. Mem. Westchester County Sch. Music Assn. (exec. bd.), Scarsdale Tchrs. Assn. (exec. bd.), Music Educators Nat. Conf. Democrat. Roman Catholic. Avocations: swimming, reading, walking, organic cooking, concerts. Office: Scarsdale Mid Sch Mamaroneck Rd Scarsdale NY 10583-5008

BROOKS, MARIAN, retired comptroller and credit manager; b. Baker, Oreg., Nov. 23, 1930; d. Paul and Florence (Cornman) Seiffert; m. Gregg Brooks, Oct. 29, 1955; 1 child, Wayne. Office mgr. Redmond (Oreg.) Motor Co., 1952-53, Morris-Nelson Pontiac, Redmond, 1953-54; comptr., credit mag. McCaulou's Inc., Madras, Oreg., 1955-1994; ret., 1994—; past pres. bd. dirs. Consumer Credit Counseling Svc. Oreg., Bend. Bd. dirs. United Way Jefferson County, Madras, 1985-96. Mem. Internat. Credit Assn. Ctrl. Orgn. (pres.), Credit Assn. Oreg. (hon. life, past pres. bd. dirs.), Soc. Cert. Credit Execs. Avocations: travel, reading. Home: 743 SE Hull St Madras OR 97741-1579

BROOKS, MARK HUNTER, systems engineering manager, consultant; b. Pinehurst, N.C., Mar. 14, 1960; s. Brady Hunter and Mary Ann Brooks; m. Selina Malherbe, June 30, 1984; 1 child, Meredith. BS in Textile Mgmt., N.C. State U., 1982; MBA in Info. Systems, NYU, 1992. Asst. dir. R & D Reliance Cons. Group, N.Y.C., 1982-86; network planning analyst Sterling Drug Inc., N.Y.C., 1986-90; sr. systems engr. Chase Manhattan Bank, N.A., N.Y.C., 1990-91; sr. LAN specialist TIAA-CREF, N.Y.C., 1991-96, tech. engring. cons., 1997-98, sr. tech. engring. cons. architecture group, 1998—, connectivity supr., 1998, environ. mgr. yr. 2000 testing team, 1998—; mem.-at-large bd. dirs. N.Am. region NetWare Users Internat., 1991, v.p., pres.-elect, 1992, pres., 1993, advisor to bd. dirs., 1994, chmn. leadership devel. and election com. 1995; founder, pres. N.Y. LAN Assn., Inc., N.Y.C., 1990-91; adv. bd. Networld Boston, 1993, Networld Dallas, 1993; readers adv. bd. LAN Times, 1993-96, 98—; corp. adv. bd. Tech. Mgrs. Forum Internat., 1996—; program adv. bd. UNIX Expo, N.Y., 1996; coord. ann. conf. Conservative Bapt. Assn.-N.Y., 1998. Chmn. fin. com. Metro Bapt. Ch., N.Y.C., 1986-88, trustee, 1988-90, vice chmn. bd. trustees, 1990; mem. missions com. Harmony Bapt. Ch., Middletown, N.Y., 1997—. Recipient Disting. Recent Alumnus award NYU, 1994, Excellence in Fin. and Adminstrn. award Am. Soc. Assn. Execs., 1994. Democrat. Baptist. Avocations: aviation, rocketry.

BROOKS, MEL, producer, director, writer, actor; b. June 28, 1926. Author: sketch Of Fathers and Sons in New Faces of 1952, 1952; co-author: sketch All American, 1962; writer for TV series Your Show of Shows; also Caesar's Hour; co-creator TV series Get Smart; recs. include 2000 Year Old Man, 2000 and One Years, 2000 and Thirteen Years, 2000 Year Old Man in the Year 2000, 1997 (Grammy award for Best Spoken Word Album Comedy 1999); writer, dir., star motion pictures including Producers, 1968 (Acad. award for Best Original Screenplay), The Twelve Chairs, 1970; co-writer, dir., star Blazing Saddles, 1973; co-writer, dir. Young Frankenstein, 1974; co-writer, dir., prodr. Robin Hood: Men In Tights, 1993, Dracula: Dead and Loving It, 1995; co-writer, dir., star Silent Movie, 1976; prodr., dir., co-writer and star High Anxiety, 1977, Spaceballs, 1987, Life Stinks, 1991; writer, dir., prodr., star History of the World-Part I, 1981; actor, prodr. To Be or Not to Be, 1983; prodr. 84 Charing Cross Road, 1987, The Elephant Man, 1980, Frances, 1982, My Favorite Year, 1982, Fly I, 1986, Fly II, 1989. Office: c/o The Culver Studios 9336 Washington Blvd Culver City CA 90232-2628

BROOKS, MICHAEL, broadcast executive. BA in Comm., Washington and Lee U., 1972. Gen. mgr. Sta. WHOA-TV, Montgomery, Ala., 1995—. Office: Sta WHOA-TV 3251 Harrison Rd Montgomery AL 36109-4321*

BROOKS, MICHAEL PAUL, urban planning educator; b. Topeka, Kans., June 13, 1937; s. Paul Edward and Gladys Leora (Nansen) B.; m. Shirley Birdeen Rhoad, June 8, 1958 (div. Aug. 1983); children: David, Timothy, Susan; m. Ann DeWitt Watts, Feb. 18, 1984. BA magna cum laude, Colgate U., 1959; M in City Planning, Harvard U., 1961; PhD, U. N.C., 1970. Dir. rsch. The N.C. Fund, Durham, 1963-66, dir. planning and program devel., 1966-67; lectr. dept. city and regional planning U. N.C., Chapel Hill, 1967-70; assoc. prof. U. N.C., 1970-71; prof. dept. urban and regional planning U. Ill., Urbana, 1971-78; head dept. U. Ill., 1971-78; dir. Bur. Urban and Regional Planning Rsch., 1971-77; dean Coll. Design, Iowa State U., Ames, 1978-84, Sch. Architecture and Environ. Design, SUNY, Buffalo, 1984-87; dean Sch. Community and Pub. Affairs, Va. Commonwealth U., Richmond, 1987-91, spl. asst. to provost for strategic planning, 1992-93; prof. dept. urban studies and planning, 1993—; cons. in field. Commr. Research Triangle Regional Planning Commn., Chapel Hill, N.C., 1969-71. Mem. Am. Planning Assn. (pres. 1979-80), Am. Inst. Cert. Planners, Assn. Collegiate Schs. Planning (pres. 1976-77). Democrat.

BROOKS, NEIL H., physician; b. Manchester, Conn., Nov. 17, 1942; m. Sandi; 1 child, David A. BS, Rensselaer Poly. Inst., 1964; MD, Hahnemann Med. Coll., 1968. Diplomate Am. Bd. Family Practice. Intern Phila. Gen. Hosp., 1968-69; chief med. svcs. Ashland Fed. Youth Ctr., 1969-71; mem. staff Rockville (Conn.) Gen. Hosp., 1970—, chief of staff, 1975-78, chair dept. family practice, 1978-84, vice chief of staff, 1984-85, corporator, 1986—; pvt. practice Rockville Family Physicians, Vernon, Conn.; preceptor U. Conn. Med. Sch.; bd. dirs. Constn. Health Care, chair, 1994-95; med. dir. Vernon Manor Nursing Home, 1984—; exec. com. Core Content Rev. Family Practice, 1984—. Contbr. articles to profl. jours. Bd. dirs. Congregation B'Nai Israel, 1972—, chair fund raising, 1973—, pres., 1978-80, Cmty. Svc. Ctr., 1974-76; mem. coms. Hartford Jewish Fedn. Fellow Am. Acad. Family Physicians (alt. del. to Congress of Dels., 1985-90, com. metnal health, 1987-89, chair subdom. mental health and substance abuse, 1989—, commn. pub. health scientific affairs, 1989-91, liaison Am. Psychiat. Assn., 1989-91, commn. spl. issues and clin. issues, 1991-92); mem. AMA (alt. del. to Ho. of Dels. 1989—), COMPAC (bd. dirs. 1990—), CMMI (bd. dirs. 1990-93), Conn. Acad. Family Physicians (bd. dirs. 1978-92, sec. 1981, pres.-elect 1982, pres. 1983, med. econs. com. 1983, chair resident Liaison com. 1983, legis. com. 1983, membership com. 1983, pub. rels. com. 1983), Conn. State Med. Soc. (rural health com. 1970—, Aetna malpractice panel 1970—, Medicare assignment com. 1970—, chair liaison com. Dept. Income Maintenance 1970—, coun. 1989—, vice spkr. 1992-94, spkr. 1994-95), Tolland County Med. Soc. (med. ethics com. 1970—, HMO/IPA com. 1970—, liaison HCMS 1970—), Capital Area Ind. Practice Assn. (v.p. 1983-91, pres. 1991—, chiar utilaztion rev./quality assurance 1984-91). Avocations: golfing, traveling. Office: Rockville Family Physicians 1 Ellington Ave Vernon Rockville CT 06066*

BROOKS, NORMA NEWTON, legal assistant; b. Granite, Okla., Oct. 30, 1936; d. Ralph David and Bessie M. (Elkins) Newton; m. Rex Dwain Brooks, May 16, 1964; children: Jonathan Douglas, Elizabeth Ann. Student, U. Okla., 1979, BS in Edn., 1970; MEd, Ctrl. State U., 1972. Cert. secondary sch. tchr., Okla. Legal asst. Rex D. Brooks Atty.-At-Law, Oklahoma City, 1974—. Mem. Am. Home Econs. Assn., Women in the Arts, Kappa Delta Pi. Baptist. Avocations: art, education. Home: 2323 N Indiana Ave Oklahoma City OK 73106-1632 Office: Rex D Brooks Atty-At-Law 1900 NW 23rd St Oklahoma City OK 73106-1202

BROOKS, PATRICK WILLIAM, lawyer; b. Grinnell, Iowa, May 11, 1943; s. Mark Dana and Madge Ellen (Walker) B.; m. Mary Jane Davey, Dec. 17, 1966; children: Carolyn Walker, Mark William. BA, State Coll. Iowa, 1966; JD, U. Iowa, 1971. Bar: Iowa 1971, U.S. Dist. Ct. (so. dist.) Iowa 1972, U.S. dist. ct. (no. dist.) Iowa 1971, U.S. Sup. Ct. 1974, U.S. Ct. Apls. (8th cir.) 1979. Tchr., Waterloo (Iowa) Community Schs., 1966-68; mem. staff Donahue & Brooks, West Union, Iowa, 1971-72; ptnr. Mowry, Irvine, Brooks & Ward, Marshalltown, Iowa, 1972-84, 1992—, Brooks, Ward & Trout, Marshalltown, 1984-92. Mem. Fayette County (Iowa) Republican Central Com., chmn. platform resolutions com., 1971-72; pres. Marshall County (Iowa) Young Reps., 1974; trustee Iowa Law Sch. Found., 1970-71; bd. dirs. Iowa Hist. Found., 1991-96. Mem. Am. Judicature Soc., Iowa Bar Assn., Marshall County Bar Assn. (pres. 1985-86), Iowa Trial Lawyers Assn., Iowa Def. Counsel Assn. Lutheran. Clubs: Buick Am., Elks. Office: Box 908 6 W Main St Marshalltown IA 50158-4941

BROOKS, PAULA, advertising executive. Dir. media svcs. Margeotes Fertitta & Ptnrs. Inc., N.Y.C., 1991—, dir. media svcs., mng. ptnr., 1994—. Office: Margeotes Fertitta & Ptnrs Inc 411 Lafayette St New York NY 10003-7032*

BROOKS, PETER (PRESTON), French and comparative literature educator, writer; b. N.Y.C., Apr. 19, 1938; s. Ernest and Mary Caroline (Schoyer) B.; m. Margaret Elisabeth Waters, July 18, 1959 (div. 1995); 3 children. BA, Harvard U., 1959, PhD, 1965; postgrad., U. Coll. London, 1959-60, U. Paris, 1962-63; MA (hon.), Yale U., 1975; Doctor (hon.), Ecole Normale Supérieure, 1997. Instr. French Yale U., 1965-67, asst. prof., 1967-72, assoc. prof., 1972-75, prof. French and comparative lit., 1975—, Chester D. Tripp prof. humanities, 1980—, dir. The Lit. Major, 1974-79, dir. Whitney Humanities Ctr., 1980-91, 96—, chmn. dept. French, 1983-88, chmn. dept. comparative lit., 1991-97. Author: The Novel of Worldliness, 1969, The Child's Part, 1972, The Melodramatic Imagination, 1976, Reading for the Plot, 1984, Body Work, 1993, Psychoanalysts and Storytelling, 1994, World Elsewhere, 1999; co-editor: Law's Stories, 1996; exec. co-editor: Cambridge History of Literary Criticism; contbg. editor Partisan Rev., 1972-88; mem. editl. bd. Yale French Studies, 1966—; chmn. Yale Jour. Criticism, 1987—. Acad. advisor Marlboro Co., 1975—; regional chmn. Mellon Fellowships in Humanities, 1982-84; trustee Hopkins Sch., New Haven, 1983-88; adv. coun. West European program The Wilson Ctr.; adv. bd. Stanford Humanities Ctr. Decorated Officier des Palmes Académiques, 1986; Marshall fellow, 1959, Morse fellow, 1967, Guggenheim fellow, 1973, Am. Coun. Learned Socs. fellow, 1980, NEH fellow, 1988. Fellow Am. Acad. Arts and Scis.; mem. MLA (exec. coun. 1993-97), Authors Guild, Yale Club, Elizabethan Club (New Haven), Century Assn. Democrat. Office: Yale U Whitney Humanities Ctr PO Box 208298 New Haven CT 06520-8298

BROOKS, PHILIP RUSSELL, chemistry educator, researcher; b. Chgo., Dec. 31, 1938; s. John Russell and Louise Jane B.; children: Scott, Robin, Christopher, Steven. BS, Calif. Inst. Tech., 1960; PhD, U. Calif., Berkeley, 1964. Rsch. assoc. physics dept. U. Chgo., 1964; from asst. to assoc. prof. chemistry Rice U., Houston, 1964-75, prof., 1975—. Editor: State-to-State Chemistry, 1977. Vol. Boy Scouts Am., Houston, 1970—. Recipient Humboldt prize Alexander von Humboldt Found., 1985; predoctoral fellow NSF, 1960-63, postdoctoral fellow, 1963-64, Alfred P. Sloan fellow, 1970-74, John Simon Guggenheim fellow, 1974-75, Vis. Erskine fellow U. Canterbury, 1991, JSPS fellow Japan Soc. Promotion Sci., 1992. Fellow Am. Phys. Soc.; mem. Am. Chem. Soc. Achievements include research on chemical reaction dynamics. Home: 1026 Glourie Cir Houston TX 77055-7504 Office: Rice U Chemistry Dept MS60 6100 Main St Houston TX 77005-1892

BROOKS, REUBEN B., federal judge. Apptd. magistrate judge so. dist. U.S. Dist. Ct. Calif. Fax: (619) 702-9940. Office: US Courthouse 940 Front St San Diego CA 92101-8994

BROOKS, RICHARD DICKINSON, lawyer; b. Daytona Beach, Fla., Sept. 17, 1944; s. Richard D. Brooks and Violet (Hamilton) Christenson; m. Betty Jane Huba, Aug. 28, 1971; children: Hillary Ann, Richard Jason. BA, Marietta (Ohio) Coll., 1967; JD, Case Western Res. U., 1972. Bar: Ohio 1972, U.S. Dist. Ct. (so. dist.) Ohio 1975, U.S. Ct. Appeals (6th cir.) 1993. Assoc., ptnr. Bridgewater Robe Brooks & Keifer, Athens, Ohio, 1972-87; of counsel Arter & Hadden, Columbus, Ohio, 1987; ptnr. Arter & Hadden, Columbus, 1988—. Coach Upper Arlington Cub Scout Baseball, Columbus, 1989-90; pres. A.T.C.O. Inc. Sheltered Workshop, Athens, 1986; chmn. com. Athens Kiwanis, 1977-87; bd.d irs. Athens C. of C., 1984-87. Sgt. U.S. Army, 1968-70, Vietnam. Fellow Am. Bar Found., Ohio Bar Found. (pres. 1988); mem. ABA, Ohio Bar Assn. (exec. com. 1979-83), Columbus Bar Assn. (environ. law com.), Athens County Bar Assn. (pres. 1978-79), Ohio CLE Inst. (bd. dirs. 1989-90), Ohio State Legal Svcs. Assn. (bd. dirs. 1982—). Avocations: basketball, tennis, fishing, furniture restoration. Office: Arter & Hadden 10 W Broad St Ste 2100 Columbus OH 43215-3422

BROOKS, RICHARD EUGENE, cultural affairs administrator; b. Keokuk, Iowa, June 21, 1949; s. George Milton Brooks and Doris Maxine Brilon; m. Mary Oestriech Brooks, Mar. 18, 1972 (div. Oct. 1994); children: Heather, Jeremy, Amanda. AA, Southeastern Iowa Area C.C., Keokuk, 1969; BA, Truman U., 1971. Cert. tchr., Mo. Tchr. Francis Howell Sch. Dist., St. Charles, Mo., 1971-76; mgr. Aey Art Craft and Model Materials, St. Charles, 1976-77; dir. cmty. rels. City of St. Peters, Mo., 1977-95, dir. cultural affairs, 1995—. Bd. dirs. Hoina Orphanages, India and U.S., 1994—, Mosaics Art Festival, St. Charles, 1995—, St. Louis Gallery Assoc., 1986—; mem. St. Louis 2004 Arts Task Force, 1997—, Homeless Task Force, St. Charles, 1998—; pres. St. Charles County Arts Coun., 1988—; regional v.p. Mo. Citizens for Arts, St. Louis, 1992-97; pres. Cmty. Svc./Pub. Rels. Coun., St. Louis, 1986. Named Mo. Vol. of Yr., Mo. Vols., 1992; recipient Achievement award Mo. Waste Control Coalition, 1994, Point Sable award Frenchtown Mus., 1997, Livetime Achievement award St. Charles County Arts Coun., 1998. Mem. Oak Leaf Artist Guild, Mo. Assn. Cmty. Arts Agys. Democrat. Lutheran. Avocations: art, walking, writing poetry, hosting art shows, art therapy. E-mail: rbrooks650@aol.com. Home: 150 Birchleaf Dr Saint Peters MO 63376 Office: City of St Peters 3960 Mexico Rd Saint Peters MO 63376

BROOKS, ROBERT EUGENE, management consultant; b. Chgo., June 13, 1946; s. Robert Eugene and Shirley Mae (Kunkel) B.; m. Tonya Thompson, Aug. 19, 1969; children: Shannon, Gabriel, Cyrus, Aleisha, Aaron, Ethan, David. AB in Arts and Scis., U. Calif., Berkeley, 1968; MA in Physics, U. Tex., 1972; PhD in Mgmt., MIT, 1975. Asst. prof. bus. U. So. Calif., Los Angeles, 1975-76; prin. Robert Brooks & Assocs., Norwalk, Calif., 1976-79; v.p. Transportation and Econ. Research Assocs., Washington, 1979-82; pres. RBA Cons., Los Angeles, 1982-84; v.p. software devel. Profit Mgmt. Devel. Inc., Los Angeles, 1984-87; ind. cons., 1987—; cons. Arthur D. Little, Inc., Cambridge, Mass., 1972-75, Chase Econometrics, Bala Cynwyd, Pa., 1976, Mathematica, Inc., Princeton, N.J., 1977-78, 82, McDonnell-Douglas Corp., 1987-97, fed. and state govts., Washington, Sacramento, Austin, Tex., 1976-83, Logistic Solutions, 1990-95, Ventana Systems, 1987-97. Author: (computer models) GASNET, 1976, GASNET2, 1977, NETS, 1981, CMOTSIM, 1982; Profit Maker, 1986, GPCM, 1987. Mem. Inst. Mgmt. Scis. Mem. Ch. Scientology. Avocations: sports, music, new mathematics. Home: 2150 Micheltorena St Los Angeles CA 90039-3019 Office: Leahy & Associates Inc 19131 Enadia Way Reseda CA 91335-3828

BROOKS, ROBERT FRANKLIN, SR., lawyer; b. Richmond, Va., July 13, 1939; s. Robert Noel Brooks and Annie Mae (Edwards) Miles; m. Patricia Wilson, May 6, 1972; children: Robert Franklin Jr., Thomas Noel, Courtenay M. Brooks Rainey. BA, U. Richmond, 1961, M of Humanities, 1993; JD, 1964. Bar: Va. 1964, N.Y. 1985, U.S. Dist. Ct. (ea. and we. dists.) Va. 1964, U.S. Ct. Appeals (4th cir.) 1965, U.S. Ct. Appeals (5th cir.) 1972, (2d cir.) 1979, (11th cir.) 1981, D.C. 1977, U.S. Supreme Ct. 1979. Assoc. Hunton & Williams, Richmond, 1964-71, ptnr., 1971—; chmn. sect. II 3d Dist. Com., 1983; mem. rules evidence com. Supreme Ct. Va., 1984-85; mem. Fourth Cir. Judicial Conf. Trustee U. Richmond. Fellow ABA, Am. Coll. Trial Lawyers (com. atty.-client relationships 1983-91, chmn. Va. state com. 1993-94), Am. Bar Found., Va. Law Found.; mem. N.Y. Bar Assn., D.C. Bar Assn., Va. State Bar (coun. 1986—, bd. govs. litigation sect. 1984-90, sec. 1985-86, chmn. 1986-87, com. lawyer fin. responsibility 1986-89, nominating com. 1990, spl. com. election methods 1989, chmn. bench-bar rels. com. 1987-88, faculty professionalism course 1988-90, governance com. 1990-91), Richmond Bar Assn. (chmn. judiciary com. 1985-87, chmn. com. on unprofl. conduct 1979-80, com. on improvement of adminstrn. of justice 1981-84), Va. Bar Assn. (profl. responsibility com. 1981-84). Home: 500 Kilmarnock Dr Richmond VA 23229-8102 Office: Hunton & Williams Riverfront Plz East Tower 951 E Byrd St Richmond VA 23219*

BROOKS, ROBERT LESLIE, bank executive; b. Kelvington, Sask., Can., June 2, 1944; s. Allan and Edith Brooks; m. Brenda Mary Griffin, Dec. 28, 1968; children: Derek, Keith, Ian. BSc, U. Man., Can., 1965; MBA, U. Western Onc., Can., 1968. Sys. comptr. Bank of N.S., Toronto, Ont., 1971-72, supr. sys. planning, 1972-73, chief acct., 1973-78, comptr., chief acct., 1978-80, gen. mgr. fin. and adminstr., 1980-83, sr. v.p. mgmt. and fin. info. sys., 1983-85, exec. v.p., gen. mgr. fin. and adminstrn., 1985-86, exec. v.p. investment banking, 1986-98, exec.v.p., group treas., 1998—; bd. dirs. Scotia Realty Ltd., ScotiaMcLeod Inc., Scotia Discount Brokerage Inc., Helix Investments Inc., Scotia McLeod Holdings Inc., Scotia Securities Inc., Scotia Cassels Investment Counsel Ltd., Scotia Properties Quebec Inc.; chmn., dir. Scotiabank (Ireland) Ltd. Vol. chair bd. Heart and Stroke Found. Ont. Mem. Fin. Execs. Inst., Nat. Club, Empire Club Can. (past pres.). Home: 2061 Lakeshore Rd E, Oakville, ON Canada L6J 1M4 Office: Bank NS Exec Offices, Scotia Plz 40 King St W, Toronto, ON Canada M5H 1H1

BROOKS, ROGER KAY, insurance company executive; b. Clarion, Iowa, Apr. 30, 1937; s. Edgar Sherman and Hazel (Whipple) B.; m. Marcia Rae Ramsay, Nov. 19, 1955 (div. Sept. 1989); children: Michael, Jeffrey, David; m. Saulene Richer, Mar. 17, 1990. B.A. magna cum laude, U. Iowa, 1959. With AmerUs Grp., Des Moines, 1964—; asst. sec. Central Life Assurance Co., 1964-68, v.p., 1968-70, exec. v.p., 1970-72, pres., 1972-92, chmn., 1992—; chmn. AmerUs Savings Bank. Mem. Des Moines Devel. Com. Fellow Soc. Actuaries; mem. Greater Des Moines C. of C. (past chmn.), Actuaries Club of Des Moines (past pres.), Iowa Ins. Hall of Fame, Phi Beta Kappa. Presbyterian (elder). Club: Des Moines (past pres.). Home: 300 Walnut St Des Moines IA 50309-2239 Office: AmerUs Group PO Box 1555 Des Moines IA 50306-1555

BROOKS, ROGER LEON, university president; b. El Dorado, Ark., Apr. 14, 1927; s. Roger Spurgeon and Lumae (Jackson) B.; m. Martha Edwina Withers, Aug. 25, 1950; children:Leslie, Roger, Geoffrey, Stephen, Douglas. BA, Baylor U., 1949; MA, U. Ill., 1950; PhD, U. Colo., 1959. Instr. English U. Colo., 1955-57, 58-60; prof. Tex. Tech U., Lubbock, 1960-64, assoc. dean Grad. Sch., 1964-67; dean Coll. Arts and Scis., East Tex.

State U., Commerce, 1967-72; pres. Howard Payne U., Brownwood, Tex., 1972-79; v.p. adminstrv. affairs Houston Bapt. U., 1979-87; dir. Armstrong Browning Libr., Baylor U., 1987-96; cons. Victorian Studies, 1967, Choice, 1970, Can. Coun., 1971. Editor: Studies in Browning and His Circle, 1987, Robert Browning and Victorian Culture, 1993; contbr. articles to profl. jours. With USNR, 1945-51; lt. col. USMCR (ret.). Rsch. grantee U. Colo. at Oxford and Brit. Mus., 1957-58, Tex. Tech. U. at Bibliotheque Nationale, Paris, 1964, Am. Philos Soc. at N.Y. Public Libr., 1963, Brit. Mus., 1980. Mem. London Browning Soc., Manuscript Soc., Grolier Club. Office: Baylor U Armstrong Browning Lib Waco TX 76798

BROOKS, SIDNEY B., bankruptcy judge; b. 1945; married; 2 children. BA in Polit. Sci., U. Colo.; JD, U. Denver Coll. Law. Assoc. atty. Nelson and Haridng, Denver, 1971-73; asst. atty. gen. Office of Atty. Gen., Denver, 1973-75; ptnr. Nelson & Harding, Denver, 1975-80, Smart DeFurio Brooks Eklund and McClure, Denver, 1980-84; pres. Brooks and Krieger P.C., 1984-87; judge U.S. Bankruptcy Ct. Colo., 1988—; guest spkr. Russian Law Conf., Russian Rsch. Ctr., Harvard U. Law Sch., 1994, Russian Bankruptcy Conf., Moscow, 1994; participant Conf. on Chinese Bankruptcy Law Reform, Internat. Rep. Inst., Beijing, 1995; cons. World Bank Legal Advisors, USAID, Orgn. Econ. Corp. and Devel., Internat. Jud. Rels. Com. of U.S. Jud. Conf.; advisor/cons. on jud. tng. and comml. ct. programs various countries; mem. and advisor Am. Law Inst.; spkr./lectr. for Fed. Jud. Ctr., Nat. Conf. of Bankrupty Judges and Am. Bankruptcy Inst., 1997-98. Contbr. over 50 articles to profl. jours. Office: US Bankruptcy Ct Colo 721 19th St Rm 560 Denver CO 80202-2508

BROOKS, STEVEN R., architect; b. N.Y.C., June 11, 1949; s. Kenneth E. and Helen R. (Wilson) Brooks; m. Monique M. Corbat-Brooks, June 22, 1974; 1 child, Michelle. B Indsl. Design with honors, Pratt Inst., 1971. Designer Warren Platner Architects, New Haven, Conn., 1971-78; owner Steven Brooks Design, New Haven, Conn., 1978-80, dePolo/Dunbar, Inc., LB Architects PC, N.Y.C., 1980—; tchr. Paier Sch. of Art, New Haven, 1981-82, Parsons Sch. of Art, N.Y.C., 1985; prof. N.Y. Sch. of Design, N.Y., 1988-90. Mem. AIA, ASID. Avocations: travel, lit. Office: Loffredo Brooks Archs PC 37 W 28th St New York NY 10001-4202

BROOKS, STUART DALE, building consultant; b. Honolulu, July 5, 1952; s. Clarence Mathew and Beatrice Miyoko (Okamoto) B.; m. Charlene Naomi Juarez, Aug. 25, 1973; children: Kaleinani S., Stuart K. AS in Drafting Tech., U. Hawaii, 1973; BS in Bus. and Constrn., U. Oreg., 1980. Cert. bldg. inspector. Archtl. draftsman Honolulu, 1972-75; archtl. designer Brooks & Assoc., Eugene, Oreg., 1980-82; sr. cost estimator Hanscomb Assoc., Inc., Anchorage, Alaska, 1983-84; energy programs mgr. State of Alaska, Anchorage, 1984-92; pres., CEO Energy Design Assocs., Inc., Eagle River, Alaska, 1992—; tech. advisor Energy Rated Homes of Alaska, Anchorage, 1985-90; tech. energy advisor Alaska Housing Fin. Corp., Anchorage, 1995-96. Author: State of Alaska Building Energy Efficiency Standard, 1992; tech. advisor, editor: State of Alaska Energy Conservation Work Book, 1988. Founder, bd. dirs. Alaska Craftsman Home Program, 1986-87. Mem. Internat. Conf. Bldg. Ofcls., Alaska Ctr. for Appropriate Tech. Office: Energy Design Assocs Inc 17526 Rachel Cir Eagle River AK 99577-7512

BROOKS, STUART MERRILL, medical educator; b. Apr. 28, 1936. BS, U. Cin., 1958, MD, 1962. Asst. prof. medicine U. Cin., 1969-73, asst. prof. environ. health, 1970-73, assoc. prof. medicine and environ. health, 1973-79, prof. environ. health and internal medicine, 1979-86; prof. and dir. occupl. and environ. medicine residency U. S. Fla., Tampa, 1986—. Fax: 813-974-7544. E-mail: sbrooks@hsc.usf.edu. Office: U S Fla Coll Pub Health MDC Box 56 13201 Bruce B Downs Blvd Tampa FL 33612

BROOKS, TERRY, lawyer, author; b. Sterling, Ill., Jan. 8, 1944; s. Dean Oliver and Marjorie Iantha (Gleason) B.; m. Barbara Ann Groth, Apr. 23, 1972; children: Amanda Leigh, Alexander Stephen. A.B., Hamilton Coll., 1966; LL.B., Washington and Lee U., 1969. Bar: bar. Mem. firm Besse, Frye, Arnold, Brooks & Miller Sterling, 1969—. Author: The Sword of Shannara, 1977, The Sword of Shannara: Panamon Creel and Keltset (rec.), 1978, The Elfstones of Shannara, 1982, The Wishsong of Shannara, 1985, Magic Kingdom for Sale/Sold, 1986, The Tangle Box: A Magic Kingdom of Landover Novel, 1994. Mem. Am., Ill., Whiteside County bar assns.. Home: 1310 Sinnissippi Park Rd Sterling IL 61081-4127 Office: Central Nat Bank Bldg Sterling IL 61081

BROOKS, THOMAS ALOYSIUS, III, retired naval officer, telecommunications company executive; b. N.Y.C., Apr. 2, 1937; s. Tom Aloysius and Fredrica (Ritter) B.; m. Clare Codyre, Mar. 20, 1965; children: Thomas Aloysius IV, Patrick, Christopher. BS in Polit. Sci., Fordham U., 1958; MBA magna cum laude, Fairleigh Dickinson U., 1971. Advanced through grades to rear adm. USN, 1988; counterintelligence coord. Naval Investigative Svc., Alexandria, Va., 1974-75; head Chief Naval Ops. Intelligence Plot, Washington, 1975-76; asst. chief of staff for intelligence comdr. Second Fleet, Norfolk, Va., 1976-78; officer in charge Fleet Ocean Surveillance Info. Ctr., Norfolk, 1978-79; comdg. officer Navy Field Operational Intelligence Office, Fort Meade, Mo., 1979-82; asst. chief of staff for intelligence Comdr. in Chief, Atlantic, Norfolk, 1982-85; dep. dir. Joint Chiefs of Staff Support Def. Intelligence Agy., Washington, 1985-88, dir. naval intelligence, 1988-91; ret. USN, 1991; govt. ops. v.p. AT&T; pres. AT&T Tech. Svcs. Co. Contbr. articles on Soviet navy to profl. and mass circulation jours. With USN, 1958-91. Decorated Bronze star with Combat V, Legion of Merit, Def. Disting. Svc. Medal, Navy Disting. Svc. medal. Mem. Nat. Mil. Intelligen Assn. (pres. 1981-82, bd. dirs.), Naval Intelligence Profls. (bd. dirs.), Navy Mutual Aid Assn. (bd. dirs.). Roman Catholic. Avocation: collecting antique automobiles (Packards).

BROOKS, TIMOTHY H., media executive; b. Exeter, N.H., Apr. 18, 1942; s. John W. R. and Olive P. (Bradbury) B. BA, Dartmouth Coll., 1964; MS, Syracuse U., 1969. Promotion asst. Sta. WTEN-TV, Albany, N.Y., 1966-68; sales promotion supr. Sta. WCBS-TV, N.Y.C., 1969-70; sr. rsch. analyst NBC Owned Stas. Div., N.Y.C., 1970-72; mgr. ratings rsch. NBC-TV Network, N.Y.C., 1972-76, dir. TV network rsch., 1978-82, dir. program rsch., 1982-88; asst. dir. rsch. and mktg. TV Advt. Reps., Inc., N.Y.C., 1976-77; sr. v.p., media rsch. dir. N.W. Ayer Inc., N.Y.C., 1989-90; v.p. rsch. USA Networks, N.Y.C., 1991-94, sr. v.p. rsch., 1994—; adj. prof. communications L.I. Univ., Greenvale, N.Y., 1979-88. Author: The Complete Directory to Prime Time TV Stars, 1987; co-author: The Complete Directory to Prime Time Network TV Shows, 1946-Present, 1979 (Am. Book award 1980, Broadcast Preceptor award San Francisco State U. 1981), TV's Greatest Hits, 1985, TV in the '60s, 1985, The Columbia Master Book Discography, 1999; also numerous articles on history of TV and recording industry. Capt. U.S. Army, 1964-66, Vietnam, USAR, 1966-74. Mem. Assn. for Recorded Sound Collections (bd. dirs. 1979-97, pres. 1982-84, contbg. editor jour. 1986—, compiler Current Bibliography 1979—, founder ARSC awards for excellence in pub. rsch. on recs., chmn. awards com. 1989-97), Media Rating Coun. (exec. com., chmn. cable comm. 1993-96, chmn. 1997-99), Advt. Rsch. Found. (bd. dirs. 1995—, chmn. video electronic media coun. 1995—, chmn. 1998-99), Radio-TV Rsch. Coun., Cabletelevision Adminstrn. and Mktg. Assn., Cabletelevision Advt. Bur. (mem. rsch. com. 1991—), Record Rsch. Assocs., City of London Phonograph and Gramophone Soc., TV Assn. Progammers L.Am. (founding mem.). Avocations: hiking, camping. Office: USA Networks 1230 Avenue Of The Americas New York NY 10020-1513

BROOKS, TIMOTHY JOE, career military officer; b. Marietta, Ohio, Mar. 17, 1954; s. Joseph Canada and Katherine (Harris) B.; m. Suzanne Rene Craig, Aug. 15, 1982; children: Thomas Joe, Patrick Craig. BS in Recreation, Ind. State U., 1976; AS in Aviation Tech., Thomas A. Edison State U., 1994. Cert. Comml. helicopter pilot FAA. Commd. 2d lt. U.S. Army, 1976, advanced through grades to lt. col., 1995. Vol. Boy Scouts Am.; scoutmaster Troop 181, 375, Security, Colo. 1997-99. Recipient Bronze Order of St. Michael award. Mem. Army Aviation Assn. Am. (v.p. programs Calif. chpt., treas. Pike's Peak chpt. Colo., life mem.), Res. Officers Assn. (v.p. Conn. chpt. 1991-92, life), Masons, Scottish Rite, Eastern Star, Phi Delta Theta. Baptist. Avocations: hunting, fishing, camping, horsemanship, genealogy. Home: 5560 Pickering Ct Colorado Springs CO 80911-3147

BROOKS, TORREY D., real estate executive; b. N.Y.C., Dec. 9, 1954; s. B.V. and Audrey (Stephenson) B.; m. Lauren F. Faxon, Mar. 16, 1985; children: Brody, Brandon. AB, Dartmouth Coll., 1976; MBA, Stanford U., 1979; CPM, Inst. Real Estate Mgmt., 1997. Product mgr. Progressive Casualty Ins. Co., Cleve., 1979-82; v.p. Western Lodging Group, Yountville, Calif., 1982-84; exec. v.p. Calif. Footwear, Redwood City; v.p. Brooks, Torrey & Scott, Inc., Norwalk, Conn., 1985—; founder, pres. Brody Realty Corp., Greenwich, Conn., 1986—; mem. Granite Nat. Realty, LLC, Norwalk, 1997—. Recipient awards Comml. and Investment Real Estate Inst., Chgo., 1998, Real Estate Cyberspace Soc., Boston, 1998. Mem. Greenwich Country Club (tennis club champion 1990-97). Avocations: golf, tennis. E-mail: tdbrooks@ccim.net. Fax: 203-840-4848. Office: Brooks Torrey & Scott Inc 542 Westport Ave Norwalk CT 06851

BROOKS, WALTER S., dermatologist; b. Cleve., July 16, 1956; s. John R. and Christel W. (Plogsties) B.; m. Debra A. HArt, Aug. 29, 1981; children: Aaron S., David J.H., Arielle N. BA magna cum laude, U. Rochester, 1978, MD, 1982. Resident in internal medicine Rochester (N.Y.) Gen. Hosp., 1982-85; resident in dermatology U. Pitts., 1985-88; clin. instr. dermatology to clin. asst. prof. dermatology U. Rochester, 1989—; dermatologist pvt. practice, Rochester, 1988—. Bd. trustees Rochester Acad. Medicine, 1996—; vice-chair campaign of the Leaders Soc. of the Dermatology Found., 1997. Recipient Leadership award Dermatology Found. Soc., 1995. Fellow Am. Acad. Dermatology; mem. Nat. Bd. Med. Examiners, Buffalo-Rochester Dermatol. Assn. (pres. 1995-96), Rochester Dermatol. Soc. (pres. 1996—). Avocations: bicycling, photography. Home: 22 Silver Fox Dr Fairport NY 14450-8666 Office: 1561 Long Pond Rd Ste 408 Rochester NY 14626-4135

BROOKS, WILLIAM GEORGE, aeronautical engineer; b. Calgary, Alta., Can., June 6, 1940; came to U.S., 1965; s. William Henry Charles and Mary Robertson (Henderson) B.; m. Lynn Chung. BS in Aero. Engring., Wichita State U., 1963, BSME, 1965; MBA, Pepperdine U., 1978. Engr. Sun Oil Co., Estevan, Sask., Can., 1964; design engr. The Carlson Co., Wichita, Kans., 1965-66; engr. United Airlines, San Francisco, 1966-67, aero. engr. B, 1967-70, aero. engr. A, 1970-71, aircraft engr. A, 1971-84, staff engr., 1984-91, sr. staff rep. engring., 1991—. Mem. ASME, Soc. Automotive Engrs. Internat. Avocations: walking, hiking. Home: 1001 Sandhurst Dr Vallejo CA 94591-6881 Office: United Airlines San Francisco Int Airport San Francisco CA 94128-3800

BROOKSHIRE, JAMES KNOX, JR., transportation facility administrator; b. Athens, Ga., Apr. 6, 1941; s. James Knox and Leclare (Hardman) B.; m. Marilyn Coile Brown, June 29, 1963; children: James Knox III, Sara Denise Brookshire Mitchell. B in Civil Engring., Ga. Inst. Technology, 1963. Registered profl. engr., Va. From engr. trainee to asst. dir. tunnels & tolls Va. Dept. Transportation, Richmond, Hampton, 1963-77; dir. ops. and engring. Richmond Metro. Auth., 1977-80; dep. dir., chief engr. Chesapeake Bay Bridge and Tunnel Dist., Cape Charles, Va., 1980-83, exec. dir., 1983—. Mem. Internat. Bridge, Tunnel & Turnpike Assn. (mgmt. coms. 1980—, vice chair adminstrn. com. 1986-87, internat. task force 1996—, budget task force 1991—, bd. dirs. 1987-95, exec. com. 1996—, 2d v.p. 1996, 1st v.p. 1997), Va. Hosp. and Travel Assn. (bd. dirs. 1994—, pres. travel coun. 1994, exec. com. 1994), Va. Travel Coun. (bd. dirs. 1989-93, exec. com. 1989-93, v.p. Eastern shore region 1989-91, 2d v.p. 1992, 1st v.p. 1993), Va. Hospitality and Travel Assn. Charitable Found. (bd. dirs. 1996—), Eastern Shore Va. Tourism Commn. (bd. dirs. 1984-94), Va. State C. of C. (bd. dirs. 1990-93). Methodist. Avocations: gardening, fishing. Office: Chesapeake Bay Bridge and Tunnel Dist PO Box 111 Cape Charles VA 23310-0111*

BROOKS SHOEMAKER, VIRGINIA LEE, volunteer, librarian; b. Oklahoma City, Sept. 16, 1944; d. Leo B. and Eloise Gilreath; m. Phil Ashley Brooks, Aug. 10, 1972 (dec. Oct. 1982); 1 child, Philip Brooks; m. Gene Darrell Shoemaker, Feb. 16, 1986; children: Rob, Julie, Donna, Gary. BS, U. Ctrl. Okla., 1988, M in Sch. Media, 1991. With Dept. Human Svcs., Oklahoma City, 1970-75, State Dept. Librs., Oklahoma City, 1980-87; substitute tchr. Oklahoma City Schs., 1989-91; vol. libr. Children's Hosp., Oklahoma City, 1992—; libr. vol. Corpus Christi Sch. Libr., 1998—. *Volunteer Children's Hospital librarian. Feels strongly that well-written, illustrated children's books have healing and enjoyable value for all ages. Certified in school media, 1998. Strong graduate background in Special Education and children's literature. Value many rewards in volunteer work above paid jobs; most valued mentors are son's graduate school friend, first grade teacher, therapist, pastor, and Fran Wilkinson, who died at 49 encouraging me through graduate school, and raising only son, Philip. Value mothers spending time with and reading to children. Son, Philip, 22, won Eva Reeves Scholarship as most outstanding senior. Life member of historic 108 year old First Baptist Church.* Sponsor World Vision, Seattle, 1994—; active Cub Scouts, Meth. Ch. of the Servant. Recipient Adopt-a-Park awards Oklahoma City, 1986-89. Mem. Coun. for Exceptional Children, U. Ctrl. Okla. Alumni Assn., Classen Alumni Assn. Baptist, Methodist. Avocations: piano, children's books to be published and art, sewing, reading biographies, writing dogs as companions.

BROOME, BURTON EDWARD, insurance company executive; b. N.Y.C., July 10, 1935; s. Burton Edward and Ann Loretta (Wall) B.; m. Anne Curtis, June 21, 1974; 1 child, Chelsea Anne. BSc, Fordham U., 1963; MBA, U. Calif., Berkeley, 1964. Ins. examiner Crum & Forster, N.Y.C., 1956-60; audit mgr. Price Waterhouse, N.Y.C., 1960-74; v.p., contr. Transamerica Corp., San Francisco, 1974—; mem. oper. com. ARC Reins. Corp., Honolulu, 1993—; mem. profl. acctg. program U. Calif., Berkeley, 1982—; bd. dirs. Transamerica HomeFirst Corp., San Francisco. Chmn. adv. coun. SEC and Fin. Reporting Inst., U. So. Calif., L.A., 1982—. With U.S. Army, 1954-55. Mem. AICPA, Fin. Exec. Inst., Calif. Soc. CPAs, Commonwealth Club Calif. Office: Transamerica Corp 600 Montgomery St San Francisco CA 94111*

BROOME, CLAIRE VERONICA, epidemiologist, researcher; b. Tunbridge Wells, Kent, England, Aug. 24, 1949; came to U.S., 1951; d. Kenneth R. and Heather C. (Platt) B.; m. John F. Head, Apr. 2, 1988; children: Gabriel K., Steven G. BA, Harvard U., 1970, MD, 1975. Diplomate Am. Bd. Internal Medicine. Dep. chief spl. pathogens br. Ctrs. for Disease Control, Atlanta, 1979-80, chief meningitis, spl. pathogens br., 1981-90, assoc. dir. sci., 1991-94, acting dir., nat. ctr. injury prevention and control, 1992-93, dep. dir., 1994—; cons. vaccine devel. AID, 1988—, WHO, NIH, various univs.; mem. steering com. on encapsulated bacterial vaccines, WHO, Geneva, 1989-91, chmn., 1992-96; mem. adv. com. on vaccines FDA, Washington, 1990-94; mem. sci. adv. group experts global program on vaccines and immunizations World Health Orgn., 1996—. Contbr. numerous articles to profl. jours. Recipient M. C. Rockefeller fellowship, 1970-71, Meritorious Svc. medal USPHS, 1986, Disting. Svc. medal USPHS, 1996, rsch. grants NIH, FDA, Dept. of State. Fellow Infectious Diseases Soc. Am. (Bristol-Myers Squibb award 1993); mem. ACP, Inst. of Medicine, Am. Epidemiologic Soc., Am. Soc. Microbiology, Common Cause, Phi Beta Kappa, Alpha Omega Alpha. Avocation: tennis. Office: Ctrs for Disease Control # D14 Atlanta GA 30333

BROOME, JOHN WILLIAM, retired architect; b. Middle Haddam, Conn., Mar. 7, 1923; s. Bertram Clinton and Helen Millington (Connery) B.; m. Althea Pratt, May 31, 1980; children: Bertram Vedeler, Sheryl Lynn. B.Arch., U. Oreg., 1951. Archtl. work in Oslo, Norway, 1951-54; planning technician Vancouver (Wash.) Housing Authority, 1954-56; archtl. designer Edmundson, Kochendoerfer & Kennedy, Portland, Oreg., 1956-58; ptnr. Broome, Oringdulph, O'Toole & Rudolf & Assos., Portland, 1958-85, ret., 1985. Mem. Gov. Oreg. Com. for Livable Oreg., 1967-71; commr. Oreg. Coastal Conservation and Devel. Commn., 1971-75; pres. The Wetlands Conservancy; trustee Meridian Park Hosp., Healthlink, Inc. Served with USMC, 1942-46. Decorated Air medal with 2 gold stars; recipient Regional Conservation award U.S. Fish & Wildlife Svc., 1990, Nat. Conservation award Environ. Law Inst., 1991, State Disting. Svc. award Oreg. Shores Conservation Coalition, 1992. Fellow AIA (pres. Portland 1966, Oreg. council 1967); mem. Phi Kappa Psi. Democrat. Address: PO Box 236 Tualatin OR 97062-0236

BROOME, KATHRYN, secondary education educator; b. Natchez, Miss., Dec. 7, 1950; d. Jackson Daniel and Edna Louise (Barrett) B.; m. John Bridges, Dec. 23, 1997. BS, Miss. State Coll. for Women, 1973; M English Edn., Miss. Coll., 1995. Tchr. Columbia (Miss.) Pub. Schs., 1973-74, Larmar County Schs., Hattiesburg, Miss., 1974-77, Monroe County Schs., Hamilton, Miss., 1977-84, Jackson (Miss.) Pub. Schs., 1984—; real estate agt. Century 21 Eddie Rosamond Realty, Jackson, 1997-98, Re/Max Properties, Jackson, 1998—; student coun. sponsor Powell Middle Sch., Jackson, Miss., 1991—, team leader 8th grade 1991-92; varsity cheerleader sponsor Hamilton H.S., 1979-80, 95. Mem. Jackson pub. schs. supts. orgn. for student coun. Jackson Pub. Schs., 1991-93; rep. Parent/Tchr. Student Assn., Jackson, 1997; supporter United Way. Grantee IBM, 1996, Jackson Pub. Schs., 1997, Entergy, 1997, Tchr. Talk, 1997, Bell South, 1997, Jr. League, 1997. Mem. NEA, Miss. Assn. of Educators, Jackson Assn. of Realtors, Jr. Beta Club, Sigma Tau Delta. Republican. Baptist. Avocations: people, animals, swimming, painting, cooking. Home: 5151 Sycamore Dr Jackson MS 39212-5772 Office: Jackson Public Schs 662 S President St Jackson MS 39201-5601

BROOME, MICHAEL CORTES, college administrator; b. Ringgold, Ga., Apr. 28, 1948; s. Cortes Carna and Frances Margaret (Lockhart) B.; m. Charlotte Lou Stackhouse, Aug. 6, 1989; children from previous marriage: Stephen, Paul. BA, U. Tenn., 1970; MA, Fla. State U., 1972; PhD, U. S.C., 1988. Law clk., proofreader Swafford and Taylor, Chattanooga, Tenn., 1967-70; instr., asst. prof. English dept. Columbia (S.C.) Coll., 1973-82, assoc. prof., 1986-92, assoc. dean, 1992—, dean Grad. Sch. Acad. Svcs., 1998—; dir. tng. devel. Nat. Guard Prof. Edn. Ctr., North Little Rock, Ark., 1982-85; editor The Stelter Co., Des Moines, 1989-90; cons. interdis. writing Williamsburg Tech. Coll., Kingstree, 1990; cons. strategic planning Am. Ins. Agy., Fort Mill, S.C., 1992; cons. State Pers. Tng. Dept., 1978-81. Author: (with others) The Vanity Fair Gallery, 1979, A Literary Map of South Carolina, 1993. Big Bro., interviewer Richland County Family Ct., Columbia, 1974-75; vol. trainer United Way of S.C., Columbia, 1990; mem. bicentennial steering com. Washington St. United Meth. Ch. With S.C. Nat. Guard, 1974-95, ret. lt. col. Named Outstanding Tchg. Asst. English Dept. Fla. State, 1973; named Outstanding Young Men of Am. U.S. C. of C., 1976, Ky. Col. Gov. of Ky., 1985. Mem. S.C. Assn. of Developmental Educators (pres. 1982), Nat. Coun. of Tchr. of English, Nat. Guard Assn. of S.C., Nat. Guard Assn. of U.S., S.C. Higher Edn. Assessment Network (chair fiscal adv. com. 1995). Democrat. Avocations: golf, tennis, Civil war history, baseball card collecting. Home: 6118 Hampton Leas Ln Columbia SC 29209-1952 Office: Columbia Coll 1301 Columbia College Dr Columbia SC 29203-5949

BROOME, OSCAR WHITFIELD, JR., accounting educator, administrator; b. Monroe, N.C., Feb. 3, 1940; s. Oscar Whitfield and Irma (Hinson) B.; m. Julia Carol Renegar, June 14, 1964; children: Christine Irma, Michael Whitfield. A.B., Duke U., 1962; M.S., U. Ill., 1964, Ph.D., 1971. Prof. acctg. U. Va., Charlottesville, 1967-91, Frank S. Kaulback Jr. prof. commerce, 1991—, assoc. dean, 1992-98, interim dean, 1997, dir. grad. studies, 1986-92; exec. dir. Inst. Chartered Fin. Analysts, Charlottesville, 1978-84; faculty fellow Price Waterhouse & Co., N.Y.C., 1964; vis. prof. U. Tex., Austin, 1975, Duke U., Durham, N.C., 1977-78; vis. rsch. scholar, Lancaster (Eng.) U., 1994; adminstr. exams. Inst. CFAs, 1973-77; bd. regents Coll. Fin. Planning, 1984-89, chmn., 1987-89; mem. CPA Exam. Rev. Bd., 1984-87, chmn., 1986-87; mem. exams. com. Nat. Assn. State Bds. Accountancy, 1995—; bd. dirs. Internat. Bd. Stds. and Practices for CFPs, 1989-91; mem. vis. adv. com. DePaul U. Sch. Accountancy, 1991-97. Named Outstanding Educator Va. Soc. C.P.A.'s, 1979; recipient Disting. Faculty award Z Soc., 1988. Mem. AICPA (bd. examiners 1977-82), Assn. for Investment Mgmt. and Rsch. (investment analysis stds. bd. 1984-86), Nat. Assn. Accts. (pres. chpt. 1974), Phi Beta Kappa, Phi Kappa Phi, Beta Gamma Sigma, Beta Alpha Psi, Omicron Delta Kappa. Office: McIntire Sch Commerce Univ Va Charlottesville VA 22903

BROOME, PAUL WALLACE, engineering research and development executive; b. Oakdale, Pa., Jan. 17, 1932; s. Paul Wallace and Mona Isabel (Lynch) B.; m. Joan Brown, Jan. 19, 1957; children: Ronald W., Virginia K., Paul W., Barbara G. B.S., Carnegie Inst. Tech., 1954, M.S., 1955, Ph.D. (Brown Instrument fellow), 1960. Sr. engr. Gen. Dynamics, San Diego, Calif., 1958-62; sr. staff scientist Pan Am. World Airways, Cocoa Beach, Fla., 1962-64; mgr. applied research Teledyne, Inc., Earth Sci. Div., Alexandria, Va., 1964-69; founder ENSCO, Inc., Springfield, Va., 1969; pres. ENSCO, Inc., Springfield, 1969-89, chmn., 1969-98; chmn. emeritus ENSCO, Inc., Springfield, Va., 1998—. Mem. IEEE, Am. Mgmt. Assn., Sigma Xi; Mem. Eta Kappa Nu. Home: PO Box 2970 Winter Park CO 80482-2970 Office: 5400 Port Royal Rd Springfield VA 22151-2301

BROOME, RANDALL, evangelist; b. Hattiesburg, Miss., June 9, 1954; s. Eugene Wallace and Doris Vonceil (Lucas) B.; m. Barbara Ann Kelly, Dec. 18, 1976; children: Christopher Randall, Kelli Kristi Anna. BMin, Fla. Bapt. Theol. Coll., Graceville, Fla., 1981; MDiv, New Orleans Bapt. Sem., 1984, DMin, 1996. Lic. to ministry So. Bapt. Conv., 1976, ordained to ministry So. Bapt. Conv., 1979. Pastor Unity Bapt. Ch., Chipley, Fla., 1979-81, Good Hope Bapt. Ch., Franklinton, La., 1983-84, Oconee Bapt. Ch., Commerce, Ga., 1984-87, 1st Bapt. Ch. of Arabi, La., 1987-90; evangelist, pres. World Evangelism, Inc., Chalmette, La., 1990—. Contbr. articles to religion mags. With U.S. Air Force, 1973-75. Mem. Living Dividends Investment Club (founder, presiding officer 1989-90). Republican. Home and Office: 2208 Legend Dr Meraux LA 70075-2829 *Circumstances of life are constantly changing, and we are constantly developing as persons. God has made life and living beings to function in that manner. This an absolute axiom. When a living organism ceases to change it dies, which is itself a change. Since I cannot remain the same, I have a responsibility to become everything that God intends me to be.*

BROOME, ROGER GREVILLE BROOKE, IV, fundraiser; b. Newport, R.I., Apr. 15, 1943; s. Roger G.B. III and Jane Louise (Leininger) B.; m. Judith C. Lawson, May 27, 1994; children from previous marriage: Roger V, Elisabeth. BA, U. Va., 1965; attended, Harvard Bus. Sch. Dir. corp. rels. Lincoln Ctr., N.Y.C., 1970-72; dir. devel. N.E. Conservatory, Boston, 1972-77, A Better Chance Inc., Boston, 1977-80; v.p. Tufts U., Medford, Mass., 1980-93; fundraising cons., 1993-95; pres. Broome & Lawson Inc., Essex, Mass., 1995—. Mem. Nat. Soc. Fund Raising Execs., Coun. for Advancement and Support of Edn., Soc. for Nonprofit Orgns. E-mail: jlawson@gis.net. Home: 50 Southern Ave Essex MA 01929-1401 Office: Broome & Lawson Inc 50 Southern Ave Essex MA 01929-1401

BROOMES, SHELLY LORI, human resources professional; b. Apr. 16, 1974. BA, Columbia U., N.Y.C., 1996; MPA, Clark Atlanta U., 1998. Rschr. So. Ctr. for Studies in Pub. Policy, Atlanta, 1997; asst. to coord. Mayor's Exec. Office, City of Atlanta, 1997-98; sr. pers. adminstr. N.Y. State Dept. Edn., Albany, 1998—. E-mail: sbroomes@mail.nysed.gov.

BROOMFIELD, ROBERT CAMERON, federal judge; b. Detroit, June 18, 1933; s. David Campbell and Mabel Margaret (Van Deventer) B.; m. Cuma Lorena Cecil, Aug. 3, 1958; children: Robert Cameron Jr., Alyson Paige, Scott McKinley. BS, Pa. State U., 1955; LLB, U. Ariz., 1961. Bar: Ariz. 1961, U.S. Dist. Ct. Ariz. 1961. Assoc. Carson, Messinger, Elliot, Laughlin & Ragan, Phoenix, 1962-65, ptnr., 1966-71; judge Ariz. Superior Ct., Phoenix, 1971-85; judge U.S. Dist. Ct. Ariz., Phoenix, 1985—, chief judge, 1994—; faculty Nat. Jud. Coll., Reno, 1975-82. Contbr. articles to profl. jours. Adv. bd. Boy Scouts Am., Phoenix, 1968-75; tng. com. Ariz. Acad., Phoenix, 1980—; pres. Paradise Valley Sch. Bd., Phoenix, 1969-70; bd. dirs. Phoenix Together, 1982—, Crisis Nursery, Phoenix, 1976-81; chmn. 9th Cir. Task Force on Ct. Reporting, 1988—; space and facilities com. U.S. Jud. Conf., 1987-93, chmn., 1989-93, chmn. security, space and facilities com., 1993-95, budget com., 1997—. Recipient Faculty award Nat. Jud. Coll., 1979, Disting. Jurist award Miss. State U., 1986. Mem. ABA (chmn. Nat. Conf. State Trial Judges 1983-84, pres. Nat. Conf. Met. Cts. 1978-79, chmn. bd. dirs. 1980-82, Justice Tom Clark award 1980, bd. dirs. Nat. Ctr. for State Cts. 1980-85, Disting. Svc. award 1986), Ariz. Bar Assn., Maricopa County Bar Assn. (Disting. Pub. Svc. award 1980), Ariz. Judges Assn. (pres. 1981-82), Am. Judicature Soc. (spl. citation 1985), Maricopa County Med. Soc. (Disting. Svc. medal 1979). Lodge: Rotary. Office: US Dist Ct US Courthouse & Fed Bldg 230 N 1st Ave Ste 7025 Phoenix AZ 85025-0008

BROOTEN, DOROTHY, nursing educator; b. Hazleton, Pa.; married; two children. BSN, U. Pa., 1966, MSN, 1970, PhD in Ednl. Adminstrn., 1980. Assoc. prof. nursing Thomas Jefferson U., 1972-77; from asst. to assoc. prof. nursing U. Pa., 1977-88, prof. nursing, chair Health Care of Women &

Childbearing, 1980-93, dir. Ctr. for Low Birthweight, Sch. Nursing, 1990-96, Overseers prof. perinatal nursing, 1990-96; dean, prof. nursing Frances Payne Bolton Sch. Nursing Case Western Res. U., Cleve., 1998—; cons. Sch. Medicine, U. Utrecht, The Netherlands, 1989, Ministry of Health, Malawi, Africa, 1991. Recipient Contbrn. to Nursing Sci. award ANA, 1988. Mem. Inst. Medicine-NAS, Am. Acad. Nursing (mem. gov. coun. 1988-91). Achievements include research on low birthweight prevention, postdischarge care of low birthweight infants, health care delivery. Office: Case Western Res Univ FP Bolton Sch Nursing 10900 Euclid Ave Cleveland OH 44106-4901

BROOTEN, KENNETH EDWARD, JR., lawyer; b. Kirkland, Wash., Oct. 17, 1942; s. Kenneth Edward Sr. and Sadie Josephine (Assad) B.; m. Patricia Anne Folsom, Aug. 29, 1965 (div. Apr. 1986); children: Michelle Catherine, Justin Kenneth. Diploma, Lewis Sch. Hotel, Restaurant and Club Mgmt., Washington, 1963; student, U. Md., 1964-66; AA, Santa Fe C.C., Gainesville, Fla., 1969; BS in Journalism with highest honors, U. Fla., 1971, MA in Journalism and Communications with highest honors, 1972, JD with honors, 1975; law student, U. Idaho, 1972-73; diploma in internat. law, Polish Acad. Scis., Warsaw, 1974; postgrad., Cambridge (Eng.) U., Eng., 1974. Bar: Fla., D.C., U.S. Dist. Ct. (no., mid. and so. dists.) Fla., U.S. Dist. Ct. D.C., U.S. Tax Ct., U.S. Ct. Appeals (5th, 9th, 11th and D.C. circs.), U.S. Supreme Ct., Trial Counsel Her Majesty's Govt. of United Kingdom. Asst. to several congressmen U.S. Ho. of Reps., Washington, 1962-67; adminstrv. asst. VA Cen. Office, Washington, 1967; adminstrv. officer VA Hosp., Gainesville, Fla., 1967-72; ptnr. Carter & Brooten, P.A., Gainesville, Fla., 1975-78, Brooten & Fleisher, Chartered, Washington and Gainesville, Fla., 1978-80; pvt. practice, Washington and Gainesville, 1980-86, Washington, 1987-88, Washington and Orlando, Fla., 1988-91, Washington and Winter Park, Fla., 1991—; permanent spl. counsel, acting chief counsel, dir. Select Com. Assassinations U.S. Ho. of Reps., 1976-77; counsel Her Majesty's Govt. of U.K. (in U.S.). Author: Malpractice Guide to Avoidance and Treatment, 1987; episode writer TV series Simon and Simon; nat. columnist Pvt. Practice, 1988-90, Physicians Mgmt., 1991-93; commentator Med. News Network, 1993-94; contbr. more than 200 articles to profl. jours. Served with USCGR, 1960-68. Named one of Outstanding Young Men Am., U.S. Jaycees, 1977. Mem. Fla. Bar Assn., D.C. Bar Assn., Am. Coll. Legal Medicine, Sigma Delta Chi. Roman Catholic. Avocations: writing, marksmanship, dangerous game hunting. Office: 631 W Fairbanks Ave Winter Park FL 32789-4710 also: 1817 19th St NW Unit G Washington DC 20009-5519

BROPHY, DEBRA ELISSE, rehabilitation and orthopaedics nurse; b. Paterson, N.J., Nov. 17, 1964; d. Timothy Edward and Marie Ann (Alexander) B. BS in Health, Physical Edn., Kent State U., 1986; AAS, Bergen C.C., Paramus, N.J. RN, N.J.; cert. in CPR, intravenous therapy, orthopedics, sports medicine, trauma, spinal surgery. Nursing asst. Wayne (N.J.) Gen. Hosp.; staff nurse orthopaedic unit Hackensack (N.J.) Med. Ctr. Athletic and acad. scholar Kent. State U., 1982-86. Mem. Nat. Orthopaedic Nurses Assn. Home: 90 E Woodcliff Ave Little Falls NJ 07424-1213

BROPHY, DENNIS RICHARD, psychology and philosophy educator, administrator, clergyman; b. Milw., Aug. 6, 1945; s. Floyd Herbert and Phyllis Marie (Ingram) B.; BA, Washington U., St. Louis, 1967, MA, 1968; M.Div., Pacific Sch. Religion, 1971; PhD in Indstrl. and Orgnl. Psychology, Texas A & M U., 1995. Cert. coll. tchr., Calif. Edn. rschr. IBM Corp., White Plains, N.Y., 1968-71; edn. minister Cmty. Congl. Ch., Port Huron, Mich., 1971-72, Bethlehem United Ch. of Christ, Ann Arbor, Mich., 1972-73, Cmty. Congl. Ch., Chula Vista, Calif., 1974; philosophy instr. Southwestern Coll., Chula Vista, 1975; assoc. prof. psychology and philosophy Northwest Coll., Powell, Wyo., 1975-96, prof., 1996—, chmn. social sci. divsn., 1992-95; religious edn. cons. Mont.-No. Wyo. Conf. United Ch. of Christ. Mem. APA (Daniel Berlyne award 1996), Wyo. Coun. for Humanities, Soc. Indsl. Orgnl. Psychology, Yellowstone Assn. of United Ch. of Christ, Phi Kappa Phi, Phi Beta Kappa, Sigma Xi, Omicron Delta Kappa, Theta Xi, Golden Key Nat. Honor Soc. Home: 533 Avenue C Powell WY 82435-2401 Office: Northwest Coll 231 W 6th St Powell WY 82435-1898

BROPHY, GILBERT THOMAS, lawyer; b. Southampton, N.Y., July 15, 1926; s. Joseph Lester and Helen Veronica (Scholtz) B.; m. Canora Woodham Brophy, Sept. 3, 1957; m. Isabel Blair Porter; children: Laure Porter Thompson, Erin Brophy Caraballo. BS with high honors, U. Fla., 1949, LLB, George Washington U., 1960; postgrad., U. Miami, 1970-73. Bar: Fla. 1960, U.S. Supreme Ct. 1965, U.S. Dist. Ct. D.C. 1970, D.C. 1974. Title examiner Jesse Phillips Klinge & Kendrick, Arlington, Va., 1959-60; ptnr. Beall, Beall & Brophy, Palm Beach, Fla., 1962-65; asst. city atty. West Palm Beach, Fla., 1965-67; ptnr. Brophy & Skrandel, Palm Beach, 1968-70, Brophy & Aksomitas, Tequesta, Fla., 1974-75, Brophy, Genovese & Sayler, Jupiter, Fla., 1977-78, Brophy & Genovese, 1978-83; town atty. Lantana, Fla., 1967-70; judge ad litem Village of Tequesta, 1970-72; town atty. Jupiter, 1974-75. Bd. dirs., disaster chmn. ARC, Palm Beach; past corr. sec. Palm Beach County Hist. Soc.; del. Fla. Caucus for Presidency, 1979, 87; mem. Rep. Com. Martin County, 1984-87. With AUS, 1944-46, ETO, 1951-54, Japan and Korea. Recipient Dedicated Svc. plaque Town of Jupiter, 1975. Mem. NRA (endowment), Nat. CIC Assn., Assn. Former Intelligence Officers (life), Attys. Title Ins. Fund, Fla. Bar Assn., Palm Beach County Bar Assn., Attys. Bar Assn. Palm Beach County, Challenge Inc., Rotary Club (pres. 1977-78, dist. 6930 ethics chair-4 way test, Paul Harris fellow), Univ. Club (Washington), Elks, Everglades Rifle and Pistol Club (hon. life), Kappa Sigma Alumni. Home: 717 S US Highway 1-504 Jupiter FL 33477-5905 Office: 810 Saturn St Ste 16 Jupiter FL 33477-4456

BROPHY, JAMES DAVID, JR., humanities educator; b. Mt. Vernon, N.Y., Oct. 5, 1926; s. James David and Mildred (Stall) B.; m. Elizabeth Bergen, Mar. 26, 1951; children: Sheila, David, Katharine, Elizabeth, James Mark. Student, MIT, 1944-45; BA, Amherst Coll., 1949; MA, Columbia U., 1950, PhD, 1965; postgrad., U. Dijon, 1950-51. Instr. English Iona Coll., New Rochelle, N.Y., 1951-58; asst. prof. Iona Coll., 1958-64, asso. prof., 1964-68, prof., 1968—, chmn. dept., 1968-71, 80-82, emeritus prof., 1992—. Author: Edith Sitwell, 1968, W.H. Auden, 1970; Editor: The Achievement of Galileo, 1962, Modern Irish Literature, 1972, Contemporary Irish Writing, 1983, New Irish Writing, 1988. Served with USNR, 1945-46. Fulbright fellow France, 1950-51; N.Y. State scholar in internat. studies, 1965; recipient Pro Operis medal Iona Coll., 1971, Bene Merenti award, 1981, Pro Multis Annis award, 1991; Nat. Endowment for Humanities grantee, 1973; Wilton Park asso., 1979. Mem. Milton Soc. Am., English Inst. Home: 39 Oceanview Dr Southampton NY 11968-4215

BROPHY, JERE EDWARD, education educator, researcher; b. Chgo., June 11, 1940; s. Joseph Thomas and Eileen Marie (Sullivan) B.; m. Arlene Marie Pintozzi, Sept. 21, 1963; children: Cheryl, Joseph. BS in Psychology, Loyola U., Chgo., 1962; MA in Human Devel., U. Chgo., 1965, PhD in Human Devel., 1967. Rsch. assoc., asst. prof. U. Chgo., 1967-68; from asst. to assoc. prof. U. Tex., Austin, 1968-76; staff devel. coord. S.W. Ednl. Devel. Lab., Austin, 1970-72; prof. Mich. State U., East Lansing, 1976-92, co-dir. Inst. for Rsch. on Tchg., 1981-93, univ. disting. prof., 1993—. Co-author: Teacher-Student Relationships: Causes and Consequences, 1974; editor (book series) Advances in Research on Teaching, 1989—. Fellow Ctr. for Advanced Study in the Behavioral Scis., 1994. Fellow APA, Am. Psychol. Soc., Internat. Acad. Edn.; mem. Am. Ednl. Rsch. Assn. (Palmer O. Johnson award 1983, Presdl. citation 1995), Nat. Coun. for the Social Studies, Nat. Soc. for the Study of Edn. Office: Mich State U 115D Erickson Hall East Lansing MI 48824-1034

BROPHY, JERE HALL, manufacturing company executive; b. Schenectady, Mar. 11, 1934; s. Gerald Robert and Helen Dorothy (Hall) B.; m. Joyce Elaine Wright, Aug. 18, 1956; children: Jennifer, Carolyn, Jere. B.S. in Chem. Enging, U. Mich., 1956, B.S. in Metall. Enging, 1956, M.S., 1957, Ph.D., 1958. Asst. prof. Mass. Inst. Tech., 1958-63; sect. supr. nickel alloys sect. Paul D. Merica Research Lab., Inco, Inc., Suffern, N.Y., 1963-67; research mgr. non-ferrous group Paul D. Merica Research Lab., Inco, Inc., 1967-72, asst. mgr., 1972-73, mgr., 1973-77; dir. research and devel. and dir. Paul D. Merica Research Lab., Inco, Inc. (Inco Research and Devel. Center), 1978-80; dir. advanced tech. initiation INCO Ltd., N.Y.C., 1980-82; v.p., dir. Materials and Mfg. Tech. Ctr. TRW Inc., Cleve., 1982-86, v.p. mfg. and materials devel. automotive sect., 1986-88; v.p. technology Brush Wellman Inc., Cleve., 1988-96; cons., 1996—. Author: (with J. Wolff) Thermodynamics of Structure; Contbr. (with J. Wolff) tech. articles to profl. jours. Fellow Am. Soc. Metals, AAAS; mem. Am. Inst. Mining and Metall. Engrs. (dir. IMD div. 1973-76), Am. Mgmt. Assn. (research and devel. council 1975-87). Episcopalian. Club: Edgewater Yacht. Home and Office: 31905 Jackson Rd Chagrin Falls OH 44022-1707

BROPHY, JEREMIAH JOSEPH, financial company official, former army officer; b. N.Y.C., Mar. 19, 1930; s. John Joseph and Mary Margaret (Moran) B.; m. Jane Guthrie, June 4, 1955; children: John, Sandy, Greg, Elizabeth, Diane, Stephen. *John, married to Claire Slade Brophy, is a neurosurgeon in Memphis, TN. Sandy, wife of Assistant U.S. Attorney Donald Q. Cochran, is Executive Vice-President of Books-A-Million, Inc. Greg is married to Cristina Bond Brophy. He is a partner in Atlanta Law Firm, Alston & Bird. Elizabeth is married to Fabian Unterzaucher a hotelier with the Four Seasons Group. Elizabeth owns and operates Viaticum Travel Service. Diane is Manager of Sales Operations for Eclipsys Corp., Delray Beach, Florida. Stephen is Projects Director for Senator Fred Thompson, Washington, D.C.* Student, Manhattan Coll., 1947-48; BS, U.S. Mil. Acad., 1953; postgrad., Army War Coll., 1969, Monmouth Coll., 1981. CFP. Commd. 2d lt. U.S. Army, 1953; advanced through grades to brig. gen., 1976; advisor 12th Vietnamese Inf. Rgt., Vietnam, 1963-64; comdr. 1st Bn., 327th Inf. 101st Airborne Divsn., Vietnam, 1969-70; comdr. U.S. garrison Aschaffenburg, Fed. Republic Germany; comdr. 3d Brigade, 3d Inf. divsn., 1973-75; comdr. U.S. garrison Baumholder, Fed. Republic Germany; asst. comdr. 8th Inf. div., 1976-78, dep. comdr. Combined Arms Tng. Devels. Agy., 1978-80; dep. comdr. U.S. Army Tng. Ctr. Ft. Dix, N.J., 1980-83; stockbroker Merrill, Lynch, Pierce, Fenner & Smith, Nashville, Tenn.; agt. Franklin Life Ins. Co.; exec. v.p. Gen. Trust Co.; divsn. mgr. Waddell & Reed Inc., Nashville, 1983-94; CFP BMA Svcs. Inc., Nashville, Tenn., 1995—. Decorated D.S.M., Bronze Star with oak leaf cluster, Purple Heart, Legion of Merit with oak leaf cluster, Vietnamese Cross of Gallantry (3 awards), Meritorious Svc. medal. Mem. Assn. Grad. U.S. Mil. Acad., West Point Soc. Mid. Tenn., Mid. Tenn. Ret. Officers Assn. (bd. dirs., pres. 1998). Roman Catholic. Home: 6071 Bethany Blvd Nashville TN 37221-4314

BROPHY, JOSEPH THOMAS, information company executive; b. N.Y.C., Oct. 25, 1933; s. Joseph R. and Mary (Mitchell) B.; m. Carole A. Johnson, June 8, 1957; children: Thomas J., David W., Patricia J., Maureen A., Kathleen M. BS cum laude, Fordham U., 1957; grad. sr. exec. program, MIT, 1987. Paramedic St. Clares Med. Ctr., N.Y.C., 1955-57; mathematician Vitro Labs., West Orange, N.J., 1957; dir. mgmt. info. systems Prudential Ins. Co., Newark, 1957-67; v.p. Huggins & Co. (cons. actuaries and mgmt. cons.), Phila., 1967-68; v.p., chief actuary Bankers Nat. Life Ins. Co., 1968-72; pres. Travelers Ins. Co., Hartford, Conn., 1972-93; chmn. Workgroup on Elect Data Interchange, Washington, 1992-95; cons. Actuarial Scis. Assocs., Somerset, N.J., 1993—; owner, dir. Solution Point, 1996—; bd. dirs. Engineered Bus. Sys., Travtech, Inc., Travelers TPA, Inc., Ctr. Corp. Health, U.S. Behavioral Health, Travelers Health Sys., Conservco, Accent Color Scis.; cons. in field, 1967—; enrolled actuary Employee Retirement Income Security Act (ERISA). Author: A User's Guide to Project Management. Tech. editor: Actuarial Digest. Pres. St. Patrick's Pipe Band, Inc.; bd. dirs. Cath. Family Svcs., Conn. Opera, Conn. Acad. for Edn. in Math., Sci. and Tech., Hartford Grad. Ctr.; corporator St. Francis Hosp.; chmn. adv. bd. info. scis. Grad. Bus. Sch., Fordham U., Bronx, N.Y.; advisor Actuarial Studies, Hartford U., Sch. Pub. Health, Harvard U.; trustee St. Joseph Coll., Conn. With USMCR, 1949-50, AUS, 1952-54. Recipient Disting. Info. Sci. award Data Processing Mgmt. Assn., 1986. Fellow Soc. Actuaries; mem. Am. Acad. Actuaries, Acoustical Soc. Am., Hartford Actuaries Club, N.Y. Actuaries Club, Am. Arbitration Soc. (arbitrator), Greater Hartford C. of C. (bd. dirs.), Hartford Club, Internat. Brotherhood of Magicians, Telemedicine 200, Lake Sunapee Yacht Club. Home: 154 Garnet Hill Rd PO Box 701 Sunapee NH 03782-0701 Office: Actuarial Scis Assocs 270 Davidson Ave Somerset NJ 08873-4140

BROPHY, MARY O'REILLY, industrial hygienist; b. N.Y.C., Aug. 3, 1948; d. Luke Edward and Regina (Mahoney) O'Reilly; children: Robert, Sara, Lena. Student, Fordham U., 1966-68; BS, U. Mich., 1970, MS, 1972, PhD, 1979. Rsch. asst. prof. Health Sci. Ctr., Syracuse, N.Y., 1979-84; environ. toxicologist Syracuse Rsch. Corp., 1984-86; pres. ARLS Cons., Inc., Syracuse, 1991—; sr. indsl. hygienist N.Y. State Dept. Labor, Syracuse, 1987—; adj. asst. prof. SUNY Sch. Pub. Health, Albany, 1990—; dir. Am. Bd. Indsl. Hygiene, Lansing, Mich., 1995—. Author: An Ergonomics Guide to VDTs, 1994, (with others) Occupational Ergonomics, 1996; contbr.: ILO's Encyclopedia of Occupational Health and Safety, 1998. Mem. Am. Indsl. Hygiene Assn. (treas. ctrl. N.Y. chpt. 1991-93), Am. Conf. Govtl. Indsl. Hygienists (ergonomic com. 1991-94, 95—, risk assessment com. 1996—). Avocations: Karate, fly-fishing, dance, folk harp. Home: 5954 Smith Rd North Syracuse NY 13212

BROPHY, SUSAN DOROTHY, adapted physical education educator; b. Waltham, Mass., Nov. 9, 1954; d. Lawrence A. and Dorothy M. (Furbush) B. BS, U. Mass., 1976; MS, U. Wis. La Crosse, 1981. Cert. tchr. phys. edn., adapted phys. edn. tchr., Mass. Substitute tchr. Waltham, Weston and Lexington (Mass.) Sch. Depts., 1976-77; supr. recreation, in-svc. trainer W. E. Fernald State Sch., Waltham, 1978-80; cons. adapted phys. edn. East Cen. Ohio Spl. Edn. Regional Resource Ctr., Dover, 1981-82; tchr. adapted phys. edn. Heartland Area Edn. Agy., Newton, Iowa, 1982-86, Lawrence (Mass.) Sch. Dept., 1986—; co-chmn. Adapted Phys. Edn. State Com., Mass., 1986—, cert. com. phys. edn. Dept. Edn., Mass., 1989-92. Co-author: (assessment test) Heartland Gross Motor Evaluation, 1985. Coach Newton YMCA Swim Team, 1985-86, Waltham (Mass.) Youth Basketball Assn., 1993—; co-founder Stephanie's Toy Box, Newton, 1984. Fed. Govt. grantee, 1980-81, Horace Mann grantee, 1988-89. Mem. AAHPERD, Am. Diabetes Assn. (mem. local arrangements com. 1998-99), Mass. Assn. Health, Phys. Edn., Recreation and Dance (co-chair com. adapted phys. edn. 1989—). Avocations: horticulture, antiques, bicycling, traveling. Home: 48 Marianne Rd Waltham MA 02452-6218 Office: Lawrence Comprehensive Early Childhood Ctr 114 Osgood St Lawrence MA 01843-2337

BRORBY, WADE, federal judge; b. 1934. BS, U. Wyo., 1956, JD with honor, 1958. Bar: Wyo. County and prosecuting atty. Campbell County, Wyo., 1963-70; ptnr. Morgan Brorby Price and Arp, Gillette, Wyo., 1961-88; judge U.S. Ct. Appeals (10th cir.), Cheyenne, Wyo., 1988—. With USAF, 1958-61. Mem. ABA, Campbell County Bar Assn., Am. Judicature Soc., Def. Lawyers Wyo., Wyo Bar Assn. (commr. 1968-70). Office: US Ct Appeals 10th Cir O'Mahoney Fed Bldg Rm 2018 PO Box 1028 Cheyenne WY 82003-1028

BROSDA, ALEXANDER CHRISTIAN, investment banker; b. Huckeswagen, N. Rhine, Germany, Apr. 26, 1970; came to U.S., 1994; s. Christian-George and Emmi-Martina (Laugallies) B. Diploma, Humanistic-Classical and, Econ. Sch., Wuppertal, Germany, 1991. Investment banker various, Dusseldorf, Germany, 1991-92; exec. product mgr., sales trainer AWD, Hanover, Germany, 1992-93; chmn., CEO ABMK & Co. Internat. Ent., Inc., N.Y.C., 1994; v.p., mktg. dir. Lyon Mountain Spring Water, Inc., Stamford, N.Y., 1994—; shareholder, 1994; bd. dirs. The Maui Inst., Hawaii, 1994—; pres. A.B.A. Enterprises, Inc., Stamford, N.Y., 1995—, Stamford Inst. for Rsch., Consulting and Internat. Comm., 1995—; CEO and chmn. bd. Stamford Fin. Theatrical Fund, Inc., 1995—; pres. and CEO of Royal Investment and Fin. Consulting, Ludwigshafen, Germany, Apollo Noble House AG, Hamburg, v.p. investor relations, Hybrids Internat., Ltd. Kan.,; exec. v.p., treas. European Mkt. Stamford Fin., Inc., N.Y., 1994—; chmn., CFO Taurus Internat. Investments, Inc., 1995; mem. sponsor N.Y.C. Venture Capital Group, Hofstra Univ. Club, Long Island; mem. Conn. Venture Capital Group; v.p. Crossroads Environ. Corp., Conore, Tex., B.G. Banking Equipment, Inc., Bowling Green U. *Hon. Alexander C. Brosda is an internationally acclaimed investment banker and money market manager. His expertise lies in identification and rapid development of new and small companies which show significant growth potential, the trainingand direction of sales forces, and the development of marketing and sales strategies. He also specializes in the acquisition and investment of growth capital. He is an exceptionally predominant negotiator with internationally diverse experience.* Chmn. ball com. Christmas Feeling Fund, Stamford, N.Y., vice chmn. of Fund; mem. econ. devel. coun., Del. County, N.Y. Recipient 20th Achievement award U.S. Libr. Congress, Degree of Merit for outstanding contribution to Finance and Industry, Melrose Press Ltd.; named Hon. Consul Sao Tome e Principe, Portugal (Inst. Collaboration and Cooperation with Portugese Africa), Man of Yr., ABI, 1996, Hon. Dep. Gov., ABIRA; selected fgn. exchange invitee to Univ. Oman, South Arabia. Mem. Club of Intellectuals, Cambridge, England, C. of C., Stamford, N.Y. (spokesman pub. rels.), New York Bar Assn. at the United Nations (mem. Hall of Fame), Congressional Group, German-American C. of C., European-American C. of C., Rotary Internat., Stamford Country Club, Saratoga Polo and Golf Assn. N.Y., Monte Carlo Country Club, Police Benevolent Assn. (hon.). Roman Catholic. Avocations: golf, reading, sailing, racing, diving.

BROSE, CATHY, principal. Prin. Pomerado elem. sch.; co-prin. Highland Ranch Eler Sch., San Diego, 1997-98; prin. Sch. Creek Elem. Sch., San Diego, 1998—. Recipient Elem. Sch. Recognition award U.S. Dept. Edn., 1989-90. Office: Shoal Creek Elem Sch 11775 Shoal Creek Dr San Diego CA 92128-4753*

BROSELOW, LINDA LATT, medical office technician, aviculturist; b. Harrisburg, Pa., July 9, 1940; d. Herman and Ricci (Buch) Latt; m. Robert Joel Broselow, Nov. 26, 1966; children: Andrew M., Katherine, Jordan. BS, Pa. State U., 1962; MA, Columbia U., 1965. Vol. Peace Corps, Ankara, Turkey, 1962-64; office mgr. Robert J. Broselow, M.D., Lubbock, Tex., 1984-88, med. office technician, 1990-98. Vol. South Park Hosp., Lubbock, 1986-87, Ronald McDonald House, Lubbock, 1990-92. Mem. MADD, Am. Diabetes Assn., Am. Assn. Ret. Persons, Humane Soc. U.S., Audubon Soc., Arkadashlar, Assn. of Univ. Women. Avocation: reading. Home: 4609 9th St Lubbock TX 79416-4710 Office: 3506 21st St Ste 506 Lubbock TX 79410-1200

BROSH, RITA, performing company executive. Trained with, Margaret Craske, Sallie Wilson, Ron Bostik, Patsy Swayze, Ron Sequoio, Robert Joffrey, Edith Stephen, Margo Marshall; student, Nat. Ballet Sch., Can. Asst. choreographer Beauty & the Beast Off Broadway, N.Y.C., 1976; artistic dir. S.W. Jazz Ballet Co., Houston, 1977—, choreographer, 1977—; artistic dir. Rita Brosh Sch. Dance, 1979—; dir. Am. in Concert Tours, 1980-92, Stars n Stripes, 1992-95. Performed in shows at Can. Nat. Exhbn., Edith Stephen Theatre Dance Co., Manhattan Festival Ballet Co., U.S. and Can. Nat. Tour, Balt. Ballet Co., Pocono's Equity Tour, San Antonio Festival Ballet, Ballet Western Reserve, U.S. Naval Acad., Miller Outdoor Theatre, numerous others. Office: SW Jazz Ballet Co PO Box 38233 720 1/2 Pinemont Dr Houston TX 77018

BROSHAR, ROBERT CLARE, architect; b. Waterloo, Iowa, May 20, 1931; s. Clare McDanel and Stella Mae (Scott) B.; m. Joyce Elaine Lukes, June 27, 1953; children: Scott, Michael, Matthew, Patrick, Elizabeth. B.Arch., Iowa State U., 1954. Ptnr. Henry & Broshar, 1960-62, Thorson, Brom, Broshar, Snyder (architects), Waterloo, 1963-96. Bd. dirs., pres. Blackhawk County YMCA, 1972-75; chmn. bd. dirs. Goodwill Industries, 1995-96; mem. Gov.'s Com. Employment of Handicapped, 1975-79. 1st lt. AUS, 1954-56. Recipient Disting. Svc. award Iowa Easter Seal Soc., 1976, Leon Chatelain award Nat. Easter Seal Soc., 1983, Iowa State U. Alumni Achievement award, 1982; named Iowa State U. Parent of Yr., 1980. Fellow AIA (Iowa pres. 1972, nat. dir. 1975-78, nat. v.p. 1979-81, 82, nat. pres. 1983, Iowa Medal of Honor 1992), Royal Archtl. Inst. Can. (hon.); mem. Soc. Architects Mex. (hon.), Soc. Architects Guatemala (hon.), Rotary, ISU Order of Knoll, Knight of St. Patrick, Tau Beta Pi, Delta Upsilon, Tau Sigma Delta, Phi Kappa Phi. Republican. Methodist. Home: 15340 Dodge Ave Clear Lake IA 50428-8773

BROSI, GEORGE RALPH, small business owner; b. Providence, Aug. 5, 1942; s. Albert Ralph and May Pauline (Potter) B.; m. Connie Carol Fearington, June 12, 1971; children: Brook, Berry, Blossom, Sunshine, Sky, Glade, Eagle. BA, Carleton Coll., 1965; MAEd, Western Carolina U., 1991. Peace intern Am. Friends Svc. Com., Dayton, Ohio, 1966; founder Vocations for Social Change, Canyon, Calif., 1968-70; Appalachian region staff Episc. Ch. Youth Program, Sequatchie, Tenn., 1971-74; with U.S. Post Office, Whitwell, Tenn., 1975-76; So. Tenn. coalfields organizer Save Our Cumberland Mountains, Sequatchie, 1977; program dir. Mountain Cmty. Union, Morgantown, W.Va., 1978; bookstore mgr. Coun. of the So. Mountains, Berea, Ky., 1979-82; sole proprietor Appalachian Mountain Books, Berea and Whittier, N.C., 1982—; part-time instr. So. Reg. Electronic Campus, Atlanta, 1998—, U. Ky., Lexington, 1995—, Ea. Ky. U., Richmond, 1991—, Somerset (Ky.) C.C., 1991—; faculty cons. Ednl. Testing Svc., Princeton, N.J., 1994—. Author: The Literature of the Appalachian South, 1992, Kentucky Literature, 1994; co-author: Jesse Stuart: The Man and His Books, 1988; new books columnist Appalachian Heritage Quar., 1986—. Staff So. Christian Leadership Conf., Atlanta, 1970, New Mobilization Com. to End War in Vietnam, Washington, 1970, So. Student Organizing Com., Nashville, 1965-66, Students for a Democratic Soc., Ann Arbor, Chgo., 1964-65. Mem. Appalachian Studies Assn., Phi Kappa Phi. E-mail: www.Appalachianbooks.com. Home: 123 Walnut St Berea KY 40403-1628

BROSILOW, COLEMAN BERNARD, chemical engineering educator; b. Phila., Nov. 14, 1934; s. Samuel and Ethel (Stein) B.; m. Rosalie Ziegleman, Feb. 18, 1962; children—Rachelle, Benjamin. B.S., Drexel U., 1957; M.Ch.E., Poly. Inst. N.Y., 1959, Ph.D., 1962. Systems engr. Am. Cyanamid Co., Process Analysis Group, Wayne, N.J., 1962-63; asst. prof. chem. engring. Case Western Res. U., Cleve., 1963-67; assoc. prof. Case Western Res. U., 1967-73, prof. chem. engring., 1973—, chmn. dept. chem. engring., 1980-84; chmn. bd. Control Soft Corp., 1985—; vis. prof. chem. engring. The Technion, Haifa, Israel, 1971-72; cons. in field. Contbr. articles to profl. jours.; editorial bd.: Am. Inst. Chem. Engrs. Jour, 1980-85. Founding mem. bd. trustees Solomon Schecter Day Sch. of Cleve., 1978—, pres., 1978-84. . Fellow AIChE (computing in chem. engring. award 1989); mem. Sigma Xi, Tau Beta Pi, Phi Lambda Upsilon. Jewish. Patentee in field. Home: 2408 Lalemont Rd University Ht OH 44118-4506 Office: Case Western Res Univ Chem Enging Dept A W Smith Bldg Cleveland OH 44106

BROSIN, HENRY WALTER, psychiatrist, educator; b. Blackwood, Va., July 6, 1904; s. Martin and Marie (Danowski) B.; m. Ruth Hatfield, 1949; 1 son, Lloyd Wisdom. A.B., U. Wis., 1927, M.D., 1933; postgrad. (Commonwealth Fund fellow in Psychiatry), U. Colo., 1934-37; postgrad. (Rockefeller fellow), Inst. Psychoanalysis, Chgo., 1937-40. Diplomate: Am. Bd. Psychiatry and Neurology (pres. 1961). Rotating intern Cin. Gen. Hosp., 1933-34; fellow Colo. Psychopathic Hosp., Denver, 1934-37; staff div. psychiatry U. Chgo., 1937-41, prof., head div., 1946-50; dir. Western Psychiat. Inst. and Clinics, 1951-69; psychiat. cons. Office Surgeon Gen., Washington, 1944-66; prof., chmn. dept. psychiatry U. Pitts., 1951-69; prof. psychiatry U. Ariz. Coll. Medicine, Tucson, 1970-90; Mem. Social Sci. Research Council; fellow Center Advanced Study Behavioral Scis., 1956-66; mem. div. med. scis. Nat. Acad. Sci., NRC, 1958-68, mem. naval med. research com. Asso. edit.: Am. Jour. Psychiatry, 1965-73; Contbr. articles to profl. jours. Served as col. M.C. AUS, 1941-46. Decorated Legion of Merit; recipient Distinguished Service award U. Chgo. Sch. Medicine, 1952; Med. Alumni citation U. Wis., 1962; Col. Wm. S. Porter award Assn. Mil. Surgeons U.S., 1967. Fellow Am. Acad. Arts and Scis., Rorschach Inst., A.C.P., Am. Psychiat. Assn. (councillor 1948-51, pres. 1967-68); mem. AMA, Phila. Psychoanalytic Assn., v.p. (1960-61, Chgo. Psychoanalytic Assns.), AAAS, Am. Psychol. Assn., Am. Coll. Psychiatrists (pres. 1970-71, Bowis award 1975), Am. Soc. Research Psychosomatic Problems (councillor), Assn. Research Nervous and Mental Diseases, Pitts. Neuropsychiat. Soc., Pitts. Psychoanalytic Inst. and Soc., Allegheny County Med. Soc., Group Advancement Psychiatry (pres. 1961-63), Nat. Assn. Mental Health, Soc. Biol. Psychiatry, Royal Psychol. Assn. (hon), Sigma Xi, Alpha Omega Alpha. Club: Cosmos. Home: 1580 E River Rd Apt 505 Tucson AZ 85718-7630

BROSIUS, SCOTT DAVID, professional baseball player; b. Hillsboro, Oreg., Aug. 15, 1966; m. Jennifer; children: Allison, Megan, David. Student, Linfield (Oreg.) Coll. 3d baseman Oakland (Calif.) Athletics, 1987-97, N.Y. Yankees, 1998—. Office: c/o NY Yankees Yankee Stadium E 161st St and River Ave Bronx NY 10451*

BROSKI, DAVID C., chancellor; b. Dec. 12, 1945. BA in Bus. Adminstrn., Mich. State U., 1969, MA in Ednl. Adminstrn., 1971, PhD in Instrnl. Sys.

Devel., 1974; DSc honoris causa, Thomas Jefferson U., 1997; LLD honoris causa, Chosun U., Republic of Korea, 1998. From asst. to assoc. prof. Sch. Allied Med. Professions Coll. Medicine, Ohio State U., Columbus, 1974-83, from asst. to assoc. dir., dir. grad. studies, 1974-83; dean Coll. Associated Health Professions U. Ill., Chgo., 1983-91, provost, vice chancellor for acad. affairs, 1991-96, chancellor, 1995—. E-mail: broski@uic.edu. Office: M/C 102 601 S Morgan St Chicago IL 60607-7128

BROSMAN, CATHARINE SAVAGE, French language educator, poet; b. Denver, June 7, 1934; d. Paul Victor and Della (Stanforth) Hill; m. Patric Savage, 1955 (div. 1964); m. Paul William Brosman Jr., Aug. 21, 1970 (div. 1993); 1 child, Katherine Elliott. BA, Rice U., 1955, MA, 1957, PhD, 1960. Instr. in French Rice U., Houston, 1960-62; asst. prof. French Sweet Briar (Va.) Coll., 1962-63, U. Fla., Gainesville, 1963-66; assoc. prof. French Mary Baldwin Coll., Staunton, Va., 1966-68; vis. assoc. prof. U. Waterloo, Ont., Can., 1970; assoc. prof. French Tulane U., New Orleans, 1968-72, prof. French, 1972-92, Kathryn B. Gore prof. French, 1992-96, prof. emerita, 1997—; De Velling & Willis vis. prof. U. Sheffield, U.K., 1996. Author: André Gide: L'évolution de sa pensée religieuse, 1962, Malraux, Sartre, and Aragon as Political Novelists, 1964, Roger Martin du Gard, 1968, Watering, 1972, Jean-Paul Sartre, 1983, Abiding Winter, 1983, Jules Roy, 1988, Art as Testimony: The Work of Jules Roy, 1989, An Annotated Bibliography...on André Gide, 1990, Journeying from Canyon de Chelly, 1990, Simone de Beauvoir Revisited, 1991, The Shimmering Maya and Other Essays, 1994, French Culture 1900-1975, 1994, Passages, 1996, Visions of War in France, 1999; editor: French Novelists 1900-1930, 1988, French Novelists 1930-1960, 1989, French Novelists Since 1960, 1989, Nineteenth-Century French Fiction Writers...1800-1860, 1992, Nineteenth-Century French Fiction Writers...1860-1900, 1992; asst. editor French Rev., 1974-77, 84-96, mng. editor, 1977-80. Home: 1550 2nd St Apt 7I New Orleans LA 70130-5943

BROSNAHAN, LEGER NICHOLAS, English educator; b. Kansas City, Mo., Dec. 11, 1929; s. Earl Francis and Helen Rose Mottin Brosnahan; m. Irene Teoh, Nov. 4, 1967; children: L. Nicholas Jr., Jennifer Ru-chao. AB, Georgetown U., 1951; MA, Harvard U., 1952, PhD, 1957. Instr. Northwestern U., Evanston, Ill., 1957-61; asst. prof. Hawaii U., Honolulu, 1961-63; rschr. U. Paris, 1963-64; vis. prof. U. Lyons, France, 1964-65; asst. prof. U. Md., College Park, 1965-68; from assoc. prof. to prof. Ill. State U., Normal, 1968—; vis. prof. Myagi-Kyoiku Dai, Sendai, Japan, 1968-69, Moscow Linguistics U., 1992-93, Changshin Coll., Masan, Korea, 1996; rschr. Usedcom, Tokyo, 1969-70. Author: Japanese and English Gesture, 1990, Chinese and English Gesture, 1991, Standard American English Behavior, 1997. Sgt. U.S. Army, 1952-54. Office: Ill State U Dept English Normal IL 61790-4240

BROSNAHAN, ROGER PAUL, lawyer; b. Kansas City, Mo., Aug. 9, 1935; s. Earl and Helen (Mottin) B.; m. Jill Farley, Aug. 2, 1958; children: Paul, Connor, Helen, Farley, Tracy, Hugh, Lee. BS, St. Louis U., 1956; LLB, Mich. U., 1959. Bar: Mo. 1959, Minn. 1959, U.S. Supreme Ct. 1971, U.S. Ct. Appeals (8th cir.) 1975. Ptnr. Streater, Murphy, Brosnahan & Langford, Winona, Minn., 1959-78, Kutak, Rock & Huie, Mpls., 1979-82, Robins, Kaplan, Miller & Ciresi, Mpls., 1982-93, Brosnahan, Joseph & Suggs P.A., Mpls., 1993—. Mem. ABA (state del. 1976-88), Minn. Bar Assn. (pres. 1974-75), Ramsey County Bar Assn., Hennepin County Bar Assn., Nat. Conf. Bar Pres. (pres. 1980-81). Democrat. Roman Catholic. Home: 1343 S River Rd Buffalo City WI 54622-7205 Office: Brosnahan Joseph & Suggs PA 701 4th Ave S Ste 500 Minneapolis MN 55415-1810

BROSNAN, CAROL RAPHAEL SARAH, retired arts administrator, musician; b. Paterson, N.J., July 19, 1931; d. Basil Roger and Mary Ellen Carroll (McDonald) B. Student, George Washington U., Washington, 1956-61, U. Va., 1975, U. Oxford (Eng.), 1975; BA in History, George Washington U., 1981, postgrad., 1983-87; piano student of, Iris Brussels, 1940-53. Adminstrv. clk. Dept. of Army, Def., Pentagon, Office of asst. chief of staff intelligence, Washington, 1955-58; clk. fgn. sci. info. program NSF, Washington, 1958-60, adminstrv. clk., 1960-65, adminstrv. fellowship clk. grad. fellowship program, 1965-72; staff asst. to Jane Alexander, chmn. Nat. Endowment for the Arts, Washington, 1972-94; ret., 1994; music tchr. piano, Paterson, N.J., 1945-53; piano recitalist U.S., Heidelberg, W. Ger. Served with WAC, 1953-55. Recipient Young People's Concerts award, 1945. Hon. fellow Harry S. Truman Libr. Inst. Nat. and Internat. Affairs, 1975. Mem. Am. Hist. Assn., Nat. Assn. Uniformed Svcs., Acad. Polit. Sci. (contbg. 1978-81), Am. Classical League, Friends of Bodleian Libr. (Oxford U.), Luther Rice Soc. of George Washington U. (life), Phi Alpha Theta. Home: 6030 Sunset Ridge Ct Centreville VA 20121-3051 Office: Nat Endowment for Arts 1100 Pennsylvania Ave NW Washington DC 20004-2501

BROSNAN, DAVID PATRICK, structural engineer; b. Medford, Ma., Feb. 5, 1962; s. David and Teresa Margaret (Keenan) B. BSCE, Tufts U., 1984; MSCE, Northeastern U., 1992. Registered profl. engr., Mass. Structural engr. Aberjona Engring. Inc., Winchester, Mass., 1984-91, C/BI Consulting Inc., Boston, 1991-92, Souza, True & Ptnrs., Inc., Watertown, Mass., 1992—; instr. Boston Archtl. Ctr., 1997—. Bd. dirs. Medford Cmty. Housing Inc. Mem. ASCE, Am. Concrete Inst., Boston Soc. Civil Engrs. Democrat. Roman Catholic. Home: 32 Cotting St Medford MA 02155-4302

BROSNAN, PETER LAWRENCE, documentary filmmaker; b. Bklyn., July 6, 1952; s. John Joseph and Audrey Barbara (Holran) B. BFA, NYU, N.Y.C., 1974; MA, U. So. Calif., 1979, Pepperdine U., 1995. Documentary filmmaker, writer L.A., 1980—; dir. DeMille Project, Hollywood Heritage, L.A., 1988—. Author: (screenplays) Heart of Darkness, 1992, The Ark, 1994, Perfect Target, 1996; co-author: (book) PML Report, 1989; writer: (documentary film) Ghosts of Cape Horn, 1980 (World Ship Trust award); prodr., dir.: (TV documentary) The Lost City, 1992; writer, segment prodr.: (PBS series) Faces of Culture, 1983-84 (Emmy award 1984), Writer Marketing, 1984 (Emmy award 1985); dir.: (documentary) Sand Castles, 1995. Democrat.

BROSNAN, PIERCE, actor; b. Navan, County Meath, Ireland, May 16, 1953; m. Cassandra Harris, 1977 (dec. 1991). Stage appearances include Wait Until Dark, The Red Devil Battery Sign, Filumena, (London); film appearances include The Mirror Crack'd, The Long Good Friday, 1982, Nomads, 1986, The Fourth Protocol, 1987, The Deceivers, 1988, Mr. Johnson, 1989, The Lawnmower Man, 1991, Mrs. Doubtfire, 1993, Love Affair, 1994, Robinson Crusoe, 1995, Goldeneye, 1995, Mars Attacks!, 1996, The Mirror Has Two Faces, 1996, Dante's Peak, 1997, Tomorrow Never Dies, 1997, The Nephew, 1998, (voice) The Quest for Camelot, 1998, Grey Owl, 1999, The Thomas Crown Affair, 1999, The World is Not Enough, 1999, others; TV appearances include Murphy's Stroke, The Manions of America, Nancy Astor, Remington Steele, Noble House, Around The World in 80 Days, 1989, Murder 101, 1991; prodr. The Nephew, 1999, The Thomas Crown Affair, 1999; TV guest appearances include The Professionals, 1977, Moonlighting, 1985, Muppets Tonight!, 1996. *

BROSS, IRWIN DUDLEY JACKSON, biostatistician; b. Halloway, Ohio, Nov. 13, 1921; s. Samuel and Mina (Jackson) B.; m. Rida Singer, Aug. 6, 1949; children: Dean, Valerie, Neal. B.A. in Math, UCLA, 1942; M.A. in Exptl. Stats, N.C. State U., 1948, Ph.D. in Exptl. Stats, 1949. Research asso. dept. biostatistics Johns Hopkins U., 1949-52; asst. prof. public health and preventive medicine Cornell U., 1952-59; head research, design and analysis Sloan Kettering Inst., 1952-59; dir. biostatistics Roswell Park Meml. Inst., Buffalo, N.Y., 1959-83; pres. Biomed. Metatech., Inc., 1983—; research prof. biostatistics State U. N.Y. at Buffalo, 1961-83; asso. dept. epidemiology Johns Hopkins U., 1971-85. Author: Design for Decision, 1953, Scientific Strategies in Human Affairs: To Tell the Truth, 1975, Scientific Strategies to Save Your Life, 1981, Crimes of Official Science: A Casebook, 1988, Scientific Fraud vs. Scientific Truth, 1992, Fifty Years of Folly and Fraud in the Name of Science, 1994, (CD-ROM, 6 books) History of U.S. Science and Medicine in the Cold War, 1996; contbr. numerous articles in field to profl. jours. Served with U.S. Army, 1941-45. Mem. AAAS, Am. Statis. Assn., Biometric Soc., Am. Coll. Epidemiol. Home and Office: 109 Maynard Dr Buffalo NY 14226-3365

BROSS, STEWARD RICHARD, JR., lawyer; b. Lancaster, Pa., Oct. 25, 1922; s. Steward Richard and Katherine Mauk (Hoover) B.; m. Isabel Florence Kenney, May 10, 1943; 1 dau., Donna Isabel Bross Campagna. Student, McGill U., Montreal, Can., 1940-42; LLB, Columbia U., 1948. Bar: N.Y. 1948. Pvt. practice N.Y.C.; ptnr. Cravath, Swaine & Moore, 1958-92, ret., 1992; adv. com. fgn. direct investment program Office of Sec. Dept. Commerce, 1969; adv. com. regulations Office Fgn. Direct Investment, 1968-70. Regent, trustee emeritus The Cathedral Ch. of St. John the Divine, N.Y.C.; warden emeritus Trinity Ch., N.Y.C. Served as officer Canadian Navy, 1942-45. Mem. ABA, N.Y. State Bar Assn., Assn. of Bar of City of N.Y., Pilgrims U.S., Econ. Club N.Y., Union Club, Rockefeller Center Club, Links Club, Univ. Club N.Y. Home: 215 E 68th St New York NY 10021-5718 also: Ashgrove 130 Litchfield Rd Norfolk CT 06058-1252 also: 3200 Wailea Alanui Dr Apt 1101 Kihei HI 96753-7757 Office: Cravath Swaine & Moore 825 8th Ave New York NY 10019-7475

BROSTERMAN, MELVIN A., lawyer; b. Bklyn., June 25, 1949. BA, SUNY, Albany, 1971; JD, Bklyn. Law Sch., 1974. Bar: N.Y. 1975, U.S. Ct. Appeals (2d cir.) 1976, U.S. Supreme Ct. 1982. Atty. office gen. counsel SEC, 1974-77; mem. Stroock & Stroock & Lavan, N.Y.C., 1977—. Editor Bklyn. Law Rev., 1973-74. Mem. ABA, FBA, N.Y. State Bar Assn., Assn. Bar City N.Y. (com. fed. cts. 1981-83). Office: Stroock & Stroock & Lavan LLP 180 Maiden Ln New York NY 10038-4925

BROSZ, MARGARET HEADLEY, pediatrics nurse; b. Dover, N.J., Dec. 31, 1951; d. Charles E. and Carolyn (Cobb) H.; m. Walter J. Brosz, May 28, 1978. Student, Douglass Coll., New Brunswick, N.J., 1970-72; BS in Nursing, Cornell U., 1974; MS, Boston Coll., Chestnut Hill, Mass., 1978. Cert. trainer medication adminstrs. Nurse Vis. Nurse Assn. Boston, 1974-76; pediatric nurse practitioner Wrentham (Mass.) State Sch., Boston Children's Hosp., 1978-80; staff nurse pediatrics ICU Thomas Jefferson U. Hosp., Phila., 1980-81; employee health clinician Children's Hosp. Phila., 1981-83; unit nurse, campus nurse The Woods Svcs., Langhorne, Pa., 1983—. Vol. interpreter Pennsbury Manor, Morrisville, Pa., bd. dirs. Pennsbury Soc. Mem. Devel. Disabilities Nurses Assn.

BROTEN, JAMES M., accountant; b. Norwich, N.Y., Dec. 9, 1960; s. Robert Alton and Helen Marilyn Broten; children: Elizabeth, Jackie. BS in Acctg., Bob Jones U., 1982; MPA, Sage Grad. Sch., 1995. CPA, N.Y. Staff acct. Talevi and Parlato, P.C., Oneonta, N.Y., 1982-83; sr. acct. Bach and Fiddler, CPAs, P.C., Norwich, 1983-84; asst. v.p. fin., fin. analyst, internal auditor Del. Otsego Corp. and Subs., Cooperstown, N.Y., 1984-88; pvt. practice Cooperstown, Norwich, 1987—; fee acct. Town of Oxford, Town of Guilford, N.Y., 1989—; exec. dir. Home Baseball Charitable Trust, Cooperstown, 1990—; adj. prof. SUNY, Norwich, 1994—. Mem. AICPA, Nat. Eagle Scout Assn., Nat. Intercollegiate Soccer Officials Assn., U.S. Soccer Fedn. (state referee, referee instr., state referee assessor, asst. state referee adminstr. N.Y. state), U.S. Fusal Fedn. (nat. referee), Am. youth Soccer Orgn. (regional referee, state dir. instrn.), N.Y. Soc. CPA (mem. govtl. acctg. com. 1991-93, pub. sch. acctg. com. 1991-95, mem. fin. acctg. stds. com. 1993-94), N.Y. State Govt. Fin. Officers Assn., N.Y. State Assn. Sch. Bus. Officers. Office: 21 Front St Norwich NY 13815

BROTH, RAY, retail executive; b. N.Y.C., Jan. 27, 1930; s. Abraham Lewis and Dorothy (Rand) B.; m. Beverly Rosenblatt, June 30, 1951; children: Penny Cheryl, Caryn, Donna Elyse, Fran Susan. Grad. high sch. Receiving & inventory clk. Peerless Camera Stores, N.Y.C., 1952, repair svcs. clk., 1953, salesman, 1954-55, buyer, 1956, sales mgr., 1958; pres. Scopus, Inc., N.Y.C., 1957; store mgr. Peerless Camera Stores, Pitts., 1959-60; exec. v.p. Willoughby/Peerless Camera Stores, N.Y.C., 1961-76; pres., chief exec. officer Sarasota (Fla.) Camera Exch. & Video Ctr., 1976-97; trustee Photo Mktg. Assocs.; charter mem. Eastman Kodak Medalist Bd., 1989. Bd. dirs. Sarasota Manatee Community Orch., 1990—. Staff sgt. USMC, 1948-52. Named Dealer of Yr. by Photo Trade News-Dealer Publ., 1988, Bus. Person of Yr. by Sarasota County C. of C., 1989; named to Hon. Order of Ky. Cols., 1989; inducted into Photo Trade News-Dealer Publ. Hall of Fame, 1998.

BROTHERS, BARBARA, English language educator; b. Youngstown, Ohio, Nov. 27, 1937; d. William Price and Mary Ella (Bingham) Hoover; m. Don R. Brothers, June 1959 (div.); children: Mark Richard, Jill Ann; m. Lawrence J. Haims, Apr. 1980. AB, Youngstown U., 1958; MA, Western Res. U., 1962; PhD, Kent State U., 1973. English tchr. Austintown Fitch, Youngstown, 1958-60; from adj. faculty to asst. prof. Youngstown State U., 1960-73, asst. to prof., 1973-83, chairperson English dept., 1974-93, acting dean grad. sch., 1993, dean coll. arts and scis., 1993—; cons. NEH, numerous university and local sch. dists.; cons. North Ctrl. Evaluator. Co-editor: Dictionary of Literary Biography 174: British Travel Writers 1876-1909, 1997, Dictionary of Literary Biography 166: British Travel Writers 1837-1875, 1996, Dictionary of Literary Biography 195: British Travel Writers 1910-1939, 1998; Reading and Writing Women's Lives, 1990; contbr. chpts. in books and articles to profl. jours. Mem. Coll. English Assn. (co-editor publs. 1988-93, exec. com. 1988-93, pres. 1989-90), MLA (organizing com. 1989-91), Nat. Coun. Tchrs. English, Women's Caucus Modern Lang. Assn., Assn. Depts. of English (exec. com. 1981-84), Virginia Woolf Soc., Midwest Modern Lang. Assn., Coll. English Assn. Ohio (pres. 1981-82), Ohio Humanities Coun. (state-based NEH program 1979-85), Phi Kappa Phi (pres. 1985-86). Office: Youngstown State U Coll Arts And Scis Youngstown OH 44555

BROTHERS, CHERYL MARIANNE MORRIS, school superintendent. Supt. Happy Valley Elem. Sch., Santa Cruz, Calif. Recipient Leadership for Learning award, Amer. Assn. of Sch. Admin., 1994. Office: Happy Valley Elem Sch Dist 3125 Branciforte Dr Santa Cruz CA 95065-9661

BROTHERS, JOHN ALFRED, oil company executive; b. Huntington, W.Va., Nov. 10, 1940; s. John Luther and Genevieve (Monti) B.; m. Paula Sprague Benson, June 21, 1975. B.S., Va. Poly. Inst., 1962, M.S., 1965, Ph.D., 1966; postgrad advanced mgmt. program, Harvard U., 1981. With Internat. Nickel Co., 1962-64; with Ashland Oil, Inc., Ky., 1966—; sr. v.p. Ashland Oil, Inc., 1983-87; sr. v.p., group operating officer Ashland Oil Inc., 1987-97; with Ashland Chem. Co., Columbus, Ohio, 1974-88; pres. Ashland Chem. Co., Columbus, 1983-88; exec. v.p. Ashland, Inc., 1997—; bd. dirs. Geon Co., Cleve., GTS Duratk, Inc., Columbia, Md.; adj. prof. engring. Ohio State U., 1978—; pres. bus. adv. coun., 1981—. Bd. dirs. Columbus Mus. Art, Columbus Children's Hosp., Ohio Dominican Coll., 1984—. NSF fellow, 1965-66; named Outstanding Young Man U.S. C. of C., 1972. Mem. Am. Petroleum Inst., Chem. Mfrs. Assn., Columbus C. of C. (bd. dirs.), Tau Beta Pi, Phi Kappa Phi. Republican. Clubs: Scioto Country, Rolling Rock, Muirfield Country, Mill Reef, Columbus. Office: Ashland Inc PO Box 391 Covington KY 41012-0391

BROTHERS, JOYCE DIANE, television personality, psychologist; b. N.Y.C.; d. Morris K. and Estelle (Rapoport) Bauer; m. Milton Brothers, July 4, 1949; 1 child, Lisa Robin. BS, Cornell U., 1947; MA, Columbia U., 1950, PhD, 1953; LHD (hon.), Franklin Pierce Coll., Gettysburg Coll., Lehigh U., 1994, Mt. St. Mary Coll., 1998. Asst. in psychology Columbia U., N.Y.C., 1948-52; instr. psychology Hunter Coll., N.Y.C., 1948-52; ind. psychologist, writer, 1952—. Co-host: TV program Sports Showcase, 1956; appearances: TV program Dr. Joyce Brothers, 1958-63, Consult Dr. Brothers, 1960-66, Ask Dr. Brothers, 1965-75; hostess (TV syndication) Living Easy with Dr. Joyce Brothers, 1972-75; columnist TV syndication, N.Am. Newspaper Alliance, 1961-71, Bell-McClure Syndicate, 1963-71, King Features Syndicate, 1972—, Good Housekeeping mag., 1962—; appearances Sta. WNBC, 1966-70; radio program Emphasis, 1966-75, Monitor, 1967-75, Sta. WMCA, 1970-73, ABC Reports, 1966-67, NBC Radio Network Newsline, 1975—; news analyst radio program, Metro Media-TV, 1975-76, news corr., TVN, Inc., 1975-76, Sta. KABC-TV, 1977-82, Sta. WABC-TV, 1980-82, , 86-88, Sta. WLS-TV, 1980-82, NIWS Syndicated News Service, 1982-84, The Dr. Joyce Brothers Program, The Disney Channel, 1985, Sta. KCBS-TV News, 1987—; spl. feature writer Hearst papers, UPI; current affairs spl. corr. Fox TV Syndication, 1990-97; featured on A&E's Biography, 1999; author: Ten Days to a Successful Memory, 1959, Woman, 1961, The Brothers System for Liberated Love and Marriage, 1975, How to Get Whatever You Want Out of Life, 1978, What Every Woman Should Know About Men, 1982, What Every Woman Ought to Know About Love and Marriage, 1988, The Successful Woman, 1989, Widowed, 1990, Positive Plus: The Practical Plan to Liking Yourself Better, 1994. Co-chmn. sports com. Lighthouse for Blind; door-to-door chmn. Fedn. Jewish Philanthropies, N.Y.C.; mem. fund raising com. Olympic Fund; mem. People-to-People Program. Winner $64,000 Question TV Program, 1956, $64,000 Challenge, 1957; recipient Mennen Baby Found. award, 1959, Newhouse Newspaper award, 1959, Am. Acad. Achievement award, Am. Parkinson Disease Assn. award, 1971, Deadline award Sigma Delta Chi, 1971, Pres.'s Cabinet award U. Detroit, 1975, Woman of Achievement award Women's City Club Cleve., 1981, award Calif. Home Econs. Assn., 1981, award Distrubutive Edn. Clubs Am., 1981, Golden Gavel Excellence in Comm. award Toastmasters, 1982, Pub. Svc. award Ridgewood Women's Club, 1987, Women Who Make a Difference award Sen. Bill Bradley, 1990, Gt. Am. award Bards of Bohemia, 1993, Diamond award, 1994, George M. and Mary Jane Leader Healthcare Achievement award, 1995, Nat. Cmty. Svc. award McQuade Children Svcs., 1998. Mem. Sigma Xi. Office: NBC Westwood One Radio Network 1700 Broadway New York NY 10019-5905

BROTHERS, JUNE ESTERNAUX SCOTT, forest products company executive; b. Bend, Oreg., June 4, 1936; d. Frank Aaron and Blanche Angeline (Esternaux) Scott; m. Charles Paskel Brothers, June 22, 1957; children: Charles Jr., Theodore Edwin, Sandra Zoe, Lorna Scott. AS, Ctrl. Oreg. C.C., 1955; BS, U. Oreg., 1957; Masters in Mgmt., Willamette U., 1984. Cert. safety profl. News editor Redmond (Oreg.) Spokesman, 1966-67, editor, 1970-75; staff writer The Sumter (S.C.) Daily News, 1967-68; cmty. ctrs. dir. Sumter County Econ. Opportunity Corp., 1968-70; asst. adminstr. Accident Prevention Divsn. Oreg. Workers Comp. Dept., Salem, 1975-88; safety dir. Georgia-Pacific Corp., Toledo, Oreg., 1988-90; sr. mgr. human resources Georgia-Pacific Corp., Atlanta, 1991-98, group dir. human resources, 1998—. Pres. PTA, Commercr City, Colo., 1965-66; trustee Ctrl. Oreg. C.C. Found., Bend, 1975-78; bd. govs. Theatre of Cascades, Bend, 1975-78. Recipient Woman Achievement award YWCA, Atlanta, 1995, Outstanding Achievement award Nat. Fedn. Press Women, 1974, Outstanding Soil Cons. Svc. Comm. award U.S. Dept. Agrl., 1973, Outstanding Citizen award Redmond C. of C., 1973. Mem. Am. Soc. Safety Engrs. (cert. com. chair 1986-88), Orgn. Devel. Network, Vets. Safety (life cert.), Vol. Protection Program Participants Assn. (nat. bd. dirs. 1996—). Republican. Home: 2081 Kincaid Cv Marietta GA 30066-6580 Office: Georgia-Pacific Corp 133 Peachtree St NE Atlanta GA 30303-1847

BROTHERSTON, LEZ, set designer, costumer. Degree in Theatre Design, Ctrl. Sch. Art and Design, 1984. Set designer: Letter to Brezhnev, Highland Fling, Cinderella (1998 Olivier Award for outstanding achievement in dance), Swan Lake (Olivier Award), The Hunchback of Notre Dame, Giselle, Dracula, The Brontes, Strange Meeting, Romeo and Juliet, A Christmas Carol; other recent dance designs include: Just Scratchin' the Surface, Greymatter, David Copperfield, Northanger Abbey, The Last Romantics, Handling Bach, The Prisoner of Zenda, The Eleventh Commandment, Hindle Wakes (Manchester Royal Exch., Manchester Evening News and Brit. Reg. Theatre award nominations), The Schoolmistress, Alarms and Excursions, Jane Eyre, The Sisters Rosenweig, Neville's Island (1995 Olivier Award nomination for best set design), Rosencrantz and Guildenstern Are Dead; opera designs include prodns. for Opera Zuld, Hong Kong Arts Festival, Opera North, Glyndebourne Touring Opera, Teatro Bellini, Royal Danish Opera and De Vlaamse Opera; musicals include: Side by Side by Sondheim, Maria Friedman by Special Arrangement. Winner 1999 Tony award for Swanlater for set and costume design. Office: Mayer & Eden Ltd, 34 Kingley Ct, London W1R 5Le, England*

BROTMAN, BARBARA LOUISE, columnist, writer; b. N.Y.C., Feb. 23, 1956; d. Oscar J. and Ruth (Branchor) Brotman; m. Chuck Berman, Aug. 28, 1983; children: Robin, Nina. BA, Queens Coll., 1978. Writer, columnist Chgo. Tribune, 1978—. Recipient Ill. Newspapers Column Writing award UPI, 1984, Peter Lisagor award Sigma Delta Chi, 1984. Avocation: broomball. Office: Chgo Tribune Co 435 N Michigan Ave Chicago IL 60611-4066*

BROTMAN, DAVID JOEL, architectural firm executive; b. Balt., Jan. 21, 1945. BS in Architecture, U. Cin., 1968. Registered architect, Ariz., Calif., Colo., D.C., Fla., Ga., Hawaii, La., Md., N.J., N.Y., Nev., Ohio, Oreg., Tex., Utah, Guam, No. Mariana Islands. Arch. Locke & Jackson, Balt., 1968, The Archtl. Affiliation, Towson, Md., 1968-75; joined RTKL, Balt., 1975—; arch. RTKL, Dallas, 1979-90, v.p., 1984-90; exec. v.p., mng. dir. RTKL, L.A., 1990—, vice chmn., 1994—; tchr. U. Tex. Sch. Architecture, Arlington, Catonsville (Md.) C.C.; arbitrator Am. Stock Exch., N.Y. Stock Exch., Nat. Assn. Security Dealers. Prin. works include Fortunoff, Paramus, N.J., Penn Sq. Mall, Oklahoma City, Galleria at South Bay, Redondo Beach, Calif., Eton Sq. (Design award Tex. Soc. Archs., 1986), Computer Sci. Corp., Fairfax County, Va., AT&T Customer Tech. Ctr., Dallas (Honor award Dallas chpt. AIA, 1988), CrossRoads of San Antonio (Design award Monitor Ctrs. and Stores of Excellence, 1988), Canal Pl., New Orleans, Menlo Park, Edison Twsp., N.J. (New Enclosed Mall co-winner Monitor Ctrs. and Stores of Excellence, 1992), Tysons Corner Ctr., McLean, Va. (Design award Monitor Ctrs. and Stores of Excellence 1989, Design award Internat. Coun. Shopping Ctrs. 1989, Exceptional Design award Fairfax County, Va., 1990, Modernization Excellence award Bldgs., 1990, Excellence award Urban Land Inst., 1992), St. Andrews (Scotland) Old Course Hotel, Tower City Ctr., Cleve., Paramount, Manila, The Philippines, Eastland Shopping Ctr., Melbourne, Australia, Morley City Shopping Ctr., Perth, Australia, Dong An Market, Beijing, China, EDSA Plz., Manila, many others; contbr. articles to profl. jours. Mem. AIA, Constrn. Specifications Inst., Internat. Coun. Shopping Ctrs., Internat. Assn. Corp. Real Estate Execs., Nat. Coun. Archtl. Registration Bds., World Trade Ctr. Inst., Urban Land Inst., World Affairs Coun. Office: RTKL Assocs Inc 333 S Hope St Los Angeles CA 90071-1406

BROTMAN, JEFFREY H., variety stores executive; b. 1942. JD, U. Wash., 1967. Ptnr. Lasher-Brotman & Sweet, 1967-74; with ENI Exploration Co., 1975-83; co-founder Costco Wholesale Corp., 1983, chmn. bd., chief exec. officer, 1983-88, chmn. bd., 1988—. Office: Costco Wholesale PO Box 34331 Issaquah WA 98027

BROTMAN, RICHARD DENNIS, counselor; b. Detroit, Nov. 2, 1952; s. Alfred David and Dorothy G. (Mansfield) B.; m. Debra Louise Hobold, Sept. 9, 1979. AA, East L.A. Jr. Coll., 1972; AB, U. So. Calif., 1974, Ms, 1976. Lic. marriage, family and child counselor, Calif.; cert. counselor, Calif. Instructional media coord. Audiovisual divsn. Pub. Libr., City of Alhambra, Calif., 1971-78; clin. supr. Hollywood-Sunset Cmty. Clinic, L.A., 1976—; client program coord. North Los Angles County Regional Ctr. for Devel. Disabled, 1978-81; sr. counselor Eastern L.A. Regional Ctr. for Devel. Disabled, 1981-85; dir. cmty. svcs. Almansor Edn. Ctr., 1985-87; tng. and resource devel. Children's Home Soc. Calif., 1987-90; program supr. Pacific Clinics-East, 1990-94; dir. clin. svcs. Alma Family Svcs., 1994—; probable cause hearing officer Orange County (Calif.) Healthcare Agy., 1986—. Corp. dir. San Gabriel Mission Players, 1973-75. Mem. Am. Assn. for Marriage and Family Therapy (approved supr.), Calif. Pers. and Guidance Assn., Calif. Rehab. Counselors Assn. (officer), San Fernando Valley Consortium of Agys. Serving Devel. Disabled Citizens (chmn. recreation subcom), L.A. Aquarium Soc. Democrat. E-mail: BRIEFTherapy@compuserve.com. Home: 3515 Brandon St Pasadena CA 91107-4542 Office: Alma Family Svcs 9140 Whittier Blvd Pico Rivera CA 90660

BROTMAN, STANLEY SEYMOUR, federal judge; b. Vineland, N.J., July 27, 1924; s. Herman Nathaniel and Fanny (Melletz) B.; m. Suzanne M. Simon, Sept. 9, 1951; children: Richard A., Alison B. BA, Yale U., 1947; LLB, Harvard U., 1950. Bar: N.J. 1950, D.C. 1951. Pvt. practice Vineland, 1952-57; ptnr. Shapiro, Brotman, Eisenstat & Capizola, Vineland, 1957-75; judge U.S. Dist. Ct. N.J., Camden, 1975—; acting chief judge Dist. Ct. of V.I., 1989-92; mem. N.J. Bd. Bar Examiners, 1970-74. Chmn. editl. bd. N.J. State Bar Jour, 1969-74; contbr. articles to profl. jours. Trustee Newcomb Hosp., Vineland, 1953-68; v.p. Fed. Judges Assn., 1993-97. With U.S. Army, 1943-45, 51-52. Fellow Am. Bar Found., Jud. Conf. U.S. (space and facilities com. 1987-93); mem. ABA (ho. of dels. 1975-80, state del. 1982-93), Nat. Conf. Fed. Trial Judges (exec. com. 1984-87, chmn.-elect 1986-87, chmn. 1987-88, chmn. standing com. jud. selection, tenure and compensation 1988-92, chmn. steering com. of nominating com. 1992-93, standing com. Fed. Jud. Improvements 1992-96), Am. Judicature Soc. (dir. 1995—), ABA

Judicial Immigration Edn. Proj. (chmn. adv. com. 1996—), Fed. Bar Assn., N.J. State Bar Assn. (pres. 1974-75), Cumberland County Bar Assn. (pres. 1969-70), Assn. of Fed. Bar of State of N.J., Harvard U. Law Sch. Assn. N.J. (pres. 1974-75), Fed. Judges Assn. (v.p. 1993-97), Yale U. Alumni Assn., Am. Legion, Jewish War Vets., Yale Club, B'nai B'rith, Masons, Shriners. Office: MH Cohen US Courthouse 1 John F Gerry Plz PO Box 1029 Camden NJ 08101-1029

BROTMAN, STUART NEIL, management consultant, lawyer, educator; b. Passaic, N.J., Dec. 5, 1952; s. William and Edith (Berkowitz) B.; m. Gloria Z. Greenfield, June 9, 1985; children: Daniel Greenfield, Rachel Greenfield, Gabriel Greenfield. BS, Northwestern U., 1974; MA, U. Wis., 1975; JD, U. Calif.-Berkeley, 1978. Bar: Calif. 1978. Spl. asst. to the asst. sec. of commerce for comm. and info. Nat. Telecom. and Info. Adminstrn., Washington, 1978-81; pres. Comm. Strategies Inc., Cambridge, Mass., 1981-84; pres. Stuart N. Brotman Comm., Lexington, Mass., 1984—; adj. assoc. prof. Boston U. Sch. Law, 1990—; adj. prof. internat. law Fletcher Sch. Law and Diplomacy, Tufts U., 1990-97; lectr. comm. policy studies, Annenberg, Washington, 1988-96; lectr. Harvard Law Sch., 1997—; adj. fellow Ctr. for Strategic and Internat. Studies, 1999—; mem. editl. adv. com. Fed. Comm. Law Jour., 1986-94, EuroWatch: Econs., Policy and Law in the New Europe, 1992—, Transnat. Data and Comm. Report, 1991-94; counsel Winthrop, Stimson, Putnam & Roberts, N.Y. 1993-95. Mem. adv. com. UCLA Comm. Law Program, 1986-92; mem. nat. adv. coun. Northwestern U. Sch. Speech, 1990—. Editor: The Telecom. Deregulation Sourcebook, 1987, Telephone Company and Cable Television Competition, 1990; co-author, Comm. Law and Practice, 1995; editl. adv. bd. BNA Info. Law and Policy Report, 1996—, World Telecom. Law Report, 1998—, Internat. Jour. Comm. Law and Policy, 1999—; contbg. editor Cable Comm., Kitchener, Ont., Can., 1983-95, Cable Comm. Mag.; adv. bd. Jour. Sci. and Tech. Law, 1996—; contbr. articles to profl. jours. Annenberg Washington Program sr. fellow, 1988-94, sr. fellow Edward R. Murrow Ctr. for Internat. Comm., 1994-97. Mem. ABA (chmn. internat. comm. law com. internat. law and practice sect., 1992-95), Fed. Comm. Bar Assn., Northwestern U. Alumni Assn. (Merit award 1996). Democrat. Jewish.

BROTT, IRVING DEERIN, JR., lawyer, judge; b. Buffalo, June 28, 1930; s. Irving Deerin and Lillian May (Cooke) B.; m. Suzanne Hunt, July 11, 1959 (dec. Sept. 1979); children: Megan Cooke, Meryl Hunt, Gordon Alexander MacDonald; m. Donna Rey Kohl, Apr. 19, 1986. BS, Bowling Green State U., 1952; JD, U. Buffalo, 1955. Bar: N.Y. 1955. Assoc. Phillips, Lytle, Hitchcock, Blaine & Huber, Buffalo, 1957-68, ptnr., 1968-94; retired, 1995. Town justice Town of Aurora Ct., East Aurora, N.Y., 1966-94; asst. treas., treas., chmn. fin. com. Camp Fire Girls Buffalo and Erie County, 1966-79; bd. dirs. N.Y. Employee Benefits Conf., 1979-94, v.p., 1993-94. Mem. ABA, N.Y. State Bar Assn., Erie County Bar Assn., N.Y. State Magistrates Assn., Am. Pension Conf., East Aurora Country Club. Avocations: golf, tennis. Home: 30 Canterbury Ln East Aurora NY 14052-1358

BROTT, M. PAUL, architectural firm executive. BArch cum laude, Howard U., 1957; postgrad., U. Va., 1954. Registered architect Va., Conn., Washington, Md., Pa., N.J. Chmn. bd., CEO Ewing Cole Cherry Brott, Phila., 1993—. Fellow Soc. Am. Mil. Engrs., Royal Soc. Health, NAt. Trust Historic Preservation; mem. AIA (nat. del.), Tau Beta Pi. Office: Ewing Cole Cherry Brott Fed Res Bldg 100 N 6th St Philadelphia PA 19106-1590*

BROTT, THOMAS GORDON, neurologist; b. Chgo., Feb. 22, 1947; s. Paul B. and Marion Wallgron; n. Kaen Thalinger; children: Brian, David, Emily. AB cum laude, Harvard U., 1969; MD, U. Chgo., 1974. Intern Harvard Med. Svc., Boston, 1974-75; asst. prof. neurology U. Cin. Coll. Medicine, 1981-88, assoc. prof. neurology, 1988-93, vice chmn. dept. neurology, 1992—, prof. neurology, 1993—; sr. assoc. cons. Mayo Clinic, Jacksonville, Fla., 1998; clin. neurologist Cin. Neurol. Assocs., Inc. Contbr. articles to profl. jours. Neurology fellow Harvard U., 1975-78. Fellow Am. Acad. Neurology; mem. Am. Heart Assn. (pres. Southwestern Ohio area 1990-92), Am. Neurol. Assn., Alpha Omega Alpha. Office: Mayo Clinic 4500 San Pablo Rd Jacksonville FL 32224

BROTTMAN, MIKITA, humanities educator, writer; b. Sheffield, Eng., Oct. 30, 1966; came to U.S., 1998; d. Michael David and Linda Hoy; m. David Michael Brottman, July 17, 1995 (separated). BA with honors, St. Hilda's Coll., Oxford, Eng., 1987, MA, 1990; PhD, St. Hugh's Coll., Oxford, 1994. Asst. prof., dir. grad. studies English Ea. Mediterranean U., Gazi Magusa, No. Cyprus, 1992-94; asst. prof. comm. studies U. E. London, 1994-98; asst. prof. dept. comparative lit. Ind. U., Bloomington, 1998—. Author: Offensive Films, 1997, Meat is Murder, 1998, Hollywood Hex, 1999; film reviewer Spectator, 1998—. Nielson scholar St. Hilda's Coll., Oxford, 1987-90. E-mail: mbrottma@indiana.edu. Office: Ind U Dept Comparative Lit Ballantine Hall Bloomington IN 47405

BROTZEN, FRANZ RICHARD, materials science educator; b. Berlin, July 4, 1915; came to U.S., 1941; s. Georg and Lena (Paculty) B.; m. Frances Burke Ridgway, Jan. 31, 1950; children: Franz Ridgway, Julie Ridgway. B.S. in Metall. Engring., Case Inst. Tech., 1950, M.S., 1953, Ph.D., 1954. Salesman a Quimica Bayer Ltda., Rio de Janeiro, Brazil, 1934-41; mfrs. rep. R.G. Le Tourneau, Inc., Longview, Tex., 1947-48; sr. research assoc. Case Inst. Tech., Cleve., 1951-54; mem. faculty Rice U., Houston, 1954—, prof. materials sci., 1959-88, prof. emeritus, 1988—, dean engring., 1962-66, master Brown Coll., 1977-82; vis. prof. Max Planck Inst., Stuttgart, W.Ger., 1960-61, 73-74, Fed. Poly. Inst., Zurich, Switzerland, 1966-67, U. Lausanne, (Switzerland), 1981. Author papers in field. Chmn. Houston Contemporary Arts Assn., 1964-65. Served to 1st lt. AUS, 1942-46. Recipient Sr. Scientist award W. German Govt., 1973-74; Guggenheim fellow, 1960-61. Fellow Am. Soc. Metals (chmn. Houston chpt. 1980-81); mem. AIME, Am. Phys. Soc., Soc. Engring. Sci., Sigma Xi, Tau Beta Pi. Home: 2701 Bellefontaine St # H Houston TX 77025 Office: Rice U Dept Materials Sci PO Box 1892 Houston TX 77251-1892

BROTZMAN, DONALD GLENN, government official, lawyer; b. Logan County, Colo., June 28, 1922; s. Harry and Priscilla Ruth (Kittle) B.; m. Louise Love Reed, Apr. 9, 1944 (dec. Jan. 1995); children: Kathleen Love, Donald Glenn Jr.; m. Gwendolyn L. Davis, Aug. 3, 1996. BBS, JD, U. Colo., 1949. Bar: Colo. 1950, D.C., 1977. Since practiced in Boulder; mem. Colo. Ho. of Reps., 1950-52, Colo. Senate, 1952-56; U.S. atty. Dist. Colo., 1959-61; mem. 88th, 90th-93d congresses from 2d Dist. Colo., Washington, mem. ways and means com.; asst. sec. army for manpower and res. affairs, 1975-77; of counsel Hopkins and Sutter (and predecessors), Chgo., Washington and Dallas, 1989—; Mem. Colo. Crime Commn., 1952-56; Colo. mem. Commn. Uniform State Laws, 1954-56. Colo. chmn. Easter Seal and Colo. Highlander Boys Club drives, 1958, Youth in Govt. program, YMCA, 1958-62; Republican candidate for gov. of Colo., 1954, 56; chmn. Indsl. Energy Users Forum, Washington; pres. Washington Indsl. Round Table; bd. visitors USAF Acad., 1966-72; mem. Golden Spike Commn., 1969-70. Served to 1st lt., inf. AUS, 1942-46, PTO. Selected by Colo. press as Outstanding Freshman Mem. of House, 1951; as Outstanding Freshman Senator, 1953; recipient Disting. Svc. award Colo. Jaycees, 1954, Disting. Alumnus award Coll. Bus. and Adminstrn. U. Colo., 1975; named to U. Colo. Hall of Fame, 1976. Mem. ABA, Fed. Bar Assn., Colo. Bar Assn., Boulder County Bar Assn., Rubber Mfrs. Assn. (pres.), Natural Rubber Shippers Assn. (pres.), Tire Industry Safety Coun. (chmn.), Former Mems. of Congress Assn. (bd. dirs. 1993—), Am. Legion, VFW, Res. Officers Assn., Boulder C. of C., Masons (33 deg., medal of honor 1990), Rotary (bd. dirs. Boulder club), Beta Theta Pi, Phi Delta Phi (past magister). Methodist (trustee). Home: 400 Madison St Apt 1604 Alexandria VA 22314-1727 Office: 888 16th St NW Washington DC 20006-4103

BROUCEK, WILLIAM SAMUEL, printing plant executive; b. Statesboro, Ga., July 27, 1950; s. Jack Wolf and Emily Louise (Kupferschmid) B.; m. Sara Carolyn Bennett, May 10, 1975; children: Samuel Josiah, William Bennett. BBA, Ga. So. U., 1972. Adminstr. Willingway Hosp., Statesboro, Ga., 1972-73; dept. mgr. Deluxe Check Printers, Inc., Jacksonville, Fla., 1975-78, asst. prodn. mgr., 1978-82, asst. plant mgr., 1982-83, mgr. Atlanta plant, 1984-96, prodn. mgr. Atlanta plant, 1996-97, owner Global Signs, Norcross, Ga., 1997—. Bd. dirs. Ga. So. U. Alumni Assn., Statesboro, 1980-81; vol. Am. Cancer Soc., Jacksonville, 1981-83, Leadership Dekalb, 1992-93, bd. dirs. 1994-97, Gwinnett Initiative, 1993—; elder, trustee Eastminster Presbyn. Ch.; bd. dirs. Am. Heart Assn. Mem. Stone Mountain Indsl. Park Assn., DeKalb County C. of C., Aircraft Owners and Pilots Assn., Nantucket Swim and Racquet Club (Lilburn, Ga.). Republican. Avocations: aviation, old cars. Home: PO Box 1337 Tucker GA 30085-1337

BROUDE, RICHARD FREDERICK, lawyer, educator; b. L.A., June 6, 1936; s. Leo Martin and Frances (Goldman) B.; m. Paula Louise Galnick, June 8, 1958; children: Julie Sue, James Matthew, Mark Allen. BS, Washington U., St Louis, 1957; JD, U. Chgo., 1961. Bar: Ill. 1961, Calif. 1971, N.Y. 1989. Prof. law U. Nebr., Lincoln, 1966-69, Georgetown U., Washington, 1969-71; ptnr. Commons & Broude, L.A., 1974-77, Irell & Manella, L.A., 1977-80, Sidley & Austin, L.A., 1980-87, White & Case, L.A., 1987-90, Mayer, Brown & Platt, N.Y.C., 1990—; adj. prof. law U. So. Calif., L.A., 1978-90. Author: Reorganizations Under Chapter 11, 1986-99, Cases and Materials on Land Financing, 3d edit., 1985; editor: Insolvency and Finance in the Transportation Industry, 1993; mem. bd. editors Collier on Bankruptcy; contbg. editor Collier Bankruptcy Practice Guide. Fellow Am. Bar Found., Am. Coll. Bankruptcy; mem. ABA (com. on bus. bankruptcy), Am. Law Inst. (advisor Transnat. Insolvency Project), Internat. Bar Assn. (chair insolvency and credit rights com.), Bar Assn. of City of N.Y., Calif. Bar Assn., Nat. Bankruptcy Conf. (conferee, chair com. on internat. aspects). Office: Mayer Brown & Platt 1675 Broadway Ste 1900 New York NY 10019-5820

BROUDE, RONALD, music publisher; b. N.Y.C., Oct. 15, 1941; s. Irving and Anne Broude; m. Janyce Ingalls, Aug. 19, 1982. AB, Columbia Coll., 1962; MA, Columbia U., 1962, PhD, 1967. Pres., exec. editor Broude Bros. Ltd., N.Y.C. and Williamstown, Mass., 1973—; trustee Broude Trust for the publ. musicological editions, N.Y.C., 1981—; mem. exec. bd. Soc. for Textual Scholarship, 1989—, Early Music Am., 1994—.

BROUDER, GERALD T., academic administrator. Interim chancellor, provost Columbia (Mo.) Coll., 1992-95, pres., 1995—. Office: Columbia Coll 1001 Rogers St Columbia MO 65216*

BROUGH, BRUCE ALVIN, public relations and communications executive; b. Wayland, N.Y., Nov. 22, 1937; s. Alvin Elroy and Marjorie Huberta (McDowell) B.; m. Jane Virginia Koethen, Aug. 9, 1958; children: John David, Pamela Marjorie, Robert Bruce. BS in Pub. Rels., U. Md., 1960; MS in Mass Comm., Am. U., Washington, 1967. Comm. mgr. IBM Corp., various locations, 1965-74; owner, pres. Bruce Brough Assocs., Inc., Boca Raton, Fla., 1974-75; worldwide press rels. rep. Tex. Instruments Inc., 1975-76; v.p. pub. rels. Regis McKenna Inc., 1976-77; pres., prin. Pease/Brough Assocs., Inc., Palo Alto, Calif., 1978-80, Franson/Brough Assocs., Inc., San Jose, Calif., 1980-81; sr. v.p., dir. Advanced Tech. Network Hill and Knowlton, Inc., San Jose, Calif., 1981-86; sr. v.p., gen. mgr. Hill and Knowlton, Inc., Santa Clara, Calif., 1989; mgr. corp. pub. rels. Signetics Corp., 1986-87; mktg. comm. mgr. Corp. Ctr. Philips Components divsn. Philips Internat., B.V., Eindhoven, The Netherlands, 1987-89; dir. corp. comm. Centigram Comm. Corp., San Jose, Calif., 1989-90; prin. Brough Comm., Santa Cruz, Calif., 1994—; dir. pub. rels. Acer Am. Corp., San Jose, 1998—; dir. Pub. Rels. Acer Am. Corp., San Jose, 1998—; lectr. San Jose State U., 1977-83, 91—; cons. comm. and pub. rels., 1986—. Author: Publicity and Public Relations Guide for Business, 1984, revised edit., 1986, The Same Yesterday, Today and Forever, 1986; contbg. editor Family Bible Ency., 1973. Recipient Sustained Superior Performance award NASA, 1964, award Freedom's Found., 1963. Mem. Pub. Rels. Soc. Am. (accredited), Soc. Tech. Comm., Nat. Press Club, Sigma Delta Chi. Republican. Roman Catholic. Avocations: writing, fishing, skiing, boating, travel. Fax: 408-922-2949. E-mail: brucebrough@acer.com. Home: 155 Rabbits Run Rd Santa Cruz CA 95060-1526 Office: Acer Am Corp 2641 Orchard Pkwy San Jose CA 95134

BROUGH, JAMES A., airport terminal executive; b. 1938. BBA, Tex. A & M Coll., 1960. Commd. officer U.S. Navy, 1961-68; with Lockheed-GA, Marietta, Ga., 1968-69, RCA, West Palm Beach, Fla., 1969-71, Holland Oil, Fort Worth, 1971-72, Indpls. Airport Authority, Indpls., 1972-73, La Crosse (Wis.) Airport, 1973-75; exec. dir. Lexington-Fayette Union County Airport Bd., Lexington, Ky., 1975-87; with Birmingham (Ala.) Airport Authority, 1987—, now exec. dir., 1987—. Office: Birmingham Internat Airport 5900 Messer Airport Hwy Birmingham AL 35212-1057*

BROUGHTON, CAROLYN MILES, public relations executive; b. Cambridge, Mass., Mar. 2, 1958; d. David Alan and Martha Jean (Butler) Miles; m. Georg C. Broughton, May 7, 1988; 1 child, Christiana Marie. AA, Am. Coll., Paris, 1979; BA in Radio and TV Communications, George Washington U., 1982; MA in Human Resources Devel., Webster U., 1996. TV reporter Sta. WHSV-TV3, Harrisonburg, Va., 1981-82, Sta. WJKS-TV17, Jacksonville, Fla., 1982-85, Sta. WJXT-TV4, Jacksonville, 1985-89; pub. rels. coord. City of Jacksonville, 1989—; v.p. The Broughton Group, Disabilities Cons., Middleburg, Fla., 1994—. Bd. dirs., mem. pub. rels. com. P.A.C.E. Ctr. for Girls, Jacksonville, 1989—; vol., Webmaster All Sts. Early Learning Ctr., Jacksonville, 1991-97; city coord. dept. adminstrn. United Way, Jacksonville, 1993; city coord. Food Drive/Food Bank, Jacksonville, 1992. Recipient Cmty. Svc. Fla. Emmy award, 1987, Golden Palm award (2), 1997, Image award (3), 1998, Image Awds. (6), 1999, Silver Quill Awd., 1998. Mem. City County Communicators and Mktg., Fla. Govt. Communicators, Internat. TV and Video Assn., U.S. Fencing Assn. Avocations: Internet, Web content and design, photography, fencing, volunteerism.

BROUGHTON, PHILLIP CHARLES, lawyer; b. Findlay, Ohio, Sept. 21, 1930; s. Harold C. and Marian (Pierson) B.; children: Margaret Crockett, Phillip Charles, Anne Duvall, Elizabeth Cox. B.A., Bowling Green U., 1953; LL.B., U. Mich., 1957; LL.M., N.Y. U., 1962. Bar: N.Y. 1957. Practiced in N.Y.C., 1957—; mem. firm Thacher, Proffitt and Wood, 1957-93, of counsel, 1993—. Pres., bd. dirs. Midgard Found., N.Y.C.; pres., bd. trustees Asheville (N.C.) Art Mus.; trustee Newstead Found., U. N.C. Asheville Found., Preservation N.C. Mem. ABA, N.Y. State Bar Assn. Office: Thacher Proffitt & Wood 2 World Trade Ctr New York NY 10048-0203

BROUGHTON, RAY MONROE, economic consultant; b. Seattle, Mar. 2, 1922; s. Arthur Charles and Elizabeth C. (Young) B.; BA, U. Wash., 1947, MBA, 1960; m. Margret Ellen Ryno, July 10, 1944 (dec.); children: Linda Rae Broughton Silk, Mary Catherine Broughton Boutin; m. Carole Jean Packer, 1980. Mgr. communications and managerial devel. Gen. Electric Co., Hanford Atomic Products Ops., Richland, Wash., 1948-59; mktg. mgr., asst. to pres. Smyth Enterprises, Seattle, 1960-62; dir. rsch. Seattle Area Indsl. Council, 1962-65; v.p., economist (mgr. econ. rsch. dept.) First Interstate Bank of Oreg., N.A., Portland, 1965-87; ind. economic cons., 1987—; mem. econ. adv. com. to Am. Bankers Assn., 1980-83; mem. Gov.'s Econ. Adv. Council, 1981-88; dir. Oregonians for Cost Effective Govt., 1989-90; instr. bus. communications U. Wash., Richland, 1956-57. Treas., dir. Oreg. affiliate Am. Heart Assn., 1972-78, chmn., 1980-81, dir., 1980-84. Served to 1st lt. U.S. Army, 1943-46; ETO. Mem. Western Econ. Assn., Pacific N.W. Regional Econ. Conf. (dir. 1967-94), Nat. Assn. Bus. Economists (co-founder chpt. 1971), Am. Mktg. Assn. (pres. chpt. 1971-72), Alpha Delta Sigma. Author: Trends and Forces of Change in the Payments System and the Impact on Commercial Banking, 1972; contbg. editor Pacific Banker and Bus. mag., 1974-80. Home and Office: 10127 SW Lancaster Rd Portland OR 97219-6302

BROUGHTON, ROBERT STEPHEN, irrigation and drainage engineering educator, consultant; b. Corbetton, Ont., Can., June 29, 1934; s. Arthur Stephen and Luella Margaret (Gray) B.; m. Ruth Mabel Smith, May 11, 1957; children: G. Anne, Sharon Mae, Heather Louise, Stephen Russell. BS in Agr., U. Toronto, 1956, B in Applied Sci., 1957; MCE, MIT, 1959; PhD in Drainage Engring., McGill U., Montreal, 1972; LLD (hon.), Dalhousie U., Halifax, N.S., Can., 1989. Cert. profl. engr., Ont., Que. Jr. engr. John Deere Plow Co., Welland, Ont., 1956; rsch. asst. MIT, Cambridge, 1957-59; hydraulic engr. conservation br. Ont. Govt., Toronto, 1959-61; lectr. in agrl. engring. McGill U., 1962-63, asst. prof. agrl. engring., 1963-66, assoc. prof., 1966-74, prof., 1974-78, prof. emeritus, 1998—; from v.p. to pres. Can. Soc. Agrl. Engring., 1968-75, chmn. drainage rsch. com.; speaker farmers' meetings. Author, editor book in field; contbr. over 130 articles to publs. Tchr. Sunday sch. Beaurepaire United Ch., Beaconsfield, Que., 1965-72, clk. of session, 1973-78. Recipient Internat. Achievement award Can. nat. com. Internat. Commn. Irrigation and Drainage, 1993, Genie award, 1994, Mastery for Svc. award Mc Gill U., 1995; named to Internat. Drainage Hall of Fame, 1994. Fellow Can. Soc. Agrl. Engring. (Maple Leaf award 1978, James Beamish award 1989), Am. Soc. Agrl. Engrs., Ordre des Ingénieurs du Que.; mem. Assn. Profl. Engrs. Ont., Corrugated Plastic Pipe Assn. (life). Mem. United Ch. Can. Achievements include research on design and construction of subsurface drainage systems for control of waterlogging and salinity of irrigated lands, assisted with irrigation and drainage projects in India, Pakistan, Egypt, Trinidad, El Salvador, Barbados, Canada, etc. Office: McGill U Ctr Drainage Stds, Macdonald Campus, Sainte Anne de Bellevue, PQ Canada H9X 3V9

BROUILLETTE, YVES, insurance company executive; b. Ste.-Geneviève de Batiscan, Que., Can., May 2, 1951; s. Wallace and Mariette (Jacob) B.; m. Dominique Savard, Dec. 30, 1972; children: Benoit, Luc, Catherine. BS in Actuarial Sci., Laval U., Que., 1972; grad. advanced mgmt. program, Harvard U., 1987. Rsch. asst. Gauvin study com. on automobile ins. Govt. of Que., 1972-74; actuary Commerce Group Ins. Co., St.-Hyacinthe, Que., 1974-84, v.p., 1978-84, exec. v.p. personal lines, 1984-90, pres., CEO, 1990—; pres., CEO ING Can., 1990—; gen. mgr., country coord. ING Fin. Svcs. Internat.; chmn. Que. com. Ins. Bur. Can.; mem. several ins. industry bds., including Commerce Group and of Commassur, Inc.; apptd. gen. mgr., county coord. ING-FSI, NA. Fellow Can. Inst. Actuaries, Casualty Actuarial Soc. N.Y.; mem. Internat. Assn. Actuaries, Mt. Royal Club, others. Avocations: badminton, skiing, tennis. Fax: 416-444-6911. *

BROUMAS, JOHN GEORGE, retired banker, retired theatre owner; b. Youngstown, Ohio, Oct. 12, 1917; s. George Elias Broumas and Evelyn Vaveris; m. Ruth Darr, Sept. 16, 1944; children: Carole Ann, Sue Ann. Chem. warfare officer, Officer Candidate Sch., Edgewood Arsenal, Md., 1944; mem. class 1954 (hon.), West Point (N.Y.) Mil. Acad., 1975. Gen. mgr. Roth Theatres, Washington, 1946-54; chmn., pres. Broumas Showcase Theatres, Washington, 1954-83; dir. McLean and Madison Bank Va., 1975-91, chmn. of bd., 1983-91; chmn. of bd., pres. Madison Nat. Bank Va., 1986-91; actor, model motion pictures, commercials, 1992—; dir. asst. to pres. Theatre Owners of Am., 1958-68; dir. v.p. Nat. Assn. of Theatre Owners, 1968-82; chmn., pres., dir. Md. Theatre Owners Assn.; v.p., dir. Va. Theatre Owners Assn.; dir. Washington D.C. Theatre Owners Assn., 1966-80, Ohio Theatre Owners Assn., 1966-80; chmn. bd. dirs. Grey Eagle, Ltd., 1992—; chmn. Caledonia Assocs.; lectr. motion pictures and film making Georgetown U., 1972-78; chmn. exec. com Madison Nat. Bank Va., 1987-91; dir. James Madison Ltd., Washington, 1987-90; dir. Potomac Fin. Group, 1991—; chmn. Hellenic studies Md. U., 1989-90. Trustee Leukemia Soc. Am., 1988, Edn. and Tng. Found. Ptnrs. Am. Vocat. Edn., 1991—; dir. USO, 1956-80, Found. Religious Action, 1965-76, Washington chpt. Coll. Football Hall of Fame, 1989 (appreciation award 1989); adv. coun., chmn. D.C. area Will Rogers Hosp., 1968-78; exec. com. East Coast div. Child Help U.S.A., 1989; vol. Am. Cancer Soc., Kidney Found., United Way, Salvation Army, Boy Scouts Am., others. Maj. U.S. Army, 1941-46. Recipient Presdl. Disting. Svc. medal Cath. U., 1989, Ahepa Achievement of Excellence award, 1981, Gold Reel award 50 Yrs. Motion Picture Industry, 1978, Outstanding Svc. award, 1978, Gold medal, 1978, Fairfax County, Va. Sch. Patrol Appreciation award, 1977, Good Guy award Motion Picture Industry, 1974, Humanitarian award Local Area Motion Picture Industry, 1972, Muscular Dystrophy Appreciation award Jerry Lewis Telethon, 1972, and others; named to Order of St. Andrew, Greek Orthodox Ch., 1987. Mem. SAG, Res. Officers Assn. (life), Fightin Frogs (hon. mem. 4th regiment 1992), Variety Club Internat. (Variety medal 1985, Life Liner award 1985, Humanitarian award 1965-66, 78-79), The Motion Picture Pioneers (dir. 1953-86), Touchdown Club, Georgetown Club, West Point Soc. D.C. (mem. leadership coun. 1994), West Point Alumni Assn. Republican. Avocations: sports, writing, travel, charity work, movies. Home: 5505 Grove St Chevy Chase MD 20815-3422

BROUN, ELIZABETH, art historian, museum administrator; b. Kansas City, Mo., Dec. 15, 1946; d. Augustine Hughes and Roberta Catherine (Hayden) Gibson. B.A., U. Kans., 1968, Ph.D., 1976; cert. advanced study, U. Bordeaux, France, 1967. Curator prints and drawings Spencer Mus. Art, Lawrence, Kans., 1976-83; asst. prof. U. Kans., Lawrence, 1978-83; asst. dir. chief curator Nat. Mus. Am. Art, Washington, 1983-88; acting dir., 1988-89; dir. Nat. Mus. Am. Art, Washington, 1989—. Author: exhbn. catalogues Prints of Zorn, 1979, Prints and Drawings of Pat Steir, 1983, Patrick Ireland; Drawings 1965-85, 1986, Albert Pinkham Ryder, 1989; co-author: Benton's Bentons, 1980, Engravings of Marcantonio Raimondi, 1981. Woodrow Wilson fellow, 1968-69; Ford. Found. fellow, 1970-72. Mem. Phi Beta Kappa. Office: Nat Mus Am Art 8th & G Sts NW Washington DC 20560

BROUN, KENNETH STANLEY, lawyer, educator; b. Chgo., July 26, 1939; s. Fred G. and Helene (Smith) B.; m. Marjorie Enid Shagam, Jan. 29, 1961; children: Jonathan, Daniel. BS, U. Ill., 1960, JD, 1963. Bar: Ill. 1963, N.C. 1976. From assoc. prof. to prof. U. N.C. Law Sch., Chapel Hill, 1969—, hon. Brandis prof. law, 1990—; dir. Nat. Inst. Trial Advocacy, Chapel Hill, 1976-79; dean Sch. Law U.N.C., Chapel Hill, 1979-87; of counsel Petree & Stockton, Raleigh, N.C., 1988-94; mayor Town Chapel Hill, N.C., 1991-95; co-dir. program in trial advocacy Black Lawyers Assn. South Africa; mem. Adv. Com. on Fed. Rules of Evidence. Author: (with J. Seckinger) Materials in Trial Advocacy, 1988, (with F. Meisenholder et al) Problems in evidence, 1973, 3d rev. edit., 1988, (with E. Cleary et al) Handbook of Evidence, 4th edit., 1992, Brandis and Broun, North Carolina Evidence, 1998, (with J. Strong et al) Cases and Materials in Evidence, 1995. Recipient award for teaching excellence U. N.C., 1978; fellow Internat. Soc. Barristers, 1978. Fellow Am. Bar Found., Internat. Soc. Barristers; mem. ABA, Nat. Inst. Trial Advocacy (chmn. 1993-94), N.C. Bar Assn. (v.p. 1991-92), Order of Coif. Home: 414 Whitehead Cir Chapel Hill NC 27514-4833 Office: U NC Law Sch CB # 3380 Chapel Hill NC 27599-3380

BROUN, RICHARD HADAS, government administrator; b. New Rochelle, N.Y., Sept. 6, 1930; s. Saul Mark and Rachel (Hadas) B.; m. Judith June Alter, Aug. 28, 1952 (wid. Aug. 1988); children: Robin, Kevin; m. Karen Elsie Daly, Oct. 10, 1993. AB, Columbia Coll., 1952; BArch, Ill. Inst. of Tech., 1956. Housing and urban planning cons. Scranton, Pa., Meriden, Conn., 1956-61; dir. cmty. renewal program City of New Haven, Conn., 1961-64, City of Stamford, Conn., 1964-67; dep. dir. Met. area Analysis Divsn. US Dept. HUD, Washington, 1968-71, dir. Environ. and Land Use Divsn., 1971-75, dir. Office of Environ. Quality, 1975-81, dir. Office of Environ. and Energy, 1981-95, dir. Office of Cmty. Viability, 1995—. Mem. AICP (life), Am. Planning Assn. Office: US Dept Housing/Urban Devel 451 7th St SW Washington DC 20410-0001

BROUNTAS, PAUL PETER, lawyer; b. Bangor, Maine, Mar. 19, 1932; s. Peter Nicholas and Penelope (Spiropoulos) B.; m. Lynn Barrett Thurston, Sept. 7, 1963; children—Paul Peter, Jennifer VanWoert, Barrett Penelope. AB summa cum laude, Bowdoin Coll., 1954; BA, Oxford (Eng.) U., 1956, MA, 1960; LLB, Harvard U., 1960. Bar: Mass. 1960. Assoc. Hale and Dorr LLP, Boston, 1960-64, jr. ptnr., 1964-68, sr. ptnr., 1968—; guest presenter Harvard U. Bus. Sch., Cambridge, Mass., 1981-87; corp. sec. various corps.; panelist, lectr. corp., venture capital and securities law. Overseer Bowdoin Coll., Brunswick, Maine, 1974-82, pres. bd. overseers, 1979-82, trustee, 1983-96, chmn. bd. trustees, 1993-96; chmn. com. for Michael S. Dukakis Gov. of Mass., 1976-88; chmn. Dukakis for Pres. Com., 1987-88; mem. corp. Children's Hosp. Med. Ctr., Boston, 1965-87, Boston Mus. Sci., 1966-91, Mass. Gen. Hosp., Boston, 1983-94; mem. bd. overseers Newton Wellesley Hosp., 1990-96; mem. Marshall Scholar Selection Com. N.E. Region, 1973-75, 88-92; mem. Weston Planning Bd., Mass., 1967-72, chmn., 1970-72; chmn. Met. Boston Citizen's Coalition for Cleaner Air, 1969-71; bd. dirs. Mass. Ctrs. of Excellence Corp., 1985-87. Served with U.S. Army, 1956-58. Marshall scholar, 1954. Mem. ABA, Mass. Bar Assn., Boston Bar Assn., Assn. Marshall Scholars and Alumni (treas. 1965-71, bd. dirs. 1988-90). Avocations: skiing, golf. Office: Hale and Dorr LLP 60 State St Boston MA 02109-1816

BROUS, THOMAS RICHARD, lawyer; b. Fulton, Mo., Jan. 7, 1943; s. Richard Pendleton and Augusta (Gilpin) B.; m. Patricia Catlin, Sept. 12, 1964; children: Anna Catlin Brous, Joel Pendleton Brous. BSBA, Northwestern U., 1965; JD cum laude, U. Mich., 1968. Bar: Mo. 1968, U.S.

Dist. Ct. (we. dist.) Mo. 1968, U.S. Ct. Mil. Appeals 1968, U.S. Supreme Ct. 1971. Assoc. Watson & Marshall L.C., Kansas City, Mo., 1968-78, ptnr., 1978-96, mng. ptnr., 1992-94; shareholder Stinson, Mag & Fizzell, P.C., Kansas City, Mo., 1996—; mem. steering com. U. Mo. Kansas City Law Sch. Employee Benefits Inst., 1990—, chmn. 1992-93; mid-states key dist. EP/EO coun. IRS, 1997—. Author: Chapter 26, III Missouri Business Organizations, 1998; asst. editor Mich. Law Rev., 1966-68. Mem. vestry St. Andrews Episcopal Ch., Kansas City, 1974-77, Grace & Holy Trinity Cathedral, 1994—, chancellor, 1998—; trustee Mo. Repertory Theatre, Inc., Kansas City, 1990—, pres., 1995-98; v.p., treas. Barstow Sch., Kansas City, 1982-86; dir. Met. Orgn. to Counter Sexual Abuse, Kansas City, 1992-95. Capt. U.S. Army, 1968-72. Mem. ABA, Univ. Club (pres. 1988-89), Greater Kansas City Soc. Hosp. Attys., Kansas City Met. Bar Assn., Heart of Am. Employee Benefit Conf., The Mo. Bar Assn. (vice-chair employee benefits com. 1997—), Mo. Soc. Hosp. Attys., Delta Upsilon, Beta Gamma Sigma. Episcopalian. Avocations: reading, hiking, gardening. Office: Stinson Mag & Fizzell PC PO Box 419251 Kansas City MO 64141-6251

BROUSE, JOHN AMMON, JR., fiber optics engineer; b. Lewisburg, Pa., Oct. 6, 1948; s. John A. Sr. and Dotty I. Brouse; m. Suzanne Cardenas, Dec. 1, 1979; children: Jesse P., Jason P. BS in Meterology, U. Utah, 1974; MS in Telecom., U.S. Naval Postgrad. Sch., Monterey, Calif., 1984. Mil. officer USN, various locations, 1968-88; sys. engring. mgr. Jones Intercable, Ft. Lauderdale, Fla., 1988-91; sr. engr. Jones Intercable, Denver, 1991-92, mgr. advanced applications, 1992-93, dir. network devel., 1993-95, engring. dir., 1995-96, v.p. engring., 1996-97; v.p. engring. 21st Century, Chgo., 1997—; mem. curriculum adv. bd. U. Denver, 1995-97. Contbr. articles to profl. jours. Mem. Soc. Cable Telecom. Engrs. (chair scholarship com. 1995-97, Polaris award 1996), Internat. Engring. Consortium (exec. advisory bd.). Lutheran. Office: 21st Century Ste 600 350 N Orleans St Chicago IL 60654

BROUSSARD, CAROL MADELINE, writer, literary consulting agent, photographer; b. Albany, Calif.; d. Roy E. Avila and Adele (Belfils) Cazet; children: Valerie Madeline, Sean Hunter Rutledge. Student, West Hill Coll., Coalinga, Calif., Coll. Sequoias, Visalia, Calif., Inst. Metaphysics, La Brea, Calif., Fresno City Coll., 1995-97. Cert. human svcs. Former pub. and investigative journalist; pub. TV Watch, Tyler, Tex., 1969-74; resource sec. John C. Fremont Sch., Corcoran, Calif., 1974-77; editor Coalinga (Calif.) Record, 1978-81; pub., prodn. mgr. Kern Valley Chronicle, Lake Isabella, Calif., 1981-84; freelance writer, 1990—; featured TV show Writing Procedures, 1992; instr. home pub. Calif. State U. Adult Edn., Fresno, 1992, 95; instr. photography Clovis (Calif.) Adult Edn., 1993—, instr. ethnic watercolors, 1993-94, instr. investigative photo-journalism. 1994, instr. freelance photo-journalism, 1995; tchr. photog. lab. Clovis Teen Summer Sch., 1992. Author poetry; composer lyrics for Cajun Hoedown Man Century T.V., summer 1990, theme song Karma for Cinnimin Skin, Lance Mungia film, 1994. Vol., Literacy Program for WIN/WIN, Fresno Unified Sch. Dist., 1992, Trained Domestic Violence Response Team, Marjoree Mason Ctr., 1996-97; vol. mgr., receptionist Residential Shelter for Abused Women and Children; crisis hotline counselor, adv. Recipient Photo-Journalist award Calif. Newspaper Assn., 1983, Best Feature Photo award Calif. Justice System, 1984, World of Child Photo award Fresno City and County Offices, 1980, Poetic Achievement award Amherst Soc., 1990, award of merit World of Poetry, 1990, Golden Poet award, 1990, 91, Iliad Literary award, 1990, Poetry Editor's Choice award, 1992-93; spotlight interview Writers' Journal, 1992. Mem. Writers Internat. Network (speaker 1991, 92, coord. Vols. Conf. awards 1991). Republican. Avocation: writing.

BROUSSARD, FRANCIS PETER, English educator; b. Lafayette, La., Aug. 27, 1941; s. Francis Peter and Florence Marie (Gladu) B.; m. Carmen Mary Lafosse, Sept. 18, 1964 (div. 1975). BA in English, U. Southwestern La., 1962; MA in English, Tulane U., 1970. Tchg. asst. Tulane U., New Orleans, 1971-75; glazer Ryder's Stained Glass Studio, Opelousas, La., 1976-77; asst. editor Internat. Cmty. of Christ, Reno, 1978-79; GED instr. Sierra Nev. Job Corps-Stead Facility, Reno, 1979-81; glazer, craftsman Beau Soleil Stained Glass Studio, Opelousas, 1981-83; pvt. practice Abita Springs, La., 1984-89; English instr. Delgado C.C., Slidell, La., 1989-96, Southeastern La. U., Hammond, 1996—; chairperson GED dept. Sierra Nev. Job Corps, Stead Facility, Reno, 1980-81. Author of poetry. Narrator Creative Dance Ctr., Covington, La., 1985-99. With U.S. Army, 1965-69, Vietnam, 97-98. Mem. Nat. Coun. Tchrs. English, La. Archaeol. Assn. Avocations: amateur archeologist, gardening. Home: 72562 Indian Trail Rd Abita Springs LA 70420-2444 Office: Southeastern La Univ PO Box 304 Hammond LA 70404-0304

BROUSSARD, THOMAS ROLLINS, lawyer; b. Houston, May 30, 1943; s. Charles Hugh and Ethel (Rollins) B.; m. Mollie Brewster, Jan. 13, 1968. B.S. cum laude in Econs., U. Pa., 1964; J.D. cum laude, Harvard U., 1967. Bar: N.Y. 1968, Calif. 1973. Tax atty. Esso Standard Eastern, Inc., N.Y.C., 1967-70; gen. tax counsel Atlantic Richfield Co., N.Y.C., Los Angeles, 1970-74; v.p. corp. affairs, sec., gen. counsel Technicolor, Inc., Los Angeles, 1974-80; mem. firm Nelson & Broussard, Los Angeles, 1980-81; pres. Thomas R. Broussard, Ltd., P.C., Los Angeles, 1981—. Mem. ABA, Calif., Los Angeles County bar assns., Assn. of the Bar of the City of N.Y. Office: 5757 Wilshire Blvd Ste 648 Los Angeles CA 90036-3686

BROUSSEAU, CATHERINE F., school health services director; b. Lowell, Mass., Oct. 24, 1942; d. Martin J. and Beatrice M. (Moynihan) Dalton; m. Richard C.J. Brousseau, Sept. 6, 1965; 1 child, Margaret E. Diploma, St. Josephs Hosp., Lowell, 1963; BA, New Eng. Coll., Henniker, N.H., 1977, MS, 1982. Cert. AIDS facilitator; cert. sch. nurse. Emergency rm. charge nurse St. Josephs Hosp., 1963-78; pub. health nurse City of Lowell, 1994—, school health svcs. program dir., 1994—. Author articles and manual. Mem. Mass. Pub. Health Assn., Mass. Sch. Nurses Assn., Am. Sch. Health Assn., Nat. Sch. Nurses Assn., Sigma Theta Tau. Home: 467 Arlington St Dracut MA 01826-5228

BROUWER, BERT, art educator; b. Apr. 13, 1946. BS, U. Wis., 1972, MFA, 1976. From asst. to assoc. prof. Ind. State U., 1981-86; assoc. prof. Albright Coll., Reading, Pa., 1987-94; mem. faculty U. Wis., 1994-97; prof., chmn. dept. art and art history U. Ala., Birmingham, 1997—; vis. assoc. prof. Cornell U., Ithaca, N.Y., 1986-87. E-mail: bbrouwer@uab.edu. Office: U Ala Dept Art-Art History 900 13th Ave S Birmingham AL 35294

BROUWER, MARK NICHOLAS, publisher, newspaper, retired; b. Lynden, Wash., June 19, 1913; s. Jacob George and Kate (Prakken) B.; m. Cornelia Ella Stryker, July 7, 1937; 1 child, Margaret Lee. AB, Hope Coll., 1935; MA, U. Mich., 1941. Asst. pub. State Jour., Lansing, Mich., 1948-57; editor, pub. Willard (Ohio) Times, 1957-80, Crestline (Ohio) Advocate, 1984—; editor, pub. Reading (Mich.) Hustler, 1942-57; bd. dirs. Ohio Newspapers Assn., Columbus, 1968-80, pres., 1978-79. Mem. U.S. Power Squadrons, Crestline Area C. of C. (pres. 1986), Sandusky Sailing Club, Sandusky Yacht Club. Presbyterian. Avocations: golf, sailing, music, reading. Office: Crestline Advocate 312 N Seltzer St Crestline OH 44827-1403

BROUWER, WAYNE ALLEN, clergyman, writer; b. Willmar, Minn., Aug. 9, 1954; s. Lester and Eva Jane (Hoogeveen) B.; m. Brenda Doreen Karsten, Apr. 11, 1982; children: Kristyn, Kimberly, Kaitlyn. BA, Dordt Coll., 1976; MDiv, Calvin Theol. Sem., Grand Rapids, Mich., 1980, ThM, 1985; MA, McMaster U., Hamilton, Ont., Can., 1989, PhD, 1999. Ordained to ministry Christian Ref. Ch., 1980. Pastor Iron Springs (Alta., Can.) Christian Ref. Ch., 1980-85, 1st Christian Ref. Ch., London, Ont., 1985-86; tchr. Ref. Theol. Coll. Nigeria, Mkar, 1985-86; sr. pastor Harderwyk Christian Ref. Ch., Holland, Mich., 1994—; lectr. theology Redeemer Christian Coll., Ancaster, Ont., 1989; chmn. worship com. Christian Ref. Ch. in N.Am., Grand Rapids, 1988-94, chmn. publs., 1990-94, clk. of synod, 1994, v.p. synod, 1997. Author: Walking on Water, 1993, With New and Open Eyes, 1994, Hear Me, O God, 1995; contbr. over 450 articles to theol. jours. Bd. govs. Kings Univ. Coll., Edmonton, Alta., Can., 1982-85. Avocations: reading, writing, travel, lawn and garden care. Office: Harderwyk Christian Ref Ch 1627 W Lakewood Blvd Holland MI 49424-6241

BROVITZ, RICHARD STUART, lawyer; b. Rochester, N.Y., Aug. 20, 1951; s. Murray H. and Rifka R. (Rotenberg) B.; m. Joan F. Zarkower, Aug. 11, 1974; children—Justin, Jessica. B.S. cum laude with honors in Acctg., Sch. Mgmt., Syracuse U., 1973, M.S., 1973, J.D. cum laude, Coll. Law, 1976. Bar: N.Y. 1977, U.S. Dist. Ct. (we. dist.) N.Y. 1977, U.S. Tax Ct. 1979. Assoc. Wegman, Mayberry, Burgess & Feldstein, Rochester, 1977-79; assoc. Fix Spindelman, Turk, Himelein & Shukoff, Rochester, 1979-81, ptnr., 1982—, mng. principal, 1985—. Pi Mu Epsilon math. scholar Syracuse U. Mem. ABA, N.Y. State Bar Assn., Monroe County Bar Assn. (chmn. Rochester life underwriters com.), Justinian Hon. Law Soc., Beta Gamma Sigma, Beta Alpha Psi, Phi Kappa Phi. Office: Fix Spindelman Brovitz Turk Himelein & Shukoff Two State St Rochester NY 14614

BROWAR, LISA MURIEL, librarian; b. N.Y.C., Jan. 22, 1951; d. Elliott Andrew and Shirley (Kahn) B. B in English Lit., Ind. U., 1973, MLS, 1977; M in English Lit., U. Kans., 1976. Asst. curator Beinecke Libr. Yale U., New Haven, Conn., 1979-81, archivist Sterling Meml. Libr., 1981-82; curator spl. collections Vassar Coll. Libr., Poughkeepsie, N.Y., 1982-87; asst. dir. rare books and manuscripts N.Y. Pub. Libr., N.Y.C., 1987-96; dir. The Lilly Libr., Ind. U., Bloomington, 1996—. Editor Rare Books and Manuscripts Librarianship, 1999—. Mem. ALA, Assn. Coll. and Rsch. Librs. (sec. rare books and manuscripts sect. 1987-89, chair, 1994-95, editor 1999—), Soc. Am. Archivists, Bibliog. Soc. Am., Grolier Club. Democrat. Avocations: opera, theatre, motion pictures, photography, singing. Office: The Lilly Libr Indiana Univ Bloomington IN 47405

BROWDE, ANATOLE, electronics company executive, consultant; b. Berlin, June 10, 1925; came to U.S., 1940, naturalized, 1946; s. Alexander and Rebecca (Braude) Kutisker; m. Jacqueline Rousseau, Mar. 10, 1973; children: David, Elizabeth, Richard. BEE, Cornell U., 1948; postgrad., Northwestern U., 1948, Columbia U., 1951-52; MLA, Washington U., St. Louis, 1994, MA, 1996. Engr. Capehart-Farnsworth Corp., Ft. Wayne, Ind., 1948-51, Arma Corp., Bklyn., 1951-53; project engr. BOMARC, Westinghouse Electric Co., Balt., 1953-55; assoc. dir. missile dept. Avco Corp., Cin., 1955-59; with McDonnell Douglas Corp., 1959-90, v.p. engring. and mktg., 1979-81; v.p., gen. mgr. info. systems div. McDonnell Douglas Electronics Co., St. Charles, Mo., 1981-82, v.p. Microelectronics Ctr., 1982-87; v.p. ops. McDonnell Douglas Electronics Systems Co., 1987-89, dir. ops. integration, 1989-90; pres. Browde Cons. Inc., St. Louis, 1990—. Chmn. secondary schs. com. Cornell U., 1968—, mem. univ. council, 1971-77, 79—; trustee First Unitarian Ch., St. Louis, 1977-80, chmn., 1979-80, chmn. fin. com., 1985—. Republican. Unitarian. Clubs: Cornell (St. Louis), Cornell U. Coun. Developed Mercury, Gemini Spacecraft electronics, 1961-68, airborne collision avoidance system, 1968-72. Home: 12031 Carberry Pl Saint Louis MO 63131-3124

BROWDER, FELIX EARL, mathematician, educator; b. Moscow, July 31, 1927; s. Earl and Raissa (Berkmann) B.; m. Eva Tislowitz, Oct. 5, 1949; children: Thomas, William. SB, MIT, 1946; PhD, Princeton U., 1948; MA (hon.), Yale U., 1962; D (hon.), U. Paris, 1990. C.L.E. Moore instr. math. MIT, 1948-51, vis. assoc. prof., 1961-62, vis. prof., 1977-78; instr. Boston U., 1951-53; asst. prof. Brandeis U., 1955-56; from asst. prof. to prof. Yale U., 1956-63; prof. math. U. Chgo., 1963-72, Louis Block prof. math., 1972-82, Max Mason disting. svc. prof., 1982-87, chmn. dept., 1972-77, 80-85; v.p. rsch. Rutgers, The State U. N.J., 1986-91; univ. prof. Rutgers U., New Brunswick, 1986—; vis. mem. Inst. Advanced Study, Princeton (N.J.) U., 1953-54, 63-64; vis. prof. Princeton U., 1968, Inst. Pure and Applied Math., Rio de Janeiro, 1960, U. Paris, 1973, 75, 78, 81, 83, 85; sr. rsch. fellow U. Sussex, Eng., 1970, 76; Fairchild Disting. visitor Calif. Inst. Tech., Pasadena, 1975-76; invited speaker Internat. Congress of Math., 1970, Sci. Bd. Santa Fe Inst., 1986-98. Contbr. theorems to books, including Nonlinear Problems, 1966, Functional Analysis and Related Fields, 1970, Nonlinear Operators and Nonlinear Equations of Evolution in Banach Spaces, 1976, Nonlinear Functional Analysis and Its Applications, 1986. With AUS, 1953-55. Guggenheim fellow, 1953-54, 66-67, Sloan Found. fellow, 1959-63, NSF sr. postdoctoral fellow, 1957-58. Fellow AAAS (chmn. sect. A 1982-83), NAS (coun. mem. 1992-95), Am. Acad. Arts and Scis., Am. Math. Soc. (editor bull. 1959-68, 78-83, mem. coun. 1959-72, 78-83, mng. editor 1964-68, 80, exec. com. coun. 1979-80, colloquium lectr. 1970, pres. 1999—), Math. Assn. Am., Sigma Xi (pres. chpt. 1985-86). Achievements include development of linear and nonlinear partial differential equations, nonlinear functional analysis and fixed point and mapping theorems.

BROWDER, GEORGE CLARK, history educator, writer; b. Balt., Mar. 14, 1939; s. Francis Gilmer and Elma (Clark) B.; m. Etta Lee Mellard, June 16, 1959; children: Bruce Wayne, Brian Scott, Christopher Todd. BS, Memphis State U., 1961; MA, U. Wis., 1966, PhD, 1968. Asst. prof. to prof. SUNY, Fredonia, 1968-90, prof., 1990—. Author: Foundations of the Nazi Police State, 1990, Hitler's Enforcers, 1996. 1st lt., USAF, 1961-64. Office: SUNY Dept History Fredonia NY 14063

BROWDER, JOHN GLEN, former congressman, educator; b. Sumter, SC, Jan. 15, 1943; s. Archie Calvin and Ila (Frierson); m. Sara Rebecca Moore; 1 child, Jenny Rebecca. BA in History, Presbyn. Coll., 1965; MA in Polit. Sci., Emory U., 1971, PhD in Polit. Sci., 1971. Asst. in pub. relations Presbyn. Coll., Clinton, S.C., 1965; sportswriter The Atlanta Jour., 1966; investigator U.S. Civil Service Commn., Atlanta, 1966-68; prof. polit. sci. Jacksonville (Ala.) State U., 1971-87; mem. Ala. Ho. of Reps., Montgomery, 1982-86; sec. of state State of Ala., Montgomery, 1987-89; mem. 101st-104th Congresses from 3d Ala. dist., Washington, 1989-96; disting. vis. prof. nat. security affairs Naval Postgrad. Sch., Monterey, Calif., 1997—. Mem. Am. Polit. Sci. Assn., So. Polit. Sci. Assn. Democrat. Methodist. Home: 517 Pelham Rd N Jacksonville AL 36265-1825*

BROWDER, OLIN LORRAINE, legal educator; b. Urbana, Ill., Dec. 19, 1913; s. Olin Lorraine and Nellie (Taylor) B.; m. Edna Olive Forsythe, Sept. 9 1939 (dec. Nov. 1993); children: Ann Browder Sorensen, Catherine Browder Morris, John; m. Aleeta Swantner, May 17, 1997. A.B., U. Ill., 1935, LL.B., 1937; S.J.D., U. Mich., 1941. Bar: Ill. 1939. Practiced in Chgo., 1938-39; asst. prof. bus. law U. Ala., 1939-41; asst. prof. law U. Tenn., 1941-42; mem. legal dept. TVA, 1942-43; spl. agt. FBI, 1943-45; prof. law U. Okla., 1946-53, U. Mich., Ann Arbor, 1953-79; James V. Campbell prof. law U. Mich., 1979-84, prof. emeritus, 1984—. Author: (with others) American Law of Property, 1953, (with L.W. Waggoner) Family Property Transactions, 1965, 3d edit., 1980, (with R. A. Cunningham, G.S. Nelson, W.B. Stoebuck, D.A. Whitman) Basic Property Law, 1966, 5th edit., 1989, (with L. W. Waggoner and R. V. Wellman) Palmer's Cases on Trusts and Succession, 4th edit., 1983. Mem. Am. Bar Assn., Order of Coif, Phi Beta Kappa, Beta Theta Phi, Phi Alpha Delta, Phi Kappa Phi. Home: 1520 Edinborough Rd Ann Arbor MI 48104-4128

BROWDER, WILLIAM, mathematician, educator; b. N.Y.C., Jan. 6, 1934; s. Earl and Raissa B. B.S., MIT, 1954; Ph.D., Princeton U., 1958. Instr. U. Rochester, 1957-58; from instr. to assoc. prof. math. Cornell U., 1958-63; prof. math. Princeton U., 1964—, chmn. dept., 1971-73; vis. fellow Math. Inst. and Magdalen Coll., Oxford U. (Eng.), 1978-79; mem. Inst. Advanced Study, 1963-64, 83; prof. associe U. Paris, 1967-68; chmn. office Math. Scis. NAS-NRC, 1978-83; chmn. briefing panel for math. office of Sci. and Tech. Policy, 1983. NSF postdoctoral fellow, 1959-60; Guggenheim fellow, 1974-75. Mem. NAS, Am. Math. Soc. (v.p. 1977-78, pres. 1989-92), Am. Acad. Arts and Scis. Office: Dept Math Princeton U Princeton NJ 08540

BROWDY, JOSEPH EUGENE, lawyer; b. Bklyn., July 23, 1937; s. Philip and Fannie (Asherowitz) B.; m. Anita Sue Rubenstein, June 18, 1958; childrenF: Jennifer, Daniel. BA, Oberlin Coll., 1958; LLB, NYU, 1961. Bar: N.Y. 1962, D.C. 1982. Assoc. Paul, Weiss, Rifkind, Wharton & Garrison, N.Y.C., 1962-71, ptnr., 1972-97, of counsel, 1998—; adj. asst. prof. real estate NYU, 1976-86; lectr. in field. With U.S. Army Res., 1961-62. Mem. Assn. of Bar of City of N.Y. (com. real property law, chmn. subcom. on leasing 1989-92), Am. Coll. Real Estate Lawyers, Order of Coif, Phi Beta Kappa. Office: Paul Weiss Rifkind Wharton & Garrison 1285 Avenue of the Americas New York NY 10019-6065

BROWER, CHARLES NELSON, lawyer, judge; b. Plainfield, N.J., June 5, 1935; s. Charles Hendrickson and Mary Elizabeth (Nelson) B.; m. Carmen Elena Wiechmann-Yañez, May 23, 1987; children: Michael Claudio Joseph Hutchings, Carmen Désirée Ponti, Frederica Anne Amity, Jasmin Maria Ponti, Charles Hendrickson II. BA cum laude, Harvard U., 1957, JD, 1961; cert. Parker Sch. Comp. & Internat. Law, Columbia U., 1962. Bar: N.Y. 1962, D.C. 1970, U.S. Supreme Ct. 1967, U.S. Ct. Appeals (D.C. cir., 2d, 5th, 6th, 7th, 8th, 9th, 11th and fed. cirs.), U.S. Ct. Inernat. Trade, U.S. Dist. Ct. (so. and ea. dists.) N.Y., U.S. Dist. Ct. D.C. Assoc., then ptnr. White & Case, N.Y.C., 1961-69; asst. legal adviser European affairs Dept. State, Washington, 1969-71, dep. legal adviser, 1971-73, acting legal adviser, 1973; ptnr. White & Case, Washington, 1973-84, 88—; judge Iran-U.S. Claims Tribunal, The Hague, 1984-88, substitute judge, 1983-84, 88—; dep. spl. counselor to the Pres., Washington, 1987; counsel and advocate for U.S., 1992, Costa Rica, 1998, Internat. Ct. Justice, The Hague, 1992; mem. Register of Experts, UN Compensation Commn., 1991—; mem. sec. of state adv. com. on internat. law, 1996—; mem. panel of arbitrators and conciliators Internat. Ctr. for Settlement of Investment Disputes. Fulbright scholar Rheinische Friedrich-Wilhelms-Universitaet, Bonn, and Hochschule fuer Politik, Berlin, 1957-78. Mem. ABA (chmn. sect. internat. law 1981-82, mem. ho. of dels. 1982, 84-98, bd. govs. 1985-88, mem. nominating com. 1992-94), Internat. Law Assn. (hon. v.p. Am. br.), Internat. Bar Assn., Am. Soc. Internat. Law (v.p. 1994-96, pres. 1996-98, hon. v.p. 1998—), Am. Law Inst., Assn. of Bar of City of N.Y., Coun. Fgn. Rels., Inst. Transnat. Arbitration (chmn. adv. bd. 1994—), Southwestern Legal Found. (trustee 1996—), Met. Club, Chevy Chase Club. Episcopalian.

BROWER, DAVID CHARLES, transportation executive; b. Glens Falls, N.Y., Oct. 3, 1945; s. Charles William and Doris Mae (Hubbell) B.; m. Eloise Mary O'Neil, Sept. 11, 1965 (div. 1986); children: Benjamin, Daniel; m. Jeanne M. Douglass, July 23, 1988. BBA, U. Vt., 1970. Indsl. engr. IBM Corp., Burlington, Vt., 1970-71; mktg. rep. IBM Corp., Albany, N.Y., 1971-77; sr. sales rep. Digital Equipment Corp., Syracuse, N.Y., 1977-79; corp. order adminstrn. cons. Digital Equipment Corp., Maynard, Mass., 1979-83; from sales ops. cons. to dist. ops. mgr. Digital Equipment Corp., Marlborough, Mass., 1983-88, product ops. mgr., 1988-90; pres. Marlboro Transp., Marlborough, 1991—. Mem. Rotary (Marlboro pres., 1996-97), Marlboro C. of C. (bd. dirs.). Office: Marlboro Transp 455 Elm St Marlborough MA 01752-1802

BROWER, DAVID JOHN, lawyer, urban planner, educator; b. Holland, Mich., Sept. 11, 1930; s. John J. and Helen (Olson) B.; m. Lou Ann Brown, Nov. 26, 1960; children: Timothy Seth, David John, II, Ann Lacey. B.A., U. Mich., 1956, J.D., 1960. Bar: Ill. 1960, Mich. 1961, Ind. 1961, U.S. Supreme Ct. 1971. Asst. dir. div. community planning Ind. U., Bloomington, 1960-70; rsch. prof. dept. city and regional planning U. N.C., Chapel Hill, 1970—, assoc. dir. Ctr. for Urban and Regional Studies, 1970-94; pres. Coastal Resources Collaborative, Ltd., Chapel Hill and Manteo, N.C., 1980—; counsel Robinson & Cole, Hartford, Conn., 1986—; vis. prof., Vt. Law Sch., South Royalton, summers, 1994—. Author: (with others) Constitutional Issues of Growth Management, 1978; Growth Management, 1984, Managing Development in Small Towns, 1984, Special Area Management, 1985, Catastrophic Coastal Storms, 1989, Understanding Growth Management, 1989, Coastal Zone Management: An Evaluation, 1991, An Introduction to Coastal Zone Management, 1994. Mem. Am. Planning Assn. (bd. dirs. 1982-85, chmn.-founder planning and law div. 1978, co-chmn. substainable devel. group 1995—), Am. Inst. Cert. Planners. Democrat. Episcopalian. Home: 612 Shadylawn Rd Chapel Hill NC 27514-2009 Office: U NC CB # 3140 Chapel Hill NC 27599-3140

BROWER, DAVID ROSS, conservationist; b. Berkeley, Calif., July 1, 1912; s. Ross J. and Mary Grace (Barlow) B.; m. Anne Hus, May 1, 1943; children: Kenneth David, Robert Irish, Barbara Anne, John Stewart. Student, U. Calif., 1929-31; DSc (hon.), Hobart and William Smith Colls., 1967; DHL (hon.), Claremont Colls. Grad. Sch., 1971, Starr King Sch. for Ministry, 1971, U. Md., 1973; PhD in Ecology (hon.), U. San Francisco, 1973, Colo. Coll., 1977; other hon. degrees, New Sch. for Social Rsch., 1984, Sierra Nev. Coll., 1985, Unity Coll., Maine, 1989. Editor U. Calif. Press, 1941-52; exec. dir. Sierra Club, 1952-69, also bd. dirs., mem. editorial bd., 1935-69, hon. v.p., 1972—; dir. John Muir Inst. Environ. Studies, 1969-71, v.p., 1968-72; pres. Friends of the Earth, 1969-79; founder, chmn. Friends of the Earth Found., 1972-84, bd. dirs.; founder Environ. Liaison Ctr., Nairobi, 1974; founder, chmn. Earth Island Inst., San Francisco, 1982—; founder, pres. Earth Island Action Group, 1989; founder biennial Fate and Hope of the Earth Confs., N.Y.C., 1982, Washington, 1984, Ottawa, 1986, Managua, 1989; activist in conservation campaigns, Kings Canyon Nat. Pk., 1938-40, Dinosaur Nat. Monument, 1952-56, Alaska parks and forests, 1954—, North Cascades Nat. Pk., 1955-94, Cape Cod, Fire Island, Point Reyes nat. seashores, 1960-68, Redwood Nat. Pk., 1963-68, Great Basin Nat. Park, 1965, Galapagos Islands World Heritage, 1965-68, Grand Canyon 1952-68, Snowdonia Nat. Park, 1970, 71, population and growth control and nuclear proliferation issues, Nat. Wilderness Preservation System, 1951-64, James Bay defense, 1991-94, conservation lectr., U.S., 1939—, Finland, 1971, Sweden, 1972, Kenya, 1972, 74, Italy, 1972, 74, 79, 82, 91, 94, Australia and N.Z., 1974, Japan, 1976, 78, 90, 92, U.K., 1968, 70, 93, USSR, 1985, 88, 90, 91, 92, France, 1970, 90-91, Fed. Republic Germany, 1989, Berlin, 1990, Nicaragua, 1988, 89, Brazil, 1992, The Netherlands, 1993-94; founder Trustees for Conservation, 1954, sec., 1960-61, 64-65; founder Sierra Club Found., 1960; bd. dirs. Citizens Com. Natural Resources, 1955-78; chmn. Natural Resources Coun. Am., 1955-57; bd. dirs. North Cascades Conservation Coun., from 1957, Rachel Carson Trust for Living Environment, 1966-72, cons. expert, from 1973; founder, steering com. League Conservation Voters, 1969-80; founder Les Amis de la Terre, Paris, 1970; founder, guarantor Friends of the Earth U.K., 1970-88; chmn. Earth Island Ltd., London, 1971-74; active Restoring-the-Earth movement, from 1986, founder Global CPR Svc., 1990, leader del. to Lake Baikal, Siberia, 1988, 90, 91, 92, mem. various adv. bds. including Found. on Econ. Trends, Nat. Strategy, Coun. Econ. Priorities, Zero Population Growth, Yosemite Concessions Svc., Earth Day 1990, 94; mem. Com. on Nat. Security; adv. to pres. Interface, Inc., 1997—. Initiator, designer, gen. editor: Sierra Club Exhibit Format Series, 20 vols., 1960-68, Friends of the Earth series The Earth's Wild Places, 10 vols., 1970-77, Celebrating the Earth series, 3 vols., 1972-73; numerous other films and books, biographee in Encounters with the Archdruid (John McPhee), 1970; (autobiography) Vol. 1, For Earth's Sake: The Life and Times of David Brower, 1990, Vol. 2, Work in Progress, 1991; co-author: (Steve Chapple) Let the Mountains Talk, Let the Rivers Run, 1995; contbr. articles to nat. mags., profl. publs., others; subject video documentary produced for Sta. KCTS, Seattle, shown nationally on PBS; contbr. to U.S. Army mountain manuals, instruction, 1943-45. Participant in planning for 1992 UN Conf. on Environment, Rio de Janeiro, 1987-92. Served as 1st lt. with 10th Mountain div. Inf. AUS, 1943-45; maj. Inf.-Res. ret. Decorated Bronze Star; recipient awards Calif. Conservation Coun., 1953, Nat. Parks Assn., 1956, Bklyn. Coll. Libr. Assn., 1970, also Carey-Thomas award, 1964, Paul Bartsch award Audubon Naturalist Soc. of Cen. Atlantic States, 1967, Golden Ark award the Prince of The Netherlands, 1979, Golden Gadfly award Media Alliance, San Francisco, 1984, Rose award World Environment Festival, Ottawa, Can., 1986, Strong Oak award New Renaissance Ctr., 1987, Lewis Mumford award Architects Designers Planners for Social Responsibility, 1991, Robert Marshall award, 1994, Blue Planet prize Asahi Glass Found., Japan, 1998; hon. fellow John Muir Coll., U. Calif., San Diego, 1986; nominated Nobel Peace Prize, 1978, 79, 98. Mem. Nat. Parks and Conservation Assn. (hon.), The Mountaineers (hon.), Appalachian Mountain Club (hon.), Sierra Club (1933—, John Muir award 1977), Am. Alpine Club (hon.). Many first ascents, 70 in Mountain Ranges in Sierra Nevada, 1934-41, 3 in Pinnacles, N.Mon., 1934-35, Shiprock, N. Mex., 1939. Office: Earth Island 300 Broadway St Ste 28 San Francisco CA 94133-4545 *It is true that some major resources of wildlife and wilderness, and all they mean to people, are still intact thanks to conservation battles I have shared. For this I can only be grateful—for the help, and the hope that future battles for these irreplaceable things will be as successful as well as the global efforts to restore what we can. They will succeed if enough people realize that this generation is not required to race through all the resources it can find, if humanity comprehends that this is the only earth, and there is no spare.*

BROWER, FORREST ALLEN, retired health facility administrator; b. Far Rockaway, N.Y., Oct. 22, 1930; s. Walter Kimball and Willa May B.; m. Mary Jo Coulter, Dec. 28, 1951; children: Catherine Lee Brower Zettler, Todd Coulter. BA, Ohio Wesleyan U., 1952; MS, Columbia U., 1956. Adminstrv. resident Harper Hosp., Detroit, Mich., 1955; adminstrv. asst. East Orange (N.J.) Gen. Hosp., 1956-57, asst. dir., 1958-64, dir., 1965-76, pres., CEO, 1977-85; group v.p. N.J. Hosp. Assn., Princeton, 1986-94; COO Health Rsch. & Edn. Trust N.J., Princeton, 1986-94; ret., 1994; trustee N.J. Hosp. Assn., 1971-72, 75-79, 81-85, 86-93; trustee Mercer Med. Ctr.,

Trenton, N.J., 1994-97; bd. dirs. Capital Health Sys., 1998—. Trustee, vice chmn. Voices, Pennington, N.J., 1988-93; active Glenridge (N.J.) Bd. Edn., 1971-74, Bd. United Fund, Glen Ridge, N.J., 1968-72; bd. dirs. Community Health Care N.J., 1963-86, pres., 1968-72; bd. trustees United Meth. Homes N.J., 1976-88, United Meth. Homes N.J. Found., 1992-98. 1st lt. USAF, 1952-54, Japan. Fellow Am. Coll. Healthcare Execs.; mem. Am. Hosp. Assn., N.J. Hosp. Assn., N.J. Hosp. Adminstrs. Forum, Nassau Club. Avocations: geneaology, piano, opera, jogging, swimming.

BROWER, JAMES CALVIN, graphic artist, painter; b. Clarksburg, W.Va., Dec. 30, 1914; s. Leroy Cooper and Margaret Wood (Watkins) B.; m. Elsie Margaret Day, Sept. 19, 1936; children: James Lawrence, Sandra Joan, Margaret, Linda Ann, Beth. Grad. high sch., Charleston, W.Va., 1932. Pvt. practice Huntington, W.Va., 1933-43, Toledo, 1952—; ptnr., art dir. Brower, Brownsberger and Burda, Toledo, 1944-51; dir. art and design Meeks Heit Pub. Co., 1992—. Illustrator: Education for Sexuality, 1970, Human Sexuality, 1982, Education for Sexuality and HIV/AIDS, 1993; paintings featured in The Creative Artist, 1990, The Best of Watercolor 2, 1997, The Best of Watercolor Composition, 1997. Recipient Pres. award Okla. Watercolor Soc., 1987, Past Pres. award San Diego Watercolor Soc. Internat. Exhbn., 1989. Mem. Ohio Watercolor Soc. (bd. dirs. 1986-92, publicity chmn. 1986-92, Gold medal 1984, Charles Burchfield Meml. award 1991, Exhbn. award 1992), Northwestern Ohio Water Color Soc. (pres. 1983-84), Nat. Water Color Soc. (Artist's Mag./Liquitex award 1990, Mem.'s Exhbn. awards 1996, 98), Ky. Watercolor Soc. (artist mem.), Ga. Watercolor Soc. (Gold award Nat. Exhbn. 1990), Toledo Fedn. Art Soc. (pres. 1987-88), Tile Club Toledo. Republican. Presbyterian. Avocations: chess, bridge. Home and Office: 2222 Grecourt Dr Toledo OH 43615-2918

BROWER, JANICE KATHLEEN, library technician; b. Chgo., July 29, 1952; d. Gerald B. and Emily (Kavicky) B. AA, Lincoln Coll., 1973; BS, Ill. State U., 1975; postgrad., U. Okla., 1984-86. Libr. assoc. Chgo. Pub. Libr., 1975-80, 81-83; libr. technician U. Okla. Biol. Sta., Norman, 1987; libr. technician Jim E. Hamilton Correctional Ctr. Okla. Dept. of Corrections, Hodgen, 1987—. Lutheran. Avocations: reading, walking, visiting historical sites and museums, architecture. Office: Jim E Hamilton Correctional Ctr HC 63 Box 5390 Hodgen OK 74939-9712

BROWER, ROBERT CHARLES, rehabilitation counselor, small business owner; b. Allendale, N.J.; s. William P. and Adele (Braun) B.; m. Hilja Kristiansen, Dec. 21, 1963; children: Robert K., Kristine D. BA in Psychology, Rutgers U., 1963; MDiv, Luth. Theol. Sem., Phila., 1966; postgrad. in counselign, Princeton Theol. Sem., 1970-71; postgrad. in Bus. Adminstrn., N.Y. Inst. Tech., 1993—. Cert. rehab. counselor, disability mgmt. specialist, case mgr., N.Y., U.S. Dept. Labor; ordained to ministry Lutheran Ch., 1966. Pastor St. Paul Luth. Ch., E. Windsor, N.J., 1966-71; psychiatric rehab. counselor N.Y. State Office of Vocations., Cen. Islip, 1971-73; coord. Rehab. Inst., Mineola, St. James, N.Y., 1973-74; program dir. and mental health clinic adminstr. Skills Unlimited, Oakdale, N.Y., 1974-78; dist. mgr. Intracorp subs. CIGNA, Woodbury, White Plains, N.Y., 1978-83; mgr. disability mgmt. svcs. Nat. Ctr. Disability Svcs. (formerly Human Resources Ctr.), Albertson, N.Y., 1984-90; pres. Brower Rehab. Svcs., Inc., Medford, N.Y., 1990—; adj. prof. Sch. Counseling, Rsch., Spl. Edn. and Rehab., Hofstra U., Uniondale, N.Y., 1988—; speaker in field. Bd. dirs. Cert. Ins. Rehab. Specialist Commn., rep. to Found. for Rehab. Cert., Edn. and Rsch., 1993—, treas. found., treas. commn., 1993-94, vice chair, 1994-95, chair, 1995-96. Mem. AAUP, Nat. Rehab. Assn. (chmn. commn. for certification of disability mgmt. specialists commn.), Nat. Rehab. Profls. in Pvt. Sector, Profl. Rehab. Assn. L.I. and N.Y.C. (Rehab. Profl. of Yr. in Ancillary Care 1994), Delta Mu Delta. Avocations: sailing, photography. Home: 37 Crooked Pine Dr Medford NY 11763-4329

BROWER, SARA E. MASKELL, elementary education educator; b. Des Moines, Aug. 27, 1952; d. Thomas Paul and Jacqueline Zzis Maskell; children: Lauren Elizabeth, Matthew V.P. BA in Early Childhood Edn. and Sociology, Hood Coll., 1974; MEd in Sch. Improvement Leadership, Goucher Coll., 1998. Cert. elem. tchr., Md., advanced profl., early childhood edn. Tech. tng. specialist RMS, Catonsville, Md., 1991-92; workshop facilitator Dundalk (Md.) C.C., 1992-93; elem. tchr. Balt. County Pub. Schs., 1993—; rep. Ctrl. Area Tchrs. Coun., 1993-94; mentor students Towson State, 1996-97. Mem. PTA; sustaining mem. Jr. League. Mem. ASCD, Phi Lambda Theta.

BROWMAN, DAVID L(UDVIG), archaeologist; b. Dec. 9, 1941; s. Ludvig G. and Audra (Arnold) B.; m. M. Jane Fox, Apr. 24, 1965; children: Lisa, Tina, Becky. BA, U. Mont., 1963; MA, U. Wash., 1966; PhD, Harvard U., 1970. Hwy. archeologist Wash. State Hwy. Dept., Olympia, 1964-66; field dir. Yale U., New Haven, Conn., 1968-69; tutor Harvard U., 1969-70; mem. faculty Washington U., St. Louis, 1970—, prof. archeology, 1984—, chmn., 1986—; dir. Cons. Survey Archeology, St. Louis, 1976—, Inst. Study of Plants, Food and Man, Kirkwood, Mo. 1979-84: cons. St. Louis Dept. Parks and Recreation, 1978—. Editor/author: Advances in Andean Archeology, 1978; Economic Organization of Prehispanic Peru, 1984; Risk Management and Arid Land Use Strategies in the Andes, 1986; editor: Cultural Continuity in Mesoamerica, 1979; Early Native Americans, 1980. Charter mem. Confluence St. Louis, 1983; mem. Gov.'s Adv. Coun. Hist. Preservation, 1982-89, sec. 1989-91. NSF fellow, 1967, grantee, 1974-75, 85—. Fellow AAAS; mem. Soc. Profl. Archeologists (sec.-treas. 1981-83, grievance coord. 1997-98), AAPA (chpt. pres. 1980-82), Registry Profl. Archaeologists (grievance coord. 1998-99), Mo. Assn. Profl. Archeologists (v.p. 1981-82), Mo. Archeology Soc. (trustee 1977—), Sigma Xi (chpt. pres. 1985-). Roman Catholic. Avocations: hiking, gardening. Office: Campus Box 1114 Washington U Saint Louis MO 63130

BROWN, ALAN ANTHONY, marketing executive; b. Winthrop, Mass., Feb. 6, 1936; s. Joseph Raymond and Harriet (Taylor) B.; m. Margret Egan, Aug. 8, 1961 (div. Feb. 1971); 1 child, Alan Jr.; m. Virginia A. Preno, Apr. 12, 1975; children: Linda, Diane, Michael, Sandra. *Son Alan Jr., BS 1985 from Stanford University, California, is Vice President ofInternational Marketing at Mastercard. Son Michael, BS 1998 from Franklin PierceCollege, New Hampshire, is a Financial Specialist for Fidelity Investments. Daughter Sandra is a manager for Holiday Inns.* BBA, Suffolk U., 1981, MBA, 1984. Test methods engr. RCA, Burlington, Mass., 1964-68; field svc. engr. BLH Electronics, Waltham, Mass., 1968; sales engr. AVCO Corp., Wilmington, Mass., 1968-71; sales rep. ITT Tech. Inst., Chelsea, Mass., 1971-75; dist. mgr. Continental Resources, Bedford, Mass., 1975-78; area mgr. Philips Test & Measurement, Woburn, Mass., 1978-81; distributor sales mgr. Hayes InstSer Inc., Billerica, Mass., 1981-85; sr. sales engr. Eaton Corp., Beverly, Mass., 1985-86; v.p. mktg. Hayes Instrument Svc. Inc., Billerica, Mass., 1986-92; svc. mgr. EIL Instruments Inc., Burlington, Mass., 1992-94; pres., CEO Viking Enterprise, Winthrop, Mass., 1994—; del. Nat. Conf. of Standards Lab., Boulder, Colo., 1985—. Campaign worker Richard Deminto, Winthrop, 1988. Recipient Acad. Achievement award Sch. of Mgmt., 1983. Mem. Assn. MBAs, IEEE, Winthrop Lodge of Elks, VFW Post #6712,, Delta Mu Delta. Avocations: baseball cards, autographs. Home: 57 Central St Winthrop MA 02152-1633 Office: Viking Enterprise 57 Central St Winthrop MA 02152-1633

BROWN, ALAN CHARLTON, retired aeronautical engineer; b. Whitley Bay, England, Dec. 5, 1929; came to U.S., 1956; s. Stanley and Dorothy (Charlton) B.; m. Gweneth Evelyn Bowler, July 26, 1952; children: Yvonne, Christine, Diane, Maureen. Diploma aeronautics, Hull (Eng.) Tech. Coll., 1950; MS, Cranfield (Eng.) Inst Tech., 1952, Stanford U., 1965. Apprentice Blackburn Aircraft Ltd., Brough, Eng., 1945-50; aerodynamicist Bristol (Eng.) Aeroplane Co., 1952-56; rsch. scientist U. So. Calif., L.A., 1956-58, Wiancko Engring. Co., Pasadena, Calif., 1958-60, Lockheed Missiles & Space Co., Palo Alto, Calif., 1960-66; group leader Lockheed Aeronautical Systems Co., Burbank, Calif., 1966-69; dept. mgr. Lockheed Aeronautical Sys. Co., Burbank, Calif., 1969-78; chief engr. F-117A Lockheed Aerospace Systems Co., Burbank, Calif., 1978-82, dir. stealth tech., 1982-89; dir. engring. Lockheed Corp., Calabasas, Calif., 1989-92. Fellow AIAA (Aircraft Design award 1990), NAE, Royal Aero. Soc. Democrat. Avocations: music, tennis, chess, model aircraft. Home: 388 Aptos Ridge Cir Watsonville CA 95076-8518

BROWN, ALAN CRAWFORD, lawyer; b. Rockford, Ill., May 12, 1956; s. Gerald Crawford and Jane Ella (Herzberger) B.; m. Dawn Lestrud, Apr. 16, 1998; children: Parker Crawford, Sydney Danielle, Sarah Kate, Drew Kristen. BA magna cum laude, Miami U., Oxford, Ohio, 1978; JD with honors, U. Chgo., 1981. Bar: Ill. 1981, U.S. Dist. Ct. (no. dist.) Ill. 1981, U.S. Tax Ct. 1986. Assoc. Kirkland & Ellis, Chgo., 1981-87; sr. assoc. Coffield Ungaretti Harris & Slavin, Chgo., 1987-89; ptnr. McDermott, Will & Emery, Chgo., 1989—. Deacon Northminster Presbyn. Ch., Evanston, Ill., 1989-92; apiarist Chgo. Botanic Garden, Glencoe, Ill., 1988-97. Mem. Order of Coif, Phi Beta Kappa. Office: McDermott Will & Emery 227 W Monroe St Ste 3100 Chicago IL 60606-5096

BROWN, ALAN J., electrical engineer; b. San Diego, Nov. 8, 1963; s. Vance E. and Doris C. B. BSEE, Calif. State U., Sacramento, 1987; MBA, U. San Diego, 1992. Registered profl. engr., Calif., Nev., Ariz. From engr. to pres. BSE Engring. (formerly Brown and Zammit Engring.), San Diego, 1987—. Mem. IEEE, Inst. Mgmt. Accts., Illuminating Engring. Soc. (pres. San Diego chpt. 1991-92), Soc. Mil. Engrs. (pres. San Diego post 1996-97), Internat. Assn. Electrical Inspectors. Office: BSE Engring 9620 Chesapeake Dr Ste 108 San Diego CA 92123-1324*

BROWN, ALAN WHITTAKER, accountant; b. Pullman, Wash., Mar. 21, 1950; s. Richard Maurice and Kathryn (Doane) B.; adopted s. Waynona (Newcom) B; m. Carmen Lee Morales, Oct. 13, 1990. BS, U. Ill., 1987. CPA, Calif. Sr. staff acct. Brookside Hosp., San Pablo, Calif., 1987-90; acct. S.J. Gallina & Co., Walnut Creek, Calif., 1990-94; fin. analyst Kaiser Permanente, Oakland, Calif., 1994-97; comptr. Nat. Ctr. Genome Resources, Santa Fe, N.Mex., 1997—. Mem. AICPA, Balloon Fedn. Am. Avocations: hot-air ballooning, gourmet cooking. Office: NCGR 1800-A Old Pecos Trail Santa Fe NM 87505

BROWN, ALICE ELSTE, artist; b. Balt., Nov. 5, 1922; d. Albert John and Anna Emily (Rosenbauer) Elste; m. Charles Hammond Brown, Nov. 30, 1946 (dec. Sept. 1994); children: Charles Hammond Jr., Barbara Brown Lander, Laurie Ellen. RN, U. Md., 1944; BS in Nursing Edn., Johns Hopkins U., 1950; BA in Art, Coll. Notre Dame, Balt., 1978; MA in Painting and Art Edn., Towson U., 1984. Nurse, head nurse U.S. Army Nurse Corps, U.S., Europe, 1944-46; pub. health nurse Balt. Health Dept., 1950-52; artist Balt., 1960—; artist-in-residence Pyramid-Atlantic Studios, Balt., 1987-92; adj. instr. drawing and design, Coll. Notre Dame, 1980. One-woman exhbns. include Roland Park Libr., 1965, Greater Balt. Med. Ctr., 1964; group exhbns. include Md. Towson YMCA Fedn. Art Juried Show, 1974 (Best of Show), Jewish Cmty. Ctr., 1970s, Towson YMCA, 1960s, Easton (Md.) Acad. Arts 13th Ann. Juried Show, 1977, Coll. Notre Dame Invitational Drawing and Print Show, 1980, Western Md. Coll. 3 Artist Show, Westminster, 1990, Mechanic Theatre, Balt., 1990, 2 Artist Show, Katzenstein Gallery, Balt., 1991, Pyramid Atlantic, Washington, 1990, Rehoboth (Del.) Art League, 1996, 97. Home nursing tchr. ARC, Balt., 1950s; asst. leader, leader Girl Scouts Am., Balt., 1960s; vol. docent Balt. Mus. Art, 1970s. 1st lt., U.S. Army Nurse Corps, 1944-46. Recipient Steinbugler award in art, Coll. Notre Dame, 1978. Mem. Nat. Mus. Women in the Arts (charter mem.), Md. Art Place, Rehoboth Art League (Thomas McFarland Skelly Meml. award 1998), Johns Hopkins U. Alumni Club, Pi Lambda Theta. Democrat. Avocations: walking, biking, reading, archaeology, environmental concerns.

BROWN, ALVIN, housing and urban development administrator; m. Santhea Hicks. Grad. in Philosophy, Jacksonville U., MBA; postgrad., Harvard U. Sr. advisor for econ. devel. U.S. Dept. Commerce, Washington; dep. adminstr. for rural bus. USDA, Washington; dir. Pres.'s Empowerment Zone and Enterprise Cmty. Program, Washington; dir. Spl. Actions Office, Office of the Sec., U.S. Dept. Housing and Urban Devel., Washington; exec. asst. Pres.-Elect Clinton/Gore Transition Team, The White House, 1992, dep. assoc. dir. Office of Presdl. Personnel; rep. V.P.'s Cmty. Empowerment Bd. FAX: 202-708-4087. Office: Dept Housing and Urban Devel Office of the Sec 451 7th St SW Washington DC 20410-0002

BROWN, AMOS CLEOPHILUS, minister; b. Jackson, Miss., Feb. 20, 1941; s. Louetta Robinson Brown; m. Jane Evangeline Smith, June 25, 1966; children: Amos Cleophilus, David Josephus, Kizzie Maria. BA, Morehouse Coll., Atlanta, 1964; MDiv, Crozer Sem., Chester, Pa., 1968; DMin, United Sem., Dayton, Ohio, 1990; DDiv, Va. Sem., Lynchburg, 1984. Ordained to ministry, Am. Bapt. Chs. and Nat. Bapt. USA, Inc., 1965. Pastor St. Paul's Bapt. Ch., West Chester, Pa., 1966-70, Pilgrim Bapt. Ch., St. Paul, 1970-76, Third Bapt. Ch., San Francisco, 1976—; mem. City and County of San Francisco Bd. Suprs., 1996—; instr. philosophy Cheyney (Pa.) State Coll., 1968-70; nat. chmn. Nat. Bapt. Conven. on Civil Rights and Human Svcs., 1982—; chmn. Bay Area Ecumenical Pastors Conf., 1980—. Vice pres. governing bd. San Francisco Community Coll., 1987-89. Recipient Martin Luther King Ministerial award, Colgate Rochester Div. Sch., 1984, Man of the Yr., San Francisco Bus. and Profl. Women's Clubs, 1985. Mem. NAACP, Rotary, Masons, Alpha Phi Alpha. Democrat. Office: Third Bapt Ch 13499 McAllister St San Francisco CA 94117 also: Board of Suprs City Hall 1 Dr Carlton B Goodlett Pl San Francisco CA 94102-4603

BROWN, ANDREA LYNN, executive recruiter; b. Portland, Maine, Dec. 22, 1967; d. Thomas Joseph and Denise Katherine (Brown) B. BS in Acctg., U. So. Maine, 1990. CPA, Maine. Asst. dept. mgr. Levinsky's, Portland, 1985-91; sr. auditor Baker Newman & Noyes, Portland, 1991-95; placement cons. Pro Search, Inc., Portland, 1995—; adj. faculty Andover Coll., Portland, 1996-97. Mem. Inst. Mgmt. Accts., Maine State Soc. Cert. Pub. Accts. Avocations: skiing, reading, boating, running. Office: Pro Search Inc 70 Center St Portland ME 04101-3935

BROWN, ANDREAS LE, book store and art gallery executive; b. Coronado, Calif., Apr. 29, 1933; s. Harvey Clair and Helene Celeste (Kimball) B. AB, Calif. State U., San Diego, 1955; postgrad., Stanford U., 1955-57. Mem. faculty Calif. State U., 1960-63; staff rsch. fellow Humanities Rsch. Ctr., U. Tex., 1963-65; appraiser rare books, 1965-67; owner, pres. Gotham Book Mart & Gallery Inc., N.Y.C., 1967—, Sorer Realty Corp., N.Y.C., 1989—. Author: A Creative Century, 1970, (with Hal Morgan) Prairie Fires and Paper Moons, 1981; mem. adv. bd. Paris Rev. Served with AUS, 1958-59. Mem. Manuscript Soc., Antiquarian Booksellers Assn. Am., Am. Booksellers Assn., Internat. League Antiquarian Booksellers, Sigma Chi, Grolier Club (N.Y.). Specialist in modern rare books and manuscripts. Home and Office: 41 W 47th St New York NY 10036-2838

BROWN, ANITA LANIER, women's health nurse; b. Portsmouth, Va., May 15, 1961; d. Samuel Edward and Elna Carlene (Crumpler) Lanier; m. Sam James Brown, June 16, 1979; children: Catherine Grace, Rebecca Faye. ADN, Coastal Carolina Community Coll., Jacksonville, N.C., 1982; BSN, U. N.C., Wilmington, 1995; MSN, U. N.C., Chapel Hill, 1997. Cert. womens health nurse practitioner, BCLS, Aspo/Lamaze cert. childbirth educator. Staff nurse ob-gyn. U.S. Naval Hosp. Cherry Point Med. Ctr., Havelock, N.C.; staff nurse operating room and ob-gyn. Duplin Gen. Hosp., Kenansville, N.C.; asst. to charge nurse ob-gyn. clinic, staff nurse labor and delivery U.S. Naval Hosp. Camp Lejeune, Jacksonville, N.C.; Cape Fear Ob-Gyn.; tchg. asst. U. N.C. Sch. Nursing, Chapel Hill, 1995-97. Mem. ANA, Assn. Women's Health, Obstetric, and Neonatal Nurses, Aspo/Lamaze, Sigma Theta Tau (N.C. nurse scholar). Home: 2253 Fountaintown Rd Chinquapin NC 28521-8713

BROWN, ANN, federal agency administrator; m. Donald Brown, 1959; 2 children. Student, Smith Coll., 1955-58; BA, George Washington U., 1959. Past v.p. Consumer Fedn. Am.; chmn. bd. Pub. Voice, 1983—; chmn. U.S. Consumer Product Safety Commn., 1994—; nat. and local chmn. consumer affairs com. Ams. for Dem. Action; past chmn. adv. bd. Washington Consumer Protection Office. Named Washingtonian of Yr., Washingtonian mag., 1989; recipient Merit award Washington City Coun., Mem. of Yr. award Ams. for Dem. Action, Golden Trumpet award publicity Club Chgo., 1996. Mem. Colaition for Consumer Health and Safety. AvocationsL tennis, movies. Office: US Consumer Product Safety Commn 4330 East West Hwy Bethesda MD 20814-4408*

BROWN, ANN BARTON, museum director. BA in Am. History, Sweet Briar Coll., 1972; MA in Am. History/Mus. Studies, U. Del., 1973; postgrad., Mus. Mgmt. Inst./U. Calif., Berkeley, 1984. Rsch. assoc. Abby Aldrich Rockefeller Folk Art Ctr., Williamsburg, Va., 1973-77; curator of collections Brandywine River Mus., Chadds Ford, Pa., 1977-84; assoc. dir. museum and collections Chester County Hist. Soc., West Chester, Pa., 1984-88; exec. dir. Am. Swedish Hist. Mus., Phila., 1989—; now mng. dir. Valley Forge Hist. Mus.; grant developer various agys., including, The Annenberg Found., 1995-97, Arronson Found., 1989-97, Elizabeth Ellis Found. Trust, 1989-97, Independence Found., 1996—, Inst. of Mus. Svcs., 1987, Kohn Found., 1993-97, Pa. Coun. on the Arts, 1985-95, others; cons. Am. Assn. of Mus., 1986—, Inst. of Mus. Svcs., 1987—, Pennsbury Land Trust, 1996—, Pa. Coun. on the Arts, 1988-90, Pa. Hist. and Mus. Commn., 1989-91; participant Seminar for Hist. Adminstrs., Williamsburg, 1975. Mem. Am. Assn. Museums, Am. Assn. State and Local History, Del. Agr. Mus., Fairmount Park Coun. for Hist. Sites (bd. dirs. 1989—), Mid-Atlantic Assn. for Museums (bd. dirs. 1982-91, treas. 1988-91), Mus. Coun. of Phila. (bd. dirs. 1980-82), Swedish Coun. of Am. (bd. dirs. 1989—), others. *

BROWN, ANN CATHERINE, investment company executive; b. St. Louis, Aug. 12, 1935; d. George Hay and Catherine Doratha (Smith) B. B.A., Northwestern U., 1956; M.B.A., U. Mich., 1958. Copywriter Fred Gardner Advt. Co., N.Y.C., 1959-61, Batten, Barton, Durstine & Osborn, N.Y.C., 1961-63, Ogilvy & Mather Co., N.Y.C., 1963-64; copy group head Benton & Bowles Co., N.Y.C., 1964-66; pvt. investor, 1966-69; with Baker, Weeks & Co., Inc., N.Y.C., 1969-76; v.p. Baker, Weeks & Co., Inc., 1973-76; exec. v.p., dir. Melhado, Flynn & Assocs., Inc., N.Y.C., 1976-83; chmn., investment exec. A.C. Brown & Assocs. Inc., 1983—. Columnist Forbes mag., 1976-90. Home: PO Box 30098 Sea Island GA 31561-0098

BROWN, ANN LENORA, community economic development professional; b. Austin, Tex., Aug. 29, 1955; d. William Alley and Ann Dyke (Shafer) B.; m. Robert William Lukeman, May 21, 1988; 1 child, Dancy Ann Lukeman. BArch, U. Tex., 1983. Main St. project dir. City of Brenham, Tex., 1983-86; owner, cons. TEXANA Cmty. Cons., LaGrange, Tex., 1980-91; dir. residential programs and arch. svcs. Galveston Hist. Found., 1988-91; realtor Barney Rapp, Inc. Realtors, Galveston, 1995-96; urban planner City of Galveston, 1996; exec. dir. Colorado City Econ. Devel. Orgn., Inc., 1998—; cmty. devel. cons. hist. neighborhoods and comml. dists., 1991-98; faculty mem. Coll. Arch., U. Houston hist. preservation program, 1991-93. Archtl. illustrator calendar U. Tex. Med. br., Galveston, 1991. Chair Broadway Redevel. Com., Galveston, 1990-93; founder, exec. dir. Galveston Cmty. Devel. Corp., 1991-96; bd. dirs., pres. Galveston Housing Fin. Corp., 1992-97. Recipient Preservation award Tex. Hist. Commn., 1986. Mem. AIA (assoc., tri-chair urban design 1991, chair hist. resources 1990-93), Tex. Cmty. Devel. Assn. Tex. (steering com. Tex. Devel. Inst. 1991-92). Episcopalian. Avocations: antiques, needlework, photography.

BROWN, ANNE RHODA WIESEN, civic worker; b. Medford, N.J., Nov. 27, 1926; d. George William and Mary Rebecca (Hattman) W.; m. Richard C. Brown, Aug., 1995. BS, U. N.H., 1948; MRE, Andover Newton Theol. Sch., 1950. Cert. community coll. instr., Calif. Dir. Christian edn. Bapt. chs., Mass., R.I., 1950-54; tchr., recreator World Coun. Chs., France, 1955; dir. Christian edn. Bapt. chs., Norristown, Wayne, Pa., 1956-62; recreation worker U.S. mil. hosps. ARC, 1962-64, recreation supr. U.S. mil. hosps. and bases, 1964-1976; field dir. ARC, Wright Patterson AFB, Ohio, 1976-79; sta. dir. ARC, Osan AFB, Republic of Korea, 1979-80; asst. dist. dir. ARC, Camp Zama, Japan, 1981-83, March AFB, Calif., 1983-84; sta. mgr. ARC, Camp Pendleton, Calif., 1985-86; vol. resource assoc. ARC, Stuttgart, Germany, 1986-88; sec. European Recreation Soc., Heidelberg, Germany, 1973-74. Author: Children Around the World, 1960. Bd. dirs. Project Pup, 1993-95. Recipient medal for civilian svcs. in Vietnam, U.S. Govt., 1968. Mem. AAUW (v.p. 1991-93), Tiger Bay Club (bd. dirs.). Democrat. Baptist. Avocations: handpainted eggs, animals, travel, hot air balloons.

BROWN, ANNE SHERWIN, speech pathologist; b. Denver, Oct. 15, 1952; d. John Frederick and Barbara Toft Sherwin; m. Max Dennis Brown, June 15, 1985; childre: Jack Steven, Michael Patrick. BA, Adams State Coll., 1974, MA, 1975. Tchr. Aurora (Colo.) Pub. Schs., 1978—. Author: Adopt-A-Cop, 1994. Bd. mgrs. YMCA, Aurora, 1996-98. Pub. Svc. Co. grantee, Denver, 1996-97, 98-99. Mem. ASCD, Aurora Edn. Assn., Internat. Reading Assn. Avocations: reading, dancing, sewing, guitar, motorcycles. Home: 416 S Victor Way Aurora CO 80012 Office: Aurora Pub Schs 395 S Troy St Aurora CO 90012

BROWN, ARNOLD, physical therapy consultant; b. N.Y.C., Apr. 8, 1930; s. Murray and Tessie Brown; m. Alice L. Kahn, July 31, 1955; 1 child, Alan. BS in Edn., Panzer Coll., 1951; cert. in phys. therapy, Columbia U., 1952; MA in Psychology, Ball State U., 1972. Lic. phys. therapist, Ind. Staff phys. therapist VA Hosp., East Orange, N.J., 1954-55; sr. phys. therapist Cerebral Palsy Clinic, Union City, N.J., 1955-56; chief phys. therapist Mobility, Inc., New Rochelle, N.Y., 1956-57, Inland Steel Co. Hosp., East Chicago, Ind., 1957-67, Ball Meml. Hosp., Muncie, Ind., 1967-84; dir. phys. therapy Profl. Med. Svc., Clay County, Ind., 1984-86, St. Anthony Hosp., Michigan City, Ind., 1986-93; ret., 1993, cons. physical therapy, 1993-96; cons. Lake County Assn. Retarded Children, Gary, Ind., 1963-67; insvc. instr. Ball Meml., St. Anthony Hosp., 1967-93; instr. Michigan City High Schs., Health Care Practicum, 1987-93; adj. clin. prof. phys. therapy Andrews U., Berrien Springs, Mich., 1987-93; clin. supr. student affiliations Ball State U., 1975-83, clin. instr. Ball State U., 1981-83; clin. supr. student affiliations Ind. U., 1975-83; mem. adv. bd. Vis. Nurse Assn., Muncie, 1972-78; tchr. health care practicum Michigan City H.S.'s, 1987-93. Author: Physiological and Psychological Considerations in Management of Stroke, 1976; author/instr.: Orientation to Physical Therapy, 1979, Body Mechanics, 1987(videotapes); contbr. to profl. jours. Bd. dirs. Nat. Multiple Sclerosis Soc., 1974-77, Easter Seal Soc., Muncie, 1976-78. With U.S. Army, 1952-54. Recipient Vocat. Dirs. award A.K. Smith Career Ctr., Michigan City, 1993. Mem. Am. Phys. Therapy Assn. (mgmt. sect.). Avocations: piano, walking, exercise, reading. Home: 2 Buckingham Ct Apt 2 Michigan City IN 46360-1588

BROWN, ARNOLD, management consultant; b. Boston, Aug. 18, 1927; s. Frank and Frances B.; children: Pamela, Cynthia, Derek. BA with honors, UCLA, 1950. Asst. dir. sales promotion Mut. Benefit Life Ins. Co., Newark, 1957-61; v.p. Inst. Life Ins., N.Y.C., 1961-77; chmn. Weiner, Edrich, Brown, Inc., N.Y.C., 1977—; guest lectr. Harvard Bus. Sch., Duke U., Wharton Sch. Co-author: Supermanaging, 1984, Office Biology, 1993, Insider's Guide to the Future, 1997; mem. editl. bd. MacMillan Encyclopedia of the Future, On the Horizon mag.; contbr. articles to profl. jours. Served with USN, 1944-46. Office: 200 E 33rd St New York NY 10016-4874

BROWN, ARNOLD LANEHART, JR., pathologist, educator, university dean; b. Wooster, Ohio, Jan. 26, 1926; s. Arnold Lanehart and Wilda (Woods) B.; m. Betty Jane Simpson, Oct. 2, 1949; children—Arnold III, Anthony, Allen, Fletcher, Lisa. Student, U. Richmond, 1943-45; M.D., Med. Coll. Va., 1949. Diplomate: Am. Bd. Pathology. Intern Presbyn.-St. Luke's Hosp., Chgo., 1949-50; resident Presbyn.-St. Luke's Hosp., 1950-51, 53-56, asst. attending pathologist, 1957-59; practice medicine specializing in pathology Rochester, Minn., 1959-78; cons. exptl. pathology, anatomy Mayo Clinic, Rochester, 1959-78; also prof., chmn. dept. Mayo Clinic, 1968-78; prof. pathology U. Wis., Madison, 1978—, dean Med. Sch., 1978-91; mem. nat. cancer adv. council NIH, 1971-74, HEW, 1972-74; chmn. clearing house on environ. carcinogens Nat. Cancer Inst., 1976-80, chmn. com. to study carcinogenicity of cyclamate, 1975-76; mem. Nat. Com. on Heart Disease, Cancer and Stroke, 1975-79; mem. com. on safe drinking water NRC, 1976-77; mem. award assembly Gen. Motors Cancer Research Found., 1978-83, vice chmn., 1982-83; co-chmn. panel on geochemistry of fibrous materials related to health risks Nat. Acad. Scis.-NRC, 1978-80; chair working group Internat. Agy. for Research on Cancer, Lyon, France, 1979, 83, 87. Contbr. articles to profl. jours. Bd. sci. counselors Nat. Inst. Environ. Health Scis., NIH Nat. Toxicology Program, 1992—. With USNR, 1943-45, 51-53. Nat. Heart Inst. postdoctoral fellow, 1956-59. Mem. Am. Soc. Exptl. Pathology, Internat. Acad. Pathology, Assn. Am. Med. Colls. (chmn. council deans 1984-85). Home: 2822 Marshall Ct Madison WI 53705-2271 Office: 1300 University Ave Madison WI 53706-1510

BROWN, ARTHUR CARL, JR., retired minister; b. Stockton, Calif., Dec. 16, 1915; s. Arthur Carl and Maud (Twitchings) B.; m. Inez Lundquist, May 10, 1940 (dec. Aug. 1982); 1 child, Arthur Carl III. BA, Coll. of the Pacific, 1937; MA, San Francisco Theol. Sem., 1939, BD with honors, 1940; postgrad., Stanford U., 1949-50. Ordained to ministry Presbyn. Ch., 1940. Pastor Presbyn. Ch., Sedro Woolley, Wash., 1940-44, Community Ch., Santa Clara, Calif., 1944-46; assoc. pastor First Presbyn. Ch., San Jose, Calif., 1946-49; minister edn. First Presbyn. Ch., Palo Alto, Calif., 1949-51; organizing pastor Covenant Presbyn. Ch., Palo Alto, 1951-74; pastor Trinity Presbyn. Ch., Santa Cruz, Calif., 1974-78; outreach assoc. Los Gatos (Calif.) Presbyn. Ch., 1978-81; commr. to gen. assembly United Presbyn. Ch., 1947, 52, 59; moderator San Jose Presbytery, 1950, chmn. various coms., 1950-78; mem. Synod Golden Gate and Synod of Pacific coms. Synod of Calif., 1947-82; pastor emeritus Covenant Presbyn. Ch. Treas., chmn. fin. com., bd. dirs. Internat. House, Davis, Calif., 1984-90, chmn. nominating com., 1990-96, mem. devel. com., 1991097. Avocations: gardening, sports, study of Greek words in New Testament, writing, family history. Home: 4414 San Ramon Dr Davis CA 95616-5018

BROWN, ARTHUR EDMON, JR., retired army officer; b. Manila, Nov. 21, 1929; s. Arthur Edmon and Grace E. M. (Montgomery) B.; m. Jerry Deane Cook, June 6, 1953; children: Marian Brown Shope, Nan Brown Irick, Arthur Edmon III. B.S., U.S. Mil. Acad., 1953; M.Public and Internat. Affairs, U. Pitts., 1965. Commd. 2d lt. U.S. Army, advanced through grades to gen.; mem. faculty U.S. Army War Coll., 1970-73; comdr. 1st Brigade, 1st Infantry Div. Fort Riley, Kans., 1973-75; mem. gen. staff Dept. Army, Washington, 1975-78; asst. div. comdr. 25th Infantry Div. Hawaii, 1978-80; dep. supt. U.S. Mil. Acad., West Point, 1980-81; comdr. U.S. Army Readiness and Moblzn., Region IV, Fort Gillem, Ga., 1981-83; dir. army staff Dept. Army, Washington, 1983-87; vice chief of staff U.S. Army, 1987-89, retired. Decorated Def. D.S.M., Army D.S.M. with oak leaf cluster, Bronze Star with 3 oak leaf clusters, Silver Star, Legion of Merit with 3 oak leaf clusters. Episcopalian. Home: 35 Fairway Winds Pl Hilton Head Island SC 29928-5547 also: 3302 N St NW Washington DC 20007-2807

BROWN, ARTHUR R., state agency administrator; b. Fulton, N.Y.. BS in Animal Sci., U. Mass.; MS in Horticulture, Cook Coll./Rutgers U., 1977. County agr. agt., 11 yrs.; prof. Cook Coll.; sec. of agr. State of N.J., Trenton. Trustee So. N.J. Devel. Coun.; chmn. census adv. com. U.S. Dept. Agr.; mem. bd. mgrs. N.J. Agrl. Expt. Sta., Eastern U.S. Agrl. and Food Export Coun., N.J. Dist. Export Coun./U.S. Dept. Commerce; mem. N.J. State Planning Commn. Recipient Hon. Am. Farmer degree Nat. Future Farmers Assn., Statesman award N.J. Devel. Coun., Golden Flower award N.J. State Florists Assn. Mem. Nat. Assn. State Depts. Agr. (chmn. agrl. rsch. task force), N.J. State Agrl. Devel. Com. Office: NJ Dept Agr PO Box 330 Trenton NJ 08625

BROWN, AUTRY, psychology educator, clergyman; b. Watson, Okla., May 1, 1924; s. Solon Lemley and Bessie Jane (Wilhelm) B.; m. Opal Irene Landers, Sept.5, 1942; children: Juanice, Rebecca, Steven, Deborah. BA, Eastern N.M. U., 1950; M of Div., New Orleans Bapt. Theol. Sem., 1955, MRE, 1956, EdD, 1968; postgrad., Colo. State U., 1970, Southwest Mo. State U., 1985. Ordained to ministry Bapt. Ch., 1942. Pastor Bookcliff Bapt. Ch., Grand Junction, Colo., 1957-61, Carrollton Ave. Bapt. Ch., New Orleans, 1962-64, Immanuel Bapt. Ch., Ft. Collins, Colo., 1964-72; asst. prof. psychology Mo. Bapt. U., St. Louis, 1972-74; asst. prof. psychology Southwest Bapt. U., Bolivar, Mo., 1974-76, prof. psychology, 1978-89, dir. counseling services, 1978-89; disting. prof. psychology, 1989—; cons. family ministry Colo. Bapt. Gen. Conv., Denver, 1976-78. Author: Church Family Life Conference Guidebook, 1973; contbr. books, profl. jour. Recipient Spl. Services award Bd. Trustees New Orleans Bapt. Theol. Sem., 1972. Mem. Am. Assn. Marriage and Family Therapy, Mo. Assn. Marriage and Family Therapy (Spl. Service award 1984, treas. state exec. bd. 1979-83), Ozark Assn. Marriage and Family Therapy (pres. 1985-86), Mo. Assn. Counseling and Devel., Fellows Menniger Found. Avocation: collecting antique barbed wire. Home: 1223 Woodland Cir Bolivar MO 65613-3351 Office: Christian Tng Inst 1223 Woodland Cir Bolivar MO 65613-3351

BROWN, BAILEY, federal judge; b. Memphis, June 16, 1917; s. Joshua Goodlett and Lillian (Pearcy) B.; m. Doris Frances Lawhorn., Dec. 24, 1964; 1 son, Bailey, Jr. A.B., U. Mich., 1939; LL.B., Harvard U., 1942. Bar: Tenn. 1941. Ptnr. Burch, Porter, Johnson & Brown, Memphis, 1946-61; judge U.S. Dist. Ct. (we. dist.) Tenn., Memphis, 1961-79, chief judge, 1966-79; sr. judge (6th cir.) U.S. Ct. Appeals, 1979—; mem. Jud. Conf. Com. on Ct. Adminstrn., 1969-75, 78-84; past chmn. Subcom. on Judicial Improvements; past mem. ad hoc com. studying Cameras in the Courtroom; guest lectr. Rhodes Coll., Memphis. Pres. Memphis Symphony, 1958-60, Memphis Pub. Affairs Forum, 1955. Lt. USNR, 1942-46. Recipient Charles A. Rond Outstanding Judge of Yr. award Young Lawyers Memphis and Shelby County Bar Assns., 1977. Mem. Memphis Bar Assn. (Lawyer's Lawyer award 1996) Shelby County Bar Assn. (Liberty Bell award 1971, Ann. Dedication and Achievement award Criminal Law Sect. 1979). Episcopalian (vestryman). Home: 115 Morning Side Pl Memphis TN 38104-3037

BROWN, BARBARA JEAN, special and secondary education educator; b. Midland, Tex., Nov. 3, 1945; d. John Joseph and Sarah Beryl (Seely) Sury; m. Samuel Bradford Brown III, June 30, 1984. BA in English, U. Tex., Arlington, 1967, MAT in English and Humanities, 1979. Cert. gifted and English tchr., Tex., Fla. With Euless (Tex.) Jr. H.S./Hurst-Euless-Bedford Ind. Sch. Dist., 1967-84, Edgewater High Sch./Orange County Sch. Bd., Orlando, Fla., 1984-86; tchr. Lakeview Mid. Sch./Seminole County Sch. Bd., Sanford, Fla., 1986-98, Lake Mary (Fla.) H.S./ Seminole County Sch. Bd., 1998—; curriculum writer Hurst-Euless-Bedford Ind. Sch. Dist., Hurst, mem. curriculum and dist. policy devel. com.; curriculum writer Seminole County Sch. Bd.; presenter Tex. Gifted Conf., Houston. Seminole County Sch. Bd. grantee, 1987-88, Svc. award, 1991, finalist, 1989-93; recipient Tchr. Merit award Walt Disney World Co., 1990-92; named Prominent Educator of Tex., 1983, Tchr. of the Yr., Coun. for Exceptional Children, 1991. Mem. NEA, PTA, Nat. Assn. Gifted Children, Seminole County Tchrs. English, Coun. Reading Tchrs., Fla. Scholastic Press Assn., Orlando Area City Panhellenic, Phi Mu (pres. Winter Park-Orlando chpt. 1988-91, nat. state day chmn. 1993-94), Sigma Tau Delta, Sigma Delta Phi. Roman Catholic. Home: 107 Hatfield Ct Longwood FL 32779-4606 Office: Lake Mary High School 655 Longwood Lake Mary Rd Lake Mary FL 32746

BROWN, BARBARA JUNE, hospital and nursing administrator; b. Milw., Aug. 17, 1933; d. Carl W. and Nora Anne (Damrow) Rydberg; children: Deborah, Robert, Andrea, Michael, Steven, Jeffrey. BSN, Marquette U., Milw., 1955, MSN, 1960, EdD, 1970. RN, Wash., Wis.; cert. nurse adminstr. advanced. Adminstr. patient care Family Hosp., Milw., 1973-78; assoc. clin. prof. U. Wash., Seattle, 1980-87; assoc. adminstr. nursing Virginia Mason Hosp., Seattle, 1980-87; assoc. exec. dir. King Faisal Specialist Hosp., Riyadh, Saudi Arabia, 1987-91; project dir. NIH, Sexual Assault Treatment Ctr., Milw., 1975-78; lectr., cons., 1974—. Founder, editor Nursing Administration Quarterly, 1976—. Vol. ski instr. for disabled, Winter Park, Colo. Fellow Am. Acad. Nursing (governing coun.), Nat. Acad. Practice; mem. ANA, Am. Orgn. Nurse Execs., Nat. League Nursing (bd. dirs.), Grand County Pub. Health and Emergency Svcs. (chmn. health adv. com. 1994-96), Sigma Theta Tau.

BROWN, BARBARA MAHONE, communications educator, poet, consultant; b. Chgo., Feb. 27, 1944; d. Loniel Atticus and Anne (Savage) Mahone. BA, Wash. State U., 1968; MBA, U. Chgo., 1975; PhD, Stanford U., 1988. Dir. corp. comm. NBC, N.Y.C., 1975-77; assoc. prof. dept. bus. adminstrn. and econs. Clark Coll., Atlanta, 1978-84; assoc. prof. depts. journalism and advt. U. Tex., Austin, 1988-91; assoc. prof. dept. mktg. San Jose (Calif.) State U., 1990—; pres. Elbow Room Cons., 1994—; cons. The Fielding Inst., Santa Barbara, Calif., 1995—; evaluator Western Assn. Schs. and Colls., Oakland, Calif., 1993—; cons. KQED-TV (PBS), San Francisco, 1991; OBAC Poet, Orgn. Black Am. Culture, Chgo., 1970-75; mentor Ctr. for Devel. Women Entrepreneurs, 1995-97; founding faculty Fielding Inst. ODE Program, 1996. Author: (vol. poetry) Sugarfields, 1970; writer-rschr. pub. affairs documentary, WMAQ-TV (NBC Chgo.) 1973, WNET-TV (PBS N.Y.C.) 1971; contbr. articles to profl. acad. jours. Bd. dirs. Kids in Common, San Jose, 1997—; trustee Hillbrook Sch., Los Gatos, Calif., 1996—; vestry St. Edward's Episcopal Ch., San Jose, 1994-96; steering com. UN Mid-Decade of Women, Southeast Regional Conf., 1980. Regents fellow in comm., U. Tex. at Austin, 1989; tchr.-scholar San Jose State U., 1993. Mem. Delta Sigma Pi, Beta Gamma Sigma. Episcopalian. Avocations: art, literature, orchids, photography. Office: San Jose State U BT-750 One Washington Sq San Jose CA 95192-0069

BROWN, BARBARA S., environmental scientist; b. Newark, Aug. 5, 1951; d. Louis and Louise (Mumper) Stein; children: Kristin Leigh, Andrew Hayden. Student Am. U., 1969-71; BS in Biology, U. Miami, 1976, postgrad. Staff scientist Environ. Sci. and Engring., Inc., Miami, 1978-86; dir. environ. crimes unit Dade County Environ. Resource Mgmt., 1986—. Mem. Nat. Assn. Environ. Profls.

BROWN, BENJAMIN A., gas, oil industry executive; b. N.Y.C., Feb. 13, 1943; s. Horace A. and Lillian A. (Hurwitz) B.; m. Elinore Carole Abravanel, Aug. 8, 1968; children—Adam Howard, Dina Lauren. B.B.A. in Acctg., Adelphi U., 1964; M.B.A. in Fin. and Investments, Baruch Coll. CUNY, 1971. Acct. Samuel Greiff C.P.A., Atty., Forest Hills, N.Y., 1963-66; v.p. research dept. Walston & Co., N.Y.C., 1967-73; treas. ENSERCH Corp., Dallas, 1974-78, v.p. fin., 1978-82, v.p. fin. relations, 1982-96; v.p. Enserch Exploration, Inc., 1995-96; v.p. fin. rels., investor EEX Corp., 1997—. Mem. N.Y. Soc. Security Analysts, Petroleum Investor Rels. Assn., DAC Country Club, Univ. Club. Avocations: walking, golf, numismatist, oenophile. Home: 2727 Elmside Dr Apt 311 Houston TX 77042-3965 Office: EEX Corp 2500 Citywest Blvd Ste 1400 Houston TX 77042-3024 *I strive everyday to give more than I take and spend less than I make. My success and happiness are entirely attributable to a very loving and supportive family, including a perfect mate for more than 30 years, two children that reflect the best qualities parents could wish for, a mother and brother that are always there for me, and in-laws that most can only dream about.*

BROWN, BENJAMIN ANDREW, journalist; b. Red House, W.Va., Apr. 30, 1933; s. Albert Miller and Mary Agnes (Donegan) B.; m. Joanne Gretchen Harder, May 22, 1956; children: Benjamin Andrew, Gretchen, Mark, Betsy Brown Larson. BS in Journalism, Fla. State U., 1955. Sportswriter Charleston (W.Va.) Daily Mail, 1955-57; with AP, 1957-93; gen. exec. AP, N.Y.C., 1976-78, 82-93; chief bur. AP, Los Angeles, 1978-82; assoc. Am. Newspapers Cons., Ltd., Milw., 1993-95; bd. dirs. Last Chance Press Club, Helena, Mont., 1969; v.p. Minn. Press Club, 1975. Office: PO Box 3012 Paso Robles CA 93447-3012

BROWN, BETSY S., hotel executive; b. Raleigh, N.C.; m. Reg Brown; children: Treg, Paige, Lance. Student, East Carolina U. Corp. sec. Hospitality Internat., Inc., Tucker, Ga., 1982—, treas., 1994—, pres., 1998—. Office: Hospitality Internat Inc 1726 Montreal Cir Tucker GA 30084-6809

BROWN, BETTY MARIE, government agency administrator; b. Siler City, N.C., June 11, 1952; d. Ardentries and Emma (Peoples) Mason; m. Tommy E. Brown, Aug. 8, 1968 (dec.); 1 child, Christopher T.; m. Roger L. Cook, June 10, 1973 (dec. Feb. 1981); 1 child, Felicia M. AAS, Phila. Community Coll., 1981; BS, Drexel U., 1986. Cert. early childhood edn. tchr., elem. edn. tchr., Pa. Mgr. Mr. Gourmet Deli, Phila., 1977-80; pres. Parents, Friends and Vols. Community Svc. Orgn., Phila., 1983—; tchr. Phila. Sch. Dist., 1988-89; remittance perfection clk. IRS, Phila., 1990-92; account analyst IRS-Automated Collection Sys., Phila., 1992—; with Census Bur./Dept. Commerce, 1980; tchr. Mid City YWCA, Phila., 1983-88. Sec. support community outreach project Dept. Human Svcs., Phila., 1990-91. Recipient Community Svc. award Dept. Human Svc., 1988. Baptist. Avocations: reading, swimming, dancing, flying, tennis. Home and Office: Parents of the 39th Dist 1132 Easton Rd Apt B Philadelphia PA 19150-2708

BROWN, BILLY CHARLIE, secondary school educator; b. Cookeville, Tenn., Feb. 20, 1947; s. Joe Homer and Sallie Mable (Hendrickson) B. BS in Forestry, BS in Edn., U. Tenn., 1969, EdD in Curriculum and Instruction, 1979; MA in Secondary Sci. Edn., Tenn. Tech. U., 1973, EdS in Secondary Sci. Edn., 1976. Cert. secondary sci. tchr., Ga., Tenn., Ky. Tchr., dept. chair Westwood Jr. High Sch., Manchester, Tenn., 1970-77; tchr., coach Feldwood High Sch., College Park, Ga., 1979-84; tchr., sci. Shiloh High Sch., Lithonia, Ga., 1984-87; coord. environ. energy sci. edn. ctr. U. Tenn., Knoxville, 1987-88; assoc. prof. Ky. Wesleyan Coll., Owensboro, 1990-93; with Cobb County Schs., Marietta, Ga., 1993—; sci. edn. cons. Oak Ridge Nat. Lab., 1993—; assoc. prof. edn. Lindsey Wilson Coll., Columbia, Ky., 1999—; vis. asst. prof. U. Tenn., Knoxville, 1988-90; co-dir. Ctr. for Environ./Energy/Sci. Edn., U. Tenn., Knoxville, 1988-90; sci. cons. area sch. dists. Ky. Wesleyan Coll., Owensboro, 1990-93; dir. Elem. Sci. Leadership Inst., Oak Ridge Nat. Lab., 1993—. Contbr. articles to profl. jours. Named Outstanding Classroom Tchr., Tenn. Edn. Assn., 1975. Mem. Nat. Sci. Tchr. Assn. (Outstanding Sci. Educator nominee 1991), Nat. Coun. Tchrs. Math., Mid-East Regional Assn. Educators Tchrs. Sci. Avocations: cultural music, sports coaching, writing, hiking. Home: 621 Dale Ave Apt 320 Knoxville TN 37921-6797

BROWN, BILLYE JEAN, retired nursing educator; b. Damascus, Ark., Oct. 29, 1925; d. William A. and Dora (Megee) B. BSNEd, U. Tex. Med. Br., Galveston, 1953; MSNEd, St. Louis U., 1958; EdD, Baylor U., 1975. Asst. prof. U. Tex. Med. Br. Sch. Nursing, 1958-60; assoc. prof. U. Tex. Nursing Sch., Austin, 1960-67; assoc. dean, prof. U. Tex. Nursing Sch., 1968-72, dean, prof., 1972-89; prof. emeritus Sch. Nursing U. Tex., 1989—; mem. Nat. Adv. Council Nurse Tng., 1982-87. Nat. League for Nursing fellow, 1957-58; recipient Alumni Merit award St. Louis U., 1981; Am. Acad. Nursing fellow, 1984. Mem. ANA, Am. Assn. Colls. Nursing (pres. 1982-84), Tex. League Nursing, Tex. Nurses Assn. (Nurse of Yr. 1980), Sigma Theta Tau (pres. 1989-91), Phi Kappa Phi (life).

BROWN, BOBBY R., retired coal company executive; b. 1932; m. Wanda Brown; children: Deede Lundeen, Laura Price, Paul. B.S., U. Ark., 1958. Sr. v.p. CONOCO, 1975-77; chmn. CONSOL Inc. (owned by DuPont and Rheinbraun), Pitts., 1977-99; bd. dirs. PNC Bank, Remington Arms Co., Inc.; mem. coal industry adv. bd. DINAMO; sec. Energy Adv. Bd.; mem. Va. Coalfield Econ. Devel. Authority. Mem. Bituminous Coal Operators Assn., Nat. Mining Assn., U.S.C. of C. (energy and natural resource com.), Ctr. for Energy and Econ. Devel. Office: CONSOL Inc 1800 Washington Rd Pittsburgh PA 15241-1405

BROWN, BONNIE, Canadian parliamentarian; m. Ron Coupland; 7 children. Elected mem. Parliament House of Commons, Oakville, Ont., Can., 1993—; mem. standing com. on industry, past mem. com. on Can. heritage, com. on pub. accounts, vice chair standing com. for human resources devel., chairperson social policy caucus, past chairperson parliamentary steel caucus, nat. caucus com. on social policy Ho. of Commons. Councillor, Regional Municipality of Halton, Town of Oakville; trustee separate sch. bd., Halton; exec. dir. parental stress svcs. Parents Anonymous; chairperson Halton Dist. Health Coun., Halton Child Abuse Coun.; chairperson steering coms. Halton Children's Mental Health and Cancer Study; past bd. dirs. Oakville-Trafalgar Meml. Hosp., Oakville United Way, Halton Children's Aid Soc., Halton Alcohol and Drug Addiction Program. Office: Ho Commons Parliamntry Offc, Rm 147 Confederation Bldg, Ottawa, ON Canada K1A 0A6 also: Ho Commons Constituence Ofc, 2421 Marine Dr, Oakville, ON Canada L6L 1C6*

BROWN, BONNIE MARYETTA, lawyer; b. North Plainfield, N.J., Oct. 31, 1953; d. Robert Jeffrey and Diana (Parket) B. AB, Washington U., St. Louis, 1975; JD, U. Louisville, 1978. Bar: Ky. 1978, U.S. Dist. Ct. (we. dist.) Ky. 1979, U.S. Dist. Ct. (ea. dist.) Ky. 1993. Pvt. practice Louisville, 1978—; of counsel Morris, Garlove, Waterman and Johnson PLLC, 1998—; lectr., seminar leader various profl., ednl., govtl. and civic groups; cons. marital rape; registered lobbyist 1994 Ky. Gen. Assembly for Ky. Assn. Marriage and Family Therapy. Editor Ky. Appellate Handbook, 1985; contbr. articles to profl. jours. Vol. legal panel Ky. Civil Liberties Union, Louisville, 1984—; author, chief lobbyist Marital Rape Bill, Ky. Coalition Against Rape and Sexual Assault, 1982—, Sexual Harassment bill, 1996; vol. advisor Louisville RAPE Relief Ctr., 1975—; treas. Family Support Group/ Family Readiness Program. of USAR, 1994-96, 3d Bat., 2nd. bge, 87th divsn., 1996-99, acting coord. 10th bat., 6th bge, 100th divsn. Recipient Cert. Spl. Recognition RAPE Relief Ctr., 1980, Cert. Outstanding Contbn., Louisville YMCA, 1983, Cert. of Appreciation, James Graham Brown Cancer Ctr., 1984, Decade of Svc. award YMCA/Rape Relief Ctr., Outstanding Victim Adv. award Fayette County Govt., 1990, cert. of Recognition Jefferson County Family Ct., 1995. Mem. ABA (family law sect., apptd. to appellate handbook com., jud. adminstrn. divsn. lawyers conf.), Am. Acad. Matrimonial Lawyers, Ky. Bar Assn. (family law sect. vice-chair 1994-95, chair-elect 1995-96, chair 1996-97, seminar spkr., task force solo practitioners and small law firms 1992, chair subcom. on law office automation and networking, solo practitioner and small Law Firm sect. chmn. elect 1998-99, chmn. 1999—, CLE award 1981, 93, 97, 98, 99), Louisville Bar Assn. (liaison to mental health sect., organizer marital rape seminar, chmn. family law sect., mediation com. property divsn., seminar spkr., organizer joint custody child abuse seminars, solo practitioner and small law firm sect., chair 1995, pro bono consortium), Ky. Acad. Trial Attys. (spkr. seminar, editor The Advocate family law sect. 1995-99), Bus. and Profl. Women (pres. River City chpt.), Ky. Fedn. (legis. chair 1986-87, 90-92, legal counsel 1992, 96, 97, 99, lobby corps chair 1993-95), Louisville Internat. Cultural Ctr., Women Lawyers Assn. Jefferson County. Republican. Avocations: basketball fan, classic cars. Office: Ste 1000 One Riverfront Plz Louisville KY 40202

BROWN, BRADFORD CLEMENT, government relations public affairs executive; b. Waterbury, Conn., Feb. 17, 1958; s. Richard Clement and Diane Elizabeth B.; m. Alicia A. Billings. BA, Providence Coll., 1980; MA, Harvard U., 1982; JD, Catholic U. Am., 1986. Asst. to chief counsel technology U.S. Dept. Commerce, Washington, 1990-91, chief counsel technology, 1991-93; prin. Hagerty, Peterson LLP Mgmt. Adv. Group, Washington, 1994-95; pres. Western Strategies (divsn. Nelson Comm. Group), Washington, Sacramento, Calif., 1995-96; sr. v.p. tech. affairs Shandwick Pub. Affairs, Washington, 1996-98, exec. v.p. tech. affairs, dep. mng. dir., 1998—; Bd. advisors Affinity Ptnrs., N.Y.C.; bd. dirs. Columbia Hosp. Women, Washington, exec. coun.; bd. dirs. Nat. Ctr. Tech. & Law George Mason U., Arlington, Va. Co-author: Attorney Desk Library Series—Contracts, 1994. Mem. ABA (co-chmn. legislation sec. sci. and tech. 1992-96). Avocations: golf, painting. Office: Ronald Reagan Internat Trade Ctr 6th Fl 1300 Pennsylvania Ave NW Washington DC 20004-3023

BROWN, BRITT, retired publishing company executive; b. Long Beach, Calif., Apr. 23, 1927; s. Harry Britton and Victoria (Eaton) B.; m. Anne Louise McCarthy, June 19, 1948; children—Cathy Lynn, Cynthia Ann, Britt Murdock, Bruce McCarthy. Student, U. So. Calif., 1944-46; B.A., U. Kans., 1947. Classified advt. salesman Wichita (Kans.) Eagle (now Wichita Eagle & Beacon Pub. Co.), 1947-50, classified mgr., 1952-55, advt. dir., 1956-62, v.p., sec., 1963-71, pub., pres., from 1971, chmn., 1973-79. Served with USMCR, 1944-46, 50-51. Mem. Sigma Delta Chi, Kappa Alpha.

BROWN, BRUCE HARDING, naval officer; b. Gary, Ind., Nov. 27, 1954; s. Russell Harding and Dorothy Jane (Schaeffer) B.; m. Laurie Marshall McPhillips, Sept. 12, 1981; children: Brendan Harding, Colin Campbell. Student, Cambridge U., 1975; BA in Polit. Sci., Ind. U., 1977; MA in Mgmt., Nat. U., San Diego, 1988. Counselor Lake County Juvenile Ctr., Crown Point, Ind., 1978; commd. ensign USN, 1979, advanced through grades to lt. comdr., 1989; comm. officer USS St. Louis, San Diego, 1980-83; 1st lt. USS Jouett, San Diego, 1983-85; exec. officer Spl. Boat Unit 13, Coronado, Calif., 1985-89; asst. officer in charge USS Alamo, San Diego, 1989-90; 1st lt. USS Tuscaloosa, San Diego, 1990-92; commdg. officer Naval and Marine Corps Res. Ctr., South Bend, Ind., 1992-94; engr. CSX Corp., Garrett, Ind., 1995-96; co. ofcl. CSX Corp., Chgo., 1996—; lectr. U. Notre Dame, South Bend, 1992. Coord. Navy Relief Soc., San Diego, 1989, Combined Fed. Campaign, South Bend, 1992; asst. scoutmaster Boy Scouts Am., 1992. Mem. Naval Res. Assn. (life), U.S. Naval Inst., Masons, Shrine. Republican. Methodist. Avocations: triathlon, rugby, swimming, golf, scuba diving. Home: 2371 Four Seasons Pkwy Crown Point IN 46307-9342 Office: CSX Corp 13600 S Halsted St Riverdale IL 60827-1123 Office: CSX Corp 500 Junction St Plymouth MI 48170-1229

BROWN, BRYAN D., career officer; b. Oct. 20, 1948. Commd. U.S. Army, advanced through grades to maj. gen., 1998; dir. requirements and strategic assessments U.S. Spl. Ops. Command, MacDill AFB, Fla., 1996-98; comdg. gen. Joint Spl. Ops. Command, Ft. Bragg, N.C., 1998—. Office: Joint Spl Ops Command PO Box 70239 Fort Bragg NC 28307

BROWN, BYRON WILLIAM, JR., biostatistician, educator; b. Chgo., Apr. 21, 1930; s. Byron William and Ruth (Munson) B.; m. Janet Louise Hyde, July 30, 1949; children: Byron William III, Eric Paul, Alan Thomas, Madeleine McGill, Mark Andrew, Lisa Anne. BA in Math., U. Minn., 1952, MS in Stats., 1955, PhD in Biostats., 1959. Asst. prof. biostats. Med. Sch. La. State U., New Orleans, 1956-57; from lectr. to prof. Sch. Pub. Health U. Minn., Mpls., 1957-65, prof., head biostats., 1965-68; prof., head divsn. Stanford (Calif.) U., 1968-98, chmn. dept. health rsch. and policy, 1988-96, prof. emeritus, 1998—; cons. govt. and industry. Author, co-author books, book chpts., and articles in profl. jours. and encys. With USAF, 1949. Fellow AAAS, Am. Statis. Assn. (sect. pres., assoc. editor Jour.), Am. Heart Assn.; mem. Inst. Medicine (elected), Biometrics Soc. (pres. Western N.Am. region 1978), Inst. Math. Stats., Soc. for Clin. Trials (pres. 1988), Internat. Stats. Inst. (elected), Phi Beta Kappa, Sigma Xi. Home: 981 Cottrell Way Stanford CA 94305-1057

BROWN, C. HAROLD, lawyer; b. Mendenhall, Ms., July 28, 1931; m. Alicia Brown; children: Tracey Gwen, Terry Lynne, Allison Anne, Harold Allen. BA, Vanderbilt U., 1957; LLB, U. Tex., 1960. Bar: Tex. 1960. Sr. ptnr. Brown Thompson Pruitt & Peterson, P.C., Ft. Worth, 1960—; pres. A.J. and Jessie Duncan Found. Past chmn. Ft. Worth Civil Svc. Commn.; past chmn. bd. dirs., past pres. Tarrant County Conv. Ctr., 1980; mem. Com. for Greater Tarrant County; past bd. dirs. Ft. Worth Camp Fire Girls; past bd. dirs. Nat. Com. for Adoption, The Gladney Ctr., Adopt a Spl. Kid/Tex.; past bd. dirs. Tex. Assn. Licensed Children's Svcs.; mgr. campaign R.M. Stovall for Mayor of Ft. Worth, 1969, 71, 73, Richard T. Andersen for Tarrant County Commr., 1972, 76, 80, 84, Senator Al Gore for Pres. (Tarrant County, Tex.), 1988; former deacon Univ. Christian Ch., Ft. Worth. Sgt. U.S. Army, 1953-55. Recipient Carnegie Hero Cert. Carnegie Hero Fund Commn., 1972; named Outstanding Young Texan, 1976. Fellow Tex. Bar Found. (life), Southwestern Legal Found., Ft. Worth-Tarrant County Bar Assn. (charter, bd. dirs. family law sect. 1978-80); mem. ABA, Tex. Bar Assn., Tarrant County Probate Bar, Ft. Worth Jr. Bar Assn. (pres. 1963), Am. Acad. Adoption Attys., Am. Acad. Hosp. Attys., Nat. Health Lawyers Assn., Pro Bono Coll. of State Bar of Tex., Badge and Shield, Vanderbilt U. Alumni Assn. (pres. 1966-67), Am. Brittany Club (Hall of Fame), Ridotto Club (pres. 1974), Petroleum Club, River Crest Country Club, Steeplechase Club, Nat. Commodore Club (adm.), Rotary, Masons, Shriners, Jesters, Alpha Tau Omega, Phi Delta Phi. Office: Brown Thompson Pruitt & Peterson 500 Throckmorton St Ste 3030 Fort Worth TX 76102-3817

BROWN, CABOT, private equity investor; b. San Francisco, Aug. 24, 1961; s. Stephen Cabot and Caludine (Montgomery) B.; m. Mollie Ward, Aug. 6, 1988; children: Parker, Harrison, Madeline, Stuart. AB, Harvard U., 1983, MBA, 1987. Fin. analyst Lehman Bros., N.Y.C., 1983-85; assoc. Volpe, Welty & Co., San Francisco, 1987-89, gen. ptnr., 1990-95; founder, mng. dir. Brown, McMillan & Co., San Francisco, 1996—; bd. dirs. Critical Care Concepts, Inc., Norcross, Ga., Wham-O, Inc., San Francisco. Contbr. articles to L.A. Times and Rolling Stone Mag. Democrat. Avocations: mountaineering, running, politics. Email: cbrown2744@aol.com. Home: 2744 Steiner St San Francisco CA 94123 Office: Brown McMillan & Co LLC 820 Montgomery St San Francisco CA 94133

BROWN, CAMERON, insurance company consultant; b. Chgo., Sept. 29, 1914; s. George Frederic and Irene (Larmon) B.; m. Dorothea Fruechtenicht, May 10, 1947 (div. Feb. 1965); children: Reid L., Deborah Sue; m. Jean McGrew, Dec. 22, 1965; 1 dau., Sophia Lyn. AB, U. Ill., 1937; grad., Indsl. Coll. Armed Forces, 1941. Vice pres. R. B. Jones & Sons, Inc., 1938-41; dir. Geo. F. Brown & Sons, Inc., Chgo., 1947-79; v.p. Geo. F. Brown & Sons, Inc., 1947-50, exec. v.p., 1950-53, pres., 1953-64, chmn., chief exec. officer, 1964-76; dir. Interstate Nat. Corp., 1968-79, pres., 1968-74, chmn., 1970-76; dir. Nat. Student Mktg. Corp., 1970-79, pres., 1970-71, chmn., 1970-75; dir. Interstate Fire & Casualty Co., 1952-79, exec. v.p., 1953-56, pres., 1956-74, chmn., 1970-76; dir. Chgo. Ins. Co., 1957-79, pres., 1957-74, chmn., 1970-76;

dir. Interstate Reins. Corp., 1957-79; pres. Cameron Brown Ltd., 1976—; underwriting mem. Lloyd's of London, 1971-95; sec., dir. Ill. Ins. Info. Svc., 1967-76. Contbg. author: Property and Liability Handbook, 1965. Pres. Chgo. area Planned Parenthood Assn., 1969-72; bd. dirs. Planned Parenthood Fedn. Am., 1976-79; active John Evans Club, Northwestern U., U. Ill., Pres.'s Club, U. Ill. Found., U. Chgo. Pres.'s Club. Lt. col. Gen. Staff Corps AUS, 1941-45. Decorated Bronze Star with oak leaf cluster. Mem. Lloyd's Broker Assn. (chmn. 1959-60), Nat. Assn. Ind. Insurers (bd. govs. 1961-77). Ill. St. Andrews Soc., Surplus Line Brokers Assn. (chmn. 1954), Confrerie des Chevaliers du Tastevin (officer-comdr. Chgo. and L.A.), Commanderie de Bordeaux (Maitre emeritus at Chgo., Santa Barbara, bd. govs. 1973—), Conseiller de Bordeaux, Chgo. Club, Exec. Club (dir. 1969-73, 1st v.p. 1970-71), Econ. Club, Mid-Am. Club, Casino Club Chgo., Army-Navy Country Club, Old Elm Club, Shoreacres Club, Onwentsia Club, Pine Valley Golf Club, Birnam Wood Golf Club, The Valley Club, Hon. Co. Edinburgh Golfers, Royal and Ancient Golf Club St. Andrews, Psi Upsilon. Home: 1400 N Green Bay Rd Lake Forest IL 60045-1110 also: 2004 Sandy Pl Santa Barbara CA 93108-2226

BROWN, CAROL (ROSE), artist; b. Rockville Ctr., N.Y., July 15, 1937; d. James Joseph and Rose (Ferme) Anderson; m. J. Dean Brown, Aug. 20, 1960 (dec. July 1973); m. Howard N. Schwartz, Mar. 20, 1994; stepchildren: Laura Ederer, Margot Ederer. BFA, Cornell U., 1957. One woman shows include The Roko Gallery, N.y.C., 1972, The Witkin Gallery, N.Y.C., 1983, 87, Charles Lucien Gallery, N.Y.C., 1990, Rettig Y Martinez, Santa Fe, 1992, The Little Gallery, Ithaca, N.Y., 1994; exhibited in group shows at Sidney Janis Gallery, N.Y.C., 1967, Finch Coll. Mus., N.Y.C., 1968, Bklyn. Mus., 1968, Richard Feigen Downtown Gallery, N.Y.C., 1968, La Jolla (Calif.) Mus., 1969, N.J. State Mus., Trenton, 1969, Alan Stone Gallery, N.Y.C., 1970, Elaine Horwitch Gallery, Scottsdale, Ariz., 1974, Rutgers U., N.J., 1983, NYU, 1984, Kleinert Gallery, Woodstock, N.Y., 1984, 55 Mercer St. Gallery, N.Y.C., 1985, Drew U., Madison, N.J., 1985, Ohio Wesleyan U. Art Gallery, Del., 1988, Etherton-Stern Gallery, Tucson, 1990, 92, Missoula (Mnt.) Mus. Fine Arts, 1991, Parrish Mus., Southampton, N.Y., 1992, Provincetown (Mass.) Art Assn. and Mus., 1993, Whitney Mus. at Stamford (Conn.), 1997; represented in collections U.S. Embassy, Athens, Greece, Rabat, Morrocco. Individual fellow Nat. Endowment for the Arts, 1994.

BROWN, CAROLYN RICE, dancer, choreographer; b. Fitchburg, Mass., Sept. 26, 1927; d. James Parker and Marion Burbank (Stevens) Rice; m. Earle Brown, June 28, 1950 (div.). BA cum laude, Wheaton Col., 1950; student, Marion Rice Studio of Dance, Fitchburg, Mass., 1931-46, Julliard, N.Y.C., 1952-53, Metropolitan Opera Ballet Sch., N.Y.C., 1953-65, Merce Cunningham Studio, N.Y.C., 1952-72; Doctor Fine Arts (honorary), Wheaton Col., 1974. Principal dancer Merce Cunningham Dance Co., N.Y.C., 1953-73; freelance choreographer and tchr. various cities and countries, 1973-90; self-employed filmmaker, 1975-78; choreographer Centre Choreographique, Anger, France, 1976; dean of dance Sch. of Arts, SUNY, Purchase, 1980-82; guest artist Die Palucca Schule, Dresden, East Germany, 1985, Bartholin Internat. Ballet, Copenhagen, Denmark, 1987; sr. fellow Dept. Theatre Arts U. Minn., Mpls., 1988-89, 90; regents lectr. Dept. Dramatic Art U. Calif., Berkeley. Choreographer numerous works, 1967-90; contbr. articles to profl. jours.; producer: (film) Dune Dance, 1978. Recipient Dance Magazine award, 1969, 100th Anniversary Disting. Svc. award Wheaton Col., 1970, Choreography awards Nat. Endowment for the Arts, 1973, 75, 76, choreography fellowship John Simon Guggenheim Found., 1983. Mem. Found. for Contemporary Performance Arts, Merce Cunningham Dance Found. Office: Cunningham Dance Found 463 West St New York NY 10014-2010

BROWN, CARROLL, diplomat, association executive; b. Selma, Ala., Oct. 5, 1928; s. Jack Crisman and Bessie (Bedsole) B.; m. Elvira DiMiceli, Apr. 2, 1953; children: David, Suzanne. AB, Columbia U., 1951, MA, 1953; postgrad., Johns Hopkins U., 1964-65. Joined Fgn. Service, 1957; posts include Yugoslavia, Poland, Washington; counselor embassy Vienna, Austria, 1968-73; dep. dir. for Eastern European affairs Dept. State, Washington, 1974-76; dep. chief mission Am. embassy, Warsaw, 1976-79; consul gen. Düsseldorf, Fed. Republic Germany, 1979-81, Munich, Fed. Republic Germany, 1981-84; dir. Office Can. Affairs Dept. State, Washington, 1984-86; acting dep. asst. sec. Dept. State, 1986; mem. U.S. delegation to 41st and 42nd UN Gen. Assemblies, N.Y.C., 1986; named pres. Am. Council on Germany, 1988, also bd. dirs.; bd. dirs. Dresdner RCM European Fund., John J. McCloy Fund. Adv. bd. World Policy Inst. Officer with USN, 1953-57. Decorated comdr.'s cross Order of Merit (Germany); recipient Meritorious Honor award and Superior Honor award U.S. Dept. State. Mem. Fgn. Svc. Assn., Diplomatic and Consular Officers, Ret., Coun. Fgn. Rels., Army-Navy Club, Univ. Club. Office: 14 E 60th St Ste 606 New York NY 10022-1006

BROWN, CARRYE BURLEY, federal agency administrator. BA, Stephen F. Austin State U.; MA, Tex. Woman's U.; postgrad. studies, Oxford (Eng.) U. Mem. sci., space and tech. com. U.S. Ho. Reps., Washington; adminstr. U.S. Fire Adminstrn. FEMA, Washington, 1994—. Office: FEMA US Fire Adminstrn 16825 S Seton Ave Emmitsburg MD 21727-6995

BROWN, CHADWICK EVERETT, football player; b. Pasadena, Calif., July 12, 1970. Degree in mktg., U. Colo., 1992. Linebacker Pitt. Steelers, 1993-97; owner Pro Exotics, Boulder, Colo.; linebacker Seattle Seahawks, 1997—. Named to Pro Bowl, 1996. Office: care Seattle Seahawks 11220 NE 53d St Kirkland WA 98033*

BROWN, CHARLES DODGSON, lawyer; b. N.Y.C., Dec. 31, 1928; s. James Dodgson and Leonora Rose (Nichols) B.; m. Martha Lockhart Spindler, Apr. 5, 1963; children: Gregory Spindler, William Howard. BA, NYU, 1949, JD, 1952. Bar: N.Y. 1952, U.S. Dist. Ct. (so. and ea. dists.) N.Y. 1955, U.S. Supreme Ct. 1958, U.S. Ct. Appeals (2d cir.) 1988. Counsel, former ptnr. Thacher Proffitt & Wood, N.Y.C., 1954—. Co-author: Equipment Leasing, 1995—. Chmn. zoning bd. Asharoken, N.Y., 1965, alt. chmn. environ. bd., 1967, trustee, 1967, village justice, 1980—; chmn. Boy Scout Am., Northport, N.Y., 1989—; elder 1st Presbyn. Ch., Northport. With U.S. Army, 1952-54. Mem. ABA, N.Y. Bar Assn., Maritime Law Assn. U.S. (proctor in Admiralty 1956, chair to marine fin. com. 1996—), N.Y. State Magistrate Assn., Suffolk County Magistrate Assn., Northport Tennis Club. Republican. Avocations: scuba diving, wind surfing, tennis. Office: Thacher Proffitt & Wood 2 World Trade Ctr New York NY 10048-0203

BROWN, CHARLES EARL, lawyer; b. Columbus, Ohio, June 6, 1919; s. Anderson and Ruth (Keeran) B.; m. Mary Elizabeth Hiett, May 23, 1959; children: Douglas Charles, Rebecca Ruth. AB, Ohio Wesleyan U., 1941; JD, U. Mich., 1949. Bar: Ohio 1949. Pvt. practice Toledo; assoc. Zachman, Boxell, Bebout & Torbet, 1950-53; ptnr. Shindler, Neff, Holmes & Schlageter (and predecessors), 1953-90, of counsel, 1991—; chmn. steering and exec. coms. Auto Trim Wholesalers div. Automotive Service Industry Assn., 1960-68. Lucas County Rep. Exec. Com., 1968-92. Capt. AUS, 1941-46; col. Res. ret. Decorated Bronze Star; recipient John J. Pershing award U.S. Army Command and Gen. Staff Coll., 1963. Fellow Am. Bar Found. (state chmn. 1978-84), Ohio State Bar Found. (trustee 1987-92), Am. Coll. Trust and Estate Counsel; mem. ABA, Ohio Bar Assn. (bd. govs. real property sect. 1953-76, coun. of dels. 1973-84, exec. com. 1984-87), Toledo Bar Assn. (past mem. exec. com.), Sixth Cir. Jud. Conf. (life), Toledo Area C. of C. (past trustee, com. chmn.), Res. Officers Assn., Assn. U.S. Army, Phi Beta Kappa. Congregationalist (past chmn. trustees). Lodge: Masons (32 deg.). Home: 3758 Brookside Rd Toledo OH 43606-2614 Office: 1200 Edison Plaza 300 Madison Ave Toledo OH 43604-1561

BROWN, CHARLES ERIC, health facility administrator, biochemist; b. Nov. 23, 1946; s. Charles E. and Dorothy R. (Riddle) B.; m. Kathy Louise Houck, July 24, 1971; 1 child, Eric Nathaniel. BA in Chemistry, SUNY, Buffalo, 1968; PhD in Biochemistry, Northwestern U., 1973. Instr., fellow depts. chemistry, biochemistry, molec. biol. Northwestern U., Evanston, Ill., 1973-75; rsch. fellow Roche Inst. Molecular Biology, Nutley, N.J., 1975-77; from asst. prof. biochemistry to assoc. prof. Med. Coll. Wis., Milw., 1977-88; analytical rsch. mgr. BP Chems. Ltd., 1992-94; dir. Rsch. Resources Ctr. U. Ill., Chgo., 1994—; adj. prof. chemistry U. Ill., Chgo., 1994—, adj. prof. mech. engring., 1998—; cons. Nicolet Instrument Corp., Metriflow, Inc., 1984-88. Contbr. articles in field to profl. jours., chpts. to books; developer biomedical and petrochemical equipment and techniques; patentee in field. Recipient Tech. Merit award Johnson Wax, 1987; NIH predoctoral fellow, 1968-72; Cottrell Rsch. grantee, 1979-82, Arthritis Found. grantee, 1984, Retirement Rsch. Found. grantee, 1987-88. Fellow Royal Soc. Chemistry; mem. AAAS, Internat. Soc. Magnetic Resonance, Soc. Neurosci., Am. Chem. Soc., Am. Soc. Pharmacology and Exptl. Therapeutics, Am. Soc. for Mass Spectrometry, Sigma Xi, Phi Lambda Upsilon. Office: Rsch Resources Ctr U Ill 901 S Wolcott Ave # E102 Msb Chicago IL 60612-7307

BROWN, CHARLES EUGENE, retired electronics company executive; b. Huntingburg, Ind., Oct. 31, 1921; s. Lemuel C. and Bertha (McCormack) B.; m. Elizabeth Sherman McAllister, Aug. 16, 1952; children—Deborah, Judith, Robert, Sarah. B.S., Ind. U., 1948, M.B.A., 1950. Corp. staff Glidden Co., Cleve., 1949-59; dir. indsl. relations Cleve. Pneumatic Tool Co., 1959-62; dir. indsl. relations Honeywell, Inc., Mpls., 1962-73, v.p. employee relations, 1973-80, v.p. exec. human resources, 1980-85, sr. staff v.p., 1985-86. Bd. dirs. Family and Children's Services, Mpls., Honeywell Retiree Vol. Program. Served with U.S. Army, 1942-45, ETO. Decorated Purple Heart. Clubs: Minneapolis, Interlachen Country. Home: 5029 Bruce Pl Edina MN 55424-1321

BROWN, CHARLES FREEMAN, II, lawyer; b. Boston, Mar. 7, 1914; s. Arthur Harrison and Nellie Abigail (Kenney) B.; m. Caroline Gotzian Tighe, Nov. 12, 1949 (dec. Jan. 1951); m. Pamela Judith Wedd, Nov. 29, 1952; children—Penelope Susan, Nicholas Wedd. A.B., Harvard U., 1936, LL.B., 1941. Bar: Mass. 1941. Assoc. atty. Sherburne, Powers & Needham, Boston, 1941-43; asst. gen. counsel, gen. counsel OSRD, Washington, 1943-47; counsel Research and Devel. Bd. and Mil. Liaison Com.; mem. Govt. Patents Bd., Office Sec. Def.; counsel Def. Prodn. Bd., NATO; dep. asst. sec. gen. for prodn. and logistics NATO detailed from Office Sec. Def., Washington, London, Paris, 1947-53; asst. to pres. Hydrofoil Corp., Annapolis, Md., 1953-54; asso. gen. counsel CIA, Washington, 1954-60; v.p., treas. Sci. Engring. Inst., Waltham, Mass., 1960-66; dep. gen. counsel NSF, Washington, 1966-73; gen. counsel NSF, 1973-76, chmn. interim compliance panel, 1970-71; cons., 1976—. Trustee Belmont (Mass.) Day Sch., 1963-66; bd. dirs. Hillcrest Children's Ctr., Washington, 1978-87, pres., 1980-83; pres. Cleveland Park Book Club, 1980-83, 91-94; bd. dirs. Cleveland Park Hist. Soc. Recipient Disting. Service award NSF. Mem. Fed. Bar Assn., Cosmos Club. Home and Office: 3500 Macomb St NW Washington DC 20016-3162

BROWN, CINDY LYNN, critical care nurse, emergency nurse, family nurse practitioner; b. Washington, July 11, 1956; d. Harry Carl and Betty (Gable) Sampson; m. Wayne Brown, 1998; children: Justin, Jesse. BSN, George Mason U., 1991; MSN, Marymount U., 1995. RN, Va.; CCRN; cert. family nurse practitioner; cert. clin. nurse specialist in critical care; cert. prescriptive authority; cert. ACLS, CPR instr./trainer, EMT; cert. chemotherapy adminstr. Coord. ARC, Honesdale, Pa., 1985-88; instr. CPR Fair Oaks Hosp., Fairfax, Va., 1988-97, extern critical care, 1990-91, trainer CPR instrn., 1991—; nurse critical care Washington Hosp. Ctr., 1991-94; flight nurse World Access Inc., 1993-94; emergency dept. nurse Mt. Vernon Hosp., Alexandria, Va., 1994-96; emergency nurse practitioner Potomac Hosp., Woodbridge, Va., 1996-97; family practice nurse practitioner Advanced Med. Ctr., Naples, Fla., 1997—; lectr. in field; instr. sign lang. Fairfax County Schs., 1989-90; tissue and organ donation educator Nat. Student Nurses Assn., George Mason U., 1990-91, pres., 1990-91; 1st aid corps mem. ARC, Fairfax, 1988—. Active nat. disaster relief health svc. team for Hurricane Andrew, ARC, Homestead, Fla., 1992, Miss. River Flood, 1993, Hurricane Marilyn, St. Thomas, V.I., 1995, Tropical Storm Jerry, Bonita Springs, Fla., 1995, Hurricane Fran, N.C., 1996, Hurricane George, Naples, Fla., 1998. Named Nursing Student of Yr. Nursing Student Assn. Va., 1991, Student Leader of Yr. George Mason U., 1991. Mem. AACN (Essay award 1991), D.C. Nursing Assn., Va. Nurses Assn., Golden Key Honor Soc., Sigma Theta Tau (Leadership award Epsilon Zeta chpt. 1991), Alpha Chi, Delta Epsilon Sigma. Avocations: country western dancing, water sports. Home: PO Box 12036 Naples FL 34101-2036

BROWN, CLANCY, actor, publishing executive; b. Urbana, Ohio, Jan. 5, 1959; s. Clarence J. and Joyce (Eldridge) B.; m. Jeanne Ellen Johnson, June 26, 1993; 1 child, Rose Beth Johnson-Brown. BS in Speech, Northwestern U., 1981. bd. dirs. Brown Pub. Co., Cin.; mng. ptnr. The B's Nest Ohio Partnership, Urbana. Appeared in films, including Bad Boys, 1983, Adventures of Buckaroo Bonzai, 1984, The Bride, 1985, Thunder Alley, 1985, The Highlander, 1986, Extreme Prejudice, 1987, Shoot to Kill, 1988, Season of Fear, 1989, Waiting for the Light, 1990, Blue Steel, 1990, Ambition, 1991, Pet Sematary II, 1992, The Shawshank Redemption, 1994, Gargoyles: The Heroes Awaken (voice), 1994, Donor Unknown, 1995, Dead Man Walking, 1995, Female Perversions, 1996, Fallout (voice), 1997, Annabelle's Wish, 1997, Starship Troopers, 1997, Flubber, 1997; TV movies include The Room Upstairs, 1987, The Man Who Broke 1,000 Chains, 1987, Johnny Ryan, 1990, Love, Lies and Murder, 1991, Cast a Deadly Spell, 1991, Past Midnight, 1992, Desperate Rescue: The Cathy Mahone Story, 1992, Bloodlines: Murder in the Family, 1993, Last Light, 1993, Earth 2, 1994, Radiant City, 1996, The Patron Saint of Liars, 1998; TV series include Earth 2, 1994, Mortal Kombat: The Animated Series (voice) 1995, Might Ducks (voice), 1996, Superman (voice), 1996, ER, 1997—, The New Batman/Superman Adventures (voice), 1997, The Legend of Calamity Jane (voice), 1997. Mem. Northwestern Entertainment Alliance. Address: care The Gersh Agy 232 N Canon Dr Beverly Hills CA 90210*

BROWN, COLIN W(EGAND), lawyer, diversified company executive; b. Port Jefferson, N.Y., Mar. 26, 1949; s. Keirn C. and Jane (Schuhl) B.; m. Cynthia Porter , Aug. 21, 1971; children: Courtney, Alec, Seth. BA, Williams Coll., 1971; JD, Duke U., 1974. Bar: N.Y. 1975, N.C. 1983, Ga. 1991. Assoc. Simpson Thacher & Bartlett, N.Y.C., 1974-81; sr. v.p., gen. counsel Cannon Mills Co., Kannapolis, N.C., 1981-82; sr. v.p., gen. counsel, corp. sec. Fuqua Industries, Inc., Atlanta, 1982-90, sr. v.p., gen. counsel, sec., 1990-91; chmn. bd. Am. Funeral Co., Atlanta, 1991-92; from v.p. to gen. counsel J.M. Family Enterprises, Inc., Deerfield Beach, Fla., 1992-94, COO, 1997—. Adv. bd. mem. Atlanta Legal Aid Soc., 1988-91, Pine Crest Schs., 1996; bd. dirs. Fulton County Heart Assn., 1988-92, Spl. Audiences, Inc., 1989-92; exec. bd. Egleston Hosp., 1989-92. Mem. ABA, Am. Corp. Counsel Assn. (pres. Ga. chpt. 1987-90). Office: JM Family Enterprises Inc PO Box 1160 Deerfield Beach FL 33443-1160*

BROWN, COLLEEN, broadcast executice. Grad., U. Colo. Gen. mgr. Sta. KPNX-TV, Phoenix, till 1998; v.p. broadcast Lee Enterprises, 1998—. Mem. March of Dimes. Mem. Young Press Assn. Office: Lee Enterprises 215 N Main St Davenport IA 52801*

BROWN, CONNELL JEAN, retired animal science educator; b. Everton, Ark., Mar. 6, 1924; s. Clarence Jackson and Winnie Dee (Trammell) B.; m. Erma Dexter (Taylor), May 19, 1946; children—Craig Jay, Mark Allen. B.S.A., U. Ark., 1948; M.S., Okla. State U., 1950, Ph.D., 1956. Asst. prof. dept. animal sci. U. Ark., Fayetteville, 1950-57; assoc. prof. U. Ark., 1957-62, livestock sect. leader, 1978-81, prof., 1962-86, Univ. prof., 1986-90, prof. emeritus, 1990—; lectr. Internat. Stockmans Short course, 1980. Contbr. articles to profl. jours. Served with USAAF, 1943-46; PTO. Recipient Rsch. award Performance Registry Internat., 1977, U. Ark. Coll. Agr. Rsch. award, 1981, Disting. Svc. award Ark. Cattlemans Assn., 1985; named to Am. Polled Hereford Assn. Hall of Merit, 1986, Ark. Agrl. Hall of Fame, 1994. Fellow AAAS, Am. Soc. Animal Sci. (pres. so. sect. 1975, leadership award so. sect. 1975); mem. Am. Genetics Assn., N.Y. Acad. Scis., So. Assn. Agrl. Scientists (bd. dirs.), Am. Registry Profl. Animal Scientists (pres. Ark. chpt. 1989), Kiwanis (dist. pres. 1984-85, lt. gov. 1992-93), Sigma Xi (pres. 1986-87), Gamma Sigma Delta (pres. 1967-68). Home: 2583 N Elizabeth Ave Fayetteville AR 72703-3710

BROWN, CORRINE, congresswoman; b. Jacksonville, Fla., Nov. 11, 1946; 1 child, Shantrel. BS, Fla. A & M U., 1969; EdS, U. Fla., 1974. Former mem. Fla. Ho. of Reps; del. Nat. Dem. Conv., 1988; mem. 103rd-105th Congress from 3rd Fla. dist., 1993, mem. transp. and infrastructure com. aviation, surface transp., mem. VA com. hosp. and health care; VA, transp. and infrastructure coms. 105th Congress. Mem. Sigma Gamma Rho. Baptist. Home: 314 Palmetto St Jacksonville FL 32202-2619 Office: US Ho of Reps 2444 Rayburn HOB Washington DC 20515-0903*

BROWN, CRAIG, advertising agency executive; b. 1951. BA in Acctg., Mich. State U., 1973. With Arthur Andersen & Co., Detroit, 1973-80, D'Arcy MacManus Masius, Inc., N.Y.C., 1980-85; exec. v.p., CFO D'Arcy Masius Benton & Bowles, N.Y.C., 1985-97; CFO DMB&B Comms. (formerly D'Arcy Masius Benton & Bowles), N.Y.C., 1997-98, exec. v.p., 1996-98; vice chmn., COO, CFO MacManus Group, N.Y.C., 1997—. Office: DMB&B Comms 1675 Broadway New York NY 10019-5820*

BROWN, CRAIG JAY, ophthalmologist; b. Fayetteville, Ark., Feb. 11, 1951; s. Connell Jean and Erma Dexter (Taylor) B.; m. Patricia Ruth Davis, Aug. 31, 1974. BS in Zoology, U. Ark., 1973, MD, 1977. Diplomate Am. Bd. Ophthalmology. Intern Bapt. Med. Ctr., Nalerigu, Ghana, 1977-78; resident in ophthalmology U. Mo., Columbia, 1978-81; practice medicine specializing in ophthalmology, Fayetteville, 1981—; attending physician Washington Regional Hosp., Fayetteville, 1981—. Contbr. articles to profl. jours. Justice of Peace for Washington County, Ark., 1972. Fellow Am. Coll. of Surgeons, Am. Acad. Ophthalmology, Royal Soc. Medicine; mem. AMA, Ark. Med. Soc. Methodist. Avocations: invertebrate paleontology. Home: 2733 W Salem Rd Fayetteville AR 72704 Office: 594 Millsap Rd Fayetteville AR 72703-4096

BROWN, CRAIG WILLIAM, physical chemist; b. Denver, Aug. 3, 1953; s. Clarence William and Gail Margaret (Farthing) B.; 1 child, Russell Corey. BS in Chemistry, Colo. State U., 1975; MS, Fla. State U., 1977, PhD, 1980. Dep. dir. picosecond and quantum radiation lab. Tex. Tech. U., Lubbock, 1980-83; systems engr. Internat. Marine Systems, Inc., Seattle, 1983-87; freelance cons., 1987-88; staff scientist Heart Interface Corp., Kent, Wash., 1988-91, sr. project engr., 1991-93; cons. scientist Brooks Rand Ltd., Seattle, 1992-93, sr. scientist, 1993-99; cons. Environ. Protection Agy., Dept. Energy, 1995-97; mgr. rsch. N.W. Aluminum Techs., 1999—; mem. battery charger/inverter project tech. com. Am. Boat and Yacht Coun., Edgewater, Md., 1989-92; cons. on mercury speciation Environ. Protection and Dept. Energy, 1995-97; mgr. of inert anode aluminum prodn. rsch. project, 1996—. Contbr. articles to Phys. Rev. Letters, Jour. Chem. Physics, Jour. of the Minerals, Metals and Materials Soc.; contbr. book revs. to Photochemistry and Photobiology; contbr. to conf. proceedings. Whiteford scholar Colo. State U., 1974-75, Honors scholar U. Denver, 1971-72, Gustavson fellow Colo. State U., 1974-75, Welch postdoctoral fellow Tex. Tech U., 1980-83; Dept. Energy rsch. grantee, 1994-96, innovative concepts program awardee, 1997-98. Mem. AAAS, Am. Chem. Soc., N.Y. Acad. Scis., Internat. Platform Assn. Achievements include patent for switched multi-tapped transformer power conversion method and apparatus; patent for fluorescent spectrophotometer system with automatic calibration and improved optics block; designed power inverters and battery chargers; designed spectrophotometric instruments; research in chemical physics, atomic and molecular spectroscopy, chemical sensors, aluminum production. Avocations: playing guitar, songwriting. Office: Northwest Aluminum Techs care Brooks Rand Ltd 3950 6th Ave NW Seattle WA 98107-5056

BROWN, D. DAVID, performing company executive. Gen. mgr. Boston Ballet. Office: Boston Ballet 19 Clarendon St Boston MA 02116-6100

BROWN, D. ROBIN, elementary school educator; b. Cleve., Oct. 31, 1949; d. William Michael and Darla G. (Carlson) Linsenmann; m. Ross H. Brown, Aug. 21, 1971. BA cum laude, W.Va. Wesleyan U., 1971; MA, Ashland U., 1988, postgrad., 1988-90; postgrad., Ohio State U., 1989-90. Cert. elem. tchr., Ohio, W.Va. Tchr. Lost Creek Elem. Sch., Clarksburg, W.Va., 1971-72, Leesburg (Va.) Middle Sch., 1972-75, Northmoor Elem. Sch., Dayton, Ohio, 1975-79, Jonathan Alder Local Schs., Plain City, Ohio, 1979—. Active TWIG # 158, Columbus, Ohio, 1990—, Salvation Army, Columbus, 1990—, Worthington Hills Women's Club, Columbus, 1985—. Recipient Sci. award Exxon, 1974. Mem. Internat. Reading Assn., Reading Recovery, Kappa Delta Pi, Sigma Eta Sigma, Pi Gamma Mu, Tri Beta. Avocations: golf, reading, travel, sports, volunteer work. Home: 825 Highview Dr West Worthington OH 43235-1232 Office: Jonathan Alder Local Schs 4331 Kilbury Huber Rd Plain City OH 43064-9064

BROWN, DALE, JR., obstetrician, educator, health facility adminstrator; b. Balt., Oct. 14, 1937; s. Dale and Louise (McCormick) B.; m. Eleanor Bartlett Moore, 1965; children: Stephen, Chris (dec.). BS, U. N.Mex., 1959, postgrad., 1960; MD, U. Tex., Galveston, 1964. Diplomate Am. Bd. Ob-Gyn (examiner 1991—). Intern Charity Hosp., New Orleans, 1964-65, resident, 1965-68; pvt. practice Amarillo, Tex., 1970-71, Houston, 1971-76, 1977—; mem. staff The Meth. Hosp.; assoc. chief ob-gyn, chief obstetrics St. Luke's Episcopal Hosp., 1984—, head residents, 1992—, chief staff, 1995-97; clin. instr. Tulane Med. Sch., 1967-68; from instr. to assoc. clin. prof. Baylor Coll. Medicine, 1972-91, clin. prof., 1991—; cons. neonatal mortality com. Tex. Children's Hosp., 1986—. Contbr. articles to profl. jours. Mem. bd. deacons First Prebyn. Ch., 1976-86, chmn. diaconate bd., 1985-86, mem. bd. elders, 1987—; Active Audubon Soc., 1978—, Wilderness Soc., 1981—. Mem. AMA (Recognition award 1982-95, 85-88, 88-91, 91-94, 94-97), ACOG (Recoginition award 1982-85, 85-88, 88-91, 91-94), ACS, Internat. Coll. Surgeons, Internat. Soc. Advancement Humanistic Studies Gynecology, Internat. Soc. Study of Vulvovaginal Disease (asst. sec., treas. 1979-87, sec. gen. 1987-93, pres. elect 1993-95, pres. 1995-97),Am. Fertility Soc., Inst. Study of Vulvar Disease (bd. dirs., treas. 1988—), Ctrl. Assn. Obstreticians and Gynecologists (chmn. local arrangements com. 1976, mem. selection and presentation of papers com. 1980), So. Med. Assn., Tex. Med. Assn., Tex. Obstet. and Gynecol. Soc., Houston Obstet. and Gynecol. Soc., Houston Surgical Soc., Harris County Med. Assn., Seward Wills Obstet. and Gynecol. Soc., Conrad Collins and Pernol Ob-Gyn Soc., Tex. Flyfishing Club, Doctor's Club, Houston City Club, River Oaks Country Club, Mu Delta. Office: 6624 Fannin St Ste 2180 Houston TX 77030-2341*

BROWN, DALE PATRICK, retired advertising executive; b. Richmond, Va., Aug. 11, 1947; d. Thomas Windom and Helen (Curtis) Patrick. BA in Journalism, U. Richmond, 1968, MA in English, 1978. Reporter city news sect. Richmond Times-Dispatch, 1968-71; free-lance writer, 1971-73; v.p., supr. pub. rels. account The Martin Agy., Richmond, 1973-77, account supr. advt., v.p., 1977-79, v.p., supr. advt. account, then group v.p. and sr. v.p., 1983-89; mgr. communications svcs. Mobil Chem. Co., Richmond, 1979-81; mgr. communications Whittaker Gen. Med., Richmond, 1981-83; exec. v.p. The Stenrich Group, Richmond, 1989-90; pres., chief exec. officer Sive/Young & Rubicam, Cin., 1992-98. Trustee U. Richmond, 1992—; mem. devel. bd. Good Samaritan Hosp., 1992-95, Leadership Cin.; bd. dirs. Met. Growth Alliance, Downtown Cin. Inc., Midwest Strategic Trust, 1993-97, Ohio Nat. Life Ins. (exec. com.), Cin. C. of C.; chair Acad. Career Women of Achievement, 1996—; bd. govs. Cin. chpt. Am. Assn. Advt. Agys. Recipient 2 AAF Silver medals, 1988, 96, Richmond Advt. Person of Yr. award Advt. Club Richmond, 1988, Woman of Achievement award Cin. YWCA, 1993, Human Rels. award Am. Jewish Com., Cin. chpt., 1996, various others including Addy, Effie, Clio awards N.Y. Art Dirs. Club. Mem. Pub. Rels. Soc. Am., Cin. C. of C., Advt. Club Cin., Queen City Club (bd. dirs.), Comml. Club of Cin. Avocations: reading, travel, arts. Home: 1231 Martin Dr Cincinnati OH 45202-1737

BROWN, DALE SUSAN, government administrator, educational program director, writer; b. N.Y.C., May 2, 1954; d. Bertram S. and Beatrice Joy (Gilman) B. BA, Antioch Coll., 1976. Rsch. asst. Am. Occupational Therapy Assn., Rockville, Md., 1976-79; writer Pres.' Com. on Employment of People with Disabilities, Washington, 1979-82, program mgr., 1982—; program mgr. labor com. Pres.' Com. on Employment of People with Disabilities, 1985, 96-98, program mgr. work environment and tech. com., 1988-94; program mgr. work environment and tech. com. Ams. with Disabilities Act, 1986-94; program com. on libr. and info. svcs. Pres.' Com. on Employment of People with Disabilities, 1984-86, youth devel com., 1986-88, new products devel. team, 1987-90, agy. rep., 1991-93, with interagy. tech. assistance coordinating team, 1992-94; program mgr. Job Accomodation Network, 1998—; program mgr. Job Accommodation Network, 1997; cons. in field, gen. assembly speaker nat. conv. Gen. Fedn. Women's Clubs, 1981, mem. Rehab Svcs. Adminstrn. Task Force on Learning Disabilities, 1981-83. *Dale S. Brown has been a program manager on the President's Committee on Employment of People with Disabilities since 1979. She is project coordinator of the Job Accommodation Network, a free, confidential telephone consultation service for people who need information on how to accomodate people with dissabilities on the job. Outside of her work, she writes books,* *including I Know I Can Climb the Mountain, a book of poetry, Learning Disabilities and Employment, a research compendium coauthored with Paul Gerber, and Steps to Independence for People with Learning Disabilities, a self-remediation handbook. She is a well-known speaker.* Author: Steps to Independence for People with Learning Disabilities, 1980, Pathways to Employment for People with Learning Disabilities, 1991, Working Effectively with People Who Have Learning Disabilities and Attention Deficit Hyperactivity Disorder, 1995, I Know I can Climb the Mountain, 1995, Learning Disabilities and Employment, 1997; writer film: They Could Have Saved Their Homes, 1982; dir. videotape Part of the Team People with Disabilities in the Workforce, 1990; editorial bd. Perceptions, 1981-83, Learning Disabilities Focus, 1988-90, In the Mainstream, 1994-98; co-editor Learning Disabilities and Employment; cons. editor Learning Disabilities Rsch. and Practice, 1990—. Pres. Assn. Learning Disabled Adults, Washington, 1979-80, bd. dirs. Closer Look Nat. Info. Ctr., Washington, 1980-83, Am. Coalition fo Citizens with Disabilities, 1985-86, chair 5th ann. conf. on Info. Tech. for User With Disabilities, 1989, spl. asst. for people with disabilities Federally Employed Women, 1991-92, mem. congrl. task force Rights and Empowerment of Ams. with Disabilities, 1988-90, mem. blue ribbon panel on Nat. Telecommunications Access for People with Disabilities, 1989-94, profl. adv. bd. Nat. Attention Deficit Disorder Assn., 1996—; del. Nat. Writer's Union, 1999. Grantee Found. for Children with Learning Disabilities, 1982; recipient Margaret Byrd Rawson award, 1989, Personal Achievement award Women's Program USDOL, 1989, Individual Achievement award Nat. Coun. on Communication Disorders, 1991, Spl. Acievement award Pres.'s Com. on Employment of People with Disabilities, 1991, Gold Screen award Nat. Assn. Gov. Communicators, 1991, Arthur S. Fleming award, 1992, 94; named One of Ten Outstanding Young Ams. U.S. Jr. C. of C., 1984, Jaycees, 1994. Mem. Nat. Network of Learning Disabled Adults (founder, pres., 1980-81, rep. Inter-agy. com. on computer support handicapped emploees 1998—), Nat. Assn. Govt. Communicators (Blue Pencil award 1986, rep. inter-agy. com. on handicapped employees 1989—), Learning Disabilities Assn. (bd. dirs. 1986-91), ALA. Democrat. Jewish. Office: Pres' Com Employment of People with Disabilities 1331 F St NW Washington DC 20004-1107

BROWN, DALE WEAVER, clergyman, theologian, educator; b. Wichita, Kans., Jan. 12, 1926; s. Harlow J. and Cora Elisa (Weaver) B.; m. Lois D. Kauffman, Aug. 17, 1947; children: Deanna Gae, Dennis Dale, Kevin Ken. A.B., McPherson Coll., 1946; B.D., Bethany Theol. Sem., 1949; postgrad., Drake U., 1954-56, Northwestern U. and Garrett Bibl. Inst., 1956-58; Ph.D., Northwestern U., 1962. Ordained to ministry Ch. of Brethren, 1946; pastor Stover Meml. Ch. of Brethren, Des Moines, 1949-56; dir. religious life, asst. prof. philosophy and religion McPherson Coll., 1958-62; assoc. prof. Christian theology Bethany Theol. Sem., Oak Brook, Ill., 1962-70; prof. Christian theology Bethany Theol. Sem., 1970-94; Del. standing com. Ch. of Brethren, 1954; moderator Middle Iowa Dist., 1952-53, mem. dist. and regional bds., gen. bd., 1960-62, moderator-elect ann. conf., 1970-71, moderator, 1971-72. Author: In Christ Jesus: The Significance of Jesus as the Christ, 1965, Four Words for World, 1968, So Send I You, 1969, Brethren and Pacifism, 1970, The Christian Revolutionary, 1971, Flamed by the Spirit, 1978, Understanding Pietism, 1978, revised edit., 1996, Berea College: Spiritual and Intellectual Roots, 1982; What About the Russians, 1984; Biblical Pacifism, 1986. Mem. Am. Acad. Religion, Internat. Bonhoeffer Soc., Fellowship of Reconciliation, Am. Theol. Soc. Home: 1101 College Ave Elizabethtown PA 17022-2236

BROWN, DALLAS COVERDALE, JR., retired army officer, retired history educator; b. New Orleans, Aug. 21, 1932; s. Dallas Coverdale and Rita Sydney (Taylor) B.; m. Joyce Regina Bush, July 26, 1955, (div. Aug. 1985); children: Dallas Coverdale, III, Leonard, Jan, Karen, Barbara; m. Elizabeth Taylor Vance, Sept. 3, 1985. B.A. in History and Polit. Sci. (Disting. Mil. Grad. 1954), W.Va. State Coll., 1954; M.A. in Govt., Ind. U., 1967, postgrad. in Def. Lang. Inst., 1966; grad., Command and Gen. Staff Coll., 1968, USA Russian Inst., 1970, Naval War Coll., 1974. Commd. 2d lt. U.S. Army, 1954, advanced through grades to brig. gen., 1978; service in Korea, W. Ger., Vietnam; dep. chief staff intelligence U.S. Army Forces Command, 1978-79; dep. vice dir. fgn. intelligence Def. Intelligence Agy., 1979-80; dep. comdr. U.S. Army War Coll., Carlisle Barracks, Pa., 1980-84; ret., 1984; assoc. prof. history W.Va. State Coll., Institute, 1984-96; mem. bd. advisors W.Va. State Coll., 1990-91; mem. W.Va. Gov.'s Higher Edn. Advocacy Team, 1992-93; bd. dirs. WPBY-TV (PBS), 1995-96. Constituent U.S. Army War Coll. Found.; mem. Mil. Adv. Coun., Ctr. for Def. Info. Decorated Def. Superior Service medal, Meritorious Service medal (2), Joint Service Commendation medal, Army Commendation medal, Master Parachutist badge, Aircraft Crewman badge; named Alumnus of Yr. W.Va. State Coll., 1978; named to W.Va. State Coll. ROTC Hall of Fame, 1980. Mem. Assn. U.S. Army, Ret. Officers Assn., Nat. Eagle Scout Assn., Sun City Vets. Assn. (comdr. 1999—), W.Va. State Coll. Alumni Assn., Alpha Phi Alpha, Alpha Lambda Boule, Sigma Pi Phi, Pi Alpha Theta, Pi Sigma Alpha, Rocks Club. Unitarian. Home: Sun City Hilton Head 17 Devant Dr E Bluffton SC 29910-4537

BROWN, DANIEL, independent art consultant, critic, writer; b. Cin., Nov. 4, 1946; s. Sidney H. and Genevieve Florence (Elbaum) B. AB cum laude, Middlebury Coll., 1968; AM, U. Mich., 1970; postgrad., Princeton U., 1971-72. Dir. cultural events U. Cin., 1972, spl. asst. to pres., 1973; v.p., corp. sec. Brockton Shoe Trimming Co., Cin., 1974—, sec. treas., 1997—; instr. Art Acad. Cin, 1980, 88—; prin. Daniel Brown, Inc., Cin. and Columbus, 19990; panel leader, mem. Midwest Coll. Art Assn. Conv., 1995; curator KZF Gallery, Cin., 1987-94, U. Clubs Ann. Art Exhibit, Christ Hosp. Art in the Lobby Program, all exhibits at Bittner's Antique & Design Studios, 1999—; co-curator Katz and Dawgs Gallery, 1989-90, exhbns. of regional artists Christ Hosp., Cin., 1999—; art critic Cin. Mag., 1980-83, Cin. Herald, 1992, Cin. Art Acad. Newsletter, Provincetown Arts, 1988-90, The Cin. Herald, 1992-94, Everybody's News, 1993-94; editor-in-chief Antenna Arts Mag., 1996-98; regular curator Bittner's Antiques Design Ctr, 1998—; co-editor, co-pub., co-owner The Blue Book of Cin., 1998—; commentator Sta. WKRC-TV, Cin.; art and music critic Sta. WCPO-TV, Cin., 1986-88; art critic USA Arts, The Cin. Herald, 1992-94; arts editor, essayist Cin. City Beat, 1994-95; guest lectr. dept. fine arts and dept. psychiatry U. Cin., 1990, lectr. English and art history, 1993—; guest lectr. dept. fine arts U. Ky., 1990—; guest curator New Art from Academe: An Overview The Cen. Exchange, Kansas City, Mo., 1988, Figure it Out! inaugural exhbn. Katz and Dawgs Gallery, Columbus, Ohio, 1988, Lyrical Abstractions, 1989, Design of the Future, 1989, Contemporary Landscape Kencabco Co., Cin., 1988, A Critic's Choice: Art of the '90's, No. Ky. U., 1989, Katz and Dawys Decorative Arts: Wave of the Future, 1989, The Arts Consortium, 1991-92, 93-94, Cuba Now Carnegie Arts Ctr., 1996; guest co-curator Cin. Yesterday and Today Tangeman Fine Arts Gallery, U. Cin., 1987, guest curator, 1988; frequent guest lectr. on arts; permanent curator The KZF Art Gallery, Cin., 1987-95; guest co-curator The Artist at Mid-Career: A Dialogue Between Columbus and Cin., 1989-90; curator for exhbns. at Liberties Restaurant, Cin., 1990-93, Fifth Third Bank, Cin., 1991-92; curator African-Am. Mus., 1992, 93, African Am. Artists, 1994; guest spkr. Arts Consortium, 1994; guest critic dept. painting and drawing U. Cin., 1993—; corr. editor: Dialogue Mag., 1986-90, art reviewer, 1983—; lead editorialist: The Arts Consortium Newsletter, 1992; monthly editorialist Antenna Newspaper, 1995—. Author: David Bumbeck: The Romantic Classicist, 1989, Tom Bacher: High Tech American Impressionist, 1989, The Universe Watching: The Art of Nancy Fletcher Cassell, 1990, John Stewart: A Retrospective, 1991, Bukang Kim: Journey to the East, 1992, Hustlers, 1992, 93, The Evolution of Form, Bukang Kim: A Retrospective, 1995; columnist Art Acad. News, 1990-94; monthly guest columnist The Cin. Post, 1991, The Downtowner, 1991-95; occasional columnist, 1991—; monthly columnist Everybody's News, 1994; editor Antenna Arts mag., 1996—. Mem. exhbns com. Contemporary Arts Ctr.; sec., bd. dirs. Mercantile Libr., 1985-91, treas., 1986, chmn. programs com., 1987—, Young Wing; trustee Contempory Arts Ctr., 1984-87, co-chmn. artists adv. bd., 1987, Vocal Arts Ensemble, 1984, Enjoy the Arts, 1985-88, v.p., 1986; mem. bd. advisors Cin. Artists Group Effort, 1986-88; guest curator Carnegie Arts Ctr., Covington, Ky., 1986—; juror art competitions, Cin. and Columbus, Ohio, 1986-87, Mansfield, Ohio, Kansas City, Mo.; mem. citizens' adv. com. Art Acad. of Cin., 1989—, trustee, 1991—; trustee Art Acad. Cin. Coop. Gallery, 1990; co-chmn. fine art com. The Arts Consortium, cin., 1990—, curator, 1991—; sole juror Art Acad. Alumni Juried Exhbn., 1992; trustee UMOJA Artists' Group, 1994. Recipient The Critic's Purse award Dialogue mag., 1985. Mem. Internat. Soc. Art Critics (N.Y. and Paris chpts.), Univ. Club (art com. 1990-91, guest curator 1992). Home: 2200 Victory Pkwy Apt 809 Cincinnati OH 45206-2823

BROWN, DANIEL G., military officer; b. Apr. 30, 1946; s. John W. Jr. and Josephine G. Brown; m. Jane T. Agnew; children: Dan, Tim, Jennifer. BA in Polit. Sci., Furman U.; MS in Transp. Mgmt., Fla. Inst. Tech.; grad., Armed Forces Staff Coll., Indsl. Coll. Armed Forces. Commd. 2d lt. U.S. Army, 1968, advanced through grades to maj. gen., 1995; comdr. 527th Transp. Co., Stuttgart, Germany, 1098th Transp. Co., 10 Transp. Bn., Ft. Eustis, Va., 155th Transp. Co., 10th Transp. Bn., Ft. Eustis, Mil. Traffic Mgmt. Bn., Pusan, Korea, 7th Transp. Group, Operation Desert Storm, Saudi Arabia; chief strategic mobility divsn. U.S. Army Staff; chief transp. assignments br. U.S. Army Pers. Command; various strategic mobility assignments Joint Deployment Agy. and U.S. Readiness Command; chief combined arms assessment team Operation Restore Hope, Somalia; commdg. gen. 19th Theater Army Area Command, Korea. Decorated Legion of Merit with oak leaf cluster, Bronze Star with oak leaf cluster, Army Commendation medal with two oak leaf clusters, Army Expeditionary medal. Office: US Army Transp Unit 15015 Center & Ft Eustis Fort Eustis VA 23604-5078

BROWN, DANIEL STEWART, JR., communications educator, university official; b. Abington, Pa., June 9, 1959; s. Daniel Stewart and Lucille Mae (Freeman) B.; m. Susan Kay Shrum, Dec. 31, 1988. BA, Bob Jones U., 1982; MA, Miami U., Oxford, Ohio, 1983; PhD, La. State U. and A&M Coll., 1987. Instr. speech Pensacola (Fla.) Christian Coll., 1983-84; asst. prof. comm. Miami U., 1987-88; dir. devel. Maranatha Christian Schs., Columbus, Ohio, 1988-90; asst. prof. comm. arts Bryan Coll., Dayton, Tenn., 1990-94, assoc. prof., 1994-97, chmn. divsn. humanities, 1993-97, dir. honors program, 1995-97; assoc. prof. comm., dir. Ind. Wesleyan U., Indpls., 1997—. Contbr. articles and book revs. to profl. publs.; dir. Destiny in Dayton, 1991, 92. Mem. planning com. Tenn. Strawberry Festival, Dayton, 1993; mem. devel. dist. planning com. Tenn. Humanities Coun., 1996; vol., bd. dirs. Women's Care Ctr., 1995—, chmn., 1996-97. Recipient Apex award Comm. Concepts, 1991. Mem. Nat. Comm. Assn., Religious Comm. Assn., Kiwanis (v.p. Dayton, Tenn. 1994-95, pres. 1995-96, bd. dirs. Noblesville-Sunrisers 1999—), Phi Delta Kappa. Republican. Presbyterian. Avocations: landscaping, cooking. E-mail: dbrown@indwes.edu. Office: Ind Wesleyan U 3777 Priority Way South Dr Indianapolis IN 46240

BROWN, DARRELL, broadcast executive. BA in Comm., Brigham Young U. V.p., gen. mgr. Sta. KGTV-TV, San Diego, 1995—. Office: Sta KGTV-TV 4600 Air Way # San Diego CA 92102-2528*

BROWN, DARRELL JAMES, publishing executive; b. Abilene, Tex., Feb. 13, 1959; s. Don J. and Alma K. Brown; m. Patricia Lee Stevens, Apr. 2, 1983; children: Tova Lee, Devon Justice. BS in Psychology, U. Mo., 1981. Dir. retail dept. The May Cos., St. Louis, 1981; vice chmn., exec. editor LEADERS Mag., N.Y.C., 1981—; v.p. Dormann Pub., Inc., N.Y.C., 1984—; v.p., sec. SIPA News Svc., N.Y.C., 1984—, Internat. Bd. Indsl. Advisors, N.Y.C., 1984—; pres. Global Change Inc., 1996—; lectr., career guidance counselor in field. Mem. editl. bd. The Scottish Rite Jour. Founding exec. bd. mem., sec., treas. Acacia Frat., U. Mo., Columbia. Mem. The Found. for Family Values (founding bd. mem., v.p.), The Young People's Leadership Found. (pres.), Princess Elizabeth of Yugoslavia Found. (inat. adv. bd.), Scottish Rite Mason (33rd degree), Order of De Molay (Legion of Honor). Avocations: tennis, skiing. Office: Leaders Mag 59 E 54th St New York NY 10022-4211

BROWN, DAVID, motion picture producer, writer; b. N.Y.C., July 28, 1916; s. Edward Fisher and Lillian (Baren) B.; m. Liberty LeGacy, Apr. 15, 1940 (div. 1951); 1 son, Bruce LeGacy; m. Wayne Clark, May 25, 1951 (div. 1957); m. Helen Gurley, Sept. 25, 1959. AB, Stanford U., 1936; MS, Columbia U., 1937. Apprentice San Francisco News and Wall St. Jour., 1936; night editor, asst. drama critic Fairchild Publs., 1937-39; editorial dir. Milk Research Council, 1939-40; assoc. editor Street & Smith Publs., 1940-43; assoc. editor, exec. editor, editor-in-chief Liberty mag., 1943-49; editorial dir. Nat. Edn. Campaign, A.M.A., 1949; assoc. editor, mng. editor Cosmopolitan mag., 1949-52; mng. editor, story editor, head scenario dept. 20th Century-Fox Film Corp. Studios, Beverly Hills, Calif., 1952-56, mem. studio exec. com., 1956-60, producer, 1960-62; v.p., dir. story operation 20th Century Fox Film Corp., Beverly Hills, Calif., 1964-69, exec. v.p. creative operations, 1969-70, dir., 1968-70; exec. v.p. creative operations, dir. Warner Bros., 1971-72; ptnr. Zanuck/Brown Co., N.Y.C., 1972-87; pres. Manhattan Project Ltd., 1987—, Island World, 1990-92; exec. story editor, head scenario dept., editorial v.p. New Am. Library World Lit., Inc., 1963-64; final judge for best short story pub. in mags. Benjamin Franklin Mag. ann. awards, 1955-58. Author: Brown's Guide to Growing Gray, 1987, Let Me Entertain You, 1990, The Rest of your Life is the Best of Your Life, 1991; contbr. articles to Am. mag., Collier's, Harpers, Sat. Evening Post, Reader's Digest, others; editor: I Can Tell It Now, 1964, How I Got That Story, 1967; contbr.: Journalists in Action, 1963; prodr.: (films) The Sting, 1973, The Sugarland Express, 1974, The Eiger Sanction, 1975, Jaws, 1977, MacArthur, 1977, Jaws II, 1978, The Island, 1980, Neighbors, 1981, The Verdict, 1982, Target, 1985, Cocoon, 1985; exec. prodr. Driving Miss Daisy, HBO Women and Men, 1 and 2, 1990, 91, The Player, 1992, A Few Good Men, 1992, Watch It, 1993, The Cemetery Club, 1993, Canadian Bacon, 1994, Kiss The Girls, 1997, The Saint, 1997, Deep Impact, 1998, Angela's Ashes, 1999. Trustee com. on film Mus. Modern Art, N.Y.C. Served as 1st lt., M.I. AUS, World War II. Mem. Acad. Motion Picture Arts and Scis. (recipient Irving G. Thalberg Meml. award 1991), Producers Guild Am. (David O. Selznick Lifetime Achievement award 1993), Nat. Press Club (Washington), Coffee Ho. Club (N.Y.C.), Bd. of Visitors Columbia U. Grad Sch. of Journalism, Players Club (N.Y.C., Dutch Treat (N.Y.C.), Century Assn. (N.Y.C.), N.Y. Friars Club. Office: Manhattan Project Ltd 1775 Broadway Ste 410 New York NY 10019-1903 *Success, after all, is no more and no less than doing well what one wants to do most-regardless of where such an endeavor places one in the hierarchy of society.*

BROWN, DAVID A.B., strategy consultant; b. Newcastle Upon Tyne, Eng., Nov. 6, 1943; came to U.S., 1968; s. David Lumsden and Joyce Ethel (Johnstone) B.; m. Karin Monica Wenham, Aug. 3, 1968; children: Sanford, Andrew. B Commerce, McGill U., Montreal, Que., Can., 1966, lic. in acctg., 1968; MBA with distinction, Harvard U., 1970. Chartered acct., Can. Dir. Boston Cons. Group, 1970-78; dir. planning Teradyne Inc., Boston, 1978-79; ptnr. Braxton Assocs., Boston, 1980-84; pres. Windsor Group, Inc., Boston, 1984—; bd. dirs. BTU Internat., Inc., Billerica, Mass., Marine Drilling Cos., Houston, Emcor Corp., Norwalk, Conn., Tech. Comm. Corp., Concord, Mass.; bd. dirs. Comstock Group, Danbury, Conn., 1984-90, chmn., 1989-90. Mem. Vineyard Haven Yacht Club (commodore 1991-93), Psi Upsilon (bd. govs. 1979—, treas. Found. 1983—, pres. 1994-98). Home: 31 Everett Ave Winchester MA 01890-3544

BROWN, DAVID G., academic administrator. AB in Econs. with honors, Denison U., 1958; PhD, MA in Econs., Princeton U., 1961. From asst. to assoc. prof. econs. U. N.C., Chapel Hill, 1961-66; Am. Coun. on Edn. fellow U. Minn., 1966-67; provost, v.p. for acad. affairs Drake U., 1967-70; provost, exec. v.p. for acad. affairs Miami U., 1970-82; pres. Transylvania U., 1982-83; spl. cons. Assn. Governing Bds., 1983-84; chancellor U. N.C., Asheville, 1984-90; provost Wake Forest U., Winston-Salem, N.C., 1990-98, v.p., dean Internat. Ctr. for Computer Enhanced Learning, 1998—; chair Asheville's Econ. Devel. Summit, 1986, Nat. Small Pub. Ivys Conf., 1988; presenter in field; leader numerous workshops. Author: The Market for College Teachers, 1965, The Mobile Professors, 1967, Leadership Vitality, 1979, Leadership Roles of Chief Academic Officers, 1984, (monograph) Economic Development: 1987 and Beyond, 1986; contbr. articles and papers to profl. bulls. and jours., also book chpts. Recipient Big A award Asheville Area C. of C., 1990; named one of 100 Young Leaders of the Acad., Change Mag., 1978; rsch. grantee Carnegie, 1979, U.S. Dept. Edn., 1965, NSF, 1965. Mem. Nat. Assn. State Univs. and Land Grant Colls. (chair coun. on acad. affairs 1975-76), Nat. Coun. Chief Acad. Officers (chair ACE 1978-80), Nat. Am. Assn. for Higher Edn. (chair 1981-82), Nat. Higher Edn. Colloquium (chair 1984-86), Phi Beta Kappa, Omicron Delta Kappa. Fax: (336) 758-4875. E-mail: brown@wfu.edu. Office: Wake Forest U PO Box 7328 Winston Salem NC 27109

BROWN, DAVID GRANT, university president; b. Chgo., Feb. 19, 1936; s. Wendell J. and Margaret (James) B.; m. Eleanor Rosene, Aug. 16, 1958; children: Alison, Dirksen. A.B., Denison U., 1958; M.A., Princeton U., 1960, Ph.D., 1961. Research asst. Indsl. Relations Center, Princeton, summers 1959-60; asst. prof., asso. prof. econs., dir. academic labor market study, gen. coll. adviser U. N.C., 1961-66; faculty St. Augustines Coll., N.C. Coll., 1961-66; Am. Council on Edn. intern in academics adminstrn. U. Minn., 1966-67; provost, v.p. academic affairs Drake U., 1967-70; exec. v.p., provost Miami U., Oxford, Ohio, 1970-82; pres. Transylvania U., Lexington, Ky., 1982-83; spl. cons. Assn. Governing Bds. Study on Strengthening Coll. Presidency, 1983-84; chancellor U.N.C.-Asheville, 1984-90; provost Wake Forest U., Winston-Salem, N.C., 1990—; dir. Leadership Vitality Project, 1978-79. Author: The Market for College Teachers, 1965, The Mobile Professors, 1967, Leadership Vitality Workbook, 1979, Leadership Roles of Chief Academic Officers, 1984; contbr. articles to profl. jours. U. N.C. Research Council grantee, 1961-63; recipient Tanner teaching award, 1965; Dept. Labor grantee, 1964; NSF grantee, 1965; U.S. Office Edn. grantee, 1965; Harold Dodds fellow, 1960-61. Mem. Nat. Assn. State Univs. and Land Grant Colls. (chmn. coun. acad. affairs 1975, exec. com. 1978-80), Am. Coun. on Edn. (chmn. coun. of chief acad. officers 1979-80), Am. Assn. Higher Edn. (chmn. 1981-82), Ohio Provosts (chmn. 1977-78), Ohio Com. Univ. Autonomy (chmn. 1977), Assn. Am. Colls. (commn. on nat. affairs), Higher Edn. Colloquium (chmn. 1984-86), Blue Key, Phi Beta Kappa, Phi Kappa Phi, Beta Gamma Sigma, Phi Delta Kappa, Omicron Delta Kappa.

BROWN, DAVID HARRY, speech educator; b. Cleve., Jan. 15, 1926; s. Joseph M. and Rose (Wolchok) B.; m. Marilyn Nathan Brown, Jan. 29, 1951 (dec. Dec. 1990); children: Holly, Mark; m. Rose Sanker, Jul. 10, 1994. AB in journalism/speech, Cleveland Coll., 1950; MS in pub. rels., Am. U., 1980; grad. Leadership Devel. Inst., Montgomery Coll. Reporter The Cleveland Press, Cleveland, Ohio, 1950-51; sales correspondent Serbin, Inc., Miami, Fla., 1951-54; reporter The Circleville (Ohio) Herald, 1954-56; state editor The Columbus Citizen, 1956-59; reporter The Cleveland Press, 1959-67; asst. dir. pub. info. The Dept. Justice, Washington, 1967-69; pub. info. officer Fed. Av. Adminstr., Washington, 1969-71, Dept. Transp., Washington, 1971-74, Govt. Printing Office, Washington, 1974-91; adj. prof. speech Montgomery Coll., Rockville, Md., 1991-98; media columnist The Montgomery Jour., 1998—; pres. Brown Speak Comms., Rockville, 1994—; presenter at numerous conv. and confs.; cons./trainer verbal comms. and media rels. Author: I Would Rather Be Audited By the IRS Than Give A Speech, 1995; columnist Montgomery Jour., 1998—. Mem. planning commn., bd. zoning appeals, city councilman University Heights, Ohio, 1962-67; chmn. bd. appeals, Rockville, 1976-79. With U.S. Army, WWII, lt. col. Res., 1950-78. Decorated Meritorious Svc. medal U.S. Army Res., 1978; recipient Excellence award Nat. Inst. for Staff and Orgnl. Devel., U. Tex., Dalton Pen award, 1997. Mem. Montgomery Coll. Found. (bd. dirs.), Nat. Assn. Govt. Comm. (founding pres.). Home: 5809 Nicholson Ln Apt 1116 Rockville MD 20852-5714 Office: Brown Speak Communications 5809 Nicholson Ln Apt 1116 Rockville MD 20852-5714

BROWN, DAVID M., physician, educator, dean; b. Chgo., Nov. 11, 1935; m. Sandra Miriam Brown. B.S., U. Ill., Urban, 1956; M.D., U. Ill., Chgo., 1960. Intern U. Ill. Research-Edn. Hosp., Chgo., 1960-61; resident in pediatrics U. Minn., Mpls., 1961-63; fellow in endocrinology and metabolism U. Minn., 1963-65; attending staff pediatric concrinology USAF Hosp., San Antonio, 1965-67; asst. prof. pediatrics, lab. medicine and pathology U. Minn., Mpls., 1967-70, assoc. prof., 1970-73, dir. clin. labs., 1970-84, prof. pediatrics, lab. medicine and pathology, 1974—, dean. Med. Sch., 1984-93, dir. Gen. clin. Rsch. Ctr., med. dir. clin. trials unit; mem. adv. com. on rsch. on women's health NIH, 1995—; co-chair orgainzing com. 7th Internat. Symposium on Basement Membranes, 1995; mem. planning com. NIH 3d Internat. Symposium on Kidney Disease of Diabetes Mellitus, 1991. With USAF, 1965-67. Recipient USPHS Research Career Devel. award, 1968-73. Mem. AAAS, Acad. Clin. Lab. Physicians and Scientists, Am. Diabetes Assn., Am. Pediatric Soc., Am. Physiol. Soc., Am. Soc. Clin. Pathology, Am. Soc. Nephrology, Am. Soc. Pediatric Nephrology, Central Soc. for Clin. Research, Endocrine Soc., Internat. Soc. Nephrology, Lawson Wilkins Soc. Pediatric Endocrinology, Mpls. Pediatris Soc., Orthopaedic Research Soc., Soc. Pediatric Nephrology, Soc. Pediatric Research, Am. Assn. Pathologists, Am. Soc. Bone and Mineral Research, Internat. Acad. Pathology, Assn. Am. Med. Colls. (chmn. council acad. Socs.), Am. Assn. Pathologists, Am. Soc. Cell Biology, Minn. Soc. Clin. Pathology, Alpha Omega Alpha. Home: 2571 Abbey Hill Dr Hopkins MN 55305-2332 Office: PO Box 404 516 Delaware St SE Minneapolis MN 55455-0356

BROWN, DAVID NELSON, lawyer; b. Harrodsburg, Ky., May 29, 1940; s. Irmel Nelson and Pauline (Harmon) B.; m. Lois Aileen Everett, June 20, 1964; 1 child, Ian Richard. A.B., Cornell U., 1963; J.D., U. Chgo., 1966; Bar: D.C. 1967. Assoc., Covington & Burling, Washington, 1966-74, ptnr., 1974—. mgmt. com. Covington & Burling, 1989-93. Comment editor U. Chgo. Law Rev. Mem. ABA, Order of Coif, Cosmos Club. Episcopalian. Office: Covington & Burling PO Box 7566 1201 Pennsylvania Ave NW Washington DC 20044

BROWN, DAVID P., public relations executive. MS, Syracuse U. Exec. Sunday editor, exec. news editor Albany (N.Y.) Times Union; pres. Sawchuk, Brown Assocs., Albany; coord. H&K Assocs. Group; lectr. SUNY, Albany, Union Coll., Russel Sage Coll., Coll. St. Rose; dir. Ctr. Econ. Growth. Contbr. articles profl. jours. Pres. Rensselaer County Hist. Soc., 1998—, bd. dirs.; bd. dirs. Albany Pub. Libr., ARC. Recipient Presdl. Citation Pub. Rels. Soc. Am. Mem. Internat. Assn. Bus. Communicators (pres. northeaster N.Y. chpt.). Fax: 518-462-6988. E-mail: info@sawchuk-brown.com. Office: Sawchuck Brown Assocs 41 State Street Ste 500 Albany NY 12207-3279

BROWN, DAVID R., academic administrator. Pres., dir. Art Ctr. Coll. Design, Pasadena, Calif., 1985—. Office: Art Ctr Coll of Design Office of Pres 1700 Lida St Pasadena CA 91103-1924*

BROWN, DAVID R., think-tank executive. Chmn. Heritage Found., Wash., D.C.

BROWN, DAVID RANDOLPH, electrical engineer; b. L.A., Oct. 31, 1923; s. Gilbert and Blanche Mabel (Phillips) B.; m. Sally England, Dec. 17, 1944; children: Philip, Ellen, Polly, Ann. BSEE, U. Wash., 1944; SMEE, MIT, 1947. Group leader MIT Lincoln Lab., Lexington, Mass., 1951-58; assoc. tech. dir. MITRE Corp., Bedford, Mass., 1958-63; lab. dir. SRI Internat., Menlo Park, Calif., 1963-85, staff scientist, 1985-93. Fellow IEEE. Avocation: genealogy. Home: 1470 Sand Hill Rd Apt 309 Palo Alto CA 94304-2029

BROWN, DAVID RUPERT, engineering executive; b. Chgo., Sept. 11, 1934; s. Hugh Stewart and Sara (Daniels) B.; m. Mary Heaton Nicolaus, Sept. 6, 1958; children: David R. Jr., Robert N., Sara D. BSME, Purdue U., 1956; MBA, U. Akron, 1968. V.p. engring. Diamond Power Specialty Co., Lancaster, Ohio, 1974-77, v.p. ops., 1977-80, pres., 1980-82; sr. v.p., group exec. Babcock & Wilcox, Lancaster, 1982-85, Barberton, Ohio, 1985-87; v.p., gen. mgr. Babcock & Wilcox, Barberton, 1987; with Worldwide Procurement Inc., Akron, Ohio, 1987-90; v.p. mktg. Stock Equipment Co., Chagrin Falls, Ohio, 1990-95. With U.S. Army, 1957-58. Mem. ASME, Fairlawn Country Club, Pi Tau Sigma, Tau Beta Pi. Home: 1717 Brookwood Dr Akron OH 44313-5072

BROWN, DAVID WARFIELD, management educator; b. Evanston, Ill., Aug. 16, 1937; s. Lloyd Warfield and Nancy (Coleman) B.; m. Alice Bean, Feb. 29, 1964; children: Peter Bean, Sarah Alice. BA, Princeton U., 1959; JD, Harvard U., 1963. Bar: N.Y. 1966. Assoc. Patterson, Belknap & Webb, N.Y.C., 1966-69; chief-of-staff Congressman Edward I. Koch, Washington and N.Y.C., 1969-74; v.p. Rand Inst., N.Y.C., 1974-75; chmn. N.Y. State Commn. Investigation, N.Y.C., 1975-78; dep. mayor City of N.Y., 1978-79; commr. Met. Transp. Authority, N.Y.C., 1979-85; ptnr. Hawkins, Delafield & Wood, N.Y.C., 1980; pres. Blackburn Coll., Carlinville, Ill., 1989-91; prof. profl. practice (mgmt.) Milano Grad. Sch. Mgmt. and Urban Policy, N.Y.C., 1996—; lectr., adj. prof. pub. mgmt. Sch. Mgmt., Yale U., New Haven, 1979-89. Author: When Strangers Cooperate: Using Social Conventions to Govern Ourselves, 1995; co-editor Higher Edn. Exch.;

contbr. articles to profl. jours. Capt. USAR, 1963-65. English Speaking Union scholar, London, 1959-60. Mem. Assn. of Bar of City of N.Y., Kettering Found. (assoc., vis. scholar 1991-92). Democrat. Presbyterian. Home: 40 E 94th St Apt 12D New York NY 10128-0726

BROWN, DEAN NAOMI, state official, geologist; b. Fairbanks, Alaska, Mar. 9, 1944; d. James Heuston and Betty (Jefford) Alexander; m. Jim McCaslin Brown, Sept. 1, 1963 (div. 1987); children: Robin Wendy, Shelly Reneé. BS in Geology, U. Wis., 1967. Lectr. geology U. Ind., Kokomo, 1971-72; geologist, landman Amax Coal Co., Indpls., 1974; asst. and field constrn. engr. Trans-Alaska pipeline Fluor Alaska, Inc., 1975-76; environ. geologist Civil Engrs./Alaska, Wasilla, 1977; various positions to acting dir. agr. Alaska Dept. Natural Resources, 1978-87; office mgr. Northwind Aviation, Anchorage, 1987-88; geologist Placer Dome U.S., Inc., Nome, Alaska, 1988; journeyman carpenter Ensearch Corp., Bradley Lake, Alaska, 1989; no. regional mgr. div. land and water mgmt. Alaska Dept. Natural Resources, Fairbanks, 1990; dep. dir. forestry Alaska Dept. Natural Resources, Anchorage, 1990-93, acting state forester, 1993, dep. state forester fire aviation resources mgmt., 1993-97, acting state forester, 1997, dep. state forester, 1997—; adj. prof. natural resource econs. Alaska Pacific U., 1991, 93; vice-chair Alaskan-Chinese Timber Commn., 1993, Gov.'s Mktg. Alaska Forest Products Coun.; del. Coun. Western State Foresters, 1994-95, Nat. Assn. State Foresters, 1994; co-chair Dept. Nat. Resources Computer Group, 1996—; des. Statewide Emergency Response Commission, 1997—; mem. AK Wildland Fire Coord. Group, 1996—, chair, 1999—. Vol. Iditarod Trail Com. Recipient cert. of appreciation City of Valdez, Alaska, 1976, Anchorage Sch. Dist., 1983, 4-H Leaders, Palmer, Alaska, 1987, cert. of achievement Susitna coun. Girl Scouts U.S.A., 1982, Outstanding Achievement award Alaska Dept. Natural Resources, 1986. Mem. Aircraft Owners and Pilots Assn., Alaska Airman's Assn., Pacific Rim Arabian Horse Assn. (charter mem. 1997—), Alaska Horse Breeders Assn. (bd. dirs. 1984-90), Ninety-Nines. Avocations: flying, horse breeding and showing, painting, photography, gold mining. Home: PO Box 870366 Wasilla AK 99687-0366 Office: Alaska Dept Natural Resources 3601 C St Ste 1058 Anchorage AK 99503-5925

BROWN, DEBORAH ELIZABETH, television producer; b. Aledo, Ill., Nov. 29, 1952; d. Kenneth M. and Mary Esther (Gilmore) B.; m. K. J. Lester, Nov. 28, 1975 (dec. Mar. 1982); children: Rebekah Jean, Aaron Mark, Jonathan Caleb. Student, Letourneau Coll., 1970; BA in Theater Arts, Sterling Coll., 1974; MA in Comm., Wheaton Coll., 1977. Producer, dir. Sta. WCFC-TV, Chgo., 1978-80; sales mgr. SNG Enterprises, St. Charles, Ill., 1980-82; pres., CEO Circle Family Video Stores, Niles, Mich., 1982-87; exec. producer Picture Radio Pictures, Portland, Oreg., 1987-93, 98; mgr. Computer Keyboard, Portland, Oreg., 1993-96, Michelle's Piano and Organ Co., Portland, 1996-98; vis. prof. comm. Wheaton (Ill.) Coll., 1980; video cons. Spring Arbor Distbrs., Belleville, Mich., 1985, Gospel Films, Muskegan, Mich., 1985. Producer, dir., writer (TV program and book) Crafts With Emilie, 1979 (Spl. Emmy nomination); video contbg. editor Christian Booksellers Assn. jour., 1984-85; set decorator Cindy Williams Comedy Spl., 1993. Corp. sponsor Pregnancy Care Ctr., Niles, 1985-87; producer Four Flags Area Apple Festival, Niles, 1987. Mem. ISGI Internat. (dir. 1998—), Fellowship of Christians in Arts, Media and Entertainment, Christian Video Retailers Assn. (exec. dir. 1985-87). Baptist. Fax: (503) 408-1829. Office: Picture Radio Pictures PO Box 33150 Portland OR 97292

BROWN, DEE ALEXANDER, author; b. La., 1908; s. Daniel Alexander and Lulu (Cranford) B.; m. Sara B. Stroud, Aug. 1, 1934; children—James Mitchell, Linda. B.S., George Washington U., 1937; M.S., U. Ill., 1951. Librarian Dept. Agr., Washington, 1934-42, Aberdeen Proving Ground, Md., 1945-48; agrl. librarian U. Ill. at Urbana, 1948-72, prof., 1962-75; on-camera narrator The Wild West, 1993, The Real West series, 1993-95, others. Author: Wave High the Banner, 1942, reprint, 1999, Grierson's Raid, 1954, Yellowhorse, 1956, Cavalry Scout, 1957, The Gentle Tamers: Women of the Old Wild West, 1958, The Bold Cavaliers, 1959, They Went Thataway, 1960, (with M.F. Schmitt) Fighting Indians of the West, 1948, Trail Driving Days, 1952, The Settler's West, 1955, Fort Phil Kearny, 1962, The Galvanized Yankees, 1963, Showdown at Little Big Horn, 1964, The Girl from Fort Wicked, 1964, The Year of the Century, 1966, Action at Beecher Island, 1967, Bury My Heart at Wounded Knee, 1971, Andrew Jackson and the Battle of New Orleans, 1972, The Westerners, 1974, Tepee Tales, 1979, Creek Mary's Blood, 1980, The American Spa, 1982, Killdeer Mountain, 1983, Conspiracy of Knaves, 1987, Wondrous Times on the Frontier, 1991, When the Century Was Young, 1993, The American West, 1994, (with Mort Künstler) Images of the Old West, 1996, Best of the West, 1998, The Way to Bright Star, 1998, Civil War Anthology, 1998; on-camera narrator: The Wild West, 1993, The Real West, 1993-95, other documentaries of the Am. West; contbr.: Growing Up Western, 1990; editor: Agricultural History, 1956-58, Pawnee, Blackfoot and Cheyenne, 1961. Served with AUS, 1942-45. Recipient A.L.A. Clarence Day award, 1971, Christopher award, 1971, Illinoisian of Yr., Ill. News Broadcasters Assn., 1972, W.W.A. Golden Saddleman award, 1984. Mem. Authors Guild, Soc. Am. Historians, Western Writers Am., Beta Phi Mu. Home: 7 Overlook Dr Little Rock AR 72207-1619

BROWN, DELORES, academic administrator; b. Detroit, Nov. 12, 1948; d. Lloyd and Sallie Gillum; m. Jesse Brown; 1 child, Khalilah. BS in English, Fisk U., 1970; MS in Reading Edn. magna cum laude, Syracuse U., 1972; postgrad., U. Ill., Chgo., 1997—. Tchr. reading Roosevelt Jr. H.S., Syracuse, 1970-71; tchr. English Woodrow Wilson H.S., Washington, D.C., 1971-74; program dir. Sch. Medicine Georgetown U., Washington, D.C., 1974-79, co-prin. investigator, proj. dir. Sch. Medicine, 1984-85; dir. health edn. Howard U. Cancer Ctr., Washington, D.C., 1979-84; freelance writer Brussels, 1985-87; asst. to assoc. dean endl. programs Med. Sch. Northwestern U., Chgo., 1987-89, asst. dean minority affairs, dir. admissions Med. Sch., 1989-91, asst. dean admissions Med. Sch., 1991—. Contbr. articles to profl. jours. chair bd. dirs. Project Heart, 1989-92; chpt. pres. LINKS, Inc., 1990—; bd. dirs. Kidshelp, 1996—, JCA Acad., 1996—; mem. Jack and Jill, Inc., 1989—. Recipient Cert. of Appreciation People United to Save Humanity, 1980, D.C. Clergy, 1982, Outstanding Contbn. Health Edn. award D.C. Pub. Assn., 1981, Significant Contbn. Pub. Health award Metro. Washington Pub. Health Assn., 1982; Women's Studies fellow U. Calif., Berkeley, 1980. Mem. AAUW, NAACP, Nat. Youth Leadership Forum Medicine (bd. dirs. 1997—), Nat. Assn. Med. Minority Educators (chair budget/fin. 1995-97), Nat. Assn. Advisors Health Profession, Assn. Am. Med. Colls., Nat. Urban League, Ill. Assn. Women Higher Edn. Office: Northwestern U Med Sch 303 E Chicago Ave Chicago IL 60611-3072

BROWN, DEMING BRONSON, Slavic languages and literature educator; b. Seattle, Jan. 26, 1919; s. Kirk Charles and Lois (Bronson) B.; m. Glenora Washington, June 18, 1941; children: Kate Deming, Sarah Fuller. A.B., U. Wash., Seattle, 1940, M.A., 1942; postgrad., Cornell U., 1945-46; Ph.D. (Rockefeller fellow 1946-48), Columbia U., 1951. Instr., then asst. prof. Russian lang. and lit. Northwestern U., Evanston, Ill., 1948-57; mem. faculty U. Mich., Ann Arbor, 1957—; prof. Slavic lang. and lit. U. Mich., 1959—, chmn. dept. Slavic lang. and lit., 1957-61, dir. Center Russian and E. European Studies, 1978-80; mem. joint com. Slavic studies Am. Council Learned Socs.-Social Sci. Research Council, 1960-64. Author: Soviet Attitudes Towards American Writing, 1962, Soviet Russian Literature Since Stalin, 1978, A Guide to Soviet Russian Translations of American Literature, 1917-47, 1954, The Last Years of Soviet Russian Literature, 1975-91, 1993. Served with AUS, 1943-45. Research fellow Am. Council Learned Socs.-Social Sci. Research Council, 1964; Fulbright-Hays fellow, 1969. Mem. Am. Assn. Slavic Studies (exec. council 1961-63), MLA, Am. Assn. Tchrs. Slavic and E. European Langs. Home: 1050 Wall St Apt 8D Ann Arbor MI 48105-1983 *Died Feb. 5, 1999.*

BROWN, DENISE SCOTT, architect, urban planner; b. Nkana, Zambia, Oct. 3, 1931; came to U.S., 1958; d. Simon and Phyllis (Hepker) Lakofski; m. Robert Scott Brown, July 21, 1955 (dec. 1959); m. Robert Charles Venturi, July 23, 1967; 1 child, James C. Student, U. Witwatersrand, South Africa, 1948-51; diploma, Archtl. Assn., London, 1955; M of City Planning, U. Pa., 1960, MArch, 1965, DFA (hon.), 1994; DFA (hon.), Oberlin Coll., 1977, Phila. Coll. Art, 1985, Parsons Sch. Design, 1985; LHD (hon.), N.J. Inst. Tech., 1984, Phila. Coll. Textiles and Sci., 1992; DEng (hon.), Tech. U. N.S., 1991; HHD (hon.), Pratt Inst., 1992; DFA (hon.), U. Pa., 1994; LittD (hon.), U. Nev., 1998; D. Arch.(hon.), U. Miami, 1997. Registered architect, U.K. Asst. prof. U. Pa., Phila., 1960-65; assoc. prof., head urban design program UCLA, 1965-68; with Venturi, Rauch and Scott Brown, Phila., 1967—, ptnr., 1969-89; prin. Venturi, Scott Brown and Assocs. Inc., Phila., 1989—; vis. prof. arch. U. Calif., Berkeley, 1965, Yale U., 1967-70; asst. prof. U. Pa., 1960-65, vis. prof. Sch. Fine Arts, 1982, 83; Eliot Noyes design critic in arch. Harvard U., Cambridge, Mass., 1989-90; mem. visitors com. MIT, 1973-83; mem. adv. com. dept. arch. Temple U., 1980—; cons. to dean search com. Sch. Arch., Washington U., St. Louis, 1992; mem. adv. bd. dept. arch. Carnegie Mellon U., 1992-96; mem. jury Prince of Wales Prize in Urban Design, Grad. Sch. Design Harvard U., Cambridge, 1993; bd. overseers Univ. Librs., U. Pa., 1995—. Author: Urban Concepts, 1990; co-author: Learning from Las Vegas, 1972, rev. edit., 1977, A View from the Campidoglio: Selected Essays, 1953-84, 85, On Houses and Housing, 1992; contbr. numerous articles to profl. jours. Mem. curriculum com. Phila. Jewish Children's Folkshul, 1980-86; policy panelist design arts program NEA, 1981-83; mem. bd. advisors Architects, Designers and Planners for Social Responsibility, 1982—; mem. capitol preservation com. Commonwealth of Pa., Harrisburg, 1983-87; bd. dirs. Ctrl. Phila. Devel. Corp., 1985—, Urban Affairs Partnership, Phila., 1987-91; trustee Chestnut Hill Acad., Phila., 1985-89; mem., bd. of overseers U. Librs., U. Pa., 1995—. Decorated commendatore Order of Merit (Italy); recipient numerous awards, citations, commendations for designs and urban planning, including Chgo. Architecture award, 1987, U.S. Presdl. award nat. medal of Arts, 1992, Hall of Fame award Interior Design mag., 1992, (with Robert Venturi) The Phila. award, 1993, The Benjamin Franklin medal Royal Soc. for Encouragement of Arts, Mfg. and Commerce, 1993, Am. Coll. Schs. of Architecture/AIA Topaz medallion, 1996. Mem. Royal Inst. Brit. Archs., Am. Acad. Arts and Scis., Archs. Designers and Planners for Social Responsibility, Am. Planning Assn, Archtl. Assn. London, Internat. Women's Forum, Soc. Coll. and U. Planning, Soc. Archtl. Historians (bd. dirs. 1981-84), Carpenters Co. of City and County of Phila., Athenaeum of Phila., Royal Soc. Encouragement of Arts, Mfr. and Commerce. Democrat. Jewish. Office: Venturi Scott Brown & Assocs Inc 4236 Main St Philadelphia PA 19127-1603

BROWN, DON, museum director. Dir. Internat. Wildlife Mus., Tucson, Ariz. Office: Internat Wildlife Mus 4800 W Gates Pass Rd Tucson AZ 85745-9600*

BROWN, DONALD ARTHUR, lawyer; b. Washington, Feb. 1, 1929; s. Louis S. and Rose (Kliban) B.; m. Ann Winkelman, July 13, 1959; children: Cathy, Laura. B.A. in Econs., George Washington U., 1949, LL.B. (Case Club oral argument competition winner), 1952, LL.M., 1958. Bar: D.C. 1952. Sr. partner Brown, Gildenhorn & Jacobs (and predecessor), Washington, 1955—; mem. faculty Practising Law Inst.; faculty Harvard U. Sch. Bus., Cambridge, Mass., 1984-93, Yale U. Sch. Mgmt., New Haven, 1986, George Washington U. Sch. Bus., Washington, 1994—; guest lectr. Am. U., Nat. Assn. Real Estate Counselors, Nat. Assn. Real Estate Investors; pres., sec. JBG Constrn., Inc.; partner JBG Assocs.; v.p., treas. JBG Properties, Inc.; trustee, gen. counsel Nat. Bank Rosslyn, Arlington, Va.; mem. minority enterprises com. SBA; finance com. Housing Devel. Corp.; mem. Model Cities Com. D.C.; apptd. by Pres. of U.S. commr. Internat. Cultural and Trade Ctr., 1988. Co-author: Understanding Real Estate Investments, 1967; contbr. articles to profl. jours. Exec. bd. Forest Hills Citizens Assn.; bd. dirs. D.C. Jr. C. of C.; mem. Friends Kennedy Center, Friends Corcoran Gallery, Big Bros. Orgn. D.C.; bd. dirs. Washington Area Tennis Patrons Found., 1964—, pres., 1973-75, Fed. city council; trustee Woodley House, psychiat. half-way house, Washington, 1973—, pres. bd. dirs., 1975—; trustee U. D.C., Sidwell Friends Sch., The Phillips Collection, 1984—; mem. art adv. council Washington Conv. Ctr. com. D.C. Conv. Ctr. Served as officer USNR, 1952-55. Named Washingtonian of Yr., Washingtonian mag., 1989. Mem. ABA, Fed. Bar Assn., D.C. Bar Assn., Washington Bd. Realtors (chmn. lawyer-realtor liaison com. 1972, chmn. investment property com. 1970), Economics Club of Washington, Burning Tree Club. Jewish (bd. mgrs. congregation 1962, treas. 1965). Club: Georgetown (Washington). Home: 3005 Audubon Ter NW Washington DC 20008-2313 Office: Brown Gildenhorn & Jacobs 1250 Connecticut Ave NW Washington DC 20036-2603

BROWN, DONALD DAVID, biology educator; b. Cin., Dec. 30, 1931; s. Albert Louis and Louise (Rauh) B.; m. Linda Jane Weil, July 2, 1957; children: Deborah Lin, Christopher Charles, Sharon Elizabeth. M.S., U. Chgo., 1956, M.D., 1956, D.Sc. (hon.), 1976; D.Sc. (hon.), U. Md., 1983; DSc (hon.), U. Cin., 1992. Staff mem. dept. embryology Carnegie Instn. of Washington, Balt., 1963—; dir. Carnegie Instn. of Washington, 1976-94; prof. dept. biology Johns Hopkins U., 1968—. Pres. Life Scis. Research Found. Served with USPHS, 1957-59. Recipient U.S. Steel Found. award for molecular biology, 1973, V.D. Mattia award Roche Inst., 1975, Boris Pregel award for biology N.Y. Acad. Scis., 1976, Ross G. Harrison award Internat. Soc. Developmental Biology, 1981, Bertner Found. award, 1982, Rosenstiel award for biomed. sci., 1985, Louisa Gross Horwitz award, 1985, Feodor Lynen award U. Miami Winter Symposium, 1987. Fellow Am. Acad. Arts and Scis., AAAS; mem. Nat. Acad. Scis. (mem. coun. 1994-97), Soc. Devel. Biology (pres. 1975), Am. Soc. Biol. Chemists, Am. Soc. Cell Biology (pres. 1992, E.B. Wilson award 1996), Am. Philos. Soc. Home: 5721 Oakshire Rd Baltimore MD 21209-4217 Office: Carnegie Instn Washington 115 W University Pky Baltimore MD 21210-3301

BROWN, DONALD DOUGLAS, transportation company executive, retired air force officer, consultant; b. Montreal, Que., Can., Aug. 1, 1931; came to U.S., 1938; s. Donald Bannerman and Hilda Taylor (Noel) B.; m. Joan Teresa McAndrews, Aug. 7, 1954; children—Cathy J. Brown Peinhardt, James D., Nancy J. Brown May. B.A., Columbia U., 1954; M.B.A., Syracuse U., 1965. Commd. officer U.S. Air Force, 1955, advanced through grades to maj. gen., 1979, ret., 1987; wing chief aircrew standardization U.S. Air Force, Phan Rang Air Base, Vietnam, 1968-69; chief Weapon System Support div. in Directorate of Supply, then dir. logistics plans U.S. Air Force, Scott AFB, Ill., 1973-75, asst. dep. chief of staff for logistics, 1975-76; from vice comdr. to comdr. U.S. Air Force, McChord AFB, Wash., 1976-77; asst. dep. chief of staff for ops. Mil. Airlift Command U.S. Air Force, Scott AFB, Ill., 1979-80, dep. chief of staff for plans, 1980-83, dep. chief of staff for ops. Mil. Airlift Command, 1983-84; comdr. 22d Air Force, Mil. Airlift Command U.S. Air Force, Travis AFB, Calif., 1984-87; ret. U.S. Air Force, 1987; chmn. bd. Evergreen Air Ctr. Inc.; cons. in aviation/logistics mgmt. Decorated Disting. Service medal with oak leaf cluster, Legion of Merit with oak leaf cluster, D.F.C. with oak leaf cluster, Bronze Star, Air medal with 4 oak leaf clusters, Republic of Vietnam Cross of Gallantry with palm. Mem. Air Force Assn., Nat. Def. Transp. Assn. (appted. to bus. practices com.), Beta Gamma Sigma.

BROWN, DONALD JAMES, JR., insurance company executive; b. Inglewood, Calif., Sept. 30, 1955; s. Donald James and Kathleen Elizabeth (McKillips) B.; m. Joan Colleen Brewer, June 25, 1977 (div. May 1985); 1 child, Randy. BA, Calif. State U., Long Beach, 1979. Estimator, supt. Home Improvement Builders, Santa Ana, Calif., 1979; asst. supt. Village Home of Calif., Santa Ana, 1980; claim rep. Aetna Life & Casualty, Orange, Calif., 1980-82, sr. claim rep., 1982-85; property specialist Aetna Life & Casualty, Woodland Hills, Calif., 1985-86; regional supr. United Pacific Ins. Co., Glendale, Calif., 1986-88; regional gen. adjuster Reliance Ins. Co., Glendale, 1988-90; regional property examiner Reliance Ins. Co., Durham, N.C., 1990-92; property claim mgr. Home Ins. Co., Maitland, Fla., 1992-95; gen. adjuster Zurich U.S., Longwood, Fla., 1995—; mem. membership com. Orange County Adjuster's Assn., Anaheim, Calif., 1983-84. Republican. Avocations: whitewater rafting, fishing, camping, sailing, motorcycle touring. Office: Zurich Ins Co PO Box 915245 Longwood FL 32791-5245

BROWN, DONALD JAMES, JR., lawyer; b. Chgo., Apr. 21, 1948; s. Donald James Sr. and Marian Constance (Scimeca) B.; m. Donna Bowen, Jan. 15, 1972; children: Megan, Maura. AB, John Carroll U., 1970; JD, Loyola U., Chgo., 1973. Bar: Ill. 1973, U.S. Dist. Ct. (no. dist.) Ill. 1973, U.S. Tax Ct. 1982. Asst. to state's atty. Cook County, Ill., 1973-75; assoc. Baker & McKenzie, Chgo., 1975-82, ptnr., 1982-95; ptnr. Donohue, Brown, Mathewson & Smyth, Chgo., 1995—. Office: Donohue Brown et al 140 S Dearborn St Chicago IL 60603-5202

BROWN, DONALD VAUGHN, technical educator, engineering consultant; b. Fairfield, Maine, May 16, 1919; s. Walter C. and Hazel (Fogg) B.; m. Christine R. Bishop, Mar. 14, 1945; 1 child, Donald V. Jr. BS, U. Maine, Orono, 1943; MS, Brigham Young U., 1963; EdD, Utah State U., 1965. Registered profl. engr., Maine. Apprentice engr. U.S. Steel Corp., Elwood City, Pa., 1943-47; works metallurgist Aluminum Co. of Am., Alcoa, Tenn., 1947-55; asst. v.p. Penobscot Fibre Co., Old Town, Maine, 1955-60; assoc. prof. Inst. Paper Chemistry, Appleton, Wis., 1960-62; instr. Brigham Young U., Provo, Utah, 1962-63, Utah State U., Logan, 1963-65; dean Fla. Keys C.C., Key West, 1965-66; dean, prof. Western Piedmont C.C., Morganton, N.C., 1967; prof. U. Tenn., Knoxville, 1968—; bd. trustees Hinkley (Maine) Sch., 1976—; cons. Assn. Am. States, Washington, 1976—, San Jose Costa Rica, S.A., Tenn. State Dept. Edn., Nashville, 1970-84, Maine State Libr., Augusta, 1982-97, Am. Adventure Inc., Orlando, Fla., 1986-96, Thousand Trails Resorts, 1989-95, Coast to Coast Camping, Inc., Washington, 1986, Lincoln Acad., New Castle, Maine, 1994. Author: A Teaching Partnership, 1972, Metallurgy Basics, 1978; contbr. articles to profl. jours.; patentee 4 chemical processes. Scoutmaster Boy Scouts Am., Elwood City, Pa. and Alcoa, Tenn., 1946-52, scout commr., Massena, N.Y. and Orono, Maine, 1952-60. Lt. USN, 1944-46, 50-52, PTO, WW II, Korean War. Recipient Presdl. USN Unit citation, 1945. Mem. Am. Vocat. Assn., Am. Tech. Edn. Assn., Engring. Edn. Assn. (editing bd. 1968-79). Avocations: photography, sailing, hiking, camping. Home: 409 E 2nd Ave Lenoir City TN 37771-2513

BROWN, DONALD WESLEY, lawyer; b. Cleve., Jan. 2, 1953; s. Lloyd Elton Brown and Nancy Jeanne Hudson. AB summa cum laude, Ohio U., 1975; JD, Yale U., 1978. Bar: Calif. 1978, U.S. Dist. Ct. (no. dist.) Calif. 1978, U.S. Dist. Ct. (cen. dist.) Calif. 1990. Assoc. Brobeck, Phleger & Harrison, San Francisco, 1978-85, ptnr., 1985—. Democrat. Home: 2419 Vallejo St San Francisco CA 94123-4638 Office: Brobeck Phleger & Harrison Spear St Tower 1 Market St San Francisco CA 94105-1420

BROWN, DOREEN LEAH HURWITZ, development company executive; b. Marseille, France, June 11, 1927; came to U.S., 1939, naturalized, 1941; d. Nathan and Anne (Silverstone) Hurwitz; m. Donald L. Brown, Dec. 30, 1951 (dec.); children: Claudia Geraldine, Nicole Deborah. BA cum laude, Bryn Mawr Coll., 1947. Adminstrv. asst., interpreter, translator FAO, Washington, 1949-51; exec. Aldon Constrn. & Mgmt. Corp., Washington, 1951—, v.p., exec. officer, 1977—; consumer liaison NAS, 1973; del. ann. US-EC conf. on agr. C. of C., U.S.-Japan Conf.; mem. Pres.'s Adv. Com. for Trade Policy and Negotiations, 1992-94. Author: Window on Washington, The Trade Deficit. Nat. chmn. nat affairs Nat. Coun. Jewish Women, N.Y.C., 1971-75; pres. Consumer Edn. Coun. on World Trade, 1973-78, Consumers for World Trade, Washington, 1977—; mem. Women's Nat. Dem. Club, 1960—. Mem. Bryn Mawr Coll. Alumnae Assn., World Trade Forum. Democrat. Jewish. Avocations: farming, theater, writing, reading, golf. Office: Consumers for World Trade 2000 L St NW Ste 200 Washington DC 20036-4924

BROWN, DOROTHY HOWARD, medical practice administrator; b. Marion, Va., May 12, 1940; d. Charles Dean and Sue Emma (Huskins) Howard; m. J. Freeland Brown, Nov. 25, 1969; children: Joseph Dean, Edith Suzanne. Diploma, N.C. Bapt. Hosp., Winston-Salem, 1961; student, Darton Coll., Albany, Ga., 1990-94. Charge nurse N.C. Bapt. Hosp., Winston-Salem, 1961-64; head nurse mgr. Phoebe Putney Meml. Hosp., Albany, 1966-70, 75-85, asst. DON, 1985-95, dir. physician practice support, 1995—. 1st lt. USAF, 1964-66, 94-96. Mem. Ga. Med. Group Mgmt. Assn., Healthcare Fin. Mgmt. Assn.

BROWN, DUDLEY EARL, JR., psychiatrist, educator, health executive, former federal agency administrator, former naval officer; b. Berryville, Va., Apr. 10, 1928; s. Dudley Earl and Rosa Lee (Costello) B.; m. Lelia Adrienne Motley, June 22, 1953; children—Lelia Brown Farr, David, Kevin. B.A., Washington and Lee U., 1949; M.D., Med. Coll. Va., 1953. Diplomate: Am. Bd. Psychiatry and Neurology. Commd. lt. (j.g.) M.C. U.S. Navy, 1953, advanced through grades to rear adm., 1974; intern Naval Hosp., Portsmouth, Va., 1953-54; resident in neuropsychiatry Naval Hosp., Bethesda, Md., 1957-60; service in Vietnam; comdg. officer Nat. Naval Med. Center, Bethesda, 1975-76, Naval Regional Med. Center, San Diego, 1976-78; fleet surgeon U.S. Pacific Fleet and staff surgeon, comdr.-in-chief U.S. Forces, Pacific, Pearl Harbor, Hawaii, 1978-80; ret., 1980; dep. asst. chief med. dir. for profl. services VA Central Office, Washington, 1980-82; assoc. dep. chief med. dir. VA, Washington, 1982-87; asst. prof. clin. psychiatry U. Pa. Med. Sch., 1967-70; prof. clin. psychiatry Uniformed Svcs. U. Health Scis., Bethesda, Md., 1981—, Med. Coll. Va., Va. Commonwealth U., Richmond, 1987—; dir. health policy studies, dir. Washington office Abt Assocs. Inc., 1987-93, v.p., 1992—, mng. v.p., 1993—; sci. adv. bd. Ctr. Prisoner of War Studies, 1998—. Contbr. to med. jours. Decorated Legion of Merit; recipient Meritorious Svc. medal, Navy Commendation medal, VA Disting. Svc. medal, Disting. Alumnus Med. Coll. Va., 1993. Fellow ACP, Am. Psychiat. Assn., Am. Coll. Psychiatrists; mem. Washington Psychiat. Soc., Nat. Health Coun. (bd. dirs. 1989-94), Assn. Mil. Surgeons U.S., Soc. Med. Cons. to Armed Forces (v.p. 1988-89, pres. 1989-90), Phi Gamma Delta, Alpha Epsilon Delta. Presbyterian. Home: 2415 Black Cap Ln Reston VA 20191-3027 Office: Abt Assocs Inc 4800 Montgomery Ln Ste 600 Bethesda MD 20814-3460

BROWN, EARL KENT, historian, clergyman; b. Kent, Ohio, July 26, 1925; s. Earl Royal and Bernice Blanche (Howard) B. B.A., Columbia U., 1948; S.T.B., Boston U., 1953, Ph.D. (Howard fellow 1953-54, United Methodist Ch. Dempster fellow 1954-55), 1956. Ordained to ministry United Meth. Ch., 1957. Asst. prof. history Baldwin Wallace Coll., 1956-63, asso. prof., 1963; asso. prof. church history Boston U., 1963-70, prof., 1970-86, prof. emeritus, 1986—; vis. prof. Case Western Res. U., 1961, Union Theol. Sem., Manila, 1970, United Theol. Coll., Bangalore, India, 1978, U. Manchester, Eng., 1979. Author: Women of Mr. Wesley's Methodism, 1983; Contbr. articles to acad. jours., religious periodicals. Fulbright fellow, 1962. Mem. Phi Beta Kappa. Home: Tropicana Park 161 Jasmine Dr Fort Myers FL 33908-3846

BROWN, EARLE PALMER, advertising agency executive; b. Manhasset, N.Y., Mar. 15, 1922; s. Palmer and Bessie (Twombley) B.; m. Barbara Mac Laughlin, July 1, 1946 (div. May 1984); children: Jeremy, Andrea (dec.), Scott, Alison, Gillian, Meredith; m. Joyce P. Baker, June 29, 1984. AB in Journalism, Washington and Lee U., 1944. Reporter News Leader, Richmond, Va.,,1949; exec. sec. Soc. Indsl. Realtors, Washington, 1950-51; assoc. editor Archtl. Forum, N.Y.C., 1952; founder, pres. Earle Palmer Brown Assocs., Washington, 1953-73; chmn. bd. Earle Palmer Brown Assocs., Bethesda, Md., 1974—; columnist Gazette Papers, 1988—; lectr. in field. Founder, 2d pres. Washington Area Tennis Patrons'; mem. bd. regents U. Md. System; bd. dirs. Smithsonian Ctr. for Advt. History; advisor Washington and Lee U. Sch. Bus.; campaign advisor, media cons. various pub. ofcls.; pres. Nat. Capital Area coun. Boy Scouts Am., 1991. Served with USN, WWII. Decorated Bronze Star with Combat V; recipient Silver Beaver and Disting. Eagle Scout award Boy Scouts Am., 1965, Citizen of Yr. award, 1990; citation USIA; named to Washington Bus. Hall of Fame, 1992. Mem. Am. Assn. Advt. Agys. (past chmn. Mid. Atlantic coun.), Am. Advt. Fedn. (Silver medal 1981), Nat. Fedn. Advt. Agys. (pres. 1967-68), Harness Tracks Am. (pres. 1978-80), Md. C. of C. (chmn. 1988-90), Met. Washington Tennis Assn. (past pres.), Congrl. Country Club (pres. 1994-95), Coral Beach Club, Capitol Hill Club, Omicron Delta Kappa. Avocation: tennis. Home: 9308 Mercy Hollow Ln Rockville MD 20854-4525 Office: Earle Palmer Brown PR 6400 Goldsboro Rd Bethesda MD 20817-5826 *If I had my life to live over, I'd do almost everything the same way. Same college, same career, same branch of service. Only two changes--I'd learn to type and start playing tennis sooner.*

BROWN, EDGAR CARY, retired economics educator; b. Bakersfield, Calif., Apr. 14, 1916; s. Verne Brainard and Ruth (Cary) B.; m. Tomlin Edwards, May 28, 1937 (div.); children: Rebecca, Gretchen; m. Margaret Durham, June 6, 1969 (div.); children: Elizabeth, Robert. B.S., U. Calif., Berkeley, 1937; Ph.D., Harvard U., 1948. Teaching fellow U. Calif. at Berkeley, 1937-39; economist U.S. WPB, 1940-41; teaching fellow Harvard U., 1941-42; economist U.S. Treasury Dept., 1942-47; prof. econs. MIT, Cambridge, 1947-86; head dept. MIT, 1965-83, 84-85, assoc. dean, head fgn. langs. and lits., 1985-86, prof. emeritus, 1986—; vis. prof. econs. Yale U., 1953-54, U.

Chgo., 1963-64; cons. various govt. agys., Brookings Instn., N.Y. State Regents Commn. on Higher Edn., 1992-93. Author: Financing Defense, 1951, Depreciation Adjustments for Price Changes, 1952, Studies in Economic Stabilization, 1967, Paul Samuelson and Modern Economic Theory, 1983; acting editor: Nat. Tax Jour, 1958-59; asso. editor: Jour. Pub. Econs, 1972-81. Guggenheim fellow, 1957; Ford Found. Faculty Research fellow, 1956-57. Mem. Nat. Tax Assn., Am. Econ. Assn., Am. Acad. Arts and Scis., Phi Beta Kappa, Beta Gamma Sigma. Home: 163 The Valley Rd Concord MA 01742-4900 Office: MIT Dept Econs Cambridge MA 02139

BROWN, EDGAR HENRY, JR., mathematician, educator; b. Chgo., Dec. 27, 1926; s. Edgar Henry and Viola (Offen) B.; m. Gail Hamilton, June 13, 1954; children: Jessica, Nicholas. BS, U. Wis., 1949; MS, Wash. State U., 1951; PhD, MIT, 1954. Instr. Washington U., St. Louis, 1954-55, U. Chgo., 1955-57; Office Naval Res. fellow Brown U., 1957-58; faculty Brandeis U., 1958—, prof. math., 1963—; vis. prof. Yale U., 1993, Math. Inst., Oxford, 1994. Served with USNR, 1944-46. NSF fellow, 1962-63; Guggenheim fellow, 1965-66; Brit. Sci. Research Council fellow, 1973-74, 82-83; sr. research fellow Jesus Coll., Oxford, 1986-87. Mem. Am. Math. Soc., Am. Acad. Arts and Sci. Home: 32 Fisher Ave Newton MA 02461-1117 Office: Brandeis U Dept Math Waltham MA 02154

BROWN, EDITH TOLIVER, retired educator; b. Mize, Ky.; d. Manford Clarence and Snowy May (McGuire) Toliver; m. James Link Brown, Mar. 14, 1948; 1 child, Pamela Jo Brown Elick. BA in Elem. Edn., Ky. Weslyan U., 1947. Permanent tchr. cert., Ohio. Tchr. Mapleton Elem. Sch., Mt. Sterling, Ky., 1939-44; chief of personnel records sect. Office of InterAm. Affairs, Washington, 1944-46; personnel staff Lockbourne (Ohio) AFB, 1951; tchr. Groveport (Ohio) Elem. Sch., 1957-73; substitute tchr. Pickaway and Franklin Counties, 1973-77; chmn. Textbook Com. Groveport (Ohio) Elem. Sch., 1960-65; mem. Curriculum Guide com., Columbus, Ohio, 1965-66. Trustee United Way of Pickaway County, 1984-87; chmn. Cancer Crusade Madison Twp., Heart Fund Drive, Madison Twp.; counselor Buckeye Girls' State, Columbus, 1955; hosp. vol., 1992-94; poll worker, 1990-93; mem. edn. com., adminstrv. bd. Hedges Chapel United Meth. Ch., 1990-94; vol. community kitchen, 1993-94. Named Ky. Col. by Ky. Gov. Brown, 1982. Mem. AAUW, Ohio Ret. Tchrs. Assn. (pres. 1989), Pickaway County Ret. Tchrs. Assn. (v.p. 1992-93, 95-96), Am. Legion Aux. #730, Nat. Ret. Tchrs. Assn. (del. to 5 convs. AARP). Democrat. Methodist. Avocations: reading, caring for elderly, grandchildren, travel. Home: 6341 Perrill Rd Ashville OH 43103-9529

BROWN, EDMUND GERALD, JR. (JERRY BROWN), mayor, former governor; b. San Francisco, Apr. 7, 1938; s. Edmund Gerald and Bernice (Layne) B. B.A., U. Calif.-Berkeley, 1961; J.D., Yale U., 1964. Bar: Calif. 1965. Research atty. Calif. Supreme Ct., 1964-65; atty. Tuttle & Taylor, Los Angeles, 1966-69; sec. state Calif., 1970-74; gov. State of Calif., 1975-83; chmn. Calif. Dem. Party, 1989-90; Dem. candidate for Pres. of United States, 1992; mayor Oakland, Calif., 1999—. Trustee Los Angeles Community Colls., 1969. Address: One Frank Ogawa Plaza 1 City Hall Plaza 3rd Flr Oakland CA 94612*

BROWN, EDWARD JAMES, SR., utility executive; b. Ft. Wayne, Ind., Sept. 30, 1937; s. William Theodore and Jane Elizabeth (Dix) B.; m. Margaret Bessey, June 17, 1989; children: Edward James Jr., Elena Emily. BA, Yale U., 1959; MA, Fordham U., 1962. Chartered fin. analyst. Fin. writer E.F. Hutton & Co., N.Y.C., 1970-71; economist N.Y. Power Authority, N.Y.C., 1971-74, prin. economist, 1974-80, mgr., customer svcs., 1980-83, mgr. spl. projects, 1983-86, dir. strategic planning, 1986-93, dir. new bus., 1993-94; mem. mgmt. com. Iroquois Gas Transmission System, 1989-94. Pres. Park Ave. Meth. Trust, N.Y.C., 1981—; pres. Friends of the Shakers, Inc., Sabathday Lake, Maine, 1982-84, dir., 1980—, treas., 1995—; trustee United Soc. of Shakers, Sabathday Lake, 1982-84, 95—, John St. Meth. Episcopal Trust Soc., N.Y.C., 1982—; bd. dirs. Meth. Ch. Home for Aged, Riverdale, N.Y., 1995—, mem. investment com., 1983—, co-chmn., 1994—, treas., 1996—; pres. Meth. Ch. Home Fund, 1996—; bd. dirs. Yorkville Emergency Alliance, N.Y.C., 1982-88; internat. adv. coun. Mus. of Am. Folk Art, N.Y.C., 1988—; dir., chmn. investment com. United Meth. City Soc., N.Y.C., 1999—. Mem. N.Y. Soc. Security Analysts, Assn. Investment Mgmt. and Rsch. Home: 500 E 85th St New York NY 10028-7407

BROWN, EDWARD MAURICE, retired lawyer, business executive; b. Watertown, N.Y., Aug. 22, 1909; s. Ernest E. and Eunice (Lewis) B.; m. Anne Amos, Oct. 2, 1937; children—Edward Dustin, Ernest Amos. *Edward Brown's ancestor, Thomas Dustin, came to America with the Trelawney Expedition in 1633. His son and daughter-in-law, Hannah, settled near Haverhill, Massachusetts Bay Province. In March 1697, Indians raided the area, taking 15 captives, including Mrs. Dustin, her nurse and a boy. They slaughtered 27 people, among them Hannah's newly-born infant. The story of her ordeal and escape fifteen days later, after killing and scalping her captors was chronicled by Cotton Mather, John Greenleaf Whittier, Nathaniel Hawthorne, and Henry David Thoreau. Hannah Dustin was the first woman ever honored with a monument in the U.S.* AB magna cum laude, Miami U., 1931, LLD, 1972; JD, Harvard U., 1934. Bar: Ohio 1934, N.Y. 1948, U.S. Supreme Ct. 1941. Assoc. Nichols, Wood, Marx & Ginter, 1934-47; asst. to pres. McCall Corp., N.Y.C., 1947-49, v.p., asst. sec., 1949-51, v.p., sec., dir., 1951-57; treas. Sperry Gyroscope Co. div. Sperry Rand Corp., 1958-59, v.p., treas., 1959-60, v.p., adminstr., 1960-65; v.p. Sperry Group, 1965-68; asst. treas. Sperry Rand Corp., 1958-68; group exec. of Teledyne, Inc., 1968-80; chmn. bd. Teledyne Can. Ltd., 1971-81. Trustee Village of Pelham Manor, N.Y., 1961-65, village mayor, 1965-67; mem. bd. govs. Nat. Ctr. for Disability Svcs., 1965-93. Lt. comdr. USNR, 1942-45. Decorated Bronze Star with Combat "V" award for svc. Mem. ABA, Phi Beta Kappa, Phi Eta Sigma, Phi Sigma, Beta Theta Pi. Republican. Episcopalian. Home: 165 Shadowy Hills Dr Oxford OH 45056-1440

BROWN, EDWARD SHERMAN, computer company executive; b. Lansing, Mich., May 6, 1940; s. Raymond Edward and Jennie W. (Maki) B.; AA, Compton (Calif.) Coll., 1970; AA in Bus. Adminstrn., Santa Ana Coll., 1975; BA in Mktg., Fullerton State U., 1976, MS in Mgmt., Cardinal Stritch Coll., 1985; m. Edith Volk; 1 child, Angela Renee. Sr. R&D technician Rockwell Internat., Anaheim, Calif., 1962-69; group leader R&D Hughes Aircraft Co., Fullerton, Calif., 1969-70; engr. spl. systems Gen. Automation, Anaheim, 1970-76, engring. mgr., 1976-77, sales mgr., 1977-78, sales mgr. computer systems, Milw., 1978-80; sales engr. computer systems div. Perkin-Elmer, Brookfield, Wis., 1980-82, sales mgr. data systems div., Overland Park, Kans., 1982-83; sr. sales rep. tech. computer systems Digital Equipment Corp., Brookfield, Wis., 1983-93; regional mgr. Globe-Tek Systems, Inc., Milw., 1993—; br. mgr. Jasper Engring. & Equipment Co., Milw., 1994-95; v.p. Process Control Sys., Inc., 1995—, Warehouse Software RF/DC Sys., 1995—; cons. in field. Recipient Proclamation for Decade of Pub. Svc. Programs, Milw. mayor. Author: A Collector's View of 19th Century Winchesters 1860-1900, 1992, In the Clouds, 1995. With U.S. Army, 1959-62. Mem. Cen. Mich. Rocket Soc. (past v.p.), Sales Mktg. Execs. (Dist. Sales award 1997) Kansas City, Mid-Am. Masters Track and Field Assn. (race dir.), Variety Club (dir. Wis. chpt., Vol of Yr. 1990), Christie Lodge Owner's Assn. (dir., v.p. Avon, Colo. chpt.), Coun. Logistics Mgmt. (dir. Milw. 1996), Sales Mktg. Execs., Pi Sigma Epsilon, Alpha Gamma Sigma. Office: Process Control Sys Inc 1300 S Calhoun Rd Brookfield WI 53005-6897

BROWN, EDWIN WILSON, JR., physician, educator; b. Youngstown, Ohio, Mar. 6, 1926; s. Edwin Wilson and Doris (McClellan) B.; m. Patricia Ann Currier, Aug. 9, 1952; children: Edwin Wilson, John Currier, Wende Patricia. Student, Carnegie Inst. Tech., 1943, Houghton Coll., 1946-47, Amherst Coll., 1943-44; M.D., Harvard U., 1953, M.P.H. (Nat. Found. fellow), 1957. Research fellow U. Buffalo, 1953-54; intern E.J. Meyer Meml. Hosp., Buffalo, 1954-55; resident pub. health Va. Dept. Health, 1955-56; tchr. medicine specializing in preventive medicine Boston, 1958-61, Hyderabad, India, 1961-63; assoc. med. dir. People-to-People Health Found., Washington, 1965-66; assoc. prof. medicine Ind. U.-Purdue U., Indpls., 1966-85, dir. div. internat. affairs, 1966-74, assoc. dean student services, dir. internat. services, 1979-85; pres. Global Health Svcs., Inc., Indpls., 1986—; med. dir. Ind. Dept. Correction, 1974-76; sr. med. edn. advisor King Faisal U., Dammam, Saudi Arabia, 1977-78; field dir. Harvard Epidemiol. Project, Egedesminde, Greenland, 1956-57; asst. prof. preventive medicine Sch. Medicine Tufts U., 1958-61; dep. chief staff Boston Dispensary, 1961; vis. prof. preventive medicine Osmania Med. Coll., Hyderabad, India, 1961-63; asst. dir. div. internat. med. edn., dir. AAMC-AID project internat. med. edn. Assn. Am. Med. Colls., Evanston, 1963-65; exec. sec. Study Group on Childhood Accidents, Boston, 1959-61; research asso. Sch. Pub. Health, Harvard U., 1959-60; dir. Curtis Pub. Co., Inc.; cons. Boston City Health Dept., 1959-60, WHO, 1973-74; chmn. bd. dirs. Med. Assistance Programs, Inc. Contbr. articles to profl. jours. Bd. dirs. Paul Carlson Found., Campus Teams, Iran Found., CARE/MEDICO, Internat. Students Inc. Served with AUS, 1944-46, ETO. Recipient Pub. Svc. award Vets. Day Coun. Indpls., 1996, Patriarch of Antioch's award Knight Comdr. of Order of St. Mark, 1998. Fellow Am. Pub. Health Assn.; mem. Assn. Tchrs. Preventive Medicine, Indian Assn. Advancement Med. Edn., Mass. Med. Soc., Internat. Policy Forum (bd. govs.), Nat. Policy Coun., Rotary Internat., Sigma Xi. Home: 8153 Oakland Rd Indianapolis IN 46240-2747 Office: PO Box 40951 Indianapolis IN 46240-0951

BROWN, ELI MATTHEW, anesthesiologist; b. Balt., Apr. 24, 1923; s. Morris and Dora (Poliakoff) B.; m. Estelle Tamus Neidish, May 26, 1948; children: Otto, Morris, Jacqueline Brown Rosenblatt, Barbara Brown Smith. BS, U. Md., 1943; MD, U. Md., Balt., 1946. Diplomate Am. Bd. Anesthesiologists. Intern Jewish Hosp. Bklyn., 1946-47, resident, 1947-48; resident Valley Forge Gen. Hosp., Phoenixville, Pa., 1948-49; asst. prof. anesthesiology SUNY-Downstate, Bklyn., 1952-54; clin. asst. prof. Wayne State U., Detroit, 1957-61, clin. assoc. prof., 1961-73, prof., 1975-76, chmn., 1976-98, prof. emeritus, 1998—; chmn. dept. anesthesia Sinai Hosp. Detroit, 1954-91. Contbr. articles to profl. jours. Maj. U.S. Army, 1948-51. Mem. AMA, Am. Soc. Anesthesiologists (pres. Ill. chpt. 1980-81), World Fedn. Soc. Anesthesiologists (del. 1978—), Am. Coll. Grad. Med. Edn., Assn. Univ. Anesthetists, Soc. Acad. Anesthesia Chmn. Avocations: golf, tennis.

BROWN, ELIZABETH ANN, foreign service officer; b. Portland, Oreg., Aug. 15, 1918; d. Edwin Keith and Grace Viola (Foss) B. A.B., Reed Coll., 1940; postgrad. (teaching fellow), Wash. State Coll., 1940-41; A.M., Columbia, 1943. Exec. asst. to chmn. 12th region WLB, Seattle, 1943-45; internat. affairs officer Dept. State, 1946-56; joined U.S. Fgn. Service, 1956; assigned Office UN Polit. Affairs, Dept. State, 1956-60; 1st sec. Am. embassy, Bonn, Germany, 1960-63; dep. dir. Office UN Polit. Affairs, 1963-65, dir., 1965-69; mem. State Dept. Sr. Seminar in Fgn. Policy, 1969-70; counselor for polit. affairs Am. embassy, Athens, Greece, 1970-75; dep. chief mission Am. embassy, The Hague, Netherlands, 1975-78; sr. insp. Dept. State, 1978-79, cons., 1980—; ret., 1979; adviser U.S. del. UN Gen. Assembly, 1946-50, 53, 55, 57-59, 64-65. Recipient 7th ann. Fed. Woman's award, 1967. Mem. Am. Fgn. Service Assn., Phi Beta Kappa. Home: 4848 Reservoir Rd NW Washington DC 20007-1561 Office: Dept State Washington DC 20007

BROWN, ELIZABETH ANNE, elementary educator; b. East Liverpool, Ohio, Jan. 10, 1957; d. Howard Junior and Hazel Marie (Springer) Welch; m. Lee Allen Brown, June 28, 1980; children: Ryan Matthew, Dustin Marshall. BA, Mt. Union Coll., 1979; MA, Ashland U., 1991. Cert. tchr., Ohio. Middle sch. math. tchr. grade 6 Alliance (Ohio) City Schs., 1979—; trainer software use, cons. Aurbach & Co., Inc., St. Louis, 1995—; east region math. edn. trainer Ohio Sci. and Math. Project Discovery, Ohio Dept. Edn., Columbus, 1996—. Mem. ASCD, Phi Delta Kappa, Alpha Xi Delta. Methodist. Avocations: reading, computers, travel. Home: 1104 Oakwood Dr Alliance OH 44601-5446 Office: BF Stanton Middle Sch South Union Ave Alliance OH 44601

BROWN, ELLEN HYNES, nursing administrator; b. Boston, Aug. 7, 1956; d. Patrick Joseph and Helen Elizabeth (Hoosen) Hynes; m. Donald E. Brown, May 30, 1992. BSN with honors, Northeastern U., 1981; MS in Primary Care Nursing, Simmons Coll., 1996. RN, Mass.; cert. adult nurse practitioner; cert. BLS, BLS instr., ACLS. Co-op gen. med. unit Carney Hosp., Dorchester, Mass., 1977; co-op cardiac stepdown unit Mt. Auburn Hosp., Cambridge, Mass., 1978-81; co-op health clinic John Hancock Ins. Co., Boston, 1981; staff nurse, gen. surg. unit Mass. Gen. Hosp., Boston, 1981-82; staff nurse, cardiac stepdown unit Mercy Hosp., New Orleans, 1982, Community Hosp. of S. Broward, Hallendale, Fla., 1983; staff nurse, SICU North Broward Med. Ctr., Pompano Beach, Fla., 1983-84; staff nurse, MICU/CCU Mass. Gen. Hosp., Boston, 1984-87, clin. supr. med. and emergency nursing, 1987—; occupl. health nurse practitioner Children's Hosp. Med. Ctr., Boston, 1996-97; adj. clin. faculty Quincy (Mass.) Coll. Nursing Program, 1997-98; occupl. health nurse practitioner Jordan Hosp., Plymouth, Mass., 1998—; instr. BLS, Mass. Gen. Hosp., Boston, 1991-93. Mem. Sigma Theta Tau. Roman Catholic. Avocations: cooking, in-line skating, antiquing, gardening, quilting. Home: 250 Court St Plymouth MA 02360-4038 Office: Mass Gen Hosp Fruit St Boston MA 02114

BROWN, ELLIOTT ROWE, physicist; b. L.A., Oct. 4, 1955; s. LaMonte Russell and Barbara Lee B.; m. Elayne Beth Reback, Aug. 2, 1981. BS, UCLA, 1979; MS, Calif. Inst. Tech., Pasadena, 1981, DS, 1985. Bachelors fellow Hughes Aircraft Co., El Segundo, Calif., 1977-79, Masters fellow, 1979-81; rsch. staff mem. MIT Lincoln Lab., Lexington, Mass., 1985-92, program mgr., 1992-94, asst. group leader, 1994-96; program mgr. Def. Advanced Rsch. Projects Agy., Arlington, Va., 1996-98; prof. elec. enging. UCLA, 1998—. Contbg. author: Hot Carriers in Semiconductor Nanostructures, 1992, Heterostructure and Quantum Devices, 1994; contbr. over 100 articles to profl. jours. Recipient Achievement Rewards for Coll. Scientists Found., Pasadena, 1983-85, Outstanding Achievement award Office of Sec. of Def., 1998, also other honors. Mem. IEEE, Am. Phys. Soc. (sr.), Materials Rsch. Soc., Phi Beta Kappa. Achievements include invention of highest frequency solid-state oscillator of electronic variety, most efficient planar antenna on a high-dielectric substrate; development of highest tunable CW power and frequency generated by optoelectronic techniques, and first remote sensing technique to unambiguously determine the thickness of oil slicks on water; patents in field. E-mail: erbrown@ee.ucla.edu. Office: UCAL Dept Elec Engring Mail Code 951594 Los Angeles CA 90095-1594

BROWN, EPHRAIM TAYLOR, JR., lawyer; b. Birmingham, Ala., Aug. 31, 1920; s. Ephraim Taylor and Lida (Otts) B.; m. Clara DeBardeleben Ebaugh, Oct. 21, 1949; children: Ephraim Taylor III, Clara DeBardeleben, Lida Otts. AB, Princeton U., 1941; LLB, Cornell U., 1943. Bar: Ala. 1943. Pvt. practice Birmingham; assoc. Cabaniss, Johnston, Gardner, Dumas & O'Neal, 1943-52, ptnr., 1952-91; of counsel, 1992—; chmn. spl. com. Revision Probate Laws Ala., 1967; chmn. bd. bar examiners Ala. State Bar, 1967-79. Bd. dirs. Childrens Fresh Air Farm; trustee, elder, deacon local Presbyn. ch. Fellow Am. Coll. Trust and Estate Counsel; mem. ABA, Ala. Bar Assn. (pres.), Birmingham Bar Assn., Ala. Law Inst. (mem. counsel), Birmingham Country Club, Sigma Alpha Epsilon. Home: 12 Cross Creek Park Birmingham AL 35213-2302 Office: PO Box 830612 2001 Park Pl Ste 700 Birmingham AL 35203-4804

BROWN, ERIC, art gallery director, art dealer; b. N.Y.C., Sept. 5, 1967; s. Neal Arthur and Carol (Kirchhofer) B. BA, Vassar Coll., 1990. Archivist, asst. to artist Nell Blaine N.Y.C., Gloucester, Mass., 1986-91; Mem. bd. Frances Lehman Loeb Art Ctr. Vassar Coll., Poughkeepsie, N.Y., 1994—. Fellow at the Morgan Libr., N.Y.C., 1994—. Avocations: painting, stamp collecting. Office: Tibor de Nagy Gallery 724 5th Ave New York NY 10019-4106

BROWN, ERIC JOEL, biomedical researcher; b. Ann Arbor, Mich., Sept. 27, 1950; s. Bernard and Shirley (Mark) B.; m. Marion Glynn Peters, Apr. 2, 1983; 1 child, Abigail. AB, Harvard Coll., 1971; MD, Harvard Med. Sch., 1975. Intern, then resident Beth Israel Hosp., Boston, 1975-77; clin. assoc. LCI/NIAID/NIH, Bethesda, Md., 1977-79, expert, 1979-81, sr. investigator, 1981-85; assoc. prof. Washington U., St. Louis, 1985-90, co-dir. divsn. infectious diseases, 1989-99, prof., 1990-99; prof. medicine and immunology U. Calif., San Francisco, 1999—. With USPHS, 1981-85. Fellow Infectious Diseases Soc.; mem. Soc. for Clin. Investigation, Am. Assn. Physicians. Office: Univ Calif San Francisco 513 Parnassus Ave Box 0513 San Francisco CA 94143*

BROWN, FAITH A., communications executive. BA in English with distinction, U. Mich., 1969. Editl. asst., prodn. mgr. Music Educators Jour., Washington, 1970-74; prodn. editor Social Edn., Washington, 1974-75, Big Farmer, Frankfort, Ill., 1976; mng. editor Am. Printer, 1976-79; dir. pub. rels., pubs. mgr. Triton Coll., River Grove, Ill., 1979-84; employee comm. mgr. Chgo. Tribune Co., 1984-90; employee comm. mgr. Tribune Co., 1990-92, corp. comm. mgr., 1992-98, corp. comm. dir., 1998—. Office: Tribune Co 435 N Michigan Ave Chicago IL 60611-4066

BROWN, FERMON, photographer, advertising professional; b. Nevada, Mo., Apr. 6, 1951; s. Roy and Lena Blossom (Reynolds) B.; m. Jana Ireland, 1971 (div. 1973); 1 child, Caleb; m. Wendy Dawson; 1 child, Jacob. Student, Mo. So. Coll., Joplin, 1970-71. Dir. advt. Ortho-Flex Saddle Co., Nevada, 1991—; owner Tree Fingers Photos, Nevada, 1992—, Ad Ventures, Nevada, 1996—. Photographer: (books) For the Sake of Our Horses, 1992, Saddling for the 21st Century, 1992, (catalog set) Ortho Flex Saddle Catalogs, 1995 (Pewter award Nat. Gold Ink Awards, Chgo. 1995, Cert. of Merit, Profl. Printing Industries of Am. 1995). Recipient Advt. Achievement award Readex Corp., 1995; named Outstanding Advertiser, Horse & Rider Mag., 1995. Avocations: poetry, art. Office: Ad Ventures 1103 N Colorado St Nevada MO 64772-1619

BROWN, FRANCES LOUISE (GRANDMA FRAN BROWN), artist, art gallery owner; b. Indpls., Oct. 19, 1925; d. Harley and Lenore (Spencer) Netherland; m. C.G. Clarkson, July 24, 1943 (div. Aug. 1967); children: James E. Clarkson, John B. Clarkson, Deborah L. Cromis. Thomas L. Currey, June 9, 1972 (dec. May 1978); m. George L. Brown, Jr., Mar. 3, 1982; 1 stepchild, Nancy Snow. BS in Edn., Miami U., 1968; MA in Edn., Ball State U., 1970. Elem. sch. tchr. Liberty (Ind.) Elem. Sch., 1968-71; tchr. Ball State U., Muncie, Ind., 1971-72; instr. Colby (Kans.) C.C., 1972-75; gallery owner, primitive artist Currey Studio Gallery, Berryville, Ark., 1975—. Author: Now Hear This, 1974; works exhibited at Nat. Mus. Am. Art, Washington, Mus. Am. Folk Art, N.Y.C., Wichita (Kans.) Art Assn. Gallery, Ark. Coll., Batesville, South Ark. Art Ctr., El Dorado, Harding Coll., Searcy, Ark., U. Ark., Fayetteville, Eureka Springs (Ark.) Hist. Mus., Western State Coll. Colo., Gunnison, MacMurray Coll., Jacksonville, Ill., Colby (Kans.) Coll., Claremore (Okla.) Coll., Warren Hall Coutts, III, Meml. Art Gallery, Inc., El Dorado, Kans., Masur Mus. Art, Monroe, La., Nebr. State Hist. Soc. Mus., Lincoln, Ind. State Mus., Indpls., Ozark Folk Ctr., Mountain View, Ark., Ft. Smith (Ark.) Art Ctr., Ctr. for So. Folklore, Memphis, Rogers (Ark.) Hist. Mus., Albrecht Art Mus., St. Joseph, Mo., Shiloh Mus., Springdale, Ark., Internat. Ctr. Contemporary Art, Paris, John Judkyn Meml. Mus., Eng., Mykonos (Greece) Folklore Mus., Musees Royaux des Beaux-Arts de Belgique, Brussels, Setagaya Art Mus., Tokyo; represented in permanent collections Smithsonian Instn., Washington, Mus. Am. Folk Art, N.Y.C., Nebr. State Hist. Soc. Mus., Lincoln, Ind. State Mus., Indpls., Ozark Mountain Folk Ctr., Mountain View, Ctr. for So. Folklore, Memphis, others; paintings recognized in various books, newspapers and articles. Avocations: pilot, sewing, reading, fishing, cooking. Home and Office: Currey Studio Gallery 3331 Highway 62 W Berryville AR 72616-8948

BROWN, FRANK, social science educator; b. Gallian, Ala., May 1, 1935; s. Tom and Ora L. (Lomax) B.; m. Joan Drake, July 6, 1963; children: Frank G., Monica J. BS, Ala. State U., 1957; MS, Oreg. State U., 1962; MA, U. Calif., Berkeley, 1969, PhD, 1970. Sci. tchr. Oakland Pub. Schs. (Calif.), 1962-68; assoc. dir. N.Y. Com. on Edn., N.Y.C., 1970-72; dir. Urban Inst. CCNY, 1971-72; prof., coll. master SUNY, Buffalo, 1972-77; dean U. N.C., Chapel Hill, 1983-90, Cary C. Boshamer prof. edn., dir. ednl. rsch. and policy project studies for rsch. in social sci., 1990—; vis. scholar U. Calif., Berkeley, 1990-91; project dir. Ford Found., N.Y.C., 1973-76, Spencer Found., Buffalo, 1976-78, NSF, Washington, 1979-80. Author: (with others) Fleischmann Commn. Report, 1973, Minority Enrollment in U.S. Institutions of Higher Education, 1977; contbr. articles to Ednl. Forum, Ednl. Researcher, Jour. Negro Edn., Jour. Black Studies, Am. Sch. Bd. Jour., numerous others; book series editor: Excellence Equity, Diversity, 1992—; editor: Emergent Leadership, 1976-80; guest editor: Edn. and Urban Soc., 1978, 89; editorial bds. Jour. Negro Edn., Jour. Ednl. Policy, Edn. and Urban Soc., Jour. Equity and Leadership, NABSE Jour., others. Bd. dirs. Buffalo Urban League, 1976-82; trustee White Rock Bapt. Ch., Durham, N.C., 1990—; chair Black Faculty/Staff caucus U. N.C., Chapel Hill, 1993-94. Grad. fellow Washington U., St. Louis, 1958, Oreg. State U., 1961, U. Calif.-Berkeley, 1968, fellow Rockefeller Found., 1979. Mem. Am. Ednl. Rsch. Assn. (sec. div. A 1980-82, v.p. 1986-88), Nat. Orgn. Legal Problems of Edn. (editorial bd. 1979-80, bd. dirs. 1990—), Assn. Social and Behavioral Scientists, Am. Assn. Colls. for Tchr. Edn. (bd. dirs. 1988—), Nat. Assn. Multicultural Edn., Assn. Sch. Bus. Ofcls. Internat., Am. Ednl. Fin. Assn., Am. Ednl. Rsch. Assn. (com. on minority affairs 1998—), Phi Delta Kappa, Alpha Phi Alpha (chpt. pres. 1977-78). Democrat. Baptist. Office: U NC Peabody Hall CB 3500 Chapel Hill NC 27599-3355

BROWN, FRANK BEVERLY, IV, lawyer; b. Bryan, Tex., June 1, 1945; s. Frank B. III and Kathleen (Mangum) B.; m. Janice Parks, July 19, 1980; children: Frank Parks, Caroline Paige. BBA, U. Tex., 1967, JD, 1975. Bar: Tex. 1976. Assoc. Daugherty, Kuperman, Golden & Morehead, Austin, Tex., 1976-80, ptnr., 1980-84; ptnr. Armburst & Brown, Austin, 1984-90, Strasburger & Price, Austin, 1990-97, Armbrust, Brown & Davis, 1997—. Capt. USAF, 1967-73. Mem. ABA (tax sect., bus. law sect.), Tex. Bar Assn. (tax sect., bus. law sect.), Travis County Bar Assn. (corp. and real estate sects.), Austin C. of C. (mil. affairs coun. 1989—). Presbyterian. Avocations: racquetball, skiing, flying. Office: Armbrust Brown & Davis Ste 1300 100 Congress Ave Austin TX 78701-4042

BROWN, FRANK DOUGLAS, academic administrator; b. Century, Fla., Jan. 18, 1941; m. Jo Ann N.; children: Jo April, Jay Douglas. ABA, N.W. Miss. Jr. Coll., 1961; BS in Bus. Adminstrn., U. So. Miss., 1963; MBA, U. Ala., 1969; PhD, Fla. State U., 1974. Computer programmer, systems analyst VF Corp., Monroeville, Ala., 1964-66; dir. data processing Livingston (Ala.) U., Livingston, 1966-68; grad. student U. Ala., Tuscaloosa, Ala., 1968-69; systems engr., mktg. rep. IBM, Montgomery, Ala., 1969-72; postgrad. Fla. State U., Tallahassee, 1971-74; assoc. exec. dir. Ala. Commn. on Higher Edn., Montgomery, 1974-78; asst. vice chancellor U. Houston, Tex., 1978-80, interim vice chancellor, 1980-81; v.p., assoc. prof. mgmt. Columbus State U., Ga., 1981-87, pres., 1988—; founding chmn. So. States Higher Edn. Fin. Officers Assn., 1977. Bd. dirs. ARC, Southeastern Mus. Ctr., United Way, Columbus Arts Council, 1983-85, Columbus Symphony Orch.; trustee, treas. Bradley Ctr.; chmn. bd. deacons Sunday Sch., 1989-91, dir., past pres. Bapt. Men, Bapt. Ch. Mem. Am. Assn. Higher Edn., Council for Advancement and Support Edn, Nat. Assn. Coll. and Univ. Bus. Officers, So. Assn. Coll. and Univ. Bus. Officers, Rotary Club, Phi Kappa Phi (v.p. 1987-88). Baptist. Home: Columbus GA 31907-1720 Office: Columbus State U Office of Pres 4225 University Ave Columbus GA 31907-5679*

BROWN, FRED ELMORE, investment executive; b. Muskogee, Okla., July 20, 1913; s. Fred E. and Alice (Washington) B.; m. Margaret Ann Gillham, Nov. 15, 1941 (dec.); 1 child, Frederick Elmore; m. Enid Sillcox Darlington, Dec. 22, 1977. B.S., U. Okla., 1934; M.B.A., Harvard U., 1936; LHD (hon.), U. Okla., 1994. Sr. ptnr. J. & W. Seligman & Co., 1955-81; chmn., chief exec. officer J. & W. Seligman & Co. Inc., 1981-89, sr. advisor, dir., 1989-93, cons., dir., 1994—. Trustee Adirondack Cmty. Trust, Lake Placid Edn. Found., Lake Placid Ctr. for the Arts; hon. trustee Trudeau Inst.; sr. mem. adv. com. Coll. Bus. Adminstrn., U. Okla.; bd. dirs. Bizzell Libr. Soc. Lt. col. OQMG AUS, 1942-46. Decorated Legion of Merit; recipient Disting. Svc. citation, 1982, Regents Alumni award U. Okla., 1985; Arthur Barto Adams fellow, 1993; inducted Okla. Hall of Fame, 1982. Mem. Union Club, Beta Theta Pi, Beta Gamma Sigma. Episcopalian. Fred E. Brown chair in bus. named in his honor, Coll. Bus. Adminstrn., U. Okla. Home: 580 Park Ave New York NY 10021-7313 Office: J & W Seligman & Co Inc 100 Park Ave Fl 7 New York NY 10017-5598

BROWN, FREDERIC JOSEPH, army officer; b. Fort Sill, Okla., July 18, 1934; s. Frederic Joseph and Kathryn (Richardson) B.; m. Harriette Anne Upham, July 7, 1956; children: Kathryn, Harriette, Judith. B.S., U.S. Military Acad., 1956; M.A., Grad. Inst. Internat. Studies, U. Geneva, Switzerland, 1963, Ph.D., 1967. Commd. officer U.S. Army; advanced through grades to lt. gen.; comdr. 1st squadron 4th cavalry U.S. Army, Vietnam, 1969-70; mem. staff Nat. Security Council, 1972-73; comdr. 1st Tiger brigade 2d Armored Divsn., Ft. Hood, Tex., 1975-76; comdr. U.S. Army Tng. Center Armor, Ft. Knox, Ky., 1977-78; asst. div. comdr. 8th Inf. Div. Baumholder, W. Ger., 1978-81; dep. chief of staff tng. U.S. Army Tng. and

Doctrine Command, Ft. Monroe, Va., 1981-82; comdg. gen., chief armor U.S. Army Armor Ctr., Ft. Knox, Ky., 1983-86; comdr. 4th U.S. Army, Ft. Sheridan, Ill., 1986-89; asst. prof. dept. polit. scis. U.S. Mil. Acad., West Point, N.Y.; mem. adj. rsch. staff Inst. for Def. Analyses; cons. in tng. tech. and devel.; advisor to Dept. Def. tng. of fgn. armies, 1995—; advisor to Dept. of Army design of advanced learning for future Army, 1997—. Author: Chemical Warfare--A Study in Restraints, 1968 The United States Army in Transition II: Landpower in the Information Age, 1993; co-author: The United States Army in Transition, 1973; author numerous papers on info. age tng. for Inst. for Def. Analyses, 1989-98; co-producer TV series on U.S. Army post-Vietnam All That It Can Be, 1995—; developer advanced tng. policies and programs for U.S. Army Force XXI, 1996-98. Decorated D.S.M. with oak leaf cluster, Silver Star, Legion of Merit; Olmsted scholar, 1961-63. Mem. Council Fgn. Relations, Internat. Inst. Strategic Studies. Episcopalian. Home: 6317 Stoneham Ln Mc Lean VA 22101-2346 Office: Inst for Defense Analyses Simulation Lab 1801 N Beauregard St Alexandria VA 22311-1733 *The essence of satisfaction is service to others. In my case, the opportunity to defend the values and wealth of our great nation.*

BROWN, FREDERICK CALVIN, physicist, educator; b. Seattle, July 6, 1924; s. Fred Charles and Rose (Mueller) B.; m. Joan Schauble, Aug. 9, 1952; children—Susan, Gail, Derek. B.S., Harvard U., 1945, M.S., 1947, Ph.D., 1950. Physicist Systems Research Lab., Harvard (NDRC), 1945-46; staff physicist Naval Research Lab., Washington, 1950; physicist Applied Physics Lab., U. Wash., 1950-51; asst. prof. Reed Coll., Portland, Oreg., 1951-55, U. Ill., Urbana, 1955-58; assoc. prof. U. Ill., 1958-61, prof., 1961-87, prof. emeritus, 1987—; assoc. Center for Advanced Study, 1969-70; prin. scientist, area mgr. Xerox Palo Alto Research Center, 1973-74; prof. U. Wash., Seattle, 1987; cons. prof., applied physics dept. Stanford, 1973-74. Author: The Physics of Solids-Ionic Crystals, Lattice Vibrations and Imperfections, 1967; Contbr. articles profl. jours. Recipient Alexander von Humboldt sr. scientist award U. Kiel, 1978; NSF sr. postdoctoral fellow Clarendon Lab., Oxford, 1964-65. Fellow Am. Phys. Soc. Achievements include innovator use of synchrotron radiation for spectroscopy. Home: 5915 25th Ave W Everett WA 98203-1468 Office: U Wash Dept Physics PO Box 351560 Seattle WA 98195-1560

BROWN, FREDERICK COURTNEY, writer; b. N.Y.C., May 30, 1953; s. Coley and Odell Brown; m. Elizabeth D. Hatton, June 19, 1979 (div. Dec. 1981); 1 child, Frederick C.D. Student, Loma Linda U., 1979-81; BA in Journalism and Mass. Comms., Benedict Coll., 1985. Master control switcher WLTX TV Sta., Columbia, 1982-83; announcer Sta. WCEZ Radio, Columbia, S.C., 1982-84, Sta. WCOS Radio, Columbia, 1984-86; consignment assoc. customer svc. Smith's Consignment Inc., Columbia, 1992—. Author screenplays: Order of the Arrow, 1992, O-Plan, Tango, A Thief in Paradise, Africa; author children's book: The Frog and The Stone, 1993. With USAF, 1978-80. Mem. VFW, Arthritis Found. Avocations: horseback riding, fishing, photography, swimming. Home: PO Box 8775 Moreno Valley CA 92552-8775

BROWN, FREDERICK LEE, health care executive; b. Clarksburg, W.Va., Oct. 22, 1940; s. Claude Raymond and Anne Elizabeth (Kiddy) B.; children: Gregory Lee, Michael Owen-Price. BA in Psychology, Northwestern U., 1962; MBA in Health Care Adminstrn., George Washington U., 1966. Vocat. counselor Cook County Dept. Pub. Aid, Chgo., 1962-64; adminstrv. resident Meth. Hosp. Ind., Inc., Indpls., 1965-66, adminstrv. asst., 1966, asst. adminstr., 1966-71, assoc. adminstr., 1971-72, v.p. ops., 1972-74; exec. v.p., chief operating officer Meml. Hosp. DuPage County, Elmhurst, Ill., 1974-82, Meml. Health Svcs., Elmhurst, 1980-82; pres., chief executive officer Christian Hosp. NW-NW, St. Louis, 1982-89; pres., chief exec. officer CH Health Techs., Inc., St. Louis, 1983-93, Christian Health Svcs., St. Louis, 1986-93, CH Allied Svcs., Inc., St. Louis, 1988-93; pres. BJC Health System, St. Louis, 1993—, CEO, 1993-98, vice-chmn, 1999—; adj. instr. Washington U. Sch. Medicine, St. Louis, 1982—; mem. chancellor's coun. U. Mo., St. Louis, 1990—; bd. dirs. HealthLink, Inc., 1985-92, mem. exec. com., 1986-92, chmn. bd., 1989-91; pres., chief exec. officer Village North, Inc., 1986-93; bd. dirs. Am. Healthcare Systems, Inc., chmn. shareholder communications com., 1985-86, v. chmn. 1992; bd. dirs. Commerce Bank St. Louis, Am. Excess Ins. Ltd.; mem. corp. assembly Blue Cross Blue Shield Mo., 1991—. Contbr. articles to profl. jours. Co-chmn. hosp. div. United Way Greater St. Louis, 1983, chmn., 1984, chmn. health svcs. div., 1985-86, vice chmn. region, 1988—, bd. dirs., 1986, Kammergild Chamber Orch., 1984-88, v.p., 1985-88, Mo. Heart Inst., 1988-92, Alton Meml. Hosp., 1987-91, bd. dirs., 1987-91; mem. exec. bd. St. Louis Area coun. Boy Scouts Am. Northstar chpt., 1989, activities coun. chmn. 1993—, bd. trustees 1990-92, chmn. Friends of Scouting Campaign, 1991-92; communion steward Webster Hills Meth. Ch., 1987—; mem. medicaid budget task force Mo. Dept. Social Svcs., 1990; mem. emergency rm. svcs. task force St. Louis Regional Med. Ctr., 1985; mem. corp. assembly Blue Cross Blue Shield of Mo., 1991; bd. dirs. Sold on St. Louis, 1991-93; St. Louis Reg. Commerce & Growth Assn., 1993—; mem. St. Louis City and County Task Force, 1991—. Fellow Am. Coll. Healthcare Execs. (chmn. credentials com. 1978, task force governance and constituencies 1986-88; mem. Gold Medal award com. 1985, chmn. task force on governance and constituencies 1986-87, com. on ethics 1989-91, chmn. awards & testamonials com., 1992—, bd. regents 1991-93); gov. dist V, mem. Am. Acad. Med. Adminstrs. (life, state dir. 1988—, Health Care Exec. of Yr. 1990, Statesman in Healthcare, 1992), Hosp. Pres.'s Assn., Advt. Club Greater St. Louis, Am. Hosp. Assn. (coun. on mgmt. 1987, alt. del. for healthcare systems 1988-90, del. to ho. of dels. for health care systems 1991, fin. com. chair 1995, chair-elect 1998, chmn. 1999), Am. Pub. Health Assn., George Washington U. Alumni Assn. for Health Svcs. Adminstrn. (preceptor 1975—, Alumnus of Yr. award 1981, Frederick Gibbs award, 1993), Hosp. Assn. Met. St. Louis (bd. dirs. 1984—, chmn. bd. 1988-89, sec. 1985-86, treas. 1987, chmn. coun. on pub. affairs and communications 1985, vice chmn. 1987, various coms.), Greater St. Louis Health Care Alliance (co-chair 1992—), Mo. Hosp. Assn. (mem. coun. on rsch. and policy devel. 1983-88, chmn. coun. on multi-instnl. hosps. 1986-88, mem. dist. coun. pres.'s 1986-89, bd. dirs. 1988-92, chmn. bd. trustees 1990), Cen. Ea. Profl. Rev. Orgn. (bd. dirs. 1982-85, various coms.), St. Louis Met. Med. Soc. (lay advisor 1990-92), Healthcare Execs. Study Soc., Internat. Health Policy and Mgmt. Inst. (bd. dirs. 1988—), Am. Protestant Health Assn. (bd. dirs. 1988-93, chmn. 1992-93), St. Louis Club, Algonquin Golf Club, Arena Club, Stadium Club (St. Louis), Rotary. Republican. Office: BJC Health System Ste 1200 120 S Central Saint Louis MO 63108-2297

BROWN, FREEZELL, JR., private school educator; b. Indpls., Aug. 19, 1957; s. Freezell Brown and Alice Samuel. BA in Religion, Carroll Coll., Waukesha, Wis., 1979; MA in Religious Edn., Christian Theol. Sem., Indpls., 1984; M. Theol. Studies in Social Ethics, Garrett-Evang. Theol. Sem., 1988; postgrad., Ind. U.-Purdue, U. Indpls.; postgrad. in edn., Walden U. Consecrated diaconal minister United Methodist Ch., 1985. Youth dir. YMCA, Waukesha, 1980-81; minister with youth N. United Meth. Ch., Indpls., 1983, min. with youth and community, 1984-87; program coord. Crooked Creek Multi-Svc. Ctr., 1990-91; instr. PSI Inst. of Indpls., Indpls., 1991; trainer Training, Inc., 1991-92; tchr. religion and English, coord. diversity concerns Brebeuf Prep. Sch., Indpls., 1992-95; dir. diversity Brebeuf Prep Sch., Indpls., 1995—; mem. com. Religion and Race So. Ind. Conf. United Meth. Ch., alt. com. investigation; mem. adv. bd. Metro. Adv. Ministry, Butler U. Campus Ministry, Indpls.; bd. dirs. Ind. Writer's Ctr.; mem. adj. faculty Advance Coll. Project Ind. U., dept. edn. U. Indpls., 1997—; adj. faculty U. Indpls., 1996—. Contbr. book revs. to Christian Century, Christian Ministry; editor Connections newsletter; spl. corr. Indpls. Recorder. Mem. neighborhood adv. bd. Indpls. Children's Mus.; mem. profl. adv. bd. Buchanan Counseling Ctr.; mem. adv. bd. Coll. Ave. Youth Behavior Acad.; mem. Christian Educators Fellowship of United Meth. Ch.; program coord. Crooked Creek Multi-Svc. Ctr., 1990; bd. dirs. The Writers' Ctr. of Indpls.; ctrl. region diversity coord. Jesuit Secondary Edn. Assn. Mem. Nat. Coun. Tchrs. English, So. Poverty Law Ctr., Ind. Interreligious Commn. on Human Equality, Ind. Schs. Assn. of Ctrl. States (midwest diversity com. Ind. chpt.), Jesuit Secondary Edn. Assn. Democrat. Avocations: painting, music composition and performance, drama, reading, writing. Home: 5704 Carrousel Dr Indianapolis IN 46254-1666

BROWN, GARDNER RUSSELL, engineering executive; b. Sterling, Mass., Nov. 3, 1927; m. Sondra Jupin Gillice, Jan. 12, 1980; children: Kevin, Stephen, Thomas. BS in Mech. and Nuclear Engring., USN, 1955. Project mgr U.S. AEC, Washington, 1953-71; mgr. Northeast Utilities Svc. Co., Berlin, Conn., 1971-73; dept. head Potomac Electric Power Co., Washington, 1971-88; CEO RusSon, Inc., Engrs. and Ind. Power Developers, Arlington, Va., 1981—. Asst. to chmn. Rep. Nat. Com. Conv., Dallas, 1984. Comdr. USN, 1945-70, PTO, Korea. Decorated Purple Hearts. Mem. Am. Nuclear Soc., U.S. Mex. C. of C., Explorers Club, Edgartown Yacht Club, Army Navy Club, Army Navy Country Club. Republican. Episcopalian. Achievements include patent in field. Office: RusSon Inc Ste 1112 1101 S Arlington Ridge Rd Arlington VA 22202-1929

BROWN, GARY SANDY, electrical engineering educator; b. Jackson, Miss., Apr. 13, 1940; s. John Leo and Welma (Kelley) B.; m. Mary Kathleen Connaughton, Mar. 16, 1970; children: Joshua John, Nathan Matthew. BSEE, U. Ill., 1963, MS, 1964, PhDEE, 1967. Grad. rsch. asst. Antenna Lab. U. Ill., Urbana, 1963-67; mem. tech. staff TRW Systems Group, Redondo Beach, Calif., 1969-70; sr. engr. Rsch. Triangle Inst., Durham, N.C., 1970-73; sr. scientist Applied Sci. Assocs., Apex, N.C., 1973-85; prof. elect. engring. Va. Poly. Inst. and State U., Blacksburg, 1985—; with Wallops Flight Facility, NASA, Wallops Island, Va., 1974; cons. Naval Rsch. Lab., Washington, 1988-91, Decision Scis. Applications, Arlington, Va., 1988-91, DTI Inc., Torrance, Calif., 1987-91, Applied Physics Lab., Laurel, Md., 1987-88, Waste Policy Inst., Blacksburg, Va., 1991—, Motorola Corp., Chandler, Ariz., 1991-93; mem. NATO AGARD Electromagnetic Propogation Panel, 1993—; dir. Electromagnetic Interactions Lab. Contbr. chpts. to books, articles to profl. jours. Capt. U.S. Army, 1967-69. Recipient Best Paper awards R.W.P. King, 1978, Schelkunoff, 1999. Fellow IEEE; mem. Antennas and Propagation Soc. of IEEE (pres. 1988), Am. Geophys. Union (editor's citation Radio Sci., Am. sects. 1986), Internat. Union of Radio Sci. (mem.-at-large 1987, sec. U.S. nat. com. 1997—), NATO AGARD Sensors and Propagation Panel. Avocations: backpacking, jogging. Office: Va Poly Inst & State U Bradley Dept Elec Engr Blacksburg VA 24061

BROWN, GENE W., steel company executive; b. Warsaw, Ind., Feb. 16, 1936; s. Dean L. and Ilean (Clase) B.; m. Beverly A. Sink, Feb. 25, 1956; children: Lisa Jo, Scott Eugene. BSME, Purdue U., 1960; MBA, Northwestern U., 1967. Engr. Ill. Tool Works, Chgo., 1957-67; gen. mgr. Chgo. Gasket Co., 1967-69; ops. mgr. Maremont Corp., Harvey, Ill., 1969-74; gen. mgr. Marmon Group, Chgo., 1974-77; pres. Whittar Steel Strip, Detroit, 1977-88, Lisco Inc., Detroit, 1979—. Home: 6322 Palma Del Mar Blvd S # 9024 Saint Petersburg FL 33715-2700 also (summer): 677N-175W Valparaiso IN 46383 Office: Brownco Inc 277 Melton Rd Chesterton IN 46304-9746

BROWN, GEOFFREY FRANCIS, public defender, lawyer; b. San Francisco, May 20, 1943; m. Wai Yung, 1973; children: Miranda, Simone, Olivia. BA in Polit. Sci., U. Calif., Berkeley, 1964; JD, San Francisco Law Sch., 1970. Bar: Calif. 1971, U.S. Dist. Ct. (no. dist.) Calif. 1971, U.S. Ct. of Appeals (9th cir.) 1971. Dep. pub. defender City of San Francisco, 1971-77, elected pub. defender, 1978—; adj. prof. law New Coll. Calif. Sch. of Law; legal expert KRON-TV and Bay TV, 1995-97; cons. US AID in Italy, 1985, Bolivia, 1991, Argentina, 1995; bd. dirs. San Francisco Law Sch., 1998—; mem. human rsch. com. U. Calif., San Francisco, 1998—. Contbr. numerous articles to profl. jours. and newspapers, presented papers at legal symposia. Mem. Mayor's Task Force on Jail Overcrowding, 1979-95, Mayor's Coun. on Criminal Justice, 1979—; bd. dirs. San Francisco Neighborhood Legal Assistance Found., 1988-96. Mem. Calif Pub. Defenders Assn. (bd. dirs. 1979—, pres. 1984), Nat. Legal Aid and Defenders Assn. (defender com. 1981-82). Office: City & County San Francisco Pub Defender's Office 555 7th St San Francisco CA 94103-4732

BROWN, GEORGE, research forester and educator; b. Warrensburg, Mo., Jan. 31, 1939; married, 1964; 2 children. BS, Colo. State U., 1960, MS, 1962; PhD in Forest Hyrdology, Oreg. State U., 1967. Prof. forest hydrology Oreg. State U., Corvallis, 1966—; head dept. forest engring. Oreg. State U., 1973-86; assoc. dean rsch. Oreg. State U., Corvallis, 1986-90, dean, 1990—; cons. hydrologist Weyerhaeuser Co., 1973; prin. engr. Forest Svc. USDA, 1981. Mem. Soc. Am. Foresters, Forest Prod. Soc. Research in research administration; temperature, sediment, dissolved oxygen. Office: Oreg State U Coll Forestry Forest Rsch Lab Corvallis OR 97331-5704*

BROWN, GEORGE E., judge, educator; b. Hammond, Ind., July 27, 1947; s. George E. and Violet M. (Matlon) B.; m. Patricia A. Schneider, June 6, 1970; children: Janet M., Elizabeth A. BS, Ball State U., 1969; JD, DePaul U., 1974; grad., Ind. Jud. Coll., 1996. Bar: Ind. 1974, Ill. 1974, U.S. Dist. Ct. (no. dist.) Ind. 1979, U.S. Supreme Ct. 1977, U.S. Tax Ct. 1977. Pvt. practice LaGrange & Lake Counties, Ind., 1974-84; judge LaGrange County Ct., 1984-87, LaGrange Superior Ct., 1988—; part-time chief dep. prosecutor LaGrange County, 1975-77; adj. faculty Tri-State U., Angola, Ind., 1991—. Vol. Jr. Achievement, 1997—. Mem. ABA, Ind. State Bar Assn. (ho. of dels., com. on written pub.), LaGrange County Bar Assn. (pres. 1978), Ind. Judges Assn., Nat. Conf. State Trial Judges, LaGrange Rotary (past dir., v.p. 1999—). Office: Lagrange Superior Ct Courthouse Lagrange IN 46761

BROWN, GEORGE LESLIE, legislative affairs and business development consultant, former manufacturing company executive, former lieutenant governor; b. Lawrence, Kans., July 1, 1926; s. George L. and Harriett Alberta (Watson) B.; m. Modeen; children: Gail Brown Chandler, Laura Nicole, Kim Doreen, Cynthia Renee; stepchildren: Ronnie, Carol, Angela, Sharolyn, Nyra. BJ, U. Kans., 1950; postgrad., U. Colo., 1950-51; A.M.P., Harvard Bus. Sch., 1980. Mem. writing staff Denver Post, 1950-65; asst. exec. dir. Denver Housing Authority, 1965-69; exec. dir. Met. Denver Urban Coalition, 1969-75; lt. gov. Colo. Denver, 1974-79; v.p. Grumman Corp., N.Y., 1979-90; assoc. Whitten & Diamond (formerly Lipsen, Whitten & Diamond), Washington, 1990-94; dir. Prudential Securities, 1994-97; of counsel Moser and Moser Law Firm, 1994—; v.p. L. Robert Kimball, Archtl. Engrs.; sr. v.p. Greenwich Ptnrs.; Bd. dirs. Davis and Elkins Coll., Washington Trade Ctr., Joint Ctr. for Polit. Studies, Boys Choir of Harlem, Coll. Aeros., Air Force Meml. Found. Mem. Colo. Ho. of Reps., 1955, Colo. Senate, 1956-74. Served with USAAF, 1944-46. Recipient Adam Clayton Powell award for polit. achievement, 1975, Opportunities Industrialization Center Nat. Govt. award, 1975; George Brown Urban Journalism scholarship established at U. Kans. William Allen White Sch. Journalism, 1976. Mem. Kappa Alpha Psi. Office: Greenwich Partners 1090 Vermont Ave NW Ste 800 Washington DC 20005-4905

BROWN, GERALD CURTIS, retired army officer, engineering executive; b. Worcester, Mass., Aug. 10, 1942; s. Victor Curtis and Ethel (Dean) B.; m. Alelaide M. Forshey, June 28, 1964 (div.); children: Deborah Ann, Suzanne Marie; m. Jean Jennings, Aug. 1, 1998. BS, U.S. Mil. Acad., West Point, N.Y., 1964; MS, U. Ill., 1970. Registered profl. engr., Tex., Md. Commd. 2d. lt. U.S. Army, 1964, advanced through grades to brig. gen., 1988; capt. 18th Engr. Brigade, Vietnam, 1966-67; maj. 1st Air Cavalry Div., Vietnam, 1970-71; assoc. prof. history U.S. Mil. Acad., West Point, 1974-77; bn. comdr. 82d Combat Engr. Bn., Bamberg, Fed. Republic Germany, 1978-80; dist. engr. Balt. Dist., Corps Engrs., 1982-84; staff engr. U.S. Army Tng. and Doctrine Command, Ft. Monroe, Va., 1984-86; mil. exec. Office Undersec. Army, Washington, 1986-88; fellow Harvard U., Cambridge, 1988-89; comdg. gen. U.S. Army Corps Engrs., North Atlantic Div., N.Y.C., 1989-92; dir. Environ. programs Dept. of Army, The Pentagon, Washington, 1992-94; ret. U.S. Army, 1994; v.p. Svedrup Civil, Inc., Falls Church, Va., 1994-95; v.p., mgr. Ea. Ops. Sverdrup Environ., Inc., Balt., 1995-98; vice pres. Sverdrup Civil, Inc., Falls Church, VA, 1998—; Natl. Defense Exec. Reserve; Fed. Emerg. Mgmt. Agency, chmn. bd. of vis., fed. Emerg. Mgmt. Inst., Maryland. Contbr. articles to mil. jours. Fellow Soc. Am. Mil. Engrs. (v.p. 1989-92, bd. dirs. 1993-96, chmn. Acad. Fellows 1995-96); mem. ASCE, Harvard Club (Washington), Nat. Press Club (Washington), Army and Navy Club (Washington). Avocations: running, squash, skiing. Home: 2670 Hillsman St Falls Church VA 22043 Office: Sverdrup Civil Inc 7600 Leesburg Pike Falls Church VA 22043

BROWN, GERALD EDWARD, physicist, educator; b. Brookings, S.D., July 22, 1926. BA, U. Wis., 1946; MS, Yale U., 1948; PhD, U. Birmingham, 1950, DSc, 1957; DSc (hon.), U. Helsinki, 1982, U. Birmingham, 1990. Prof. physics U. Birmingham, 1959-60, Nordic Inst. Theoretic Atomic Physics, 1960-85, Princeton U., 1964-68; prof. physics SUNY, Stony Brook, 1968-74, leading prof., 1974-88, dist. prof. physics, 1988—; lectr. math physics, 1955-58; reader U. Birmingham, 1958-59; dir. nuclear astrophysics Inst. Theoretical Physics NSF, U. Calif., 1960. Recipient Boris Pregel award N.Y. Acad. Sci., 1976, Tom W. Bonner prize Nuclear Physics, 1982, Sr. Dist. Sci. award Alexander von Humboldt Found., 1987, John Price Wetherill medal Franklin Inst., Phila., 1992, Max-Planck medaille German Phys. Soc., 1997. Office: SUNY Inst Theoretical Physics Stony Brook NY 11794

BROWN, GERALDINE, nurse, freelance writer; b. Clemson, S.C.; d. Isaac and Gladys (Patterson) B. AS in Nursing, U. D.C., Washington, 1973; real estate cert., Long and Foster Inst., College Park, Md., 1984; cert. in TV broadcasting, Columbia Sch., Bailey's Crossroads, Va., 1987; BSN, Bowie State U., 1989, MA in Comm., 1991, MSN, 1997; PhD, Howard U., 1994. RN, D.C., FCC Third Class License. Supr. staff nurse Walter Reed Hosp., Washington, 1970-76; supr. clin. nurse Dept. Human Svcs., Washington, 1976-78, cmty. health nurse, 1978-84; nursing instr. Phillips Bus. Sch., Alexandria, Va., 1984-85; pvt. nurse Washington, 1973—; faculty Howard U. Coll. Nursing, 1994—; dir. pub. affairs Bible Way Chs. Worldwide, Inc., Washington, 1978-91; soc. columnist As It Happens, Charlotte (N.C.) Post, 1964-66; soc. editor Washington Cafe Soc. mag, 1971; contbr. feature stories Capital Spotlight newspaper, 1978—; mem. faculty Coll. Nursing, Howard U., 1994—. Asst. organizer DC Mayor's United Nations Day, 1980; vol. Met. Boys and Girls Clubs, Washington, 1980—; vol. Nursing Instr., The Washington Saturday Coll., 1982-84; Co. ARC, 1973—, Big Sisters of the Washington Met. Area, 1988—. Recipient certs. of excellence Govt. of D.C., 1978-84; cert. of appreciation Mayor of D.C., 1980, Meritorious Pub. Svc. award, 1980; svc. trophy Washington Saturday Coll., 1984. Mem. ANA, NAACP, Nat. Coun. Negro Women, Smithsonian Inst. (assoc.), Nat. Black Nurses Assn., Washington Urban League, Chi Eta Phi, Sigma Theta Tau. Democrat. Avocations: stamp collecting, traveling, writing poetry.

BROWN, GERALDINE REED, lawyer, consulting executive; b. L.A., Feb. 18, 1947; d. William Penn and Alberta Vernice (Coleman) Reed; m. Ronald Wellington Brown, Aug. 20, 1972; children: Kimberly Diana, Michael David. BA summa cum laude, Fisk U., 1968; JD, Harvard U., 1971, MBA, 1973. Bar: N.Y. 1974, U.S. Dist. Ct. (so. and ea. dists.) N.Y. 1974, U.S. Ct. Appeals (2d cir.) 1974, U.S. Supreme Ct. 1977, N.J. 1992, U.S. Dist. Ct. N.J. 1992, Pa. 1993. Assoc. White & Case, N.Y.C., 1973-78; atty. J.C. Penney Co., Inc., N.Y.C., 1978-88; pres. The Reed-Brown Cons. Group., Montclair, N.J., 1989—; counsel Spooner & Burnett, N.Y.C., 1993-98; asst. prof. bus. law Montclair State Coll., 1990-92; adj. prof. bus. law Kean Coll. N.J., 1989-94; adj. prof. Law Sch. Seton Hall, 1995—; dir. Renaissance Jr. Golf, Inc., Newark. Bd. dirs. Coun. Concerned Black Execs., N.Y.C., 1977-88, Studio Mus. in Harlem, N.Y.C., 1980-81; mem. Montclair (N.J.) Devel. Bd., 1985-88, ad hoc com. on Montclair Econ. Devel. Corp., 1985-88; sec. bd. trustee Montclair YWCA, 1989-97, United Hosps. Med. Ctr., vice chmn., 1991-93, trustee, exec. com., chair bylaws com., chair strategic planning com., pers. com.; sec. bd. trustees Ramapo Coll.; chair bylaws com. N.J. United Minority Bus. Brain Trust.; trustee Essex County Ct. Apptd. Spl. Advocates, 1989-93, Jr. League of Montclair, Newark, Mental Health Resources Ctr., Montclair, N.J., 1991-96; trustee, sec. Montclair Early Childhood Corp., 1997-98; trustee St. Marks United Meth. Ch. Mem. ABA (several coms. sect. corp., banking and bus. law, sect. internat. law and practice), N.J. Bar Assn. (mem. bus. orgns. com.), Essex County Bar Assn., N.Y. State Bar Assn. (continuing legal edn. com., legis. liason 1981-90, vice chmn. 1988-90, exec. com. of corp. counsel sect., chmn. com. on SEC, fin. corp. law and governance, chair com. atty. professionalism, mem. task force on profession, com. rev. of cts. and professions), Assn. of Bar of City of N.Y. (corp. law com. 1978-81), N.Y. County Lawyers Assn. (corp. law com.), Exec. Women of N.J., Harvard Bus. Sch. Club, Harvard Law Sch. Assn. (trustee N.J. chpt.), Coalition 100 Black Women, Harvard Bus. Sch. Black Alumni Assn., Harvard Law Sch. Black Alumni Assn., Harvard Club (N.Y.C.), Phi Beta Kappa, Delta Sigma Theta (past chair social action com. Montclair alumnae chpt., chair rules com., parlimentarian). Home and Office: The Reed-Brown Cons Group 180 Union St Montclair NJ 07042-2125

BROWN, GERRI ANN, physical therapist; b. N.Y.C., May 1, 1948; d. S. Stanley and Corinne (Carlin) Schkurman; m. Michael Edward Brown, Oct. 2, 1971. BS in Phys. Therapy, Ithaca Coll., 1969. Registered phys. therapist, Colo., N.Y. Lectr. U. Colo. Med. Sch., Denver, 1970-81; dir. phys. therapy and team facilitator Wheatridge (Colo.) Regional Ctr., 1969-81; phys. therapist Ptnrs. Home Health Care, Lakewood, Colo., 1982-83, Mt. Evans Home Health Care, Evergreen, Colo., 1983-88, Western Home Health, Arvada, Colo., 1988-93, ICON Home Care, Lakewood, 1993-97, Vis. Nurse Assn., Denver, 1995—, 1995—; lectr. U. Colo., Denver, 1970-81, U. No. Colo., Greeley, 1977-81; tchr., cons. ICON Home Care, Lakewood, 1993-97, Western Home Health Care, Arvada, 1988-93, Mt. Evans Health Care, 1983-88, Vis. Nurses Denver, 1996—; chairperson task force State of Colo., Denver, 1972-73. Mem. Citizens for Action, Idledale, Colo., 1975-76. Mem. Am. Phys. Therapy Assn. (sect. on geriatrics and home health care), Hiwan Golf Club. Avocations: golf, travel, music. Home: PO Box 88 Idledale CO 80453-0088

BROWN, GILES TYLER, history educator, lecturer; b. Marshall, Mich., Apr. 21, 1916; s. A. Watson and Ettroile (Kent) B.; m. Crysta Beth Cosner, Nov. 21, 1951 (dec. July 1992). AB, San Diego State Coll., 1937; MA, U. Calif.-Berkeley, 1941; PhD, Claremont Grad. Sch., 1948; post-doctoral seminar, U. Edinburgh, Scotland, 1949. Tchr., counselor, Binet intelligence tester San Diego City Schs., 1937-46; chmn. social sci. div. Orange Coast Coll., Newport Beach, Calif., 1948-60; prof. history, chmn. social sci. div. Calif. State U., Fullerton, 1961-66; also chmn. history dept., dean grad. studies Calif. State U., 1967-83, assoc. v.p. acad. programs, 1979-83; pub. lectr. nat., internat. affairs, 1951—; also cons. gerontology; participant Wilton Park Conf., Eng., 1976; mem. instl. rsch. bd. So. Calif. Coll. Optometry, 1980—; past chmn. Hist. Landmarks Com. Orange County; mem. nat. task force Assessment Quality Masters' Degree, Coun. Grad. Schs., 1981-83. Author: Ships That Sail No More, 1966; Contbr. to: Help in Troubled Times, 1962; contbr. articles, book reviews to profl. jours. Trustee, past pres., past chmn. bd. World Affairs Coun. Orange County; past pres. U. Calif.-Irvine Friends Libr.; nat. bd. dirs., past nat. pres. Travelers Century Club; mem. grad. fellowship adv. com. State of Calif., 1980, Orange County Bd. The National Conf., 1984—; emeritus bd. dirs. Pacific Symphony Orch. Recipient Pacific History award Pacific Coast br. Am. Hist. Assn., 1950; hon. medal DAR, 1977; named Outstanding Prof. Calif. State U., 1966, Hon. Citizen of Orange County, 1969, Citizen of Yr., Orange Coast Coll., 1993; hon. medal Nat. Soc. Daus. Colonial Wars, 1984. Mem. AAAS, SAR, Am. Hist. Assn., Western Assn. Grad. Schs. (exec. com. 1981-83), Wisdom Soc. (adv. bd.), Phi Beta Kappa, Phi Delta Kappa, Phi Alpha Theta, Phi Beta Delta (hon. internat. scholar), Kappa Delta Pi, Explorers, Masons. Baptist. Home: 413 Catalina Dr Newport Beach CA 92663-4105

BROWN, GLENDA ANN WALTERS, ballet director; b. Buna, Tex., July 22, 1937; d. Jesse Olaf and Kathryn Jeanette (Rogers) Walters; m. David Dann Brown, Dec. 13, 1958 (div. 1994); children: Kathryn, Jean, Vanessa Lea. Grad. H.S., Beaumont, Tex. Mem. Melody Maids, Beaumont, 1950-60; asst. tchr. Widman Sch., Beaumont, 1952-55; owner, tchr. Walters Sch. of Dance, Jasper, Tex., 1955-59; assoc. tchr. Emmamae Horn Sch., Jasper, 1964-81, artistic dir., 1981—; dir. Nat. Craft of Choreography Conf., Jasper, 1987—; owner, dir. Allegro Ballet, Houston, 1974-81, artistic dir., 1981—; dir. Nat. Choreography Conf., 1987—; mem. adv. bd. Dance Tchr. mag., 1998. Mem. dance panel Cultural Arts Coun., Houston, 1979, Tex. Commn. on the Arts, 1988-90; sec. Riedel Estates Civic Club, Houston, 1975-78; Rep. poll worker, Houston, 1970-81; bd. dirs. Austrian Alps Performing Arts Festival, 1996-98; coord. First Nat. Regional Dance Am. Festival, 1997, bd. dirs. Tanzsommer/Austria '98. Mem. Dance Masters Am. (exam. chmn. chpt. 3 1980-86), Regional Dance Am. S.W. (exec. v.p. 1981—), Dance Am., Nat. Assn. Regional Ballet (bd. dirs. 1985-88), Regional Dance Am. (nat. bd. dirs., v.p. 1988-95, pres. 1995—). Methodist. Avocations: camping, singing, golf, travel. Office: Allegro Ballet and Dance Acad Ste 200 1570 S Dairy Ashford Rd Houston TX 77077-3869

BROWN, GLORIA VASQUEZ, banker; b. Alice, Tex., Aug. 7, 1945; d. Mauro and Aurora (Canales) Vasquez; m. Larry R. Brown, July 5, 1986. BA in Math., Tex. Woman's U., 1967; postgrad., U. Tex., San Antonio, 1979. Tchr. math. Corpus Christi (Tex.) Ind. Sch. Dist., 1967-69, Columbus (Ohio) Ind. Sch. Dist., 1969-70; with Urban Mass Transp., Washington, 1971-77; owner/operator Derma Clinic, San Antonio, 1977-79; field svcs. officer Neighborhood Reinvestment Co., Dallas, 1979-89, spl. projects officer, 1989-91; cmty. affairs officer Fed. Res. Bank of Dallas, 1991-96, v.p. pub. affairs, 1997—; lectr. in field; instr. So. Meth. U./Southwestern Grad. Sch. Banking. Creator: Breaking Ground, 1995 (Merit award 1995); creator/editor Banking and Cmty. Perspectives, 1992. Bd. dirs. Arts Dist. Friends, Dallas, 1991-94, Shared Housing Ctr., 1997—; mem. Region VI adv. coun. U.S. SBA, Dallas, 1992—; mem. program com. Dallas Nonprofit Capacity Bldg. Program, 1994-96; vice chair IMAGE de Dallas, 1993-94; mem. Hispanic 50, Dallas Friday Group. Recipient Women Making a Difference award Minority Bus. News, Dallas, 1995, Key to the City, City Coun. of Lafayette, La., 1980's; Leadership Tex. Found. for Women's Resources, Austin, 1996. Mem. Greater Dallas C. of C. (women's bus. issues adv. coun. 1994—, finalist Athena award 1998), Tex. Woman's U. Alumnae Assn., Hispanic Bankers Assn. Roman Catholic. Avocations: movies, travel, card games, walking. Home: 7107 Judi Ct Dallas TX 75252 Office: Federal Reserve Bank Dallas 2200 N Pearl St Dallas TX 75201-2272

BROWN, GREGORY K., lawyer; b. Warren, Ohio, Dec. 9, 1951; s. George K. and Dorothy H. (Gaynor) B.; m. Joy M. Feinberg, Apr. 10, 1976. BS in Bus. & Econs., U. Ky., 1973; JD, U. Ill., 1976. Bar: Ill. 1976. Assoc. atty. McDermott, Will & Emery, Chgo., 1976-80, Mayer, Brown & Platt, Chgo., 1980-84; ptnr. Keck, Mahin & Cate, Chgo., 1984-93, Oppenheimer Wolff & Donnelly, Chgo., 1994-97, Seyfarth, Shaw, Fairweather & Geraldson, Chgo., 1997—. Contbg. author: The Handbook of Employee Ownership Plans, 1989, Employee Stock Ownership Plans, 1989. Active Chgo. Coun. Fgn. Rels. Named One of the Top Benefits Lawyers Nat. Law Jour., 1998. Mem. ABA (chair Employee Stock Ownership Plan com. real property, probate and trust law sect., Nat. Ctr. Employee Ownership, Employee Stock Ownership Plan Assn. (chair legis. and regulatory adv. com.), Chgo. Bar Assn. (chmn. employee benefits com. 1988-89). Avocations: basketball, bicycling, golf, opera, theatre. E-mail: browngr@seyfarth.com. Office: Seyfarth Shaw Fairweather & Geraldson 55 E Monroe St Ste 4200 Chicago IL 60603-5713*

BROWN, GREGORY MICHAEL, psychiatrist, educator, researcher; b. Toronto, Mar. 27, 1934; s. Norbert Joseph and Nellie Shaw (Diack) B.; m. Audrey Christina Shute, June 18, 1960; children: Jacqueline Anne Embleton, David Michael, Mary Catherine, Paul Douglas, Barbara Suzanne French, Joyce Christina, Patricia Elizabeth, Anne Marie. BA, U. Toronto, 1955, MD, 1959, diploma in Psychiatry, 1964; PhD, U. Rochester, 1971. Intern St. Michael's Hosp., 1959-60; resident in medicine Shaughnessy Hosp., Vancouver, 1960-61; resident in psychiatry various hosps., Ont., 1961-64; ward physician Toronto Psychiat. Hosp., 1964-66; courtesy staff Peel Meml. Hosp., Brampton, Ont., 1964-66; fellow in clin. investigation dept. psychiatry U. Toronto, 1964-66, clin. tchr. in psychiatry, 1968-69, asst. prof. to assoc. prof., 1969-75, prof., 1975-77, prof. dept psychiatry, prof. dept. physiology, 1989—, prof. Inst. Med. Sci., 1991—; prof. depts. neurosci. and psychiatry McMaster U., 1977-87; staff psychiatrist Med. Ctr. McMaster U., Hamilton, Ont., 1977—; chmn. dept. neurosci. McMaster U., 1977-87, prof. dept. neurosci., 1987-88, prof. dept. biomed. scis., 1988-89, prof. emeritus, 1989—; external examiner dept physiology U. Hong Kong, 1990-92; instr. medicine and psychiatry U. Rochester Sch. Medicine, N.Y., 1966-69; staff psychiatrist Clarke Inst. Psychiatry, Toronto, 1968-77, 90—, dir. rsch., 1990—, v.p. rsch., 1995-96, head neuroendocrinology rsch. sect., 1996—. Co-author: Frontiers in Neurology and Neuroscience Research, 1974, Clinical Neuroendocrinology, 1977, Neuroendocrinology and Psychiatric Disorder, 1984, The Pineal Gland: Endocrine Aspects, Advances in the Biosciences, 1985, Clinical Neuroendocrinology, 1988; assoc. editor Can. Jour. Physiology and Pharmacology, 1973-78; mem. editorial bd. Psychoneuroendocrinology, 1978-89, Jour. Pineal Rsch., 1981-89, Psychiatry Rsch., 1979—, Jour. Psychiatry and Neuroscience, 1990—; mem. exec. editorial bd. Progress in Neuro-Psychopharmacology and Biological Psychiatry, 1989—; mem. editorial bd. Biological Signals, 1991—; contbr. to books; contbr. articles to profl. jours. Named Rsch. assoc. Ont. Mental Health Found., 1968—, Traveling fellow Ont. Mental Health Found., 1966-68; recipient numerous rsch. awards, McNeil Lab. award, 1975, John Dewan award Ont. Mental Health Found., 1980, Heinz Lehmann award Can. Coll. Neuropsychopharmacology, 1983. Fellow APA, Royal Coll. Physicians; mem. Can. Psychiat. Assn., Ont. Psychiat. Assn., Am. Psychosomatic Soc. (councillor 1978-82), Can. Med. Assn., Ont. Med. Assn., Soc. Psychoneuroendocrinology (councillor 1981-87), Endocrine Soc., Can. Coll. Neuropsychopharmacology (chmn. publ. com. 1986-89), Can. Soc. Endocrinology and Metabolism (councillor 1981-83), Can. Soc. Clin. Investigation. Roman Catholic. Avocations: photography, music, theatre. Home: 1382 Crestdale Rd, Mississauga, ON Canada L5H 1X7 Office: Clarke Inst of Psychiatry, 250 College St, Toronto, ON Canada M5T 1R8*

BROWN, GREGORY NEIL, university administrator, forest physiology educator; b. Detroit, Feb. 10, 1938; s. Robert Octavus and Dorothy Etta May (Kingsbury) B.; m. Patricia Lee Talbott, Dec. 16, 1961 (div. 1974); children: Kathryn Duket, Julie Ann, Deborah Louise; m. Janeth Christine Hartman, May 24, 1974 (dec. 1997); children: Kimberly Suzanne, Kevin Scott; m. Laura Jean Dale, June 27, 1998. B.S., Iowa State U., 1959; M.F., Yale U., 1960; D.F., Duke U., 1963. Plant physiologist Oak Ridge Nat. Lab., 1963-66; asst. prof. forestry to prof. U. Mo.-Columbia, 1966-77, dir. grad. studies Sch. Forestry, 1969-74; prof. Iowa State U., Ames, 1977-78; dept. head, prof. U. Minn.-St. Paul, 1978-83; dean, prof. U. Maine-Orono, 1983-86, acting v.p. acad. affairs, 1986-87, 91-92, v.p. research and pub. service, 1987-92; dean, prof. Va. Poly. Inst. and State U., Blacksburg, 1992—; assoc. dir. Maine Agrl. Exptl. Sta., Orono, 1983-86, acting pres., 1992; assoc. dir. Va. Agrl. Exptl. Sta., Blacksburg, 1992—, interim provost, 1995; chair, bd. dirs. Powell River Project, 1996—. Author-editor: Seedling Physiology and Reforestation Success, 1984; editor: International Directory of Woody Plant Physiologists, 1974-84, Jour. Forest Sci., 1979-82. Contbr. articles to profl. jours. Scoutmaster Boy Scouts Am., 1965-66. Mem. Soc. Am. Foresters (chmn. physiology working group 1983-84), Nat. Assn. Profl. Forestry Schs. and Colls. (north Ctrl. rsch. chmn. 1981-82, nat. sec. treas. 1984-85, nat. pres. elect 1986-87, 94-95, pres. 1996-97), Internat. Union Forest Orgns. (chmn. working parties 1970-86), Nat. Assn. State Univs. and Land-Grant Colls. (chair bd. on natural resources 1997, chair U.S. geol. survey partnership com. 1997—), Soc. for Preservation and Encouragement of Barbershop Quartet Singing in Am. (pres. 1973-74), Sigma Xi, Xi Sigma Pi, Gamma Sigma Delta (jr. faculty award 1971). Lutheran. Home: 1810 Mountainside Dr Blacksburg VA 24060-5118 Office: Va Poly Inst and State U Coll Forestry & Wildlife 324 Cheatham Hall Blacksburg VA 24061

BROWN, HANK, former senator, university administrator; b. Denver, Feb. 12, 1940; s. Harry W. and Anna M. (Hanks) B.; m. Nana Morrison, Aug. 27, 1967; children: Harry, Christy, Lori. BS, U. Colo., 1961, JD, 1969; LLM, George Washington U., 1986, M in Tax Law, 1986. Bar: Colo. 1969; CPA, 1988. Tax acct. Arthur Andersen, 1967-68; asst. pres. Monfort of Colo., Inc., Greeley, 1969-70; corp. counsel Monfort of Colo., Inc., 1970-71; v.p. Monfort Food Distbg., 1971-72, v.p. corp. devel., 1973-75, v.p. internat. ops., 1975-78, v.p. lamb div., 1978-80; mem. 97th-101st Congresses from Colo. 4th dist., 1981-90; mem. Colo. State Senate, 1972-76, asst. majority leader, 1974-76; U.S senator from Colo. Washington, 1991-96; co-dir. Ctr. for Pub. Policy and Contemporary Policies, U. Denver, 1997-98; pres. U. No. Colo., Greeley, 1998—; chmn. Fgn. Rel. subcom. Near Ea. and South Asian affairs, Judiciary subcom. on constl. law. With USN, 1962-66. Decorated Air medal, Vietnam Svc. medal, Nat. Defense medal, Naval Unit citation. Republican. Congregationalist. Office: Univ of Northern Colorado Office of the Pres Greeley CO 80639

BROWN, HARDIN, occupational health nurse; b. Memphis, July 6, 1955. ADN, Memphis State U., 1976; BSN, U. Neb. Med. Ctr., 1978; MPA, Portland (Oreg.) State U., 1984; MSN, Oreg. Health Scis. U., 1985. RN, Oreg., Tenn. DON svcs. Beverly Enterprises, Portland, 1981-82; instr. Meth. Sch. Nursing, Memphis, 1992-94, occupational health nurse, 1994—; rsch. assessment of staff turnover nursing assts. Oreg. Geriatric Nursing Homes. Mem. ARC. Lt. USN, 1985-90, USNR, 1990-92. Mem. Am. Assn. Occupational Health Nurses, Sigma Theta Tau.

BROWN, HAROLD, former secretary of defense, corporate director; b. N.Y.C., Sept. 19, 1927; s. A.H. and Gertrude (Cohen) B.; m. Colene Dunning McDowell, Oct. 29, 1953; children: Deborah Ruth (Mrs. Eric Ploumis), Ellen Dunning (Mrs. Ray Merewether). A.B., Columbia U., 1945, A.M., 1946, Ph.D. in Physics (Lydig fellow 1948-49), 1949; 11 hon. degrees. Research scientist Columbia U., 1945-50, lectr. physics, 1947-48; lectr. physics Stevens Inst. Tech., 1949-50; divsn. leader E.O. Lawrence Radiation Lab. U. Calif., Berkeley, 1950-60, staff mem., group leader E.O. Lawrence Radiation Lab., 1952-60; dir. Lawrence Livermore (Calif.) Lab., 1960-61; dir. def. rsch. and engring. Dept. Def., Washington, 1961-65; sec. Dept. Air Force, Washington, 1965-69; pres. Calif. Inst. Tech., Pasadena, 1969-77; sec. def. Washington, 1977-81; disting. vis. prof. Sch. Advanced Internat. Studies Johns Hopkins U., Md., 1981-84, chmn. Fgn. Policy Inst., 1984-92, counselor, Ctr. Strategic & Internat. Studies, 1992—; ptnr. Warburg, Pincus & Co., N.Y.C., 1990—; bd. dirs. Philip Morris Inc., Cummins Engine Co., Mattel, Inc., Evergreen Holdings, Inc.; mem. Polaris Steering Com., 1956-58; mem. Pres.'s Sci. Adv. Com., 1960-61; sr. sci. advisor Conf. Discontinuance Nuclear Tests, 1958-59; U.S. del. SALT, Helsinki, Vienna and Geneva, 1969-77; chmn. Tech. Assessment Adv. Coun. to U.S. Congress, 1974-77; chmn. Commn. on Roles and Capabilities of U.S. Intelligence Comty., 1995-96; mem. exec. com. Trilateral Commn., 1973-76, trustee, 1992—; trustee Rand Corp., 1983-92, 94—. Author: Thinking About National Security: Defense and Foreign Policy in a Dangerous World, 1983. Trustee Beckman Found., 1982-85, chmn., 1993-95; trustee Rockefeller Found., 1983-93. Decorated Medal of Freedom; named One of 10 Outstanding Young Men U.S. Jaycees, 1961; recipient Medal of Excellence Columbia U., 1963; Joseph C. Wilson award in internat. affairs, 1976, Enrico Fermi award U.S. Dept. Energy, 1992. Mem. NAE, NAS, Am. Phys. Soc., Am. Acad. Arts and Scis., Bohemian Club, River Club, Met. Club, Phi Beta Kappa. Office: Ctr for Strategic & Intl Studies 1800 K St NW Ste 400 Washington DC 20006-2202

BROWN, HAROLD EUGENE, magistrate; b. Damascus, Ark., Jan. 6, 1935; s. Amos Eugene and Hazel Gladys (Thomas) B.; m. Carolyn Marie Sanders, Aug. 26, 1972; children: James Daryl, Deena Leigh, Cynthia Marie. Student, U. Md. Overseas div. Verdun, France, 1962-64, Germanna Community Coll., 1978-84. Enlisted U.S. Army, 1954, advanced through grades to sgt. maj., 1977; White House liaison Chief of Staff Army, Washington, 1969-73; dep. dir. Def. Coop. Agy., New Delhi, India, 1973-77; post sgt. maj., co. comdr. Fort A.P. Hill, Bowling Green, Va., 1977-81; district chief magistrate 15th dist. Supreme Ct. Va., Fredericksburg, 1982—, apptd. chief magistrate, 1987—. Bd. dirs. Rappahannock Coun. Domestic Violence, Rappahannock United Way. Decorated Cross Gallantry Rep. Vietnam, 1969. Mem. Am. Judges Assn., Va. Magistrates Assn., Va. Cmty. Criminal Justice Assn., Ret. Sgts. Maj. Assn. Avocations: golf, photography, computer programming. Home: PO Box 5431 Fredericksburg VA 22403-0431 Office: 2124 Jefferson Davis Hwy Stafford VA 22554-7264

BROWN, HELEN GURLEY, editor, writer; b. Green Forest, Ark., Feb. 18, 1922; d. Ira M. and Cleo (Sisco) Gurley; m. David Brown, Sept. 25, 1959. Student, Tex. State Coll. for Women, 1939-41, Woodbury Coll., 1942; LLD, Woodbury U., 1987; DLitt, L.I. U., 1993. Exec. sec. Music Corp. Am., 1942-45, William Morris Agy., 1945-47; copywriter Foote, Cone & Belding (advt. agy.), Los Angeles, 1948-58; advt. writer, account exec. Kenyon & Eckhardt (advt. agy.), Hollywood, Calif., 1958-62; editor-in-chief Cosmopolitan mag., 1965-97; editorial dir. Cosmopolitan Internat. Edits., 1972—; editor-in-chief Cosmopolitan Internat. Edits, 1997—. Author: Sex and the Single Girl, 1962, Sex and the Office, 1965, Outrageous Opinions, 1967, Helen Gurley Brown's Single Girl's Cook Book, 1969, Sex and the New Single Girl, 1970, Having It All, 1982, The Late Show, 1993, The Writer's Rules, 1998. Named 1 of 25 most influential women in U.S., World Almanac, 1976-81; recipient Francis Holmes Achievement award for outstanding work in advt., 1956-59, Disting. Achievement award U. So. Calif. Sch. Journalism, 1971, Spl. award for editl. leadership Am. Newspaper Woman's Club, Washington, 1972, Disting. Achievement award in journalism Stanford U., 1977, Matrix award in matg. category N.Y. Women in Comm., 1985, Henry Johnson Fisher award Mag. Pubs. of Am., 1995; Helen Gurley Brown Rsch. Professorship established in her name Northwestern U. Medill Sch. Journalism, 1986; inducted into Pubs.' Hall of Fame, 1988. Mem. Authors League Am., Am. Soc. Mag. Editors (Hall of Fame award 1996), AFTRA, Eta Upsilon Gamma. Office: Cosmopolitan The Hearst Corp 959 8th Ave New York NY 10019-3737

BROWN, HELEN SAUER, fund raising executive; b. Findlay, Ohio, Feb. 7, 1923; d. Joseph Thomas and Mary Magdalene (Sweeney) Sauer; m. Thomas Francis Brown, June 10, 1944; children: Mary Helen Anne, Thomas F., Joachim J., Mary Christine, Mary Kathleen, Mary Elizabeth, Timothy J., Martin J., John Fitzgerald Kennedy. BA magna cum laude, Mundelein Coll. for Women, 1944, MA summa cum laude, 1970. V.p. T.F. Brown Co., Chgo., 1962-84; tchr. Nazareth Acad., La Grange Park, Ill., 1968-72; pastoral min. Ill., 1970—; dir. religious edn. Divine Savior Parish, Downers Grove, Ill., 1972-76; pres. Herself's Doings Ltd., La Grange, Ill., 1972—; retail store owner/mgr. Nettle Creek Shop, La Grange, 1976-85; dir. resource devel. Cmty. Family Svc. & Mental Health Assn., Lyons and Riverside Townships, Ill., 1986—; cons., spkr. in field; pres. Religious Edn. Svcs., La Grange, 1972-86; adv. coun. U. Notre Dame Sch. of Theology, 1970-72; chair, resident Coun. Bethlehem Woods, 1997—. Author: Community and Social Justice, 1974. Trustee Mundelein Coll., Chgo., 1970-90; organizer ERA, Springfield, Ill., 1968—; peace activist, Washington, 1966—; commr. Lyons (Ill.) Mental Health Commn., 1978-80; commr. econ. devel. Village of La Grange, 1983-93; commr. program rev. Pvt. Industry Coun., Cook County, Ill., 1984-94; dir. Ill. Retirement Home Assn., Hinsdale, 1993—; chair Resident Coun., Bethlehem Woods. Recipient Welford award for disting. svc. to mental health, 1983; Cardinal Meyer scholar Archdiocese of Chgo., 1970. Mem. NAACP, AAUW, LWV, Nat. Soc. Fund Raising Execs. (cert. 1991), La Grange West Suburban C. of C. (chair pres.'s coun. 1985-96, pres. 1986-87, Woman of Yr. 1983), Women for Peace, Amnesty Internat., Bus. and Profl. Women/USA (Outstanding Working Woman Ill. chpt. 1993), Phoenix Soc., Women's Bd., Clergy and Laity Concerned for Justice and Peace, Gannon Ctr. Women and Leadership, Mundelein Coll. Alumnae, La Grange Cath. Women's Club, Kappa Gamma Pi. Democrat. Roman Catholic. Avocations: book reviewing, public opinion research, liturgical planning, philosophy, word puzzles. Home: 1571 W Ogden Ave Apt 2626 La Grange Park IL 60526

BROWN, HENRY, chemist; b. Jersey City, Apr. 5, 1907; s. Mayer and Kate (Hearsh) B.; m. Harriet Stone; children: Paula, Dennis. AB, U. Kans., 1928; MS, PhD, U. Mich., 1933. Chemist Udylite Corp., Detroit, 1934-50, dir. rsch., 1950-72; rsch. chemist Manhattan Project Columbia U., N.Y.C., 1943-45. Author: (with others) Modern Electroplating 3rd edit., 1974; contbr. numerous articles to profl. jours., 1932-71. Bd. dirs. Sinai Hosp., Detroit, 1965. Recipient Carl Heussner award Am. Electroplaters Soc., Detroit, 1953, George Hogaboom award, 1963, AES Sci. Achievement award, 1968, Westinghouse prize Inst. of Metal Finishing of Great Britain, 1970; named to Outstanding Inventors List, State of Mich. 1968. Fellow Am. Inst. Chemists; mem. N.Y. Acad. Scis, Am. Chem. Soc. (Midgely Gold Medal 1971), Sigma Xi. Jewish. Achievements include 96 U.S. patents, 250 foreign patents; development of high speed brass electroplating of steel shell casings used during World War II to prevent the sticking of the shell cases inside the cannon after firing, of copper alloy plating for steel pennies during World War II, of high speed electroposition of silver for sleeve linings for Allison airplane engines, of use of perfluoro octane sulfonic acid for the complete suppression of toxic spray during chromium plating; discovery of unsaturated organic addition agents which form the basis of modern brilliant nickel electroplating which underlies the final thin, hard chromium plate. Home: Apt 502 5270 Gulf Of Mexico Dr Longboat Key FL 34228-2018

BROWN, HENRY, surgeon; b. Feb. 20, 1920; m. Julie Brown, June 29, 1945; 5 children. AB, U. Mich.; MD, U. Pa., postgrad.; postgrad., Cambridge (Eng.) U. Diplomate Am. Bd. Surgery. with divsn. plastic surgery Harvard U. Sch. Medicine, Boston, Brigham and Women's Hosp., Boston. Author, editor books; contbr. articles to med. jours. Lt. comdr. M.C., USN, . Recipient Graye Simpson Priestley award for rsch. Mem. Am. Physiol. Soc. (chmn. interest in history group), Am. Chem. Soc. (bd. dirs. northeastern sect.), Boston Hand Soc. (founder).

BROWN, HENRY BEDINGER RUST, financial management company executive; b. Pitts., Feb. 13, 1926; s. Stanley Noel and Elizabeth Fitzhugh (Rust) B.; m. Betsey Jean Smith, Mar. 27, 1954; children—Peter, Alexander, Elizabeth, Harriet. A.B., Harvard U., 1948. Asst. v.p. Citibank, N.Y.C., 1954-63; 2d v.p. Tchrs. Ins. & Annunity Assn., N.Y.C., 1963-68; chmn. Res. Fund, N.Y.C., 1970-83; pres. Res. Mgmt. Co., Inc., N.Y.C., 1984-98, Transfer Solutions Inc., Leesburg, Va., 1998—. Councilman Town of Westfield, N.J., 1982-84. Served with USNR, 1944-46. Creator first money mkt. fund.

BROWN, HERBERT CHARLES, chemistry educator; b. London, May 22, 1912; came to U.S., 1914; s. Charles and Pearl (Gorinstein) B.; m. Sarah Baylen, Feb. 6, 1937; 1 son, Charles Allan. AS, Wright Jr. Coll., Chgo., 1935; BS, U. Chgo., 1936, PhD, 1938, DSc (hon.), 1968; hon. doctorate, Wayne State U., 1980, Lebanon Valley Coll., 1980, L.I. U., 1980, Hebrew U. Jerusalem, 1980, Pontificia Universidad de Chile, 1980, Purdue U., 1980; hon. doctorates, U. Wales, 1981, U. Paris, 1982, Butler U., 1982, Ball State U., 1985. Asst. chemistry U. Chgo., 1936-38, Eli Lilly post-doctorate rsch. fellow, 1938-39, instr., 1939-43; asst. prof. chemistry Wayne U., 1943-46, assoc. prof., 1946-47; prof. inorganic chemistry Purdue U., 1947-59, Richard B. Wetherill prof. chemistry, 1959, Richard B. Wetherill rsch. prof., 1960-78, emeritus, 1978—; vis. prof. UCLA, 1951, Ohio State U., 1952, U. Mexico, 1954, U. Calif. at Berkeley, 1957, U. Colo., 1958, U. Heidelberg, 1963, SUNY, Stonybrook, 1966, U. Calif., Santa Barbara, 1967, Hebrew U., Jerusalem, 1969, U. Wales, Swansea, 1973, U. Cape Town, South Africa, 1974, U. Calif., San Diego, 1979; Harrison Howe lectr., 1953, Friend E. Clark lectr., 1953, Freud-McCormack lectr., 1954, Centenary lectr., Eng., 1955, Thomas W. Talley lectr., 1956, Falk-Plaut lectr., 1957, Julius Stieglitz lectr., 1958, Max Tishler lectr., 1958, Kekule-Couper Centenary lectr., 1958, E.C. Franklin lectr., 1960, Ira Remsen lectr., 1961, Edgar Fahs Smith lectr., 1962, Seydel-Wooley lectr., 1966, Baker lectr., 1969, Benjamin Rush lectr., 1971, Chem. Soc. lectr., Australia, 1972, Armes lectr., 1973, Henry Gilman lectr., 1975, others; hon. prof. Organomet Chem., Chinese Acad. Scis., 1994; chem. cons. to indsl. corps; rschr. in phys., organic and inorganic chemistry relating chem. behavior to molecular structure, selective reductions, hydroboration and chemistry of organoboranes. Author: Hydroboration, 1962, Boranes in Organic Chemistry, 1972, Organic Synthesis via Boranes, 1975, The Nonclassical Ion Problem, 1977, (with A.W. Pelter and K. Smith) Borane Reagents, 1988; contbr. articles to chem. jours. Bd. govs. Hebrew U., 1969-90; co-dir. war rsch. projects U. Chgo. for U.S. Army, Nat. Def. Rsch. Com., Manhattan Project, 1940-43. Decorated Order of the Rising Sun, Gold and Silver Star (Japan); recipient Purdue Sigma Xi rsch. award, 1951, Nichols medal, 1959, award Am. Chem. Soc., 1960, S.O.C.M.A. medal, 1960, H.N. McCoy award, 1965, Linus Pauling medal, 1968, Nat. Medal of Sci., 1969, Roger Adams medal, 1971, Charles Frederick Chandler medal, 1973, Chem. Pioneer award, 1975, CUNY medal for sci. achievement, 1976 Elliott Cresson medal, 1978, C.K. Ingold medal, 1978, Nobel prize in chemistry, 1979, Priestley medal, 1981, Perkin medal, 1982, Gold medal award Am. Int. Chemists, 1985, G.M. Kosolapoff medal, 1987, NAS award in chem. scis., 1987, Oesper award Cin. sect.-Am. Chem. Soc., 1990, Herbert C. Brown medal and award for creative rsch. in synthetic methods Am. Chem. Soc., 1998; Hon. fellow U. Wales Swansea, 1994; named One of Top 75 Disting. Contbrs. to Chem. Enterprise Chem. & Engring. News, 1998. Fellow AAAS, Royal Soc. Chemistry (hon.), Indian Nat. Sci. Acad. (fgn.); mem. NAS, Am. Acad. Arts and Sci., Am. Chem. Soc. (chmn. Purdue sect. 1955-56), Chem. Soc. Japan (hon.), Pharm. Soc. Japan (hon.), Ind. Acad Sci., Chinese Acad. Sci. (hon. prof. 1994), Phi Beta Kappa, Sigma Xi, Alpha Chi Sigma, Phi Lambda Upsilon (hon.). Office: Purdue U Dept Chemistry Purdue University IN 47907

BROWN, HERBERT RUSSELL, lawyer, writer; b. Columbus, Ohio, Sept. 27, 1931; s. Thomas Newton and Irene (Hankinson) B.; m. Beverly Ann Jenkins, Dec. 2, 1967; children: David Herbert, Andrew Jenkins. BA, Denison U., 1953; JD, U. Mich., 1956. Assoc. Vorys, Sater, Seymour and Pease, Columbus, Ohio, 1956, 60-64, ptnr., 1965-82; treas. Sunday Creek Coal Co., Columbus, 1970-86; assoc. justice Ohio Supreme Ct., Columbus, 1987-93; examiner Ohio Bar, 1967-72, Multi-State Bar, 1971-76, Dist. Ct. Bar, 1968-71; commr. Fed. Lands, Columbus, 1967-68, Lake Lands, Columbus, 1981; bd. dirs. Thurber House, 1992-94, Sunday Creek Coal Co.; adj. prof. Ohio State U. Coll. Law, 1997—; panelist Am. Arbitration Assn., 1993—. Author: (novel) Presumption of Guilt, 1991, Shadows of Doubt, 1994; mem. editl. bd. U. Mich. Law Rev., 1955-56. Bd. dirs. Ctrl. Cmty. House Columbus, 1967-75; deacon, mem. governing bd. 1st Cmty. Ch., 1966-80; trustee Columbus Bar Found., 1993—; candidate Ohio State Legis., 1966. Capt. JAGC, U.S. Army, 1956-57. Fellow Am. Coll. Trial Lawyers; mem. Ohio Bar Assn., Columbus Bar Assn. Democrat. Office: 145 N High St Columbus OH 43215-3006

BROWN, HERMIONE KOPP, lawyer; b. Syracuse, N.Y., Sept. 29, 1915; d. Harold H. and Frances (Burger) Kopp; m. Louis M. Brown, May 30, 1937 (dec. Sept. 1996); children—Lawrence D., Marshall J., Harold A. BA, Wellesley Coll., 1934; LLB, U. So. Calif., 1947. Bar: Calif. 1947. Story analyst 20th Century-Fox Film Corp., 1935-42; assoc. Gang, Kopp & Tyre, Los Angeles, 1947-52; ptnr. to sr. ptnr. Gang, Tyre, Ramer & Brown, Inc., Los Angeles, 1952—; lectr. copyright and entertainment law U. So. Calif. Law Sch., 1974-77. Contbr. to profl. pubs. Fellow Am. Coll. Trust and Estate Coun.; mem. Calif. Bar Assn. (chair probate law cons. group nd. legal specialization 1977-82, trust and probate law sect., exec. com. 1983-86, advisor 1986-89), L.A. Copyright Soc. (pres. 1979-80), Order of Coif, Phi Beta Kappa. Avocations: literature, theatre, music. Office: Gang Tyre Ramer & Brown Inc 132 S Rodeo Dr Beverly Hills CA 90212-2415

BROWN, HERSHEL M., retired newspaper publisher; b. Phila., Jan. 7, 1923; s. Paul and Sarah (Magil) B.; m. Lorraine Rose Blofson, Apr. 21, 1944; children: Susan R., Stephen J., Adam L. Student, U. Pa., Phila., 1940-42; BS in Bus., Northwestern U., Evanston, Ill., 1944; MS in Journalism, Northwestern U., 1947. Reporter, editorial writer, music critic Globe Times, Bethlehem, Pa., 1947-48; rewrite asst. to Sunday editor, music critic Post Gazette, Pitts., 1949-50; advt. copywriter, account exec., plans bd. chmn., v.p./exec. supr. Al Paul Lefton Co. Inc., Phila., Chgo., L.A., 1950-68; pub. Register News, Bordentown, N.J., 1968-96; pres. Lorraine Pub. Inc., Bordentown, N.J., 1968-96. V.p., trustee Jenkintown (Pa.) Music Sch.; pub. rels. dir. Co-Opera Co. Phila., 1950-57; bd. mem. Farnsworth Ave. Revitalization Project, Bordentown, N.J., 1984-90; mem. artists selection com. Cmty. Concerts Bordentown, Inc., 1982-96. Lt. USNR, 1944-46. Recipient 1st pl. awards Pa. Newspaper Pubs., 1948, N.J. Press Assn., 1971, 78. Mem. Merchandising Execs. Club Chgo., Am. Newspaper Guild, Sigma Delta Chi. Jewish. Avocations: piano, cello, concerts, theater, record collecting, swimmming. Home: 379 Landing St Mount Holly NJ 08060-4525

BROWN, HILTON, visual arts educator, artist; b. Momence, Ill., Sept. 22, 1938; s. Oswald E. and Maud M. (Shronts) B. Student, Art Inst. Chgo., 1956-58, U. Chgo., 1959-60, U. Ill., Chgo., 1961-62; BFA in Painting, Sch. of Art Inst. Chgo., 1962, MFA in Painting, 1963. Instr. drawing/painting Sch. Art Inst. Chgo., 1962-65; asst. prof. fine art Sch. Fine Arts Washington U., St. Louis, 1965-68; asst. prof. fine arts Goucher Coll., Towson, Md., 1968-70, assoc. prof. fine arts, 1970-75, prof. and chair dept. visual arts, 1975-78; vis. assoc. prof. art history U. Del., 1974-78; prof. art conservation U. Del., Newark, 1978-84, Mayer prof. artists techniques, 1984-88, prof. art, art history and art conservation, 1988-92, Harriet T. Baily prof. art, art conservation, art history and mus. studies, 1992—; cons., lectr. Nat. Tchr. Inst./Nat. Gallery of Art, Washington, 1990—. Author: (exhbn. catalog) The Art and Archives of Ralph Mayer, 1984; one person show Susan Isaacs Gallery, Wilmington, Del., 1990, work in mus. collections Balt. Mus. of Art. Sec. bd. dirs. Gay and Lesbian Alliance of Del., Wilmington, 1991-93; co-chair Lesbian, Gay, Bisexual Caucus of Commn. to Promote Racial and Cultural Diversity, U. Del., 1992—, chair faculty senate com. on diversity and affirmative action, 1993-95, 97-98. Democrat. Anglican Catholic. Avocations: reading, gardening. E-mail: Hilton.Brown@MVS.UDEL.EDU. Office: Univ of Delaware Mus Studies 301 Old College Hall Newark DE 19716

BROWN, HOBSON, JR., executive recruiting consultant; b. San Francisco, Jan. 2, 1942; s. Hobson and Rita (Piel) B.; m. Erwin Parrott, Aug. 7, 1965; children: Erwin Carter, Hobson III. BA in Econs., U. N.C., 1964; MBA in Fin., U. Pa., 1969. Corp. fin. assoc. Dominick & Dominick, N.Y.C., 1969-70; v.p. Morgan Guaranty Trust Co., N.Y.C., 1970-77; v.p. Russell Reynolds Assocs., Inc., N.Y.C., 1977-81, sr. v.p., 1981-83, mng. dir., 1983-87, pres., 1987—, CEO, 1991—. With USNR, 1964-67. Mem. Blooming Grove (Hawley, Pa.), The Links, Union, Sky Club, Westminster Kennel Club, Anglers' (N.Y.C.), Hillsboro Club (Pompano Beach, Fla.). Avocations: hunting, fishing. Address: 170 E 87th St New York NY 10128-2211

BROWN, HOWARD JORDAN, newspaper publisher; b. Chgo., July 31, 1923; s. Isidore and Gladys B.; m. Elizabeth Kassel, Mar. 2, 1960; children: Lucille Minn, Sarah Tuchler, Amy Russ. BA, Princeton U., 1946; MS, Columbia U., 1948. Fgn. correspondent Chgo. Sun Times, 1948-49; with Cleve. Plain Dealer, 1950-59, Ottaway Newspapers, Campbell Hall, N.Y., 1959-62, Kenosha (Wis.) News, 1962—; pres. United Comm. Corp., Kenosha, 1969—; owner Kenosha News, Attleboro, Mass., Sun Chronicle, KEYC-TV12, Mankato, Minn., WWNY-TV7, Watertown, N.Y., also several weeklies. Bd. dirs. Kenosha Jewish Welfare Fund, 1963—, Kenosha Youth Found., 1964—; pres. Kenosha Christmas Charities, 1980—; trustee Carthage Coll., Kenosha, Wis., 1987—. With U.S. Army Infantry, 1943-46, ETO. Jewish. Avocation: tennis. Office: Kenosha News 715 58th St Kenosha WI 53140-4136

BROWN, ILENE DE LOIS, special education educator; b. Wichita, Kans., Aug. 17, 1947; d. Homer DeWitt and Estella Lenora (Cleland) Rusco; m. Gale Robert Aaroe, Nov. 23, 1967 (div. July 1983); 1 child, Candice Yvonne. BEd in Elem. Edn., Washburn U., Topeka, 1969; MS, Nazareth Coll. Rochester, 1979. Cert. tchr. Idaho. Emotionally disturbed trainer Rochester Mental Health Ctr., Greece, N.Y., 1970-71, West Ridge, Greece, 1971-72; tutor kindergarten through grades 6 Craig Hill, Greece, 1978-79; resource rm. tchr. math. English Village, Greece, 1979-80; resource rm. tchr. grades 4-6 Lakeshore, Greece, 1980; tutor, translator Guadalajara, Mex., 1980-82; tchr. grade 1 English John F. Kennedy Sch., Guadalajara, 1982-83; tchr. various grades Greenleaf (Idaho) Friends Acad., 1983-89; resource tchr., high sch. spl. edn. community work coord. Middleton (Idaho) Primary Sch., 1989-91, tchr., 1991—, tchr. 2d grade, 1990—. Sunday sch. tchr. Mem. Coun. for Exceptional Children, Coun. for Children with Behavior Disorders and Learning Disabilities (officer, sec. state chpt. 1991-92), Middleton Profl. Devel. Com. (chairperson profl. devel. com. 1992-95—), Idaho Edn. Assn., Middleton Edn. Assn., Phi Delta Kappa. Avocations: bicycling, traveling, reading, birdwatching. Office: Mill Creek Primary Sch 500 N Middleton Rd Middleton ID 83644-5499

BROWN, J. E. (BUSTER BROWN), state senator, lawyer; b. Dec. 10, 1940. B.S., Tex. A&I U.; J.D., U. Tex. Mem. Tex. Senate; chmn. Senate Natural Resources Com., Sunset Adv. Com., Natural Resources Interim Com., Water Resources Devel. and Mgmt. Com., Gulf States Marine Fisheries Commn. Mem. Criminal Justice Com., So. Legis. Conf. Energy Comm., Am. Legis. Exchange Coun. Telecommunications Comm., Nat. Conf. State Legis. Comm. and Info. Policy, Legis. and Congl. Redistricting Com., Fin. Com., Nominations Com., Vets. Affairs and Mil. Installations Com.; mem. Fin. Com., alt. Environ. Com., mem. of Legal Com. of Interstate Oil and Gas Compact Commn.; past chmn. Energy Coun.; adj. prof. U. Tex. Sch. Law. Office: Tex Senate PO Box 12068 Austin TX 78711-2068

BROWN, JACK, magazine editor; b. Los Angeles, Aug. 6, 1927; s. George Wesley and Harriett Isabel (Barton) B.; m. Arlyne Reddick, 1950 (div. 1962); children: Gregg Richard (dec.), Jeffrey Loren, Jan Patrice; m. Patricia Willard, 1963 (div. 1976); 1 child, Jack B. Jr.; m. Lynn Johannsen, 1986. AS, Los Angeles City Coll., 1948; BA, UCLA, 1950. Asst. polit. editor Los Angeles Examiner, 1960-62; exec. asst. Office Mayor, Los Angeles, 1962-69; polit. editor Los Angeles Herald Examiner, 1970-77; assoc. pub. Met. News, Los Angeles, 1977-81; editor Western Outdoors, Costa Mesa, Calif., 1981—; faculty Reader's Digest Writers Workshops. Co-editor: Outdoor Writers Association of America Style Manual, 1992, rev. 1995; contbr. articles to profl. jours. With USN, 1945-46. Recipient Resolution Commendation award Calif. State Senate, 1962. Mem. Outdoor Writers Assn. Am., Outdoor Writers Calif. (bd. dirs. 1990-91), Pacific Northwest Outdoor Writers, Soc. Outdoor Mag. Editors (founding pres. 1990-91). Avocations: boating, fishing, silhouette shooting, upland game hunting. Home: 3515 Landsford Way Carlsbad CA 92008-7047

BROWN, JACK D(ELBERT), chemist, researcher; b. Boise, Idaho, June 21, 1954; s. Robert and Shirley Fay (Piper) B.; m. Leslie Anne Terry, June 12, 1981; children: Lauren Anne, Justin Andrew. Student, Boise State U., 1973-76; BS, Utah State U., 1983, PhD, 1987. Post-doctoral researcher Colo. State U., Ft. Collins, 1986-88; sr. rsch. chemist Syntex Chemicals Inc., Boulder, Colo., 1988-90; prin. rsch. chemist, Tech. Ctr. Syntex Chemicals Inc., Boulder, 1990—, Roche Colo. Corp., Boulder, 1998—. Co-author: (book chpt.) Metabolism of Food Disaccharides, 1983; co-inventor; contbr. articles to profl. jours. Explorer Scout advisor Boy Scouts Am., Boulder, 1991. Mem. AAAS, Am. Chem. Soc., N.Y. Acad. Scis., Sigma Xi. Home: 11329 Chase Way Westminster CO 80020-6811 Office: Roche Colo Corp 2075 55th St Boulder CO 80301-2803

BROWN, JACK H., supermarket company executive; b. San Bernardino, Calif., June 14, 1939. Student, San Jose State U., UCLA. V.p. Sages Complete Markets, San Bernardino, 1960-71, Marsh Supermarkets, Yorktown, Ind., 1971-77; pres. Pantry Supermarkets, Pasadena, Calif., 1977-79; pres. mid-west div. Cullum Cos., Dallas, 1979-81; pres., chief exec. officer Stater Bros. Markets, Colton, Calif., 1981—; chmn. bd. dirs. Stater Bros. Inc., 1986—; dir. Life Savs. & Loan Assn., San Bernardino. Trustee, U. Redlands, Calif.; bd. dirs. Goodwill Industries of Inland Empire, San Bernardino; bd. councillors Calif. State U., San Bernardino. With USNR, 1956-62. Named Sagamore of the Wabash, Gov. Ind., 1978. Recipient Horatio Alger award of Disting. Ams., 1992, Bus. Exec. of Yr. award U. So. Calif., 1993; Calif. State U., San Bernadino Sch. Bus. named in his honor, 1992. Mem. Western Assn. Food Chains (v.p., bd. dirs., pres. 1987-88), Calif. Retailers Assn. (bd. dirs.), Food Mktg. Inst. (vice chmn.), So. Calif. Grocers Assn., Food Employers Council (bd. govs.), Elks. Republican. Presbyterian. Office: Stater Bros Markets 21700 Barton Rd Colton CA 92324-4401*

BROWN, JACK HAROLD UPTON, physiology educator, university official, biomedical engineer; b. Nixon, Tex., Nov. 16, 1918; s. Gilmer W. and Thelma (Patton) B.; m. Jessie Carolyn Schulz, Apr. 14, 1943. B.S., S.W. Tex. State U., 1939; postgrad., U. Tex., 1939-41; Ph.D., Rutgers U., 1948. Lectr. physics Southwest Tex. State U., San Marcos, 1943-44; instr. phys. chemistry Rutgers U., New Brunswick, N.J., 1944-45, rsch. assoc., 1944-48; lectr. U. Pitts., 1948-50; head biol. scis. Mellon Inst., Pitts., 1948-50; asst. prof. physiology U. N.C., Chapel Hill, 1950-52; scientist, prof. biology Oak Ridge Inst. Nuclear Studies, 1952; assoc. prof. physiology Emory U. Med. Sch., Atlanta, 1952-58, prof., 1959-60, acting chmn. dept. physiology, 1958-60; lectr. physiology George Washington U. and Georgetown U. med. schs., Washington, 1960-65; exec. sec. biomed. engring. and physiology tng. coms. Nat. Inst. Gen. Med. Scis., NIH, Bethesda, Md., 1960-62; chief spl. rsch. br. div. Rsch. Facilities and Resources NIH, 1962-63, acting chief gen. clin. rsch. ctrs. br., 1963-64, asst. dir. ops. Div. Research Facilities and Resources, 1964-65; acting program dir. pharmacology/toxicology program Nat. Inst. Gen. Med. Scis., NIH, 1966-70, asst. dir. ops., 1965-66, assoc. dir. sci. programs, 1967-70, acting dir., 1970; spl. asst. to adminstr. Health Services and Mental Health Adminstrn., USPHS, Rockville, Md., 1971-72; assoc. dep. adminstr. for devel. Health Svcs. and Mental Health Adminstrn., USPHS, 1972-73; spl. asst. to adminstr. Health Resources Adminstrn., 1973-78; coord. Southwest Rsch. Consortium, San Antonio, 1974-78; prof. physiology U. Tex. Med. Sch., San Antonio, 1974-78; prof. environ. scis. U. Tex. at San Antonio, 1974-78; adj. prof. health svcs. adminstrn. Trinity U., 1975-78; assoc. provost rsch. and advanced edn. U. Houston, 1978-80, prof. biology, 1980-89, prof. emeritus, 1990—; adj. prof. U. Tex. Sch. Public Health, 1978—; prof. public adminstrn. Tex. Women's U., 1978—; adj. prof. community medicine Baylor Coll. Medicine, Houston, 1986-89; vice-chmn. SCORE (Svc. Corps of Retired Execs.), 1993-96; chmn., 1997; regional editor Savant, 1996—, dist. mgr., 1997—; Fulbright lectr. U. Rangoon, 1950; cons. health systems WHO, Oak Ridge Inst. Nuclear Studies, Lockhead Aircraft Co., Drexel Inst. Tech., NASA, Vassar Coll., TelTech; mem. adv. bd. Ctr. for Cancer Therapy, San Antonio, 1974—; bd. dirs. South Tex. Health Edn. Ctr.; mem. Tel-Tech, cons., Univ. Tex. Health Sci. Ctr., Sumitomo Corp., Tokyo. Author: Physiology of Man in Space, 1963, (with S.B. Barker) Basic Endocrinology, 1966, 2d edit., 1970, (with J.F. Dickson) Future Goals of Engineering in Biology and Medicine, 1968, Advances in Biomedical Engineering, vol. II, 1972, vols. III, IV, 1973, vol. V, 1974, vol. VI, 1976, Vol. VII, 1978, (with J.E. Jacobs and L.E. Stark) Biomedical Engineering, 1972, (with D.E. Gann) Engineering Principles in Physiology, vols. I, II, 1973, The Health Care Dilemma, 1977, Integration and Control of Biol. Processes, 1978, Politics and Health Care, 1978, Telecommunications in Health Care, 1981, Management in Health Care Systems, 1983, A Laboratory Manual in Animal Physiology, 1984, 3d edit., 1988, High Cost of Healing, 1985, (with J. Comolo) Productivity in Health Care Systems, 1987, Guide to Collecting Fine Prints, 1989, (with J. Cumolo) Educating for Excellence, 1991, Footsteps in Sci., 1993, Revisions of Starting and Running a Small Business, 1994, Records for Small Business, 1995; editor: (with Ferguson) Blood and Body Functions, 1966, (with Miller) Exercise Physiology, 1966, Life Into Space, (Wunder), 1968; contbr. numerous articles on biomed. engring. to sci. jours. Mem. adv. bd. San Antonio Mus. Assn.; mem. spl. effects com. Tex. Sesquicentennial; bd. dirs. Inst. for Health Policy, U. Tex. Health Sci. Ctr. Served with USNR, 1941. Recipient cert. appreciation NIH, 1969, 1st pl. award Atlanta Internat. Film Festival, 1970, spl. team award NASA, 1978, recognition award Emergency Med. Care, 1980, Best Tchr. award Nat. Mortar Bd., 1986, Most Disting. Alumni award S.W. Tex. State U., 1986; Gerard Swope fellow Gen. Electric Co., 1946-48; Fulbright grantee, 1950; Dept. of Def. grantee, 1950-52; NIH grantee, 1950-60; Cancer Soc. grantee, 1958; Damon Runyon Cancer award grantee, 1959; Dept. Energy grantee, 1980-81; NASA grantee, 1987-89. Fellow AAAS, Nat. Acad. Engring., IEEE (joint com. engring. in medicine and biology 1966—); mem. Am. Chem. Soc. (sr.), Biomed. Engring. Soc. (pres. 1969-70, dir. 1968-69), Inst. Radio Engrs. (nat. sec. profl. group biomed. engring. 1962-64), N.Y. Acad. Scis., Endocrine Soc., Am. Physiol. Soc. (com. mem. 1959-63, nat. com. on animals in research 1985—), Tex. Print Soc. (founder, pres.), Soc. for Exptl. Biology and Medicine, Svc. Corps Ret. Execs. (vice chmn. 1994-95, chmn. 1995—), Sigma Xi (research award 1961, founder, pres. Alamo chpt. 1977-78), Council Biology Editors, Soc. Research Adminstrn., Pi Kappa Delta, Phi Lambda Upsilon, Alpha Chi. Club: Cosmos. Inventor capsule manometer, respirator for small animals and basal metabolic apparatus for small animals, dust sampler, apparatus for partitioning human lung volumes, laser credit card patient record system, Warburg apparatus calibrator. Home: 2908 Whisper View St San Antonio TX 78230-3743 Office: 8100 Cambridge St Apt 10 Houston TX 77054-3105

BROWN, JACK WYMAN, architect; b. Detroit, Oct. 17, 1922; s. Ernest E. and Mary Morse (Jones) B.; m. Joan M. Graham, Oct. 4, 1971; 1 dau., Elizabeth. B.S., U. Mich., 1945. Designer Odell, Hewlett & Luckenbach, Inc., Birmingham, Mich., 1952-57; pres. Brown Assocs. Architects, Inc., Bloomfield Hills, Mich., 1957—; part-time instr. design Lawrence Inst. Tech., 1959. Mem. Mayor Detroit Task Force, 1969-70. Served with USNR, 1943-46. Co-recipient 1st prize nat. competition design Nat. Cowboy Hall Fame, 1967; recipient Institutions mag. award, 1980. Mem. AIA (chmn. working coms.), Am. Soc. Ch. Architecture (dir. 1960-64, 72—), Mich. Soc. Architects (design award St. Regis Ch. 1969, Fox Hills Elem. Sch. 1970, Andor Office Bldg. 1972, CAM Design award 1992). Home: 5980 Braemoor Rd Bloomfield Hills MI 48301-1419 Office: Brown Teefey Assocs Archs Inc 4190 Telegraph Rd Bloomfield Hills MI 48302-2079

BROWN, JACQUELINE LEY WHITE, retired lawyer; b. Blue Island, Ill., Apr. 14, 1948; d. William Raymond and June Irene (Cowing) L.; m. Arthur Lee White, May 2, 1970 (div. Mar. 1982); m. William John Brown, May 7, 1988. BA, U. Fla., 1969; MA, Rider Coll., 1977; JD, Stetson U., 1992. Bar: Fla. 1993. From supr. to dir. social services Steuben County (N.Y.) Dept. Social Svcs., Bath, N.Y., 1970-75; from sr. to prin. N.J. Dept. Pub. Welfare, Trenton, N.J., 1975-78; mgmt. cons., nat. seminar leader sales and mktg. Nathaniel Hills & Assocs., Raleigh, N.C., 1978-79; from dir. mktg. to v.p. Concord Mgmt. Sys., Tampa, Fla., 1979-88; labor and employment def. atty. Zinober & McCrea, P.A., Tampa, 1993-98; of counsel Zinober & McCrea, 1998; ret.; bd. dirs. Tex. Instruments Users Group, 1983-84; pres. Data Bus., St. Petersburg, 1985-88; bd. trustees Am. Stage, 1997-98; speaker in field. Contbr. articles to profl. jours. Vol. docent Mus. of Fine Arts, St. Petersburg, 1998—. Mem. ABA (labor and employment law sect.), Fla. Bar Assn., Indsl. Labor Rels. Rsch. Assn. Democrat. Methodist. Avocations: swimming, cooking, sailing. Home: 1 Beach Dr SE Apt 2101-02 Saint Petersburg FL 33701-3963

BROWN, JAMES ANDREW, naval architect; b. Columbia, Tenn., Aug. 19, 1914; s. Charles Allen and Martha (Crawford) B.; m. Frances Adelaide Jones, June 7, 1941 (dec.); children: James Andrew, Martha Janet; m. Mary Julia Hargroves Greene, Feb. 16, 1973. BS, U.S. Naval Acad., 1936; MS, MIT, 1941. Registered profl. engr., Va. Commd. ensign U.S. Navy, 1936, advanced through grades to rear adm., 1963; jr. officer in USS W.Va., 1936-38; asst. hull supt. charge new constrn. Boston Naval Shipyard, 1942-45; mem. staff Comdr. Service Force Pacific, 1945-47; with Bur. Ships, Dept. Navy, 1947-50, project officer destroyer types, 1950-51, head hull design, 1955-59, asst. chief design, shipbldg. and fleet maintenance, 1963-65; prof. naval architecture MIT, Cambridge, 1951-54; comdg. officer ship repair facility Subic Bay, P.I., 1954-55; planning officer N.Y. Naval Shipyard, 1959, prodn. officer, 1959-61; supr. shipbldg. U.S. Navy, Camden, N.J., 1961-63; comdr. Norfolk Naval Shipyard; also supr. shipbldg. 5th Naval Dist., Portsmouth, Va., 1965-70; ret., 1970; prodn. mgr. J.L. Smith Constrn. Co., Portsmouth, 1970-77; pres. CDI Marine of Va., 1978-81; mgr. Hampton (Va.) Office, 1979-80; sr. engr. QED Systems Inc., 1981-87, chief engr. ship-systems group, 1987-90. Pres. Tidewater Fed. Exec. Agy., 1968; exec. bd. Inter Agy. Bd. Examiners Civil Service for Va., 1968-70; mem. Supplemental Fire and Police Retirement Bd., City of Portsmouth, 1978-86, chmn., 1980-86; bd. dirs. Portsmouth Community Action, 1969-70, 78-79; mem. Panel Spl. Advisers Auditor Gen. U.S.A., 1972, citizen adv. com. transit devel. study Southeastern Va. Planning Dist. Commn.; commr. Tidewater Transit Dist. Commn., 1978-86; bd. dirs. Portsmouth United Fund, 1965-77; coord. for vol. tutors, Portsmouth Sch. Bd., 1991-92. Decorated Legion of Merit; recipient Commendation medal Sec. of Navy; named Disting. Grad. Class of '31 Peabody Demonstration Sch., Nashville, 1986. Mem. Am. Soc. Naval Engrs. (coun. 1959), Naval Inst., Naval Archs. and Marine Engrs. (coun. 1968-69, chmn. Chesapeake sect. 1959, chmn. Hampton Rds. sect. 1969-70, v.p. 1969-70), Am. Philatelic Soc., World Affairs Coun. Greater Hampton Rds. (v.p. 1969-70, pres. 1971, 72), English Speaking Union, Portsmouth Hist. Soc. (hon., dir. 1977—, 1st v.p. 1987—), Portsmouth C. of C. (chmn. urban affairs com., v.p. for urban affairs 1972-73, chmn. com. hwys. and mass transit 1974-75, 76-78, bd. dirs. 1971-73, 79-82), Portsmouth C. of C. (mil. affairs com. 1970-95, transp. com. 1983-87), Navy League, Portsmouth Execs. Club (bd. dirs. 1975-76, 78-79, 79-82, 83-87, mem. ship structure com. 1963-65, chmn. subcom. 1955-59, 87-88), Sigma Xi. Home: 4260 Hatton Point Rd Portsmouth VA 23703-4000

BROWN, JAMES CARRINGTON, III (BING BROWN), public relations and communications executive; b. Wilmington, Del., May 17, 1939; s. James Carrington Jr. and Virginia Helen (Miller); m. Carol Osman, Nov. 3, 1961. Grad. security mgmt. group, Indsl. Coll. of the Armed Forces; BBS, Ariz. State U., 1984. Accredited, Pub. Rels. Soc. Am., 1988. Newsman, disc jockey, program dir. various radio stas., Ariz., 1955-60; morning news editor Sta. KOY, Phoenix, 1960-61; staff writer, photographer Prescott (Ariz.) Evening Courier, 1961; bus. editor, staff writer, photographer Phoenix Gazette, 1961-65; various communications positions Salt River Project, Phoenix, 1965-89; pres. Carrington Communications, Phoenix, 1989—; cons. comm., freelance writing, photography The Browns, Phoenix, 1965—; pub. info. officer Water Svcs. Dept., City of Phoenix, 1991—; instr. Rio Salado C.C., Phoenix, 1989-93; guest lectr. various colls. and univs., 1975—; prof. Walter Cronkite Sch. Journalism and Telecomm., Ariz. State U., 1990—; exec. prodr., prodr., asst. prodr. various ednl. videos. Bd. dirs. Grand Canyon coun. Boy Scouts Am., 1985-89, mem. adv. coun., 1990—; mem. exec. com. Cmty. Svc. Fund Drive, 1992—; mem. environment com. Phoenix Futures Forum, 1991-93; mem. project adv. com. for Am. Waterworks Assn. Rsch. Found. study of Pub. Involvement Strategies, 1994-95; deacon Meml. Presbyn. Ch., 1980-82, elder, 1985-87; mem. spl. gifts com. United Way, Phoenix, 1986-89. Recipient Golden Eagle award Boy Scouts Am., 1992. Mem. Pub. Rels. Soc. Am. (Percy award Sun chpt. 1986), Western Systems Coord. Coun. (chmn. pub. info. com. 1969-89), Ariz. Newspapers Assn. (Billy Goat award, Allied Mem. of Yr. 1985), Ariz. Broadcasters Assn., Western Coalition Arid States (chmn. comm. subcom. 1991-93, chmn. com. and mem. com. 1993—, editor WESTCAS News 1991—, Disting. Performance award 1996), Western Energy Supply and Transmission Assocs. (mem. pub. info. com. 1967-89), Phoenix Press Club (pres. 1982-83), PRSA, Nat. Acad. TV Arts/Scis., Ariz. Zool. Soc., Heard Mus. Anthropology and Primitive Art, Nature Conservancy, Jazz in Ariz., World Affairs Coun., City, County Comms. and Mktg. Assn. (Savvy award for outstanding video 1995—). Republican. Avocations: fly fishing, golf, photography, reading, cooking. Home and Office: Carrington Comm 3734 E Campbell Ave Phoenix AZ 85018-3507 also: Phoenix Water Svcs Dept 200 W Washington St Phoenix AZ 85003-1611

BROWN, JAMES EDWARD, safety engineer; b. Toledo, Ohio, Mar. 25, 1948; s. Kenneth E. and Helen M. (Wineland) B.; m. Debra Jean Mesteller, May 4, 1973; 1 child, Daniel James Mesteller. A in Engring. Tech., U. Toledo, 1971, B in Engring. Tech., 1995. Cert. quality engr.; cert. quality technician; registered quality sys. auditor. Sr. lab. technician Libbey Owens Ford, Toledo, 1970-73; electronic test engr. Prestolite Electric Inc., Toledo, 1973-90; quality supr. Rowe Industries, Toledo, 1990-93; project engr. Jobst Industries, Toledo, 1994; quality engr. Toledo Molding and Die, Inc., 1994—, corp. safety engr., 1997—. Pres. Toledo Friends of Libr., 1990; chmn. Oregon (Ohio) Rep. Party, 1995; chmn. Oregon Fest, City of Oregon, 1995-99; bd. dirs. Genealogy by Computer, Toledo, 1996-97. Named One of Ten Outstanding Men of Yr., Jr. C. of C., Toledo, 1978. Mem. IEEE (vice chmn. 1990-93), Am. Soc. Quality (chmn. sect. mgmt. plan 1997), Am. Soc. Safety Engrs. (newsletter editor 1999—). Republican. Avocation: genealogy. Home: 123 S Berlin Ave Oregon OH 43616-2134 Office: Toledo Molding and Die Inc 424 Coining Dr Toledo OH 43612-2932

BROWN, JAMES H., JR., state insurance commissioner, lawyer; b. May 6, 1940. BA, U. N.C.; JD, Tulane U. Bar: La. 1966. Pvt. practice, 1966—; mem. La. State Senate, 1972-80; sec. of state State of La., 1980-87; mem. Brook, Morial, Cassibry, Fraiche, Pizza, Baton Rouge/New Orleans, 1987-91; commr. ins. State of La., 1991—. Del. La. Constl. Conv., 1973. Democrat. Presbyterian.

BROWN, JAMES ISAAC, rhetoric educator; b. Tarkio, Mo., Dec. 15, 1908; s. John Vallance and Ada (Moore) B.; m. Ruth Bernice Sam, Sept. 19, 1942; children: Katherine Ada, Susan Phyllis. B.A., Tarkio Coll., 1930, D.H.L. (hon.), 1976; M.A., U. Chgo., 1933; Ph.D., U. Colo., 1949. Instr. English Monmouth Coll., 1933-34; faculty U. Minn., 1934—, successively instr., asst. prof., assoc. prof., 1934-77, prof. rhetoric, 1954-77, acting chief rhetoric, 1947-48; instr. English, Yavapai Coll., 1982-84; vis. lectr. U. Colo., summers 1950, 52, 54, U. Utah, summer 1955; staff mem. Effective Communication in Industry Course, summer 1954, 55; instituted Reading Efficiency Program in Industry, summers 1957, 58; conf. leader Mgmt. Clinic, Hot Springs, Va., 1956; communications cons. Minn. Mining & Mfg. and Caterpillar Tractor Cos., 1964. *While teaching reading improvement classes to university students in 1946, Brown recognized unmet adult needs by starting adult classes in 1950. With no available text, he wrote "Efficient Reading" in 1952 (now in its 8th edition). Widespread adult interest led to the development of five educational TV offerings, enrolling over 50,000 students, and to devising two home-study courses, one awarded a Certificate of Honor by the Independent Study Division, National University Extension Association in 1972. His "Reading Power" text followed (now in its 6th edition). His reading text sales now total well over a million. His newest project, a CD-ROM self-help reading program for a Belgian company, is now completed (1999).* Author: Efficient Reading, 1952, (with G. Robert Carlsen) Brown-Carlsen Listening Comprehension Test, 1954, Lex-o-Gram, 1954, (with Eugene S. Wright) Minnesota Efficient Reading Tachistolide Series, Minnesota Clerical Training Tachistoslide Series and Minnesota Timing Series, 1955, Revision of Nelson Denny Reading Test, 1960, (with Rachel Salisbury) Building a Better Vocabulary, 1959, Explorations in College Reading, 1959, Exercise Manual for Explorations in College Reading, 1959, (with George Sanderlin) Effective Writing and Reading, 1962, Pyramid, 1963, Programmed Vocabulary (TV edit., coll. edit. and high sch. edn.), 1964, 3d edit., 1980, Guide to Effective Reading, 1966, (with O.M. Haugh) College English Placement Test, 1969, Accelerad System, 1970, also the visual-linguistic basic reading series, 1966—, Efficient Reading, Revised Form A, 1971, Revised Form B, 1976, 6th edit., 1984, 7th edit., 1993, 8th edit., 1997, Forms C and D, Nelson-Denny Reading Test, 1973; Forms E and F, Nelson-Denny Reading Test, 1981, Forms G and H, 1992; Reading Power, 1975, alt. edit., 1978, 2d edit., 1983, 3d edit., 1987, 4th edit., 1991, 5th edit., 1995 (with Thomas E. Pearsall) Better Spelling, 1971, 2d edit., 1978, 3d edit, 1985, 4th edit., 1991, 5th edit., 1996, Word Power, 1982, EyeSCAN, 1999; mem. adv. bd., cons. ednl. edit. Reader's Digest, 1957; courses ednl. TV Success thru Better Spelling; tapes Putting Words to Work, for U.S. Dept. Edn.; cons. editor Jour. Internat. Listening Assn., 1986. Mem. visitor bd. Embry-Riddle Aeronautical U., Ariz., 1996—. Served with AUS, 1943-45, ETO. Recipient Tarkio Coll. Student Assn. Hall of Fame Award, 1965, Certificate of Merit in recognition outstanding ind. study course Efficient Reading Nat. Extension Assn., 1972, award of merit Gamma Sigma Delta, 1977, Winston Churchill Medal of Wisdom, 1988, Eisenhower Am. Achievement Honor award, 1989; named to Listening Hall of Fame, 1980. Mem. AAUP, Internat. Platform Assn., Nat. Council Tchrs. English, Nat. Soc. Study Communication (exec. sec. 1951, chmn. com. on reading comprehension 1951-63, pres.), Internat. Reading Assn., Conf. Coll. Composition and Communication, Speech Assn. Am., Am. Council Edn., Yavapai Symphony Assn. (pres. 1988-91), Phi Delta Kappa. Episcopalian (vestry mem. 1982-86, sr. warden 1984-86). Home: 1030 Scott Dr Unit C27 Prescott AZ 86301-1754

BROWN, JAMES JOSEPH, manufacturing company executive; b. N.Y.C., Apr. 4, 1928; s. Peter J. and Mary (O'Neil) B.; m. Mary E. McKeon, Dec. 30, 1961; children: Patricia, James, Carolyn, Denise, Erin. B.S., Fordham U., 1952. C.P.A., N.Y. Acct. Touche, Ross, Bailey & Smart (C.P.A.s), N.Y.C., 1952-54; sr. acct. Price Waterhouse & Co. (C.P.A.s), Caracas, Venezuela and N.Y.C., 1954-63; mgr. internal audit Litton Industries, 1963-65; sr. v.p., chief fin. officer dir. Kidde, Inc., 1965-82; chmn. bd. Am. Desk Mfg. Co., 1982-97. Served with AUS, 1946-48. Named Alumni Man of Year, Fordham U. Coll. Bus. Adminstrn., 1971. Mem. AICPA, N.Y. State Soc. CPAs, Econ. Club N.Y. Clubs: Treasurers of N.Y., Ridgewood Country, N.Y. Athletic. Office: 441 Weymouth Dr Wyckoff NJ 07481-1216

BROWN, JAMES KEVIN, professional baseball player; b. McIntyre, Ga., Mar. 14, 1965. Student, Ga. Tech. Inst. With Tex. Rangers, 1986-94, Balt. Orioles, 1995, Fla. Marlins, Miami, 1996-97, San Diego Padres, 1997-98; pitcher L.A. Dodgers, 1998—. Named Sporting News Coll. All-Am. Team, 1986, Am. League All-Star Game, 1992, Nat. League All-Star Team, 1996. Ranked 2nd in Am. League in victories, 1992. Office: LA dodgers 1000 Elysian Park Ave Los Angeles CA 90012*

BROWN, JAMES KNIGHT, lawyer; b. Rainelle, W.Va., Sept. 25, 1929; s. Hugh Allen and Florence Catherine (Knight) B.; m. Sarah Elizabeth Droste, June 21, 1952; children: Carolyn, Patricia, Julia. BS, W.Va. U., 1951, LLB, 1956. Bar: W.Va. 1956, U.S. Ct. Appeals (4th and 6th cir.), U.S. Supreme Ct. Assoc. Jackson & Kelly, Charleston, W.Va., 1956-62, ptnr., 1962-98; mem. Jackson & Kelly PLLC, Charleston, 1999—; bd. dirs. One Valley Bancorp., Inc., Charleston. 1st lt. USAF, 1951-53. Fellow Am. Bar Found.; mem. ABA, W.Va. State Bar (pres. 1975-76), Order of Coif, Phi Beta Kappa. Democrat. Presbyterian. Avocations: woodworking, golf. Office: Jackson & Kelly PLLC 1600 Laidley Tower Charleston WV 25301-2189

BROWN, JAMES NELSON, JR., accountant; b. Bronx, N.Y., Apr. 17, 1929; s. James Nelson and Agnes Mary (Cummins) B.; m. Lila Barbara Watt, Dec. 12, 1950; children: Constance Ellen Brown Buttacavole, Nelson Arthur, Richard John. BSBA, Drake U., 1956. CPA; cert. internal auditor, fraud examiner. Sr. acct. Arthur Andersen & Co., N.Y.C., 1956-61; asst. v.p., dir. internal auditing Salomon Inc., N.Y.C., 1961-86, asst. v.p., dir. projects mgmt. dept., 1986-91; asst. v.p. environ. litigation dept. Salomon Inc., 1991-93, v.p., mgr. environ. litig. dept., 1994-97; cons. environ. litig. dept. Citigroup, Inc., N.Y.C., 1998—. Com. chmn. Cub Scouts, 1973-75; troop com. chmn. Boy Scouts Am., Carteret, N.J., 1976-77, 88-90, com. mem., 1978-87. Sgt. AUS, 1947-52. Mem. AICPA, VFW, Am. Mgmt. Assn., N.J. Soc. CPAs, Nat. Assn. Cert. Fraud Examiners, Inst. Internal Auditors, Am. Legion, Elks. Republican. Roman Catholic. Home: 224 Wagon Wheel Ln Columbus NJ 08022-1119 Office: 388 Greenwich St New York NY 10013-2362

BROWN, JAMES RANDALL, mechanical engineer; b. Aug. 12, 1958; m. Reina Telles, June 1995; children: Jacqueline, Sonya, Danielle. BS in mech. engring., Rensselaer Poly. Inst., 1983; BS in computer sci., U. N.C., 1986. Engr. Stone & Webster Engring. Corp., Boston, 1981-83; mfg. engr. Digital Equipment Corp., Maynard, Mass., 1988-94; engr. PRI Automation, Inc., Billerica, Mass., 1994-97; sr. product engr. Honeywell, Inc., Mpls., 1997—.

Mem. ASME, ACM, IEEE, SME. Home: 6401 Prairie Sage Dr NW Albuquerque NM 87120-2576

BROWN, JAMES ROBERT, retired air force officer; b. Bozeman, Mont., June 17, 1930; s. Marley Robert and Ann Louise (Pace) B.; m. Sandra Shores, Dec. 19, 1964; children: James V., Brian R. B.S., Mont. State U., 1953; grad., Squadron Officer Sch., 1962, Air Command and Staff Coll., 1964, Indsl. Coll. of Armed Forces, 1974. Commd. 2d lt. U.S. Air Force, 1953, advanced through grades to lt. gen., 1984; undergrad. pilot tng. program U.S. Air Force, Williams AFB, Ariz., 1954-54; bomb comdr., intelligence officer 20th Fighter-Bomber Wing U.S. Air Force, Royal Air Force Station Wethersfield, Eng., 1955-58; fighter gunnery, instr. pilot, acad. instr. U.S. Air Force, Nellis AFB, Nev., 1958-62; flight evaluator Tactical Air Command U.S. Air Force, Langley AFB, Va., 1962-63; flight comdr., instr. pilot U.S. Air Force, Davis-Monthan AFB, Ariz., 1964-66; tour duty U.S. Air Force, Vietnam, 1966-67; dir. tng. analysis and devel. U.S. Air Force, Davis-Monthan AFB, Ariz., 1967-71; staff action officer tactics br. chief, acting chief tactical div. for Directorate of Plans and ops. U.S. Air Force, Washington, 1971-75; dir. ops. 388th Tactical Fighter Wing U.S. Air Force, Korat Royal Thai AFB, Thailand, 1975-76; vice comdr. 3d Tactical Fighter Wing U.S. Air Force, Clark Air Base, Philippines, 1976, comdr. 3d Tactical Fighter Wing, 1976-78; comdr. 313th Air div. and 18th Tactical Fighter Wing U.S. Air Force, Kadena Air Base, Japan, 1978-81; dep. chief of staff for ops. U.S. Air Force, Ramstein Air Base, Ger., 1981; asst. chief staff ops. Supreme Hdqrs. Allied Powers, Europe U.S. Air Force, Mons, Belgium, 1981-84; comdr. Allied Air Forces So. Europe, dep. comdr. in chief U.S. Air Forces in Europe U.S. Air Force, Naples, Italy, 1984-86; vice comdr. Langley AFB Tactical Air Command, Va., 1986-88; ret., 1988; dir. aviation programs East Inc., Chantilly, Va., 1991-94, 97—. Decorated D.D.S.M., D.S.S.M., Legion of Merit with oak leaf cluster, Bronze Star medal, Air Medal with four oak leaf clusters, Air Force Commendation medal with oak leaf cluster, Def. Superior Service medal. Avocations: golf, bike riding, walking, horseback riding. Home: 1591 Stowe Rd Reston VA 20194-1602

BROWN, JAMES ROY, retail executive; b. Broken Arrow, Okla., Nov. 24, 1950; s. Roy Thelbert and Betty Anne (Ice) B.; m. Eva Jane Boggs, June 25, 1970; children: Courtney James, Ava Lauren. AA in Fine Arts, Tulsa Jr. Coll., 1971. Stocker Doc's Food Stores, Inc., Bixby, Okla., 1962-69, produce mgr., 1969-72, meat mgr., 1972, store mgr., 1972-85, v.p., 1979, pres. and owner, 1983—; pres. and owner Bixby True Value, 1986-92. Mem. adv. com. for vocat. edn. Bixby High Sch., 1986-87; mem. bd. Family YMCA, 1988, chmn. bldg. fund; v.p. Bixby Endowment Fund, 1991—; bd. dirs. Okla. Grocers Edn. Found., 1991. treas., 1995, chmn. elect., 1996, chmn., 1997-98. Named Outstanding Employer Okla. chpt. Distributive Edn. Clubs Am., 1986. Mem. Okla. Grocers Assn. (bd. dirs. 1989, treas. 1996, chmn. elect, 1997, chmn., 1998), Bixby C. of C. (v.p. 1971-72, 87-88, pres. 1973, 88-89), Bixby Jaycees (Jaycee of Month award 1971, Jaycee of Quarter award 1982), Optimists (v.p. 1982, Optimist of Yr. award 1976). Democrat. Baptist. Avocations: snow skiing, golfing, tennis, water skiing. Home: 45 W 5th St Bixby OK 74008-4536 Office: Doc's Food Stores Inc 211 N Cabaniss Ave Bixby OK 74008-4390

BROWN, JAMES SHELLY, lawyer; b. Trenton, N.J., May 5, 1945; s. Alexander Aloysius and Madlyn (Shelly) B.; m. Margaret Lee Martin, June 6, 1987; children: Elizabeth Paige, Kristen Blaire. BA, Hoftsra u., 1968; JD, Fordham U., 1972. Bar: N.Y. 1973. Asst. dist. atty. County of N.Y., N.Y.C., 1972-78; ptnr. Wilson, Eiser, Moskowitz, Edelman and Dicker, N.Y.C., 1994—. Mem. N.Y. State Bar Assn., Assn. of Bar of City of N.Y. Avocation: tennis. Home: 31 Old Parish Rd Darien CT 06820-4319*

BROWN, JAMES THOMPSON, JR., computer information scientist, logistics specialist; b. Orange, N.J., Jan. 3, 1935; s. James Thompson and Marjorie (Hale) B.; m. Alice Beasley, Oct. 3, 1959; children—Kathryn, James. B.M.E., Cornell U., 1957; M.S., Stanford U., 1964. Applied sci. rep. IBM Corp., Schenectady, N.Y., 1957-59, corp. staff mem., White Plains, N.Y., 1960-68; cons. Case & Co., Stamford, Conn., 1969-74, dir., 1975-83, pres., 1983-84; pres. Tom Brown & Co., Wilton, Conn., 1985—; advisor Russian Fedn. Customs Svc. Developer inventory mgmt. systems and svc. pricing techniques. Life mem. Rep. Inner Circle. Mem. Internat. Assn. Chain Stores (adviser, speaker 1971—), Nat. Grocers Assn. (adviser 1983—), Am. Inst. Indsl. Engrs. (sr. mem.), Inst. Ops. Rsch. and Mgmt. Scis., Landmark Club, Cornell Club (N.Y.), Capitol Hill Club. Republican. Home: 135 Middlebrook Farm Rd Wilton CT 06897-2019 Office: Tom Brown & Co PO Box 431 Wilton CT 06897-0431 *One of my guiding principles is not to try to solve a problem until I understand it. Understanding often means getting your hands dirty. And when I do understand, take the time to carefully think out the solution.*

BROWN, JAMES WALKER, JR., city government planning and development administrator; b. Boston, Oct. 26, 1948; s. James and Anna L. (Greenlaw) B.; m. Sharon Jean Scott, June 6, 1970; children: Allison, Hannah. BA, U. Maine, Presque Isle, 1973. Emergency med. technician, asst. dir. Houlton (Maine) Ambulance Svc., 1971-76; regional coord. Maine Emergency Med. Svcs. Project, Presque Isle, 1976-79; devel. specialist Maine Hypertension Control Project, Presque Isle, 1980-82; emergency med. technician Lamb's Ambulance Svc., Presque Isle, 1982-83; project coord., planner City of Presque Isle, 1984-92, dir. planning & devel., 1992—; adv. com. Maine Dept. Transportation, Caribou, 1993-97; Crown ambulance com. Aroostook Med. Ctr., Presque Isle, 1988—. Mem. mcpl. charter commn. City Presque Isle, 1992-92; bd. dirs. Maine Sch. Adminstrv. Dist. 1, Presque Isle, 1981-82, Aroostook County Action Program, 1996—, Aroostook Regional Trans. Sys., Inc., 1998—; support team Nat. Envirothon, Mapleton, Maine, 1991. Mem. Am. Inst. Cert. Planners, Am. Planning Assn., Maine Assn. Planners, Maine Cmty. Devel. Assn. Office: City of Presque Dept Econ and Cmty Devel 12 2nd St Presque Isle ME 04769-2459

BROWN, JAMES WARD, mathematician, educator, author; b. Phila., Jan. 15, 1934; s. George Harold and Julia Elizabeth (Ward) B.; m. Jacqueline Read, Sept. 3, 1957; children: Scott Cameron, Gordon Elliot. AB, Harvard U., 1955; MA, U. Mich., 1958, Ph.D. (Inst. Sci and Tech. predoctoral fellow), 1964. Asst. prof. math. U. Mich., Dearborn, 1964-66, assoc. prof., 1968-71, prof., 1971—, acting chmn. dept., 1974, 85; asst. prof. Oberlin Coll., 1966-68; editorial cons. Math. Rev., 1970-85; dir. NSF Grant, 1969. Author: (with R.V. Churchill) Complex Variables and Applications, 6th edit., 1996, Internat. Student edit., 1996, Japanese edit., 1995, Spanish edit., 1978, Chinese edit., 1985, Korean edit., 1992, Greek edit., 1993, Fourier Series and Boundary Value Problems, 5th edit., 1993, internat. student edit., 1993, Japanese edit., 1980; contbr. articles to U.S. and fgn. sci. jours. Recipient Disting. Faculty award U. Mich.-Dearborn, 1976, Disting. Faculty award Mich. Assn. Governing Bds. Colls. and Univs., 1983. Mem. Am. Math. Soc., Research Club of U. Mich., Sigma Xi. Home: 1710 Morton Ave Ann Arbor MI 48104-4522 Office: 4901 Evergreen Rd Dearborn MI 48128-2406

BROWN, J'AMY MARONEY, journalist, media relations consultant, investor; b. L.A., Oct. 30, 1945; d. Roland Francis and Jeanne (Wilbur) Maroney; m. James Raphael Brown, Jr., Nov. 5, 1967 (dec. July 1982); children: James Roland Francis, Jeanne Raphael. Attended U. So. Calif., 1963-67. Reporter L.A. Herald Examiner, 1966-67, Lewisville Leader, Dallas, 1980-81; editor First Person Mag., Dallas, 1981-82; journalism dir. Pacific Palisades Sch., L.A., 1983-84; free-lance writer, media cons., 1984-88; press liaison U.S. papal visit, L.A., 1987; media dir., chief media strategist Tellem Inc., 1990-92, comm. cons., issues mgr. 1992—; pres., CEO and owner PRformance Group Comm., 1995—; auction chmn. Assn. Pub. Broadcasting, Houston, 1974, 75; vice chmn. Dallas Arts Council, 1976-80; vice chmn. Met. March of Dimes, Dallas, 1980-82; del. Dallas Council PTAs, 1976-80; bd. dirs. Santa Barbara City Coll. Bus. and Industry Coun.; mem. core-coun. Santa Barbara Coun. on Self-Esteem; coord. specialist World Cup Soccer Organizing Com. Recipient UPI Editors award for investigative reporting, 1981. Mem. NAFE, Pub. Rels. Soc. Am. (accredited), Women Meeting Women, Women in Comm., Am. Bus. Women's Assn., Santa Barbara C. of C. (media com.). Republican. Roman Catholic. Home: 1143 High Rd Santa Barbara CA 93108-2430

BROWN, JAN WHITNEY, small business owner; b. Roundup, Mont., Mar. 16, 1942; d. John Estes and Janet Lillian (Snyder) Dahl; m. William A. Brown III; children: Erik Lane, Kimberly Elise. BA in Sociology, Social Work, Carroll Coll., 1976. Sec. 1st Nat. Bank, Bozeman, Mont., 1962, Office of Gov., Helena, Mont., 1963-69; pub. info. coord. Helena Model City Program, 1969-73; pub. relations and assn. mgmt. Mont. Bar Assn., Helena, 1973-76, Mont. Assn. Life Underwriters, Helena, 1973-76; legis. liaison Mont. Religious Legis. Coalition, Helena, 1975-81; exec. dir. Helena Food Share Inc., 1987; co-owner Jorud Photo and Gifts, Helena, 1971—; legislator Mont. St. Legislature, Helena, 1983-92; mem. legis. coun. Helena, 1989-92; bd. dirs. Helena Food Share, Inc., Bus. Improvement Dist.; chmn. state adminstrn. com. Mont. Ho. of Reps., 1989-92. Chmn. Mont. Medal of Valor Com., Helena, 1986-93; pres. United Way, Helena, 1982; bd. dirs. Mont. Area Health Edn. Ctr., Bozeman, 1988-93, Mont. Hunger Coalition, Helena, 1988-89, St. Peter's Cmty. Hosp. Found. Bd., 1994-96, 97—, St. Peter's Hosp., 1994—, chair bd. dirs., 1997—; Helena City Commr., 1993; vice chair Helena Citizens Coun., 1994-96; mem. cmty. adv. bd. U.S. Bank, 1994—; sec.-treas. Mt. Soc. for Hosp. Governance, 1995-97; mem. visions com. United Way, 1997-98; mem. diocesan coun. Episcopal Diocese of Mont., 1997—. Recipient Disting. Svc. award Mental Health Assn., 1976, Disting. Cmty. Svc. award Jaycees, 1982, Ann. Appreciation award Child Support Enforcement, 1985, United Way award, 1988, Cmty. Svc. award VFW, 1988. Mem. Helena Unlimited. Democrat. Episcopalian. Avocations: symphony, choir. Office: Jorud Photo and Gifts 327 N Last Chance Gulch St Helena MT 59601-5013

BROWN, JANE COMFORT BRENNAN, educator, language and movement therapist; b. Mt. Kisco, N.Y., June 5, 1931; d. Richard Francis and Marjorie Barnard (Collins) Brennan; m. William Joseph Brown, June 19, 1954 (dec. Oct. 1992); children: William Joseph Jr., Gerald Francis. BA in Edn., U. Del., 1954; MEd in Spl. Edn., Learning Disabilities, Am. U., 1985; cert. tchr. Alexander Technique, Alexander Found., Phila., 1988. Primary tchr. Newark (Del.) Pub. Sch. Sys., 1954-55; asst. to dir. Penland (N.C.) Sch. Crafts, 1962-83; founder Penland Sch. Creative Movement Prog.; pvt. tutor Mitchell County Public Schs., N.C., 1964-80, 85-89; mem. adj. faculty, teacher of the Alexander Technique Appalachian State U. Sch. Music, Boone, N.C., 1988—; tchg. mem. Alexander Technique Internat., Cambridge, Mass.; spkr., tchr., trainer in field of dyslexia, 1967—, organizer Dyslexia-June L. Orton tchr. tng. workshops, Penland Sch. of Crafts, summers 1967-70; condr. numerous workshops on Alexander Technique in S.E., 1988—. Bd. dirs. Arthur Morgan Sch., N.C., 1967-68. Grantee Hillsdale Fund, Inc., 1984, Ella Lyman Cabot Trust, 1984, Kittredge Fund, 1984, also pvt. grantee, 1984. Fellow Orton-Gillingham Practitioners and Educators; mem. Internat. Somatic Movement Educators and Therapy Assn. (registered movement therapist), Orton Dyslexia Soc. (bd. dirs. Carolinas br. 1986, founding bd. dirs. N.C. br. 1986-95, v.p. bd. 1993-95), Internat. Dyslexia Assn. (adv. bd. dirs. 1998—). Episcopalian. Home: 561 Conley Ridge Rd Bakersville NC 28705 Office: Appalachian State U Sch Music Boone NC 28608

BROWN, JANET MCNALLEY, retirement plan consultant; b. Denver, May 16, 1960; d. Michael Collins and Sharon Bess (Cook) McNalley. Student, Mt. Holyoke Coll., 1978-79; BA in Econs. with honors, Mills Coll., Oakland, Calif., 1982; MA in Social Scis., U. Calif., Irvine, 1987, elem. teaching credential, 1988. Teaching asst. U. Calif., Irvine, 1986-88; employee benefits adminstr. Western Co. N.Am., Ft. Worth, 1988-89; trust officer Ameritrust Tex. N.A., Ft. Worth, 1989-90; thrift and profit sharing analyst Burlington No. R.R., Ft. Worth, 1990-93; assoc. human resources group Coopers & Lybrand, Dallas, 1993-94; pension coord. Bell Helicopter Textron, Inc., Ft. Worth, 1994-95; adminstr., cons. Rogers & Assocs., Ft. Worth, 1995-97; pvt. practice Ft. Worth, 1997—; owner Retirement Plan Mgmt., 1997—. Dem. del., Ft. Worth, 1990; mem. Liberty Coalition, Bluebonnet Pl. Neighborhood Assn. (newsletter editor); neighborhood crime prevention coord. Citizens on Patrol. Mem. AAUW (membership v.p. 1990-92, charter Eleanor Roosevelt Fund. 1990-92), Am. Soc. pension Actuaries (qualified pension adminstr., cert. pension cons.). Avocations: dance, sewing, travel. Home and Office: 3408 Cockrell Ave Fort Worth TX 76109-3003

BROWN, JANICE ROGERS, state supreme court justice. Assoc. justice Calif. Supreme Ct., San Francisco. Office: Calif Supreme Ct 303 2d St South Tower San Francisco CA 94107-3600*

BROWN, JARED, theater director, educator, writer. BFA, Ithaca Coll., 1960; MA Theatre, San Francisco State Coll., 1962; PhD Theatre, U. Minn., 1967. Instr. creative writing St. Paul Pub. Sch. System, 1962-63; teaching asst. U. Minn., 1963-64, instr. Communication Dept., 1964-65; from asst. prof. to prof. dept. theatre Western Ill. U., 1965-89, acad. dir. Semester in London, 1979-80; dir. Sch. Theatre Arts, Prof. Theatre Arts Ill. Wesleyan U., 1989—; aided devel. (policies, curriculum), Theatre Dept. Western Ill. U., 1971; panel discussant Western Ill. U., 1973, 1974; chmn. panel Ill. Theatre Assn. Convention, 1976; panel discussant Assn. Theatre in Higher Edn. Convention, 1987; disting. faculty lectr. Western Ill. U., 1986, dir. grad. program dept. theatre, 1975-89, chmn. directing, theatre history and playwriting programs, dept. theatre, 1972-89; mem. panel judges to award NEH Summer Stipends, Ill., 1990; judge Am. Coll. Theatre Festival, 1973-74, 89-90; mem. various theatre coms. Ill. Wesleyan U.; mem. various coms. Univ., Coll. Fine Arts, Dept. Theatre Western Ill. U.; spkr., presenter in field. Author: The Fabulous Lunts, A Biography of Alfred Lunt and Lynn Fontanne, 1986, (Barnard Hewitt award 1987), Zero Mostel: A Biography, 1989, The Theatre in America During the Revolution, 1995; dir. plays including The Merchant of Venice, Hedda Gabler, Henry IV, La Ronde, Death of a Salesman, Cat on a Hot Tin Roof, A Streetcar Named Desire, Who's Afraid of Virginia Woolf, You Can't Take It With You, Brighton Beach Memoirs, Inherit the Wind, Peter Pan, Bye Bye Birdie, Guys and Dolls, Kiss Me Kate, 110 In The Shade, Annie, Funny Girl, Broadway Bound, Tartuffe, Antigone, She Loves Me, Noises Off, Sight Unseen, Bedroom Farce; appeared in My Fair Lady, Western Ill. U., 1978, On The Twentieth Century, 1986, various radio and TV programs; contbr. chpts. to texts, articles to profl. jours. Recipient stipend NEH, 1988, DuPont award for tchg. excellence, 1997; named Best Dir., The Pantagraph, 1991, 92, 94, 96; grantee Ill. Arts Coun., 1980, 81, 87, Western Ill. U., 1983-85, 86-87, 89, Cultural Arts Devel. Fund, 1980-89, Ill. Wesleyan U., 1990, Artistic/Scholarly Devel. grantee, 1999. Mem. Nat. Collegiate Players, Phi Kappa Phi, Theta Alpha Phi. Home: 18 Chatsford Ct Bloomington IL 61704-6220 Office: Sch Theatre Arts Ill Wesleyan U Bloomington IL 61702

BROWN, JASON ROBERT, composer, arranger. Composer, arranger: Parade, Songs for a New World; arranger: William Finn's A New Brain, Dinah Was, Paul Robeson: All American; orchestrator: Andrew Lippa's John and jen, Yoko Ono's New York Rock, Love's Fire, Sondheim: A Celebration at Carnegie Hall; mus. dir.: The Petrified Prince, When Pigs Fly. Winner 1999 Tony for original score in Parade, Gilman and Gonzalez-Falla Mus. Theatre award, 1996. Office: Screen Composers of Am 2451 Nichols Canyon Rd Los Angeles CA 90046-1798*

BROWN, JASON WALTER, neurologist, educator, researcher; b. N.Y.C., Apr. 14, 1938; s. Samuel Robert and Sylvia (Brown) B.; children: Jonathan Schilder, Jovana Millay; m. Carine Brown; 1 child, Ilya. B.A., U. Calif.-Berkeley, 1959; M.D., U.S.C., 1963. Intern St. Elizabeth's Hosp., Washington, 1963-64; resident in neurology UCLA, 1964-67; practice medicine specializing in neurology N.Y.C., 1970—; instr. Boston U. Med. Sch., 1969-70; asst. clin. prof. Columbia-Presbyn. Hosp., N.Y.C., 1970-75; vis. asst. prof. neurology Albert Einstein Coll. Medicine, N.Y.C., 1972-75; vis. assoc. prof. Rockefeller U., N.Y.C., 1978-79; clin. assoc. prof. neurology NYU, 1975-79, clin. prof., 1979—; pres. Inst. Research in Behavioral Neurosci.; vis. scholar N.Y. Psychoanalytic Inst., 1993—. Author: Aphasia, Apraxia and Agnosia, 1972, Mind, Brain and Consciousness, 1977, Life of the Mind, 1988; editor: Jargonaphasia, 1982; English Translation of Aphasie by Arnold Pick (Aphasia), 1973, Neuropsychology of Visual Perception, 1989, Classics in Neuropsychology: Apraxia and Agnosia, Self and Process, 1991, Time, Will and Mental Process, 1996, The Mind of Nature, 1999; contbr. numerous articles on neurology to med. jours.; mem. editl. bd. Jour. Nervous and Mental Disease, Aphasiology, Advances in Neurolinguistics. Grantee NIH; fellow Alexander von Humboldt Found., 1979—, World Rehab. Fund, 1982, Founds. Fund for Research in Psychiatry, 1974-75. Jewish. Home and Office: 66 E 79th St New York NY 10021-0217

BROWN, JAY MARSHALL, retired secondary education educator; b. Bklyn., July 26, 1933; s. Sidney and Bertha (Swirsky) B.; m. Merle Thelma Kaminsky, Nov. 4, 1956; children: Sidney Matthew, Ellen Beth Factor. BS in Journalism, NYU, 1955, MA in Am. Civilization, 1960; postgrad., Yeshiva U., 1958-60, U. Conn., West Hartford, 1968-70; 6th yr. profl. diploma, So. Conn. State Coll., 1977. Pub. relations dir, asst. credit mgr. Colonial Sand & Stone Co., N.Y.C., 1955-60; employment counselor N.Y.C. Dept. Welfare, 1960-63; attendance tchr. Bd. Edn., N.Y.C., 1963-65; youth dir. Jewish Community Ctr., Rochester, N.Y., 1965-67; exec. dir. Conn. Valley Regional B'nai B'rith Youth, New Haven, 1967-70; resource tchr. Sheridan Middle Sch., Bd. Edn., New Haven, 1970-72; learning ctr. tchr. Bd. Edn., New Haven, 1972-74; social studies tchr. Troup Middle Sch., Bd. Edn., New Haven, 1974-80; history tchr. Hillhouse High Sch., Bd. Edn., New Haven, 1980-93; U.S. history tchr. New Eng. Acad. for Jewish Studies, New Haven, 1984-85; audio-visual and media specialists Quinnipiac Coll., Hamden, Conn., 1982. Contbr. articles to profl. jour.; editor BBYO Bd. dirs. newsletter, Bklyn., 1961-62; columnist The Luna Spark, Bklyn., 1961-63. Chmn. clear sch. mission com. Hillhouse H.S., 1984, mem. effective sch. steering com., 1984, mem. sch. planning and mgmt. team, 1988-91, coord. teenagers adv. program, 1989-91, mem. faculty senate, 1991-93; bd. dirs. Citizen TV, Inc., 1991-93; acting pres. Alliance for Mentally Ill, 1993-94, pres., 1995—; pres. Brotherhood of Mishkan Israel, 1976-78, 83-84, 88-89, sec., 1997-98, treas., 1998—; asst. treas. Congregation Mishkan Israel, 1983-84, budget chmn., 1987-88, chmn. house and property com., 1979-84, trustee, 1978-84, 86-92, 94—, mem. pers. com., 1996—, mem. abatement com., 1997-98, libr. and archivist, 1981-84; past chmn. Hamden Cmty. Devel. Action Planning Com. on Youth Svcs.; past sec. Hamden Anti-Drug Task Force; mem. Hamden Dem. Town Com., 1974-76; corr. sec. Jewish Hist. Soc., New Haven, 1980-81; v.p. Regency Hills Condo Assn., 1994-95; active Mental Health Month Com., 1995—, Family Resource Ctr. com. Consultation Ctr., 1994-98; coord. Mental Health Network Speakers Bur., 1996-97, 98; facilitator Journey of Hope Ednl. Program, 1995-98; mem. Regional Mental Health Bd., Catchment Area 7, 1996-97, vice chmn., 1997—; mem. review and evaluation team State Regional Mental Health Bd. Dist. 2, 1996—, vice chmn., 1997—; bd. govs. Inst. Learning and Retirement, 1998—; treas. Nat. Alliance Mentally Ill, 1998-99. Recipient Man of Yr. award of merit Congregation Mishkan Israel's Brotherhood, 1978; named Outstanding Profl. in Human Svcs., 1974-75. Mem. New Haven County Ret. Tchr. Assn. (v.p. 1994-95, sec. 1997—), Regency Hills Condo Assn. (pres. 1995-96), Phi Delta Kappa. Democrat. Jewish. Avocations: philately, polit. items, sports items, community svc. Home: 25 Wright Ln Hamden CT 06517-2126

BROWN, JEAN GAYLE, social worker; b. St. Joseph, Mo., May 22, 1953; d. Forrest Dale and Mildred M. (Benner) Paden; m. William G. Brown, Aug. 3, 1973; children: Abigail, Adam. BSW, Mo. Western State Coll., 1973; MSW, W.Va. U., 1976. Social worker Family Guidance Ctr., St. Joseph, 1973-77, family planning dir., 1977-83; adminstr. Family Guidance Ctr., St. Joseph, Mo., 1983-95; exec. dir. YWCA, St. Joseph, 1995—. Author: Parent-Child Sex Education: A Training Module, 1976, Sexuality Education: A Curriculum for Parent-Child Programs, 1982, (with others) Sexuality Education: A Resource Book, 1989. Pres. Midland Empire Girl Scout Coun., St. Joseph, 1986-90. Named one of Disting. Alumni Mo. Western State Coll., 1989. Mem. NASW, Acad. Cert. Social Workers, Am. Assn. Sex Educators, Counselors and Therapists (cert. sex educator). Mem. Christian Ch. Home: 5605 Pleasant Ave Saint Joseph MO 64503-2275 Office: YWCA St Joseph 304 N 8th St Saint Joseph MO 64501-1988

BROWN, JEANETTE GRASSELLI, university official; b. Cleve., Aug. 4, 1928; d. Nicholas W. and Veronica (Varga) Gecsy; m. Glenn R. Brown, Aug. 1, 1987. BS summa cum laude, Ohio U., 1950, DSc (hon.), 1978; MS, Western Res. U., 1958, DSc (hon.), 1995; DSc (hon.), Clarkson U., 1986; D Engring. (hon.), Mich. Tech. U., 1989; DSc (hon.), Wilson Coll., 1994, Notre Dame Coll., 1995, Kenyon Coll., 1995, Mt. Union Coll., 1996. Project leader, assoc. Infrared Spectroscopist, Cleve., 1950-78; mgr. analytical sci. lab. Standard Oil (name changed to BP Am., Inc. 1985), Cleve., 1978-83, dir. technol. support dept., 1983-85, dir. corp. rsch. and analytical scis., 1985-88; disting. vis. prof., dir. rsch. enhancement Ohio U., Athens, 1989-95; bd. dirs. B.F. Goodrich Co., AGA Gas, Inc., USX Corp., Inc.; mem. bd. on chem. sci. and tech. NRC, 1986-91; chmn. U.S. Nat. Com. to Internat. Union of Pure and Applied Chemistry, 1992-94; mem. joint high level adv. panel U.S.-Japan Sci. and Tech., 1994—, Ohio Bd. Regents, 1995—, vice-chair, 1999—. Author, editor 8 books; editor: Vibrational Spectroscopy; contbr. numerous articles on molecular spectroscopy to profl. jours.; patentee naphthalene extraction process. Bd. dirs. N.E. Ohio Sci. and Engring. Fair, Cleve., 1977—; trustee Holden Arboretum, Cleve., 1988—, Edison Biotech Ctr., Cleve., 1988-95, Cleve. Playhouse, 1990-96, Garden Ctr. Greater Cleve., 1990-93, Mus. Arts Assn., 1991—, Gt. Lakes Sci. Ctr., 1991—, Rainbow Babies and Children's Hosp., 1992-95, Nat. Inventors' Hall of Fame, 1993—; trustee Ohio U., 1985-94, chmn. 1991-92; chair Cleve. Scholarship Programs, 1995—; chair steering com. Mellen Ctr. Cleve. Clinic, 1996—. Recipient Disting. Svc. award Cleve. Tech. Soc. Coun., 1985; named Woman of Yr. YWCA, 1980; named to Ohio Women's Hall of Fame State of Ohio, 1989, Ohio Sci. & Tech. Hall of Fame, 1991. Mem. Am. Chem. Soc. (chair analytical divsn. 1990-91, Garvan medal 1986, Analytical Chem. award 1993, Encouraging Women into Careers in Sci. award 1999), Soc. for Applied Spectroscopy (pres. 1970, Disting. Svc. award 1983), Coblentz Soc. (bd. govs. 1968-71, William Wright award 1980), Royal Soc. Chemistry (Theophilus Redwood lectr. 1994), Phi Beta Kappa, Iota Sigma Pi (pres. fluorine chpt. 1957-60, nat. hon. mem. 1987). Republican. Roman Catholic. Avocations: swimming, dance, music. Home: 150 Greentree Rd Chagrin Falls OH 44022-2424

BROWN, JEANETTE L., environmental protection administrator. BBA, Morgan State U., 1980; postgrad., Am. U., Washington. Intern Navy Regional Contracting Ctr., Washington, 1978; with Navy Automatic Data Processing Selection Office, Joint Cruise Missile Project/NAV AIR; dep. dir. Office of Small and Disadvantaged Bus. Utilization, EPA, Washington, dep. dir. Office of Acquisition Mgmt., dir. Office of Acquisition Mgmt.,. FAX: 202-401-1080. Office: US EPA Samll and Disadvantaged Bus 401 M St SW Washington DC 20024-2610

BROWN, JERROLD STANLEY, lawyer; b. Little Falls, N.Y., Nov. 8, 1953; s. Stanley Clayton and Ruth Jane Brown; m. Catherine M. Agnello, Aug. 2, 1980. BA, SUNY, Albany, 1975; JD, Union U., 1979. Bar: N.Y. 1980, U.S. Dist. Ct. (no. dist.) N.Y. 1980, U.S. Dist. Ct. (we. dist.) N.Y. 1982, U.S. Ct. Appeals (2nd cir.) 1983, U.S. Supreme Ct. 1989. Law clk. to judge N.Y. Ct. Appeals, Albany, 1979-81; assoc. Hodgson, Russ, Andrews, Woods & Goodyear, Buffalo, 1981-85, ptnr., 1986—; mem. adv. panel N.Y. Clean Air Act, 1996—, bd. dirs., Studio Arena Theatre, 1999—, bd. dirs., Shakespeare in Delaware Park, 1999—. Note and comment editor Albany Law Rev., 1978-79. Trustee Westminster Presbyn. Ch., Buffalo, 1986, pres., 1988, elder, 1992-93, 97—; bd. dirs. Homespace, Inc., 1998—, Shakespeare in Del. Pk., 1999—, Studio Arena Theater, 1999—; ward leader Del. Dist. Rep. Party, 1992; mem. adv. bd. Salvation Army, Buffalo Area, 1999—. Mem. N.Y. State Bar Assn. (task force on commerce and industry 1998—). Office: Hodgson Russ Andrews Woods & Goodyear Ste 2000 One M & T Plz Buffalo NY 14203

BROWN, JERRY See BROWN, EDMUND GERALD, JR.

BROWN, JERRY A., federal judge; b. 1932. BA, Murray State Coll., 1954; LLB, Tulane U., 1959. Law clk. to Hon. John Minor Wisdom U.S. Ct. Appeals (5th cir.), 1959-60; assoc. Monroe & Lemann, New Orleans, 1960-63, ptnr., 1963-90; assoc. Bronfin & Heller, New Orleans, 1991-92; bankruptcy judge U.S. Dist. Ct. (ea. dist.) La., New Orleans, 1992—. With U.S. Army, 1954-56. Office: US Dist Ct (ea dist) La 501 Magazine St Rm 741A New Orleans LA 70130

BROWN, JIM (JAMES NATHANIEL BROWN), film actor, former professional football player; b. St. Simon's Island, Ga., Feb. 17, 1936; s. Swinton and Theresa B.; m. Sue Jones, 1958 (div.); children: Kim and Kevin (twins), Jim; m. Monique Gunthrop. BA, Syracuse U., 1957. Fullback Cleve. Browns Profl. Football Team, 1957-65; founder Negro Industrial Economic Union (now Black Economic Union), 1965—, Vital Issues, 1986—, Amer-I-can, 1989—; spl. con. Cleve. Browns, 1993—. Now film actor: appeared in Rio Conchos, 1964, The Dirty Dozen, 1967, Ice Station

Zebra, 1969, The Split, 1968, Riot, 1969, 100 Rifles, 1969, Kenner, 1971, Slaughter, 1972, Slaughter's Big Rip-off, 1973, I Escaped from Devil's Island, 1973, The Slams, 1973, Three the Hard Way, 1974, Take a Hard Ride, 1975, Adios Amigo, 1976, Gus, 1976, I Will, I Will . . . For Now, 1976, Fingers, 1977, Superbug, The Wild One, 1977, One Down, Two to Go, 1982, The Running Man, 1987, I'm Gonna Git You Sucka, 1988, Crack House, 1989, Twisted Justice, 1990, Original Gangstas, 1996, Mars Attacks!, 1996, He Got Game, 1998, Small Soldiers (voice), 1998, Any Given Sunday, 1999, others; author: Off My Chest, 1964, Out of Bounds, 1989. Founder Black Economic Union. Recipient numerous Nat. Football League awards including Rookie of the Year, 1958, Player of Year, 1959, 64, Jim Thorpe Trophy, 1959, Back of the Decade, 1960; Hickock Belt as Profl. Athlete of Yr., 1964; named to Pro Bowl 1958-65; recipient Bert Bell Memorial Award, 1964; named to Pro Football Hall of Fame, 1971, Coll. Football Hall of Fame, 1995. *

BROWN, JOBETH GOODE, food products executive, lawyer; b. Oakdale, La., Sept. 15, 1950; d. Samuel C. Goode and Elizabeth E. (Twiner) Baker; m. H. William Brown, Aug. 4, 1973; 1 child, Kevin William. BA, Newcomb Coll. Tulane U., 1972; JD, Wash. U., 1979. Assoc. Coburn, Croft & Putzell, St. Louis, 1979-80; staff atty. Anheuser-Busch Cos. Inc., St. Louis, 1980-81, exec. asst. to v.p. sec., 1982-83, asst. sec., 1983-89, sec., v.p., 1989—. Trustee Anheuser-Busch Found., St. Louis, 1989—, St. Louis Sci. Ctr.; dir. Girl Scouts USA Coun., Greater St. Louis, 1991-; bd. dirs. St. Louis Zoo Friends. Mem. ABA, Mo. Women's Forum, Mo. Bar Assn., Bar Assn. Met. St. Louis, Am. Soc. Corp. Secs. (pres. 1992), Algonquin Golf Club, Order of Coif. Republican. Presbyterian. Office: Anheuser-Busch Cos Inc 1 Busch Pl Saint Louis MO 63118-1852

BROWN, JOE BLACKBURN, judge; b. Louisville, Dec. 9, 1940; s. Knox and Miriam (Blackburn) B.; m. Marilyn McGowen, Aug. 10, 1963; children: Jennifer Knox, Michael McGowen. BA cum laude, Vanderbilt U., 1962, JD, 1965. Bar: Ky. 1965, Tenn. 1972, U.S. Supreme Ct. 1979. Asst. U.S. atty. Dept. Justice, Nashville, 1971-73, 1st asst. U.S. atty., 1974-81, U.S. atty., 1981-91, spl. asst. U.S. trustee, 1991-98; U.S. magistrate judge, U.S. Dist. Ct. (mid. dist.) Tenn., Nashville, 1998—; lectr. law Atty. Gen.'s Advocacy Inst., 1982—, (hon.) Nashville Sch. Lab, 1999—; vice chmn. Atty. Gen.'s Adv. Com., 1986-87, chmn. subcom. on sentencing guidelines, mem. subcom. on budget and office mgmt., 1982-91; instr. math. and bus. law Augusta (Ga.) Coll., 1966-69; instr. law Nashville Sch. Law, 1999—. Contbr. articles to legal jours. Bd. dirs. Mid-Cumberland Drug Abuse Coun., Nashville, 1977-86; asst. scoutmastr Boy Scouts Am.; vestryman St. David's Episcopal Ch., sr. warden, 1982, 90; ch. atty. Episcopal Diocese of Tenn., 1995-98; lt. col. CAP, 1996—. Maj. U.S. Army, 1965-71; col. JAGC, USAR ret. Decorated Legion of Merit, Meritorious Svc. medal with 3 oak leaf clusters; recipient Disting. Svc. award Atty. Gen.'s Adv. Com., 1988. Fellow Tenn. Bar Assn., Nashville Bar Found.; mem. FBA (treas. 1978), Nashville Bar Assn. (bd. dirs. 1995-97, exec. com. 1996-97, v.p. 1997), Radio Amateur Transmitting Soc. (pres. 1997-98), Nat. Assn. Flight Instrs., Profl. Assn. Div Instrs., Ky. Bar Assn., NRA (life, Disting. Rifleman award), Harry Phillip Inn of Ct. (master of bench and bar 1994—), Order of Coif, Phi Beta Kappa. Republican. Home: 3427 Woodmont Blvd Nashville TN 37215-1421 Office: US Courthouse 801 Broadway Nashville TN 37203-3816

BROWN, JOHN CARTER, art and education consultant, federal agency administrator; b. Providence, Oct. 8, 1934; s. John Nicholas and Anne (Kinsolving) B.; m. Pamela Braga, 1976 (div. 1991); children: John Carter IV, Elissa Lucinda Rionda. AB summa cum laude, Harvard U., 1956, MBA, 1958; postgrad., U. Munich, 1958; studied with Bernard Berenson, Florence, Italy, 1958; mus. tng. course, Ecole du Louvre, Paris, 1958-59, The Netherlands Inst. Art History, 1960; MA, Inst. Fine Arts, N.Y. U., 1961; LLD (hon.), Brown U., 1970; LHD (hon.), Mt. St. Mary's Coll., 1974, Georgetown U., 1975, George Washington U., 1978; DFA (hon.), Roger Williams Coll., 1978, Coll. William and Mary, 1984, RISD, 1984, Phila. Coll. Art, 1987, Marquette U., 1988, Washington Coll., 1993; DPS (hon.), Bowling Green State U., 1979, U. Mich., 1992; DHL (hon.), Mt. Vernon Coll., 1987, U. Md., 1990, Tougaloo Coll., 1994. Asst. to dir. Nat. Gallery Art, Washington, 1961-63, asst. dir., 1964-68, dep. dir., 1968-69, dir., 1969-92, dir. emeritus, 1992—; chmn. Pritzker Architecture Prize Jury, 1979—, Leadership Coun., Nat. Cultural Alliance, 1992—, U.S. Commn. of Fine Arts, Ovation, Inc., The Arts Network, 1993—; bd. govs. John Carter Brown Libr., Brown U.; bd. dirs. Nordstern Ins. Co. Am. Author, dir. (film) The American Vision, 1965, (exhbn.) Rings: Five Passions in World Art, 1996; contbr. articles to profl. jours. Trustee Brown U., Morris and Gwendolyn Catritz Found., Doris Duke Charitable Found., Vira I Heinz Endowment, John F. Kennedy Ctr. for Performing Arts, Am. Acad. in Rome, Nat. Geog. Soc., Storm King Art Ctr., World Monuments Fund, Am. Fedn. Arts, John Nicholas Brown Ctr. for Study of Am. Civilization, Fed. City Coun.; treas. White House Hist. Assn., Fed. Coun. on the Arts and Humanities; mem. Com. for the Preservation of the White House, Fed. Coun. on the Arts and Humanities, Nat. Adv. Coun. Leonard Bernstein Ctr. for Edn. through the Arts, State Hermitage Mus. Adv. Bd. Decorated comdr. Ordre des Arts et des Lettres (France), 1975; knight Légion d'Honneur (France), 1976; comdr. Order Republic of Egypt, 1979; comdr. Order of Orange-Nassau (The Netherlands), 1982; commendatore Order of Merit of Italian Republic, 1984; knight Order of St. Olav (Norway), 1979; knight comdr. Order of Isabel la Católica (Spain), 1985; grande oficial Order of Prince Henry the Navigator (Portugal), 1992; Austrian Cross of Honor for Arts and Letters; comdr. Royal Order of Polar Star (Sweden), 1988; comdr. of British Empire (U.K.), 1993; recipient Gold medal of honor Nat. Arts Soc., 1972, Disting. Grotonian award Groton (Mass.) Sch., 1986, Gold medal Nat. Inst. Social Scis., 1987, Nat. Medal of Arts U.S., 1991, Disting. Svc. award Am. Assn. Mus., 1993; named Washingtonian of Yr., Washingtonian mag., 1977. Fellow Royal Acad. Arts (hon.), Am. Acad. Arts and Scis., Nat. Acad. Design; mem. AIA (hon.), Am. Philos. Soc., Assn. Art Mus. Dirs. (hon. trustee for life), Touro Synagogue Nat. Heritage Trust(hon. trustee), Phi Beta Kappa. Episcopalian. Avocations: sailing, photography, music. Office: Ste 621 1201 Pennsylvania Ave NW Washington DC 20004-2401*

BROWN, JOHN EUGENE, social science educator, retired minister; b. Ft. Wayne, Ind., July 3, 1931; s. Clifford Leo and Edith Eunice (Bolinger) B.; m. Edith Ann Beer, June 5, 1953 (div. May 1981); children: Beth Ann Brown-Reinsel, Lisa Suzanne, Christine Louise Brown St. Ours, John Jefferson; m. Gloria Margaret Limberg Hastings, Aug. 1, 1981; 3 stepchildren. BA, DePauw U., 1954; BDiv, San Francisco Theol. Sem., 1957; MA, Johns Hopkins U., 1959; PhD, Ball State U., 1970. Ordained min. Presbyn. Ch., 1961. Univ. chaplain's asst. Johns Hopkins U., Balt., 1958-60; asst. prof. religion Alma (Mich.) Coll., 1960-64; min. Christian edn. Grace Presbyn. Ch., Jenkintown, Pa., 1964-66; vis. asst. prof. history Centre Coll. of Ky., Danville, 1967; tchg. asst. in history Ball State U., Muncie, Ind., 1967-70; prof. history, philosophy and religion Harford C.C., Bel Air, Md., 1970-96; ret., 1996; mem. Presbytery of Balt., 1970-96, honorably ret., 1996. Contbr. articles to profl. jours.; editor Harford Hist. Bull., 1982-85. Commr. Historic Preservation Commn., Harford County, Md., 1994-96; bd. dirs. Mus. Colquitt County History, Ga. Rsch. grantee on Havre de Grace Md., NEH and MD. Humanities Coun., Balt., 1985. Mem. Orgn. Am. Historians, Md. Hist. Soc., Ind. Hist. Soc., Hist. Soc. Harford County Md. (pres. 1986-88), Ga. Hist. Soc., Colquitt County Hist. Soc. (bd. dirs.), Kiwanis Club Moultrie Ga. (bd. dirs.), Bel Air Am. History Club (v.p. 1985-90). Presbyterian. Avocations: history writing, computers, opera, symphony, piano. Home: 1209 2d St SE Moultrie GA 31768-5913

BROWN, JOHN FRED, steel company executive; b. Floydada, Tex., May 20, 1941; s. Rex. R. Brown and Martha L. (McCleskey) Mayfield; m. Karolyn Kay Robertson, July 31, 1960; children: John Robert, Jonathan David, William Charles. BSME, U. Wis., 1968; MBA, Tex. Tech U., 1978. Staff engr. Continental Oil Co., Houston, 1971-73; sr. buyer Continental Oil Co., Lake Charles, La., 1973-74; v.p. WedgeCor, Inc., Billings, Mont., 1974-76; chmn., CEO Tri-Steel Structures, Inc., Denton, Tex., 1976—, Hawk Industries, Inc., Denton, 1978—; chmn. Advanced Framing System, Inc., Conyers, Ga., 1989—. Contbg. author: Steel Homes, 1985. Mem. Rep. Senatorial Inner Circle. With U.S. Army, 1968-69, Vietnam. Decorated Bronze Star. Mem. Ctr. for Entrepreneurial Mgmt., CEO Club, Mensa, Presdl. Roundtable. Mem. Ch. of Christ. Club: Denton Country. Avocations: golf, travel, photography, lic. comml. pilot. Home: RR 1 Box 362E Denton TX 76207-9202 Office: 5400 S Stemmons St Denton TX 76205-2338

BROWN, JOHN HOWARD, economics educator; b. Warren, Ohio, Feb. 4, 1952; s. Howard Graham and Mary Elizabeth (Longfellow) B.; m. Joan Ellen Broome, Dec. 14, 1978; 1 child, Paul Joseph. BA, Buchtel Coll. Arts & Scis., 1978, MA, 1982; PhD in Econs., Mich. State U., 1989. Vis. instr. U. Akron, Ohio, 1983-84, Albion (Mich.) Coll., 1987-88; vis. lectr. Mich. State U., East Lansing, 1988-89; asst. prof. econs. U. Nev., Las Vegas, 1989-94, Ga. So. U., Statesboro, 1994—; mem. 3d World Cliometric Congress, Munich, 1997. Contbr. articles to profl. publs. Bus. and econs. fellow U. Pitts., Czech Republic, 1993. Mem. Am. Econ. Assn., Indsl. Orgn. Soc., Am. Law and Econs. Assn. (presenter ann. meetings 1999), Cliometric Soc. Avocations: golf. Office: Ga So Univ Dept Fin and Econs PO Box 8151 Statesboro GA 30460-1000

BROWN, JOHN LAWRENCE, JR., electrical engineering educator; b. Ellenville, N.Y., Mar. 6, 1925; s. John Lawrence and Grace Evelyn (Freer) B.; m. Marjorie Anne Schnelle, June 15, 1957 (div. Mar. 1969). BS, Ohio U., 1948; PhD, Brown U., 1953. Asst. prof. Pa. State U., State College, 1951-53, assoc. prof., 1953-60, prof. engring. rsch., 1960-69, prof. elec. engring., 1969-88, prof. emeritus, 1988—; Stocker vis. prof. Ohio U., Athens, Ohio, 1988-90. Author numerous papers in profl. jours. With U.S. Army, 1943-46,. Prince vis. fellow Ariz. State U., Phoenix, 1982-83, Gen. Lew Allen Rsch. Chair Air Force Inst. Tech., Dayton, Ohio, 1984-85. Fellow IEEE; mem. Math. Assn. Am., Acoustical Soc. Am. Avocations: tennis, book collecting. Home: 1431 Curtin St State College PA 16803-3020 Office: Pa State Univ 121 Electrical Engineering E University Park PA 16802-2705

BROWN, JOHN LOTT, educator; b. Phila., Dec. 3, 1924; s. John Lott and Carolyn Emma (Francis) B.; m. Catharine Hertfelder, June 11, 1948; children: Patricia Carolyn, Judith Elliott, Anderson Graham, Barbara Smith. B.S. in Elec. Engring, Worcester (Mass.) Poly. Inst., 1945, D.Sc. (hon.), 1984; M.A., Temple U., 1949; Ph.D., Columbia U., 1952. Personnel tng. and personnel mgr. Olney foundry Link-Belt Co., Phila., 1948-50; tech. dir. air force contract, dept. psychology Columbia U., 1952-54; head psychology div., aviation med. lab. Naval Air Devel. Center, Johnsville, Pa., 1954-59; dir. grad. tng. program physiology, 1962-65; asst., then asso. prof. physiology U. Pa. Med. Sch., 1955-65; prof. physiology and psychology Kans. State U., 1965-69; dean Grad. Sch., 1965-66, v.p. acad. affairs, 1966-69; prof. optics and psychology, dir. center visual sci. U. Rochester, N.Y., 1969-78; pres. U. South Fla., Tampa, 1978-88, prof. psychology, physiology and opthalmology, 1978-92, prof. indsl. engring., 1988-92, interim dir. Ctr. for Micoelectronic Rsch., 1993-94, pres. emeritus, 1988—; interim pres. Worcester Poly. Inst., 1994-95; chmn. com. vision NRC-Nat. Acad. Scis., 1965-70; chmn. vision rsch. program com. Nat. Eye Inst., 1975-78; trustee Worcester Poly. Inst., 1970-83, mem. alumni coun., 1975-76; trustee Illuminating Engring. Rsch. Inst., 1974-79; mem. U.S. nat. com. Internat. Commn. Optics, 1977. Author chpts. in books, also monographs, articles, 1953—; cons. editor: Perception and Psychophysics, 1972-90; editorial adv. bd.: Vision Research, 1971-77. Bd. dirs. Pub. Broadcasting Service, 1980-83, Mid-Am. Inst. Profl. Devel., 1980-82, Fla. Gulf Symphony, 1979-81, Tampa Gen. Hosp. Found., 1980-81, Smith-Kettlewell Eye Rsch. Inst., 1991-97; mem. Fla. Council 100, 1978-88; mem. corp. bd. Tampa Performing Arts Hall, 1980-88; chmn. Tampa Bay Area Research and Devel. Authority, 1979-86, Tampa Bay Area Fgn. Affairs Com., 1979-92; chmn. bd. dirs. H. Lee Moffitt Cancer Ctr. and Rsch. Inst., 1984-88, Exec. Svc. Corp. of Tampa Bay, 1989-97, pres., 1994. Served with USNR, 1943-46. Recipient Research Career Devel. award NIH, 1961-62, Robert Goddard award Worcester Poly. Inst., 1969; sr. research fellow USPHS, 1959-61; grantee NIH; grantee NSF; grantee Office Naval Research; grantee Nat. Eye Inst.; grantee NIMH; grantee NASA. Fellow Optical Soc. Am. (exec. coun. Rochester chpt. 1975-76, assoc. editor jour. 1972-77), Am. Psychol. Assn., AAAS; mem. Assn. Rsch. Vision and Ophthalmology (pres. 1978), Soc. Neurosci., Psychonomic Soc., Fla. Assn. Colls. and Univs. (pres. 1988-89), Sigma Xi, Tau Beta Pi, Psi Chi, Phi Eta Sigma, Phi Kappa Phi, Omicron Delta Kappa, Phi Gamma Delta. Quaker. Home: 105 Kendal Dr Oberlin OH 44074-1905

BROWN, JOHN O., banker; b. Kansas City, Mo., Jan. 15, 1934; s. O.L. and Harriett M. (Baker) B.; m. Peggy, Sept. 16, 1955; children—Anne, J. David, Carol, J. Alan. BS in Bus. Adminstrn, U. Kans., 1955. Vice chmn. Commerce Bancshares, Inc., Commerce Bank NA; bd. dirs. Key Industries, Inc. Mem. Robert Morris Assos. Presbyterian. Club: University. Home: 4809 W 81st St Shawnee Mission KS 66208-5031 Office: Commerce Bank 10th Walnut St Kansas City MO 64106

BROWN, JOHN PATRICK, newspaper executive, financial consultant; b. N.Y.C., Oct. 14, 1925; s. Patrick and Emma A (McCarrick) B.; m. Caroline T. Hopkins, Oct. 17, 1959; children: John Patrick, Anne B. Loftus. B.B.A., St. John's U., Jamaica, N.Y., 1949; M.B.A., N.Y.U., 1960. C.P.A., N.Y. Accountant Arthur Young & Co., C.P.A.s, N.Y.C., 1950-58; asst. treas. Paramount Pictures Corp., 1962-65; controller, treas. Washington Star, 1966-76; v.p. fin., treas. Bergen Evening Record Corp., N.J., 1976-82; dir. fin. and adminstrn. Washington Times, 1982-88; adj. prof. acctg. Am. U., U. Va., Va. Tech. Served with AUS, 1944-46. Mem. AICPA, Fin. Execs. Inst., Internat. Newspaper Fin. Execs. Roman Catholic. Club: Metropolitan (Washington). Home and Office: 4230 Embassy Park Dr NW Washington DC 20016-3619

BROWN, JOHN ROBERT, lawyer, priest, philanthropist; b. Muskogee, Okla., Apr. 22, 1948; s. John Robert and Betty Jane (Singleterry) B. BA, MA, Cambridge U., 1972; STB, Gen. Theol. Sem., 1973; STM, Union Theol. Sem., 1978, Harvard U., 1981; MA, STL, U. Louvain, Belgium, 1983; JD, Howard U., 1991. Bar: Ga. 1991, D.C. 1991, U.S. Supreme Ct. 1997; ordained priest Episcopal Ch., 1972. Tchr., headmaster St. John's Sch., Oklahoma City, 1973-77; novice Soc. St. John the Evangelist, Cambridge, Mass., 1979-81; minor canon Pro-Cathedral of Holy Trinity, Brussels, Belgium, 1981-83; assoc. rector St. James Ch., L.A., 1983-87; hon. assisting priest Ch. of the Ascension and St. Agnes, Washington, 1987-91; legis. aide U.S. Ho. of Reps., Washington, 1987-91; hon. asst. priest Ch. of Our Savior, Atlanta, 1991—; staff atty. Ga. Legal Svcs., Atlanta, 1991-1995; asst. gen. counsel State Bar Ga., Atlanta, 1996—; reader Ecumenical Inst. World Coun. Ch., Geneva, 1978, Huntington Libr., San Marino, Calif., 1985-86, Coll. of Preachers, Nat. Cathedral, Washington, 1987, fellow, Center for Ethics in Public Policy and the Professions, Emory U., 1996-98. Contbr. articles to profl. jours. Bd. dirs. S.W. Assn. Episcopal Schs., 1974-77, Anglican Roman Cath. Commn. of Beligum, 1981-83, Cmty. Counseling Svc., L.A., 1983-86, Acad. Performing Arts, L.A., 1984-85, Cape Coast Outreach Found., 1984-86, Coun. Battered Women, Atlanta, 1991-94, AID Atlanta, 1993—, Atlanta Opera, 1993—, ACLU of Ga., 1994—, Fund for So. Cmtys., 1995-98, OUT Fund for Lesbian and Gay Liberation, 1996-99, Funding Exch., 1997—, Cathedral of St. Philip Bookstore, 1998—; vol. NIH. 1987-88. Fed. Charitable Campaign, Washington, 1988-89, Atlanta Project, 1991-96; spiritual adv. com. AIDS Project, L.A., 1984-86; Mayor's Task Force on Family Diversity, 1984-86, Mcpl. Elections Com. L.A., 1984-86; governing bd. Robert Wood Johnson Homeless Care Project, L.A., 1985-87; trustees com. Opera Am., 1994-97; co-trustee Freeman Found., 1994-97; adv. bd. Caring Hands Programs, 1983-87; United Way of Metro Atlanta, 1993-97, Metro Atlanta Cmty. Found., 1994-97; chmn. social justice grants com. Threshold Found., 1994-96; chaplain Most Venerable Order of St. John of Jerusalem, 1996—; capt. The Old Guard of Atlanta, 1998—. Named one of Outstanding Young Men of Am., 1974; Yale U. rsch. fellow, 1983; recipient Mayor's Phoenix award, Atlanta, 1997. Fellow Georgia Bar Found. (life); mem. ABA (vice-chmn. fed. legis. com. gen. practice sect. 1989-91), Nat. Lawyers Guild, Nat. Network Grantmakers, Lambda Legal Def. and Edn. Fund, Lesbian and Gay Victory Fund, Met. Opera Guild, Patrons of the Vatican Mus., United Oxford and Cambridge U. Club (London), Harvard Club (Washington), City Tavern (Washington), Lawyers Club (Atlanta). Office: The Hurt Bldg # 800 50 Hurt Plz SE Atlanta GA 30303-2914

BROWN, JOHN ROBERT, computer company executive; b. Humboldt, Tenn., Dec. 11, 1952; s. Robert Henry and Lenora B.; m. Debbie Fay Thompson, June 4, 1976. AS, Jackson State, 1978; BS, U. Tenn., 1982. Enlisted man USN, 1970, advanced through grades to E-5, 1974; resigned, 1979; carrier U.S. Postal Svc., Camden, Tenn., 1978-89; owner Compu-Pals, Camden, 1989—. Chmn. ARC, Benton County, 1991-97. Mem. Masons. Avocations: hunting, camping, boating, planes. Home: 167 Doty St Camden TN 38320-1513 Office: Compu-Pals 309 Highway 641 N Camden TN 38320-3011

BROWN, JOHN WALTER, vocational education supervisor; b. Waverly, Va., Dec. 13, 1937; s. Wilburt Herman and Martha Ann (Holmes) B. BS in Vocat. Indsl. Edn., Va. State U., 1968; MEd in Vocat. Indsl. Edn., Pa. State U., 1970; cert. advanced study in edn., Johns Hopkins U., 1973; PhD in Vocat. Indsl. Edn., Pa. State U., 1976. Cert. tchr., advanced profl., prin., supr., supt., vocat. edn., Md. and Pa. Drafting instr. Peabody Sr. High Sch., Petersburg, Va., 1962-63; electronics instr. Hampstead Hill Jr. High Sch., Balt., 1965-66; electronics instr. Calverton Jr. High Sch., Balt., 1966-73, dep. prin., 1975-80; vice prin. Carver Vocat. Tech. Sr. High Sch., Balt., 1975; ednl. specialist Balt. City Pub. Schs., 1974, coord., 1980-84, div. specialist, 1984-89, curriculum specialist, 1989-93; prin. House One Rowland Intermediate Sch., Harrisburg, Pa., 1993-94; coord. profl. pers. devel. Pa. State Dept. of Edn., Harrisburg, 1994—; instr. Va. State U., Petersburg, 1962-63, Coppin State Coll., Balt., 1972-73; mem. Balt. City Adv. Coun. on Vocat. Edn. and trade adv. subcoms. With U.S. Army, 1963-65. Mem. Am. Vocat. Edn. Assn., Nat. Assn. Indsl. and Tech. Edn., Pub. Schs. Adminstrs. and Suprs. Assn., Johns Hopkins Alumni Assn., Pa. State U. Alumni Assn., Va. State U. Alumni Assn., Iota Lambda Sigma, Phi Delta Kappa. Methodist. Avocations: sports, reading, traveling, writing, gardening. Home: 5914 Charnwood Rd Baltimore MD 21228-1205 Office: Pa State Dept Edn Bur of Vocat Tech Edn 333 Market St Harrisburg PA 17101-2210

BROWN, JOHN WILFORD, surgical/medical company executive; b. Paris, Tenn., Sept. 15, 1934; s. Albert T. and Treva (Moody) B.; m. Rosemary Kopel, June 7, 1957; children: Sarah Beth, Janine. BSChemE, Auburn U., 1957. Process engr. Ormet Corp., Hannibal, Ohio, 1958-62; sr. engr. Thiokol Chem. Corp., Marshall, Tex., 1962-65; with Squibb Corp., Princeton, n.J., 1965-72, asst. to pros., 1970-72; pres. Edward Weck & Co. divsn. Squibb Corp., N.Y.C., 1972-77; chmn. bd. dirs., pres., CEO Stryker Corp., Kalamazoo, Mich., 1979—. Mem. Am. Chem. Soc., Health Industries Mfg. Assn. (bd. dirs.). Democrat. Mem. Ch. of Christ. Office: Stryker Corp 2725 Fairfield Rd Portage MI 49002-1753*

BROWN, JOHN Y., III, state official. BA in History magna cum laude, Bellarmine Coll., Louisville, Ky., 1988; JD with distinction, U. Ky. Coll. Law, Lexington, 1992. Summer assoc. Stoll, Keenon & Park Law Firm, Lexington, Ky., 1990, Brown, Todd & Heyburn Law Firm, Louisville, Ky., 1991; dir. franchising Roasters Franchise Corp., Fort Lauderdale, Fla., 1992-94; sec. of state Commonwealth of Ky., Frankfort, 1996—; grad. asst. Dale Carnegie Tng., 1987-92. Mem. ABA, Ky. Bar Assn. Home: 6910 Windham Pkwy Prospect KY 40059-8863 Office: 700 Capitol Ave Frankfort KY 40601-3410

BROWN, JONATHAN, art historian, fine arts educator; b. Springfield, Mass., July 15, 1939; s. Leonard Melvin and Jeanette (Levy) B.; m. Sandra Backer, July 22, 1966; children: Claire, Michael, Daniel. A.B., Dartmouth Coll., 1960; M.F.A., Princeton U., 1963, Ph.D., 1964; M.A. (hon.), Oxford U., 1981. Mem. faculty Princeton, 1965-73, asso. prof. art and archaeology, 1971-73; asso. prof. art NYU, 1973-75, prof., 1976-84, Carroll and Milton Petrie prof., 1984—; dir. Inst. Fine Arts, 1973-78; Slade prof. fine arts Oxford (Eng.) U., 1981-82; vis. mem. Inst. Advanced Study, Princeton, N.J., 1978-79; adv. com. dept. European paintings Met. Mus. Art, 1974-79; adv. bd. Master Drawings jour.; bd. dirs. Fundacion Duques de Soria, 1990—; curator Am. Phil. Soc., 1992—; Andrew W. Mellon lectr. in fine arts Nat. Gallery of Art, 1994; adv. com. Mus. del Prado. Author: Prints and Drawings by Jusepe de Ribera, 1973, Zurbaran, 1973, Murillo and His Drawings, 1976, Images and Ideas in Seventeenth Century Spanish Painting, 1978, A Palace for a King: The Buen Retiro and the Court of Philip IV, 1980; (with J.H. Elliott) also articles on Spanish art, (with others) El Greco of Toledo, 1982, Velazquez, Painter and Courtier, 1986, (with R.G. Mann) Spanish Paintings of the Fifteenth through Nineteenth Centuries, National Gallery of Art, 1990, The Golden Age of Painting in Spain, 1991, Kings and Connoisseurs: Collecting Art in 17th Century Europe, 1995, (with C. Garrido) Velázquez. The Technique of Genius, 1998, Painting in Spain, 1500-1700, 1998; editor: Picasso and the Spanish Tradition, 1996, Franklin and Condorcet: Two Portraits from the American Philosophical Society, 1997; co-editor: Sources and Documents in the History of Art: Italy and Spain 1600-1750, 1970. Recipient Medalla de Oro de Bellas Artes, Gov. of Spain, 1986; Fulbright fellow, 1964-65; Am. Council Learned Socs. fellow, 1968-69; Nat. Endowment Humanities fellow, 1978-79; Guggenheim fellow, 1980-81; Order of Isabel la Catolica, 1986, Gran Cruz de Alfonso X el Sabio, 1996, Premio Elio Antonio Nebrija U. de Salamanca, 1997. Mem. AAAS, Coll. Art Assn. Am. (Arthur Kingsley Porter prize 1971), Hispanic Soc. Am. (corr.), Am. Philos. Soc., Real Academia de Bella Artes (Madrid, corr.). Home: 71 Battle Rd Princeton NJ 08540-4945 Office: 1 E 78th St New York NY 10021-0102

BROWN, JOSEPH W., JR. (JAY BROWN), insurance company executive. Various positions to chief exec. Fireman's Fund Ins. Cos., 1975-92; chmn. Talegen Holdings, Inc., 1992-98; chmn., chief exec. MBIA Inc., 1998—, MBIA Ins. Cos., 1998—. *

BROWN, JUDITH OLANS, lawyer, educator; b. Boston, May 29, 1941; d. Sidney and Evelyn R. (Lefkovitz) Olans; m. James K. Brown, Oct. 5, 1969. A.B. magna cum laude with distinction, Mt. Holyoke Coll., 1962; LL.B. cum laude, Boston Coll., 1965. Bar: Mass. 1965. Law clk. Supreme Jud. Ct., 1965-66; assoc. Foley, Hoag and Eliot, Boston, 1966-69; chief counsel Mass. Dept. Community Affairs, Boston, 1969-70; atty. adv. Office of Regional Counsel, HUD, Boston, 1970; asst. regional counsel Office of Regional Counsel, HUD, Boston, 1971, assoc. regional counsel, 1971-72; instr. Boston U. Law Sch., 1971; instr. Northeastern U. Sch. Law, Boston, 1972, assoc. prof., 1972-75, prof., 1975-98, prof. emerita, 1998—; vis. prof. Law Sch., Boston Coll., 1992. Contbr. articles to legal jours.; article and book rev. editor: Boston Coll. Indsl. and Comml. Law Rev., 1964-65. Mem. steering com. Lawyers Com. for Civil Rights under Law; trustee Kimball Union Acad. Loeb fellow, 1972-73. Mem. Order of Coif, Phi Beta Kappa. Home: PO Box 82 Plainfield NH 03781-0082 Office: 400 Huntington Ave Boston MA 02115-5005

BROWN, JUNE GIBBS, government official; b. Cleve., Oct. 5, 1933; d. Thomas D. and Lorna M. Gibbs; children: Ellen Rosenthal, Linda Windsor, Victor Janezic, Carol Janezic. BBA summa cum laude, Cleve. State U., 1971, MBA, 1972; postgrad., Cleve. Marshall Law Sch., 1973-74; JD, U. Denver, 1978; postgrad. Advanced Mgmt. Program, Harvard U., 1983. Cert. govt. fin. mgr., 1995; CPA. Real estate broker, officer mgr. N.E. Realty, Cleve., 1963-68; staff acct. Frank T. Cicirelli, C.P.A., Cleve., 1970-71; asst. to comptr. S.M. Hexter Co., Cleve., 1971; grad. tchg. fellow Cleve. State U., 1971-72; dir. internal audit Navy Fin. Ctr., Cleve., 1972-75; dir. fin. sys. design Bur. of Land Mgmt., Denver, 1975-76; project mgr. Bur. of Reclamation, 1976-79; insp. gen. Dept. Interior, Washington, 1979-81, NASA, Washington, 1981-85; v.p. fin. and adminstrn. Sys. Devel. Corp., a Burroughs Co., 1985-86; assoc. adminstr. for mgmt. NASA, 1986-87; insp. gen. U.S. Dept. Def., Arlington, Va., 1987-90; dep. insp. gen. USN-CINCPACFLT, 1990; insp. gen. USN Pacific Fleet, Pearl Harbor, Hawaii, 1991-93, HHS, Washington, 1993—; inspector gen. HHS, SSA, Washington, 1995-96; bd. dirs. Fed. Law Enforcement Tng. Ctr., 1984-85, Interagy. Auditor Tng. program Dept. Agr. Grad. Sch., 1983-85; chmn. interagy. com. on Info. Resource Mgmt., 1984-85; mem. bd. advisors Nat. Contract Mgmt. Assn., 1987-89; mem. Pres.'s Coun. on Integrity and Efficiency, 1993—, vice chair, 1994-97, rep. Nat. Intergovtl. Audit Forum, 1994-98, mem. adv. coun. Govt. Auditing Stds., 1996—; bd. dirs. Inspectors Gen. Auditor Tng. Inst. Mem. bd. advisors Howard U. Sch. Bus., 1987-89. Recipient award Am. Soc. Women Accts., 1969, 70, 71, Raulston award Cleve. State U., 1971, Pres.'s award Cleve. State U., 1971, Outstanding Achievement award U.S. Navy, 1973, Career Svc. award Chgo. region Fed. Exec. Bd., 1974, Outstanding Contbn. to Fin. Mgmt. award Denver region Fed. Exec. Bd., 1977, Donald L. Scantlebury award Joint Fin. Mgmt. Improvement Program, 1980, Outstanding Svc. award Nat. Assn. Minority CPA Firms, 1980, NASA Exceptional Svc. medal, 1985, Outstanding Achievement in Aerospace award, 1987, Woman of Yr. award, YWCA 1988, Bur. Land Mgmt., Dept. Interior, 1975, Disting. Pub. Svc. award Dept. Def., 1989, Meritorious Civilian Svc. award U.S. Navy, 1993, Nat. Capital Area chpt./Govt. Exec. Mag. award for leadership, 1994, George Washington U. Pi Alpha Alpha Pub. Svc. award, 1996; named Disting. Alumni Cleve. State U., 1990. Fellow Nat. Acad. Pub. Adminstrn. (standing panel exec. orgn. and mgmt., pub. svc. panel); mem. AICPAs, Assn. Govt. Accts. (nat. pres. 1985-86, nat. exec. com. 1977-87, vice chmn. nat. ethics com. 1978-80, 90, chmn. fin.

mgmt. standards bd. 1981-82, service award 1973, 76, 93, outstanding achievement award 1979, Robert W. King Meml. award 1988, dir. Hawaii chpt. 1991-93, disting. fed. leadership award 1998, Disting. Fed. Leadership award 1998), Hawaii Soc. CPAs (bd. dirs. 1991-93), Am. Accts. Assn., Nat. Contract Mgmt. Assn. (bd. advisors 1988-90), NASA Alumni Assn., Women in Aerospace, ASPA (at-large mem. nat. coun. 1994-98, Profl. Responsibility Exemplary Practice award 1990, pres.-nat. capital area chpt. 1989), Exec. Women in Govt., Beta Alpha Psi. Office: HHS Inspector Gen 330 Independence Ave SW Washington DC 20201-0001

BROWN, KAREN K., federal judge; b. 1947. BA, U. Pa., 1970; JD, U. Houston, 1973. Bar: Tex. 1974, U.S. Dist. Ct. (so. dist.) Tex. 1974, U.S. Ct. Appeals (5th cir.) 1974, U.S. Dist. Ct. (we. dist.) Tex. 1978. Law clk. to Hon. John Brown U.S. Ct. Appeals (5th cir.), 1973-75; law clk. to Hon. Woodrow Seals U.S. Dist. Ct., 1975-76; mem. staff Fed. Pub. Defenders Office, 1976-82; pvt. practice Houston, 1982-83; magistrate judge U.S. Dist. Ct. (so. dist.) Tex., 1984-90; bankruptcy judge U.S. Dist. Ct. (so. dist.) Tex., Houston, 1990—. Office: US Dist Ct So Dist Tex 10501 Fed Bldg 515 Rusk Ave Houston TX 77202

BROWN, KAREN RIMA, orchestra manager, Spanish language educator; b. N.Y.C., Apr. 26, 1943; d. Alexander and Leona (Rosenfeld) Jaffe; m. Russell Vernon Brown, Aug. 13, 1966; children: Stephanie Leona and Gregory Russell. BA, Colby Coll., 1965; MA, U. Wis., 1966. Teaching asst. U. Wis., Madison, 1965-66; instr. Spanish U. Wis., Janesville, 1966-68, Baraboo, 1968-70, Eau Claire, 1970-71; instr. Spanish Ohio U., Zanesville, 1978-98, assoc. prof., 1998—; mgr. Southeastern Ohio Symphony, New Concord, 1977—; lectr. Spanish Muskingum Coll., New Concord, 1984, 97—; mem., music panelist Ohio Arts Coun., Columbus, 1979-83, 90-93; pres. S.E. Ohio Regional Arts Coun., Zanesville, 1978-80. Bd. dirs. Muskingum County Visitors and Conv. Bur., Zanesville, 1987-90, bd. sec., 1989-90; bd. dirs. Assn. of Two Toledos, 1984-87, Ohio Citizens Com. for Arts, Canton, 1979-84; regional coord. Ohio Citizens for the Arts, 1995—. Mem. Am. Assn. Tchrs. Spanish and Portuguese, Ohio Valley Fgn. Lang. Assn., Bus. and Profl. Women, Phi Beta Kappa, Phi Sigma Iota, Sigma Delta Pi (hon.). Democrat. Avocations: travel, consultant to arts organizations, mentor for gifted high school students. Office: Southeastern Ohio Sym Orch PO Box 42 New Concord OH 43762-0042

BROWN, KATE, state legislator; b. Torrejon de Ardoth, Spain, 1960. BA, U. Colo.; JD, Lewis and Clark Northwestern. Mem. Oreg. Ho. of Reps., 1991-96, Oreg. Senate, 1996—; atty. Democrat. Address: PO Box 82699 Portland OR 97282-0699 Office: Oreg State Senate State Capitol S-323 State Capitol Salem OR 97310

BROWN, KATHERINE JANE, editor, retired, chamber of commerce executive; b. Corinth, Miss., Jan. 17, 1924; d. William Lloyd and Sara Camille (Ray) Parker; m. Frederic Warren Brown, July 9, 1944; children: Kathy Lee Clementz, Melanie Sue Peters, Robin Eric, Frederic Warren II. Diploma, Palestine Twp. H.S., 1942. Postal clk. U.S. Post Office, Palestine, Ill., 1942; sec. import-export mgr. John Oster Mfg. Co., Genoa, Ill., 1944; owner boutique Jane's in Genoa, Ill., 1961-64; state editor, retired Daily Gazette, Sterling, Ill., 1964-71; sec.-mgr. Genoa C. of C., 1971-78. Editor Parker Pathways newsletter, 1986—. Recipient Hon. Mention award Heart of Am. Geneol. Soc. & Libr. Inc., 1997. Fellow Kishwaukee Valley Heritage Mus. Soc. (sec. 1989-90). Mem. Pentecostal Ch. Avocations: art collection, cooking, geneology. Home and Office: 32785 Genoa Rd Genoa IL 60135-8229

BROWN, KATHLEEN, state treasurer, lawyer; d. Edmund G. and Bernice Brown; m. George Rice (div. 1979); children: Hilary, Alexandra, Zebediah; m. Van Gordon Sauter, 1980; 2 stepsons. BA in History, Stanford U., 1969; grad., Fordham U. Sch. Law. Mem. L.A. Bd. Edn., 1975-80; with O'Melveny & Myers, N.Y.C., then L.A.; commr. L.A. Bd. Pub. Works, 1987-89; elected Treas. of Calif., 1990-94; exec. v.p. Bank of Am., L.A., 1994-99; pres. Pvt. Bank West, L.A., 1999—. Democrat. Office: Bank of Am 555 S Flower St Fl 51 Los Angeles CA 90071-2300*

BROWN, KATHRYN ELIZABETH, development director; b. Charleston, W.Va., May 7, 1973; d. Harold Eugene and Betty Lou (Keeney) B.; m. Michael L. Reed, Oct. 18, 1997. BA, U. Charleston, 1995, postgrad. Exec. prodr., host WVLC Channel 11, Charleston, 1994-96; physician placement coord. Charleston Area Med. Ctr., 1995-96; dir. annual giving, alumni rels. U. Charleston, 1996—. Host, prodr. (TV program) Petagree, 1994-96. Chair Charleston Jr. League Publs. Mem. Nat. Soc. Fundraising Execs., Coun. Advancement Support Edn., U. Charleston Alumni Assn. (exec. dir. 1996—), Jr. League Charleston. Presbyterian. Avocations: cooking, traveling, animals. Home: 631 Gordon Dr Charleston WV 25314-1751 Office: U Charleston 2300 Maccorkle Ave SE Charleston WV 25304-1045

BROWN, KEITH, musician, educator; b. Colorado Springs, Colo., Oct. 21, 1933; s. Kenneth Vernon and Audrey Lucille (Nelson) B.; m. Leslee Joanne Scullin, June 13, 1954 (div. Jan. 1991); children: Robert Vernon, Lise Joanne, Kristin Patricia; m. Joann Alexander, May 14, 1994. B.Mus., U. So. Calif., 1957; M.Mus., Manhattan Sch. Music, 1964. Trombonist Indpls. Symphony Orch., 1957-58; mem. faculty, solo trombonist Aspen Festival, 1957-69; trombonist N.Y. Brass Quintet, 1958-59; prin. trombonist Casals Festival, San Juan, P.R., 1958-80; assoc. prin. trombonist Phila. Orch., 1959-62; prin. trombonist Met. Opera Orch., 1962-65; performed with Chamber Music Soc. of Lincoln Ctr., 1969-88; participant Marlboro Festival, 1970-73; dir. instrumental activities, prof. music, condr. univ. orch. Temple U., Phila., 1965-71; prof. emeritus, condr. Ind. U., Bloomington, 1971-97; condr., music dir. Bloomington Symphony Orch., 1975-80; chmn. brass dept., condr. Music Acad. of West, 1978-82, 85-87; co-founder Ensemble Mediation, 1998—; artistic dir., condr. Camerata Orch., Bloomington, 1989-96; artistic/mus. dir. InterAm. Youth Orch. of the Festival Casals, San Juan, P.R., 1989-91. Regular guest condr. Orquesta Sinfonica Venezuela, coach, adv., guest condr. Orquesta Nacional Juvenil Simón Bolívar, Caracas, 1979—; coach, adviser Joven Orquesta Nacional de Espana, 1984-94; bd. advisers N.Y. Cornet and Sacbut Ensemble, 1984—; tchr. master classes, lectr., recitalist (1st western trombonist), conservatories in Beijing and Shanghai, China, 1982, Beijing, 1988; guest condr. Sapporo (Japan) Symphony Orch., 1990, Orquesta del Principado de Asturias, Spain, 1991; author 10 vols. orchestral studies for trombone and tuba, numerous edits. of solos, brass ensembles, study materials, 1960—. Served with U.S. Army, 1953-56. Recipient spl. award Asociacion Musical, Caracas, Venezuela, 1979, Alumni award U. So. Calif. Sch. Music, 1957; Nat. Arts assoc. Sigma Alpha Iota, 1995. Mem. Internat. Trombone Assn., Phi Mu Alpha Sinfonia, Pi Kappa Lambda, Kappa Kappa Psi (hon.). Methodist. Club: Rotary. Avocations: tennis, sailing. Home: 2925 Olcott Blvd Bloomington IN 47401-2403

BROWN, KEITH LAPHAM, retired ambassador; b. Sterling, Ill., June 18, 1925; s. Lloyd Heman and Marguerite (Briggs) B.; m. Carol Louise Liebmann, Oct. 1, 1949; children: Susan, Briggs (dec.), Linda, Benjamin. Student, U. Ill., 1943-44, Northwestern U., 1946-47; LLB, U. Tex., 1949. Bar: Tex., Okla., Colo. Assoc. Lang, Byrd, Cross & Ladon, San Antonio, 1949-55; v.p., gen. counsel Caulkins Oil Co., Oklahoma City, 1955-70, Denver, 1955-70; founder, developer Vail Assocs., Colo., 1962; pres. Brown Investment Corp., Denver, 1970-87; developer Colo. State Bank Bldg., Denver, 1971; amb. to Lesotho Dept. State, 1982-84; amb. to Denmark Dept. State, Copenhagen, 1988-92; ret., 1992; chmn. Brown Investment Corp., Denver, 1993—. Chmn. Rep. Nat. Fin. Com., 1985-88; hon. trustee, past pres. bd. Colo. Acad. Served with USN, 1943-46. Mem. Denver Country Club, San Antonio Country Club, Univ. Club, Bohemian Club. Presbyterian. Address: PO Box 1172 Edwards CO 81632-1172 also: 11 Auburn Pl San Antonio TX 78209-4739 Office: 1490 Colo State Bank Bldg 1600 Broadway Denver CO 80202-4927

BROWN, KENNETH CHARLES, manufacturing company executive; b. Ft. Collins, Colo., July 9, 1952; s. Charles Calvin and Barbara Ann (Brookhart) B.; m. Victoria Marie Martin, July 27, 1984; children: Bryson John Kenneth, Charles Brookhart, Theodore McFarlane, Kenneth Cashin. BSME, Cornell U., 1974; MA in Engring. Sci. and Econs., Oxford U., Eng., 1977. Registered profl. engr., Colo. Assoc. engr. Stone & Webster Engring. Corp., Boston, 1974-75; with Solar Energy Rsch. Inst., Golden, Colo., 1977-79, sr. engr., 1979-80, mgr., 1980; mgr. Sci. Applications Internat., Golden, 1980-82; mgr. Price Waterhouse, Denver, 1982-84, sr. mgr., 1984; v.p. Inspiration Resources Corp., N.Y.C., 1985-91; gen. mgr. GE Co., Plainville, Conn., 1992-93; nat. exec., CEO GE Mex., Mexico City, 1994-95; pres. GE Southeast Asia, Singapore, 1996-99, Skidmore, Owings & Merrill LLP, N.Y.C., 1999—. Contbr. chpts. to books. Mem. Cornell U. Council, 1979-83, Rhodes Scholarship Selection Com., Topka, Mpls., 1978-84. Recipient World Rowing Championship Gold medal, Fedn. Internat. Soc. d'Aviron, 1974; Rhodes scholar, 1975. Mem. Am. C. of C. Mex. (v.p. 1995), Am. C. of C. Thailand, Cornell Soc. Engrs., Cornell Club N.Y. Episcopalian. Avocations: skiing, horseback riding, diving. Home: GE Internat Singapore #42 32 Sawmill Ln Greenwich CT 06830 Office: Skidmore Owings & Merrill 14 Wall St New York NY 10005

BROWN, KENNETH LLOYD, lawyer; b. N.Y.C., Sept. 28, 1927; s. Edythe Schneider; m. Freya Dorothy Finkelstein, July 10, 1954; children: Ivy Hope Brown Hill, Patrice Shari. BS, NYU, 1951; LLB, St. John's U., Bklyn., 1954. Bar: N.Y. 1955. Pvt. practice Forest Hills, N.Y., 1955-61; asst. corp. counsel City of N.Y., 1962-78; ptnr. Rivkin, Radler & Kremer and predecessor firms, Uniondale, N.Y., 1977-98; pvt. practice Jamaica, N.Y., 1998—. Dem. dist. leader Queens County Dem. Orgn., Forest Hills, until 1982; mem. Forest Hills Jewish Ctr. With U.S. Army, 1945-47. Mem. Queens County Bar Assn. (various coms.), Am. Legion, Jewish War Vet. Post, B'nai B'rith, Masons, Knights of Pythias. Avocation: politics. Home: PO Box 457 Flushing NY 11375-0457

BROWN, KENNETH RAY, banker; b. Cherokee, Okla., July 6, 1936; s. Tom Melton and Mary Elizabeth (Foster) B.; m. Elizabeth Kay Callahan, Oct. 17, 1964; children—Kathryn Sue, Elizabeth Ann, Angela Kay. B.B.A., U. Okla., 1957. Vice pres., then sr. v.p., sr. investment officer Bank One Okla., N.A., Oklahoma City, 1965-79, exec. v.p., 1979—. Mem. Inst. Chartered Fin. Analysts, Okla. Soc. Fin. Analysts, Econ. Club Okla. Presbyterian. Office: Bank One Okla NA 100 Broadway Cir Oklahoma City OK 73170-7220

BROWN, KENT LOUIS, JR., magazine editor; b. Cleve., Nov. 24, 1943; s. Kent L. and Elizabeth (Myers) B.; m. Jolyn Taylor; children: Maj Turi, Boyd Benjamin, George Kent. Student, U. Hawaii, 1963-65; BA in English, Hobart Coll., 1967; postgrad., SUNY-Oswego, 1969; MS in English Edn., Syracuse U., 1971; D in Herbopsychiatry, Am. Inst. Herbopsychiatry, 1985. Cert. tchr., N.Y. Mgmt. trainee Agway, Inc., Phelps, N.Y., 1967-68; vegetable grower Clyde, N.Y., 1968-71; tchr. Lyons Cen. Sch., N.Y., 1969-71; asst. editor Highlights for Children, Honesdale, Pa., 1971-76; mng. editor Highlights for Children, Honesdale, 1976-78, editor, 1978—, dir., 1976—, v.p., 1979—; pub. Boyd Mills Press, 1990—; chmn. bd. Serendipity Ctr., Inc., Honesdale, 1971-72; sec., treas. Fox Hill Lumber Co., 1977—. Mem. Coop. Extension Assn., Wayne Conty, Pa., 1979-81; exec. dir. Highlights Found., 1988—; dir. Wayne County Agrl. Land Preservation Bd. With U.S. Army, 1963-65. Recipient Honesdale Jaycees Boss of Yr. award, 1990. Mem. ALA, Am. Soc. Mag. Editors, Ednl. Press Assn. Am. (pres. 1986-87), N.Y. Reading Assn. (N.Y. State Reading Friend of Literacy award 1994), Wayne County Farmers Assn., Internat. Reading Assn., Nat. Coun. Tchrs. English, Nat. Press Club. Republican. Club: Honesdale Country (dir. 1981-82). Office: Highlights for Children 803 Church St Honesdale PA 18431-1895*

BROWN, KENT NEWVILLE, ambassador; b. Oakland, Calif., May 7, 1944; s. Victor B. and Mary E. (Shaver) B.; m. Norma Giorno, Dec. 29, 1995; children from previous marriage: Steven D., Karen E. BA, U. Calif., Davis, 1964, MA, 1966. 3rd sec. U.S. Embassy, Panama, 1967-69; 2nd sec. U.S. Embassy, Prague, Czechoslovakia, 1970-73; watch officer to exec. secretariat U.S. Dept. of State, Washington, 1973-74; fellow Hoover Instn., Stanford, Calif., 1974-75; officer Soviet desk U.S. Dept. of State, Washington, 1976-80; 1st sec. U.S. Embassy, Moscow, 1980-83; sr. advisor U.S. Arms Control Del., Vienna, Austria, 1984-88; office dir. Strategic Nuc. Policy U.S. Dept. of State, Washington, 1989-90; polit. advisor Supreme Allied Comdr. Europe, Belgium, 1990-92; amb. U.S. Embassy, Tbilisi, Georgia, 1992-95; dir. pers. U.S. Dept. of State, Washington, 1995-96; v.p. govt. rels. Ea. Europe J.T. Internat., Geneva, 1996—; bd. dirs. NATO workshop, Menlo Park, Calif. Bd. dirs. U.S.-Russia Bus. Coun. Mem. Internat. Inst. for Strategic Studies. Office: 12 Ch de Rieu, Geneva 17, Switzerland

BROWN, KEVIN, writer; b. Kansas City, Mo., Sept. 3, 1960; s. John and Duane (Nimmons) B. BA, Columbia U., 1988. Author: Romare Bearden, 1994, Malcolm X, 1995; contbg. editor: New York Public Library African-American Desk Reference, 1999; contbr. articles to profl. jours. including London Times Lit. Supplement, Washington Post Bookworld, others. Gen. Studies scholar Columbia U., 1988. Mem. PEN Am. Ctr. Roman Catholic. Avocations: travel, music, fine arts, wines, cooking. Home: 65-60 Booth St Apt 2E Rego Park NY 11374

BROWN, KEVIN JAMES, real estate broker, consultant; b. Sheboygan, Wis., July 12, 1952; s. Keith Hammond and Jean Lois (Van Ouwerkerk) B.; m. Ana Ligia Arevalo, Mar. 14, 1986 (div. Sept. 6, 1997). BA in English, Denison U., 1974; doctoral candidate, U. Pitts., 1997; MBA in Mgmt., Pepperdine U., 1980. Mgr. Flying Tiger Line, San Francisco, 1978-81; founder, pres. Angel Enterprises, Foster City, Calif., 1981-83; mgr. aerospace mktg. CF Airfreight, Inglewood, Calif., 1983-85; regional mgr. TNT Express divsn. Kwikasair, Inglewood, Calif., 1985; gen. mgr. Three Way Corp., Hawthorne, Calif., 1985-86; v.p. ops. Boardroom Bus. Products, Costa Mesa, Calif., 1986-88; dist. mgr. Nat. Inst. Bus. Mgmt., L.A., 1988; ind. contractor, realtor, broker Culver City, Calif., 1988-91; mng. broker. br. mgr. Vol. Realty Co., Knoxville, Tenn., 1991-93; franchise devel. sr. market analyst Coldwell Banker Residential Affiliates, Mission Viejo, Calif., 1993-96. Featured guest Sta. WIVK, 1992; contbr. articles to profl. jours. Named Hon. Ky. Col., 1993. Mem. ACLU, Am. Polic. Sci. Assn., Acad. Polit. Sci., Soc. Study Social Problems, Acad. Mktg. Sci., Policy Studies Orgn., Pub. Citizen, World Future Soc., Wolf Edn. and Rsch. Ctr., Common Cause, Denison U. Alumni Assn., Pepperdine U. Alumni Assn., Silver Saddle Homeowners Assn., So. Poverty Law Ctr. Democrat. Avocations: reading, music, pets, computers, genealogy. Home: 7070 Forward Ave Apt 102 Pittsburgh PA 15217-2549

BROWN, KRISTI, principal. Prin. Holy Rosary Sch, Seattle. Recipient Elem. Sch. Recognition award U.S. Dept. Edn., 1989-90. Office: Holy Rosary Sch 4142 42nd Ave SW Seattle WA 98116-4202

BROWN, L(ARRY) EDDIE, tax accountant, real estate broker, financial planner; b. Hanging Limb, Tenn., Aug. 31, 1941; s. Earl and Lois Ovoca (Norrod) B.; m. Lillian Virginia Edwards, Feb. 9, 1965; children: Clifford Bruce, Michael Dwayne, Jennifer Noelle. BBA, Ga. State U., 1974, MBA, 1976. Cert. tax profl.; accredited tax advisor, enrolled agent. Mgmt. trainee Citizens Bank, Cookeville, Tenn., 1963-65; office mgr. Redisco, Tampa, Fla., 1965-67; methods analyst Delta Air Lines, Atlanta, 1967-83; owner Brown Enterprises, College Park, Ga., 1971—; pres. So. Heritage Properties, Inc., 1984—; instr. Ga. State U., 1976-80. Bd. dirs. Ga. Spl. Olympics, Atlanta, 1983-90; Ga. del. White House Conf. on Small Bus., 1995, Congl. Small Bus. Summit, 1998. With USAF, 1959-63. Mem. Nat. Soc. Tax Profls. (Ga. state com. 1994—), Nat. Assn. Tax Practitioners (Ga. bd. dirs. 1994-98), Nat. Soc. Pub. Accts., Ga. Assn. Pub. Accts. (pres. So. Cres. chpt. 1993-95, bd. govs. 1994—, 1st v.p. 1996-97, pres. 1997-99), Internat. Assn. Fin. Planners, Nat. Assn. Securities Dealers, Atlanta Bd. Realtors. Mormon. Clubs: Civitan (pres. Airport-Southside, Atlanta 1982-83, treas. Airport Area, Atlanta 1979-81, Civitan of Yr. chpt. 1982, bd. dirs. Ga. dist. north 1984-86, trustee Ga. dist. North Found. 1985-88), Masons. Office: Brown Enterprises 392 Glynn St N Fayetteville GA 30214-1191

BROWN, LARRY R., lawyer; m. Priscilla Ann Long, Aug. 3, 1958; children: Cynthia E. DeLoach, Scott D. BSc in Bus. Adminstrn., Ohio State U., 1957, JD summa cum laude, 1960. With Day, Ketterer, Raley, Wright & Rybolt, Canton, Ohio, 1960-90, mng. ptnr., 1985-90; sr. v.p., gen. counsel Timken Co., Canton, Ohio, 1990—. Office: Timken Co 1835 Dueber Ave SW Canton OH 44706-2798

BROWN, LAURENCE DAVID, retired bishop; b. Fargo, N.D., Feb. 16, 1926; s. John Nicolai and Ada Amelia (Johnson) B.; m. Virginia Ann Allen, Sept. 6, 1950; children: Patricia Ann, Julia Louise, Claudia Ruth. BS, U. Minn., 1946; BA, Concordia Coll., 1948; M of Theology, Luther Theol. Sem., 1951. Ordained to ministry Evang. Luth. Ch., 1951. Pastor Our Savior's Luth. Ch., New Ulm, Minn., 1951-55; nat. assoc. youth dir. Evang. Luth. Ch., Mpls., 1955-60; nat. youth dir. Am. Luth. Ch., Mpls., 1960-68; instn. dir. Tchr. Tng., U. Minn., Mpls., 1968-69; exec. dir. Freedom from Hunger Found., Washington, 1969-73; sr. pastor St. Paul Luth. Ch., Waverly, Iowa, 1973-79; bishop Iowa Dist. Am. Luth. Ch., Des Moines, 1979-89, N.E. Iowa Synod, Evang. Luth. Ch. in Am., Waverly, 1989-92; prof. religion Wartburg Coll., Waverly, Iowa, 1992-93; interim sr. pastor Ctrl. Luth. Ch., Mpls., 1994-95, Calvary Luth. Ch., Mpls., 1996-97; bd. regents Luther Coll., Decorah, Iowa, 1989-92, Wartburg Coll., 1988-92, Wartburg Theol. Sem., Dubuque, Iowa, 1988-91, Self-Help, Inc., 1989-94. Author: Take Care: A Guide for Responsible Living, 1983; contbr. articles to profl. jours. Lt. USN, 1943-46. Lutheran. Avocation: reading. Home: 7201 York Ave S Apt 514 Edina MN 55435-4444

BROWN, LAWRENCE HAAS, banker; b. Evanston, Ill., July 29, 1934; s. Robert C. and Alice (Haas) B.; m. Ann Ferguson, June 23, 1956; children—Michael, Kenneth, Russell. Student, Cornell U., Ithaca, N.Y., 1952-54; B.B.A., U. Mich., 1956. Sr. v.p. No. Trust Co., Chgo., 1958-89, ret., 1989; chmn. Pub. Securities Assn., N.Y.C., 1980; vice chmn. Mcpl. Securities Rulemaking Bd., Washington, 1982; bd. dirs. Nuveen Open-end and Exch. Traded Funds. Pres. Highwood (Ill.) Pub. Libr., 1993-97. Lt. USN, 1956-58. Republican. Presbyterian. Clubs: Exmoor Country (Highland Park, Ill.) (pres. 1984-85); Municipal Bond (pres. 1977). Avocations: tennis; curling; golf. Home: 201 Michigan Ave Highwood IL 60040-1808

BROWN, LAWRENCE HARVEY (LARRY BROWN), basketball coach; b. Brooklyn, NY, Sept. 14, 1940. Student, U. North Carolina, Chapel Hill, NC, 1959-63. Amateur basketball player Akron Goodyears, Akron, OH, 1963-65; asst. coach U. North Carolina, Chapel Hill, NC, 1965-67; player New Orleans (ABA), New Orleans, LA, 1967-68, Oakland (ABA), Oakland, CA, 1968-69, Washington (ABA), 1969-70, Virgina Squires (ABA) - Denver Nuggets (ABA), 1970-71, Denver Nuggets (ABA), Denver, CO, 1971-73; head coach Carolina Cougars (ABA), 1972-74, Denver Nuggets (ABA), 1974-76, Denver Nuggets (NBA), Denver, CO, 1976-79, UCLA, Los Angeles, CA, 1979-81, New Jersey Nets (NBA), Newark, NJ, 1981-83, U. Kansas, Lawrence, KS, 1983-88, San Antonio Spurs (NBA), San Antonio, TX, 1988-92, Los Angeles Clippers (NBA), Los Angeles, CA, 1992-93, Indiana Pacers (NBA), Indpls., 1993-97, Phila. 76ers (NBA), 1997—; mem. Am. Basketball Assn. All-Star Team, 1968-70; led Am. Basketball Assn. in assists, 1968-70, coached team to NCAA Basketball Finals, 1980; mem. U.S. Olympic Team, 1964, Am. Basketball Assn. Championship Team, 1969. Named Most Valuable Player ABA All-Star Game, 1968, ABA Coach of the Yr., 1973, 75. Office: Phila 76ers First Union Ctr 3601 S Broad St Philadelphia PA 19148*

BROWN, LEE PATRICK, federal official, law enforcement educator; b. Wewoka, Okla., Oct. 4, 1937; s. Andrew and Zelma (Edwards) B.; m. Yvonne Carolyn Streets, July 14, 1958 (dec.); children: Patrick, Torri, Robyn, Jenna; m. Frances M. Young, Dec. 29, 1996. BA, Fresno State U., 1960; MA, San Jose State U., 1964; MS, U. Calif., 1968, D in Criminoloy, 1970; D of Pub. Affairs (hon.), Fla. Internat. U., 1982; LLD (hon.), John Jay Coll., 1985; HHD (hon.), Portland State U., 1990; LHD (hon.), Fresno State U., 1994; LLD (hon.), SUNY Brockport, 1995. Officer San Jose (Calif.) Police Dept., 1960-68; prof. Portland (Oreg.) State U., 1968-72; assoc. dir. Urban Affairs Inst. Howard Inst., Washington, 1972-75; sheriff Sheriff's Dept., Mulnomah County, Oreg., 1975-76; dir. Dept. Justice Services, Mulnomah County, 1976-78; commr. Dept. Pub. Safety, Atlanta, 1978-82; chief of police Houston Police Dept., 1982-90; police commr. N.Y.C., 1990-92; prof. Tex. So. Univ., 1992—; dir. Nat. Drug Control Policy, Washington, DC, 1993-96; mem. Pres. Cabinet, 1993-96; prof. Rice Univ., HOuston, 1996-98; mayor City of Houston, 1998—; adj. prof. U. Houston, U. Tex. Health Sci. Ctr., Houston, Tex. So. U., Houston; cons. U.S. Dept. Justice, Washington, Police Found., Washington, various state and local govts., Houston; chmn. Nat. Minority Adv. Council on Criminal Justice; mem. Nat. Adv. Commn. on Criminal Justice Standards and Goals, Washington, Nat. Commn. on Higher Edn. for Police, Washington, Commn. on Accreditation for Law Enforcement Agencies, Washington, Presdl. Task Force, 1993—. Co-author: Attitudes of Black Police Officers, 1976, Police and Society, 1981; editor: Neighborhood Team Policing, 1976, Violent Crime, 1981; author of numerous articles and book chpts. Bd. dirs. Boy Scouts Am., United Way, Urban League, Blue Bonnet Bowl, "Just Say No", Peoples Workshop for Visual and Performing Arts, Houston, 1987—, Nat. Black Child Devel. Inst., Washington, 1987—, Nat. Alliance Against Violence, N.Y., 1986—, Sheltering Arms, Houston, 1985—; task forcemem. Nat. Ctr. for Missing and Exploited Children, Washington, 1986—; adv. bd. Nat. Inst. Against Prejudice and Violence, Balt., 1987—; mem. Police Activities League, Houston, 1987—; mem. adv. policy bd. Nat. Incident Based Reporting System, 1988—. Recipient Peace and Justice award Martin Luther King Jr., 1981, Nat. Law Enforcement award Nat. Black Police Assn., 1982, Disting. Alumnus award Fresno State U., 1983, Police Leadership award, Police Exec. Research Forum, 1987, Liberty Bell award Houston Young Lawyers Assn., 1987, August Vollmer award Am. Soc. Criminology, 1988, Cartier Pasha award Cartier Internat., 1992, Exemplary Leader award Am. Leadership Forum, 1994; named to Gallup Hall of Fame by Gallup, Inc., 1993; named Mgr. of Yr., Nat. Mgmt. Assn., Practitioner of Yr., Nat. Assn. of Blacks Criminal Justice, 1984, Communicator of Yr. Washington News Service, 1986, Father of Yr. Nat. Father's Day com., 1991; rsch. fellow Harvard U., 1988. Mem. Internat. Assn. Chiefs of Police (past pres.), Nat. Orgn. of Black Law Enforcement Execs. (v.p. 1985, Robert Lamb Jr. Humanitarian award 1987), Police Exec. Research Forum, Internat. Narcotic Enforcement Officers Assn., Nat. Forum for Black Pub. Adminstrs., N.Y. Police Chiefs Assn., Tex. Police Assn., Tex. Criminal Justice Task Force, Nat. Police Athletic League, Mich. State U. (adv. council nat. neighborhood foot patrol ctr.), Nat. Research Council (com. on research on law enforcement and the adminstrn. of justice, com. on status of Black Ams.), Harvard U. (com. exec. session on community policing), Nat. Council on Crime and Delinquency (bd. dirs.), Nat. Acad. Pub. Adminstrn. (Nat. Pub. Svc. award 1988), Am. Soc. Pub. Adminstrn. (Nat. Pub. Svc. award 1988), Am. Leadership Forum, Forum Club of Houston (bd. dirs. 1987—), Calif. Alumni Club of Tex., Houston Bus. and Profl. Men's Club, Alpha Phi Alpha, Sigma Pi Phi. Democrat. Avocations: travel, reading. Office: City Hall 901 Bagby St Fl 3 Houston TX 77002-2526*

BROWN, LEON CARL, history educator; b. Mayfield, Ky., Apr. 22, 1928; s. Leon Carl and Gwendolyn (Travis) B.; m. Anne Winchester Stokes, Aug. 29, 1953; children: Elizabeth Boone, Joseph Winchester, Jefferson Travis. B.A., Vanderbilt U., 1950; postgrad., U. Va., 1950-51, London Sch. Econs., 1951-52; Ph.D., Harvard, 1962. Fgn. Svc. officer. Beirut, 1954-55, Khartoum, Sudan, 1956-58; asst. prof. Mid. Ea. studies Harvard U., Cambridge, Mass., 1962-66; assoc. prof. Nr. Ea. history and civilization Princeton (N.J.) U., 1966-70, Garrett prof. fgn. affairs, 1970-93, Garrett prof. emeritus, 1993—, chmn. dept. Nr. Ea. studies, 1969-73, dir. program Nr. Ea. studies, 1969-73, 80-93. Author: (with C.A. Micaud and C.H. Moore) Tunisia: The Politics of Modernization, 1964, The Tunisia of Ahmad Bey, 1974, International Politics and the Middle East, 1984; editor: State and Society in Independent North Africa, 1966, From Madina to Metropolis: Heritage and Change in the Near Eastern City, 1973, (with Norman Itzkowitz) Psychological Dimensions of Near Eastern Studies, 1977, Centerstage: American Diplomacy Since World War II, 1990, (with Cyril E. Black) Modernization in the Middle East, 1992, Imperial Legacy: The Ottoman Impact On The Balkans & The Middle East, (with Matthew Gordon) Franco-Arab Encounters, 1996; translator with commentary: The Surest Path; The Political Treatise of a 19th Century Muslim Statesman, 1967. Served with USAAF, 1945-46. Mem. Middle East Studies Assn. (pres. 1975-76). Home: 191 Hartley Ave Princeton NJ 08540-5613

BROWN, LES (LESTER LOUIS), journalist; b. Indiana Harbor, Ind., Dec. 20, 1928; s. Irving H. and Helen (Feigenbaum) B.; m. Jean Rosalie Slaymaker, June 12, 1959; children: Jessica, Joshua, Rebecca. B.A. in English, Roosevelt U., Chgo., 1950. Entertainment industry reporter, reviewer theatrical events Chgo. bur. Variety, 1953-55; asso. editor Downbeat mag., 1955; co-founder, operator folk music cabaret The Gate of Horn, Chgo., 1956; Chgo. bur. mgr. Variety, 1957-65; editor radio-TV dept. N.Y.C., 1965-73, asst. mng. editor, 1973; radio-TV corr. N.Y. Times, 1973-80; editor in chief Channels mag., 1980-87; sr. v.p. editorial devel. C.C. Pub., N.Y.C., 1987-91; pub. TV Bus. Internat. mag., 1988-91, editor in chief, 1990-91; columnist, 1992—; pub. World Guide, 1990; editorial cons. Ctr. for Communication, N.Y.C., 1991—; cons. Revson Found., 1978, World Alliance TV for Children, 1993—, Golden Rose Montreux TV Festival, 1994—, Monte Carlo TV Festival, 1994—; lectr. creative writing and entertainment industries Columbia Coll., Chgo., 1959-62, scholar-in-residence, 1985; lectr. comm. Hunter Coll., N.Y.C., 1973-75, New Sch., N.Y.C., 1977-83, Columbia U., 1994-96; lectr. Fordham U., 1995—, dir. The TV Pantheon Oral History Project, 1996; Poynter fellow in modern journalism Yale U., 1977, lectr., 1978-80; assoc. fellow Morse Coll., 1978-86; Presdl. fellow Aspen Inst., 1978; mem. bd. Humanitas Prize, 1980-87, Peabody Awards, 1983-88, Dore Schary Awards, 1987—, World TV and Radio Coun. UNESCO; sr. fellow Freedom Forum Media Studies Ctr. Columbia U., 1992-93. Author: lyrics Abilene, 1963, Television: The Business Behind The Box, 1971, Electric Media, 1973, New York Times Encyclopedia of Television, 1977, Keeping Your Eye on Television, 1979; Les Brown's Encyclopedia of Television, 1982, Fast Forward: The New Television and American Society, 1983, Les Brown's Encyclopedia of Television, 1992; also articles. Mem. Film-TV adv. bd. N.Y. State Coun. on Arts, 1975; pres. Media Commentary Coun. Inc. With AUS, 1951-53. Recipient Silver Cir. award N.Y. Chpt. Nat. Acad. TV Arts and Scis., 1996; Ctr. Digital Future fellow. Office: Ctr for Communication 271 Madison Ave New York NY 10016-1001

BROWN, LESTER RUSSELL, research institute executive; b. Bridgeton, N.J., Mar. 28, 1934; s. Calvin C. and Delia (Smith) B.; m. Shirley Ann Woolington, June 12, 1960 (div.); children: Brian, Brenda. BS in Agrl. Sci., Rutgers U., 1955; MA in Agrl. Econs., U. Md., 1959; MPA, Harvard U., 1962; hon. degree, Dickinson Coll., U. Md., Franklin Coll., Williams Coll., Rutgers U., Glassboro State Coll., Tufts U., Coll. of Wooster, Clark U., Ripon Coll., Otterbein Coll., U. Pisa, McGill U., U. Notre Dame, Northland Coll., St. Lawrence U.; hon. deg., Claremont Coll., Villanova U., Westminster Coll. With Dept. of Agr., 1959-69, adminstr. internat. agr. devel. service, 1966-69; sr. fellow Overseas Devel. Council, 1969-74; pres. Worldwatch Inst., Washington, 1974—; mem. faculty Salzburg Seminar in Am. Studies, summer 1971, 74; guest scholar Aspen Inst., summers 1972-74; project dir., co-author State of the World, 1984-95; adv. com. mem. Population Reference Bur., Inst. for Internat. Econs. Author: Man, Land and Food, 1963, Increasing World Food Output, 1965, Seeds of Change, 1970, World Without Borders, 1972, In the Human Interest, 1974, (with Erik Eckholm) By Bread Alone, 1974 (Christopher award), The Twenty-Ninth Day, 1978 (Ecologia Firenze award), (with Colin Norman and Christopher Flavin) Running on Empty, 1979, Building a Sustainable Society, 1981, State of the World, 1984—, (with others) Vital Signs, 1992—, Full House, 1994, Who Will Feed China?, 1995, Tough Choices: Facing the Challenge of Global Food Scarcity, 1996; editor: (with Ed Ayres) World Watch Reader, 1998, (with Flavin and Sandra Postel) Saving the Planet, 1991, (with Gardner and Halweil) Beyond Malthus, 1999, numerous others; also articles. Mem. adv. com. Inst. Internat. Econs., Com. for Nat. Insts. for Environ., UN Found., Eco-Policy Ctr./Rutgers U.; mem. bd. advisors Internat. Fund for China's Environment; mem. internat. coun. Earth Day 2000; mem. internat. adv. com. Asahi Shimbun Create 21; bd. dirs. N.W. Environment Watch, Inst. for Sustainable Devel., Poland; mem. adv. coun. Internat. Fund for Agrl. Rsch.; advisor Clean Up the World Project, Australia, Internat. Coun. Earth Day 2000; mem. adv. bd. Ctr. for a New Am. Dream. Recipient Superior Svc. award Dept. Agr., 1965, Arthur S. Flemming award, 1965, A.H. Boerma award UN Food and Agrl. Orgn., 1981, Lorax award Global Tomorrow Coalition, 1985, award World Wildlife Fund for Nature Internat., 1989, UN Environment prize, 1989, A Bizzozero award U. Parma, 1990, Humanist of Yr. award, 1991, Pro Mundo Habitabili award King Carl XVI Gustaf, Sweden, 1991, Delphi Internat. Cooperation award, 1991, Robert Rodale Lectr. award, 1992, Environmentalist of Yr. award Japan Jaycees, 1992, Cert. Spl. Recognition Assn. Am. Geographers, 1993, Blue Planet prize Asahi Glass Found., 1994, J. Sterling Morton Arbor Day award, 1995, Pub. Svc. award Fedn. Am. Scientists, 1995, Disting. Achievement award Heylar House Alumni Assn. Rutgers U., 1995; selected as 100 Who Made A Difference The Earth Times, 1995, 100 Champions of Conservation Audubon Soc., 1998. Mem. Coun. Fgn. Rels., Zero Population Growth (nat. adv. bd.), World Future Soc., Cosmos Club. Office: Worldwatch Inst Ste 800 1776 Massachusetts Ave NW Washington DC 20036-1995

BROWN, LILLIAN HILL, retired educator; b. Newport News, Va., Nov. 24, 1932; d. Charlie Wyatt and Caroline Melinda (Rowlett) Hill; m. Louis Franklin Brown, June 30, 1956; children: Avery L., Colin H. BS, Va. State Univ., 1955; MS, U. Bridgeport, 1967, profl. diploma advanced study, 1983; post grad., So. Conn. State Univ., 1985. Chmn. guidance and pers. svcs. Wilby H.S., Waterbury, Conn., team mem. student assistance team, coord. natural helpers program, proctor SAT coll. bds. prog.; mem. pres.'s adv. bd. Teikyo Post U.; admission advisor com. Naugatuck Valley Comty.-Tech. Coll.; adv. bd. to bd. govs. for higher edn. in Waterbury; adv. panel Racial Imbalance Regulations of Pub. Schs. in Conn.; regional adv. bd. dirs. Bank Boston. Bd. trustees St. Margaret's-McTernan Sch.; bd. dirs., chmn. nominating com. Waterbury Symphony Orch.; trustee, chair nominating com. The Antiquarian and Landmark Soc.; bd. dirs. Children's Comty. Sch.; chmn. bd. dirs. Waterbury chpt. ARC; bd. trustees, chmn. scholarship com. The Waterbury Found.; bd. mgrs., mem. The Waterbury Club; mem. devel. com. Waterbury Hosp. Health Network, Inc.-Waterbury Hosp.; vestry bd., chalice bearer St. John's Episcopal Ch.; life mem. NAACP; mem. Waterbury chorale; co-founder In Search of Excellence A Scholarship Fund for African Am. Students; incorporator Child Guidance Clinic. Recipient Plaque for Outstanding Leadership in Comty., Tribute to Conn. Women, Plaque for Outstanding Leadership in Comty., Alpha Kappa Alpha, Achievement award Nat. Assn. Negro Bus. and Profl. Woman's Clubs, Inc., Comty. Svc. award Waterbury Jaycees, 1991, St. John's Order of the Eagle, 1995. Mem. NEA (life), Conn. Edn. Assn., Waterbury Tchr. Assn., Pupil Pers. and Guidance Assn., The Sch. Counselor (Conn. chpt.), Phi Delta Kappa (Plaque for Dedicated Svc. to U. of Conn. chpt. 1993), Delta Sigma Theta (charter mem. New Haven alumnae chpt.), The Links, Inc. (charter mem. Waterbury chpt.). Avocations: domestic and foreign travel, collecting Llardo porcelain. Home: 59 Timber Ln Waterbury CT 06705-3608

BROWN, LINDA LOCKETT, nutrition management executive, nutrition consultant; b. Jacksonville, Fla., Jan. 8, 1954; d. Willie James and Katie Lee (Taylor) Lockett; m. Thomas Lee Brown, Dec. 18, 1982; children: Ashanti, William, Timothy. BS in Agr., U. Fla., 1975, M of Agr., 1981. Lic. profl. nutritionist; cert. food svc. dir. III; registered dietitian; cert. lifestyle counselor in stress and weight management. Chemist/microbiologist Green Giant Co., Alachua, Fla., 1975-77; lab. technologist II U. Fla., Gainesville, 1977-81, extension agt. I, Ft. Myers, 1981-85, extension agt. II, 1985-87, West Palm Beach, 1987-88; pres. CINET, Inc., 1985—, nutritionist head start, Jacksonville Fla.; area supr. Palm Beach County Sch. Food Svc., 1988-90; adj. prof. Palm Beach Community coll., 1990, Fla. C.C., Jacksonville, 1993—; dir. sch. food svc. St. Johns County, 1990—; nutrition cons. Congregate Meals, Ft. Myers, 1984-87, Serenity House, Ft. Myers, 1985-87; cons. Performax, 1989—; vis. prof. U. Fla. Coop. Ext. Svc., Clay County, 1996—; treas. St. Augustine chpt. Internat. Food Svc. Execs. Assn., 1993—; apptd. by gov. Fla. Health and Human Svcs. Bd., elected vice chair, 1993-94, chair, 1994-96. Columnist Palm Beach Post, 1989—; diabetes educator Diabetes Treatment Ctr. Am., Jacksonville, 1997—. Contbr. articles to profl. jours.; host nutrition digest radio show Sta. WZNZ-AM, Jacksonville, Fla., 1996—. Mem. exec. bd. Community Coordinating Coun., Ft. Myers, 1985; Am. Heart Assn., Palm Beach, 1989-90; co-founder Friends of Hearing Impaired Youth, Gainesville, 1976; tutor-coord. Sampson, Gainesville, 1973; mem. Jr. League, Ft. Myers, 1987; mem. Jr. League, Palm Beach, Fla., 1987-90, mem. edn. tng. com., community rsch. com. 1989-90; mem. nutrition com. Am. Heart Assn., Palm Beach, 1989—. State U. System Bd. Regents grantee, 1980. Mem. NAFE, Soc. Nutrition Edn. (legis. network chmn.), Am. Diabetes Assn. (mem. profl. adv. com. Jacksonville affiliate 1996), Am. Dietetic Assn. (network of blacks in nutrition, chair legis. com. 1988-89, chair nominating 1989, sec. 1989-90, state profl. recruitment coord.), Fla. Dietetic Assn. (chair minority issues com., chair membership 1987-88, chair edn. and registration 1988-90, state profl. recruitment coord. rep. Fla. chpt., chair nominating com. 1994—), Palm Beach Dietetic Assn. (community nutrition chair 1988-89, chair legis. com. 1989-90), Caloosa Dietetic Assn. (sec.), Nat. Speakers Assn., Sch. Food Svcs. Assn. (1988—), Nat. Assn. Extension Home Econs. Agts., Internat. Platform Assn., Jacksonville Dietetic Assn., Nutrition Today Soc., Alpha Zeta, Epsilon Sigma Phi. Club: Greater Palm Beaches Bus. and Profl. Women (minority student mentor, role model mentor), Nat. Speakers Assn., N. Fla. Profl. Speakers Assn. Avocations: singing, violin. Office: 2717 Cedarcrest Dr Orange Park FL 32073-6509

BROWN, LINDA M., neurologist; b. July 11, 1950. MD, Medical Coll. Pa., 1976. Dir. Maine Medical Ctr. Epilepsy Program, Portland, 1991—. Office: Maine Medical Coll 930 Congress St Portland ME 04102-3032

BROWN, LINDA MEGGETT, reporter; b. Charleston, S.C.; d. James Lee and Arabell (Cohen) M. BA in Journalism, Marshall U., 1985. Reporter Herald Dispatch, Huntington, W.Va., 1985-88, Desert Sun, Palm Springs, Calif., 1988-90; reporter govt. Santa Barbara (Calif.) News-Press, 1990-92; reporter gen. assignment Post and Courier, Charleston, S.C., 1992—. Author: Black Issues in Higher Education, 1994—, U.S. Black Engineer and Information Technology, 1997-99. Planning com. mem. YWCA, Charleston, 1994-97. Mem. Nat. Assn. Black Journalists, S.C. Coastal Assn. Black Journalists (treas. 1993-97, pres. 1998-2000), Sigma Gamma Rho (v.p. Delta Iota Sigma chpt. 1996-97). Methodist. Avocations: travel, reading, exercise. Home: 7121 Highway 162 Hollywood SC 29449-5603 Office: Post and Courier 134 Columbus St Charleston SC 29403-4800

BROWN, LINDA WEAVER, academic administrator; b. Pottsville, Pa., Aug. 29, 1941; d. Robert Roland and Blanche (Cox) Weaver; m. Harold Lewis Brown Jr., June 9, 1962; children: Garth Weaver, Blythe Elizabeth, Grant Christian. BA, Gettysburg Coll., 1963; MEd, U. Hawaii, 1965; MA, Carnegie-Mellon U., 1970, PhD, 1972. Faculty Point Park Coll., Pitts., 1967-68, asst. dean admissions, 1968-69; faculty Allegheny C.C., Pitts., 1969-72, U. Santa Clara, Calif., 1976-80, Bentley Coll., Waltham, Mass., 1986-88; chair humanities Endicott Coll., Beverly, Mass., 1988-89; v.p. comms. Brown Assoc., Concord, Mass., 1989-91; dir. edn. Bunsai Gakuen Boston Inst Intercultural Comm., Lincoln, Mass., 1991-93; divsn. chair English and ESL Roxbury C.C., Boston, 1994-96; v.p. Brown Assocs., Concord, Mass., 1997—; cons., spkr. in field. Author book rev. New Perspectives on Down Syndrome, 1989. Bd. dirs. Mental Health Assoc., Middlesex County, 1985-89, Minuteman Assn. for Retarded Citizens, Concord, 1990-92. Named Outstanding Young Woman from Hawaii, Bus. and Profl. Women, 1966; faculty grantee Allegheny C.C., 1969, 70, 71, U. Santa Clara, 1978, 79, 80. Mem. AAUP, AAUW, Alpha Psi Omega. Avocations: music, advocacy, reading, cross cultural studies. Home: 384 Caterina Hts Concord MA 01742-4752 Office: Brown Assocs 384 Caterina Hts Concord MA 01742-4752

BROWN, LISA ROCHELL, academic administrator; b. Akron, Ohio, Feb. 14, 1962; d. James Allen and Elaine (Foster) B.; 1 child, Bridjette Nicole. BS in Biology, U. Akron, 1986, MPA, 1991. Coord. peer counseling program U. Akron, 1986-90, rsch. assoc., 1991-92; coord. minority admissions and retention programs Miami U., Oxford, Ohio, 1990-91; dir. intercultural rels. Edinboro U. of Pa., 1992—; ind. cons. Lorain (Ohio) County C.C., 1992—; faculty advisor Alliance for Racial Identity and Cultural Acceptance, Intercultural Diplomats. Bd. dirs. Booker T. Washington Ctr., Hamilton, 1990-91, Walking in Black History, JFK Cmty. Ctr., Erie, Pa., 1998; chair scholarship com. Arlington Christian Acad., Akron, 1991-93; chair Met. Erie Intervention Program, 1994—. Recipient Dr. MLK Jr. Day of Svc. award Corp. for Nat. Svc., 1998; grantee Erie Ins. Group Inc., 1996-98, Erie Cmty. Found., 1997, Pa. State Sys. Higher Edn., 1997. Mem. Alpha Kappa Alpha. Mem. Ch. of God. Avocations: aerobics, singing, exercise, reading, basketball. Office: Edinboro U Pa 201 University Ctr Edinboro PA 16444

BROWN, LLOYD DAVID, association executive, management educator; b. New Haven, Conn., Mar. 22, 1941; s. Lloyd and Laura Whitney (Dodge) B.; m. Jane Gibson Covey, June 14, 1969; children: Rachel Covey, Nathan Lloyd. BA in Social Rels., Harvard Coll., 1963; LLB, Yale U., 1969, MPhil in Organizational Behavior, 1969, PhD in Organizational Behavior, 1971. Community organizer Peace Corps, Dessie, Ethiopia, 1963-65; from asst. to assoc. prof. organizational behavior Case Western Res. U., Cleve., 1971-80; pres. Inst. Devel. Rsch., Boston, 1980—; from assoc. to full prof. Boston U. Sch. Mgmt., 1981—, chmn. organizational behavior, 1981-86, 97-99, faculty dir. doctoral program, 1993-95; Fulbright vis. lectr. Pub. Enterprise Ctr. for Continuing Edn., New Delhi, India, 1979-80; cons. Ford Found., WHO, World Bank, USAID, Asia and Africa, 1980—; vis. prof. pub. policy Kennedy Sch. Govt., Harvard U., 1999—, assoc. dir. internat. programs Hauser Ctr. for Non-Profit Orgn., 1999—. Author: Learning From Changing, 1974, Managing Conflict at Organizational Interfaces, 1983, The Struggle for Accountability: NGO'S, Social Movements and the World Bank, 1998; contbr. articles to profl. jours. Assoc. Synergos Inst., N.Y.C., 1987—; mem. adv. coun. Vol. Fgn. Aid, Washington, 1997—. Mem. Nat. Inst. Applied Behavioral Sci. (bd. dirs. 1981-84), Acad. Mgmt. (pres. organizational devel. div. 1982-85). Democrat. Avocations: skiing, tennis, science fiction. Office: Inst Devel Rsch 44 Farnsworth St Boston MA 02210 also: Boston U 595 Commonwealth Ave Boston MA 02215

BROWN, LLOYD HARCOURT, JR., newspaper editor; b. Jacksonville, Fla., Sept. 28, 1939; s. Lloyd H. and Zada Elizabeth (Bentley) B.; m. Geraldine Raulerson (div. 1975); children: Lloyd H. III, Lori; m. Patricia Levine; 1 child, Amanda Dale. BA, U. North Fla., 1980. Copy boy Jacksonville Jour., 1957-59, reporter, 1959-79, editor, 1979-81, editorial writer, 1982-83; editorial writer Fla. Times-Union, Jacksonville, 1983-93, editor editorial page, 1993—. Bd. dirs. Goodwill Industries, Jacksonville, 1994; mem. Fla. Bar Grievance Com., Jacksonville, 1994. With USAR and USMC, 1963-93. Avocation: golf. Home: 2833 Doric Ave Jacksonville FL 32210-4318 Office: Fla Times-Union 1 Riverside Ave Jacksonville FL 32202-4904

BROWN, LOIS HEFFINGTON, health facility administrator; b. Little Rock, Mar. 28, 1940; d. Carl Otis and Opal (Shock) Heffington; M. Ivy Roy Brown, June 21, 1984; children: Carletta Jo Rice, Roby Lynn Rice, Pherby Allison Graham, Phelan Missy Graham. Student, Guilford Tech. Community Coll., Jamestown, N.C., 1974-75, 77, 80. Cert. hearing aid specialist. Sec. Berger Enterprises, West Memphis, Ark., 1962-65; office mgr. Beltone Hearing Aid Ctr., Greensboro, N.C., 1975-81; owner Hearing Care Ctr., Cullman, Ala., 1982-85, Miracle-Ear Ctr., Cullman, Decatur, Fultondale, Jasper and Birmingham, Ala., 1985-87; pres. L&I Corp., Cullman, Decatur, Fultondale, Jasper and Birmingham, 1987-90, L & I Corp. Miracle Ear Ctr., Cullman, Decatur, Jasper, Ala., 1991-93; owner Conway (Ark.) Hearing Aid Ctr., 1994—, Beltone Hearing Aid Ctr., Conway, 1995-96; distbr. Showcase Distbg. Co., Conway, North Little Rock, Ark. Gov.-appointed Ala. Bd. Hearing, chmn. of the bd., 1989-91. Mem. Nat. Hearing Aid Soc., Ark. Hearing Soc. (sec. 1996—), Ala. Hearing Aid Dealers Assn. (sec. 1984-86, v.p. 1986-88, bd. dirs. 1988-91), Ark. Hearing Aid Dealers Assn., Women of the Moose. Republican. Baptist. Avocations: music, swimming, gardening, tennis. Home: 199 Highway 107 Enola AR 72047-8101

BROWN, LOMAS, JR., professional football player; b. Miami, Fla., Mar. 30, 1963. Student, U. Fla. Offensive tackle Detroit Lions, 1985-95, Arizona Cardinals, 1996-98, Cleve. Browns, 1999—. Founder Lomas Brown, Jr. Found., 1991. Played in Pro Bowl, 1990-93; named tackle The Sporting News All-America team, 1984, offensive tackle The Sporting News All-Pro team, 1992. Office: Cleve Browns 76 Lou Groza Blvd Berea OH 44017*

BROWN, LOREN DENNIS, internist, educator; b. Des Moines, Feb. 21, 1949; s. Wendell James and Vivian Rose (Young) B.; m. Debra Dee Winders, Feb. 27, 1971; children—Marcus Loren, Melissa Lynn, Katherine Megan. B.A., U. Iowa, 1971; D.O., Coll. Osteo. Medicine and Surgery, Des Moines, 1974. Diplomate: Nat. Bd. Examiners for Osteo. Physicians and Surgeons; bd. cert. internal medicine and med. oncology. Intern, Des Moines Gen. Hosp., 1974-75; resident in internal medicine Chgo. Osteo. Hosp., 1975-76, Youngstown Osteo. Hosp., 1976-77; fellow hematology/med. oncology Cleve. Clinic Found., 1977-79; practice medicine specializing in hematology/med. oncology Ctrl. Iowa Oncology & Hematology Assn. P.C., Des Moines, 1979—, Assoc. Med. Clinic, Des Moines, 1979—; assoc. prof. medicine U. Osteo. Medicine and Health Scis., Des Moines, 1979-96, prof. medicine, 1996—; assoc. investigator North Central Cancer Treatment Grup/Iowa Oncology Research Assn., Des Moines, 1980—. Mem. Am. Osteo. Assn., Am. Coll. Osteo. Internists, Am. Soc. Clin. Oncology, Am. Soc. Hematology, Iowa Soc. Osteo. Physicians and Surgeons, Iowa Oncology Research Assn. (co-prin. investigator 1984-90). Roman Catholic. Address: Ctrl Iowa Oncology 411 Laurel St Des Moines IA 50314-3005*

BROWN, LORENE B(YRON), library educator, educational administrator; b. Plant City, Fla., Nov. 9, 1933; d. Benjamin and Sallie (Barton) Byron; m. Paul L. Brown, Aug. 1, 1974. B.S., Fort Valley State Coll., 1955; M.S.L.S., Atlanta U., 1956; Ph.D., U. Wis., 1974. Cataloguer N.C. Central U., Durham, 1956-58, Gibbs Jr. Coll., St. Petersburg, Fla., 1958-60, Fort Valley State Coll., Ga., 1960-65, Norfolk State U., Va., 1965-70; assoc. prof., dean Atlanta U., 1970-89, prof., 1989—; dir. Info. Retrieval Workshops, Atlanta, 1976-78; evaluator Coop. Coll. Library Ctr., Atlanta, 1979-82; cons. United Bd. Coll. Devel., Atlanta, 1976-79. Author: Subject Access for African American Material, 1995. Mem. Friends of Library, Atlanta, 1982. Recipient Rachel Schenk award Library Sch. U. Wis., Madison, 1971; So. Fellowship Found. fellow Atlanta, 1972-74. Mem. ALA, Am. Soc. for Info. Sci., Assn. Library and Info. Sci. Edn., Ga. Library Assn., Met Atlanta Library Assn., Beta Phi Mu. Democrat. Baptist. Home: 855 Flamingo Dr SW Atlanta GA 30311-2402 Office: Atlanta U Sch Libr and Info Studies 223 James P Brawley Dr SW Atlanta GA 30314-4358

BROWN, LORETTA ANN PORT, physician, geneticist; b. Kingston, N.Y., July 30, 1945; d. Frank and Sophie (Hormann) Port; m. Robert Don Brown, Aug. 22, 1970; 1 child, Adrian Robert. BS, SUNY, New Paltz, 1967; MS, U. Mich., 1968, postgrad., 1969; MD, Ea. Va. Med. Sch., Norfolk, 1981. Diplomate Am. Bd. Med. Examiners. Lab. tech. U. Mich., Ann Arbor, 1969-70; rsch. asst. M.D. Anderson Hosp. and Tumor Inst., Houston, 1970; rsch. instr. Baylor Coll. Medicine, Houston, 1971-76; resident internal medicine Ea. Va. Med. Sch., Norfolk, 1981-84; asst. prof. medicine Med. Coll. Hampton Rd, Norfolk, 1984—; physician Health America, Hampton, Va., 1984-87, Tidewater Pulmonary Assocs., Newport News, Va., 1987-88; chief, admitting and screening VA Med Ctr., Hampton, 1988-92, staff physician, 1988—; trainee genetics USPHS, Ann Arbor, Mich., 1967-69; rsch. participant NSF, Albion, Mich., 1966; cons. VA Med. Ctr., 1984-88. Contbr. articles to profl. jours. Recipient Achievement award Am. Med. Women's Assn., 1981, Am. Chem. Soc., 1966. Mem. Am. Morgan Horse Assn., Am. Horse Show Assn. (Morgan judge 1990—), Old Dominion Morgan Horse Assn. (v.p. 1987-89), Va. Carolina Morgan Horse Assn., Nu Pi Sigma. Roman Catholic. Avocations: horses, orchids. Office: VA Medical Ctr 590 170 Hampton VA 23667

BROWN, LORI LIPMAN, secondary school educator; b. Bklyn., June 17, 1958; d. Melvin S. and Anita (Orlen) Lipman; m. Paul R. Brown, June 7, 1986. BA in Communications, U. Nev., Las Vegas, 1981; JD, Southwestern U., Los Angeles, 1983. Bar: Calif. 1983, Nev. 1984, Ariz. 1985. Atty. Melvin S. Lipman, Las Vegas; tchr. speech and drama Eldorado H.S./Clark County Sch. Dist., Las Vegas; state senator dist. 7, Nev., 1992-94; selected for NEA diversity cadre, 1997-99. Corr. sec. Jewish Cmty. Ctr., 1995-96; parliamentarian, nominating com. chair Hadassah Shoshanim Group, Las Vegas, 1995-96; bd. dirs. Planned Parenthood So. Nev., 1993-95, Aid for AIDS Nev., 1993-94. Named Civil Libertarian of Yr. ACLU, 1994; recipient Spotlight Honor Women's Dem. Club, 1993, Legislative Excellence award Citizens Against Nuclear Waste, Nev., 1993, Most Valuable Prisoner award March of Dimes Jail and Bail, 1993, Legislator of Year award Nat. Assn. Social Workers, Nev., 1994, Friend of the Ctr. award Gay and Lesbian Cmty. Ctr. of So. Nev., 1998; honoree Valley Outreach Synagogue, 1999. Mem. Nev. Tchrs. English (Best New Tchr. award 1989), Nev. State Edn. Assn. (mentor tchr. for urban tchr. partnership 1998—, celebration of excellence 1990, English curriculum task force 1991, Excellence in Edn. award 1992), Clark County Classroom Tchrs. Assn., Las Vegas Bus. and Profl. Women (v.p. membership 1995-96. Home: 5408 Bernadette St Las Vegas NV 89122-6906

BROWN, LORRAINE ANN, office manager; b. Providence, Mar. 15, 1947; d. Leonard Francis and Elaine Frances (Pettis) Millen; m. Jeffrey Schofield Brown, May 22, 1976 (div. 1983); 1 child, Kaneeta Sage; m. Dieter Paul Wuennenberg, July 14, 1965; 1 child, Desirée Jacqueline Wuennenberg. Student, Manhattan Sch. Printing, 1972, L.A. Trade Tch. Coll., 1981-83; BA in Bus., Antioch U., 1996. Comms. rep. TransAmerica Occidental, Los Angeles, 1973-77; owner, jewelry designer The Lorraine Brown Co., El Segundo, Calif., 1979-83; mgr. Silk Lingerie Outlet, Sherman Oaks, Calif., 1982-83; office mgr. Am. Silk Label, L.A., 1984; asst. prodn. coordinator Pacific Coast Mills, L.A., 1984-85; asst. designer jr. wear Judy Knapp Inc., L.A., 1986-87; sales exec. Integrated Aquatic Systems, Marina Del Rey, Calif., 1987-88; adminstrv. svcs. coord. GTE Govt. Svcs., El Segundo, Calif., 1988-94; event coord. Jackson Nat. Life Dist., Westwood, 1995-96; office mgr. Ind. Jour. Newspapers, 1996-97; project coord. Complex Legal Svcs., El Segundo, Calif., 1997-98; owner, organizer, event coord., Reiki master, tchr. El Segundo, 1997—. Asst. leader Girl Scouts U.S., El Segundo, 1985-87; P.V.P. leader 4-H, 1991-94; vol. Tree Muskateers and Swift Project. Mem. Am. Bus. Women's Assn., Svcs. Employees Assn. (pres.), Young Exec. Singles, Advanced Degrees, Sierra Singles, Redbird, Art of Living Found. Avocations: gardening, decorating, floral designing, catering. Home: 756 Main St El Segundo CA 90245-3051

BROWN, LOUIS, physicist, researcher; b. San Angelo, Tex., Jan. 7, 1929; s. Metz and Sadie (Johnson) Bishop; m. Lore Elisabeth Frick, July 24, 1952. BS, St. Mary's U., 1950; PhD, U. Tex., 1958. Teaching asst. dept. physics U. Tex. Austin, 1952-58; rsch. asst. dept. physics U. Basle, Switzerland, 1958-61; postdoctoral fellow dept. terrestrial magnetism Carnegie Instn., Washington, 1961-63, staff assoc., 1963-69, staff scientist, 1969-94; emeritus, 1994—; electronics designer Mil. Physics Lab., Austin, 1955-57; acting dir. dept. terrestrial magnetism Carnegie Instn., 1991-92. Contbr. numerous articles to profl. jours. With U.S. Army, 1950-52. Recipient Amerbach prize U. Basle, 1963. Fellow Am. Phys. Soc.; mem. AAAS, Am. Geophysical Union. Achievements include collaboration on building of first operating source of polarized ions, on development of techniques for measuring the cosmogenic isotope 10Be in natural materials, on clarifying nature of threshold state in Be-8, and on demonstrating that lavas from island-arc volcanoes have a sedimentary component. Office: Carnegie Inst Washington Dept Terrestrial Magnetism 5241 Broad Branch Rd NW Washington DC 20015-1305*

BROWN, LOWELL SEVERT, physicist, educator; b. Visalia, Calif., Feb. 15, 1934; s. Volney Clifford and Anna Marie Evelyn (Jacobson) B.; m. Shirley Isabel Mitchell, June 23, 1956; 1 son, Stephen Clifford. AB, U. Calif., Berkeley, 1956; Ph.D. (NSF predoctoral fellow 1956-61), Harvard U., 1961; postgrad., U. Rome, 1961-62, Imperial Coll., London, 1962-63. From research asso. to asso. prof. physics Yale U., 1963-68; mem. faculty U. Wash., Seattle, 1968—; prof. physics U. Wash., 1970—; vis. prof. Imperial Coll., London, 1971-72, Columbia U., N.Y.C., 1990; vis. scientist Brookhaven Nat. Lab., summer, 1965-68, Lawrence Berkeley Lab., summer 1966, Stanford Accelerator Ctr., summer, 1967, CERN, Geneva, summer, 1979, Inst. for Theoretical Physics, U. Calif., Santa Barbara, winter 1999; mem. Inst. Advanced Study, Princeton, N.J., 1979-80; cons. Los Alamos Nat. Lab., spring 1999, vis. scientist, 1991; vis. physicist Deutches Elektronen-Synchrotron, Hamburg, 1986;. Author: Quantum Field Theory, 1992; mem. editl. bd. Phys. Rev., 1978-81; editor Phys. Rev. D, 1987-95; contbr. articles to profl. publs. Trustee Seattle Youth Symphony Orch., 1986-95. Postdoctoral fellow NSF, 1961-63; sr. post-doctoral fellow, 1971-72; Guggenheim fellow, 1979-80. Mem. Ferrari Club of Am. (dir. Northwest region 1999—). Home: 1157 Federal Ave E Seattle WA 98102-4314 Office: U Wash Dept Physics Seattle WA 98195

BROWN, LYNETTE RALYA, journalist, publicist; b. Beloit, Wis., Dec. 15, 1926; d. Lynn Louis and Ethel Clara (Meeker) Ralya; m. Donald Adair Brown, Jr., Dec. 20, 1947; children: Donald Adair III, Alison Laura, Julia Carol. BA in Journalism, Mich. State U., 1948; MA in Journalism, Michigan State U., 1985; MA in Mass Comm., Wayne State U., 1983. Actress, publicist Grand Traverse Playhouse, Traverse City, Mich., 1946 (summer), N.Y. Summer Playhouse, Mackinac Island, Mich., 1947 (summer); writer WILS Radio, Lansing, Mich., 1947-48; writer, performer WJBK Radio, TV, Detroit, 1948-49; editor Denby Ctr. News, Detroit, 1949-51; freelance writer Oakland County, Mich., 1952-78; editor Henry Ford Mus., Dearborn, Mich., 1979-81; writer, reporter Legal Advertiser Newspaper, Detroit, 1983-85; publicist Bloomfield (Mich.) and Birmingham (Mich.) Pub.

Librs., 1986-89; freelance writer, publicist Lynette Brown Comm., Birmingham, Mich., 1989—. Columnist: (newspaper) At the Libraries, 1986-89; solo performer Elizabeth Cady Stanton, 1995—. Probation sponsor Dist. Ct. Mich., 1960-70; publicist Oakland County Vol. Bur., 1979-82; leader sr. high/jr. high youth group Drayton Ave. Presbyn. Ch., Oakland County, 1952-54, 62-66, Pine Hill Congl. Ch., Oakland County, 1968-71, Northbrook Presbyn. Ch., Oakland County, 1976-77; polit. campaign worker Rep. candidates and non-partisan jud. candidates, 1952—; Cub Scout leader Royal Oak Emerson Sch., Oakland County, 1961-64; Girl Scout troop leader Bloomfield Twp. Meadow Lake Sch., Oakland County, 1966-71. Grantee N.Y. State's Thanks Be To Grandmother Winifred Found., 1996. Mem. AAUW (chair women's issues, pub. info. dir. 1995—), Oakland County C. of C. (Athena award 1995). Home and Office: 6120 Westmoor Rd Bloomfield Hills MI 48301

BROWN, MABEL WELTON, lawyer; b. Geneseo, Ill., Dec. 7, 1916; d. Harry E. and Mabel (Welton) B. BA, Oberlin Coll., 1938; JD, U. Chgo., 1941. Bar: Ill. Ptnr. Brown and Brown, Geneseo, 1941-44; sole owner Brown & Brown, Geneseo, 1944-81; sr. ptnr. Brown and Ray, Geneseo, 1981—; atty. Green River Spl. Drainage Dist., Henry and Bureau Counties, Ill.; chmn. Geneseo Planning Commn., 1961-68. Mem. ABA, Ill. Bar Assn., Henry County Bar Assn. (pres. 1973-76). Republican. Methodist. Office: Brown and Ray 115 N State St Geneseo IL 61254-1345

BROWN, MARCIA JOAN, author, artist, photographer; b. Rochester, N.Y., July 13, 1918; d. Clarence Edward and Adelaide Elizabeth (Zimber) B. Student, Woodstock Sch. Painting, summers 1938, 39; student painting, New Sch. Social Research, Art Students League; BA, N.Y. State Coll. Tchrs., 1940; student Chinese calligraphy, painting, Zhejiang Acad. Fine Arts, Hangzhou, Peoples Republic China, 1985, 87; studied painting with Judson Smith, Stuart Davis, Yasuo Kuniyoshi, Julian Levi; LHD (hon.), SUNY, Albany, 1996. Tchr. English, dramatics Cornwall (N.Y.) High Sch., 1940-43; library asst. N.Y. Pub. Library, 1943-49; tchr. puppetry extra-mural dept. U. Coll. West Indies, Jamaica, B.W.I., 1953; tchr. workshop on picture book U. Minn.-Split Rock Arts Program, Duluth, 1986, workshop on Chinese brush painting Brush Artists Guild, 1988; sponsor Chinese landscape painting workshops with Zhuo HeJun, 1988-89; sponsored workshops Chinese caligraphy with A. Wang Dong Ling, 1989, 90, 92; invited speaker exhbn. illustrations, Japan, 1990, 94. Illustrator: The Trail of Courage (Virginia Watson), 1948, The Steadfast Tin Soldier (Hans Christian Andersen), 1953 (Caldecott Honor Book award), Anansi (Philip Sherlock), 1954, The Three Billy Goats Gruff (Asbjornsen and Moe), 1957, Peter Piper's Alphabet, 1959, The Wild Swans (Hans Christian Andersen), 1963, Giselle (Théophile Gautier), 1970, The Snow Queen (Hans Christian Andersen), 1972, Shadow (Blaise Cendrars), 1982 (Caldecott award 1983), How the Ostrich Got His Long Neck (Aardema, Mainichi Japan Picture Book award 1997, Tranlation Winner' prize Mainichi Newspapers and Sch. Libr. Assn. 1997), 1995, (with others) Sing a Song of Popcorn, 1988, Of Swans, Sugar Plums and Satin Slippers (Violette Verdy); author, illustrator: The Little Carousel, 1946, Stone Soup, 1947 (Caldecott Honor Book award), Henry Fisherman, 1949 (Caldecott Honor Book award), Dick Whittington and His Cat (retold), 1950 (Caldecott Honor Book award), Skipper John's Cook, 1951 (Caldecott Honor Book award), The Flying Carpet (retold), 1956, Felice, 1958, Tamarindo, 1960, Once a Mouse (retold), 1961 (Caldecott award), Backbone of the King, 1966, The Neighbors, 1967, The Bun (retold), 1972, All Butterflies, 1974 (Boston Globe Honor Book, Horn Book), The Blue Jackal (retold), 1977, Walk Through Your Eyes, 1979, (with photographs) Touch Will Tell, 1979, (with photographs) Listen to a Shape, 1979, Lotus Seeds; Children, Pictures and Books, 1985, (with others) From Sea to Shining Sea, 1993; translator. illustrator: Puss in Boots, 1952 (Caldecott Honor Book award), Cinderella (Charles Perrault), 1954 (Caldecott award 1955), How, Hippo!, 1969 (honor book Book World Spring Book Festival); author, photographer: film strip The Crystal Cavern, 1974; woodcut prints exhibited, Bklyn. Mus., Peridot Gallery, Hacker Gallery, Library Congress, Carnegie Inst., Phila. Print Club; Chinese brush painting and calligraphy exhibited at Hammond Mus., North Salem, N.Y., 1988, one woman show, U. Albany, SUNY, 1997; prints in permanent collection, Library of Congress, N.Y. Pub. Library, pvt. collections; art work in Mazza Gallery Findlay (Ohio) Coll.; traveling exhibition, lectrs. illustration Japan, 1990, 94. Recipient Disting. Svc. to Children's Lit. award, U. So. Miss., 1972, Regina medal Cath. Libr. Assn., 1977, Disting. Alumnus medal SUNY, 1969, Laura Ingalls Wilder award, 1992; U.S. nominee Internat. Hans Andersen award illustration, 1966, 76; career rsch. material in spl. libr. collection, SUNY, Albany, de Grummond Collection, U. So. Miss., Hattiesburg, Kerlan Collection, U. Minn. Fellow Internat. Inst. Arts and Letters (life); mem. Author's Guild, Print Coun. Am., Art Students League, Oriental Brush Artists Guild, Sumi-e Soc. Am, Am. Artists of Chinese Brush Painting.

BROWN, MARGUERITE JOHNSON, music educator; b. El Paso, Tex., Mar. 31, 1940; d. Don Lee and Eloise (Watson) Johnson; m. R. Don Lumley, Dec. 1961 (div. July 1982); children: Jessica Lumley Rodela, Jeffrey Tate; m. Gilbert Bivins Brown, Oct. 27, 1989; stepson, Erich Michael. MusB in Piano Pedagogy (hons.), U. Tex., 1962; M in Liberal Arts (hons.), So. Meth. U., 1974. Tchr., group piano Dallas Ind. Sch. Dist., 1965-72; tchr. music theory Canal Zone Coll., Panama Canal Zone, 1977-79, musical theater accompanist, 1975-79; tchr. class piano Del Mar Coll., Corpus Christi, Tex., 1980-82; tchr., edn. dir. piano & keyboard Coast Music Co., Corpus Christi, Tex., 1982-87; tchr. class piano, theory Del Mar Coll., Corpus Christi, Tex., 1987-90, performance accompanist, 1993-94; owner, piano tchr. pvt. Studio 88, Corpus Christi, Tex., 1994—. Mem. Nat. Fedn. Music Clubs, Corpus Christi Music Tchrs. Assn. (pres. 1995-97), Music Tchrs. Nat. Assn., Dallas Music Edn. Assn. (pres. 1969-71), Music Educators Nat. Conf., Thursday Music Club. Episcopalian. Home: 1202 Harbor Lights Dr Corpus Christi TX 78412-5339 Office: Studio 88 1241 Nile Dr Corpus Christi TX 78412-4120

BROWN, MARILYNNE JOYCE, emergency nurse; b. Algona, Iowa, Sept. 26, 1932; d. Michael Henry and Enid Hazel (Bonnet) Miller; m. Vaughn Hardgrove Brown; children: Jeffrey Von, Steven Michael, Sindy Lynne, Timothy Ralph. Diploma in Nursing, St. Mary's Sch. Nursing, Rochester, Minn., 1953; AA, Grossmont C.C., El Cajon, Calif., 1981; BS in Health Sci. Edn., San Diego State U., 1983. Cert. emergency nurse; cert. tchr., Calif.. Dir. Algona Osteo. Clinic, 1953-55; staff nurse St. Ann's Hosp., Algona, 1955-60; emergency/relief charge nurse El Cajon Valley Hosp., 1960-65; emergency nurse, mobile intensive care nurse Grossmont Hosp., La Mesa, Calif., 1965-90; ret.; coord. EMT program Grossmont C.C., El Cajon, 1970-83; cons. and lectr. in field. Mem. Emergency Nurses Assn. (life; past sec., v.p. and pres. San Diego County chpt.), Beta Sigma Phi (life). Home: 596 Dichter St El Cajon CA 92019-2572

BROWN, MARION LIPSCOMB, JR., publisher, retired chemical company executive; b. Greenwood, Miss., Aug. 1, 1925; s. Marion Lipscomb and Martha Helen (Wheeler) B.; m. Dorothy Dell Tramel, Aug. 28, 1948; children: Paul Thomas, Marion Lipscomb III, Janet Marie, Jeffrey Robert. BSChemE, Miss. State U., 1950; cert. in exec. devel. La. State U., 1969. Rsch. engr. Cities Service Corp., Lake Charles, La., 1951-53; with Miss. Chem. Corp., Yazoo City, 1953-87, v.p. rsch. and engring., 1972-74, v.p. research and devel., 1974-87; exhibiting photographer in maj. mus. collections of world, tchr. photography; pub. Jour. Creative Photography, 1989-95. Author: Fertilizer Formulation Manual, 1967; contbr. articles to profl. jours.; patentee in fertilizer tech. Dir., coach Little Boys and Youth Baseball, 1958-68; engring. adviser Miss. State U., 1972—, also vice chmn., chmn. adv. com. Served with USN, 1943-46, PTO. Named Photographer of Yr. award Miss. Inst. Arts and Letters, 1996. Mem. Am. Chem. Soc., Creative Edn. Found., Miss. State U. Dist. Alumni Assn. (pres. 1966). Methodist. Home: 315 E Nineteenth St Yazoo City MS 39194-2340

BROWN, MARION MARSH, author, educator; b. Brownville, Nebr., July 22, 1908; d. Cassius Henry and Jenevie (Hairgrove) Marsh; m. Gilbert Silas Brown, June 11, 1937; 1 child, Paul. AB, Peru State Coll., 1925; MA, U. Nebr., 1936; MA (hon.), Peru State U., 1997; postgrad., U. Minn.; D (hon.), Peru State Coll. Instr. writing courses Peru (Nebr.) State U., 1930-36; prof. U. Nebr., Omaha, 1940-68. Author: Young Nathan, 1949 (Jr. Lit. Guild Selection), Swamp Fox, 1950 (Boys' Club of Am. Seal), Frontier Beacon, 1953, 2nd edit. (Stuart's Landing), 1968, Broad Stripes and Bright Stars, 1955 (Catholic Children's Book Club Selection), Prairie Teacher, 1957, Learning Words in Context, 1961, 2nd rev. edit. 1974, A Nurse Abroad, 1963, Marnie, 1971, The Pauper Prince, 1973, The Brownville Story, 1974, Homeward the Arrow's Flight, 1980, reprint, 1995, Dreamcatcher: The Life of John Neihardt, 1983, 2d edit. 1993, Susette La Flesche, 1992; co-author: (with Ruth Crone) The Silent Storm, 1963, 2d edit. 1985 (Jr. Literary Guild Selection, Neb. Presswomen award, Nat. Presswomen award), Willa Cather: The Woman and Her Works, 1970, Only One Point of the Compass: Willa Cather in the Northeast; contbr. articles magazines and newspapers. Recipient Outstanding Woman of Achievement award YWCA, Pen and Scroll Lewis Central H.S., Fellowship named after Marion Brown AAUW, Admiral in Neb. Navy, Sandoz award Neb. State Lib. Assn., Sower award Neb. Humanities Coun. Mem. Nat. League of Am. Penwomen, Inc. (sec. Omaha chpt.), Neb. Writers Guild (past pres., bd. life mem., chmn. 50th Yr. Celebration, 1975, historian), Neb. Coun. Tchrs. in English, Western Writers of Am. Republican. Presbyterian. Home: 12856 Deauville Dr Omaha NE 68137

BROWN, MARK MALLOCH, bank executive. Grad. in History, Cambridge (Eng.) U.; M in Polit. Sci., U. Mich. With UN High Commr. for Refugees, 1979-83; founder, editor The Economist Devel. Report, 1983-86; ptnr. internat. consulting firm; dir. external affairs World Bank, Washington, 1994-96, v.p. external affairs, 1996—; dir. field ops. for Cambodian refugees, Thailand, 1979-81; dep. chief emergency unit, Geneva, 1981; vice-chmn. Bd. Refugees Internat., Washington; mem. Soros Adv. Com., Bosnia, 1993-94. Contbr. articles to profl. jours. Recipient (UN High Commr. for Refugees and staff) Nobel Peace prize, 1981. FAX: 202-522-2644. Office: The World Bank External Affairs 1818 H St NW Washington DC 20433-0002

BROWN, MARK RANSOM, financial advisor; b. L.A., Jan. 20, 1959; s. Peter Ransom Brown and Virginia (Beard) Pitt. Student, Pepperdine U., 1977-78; BS in Bus., U. Colo., 1981. Fin. advisor Planning Svcs., Inc., Denver, 1983-88; co-owner Brown & Tedstrom, Inc., Denver, 1988—. Mem. Inst. CFPs, Nat. Fedn. Ind. Bus. Owners, Internat. Assn. Fin. Planners, Colo. Assn. Commerce and Industry, Denver C. of C., Rotary (bd. dirs. S.E. Denver 1997—, pres. 1999—). Avocations: skiing, travel, cooking, reading, golf. Office: Brown & Tedstrom Inc 1700 Broadway Ste 500 Denver CO 80290-0500

BROWN, MARK WALDEN, artist; b. Lexington, Ky., Oct. 8, 1949; s. Richard Walden and Gene Elizabeth (Miracle) B.; m. Catherine Ann Kiffney, Apr. 2, 1994. BA, U. Ky., 1972; MFA, U. N.C., Chapel Hill, 1983. Decorative painting contractor self employed, Chapel Hill, N.C., 1983—; instr. painting Rowan Tech. Coll., Salisbury, N.C., 1981; vis. asst. prof. photography Ky. State U., Frankfort, 1979; mem. MFA candidates critique panel U. N.C., Chapel Hill, 1995, vis. asst. prof. painting., 1997. Exhibited works in solo show at E.S. Vandam Gallery, N.Y.C., 1994, Marita Gilliam Gallery, Raleigh, 1994, Duke Inst. for the Arts, Durham, 1993; group shows include Triennial Exhbn. of N.C. Artists, N.C. Mus. Art, 1984, 93, S.E. Ctr. for Contemporary Art, Winston-Salem, 1983, Ackland Art Mus., Chapel Hill, 1983, Davidson (N.C.) Coll., 1992, Duke U. Mus. Art, Durham, 1994, Modern Mus., Durham, 1997. Precinct capt. Dem. Party, Lexington, 1972; active ACLU. Grantee Smith Fund, U. N.C., 1983, N.C. Arts Coun., 1992. Avocation: paleolithic art. Home: 3707 Hawk Ridge Rd Chapel Hill NC 27516-5737 Office: White Cross Sch 3501 Hwy 54 West Studio AA Chapel Hill NC 27516

BROWN, MARTIN HOWARD, physician; b. Bklyn., Feb. 21, 1953; s. Alan Aaron and Clarice (Steinberg) B.; m. Rebecca Jeanne Sarley; children: Meghan E., Elliott A. BS with honors, George Washington U., 1974, MD, 1978. Chief med. resident George Washington U. Hosp., Washington, 1981-82; staff physician Emergency Medicine Assocs., Bethesda, Md., 1982-83; asst. prof. medicine George Washington U. Med. Ctr., 1983—; aeromed. dir. Worldcare Travel Assistance Assn., Washington, 1985-88; vice chmn. dept. emergency medicine Nat. Hosp., Arlington, Va., 1985-87, chmn. dept., 1987-91; asst. prof. medicine Georgetown U. Hosp., Washington, 1988—; med. dir. USASSIST, Washington, 1988-98; chmn. dept. emergency medicine Washington Adventist Hosp., 1991—; med. dir. Md. Ambulance Svc., 1995—, AXA Assistance, Chgo., 1998; trauma ctr. site reviewer State of Va.; mem. adv. com. Emergency Med. Svcs. Curriculum, No. Va. Community Coll., 1990-92; cons. in field. Trustee Nat. Hosp. Bd. Trustees, 1987-96; mem. adv. com. emergency med. svcs. Arlington County Bd., 1987-91, chmn. adv. com., 1991. Fellow Am. Coll. Emergency Physicians, Am. Coll. Physician Execs., Alpha Omega Alpha. Jewish. Home: 10901 Cripplegate Rd Potomac MD 20854-1628 Office: Emergency Medicine Assocs 9210 Corporate Blvd Rockville MD 20850-4608

BROWN, MARY JEAN, public health nurse; b. Ft. Knox, Ky., June 8, 1950; d. Hugh Mack Brown and Margaret (McHugh) Salter; Robert Muhlhan, Feb. 2, 1969 (div. Feb. 1979); children: Roseanne, Justine; m. Kevin Joseph McCarthy, Sept. 9, 1982; 1 child, Thomas Joseph. ADN, Cuyahoga C.C., 1979; BS, Boston Coll., 1982; MS, Harvard U., 1996. Registered nurse, Mass. Staff nurse Met. Gen. Hosp., Cleve., 1977-80, Mt. Auburn Hosp., Cambridge, Mass., 1980-82; pub. health nursing coord. Dept. Pub. Health, Boston, 1982-90, asst. dir. - lead program, 1990-96, pub. health nursing advisor, 1996—; tchg. asst. Harvard U., Boston, 1996—; tech. advisor Emergency Med. Svcs., Boston, 1993—; mem. Atty. Gen.'s Task Force, 1992-93. Contbr. articles to profl. jours. Tech. advisor Alliance to End Lead Poisoning, Washington, 1990—. Taplin fellow Harvard U., 1996, 97. Mem. Am. Pub. Health Assn., Mass. Lead Nurses Assn., Mass. Nurses Assn. (bd. dirs. 1996, Leadership award 1995), Nat. Ctr. Lead Safe Nursing (bd. dirs. 1999). Home: 20 Emerald St Newton MA 02458-1214 Office: State Lab Inst 305 South St Jamaica Plain MA 02130-3515

BROWN, MARY WILLOUGHBY, health facilities administrator; b. Louisville, July 7, 1950; d. Willoughby Randolph and Emma Madelein (Geissinger) B.; m. Richard Frederick Teichgraeber III, June 23, 1974; children: Rebecca Flynn, Erin Marie. Student, Smith Coll., 1968-70; BA, Williams Coll., 1972; MEd, Northeastern U., Boston, 1973; MBA, U. Pa., 1977. Mental health worker McLean Hosp., Belmont, Mass., 1973-74, asst. social worker, 1974-75; dir. adminstrv. services mental health ctr. Peninsula Hosp., Burlingame, Calif., 1977-79; resource adminstr. Ochsner Found. Hosp., New Orleans, 1979-81, adminstrv. assoc., 1981-83, asst. hosp. dir., 1983-86, assoc. hosp. dir., 1986-95, sr. v.p., hosp. COO, 1995—; bd. dirs. Ochsner Home Health Services Inc., New Orleans. Bd. dirs. Hospice New Orleans, 1985-95, East Jefferson Cmty. Health Ctr. Mem. Am. Coll. Healthcare Execs. (regent at-large 1995—), New Health Care Mgrs. Assn. (bd. dirs. 1983-86), Women's Health Care Exec. Network (founding), Am. Hosp. Assn. (adv. panel clin. svcs. and tech. 1988—, faculty 1988—). Democrat. Episcopalian. Office: Ochsner Found Hosp 1516 Jefferson Hwy New Orleans LA 70121-2429

BROWN, MATTHEW, lawyer; b. N.Y.C., Mar. 26, 1905; s. Jack Goddard and Pauline B. (Roth) B.; m. Edna Goodrich, Nov. 8, 1932; 1 child, Patricia Brown Specter. BS, NYU, 1925; LLB, Harvard U., 1928; LLD (hon.), Suffolk U., 1983. Bar: Mass. 1928, U.S. Supreme Ct. 1935. Sr. ptnr. Brown, Rudnick, Freed & Gesmer, Boston, 1940-88, counsel, 1988—; spl. justice Boston Mcpl. Ct., 1962-72; chmn. Boston Broadcasters, 1972-81. Selectman Town of Brookline, Mass., 1953-64; trustee New Eng. Aquarium, Boston, 1981-88; mem. Nat. Jewish Coalition, Boston, 1984, Holocaust Meml. Coun., Washington. Fellow Brandeis U., Waltham, Mass., 1985 (hon.). Mem. ABA, Mass. Bar Assn., Boston Bar Assn., Am. Jewish Com. (hon. v.p.), Combined Jewish Philanthropies (hon. trustee, life), Belmont Country Club. Summer Address: 180 Beacon St # 11G Boston MA 02116-1401 Office: Brown Rudnick Freed Gesmer One Fin Ctr Boston MA 02111 Winter Address: 130 Sunrise Ave Palm Beach FL 33480-3961

BROWN, MELVIN F., corporate executive; b. Carlinville, Ill., June 4, 1935; s. Ben and Selma (Frommel) B.; m. Jacqueline Sue Hirsch, Sept. 2, 1962 (dec.); children: Benjamin Andrew, Mark Steven; m. Pamela Turken, Sept. 12, 1992. AB, Washington U., 1957, JD, 1961. Bar: Mo. 1961. Pvt. practice St. Louis, 1961-62; asst. to gen. counsel Union Elec. Co., St. Louis, 1962-65; sec., atty. ITT Aetna Corp., St. Louis, 1965-72; v.p., gen. counsel ITT Aetna Corp., 1972; also dir.; corp. sec., gen. counsel ITT Fin. Corp., 1974-77, exec. v.p., 1977-95; pres. ITT Comml. Fin. Corp., 1977-95, St. Louis, 1977-95; pres., CEO Deutsche Fin. Svcs., 1995-96, vice chmn., 1997-98; bd. dirs. Falcon Products, Foundors Bancshares. Mem. Mo. Commn. Dem. Party Constn. By-Laws and Party Structure, 1969-70, Mo. Dem. Platform Com., 1966, 68; mem. bd. adjustment City of Clayton, Mo., 1974—; chmn. St. Louis chpt. Am. Jewish Com., 1968—; mem. nat. coun. Washington U. Sch. Law; bd. trustees Mo. Hist. Soc.; trustee Whitaker Charitable Found.; trustee Maryville U., St. Louis Symphony Soc.; pres. Gateway chpt. Leukemia Soc.; mem. Rsch. Hon. col. Mo. Gov.'s Staff. Capt. AUS, 1957-64. Mem. Bar Assn. Met. St. Louis (pres. young lawyers sect. 1965-66), Mo. Bar Assn.. Office: Deutsche Fin Svcs 655 Maryville Centre Dr Saint Louis MO 63141-5815

BROWN, MEREDITH M., lawyer; b. N.Y.C., Oct. 18, 1940; s. John Mason Brown and Catherine (Screven) Meredith; m. Sylvia Lawrence Barnard, July 17, 1965; 1 child, Mason Barnard. AB, Harvard U., 1962, JD, 1965. Bar: N.Y. 1965, U.S. Ct. Appeals (2d cir.) 1966, U.S. Dist. Ct. (so. dist.) N.Y. 1976. Law clk. to Hon. Leonard P. Moore U.S. Ct. Appeals (2d cir.), N.Y.C., 1965-66; assoc. Debevoise & Plimpton, N.Y.C., 1966-72, ptnr., 1973—, co-chair corp. dept., 1993—. Author: (with others) Takeovers: A Strategist's Manual for Business Combinations, 2d edit., 1993, Global Offerings, 1994, Privatisations, 1994, Mechanics of Global Equity Offerings, 1995, International Mergers and Acquisitions: An Introduction, 1999; contbr. articles to profl. publs. Mem. ABA (fed. regulation of securities com., bus. law sect.), Assn. of Bar of City of N.Y. (chmn. profl. responsibility com. 1987-90), Internat. Bar Assn. (co-chmn. com. on issues and trading of securities, sect. on bus. law 1994-98, co-chmn. capital markets forum, sec. bus. law 1998—). E-mail: mmbrown@debevoise.com. Home: 1021 Park Ave New York NY 10028-0959 Office: Debevoise & Plimpton 875 3rd Ave Fl 23 New York NY 10022-6256

BROWN, MICHAEL, information technology executive; b. Williamsport, Pa., Oct. 28, 1943; s. Irwin and Helen (Shuster) B.; m. Candance Carver, Apr. 8, 1967 (div. 1979); children: Kristin, Brett, Lee; m. Stephanie Barry, Apr. 21, 1984. BS, U.S. Naval Acad., 1966. Systems engr. Electronic Data Systems, Dallas, 1970-72; exec. v.p., chief info. officer New Eng. Life Ins. Co., Boston, 1972-93; sr. v.p. Fidelity Investments, Boston, 1993—. Bd. dirs., treas. Inroads, Inc., Boston. With USN, 1966-70. Roman Catholic. Avocations: skiing, weight training. Office: Fidelity Investments 82 Devonshire St Boston MA 02109-3614

BROWN, MICHAEL A., computer hardware company executive; b. 1958. BA in Econs., Harvard U.; MBA, Stanford U. Rsch. assoc. Braxton Assocs., strategic planning cons., 1982-84; various mktg. positions Quantum Corp., Milpitas, Calif., 1984-89, dir. product mktg., 1989-90, v.p. mktg., 1990-92, exec. v.p. responsible for hard drive bus., 1992-93, COO, 1993, pres. desktop and portable storage group, 1993-95, CEO, 1995—, also chmn. Office: Quantum Corp 500 McCarthy Blvd Milpitas CA 95035

BROWN, MICHAEL ARTHUR, lawyer; b. San Angelo, Tex., Oct. 15, 1938; s. Edwin Michael and Sadie Beatrice (Johnson) B.; m. Carol Ann Campbell, Dec. 20, 1958 (div. Mar. 1978); children: Michael Paul, Michele Louise; m. Teresa Ann Boyd, Feb. 24, 1979; 1 child, Matthew Arthur. BBA, St. Mary's U., 1961, LLB magna cum laude, 1961; LLM, Georgetown U., 1970. Bar: Tex. 1962, U.S. Supreme Ct. 1967, D.C. 1974, U.S. Ct. Appeals (5th cir.) 1975. Commd. 2d lt. U.S. Army, 1961, advanced through grades to maj., 1966, resigned, 1969; ret. as Col. USAR, 1991; dep. asst. gen. counsel U.S. Dept. Commerce, Washington, 1969-73; gen. counsel U.S. Consumer Product Safety Commn., Washington, 1973-76, exec. dir., 1976-79; dep. gen./enforcement counsel U.S. EPA, Washington, 1982-83; ptnr. Schmeltzer, Aptaker & Sheppard, Washington, 1979-82, 84-90, Thelen, Marrin, Johnson, Washington, 1990-91, McCutchen, Doyle, Brown & Enersen, Washington, 1991-97, Brown & Freeston, Washington, 1997—. Named one of Outstanding Young Lawyers U.S., Jr. C. of C., 1969. Mem. D.C. Bar Assn., Tex. Bar Assn. Avocations: snow and water skiing. Office: Brown and Freeston 3201 New Mexico Ave NW Washington DC 20016-2756

BROWN, MICHAEL DEWAYNE, lawyer; b. Guymon, Okla., Nov. 11, 1954; s. Wayne E. and R. Eloise (Ferguson) B.; m. Tamara Ann Oxley, July 19, 1973; children: Jared Michael, Amy Aryann. Student, Southeastern State Coll., 1973-75; BA in Polit. Sci. and English, Cen. State U., Edmond, Okla., 1978; JD, Oklahoma City U., 1981. Bar: Okla. 1982, Colo. 1992, U.S. Dist. Ct. (no. and we. dists.) Okla. 1982, U.S. Ct. Appeals (10th cir.) 1982, U.S. Ct. Appeals (D.C. cir.) 1987. Assoc. Long, Ford, Lester & Brown, Enid, Okla., 1982-87; sole practice Enid, 1987—; adj. prof. state and local govt. law legis. Oklahoma City U.; cons. No. Okla. Devel. Assn., Enid, 1983-91; gen. counsel Alpha Oil Co., Duncan, Okla., 1985—, Physicians Mgmt. Svc. Corps., 1985-90, Physicians of Okla., Inc., Physicians Med. Plan Okla., Inc., City Nat. Bank & Trust Co., 1987-88, Stanfield Printing Co., 1987—, Hammell Newspapers, Inc., 1987-90, Dillingham Ins., 1989-91, Suits Rig Corp., Suits Drilling Co., 1989-91; chmn. bd. dirs. Okla. Mcpl. Power Authority, Edmond, 1982-88, judges & stewards commr. Internat. Arabian Horse Assn., 1991—. Councilman City of Edmond, 1981; cons. Okla. Reps., Oklahoma City, 1983; bd. dirs. Okla. Christian Home, Edmond, 1985; Rep. nominee 6th Dist. U.S. Congress, 1988; co-chmn. Nat. Challengers Polit. Coalition, 1989-91; trustee, co-chair fin. com. Theodore Roosevelt Assn., 1994—. Michael D. Brown Hydroelectric Power Plant and Dam named in his honor, Kaw Reservoir, Okla., 1987. Mem. Okla. Bar Assn. (assoc. bar examiner 1984—), MD Physicians Okla., Ariz. and La., MD Physicians of Tulsa. Mem. Christian Ch. (Disciples of Christ). Avocations: travel, photography, reading, wilderness adventures, swimming. Home and Office: 2 Eagle Nest Ln PO Box 936 Lyons CO 80540-0936

BROWN, MICHAEL RICHARD, minister; b. Columbus, Ohio, Mar. 2, 1959; s. Cornelius Paul Brown and Pearl Elizabeth (Baker) Buck; m. Christine Elaine Stanley, Aug. 23, 1980; 1 child, Stephanie Nicole. BA in Bible and Religion, Huntington Coll., 1981, M in Ministry, 1983, postgrad., 1984. Ordained to ministry Ch. of United Brethren in Christ, 1983. Minister Monroe (Ind.) United Brethren Ch., 1982-89, Franklin United Brethern Ch., New Albany, Ohio, 1989—. Dir. Adams County Soccer Clinic, Decatur, Ind., 1984-85; chmn. Adams County Child Protection Team, Decatur, 1985; v.p. Adams County Energy Assistance Inc., 1986; mem. Hoosiers for Better Schs., A-Plus Program; soccer coach New Albany Mid. Sch., 1989-91, 96; bd. dirs. Camp COTUBIC. Named one of Outstanding Young Men of Am., 1985. Mem. New Albany Ministerial Assn. (v.p. 1994, pres. 1991, 94, conf. supt. Columbus dist. 1995-97). Republican. Avocations: soccer coach, running. Home: 6695 Albanyview Rd Westerville OH 43081-9236 Office: Franklin United Brethren Ch 7171 Central College Rd New Albany OH 43054-9303

BROWN, MICHAEL ROBERT, finance specialist; b. Joliet, Ill., Aug. 9, 1960; s. Robert Raymond and Virginia A. (Bianchi) B. AAS, Joliet Jr. Coll., 1980; BS, No. Ill. U., 1983, MBA, 1996. Acctg. supr. northern region DeKalb (Ill.) Genetics, 1982-85; fin. analyst Baxter Healthcare Corp., Deerfield, Ill., 1985, sr. fin. analyst, 1985-87, sr. consols. analyst, 1987-88, mgr. acctg. svcs., 1988-89, mgr. corp. acctg., 1989-93; dir. fin. planning Baxter Healthcare Corp., McGaw Park, Ill., 1993-95, asst. contr. renal divsn., 1995—. Vol. Jr. Achievement, United Way; bd. exec. advisors No. Ill. U. Mem. Inst. Mgmt. Accts., Chgo. Coun. Fgn. Rels., No. Ill. U. Alumni Assn., No. Ill. U. Exec. Club. Avocations: music, tennis.

BROWN, MICHAEL ROBERT, lawyer; b. Worcester, Mass., Apr. 5, 1938; s. Walter David and Ethel Fay (Berman) B.; m. Susan Fay Lappin, July 8, 1962; children: Laura, Pamela. BA, Bowdoin Coll., 1959; JD, Columbia U., 1962. Bar: Mass. 1963, N.Y. 1968. Staff atty. NLRB, Washington, 1963-66; assoc. Simpson, Thacher & Bartlett, N.Y.C., 1966-70; ptnr. Herrick & Smith, Boston, 1970-84, Goldstein & Manello, Boston, 1984-90, Palmer & Dodge, Boston, 1990—; adj. prof. employment law Sch. Law Suffolk U., Boston,. Selectman, Wellesley, Mass., 1992-95. Fellow Coll. Labor and Employment Lawyers; mem. ABA, Mass. Bar Assn., Boston Bar Assn. Office: Palmer & Dodge 1 Beacon St Ste 22 Boston MA 02108-3190

BROWN, MICHAEL STUART, geneticist, educator, administrator; b. N.Y.C., N.Y., Apr. 13, 1941; s. Harvey and Evelyn (Katz) B.; m. Alice Lapin, June 21, 1964; children: Elizabeth Jane, Sara Ellen. BA, U. Pa., 1962, MD, 1966; DSc (hon.), Rensselaer Poly. Inst., 1982, U. Chgo., 1982, U. Pa., 1986, U. Buenos Aires, 1988, U. Paris, 1988, So. Meth. U., 1993, U.

Miami, 1996. Intern, then resident in medicine Mass. Gen. Hosp., Boston, 1966-68; served with USPHS, 1968-70; clin. assoc. NIH, 1968-71; asst. prof. U. Tex. Southwestern Med. Sch., Dallas, 1971-74; Paul J. Thomas prof. genetics, dir. Ctr. for Molecular Genetics, 1977—; mem. med. adv. bd. Scripps Inst., Salk Inst.; dir. Pfizer, Inc., Regeneron, Inc. Co-editor: The Metabolic Basis of Inherited Disease, 1983. Trustee U. Pa., Lamplighter Sch. Recipient Pfizer award Am. Chem. Soc., 1976, Passano award Passano Found., 1978, Lounsbery award U.S. Nat. Acad. Scis., 1979; Lita Annenberg Hazen award, 1982, Albert Lasker Med. Rsch. award, 1985, Horwitz prize, 1985, Nobel Prize in Medicine or Physiology, 1985, Nat. Medal of Sci. U.S., 1988. Mem. Nat. Acad. Scis., Am. Soc. Clin. Investigation, Assn. Am. Physicians, Harvey Soc., Royal Acad. Scis. (fgn. mem.). Office: U Tex Health Sci Ctr Dept Molecular Genetics 5323 Harry Hines Blvd Dallas TX 75235-8850*

BROWN, MIKE, professional sports team executive. Gen. mgr., v.p. Cin. Bengals, now pres., gen. mgr. Address: Cincinnati Bengals Cinergy Field One Bengals Dr Cincinnati OH 45204*

BROWN, MORRIS, lawyer; b. Rahway, N.J., Mar. 16, 1928; s. Frank and Celia (Roth) B.; m. Sylvia Cohen, Aug. 2, 1953; children: David H., Alan S. BA, George Washington U., 1951; LLB, Harvard U., 1955. Bar: N.J. 1956, U.S. Dist. Ct. N.J. 1956. Law clk. to Judge Thomas F. Meaney U.S. Dist. Ct. for N.J., 1955-56; assoc. Wilentz, Goldman & Spitzer, Woodbridge, N.J., 1956-67, ptnr., 1967—; Mem. adv. commn. on profl. ethics N.J. Supreme Ct., 1983-95. Assoc. editor N.J. Law Jour., 1985-91. V.p. Temple Neve Shalom, Metuchen, N.J., 1971-73, bd. dirs. 1973, 75; co-chmn. United Jewish Appeal, 1971; v.p. No. Middlesex County YMHA, 1972-73; interim pres. Jewish Fedn. No. Middlesex County, 1975; trustee John F. Kennedy Med. Ctr. Edison, N.J., 1975—. with USN, 1946-48. Mem. ATLA-N.J. (pres. 1976-77), N.J. State Bar Assn., N.J. Trial Lawyers Assn., Middlesex County Bar Assn., Middlesex County Trial Lawyers Assn. (pres. 1970-72), Am. Bd. Trial Attys., Am. Coll. Trial Lawyers. Democrat. Home: 9 Fairway Ln Ocean Township NJ 07712-3634 Office: Wilentz Goldman & Spitzer PA PO Box 10 90 Woodbridge Ctr Woodbridge NJ 07095-1304

BROWN, MORTON B., biostatistics educator; b. Montreal, Que., Can., Dec. 15, 1941; s. Israel I. and Leah (Shaikovitch) B.; m. Raya Sobol, Oct. 16, 1969; children—Danit, Alon. B.Sc., McGill U., 1962; M.A., Princeton U., 1964, Ph.D., 1965. Asst. research statistician UCLA, 1965-68, assoc. research statistician, 1975-77; vis. lectr. Tel Aviv U., 1968-69, sr. lectr., 1969-75, assoc. prof. stats., 1975-81; prof. biostatistics U. Mich., Ann Arbor, 1981—; chmn. dept. U. Mich., 1984-87. Editor: BMDP Statistical Software, 1977. Fellow Royal Statis. Soc.; mem. Internat. Statis. Inst., Am. Statis. Assn., Biometric Soc., Inst. Math. Stats. Office: U Mich Dept Biostats Ann Arbor MI 48109-2029

BROWN, MYRA SUZANNE, librarian; b. Gainesville, Fla., Jan. 6, 1949; d. Samuel Jackson and Myra Frances (Whiddon) B.; m. Roman Jonas Yoder, Jan. 5, 1973; m. Jeremy Gallaudet Hole, May 3, 1986. Student European divsn., U. Md., West Berlin, 1967-69; BA, U. South Fla., 1971; MSLS, Fla. State U., 1972; postgrad., U. Cin., 1974. Libr. asst. Strozier Libr., Fla. State U., Tallahassee, 1973, libr. serials dept., 1973; libr. sci. and tech. dept. Pub. Libr. of Cin. and Hamilton County, 1973-74; libr. assoc. II Coll. Design, Architecture and Art Libr. U. Cin., 1975-77; assoc. univ. libr. State U. Sys. of Fla. Extension Libr., St. Petersburg, Fla., 1979-81; assoc. univ. libr. Edn. Libr. U. Fla. Librs., Gainesville, 1982-84, head and edn. bibliographer, 1984-90; asst. dept. chair humanities and social scis. svcs. dept. Smathers Librs. U. Fla., Gainesville, 1990-92, head and edn. bibliographer Edn. Libr., 1992—; mem. reference liaisons discussion group Rsch. Librs. Group, Inc., 1990-92; reviewer Gale Rsch. Co., Inc., 1988—; participant rsch. panel Univ. Microfilms Internat., 1992; mem. nat. user group Libr. of Congress Cataloging Distbn. Svc., 1992-96; cons. Mus. Fine Arts Libr., St. Petersburg, Fla., 1981-82, Design, Architecture and Art Libr., U. Cin., 1975-77. Contbr.: World Architecture Index: A Guide to Illustrations, 1991; contbr. articles to profl. jours. Aux. mem., vol. Shands Hops. of U. Fla., Gainesville, 1993—, nominating com., 1995-96; advocate for homeless; mem. outreach com. Holy Trinity Episcopal Ch.; advocate for animal rights. Mem. ALA (reference svcs. in medium-sized rsch. librs. discussion group 1992—), Libr. Adminstrn. and Mgmt. Assn. (mem. econ. status and staff welfare com., 1993-95, staff devel. com. 1994-98, publs. com. 1999—), Spl. Librs. Assn. (info. tech. divsn., 1979-93, edn. divsn. Fla. chpt. 1979—, list svc. mgr. 1994—), Am. Ednl. Rsch. Assn. (divsn. E counseling and human devel. 1989-90, 92—, divsn. K. tchr. edn. 1994—), Fla. Ednl. Rsch. Assn., U. Fla. Librs. Assn. (v.p. 1983-84), Phi Delta Kappa (historian 1993-94). Democrat. Episcopalian. Avocations: church choir, hospital volunteering, animal welfare concerns, painting. Office: Smathers Librs of U Fla Edn Libr 1500 Norman Hall PO Box 117016 Gainesville FL 32611-7016

BROWN, NANCY CHILDS, marriage and family therapist; b. Butler, Ga., Feb. 17, 1938; d. Preston Bussey and Essie Lou (Jones) Childs; m. Luther Edward Brown (dec. Oct. 6, 1988); children: Melanie B. Ketchum, Catherine B. Tucker, Anthony E. Brown. BA in English with honors, Mercer U., 1960, MS, 1998. Lic. assoc. marraige and family therapist. Stockbroker/sales asst. Evans & Co./Robinson-Humphrey Co., Augusta, Ga., 1961-64; real estate owner/mgr. Macon, Ga., 1975-98; exec. dir. Macon Arts Alliance, 1985-92; assoc. marriage and family therapist in pvt. practice, 1998—; bd. leaders Atlanta Internat. Mus. Art and Design, 1994—; bd. dirs. Ga. Coun. for the Arts (gov. appointee), 1994-97. Treas. Hay House, 1995-96; pres. Macon Heritage Found., 1979-80; mem. founding bd. City Club of Macon, 1989-91; v.p. legislation Assocs. to Ga., Soc. Ophthalmology, 1985; chmn. City of Macon Cmty. Devel. Inner City Adv. Com., 1979-82; bd. dirs. tourism devel. com. Macon Conv. and Visitors Bur.; mem. MAPS (City of Macon) Policy Com. (mayoral appointee ward 3), 1994—; former pres. Bibb County Med. Soc. Alliance; choir of Vineville United Meth. Ch., 1988—; bd. dirs. Macon Symphony Orch., 1998—. Recipient Macon Cultural award Macon Arts Alliance and City of Macon, 1992; named Woman of Achievement Career Women's Network, Macon, 1990; winner Algernon Sydney Sullivan award, 1960, Alumni Meritorious Svc. award Mercer U., 1977. Mem. Career Women's Network, City Club of Macon, Ga. Trust for Hist. Preservation, Am. Assn. for Marriage and Family Therapy, Phi Kappa Phi. Avocations: singing, golf, culinary arts, piano playing, travel. Home: 937 Walnut St Macon GA 31201-1918

BROWN, NANCY FIELD, editor; b. Troy, N.Y., Feb. 20, 1951; d. Robert Grant and Barbara Katherine (Field) B. BS in Journalism, Mich. State U., East Lansing, 1974. Asst. editor Mich. Am. Legion, Lansing, 1974-76; asst. editor State Bar of Mich., Lansing, 1976-78, editor, 1976—, sr. dir. pubs., 1995-98, asst. exec. dir. publs., 1998—. Mem. Nat. Assn. Bar Execs. (cons. pubs. com. Chgo. chpt. 1989—), Mich. State U. Alumni Assn., Nat. Assn. Desktop Pubs., Am. Soc. Assn. Execs. Presbyterian. Avocations: reading, writing, photography, travel. Office: State Bar of Mich 306 Townsend St Lansing MI 48933-2012

BROWN, NORMAN ALLEN, consultant, educator; b. Temperance, Mich., Oct. 18, 1938; s. Wilfred b. and Vivian Ione (Allen) B.; m. Bernice J. Treadway, Jan. 2, 1960; children: Barry N., Judi A., Rebecca L., Douglas K. BS, Mich. State U., 1961, MA, 1965, PhD, 1970; LLD (hon.), U. Natal, South Africa. Rural youth specialist U.S. Dept. State, Far East, 1958-59; tchr. Bath (Mich.) Schs., 1960-63; extension agt. Mich. State U., East Lansing, 1963-64, coord. student programs, 1964-69, asst. dir. acad. programs, 1969-72, state 4-H dir., 1973-80; dean, dir. extension svc. U. Minn., St. Paul, 1980-84; exec. v.p., program dir. W.K. Kellogg Found., Battle Creek, Mich., 1984-86, pres., 1987-94, pres. emeritus, 1995—; cons. Ptnrs. of Ams., Washington, 1974-84; pres. bd. trustee Coll. Agr. for Humid Tropics, San Jose, Costa Rica, 1986—; bd. dirs., vice chmn. Ind. Sector, Washington; dir. Coun. on Founds., Washington; adj. prof. Mich. State U., We. Mich. U. Trustee Bath Bd. Edn., 1978-80; mem. Pres. Bush's Points of Light Com., Washington, 1989-90; trustee Points of Light Found., 1991—. Recipient Superior Svc. award USDA, 1978, Disting. Alumni award Mich. State U., 1996. Mem. Mich. State U. Alumni Assn. (bd. dirs), Phi Kappa Phi. Baptist. Office: 1424 K St NW Ste 700 Washington DC 20005-2410

BROWN, NORMAN DONALD, history educator; b. Pitts., June 28, 1935; s. Donald Madden and Regina Deborah (Koehler) B.; m. Betty Jane Aldrich, Apr. 2, 1966; children: David, Tracy. BA summa cum laude, Ind. U., 1957; MA, U. N.C., 1959, PhD, 1963. Instr. history U. Tex., Austin, 1962-65, asst. prof., 1965-69, assoc. prof., 1969-83, prof., 1983-84, Barbara White Stuart Centennial prof. Tex. history, 1984—. Author: Daniel Webster and the Politics of Availability, 1969, Edward Stanly, 1974, Hood, Bonnet, and Little Brown Jug, 1984; editor: One of Cleburne's Command, 1980, Journey to Pleasant Hill, 1982. Woodrow Wilson fellow, 1957. Fellow Tex. State Hist. Assn. (coun. 1989-93, 2d v.p. 1997-98, 1st v.p. 1998-99, pres. 1999—); mem. Orgn. Am. Historians, So. Hist. Assn., Soc. Historians Early Am. Republic, Soc. Civil War Historians (coun. 1986—), Civil War Round Table Assocs., Phi Beta Kappa, Phi Alpha Theta, Phi Kappa Phi. Democrat. United Methodist. Avocations: book and stamp collecting. Home: 2607 Barton Skyway Austin TX 78704-4602 Office: Univ Tex Dept History Austin TX 78712

BROWN, NORMAN JAMES, financial manager; b. Concord, N.H., May 12, 1942; s. Gilman D. and Katherine (Tucker) B.; m. Catherine Murphy, Sept. 17, 1983. BBS cum laude, N.H. Coll., 1968. CPA, Tenn. Acct. Peat Marwick Mitchell & Co., Portland, Me., 1968-69; audit mgr. Internal Audit Service div. VA, Washington, 1969-77; fin. mgr. regional office VA, Nashville, 1980—; supr. auditor Office Inspector Gen., Austin, Tex., 1977-80. With USAF, 1960-64. Mem. Assn. Govtl. Accts., Mid. Tenn. Fed. Exec. Assn., Moose. Republican. Mem. LDS Ch. Home: PO Box 22604 Nashville TN 37202-2604 Office: VA Regional Office 110 9th Ave S Nashville TN 37203-3817

BROWN, OLEN RAY, medical microbiology research educator; b. Hastings, Okla., Aug. 18, 1935; s. Willis Edward and Rosa Nell (Fulton) B.; m. Pollyana June King, Aug. 30, 1958; children: Barbara Kathryn, Diana Carol, David Gregory. BS in Lab. Tech., Okla. U., 1958, MS in Bacteriology, 1960, PhD in Microbiology, 1964. Diplomate Am. Bd. Toxicology, Am. Bd. Forensic Examiners. Instr. Sch. Medicine, U. Mo., Columbia, 1964-65, asst. prof., 1965-70, assoc. prof., 1970-77, prof. dept. molecular microbiology and immunology, 1981-96; rsch. prof. Sch. Medicine, U. Mo., 1996—; joint appointments, prof. depts. microbiology and biomed. scis. Coll. Vet. Medicine, U. Mo., 1977-96, prof. biomed. scis., 1987-96; guest lectr. Ross U., St. Kitts, W.I., 1984, 88; asst. dir. Dalton Rsch. Ctr., U. Mo., 1974-78, Dalton rsch. investigator grad. sch., 1968—; grant peer reviewer for program projects SCOR and Superfund grants NIH, 1979, Nat. Inst. Environ. Health Scis., Dept. Commerce, EPA, 1986, 90-99, Am. Inst. Biol. Scis. for Dept. Def., USAMRMC; cons. drug abuse policy office White House, 1982, Immunol. Vaccines, Inc., Columbia, 1984—, Lab. Support, Inc., Chgo., 1988-89, Ea. Rsch. Group, Lexington, Mass., 1991—, Teltech, Mpls., 1992—, Scis. Internat., Inc., Alexandria, Va.; judge top 100 products for 1996, 99, Rsch. and Devel. Mag. Author: Laboratory Manual for Veterinary Microbiology, 1973, The Expert Witness: A Manual for Attorneys and Professionals Under Contract; co-author: elem. and advanced lab. manuals for med. microbiology, 2 vols., 1978, 79; contbr. Progress in Clinical Research, Vol. 21, 1978, 79, Oxygen, 5th Internat. Hyperbaric Conf., Vols. I, II, 1974, 79, numerous articles to profl. jours.; book and film critic AAAS, Washington, 1986—; item preparer Am. Coll. Test, Med. Coll. Admissions Test, 1981—; mem. editorial staff Biomed. Letters, 1981—; responder Sci. and Math. Helpline for Mus. Sci. Discovery, Harrisburg, Pa., 1996—, reviewer profl. jours. Track and field ofcl. U. Mo. and Big Eight Conf., Columbia, 1979-86. Investigative rsch. grantee Office Naval Rsch., Dept. Def., 1968-81, NIH, 1976-88, NIEHS, 1981-94, 95—, USAID, 1983-86, Nat. Inst. Dental Health Scis., 1989-92. Fellow Am. Inst. Chemists (cert. chemistry and chem engring., profl. program bd. 1989-90, sd com. chemistry and environ. concerns); mem. Top One Percent Soc., Soc. Toxicology, Internat. Soc. Study Xenobiotics, Am. Chem. Soc., Am. Heart Assn., Internat. Soc. Exposure Analysts, Nat. Space Soc., Oxygen Soc., Columbia Track Club (sec.-treas. 1979-82). Avocations: long-distance running, oil painting. Office: U Mo Dalton Rsch Ctr Columbia MO 65211

BROWN, OMER FORREST, II, lawyer; b. Somerville, N.J., Mar. 4, 1947; s. George Alvin and Frances (Schnitzler) B.; m. Sandra J. Cannon, Apr. 3, 1982. AB, Rutgers U., 1969; JD, Cornell U., 1972. Bar: N.J. 1972, D.C. 1974, U.S. Supreme Ct. 1976. Dept. atty. gen. dept. law and pub. safety State of N.J., Trenton, 1972-75; sr. trial atty. U.S. Dept. Energy, Washington, 1979-83; ptnr. Davis Wright Tremaine, Washington, 1987-96, Harmon & Wilmot, L.L.P., Washington, 1997—; bd. dirs., sec. VideoTakes, Inc., Arlington, Va., 1986—; mem. OECD Contact Group on Nuclear Safety Assistance for Eastern Europe, 1994—; mem. G-7 Joint Task Force on Ukrainian Nuclear Legislation, 1996—. Contbr. numerous articles on energy, enviro. and ins. law to legal jours. Capt. USAR, 1969-75. Recipient Class of 1931 award Rutgers U. Alumni Assn., 1979, Loyal Son of Rutgers award, 1980. Mem. ABA (various offices tort and ins. practice sect. 1981-96, coord. group on energy law 1995-99), Internat. Bar Assn., Internat. Nuclear Law Assn., Fed. Bar Assn., Univ. Club of Washington, D.C. Democrat. Roman Catholic. Address: PO Box 419 Saint Michaels MD 21663-0419

BROWN, OPAL DIANN, medical technologist, nurse; b. Gassaway, W.Va., Aug. 9, 1958; d. Albert Lee and Elizabeth Lee (Kidd) Persinger; m. Thomas David Brown, July 31,1993. BS in Med. Tech., W.Va. U., 1981; BSN, U. S.C., 1993. Med. technologist Biomed. Reference Labs., Fairmont, W.Va., 1981-82, Fairmont Gen. Hosp., 1982, B.G. Thimmappa, M.D., Inc., Bridgeport, W.Va., 1982-83, Pocahontas Meml. Hosp., Marlinton, W.Va., 1984-87, Alexandria (Va.) Hosp., 1987-88, Richland Meml. Hosp., Columbia, S.C., 1988-97; RN ATC Healthcare Svcs., Inc., West Columbia, S.C., 1997—; part-time RN Midlands Regional Ctr., S.C. Dept. of Disabilities and Spl. Needs, Columbia, 1994—; Excel Ind. rep. Mem. Am. Soc. Clin. Pathologists, Sigma Theta Tau. Democrat. Presbyterian. Avocations: skiing, reading, watching TV, working with children. Home: 232 Laurel Meadows Dr West Columbia SC 29169-2361

BROWN, PAMELA WEDD, artist; b. Cauderan, Gironde, France, Nov. 21, 1928; came to U.S., 1953; d. William Basil and Nora Marsh (van Nostrand) Wedd; m. Charles Freeman Brown, Nov. 29, 1952; children: Penelope Susan, Nicholas Wedd. Student, Ecole des Beaux Arts, Paris, 1947-48, Academie Julian, Paris, 1946-51. Free lance fashion illustrator Paris, 1947-48; dir. arts and crafts YWCA, Toronto, Ont., Can., 1951; dir. Washington Womens Arts Ctr., 1987-88; dir., pres. Washington Printmakers Gallery, 1990-91; co-pres. Studio Gallery, 1992-94; artist in residence The Art Barn, Washington, 1986. Designer book plate Nat. Mus. Women in Arts Libr., 1985; represented in permanent collections Libr. of Congress, NIH, Nat. Mus. Am. History, Nat. Mus. Women in Arts. Precinct capt. Bd. of Elections and Ethics, Washington, 1970-80. Recipient First Prize Drawing, Academie Julian, Paris, 1947, Purchase award The Jr. League, Newport News, Va., 1971, Equal awards The Art League, Alexandria, Va., 1980, 82, 85, 88. Mem. Studio Gallery D.C., The Art League, Artists' Equity, Woman's Nat. Dem. Club. Avocations: music, tennis, sailing, dance. Home: 3500 Macomb St NW Washington DC 20016-3162

BROWN, PATRICIA ANITA, university official; b. Williamson, W.Va., Feb. 27, 1960; d. Lonnie and Juanita June (Wise) Parsley; m. Garland Nuel Brown, Oct. 21, 1989 (div.); 1 child, Laura Nicole. AA, Ea. Ky. U., 1980; BA with highest distinction, U. N.C., 1996. Office mgr. The Man's Shop, Williamson, W.Va., 1982-85; adminstrv. sec. of devel. Duke U., Durham, N.C., 1985-87, staff asst. Sch. Law, 1987-88, major projects coord. Sch. Law, 1988-95, dir. devel. svcs., 1995-96, dir. ann. fund, 1996-97, dir. ann. fund and alumni rels. Sch. Law., 1997-98, dir. ann. fund and special projects, 1998—. Mem. Am. Assn. Law Schs. (sect. mem.), Coun. for Advancement and Support of Edn., Ky. Cols., Phi Beta Kappa. Democrat. Avocations: music, reading. Office: Duke Univ Sch Law PO Box 90389 Durham NC 27708-0389

BROWN, PATRICIA IRENE, lawyer, retired law librarian; b. Boston; d. Joseph Raymond and Harriet A. (Taylor) B. BA, Suffolk U., 1955, JD, 1965, MBA, 1970; MST, Gordon Conwell Theol. Sem., 1977. Bar: Mass. 1965. Libr. asst. Suffolk U., Boston, 1951-60, asst. libr., 1960-65, asst. law libr., 1965-85, assoc. law libr., 1985-92; human resources counselor Winthrop (Mass.) Sr. Ctr., 1993—. Dir. Referral/Resource Ctr., Union Congl. Ch., Winthrop, Mass.; vol. health benefits counselor Mass. Dept. Elder Affairs, 1994—. First Woman inducted into Nat. Baseball Hall of Fame, Cooperstown, N.Y., 1988, All- Am. Girls Profl. Baseball League, 1950-51. Mem. Assn. Am. Law Librs., Am. Congl. Assn. (bd. dirs. 1992—), Mass. Bar Assn. Avocations: television and movie history, walking, computers. Home: 1100 Governors Dr Apt 26 Winthrop MA 02152-3254

BROWN, PATRICIA TILLEY, pharmacist; b. Hobbs, N.Mex., Apr. 28, 1966; m. Mark R. Brown; 1 child, Cameron J. BS, U. Houston, 1989. Cert. pharmacist. Pharmacist in charge Eckerd Drug Co., Houston, 1990-96; pharmacist Tex. Children's Hosp., Houston, 1996—. Mem. Am. Pharm. Assn. Home: 407 Mcconn Ct Webster TX 77598-2021 Office: Tex Childrens Hosp 6621 Fannin St Houston TX 77030-2303

BROWN, PAUL, publishing executive. V.p., gen. mgr. legal info. svcs. Lexis-Nexis, Dayton, Ohio, 1994-96, COO legal info. svcs., 1996—. Office: Matthew Bender Inc 2 Park Ave New York NY 10016-5675*

BROWN, PAUL BRADLEY, architect; b. Lake City, Minn., Apr. 20, 1912; s. Clark William and Belle (Patton) B.; m. Betty V. Padou, Dec. 29, 1945 (dec. May 1989); children: Barry, Bennett, Bradley. A.B., Oberlin Coll., 1933; B.Arch., U. Mich., 1936. Draftsman Hugh Keyes (Architet), Detroit, 1936-37; designer I.M. Lewis (Architect), Detroit, 1937-39, Harley Ellington Assos. Inc., Detroit, 1939-48; project architect Harley Ellington Assos. Inc., 1948-55, prin., 1955-70; exec. partner Harley Ellington Pierce Yee & Assos., 1970-82. Pres. Birmingham (Mich.) Planning Commn., 1956-58; pres. Forum for Detroit Area Met. Goals, 1962-67. Served with USNR, 1943-45. Fellow AIA (pres. Detroit chpt. 1961-63, Gold medal Detroit chpt.), Engring. Soc. Detroit (Gold medal); mem. Mich. Soc. Architects (dir. 1964-65). Home: 4586 Paper Birch Ln Traverse City MI 49686-3826

BROWN, PAUL EDMONDSON, lawyer; b. Van Buren County, Iowa, Dec. 24, 1915; s. William Allen and Margaret (Edmondson) B.; m. Lorraine Hill, Jan. 9, 1944; 1 child, Scott. BA, U. Iowa, 1938, JD with distinction, 1941. Bar: Iowa 1941, U.S. Supreme Ct. 1966. Ptnr. Mahoney, Brown, Mahoney, Boone, Iowa, 1946-52; v.p., counsel Bankers Life Co. (now Prin. Fin. Group), Des Moines, 1952-80; of counsel Grefe & Sidney, Des Moines, 1980-84, Davis, Hockensberg, Wine, Brown, Koehn, Shors, Des Moines, 1984-91; pvt. practice Des Moines, 1991—; atty. County of Boone, Iowa, 1948-52; pres. Iowa Life Ins. Assn., Des Moines, 1980-85. With U.S. Army, 1942-46, col. USAR, 1946-70. Named Outstanding Young Man of Iowa, Iowa State Jr. C. of C., 1948. Mem. ABA, FBA, Iowa Bar Assn., Polk County Bar Assn., Assn. Life Ins. Counsel, U. Iowa Alumni Assn. (mem. Pres.' Club and various coms.), Civil War Roundtable, World War II State Monument Com., Downtown Des Moines Kiwanis Club (pres. 1961, Hixson fellow 1999). Republican. Congregationalist. Home and Office: 5804 Harwood Dr Des Moines IA 50312-1206

BROWN, PAUL FREMONT, aerospace engineer, educator; b. Osage, Iowa, Mar. 10, 1921; s. Charles Fremont and Florence Alma (Olson) B.; m. Alice Marie Culver, Dec. 5, 1943; children—Diane, Darrell, Judith, Jana. BA in Edn. and Natural Sci., Dickinson State Coll., 1942; BS in Mech. Engring., U. Wash., 1948; MS in Cybernetic Systems, San Jose State U., 1971. Profl. quality engr., Calif., 1978; cert. reliability engr., Am. Soc. Quality Control, 1976. Test engr., supr. Boeing Aircraft Corp., Seattle, 1948-56; design specialist, propulsion systems, Lockheed Missiles and Space Co., Sunnyvale, Calif., 1956-59; supr. system effectiveness, 1959-66, staff engr., 1966-76, mgr. product assurance Hubble Space Telescope Program, 1976-83; v.p. research, devel. Gen. Agriponics Inc. of Hawaii, 1971-76; owner Diversatek Engring. and Product Assurance Conss., 1983—; coll. instr., lectr., San Jose State U. Active in United Presbyn. Ch., 1965—; scoutmaster, Boy Scouts Am., 1963-65. Served to 1st lt., USAF, 1943-46. Recipient awards for tech. papers, Lockheed Missiles and Space Co., 1973-75. Mem. Am. Soc. Quality Control, AIAA. Clubs: Toastmasters (Sunnyvale, Calif.), Calif. Writers' (pres. South Bay br. 1993-94). Author: From Here to Retirement, 1988; contbr. articles to profl. jours. Home and Office: 19608 Braemar Dr Saratoga CA 95070-5046

BROWN, PAUL M., lawyer; b. N.Y.C., Jan. 10, 1938; s. I. Harry and Rose L. (Kresge) B.; m. Helga J. Fischer, Aug. 4, 1962 (div. 1977); children: Stephanie J., William A.; m. Ruth Reiter, June 28, 1986. Student, Williams Coll., 1955-57; BS in Econs., U. Pa., 1959; LLB, Columbia U., 1962. Bar: N.Y. 1963, U.S. Ct. Appeals (2d cir.) 1963, U.S. Dist. Ct. (so. and ea. dists.) N.Y. 1964, U.S. Dist. Ct. Mass. 1981, U.S. Ct. Appeals (3d cir.), U.S. Ct. Appeals (1st cir.) 1982, U.S. Dist. Ct. (we. dist.) N.Y. 1983, U.S. Ct. Appeals (6th cir.) 1983, U.S. Dist. Ct. R.I. 1985, U.S. Dist. Ct. (ea. dist.) Mich. 1986. Assoc. Berman & Frost, N.Y.C., 1963-66; ptnr. Havens, Wandless, Stitt & Tighe, N.Y.C., 1966-76, Whitman & Ransom, N.Y.C., 1976-93; ptnr. Parson & Brown, N.Y.C., 1994—. Councilman, Closter, N.J., 1970-74; police commr. Closter, 1970-73; trustee Northern Valley Regional High Sch., Demarest, N.J., 1972. Served with USAR, 1962-68. Mem. Assn. of Bar of City N.Y., N.Y. State Bar Assn., Fed. Bar Council, Am. Arbitration Assn. (panel of arbitrators). Democrat. Clubs: University (N.Y.), Columbia Golf & Country, Las Campanas (N.Mex.). Office: Parson & Brown 666 3rd Ave New York NY 10017-4011

BROWN, PAUL NEELEY, federal judge; b. Denison, Tex., Oct. 4, 1926; s. Arthur Chester and Nora Frances (Hunter) B.; m. Frances Morehead, May 8, 1955; children: Paul Gregory, David H. II. JD, U. Tex., 1950. Assoc. Keith & Brown, Sherman, Tex., 1951-53; ptnr. Brown & Brown, Sherman, 1953; asst. U.S. atty. for Ea. Dist. Tex. Texarkana and Tyler, Tex., 1953-59; U.S. atty. Ea. Dist. Tex., Tyler, 1959-61; ptnr. Brown & Brown and Brown Brothers & Perkins, Sherman, 1961-65, Brown and Perkins, Sherman, 1965; sole practice, Sherman, 1965-67; ptnr. Brown & Hill, Sherman, 1967, Brown Kennedy Hill & Minshew, Sherman, 1967-71, Brown & Hill, Sherman, 1971-76, Brown Hill Ellis & Brown, Sherman, 1976-85; U.S. dist. judge U.S. Dist. Ct. (ea. dist.) Tex., Sherman, 1985—. Served with USN, 1944-46, 50-51. Fellow Tex. Bar Found.; mem. Rotary. Presbyterian. Office: US Dist Ct Fed Bldg 101 E Pecan St # 9 Sherman TX 75090-5989

BROWN, PAUL WILLIAM, publishing executive. MA, U. Cambridge, Eng., 1976. V.p., gen. mgr. legal info svcs. Lexis-Nexis, Dayton, Ohio, 1994-96, COO legal info. svcs., 1996—. Office: Lexis-Nexis 9443 Springboro Pike Miamisburg OH 45401*

BROWN, PAULA KINNEY, heating and air conditioning contractor; b. Portsmith, Va., June 19, 1953; d. Curtis Wade and Joan (Glascoe) Kinney; m. Wayne Howard Brown, Feb. 12, 1983; children: Rebecca Jo, Raina Jaye. AS, Lake Sumter C.C., 1977; student, lake County Area Vocat. Ctr., 1979-80. Cert. air conditioning and heating contractor. Pres. kinney's Air Conditioning and Heating, Leesburg, Fla., 1981-97, head computer sys. operator, 1986-97, office mgr.; sec.-treas. Wayne's Paint and Body Inc., Leesburg, 1995—; title clk., office mgr., sec.-treas., Wayne's Paint & Body & Auto Sales, 1999—, Mid-Fla. Svc. Experts, Ocala, 1999—; dist. mgr. Leesburg br. CSG Mgmt. Inc., dba Authorized Air of Cen. Fla., 1997-98. Home: 5 Lonesome Pine Trl Yalaha FL 34797-3058 also: Wayne's Paint & Body Inc 3831 W Main St Leesburg FL 34748-9716

BROWN, PEGGY ANN, artist; b. Ft. Wayne, Ind., Mar. 15, 1934; d. Nicholas Henry and Stella Jo (Meiners) Mattes; m. James Russel Brown, Oct. 4, 1958; children: Kurt R., James L., Nick W. BS in Journalism, Marquette U., 1956. Writer, prodr. WOWO Radio, Ft. Wayne, 1956-58; artist Nashville, Ind., 1970—. Mem. Am. Watercolor Soc. (bd. dirs. 1990-92, award 1980), Midwest Watercolor Soc. (bd. dirs. 1977-79), Nat. Watercolor Soc. (Best Show award 1993), Watercolor USA Hon. Soc. (Merit award 1994), Allied Artists Am. (gold medal 1978), Rocky Mt. Watercolor Soc. (Merit award 1994), Watercolor Soc. Ind. (Best Show award 1992, 94). Avocations: camping, hiking, golfing, gardening, stitching. Home and Office: 1541 Clay Lick Rd Nashville IN 47448-8641

BROWN, PERRY JOE, university dean. Student, Foothill Coll., Los Altos, Calif., 1962-63; BS in Forestry, Utah State U., 1967, MS in Forest Recreation, 1968, PhD in Outdoor Recreation & Social Psych, 1971; postgrad., U. Mich., 1968, 69-70. Lectr. forest sci. Utah State U., Logan, 1968-71, asst. prof. forest sci., 1971-73; asst. prof. recreatin resources Colo. State U., 1973-74, assoc. prof. recreation resources, 1974-79, prof., dept. head forest recreation resources, 1979-88, asst. dean Coll. Forestry, 1982-84, assoc. dean instrn., continuing edn. and internat. programs, 1988-94; dean Sch. Forestry, prof. forest resources U. Mont., Missoula, 1994—, dir. Mont. Forest and Conservation Expt. Sta., 1994—; social sci. project leader Oreg.

State U.-Nat. Park Svc. Coop. Park Studies Unit, 1990-93; interim dir. Oreg. Tourism Inst., Oreg. State Sys. Higher Edn., 1987-89; mem. adv. bd. Va. Poly. Inst. and State U. Coll. Forestry and Wildlife; mem. numerous panels and task forces NAS, regional planning commns., fed. and state agys. and domestic and internat. profl. orgns.; profl. cons. to numerous fed., state and internat. land mgmt. agys., univs., cos. and the Forest Ecosystem Mgmt. Assessment Team social sci. team. Editor Utah Tourism and Recreation Rev., 1972-73; assoc. editor Jour. Leisure Rsch., 1977-79, Jour. Leisure Scis., 1982-85; mem. editl. bd. Jour. Forest and Landscape Rsch., 1993-99; author over 110 books, articles, papers and reports including 2 books and 16 book chpts. Recipient Cert. of Appreciation, USDA Forest Svc., 1988. Fellow Acad. Leisure Scis.; mem. Soc. Am. Foresters, Human Dimensions in Wildlife Study Group, Internat. Union Forestry Rsch. Orgns. (leader forest recreation, landscape planning and nature conservation sect. 1986-96, dep. coord. divsn. 6 1996—), Nat. Assn. Profl. Forestry Schs. and Colls. (western region chair, exec. bd. 1996-97, pres.-elect 1998—). Office: U Mont Sch Forestry Missoula MT 59812

BROWN, PETER GILBERT, philosopher, educator, tree farmer; b. New Haven, Jan. 15, 1940; s. C. Victor and Margaret Elizabeth (Tullock) B.; children: David, Ethan, Margaret. BA, Haverford Coll., 1961; MA, Columbia U., 1964, PhD, 1969. Tutor St. John's Coll., Annapolis, Md., 1965-70; asst. v.p. for research Urban Inst., Washington, 1970-73; vis. fellow Battelle Seattle Research Center, 1973-74; fellow Acad. Contemporary Problems, Washington, 1974-76; dir. Ctr. Philosophy and Pub. Policy U. Md., 1976-81, acting dean/assoc. dean Sch. Pub. Affairs, 1980-84; asst. exec. v.p. U. Md. System, 1984-86; prof. pub. affairs U. Md., 1984-99, dir. environ. programs Sch. Pub. Affairs, 1989-97; vis. prof. Woodrow Wilson Sch., Princeton U., fall 1986, spring 1988, prof., dir. McGill Sch. Environment, 1999—. Author/editor books and monographs including Restoring the Public Trust, Ethics, Economics and International Relations; contbr. articles to profl. jours. Bd. dirs. Blue Hill Heritage Trust. Fellow Inst. Soc. Ethics and Life Scis. Home: PO Box 268 Sargentville ME 04673 Office: U Md, McGill Sch Environment, 3534 University Ave, Montreal, PQ Canada H3A 2A7 *Over the past thirty years I have endeavored to broaden and deepen our ideas about policy-oriented research. We need to examine our basic moral concepts as they apply to public policy. Without examining these concepts and the obligations they imply we are without standards to judge the legitimacy of our policies and the means to determine the ideals to which we should aspire as a nation and as individuals.*

BROWN, PHILIP ALBERT, lawyer; b. Gettysburg, Pa., June 12, 1949; s. Clyde Raynor and Jean (McCullough) B.; m. Donna Leslie Lohr, May 25, 1985; 1 child, Andrew Raynor. BA in History, George Washington U., 1971; JD, U. Mich., 1974. Bar: Ohio 1974. Assoc. Vorys, Sater, Seymour & Pease, Columbus, Ohio, 1974-81, ptnr., 1981—; arbitrator Nat. Assn. Security Dealers: mem. Ohio civil legal needs assessment implementation com. Ohio Supreme Ct., 1991-94. Trustee Legal Aid Soc. Columbus, 1985-91, pres. 1989-90; trustee Ohio State Legal Svcs. Assn., 1994—; mem. Nat. Coun. for Arts and Scis. of George Washington U. Fellow Columbus Bar Found.; mem. Phi Beta Kappa. Avocation: fishing. Office: Vorys Sater Seymour & Pease 52 E Gay St Columbus OH 43215-3161

BROWN, PHILLIP JAMES, systems engineer; b. Dayton, Ohio, Jan. 4, 1942; s. Willis James and Evelyn Sylvia (Nyberg) B.; m. Mary Christine Isham, Jan. 2, 1971; children: Charlotte Marie, Susan Elizabeth. BCE, Ga. Inst. Tech., 1964; MS, Ohio State U., 1966. Registered profl. engr., Tex. Engr.-in-tng. State Rd. Commn. W.Va., Charleston, 1964; rsch. asst. Ohio State U. Sys. Rsch. Group, Columbus, 1965-66; weapon sys. engr. LTV Aerospace Corp., Dallas, 1966-71, lead weapon sys. engr., 1972-75; tech. specialist Vought Corp., Dallas, 1976-83; hypervelocity missile chief analyst LTV Aerospace & Def., Dallas, 1984-92; tech. project mgr. Loral Vought Sys., Dallas, 1992-96, Lockheed Martin Vought Sys., Dallas, 1996-98; dir. engring. Sys. Engrs. Assocs., Inc., Dallas, 1998—. Contrib. articles to engring. journals. Coach, assn. officer Grand Prairie (Tex.) Soccer Assn., 1981-86; publicity chmn. Jackson Mid. Sch. PTA, Grand Prairie, 1991-92; coll. fair recruiter Ga. Tech. Alumni Assn., Grand Prairie, 1991—. Mem. NSPE, Inst. for Ops. Rsch. and the Mgmt. Scis., Internat. Coun. Sys. Engring. (metrics com. 1993-96, edn. and rsch. com. 1995—, co-chair 1998—), Tex. Soc. Profl. Engrs. (scholarship com. Mid-Cities chpt. 1994-98, bd. dirs. 1995—, state scholarship chair 1998—), Alpha Pi Mu. Achievements include development of procedures for integrating software development processes into a test focused organizational culture; developing web-based collaboration tool for improving integrated product team productivity. Home: 3726 Green Hollow Dr Grand Prairie TX 75052-6717 Office: Sys Engring Assocs PO Box 650003 Dallas TX 75265-0003

BROWN, PRESTON, lawyer; b. N.Y.C., Oct. 6, 1936; s. John Mason and Catherine (Meredith) B.; m. Betsey G. Pinckney, Oct. 9, 1965 (div. Mar. 1982); children: Catherine St. George, John Preston. AB, Harvard U., 1958, LLB, 1961. Bar: N.Y. 1962, D.C. 1969, U.S. Supreme Ct. 1974. Assoc. Davis, Polk & Wardwell, N.Y.C., 1961-67; adminstrv. asst., del N.Y. State Constl. Conv., Albany, 1967; spl. asst. to under sec. HUD, Washington, 1967-69; resident counsel Curtis, Mallet-Prevost, Colt & Mosle, Washington, 1969-75, ptnr., 1975—. Contbr. articles to profl. jours. Bd. dirs. Goodwill Industries Am., Washington, 1969-75, Young Audiences of D.C., 1985-92, 93—, pres., 1989-92. Mem. ABA, Knickerbocker Club (N.Y.C.). Democrat. Episcopalian. Home: 2231 48th St NW Washington DC 20007-1036 Office: Curtis Mallet-Prevost Colt & Mosle 1801 K St NW Ste 1205 L Washington DC 20006-1301

BROWN, QUINCALEE, professional society administrator; b. Wichita, Kans., Nov. 9, 1939; d. Quincy Lee and Lorene (York) B.; m. James Parson Simsarian, June 24, 1978. BA, Wichita State U., 1961; MA, U. Pitts., 1963; PhD, U. Kans., 1975. Asst. prof. speech communications, dir. debate Wichita State U., 1963-69, Ottawa U., 1970-73; adminstrv. asst. Montgomery County (Md.) Commn. for Women, 1973-74, exec. dir., 1975-80; mgr. fed. women's program Govt. Printing Office, Washington, 1974-75; exec. dir. AAUW, Washington, 1980-85, Gen. Fedn. of Women's Clubs, 1986, Water Pollution Control Fedn. (name now Water Environment Fedn.), 1986—. Contbr. articles to profl. jours. Bd. dirs. Greater Washington Soc. Assn. Execs. Found., 1996-99, Am. Inst. for Pollution Prevention, 1996-97, Alexandria (Va.) Econ. Devel. Partnership, 1997—. Recipient Contbn. to Pub. Svc. award Montgomery County Govt., 1975, Outstanding Contbn. to Sex Equity, 1979, Career Achievement award Profl. Fraternity Assn., 1981, Frances E. Willard award Alpha Phi Fraternity, 1994, ASAE Key award, 1995. Fellow Am. Soc. Assn. Execs. (bd. dirs. 1985-88, vice chmn. 1990-91, chmn. elect 1991-92, chmn. 1992-93, cert. assn. exec.); mem. AAUW, Greater Washington Soc. Assn. Execs. (chmn. bd. dirs. leadership found. 1997-98), Speech Comms. Assn., Kappa Delta Epsilon (hon.), Zeta Phi Eta (Outstanding Svc. award 1975), Alpha Phi (Francis E. Willard award of achievement 1994). Office: WEF 601 Wythe St Alexandria VA 22314-1994

BROWN, RALPH SAWYER, JR., retired lawyer, business executive; b. Cohasset, Mass., July 21, 1931; s. Ralph Sawyer and Rosemary (Wyman) B.; m. Elizabeth Atkinson Rash, June 12, 1953; children—Lucy Victoria Phillips, Alexander Sawyer Batson. BA, Swarthmore Coll., 1954; LLB, Harvard U., 1957. Bar: Mass. bar 1957, N.Y. State bar 1963. Assoc. Hutchins & Wheeler, Boston, 1957-62, Carter, Ledyard & Milburn, N.Y.C., 1962-68; ptnr. Janklow & Traum, N.Y.C., 1968-71; sec., asst. gen. counsel Indian Head, Inc., N.Y.C., 1971-76, v.p., treas., 1976-79; v.p., gen. counsel, sec. Esquire, Inc., N.Y.C., 1979-83, sr. v.p., gen. counsel, sec., 1983-84; assoc. counsel Paramount Communications Inc., N.Y.C., 1984-93, sr. counsel, 1993-94. Mem. Phi Beta Kappa. Home: 390 West End Ave New York NY 10024-6107

BROWN, RAY KENT, biochemist, physician, educator; b. Columbus, Ohio, Apr. 7, 1924; s. Ray Stemen and Grace (Nunemaker) B.; m. Gertrude Lydia Harris, Jan. 25, 1947 (dec. Feb. 1998); children—Kimberly Brown, Kitene Kading, Kevin; m. Dorothy Skinner, Mar. 19, 1998. B.A., Ohio State U., 1944, M.D., 1947, M.S., 1948; Ph.D., Harvard U., 1951. Intern Boston City Hosp., 1947-48; sr. asst. surgeon USPHS, Bethesda, Md., 1951-53; asst. dir. div. labs. and research N.Y. State Dept. Health, Albany, 1953-59, assoc. dir. div., 1959-63; asst. prof. biochemistry Albany Med. Coll., 1954-56, assoc. prof., 1956-61, prof., 1961-63; prof. Wayne State U. Sch. Medicine, 1963-96, chmn. dept. biochemistry, 1963-87, prof. emeritus, 1996—. Mem. Highland Twp. (Mich.) Planning Commn., 1968-96. Served with U.S. Army, 1943-45, with USPHS, 1951-53. Mem. Am. Soc. Biol. Chemistry (Travel award 1958, 61, 64), Am. Assn. Immunologists, Biochem. Soc. Gt. Britain, Am. Chem. Soc. Home: 3820 Middle Rd Highland MI 48357

BROWN, RAYMOND JESSIE, financial and insurance company executive; b. La., Nov. 29, 1944; s. Clarence and Katherine (Foster) B.; m. Syndee D. Williams, July 26, 1992; children: Shawn, Carmen. BA in Govt. and Speech, Southeastern U., Hammond, La., 1967; postgrad., La. State U. Cert. internat. financier. Asst. mgr. CIT, Baton Rouge, 1967-71, Thrift Funds, Baton Rouge, 1971-72; mgr. Blazer Fin., Baton Rouge, 1972-73; v.p. Fidelity Fin. Svc., Baton Rouge, 1973-82; chief exec. officer CFC-City Fin. Corp., Baton Rouge, 1982—; pres., chief exec. officer City Life and Casualty, Baton Rouge; pres. Ray Brown and Assocs.; treas. Baton Rouge Lenders Exchange, 1982, pres., 1983. Mem. La. Ind. Fin. Assn. (bd. govs. 1984-88, exec. com. 1988—, pres. 1995-96). Republican. Roman Catholic. Avocations: pumping iron, jogging, reading. Office: City Fin Corp 5235 Florida Blvd # E Baton Rouge LA 70806-4149

BROWN, RHONDA ROCHELLE, chemist, health facility administrator, lawyer; b. Shelbyville, Ky., July 13, 1956; d. Clifton Theophilus and Fannie Mae (Lawson) B. BA in Chemistry, U. Md., 1978; MA, Central Mich. U., 1983; JD, No. Va. Law Sch., 1992. Bar: Wash. 1998. Analytical chemist Dept. Health and Mental Hygiene, Annapolis, Md., 1978-83; epidemiologist Dept. Health and Mental Hygiene, Balt., 1983-88; patent examiner U.S. Patent and Trademark Office, Xtal City, Va., 1989-90; freelance researcher New Carrollton, Md., 1990—; lawyer, pvt. practice Washington, 1998—; mem. Am. Chem. Soc., Washington, 1978-82; mem., exec. bd. Nat. Lawyers Guild, Washington, 1987—; pres. Voucher Express, 1993—; mediator Superior Ct., Washington, 1993—; legal advt. mgr. Sentinel Newspaper. subcommittee chmn. Anne Arundel County Task Force for Drug and Alcohol Abuse, 1979-80; pres., bd. mem. Md. Ornithological Soc., 1979-82; mem., exec. bd. Md. Condominium and Homeowners Assn., Rockville, Md., 1988-91. Named Outstanding Young Women of Am., 1983. Mem. Nat. Intellectual Propery Law Assn., Anne Arundel County Tennis Assn., Sigma Iota Epsilon.

BROWN, RICHARD ALEXANDER, chemist; b. Waterbury, Conn., Aug. 16, 1949; s. Spenser Allen and Helen (Pendo) B.; m. Susan Eileen Haringa, June 26, 1976; children: Jeffrey, Michele, Robert. AB, Harvard Coll., 1971; MS, Cornell U., 1974, PhD, 1977. Rsch. chemist FMC Corp., Princeton, N.J., 1976-81, group leader, 1981-84, tech. mgr. aquifer remediation, 1984-86; dir. bus. devel. Cambridge Analytical Assocs., Princeton, 1987; regional mgr. bioremediation Groundwater Tech., Inc., Trenton, N.J., 1988-89, dir. chem. treatment, 1990-91, v.p. remediation tech., 1992-98; sr. tech. cons. IT Corp., 1998-99; dir. tech. devel. ERM Inc., 1999—. Author: Handbook of Bioremediation, 1994; contbr. chpts.: Bioremediation: Field Experience, 1994, Air Sparging for Site Remediation, 1994. Chmn. local com. Intervarsity Christian Fellowship, N.J., 1988-92. Recipient award for editl. excellence Pollution Engring., 1992. Mem. Am. Chem. Soc., Water Environment Fedn., Assn. Groundwater Scientists and Engrs. Democrat. Presbyterian. Achievements include patents for method for decontamination of subterranean formations, stimulation of bioxidation in subterranean formation, composition and method for treating a subterranean formation, oxidation of sulfides. Home: 42 W Long Dr Lawrenceville NJ 08648-2714 Office: ERM Inc 250 Phillips Blvd Ste 280 Ewing NJ 08618

BROWN, RICHARD CARLOS, journalism educator, editor; b. Charleston, W.Va.; s. Buster Keaton and Betty Jo (Hill) B. BA in Christian Edn., Gateway Coll. Evangelism, 1991. Christian Educator's cert. Accelerated Christian Edn. Headmaster Auburndale (Fla.) Christian Acad., 1991-92; mng. editor Apostolic Info. Svc., Indpls., 1993—; journalism instr. Ind. Bible Coll., Indpls., 1995—. Freelance religion writer, 1983-93. Mem. Soc. Profl. Journalists (assoc.). Republican. United Pentecostal. Avocations: shortwave radio, collecting vintage 1960's and 1970's GI Joes.

BROWN, RICHARD CHRISTOPHER, epidemiologist; b. Gainesville, Fla., Jan. 16, 1932; s. Joseph P. and Mildred Smith Brown; m. Linda Dickinson, July 2, 1960 (div. Dec. 1984); children: Douglas R., Jennifer Brown Kirkham. AB, Western Res. U., 1953; MD, U. Fla., 1962; MPH, U. Calif., Berkeley, 1967. Diplomate Am. Bd. Preventive Medicine. Pub. health inspector Polk County Health Dept., Lakeland, Fla., 1956-57; rotating intern Va. Mason Hosp., Seattle, 1962-63; resident in preventive medicine Fla. Dept. Health, West Palm Beach, Fla., 1963-64; resident in internal medicine U.S. VA Hosp., Portland, Oreg., 1964-66; epidemiologist USPHS, Window Rock, Ariz., 1967-68; asst. prof. preventive medicine U. Okla. Med. Sch., Oklahoma City, 1967-68; staff physician Morton Plant Hosp., Clearwater, Fla., 1968-91, Bay Pines (Fla.) VA Med. Ctr., 1991—; dir. Hernando County Health Dept., Brooksville, Fla., 1987-88. Contbr. articles to profl. jours. Bd. dirs. ARC, Clearwater, Fla., 1970; spl. expert witness Agy. for Health Care Adminstrn., State of Fla. Bd. Medicine, Tallahassee, 1997-98. Asst. surgeon USPHS, 1962-67. Recipient Rsch. award Am. Geriatrics Soc., Lederle Lab., 1965, Physician Recognition award AMA, 1969. Fellow Am. Coll. Preventive Medicine; mem. Am. Coll. Epidemiology, Fla. Soc. Preventive Medicine (past pres.), Delta Tau Delta. Democrat. Episcopalian. Avocations: triathlon and marathon running. Home: 1157 Granada St Clearwater FL 33755 Office: VA Primary Care Clinic Oakbrook Plz 2465 McMullen Booth Rd Clearwater FL 34619

BROWN, RICHARD E., state legislator. Gen. agt. Sioux Falls, S.D.; mem. S.D. Ho. of Reps., Pierre; mem. edn. and taxation coms., S.D. Ho. of Reps.

BROWN, RICHARD E., III, military officer. BA in Psychology and History, Tex. Christian U., 1970; grad., Squadron Officer Sch., 1975; MA in Guidance and Counseling, U. Okla., 1977; disting. grad., Air Command and Staff Coll., 1983; nat. security mgmt. course, 1987; grad., Air War Coll., 1991, Armed Forces Staff Coll., 1993. Commd. 2d lt. USAF, 1970, advanced through grades to maj. gen., 1999; student pilot 3640th Flying Tng. Wing, Laredo AFB, Tex., 1970-71; A-1 skyraider pilot Nakon Phanom, RT AFB, Thailand, 1971-72; T-37 instr., flight examiner 80th Flying Tng. Wing, Sheppard AFB, Tex., 1973-77; A-7D fighter pilot 75th Tactical Flying Tng. Wing, England AFB, La., 1977-80; pers. staff officer Fighter Assignments Sect. Air Force Manpower and Pers. Ctr., Randolph AFB, Tex., 1980-82; F16 fighter pilot, ops. officer, squadron comdr. 50th Fighter Wing, Hahn Air Base, Germany, 1983-88; vice comdr. Warrior Prep. Ctr. USAF and U.S. Army Forces in Europe, Ramstein Air Base, West Germany, 1988-90; vice comdr. 56th Fighter Wing, MacDill AFB, Fla., 1991-92; chief air ops. sect., joint ops. and plans sect. Supreme Hdqs. Allied Powers Europe, NATO, Mons, Belgium, 1992-94; wing comdr. 24th Wing, comdr. U.S. So. Command Air Forces Forward, Howard AFB, Panama, 1994-95; wing comdr. 354th Fighter Wing, Eielson AFB, Ala., 1995-97; dir. logistics Hdqs. Pacific Air Forces, Hickam AFB, Hawaii, 1997-98; dir. joint matters Dep. Chief of Staff Air and Space Ops. Hdqs. USAF, Washington, 1998—. Decorated Silver Star with 2 oak leaf clusters, Legion of Merit, Def. Superior Svc. medal, D.F.C. with 7 oak leaf clusters, Meritorious Svc. medal with 3 oak leaf clusters. Office: HQ USAF/XOJ 1480 Air Force Pentagon Washington DC 20330-1480

BROWN, RICHARD FRANCIS, command and control systems engineer, military off; b. Newton, Mass., Sept. 17, 1945; s. Francis Healey and Kathryn Ellenor (Morrissey) B.; m. Mary Ellen Laird, June 12, 1972; 1 child, Patrick Aaron. BS, U. Mass., 1967. Field artillery officer U.S. Army, 1967-75; field artillery specialist tactical data systems U.S. Army Field Artillery Sch., Ft. Sill., Okla., 1975-87; telecomm. mgr. U.S. Army Combined Arms Command, Ft. Leavenworth, Kans., 1987—; spl. staff asst. U.S. Army Sci. Bd., Washington, 1996-97. Contbr. articles to profl. jours. Lt. col. U.S. Army, 1967-97. Decorated Bronze Star with 2 oak leaf clusters, U.S. Army, Vietnam, 1969-70, Purple Heart, 1969-70, Army Commendation medal with V device, 1969-70. Mem. Armed Forces Comm.-Electronics Assn. (pres. Kansas City chpt. 1988-91, v.p. 1992—), Leavenworth Bicycle Club (v.p. 1996—). Avocations: bicycling, swimming, photography. Home: PO Box 3318 Fort Leavenworth KS 66027-0318 Office: Tradoc Program Integration Office-ABCS 415 Sheridan Ave Fort Leavenworth KS 66027

BROWN, RICHARD HARRIS, information technology executive; b. New Brunswick, N.J., June 3, 1947; s. Harris Ransford and Winifred (Clelland) B.; m. Christine Demler, Sept. 27, 1969; children: Ryan, Allison. BS in Communications, Ohio U., 1969. Comml. rep. Ohio Bell, Columbus, 1969-71, comml. mgr., 1971-74; dist. comml. mgr. Ohio Bell, Toledo and Cleve., 1974-80; div. mgr. Ohio Bell, Cleve., 1980-81; v.p. engring. & ops. United Telephone System, Inc. subs. United Telecommunications, Inc., Westwood, Kans., 1981-82; v.p. ops. United Telephone Co. of Midwest, Overland Park, Kans., 1982-83; v.p., COO United Telephone Co. of Fla., Apopka, 1983-87; sr. v.p. human resources & adminstrn. United Telecommunications, Inc., Shawnee Mission, Kans., 1987, sr. v.p. ops., 1987-89, exec. v.p., chief info. & planning officer, 1989; vice chmn., bd. dirs. Ameritech, 1993-95, Chgo., 1993-95; pres., CEO H&R Block, Inc., Kansas City, Mo., 1995-96; CEO, bd. dirs. Cable and Wireless PLC, London, 1996-99; chmn., ceo EDS (Elec. Data Systems), Plano, TX, 1999—; bd. dirs. Pharmacia and Upjohn Inc., London, The Seagram Co. Ltd.; chmn. Hong Kong Telecomm., bd. dirs., The Seagram Co., Ltd. Trustee, vice-chmn. Ohio U. Found., Athens, 1989—; vice chmn. Chgo. United Way Campaign, 1994. With USNG, 1969-74. Named Outstanding Alumnus, Coll. of Interpersonal Comms., Ohio U., 1988. Mem. Chgo. Club, Shoreacres Country Club, Coml. Club, Econ. Club, Northwestern U. Assocs. Execs. Club, The Bus. Roundtable, 1999. Office: EDS (Electronic Data Systems) 5400 Legacy Drive Plano TX 75024

BROWN, RICHARD HOLBROOK, library administrator, historian; b. Boston, Sept. 25, 1927; s. Joseph Richard and Sylvia (Cook) B. B.A., Yale U., 1949, M.A., 1952, Ph.D., 1955. Instr. history U. Mass., Amherst, 1955-59, asst. prof., 1959-62; assoc. prof. history No. Ill. U., De Kalb, 1962-64; dir. The Amherst Project, Amherst and Chgo., 1964-72; dir. research and edn. Newberry Library, Chgo., 1972-83, acad. v.p., 1983-94; sr. rsch. fellow, 1994—; mem. Ill. Humanities Council., 1980-86, chmn., 1982-83; cons. Nat. Endowment Humanities, 1977—; bd. dirs. Chgo. Metro History Fair, 1977—, pres., 1984-91; nat. adv. bd. Ctr. Study of So. Culture, U. Miss., 1979—; vis. prof. history and edn. Northwestern U., Evanston, Ill., 1971-84. Author: The Hero and the People, 1964, The Missouri Compromise: Political Statesmanship or Unwise Evasion?, 1964; gen. editor: Amherst Project Units in American History, 25 vols., 1964-75. Recipient George Washington Egleston prize Yale U., 1955; Andrew Mellon post doctoral fellow, 1960-61. Mem. Am. Antiquarian Soc., Social Sci. Edn. Consortium (pres. 1975-77), Orgn. Am. Historians. Democrat. Roman Catholic. Office: The Newberry Libr 60 W Walton St Chicago IL 60610-3380

BROWN, RICHARD LAWRENCE, lawyer; b. Evansville, Ind., Dec. 8, 1932; s. William S. and Mildred (Tenbarge) B.; m. Alice Rae Costello, June 14, 1957; children: Richard, Catherine, Vanessa, Mary, James. AA, Vincennes U., 1953; BA, Ind. State U., 1957; JD, Ind. U., 1960. Bar: Ind., 1960, U.S. dist. ct. (so. dist.) Ind., 1961, U.S. Ct. Apls. (7th cir.), 1972, U.S. Sup. Ct., 1972. Mng. ptnr. Butler, Brown, Hahn and Little, and predecessor firms, Indpls., 1961-85, Butler, Brown and Blythe, Indpls., 1985-94; city atty. City of Beech Grove, Ind., 1967—; pvt. practice Beech Grove, Ind., 1992—; of counsel Blythe & Ost, Indpls., 1994-96, Holwager, Byers & Caughby, Beech Grove, 1996—; sec., treas. Internat. Bus. Inst., Dayton, Ohio, 1987-96, Internat. Pub. Inst., Dayton, 1987-96; bd. dirs. Vincennes U. Found. Editor: Indiana Municipal Lawyers Assn. Newsletter, 1985—. Chmn. bd. zoning appeals small cities and towns Marion County, Ind., 1965-66; gen. counsel Habitat for Humanity Greater Indpls., 1985-95; parish chmn. St. Jude's Ch. With U.S. Army, 1953-55. Fellow Indpls. Bar Assn.; mem. ABA, Ind. Bar Assn., Ind. Mcpls. Lawyers Assn. (co-editor newsletter, bd. dirs., pres. 1987-88), Vincennes U. Alumni Assn. (pres., bd. dirs. 1990-92), KC, Delta Theta Phi. Roman Catholic. Avocation: golf. Office: 1818 Main St Beech Grove IN 46107-1418

BROWN, RICHARD LEE, lawyer; b. Ft. Worth, Dec. 7, 1925; s. Marvin H. and Janie (McIntosh) B.; m. Elizabeth McPherson, Nov. 19, 1949; children: Beverly Elizabeth, Leigh Ann (dec.). Student, Rice U., 1942-43; LLB, U. Tex., 1949; LLM, George Washington U., 1954. Bar: Tex. 1949. Asst. dist. atty. Tarrant County, 1949- 50; spl. atty. Chief Counsel's Office, IRS, Washington, 1953-56; partner Friedman & Brown, 1956-60, Stone, Parker, Snakard & Brown, 1961-66, Law, Snakard, Brown & Gambill, 1967-81, 83-84; of counsel Bishop Payne & Werley, Ft. Worth, 1984-89, 91—; judge Ct. Appeals Tex. 2d Dist., 1981-83; chief civil div. Tarrant County Dist. Atty's Office, 1989-91. Former mem. bd. commrs. Pub. Housing Authority Ft. Worth, chmn., 1976-77; Chmn. bd., chmn. competition Van Cliburn Internat. Piano Competition, 1966-69. Served with U.S. Army, 1944-46; Served with U.S. Army, 1950-53. Decorated Bronze Star medal, Combat Infantry badge and 3 battle stars. Fellow Tex. Bar Found. (life); mem. Tex. Bar Assn., Tarrant County Bar Assn. (pres. 1977-78). Office: Bank of America 500 W 7th St Fort Worth TX 76102-4700

BROWN, RICHARD P., JR., lawyer; b. Phila., Dec. 21, 1920; s. Richard P. and Edith (Gillette) B.; m. Virginia M. Hanavan Curtin, Nov. 12, 1965. A.B., Princeton U., 1942; LL.B., U. Pa., 1948. Bar: Pa. 1949, U.S. Supreme Ct. 1957. Assoc. Morgan, Lewis & Bockius, Phila., 1948-56, ptnr., 1956-88, counsel, 1988—; chmn. WHYY Inc., 1982-86, also bd. dirs.; dir. Univ. City Assocs. Pres. Phila. Council for Internat. Visitors, 1966-67; chmn. World Affairs Council, Phila., 1968-70; mem. Council Fgn. Relations, N.Y.C., 1975—; bd. dirs. Internat. Peace Acad., 1977—, Greater Phila. Partnership (now Greater Phila. Urban Affairs Partnership), 1968—; bd. overseers U. Pa. Law Sch., 1969-87, William Penn Charter Sch., Phila., 1969—; trustee U. Pa., 1979-91, trustee emeritus , 1991—, vice chmn., 1989-91; chmn. U. Pa. Med. Ctr., 1987-91, chmn. emeritus 1991—, U. Pa. Inst. Aging, 1991—, Annenberg Sch. Comm., 1984-94; bd. mgrs. U. Pa. Mus., 1967-82, St. Christopher's Hosp. for Children, Phila., 1977-80; vice chmn. United Hosp., 1980-87; trustee Eisenhower Exchange Fellowships, 1982—, Hosp. Assn. Pa., 1989-92, Del. Valley Hosp. Coun., 1990-96. Fellow Am. Coll. Trial Lawyers, Am. Bar Found.; mem. ABA (chmn. sect. internat. law 1975-76), Phila. Bar Assn., Order of Coif. Home: 8800 Towanda St Philadelphia PA 19118-3628 Office: Morgan Lewis & Bockius LLP 1701 Market St Philadelphia PA 19103-2921

BROWN, RITA MAE, author; b. Hanover, Pa., Nov. 28, 1944; d. Ralph and Julia Ellen B. AA, Broward Jr. Coll., 1965; BA, NYU, 1968; cinematography degree, Sch. Visual Arts, N.Y.C., 1968; PhD, Inst. Policy Studies, 1976. Photo editor Sterling Pub., N.Y.C., 1969-70; lectr. Fed. City Coll., Washington, 1970-71; rsch. fellow Inst. Policy Studies, Washington, 1971-73; pres. Am. Artists Inc., Charlottesville, Va., 1980—; vis. mem. faculty in feminist studies Goddard Coll., Plainfield, Vt., 1973—; mem. lit. panel NEA, 1978-81; Hemingway judge for 1st fiction PEN Internat., 1983; blue ribbon panelist Prime Time Emmy Awards, 1984, 86. Author: (translator) Hrotsvitra: Six Medieval Plays, 1971, (novels) The Hand That Cradles the Rock, 1971, Songs to a Handsome Woman, 1973, In Her Day, 1976, Southern Discomfort, 1982, Sudden Death, 1983, High Hearts, 1986, Bingo, 1988, Venus Envy, 1993, Dolley, 1994, Paydirt, 1995, Riding Shotgun, 1996, Murder, She Meowed, 1996, The Plain Brown Rapper, 1972, Rubyfruit Jungle, 1974, Six of One, 1977, Starting from Scratch, 1987, Wish You Were Here, 1989, Rest in Pieces, 1991, Murder at Monticello, 1993, others; (poetry) The Poems of Rita Mae Brown, 1987; TV series include I Love Liberty, 1982, Long Hot Summer, 1985, My Two Loves, 1986, The Alice Marble Story, 1986, Southern Exposure, 1990; TV films include The Firls of Summer, 1989, Selma, Lord, Selma, 1989, Passing Through, 1993, A Family Again, 1994, others; (cable TV) The Mists of Avalon, 1986, The Nat Turner Story-African American Anthology, 1993, The Wall, K-9, 1993; (films) Slumber Party Massacre, 1982, Sweet Surrender, 20th Century Fox, 1986, Table Dancing, 1987. Former exec. officer NOW; bd. dirs. Human Rights Campaign Fund, N.Y.C., 1986; co-founder Radical Lesbians; founder Redstockings Radical Feminist Group, Nat. Gay Task Force, Nat. Women's Polit. Caucus. Recipient Award for Best Variety Show on TV Writers Guild Am., 1982, Literary Lion award N.Y. Pub. Library, 1986, Emmy award nomination for The Long Hot Summer, ABC mini-series, 1985; Emmy nomination for best variety show I Love Liberty, 1982; named Charlottesville favorite author The Observer, 1990, Athlete of the Week, The Observer, 1990. Mem. PEN Internat., Oak Ridge Foxhunt Club (Master of Foxhounds). Office: care of The Wendy Weil Agy 232 Madison Ave New York NY 10016-2901*

BROWN, ROBERT ALAN, retired construction materials company executive; b. Mt. Vernon, Ill., July 20, 1930; s. Herbert E. and Opal (Clayborn) B.;

m. Norma Jean Falz, June 16, 1953; children: Carla, Todd, Scott, David. B.B.A., U. Minn., 1953; postgrad., Harvard U. Bus. Sch., 1971. With Firestone Tire & Rubber Co., 1953-73; plant mgr. Firestone Tire & Rubber Co., Albany, Ga., 1967-73; asst. to v.p. Firestone Tire & Rubber Co., Akron, Ohio, 1973; dir. mfg. Firestone Internat. Co., Akron, 1973-75; exec. v.p. Firestone Can. Ltd., Hamilton, Ont., Can., 1975-78; pres. Carlisle Tire & Rubber Co., Pa., 1978-82, Carlisle Syntec Sys. (Pa.), 1982-94. Served with U.S. Navy, 1948-49. Presbyterian. Home: 1193 Peninsula Dr Central City PA 15926-9119

BROWN, ROBERT ARTHUR, chemical engineering educator; b. San Antonio, July 22, 1951; s. Ralph and Lillian (Rilling) B.; m. Beverly Ann Lamb, June 22, 1972; children: Ryan Arthur, Keith Andrew. BS, U. Tex., 1973, MS, 1975; PhD, U. Minn., 1979. Instr. U. Minn., Mpls., 1978; asst. prof. MIT, Cambridge, 1979-82, assoc. prof., 1982-84, prof., 1984—, Warren K. Lewis prof., 1992—, exec. officer dept. chem. engring., 1987-88, head dept. chem. engring., 1989-96, dean Sch. of Engring., 1996-98, co-dir. supercomputer facility, 1989-94, provost, 1998—; cons. Lincoln Labs., Lexington, Mass., 1985-87, Mobil Solar Energy, Waltham, Mass., 1982-93. Contbr. over 160 articles to profl. jours. Recipient Outstanding Jr. Faculty award Amoco Oil Co., 1981, Camille and Henry Dreyfus Tchr.-Scholar award 1983; named one of Outstanding Young Texaxs-Execs. U. Tex., 1991. Mem. AAAS, NAE, AIChE (Allen P. Colburn award 1986, Profl. Progress award 1996), Soc. Indsl. and Applied Math., Am. Assn. Crystal Growth (Young Author award 1985), Am. Phys. Soc., Am. Acad. Arts and Scis. Office: MIT 3-208 Cambridge MA 02139

BROWN, ROBERT CARROLL, lawyer; b. Ridley Park, Pa., June 24, 1948; s. Robert Carroll Sr. and Marjorie Elizabeth (Nowell) B.; m. Charlene M. Lipp, Oct. 4, 1986; children: Robert Charles, Gregory Scott, Michael Joseph. AB in Polit. Sci., Pa. State U., 1970; JD, Temple U., 1973. Bar: Pa.; U.S. Dist. Ct. (ea. dist.) Pa. 1977, Pa. Supreme Ct. 1973, U.S. Ct. Appeals (3d cir.) 1980. Judicial law clk. Ct. Common Pleas/Northampton County, Easton, Pa., 1973-74; assoc. Fox & Oldt, Easton, 1974-82; ptnr. Fox, Oldt & Brown, Easton, 1982—. Sec. Greater Easton Corp., 1977-82, Two Rivers Area Commerce Coun., Easton, 1983-85; officer Lehigh Valley Flying Club, Allentown, Pa., 1979-99. Mem. Northampton County Bar Assn. (sec. 1983-84), Pa. Bar Assn., Pa. Trial Lawyers Assn., Pa. Def. Inst. Republican. Presbyterian. Avocations: pvt. pilot, sports cars, golf, spectator sports. Home: 420 Wedgewood Dr Easton PA 18045-5753 Office: Fox Oldt & Brown 6 S 3rd St Ste 508 Easton PA 18042-4591

BROWN, ROBERT CLARK, JR., sales executive; b. Akron, Ohio, Feb. 16, 1952; s. Robert Clark and Virginia Elizabeth (Raymont) B.; m. Patricia Ann Ream, Aug. 16, 1970; children: Stephen Clark, Melissa Kelly. BSBA, Bowling Green State U., 1974. Dist. scout exec. Boy Scouts Am., Ft. Wayne, Ind., 1974-76; agt. Res. Life Ins. Co., Ft. Wayne, Ind., 1976-77; v.p. Lehman Electric and Plbg., Inc., Huntington, Ind., 1977-88; sales exec. Felton Electronics, Inc., Huntington, Ind., 1986; agt. Landmark Ins. Agy., Huntington, Ind., 1989-92; mem. dealer rels. staff E.C.P. Inc., Huntington, Ind., 1992-96; sales exec. Sees Equipment & Supply Co., Inc., Huntington, Ind., 1996. Mem. common coun., City of Huntington, 1986—, pres. pro tempore, 1995-96, pres. bd. fin., 1986-87; chair Huntington County Solid Waste Mgmt. Dist., 1993, 97, vice chair, 1992, 96, sec., 1990-91, dir., 1990—; chair Rep. County Com. Huntington County, 1998—, precinct committeeman, 1983—; elder First Presbyn. Ch., Huntington, 1986—; bd. dirs. Samaritan Ctr., Huntington, 1982-84, pres., 1984; dir. Region IIIA Regional Econ. Devel. and Planning Agy., Kendallville, Ind., 1996-98; bd. dirs. Fed. Emergency Mgmt. Local Providers, Huntington, 1989—. Mem. Masons (past master 1986, Amith Lodge F&AM #483). Avocations: politics, electronics, golf, reading. Home: 2027 Camden Ct Huntington IN 46750 Office: Sees Equipment & Supply Co Inc 15 Commercial Rd Huntington IN 46750

BROWN, ROBERT ELLIOTT, lawyer; b. Ann Arbor, Mich., Apr. 23, 1934; s. Carl Richards and Ruth Adams Brown; m. Agnes Chen, Feb. 15, 1990. AB in Econs., U. Mich., 1955, JD, 1958, MBA, 1961. Bar: Mich., Calif. Atty. Calif. Dept. Transp., San Francisco, 1961-98. With U.S. Army, 1958-60. Avocations: backpacking, skiing, basketball, softball, tennis. Home: 1301 Clay # 4 San Francisco CA 94109

BROWN, ROBERT FREDERICK, industrial systems engineer, technology applications, industrial systems and management systems consultant; b. N.Y.C., Nov. 8, 1944; s. Robert Joseph and Ruth Mildred (Mueller) B.; children: Dana Marguerite, Cristina Ruth. BS, Kans. State U., 1970, MS, 1971; MBA, U. Richmond, 1976. Cert. master hazardous materials mgr., cert. plant engr.; reg. profl. engr., Tenn. Indsl. engr. Philip Morris USA, Richmond, Va., 1972-77; mgr. indsl. engring. Consolidated Aluminum, St. Louis, 1977-78; mgr. system engr. System Devel. Corp., Oak Ridge, Tenn., 1978-84; project dir. Roy F. Weston Inc., West Chester, Pa., 1984-86; project mgr. Systematic Mgmt. Svcs., Inc., Oak Ridge, Tenn., 1986-88; v.p. Systematic Mgmt. Svcs., Inc., Oak Ridge, 1988-91; mgr. Tenera, L.P., 1991-92; regional dir. Pragmatics Inc., Oak Ridge, 1992-95; ind. cons., 1996-99; ops. mgr. Cambridge Mgmt. Cons., 1999—. Pres. Crestwood Farms Resident Assn., Richmond, 1976; coun. chmn. Knoxville Ctr. Kairos Found. With U.S. Army, 1966-69, Vietnam. Mem. NSPE, Am. Soc. Engring. Mgmt., Inst. Indsl. Engrs. (cert. sys. imtegration, chpt. pres. 1969—), Am. Soc. Cost Engrs., U.S. Power Squadron (comdr. 1984-85), Nat. Contract Mgmt. Assn., Project Mgmt. Inst. (cert. project mgmt. profl.), Nat. Corvette Restorers Soc., Am. Soc. Quality Control, Soc. Am. Value Engrs., Am. Nuclear Soc., Nat. Coun. Sys. Engring., Order of Engr., Am. Mensa, Rotary. Avocations: scuba, sailing, skiing, racquetball, auto restoration. Office: 118 Ridgeway Ctr Oak Ridge TN 37830-6926

BROWN, ROBERT G., lawyer; b. Boston, Apr. 29, 1956; s. Roger Ellis and Ida Margaret (Roherty) B.; m. Margaret H. Brown Dec. 11, 1991. AA, Cape Cod C.C., 1976; BA, Northeastern U., 1979; JD, Suffolk U., 1982. Counsel Barnstable Conservation Found., Inc., 1983-1990, Hyannis (Mass.) Fire Dist., 1985-93, Cotuit (Mass.) Fire Dist., 1985-88, West Barnstable (Mass.) Fire Dist., 1987—, Old King's Hwy Region Hist. Dist. Com., 1987—, Mass. Dept. Correction, Boston, 1989-95; dir. Barnstable Conservation Found. Inc., 1983-85. Mem. Barnstable Town Meeting, 1975-87, Barnstable Planning Com., Barnstable Charter Com., 1976-77, Barnstable Planning Bd., 1979-85. Mem. Mass. Bar Assn. (small firm mgmt. sect. coun. 1991-93), Mass. Acad. Trial Attys., Barnstable County Bar Assn., Phi Alpha Delta. Office: 86 Willow St Yarmouthport MA 92675

BROWN, ROBERT GROVER, engineering educator; b. Shenandoah, Iowa, Apr. 25, 1926; s. Grover Whitney and Irene (Frink) B. BS, Iowa State Coll., 1948, MS, 1951, PhD, 1956. Instr. Iowa State Coll., Ames, 1948-51, 53-55, asst. prof., 1955-56, assoc. prof., 1956-59, prof., 1959-76, Disting. prof., 1976-88; Disting. prof. emeritus Iowa State Coll., 1988—; research engr. N. Am. Aviation, Downey, Calif., 1951-53; cons. various aerospace engring. firms., 1956—. Author: (with R.A. Sharpe, W.L. Hughes) Lines, Waves and Antennas, 1961, (with J.W. Nilsson) Linear Systems Analysis, 1962, (with Patrick Y.C. Hwang) Introduction to Random Signals and Applied Kalman Filtering with MATLAB Exercises and Solutions, 3d edit., 1997. Fellow IEEE, Inst. Navigation (Burka award 1978, 84, Weems award 1994). Office: Iowa State U Dept Engring Ames IA 50011

BROWN, ROBERT LAIDLAW, state supreme court justice; b. Houston, June 30, 1941; s. Robert Raymond and Warwick (Rust) B.; m. Charlotte Banks, June 18, 1966; 1 child, Stuart Laidlaw. BA, U. of the South, 1963; MA in English and Comparative Lit., Columbia U., 1965; JD, U. Va., 1968. Bar: Ark. 1968, U.S. Dist. Ct. (ea. and we. divs.) Ark. 1968. Assoc. Chowning, Mitchell, Hamilton & Burrow, Little Rock, 1968-71; dep. prosecuting atty. 6th Jud. Dist., Prosecuting Atty. Office, Little Rock, 1971-72; legal aide Office Gov. Dale Bumpers, Little Rock, 1972-74; legis. asst. U.S. Senator Dale Bumpers, Washington, 1975-76; adminstrv. asst. Congressman Jim Guy Tucker, Washington, 1977-78; ptnr. Harrison & Brown, P.A., Little Rock, 1978-85; pvt. practice law, 1985-90; assoc. justice Ark. Supreme Ct., Little Rock, 1991—. Contbr. articles to profl. jours. Trustee U. of the South, Sewanee, Tenn., 1983-89, bd. regents, 1989-95. Fellow ABA, Ark. Bar Found (cert. of recognition 1981); mem. Ark. Bar Assn. Episcopalian.

BROWN, ROBERT LYLE, foreign affairs consultant; b. Dayton, Ohio, July 21, 1920; s. Joseph Sebastian and Elsie Lenore (Miller) B.; m. Marion Jean Jenkin, Nov. 14, 1947; 1 son, Garry Lyle. AB, Syracuse U., 1943; postgrad., Northwestern U., 1950-51, George Washington U., 1963-65. Corp. officer Evered, Inc., Camden, N.J., 1943-44; officer-in-charge consulate Noumea, 1944-48; vice consul, chief econ. sect., consulate gen. Casablanca, 1948-50; vice consul, chief econ. sect. Kobe and Osaka, 1951-54; consul, 2d sec., chief econ. sect., asst. comml. attache embassy Brussels, 1954-58; alt. U.S. observer Customs Coop. Council, 1954; acting U.S. commr. gen. Brussels World Fair, 1958; chief loan coordination br. econ. devel. div. Customs Coop. Council, 1959-62; dep. U.S. rep. Tripartite Gold Commn., Belgium; adviser U.S. dels. com. trade, com. industry and natural resources UN Econ. Commn. Asia and Far East, 18th Session, Bangkok; adviser U.S. del. Econ. Commn. Asia and Far East, Tokyo, 1962; mem. Sr. Seminar in Fgn. Policy, 1962-63; chief European personnel ops., 1963-65; counselor econ. affairs Am. embassy, Taipei, Republic China, 1965-68; dir. AID, Republic of China, 1966-67; dep. exec. sec. to 2 sec. State, 1968-71; dep. dir. Office Personnel Dept. State, 1972-75; minister, polit. adviser to Supreme Allied Comdr. Europe, 1975-79; sr. insp. Fgn. Service, 1979-80; insp. gen. Dept. State and Fgn. Service, 1981-83; assoc., cons. Worldwide Assn. Office of Gen. Alexander Haig, Hudson Inst., 1983-85; cons. State Dept., 1983-88, Betac Corp., Washington, Mgmt. Logistics Internat., 1983-85, Worldwide Assocs., Hudson Inst.; treas. Com. for Am., 1986; adviser U.S. del. 24th Gen. Assembly UN, 1969; spl. asst. to sec. State for UN 25th Anniversary, 1970; observer N. Atlantic Assembly, 1976-79, Western European Union, 1979; mem. Pres.'s Council on Integrity and Efficiency, 1981-83. Coord. Dept. State United Givers Fund campaign, 1960; bd. dirs. Internat. Sch., Brussels, Fulbright Com., Republic of China, 1965-68; v.p. Arlington dist. United Meth. Ch.; mem.-at-large adminstrv. bd. Walker Chapel, 1992-95. With USNR, 1943. Mem. U.S. Washington fgn. svc. assns., SHAPE Officers Assn., Delta Sigma Rho. Address: 3021 N Peary St Arlington VA 22207-5326

BROWN, ROBERT MCAFEE, minister, religion educator; b. Carthage, Ill., May 28, 1920; s. George William and Ruth Myrtle (McAfee) B.; m. Sydney Thomson Brown, June 21, 1944; children: Peter Thomson, Mark McAfee, Alison McAfee, Thomas Seabury. B.A., Amherst Coll., 1943, D.D., 1958; M. Div., Union Theol. Sem., N.Y.C., 1945; Ph.D., Columbia, 1951; postgrad., Mansfield Coll., Oxford (Eng.) U., 1949-50, St. Mary's Coll., 1959, St. Andrews (Scotland) U., 1959-60; Litt.D., U. San Francisco, 1964; L.H.D., Lewis and Clark Coll., 1964, St. Louis U., 1966, Hebrew Union Coll., 1982; LL.D., U. Notre Dame, 1965, Loyola U., 1963, Boston Coll., 1965, St. Mary's Coll., 1968, Kenyon Coll., 1981, Lehigh U., 1988; D.D., Hamilton Coll., 1968, Pacific Sch. Religion, 1967, Kalamazoo Coll., 1980, Macalester Coll., 1985, Carleton Coll., 1993. Ordained to ministry Presbyn. Ch., 1944. Asst. chaplain Amherst Coll., 1946-48; prof. religion, chmn. dept. Macalester Coll., St. Paul, 1951-53; faculty Union Theol. Sem., N.Y.C., 1953-62, prof. systematic theology, 1962-76, prof. ecumenics and world Christianity, 1976-79; prof. religion Stanford U., 1962-76; prof. theology and ethics Pacific Sch. Religion, Berkeley, 1979-85; Hanley Disting. prof. Santa Clara (Calif.) U., 1990; Montgomery fellow Dartmouth Coll., 1985; Benedict Disting. vis. prof. Carleton Coll., 1987. Author: P.T. Forsyth: Prophet for Today, 1952, The Bible Speaks to You, 1955, The Significance of the Church, 1956, (with Gustave Weigel) An American Dialogue, 1960, The Spirit of Protestantism, 1961, Observer in Rome: A Protestant Report on the Vatican Council, 1964, The Collected Writings of St. Hereticus, 1964, The Ecumenical Revolution, 1967, Vietnam: Crisis of Conscience, 1967, The Pseudonyms of God, 1972, Religion and Violence, 1973, Frontiers for the Church Today, 1973, Is Faith Obsolete?, 1974, Theology in a New Key: Responding to Liberation Themes, 1978, The Hereticus Papers, 1979, Creative Dislocation—The Movement of Grace, 1980, Gustavo Gutierrez, 1980, Making Peace in the Global Village, 1981, Elie Wiesel: Messenger to all Humanity, 1983, Unexpected News: Reading the Bible with Third World Eyes, 1984, Saying Yes and Saying No: On Rendering to God and Caesar, 1986, Spirituality and Liberation, 1988, Gustavo Gutierrez: an Introduction to Liberation Theology, 1990, Persuade Us to Rejoice: The Liberating Power of Fiction, 1992, Liberation Theology: An Introductory Guide, 1993, Reclaiming the Bible: Words for the Nineties, 1994, Dark the Night, Wild the Sea, 1998; gen. editor: The Layman's Theological Library, 12 volumes, 1956-58; translator: (deDietrich): God's Unfolding Purpose, 1960; (Casalis), Portrait of Karl Barth, 1963; (Dumas), Dietrich Bonhoeffer: Theologian of Reality, 1971; editor: (with David Scott) The Challenge to Reunion, 1963, The Essential Reinhold Niebuhr, 1986, (with Sydney Brown) A Cry for Justice: The Churches and Synagogues Speak, 1989, Kairos: Three Prophetic Challenges to the Church, 1990; contbr. to books; mem. editorial bd. various mags. and jours. Served as chaplain USNR, 1945-46. Mem. Am. Theol. Soc., Soc. Theol. Discussion, Phi Beta Kappa. Home: 2090 Columbia St Palo Alto CA 94306-1230

BROWN, ROBERT MUNRO, museum director; b. Riverside, N.J., Mar. 4, 1952; s. James Wendell and Janet Elizabeth (Munro) B.; m. Mary Ann Noel, June, 1973 (div. 1977); m. Claudia Leslie Haskell, Jan. 14, 1978. BA in Polit. Sci. cum laude, Ursinus Coll., 1973; MA in Social Scis., Rivier Coll., 1978; PhD in Early Am. History, U. N.H., 1983. Grad. asst. dept. history U. N.H., Durham, 1979-83, instr., 1983-84; site curator T.C. Steele State Hist. Site Ind. State Mus. System, Nashville, Ind., 1984-91; exec. dir. Hist. Mus. at Ft. Missoula, Mont., 1991—; hist. interpreter Strawberry Banke, Portsmouth, N.H., 1980-83; instr. Rivier Coll., Nashua, N.H., 1986-91, N.H. Coll., Nashua and Salem, 1986-91; supr. pub. programs Mus. Am. Textile History, North Andover, Mass., 1985-91; sec.-treas. Western Mont. Heritage Ctr./No. Rockies Heritage Ctr., 1992-93; mem. grad. com. U. Mont., 1993; mem. steering com. Ft. Missoula, 1993; reviewer Inst. Mus. Svcs., 1993, 94, 95, 97, 98; reviewer Am. Assn. Mus.-Mus. Asessment Programs, 1997—; mem. Mont. Com. of the Humanities Spkrs. Bur., 1995—; lectr., presenter, chair panels in field. Contbr. articles to profl. jours. Trustee Historic Harrisville, N.H., 1989-91; bd. dirs. United Peoples Found., 1991-93, v.p., 1993; mem. planning com. Western Mont. Heritage Ctr., 1991, U. Mont. Centennial Celebration, 1992, Leadership Missoula, 1992; active open space, parks and resource planning and mgmt. project team City of Missoula, 1993; mem. blue ribbon task force Five Valleys Luth. Retirement Community Planning Com., 1994. Scholar U. N.H., 1979-83, rsch. grantee, 1982; grantee Mass. Coun. on Arts and Humanities, 1986, 87, 88, Int. Mus. Svcs., 1988, 89, 90, 91, 93, 95, 97, AT&T, 1988, Am. Wool Coun., 1988, BayBank, 1989, Am. Yarn Assn., 1989, North Andover Arts Lottery Coun., 1989, 90, Mass. Cultural Coun., 1990, Greater Lawrence Cmty. Found., 1991, Mass. Arts Lottery Coun., 1991, Gallery Assn. for Greater Art, 1991, 92, 94, 95, 96, 97, 98, Mont. Com. for Humanities, 1991, 92, 93, 94, 95, 96, 97, 98, Sinclair Oil Co., 1991, Mont. Rail Link, 1992, 98, U. Mont. Found., 1992, Pepsi-Cola Co., 1992, 93, 94, 95, 96, 97, Coca-Cola Bottling Co., 1998, Cmty. Med. Ctr., 1999, St. Patrick Hosp., 1999, U.S. WEST Found., 1992, 95, The Missoulian, 1992, 95, Champion Internat., 1992, Mont. Cultural Trust, 1993, 95, 97, Missoula Rotary, 1993, Tex. Mus. Assn., 1993, Inst. Mus. Svcs., 1993, 95, Zip Beverage Co., 1994, Bitterroot Motors, 1994, 95, 96, 97, 98, Grizzly Hackle, 1994, University Motors, 1995, 96, Earl's Distributing, 1996, Norwest Bank, 1996, 97, 98; Kellogg Found. fellow, 1987. Mem. Am. Assn. Mus., Am. Assn. State and Local History (state membership rep. 1996-98), Am. Hist. Assn., Assn. Records Mgrs. and Adminstrs. (charter Big Sky chpt. 1992-94), Mont. Hist. Soc., Mus. Assn. Mont. (panelist 1994), Western Mont. Fundraisers Assn. (charter 1991, v.p. 1993-95, pres. 1995-97), Mtn. Plains Mus. Assn. (Mont. state rep. 1995-97, ann. meeting local arrangements chair 1997, chmn. scholarship com. 1998, 99, sec. 1998—), Greater Boston Mus. Educator's Roundtable (steering com. 1988-90), Masons (Missoula chpt.), Kiwanis (Sentinel chpt.), Phi Alpha Theta (Psi Pi chpt.). Democrat. Avocations: canoeing, cross-country skiing, snowshoeing. Home: 216 Woodworth Ave Missoula MT 59801-6050 Office: Hist Mus at Ft Missoula Ft Missoula Bldg 322 Missoula MT 59801

BROWN, ROBERT WALLACE, mathematics educator; b. Portland, Oreg., May 20, 1925; s. Bert and Stella (Conway) B.; m. Doris Arrilda Burroughs, Sept. 4, 1948; children: Robert Wallace, Janice Dianne. BS, Pacific U., 1950; M.S., Oreg. State U., 1952, Ph.D., 1958. Mathematician, Nat. Bur. Standards, Corona, Calif., 1952-54; Mathematician Boeing Co., Seattle, 1958-66; vis. asso. prof. Oreg. State U., Corvallis, 1966-67; prof. math. U. Alaska, Fairbanks, 1967-82; head dept. U. Alaska, 1967-77, 79-82; vis. prof. math. Lewis and Clark Coll., Portland, Oreg., 1982-85. Contbg. author: Error in Digital Computation, 1965. Served with USNR, 1942-45. Mem. Math. Assn. Am., Am. Math Soc., SIAM, Sigma Xi, Pi Mu Epsilon, Sigma Pi Sigma. Home: 20755 SW Prindle Rd Tualatin OR 97062-9701

BROWN, ROBERT WAYNE, lawyer; b. Allentown, Pa., July 6, 1942; s. P.P. and Rose (Ferrara) B.; m. Rochelle Kaplan, Oct. 23, 1977; m. Shelley Sherman, Mar. 3, 1973; children: Courtney Sherman, Robin Thea, Ryan Palmer; m. Lupe Peance, Nov. 22, 1996. AB, Franklin and Marshall Coll., 1964; JD, Cornell U., 1967. Bar: Ill. 1969, Pa. 1971. VISTA atty. Cmty. Legal Svcs., Detroit, 1967-68; asst. prof. law U. Ill., 1968-70; ct. adminstr., law clk. Lehigh County Ct. Common Pleas, 1971-72; ptnr. Gross & Brown, Allentown, 1972-76; pvt. practice law Allentown, 1976-77; sr. ptnr. Brown & Brown, Allentown, 1977-82, Brown, Brown & Solt, Allentown, 1982-85, Brown, Brown, Solt & Krouse, Allentown, 1985-89, Brown, Brown, Solt & Ferretti, Allentown, 1989—; instr. bus. law Muhlenburg Coll., 1973-76; pub. defender Lehigh County, 1973-74; mem. adv. bd. PNC Bank. Mem. Rape Crisis Coun. Lehigh Valley, 1978-84, Lehigh County Pre-trial Svcs., 1975-82; bd. dirs. Hispanic Am. Orgn., 1982-90, treas., 1983-86; bd. dirs. Lehigh County Sr. Citizens, 1980-88, pres., 1984-86; bd. dirs. Lehigh County Legal Svcs., 1973-77, Boys and Girls Club Allentown, 1994—, pres., 1998—; founding trustee Robert Clemente Charter Sch., 1998—. Recipient Cmty. Svc. award Hispanic Am. Orgn., 1985, Human Rels. Commn. award, Allentown, 1986; Lindback scholar Franklin and Marshall Coll., 1963-64. Mem. ABA, Pa. Bar Assn., Lehigh County Bar Assn., Order of Coif, Rotary (bd. dirs. Allentown 1998—). Democrat. Home: 225 Parkview Ave Allentown PA 18104-5323 Office: 1425 W Hamilton St Allentown PA 18102-4224

BROWN, ROGER DALE, college dean; b. Durant, Okla., Sept. 16, 1943; s. Paul Bruce and Blanch Elizabeth (Barr) B.; m. Judie Ann MacDermott, June 18, 1944; children: Roger Dale Jr., Jeffrey Alan. BA in Edn., Southea. State U. Okla., 1967; MEd, Ctrl. State U., Edmond, Okla., 1973; EdD, East Tex. State U., 1982. Dir. choir Beaver (Okla.) Pub. Sch., 1967-70, Borger (Tex.) Pub. Sch., 1970-73; dir. choir, chairperson dept. music Frank Phillips Coll., Borger, 1973-91, dean continuing/off-campus edn., 1991—. Pres. Tri-City Concert Assn., Borger, Tex., 1976-78, Magic Plains Arts Coun., Borger, 1983-85.; U.S. fed. govt. funds to Tex. higher edn. coordinating bd. grant to Frank Phillips Coll. Carl Perkins grantee in vocat. edn., 1991—. Mem. Tex. Adminstrs. of Continuing Edn. (chmn. West Tex. region 1993-96, state bd. dirs. 1993-96, chmn. Panhandle tech-prep consortium bd. dirs. 1996—), Rotary Internat. (mem. bd. vocat. svc. Borger club 1994-95, song leader 1982-85), Phi Delta Kappa. Methodist. Avocations: reading, gardening, singing. Office: Frank Phillips Coll PO Box 5118 Borger TX 79008-5118

BROWN, RONALD DELANO, endocrinologist; b. Grosse Pointe, Mich., Dec. 28, 1936; s. Carroll Bradley and Alice Ruth (Chapper) B.; m. Marylee Ethel Lucas, July 27, 1957; children: Linda Diane, Kent William, Mark Steven. BS with distinction, U. Mich., 1959, MD with distinction, 1963. Diplomate Am. Bd. Internal Medicine, subspecialty in endocrinology and metabolism; lic. physician Mich., Calif., Tenn., Tex., Minn., Okla. Intern Detroit Gen. Hosp., 1963-64; asst. resident in medicine U. Calif. Med. Ctr., San Francisco, 1966-68; chief resident in medicine San Francisco Gen. Hosp., 1968-69; fellow in endocrinology Vanderbilt U., Nashville, 1969-71, instr. medicine, 1969-71, asst. prof. medicine, 1971-73; assoc. prof. medicine Baylor Coll. Medicine, Houston, 1973-74, Mayo Med. Sch., Rochester, Minn., 1975-80; prof. medicine Health Scis. Ctr., U. Okla., Oklahoma city, 1980-93; clin. staff St. Joseph's Mercy Hosp., Clintown Twp., Mich., 1993—; dir. U. Okla. Hypertension Ctr., 1986-93; chief clin. hypertension Health Scis. Ctr., U. Okla., 1980-93; chief hypertension VA Hosp., Oklahoma City, 1980-86; dir. multidisciplinary hypertension rsch. tng. program (NIH), Mayo Clinic, Rochester, 1977-80; chief endocrinology Ben Taub Hosp., Houston, 1973-74, assoc. dir. clin. rsch. ctr., 1973-74; coord. Tenn. Mid-South Regional Hyper-Control Program, Vanderbilt U., 1971-73; lectr. in field. Editl. bd. Jour. Clin. Endocrinology and Metabolism, 1987-91; reviewer for Life Scis., Annals of Internal Medicine, Jour. Lab. Clin. Medicine, Am. Jour. Medicine, Endocrinology, Mayo Clinic Proceedings, Steroids; contbr. 58 articles to profl. jours. Capt. USAF, 1964-66. Fellow ACP; mem. Am. Fedn. for Clin. Rsch., Endocrine Soc., Ctrl. Soc. for Clin. Rsch., Coun. for High Blood Pressure Rsch., Inter-Am. Soc. Hypertension, Am. Soc. Hypertension, Internat. Soc. on Hypertension in Blacks, Am. Diabetes Assn., Am. Assn. Clin. Endocrinologists, Am. Soc. Internal Medicine, Midwest Salt and Water Club, Phi Kappa Phi, Phi Lambda Upsilon, Alpha Omega Alpha. Avocation: tree nursery. Office: 43171 Dalcoma Dr Ste 1 Clinton Township MI 48038-6306

BROWN, RONALD JAMES, lawyer, political consultant; b. McKeesport, Pa., Nov. 4, 1951; s. James W. and Katherine V. (Amatangelo) B.; children: Claudia Jean, Jocelyn Kaye; m. Kathy E. Brown, July 6, 1996. BA, U. Pitts., 1973, JD, 1976. Bar: Pa. 1976. Assoc. firm Lucchino, Gaitens & Hough, Pitts., 1976-79; asst. dep. contr. Allegheny County Contr.'s Office, Pitts., 1979-86; ptnr. law firm Grogan, Graffam, McGinley & Lucchino, Pitts., 1986—; polit. cons. Brown-Giorgetti Cons., Pitts., 1990—. Candidate for State Senator, Dem. Party, North Hills, Pa., 1986; chmn. Nov. Caucus, Pitts., 1995—; mem. Dem. Forum of We. Pa., Pitts., 1987-91; del. Dem. Nat. Conv., 1978. Recipient Commrs. award citation of merit Allegheny County Bd. Comms., 1984. Mem. Allegheny County Bar Assn. Roman Catholic. Avocations: golf, reading, watching hockey, travel. Office: Grogan Graffam McGinley & Lucchino 3 Gateway Ctr Pittsburgh PA 15222-1000

BROWN, RONALD LAMING, lawyer; b. Springfield, Mass., Aug. 26, 1944; s. Douglas Seaton and Elizabeth Ruth (Stover) B.; m. Barbara Jo Roesler Moher, June 13, 1967 (div. Mar., 1987); children: Kimberly Lynn, Kathryn Jo, Karen Elizabeth, Kristine Ann, John Paul; m. Susan Janet Toth, Jan. 2, 1988; 1 child, Megan Christina. Chapman Coll., 1968-70; JD, Creighton U., 1972. Bar: Neb. 1973, U.S. Dist. Ct. Neb. 1973, U.S. Ct. Appeals (8th cir.) 1974, U.S. Dist. Ct. Wyo. 1974, U.S. Ct. Appeals (10th cir.) 1976, Colo. 1987, U.S. Dist. Ct. Colo. 1987. 2d v.p., comml. loan counsel Omaha Nat. Bank, Omaha, 1973-74; prosecuting atty. Natrona County Atty., Casper, Wyo., 1974-75; partner Brown, Drew, Apostolos, Massey & Sullivan, Casper, Wyo., 1975-83; shareholder Burke & Brown, Casper, Wyo., 1983-86; pvt. practice Casper, Wyo., 1986-88, Ft. Collins, Colo., 1987—; bd. dirs. Tooke Internat., Inc.; trustee Brown Investment Trust, Ventura, Calif., 1996—; lectr. Casper (Wyo.) Col., 1980. Mem. sch. bd. St. Anthony's Sch., Casper, Wyo., 1979-82, Ft. Collins (Colo.) Connections, 1995—. Sgt. USMC, 1964-68. Mem. Neb. Bar Assn., Wyo. Bar Assn., Colo. Bar Assn. Republican. Avocations: golf, motor cycling, auto restoration, reading, home repair. Home: 1400 Wildwood Rd Fort Collins CO 80521-4026 Office: 425 W Mulberry St Ste 105 Fort Collins CO 80521-2864

BROWN, RONALD LEE, lawyer; b. Ft. Worth, July 21, 1946; s. Jack Lee and Mary Elizabeth (Batton) B.; m. Sharon Elise Haralson, Aug. 31, 1968; children: Grant A., Nathan H. BA in History, Tex. Tech U., 1968; JD, So. Meth. U., Dallas, 1975. Bar: Tex. 1975, U.S. Dist. Ct. (no. dist) Tex. 1976, U.S. Tax Ct. 1976, U.S. Ct. Appeals (5th cir.) 1976. Ptnr., pres. Baker, Mills & Glast, Dallas, 1975-80; ptnr., v.p. Riddle & Brown, Dallas, 1980-88; ptnr. Butler and Binion, Dallas, 1988-90, head corp. tax sect., Dallas mng. ptnr., 1990-93; principal Glast, Phillips & Murray, P.C., Dallas, 1993—; adj. prof. Law Sch., So. Meth. U., 1981-83; bd. dirs. Benedict Optical Inc. Sr. warden St. Michael Episc. Ch., Dallas, 1985; pres. St. Michael Found., Dallas, 1986-88; dir. NCCJ, Dallas, Planned Parenthood, Dallas, 1987-90; bd. dirs. So. Meth. U. Law Alumni, 1988-90; sec. Episc. Diocese of Dallas, 1989—; bd. dirs. Profl. Devel. Inst., 1995-99, chmn., 1999; mem. Order of Hosp. of St. John, Jerusalem, Israel, 1999—. Lt. USN, 1968-72. Mem. ABA, Prestonwood Country Club. Democrat. Office: Glast Phillips & Murray 13355 Noel Rd Ste 2200 Dallas TX 75240-6612

BROWN, RONALD MALCOLM, engineering corporation executive; b. Hot Springs, S.D., Feb. 21, 1938; s. George Malcolm and Cleo Lavonne (Plumb) B.; m. Sharon Ida Brown, Nov. 14, 1964 (div. Apr. 1974); children: Michael, Troy, George, Curtis, Lisa, Brittney. AA, Southwestern Coll., 1970; BA, Chapman Coll., 1978. Commd. USN, 1956, advanced through grades to master chief, 1973, ret., 1978; engring. mgr. Beckman Inst., Fullerton, Calif., 1978-82; mech. engring. br. mgr. Northrop Corp., Hawthorne, Calif., 1982-83; dir. of ops. Transco, Marina Del Rey, Calif., 1983-85; v.p. ops. Decor Concepts, Arcadia, Calif., 1985-87; design dir. Lockheed Aircraft Corp., Ontario, Calif., 1987-97; v.p. engring., space programs Ducommon Inc., Carson, Calif., 1997—. Mem. Soc. Mfg. Engrs., Inst. Indsl. Engrs., Nat. Trust for Hist. Preservation, Fleet Res. Assn., Am. Film Inst., Nat. Mgmt. Assn. Avocations: golf, running, racquetball.

BROWN, RONALD OSBORNE, telecommunications and computer systems consultant; b. Winchester, Mass., Apr. 9, 1941; s. Herbert Walcott and Madeleine Louise (Osborne) B.; m. Annette L. Brown; children: Melinda E., Jeffrey J. BS with distinction, U. Maine, 1963; MS, Tufts U., 1965; PhD, Queens U., Kingston, Ont., 1972. Mem. tech. staff RCA Corp., Burlington, Mass., 1965-66; rsch. assoc. Queen's U., Kingston, Ont., 1966-71; mem. sci. staff BNR, Ottawa, Ont., 1971-72; sr. systems engr. GTE Corp., Needham, Mass., 1973-83; mgr. Coopers & Lybrand, Boston, 1983-87, nat. dir, 1987-88; pvt. practice cons. Melrose, Mass., 1988-91; pres. R.O. Brown Cons., Melrose, 1991—; program coord. Northeastern U., Boston, 1976-93; cons. Bell Can., 1968-71; program chmn. Networking Mgmt. Inst.; lectr. U. Wis., 1990—. Contbg. editor Networking Mgmt. Mag., 1988-93. Mem. IEEE, Assn. Profl. Engrs. Ont., Tau Beta Pi, Phi Kappa Phi, Eta Kappa Nu. Home: 864 Quaker Ridge Rd PO Box 470 South Casco ME 04077-0470 Office: 23 Baxter St Ste 2 Melrose MA 02176-3639

BROWN, RONALD REA, software engineer, artist; b. Kansas City, Mo., Mar. 20, 1944; s. Stanton Rea and Agnes S. B.; m. Josette Adella Keenan, Aug. 14, 1977; children: Nathan William, Lisette Louise, Andrew Rea. BA in Math. magna cum laude, William Jewell Coll., 1966; MA in Math., U. Kans., 1968; MEd, Montclair State Coll., 1972. Cert. secondary sch. tchr., N.J., Pa. Vol. Peace Corps, Andhra Pradesh, India, 1969-70; tchr. Alternative West H.S., Lower Merion, Pa., 1973-79; software engr. Delta Data Syss., Trevose, Pa., 1979-83; sr. software engr. Unisys, Flemington, N.J., 1983-89, Thwing-Albert Inst. Co., Phila., 1990-94; sr. engr. Catalyst, Newtown, Pa., 1994-97, Thwing-Albert Iust. Co., Phila., 1997—; Presenter in field of art. Contbr. articles to profl. jours. Vol. Peace Corps, Andhra Pradesh, India, 1969-70. Mem. Internat. Soc. for Interdisciplinary Study of Symmetry, Lehigh (Pa.) Art Alliance (sculpture award 1992), YLEM, Internat. Sculpture Ctr., Art & Sci. Collaborations, Inc. Avocations: reading, fractals, virtual reality, robotics, 2D and 3D art based on the way a knight moves on a chessboard. Home: 569 Lake Warren Rd Upper Black Eddy PA 18972-9342 Office: Thwing-Albert Inst Co 10960 Dutton Rd Philadelphia PA 19154-3204

BROWN, ROSANNA SOFIA, landscape architect; b. San Bernardino, Calif., Sept. 11, 1958; d. Donald Brown and Rosa-Alma Valade. BA, U. South Fla., 1980; MLA, U. Tex., Arlington, 1990. Landscape architect City of Ft. Worth, 1989-92, U.S. Army Corps Engrs., Ft. Worth, 1992—. Author: CELA conf. proceedings, 1990. Mem. Am. Soc. Landscape Architects (chairwoman Dallas-Ft. Worth sect. 1992-93, sec. Tex. chpt. 1993-94, pres. Tex. chpt. 1995-96). Roman Catholic.

BROWN, ROWLAND CHAUNCEY WIDRIG, information systems, strategic planning and ethics consultant; b. Detroit, Oct. 11, 1923; s. Rowland Chauncey and Rhea (Widrig) B.; m. Kathleen Heather Sayre, May 18, 1946; children: Stephanie Anne, Geoffrey Rowland Sayre (dec.), Kathleen Heather. BA cum laude, Harvard U., 1947, JD, 1950; sr. mgmt. Sloan Sch., MIT, 1969; D. Humane Letters (hon.), Ohio Dominican Coll., 1999. Bar: D.C. 1951. Counsel Econ. Sablzn. Agy., 1950-52; staff counsel SBA, 1954; counsel Machinery and Allied Products Inst., Washington, 1955-59; with Dorr Oliver, Stamford, Conn., 1959-70, pres., 1968-70; pres., chief exec. officer Buckeye Internat., Inc., Columbus, Ohio, 1970-80; chief exec. officer Online Computer Libr. Ctr., Columbus, 1980-89; adv. bd. tchg. and learning Ohio State U. Bd. visitors Oberlin Coll. Libr.; sr. internat. cons. Coun. for Ethics and Econs.; hon. trustee Columbus Cmty. Cable Access; bd. dirs., trustee, chmn. acad. affairs Ohio Dominican Coll., chmn. external adv. bd., provost Ohio State U.; mem. race rels. vision coun. United Way. Decorated Air medal (3), Purple Heart, Korean Republic citation. Mem. ALA, Am. Soc. Info. Sci., Am. Assn. for Higher Edn., N.Y. Harvard Club, Columbus Club, Torch Club, Scioto Country Club, Rotary. Home and Office: 2711 Edington Rd Columbus OH 43221-2502

BROWN, RUBEN PERNELL, football player; b. Englewood, N.J., Feb. 13, 1972. Student, U. Pitts. Guard Buffalo Bills, 1995—. Named to All-Rookie Team, Pro Football Writers of Am., 1995, Pro Bowl, 1996. Office: care Buffalo Bills 1 Bills Dr Orchard Park NY 14127-2237*

BROWN, RUBYE ELLEN, retired nursing administrator; b. Milam County, Tex., Feb. 21, 1925; d. Henry Clarence and Carrie (Kyle) Spence; m. Elbert Howard Brown, Sept. 21, 1946; 1 child, Bert. Diploma in nursing, Brackenridge Hosp., Austin, Tex., 1946. RN, Tex. County health nurse State of Tex., Cameron; county sch. nurse Milam County, Cameron; head nurse Richards Meml. Hosp., Rockdale, Tex.; ret.; nurse church camp in summers. Mem. ANA. Home: PO Box 1292 Rockdale TX 76567-1292

BROWN, RULON SPILSBURY, agricultural consultant; b. Oct. 6, 1925; married. Student, Tex. Coll. Mines, El Paso, Brigham Young U. Gen. mgr. Corralitos Ranch, Las Cruces, N.Mex., 1967-77, Taylor Ranch, Wells, Nev., 1977-93; contract cons. various agrl., farm. and coop. assns., 1993—. Fax: (801) 947-0973. E-mail: barubar@aol.com. Address: 7576 S 2300 E Salt Lake City UT 84121

BROWN, RUSHIA, basketball player; b. May 5, 1972. B of Sociology, Furman Coll., 1994. Forward-center Spain, 1994-95, Aix-en-Provence, France, 1996-97, WNBA- Cleve. Rockers, 1997—. Named First Team All-So. Conf. & MVP 1991, 92, 93, 94. Avocations: sports, football. Office: Cleve Rockers Gund Arena One Ctr Ct Cleveland OH 44115*

BROWN, SALLY ANN, research scientist; b. N.Y.C., Sept. 8, 1959; d. Richard Daniel and Joann Ellen (Detschel) B. BS in Biology, SUNY, Geneseo, 1981, MA in Biology, 1989; postgrad., Loyola Marymount U., L.A. Grad. tchg. asst. biology dept. SUNY, Geneseo, 1983; rsch. technician dept. neurology U. Rochester, N.Y., 1984-88; rsch. assoc. dept. neurogerontology U. So. Calif., L.A., 1989-95; presenter in field. Co-author: The Basal Ganglia II Structure and Function, 1987, Aging: The Universal Human Experience, 1987; contbr. articles to profl. jours.; mem. staff Internat. and Comparative Law Jour., 1996-97, sr. note and comment editor, 1997-98. Participant, tutor Literacy Vols./ESL, Rochester, 1978; active Big Bro.-Big Sister Program, Rochester, 1985-88. Leone-Haggerty Meml. scholar Miller Place (N.Y.) PTA, 1977, Regents scholar N.Y. State Bd. Regents, Albany, 1978, Am. Mensa Edn. and Rsch. Found. scholar, 1989; Sci. and Math. fellow N.Y. State Higher Edn., Albany, 1983; Mabel Wilson Richards scholar, 1997-98. Mem. ABA, St. Thomas More Law Honor Soc., Phi Delta Phi. Home: 7230 Franklin Ave Apt 327 Los Angeles CA 90046

BROWN, SAMUEL, retired corporate executive; b. Mobile, Ala., Mar. 2, 1908; s. Milton Leopold and Edna (Solomon) B.; m. Carolyn Elkan Greenfield, Nov. 2, 1930 (dec. Oct. 1989); children: Milton Leopold, Maxine Phyllis Brown Feibelman, Carol Lynn Brown Robinson. BS, U. Ala., 1929. Mng. ptnr. Brown & Brown, Mobile, 1935-42, owner, 1942-54; pres. Brown & Brown, Inc., Mobile, 1954-84; pres. Brownfield Investment Corp., Mobile, 1954, also bd. dirs.; pres. Brown and Brown of Del., Inc., Wilmington, 1984—, also bd. dirs.; pres. Greenfield Lands, Inc., Atlanta, 1981—, also bd. dirs. Author: The Rotary Club of Mobile, Alabama, 1914-1986, Brown & Brown, May 1, 1877-Sept. 29, 1996 Events During 119 Years 5 Months; also articles. Pres. Rotary, Mobile, 1955-56, bd. trustees Mobile Pub. Libr., 1964. Recipient Disting. Svc. award Ala. Soc. for Crippled Children, 1973. Mem. Indsl. Fabrics Assn. (hon. life), Mobile Country Club. Republican. Jewish. Avocation: golf.

BROWN, SANFORD DONALD, lawyer; b. Neptune, N.J., May 16, 1952; s. Richard B. and Janet (Flint) B.; m. Joan Miller, Sept. 5, 1978; children: Jennifer, Sanford Flint, Edward. BA, Brown U., 1974; JD, Seton Hall U., Newark, 1978. Bar: N.J. 1978, U.S. Dist. Ct. N.J. 1978. Law clk. to Hon. Patrick J. McGann Freehold, N.J., 1978-79; assoc. Dawes & Youssouf, Freehold, 1979-81; ptnr. Dawes & Brown, Freehold, 1981-86, Cerrato, O'Connor, Dawes, Collins et al, Freehold, 1986-89, Cerrato, Dawes, Collins et al, Freehold, 1989—; gen. counsel Manalapan-Englishtown Regional Bd. Edn., N.J., 1979-85, 87—, Monmouth Vocat. Bd. Edn., Colts Neck, N.J., 1979—, Allenhurst Bd. Edn., 1990-98, Interlaken (N.J.) Bd. Adjustment/Planning Bd., 1990—, Manasquan River Regional Sewer Authority, Howell, 1979-91, Pioneer Farm Credit, 1990—, United Meth. Homes N.J., 1992—, Ocean Twp. Bd. Adjustment Spl. Counsel, 1995—; fee arbitrator N.J. Supreme Ct., 1995—, panel chair, 1998—. Chancellor, So. N.J. Ann. Conf., United Meth. Ch., 1995—; coach Ocean Twp. (N.J.) Recreation League, 1986-97, Ocean Twp. Little League, 1992-95; chmn. bd. trustees United Meth. Ch., 1986-91; chmn. county advancement com. Boy Scouts Am., 1989-92, atty., county exec. bd., 1992—, spl. coun., 1995—, dist. chmn., 1996—, nat. rep., 1997—; gen. counsel Monmouth Presbytery Presbyn. Ch. Recipient Monmouth Legal Sec. assn. Employer of the Year award, 1993, Monmouth Coun. Boy Scouts Disting. Adult Eagle Scout award, 1997, Silver Beaver award, 1998, Dist. Award of Merit, 1999. Mem. Monmouth Bar Assn., N.J. Bar Assn., N.J. Sch. Bd. Attys. Assn. (regional v.p. 1991), Brown U. Alumni Assn. (chpt. pres. 1986-89, 95—), Wemrock Profl. Condo Assn. (pres. 1988-96, v.p. 1996—), Nat. Eagle Scout Assn. (life), United Meth. Scouters Assn. (life). Methodist. Avocation: swimming. Office: Cerrato Dawes Collins 509 Stillwells Corner Rd Freehold NJ 07728-5302

BROWN, SARAH M., artist, gallery owner, educator, publisher; b. Longview, Tex., Jan. 30, 1935; d. Phil Uhls and Fannie Belle (Keating) B. BFA, U. Chgo., 1957; student, Tulane U., 1960, Odyssey Studio, Atlanta, 1978, Nat. Watercolor Seminar, 1980. Tchr. ceramics Pensacola Fla. Jr. Coll., 1958; dir. art dept. Pensacola Fla. Adult Vocat. Sch., 1958-59; owner S. Brown Studio-Gallery, New Orleans, 1959-63, Atlanta, 1963-89, Roswell, Ga., 1986-89; owner Sarah Brown Studio-Gallery, Atlanta, 1989—; founder Sarah Brown Art Tours, 1973—, The Little Brown Press, 1976—; conductor seminars in field. One-woman shows include Longview (Tex.) Art Assn., Pensacola Art Assn., Douglasville Cultural Arts Ctr., 1995; exhibited in group shows Nat. Western Small Painting Exhbn., 1982 (Best of Show, 1st pl.), Palm Beach Galleries (3d pl. show, 1st pl. Western category), NLAPW Ga. State Competition (1st pl. oils), Midwest Armory Art Exhbn., Chgo., Johnson Galleries, Chgo., Three Arts Club, Chgo., Southside Arts Festival, Chgo., Delgado Mus., New Orleans, Pensacola Quadricentennial, Royal Orleans Hotel, New Orleans, Piedmont Art Festival, Berman Lipton Interiors, Atlanta Artists Group Show, Jr. C. of C., , Am. Painters in Paris, Winter Pk. (Fla.) Outdoor Art Festival, Festival of the Masters, Lake Buena Vista, Fla., Knickerbocker Artists 31st Annual, N.Y.C., Catherine Lorillard Wolfe Art Club Exhibit, N.Y.C., Nat. Western Small Painting Exhbn., Bosque Farms, N.Mex., Palm Beach Galleries, New Orleans, ABC Art and Frame Show, Atlanta, Ga. Wildlife Fedn., 1994, Safari Internat. Exhbn., Galleria Mall, Atlanta, 1995; commissions include A.H. Stephens Meml., Crawfordville, State of Ga., Dept. Natural Resources, Warm Springs Lodge, Elijah Clarke Mus., New Echota Historic Site, Hofwyl Plantation, Savannah, Ga.; represented in numerous pvt. and pub. collections; contbr. art to mags. Founder Mitzi Brown Drama Fund, Shamrock H.S., Atlanta, 1974. Mem. Nat. League Am. Pen Women, Nat. Mus. Women in the Arts (charter), Am. Soc. Portrait Artists, Atlanta High Mus., Atlanta Zool. Soc., Ga. Wildlife Fedn. Office: Sarah Brown Studio-Gallery 2947 Lookout Pl NE # 2 Atlanta GA 30305-3217

BROWN, SEYMOUR R., lawyer; b. Cleve., Oct. 24, 1924; s. Leonard and Ella (Rubinstein) B.; m. Madeline Kusevich, July 8, 1956; children: Frederic M., Thomas R., Barbara L. N. Rybicki. *Mr. Brown's son, Frederic, is the Director of Marketing Operations at American Greetings Corporation. His son, Thomas R., is Vice President of Key Bank and Director of Consultant Relations. His daughter, Barbara L. Rybicki, is a registered nurse. Her Husband, Dr. George Rybicki, is a nuclear physicist at Patrick Air Force Base, Florida.* B.A., Case-Western Res. U., 1948; J.D., Cleve. State U., 1953. Bar: Ohio 1953. Prin. Seymour R. Brown & Assocs., Cleve.; pres. Carnegie Fin. Corp., Cleve., 1961—; ptnr. Brown-McCallister Real Estate, Residential & Comml. Constrn., Melbourne, Fla., 1973-81; spl. counsel to atty. gen. State of Ohio, 1963-70. Editor, pub.: Gt. Lakes Architecture, 1955-59. Chmn. CSC, University Heights, Ohio, 1978-82, 84-86, mem., 1976—; mem. exec. com. Cuyahoga County Rep. Orgn., 1966—; pres. Nat. Permanent Endowment Fund, Inc., 1988-92. With AUS, 1943-45. Decorated Purple Heart, Bronze Star. Mem. ABA, Ohio Bar Assn., Cleve. Bar Assn., Am. Arbitration Assn. (comml. arbitration panel), Zeta Beta Tau (nat. dir., nat. pres. 1978-80), Masons. Home: 3718 Meadowbrook Blvd Cleveland OH 44118-4422 Office: 30100 Chagrin Blvd Cleveland OH 44124-5705 *Dedication to family, community, profession, and friends, and a willingness to be of help and assistance in the lives of others motivates me, and has contributed to whatever success I have attained in business, professional, and community life. I believe that way to lead is to participate actively in any undertaking together with others involved. If anything I am an activist, moving as vigorously as I am able to accomplish a result.*

BROWN, SEYOM, international relations educator, government consultant; b. Hightstown, N.J., May 28, 1933; s. Benjamin I. and Sarah E. (Sokolow) B.; children: Lisa, Steven, Elliot, Nell, Benjamin, Matthew, Jeremiah. B.A., U. So. Calif., 1955, M.A., 1957; Ph.D., U. Chgo., 1963. Social scientist Rand Corp., Santa Monica, Calif., 1962-69; cons. Dept. Def. and Dept. State, Washington, 1967-68; sr. fellow Brookings Instn., Washington, 1969-76; program dir. Carnegie Endowment, Washington, 1976-78; vis. prof. Harvard U., summers 1979—; vis. fellow Brookings Instn., Washington, 1999—; acting dir. Univ. Consortium for Rsch. on N.Am., Harvard U., 1983-84; assoc. Harvard Ctr. Internat. Affairs, 1985-94; prof. Brandeis U., 1978—, chair dept. politics, 1987-93; cons. Dept. Def. and Dept. State, Washington, 1967-68. Author: New Forces in World Politics, 1974, The Crises of Power, 1979, The Faces of Power, 1994, New Forces, Old Forces, and the Future of World Politics, 1995, International Relations in a Changing Global System, 1996. Mem. Internat. Studies Assn. (Harold and Margaret Sprout award 1980). Office: Brandeis U Dept Politics Waltham MA 02254-2758

BROWN, SHARON ELIZABETH, software engineer; b. Lynn, Mass., Nov. 23, 1960; d. Leland James Brown and Vail (Wilkinson) Bartelson. BSChemE, U. Mass., 1983. Software engr. K&L Automation div. Daniel Industry, Tucson, 1983-86, sr. software engr., 1986-87, asst. mgr. software systems, 1987; software mgr. Daniel Automation, Houston, 1987-91; sr. software engr. Praxis Instruments, Inc., Houston, 1991-93, Dresser Measurement, Houston, 1993-97, Dresser Roots Instruments Operation, Houston, 1997—. Mem. NSPE, ISA. Republican. Avocations: church, contemporary Jazz, fitness, computers. Home: 5735 Henniker Dr Houston TX 77041-6589 Office: Dresser Roots Instruments Operation 16503 Park Row Houston TX 77084-5016

BROWN, SHARON GAIL, company executive, consultant; b. Chgo., Dec. 25, 1941; d. Otto and Pauline (Lauer) Schumacher; B in Gen. Studies, Roosevelt U.; m. Robert B. Ringo, Aug. 2, 1984; 1 dau. by previous marriage, Susan Ann. Info. analyst Internat. Minerals & Chems., Northbrook, Ill., 1966-71, programmer analyst, 1971-74; programmer analyst Procon Internat. Inc. subs. UOP Inc., Des Plaines, Ill., 1974-76, systems analyst, 1976-77, project leader, 1977-78; mgr. adminstrv. services, 1978-82; spl. cons. to pres. IPS Internat., Ltd., 1982-83; spl. cons. to pres. CEI Supply Co. div. Sigma-Chapman, Inc., 1984-87, ptnr. and co-founder Brown, Ringo & Assocs., 1987—; data processing cons. Mem. Buffalo Grove (Ill.) Youth Commn., 1978-82; mem. adv. com. UOP Polit. Action Com., 1979-82; Mem. Rep. Senatorial Com. Inner Circle. Mem. Am. Mgmt. Assn., Chgo. Council on Fgn. Rels., Lake Forest-Lake Bluff Hist. Soc. Home: 90 Atteridge Rd Lake Forest IL 60045-1713 *NEVER GIVE UP ... To be successful at whatever you do, you must want it so badly that you make it your top priority and work as hard as it takes for as long as it takes. To remain successful, you must do everything you do with excellence and integrity.*

BROWN, SHEBA ANN, elementary education educator; b. Miss., 1951; married; 1 child, Joshua. BS in Elem. Edn., U. So. Miss., 1973. Tchr. 4th grade Biloxi (Miss.) Pub. Schs., 1973-74; tchr. 3d grade Ferncrest Acad., New Orleans, 1974-75, Cifton Ganus Pvt. Sch., New Orleans, 1975-78; tchr. 4th grade Putnam County Schs., Palatka, Fla., 1986-87; tchr. multi-age primary class Biloxi Pub. Schs., 1987—; condr. workshops; presenter in field. Recipient Beverly Briscoe award Biloxi Schs., 1990, Enhancement award City of Biloxi, 1995, Leo Seal Tchr. Recognition award, 1999; named Miss. Tchr. of Yr., 1995, Women at the Top Coast Mag., 1996. Mem. Internat. Reading Assn., Nat. Coun. Tchrs. English, Jeff Davis PTA (treas.), Delta Kappa Gamma. Home: 135 Travia Ave Biloxi MS 39531-5328

BROWN, SHELBY JEAN BAILEY, lay worker; b. Gary, W.Va., July 21, 1947; d. Irvin and Hannah (Kennedy) Roberts; m. Garry Lee Bailey, Nov. 9, 1963 (wid. May 1982); children: Patricia Lynn, Larry Lee, Melissa Pauline; m. Freddie L. Brown, June 13, 1992. BA, Bluefield State Coll., 1986; MA, U. W.Va., 1990. Cert. elem. edn. tchr., K-8, specific learning disabilities tchr./spl. edn. K-12, W.Va. Sec./treas. Bethel Assembly of God, Kimball, W.Va., 1965-78, youth dir., 1968-78; youth dir. Rolfe Pentecostal Holiness Ch., Northfork, W.Va., 1990; tchr. Sunday sch. Bethel Assembly of God and Rolfe Pentecostal Holiness Chs., 1965-91; sch. tchr. McDowell County Bd. of Edn., Welch, W.Va., 1986-93. Sponsor Fellowship of Christian Students Club, Elkhorn Jr. High, Northfork, W.Va., 1989-91. Home: 2304 Lupine Ln Christiansburg VA 24073-6038 *Although life offered many challenges, along with the challenges come opportunities to rise higher in life and become a better person. Facing life with a positive attitude and faith in God will allow life's rocks to become stepping stones to our success.*

BROWN, SHERROD, congressman, former state official; b. Mansfield, Ohio, Nov. 9, 1952; s. Charles G. and Emily (Campbell) B.; children: Emily, Elizabeth. B.A., Yale U., 1974; M.A. in Edn., Ohio State U., 1979, M.A. in Pub. Adminstrn., 1981. Mem. Ohio Ho. of Reps., Mansfield, 1975-82; Sec. of State State of Ohio, Columbus, 1983-91; mem. 103rd-105th Congresses from 13th Ohio dist., Washington, 1993—; instr. Ohio State U., Mansfield, 1978-79; com. mem. commerce, subcom. health and environment, internat. rels. com., subcom. on Asia and the Pacific. Active India Caucus. Recipient Eagle Scout Am. 1966, Friend of Edn. award, 1978. Mem. Nat. Assn. Secs. State. Democrat. Lutheran. Office: US Ho of Reps 328 Cannon Bldg Washington DC 20515-3513*

BROWN, SHIRLEY ANN, speech-language pathologist; b. Bklyn., Oct. 9, 1935; d. Hyman and Lillian (Fuhrer) Rubak; m. Ronald Wallace Brown, Sept. 29, 1956; children: Abbie Howard, Daniel Mark. BA, Bklyn. Coll., 1956, MA, 1961. Lic. speech/lang. pathologist, N.Y., N.J. Speech pathologist Richmond County CP Treatment Ctr., S.I., N.Y., 1956-59, Coney Island Hosp., Bklyn., 1959-61, Mendham Boro Schs. and Chatham Twp. Schs., 1962-67; pvt. practice home care speech pathologist various hosps. and med. facilities, 1967-79; dir. speech pathology dept. Englewood (N.J.) Hosp., 1974-92; speech pathologist Holy Name Hosp., Teaneck, N.J., 1992-96, chief speech-lang. pathology dept., 1996—; speech pathologist Home Health Care Agys., Bergen County, 1992—; clin. supr. comm. disorders grad. program Hunter Coll., N.Y.C., 1993—, Kean Coll., N.J., 1993—, Montclair State U., 1996—. Chair svc. and rehab. Am. Cancer Soc., Hackensack, N.J. Recipient Nat. Honor citation for Profl. Edn., Am. Cancer Soc., 1985, Crimson Sword award Am. Cancer Soc., 1989. Mem. Am. Speech. Lang. and Hearing Assn. (cert., congl. action com., state chair career info., Continuing Edn. award 1983—, Outstanding Clin. Achievement award 1985), N.J. Speech, Lang. and Hearing Assn. Avocation: cooking. Home: 6 Sisson Ter Tenafly NJ 07670-1810 Office: Holy Name Hosp Speech-Lang Pathology Dept 718 Teaneck Rd Teaneck NJ 07666-4245

BROWN, SHIRLEY MARGARET KERN (PEGGY BROWN), interior designer; b. Ellensburg, Wash., Mar. 30, 1948; d. Philip Brooke and Shirley (Dickson) Kern; m. Ellery Kiess Brown, Jr., Aug. 7, 1970; children; Heather Nicole Coco, Rebecca Cherise, Andrea Shirley Serene, Ellery Philip. BA in Interior Design, Wash. State U., 1973. Apprentice then interior designer L.S. Higgins & Assocs., Bellevue, Wash., 1969-72; interior designer ColorsPlus Interiors, Inc., Bellevue, Wash., 1972, Strawns Office Furniture & Interiors, Inc., Boise, 1973-75, Empire Furniture, Inc., Tulsa; owner Inside-Out Design Co., Ltd., Boise, 1973-82; interior designer Architekton, Inc., Tulsa, 1984-86, Johnson Brand Design Group, Inc., 1986-87, Ellery Brown & Assocs. Arch., 1987—, Seattle Design Ctr.-Visions & Studio Programs, Scottsdale, Ariz., 1998—, Mehagian's Fine Furniture, Scottsdale, Ariz.; lectr. in field. Contbr. articles to profl. jours. Pres. PTA, co-chair capital bond prin. sel. com., enrollment rev. com., 1989-95; bd. dirs. Paradise Valley Young Life. Mem. AAUW, Am. Soc. Interior Designers (Wash. state presdl. citation 1995, 96, 97, presdl. citation Oreg. chpt. 1977, 95-96, dir. chpt. 1976-77, chmn. Boise subchpt. 1977-79, sec. 1980-81, Wash. chpt. 2 step workshop chmn., NCIDQ chmn. 1993-97), Nat. Soc. Interior Designers, Idaho Hist. Co., Wash. State U. Alumni Assn., Jr. League Seattle, Jr. League Phoenix, Zonta, Alpha Gamma Delta. Republican. Presbyterian. Office: 16227 N 50th St Scottsdale AZ 85254-9652

BROWN, STELLA CHANEY, advertising agency executive; b. East St. Louis, Ill., Apr. 1, 1924; d. James Oscar and Lela Elizabeth (Hartill) Chaney; student Northwestern U., 1941-42, Jefferson Coll., 1942-45; m. A. Harvey Brown, Nov. 1, 1946 (div. Nov. 1960); children—Wendy Alexandra Brown Kennedy, Deborah Elisabeth Brown Garrity. Advt. mgr. Sonnenfelds, St. Louis, 1943; dir. men's wear advt. Stix, Baer & Fuller, St. Louis, 1944; account exec., copy writer Hillman Shane Breyer Agy., Los Angeles, 1945; copy dir. Harry Serwer Agy., N.Y.C., 1945-46; advt. mgr. Libson Shops, St. Louis, 1946-47; asst. advt. dir. Edison Bros. Stores, Inc., 1947-53; copy dir., account exec. Hirsch-Tamm & Ullman Agy., 1957-58; pres. Stella Chaney Brown Advt., Inc., Clayton, Mo., 1959—; dir. St. Louis Broadcasting Co., Inc.; fashion editor Prom Mag., 1946—. Mem. Am. Fedn. Astrologers. Editor: Wheelspin, 1953-58. Address: 11775C Casa Grande Dr Saint Louis MO 63146-4242

BROWN, STEPHANIE CECILE, librarian, writer; b. Pasadena, Calif., Mar. 23, 1961; d. Harry Francis and Anne Catherine (Murray) B.; m. Derek Lawrence Christiansen, Dec. 1, 1991; children: Nathaniel, Thomas. BA, Boston U., 1984; MFA, U. Iowa, 1986; MLS, U. Calif., Berkeley, 1987. Libr. specialist Orange County Pub. Libr., 1989—. Author: Allegory of the Supermarket, 1998; contbr. poetry to profl. publs. Recipient Jessica Maxwell Meml. Poetry prize Am. Poetry Rev., 1994. Roman Catholic. Office: San Juan Capistrano Regional Libr 31495 El Camino Real San Juan Capistrano CA 92675

BROWN, STEPHEN BERNARD, corporate lawyer; b. N.Y.C., Apr. 26, 1939; m. Linda S. Brown, Dec. 17, 1963; children: Allison, Jennifer. BA, Columbia U., 1960, BS, 1961; LLB, NYU, 1965. Bar: N.Y. 1965. Assoc. Gainsburg, Gottlieb, Levitan & Cole, N.Y.C., 1965-67; corp. atty. Champion Internat. Corp., Stamford, Conn., 1968-80, v.p., sr. counsel, 1980-96, sr. v.p., gen. counsel, 1997—. Office: Champion International Corp One Champion Plz Stamford CT 10128

BROWN, STEPHEN BRYAN, real estate editor; b. Denison, Tex., Mar. 15, 1955; s. Bryan Stevenson and Elizabeth Lorraine (Towns) B. BFA, So. Meth. U., 1977. News reporting intern Dallas Morning News, 1977-78, Met. reporter, 1978-80, bus. news reporter, 1980-82, real estate editor, 1982—; Dallas corr. Nat. Real Estate Investor, Atlanta, 1980—. Mem. Nat. Assn. Real Estate Editors (former dir.). Office: The Dallas Morning News 508 Young St Dallas TX 75202-4828*

BROWN, STEPHEN D., lawyer; b. Boston, 1949. BA, Williams Coll., 1971; JD, Villanova U., 1976. Bar: Mass. 1976, Pa. 1978. Law clk. to Hon. Daniel H. Huyett, 3d U.S. Dist. Ct. (ea. dist.) Pa., 1976-78; ptnr. Dechert Price & Rhoads, Phila. Editor-in-chief Villanova U. Law Rev., 1976. Office: Dechert Price & Rhoads 1717 Arch St Ste 4000 Philadelphia PA 19103-2793

BROWN, STEPHEN IRA, mathematics educator; b. Bklyn., July 14, 1938; s. Milton Frank and Ruth (Mittman) B.; m. Eileen Thaler, June 12, 1960; children: Jordan David, Sharon Jean. A.B., Columbia Coll., 1960; M.A. in Teaching (Sloan fellow 1960-61), Harvard U., 1961, Ed.D., 1967. Instr. math. and edn. Simmons Coll., Boston, 1962-65; asst. prof. edn. Harvard U., 1966-72; vis. prof. Hebrew U., Jerusalem, 1970-71; asso. prof. Syracuse (N.Y.) U., 1972-73; mem. faculty SUNY, Buffalo, 1973-98; prof. math. edn. SUNY, 1979-98, prof. philosophy of edn., 1982-98, prof. emeritus, 1998—; vis. prof. U. Ga., Athens, 1979-80; vis. scholar Harvard U., Cambridge, Mass., 1993-94; participant ethics workshops Coll. Jewish Studies, Buffalo, 1974-76. Author: Some Prime Comparisions, 1978, Student Generations, 1987, Posing Mathematically, 1996; co-author: The Art of Problem Posing, 1983, rev. edit., 1990; co-author: Mathematics, Pedagogy and Secondary Teacher Education, 1996; co-editor: Progressive Education: A Movement and Its Professional Journal, 1988, Problem Posing: Reflections and Applications, 1993; editor: Creative Problem Solving, 1989; mem. rev. bd. Ednl. Theory, 1983-87; mem. editorial bd. Math. Tchr., 1977-70, For Learning of Math., 1980—; mem. adv. bd. Humanistic Math. Network Jour., 1995—; contbr. articles to profl. jours. Mem. adv. council Inst. Jewish Life, 1973-75. Grantee Dewey Found., 1979-80, NSF, 1983-86, 90-97; John Dewey sr. fellow, 1986-87. Fellow Philosophy Edn. Soc.; mem. John Dewey Soc. (bd. dirs. 1976-78), Math. Assn. Am., Nat. Council Tchrs. Math., Phi Beta

Kappa, Phi Delta Kappa. Home: 86 Sherbrooke Ave Amherst NY 14221-4606 Office: SUNY Buffalo Grad Sch Edn Amherst NY 14260 *I attribute a large part of my success to lack of clarity and specificity with regard to goals, to ambiguity and vagueness with regard to principles, to a sense of humor which provides distance between a taken for granted reality and my personal world, and to a general disinclination to analyze what accounts for my success.*

BROWN, STEPHEN LAWRENCE, environmental consultant; b. San Francisco, Feb. 16, 1937; s. Bonnar and Martha (Clendenin) B.; m. Ann Goldsberry, Aug. 13, 1961; children: Lisa, Travis, Meredith. BS in Engring. Sci., Stanford U., 1958, MS in Physics, 1961; PhD in Physics, Purdue U., 1963. Ops. analyst Stanford Rsch. Inst., Menlo Park, Calif., 1963-74, program mgr., 1974-77, dir. Ctr. Resource and Environ. Systems Studies, 1977-80, dir. Ctr. Health and Environ. Rsch., 1980-83; assoc. dir. Commn. on Life Scis. NAS, Washington, 1983-86; prin. Environ Corp., Arlington, Va., 1986-91; mgr. risk assessment ENSR Cons. and Engring., Alameda, Calif., 1992-93; dir. Risks of Radiation and Chem. Compounds (R2C2), Oakland, Calif., 1993—; mem. sci. adv. bd. EPA, Washington, 1991—; mem. coms. SAB, NAS, 1980-87. Contbr. over 20 articles to profl. jours., chpts. to books; author over 100 reports in field. Mem. Internat. Soc. Exposure Assessment, Soc. for Risk Analysis, Phi Beta Kappa, Sigma Xi, Sigma Pi Sigma, Tau Beta Pi. Office: R2C2 4700 Grass Valley Rd Oakland CA 94605-5622

BROWN, STEPHEN LEE, insurance company executive; b. Providence, July 6, 1937. AB, Middlebury Coll., 1958. CLU, FSA. With John Hancock Mut. Life Ins. Co., Boston, 1958—, asst. actuary, 1963-67, assoc. actuary, 1967-70, 2d v.p., 1970-73, v.p., actuary, 1973-77, sr. v.p., treas., 1977-81, exec. v.p., 1981-87, pres., chief ops. officer, vice chmn. bd., 1987-92, chmn., CEO, 1992—, also bd. dirs.; bd. dirs. John Hancock Subs., Inc., The Berkeley Fin. Group, Fed. Res. Bank of Boston, CareGroup; mem. tax com. Mut. Life Ins. Co. Bd. dirs. Jobs for Mass., Alfred P. Sloan Found., Com. for Econ. Devel.; trustee Wang Ctr. for Performing Arts; chmn. Boston Coord. Com. (The Vault). 1st lt. U.S. Army, 1956-59. Fellow Soc. Actuaries; mem. Am. Coun. Life Ins. (bd. dirs.), Life Ins. Assn. Mass. (bd. dirs.), Boston Life Underwriters Assn., Am. Acad. Actuaries, Actuaries Club Boston, Algonquin Club, Comml. Club (pres. 1994-96). Office: John Hancock Mut Life Ins John Hancock Place PO Box 111 Boston MA 02117-0111

BROWN, STEPHEN NEAL, computer engineer; b. Austin, Tex., July 30, 1952; s. Edward James and Alice Marie (Stewart) B. BS in Mech. Engring., U. Tex., 1975, MS in Mech. Engring., 1978, MS in Elec. Engring., 1984, PhD in Computer Engring., 1989. Registered profl. engr., Tex. Jr. engr. IBM, Austin, 1975-76, assoc. engr., scientist, 1976-79, sr. assoc. engr., scientist, 1979-89, devel. staff engr., 1989-92; pres. Knowledge Innovations, Inc., Austin, 1992—; grad. rsch. asst. II, U. Tex.-Austin, 1984-85. Team leader CD, San Antonio, 1969; aquatic dir. summer camp Boy Scouts Am., Kerrville, Tex., 1973. Recipient Eagle Scout award Boy Scouts Am., 1969. Mem. IEEE Computer Soc., Assn. Computing Machinery, ASME (1st Place award for paper 1975), Tau Beta Pi, Eta Kappa Nu. Avocation: travel. Home: 14307 Richard Walker Blvd Austin TX 78728-6863 Office: Knowledge Innovations Inc 14307 Richard Walker Blvd Austin TX 78728-6863

BROWN, STEPHEN THOMAS, magistrate judge; b. N.Y.C., Feb. 1, 1947; s. Albert and Ruth Hope (Kaff) B.; m. Yvonne Tobias Brown, Aug. 10, 1968. BS, Fla. State U., 1968; JD, U. Miami, Fla., 1972. Bar: Fla. 1972, U.S. Dist. Ct. (so. dist.) Fla. 1973, U.S. Dist. Ct. (mid. dist.) Fla. 1989, U.S. Ct. Appeals (11th cir.) 1973, U.S. Supreme Ct. 1976. Atty. Preddy, Kutner & Hardy, Miami, Fla., 1972-77; ptnr. Preddy, Kutner & Hardy, 1977-86, Preddy, Kutner, Hardy, Rubinoff, Brown & Thompson, Miami, 1986-91; U.S. magistrate judge U.S. Dist. Ct. (so. dist.) Fla., Miami, 1991—; adj. prof. U. Miami Sch. Law, 1983-84; vice chmn. auto ins. com. Fla. Bar, 1979-80, chmn. grievance com., 1981-84; mem. adv. com. on rules and procedures So. Dist. Fla., 1995—; mem. leadership coun. Fla. State U. Sch. of Arts & Scis. Mem. ABA, Acad. Fla. Trial Lawyers, Dade County Bar Assn., Fla. State U. Alumni Assn. (dist. v.p. 1993—), Seminole Boosters Inc. (bd. dirs. 1988-93), Seminole Club Dade County (pres. 1984-87), U. Miami Law Sch. Alumni Assn. (bd. dirs. 1994—). Avocations: snow skiing, fishing, golf. Office: US Dist Ct 300 NE 1st Ave Miami FL 33132-2126

BROWN, STEVEN BRIEN, radiologist; b. Ft. Collins, Colo., Jan. 18, 1952; s. Allen Jenkins and Shirley Irene (O'Brien) B.; m. Susan Jane DiTomaso, Sept. 10, 1983; children: Allison Grace, Laura Anne. BS, Colo. State U., 1974; MD, U. Calif., San Diego, 1978. Diplomate Am. Bd. Radiology, Am. Bd. Neuroradiology and Vascularand Interventional Radiology. Intern U. Wash., Seattle, 1978-79; resident in radiology Stanford (Calif.) U., 1979-82; fellow in interventional and neuro-radiology Wilford Hall, USAF Med Ctr., San Antonio, 1982-83; staff radiologist Wilford Hall, USAF Med Ctr., 1983-86; staff radiologist Luth. Med. Ctr., Wheat Ridge, Colo., 1986—, chief angiography and interventional radiology, 1987-94; chief dept. med. imaging Luth. Med. Ctr. Joint Venture, Wheat Ridge, Colo., 1994-96; pres. Luth. Med. Ctr. Joint Venture, 1992-95; mem. bd. mgrs. Primera HealthCare LLC, 1995-97; pres. HealthCare Select Inc., 1995—. Contbr. articles to profl. jours. Mem. Rep. Nat. Com., Washington, 1984—, Nat. Rep. Senatorial Com., 1985—, Rep. Presdl. Task Force, 1986—; bd. dirs. The Health Care Initiative. Maj. USAF, 1982-86. Fellow Radiol. Soc. N.Am.; mem. Colo. Radiol. Soc. (pres. 1995-96), Rocky Mt. Radiol. Soc. (pres. 1994-95), Am. Coll. Radiology (exec. com. intersoc. commn. 1996—), Soc. Cardiovasc. and Interventional Radiology, Western Neuroradiol. Soc., Am. Soc. Neuroradiology, Colo. Preferred Physicians Orgn. (bd. dirs. 1987—), World Wildlife Orgn., Colo. Angio Club. Republican. Presbyterian. Avocations: skiing, sailing, gardening. Office: Luth Med Center 8300 W 38th Ave Wheat Ridge CO 80033-6005

BROWN, STEVEN HARRY, corporation health physicist, consultant; b. Phila., Sept. 16, 1948; s. Robert Martin and Vera Ethel (Lipovsky) B.; m. Kathryn Helena Vassie, May 24, 1970; children: Chad, Joshua, Sean. A.B.S., Temple U., 1970, B.S., 1971; M.A., West Chester (Pa.) U., 1974. Diplomate Am. Acad. Health Physics (panel examiner 1988-91). Health physicist Temple U., Phila., 1969-71; tchr. phys. sci. Phila. Sch. Dist., 1971-76; mgr. radiation protection Westinghouse Electric Corp., Lakewood, Colo., 1976-80; mgr. western regional office Radiation Mgmt. Corp., Phila., 1980-82; prin. safety analysis engr. Rockwell Internat., Golden, Colo., 1982-83, program mgr. waste isolation pilot project, 1983-85; sr. project mgr. West Valley Demonstration Project Dames and Moore, West Valley, N.Y., 1985-87; dir. Radiol. Svcs., 1987-92; dir. Dept. of Energy programs Western U.S. Internat. Tech. Corp., Englewood, Colo., 1992—; U.S. rep. Internat. Conf. on Radiation Hazards in Mining, Beijing, 1986. Mem. Nat. Health Physics Soc. (pres. Rocky Mountain chpt. 1982-83), Am. Nuclear Soc. Office: IT Corp 5200 S Quebec St Englewood CO 80111-2100

BROWN, STEVEN L., art educator; b. Chickasha, Okla., Nov. 26, 1951; s. Wendell Vinton and Beverly Jean (Holcombe) B.; m. Carrie Ann Meeks, Nov. 26, 1960; children: Mat, Sean. BA, Okla. Coll. Liberal Arts, 1974; BFA, U. Okla., 1976; MFA, U. Ohio, 1978. Asst. prof. U. Americas, Puebla, Mex., 1978-79; instr. art U. Scis & Arts Okla., Chickasha, 1980-88, asst. prof. art, 1988-92, assoc. prof. art, 1992—; adv. panelist Okla. State Arts Coun., Oklahoma City, 1988-94. Mem. Individual Artists of Okla., Okla. Visual Arts Coalition. Avocations: art history, anthropology, philosophy. Home: 119 Skyline Dr Chickasha OK 73018-7265 Office: U Sci & Arts Okla PO Box 82345 Chickasha OK 73018

BROWN, STEVEN SPENCER, lawyer; b. Manhattan, Kans., Feb. 26, 1948; s. Gerald James and Buelah Marie (Spencer) B. BBA, U. Mo., 1970, JD, 1973. Bar: Mo. 1973, U.S. Tax Ct. 1974, Ill. 1977, U.S. Dist. Ct. (no. dist.) Ill. 1979, U.S. Ct. Appeals (7th cir.) 1980, U.S. Ct. Claims 1986, Calif. 1989, U.S. Ct. Appeals (11th cir.) 1989. Trial atty. IRS Regional Counsel, Chgo., 1973-78; sr. trial atty. IRS Dist. Counsel, Chgo., 1978-79; assoc. Silets & Martin Ltd., Chgo., 1979-85, ptnr., 1985-92; ptnr. Martin, Brown & Sullivan Ltd., Chgo., 1992—; adj. prof. John Marshall, Chgo., 1985—. Republican. Presbyterian. Avocations: golf, tennis. Home: 1340 N Astor St Apt 2903 Chicago IL 60610-8438 Office: Martin Brown & Sullivan Ltd 10th Fl 321 S Plymouth Ct Chicago IL 60604-3912

BROWN, STEVEN THOMAS, communications company official; b. Monticello, Fla., Mar. 31, 1961; s. Homer Thomas and Brenda (Leviner) B.; m. Alisa Walleen Senterfit, Feb. 28, 1987; children: David Gregory, Emily Kaytlin, Austin Thomas. AA in Bus. Adminstrn., Tallahassee C.C., 1981; BA in Econs., Fla. State U., 1983, BA in Internat. Affairs, 1983; MBA, Nova Southeastern U., 1992. Fiscal clk. II Dept. Adminstrn. State of Fla., Tallahassee, 1983-84; mgr. trainee Winn Dixe Inc., Tallahassee, 1982-86; pers. aide Dept. Adminstrn. State of Fla., Tallahassee, 1984-85, benefit cal. specialist, 1986-88; regulatory analyst I Fla. Pub. Svc. Commn., Tallahassee, 1988-89, regulatory analyst II, 1989-91, regulatory analyst III, 1991-92, regulatory analyst supr., 1992-96; sr. dir. regulatory analysis and compliance Intermedia Comm., Tampa, Fla., 1996—. Avocations: softball, golf, reading, gardening. Home: 2108 Golf Manor Blvd Valrico FL 33594-7290 Office: Intermedia Comm Corp Hdqs 3625 Queen Palm Dr Tampa FL 33619-1309

BROWN, STRATTON SHARTEL, lawyer; b. Ann Arbor, Mich., Sept. 13, 1923; s. William Ellis and Eleanor York (Shartel) B.; m. Joyce Laughlin Hall; children: Paula Brown Gray, Duncan Hall. BA, U. Mich., 1947, JD, 1949. Bar: Mich. 1949. Instr. USN Midshipman Sch., Columbia U., N.Y.C., 1944; assoc. Miller, Canfield, Paddock and Stone P.L.C., Detroit, 1949-58; ptnr. Miller, Canfield, Paddock & Stone, Detroit, 1958-89, mng. ptnr., 1973-81, adminstrv. ptnr., 1978, of counsel, 1989—. Mem. Gov.'s Commn. on Bed Reduction, Lansing, Mich., 1979, Mayor's Fiscal Stabilization Commn., Detroit, 1981; gen. sec. Southeastern Mich. Regional Transp. Coord. Coun. Lt. (j.g.) USNR. Mem. ABA (chmn. transp. subcom. urban law), State Bar Mich., Detroit Bar Assn., Govt. Fin. Officers Assn., Nat. Inst. Mcpl. Law Officers, Nat. Assn. Bond Lawyers, Orchard Lake Country Club, Belvedere Country Club, Order of the Coif. Episcopal. Office: Miller Canfield Paddock & Stone PLC 150 W Jefferson Ave Fl 25th Detroit MI 48226-4432 *As a lawyer for almost 50 years I view myself in drafting documents, briefs and legislation as a tranferer of ideas and thoughts, mine and others. To do so effectively, I believe in keeping this short and simple.*

BROWN, STUART I., ophthalmologist, educator; b. Chgo., Mar. 1, 1933; s. Leonard and Ann (Gladin) B.; m. Isabel Bodor; children: Sarah, Emily. B.M.S., U. Ill.-Chgo., 1955, M.D., 1957. Intern Jackson Meml. Hosp., Miami, Fla., 1957-58; resident in opthalmology, Eye, Ear, Nose and Throat Hosp., Tulane Med.Sch., New Orleans, 1961; fellow in cornea Mass. Eye and Ear Infirmary, Boston, 1962-66; clin. asst. prof. dept. opthalmology N.Y. Hosp.-Cornell Med. Ctr., N.Y.C., 1966, dir. cornea services cornea research lab, 1966-69, clin. assoc. prof., 1970-73; chmn., prof. dept. opthalmology U. Pitts. Sch. Medicine, 1974-82, U. Calif. Sch. Medicine-San Diego, 1983—; bd. dirs. nat. adv. commn. Nat. Eye Bank, Inc. Recipient Heed Ophthalmic Found. award, 1976. Mem. Am. Acad. Ophthalmology, AMA, Assn. Research in Vision and Ophthalmology, Assn. U. Profs. Ophthalmology, Internat. Soc. Eye Research, Internat. Corneal Soc. (pres.). Office: U Calif San Diego Shiley Eye Ctr - Ophthalmol 9415 Campus Dr La Jolla CA 92093-0946

BROWN, STUART L., tax specialist. BA, Yale Coll., 1972; JD, Harvard U., 1975. Law clk. to Judge Arnold Raum U.S. Tax Ct., Washington, 1975-77; atty. Caplin & Drysdale, Chartered, Washington; dp. chief of staff Joint Com. on Taxation, IRS, Washington, 1989-91, assoc. chief counsel, 1991-94, chief counsel, 1994—; instr. corp. taxation Am. U. Law Sch., Washington, 1981; adj. prof. grad. tax program Georgetown U. Law Ctr., Washington, 1982-89. Office: Dept of Treasury Office of Chief Counsel 1111 Constitution Ave NW Washington DC 20224-0001

BROWN, SUE, foundation executive; b. Ft. Bragg, N.C., July 13, 1945; d. Gifford Wesley and Carol Claire (Mathwig) Zimmerman; m. Richard Ellsworth Brown, June 17, 1967; children: Matthew M., Terra L., Jennifer B. BA, Lawrence U., 1967. Sec. U.S Congressman Tom Railsback, Washington, 1967-68; mgmt. intern HUD, Washington, 1968-69, housing/community devel. specialist, 1969-79; pvt. practice Sioux Falls, S.D., 1979-84. Rep. Lutheran Brotherhood, 1989-92; bd. dirs., officer S.D. Housing Authority, Sioux Falls Housing Authority, United Way, YWCA, Turning Point, Habitat Humanity, Mundt Found., others; mem. Sioux Falls Sch. Bd., 1983-89. Republican. Lutheran. Home: 9 Elkjer Cir Sioux Falls SD 57103-4338 Office: Sioux Falls Area Found 1000 N West Ave Sioux Falls SD 57104-1332

BROWN, SUSAN THOMAS, research scientist; b. Chester, Pa., Mar. 20, 1953; d. Wesley J. and Althea (Jackson) Thomas; m. Paul Edward Rittenhouse, Apr. 5, 1997; children: Naomi, Eden, Bethel. BS in Chem. Engring., U. Wis., 1980; diploma with honors, VonKarman Inst., Belgium, 1982; PhD, Free U. Brussels, Belgium, 1985. Rsch. scientist Norsk Hydro, Norway, 1986-89; sr. rsch. scientist Battelle, Columbus, Ohio, 1989-97, tech. access leader, 1997—; allocations chmn. Ohio Supercomputer Ctr., Columbus, 1993—; chem. expert United Nations Spl. Com., N.Y.C., 1996-98. Recipient R & D 100 award, 1997. Mem. Battelles Spkrs. Bur., Moose Lodge, Apha Gamma Sigma. Achievements include 2 patents for non-intrusive pressure sensor. Office: Battelle 505 King Ave Columbus OH 43201-2693

BROWN, SUSIE WARRINGTON, foundation executive; b. Lambert, Miss., Apr. 18, 1952; d. Richard Leon and Mary Josephine (White) Warrington; children: Melissa Jo, Ronny Leon. BBA, Delta State U., 1985; M of Health Sci., Wichita State U., 1987. Exec. dir. Harvey County United Way, Halstead, Kans., 1985-87, United Way Washington County, Greenville, Miss., 1987-90, United Way Kankakee (Ill.) County, 1991-94, United Way of Greater Utica, N.Y., 1994-97; human svcs. coord. County of Oneida, Utica, N.Y., 1997-98; v.p. resource devel. United Way Somerset County, Somerville, 1998—; co-founder, dir. Christmas in Apr., Kankakee, 1991—; dir. Cmty. Resource Ctr., Kankakee, 1992—; chmn. mayor's adv. com. Cmty. Econ. Devel., Kankakee, 1994; founder Blueprint, 1994, Success by Six, 1995. Treas. Eastside Bus. Coun., Kankakee, 1991—; bd. dirs. Land of Oneida Boy Scouts Am., leadership giving chair, v.p., 1997-98. Recipient Point of Light award Pres. George Bush, 1990, Key to the City award Mayor Frank Self, 1992, Larry Power Comty. Excellence award Bourbonnais C. of C., 1994, Point of Light award Congressman Tom Ewing, 1992; Gus Shea Meml. scholar United Way Am., 1993. Mem. Manteno C. of C. (bd. dirs. 1992—), Kiwanis (com. chair 1991—), Rotary. Baptist. Avocations: reading, walking, community theater, collecting National Geographic magazines. E-mail: swb@uwscty.org. Fax: (908) 725-5598. Home: Staee Hill Rd Califon NY 07830 Office: United Way Somerset County 205 W Main St Somerville NJ 08876

BROWN, SUZANNE WILEY, museum director; b. Cheyenne, Wyo., Aug. 28, 1938; d. Robert James and Catharine Helen (Schroeder) Wiley; BS with honors, U. Wyo., 1960, MS, 1964; postgrad. U. Cin. Med. Sch., 1965-66, U. Ill., 1969-72; m. Ralph E. Brown, July 19, 1968; 1 dau., Nina M. Rsch. asst. Harvard Med. Sch., 1962-63; rsch. asst. U. Cin. Med. Sch., 1964-65; sr. lab. asst. U. Chgo., 1966-67; rsch. assoc. U. Colo. Med. Sch., 1968; teaching asst. U. Ill., 1971-73; exec. asst. Chgo. Acad. Scis., 1974-82, asst. dir., 1982-84, assoc. dir., 1984-90, ret.; mem. adv. bd. Mitchell Indian Mus., Evanston, Ill., Fechin Inst., Taos, N.Mex.; mem. collectors com. Field Mus., Chgo. NDEA fellow, 1960-62. Mem. Achievement Rewards Coll. Scis., Brookfield Zool. Soc. (bd. govs.), Phi Beta Kappa, Sigma Xi, Phi Kappa Phi.

BROWN, TED LEON, JR., investment company executive; b. Lawrence, Kans., Jan. 14, 1956; s. Ted Leon and Simona (Garcia) B.; m. Cynthia Marie Fulmer, Jan. 26, 1974 (div. 1983); children: Chauntel M., Donald E.; m. Cynthia Jean Ford (div. 1993); children: Mark W. Kurta, Jennifer L. Kurta; m. Anne E. Scott, Aug. 19, 1995; 1 child, Amber Scott. Grad. high sch. Produce mgr. Pantry Pride, Lauderhill, Fla., 1971-77; asst. grocery mgr. Albertsons South Co., Plantation, Fla., 1977-79; pres. Brown & Brown Investments Inc., Ft. Lauderdale, Fla., 1980-91, Advent Investments Inc., Tamarac, 1990-92, Safeguard Investments Inc., Coral Springs, Fla., 1995-98; property mgr. Shaker Village, Tamarac, 1998—. Chmn. adv. bd. Pinewood Elem. Sch., North Lauderdale, 1987-89; exec. dir. Fla. Lions Eye Bank, Miami, 1989-91; chmn. Boy Scouts Am., North Lauderdale, 1987. Recipient Landscape Excellence award,, City of Boca Raton, 1989, Landscape Maint. award, Tishman Speyer Properties, 1990, Gov.'s Achievement award, Lions, 1989. Mem. Lions (pres. Tamarac 1990-91). Home: 12162 NW 23rd Mnr Coral Springs FL 33065-3282 Office: Shaker Village 40 Meacham Ln Tamarac FL 33319-2416

BROWN, TERRENCE CHARLES, art association executive, researcher, lecturer; b. N.Y.C., Oct. 2, 1949; s. Robert Carl and Ruth Carothers Johnson; m. Catherine Simms Citarella, Apr. 24, 1982; children: Peter Huston, Christopher Simms. B.A., Vanderbilt U., Nashville, 1971. Curator Soc. Illustrators Mus. Am. Illustration, N.Y.C., 1972-83; dir. Soc. Illustrators, N.Y.C., 1983—; instr. Sch. of Visual Arts, N.Y.C., 1995—. Contbr.: 200 Years of American Illustration, 1976, The Illustrator in America: 1880-1980, 1984. Served to capt. USAR, 1971-79. Office: Soc of Illustrators 128 E 63rd St New York NY 10021-7303

BROWN, TERRENCE J., federal agency administrator; b. Sarnia, Ont., Can., July 29, 1947; m. LInda Whitlock; children from previous marriage: Allison, Tristan. B in Polit. Sci., Kalamazoo Coll.; M in Internat. Devel. and Law, Fletcher Sch. Law & Diplomacy. With USAID, 1971—; chief project office USAID, Bolivia, 1979-80; dep. dir. regional devel. office USAID, Caribbean, 1981-85; dir. Office of Devel. Resources for L.Am. and Caribbean USAID, 1986-90; mission dir. USAID, Guatemala, 1990-93; asst. to adminstr. for policy and program coordination USAID, 1993-95, dep. asst. adminstr. for Asia and Near East, 1995-97, asst. adminstr. for mgmt., 1997—; career min. Sr. Fgn. Svc. Office: USAID RRB 1300 Pennsylvania Ave NW Washington DC 20523

BROWN, THEODORE LAWRENCE, chemistry educator; b. Green Bay, Wis., Oct. 15, 1928; s. Lawrence A. and Martha E. (Kedinger) B.; m. Audrey Catherine Brockman, Jan. 6, 1951; children: Mary Margaret, Karen Anne, Jennifer Gerarda, Philip Matthew (dec.), Andrew Lawrence. BS in Chemistry, Ill. Inst. Tech., 1950; PhD, Mich. State U., 1956. Mem. faculty U. Ill., Urbana, 1956—, prof. chemistry, 1965-93, prof. chemistry emeritus, 1993—, vice chancellor for rsch., dean Grad. Coll., 1980-86, dir.Beckman Inst. for Advanced Sci. and Tech., 1987-93; vis. scientist Internat. Meteorol. Inst., Stockholm, 1972; Boomer lectr. U. Alta., Edmonton, Can., 1975; Firth vis. prof. U. Sheffield, Eng., 1977; mem. bd. govs. Argonne Nat. Lab., 1982-88, Mercy Hosp., Urbana, 1985-89, Chem. Abstracts Svc., 1991-96, Arnold and Makel Beckman Found., 1994—, Am. Chem. Soc. Pub., 1996—. Author: (with R.S. Drago) Experiments in General Chemistry, 3d edit., 1970, General Chemistry, 2d edit., 1968, Energy and the Environment, 1971, (with H.E. LeMay and B.E. Bursten) Chemistry: The Central Science, 1977, 8th edit., 1999; assoc. editor Inorganic Chemistry, 1969-78; contbr. articles to profl. publs. Mem. Govt.-Univ.-Industry Roundtable Coun., 1989-94; bd. dirs. Champaign County Opportunities Industrialization Ctr., 1970-79, chmn. bd. dirs., 1975-78. With USN, 1950-53. Sloan rsch. fellow, 1962-66, NSF sr. postdoctoral fellow, 1964-65, Guggenheim fellow, 1979. Fellow AAAS, Am. Acad. Arts and Scis.; mem. Am. Chem. Soc. (award in inorganic chemistry 1972, award for disting. svc. in advancement of inorganic chemistry 1993), Sigma Xi, Alpha Chi Sigma. Home: 309 Yankee Ridge Ln Urbana IL 61802-7115 Office: U Ill 426A CLSL Box 13-6 601 S Goodwin Ave Urbana IL 61801-3709

BROWN, THEODORE M., history educator, curator, historical consultant; b. N.Y.C., May 12, 1942; s. Philip and Anne (Rabinowitz) B.; m. Danielle Fraenkel, Dec. 21, 1963 (div. Dec. 1981); children: Elena Julienne, David Avram; m. Corinne Sutter, Nov. 2, 1994. BA in History, CCNY, 1963; MA, Princeton U., 1965, PhD in History of Sci., 1968. Postdoctoral fellow Inst. History of Medicine/Johns Hopkins U., Balt., 1969; asst. prof. history Princeton U., 1969-71; asst. prof. then assoc. prof. history City Coll. of CUNY, N.Y.C., 1972-77; from assoc. prof. to prof. history and cmty. and prev. med. U. Rochester, N.Y., 1977—, Mercer Brugler disting. tchg. prof., 1979-82; vis. curator, hist. cons. Nat. Libr. of Medicine, Bethesda, Md., 1995-97. Author, co-editor: Making Medical History: The Life and Times of Henry E. Sigerist, 1997; author exhbn. catalog. Sec.-treas. Sigerist Circle (of Med. Historians and Health Activists), 1994-97. Herodotus fellow Inst. for Advanced Study, Princeton, N.J., 1972-73. Mem. Am. Assn. for the History of Medicine (chmn. Welch medal com. 1991-93). Office: U Rochester Dept History Rochester NY 14627

BROWN, THEODORE MOREY, art history educator; b. Winthrop, Mass., Nov. 11, 1925; s. Isydor and Nettie (Schwartz) B.; m. Barbara M. Rome, May 29, 1951; children: Lisa N., David O. B.Arch., M.I.T., 1953; M.A., Harvard U., 1956; Ph.D., U. Utrecht, The Netherlands, 1958. Asst. prof. history of art U. Louisville, 1958-62, asso. prof., 1962-67; prof. history art Cornell U., 1967-88, prof. emeritus, 1988—; cons. in field. Author: The Work of G.T. Rietveld, Architect, 1958, Margaret Bourke-White Photojournalist, 1972. Served with USN, 1943-46. Home: 92 Ithaca Rd Ithaca NY 14850-6102 Office: Cornell Univ Dept History Of Art Ithaca NY 14850

BROWN, THOMAS ANDREW, retired aircraft/weaponry manufacturing executive; b. Iowa City, Iowa, July 24, 1932; s. Charles Valentine and Mary Clementine (Proestler) B.; m. Louise Grafton Baggott, Aug. 31, 1957; children: James, Mary, Catherine. B.A., State U. Iowa, 1953; B.A. with honors, Oxford U., 1955; M.A., Harvard U., 1958, Ph.D., 1962. With Rand Corp., 1962-74, assoc. head info. sci., 1966-74; dir. strategic studies Rand Corp., Washington, 1983-85; asst. v.p. Sci. Applications, Inc., Los Angeles, 1974-77; dep. asst. sec. of def. program analysis and evaluation Dept. Def., Washington, 1977-81; ptnr. Booz, Allen & Hamilton, Bethesda, Md., 1981-83; mgr. strategic studies Northrop Corp., 1985-94. Served with USAF, 1955-57. Recipient Disting. Pub. Svc. medal Dept. Def., 1981; Rhodes scholar, 1953-55; NSF fellow, 1957-61. Home: 21912 234th Ave SE Maple Valley WA 98038-8423

BROWN, THOMAS CARTMEL, JR., lawyer; b. Marion, Va., June 20, 1945; m. Sally Guy Lynch; children: Sarah Preston, Taylor Cardwell. AB, Davidson Coll., 1967; JD, U. Va., 1970. Bar: Va. 1971. Assoc. Boothe, Prichard & Dudley, Alexandria, Va., 1971-76; ptnr. Boothe, Prichard & Dudley, Alexandria, 1976-86, McGuire Woods Battle & Boothe L.L.P. and predecessors, McLean, Va., 1986—; chmn. bd. trustees HCA Dominion Hosp., Falls Church, Va., 1990-93; mem. lawyers com. Nat. Ctr. for State Cts., 1993—; sec., gen. counsel Potomac KnowledgeWay, Inc., 1995—. Mem. Va. Child Day-Care Coun., Richmond, 1987-91, No. Va. Roundtable, 1995—; bd. dirs. Alexandria chpt. ARC, 1982-88. Fellow Am. Bar Found., Va. Law Found. (bd. dirs. 1997—); mem. Va. Bar Assn. (pres. 1992), Va. State Bar (chmn. bus. law sect. 1987-88), Alexandria C. of C. (counsel 1987-89), Omicron Delta Kappa. Office: McGuire Woods Battle & Boothe LLP 1750 Tysons Blvd Ste 1800 Mc Lean VA 22102

BROWN, THOMAS EDWARD, information systems executive; b. Laredo, Tex., July 23, 1968; s. Thomas Edward and Elia Ester Brown; m. Shawnie Jo Wilcox, May 10, 1998. AA, U. Md., Munich, Germany, 1989; B in Bus. Mgmt. Sci., U. Tex., San Antonio, 1995. Intern Grtr. D.C. Cares, Washington, 1995; staff asst. U. Tex., San Antonio, 1992-97; Internet mgr. Gillespie Ford, San Antonio, 1997—; cons., San Antonio, 1998—. Bd. dirs. Christmas in April, San Antonio, 1993—; vol. coord. U. Tex. San Anotnio Assn. Balloon Fest, 1997—. Mem. NRA, Bus. Vol. Coun., Alpha Phi Omega. Avocations: computers, volunteering, reading, outdoor activities. E-mail: tombrown@gillespieford.com. Office: Gillespie Ford 7111 NW Loop 410 San Antonio TX 78238

BROWN, THOMAS HUNTINGTON, neuroscientist; b. N.Y.C., June 13, 1945; s. Thomas Huntington and Elvira R. (Crandall) B. BA in Molecular Biology, Calif. State U.-San Jose, 1972, MA in Psychology, 1972; PhD in Neurosic., Stanford U., 1977. Postdoctoral fellow Stanford U., Calif., 1977-79; asst. rsch. scientist Beckman Rsch. Inst., Duarte, Calif., 1979-82, assoc. rsch. scientist, 1982-86; rsch. scientist Beckman Rsch. Inst., Duarte, 1986-88; prof. dept. psychology Yale U., New Haven, 1988—; mem. joint appt. dept. cellular molecular physiology Yale U., 1992—, dir. Ctr. for Theoretical and Applied Neurosci., 1992-96; adviser NIH, NIMH study sects., 1982-83, 89-94, 94-98, mem. NIH-IFCN5 study sect., IFCN1 study sect., 1998—. Mem. editl. bd. Behavioral Neurosci. Jour., 1983-89, Network: Computation in Neural Systems, 1990-92, Synapse, 1990—, Hippocampus, 1990-93, Psychobiology, 1997—; contbr. articles to sci. jours., 1976—. Recipient Epilepsy Found. Am. award, 1980, McKnight Found. Scholar's award, 1981, McKnight Found. Career Devel. award 1984, Muscular Dystrophy Found. fellow, 1977, NIH fellow, 1978; grantee in field, 1980—. Mem. AAAS, Am. Psychol. Soc., N.Y. Acad. Scis., Conn. Acad. Sci. Engring., Soc. Neurosci., Internat. Neurol. Network Soc. Office: Yale U Dept Psychology PO Box 208205 New Haven CT 06520-8205

BROWN, THOMAS PHILIP, III, lawyer; b. Washington, Dec. 18, 1931; s. Raymond T. and Beatrice (Cullen) B.; m. Alicia A. Sexton, July 28, 1955; children: Thomas, Mark, Alicia, Maria, Beatrice. B.S., Georgetown U., 1953, LL.B., 1956. Bar: D.C., Md. Pvt. practice law, 1958—. Author monograph and articles on legal malpractice. Pres. Cath. Youth Orgn. of Washington, 1972. Served to 1st lt. USMCR, 1955-58. Mem. Bar Assn. D.C. (pres. 1986, bd. dirs. 1987), Barristers Club, Columbia Country Club. Home: 5210 Norway Dr Chevy Chase MD 20815-6672 Office: 4948 Saint Elmo Ave Bethesda MD 20814-6013

BROWN, TIMOTHY ALLEN, executive search consulting company executive; b. Spearman, Tex., Sept. 22, 1965; s. Henry Roger Brown and Nellie Brown Wilkirson; m. Ivette Lozano, Oct. 25, 1997; 1 child, Taite Ivette. BS, Tex. Christian U., 1988, MS, 1990. Rsch. analyst Ray & Bernotson, Ft. Worth, 1989-93; assoc. LAI Worldwide, Dallas, 1995-97, prin., 1997—; cons. Ray & Bernotson, N.Y.C., 1993-95. Mem. N.Y. Tex. Exes, N.Y.C., 1993-95; v.p. Ft. Worth Housing Corp., 1993; vol. Big Bros.-Big Sisters, Dallas, 1995—. Mem. Assn. Exec. Search Cons., Tex. Christian U. Frog Club. Republican. Avocations: golf, biking, fly fishing. E-mail: tbrown@laix.com. Home: 6151 La Vista Dr Dallas TX 75214 Office: LAI Worldwide 1601 Elm St Ste 4150 Dallas TX 75201

BROWN, TINA, magazine editor; b. Maidenhead, Eng., Nov. 21, 1953; d. George Hambley and Bettina Iris Mary (Kohr) B.; m. Harold Evans, Aug. 20, 1981; children: George Frederick, Isabel Harriet. M.A., Oxford U. Columnist Punch Mag., London, 1978; editor in chief Tatler Mag., London, 1979-83, Vanity Fair Mag., N.Y.C., 1984-92; editor New Yorker mag., N.Y.C., 1992-98; chmn. Miramax/Talk Media, 1998—. Author: (play) Under the Bamboo Tree, 1973 (Sunday Times Drama award), (play) Happy Yellow, 1977, (book) Loose Talk, 1979, (book) Life As A Party, 1983; editor Talk mag., N.Y.C., 1998—. Named Most Promising Female Journalist, recipient Kathrine Pakenham prize Sunday London Times, 1973; named Young Journalist of Yr., 1978, Mag. Editor of Yr. Advt. Age mag., 1988.recipient USC Distinguished Achievement in Journalism Award, USC Journalism Alumni Assoc., 1994. Fax: 212-830-5838. *

BROWN, TOD DAVID, bishop; b. San Francisco, Nov. 15, 1936; s. George Wilson and Edna Anne (Dunn) B. BA, St. John's Coll., 1958; STB, Gregorian U., Rome, 1960; MA in Theology, U. San Francisco, 1970, MAT in Edn., 1976. Dir. edn. Diocese of Monterey, Calif., 1970-80, vicar gen., clergy, 1980-82, chancellor, 1982-89, vicar gen., chancellor, 1983-89; pastor St. Francis Xavier, Seaside, Calif., 1977-82; bishop Roman Catholic Diocese of Boise, Idaho, 1989-98; appointed and installed bishop Roman Cath. Diocese of Orange, Calif., 1998; mem. subcom. on laity, mem. 3d millenium com. Nat. Conf. Cath. Bishops; mem. episcopal bd. govs. N.Am. Coll. Named Papal Chaplain Pope Paul VI, 1975. Mem. Cath. Theol. Soc. Am., Cath. Biblical Assn., Canon Law Soc. Am., Equestrian Order of the Holy Sepulchre in Jerusalem. Avocations: films, travel, reading, exercise. Office: Diocese of Orange Marywood Ctr 2811 E Villa Real Dr Orange CA 92867-1932*

BROWN, TOM, publishing executive. V.p., pub. Golf Digest N.Y. Times Co. Mag. Group, N.Y.C., Conn. Office: NY Times Co Mag Group 1120 Ave of Americas 8th Fl New York NY 10036*

BROWN, TOM CHRISTIAN, newspaper publisher; b. Nampa, Idaho, July 24, 1947; s. Frank Thomas and Esther (Ulrich) B.; m. Carol Burroughs, May 31, 1969; children: Brian J., Maree C. BA in History with honors, Oreg. State U., 1969; MS in Journalism, Northwestern U., 1970. Reporter Corvallis (Oreg.) Gazette-Times, 1969; reporter, asst. city editor Billings (Mont.) Gazette, 1970-74; ops. mgr. Mont. Std., Butte, 1974-76; gen. mgr. Missoulian, Missoula, Mont., 1976-80, pub., 1980-86; pub. Concord (N.H.) Monitor, 1987—; bd. dirs. Newspapers of New Eng., Concord; pres. Page Buying Coop, Phila., 1994-96, chmn. bd., 1996—. Bd. dirs. United Way, Concord, 1989-96, Capital Ctr. for Arts, 1998—, Missoula YMCA, 1984-86; pres. Missoula Symphony, 1985, Mont. Press Assn., Helena, 1985; v.p. N.H. BBB, Concord, 1995—; 2d v.p. Pacific N.W. Newspaper Assn., Portland, 1986; mem. Concord Task Force on Racism. Mem. Newspaper Assn. Am., New England Newspaper Assn. (com. chair 1994—), Merrimack C. of C. (bd. dirs. 1993-98), Missoula C. of C. (bd. dirs. 1977-84, v.p. 1983), Rotary (bd. dirs. Missoula chpt. 1976-79), Sigma Delta Chi. Avocations: running marathons, skiing, hiking, climbing, reading. Home: 15 Dwinell Dr Concord NH 03301-2542

BROWN, TONI CYD, elementary, middle, and secondary school educator; b. Billings, Mont., Apr. 22, 1950; d. Alec Wilbert and Ruth Isabel (Uline) Brown; children: Marykitt, Elizabeth. BA in English, U. Wyo., 1972; MA in English, 1979, BA in Elem. Edn., 1988. Cert. Comml. pilot, 1995, instrument ground instr. Tchr. Billings Sch. Dist. #2, 1973-77; admissions counselor Rocky Mt. Coll., Billings, 1977-78; tchr. Gillette Campus No. Wyo. Community Coll., 1979-80, dir. Region III Developmentally Delayed Presch. Prog., 1980; tchr. various grades Campbell County Sch. Dist., Gillette, Wyo., 1980-88; tchr. gifted resource rm. Campbell County Sch. Dist., Gillette, 1988-89; tchr. mid. sch. English comm., career, acad. competition, 1989—; cons. in field; lectr. in aerospace edn. Chairman bd. dirs. High Plains Energy Tech. Ctr. Found. Named Campbell County Am. Legion Educator of the Yr., 1988, Outstanding Educator of Yr. Fed. Aviation Adminstrn., 1990, Crossfield Tchr. of Yr. finalist, 1993, Air Force Assn. Rocky Mountain Region Tchr. of Yr., 1995, Nat. Air Force Assn. McAuliffe award; Space Acad. grantee Internat. Ninety-Nines, 1987; Wyo. Christa McAuliffe fellow, 1990; recipient Civil Air Patrol Rocky Mountain Region Brewer award, 1994. Mem. Am. Quarter Hourse Assn., Internat. Arabian Horse Assn., Campbell County Reading Assn., Wyo. Reading Assn., Wyo. Sci. Tchrs. Assn. (Elem. Sci. Tchr. of Yr. 1988), Aircraft Owners and Pilots Assn., Civil Air Patrol, Exptl. Aircraft Assn., Ninety Nines, Inc., U. Wyo. Alumni Assn., Women's Sports Found., Wyo. Writers/Poets. Avocation: flying. E-mail: tcb@ucn.com. Home and Office: 2610 S Douglas Hwy Ste 180-326 Gillette WY 82718-6468

BROWN, TONY ERSIC, record company executive; b. Greensboro, N.C., Dec. 11, 1946; s. Floyd Everett and Mattie Agnes (Nance) B.; m. Janie Breeding (div. July 1975); children: Brandi, Brennan; m. Gina Lou Morrison, Apr. 19, 1979 (div. Apr. 1992). Grad. high sch., Durham, S.C. Mem. band Oak Ridge Boys, Nashville, 1972-75, Elvis Presley, Nashville, 1975-77, Emmylou Harris, Nashville, 1977-80; mgr. artists and repertoire RCA Records, Hollywood, Calif., 1978-80; dir. artists and repertoire Nashville, 1983-84; mem. band Rosanne Cash, Nashville, 1980-83; sr. v.p. artists and repertoire MCA Records, Nashville, 1984-87, exec. v.p., head of A & R, 1987—; now pres. MCA Records; songwriter Silverline Music, 1972—. Active Leadership Nashville, 1987. Mem. Nat. Acad. Rec. Arts and Scis. (bd. dirs., Grammy award 1980, 83, 85, Producer of Yr. 1991), Country Music Assn., Acad. Country Music, Nashville Entertainment Assn., Gospel Music Assn. (Dove award 1972). Office: MCA Records 60 Music Sq E Nashville TN 37203-4325*

BROWN, TREVOR, dean. Dean journalism Ind. U., Bloomington. Office: Ind U Sch Journalism Ernie Pyle Hall Rm 200 940 E 7th St Bloomington IN 47405-6200*

BROWN, TRISHA, dancer; b. Aberdeen, Wash., Nov. 25, 1936. BA in Dance, Mills Coll., 1958; hon. doctorate, Mills Coll., 1997; PhD hon. in Fine Arts, Oberlin Coll.; hon. degree, Mills Coll., 1997. Founder, pres. Trisha Brown Dance Co., New York, NY, 1970—; founding mem. Judson Dance Theater; choreographer Grand Union Improvisation Group, 1970-76; lectr. Mills Coll., Calif., Reed Coll., Oreg., NYU, Goucher Coll., Md., Carnegie Mellon U., Pa.; conductor workshops and seminars throughout world. Dancer worldwide; choreographer: Untitled, 1961, Trillium, 1962, Lightfall, 1963, Untitled Duet, 1963, Part of a Tango, 1963, Target, 1964, Rulegame Five, 1964, Motor, 1965, Homemade, 1965, Inside, 1966, Skunk Cabbage, 1967, Saltgrass and Waders, 1967, Medicine Dance, 1967, Snapshots, 1968, Ballet, 1968, Falling Duet, 1968, Sky Map, 1969, Dance with Duck's Head, 1968, Yellow Belly, 1969, Leaning Duets, 1970, The Stream, 1970, Man Walking Down the Side of a Building, 1970, Accumulation 4 1/2, 1971, Walking on the Wall, 1971, Leaning Duets II, 1971, Falling Duet II, 1971, Rummage Sale and the Floor of the Forest, 1971, Planes, 1968, Roof Piece, 1971, Primary Accumulation, 1972, Accumulating Pieces, 1973, Group Accumulation, 1973, Roof and Fire Piece, 1973, Spanish Dance, 1973, Structured Pieces, 1973, Figure 8, 1974, Drift, 1974, Spiral, 1974, Pamplona Stones, 1974, Locus, 1975, Line Up, 1976, Water Motor and Splang, 1978, Glacial Decoy, 1979, Opal Loop, 1980, Son of Gone Fishin', 1981, Set and Reset, 1983 (N.Y. Dance and Performance award 1984), Lateral Pass, 1985 (N.Y. Dance and Performance award 1986), Carmen, 1986, Newark, 1987, Astral Convertible, 1989, For M.G.: The Movie, 1991, Astral Converted, 1991, Another Story as in Falling, 1993, If you couldn't see me, 1994, Foray Forêt, 1990, You Can See Us, 1995, M.O., 1995, Twelve Ton Rose, 1996; featured TV show, M.O., Sta. WNET-TV, N.Y.C., Dance in America, Sta. WGBH-TV, Boston, Dancing on the Edge, Sta. WGBH-TV, Boston, Making Dances, Sta. WGBH-TV, Boston; drawings exhibited Venice Biennale, Toulon Museum; group exhibition: Musées de Marseille, Numerals: Mathematical Concepts in Contemporary Art, Drawings: The Pluralist Decade, New Notes for New Dance, Art and Dance: Images From the Modern Dialogue; Avant-garde Theater and Dance Notes & Scores curated by Robert Rauschenberg; film Accumulation with Talking plus Watermotor, KCET, Los Angeles, and KTCA, Mpls. Fellow Guggenheim Found., 1975, 84, NEA Creative Artists Svc. Progam, 1977, 81-84, MacArthur fellow, 1991; grantee NEA, N.Y. State Coun. on Arts, others founds. and corps.; recipient creative arts award Brandeis U., 1982, Dance Mag., 1987, Chevalier dans L'Ordre des Arts et des Lettres, Govt. France, 1988, Samuel H. Scripps Am. Dance Festival award, 1994, Prix de la Danse la Société des Auteurs et Compositeurs Dramatiques award, 1996; appointed to Nat. Coun. on the Arts by Pres. Clinton, 1994; inducted into Am. Acad. Arts and Letters, 1997. Mem. Am. Acad. Arts and Letters. Office: Trisha Brown Co c/o Christopher Johnson 211 W 61st St Fl 4 New York NY 10023-7832*

BROWN, TROY ANDERSON, JR., electrical distributing company executive; b. Tampa, Fla., July 7, 1934; s. Troy Anderson and Valerie Aldona (Mohler) B.; m. Jean Thompson, Aug. 22, 1962; children: Troy Anderson, III, George Albert, Douglas Alan. AB, Harvard U., 1956; JD, U. N.C., 1959. Bar: Fla. bar 1959. With Raybro Electric Supplies Inc., Tampa, 1960—; exec. v.p. Raybro Electric Supplies Inc., 1964-74, pres., 1974—. Mem. exec. com. Tampa Com. 100, 1975, U. S.Fla. Found., 1974-75; chmn. bd. fellow U. Tampa, 1978; bd. dirs., vice chmn. Tampa Mus., 1977-79; bd. dirs. Tampa YMCA, 1977-79, Tampa Marine Inst., 1976-77. With USAFR, 1959. Mem. Fla. Bar Assn., Nat. Assn. Elec. Distbrs. (bd. dirs. 1989-91), Young Pres. Orgn., Greater Tampa C. of C. (gov. 1968-74), Exchange Club Tampa (pres. 1970), Presidents Round Table Tampa (pres. 1971), Tampa Mchts. Assn. (dir. 1980). Episcopalian. Clubs: Ye Mystic Krewe Gasparilla, Tampa Yacht and Country, Univ. (bd. dirs. 1982-83), Tampa, Palma Ceia Golf and Country, Shriners, Jesters, University; Harvard of Fla. (pres. 1984); Harvard (N.Y.C.). Home: 1013 S Skokie St Tampa FL 33629-5237 Office: Raybro/CED PO Box 1351 Tampa FL 33601-1351

BROWN, VALERIE ANNE, psychiatric social worker, educator; b. Elizabeth, N.J., Feb. 28, 1951; d. William John and Adelaide Elizabeth (Krasa) B.; BA summa cum laude (fellow), C.W. Post Coll., 1972; MSW (Silberman scholar), Hunter Coll., 1975; PhD, Am. Internat. U., 1996; Diplomate Am. Bd. Examiners, Am. Bd. Clin. Social Work, Nat. Assn. Soc. Work; cert. addictions specialist, cert. master hypnotherapist. Social work intern Greenwich House Counseling Center, N.Y.C., 1973-74, Metro Cons. Center, N.Y.C., 1974-75; sr. psychiat. social worker, co-adminstr. Essex County Guidance Center, East Orange, N.J., 1975-80; pvt. practice psychiat. social work, psychotherapy, 1979—; sr. psychiat social worker John E. Runnells Hosp., Berkeley Heights, N.J., 1980-86; dir. social work Northfield Manor, West Orange, N.J., 1987; clin. coord. Project Portals East Orange Gen. Hosp., 1987-88; asst. dir. ARS/Century House Riverview Med. Ctr., Red Bank, N.J., 1988-93; sr. clin. case mgmt. specialist Prudential Ins. Co., Woodbridge, N.J., 1993-93; clin. dir. Greenhouse-KMC, Lakewood, N.J., 1994—, Shoreline-KBH, Toms River, N.J., 1996—; tech. advisor Nat. Comm. Network, 1988—; instr. Brookdale Coll., 1991—; co-founder Women's Growth Ctr., Cedar Grove, N.J., 1979; counselor Passaic Drug Clinic, 1978-80; field instr. Fairleigh Dickinson U., Madison, N.J., 1981-86, Brookdale Coll., 1989-92; field supr. Union Coll., Cranford, N.J., 1986; instr. Sch. Social Work, NYU, N.Y.C., 1980-83, asst. prof., 1983-85; evaluator Intoxicated Driver Resource Ctr., Essex County, N.J., 1987-88. Alt. Monmouth County profl. adv. bd. Named Dist. Alumnae Mother Seton Regional H.S., Clark, N.J., 1997. Mem. NASW (Whittman Lifetime Achievement nominee 1997—), Psi Chi, Pi Gamma Mu, Sigma Tau Delta. Avocations: reading, swimming, travel. Office: 20 Ellsworth Ct Red Bank NJ 07701-5403

BROWN, W. MICHAEL, publishing company executive. Deputy chmn. Thomson Corp., Toronto, Ont., Can. Office: The Thomson Corp Metro Ctr 1 Station Pl Ste 6 Stamford CT 06902-6800*

BROWN, W. VIRGIL, internal medicine educator; b. Royston, Ga., Sept. 25, 1938; m. Alice; 2 children. BA in Physics and Chemistry, Emory U., 1960; MD, Yale U., 1964. Diplomate Am. Bd. Internal Medicine, Am. Bd. Endocrinology. Intern, asst. resident Osler Med. Svc. Johns Hopkins Hosp., Balt., 1964-66; clin. assoc. Nat. Heart and Lung Inst., Bethesda, Md., 1966-69; fellow in endocrinology and metabolism Yale-New Haven Hosp., 1969-70; asst. prof. medicine U. Calif. Dept. Medicine, San Diego, 1970-74, assoc. prof. medicine, 1974-78; dir. lipid rsch. clinic U. Calif., San Diego, 1972-78; prof. medicine Mt. Sinai Sch. Medicine, N.Y.C., 1978-87, dir. divsn. arteriosclerosis and metabolism, 1991-94; pres., CEO Medlantic Rsch. Found., Washington, 1987-91; Charles Howard Candler prof. internal medicine, dir. divsn. arteriosclerosis and lipid metabolism Emory U., Atlanta, 1991—; chief of medicine Atlanta VA Hosp. Mem. editl. bd. Jour. Lipid Rsch., 1977-81, 91-95. Alexander von Humboldt fellow. Fellow ACP (master physician); mem. Am. Heart Assn. (mem. physiology study sect. 1978-80, mem. credentials com. arteriosclerosis coun. 1978-80, chmn. credentials com. arteriosclerosis coun. 1979-82, mem. nutrition com. 1981-86, mem. several rsch. coms., chmn. nutrition com. 1982-86, bd. dirs. 1983, vice-chmn. edn. and cmty. program com., pres.-elect 1990-91, pres. 1991-92, gold heart award 1996, fellow arteriosclerosis coun., fellow epidemiology and preventive cardiology coun., numerous others), Am. Fedn. Clin. Rsch., Am. Soc. Clin. Investigation, Am. Soc. Exptl. Biology, Southeastern Lipid Conf., Am. Bd. Bioanalysis (high-complexity clin. lab. dir.), Phi Beta Kappa, Alpha Omega Alpha. Achievements include research in study of the structure and metabolism of lipoproteins, study of the lipolytic enzymes, including their molecular and kinetic characteristics, diagnosis and treatment of the hyperlipoproteinemias, the relationship of lipoprotein metabolism to atheromatous vascular disorders. Fax: (404) 235-3005. Office: Atlanta VA Hosp 1670 Clairmont Rd Decatur GA 30033-4004

BROWN, WALSTON SHEPARD, lawyer; b. Darien, Conn., Jan. 20, 1908; s. Clarence Shepard and Alma Mary (Mitchell) B.; m. Ellen F. Regan, August 13, 1955. A.B., Leland Stanford U., 1930; student, L'Ecole Libre des Science Politiques, Paris, 1931-32; LL.B., Harvard U., 1935. Bar: D.C. 1936. Atty. various govt. depts., 1935-40; asst. gen. counsel U.S. Maritime Commn., also mem. various adv. coms. on drafting, reconversion and contract termination legislation, 1940-45; practiced in N.Y.C., 1945—; ptnr., counsel Willkie Farr & Gallagher and predecessors. Mam. ABA, S.R., Phi Beta Kappa. Unitarian. Clubs: River (N.Y.C.), Tuxedo (N.Y.). Home: Mountain Farm Rd PO Box 772 Tuxedo Park NY 10987-0772

BROWN, WALTER CREIGHTON, biologist; b. Butte, Mont., Aug. 18, 1913; s. D. Frank and Isabella (Creighton) B.; m. Jeanette Snyder, Aug. 20, 1950; children: Pamela Hawley, James Creighton, Julia Elizabeth. AB, Coll. Puget Sound, 1935, MA, 1938; PhD, Stanford U., 1950. Chmn. dept. Clover Park High Sch., Tacoma, Wash., 1938-42; acting instr. Stanford U., Calif., 1949-50; instr. Northwestern U., Evanston, Ill., 1950-53; dean sci. Menlo Coll., Menlo Park, Calif., 1955-66, dean instrn., 1966-75; rsch. assoc., fellow Calif. Acad. Sci., San Francisco, 1978—; lectr. Sillman U., Philippines, 1954-55, dir. rsch. Program on Ecology and Systematics of Philippine Amphibians and Reptiles, 1958-74; rschr. rels. of amphibian faunas of Philippines & Indo-Australian Archipelago; vis. prof. biology Stanford U., 1962, 64, 66, 68, Harvard U., Cambridge, Mass., 1969, 72. Author: Philippine Lizards of the Family Gekkonidae, 1978, Philippine Lizards of the Family Scincidae, 1980, Lizards of the Genus Emoia (Scincidae) with Observations of Their Evolution and Biogeography, 1991, Philippine Amphibians: An Illustrated Field Guide ; contbr. over 80 articles to profl. jours. Served with U.S. Army, 1942-46. Fellow AAAS; mem. Am. Soc. Ichthyologists and Herpetologists, Am. Inst. Biol. Scis., Sigma Xi. Office: Calif Acad Scis Dept Herpetology Golden Gate Park San Francisco CA 94118

BROWN, WALTER H., investment company executive. Gen. ptnr. Brown Bros. Harriman & Co., N.Y.C., 1968-98, ltd. ptnr., 1998—. Office: Brown Bros Harriman & Co 59 Wall St New York NY 10005-2818*

BROWN, WALTER REDVERS JOHN, physicist; b. Toronto, Ont., Can., Aug. 22, 1925; s. Ernest Redvers and Rita Mary (Brooks) B.; m. Anita Catherine Goggio, June 5, 1948 (div. 1972); children: Paul, Susan, Patricia, Judith; m. Beth Susan Southard, Oct. 12, 1974; 1 child, Amy. BS, U. Toronto, 1947, MS, U. Rochester, 1949. Sr. physicist Eastman Kodak Co., Rochester, N.Y., 1947-55; rsch. assoc. Boston U., 1955-57; asst. to dir. rsch. Itek Corp., Lexington, Mass., 1957-62; v.p. R & D United Carr Inc., Boston, 1962-69; exec. v.p. Ealing Corp., Cambridge, Mass., 1969-71; pres. Daedalon Corp., Salem, Mass., 1971—. Patentee in field. Fellow Optical Soc. Am. (Adolph Lomb medal 1956); mem. Eastern Yacht Club, St. Botolph Club. Roman Catholic. Home: 120 Atlantic Ave Marblehead MA 01945-3049 Office: Daedalon Corp PO Box 2028 Salem MA 01970-6228

BROWN, WARREN JOSEPH, physician; b. Bklyn., July 17, 1924; s. Benjamin Oscar and Angela Marie (Cahill) B.; m. Greet Roos, July 3, 1970; children—Warren James, Robert E., Suzanne J., Annemarie, Eric Jan. Student, Ursinus Coll., 1942-43; B.S., Bethany Coll., 1945; M.D., Ohio State U., 1949. Diplomate Am. Bd. Family Practice. Intern U.S. Naval Hosp., Long Beach and Oceanside, Calif.; resident Pottstown Hosp., Pa., 1950-51; assoc. Roos Loos Med. Group, Alhambra, Calif., 1951; practice medicine specializing in family practice Largo, Fla., 1953—; sr. civilian flight surgeon FAA, 1964—; pres. Aero-Med. Consultants, Inc., Largo, 1969—. Author: Florida's Aviation History, 1980, 2d edit., 1993, Child Yank Over the Rainbow, 1977, Patients' Guide to Medicine, 10th edit., 1987, The World's First Airline: The St. Petersburg-Tampa Airboat Line, 1914, 1981, 2d edit., 1984. Historian Fla. Aviation Hist. Soc., 1978—, St. Petersburg-Clearwater-Tampa Hangar Order of Quiet Birdmen, 1969—. With USN, 1943-45, 49-50, 51-53. Fellow Am. Acad. Family Physicians; mem. Pinellas County Med. Assn., Fla. Med. Assn., Aircraft Owners and Pilots Assn., Am. Radio Relay League, Med. Amateur Radio Coun. (Southeastern, USA dir.). Home: 14607 Brewster Dr Largo FL 33774-4822 Office: 10912 Hamlin Blvd Largo FL 33774-5044

BROWN, WAYNE J., mayor; b. 1936. BS, Ariz. State U. Staff acct. Arthur Andersen & Co. CPA's, 1960-63; mng. ptnr. Wayne Brown & Co. CPA's, 1964-79; dir. acctg. Ariz. State Dept. Adminstrn., 1979-80; chmn. Brown Evans Distbg. Co., Mesa, Ariz., 1980—; mayor City of Mesa, 1996—. Office: Office of the Mayor PO Box 1466 Mesa AZ 85211-1466*

BROWN, WENDY WEINSTOCK, nephrologist, educator; b. N.Y.C., Dec. 9, 1944; d. Irving and Pearl (Levack) Weinstock; m. Barry David Brown, May 2, 1971 (div. Sept. 1995); children: Jennifer Faye, Joshua Reuben, Julie Aviva, Rachel Ann. BA, U. Mass., 1966; MD, Med. Coll. of Pa., 1970; MPH, St. Louis U., 1999. Am. Bd. Internal Medicine, 1977. Intern U. Ill. Affiliated Hosps., Chgo., 1970-71; resident in internal medicine The Med. Coll. Wis. Affiliated Hosps., Milw., 1971-74; gen. practitioner Vogelweh (W. Germany) Health Clinics, 1975-76; fellow in nephrology Med. Coll. of Wis. Milw. County Med. Complex, Milw., 1976-78; staff physician St. Louis VA Med Ctr., 1978—, acting chief, hemodialysis sect., 1983-85, chief dialysis/renal sect., 1985-90; dir. clin. nephrology, 1990—; staff physician St. Louis U. Hosps., 1978—, St. Louis City Hosp., 1982-85, St Mary's Health Ctr., St. Louis, 1994—; assoc. prof. internal medicine St. Louis U. Health Sci. Ctr., 1985-98, prof. internal medicine, 1998—. Reviewer Clin. Nephrology, Am. Jour. Kidney Disease, Jour Am. Geriatric Soc., Jour. Jour. Renal Replacement Therapy, Jour. Am. Soc. Nephrology, Geriatric Nephrology and Urology; med. editor NKF Family Focus; mem. editl. bd. Clin. Nephrology, Geriatric Nephrology, Advances in Renal Replacement Therapy; contbr. articles to profl. jours. Mem. adv. coun. Mo. Kidney Program, 1985-91, chmn., 1988-89; numerous positions Nat. Kidney Found., 1984—, nat. chmn., 1995-97; bd. dirs. Nat. Kidney Found. Ea. Mo. and Metro East, Inc., 1980-94; bd. dirs. Combined Health Appeal Greater St. Louis, Inc., 1988, pres., 1989-92; bd. dirs. Combined Health Appeal Am., 1991-98, sec., 1992-96, vice chmn., 1996-98. Recipient Upjohn Achievement award Med. Coll. Wis. Affiliated Hosps. 1972, St. Louis YWCA Cert. of Leadership 1989, Chmn.'s award Nat. Kidney Found. of Ea. Mo. and Metro East 1990, Nat. Kidney Found., Washington 1990; named Casual Corner Career Woman of the Yr. 1986, Combined Health Appeal of Am. Vol. of Yr. 1991, Olympic Torch Bearer, 1996, St. Louis Health Profl. of Yr., 1997. Fellow ACP; mem. Am. Soc. Nephrology, Internat. Soc. Nephrology, Coun. on Kidney in Cardiovascular Disease, Am. Heart Assn., St. Louis Soc. Am. Med. Women's Assn., St. Louis Internists (v.p. 1983-84, pres. 1984-85), Women in Nephrology, Internat. Soc. for Peritoneal Dialysis, Am. Geriatrics Soc., Alpha Omega Alpha. Home: 100 Frontenac Frst Saint Louis MO 63131-3235 Office: Saint Louis VAMC 915 N Grand Blvd Saint Louis MO 63106-1621

BROWN, WESLEY ERNEST, federal judge; b. Hutchinson, Kans., June 22, 1907; s. Morrison H. H. and Julia (Wesley) B.; m. Mary A. Miller, Nov. 30, 1934 (dec.); children: Wesley Miller, Loy B. Wiley; m. Thadene N. Moore. Student, Kans. U., 1925-28; LLB, Kansas City Law Sch., 1933. Bar: Kans. 1933, Mo. 1933. Pvt. practice Hutchinson, 1933-58; county atty. Reno County, Kans., 1935-39; referee in bankruptcy U.S. Dist. Ct. Kans., 1958-62, judge, 1962-79, sr. judge, 1979—; apptd. Temporary Emergency Ct. of Appeals of U.S., 1980-93; dir. Nat. Assn. Referees in Bankruptcy, 1959-62; mem. bankruptcy divsn. Jud. Conf., 1963-70; mem. Jud. Conf., U.S., 1976-79. With USN, 1944-46. Mem. ABA, Kans. Bar Assn. (exec. council 1950-62, pres. 1964-65), Reno County Bar Assn. (pres. 1947), Wichita Bar Assn., S.W. Bar Assn., Delta Theta Phi. Office: US Dist Ct 414 US Courthouse 401 N Market St Wichita KS 67202

BROWN, WILLIAM A., lawyer; b. Memphis, Nov. 6, 1957; s. Winn D. Sr. and Annie Ruth (Hurt) B.; m. Mary Lee Walker, Dec. 27, 1980. BBA, U. Miss., 1978, JD, 1981. Bar: Miss. 1981, U.S. Dist. Ct. (no. and so. dists.) Miss. 1981, U.S. Dist. Ct. (we. dist.) Tenn. 1987. Ptnr., pres. Walker, Brown & Brown, P.A., Hernando, Miss., 1981—. Pres. DeSoto Literacy Coun., Hernando, 1988, Am. Cancer Soc., Hernando, 1988, DeSoto County Econ. Devel. Coun., 1995-96; mem. Leadership 2000, 1990-91; vice-chmn. Hernando Preservation Commn., 1997—; chmn. design com. Main Street Project, 1997—. James O. Eastland scholar, 1978-81; Paul Harris fellow Rotary Internat., 1997. Mem. Miss. Bar Assn. (bd. dirs. young lawyers sect. 1988-89), DeSoto County Bar Assn. (v.p. 1988-89, pres. 1996-98), Rotary (pres. Hernando chpt. 1989-90), Boy Scouts Am., N.W. Miss. (membership chmn. 1990, activities chmn. 1991), Am. Arbitration Assn. Methodist. Avocations: gardening, design and construction projects. Home: PO Box 276 Hernando MS 38632-0276 Office: Walker Brown & Brown PA PO Box 276 Hernando MS 38632-0276

BROWN, WILLIAM ANTHONY (TONY), broadcast executive; b. Charleston, W.Va., Apr. 11, 1933; s. Royal and Catherine (Davis) B.; 1 child, Byron Anthony. BS in Sociology, Wayne State U., 1959, MS in Psychiat. Social Work, 1961. Social worker, drama critic, city editor Detroit Courier; programming staff WTVS, Detroit; prod. Colored People's Time, Detroit; exec. prod. Black Jour., N.Y.C., 1968-77, Tony Brown's Jour., N.Y.C., 1977—; pres. Tony Brown Prodns., N.Y.C., 1977—; founder Sch. Comm. Howard U., Washington, 1971, dean, 1974; host call-in radio program Tony Brown, WLIB-AM, N.Y.C., 1995—. Author: Black Lies, White Lies: The Truth According to Tony Brown, 1995, Empower the People: A 7-Step Plan to Overthrow the Conspiracy That is Stealing Your Money and Freedom; author, dir., prodr, distbr. (film) The White Girl, 1990. Hon. chairperson Nat. Orgn. Black Coll. Alumni, Inc., founded ann. Black Coll. Day, 1980; mem. bd. trustees Shaw Divinity Sch.; bd. dirs. Assn. Study Afro-Am. Life and History; mem. nat. adv. bd. Rep. Mainstream Com., Nat. Am. Slavery Meml. Bd.; adviser Harvard Found. for Intercultural and Race Rels. Recipient Operation Push's Communicator for Freedom award, 1973, Frederick Douglass Liberation award, 1974, Nat. Urban League's Pub. Svc. award, 1977, Black Psychologists' Cmty. Svc. award, 1988, Am. Psychiat. Assn.'s Colomon Carter Fuller award, 1989, NAACP Image award, 1991, Black Emmy award, 1993, Sales and Mktg. Execs. Internat. Acad. Achievement's Amb. of Free Enterprise award, Communicator or Yr. award,

1994, Educator of Yr. award, 1995, So. Christian Leadership Conf.'s Econ. Empowerment award. Mem. Nat. Assn. Black Media Prodrs. (founder), Coun. Econ. Devel. Black Ams. (founder), Nat. Assn. Black TV & Film Prodrs., Nat. Comm. Coun. Office: Tony Browns Prodn 1501 Broadway Ste 412 New York NY 10036-5501*

BROWN, WILLIAM DOUGLAS, pediatric neurologist; b. Pasadena, Calif., Sept. 13, 1961; s. Alan Douglas Brown and Anne Arvilla Dixon; m. Mara Genevieve Coyle, May 30, 1992; children: Ryan Douglas, Nathan Alexander. AB in English and Am. Lit., Brown U., 1983, AB in Biology, 1983, MD, 1987. Diplomate Am. Bd. Pediats., Am. Bd. Psychiatry and Neurology. Resident in pediats. R.I. Hosp., Providence, 1987-90; fellow in child neurology Childrens Hosp. L.A., 1990-93, rsch. fellow in neuropathology, 1993-95; asst. prof. pediats. and clin. neuroscis. Brown U., Providence, 1995—; attending physician dept. pediats. and dept. neurology R.I. Hosp., 1995—. Contbr. articles to med. jours. including Pediat. Neurology, Neurosurgery, Jour. Neuropathology Experimental Neurology. Bd. dirs. Am. Friends of Coll. Cevenol, N.Y., 1982—. Fellow Am. Acad. Pediats.; mem. AMA, Am. Acad. Neurology, Child Neurology Soc. Democrat. Congregational. Office: R I Hosp Dept Pediats 593 Eddy St Providence RI 02903

BROWN, WILLIAM ERNEST, dentist; b. Benton Harbor, Mich., Aug. 29, 1922; s. William Ernest and Gertrude (Eliot) B.; m. T.N. McDonald, Oct. 21, 1944 (dec. July 1969); children: Judith M. Brown Smith, Wendy E. Brown Kerschbaum, Terrence N.; m. E.M. Tyree, Sept. 11, 1970. D.D.S., U. Mich., 1945, M.S., 1947. Practice pediatric dentistry Ann Arbor, Mich., 1947-62; part-time tchr. U. Mich., 1947-62; asst., then asso. prof. dentistry, asso. dir. W.K. Kellogg Found. Inst. Grad. and Postgrad. Dentistry, 1962-69; dean Coll. Dentistry, U. Okla., Oklahoma City, 1969-87; acting provost Health Scis. Ctr. U. Okla., 1973-75. Author: Oral Health, Dentistry and the American Public, 1974, Dental Education in the United States, 1976. Mem. City of Ann Arbor Human Rels. Commn., 1960-66, chmn., 1965-66; chmn. bd. dirs. ARC, Oklahoma County chpt., 1991-93, Cmty. Coun. Ctrl. Okla., (pres. 1998—). Recipient Gies Editorial award, 1965, 67. Mem. ADA, Am. Assn. Dental Schs. (pres. 1984-85), Am. Acad. Pediatric Dentistry, Am. Soc. Dentistry for Children. Home: 24 S Easy St Edmond OK 73003-4532

BROWN, WILLIAM FREDRICK, art educator; b. Evansville, Ind., June 21, 1947; s. Joseph Carl and Annette Elizabeth (Steinbach) B.; m. Laura Marie Nagy, June 29, 1969; children: Christopher Allen, Ryan Patrick. BS in art, Ind. State U., 1969; MFA, Sch. of the Art Inst. of Chgo., 1975. Instr. Henderson State U., Arkadelphia, Ark., 1975-77; asst. prof. Marshall U., Huntington, W.Va., 1977-80; prof. art U. Evansville (Ind.), 1980—. Roman Catholic. Avocation: travel. Home: 724 Hillcrest Dr Newburgh IN 47630-1359 Office: U Evansville 1800 Lincoln Ave Evansville IN 47714-1506

BROWN, WILLIAM HILL, III, lawyer; b. Phila., Jan. 19, 1928; s. William H. Jr. and Ethel L. (Washington) B.; m. Sonya Morgan Brown, Aug. 29, 1952 (div. 1975); 1 child, Michele D.; m. D. June Hairston, July 29, 1975; 1 child, Jeanne-Marie. BS, Temple U., 1952; JD, U. Pa., 1955. Bar: Pa. 1956, D.C. 1972, U.S. Ct. Appeals (3d cir.) 1959, U.S. Ct. Appeals (4th cir.) 1978, U.S. Dist. Ct. (ea. dist.) Pa. 1957, U.S. Ct. Appeals (10th cir.) 1986, U.S. Ct. Appeals (5th cir.) 1988, U.S. Dist. Ct. D.C. 1994, U.S. Ct. Appeals (D.C. cir.) 1994, U.S. Ct. Appeals (fed. cir.) 1997. Assoc. Norris, Schmidt, Phila., 1955-62; ptnr. Norris, Brown, Hall, Phila., 1962-68; ptnr. Schnader, Harrison, Segal & Lewis, Phila., 1974—, mem. exec. com., 1983-87; chief of frauds Dist. Atty.'s Office, 1968, dep. dist. atty., 1968; commr. EEOC, Washington, 1968-69; chmn. EEOC, 1969-73; lectr. S.W. Legal Found., Practising Law Inst., Nat. Inst. Trial Advocacy; bd. dirs. United Parcel Svc., Inc., 1983—, Lawyers Com. Civil Rights Under Law; chmn. Phila. Spl. Investigation Commn. MOVE; pres. Nat. Black Child Devel., Inc., 1986-90; bd. dirs. Cmty. Legal Svcs., 1986—; mem. exec. com. Schnader, Harrison, Segal & Lewis, 1983-87; bd. dirs., mem. exec. com. Lawyers Com. Civil Rights Under law, 1977—, co-chair, 1991-93; mem. Commn. on Comml. Operation of U.S. Customs Svc., 1994-98. Contbr. articles to profl. jours. Bd. dirs. Mid. States Colls. and Secondary Schs., 1983-89, Main Line Acad., 1982—, Nat. Sr. Citizens Law Ctr., 1988-94; mem. nat. bd. govs. Am. Heart Assn., 1994-96, mem. audit com., mem. pub. affairs policy com., bd. dirs., 1986-94, mem. audit com., mem. pub. affairs policy com.; mem. adv. com. on appellate ct. rules Supreme Ct. Pa., 1989-95. With USAF, 1946-48. Recipient award of merit Fed. Bar Assn., Columbus, 1971, NAACP award, 1971, Dr. Edward S. Cooper award Am. Heart Assn., 1995, Whitney M. Young Jr. Leadership award Urban League, 1996, Whitney North Seymor award Lawyers Com. for Civil Rights Under Law, 1996, Champions for Social Justice and Equality award Black Law Students Assn. Rutgers-Camden, 1997, Earl G. Harrison Pro Bono award, 1998. Fellow Am. Law Inst.; mem. ABA, Phila. Bar Assn. (Fidelity award 1990), D.C. Bar Assn., Pa. Bar Assn., Fed. Bar Assn., Nat. Bar Assn., Inter-Am. Bar Assn., World Assn. Lawyers (founding mem.), Am. Arbitration Assn. (past bd. dirs.), Barrister's Assn. Phila., Inc. (J. Austin Norris award 1987), Citizens Commn. on Civil Rights, NAACP (bd. dirs. legal def. and ednl. fund), Alpha Phi Alpha (Recognition award 1969). Republican. Episcopalian. Office: Schnader Harrison Segal & Lewis 1600 Market St Ste 3600 Philadelphia PA 19103-7240

BROWN, WILLIAM HOUSTON, lawyer; b. Apr. 14, 1941; s. George Leon and Hattie Lou (Stubblefield) B.; m. Deborah Kay Wallace, Dec. 10, 1982; children: Shaun Alan, Ward Houston. BA, Union U., Jackson, Tenn., 1963; MA, Mid. Tenn. State U., 1967; JD, U. Tenn., 1972. Bar: Tenn. 1972, U.S. Dist. Ct. (we. dist.) Tenn. 1973, U.S. Ct. Appeals (6th cir.) 1973. Asst. dean U. Tenn. Coll. Law, Knoxville, 1972-73; prvt. practice Jackson, 1973-79; sr. ptnr. Brown, Holmes & Rich, Jackson, 1979-83, Brown & Larson, Jackson, 1983-85; assoc. prof. law Coll. Law U. Wyo., Laramie, 1984-85, Coll. Law U. Miss., 1985—; dir. Western Trial Advocacy Inst., Laramie, 1984-85. Contbg. author: Bankruptcy Exemption Manual, 1998, Bankruptcy Jury Manual, 1998. Bd. dirs. West Tenn. Legal Svcs., Inc., Jackson, 1975-80; pres. Jackson Theatre Guild, 1982. Woodrow Wilson fellow, 1963. Fellow Am. Coll. Bankruptcy, Tenn. Bar Found.; mem. Am. Bankruptcy Inst., Nat. Conf. Bankruptcy Judges, Order Coif. Democrat. Baptist. Office: US Courthouse 200 Jefferson Ave Ste 675 Memphis TN 38103-2328

BROWN, WILLIAM JOHN, computer scientist; b. McMinnville, Oreg., Oct. 2, 1954; s. John Daniel and Betty Jean (Johnson) B. BS in Zoology, Oreg. State Univ., 1977; MBA in Fin., Univ. Oreg., 1980; MS in Computer Sci., U. N.C., 1990. Actuarial technician Standard Ins. Co., Portland, Oreg., 1982-84; programmer analyst Standard Ins. Co., Portland, 1984, Pacific Power and Light, Portland, 1984-87; sr. programmer analyst Eddie Bauer, Richmond, Wash., 1987-88; summer intern IBM Rsch., Hawthorne, N.Y., 1990; computing sys. analyst Boeing Comml. Airplane, Everett, Wash., 1991-94; advanced tech. specialist Boeing Info. and Support Svcs., Bellevue, Wash., 1994—; rsch. asst. U. N.C., Chapel Hill, 1988-90, rsch. assoc., 1990-91; adminstrv. v.p. Willamette Valley ACM, Portland, 1986; mem. program com. Virtual Reality Ann. Internat. Symposium '93, Seattle, 1993. Vol. Oxfam Am., Seattle, 1988-95; tutor Lego/Logo class for inner city youth, Seattle, 1993. Mem. Sunrise Toastmasters (pres. 1986, Toastmaster of Yr., 1986), U. N.C. Puget Sound Alumni (treas. 1991—). Democrat. Avocations: contradancing, master's swimming. Address: PO Box 3707 M/S 7L-48 Seattle WA 98124

BROWN, WILLIAM L., banker; b. Hendersonville, N.C., Feb. 1, 1922; s. William W. and Sarah (Maxwell) B.; m. Helen Presbrey, August, 1947; children: Kathryn H., Richard P., Steven J., Melissa M. Student, Mars Hill Coll., Newbury Coll.; M.B.A., Harvard, 1947. With First Nat. Bank Boston/Bank of Boston Corp., 1949-89, asst. v.p., 1949-59, v.p., 1959-66, sr. v.p., 1966-69, exec. v.p., 1969-71, bd. dirs., 1969-92, dir. of corp., 1970-92, pres., COO, 1971-83, chmn., CEO, 1983-87, ret., 1989; bd. dirs. Gen. Cinema Corp., Chestnut Hill, Mass., Ionics, Inc., Watertown, Mass., N.Am. Mortgage Co., Santa Rosa, Calif.; trustee Bradley Real Estate Trust, Boston. Hon. life overseer Children's Hosp. Med. Ctr., Boston; trustee assoc. Boston Coll., Marine Biol. Lab., Woods Hole, Mass.; trustee, mem. corp. Mus. Sci.; bd. dirs. Jobs for Mass., Inc., John F. Kennedy Libr. Found., Ret. Artery Bus. Com., Ret. Friends of Post Office Sq.; mem. corp. Northeastern U. Lt. USNR, World War II. Office: Bank of Boston MS/01-28-02 100 Federal St Fl 8 Boston MA 02110-1898

BROWN, WILLIAM RANDALL, geology educator; b. Staunton, Va., Oct. 31, 1913; s. Thornton Lee and Ellen (Greer) B.; m. Elizabeth Blessing Whitmore, Aug. 20, 1942; children—Elizabeth Dudley, Denison Greer, Elaine Daingerfield. B.S. with final honors, U. Va., 1938, M.A., 1939; Ph.D., Cornell U., 1942. Geologist Va. Geol. Survey, Charlottesville, 1942-45; mem. faculty dept. geology U. Ky., 1945—, assoc. prof., 1947-50, prof., 1950-84, prof. emeritus, 1984—; geologist U.S. Geol. Survey, 1965-76; rep. Am. Geol. Inst. to Internat. Field. Inst., Japan, 1967. Contbr. articles to profl. jours. Fellow Geol. Soc. Am. (chmn. S.E. sect. 1970-71); mem. Am. Assn. Petroleum Geologists, Sigma Xi. Home: 253 Shady Ln Lexington KY 40503-2034 Office: U Ky Dept Geol Scis Lexington KY 40506

BROWN, WILLIAM ROBERT, association executive, consultant; b. Delaware, Ohio, Jan. 19, 1926; s. Omar Lloyd and Olive Ida (Johnson) B.; m. Dorothy Judd Curtis, Dec. 30, 1950; children—Darmae Judd, Ann Barlett Brown Nutt. B.A., Ohio Wesleyan U., 1948; M.A.; research scholar, Ohio State U., 1949. Asst. Inst. Practical Politics, Ohio Wesleyan U., 1947-48; research dir. Mo. State C. of C., 1950-64; govtl. research dir. Del. State C. of C., 1964-65; assoc. research dir. Council of State Chambers of Commerce, Washington, 1965-78, pres., 1979-90; pres. Commerce Service Ctr., Inc., 1986-90; cons., 1991—. Editor: State Tax Report, 1969-81, Jud. Report, 1969-81, Property Tax Report, 1979, State UC Report, 1984-90, State Chamber News, 1988-90. Trustee Nat. Found. for Unemployment Compensation and Workers Compensation; precinct chmn. Rep. Party, 1968-70; pres. Friends of the Railroad, 1980-89. Mem. Nat. Tax Assn., Estero (Fla.) C. of C. (exec. dir. 1998—), Phi Beta Kappa, Pi Sigma Alpha, Kappa Delta Pi, Sigma Chi. Methodist. Home: 4061 Gunnison Ct # 821 Estero FL 33288

BROWN, WILLIAM SAMUEL, JR., communication sciences and disorders educator; b. Pottstown, Penn., Apr. 25, 1940; s. William Samuel and Elizabeth (Gallager) B.; m. Elaine Kay Whitehouse, Aug. 18, 1962; children: William Samuel III, Allen Reed. MA, SUNY, Buffalo, 1967, PhD, 1969. Speech therapist Crawford Cty. Schools, Meadville, Penn., 1962-65; rsch. asst. SUNY, Buffalo, N.Y., 1965-68; prof. U. Fla., Gainesville, Fla., 1970—; Contrib. numerous publications to scientific jours. Postdoctoral fellow U. Fla, Gainsville, 1968-70. Fellow Internat. Soc. Phonetic Sci. (coun. rep. 1980—), Am. Speech-Lang.-Hearing Assn., Acoustical Soc. Am.; mem. Am. Assn. Phonetic Sci. (exec. sec. 1980—). Republican. Presbyterian. Office: U Fla IASCP Dauer 63 Gainesville FL 32611

BROWN, WILLIE LEWIS, JR., mayor, former state legislator, lawyer; b. Mineola, Tex., Mar. 20, 1934; s. Willie Lewis and Minnie (Boyd) B.; children: Susan, Robin, Michael. B.A., San Francisco State Coll., 1955; LL.D., Hastings Coll. Law, 1958; postgrad. fellow, Crown Coll., 1970, U. Calif.-Santa Cruz, 1970. Bar: Calif. 1959. Mem. Calif. State Assembly, Sacramento, 1964-95; speaker Calif. State Assembly, 1980-95, chmn. Ways and Means Com., 1971-74; chmn. revenue and taxation com., 1976-79; Democratic Whip Calif. State Assembly, 1969-70, majority floor leader, 1979-80, chmn. legis. black caucus, 1980, chmn. govtl. efficiency and economy com., 1968-84; mayor San Francisco, 1995—. Mem. U. Calif. bd. regents, 1972, Dem. Nat. Com., 1989-90; co-chmn. Calif. del. to Nat. Black Polit. Conv., 1972, Calif. del. to Nat. Dem. Conv., 1980; nat. campaign chmn. Jesse Jackson for Pres., 1988. Mem. State Legis. Leaders Found. (dir.), Nat. Conf. State Legislatures, NAACP, Black Am. Polit. Assn. Calif. (co-founder, past chmn.), Calif. Bar Assn., Alpha Phi Alpha, Phi Alpha Delta. Democrat. Methodist. Office: Office of the Mayor City Hall Rm 200 1 Dr Carlton B Goodlett Pl San Francisco CA 94102 also: 1388 Sutter St Ste 820 San Francisco CA 94109-5453*

BROWN, ZANIA FAYE, elementary education educator; b. Muskogee, Okla., Sept. 22, 1954; d. Aaron L.Z. and Teleatha (Sanford) Mahone; m. Benjamin Brown Jr., Oct. 5, 1985. BA in Elem. Edn., U. Mo., 1976, MA in Reading Edn., 1980. Cert. elem. edn. and reading edn. tchr., Mo. Elem. tchr. Kansas City (Mo.) Sch. Dist., 1977—, tchr. chpt. I basic skills, 1990—; Title 1 instrnl. facilitator Kansas City (Mo.) Sch.Dist., 1995-96, mem. profl. devel. team, 1995-96, 97—, Title 1 instnl. facilitator, 1997—; mem. Kansas City Equity Cadre, 1996—, profl. devel. team, 1997, co-sec. mentor steering com. for new and beginning tchrs., 1997—; presenter classroom mgmt. for profl. devel. for new and beginning tchrs., 1997—; reading recovery tchr., 1999. Site coord. Reading Is Fundamental, 1995—. Recipient For Kids' Sake Caring award Kansas City TV 5, 1990; named one of Outstanding Young Women of Am., 1980. Mem. Internat. Reading Assn., Nat. Assn. Negro Profl. and Bus. Women, Alpha Kappa Alpha (corr. sec. Kansas City chpg. 1986-88, treas. 1976, sgt.-at-arms 1984-85), Nat. Sorority of Phi Delta Kappa (v.p. 1993, reading power chairperson 1984, 97, 99, sec. 1991, corr. sec. 1992-93, pres. 1995-97, exec. advisor 1997—). Office: 1211 Mcgee St Kansas City MO 64106-2416

BROWNBACK, SAM, senator; b. Parker, Kans.; m. Mary; children: Abby, Andy, Liz. BS in Agrl. Econs. with honors, Kan. State U.; JD, U. Kans. Farm broadcaster KKSU; ptnr. law firm, N.Y.C.; instr. law Kans. State U.; city atty. Ogden and Leonardville, Kans.; sec. agr., Washington; mem. 104th Congress from 2nd Kans. dist., Washington, 1994-96, U.S. Senate, Washington, 1996—; mem. com., sci.. and transp., fgn. rels., govtl. affairs, joint econ. coms.; fellow U.S. Trade Rep. Carla Hills, 1990-91, mem. intergovtl. adv. com.; spkr. on trade, agr., leadership, motivation, mem. com. health, edn., labor and pensions. Co-author: 2 books; contbr. numerous articles. Pres. Kans. Prayer Breakfast; developer Family Impact Statement; vice chmn. Riley County Rep. Com. Recipient Hon. Am. Farmer degree, FFA; named Outstanding Young Person, Osaka, Japan Jaycees, Kansan of Distinction, 1988. Office: US Senate 303 Hart Senate Office Bldg Washington DC 20510*

BROWN-CHRISTOPHER, CHERYL DENISE, physician; b. Washington, Dec. 4, 1954; d. Samuel and Cornelia Lela (Banks) Brown; m. Joseph William Christopher, Feb. 14, 1981; children: Jeremy, Callye Joelle. MD, Howard U., 1978. Intern Howard U., Washington, 1978-79, resident, 1982; physician pvt. practice, Annapolis, Md., 1982—; v.p. Back Pain Assn., Pasadena, Md., 1995—. Tchr. jr. dept. Sunday Sch. Vt. Ave Bapt. Ch., 1990—choir mem., 1978—; ethics com. Md. State MEd. and Chirurgical Faculty, 1986, medicine and religion com., 1984-86. Washington Heart Assn. Summer rsch. fellow, 1970; recipient AMA Physicians Recognition award 1981, 84, 90, 93, Vt. Ave. Bapt. Ch. Health Fair award, Washington, 1985. Fellow Am. Acad. Family Physicians; mem. Am. Osteo. Acad. Sclerotherapy, Am. Acad. Pain Mgmt. (diplomate, bd. cert.), Am. Coll. Advancement of Medicine, Am. Soc. Clin. Hypnosis, So. Med. Assn., Order of Eastern Star. Avocations: classical piano, swimming. Office: Lifestyle Med Ctr 1419 Forest Dr Ste 202 Annapolis MD 21403-1473

BROWNE, ARTHUR, newspaper editor. Editorial page editor The Daily News, N.Y.C., mng. editor, 1995—. Office: NY News Inc 450 W 33rd St New York NY 10001-2603*

BROWNE, CORNELIUS PAYNE, physics educator; b. Madison, Wis., Oct. 30, 1923; s. Frederick Lincoln and Vera (Payne) B.; m. Cynthia Cochrane, July 6, 1957 (dec. 1990); children: Margaret, Cornelius. B.A., U. Wis., 1946, Ph.D., 1951. Rsch. assoc. MIT, Cambridge, 1951-56; prof. physics U. Notre Dame, Ind., 1956—; cons. Argonne Nat. Lab., 1961-66, Los Alamos Nat. Lab., 1963-66; vis. prof. U. Tex., Austin, 1972, U. Wis., summers 1959-61; program officer for nuclear physics NSF, 1980-81; chmn. manpower subcom. NSF-Dept. Energy Nuclear Sci. Adv. Com., 1984-87. Contbr. articles profl. jours. Chpt. mem. Episcopalian Ch., 1968-70, 74, mem. vestry, 1991-93. Fellow Am. Phys. Soc. (div. nuclear physics program com. 1972-73, nominating com. 1973-74); mem. Am. Assn. Physics Tchrs., Eagle Lake Yacht Club (bd. dirs. 1968-70, 73-76, commodore 1974-75), Sigma Xi (pres. chpt. 1969-70), Phi Beta Kappa, Theta Delta Chi. Research in nuclear reactions and excitation levels Browne-Buechner broad-range magnetic spectrograph. Home: 1606 E Washington St South Bend IN 46617-3415 Office: U Notre Dame Nuclear Structure Lab Physics Dept Notre Dame IN 46556*

BROWNE, DIANA GAYLE, artist, social services; b. San Francisco, Aug. 31, 1924; d. Clarence Luther and Elsa Henrietta (Ericson) Sidelinger; m. Alfred B. Britton Jr., Sept. 2, 1942 (div. 1960); children: Alfred B. Britton III, Kathryn H. Lumbert, Patrick Luther Britton; m. James Stuart Browne M.D., May 19, 1963; children: Bruce Petter Browne, Julia Regina Browne. Student, Stanford U., 1947; BA magnum cum laude, San Jose State U., 1949; MSW, U. Calif., 1958; BFA, San Francisco Art Inst., 1973. Lic. Clinical Social Worker, Calif. Clinical social worker Dept. of Mental Health, Sacramento, 1958-59; clin. social worker U. Calif. Med. Ctr., San Francisco, 1960-61, Langley Porter Neuropsych. Inst., San Francisco, 1961-65, Napa State Hosp., 1980-85; postgrad. Inst. for Clin. Social Work, Berkeley, 1981-83; freelance artist Mill Valley, Calif., 1966-80, Mill Valley, 1985—; mem. Acci Gallery, Berkeley, 1977-91, Alliance Women Artists, 1988-89. Recipient Merit award Calif. State Fair Fine Arts Div., 1989, Marin Arts Guild, Larkspur, Calif., 1977-79, Best of Show, Merit award (7s), Marin County Fair Photo and Fine Arts Divs., San Rafael, Calif., 1977-78, 89, 90. Mem. AAUW (v.p. San Francisco chpt. 1963), Calif. Soc. Printmakers, Marin Soc. Artists (signature mem., adv. coun. 1987-89, 91-92, bd. dirs. 1994-95, cash and merit awards 1974-79, 90), San Francisco Women Artists (sec. 1978-79), Calif. Watercolor Assn. (signature mem., membership chmn. 1986-88, merit award 1987), Outdoor Art Club, Marin Watercolor Soc., Alpha Chi Omega (pres. Santa Clara County alumnae 1949-51, Marin County alumnae 1966-68). Avocations: computer graphics, photography.

BROWNE, DONALD ROGER, speech communication educator; b. Detroit, Mar. 13, 1934; s. A. and L. Browne; m. Mary Jo Rowell, Aug. 23, 1958; children: Mary Kathleen, Stuart Roger, Steven Rowell. BA, U. Mich., 1955, MA, 1958, PhD, 1961. Corr. Voice of Am., fgn. service officer U.S. Info. Agy., Tunis, Tunisia and Conakry, Guinea, 1960-63; asst. prof. broadcasting Boston U., 1963-65; asst. prof. speech Purdue U., West Lafayette, Ind., 1965-66; assoc. prof. U. Minn., Mpls., 1966-70, prof., 1970—, dept. chair, 1989-93, 96-99; Fulbright lectr., Beirut, 1973-74; vis. lectr. Lund U., Sweden, spring 1993. Author: International Radio Broadcasting, 1982, Comparing Broadcast Systems, 1989 (BEA/NAB Electronic Media Book of Yr. award 1989, Outstanding Acad. Book in Comm. Category, Choice, 1990), Television/Radio News & Minorities, 1994, Electronic Media and Indigenous Peoples, 1996, Electronic Media and Industrialized Nations, 1999. Mem.Civic Orch. Mpls., 1966—. Served with U.S. Army, 1955-57. NATO fellow, Brussels, 1980; named Outstanding Young Tchr., Cen. States Speech Assn., 1968. Mem. Broadcast Edn. Assn., Assn. for Edn. in Journalism and Mass Communication, Internat. Inst. Communication. Episcopalian. Avocation: playing trombone. Office: Univ of Minn Dept of Speech-Communication 460 Folwell Hall Minneapolis MN 55455

BROWNE, EDMUND JOHN PHILLIP, oil company executive; b. Hamburg, Germany, Feb. 20, 1948; came to U.S., 1986; s. Edmund and Paula Browne. MA in Physics, Cambridge U., Eng., 1969; MS in Bus., Stanford (Calif.) U., 1981; DEng (hon.), Heriott Watt U.; DTech (hon.), Robert Gordon U. Registered profl. engr., U.K. Petroleum engr. Brit. Petroleum Co., London, N.Y., Calif. and Alaska, 1969-79; regional petroleum engr. Brit. Petroleum Co., London, 1979-80, comml. mgr., 1981-83, group treas., 1984-86; mgr. forties field Brit. Petroleum Co., Aberdeen, Scotland, 1983-84; exec. v.p., CFO, CEO Standard Oil Co. of Ohio, Cleve., 1986—; CEO Standard Oil Prodn. Co., 1987—; chief fin. officer BP America, Inc., Cleve., 1987-89; mng. dir., chief exec. officer BP Exploration, London, 1989-95; mng. dir., bd. The British Petroleum Co., PLC, 1991, group chief exec., 1995—; CEO BP Amoco, 1998—; nonexec. dir. Redland PLC, 1992-96, Smithkine Beecham, 1995—, Intel Corp., 1997—; bd. dirs. Brit. Petroleum Co. plc.; mem. internat. adv. bd. Daimler-Benz, 1997—. Emeritus chmn. adv. bd. Stanford Grad. Sch. Bus., 1997; trustee Brit. Mus., 1995—, Conf. Bd., Inc.; mem. governing body London Bus. Sch., 1996—; v.p., bd. dirs. Prince of Wales Bus. Leaders Forum; hon. fellow St. John's Coll., Cambridge. Knighted, 1998; Trevelyan open scholar. Fellow Royal Acad. Engring., Inst. Mining and Metallurgy, Inst. Chem. Engrs. (hon.); mem. Athenaeum Club (London). Avocations: ballet, opera, tennis, photography, pre-Columbian art.

BROWNE, G.M. WALTER SHAWN BROWNE, journalist, chess player; b. Sydney, Australia, Jan. 10, 1949; s. Walter Francis and Hilda Louise (Leahy) B.; m. Raquel Emilse Facal, Mar. 9, 1973; 1 stepson, Marcello Garcia. Grad. high sch. Chess player, 1957—, U.S. jr. champion, 1966, Australian champion, 1968-69, U.S. Open champion, 1971-73, Nat. Open champion, 1971-73, 75, 84, 86-87, 91, 94-95, U.S. champion, 1974-78, 80-83, Pan-Am. champion, 1974, Internat. German champion, 1975, mem. U.S. Olympic Team, 1974, 78, 82, 84, Nat. and U.S. Open Blitz chess champion, 1989, Pan-Pacific Blitz chess champion, 1991; columnist Chess Life & Rev., Berkeley, Calif., 1973—; lectr. in field. Publisher: Strongest International Chess Tourneys, 1978-85. Named Internat. Master Fedn. Internat. des Eshecs, 1969, Internat. Grandmaster, 1969; 1st pl. Venice, 1971; 1st pl. Rejkavik, Iceland, 1978; 1st pl. Wijk Am. Zee, Holland, 1974, 80; 1st pl. Indonesia, 1982, 2d-3d World Open, Phila., 1988; only 10 time winner Nat. Open, Can. Open champion, 1991, U.S. class champion, 1991, 7 time Am. Open champion; winner N.Am. Open 1991, 93, 94, 96. Mem. World Blitz Chess Assn. (pres., founder, pub., editor quar. mag. Blitz Chess 1988—). Performer simultaneous chess exhbns., including world record of 29-0 in 45 minutes, Adelaide, Austrlia, 1971. Played 106 competitors, including a computer, for a world record score of 94 wins, 9 draws, and 3 losses, and time of 7 hours, 20 minutes, N.Y.C., 1973, 1st pl., Gjovik, Norway, 1983, 1st pl., Naestved, Denmark, 1985; 1st pl. World Blitz Chess Assn.-Software Blitz Chess, Long Beach, Calif., 1988; defeated World Blitz champion, Mikhail Tal by a score of 2 1/2-1/2. 5-time Western Class champion, Concord and L.A.; 2-time Western States champion, Reno. Address: 8 Parnassus Rd Berkeley CA 94708-2041*

BROWNE, JEFFREY FRANCIS, lawyer; b. Clare, South Australia, Australia, Mar. 1, 1944; came to U.S., 1975; s. Patrick Joseph and Irene Kathleen (Cormack) B.; m. Deborah Mary Christine West, Aug. 28, 1971; children: Veronique Namur Irene, Jeffrey James, Nicholas Patrick, Sophie Christina, Amy Elizabeth. LLB, Adelaide U., South Australia, 1966; LLM, Sydney U., Australia, 1968, Harvard U., 1976. Bar: South Australia 1969, Australian Capital Territory 1973, N.Y. 1978, Victoria 1982, New South Wales 1983, Western Australia 1983. Assoc. High Ct. Australia, Canberra, Australian Capital Territory, 1967-68; diplomat Dept. Fgn. Affairs, Canberra, 1969; 2d sec. Australian High Commn., London and Malaysia, 1970-71; acting high commr. Australian High Commn., Ghana, 1972; counsel nuclear tests case Internat. Ct. Justice, 1973-74; assoc. Sullivan & Cromwell, N.Y.C., 1976-81, ptnr., 1983—; gen. counsel Alcoa of Australia, Melbourne, 1981-82; bd. dirs. Compinvest Pty. Ltd. Mem. Law Inst. Victoria, Australian Mining and Petroleum Law Assn., Law Coun. Australia (chmn. fin. and securities subcom., internat. trade and bus. law com.), Inst. Dirs. of Australia, Internat. Bar Assn. (sect. on energy and natural resources), Am. C. of C. in Australia (bd. dirs.), Am. Soc. Internat. Law, N.Y. Yacht Club, Melbourne Club. Office: Sullivan & Cromwell 125 Broad St Fl 28 New York NY 10004-2489 also: 101 Collins St, Melbourne Victoria 3000, Australia*

BROWNE, JOHN ROBINSON, banker; b. Ft. Worth, Aug. 29, 1914; s. Virgil and Maimee Lee (Robinson) B.; m. Elizabeth Anne Hargett, Sept. 1, 1945 (dec. June 1990); children: John Robinson, Ann Browne (Mrs. John M. Dunker); stepchildren: Bob Allen Street, David H. Street; m. Christine H. Anthony, Mar. 20, 1992 (dec. May 1993); m. Barbara C. (Conner) Edwards, Nov. 18, 1994. A.B., Okla. U., 1938, J.D., 1939; postgrad., Harvard Grad. Sch. Bus. Adminstrn., 1939-40; grad., Stonier Grad. Sch. Banking, Rutgers U., 1965. Bar: Okla. bar 1939. With Liberty Nat. Bank & Trust Co., Oklahoma City, 1945-46, 60-71; sr. v.p. Liberty Nat. Bank & Trust Co., 1960-71; gen. mgr. Coca-Cola Bottling Co., Colorado Springs and Pueblo, Colo., 1946-59; mgr. credit dept. Bank of Mid-Am., Oklahoma City, 1959-60; pres., chmn. bd., chief exec. officer Security Nat. Bank, Cairo, Ill., 1959-62; chief exec. officer Union Bancorp., Inc., Oklahoma City, 1971-89; chmn. bd. dirs. Sterling Sugars Co., Franklin, La., 1989-96, Cheyenne Propagation Co., Colo. Springs, Colo., 1989—; mng. gen. ptnr. Glencoe-Vacherie Plantation Ltd., Okla., 1972—. Pres. Community Chest, Colorado Springs.; former trustee Deaconess Hosp.; past bd. dirs. Trust Co. of Okla. Served from 2d lt. to lt. col., F.A. AUS, 1940-45. Mem. Okla. Bar Assn. Presbyterian (elder, trustee). Clubs: Oklahoma City Golf and Country (Oklahoma City); Garden of the Gods (Colorado Springs, Colo.). Home: 4029 Neptune Dr Oklahoma City OK 73116-1659 Office: Colcord Bldg 15 N Robinson Ave Oklahoma City OK 73102-5405*

BROWNE, JOSEPH PETER, retired librarian; b. Detroit, June 12, 1929; s. George and Mary Bridget (Fahy) B.; A.B., U. Notre Dame, 1951; S.T.L., Pontificium Athenaeum Angelicum, Rome, 1957, S.T.D., 1960; MS in L.S., Cath. U. Am., 1965. Joined Congregation of Holy Cross, Roman Cath. Ch., 1947, ordained priest, 1955; asst. pastor Holy Cross Ch., South Bend, Ind., 1955-56; libr., prof. moral theology Holy Cross Coll., Washington, 1959-64; mem. faculty U. Portland (Oreg.), 1964-73, 75—, dir. libr., 1966-70, 76-94, dean Coll. Arts and Scis., 1970-73, assoc. prof. libr. sci. 1967-95, prof. emeritus, 1995—, regent, 1969-70, 77-81, chmn. acad. senate, 1968-70, 1987-88; prof., head dept. libr. sci. Our Lady of Lake Coll., San Antonio, 1973-75; chmn. Interstate Libr. Planning Coun., 1977-79. Mem. Columbia River chpt. Huntington's Disease Soc. Am., 1975-90, pres., 1979-82; pastor St. Birgitta Ch., Portland, 1993—; chmn. Archdiocesan Presbyteral Coun., 1994-98; mem. coll. of cons. Archdiocese of Portland, 1995—. Recipient Culligan award U. Portland, 1979. Mem. Cath. Libr. Assn. (life, pres. 1971-73), ALA, Cath. Theol. Soc. Am., Pacific N.W. Libr. Assn. (pres. 1985-86), Oreg. Libr. Assn. (life, pres. 1967-68), Nat. Assn. Parliamentarians, Oreg. Assn. Parliamentarians (pres. 1985-87), Mensa Internat., All-Ireland Cultural Soc. Oreg. (pres. 1984-85). Democrat. Club: KC. Home: 11820 NW Saint Helens Rd Portland OR 97231-2319

BROWNE, JOY, psychologist; b. New Orleans, Oct. 24, 1950; d. Nelson and Ruth (Strauss) B.; Carter Thweatt, June 9, 1966 (div. 1979); 1 child, Patience. BA, Rice U.; PhD, Northeastern U.; postgrad., Tufts U. Registered psychologist, Mass. With rsch./optics dept. Sperry Rand, Boston, 1966-68; engr. space program Itek, Boston, 1968-70; head social svcs. dept. Boston Redevel. Authority, 1970-71; staff psychologist South Shore Counselling Assocs., Boston, 1971-82; on-the-air psychologist Sta. WITS, Boston, 1978-82, Sta. KGO, San Francisco, 1982-84; host, news Sta. KCBS, San Francisco, 1984-85; on-air psychologist Sta. WABC, N.Y.C., 1985-87, ABC Talkradio, N.Y.C., 1987-92, WOR Radio Network, N.Y.C., 1992—, Sta. WABC-TV, 1995-97, Dr. Joy Browne Show, Syndicated Eyemark Entertainment, 1999—; on-air psychologist WCBS-TV Five O'Clock News, 1999; dir. Town of Hull Adolescent Outreach Program; cons. human sexuality PBS, 1994—. Author: The Used Car Game, 1971, The Research Experience, 1976, Nobody's Perfect, 1988, Why They Don't Call When They Say They Will and Other Mixed Signals, 1989, Dating for Dummies, 1998, 9 Fantasies That Will Ruin Your Life, 1998. Named One of 25 Outstanding Broadcasters USA Today, 1995-96, 100 Most Influential Talkers, Legend La., 1996, Best Female Talk Show Host, Nartash, 1996, 97, Female Talk Show Host of Yr., Vanity Fair Hall of Fame, 1996. Mem. APA (bd. dirs. 1994-97), Phi Kappa Phi (Communicator of Yr. award 1992). Office: WOR Radio Network 1440 Broadway Fl 23 New York NY 10018-2390

BROWNE, KINGSBURY, lawyer; b. Brookline, Mass., Nov. 18, 1922; s. Kingsbury and Sophie (Acheson) B.; m. Annette Wright Upson, June 11, 1949; children: Annette, Kingsbury, Mark, Christopher, Juliet, Gabriella. AB cum laude, Harvard U., 1944, LLB, 1950. Bar: Mass. 1950. Law clk. Judge of U.S. Tax Ct., Washington, 1950-53; ptnr. Hill & Barlow, Boston, 1965-92, of counsel, 1992—; mem. faculty Northeastern U. Law Sch., Boston, 1955, Suffolk Law Sch., Boston, 1956, Boston U. Grad. Tax Program, 1957; tax. cons. nat. and regional environ. orgns., govtl. agys.; dir. Guilford Industries, Maine, 1960-82, Sugarloaf Mountain Corp., Maine, 1965-78, Boston & Worcester Corp., Mass., 1970-79; mem. corp. Brookline Savs. Bank, 1966-83; fellow Lincoln Inst. of Land Policy; vis. scholar Harvard U. Law Sch., 1980; mem. nat. adv. coun. Trust for Pub. Land, 1988—; chmn. Brookline Coun. for Planning and Renewal, 1954-56; mem. Selectmen's Com. for Study of Legal Svcs., 1974-75, Corporator Boston Hosp. Women, 1973-78; mem. Corp. Winsor Sch., 1963-85, exec. com., 1967-70; trustee Skowhegan Sch. Sculpture and Painting, 1966-86; overseer Plymouth Plantation, 1978—; mem. vis. com. Sch. Visual Arts, Boston U., 1975-80, Peabody Mus. Archaeology and Ethnology Harvard U., 1976-83. Contbr. articles to profl. jours. Former bd dirs. Mus. Sch. Boston Mus. Fine Arts, Miramichi Salmon Assn., N.B., Can., 1968-79. Served to capt. USAAF, 1943-46. Mem. ABA, Mass. Bar Assn., Boston Bar Assn., Am. Law Inst., Am. Bar Found. Home: PO Box 602A Kennebunkport ME 04046-1602 Office: 1 International Pl Boston MA 02110-2602

BROWNE, M. LYNNE, artist, optician; b. Houston, Sept. 15, 1958; d. Drew Arthur Browne and Marlena Kay Shofner. Student, Tex. Woman's U. Cert. dispensing optician. Optician Tex. State Optical, Lewisville, 1986—; freelance artist. Mem. Nat. Mus. Women in the Arts. Mem. NAFE. Avocations: reading, photography, flowers, animals. Office: Tex State Optical 1124 W Main St Lewisville TX 75067-3469

BROWNE, MALCOLM WILDE, journalist; b. N.Y.C., Apr. 17, 1931; s. Douglas Granzow and Dorothy Rutledge (Wilde) B.; m. Huynh thi Le Lieu, July 18, 1966. Student, Swarthmore Coll., 1948-50, N.Y.U., 1950-52. Cons. chemist, tech. writer, 1952-56; newsman, copy editor Middletown (N.Y.) Daily Record, 1958-60; with Balt. bur. A.P., 1960-61; chief Indochina corr., 1961-65; Saigon corr. ABC, 1965-66; freelance writer and corr. N.Y.C., 1966-68; corr. New York Times in, Buenos Aires, 1968-71, in S. Asia, 1971-73, in Eastern Europe, 1973-77; sci. corr. New York Times in, 1977-81; sr. editor Discover mag., 1981-84; sci writer N.Y. Times, 1985—; McGraw prof. writing Princeton (N.J.) U., 1995-96. Author: The New Face of War, 1965, Muddy Boots and Red Socks, 1993, also numerous articles. Served with AUS, 1956-58. Recipient First prize World Press Photo award The Hague, 1963, Pulitzer prize fgn. corr., 1964, Overseas Press Club award, 1964, Sigma Delta Chi award, 1964, Louis M. Lyons award, 1964, Nat. Headliners Club award, 1964; A.P. Mng. Editors award, 1964, Grady-Stack medal Am. Chem. Soc., 1992; Edward R. Murrow Meml. fellow Coun. on Fgn. Rels., 1966-67. Address: 36 E 36th St New York NY 10016-3463

BROWNE, RAY BROADUS, popular culture educator; b. Millport, Ala., Jan. 15, 1922; s. Garfield and Annie Nola (Trull) B.; m. Olwyn Orde, Aug. 21, 1952 (dec.); children—Glenn, Kevin; m. Alice Pat Matthews, Aug. 25, 1965; 1 child, Alicia. A.B., U. Ala., 1943; A.M., Columbia U., 1947; Ph.D., UCLA, 1956. Instr. U. Nebr., Lincoln, 1947-50; instr. U. Md., College Park, 1956-60; asst. prof., assoc. prof. Purdue U., Lafayette, Ind., 1960-67; prof. popular culture Bowling Green (Ohio) State U., 1967—, Univ. disting. prof., 1975—. Author, editor over 50 books, including Melville's Drive to Humanism, 1971, Popular Culture and the Expanding Consciousness, 1973, The Constitution and Popular Culture, 1975, Dominant Symbols in Popular Culture, 1990, The Many Tongues of Literacy, 1992, Continuities in Popular Culture, 1993, The Cultures of Celebrations, 1994, Preview 2001 : Popular Culture Studies in the Future, 1996, Lincoln-Lore: Lincoln in Contemporary Popular Culture, 1996, Pioneers in Popular Culture Studies, 1998, Paying Back: Remorse and Atonement in Native American Crime Fiction, 1999; creator, editor Jour. Popular Culture, 1967—, Jour. Am. Culture, 1977. Served with U.S. Army, 1942-46. Mem. Popular Culture Assn. (founder, sec., treas. 1970—), Am. Culture Assn. (sec.-treas. 1977—). Democrat. Avocation: scholarly research. Home: 210 N Grove St Bowling Green OH 43402-2335 Office: Bowling Green U Jour Popular Culture Bowling Green OH 43403

BROWNE, RICHARD CULLEN, lawyer; b. Akron, Ohio, Nov. 21, 1938; s. Francis Cedric and Elizabeth Ann (Cullen) B.; m. Patricia Anne Winkler, Apr. 23, 1962; children: Richard Cullen, Catherine Anne, Paulette Elizabeth, Maureen Frances, Colleen Marie. BS in Econs., Holy Cross Coll., 1960; JD Catholic U. Am., 1963. Bar: Va. 1963, U.S. Ct. Claims 1963, U.S. Ct. Customs and Patent Appeals 1963, D.C. 1964, U.S. Ct. Mil. Appeals, 1963, U.S. Ct. Appeals (D.C. cir.) 1964, U.S. Supreme Ct. 1966, U.S. Ct. Appeals (fed. cir.) 1982, U.S. Ct. Appeals (9th cir.) 1983, U.S. Ct. Appeals (6th cir.) 1991, U.S. Ct. Appeals (7th cir.) 1998. Assoc. Browne, Beveridge, DeGrandi & Kline, Washington, 1963-68, ptnr., 1968-72; ptnr. Shaffert, Miller & Browne, Washington, 1972-74; sr. counsel Office of Enforcement, EPA, Washington, 1974-76; asst. chief hearing counsel U.S. Nuc. Regulatory Commn., Washington, 1976-78; sole practice, Washington, 1978-79; ptnr. Winston & Strawn, and predecessor firms, 1980—; lectr. U. R.I., 1975, Washburn U., 1978, Legal Inst., CSC, 1975-78, Hofstra U., 1987—, Nat. Inst. for Trial Advocacy, 1986—. Del., Montgomery County Civic Fedn., 1970-74; chmn. Citizens Adv. Com. on Rockville Corridor, 1972-77; mem. Montgomery County Potomac River Basin Adv. Com., 1972-74. Served to capt. USAF JAGC, 1963-66, USAFR, 1966-69. Named Disting. Mil. grad. Holy Cross Coll., 1960. Mem. Coll. Holy Cross Alumni Assn. (bd. dirs. 1971-78, 98—, alumni senate 1978-97, mem. nominations and elections com. 1995—,), Cath. U. Law Sch. Alumni Soc. (pres. 1992-93, dir. 1991—, bd. visitors 1998—), Cath. U. Gen. Alumni Assn. (bd. govs. 1992—, co-chair Gibbons medal com. 1995—, exec. com. 1995—, chmn. Cath. U. Am. Fund 1996—). Republican. Roman Catholic. Clubs: Holy Cross (pres. Washington 1968-69, 1973-74), Kenwood (Md.), Cosmos Club (Washington), Cripple Creek (Del.). Bd. editors Cath. U. Law Rev., 1962-63. Home: 7203 Old Stage Rd Rockville MD 20852-4438 Office: Winston & Strawn 1400 L St NW Ste 800 Washington DC 20005-3508

BROWNE, RICHARD HAROLD, statistician, consultant; b. St. Louis, Sept. 24, 1946; s. Basil Campbell and Evelyn Beatrice (Biver) B.; m. Dennise Marie Richardson, Aug. 10, 1970. AS, Meramec C.C., 1966; BS, U. Mo.-Rolla, 1968; MS, Okla. State U., 1970, PhD, 1973. Statistician M.D. Anderson Hosp., Houston, 1971-72; asst. prof. U. Tex. Health Sci. Ctr., Dallas, 1973-79; statistician Criterion Inc., Dallas, 1979-81; sr. mgmt. analyst Sun Co., Dallas, 1981-83; sr. biostatistician Teams, Inc., Dallas, 1983-85; sr. cons. RHB Cons. Svcs., Dallas, 1979—; adminstrv. dir. rsch. Tex. Scottish Rite Hosp., Dallas, 1988—; adj. asst. prof. So. Meth. U., Dallas, 1974-77, Health Sci. Ctr., U. Tex.-Dallas, 1979-82; adj. assoc. prof. Tex. Women's U., Dallas, 1984-95; asst. prof. U. Tex. Southwestern Med. Ctr., 1997—. Contbr. articles to profl. jours. Active People to People Internat. Mem. Am. Statis. Assn. (North Tex. chpt. pres.), Biometric Soc., Nat. Coun. Univ. Rsch. Adminstrs., North Tex. SAS Users Group (treas.), Dallas Camera Club, Alzheimer's Assn. (group leader), North Tex. PC Users Club, Pediatric Orthopaedic Soc. of N.Am., Phi Kappa Phi. Republican. Avocation: photography. Home: 12045 Inwood Rd Dallas TX 75244-8016 *Success in school is 90% academics and 10% social skills. What few realize is that after graduation, success is 90% social skills and 10% academics.*

BROWNE, SPENCER I., mortgage company executive; b. 1949; married. BS, U. Pa., 1971; JD, Villanova U., 1974. Ptnr. Brownstein Hyatt Farber & Madden, Denver, 1983-84; pres., dir. MDC Holdings, Inc., 1984-96; pres., CEO, dir. Asset Investors Corp., 1988-96; pres., CEO & dir. Comml. Assets, Inc., 1994-96; with Strategic Asset Mgmt. LLC, Denver, 1996—; bd. dirs. Mego Mortgage Corp., Annaly Mortgage Mgmt., Convergent Comm., Inc. Office: Strategic Asset Mgmt LLC 650 S Cherry St Ste 420 Denver CO 80246-1806

BROWNE, STANHOPE STRYKER, lawyer; b. Colorado Springs, Colo., July 22, 1931; s. Samuel Stanhope Stryker and Florence Jeanette (Reynolds) B.; m. Elizabeth Whitney Sturges, Sept. 12, 1964; children: Katrina C., Whitney R. A.B., Princeton U., 1953; LL.B., Harvard U., 1956. Bar: Pa. 1957. Assoc. Dechert Price & Rhoads, Phila., 1956-65, ptnr., 1965-97; of counsel, 1998—; resident ptnr. Dechert Price & Rhoads, Brussels, Belgium, 1972-76; lectr. internat. law. Contbr. articles to profl. jours. Chmn. Penn's Landing Corp., Phila., 1981-97, Com. to Preserve Am.'s Birthplace, 1965-72; vice chmn. World Affairs Council, 1978-90; bd. dirs. Phila. 1976 Bicentennial Corp., 1971-72, Greater Phila. Movement, 1970-71, Phila. Port Corp., 1984-90, Ecole Française Internationale de Philadelphie, 1991—, The Ch. Found., 1998—, Friends of Vieilles Maisons Françaises, Inc., 1999—; mem. exec. com. Cen. Phila. Devel. Corp., 1968-72, 77-99; mem. Phila. Dist. Export Council U.S. Dept. Commerce, 1983-96; vice pres. Pa. Prison Soc., 1962-69; pres. Greater Phila. Council of Chs., 1966-67; mem. Diocesan coun. Episcopal Diocese of Pa., 1967-71; rector's warden St. Peter's Ch., 1983-90; chmn. Democrats Abroad, Belgium, 1975-76, Pa. Internat. Trade Conf., 1977-79; mem. adv. commn. Independence Nat. Hist. Park, Phila., 1969-72; hon. consul of France in Phila., 1986-96. Recipient Pub. Service and Polit. Courage award Southeastern Pa. chpt. Ams. for Democratic Action, 1965; decorated Nat. Order of Merit, France, 1998. Mem. ABA (vice chmn. com. on fgn. investment in U.S. 1981-88), Phila. Bar Assn., Internat. Bar Assn., French-Am. C. of C. (bd. dirs. Phila. chpt. 1989—), Independence Hall Assn. (bd. dirs. 1978-90, adv. com. 1990—), Phila. Com. on Fgn. Rels., Brook Club (N.Y.C.), Phila. Club (bd. dirs. 1988-92), Phi Beta Kappa. Democrat. Episcopalian. Home: 306 S 2nd St Philadelphia PA 19106-4302 Office: Dechert Price & Rhoads 4000 Bell Atlantic Tower 1717 Arch St Philadelphia PA 19103-2793

BROWNE, THOMAS REED, neurologist, researcher, educator; b. Lakewood, N.J., Aug. 10, 1943; s. Thomas Reed and Margaret (King) B.; m. Lynne Van Beuren, Mar. 27, 1969; children: Hilary Katherine, David Gerard. BA cum laude, Princeton U., 1965; MD with honors, U. Rochester, 1969. Diplomate Am. Bd. Psychiatry and Neurology, Am. Bd. Clin. Neurophysiology. Intern in medicine Cornell U. Med. Ctr., N.Y.C., 1969-70; staff assoc. epilepsy NIH, Bethesda, Md., 1970-72; resident in neurology Mass. Gen. Hosp., Boston, 1972-75; fellow in epilepsy Childrens Hosp., Boston, 1975-76; asst. prof. neurology Boston U. Sch. Medicine, Boston, 1976-80, assoc. prof. neurology, 1980-84, prof. neurology, 1984—, vice-chmn. dept. neurology, 1987—; clin. instr. in neurology Harvard Med. Sch., 1976-86; lectr. neurology Harvard Med. Sch., Boston, 1987—; assoc. chief neurology svc. VA Med. Ctr., Boston, 1987-97, chief neurology svc., 1997—. Editor: Epilepsy: Diagnosis and Management, 1983, 5th Frontiers of Pharmacology Symposium, Stable Isotopes in Pharm. Res., 1987, Handbook of Epilepsy, 1997, 2d edit. 1999, Stable Isotopes in Pharmaceutical Research, 1997; sect. editor Jour. Clin. Pharmacol., 1987—, Pharmacotherapy, 1982—, Am. Jour. Therapeutics, 1994—; contbr. 180 articles to profl. jours. Recipient Ciba Geigy award Internat. League Epilepsy, 1985. Fellow Am. Coll. Clin. Pharm. (regent 1985-90, McKeen Cattell award 1993), Am. Acad. Neurology, Am. EEG Soc.; mem. Am. soc. Clin. Pharmacol. Therapy, Mass. Epilepsy Soc. (profl. adv. bd.). Achievements includes development of stable isotope tracer methods for human pharmacology studies. Avocations: sailboat racing, model railroading.

BROWNE, WILLIAM BITNER, lawyer; b. Springfield, Ohio, Nov. 23, 1914; s. John Franklin and Etta Blanche (Bitner) B.; m. Dorothy Ruth Gilbert, Aug. 31, 1939; children: Franklin G., Dale Ann Browne Compton. AB, Wittenberg U., 1935, LLD (hon.), 1970; postgrad., U. Bordeaux, 1935-36; JD cum laude, Harvard U., 1939. Bar: Ohio 1939, U.S. Dist. Ct. (so. dist.) Ohio 1941, U.S. Ct. Appeals (6th cir.) 1950, U.S. Supreme Ct. 1970. Assoc. Donovan, Leisure, Newton & Lumbard, N.Y.C., 1939-40; assoc. Corry, Durfey & Martin, Springfield, Ohio, 1940-48; ptnr. Corry, Durfey, Martin & Browne and successors, Springfield, Ohio, 1948-88; of counsel Martin, Browne, Hull & Harper, Springfield, 1988-94. Contbr. (articles to legal jours.). Bd. dirs. Wittenberg U., 1955-89; pres. Greater Springfield & Clark County Assn., 1948-49; vice chmn. Clark County Republican Central and Exec. coms., 1948-52; mem. Springfield City Bd. Edn., 1950-53; mem. exec. com. United Appeals Clark County, 1956-62. Capt. OSS Signal Corps, U.S. Army, 1942-46. Decorated Bronze Star; decorated Croix de Guerre with palm, Medaille de Reconnaisance Francaise. Fellow Am. Coll. Trial Lawyers (ret.), Am. Bar Found., Am. Coll. Trust and Estate Counsel (ret.), Ohio Bar Found. (pres. 1979, Fellows rsch. and svc. award 1976); mem. ABA (del. 1971-76), Ohio Bar Assn. (pres. 1969-70, medal of honor 1973), Springfield Bar Assn. (pres. 1967), Springfield C. of C. (pres. 1961-62), Zanesfield Rod and Gun Club, Springfield Country Club, Rotary, Masons. Episcopalian. Office: Martin Browne Hull & Harper 1 S Limestone St PO Box 1488 Springfield OH 45501-1488

BROWNELL, BLAINE ALLISON, university administrator, history educator; b. Birmingham, Ala., Nov. 12, 1942; s. Blaine Jr. and Annette (Holmes) B.; m. Mardi Ann Taylor, Aug. 21, 1964; children—Blaine, Allison. BA, Washington and Lee U., 1965; MA, U. N.C., 1967, PhD, 1969. Asst. prof. Purdue U., West Lafayette, Ind., 1969-74; assoc. prof., chmn. dept. U. Ala., Birmingham, 1974-78, prof., 1980-90, dean grad. sch., 1978-84, dean social and behavioral scis., 1984-90; provost, v.p. for acad. affairs U. North Tex., Denton, 1990-98; exec. dir. Ctr. Internat. Programs and Svcs. U. Memphis, 1998—; sr. fellow Johns Hopkins U., Balt., 1971-72; Fulbright lectr. Hiroshima U., Japan, 1977-78; dir. U. Ala. Ctr. Internat. Programs, 1980-90. Author: The Urban Ethos...., 1975, City in Southern History, 1977, Urban America, 1979, 2d edit., 1990, The Urban Nation 1920-80, 1981; editor Jour. Urban History, 1976-90, assoc. editor, 1990-95. Mem. Birmingham City Planning Commn., 1975-77, Jefferson County Planning Commn., 1975-77, Dallas Com. Fgn. Rels., 1990-98; chmn. Birmingham Coun. on Fgn. Rels., 1988-90. Mem. Am. Hist. Assn., Orgn. Am. Historians, So. Hist. Assn., Philos. Soc. Tex., Memphis Rotary Club. Democrat. Presbyterian. Avocations: microcomputers; photography. Office: U Memphis Ctr Internat Programs Svcs Memphis TN 38152

BROWNELL, EDWIN ROWLAND, banker, civil engineer, land surveyor; b. Tampa, Fla., Sept. 19, 1924; s. Clarence DeWolf and Helen Lucy (Hill) B.; m. Helen Marie Kegel, Jan. 22, 1948 (dec. Apr. 1967); 1 child, Nancy; m. Blanche Rosina Parisi, Dec. 26, 1967; children: Elizabeth, Elaine, Evelyn. BCE, U. Fla., 1947. Registered profl. surveyor, Fla., Ark., Ga., Miss., Nev., N.D., S.D., S.C., Tenn., W.Va. Cadastral engr. City of Miami, Fla., 1948-53; pres., CEO, chmn. E.R. Brownell & Assocs., Inc., Miami, 1953-93, real estate salesman, 1975—; pres., chief exec. officer, chmn. Brickellbanc Savs. Assn., Miami, 1985-89, also bd. dirs.; pres. Tri-County Engring. Co., 1983-89, Naples (Fla.) Title and Abstract Co., 1st Title and Abstract Co.; chmn. surveying com. U. Fla., Gainesville, 1974—, mem. pres.'s coun.; mem. nat. engring. degree accreditation team Nat. Coun. Engring. Examiners, Md., 1985-95, mem. team evaluating engring. readiness U.S. Armed Forces, 1980-81; chmn. engring. adv. com. Fla. Bd. Regents, Tallahassee, 1982-85; vice-chmn. legal grievance com. Fla. Bar, 1992-94. Elected county surveyor State of Fla., Dade County, 1956-60; chmn. Zoning Bd. Adjustment, Coral Gables, Fla., 1978-87; chmn. Coral Gables Planning and Zoning Bd., 1987-95; mem. Coral Gables Code Enforcement Bd., 1995-97, City of Coral Gables Historic Preservation Com., 1997, City of Coral Gables Constrn. Regulation Bd., 1997—; bd. dirs. Boys Club of Miami, 1980-83, Salvation Army South Fla., 1990-94. Named Man of Yr., Dade County, Fla., 1989. Fellow Am. Congress Surveying and Mapping (pres. 1980-81, Surveying Excellence award 1977, Miami Man Yr. 1990, Presdl. award 1994), NSPE, Nat. Soc. Profl. Surveyors (pres. 1978-79), Fla. Soc. Profl. Land Surveyors (hon. life mem., Fla. Land Surveyor of Yr. 1973, pres. 1978-79, pres. Dade County chpt. 1965-69, hon. life mem. Dade County chpt. 1993); mem. AIA, NSF, Profl. Surveyors of Fla. (bd. dirs., chmn. 1993-94), Am. Soc. Photogrammetry and Remote Sensing (Presdl. citation 1982, 91, Merit award 1992), Am. Soc. Photogrammetry Found. (vice chmn. 1985-91), Am. Mil. Engrs., Am. Planning Assn., Internat. Geog. Info. Found. (vice-chmn.), Miami Bd. Realtors, Fla. Engring. Soc. (bd. dirs. 1992-94), Fla. Planning and Zoning Assn. (S. Fla. chpt.), Fla. Assn. Cadastral Mappers, Bus. Inc., Fla. Surveying and Mapping Soc. (hon. life mem.), Sierra Club (pres. 1977), Am. Contract Bridge Assn., Com. of 100, Bus. Inc., Granada Golf Assn., 10th Holers Golf Assn. (treas. 1995-96, pres. 1996-97), Coral Gables Country Club Fleet, Coral Gables 30 Yr. Club, Coral Gables Fin. Club (pres. 1998—), Century Club of Coral Gables (exec. sec., treas. 1993-96), Coral Gables Country Club (dir., pres. 1991-97, chmn., vice chmn. found. 1992-94, pres. fin. club 1998—), Riviera Country Club, Holly Hills Country Club (N.C.), Computer Club Coral Gables (bd. dirs.), Kiwanis (pres. Southwest Miami chpt. 1979-81), Elks (Lodge #948), Lambda Alpha Internat., Kappa Alpha. Republican. Roman Catholic. Avocations: golf, bridge. Home: 1207 Sorolla Ave Coral Gables FL 33134-3515 Office: E R Brownell & Assocs Inc 3152 Coral Way Miami FL 33145-3210

BROWNELL, GORDON LEE, physicist, educator; b. Duncan, Okla., Apr. 8, 1922; s. Roscoe David and Mabel (Gourley) B.; m. Anna-Liisa Kairento; children: Wendy Silverman, Peter G., David L., James K., Piia Kairento, Janne Kairento. B.S., Bucknell U., Lewisburg, Pa., 1944; Ph.D., Mass. Inst. Tech., 1950. Mem. faculty Mass. Inst. Tech., 1950—, prof., 1970—; dir. Physics Research Lab. Mass. Gen. Hosp., Boston, 1950—; trustee Retina Found.; bd. dirs. Boston Biomed. Found., Neuroresearch Fund. Served to lt. (j.g.) USNR, 1944-46. Fellow Am. Phys. Soc., Am. Nuclear Soc., Am. Coll. Radiology (hon.); mem. Am. Assn. Physicists in Medicine (Coolidge award 1987), Soc. Nuclear Medicine (Paul C. Aebersold award 1975), European Soc. Nuclear Medicine (de Hevesy medal 1979). Clubs: Union Boat (Boston); Cambridge (Mass.); Tennis. Home: 45 Warren St Salem MA 01970-3132 Office: Mass Gen Hosp Physics Rsch Lab Boston MA 02114 also: MIT Cambridge MA 02139

BROWNELL, KELLY DAVID, psychologist, educator; b. Evansville, Ind., Oct. 31, 1951; s. Arnold Buffum and Margaret Elizabeth (Egly) B.; m. Mary Jo Gabriele, Aug. 20, 1977; children: Matthew Joseph, Kevin David, Kristy Elizabeth. BA, Purdue U., 1973; PhD, Rutgers U., 1977. Lic. clin. psychologist, Pa., Conn. Postdoctoral fellow Brown U., Providence, 1977; asst. prof. U. Pa., Phila., 1977-82, assoc. prof., 1982-87, prof., 1987-90; prof. psychology Yale U., New Haven, Conn., 1991—; prof. epidemiology and pub. health Yale U., New Haven, dir. Yale Ctr. for Eating and Weight Disorders; master of Silliman Coll. Author: Handbook of Behavioral Medicine, 1988, Handbook of Eating Disorders, 1986, Eating Disorders in Athletes, 1991, Eating Disorders and Obesity, 1995;; contbr. more than 200 articles to profl. jours. Recipient Cattell award N.Y. Acad. Scis., 1978, Choice award ALA, 1989. Fellow Am. Psychol. Assn. (pres. div. health psychology 1989-90), Soc. Behavioral Medicine (pres. 1988-89), Acad. Behavioral Medicine Rsch.; mem. Assn. for Advancement Behavior Therapy (pres. 1988-89). Office: Yale U Dept Psychology Box 208205 Yale Sta New Haven CT 06520-8205

BROWNELL, WILLIAM S., federal judge; b. 1946. BA, U. Maine, 1968, JD, 1971. Bar: Maine 1971. Law clk. to Hon. Randolph A. Weatherbee, Supreme Jud. Ct., Portland, Maine, 1971-72; chief dep. clk. U.S. Dist. Ct. for Dist. Maine, Portland, 1973-78, clk., 1979—; part-time magistrate judge U.S. Magistrate Ct., Portland, 1979—. Office: 156 Federal St Portland ME 04101-4152

BROWNER, CAROL, federal agency administrator; d. Michael Browner and Isabella Harty Hugues; m. Michael Podhorzer; 1 child, Zachary. Grad., U. Fla., 1977, JD, 1979. Gen. counsel govt. ops. com. Fla. Ho. of Reps.; with Citizen Action, Washington; chief legis. aide environ. issues to Sen. Lawton Chiles, legis. dir. to Sen. Al Gore, Jr., 1988-91; sec. Dept. Environ. Regulation, Fla., 1991-93; administr. EPA, Washington, 1993—. Office: Environmental Protection Agency Office of the Administrator 401 M St SW # Mc1101 Washington DC 20460-0003

BROWNFELD, ALLAN CHARLES, columnist; b. N.Y.C., Nov. 26, 1939; s. Benjamin and Estelle (Snyder) B.; m. Solveig Eggerz, June 2, 1970; children: Alexandra, Peter, Burke. BA, Coll. of William and Mary, 1961, JD, 1964; MA, U. Md., 1968. Faculty St. Stephen's Episcopal Sch., Alexandria, Va., 1964-65, U. Md., College Park, 1965-66; spl. asst. internal security com. U.S. Senate, Washington, 1967-69; asst. to rsch. dir. Rep. Conf. Ho. of Reps., Washington, 1970; spl. asst. Rep. Philip M. Crane, Washington, 1970-73; legis. asst. Rep. William Scherle, Washington, 1973-74; editor The New Guard, Washington, 1968-69; Washington editor Private Practice, 1970-75; assoc. editor The Lincoln Rev., Washington, 1984—; editor Issues, Washington, 1989—; cons. Accuracy in Media, Washington, 1984—; mem. pres. Ronald Reagan's transition team EEOC, 1980. Author: Hung Up on Freedom, 1969, Dossier on Douglas, 1970, (U.S. Senate subcom. internal security study) The New Left, 1968; co-author: What the Negro Can Do About Crime, 1974, The Revolution Lobby, 1984. Bd. dirs. Coun. for Def. of Freedom, Washington, 1984—. Recipient Wall St. Jour. Found. award, 1963; decorated George Washington medal Freedoms Found., 1970, 71, 72, 73, 77, 84; named Disting. Lectr. U.S. Air Force Spl. Ops. Sch., 1970. Office: PO Box 9009 Alexandria VA 22304-0009

BROWNFIELD, SHELBY HAROLD, soil scientist; b. Ava, Ill., June 12, 1931; s. William Edward and Mabel (Ditzler) B.; m. Lois Marie Landreth, Apr. 27, 1952 (dec. 1991); children: Susan, Nancy, David, Judy, Lori; m. Joyce Marilyn Bland-Gasperson, Dec. 11, 1993. BS in Agriculture, U. Ill., 1954; postgrad., Iowa State U., 1968. Lab. tech. USDA, Urbana, Ill., 1952-54; soil conservation tech. USDA, Joliet, Ill., 1954; soil scientist soil conservation svc. USDA, Greencastle, Ind., 1954-56, Spencer, Ind., 1957-60; soil survey party leader USDA, Franklin, Ind., 1960-65, Shelbyville, Ind., 1965-67, North Vernon, Ind., 1967-72; area soil scientist and party leader USDA, Kendallville, Ind., 1972; soil correlator USDA, Bozeman, Mont., 1972-77; state soil scientist USDA, Boise, 1977-86; cons. soil scientist Idaho Divsn. Environ. Quality, Boise, 1986-88, Associated Earth Scis., Boise, 1988—; Author: Soil Survey of Shelby County, Indiana, 1968, Soil Survey of Bartholomew County, Indiana, 1972; co-author: Soil Survey of Owen County, Indiana, 1960; contbr. articles to profl. jours. Mem. Am. Soc. Agronomy, Idaho Soil Scientist Assn. (pres. 1993), Masons, Elks. Baptist. Avocation: travel. Home and Office: 7689 Stirrup Ave Boise ID 83709-6466 also: PO Box 418 Bunker Hill IL 62014-0418

BROWN-GATTA, LINDA MARION, women's health nurse; b. Phila., Apr. 25, 1967; d. James E. and Marion (Miles) B.; m. Jon Gatta, Oct. 17, 1992; children: Kevin, Matthew, James. Diploma in nursing, Frankford Hosp.,

Phila., 1988; AA, Pa. State U., Rydel, 1988; BSN cum laude, Thomas Jefferson U., 1990. RN, Pa. Nurse Thomas Jefferson U. Hosp., Phila., 1990—. Mem. ANA, Sigma Theta Tau. Home: 162 Wildflower Dr Plymouth Meeting PA 19462-1522 Office: Thomas Jefferson U Hosp 11th And Walnut St Philadelphia PA 19107

BROWNING, CHARLES, publishing executive; b. Washington, Mar. 14, 1949; s. Robert and Carolyn Browning; m. Lani F. Brownig, Oct. 24, 1972; children: Skylar, Lilia S. BA, Wasington & Lee U., 1972. Pub. New Homes Guide, Vienna, 1979—. Office: New Homes Guide 1980 Gallows Rd Ste 200 Vienna VA 22182-3913

BROWNING, CHARLES BENTON, retired university dean, agricultural educator; b. Houston, Sept. 16, 1931; s. Earl William and Emma (Summerlin) B.; m. Magda Luest, Jan. 14, 1956; children: Susan Elaine Browning Kreps, Charles Benton Jr., Steven Randolph, Karen Diane Browning Bassetti, Heidi Charlene, Browning Dahlander, Gary Thomas. B.S. in Animal Sci., Tex. Tech., 1955; M.S. in Dairy Sci., Kans. State U., 1956, Ph.D. in Animal Nutrition, 1958. Asst. prof. Miss. State U., State Coll., 1958-60, assoc. prof., 1960-61, prof., 1961-66; head dept. dairy sci. U. Fla., Gainesville, 1966-69, dean acad. programs, 1969-79; dean and dir. div. agr. Okla. State U., Stillwater, 1979-97; dean, dir. emeritus Okla. State U., 1997—; mem. numerous state agrl. coms.; head team to rev. agrl. problems and programs of Jamaica for AID, 1978, team to rev. agrl. edn. programs in Honduras, 1983, MIAC team to rev. agrl. project in Morocco, 1985, 86, 89, in Tunisia, 1988, in Kenya, 1989, Gov.'s Reverse Trade Mission to Japan, 1986; mem. USDA, SEA Joint Council on Food and Agrl. Scis., 1977; cons. Dept. State Internat. Communication Agy., Venezuela, 1978; del. 6th Working Conf. of Reps., Paris, 1978. Named Outstanding Prof. Alpha Zeta, 1966; recipient Z.W. Craine Research award Nat. Silo Assn., 1967, Disting. Agriculture Alumnus award Tex. Tech U., 1985; named to Okla. Higher Edn. Hall of Fame, 1997. Mem. Am. Dairy Sci. Assn., Am. Soc. Animal Sci., Am. Grassland Council, AAAS, Sigma Xi, Phi Kappa Phi, Omicron Delta Kappa, Gamma Sigma Delta, Alpha Zeta. Episcopalian. Home: 6505 Coventry Dr Stillwater OK 74074-1024 Office: Okla State U 139 Agriculture Hall Stillwater OK 74078-6015

BROWNING, CHRISTOPHER R., historian, educator; b. Durham, N.C., May 22, 1944; s. Robert Willard and Eleanor (Oechsli) B.; m. Jennifer Jane Horn; children: Kathryn, Anne. BA, Oberlin Coll., 1967; MA, U. Wis., 1968, PhD, 1975. Instr. history Allegheny Coll., Meadville, Pa., 1969-71; asst. prof. history Pacific Luth. U., Tacoma, 1974-79, assoc. prof., 1979-84, prof., 1984-97, disting. univ. prof., 1997-99; Frank Porter Graham prof. history U. N.C., Chapel Hill, 1999—; J.B. and Maurice C. Shapiro sr. scholar in residence U.S. Holocaust Mus., 1996; George Macaulay Trevelyan lectr. Cambridge U., 1999. Author: The Final Solution and the German Foreign Office, 1978, Fateful Months, 1985, Ordinary Men, 1992 (Nat. Jewish Book award 1993), The Path to Genocide, 1992. Woodrow Wilson fellow, 1967-68; Alexander von Humboldt fellow, Germany, 1980-81; Fulbright rsch. fellow, Israel, 1989; Inst. for Advanced Studies fellow, Princeton, N.J., 1995. Office: Dept History Pacific Luth U Tacoma WA 98447-0014

BROWNING, COLIN ARROTT, retired banker; b. Jersey City, June 24, 1935; s. Colin John Herbert and Ellenor May (Coughlin) B.; m. Ellen Miriam McNeill, July 18, 1964; children: Colin Robertson, Paul William. BA, Cornell U., 1957; MBA, NYU, 1964. Trust adminstr. Chase Manhattan Bank, N.Y.C., 1960-64; v.p. Midlantic Bank, Newark, 1964-70; v.p. IBJ Schroder Bank and Trust Co., N.Y.C., 1970-71, sr. trust officer, 1971-72, sr. v.p., 1972-77, exec. v.p., mem. exec. com., 1977-93; chmn., pres. IBJ Schroder Internat. Bank and Trust Co., Miami, 1985-93, ret. Trustee Upper N.J. chpt. Multiple Sclerosis Soc., Newark, 1965-72, pres., 1969-70; trustee N.J. Shakespeare Festival, 1988-91; trustee Fla. Zool. Soc., 1995—, pres. docent coun., 1997—. Mem. Corp. Fiduciaries Assn., Am. Lepidopterists Soc., Am. Orchid Soc., Xerces Soc., The Explorers Club, Pi Kappa Alpha, Beta Theta. Avocations: fly fishing, orchid growing.

BROWNING, DON SPENCER, religion educator; b. Trenton, Mo., Jan. 13, 1934; s. Robert W. and Nelle J. (Trotter) B.; m. Carol Kohl, Sept. 27, 1958; children: Elizabeth Dell, and Christopher Robert. A.B., Central Methodist Coll., 1956; B.D., U. Chgo. Div. Sch., 1959, M.A., 1962, Ph.D., 1964; DD (hon.), U. Glasgow, Scotland, 1998. Asst. prof. Grad. Sem. Phillips U., Enid, Okla., 1963-65; instr. religion and personality U. Chgo. Div. Sch., 1965-66, asst. prof., 1967-68, assoc. prof., 1968-77, prof., 1977-80, Alexander Campbell prof., 1980—; dean Disciples Divinity House U. Chgo., 1977-83. Author: Atonement and Psychotherapy, 1966, Generative Man, 1973, The Moral Context of Pastoral Care, 1976, Pluralism and Personality, 1980, Practical Theology, 1983, Religious Ethics and Pastoral Care, 1983, Religious Thought and The Modern Psychologies, 1987, A Fundamental Practical Theology, 1991; co-author: From Culture Ways to Common Ground: Religion and the American Family Debate, 1997; gen. editor: Studies in Family, Religion and Culture (10 vols.); assoc. editor: Zygon Jour.; editor: Jour. of Religion; mem. editl. bd. Jour. of Pastoral Care, Pastoral Psychology, Toronto Jour. of Theology. Nat. Book award finalist, 1974; Guggenheim fellow, 1975-76; recipient Oskar Pfister award Am. Psychiat. Assn., 1999. Mem. Am. Acad. Religion, Assn. Practical Theology, Itnernat. Acad. Practical Theology (pres. 1991-95), Soc. Sci. Study Religion, Assn. Christain Ethics. Office: Univ Chgo 1025 E 58th St Chicago IL 60637-1509

BROWNING, EDMOND LEE, retired bishop; b. Corpus Christi, Tex.; s. Edmond Lucian and Cora Mae (Lee) B.; m. Patricia Sparks, Sept. 10, 1953; children: Robert Mark, Patricia Paige, Philip Myles, Peter Sparks, John Charles. B.A., U. of South, 1952, B.D., 1954, D.D., 1970; D.D., Gen. Theological Seminary, 1986, Ch. Divinity Sch. of Pacific, 1987, Seabury Western Seminary, 1987, Trinity Coll., Hartford, Conn., 1988, Va. Theol. Sch., 1989; DHL, Chaminade U., Honolulu, 1985, St. Paul's Coll., Lawrenceville, Va., 1987. Ordained priest Episcopal Ch., 1954, named bishop, 1968; curate Ch. of the Good Shepherd, Corpus Christi, 1954-56; rector Redeemer Ch., Eagle Pass, Tex., 1956-59, All Souls Ch., Okinawa, 1959-63, St. Matthews Ch., Okinawa, 1965-67; archdeacon Okinawa Episcopal Ch., 1965-67, 1st missionary bishop of Okinawa, 1968-71; bishop of convocation Episcopal Chs. in Europe, 1971-74; exec. Nat. and World Mission Exec. Council, N.Y.C., 1974-76, 82-83; bishop of Hawaii, 1976-85; presiding bishop Episcopal Ch., 1986-98; bd. dirs. Anglican Center, Rome, 1971-74, St. Stephens Sch., Rome, 1971-74; mem. Anglican Consultative Council, 1982-91. Named hon. canon St. Michaels Cathedral Kobe, Japan, St. George's Cathedral, Jerusalem. Address: 5164 Imai Rd Hood River OR 97031-9442*

BROWNING, JAMES FRANKLIN, professional society executive; b. Tonawanda, N.Y., Feb. 19, 1923; s. Charles Oscar and Gertrude (Keller) B. Student, La. State U., 1943, U. Buffalo, 1948-49; pvt. study music, 1942—. Regional dir. Civic Concert Services, N.Y. C., 1954-57; asst. mgr. Pitts. Symphony Orch., 1957-59; adminstr. Met. Opera Nat. Council, N.Y.C., 1959-62; spl. rep. to chmn. John F. Kennedy Center Performing Arts, 1962-63; gen. mgr. Am. Music Center, N.Y.C., 1963-72; exec. sec. Nat. Music Council, N.Y.C., 1965-72, Nat. Assn. Tchrs. Singing, 1973-85; tech. cons. N.Y. State Coun. of Arts 1963—; sec. Pioneer Editions, N.Y.C., 1965-67; mem. exec. com. Nat. Coun. ARts and Govt., N.Y.C., 1964-73; treas. Arlington (Va.) Opera Theatre, 1962-63; bd. dirs. U.S. Inst. Theatre Tech., 1960-62; U.S. rep. Internat. Music Coun. Congress, Rotterdam, Holland, 1966, Internat. Rostrum Composers, Paris, 1966; adv. bd. Musicians Club Fla., 1969—; apptd. cons. Greater Buffalo (N.Y.) Opera Co. Contbr. to publs. in field.; editor: Music Today Newsletter, 1963-72, Nat. Music Coun. Bull., 1965-72; assoc. editor: Aria Mag., 1983-86; mem. adv. coun. Music Jour., 1964-84. Bd. dirs. Symphony of New World, 1973-76. Served with USAAF, 1943-46. Life mem. NAACP; mem. Contemporary Music Soc. (dir. 1968—); life hon. profl. mem. Phi Mu Alpha. Home and Office: 120 Ellicott Creek Rd # 15 Tonawanda NY 14150-4000

BROWNING, JAMES ROBERT, federal judge; b. Great Falls, Mont., Oct. 1, 1918; s. Nicholas Henry and Minnie Sally (Foley) B.; m. Marie Rose Chapell. BA, Mont. State U., Missoula, 1938; LLB with honors, U. Mont., 1941, LLD (hon.), 1961; LLD (hon.), Santa Clara U., 1989. Bar: Mont. 1941, D.C. 1950, U.S. Supreme Ct. 1952. Spl. atty. antitrust div. Dept. Justice, 1941-43, spl. atty. gen. litigation sect. antitrust div., 1946-48, chief antitrust dept. N.W. regional office, 1948-49; asst. chief gen. litigation sect. antitrust div. Dept. Justice (N.W. regional office), 1949-51, 1st asst. civil div., 1951-52; exec. asst. to atty. gen. U.S., 1952-53; chief U.S. (Exec. Office for U.S. Attys.), 1953; pvt. practice Washington, 1953-58; lectr. N.Y.U. Sch. Law, 1953, Georgetown U. Law Center, 1957-58; clk. Supreme Ct. U.S., 1958-61; judge U.S. Ct. Appeals 9th Circuit, 1961-76, chief judge, 1976-88, judge, 1988—; mem. Jud. Conf. of U.S., 1976-88, exec. com. of conf., 1978-87, com. on internat. conf. of appellate judges, 1987-90, com. on ct. adminstrn., 1969-71, chmn. subcom. on jud. stats., 1969-71, com. on the budget, 1971-77, adminstrn. office, subom. on budget, 1974-76, com. to study U.S. jud. conf., 1986-88, com. to study the illustrative rules of jud. misconduct, 1985-87, com. on formulation of standard of conduct of fed. judges, 1969, Reed justice com. on cont. edn., tng. and adminstrn., 1967-68; David T. Lewis Disting. Judge-in-residence, U. Utah, 1987; Blankenbaker lectr. U. Mont., 1987, Sibley lectr. U. Ga., 1987, lectr. Human Rights Inst. Santa Clara U. Sch. Law, Strasbourg. Editor-in-chief, Mont. Law Rev. Dir. Western Justice Found.; chmn. 9th Cir. Hist. Soc. 1st lt. U.S. Army, 1943-46. Decorated Bronze Star; named to Order of the Grizzly, U. Mont., 1973; scholar in residence Santa Clara U., 1989, U. Mont., 1991; recipient Devitt Disting. Svc. to Justice award, 1990. Fellow ABA (judge adv. com. to standing com. on Ethics and Profl. Responsibility 1973-75); mem. D.C. Bar Assn., Mont. Bar Assn., Am. Law Inst., Fed. Bar Assn. (bd. dirs 1945-61, Nat. council 1958-62), Inst. Jud. Adminstrn., Am. Judicature Soc. (chmn. com. on fed. judiciary 1973-74, bd. dirs. 1972-75), Herbert Harley award 1984), Am. Soc. Legal History (adv. bd. jour.), Nat Lawyers Club (bd. govs. 1959-63). Office: US Ct Appeals 9th Cir PO Box 193939 San Francisco CA 94119-3939 *Notable cases include: pro bono case Bell vs. U.S., 349 U.S. 81, 1955.*

BROWNING, JOHN, pianist; b. Denver, May 23, 1933; s. John and Esther (Green) B. Student, Occidental Coll., D.Mus. (hon.), 1975; student, Juilliard Sch. Music; D.Mus. (hon.), Ithaca Coll.; student, Lee Pattison, Calif., Rosina Lhevinne, N.Y.C. Debut, Denver, 1943; N.Y.C. debut N.Y. Philharmonic Orch. at Carnegie Hall, 1956; appearances with numerous orchs., U.S., Europe, Mexico, Russia, Eng.; recitalist; pianist: for world premiere performance Samuel Barber's First Piano Concerto with Boston Symphony Orch; pianist with Cleve. Orch. on Dept. State tour to USSR, 1965; rep., Am. govt. World's Fair, Brussels, 1968, instr. master classes, Northwestern U., 1975-80, Manhattan Sch. Music, 1980-86, Juilliard Sch., 1986—; rec. artist. Served with U.S. Army. Recipient Jr. award KFI-Hollywood Bowl Young Artists Competition, 1945, Steinway Centennial award Nat. Fedn. Music Clubs, 1954, Edgar M. Leventritt award, 1955, Queen Elisabeth Internat. Concours award, 1956; Lhevinne Meml. scholar; recipient Grammy award Best Instrumental Soloist with Orch., 1992, Grammy award Best Instrumental Soloist (without Orch.) for Barber: The Complete Solo Piano Music, 1994. Mem. Pi Kappa Lambda. Office: Columbia Artist Mgmt Saldick Divsn 165 W 57th St New York NY 10019-2201*

BROWNING, KURT, figure skating champion. Champion World Figure Skating, 1989-91, 93, profl.; 1995, 96, 97; Champion World Profession, 1995, 96, 97. Record holder first man to complete Four Revolution Jump "QUAD" Guiness World Book, 1988. Office: c/o Kevin AlbrechtIMG Canada, c/o Kevin Albrect IMG Can, 1st Clair Ave E Ste 700, Toronto, ON Canada M4T2V7 also Office: Profl Skaters Assn PO Box 5904 Rochester MN 55903-5904

BROWNING, NORMA LEE (MRS. RUSSELL JOYNER OGG), journalist; b. Spickard, Mo., Nov. 24, 1914; d. Howard R. and Grace (Kennedy) B.; m. Russell Joyner Ogg, June 12, 1938. A.B., B.J., U. Mo., 1937; M.A. in English, Radcliffe Coll., 1938. Reporter Los Angeles Herald-Express, 1942-43; with Chgo. Tribune, from 1944, Hollywood columnist, 1966-75; Vis. lectr. creative writing, editorial cons., mem. nat. adv. bd. Interlochen Arts Acad., Northwood Inst. Author: City Girl in the Country, 1955, Joe Maddy of Interlochen, 1963, (with W. Clement Stone) The Other Side of the Mind, 1965, The Psychic World of Peter Hurkos, 1970, (with Louella Dirksen) The Honorable Mr. Marigold, 1972, (with Ann Miller) Miller's High Life, 1972, Peter Hurkos: I Have Many Lives, 1976, Omarr: Astrology and the Man, 1977, (with George Masters) The Masters Way to Beauty, 1977, (with Russell Ogg) He Saw A Hummingbird, 1978, (with Florence Lowell) Be A Guest At Your Own Party, 1980, Face-Lifts: Everything You Always Wanted to Know, 1981, Joe Maddy Of Interlochen: Portrait of A Legend, 1991; Contbr. articles to nat. mags. Recipient E.S. Beck award Chgo Tribune. Mem. Theta Sigma Phi, Kappa Tau Alpha. Address: 226 E Morongo Rd Palm Springs CA 92264-8402

BROWNING, PETER CRANE, packaging company executive; b. Boston, Sept. 2, 1941; s. Ralph Leslie and Nancy (Crane) B.; m. Carole Ann Shegog, Dec. 14, 1963 (div. 1974); children: Christina, Jennifer; m. Kathryn Anne Klucharich, July 27, 1974; children: Kimberly, Peter. AB in History, Colgate U., 1963; MBA, U. Chgo., 1976. Salesman, mktg. mgr. White Cap div. Continental Can, Northbrook, Ill., 1964-75; mgr. mktg. Conally Venture div. Continental Can, 1975-79; gen. mktg. and sales mgr. Bondware div. Continental Can, 1979-81, v.p., gen. mgr., 1981-84; v.p. gen. mgr. White Cap. div. Continental Can, 1984-86, exec. v.p., oper. officer, 1987-89; pres. Gold Bond Bldg. Products div. Nat. Gypsum Co., Charlotte, N.C., 1989-90; pres., CEO Nat. Gypsum Co., Dallas, 1990-93, Aancor Holdings Inc., Dallas, 1990—; chmn. bd. dirs., CEO Nat. Gypsum Co. parent co. Aancor Holdings, Inc., 1991-93; exec. v.p. Sonoco Products Co., Hartsville, S.C., 1993-96, pres., COO, 1996-98, also bd. dirs., pres., CEO, 1998—; bd. dirs. Nucor Corp., Wachovia Corp., Lowe's Cos., Inc. Mem. bd. visitors McColl Sch. Bus./Queens Coll., Davidson Coll.; mem. coun. on Grad. Sch./U. Chgo.; mem. exec. bd. Pee Dee Area coun. Boy Scouts Am.; trustee Presbyn. Hosp. Found.; bd. trustees, Coker Coll.; bd. dirs., Darlington County Cmtys. in Schs. Mem. NAM (exec. com., bd. dirs.), Conf. Bd., Quail Hollow Country Club, DeBordieu Country Club. Republican. Episcopalian. Avocations: mountain climbing, running, reading. Home: 1400 W Carolina Ave Hartsville SC 29550-4902 Office: Sonoco Products Co 1 N 2nd St Hartsville SC 29550-3305

BROWNING, ROBERT LYNN, educator, clergyman; b. Gallatin, Mo., June 19, 1924; s. Robert W. and Nelle J. (Trotter) B.; m. Jean Beatty, Dec. 27, 1947 (dec. 1977); children: Gregory, David, Peter, Lisa; m. Jackie L. Rogers, Aug. 26, 1979. BA, Mo. Valley Coll., 1945; MDiv, Union Theol. Sem., 1948; PhD, Ohio State U., 1960; postgrad., Columbia U., 1951-53, Oxford (Eng.) U., 1978-79, 84-85. Ordained to ministry Disciples of Christ Ch., 1947, transferred to United Meth. Ch., 1950. Minister edn. Old Stone Ch., Meadville, Pa., 1946-51, Cmty. Ch. at the Cir., Mt. Vernon, N.Y., 1951-53, North Broadway United Meth. Ch., Columbus, Ohio, 1953-59; prof. Christian edn. Meth. Theol. Sch., Delaware, Ohio, 1959-72, William A. Chryst prof. Christian edn., 1972-89, prof. emeritus, 1989—; sr. counselor Coun. for Ethics in Econs., 1989—; pres. Meth. Conf. on Christian Edn., 1967-69; exec. dir. Commn. on Role of The Professions in Soc., Fellow Acad. for Contemporary Problems, 1974-76, commn. bd., 1976—. Author: Communication with Junior Highs, 1968, Guidelines for Youth Ministry, 1970, What on Earth Are You Doing, 1966; (audiotape with Charles Foster) Communicating the Faith with Children, 1971, Ways the Bible Comes Alive, 1975, Ways Persons Become Christian, 1976 (with Charles Foster, Everett Tilson) Looking at Leadership with the Eyes of Biblical Faith, 1978, (with Roy Reed) The Sacraments in Religious Education and Liturgy: An Ecumenical Model, 1985, Model of Confirmation: Liturgical and Educational Issues and Designs, 1995; contbg. author: Preventing Adolescent Alienation: An Interprofessional Approach, 1983, Children, Parents and Change, 1984, Interprofessional Education, 1987, Handbook for Families, 1998; editor: Integration: Objective Studies and Practical Theology, Proc. Assn. Profl. Edn. for Ministry, 1981, The Pastor as Religious Educator, 1989; contbg. author: Congregations: Their Power to Form and Transform, 1988; contbr. articles on religious edn. to profl. jours. Bd. dirs. Southside Settlement, columbus, 1968-74, Tray-Lee Ctr., Columbus, 1955-59, Ohio State U. Wesleyan Found., 1960-78, vice chmn., 1976-78; bd. ministry ohio West Conf. United Meth. Ch., 1982-89. With USN, 1942-45. Recipient Paul Hinkhouse award Religious Pub. Rels. Coun. Am., 1971. Mem. Assn. for Profl. Edn. for Ministry (editor proc. 1980-82), Religious Edn. aSsn., Assn. for Profs. and Rschrs. in Religious Edn. (pres. 1989), United Meth. Profs. Christian Edn. Home: 6613 Hawthorne St Worthington OH 43085-3071

BROWNING, RODERICK HANSON, banker; b. Salt Lake City, Oct. 9, 1925; s. Frank M. and Eugenia H. B.; m. Mary Wadsworth, Mar. 7, 1956; children—Patricia Ann, Jonathan Wadsworth, Frank Wadsworth, Anthony Stuart, Carolyn Rae. A.B., Stanford U., 1948. Vice pres. Bank of Utah, Ogden, 1954-59; chmn. bd., pres. Bank of Utah, 1959—, Bank of Brigham City, Utah, 1973—; chmn. bd. Bank No. Utah, Clearfield, 1971—; dir. Salt Lake City br. Fed. Res. Bank San Francisco, 1969-74; Bd. dirs., treas. Ogden Indsl. Devel. Corp., Weber County (Utah) Indsl. Devel. Bur.; adv. bd. St. Benedicts Hosp.; bd. dirs. Weber State Coll., Ogden; former pres. United Fund No. Utah. Served with U.S. Army, 1948-53. Mem. Am. Bankers Assn., Utah Bankers Assn. (former mem. exec. com.), Am. Legion. Clubs: Rotary (Ogden); Weber, Alta, Ogden Golf and Country. Office: PO Box 231 Ogden UT 84402-0231

BROWNING, ROY WILSON, III, mortgage banking executive; b. Enid, Okla., Mar. 27, 1952; s. Roy W. Jr. and Geraldine L. (Green) B.; m. Ann Karlene Trousdale, May 31, 1974; children: Kamden, Karina, Christopher. BS in Acctg., Phillips U., 1974. CPA, Okla., Kans. Audit Arthur Andersen & Co., Oklahoma City, 1974-81; treas., CFO, Clements Energy, Inc., Oklahoma City, 1981-82; CFO, Atlas Investment Corp., Oklahoma City, 1982-85; exec. v.p. Metmor Fin., Inc. subs. Met. Life Ins. Co., Overland Park, Kans., 1985-95; exec v.p., cfo Greenpoint Mortgage Corp, Charlotte, NC, 1995. Trustee Phillips U., Enid, 1993—. Mem. AICPA, Kans. Soc. CPA's, Mortgage Bankers Assn. Am. (chmn. fin. mgmt. com. 1994), Hallbrook Country Club, Rotary (bd. dirs. Overland Park 1986—). Republican. Mem. Ch. of Nazarene. Avocations: golf, travel, reading. Office: GreenPoint Mortgage Corp 5032 Parkway Plaza Blvd Charlotte NC 28217-1962*

BROWNING, T. JEFF, commissioner, state and local. MS in Planning, U. Tenn., 1970. Exec. dir. Met. Planning Commn. Met. Govt. Nashville and Davidson County, 1985—. Office: City of Nashville & Davidson County Met Planning Commn 737 Second Ave S Nashville TN 37201*

BROWNING, WILLIAM DOCKER, federal judge; b. Tucson, May 19, 1931; s. Horace Benjamin and Mary Louise (Docker) B.; children: Christopher, Logan, Courtenay; m. Zerilda Sinclair, Dec. 17, 1974; 1 child, Benjamin. BBA, U. Ariz., 1954, LLB, 1960. Bar: Ariz. 1960, U.S. Dist. Ct. Ariz. 1960, U.S. Ct. Appeals (9th cir.) 1965, U.S. Supreme Ct. 1967. Pvt. practice Tucson, 1960-84; judge U.S. Dist. Ct., Tucson, 1984—; mem. jud. nominating com. appellate ct. appointments, 1975-79; mem. Commn. on Structural Alternatives, Fed. Ct. Appeals, 1997—; apptd. Commn. on Structural Alternatives for the Fed. Ctrs. of Appeals. Del. 9th Cir. Jud. Conf., 1968-77, 79-82; trustee Inst. for Ct. Mgmt., 1978-84; mem. Ctr. for Pub. Resources Legal Program. 1st lt. USAF, 1954-57, capt. USNG, 1958-61. Recipient Disting. Citizen award U. Ariz., 1995. Fellow Am. Coll. Trial Lawyers, Am. Bar Found.; mem. ABA (spl. com. housing and urban devel. law 1973-76, com. urban problems and human affairs 1978-80), Ariz. Bar Assn. (chmn. merit selection of judges com. 1973-76, bd. gove. 1968-74, pres. 1972-73, Outstanding Mem. 1980), Pima County Bar Assn. (exec. com. 1964-68, med. legal screening panel 1965-75, pres. 1967-68), Am. Bd. Trial Advocates, Am. Judicature Soc. (bd. dirs. 1975-77), Fed. Judges Assn. (bd. dirs.). Office: US Dist Ct US Courthouse Rm 301 55 E Broadway Blvd Tucson AZ 85701-1719

BROWN-KUYKENDALL, DONITA, early childhood educator; b. Edmond, Okla., Dec. 23, 1953; d. Donald Gene and Juanita (Renner) Brown; children: Kristin Kuykendall, Kaitlin Kuykendall. BS in Elem. Edn., Southeastern Okla. State U., 1975; MEd, U. Ctrl. Okla., 1989. Tchr. Keystone Sch., Tulsa, 1975-76, Mid-Del Pub. Sch. Sys., Midwest City, Okla., 1976-78, 79-81, Bur. Indian Affairs, Albuquerque, 1978-79, Vietnamese Refugee Ctr., Oklahoma City, 1981-83, Yukon (Okla.) Pub. Sch. Sys., 1985-92; supervisor early childhood practicums U. Ctrl. Okla., Edmond, 1992—; adv. bd. Ea. Okla. County Vo-Tech. Child Devel. Ctr., Choctaw, 1994—; adv. bd. Okla. State Dept. Edn., Oklahoma City, 1992-95; curriculum adv. bd. Yukon Pub. Sch. Sys. Vol. Children's Def. Fund, Washington, 1991—. Mem. Nat. Assn. Educators of Young Children, AAUW, ASCD, Okla. Assn. Children Under Six, U. Ctrl. Okla. Alumni Assn., Okla. State Reading Assn., Kappa Delta Pi, Sigma Kappa, DAR. Methodist. Avocations: reading, quilting, spectator sports, theater, concerts. Home: 6512 N Grove Ave Oklahoma City OK 73132-7719

BROWN LEATHERBERRY, THOMAS HENRY, gospel music company executive, clergy member; b. Wilmington, Del., June 24, 1930; s. Glenn Ford and Rita (Leatherberry) Brown; m. Grace L. Wilson, Mar. 1, 1950 (div. 1978); children: Linda Henry, Patricia Williams, Lucinda Brown, Martha Baccus, Tommy Jr. (dec.), Jason James. Student, Carnegie Hall Sr. Drama Sch., N.Y.C., 1961; A. in Engring. Comms., N.Y. Sch. Announcing, N.Y.C., 1968; BA in Behavioral Sci. and Bibl. Edn., U. Del.; M Bibl. Theology, Ea. Bapt. U.; DD (hon.), Trinity Coll., Knoxville, Tenn., 1970. Artist, comedian Mantan Moreland, N.Y.C., 1959-62; road mgr., negotiator Langston Hughes Prodns., N.Y.C., 1963-66; dir. music Chs. of God in Christ, Bklyn., 1968-78; dir. arts Gospel Arts Coalition, Inc., Wilmington, 1978—; pastor Bible Way House of Prayer Worldwide Inc., Wilmington, 1989—; minister of music Bibleway Mid-Atlantic Diocese, Balt., 1990—; dir. asst. Alvin Ailey Dancers, N.Y.C., 1963; disk jockey Sta. WWRL Radio, N.Y.C., 1969, tchr. Christina Cultural Arts, Wilmington, 1983-89; music dir. World Christian Fellowship, 1989—. Dir. recs. Rite Enterprise Rec. Co., 1954; actor Prodigal Son, 1963, Black Nativity, 1964; asst. to producer (TV) MD, 1967; stage dir., program mgr. Gospel Music shows, CBS-TV, 1967; author (radio) America Calls, 1967, Israel Radio Calls, 1967; dir., engr. RCA Institutes TV, Sta. ABC-TV, 1968. Program dir. Y.M.C.A., Wilmington, 1978-81; entertainer for Gov. Dupont, State of Del., 1980; dir. gospel music coun. 6602, City of Wilmington, 1983. With U.S. Army, 1950-53. Named State Leader, African Am. Proclamation Inc., Phila., 1983; recipient Attestation Pilgrimage award, Minister of Courison, Jerusalem, 1983, award of Grand Performance, Jewish Community Rels. Com., Wilmington, 1988. Mem. BMI, Am. Guild Authors and Composers, Trinity Coll. Alumni Assn., Am. Legion (chaplain Brandywine, Del.), VFW (life), Masons (grand music dir. 1989—, past worshipful master, illustrious master, imperial dep. chaplain 1997—), Holy Royal Arch Masons (past grand high priest), Order Ea. Star (past worthy patron), Shriners, Elks (appreciation award Paul Lawrence Dunbar lodge #106 1981), Heidres of Jericho (grand Joshua), Epsilon Delta Psi (life). Democrat. Avocations: football, basketball, movies, playing organ and piano. Office: NOW Gospel Arts Singers PO Box 824 Wilmington DE 19899-0824

BROWNLEE, DONALD EUGENE, II, astronomer, educator; b. Las Vegas, Nev., Dec. 21, 1943; s. Donald Eugene and Geraldine Florence (Stephen) B.; m. Paula Szkody. B.S. in Elec. Engring, U. Calif., Berkeley, 1965; Ph.D. in Astronomy, U. Wash., 1970. Research assoc. U. Wash., 1970-77, asso. prof. astronomy, 1977-89; asso. geochemistry Calif. Inst. Tech., Pasadena, 1977-82; prof. astronomy U. Wash., 1989—; cons. NASA, 1976—. Author papers in field, chpts. in books. Grantee NASA, 1975; recipient J. Lawrence Smith medal Nat. Acad. of Sciences, 1994. Mem. AAAS, Internat. Astron. Union, Am. Astron. Assn., Meteoritical Soc. (Leonard medal 1996), Com. Space Rsch. Dust, NAS (NASAPI stardust mission). Office: U Wash Dept Astronomy Seattle WA 98195

BROWNLEE, JUDITH MARILYN, priestess, psychotherapist, psychic; b. Beaumont, Tex., May 16, 1940; d. Alvin Maurice and Juanita M. (Whittington) B.; m. Theodore Blakey Peak, Apr. 12, 1974 (div. 1981); 1 child, Daniel David Brownlee Peak; m. Floyd S. Bond, Aug. 18, 1996. BA, Lamar U., Beaumont, Tex., 1962; postgrad., U. Denver, 1971, Avalon Inst., Boulder, Colo., 1989-92; student, Our Lady Perpetual Responsibility, The Silent Cir., 1975-79. Wiccan priestess. Tchr. Deer Trail (Colo.) H.S., 1963-64, Lutcher Stark H.S., Orange, Tex., 1967-69; libr. technician Denver Pub. Libr., 1970-73; bus. exec. Weight Watchers Rocky Mtn., Denver, 1974; mail order divsn. mgr. Mile High Comics and Books, Denver, 1975-81; religious tchr. The Silent Cir., Denver, 1979-83; gov. employee Colo. Atty. Gen. Office, Denver, 1983-92; minister Fortress Temple, Denver, 1984-96; psychotherapist, 1992—; pub. spkr. Spring Mysteries Festival, Seattle, 1988-92; counselor Profl. Psychic Counselors Network, 1993-96, Morningstar Inc., 1997, Psychic Choice, 1997—; pub. spkr. Denver, 1988—; workshop leader Spring Mysteries Festival, Seattle, 1988, 92, Dragonfest Pagan Festival, Denver, 1987-92; lectr. Isis Metaphys. Ctr., workshop leader, 1985—; lectr.

Raven & Rose Bookstore, Ft. Collins Colo., 1992-93, Enchanted Chalice Bookstore, 1994—, Herbs & Arts Bookstore, 1996, Spirit Ways Bookstore, 1998; organizer Front Range Pagan Festival, 1985; guest spkr. Greeley (Colo.) Unitarian Fellowship, 1992; spkr. Rocky Mountain Fiction Writers Conv., 1993; creator, dir. Edn. for Pagan Youth com. Pagan Sch., 1990-94, 96-97. Author: Pagan Parenting, 1987, The Wheel of the Year, 1988; contbr. articles to profl. jours. Interviewee KOA Radio, 1984, 92, 95, 96, KNUS and KYBG, 1992, KUSA Channel 9, 1987, 90, Rocky Mountain News, Denver, 1992, 96; cmty. prodr. Mile High Cablevision, 1987; tel. counselor Lifeline of Colo., Denver, 1988; field tng. supr. Iliff Sch. Theology, Denver, 1995-96. Recipient Hart and Crescent Disting. Youth Svc. award Covenant of the Goddess, 1995. Mem. Colo. Assn. Psychotherapists, Assn. Past Life Rsch. and Therapy, Women's Spiritual Leadership Alliance (bd. dirs. 1992—), Daus. of New Moon (founder, facilitator), Soc. for Creative Anachronism (Colo. founder, CEO 1970-73, treas. 1981-83), Denver Area Sci. Fiction Assn. (editor 1969-70, dir. 1974-75, conf. chmn. 1970-75), Denver Area Interfaith Clergy Conf., Covenant Unitarian Universalist Pagans. Avocations: reading, theatre, films, science fiction, internet. E-mail: judith1152@aol.com. Office: PO Box 172271 Denver CO 80217-2271 *The two most important issues of this decade will be the return of the Goddess (the feminine in Diety) and the re-imaging of our planet as Her Body (the Gaia Theory). We must give up our persona of "dominance over Nature" and remember again that we are part of Nature.*

BROWNLEE, PAULA PIMLOTT, educational consultant, former academic administrator; b. London, June 23, 1934; came to U.S., 1959; d. John Richard and Alice A. (Ajamian) Pimlott; m. Thomas H. Brownlee, Feb. 10, 1961; children: Kenneth Gainsford, Elizabeth Ann, Clare Louise. BA with honors, Somerville Coll., Oxford (Eng.) U., 1957; PhD in Organic Chemistry, Oxford (Eng.) U., 1959. Postdoctoral fellow U. Rochester, N.Y., 1959-61; rsch. chemist Am. Cyanamid Co., Stamford, Conn., 1961-62; lectr. U. Bridgeport, Conn., 1968-70; asst. prof., then assoc. prof. Rutgers U., N.J., 1970-76, assoc. dean, then acting dean Douglass Coll., 1972-76; dean faculty, prof. chemistry Union Coll., Schenectady, N.Y., 1976-81; pres., prof. chemistry Hollins U., Va., 1981-90; pres. Assn. Am. Colls. and Univs., Washington, 1990-98; prin. The Pres.' Group, LLC; bd. chair Acad. Search Consultation Svc. Author lab. manual; contbr. articles and chpts. to profl. publs. Bd. dirs. U. Rochester, Assn. Religion in Intellectual Life,. Hon. fellow Somerville Coll., Oxford, Eng., 1996—. Mem. Am. Chem. Soc., Cosmos Club, Sigma Xi. Episcopalian. E-mail: brownlees@worldnet.att.net.

BROWNLEE, ROBERT CALVIN, pediatrician, educator; b. Due West, S.C., Mar. 13, 1922; s. Robert Calvin and Eleanor Louise (Pressly) B.; m. Judith Frances Irby; children: Eleanor Koets, Susan, Katherine Chambers, Jonathan, Robert Calvin. AB, Erskine Coll., 1943; MD, Vanderbilt U., 1945. Diplomate Am. Bd. Pediat. (pres. 1975), Am. Bd. Family Practice. Intern Vanderbilt U. Hosp., Nashville, 1945-46, resident, 1948-49; resident U. Va., Charlottesville, 1949-50; chief resident Vanderbilt U., Nashville, 1950-51; practice medicine, specializing in pediat. Christie Pediatric Group, Greenville, S.C., 1951-70; dir. pediat. Greenville Hosp. Sys., 1970-75; assoc. exec. sec. Am. Bd. Pediat., Chapel Hill, N.C., 1976, exec. sec., 1977-87, pres., 1987-92; clin. prof. pediat. U. Pa., 1976-78; prof. Med. U. S.C., 1971-75; clin. prof. U. N.C., 1978-96. Contbr. articles to med. jours. With AUS, 1943-45; with M.C. USAF, 1946-48, 53. Mem. Am. Acad. Pediat., Ambulatory Pediat. Assn., So. Soc. Pediat. Rsch. Presbyterian. Home: 120 Sheffield Cir Chapel Hill NC 27514-6514

BROWNLEE, ROBERT HAMMEL, lawyer; b. Chester, Ill., Dec. 15, 1951; s. Robert Mathis and Geneva (Hammel) B.; m. Sue F., June 17, 1978. BS, So. Ill. U., Carbondale, 1973; JD, Vanderbilt U., Nashville, 1976. Bar: Mo. 1976, Ill. 1977, U.S. Dist. Ct. (ea. and we. dists.) Mo. 1976, U.S. Dist. Ct. (so. and cen. dists.) Ill. 1977, U.S. Ct. Appeals (8th cir.) 1979, Ky. 1998. Assoc. Thompson & Mitchell, St. Louis, 1976-82; ptnr. Thompson Coburn, St. Louis, 1982—; mng. editor Vanderbilt Law Review, Nashville, 1975-76; mem. Bar Assn. of Met. St. Louis, 1976—, Ill. State Bar Assn., Springfield, Ill., 1977—, Am. Bankruptcy Inst., 1988—. Co-author: (books) Rights of Secured Creditors in Bankruptcy, 1987, Lender Liability in Missouri, 1988, Protection of Secured Interests in Bankruptcy, 1989, Litigation in Bankruptcy Proceedings, 1994, Interlocutory Appeal Issues Before the Bankruptcy Reform Commission, 1996, Bankruptcy Impact on Commercial Leases, Advanced Missouri Real Estate Law, 1997, Impact of the Bankruptcy Review Commissions Report on Creditor Issues, 1997. Mem. Friends of the St. Louis Zoo., 1986—, St. Louis Bot. Garden Sponsors, 1987—; builder of the community United Way of Greater St. Louis, 1988—. Mem. ABA (litigation sec. 1976—, co-chair jury instrn. subcom. of bankruptcy and insolvency com. 1994—), Mo. Athletic Club, Mo. Bankers Assn. (chmn. legal adv. bd. 1997-98). Avocations: fishing, american art pottery, antiques, gardening. Office: Thompson Coburn 1 Mercantile Ctr Ste 3500 Saint Louis MO 63101-1643*

BROWNLEE, SARAH HALE, elementary special education educator; b. N.Y.C., Feb. 4, 1938; d. Ralph Cochran and Maud Catherine (Welfley) Hale; m. John Malcolm Brownlee Jr., Sept. 2, 1961; children: Hale Perry, John Malcolm. BArch., Va. Poly. Inst. and State U., 1960; MEd, State U. West Ga., 1993. Registered architect, Ga.; cert. tchr., N.C. Archtl. intern Baskervill & Son Architects, Richmond, Va., 1962-65, Rabun Hatch, Architects, Atlanta, 1984-86; ednl. missionary Presbyn. Ch. U.S.A., Yogyakarta, Indonesia, 1973-84; architect Spangler & Manley, Architects, Griffin, Ga., 1988-90; exceptional children's tchr. Pike County Elem. Sch., Zebulon, Ga., 1992-93, Harrisburg (N.C.) Elem. Sch., 1994-98; owner, mgr. tutoring svcs. Sarah's Study, Huntersville, 1998—. Mem. presch. bd. Ramah Presbyn. Ch., Huntersville, N.C., 1995—. Bright Ideas grantee Carolina Elec. Coops. & Union EMC, 1996. Mem. Coun. for Exceptional Children, Children and Adults with Attention Deficit Disorders, Nat. Trust for Hist. Preservation, Tau Sigma Delta, Phi Kappa Phi. Home and office: 14401 Ramah Church Rd Huntersville NC 28078-4008

BROWNLEE, THOMAS MARSHALL, lighting manufacturing company executive; b. Omaha, Oct. 11, 1926; s. John Templeton and Reed (Marshall) B.; children: Linda Sue, Thomas John, Curtis Marshall, Reed Ann; m. Lenora A. Hollingsworth, Mar. 31, 1994. BSBA, U. Nebr., 1950. Asst. mgr. Daytona Beach (Fla.) C. of C., 1950, Tampa (Fla.) C. of C., 1952-53; exec. mgr. Tallahassee C. of C., 1953-58; exec. v.p. Greater Columbia (S.C.) C. of C., 1959-63, Winston-Salem (N.C.) C. of C., 1963-64, Orlando Area (Fla.) C. of C., 1964-78; chmn. Brownlee Lighting Co., Orlando, 1978—; mem. energy policy com. Orange County (Fla.) Schs.; mem. Fla. Energy Action Com.; mem. energy com. Nat. League Cities. Contbr. articles to profl. jours. Bd. dirs. Loch Haven Art Mus.; bd. dirs. Chamber Inst., U. Ga.; mem. Orlando City Council.; pres. Christian Service Ctrs. Daily Bread. Served with USNR, 1944-46; as 1st lt. AUS, 1951-52. Mem. Fla. Energy Mgmt. Assn. (pres.), Illuminating Engring. Soc. (pres. Ctrl. Fla. chpt., bd. dirs., pres. internat. soc. 1996), Am. C. of C. Execs. Assn. (hon., pres. 1966), S.C. C. of C. Execs. Assn., Fla. C. of C. Execs. Assn. (pres. 1971), Better Bus. Bur. Ctrl. Fla. (chmn.), Scottish-Am. Soc. Ctrl. Fla. (bd. dirs.), Orlando Scottish Games (exec. coun.), St. Andrews Soc. Ctrl. Fla. (pres.), Country Club Orlando, Univ. Club, Tiger Bay Club (pres.), Clan Hamilton Soc. (Fla. commr.), Rotary, Phi Delta Theta. Presbyterian (deacon). Office: Brownlee Lighting 4600 Dardanelle Dr Orlando FL 32808-3832

BROWNLEE, WILSON ELLIOT, JR., history educator; b. Lacrosse, Wis., May 10, 1941; s. Wilson Elliot Sr. and Pearl (Woodings) B.; m. Mary Margaret Cochran, June 25, 1966; children: Charlotte Louise, Martin Elliot. BA, Harvard U., 1963; MA, U. Wis., 1965, PhD, 1969. Asst. prof. U. Calif., Santa Barbara, 1967-74, assoc. prof., 1974-80, prof. history, 1980—, spl. advisor to systemwide provost, 1995, assoc. systemwide provost, 1996; vis. prof. Princeton (N.J.) U., 1980-81; chmn. dept. history U. Calif., Santa Barbara, 1984-87, acad. senate, 1983-84, 88-90, systemwide acad. senate, 1992-93; dir. U. Calif.-Santa Barbara Ctr., Washington, 1990-91; chmn. exec. com. dels. Am. Coun. Learned Socs., N.Y.C., 1988-90, bd. dirs.; bd. dirs. Nat. Coun. on Pub. History, Boston; bicentennial lectr. U.S. Dept. Treasury, 1989; faculty rep. U. Calif. Bd. Regents, 1991-93; adj. prof. history Calif. State U., Sacto., 1997-99; mem. bd. control, U. Claif. Press, 1996—. Author: Dynamics of Ascent, 1974, 2nd edit., 1979, Progressivism and Economic Growth, 1974, Federal Taxation in America: A Short History, 1996; co-author: Essentials of American History, 1976, 4th edit., 1986, America's History, 1987, 3rd edit., 1997; editor: Women in the American Economy 1976, Funding the American State, 1996; contbr. numerous articles to profl. jours., chpts. to books. Chmn. schs. com. Harvard Club, Santa Barbara, 1971-80, 85, 86; pres. Assn. for Retarded Citizens, Santa Barbara, 1982-84; 1st v.p. Assn. for Retarded Citizens Calif., Sacramento, 1983-84; pres. Santa Barbara Trust for Hist. Preservation, 1986-87, 95-97; trustee Las Trampas Inc., 1994-97. Charles Warren fellow Harvard U., 1978-79, fellow Woodrow Wilson Ctr., Washington, 1987-88; recipient Spl. Commendation, Calif. Dept. Pks. and Recreation, 1988, Oliver Johnson award for Disting. Svc. U. Calif. Acad. Senate, 1998. Mem. Am. Hist. Assn., Orgn. Am. Historians, Econ. History Assn., Am. Tax Policy Inst. Office: U Calif Dept History Santa Barbara CA 93106

BROWNLOW, DONALD GREY, private school educator; b. Germantown, Pa., Jan. 17, 1923; s. John Charles Victor and Ruth (Hutchinson) B.; m. Sandra Barbara Dobbs, July 16, 1987; children; Kendall Jutchinson, pamela Cooke, Douglas Grey, Priscilla Dobbs. Student, U. Zurich, 1946-47; BA, U. Pa., 1948, MA, 1949. Rsch. libr. Presbyn. Hist. Soc., Phila., 1949-50; master Am. history and inernat. rels. Haverford (Pa.) Sch., 1951—; dir. Haverford Tours, 1956-75, 81—; charter mem. World War II Meml. Soc.; mem. faculty grad. divsn. Pa. State U., 1966—; cons. Imperial War Mus., London. Author: Documentary History of the Paoli Massacre, 1952, Documentary History of the Battle of Germantown, 1955; The Battle of Brandywine, 1957, The Accused: The Ordeal of Rear Admiral Husband E. Kimmel, USN, 1968; Panzer Baron: The Military Exploits of General Hasso von Manteuffel, 1975, Checkmate at Ruweisat: Auchinleck's Finest Hour, 1977, Hell Was My Home, 1983, The Life and Times of Horst Wessel, 1995; author, producer Haverford School Faces the Cold War, Vol. 1, 1962, Vol. 2, 1963. Chmn. Planning Bd. West Nantmeal Twp., 1964-71; mem. Emergency Com. Chinese Refugees, 1962, Com. of One Million; chmn. Zoning Hearing Bd., Warwick Twp., 1976-84; bd. dirs. Gt. Valley Assn., 1959-62; mem. planning bd. Ctr. Teaching Ams., Immaculata Coll., 1961-69; eagle scout Boy Scouts Am., 1939, qUARTERMASTER SEA SCOUT, 1973; active French and Pickering Creeks Conservation Trust; mem. U.S. Holocaust Meml. Coun. Maj. U.S. Army, 1942-64. Recipient Valley Forge Freedoms Found. medal 1962, Suez medal from gov. Suez, UAR, 1966; named Citizen of Honor of Utah Beach, Mayor of Sainte-Marie-du-Mont, France, 1975, name placed on Wall of Liberty by the Battle of Normandy Found., 1994. Mem. VFW (life), Am. Hist. Assn., Paoli Meml. Assn. (life), Germantown Hist. Soc., Chester County Hist. Soc., Smithsonian Assocs., Geneal. Soc. Pa., Pa. Soc., Am. Mus. Natural History, Res. Officers Assn. (life), Soc. Am. Magicians, Nat. Wildlife Fedn., Nat. Audubon Soc., Nat. Trust for Hist. Preservation, Libr. Congress Assocs., U.S. Holocaust Meml. Mus. Simon Wiiesenthal Ctr., World Wildlife Fund, Pa. Sheriff's Assn., Zool. Soc. Phila., Am. Legion (life), Acad. Natural Scis. Phila., Nature Conservancy, Wilderness Soc., Franklin Inst. Ssi., Us., Charles Custis Harrison Soc., Reading Pub. Mus. Republican. Episcopalian. Home: PO Box 468 Elverson PA 19520-0468 Office: Haverford Sch Haverford PA 19041

BROWNLOW, FRANK WALSH, English language educator; b. Dundonald, Northern Ireland, Sept. 2, 1934; came to U.S., 1959; s. Frank and Katherine Georgina (Darroch) B.; m. Jeanne Brockway Piazza, 1961; 1 child, Nicholas Darroch. BA, Liverpool (Eng.) U., 1956; PhD, U. Birmingham, Eng., 1963. From instr. to assoc. prof. English U. Mich., Ann Arbor, 1959-61, 63-69; lectr. U. Western Ont., London, Can., 1961-63; from assoc. prof. to prof. Mt. Holyoke Coll., South Hadley, Mass., 1969—; vis. assoc. prof. Dartmouth Coll., Hanover, Mass., 1968-69. Author: Two Shakespearan Sequences, 1977, Shakespeare, Harsnett and the Devils of Denham, 1993, Robert Southwell, 1996; editor: John Skelton: The Book of the Laurel, 1991; contbr. articles on Shakespeare, Skelton, Byron, Herbert, Chesterton, also others, to profl. jours. Mem. Renaissance Soc. Am., Shakespeare Assn. Am., Byron Soc., Main St. Com. of the Rockford Inst. Avocation: music. Office: Mt Holyoke Coll Dept English South Hadley MA 01075*

BROWNLOW, WILFRED J., retired physician; b. Zion, Ill., Feb. 26, 1931; s. Wilfred J. and Ruth M. Brownlow; m. Kathryn J. Klettke, Dec. 26, 1954 (div. Jan. 1978); children: James A., Edward A., William J.; m. Barbara Lee Szczepanek, May 16, 1994. BS, U. Wis., 1952, MS, 1954; MD, U. Md., 1966; MPH, Johns Hopkins U., 1968. Diplomate Am. Bd. Preventive Medicine, Am. Bd. Occupl. Medicine. Commd. ensign Med. Svc. Corp. USN, 1954, advanced through grades to capt., 1977, ret., 1979; intern rotating USN Med. Ctr., Bethesda, Md., 1966-67; resident Sch. Hygiene and Pub. Health Johns Hopkins U., 1967-69; corp. physician Sohio, BP Am., Cleve., 1980-90; med. dir. BP Oil Co., Cleve., 1991-93; pres., med. cons. Bus. Med. Strategies, Inc., Huron, Ohio, 1994-98; ret., 1999. Contbr. articles to profl. jours. Office: Bus Med Strategies Po Box 459 Huron OH 44839

BROWN-OLMSTEAD, AMANDA, public relations executive; b. Jackson, Miss., Oct. 7, 1943; d. J.A. and Iris (Williamson) Brown; m. George T. Olmstead; children: Vanessa, Blake, Jamie. Student in Liberal Arts, U. Miss., 1965. In pub. relations, fashion direction and coordination Rich's, J.P. Allen, and Saks Fifth Ave., 1965-71; founder, pres., owner A. Brown-Olmstead Assocs., Atlanta, 1972—; former v.p. Pinnacle Group; instr. courses Emory U. and SBA. Bd. dirs. Atlanta chpt. Muscular Dystrophy, 1968-73, pres., 1972-73; adv. bd. YMCA Women of Achievement, 1983; founder Young Careers div. High Mus. Art, 1970; mem. annual ball com. Bot. Gardens, 1981-82, Piedmont Ball Com., 1975, 78; mem. adv. bd. Shepherd Spinal Ctr., Bus. Sch. U. Miss., Ga. chpt. Nat. Osteoporosis Found., Ga. State Sch. of Bus., U. Miss. Bus. Sch., Internat. Women's Forum; mem. adv. guild Clark U.; bd. councillors Carter Ctr.; bd. dirs. Atlanta Botanical Gardens; pres. exec. com. Counselor's Acad. of PRSA; mem. Coun. of Growing Co.; bd. vis. Emory U.; mem. Atlanta Clean City Commn., 1978-81, Leadership Atlanta, 1978, Central Atlanta Progress, 1983, Paralympics Congress, Centennial Olympics Park Leadership Com., Am. Project Brit.-Am. Group, Ole Miss Pres. Coun.; active Atlanta Ballet, 1969-76. Recipient Gold Medal N.Y. Film and TV Festival, 1968; named one of Ten Outstanding Young People of Atlanta, 1976; featured as one of six young tycoons in fashion in U.S., Mademoiselle mag., 1970. Mem. Pub. Relations Soc. Am. (honors and awards com., bd. dirs. Counselors Acad., del. at large nat. assembly), Fashion Group, ODK (nat. spkr., hon.), Internat. Women's Forum (pres. Ga. chpt. 1996), Atlanta C. of C. (Phoenix House award adv. bd. 1983, bd. dirs., pres. intown branch). Democrat. Episcopalian. Clubs: Atlanta City, World Trade. Writer, dir. TV spl.: The Land of Cotton, 1968. Office: A Brown-Olmstead Assocs Ste 312 75 John Wesley Dobbs Atlanta GA 30303-1800*

BROWNRIDGE, J. PAUL, city manager; b. Macon, Miss., June 10, 1945. BS, U. Akron, 1970, JD, 1973; postgrad., Ind. U., Harvard U. Bar: Colo., Ill., Mich. Acct. Goodyear Tire; sr. tax atty. Phillips Petroleum; dir. revenue City Chgo.; treas. City and County Denver, City of Grand Rapids, Mich.; city treas. City of L.A., 1991—; vis. prof. numerous colls. and univs.; spkr. ednl. confs. Author: The Kings & I, 1998. Fundraising chmn. Black Patriots Found.'s Presdl./Congl., Nat. Monument dedicated to Black Patriots of the Am. Revolution, Washington; mem. Rebuild L.A. Fin. Com., Calif. Gen. Assembly Commn. on Emerging Bus. Enterprises; bd. dirs. several non-profit corps. With U.S. Army, Vietnam. Named one of top 650 Pub. Sector Decision Makers Governing Mag. Sourcebook, 1997. Mem. Govt. Fin. Officers Assn. (exec. bd. dirs., cash mgmt. com., awards for excellence rev. com. for capital financing and debt adminstrn., issues focal team), Mcpl. Treas. Assn. Office: Office of the Treasurer City of LA 295 City Hall 200 N Spring St Los Angeles CA 90012-4801*

BROWNRIGG, JOHN CLINTON, lawyer; b. Detroit, Aug. 7, 1948; s. John Arthur and Sheila Pauline (Taffe) B.; m. Elizabeth Thurmond, Apr. 30, 1976; children: Brian M., Jennifer A., Katharine T. BA, Rockhurst Coll., 1970; JD cum laude, Creighton U., 1974. Bar: Nebr. 1974, U.S. Dist. Ct. Nebr. 1974, U.S. Tax Ct. 1977, U.S. Ct. Appeals (8th cir.) 1990. Ptnr. Eisenstatt, Higgins, Kinnamon, Okun & Brownrigg, P.C., Omaha, 1974-80, Erickson & Sederstrom, P.C., Omaha, 1980—; lectr. in law trial practice Creighton U. Sch. Law, Omaha, 1978-83; dir. Legal Aid Soc., Inc., Omaha, 1982-88, pres., 1987-88, mem. devel. coun., 1989—; dir. Nebr. Continuing Legal Edn., Inc., Lincoln, 1991-93. Chmn. law sect. Archbishop's Capital Campaign, Omaha, 1991. Sgt. USAR, 1970-76. Fellow Nebr. State Bar Found. (dir. 1991-93); mem. Nebr. State Bar Assn. (pres. 1992-93), Nebr. Assn. Trial Attys., Omaha Bar Assn. (pres. 1990-91). Avocations: golf, bicycling, reading. Office: Erickson & Sederstrom PC Ste 100 10330 Regency Parkway Dr Omaha NE 68114-3761*

BROWNRIGG, WALTER GRANT, cartoonist, corporate executive; b. Boston, Oct. 26, 1940; s. Philip Parker and Mary Jane (Grant) B.; children by previous marriage: Elizabeth Grant, Christopher Hertel; m. Judith Courtney Hamilton, Apr. 28, 1984; children: Carter Grant, Taylor Hamilton, Kelsey Anderson. A.B. in History cum laude, Princeton U., 1962; M.B.A., Columbia U., 1964. Asst. plant mgr. Berwick Weaving, Inc., Pa., 1964-72; asst. to v.p. Frank & Stessel, Inc., N.Y.C., 1972-73; sr. assoc. Drake Sheahan/Stewart Dougall, Inc., N.Y.C., 1973-76; exec. dir. Greater Hartford (Conn.) Arts Council, 1976-79; dir. Am. Council Arts, N.Y.C., 1979-83; greeting card designer, 1983—; cartoonist, creator Grantland, 1984—, creator Corp-A-Copia, 1990; pres. Grantland Enterprises, Inc., 1991; spkr., cons. in field. Author: Effective Corporate Fundraising, Corporate Fundraising: A Practical Plan of Action. Chmn. St. Cassian Pastoral Coun., 1992-94. Mem. Beta Gamma Sigma. Roman Catholic. Home: 2408 Brook Rd Charlottesville VA 22901

BROWNSBERGER, SUSAN CAMPBELL, translator; b. Melrose, Mass., Apr. 16, 1935; d. William Charles Campbell and Lillian Louise Crosscup; m. Carl Nordyke Brownsberger, June 10, 1955; children: William Nordyke, Sarah McFarland. AB, Radcliffe Coll., 1956; AM, Boston Coll., 1974. V.p. translation The Word Guild, Cambridge, Mass., 1974-75; freelance translator Watertown, Mass., 1976—. Translator: (books) The History of a Town or The Chronicles of Foolov, 1982, Sandro of Chegem, 1983, It's Me, Eddie, 1983, The Gospel According to Chegem, 1984, Pushkin House, 1987, The Fur Hat, 1989, The Hand, 1989, A Captive of the Caucasus, 1992, The Monkey Link, 1995, Life Without Us, 1999, others. Chair edn. com. Charrette, Watertown, 1970. Mem. Am. Translators Assn., Am. Literary Translators Assn., Am. Assn. Tchrs. Slavic & East European Langs., Modern Lang. Assn. Avocations: ballroom dancing, ballet, swimming. E-mail: brownsberger@mediaone.net. Home: 25 Russell Ave Watertown MA 02472-3452

BROWNSON, ANNA LOUISE HARSHMAN, publishing executive, editor; b. Indpls., May 4, 1926; d. Walter W. and Jennie Andrea (Jensen) Harshman; m. Charles B. Brownson (dec.); children: Dwight, Bruce, David, Catharine, Scott. BA, Butler U., 1949, postgrad., 1950-51. Asst. biochemistry lab. Ind. U. Med. Sch., Indpls., 1944-47; grad. asst. Butler U., Indpls., 1949-51; adminstrv. asst. to U.S. congressman from 11th Dist. Ind. Indpls., 1951-58; assoc. editor, treas. Congl. Staff Directory, Ltd., 1959-79, pres., 1980-96, pub. emeritus, 1996—; pub., owner, editor Advance Locator for Capitol Hill, 1963-82, Election Index Congl. Staff Directory, 1966-82, Fed. Staff Directory, 1982-96, Jud. Staff Directory, 1987-96; gen. ptnr. Brownson Partnership Corr. sec. Fusaliers; past pres., former mem. Congress Aux.; exec. com., trustee George C. Marshall Found. Bd. dirs. Madison Coun. The Libr. of Congress, Accokeek Found., Nat. Colonial Farm; sec. Va. Asn. Mus.; v.p. Nat. Capitol area Boy Scouts Am. (silver Beaver award); active Mt. Vernon Life Guard, Internat. Oceanographic Found., World Affairs Coun. Washington, Fairchild Gardens, Mount Vernon 100. Mem. Internat. Palm Soc., Potomac River Basin Consortium, Capitol Hill Club, Nature Conservancy, U.S. Capitol Hist. Soc., Kappa Alpha Theta (treas. Zeta Iota House Corp.). Presbyterian. Home: 1261 S Alhambra Cir Coral Gables FL 33146-3104 Office: PO Box 17 Mount Vernon VA 22121-0017

BROWNSON, E. RAMONA LIDSTONE BRADY, secretary; b. Big Sandy, Mont., May 13, 1930; d. Elmer Gordon and Ethel Mercy (Kuhl) Lidstone; m. William Chauvin Brady, Oct. 10, 1949 (div. 1976); children: William Kim Brady, Colleen Kay Brady, Scott Patrick C. Brady; m. Elwyn James Brownson, Nov. 14, 1980. AS with honors, Mont. State U. No., 1976, BA with honors, 1977. Owner/operator Pep's Bar & Bowling Lanes, Big Sandy, 1954-76; guidance sec./registrar Havre (Mont.) High Sch., 1976-77; sec. to asst. supt. Havre Pub. Schs., 1977-78; sec./bookkeeper Bear Paw Devel. Corp., Havre, 1978-79; new accts./vault cash teller Great Am. Savings Bank, Havre, 1979-88; sec. to ombudsman U. Nebr., Lincoln, 1989-92, receptionist, sec. dept. human resources, 1992-97, ret., 1997. Active Dems. Hill County, Mont., 1977-88, Nebr., 1988—; polit. precinct committeewoman Hill County, Mont., 1980-88; life mem. P.E.I. Hist. Soc., Can., Lidstone Soc., Plymouth, Eng.; charter mem. Big Sandy, Mont. Hist. Soc. Recipient Toastmasters' Internat. Speechcraft cert., 1979; No. Mont. Coll. scholar, 1949-50, 75-76. Mem. AAUW (internat. affairs chair 1986-88, booksale co-chair 1986), AARP, Nat. Assn. Edn. Office Pers., Cert. Ednl. Office Employee (cert. 1993), Nebr. Ednl. Office Pers., U. Nebr. Office Pers. (membership chair 1991-92), Mont. State U. No. Alumni, Lincoln Lancaster County Geneal. Soc., Assinboine Geneal. Soc. (charter), Irish/Scotch Soc., Eagles Aux. Lodge, VFW Aux., Am. Legion Aux., The Westerners. Avocations: reading, dancing, genealogy/history, movies/theatre, travel. Home: 2205 Southwood Pl Lincoln NE 68512-1375 Office: U Nebr Dept Human Resources 407 Administrn Bldg Lincoln NE 68588-0438

BROWNSON, ELWYN JAMES, artist, educator, art therapist; b. Lincoln, Nebr., Sept. 30, 1920; s. Elwyn James and Julia Margaret (Hall) B.; m. Mary Lou Poppe, Dec. 30, 1950 (div. 1978); children: Elwyn James, Richard Louis, Matthew Lynn, Mary Laine; m. Edna Ramona Lidstone, Nov. 11, 14, 1980. *Son, Richard Brownson is in construction management and is a ski instructor during the ski season in Sun Valley, ID. Son Matthew Brownson is a commercial artist in the Denver, CO area. Daughter, Mary Laine Brownson is in the human resources and marketing division for Albertson's Corporate Office in Boise, ID. Son, E. James Brownson, Jr.'s whereabouts are unknown.* BA in Edn., U. Nebr., 1948; MS, Ohio State, 1951; ABD, Pa. State U., 1970; postgrad., Cranbrook Acad. Art, Cleve. Inst. Art. Asst. prof. art Wittenberg U., Springfield, Ohio, 1951-55; owner Ceramic Ctr., Lincoln, Nebr., 1955-58; assoc. prof. art No. Mont. Coll., Havre, 1958-87; art therapist Lincoln, 1989-95; art therapist Golden Triangle Mental Health, Havre, 1984-86. *During military service as a U.S. Marine Corporal (1942-46), E. James Brownson was assigned duties such as Field Music, S-2 Intelligence (map drawing) and chaplain's assistant. Attended Cranbrook Academy of Art for 36 credit hours in Bloomfield, MI. His course work was in sculpture, drawing, survey of art and ceramics. Also attended Cleveland Institute of Art in Cleveland, OH for 15 credit hours. There he took course work in ceramics and sculpture. He also received first place award in ceramics.* Artist: (logo) Hill County Logo, 1986; potter wheel-thrown pottery, Columbus Art Gallery, 1952 (first place). Pres., bd. dirs. District 4 Human Resources Devel. Coun., 1978-88; contest chmn. Mont. Assn. for Vocat. Indsl. Clubs of Am., 1979-87; mem., state bd. dirs. Nat. Multiple Sclerosis Soc., 1979; co-chair, bd. dirs. tutor Literacy Vols. of Am. Robins Sch, Havre, 1988; bd. dirs. hosp. bd. Northern Mont. Health Care, Inc., 1986-88; bd. dirs., pres. Human Resource Devel. Coun., Havre, 1987. Corp. USMC, 1942-46, PTO; alcohol adv. com. Lincoln Lancaster Justice Coun., 1989; manic depressive support group, Bryan Meml. Hosp., Lincoln, Neb., 1989; bd. dirs. Havre Day Activity Ctr. Mem. ACS (Lancaster nom. com.), VFW (life), Nat. Art Edn. Assn., Alliance for Mentally Ill, Mental Health Assn. Mont. (Havre chpt.), Lincoln Artists Guild, Nat. Art Edn. Assn., Toastmasters Internat. (CTM cert.), Am. Legion (life), Marine Corp League, Elks, Eagles, Phi Delta Kappa (past pres.). Unitarian. Avocations: sculpture, pottery, painting, tennis, bowling. Home: 2205 Southwood Pl Lincoln NE 68512-1375

BROWNSON, JACQUES CALMON, architect; b. Aurora, Ill., Aug. 3, 1923; s. Clyde Arthur and Iva Kline (Felter) B.; m. Doris L. Curry, 1946; children—Joel C., Lorre J., Daniel J. BS in Architecture, Ill. Inst. Tech., 1948, MS, 1954. Instr., asst. prof. architecture Ill. Inst. Tech., 1949-59; prof. architecture, chmn. dept. U. Mich., 1966-68; chief design C.F. Murphy Assocs., Chgo., 1959-61; project architect, chief designer Chgo. Civic Ctr. Architects, 1961-68; dir. state bldg. div. State of Colo., Denver, 1986-88; pvt. practice Denver, 1988—; guest lectr. architect Chgo. Pub. Bldg. Commn.; past dir. planning and devel. Auraria Ctr. for Higher Edn., Denver; bd. dirs. Capital Constrn., Denver; guest lectr. architecture in U.S. and Europe. Prin. works include Chgo. Civic Ctr., Lake Denver, Colo., 1985, Chgo. Tribune/Cabrini Green Housing, 1993; author: History of Chicago Architects, 1996, Oral History of Jacques Calmon Brownson, 1996. Recipient award for Geneva House Archtl. Record mag., 1956; Design award for steel framed factory Progressive Architecture mag., 1957. Home and Office: 659 Josephine St Denver CO 80206-3722

BROWNSTEIN, BARBARA LAVIN, geneticist, educator, university official; b. Phila., Sept. 8, 1931; d. Edward A. and Rose (Silverstein) Lavin; m. Melvin Brownstein, June 1949 (div. 1955); children: Judith Brownstein Kaufmann, Dena. Asst. editor Biol. Abstracts, Phila., 1957-58; research fellow dept. microbial genetics Karolinska Inst., Stockholm, 1962-64; assoc. Wistar Inst., Phila., 1964-68; assoc. prof. molecular biology, dept. biology Temple U., Phila., 1968-74; prof. Temple U., 1974-96; prof. emeritus U. Wash., Seattle, 1996—; chmn. dept. Temple U., 1978-81, provost, 1983-90; vis. scientist dept. tumor cell biology Imperial Cancer Rsch. Fund Labs., London, 1973-74; bd. dirs. Univ. City Sci. Ctr., Greater Phila. Econ. Devel. Coun., Forum Exec. Women; program officer NSF, 1992-93; sr. assoc. Ctr. for Ednl. Renewal U. Wash., Seattle, 1994—. Recipient Liberal Arts Alumni award for excellence in teaching Temple U., 1980; recipient Outstanding Faculty Woman award Temple U., 1980. Fellow AAAS; mem. Am. Soc. Cell Biology, N.Y. Acad. Sci., Assn. Women in Sci., NSF (program officer 1992-93). Home: 906 Lake Washington Blvd S Seattle WA 98144-3314 Office: Ctr for Ednl Renewal Univ Wash Seattle WA 98195-3600*

BROWNSTEIN, JULIAN M., advertising and public relations executive; b. Providence, R.I., Apr. 4, 1927; s. Harry and Ann Ruth (Bernstein) B.; m. Geraldine Mark, Apr. 8, 1951 (div. Nov. 1965); children: Marcia, William, Jeffrey; m. Joan Carol Balash, Nov. 24, 1965; children: Ellen, Beth, Maureen. BA, Brown U., 1947; BS, Bryant Coll., 1949. Account exec., nat. sales mgr. various radio stas., 1953-67; exec. v.p., gen. mgr. Sta. WMMW, Meriden, Conn., 1967-70; gen. mgr. Sta. WORC, Worcester, Mass., 1970-72; owner Sta. WCDQ, Hamden, Conn., 1972-76; mgr. advt. and mktg. Corp. Resource Group, Hartford, Conn., 1976-80; exec. v.p. advt. and mktg. Mgmt. Res. Group, New Haven, 1980-82; pres. Julian Assocs., Inc., Newington, Conn., 1982—; adj. prof. U. New Haven, 1973-75. With USNR, 1945-47. Mem. N.E. Broadcast Assn., Conn. Broadcast Assn., Conn. Assn. Press, Advt. Club Greater Hartford, Am. Mktg. Assn., Conn. Assn. Pers. Cons., Nat. Assn. Exec. Recruiters, B'nai B'rith, Rotary, Kiwanis. Home: 105 Brittany Farms Rd # D New Britain CT 06053-1132 Office: Julian Assocs Inc 105 Brittany Farms Rd Apt D New Britain CT 06053-1132

BROWNSTEIN, MARTIN HERBERT, dermatopathologist; b. N.Y.C., Aug. 20, 1935; s. Samuel C. and Florence (Sturm) B.; m. Ann Lehman, June 23, 1964 (div. Aug. 1993); children: Sara Leah, Michael Ari; m. Barbara Boltax, Sept. 19, 1993. AB, Harvard U., 1956; MD, Albert Einstein Coll. Medicine, 1961. Intern Lenox Hill Hosp., N.Y.C., 1961-62; resident in internal medicine VA Hosps., N.Y.C., 1962-65; resident in dermatology NYU, N.Y.C., 1965-66; pvt. practice medicine specializing in dermatopathology N.Y.C., 1970-72, Great Neck, N.Y., 1972-84, Port Washington, N.Y., 1984—; Osborne fellow Armed Forces Inst. Pathology, Washington, 1968-69; asst. clin. prof. dermatology N.Y. Med. Coll., N.Y.C., 1970-73, clin. assoc. prof. dermatology, 1973-78, clin. prof. dermatology, 1978-83; clin. prof. dermatology Mt. Sinai Med. Ctr., N.Y.C., 1983—. Chief editor Jour. Cutaneous Pathology, 1984; contbr. articles to profl. jours. Trustee North Shore Hebrew Acad., Great Neck, N.Y., 1979-80; hon. trustee Great Neck Synagogue, 1986-88; sec. Ramot Shapira World Youth Ctr., bd. dirs., chmn. Chabad, Port Washington, N.Y., bd. dirs. Nat. Com. Futherance Jewish Edn., Nassau County. With M.C. U.S. Army, 1966-68. Recipient Pres.'s award Union Orthodox Jewish Congregations of Am., 1983. Mem. ACP, AMA, Am. Soc. Dermatopathology (pres. 1983-84), N.Y. State Soc. Dermatology, Am. Acad. Dermatology (chmn. com. on pathology 1980-82), Med. Soc. N.Y. State, Med. Soc. N.Y. County, Dermatol. Soc. Greater N.Y. (pres. 1978-79), L.I. Dermatology Soc. (pres. 1992-94), N.Y. Acad. Medicine. Office: 2 N Plandome Rd Port Washington NY 11050-3443*

BROWNSTEIN, MARTIN LEWIS, political science educator; b. Bklyn., July 23, 1942; s. Max and Beatrice (Hutter) B. BA, CUNY, 1963; MA, Yale U., 1966, MPhil, 1968. Assoc. prof. dept. politics Ithaca (N.Y.) Coll., 1970—, chmn. dept., 1995-98. Mem. Phi Beta Kappa. Democrat. Jewish. Home: 123 E King Rd Apt A-4 Ithaca NY 14850-9478 Office: Ithaca Coll Dept Politics 307 Muller Faculty Ctr Ithaca NY 14850

BROWNSTEIN, PHILIP NATHAN, lawyer; b. Ober, Ind., Feb. 14, 1917; s. Max and Anna (Katz) B.; m. Esther Savelle, Sept. 4, 1938; 1 child, Michael. Student, George Washington U., 1937-38; LLB, Columbus U. (now Cath. U.), Washington, 1940, LLM, 1941. Bar: D.C. 1940. With FHA, Washington, 1935-44, commr., 1963-69; with VA, Washington, 1946-63, dir. loan guaranty service, 1956-61, chief benefits dir., 1961-63; asst. sec. mortgage credit HUD, Washington, 1966-69; ptnr. Brownstein and Zeidman, Washington, 1969-92, of counsel, 1992-96; sr. counsel Swidler Berlin Shereff Friedman, LLP, 1996—; mem. Pres.'s Task Force on Low Income Housing, 1970, Sec.'s Task Force on Role of Fed. Housing Adminstrn., 1977-78, HUD Task Force on Center for Housing Mgmt., 1980, Pres.'s Adv. Com. on Housing, 1980; Bd. dirs. Fed. Nat. Mortgage Assn., 1963-69, 70-72; bd. dirs. Nat. Commn. against Discrimination in Housing, 1972-87; dir. Nat. Housing Conf., 1969-96 , vice chmn., 1969-85, life dir. 1996—. Prin. Ctr. for Excellence in Govt., 1986—; bd. dirs. Ctr. for Housing Policy, 1993—. Served with USMC, World War II. Recipient Exceptional Service award VA, 1960, Top Performer in Housing award House and Home, 1964, Career Service award Nat. Civil Service League, 1967, Isaac Shallcross award U.S. League Savs. Assns., 1982; named to Nat. Assn. Home Builders Housing Hall of Fame, 1984, named Housing Person of Yr. Nat. Housing Conf., 1982. Home: 550 N St SW Washington DC 20024-4643 Office: 3000 K St NW Washington DC 20007-5109

BROWN-STIGGER, ALBERTA MAE, nurse; b. Columbus, Ohio, Nov. 11, 1932; d. Sylvester Clarence and Malinda (Mason) Angel; grad. Antelope Valley Coll., 1961; AA, L.A. Valley Coll., 1975; BS, Calif. State U., Dominguez Hills, 1981; m. Norman Brown, Dec. 29, 1967 (dec. Jan. 1989); children: Charon, Charles, Stevan, Carole; m. A.C. Stigger, June 14, 1992. RN, Calif.; lic. vocat. nurse. Nurses aid, vocat. nurse, respiratory therapist St. Bernardines Hosp., 1965-69, Good Samaritan Hosp., L.A., 1969-70, Midway Hosp., L.A., 1973-81; allergy nurse, instr. respiratory therapy VA Hosp., L.A., 1970-93, also acting dept. head; nurse, respiratory splty. unit Jerry L. Pettis Meml. Hosp., Loma Linda, Calif., 1984-93; with Wadley Regional Med. Ctr., Texarkana, Tex., 1993-94; rehab. nurse Robert H. Ballard Rehab. Hosp., San Bernardino, Calif., 1994-98; instr. L.A. Valley Med. Technoogists Sch., Compton Coll. seminar instr., 1979. Active Arrowhead Allied Arts Coun. of San Bernardino; CPR instr. Am. Heart Assn. Mem. Am. Assn. Respiratory Therapy, Nat. Honor Soc., Eta Phi Beta. Democrat. Baptist. Clubs: Social-Lites, Inc. of San Bernardino, Order Ea. Star. Patentee disposable/replaceable tubing for stethoscope. Home: Orangewood Estates 1545 Hancock St San Bernardino CA 92411-1667

BROWNSTONE, PAUL LOTAN, retired speech communications and drama educator; b. N.Y.C., Jan. 21, 1923; s. Harry and Mollie B.; m. Enid Barbara Klein, Nov. 6, 1955 (div. 1988); children: Hugh M., Susan L., Karen A. B.A., Bklyn. Coll., 1947; M.A., U. Denver, 1948; Ph.D., Pa. State U., 1960. Mem. faculty dept. speech and theatre Bklyn. Coll., 1953-69, asst. prof., 1960-69; prof., chmn. dept. speech and theatre, dir. humanities div. L.I.U.-Bklyn. Center, 1969-74, sr. prof. humanities, 1974-89, prof. emeritus, 1989—, chmn. dept. speech communication, 1979-85; assigned to C.W. Post Component Campus, Nassau County, 1974-76; cons. leadership tng. center U. Calif. at Berkeley, 1960. Contbr. articles to profl. jours. Named one of Outstanding Educator of Am., 1971. Mem. Speech Assn. Am. (del. legis. assembly 1966-68), Speech Assn. Eastern States (pres. 1970-71, program chmn. conv. 1977), N.Y. State Speech Assn., Lawrence Assn. (gov. 1975-80), AAUP, United Fedn. Coll. Tchrs. Home: Lido Beach Towers Apt 3Q 2 Richmond Rd Lido Beach NY 11561 Office: LI U Brooklyn Campus Dept Speech Communication University Plz Brooklyn NY 11201-5372

BROWNWOOD, DAVID OWEN, lawyer; b. L.A., May 24, 1935; s. Robert Scott Osgood and Ruth Elizabeth (Bellamy) B.; m. Sigrid Carlson, Mar. 3, 1956 (div. 1972); children: Jeffrey Owen, Kirsten, Scott David, Daniel Stuart; m. Susan Sloane Jannicky, July 4, 1975; 1 child, Mary Ruth Bellamy; stepchildren: Bradbury, Stephanie Ellington. AB with distinction, Stanford U., 1956; LLB magna cum laude, Harvard U., 1964. Bar: Calif. 1965, N.Y. 1969. Law clk. Ropes & Gray, Boston, 1963; assoc. McCutchen, Doyle, Brown & Enersen, San Francisco, 1964-66; lectr. law U. Khartoum, Sudan, 1966-67, Kenya Inst. Adminstrn., Lower Kabete, 1967-68; assoc. Cravath, Swaine & Moore, N.Y.C., 1968-72, ptnr., 1973—, recruiting ptnr., 1978-82, mng. ptnr. for legal staff, 1983-86; ptnr. in charge London office, 1995—; treas. N.Y. Law Inst., 1978-83, chmn. exec. com., 1983-88, pres., 1988-93. Mem. editorial bd. Harvard U. Law Rev., 1963-64. Dir. Literacy Assistance Ctr., N.Y.C., 1983-94, co-chmn. bd. dirs. 1987-94; trustee Greenwich (Conn.) Country Day Sch., 1985-92, v.p., 1986-88, pres., chmn. bd. trustees, 1988-92; co-chmn. Harvard U. Law Sch. 25th Reunion Gift, 1988-89; nat. chair Harvard Law Sch. Fund, 1991-93; N.Y. regional com. campaign for Harvard Law Sch., 1991-95; com. on univ. resources Harvard U., 1991—, mem. Harvard law sch. vis. com., 1995—; keystone regional vice chair centennial campaign Stanford U., 1986-92; exec. com. Stanford U. N.Y. Coun., 1992-95; vice chmn. Stanford U. N.Y. Major Gifts Com., 1993-95; co-chair Stanford U. Ea. Coun., 1993; bd. govs. Stanford Assocs., 1993-95, pres., chmn. bd. govs., 1994-95; bd. advisors Stanford Trust (U.K.), 1995—; mem. nat. adv. bd. Outward Bound USA, 1993-96. 1st lt. USAF, 1956-61, fighter pilot Air Def. Command, capt. USAFR, Mass. Air N.G., 1961-66. Recipient Centennial medallion Stanford U., Stanford Assocs. award. Fellow Am. Bar Found., N.Y. State Bar Found.; mem. ABA, Internat. Bar Assn., N.Y. State Bar Assn., Assn. Bar City N.Y., Round Hill Club (Greenwich), Field Club (Greenwich), Sankaty Head Club (Nantucket), Siasconset Casino Assn. (Nantucket), Harvard Club (N.Y.C.). Home: 19 Pelham Crescent, London SW7 2NR, England also: 39 Baxter Rd Siasconset MA 02564 Office: Cravath Swaine & Moore, 33 King William St, London EC4R 9DU, England also: Cravath Swaine & Moore 825 8th Ave New York NY 10019-7416

BROXMEYER, HAL EDWARD, medical educator; b. Bklyn., Nov. 27, 1944; s. David and Anna (Gurman) B.; m. C. Beth Biller, 1969; children: Eric Jay, Jeffrey Daniel. BS, Bklyn. Coll., 1966; MS, L.I. U., 1969; PhD, NYU, 1973. Postdoctoral student Queens U., Kingston, Ont., Can., 1973-75; assoc. researcher, rsch. assoc. Meml. Sloan Kettering Cancer Ctr., N.Y.C., 1975-78, assoc., 1978-83, assoc. mem., 1983; asst. prof. Cornell U. Grad. Sch., N.Y.C., 1980-83; assoc. prof. Ind. U. Sch. Medicine, Indpls., 1983-86, prof. medicine, microbiology and immunology, 1986—; sci. dir. Walther Oncology Ctr., Indpls., 1988—, chmn. microbiology and immunology, 1997—; mem. hematology II study sect. NIH, Bethesda, Md., 1981-86, 95—, chair, 1997—; adv. com. NHLBI, NIH, Bethesda, 1991-94; chmn. bd. sci. counselors Nat. Space Biomed. Rsch. Inst., 1998—. Assoc. editor Exptl. Hematology, 1981-90, Jour. Immunology, 1987-92, Stem Cells, 1996-97, Brit. Jour. Haematology, 1998—; editor Jour. LeuKocyte Biology, 1995—; mem. editl. bd. Blood, 1983-87, Biotech. Therapeutics, 1988—, Internat. Jour. Hematology, 1991—, Jour. Lab. Clin. Medicine, 1992—, Jour. Exptl. Medicine, 1992—, Annals Hematology, 1993—, Cell Transplantation, 1994—, Critical Rev. Oncology/Hematology, 1995—, Stem Cells, 1998—, Jour. Blood and Marrow Transplantations, 1998—, Cytokines, Cellular and Molecular Therapy, 1998—. Mem. ednl. com. Leukemia Soc. Am., Indpls., 1983—, nat. study sect., N.Y., 1991-95. Recipient Merit award Nat. Cancer Inst., 1987-95, Spl. Fellow award, 1976-78, and Scholar award, 1978-83, Leukemia Soc. Am. Mem. AAAS, N.Y. Acad. Scis., Soc. for Leukocyte Biology, Am. Assn. Cancer Rsch., Am. Assn. Immunologists, Internat. Soc. Exptl. Hematology (pres. 1990-91), Am. Soc. Hematology, Am. Fedn. Clin. Rsch., Am. Soc. Blood and Marrow Transplantation. Avocations: competitive Olympic-style weightlifting (nat. master's champion 50-54 age group 76 kg. class, 1994, 97), running. E-mail: hbroxmey@iupui.edu. Fax: 317-274-7592. Home: 1210 Chessington Rd Indianapolis IN 46260-1630 Office: Ind U Sch Medicine 1044 W Walnut St Rm 302 Indianapolis IN 46202-5254

BROYLES, STEPHEN DOUGLAS, public administrator; b. Columbus, Ohio, Sept. 7, 1947; s. Enoch Ernest and Georgina Marie (Weaver) B; m. Kay Lyn Porter, May 31, 1968; children: Paul Douglas, Leora Marie. BA, Ohio State U., 1969; MA, Webster Coll., 1978; DPA, U. Ala., 1995. Commd. 2d lt. U.S. Air Force, 1969, advanced through gades to lt. col., 1989; chief mgmt. support divsn. Def. Comms. Agy., Stuttgart, West Germany, 1983-87; dep. base comdr. USAFE, San Vito Air Base, Italy, 1987-89; chief seminar divsn. Air U., Maxwell AFB, Ala., 1989-92; ret. U.S. Air Force, 1992; asst. mgr. Pizza Hut Delivery, Montgomery, Ala., 1993-94; city adminstr. City of Muenster, Tex., 1995—. Mem. Am. Soc. Pub. Adminstrs., Kiwanis (pres. 1996-98). Avocations: reading, Tai Chi, swimming, hiking. Home: 407 W 9th St Muenster TX 76252-2241 Office: City Hall PO Box 208 Muenster TX 76252-0208

BROZAK-MCMANN, EDITH MAY, performing and visual artist; b. Totowa, N.J., Mar. 26, 1929; d. Henry and Lena (Ulmer) Brozek; m. Frank Richard McMann, May 26, 1957; children: Robert, Stephen. Dance student, Sch. Am. Ballet, N.Y.C., 1945-57; art student, Westchester Art Workshop, Art Students League, N.Y.C., 1976-84; B in Profl. Studies in Dance and Visual Arts, SUNY, 1984; MS in Studio Art, Coll. of New Rochelle, 1989. Performing artist Alicia Alonso's Nat. Ballet Cuba tours, Mex., C.Am., S.Am., 1948-50, N.Y.C. Ballet, 1950-57; visual artist N.Y.C., 1970—; intern Silvermine Coll. Art, 1989. Solo exhibits include Dance in Art, Greenburgh Libr., White Plains, 1976, Gutman Gallery, White Plains, 1990; groups exhbns. include Xavier Gallery, New Rochelle, N.Y., 1989-94, Mamaroneck Artist Guild Gallery, Larchmont, N.Y., 1990—, Beaux Arts Exhibits, 1991-94, Manhattanville Coll., Purchase, N.Y., 1991, Town Ctr. Gallery, Mamaroneck, 1993—, N.Y.C. Ballet, Lincoln Center, N.Y., 1993, Westbeth Gallery, N.Y.C., 1994, Hammond Mus., Salem, N.Y., 1994; represented in archives Dance Libr., Lincoln Ctr., N.Y.C., Nat. Mus. for Women in Arts, Washington, also in public and pvt. collections, U.S., abroad; performing artist in Alicia Alonso's Nat. Ballet Cuba, touring Mex., C.Am. and S.Am., 1948-50, including roles in Apollo, Sleeping Beauty, Pas de Quatre, Ensayo Symphonica; performing arts in George Balanchine's N.Y.C. Ballet, 1950-57, touring U.S., Europe and Can. with roles in Nutcracker, Swan Lake, Symphony C, Con Amore, etc. Recipient numerous awards for sculpture, painting and graphics including Cert. of Merit U.S. Senator-N. Spano, 1989, U.S. State Assemblyman-R. Brodsky, 1989, Letter of Appreciation U.S. Senator Pat Moynihan, 1989, Letter of Congratulations U.S. Congressman - B. Gilman, 1989. Mem. Allied Artist of Am., Hudson River Contemporary Artists, Nat. Mus. for Women in ARt, Silvermine Guild of Artists, Scarsdale Art Soc., Mamaroneck Artists Guild (bd. dirs. assoc. rep. 1990-91, receiving com. 1992). Home: 10 Burkewood Rd Hartsdale NY 10530-2933

BROZMAN, TINA L., federal judge; b. 1952. BA, NYU, 1973; JD, Fordham U., 1976. Ptnr. Anderson Russell Kill & Olick, 1976-85; bankruptcy judge U.S. Ct. So. Dist. N.Y., N.Y.C., 1985—; lectr. Practicing Law Inst., 1987. Mem. Assn. of Bar of City of N.Y. Office: US Dist Ct Alexander Hamilton Custom House 1 Bowling Grn New York NY 10004-1415

BROZOVSKY, JOHN A., accounting educator; b. Spokane, Wash., Apr. 30, 1951; s. Victor Jerald and Orise (Watson) B.; m. Sue Ellen King, Apr. 14, 1984; 1 child, Joseph Victor. AAS, Spokane C.C., 1971; BBA, U. Tex., 1975, M in Profl. Acctg., 1978; PhD in Bus. Adminstrn., U. Colo., 1990. CPA, Tex.; cert. data processor; cert. computer programmer. Computer programmer U. Tex., Austin, 1974-77; computer programmer II Tex. State Health Dept., Austin, 1978-80; EDP auditor City of Austin, 1980-81; sr. internal auditor Enserch Corp., Dallas, 1981-83; lectr. Calif. State U., Fresno, 1983-86; rsch. and teaching asst U. Colo., Boulder, 1986-89; asst. prof. Va. Tech., Blacksburg, 1989-96, assoc. prof., 1996—; presenter in field. Contbr. articles to profl. jours. Am. Accctg. Assn. fellow, 1986, Gerald Hart fellow, 1987; grantee Calif. CPA Found., 1986-89, AICPA, 1988, Pamplin, 1992. Mem. Am. Acctg. Assn., Am. Econ. Assn., Am. Tax Assn., Nat. Tax Assn., Inst. Mgmt. Accts. (coach nat. championship team student case competition 1995, nat. finalists 1996, 1997, nat. semifinalists, 1998, v.p. profl. edn. Roanoke chpt. 1997-98). Avocation: stamp collecting. Home: 9000 Newport Rd Catawba VA 24070-3018 Office: Va Tech Pamplin # 3007 Blacksburg VA 24061

BROZOWSKI, LAURA ADRIENNE, mechanical engineer; b. Yokohama, Japan, May 12, 1960; came to U.S., 1961; d. John and Muriel Sydney (Jackson) B. BSME, U. Calif., 1982; MSME, Calif. State U., 1987; MBA, Pepperdine U., 1988. Registered profl. engr., Calif.; cert. profl. mgr. Inst. Cert. Profl. Mgrs. Engring. specialist Rocketdyne Propulsion and Power Boeing Co., Canoga Park, Calif., 1982—. Author in field. Fellow Inst. Advancement Engring.; mem. ASME, NSPE, Nat. Mgmt. Assn. Avocations: music, continuing education, violin. Home: 22036 Collins St Apt 230-N Woodland Hills CA 91367-4730

BRUBAKER, CHARLES WILLIAM, architect; b. South Bend, Ind., Sept. 28, 1926; s. Ralph and Mary (Holderman) B.; m. Elizabeth Allen Rogers, June 25, 1955; children: William Rogers, Elizabeth Allen, Robert Andrew. Student, Purdue U., 1945; BArch, U. Tex., 1950. Registered architect Calif., Colo. Fla., Ill., Ind., Iowa, Mich., Nev., N.Mex., N.Y., N.C., N.Dak., Ohio, Pa., S.C., Tex. Wash., Wis. Architect Perkins & Will, Architects, Chgo., 1950-58, ptnr., 1958-70; v.p. Perkins & Will, Inc., Chgo., 1970-85, pres., 1985-86, vice chmn., 1986—; bd. dirs. Chgo. Architecture Found., 1976—; mem. bd. govs. Met. Planning Coun., Chgo., 1976—. Prin. works include Capital High Sch., Santa Fe, New Mex., Richland Coll., Dallas, First Nat. Bank Chgo.; author: Planning Flexible Learning Places, 1977. V.p. Greater North Michigan Ave. Assn., Chgo., 1986-88; commr. Shoreline Protection Commn., Chgo., 1987-88; mem. Winnetka (Ill.) Plan Commn., 1979-82. With USN, 1945-46. Named Planner of Yr., Coun. Ednl. Facility Planners, 1984. Fellow AIA (chancellor 1988, Disting. Svc. award 1987); mem. Soc. for Coll. and Univ. Planning, Chgo. Yacht Club, Lambda Alpha (pres. 1983-84). Avocations: sketching, music. Home: 82 Essex Rd Winnetka IL 60093-4259 Office: Perkins & Will Inc 330 N Wabash Ave Chicago IL 60611-3603

BRUBAKER, CRAWFORD FRANCIS, JR., government official, aerospace consultant; b. Fruitland, Idaho, Apr. 23, 1924; s. Crawford Francis and Cora Susan (Flora) B.; m. Lucile May Christensen, May 5, 1945; children: Eric Stephen, Alan Kenneth, Craig Martin, Paul David. BA, Pomona Coll., 1946; MBA, U. Pa., 1948. Office mgr. Lockheed Calif. Co., Burbank, 1948-54, sales adminstr., 1954-57, with fighter contracts div., field office rep., 1959-65, asst. dir. fighter sales, 1965-69, dep. mgr. bid and proposals, 1969-74, mgr. govt. sales, 1974-76; dir. internat. mktg. devel. and policy Lockheed Corp., Burbank, 1976-83; dep. asst. sec. for aerospace U.S. Dept. Commerce, Washington, 1983-87; internat. aerospace cons., 1987—; bd. dirs. So. Calif. Presbyn. Homes; vice chmn. Industry Sector Adv. Com., Washington, 1979-83; mem. Aero. Policy Rev. Com., Washington, 1983-87. Vice chmn. So. Calif. Dist. Export Coun., L.A., 1980-83, 88-91, chmn., 1992-93. Lt. (j.g.) USN, 1943-45, PTO. Mem. AIAA, Am. Defense Preparedness Assn., Kiwanis, Sigma Alpha Epsilon. Republican. Presbyterian. Avocations: numismatics; golf; fishing; photography.

BRUBAKER, JAMES CLARK, construction executive; b. Normal, Ill., Mar. 22, 1947; s. Walter Clark and Vernie Helen (Rubenaker) B.; m. Celeste Renee Rohling, Jan. 16, 1971; children: Elizabeth, Andrew. BS in Communications, U. Ill., 1969. Lic. real estate agt. Sales mgr. Proctor & Gamble, Chgo., 1969-71, Johnson & Johnson, St. Louis, 1971-74; v.p. sales Omega Sports, St. Louis, 1976-79; exec. v.p. Thomas Constrn., St. Louis, 1982-89; chief exec. officer Permastone, Inc., St. Louis, 1987-90; pres. Encore Enterprises, Inc., St. Louis, 1987—, Omega Ventures, Inc., 1999—; bd. dirs. Constrn. Industry Arbitration and Mediation. Dir. Grace Ch. of Mid-Mo., Columbia, 1986-89; bd. dirs. Citadel Christian Sch., 1992-96. Mem. Profl. Remodeler's Assn. (bd. dirs. 1988-93). Republican. Fundamentalist. Avocations: reading, bible study, physical fitness, racquetball, running. Home: 3411 Erman Dr Bridgeton MO 63044-3073 Office: Encore Enterprises Inc 1030 N Lindbergh Blvd Saint Louis MO 63132-2912

BRUBAKER, KAREN SUE, manufacturing executive; b. Ashland, Ohio, Feb. 5, 1953; d. Robert Eugene and Dora Louise (Camp) B. BSBA, Ashland Coll., 1975; MBA, Bowling Green State U., 1976. Supr. tire ctr. ops. B.F. Goodrich Co., Akron, Ohio, 1976-77, supr. tire ctr. acctg., 1977-79, asst. product mgr. radial passenger tires, 1979-80, product mgr. broadline passenger tires, 1980-81, group product mgr. broadline passenger and light truck tires, 1981-83, mktg. mgr. T/A high tech radials, 1983-86; product mktg. mgr. B.F. Goodrich T/A radials The Uniroyal Goodrich Tire Co., Akron, Ohio, 1986-91; product mktg. mgr. Michelin performance tires Michelin Americas Small Tires, Akron, Ohio, 1991-95; ind. Alpine distbr. Indoor Air Repair, Fairlawn, Ohio, 1996—; charter exec. Big Planet Inc., Fairlawn, Ohio, 1998—. Sect. chmn. indsl. divsn. United Way, Akron, 1983-86; mem. adv. coun. to trustees Coll. Bus. and Econs, Ashland U., 1990-92; vol. Hospice Vis. Nurses Svcs.; fund raiser Nat. Heart Assist and Transplant Fund/Judi Reali Transplant Fund, 1996. Recipient Alumni Disting. Service award Ashland Coll., 1986; Alpha Phi Clara Bradley Burdette scholar, 1975. Mem. Am. Mktg. Assn. (pres. Akron/Canton chpt. 1982-83, Highest Honors award 1983, nat. bd. dirs., v.p. bus. mktg. 1984-86, v.p. profl. chpts. 1987-89), Sales and Mktg. Execs. (v.p. membership, 1998-99), Akron Women's Network, Zonta, Beta Gamma Sigma, Omicron Delta Epsilon. Home: 822 Village Pkwy Fairlawn OH 44333-3297

BRUBAKER, LAUREN EDGAR, minister, educator; b. Birmingham, Ala., Oct. 8, 1914; s. Lauren Edgar and Nora (Drake) B.; m. Leonte Saye, June 6, 1944; children: Lauren Eugene, Edward Saye; m. Patricia Barnett, July 23, 1994. AB, Birmingham So. Coll., 1935; MDiv, Princeton Theol. Sem., 1938, postdoctoral, 1946-47; STM, Union Theol. Sem., N.Y., 1942, ThD, 1944. Ordained to ministry Presbyn. Ch., 1938. Asst. pastor in Parkersburg, W.Va., 1938-41; grad. asst. Union Theol. Sem., 1941-43; chaplain U.S. Army, 1943-46; grad. instr. Princeton Theol. Sem., 1946-47; prof. philosophy and religion, chaplain Parsons Coll., Fairfield, Iowa, 1947-49; assoc. prof. U. S.C., Columbia, 1949-58, prof., 1958-79, Disting. prof., 1979-80, Disting. prof. emeritus, 1980—, univ. chaplain, 1949-94, chmn. dept. religious studies, 1949-80; adj. prof. Luth. Theol. So. Sem.; moderator Univ. Forum on S.C. Ednl. TV, 1965-73. Contbr. articles to profl. jours. Dir. S.C. Council Human Relations, 1966-69; exec. committeeman Columbia and Richland County Democratic party, 1950-60. Served to maj. AUS, 1943-46. Mem. Inst. Religion (dir. 1960-63), S.C. Acad. Religion (founder 1968, pres. 1968), Am. Acad. Religion (pres. 1959), Presbyn. Edn. Assn. South, Columbia Ministers Assn. (pres. 1972), Assn. for Coll. and Univ. Religious Affairs (bd. dirs. 1985-86), AAUP (past officer), Columbia Forum on Internat. Affairs (pres. 1971), Columbia Coun. for Internats. (bd. dirs., pres. 1986, 87), Nat. Assn. Coll. and Univ. Chaplains, Soc. Bibl. Lit. (past officer), Christian Jewish Congress S.C. (sec. 1982-90), Columbia CROP WALK (treas. 1983-98), Common Cause of S.C. (dir. 1988—, sec. 1989-96), Omicron Delta Kappa (faculty adviser 1968-71), Pi Gamma Mu, Phi Kappa Phi, Tau Kappa Alpha. Club: Executive of Columbia (pres. 1960-61). Lodge: Kiwanis (pres. 1986-87). Research teaching religion in accredited colls. and univs. Home: 9 Churchill Cir Columbia SC 29206-4412

BRUBAKER, LOU ANN, advertising executive, consultant; b. Mansfield, Ohio, Apr. 29, 1957; d. Louis Stanley and Doris Ellen (Schneider) B. BA in Polit. Sci. and Urban Planning, Kent State U., 1981. Zoning adminstr. City of Cuyahoga Falls (Ohio), 1980-81; v.p. mktg. Nat. Mgmt. and Mktg., Columbus, Ohio, 1981-86; dir. advt. Drustar Drug Control Systems, Grove City, Ohio, 1986-88; program dir. STN Internat. Chem. Abstract Svcs., Columbus, 1988-91; pres. Brubaker Professional Develop. Seminars, Laurel, Md., 1991—; bd. dirs. Woman Rising Inc., Balt. Avocations: public speaking, training seminars developer, tennis, travel. Home and Office: Brubaker Prof Develop Sems 10422 Churchill Way Laurel MD 20723-5749

BRUBAKER, ROBERT LORING, lawyer; b. Louisville, May 22, 1947; s. Robert Lee and Betty (Brock) B.; m Jeannette Marie Montgomery, Dec. 21, 1968; children: Benjamin Brock, Anne Montgomery. BA, Earlham Coll., 1969; JD, U. Chgo., 1972. Bar: Ohio 1972, U.S. Dist. Ct. (so. dist.) Ohio 1973, U.S. Ct. Appeals (6th cir.) 1975, U.S. Supreme Ct. 1978, U.S. Ct. Appeals (D.C. cir.) 1979, U.S. Ct. Appeals (3d, 4th and 7th cirs.) 1995. Asst. atty. gen. Atty. Gen.'s Office State of Ohio, Columbus, 1972-76; assoc. Porter Wright Morris & Arthur, Columbus, 1976-78, ptnr., 1979—. Editor: Ohio Environmental Law Handbook, 1990, 2d edit., 1992, 3d edit., 1994, Deposition Strategy, Law and Forms: Environmental Law; assoc. editor Ohio Environ. Law Letter, 1991. Mem. ABA (natural resources, energy and environ. law sect.), Ohio Bar Assn. (environ. law com.), Air and Waste Mgmt. Assn. (chmn. S.W. Ohio chpt. 1990-91, chmn. East Ctrl. sect. 1991-92), Columbus Bar Assn. (environ. law com.), Nat. Coal Coun. Home: 2661 Wexford Rd Columbus OH 43221-3217 Office: Porter Wright Morris & Arthur 41 S High St Ste 2800 Columbus OH 43215-6194

BRUBAKER, ROBERT PAUL, food products executive; b. Sturgis, Mich., Oct. 6, 1934; s. Leland C. and Ruth (Cunningham) B.; m. Carol Cowart Highsmith, Nov. 14, 1998; children: Susan, Beverly, Thomas. BA, Mich. State U., 1956. With product mgmt. Gen. Foods Corp., White Plains, N.Y., 1959-67; exec. v.p. King Shrimp Co. Inc., Brunswick, Ga., 1967-80; pres. King & Prince Seafood Corp. (formerly King Shrimp Co. Inc.), Brunswick,

Ga., 1980—, CEO, 1993—, chmn., 1995—. Bd. dirs. United Way, Brunswick, Ga., 1985—; organizing sponsor No Is OK Youth Group, Brunswick, 1984-85. Lt. USAF, 1956-59. Mem. Soc. Internat. Bus. Fellows, Nat. Shrimp Breaders and Processors Assn. (pres., chmn. 1979-83), Nat. Fisheries Inst. (regional v.p. 1981-82, dir., sec. 1982-86, v.p., pres., chmn. 1986-89), Brunswick C. of C. (v.p. edn., dir. 1985-86, 88-89, 94-95), Sea Island Golf Club, Rotary. Republican. Presbyterian. Avocations: golf, tennis, travel. Home: 206 Settler's Rd Saint Simons Is GA 31522-1943 Office: King & Prince Seafood Corp PO Box 899 1 King & Prince Blvd Brunswick GA 31520-8603

BRUBAKER, WILLIAM ROGERS, sociology educator; b. Evanston, Ill., June 8, 1956; s. Charles William and Elizabeth (Rogers) B. BA summa cum laude, Harvard U., 1979; MA, Sussex U., Eng., 1980; PhD, Columbia U., 1990. Prof. UCLA, 1994—, assoc. prof. sociology, 1991-94. Author: The Limits of Rationality, 1984, Citizenship and Nationhood in France and Germany, 1992, Nationalism Reframed, 1996; editor: Immigration and Politics of Citizenship in Europe and North America, 1989. Jr. fellow Soc. Fellows Harvard U., 1988-91; MacArthur fellow, 1994—; NSF Young Investigator awardee. Office: U Calif Dept Sociology 2201 Hershey Hall 610 Charles E Young Dr Los Angeles CA 90095*

BRUCCOLI, MATTHEW JOSEPH, English educator, publisher; b. N.Y.C., Aug. 21, 1931; s. Joseph M. and Mary (Gervasi) B.; m. Arlyn Shuey Firkins, Oct. 5, 1957; children: Mary Firkins, Joseph Matthew, Josephine Arlyn, Arlyn Barbara. B.A., Yale U., 1953; M.A., U. Va., 1956, Ph.D., 1961. Prof. English U. S.C., Columbia, 1969—; Jefferies prof. English U. S.C., 1976—; dir. Ctr. for Edits. of Am. Authors, 1969-76; pres. Bruccoli Clark Layman, Pubs., 1976—. Author: The Composition of Tender Is the Night, 1963, The Last of the Novelists, 1977, The O'Hara Concern, 1975, Scott and Ernest, 1978, Some Sort of Epic Grandeur: The Life of F. Scott Fitzgerald, 1981, James Gould Cozzens, 1983, Ross Macdonald, 1984, The Fortunes of Mitchell Kennerley, Bookman, 1986, F. Scott Fitzgerald and Hemingway, 1994, Reader's Companion to Tender Is the Night, 1996; editor: Fitzgerald/Hemingway Annual, 1969-70; series editor Dictionary of Literary Biography, 1978—, Lost Am. Fiction, 1972-80, Pittsburgh Series in Bibliography, 1971—, Selected Letters of John O'Hara, 1978, Just Representations: A James Gould Cozzens Reader, 1978, Correspondence of F. Scott Fitzgerald, 1980, Understanding Contemporary American Literature, 1985—, Understanding Contemporary British Literature, 1989—, The Cambridge Edition of the Works of F. Scott Fitzgerald, 1991-93, Zelda Fitzgerald The Collected Writings, 1991, F. Scott Fitzgerald A Life in Letters, 1994, F. Scott Fitzgerald's Tender Is the Night, 1995, F. Scott Fitzgerald on Authorship, 1996, The Only Thing that Counts, 1996, American Expatriate Writers: Paris in the Twenties, 1997. Guggenheim fellow, 1973. Club: Yale, Century (N.Y.C.). Home: 31 Heathwood Cir Columbia SC 29205-1946 Office: U SC Dept English Columbia SC 29208

BRUCE, DAVID LIONEL, retired anesthesiologist, educator; b. Champaign, Ill., Oct. 27, 1933; s. Lionel Harry and Freda Eleanor (Tipsword) B.; m. Geraldine Zawasky, Nov. 24, 1956 (div. 1967); children: Ellen Marie, Brian David; m. Sharon Jean Wells, Jan. 18, 1985. Student, U. Ill., 1951-54, MD, 1960. Diplomate Am. Bd. Anesthesiology. Intern Ill. Rsch. and Ednl. Hosp., Chgo., 1960-61; resident U. Pa., Phila., 1961-64; asst. prof. anesthesiology U. Ky. Med. Ctr., Lexington, 1964-66; from asst. prof. to prof. Northwestern U. Med. Sch., Chgo., 1966-77; prof. U. Calif., Irvine, 1977-81; prof. anesthesiology NYU Med. Sch., 1981-84; prof. U. Miss. Med. Ctr., Jackson, 1984-90, chmn. dept., 1985-90; dir. outpatient surgery Athens (Ga.) Regional Med. Cr., 1990-92; prof. anesthesiology U. South Fla., Tampa Gen. Hosp., 1992-93; med. dir. surg. svcs. Tampa Gen. Hosp., 1993; med. dir. outpatient surgery ctr. Athens (Ga.) Regional Med. Ctr., 1993-95; cons. FDA, Rockville, Md., 1972-75, mem. adv. com., Bethesda, Md., 1973-77. Contbr. numerous articles to profl. jours. Cpl. U.S. Army, 1954-56. Recipient Rsch. Career Devel. award USPHS, 1967-72. Fellow Royal Soc. Medicine (Eng.) (travelling fellow 1975); mem. Am. Soc. Anesthesiologists. Avocations: music, writing fiction. Home and Office: 201 McNeil Rd Argyle NY 12809-1421

BRUCE, DEBRA M., poet, English language educator; b. Bristol, Conn., Apr. 4, 1951; d. Willard Arthur Bruce and Mary Elizabeth Conlin; m. Rick Kinnebrew, Aut. 21, 1981; 1 child, Kevin Kinnebrew. BA summa cum laude, U. Mass., 1974; MA, Brown U., 1978; MFA, U. Iowa, 1978. Instr. English Old Dominion U., Norfolk, Va., 1978-84; prof. English Northeastern Ill. U., Chgo., 1984—. Author: (books of poetry) Pure Daughter, 1983, Sudden Hunger, 1988, What Wind Will Do, 1997, (chapbook) Dissolves, 1977; contbr. poetry to anthologies including A Century in Two Decades, Naming the Daytime Moon, The Virago Book of Wicked Press, also mags. Creative writing fellow NEA, 1982, scriptwriting fellow, 1982, creative writing fellow Ill. Arts Coun., 1986, 99, Carl Sandburg Poetry award Chgo. Pub. Libr., 1989. Mem. Acad. Am. Poets, Associated Writing Programs, Poetry Soc. Am. (Gustave Davidson award 1989). Office: Northeastern Ill I English Dept 5500 N St Louis Ave Chicago IL 60645

BRUCE, DOUGLAS E., real estate investor; b. L.A., Aug. 26, 1949; s. Carl Edward and Marjorie Louise (Atkinson) B. BA, Pomona Coll., 1970; JD, U. So. Calif., 1973. Bar: Calif. 1973. Dep. dist. atty. L.A. county, 1973-79; pvt. practice real estate investor, 1975—. Author Colo. state constl. amendment limiting state and local govt. taxes, revenue and debt, 1992, Colorado Springs tax cuts, 1991, capital improvements petition, 1997, state constl. amendment to cut state and local taxes for Nov. 2000 election. Named Coloradoan of the Yr. Rocky Moutain News, 1992, Friend of Liberty Colo. Libertarian Party, 1993, 95. Republican. Avocations: classical music, travel, chess, bridge, poker, old houses. E-mail: taxcutter@msn.com. Office: PO Box 26018 Colorado Springs CO 80936-6018

BRUCE, E(STEL) EDWARD, lawyer; b. Hutchinson, Kans., Nov. 23, 1938; s. Kenneth Dean and Josephine (Vigna) B.; m. Marnell Elaine Higley, Aug. 9, 1960; children: Anthony Dean, Caroline Summers. BA summa cum laude, Yale U., 1960, LLB magna cum laude, 1966. Bar: D.C. 1967, U.S. Ct. Appeals (1st, 2d, 3d, 5th, 6th, 9th, 10th, D.C. and Fed. cirs.), U.S. Supreme Ct. Law clk. U.S. Supreme Ct., Washington, 1966-67; assoc. Covington & Burling, Washington, 1967-73; ptnr. Covington & Burling, 1973—; adj. prof. constitutional law Georgetown U. Law Center, 1970-75; mem. Appellate Judges Conf., Com. on Appellate Practice, 1993—; mem. faculty ABA Appellate Inst., 1992—. Mem. adminstrv. bd. Cornell Lab. Ornithology, 1998—; bd. dirs. Washington Area Lawyers for the Arts, 1993—, Yale Law Sch. Fund, 1992-98, Audubon Nat. Soc., 1986-92. Mem. ABA, Am. Law Inst., Am. Acad. Appellate Lawyers, D.C. Bar Assn., Order of Coif, Phi Beta Kappa, Met. Club, Chevy Chase Club. Home: 2701 Foxhall Rd NW Washington DC 20007-1128 Office: Covington & Burling 1201 Pennsylvania Ave NW PO Box 7566 Washington DC 20044-7566

BRUCE, JACKSON MARTIN, JR., lawyer; b. Milw., Apr. 10, 1931; s. Jackson Martin and Harriet (Edgell) B.; m. Lilias M. Morehouse, June 30, 1954; children: Lilias Stephanie, Andrew Edgell. AB magna cum laude, Harvard U., 1953, JD cum laude, 1957; MA with 1st class honors in Law, Cambridge U., 1955. Bar: Wis. 1957, Fla. 1973. Assoc. Quarles & Brady, Milw., 1957-64, ptnr., 1964-96; shareholder Dunwody, White & Landon, Naples, Fla., 1996—; counsel Michael Best & Friedrich, Milw., 1996—. Mem. joint editorial bd. Uniform Probate Code; contbr. articles to profl. jours. Bd. dirs. Living Ch. Found., Inc., 1965-98; trustee Univ. Sch. Milw., 1973-79. Fellow Am. Coll. Trust and Estate Counsel (bd. regents 1976-82, treas. 1990-91, sec. 1991-92, v.p. 1992-93, pres. 1994-95); mem. ABA (bd. govs. 1994-97, chmn. sect. real property, probate and trust law 1984-85, ho. dels., ethics com. 1998—), State Bar Wis. (chmn. bd. govs. 1979-80), Am. Bar Found., Am. Law Inst., Internat. Acad. Estate and Trust Law (mem. exec. coun. 1980-86), Nat. Conf. Bar Pres., Nat. Conf. Lawyers and Corp. Fiduciaries (chmn. 1984-90), Town Club, Milw. Club (bd. dirs.), The Club Pelican Bay. Home: 9008 N Bayside Dr Milwaukee WI 53217-1913 also: 6101 Pelican Bay Blvd Apt 904 Naples FL 34108-8183 Office: Michael Best & Friedrich 100 E Wisconsin Ave Ste 3300 Milwaukee WI 53202-4108 also: Dunwody White & Landon 4001 Tamiami Trl N Ste 300 Naples FL 34103-3591

BRUCE, JAMES DONALD, academic administrator; b. Livingston, Tex., June 28, 1936; s. Vivian Eugene and Edna Lee (St. Clair) B.; m. Eleanor MacLaren, Nov. 25, 1959; children: David MacLaren, Heather MacLaren, Nathaniel MacLaren. BSEE, Lamar State Coll. Tech., Beaumont, Tex., 1958, BS in Math., 1958; SMEE, MIT, 1960, ScD, 1964. Mem. faculty MIT, Cambridge, 1964—, assoc. dean engring., 1971-78, acting dean, 1977-78, prof. elec. engring., 1973—, dir. indsl. liaison, 1979-82, dir. info. sys., 1983-86, v.p. for info. sys., chief info. officer, 1986—, program mgr. reengring adminstrv. process, 1994-98; found., mem. steering com. New Eng. Acad. and Rsch. Network (NEARnet), 1988-95; bd. dirs. BBN Tech. Svcs., Inc., 1993-95; cons. to govt. and industry; mem. adv. com. elec. engring. Lamar U., 1993—; mem. tech. adv. com. Mass. Divsn. Capital Planning and Ops., 1993-95; mem. total quality edn. com. to sec. edn. Commonwealth of Mass., 1993-95; founder, bd. dirs., treas. Marketplace Network, Inc., 1993—. Trustee Harvard Coop. Soc., 1974-84, 93-96; trustee Park St. Congrl. Ch., Boston, 1977-83, vice chmn. bd. trustees, 1979-81, chmn., 1981-83, deacon, 1985-96, elder, 1997-99. Ford Found. postdoctoral fellow, 1964-65. Sr. mem. IEEE; mem. Am. Soc. Engring. Edn., Consortium for Sci. Computing (trustee, mem. exec. com., 1984-90, vice chmn. 1986-88), Eta Kappa Nu, Tau Beta Pi. Home: 12 Woodpark Cir Lexington MA 02421-7208 Office: MIT 77 Massachusetts Ave Rm 10-219 Cambridge MA 02139-4307

BRUCE, JAMES EDMUND, retired utility company executive; b. Boise, Idaho, June 23, 1920; s. James E. and Bessie (Barcus) B.; m. Lois I. Stevens, Aug. 24, 1946; children: James E., IV, Steven, Robert, David. Student, Coll. Idaho, 1937-39; BA, Portland U., 1941; postgrad., Georgetown U., 1941-42; LLB, U. Idaho, 1949. Bar: Idaho 1948. Asst. atty. gen. State of Idaho, 1948-49; dep. pros. atty. Ada County, Idaho, 1949-51; with Idaho Power Co., Boise, 1951-87, v.p., 1968-74, pres., chief operating officer, 1974-76, pres., chief exec. officer, 1976-85, chmn., 1985-87, ret., 1987; dir. Albertson's Inc., First Security Corp., 1981-93; chmn. Blue Cross of Idaho, 1988-90. Bd. dirs. Mountain States Legal Found., 1977-88; mem. St. Alphonsus Found., Boise State U. Found., Bishop Kelly Found., Boise Park Bd., 1958-78; chmn. Idaho State Lottery; Idaho chmn. U.S. Savs. Bonds, 1976-85; chmn. bd. trustees St. Alphonsus, 1985-86; trustee Coll. Idaho, YMCA, Idaho Nature Conservancy; pres. Ada County Hwy. Dist. Commn. With U.S. Army, 1942-46. Mem. ABA, Boise Execs. Assn., Edison Electric Assn. (dir. 1978-85), N.W. Electric Light and Power Assn. (pres. 1982), Boise C. of C., Arid Club, Crane Creek Country Club, Rotary, Elks, K.C. Roman Catholic.

BRUCE, JOHN ALLEN, foundation executive, educator; b. Kansas City, Mo., Sept. 17, 1934. BA, Wesleyan U., Middletown, Conn., 1956; MDiv., Gen. Theol. Sem., N.Y.C., 1959; PhD, U. Minn., 1972. Ordained to ministry Episcopal Ch., 1959. Clergyman, 1959-68; prof. U. Ala., Tuscaloosa, 1972-74; exec. dir. E.C. Brown Found., Portland, Oreg., 1974-98; cons. to philanthropies and corp. programs; clin. prof. community medicine Sch. Medicine, Oreg. Health Scis. U., Portland, 1976-98. Author, editor various scholarly publs.; exec. prodr. ednl. films on family life, health and values. Bd. dirs., officer various cmty. orgns. Served to lt. USN, 1964-67. Recipient awards and grants from med. orgns. and related groups. Mem. Nat. Coun. on Family Rels. (Disting. Svc. to Families award 1979), Oreg. Coun. on Family Rels. (pres. 1981), Cosmos Club. Republica. Home: 2990 NW 151st Pl Beaverton OR 97006-5455

BRUCE, RACHEL MARY CONDON, nurse practitioner; b. Bklyn., Dec. 18, 1940; d. Bernard Francis Sr. and Rachel Evelyn (Riggott) Condon; m. Donald Eugene Bruce, Sept. 27, 1966; children: Donald Eugene, Kevin Francis, Rachel Janine. BS in Nursing, Molloy Cath. Coll., 1962; MEd in Counselor Edn., U. Guam, Mangilao, 1975; cert. sch. nurse practitioner, U. Colo., 1984, cert. pediatric nurse practitioner, 1985. RN, N.Y., Tex.; cert. sch. nurse practitioner, pediatric nurse practitioner ANCC. Asst. head nurse med.-surg. unit Bklyn. Hosp., 1962-64; part-time med.-surg. nurse Guam Meml. Hosp., Tamuning, 1971-72; sch. health counselor IV, Dededo Jr. H.S., Dept. Edn., Guam, 1973-76; asst. prof. nursing U. Guam, Mangilao, 1976-80; vis. nurse Indiana (Pa.) Vis. Nuses Assn., 1980-81; instr. first responder Police Acad. Guam C.C., Mangilao, 1981-84, prof., sch. health counselor, nurse practitioner Student Health Ctr., 1982-94; ednl. health cons., Mangilao, 1994-96; asst. prof. tng. project Peace Corps, Tumon, Guam, summer 1978; part-time pediatric nurse practitioner Family Med. Clinic, Tamuning, 1988-90; mem. adv. com. preparing Guam Nurse Practice Act, Nurse Practitioner Task Force, 1985-87, mem. revision com., 1993-96; mem. com. on family planning Guam Health Objectives for 1990, 1986-87; mem. grant writing com. Fipse (drug awareness) Guam C.C., 1989-91; Guam C.C. rep. to CEO's Task Force on Health Issues, 1989-90; lic. ednl. cons. sch. health, pediatrics, adolescent health and teen pregnancy. Co-author: (booklet) Growing Together, 1987, (revised) Growing Together, 1995. CPR instr. ARC, Guam, 1978-81; BCLS instr. Guam Heart Assn., 1981-84; vol. sexual assault counselor Counseling Advs. Reaching Out, Guam, 1982-84; founding bd. mem., co-vice chair Guam Arthritis Found., 1989; singer Guam Symphony Chorale, 1987-95; sponsor Houston Symphony Soc., 1997-99; vol. Cynthia Woods Mitchell Pavillion, Woodlands, Tex., 1997-99. 1st lt. USAF Nurse Corps, 1964-66. Recipient proclomation for outstanding svc. in nursing Guam Legislature, 1988, for outstanding profl. and cmty. svc., 1989, Governor's merit award for distinguished performance, 1987, Governor's merit award for distinguished performance employee of yr. award, 1993. Mem. ANA (nat. disting. svc. register 1988), AAUW (past pub. rels. officer, pub. pol. chair, 1998-99, v.p. programs 1999—), Tex. Nurses Assn., Nat. Assn. Sch. Nurses, Tex. Assn. Sch. Nurses, Am. Acad. Nurse Practitioners (state award for excellence of care and outstnding contbn. in practice 1991), Internat. Reading Assn. (grantee 1992), People to People Internat. (sch. health del. to Ea. Europe 1994), scuba diving team Kosrae Reef Preservation Project, 1998. Roman Catholic. Avocations: scuba diving, travel, gardening, fitness walking, grandmothering. Home: 11 Timber Ln Conroe TX 77384-3159

BRUCE, ROBERT JAMES, university president; b. Aug. 12, 1937; s. Andrew Carson and Ruth Lillian (Barr) B.; m. Judith Ann Garland, Aug. 29, 1959; children: Kimberley Bruce Campbell, Scott Garland. AB, Colby Coll., 1959; MA, U. Mass., Boston, 1964; postgrad., Boston U., 1964; LHD, Widener U., 1992. Devel. officer Colby Coll., Waterville, Maine, 1965-70; v.p. Bard Coll., Annandale-on-Hudson, N.Y., 1970-74, acting pres., 1974; v.p. univ. rels. Clark U., Worcester, Mass., 1975; v.p. devel. Widener U., Chester, Pa., 1975-81, pres., 1981—, also trustee; lectr. Queen Anne's Coll., U.K., Chorley Tchrs. Coll., U.K.; instr. Colby Coll.; chmn. Crozer-Keystone Health System; chmn. RDC, Inc. Recipient Bard Coll. medal, 1975, Disting. Alumnus award Colby Coll., 1985, Liberty Bell award; Fulbright grantee U.K., 1964-65. Mem. Am. Assn. Colls., Nat. Assn. Ind. Colls. and Univs. (past chmn. bd.), Am. Assn. Higher Edn., Pa. Assn. Colls. and Univs., Pa. Commn. for Ind. Colls. and Univs. (exec. com.), Univ. Club (N.Y.C.), Union League (Phila.), Univ. and Whist Club (Wilmington, Del.), St. Andrew's Soc. Pa., Springhaven Club, Rodney Square Club (Del.), Winter Harbor (Maine) Yacht Club, Castine Golf Club (Maine), Phi Kappa Phi. Episcopalian. Home: 10 Church Rd Wallingford PA 19086-6210 Office: Widener U Office Pres Chester PA 19013

BRUCE, ROBERT ROCKWELL, lawyer; b. Mt. Kisco, N.Y., Mar. 8, 1944; s. Robert R. and Nona (Burtch) B.; m. Collot Guerard, Aug. 30, 1969 (div. Sept. 1983); 1 child, Benjamin; m. Kathryn Stearns, Jan. 2, 1988; children: Hannah, David. B.A. magna cum laude, Harvard U., 1966, J.D., 1970; M.P.A., Kennedy Sch. Govt., 1970. Bar: D.C. 1972. Dir. communications planning Public Broadcasting Service, 1970-72; asso. firm Hogan & Hartson, Washington, 1972-77; gen. counsel FCC, Washington, 1977-81; ptnr. firm Leva, Hawes, Symington, Martin & Oppenheimer, Washington, 1981-83, Debevoise & Plimpton, 1983—. Office: Debevoise & Plimpton, Old Broad St, London EC2M 1HQ, England also: Debevoise & Plimpton 875 3rd Ave New York NY 10022-6225

BRUCE, ROBERT VANCE, historian, educator; b. Malden, Mass., Dec. 19, 1923; s. Robert Gilbert and Bernice Irene (May) B. Student, MIT, 1941-43; BS, U. N.H., 1945; MA, Boston U., 1947, PhD, 1953. Instr. U. Bridgeport, Conn., 1947-48; master Lawrence Acad., Groton, Mass., 1948-51; research asst. to Benjamin P. Thomas, Washington, 1953-54; mem. faculty Boston U., 1955—, assoc. prof. history, 1960-66, prof., 1966-84, prof. emeritus, 1984—; vis. prof. U. Wis., Madison, 1962-63. Author: Lincoln and the Tools of War, 3d edit., 1989, 1877, Year of Violence, 3d edit., 1989, Bell: Alexander Graham Bell and the Conquest of Solitude, 3d edit., 1995, Brit. edit., 1973, Japanese edit., 1991, Lincoln and the Riddle of Death, 1982, The Launching of Modern American Science, 2d edit., 1988 (Pulitzer prize 1988); contbg. author: Lincoln the War President, 1992, Feeding Mars, 1993, War Comes Again, 1995; contbr. articles to profl. jours. With AUS, 1943-46. Guggenheim fellow, 1957-58; Henry E. Huntington fellow, 1966; recipient Pulitzer Prize in history, 1988. Fellow AAAS, Soc. Am. Historians; mem. Orgn. Am. Historians (life mem.), AAAS, Lincoln Group of Boston (pres. 1969-74), Phi Beta Kappa. Democrat. Home: 28 Evans Rd Madbury NH 03820-7000

BRUCE, THOMAS ALLEN, retired physician, philanthropist, educator; b. Mountain Home, Ark., Dec. 22, 1930; s. Rex Floyd and Dora Madeline (Fee) B.; m. Dolores Fay Montgomery, May 28, 1960; children: T.K. Montgomery, Dana Fee Thomas. B.S.M., M.D., U. Ark., 1955, DSc (hon.), 1995. Intern Duke Hosp., 1956-57; resident medicine Bellevue Hosp., N.Y.C., 1957, Meml. Center Cancer and Allied Diseases, N.Y.C., 1958, Parkland Meml. Hosp., Dallas, 1958-59; cardiopulmonary trainee Southwestern Med. Sch. of U. Tex., 1959-60; cardiac research fellow Hammersmith Hosp. and U. London Postgrad. Med. Sch., London, 1960-61, Harvard Bus. Sch., 1974; from instr. to prof. medicine Wayne State U., 1961-68, also asst. dean Sch. of Medicine; prof. medicine, head cardiovascular sect. U. Okla. Med. Center, 1968-74; prof. medicine, dean Coll. Medicine, U. Ark. Med. Scis., 1974-85, emeritus prof., 1997—; med. dir. Barton Research Inst., 1974-85; coordinator Sino-Am. Med. Exchange Program, 1979-85; mem. research support rev. com. NIH, 1983-85; program dir. in health W.K. Kellogg Found., 1985-97, program cons. and advisor, 1997—; bd. dirs. Grantmakers in Health, 1986-94; co-chair session 312 Salzburg Seminar, Austria; mem. nat. adv. com. Native Am. Substance Abuse Prevention Initiative, Robert Wood Johnson Found., History of Medicine Assocs.; nat. adv. bd. cmty. health leadership program Robert Wood Johnson Found.; mem. policy adv. bd. Ctr. for Health Improvement U. Ark. for Med. Scis.; mem. program adv. com. Found. for the Midsouth; advisor group XVI Kellogg Nat. Leadership Program, Coalition for Healthier Cities and Communities in U.S.; bd. dirs. Ctr. Advancement of Cmty.-Based Pub. Health, Founder's Soc., U. Ark. Coll. Medicine, Watershed Human Svcs. Agy., Heifer Project Internat., Ark. Grantmakers Assn.; adj. staff Ark. Cmty. Found. Bruce Soc. Am. Rsch. and publs. on cardiovascular disease including left ventricular function in cardiac denervation, coronary heart disease, myocardial metabolism relating to phospholipids in graded cardiac ischmia, med. edn. with particular reference to rural health care, health promotion and disease prevention, primary health care, community-based pub. health. master gardener, chmn. garden docents Wildwood Pk. Performing Arts. Recipient Ark. Gov.'s Meritorious Achievement award. Fellow ACP, Am. Coll. Cardiology; mem. APHA, AMA, Assn. Am. Med. Colls., Ark. Caduceus Club, Leila Arboretum Soc. (pres. 1989-92), Sigma Xi, Alpha Omega Alpha. Home: 6 Spy Glass Ln Little Rock AR 72212-4418

BRUCE, WILLIAM A., airport executive. BS in Polit. Sci., UCLA, 1967; MPA, Calif. State U., L.A., 1971. Budget analyst, chief negotiator employee rels. City of L.A., 1969-80, various other positions, 1980-99; dir. airports adminstrn. L.A. World Airports, 1999—. Office: Los Angeles Dept Airports 1 World Way Los Angeles CA 90045-5803*

BRUCE, WILLIAM ROBERT, physician, educator; b. Hamhung, Korea, May 26, 1929; s. George Findlay and Ellen (Tate) B.; m. Margaret MacFarlane, June 15, 1957; children: Graham Douglas, Lynda Jeanne, Kevin Robert. B.Sc., U. Alta., 1950; Ph.D., U. Sask., 1956; M.D., U. Chgo., 1958. Intern Billings Hosp., Chgo., 1958-59; mem. faculty U. Toronto, Can., 1959; prof. biophysics U. Toronto, 1966—; mem. epidemiology sect. Ont. Cancer Inst., Toronto, 1959-81, sr. scientist epidemiology sect., 1989—; dir. Ludwig Inst. for Cancer Research, Toronto, 1981-88. Fellow Royal Coll. Physicians (Can.), Royal Soc. Can.; mem. Assn. Cancer Research. Research, publs. on X-ray and gamma ray penetration, control red blood cell prodn., action of anti-cancer agts. on normal and tumor cells, sperm prodn., computers in med. records, origins of human cancer. Home: 4 Marshfield Ct, Don Mills, ON Canada M3C 2E3 Office: U Toronto Dept Nutritional Scis, 150 College St, Toronto, ON Canada M5X 1A8

BRUCH, BARBARA RAE, artist, educator; b. Seattle, Apr. 15, 1940; d. Willard Ray and Zephyr Eloise (Tull) B. BA, U. Wash., 1962, MFA, 1964. Children's art instr. Cornish Coll. Art, Seattle, 1965-67; artist-in-residence City of Seattle, 1967-78; lectr. art Seattle Pacific U., 1974-78; gallery dir. Husted Gallery, Seattle, 1978-94; art instr. Sev-Shoon Art Ctr., Seattle, 1994—; recording agt. Kappeler Inst., Seattle, 1995—; art restorer Husted Gallery/Studio Tara, 1978—; gallery coord. A New Space Gallery, Seattle, 1986-88; condr. art workshops. Illustrator: Stocks and Commodities mag., 1994—; one woman exhbns. include Seattle Pacific U., 1993, New Space Gallery, 1986, Husted Gallery, 1983, 85. Illustrator/mem. Friends of the Earth, Seattle, 1972-76, Wash. Wildlife Study Coun., Seattle, 1974-76. Recipient Editor's Choice award Nat. Libr. Poetry, 1995; Bank of Am. scholar, 1958. Mem. Seattle Women's Caucus for Art (pres. 1991-94, Kathe Kollwitz award 1996), No Limits for Women Artists. Avocations: reading, hiking, making jewelry. Office: Kappeler Inst PO Box 9229 Seattle WA 98109-0229

BRUCH, CAROL SOPHIE, lawyer, educator; b. Rockford, Ill., June 11, 1941; d. Ernest and Margarete (Willstätter) B.; m. Jack E. Myers, 1960 (div. 1973); children: Margarete Louise Myers, Kurt Randall Myers. A.B., Shimer Coll., 1960; J.D., U. Calif.-Berkeley, 1972. Bar: Calif. 1973, U.S. Supreme Ct. 1980. Law clk. to Justice William O. Douglas U.S. Supreme Ct., 1972-73; acting prof. law U. Calif.-Davis, 1973-78, prof., 1978—, chair doctoral program in human devel., 1996—; acad. vis. law dept. U. Munich, 1978-79, 92, U. Cologne, 1990, U. Cambridge, 1990, London Sch. Econs. and Polit. Sci., 1991, Kings Coll., London, 1991; vis. prof. U. Calif., Berkeley, 1983, Columbia U., 1986, U. Basel, 1994, vis. Fulbright prof. Hebrew U., Jerusalem, 1996-97; vis. fellow Fitzwilliam Coll., Cambridge, Eng., 1990, U. Calif. Humanities Rsch. Inst., Irvine, 1999; cons. to Ctr. for Family in Transition, 1981, Calif. Law Revision Commn., 1979-82, NOW Legal Def. and Edn. Fund, 1980-81; lectr., legis. drafting and testimony, 1976—; mem. U.S. del. 4th Inter-Am. Specialized Conf. on Pvt. Internat. Law, OAS, 1989. Contbr. articles to legal jours. Editor Calif. Law Rev., 1971; editorial Bd. Family Law Quar., 1980-87. Mem. adv. com. child support and child custody Calif. Commn. on Status of Women, 1981-83; host parent Am. Field Service, Davis, 1977-78. Max Rheinstein sr. rsch. fellow Alexander von Humboldt Found., Fed. Republic Germany, 1978-79, 92, Fulbright fellow, Western Europe, 1990, Israel, 1997. Mem. ABA, Calif. State Bar Assn. (inactive), Am. Law Inst., Internat. Soc. Family Law (exec. coun. 1994—), Order of Coif. Democrat. Jewish. Office: U Calif Sch of Law Davis CA 95616

BRUCK, ARLENE LORRAINE, secondary education educator; b. Kingston, N.Y., June 26, 1945; d. Machileo and Lillian (Turco) Forte; m. Laurence J. Bruck; children: Jennifer Lynn, Jason Scott. BA in Latin, Coll. Mt. St. Vincent, Riverdale, N.Y., 1967; MS in Psychology, SUNY, New Paltz, 1971. Cert. in social studies, Latin, elem. edn. Tchr. 2d grade Kingston Schs. Consol., 1967-74, tchr. Latin, psychology and sociology, 1984—; mem. Mid-Hudson Social Studies Coun., 1992—. Placement chair Jr. League, Kingston, 1982-84; vol. Girl Scouts, Tillson, N.Y., 1981-86, Athletes Against Drugs, Kingston, 1984-87. Recipient Mary Dodge McCarthy award for gen. excellence, 1967, Mid-Hudson Social Studies Coun. Excellence in Tchg. award, 1994; named Outstanding Young Woman, 1974; N.Y. State Regents scholar, 1963-67, AAUW scholar, 1963-67; NEH fellow, 1992. Mem. APA, AAUW (v.p. 1970-74, sec. 1975-77, pres. program 1994, pres. 1995-96), N.Y. State Assn. Fgn. Lang. Tchrs. Roman Catholic. Avocations: reading, gourmet cooking, travel. Home: 39 Beth Dr Kingston NY 12401-6148 Office: Kingston High Sch 403 Broadway Kingston NY 12401-4617

BRUCK, PHOEBE ANN MASON, landscape architect; b. Highland Park, Ill., Nov. 26, 1928; d. George Allen and Louise Townsend (Barnard) Mason; m. F. Frederick Bruck, June 30, 1956 (dec. May 1997). Student Bard Coll., 1946-49; BS, Ill. Inst. Tech., 1954; MLA, Harvard U., 1963. Trainee, Nat. Gallery of Art, Washington, 1947, Mus. Modern Art, N.Y.C., 1948; head design dept. Design Research Inc., Cambridge, Mass., 1955-60; cons. The Architects Collaborative & Sert, Jackson Assocs., Inc., 1960-63; v.p. F. Frederick Bruck, Architect & Assoc., Inc., Cambridge, pres., 1993-96; vis. design critic dept. landscape architecture Harvard U. Grad. Sch. Design, 1971-79; v.p. The Buccaneers Co., 1989—, also bd. dirs; cons. The arts at

Harvard and Radcliff, 1995—. Contbr. to New Landscapes for Living, 1980. Judge, New Eng. Flower Show, Mass. Hort. Soc., 1971-79, Thoreau Awards, Assn. Landscape Contractors, 1980; mem. Sci. Adv. Group for Edn., Cambridge Pub. Schs., 1981-82; chair Harvard Sq. Adv. Commn., 1986—; co-chair Quincy Sq. Design Com., 1991-97. Mem. Mass. Bd. Registration of Landscape Architects (chair 1992-95), Am. Arbitration Assn., Am. Soc. Landscape Architects, Boston Soc. Landscape Architects (pres. 1973-75, examining bd. 1978-81), Mass. Soc. Mayflower Descendants, Harvard Sq. Def. Fund (chmn. adv. ocm. 1987, bd. dirs. 1984-85, pres. 1985-86), Harvard U. Grad. Sch. Design Alumni Assn. (officer 1972-78), Soc. for Protection of New Eng. Antiquities (design adv. com). Episcopalian. Home and Office: 148 Coolidge Hl Cambridge MA 02138-5521

BRUCK, WILLIAM, company executive, educator; b. Dayton, Ohio, Aug. 1, 1951; s. Emil J. and Lucy A. (Lombardi) B.; m. Jacqueline Youden, June 6, 1984 (div. Dec. 1987); m. Anita M. Brack, June 15, 1996. AB, Brown U., 1973; MA, Duquesne U., 1974; PhD, U. Fla., 1977. Lic. clin. psychologist, Va.; nat. cert. counselor. Asst. prof. psychology Seattle U., 1978-79, West Ga. Coll., Carrollton, 1979-81; prin. Leadership Resources, Inc., Fairfax, Va., 1981-83; assoc. prof. psychology Marymount U., Arlington, Va., 1983-91, dir. instnl. rsch., 1986-91, prof. psychology, 1991-99; owner/operator Bill Bruck & Assocs., Falls Church, Va., 1986—; chief oper. officer Caucsu Sys. Inc., 1999—. Author: Special Edition Using WordPerfect Office, 1994, Special Edition Using PerfectOffice 3, 1995, Special Edition Using Novell GroupWise 4, 1995, Using Corel WordPerfect Suite 7, 1996, Using Corel WordPerfect Suite 8, 1997, The Essential Book for Microsoft Office 95, 1996, The Essential Book for Microsoft Office 97, 1997. Mem. APA, Am. Counseling Assn., Assn. of Specialists in Group Work, Am. Soc. Tng. and Devel., Orgn. Devel. Network, Internat. Ctr. for Study of Psychiatry and Psychology (chmn. bd. dirs. 1993—). Avocations: martial arts (Black belt in karate 1972, 2d deg. black belt in Aikido 1992), racquetball, folk music, gardening. Office: Caucus Sys Inc 2000 N 15th St Ste 103 Arlington VA 22201

BRUCKEN, ROBERT MATTHEW, lawyer; b. Akron, Ohio, Sept. 15, 1934; s. Harold M. and Eunice B. (Boesel) B.; m. Lois R. Gilbert, June 30, 1960; children: Nancy, Elizabeth, Rowland, Gilbert. AB, Marietta Coll., 1956; JD, U. Mich., 1959. Bar: Ohio 1960. Assoc., Baker & Hostetler, Cleve., 1960-69, ptnr., 1970—. Trustee Lakeside Assn., 1979-97, Marietta Coll., 1983—; sec., treas. Leader Shape, Inc., 1990—. Served with AUS, 1959-60. Mem. ABA, Ohio State Bar Assn. (chmn. probate and trust law sect. 1981-83), Cleve. Bar Assn. (chmn. probate ct. com. 1973-75), Am. Coll. Trust and Estate Counsel, Phi Beta Kappa. Congregationalist. Office: Baker & Hostetler 3200 Nat City Ctr 1900 E 9th St Ste 3200 Cleveland OH 44114-3475

BRUCKENSTEIN, JOEL P., investment company executive, financial planner; b. N.Y.C., Jan. 18, 1956; s. Bernard and Anita B.; m. Viviana Srolovich, Sept. 18, 1990; children: Kevin, Alan, Eric. BA magna cum laude, SUNY, New Paltz, 1979. V.p. Kobayashi & Co., Tokyo, 1988-90, Bierbaum-Martin, Inc., N.Y.C., 1990-95; pres. Global Fin. Advisors, Inc., Pleasantville, N.Y., 1995—; mem. adv. bd. Schwab Inst. Emerging Practices Adv. Coun. Mem. Internat. Assn. Fin. Planning, Inst. Cert. Fin. Planners (pres.-elect 1999—, dir. tech. 1998—), Inst. Bus. & Fin. Avocations: scuba diving, reading. Office: Global Fin Advisors Inc 139 Mountain Rd Pleasantville NY 10570-1913

BRUCKER, JANET MARY, nurse; b. London, May 26, 1946; came to U.S., 1953; d. George Edward and Elsie Maud (Sharp) Blain; m. Dennis Jack Brucker, July 8, 1967 (div. 1978); children: Stephen Jack (dec.), Denise Michelle. Diploma in nursing, M.B. Johnson Sch. Nursing, 1967; student, San Jacinto Coll., 1979-82; BSN, U. Tex., Houston, 1984; MS in Nursing Adminstrn., Tex. Woman's U., 1988. RN, Tex.; cert. neuroscience nurse. Staff nurse pediatrics Mount Sinai Hosp., Cleve., 1967-71; staff nurse Rainbow Babies and Children's Hosp., Cleve., 1971-73; night charge nurse pediatrics Clear Lake (Tex.) Hosp., 1973; head nurse Bay Area Pediatric Assocs., Clear Lake City, 1973-78; staff nurse, night charge nurse pediatric intensive care Tex. Children's Hosp., Houston, 1978, unit tchr., pediatric intensive care, 1978-79, charge nurse Jr. League Clinic, 1979-80, asst. nurse mgr. pediatric neurosurgery/neurology, 1980-86, staff devel. coord., 1986-90, asst. dir. nursing, 1990-99; asst. dir. clin. svcs. Tex. Children's Cancer Ctr., Houston, 1999—; clin. instr. pediatrics Houston Bapt. U., 1988—, U. Tex. Health Sci. Ctr. Sch. Nursing, Houston, 1988—; speaker in field. Co-author: Manual of Pediatric Nursing, 1996; contbr. numerous articles to profl. jours. Mem. NAFE, Am. Assn. Neurosci. Nurses (chmn. social activities S.E. Tex. chpt. 1985, membership chmn. 1984), Continuing Edn. League, Health Meeting Planners Houston, Soc. Pediatric Nurses (nat. bd. mem. 1993-95, v.p. 1995-98), Am. Assn. Neurol. Surgeons (assoc.), Epilepsy Assn. (sec., profl. adv. bd., 1995—), Sigma Theta Tau (pres. Eta Phi chpt. 1992-94). Episcopalian. Avocations: summer sports, sewing. Home: 2326 Swift Blvd Houston TX 77030-1117 Office: Tex Children's Hosp 6621 Fannin St Houston TX 77030-2303

BRUCKER, PAUL C., academic administrator, physician. Pres. Thomas Jefferson U., Phila. Office: Thomas Jefferson U Office of President 1020 Walnut St Philadelphia PA 19107-5585

BRUCKER, WILBER MARION, retired lawyer; b. Saginaw, Mich., Apr. 13, 1926; s. Wilber Marion and Clara (Hantel) B.; m. Doris Ann Shover, June 23, 1951; children: Barbara Ann, Wilber Marion, Paul Bradford. Student, Wayne State U., 1943; AB, Princeton U., 1949; JD, U. Mich., 1952. Bar: Mich. 1953. Assoc. Clark, Klein, Brucker & Waples, Detroit, 1952-58; pvt. practice Detroit, 1958-61; ptnr. Brucker & Brucker, Detroit, 1961-67, McInally, Rockwell & Brucker, Detroit, 1968-78, McInally, Brucker, Newcombe, Wilke and DeBona, Detroit, 1978-86; pres. Alliance Fin. Corp., 1986-89; sr. legal counsel Riley and Roumell, Detroit, 1990-96; dir. Bank of Dearborn, Mich., 1970-89, Alliance Fin. Corp., 1982-89; ret.; legal counsel Econ. Club Detroit, 1968-86; arbitrator Am. Arbitration Assn., 1965-79; bd. dirs. Cmty. Bank Dearborn. Bd. govs. Wayne State U., Detroit, 1967-78, chmn. bd. govs., 1972; pres. bd. trustees Arnold Home, 1968-96; mem. Whtanagamote, 1956—, Centurions, 1977-96, Woodworkers, 1991—; mem. bd. canvassers City of Grosse Pointe Farms, Mich., 1972-74; pres. Grosse Pointe Sr. Mens Club, 1998—. Mem. ABA, Mich. Bar Assn., Country Club of Detroit, Masons. Home: 253 Touraine Rd Grosse Pointe MI 48236-3308

BRUCKHEIMER, JERRY, producer; b. Detroit, 1945. Grad., U. Ariz. Former prodr., art dir. advt. agy.; co-founder Don Simpson/Jerry Bruckheimer Films, 1983. Assoc. prodr. (films) Culpepper Cattle Company, 1972, Rafferty and the Gold Dust Twins, 1975; prodr. (films) American Gigolo, 1980, Young Doctors in Love, 1982; (with George Pappas) Farewell My Lovely, 1975; (with Dick Richards) March or Die, 1977; (with William S. Gillmore) Defiance, 1980; (with Ronnie Caan) Thief, 1981, Cat People, 1982; (with Don Simpson) Flashdance, 1983, Beverly Hills Cop, 1984, Thief of Hearts, 1984, Top Gun, 1986, Beverly Hills Cop II, 1987, Days of Thunder, 1990, The Ref, 1994, Bad Boys, 1995, Crimson Tide, 1995, Dangerous Minds, 1995; The Rock, 1996, Con Air, 1997, Armageddon, 1998, Enemy of the State, 1998; exec. prodr. Dangerous Minds-TV, 1996, Soldier of Fortune-TV, 1997, Enemy of the State, 1998, Armageddon, 1998, Max Q, 1998 (TV, exec.), The Rock Star, 1999 (exec.), Swing Vote, 1999 (TV, exec.). Recipient ShoWest award Prodr. of Yr., 1999. Office: Jerry Bruckheimer Films 1631 10th St Santa Monica CA 90404-3705

BRUCK LIEB PORT, LILLY, retired consumer advisor, broadcaster, columnist; b. Vienna, Austria, May 13, 1918; came to U.S., 1941, naturalized, 1944; d. Max and Sophie M. Hahn; m. Sandor Bruck, Mar. 7, 1943; 1 child, Sandra Lee (Mrs. John David Evans III); m. David L. Lieb, Dec. 7, 1985; m. Charles S. Port, Nov. 22, 1998. PhD in Econs., U. Vienna; postgrad., Sorbonne, Paris, Sch. of Econs., London, Sch. of Bus., Columbia U., 1941-42, Sch. of Social Work, NYU, 1964-66. Dir. consumer edn. Dept. Consumer Affairs, City of N.Y., 1969-78; project dir. Am. Coalition of Citizens with Disabilities, 1977-78; consumer advisor, broadcaster In Touch Networks, N.Y.C., 1978-90; consumer affairs commentator Nat. Pub. Radio, 1980-82; ret. Author: Access, The Guide to a Better Life for Disabled Americans, 1978; contbr. articles to disability and rehab. to books, ency. and mag. Presid. Scarsdale Hadassah, 1960-88. Chmn. Westchester county, Bonds for Israel, 1960-64; trustee Kol AMI-JCC, White Plains, N.Y.; assoc. Jewish Mus.; sponsor Lilly Bruck Lieb Creative Writing Program, Purchase Coll., SUNY; mem. pres.'s coun. White Plains (N.Y.) Hosp. Recipient Woman of Yr. award Anti Defamation League, 1972. Democrat. E-mail: lblone@aol.com. Home: 25 Murray Hill Rd Scarsdale NY 10583-2829

BRUCKMANN, DONALD JOHN, investment banker; b. Montclair, N.J., Jan. 4, 1929; s. William A. and Elizabeth M. (Fullmer) B.; m. Mary Thudium, June 1, 1957. B.A., Lafayette Coll., Easton, Pa., 1950; LL.B., Columbia U., 1955. Bar: N.Y. 1955. Assoc. Simpson, Thacher & Bartlett, N.Y.C., to 1960; sr. v.p., dir. Smith Barney, Harris Upham & Co., investment bankers, 1963-73, Dean Witter Reynolds Inc., N.Y.C., 1973-83; pres., chief exec. officer Dean Witter Reynolds Internat. Inc., 1974-83; dir., fin. adviser Bank Audi (USA), N.Y.C., 1986-94, mem. adv. bd., 1995-96; chmn. bd. Animal Med. Ctr., 1996—. Chmn. bd. mgrs. N.Y. Bot. Garden, 1976-86, trustee, 1973—; mem. coun., trustee Cooper-Hewitt Mus., N.Y.C., 1987—, chmn., 1990-93; bd. dirs. Morningside House, N.Y.C., 1960-80; bd. dirs. Pa. Ave. Devel. Corp., Washington, 1973-81, vice chmn., 1973-79; trustee Cen. Park Conservancy, N.Y.C., 1980-93; mem. internat. capital mkts. adv. com. N.Y. Stock Exch., 1980-86; trustee Animal Med. Ctr., N.Y.C., 1990—; v.p., East Hampton Beach Preservation Soc., 1982—, bd. dirs., 1988—; trustee Village Preservation Soc., founding trustee Garden Conservancy, 1989—. 1st lt. U.S. Army, 1950-52. Mem. Assn. of Bar of City of N.Y., Asia Soc. (vice chmn., bd. dirs. 1983-89), Bond Club N.Y.C., Maidstone Club, Knickerbocker Club, Devon Yacht Club. Republican. Address: Lily Pond Ln East Hampton NY 11937

BRUCKNER, LYNNE DICKSON, English educator; b. Oct. 12, 1963; m. Donald Walter Bruckner, Aug. 22, 1998. BA cum laude, Middlebury Coll., 1986; MA, Rutgers U., 1989, PhD, 1997. Asst. prof. English, Chatham Coll., Pitts., 1993—. E-mail: dickson@chatham.edu. Home: 235 Edmond St Pittsburgh PA 15232 Office: Chatham Coll CPO Box 20 Pittsburgh PA 15230-0020

BRUCKNER, MICHAEL STEWART, college official; b. New London, Conn., Sept. 12, 1956; s. Martin and Selma G. Bruckner; m. Jane Stoecker, July 11, 1981; children: Katie Lynn, Jennifer Lee. BA, U. R.I., 1978. Dir. sports info. U. N.H., Durham, 1979-91; account exec. Gehrung Assocs., Keene, N.H., 1991-96; with pub. rels. dept. Muhlenberg Coll., Allentown, Pa., 1996—. Active South Parkland Youth Assn., Allentown, 1996—. Mem. Coun. for Advancement and Support Edn. Avocations: family, sports. E-mail: bruckner@muhlenberg.edu. Office: Muhlenberg Coll 2400 Chew St Allentown PA 18104

BRUCKNER, WILLIAM J., lawyer; b. Atlanta, Mar. 28, 1944; s. William Paul and Ruth (Seibert) B.; m. Lucy Clark, June 27, 1970; children: Heather, Christina. BS, The Citadel, 1966; JD, U. Ga., 1969. Bar: Ga. 1970, S.C. 1982, U.S. Dist. Ct. (no. and mid. dists.) Ga., U.S. Ct. Appeals (5th cir.), U.S. Supreme Ct. Asst. solicitor Solicitor's Office County of Fulton, Atlanta, 1971-73; labor solicitor So. Bell, Atlanta, 1973-82; gen. atty. So. Bell, Columbia, S.C., 1982-83, Atlanta, 1983-86; ops. and litigation counsel BellSouth Enterprises, Atlanta, 1986; assoc. gen. counsel Bell South Enterprises, Atlanta, 1990—; gen. atty. human resources divsn. Bell South Corp., Atlanta, 1986-90, assoc. gen. counsel, 1993—. Mem. Atlanta Soc., 1990—; bd. dirs. Ashford-Dunwoody YMCA, Atlanta, 1986-87, Horizon Theater, Atlanta, 1990—. Capt. U.S. Army, 1970-71. Mem. Atlanta Lawyers Club, Greater Atlanta U. Ga. Club (pres. 1990, trustee Ga. Student Ednl. Fund, chmn. ACCA legal office mgmt. com.), Buckhead Club. Roman Catholic. Avocations: photography, sports. Home: 11315 Bowen Rd Roswell GA 30075-2238 Office: Bell South Corp 1155 Peachtree St NE Ste 1700 Atlanta GA 30309-3610

BRUCKSTEIN, ALEX HARRY, internist, gastroenterologist, geriatrician; b. Germany, Dec. 2, 1949; came to U.S., 1950; s. Jacob and Rose B., m. Dorothy Krausman, Mar. 23, 1973; children: Tammy, Sharon, Sarah, Michael. BS in Chemistry, CCNY, 1971; MD, Albert Einstein Coll. Medicine, 1975. Diplomate Am. Bd. Internal Medicine, Am. Bd. Gastroenterology, Am. Bd. Internal Medicine- Geriatrics. Intern in internal medicine Roosvelt Hosp., N.Y.C.; resident in internal medicine St. Luke's Hosp., N.Y.C.; resident in gastroenterology VA Hosp., N.Y.U., N.Y.C.; pvt. practice internal medicine, gastroenterology Staten Island, N.Y.; hosp. affiliations: Doctors' Hosp. Staten Island, N.Y., Staten Island U. Hosp. N., Staten Island U. Hosp. S., St. Vincent's Hosp., Staten Island; vis. clin. fellow Columbia U. Dept. Medicine, 1975-78, NYU Dept. Medicine, 1978-80; clin. asst. prof. medicine N.Y. Med. Coll., 1983-90, SUNY Health Sci. Ctr. at Bklyn., 1990—. Fellow ACP, Am. Coll. Gastroenterology; mem. AMA, Med. Soc. State N.Y., Richmond County Med. Soc., Am. Gastroent. Assn., N.Y. Soc. Gastrointestinal Endoscopy, N.Y. Acad. Gastroenterology, Am. Geriatrics Assn. Office: 2627 Hylan Blvd Staten Island NY 10306-4339

BRUDER, CHARLES IRWIN, psychologist, researcher; b. N.Y.C., Nov. 10, 1950; s. Samuel Hank and Janet Natalie (Weltman) B.; children: Benjamin, Rachel. BA, U. Rochester, 1972; M in Philosophy, George Washington U., 1978, PhD, 1980. Lic. clin. psychologist, Conn. Dir. psychiatric emergency unit Montgomery Gen. Hosp., Olney, Md., 1974-76; sr. rsch. assoc. George Washington U. Med. Sch., Washington, 1976-77; dir. emergency svcs. Prince William County, Manassas, Va., 1977-80; asst. prof. psychiatry Yale U. Sch. Med., New Haven, 1980-85, asst. clin. prof. psychiatry, 1985-91; pvt. practice New Haven, Madison, Conn., 1980—; disaster mental health specialist ARC, New Haven, 1991—; vice chmn., chmn. quality assurance com. Conn. Disaster Mental Health Svc., New Haven, 1993—; employee asst. cons. ETP, Inc., East Hartford, 1993—; critical incident cons. Value Behavioral Health, Inc., Boston, 1996—. Contbr. articles to profl. jours. Comm. dir. Madison Emergency Preparedness, 1985—; dep. commr. Spl. Olympics World Games, New Haven, 1993-95. Mem. Am. Psychol. Assn., Conn. Psychol. Assn. Democrat. Avocations: high fidelity audio, skiing, sailing, golfing. Office: 45 Trumbull St New Haven CT 06510-1003

BRUDER, GEORGE FREDERICK, lawyer; b. Ann Arbor, Mich., June 4, 1938; s. George G. and Mary Louise (Pfisterer) B.; m. Jean Riley, July 10, 1965; children: Roxanne, Stephanie. AB, Dartmouth Coll., 1960; JD, U. Chgo., 1963. Bar: D.C. 1964. Atty. FPC, Washington, 1964-67; atty. long lines dept. AT&T, Washington, 1967-68; assoc. Debevoise & Liberman, Washington, 1968-70, ptnr, 1971-75; ptnr. Bruder, Gentile & Marcoux, Washington, 1976-97. Mem. Fed. Energy Bar Assn. (pres. 1984-85), ABA. Democrat. Episcopalian. Home: 8 E Lenox St Chevy Chase MD 20815-4211

BRUDER, HAROLD JACOB, artist, educator; b. N.Y.C., Aug. 31, 1930; s. Julius and Della (Wlodinger) B.; m. Anet Sirna, July 15, 1979; 1 child, Dellan; children from previous marriage: David, Shari. Cert., Cooper Union, 1951. Mem. faculty Kansas City Art Inst., 1963-65, Pratt Inst., 1965-66; prof. art Queens Coll., Flushing, N.Y., 1965-95, chmn. art dept., 1982-85, prof. emeritus, 1995—. Artist-in-residence, Aspen, Colo., 1967; One-man shows include, Robert Isaacson Gallery, N.Y.C., 1962, Forum Gallery, N.Y.C., 1968, 69, 72, 76, 79, Durlacher Bros., N.Y.C., 1964, 1967, William and Mary Coll., 1979, Queens Coll., N.Y.C., 1974, Queens Mus., N.Y.C., 1982, Armstrong Gallery, N.Y.C., 1984, 86, Contemporary Realist Gallery, San Francisco, 1988; group exhbns. include, Whitney Mus., 1970, Balt. Mus., 1970, Butler Inst., 1972, Cleve. Mus., 1974, Phila. Mus., 1976, represented in permanent collections, Hirshhorn Mus., Washington, Sheldon Meml. Gallery, Lincoln, Nebr., N.J. State Mus., Trenton; contbr. articles to profl. jours. NEA grantee, 1985. Home: 165 W End Ave Apt 3N New York NY 10023-5505

BRUDER, JUDITH, writer; b. Bklyn., Nov. 6, 1934; d. Harry and Libby Mandell; m. Franklin Bruder, Feb. 28, 1960; children: Jane Kennedy, John Bruder. BA with honors, Wellesley Coll., 1956; MA, L.I. U., 1973. Assoc. editor Merrill Lynch, N.Y.C., 1956-62; campus min. Fordham at Lincoln Ctr., N.Y.C., 1989-97; adj. instr. SUNY, Stony Brook, 1975-79. Author: Going to Jerusalem, 1979, Convergence, 1993; contbr. articles to profl. publs. Creative fellow AAUW, 1979. Mem. Jane Austen Soc. (life), Friends of Uther Pendragon (co-founder). Avocations: reading, traveling. E-mail: jbruder1@earthlink.net. Home: 132 Wagon Rd Roslyn Heights NY 11577

BRUDNER, HARVEY JEROME, physicist; b. N.Y.C., May 29, 1931; s. Joseph and Anna (Fiddelman) B.; m. Helen Gross, Dec. 18, 1963; children: Mae Ann, Terry Joseph, Jay Scott. BS in Engring. and Physics, NYU, 1952, MS, 1954, PhD, 1959; postgrad., U. Md., 1954-56, CCNY, 1958, Columbia U., 1959-61. Electronics engr. Bendix Corp., Teterboro, N.J., 1952; physicist U.S. Naval Ordnance Lab., White Oak, Md., 1953-54; sr. physicist Emerson Rsch. Labs., Washington, 1954-57; prin. physicist Emerson Radio, Jersey City, 1957-61; rsch. assoc. NYU Inst. Math. Scis., N.Y.C., 1957-60; guest scientist Rockefeller Inst. for Med. Rsch., N.Y.C., 1960-61; sr. rsch. assoc. Am. Can Co., Princeton (N.J.) Lab., 1964-67; v.p. R & D Westinghouse Learning Corp., N.Y.C., 1967-71; pres. Westinghouse Learning Corp., 1971-76; also dir.; mem. adminstrv. com. Westinghouse Electric Corp., Pitts., 1971-76; pres. Westinghouse Electric Corp. (Westinghouse Learning Group), 1971-76, H.J.B. Enterprises, N.Y.C., 1961—, Med. Devel., Inc., N.Y.C., 1962; dir. Ideal Sch. Supply Corp., Ednl. Products, Inc., Document Reading Svcs., Ltd., Linguaphone Inst. Ltd., Info. Synergy, Inc., Cambridge Learning Connection, Inc.; chmn. new devels. com. Project Aristotle; acting dir. Gottscho Info. Center, Coll. Engring., Rutgers U.; prof. math., physics, dean sci. and tech. N.Y. Inst. Tech., 1962-64; instr. atomic physics N.Y. U., 1953-54; cons. Nat. Inst. Edn., Mass. Inst. Tech., Rutgers U., Worcester Poly. Inst., Poly. Inst. N.Y., Nat. Inst. Community Devel., U.S. Ho. of Reps. Com. on Sci. and Tech.; mem. adv. com. Middlesex County Coll., 1966—, Paterson State Coll., 1975; mem. exec. planning com. tng. adv. sect. Nat. Security Indsl. Assn., 1966; nat. adv. bd. Am. Coll. in Jerusalem; dir. computers in edn. study Nat. Inst. Edn., 1979; bd. dirs. World Learning and Communications, 1978—. Editl. commentator Another Opinion, Sta. WCBS, N.Y.C., N.Y. Power Authority; author: Semiconductor Physics, 1954, College Technical Mathematics, 1967, On Fermat's Last Theorem, 1979, Fermat and The Missing Numbers, 1994; columnist Light-On Series: Ednl. Tech. Mag., Source Data: Datamation Mag.; chmn. editl. adv. bd. Tech. Horizons in Edn. Jour.; contbr. rsch. articles on atomic physics, radar, ednl., med., energy, electronic sys., biol. effects of radiation, laser tech., others, to various publs. Mem. steering com. Project PROCEED, NSF, Mcpl. Alliance Com., Highland Park, 1990—; capt. long-range planning com. Highland Park Sch. Bd.; trustee Ross Hall Heights Assn., 1966; chmn. Joyce Kilmer Authority, New Brunswick, N.J., 1985—, Joyce Kilmer Centennial Commn., Inc., 1986—; coord. WABC-TV News, N.Y.C., Joyce Kilmer Trees, 1994; coord. program Fermat and Babylonian Rectangles, Sta. WCTC, 1994; apptd. to Mcpl. Alliance Against Drugs and Alcohol, 1990-99, Middlesex County Mcpl. Alliance Network, 1995—; coord. Project DATE (Drugs, Alcohol, Tobacco, Education), Rutgers U. N.J. Forum, 1995—. Recipient Cert. Americanism Vets. Alliance of Raritan Valley, 1992, Kiwanis Internat. award 1993; Raritan-Millstone Heritage Alliance, 1998; named Knight, Order of the Swan, 1996. Fellow IEEE (life, adminstrn. com., solar standards com., photovoltaic subcom.), mem., Am. Phys. Soc., Soc. Motion Picture and TV Engrs., Internat. Fedn. Med. Electronics, AAAS, Electronic Industries Assn. (edn. com.), Am. Ednl. Research Assn., Adult Edn. Assn. U.S.A., N.Y. Acad. Scis., Am. Mgmt. Assn. (ednl. adv. com.), Math. Assn. Am., Am. Soc. Tng. and Devel., Council Ams., Am. Judicature Soc., Am. Math. Soc., Am. Soc. Curriculum Devel., Knight, Order of the Swan, Sigma Xi, Sigma Pi Sigma, Tau Beta Pi. Clubs: Chemists (N.Y.C.); N.Y. Univ., The Midtown Exec. and Chemists' Club, N.Y.C., Toastmasters. Home: 812 Abbott St Highland Park NJ 08904-2909 *I have tried: to play a constructive part in permitting others to make a positive contribution to society; to achieve a proper mix of idealism, reason, and faith in my decision making; to apply science and technology for the betterment of humanity.*

BRUDNER, HELEN GROSS, social sciences educator; b. N.Y.C.; d. Nathan and Mae (Grichtman) Gross; m. Harvey Jerome Brudner, Dec. 18, 1963; children: Mae Ann, Terry Joseph, Jay Scott. BS, NYU, 1959, MA, 1960, PhD, 1973. Tchr. N.Y.C. Bd. Edn., 1959-60; instr. Pratt Inst., Bklyn., 1959-61; asst. prof. history N.Y. Inst. Tech., N.Y.C., 1961-63, dir. guidance, 1962-63; assoc. prof. Fairleigh Dickinson U., Rutherford, N.J., 1963-73; prof. history and polit. sci. Fairleigh Dickinson U., Teaneck, N.J., 1974—; dir. Honors Coll. Fairleigh Dickinson U., Rutherford, N.J., 1972-84, chmn. dept. social sci., 1980-88, pres. univ. senate, 1975-78, asst. provost, 1983—, dean, 1984, dir. grad. programs, assoc. dir. Sch. Polit. Studies, 1995—, internat. studies dir. lang. grad. studies, pres. acad. senate, 1996—; v.p. HJB Enterprises, Highland Park, N.J., 1970—; vice chmn. bd. dirs. WLC Inc., Highland Park, 1990—; cons. auto ednl. systems, 1971—; participant bd. trustees F.D.U. Contbr. articles to profl. jours. on constl. law, transfer of tech., futurism. Active women in politics project NSF, 1981; active consortium project women in Am. history NEH and Woodrow Wilson Found., 1980, Consortium on Global Interdependence, Princeton, 1984; bd. dirs. Options Spkrs. Bur., N.J. Credit Union League, N.J. Credit Union Shared Network, WLC Inc.; mem. Mcpl. Alliance Highland Park, Hist. Preservation Commn., Highland Park; chmn. bd. dirs. Fairleigh Dickinson U. Fed. Credit Union, 1987—; mem. N.J. Gov.'s Com. on Women Vets., 1993—; design selection com. N.J. Korean Vets. Meml. Recipient Woman of Yr. award Am. Businesswomen's Assn., 1980, Meritorious Svc. award N.J. Credit Union League, 1997. Mem. Am. Judicature Soc., Am. Hist. Soc., Acad. Polit. Sci., Phi Alpha Theta, Phi Sigma Alpha. Office: Fairleigh Dickinson U Sch Polit Internat Studies Dept History And Sci Teaneck NJ 07666

BRUDVIG, GLENN LOWELL, retired library director; b. Kenosha, Wis., Oct. 14, 1931; s. Lars L. Brudvig and Anna Elizabeth (Hillesland) B. Lovejoy; m. Myrna Winifred Michael, Oct. 1, 1953; children—Gary Wayne, Lee Anthony, James Lowell, Kristin Elizabeth. BA in Edn., U. N.D., 1954, MA, 1956; MALS, U. Minn., 1962. Tchr. pub. schs. Mahnomen and Herman, Minn., 1954-55, 56-58; librarian, archivist U. N.D., Grand Forks, 1958-62; asst. librarian U. N.D., 1962-63; supr. dept. libraries U. Minn., Mpls., 1964; dir. bio-med. libr. U. Minn., 1964-83; dir. librs. Calif. Inst. Tech., Pasadena, 1983-95, ret., 1995; instr. library sci. U. N.D., Grand Forks, 1962-63; asst. dir. for research and devel. U. Minn., Mpls., 1968-79, instr. library sci., 1968-71, dir. Inst. Tech. Libraries, 1982-83; cons. Nat. Library of Medicine, Bethesda, Md., 1971-75. Contbr. articles to profl. jours. Served with U.S. Army, 1951-52. Nat. Library of Medicine grantee, 1967-79. Home: 15 Eagle Ridge Rd Saint Paul MN 55127-6411

BRUDVIG, JON LARSEN, educator, historian; b. Kenosha, Wis., Mar. 6, 1965; s. Manley Hale and Mary Ann Brudvig; m. Sandra Jean Swift, Oct. 10, 1987. BA, Marquette U., 1987, MA, 1989; PhD, Coll. of William and Mary, 1996. Instr. Thomas Nelson C.C., Hampton, Va., 1992-96; asst. prof. St. Leo Coll., Langley AFB, Va., 1994-96, U. Mary, Bismarck, N.D., 1996—. Contbr. articles to profl. jours. Vol. ARC, Fort Eustis, Va., 1994-96, State Hist. Soc., Bismarck, N.D., 1996-98. Va. Commonwealth fellow State Coun. of Higher Edn., 1993-94, rsch. fellowship Commonwealth Ctr., 1992-93; Bicknell scholarship Nat. Sons and Daus. of the Pilgrims, 1991-92. Mem. SAR, Hist. Soc., Loyal Order of Moose, Elks, Phi Beta Kappa. Roman Catholic. Avocations: fishing, running. E-mail: jlbrud@umary.edu. Office: U of Mary 7500 University Dr Bismarck ND 58504

BRUECHERT, BEVERLY ANN, interior design consultant, recording artist, pianist; b. Oregon City, Oreg., May 3, 1960; d. Robert Wayne and Bonnie Helen (Troutner) B. BS in Applied Design with honors, Portland State U., 1986. Sales exec. iin interior furnishing MW End Store, Portland, Oreg.; fabric designer Daisy Kingdom, Portland; sales exec. in design firm Chase Internat., Portland; music dir. Waverly United Ch. of Christ, Portland; asst. music dir. Sunset Presbyn. Ch., Portland. Recorded album/CD, Twilight, a solo piano experience, 1994; vocal and piano compositions; featured artist KINK Radio, Lights Out VI album, Oreg. Food Bank benefit, 1997; rec. album/CD Daybreak, 1999. Mem. Fashion Group Internat. Republican. Christian. Avocations: music, sports, travel, sewing. Home: 6645 W Burnside Rd Apt 524 Portland OR 97210-6645

BRUECKNER, LAWRENCE TERENCE, orthopedic surgeon; b. Casper, Wyo., Jan. 24, 1945; s. Lawrence W. and Jayne Anne (Dennis) B.; m. Mary Ellen Coleman, May 11, 1974; children: Ellen, Amanda, Chris. MD, Creighton U., 1970. Diplomate Am. Bd. Orthop. Surgery. Intern S.I. Hosp., N.Y.C., 1974-77; resident Hosp. for Joint Disease, N.Y.C., 1977; orthop. surgeon Gwinnett Orthop. Ctr., Snellville, Ga., 1977—. Capt. U.S. Army, 1971-73. Fellow Am. Acad. Orthop. Surgeons; mem. AMA, Med. Assn. Ga., Atlanta Orthop. Soc., Orthop. Rsch. and Edn. Found., Alpha Omega Alpha. Office: Gwinnett Orthop Ctr 2121 Fountain Dr Ste E Snellville GA 30078-2900

BRUEMMER, FRED, writer, photographer; b. Riga, Latvia, June 26, 1929; emigrated to Can., 1951, naturalized, 1956; s. Arist and Dorothea (Wahl)

B.; m. Maud van den Berg, Mar. 31, 1962; children: Aurel, Rene. Student Fed. Republic Germany schs.; DLitt (hon.), U. N.B., Can., 1989. Self-employed writer-photographer specializing in arctic and antarctic regions, 1961—; books include The Long Hunt, 1969, Seasons of the Eskimo, 1971, Encounters with Arctic Animals, 1972, The Arctic, 1974, The Life of the Harp Seal, 1977, Children of the North, 1979, Summer at Bear River, 1980, The Arctic of the World, 1985, Arctic Animals, 1986, Seasons of the Seal, 1988, World of the Polar Bear, 1989, (with Eric S. Grace) Seals, 1991, The Narwhal, 1993, (with Angèle Delaunois), Les Animaux du Grand Nord, 1993, (with Karen Pandell) Land of Dark, Land of Light, 1993, Arctic Memoires: Living with the Inuit, 1993, (with Angèle Delaunois) Nanook and Naoya: The Polar Bear Cubs, 1995, Kotik: The Baby Seal, 1995, (with Thomas D. Mangelsen) Polar Dance, 1996, Seals in the Wild, 1998. Decorated Order of Can.; Recipient Queen Elizabeth II Silver Jubilee medal, 1978, Canadian Anniversary Commemorative medal, 1993. Fellow Arctic Inst. N.Am., Royal Can. Acad. Art, Travel Journalists Guild. Address: 2 Strathearn South, Montreal West, Montreal, PQ Canada H4X 1X4

BRUEMMER, LORRAINE VENSKUNAS, funeral director, real estate broker, nurse; b. Waterbury, Conn., Jan. 25; d. Anthony George and Mary Agnes (Kritchman) Venskunas; m. Jay Porter Bruemmer, Oct. 28, 1973; 1 child by previous marriage: Linda L. Rocco Sovak. R.N., St. Francis Hosp. Sch. Nursing, 1950; B.S., Columbia U., 1958; M.Ed., U. Hartford, 1961. Head nurse pediatrics Cook Hosp., Hartford, Conn., 1953-56; instr. pediatrics Bellevue Hosp., N.Y.C., 1958-59; instr. med. surg. nursing New Britain Gen. Hosp., 1959-62; hosp. supr. New Britain Gen. Hosp., 1962-63; owner Venskunas Funeral Home, New Britain, 1962—; owner Bruemmer Venskunas Real Estate, New Britain, 1974—, Stanley Monumental Co., 1993—; commr. New Britain Health Dept., 1965-74; nurse blood bank ARC, N.Y.C., 1957-59, New Britain, 1960-69. Vol. Republican Party, New Britain. Mem. New Britain Funeral Dis. Assn. (pres. 1975-78), Conn. Funeral Dirs., Nat. Funeral Dirs., New Britain Bd. Realtors, Hartford Bd. Realtors, Nat. Bd. Realtors, Multiple Listing Service Greater Hartford. Roman Catholic. Clubs: Ladies Guild (pres. 1969), Shuttle Meadow Country. Avocations: antiques; golf; tennis; swimming; bicycling; gardening. Home: 36 Roslyn Dr New Britain CT 06052-1824 Office: Venskunas Funeral Home 665 Stanley St Ste 1612 New Britain CT 06051-2736

BRUEN, JAMES A., lawyer; b. South Hampton, N.Y., Nov. 29, 1943; s. John Francis and Kathryn Jewell (Arthur) B.; m. Carol Lynn Heller, June 13, 1968; children: Jennifer Lynn, Garrett John. BA cum laude, Claremont Men's Coll., 1965; JD, Stanford U., 1968. Bar: Calif. 1968, U.S. Dist. Ct. (no., ea., so. and cen. dists.) Calif. 1970, U.S. Ct. Claims 1972, U.S. Tax Ct. 1972, U.S. Ct. Appeals (9th cir.) 1972, U.S. Supreme Ct. 1973, Ariz. 1993. Atty. FCC, Washington, 1968-70; asst. U.S. atty. criminal div. Office of US. Atty., San Francisco, 1970-73, asst. U.S. atty. civil div., 1973-75, chief of civil div., 1975-77; ptnr. Landels, Ripley & Diamond, San Francisco, 1977—; mem. faculty Nat. Jud. Coll. ABA; lectr. Am. Law Inst. Am. Bd. Trial Advocates, Practising Law Inst. Def. Rsch. Inst., others. Co-author: Pharmaceutical Products Liability, 1989; contbg. editor: Hazardous Waste and Toxic Torts Law and Strategy, 1987-92; contbr. numerous articles to profl. jours. Mem. ABA (vice chmn. environ. quality com. nat. resources sect. 1989-93, co-chmn. enforment litigation subcom. environ. litigation com. litigation sect. 1990-92), Am. Inn of Ct. (master-at-large), Internat. Soc. for Environ. Epidemiology. Avocations: scuba diving, travel. Office: Landels Ripley & Diamond 350 The Embarcadero San Francisco CA 94105-1250

BRUEN, JOHN DERMOT, business management consultant; b. Glen Cove, N.Y., Oct. 19, 1930; s. John D. and Kathleen M. (Halferty) B.; m. Ann Theone Lee, June 22, 1957; children: Michael J., Kathleen A., Thomas L., Lisa M. B.S. in Mil. Sci, U. Md., 1959; MBA, U. Pitts., 1963; grad., Naval War Coll. Command and Staff Course, 1966, Army War Coll., 1972. Enlisted in U.S. Army, 1948, commd. 2d lt., 1953, advanced through grades to lt. gen., 1983; service in Korea, Germany, Azores, Thailand and Vietnam; dir. resources and mgmt. Office Dep. Chief Staff Logistics, 1977-79; comdr. Mil. Traffic Mgmt. Command Washington, 1979-83; comdr. 21st Support Command Europe, 1983-86; ret., 1986; pres. Bruen & Assocs., Springfield, Va., 1986—; vice chmn. internat. US CALS Industry Steering Group, 1991-95; hon. col. US Army Transp. Corps Regiments, 1997—. Contbr. articles on leadership, mgmt. to profl. jours. Decorated Def. D.S.M., Army D.S.M., Legion of Merit with two oak leaf clusters, Bronze Star with one oak leaf cluster, Meritorious Svc. medal with one oak leaf cluster, Army Commendation medal with one oak leaf cluster; named to U.S. Inf. Hall of Fame, 1979; named Grand Officer of the Order of the Crown, Belgium, 1986. Mem. OCS, U.S. Army Transp. Corps Assn. (pres. 1997—), Nat. Def. Transp. Assn., Assn. U.S. Army, The Retired Officer's Assn. (bd. dirs.). Roman Catholic. Office: 6104 Greenlawn Ct Springfield VA 22152-1314

BRUENE, WARREN BENZ, electronic engineer; b. Beaman, Iowa, Nov. 1, 1916; s. Fred Karl and Luella Lydia (Benz) B.; m. Mildred Clare Meyer, July 13, 1941; children: Julia Beth Bruene Thomas, Jo Carol Bruene Lilley. BSEE, Iowa State U., 1938. Registered profl. engr., Tex. Design engr. Collins Radio Co., Cedar Rapids, Iowa, 1939-46, project engr., 1946-54, group head, 1954-57, dept. staff, 1957-60, dept. head, 1960-61, div. staff, Richardson, Tex., 1961-73; div. staff Rockwell Internat., Richardson, 1973-84; sr. engr. Electrospace Systems, Inc., Richardson, 1984-90; pvt. practice radio engrng. cons. Dallas, 1990—; vis. com. U. Tex., Austin, 1966-72. Co-author 7 tech. books; contbr. articles to profl. jours. Inventor 22 patents. Named Engr. of Yr., Preston Trail chpt. Tex. Soc. Profl. Engrs., 1975, profl. achievement citation in engrng. Iowa State U., 1993. Fellow IEEE (sect. chmn. 1958-59, region dir. 1962-63), Toastmasters (Richardson) (area gov. 1969). Republican. Methodist. Avocations: economics, amateur radio, technical writing. Home: 7805 Chattington Dr Dallas TX 75248-5307

BRUENER, JAMES WILLIAM, fundraiser; b. Port Edwards, Wis., July 4, 1950; s. William John and Dorothy Anne (Lobner) B.; life ptnr. Clifford Goltz, Aug. 1, 1992. BA, U. Minn., 1972. Fundraiser Friends for a Non-Violent World, Mpls., 1992—. Mem. Soc. of Friends. Avocations: theater, symphonic performances, opera, art museums. Home: 1179 Edmund Ave Saint Paul MN 55104-2523

BRUENING, GEORGE E., virologist; b. Chgo., Aug. 10, 1938. Diploma, Carroll Coll., 1960; MS, U. Wis., 1963, PhD in Biochemistry, 1965. Guggenheim Meml. Found. fellow, 1974-75; prof. U. Calif., Davis; vis. scientist plant path., Cornell U., Ithaca, N.Y., 1974-75, vis. scientist biochemistry, U. Adelaide, Australia, 1981; vis. scientist plant indsl. CSIRO, Canberra, Australia, 1989. Fellow Am. Phytopath Soc.; mem. Nat. Acad. Sci., Am. Soc. Biochem. and Molecular Biology, Soc. Microbiol. UK, AAAS. Office: Dept Plant Pathology U Calif Davis Davis CA 95616*

BRUENING, RICHARD P(ATRICK), lawyer; b. Kansas City, Mo., Mar. 17, 1939; s. Arthur Louis, Jr. and Lorraine Elizabeth (Gamble) B.; m. Jane Marie Egender, Aug. 25, 1962; children—Christiana G., Paul R., Erin E. AB, Rockhurst Coll., 1960; JD, U. Mo. at Kansas City, 1963. Bar: Mo. bar 1963. Since practiced in Kansas City; law clk. U.S. Dist. Judge R.M., Duncan, 1963-65; assoc. firm Houts, James, McCanse & Larison, 1965-68; gen. atty. Kansas City So. Ry. Co., 1969; asst. gen. counsel Kansas City So. Industries, Inc., 1970-76, gen. counsel, 1976-82, v.p., gen. counsel, 1982—, sr. v.p., gen. counsel Transp. Group, 1992—; bd. dirs. Kansas City So. Ry. Co.; mem. Mo. Press-Bar Commn., 1981-85, Mo. Rail Improvement Authority, 1984-86, chmn., 1984-85; mem. bd. commrs. Port Authority Kansas City, 1995-98; mem. Mo. Total Transp. Commn., 1997—. Bd. dirs. Friends of Zoo, Inc., 1987-98, Heart of Am. Shakespeare Festival, 1995—, Performing Arts Found./Folly Theatre, 1983-90, sec., 1984-90; exec. com., bd. trustees Conservatory Music, U. Mo., Kansas City. Mem. ABA, Mo. Bar Assn., Kansas City Bar Assn., Lawyers Assn. Kansas City, Nat. Assn. R.R. Trial Counsel (exec. com.), Practising Law Inst., Kansas City Country Club, Kansas City Club, The River Club, Phi Delta Phi, Omicron Delta Kappa. Roman Catholic. Home: 606 W Meyer Blvd Kansas City MO 64113-1544 Office: Kans City So Industries Inc 114 W 11th St Kansas City MO 64105-1804

BRUES, ALICE MOSSIE, physical anthropologist, educator; b. Boston, Oct. 9, 1913; d. Charles Thomas and Beirne (Barrett) B. A.B., Bryn Mawr Coll., 1933; Ph.D., Radcliffe Coll., 1940. Faculty U. Okla. Sch. Medicine, 1946-65, prof., 1960-65; vis. prof. anthropology U. Colo., Boulder, 1965-66; prof. U. Colo., 1966—, chmn. dept. anthropology, 1969-71. Asso. editor: Am. Jour. Phys. Anthropology, 1962-66; Author: People and Races, 1977, contbr. articles to profl. jours. Mem. Am. Assn. Phys. Anthropologists (v.p. 1966-68, pres. 1971-73), Soc. Study Evolution, Am. Acad. Forensic Scis., Soc. Naturalists, Sigma Xi. Home: 4325 Prado Dr Boulder CO 80303-9629

BRUESCHKE, ERICH EDWARD, physician, researcher, educator; b. nr. Eagle Butte, S.D., July 17, 1933; s. Erich Herman and Eva Johanna (Joens) B.; m. Frances Marie Bryan, Mar. 25, 1967; children: Erich Raymond, Jason Douglas, Tina Marie, Patricia Frances, Susan Eva. B.S. in Elec. Engring, S.D. Sch. Mines and Tech., 1956; postgrad., U. So. Calif., 1960-61; M.D., Temple U., 1965. Diplomate Am. Bd. Family Practice, also cert. in geriatrics. Intern Germantown Dispensary and Hosp., Phila., 1965-66; mem. tech. staff Hughes Research and Devel. Labs., Culver City, Calif., 1956-61; practiced gen. medicine Fullerton, Calif., 1968-69; dir. research Ill. Inst. Tech. Research Inst., Chgo., 1970-76; research asst. prof. Temple U. Sch. Medicine, 1965-69; mem. staff Mercy Hosp. and Med. Center, Chgo., 1970-76; vis. prof. Rush Med. Coll., Chgo., 1974-76, prof., chmn. dept. family practice, 1976—, program dir. Rush. Christ family practice residency, 1978-93, vice dean, 1992—, acting dean, 1993-94; dean, 1994—; trustee Anchor HMO, 1976—, v.p. med. and acad. affairs, 1981—; trustee Synergon Health Systems, 1993—; vice chmn., bd. dirs. Rush Presbyn. St. Lukes Health Assocs.; sr. attending Presbyn.-St. Luke's Hosp., Chgo., 1976—; med. dir. Chgo. Bd. of Health West Side Hypertension Center, 1974-78; Bd. dirs. Comprehensive Health Planning Met. Chgo., 1971-74. Assoc. editor Primary Cardiology, 1979-85; cons. editor for family practice Hosp. Medicine, 1986—; med. editor World Book/Rush Presbyn. St. Lukes/Med. Ency., 1987—; contbr. articles to profl. jours. Served with USAF, 1966-68. Named Physician Tchr. of Yr. Ill. Acad. Family Physicians, 1988, alumni of yr. Temple U. Sch. Medicine, 1996. Fellow Am. Acad. Family Physicians, Inst. of Medicine of Chgo.; mem. IEEE (chmn. Chgo. sect. Engrng. in Medicine and Biology group 1974-75), Internat. Soc. for Artificial Internal Organs, Am. Fertility Soc., Am. Occupational Med. Assn. (recipient Physician's recognition award 1969, 72, 75), Chgo. Med. Soc., Am. Heart Assn., Assn. for Advancement Med. Instrumentation, N.Y. Acad. Scis., Sigma Xi, Phi Rho Sigma, Eta Kappa Nu, Alpha Omega Alpha. Home: 319 N Lincoln St Hinsdale IL 60521-3442 Office: Rush Medical College of Rush Univ 600 S Paulina St Chicago IL 60612-3806 *It is important to be courageous and do what you really want to do rather than what is expected or what seems to be currently popular. If life is approached with a spirit of goodwill and one is strong enough to follow one's own desires, then the contribution made and the success achieved can be a credit to humanity and also a source of endless enjoyment. The real secret of life is self-discipline; this allows the tempering of short-term needs with the necessary long-term planning to achieve a stable life and a meaningful contribution to humankind.*

BRUESEKE, HAROLD EDWARD, magistrate; b. Sandusky, Ohio, Mar. 19, 1943; s. Edward W. and Jolanda (Sommer) B.; m. Bonnie A. Beaver, Aug. 12, 1967; children: Matthew E., Michael A. BA with honors, Elmhurst Coll., 1965; JD, Ind. U., 1968. Bar: Ind., 1968, U.S. Dist. Ct. (no. and so. dists.) 1968, U.S. Supreme Ct. 1978; lic. real estate broker, Ind. Staff atty. Legal Svcs./Legal Edn., South Bend, Ind., 1968-70; pvt. practice South Bend, 1971-92; dep. pros. atty. St. Joseph County, South Bend, 1971-73; juvenile referee St. Joseph Probate Ct., South Bend, 1973-92, judge pro tem, 1993, magistrate, 1993—. Contbg. author: Juvenile Benchbook, 1980-92. Bd. dirs. Eden Theol. Sem., St. Louis, 1989—, various other civic orgns., South Bend, 1968—; bd. dirs., elder Zion United Ch. of Christ, South Bend, 1994-96. Mem. ABA, Ind. State Bar Assn., St. Joseph County Bar Assn., Nat. Coun. Juvenile and Family Ct. Judges, Ind. Coun. Juvenile and Family Ct. Judges (bd. dirs., sec., v.p. pres. 1980—), Judicial Conf. Ind. (dir. 1998—). Avocations: amateur radio, recreational vehicles, computers. Home: 52741 Arbor Dr South Bend IN 46635-1205 Office: Juvenile Justice Ctr 1000 S Michigan St South Bend IN 46601-3426

BRUESKE, CHARLOTTE, poet, composer; b. Plainview Township, Minn., Jan. 1, 1934; d. Layton Floyd and Berneta Dallas (Thompson) B. AA, Pasadena City Coll., 1976; BA, Calif. State U., Fullerton, 1984; postgrad., Fuller Theol. Sem. Author: Once in a Coon's Age, 1989, The Ancestors of Gottlob August Bruss and Bertha Pauline Goede, 1989, A Search for the Records of the Orphans of Dannan, 1990; composer, lyricist numerous works, including Evergreen, 1990, Every New Day, 1991, Lift Up One Another, 1991, Where the Red Ferns Abound, 1995, To Touch This World by Love, 1996, Because of Love, 1997, Poems of the Seasons, To Every Life, 1998; co-author: (with J'hana Brueske) I Heard a Robin Sing Today, 1997, Consider the Lilies, 1997, Life Friend, 1998, Where Love Abides, 1998. Recipient Cert. of Merit Virginia Baldwin/Talent Assocs., 1977. Democrat. Presbyterian. Home: 260 Streamwood Irvine CA 92620-1966

BRUESS, CHARLES EDWARD, lawyer; b. St. Paul, Oct. 15, 1938; s. Edward Charles and Eleanor Mabel (Hammersten) B.; m. Jean Ellen Gustafson, Aug. 26, 1962; children: Steven Charles, Karen Jean. BA, U. Minn., 1959; student, Ohio U., 1959-60; JD, Ind. U., 1963. Bar: Ind. 1963, U.S. Dist. Ct. (so. dist.) Ind. 1968, U.S. Supreme Ct. 1966. Assoc. Barnes, Hickam, Pantzer & Boyd, Indpls., 1967-71; ptnr. Barnes & Thornburg (formerly Barnes, Hickam, Pantzer & Boyd), Indpls., 1972-94, of counsel, 1995-96, ret., 1996; dep. clk. U.S. Dist. Ct. (so. dist.) Ind., 1999—. Trustee Eagle-Union Community Sch. Corp., Zionsville, Ind., 1978-90; dir. Tri-County Ctr. Inc., 1991-94, dir., sec. Zionsville Pub. Libr., Leasing Corp., 1992—; bd. dirs. Hussey-Mayfield Meml. Pub. Libr. Found., 1999—. Fellow Ind. Bar Found.; mem. Ind. Bar Assn., Lawyers Club (Indpls.). Republican. Methodist. Home: 720 Pineview Dr Zionsville IN 46077-9326

BRUETT, KAREN DIESL, sales and fundraising consultant; b. N.Y.C., May 15, 1945; d. Francis J. and Dorothy (Peterson) Diesl; m. William H. Bruett, Jr., Mar. 18, 1967; 1 child, Lindsey Diesl. BA in English, St. Lawrence U., 1966; MA, Hunter Coll., 1971. Tchr. English Freeport (N.Y.) pub. schs., 1966-70; exec. interviewer, researcher Louis Harris & Assocs., N.Y.C., 1970-72; dir. adult edn. West Side YMCA, 1972-76, mem. bd. mgrs., 1978-83; v.p. new bus. devel. Gaylord Adams & Assocs., Inc., N.Y.C., 1976-81; account exec. John Blair Mktg., N.Y.C., 1981-83, v.p. sales, 1983-84, sr. v.p., gen. sales mgr., 1984-86; ind. sales and fundraising cons.; bd. dirs. Resolution, Inc., S. Burlington, Vt., Kendall Mktg. Assocs., Inc., Cambridge, Mass. Trustee St. Lawrence U., 1978-99, vice-chair trustees, 1995—, chair alumni fund, 1983-84, chair annual giving, 1984-88, chair planning com., 1987-88, chair presidential search com., 1994-95, mem. exec. com., 1987—, chair devel. com., 1988-95; trustee Vt. Coun. on Arts, 1986-91, vice-chair bd. trustees, chair devel. com., 1988-91; bd. advisors Somerset Hills Edn. Found., 1997—; del. Am.-Soviet Youth Forum, Baku, USSR, 1974. Mem. Internat. Women's Forum, 1991—. Home and Office: 110 Mosle Rd Far Hills NJ 07931-2229

BRUFF, BEVERLY OLIVE, public relations consultant; b. San Antonio, Dec. 15, 1926; d. Albert Griffith and Hazel Olive (Smith) B. BA, Tulane U., 1948; postgrad., Our Lady of Lake Coll., 1956, Okla. Ctr. for Continuing Edn., 1960-70. Asst. dir. New Orleans Theatre Guild, 1948-50; dist. dir. San Antonio Area coun. Girl Scouts U.S.A., 1958-70, pub. rels. dir., 1970-83; freelance pub. rels., San Antonio, 1983—; mem. Coun. of Pres., v.p., 1981-82, 84-86; mem. Coun. of Internat. Rels. Zoning commr. Hill Country Village, Tex., 1973-76, 83-85, 88—; councilwoman Hill Country Village, 1985-88; bd. dirs. Animal Def. League, Camp Fire, Inc. Mem. Pub. Rels. Soc. Am., Woman in Comm. (historian 1969-70, v.p. 1970-71, treas. 1971-73), Nat. Fedn. Press Women, Am. Women in Radio and TV (chpt. bd. dirs. 1974, sec. 1975, pres. 1979-80), Internat. Assn. Bus. Communicators, Tex. Pub. Rels. Assn. (Silver Spur award), Tex. Press Women (exec. bd. dirs. 1970-71, 73-74, dist. treas. 1972-73, dist. v.p. 1972-73, state writing contest awards 1971-74), Speech Arts San Antonio (pres. 1964-66, 70-72, 84-86, bd. dirs. 1964-72, 88—, chmn. bd. dirs. 1966-69), San Antonio Soc. Fund Raising Execs. Home: 508 Tomahawk Trail San Antonio TX 78232-3620

BRUGGEMAN, TERRANCE JOHN, financial corporate executive; b. Mandan, N.D., Oct. 20, 1946; s. George Edward and Marcella Merle (Gray) B.; m. Nancy Ellen Hohman, June 28, 1969; children: Todd M., Megan P. B.A., U. Notre Dame, 1968; postgrad. bus. adminstrn., U. Chgo., 1968-70. Div. mgr., v.p. Continental Ill. Nat. Bank, Chgo., 1968-77; asst. treas. Gould Inc., Rolling Meadows, Ill., 1977-78, treas., 1978-80, v.p., treas., 1980-81; chmn. Gould Fin. Inc., Rolling Meadows, 1978-81; v.p. fin. and adminstrn. AM Internat., Inc., Chgo., 1981-85; mng. dir. Dean Witter Reynolds, Inc., 1985-86; sr. mng. dir. Bear, Stearns and Co., Inc., N.Y.C., 1986-89; sr. v.p., bd. mem., chief ops. officer Lear Siegler Inc., Livingston, N.J., 1989-90; sr. v.p., bd. dirs., chief fin. officer chief ops. officer Grimes Aerospace and FL Industries, Livingston, 1989-90; mng. ptnr. Three Cities Rsch., Inc., N.Y.C., 1990-93; chmn., pres. and CEO Network Mgmt. Inc., Fairfax, Va., 1993-97; chmn., CEO Piatl Holdings Inc., Mt. Laurel, N.J., 1993—; chmn., pres., CEO Syscon Corp., Falls Church, Va., 1995-96; chmn., CEO Norcross Safety Products, Oak Brook, Ill., 1996, Red Ball Inc., Louisville, 1996, So. Cross O'Fallon Bldg. Products, St. Louis, 1996, Red Giraffe, Louisville, 1996; chmn., CEO, pres. Diversa Corp., 1996—; bd. dirs. Harnifschfeger Industries, Inc., SGI, Inc., Silver Eagle Transport, Inc., Stationers Distbg., Inc., Alpha Wire Inc., Miss Erika Inc., Garden Ridge Pottery Corp., Pameco Holding Inc., Curtis Industries Inc., Gulf Coast Lubrication. Bd. dirs. Lincoln Park Zool. Soc., 1972—, pres., CEO, 1984-87; bd. dirs. North Shore Youth Health Svc., 1979-80, N.Y. Zool. Soc./The Wildlife Conservation Soc., 1987-96, Biocom, 1999. Mem. Fin. Execs. Inst., Am. Bankruptcy Inst., Am. Assn. Zool. Parks and Aquariums, Chgo. Club, Notre Dame Club. Home: 5240 Fiore Ter Apt J-215 San Diego CA 92122-5636 Office: 10665 Sorrento Valley Rd San Diego CA 92121-1609

BRUGGER, GEORGE ALBERT, lawyer; b. Erie, Pa., Jan. 19, 1941; s. Albert F. and Georgia V. (Bach) B.; children from previous marriage: Laura, Linda, Mark; m. Ann Rosenberg. BA, Gannon Coll., 1963; JD, Georgetown U., 1967. Bar: Md. 1968, U.S. Dist. Ct. Md. 1972, U.S. Supreme Ct. 1972. Law clk. to U.S. asst. atty. gen. U.S. Dept. of Justice, Washington, 1963-66; mgr. pub. affairs Air Transport Assn. of Am., Washington, 1966-68; ptnr. Beatty & McNamee, Hyattsville, Md., 1968-75; sr. ptnr., pres. Fossett & Brugger, Chartered, Seabrook, Md., 1975—; bd. dirs. Prince George's County Fin. Svcs. Corp. Chmn. bd. dirs. Prince George's Econ. Devel. Corp.; pres. Laurel Regional Hosp. Found. Recipient Disting. alumni award Gannon Coll. Fellow Md. Bar Found.; mem. ABA (chmn. land use regulation com.), Md. Bar Assn. (bd. dirs.), Prince George's County Bar Assn. (pres. 1982), Prince George's Law Found., (bd. dirs.), Prince George's County C. of C. (Disting. Svc. award 1980, 83, 85), Fed. Bar Assn. (dir.). Roman Catholic. Avocations: collecting classic sports cars, marine tropical fish. Home: The Colonnade 2801 New Mexico Ave NW Washington DC 20007 Office: Fossett & Brugger Chartered 6404 Ivy Ln Ste 720 Greenbelt MD 20770

BRUGGINK, ERIC G., federal judge; b. Kalidjati, Indonesia, Sept. 11, 1949; naturalized citizen U.S., 1961; m. Melinda Harris; children: John, David. BA in Sociology cum laude, Auburn U., 1971, MA in Speech, 1972; JD, U. Ala., 1975. Bar: Ala., D.C. Law clk. to chief judge U.S. Dist. Ct. (no. dist.) Ala., 1975-76; assoc. Hardwick, Hause & Segrest, Dothan, Ala., 1976-77; asst. dir. Ala. Law Inst., 1977-79; assoc. Steiner, Crum & Baker, Montgomery, Ala., 1979-82; dir. Office of Appeals Counsel Merit Systems Protection Bd., 1982-86; judge U.S. Ct. Fed. Claims, Washington, 1986—. Office: US Ct Fed Claims 717 Madison Pl NW Washington DC 20005-1011*

BRUGGINK, HERMAN, publishing executive; b. 1946. Pub. Wolters Kluwer, 1976-88; mng. dir. Markgraaf B.V., 1988-91; dir. Elsevier and Reed Elsevier, 1993—; chmn. bd. Elsevier and Reed Elsevier, Amsterdam, 1995—. Office: Reed Elsevier, Van de Sande Bakhuyzenstr 4, 1061 AG Amsterdam The Netherlands

BRUGH, REX, urologist; b. Takoma Park, Md., July 27, 1945; s. Rex Sr. Brugh and Pearl Atland Baird; m. Janet Alma McLain, Aug. 15, 1970 (div. 1989); m. Rhonda Lewis Holland, July 28, 1990; children: Laura Anne, Michael Rex, Heath. BS, Va. Inst. Tech., 1967; MD, Med. Coll. Va., 1971. Diplomate Am. Bd. Urology. Urologist S.C. Urol. Cons., Columbia. Contbr. articles to med. jours. Maj. USAF, 1973-75. Mem. ACS, Internat. Coll. Surgeons, Columbia Med. Soc., Am. Urol. Assn., S.C. Med. Soc., S.C. Urol. Assn., Lexington Med. Soc. Avocations: golf, gardening, fishing, herpeticulture. Office: SC Urol Cons 9 Med Park Rd Ste 500 Columbia SC 29203

BRUGIONI, DAVID MICHAEL, graphic designer, illustrator, artist; b. Gary, Ind., Sept. 21, 1956; s. Dominic and Delores Brugioni; m. Nancy Tarr, Nov. 2, 1985; children: Heather, Catherine. Student, W.Va. No. C.C., Wheeling, 1986, 87. Percussionist various club bands Wheeling, 1980—; digital photo editor The Times Leader News, Martins Ferry, Ohio, 1990—. Illustrator: editl. cartoons, 1993, 94, 97. Recipient 2nd pl. award of merit for editl. cartoon AP Ohio, 1999. Avocation: art, playing drums.

BRUHN, PAUL ROBERT, principal; b. Elgin, Ill., Jan. 6, 1956; s. Robert Ernest and Elizabeth Julia (Wittlief) B.; m. Deborah U. Bruhn, Aug. 10, 1979; children: George, Patrick. BS in Edn., Concordia Tchrs. Coll., 1978; MEd, John Carroll U., 1982; PhD, Case Western U., 1990. Cert. tchr. Ohio. Tchr. Luth. H.S. East, Cleveland Heights, Ohio, 1978-93, prin., 1993—. Ch. bd. of edn. St John Luth. Ch., South Euclid, Ohio, 1993-96, vice chmn. of congregation; chmn. of congregation Mt. Olive Luth. Ch., Cleveland Heights, 1986-90. Mem. ASCD, Ohio Assn. of Secondary Sch. Adminstrs., Assn. of Luth. Secondary Schs. Office: Lutheran High Sch East 3565 Mayfield Rd Cleveland Heights OH 44118

BRUICE, THOMAS C., chemist, educator. PhD, U. So. Calif., 1954. Prof. chemistry U. Calif., Santa Barbara, 1964—. Contbr. articles to profl. jours. Recipient Career Devel. award NIH, 1979, Lifetime Investigator award, 1979, MERIT award, 1979, Richard C. Tolman medal, 1979, Arthur C. Scope Scholar award Am. Chem. Soc., 1987, Repligan medal, 1987, Alfred Bader medal, 1988, James Flack Norris award, 1996; Guggenheim fellow, 1979. Fellow AAAS, Royal Soc. Chemistry, Am. Acad. Arts and Scis.; mem. NAS. Office: U Calif Santa Barbara Dept Chemistry Santa Barbara CA 93106-9510

BRUINSMA, THEODORE AUGUST, retired business executive; b. Prospect Park, N.J., Aug. 3, 1921; s. Theodore and Ella (Ullman) B.; m. Edith Moog, July 16, 1943; children—Tim Charles, Lynn Ellen, Dayle. BA, Washington and Lee U., 1941; IA, Bus. Sch., Harvard U., 1943, LLB, 1948. Bar: N.Y. bar 1949, U.S. Dist. Ct. 1949, Ga. bar 1953, U.S. Supreme Ct. bar 1980. Atty. Whitman Ransom & Coulson, N.Y.C., 1948-56; v.p., gen. counsel McCall Corp., N.Y.C., 1956-58; pres. Systematics, Inc., N.Y.C., 1958-61, Lear Jet, Inc., Wichita, Kans., 1966-67; also dir.; pres. Harvest Industries, Inc., Los Angeles, 1969-78; also dir.; exec. v.p. Capital for Tech. Industries, Santa Monica, Calif., 1963-65, Packard Bell Electric, Los Angeles, 1965-66; Councilman Glen Rock, N.J., 1956-60; dean Law Sch., Loyola U., Los Angeles, 1979-81; pres. Los Angeles C. of C., 1983-84, Univ. Ventures, Los Angeles, 1984-90; ret.; state chmn. Job Tng. Coun., State of Calif., 1982-85, mem. Industry/Edn. Council, 1983-86, mem. Calif. Econ. Devel. Task Force, 1983-86; Gov.'s appointment sec., 1984; mem. Los Angeles County Economy and Efficiency Commn., 1985-88; vis. scholar Claremont (Calif.) Grad. Sch., 1991-93. Author: Foresight Capacity, 1996, A Special Place, 1997, Our Peninsula, 1999. Mem. L.A. Republican Ctrl. Com.; bd. dirs. San Pedro (Calif.) YMCA, 1964-66, Am. Edn. League, 1979-82, San Pedro Hosp., 1987-91; trustee Boy Scouts Am., San Pedro, 1965-66; Calif. chmn. Assembly Rep. Polit. Action Com., 1978; founder L.A. Polit. Affairs Coun., 1977, Rep. candidate for U.S. Senate, 1982; trustee Calif. State U., 1986-89. Served to lt. comdr. USNR, 1943-46, 50-51, PTO. Recipient award Freedoms Found., 1978. Mem. Copyright Soc. U.S.A. (original trustee 1949-56).

BRULEY, DUANE FREDERICK, academic administrator, consultant, engineer; b. Chippewa Falls, Wis., Aug. 3, 1933; s. Casper Sepharald and Hazel Ella (Kuehn) B.; m. Suzanne Bigler, June 14, 1959; children: Scott, Randall, Mark. Student, Eau Claire (Wis.) State U., 1951-53; BSChemE, U. Wis., 1956; student, Oak Ridge (Tenn.) Sch. of Reactor Tech., 1957; M in Mech. Engring., Stanford U., 1959; PhD in Chem. Engring., U. Tenn., 1962. Registered profl. engr., S.C. Nuclear engr. Union Carbide Nuclear Co., Oak Ridge, Tenn., 1956-59; head tennis coach U. Tenn., 1961; prof. chem. engrng., head tennis coach Clemson (S.C.) U., 1962-73; head chem. engrng., head tennis coach Tulane U., New Orleans, 1973-77; head tennis profl. Timberlane Country Club, Gretna, La., 1973-76; v.p. acad. affairs, asst. tennis coach Rose Hulman Inst. Tech., Terre Haute, Ind., 1977-81; head biomed. engrng., dir. rehab. engrng. ctr. La. Tech. U., Ruston, 1981-84; dean sch. of engrng., prof. engrng. sci. Calif. Poly U., San Luis Obispo,

1984-91; program dir. biochem. and biomass engring. NSF, Washington, 1987-90; sect. head bioengring. and environ. systems NSF, 1989-90; pres. Synthesizer, Inc., 1988—; dean engring. U. Md., Baltimore County, 1991-94; dir. bioengring. U. Md., Baltimore County, 1994—; vis. prof. Princeton (N.J.) U., fall 1970, U. Yamagata (Japan), U. Hokkido, summer 1975; vis. prof. U. Minn., 1997; cons. Westvaco, Charleston, S.C., 1964-67, DuPont, Ponchartrain, La., 1974-79, Am. Enka Corp., 1970-71, Milliken and Co., 1978-79, Exxon, Baton Rouge, La., 1978-79, El Paso Products Co., 1980-82, Electronics Assocs., Inc., Long Branch, N.J., 1984-88, CRAY Rsch., 1986; varsity football and varsity tennis U. Wis., Eau Claire; semi profl. football Chippewa Marines, 1951-52; co-program dir. Nat. Heat Transfer Conf., Balt., 1997, chmn. conf. coord. com., 1998; chmn. nat. heat transfer coord. com. AIChE/ASME, 1998, Nat. Heat Transfer Ann. Conf., 1999. Author: (chpt.) Mathematics of Microcirculation, 1980; editor: Oxygen Supply, 1973, Oxygen Transport to Tissue, 1973, 83, 88, 91, 92, 94, 98, Hyperthermia, 1988, Protein C and Related Anticoagulants, 1990; rsch. editorial bd.: Biomedical Instrumentation and Technology, 1993-97; contbr. numerous articles to profl. jours.; co-developer BWK Technique for high speed numerical integration, 1982. Cons. ARC; narrator five part TV series on biomed. engring., 1982, TV Biomed. Engring. Sta. WEAU, Eau Clare, Wis., 1982; keynote spkr. First Cray Acd.; recorded for Wis. Pub. TV Network Biotechnology/Bioengring.; head tennis profl. Montebello Tennis Club, 1989-90; referee Sunshine Cup Internat. Jr. Tennis Tournament, Miami, 1966-69. Recipient Ann. Rsch. award La. Tech. U., 1983, Gold medal downhill skiing Nat. Standard Race, 1987, Alumni Disting. Svc. award U. Wis., Eau Claire, 1992, Spl. Opportunity award in Bioengring. The Whitaker Found., 1994—; named 2d Winningest Tennis Coach in Atlantic Coast Conf. history, 1990, one of Outstanding Educators of Am., 1972. Fellow AIChE (chmn. heat transfer energy conversion divsn., chmn. com. for Donald Q. Kern award 1997, chmn. com. for Max Jakob Meml. award 1997, Disting. spkr.), Am. Inst. Med. and Biol. Engring. (founding fellow); mem. ASME (exec. bd., bioprocess engring. program, chmn. bioprocess engring. subdivsn., Disting. spkr.), Internat. Soc. on Oxygen Transport Tissue (co-founder 1973, pres. 1983, exec. com., founder, chmn. com. Melvin H. Knisely award 1983—, keynote spkr. 25th anniversary 1997, 26th ann. meeting, Budapest, Hungary 1998), N.Y. Acad. Scis., Calif. Soc. Profl. Engrs. (hon.), Soc. Automotive Engrs. (Ralph R. Teetor Ednl. award 1986), Nat. Soc. Profl. Engrs., Am. Soc. Engring. Edn. (1st Pl. Rsch. award 1967, Biomed. Instrumentation and Tech. Outstanding Rsch. Paper award 1966, 97), La. Engring. Soc. (Charles M. Kerr Pub. Rels. award 1983), U.S. Profl. Tennis Assn., U.S. Tennis Assn. (hon. life mem., player ranking 5.5-3.5), Sigma Xi, Tau Beta Pi. Home: 7345 Swan Point Way Columbia MD 21045-5010

BRULLO, ROBERT ANGELO, chemical company executive; b. Chgo., Aug. 20, 1948; s. Ralph V. and Vicky M. (Santapa) B.; m. Kathleen M. Peltier, Feb. 27, 1993; children: Jennifer, Amy, Dawn. BSChemE, Ill. Inst. Tech., 1970; MBA, U. St. Thomas, 1976. Sr. analyst corp. mktg. 3M Co., St. Paul, 1977-78, supr. market devel. comml. chems. divsn., 1978-80; sr. account rep. comml. chems. divsn. 3M Co., Detroit, 1980-82; mgr. market devel. comml. chems. divsn. 3M Co., St. Paul, 1982-86, global mktg. mgr. indsl. chem. products divsn., 1986-88, global bus. mgr. indsl. chem. products divsn., 1988-92, dept. gen. mgr. specialty fluoropolymers dept., 1993-96; pres., CEO, bd. dirs. Dyneon LLC (3M/Hoechst JV), 1996—; bd. dirs., vice chmn. Alventia LLC (Dyneon/Solvay JV). Patentee in field. Mem. Rubber Mfrs. Assn., Am. Chem. Soc. (bd. dirs. rubber div. area 1986-88), Twin Cities Rubber Group (sec. 1979-80), Ft. Wayne Rubber Group, Soc. Plastics Industry (fluoropolymers div.), Chem. Mfrs. Assn. Lutheran. Home: 13877 Ozark Avenue Ct N Stillwater MN 55082-3411 Office: c/o Dyneon LLC 6744 33d St N Oakdale MN 55128

BRUM, BRENDA, state legislator, librarian; b. Parkersburg, W.Va., Jan. 3, 1954; d. Carl Henry Ogilvie and Helen Mae (Camp) B. BS, W.Va. U., 1975, MA, 1978. Libr., tchr. English, Hamilton Jr. H.S., Parkersburg, 1976-85; libr. Parkersburg South H.S., 1985—; mem. W.Va. Ho. of Dels., 1991-92, 93-94. Bd. dirs. Wood County chpt. Am. Cancer Soc.; foster parent Try Again Homes; mem. adv. bd. Wood County Vocat. Nursing. Mem. LWV, Wood County Edn. Assn. (past treas., exec. com.). Democrat. Avocations: water and snow skiing. Home: 2600 17th Ave Parkersburg WV 26101-6419

BRUMAGHIM, PAUL, small business owner; b. Gloversville, N.Y., June 26, 1926; s. William and Lydia (Slack) B.; children: Sheryl A. Petersen, Todd. Grad., Real Estate Inst., Peoria, Ill. Staff. sgt. USAF, U.S.A., 1944-52; with acctg. sales Nat. Cash Register Co., Danville, Ill., 1952-57; v.p. sales mgr. Danville Community Homes, 1957-62; real estate sales Montgomery Realty Co., Danville, 1962-64; owner-realtor ins. appraiser Brumaghim Real Estate, Danville, 1964—. Pres. bd. dirs. YMCA, Danville, 1968; chmn. bd. Vermillion County Red Cross, Danville, 1970-91; bd. commr. Danville Housing Authority, 1999. Recipient House Resolution 885 award House of Rep., Springfield, Ill., 1980, Hall of Fame award ARC, Shelter Ins. Co., Danville, 1987. Mem. NAREA (pres. ctrl. Ill. divsn. 1995-96), Danville Area Bd. Realtors (pres. 1978, 81, Realtor Yr. 1981), Ill. State Bd. Realtors (dist. v.p., Danville Life Underwriters pres. 1987—), Danville Archtl. Control Bd., First Ill. Credit Union (bd. dirs.), Am. Legion, Elks, Kiwanis (pres. 1967, lt. gov. 1970). Republican. Avocation: golf, traveling. Office: Brumaghim Real Estate 408 Sheridan PO Box 753 Danville IL 61834-0753

BRUMBACK, CHARLES TIEDTKE, retired newpaper executive; b. Toledo, Sept. 27, 1928; s. John Sanford and Frances Hannah (Tiedtke) B.; m. Mary Louise Howe, July 7, 1951; children: Charles Tiedtke Jr., Anne Meyer, Wesley W., Ellen Allen. BA in Econs., Princeton U., 1950; postgrad., U. Toledo, 1953-54. CPA, Ohio, Fla. With Arthur Young & Co., CPAs, 1950-57; bus. mgr., v.p., treas., pres., CEO Sentinel Star Co. subs. Tribune Co., Orlando, Fla., 1957-81; pres., CEO Chgo. Tribune subs. Tribune Co., 1981-88, pres., COO, 1988-90, CEO, 1990-95, chmn., 1993-95, bd. dirs., 1981-96; bd. dirs. Avid Tech., Inc., Spyglass, Inc. Bd. dirs. Robert R. McCormick Tribune Found.; life trustee Northwestern U., Chgo. Symphony Orch.; trustee Culver Ednl. Found., Chgo. Hist. Soc., Northwestern Meml. Hosp., chmn., 1987-90. 1st lt. U.S. Army, 1951-53. Decorated Bronze star. Mem. AICPA, Fla. Press Assn. (treas. 1969-76, pres. 1980, bd. dirs.), Am. Newspaper Pubs. Assn. (bd. dirs., treas. 1991-92), Newspaper Assn. Am. (bd. dirs., sec., 1992-93, vice chmn. 1993-94, chmn. 1994-95), Comml. Club Chgo., Chgo. Club, Tavern Club. Home: 1500 N Lake Shore Dr Chicago IL 60610-6657 Office: Tribune Co 435 N Michigan Ave Chicago IL 60611-4066

BRUMBACK, CLARENCE LANDEN, physician; b. Denver, Apr. 19, 1914; s. Carl Alvin and Hildur Athelia (Landen) B.; m. Lucile Leslie Gillie, June 17, 1943; children—Richard, Carl. AB, U. Kans., 1936, MD, 1943; MPH, U. Mich., 1948. Diplomate Am. Bd. Preventive Medicine. Intern U.S. Marine Hosp., San Francisco, 1943-44; dir. pub. health Laclede County, Mo., 1947, AEC, Oak Ridge, 1948-50; dir. Palm Beach County (Fla.) Health Dept., 1950-86; coord. grad. edn. Palm Beach County Health Dept., 1986—; clin. prof. U. Miami; adj. prof. Fla. Atlantic U., Boca Raton, Fla. Mem. editl. bd. Jour. Public Health Policy, 1981-88; contbr. articles to profl. jours. Bd. dirs. Palm Beach County chpt. A.R.C., Am. Lung Assn. S.E. Fla., Heart Assn. Palm Beach County, Community Mental Health Center Palm Beach County, Palm Beach County unit Am. Cancer Soc., Palm Beach County Mental Health Assn., Palm Beach County Health Dept., 1950-86; pres. YMCA of Palm Beaches, 1970. With AUS, 1944-47. Recipient Meritorious Svc. award Fla. Public Health Assn., 1968; Merit award State of Fla., 1972; Physician of Yr. award Am. Assn. Public Health Physicians, 1975. Fellow APHA (Sedgwick Meml. medal 1989), Am. Coll. Preventive Medicine, Royal Soc. Health; mem. AMA (Dr. Nathan Davis award 1993), Fla. Med. Assn. (cert. of Merit award 1995), Palm Beach County Med. Soc., Rotary, Elks. Democrat. Lutheran. Home: PO Box 6512 West Palm Beach FL 33405-6512 Office: 826 Evernia St West Palm Beach FL 33401-5708

BRUMBACK, ROGER ALAN, neuropathologist, researcher; b. Washington, Feb. 15, 1948; s. Oscar Benjamin and Frances Elaine (Neufeld) B.; m. Mary Helen Skinner, Apr. 26, 1969; children: Darryl Wyatt, Audrey Christine, Owen Eliot. BS, Pa. State U., 1967; MD, Pa. State U., Hershey, 1971. Diplomate Nat. Bd. Med. Examiners, Am. Bd. Pediatrics, Am. Bd. Psychiatry and Neurology, Am. Bd. Pathology; cert. clin. electroencephalography. Pediatric intern Johns Hopkins Hosp., Balt., 1971-72, pediatric asst. resident, 1972-73; fellow in pediatrics Johns Hopkins U. Sch. Medicine, Balt., 1971-73; asst. resident neurology Barnes Hosp., St. Louis, 1973-74; fellow in pediatric neurology Washington U., St. Louis Children's Hosp., 1973-75; clin. assoc. neurology and exptl. neuropathology med. neurology br. Nat. Inst. Neurol. and Communicative Disorders and Stroke, Nat. Insts. of Health, Bethesda, Md., 1975-77; clin. instr. neurology and pediatrics U. Pitts., 1977-78; asst. prof. neurology U. N.D., Fargo, 1978-79, asst. prof. pediatrics, 1978-82, assoc. prof. neurology, 1980-82; resident/fellow anatomic pathology and neuropathology svcs. Strong Meml. Hosp., U. Rochester (N.Y.), 1982-86; assoc. prof. pathology U. Okla., Oklahoma City, 1986-89, chief neuropathology sect. Health Scis. Ctr., 1987—, prof. pathology, 1989—, interim chmn., dept. pathology, 1999—; chief neurology svc. V.A. Med. Ctr., Fargo, 1978-82; dir. Muscular Dystrophy Assn. Clinic, Fargo, 1978-82, co-dir., Oklahoma City, 1988-91; adj. assoc. prof. pediatrics U. Okla., 1986-90, adj. assoc. prof. psychiatry and behavioral scis., 1986-91, adj. prof. pediatrics, 1990—, adj. prof. psychiatry and behavioral sci., 1991—, adj. prof. neurology 1991—, adj. prof. orthopaedic surgery, 1996—, David Ross Boyd prof. pathology, 1997—, adj. prof. geriatric medicine, 1998—; clin. care cons. dermatology br. Nat. Cancer Inst., 1987—. Author: (with W.H. Olson, G. Gascon, L.A. Christoferson) Practical Neurology for the Primary Care Physician, 1981, (with J.W. Gerst) The Neuromuscular Junction, 1984, (with R.W. Leech) Color Atlas of Muscle Histochemistry, 1984, (with R.M. Herndon) The Cerebrospinal Fluid, 1989, (with M.H. Brumback) The Dietary Fiber Weight Control Handbook, 1989, (with R.W. Leech) Hydrocephalus: Current Clinical Concepts, 1991, Neurology and Clinical Neuroscience, 1993, (with W.H. Olson, G. Gascon, V. Iyer) Handbook of Symptom-Oriented Neurology, 2nd edit., 1994, (with R.W. Leech) Neuropathology and Basic Neuroscience, 1995, (with C.E. Coffey) Textbook of Pediatric Neuropsychiatry, 1998; chief editor Jour. Child Neurology, 1986—; mem. editorial bd. Jour. Geriatric Psychiatry and Neurology, 1990—, Biomed. Rsch. India, 1990—, Neuropsychiatry, Neuropsychology and Behavioral Neurology, 1994—. With USPHS, 1975-77. Mem. Am. Acad. Neurology, Am. Assn. Electrodiagnostic Medicine, Am. Assn. Neuropathologists, Am. Acad. Pediats., Am. Neurol. Assn., Child Neurology Soc., Coun. Biology Editors, Coll. Am. Pathologists, Internat. Child Neurology Assn., Soc. for Exptl. Neuropathology (sec.-treas. 1988-93, pres. 1995-97), Behavioral Neurology Soc. (councillor 1990-91, sec.-treas. 1991-93, pres. 1993-95). Republican. Lutheran. Home: 4014 Hidden Hill Rd Norman OK 73072-3013 Office: Okla U Health Sci Ctr PO Box 26901 Oklahoma City OK 73126-0901

BRUMBACK PATTERSON, CATHY JEAN, psychologist; b. Birmingham, Ala., Oct. 15, 1953; d. Roy Clifton and Violet Lorraine (Wesley) Brumback; m. Louis Loomis Patterson, June 10, 1987; children: Catherine Elizabeth Patterson, Allyson Brumback Patterson. BA, U. Ala., Tuscaloosa, 1975; MA, U. Ala., Birmingham, 1977; EdS, Ga. State U., 1985, PhD, 1986. Diplomate Am. Bd. Profl. Psychology, Am. Bd. Forensic Examiners; lic. psychologist; cert. sch. psychologist. Tchr. Jefferson County Bd. Edn., Birmingham, 1975-76, Birmingham (Ala.) Bd. Edn., 1976-77, Baldwin County Bd. Edn., Bay Minette, Ala., 1977-79; psychometrist Regional Edn. Svc. Ctr., Bartlesville, Okla., 1979-81, Union Pub. Schs., Tulsa, 1981-82, Forsyth County Schs., 1982-84; sch. psychologist Atlanta (Ga.) Pub. Schs., 1984-87; pvt. practice psychologist Northport, Ala., 1987-94, Fairhope, Ala., 1994—; grad. rsch. asst. Ga. State U., Atlanta, 1982, 85, instr., 1986; instr. U. Ala., Tuscaloosa, 1988-90. Named Mrs. Ala., Mrs. Am. Assn., 1979, Outstanding Young Women of Am., 1982, 87, 89; recipient Outstanding Doctoral Student award Ga. Assn. Sch. Psychologists, 1987. Fellow Am. Acad. Sch. Psychology; mem. AAUW, APA, Ala. Psychol. Assn., Nat. Regiter Health Svc. Providers, Montrose Garden Club, St. Paul's Parents' Orgn., Rock Creek Country Club, Rotary, Phi Delta Kappa, Kappa Delta Pi. Avocations: writing, singing, playing piano, traveling, reading. Home: PO Box 687 Montrose AL 36559-0687 Office: 22787 Highway 98 Bldg A Fairhope AL 36532-3339

BRUMBAUGH, JOHN A., JR., electrical engineer; b. Pittsburg, Kans., Aug. 23, 1927; s. John A. and Leona G. (Finley) B.; m. Shirley Jean Ellis, July 8, 1950; children: Mark Alan, Steven Thomas, Scott Andrew. Design engr. McNally Pitts. Mfg. Co., Pittsburg, 1949-55; plant engr. Morton Salt Co., Hutchinson, Kans., 1955-59; asst. plant mgr. Morton Salt Co., Port Huron, Mich., 1959-65; plant mgr. Morton Salt Co., Grand Salne, Tex., 1965-70; facility mgr. Morton Salt Co., Hutchinson, Kans., 1970-84, Morton Salt div. Morton Internat., Inc., Rittman, Ohio, 1984-89; ret. Lt. USNR, 1945-46. Recipient Boss of Yr. award Bus. and Profl. Women, 1979. Mem. Kans. Assn. Commerce, Assn. Commerce and Industry (dir. 1974-84), Tex. Mfs. Assn., (dir. Dallas chpt. 1966-70), East Tex. C. of C. (dir. 1968-70), Am. Legion, Lions (pres. local club 1964-65). Avocations: golfing, hunting, fishing, boating, hiking. Home: 431 Allen Dr Wadsworth OH 44281-2120

BRUMBAUGH, JOHN MAYNARD, lawyer, educator; b. Annapolis, Md., Feb. 9, 1927; s. Heber Byron and Nina Elizabeth (Maynard) B.; m. Alice Austin Soled, 1983. B.A., Swarthmore Coll., 1948; J.D., Harvard U., 1951. Law clk. firm Haight, Deming, Gardner, Poor & Havens, N.Y.C., 1951, 53-55; teaching fellow Harvard U., 1955-56; asst. prof. law U. Md., Balt., 1956-59, assoc. prof., 1959-63, prof., 1963-96; prof. emeritus, 1996—; Wharton, Levin, Ehrmantraut, Klein & Nash disting. svc. scholar, 1993-96, scholar emeritus, 1996—. Author: Cases and Materials on Criminal Law and Approaches to the Study of Law; contbr. articles to profl. jours. Mem. ABA, Md. Bar Assn., Am. Law Inst., Wranglers Club. Office: 500 W Baltimore St Baltimore MD 21201-1701

BRUMBAUGH, ROLAND JOHN, bankruptcy judge; b. Pueblo, Colo., Jan. 21, 1940; s. Leo Allen and Ethel Marie (Brummett) B.; m. Pamela Marie Hultman, Sept. 8, 1967; children: Kenneth Allen, Kimberly Marie. BS in Bus. with honors, U. Colo., 1968, JD, 1971. Bar: Colo. 1971, U.S. Dist. Ct. Colo. 1972, U.S. Ct. Appeals (10th cir.) 1973, U.S. Supreme Ct. 1980. Legal intern HUD, Denver, 1971-72; sole practice Denver, 1972-75; chief dep. city atty. City of Lakewood, Colo., 1975; dep. dir. Colo. Dept. of Revenue, Denver, 1975-78; asst. U.S. atty. Dist. of Colo., Denver, 1978-82; judge U.S. Bankruptcy Ct. Dist. of Colo., Denver, 1982—; lectr. in field. Author: Colorado Liquor and Beer Licensing-Law and Practice, 1970; Handbook for Municipal Clerks, 1972. Contbr. articles to profl. jours. Served with USAF, 1962-65. Recipient numerous awards for excellence in law. Mem. Colo. Bar Assn., Alpha Kappa Psi, Beta Gamma Sigma, Rho Epsilon, Sigma Iota. Home: 1845 Sherman St Ste 400 Denver CO 80203-1167 Office: US Custom House 721 19th St Denver CO 80202-2508*

BRUMBERG, G. DAVID, history bibliographer; b. Ironton, Ohio, June 7, 1939; s. Z. Dewey and Lizzetta Louise (Kurtz) B.; m. Joan Jacobs, Dec. 23, 1972; 1 child, Adam. B.S. in Econs., U. Pa., 1961; M.A. in History, Miami U., Oxford, Ohio, 1968, Ph.D. in History, 1977. Archivist, Nat. Archives Ctr. for Documentary Study of Am. Revolution, Washington, 1971-73; dir. Geneva Hist. Soc., N.Y., 1973-76; dir. N.Y. Hist. Resources Ctr., Cornell U., Ithaca, N.Y., 1977-90; history bibliographer collection devel. dept. Olin Libr., Cornell U., 1990—; organizer co-conf. Conf. on N.Y. State History, 1986—. Author: The Making of an Upstate Community: Geneva, New York, 1976; (with others) History for the Public, 1984 (Regional Conf. of Hist. Agys. Merit award 1985). Treas. Hist. Ithaca and Tompkins County, Inc., Ithaca, 1983-86. 1st lt., U.S. Army, 1962-64. Mem. Am. Assn. for State and Local History (seminar for hist. adminstrs. 1972), N.Y. State Studies Group (coordinator 1980-85), Lake Ontario Archives Conf. (co-treas. 1981-83). Democrat. Jewish. Avocations: sailing, music, travel, art, golf.

BRUMELLE, KENNETH COY, retail store owner; b. Odessa, Tex., Mar. 18, 1945; s. Clarence Lee and Leota (Jones) B.; m. Sharon Jean Suther, Dec. 21, 1967; 1 child Jenni Rebecca. AS, Odessa Coll., 1966; BBA, Tex. Tech U., 1968. Buyer trainee Sanger Harris, Dallas, 1969-71, buyer, 1971-73; buyer White House Dept. Stores, Beaumont, Tex., 1973-74; mdse. mgr. White House Dept. Stores, Beaumont, 1974-77; owner Outlaw Jean Store, Odessa, Tex., 1977-97; pres. COLAM, Inc. Bd. dirs. Better Bus. Bur., 1991—. With U.S. Army, 1968-69, Tex. N.G., 1969-74. Mem. Nat. Fedn. Ind. Bus., Tex. Retail Mchts. Assn. (bd. dirs. 1987—), Tex. Retail Assn. (state chmn. membership com. 1991—), Odessa C. of C., Optimist (v.p. Odessa club), Masons. Republican. Methodist. Home: 1809 E 52nd St Odessa TX 79762-4547 Office: COLAM Inc 4526 E Univ Bldg 5 Odessa TX 79762

BRUMIT, LAWRENCE EDWARD, III, oil field service company executive; b. Brunswick, Ga., Feb. 5, 1950; s. Lawrence Edward Jr. and Felicite (Smith) B.; m. Leila Ann Parker, Feb. 21, 1976; children: Mary Louise, Lawrence Edward IV. BS in Petroleum Engring., Mont. Tech., 1974. Field engr. Dowell, Farmington, N. Mex., 1974; service engr. Dowell Schlumberger, Warri, Nigeria, 1975, mgr., Cork, Ireland, 1976, tech. engr., Galeota, Trinidad, 1977, mgr., San Fernando, Trinidad, 1978-79, tng. ctr. mgr., Pau, France, 1980, div. mgr. S.W. Africa, Luanda, Angola, 1981-82, tech. mktg. mgr., Paris, 1983-84, v.p., region mgr., Paris, 1984-86, pres. compagnie de services, 1985—, mgr., v.p. Europe Africa, 1986-88; dir. personnel Schlumberger Ltd. Drilling and Pumping Svcs., Paris, 1988-90; v.p., gen. mgr. Dowell Schumberger North Am., Houston, 1991-95, rancher Flying "B" Ranch, 1995—; bd. dirs. Mont. Tech. Found., 1993-96. Recipient All Conf. Baseball Outstanding Coll. Athlete of Am. award Frontier Conf., 1969-71, 72, No. 1 Player and Capt. award, 1971. Mem. Soc. Petroleum Engrs. Episcopalian. Avocations: flying; golf. Home: 4425 Sundown Rd Missoula MT 59804-7109

BRUMM, JAMES EARL, lawyer, trading company executive; b. San Antonio, Dec. 19, 1942; s. John Edward and Marie Oletha (Gault) B.; m. Alicia Joan Pine, Aug. 17, 1968 (div. Mar. 1991); children: Christopher Kenji, Jennifer Kimiko, Laurie Kiyoko; m. Yuko Tsuchida, Apr. 17, 1991. AB, Calif. State U., Fresno, 1965; LLB, Columbia U., 1968. Bar: N.Y. 1969. Assoc. Reid & Priest, N.Y.C., 1968-72, Logan, Takashima & Nemoto, Tokyo, 1973-76; exec. v.p., gen. counsel, dir. Mitsubishi Internat. Corp., N.Y.C., 1977—; pres. Mitsubishi Internat. Corp. Found., N.Y.C., 1992—; dir. Mitsubishi Corp., Japan, N.Y.C., 1995—; bd. dirs. Brunei LNG, Tembec, Inc. Trustee Spuyten Duyvil Nursery Sch., Bronx, N.Y., 1991-95; mem. lawyers com. for human rights, steering com. Internat. Rule of Law Coun., 1993—; bd. dirs. Jr. Achievement Internat., 1997—, Internat. Sch. Svcs., 1997—; mem. adv. coun. Sanctuary for Families, Ctr. for Battered Women's Legal Svcs., 1997—; bd. vis. Columbia Law Sch., 1998—. Mem. ABA, Assn. Bar City N.Y. (chmn. com. on internat. trade 1990-93, chmn. task force on internat. legal svcs. 1998—), Univ. Club, Nippon Club. Home: 255 W 84th St Apt 6C New York NY 10024-4327 Office: Mitsubishi Internat Corp 520 Madison Ave New York NY 10022-4213

BRUMM, PAUL MICHAEL, banker; b. Cin., Oct. 18, 1947; s. Paul Frederick and Jeane (Faine) B.; m. Linda Ann Phillips, Dec. 28, 1968 (div. Dec. 1982); children: Anna Ulrika, Nicholas David. Jaqualine Dorothy Speier, June 25, 1983. BA in Econs., U. Cin., 1969, MBA in Fin., 1976. With The Fifth Third Bank, Cin., 1966-77, v.p., 1981-85, v.p., treas., trust officer, 1985-87; treas. Fifth Third Bancorp, Cin., 1985-89, sr. v.p., trust officer, chief investment officer, 1987-90, sr. v.p., CFO, 1990-95, exec. v.p., CFO, 1995-97, exec. v.p., corp. devel., 1997—; mem. Bankers roundtable, Banking & Fin. Mkts. Com. Past chmn. The Salvation Army Bus. Adv. Bd., Cin.; trustee Cath. Healthcare Ptnrs. Mem. Univ. Club, Cin. Athletic Club, Coldstream Country Club, Delta Mu Delta. Republican. Roman Catholic. Avocation: golf. Home: 1428 Apple Hill Rd Cincinnati OH 45230-5113 Office: Fifth Third Bank 38 Fountain Square Plz Cincinnati OH 45263-0001

BRUMMEL, MARK JOSEPH, magazine editor; b. Chgo., Oct. 28, 1933; s. Anthony William and Mary (Helmreich) B. BA, Cath. U. Am., 1956, STL, 1961, MSLS, 1964. Joined Order of Claretians, Roman Cath. Ch., 1952; ordained priest Order of Caretians, Roman Cath. Ch., 1960; librarian, tchr. St. Jude Sem., Momence, Ill., 1961-70; asso. editor U.S. Cath. mag., Chgo., 1971-72; editor U.S. Cath. Mag., 1970—; dir. St. Jude League, Chgo., 1970—; treas. Eastern Province Claretians, 8th Day Ctr., 1998—, also bd. dirs.; bd. dirs. Chgo. Family Health Ctr. Editor Today mag., 1970-71; contbr. article to publ. Chmn. bd. Eighth Day Ctr. for Justice, Chgo., 1988-92; bd. dirs. Assn. of Chgo. Priests, 1994-96; mem. Ill. Cath. Conf., 1993-96. Mem. Cath. Press Assn. (v.p. 1985-87, St. Francis De Sales award 1996), Associated Ch. Press. Avocation: photography. Home: 3200 E 91st St Chicago IL 60617-4496 Office: US Cath 205 W Monroe St Fl 7 Chicago IL 60606-5033

BRUMMER, STEVEN E., police chief. Chief of police Bakersfield, Calif. Office: PO Box 59 1601 Truxtun Ave Bakersfield CA 93302

BRUN, HENRY, publishing executive; b. N.Y.C., Feb. 11, 1940. BA, Bklyn. Coll., 1958-62; MS, Pace U., 1975. Supr. N.Y.C. Sch. Sys., 1962-90; prin. John Jay H.S., Bklyn., 1990-94; COO Amsco Sch. Pubs. Inc., N.Y.C., 1994-95, pres., 1995—. Mem. Am. Archaeological Assn., Soc. Antiquaries New Castle upon Tyne, Soc. Promotion Roman Architecture. Office: Amsco Sch Pubs Inc 315 Hudson St New York NY 10013-1009*

BRUN, JUDITH, principal. Prin. St. Joseph's Acad., Baton Rouge, 1981—. Recipient Blue Ribbon Sch. award U.S. Dept. Edn., 1990-91. Office: Saint Josephs Acad 3015 Broussard St Baton Rouge LA 70808-1198*

BRUNACINI, ALAN VINCENT, fire chief; b. Jamestown, N.Y., Apr. 18, 1937; s. John N. and Mary T. Brunacini; B.S., Ariz. State U., 1970, M.P.A., 1975; m. Rita McDaugh, Feb. 14, 1959; children—Robert Nicholas, John Nicholas, Mary Candice. Mem. Phoenix Fire Dept., 1959—, bn. chief, then asst. fire chief, 1971-78, fire chief, 1978—; condr. nat. seminar on fire dept. mgmt., 1970—. Redford scholar, 1968. Mem. Am. Soc. Public Adminstrn. (Superior Service award 1980), Nat. Fire Protection Assn. (chmn. fire service sect. 1974-78, dir. 1978), Internat. Assn. Fire Chiefs, Soc. Fire Service Instrs. Author: Fireground Command; also articles in field. Office: Office of Fire Chief 455 N Fifth St Phoenix AZ 85004-2301

BRUNALE, VITO JOHN, aerospace engineer; b. Mt. Vernon, N.Y., July 2, 1925; s. Donato and Antoinette (Wool) B.; m. Joan Florence Montuori, Apr. 23, 1949; 1 child, Stephen. AAS, Stewart Aero. Inst., 1948; BSAE, Tri-State U., 1958; MSME, U. Bridgeport, 1966; DSc, Nev. Inst. Tech., 1973; PhD (hon.), Internat. U., Spain, 1987; DSc, Pacific Western U., 1984. Rsch. engr. Norden Labs., White Plains, N.Y., 1948-55; instr. Tri-State U., Angola, Ind., 1955-58; engring. cons. Norden Div. United Aircraft, Norwalk, Conn., 1958-67; chief engring. cons. Singer-Kearfott Corp., Pleasantville, N.Y., 1967-73; chief engr. Diagnostic/Retrieval Systems, Mt. Vernon, N.Y., 1973-76; tech. problem mgr. Fairchild Republic Co., Farmingdale, N.Y., 1977-87; sr. tech. expert Sikorsky Aircraft, 1987—; cons. in field; engring. tutor to coll. students; v.p. Lithoway, Inc., 1969-73; lectr. in field; tech. guest speaker numerous tech. soc. meetings.; participant engring. exchange program, USSR, People's Republic China. Contbr. articles to profl. jours. including Product Engring., Aviation Week, Environ. Scis. Participant U.S.A. Citizen Amb. Program. Served with USAAF, 1943-45. Decorated Purple Heart (3), Air medals, D.F.C. Tri-State U. teaching fellow, 1955-58; NSF grantee; recipient Aircraft Design award, 1948, Inst. Aero. Sci. Lecture award, 1948, Norden Rsch. award, 1963, Cost Reduction award, 1965, Singer Engring. award, 1970, 72, Fairchild outstanding achievement award, 1985, 86, 87, Fairchild award of excellence, 1984, Am. Biographical Inst. and Research Assn. Outstanding Performance award, 1989, Aircraft Recognition award, 1986, citation N.Y. State Assembly, 1988, Conspicuous Service Cross N.Y. State, 1988, Prisoner of War medal, 1988, others; named to Wisdom Hall of Fame, 1998. Mem. AIAA (award 1973, Aviation award 1994, Sr. Mem. award 1994, Merit award 1998, membership award 1998, award 1998), VFW, DAV, K.C., U.S. Naval Inst., Air Force Assn., Am. Ordnance Asssn., Inst. Environ. Sci., Nat Space Inst., Newman Club, Internat. Students Assn., Internat. Platform Assn., World Inst. of Achievement. Roman Catholic. Achievements include patent (with others) for Bearing Spin Rail Test; development of method of discriminate displacement for equilibrium of structures, of the position point vibration isolation technique, of the vapress vibration system, of advanced techniques for structural and vibration analyses, of the Doppler-Inertial-Loran system, of state of the art mathematical and structural analyses techniques, of Mars Doppler Lander system, computer time studies, anti-corrosion methods; resolution of 140 technical problems on the Fairchild A-10 aircraft, of more than 30 technical problems with the Saab-Fairchild 340; solution of Grumman A-6A radar tracking problem in Vietnam; elimination of technical problems on LEM inertial guidance; rsch. in mfg. productivity, co-planer structural analyses. Home: 459 Bronxville Rd Bronxville NY 10708-1102 Office: Main St Bridgeport CT 06606

BRUNDAGE, RUSSELL ARCHIBALD, retired data processing executive; b. N.Y.C., Feb. 16, 1929; s. Eugene Columbus and Sophia Catherine (Gillies) B.; m. Barbara Jane Nelson, May 18, 1958; children: Russell Archibald, Nelson David, Beth Ellen, Paul Winston. B.A., Washington Sq. Coll., NYU, 1957. With U.S. Fgn. Service, State Dept., 1950-55; applied sci. writer

IBM Corp., N.Y.C. and White Plains, N.Y., 1957-60; with Colonial Penn Group, Phila., 1960-81, v.p., 1972-81; pres. Colonial Penn Group Data Corp., 1970-77; v.p. Nat. Assn. Plans, Inc., 1971-81; v.p. data processing SAI Group, Inc., 1982; pres. SAI Data Services Div., 1983-86; v.p. MIS Mut. Assurance Co., Phila., 1989-94; v.p. Green Tree Ins. Co., Phila., 1989-94; v.p., bd. dirs. Valley Ins. Co., Phila., 1990-92, Green Tree Ins. Co., Phila., 1992-94; v.p. Am. Loyalty Ins. Co., Gahanna, Ohio, 1989-94, also bd. dirs.; v.p., sec. Mut. Assurance Co., Green Tree Ins. Co., Am. Loyalty Ins. Co., 1991-94. Chmn. Lee Magisterial Dist. Republican Com., Fairfax County, Va., 1966; bd. dirs. S.E. Pa. chpt. Am. Heart Assn., 1993-96. Served with USAF, 1947-50. Mem. Vets. 7th Regt. N.Y. Republican. Presbyterian. (ret. elder). Home: 23 Wincrest Dr Phoenixville PA 19460-5735

BRUNDIGE, ROBERT WILLIAM, JR., lawyer; b. Dayton, Ohio, Feb. 4, 1944; s. Robert W. and Elizabeth (Marquardt) B.; m. Katherine D. Muller, Dec. 18, 1971; children: Elizabeth, Allyson. BA, Yale U., 1966; JD, Vanderbilt U., 1969. Bar: N.Y. 1970, U.S. Dist. Ct. (so. and ea. dists.) N.Y. 1972, U.S. Tax Ct. 1973, U.S. Ct. Appeals (2d cir.) 1975, U.S. Ct. Appeals (11th cir.) 1983, U.S. Ct. Appeals (5th cir.) 1985, U.S. Supreme Ct. 1996, N.J. 1997, U.S. Dist. Ct. N.J. 1997. Assoc. Sage, Gray, Todd & Sims, N.Y.C., 1969-75, ptnr., 1976-86; ptnr. Hughes, Hubbard & Reed, N.Y.C., 1987—; mem. Vanderbilt Law Sch. Nat. Alumni Bd., Nashville, 1993—; del. Yale U. Assn. of Yale Alumni, 1994—; presenter in field. Author: (with others) The McGraw-Hill Construction Business Handbook, 2d edit., 1985; contbr. article to profl. jours. Trustee Ridgewood Pub. Edn. Found., 1990—, pres., 1990-93; pres. dean's coun. Vanderbilt U. Law Sch., Nashville, 1996—. Recipient Disting. Svc. award Vanderbilt Law Sch., 1995. Mem. ABA (sect. litigation, chmn. subcom. on commodities 1984-86). Episcopalian. Avocation: tennis. Home: 251 Palmer Ct Ridgewood NJ 07450-2316 Office: Hughes Hubbard & Reed 1 Battery Park Plz Fl 12 New York NY 10004-1482

BRUNE, DAVID HAMILTON, financial corporation executive, lawyer; b. Long Beach, Calif., Apr. 23, 1930; s. Stephen J. and Rebecca (Welch) B.; m. Eleanor Goode, Jan. 29, 1957; children: Claudia Ann, Elizabeth Burr. Student, Tex. Christian U., 1948-50; BA, U. Tex., 1953, JD, 1958. Bar: Tex. 1958. From assoc. to ptnr. Sawtelle, Hardy, Davis & Goode, San Antonio, 1958-62; gen. counsel San Antonio River Authority, 1963-66, mgr., 1966-68; gen. mgr. Trinity River Authority, Arlington, Tex., 1968-79; exec. officer, bd. dirs. Southland Fin. Corp. and 2 key subs. (Las Colinas Corp., Southland Land & Cattle Co.), 1979-89; exec. v.p., chief devel. officer, gen. counsel Las Colinas, Inc., Irving, Tex., 1989-92; assoc. Hutchison Boyle Brooks & Fisher, 1992; mng. dir. and corp. counsel Faison-Stone Las Colinas, Inc., Irving, 1993—. Pres.-elect Tex. Water Conservation Assn., Austin, 1978-79; bd. dirs. North Tex. Commn., 1984-88, 91-92; pres., CEO, Dallas County Utility and Reclamation Dist., 1981—; bd. councillors U. Dallas. Decorated knight grand cross Order Holy Sepulchre (Jerusalem); recipient Preservation, Conservation & Utilization award San Antonio Conservation Soc., 1966, Unselfish Svc. award Soil Conservation Soc. Am., 1966, Hon. Membership award, 1971. Mem. ABA, State Bar Tex., Dallas Bar Assn., Greater Dallas C. of C. (bd. dirs. 1980-84), Irving C. of C. (bd. dirs. 1990-94, chmn.-elect 1991-92, chmn. 1992-93), U. Dallas Serra Club (past pres.), Las Colinas Country Club, LaCima Club, Phi Alpha Delta. Roman Catholic.

BRUNE, EVA, fundraiser; b. Bklyn., Apr. 20, 1952; d. Paul Mass and Edythe Siegel; m. David H. Brune, Oct. 30, 1988; children: Jared Alexander, Isaac Nicolai. BFA, Calif. Coll. Arts and Crafts, Oakland, 1978. Visual arts dir. Sonoma (Calif.) County Arts Commn., 1980-82; assoc. dir. Visual Arts Ctr. of Alaska, Anchorage, 1982-83; program dir. Internat. Sculpture Ctr., Washington, 1983; dir. Pro Arts, Oakland, 1983-85; devel. dir. A Traveling Jewish Theater, San Francisco, 1985-88; mng. dir. INTAR Hispanic Arts. Ctr., N.Y.C., 1988-94; dir. ann. fund The Big Apple Circus, N.Y.C., 1994-96; exec. dir. CityKids Found., N.Y.C., 1996-98; nat. dir. instnl. advancement Young Audiences, Inc., N.Y.C., 1998—; instr. Calif. Coll. Arts and Crafts, Oakland, 1978-79. Past bd. dirs. Alliance Resident Theaters, N.Y.C., Citiarts, N.Y.C.; former panelist theater program Nat. Endowment for Arts, Washington, OPERA Am., Fla. State Coun. on Arts, Westchester County Coun. on Arts, N.Y.; panelist N.J. State Coun. on Arts. Recipient fellowships Nat. Endowment for the Arts, Washington, 1980, 82. Jewish. Avocations: piano, furniture building, writing. E-mail: eva@ya.org.

BRUNEAU, MARIE-FLORINE, French educator; b. Casablanca, Morocco, May 18, 1943; came to U.S., 1970; d. Louis and Lucienne (Bois) B.; m. Michael Paine, Dec. 22, 1969 (div. Oct. 1989); m. Charles A. Krance, Nov. 11, 1989. BA, U. Calif., Berkeley, 1973, MA, 1975, PhD, 1980. Asst. prof. French U. So. Calif., L.A., 1980-86, assoc. prof. French, 1986-96, prof. French, 1996—; vis. assoc. prof. U. Chgo., 1988. Author: Racine, Jansénisme et modernity, 1986, Women Mystics Confront the Modern World, 1998; contbr. articles to profl. publs. Grantee Burlington No. Found., 1986, NEH, 1989-90, U. So. Calif., 1988; named Taft lectr. U. Cin., 1991. Mem. MLA (exec. com. sect. XVII Century French lit. 1992-94), NOW, Midwest MLA, Am. Assn. Tchrs. of French, Phi Beta Kappa. Office: U So Calif Dept French And Italia Los Angeles CA 90089-0359

BRUNEAU, WILLIAM JOSEPH, JR., minister, career counselor; b. New Haven, Feb. 27, 1947; s. William Joseph Bruneau and Erma Luca Schipritt; m. Barbara Boynton, Mar. 28, 1970; children: Heidi Bruneau Hayes, Michael William. BA in Bibl. Studies, Breadloaf Bible Coll., Burlington, N.C., 1985; MDiv, Earlham Sch. Religion, Richmond, Ind., 1994. Ordained to ministry Elim Fellowship, 1981, The Christian and Missionary Alliance, 1987. Vice pres. World Harvest Evangelism of New Eng., Durham, Conn., 1977-80; founder, dir. The Storefront St. Ministry, Meriden, Conn., 1981—; assoc. pastor The Ch. of the Living God, Farmington, Conn., 1981-85; pastor The Community Ch. of the Cross, Richmond, Ind., 1985-91, Moreland (Ind.) Friends Meeting, 1991-95; sr. career advisor Bernard Haldane Assocs., Indpls., 1995-98; sr. pastor Penn Friends Ch., Cassopolis, Mich., 1998—; chaplain Cass County Sheriff's Dept., 1998—; evangelist World Harvest Evangelism, Madurai, India, 1979; chmn. Christian Life and Witness, So. New Eng. Billy Graham Crusade, 1984-85; chaplain Wayne County Jail, Richmond, 1986-94; founder, dir. The "Fire Escape" radio/concert ministry, Richmond, 1987—. Columnist Sr. Life Mag., 1990-95. Bd. dirs. Richmond Jr. Players, 1987, Mental Health Assn. Wayne County, Richmond, 1990—95. William W. Wildman Found. scholar, 1991. Mem. ASTD, Richmond Ministerial Assn. (bd. dirs., pres. 1987), Wayne County C. of C. (co-chmn. promotion and advt. devel. 1987, chmn. Quality of Life Com. 1988). Home: 509 E State St Cassopolis MI 49031-1132 Office: Penn Friends Ch 19107 Quaker St Cassopolis MI 49031-9492 *The Church must not live in isolation from its surroundings. If we expect our communities to hear and respond to the message of Christ, then the church must hear and respond to the voice of its community. To be heard we must also hear.*

BRUNELL, MARK ALLEN, football player; b. L.A., July 17, 1970; m. Stacy; children: Caitlin, Jacob. BA in History, 1992. 2nd quarterback Green Bay Packers, 1994-95; quarterback Jacksonville Jaguars, 1995—. Staged inaugural Mark Brunell Charity Golf Tournament to benefit Wolfson Children's Hosp.; spokesman Leukemia Soc. Am., 1996; active Fellowship Christian Athletes. Named Most Valuable Player Rose Bowl, 1991, NFL Offensive Player of Week, 1996, AFC Offensive Player of Week, 1996, Pro Bowl AFC, 1997. Avocations: hunting, fishing, golf. Office: 1 Alltel Stadium Pl Jacksonville FL 32202-1928*

BRUNELL, PHILIP ALFRED, physician; b. N.Y.C., Feb. 1, 1931; s. Irving and Rose Brunell; children: Wayne, Robert, Rhonda. B.S., CCNY, 1950; postgrad., N.Y.U., 1950-51; M.S. in Physiology, U. Ill., 1952; M.D., U. Buffalo, 1957. Diplomate in pediatric and pediatric infectious diseases Am. Bd. Pediatrics. Research asst. physiology U. Ill., 1951-52, teaching asst., 1952-53; intern E.J. Meyer Meml. Hosp., Buffalo, 1957-58; resident in pediatrics Children's Hosp., Buffalo, 1958-60; asst. in pediatrics Cornell U., 1960-61; instr. pediatrics Emory U., 1961-64; asst. prof. pediatrics N.Y. U. Sch. Medicine, 1964-71, assoc. prof., 1971-75; prof., chmn. dept. pediatrics U. Tex. Health Sci. Center, San Antonio, 1975-81; prof., head div. infectious diseases dept. pediatrics U. Tex. Health Sci. Center, 1981-87; attending physician Santa Rosa Children's Hosp., San Antonio, 1975-81; prof. pediatrics UCLA; chief pediatrics Bexar County Hosp. Dist. Teaching Hosps., San Antonio, 1975-81; vice chmn. Cedars Sinai Med. Ctr., L.A., 1987-96, cons. in pediat., 1997—; cons. Brooke Army Med. Ctr., Wilford Hall USAF Med. Ctr., 1977-81; mem. cons. group on vaccine devel., 1991-94; cons. FDA, 1994-96; vis. rschr. Nat. Inst. Allergy and Infectious Diseases, 1995; spl. expert Lab. Clin. Investigation Nat. Inst. Allergy and Infectious Dis., NIH, 1998—. Chief med. editor Infectious Diseases of Children, 1987—; contbr. chpts. to books; contbr. articles to med. jours. Chmn. Internat. Year of Child, San Antonio, 1979-80; bd. dirs. Santa Rosa Children's Hosp. Found. Served with USPHS, 1961-64. USPHS fellow, 1971-72. Fellow Infectious Diseases Soc. Am. (awards com. 1979, chmn. 1982); mem. Am. Acad. Pediatrics (chmn. com. pediatric research 1977-78, chmn. com. infectious diseases 1978-85), Am. Soc. Microbiology, Am. Acad. Microbiology, Am. Pediatric Soc., Soc. Pediatric Infectious Diseases (council 1984, pres. 1987-89), World Pediatric Infectious Diseases Soc. (sec. 1996—, pres. 2d internat. conf.), Soc. Pediatric Research, San Antonio Pediatric Soc., Tex. Pediatrics Soc. (awards com.), Council Tex. Pediatric Dept. Chmn. (chmn. 1978-81), Tex. Med. Assn. (sec. treas. pediatric sect. 1979-80, pres. 1980-81), Bexar County Med. Soc., Tex. Infectious Disease Soc., Western Soc. Pediatric Rsch., L.A. Pediatric Soc. Home: # 416 4903 Edgemoor Ln Apt 416 Bethesda MD 20814-5346 Office: NIAID NIH Lab of Clin Investigation Bldg 10 Rm 11N229 Bethesda MD 20892

BRUNELLE, EUGENE JOHN, JR., mechanical engineering educator; b. Montpelier, Vt., Mar. 17, 1932; s. Eugene John Sr. Brunelle and Maxine Gertrude (Chatfield) Corson; m. Raylene Julia Clark, June 12, 1955 (div. Sept. 1967); children: Steven, Alison, Holly. BS in Engring., U. Mich., 1953, MS in Engring., 1955; ScD, MIT, 1962. Asst. prof. Princeton (N.J.) U., 1960-64; assoc. prof. Rensselaer Poly. Inst., Troy, N.Y., 1964-98, prof. emeritus, 1998—; vis. prof. Air Force Inst. Tech., Dayton, Ohio, 1983-85; cons. aerospace firms, 1958—. Contbr. chpt. Principles of Aeroelasticity, 1962; contbr. over 70 papers to profl. jours., also reviewer. Patron Challenger Space Ctrs., 1988—. Fellow Boeing Aerospace Co., 1959; grantee NSF, 1967, NASA, 1975-83. Mem. ASME, AIAA, Am. Acad. Mechs. (founding), Soc. Indsl. and Applied Maths., Am. Math. Soc. Achievements include discovery of similarity rules and scaling laws for composite structures, of affine transformations for all the field equations of classical physics and mechanics; discovery of fundamental solution properties of classical linear elasticity. Home: 66 Thimbleberry Rd Ballston Spa NY 12020-4360 Office: Rensselaer Poly Inst 4006 Jonsson Engring Ctr Troy NY 12180-3590

BRUNELLE, ROBERT L., retired state education director; b. Somersworth, N.H., Sept. 19, 1924; s. Lorenzo A. and Laomie (Carter) B.; m. Diane P. Gagnon, June 14, 1947; children—Roberta, Marc. B.Edn., U. N.H., M.Edn., 1958; Ed.D., Boston U., 1972. Prin. Elem. Schs., Somersworth, N.H., 1952-58; supt. schs. Somersworth Schs., Somersworth, N.H., 1958-68; dep. commr. edn. State Dept. Edn., Concord, N.H., 1968-76, commr. edn., 1976-86, exec. dir. Gov.'s Excellence in Edn. Program, 1986-88; ret., 1988; Trustee U. N.H., 1976-86. Chmn. state employees div. United Way Fund of Greater Concord, 1971-72; v.p. Daniel Webster coun. Boy Scouts Am., 1978-88; awards chmn. Philbrook Children's Found., 1991-95, Ch. Coun., 1992-93; mem. programs and svcs. com. Croched Mountain Found. With USN, 1944-53. Recipient Award of Excellence, Pa. Sch. Bds. Assn.; Sears Found. scholar. Mem. Am. Assn. Sch. Adminstrs., N.E. Regional Exch. (chmn. 1984-85), Am. Automobile Assn. (chmn. 1984-87), Ret. Adminstrs. (chmn. 1992-94), Am. Legion, Phi Delta Kappa, Kiwanis (v.p. 1958-59, pres. 1959-60). Roman Catholic. Home: 83 Rockingham St Concord NH 03301-2649

BRUNELLO-MCCAY, ROSANNE, sales executive; b. Cleve., Aug. 26, 1960; d. Carl Carmello and Vivan Lucille (Caranna) B.; m. Walter B. McCay, Feb. 26, 1994 (div. 1998); 1 child, Angela Breanna. Student, U. Cin., 1978-81, Cleve. State U., 1981-82. Indsl. sales engr. Alta Machine Tool, Denver, 1982; mem. sales./purchases Ford Tool & Machine, Denver, 1982-84; sales/ptnr. Mountain Rep. Enterprises, Denver, 1984-86; pres., owner Mountain Rep. Ariz., Phoenix, 1986—; pres. Mountain Rep. Oreg., Portland, 1990—, Mountain Rep. Wash., 1991—; pres. Mountain Rep. Calif., Sunnyvale, 1997—, San Clemente, 1998—, Port Clinton, Ohio, 1999—, Milford, Ohio, 1999—; sec. Computer & Automated Systems Assoc., 1987, vice chmn., 1988, chmn., 1989. Active mem. Rep. Party, 1985—; mem. Phoenix Art Mus., Grand Canyon Minority Coun., 1994; vol. Make-A-Wish Found. fund raiser, 1995-99. Named Mrs. Chandler Internat. by Mrs. Ariz. Internat. orgn., 1996, Mrs. East Valley U.S., 1997; finalist Mrs. Ariz. Internat., 1996. Mem. NAFE, Soc. Mfg. Engrs. (pres. award 1988), Computer Automated Assn. (sec. 1987, vice chmn. 1988 chmn. 1989), Nat. Hist. Soc., Italian Cultural Soc., Tempe C. of C., Vocat. Ednl. Club Am. (mem. exec. bd., pres. 1987—). Roman Catholic. Avocations: sports, aerobics, dancing, skiing, golfing, tennis. E-mail: rosanne@mtnrep.com. Office: Mountain Rep Ariz 410 S Jay St Chandler AZ 85224-7668

BRUNER, CHARLOTTE HUGHES, French language educator; b. Urbana, Ill., May 8, 1917; d. Charles Hughes and Nell Converse (Bomar) Johnston; m. David Kincaid Bruner, July 16, 1939; children: Nell Kincaid Bruner Sedransk, Charles Hughes. B.A., U. Ill., 1938; M.A., Columbia U., 1939. Tchr. French Iowa State U., 1942-44, 55—, prof., 1980-87, prof. emeritus, 1987—; instr. U. Ill., 1944-45. Writer, dir. radio series, 1974, 79, 80-86; editor: Unwinding Threads: Writing by Women in Africa, 1983, The Heinemann Book of African Women's Writing, 1993; consulting editor for Africa: The Feminist Companion to Literature in English, 1990; contbr. articles to profl. jours. Named to Iowa Women's Hall of Fame, 1997. Mem. MLA, African Lit. Assn. (vice chmn. 1978-79), Am. Tchrs. French, Coll. Lang. Assn., Phi Beta Kappa, Phi Kappa Phi, Phi Sigma Iota, Pi Delta Pi. Home: 4625 Westbend Dr Ames IA 50014-3662 Office: Iowa State U Dept Fgn Langs and Lits Ames IA 50011

BRUNER, EVANS, management consultant. BS in applied Math., MBA in Fin. Pres. Bruner Cons. Assocs., Inc., Bridgeport, Conn., 1980—. Mem. Ind. Computer Cons. Assn. (pres. Conn. chpt. 1983-84, cert., nat. pres. 1989-90), Data Processing Mgmt. Assn. (pres. 1985), Inst. Mgmt. Cons. (cert., pres. Fairfield/Westchester chpt. 1994-97). Office: Bruner Cons Assocs Inc 1069 Briarwood Ave Bridgeport CT 06604

BRUNER, JEFFREY BENHAM, foreign language educator; b. Holdenville, Okla., Mar. 20, 1961; s. Eugene and Billye Jo B.; m. Deborah Elaine Wilkinson, June 16, 1984 (div. Feb. 1995); m. Twyla Anne Meding, Dec. 22, 1995. BA in Spanish, Okla. Bapt. U., 1983; MA in Spanish, Rutgers U., 1986, PhD in Spanish, 1990. Asst. prof. Trenton (N.J.) State Coll., 1988-90; asst. prof. W.Va. U., Morgantown, 1990-96, assoc. prof., 1996—; mem. adv. bd. W.Va. U. Phil. Papers, 1994—. Contbr. articles to profl. jours. V.p., bd. dirs. Maintain People's Coop., Morgantown, 1996—. Recipient Radiol. Cons. Assn. award, Morgantown, 1992; Riggle fellow, W.Va. U., 1992. Mem. Northeast Modern Lang. Assn., So. Comparative Lit. Assn., Modern Lang. Assn., 20th Century Spanish Soc. Avocations: cross country skiing, cycling, hiking, travel. Office: WVa U Dept Fgn Langs Chitwood Hall Morgantown WV 26506-6298

BRUNER, PHILIP LANE, lawyer; b. Chgo., Sept. 26, 1939; s. Henry Pfeiffer and Mary Marjorie (Williamson) B.; m. Ellen Carole Germann, Mar. 21, 1964; children: Philip Richard, Stephen Reed, Carolyn Anne. AB, Princeton U., 1961; JD, U. Mich., 1964; MBA, Syracuse U., 1967. Bar: Wis. 1964, Minn. 1968. Mem. Briggs and Morgan P.A., Mpls., St. Paul, 1967-83; founding shareholder Hart, Bruner and O'Brien P.A., Mpls., 1983-90; ptnr., head constrn. law group Faegre & Benson, Mpls., 1991—; adj. prof. William Mitchell Coll. Law, St. Paul, 1970-76; lectr. law seminars, univs., bar assns. and industry; chmn. Supreme Ct. Minn. Bd. Continuing Legal Edn., 1994-98. Contbr. articles to profl. jours. Mem. Bd. Edn., Mahtomedi Ind. Sch. Dist. 832, 1978-86; bd. dirs. Mahtomedi Area Ednl. Found., 1988-94, pres., 1988-91; bd. dirs. Minn. Ch. Found., 1975—, pres., 1989-97; chmn. Constrn. Ind. adv. bd., Fedl. Pub., Inc., 1991—. Capt. USAF, 1964-67. Decorated Air Force Commendation Medal; recipient Disting. Service award St. Paul Jaycees, 1974; named One of Ten Outstanding Young Minnesotans, Minn. Jaycees, 1975. Fellow Am. Coll. Constrn. Lawyers (founding mem., bd. govs.), Nat. Contract Mgmt. Assn., Am. Bar Found.; mem. ABA (chmn. internat. constrn. divsn. forum com. on constrn. industry 1989-91, chmn. fidelity and surety law com. 1994-95, regional chmn. pub. contract law sect. 1990-96), Internat. Bar Assn., Inter-Pacific Bar Assn. (vice chmn. internat. constrn. com. 1995-97), Fed. Bar Assn., Minn. Bar Assn. (vice chmn. litigation sect. 1979-81), Wis. Bar Assn., Hennepin Bar Assn., Internat. Assn. Def. Counsel, Am. Arbitration Assn. (nat. panel arbitrators), Mpls. Club. Presbyterian. Home: 8432 80th St N Stillwater MN 55082-9331 Office: Faegre & Benson 2200 Norwest Ctr 90 S 7th St Ste 2200 Minneapolis MN 55402-3901

BRUNER, ROBERT B., hospital consultant; b. N.Y.C., Aug. 4, 1933; s. Samuel Wolf and Pauline (Rothstein) B.; m. Janet Bergman, Aug. 26, 1956; children: Steven Wayne, Marc Richard. Student, NYU, 1950-53; BA cum laude, L.I. U., 1956; MS, 1959. Adminstrv. asst., asst. adminstr. Bklyn. Hebrew Home and Hosp. for Aged, 1958-62; asst. adminstr. Montefiore Hosp., Bronx, N.Y., 1962-64, L.I. Jewish Hosp., New Hyde Park, N.Y., 1964-66; adminstr. L.I. Jewish Hosp., Queens, 1966-69, Univ. Hosp., SUNY, Stony Brook, 1969-71; exec. dir., pres. Mt. Sinai Hosp., Hartford, Conn., 1971-91; cons., 1990-93; prin. Healthcare Practice, The Futures Group, 1993-96; pres. Conn. Sinai Corp., 1984-90, Blueridge Health Svcs., 1984-91, Mt. Sinai Hosp. Found., 1984—; sr. cons. The Future Group, Signal Med. Svcs., Staff Builders, Cornerstone Health Svcs.; trustee People's Bank Holding Co., Bridgeport; adj. faculty U. Hartford; asst. prof. SUNY, 1969-71; prof. NYU, 1973-75; preceptor Yale Sch. Pub. Health; commr. Conn. Commn. on Hosps. and Health Care, 1976-81; mem. Nat. Commn. on Certification of Physicians Assts., 1976-84, pres., 1981-84; chmn. blue ribbon com. New Eng. Hosp. Assembly, 1979-91; pres. Combined Hosps. Alcoholism program, 1977-79; v.p. Capital Area Health Consortium, 1978-79, pres., 1982-84; vice chmn. Health Sys. Agy. Bd. dirs. Premier Health System, 1986-88. Recipient E. Clayton Gengras Humanitarian award Nat. Multiple Sclerosis Soc., 1987, Disting. Svc. award Capital Area Health Consortium, 1988; named Boss of Yr., Greater Hartford Jaycees, 1977. Fellow APHA, Am. Coll. Healthcare Adminstrn. (recert. 1989), Royal Soc. Health, Am. Acad. Med. Adminstrn.; mem. AAAS, N.Y. Acad. Sci. (coun. teaching hosps., del. to Assn. Am. Med. Colls.), Conn. Hosp. Assn. (trustee T.S. Hamilton Disting. Svc. award, chmn.-elect 1985, chmn. 1986), Am. Hosp. Assn. (alt. del. regional planning bd. I, del. 1992), Am. Hosp. Assn. Planning, Greater Hartford C. of C. (futures com., bd. dirs.), Hosp. Execs., Healthcare Study Soc. Home: 141 Sunny Reach Dr Hartford CT 06117-1534

BRUNER, STEPHEN C., lawyer; b. Chgo., Nov. 11, 1941; s. Henry Pfeiffer and Mary Marjorie (Williamson) B.; m. Elizabeth Erskine Osborn, Apr. 7, 1973; children: Elizabeth, David. B.A. summa cum laude, Yale U., 1963; J.D. cum laude, Harvard U., 1967. Bar: Ill. 1967, U.S. Dist. Ct. (no. dist.) Ill. 1971, U.S. Ct. Appeals (7th cir.) 1983, U.S. Supreme Ct. 1988. Assoc. Winston & Strawn, Chgo., 1971-76, ptnr., 1976—, capital ptnr., 1982—; lectr. Northwestern U. Sch. of Law, 1983-84; cons. Commn. on Govt. Procurement, 1972; mem. Landmarks Commn., Oak Park, Ill., 1978-81; bd. govs. Oak Park-River Forest Community Chest, 1985-90; elected mem. Bd. Edn. Oak Park and River Forest High Sch., 1993—. Served to lt. USN, 1968-71. Recipient Navy Achievement medal; Corning Found. travelling fellow, 1963-64. Mem. ABA (litigation and pub. contracts sects.), Chgo. Bar Assn., Am. Arbitration Assn. (panel of arbitrators), Chgo. Coun. on Fgn. Rels., Econ. Club, Univ. Club, Yale Club, Harvard Club (Chgo.). Office: Winston & Strawn 35 W Wacker Dr Ste 4200 Chicago IL 60601-1695*

BRUNER, WILLIAM GWATHMEY, III, lawyer; b. Gadsden, Ala., Nov. 29, 1951; s. William G. and Nicolette A. (Diprima) B.; m. Eloisa Fernandez, Aug. 7, 1976; children: Nicolette, Virginia, William, Weston. BSE, U. Mich., 1973; JD, U. Va., 1976. Bar: Ind., Pa. Assoc. Bingham, Summers, Indpls., 1976-78; corp. counsel Scott Paper Co., Phila., 1978-86; group counsel Emhart Corp., Farmington, Conn., 1986-89; corp. counsel Black & Decker, Towson, Md., 1989-93, sr. corp. counsel, 1994—. Mem. ABA (EEO com. labor and employment law sect., taxation sect.). Republican. Roman Catholic. Office: Black & Decker Corp 701 E Joppa Rd Baltimore MD 21286-5559

BRUNET, JAMES ROBERT, public administration research associate; b. Queens, N.Y., Nov. 6, 1966; s. Joseph Robert Brunet and Margaret Delabo; m. Greta C. Larkin, Sept. 19, 1992. BA, Siena Coll., 1988; MPA, U. Conn., 1990. Asst. project mgr. Gov.'s Mgmt. and Productivity Office, Albany, N.Y., 1990-92; budget examiner N.Y. State Divsn. Budget, Albany, 1992-93; asst. dir. Cmty. Justice Resource Ctr. Guilford Coll., Greensboro, N.C., 1994-96; rsch. assoc. N.C. State U., Raleigh, 1998—. Mem. ASPA, Am. Polit. Sci. Assn. Roman Catholic. Avocations: Civil War history, bass guitar. E-mail: jimúbrunet@ncsu.edu. Home: Apt MM-11 605 Jones Ferry Rd Carrboro NC 27510

BRUNETT, ALEXANDER J., bishop; b. Detroit, MI, Jan. 13, 1958. ordained priest July 13, 1958. Ordained bishop Diocese of Helena, 1994; archbishop Diocese of Seattle, 1997—. Office: Chancery Office 910 Marion St Seattle WA 98104-1274*

BRUNETTI, MELVIN T., federal judge; b. 1933; m. Gail Dian Buchanan; children: Nancy, Bradley, Melvin Jr. Student, U. Nev.; JD, U. Calif., San Francisco, 1964. Mem. firm Vargas, Bartlett & Dixon, 1964-69, Laxalt, Bell, Allison & Lebaron, 1970-78, Allison, Brunetti, MacKenzie, Hartman, Soumbeniotis & Russell, 1978-85; judge U.S. Ct. Appeals (9th cir.), Reno, 1985—. Mem. Council of Legal Advisors, Rep. Nat. Com., 1982-85. Served with U.S. Army N.G., 1954-56. Mem. ABA, State Bar of Nev. (pres. 1984-85, bd. govs. 1975-84). Office: US Ct Appeals US Courthouse 400 S Virginia St Ste 506 Reno NV 89501-2194

BRÜNGER, AXEL THOMAS, biophysicist, researcher, educator; b. Leipzig, Germany, Nov. 25, 1956; came to U.S., 1982; s. Hans and Hildegard (Müller) B. Diploma, U. Hamburg (Germany), 1980; PhD, Tech. U. Munich, 1982. Postdoctoral fellow Max-Planck Inst., Martinsried, Germany, 1984; rsch. assoc. Harvard U., Cambridge, Mass., 1982-83, 85-87; asst. investigator Howard Hughes Med. Inst., New Haven, 1987-92, assoc. investigator, 1992-95, investigator, 1995—; asst. prof. Yale U., New Haven, 1987-91, assoc. prof., 1991-93, prof., 1993—. Recipient Röntgen prize for bioscis. Würzburg U., 1995; NATO postdoctoral fellow Deutscher Akademischer Austauschdienst, Bonn, Germany, 1982-83. Mem. AAAS, Am. Crystallographic Assn., Am. Chem. Soc., Protein Soc. Achievements include studies of protein structure and function, developments in macromolecular x-ray crystallography and solution NMR spectroscopy. Office: Yale U 266 Whitney Ave New Haven CT 06511-8902

BRUNGS, ROBERT ANTHONY, theology educator, institute director; b. Cin., July 7, 1931; s. Adolph and Helen (Klosterman) B. AB, Bellarmine Coll., Plattsburgh, N.Y., 1955; Licentiate in Philosophy, Fordham U., 1956; PhD in Physics, St. Louis U., 1962; Sacred Theology Licentiae, Woodstock (Md.) Coll., 1965. Asst. prof. physics St. Louis U., 1970-75, assoc. prof. physics, 1975-83; dir. Inst. for Theol. Encounter with Sci. and Tech., St. Louis, 1968—; cons. Vatican, Rome, 1973-84, Council Cath. Bishops, Washington, 1973—; mem. adv. bd. Zygon Mag., Chgo., 1975—. Exec. producer video program DECISION, 1987, Lights Breaking, 1985; author: Building the City,1 967, A Priestly People, 1968, You See Lights Breaking Upon Us: Doctrinal Perspectives on Biological Advance, 1989; contbr. 60 articles to mags., newspapers, profl. jours. Mem. AAAS, Am. Phys. Soc., Sigma Xi, Phi Beta Kappa. Fax: 314-977-7264. E-mail: brungsr@slu.edu. Office: Inst for Theol Encounter with Sci and Tech 221 N Grand Blvd Saint Louis MO 63103-2006

BRUNI, STEPHEN THOMAS, art museum director; b. Phila., Feb. 3, 1949; s. Eugene Thomas and Frances Isabel (McMorran) B.; m. Barbara Natalie Plunket, May 13, 1949; children: Christopher Stephen, Katherine Elizabeth. BA, George Washington U., 1971. Curatorial asst. Del. Art Mus., Wilmington, 1972-74, program asst., 1974-77, adminstrv. asst., 1977-79, mgr. support svcs., 1979-82, asst. dir. adminstrn., 1982-84, dep. dir. adminstrn., 1984-85, acting dir. adminstrn., 1985-86, exec. dir., 1986—; mem. arts selection com. Del State Arts Coun., 1985-86, State Divsn. Librs., 1984-86; mem. Gov.'s Arts Adv. Com., 1983-85; mem. adv. bd. Siena Hall and Seton Villa, Creative Artists Network; bd. dirs. Studio Group, Inc. Mem. bd. Literacy Vols. Am. (affiliate Wilmington Libr.). Mem. Am. Assn. Mus., Assn. Art Mus. Dirs., Bd. Greater Wilmington Conv. and Visitors Bur. Avocations: skiing, racquet sports, golf, cycling. Office: Del Art Mus 2301 Kentmere Pky Wilmington DE 19806-2019

BRUNIE, CHARLES HENRY, investment manager; b. N.Y.C., July 17, 1930; s. Charles Henry and Olivia (Swanston) B.; m. Jean Isbell Corley, June 23, 1965; stepchildren: William Corley, Jean Corley Yankus, Ellen Corley. B.A., Amherst Coll., 1952; M.B.A., Columbia, 1956. Analyst N.Y. Life Ins. Co., N.Y.C., 1956-60, Faulkner, Dawkins & Sullivan, 1960-63, Oppenheimer & Co., N.Y.C., 1963-65; gen. ptnr. Oppenheimer & Co., 1965-82, mem. exec. com., 1969-82; chmn. Oppenheimer Capital, 1969-96, chmn. emeritus, 1996—; trustee Manhattan Inst., 1978—, chmn. bd., 1980-1990, chmn. emeritus, 1990—. Served with AUS, 1952-54. Mem. N.Y. Soc. Security Analysts, Chartered Financial Analysts, Mont Pelerin Soc., Delta Upsilon. Clubs: Knickerbocker (N.Y.C.), Doubles (N.Y.C.), Annabell's (London), Bronxville Field, Siwanoy Country (Bronxville). Home: 21 Elm Rock Rd Bronxville NY 10708-4202 Office: Oppenheimer Capital Oppenheimer Tower 200 Liberty St Fl 37 New York NY 10281-3797

BRUNING, JAMES LEON, university official, educator; b. Bruning, Nebr., Apr. 1, 1938; s. Leon G. and Delma Dorothy (Middendorf) B.; m. E. Marlene Schaff, Aug. 24, 1958; children: Michael, Stephen, Kathleen. B.A., Doane Coll., 1959; M.A., U. Iowa, 1961, Ph.D., 1962. Chmn. dept psychology Ohio U., Athens, 1972-76, acting dean arts and scis., 1976-77, assoc. dean, 1977-78, vice provost, 1978-81, provost, 1981-93, trustee prof., 1993—; provost Shawnee (Ohio) State U., 1996; v.p. regional higher edn. Ohio U., 1998-99; planning cons. NCHEMS, Boulder, Colo., 1979-80. Author: Computational Handbook of Statistics, 1968, Research in Psychology, 1970; contbr. over 70 articles to profl. jours. Chair task force Ohio Bd. Regents, 1994-95. Grantee Esso., 1963-64, NIMH, 1963-66, EPDA, 1974-75, OBOR, 1989-91. Mem. Am. psychol. Assn. (vis. scientist), Midwestern Psychol. Assn., AAAS, Sigma Xi. Democrat. Lutheran. Home: 6148 Melnor Dr Athens OH 45701-3577 Office: Ohio U Psychology Dept Athens OH 45701

BRUNK, SAMUEL FREDERICK, oncologist; b. Harrisonburg, Va., Dec. 21, 1932; s. Harry Anthony and Lena Gertrude (Burkholder) B.; m. Mary Priscilla Bauman, June 24, 1976; children: Samuel, Jill, Geoffrey, Heather, Kirsten, Peter, Christopher, Andrew, Paul, Barbara. BS, Ea. Mennonite Coll., 1955; MD, U. Va., 1959; MS in Pharmacology, U. Iowa, 1967. Diplomate Am. Bd. Internal Medicine, Am. Bd. Internal Medicine in Med. Oncology. Straight med. intern U. Va., Charlottesville, 1959-60; resident in chest diseases Blue Ridge Sanatorium, Charlottesville, 1960-61; resident in internal medicine U. Iowa, Iowa City, 1962-64, fellow in clin. pharmacology (oncology), 1964-65, 66-67, asst. prof. internal medicine, 1967-72; assoc. prof. internal medicine, 1972-76; fellow in medicine (oncology) Johns Hopkins U., Balt., 1965-66; clin. assoc. prof. med. Okla. State U. Coll. Osteo; vis. physician bone marrow transplantation unit Fred Hutchinson Cancer Treatment Ctr., U. Wash., Seattle, 1975; practice medicine specializing in med. oncology Des Moines, 1976-94; attending physician Iowa Luth. Hosp., 1976-94, Iowa Meth. Med. Ctr., 1976-94, Charter Hosp., 1976-94, Mercy Hosp. Med. Ctr., 1976-94; dir. med. oncology Hahne Regional Cancer Ctr., DuBois, Pa., 1994; attending physician DuBois Regional Med. Ctr., 1994; dir. Pa. Cmty. Cancer Care, 1995; attending physician St. Mary's Regional Med. Ctr., 1994; med. oncologist Cancer Treatment Ctr., Tulsa, Okla., 1995—; attending physician Meml. Med. Ctr., Tulsa, Okla., 1995—; chief of staff Iowa Luth. Hosp., 1990, chmn. dept. internal medicine, 1988; cons. physician Des Moines Gen. Osteo. Hosp., 1976-94; prin. investigator Iowa Oncology Rsch. Assn. in assn. with N. Cen. Cancer Treatment Group and Ea. Coop. Oncology Group, 1978-83; prin. investigator Iowa Oncology Rsch. Assn. Cmty. Clin. Oncology Program, 1983-84; mem. cancer care com. St, Mary's, Pa., 1995. Contbr. articles to profl. jours. Bd. dirs. Iowa div. Am. Cancer Soc., 1971-89, Johnson County chpt., 1968-72. Mosby scholar, U. Va., 1959. Fellow ACP, Am. Coll. Clin. Pharmacology; mem. AMA, Okla. Medical Soc., Tulsa County Medical Soc., Iowa Thoracic Soc., Am. Thoracic Soc., Iowa Clin. Med. Soc., Am. Fedn. Clin. Rsch., Iowa Heart Assn., Am. Assn. Cancer Edn., Am. Soc. Hematology, Am. Soc. Clin. Pharmacology and Therapeutics, Cen. Soc. Clin. Rsch., Raven Soc., Alpha Omega Alpha. Roman Catholic. Home: 2929 E 69th St Tulsa OK 74136-4541

BRUNK, WILLIAM EDWARD, astronomer; b. Cleve., Nov. 24, 1928; s. Edgar Rea and Mabel Mowbray (Pearson) B.; 1 dau., Anna Kathryn. B.S., Case Inst. Tech., 1952, M.S., 1954, Ph.D., 1963. Aero. research scientist Lewis Flight Propulsion Lab., NACA, Cleve., 1954-58; aerospace engr. Lewis Research Center, NASA, Cleve., 1958-64; staff scientist for planetary astronomy NASA Hdqrs., Washington, 1964-65, program chief planetary astronomy, 1965-77, discipline scientist planetary astronomy, 1977-82, chief planetary sci. br., 1982-85; mgr. solar system sci. Univ. Space Rsch. Assn., Washington, 1985-94; ret., 1994. Recipient Exceptional Service medal NASA, 1985. Fellow AAAS; mem. Am. Astron. Soc. (Harold Mazursky Meritorious Svc. award 1995), Internat. Astron. Union; Mem. Sigma Xi. Home: PO Box 3466 Annapolis MD 21403-0466

BRUNKEN, GERALD WALTER, SR., manufacturing company executive; b. Oak Park, Ill., May 31, 1938; s. Walter Richard and Elenore (Troost) B.; m. Louise Nunziato, June 29, 1968; children: Gerald Jr., Patrick. BS, Lincoln Coll., 1958; BA in Econs., Baker U., 1961. Br. coord. A.M. Castle, Franklin Park, Ill., 1961-62; sales rep. Proviso West Realty, Berkley, Ill., 1962-65; CEO Addison (Ill.) Machine Engring., 1965—, CEO, pres., 1995—; pres. Sci. Tube Inc., Addison, 1971-95. One man show, Addison, 1971; contbr. articles to profl. jours. Cub master Boy Scouts Am., Addison, 1976-78; athletic dir. St. Philip the Apostle Sch., Addison, 1982-84; pres. Driscoll Cath. High Booster Club, 1985-86. Mem. Fabricating Mfrs. Assn. (speaker, panelist), Am. Tube Assn. (speaker, panelist), Ducks Unlimited (treas. Salt Creek chpt. 1982-90, zone chmn. State of Ill. 1990—, Spl. Projects awards 1987, 88, 89, 90), KC. Roman Catholic. Avocations: painting, writing, hunting, fishing. Home: 4444 N Ann Ct Addison IL 60101

BRUNNER, ELIZABETH KING, health facility administrator, consultant; b. Milw., Feb. 9, 1947; d. Harvey King and Elizabeth Vogt; m. Dale Brunner, Aug. 10, 1968; children: Robert, Kelly, Kate. ADN, Cardinal Stritch Coll., 1982, BS in Mgmt., 1989. Lic. Nursing Home Adminstr. Dir. nursing Hearthside Rehab. Ctr., Milw., 1983-85, Oakland Manor, Shorewood, Wis., 1986, St. Camillus Campus, Wauwatosa, Wis., 1989; adminstr. Roseville Manor nursing home, Milw., 1989; nurse, cons. McKnight & Assocs., Milw., 1990-96; dir. nursing Mequon (Wis.) Care Ctr., Mequon, ., 1997-98; regional nurse cons. Extendicare Health Facilities Inc., 1999—; sr. clin. cons. Hoffman and Assocs. Mem. Long Term Care Dirs. of Greater Milw. (pres. 1985-87), Wis. Dirs. of Nursing Coun. (vice chairperson bd. dirs. 1989, 91-92, pres., dir. nursing coun. 1992-96). Home: N170 W 21801 Rosewood Ln Jackson WI 53037

BRUNNER, GEORGE MATTHEW, management consultant, former business executive; b. Newark, Jan. 17, 1925; s. Mathias J. and Mary E. (Fuith) B.; m. Ruth E. Owens, Nov. 16, 1953. AB in Chemistry, Columbia U., 1949, MChemE, 1950. Devel. engr. J.T. Baker Chem. Co., Phillipsburg, N.J., 1950-53; plant mgr. Internat. Minerals & Chem. Corp., Niagara Falls, N.Y. and Houston, 1953-62; mfg. engring. mgr. Gen. Foods Corp., Hoboken, N.J., Houston and Lafayette, Ind., 1962-71; v.p. mfg. W.R. Grace & Co., St. Simons Islands, Ga., 1971-73; pres., chief exec. officer S.A. Schonbrunn & Co., Inc., Palisades Park, N.J., 1973-82; v.p. ops. Am. Maize Products Co., Stamford, Conn., 1982-84; mgmt. cons., 1984—. Served with AUS, 1943-45. Decorated Purple Heart. Mem. Nat. Coffee Assn. (dir.), Pres.'s Assn., Am. Chem. Soc., Am. Inst. Chem. Engrs., Electrochem. Soc., 5th Armored Div. Assn. (pres. 1980-81). Patentee in field. Home and Office: 1221 Clays Trl Oldsmar FL 34677-4866

BRUNNER, JANET LEE, physician assistant; b. Milw., Sept. 15, 1955; d. Donald Edward and Carol Louise (Radtke) B. BA in Biology, Luther Coll., 1977; MA in Edn., Ctrl. Mich. U., 1984; BS in Physician Assistance, U. Iowa, 1989. Cert. physician asst., Pa. Nat. Commn. on Certification of Physician Assts; registered med. technologist. Staff med. technologist St. Joseph's Hosp., Milw., 1977-79, 81-87, Hosp. Castañer (P.R.), 1979-81; physician asst. med. oncology Med. Coll. Wis., Milw., 1989-92; physician asst. bone marrow transplant Med. Coll. Wis., 1992-94, sr. coord. bone marrow transplant program, 1993-94; physician asst., sr. coord. bone marrow transplant program Thomas Jefferson U. Hosp., Phila., 1995—; lab. cons. Am. Immediate Care, Chgo., 1984; guest lectr. Allentown Coll., Center Valley, Pa., 1996-98. Sec. bd. dirs. Wis. Interfaith Com. on Ctrl. Am., Milw., 1992-94; election observer U.S. Citizens Election Observer Mission, El Salvador, 1994; mem. coun. Prince of Peace Luth. Ch., 1997-99. Fellow Am. Acad. Physician Assts.; mem. Pa. Soc. Physician Assts. Avocations: aerobics, travel, bicycling. Home: 47 Lavister Dr Mount Laurel NJ 08054-2642 Office: Thomas Jefferson U Hosp 130 S 9th St Ste 400 Philadelphia PA 19107-5233

BRUNNER, KIRSTIN ELLEN, pediatrician, psychiatrist; b. Allentown, Pa., July 26, 1959; d. John Wilson and Ingrid Ulla Brita (Arvide) B. BS, Muhlenberg Coll., Allentown, Pa., 1981; DO, Phila. Coll. Osteo. Medicine, 1986. Diplomate Am. Bd. Pediatrics, Am. Bd. Psychiatry and Neurology in child and adolescent psychiatry and adult psychiatry. Resident U. Ky., 1992; dept. dir. Integra Health Family Devel. Ctr., Cedar Rapids, Iowa, 1993-98; with Hamot Inst. for Behavioral Health, Erie, Pa., 1998—. Fellow Am. Acad. Pediatrics; mem. AMA, Am. Acad. Child and Adolescent Psychiatry, Am. Psychiat. Assn. Avocations: cross country skiing, soccer (outdoor and indoor). Office: Hamot Inst Behavioral Health 118 E 2d St Erie PA 16507-1507

BRUNNER, LILLIAN SHOLTIS, nurse, author; b. Freeland, Pa.; d. Andrew J. and Anna (Tomasko) Sholtis; m. Mathias J. Brunner, Sept. 8, 1951; children: Janet Brunner Cramer, Carol Ann Brunner Burns, Douglas Mathias. RN, diploma, U. Pa., 1940, BS, 1945, LittD (hon.), 1985; MS in Nursing, Case-Western Res. U., 1947; ScD (hon.), Cedar Crest Coll., 1978. RN, Pa. Head nurse U. Pa. Hosp., Phila., 1940-42, operating room supr., 1942-44; head, fundamentals of nursing dept. U. Pa. Hosp., 1944-46; asst. prof. surgical nursing Yale U. Sch. Nursing, New Haven, Conn., 1947-51; surgical supr. Yale-New Haven Hosp., 1947-51; rsch. project dir. Sch. Nursing Bryn Mawr (Pa.) Hosp., 1973-77; co-founder History of Nursing Mus., Pa. Hosp., Phila., 1974; mem. bd. overseers Sch. Nursing U. Pa., 1982-88; bd. overseers emeritus, 1988—; chmn. nursing adv. Presbyn.-U. Pa. Med. Ctr., Phila., 1970-88, 90-93, trustee, 1976-88, 90-95, vice chmn. bd. trustees, 1985-88; mem. com., profl. advisor Vis. Nurse Assn., Lancaster, Pa., 1996—; sec. Glen Coun., Willow Valley Manor North, 1999—. *With a rich background including clinical experience, teaching and writing, Dr. Brunner stands tall as a leader and role model in professional nursing. Her major contribution includes senior-author of the Textbook of Medical-Surgical Nursing, revised eight times since 1964 and known lovingly by students as the "bible" in nursing. Another volume is the Lippincott Manual of Nursing Practice. Both books have been translated into at least eight languages. Being a strong proponent of "excellence in nursing practice," she served in many professional organizations and has been the recipient of numerous honors. Currently she is an Overseer Emerita at the top-ranking University of Pennsylvania School of Nursing.* Author: Manual of Operating Room Technology, 1966, (with others) Lippincott Manual of Nursing Practice, 1974, 4th edit., 1986, Textbook of Medical and Surgical Nursing, 1964, 6th edit., 1988; editl. bd. Jour. Nursing and Health Care, Nursing 2000, Nursing Photobook Series, 1978-90. Bd. dirs. Presbyn. Found. for Phila., 1995-. Recipient Disting. Alumnus award Frances Payne Bolton Sch. Nursing, Case Western Res. U., 1980, Alumni award for merit Soc. Alumni Assns., U. Pa., and Am. Dream Achievement award Class of '45, U. Pa., 1995. Fellow Am. Acad. Nursing; mem. ANA, Nat. League for Nursing (judge nat. writing contest 1982-84, Disting. Svc. award 1979), Nat. League Am. Pen Women (sec. Phila. chpt. 1972-76, nat. sec. 1984-86), Nurses Alumni Assn. U. Pa. Hosp., Ben Franklin Soc., Internat. Old Lacers Soc., Sigma Theta Tau, Pi Gamma Mu, Pi Lambda Theta. Home and Office: Apt J-411 645 Willow Valley Sq Lancaster PA 17602-4871

BRUNNER, ROBERT FRANCIS, composer, conductor; b. Pasadena, Calif., Jan. 9, 1938; s. Francis Rudolph and Barbara Jeanne (Reese) B. Student, UCLA, 1955-56; pvt. studies, 1942-63. Bass player, vocalist The Rhythm Rangers, L.A., 1949-52; leader, pianist, arranger, vocalist Bob Brunner & His Orchestra, L.A., 1951-64; bass player Brentwood Symphony Orch., L.A., 1956-62; bass player, solo pianist Santa Monica (Calif.) Civic Symphonic Band, 1956-61; free lance arranger L.A., 1956-64; recording background vocalist various TV, motion pictures and records, Hollywood, Calif., 1961-65; composer, conductor, arranger, songwriter Walt Disney Prodns., Inc., Burbank, Calif., 1963-80; musical dir. New Mickey Mouse Club, 1976-78; free-lance composer, conductor, arranger, songwriter, record producer, pub. various entertainment industry projects, 1980—; owner Brunner Mus. Pub. Co., 1973—; historic music advisor San Diego Yacht Club, 1985; mem. adv. bd. music dept. L.A. City Coll., 1986—; mus. dir. Hollywood Bowl Easter Sunrise Svcs., 1988; cons. Saundra's Story Books, Inc., 1987—; guest lectr. film scoring and musicology Otis Art Inst., Utah State U., U. Utah, Brigham Young U., UCLA, U. Calif.-Santa Barbara, Calif. Poly. Coll., Pomona, Claremont Men's Coll., Calif. State U., Long Beach, UCLA Internat. Vis. Fulbright Scholars Program, Composers Guild, Sempre Musica Soc. So. Calif., Wednesday Club of San Diego. Composer, condr., songwriter for motion pictures, TV, stage plays, musical theater, theme parks, audio-animatronic showcases, LDS Ch., Walt Disney Prodns., Inc., Roy Edward Disney Prodns., Don Bluth Prodns.; composer (patriotic anthem) So Many Voices Sing America's Song; film scores include That Darn Cat!, 1965, Lt. Robin Crusoe, U.S.N., 1966, Monkeys, Go Home!, 1967, Blackbeard's Ghost, 1968, Never a Dull Moment, 1968, The Computer Wore Tennis Shoes, 1969, Smith!, 1969, The Boatniks, 1970, Barefoot Executive, 1971, The Wild Country, 1971, The Busciut eater, 1972, Now You See Him, Now You Don't, 1972, The Snowball Express, 1972, Teh Castaway Cowboy, 1974, The Strongest Man in the World, 1975, Gus, 1976, The North Avenue Irregulars, 1979, Amy, 1981. Capt. USAF; conductor & comdg. officer 562nd Calif. Air Nat. Guard Band, 1956-71. Recipient Achievement award Bank of Am., 1955, Spl. Talent award Mickey Mouse Club, 1955, Harmony award The Young Musicians Found., 1961, award for outstanding classical composition for symphony orch. U. Redlands, 1961, 62, Acad. award nomination Acad. Motion Picture Arts and Scis., 1974, Emmy award nomination Acad. TV Arts and Scis., 1978, Outstanding Achievement in Songwriting award So. Calif. Motion Picture Coun., 1981, Recognition for Outstanding Achievement in Songwriting from Internat. Luth. Deaf Assn., 1981, Award for Outstanding Achievment Nat. Soc. DAR, 1987, George Washington Honor Medal for Excellence in Individual Achievement Freedoms Found. at Valley Forge, 1988. Mem. ASCAP (mem. West Coast writers adv. bd. 1974-77, ASCAP awards 1987, 88), AFTRA, SAG, Screen Composers Assn. (bd. dirs. 1970-76), Acad. Motion Picture Arts and Scis. (exec. com. music br. 1971-74), Songwriters Guild Am., Soc. Composers and Lyricists, Acad. TV Arts and Scis., Am. Guild Mus. Artists, Am. Fedn. Musicians (life), Assoc. Latter-Day Media Artists, Sons of Utah Pioneers (life), Dramatists Guild. Republican. Mem. LDS Church. Avocations: skiing, swimming, tennis, horseback riding, photography. Home and Office: 7236 Imbach Pl Moorpark CA 93021-3262 also: ASCAP 6430 W Sunset Blvd Ste 1002 Los Angeles CA 90028-7913

BRUNNER, ROBERT VINCENT, JR., civil engineer; b. Binghamton, N.Y., Jan. 18, 1961; s. Robert Vincent, Sr. and Patricia Jean (Brace) B.; m. Mary Ellen Pace Giovannetti, Feb. 17, 1983 (div. May, 1989); children: Erica, Steven,; m. Cheryl Anne Stec, June 27, 1992; children: Allison, Paige. BSCE, Clarkson U., 1983. Jr. engr. N.Y. State Dept. Transp., Albany, 1983-84, asst. civil engr., 1984-88, sr. civil engr., 1988; bridge safety and inspection engr. N.Y. State Thruway Authority, Albany, 1988-91, design supr., structural design bur., 1991-96, asst. dir., structural design bur., 1996-97, dir. architectural design bur., 1998—. Com. Schenectady County Rep. Com., N.Y., 1993-96. Avocation: woodworking. Office: NY State Thruway Authority PO Box 189 Albany NY 12201-0189

BRUNNETT, KATHLEEN SHANNON, secondary educator; b. Balt., Aug. 10, 1968; d. Robert Paul and Marie Louise (Cassel) Anderson; m. James Douglas, July 15, 1995. BA, Shippensburg U. of Pa., 1990; MS, Western Md. Coll., 1998. English tchr. Carroll County Pub. Schs., Sykesville, Md., 1994—; English curriculum writing team CC Public Schs., Westminster, 1996, 99. Founding mem. MADD of Carroll County, Westminster; co-chair S.C. Middle States Evaluation Effort. Mem. NEA, ASCD, Nat. Coun. of Tchrs. of English, Alpha Sigma Tau. Roman Catholic.

BRUNO, ANTHONY D., lawyer; b. Newark, N.J., May 3, 1956; s. Frank and Delores (Fleming) B.; m. Gina Mabey, Aug. 1982; children: Chris, Dan, Will. BA in Polit. Sci., Syracuse U., 1978; JD, George Washington U., 1981. Bar: N.Y. 1981, N.J. 1981. Atty. Shearman & Sterling, N.Y.C., 1981-84; assoc. gen. counsel Warner-Lambert, Morris Plains, N.J., 1984—. Office: 201 Tabor Rd Morris Plains NJ 07950*

BRUNO, BARBARA ALTMAN, social worker; b. N.Y.C., May 26, 1947; m. Joseph Peter Bruno, Oct. 2, 1977. AB in English, Cornell U., 1969; MSW in Psychiat. Social Work, Calif. State U., Sacramento, 1974; PhD in Psychology, Columbia Pacific U., 1987. Diplomate clin. social work; cert. social worker, N.Y. Group facilitator San Francisco DWI Sch., 1975-76; social svc. coord. Kosher Nutrition Project, San Francisco, 1975-76; counselor SUNY, Purchase, 1980-81, Pace U. Counseling Ctr., N.Y.C., 1981-84; group leader No. Westchester YMHA/YWHA, Pleasantville, N.Y., 1981-91; pvt. practice psychotherapy Pleasantville, 1984—; adj. faculty Westchester Community Coll., Valhalla, N.Y., 1990—, COED program, Pleasantville, 1988-92; founder Weight Release Svcs., Pleasantville, 1989—, Thinside Out, Pleasantville, 1985-90. Author: Quakers, 1985, Worth Your Weight, 1996; editor Roundup, 1990-98; well being columnist Dimensions mag.; contbr. articles to profl. jours. Fellow Soc. Clin. Social Work Psychotherapists (cert.), Nat. Assn. to Advance Fat Acceptance (chair Westchester-Rockland chpt. 1989-91, nat. bd. dirs. 1991-97, mental health advisor 1991—); mem. Acad. Cert. Social Workers, Assn. for Health Enrichment of Large People (founding mem.).

BRUNO, CATHY EILEEN, management consultant, former state official; b. Binghamton, N.Y. d. Martin Frank and Beverly Carolyn (Hamlin) Piza; m. Frank L. Delaney (div.); m. Paul R. Bruno, May 5, 1990. BA, SUNY, Binghamton; MSW, Syracuse U. Psychiat. social worker Willard (N.Y.) Psychiat. Ctr., 1968-73, Broome Devel. Ctr., Binghamton, 1973-74, 76; congl. legis. aide, 1975; asst. dir. Bur. Program and Fiscal audits N.Y. State Office Mental Retardation and Devel. Disabilities, Albany, 1976-80, statewide coord. Intermediate Care Facilities for Developmentally Disabled, 1980, cert. coord. Western County Svc. Group, 1980-83, Upstate unit dir. Bur. Cert. Control, 1983-85; dir. ICF/DD Survey and Rev., 1985-89; area dir. Bur. Program Cert., 1989-95; dir. Bur. Transitional Svcs., 1995-97; mgmt. cons., 1997—; adj. instr. SUNY Sch. Social Welfare, Albany, 1982-83. Grantee HEW, 1975-76. Mem. Am. Mgmt. Assn.

BRUNO, E., bank company executive. CEO Credito Italiano, Milan. Office: Credito Italiano, Piazzo Cordusio, 20123 Milan Italy

BRUNO, FRANK A., film producer; b. Bklyn., Jan. 10, 1962; s. Daniel F. and Gloria (Perrone) B.; m. Paula J. Laterza, June 8, 1985. BS in Film, Radio and TV Prodn., Syracuse U., 1984; postgrad. in music rec., Inst. Audio Rsch., 1985. Audio engr. Nat. Pub. Radio, N.Y.C., 1986, WNYU Radio, N.Y.C., 1988-90; audio technician NYU, N.Y.C., 1986-88; ind. producer Greensboro, N.C., 1990—; tchr. NYU, N.Y.C., 1989-90. Sound rec. engr. films: Morning Becomes Electra, 1987, Slave, 1988, The Cradle Will Fall, 1988, The Fifth Season, 1989-90, The Game, 1989; producer, engr. record album: The Pan, 1990. Mem. Audio Engring. Soc., Soc. Broadcast Engrs., Assn. Ind. Video and Filmmakers, Ind. Feature Project. Avocations: sports, computers, books, music, films. Home and Office: 7676 Anthony Rd Kernersville NC 27284-8720

BRUNO, FRANK EUGENE, television producer, videotape editor, telecine colorist; b. Newark, June 3, 1945; s. Frank Eugene and Libby Maria (D'Arpino) B.; m. Melanie Noreen Giambattista, Apr. 1, 1967 (div. Sept. 1997); children: Patrick, Theresa. Grad. high sch., Orange, N.J., 1963. Cert. videotape editing, telecine coloring, cinematography. Freelance wedding photographer West Orange, N.J., Newhall, Calif., 1960-81; photo chem. mixer Quality Color Labs, Orange, N.J., 1962-63; asst. mgr. Interstate Camera Stores, Orange, 1963-66; asst. theater mgr. Gen. Cinema Corp., West Orange, 1966-67; film expeditor Du Art Color Labs, N.Y.C., 1966; theatrical film booker Warner Bros. Pictures Distributing Corp., N.Y.C, L.A., 1966-67; head theatrical film booker 20th Century Fox Film Corp., San Francisco, 1967-70; film buyer Nat. Gen. Theatres, San Francisco, L.A., 1970-73; pres., TV producer Continental Am. Pictures Corp., Santa Clarita, Calif., 1973—; western div. mgr. New World Pictures, L.A., 1973-75; n.w. territory mgr. Columbia Pictures, L.A., 1975-78; coord. promotional material Walt Disney Pictures/Buena Vista Distbn., Burbank, Calif., 1978-89; videotape editor, telecine colorist The Video Tape Co./Western World Telefilm, North Hollywood, Calif., 1981-89, Dubs, Inc., Hollywood, Calif., 1989—; guest speaker U. Calif., Irvine, 1974. Prodr. rep. Roberto Rossellini's The Messiah, 1997—; writer, producer, dir. (TV series) Whistle Stop, 1986, The Best of Whistle Stop, 1988. Mem. Soc. Motion Picture and TV Engrs. Republican. Catholic. Avocations: photography, flying, model railroading, swimming, movie and TV nostalgia. Office: Frank Bruno Prodns 23450 San Fernando Rd Spc 16 Santa Clarita CA 91321-3101

BRUNO, GRACE ANGELIA, accountant, retired educator; b. St. Louis, Oct. 11, 1935; d. John E. and Rose (Goodwin) B. BA, Notre Dame Coll., 1966; MEd, So. Ill. U., 1972; MAS, Johns Hopkins U., 1983; PhD, Walden U., 1985. CPA, Mo., Md., N.J. Tchr. Sch. Sisters of Notre Dame (SSND) of St. Louis, 1962-80; pres. Bruno-Potter, Inc., Avon By The Sea, N.J., 1981—; asst. treas., instr. acctg. Coll. of Notre Dame of Md., Balt., 1978-80, treas., 1979-80; asst. prof. acctg. Georgian Ct. Coll., Lakewood, N.J., 1985-91; fin. advisor James Harry Potter gold medal award ASME, N.Y.C., 1980—. Elected to Internat. Platform Assn., 1987. Mem. AICPA, N.J. Soc. CPAs, St. Louis Bus. Educators (treas. 1972-73), Inst. Bus. Appraisers, Inc., Johns Hopkins Univ. Faculty Club. Democrat. Roman Catholic. Home and Office: 419 3rd Ave Avon By The Sea NJ 07717-1244

BRUNO, HAROLD ROBINSON, JR., retired journalist, educator, writer; b. Chgo., Oct. 25, 1928; s. Harold R. and Tallulah H. (Kandel) B.; m. Margaret E. Christian, Nov. 12, 1959; children: Harold, Daniel. BS in Journalism, U. Ill., 1950. Reporter Advt. Age, Chgo., 1950; sports editor DeKalb (Ill.) Chronicle, 1950-51; reporter City News Bur., Chgo., 1953-54, Chgo. American, 1954-60, Newsweek mag., 1960-63; bur. chief Newsweek mag., Chgo., 1963-66; news editor Newsweek mag., N.Y.C., 1966-71; chief polit. corr. Newsweek mag., Washington, 1971-78; polit. dir. ABC News, Washington, 1978-97, polit. analyst, 1997-98; ret., 1998; adv. bd. Internat. Programs and Studies, U. Ill., Washington Ctr. for Politics and Journalism; moderator Vice Presdl., 1992. Columnist Firehouse mag; Contbr. articles to various publs. Bd. dirs. Chevy Chase Fire Dept.; adv. bd. Presdl. Classroom for Young Ams.; mem. Port Chester (N.Y.) Vol. Fire Dept.; dir. Fallen Firefighters Meml. Nat. Fire Acad. With U.S. Army, 1951-53. Recipient Lowell Thomas award Internat. Platform Assn., 1984; Fulbright scholar, 1956-57; named Fire Svc. Person of Yr. Cong. Fire Svc. Inst., 1995. Mem. Nat. Fire Protection Assn., Nat. Vol. Fire Coun., AFTRA, Chgo. Newspaper Reporters Assn., Friendship Fire Assn., U. Ill. Alumni Assn. (bd. dirs., Illini achievement award 1984), Bethesda-Chevy Chase Rescue Squad Alumni, Soc. Profl. Journalists, Chgo. Press Vets. Assn., Internat. Assn. Fire Fighters (hon.), Tau Delta Phi. Jewish. Home: 3414 Cummings Ln Chevy Chase MD 20815-3238

BRUNO, JUDYTH ANN, chiropractor; b. Eureka, Calif., Feb. 16, 1944; d. Harold Oscar and Shirley Alma (Farnsworth) Nelson; m. Thomas Glenn Bruno, June 1, 1968; 1 child, Christina Elizabeth. AS, Sierra Coll., 1982; D of Chiropractic, Palmer Coll. of Chiropractic West, Sunnyvale, Calif., 1986. Diplomate Nat. Bd. Chiropractic Examiners. Sec. Bank Am., San Jose, Calif., 1965-67; marketer Memorex, Santa Clara, Calif., 1967-74; order entry clk. John Deere, Milan, Ill., 1977; system analyst Four Phase, Cupertino, Calif., 1977-78; chiropractic asst. Dr. Thomas Bruno, Nevada City, Calif., 1978-81; chiropractor Chiropractic Health Care Ctr., Nevada City, 1987—; pvt. practice Cedar Ridge, Calif., 1991—. Area dir. Cultural Awareness Coun., Grass Valley, Calif., 1977—; vol. Nevada County Libr., Nevada City, 1987-88, Decide Team II, Nevada County, 1987-92, Active Parenting of Teen Facilitator Nev. Union H.S., 1989-93, judge sr. projects, 1992—. Recipient Bus. and Profl. Woman of Yr. award No. Mines, 1997. Mem. Women Health Practitioners of Nevada County (founder 1993—), Nevada County C. of C. (vol. task force health care 1993), Toastmasters (sec. 1988, pres. 1989, 98, edn. v.p. 1990, Early Risers Toastmaster of Yr. 1998). Republican. Avocations: spiritual growth, skiing, origami, ecology. Office: Chiropractor Health Care PO Box 1718 Cedar Ridge CA 95924-1718

BRUNO, MICHAEL STEPHEN, ocean engineering educator, researcher; b. Nutley, N.J., Apr. 16, 1958; s. Frank Joseph and Annie Marie (Golden) B. BS, N.J. Inst. Tech., 1980; MS, U. Calif., Berkeley, 1981; PhD, MIT,

1986. Registered profl. engr., N.J. Prin. engr. N.J. Dept. Environ. Protection, Toms River, 1981-82; rsch. asst. MIT, Cambridge, 1982-86; asst. prof. N.J. Inst. Tech., Newark, 1986-89; assoc. prof., dir. Davidson Lab. Stevens Inst. Tech., Hoboken, N.J., 1989-98; prof. Stevens Inst. Tech, Hoboken, NJ, 1998—; young investigator Office of Naval Rsch., Washington, 1991. Editor-in-chief Jour. Marine Environ. Engring., 1991—; contbr. articles to profl. jours. Mem. Planning Bd., West Caldwell, N.J., 1990—. Recipient Fulbright Scholar, 1996. Mem. ASCE (Outstanding Svc. award 1987), ASME, Am. Geophys. Union, Pan Am. Fedn. Ocean Engrs. (sec.-gen. 1990—), Soc. Naval Architects and Marine Engrs., Tau Beta Pi. Office: Stevens Institute of Technology Castle Point Sta Hoboken NJ 07030-5907

BRUNO, RONALD G., food service executive; b. 1951; married. BS, U. Ala., 1974. With Bruno's Inc., Birmingham, Ala., chmn. bd., CEO, 1990-98; pres. Bruno Capital Management Corp, 1998—. Office: Bruno Capital Management Corp Two Perimeter Pk S Ste 300E Birmingham AL 35243*

BRUNS, BILLY LEE, consulting electrical engineer; b. St. Louis, Nov. 21, 1925; s. Henry Lee and Violet Jean (Williams) B.; BA, Washington U., St. Louis, 1949, postgrad. Sch. Engring., 1959-62; EE, ICS, Scranton, Pa., 1954; m. Lillian Colleen Mobley, Sept. 6, 1947; children: Holly Rene, Kerry Alan, Barry Lee, Terrence William. Supt., engr., estimator Schneider Electric Co., St. Louis, 1950-54, Ledbetter Electric Co., 1954-57; tchr. indsl. electricity St. Louis Bd. Edn., 1957-71; pres. B.L. Bruns & Assos., cons. engrs., St. Louis, 1963-72; v.p., chief engr. Hosp. Bldg. & Equipment Co., St. Louis, 1972-76; pres., prin. B. L. Bruns & Assos. cons. engrs., St. Louis, 1976—; tchr. elec. engring. U. Mo. St. Louis extension, 1975-76. Mem. Mo. Adv. Council on Vocat. Edn., 1969-76, chmn., 1975-76; leader Explorer post Boy Scouts Am., 1950-57. Served with AUS, 1944-46: PTO, Okinawa. Decorated Purple Heart. Registered profl. engr., Mo., Ill., Wash., Fla., La., Wis., Minn., N.Y., N.C., Iowa, Pa., Miss., Ind., Ala., Ga., Va., R.I. Mem. Nat. Soc. Profl. Engrs., Mo. Soc. Profl. Engrs., Profl. Engrs. in Pvt. Practice, Am. Soc. Heating, Refrigeration and Air Conditioning Engrs., Illuminating Engrs. Soc., Am. Mgmt. Assn., Nat. Fire Protection Assn. (health care div., archtl./engr. div.), Masons. Baptist. Tech. editor The National Electrical Code and Blueprint Reading, Am. Tech. Soc., 1959-65. Home: 1243 Hobson Dr Ferguson MO 63135-1422 Office: 400 Brookes Dr Ste 203 Hazelwood MO 63042-2745

BRUNS, NICOLAUS, JR., retired agricultural chemicals company executive, lawyer; b. N.Y.C., Sept. 27, 1926; s. Nicolaus and Emily Marie (Hawkins) B.; m. Joan-Carol Littleton, Aug. 29, 1959; children: Nicolaus III, Gregory. B.S., U. Miami, Fla., 1947; J.D., Georgetown U., 1949, LL.M., 1952. Bar: D.C. 1950, ILL. 1965, U.S. Supreme Ct. 1965, N.Y. 1980. Spl. asst. U.S. Navy Dept., Washington, 1950-57; sr. trial atty. U.S. Dept. Justice, Washington, 1957-65; sr. atty. Internat. Minerals and Chem. Corp., Skokie, Ill., 1965-70, asst. gen. counsel, 1970-74, gen. counsel ops., 1974-79; v.p., sec., assoc. gen. counsel Internat. Minerals and Chem. Corp., Northbrook, Ill., 1979-87; sr. v.p., sec., gen. counsel IMC Fertilizer Group Inc., Northbrook, 1987-90; antitrust policy counsel U.S. C. of C., Washington, 1981-90; adj. prof. Loyola U., Chgo., 1980-81, Lake Forest Grad. Sch. Mgmt., Ill., 1981—. Adminstrv. asst. to v.p. Boy Scouts Am., N.E. Ill. area, 1967, 80; pres. Fund for Perceptually Handicapped, Skokie, Ill., 1976, Concerned Help in Learning Devel., Highland Park, Ill., 1974-75. With U.S. Army, 1945-46. Mem. ABA (antitrust and securities com.), Chgo. Bar Assn., Fed. Bar Assn., Am. Soc. Corp. Secs. (bd. dirs. 1985-87, pres. Midwest region 1984), K.C. (past grand knight Washington coun.), Mich. Shore Club (Wilmette, Ill.), Harbour Ridge Club (Stuart, Fla.). Republican. Roman Catholic. Home: 8 Regentwood Rd Northfield IL 60093-2728 also: Harbour Ridge 2532 NW Seagrass Dr Palm City FL 34990-4884

BRUNS, WILLIAM JOHN, JR., business administration educator; b. Pasadena, Calif., July 13, 1935; s. William John and Carol Jane (Stalder) B.; m. Barbara Jean Dodge, Apr. 12, 1957 (div. 1980); children: Robert William, John Richard, David James, Michael Alan.; m. Sharon Merle McKinnon, July 16, 1982. B.A., U. Redlands, Calif., 1957, D.B.A. (hon.), 1976; M.B.A., Harvard U., 1959; Ph.D., U. Calif. at Berkeley, 1963. Asst. prof. econs., then asst. prof. econs. and indsl. adminstrn. Yale U., 1962-66; asso. prof., then prof. accounting U. Wash., 1966-72; prof. bus. adminstrn. Harvard U., 1972-93, Henry R. Byers prof. bus. adminstrn., 1993—; cons. to industry. Author: Accounting for Decisions: A Business Game, 1966, Accounting and Its Behavioral Implications, 1969, Introduction to Accounting: Economic Measurement for Decisions, 1971, A Primer on Replacement Cost Accounting, 1976, Cases in Management Accounting, 1981, 85, Accounting and Management: Field Study Perspectives, 1987, Performance Measurement, Evaluation, and Incentives, 1992, The Information Mosaic, 1992, Accounting for Managers: Text and Cases, 1994, 99; book rev. editor: Accounting Rev, 1967-69; mem. editorial bd., 1969-72, 76-78; advisory editor: Addison-Wesley Pub. Co; mem. editorial bd.: Accounting, Orgns., and Soc, 1975-79, Jour. of Managerial Issues, 1993—. Mem. Quinnipiac council Boy Scouts Am., 1964-66; Chief Seattle council, 1966-72, Algonquin council, 1972-81. Danforth grad. fellow, 1957-62; Danforth assoc., 1967-89. Mem. Am. Acctg. Assn., Inst. Mgmt. Accts. Home: 46 Garden Rd Wellesley MA 02481-3015 Office: Harvard Bus Sch Soldiers Fld Boston MA 02163-1317

BRUNSON, BURLIE ALLEN, aerospace executive; b. Bakersfield, Calif., Apr. 28, 1945; s. Burlie B. and Mary Helen (Self) B.; m. Lois L. Corbett, Apr. 25, 1968; children: Marci L., Meredith L. BS, U.S. Naval Acad., 1967; Fulbright Scholar, Cen. U., Quito, Ecuador, 1968; MS, Oreg. State U., 1972, PhD, 1983; MBA, George Washington U., 1995. Commissioned officer USN, Pensacola, Fla., 1968-70; research asst. Oreg. State U., Corvallis, 1970-72; research oceanographer Naval Ocean Systems Ctr., San Diego, 1972-78; research physicist Naval Ocean Research & Devel. Activity, Bay St. Louis, 1978-81; prin. scientist Planning Systems Inc., McLean, Va., 1981-86; v.p. Planning Systems Inc., McLean, 1986-88, sr. v.p., tech. dir., 1988-89; exec. v.p., chief operating officer, 1989-91; v.p., ASW Lockheed Sanders Inc., Nashua, N.H., 1991-92; dir. Maritime Systems Lockheed Corp., Calabasas, Calif., 1992-94; v.p. Washington ops. Lockheed Martin Corp., Bethesda, Md., 1995-99, v.p. program devel., 1999—. Patentee in field; contbr. various articles to profl. jours. Mem. Acoustical Soc. Am. (tech. reviewer 1980—), Am. Geophys. Union, Nat. Def. Indsl. Assn., Am. Mgmt. Assn., Sigma Xi, Phi Kappa Phi, Beta Gamma Sigma. Republican. Presbyterian. Home: 711 Potomac Knolls Dr Mc Lean VA 22102-1421 Office: Lockheed Martin Corp 6801 Rockledge Dr Bethesda MD 20817

BRUNSON, DOROTHY EDWARDS, broadcasting executive; b. Glensville, Ga., Mar. 13, 1938; d. Wadis and Naomi (Ross) Edwards; children: Edward, Daniel. BS, Empire State Coll.; doctorate (hon.), Clark Atlanta U., 1989. Entered print communications industry, 1960-62; asst. gen. mgr. radio sta. WWRL, N.Y.C., 1964-68, corp. coord., liason dir., 1968-72; v.p. Howard Sanders Advt., Inc., N.Y.C., 1972-79; corp. v.p. Inner City Broadcasting Corp., N.Y.C., 1973-79, corp. gen. mgr., 1979; owner Sta. WGTW-TV, Phila., 1979—; lectr., speaker bus., econ. devel., affirmative action, comm., women's rights, religious and human issues throughout country; panelist bus. and comm. U.S. Congress, 1995. Contbr. articles to Vogue, Black Enterprise, Newsweek. Recipient awards including citation NCCJ. Methodist. Office: Brunson Communication Inc PO Box 67771 Baltimore MD 21215-0019 also: 3900 Main St Philadelphia PA 19127-2110

BRUNSON, JOHN SOLES, lawyer; b. Houston, Jan. 8, 1934; s. Nathan Bryant and Jonnie E. (McMillian) B.; m. Joan Erwin, Dec. 26, 1953; children: W. Mark, Dana Ruth. BBA, Baylor U., 1956, LLB, 1958, JD, 1965. Bar: Tex., 1958, U.S. Supreme Ct., 1961. Assoc. Dillingham, Schleider & Lewis, Houston, 1958-64; ptnr. Brunson & Brill, Houston, 1964-70, Baker, Heard & Brunson, Houston, 1970-72, Brunson & Erwin, Houston, 1972-84; pres. New Asia Products, Inc., 1982—; chmn. Clavis Investment Corp., 1984—; bd. dirs. Ridgewood Devel. Mem. Harris County (Tex.) Dem. Exec. Com., 1959-65, Tex. Dem. Exec. Com., 1963-74; mem. exec. bd. Bapt. Gen. Conv. Tex., 1988-94; trustee First Bapt. Acad., Houston Christian H.S. Mem. ABA, State Bar Tex., Houston Bar Assn. Office: 7555 Katy Fwy Apt 70 Houston TX 77024-2119

BRUNSON, KENNETH WAYNE, cancer biologist; b. Chico, Tex., Sept. 18, 1936; s. George Starr and Gwendolyn Laverne (Wood) B.; m. Myrna Marquerite Lapré, Jan. 26, 1963; children: Gregory Sean, Geoffrey Gordon. BA in Biology, Chemistry, U. N. Tex., 1964, MA in Biology, Biochemistry, 1966; PhD in Microbiology, Biochemistry, U. Minn., 1973; postdoctoral Tumor Biology, The Salk Inst., San Diego, Calif., 1974-77. Lectr. U. Calif., Riverside, 1974-75; rsch. assoc. The Salk Inst., La Jolla, Calif., 1974-77; asst. specialist U. Calif., Irvine, 1977-79; asst. prof. Sch. Medicine Ind. U., Indpls., Gary, 1979-84; assoc. mem. grad. sch. Ind. U., Bloomington, 1979-84; sr. rsch scientist Pfizer Inc, Groton, Conn., 1984-91; assoc. prof. Sch. Medicine U. Pitts., 1991—; affiliate mem. U. Pitts. Cancer Inst., 1991-94, mem., 1994—, dir. Tumor Model Lab., 1995—, dir. in vivo preclin. rsch. for health scis., 1996-99; bd. dirs. Am. Cancer Soc., Merrillville, Ind., 1981-84, Pa. Soc. for Biomed. Rsch., 1997—; mem. expert panel workshop Exptl. Metastasis: Designing New Strategies, 1988; founding mem. sci. edn. com., Pfizer, Inc. Groton, Conn., 1987-91. Sci. advisor 10-vol. treatise Cancer Growth and Progression, 1986-89; editor: (book) Local Invasion and Spread of Cancer, 1989; contbr. (jour.) Current Opinion in Oncology, Jour. Nat. Cancer Inst., Cancer Rsch., In Vivo. Mem. planning com. Regional Health Adminstrn. Conf., Ind., 1984, exec. bd. Shadyside Action Coalition, Pitts., 1993-96, chmn. parking and transp. com., 1993-95. With U.S. Army, 1958-61. Recipient XVI Internat. Cancer Congress award Internat. Union Against Cancer, New Delhi, India, 1994. Mem. Am. Assn. for Cancer Rsch., Am. Assn. Immunologists, Am. Soc. Cell Biology, Metastasis Rsch. Soc., Am. Soc. for Microbiology, (chmn. edn. com., Ind. br.), Am. Inst. Biol. Scis., Pa. Soc. Biomed. Rsch. (bd. dirs. 1997—). Achievements include pioneering research in cancer metastasis models, some of which has been described in Sci. Am., Mar., 1979, Proceedings of Nat. Acad. of Sci. , 1980, Cancer Growth and Progression, 1989, and Biologic Therapy of Cancer, 1995. Home: 422 Noble St Pittsburgh PA 15232-1618 Office: U Pitts Cancer Inst Divsn Basic Rsch Biomed Sci Tower W940 200 Lothrop St Pittsburgh PA 15213-2546

BRUNSON, MABEL (DIPPER), researcher; b. Oshoto, Wyo., Mar. 24, 1934; d. Robert Emmett and Gennevieve Mae (Irwin) Brislawn; m. Donald George Brunson, Jan. 1, 1959; children: Daniel F., David G. Student, Nieman's Bus. Coll., 1956. Rschr., sec. Bob Brislawn, Spanish Mustang Registry Inc., Oshoto, 1943-79; legal sec. Scotty Gladstone/Richard Macy law offices, Sundance, Wyo., 1957-58; cons. Bob Brislawn, Spanish Mustang Registry Inc., 1957-79; sec., clk. Farmers Home Adminstrn., Sundance, 1958-59, Soil Conservation Svc., Sundance, 1975-82. Co-author: Spanish Mustang Registry, Inc., 1996; author: Mr. Mustang and the Spanish Pony, Life of Bob Brislawn, 1999; also author brochures. Sec., treas. Homemaker's Clubs, Wyo., 1959-76; religious tchr. Cath. Chs., Upton and Sundance, Wyo., 1965-80, eucharistic min., Sundance, 1984-99; cub scout leader Boy Scouts Am., Sundance, 1972-79. Recipient Svc. award Boy Scouts Am., 1979; named Centennial Woman of Yr. St. Paul's Cath. Ch., 1990. Avocations: history, genealogy, western art, writing. Office: Brunson Enterprises 1310 Oak Creek Rd Aladdin WY 82710-9729

BRUNSTETTER, PETER SAMUEL, lawyer; b. San Francisco, Feb. 28, 1956; s. Richard Worstall and Roberta Sandra (Bessin) B.; m. Jodie Bray, July 1, 1978; children: Peter Jr., Rebecca, Daniel, Timothy. BA, Tulane U., 1977; JD, U. Va., 1984. Bar: Va. 1984, D.C. 1985, N.C. 1986. Assoc. McGuire, Woods & Battle, Richmond, Va., 1984-85; assoc., then ptnr. Kilpatrick Stockton LLP, Winston-Salem, N.C., 1985—. Chmn. Forsyth County (N.C.) Bd. Elections, 1990-91; mem. Forsyth County Bd. Commrs., 1991—, chmn., 1994—; bd. visitors N.C. State U., Raleigh, 1997, U. N.C., Wilmington, 1998—; trustee Novant Health, Inc., Winston-Salem, 1997; mem. state health coord. coun., 1998—; mem. Piedmont Triad Internat. Airport Authority, 1999—. Lt. USN, 1977-81. Named fellow N.C. Inst. Polit. Leadership, 1988, one of Emerging Leaders of South, Lamar Soc., 1995. Mem. N.C. State Bar, Order of Coif, Winston-Salem Downtown Rotary. Republican. So. Bapt. Avocation: flying (licensed and instrument-rated multi-engine pilot). Home: 3641 Will Scarlet Rd Winston Salem NC 27104 Office: Kilpatrick Stockton LLP 1001 W 4th St Winston Salem NC 27101

BRUNSVOLD, BRIAN GARRETT, lawyer, educator; b. Mason City, Iowa, Apr. 10, 1938; s. P.O. and Arlene J. (Garrett) B.; m. Mary Sue Willey, Nov. 28, 1963; 1 child, Laura Ann. BS in Chem.Engring., Iowa State U., 1960; JD, George Washington U., 1967. Bar: Va. 1967, D.C. 1967. Law clk. U.S. Ct. Claims, Washington, 1966-67; atty. firm Finnegan, Henderson, Farabow, Garrett & Dunner, Washington, 1967—; professorial lectr. in law George Washington U., Washington, 1975-96. Co-author: Drafting Patent License Agreements, 1984, 91, 98. 1st lt. C.E., U.S. Army, 1961-63, Korea. Mem. Licensing Execs. Soc. (trustee 1987-89, Cert. of Merit 1988). Avocations: tennis, hunting, fishing. Office: Finnegan Henderson Farabow Garrett & Dunner 1300 I St NW Fl 6-8 Washington DC 20005-3315

BRUNSWIG, JESSIE, executive assistant; b. Leone, Am. Samoa, Aug. 24, 1943; came to U.S., 1949; d. Harold Edwin Miller and Juliana (Toilolo) Copeland; m. William Lloyd Brunswig, July 17, 1989; children: Jennifer, Jeffrey, Eric, Kirk. Student, Washington State U., 1961, Lower Columbia Coll., 1964, Centralia Coll., 1988; diploma, Police Dept. Citizen's Acad., Centralia, 1996. Legal asst./paralegal Thurston County Prosecutor's Office, 1985-89; confidential sec. State Bd. of Health, 1989-91; adminstrv. asst. Wash. State Dept. Health, 1991-93; exec. asst. Wash. State Gov.'s Office, 1993-98; staff Gov.'s Health Policy Group, 1993-98; spkr. Centralia Coll. Citizenship Class, 1997—; Mayor city of Centralia, Wash., 1997—. Councilor Centralia City Coun., 1993—; staff Gov.'s Task Force on Higher Edn., 1995-96, Exec.-Joint Legis. Task Force on Long Term Care, 1997-98; mem. Cascadia Mayor's Coun., 1998—; pres. small cities adv. coun., 1997-99; bd. dirs. Lewis County Cmty. Network, 1995-96; com. Elect Gary Alexander Rep. 20th dist., 1996-97; mayor pro-tem Centralia City Coun., 1995-96; bd. dirs. Lewis County Econ. Devel. Coun., 1995—, Lewis County Children with Spl. Needs, 1997—; Region VI adv. com. Wash. State Dept. Social and Health Svcs., 1997-98; chief police adv. panel, coun. liaison, 1995-97. Named Outstanding Young Woman in Am., 1973, Girl of Yr. Beta Sigma Phi Internat., 1978, Life Master Am. Contract Bridge League, 1976, Wash. State Legal Sec. Yr. Wash. Assn. Legal Profls., 1990. Mem. Assn. Wash. Cities (nom. com. 1999). Lutheran. Avocations: duplicate bridge, cooking, travel. Home: 615 W 3rd St Centralia WA 98531-4807

BRUNT, HARRY HERMAN, JR., psychiatrist; b. Phila., Jan. 22, 1921; s. Harry Herman and Ann (Zurbrugg) B.; m. Zoe M. Bower, July 2, 1944; children: Marianne Brunt Tallman, Margaret B. Griffin, Jane, Mary Lazar. B.S. with honors, Va. Poly. Inst., 1942; M.D., U. Pa., 1945. Diplomate: Am. Bd. Psychiatry and Neurology. Intern, Lankenau Hosp., 1946; resident psychiatry Trenton (N.J.) State Hosp., VA Hosp., Coatesville, 1948-52; practice medicine specializing in psychiatry Trenton, 1952, Princeton, N.J., 1952-54, Hammonton, N.J., 1954-69, Long Branch, N.J., 1969-74; acting asst. clin. dir. Trenton State Hosp., 1952; asst. supt. N.J. Neuropsychiat. Inst. Princeton, 1952-54; med. dir. Ancora State Hosp., 1954-69; dir. dept. psychiatry Monmouth Med. Center and Pollak Clinic, Long Branch, 1969-74, Jersey Shore Med. Ctr., 1980; pvt. practice, 1974—; assoc. prof. psychiatry Jefferson Med. Coll., 1952-66; instr. psychiatry U. Pa., 1953-65; adj. asso. prof. psychiatry Temple Med. Sch., 1968-70; prof. psychiatry Hahneman Med. Coll., 1970-74; clin. prof. psychiatry Robert Wood Johnson Med. Sch., New Brunswick, N.J., 1971-96. Cons. bur. family services Dept. Health, Edn. and Welfare Dept., 1960-68. Served to capt. M.C. AUS, 1946-48. Fellow ACP, AAAS, Am. Psychiat. Assn. (life, chmn. future planning com. assembly dist. brs., mem. policy com. area III 1968, recorder 1969, speaker 1971-72, trustee 1972-73, 74-75), Am. Geriatric Soc., Am. Coll. Psychiatrists (founding); mem. AMA, Monmouth County Med. Soc. (exec. com.), N.J. Neuropsychiat. Assn. (past pres.), Med. Soc. N.J. (chmn. coun. mental health), Beach Haven Yacht Club (commodore 1992-93), Alpha Kappa Kappa, Phi Kappa Phi. *I have obtained a great deal of satisfaction from helping others throughout my life but little of this would have been possible without my family's backing and sacrifice. The family is still what makes life worth living.*

BRUNTON, DANIEL WILLIAM, mechanical engineer; b. Ft. Wayne, Ind., Sept. 25, 1956; s. Paul Edward and Margaret Alice (Rice) B.; m. Carol Marie Pryor, Feb. 19, 1994; children: Edward Daniel, Ann Marie. BS, UCLA, 1978, MS in Engring., 1980, M of Engring., 1986. Mem. tech. staff Hughes Missiles Group, Canoga Park, Calif., 1978-89, dept. mgr., 1989-93; mech. engr. dept. mgr. Litton Itek, Lexington, Mass., 1993-94; sr. engr. Raytheon Missile Sys. Co., Tucson, 1994-97, prin. engr., 1997—. Mem. Soc. Photonic Instrumentation Engrs., Tau Beta Pi. Achievements include 4 patents filed on cryogenics, optical material testing, and mechanisms. Office: Raytheon Missile Sys Co PO Box 11337 Tucson AZ 85734-1337

BRUNTON, PAUL EDWARD, retired diversified industry executive; b. Decatur, Ind., July 8, 1922; s. John Harrison and Jessie (Holthouse) B.; m. Margaret Alice Rice, July 10, 1945; children—Patricia Ann, David John, Thomas Edward, Mary Josephine, Elizabeth Alice, Daniel William. B.S. in Fin, St. Joseph's Coll., 1944. Staff accountant Deloitte & Touche LLP, Chgo. and Mpls., 1946-48; sr. accountant Reinking Kern & Co. (CPAs), Ft. Wayne, Ind., 1948-53; controller, sec. Ft. Wayne Builders Supply Co., 1953-54; with ITT, 1954-61; controller Farnsworth Electronics, 1954-57; asst. controller ITT, Fed. div., 1958-61; dir. fin. and adminstrn. ITT, Kellogg div., 1961; with Litton Industries, Inc., 1961-75; v.p. fin., Guidance and Control Systems div. Litton Industries, Inc., Woodland Hills, Calif., 1961-66; v.p. adminstrn. Ingalls Shipbldg. div Litton Industries, Inc., Pascagoula, Miss., 1966; v.p. fin., bus. equipment group Litton Industries Inc., 1967; corp. controller Litton Industries Inc., Beverly Hills, Calif., 1967-70; pres., Louis Allis div. Litton Industries Inc., Milw., 1970-72; v.p. def. group Litton Industries Inc., Los Angeles, 1972-73; v.p. bus. equipment group Litton Industries Inc., 1973-75; sr. v.p., chief fin. officer Rohr Industries, Inc., Chula Vista, Calif., 1976-88. Served to lt. (j.g.) USNR, World War II. Mem. AICPA. Home: Apt 104 1820 Avenida del Mundo Coronado CA 92118-3013

BRUSCA, RICHARD CHARLES, zoologist, researcher, educator; b. L.A., Jan. 25, 1945; s. Finny John and Ellenora C. (McDonald) B.; m. Caren Irene Spencer, 1964 (div. 1971); m. Anna Mary Mackey, 1980 (div. 1987); children: Alec Matthew, Carlene Anne; m. Wendy Moore, 1998. BS, Calif. Poly. State U., 1967; MS, Calif. State U., L.A., 1969; PhD, U. Ariz., 1975. Curator, rschr. Aquatic Insects Lab., Calif. State U., L.A., 1969-70; resident dir. U. Ariz. and U. Sonora (Mex.) Coop. Marine Lab., Sonora, 1969-71; prof. biology U. So. Calif., L.A., 1975-86; head Invertebrate Zoology sect. Los Angeles County Mus. Natural Hist., 1984-87; Joshua L. Baily curator, chmn. dept. invertebrate zoology San Diego Natural History Mus., 1987-93; prof., dir. grad. program in marine biology U. Charleston, S.C., 1993-98, assoc. dir. Grice Marine Lab., 1993-98; sr. rsch. scientist, dir. undergrad. edn. Biospere 2 Ctr., Columbia U., N.Y.C., 1998—, dir. acad. programs, 1998—; dir. acad. program Catalina Marine Sci. Ctr., U. So. Calif.; field rschr. North, Ctrl. and South Ams., Polynesia, Australia, New Zealand, Antarctica, Sahran and Sub-Saharan Africa, Euorpe; bd. dirs. orng. for Tropical Studies, Slocum-Lunz Found., Intercultural Ctr. for the Study of Deserts and Oceans; mem. panels NAS/NSF; chairperson adv. com. Smithsonian Instn., Systematics Agenda 2000, Internat. Union for Conservation of Nature Species Survival Commn.; adj. prof. U. Ariz., 1998—. Author: Common Intertidal Invertebrates of the Gulf of California, 1980; co-author: A Naturalist's Seashore Guide, 1978, Invertebrates, 1990; contbr. over 95 articles to sci. jours. Recipient U.S. Antarctic Svc. medal, 1965, numerous rsch. awards; grantee NSF, Nat. Geog. Soc., Charles Lindberg Found, NOAA, Am. Philos. Assn., others. Mem. AAAs, Crustacean Soc. (pres.), Soc. for Systematic Biology, Willi Hinnig Soc., U. Edinburgh Biogeography Study Group, S. Am. Exploreres Club, Assn. Sea of Cortez Rschrs. (hon. life), Sigma Xi. Avocations: photography, Mesoamerican indigenous art and culture, Latin American politics. E-mail: rbrusca@bio2.edu. Office: Columbia U Biosphere 2 Ctr PO Box 689 Oracle AZ 85623-0689

BRUSCA, ROBERT ANDREW, economist; b. Detroit, Mar. 14, 1950; s. Andrew Adam and Doris Rita (Lozon) B.; m. Kathleen Hays. BA, U. Mich., 1973; MA, Mich. State U., 1976, PhD, 1977. Chief economist Fed. Res. Bank of N.Y., N.Y.C., 1977-82; economist, fedwatcher Irving Trust Co., N.Y.C., 1982-85; chief economist, exec. v.p. The Nikko Securities Co Internat., Inc., N.Y.C., 1986-99; cons. N.Y.C.; adj. prof. Columbia U., 1978—; appeared frequently on TV, radio as fin. specialist, 1983—. Author (column) Money Current, Fin. World mag., 1987-88, Econ. Currents, 1988—; contbr. articles in field. Mem. Money Marketeers NYU (bd. dirs. 1966—, pres.). Avocations: golf, basketball, reading, travel. Home: 357 West End Ave Apt One New York NY 10024-6815*

BRUSCH, JOHN LYNCH, physician; b. Boston, Nov. 3, 1943; s. Charles and Margaret Agnes (Lynch) B.; m. Patricia Gahan, May 12, 1973; children: Amy Claire, Meaghan, Patrick. BS, Tufts U., 1965, MD, 1969. Diplomate Am. Bd. Internal Medicine, Am. Bd. Infectious Disease, Am. Bd. Geriatrics. Intern New England Med. Ctr., Boston, 1969-70, resident in medicine, 1970-71, resident in infectious disease, 1971-74; asst. chief medicine Brighton Pub. Health Svc. Hosp., Boston, 1974-76; pvt. practice physician Cambridge, Mass., 1976—; chief medicine Youville Hosp., Cambridge, 1991—, dir. cmty. medicine, 1995—; clin. assoc. medicine Mass. Gen. Hosp., Boston, 1996—; med. dir. Somerville Hosp. Transitional Care Unit. Co-author: Infective Endocardits, assoc. editor Infectious Disease Practice, 1984—; contbr. articles to med. jours. Dir. North Cambridge Coop Bank, 1980—. With USPHS, 1974-76. Fellow ACP; mem. Am. Soc. Microbiology, Longwood Cricket Club. Home: 52 Radcliffe Rd Belmont MA 02478-3340 Office: Cambridge Hosp 1493 Cambridge St Cambridge MA 02139-1099

BRUSE, KRISTY DEAN, cardiovascular pharmacologist; b. Riverside, Calif., Dec. 22, 1958; d. Robert Leonard Muir and Linda Shane (Armes) Lake; m. Shannon Eric Bruse. BS in Biology, U. Mo., Kansas City, 1982; MS, S.W. Mo. State U., Springfield, 1986; PhD in Pharmacology and Toxicology, Med. Coll. Va., Richmond, 1996. Rsch. asst., lab. mgr. dept. surgery/nephrology U. Kans. Med. Ctr., Westwood, 1977-81; staff rsch. asst. dept. animal physiology U. Calif., Davis, 1987; rsch. asst. dept. cardiovascular rsch. Syntex Pharms., 1988-92; sr. rsch. assoc. dept. devel. rsch. Scios, Inc., 1992-93; vet. asst. with emergency vet. clinics, Mo., Calif., Va., 1981-83, 87-79, 95-96; postdoctoral fellow gene targeting/gene therapy dept. internal medicine U. Iowa, Iowa City, 1997—. Contbr. articles to profl. jours. Judge for sci. fairs. Recipient various awards. Mem. AAAS, Soc. for Neurosci., N.Y. Acad. Sci. Avocations: scuba diving, softball. Home: 2269 235th St Williamsburg IA 52361-9477

BRUSEWITZ, GERALD HENRY, agricultural engineering educator, researcher; b. Green Bay, Wis., June 1, 1942; s. Henry Jackson and Wardeen Mae (Thiel) B.; m. Glenna Sue Williams, May 12, 1990; children: Kelly K., Nicole J. BS in Agr., U. Wis., 1964, BSME, 1965, MSAE, 1966; PhDAE, Mich. State U., 1969. Registered profl. engr., Okla. Rsch. asst. U. Wis., Madison, 1965-66; asst. prof. Okla. State U., Stillwater, 1969-75, assoc. prof., 1975-80, prof., 1980-92, interim dept. head, 1985; regents prof., 1992—; sabbatical leave U. Calif., Davis, 1979, Cornell U., 1988; vis. engr. solar energy dept. Kuwait Inst. for Sci. Rsch., 1980; cons. Cen. Machine & Tool Co., Enid, Okla., 1986, Clements Food Co., Oklahoma City, 1986-87, Omnidata Internat. of Logan, 1990. Recipient Dist. Svc. to Students award Alpha Epsilon, Outstanding Engring. Faculty award Halliburton, 1991, Outstanding Agriculture Faculty award, 1994. Fellow Am. Soc. Agrl. Engrs. (Paper award 1990); mem. Am. Assn. Cereal Chemists, Inst. Food Technologists, Alpha Zeta. Methodist. Avocations: racquetball, cycling, hiking. Office: Okla State U Biosystems and Agrl Engring 216 Ag Hall Stillwater OK 74078-6020

BRUSH, CRAIG BALCOMBE, retired French language and computer educator; b. N.Y.C., May 28, 1930; s. John Mitchell and Josephine (Marple) B. BA, Princeton U., 1951; MA, Columbia U., 1955, PhD, 1966. Tchr. English, French Choate Sch., Wallingford, Conn., 1951-54; instr. French Columbia Coll., N.Y.C., 1955-63, asst. prof., 1963-67; asst. prof. City Coll., CUNY, 1967-70; assoc. prof. Fordham U., N.Y.C., 1970-73, prof. French, computers, 1973-95, ret., 1995. Author: Montaigne and Bayle, 1966, Selected Writings of Pierre Gassendi, 1972, From the Perspective of the Self, 1994. With NYNG, 1948-56. Fulbright fellowship, Paris, 1957-59. Mem. MLA, Société des Amis de Montaigne, Assn. for Computers and the Humanities, N.E. for Computers and the Humanities, Soc. Sr. Scholars (Columbia U.). Democrat. Avocations: music, theater, scuba diving. Home: 411 W 115th St New York NY 10025-1741

BRUSH, F(RANKLIN) ROBERT, psychobiology educator; b. Phoenixville, Pa., Nov. 24, 1929; s. Franklin Cotton and Anna (Fox) B.; m. Mary Margaret Doring, Apr. 24, 1948; children: Robert C., Elizabeth W., Suaan A. Doring, Tammy L. Michaels. BA, Princeton U., 1951; MA, Harvard U., 1953, PhD, 1956. Rsch. assoc. McGill U., Montreal, Que., Can., 1955-56; asst. prof. U. Md., College Park, 1956-59, U. Pa., Phila., 1959-65; assoc.

prof. U. Oreg. Med. Sch., Portland, 1965-67, prof., 1967-71; prof. Syracuse (N.Y.) U., 1971-80; prof. psychobiology Purdue U., West Lafayette, Ind., 1981—. Editor: Aversive Conditioning and Learning, 1971, Affect, Conditioning and Cognition, 1985, Psychoendocrinology, 1989. Rsch. grantee NIMH, 1967-71, 88-98. Fellow AAAS; mem. Internat. Behavioral Neurosci. Soc., Internat. Behavioral and Neural Genetics Soc. Avocations: skiing, swimming. E-mail: fbrush@mail.sdsu.edu. Office: Purdue U Dept Psychol Scis West Lafayette IN 47907

BRUSH, GEORGE W., college president; b. Boonton, N.J., Sept. 4, 1921; s. George W. and Adele (Tillotson) B.; m. Dorothy E. Mackallor, Sept. 27, 1942; children—Elithe, Lawrence, Kathleen, Sharon, George III, Charles, Nancy, Elizabeth. B.S., Fairleigh-Dickinson U., 1960; M.A., NYU, 1964, Ed.D., 1969. Cert. airframe and powerplant technician FAA. Dir. tng. Teterboro Sch. (N.J.), 1947-50; dir. admissions Coll. Aeros. (formerly Acad. Aero.), Flushing, N.Y., 1950-66, exec. dean, 1966-80, v.p., 1980-83, pres., 1984-90, pres. emeritus, 1990, trustee, 1990-94; cons. community colls., N.Y. and N.J., 1965—, N.Y. State Bd. Regents, 1971-85; visitor Middle States Assn. Colls. and Schs., 1975—; faculty cons. Regents Coll., Albany, N.Y. . Chair bd. trustees Plz. Bus. Coll., N.Y.C.; edn. chair bd. trustees N.J. Aviation Hall of Fame and Mus. Recipient Disting. Alumni award Coll. Aeros. Chmn., Maywood Planning Bd. (N.J.), Disting. Svc. award N.Y. State Bd. Regents, 1983; named Vol. of Yr. 1992 Bergen County; arbitrator Better Bus. Bur., Bergen County, N.J., 1976—. Served as staff sgt. U.S. Army, 1944-46. Recipient Adminstrs. award FAA, 1990. Mem. AIAA, FAA (Frank Taylor award 1995), Aviation Writers Assn., Am. Legion, Wings (bd. govs. 1986-89, chmn. edn. com.), KC, Estero (Fl.) Civic Assn. (bd. dirs.). Home & Office: 21030 Butchers Holler Estero FL 33928-2201

BRUSH, LOUIS FREDERICK, lawyer; b. Amityville, N.Y., Dec. 7, 1946; s. Frederick and Frances (Annunziata) B.; m. Eileen Forsyth, Aug. 13, 1972; children: Christopher, Brian, Stephen. BS in Acctg. and Bus. Adminstrn., L.I. U., 1971; MBA in Taxation, CCNY, 1975; JD, N.Y. Law Sch., 1980. Bar: N.Y. 1980, U.S. Dist. Ct. (so. and ea. dists.) N.Y. 1980, U.S. Tax Ct. 1980, U.S. Ct. Appeals (2d cir.) 1980. Agt. IRS, Mineola, N.Y., 1971-76; appellate conferee IRS, Carle Place, N.Y., 1976-80; sole practice Mineola, 1980—; lectr. 5th Annual Estate Planning Conf. Am. Inst. CPA's, San Francisco, 1982; dept. chmn. Bramson Tech. Coll., N.Y.C., 1980-81; part-time prof. acctg. and tax law SUNY, Farmingdale, 1974-75, Suffolk County Community Coll., Selden, N.Y., 1975-76, CUNY, Queens, 1980-81. Contbr. articles to profl. jours. Mem. N.Y. State Bar Assn. (award 1980), Nassau County Bar Assn., N.Y. State Trial Laywers Assn., N.Y. County Trial Lawyers Assn. Office: 101 Front St Mineola NY 11501-4402

BRUSH, PETER NORMAN, retired federal agency administrator, lawyer; b. St. Paul, Oct. 24, 1944; s. Robert Lee and Marjorie (Wilenchek) B.; m. Joanna Kurty, June 26, 1946; children: Christopher John, Peter Norman Jr. BA, Brown U., 1966; JD, U. Conn., West Hartford, 1969; LLM, Georgetown U., 1973. Bar: Conn. 1969, D.C. 1972. Atty. U.S. Atomic Energy Commn., Washington, 1969-75; counselor atomic energy U.S. Mission to U.N., Vienna, Austria, 1980-85; asst. gen. coun. internat. affairs U.S. Dept. Energy, Washington, 1975-80, dir. office nuclear proliferation policy, 1985-88, prin. dep. asst. sec. office of environment, safety and health, 1988-99. Contbr. articles to law jours. Chmn. exec. bd. Am. Internat. Sch., Vienna, 1981-84. Recipient Presdl. Meritorious Exec. award The White House, 1988. Mem. Conn. Bar Assn., D.C. Bar. Home: 15531 Bushy Tail Run Woodbine MD 21797-8025 Office: Office of Environment Safety & Health 1000 Independence Ave SE Washington DC 20585-0001*

BRUSHABER, GEORGE KARL, college-theological seminary president, minister; b. Milw., Dec. 15, 1938; s. Ralph E. and Marie C. (Meister) B.; m. N. Darleen Dugar, Jan. 27, 1962; children: Deanna Lyn Dalberg, Donald Paul. BA, Wheaton Coll., 1959, MA, 1962; MDiv, Gordon-Conwell Theol. Sem., 1963; PhD, Boston U., 1967. Ordained to ministry Bapt. Gen. Conf., 1966. Prof. philosophy, chair dept. Gordon Coll., Wenham, Mass., 1963-72; dir. admissions and registration Gordon-Conwell Theol. Sem., 1970-72; v.p., acad. dean Westmont Coll., Santa Barbara, Calif., 1972-75; v.p., dean of coll. Bethel. Coll., St. Paul, 1975-82; pres. Bethel Coll. & Theol. Sem., St. Paul and San Diego, 1982—; Staley Found. lectr. Anderson U., Sioux Falls Coll.; sec. for higher edn. Bapt. Gen. Conf., Arlington Heights, Ill., 1982—; cons., evaluator Minn. Humanities Commn., St. Paul. Editor Gordon Rev., 1965-70; pub., founding editor Christian Scholar's Rev., 1970-79; exec. editor Christianity Today, 1985-90, chmn. sr. editors, 1990—; contbr. articles to religious jours. Bd. dirs. Youth Leadership, Mpls., 1982—, Fairview Elders' Enterprises Found., 1989—, Scripture Press Ministries Found., 1994—; chair bd. Scripture Press Ministries, 1994—; adv. coun. Evang. Environ. Network, 1994—; mem. Commn. on Minorities in Higher Edn. Am. Coun. Edn., 1995—. Mem. Christian Environ. Assn., Christian Coll. Consortium (bd. dirs.), Nat. Assn. Evangs. (trustee 1982—), Minn. Pvt. Coll. Coun. (bd. dirs. 1982—), Minn. Consortium Theol. Sems. (bd. dirs. 1982—), Coun. Ind. Colls (bd. dirs. 1984-89), Am. Philos. Assn., Evang. Theol. Soc., Am. Assn. Higher Edn., Soc. Christian Philosophers, Cook Comm. Internat. (bd. dirs.), Fellowship Evang. Sem. Pres., Minn. Club, North Oaks Country Club. Home and Office: Bethel Coll and Theol Sem 3900 Bethel Dr Saint Paul MN 55112-6902

BRUSHWYLER, LAWRENCE RONALD, minister; b. E. Orange, N.J., Jan. 31, 1936; s. Vincent M. and Nan Josephine (Kjelstad) B.; m. Carol Valerie Kinney, June 24, 1961; children: Kevin Ross, Lisa Marlene Brushwyler Larson, Kurt Ronald. BA cum laude, Wheaton (Ill.) Coll., 1958; BD, Fuller Theol. Sem., Pasadena, 1963; STM, Andover Newton Theol. Sem., Newton Center, Mass., 1964; DMin, Bethany Theol. Sem., Oak Brook, Ill., 1983. Ordained to ministry, Am. Bapt. Chs. USA, 1965; lic. marriage, family counselor; nat. cert. counselor. Pastor Trinity Bapt. Ch., Poway, Calif., 1965-68; sr. pastor First Bapt. Ch., San Bruno, Calif., 1968-73; area minister Am. Bapt. Chs. of West, Oakland, Calif., 1973-77; exec. dir. Midwest Career Devel. Svc., Westchester, Ill., 1977—; chmn. strategy com. Ch. Career Devel. Coun., N.Y.C., 1985—; faculty pastoral leadership program Roman Cath. Diocese of Joliet, Ill., 1988—. Contbr. articles to profl. jours. Mem. Am. Assn. Marriage and Family Therapists, Am. Assn. Pastoral Counselors, Ill. Psychol. Assn., Am. Assn. Counseling Assn. Home: 633 Brighton Dr Wheaton IL 60187-8105 Office: Midwest Career Devel Svc 1840 Westchester Blvd # 7249 Westchester IL 60154-7249

BRUSILOW, SAUL, pediatrics researcher; b. Bklyn., June 7, 1927; s. Samuel Michael and Marie (Arenson) B.; m. Sallie Evans (dec.); children: William, Susan, Alexander (dec.). A.B., Princeton U., 1950; M.D., Yale U., 1954. Diplomate: Am. Bd. Pediatrics, Am. Bd. Pediatric Nephrology. Intern, asst. resident Grace-New Haven Hosp., 1954-56; asst. resident Johns Hopkins Hosp., Balt., 1956-57; research fellow Johns Hopkins U., Balt., 1957-59, instr., 1959-60, asst. prof., 1960-64, assoc. prof., 1964-74, prof., 1974—. Contbr. articles on pediatrics to profl. jours.; patentee in field; author: Inborn Errors of Metabolism. Served with USNR, 1945-46. Recipient Sci. Rsch. award Joseph P. Kennedy Jr. Found., 1995; grantee NIH, 1959—. Mem. Soc. Pediatric Research, Am. Fedn. Clin. Research, Am. Physiol. Soc., Am. Pediatric Soc. Democrat. Jewish. Fax: (410) 955-0885. E-mail: sbru@welchlink.welch.jhu.edu. Home: 4804 Keswick Rd Baltimore MD 21210-2325 Office: Johns Hopkins U Sch Medicine 600 N Wolfe St Baltimore MD 21287-0005

BRUSKEWITZ, FABIAN W., bishop; b. Milw., Sept. 6, 1935. Ordained priest Roman Catholic Ch., 1960. Ordained priest, 1960; bishop Diocese of Lincoln, Nebr., 1992—. Office: Chancery Office PO Box 80328 3400 Sheridan Blvd Lincoln NE 68506-6125*

BRUSKI, PAUL STEVEN, marketing executive; b. Kansas City, Mo., Mar. 10, 1949; s. Paul and Elizabeth Ann (Cravens) B.; m. Mary Margaret Williams, May 3, 1980. BS in Journalism, U. Berlin, 1972. With engring. mgmt. Storage Tech. Corp., Louisville, Colo., 1973-77; dir. tech. svcs. Internat. Mktg. Communications, Denver, 1977-79; ptnr. Flack and Bruski Advt., Denver, 1979-80; pvt. practice advt. cons. Schenectady, N.Y., 1981-82; dir. tech. Services D. J. Moore Advt., Guilderland, N.Y., 1983-84; dir. mktg. Enable Software, Inc., Ballston Lake, N.Y., 1984-86; dir. corp. commnications Innovative Software Inc., Lenexa, Kans., 1986-89, Informix Software, Inc. (formerly Innovative Software, Inc.), Lenexa, 1988-89; pres. Market Rels. Cons., Olathe, Kans., 1989—, Am. Ednl. Resources, Inc., Olathe, Kans., 1989-91, MRC Cos., Olathe, 1992—; dir. Corp. Comms. & Spl. Sys. sect. Long Data Sys., Inc., Lenexa, Kans., 1992-96; v.p. mktg. and sales Visual Applications, Inc., Kansas City, Mo., 1996-97; pres. Images That Sell, Olathe, Kans., 1997; mktg. cons. Security Benefit Group of Cos., Topeka, Kans., 1997—; cons. publ. Brodock Press Inc., Utica, N.Y., 1983-86; computer cons. and freelance journalist, 1974—; mktg. cons. Security Benefit Group, Topeka, 1997-99. Author: Collected Works, 1977. With U.S. Army, 1968-72. Mem. Pub. Rels. Soc. Am. (accredited, Prism award 1989). Avocations: race car design, ski racing. Office: Market Rels Cons 15404 W 152nd St Ste F Olathe KS 66062-3085

BRUSKY, LINDA L., middle school mathematics and science educator; b. Chgo., Sept. 22, 1948; d. Ervin and Elizabeth (Martinek) Lange; m. George F. Brusky, Mar. 13, 1971. BA in Elem. Edn., Northeastern Ill. State Coll., Chgo., 1970; MA in Gen. Adminstrn., Northeastern Ill. U., 1998. Cert. tchr. K-9, Ill., gen. adminstr., Ill., 1998. Tchr. St. Mary of the Angels Sch., Chgo., 1970-98, tchr. jr. high sch. math. and sci., 1987-93, tchr. mid. sch. math., 1993-98; prin. St. James Sch., Chgo., 1998—. Charter mem. Statue of Liberty Ellis Island Found., Inc., N.Y.C., 1985—; site coord. Joyce Found. Magnet Summer Sch., 1991, DeWitt-Wallace/Readers Digest Found. Magnet Ctr. Summer Sch., 1992. Recipient Cardinal Bernadin Tchr. Achievement award 1992; Joyce Found. scholar, 1987-91, Weber H.S. Tchr. Recognition award, 1998. Fellow Nat. Assn. Watch and Clock Collectors; mem. ASCD, Ill. Assn. for Supervision and Curriculum Devel., Nat. Coun. Tchrs. Math., Nat. Cath. Edn. Assn. (Disting. Grad. award 1995), Ill. Coun. Tchrs. Math., Archdiocesan Prins. Assn., Psi Chi. Roman Catholic. Avocations: opera, collecting antique clocks and watches. Office: St James Sch 2456 N Mango Ave Chicago IL 60639-2313

BRUST, DAVID, physicist; b. Chgo., Aug. 24, 1935; s. Clifford and Ruth (Klapman) B.; BS, Calif. Inst. Tech., 1957; MS, U. Chgo., 1958, PhD, 1964. Rsch. assoc. Purdue U., Lafayette, Ind., 1963-64; rsch. assoc. Northwestern U., Evanston, Ill., 1964-65, asst. prof. physics, 1965-68; theoretical rsch. physicist U. Calif., Lawrence Radiation Lab., Livermore, Calif., 1968-73; cons. Bell Telephone Lab., Murray Hill, N.J., 1966. Campaign co-ordinator No. Calif. Scientists and Engrs. for McGovern, 1972. NSF travel grantee, 1964; NSF rsch. grantee, 1966-68. Mem. Am. Phys. Soc., Am. Assn. Coll. Profs., Internat. Solar Energy Soc., Astron. Soc. of Pacific, Nature Conservancy, Calif. Acad. Sci., Commonwealth Club of Calif., World Affairs Coun. No. Calif. Commonwealth Club Anza Borrego Desert, Natural History Assn., Planetary Soc., Sierra Club, Sigma Xi. Office: PO Box 13130 Oakland CA 94661-0130

BRUSTAD, ORIN DANIEL, lawyer; b. Chgo., Nov. 11, 1941; s. Marvin D. and Sylvia Evelyn (Peterson) B.; m. Ilona M. Fox, July 16, 1966; children: Caroline E., Katherine L., Mark D. BA in History, Yale U., 1963, MA, 1964; JD, Harvard U., 1968. Bar: Mich. 1968, U.S. Dist. Ct. (so. dist.) Mich. 1968. Assoc. Miller, Canfield, Paddock and Stone, Detroit, 1968-74, sr. ptnr., 1975—, chmn. employee benefits practice group, 1989-96, dep. chmn. tax dept., 1989-93; bd. dirs. Electrocon Internat., Inc., Ann Arbor, Mich. Mem. editl. adv. bd. Benefits Law Jour.; contbr. articles to profl. jours. Mem. ABA, Mich. Bar Assn., Detroit Bar Assn., Mich. Employee Benefits Conf. Avocations: sailing, skiing, reading, piano. Home: 1422 MacGregor Ln Ann Arbor MI 48105-2836 Office: Miller Canfield Paddock & Stone 150 W Jefferson Ave Fl 25th Detroit MI 48226-4432

BRUSTEIN, ABRAM ISAAC, insurance company executive; b. Bridgeport, Conn., Jan. 14, 1946; s. Louis and Flora (Forman) B.; m. Barbara Bederick Rudman, July 3, 1969; children: Asher Jeremey, Darrah Bethany, Garrett Michael. BA, U. Conn., 1968; MS in Mgmt., Am. Coll., 1985. CLU, chartered fin. cons. Agt. N.Y. Life Ins. Co., Stamford, Conn., 1968-70, sales mgr., 1970-75; gen. mgr. N.Y. Life Ins. Co., Amherst, N.Y., 1975-79, Bala Cynwyd, Pa., 1979-87; gen. agt. Penn Mut. Life Ins. Co., Phila., 1987-94; exec. dir. Prudential Ins. Co. Am., Lutherville, Md., 1994-95; v.p. Phoenix Home Life Ins. Co., Hartford, Conn., 1995-98; mng. dir. Mut. N.Y., Towson, Md., 1998—; mem. rev. panel Am. Coll., Bryn Mawr, Pa., 1984—, focus group mem. Masters Degree com., 1986; lectr. local univs., 1985—. Served with USAR, 1969-75. Mem. Gen. Agts. and Mgrs. Assn. (pres. 1986-87, Nat. Mgmt. award 1978-91), Am. Soc. CLUs and Chartered Fin. Cons., Phila. Assn. Life Underwriters (pres. 1988-89), Penn Mut. Agy. Assn. (pres. 1990-91), Germantown Cricket Club (Phila.), Chestnut Ridge Country Club (Lutherville, Md.). Jewish. Avocations: tennis, aerobics, skiing, bicycling. Home: 313 W Timonium Rd Timonium MD 21093-2930

BRUSTEIN, LAWRENCE, financial executive; b. Liberty, N.Y., Oct. 11, 1936; s. Leo and Rae (Smoller) B.; m. Ellen Gloria Sheppard, June 20, 1965; children: Jacqueline, Michael. BS, U. Buffalo, 1958. CPA, N.Y. With Irving Handel & Co., CPAs, N.Y.C., 1959-62, Robert Simons & Co., CPAs, N.Y.C., 1962-64, E&L Distbrs., Inc., 1964-66, Barney's, N.Y.C., 1966-68; controller Holly Stores div. K-Mart, North Bergen, N.J., 1968-70; v.p., treas. Marcade, Jersey City, 1970-86; exec. v.p. Modells, N.Y.C., 1987—. Exec. v.p. Reform Temple of East Brunswick, 1977—. Mem. AICPA, N.Y. State Soc. CPAs, Internat. Mass Retail Assn. (chmn. fin.). Home: 1 Jamestown Ct East Brunswick NJ 08816-3229 Office: Modells 498 7th Ave New York NY 10018-6701

BRUSTEIN, ROBERT SANFORD, English language educator, theatre director, author; b. N.Y.C., N.Y., Apr. 21, 1927; s. Max and Blanche (Haft) B.; m. Norma Ofstrock, Mar. 25, 1962 (dec.); children: Phillip Cates (stepson), Daniel Anton; m. Doreen Beinart, Dec. 22, 1996; stepchildren: Jean Beinart, Peter Beinart. BA, Amherst Coll., 1948, LittD; postgrad., Yale Drama Sch., 1948-49, U. Nottingham, Eng., 1953-55; MA, Columbia U., 1950, PhD, 1957; LittD, Lawrence U.; LLD, Beloit Coll., 1975; ArtsD, Bard Coll., 1981; LHD, Emory U., 1983; Arts D, Marlboro Coll., 1995, Middlebury Coll., 1996, Hebrew Coll., 1997. Instr. English Cornell U., 1955-56; instr. drama Vassar Coll., 1956-57; faculty Columbia, 1957-66, prof. English and comparative lit., 1965-66; prof. English Yale U., New Haven; dean Yale U. (Sch. Drama); founder, artistic dir. Yale Repertory Theatre, 1966-79; dir. Loeb Drama Centre; also founder, artistic dir. Am. Repertory Theatre Co.; prof. English Harvard U., 1979—; drama critic New Republic, 1959-67, 78—, contbg. editor, 1959-79; guest theatre critic London Observer, 1972-73; contbr. to N.Y. Times, 1972—; directed and adapted plays including: Ghosts, 1982, Six Characters in Search of an Author, 1984, The Changeling, 1985, Tonight We Improvise, 1986, Right You Are, 1987, The Father, 1990, When We Deal Awaken, 1992, The Seagull, 1994, The Cherry Orchard, 1995, The Wild Duck, 1996, The Master Bucker, 1999; panel mem. Nat. Endowment for Arts, 1969-72, 81-84; created, adapted Shlemiel the First, 1994. Author: The Theatre of Revolt: Studies in the Modern Drama, 1964, Seasons of Discontent: Dramatic Opinions 1959-65, 1965, The Third Theatre, 1969, Revolution as Theatre: Notes on the New Radical Style, 1971, The Culture Watch, 1975, Critical Moments, 1980, Making Scenes, 1981, Who Needs Theatre, 1987, Reimagining American Theatre, 1991, Dumbocracy in America, 1994, Cultural Calisthenics, 1998, (plays) Demons, 1995, Nobody Dies on Friday, 1996, Poker Face, 1999; editor: The Plays and Prose of Strindberg, 1964; contbr. numerous articles to profl. jours. Trustee Sarah Lawrence Coll., 1973-77. Served with U.S. Mcht. Marine, 1945-47. Recipient George Jean Nathan award dramatic criticism, 1962, 87, George Polk Meml. award outstanding criticism, 1965, Eliot Norton award, 1984, award in criticism Jersey City Jour., 1967, award Outstanding Achievement in Am. Theater, New Eng. Theater Coun., 1985, Tiffany award for excellence in theatre Internat. Soc. Performing Arts Adminstrs., 1987, Thomas De Gaetan award UITT, 1991, Disting. Svc. to Arts award Am. Acad. Arts and Letters, 1995; Fulbright fellow, 1953-55; Guggenheim fellow, 1961-62; Ford Found. fellow, 1964-65. Mem. Am. Acad. Arts and Scis., Am. Acad. Arts and Letters. Office: Harvard U Loeb Drama Center Cambridge MA 02138

BRUTON, JOHN MACAULAY, trade association executive; b. Mexico City, Nov. 13, 1937; s. Edmund Macaulay and Byrd (Grant) B.; m. Frances McMillan Marks, Nov. 25, 1960; children: Alexander, Macaulay, Brinley. BA, Duke U., 1959. Pres., gen. mgr. Grant Advt. de Panama, Panama City, 1970-72, Mexico City, 1972; comm. dir. Am. C. of C. of Mex., Mexico City, 1972-74, gen. mgr., 1974-77, exec. v.p., CEO, 1977—; v.p. exec. mgmt. Assn. Am. C. of C. in Latin Am., L.A., Washington, 1985-88, v.p. membership svc., 1988—. Bd. dirs. Am. Benevolent Soc., Mex., 1964-68, Am. Soc. Mex., 1975-78, 80-84; adv. bd. Jr. League Mexico City, 1978—; founder, bd. dirs. Jr. Achievement Mex., 1977—; bd. trustees Fomento Educacional A.C., 1988—, treas., 1993—. Mem. Univ. Mex. (bd. dirs. 1979-83, pres. 1981-82). Episcopalian. Home: Ameyalcalli, Ocotepec 80, 10200 Mexico City Mexico Office: Am C of C Mex, Lucerna 78, 06600 Mexico City Mexico

BRUYN, HENRY BICKER, physician; b. Bklyn., Jan. 24, 1918; s. Henry Bicker and Mary Janet (Retter) B.; m. Marion Helen Burkhardt, Sept. 19, 1942; children: Martha Elizabeth, Barbara Jane, Charles DeWitt, Jonathan Henry; m. Harriet Hall Brainerd, Apr. 22, 1973; m. Jennie Low, Jan. 7, 1994. B.A., Amherst Coll., 1940; M.D., Yale, 1943. Intern pediatrics New Haven Hosp., 1943-44; resident Buffalo Children's Hosp., 1944-45; fellow infectious disease U. Calif. Med. Sch., San Francisco, 1946-47, mem. faculty, 1948-98; clin. prof. medicine and pediatrics U. Calif. Med. Sch., 1969-98; chief isolation svc. San Francisco Gen. Hosp., 1950-59, chief pediatrics, 1954-59; lectr. Sch. Pub. Health, U. Calif., Berkeley, 1960-98, dir. student health svc., 1959-72; cons. City of San Francisco, 1974-91, U.S. Naval Hosp., U.S. Army Hosp., Children's Hosp. East Bay, Calif. Viral and Rickettsial Disease Lab.; mem. med. svc. com. Alameda County Coun. Social Planning, 1962-64; med. cons. Morrisonnn Ctr. Rehab., 1954-58, Medic-Alert Found., Elizabeth Kenney Found., San Francisco, 1950-52; med. dir. Drug Abuse Rehab. New Bridge Inc.; pres. Berkeley Med. Instrument Co., 1960-68. Co-author: Handbook of Pediatrics, 1st-15th edit, 1979-86, Handbook of Medical Treatment, 1972, Current Diagnosis and Therapy, 1972, Practice of Pediatrics, 1963, Drinking Among Collegians, 1970, Parents Guide to Child Raising, 1978, Parents Medical Manual, 1978; contbr. articles to profl. jours. Bd. dirs. Alameda County Council Alcoholism, 1960-70, Alameda County Suicide Prevention, 1962-70, Ronoh Sch., 1966-70, New Bridge Found., 1968—, Carmel Valley Manor, 1969-98, Goodwill Industries, 1972-92 , Com. Children's TV, 1977-79, Jack B. Goldberg Found., 1978—, Am. Found. for Traditional Chinese Medicine, 1990-98; trustee, mem. ch. council Arlington Community Ch., 1954-72. Served to lt. comdr. M.C. USNR, 1945-46, 53-54. Mem. AMA, APHA, Royal Soc. Health, Am. Coll. Health Assns. (pres. 1965-66), Pacific Coast Coll. Health Assn. (pres. 1968-69), Am. Fedn. Clin. Rsch., Western Soc. Clin. Rsch., Am. Acad. Pediatrics (chmn. cmty. svcs. com. No. Calif. sect. 1962-94), Calif. Acad. Medicine, Order Golden Bear, Delta Tau Delta, Nu Sigma Nu. Home: 432 Woodland Rd Kentfield CA 94904-2636

BRUZELIUS, NILS JOHAN AXEL, journalist; b. Stockholm, Feb. 27, 1947; came to U.S., 1958; s. Axel Sture and Constance (Brickett) B.; divorced. B.A. in History, Amherst Coll., 1968. Reporter, bur. chief Middlesex News, Framingham, Mass., 1968-70; reporter, state house corr. AP, Boston, 1970-73; med./mental health writer Boston Globe, 1973-79, investigative reporter, 1979-81, asst. met. editor, 1981-86, health and sci. editor, 1986-99, fgn. editor, 1999—. Mem. Boston Globe investigative team receiving Disting. Investigative Reporting award Investigative Reporters and Editors Assn., 1979, Disting. Journalism citation Scripps-Howard Found., 1979, Pulitzer prize for spl. local reporting, 1980; Knight Sci. Journalism fellow MIT, 1992-93. Mem. Nat. Assn. Sci. Writers. Club: Ocean Cruising. Home: PO Box 482 1973 Main Rd Westport Point MA 02791 Office: Globe Newspapers Co 135 Morrissey Blvd Dorchester MA 02107-2738

BRUZS, BORIS OLGERD, management consultant; b. Riga, Latvia, July 11, 1933; s. Boris and Zelia (Neumanis) B.; m. Anne Quoniam de Schompre, Feb. 10, 1988. Lic. es Sc., La Sorbonne, Paris; BA, Bowdoin Coll., Maine; MPC, U. Strasbourg, France. Tech. svc. mgr. Union Carbide Internat., Geneva, Switzerland, 1959-62; gen. mgr. Profile Steel Co., Detroit, 1962-64; cons. Booz, Allen & Hamilton, Zurich, 1964-66; ptnr. Booz, Allen & Hamilton, Dusseldorf, 1966-69; mng. ptnr. Booz, Allen & Hamilton, Paris, 1969-79; pres. internat. affairs Booz, Allen & Hamilton, N.Y.C., 1979-94. Mem. Inst. Mgmt. Cons., Polo Club. Home: 16 Rue Maitre Albert, 75005 Paris France Office: Booz Allen & Hamilton 101 Park Ave New York NY 10178

BRY, JEFFREY ALLEN, auditor; b. Mpls., Nov. 27, 1949; s. Allen Parnell and Alvina Clarice (Olson) B.; m. Marjorie Ann Kittridge, Dec. 4, 1971; children: Jeffrey Allen Jr., Nathan Andrew. BA in Acctg., Fin., Augsburg Coll., 1972; MA in Mgmt., Webster U., 1976. lic. pub. acct., Minn.; nat. cert. cost analyst. Cost acct. tank automotive command U.S. Dept. of Army, Warren, Mich., 1975-76; super. field auditor office insp. gen. office adult svcs. HHS, St. Paul, 1976—. Co-chair Valley Park Homeowners Assn., Lakeville, Minn., 1989—; spokesperson various citizen task forces; appointee Lakeville Strategic Growth Mgmt. Task Force; ch. lay reader. With U.S. Army, 1972-74. Mem. Assn. Govt. Accts. (vol. tax preparer for underprivileged filers), Soc. Cost Estimating and Analysis, Big Apple Toastmasters (pres. 1986). Lutheran. Avocations: theater, reading, walking. Home: 16170 Garner Ave W Rosemount MN 55068-1059 Office: HHS Audit Svcs 375 Jackson St Saint Paul MN 55101-1810

BRYAN, ALBERT V., JR., federal judge; b. Alexandria, Va., Nov. 8, 1926; m. Marilyn Morgan, Aug. 25, 1950; children: Marie, John, Vickers. Student, Va. Military Inst., 1943-44; grad., Geo. Wash. Univ., 1946; LLB, Univ. Va., 1950. Bar: Va. Practicing atty. Alexandria, Va., 1950-62; circuit judge State of Va., 1962-71; judge U.S. Dist. Ct. (ea. dist.) Va., 1971-91, sr. judge, 1991—. With USMC 1944-46, PTO. Office: US Dist Ct Ea Dist 401 Courthouse Sq Alexandria VA 22314-5704

BRYAN, A(LONZO) J(AY), service club official; b. Washington, N.J., Sept. 17, 1917; s. Alonzo J. and Anna Belle (Babcock) B.; student pub. schs.; m. Elizabeth Elfreida Koehler, June 25, 1941 (div. 1961); children: Donna Elizabeth, Alonzo Jay, Nadine; m. Janet Dorothy Onstad, Mar. 15, 1962 (div. 1977); children: Brenda Joyce, Marlowe Francis, Marilyn Janet. Engaged as retail florist, Washington, N.J., 1941-64. Fund drive chmn. ARC, 1952; bd. dirs. Washington YMCA, 1945-55, N.J. Taxpayers Assn., 1947-52; mem. Washington Bd. Edn., 1948-55. Mem. Washington Grange, Sons and Daus. of Liberty, Soc. Am. Florists, Nat. Fedn. Ind. Businessmen, Florists Telegraph Delivery Assn., C. of C. Methodist. Clubs: Masons, Tall Cedars of Lebanon, Jr. Order United Am. Mechanics, Kiwanis (pres. Washington (N.J.) 1952, lt. gov. internat. 1953-54, gov. N.J. dist. 1955, sec. N.J. dist. 1957-64, sec. S.E. area Chgo. 1965-74; editor The Jersey Kiwanian 1958-64, internat. staff 1964-85)); Breakfast (pres. 1981-82) (Chgo.); sec., treas. Rocky Mtn. Kiwanis Dist., 1989; pres. South Denver, 1990-91; editor Rocky Mountain Kiwanian, 1990-96. Home: 8115 S Poplar Way B 203 Englewood CO 80112-3174 Office: 8859 Fox Dr Ste 100 Denver CO 80221-6831

BRYAN, BARBARA DAY, retired librarian; b. Livermore Falls, Maine, May 20, 1927; d. Lorey Clifford and Olga Elvira (Bergquist) Day; m. Robert S. Bryan, June 24, 1950. BA in Psychology, U. Maine, 1948; MS in Library Sci., So. Conn. State U., 1964. Catalog dept. asst. Yale U. Library, New Haven, 1948-49; departmental library cataloger Harvard U., Cambridge, Mass., 1949-51; descriptive cataloger Yale U. Library, New Haven, 1951-52; cataloger Fairfield (Conn.) Pub. Library, 1952-54, reference librarian, 1954-57, asst. librarian, order librarian, 1957-65; asst. dir. libraries Fairfield U., 1965-74, university librarian, 1974-96, u. libr. emerita, 1996—; mem. Conn. State Libr. Bd., Hartford, 1978-82, chair, 1987-92; bd. dirs. Bibliomation, Inc., Stratford, Conn., 1987-91. Pres. Friends Nyselius Libr., Fairfield U., 1998—. Recipient Disting. Alumnus award So. Conn. State U. Sch. of Libr. Sci., 1979; named Conn. Libr. Assn. Libr. of Yr., 1988. Mem. ALA (Conn. chpt. councilor 1977-80), Assn. Coll. and Rsch. Librs. (constn. and by-laws com. 1986-90, mem. coll. libr. sect. stds. com. 1991-95), New Eng. Libr. Assn. (mem. com. 1981-85, coun. mem. 1975-77), Conn. Libr Assn., Fairfield Hist. Soc. (libr. vol.), Conn. Audubon Soc., Oak Lawn Cemetery Assn. (bd. dirs. 1994—), Assn. Conn. Libr. Bds. (bd. dirs., chair legis. com. 1996—), Inst. Ret. Profl. (adv. bd. 1998—), Phi Beta Kappa, Phi Kappa Phi. Democrat. Avocations: reading, walking. Home: 999 Merwins Ln Fairfield CT 06430-1919

BRYAN, BARRY RICHARD, lawyer; b. Orange, N.J., Sept. 5, 1930; s. Lloyd Thomas and Amy Rufe (Swank) B.; m. Margaret Susannah Elliot, July 24, 1953; children—Elliot Christopher, Peter George (dec.), Susannah Margaret, Sallie Catharine. B.A., Yale U., 1952, J.D. cum laude, 1955; diploma in comparative legal studies, Cambridge U., Eng., 1956. Bar: N.Y. 1959. Legal advisor to gen. counsel Sec. of U.S. Air Force, Washington, 1956-58; assoc. Debevoise & Plimpton, N.Y.C., 1958-62, ptnr., 1963-93, presiding ptnr., 1993-98, of counsel, 1999—. Served to 1st lt. USAF, 1956-58. Fulbright scholar Trinity Coll., Cambridge U., 1956. Mem. ABA, Assn.

of Bar of City of N.Y., Union Internationale des Avocats, Country Club of New Canaan, Polo de Paris, Fishers Island Club, Order of Coif, Phi Beta Kappa. Episcopalian. Home: PO Box 197 Isabella Beach Rd Fishers Island NY 06390 Office: Debevoise & Plimpton 875 3rd Ave Fl 23 New York NY 10022-6256

BRYAN, CAROLINE ELIZABETH, nun; b. Washington, Dec. 4, 1951; d. Carter Royston and Anna Maria (Schneider) B. BA, Vassar Coll., 1973. Programmer Santa Barbara Rsch. Ctr., Goleta, Calif., 1975-77; tester, software developer and sr. test technician Johnson Controls, Inc., Milw., 1977-85; cons. Cap Gemini Am., Cranford, N.J., 1986-90; quality assurance engr. PRC, Inc., McLean, Va., 1990-91; software quality assurance engr. Unify Corp., Sacramento, 1991-94; software engr. Objective Systems Integrators, Folsom, Calif., 1994-99; postulant Order of St. Benedict, Atchison, Kans., 1999—; cons. AT&T, Lincroft and Middletown, N.J., 1986-90. Editor (newsletter) Captain America, 1989. Fellow Murphy Ctr. for Codification of Human and Organizational Law. Democrat. Roman Catholic. Avocations: gourmet cooking, gardening, quilt design, choir. Home: 801 S 8th St Atchison KS 66002

BRYAN, COLGAN HOBSON, aerospace engineering educator; b. Trenton, S.C., Oct. 7, 1909; s. John William and Mary (Hobson) B.; m. Sara Lucille Turbeville, June 18, 1938 (dec. Nov. 17, 1975); 1 son, Colgan Hobson; m. Carol Lindsay Smelley, July 14, 1979 (dec. Sept. 20, 1993). B.S. in Elec. Engring, U. S.C., 1932; M.Ed., Duke U., 1940; M.S. in Aero. Engring, Ga. Inst. Tech., 1948. Registered profl. engr., Ala. Faculty U. Ala., 1942—, prof. aerospace engring., 1948—, chmn. dept., 1952—; research scientist NASA, 1962; on leave with U. Tenn. Space Inst., 1968-69; cons. to industry, 1941—. Mem. Ala. Aero. Commn., 1944-48. Recipient Charles Henry Ratcliff award for excellence in teaching, 1976, Outstanding Faculty award Delta Tau Delta, 1976, George H. Denny Outstanding Faculty award Sigma Chi, 1976; established Colgan H. Bryan Aerospace Engring. Scholarship, 1991. Fellow AIAA (assoc., Disting. Svc. award 1980); mem. NSPE, ASME, AAUP, NEA, Am. Soc. Engring. Edn., Am. Ordnance Assn., Ala. Soc. Profl. Engrs. (Engr. of Yr. award Tuscaloosa chpt. 1990), Ala. Edn. Assn., Acacia (life), Pi Tau Chi (faculty adviser). Episcopalian. Club: Kiwanian (pres. Tuscaloosa 1966, recipient Service award 1966, Distinguished Service award 1977). Research projects in theoretical and applied aerodynamics, energy (solar and wind). Home: 12 Lakeshore Dr Tuscaloosa AL 35404-4982 Office: U Ala PO Box 861461 Tuscaloosa AL 35486-0013

BRYAN, CYNTHIA JOAN, emergency medical science educator, special education educator; b. Kingman, Kans., Aug. 10, 1953. BE, Kans. Wesleyan U., 1978; M in ednl. psychol. with honors, Wichita (Kans.) State U., 1985; cert. in emergency mobile intensive care tech., Hutchinson Community Coll., 1987. Educator. Tchr. USD #331, Kingman, Kans., 1978-80; tchr. special edn. South Cen. Kans. Special Edn. Coop., Pratt, 1980-82; police dispatcher Kingman (Kans.) Police Dept., 1979-82; emergency medical technician Kingman Emergency Med. Svcs., 1980—; spl. edn. tchr. Three Lakes Spl. Edn. Coop., Burlington, Kans., 1982-83, South Cen. Kans. Spl. Edn. Coop., Iuka, Kans., 1983-89; paramedic Kingman Emergency Med. Svc., 1987—; emergency paramedic educator Hutchinson (Kans.) C.C., 1989-94; emergency mem. examiner Kans. Bd. Emergency Med. Svcs., Topeka, 1989—; established paramedic edn. program for Hutchinson C.C. on Wichita State U. Campus, 1991-94, establisher, lead instr. Iuka Alt. Sch., 1994—; presenter in field; EMS educator Pratt C.C., Kans., 1995—. Editor monthly newsletter. Mem. NEA, Kans. Instr./Coord. Soc. (pres.), Tchrs. Assn. Spl. Kids (pres.). Avocations: reading, quilting, swimming. Home: 827 N Spruce St Kingman KS 67068-1557 Office: South Ctrl Kans Spl Edn Coop PO Box 177 Iuka KS 67066-0177

BRYAN, ELIZABETH JOHNSON, English language educator; b. Lumberton, N.C., May 11, 1953; d. Finley S. and Christine (Johnson) B. BA summa cum laude, U. N.C., Greensboro, 1975; MA, U. Pa., 1981, PhD, 1990. Assoc. prof. English Brown U., 1997—. Vol. Peace Corps, Liberia, 1975-77. Office: Brown U PO Box 1852 Providence RI 02912-1852

BRYAN, GEORGE THOMAS, pediatrician, academic administrator; b. Sewanee, Tenn., Nov. 19, 1930; s. Lawton P. and Velma (Courtney) B.; m. Peggy Marie Graham, Dec. 19, 1952; children: Ralph T., Janice M. Student, Vanderbilt U., 1949-51; MD, U. Tenn., 1955. Intern D.C. Gen. Hosp., 1955-56; resident in pediatrics U. Iowa Hosp., Iowa City, 1956-58, fellow in pediatric endocrinology, 1958-59; clin. assoc. pediatrics, Lab. Clin. Investigation NIH, USPHS, Bethesda, Md., 1959-60, acting head pediatric svc., 1960-61, pediatrician clin. endocrinology br. Nat Heart Inst., 1961-63; asst. prof. pediatrics U. Tex. Med. Br., Galveston, 1963-67, assoc. prof., 1967-73, prof., 1973—, asst. dir. clin. study ctr., 1963-72, assoc. dir., 1972-75, assoc. dean curricular affairs, 1974-77, dean Sch. Medicine, 1977-95, dean emeritus Sch. Medicine, 1995—. Contbr. articles to profl. jours. Lt. USNR, 1956-59. Markle scholar, 1967-72. Mem. Am. Pediatric Soc., Soc. Pediatric Rsch., Am. Acad. Pediatrics, Lawson Wilkins Soc. Pediatric Endocrinology, Endocrine Soc., Am. Fedn. Clin. Rsch., So. Soc. Pediatric Rsch., AMA, Tex. Med. Assn., Galveston County Med. Soc., Am. Assn. Med. Colls., Sigma Xi. Mem. Christian Ch. Office: U Tex Med Br 301 University Blvd Galveston TX 77555-1011

BRYAN, GORDON REDMAN, JR., retired naval officer; b. Cleve., Dec. 1, 1928; s. Gordon Redman and Iola (Schecter) B.; m. Janet Louise McIntyre, Aug. 1, 1951 (div. Oct. 1985); children: Gordon L., Steven G.; m. Judith Hager, July 5, 1987. BA, Brown U., 1951; MS, George Washington U., 1970. Commd. ensign USN, 1951, advanced through grades to capt., 1971; comdg. officer 4 navy ships and 5 shore commands, 1965-78, submarine squadron, 1972-74; ret., 1978; marine design cons. various aerospace and engring. cos., Seattle, 1979-81; engring. cons. U.S. Nuc. Regulatory Commn. and U.S. Dept. Energy, Seattle, 1982-95. Decorated Legion of Merit. Mem. Am. Nuclear Soc., Am. Radio Relay League, N.Y. Acad. Scis., Rotary. Republican. Avocations: amateur radio, travel. Home and Office: SaddleBrooke Country Club 37810 S Rolling Hills Dr Tucson AZ 85739-1069 also: PO Box 1285 Bay View MI 49770

BRYAN, HENRY C(LARK), JR., lawyer; b. St. Louis, Dec. 8, 1930; s. Henry Clark and Faith (Young) B.; m. Sarah Ann McCarthy, July 28, 1956; children—Mark Pendleton, Thomas Clark, Sarah Christy Nussbaum. A.B., Washington U., St. Louis, 1952, LL.B., 1956. Bar: Mo. 1956. Law clk. to fed. judge, 1956; assoc. McDonald & Wright, St. Louis, 1956-60; ptnr. McDonald, Bernard, Wright & Timm, St. Louis, 1961-64, McDonald, Wright & Bryan, St. Louis, 1964-81, Wright, Bryan & Walsh, St. Louis, 1981-84; pvt. practice law, 1984-96, ret., 1996; v.p., dir. Harbor Point Boat & Dock Co., St. Charles, Mo., 1966-80, Merrell Ins. Agy., 1966-80. Served to 1st lt. AUS, 1952-54. Mem. ABA, Mo. Bar Assn., St. Louis Bar Assn. (past chmn. probate and trust sect., marriage and div. law com.), Kappa Sigma, Phi Delta Phi. Republican. Episcopalian. Lodge: Elks. Home: 41 Ladue Ter Saint Louis MO 63124-2047

BRYAN, HENRY COLLIER, retired secondary school educator, clergyman; b. Atlanta, Apr. 10, 1941; s. Thomas Harper and Rubye (Collier) B. Student, Temple U., 1959-63, 64, 70; BEd, Cheyney U., 1962; postgrad., Va. Union U., 1965-66; MDiv, Ea. Bapt. Theol. Sem., 1968; postgrad., Howard Law Sch., 1962-63, U. Alaska, Juneau, 1990. Cert. math. tchr., Phila.; ordained to ministry Am. Bapt. Ch., 1968. Tchr. math. Masterman Demonstration Sch., Phila., 1968-71, Phila. High Sch. for Girls, 1971-97; ret., 1997; chaplain Alpha Phi Alpha Fraternity, Phila, 1968—. Assoc. min. Zion Bapt. Ch., 1967-68; asst. min. Wynnefield United Presbyn. Ch., 1969-72; Charter mem. North br. Y's Men Assn., Phila., 1972—; bd. dirs. Cherry Hill (N.J.) Civic Assn., 1992—. Recipient Outstanding Young Men Am. award Wynnefield Presbyn. Ch., Phila., 1971. Mem. ASCD, NSTA (life), NAACP (life), Assn. Tchrs. Math. Phila. (life), Nat. Coun. Tchrs. Math. (life), Phila. Fedn. Tchrs. (bldg. rep. at Girls' H.S. 1996-97), Math. Assn. Am., Nat. Coun. Suprs. of Math., Pa. Coun. Suprs. of Math., Pa. Coun. Tchrs. Math., Am. Bapt. Mins. Coun. (life), Phila. Health Users Group (life), Phi Delta Kappa (life), Alpha Phi Alpha (life). Avocations: computers, electronics, sports, chess, world travel. Home: 17 W Brook Dr Cherry Hill NJ 08003-1109

BRYAN, JAMES LEE, oil field service company executive; b. Waco, Tex., Aug. 18, 1936; s. Andrew Walton and Thelma Lee (Clements) B.; m. Joretta Griffin, Nov. 28, 1958; children—Deborah Lee, Catherine Ann, Rebecca Kaye, Cynthia Jean. B.S. in Geology, Baylor U., 1958. Drilling fluids engr. Dresser Industries, La., 1959-61; dist. engr. Dresser Industries, Utah, 1961-62; dist. mgr. Dresser Industries, Mont., 1962-65; gen. mgr. Dresser Industries, Nigeria, 1965-67; mng. dir. Dresser Industries, Kuwait, 1967-69; area mgr. Middle and Far East Dresser Industries, 1969-72, Europe, Africa, 1972-74; v.p. Western ops. Dresser Industries, Houston, 1974-77, exec. v.p. Magcobar div., 1977-79; pres. Magcobar Group, 1980-86; pres., CEO M-I Drilling Fluids Co., 1986-90; v.p. ops. Dresser Industries, 1990-94, sr. v.p. ops., 1994-98; exec. v.p. Newpark Drilling Fluids, Inc., Houston, 1999—. Mem. Inst. Mech. Engrs., Am. Petroleum Inst., Soc. Petroleum Engrs., Petroleum Equipment Supply Assn., Nomads, Pi Epsilon Tau. Republican. Baptist. Clubs: Champions, Lochinvar, Petroleum. Office: 15810 Park Ten Pl Ste 385 Houston TX 77084

BRYAN, JEAN MARIE WEHMUELLER, nurse; b. St. Louis, Aug. 10, 1964; d. Harold Leroy and Rose Marie (Maurer) Wehmuelle; m. Michael Thomas Bryan; children: Emily, Dennis. ADN, St. Louis C.C., 1984; BSN cum laude, U. Mo., St. Louis, 1986; postgrad., Fontbanne Coll. RN, Mo. Libr. asst. St. Louis County Libr., 1980-86; charge/staff nurse Incarnate World Hosp., St. Louis, 1986-88, Alexian Bros. Hosp., St. Louis, 1988-89, Compre Health, Inc., St. Louis, 1989-91; office nurse to pvt. practice physician St. Louis, 1991-97; owner Stained Glass Classics Studio, 1992—; billing ctr. processor Am. Home Patient, Inc., 1997-98; med. cost analyst ESSE Health, 1998—. Republican. Lutheran. Home: 200 Martigney Dr Saint Louis MO 63129-3412

BRYAN, JOHN HENRY, food and consumer products company executive; b. West Point, Miss., 1936. BA in Econs. and Bus. Adminstrn, Rhodes Coll., Memphis, 1958. Joined Bryan Foods, 1960; with Sara Lee Corp. (formerly known as Consol. Food Corp.), Chgo., 1960—; from exec. v.p. to pres. Sara Lee Corp. (formerly known as Consol Food Corp.), Chgo., 1974, chief exec. officer, 1975—, chmn. bd., 1976—, also bd. dirs.; bd. dirs. Gen. Motors Corp., Amoco Corp., 1st Chgo. Corp., 1st Nat. Bank Chgo. Chmn. bus. adv. coun. Chgo. Urban League; bd. govs. Nat. Women's Econ. Alliance, Chgo.; trustee, vice-chmn., exec. com. U. Chgo., Rush-Presbyn.-St. Luke's Med. Ctr.; trustee Com. Econ. Devel.; trustee, treas. Art Inst. Chgo.; chmn. Catalyst; bd. dirs. Bus. Com. for Arts; chmn. Chgo. com. Chgo. Coun. on Fgn. Rels.; mem. trustee's coun. Nat. Gallery Art, Washington; mem. pres.'s com. on the arts and humanities; dir. bus. com. for the arts. Decorated Legion of Honor (France), Order of Orange Nassau (The Netherlands), Order of Lincoln Medallion; recipient Nat. Humanitarian award NCCJ, William H. Albers award Food Mktg. Inst., Man of Yr. award Harvard Bus. Sch. Club Chgo.; named Exec. Yr. Crain's Chgo. Bus., 1992, Jr. Achievement Chgo. Bus. Hall of Fame, 1992, Miss. Hall of Fame, 1992. Mem. Grocery Mfrs. Assn. (sr., past. chmn. bd.), Bus. Coun., Bus. Roundtable. Office: Sara Lee Corp 3 1st Nat Plz 70 W Madison St Ste 4500 Chicago IL 60602-4260*

BRYAN, JOHN RODNEY, management consultant; b. Berkeley, Calif., Dec. 29, 1953; s. Robert Richard and Eloise (Anderson) Putz; m. Karen Nelson, Jan. 20, 1990. BA in Chemistry, U. Calif., San Diego, 1975; MBA, Rutgers U., 1985. Agt. Prudential, San Diego, 1975-79; sales mgr. Herman Schlorman Showrooms, L.A., 1980-83; pvt. practice mgmt. cons. Basking Ridge, N.J., 1983-85; mgmt. cons. The Brooks Group, Hollywood, Fla., 1985-99; pvt. practice San Diego, 1988—; with Western Productivity Group, 1990-95. Elder La Jolla Presbyn. Ch., 1991—. Mem. Inst. Indsl. Engring., Rutgers Club So. Calif., Beta Gamma Sigma. Avocation: singing. Office: 6265 Hurd Ct San Diego CA 92122-2917

BRYAN, JOHN STEWART, III, newspaper publisher; b. Richmond, Va., May 4, 1938; s. David Tennant and Mary Davidson Bryan; m. Alice Pyle Zimmer, 1963 (div. 1985); children: Elizabeth Talbott, Anna Saulsbury; m. Lisa-Margaret Stevenson, 1993. BA, U. Va., 1960; LHD (hon.), Hampden-Sydney Coll., 1991. Former advt. salesman Burlington (Vt.) Free Press; former reporter The Tampa (Fla.) Times; pub. The Tampa Tribune and Times, Fla., 1976-77, Richmond Times-Dispatch, Richmond News Leader, Va., 1978—; bd. dirs. Media Gen., Inc., Richmond, 1974—, vice-chmn., exec. v.p., 1985—, chmn., pres., CEO, 1990—; bd. dirs. Mut. Ins. Co., Bermuda. Past pres. or chmn. Tampa Bay Art Ctr., Tampa Citizens Safety Coun., Tampa United Way, Gulf Coast Symphony, Va. Commonwealth U. Found., Jr. Achievement Richmond, Goodwill Industries Richmond, United Way Greater Richmond; trustee Va. Found. Ind. Coll., chmn., 1993-95; trustee Va. Hist. Soc., Inst. Bill of Rights Law, Coll. William and Mary, World Affairs Coun. Richmond, Found. Am. Communications; overseer Hoover Inst. With USMC, 1960-62. Mem. SAR, S.R., Soc. of Cin., Fla. Soc. Newspapers Editors (life), So. Newspapers Pub. Assn. (found. chmn. 1978-79, pres. 1981-82), Fla. Press Assn. (life, pres. 1971-72, Disting. Svc. award 1975), Va. Press Assn. (bd. dirs. 1980-86), Newspaper Advt. Bur. (chmn. 1991-92), Newspaper Assn. of Am., Soc. Profl. Journalists, World Bus. Coun., Va. Bus. Coun., Fla. Coun. of 100, Bohemian Club, Country Club Va., Commonwealth Club, Tampa Yacht and Country Club. Home: 4608 Sulgrave Rd Richmond VA 23221-3119 Office: Media Gen Inc PO Box 85333C Richmond VA 23293-5333

BRYAN, JOSEPH SHEPARD, JR., lawyer; b. Wilson, N.C., Nov. 8, 1922; married; five children. BS, U.S. Naval Acad., 1944; JD, Harvard U., 1950. Bar: Fla., N.C. Asst. prof. pub. law and govt. U. N.C., 1950-54; counsel Winn-Dixie Stores Inc., Jacksonville, Fla., 1954-61; gen. counsel Winn-Dixie Stores Inc., Jacksonville, Fla., 1961-66; sec. Winn-Dixie Stores Inc., Jacksonville, 1961-66, v.p., gen. counsel, sec., 1966-91; also bd. dirs. Winn-Dixie Stores Inc.; of counsel Holland & Knight, Jacksonville, 1991—; mem. adv. bd. 1st Union Nat. Bank of Fla., Inc.; bd. dirs. Shands Tchg. Hosp. Clins., Inc., Gainesville, Fla., Jacksonville Cmty. Found., Bok Tower Gardens Found., Jacksonville Symphony Assn., Cultural Coun. Greater Jacksonville, Inc.; exec. com., bd. dirs. Baptist St. Vincent's Health Sys., Jacksonville; bd. govs. The Nat. Conf. With USN, 1944-47, 51-52. Recipient Individual award Arts Assembly of Jacksonville, Inc., Humanitarian award Nat. Conf. Christians and Jews. Mem. ABA, Am. Arbitration Assn., Am. Corp. Counsel Assn., Riverside Presbyn. Ch. Home: 1651 Beach Ave Jacksonville FL 32233-5840 Office: Holland & Knight LLP PO Box 52687 50 N Laura St Jacksonville FL 32202-3664

BRYAN, JUDITH HAGER, travel consultant, educator; b. Bklyn., May 9, 1938; d. Wesley Harold and Charlotte (Sweet) Hager; m. Ralph Edward Tuggle, June 20, 1959 (div. Oct. 1986); children: David William Tuggle, Rebecca Joanne Tuggle Friendly, Robert Scott Tuggle, Kevin Bradley Tuggle; m. Gordon Redman Bryan, Jr., July 7, 1987. BA, DePauw U., 1959; postgrad., Old Dominion U., 1968-69. Tchr. Ocean Air Elem. Sch., Norfolk, Va., 1959-60, Ohau (Hawaii) Pub. Schs., 1960, Groton (Conn.) Pub. Schs., 1960, San Diego Pub. Schs., 1960-63; travel agt., cons., 1967—. Pres. Submarine Officers Wives Club, Groton, Conn., 1960-62, chair art shows, 1970; pres. U.S. Naval PG Sch. Student Wives Club, Monterey, 1965-69, USNA '59 Wives Club, Norfolk, 1966-68, PTA, San Diego, 1981-83; gray lady ARC, 1961; mem. USN Relief Assn., San Diego, 1963-65, United Meth. Chs., 1959—, Navy Officers Wives Choral Assembly, Ohau, 1965-66, Mus. Arts and Scis., Norfolk, 1969, Keynote Music Club, Monterey, Calif., 1969; youth counselor San Diego Schs., 1963-65; trustee Congl. Ch., Suquamish, Wash., 1993; hostess Adobe House Tours, Monterey, 1966, Jamestown Exposition, Norfolk, 1969, Norfolk Week house tours, 1969; leader Cub Scouts, Norfolk, 1973-75, San Diego, 1977-84, Girl Scouts, San Diego, 1983-84, Brownies, San Diego, 1980-81. Named one of Outstanding Young Women Am., 1970; recipient commendation ARC, 1961, commendation USS Pargo, USN, 1973. Mem. Bay View Assn., Kappa Kappa Gamma Alumni, P.E.O. (treas. 1981-91, chaplain 1984-85, sec. 1988-89). Methodist. Avocations: golf, travel, photography, crafts, singing. Home: 37810 S Rolling Hills Dr Tucson AZ 85739-1069 Office: Copper Travel 16150 N Oracle Rd Tucson AZ 85739-8720

BRYAN, KATHERINE BYRAM, health care executive; d. John Charles and Jane Ballew (Price) Byram; 1 child by previous marriage, George Gurley III; m. John Shelby Bryan, Mar. 12, 1982; children: Austin, Jack. BA, U. Mo., 1969, PhD in Counseling Psychology, 1979. With Corp. Health Examiners, N.Y.C., 1978—, v.p. mktg., 1980-84; mem. adv. bd. John F. Kennedy Ctr. for Performing Arts, Washington. Author articles in field. Jr. bd. dirs. Nelson Gallery, Kansas City, Mo., 1973-76; bd. dirs. Family Dynamics, N.Y., 1987-92, N.Y.C. Ballet; mem. adv. bd. Kennedy Ctr. Mem. DAR, Colonial Dames Am., Am. Psychol. Assn., Biofeedback Soc. Am. Clubs: Maidstone (East Hampton, N.Y.); River (N.Y.C.). Home: 220 E 63d St New York NY 10021

BRYAN, KIRK, JR., research meteorologist, research oceanographer; b. Albuquerque, July 21, 1929; married, 1956; 2 children. BS, Yale U., 1951; PhD in Meteorology, MIT, 1957. Rsch. assoc. meteorologist Woods Hole Oceanography Inst., 1958-61; rsch. meteorologist Gen. Circulation Rsch. Lab. U.S. Weather Bureau, 1961-68; oceanographer Geophys. Fluid Dynamics Lab., NOAA and Princeton (N.J.) U., 1968-94; vis. lectr. Princeton U., 1968-94, rsch. scientist, 1994-96, sr. rsch. scholar, 1996—; mem. panel climatic variation global atmosphere rsch. program NAS, 1972-74; chmn. working group numerical models Sci. Com. Ocean Rsch., 1975-77. Fellow Am. Meteorol. Soc., Am. Geophys. Soc., Am. Geophys. Union (pres. oceanography sect., Maurice Ewing award 1993); mem. Russian Acad. Sci. (fgn.). Achievements include research in dynamic meteorology, physical oceanography, and general circulation of the atmosphere and oceans. Home: 100 Gulick Rd Princeton NJ 08540-4114 Office: Princeton Univ Program Atmos and Ocean Sci Sayre Hall Princeton NJ 08544-1003

BRYAN, LAWRENCE DOW, college president; b. Barberton, Ohio, Jan. 30, 1945; s. W. Richard and Celia A. (Evans) B.; m. Marjorie Napier, June 15, 1968; children: Mark Evans, Alexa Marie. BA, Muskingum Coll., 1967; MDiv., Garrett Theol. Sem., 1970; PhD, Northwestern U., 1973. Tchg. asst. Nat. Coll. Edn., Evanston, Ill., 1969-71; biog. rsch. fellow Garrett Theol. Sem., Evanston, 1972-73; asst. prof. religious studies, chaplain McKendree Coll., Lebanon, Ill., 1973-77, asst. v.p. acad. affairs, 1977-78, dean, 1978-79, assoc. prof., 1978-79; prof. philosophy and religion, v.p., dean Franklin (Ind.) Coll., 1979-90; pres. Kalamazoo Coll., 1990-96, MacMurray Coll., Jacksonville, Ill., 1996—; trustee Parkstone Group of Funds. Mem. Forum for Kalamazoo County, 1990-94, Kalamazoo Symphony Orch. Bd., 1990-96; pres. Heyl Found., Kalamazoo, 1990-96; bd. dirs. Bronson Hosp., 1991-96; trustee Interlochen Ctr. for Arts, 1994-97. Mem. Am. Acad. Religion, Internat. Bonhoeffer Soc., Rotary, Phi Sigma Tau, Delta Sigma Rho-Tau Kappa Alpha, Alpha Psi Omega, Theta Alpha Phi. Methodist.

BRYAN, NORMAN E., dentist; b. South Bend, Ind., Jan. 20, 1947; s. Norman E. and Frances (Kuhn) B.; m. Constance C. Cook, Feb. 23, 1974 (div. Apr. 1985); m. Linda Markley, Dec. 31, 1986; 1 child, Noelle. AB, Ind. U., 1969; DDS, Ind. U. Purdue U., Indpls., 1973. Sr. dentist Downtown Dental Svcs., Elkhart, Ind., 1973—; specialist Temporomandibular Joint Disfunction. Author: Canine Endodontics, 1982. Mem. ADA, Ind. Dental Assn., Elkhart Dental Assn. (pres. 1976-77, 84-86), Am. Acad. Head, Neck and Facial Pain, Great Lakes Cruising Club (Chgo.), Elcona Country Club, Great Lakes Cruising Club (Chgo.). Republican. Avocations: sailor, photography, painter. Office: 505 Vistula St Elkhart IN 46516-2809

BRYAN, PAUL EDWARD, pharmacist; b. Winfield, Kans., July 23, 1944; s. Brooks Cecil and Sarah Elizabeth (Miller) B.; m. Yvonne Catherine Ritz, Dec. 4, 1971; children: Rose Marie, Joan Renae. BS in Pharmacy, N.Mex. U., 1967. Pres. Valley Drug, Inc., Valley Center, Kans., 1973—; bd. dirs. Kans. Pharmacy Svc. Corp., Topeka; bd. dirs., v.p. Wichita Acad. Pharm., 1996—, pres., 1998-99.. Treas. Valley Center Libr., 1984. Named Citizen of Yr., Interclub Coun., 1983. Mem. Valley Center Lions (sec. 1996—), Valley Center C. of C. (bd. dirs. 1994-97). Republican. Home: 301 S Dexter Ave Valley Center KS 67147-2020 Office: Valley Drug Inc PO Box 255 126 W Main St Valley Center KS 67147-2214

BRYAN, RICHARD H., senator; b. Washington, July 16, 1937; m. Bonnie Fairchild; 3 children. BA, U. Nev., 1959; LLB, U. Calif., San Francisco, 1963. Bar: Nev. 1963. Dep. dist. atty. Clark County, Nev., 1964-66; public defender Clark County, 1966-68; counsel Clark County Juvenile Ct., 1968-69; mem. Nev. Assembly, 1969-73, Nev. Senate, 1973-79; atty. gen. State Nev., 1979-83, gov., 1983-89; senator from Nevada U.S. Senate, 1989—; mem. U.S. Senate coms. on commerce, sci. and transp.; mem. Dem. Policy Com.; mem. Fin. Com.; mem. Banking, Housing and Urban Affairs Com.; mem. Sen. Nom. Steering and Coor. Com.; mem. select. Com. on Intelligence. Bd. dirs. March of Dimes; former v.p. Nev. Easter Seal Soc.; former pres. Clark County Legal Aid Soc. Served with U.S. Army, 1959-60. Recipient Disting. Svc. award Vegas Valley Jaycees. Mem. ABA, Clark County Bar Assn., Am. Judicature Soc., Council of State Govts. (past pres.), Phi Alpha Delta, Phi Alpha Theta. Democrat. Clubs: Masons, Lions, Elks. Office: US Senate 269 Russell Senate Office Bldg Washington DC 20510-2804

BRYAN, RICHARD RAY, real estate development executive, construction executive; b. Centerville, Iowa, Apr. 15, 1932; s. Ashley Chester and Celia Mildred (Wright) B.; m. Shirley Erline Wilson, Dec. 17, 1955; children: Scott Douglas, Shari Kay. BS, Tex. A&M U., 1956; MS, Stanford U., 1957; postgrad., Harvard U., 1986. Registered profl. engr., Tex. Project mgr. H.B. Zachry Co., San Antonio, 1957-63, 69-70, v.p., 1985-87, sr. v.p., mem. exec. com., 1987-93, exec. v.p., 1993, also bd. dirs., exec. com.; project mgr. Zachary Internat., Lima, Peru, 1964-68; gen. mgr. Trans-Pecos Materials Co., Odessa, Tex., 1968-69; project mgr., v.p. Gerald D. Hines Interests, Houston, 1970-75, sr. v.p., 1979-80; bd. dirs., gen. mgr. Hines Overseas Ltd., Athens, Greece, 1976-78; sr. v.p. Cadillac Fairview, Urban Devel. Inc., Houston, 1981-85; v.p., mem. exec. com. Meth. Healthcare Ministries of South Tex. Wtih USAF, 1950-52, Korea. Fellow ASCE, former mem. Constrn. Industry Inst. (adv. bd., exec. com., chmn. 1993), Natl. Geographic Soc., Giraud Club, Dominion Country Club. Home: 7618 Woodhaven St San Antonio TX 78209-2749

BRYAN, ROBERT ARMISTEAD, university administrator, educator; b. Lebanon, Pa., Apr. 26, 1926; s. Morris Armistead and Katherine (Maulfair) B.; m. Kathryn Elizabeth Williams, Feb. 3, 1953; children: Lyla, Matthew. BA, U. Miami, 1950; MA, U. Ky., 1951, PhD, 1956. Teaching asst. U. Ky. at Lexington, 1950-54, instr., 1956-57; lectr. extension div. U. Calif., Tokyo, Japan, 1955-56; dean advanced studies, dir. sponsored rsch. Fla. Atlantic U., 1969-70; mem. faculty, adminstrn. U. Fla., Gainsville, 1957-90, prof. English, 1968-90; dean faculties U. Fla., 1970-71, assoc. v.p. acad. affairs, 1971-75, v.p. acad. affairs, 1975-85, provost, 1985-89, interim pres., 1989-90, ret., 1990; interim pres. U. Cen. Fla., 1991-92, U. South Fla., 1993-94; reader Coll. Bd. Exams., Ednl. Testing Svc., 1958-61; cons. So. Assn. Schs. and Colls., 1965-73, also chmn. visitation com., 1966-67; cons. HEW, Nat. Assn. of State Univs. and Land Grant Colls., 1990-91; cons. Fla. Bd. Regents, 1994-95; trustee Bethune-Cookman Coll., 1994—; commr. Fla. Postsecondary Edn. Planning Commn., 1996—. Bibliographer: Twentieth Century Literature, 1958-61. Served with U.S. Mcht. Marine, 1944-47, with AUS, 1954-56. Decorated Royal Order North Star (Sweden). Mem. MLA, Southeastern Renaissance Conf., S. Atlantic Mod. Lang. Assn., Sigma Chi. Episcopalian. Home: 9518 SW 56th Pl Gainesville FL 32608-4332

BRYAN, ROBERT J., federal judge; b. Bremerton, Wash., Oct. 29, 1934; s. James W. and Vena Gladys (Jensen) B.; m. Cathy Ann Welander, June 14, 1958; children: Robert James, Ted Lorin, Ronald Terence. BA, U. Wash., 1956, JD, 1958. Bar: Wash. 1959, U.S. Dist. Ct. (we. dist.) Wash. 1959, U.S. Tax Ct. 1965, U.S. Ct. Appeals (9th cir.) 1985. Assoc., then ptnr. Bryan & Bryan, Bremerton, 1959-67; judge Superior Ct., Port Orchard, Wash., 1967-84; ptnr. Riddell, Williams, Bullitt & Walkinshaw, Seattle, 1984-86; judge U.S. Dist. Ct. (we. dist.) Wash., Tacoma, 1986—; mem. State Jail Comm., Olympia, Wash., 1974-76, Criminal Justice Tng. Com., Olympia, 1978-81, State Bd. on Continuing Legal Edn., Seattle, 1984-86; mem., sec. Jud. Qualifications Commn., Olympia, 1982-83; chair Wash. Fed.-State Jud. Coun., 1997-98. Author: (with others) Washington Pattern Jury Instructions (civil and criminal vols. and supplements), 1970-85, Manual of Model Criminal Jury Instructions for the Ninth Circuit, 1992, Manual of Model Civil Jury Instruction for the Ninth Circuit, 1993. Chmn. 9th Ct. Jury Com., 1991-92. Served to maj. USAR. Mem. 9th Cir. Dist. Judges Assn. (sec.-treas. 1997—). Office: US Dist Ct 1717 Pacific Ave Rm 4427 Tacoma WA 98402-3234

BRYAN, SUKEY, artist; b. Summit, N.J., Apr. 4, 1961; d. Barry Richard and Margaret Susannah (Elliot) Bryan; m. James Duane Brooks, July 8, 1989; children: Matthew Lyle Brooks, William Elliot Brooks. BA, Yale U.,

1983; MFA, Md. Inst./Coll. of Art, Balt., 1990. Artist. Solo exhbns. include Essex (Md.) C.C., 1990, 91, Johns Hopkins U., Balt., 1992, H. Pelham Curtis Gallery, New Canaan, Conn., 1992, Galerie Francoise e.s.f., Balt., 1994, C. Grimaldis Gallery, Balt., 1995, 97; exhibited in group shows The BauHouse, Balt., 1991, Ctr. for Creative Arts, Yorklyn, Del., 1992, Edinboro U. Pa., 1992, Dundalk (Md.) Art Gallery, 1993, Addison Gallery Arm Art, Andover, Mass., 1993, Kristal Gallery, Warren, Vt., 1994, Fifth Column, Washington, 1995, St. Mary's Coll. Md., 1995, Balt. Festival for the Arts, 1992, 93, 95, C. Grimaldis Gallery, 1995, 96, 97, 98, Art Sites, Rockville (Md.) Art Place, 1996, Corcoran Gallery Art, Washington, 1996, Balt. Sch. for the Arts, 1997, Goya-Girl Press, Balt., 1997, U. Pacific, Stockton, Calif., 1998, Susan Cummins Gallery, Mill Valley, Calif., 1999, Indpls. Art Ctr., 1999, others; represented in collections at Balt. Mus. of Art, Cathedral of the Incarnation, Balt., Piper & Marbury, Balt.; author, artist: Tidal Grass, 1993. Recipient Individual Artist award Md. State Arts Coun., 1991; Visual Artist fellow Nat. Endowment for Arts, 1993-94. Democrat. Episcopalian.

BRYAN, THELMA JANE, university administrator, English educator; b. Scotland, Md., Aug. 21, 1945; d. Joseph Webster and Mary Gertrude (Holley) B.; m. David George Preston, Mar. 17, 1980; 1 child, Bryan David Preston. BA, Morgan State Coll., 1970, MA, 1975; PhD, U. Md., 1982. Instr. English Coppin State Coll., Balt., 1979-82, asst. prof., 1982-87, assoc. prof., 1987-90; prof., 1990—; chair lang., lit., journalism, and philosophy Coppin State Coll., Balt., 1987-90, dean honors divsn., 1990-98, dean Coll. Arts and Scis., 1991-98; acting assoc. vice chancellor for acad. affairs U. System of Maryland, 1998-99, assoc. vice chancellor for acad. affairs, 1999—; coun. mem. preparing future faculty Assn. Am. Colls. & Univs., Washington, 1994-97; steering com. mem. Alliance for Success, Urbana-Champaign, Ill., 1989-97; dean's com. mem. African Am. Inst., N.Y.C., 1994—; scholarship com. mem. Md. Paper Box Co., Linthicum, 1984-90. Contbr. articles, poetry to profl. jours. Adv. coun. mem. campus prism Nat. Coun. Christians and Jews, Balt., 1984-85; bd. trustees Stella Maris, Inc., Towson, Md., 1996-97. Recipient Governor's Citation award State of Md., Annapolis, 1992. Mem. MLA, Am. Assn. Higher Edn., Coll. Lang. Assn., Nat. Coun. Tchrs. English, Nat. Collegiate Honors Coun., Northeast Nat. Collegiate Honors Coun. (faculty rep. 1984-95), Alpha Kappa Mu (dir. 1989-95, Outstanding Advisor award 1989, 91, Outstanding Regional Dir. award 1990-91). Democrat. Roman Catholic. Avocations: jogging, aerobic dancing, body building, reading, creative writing. Home: 1522 Woodcliff Ave Baltimore MD 21228-1056

BRYAN, THOMAS LYNN, lawyer, educator; b. Wichita, Kans., June 10, 1935; s. Herbert Thomas and Ruth Marjorie (Williams) B.; m. Virginia Alice Cooper, June 13, 1981; children from previous marriage—Victoria Lynne Hague, Douglas Edward. BA, U. Kans., 1957; LLB, Columbia U., 1960. Bar: N.Y. Assoc. Willkie Farr & Gallagher, N.Y.C., 1960-66, ptnr., 1967-92; adj. prof. Stetson U. Coll. Law, 1993-97. Co-author: Business Acquisitions, 1971, 2d edit. 1981. Mem. Longboat Key Club, Upper Ridgewood Tennis Club, Phi Beta Kappa. Republican. Avocations: tennis, sports, golf, theatre. Home: 41 N Bayard Ln Mahwah NJ 07430-2236 also: 3448 Mistletoe Ln Longboat Key FL 34228-4146

BRYAN, WENDELL HOBDY, II (HOB BRYAN), senator; b. Amory, Miss., Dec. 5, 1952; s. Wendell Hobdy and Nadine (Morgan) B. BA, Miss. State U., 1974; JD, U. Va., 1977. Bar: Miss. 1977. Pvt. practice Amory, 1977—; mem. Miss. Senate, 1984—; chmn. Senate Fin. Com., 1996—. Democrat. Baptist. Office: PO Box 75 205 Main St Amory MS 38821-0075

BRYAN, WILLIAM ROYAL, finance educator; b. Muncie, Ind., Apr. 16, 1932; s. Frank Cain and Bertha Ellen (Bishop) B.; m. Fanny Elisabeth Bennigsen, Apr. 20, 1979; 1 dau. by previous marriage—Rebecca Gay. B.S., Ball State U., 1954; M.S., U. Wis., 1958, Ph.D., 1961. Tchr. public schs. Cedar Lake, Ind., 1954-55; grad. teaching asst. U. Wis., Madison, 1957-60; sr. economist Fed. Res. Bank of St. Louis, 1960-66; vis. asst. prof. Washington U., St. Louis, 1962-66; prof. fin. U. Ill., 1966-95, chmn. dept. fin., 1977-81, 85-88, dir. Bur. Econ. and Bus. Rsch., 1988-95, assoc. dean rsch. coll. commerce, 1991-95; dean Sch. Bus. Adminstrn. Loyola U., Chgo., 1995—; cons. joint econ. com. U.S. Congress, 1977-79; vis. scholar U.S. Treasury, 1970-71; dir. United of Am. Bank, Chgo., Exch. Nat. Bank Chgo., Bank of Rantoul, Ill. Editor: Illinois Business Rev., 1978-92; contbr. articles in field. Served with USAF, 1955-57. Fed. Res. Bank of St. Louis fellow, 1959-60. Mem. Am. Econ. Assn., Assn. Univ. Bur. Econ. Rsch. (bd. dirs. 1990-92). Unitarian. Home: 9 E Huron St Chicago IL 60611-2734 Office: Loyola Univ Chgo 820 N Michigan Ave Chicago IL 60611-2103

BRYANT, ARTHUR H., lawyer; b. Harrisburg, Pa., Aug. 11, 1954; s. Albert Irwin and Marjorie (Weinrib) B.; m. Nancy Kaye Johnson, Aug. 17, 1991; 1 stepchild, Cazber Johnson; 1 child, Wallace Johnson Bryant. AB with honors, Swarthmore Coll., 1976; JD, Harvard U., 1979; D (hon.) Ripon Coll., 1998. Bar: Pa. 1981, U.S. Dist. Ct. (ea. dist.) Pa. 1981, U.S. Ct. Appeals (3d cir.) Pa. 1981, U.S. Ct. Appeals (11th cir.) Ga. 1985, U.S. Ct. Appeals (6th cir.) Ohio 1986, U.S. Ct. Appeals (D.C. cir.) 1986, U.S. Ct. Appeals (9th cir.) Calif. 1987, U.S. Ct. Appeals (7th cir.) Ill. 1988, U.S. Ct. Appeals (10th cir.) Colo. 1988, U.S. Ct. Appeals (5th cir.) Tex. 1988, D.C., 1989, U.S. Supreme Ct. 1989, U.S. Ct. Appeals (1st cir.) 1996. Intern, Rosenman, Colin & Freund, N.Y.C., 1978, N.Y. Civil Liberties Union, 1978, Cambridge & Somerville Legal Services, Cambridge, Pa., 1979; law clk. U.S. Dist. Ct. (so. dist.) Tex., 1979-80; atty. Kohn, Savett, Marion & Graf., Phila., 1980-84; staff atty. Trial Lawyers for Pub. Justice, Washington, 1984-87, exec. dir., 1987—. Named one of 20 young lawyers making a difference in the world ABA Barrister Mag., 1991, one of 50 most influential people in coll. sports Coll. Sports Mag., 1994, one of 45 lawyers whose vision and commitment are changing lives The Am. Lawyer, 1997; recipient Wasserstein Pub. Interest Law fellowship, 1996. Mem. ABA, Assn. Trial Lawyers Am. Office: Trial Lawyers Pub Justice Ste 800 1717 Massachusetts Ave NW Washington DC 20036-2006

BRYANT, ARTHUR STEVEN, public relations executive; b. Warner Robins, Ga., June 8, 1956; s. Arthur Bowman Bryant and Betty Sue (Doke) Golden; m. Demian, Sept. 1, 1981. BS in Music, Psychology and Sociology, U. State N.Y., Albany, 1987. Accredited bus. communicator. Profl. singer classical music San Francisco, 1980-85; co-dir. Ptnrs. Task Force for Gay and Lesbian Couples, Seattle, 1986—; chief creative officer Publicis Dialog, Seattle, 1986—. Bd. mem. Seafair, Seattle, 1995-96. Recipient award of merit Soc. Tech. Comm. 1988, award of merit for videotape L.A. Bus./Profl. Advt. Assn., 1988, 2d pl. for non-for-profit comm. rels. Wash. Press Assn., 1988, 3rd pl. for media kits Wash. Press Assn., 1989, 2nd pl. for one-to-three color bus. newsletters Wash. Press Assn., 1989, 1st pl. for one-to-three color bus. newsletters Wash. Press Assn., 1989, Totem award Pub. Rels. Soc. Am., 1989, award for achievement in poster design Soc. Tech. Comm. 1991-92, 3rd pl. for news releases Wash. Press Assn., 1990, 2nd pl. for advt. BioMed. Mktg. Assn., 1991, award of merit for outside newsletters Soc. Tech. Comm., 1992, Best of Show and Disting. award for newsletters Soc. Tech. Comm., 1993, 1st pl. Totem award Pub. Rels. Soc. Am., 1993, 1st pl. for original film or video Wash. Press Assn., 1993, 2nd pl. for original film or video Wash. Press Assn., 1993, 2nd pl. Totem award Pub. Rels. Soc. Am., 1993, 2nd pl. for four-color brochures Wash. Press Assn., 1993, 1st pl. for video Nat. Fedn. Press Women 1994, 1st pl. for pub. svc. Wash. Press Assn., 1994, 2nd pl for comm. rels. Wash. Press Assn., 1994, 2nd pl. for mktg. campaign for new product Wash. Press Assn., 1994, award of merit for publs. Soc. Tech. Comm., 1994-95, 1st pl. for video Pub. Rels. Soc. Am., 1995, 1st pl. for spl. print comm. Pub. Rels. Soc. Am., 1995; numerous others. Mem. Med. Mktg. Assn., Internat. Assn. Bus. Communicators (award of excellence for sales promotion brochures 1989, award of merit for tech. writing 1992, award of excellence for sales/mktg. videos 1994, award of merit 1994, award of merit for sales/mktg. videos 1994, award of merit for multimedia 1995, award of merit 1995, awards for excellence and merit for print comm. 1995, award of merit for brochure design 1995, award of merit for brochure writing 1995, awards of excellence for corp. image video, brochures and materials for spl. events and external comm. programs, awards of merit for pub. svc. announcements, sales video and pro bono video 1996). Democrat. Avocation: classical piano, ballet dancing. Office: Publicis Dialog 190 Queen Anne Ave N Ste 400 Seattle WA 98109-4900

BRYANT, BARBARA EVERITT, academic researcher, market research consultant, former federal agency administrator; b. Ann Arbor, Mich., Apr. 5, 1926; d. William Littell and Dorothy (Wallace) Everitt; m. John H. Bryant, Aug. 14, 1948; children: Linda Bryant Valentine, Randal F., Lois Bryant Chen. AB, Cornell U., 1947; MA, Mich. State U., 1967, PhD, 1970; HonD, U. Ill., 1993. Editor art Chem. Engring. mag. McGraw-Hill Pub. Co., N.Y.C., 1947-48; editl. rsch. asst. U. Ill., Urbana, 1948-49, free-lance editor, writer, 1950-61; with continuing edn. adminstrn. dept. Oakland Univ., Rochester, Mich., 1961-66; grad. rsch. asst. Mich. State U., East Lansing, 1966-70; sr. analyst to v.p. Market Opinion Rsch., Detroit, 1970-77, sr. v.p., 1977-89; dir. Bur. of the Census, U.S. Dept. Commerce, 1989-93; rsch. scientist Sch. Bus. Adminstrn., U. Mich., 1993—. Author: High School Students Look at Their World, 1970, American Women Today & Tomorrow, 1977, Moving Power and Money: The Politics of Census Taking, 1995; contbr. articles to profl. jours. Mem. U.S. Census Adv. Com., Washington, 1980-86, Mich. Job Devel. Authority, Lansing, Mich., 1980-85; state editor LWV of Mich., 1959-61. Fellow Am. Statis. Assn.; mem. Soc. for Quality Control, Women in Comms. (pres. Detroit 1974-75, Nat. Headliner award 1980), Am. Mktg. Assn. (pres. Detroit 1976-77, midwestern v.p. 1978-80, v.p. mktg. rsch. 1982-84), Am. Assn. Pub. Opinion Rsch., Cosmos Club (Washington), Cornell Club N.Y. Republican. Presbyterian. Avocation: swimming. Home: 1505 Sheridan Dr Ann Arbor MI 48104-4051 Office: U Mich Sch Bus Ann Arbor MI 48109-1234

BRYANT, BERTHA ESTELLE, retired nurse; b. Va., Jan. 11, 1927; d. E.F. and Julia B. Diploma, Sibley Meml. Hosp., Washington, 1947; B.S., Am. U., 1948; M.A., Tchrs. Coll., Columbia U., 1962. Staff nurse, head nurse NIH, Bethesda, Md., 1954-59; asst. dir. nursing USPHS Alaska Native Hosp., Mt. Edgecumbe, 1959-61; instr. Sch. Nursing, U. Mich., 1962-64; chief div. clin. nursing Bur. Nursing, D.C. Dept. Public Health, Washington, 1964-65; commd. Nurse Corps, USPHS, 1965, nurse dir., capt., 1974—; nurse cons., hosp. facilities services br., div. hosps. and med. facilities Bur. Health Services, HEW, Silver Spring; nurse cons., social analysis br., div. health services research and analysis Nat. Center Health Services Research, Health Resources Adminstrn., HEW, Rockville, Md.; nurse cons. div. extramural research Nat. Center Health Services Research, Office Asst. Sec. Health, HHS, Hyattsville, Md., 1977-81. Contbr. articles to profl. jours. Mem. AAUW, Assn. Mil. Surgeons U.S., Commd. Officers Assn. USPHS.

BRYANT, CLIFTON DOW, sociologist, educator; b. Jackson, Miss., Dec. 25, 1932; s. Clifton Edward and Helen (Dow) B.; m. Nancy Ann Arrington, Sept. 13, 1953; m. Patty Maurine Watts, Feb. 1, 1957; children: Melinda Dow, Deborah Carol, Karen Diane, Clifton Dow II. Student, U. Miss., 1950-53, B.A., 1956, M.A., 1957; postgrad., U. N.C., Chapel Hill, 1957-58, La. State U., 1958-60; Ph.D., La. State U., 1964. Vis. instr. dept. sociology and anthropology Pa. State U., summer, 1958; instr., rsch. assoc. dept. sociology and anthropology U. Ga., 1960-63; asst. prof., assoc. prof., chmn. dept. sociology and anthropology Millsaps Coll., Jackson, Miss., 1963-67; summer research participant, tng. and tech. project Oak Ridge Asso. Univs., summer 1967; prof., head dept. sociology and anthropology Western Ky. U., Bowling Green, Ky., 1967-72; prof. sociology Va. Poly. Inst. and State U., Blacksburg, 1972—; head dept. Va Poly. Inst. and State U., Blacksburg, 1972-82; vis. prof. Xavier U., Philippines, 1984-85; vis. prof., vis. rsch. scholar Miss. Alcohol Safety Edn. Program, Miss. State U., (summer), 1985; vis. Fulbright prof. dept. grad. inst. sociology Nat. Taiwan U., Taipei, Republic of China, 1987-88; vis. scientist U.S. Army summer faculty rsch. and engring. program, 1993; participant Fulbright-Hays Seminar Abroad program, Hungary, 1993. Author: Khaki-Collar Crime: Deviant Behavior in Military Context, 1979, Sexual Deviancy and Social Proscription, 1982; editor and contbr.: Deviant Behavior: Occupational and Organizational Bases, 1974, The Social Dimensions of Work, 1972, Sexual Deviancy in Social Context, 1977, Deviant Behavior: Readings in the Sociology of Norm Violations, 1990; co-editor, contbr.: Deviancy and the Family, 1973, The Rural Work Force: Nonagricultural Occupations in America, 1985; compiler: Handbook of Audio-Visual Resources to Accompany Social Problems Today, 1971; editor: Social Problems Today: Dilemmas and Dissensus, 1971; co-editor: Introductory Sociology: Selected Readings for the College Scene, 1970; editor in chief Deviant Behavior: An Interdisciplinary Jour., 1978-91; editor So. Sociologist, 1970-74; mem. editorial bd. Criminology: An Interdisciplinary Jour, 1978-91; chmn. editorial policy bd., founding editor-in-Chief Deviant Behavior: An Interdisciplinary Journal, 1992—; chmn. editorial bd. Sociol. Symposium, 1968-80; assoc. editor Sociol. Forum, 1979-80, Sociol. Spectrum, 1981-85; mem. bd. adv. editors Sociol. Inquiry, 1981-85, assoc. editor, 1997—; bd. editors Society and Animals, 1997—; assoc. editor spl. issue Marriage and Family Relations, fall 1982, Sociological Inquiry, 1997—; contbr. chpts. to books, articles, book reviews to profl. publs. Served to 1st lt., M.P. U.S. Army, 1953-55. Recipient E. Gordon Ericksen Outstanding Grad. Faculty award sociology dept. Va. Poly. Inst. and State U., 1992, 93, spl. award for continuing contbn. to undergrad. teaching enterprise, 1992, Undergraduate Tchg. Excellence award, 1995-96. Mem. Am. Sociol. Assn., Am. Soc. Criminology, So. Sociol. Soc. (pres. 1978-79), Mid-South Sociol. Assn. (pres. 1981-82, Disting. Career award 1991), Rural Sociol. Soc., Soc. Anthropology of Work, Internat. Sociol. Assn., Inter-Univ. Seminar on Armed Forces and Society, So. Assn. Agr. Scientists, Omicron Delta Kappa, Phi Kappa Phi, Alpha Phi Omega, Alpha Kappa Delta, Pi Kappa Alpha, Phi Beta Delta. Presbyterian. Home: 1724 E Ridge Dr Blacksburg VA 24060-8568 Office: Va Poly Inst State U Dept Sociology Blacksburg VA 24061*

BRYANT, CORALIE MARCUS, political science educator; b. Holland, Mich., Aug. 10, 1937; d. James J. and Helen Blanche (Rutgers) M.; married; children: Jennifer Miranda, Deborah Helen, Juliet Evelyn. BA, Barnard Coll., 1959; postgrad., Yale U., 1959-60; PhD, London Sch. Econs., 1963. Asst. prof. Sch. of Govt. Am. U., Washington, 1967-74, prof. Sch. Internat. Svc., 1974-87, co-dir. Internat. Devel. Program, 1977-87; sr. fellow Overseas Devel. Coun., Washington, 1985-89; sr. staff mem. World Bank, Washington, 1989-96; prof., dir. Econ. and Polit. Devel. Program, Columbia U., N.Y.C., 1997—; cons. USAID, UNICEF, World Bank, UN-UNA. Co-author: (textbook) Managing Development in Third World, 1982, Managing Rural Development, 1981; editor: (book) Poverty, Policy, and Food Security in Southern Africa, 1988; contbr. articles to profl. jours. Mem. gen. com. Friends Com. on Nat. Legislation, Washington, 1996-98; trustee Sidwell Friends Sch., Washington, 1976-84. Mem. Women's Fgn. Policy Group, Devel. Mgmt. Network, Am. Soc. Pub. Adminstrn. (chair sect. on internat. and pub. adminstrn. 1995-96, Riggs award). Democrat. Mem. Soc. of Friends. Avocations: mountain hiking, mountain jeeping. Office: Columbia Univ 420 W 118th St New York NY 10027-7213

BRYANT, DARYL LESLIE, painter, educator; b. L.A., Feb. 11, 1940; d. Colin Willis and Virginia Rouseau (Graves) Timmons; m. Dennis Rourke Murphy, 1960 (div. 1972); children: John Ashley, Sarah; m. Daniel Walster Bryant, 1985. Student, U. So. Calif., Acad. Arts, Florence, Italy; AA, Valley Coll., Van Nuys, Calif. Asst. designer Koret Calif., San Francisco, 1959-60; freelance artist Studiowork, Studio City, Calif.; art dir. Brentwood (Calif.) Publs., 1978-87; painter, graphic designer South Pasadena, Calif., 1987—; tchr. Creative Arts Group, Sierra Madre, Calif., 1996—. Works published in books and mags. Mem. Mid Valley Arts League (bd. dirs. 1993—), Nat. Watercolor Soc. (signature), Watercolor West (signature), Calif. Art Club (signature). Avocations: swimming, hiking, travel, journal keeping.

BRYANT, DENNIS MICHAEL, publisher, educator; b. Austin, Tex., June 30, 1947; s. L.D. and Mildred (Perkins) B.; m. Nancy Louthan, Apr. 17, 1976; children: Michael, Sarah. BS, Trinity U., 1970. Sales mgr. Southland Equipment Co., Houston, 1973-74; mgr., equipment specialist Briggs Weaver Co., San Antonio, 1974-81; life ins. specialist N.Y. Life Ins. Co., San Antonio, 1981-85; territorial ins. specialist Merrill Lynch Life Agy., San Antonio, 1985-86; life and group ins. mgr. Cen. Fin. Ins. Svcs., San Antonio, 1986—; owner Bryant Agy./Trinity Fin. Concepts, San Antonio, 1988—; chmn. Focus on Growth, 1993—; chmn. Focus on Growth, Inc. Active Project Any Baby Can, San Antonio, 1983—, pres. 1984-85. 1st lt. U.S. Army, 1971-73. Republican. Avocations: skiing, running, flying. Home: 110 Skyvue Ave New Braunfels TX 78132-4635

BRYANT, DON ESTES, economist, scientist; b. Truman, Ark., May 18, 1917; s. James Monroe and Olivia (Mayfield) B.; m. Jess Ann Chailer, Jan. 27, 1956; children: Stephen Williamson (dec.), Patrice Ann. Student, Cass Tech. Trade Coll., 1938-41. Pres., founder Consol. Aircraft Products, El Segundo, Calif., 1949-57, Trilan Corp., El Segundo, 1957-62, The Am. Inventor, Palos Verdes Estates, Calif., 1962-68; chmn., founder Message Control Crop., Palos Verdes Estates, 1968-70; scientist Econ. Rsch., Palos Verdes Estates and Lake Arrowhead, Calif., 1970—; cons. Svc. Corps. Ret. Execs. Assn.-SBA, L.A., 1965-67; founder Bryant Inst. and Club U.S.A. (United to Save Am.), 1991, J. Ayn Bryant and Assocs., 1991. Inventor missle and satellite count-down systems for USAF, 1958; formulator sci. of human econs.; host TV talk show World Peace Through Free Enterprise, 1985; author: 10-book children's series The 1, 2, 3's of Freedom and Economics, 1988. Served with USN, 1935-37. Republican. Roman Catholic. Avocations: sailing, woodworking. Home: 329 Greenview Ln Fallbrook CA 92028-1864

BRYANT, DONALD LOYD, insurance company executive; b. Orchard, Iowa, Jan. 30, 1919; s. Lester E. and Bessie (Farless) B.; m. Eileen Galloway, May 11, 1941; children: Donald Loyd, Hedy E. Bryant Garlock, Brenda K., Becky Bryant Hubert. B.Ed., So. Ill. U., 1940. With War Manpower Commn., Mt. Vernon, Ill., 1940; agt., dist. mgr. Equitable Life Assurance Soc. U.S., Elgin and Carbondale, Ill., 1946-54; agy. mgr. Equitable Life Assurance Soc. U.S., St. Louis, 1954-69; v.p., chief agy. staff ops. Equitable Life Assurance Soc. U.S., N.Y.C., 1969-71; v.p. corp. relations Equitable Life Assurance Soc. U.S., 1971-72, sr. v.p. corp. relations, 1972-74, exec. v.p., spl. asst. to pres., 1974-78, exec. v.p., 1978-81; bus exec.-in-residence Tex. Christian U., Ft. Worth, 1980—; cons. Nat. Exec. Services Corp.; bus. exec.-in-residence So. Ill. U. Served to lt. USN, 1942-46. Recipient Alumni Achievement award So. Ill. U., 1964, 88. Presbyterian. Club: Quail Ridge Golf and Tennis (Boynton Beach, Fla.). Home and Office: 1489 Partridge Pl N Boynton Beach FL 33436-5409 *On each job, behave as though you will be on that job for the remainder of your working life. In this way you avoid mistakes because you'd have to live with those mistakes. You are careful to pick good associates because you will have to live with them forever. You give security to your subordinates, command their loyalty, because they sense you'll be there forever. Ironically you'll then do such a superior job that you'll be promoted over and over while behaving as though you'll be on your job forever.*

BRYANT, DOUGLAS E., public health service official. BS in Health Edn., U. S.C., 1976, MPH, 1981. Communicable disease investigator S.C. Dept. Health & Environ. Control, 1976-78, dist. dir. Upper Savannah Health Dist., 1982-85, dir. office primary care, 1986-87, asst. to commr., 1987-93, commr., 1993—; dir. specialized health care svcs. S.C. Dept. Corrections, 1978-81; asst. adminstr. State Pk. Health Ctr., 1981-82; interim exec. dir. Orangeburg Family Health Ctrs., Inc., 1985-86; adj. prof. dept. health adminstrn. U. S.C.; mem. AHEC Rural Physician adv. bd.; mem. adv. bd. Athletic Trainers. Mem. adv. bd., bd. visitors Lander Coll. Mem. Am. Coll. Hosp. Adminstrs., S.C. Pub. Health Assn., So. Health Assn., Delta Omega. Office: Dept Health & Environ Control 2600 Bull St Columbia SC 29201-1708*

BRYANT, EDWARD, congressman; b. Jackson, Tenn., Sept. 7, 1948; m. Cyndi Bryant; 3 children. BA, U. Miss., 1970, JD, 1972. With U.S. Army Judge Advocate Gen.'s Corps, 1972-78; army prosecutor Ft. Carlson, 1975-77; legal instr. U.S. Mil. Acad., 1977-78; ptnr. Waldrop & Hall, 1978-91, 93—; U.S. atty. Western Dist. of Tenn., 1991-93; agrl. judiciary com. 104th-106th Congress from 7th Tenn. dist., 1995—; mem. dept. agrl. ops., nutrition & fgn. agriculture, risk mgmt. & specialty crops coms. and comml. & adminstrv. law, constn., immigration & claims coms. Republican. Office: US House Reps 408 Cannon Bldg Washington DC 20515-4207*

BRYANT, GARY JONES, minister; b. Stockton, Mo., Aug. 20, 1942; s. John Franklin and Imogene Eunice (Jones) B.; m. Deborah A. Brewer, Aug. 20, 1965; children: Gary Jason, Gareth Joshua. BA in Bible, Cen. Bible Coll., Springfield, Mo., 1966; BS in Religious Studies, Bethany Bible Coll., Santa Cruz, Calif., 1968; MA in Religion, Crossroad Grad. Sch. Div., Muncie, Ind., 1973, PhD in Religion, 1975. Ordained to ministry Assemblies of God, 1969, Internat. Ch. of the Foursquare Gospel, 1994. Pastor Vista (Calif.) Assembly of God Ch., 1972-75, First Assembly of God Ch., Porterville, Calif., 1976-83, Christian Life Ch., Pitts., 1982-84; dir. Heart of Am. Counseling Ctr., Kansas City, Mo., 1984-85; pastor, dir. Peoples Ch.-Peoples Counseling Ctr., Las Cruces, N.Mex., 1986-99; pastor Stream in the Desert Foursquare Gospel Ch., 1999—; Christian edn. advisor So. Calif. Dist. Assemblies of God, Costa Mesa, 1978-80, youth leader, San Diego, 1976-78, presbyter, Costa Mesa, 1980-83. Author: Flight of the Dove - Cedar County, 1975. Bd. dirs. So. Calif. Coll., Costa Mesa, 1980-83; adv. bd. Tulare County Mental Health Hosp. and Clinics, 1979-82; adv. com. Cen. Bus. Dist. Coun., Las Cruces, 1991; pastor Lighthouse Ch., Vincennes, Ind., 1996—; divsn. supt. Great Lakes Divsn. Foursquare Chs., So. Ing., 1996—. Mem. Rotary. Republican. Home: 361 N Lovekin Blvd Blythe CA 92225

BRYANT, GEORGE MACON, chemist; b. Anniston, Ala., Aug. 3, 1926; s. Fred Boyd and Jessie Elizabeth (Macon) B.; m. Mary Lee Miles, Sept. 9, 1950; children—Fred Boyd II, George Macon. B.S. in Physics, Auburn U., 1948; M.S., Inst. Textile Tech., 1950; Ph.D., Princeton U., 1954. Research chemist research and devel. ctr. Union Carbide Corp., South Charleston, W.Va., 1954-58, group leader, 1958-66, assoc. dir., 1966-75, corp. research fellow, 1975-86, cons. 1986—. Served with USN, 1944-46. Mem. Am. Chem. Soc. (award for sci. achievement 1979), Am. Assn. Textile Chemists (Milson award 1982), Fiber Soc. (award for disting. early achievement 1964), Sigma Xi, Phi Kappa Phi. Democrat. Presbyterian. Contbr. articles to profl. jours.; patentee in field. Home: 1204 Williamsburg Way Charleston WV 25314-1938

BRYANT, HUBERT HALE, lawyer; b. Tulsa, Jan. 4, 1931; s. Roscoe Conkling and Curlie Beatrice (Marshall) B.; m. Elnora Geraldine Roberson, Oct. 25, 1952; children—Cheryl Denise, Tara Kay. B.A., Fisk U., 1952; LL.B., Howard U., 1956. Bar: Okla. bar 1956, U.S. Dist. Ct. bar for No. Dist. Okla 1956, U.S. Ct. Appeals (10th cir.) 1967, U.S. Supreme Ct. bar 1980. Individual practice law Tulsa, 1956-67, 81-84, 86—; asst. city prosecutor, City of Tulsa, 1961-63, chief city prosecutor, 1963-67, asst. U.S. atty., No. Dist. Okla., 1967-77, U.S. atty., 1977-81; mcpl. ct. judge City of Tulsa, 1984-86. Trustee 1st Bapt. Ch., Tulsa, 1970-75, 96—; bd. dirs. Tulsa Urban League, 1962-64. Recipient Outstanding Alumni award Howard U. Sch. Law, 1981, 30 Yr. Outstanding African Am. Lawyer award Met. Tulsa Urban League, 1997. Mem. NAACP, Nat. Bar Assn. (Named to Hall of Fame), Okla. Bar Assn., Tulsa County Bar Assn., Okla. Trial Lawyers Assn., Nat. Set, Masons (named Mason of Yr. local chpt. 1963, Outstanding Citizen award 1978), Sigma Pi Phi, Alpha Theta Boule, Alpha Phi Alpha. Democrat. Clubs: Nat. Set, Masons (named Mason of year local chpt. 1963, Outstanding Citizen award 1978). Home: 1818 N Boston St Tulsa OK 74106 Office: 2623 N Peoria Ave Tulsa OK 74106-2512

BRYANT, JACQUELINE EOLA, educational consultant, urban specialist; b. Norfolk, Va., Oct. 26, 1949; d. James Thomas Sr. and Wincie (Jackson) B. BS, Old Dominion U.; MA, George Washington U.; postgrad., Va. Polytech. Inst., U. Va. Cons., coord, supr. Fibachu Corp., Norfolk, Va., 1978-79; tchr. English, chmn. dept. Virginia Beach (Va.) City Schs., 1981-83, lang. arts coord. Mid. Sch., 1983-90; cons., ednl. specialist Target Communications Inc., Norfolk, 1989-90; dir. reading/lang. arts Dallas Ind. Sch. Dist., 1990-94; tchr. Larkspur Mid. Sch., Virginia Beach, 1994-95; v.p. nat. key accounts coord. McDougal Littell/Houghton Mifflin Co., Evanston, Ill., 1995-97, v.p. nat. key accounts, 1997—. Contbr. articles to profl. jours. Mem. ASCD, Internat. Reading Assn., Va. Assn. Tchrs. English (pres. 1985), Nat. Coun. Tchrs. English (bd. dirs. 1984, chmn. com. to evaluate curriculum guide, mem. editl. bd. 1997—); Conf. on English Edn. (chmn. com. minority educators, mem. tchr. preparation and cert. com.), Phi Delta Kappa. Home: 4821 Gatwick Dr Virginia Beach VA 23462-6437

BRYANT, JAMES ARTHUR, painter; b. Huron, S.D., Apr. 15, 1951. Student, Omaha Art Sch. and Studio, 1969-71, Kansas City (Mo.) Art Inst., 1971-76. Impressionist/expressionist painter, photographer, sculptor Huron, S.D., 1976—. Included in: American Artists: An Illustrated Survey of Contemporary Artists, 1989,An Illustrated History of the Arts in South Dakota, 1986; cover artist: Being and Becoming, 1987; one-man shows include Cmty. Cultural Ctr., Brookings, S.D., 1987, Eros Data Ctr., Sioux Falls, S.D., 1989, Stone Ch., Huron, 1992; exhibited in group shows at

Kansas City (Mo.) Art Inst., 1971-75, Meml. Art Ctr., Brookings, 1981-82, Warren M. Lee Ctr. Fine Arts, Vermillion, S.D., 1984, Civic Fine Arts Assn., Sioux Falls, 1978-97, Huron Symphony League, 1991-95, Lincoln Ctr. for Arts, Aberdeen, S.D., S.D. Art Mus., Brookings, 1988-89, Oscar Howe Art Ctr., Mitchell, S.D., 1988-98 (juror's award 1996), Dahl Fine Arts Ctr., Rapid City, S.D., 1988-89, El Dorado Gallery, Colorado Springs, Colo., 1993 (merit award), Oscar Howe Art Ctr., Mitchell, S.D., 1994 (visitor's choice award), Margaret Harwell Art Mus., Poplar Bluff, Mo., 1995, San Bernardino (Calif.) County Mus., 1995, Cmty. Cultural Ctr., Brookings, 1984-98, Stone Ch., Huron, 1996, 98, John McEnroe Gallery, N.Y.C., Washington Pavilion of Arts and Scis., Sioux Falls, 1999; also pvt. collections in 16 states, Can. and Switzerland. Recipient artist fellowship S.D. Arts Coun., 1979, 1st pl. S.D. Outdoor Art Competition, Black Hills, Badlands and Lake Assn., 1986, S.D. selects fellowships in visual arts exhbn., 1988-89; grantee S.D. Arts Coun./Nat. Endowment for the Arts, 1999. Home: 1330 Illinois Ave SW Huron SD 57350-3517

BRYANT, J(AMES) BRUCE, lawyer; b. Dettlebach, Fed. Republic Germany, Jan. 23, 1961; came to U.S., 1964; s. John Thomas and Doris Jean (Hazenbuehler) B.; 1 child, James Bruce II. BA, Northwestern State U., Natchitoches, La., 1984; MJ, La. State, 1986; JD, Miss. Coll., 1989. Bar: Miss., Tex. 1995, U.S. Dist. Ct. (no. and so. dists.) Miss., U.S. Ct. Appeals (5th cir.) La. 1991, U.S. Dist. Ct. (we. dist.) La. 1994. With residential life La. State U., Baton Rouge, 1985-86; law libr. worker Miss. Coll. Sch. Law, Jackson, 1986-87; clk. Brunini Law Firm, Jackson, 1987-88; ptnr. Cook & Bryant, Bay St. Louis, Miss., 1989-90; assoc. Cook, Yancey, King & Galloway, Shreveport, La., 1990-93; prof. bus. law La. State U., 1991-92, prof. paralegal sci., 1994-96; staff atty. State of La. Office of Support Enforcement, Shreveport, 1993-95; atty. Storm Operating Co. Inc. of La., 1994—; sr. regional atty. State of La. Dept. Health and Hosps., Shreveport-Bossier City, La., 1995—; prof. comms. law Northwestern State U., 1996—; spl. asst. dist. atty. 1st Jud. Dist., Caddo Parish, La., 1998—; bd. dirs. Extra Mile; cons. Wyman Fed. Credit Union, Geismar, La., 1989-90, Comml. Nat. Bank, Shreveport, 1990—; owner, pres. SHOWBIZZ Entertainment Agys., Shreveport, 1992—; v.p. Godfather Prodns., Inc., Shreveport-Bossier City, La., 1994—; owner La. Ctr. for Law and Justice, 1995—; spl. asst. dist. atty. Caddo Parish, 1998—; owner, pres. Dreamworks Internat., 1999—. Editor, author (with others): Art & Bylaws for Moot Court, 1989. Del. Republican Dist. IV, 1994—; bd. dirs. Shreveport Little Theatre, 1995—, Extra Mile, 1996—. Mem. ABA, Miss. Pro Bono Project, Miss. Bar Assn., Assn. Trial Lawyers Am., La. Trial Lawyers Assn., Hancock County Bar Assn. (social chmn.), Shreveport Bar Assn. (comml. litigation sect., editor newsletter), L.A. Pro Bono Project, TKE Alumni Assn. (pres.), Univ. Club (mem. com. 1994—). Roman Catholic. Avocations: martial arts, weightlifting, skiing, shooting. Home: PO Box 444 Shreveport LA 71162-0444 also: 3012 Pines Rd Shreveport LA 71119-3502 Office: La Ctr for Law and Justice 711 Texas Advocates Bldg Shreveport LA 71120

BRYANT, JOHN, author, publisher; b. Washington, Oct. 26, 1943. Student, Antioch Coll., 1963; BA in Math., Am. U., 1968; postgrad. in philosophy of logic, Union Grad. Sch., Yellow Springs, Ohio, 1978-79. Founder, mgr. Socratic Press, St. Petersburg, Fla., 1986—, 701 Advt., St. Petersburg, 1986—. Author: The Mortal Works of J.B.R. Yant and Other Irritations, 1987, The Most Powerful Idea Ever Discovered, 1987, Success in Marriage Guaranteed, 1987, Bryant's Law and Other Broadsides, 1989, Systems Theory and Scientific Philosophy, 1991, Mortal Words Special Topics Series, 25 vols., 1994-97, others; creator Mortal Words Birds cartoon feature; columnist and cartoonist, Nationalist Times, 1994=98; contbr. articles to profl. jours. Founder, dir. extended family program Unitarian Soc. Germantown, Phila. Mem. Mensa. Avocations: computers, tennis, futures trading, pigeons. *It is nice to be loved, but it is better to be feared.*

BRYANT, JOHN BRADBURY, economics educator, consultant; b. July 7, 1947; s. Royal Calvin and Martha Preble (Jones) B.; m. Evelyn Sandra Seltzer, June 24, 1973; 1 child, Aryn Royale. BA, Oberlin Coll., 1969; MS, Carnegie-Mellon U., 1973, PhD, 1975. Economist, bd. govs. FRS, Washington, 1974-77; sr. economist Fed. Res. Bank, Mpls., 1977-81; assoc. prof. U. Fla., Gainesville, 1980-81; cons. Fed. Res. Bank, Dallas, 1983-86, 91-92; Fox assoc. prof. Rice U., Houston, 1981-84, Fox prof. econs., 1984—, prof. mgmt., 1987—; vis. scholar Hoover Inst., Stanford U., 1988-89; vis. rschr. Ctr., Tilburg U., Netherlands, 1998-99. Contbr. articles to profl. jours., books. Office: Rice U Dept Econs MS22 6100 Main St Houston TX 77005-1892

BRYANT, JOHN WILEY, former congressman; b. Lake Jackson, Tex., Feb. 22, 1947; s. Robert Link and Billie Rae (Wiley) B.; m. Janet Elizabeth Watts, Dec. 28, 1968; children: Amy, John Wiley Jr., Jordan. BA, So. Meth. U., 1969; JD, So. Meth. U., 1972. Bar: Tex. 1972. Since practiced in Dallas, 1972—; chief counsel Tex. Senate Subcom. on Consumer Protection, Austin, 1973; adminstrv. asst. Tex. Senate, Austin, Dallas, 1972-73; mem. Tex. Ho. of Reps., 1973-83, 98th-103rd Congresses from 5th Tex. dist., Washington, D.C., 1983-96; former majority whip for Tex. U.S. House; mem. House Com. on Energy and Commerce; mem. House Com. on Judiciary, ranking minority mem. judiciary subcom. on immigration and claims. Bd. dirs. Deaf Action Ctr. of Dallas. Named Hardest Working Mem. Tex. Capital Press Corps., 1977; named Outstanding Legislator Tex. Monthly Mag., 1977, 79, One of Five Outstanding Young Texans, Tex. Jaycees, 1979. Mem. Old Scyene Hist. Soc., Hist. Preservation Soc., Lions Eye Bank (Dallas) (life), Rotary. Democrat. United Methodist. Address: 1601 Elm St Ste 2000 Dallas TX 75201 Office: PO Box 140977 Dallas TX 75214-0977*

BRYANT, JOSEPH ALLEN, JR., English language educator; b. Glasgow, Ky., Nov. 26, 1919; s. Joseph Allen and Florence Morford (Rogers) B.; m. Mary Virginia Woodruff (dec.) m. Sara Coffman, March 9, 1993; children: Joseph Allen, III, Garnett Woodruff. A.B., Vanderbilt U., 1940; M.A., Vanderbilt U., 1941; Ph.D., Yale U., 1948. Instr., then assoc. prof. English Vanderbilt U., 1948-56; assoc. prof. U. South, Sewanee, Tenn., 1956-59, Duke U., 1959-61; prof., chmn. dept. U. N.C., Greensboro, 1961-68, Syracuse (N.Y.) U., 1968-71; prof. English U. Ky., Lexington, 1971-90; chmn. dept. U. Ky., 1973-81; Fulbright lectr. U. Nantes, France, 1965-66. Author: Hippolyta's View, 1961, Eudora Welty, 1968, Compassionate Satirist, 1973, Shakespeare and the Uses of Comedy, 1986, Understanding Randall Jarrell, 1986; editor: Romeo and Juliet, 1964, Twentieth-Century Southern Literature, 1997. Served to lt. (j.g.) USNR, 1942-46. Recipient Research award U. Ky., 1973; Ford fellow, 1952-53; Sewanee Rev. fellow, 1958-59. Mem. MLA, So. Atlantic MLA (Book award 1972), Southeastern Renaissance Conf., Soc. Study So. Lit. Democrat. Episcopalian. Home: 713 Old Dobbin Rd Lexington KY 40502-2851

BRYANT, JOSEPHINE HARRIET, library executive; b. Oshawa, Ont., Can., Dec. 3, 1947; d. Donald Joseph and Margaret Mary (Quilty) B.; children: David Joseph, Michael Andrew. BA, U. Toronto, Ont., 1969, BLS, 1970, MLS, 1974; diploma in Pub. Adminstrn., U. Western Ont., London, 1988. Libr. Ont. Hydro, Toronto, 1970-74; libr. supr. Brampton (Ont.) Pub. Libr. and Art Gallery, 1974-77, branch head, 1977-79; regional dir. Fairview North York (Ont.) Pub. Libr., 1983-85, mgr. cen. libr., 1986, dep. dir., 1986-88, CEO, 1988-98; city libr. Newly Amalgamated Toronto Pub. Libr., Ont., Can., 1998—. Mem. ALA, Can. Libr. Assn., Ont. Libr. Assn., Inst. Pub. Adminstrn. Avocations: tennis, golf. Office: Toronto Pub Libr, 789 Yonge St, Toronto, ON Canada M4W 2G8*

BRYANT, KAREN WORSTELL, financial advisor, investment company executive; b. Cadillac, Mich., Sept. 7, 1942; d. Harley Orville and Rose Edith (Bell) Worstell; children: Lynda Jean Bashoor, Tracey Jo Taylor, Cynthia Jill Warren, Troy Thomas; m. Robert Melvin Bryant, Nov. 29, 1968. Student, Cen. Mich. U., 1963-67, Mich. State U., 1966, Johns Hopkins U., 1982-83. Sales rep. Xerox Corp., Southfield, Mich., 1972-74; cons. and employment contracts IBM World Trade Asia, The Policy Study Grp., Johnson & Johnson Internat., Tokyo, 1974-79; area sales mgr. Universal Plastics, McLean, Va., 1979-81; exec. product mgr. The Western Union Telegraph Co., Upper Saddle River, N.J., 1981-86; dir. mktg. and sales support The Nat. Guardian Corp., Greenwich, Conn., 1986-88; first v.p. investments, fin. cons. Salomon Smith Barney, Paramus, N.J., 1988-97; 1st v.p., fin. advisor Morgan Stanley Dean Witter, Nyack, N.Y., 1997—; guest lectr. for orgns.; guest on TV documentaries. Bd. dirs. Ramapo Ctrl. Found., Hillburn, N.Y., Helen Hayes Performing Arts Ctr. Mem. World Wildlife Fedn., Nature Conservancy, Nyack C. of C. Republican. Avocations: horseback riding. Home: One Main St Clermont on the Hudson 19 Sky Meadow Rd Suffern NY 10901-2520 Office: Morgan Stanley Dean Witter Clermont on the Hudson 1 Main St Ste 1 Nyack NY 10960-3240

BRYANT, KEITH LYNN, JR., history educator; b. Oklahoma City, Nov. 6, 1937; s. Keith Lynn and Elsie L. (Furman) B.; m. Margaret A. Burum, Aug. 14, 1962; children: Jennifer Lynne, Craig Warne. BS, U. Okla., 1959, MEd, 1961; PhD, U. Mo., 1965. From asst. prof. to prof., assoc. dean U. Wis., Milw., 1965-76; prof. Coll. Liberal Arts Tex. A&M U., College Station, 1976-88, head dept. history Coll. Liberal Arts, 1976-80, dean, 1980-84; prof. history U. Akron, Ohio, 1988—, head dept., 1988-95; cons. So. Ry., NEH. Author: History of the Atchison, Topeka and Santa Fe Railway, 1974, Arthur E. Stilwell, Promoter With a Hunch, 1971, Alfalfa Bill Murray, 1968, William Merritt Chase: A Genteel Boehemian, 1991; co-author: A History of American Business, 1983; bd. editors Western Hist. Quar., 1984-87, Southwestern Hist. Quar., 1980-87; editor Railroads in the Age of Regulation, 1900-1980, 1988. Various offices local Rep. Party, Okla., Tex.; chmn. Bush for Pres., Brazos County, 1979-80. Served to 1st lt. U.S. Army, 1959-60. Recipient William H. Kiekhofer award U. Wis., 1968, George W. and Constance M. Hilton book award Ry. and Locomotive Hist. Soc., 1990, David P. Morgan award, 1998; grantee Am. Philos. Soc., 1968, NEH, 1984. Mem. So. Hist. Assn. (chmn. Frank Owsley book award com. 1988), Western History Assn., Tex. State Hist. Assn., Lexington Group, S.W. Conf. Humanities Consortium (pres. 1982-83). Presbyterian. Home: 293 Delaware Pl Akron OH 44303-1275 Office: U Akron Dept History Akron OH 44325-1902

BRYANT, KOBE, basketball player; b. Aug. 23, 1978. Student, Lower Merion (Pa.) High Sch. Player L.A. Lakers, 1996—. Named to NBA All-Rookie 2nd Team, 1996-97. Office: c/o LA Lakers 3900 W Manchester Blvd Inglewood CA 90306*

BRYANT, L. GERALD, health care administrator; b. Norman, Okla., July 27, 1942; s. Lewis Cullen and Ludie A. (Skacel) B.; m. Linda Sue Farris, June 12, 1964; children: David Graham, Heather Leigh. BBA, U. Okla., 1964; MHA, Washington U., St. Louis, 1968. Acct. Pan-Am. Petroleum Corp., Tulsa, 1964-66; adminstrv. asst. Baylor U. Med. Ctr., Dallas, 1968-70, adminstr. C.P.C.H., 1970-72, assoc. dir., 1972-75, assoc. dir. planning and budget, 1975-80, sr. v.p., 1980-81; sr. v.p. Baylor Health Care System, Dallas, 1981-84; COO, exec. v.p. Baylor Health Care System, 1984-92, exec. v.p. strategy devel., 1992—; adj. faculty Washington U. Sch. Med., St. Louis, 1983—, U. Ala., Birmingham, 1992—, Trinity U., San Antonio, 1996—; active Blue Ribbon Task Force on Health Care Reform, Tex. Hosp. Assn., 1992-93; bd. dirs. Regional Health Planning Agy., Irving, Tex., 1979-83; devel. bd. dirs. Allied Bank Dallas. Contbr. chpts. to books. Bd. dirs. Arthritis Found. Dallas, 1980-84; bd. dirs. Preservation Dallas, 1995—; deacon Wilshire Bapt. Ch., Dallas, 1976—; bd. dirs. Dallas Sci. Pl., 1995—. Fellow Am. Coll. Health Care Execs.; mem. Am. Hosp. Assn. (coun. regents 1994—, ho. of dels. 1996—, region 7 policy bd. 1994—), Tex. Hosp. Assn. (coun. on health planning 1981-84, coun. on pre-paid health plans 1984—), Am. Soc. Hosp. Planning, Am. Mgmt. Assn. Republican. Baptist. Lodge: Rotary. Avocations: antique furniture collecting, travel, gardening. Home: 8246 San Fernando Way Dallas TX 75218-4436 Office: Baylor Health Care System 3600 Gaston Ave Ste 150 Dallas TX 75246-1901*

BRYANT, LAURA MILITZER, artist; b. Detroit, Mar. 3, 1955; d. Paul Herman and Kanella (George) Militzer; m. Matthew T. Bryant, May 25, 1980. BFA summa cum laude, U. Mich., 1978. Pres., owner, founder Prism, Buffalo, 1983-92; pres., owner Prism, St. Petersburg, Fla., 1992—. Active Emily's List, 1990—, Mus. Fine Arts, St. Petersburg, 1992—, Fla. Gulf Coast Art Ctr., 1994—. Individual artist grantee State of Fla., 1994; individual artist fellow Nat. Endowment for Arts, 1992; recipient Best of Show award Hilton Head Art League, 1995, award of excellence Craft Art, 1997. Mem. Am. Craft Coun., Knitting Guild Am. (tchr. 1995-96), Nat. Needlework Assn., Fla. Craftsmen (mem. various coms. 1993—). Office: Prism 2595 30th Ave N Saint Petersburg FL 33713-2925*

BRYANT, LELAND MARSHAL, business and nonprofit executive; b. Gainesville, Ga., Apr. 28, 1950; s. William Marcus and Pierre Lou (Milner) B.; children: Shauna, Natalie, Marcus, Jacob. Student, Vanderbilt U., 1968-70; BBA with hons., U. Tex., 1972; MBA, U. Pa., 1978. CPA, Tex. Acct. Arthur Andersen and Co., Dallas, 1978-81; exec. v.p. Walter Bennet Comms., Dallas, 1981-89; pres. Grand Canyon Railway, Flagstaff, Ariz., 1989-97; v.p., CFO, Grand Canyon (Ariz.) Assn., 1997—; pres. Fray Marcos Hotel, Flagstaff, 1995-97. Bd. dirs. Grand Canyon Nat. Park Found., 1995—; nat. adv. bd. No. Ariz. U., Flagstaff, 1994-97. Mem. AICPA, Grand Canyon Assn. (bd. dirs. 1995-97), Nat. Parks Conservation Assn. (nat. adv. coun. 1995-98). Republican. Office: Grand Canyon Assn PO Box 399 Grand Canyon AZ 86023-0399

BRYANT, MAXINE L(EONA), training consultant, entrepreneur; b. Indpls., Dec. 20, 1958; d. Rufus and Leona (Christopher) Taylor; m. Johnny Bryant, Oct. 19, 1985 (div. Oct. 1990); children: Mayosha Martin-Bryant, Jonathan William Bryant. BS, Ball State U., 1981; MS, Saginaw Valley State U., 1990; postgrad., Western Mich. U., 1992—. Trainer, tchr. Saginaw (Mich.) Pub. Schs., 1985-89; program adminstr. Cmty. Treatment Ctr., Detroit, 1989-90; exec. dir. Offender Aid & Restoration, Indpls., 1990-93; tng. coord. Fairbanks Rsch. and Tng., Indpls., 1993-94; tng. mgr. Health Care Edn. & Tng., Indpls., 1994—; proprietor Bryant Edn. Seminars and Tng., Indpls., 1995—; fellow Stanley K. Lacey Leadership Series, 1993-94; chair adv. bd. Now for the Future, Indpls., 1993-96; tng. cons. Nat. Coun. Negro Women, Washington, 1995; adj. faculty Ind. Wesleyan U., Marion, 1995—; staff devel. cons. Planned Parenthood, Chgo., 1996-97; tng. cons. St. Elizabeth's Home, Indpls., 1997—. Author: Ancestrial Notes, 1996; editor, author (tng. manual) Substance Abuse Intervention, 1993-94, Ethnics of Color, 1994-95. Moderator Opportunities Indpls., 1994; mem. steering com. Ind. Gov.'s Conf. on Fatherhood, 1996-97; bd. dirs. parenting program adv. bd. YWCA, Indpls., 1994, Independent Coun. Adolescent Pregnancy, Indpls., 1995—; vol. Planned Parenthood C&S Ind., 1997; pres., bd. dirs. Ind. Coun. Adolescent Pregnancy. Mem. NAFE. Avocations: tennis, reading, speed-walking, writing poetry. Office: Bryant Ednl Seminars & Tng 8325 N Michigan Rd # 250 Indianapolis IN 46268-3635

BRYANT, PAUL THOMPSON, English language educator; b. Oklahoma City, Aug. 24, 1928; s. Paul Dewey and Lynnis (Thompson) B.; m. Genevieve Dale Bryant, Aug. 27, 1949; children: Elaine Lynette Bryant Smyth, Christopher Dale. BS, U. Okla., 1950, MS, 1952, MA, 1956; PhD, U. Ill., 1965. Editor Inst. of Tech., Wash. State U., Pullman, 1954-56, Am. Soc. Engring. Edn., Urban, Ill., 1958-64; dir engring. pubs. U. Ill., Urban, 1958-64; chmn. Dept. English Colo. State U., Ft. Collins, 1969-75, faculty English, 1964-84, assoc. dean grad. sch., 1980-84; prof. English, dean Grad. Coll. Radford (Va.) U., 1984-93; ind. scholar, writer, cons., 1993—. Author essays, poems, short stories; author: H.L. Davis, 1978; editor, compiler essay collection: Geography to Geotechnics, 1969; co-editor essay collection: Frontier Experience and the American Dream, 1989. Bd. dirs. NRV Cmty. Sentencing, Christiansburg, Va., 1985-91; trustee Sci. Mus. of Western Va., Roanoke, 1989-92; adv. coun. Assn. for the Study of Lit. and the Environment, 1994—. With U.S. Army, 1946-47. Mem. MLA, Coll. English Assn. (pres. 1982-83), Western Lit. Assn. (exec. com. 1989-91), conf. of So. Grad. Schs. (pres. 1991-92).

BRYANT, RANDAL EVERITT, computer science educator, consultant; b. Glen Ridge, N.J., Oct. 27, 1952; s. John Harold and Barbara Alice (Everitt) B.; m. Janice Lukens, May 14, 1983; children: Jacob, Claire, Elizabeth. B.S., U. Mich., 1973; S.M., MIT, 1977, E.E., 1978, PhD, 1981. Asst. prof. Calif. Inst. Tech., Pasadena, 1981-84; asst. prof. Carnegie-Mellon U., Pitts., 1984-87, assoc. prof., 1987-92, prof., 1992—, Pres. Disting. prof. computer scis., 1997—; instr., cons. Dig Equipment Corp., Hudson, Mass., 1982-83; vis. rsch. fellow Fujitsu Labs., Kawasaki, Japan, 1990-91; chmn., editor proc. 3d Caltech VLSI Conf., Calif. Inst. Tech., 1983. Contbr. articles to profl. publs. Recipient Faculty Devel. award IBM, 1983, 84; NSF fellow; Intel rsch. grantee, 1985, 97. Fellow IEEE (Best Paper award 1986, Baker prize 1989, assoc. editor Trans. on CAD/IC 1989-95, 95—); mem. Assn. Computing Machinery. Presbyterian. Avocation: bicycling. Home: 528 Briar Cliff Rd Pittsburgh PA 15221-3219*

BRYANT, ROY, SR., bishop; b. Armour, N.C., July 18, 1923; s. Augusta and Susan (Granger) B.; m. Sissieretta Burney, Oct. 11, 1942; children: Eurnetha, Roy, Larry, Ruth, Seth. DD, Fla. State Christian Coll., 1966. Ordained to ministry Bible Ch. of Christ, 1959. Elder Phila. Bible Ch., N.Y.C., 1959-61; bishop The Bible Ch. of Christ, Inc., N.Y.C., 1961—; pres. Theol. Inst., Bible Ch. of Christ, N.Y.C., 1976—, dir. Christian Bookstore, 1978—. Exec. editor The Voice; author: Manual on Demonology, 1998; producer, host Radio Ministry.

BRYANT, RUTH ALYNE, banker; b. Memphis, Jan. 12, 1924; d. James Walter and Leola (Edgar) B. Student, Rhodes Coll. (formerly Southwestern Coll.), Memphis, 1941-43; LHD (hon.), U. Mo., St. Louis, 1990. Clk. Fed. Res. Bank of St. Louis (Memphis Br.), 1943-47, exec. sec., 1947-68, asst. cashier, 1968-69, asst. v.p., 1969-73, v.p., 1973-90. Trustee chancellor's coun. U. Mo., St. Louis, 1979—, chmn., 1985-88; pres. Premiere Performances, 1990-96, vice chmn., 1996-98, bd. dirs., 1998; mem. adv. bd. Salvation Army, St. Louis, 1983-91, DePaul Health Ctr., St. Louis, 1984-87, adv. coun. Hope Ctr., St. Louis, 1987, chmn., 1990-91; chmn. adv. coun. Riverway Sch., 1989-95; bd. dirs. Assocs. of St. Louis U. Librs., 1977—, pres., 1983-85; bd. dirs. The Vanderschmidt's Sch., 1980-86, Internat. Edn. Consortium, 1988-92; bd. dirs. St. Louis Merc. Libr., 1989—, sec., 1990-92, v.p., 1992-94, pres., 1994—; trustee Mo. Coun. on Econ. Edn., 1989-93; bd. dirs. Dance St. Louis, 1992—, v.p., 1993-94, English Lang. Sch., 1993-97. Mem. Am. Inst. Banking (nat. women's com. 1962-63, pres. Memphis chpt. 1968-69), Mo. Bankers Assn. (mktg. and pub. rels. com. 1974-76), Nat. Assn. Bank Women (editor Woman Banker 1959-62, v.p. so. region 1967-68, v.p. 1969-70, pres. 1970-71, trustee ednl. found. 1974-75), English Speaking Union (bd. dirs. 1989—, v.p. 1992-96, nat. bd. dirs. 1995-96, pres. 1997—, nat. bd. dirs. 1998—), Bank Mktg. Assn. (dir. Mo.-Ill. chpt. 1976-79), Am. Soc. Arts and Letters, The Venerable Order of St. John in Jerusalem (comdr.), Univ. Club, St. Louis. Home: 625 S Skinker Blvd Apt 202 Saint Louis MO 63105-2301

BRYANT, STANLEY W., career officer; b. Detroit; m. Virginia Bryant; children: Kimberly, Scott, Jennifer, Tim. Student, Wayne State U.; grad., U.S. Naval Acad., 1969. Commd. ensign USN, 1969, advanced through grades to rear adm., 1998; flight officer VA-196 USS Enterprise, 1970; flight instr., student control officer VT-10, Pensacola, Fla.; squadron maintenance & ops. officer Attack Squadron 65 USS Ind.; squadron maintenance & ops. officer Attack Squadron 65 USS Dwight D. Eisenhower, ops. mgr. Carrier Air Wing 7; adminstrv. officer Staff Med. Attack Wing 1, 1979-80; prospective commdg. officer Warhorses Attack Squadron 55 Attack Wing 1; asst. air offier USS Nimitz, 1985-87; exec. officer Abraham Lincoln Precommng. Unit, 1987-90; commdr. USS Ponce, 1990-91; fellow Chief Naval Ops. Strategic Studies Group, Newport, R.I., 1991-92; commdr. Iceland Def. Force, 1994-96, Carrier Group 4, 1996-98; dir. resources, warfare requirements and assessments N8, U.S. Atlantic Fleet, Norfolk, Va., 1998—. Decorated Def. Superior Svc. Medal, 2 Legion Merit awards, 3 Disting. Flying Cross Medals, 2 Meritorious Svc. Medals, Individual Air Medal, 8 Strike/Flight Air Medals, Navy Achievement Medal, 18 campaign & svc. awards; recipient Commdr.'s Cross Star Icelandic Order Falcon, Govt. Iceland. Office: USN Unit 60102 FPO AE 09501-4304*

BRYANT, THOMAS EDWARD, physician, lawyer; b. Bellamy, Ala., Jan. 17, 1936; s. Howard Edward and Alibel (Nettles) B.; m. Lucie Elizabeth Thrasher, July 9, 1961; children: Thomas Edward, Evelyn Thaxton. A.B., Emory U., 1958, M.D., 1962, J.D., 1967. Bar: Ga. 1967. Intern Grady Meml. Hosp., Atlanta, 1962-63; dir. health affairs OEO, Washington, 1969-71; pres. Nat. Drug Abuse Council, 1971-79; chmn., dir. Pres.'s Commn. Mental Health, 1977-79; chmn. Aspirin Found. of Am., 1987—, Nonprofit Mgmt. Assocs., Inc., 1989—. Pres. Friends of Nat. Library of Medicine, 1985—; exec. dir. County Behavioral Health Inst., 1997—. Served with USAF, 1963-65. Recipient Exceptional Service award OEO, 1971. Mem. Ga. Bar Assn., D.C. Bar Assn., Nat. Acad. Scis., Inst. Medicine. Democrat. Clubs: Cosmos (Washington); Century Assn. (N.Y.C.). Office: Non Profit Mgmt Assocs Inc 1555 Connecticut Ave NW Ste 200 Washington DC 20036-1126

BRYANT, WAYNE RICHARD, state legislator; b. Camden, N.J., Nov. 7, 1947; s. Isaac Rutledge Sr. and Anna Mae (Jones) B.; 1 child, Wayne Richard Jr. BA, Howard U., 1969; JD, Rutgers U., 1972; LLD, Howard D., 1991. Bar: U.S. Supreme Ct. Freeholder Camden County, N.J., 1979-82; dist. 5 N.J. State Assembly, 1982-95, N.J. State Senator, 1995—; vice-chmn. transportation & comms. com., N.J. State Assembly, 1982—, ind. authorities & commn. coms., 1982—, majority leader, 1990-91; staff atty. Camden Regional Legal Svc., Inc., 1972-74; ptnr., Zeller & Bryant, 1974—. Recipient legis. achievement award N.J. Fedn. Dem. Women, 1988, equal justice award Legal Svc. N.J., 1990, Arthur Armitage disting. alumni award Rutgers U. Sch. Law, 1992. Mem. Nat. Black Caucus, ABA, N.J. Bar Assn., Camden County Bar Assn. Address: 501 Cooper St Camden NJ 08102-1210

BRYANT, WILLIAM B., federal judge; b. Wetumpka, Ala., Sept. 18, 1911; s. Benson and Alberta B.; m. Astaire A. Gonzalez, Aug. 25, 1934; children: Astaire, William B. A.B., Howard U., 1932, LL.B., 1936. Asst. U.S. atty. for D.C., 1951-54; partner firm Houston, Bryant & Gardner, 1954-65; sr. U.S. dist. judge U.S. Dist. Ct. Washington, 1965—; prof. law Howard U. Sch. Law, 1965-91. Served with AUS, 1943-47. Mem. ABA. Office: US Dist Ct US Courthouse 333 Constitution Ave NW Washington DC 20001*

BRYANT, WILLIAM BRUCE, minister; b. Tupelo, Miss., Feb. 13, 1947; s. Therman Virgil and Annie Grace (McCord) B.; m. Sue Lynne Brooks, Aug. 26, 1967; children: Kelly, Rusty. BA, Miss. Coll., 1969; MS, U. So. Miss., 1975. Tchr. Nettleton (Miss.) Line Consolidated Sch. Dist., 1969-70; adminstrv. asst., consumer protection divsn. Miss. Dept. Agr. and Commerce, Jackson, 1974-76, dir., consumer protection divsn., 1976-78; pers. officer Miss. Dept. Archives and History, Jackson, 1978-80; dir. Office of Pers., Gov.'s Office of Fed.-State Programs, Jackson, 1980-81; adminstrv. asst. to dir. Miss. Dept. Archives and History, 1982-86, pers. dir., 1986-98; min. edn. and adminstrn. 1st Bapt. Ch., Clinton, Miss., 1998—; mem. Miss. Pers. Adv. Coun., Jackson, 1993-98, Cert. Pub. Mgr. Adv. Bd., 1996-97. Mem. Hinds County Farm Bur., Raymond, Miss., 1967—. Sgt., USAF, 1971-73, U.S. Mem. Miss. Hist. Soc. Home: 1302 Arlington St Clinton MS 39056-4006 Office: 1st Bapt Ch 100 E College St Clinton MS 39056-4246

BRYANT, WINSTON, former state attorney general; b. Donaldson, Ark., Oct. 3, 1938. B.A. in Bus. Adminstrn, Ouachita Bapt. U., 1960; LL.B., U. Ark., 1963; LL.M. in Adminstrv. Law, George Washington U., 1970. Bar: Ark. 1963. Individual practice law Malvern, Ark., 1964-66, 71-75; atty. Ark. Ins. Commn., 1966; asst. U.S. atty. for Eastern Dist. Ark., 1967; legis. asst. to Senator from Ark., 1968-71; dep. pros. atty. Hot Spring County, Ark., 1971-75; mem. Ark. Ho. of Reps., 1973-76; sec. of state State of Ark., Little Rock, 1976-80; lt. gov. State of Ark., 1981-91, atty. gen., 1991-98; instr. polit. sci. Ouachita Bapt. U., 1971-73, Henderson (Ark.) State U., 1973—. Mem. Ark. Youth Svcs. Planning Adv. Coun., 1974, Ark. Gov.'s Ad Hoc Com. on Workmen's Compensation, 1975. Served to capt., inf. U.S. Army, 1963-64. Mem. ABA, Ark. Bar Assn. (ho. of dels.), Malvern C. of C. (pres. 1972), Am. Legion, Ark. Farm Bur. Baptist. *

BRYCE, WILLIAM DELF, lawyer; b. Georgetown, Tex., Aug. 7, 1932; s. D. A. Bryce and Frances Maxine (Wilson) Bryce Bakke; m. Sarah Alice Riley, Dec. 20, 1954; children: Douglas Delf, David Dickson. BA, U. Tex., 1955; LLB, Yale U., 1960. Bar: Tex. 1960, U.S. Dist. Ct. (we. dist.) Tex. 1963, U.S. Ct. Claims 1964, U.S. Supreme Ct. 1971. Briefing atty. Tex. Supreme Ct., Austin, 1960-61; sole practice, 1961—; lectr. U. Tex., 1965-66. Editor Tex. Supreme Ct. Jour. Served to 1st lt. USAF, 1955-57. Fellow Tex. Bar Found. (sustaining, life); mem. ABA, Travis County Bar Assn., Williamson County Bar Assn., State Bar Tex., Rotary Internat. (dist. 5870 gov. 1999-2000), Headliners Club (Austin), The Argyle (San Antonio). Home: 308 E University Ave Georgetown TX 78626-6813 also: 511 S Main St Georgetown TX 78626-5609

BRYCHEL, RUDOLPH MYRON, engineer, consultant; b. Milw., Dec. 4, 1934; s. Stanley Charles and Jean Ann (Weiland) B.; m. Rose Mary Simmons, Sept. 3, 1955; children: Denise, Rita, Rudolph Myron Jr., Patrick, Bradford, Matthew. Student, U. Wis., Stevens Point, 1953, U.S. Naval

Acad., 1954-55, U. Del., 1957, Colo. State U., 1969, North Park Coll., Chgo., 1973, Regis U., Denver, 1990-91. Lab. and quality tech. Thiokol Chem. Co., Elkton, Md., 1956; final test insp. Martin Aircraft Co., Middle River, Md., 1956-57; system final insp. Delco Electronics Co., Oak Creek, Wis., 1957-58; test equipment design engr. Martin Marietta Co., Littleton, Colo., 1958-64; prodn. supr. Gates Rubber Co., Denver, Colo., 1964-65; freelance mfr., quality and project engr. Denver and Boulder, Colo., Raton, N.Mex., 1965-67; quality engr. IBM, Gaithersburg (Md.), Boulder (Colo.), 1967-73; sr. quality engr. Abbott Labs., North Chicago, Ill., 1973-74; instrumentation and control engr. Stearns Roger Co., Glendale, Colo., 1974-81; staff quality engr. Storage Tech., Louisville, Colo., 1981-83; sr. quality engr. Johnson & Johnson Co., Englewood, Colo., 1983-84; quality engr., cons. Staodynamics Co., Longmont, Colo., 1984-85; sr. engr. for configuration and data mgmt. Martin Marietta Astronautics Group, Denver, 1985-91; freelance cons. Littleton, Colo., 1991—. With USN, 1953-56. Mem. Am. Soc. Quality Control (cert. quality engr.), Regulatory Affairs Profl. Soc., Soc. for Tech. Communications (regional chpt. chmn. 1970), KC. Democrat. Roman Catholic. Avocations: berry and fruit gardening. Home and Office: 203 W Rafferty Gardens Ave Littleton CO 80120-1710

BRYCHTOVA, JAROSLAVA, sculptor; b. Semily, Czechoslovakia, 1924; m. S. Libensky. Student, Acad. Applied Arts, Prague, Czechoslovakia, 1945-51, Acad. Fine Arts, Prague, 1947-50. Designer Zeleznobrodské sklo, Zelezny Brod, Czechoslovakia, 1950-84; guest lectr. Pilchuck Summer Sch., Stanwood, Wash., Ctr. Creative Studies, Detroit, others; presenter in field. Office: 7 N Saginaw St Pontiac MI 48342

BRYDGES, THOMAS EUGENE, lawyer; b. Niagara Falls, N.Y., June 1, 1942; s. Earl W. and Eleanor M. (Mahoney) B.; m. Melissa May, May 26, 1990; children: Andrew MacLeod, Elizabeth Hendricks. BA in History, Syracuse U., 1971, JD, 1973. Bar: N.Y. 1974, U.S. Dist. (we. dist.) N.Y. 1974, U.S. Ct. Appeals (2d cir.) 1978. Assoc. Jaeckle, Fleischmann & Mugel, Buffalo, 1973-78, ptnr., 1979—; bd. dirs., sec. Theodore Roosevelt Chroagurve site. Author: (with others) Employment Discrimination Law, 1980—. Trustee Daemen Coll., Amherst, N.Y., 1988—; bd. dirs., v.p. Art Park & Co., Lewiston, N.Y., 1976—. Capt. U.S. Army, 1962-68, Vietnam. Decorated Bronze Star, Air medal, Army Commendation (2). Mem. ABA (labor sect.), Erie County Bar Assn., N.Y. Bar Assn. (labor law com.). Office: Jaeckle Fleischmann & Mugel 700 Fleet Bldg Buffalo NY 14202

BRYER, LENA DOROTHY, nursing educator; b. Jersey City, Nov. 27, 1931; d. Adolph and Angelina (Schettino) Marino; m. Alfred Bryer, Oct. 31, 1954. Diploma, Jersey City Med. Ctr., 1953; BA, Jersey City State Coll., 1972, MA, 1974; postgrad., Montclair (N.J.) State Coll., 1972. RN, N.J. Nurse asst. in oral surgery dept. Jersey City; instr. in health edn. Jersey City Bd. Edn.; part-time assoc. prof. health sci. dept. Hudson County C.C., 1976—; part-time per diem nurse Local Area Hosps. Recipient Recognition award as outstanding tchr. N.J. Gov., 1988; grantee in field. Mem. NEA, N.J. Edn. Assn., Hudson County and Jersey City Edn. Assn., Jersey City Med. Ctr. Alumni Assn., Harvard Med. Sch. Rsch. for Nurses, Phi Delta Kappa.

BRYFONSKI, DEDRIA ANNE, publishing company executive; b. Utica, N.Y., Aug. 21, 1947; d. Lewis Francis and Catherine Marie (Stevens) B.; m. Alexander Burgess Cruden, May 24, 1975. B.A., Nazareth Coll., Rochester, N.Y., 1969; M.A., Fordham U., 1970. Editorial asst. Dial Press, N.Y.C., 1970-71; editor Walker & Co., N.Y.C., 1971-73; editor Gale Research Co., Detroit, 1974-79, sr. editor, 1979, v.p., assoc. editorial dir., 1979-84, sr. v.p., editorial dir., 1984-86, exec. v.p., pub., 1986-94, pres., CEO, 1995-98; pres. libr./edn. divsn. The Gale Group, Farmington Hills, Mich., 1999—. Author: The New England Beach Book, 1974; editor: Contemporary Literary Criticism, Vols. 7-14, 1977-80, Twentieth Century Literary Criticism, vols. 1-2, 1977-78, Contemporary Issues Criticism, vol. 1, 1982, Contemporary Authors Autobiography Series, vol. 1, 1984. Bd. dirs. Friends of Detroit Pub. Libr., 1980-89, pres., 1984-86; bd. dirs. Friends of Librs. U.S.A., 1995—. Mem. ALA, Assn. Am. Pubs. (chmn. libraries com. 1983-85, exec. council gen. pub. div. 1985-87, co-chmn. joint com. resources and tech. services div. 1983-85). Home: 546 Lincoln Rd Grosse Pointe MI 48230-1218 Office: The Gale Group 27500 Drake Rd Farmington Hills MI 48331-3535

BRYNING, SUSAN MARY, critical care nurse, adult nurse practitioner; b. Waltham, Mass., Oct. 8, 1949; d. James Dennis and Caroline Elizabeth (Knight) West; m. Mervin Alfred Bowman, Mar. 21, 1968 (div. Nov. 1973); 1 child, Karen Marie; m. Richard Neil Bryning, Dec. 31, 1978. LPN, Indian River C.C., Ft. Pierce, Fla., 1974; student, Pima C.C., Tucson, 1986-90; BSN, U. Ariz., 1992, MSN, 1997. RN, Ariz.; cert. critical care nurse, adult nurse practitioner. LPN staff nurse Ft. Pierce (Fla.) Meml. Hosp., 1974-75, Lawn Wood Med. Ctr., Ft. Pierce, 1975-78, Colonial Oaks Nursing Home, Metairie, La., 1978-79, La Colina Nursing Home, Tucson, 1984-88; LPN pvt. duty nurse Nursing Svc., Inc., Tucson, 1988-92; critical care staff nurse VA Med. Ctr., Tucson, 1992-98, nurse practitioner, 1998—. Vol. St. Mary's Hospice, Tucson, 1992-94. Mem. ANA, SANP (Chpt. 10), AANP, Sigma Theta Tau (Beta Mu chpt.), Nova. Republican. Avocations: doll making, hiking, camping. Office: VA Med Ctr S 6th Tucson AZ 85713

BRYNJOLFSSON, ERIK, management educator, researcher; b. Roskilde, Denmark, Apr. 14, 1962; m. Martha Pavlakis. AB, Harvard U., 1984, SM, 1984; PhD, MIT, 1991. Ptnr., co. founder Foundation Technologies, Cambridge, Mass., 1986-90; instr. Harvard U.; asst. prof. MIT Sloan Sch., Cambridge, Mass., 1990-95, assoc. prof., Douglas Drane chair, 1995—; vis. prof. Stanford (Calif.) U., 1996-98. Contbr. numerous articles to profl. jours. Office: MIT Sloan Sch 50 Memorial Dr Rm E53-313 Cambridge MA 02142-1347

BRYNN, EDWARD PAUL, former ambassador; b. Pitts., Aug. 1, 1942; s. Walter Bruggeman and Mary Margaret (Callahan) B.; m. Jane Cooke , Apr. 1, 1967; children: Sarah, Edward, Kiernan, Anne-Elizabeth, Justin-Oliver. BS in Fgn. Svc., Georgetown U., 1964; MA in History, Stanford U., 1965, Phd in History, 1968; MLitt, Trinity Coll., Dublin, Ireland, 1968, PhD in Politics, 1977. Prof. history USAF Acad., Colorado Springs, Colo., 1968-72, 76-78; polit. officer Am. Embassy, Colombo, Sri Lanka, 1973-75, Bamako, Mali, 1978-80; staff mem. Senate Select Com. on Intelligence, Washington, 1981-82; dep. chief of mission Am. Embassy, Nouakchott, Mauritania, 1982-85; charge d'affaires Am. Embassy, Moroni, Comoros, 1985-87; dep. chief of mission Am. Embassy, Yaounde, Cameroon, 1987-89; amb. Am. Embassy, Ouagadougou, Burkina Faso, 1990-93; prin. dep. asst. sec. Bur. of African Affairs, 1993-95; amb. Am. Embassy, Ghana, 1995-98. Author: Crown and Castle, 1979, Church of Ireland, 1980. Lt. col. USAFR, 1990. Mem. Am. Fgn. Svc. Assn. Home: RR 1 Box 66 Washington VT 05675-9710*

BRYNSKI, CHRISTINA HALINA, school system administrator, consultant, educator; b. Detroit, June 2, 1940; d. Halina J. (Zawadzki) B. BA, Wayne State U., 1962, MA, 1984. Cert. secondary education tchr. Lang. arts tchr. Livonia (Mich.) Pub. Schs., 1962-74, learning specialist, 1974-85, social studies coord., 1982-85, staff devel. coord., 1985—; cons. Ednl. Support Systems, Inc., Farmington Hills, Mich., 1992—; cons. Right to Read, Washington, 1971-72, Mid. Cities Assn., Lansing, Mich., 1985-89, various counties in Mich., 1985-90; adj. prof. Madonna U., Livonia, Mich., 1994—. Contbr. articles to profl. jours. Mem. ASCD, Nat. Staff Devel. Coun., Effective Instrn. Consortium, Phi Delta Kappa, Pi Lambda Theta. Avocations: knitting, reading, gardening. Home: 17547 Fairfield St Detroit MI 48221-2740

BRYSON, ARTHUR EARL, JR., retired aerospace engineering educator; b. Evanston, Ill., Oct. 7, 1925; s. Arthur Earl and Helen Elizabeth (Decker) B.; m. Helen Marie Layton, Aug. 31, 1946; children—Thomas Layton, Stephen Decker, Janet Elizabeth, Susan Mary. Student, Haverford Coll., 1942-44; BS, Iowa State U., 1946; MS, Calif. Inst. Tech., 1949, PhD in Aeros, 1951; MA (hon.), Harvard., 1956. With Container Corp. Am., 1947-48, United Aircraft Corp., 1948; research asst. aero. Calif. Inst. Tech., 1949-50; mem. tech. staff Hughes Research & Devel. Labs., 1950-53; mem. faculty Harvard, 1953-68, Gordon McKay prof. mech. engring., 1961-68; mem. faculty Stanford, 1968-93, chmn. dept. applied mechanics, 1969-71, chmn. dept. aeros. and astronautics, 1971-79, Paul Pigott prof. engring., 1972-93; Hunsaker prof. Mass. Inst. Tech., 1965-66; Mem. nat. com. Fluid Mechanics Films, 1961-68. Author: (with Y.C. Ho) Applied Optimal Control, 1969, Control of Spacecraft and Aircraft, 1994, Dynamic Optimization, 1998. Served as ensign USNR, 1944-46. Recipient Rufus Oldenberger medal ASME, 1980, Control Systems Sci. and Engrng. award IEEE, 1984, Bellman Heritage award Am. Auto Control Coun., 1990, von Karman lectureship Am. Inst. of Aeronautics and Astronautics, 1994. Fellow AIAA (hon., assoc. editor jour. 1963-65, bd. dirs. 1965-68, Pendray Award 1968, mechanics and control of flight award 1980, Dryden lectr. 1984, Von Karman lectr. 1994); mem. NAS, NAE (aero. and space engring. bd. 1970-79), Am. Acad. Arts and Scis., Am. Soc. Engring. Edn. (Westinghouse award 1969), Sigma Xi, Tau Beta Pi. Congregationalist. Office: Stanford U Durand Building Rm 279 Stanford CA 94305

BRYSON, GARY SPATH, cable television and telephone company executive; b. Longview, Wash., Nov. 8, 1943; s. Roy Griffin and Marguerite Elizabeth (Spath) B.; m. Bobbi Bryson; children: Kelly Suzanne, Lisa Christine. AB, Dartmouth Coll., 1966; MBA, Tuck Sch., 1967. With Bell & Howell Co., Chgo., 1967-79; pres. consumer and audio-visual group Bell & Howell Co., 1977-79; chmn. bd., CEO Bell & Howell Mamiya Co., Chgo., 1979-81; exec. v.p. Am. TV & Communications Corp., subs. Time, Inc., Englewood, Colo., 1981-88; v.p. diversified group US West, Englewood, 1988-89, pres. cable communications div., 1989-92; pres., CEO TeleWest Internat., 1992-93; pres. SkyConnect, Boulder, 1994-96; comm. cons., 1996—. Mem. Phi Beta Kappa, Sigma Alpha Epsilon. Republican. Lutheran. Home: 2221 Carriage Hills Dr Boulder CO 80302-9481

BRYSON, JOHN E., utilities company executive; b. N.Y.C., July 24, 1943; m. Louise Henry. B.A. with great distinction, Stanford U., 1965; student, Freie U. Berlin, Federal Republic Germany, 1965-66; J.D., Yale U., 1969. Bar: Calif., Oreg., D.C. Asst. in instrn. Law Sch., Yale U., New Haven, Conn., 1968-69; law clk. U.S. Dist. Ct., San Francisco, 1969-70; co-founder, atty. Natural Resources Def. Council, 1970-74; vice chmn. Oreg. Energy Facility Siting Council, 1975-76; assoc. Davies, Biggs, Strayer, Stoel & Boley, Portland, Oreg., 1975-76; chmn. Calif. State Water Resources Control Bd., 1976-79; vis. faculty Stanford U. Law Sch., Calif., 1977-79; pres. Calif. Pub. Utilities Commn., 1979-82; ptnr. Morrison & Foerster, San Francisco, 1983-84; sr. v.p. law and fin. So. Calif. Edison Co., Rosemead, 1984; exec. v.p., chief fin. officer Edison Internat. and So. Calif. Edison Co., 1985-90; chmn. of bd., CEO Edison Internat. and So. Calif. Edison Co., Rosemead, 1990—; lectr. on pub. utility, energy, communications law.; former mem. exec. com. Nat. Assn. Regulatory Utility Commrs., Calif. Water Rights Law Rev. Commn., Calif. Pollution Control Financing Authority; former mem. adv. bd. Solar Energy Research Inst., Electric Power Research Inst., Stanford Law Sch.; bd. dirs. Pacific Am. Income Shares Inc. Mem. bd. editors, assoc. editor: Yale U. Law Jour. Bd. dirs. World Resources Inst., Washington, Calif. Environ. Trust, Claremont U. Ctr., Grad. Sch., Stanford U. Alumni Assn.; trustee Stanford U., 1991. Woodrow Wilson fellow. Mem. Calif. Bar Assn., Oreg. Bar Assn., D.C. Bar Assn., Nat. Assn. Regulatory Utility Commrs. (exec. com. 1980-82), Stanford U. Alumni Assn. (bd. dirs. 1983-86), Phi Beta Kappa. Office: Edison Internat 2244 Walnut Grove Ave Rosemead CA 91770-3714

BRYSON, REID ALLEN, earth sciences educator; b. Detroit, June 7, 1920; s. William Riley and Elma (Turner) B.; m. Frances Edith Williamson, June, 13, 1942; children—Anne, William, Robert, Thomas. A.B., Denison U., 1941, D.Sc. (honoris causa), 1971; postgrad., U. Wis., 1941, 46; Ph.D., U. Chgo., 1948. Asst. prof. meteorology and geology U. Wis., 1946-48, asst. prof. meteorology, 1948-50, assoc. prof., 1950-56, chmn. dept., 1948-50, 52-54, prof., 1957-86, prof. emeritus, 1986—, sr. scientist, 1986—; dir. Ctr. for Climatic Rsch., Madison, 1962-70, Inst. for Environ. Studies, 1970-85; prof. U. Ariz., 1956-57; mem. various coms. NAS-NRC, 1956-57, remote sensing com., 1964-67, com. on mil. geography, 1966-69, Smithsonian Coun., 1976-79; sr. cons. UN Environ. Programme, 1975-77, Global 500 Honour Roll, 1990; trustee Univ. Corp. for Atmospheric Rsch.; councilor World Coun. for Biosphere, 1984-92. Author: Atlas of 500 mb Wind Characteristics for the Northern Hemisphere, 1958, Atlas of Five-Day Normal Sea-Level Pressure Charts for the Northern Hemisphere, 1958, Atlas of 300 mb Wind Characteristics, 1959; Editor: (with F.K. Hare) Climates of North America, 1974, Climates of Hunger, 1977 (Banta medal 1978); Contbr.articles to profl. jours. Cited by Denison U., 1966. Fellow AAAS, Am. Meteorol. Soc., Wis. Acad. Scis., Arts and Letters (past pres.); mem. Wis. Phenological Soc. (past pres.), Soc. Am. Archaeology, Am. Quaternary Assn. (pres. 1986-90), Phi Beta Kappa, Sigma Xi, Phi Kappa Phi (hon.). Achievements include application of climatology to archaeological problems; archaeoclimatic modeling; climatic changes; interdisciplinary environmental studies. Home: 11 Rosewood Cir Madison WI 53711-2723

BRYSON, VERN ELRICK, nuclear engineer; b. Woodruff, Utah, May 28, 1920; s. David Hyrum and Luella May (Eastman) B.; m. Esther Sybil de St Jeor, Oct. 14, 1942; children: Britt William, Forrest Lee, Craig Lewis, Nadine, Elaine. Commd. 2d lt. USAAF, 1941; advanced through grades to lt. col. USAF, 1960, ret., 1961; pilot, safety engr., civil engr., electronic engr., nuclear engr., chief Aeronaut. Systems div., Aircraft Nuclear Propulsion Program, Wright-Patterson AFB, Ohio, 1960-61; chief Radiation Effects Lab., also chief Radiation Effects Group Boeing Airplane Co., Seattle, 1961-65; nuclear engr. Aerospace Corp., San Bernardino, Calif., 1965-68; service engr., also head instrumentation lab., Sacramento Air Logistic Ctr. USAF, McClellan AFB, Calif., 1968-77; owner, mgr. Sylvern Valley Ranch, Calif., 1977—; Mem. panel Transient Radiation Effects on Electronics, Weapon Effects Bd., 1959-61. Contbr. research articles on radiation problems to profl. pubs. Decorated D.F.C. with oak leaf cluster, Air medal with 12 oak leaf clusters. Mem. IEEE. Mem. Ch. Jesus Christ of Latter-day Saints. Home: 1426 Caperton Ct Penryn CA 95663-9515

BRYSON, WILLIAM CURTIS, federal judge; b. 1945. B.A. magna cum laude, Harvard Coll., 1969; J.D., U. of Tex. Sch. of Law, 1973. Law clerk to Justice Henry Friendly U.S. Ct. of Appeals, 2nd Circuit, 1973-74; law clerk to Justice Thurgood Marshall U.S. Supreme Ct., 1974-75; atty. Miller, Cassidy, Larroca & Lewin, 1975-78; asst. to the Solicitor General U.S. Dept. of Justice, 1978-79; chief Appellate Section, Criminal Div., 1979-82; special counsel Organized Crime & Racketeering Section, Criminal Div., 1982-86; dep. solicitor gen., 1986-94, dep. assoc. atty. & acting assoc. atty. gen., 1994; circuit judge Federal Circuit, Washington, D.C., 1994—. Office: 717 Madison Pl NW Washington DC 20439-0002*

BRZEZINSKI, ZBIGNIEW, political science educator, author; b. Warsaw, Poland, Mar. 28, 1928; came to U.S., 1953, naturalized, 1958; s. Tadeusz and Leonia (Roman) B.; m. Emilie Anna Benes, June 11, 1955; children: Ian, Mark, Mika. B.A. with 1st class honors in Econs. and Polit. Sci., McGill U., 1949, M.A. in Polit. Sci., 1950; Ph.D., Harvard U., 1953. Inst. govt. and research fellow Russian Research Center, Harvard U., 1953-56; asst. prof. govt., research assoc. Russian Research Center and Center Internat. Affairs, Harvard U., 1956-60; assoc. prof. public law and govt. Columbia U., 1960-62, prof., 1981-89; dir. Rsch. Inst. Internat. Change, 1962-77; mem. faculty Russian Inst., 1960-77; dir. Trilateral Commn., 1973-76; asst. to pres. U.S. for nat security affairs, 1977-81; ofcl. Nat. Security Coun., 1977-81; counselor Ctr. Strategic and Internat. Studies, 1981—; prof. Nitze Sch. Advanced Internat. Studies, Johns Hopkins U., 1989—; mem. policy planning coun. U.S. Dept. State, 1966-68, Pres.'s Fgn. Intelligence Adv. Bd., 1987-91; mem. Joint Com. Contemporary China, Social Sci. Rsch. Coun., 1961-62; guest lectr. numerous pvt. and govt. instns. 1953—, participant internat. confs., 1955—. Author: The Permanent Purge-Politics in Soviet Totalitarianism, 1956, The Soviet Bloc—Unity and Conflict, 1960, Ideology and Power in Soviet Politics, 1962, Alternative to Partition, 1965, Between Two Ages, 1970, The Fragile Blossom, 1971, Power and Principle, 1983, Game Plan, 1986, The Grand Failure: The Birth and Death of Communism in the Twentieth Century, 1989, Out of Control, 1993, The Grand Chessboard, 1997; co-author: Totalitarian Dictatorship and Autocracy, 1957, Political Power: USA/USSR, 1964 (German edit. 1966), also numerous articles.; editor, co-author, contbr.: Political Controls in the Soviet Army, 1954; editor, co-author, contbr.: Africa and the Communist World, 1963, Dilemmas Of Change In Soviet Politics, 1969, Dilemmi Internationazionali In Un-epoca. Teconetronica, 1969; columnist: Newsweek, 1970-72; co-editor: Russia and the Commonwealth of Independent States: Documents, Data and Analysis, 1997. Mem. hon. steering com. Young Citizens for Johnson, 1964. Recipient Presdl. Medal of Freedom, 1981, U Thant award, 1995, Order of White Eagle, Poland, 1995. Fellow AAAS; mem. Coun. Fgn. Relations. Club: Univ. (Washington). Office: Ctr Strategic & Internat Studies 1800 K St NW Washington DC 20006-2202

BRZOSKA, DENISE JEANNE, paralegal; b. Wilmington, Del., Mar. 21, 1945; d. Eugene Joseph and Marie Jeanette (Durr) B. Student, U. Del., 1971-84; grad., Citizen's Police Acad., New Castle, Del., 1995. Cert. graphic designer; cert. paralegal. Bookkeeping clk. Del. Div. of Revenue, Wilmington, 1963-66; tech. support personnel dept. physics and astronomy U. Del., Newark, 1966-91; paralegal Wilmington Trust Co./Trust Legal, 1992—; mem. geographic adv. coun. and by-laws com. New Castle County Police, 1996. Artist representing Del. at Colliseum Arts Internat., World Trade Ctr., 1981. Campaign worker Joe Biden for U.S. Senate, Del., 1978, S.B. Woo for Lt. Gov., Del., 1984, S.B. Woo for U.S. Senate, Del., 1988; mem. geographic adv. coun., by-laws com. New Castle County Police Dept., 1996; treas. New Castle County Policy Ctrl. Dist. Adv. Coun., 1996—. Mem. Del. Paralegal Assn., Wilmington Women in Bus., Pa. Horticultural Soc., Del. Art Mus., Nat. Mus. Women in the Arts, Wilmington Garden Day. Roman Catholic. Avocations: painting, gardening, gourmet cooking, theater. Home: 422 Old Airport Rd New Castle DE 19720-1002

BRZUSTOWICZ, JOHN CINQ-MARS, lawyer; b. Rochester, N.Y., Feb. 1, 1957; s. Richard J. and Alice (Cinq-Mars) B.; m. Diane Day, Aug. 22, 1981; children: Richard Reed, Megan Day, Emily Day-Hanson. BA, Coll. Wooster, 1979; JD, Case Western Res. U., 1985; cert., Cornell Inst. Labor Rels., 1982. Bar: Pa. 1985, U.S. Dist. Ct. (we. dist.) Pa. 1985, U.S. Ct. Appeals (3d cir.) 1986, U.S. Supreme Ct. 1990. Asst. to dir. Inst. Am. Music U. Rochester, Rochester, 1979-82; assoc. Peacock, Keller, Yohe, Day & Ecker, Washington, Pa., 1985-88, Sable, Makoroff & Libenson, Pitts., 1988-90; pvt. practice Brzustowicz Law Offices, McMurray, Washington, Pa., 1990-94; shareholder Day & Brzustowicz Law Offices, P.C., McMurray, Pa., 1995—; chmn. bd. dirs. Inst. for Am. Music of Eastman Sch. Music, 1997—; bd. dirs. Hanson Inst. Am. Music of Eastman Sch. Music, 1996; chmn. law libr. Washington County ((Pa.) Bar, 1992; mem. com. Jud. Inquiry Bd., Pa., 1991—; dir. Hanson Inst. of Am. Music of the Eastman Sch. of Music, U. Rochester, 1995. Co-author: Pennsylvania School Law, 1992, Pennsylvania Adminstrative Law, 1987; editor: So You Want to Be A Lawyer, 1990; advisor on PBC documentary: Life of Howard Hanson, An American Masterpiece, 1987. V.p. Young Reps., Wooster, Ohio, 1977-79; co-founder, officer Wooster Polo and Hunt Club, 1976-79; bd. dirs. Washington County Found. Recipient Merit award Inst. Am. Music, 1981, Outstanding Scholar award Rotary. Mem. ABA, ATLA, Pa. Bar Assn. (del. 1992), Allegheny County Bar Assn., Washington County Bar Assn., Pa. Young Lawyers for Washington County (state rep. 1988), Peters Twp. C. of C. Roman Catholic. Avocations: reading, woodworking, biology. Home: 56 Mckennan Ave Washington PA 15301-3531 Office: 3821 Washington Rd Mc Murray PA 15317-2946

BRZUSTOWICZ, STANISLAW HENRY, clinical dentistry educator; b. Bklyn., Apr. 30, 1919; s. John Stanislaw and Victoria (Szutarski) B.; m. Wanda Frances Seglow, July 3, 1949; children: Robert, Thomas, Michael, Linda. BS, St. John's U., 1940; DDS, Columbia U., 1943. Pvt. practice gen. dentistry Bklyn., 1947-74, New Hyde Park, N.Y., 1963-93; prof. clin. dentistry Columbia U. Sch. Dental and Oral Surgery, N.Y.C., 1946-87, prof. emeritus clin. dentistry (operative), 1987—; course dir. preclin. operative dentistry, attending dentist Presbyn. Hosp., N.Y.C., 1974—; spl. lectr. in dentistry, 1990—; bd. dirs., v.p. Prospect Pattern & Machine Works, Inc., Bklyn., 1962-72; bd dirs., sec. to bd. Atlas Savs. & Loan Assn., Bklyn., 1962-94. Contg. author Differential Diagnosis of Mouth Diseases, 1943. Served to capt. U.S. Army, 1943-46. Mem. ADA, N.Y. State Dental Soc., 2d Dist. Dental Soc., Nat. Med. and Dental Soc., Cath. Dentist Guild (joint program dental care for indigent children with Cath. Guardian Soc. 1949-54), Roger Bacon Scientific Soc., Kosciuszko Found., Holy Name Soc., Omicron Kappa Upsilon. Republican. Roman Catholic. Home: 58 Executive Dr New Hyde Park NY 11040-1014 Office: Columbia U Sch of Dental and Oral Surgery 630 W 168th St New York NY 10032-3795

BUA, NICHOLAS JOHN, retired federal judge; b. Chgo., Feb. 9, 1925; s. Francesco and Lena (Marino) B.; m. Camille F. Scordato, Nov. 20, 1943; 1 dau., Lisa Annette. JD, DePaul U., 1953; LLD (hon.), Govs. State U., 1992. Bar: Ill. 1953. Trial atty. Chgo., 1953-63; judge Village Ct., Melrose Park, Ill., 1963-64; assoc. judge Cir. Ct. Cook County, Chgo., 1964-71; cir. judge Cir. Ct. Cook County, 1971-76; justice Appellate Ct. Ill., 1st Dist., 1976-77; judge U.S. Dist. Ct., Chgo., 1977-91; with Burke, Weaver & Prell, 1991—; spl. counsel to U.S. atty. gen., 1991-93; mem. exec. com. Jud. Conf. Ill., also mem. supreme ct. rules com., 1970-77; lectr. DePaul U.; mem. faculty Def. Tactics Seminar, Ill. Def. Counsel Seminar, 1971; fellow Nat. Coll. State Trial Judges, U. Nev., 1966. Contbr. articles to legal pubs. Bd. govs. Gottlieb Meml. Hosp., 1978-79; trustee Schwab Rehab. Hosp., 1977-78; chmn. Mayor of City of Chgo.'s Gaming Commn., 1992. With AUS, World War II. Named Man of Yr. Justinian Soc. Lawyers, 1977, Best Fed. Judge No. Dist. Ill. Chgo. Lawyer, 1989; recipient Alumni award DePaul U., 1977. Mem. Am. Justinian Soc. Jurists (pres. 1978). Clubs: Nat. Lawyers (Chgo.), Legal (Chgo.), Union League (Chgo.), Lex Legio DePaul U. (Chgo.). Office: Burke Weaver & Prell Xerox Centre 55 W Monroe St Chicago IL 60603-5001 *Notable cases include: ordered Sears, Roebuck & Co. to pay former employee Peter M. Roberts $8.1 million for willful infringement of a patent on a socket wrench he designed 18 yrs. earlier, 1982; put into receivership and froze the assets of the bus. owned by Allen Dorfman, 1982; gave Chgo. and Cook County one yr. to eliminate politically-motivated hirings, dismissals, and harassment of mcpl. workers, 1983; declared invalid two Dept. of Health and Human Svcs. regulations used to determine who qualified for disability payments, thereby allowing more than 10,000 Ill. residents new eligibility hearings, 1984.*

BUATTA, MARIO, interior designer; b. N.Y.C., Oct. 20, 1935; s. Felix and Olive B.; student Wagner Coll., 1953-54, Cooper Union, 1958-59, Parsons Sch. Design, Europe, 1961; Ph.D. (hon.), Wagner Coll. Asst. decorator B. Altman & Co., N.Y.C., 1959-61, Elisabeth Draper Inc., N.Y.C., 1961, Keith Irvine and Co., N.Y.C., 1962; pvt. practice interior decorating, N.Y.C., 1963—, works include: Protocol Offices of 1964 World's Fair, exec. offices Met. Opera House at Lincoln Center, N.Y.C.; dean of design Chgo. Merchandise Mart Design Community. Bd. dirs. East Side House Settlement, N.Y.C.; past bd. dirs. Kips Bay Boys Club, N.Y.C., Fashion Inst. Tech., N.Y.C.; work in process includes: redecoration of Blair House, the White House Guest House. Bd. dirs. Royal Oak, Nat. Trust Gt. Britain, The Hist. House Trust, N.Y.C.; chmn. Winter Antiques Show, East Side House Settlement benefit; hon. chmn. Cooper Hewitt Mus., Decorative Arts Soc. Mem. Am. Soc. Interior Designers. Designs included in numerous pubs. Inducted into Interior Design Hall of Fame. Office: 120 E 80th St New York NY 10021-0306

BUB, ALEXANDER DAVID, acoustical engineer; b. Milw., Oct. 19, 1949; s. Alex Robert and Rose (Monafo) B.; m. Kay Lynn Johannes, Jan. 5, 1982; 1 child, David. AAS in Electronic Communications, Milw. Sch. Engring., 1969, postgrad., 1993—; BA in Econs., History and Anthropology, U. Wis., Milw., 1976. Nuclear weapons specialist USAF, 1969-73; with Harley Davidson, Inc., Milw., 1977—, project mgr., 1997—, with powertrain devel. group, 1993—, sect. lead power generation, 1999—. U.S. nat. champion 410 Superbike, 1979, Mexican champion 750 Prodn. and Open Superbike, 1980, Midwest champion Supertwins and Formula Twins, 1985, 86, 87. Mem. Acoustical Soc. Am. (guest speaker conf. 1990, 92), Soc. Automotive Engrs., Western/Eastern Roadracing Assn., Am. Motorcyclist Assn. Avocations: motorcycle RR, MX, trials riding, mountain bikes, skiing, amateur radio (WA9OLH). Home: W4802 Knuth Rd Random Lake WI 53075-1355 Office: Harley Davidson Inc 11800 W Capitol Dr Wauwatosa WI 53222-1007

BUBAR, JOSEPH BEDELL, JR., church official; b. Rochester, NH, June 7, 1947. BA in History, Gordon Coll., 1968; MDiv, Trinity Evang. Divinity Sch., 1972. Sr. pastor Bethany Evan. Free Ch., La Crosse, Wis., 1980-97, Grace Bible Ch., ArroyoGrande, Calif., 1997—; bd. dirs. Bethany-St. Joe Care Ctr., La Crosse; vice chmn. Christian Svc. Brigade, Wheaton, Ill., 1980-89. Bd. dirs. Forest Lakes dist. Evan. Free Ch. of Am., 1989-91; bd. dirs., bd. chmn. Mission USA, 1989-91, vice-moderator, 1991-93, moderator, 1993-95. *

BUBASH, PATRICIA JANE, special education educator; b. St. Louis; d. Emil John and Anne Marie (Candrl) B. BA in Deaf Edn., Fontbonne Coll., 1974; postgrad., St. Louis U., 1975-76, U. Mo., Columbia, 1982-84, U. Mo., St. Louis, 1984; MA in Edn., Washington U., 1996. Life cert. K-12 tchr. of deaf, learning disabilities, emotional and behavior disorders, K-8 elem. tchr., Mo. Tchr. of deaf Spl. Sch. Dist. St. Louis County, 1974—; mem. curriculum devel. action com. Drug Free Schs.; com. mem. Drug Edn. Task Force. Mem. Jr. League St. Louis, 1989—; mem. bd. jr. divsn. St. Louis Symphony Soc., co-chmn. membership, 1991-92, 92-93; co-chmn. Gypsy Caravan Vols., St. Louis, 1991, 92-93; leader Boy Scouts Am., 1984—, Explorer Scouts, 1990, Girl Scouts U.S.A., 1984—, Just Say No Club, 1987—; mem. dance St. Louis Bravo, 1991—; mem. Step Up St. Louis, 1991—; active Alliance Francaise; mem. St. Louis-Lyon Sister Cities, Inc. Named Tchr. of Month, Spl. Sch. Dist. St. Louis County, 1987; recipient Spl. Needs Tchr. award for Classroom Boy Scouts Am., 1989, 96. Mem. Coun. for Exceptional Children, Mo. Edn. Assn., Alexander Graham Bell Assn. for Deaf, Coun. Edn. of Deaf, St. Louis Ski Club, St. Louis Skating Club. Roman Catholic. Avocations: French, dancing, swimming, tennis, snow skiing. Office: Spl Sch Dist St Louis County 12110 Clayton Rd Saint Louis MO 63131-2516

BUBE, RICHARD HOWARD, materials scientist; b. Providence, Aug. 10, 1927; s. Edward Neser and Ella Elvira (Baltteim) B.; m. Betty Jane Meeker, Oct. 9, 1948 (dec. Apr. 2, 1997); children: Mark Timothy, Kenneth Paul, Sharon Elizabeth, Meryl Lee. Sc.B., Brown U., 1946; M.A., Princeton U., 1948, Ph.D., 1950. Mem. sr. research staff RCA Labs., Princeton, N.J., 1948-62; prof. materials sci. and elec. engring. Stanford U., 1962-92, prof. emeritus, 1992—, chmn. dept., 1975-86, assoc. chmn. dept., 1990-91; cons. to industry and govt. Author: A Textbook of Christian Doctrine, 1955, Photoconductivity of Solids, 1960, The Encounter between Christianity and Science, 1968, The Human Quest: A New Look at Science and Christian Faith, 1971, Electronic Properties of Crystalline Solids, 1974, Electrons in Solids, 1981, 3d edit., 1992, Fundamentals of Solar Cells, 1983, Science and the Whole Person, 1985, Photoelectronic Properties of Semiconductors, 1992, Putting It All Together: Seven Patterns for Relating Science and Christian Faith, 1995, One Whole Life: Personal Memoirs of Richard H. Bube, 1995, Photoinduced Defects in Semiconductors, 1996, Photovoltaic Materials, 1998; also articles; editor Jour. Am. Sci. Affiliation, 1969-83; mem. editl. bd. Solid State Electronics, 1975-94, Christians in Sci.; assoc. editor Ann. Rev. Materials Sci., 1969-83. Fellow Am. Phys. Soc., AAAS, Am. Sci. Affiliation; mem. Am. Soc. Engring. Edn. (life), Internat. Solar Energy Soc., Sigma Xi. Evangelical. Home: 753 Mayfield Ave Stanford CA 94305-1043 Office: Dept Materials Sci/Engring Stanford Univ Stanford CA 94305-2205 *I find no contradiction or conflict between science and Christian faith, but rather a marvelous compatibility that touches all aspects of life.*

BUBENZER, GARY DEAN, agricultural engineering educator, researcher; b. Bicknell, Ind., Aug. 21, 1940; s. Ernest and Nelda (Telligman) B.; m. Sandra Lee Capehart, June 10, 1962; children—Nathan Edward, Brian Peter. A.S., Vincennes U., 1960; B.S., Purdue U., 1962, M.S., 1964; Ph.D., U. Ill., 1970. Registered profl. engr., Wis. Instr. agrl. engring. U. Ill., Urbana, 1964-69; asst. prof. U. Wis., Madison, 1969-74; assoc. prof. U. Wis., 1974-79, prof., 1979—, chmn. dept. agrl. engring., 1983-88; guest scholar Kyoto U., Japan, 1981. Contbr. articles to profl. jours. Named Outstanding Instr., Coll. Agr. and Life Sci., U. Wis., 1983; recipient faculty-alumni citation Vincennes U., 1984. Fellow Am. Soc. Agrl. Engrs. (chmn. soil and water div. 1983-84, engr. of the yr. Wis. sect. 1988, Honor award 1998). United Methodist. Home: 5105 Sherwood Rd Madison WI 53711-1019

BUBLITZ, DEBORAH KEIRSTEAD, pediatrician; b. Boston, Feb. 28, 1933; d. George and Dorothy (Kingsbury) Keirstead; m. Clark Bublitz, Mar. 1, 1958; children: Nancy B. Dyer, Susan B. Schooleman, Philip K. Bublitz, Caroline D. Bublitz, Elizabeth E. Bublitz. BS, Bates Coll., 1955; MD, Johns Hopkins U., 1959. Resident St. Louis Children's Hosp., 1959-60, U. Colo. Health Sci. Ctr. and Dept. Health and Hosps., Denver, 1968-74; pvt. practice Littleton, Colo., 1974—; asst. clin. prof. pediatrics U. Colo. Health Sci. Ctr. and Children's Hosp., 1975-87, assoc. clin. prof. pediatrics, 1987—; creditials com. Swedish/Porter Hosp., Englewood, Colo., 1985-87, chief dept. pediatrics, 1985-87; med. assoc., advisor LaLeche League, 1975—. Author: (with others) Clinical Pediatric Otolaryngology, 1986. Fellow Am. Acad. Pediatrics; mem. AMA, Colo. Med. Soc. (women's governing coun. 1990-96, asst. chair women's governing coun. 1993-94, chair, 1994-95), Arapahoe Med. Soc., Am. Women's Med. Assn. Episcopalian. Avocations: painting, gardening, bird watching, church choir, grandchildren. Home: 5621 Blue Sage Dr Littleton CO 80123-2713 Office: Littleton Pediatric Med Ctr 206 W County Line Rd Ste 110 Highlands Ranch CO 80126-2319

BUBRICK, MELVIN PHILLIP, surgeon; b. Chgo., June 2, 1944; m. Barbara Lynn Jacobs, Jan. 26, 1969; children: Jerome Bradley, Ellen Jeanne, Dena Beth. BA with honors, U. Ill., 1964, MD, 1968. Diplomate Am. Bd. Surgery, Am. Bd. Colon and Rectal Surgery; lic. Minn. Intern in surgery Univ. Hosps., Madison, Wis., 1968-69; resident in gen. surgery Hennepin County Gen. Hosp., Mpls., 1969-74; postdoctoral fellow colon and rectal surgery U. Minn. Health Scis. Ctr., Mpls., 1974-75; clin. instr. div. colon and rectal surgery U. Minn., Mpls., 1975-77, clin. asst. prof., 1977-78, clin. asst. prof. dept. surgery, 1978-80, asst. prof., 1980-87, assoc. prof., 1987—; chief surgery, program dir. surg. residency Hennepin County Med. Ctr., 1988-94; pres., CEO Hennepin Facility Assocs., 1995—; v.p. Mpls. Med. Rsch. Found., 1991-95; chmn. bd. dirs. Hennepin Faculty Assocs., 1991—, pres., CEO, 1995—. Author: (with others) Conn's Therapy, 1985, The Pancreas. Principles of Medical and Surgical Practice, 1985, Applied Therapeutics: The clinical use of drugs, 4th rev. edit., 1988; contbr. over 90 articles to Minn. Med. jour., Am. Surg. jour., Diseases of Colon and Rectum, Surgery, others. Bd. dirs. Mpls. Med. Rsch. Found., Inc., 1981-89. Mem. AMA, ACS, Am. Assn. Surgery of Trauma, Am. Soc. Colon and Rectal Surgeons (co-chair Self Assessment Exam. Com. 1984-85), Am. Soc. Microbiology, Assn. Program Dirs. of Surgery, Cen. Surg. Assn., Collegium Internat. Chirurgiae Digestivae, Soc. Surgery of Alimentary Tract, Minn. Assn. Pub. Teaching Hosps., Minn. Surg. Soc., Minn. Med. Assn., Mpls. Surg. Soc., Hennepin County Med. Soc. (mem. and chair various coms. 1975—, Hennepin faculty assoc. 1983—). Achievements include rsch. in assessment of bursting strength and healing of intestinal anastomoses, predictive value of surface oximetry in assessing healing in irradiated bowel, use of antibiotic microspheres for infected vascular grafts and peritonitis, clinical and anatomic assessment of first rib-clavicular decompression on subclavian catheters and pacemaker leads, influence of nutritional deficits in intestinal anastomotic strength, iron chelation with a Deferoxamine (DFO) conjugate in hemorrhagic shock.

BUC, NANCY LILLIAN, lawyer; b. Orange, N.J., July 27, 1944; d. George L. and Ethel (Rosenbaum) B. AB, Brown U., 1965, LLD (hon.), 1994; LLB, U. Va., 1969. Bar: Va. 1969, N.Y. 1977, D.C. 1978. Atty. Fed. Trade Commn., Washington, 1969-72; assoc. Weil, Gotshal & Manges, N.Y., 1972-77, ptnr., 1977-78; ptnr. Weil, Gotshal & Manges, Washington, 1978-80, 81-94, Buc & Beardsley, Washington, 1994—; chief counsel FDA, Rockville, Md., 1980-81; mem. recombinant DNA adv. com. NIH, 1990-94; consensus panelist NIH Consensus Devel. Conf. on Effective Med. Treatment of Heroin Addiction, 1997; bd. dirs. Agritope, Inc. Mem. editl. bd. Food Drug and Cosmetic Law Jour., 1981-87, 94-97, Jour. of Products Liability, 1981-92, Health Span: The Jour. of Health, Bus. & Law, 1984-95. Mem. adv. com. on new devels. in biotech. Office of Tech. Assessment, Washington, 1986-89, mem. adv. com. on govt. policies and pharm. R & D, 1989-93, mem. com. to study drug abuse medications devel. and rsch., 1993-95; mem. com. on contraceptive R & D, Inst. Medicine, Washington, 1994-96; trustee Brown U., 1998—. Recipient Disting. Svc. award Fed. Trade Commn., Washington, 1972, Award of Merit FDA, Rockville, 1981, Sec.'s Spl. citation HHS, Washington, 1981, Ind. award Associated. Alumni of Brown U., 1991. Mem. ABA (mem. spl. com. to study FTC 1988-89), Com. of 200, Va. Law Sch. Found. (bd. dirs.), Women's Legal Def. Fund (bd. dirs.). Office: Buc & Beardsley 919 18th St NW Ste 600 Washington DC 20006-5507*

BUCCIERO, JOSEPH MARIO, JR., executive consulting firm; b. Phila., Mar. 27, 1948; s. Joseph Mario Sr. and Carmela (Biscari) B.; m. Nancy Louise Arnquist, Aug. 19, 1972; children: Paul Joseph, Mark Benjamin. BS, Villanova U., 1969. Software programmer, project software engr. Leeds and Northrup Co., North Wales, Pa., 1969-72; applications engr. Leeds and Northrup Co., North Wales, 1972-74; systems cons. Macro Corp., Horsham, Pa., 1974-76; consulting engr. Macro Corp., Horsham, 1976-82, sr. consulting engr., 1982-89; strategic bus. unit mgr. Cegelec ESCA, Bellevue, Wash., 1989-90; prin. cons. KEMA-ECC, Fairfax, Va., 1990—; bus. area mgr. KEMA Consulting, Fairfax, 1991—; v.p. KEMA Consulting, Inc., Fairfax, 1992—. Contbr. articles to profl. jours. Ch. coun. pres. Little Zion Luth. Ch., Telford, Pa., 1980-85. Mem. IEEE (sr. mem.). Avocations: bowling, down hill skiing, traveling. Home: 6619 Mccambell Cluster Centreville VA 20120-3731

BUCCINO, ALPHONSE, university dean emeritus, consultant; b. N.Y.C., Mar. 14, 1931; s. Aniello and Anna (Tino) B.; m. Estelle Marie Ambrose, Mar. 22, 1953; 1 child, Daniel Laurence. BS, U. Chgo., 1958, MS, 1959, PhD, 1967. Mem. faculty Roosevelt U., Chgo., 1961-63; head math dept. DePaul U., Chgo., 1963-70; sci. edn. adminstr. NSF, Washington, 1970-84; dean edn., prof. U. Ga., Athens, 1984-94; edn. advisor Office of Sci. and Tech. Policy, Exec. Office of Pres., Washington, 1992-93; pres. Contemporary Comm. Inc., Bethesda, Md., 1994—; cons. innovation mgmt. Author, editor conception and design numerous planning and policy documents, official org. pubs. Capt. USMC, 1951-54, Korea. Woodrow Wilson Found. fellow, 1958, NSF fellow, 1959-61. Fellow AAAS; mem. Am. Math. Soc., Nat. Coun. Tchrs. of Math., Am. Ednl. Rsch. Assn. (mem. fin. com. 1976-79). Roman Catholic. Avocations: bicycling, cooking. Home and Office: 5615 Glenwood Rd Bethesda MD 20817-6727

BUCELLA, DONNA A., federal official; b. Bayside, N.Y., June 14, 1956. Student, St. John's U., 1974-76; BA in Sociology with distinction, U. Va., 1978; JD, U. Miami, 1983. Bar: Fla. 1984, U.S. Ct. Mil. Appeals 1985, Va. 1986. Paralegal Dickstein, Shapiro & Morin, Washington, 1978-80; criminal def. atty. U.S. Army Judge Advocacy Gen. Corps., Ft. Belvoir, Va., 1984-86; litigation atty. U.S. Army Judge Advocacy Gen. Corps., Washington, 1986-87; with Asst. U.S. Atty. So. Dist. Fla., 1987-93, dep. chief major crimes, 1992, dep. chief spl. investigations, 1992-93; dir. Office Legal Edn. Exec. Office U.S. Attys. U.S. Dept. Justice, Washington, 1993-94, prin. dep. dir., 1994-97, dir., 1997—; interim U.S. Atty. Mid. Dist. Fla., 1994. Mem. ABA, Fla. Bar (mil. law com. 1985-87, 93), Phi Alpha Delta. Office: Exec Office US Attys Main Justice Bldg Rm 1619 10th & Pennsylvania Ave NW Washington DC 20530

BUCHAN, ALAN BRADLEY, rail transportation executive, consultant; b. N.Y.C., Mar. 1, 1936; s. Harold Bradley and Grace Viola (Lahrs) B.; m. Janet Lucille Riemersma, Feb. 20, 1960; children: Robert Michael, Richard Steven, Kathleen Ann. BCE, Norwich U., 1957; MLA, U. Pa., 1992, cert. in Hist. Preservation, 1992. Track supr. The Pa. R.R., various locations, 1964-66; indsl. engr. The Pa. R.R., Phila., 1966-68; tng. supr. Penn Cen. Transp. Co., Phila., 1968-69; dir. tng. and safety Franklin Mint, Inc., Franklin Center, Pa., 1969-71; dir. mgmt. devel. N.Y.C. Transit Authority, Bklyn., 1971-72; sr. cons. Cole, Warren and Long, Phila., 1972-74; sr. cons. Transp. and Distbn. Assocs., Media, Pa., 1974-77, v.p., 1977-86, pres., 1986-89; pres. TSD, Inc., Phila., 1986-89; v.p. transp. Day & Zimmermann, Inc., Phila., 1986-89; prin. Alan Buchan & Assocs., Mount Laurel, N.J., 1989—; vis. lectr. U. Pa., 1993; open space program adminstr. County Burlington, N.J., 1992-98. V.p., trustee Whitesbog Preservation Trust, 1993-97; vice chmn. adv. bd. N.J. Historic Sites Coun. Capt. U.S. Army, 1957-64. Mem. N.J. Assn. of Environtl. Commns. (trustee), Chi Epsilon. Republican. Episcopalian. Avocation: model making. Home: 785 Cornwallis Dr Mount Laurel NJ 08054-3209

BUCHAN, DOUGLAS CHARLES, petroleum company executive, government official; b. Bklyn., Aug. 4, 1936; s. Charles J. and Amelia P. (Petraca) B.; student U. Fla., 1954-56; m. Beverly Ann Wilcox, Mar. 7, 1970; 1 son, Paul Douglas. Pres., Buchan Gas Co., St. Petersburg, Fla., 1955-86, Buchan Oil Co., St. Petersburg, 1966-89, Grill Parts Distbrs., 1982-86, Site Mgmt., 1983—; dep. asst. sec. energy U.S. Dept. Energy, Washington, 1989—. Pres., Pinellas County Republican Ivory Club; chmn. Fla. campaign George Bush for Pres.; chmn. Pinellas campaign Reagan-Bush; mem. U.S. Senate Bus. Adv. Com., 1984—. Served to 1st lt. U.S. Army, 1958-65. Mem. Nat. Oil Jobbers Council, Nat. Liquified Petroleum Gas Assn., Fla. Petroleum Marketers Assn. (v.p.), Oil Fuel Inst. Fla. (pres., chmn. bd.). Episcopalian. Club: St. Petersburg Yacht. Home: 1067 42nd Ave NE Saint Petersburg FL 33703-5235 Office: US Dept Energy 1000 Independence Ave SW Washington DC 20585-0001

BUCHAN, JONATHAN EDWARD, JR., lawyer; b. Mullins, S.C., Sept. 1, 1950; s. Jonathan Edward and Margaret Alice (Liles) B.; m. Suzette Rogers Phillips, Nov. 22, 1986; 1 stepchild, Geoffrey Eliot Eloge; 1 child, Caroline Phillips. AB magna cum laude, Princeton U., 1972; JD, Duke U., 1978. Bar: N.C. 1978. Co-founder, sr. editor, Osceola News Weekly, Columbia, S.C., 1973-74; govt. reporter Charlotte Observer, Columbia, S.C., 1974-75; govt. editor Charlotte (N.C.) Observer, 1983-84; assoc. Smith Helms Mulliss & Moore and predecessor Helms Mulliss & Johnston, Charlotte, 1978-83; ptnr. Smith Helms Mulliss & Moore and predecessor Helms Mulliss & Johnson, Charlotte, 1984—; mem. adj. faculty dept. mass media law Wake Forest Law Sch., 1992-94, 97-98; bd. dirs. Legal Svcs. for So. Piedmont, Inc., 1993-98. Co-author: 50-State Survey of Libel Law, N.C. Sect., 1981—; contbg. author: North Carolina Media Law Handbook, 1992. Pres., bd. dirs. Hospice at Charlotte, Inc., 1982-88. Mem. N.C. Bar Assn. (chmn. news media-adminstrn. of justice coun. 1985-87). Avocations: fly fishing, tennis, reading. Home: 2342 Thetford Ct Charlotte NC 28211-3268 Office: Smith Helms Mulliss & Moore PO Box 31247 201 N Tryon St Ste 3000 Charlotte NC 28202-1157

BUCHAN, RUSSELL PAUL, publisher, gas company executive, entrepreneur; b. St. Petersburg, Fla., May 24, 1947; s. Charles Joseph and Amelia (Petraca) B. BS in Econs. magna cum laude, Stetson U., 1969; MA, Vanderbilt U., 1975. Asst. to pub. Trend Publs., Tampa, Fla., 1971-74; book editor South Mag., Tampa, 1973-74; owner Buchan Gas Co., St. Petersburg, 1968—; pub. Buchan Publs., St. Petersburg, 1980—; pres. Buchan Gas Co., Grills Parts Dist., 1986—. Host Radio Sta. WTAN, Clearwater, Fla.; co-author: Florida: A Guide to the Best Restaurants, Resorts, Hotels, 1992, Florida Weekends, 1991, rev. edit., 1994; pub.: Florida's Best Beach Vacations, Florida County Inns, 1993. Mem. Pinellas County Gas Adv. Bd., 1979-88, vice-chmn., 1982-83, chmn. 1986-87; bd. dirs. Eckerd Coll. Library Friends, 1971-85, 91-95, chmn., 1982. Named Res. Grand champion Fla. State Barbecue Championship, 1995; Woodrow Wilson fellow, 1969. Mem. Pinellas County Gas Assn. (sec.-treas. 1977-78, pres. 1979-80), Fla. Young Gassers (dist. dir. 1979-81), Nat. LP Gas Assn., Fla. LP Gas Assn. (dir. 1979-81), Fla. Mag. Assn. (treas. 1974-75), Tampa Bay Econs. Forum, Kansas City Barbecue Soc., Internat. Wine and Food Soc. (br. chmn. St. Petersburg 1979-80), Confrerie de la Chaine des Rotisseurs, Wine Friends, WineBuffs, Brotherhood Knights of Vine, Order of Dali. Republican. Roman Catholic. Office: Buchan Gas Co 6150 49th St N Saint Petersburg FL 33709-2116

BUCHANAN, BENNIE LEE GREGORY, special education educator; b. Bells, Tenn., Mar. 24, 1928; d. Walter Homer and Hassie Mae (Herron) Gregory; m. Shannon Mill Buchanan, Sept. 10, 1951 (dec. 1989); children: Michael Keith, Shannon M. Jr., Sandra J., Greg ory E. Student, A&I State Coll., 1948-51; BA, Lane Coll., 1955; MEd, Memphis State U., 1977. Tchr. Haywood County Bd. Edn., Brownsville, Tenn., 1956-59, Hardeman County Bd. Edn., Bolivar, Tenn., 1959-89; owner, dir. Bennie's Family Day Care Home, Bolivar, 1991—, tchr. jr. high sch. spl. edn., 1972-88; owner, dir. Bennies Group Day Care Home, Bolivar, 1993—. Den leader Bolivar area Boy Scouts Am., 1972-74; chair Jr. High Band Boosters, Bolivar, 1973. Mem. ASCD, NAACP, Hardeman County Homemakers Club, Eastern Star, Daus. of Isis. Democrat. Baptist. Avocations: reading, sewing, crafts. Home: 431 S Jones St Bolivar TN 38008-2547

BUCHANAN, BRUCE, metal artist, photographer; b. Washington, Sept. 10, 1947; s. Lloyd and Marguerite Belva (Smith) B. Student, Long Beach C.C., U. New Orleans. Artist; Former deep-sea diver, pipe welder nationwide and P.R.; tchr. diving for Mexican govt., Veracruz, 1982. Mem., bd. dirs. Unitarian Universalist Ch., chmn. social action com., literacy vol.; founder Free Meal Kitchen. With U.S. Army, 1974. Mem. Art Dirs. of Portland, Artists and Blacksmiths N.Am. Avocations: taking care of abused and abandoned animals, helping disadvantaged and oppressed people, creating unique, outrageous things of beauty. Office: Big City Enterprises PO Box 556 Bar Mills ME 04004-0556

BUCHANAN, BRUCE, II, political science educator; b. Shelby, Mont., July 28, 1945; s. Neil and Dorothy Jean (Gallup) B.; m. Susan Safford Bright, June 10, 1964 (div. June 1976); m. Stephanie Ann Sokolewicz, Jan. 3, 1981; children: Kathryn Elaine, Douglas Neil, Jacqueline May. BA, Stanford U., 1967; MA, Yale U., 1969; MPhil, 1970, PhD, 1972. Prof. U. Ga., Athens, 1973-74, U. Tex., Austin, 1974—. Author: The Presidential Experience, 1978, The Citizens Presidency, 1987,Electing A President, 1991, Renewing Presidential Politics, 1996. Exec. dir. Markle Commn. on Media and Electorate, 1988-90; rsch. dir. Markle Found. Presdl. Election Study, 1992, dir. Markle Presdl. Watch, 1996. Mem. Am. Polit. Sci. Assn. (award for best paper on presidency 1997), Presidency Rsch. Group. Avocations: cello, sports, gardening. Home: 1304 Wilshire Blvd Austin TX 78722-1127 Office: U Tex Dept Govt Austin TX 78712-1087

BUCHANAN, CALVIN D., lawyer; b. Okolona, Ms., Feb. 15, 1958; m. Donna C. BA, U. Miss., 1980, JD, 1983. Bar: Miss. 1983, U.S. Mil. Ct. Rev. 1983, U.S. Dist. Ct. (no. dist.) 1983, U.S. Ct. Appeals (5th cir.) 1991. 1st Lt. MS Army NG, 1980-83; commd. U.S. Army, 1983; advanced through grades to capt., 1990; maj. Individual Ready Res., 1990—; asst. U.S. atty. No. Dist. Miss., 1990-97, U.S. atty., 1997—. Leonard B. Melvin scholar U. Miss. Sch. Law. Mem. Nat. Bar Assn., Miss. Bar Assn., Magnolia Bar Assn., Lafayette County Bar Assn., U. Miss. Alumni Assn. (mem. adv. coun. 1988-97), Inns of Court, Order of Omega, Phi Eta Sigma. Baptist. Office: US Atty No Dist Miss Federal Bldg & U.S.Courthouse PO Box 886 Oxford MS 38655-0886*

BUCHANAN, DAVID ROYAL, associate dean; b. Mansfield, Ohio, Mar. 28, 1934; s. Royal S. and Hazel M. (Sanders) B.; m. Sara M. Meister, Dec. 28, 1957; children: Susan, Linda, Ann, Christopher. BS with honors, Capital U., 1956; PhD, Ohio State U., 1962. Rsch. chemist Chemstrand Rsch. Ctr. Inc., Durham, N.C., 1962-67; sr. rsch. chemist Phillips Petroleum Co., Bartlesville, Okla., 1967-70; rsch. project mgr. Phillips Fibers Corp., Greenville, S.C., 1970-75; assoc. prof., design & environ. analysis Cornell U., Ithaca, N.Y., 1975-78; prof., dept. head, textile materials & mgmt. N.C. State U., Raleigh, 1978-83, prof., 1983-88, assoc. dean, coll. textiles, 1988—; mem. edit. bd. Jour. Nonwovens Rsch., 1989—. Editor: Robotics and Automation in the Textile and Applied Industries, 1986, Automation in the Textile Industry--from Fibers to Apparel, 1995; editor in chief Textile Progress, 1992—; contbr. articles to profl. jours. Mem. AAAS, Am. Phys. Soc. (high polymer physics), Am. Crystallography Assn., Soc. Mfg. Engrs., Textile Inst., Fiber Soc., Sigma Xi, Phi Kappa Phi, Phi Lambda Upsilon, Phi Psi. Home: 105 Lochwood Dr W Cary NC 27511-9741 Office: NC State U Coll Textiles PO Box 8301 2501 Research Dr Raleigh NC 27695-8301*

BUCHANAN, DENNIS MICHAEL, manufacturing and holding company executive; b. Houston, July 24, 1945; s. James Riley and Mary Elizabeth (Way) B.; children from previous marriage: Keith Michael, Monica Lynn. BBA in Mktg., U. Tex., Arlington, 1971; grad. advanced mgmt. program, Harvard U., 1982. Mdse. mgr. Continental Grain Co., Sao Paulo, Brazil, 1976-79; comml. mgr. Anderson Clayton S.A., Sao Paulo, Brazil, 1974-76, v.p., dir., 1979-84, exec. v.p., dir., 1984; group v.p., dir. Anderson Clayton & Co., Houston, 1984-87; pres., chief exec. officer Long Reach Holdings, Long Reach Mfg. & Rol-Lift Corp., Houston, 1987—; pres., bd. dirs. Brudi Pacific Pty. LTD, Adelaide, Australia, 1996—; bd. dirs., chmn. soybean rules com. Sao Paulo Commodity Exchange, 1981-84. Mem. Nat. Cottonseed Products Assn. (investment com. 985-87), Brazilian Oilseed Crushers Assn. (exec. dir. 1979-84), Nat. Cotton Coun., Material Handling Equipment Distbrs. Assn., Indsl. Truck Assn. (assoc.), Forum Club, Univ. Club. Republican. Methodist. Avocations: tennis, sailing, golf. Office: Long Reach Holdings PO Box 45069 Houston TX 77245*

BUCHANAN, EDNA, journalist; b. Paterson, N.J.. Journalist Miami Beach (Fla.) Daily Sun, 1965-70; became journalist The Miami (Fla.) Herald, 1970. Author: Carr: Five Years of Rape and Murder, 1979, The Corpse Had a Familiar Face: Covering America's Hottest Beat, 1987, Nobody Lives Forever, 1990, Never Let Them See You Cry: More From Miami, America's Hottest Beat, 1992, Contents Under Pressure, 1992, Miami, It's Murder, 1994; contbr. articles to popular mags. Recipient Green Eye Shade award Soc. Profl. Journalists, 1982, Pulitzer prize for gen. reporting, 1986. Mem. United Ch. of Christ. Office: care Hyperion Books 114 5th Ave New York NY 10011-5604*

BUCHANAN, EDWARD A., education educator; b. Newark, Aug. 28, 1937; s. Osborne B. and Edna Dorothy (Weber) B.; m. Gladys J. Buchanan, Aug. 28, 1965; children Roger, Becky. AB, Rutgers U., 1959; MRE, N.Y. Theol. Sem., 1962; PhD, So. Bapt. Theol. Sem., 1970. Tchr. Cen. Sch., Middlesex, N.J.; assoc. prof. psychology and edn. Grand Rapids (Mich.) Bapt. Coll.; dean of acad. affairs, prof. Lancaster (Pa.) Bible Coll.; prof. edn., dir. continuing edn. Bethel Theol. Sem., St. Paul; prof. edn. Southeastern Bapt. Theol. Sem., Wake Forest, N.C. Contbr. articles to profl. jours. Mem. bd. dirs. Trinity Acad., Raleigh, N.C. Mem. APA, ASCD, Am. Ednl. Rsch. Assn., Nat. Soc. Study of Edn. Home: 1113 Silent Brook Rd Wake Forest NC 27587-7145

BUCHANAN, ENID JANE, healthcare professional, housing administrator; b. Winnipeg, Man., Can., June 20, 1950; came to U.S., 1987; d. William Wallace and Marguerite (Oastler) B.; m. Malcolm Patrick O'Malley, Nov. 15, 1986; children: Kevin, Brian, William. BA with honours, Queen's U., Kingston, Ont.,Can., 1972; MA in Urban and Regional Planning, U. B.C., Vancouver, Can., 1979. Gen. mgr. Inuit Non Profit Housing Corp., Ottawa, Ont., 1976-78; sr. policy analyst Alta. Housing and Pub. Works, Edmonton, Can., 1978-80; sr. intergovtl. officer Fed. and Intergovtl. Affairs, Edmonton, 1980-82; dir. policy programs Ministry Lands, Parks and Housing, Victoria, B.C., 1982-85; dir. policy planning B.C. Housing and Cmty. Rels., Vancouver, 1985-90; asst. dir. housing Dept. Cmty. Trade and Econ. Devel., Olympia, Wash., 1994-97; vice chair Greater Lakes Mental Healthcare, 1997—, also bd. dirs.; bd. dirs. Wash. Cmty. Reinvestment Assocs., Wash. State Housing Fin. Commn., 1994-97. Mem. program com. Communities in Schs., Lakewood, 1997—; mem. steering com. Lakewood (Wash.) Cmty. Summit, 1992-93; mem. univ. scholarship selection com. CMHC, 1986-90, chair Can. housing awards com., 1990-91; bd. dirs. Can. Housing Design Coun., 1984-85; chmn. internat. devel. com. Edmonton YMCA, 1981-82. Can. Mortgage and Housing Corp. grad. fellow, 1975; B.C. grad fellow, 1974. Home: 12607 Gravelly Lake Dr SW Lakewood WA 98499-1425

BUCHANAN, JAMES JUNKIN, classics educator; b. Pitts., Mar. 7, 1925; s. John Grier and Charity (Packer) B.; m. Joanne Harriett Cherrington, Mar. 31, 1951; children—Susan Grier, Edison Cherrington, Constance P. Leyden, James Junkin, Charles Sturm. A.B., Princeton U., 1946, Ph.D., 1954; M.B.A., Harvard U., 1948. Investment advisor First Boston Corp, Pitts., 1948-51; asst. prof. classics Princeton U., N.J., 1953-60, dir. tchr. placement, 1957-60, sec. schs. com., 1957-60; dean Coll. Arts and Scis. So. Meth. U., Dallas, 1960-63; chmn. dept. classics Trinity U., San Antonio, 1963-64; prof. classical langs. Tulane U., New Orleans, 1964-87, prof. emeritus, 1987—. Author: Theorika, 1962; translator: Zosimus: Historia Nova, 1967; editor Ency. Americana, 1954-60; editor and translator: Boethius: Consolation of Philosophy, 1957; contbr. articles to profl. jours. Trustee, Trinity Sch., New Orleans, 1967-76. Served with USNR, 1942-43. Page fellow in classics, 1953-54. Mem. Classical Assn. Eng., Classical Assn. of Middle West and South, Archaeol. Inst. Am., Am. Philos. Assn., Colonial Club (gov. 1956-61) (Princeton), Harvard-Yale-Princeton Club (Pitts.), Princeton Club (N.Y.C.), Univ. Club (Pitts.), Boston Club (New Orleans), Phi Beta Kappa (pres. La. Alpha chpt. 1974-75, 85-87). Democrat. Episcopalian. Avocations: travel; tennis; horseback riding; music. Home: The King Edward 4609 Bayard St Apt 81 Pittsburgh PA 15213-2711

BUCHANAN, JAMES MCGILL, economist, educator; b. Murfreesboro, TN, Oct. 2, 1919; s. James McGill and Lila (Scott) B.; m. Anne Bakke, Oct. 5, 1945. BS, Middle Tenn. State Coll., 1940; MA, U. Tenn., 1941; PhD, U. Chgo., 1948; D honoris causa, U. Giessen, 1982, U. Zurich, 1984, George Mason U., U. Valencia, New U. Lisbon, 1987, Ball State U., 1988, City U., London, 1988, Lycoming Coll., 1992, Free U., Rome, 1993, U. Bucharest, 1994, Acad. Econ. Studies, Romania, 1994, U. Catania, 1994, U. Porto,

1995, U. Valladolid (Spain), 1996. Assoc. prof. U. Tenn., 1948-50, prof. econs., 1950-51; prof. Fla. State U., 1951-56; prof. U. Va., 1956-62, Paul G. McIntyre prof. econs., 1962-68, chmn. dept., 1956-62; prof. UCLA, 1968-69; univ. disting. prof. Va. Poly. Inst., 1969-83, George Mason U., 1983—; adv. dir. Ctr. for Pub. Choice, 1969—; Fulbright rsch. scholar, Italy, 1955-56; Ford Faculty rsch. fellow, 1959-60; Fulbright vis. prof. Cambridge U., 1961-62. Author: (with C.L. Allen and M.R. Colberg) Prices, Income and Public Policy, 954, Public Principles of Public Debt, 1958, The Public Finances, 1960, Fiscal Theory and Political Economy, 1960, (with G. Tullock) The Calculus of Consent, 1962, Public Finance in Democratic Process, 1966, The Demand and Supply of Public Goods, 1968, Cost and Choice, 1969, (with N. Devletoglou) Academia in Anarchy, 1970; Editor: (with R. Tollison) Theory of Public Choice, 1972, (with G.F. Thirlby) LSE Essays on Cost, 1973, The Limits of Liberty, 1975, (with R. Wagner) Democracy in Deficit, 1977, Freedom in Constitutional Contract, 1978, What Should Economists Do?, 1979, (with G. Brennan) The Power to Tax, 1980; (with G. Brennan) The Reason of Rules, 1985; Liberty Market and State, 1985, Economics: Between Predictive Science and Moral Philosophy, 1987, Explorations in Constitutional Economics, 1989, Economics and Ethics of Constitutional Order, 1991, Better than Plowing, 1992, Ethics and Economic Progress, 1994; editor: (with Yong Yoon) Return to Increasing Returns, 1994, Post-Socialist Political Economy, 1997, (with R. Congleton) Politics By Principle, Not Interest, 1998; contbr. articles to profl. jours. Lt. USNR, 1941-46. Decorated Bronze Star; recipient Seidman award, 1984, Nobel Prize in Econs., 1986. Fellow Am. Acad. Arts and Scis.; mem. Am. Econ. Assn. (exec. com. 1966-69, v.p. 1971, dist. fellow 1983—), So. Econ. Assn. (pres. 1963), Western Econ. Assn. (pres. 1983), Mt. Pelerin Soc. (pres. 1984-86). Home: PO Box 4 Blacksburg VA 24063-1021 Office: George Mason U Buchanan House Mail Stop 1 E6 Fairfax VA 22030-4443

BUCHANAN, JOHN, city official; b. Chgo., Jan. 5, 1924; m. Lorraine Halbe, 1947; children: Patricia, John. Grad., Ill. Inst. Technology, Chgo. Alderman 10th ward Chgo., 1963-71; coord. econ. devel. Office of Mayor, Chgo., 1972-77; aide Office of Alderman 10th ward, Chgo., 1981-91, alderman, 1991-99; staff mgr., title ins. rep. Metro. Life Ins. Co., Chgo., 1949-63. Bd. dirs. Southeast Devel. Commn., East Side C. of C., South Chgo. YMCA, Southeast Cmty. Youth Svc. Bd., Hegewisch C. of C., South Chgo. C. of C.; vol. Boy Scouts Am., Chgo. Assn. for Retarded. Mem. Am. Heart Assn., Chgo. Heart Assn., East Side Hist. Soc., Kiwanis. Office: 9618 S Commercial Ave Chicago IL 60617-5021

BUCHANAN, JOHN DONALD, retired health physicist, radiochemist; b. Mesa, Ariz., Oct. 1, 1927; s. John Freeborn and Marguerite (Brimhall) B.; m. Donna Marie Smith, Aug. 27, 1955; children—Margaret MacNeil, John Michael, Andrew Tierney, David Brimhall. B.S. in Chemistry, U. Ariz., 1949. Diplomate: Am. Bd. Health Physics, Nat. Cert. Commn. in Chemistry and Chem. Engring. Sr. chemist Tracerlab, Inc., Richmond, Calif., 1950-59; staff asso. Gen. Atomic div. Gen. Dynamics Corp., San Diego, 1959-62; mgr. nuclear applications and measurements Teledyne-Isotopes Co., Palo Alto, Calif., 1962-71; mgr. applied research Internat. Nutronics Inc., Palo Alto, 1971-73; supr. radiol. monitoring programs NUS Corp., Rockville, Md., 1973-75; sr. health physicist, radiochemist U.S. Nuclear Regulatory Commn., Washington, 1975-94. Author papers on radiation protection, radioanalytical chemistry, radioactivity measurements, radioisotope applications. Served with USNR, 1945-46. Recipient Meritorious Service award U.S. Nuclear Regulatory Commn., 1981. Fellow AAAS, Am. Inst. Chemists, Health Physics Soc.; mem. Am. Nuclear Soc., Am. Chem. Soc., Soc. for Risk Analysis, Am. Acad. Health Physics, Phi Lambda Upsilon, Phi Delta Theta. Home: 7508 Dew Wood Dr Rockville MD 20855-1007

BUCHANAN, JOHN E., JR., museum director; b. Nashville, July 24, 1953. Exec. dir. Portland (Oreg.) Art Mus., 1994—. Office: Portland Art Museum 1219 SW Park Ave Portland OR 97205-2486

BUCHANAN, JOHN MACHLIN, biochemistry educator; b. Winamac, Ind., Sept. 29, 1917; s. Harry James and Eunice Blanche (Miller) B.; m. Elsa Nilsby, Dec. 11, 1948; children—Claire Louise, Stephen James, Lisa Renee, Peter Nilsson. A.B., De Pauw U., 1938, D.Sc., 1975; M.S., U. Mich., 1939, D.Sc., 1961; Ph.D., Harvard, 1943. Instr. dept. physiol. chemistry Sch. Medicine U. Pa., 1943-46, asst. prof., 1946-49, asso. prof., 1949-50, prof., 1950-53; NRC fellow Med. Nobel Inst., Stockholm, 1946-48; prof., head div. biochemistry dept. biology Mass. Inst. Tech., 1953-67, Wilson prof. biochemistry, 1967-88, Wilson prof. emeritus, 1988—; lectr. Harvey Soc., 1958. Mem. editorial bd.: Jour. Biol. Chemistry, 1961-67, Jour. Am. Chemistry Soc, 1961-72, Physiol. Revs, 1957-60, 65-71. Civilian with Nat. Def. Research Com., 1943; mem. subcom. blood and related substances NRC, 1951-55, mem. med. fellowship bd., 1954—; mem. sci. adv. bd. Boston Biomed. Rsch. Inst., 1975-93, Papanicoulaou Cancer Research Inst., 1975-81. Fellow Guggenheim Meml. Found., 1964-65; leave of absence to Salk Inst. Biol. Studies LaJolla, Calif. Mem. Am. Soc. Biol. Chemists (sec. 1969-72), Am. Chem. Soc. (Eli Lilly award in biol. chemistry 1951), Internat. Union Biochemists (mem. nat. com.), Nat. Acad. Scis., Am. Acad. Arts and Scis., Sigma Xi. Home: 56 Meriam St Lexington MA 02420-3622

BUCHANAN, JOHN MACLENNAN, Canadian provincial official; b. Sydney, N.S., Can., Apr. 22, 1931; s. Murdoch William and Flora Isabel (Campbell) B.; m. Mavis Forsyth, Sept. 1, 1954; children: Murdoch, Travis, Nichola, Natalie, Natasha. BSc, Mt. Allison U., cert. engring., 1954; LLB, Dalhousie U., Halifax, N.S., 1958; DEng (hon.), N.S. Tech. Coll., 1979; LLD (hon.), St. Mary's U., 1982; DCL, Mt. Allison U., 1981; LLD (hon.), St. Francis Xavier U., 1986; D Polit. Sci. (hon.), U. de St. Anne, 1989. Bar: Called to bar, created queen's counsel 1972. Pvt. practice Halifax, 1958-71; mem. N.S. Legislative Assembly, Halifax, from 1967; min. public works, then fisheries; premier of N.S., 1978-90; created Queen's Counsel, 1972; leader Progressive Conservative Party in N.S., from 1971; elected mem. legis. assembly for Halifax-Atlantic provinces gen. election, 1967, 70, 74, 78, 81, 84, 88, apptd. Privy Coun., 1972; apptd. to Senate of Can., 1990, bd. dirs. Legal Aid for N.S. Barristers Assn. Active Boy Scouts Am., pres. exec. oun., chmn. policy bd., 1978-90. Mem. Can. Bar Assn., N.S. Barristers Assn., Can.-U.S. Parliamentary Assn. (bd. dirs.), Royal Can. Legion, Buchanan Soc. of Glasgow, Scotland (bd. dirs.), Halifax Club, City Club, Lions, Masons, Shriners, Odd Fellows. Mem. United Ch. Can. Office: The Senate, Ottawa, ON Canada

BUCHANAN, LEE ANN, public relations executive; b. Albuquerque, July 6, 1955; d. William Henry Buchanan and Juanita Irene (Pilgrim) Wood; m. Charles Stanton Wood, Jan. 17, 1987. BA, U. Calif., Irvine, 1977. Exec. asst. to Congressman William Thomas, U.S. Ho. of Reps., Washington, 1979-83; dep. chief staff Gov. George Deukmejian, Sacramento, 1983-84; sr. v.p., ptnr. Nelson Comm., Costa Mesa, Calif., 1985-95. Bd. govs. Rep. Assocs. of Orange County, 1985—; founding sec. Orange County Young Reps., 1985. Mem. Internat. Assn. Bus. Communicators, Am. Assn. Polit. Cons., Pub. Relations Soc. Am., U. Calif.-Irvine Alumni Assn. Avocations: skiing, hiking. Address: PO Box 1741 Mammoth Lakes CA 93546-1741*

BUCHANAN, LOVELL, entertainer; b. Ephrata, Pa., Mar. 22, 1949; s. Virginia (Eidemiller) Windham; m. Marie Veronica Sheetz. BS cum laude, Millersville (Pa.) U., 1977. Cert. tchr., Pa. Machinist Alcoa Corp., Lancaster, Pa., 1973-74; tchr. Manheim Twp. Sch. Dist., Lancaster, 1978-81, Downingtown (Pa.) Sch. Dist., 1982-83; tech. trainer Hamilton Tech. Co., Lancaster, 1984-88; pres. FunFoolery Prodns. Creator Dimmer the Million Dollar Robot, Prof. Funfoolery character, Chuckles the Clown (permanent collection Clown Hall of Fame, Delevan, Wis.), Whistling Willie, Chef Percy Produce, Juan D. Waiter, Monsieur Von Juggle; sculptor: It's Magic, 1978, Optical Illusions, 1998; permanent collections include Magician's Hall of Fame, Hollywood, Calif., Ripley's Believe It or Not Mus., Atlantic City, N.J. With USN, 1968-72, Vietnam. Decorated Gallantry Cross. Mem. Internat. Brotherhood Magicians, Soc. Am. Magicians, Internat. Jugglers Assn., World Clown Assn., Humane League (Appreciation award, 1985), Epsilon Pi Tau. Republican. Home: 2726 Chapel Rd Lancaster PA 17603-5917

BUCHANAN, PATRICK JOSEPH, journalist; b. Washington, Nov. 2, 1938; s. William Baldwin and Catherine E. (Crum) B.; m. Shelley Ann Scarney, May 8, 1971. A.B. in English cum laude, Georgetown U., 1961; M.S. in Journalism, Columbia U., 1962. Editorial writer St. Louis Globe Democrat, 1962-64, asst. editorial editor, 1964-66; exec. asst. to Richard M. Nixon, 1966-69; spl. asst. to Pres. Nixon, 1969-73; cons. to Presidents Nixon and Ford, 1973-74; syndicated columnist N.Y. Times Spl. Features, 1975-78, Chgo. Tribune-N.Y. News Syndicate, 1978-85, Tribune Media Svcs., 1987-91, 93-95; commentator NBC Radio Network, 1978-82; asst. to Pres., dir. communications White House, Washington, 1985-87; co-host Buchanan-Braden Show, Sta. WRC, 1978-83, Crossfire (TV show) Cable News Network, 1982-85, 87-91, 93-95, 97—; panelist The McLaughlin Group, NBC/PBS, 1982-85, 88-92, 97—; moderator Capital Gang (TV Show) Cable News Network, 1988-92; editor-in-chief newsletter PJB-From the Right, 1990-91; candidate for Rep. Nomination for Pres., 1992, 96; chmn. The Am. Cause, 1993-95, 97—, Pat Buchanan & Co., Mut. Broadcasting System, 1993-95. Author: The New Majority, 1973, Conservative Votes, Liberal Victories, 1975, Right from the Beginning, 1988, 90, (intro.) America Asleep, 1991, Barry Goldwater, The Conscience of a Conservative, 1990, The Great Betrayal, 1998. Mem. President's Commn. White House Fellowships, 1969-73; v.p. Am. Council of Young Polit. Leaders, 1974-75, 76-79. Named Knight of Malta, 1987. Republican. Roman Catholic. *

BUCHANAN, RAY ALLEN, clergyman; b. Houston, Jan. 8, 1947; s. Wilbur Allen and Louise (Zwahr) B.; m. Marian Kelly, Aug. 5, 1967; children: Peter Andrew, Amy Krysteen. BA, U. N.C., Wilmington, 1972; MDiv, Southeastern Bapt. Theol. Seminary, 1976; DD, Shenandoah Coll., 1990. Ordained to ministry United Meth. Ch., 1977. Pastor North Mecklenburg United Meth. Ch., Union Level, Va., 1973-77, Oak Hall (Va.) United Meth. Ch., 1977-79, Bedford (Va.) Cir. United Meth. Ch., 1979-81; co-founder, co-dir. Soc. St. Andrew, Big Island, Va., 1979-97; founder, dir. Stop Hunger Now, 1998—; mem. Va. ann. conf. United Meth. Ch. Co-editor Gleanings, 1986; co-author: Prepare the Way of the Coed, 1986; author: Pass the Potatoes, 1987, Bones Will Not Suffice: Poems for the Dead of Night, 1997; contbr. articles, poems to various publs. Pres. bd. trustees Sedalia Fin Arts Ctr.; chaplain Clan Buchanan Soc. in U.S.; commr. Mid-Atlantic Region Clan Buchanan Soc. Internat.; pres. Clar Innis Found.; mem. nat. com. for World Food Day; co-organizer Va. Congress on Hunger; bd. dirs. Soc. St. Andrew, Mission Caribe, Christian Alliance for Humanitarian Relief. Recipient Disting. Alumnus award U. N.C.-Wilmington, 1985, Real Am. Hero award Maxwell House, 1992, Lynchburg Humanitarian award NCCJ Assn. Christians and Jews, 1998, Nat. Humanitarian award Caring Inst., 1998. Avocations: writing, photography, outdoor activities. Home: 3082 Union Ch Rd Thaxton VA 24174 *Of all the obscenity spawned by an immoral society, nothing compares to the vulgarity of hunger. Erasing this moral outrage is the greatest challenge of our age.*

BUCHANAN, RICHARD KENT, electronics company executive; b. Schenectady, Sept. 10, 1951; s. Richard Linton and Jeanette (Dunn) B.; m. Diane Carolyn Laffler, Oct. 14, 1984; 1 child, Lindsay Sarah. BSEE, USAF Acad., 1973; MBA, Harvard U., 1980. Commd. 2d lt. USAF, 1973, advanced through grades to capt., 1976; resigned, 1978; mgmt. cons. Bain and Co., Boston, 1979-82; corp. dir. strategy Gen. Instrument Corp., N.Y.C., 1982-84; mgr. strategic planning GE Med. Systems Group, Milw., 1984-86, mgr. mktg. magnetic resonance, 1986-87, product gen. mgr. magnetic resonance bus. unit, 1987-89; dir. strategic mktg. Motorola Communications Sector, Schaumburg, Ill., 1989-91; dir. internat. networks svcs. Motorola Land Mobile Sector, Schaumburg, Ill., 1991-94; v.p., gen. mgr. Am. Parts Divsn., Motorola, Schaumburg, Ill., 1994-97, Radio Products Group, N.Am. Divsn., Motorola, Rolling Meadows, Ill., 1997—. Contbr. numerous articles on time div. multiple access comm. systems to profl. jours. Scholar NSF, 1968. Mem. IEEE, N.Y. Acad. Scis. Republican. Avocations: skiing, travel, art, swimming. Home: 1076 Aberdeen Rd Inverness IL 60067-4313 Office: Motorola 5201 Tollview Dr Rolling Meadows IL 60008-3711

BUCHANAN, RICK, press secretary; b. Oklahoma City, June 1, 1957. BA, Baylor U., 1979. Press sec. Office of the Gov., State of Okla., Oklahoma City, 1995—. Office: Press Sec Office of the Gov State Capitol Rm 212 Oklahoma City OK 73105

BUCHANAN, ROBERT ANGUS, archaeology educator; b. Sheffield, Yorkshire, U.K., June 5, 1930; s. Robert Graham and Bertha (Davis) B.; m. Brenda June Wade, Aug. 10, 1955; children—Andrew Nassau, Thomas Claridge. B.A., St. Catharine's Coll., Cambridge U., 1953, M.A., 1957, Ph.D., 1957; D.Sc. (hon.), Chalmers U., Goteborg, Sweden, 1986, Leonardo da Vinci medal of the Soc. for the History of Technology, 1989. Edn. officer St. Katharine's Found., London, 1956-60; lectr., reader U. Bath, 1960—, prof. of the Hist. of Technology, emeritus prof., 1995—; pres. Internat. Com. for the History of Tech., 1993-98. Author: Technology and Social Progress, 1965; Industrial Archaeology in Britain, 1972; History and Industrial Civilization, 1979, The Engineers: A History of the Engineering Profession in Britain, 1750-1914, 1989, The Power of the Machine, 1992. Mem. properties com. Nat. Trust, 1974—; commr. Royal Commn. Hist. Monuments, Eng., 1978-93. Served to pvt. RAOC, 1948-50. Recipient OBE, 1993. Fellow Soc. Antiquarians of London (v.p. 1994—); mem. Assn. Indsl. Archaeology (pres. 1974-77), Newcomen Soc. History of Tech. (pres. 1980-82). Office: Centre History Tech Sci & Soc, Univ Bath, Claverton Down BA2 7AY, England

BUCHANAN, ROBERT L., JR., federal judge, lawyer; b. 1951. AB, Erskine Coll., 1973; UD, U. S.C., 1976. Bar: S.C. 1976. Pvt. practice, Aiken, S.C., 1976—; part-time magistrate judge for S.C., U.S. Magistrate Ct, Columbia, 1979—. Office: 1845 Assembly St Columbia SC 29201-2455

BUCHANAN, ROBERT MCLEOD, lawyer; b. N.Y.C., Oct. 4, 1932; s. Albert William and Elizabeth (McLeod) B.; m. Jane Vidaud Britton, July 6, 1957; children: Robert M. Jr., Jamy B., Stephen S., Genevra V., Buchanan Casais. BA, Dartmouth Coll., 1954; JD, Harvard U., 1959. Bar: N.Y. 1960, Mass. 1969, U.S. Supreme Ct. 1973. Assoc. Debevoise & Plimpton, N.Y.C., 1959-68; ptnr. Sullivan & Worcester LLP, Boston, 1968—. Contbr. articles on antitrust law to profl. jours. Moderator Town of Weston, Mass., 1980—, mem., chmn. fin. com., 1975-80; chmn. weston Hist. Dist. Study Com., 1973. With U.S. Army, 1954-56. Mem. Mass. Bar Assn. (ethics com. 1986—), Boston Bar Assn. (chmn. antitrust com. 1980-86), Harvard Faculty Club. Unitarian. Avocations: reading, guitar playing, sailing. E-mail: RMB@SANDW.COM. Office: Sullivan & Worcester LLP 1 Post Office Sq Ste 2300 Boston MA 02109-2129

BUCHANAN, TERI BAILEY, communications executive; b. Long Beach, Calif., Feb. 24, 1946; d. Alton Hervey and Ruth Estelle (Thompson) Bailey; m. Robert Wayne Buchanan, Aug. 14, 1964 (div. May 1979). BA in English with highest honors, Ark. Poly. Coll., 1968. With employee communications AT&T, Kansas City, Mo., 1968-71; freelance writer Ottawa, Kans., 1971-73; publs. dir. Ottawa U., 1973-74; regional info. officer U.S. Dept. Labor, Kansas City, 1974; owner, operator PBT Communications, Kansas City, 1975-79; sr. pub. affairs rep., sr. editor, exhibit supr., communications specialist Standard Oil/Chevron, San Francisco, 1979-84; owner The Resource Group/Comms., Napa, Calif., 1984—; mem. faculty pub. rels. master's program Golden Gate U., San Francisco, 1987. Pub. rels. trainer Bus. Vols. for Arts, San Francisco, 1985-93; mem. Nat. trust for Hist. Preservation, Napa County Landmarks. Recipient Internat. Assn. Bus. Communicators Bay Area Gold and Silver awards, 1984. Mem. Yountville C. of C., North Bay Assn. Realtors. Democrat. Episcopalian. Avocations: piano, photography, travel. Office: The Resource Group 134 Golden Gate Cir Napa CA 94558-6186

BUCHANAN, THOMAS STEVEN, biomechanics educator; b. Lancaster, Calif., Aug. 18, 1958; s. Thomas Joseph and Laura Mae Buchanan; m. Gaye Rudell Hoch, Nov. 10, 1990; children: Rebecca Rudell, Stephen Thomas, Benjamin Hoch. BS in Bioengring., U. Calif., San Diego, 1980; MS in Biomed. Engring., Northwestern U., Evanston, Ill., 1982, PhD in Theoretical and Applied Mechanics, 1986. Rsch. asst. rehab. engring. Northwestern U., Chgo., 1981-85, postdoctoral assoc. dept. physiology, 1986-88, rsch. asst. prof. dept. rehab. medicine, 1989-90, asst. prof. Med. Sch., 1990-96; rsch. asst. Rehab. Inst. Chgo., 1982-85, rsch. assoc., 1986-89; postdoctoral assoc. dept. brain and cognitive scis. MIT, Cambridge, 1985-86; assoc. prof. mech. engring. and biomechanics & movement sci. U. Del., Newark, 1996—, dir. Ctr. Biomed. Engring. Rsch., 1998—; assoc. dir. sensory motor program Rehab. Inst. Chgo., 1989-96, assoc. editor Touchstone, 1992-98. Assoc. editor Touchstone, 1998—. Murphy fellow Northwestern U., 1980-81, Hearst Found. fellow Rehab. Inst. Chgo., 1983-84, Nat. Rsch. Svc. Award fellow NIH, 1988-89, Falk Med. Rsch. scholar Rehab. Inst. Chgo., 1993-94; recipient First award NIH, 1990-96. Mem. ASME (assoc.), IEEE (assoc.), Internat. Brain Rsch. Orgn., Soc. Neurosci., Am. Soc. Biomechanics, Neural Control of Movement. Eastern Orthodox. Home: 10 Springbenny Landenberg PA 19350-1311 Office: U Del 126 Spencer Lab Newark DE 19716

BUCHANAN, WILLIAM HOBART, JR., lawyer, publishing company executive; b. Summit, N.J., July 2, 1937; s. William Hobart and Margaret R. B.; m. Eleanor A. Lincoln, June 18, 1966; children: Diana A., Jessica R. A.B., Princeton U., 1959; LL.B., Harvard U., 1963. Bar: N.Y. 1964. Assoc. firm Shearman & Sterling, N.Y.C., 1963-70; v.p., sec., gen. counsel Reuben H. Donnelley Corp., N.Y.C., 1970-91, sr. v.p., chief legal counsel, 1991-97; asst. sec., assoc. gen. counsel Dun & Bradstreet Corp., N.Y.C., 1976-79, v.p., assoc. gen. counsel, 1979-91, v.p. law, 1991-96, v.p. law, sec., 1996-97; mng. dir. cor. fin. Spencer Trask Securities, Inc., N.Y.C., 1998—; pres. Spencer Trask Spin-Off Group LLC, 1998—. Served with USMCR, 1959-60. Mem. Am. Soc. Corp. Secs. (pres. N.Y. regional group 1979-80, nat. treas. 1979-83, bd. dirs. 1983-86), ABA, N.Y. State Bar Assn., Assn. Bar City N.Y. Republican. Presbyterian. Clubs: Princeton (N.Y.C.); New Canaan Field.

BUCHANAN, WILLIAM JENNINGS, lawyer, judge; b. Newberry, S.C., Oct. 2, 1948; s. James Willie and Martha Morton (Jennings) B.; m. Phyllis Kaye Brunson, June 3, 1978; children: Ashley, Whitney. BS in Mktg., U. S.C., 1983, JD, 1987. Bar: S.C. 1987, U.S. Dist. Ct. S.C. 1988. Assoc. Setzler, Chewning & Scott, West Columbia, S.C., 1988-93; pvt. practice Columbia, S.C., 1993—; assoc. judge City of Cayce, S.C., 1988-93; instr. Midlands Tech. Coll., Columbia, S.C., 1989-96. Mem. Sertoma Internat., Columbia, 1987-89, real property, probate and trust sect. Mem. ABA, S.C. Bar Assn., Richland County Bar Assn., Lexington County Law Enforcement Ofcls. Assn. Baptist. Avocations: golf, fishing, hunting, snow skiing, boating. Home: 1728 Shadowood Dr Columbia SC 29212-1318 Office: William J Buchanan PA PO Box 12292 Capitol Sta 900 Elmwood Ave Ste 102 Columbia SC 29201-2058

BUCHANAN, WILLIAM MURRAY, consulting actuary; b. Valley Junction, Iowa, Apr. 14, 1935; s. William Murray and Margaret Ann (Kehoe) B.; m. Jean Marie West, Aug. 20, 1955; children: Belinda Jean, Jennifer Sue, William Murray, Timothy John. BBA, Drake U., 1957. Actuarial assoc. Western and Southern Life Ins. Co., Cin., 1957-61; cons. actuary Nelson & Warren, Kansas City, Mo., 1961-65, Buchanan & Lewis, Dallas and Kansas City, Mo., 1966-76; pres. Knickerbocker Life Group, Austin, Tex., 1976-79; cons. actuary Buchanan & Assocs., Overland Park, Kans., 1979—; chmn., owner Unified Life Ins. Co., 1986—. Editor, commentator taped info. service Exec. Info. Service, 1981-83. Fellow Soc. Actuaries, Conf. of Consulting Actuaries; mem. Am. Acad. Actuaries. Roman Catholic. Avocations: running, theater, music. Home: 15904 Meadow Ln Shawnee Mission KS 66224-9741 Office: Buchanan and Assocs 7201 W 129th St Ste 300 Overland Park KS 66213-2628

BUCHBINDER, DARRELL BRUCE, lawyer, b. N.Y.C., Oct. 17, 1946; s. Julian and Bernice (Levy) B.; m. Janet Grey McLean, Jan. 22, 1977; children: Julian Bradford, Andrew Grey, Ian Jeffress. BA in Politics with honors, NYU, 1968, JD, 1971. Bar: N.Y. 1972, U.S. Dist. Ct. (so. and ea. dists.) N.Y. 1973. Sole practice, N.Y.C., 1972-79; atty. Port Authority of N.Y. and N.J., N.Y.C., 1979-83, prin. atty., 1983-86, dep. chief fin. div. Law Dept., 1986-92, chief pub. securities law div. Law Dept., 1992—. Served with USNR, 1968-70. Mem. Nat. Assn. Bond Lawyers, Pi Sigma Alpha. Republican. Club: Larchmont Shore. Office: Port Authority NY and NJ 1 World Trade Ctr Fl 66 New York NY 10048-0682

BUCHBINDER, SHARON BELL, health care management educator; b. Washington, Nov. 27, 1951; d. James Wright and Effie Naomi (Rhodes) Bell; m. Dale Buchbinder, May 9, 1976; 1 child, Joshua Harlow. BA in Psychology, U. Conn., 1973; MA in Psychology, U. Hartford, 1976; AAS in Nursing, SUNY, Albany, 1981; PhD iin Pub. Health Scis., U. Ill., Chgo., 1992. RN, Md. Intravenous technician dept. intravenous therapy Hartford (Conn.) Hosp., 1974-76; supr. dept. intravenous therapy Albany Med. Ctr. Hosp., N.Y., 1976-80; asst. rsch. scientist N.Y. Dept. Mental Hygiene, Albany, 1980-81; staff specialist Nat. Commn. on Nursing, Chgo., 1982-83; staff specialist divsn. nursing Am. Hosp. Assn., Chgo., 1983-84; sr. rsch. assoc. divsn. evaluation and nomenclature med. terminology and nomenclature AMA, Chgo., 1984-86, exec. asst., 1986-88, mktg. exec., 1988-89, asst. dept. dir. dept. preventive medicine, 1989-90; dir. devel. Norbel Sch., 1990-91; postdoctoral fellow in children's mental health svcs. Sch. Hygiene and Pub. Health Johns Hopkins U., Balt., 1993-94, sr. staff rsch. coord. dept. pediats. Sch. Medicine, 1994-95, rsch. assoc. dept. pediats. Sch. Medicine, 1995-96; asst. prof. dept. health scis. Towson U., Md., 1996—. Contbr. articles to profl. jours., chpts. to books; spkr. in field. Rsch. grantee Mut. Life Ins. Co. of N.Y., 1986, Faculty Devel. grantee Towson U., 1997, AHCPR, 1995; Shriver Ctr. grantee, 1999; CIAT Tech. fellow, 1999. Mem. NAFE, AAUW, APA, APHA, Acad. of Mgmt., Assn. for Health Svcs. Rsch., Phi Kappa Phi, Delta Omega (mem. Lambda chpt.), Eta Sigma Gamma (Beta Zeta chpt.). Democrat. Jewish. Avocation: fishing.

BUCHBINDER-GREEN, BARBARA JOYCE, art and architectural historian; b. Bronx, N.Y., Dec. 23, 1944; d. Michael and Esther Buchbinder; m. Raymond Jerome Green, Dec. 18, 1970. BA cum laude, Vanderbilt U., 1965; PhD, Northwestern U., 1974. Teaching asst. Northwestern U., Evanston, Ill., 1967-68; lectr. Northwestern U., Chgo., 1975; freelance researcher and writer Evanston, 1977—; editor GreenAssoc. Architects, Inc., Evanston, 1979—; cons. nomination forms Nat. Register of Historic Places, 1983—; mem. architecture adv. com. Mus. Sci. and Industry, Chgo., 1980-86; trustee Evanston Hist. Soc., 1986-92, pres., 1988-90, trustee emeritus, 1999, mem. house walk com. 1981-83, 88-90, chmn., 1988-90, mem. restoration planning com., 1980-91, editor newsletter TimeLines, 1989-92. Author: Lucy Fitch Perkins, 1984, Evanston: A Pictorial History, 1989; editor, compiler Evanstoniana, 1984; guest curator "Lucy Fitch Perkins" exhibit, 1983-84, "Photographs from Evanstoniana" exhibit, 1984-87; pub. photographer: Evanstoniana, 1984, Evanston: A Pictorial History, 1989, Victorian Details, 1990; history editor Chgo. Yacht Club Blinker, 1993-95; editor Cruising Sail Fleet, 1993-98, women's com., 1998—; contbr. articles to profl. jours. Founding mem. Preservation League Evanston, 1982; commr. Evanston Preservation Commn., 1981-89, chmn. preservations awards com., 1983-84, mem. evaln. com., 1978-92, chmn., 1985-89; mem. Citizen's Adv. Com. on Pub. Pl. Names, 1989-92; bd. dirs. Dewey Cmty. Conf., 1981-84, mem. exec. com., 1981-82, rec. sec., 1982-83. Univ. fellow Northwestern U., 1968-69, Dissertation Year fellow, 1969-70; Vanderbilt U. scholar, 1962-65. Mem. Victorian Soc. in Am. (bd. dirs. Chgo. chpt. 1978-81), Chgo. Architecture Found. Aux. Bd. (sec. 1990-91, exec. com. 1990-92, v.p. for cmty. affairs 1991-92), Archtl. Soc. Art Inst. Chgo., Soc. Archtl. Historians, Women's Archtl. League (v.p. 1980-82), Chgo. Maritime Soc., Nat. Trust for Hist. Preservation, Lake Forest Found. for Hist. Preservation, Howard Van Doren Shaw Soc., Tibetan Terrier Club Am., Cliff Dwellers Club. Avocations: sailing, photography. Home and Office: 1026 Michigan Ave Evanston IL 60202-1436

BUCHELE, WESLEY FISHER, retired agricultural engineering educator; b. Cedar Vale, Kans., Mar. 18, 1920; s. Charles John and Bessie (Fisher) B.; m. Mary Jagger, June 12, 1945; children: Rod, Marybeth, Steve, Steven. BS, Kans. State U., 1943; MS, U. Ark., 1951; PhD, Iowa State U., 1954. Registered profl. engr., Iowa, Calif. Jr. engr. John Deere Tractor Works, Waterloo, Iowa, 1946-48; asst. prof. U. Ark., Fayetteville, 1948-51; agrl. engr. USDA, Ames, Iowa, 1954-56; assoc. prof. Mich. State U., East Lansing, 1956-63; prof. Iowa State U., Ames, 1963-89, prof. emeritus, 1989—; vis. prof. U. Ghana, Legon, 1968-69, Beijing Agrl. Engring. U., 1983-84; vis. scientist Commonwealth Sci. and Indsl. Rsch. Orgn., Australia, Internat. Inst., Tropical Agr., Ibadan, Nigeria, 1979-80, Internat. Rice Rsch. Inst., Manila, 1991-92; cons. engr. Detroit Arsenal, Ordnance Corps, Waterways Exptl. Sta., Corps of Engrs., U.S. Steel Corp., GM, Detroit, 1974-76; bd. dirs. Farm Safety 4 Just Kids, Earlham, Iowa, Self-Help, Inc., Waverly, Iowa, JAC Tractor Co. Author 18 books; inventor 23 patents. Mem. Ames Energy Com., 1974-75; advisor Living History Farm, Urbandale, Iowa, 1965—, bd. govs., 1984—. Maj. U.S. Army, 1943-46, PTO; maj. Ordnance Corps, USAR, 1946-69, ret. Named Eminent Engr., Iowa

Engring. Soc., 1989. Fellow Am. Soc. Agrl. Engrs. (bd. dirs. 1978-80, McCormick-Case award 1988), Nat. Inst. Agrl. Engrs.; mem. AAAS, Soc. Automotive Engrs., Am. Soc. Agronomy (mem. com. 1961-65), Steel Ring, Internat. Assn. Mechanization of Field Experiments (v.p. 1964-93), Internat. Platform Assn., Osborne Club, Toastmasters. Avocations: photography, travel, golf, inventing, writing. Home and Office: 239 Parkridge Cir Ames IA 50014-3645

BUCHEN, JOHN GUSTAVE, retired judge; b. Sheboygan, Wis., Sept. 3, 1920; s. Gustave William and Elinor (Jung) B.; m. Anne Armstrong, Aug. 9, 1943; children: John Stephen, Laura, Elizabeth, Timothy, James. BA, U. Wis., 1942, LLB, 1948. Bar: Wis. 1948. Dist. atty. Sheboygan County, 1949-55; ptnr. Buchen & Heffernan, Sheboygan, 1955-63; asst. city atty. City of Sheboygan, 1957-63; commr. Family Ct. Sheboygan County, 1959-63; judge Sheboygan County Cir. Ct., 1963-89, res. judge, 1989—; mem. faculty Wis. Jud. Coll., 1968-78; chmn. Wis. Bd. Criminal Ct. Judges, 1977-78. With USAAF, 1944-48. Mem. ABA (1st pl. nat. award 1969), State Bar Wis., Am. Law Inst. Home: 422 St Clair Ave Sheboygan WI 53081-3563

BUCHENROTH, STEPHEN RICHARD, lawyer; b. Bellefontaine, Ohio, Feb. 8, 1948; s. Richard G. and Patricia (Muller) B.; m. Vicki Anderson, June 6, 1974; children: Matthew Brian, Sarah Elizabeth. BA, Wittenburg U., Springfield, Ohio, 1970; JD, U. Chgo., 1974. Bar: Ohio 1974, U.S. Dist. Ct. (so. and no. dists.) Ohio 1974, U.S. Ct. Appeals (6th cir.) 1974. Ptnr. Vorys, Sater, Seymour & Pease, Columbus, Ohio, 1974—. Author: Ohio Mortgage Foreclosures, 1986, Ohio Franchising Law, 1990, also chpts. in books. Trustee, v.p. Godman Guild Assn., Columbus, 1977-83; trustee, sec. Neighborhood Homes, Inc., Columbus, 1977-85; mem. bd. rev. Worthington Pers., 1981—; pres. Worthington Alliance for Quality Edn., 1989-91; chmn. bd. advisors paralegal program Capitol U. Law Sch., 1991; pres. bd. trustees Worthington Edn. Found., 1997-98; mem. Ohio Supreme Ct. Commn. on CLE, chmn., 1999; bd. advisors C.H.A.D.D. of Ctrl. Ohio, 1993-97. Recipient Cmty. Svc. award Legal Assts. Ctrl. Ohio, 1987. Mem. ABA (forum com. franchising), Ohio State Bar Assn. (coun. dels., chmn. legal assts. com., bd. govs. real property sect.), Columbus Bar Assn. (bd. govs., pres. 1992-93), Am. Coll. Real Estate Lawyers. Republican. Lutheran. Home: 2342 Collins Dr Columbus OH 43085-2810 Office: Vorys Sater Seymore & Pease 52 E Gay St PO Box 1008 Columbus OH 43215-3161

BUCHER, RICHARD DAVID, sociology educator; b. New Haven, Apr. 13, 1949; s. Charles Augustus and Jacqueline (Dubois) B.; m. Patricia Lawrence, July 28, 1973; children: James, Kathryn, Suzette. BA in Sociology, Colgate U., 1971; MA in Sociology, NYU, 1974; PhD in Sociology, Howard U., 1983. Instr. sociology Rock Valley Coll., Rockford, Ill., 1972-73; prof. sociology Balt. City C.C., 1974—, coord. sociology, 1982-89, dir. Inst. Intercultural Understanding, 1991-96; campus liaison Am. Assn. C.Cs./Kellogg Beacon Coll. project Promoting Intercultural Awareness and Understanding in Md. Cmty. Colls., 1992-94. Co-author: Recreation for Today's Society, 1974, 2d edit., 1984. Chair Carroll County Cmty. Rels. Commn. Westminster, Md., 1990-91; chair pers. parish rels. com. Wesley-Freedom Ch., Eldersburg, Md., 1982-84. Grantee Fund for Improvement Post-Secondary Edn., Washington, 1989-90; recipient tchg. excellence award Nat. Inst. Staff and Orgnl. Devel., 1994. Mem. Am. Sociol. Assn., So. Sociol. Soc., Soc. for Disability Studies. Democrat. Methodist. Avocations: walking, swimming, family recreation. Home: 2538 Vance Dr Mount Airy MD 21771-8814 Office: Balt City C C 2901 Liberty Heights Ave Baltimore MD 21215-7807

BUCHERT, RONALD V., retired military career officer; b. Norwood, Ohio, Feb. 1, 1934; s. Vincent A. and Elenora (Burns) B.; m. Shirley Ann Tyndall, June 18, 1955; children: Terrence S., Kathleen G. Buchert La Paglia, Peggy L. Buchert Miyares. BS, U. Cin., 1956; MPA, Auburn U., 1974; Diploma, Air Command and Staff Coll., 1976, Air War Coll. Commd. 2d lt. USAF, 1956, advanced through grades to col., 1977, ret., 1986; mgr. First Fla. Bank, Tampa, 1987-93; dir. adminstrv. svcs. U. Tampa, 1994-96; dean dept. profl. devel. Armed Forces Staff Coll.; faculty Air Command and Staff Coll. Pres., founder MacDill Meml. Park Found., Tampa, 1994—; v.p. for Air Force, Tampa C. of C., 1989-90; chmn., trustee Mil. Officers Benevolent Corp., Sun City Ctr., Fla., 1996—. Decorated Def. Superior Svc. medal, Disting. Flying Cross, Air medal with 4 oak leaf clusters, Meritorious Svc. medal with 3 oak leaf clusters. Mem. Ret. Officers Assn. (pres. Tampa chpt. 1991-93, pres. Fla. coun. 1996-98), Air Force Assn. Missileers, Air Force Retiree Coun., Soc. Strategic Air Command. Republican. Presbyterian. Avocations: photography, running, mil. history. Home: 14504 Thornfield Ct Tampa FL 33624-2641

BUCHHEIT, WILLIAM A., neurosurgeon, educator; b. Donora, Pa., Oct. 14, 1933; s. Barnard H. and Thelma A. Buchheit; m. Christa T. Buchheit, Jan. 22, 1983. AB, Duke U., 1955; MD, Temple U., 1960, MS in Neurosurgery, 1960. Diplomate Am. Bd. Neurosurgery. Prof., chmn. dept. neurosurgery Temple U., Phila., 1975-94; prof., chief neurosurgery fellowship U. Phila., 1994—. Home: 6014 Cricket Rd Flourtown PA 19031 Office: U Phila 1015 Chestnut Philadelphia PA 19107

BUCHHOLZ, BERNARD, retired research manager; b. Newark, May 4, 1929; s. Bernard Carl and Emma Pauline (Kuhm) B.; m. Audrey Fay Merritt, June 25, 1955; children: Douglas Bernard, Linda Susan, Carl Merritt. BA, Drew U., 1951; MS, U. Va., 1954, PhD, 1956. Sr. rsch. chemist Elf Atochem NA, Phila., 1956-66, project leader, 1966-73, group leader, 1973-83, rsch. mgr., 1983-93. Patentee in field of organo-sulfur chemistry. Newsletter editor Kiwanis Internat., Berlin, Md., 1993-95, sec., 1996-97; adminstrv. officer U.S. Power Squadrons, Ocean City, Md., 1995-96. Rsch. fellow Eli Lilly Co., 1954-56; tchg. assistantship DuPont Chem. Co., U. Va., 1951-53. Mem. Am. Chem. Soc. (mem. Phila. sect.). Republican. Presbyterian. Avocations: boating, fishing, camping, traveling, hiking. Home and Office: 5 Portside Ct Ocean Pnes Berlin MD 21811-7121

BUCHHOLZ, DAVID W., neurologist, headache specialist, educator; b. Phila., Jan. 5, 1953; s. Carl Daniel and Doris Alice (Heiss) B.; m. Stefanie Neumann, Dec. 8, 1994; children: Brittany, Alison, Maximilian. BA, U. Pa., 1977, MD, 1979. Diplomate Am. Bd. Neurology and Psychiatry. Asst. prof. neurology Johns Hopkins U., Balt., 1983-90, assoc. prof. neurology, 1990—, dir. Neurol. Consultation Clinic, 1983-97; pvt. practice Lutherville, Md., 1997—; peer reviewer numerous jours., 1985—; medicolegal cons., 1984—. Author: Controlling Your Headaches, 1999; contbr. articles to profl. jours.; mem. editl. bd. Dysphagia, 1985—. Mem. Am. Acad. Neurology, Am. Sleep Disorders Assn., Am. Assn. for the Study of Headache, Internat. Headache Soc., Sleep Rsch. Soc., Stroke Coun., Phi Beta Kappa, Alpha Omega Alpha. Avocation: ornamental gardening. Office: Johns Hopkins at Green Spring Sta 10753 Falls Rd Lutherville MD 21093

BUCHHOLZ, DONALD ALDEN, stock brokerage company executive; b. LaPorte, Tex., Mar. 10, 1929; s. Fred T. and Chrystine (McCombs) B.; m. Ruth Vernon, May 17, 1958; children: Robert, Chrystine Louise. BBA, North Tex. U., 1952. C.P.A., Tex. Acct., staff auditor Peat, Marwick & Mitchell, Dallas, 1952-54; asst. sec.-treas., chief acct. ICT Discount Corp., 1954-56; comptroller Eppler-Guerin & Turner, Inc., 1956-59; ptnr. Cheshier-Buchholz (pub. accountants), 1959-60; comptroller, sec. Parker Ford, Inc. (stock brokers), Dallas, 1960-63, also dir., 1962-63; v.p., chief adminstrv. officer, sec. Weber, Hall, Cobb & Caudle, Inc., Dallas, 1963-72, also bd. dirs.; ptnr., chmn. bd. Southwest Securities Group, 1972—; chmn. bd. Buckley Oil Co., Dallas, 1994—, First Savs. Bank, Arlington, Tex., 1994-98; bd. govs. N.Y. Stock Exch., 1969-71; assoc. mem. Am. Stock Exch.; mem. Chgo. Bd. Trade, Midwest Stock Exch.; mem. adv. bd. Security Bank N.A., Garland, Tex., 1987—; mem. found. bd. U. North Tex., 1998—. Trustee Garland Ind. Sch. Bd., 1971-74, pres., 1973-74; trustee Dallas County C.C. Dist., 1978-97, pres., 1982-84, 90-92; bd. dirs. Garland Meml. Hosp., 1981-85, Garland Meml. Hosp. Found., 1981, Alliance of Higher Edn., 1994—, Coun. for Higher Edn. Accreditation, 1996-97, Dallas Citizens Coun., Old Red Found. 1997—; mem. bus. adv. bd. Baylor U., 1991-94, pres. adv. bd. Hankamer Sch. Bus., 1995-97. Recipient U. N. Tex. Outstanding Alumnus Svc. award, 1999. Mem. Nat. Security Dealers Assn. (chmn. bus. conduct com. dist. 6 1985-87, bd. govs. 1988-91), Securities Industry Assn. (exec. com. south cen. dist. 1986—, exec. bd. 1990-93), Dallas Security Dealers Assn. (sec. 1961), Tex. Stock and Bond Dealers Assn. (treas. 1982, v.p. 1986-87, pres. 1987-88), Lakewood Country Club, Ea. Hills Country Club, City Club Dallas, Kiwanis (pres. 1957-58), Nat. Coun. of Policy Advisors. Baptist. Home: 3627 Glenbrook Ct Garland TX 75041-5101 Office: SW Securities Inc 1201 Elm St Ste 3500 Dallas TX 75270-2102

BUCHHOLZ, DOUGLAS DAVID, military officer. BS in Advt., U. Oreg.; MS in Procurement/Contract Mgmt., Fla. Inst. Tech.; grad., U.S. Army Command/Gen. Staff, Indsl. Coll. of Armed Forces. Commd. 2d lt. U.S. Army, 1968, advanced through grades to lt. gen., 1996, ret., 1998; procurement and prodn. officer U.S. Army Missile Command, Redstone Arsenal, Ala., 1974-77; procurement officer, exec. officer Office of Program Mgr. M1 Tank sys., U.S. Army Tank Automotive Command, Warren, Mich., 1981-83; chief comms. interoperability and maneuver divsn. C31 Dir. U.S. Army Combined Arms Ctr., Ft. Leavenworth, Kans., 1986-88; comdr. 3d Signal Base Ft. Hood, Tex., 1988-90; mil. sec. Mil. Comms. and Electronics Bd. Office of J-6, The Joint Staff, Washington, 1990-91; dep. dir. Unified and Specified Command, Command Control Comms. and Computers Support, J-6, The Joint Staff, Washington, 1991-93; dep. comdg. gen., asst. commandant U.S. Army Signal Ctr. and Ft. Gordon, U.S. Army Signal Sch., Ft. Gordon, Ga., 1993-94, comdg. gen., 1994-96; dir. Command, Control, Comms., and Computers Support J-6, The Joint Staff, Washington, 1996-98. Office: The Joint Staff 6000 Joint Staff Pentagon Washington DC 20318-6000

BUCHHOLZ, RONALD LEWIS, architect; b. Milw., Jan. 14, 1951; s. Raymond LeRoy and Della (Krause) B.; m. Mary Lou Stockhausen, May 20, 1972; children: Lauren Robert, Geoffrey Alan. BS in Architecture, U. Wis., Milw., 1973, cert. pub. mgr., 1995. Registered architect, Wis. Archtl. appraiser Am. Appraisal Co., Milw., 1973; plan examiner, bur. bldgs., structures Wis. Dept. Industry, Labor & Human Rels., Madison, 1973-76, staff architect, 1976, architect, adminstrv. code cons., bur. code devel., 1976-80, dep. dir., 1980-83, asst. dir., 1983-87, asst. office dor. divsn. codes & applications, 1987-89, dep. divsn. adminstr. divsn. safety & bldgs., 1989-96; dep. divsn. adminstr. divsn. safety & bldgs. Wis. Deot. Commerce, Madison, 1996—; instr. U. Wis., Madison Ext., also. state cert. courses for bldg. and dwelling insps.; mem. Wis. Bldg Code Adv. Rev. Bd., 1976-89, Fire Prevention Coun., 1978-89, adv. com. Alternative Energy Tax Credits, 1978, 80, Dept. Devel. Permit Ctr., 1984-89; mem. Interagy. Com. on Spills of Hazardous Materials, 1981-82, Flood Hazard Interagy. Coord. Coun., 1985-90; mem. adv. com. Wis. Elec. Supply, 1984-86; state rep. U.S. EPA Study Group for Underground Storage Tank Regulations, 1987-90. Author tech. reports. Vol. leader Boy Scouts Am.; coach Madison Area Youth Soccer Assn., 1984-87; basketball coach Madison Parochal Sch. League, 1984-95. With U.S. Army N.G., 1970-76. Mem. ASTM, Resdl. Facilities Coun. (exec. sec. 1976-78), Bldg. Ofcls. and Code Adminstrs. Internat., Inc., Internat. Conf. Bldg. Ofcls., Inc., Wis. Soc. Cert. Pub. Mgrs. (pres. elect 1998-99), Am. Acad. Cert. pub. Mgrs., Nat. Eagle Scout Assn., KC. Roman Catholic. Fax: (608) 266-9946. E-mail: rbuchholz@commerce.state.wi.us. Home: 4925 Knox Ln Madison WI 53711-3636 Office: 4th Fl 201 W Washington Ave Madison WI 53703 also: 5600 Fishers Ln Ste 740 Rockville MD 20857

BUCHHOLZ, WILLIAM JAMES, communications specialist, educator; b. Ladysmith, Wis., July 17, 1945; s. James Fossegard and Hazel Winnefred (Crandell) B.; m. Dorothy Ann Kostka, June 17, 1967; children: Christopher, Jeffrey. BA, U. Wis., Eau Claire, 1967; MA, Ohio U., 1968; PhD, U. Ill., 1976. Grad. asst. U. Ill., Urbana, 1972-76; asst. prof. English, bus. communication Bentley Coll., Waltham, Mass., 1976-83; assoc. prof. Bentley Coll., Waltham, 1983-91; prof. Bentley Coll., Waltham, Mass., 1991—; dir. undergrad./grad. bus. communication programs Bentley Coll., Waltham, 1988-95; co-chmn. dept. English Bentley Coll., Waltham, Mass., 1993; chmn. dept. English, 1995—; cons. in corp. comm. and internet Waltham, Mass., 1978—; mgr. pubs. Scholastech Inc., Cambridge, Mass., 1983-9; cons. in field. Author: (with others) Truth and Taste: Revisiting High Ethical Standards, 1994, Writing in Business and Manufacturing, 1998; editor, author: Communication Training and Consulting in Business, Industry and Government, 1983; co-editor, contbr.: The Challenge of Change, Managing Communications and Building Corporate Image in the 1990s, 1989, Global Communications: Applying Resources Strategically, 1990; co-editor: New Corporate Relationships, 1991; contbr. articles to profl. jours., chpts. to books. With USN, 1968-72. Grantee FIPSE, 1986, 87; fellow NDEA-IV, 1967-68, inst. fellow Bentley Coll., 1991-92. Mem. Assn. for Bus. Comm., Assn. for Profl. Writing Cons., Phi Sigma Epsilon. Roman Catholic. Avocations: personal computing, swimming, cross-country skiing, reading, travel. E-mail: wbuchholz@bentley.edu. Home: 44 Raffaele Dr Waltham MA 02452-0313 Office: Bentley Coll Grad Ctr 175 Forest St Waltham MA 02452-4713

BUCHI, MARK KEITH, lawyer; b. Salt Lake City; m. Denise Kimball, June 4, 1973; 7 children. BS, U. Utah, 1974, MBA, 1974, JD, 1978. Bar: Utah 1978. Divsn. chief tax and bus. Utah Atty. Gen. Office, Salt Lake City, 1980-83, asst. atty. gen., 1978-83; chmn. Utah Tax Commn., Salt Lake City, 1983-86; atty. Holme Roberts & Owen, Salt Lake City, 1986-88, ptnr., 1988-89, mng. ptnr., 1989-95, mem. firmwide exec. com., 1995—, ptnr., 1999—; mem. tax recodification commn. Utah State Tax Commn., Salt Lake City, 1984-91; mem. Utah Govs. Tax Rev. Commn., Salt Lake City, 1991—; mem. exec. com. Multistate Tax Commn., Boulder, Colo., 1985-86. Mem. tax platform com. Utah Rep. Party, 1986. Mem. ABA, Utah Tax Payers Assn. (chmn. 1992, bd. dirs. 1990—). Mormon. Avocations: golf, water skiing, fishing, gardening, carpentry. Office: Holme Roberts & Owen 111 E Broadway Ste 1100 Salt Lake City UT 84111-5233*

BUCHIGNANI, LEO JOSEPH, lawyer; b. Memphis, Nov. 4, 1922; s. Joseph Richard and Leonora B. (Shea) B.; m. Grace Elisabeth Crisler, Nov. 23, 1950; children—Leo, Crisler Quick, Joan Barnett. B.A., Notre Dame U., 1944; LL.B., Harvard U., 1948. Bar: Tenn., 1948, U.S. Sup. Ct., 1960, U.S. Dist. Ct., 1950. Assoc., Chandler, Shepherd, Heiskill & Williams, Memphis, 1948-50; ptnr. Buchignani & Greener, Memphis, 1950-53; ptnr. Quick, Buchignani & Greener, Memphis, 1953-58; ptnr. Buchignani & Greener, Memphis, 1958-80; ptnr. Buchignani & Neal, Memphis, 1981-83; ptnr. Buchignani, Neal & Burnham, 1983-88; co-founder, v.p., sec. Catherine's Stores, 1960-78; commr. Tenn. Jud. Standards Commn., 1971-74; commr. Tenn. Law Revision Commn., 1971-74. Mem. Tenn. Republican State Exec. Com., 1960-62. Served with USN, 1942-45. Mem. ABA, Tenn. Bar Assn., Memphis and Shelby County Bar Assn. (dir. 1959-61, sec.-treas. 1964-65, v.p. 1965-66, pres. 1966-67). Republican. Roman Catholic. Clubs: Harvard, Notre Dame, Memphis Country, Colonial Country. Home: 315 Kenilworth Pl Memphis TN 38112-5405

BUCHIN, JACQUELINE CHASE, clinical psychologist; b. Providence, Nov. 27, 1935; d. Leslie Thurber and Mary Hillyer (Lyon) Chase; m. Stanley Ira Buchin, Sept. 14, 1957; children: Linda Chase Sullivan, David Lyon, Gordon Tomlinson. BA, Wellesley Coll., 1957; MEd in Counseling Psychology, Antioch U., 1979; PsyD, Mass. Sch. Profl. Psychology, Boston, 1990. Lic. clin. psychologist, Mass. Dir., coord. emergency housing program Multi-Svc. Ctr., Newton, Mass., 1978-81; family therapy intern Newtom Guidance Clinic, 1981-82, Framingham (Mass.) Youth Guidance, 1982-84; psychology intern The Arbour Hosp., Boston, 1984-85, Solomon Carter Fuller Hosp., Boston, 1985-86, Behavior Assocs., Boston, 1986-90; staff psychologist Biobehavioral Treatment Ctr., Brookline, Mass., 1990—; fellow in clin. cognitive therapy program Mass. Gen. Hosp., Boston, 1993-95, clin. assoc., 1995—, rsch. clinician, 1995—; clin. instr. psychology dept. Havard Med. Sch., Boston, 1995—; faculty mem. Inst. Cognitive Therapy Mass. Gen. Hosp., 1996—. Mem., sec., v.p. Wellesly Jr. Svc. League, pres., 1972-73; mem., bd. dirs. Jr. League of Boston, 1975-77; bd. dirs. Wellesley Cmty. Chest and Coun., 1972-73, Wesllesley Friendly Assoc., 1972-73, Family Counseling Region West, 1969, Wellesly chpt. ARC, Wellesley Cmty. Child Care, 1976, Human Rels. Svc.; trustee Mass. Sch. Profl. Psychology, chmn. human resources com., 1991—. Mem. APA, Mass. Psychol. Assn., Assn. for Advancement of Behavior Therapy. Episcopalian. Home: Union Wharf Boston MA 02109-1206 Office: Biobehavioral Treatment Ctr 1330 Beacon St Brookline MA 02446-3202

BUCHIN, JEAN, psychologist; b. N.Y.C.; d. Mac and Celia Jacobs; BA, CUNY; MA, Columbia U.; PhD, NYU; children: Peter J., John D. Tchr. N.Y.C. Pub. Schs.; counselor, asst. prof. CUNY. Mem. Nat. Bd. Cert. Counselors, Nat. Bd. Cert. Career Counselors; asst. prof. coord. Which Way With Women program Baruch Coll.; vis. asst. prof. NYU; cons. N.Y.C. Tchrs. Consortium; mem. Spkrs. Bur., Child Abuse Ctr.; mgmt. tng. cons. Met. Life Ins. Co., N.Y.C.; cons. assessment programs N.Y.C. Divsn. Pers., Sci. and Tech. Adv. Bd.; cons. N.J. Human Resources Divsn.; career cons. AARP; lectr., leader workshops 53d St. Y., NYU, Queens Coll., A.W.E.D., leader workshops Marymount Coll.; mediator ABA; bd. dirs. Am. Coll. Forensic Examiners; cons. Child Abuse Ctr. Author: Singular Parent, Noah's Ark Minus One. Washington Sq. Coll. fellow. Mem. AAUP, APA (pres. Tri State chpt. divsn. 35), ACA, Ea. Psychol. Assn., Met. N.Y. Assn. for Applied Psychology, Bus. and Profl. Women, Career Devel. Specialists Network.

BUCHIN, STANLEY IRA, management consultant, educator; b. N.Y.C., Sept. 7, 1931; s. K. and Bertha (Handman) B.; m. Jacqueline Thurber Chase, Sept. 14, 1957; children: Linda C., David L., Gordon T. SB, MIT, 1952; MBA, Harvard U., 1956, DBA, 1962. Asst. to treas. Bay State Abrasives, 1956-58; rsch. asst. Harvard Bus. Sch., 1958-59, rsch. assoc., 1959-60, instr., 1960-61, lectr., 1961-62, asst. prof., 1962-66, assoc. prof., 1966-69; pres. Applied Decision Systems, Wellesley, Mass., 1969-78; v.p. Temple, Barker & Sloane, Inc., Lexington, Mass., 1975-80, sr. v.p., 1980-90; prin. Arthur D. Little, 1991—; pres. Boston-Bermuda Cruising Ltd., 1992-97, Gen. Ship Cruising Corp., 1994-97; vis. lectr. Templeton Coll. Oxford (Eng.), 1991-93; prof. Arthur D. Little Sch. Mgmt., 1992—; assoc. prof. Boston U., 1997—. Trustee Mass. Sch. Profl. Psychology. Served in Chem. Corps, U.S. Army, 1952-54. IBM fellow, 1962-63; George F. Baker scholar, 1956. Mem. Am. Mktg. Assn., Inst. Mgmt. Sci., Fin. Mgmt. Assn., Harvard Club Boston, Tau Beta Pi. Republican. Congregationalist. Home: Union Wharf # 304 Boston MA 02109-1206 Office: 808 Commonwealth Ave Boston MA 02215

BUCHINSKY, CHARLES See **BRONSON, CHARLES**

BUCHKO, GARTH, broadcasting executive; b. Winnipeg, MB, Canada, 1958; m. Lesley; 1 child. From acct. exec. to retail and gen. sales mgr. CJOB AM, Winnipeg, 1982-95, pres., gen. mgr., 1995—. Bd. dirs. Children's Hosp. Rsch. Found., Manitoba Spl. Olympics, Big Brothers of Manitoba; chmn. fundraising com. 1997 Manitoba Spl. Olympics Summer Games. Avocations: football, travel, golf. Office: CJOB AM, 930 Portage Ave, Winnipeg, MB Canada R3G 0P8*

BUCHMAN, ELWOOD, internist, pharmaceutical company medical director; b. Ottumwa, Iowa, June 10, 1923; s. Abe and Sarah (Redman) B.; m. Kathleen Field, June 8, 1945 (deceased); children—Elizabeth Anne, Bernard Kip; m. Eloise Marolf Schooley Buchman, June 30, 1989. B.A., U. Iowa, 1940, M.D., 1943. diplomate Am. Bd. Internal Medicine. Intern D.C. Gen. Hosp.; resident in internal medicine Wayne State U., VA Hosp., Detroit; fellow U. Pa., 1956; mem. staff Wayne State U. Med. Sch., VA Hosp., Detroit, 1946-52; assoc. prof. U. Iowa, Iowa City, from 1952; chief med. service VA Hosp., Des Moines, 1969-73; med. dir. Cintest Inc., Cin., 1980-86; former assoc. dir. Norwich Eaton Pharm. Co.; and div. dir. Merrell Pharm. Rsch. Ctr., Cin.; sr. examiner numerous ins. cos. Contbr. numerous articles to med. jours. Served to capt. M.C., U.S. Army; lt. col. USAR. Fellow Am. Coll. Gastroenterology, Am. Soc. Clin. Pharmacology and Therapeutics; mem. Am. Profl. Practice Assn., Acad. Medicine Cin., Sigma Xi, Alpha Omega Alpha. Address: 6080 Miami Rd Cincinnati OH 45243-3025

BUCHMAN, KENNETH WILLIAM, lawyer; b. Plant City, Fla., Nov. 20, 1956; s. Paul Sidney and Beryle (Solomon) B.; m. MarDee H. Buchman, May 9, 1985; 1 child, Katherine Elizabeth. AA, U. Fla., 1976, BBA, 1978, JD, 1981. Bar: Fla. 1981; U.S. Dist. Ct. (Mid. dist.) Fla. 1981; U.S. Ct. Appeals (11th cir.) 1986; U.S. Supreme Ct. 1988; bd. cert. city, county, local govt. law. Ptnr. Buchman and Buchman, Plant City, 1981-85, Buchman and Buchman, PA, Plant City, 1985-91; pvt. practice Plant City, 1991—; city atty. City of San Antonio, Fla., 1995—; asst. city atty. City of Plant City, 1982-91, city atty., 1991—; mem. exec. coun. city, county and local govt. law sect. Fla. Bar., 1997—. Mem. Fla. Mcpl. Attys. Assn. (steering com. 1997—), Attys. Title Ins. Fund, Plant City Bar Assn., Kiwanis (pres. Plant City club 1986-87), Masons. Jewish. Office: 212 N Collins St Plant City FL 33566-3314

BUCHMAN, MARK EDWARD, banker; b. Caldwell, N.J., June 19, 1937; s. Samuel Joseph and Dorothy Eunice (Friedland) B.; m. Mary Angela Dolan, June 6, 1964 (div. 1991); children: Jennifer Ann, Romy Ellen. BS, U. Pa., 1959; AMP, Harvard U., 1977. Sr. v.p., dep. gen. mgr. Mfrs. Hanover Trust Co., N.Y.C., 1962-82; exec. v.p. Union Bank, Los Angeles, 1982-88; pres. Govt. Nat. Mortgage Assn., Washington, 1988-89; prin. Buchman & Assocs., 1989-90; pres., CEO Bank of L.A., 1990-92, Liberty Bank, Honolulu, 1993-94. Mem. pres.'s council U. Pa., 1984—; Pacific Asia Mus., Pasadena, Calif., 1983-85. Served to lt. (j.g.) USN, 1959-62. Mem. Council on Fgn. Relations, Asia Soc., Japan-Am. Soc. So. Calif. (pres.), Calif. Bankers Assn. (pres. 1986-87), Assn. Res. City Bankers. Republican. Clubs: Calif., Riviera Country (Los Angeles). Avocations: tennis, skiing, golf, bridge. E-mail: shibuihito@aol.com. Home: 10701 Wilshire Blvd Apt 2202 Los Angeles CA 90024-4451

BUCHMANN, ALAN PAUL, lawyer; b. Yonkers, N.Y., Sept. 5, 1934; s. Paul John and Jessie Gow (Perkins) B.; m. Lizabeth Ann Moody, Sept. 5, 1959. BA, Yale U., 1956; postgrad, U. Munich, 1956-57; LLB, Yale U., 1960. Bar: Ohio 1960, U.S. Dist. Ct. (no. dist.) Ohio 1963, U.S. Ct. Appeals (6th cir.) 1968, U.S. Supreme Ct. 1977, Fla. 1996. Assoc. Squire, Sanders & Dempsey, Cleve., 1960-70, ptnr., 1970-96. Contbr. articles to profl. jours. State chmn. Ohio Young reps., 1970-71, nat. committeeman, 1971-74; mem. exec. com. Cuyahoga County Reps., 1969-95, fin. com., 1987-94; mem. Selective svc. Bd., 1967-75; trustee Cleve. Internat. Program, 1979-82, 94-95; pres. English Speaking Union, 1981-83. Recipient Robert A. Taft award Young Reps., 1969, Outstanding State Chmn. award, 1971, James A. Rhodes award, 1974; Fulbright fellow U. Munich, 1956-57. Mem. ABA (chmn. pub. utility law sect. 1989-90, sect. del. 1996—, mem. coord. com. on legal edn. 1991-97), Fla. Bar Assn., Ohio State Bar Assn., Cleve. Bar Assn., St. Petersburg Bar Assn., Hillsborough County Bar Assn.

BUCHMEYER, JERRY, federal judge; b. Overton, Tex., Sept. 5, 1933. Student, Kilgore Jr. Coll., 1953; B.A., U. Tex., 1955, LL.B., 1957. Bar: Tex. 1957. Assoc. Thompson, Knight, Simmons & Bullion, Dallas, 1958-63, ptnr., 1963-66, sr. ptnr., 1968-79; judge U.S. Dist. Ct. (no. dist.) Tex., Dallas, 1979-94, chief judge, 1995—. Mem. ABA, Dallas Bar Assn. (pres. 1979), State Bar Tex. (chmn. com. 1978-79, dir. 1982-84, 94-95). Office: US Dist Courthouse 1100 Commerce St Rm 15 D28A Dallas TX 75242-1027*

BUCHNESS, MICHAEL PATRICK, cardiologist, surgeon; b. Balt., Sept. 19, 1939; s. John Adam and Catherine (Horn) B.; m. Margaret A. Struble, June 11, 1966; children: Michael John, Eleanor Ann. BS, Loyola U., Balt., 1962; MD, U. Md., 1966. Diplomate Am. Bd. Surgeons, Am. Bd. Thoracic Surgery. Intern USPHS, Staten Island, N.Y., 1966-67; resident in medicine USPHS, Staten Island, 1967-68; chief outpatient clinic USPHS, Cleve., 1968-69; resident in surgery U. Md., Balt., 1969-73, asst. prof. vascular surgery, 1973-74, resident thoracic surgery, 1974-76; cardiac surgeon Peninsula Regional Med. Ctr., Salisbury, Md., 1976—; chief of surgery Peninsula Regional Med. Ctr., Salisbury, 1988-90. Mem. ACS, Am. Coll. Cardiology, Soc. for Thoracic Surgery, Ea. Vascular Soc., Chesapeake Vascular Soc. Republican. Roman Catholic. Avocations: running, skiing, bird watching. Office: Cardiovascular Surg Assocs PA 201 Pine Bluff Rd Salisbury MD 21801

BUCHOLTZ, HAROLD RONALD, lawyer; b. Newark, Jan. 24, 1952; s. Samuel and Dorothy (Sorren) B. BBA, Rutgers U., 1973; JD, U. Va., 1976; LLM in Taxation, Georgetown U., 1980. Bar: Va. 1976, D.C. 1980, U.S. Tax Ct. 1980, U.S. Supreme Ct. 1980, U.S. Ct. Appeals (fed. cir.) 1981, U.S. Ct. Appeals (D.C. cir.) 1982, U.S. Ct. Appeals (11th cir.) 1983. Atty. office of the chief counsel IRS, Washington, 1976-81; assoc. Pope, Ballard & Loos, Washington, 1981, Holland & Knight, Washington, 1982-84; ptnr. Holland & Knight LLP, Washington, 1985—. Contbr. articles to profl. jours. Mem. ABA (taxation sect.), Am. Law Inst., Va. Bar Assn., D.C. Bar Assn. Home: 1901F N Adams St Arlington VA 22201-3609 Office: Holland & Knight LLP 2100 Pennsylvania Ave NW Washington DC 20037-3295

BUCHOLZ, ARDEN KINGSBURY, historian, educator; b. Chgo., May 14, 1936; s. Arden Kingsbury and Betty (Lutz) B.; m. Sue Ann Tally, July 7, 1962; children: Merritt, Mark. AB, Dartmouth Coll., 1958; diploma, U. Vienna, Austria, 1960; AM, U. Chgo., 1965, PhD, 1972. Tchr. English Amerikan Orta Okulu, Talas-Kayseri, Turkey, 1958-60; tchr. history Latin Sch Chgo., 1965-70; prof. history SUNY, Brockport, 1970—, dir. grad. program in history, 1990-97; dir. SUNY program Brunel U., Uxbridge, Eng., 1987-88; cons. NEH, Washington, 1988—, WXXI TV, Rochester, N.Y., 1990-92, Houghton Mifflin Co., Boston, 1982-84, Harper & Row, N.Y.C., 1983-86; rsch. assoc. U.S. Army Mil. History Inst., Carlisle Barracks, Pa., 1985. Author: Hans Delbrueck and German Military Establishment, 1985, Moltke, Schliffen and Prussian War Planning, 1991, Delbrück's Modern Military History, 1997. Pres. bd. edn. Lyndonville (N.Y.) Ctrl. Sch., 1980-87. With U.S. Army, 1961-64. Recipient Chancellor's award SUNY, 1977. Mem. Phi Alpha Theta. Home: 13510 Roosevelt Hwy Waterport NY 14571-9712 Office: SUNY Dept History Brockport NY 14420

BUCHSBAUM, PETER A., lawyer; b. Bklyn., Dec. 27, 1945; s. Arnold and Rose (Chanes) B.; m. Elaine Frey, Dec. 24, 1967; children: Matthew, Andrew, Aaron. AB, Cornell U., 1967; JD, Harvard U., 1970. Bar: N.J. 1971, U.S. Dist. Ct. N.J. 1971, U.S. Ct. Appeals (3d cir.) 1986. Law sec. to chief justice Hon. Joseph Weintraub, Trenton, N.J., 1970-71; lawyer N.J. State Tax Policy Commn., Trenton, 1971-72; staff counsel ACLU, Newark, 1972-74; asst. dep. pub. adv. N.J. Dept. Pub. Adv., Trenton, 1974-79; lawyer Warren, Goldberg, & Berman, Princeton, N.J., 1979-84; ptnr. Hannoch Weisman, Princeton, 1984-91, Greenbaum, Rowe, Smith, Ravin & Davis, Woodbridge, N.J., 1991—; spl. counsel N.J. State League Mcpl., Trenton, 1988-94; counsel Boroughs of High Bridge and Flemington, N.J., redevelopment coun. Long Branch, Atlantic City, N.J.; commr. N.J. Law Rev. Commn., Newark. Columnist N.J. Reporter Mag., Princeton, 1982—, State and Local Law News ABA, 1996—; co-editor State and Regional Comprehensive Planning, 1993; contbr. articles to profl. jours. Exec. com. N.J. Assn. for Retarded Citizens, North Brunswick; bd. dirs. Hunterdon County Housing Corp., Flemington, N.J., bd. dirs. MSM (Middlesex-Somerset-Mercer) Regional Coun., Princeton. Mem. ABA (coun. state and local govt. law sect.), N.J. State Planning Commn. (regional design sys. adv. com. 1989-93), N.J. State Bar Assn. (chmn. land use law sect. 1986-87, trustee 1983-96, media award 1987). Democrat. Jewish. Avocations: hiking, writing. Home: 126 Bowne Station Rd Stockton NJ 08559-1907 Office: Greenbaum Rowe Smith Ravin Davis & Himmel Metro Corp Campus I PO Box 5600 Woodbridge NJ 07095-0988

BUCHSTEIN, FREDERICK DAVID, public relations executive; b. N.Y.C., Nov. 17, 1944; s. Nathan Buchstein and Madeline (Ginsburg) Eilbaum; m. Elizabeth Josephine Glass, June 30, 1947; children: Jessica, Joshua, Jerry, William, Rebecca. BA in Philosophy, Ohio Wesleyan U., 1966; MA in Journalism, Pa. State U., 1970. Feature writer, editor N.Y. Daily News, 1967-69; bus. editor The Cleve. Press, 1970-82; v.p. Dix & Eaton Inc., Cleve., 1982—; adj. faculty comms. John Carroll U., University Heights, 1977—, Cleve. State U., 1978-82, Case Western Res. U., 1994. Contbr. articles to profl. jours. Chmn. bd. Children's Svcs., Cleve., 1996, Applewood Ctrs. Inc., Cleve., 1997; adv. bd. Cuyahoga Cts. Dept. of Children and Family Svcs., 1997. Mem. Cleve. City Club. Avocations: jogging, swimming, Mongolian history, foster parenting. Home: 3427 E Fairfax Rd Cleveland Hts OH 44118-4209 Office: Dix & Eaton Inc 1301 E 9th St Ste 1300 Cleveland OH 44114-1820

BUCHTA, EDMUND, engineering executive; b. Wostitz, Nikolsburg, Czechoslovakia, May 11, 1928; came to U.S., 1979; Kaufmann, Deutsche Wirtschaftoberschule, Bruenn, Czechoslovakia, 1942-45. Shop foreman Messerklinger, Ernsting, Austria, 1949-51; constrn. foreman Hinteregger, U.S. Mil. Project, Salzburg, Siezenheim, Austria, 1951-52, Auserehl Constrn. Corp., N.Y.C., 1963; pres. Grout Concrete Constrn. Ltd., Edmonton, Alta., Can., 1966-73; pioneer & explorer Canol Project Parcel B and Land Ownership N.W. Can., 1968—; pres. Barbarosa Enterprises Ltd., Yellowknife, Can., 1971—; owner (with Barbarosa Enterprises Ltd.) Canol Project Parcel B, 1968—. Mem. Dem. Senatorial Campaign Com. With German Mil., 1943-45. Named Emperor of the North, McLean Mag., Can., 1976. Mem. Internat. Platform Assn., Dem. Senatorial Campaign Com. Home: PO Box 7000-713 Redondo Beach CA 90277

BUCHTEL, MICHAEL EUGENE, optical mechanical engineer; b. Denver, Jan. 29, 1939; s. William Paxton and Lorraine Edith (Hammond) B.; m. Gloria Jean Guerrero, Sept. 29, 1967. BS, West Coast U., Compton, Calif., 1972. Sr. engr. Ford Aerospace Corp., Newport Beach, Calif., 1972-92; pres. The Techtel Co., Costa Mesa, Calif., 1992—; cons. Internat. Orgn. for Standards, Pforzheim, Switzerland, 1993—. Patentee for optical scanner in U.S. and Japan. With U.S. Army, 1962-64. Mem. Internat. Soc. for Optical Engrs., Am. Soc. Design Engrs. Republican. Roman Catholic. Office: The Techtel Co 1666 Newport Blvd Costa Mesa CA 92627-3717

BUCHWALD, ART, columnist, writer; b. Mt. Vernon, N.Y., Oct. 20, 1925; s. Joseph and Helen (Kleinberger) B.; m. Ann McGarry, Oct. 11, 1952; 3 children. Student, U. So. Calif., 1945-48. Syndicated columnist, 550 newspapers throughout world; columnist Los Angeles Times Syndicate. Author: Paris After Dark, 1950, Art Buchwald's Paris, 1954, The Brave Coward, 1957, A Gift From the Boys, 1959, More Caviar, 1958, Un Cadeau Pour Le Patron (Prix de la Bonne Humeur 1958), Don't Forget to Write, 1960, Art Buchwald's Secret List to Paris, 1963, How Much Is That in Dollars?, 1961, Is It Safe to Drink the Water?, 1962, I Chose Capitol Punishment, 1963, And Then I Told the President, 1965, Son of the Great Society, 1966, Have I Ever Lied to You, 1968, The Establishment Is Alive and Well in Washington, 1969, Counting Sheep, 1970, Getting High in Government Circles, 1971, I Never Danced at the White House, 1973, The Bollo Caper, 1974, I Am Not a Crook, 1974, Irving's Delight, 1975, Washington is Leaking, 1976, Down the Seine and Up the Potomac, 1977, The Buchwald Stops Here, 1978, Laid Back in Washington, 1981, While Reagan Slept, 1983, You CAN Fool All of the People All the Time, 1985, I Think I Don't Remember, 1987, Whose Rose Garden Is It Anyway?, 1989, Lighten Up, George, 1991, Leaving Home: A Memoir, 1994, I'll Always Have Paris, 1996. Served as sgt. USMCR, 1942-45. Recipient Pulitzer prize for outstanding commentary, 1982. Mem. Am. Acad. Arts and Scis., Am. Acad. Humor Columnists. Office: Ste 3804 540 Park Ave New York NY 10021

BUCHWALD, ELIAS, public relations executive; b. N.Y.C., Feb. 5, 1924; s. Louis and Sara (Gottfried) B.; m. Oct. 25, 1952; children: Monita, Lee Ezer, Gena Golda. B. Chem Engring., Sch. Tech. CCNY, 1944. Process engr. Union Carbide, Oak Ridge, 1946-48; acct. exec. Sheldon, Morse, Hutchins & Easton, N.Y.C., 1948-50; sr. assoc. Harold Burson, Pub. Relations, N.Y.C., 1950-52; v.p. Burson-Marsteller, N.Y.C., 1952-75, vice chmn., 1975—; pres. Marsteller Found., N.Y.C., 1980—; vice chmn. Cohn & Wolfe, 1988—. Contbr. articles to profl. jours. Served with U.S. Army, 1944-46. Mem. Pub. Relations Soc. Am. (pres. N.Y. chpt. 1987-88, chmn. bd. ethics and profl. standards 1988-89, Presdl. Citation 1980-82, 1987, 88), Am. Inst. Chem. Engrs., Wellness Coun. Am. (bd. dirs.). Republican. Jewish. Home: 1020 Park Ave New York NY 10028-0913 Office: Burson Marsteller 230 Park Ave S New York NY 10003-1513

BUCHWALD, HENRY, surgeon, educator, researcher; b. Vienna, Austria, June 21, 1932; came to U.S., 1939; naturalized; s. Andor and Renee (Franzos) B.; m. Emilie D. Bix, June 6, 1954; children: Jane Nicole, Amy Elizabeth, Claire Gretchen, Dana Alexandra. BA summa cum laude, Columbia U., 1954, MD, 1957; MS in Biochemistry, PhD in Surgery, U. Minn., 1967. Diplomate Am. Bd. Surgery. Intern Columbia/Presbyn. Med. Ctr., N.Y.C., 1957-58; resident fellow in surgery U. Minn., Mpls., 1960-67; asst. prof. surgery U. Minn. Med. Sch., Mpls., 1967-70, assoc. prof., 1970-77, prof. surgery, prof. biomed. engring., 1977—, dir. grad. surg. tng., resident tng. program, in-tng. exam.; chmn. credentials com.; pres. Minn. Inventors Hall of Fame, 1989-92, chmn. bd. dirs. 1992-94; vis. prof., lectr. McLaren Gen. Hosp., Flint., Mich., 1979, Buffalo Surg. Soc., Mpls., 1980, G.P. Wratten Surg. Symposium, Washington, 1980, Frontiers of Medicine Series, Chgo., 1980, Minn. Endocrine Club, Mpls., 1980, Symposium on Surgery, Tokyo, 1980, Northwestern Med. Assn., Sun Valley, Idaho, 1981, Mayo Clinic, Rochester, Minn., 1981, BSG/Glaxo Internat. Teaching Day, Norwich, Eng., 1982, Mass. Gen. Hosp., Boston, 1983, SUNY Stony Brook, 1984, D.C. Gen. Hosp., Washington, 1984, L.A. Surg. Soc., 1987, Sch. Dentistry, Dept. Continuing Edn., U. Minn., 1988, others; Alfred Strauss vis. lectr., Chgo., 1989; spkr., cons. in field.; presenter numerous confs. and symposia. Author: (with others) Hepatic, Biliary and Pancreatic Surgery, 1980, Lipoproteins and Coronary Atherosclerosis, 1982, Atherosclerosis: Clinical Evaluation and Therapy, 1982, Nutrition and Heart Disease, 1982, Advances in Vascular Surgery, 1983, Advances in Surgery, 1984, others; contbr. Gibbon's Surgery of the Chest, 4th edit., 1983, Hardy's Textbook of Surgery, 1983, Implantable Pumps: ASAIO Primers in Artificial Organs, 1987; contbr. over 250 articles to profl. jours., trans.; mem. editorial bd. Chirurgia Generale, Jour. Clin. Surgery, Infu-Systems Internat., Diabetes, Nutrition and Metabolism, Obesity Surgery Jour. Am. Soc. Artificial Int. Orgn., Jour. Bacteriol. Surgery, Online Jour. Current Clin. Trials, also guest editor other jours. Capt. SAC, USAF, 1958-60. Recipient Inventor of Yr. award Minn. Inventors Hall of Fame, 1988, 90, Cln. Scholar award U.Minn., 1991; recipient numerous rsch. grants univs., Nat. Heart and Lung Inst., Nat. Cancer Inst., Nat. Inst. Arthritis, Metabolism and Digestive Diseases, NIH, med. founds., pharm. cos., corps., 1956—. Fellow ACS (Samuel D. Gross award 1969), Am. Surg. Assn., Soc. Univ. Surgeons, Cen. Surg. Assn. (program com. 1982-85, chmn. 1984-85, treas. 1992-94, pres. 1997-98), Assn. Acad. Surgery (Disting. Svc. award 1976), Epidemiology Coun. and Cardiovascular Coun. Am. Heart Assn. (established investigator), Am. Coll. Cardiology, Soc. Surgery Alimentary Tract, Soc. Clin. Trials (program com. 1984-85); mem. AAAS, Minn. Surg. Assn. (First Clin. Rsch. award 1965), Mpls. Surg. Assn., Minn. Heart Assn., Am. Assn. History Medicine, Am. Soc. Artificial Internal Organs (program com. 1984-87, sect. editor Trans.), Internat. Study Group Diabetes Treatment with Implantable Insulin Delivery Devices (sec.-gen. 1984-88, chmn. 1989-94), St. Paul Surg. Soc. (hon.), Am. Coll. Nutrition (mem. editorial bd.), Am. Soc. Bariatric Soc. (pres. 1998-99), Paleopathology Club, Alpha Omega Alpha. Avocations: running, riding, tennis, reading, chess. Home: 6808 Margarets Ln Minneapolis MN 55439-1019 Office: U Minn Dept Surgery PO Box 290 Minneapolis MN 55440-0290

BUCHWALD, JED ZACHARY, environmental health researcher, science history educator; b. N.Y.C., June 25, 1949. BA, Princeton U., 1971; MA, Harvard, 1973, PhD, 1974. Instr., dir. Inst. History Philosophy Sci. and Tech. U. Toronto, 1974-92; prof., dir. Dibner Inst. for History of Sci. and Tech. MIT. Author: (book) The Creation of Scientific Effects, 1994. Named MacArthur fellow John D. and Katherine T. MacArthur Foundation, 1995; recipient award for excellence in environ. health rsch. Lovelace Inst., Albuquerque, 1995. Office: MIT Dibner Inst History/Sci Bldg MIT-E56-100 38 Memorial Dr Cambridge MA 02139*

BUCHWALD, MARTYN JEREL See BALIN, MARTY

BUCHWALD, MONITA, public relations executive. Account exec. Manning, Selvage & Lee Inc., N.Y.C., 1980-83, v.p., 1983-85, dep. group mgr., 1985-86; group mgr. Manning, Selvage & Lee, Inc., N.Y.C., 1986-87, sr. v.p., 1987-88, dir. health care divsn., worldwide acct. dir., 1988-92, sr. v.p., 1992-93, joint mng. dir. N.Y., 1993-94, sr. v.p., dep. dir. creative and strategic devel., then exec. v.p., 1994-97, vice chmn., worldwide dir. strategic planning, 1997—. Office: Manning Selvage & Lee Inc 79 Madison Ave New York NY 10016-7802*

BUCHWALD, NAOMI REICE, judge; b. Kingston, N.Y., Feb. 14, 1944. BA cum laude, Brandeis U., 1965; LLB cum laude, Columbia U., 1968. Bar: N.Y. 1968, U.S. Ct. Appeals (2d cir.) 1969, U.S. Dist. Ct. (so. and ea. dists.) N.Y. 1970, U.S. Supreme Ct. 1978. Litigation assoc. Marshall, Bratter, Greene, Allison & Tucker, N.Y.C., 1968-73; asst. U.S. atty. So. Dist. N.Y., 1973-80, dep. chief civil divsn., 1976-79, chief civil divsn., 1979-80; U.S. magistrate judge U.S. Dist. Ct. (so. dist.) N.Y., N.Y.C., 1980—, chief magistrate judge, 1994-96. Editor Columbia Jour. Law and Social Problems, 1967-68. Recipient spl. citation FDA Commrs., 1978, Robert B. Fiske Jr. Assn. William B. Tendy award, Outstanding Pub. Svc. award Seymour Assn., Columbia Law Sch. Class of 1968 Excellence in Pub. Svc. award, 1998. Mem. Fed. Bar Coun. (trustee 1976-82, 97—, v.p. 1982-84), N.Y. State Bar Assn., Assn. of the Bar of the City of N.Y. (trademarks and unfair competition com. 1988-89, mem. long range planning com. 1993-95, litigation com. 1994-96, ad hoc com. on jud. conduct 1996-99), Phi Beta Kappa, Omicron Delta Epsilon. Office: US Ct House 500 Pearl St Rm 2270 New York NY 10007-1316

BUCINELL, RONALD BLAISE, mechanical engineer, educator; b. Johnson City, N.Y., Feb. 3, 1958; s. Felix James and Irene Mary (Novak) B.; m. Jill Bucinell, Aug. 24; children: Ryan Michael, Benjamin David. AAS, Rochester Inst. Tech., 1978, BS, 1981; MS, Drexel U., 1983, PhD, 1987. Registered profl. engr., N.Y. Engr. Boeing Aerospace, Seattle, 1979-80; rsch. asst. Dyna East Corp., Wynnewood, Pa., 1983-85; rsch. analyst Hercules Aerospace, Magna, Utah, 1987-89; rsch. engr. Materials Scis. Corp., Blue Bell, Pa., 1989-93; v.p. Innotech, Schenectady, N.Y., 1991—; adj. asst. prof. Temple U., Phila., 1991—, U. Utah, Salt Lake City, 1988-90; assoc. prof. Union Coll., Schenectady, 1993—; creator virtual internat. design studio. Publ. reviewer: Jour. Composite Materials, 1988—; contbr. articles to profl. jours. Initiated a pilot hands-on sci. program for 1st-5th graders, later adopted, Schenectady Schs., mem. PTO, mem. Shared Decision Making Com. Fellow NASA. Mem. ASME, ASM, ASTM (chmn. task group, vice chmn. subcom.), Am. Soc. Engring. Edn., KC (4th deg.), Sigma Xi. Achievements include the development of methodology for altering failure modes in composite overwrapped pressure vessels; scaling methodology for response of composite materials; stochastic damage progression model for composite materials; test procedures and fixtures for evaluating the behavior of composite materials; developer of the international virtual design studio concept in engineering education. Home: 1063 Merlin Dr Schenectady NY 12309-1633 Office: Union Coll Steinmetz Hall Schenectady NY 12308

BUCK, ALFRED ANDREAS, physician, epidemiologist; b. Hamburg, Germany, Mar. 9, 1921; came to U.S., 1958, naturalized, 1967; s. Heino C. and Antonie (Schwarz) B.; m. Kay A. Amann, Sept. 15, 1962; children: Suzanne Karen, Alfred Andreas. MD in Pharmacology, U. Hamburg, 1945; MPH, Johns Hopkins U., 1959, DrPH, 1961. Med. resident Univ. Hosp., Hamburg, 1945-52; physician, cons. Gen. Govt. Hosp., Makassar, Celebes, Indonesia, 1952- 55; head physician Red Cross Hosp., Pusan, Korea, 1955-58; mem. faculty Johns Hopkins U., Balt., 1963—, prof. epidemiology and internat. health, 1968-92, prof. immunology and infectious diseases, 1986-92, dir. div. bacteriology and mycology Sch. Hygiene, 1967-72, chmn. tropical medicine council, 1973-74, also research dir., geog. epidemiology group; dep. dir. Vector-Borne Disease Project, Arlington, Va.; adj. prof. immunology and infectious diseases Johns Hopkins U., Balt.; cons. AID, Ethiopia, 1962-64, West and Ctrl. Africa, 1971; mem. sr. staff WHO, Geneva, 1971-73, chief med. officer divsn. malaria and other parasitic diseases, 1974-78, chief rsch. coordination, epidemiology and tng. and sec. sci. working group for epidemiology, spl. program rsch. and tng. in tropical diseases; tropical medicine adv. Office of Health, Dept. State, AID, Washington, 1978-88; adj. prof. internat. health, molecular microbiology and immunology Johns Hopkins U.; adj. prof. tropical medicine Tulane U., 1988—; vis. prof. Sch. of Medicine Ain Shams U., Cairo; vis. prof. Sch. of Medicine, Hannover, Germany, 1991-97; expert tropical medicine NIH/NIAID; resident scientist, Cairo; mem. Steering Coms. of Sci. Working Groups "Fieldmal" and "Epidemiology" of WHO, Geneva. Author books; contbr. articles in field; assoc. editor: Tropenmedizin und Parasitologie. Recipient Meritorious Honor award Dept. State, 1980, Bernhard Nocht medal in tropical medicine, 1981, Meritorious Svc. award USAID, 1985, Superior Unit citation, 1991, AID/Dept. State Meritorious Svc. award, 1986, Spl. award DHHS/NIH, 1991, Donald Mackay medal in tropical medicine jointly Am. Soc. Tropical Medicine and Hygiene and Royal Soc. Tropical Medicine, 1995; hon. fellow in tropical medicine Faculty Liverpool Sch. Tropical Medicine, 1982. Fellow APHA, Am. Coll. Epidemiology; mem. Epidemiol. Rsch. Assn., Am. Soc. Tropical Medicine, Internat. Epidemiologic Soc., Am. Epidemiol. Soc., Tropical Medicine Assn. D.C., Delta Omega. Lutheran. Home: 1603 East Ave Mc Lean VA 22101-4105

BUCK, ALISON JENNIFER, computer programmer; b. Bangor, Maine, Dec. 11, 1952; d. George Hill and Anna (Komisaruk) B. BS, U. Maine, Orono, 1974; MA, Brigham Young U., 1978. Cert. tchr., Maine, Mass. Vol. program coordinator Head Start/Hampshire Community Action Commn., Northampton, Mass., 1980; career edn. specialist, job developer Hampshire Ednl. Collaborative, Northampton, 1981; documentation specialist Amherst (Mass.) Assocs., 1981-84; sr. tech. writer Visual Intelligence Corp., Amherst, 1984-85; tech. documentation specialist Video Communications Inc., Feeding Hills, Mass., 1986-87; contract tech. writer Digital Equipment Corp., Westfield, Mass., 1987; mktg. coordinator, tech. publs. mgr. Millitech Corp., South Deerfield, Mass., 1988; contract tech. writer Carrier Corp., Farmington, Conn., 1988-89; author computer-based tng. materials AMS Courseware Developers, Manchester, Conn., 1989-92; learning tech. Aetna Ins. Corp., Hartford, Conn., 1992-94; application developer Health New Eng., Springfield, Mass., 1994-97; programmer Myers Info. Systems, West Springfield, Mass., 1997-98; cons. computer svcs., 1998—. Co-author: The Coffee Maker Cookbook, 1988. Democrat. Avocations: music, writing, yoga, movement improvization, skiing, tennis.

BUCK, ANNE MARIE, library director, consultant; b. Birmingham, Ala., Apr. 12, 1939; d. Blaine Alexander and Marie Reynolds (McGeorge) Davis; m. Evan Buck, June 17, 1961 (div. Apr. 1977); children: Susan Elizabeth Buck Rentko, Stephen Edward. BA, Wellesley (Mass.) Coll., 1961; MLS, U. Ky., 1977. Bus. mgr. Charleston (W.Va.) Chamber Music Soc., 1972-74; dir. Dunbar (W.Va.) Pub. Libr., 1974-76; tech. reference libr. AT&T Bell Labs., Naperville, Ill., 1977-79; group supr. libr. AT&T Bell Labs., Reading, Pa., 1979-83; group supr. support svcs. AT&T Bell Labs., North Andover, Mass., 1983; dir. libr. network Bell Communications Rsch. (Bellcore), Morristown, N.J., 1983-89; dir. human resources planning Bell Communications Rsch. (Bellcore), Livingston, N.J., 1989-91; univ. libr. N.J. Inst. Tech., Newark, 1991-95, Calif. Inst. of Tech., Pasadena, 1995—; adj. prof. Rutgers U., New Brunswick, N.J., 1989-90; instr. U. Wis., Madison, 1988-90; v.p. Engring. Info. Found., N.Y.C., 1994—; mem. Engring. Info. Inc. (bd. dirs.), Castle-Point-on-the-Hudson, Hoboken, N.J., 1988-98; spkr. profl. assn. confs., 1982—; libr. cons. North Port (Fla.) Area Libr., 1990-91; co-chair Caltech Conf. on Scholarly Comm., 1997. Mem. editorial adv. bd. Highsmith Press, 1991-97; contbr. articles to profl. jours. Sect. mgr. United Way of Morris County, Cedar Knolls, N.J., 1984-95; advisor Family Svc. Transitions Coun., Morristown, 1987-90; mem. local svcs. & programs com. San Gabriel Valley (Calif.) United Way, 1998—; libr. trustee Lisle (Ill.) Pub. Libr. Dist., 1978-80; bd. dirs. Kanawha County Bicentennial Commn., Charleston, W.Va., 1974-76; personnel com., denominational affairs com., Neighborhood Ch., Pasadena, Calif., 1996—. Recipient Vol.'s Gold award United Way, 1991, Disting. Alumna award U. Ky. Sch. Libr. and Info. Sci., 1996. Mem. ALA (Grolier Nat. Libr. Week grantee 1975), Am. Soc. Info. Sci. (chpt. chmn. 1987-89, Chpt. of Yr. award 1988, treas. 1992-95), Conf. Bd. Inc. (chmn. info. svcs. adv. coun. 1987-89), Spl. Libr. Assn., Am. Soc. Engring. Edn., Archons of Colophon, Indsl. Tech. Info. Mgrs. Group, Wellesley Coll. Alumni Assn. (class rep. 1986-91), N.J. Wellesley Club (regional chmn. 1986-89, corr. sec. 1994-95), Beta Phi Mu. Unitarian. Avocations: choral singing, travel, photography. Home: 2254 Loma Vista St Pasadena CA 91104-4906 Office: Calif Inst Tech Mail Stop 1-32 Pasadena CA 91125 *Perhaps the greatest skill one can develop is the ability to identify genuine opportunities and the willingness to incur risk in pursuing them.*

BUCK, CAROL KATHLEEN, medical educator; b. London, Ont., Can., Apr. 2, 1925; d. Albert Henry and Evelyn Florence (Parsons) Whitlow; m. Robert Crawforth, June 22, 1946; children: Lucy Anne, Effie Louise. MD, U. Western Ont., 1947, PhD, 1950; DPH, London Sch. Hygiene and Tropical Medicine, 1951; LLD (hon.), Dalhousie U., 1989. Asst. prof. U. Western Ont., London, 1952-56, assoc. prof., 1956-62, prof. epidemiology, 1962-90, ret., 1990; mem. adv. com. Stats. Can., Ottawa, 1985-95; mem. occupl. disease panel Ministry of Labour, Toronto, Ont., 1988-97. Contbr. articles to profl. jours., chpts. to books. Fellow Royal Soc. Can., Am. Coll. Epidemiology, Internat. Epidemiology Assn. (pres. 1981-84); mem. John Howard Soc. Ont. (life). Mem. New Dem. Party Can. Avocations: reading, music, golf. Home: 181 Elmwood Ave, London, ON Canada N6C 1K1

BUCK, CAROLYN J., federal official. BA, U. Minn.; JD with honors, George Washington U. Chief counsel Office of Thrift Supervision, Washington, 1992—. Office: Office of Thrift Supervisin 1700 G St NW Washington DC 20552-0003

BUCK, CHRISTOPHER GEORGE, religion educator, writer; b. Quantico, Va., Oct. 11, 1950; s. George Hugh and Sandra Kay (Thompson) B.; m. Nahzy Abadi, May 26, 1984; children: Takor George, Taraz Earle. MA, U. Calgary, Alta., Can., 1991; PhD, U. Toronto, 1996. Lectr. dept. religion Carleton U., Ottawa, Ont., Can., 1994-96; asst. prof. dept. religion Millikin U., Decatur, Ill., 1997—. Author: Symbol and Secret, 1995 (Baha'i Book of Yr. 1995), Paradise and Paradigm, 1999; mem. editl. adv. bd. Assn. for Baha'i Studies, Ottawa, 1998—; contbr. articles to profl. jours. Dir. Svc. Learning Project/Luth. Sch. Assn., Decatur, 1998—. Mem. Am. Acad. Religion, Assn. for Baha'i Studies (award for excellence, 1991, 94. Baha'i Faith. Avocations: digital typography, chess, weight-lifting, distance running. Email: CBuck@Mail.Millikin.Edu. Office: Millikin U Dept Religion 1184 W Main St Decatur IL 62522-2084

BUCK, DONALD TIRRELL, finance educator; b. Manchester, N.H., Nov. 17, 1931; s. Harry Forrest and Gladys (Tirrell) B.; m. Marion Gilmour, Aug. 2, 1969; children: Marianne Elizabeth, Elizabeth Allison Tirrell. BS, U. N.H., 1955, MA, 1961. Analyst New England Mut. Life Ins. Co., Boston, 1957-59; instr. fin. U. Pa. Wharton Sch. Bus., Phila., 1961-65; asst. prof. econs. and fin. So. Conn. State Coll., New Haven, 1965-74; assoc. prof. So. Conn. State U., New Haven, 1975-80, prof., 1981-97, emeritus prof., 1998—, mem. faculty senate, 1968-76, chmn. dept. acctg. fin., 1984-85; pub. mem. investment adv. coun. to treas. State of Conn., Hartford, 1983-92. Contbr. articles to profl. publs. Mem. adv. coun. Bd. Higher Edn. State of Conn., 1983-85; participant econ. workshop hearings legis. fin. com. Gen. Assembly, Conn., 1978-83. With U.S. Army, 1955-57. Mem. AAUP (pres. So. Conn. State U. chpt. 1981-83), SAR (pres. Nathan Hale chpt. 1993-96, auditor Conn. State chpt. 1993—), Am. Econ. Assn., Soc. Colonial Wars in State of Conn. Congregationalist. Home: Old Town St Hadlyme CT 06439-0129 Office: So Conn State U 501 Crescent St New Haven CT 06515-1330

BUCK, EARL WAYNE, insurance investigator, private detective; b. La Porte City, Iowa, Jan. 15, 1939; s. Edwin Earl and Uleta Pearl (Purdy) B.; m. Maxine E. Parker, Oct. 19, 1969; children: Brian, Douglas. LLB, La Salle U., 1969. Asst. mgr. Chgo. br. Atwell, Vogel & Sterling, Scarsdale, N.Y., 1965-70; pvt. detective, Sioux City, Iowa, 1968-74; mgr. Milw. br. Atwell, Vogel & Sterling, Scarsdale, N.Y., 1970; sr. auditor Comml. Union Ins. Co., Chgo., 1970-74; police chief McHenry Shores (Ill.) Police Dept., 1973-79; self-employed ins. investigator McHenry, Ill., 1980-88, Rapid City, S.D., 1988—; owner Corral Motel, Rapid City, 1988—; liquor liability investigator for various ins. cos., 1980-88; farm owner, 1986-96; owner High Plaines Detective Agy., 1990—; ptnr. Juke Boxes, Western Fla. Chmn. McHenry Shores (Ill.) Zoning Commn., 1972, Police Support Subcom., C. of C. Pub. Safety Com.; key contact Help Abolish Legal Tyranny; active Rapid City Police Res., 1989-90, North Rapid Civic Assn., 1991-94, pres., chmn. bd., 1993-94; active Pennington County Air Quality Bd., 1990-93, chmn., 1992-93. With U.S. Army, 1957-61. Recipient Police Meritorious Service award Vill. of McHenry Shores, 1979. Mem. Midwest Inst. Auditors Assn., McHenry County Police Chief's Assn., Rapid City Police Officers Assn., Rapid City Area Hospitality Assn. (bd. dirs.), Rapid City Area C. of C. (safety com. 1989-91), Black Hills Badlands & Lakes Assn., Fed. Weed and Seed Program Rapid City (steering com.), NRA, Moose. Republican. Lutheran. Avocations: flying, amateur archaelogy, photography, fishing, hunting.

BUCK, FRANCIS SCOTT, pathologist, educator; b. Eskridge, Kans., Oct. 6, 1921; s. Robert Willard Buck and Helen Miriam Dill; m. Dorothy Irene Hollenbeck, Sept. 10, 1948; children: Ronald Scott, Richard Allen, Robert Grant, Dottiann Irene Buck. Student, Fresno State Coll., 1939-43, 45-47; DO, Coll. Osteo. Physicans/Surgeon, L.A., 1951; MD, Calif. Coll. Medicine, 1962. Cert. anatomic and clin. pathology Am. Bd. Pathology. Dir. pathology L.A. County Hosp., 1955-68; chief physician, pathologist L.A. County/U. So. Calif. Med. Ctr., L.A., 1968-85, attending physician, 1985—; mem. profl. staff assn. L.A. County/U. So. Calif. Med. Ctr., L.A., 1968-85; v.p., bd. govs. Am. Osteopathic Coll. Pathology, 1961-62. Contbr. articles to med. jours. Mem. donor recruitment com. L.A./Orange County ARC Blood Bank, 1980-81; bd. trustees Reformed Presbyn. Ch. N.Am., 1972-79; elder Reformed Presbyn. Ch. L.A., 1971—. Capt. U.S. Army Air Force,

1942-45. Mem. AMA, Calif. Med. Assn., Calif. Soc. Pathologists, L.A. Soc. Pathologists, Grad. Soc. Pathologists, L.A. County/U. So. Calif. Med. Ctr. (sec., pres. 1979-85). Republican. Avocations: theology, teaching bible, fishing, hiking, gem cutting. Home: 240 Cherry Dr Pasadena CA 91105-1325

BUCK, GENE, graphics company executive, satirist, historian; b. Seattle, July 4, 1946; s. Gene Cecil and Theodosia Ann (Burr) B. Student, U. Hawaii, 1975-76, U. Wash., 1976-79, Kingswork Inst., Honolulu, 1979-80. Owner Buck & Assocs. Advt. Agy., Monterey, Calif., 1980-85, Cypress Fine Arts, Monterey, 1981-87, Gene Buck, Publicist, Monterey, 1983-87; dir. Aaron Burr Accord, Seattle, 1987—; chmn. Aaron Burr Commemorative Stamp Com., Seattle, 1981—; owner Storyville Graphics, Seattle, 1990—; cons. Spencer Prodns., Inc., N.Y.C., 1975-98, Bing Crosby Hist. Soc., Tacoma, 1975-94; dir. Brotherhood for Respect, Elevation, and Advancement of Dishwaters, Monterey, 1983-85, founder Empire of Burravia, 1985—. Author: (children's book) On the Sidewalks of New York, 1995, ABC Color and Learn Book, 1997, (satire/cartoon book) The Penguin Papers, 1993, (with Gerald E. Mowery) Who's Who in the Slow-Lane, 1997, The Y2K Crash—Don't Blame Bill Gates!, 1998, The Secret Stamps, 1999, Back to Aaron Burr, 1999, Quotations of Aaron Burr in Exile, 1999—, Betty Oops, 1999. Chmn. Rose St. Commons, Seattle, 1992-98, Stop the Train!, Seattle, 1993-98; dir. Soc. of Disenfranchised, Seattle, 1987-96, dir., 1980-98; chmn. Goldwater Alliance, 1998—. With USNR, 1974-78. Avocation: collecting Betty Boop memorabilia. Office: Storyville Graphics PO Box 4644 Seattle WA 98104-0644

BUCK, JACK, sportscaster, broadcast executive; b. Holyoke, Mass.; m. Carol Buck. Grad., Ohio State U. Previously sportscaster baseball games Columbus, Ohio, Rochester, N.Y.; sportscaster, commentator Sta. KMOX (CBS Radio), St. Louis, 1954—, now sports dir.; announcer St. Louis Baseball Cardinals, 1954—; announcer baseball CBS-TV Sports, 1990—; sportscaster CBS Sports NFL Football, 1970-74, CBS-TV Sports NFL Football, 1978—, NBC Sports, 1975-78, CBS Radio Network Monday Night Football broadcasts, 1978—; commentator World Series Game, 1968, 82, Super Bowl Games, 1970, 78—; dir. sports operation CBS Radio. Campaign chmn. Cystic Fibrosis Found., St. Louis. Served in World War II. Decorated Purple Heart; recipient Cert. of Excellence Abe Lincoln awards. Office: KMOX AM Radio Gateway Tower 1 S Memorial Dr Saint Louis MO 63102-2425*

BUCK, JAMES E., financial exchange executive. Sr. v.p. & corp. sec. N.Y. Stock Exch., N.Y.C., 1993—. Address: NY Stock Exch Inc 11 Wall St Fl 6 New York NY 10005-1905 Address: 4 World Trade Ctr Fl 8 New York NY 10048-0899*

BUCK, JAMES MAHLON, JR., venture capital executive; b. Bryn Mawr, Pa., Apr. 27, 1925; s. J. Mahlon and Grace Irene (Knapp) B.; m. Elia Garrett Durr, Sept. 15, 1953; children: Caroline Buck Rogers, James M. III. AB in Econs., Princeton U., 1948. Ops. mgr. Smith, Kline and French, Inc., Phila., 1948-56, v.p. ops., 1956-65; chmn., chief exec. officer The Drug House, Inc., Phila., 1965-77; chmn. Alco Health Services Group, Valley Forge, Pa., 1977-83; pres., CEO TDH Capital Ptnrs., Radnor, Pa., 1977—; adv. bd. mem. Phila. Phillies, 1981—. Bd. dirs. The Bryn Mawr (Pa.) Hosp. Found., 1978—. With U.S. Army, 1943-45, ETO. Republican. Presbyterian. Clubs: Merion Golf (Ardmore, Pa.); Merion Cricket (Haverford, Pa.). Avocations: tennis, golf, music, spectator sports. Home: 121 Rose Ln Haverford PA 19041-1724 Office: TDH Capital Corp PO Box 8234/Radnor Ct 259 N Radnor Chester Rd Ste 210 Radnor PA 19087-5259 also: Phila Phillies PO Box 7575 Philadelphia PA 19101-7575

BUCK, JOHN E., sculptor, print maker, educator; b. Ames, Iowa, Feb. 14, 1946; m. Debora Butterfield; 2 children. BFA, Kans. City Art Inst., 1968; MFA, U. Calif., Davis, 1972. Instr. in sculpture Mont. State U., Bozeman, 1976-90. Sculptor and print maker: solo exhibitions include: Kans. City (Mo.) Art Inst., John Buck, 1988, Fine Arts Mus. San Francisco, John Buck: Woodblock Prints, 1993— (travels), Palm Springs Desert Mus., 1994, John Buck: Sculpture, 1994, The Contemporary Mus., Honolulu, John Buck: A Survey Exhibition, 1995; group exhibits Seattle Art Mus., Seattle, Calif. Permanent Collection, 1992, Newport Harbor Art Mus., Newport Beach, Calif., Beyond the Bay, 1993, Laguna Gloria Art Mus., Austin, Human Nature, Human Form, 1993, The Oakland (Calif.) Mus., Here and Now, 1994; commissions include: Ahmanson Commercial Devel., Chgo., 1991, Prin. Fin. Group, Des Moines, Iowa, 1989; represented by Zolla/Lieberman Gallery, Chgo., Greg Kucera Gallery, Seattle, DC Moore Gallery, N.Y.C. Recipient Individual Artist's award NEA, 1980, awards in the visual arts, Nat. Artists Award, 1984. Fax: (406) 585-9757. Office: 11229 Cottonwood Rd Bozeman MT 59718-9576

BUCK, LAWRENCE PAUL, academic administrator; b. Pittsburg, Kans., Oct. 6, 1944; m. Judy L.; children: David L., Laura T. BA, Wichita State U., 1966; MA, Ohio State U., 1967, PhD in History, 1971. Asst. prof. Widener U., Chester, Pa., 1971-77, assoc. prof. history, 1977-85, prof. history, 1985—, dean Coll. Arts and Scis., 1981-84, acad. v.p., provost, 1984—; acting pres. Widener U., 1994. Author: Die Haltung der Nurnberger Bauernschaft im Bauernkrieg, 1970, Opposition to Tithes in the Peasants' Revolt, 1973, Civil Insurrection in a Reformation City, 1976, Demands for Reform by Urban Dissidents During the German Peasants' Revolt, 1977, The Reformation, Purgatory, and Perpetual Rents in the Revolt of 1525 at Frankfurt am Main, 1985; translator: Monemvasia: The Town and Its History, 1981; co-editor: The Social History of the Reformation; contbr. articles to profl. jours., book chpts. Rsch. grantee Am. Philos. Soc., 1973, NEH, 1974. Mem. Am. Soc. Reformation Rsch., 16th Century Study Conf. Office: Widener U Office of Provost One University Pl Chester PA 19013

BUCK, LEE ALBERT, retired insurance company executive, evangelist; b. Jonesboro, Ark., July 28, 1923; s. Lee A. and Annie (Ballew) B.; m. Audrey Ruth McMurphy, Feb. 26, 1945; children—Melody Anne, Merrilee Ruth, Bonnie Sue, Lisa Carol. B.A. with honors, U. Mich., 1947, M.A. in Colonial Am. History, 1948; C.L.U., 1960. With N.Y. Life Ins. Co., 1949—, dir. agys., 1962-63, 2d v.p., 1963-64, v.p. agys., 1964-66, regional v.p. charge Southeastern U.S., 1964-67; v.p. mktg. N.Y. Life Ins. Co., N.Y.C., 1967-74; sr. v.p. group mktg. N.Y. Life Ins. Co., 1974-78, sr. v.p. mktg., 1978-83; lay evangelist St. Paul's Episcopal Ch., Darien, Conn., 1983—; chmn. Com. for Freedom (polit. action com.), Washington; bd. dirs. N.Y.C. Relief Inc., Singapore Cons. Inc.; internat. speaker and tchr. leadership principles speaker, tchr. bus. principles and practices to aid Ea. European nations. Author: Tapping Your Secret Source of Power. Past bd. dirs. Greater N.Y. councils Boy Scouts Am.; formerly bd. dirs. Ams. for Indian Opportunity; bd. dirs. Walter Hoving Home; former chmn. bd. Life Underwriter Tng. Council; trustee Regent U., Va. Beach, Va.; past trustee Barrington (R.I.) Coll.; bd. dirs. Faith Alive, Episcopal Renewal Ministries; lay evangelist Episcopal Ch. U.S.A.; nat. v.p., chmn. evangelism commn. Brotherhood of St. Andrew; bd. dirs. Washington for Jesus, Episc. Renewal Ministries; trustee Regent U.; active St. Judes Episc. Ch., Marietta, Ga. Served to lt. USNR, 1942-46, 50-52. Named Disting. Fellow Flint No. High School, 1993. Mem. Nat. Assn. Life Underwriters, Am. Soc. CLUs, Life Ins. Mktg. and Research Assn. (dir.), Agy. Mgmt. Tng. Council. Episcopalian. Home: 605 Townsend Pl NW Atlanta GA 30327-3041

BUCK, LINDA DEE, civic worker; b. San Franciso, Nov. 8, 1946; d. Sol and Shirley D. (Setterberg) Press. Student, Coll. of San Mateo, Calif., 1969-70. Head hearing and appeals br. Dept. Navy Employee Rels. Svc., The Philippines, 1974-75; dir. human resources Homestead Savs. & Loan Assn., Burlingame, Calif., 1976-77; mgr. VIP Agy., Inc., Palo Alto, Calif., 1977-78; exec, v,o,m dur, Sequent Pers. Svcs., Inc., Mountain View, Calif., 1978-83; founder, pres. Buck & Co., San Mateo, 1983-91. Publicity mgr. for No. Calif., Osteogenesis Imprfecta Found. Inc., 1970-72; cons. Am. Brittle Bone Soc., 1979-88; mem. Florence (Oreg.) Area Humane Soc., 1994—, Friends of Libr., Florence, 1994—; bd. dirs. Florence Festival Arts, 1995; bd. dirs., dir. women Rhododendron Scholarship Program, Florence, 1995. Jewish.

BUCK, LOUISE ZIERDT, psychologist; b. Edgewood, Pa., Nov. 21, 1919; d. Conrad Henry and Nancy Leora (Harshberger) Zierdt; div. 1954; children: David Randall, Susan Buck Sutton. BS, Pa. State U., 1940; MEd, U. Pitts., 1954; EdD, Columbia U., 1978; advanced cert., Bklyn. Coll., 1984. Lic. sch. psychologist, clin. psychologist, N.Y. Tchr., dir. Chatham Village Nursery Sch., Pitts., 1953-55; tchr., dir. Yellow Springs (Ohio) Community Nursery Sch., 1955-58; tchr. Oak Lane Country Day Sch., Phila., 1958-59, Walden Sch., N.Y.C., 1959-60, Bank St. Sch. for Children, N.Y.C., 1960-61; early childhood tchr., coord. sch. psychology Bd. Edn., City of N.Y., 1961-87; asst. prof. Bklyn. Coll., 1978-80; rsch. fellow Albert Einstein Coll. Medicine, Bronx, N.Y., 1988-89; psychotherapist Fifth Ave Ctr. for Psychotherapy, N.Y.C., 1989, Met. Ctr. for Mental Health, N.Y.C., 1990—; psychologist cons. Bd. Edn. City of N.Y., 1987-88; pvt. practice, N.Y.C. Contbr. articles to profl. jours. Mem. APA, N.Y. State Psychol. Assn., Soc. for Psychoanalytic Psychotherapy. Democrat. Avocations: traveling, swimming, the arts, enjoying grandchild. Home: 444 E 86th St Apt 34C New York NY 10028-6459 Office: 27 W 96th St Ste 1A New York NY 10025-6515

BUCK, RICHARD PIERSON, chemistry educator, researcher; b. L.A., July 29, 1929; s. Richard Maurice and Lucile Frances (Pierson) B.; m. Mary Ann Kenney, May 23, 1959; children: Nancy Elizabeth Buck McKenna, Pierson Kenney, Margaret Ruth. BS, Calif. Inst. Tech., 1950, MS, 1951; PhD, MIT, 1954. Teaching asst. MIT, Cambridge, 1951-52, NSF fellow, 1952-53, Dupont teaching fellow, 1953-54; rsch. chemist Chevron Rsch. Corp., Richmond, Calif., 1954-61, asst. to gen. mgr., 1956-58; prin. rsch. chemist Bell & Howell Rsch. Ctr., Pasadena, Calif., 1961-65; sr. scientist Beckman Instrument Co., Fullerton, Calif., 1965-67; assoc. prof. chemistry U. N.C., Chapel Hill, 1967-75, prof., 1975—, adj. prof. biomed. engring. and math. Sch. Medicine, 1990—, prof. emeritus, 1998—; Kenan prof.-on-leave U. Bristol, Eng., 1976-77; vis. prof. Imperial Coll., London, 1987, Bundeswehr U. Munich, 1989-91; cons. Eastman Kodak, Rochester, N.Y., 1969-77, E.I. duPont de Nemours & Co., Wilmington, Del., 1979-84; mem. adv. bd. I-Stat Corp., Princeton, N.J., 1984-90, HemoSense, Inc., San Jose, Calif, 1998—, NIH resource at Case Western Res. U., Cleve., 1977-84, Ctr. for Solid State Sensors, U. Pa. Moore Sch. Engring., Phila., 1980-84; chmn. A Nomenclature Commn., Internat. Union Pure and Applied Chemistry, 1991—. Author: (with V.V. Cosofret) Pharmaceutical Applications of Membrane Sensors, 1992; mem. editorial bd. 4 internat. chemistry jours.; contbr. chpts. to sci. jours., chpts. to numerous books. Von Humboldt grantee von Humboldt Stiftung, Bonn, Germany, 1989-91, grantee Advanced Rsch. Projects Agy., 1967-71, NSF, 1971—, N.C. Biotech. Ctr., 1990-94. Fellow Electrochem. Soc. (div. chmn., outstanding achievement award sensor divsn. 1996); mem. Am. Chem. Soc., Internat. Soc. Electrochemistry (bd. dirs. 1988-91), Bohemian Club (San Francisco). Avocations: performing chamber music, solo piano playing. Home: 101 Creekview Cir Carrboro NC 27510-4111 also: 139 Elliott Dr Menlo Park CA 94025-2622 Office: U NC Dept Chemistry CB 3290 Venable Hall Chapel Hill NC 27599-3290

BUCK, ROBERT FOLLETTE, retired banker, lawyer; b. Superior, Nebr., June 7, 1917; s. Samuel Rea and Faye (Follette) B.; m. Barbara J. Carlson, Apr. 29, 1963; children by previous marriage: Carolyn (Mrs. Robert G. Norman), Vincent Templin. B.A., U. Wash., 1938, LL.B., 1942. Bar: Wash. 1946, D.C. bar 1960. Pres. Orcas Power & Light Co., Eastsound, Wash., 1947-54; regional dir. SBA, Seattle, 1954-59; dep. adminstr. SBA, Washington, D.C., 1959-61; v.p. Rainier Nat. Bank, Seattle, 1961-66, sr. v.p., 1966-74, exec. v.p., 1974-82; of counsel Foster, Pepper and Shefelman, Seattle, 1986-95; pros. atty. San Juan County, Wash., 1947-54; pres. Pacific Northwest Trade Assn., 1969-70. Trustee Assn. Wash. Bus., 1968-95, chmn., 1978-79; v.p. Seattle Mcpl. League, 1966-67, trustee, 1964-72; trustee Econ. Devel. Coun. Puget Sound, 1970-84, pres., 1975-77, chmn., 1977-79; trustee Econ. Devel. Partnership for Wash., 1985-87; trustee Wash. State Internat. Trade Fair, 1963-90, pres., 1967-69; dir. many Seattle area musical and theatrical orgns. With USNR, 1942-46, PTO. Decorated Bronze Star medal. Mem. Seattle C. of C. (trustee 1965-66, v.p. 1968-69), Am. Bankers Assn. (dir. 1976-78), Wash. Bankers Assn. (dir. 1975-82, pres. 1978-79), Nat. Mcpl. League (regional v.p. 1977-84), Phi Gamma Delta, Phi Delta Phi. Clubs: Mason (Seattle) (32), Wash. Athletic (Seattle), Rainier (Seattle), Seattle yacht, San Juan Isl. Yacht. Home: 700 Turn Point Rd Friday Harbor WA 98250-9303

BUCK, ROBERT TREAT, JR., gallery director, former museum director, educator; b. Fall River, Mass., Feb. 16, 1939; s. Robert Treat and Hazel (Sayward) B.; m. Nicole Challamel, July 2, 1966; children: Thomas, Philip. BA, Williams Coll., 1961; student, Mus. Tng. Program Met. Mus. Art, 1963-64; MA, NYU, 1965. Lectr., researcher Toledo Mus. Art, 1964-65; asst. curator, instr. art and archaeology Washington U., St. Louis, 1965-67; dir. art gallery Washington U., 1968-70; asst. dir. Albright-Knox Art Gallery, Buffalo, 1970-73, dir., 1973-83; dir. Bklyn. Mus., 1983-96, Marlborough Gallery, N.Y.C., 1997—; adj. prof. dept. art SUNY, Buffalo, 1972-73; mem. N.Y. Coun. for Humanities, 1976-82; mem. art adv. panel IRS, 1978-82; bd. rep. Pratt Inst. Arts, 1984-96, Hirshhorn Mus., 1987-97, Am. Fedn. Arts, 1987-97, Internat. Coun. Mus. Modern Art, 1987-95. Author: Sam Francis: Paintings, 1947-1972, 1972, Diebenkorn: The Ocean Park Paintings, 1976, Sonia Delaunay: A Retrospective, 1980, Ferdinand Leger Retrospective, 1982, Leon Polk Smith: Selected Works, 1943-1992, Promised Gift to Brooklyn Museum, 1993. Mem. Assn. Art Mus. Dirs. (trustee, sect., treas., v.p., pres. 1995-96). Office: Marlborough Gallery 40 W 57th St Fl 2D New York NY 10019-4001

BUCK, ROSS WORKMAN, communication sciences educator, psychology educator, writer; b. Sewickley, Pa., Aug. 16, 1941; s. Ross Workman and Ruth Isabel (Hadley) B.; Marianne Jenney, Dec. 28, 1963; children: William, Maria, Nancy Jenney, Theodore. BA, Allegheny Coll., Meadville, Pa., 1963; MA, U. Wis., 1965; PhD, U. Pitts., 1970. Rsch. assoc. U. Pitts., 1967-70; asst. prof. Carnegie-Mellon U., Pitts., 1967-74; asst. prof. to full prof. U. Conn., Storrs, 1974—; vis. scholar Harvard U., Boston, 1980-81, VA Med. Ctr., Boston, 1980-81; vis. fellow Wolfson Coll., Oxford, Eng., 1987-88, Oxford U., 1987-88; fellow Yale U., New Haven, Conn., 1990-91; vis. prof. Brandeis U., Waltham, Mass., 1994-95. Author: Human Motivation and Emotion, 1976, The Communication of Emotion, 1984, Human Motivation and Emotion, 2d edit, 1988; co-editor: Nonverbal Communication in Clinical Content, 1986; mem. editorial bd. Psychol. Bull., 1994—, J. Personality and Social Psychology, 1989—. Grantee NIMH, 1971-72, 1987-92, Harry Frank Guggenheim Found., 1994-96, EJLB Found., 1994-98. Fellow APA, Am. Psychol. Soc., Soc. Personality Soc. Psychology; mem. Internat. Soc. Rsch. Emotions (charter mem., editor newsletter 1994-97), Internat. Soc. Rsch. Agression, Soc. Exptl. Soc. Psyc. Democrat. Avocations: photography. Home: 63 Cedar Swamp Rd Storrs Manfld CT 06268-1206 Office: U Conn Communication Scis U-85 Storrs Mansfield CT 06269

BUCK, THOMAS RANDOLPH, retired lawyer, financial services executive; b. Washington, Feb. 5, 1930; s. James Charles Francis and Mary Elizabeth (Marshall) B.; m. Alice Armistead James, June 20, 1953; children: Kathryn James, Thomas Randolph, Douglas Marshall, David Andrew; m. Sunny Clark, Sept. 15, 1971; 1 child, Carey Virginia; me. Yvonne Brackett, Nov. 27, 1981. B.A. summa cum laude, Am. U., 1951; JD, U. Va., 1954. Bar: Va. 1954, Ky. 1964, Fla. 1974. Asst. gen. atty. Seaboard Air Line R.R. Co., 1958-63; sec., gen. counsel Am. Comml. Lines. Inc., Houston, 1963-68; asst. gen. counsel Tex. Gas Transmission Corp., 1968-72; sec., gen. counsel Leadership Housing Inc., 1972-77; pres. law firm Buck and Golden, P.A., 1975-92; exec. v.p., gen. counsel Buck Fin. Svcs., Inc., Ft. Lauderdale, Fla., 1992-99; past dir. Computer Resources Inc., Ft. Lauderdale, Fla., So. Aviation Inc., Opa Locka, Fla.; chmn. Hanover Bank of Fla. Bd. dirs. Sheridan House for Youth; trustee Fla. Bapt. Found. Served to capt. USMCR, 1954-58. Mem. Assn. ICC Practitioners (nat. v.p., mem. exec. com.), Maritime Law Assn. U.S., Am. Judicature Soc., Omicron Delta Kappa, Alpha Sigma Phi, Delta Theta Phi. Clubs: Kiwanian, Propeller of U.S. Home: #101 301 N Pine Island Rd Plantation FL 33324

BUCK, WILLIAM JOSEPH, theatrical designer, educator; b. Newark, Jan. 22, 1954; s. Paul and Amelia Buck; m. Susan Conaty. BA, Glassboro State Coll., 1975; MFA, Yale U., 1984. Dir. design dept. theatre U. S.C., Columbia, 1984-88; asst. prof. Mt. Holyoke Coll., South Hadley, Mass., 1988-92; artistic dir. Children's Playshop, Harrisonburg, Va., 1994—; sch. dir. Sch. Theatre and Dance, James Madison U., Harrisonburg, 1992—; cons. in theatre Chapin (S.C.) pub. schs., Harrison Found. for the Arts, Glassboro pub. schs. Designer over 150 prodns. at univs., theater works, theatre-in-the-works, changing stages. Carolina Venture Fund grantee. Mem. United Scenic Artists (local 829), Southeastern Theatre Conf., Puppeteers of Am.

BUCKALEW, ROBERT JOSEPH, psychologist, consultant; b. Eustis, Fla., Mar. 24, 1924; s. Alfred Henry and Jessie Olive (Bowron) B.; m. Flora Jean Kissinger, Aug. 16, 1959; children: Flora C., Faye R. BS, West Chester (Pa.) U., 1948; MEd, Temple U., 1949, EdD, 1962. Cert. sch. psychologist, Pa. Group living tchr. N.J. Reformatory for Boys, Bordentown, 1948-49; social studies tchr., high sch. guidance counselor Milford (Del.) Spl. Sch. Dist., 1949-52, elem. guidance counselor, reading clinic, 1952-53; psychologist Del. Colony for the Feebleminded, Stockley, Del., 1953; guidance counselor, sr. high sch. tchr. sci., social studies Lord Balt. Cons. Schs., Millville, Del., 1953-55; spl. edn. tchr. Delhaas Sch. System, Bristol, Pa., 1955-57; asst. county supr. spl. edn. Carbon County Sch. Bd., Jim Thorpe, Pa., 1957-62; dir. rsch. and curriculum Kutztown (Pa.) U., 1962-70, prof., 1962-89; cons., past pres., mem. exec. com. Assn. of Pa. State Colls. and Univ. Ret. Faculties, Inc., 1990—. Bd. dirs. Tarsus Manor, Inc., Fleetwood, Pa., 1989-97. Maj. USAF, 1943-45. Decorated Air Medal with 2 oak leaf clusters. Mem. NEA, Am. Psychol. Assn., Pa. Psychol. Assn. (Outstanding Psychologist 1978), Berks County Psychol. Assn. (pres. 1978-79), Berks County Res. Officers Assn. (pres. 1980-83, 96—), SAR (pres. 1983-85, Silver Citizenship medal 1991), Am. Legion, Phi Delta Kappa. Republican. Avocations: history, genealogy, politics. Home: 113 N Richmond St Fleetwood PA 19522-1304

BUCKAWAY, WILLIAM ALLEN, JR., lawyer; b. Bowling Green, Ky., Dec. 3, 1934; s. William Allen and Kathryn Anne (Scoggin) B.; m. Bette Joan Cross, July 27, 1963; 1 child, William Allen III. AB, Centre Coll. of Ky., 1956; JD, U. Louisville, 1961. Bar: Ky. 1961, U.S. Dist Ct. (we. dist.) Ky. 1981, U.S. Dist. Ct. (ea. dist.) Ky. 1986, U.S. Supreme Ct. 1975. Assoc. Tilford, Dobbins, Caye & Alexander, Louisville, 1961-78; ptnr. Tilford, Dobbins, Alexander, Buckaway & Black, Louisville, 1978—; atty. Masonic Homes of Ky., Louisville, 1985—; gen. counsel Kosair Charitites; adj. John Hunt Morgan Camp, 1993-96. Elder 2d Presbyn. Ch., Louisville, 1975; emeritus mem. bd. govs. Lexington (Ky.) unit Shriners Hosp. for Cripled Children, 1986, sec., 1989-94; mem. chidren's oper. bd. Kosair Children's Hosp., 1986-99; mem. bd. govs. Norton Health Care, Louisville, 1999—. With USNR, 1956-58. Named Disting. Alumnus U. Louisville Sch. Law, 1986, Centre Coll., 1986. Mem. SAR, Soc. of the Cin. in State of Va., Sons Confederate Vets., Masons (33 deg., past master Crescent Hill lodge 1967, chmn. jurisprudence and law com. imperial coun. Shrine of N.Am. 1989-91), Kosair Shrine Temple (potentate 1986), Rotary, Soc. Colonial Wars, Soc. War of 1812 (pres. Ky. soc. 1998—), Sigma Chi, Phi Alpha Delta. Home: 1761 Sulgrave Rd Louisville KY 40205-1643

BUCKELEW, ROBIN BROWNE, aerospace engineer; b. York, Pa., Mar. 14, 1947; d. Grant Hugh and Frances (Coleman) Browne; m. William Paul Buckelew, June 5, 1971; children: Leon, Christina. BS in Aerospace Engring., U. Ala., 1970; MS in Engring., U. Ala., Huntsville, 1977, PhD in Engring., 1994. Registered profl. engr., Ala. Aerospace engr. U.S. Army Missile Command, Redstone Arsenal, Ala., 1970-74; systems engr. U.S. Army Missile Intelligence Agy., Huntsville, Ala., 1974-81; group leader air vehicle Sentry U.S. Army Ballistics Missile Def. System Command, Huntsville, 1981-83, interceptor engr. High Endoatmospheric Def. Interceptor, 1983-85; chief air vehicle div. HEDI project U.S. Army Strategic Def. Command, Huntsville, 1985-88, chief Ground Based Interceptor Experiment Office, 1988-91, chief engr. HEDI project, 1991-92; dir. Sys. Directorate, U.S. Army Space and Strategic Def. Command, Huntsville, 1993-94, dir. Engring. and Sys. Directorate, 1994-95; dir. Missile Def. Battle Integration Ctr., 1995-97; dir. Ctr. for Land Warfare Office of the Chief of Staff of the Army, Washington, D.C., 1997—. Contbr. articles to AIAA conf. proceedings. Bd. dirs. Trinity Personal Growth Ctr., Huntsville, 1990-92. Named Strategic Def. Engr. of Yr., NSPE, 1990, Disting. Engring. fellow U. Ala., 1993, State of Ala. Engring. Hall of Fame, 1995; recipient Superior Civilian Svc. award U.S. Army, 1991, Outstanding Alumna award U. Ala., Huntsville, 1996, Meritorious Civil Svc. award U.S. Army, 1997, Presdl. Rank award U.S. Govt., 1998. Fellow AIAA (assoc.); mem. Capstone Engring. Soc. (bd. dirs. at large), Ancient Order St. Barbara, Sigma Xi. Methodist. Home: 117 Bel Air Rd SE Huntsville AL 35802-3107 Office: Office of the Chief of Staff of the Army Ctr Land Warfare 200 Army Pentagon Washington DC 20310-0200

BUCKELS, MARVIN WAYNE, savings and loan executive; b. Sterling, Colo., Feb. 11, 1929; s. Harvey and Myrl (Tarr) B.; m. Doris Torrance, Aug. 1, 1959; children: Lisa K., Devon Carol. BA, U. Denver, 1951; MS, U. Wis., 1952. With Beatrice Foods, Denver, 1952-55; loan counselor Midland Fed. Savs. and Loan Assn., Denver, 1955-56, treas., 1956-62, exec. v.p., 1962-85; exec. v.p. Western Capital Investment Corp., Denver, 1985-91. Vice-chmn. Colo. Bd. Vocat. Edn., 1967; pres. Adult Edn. Coun. Met. Denver, 1970; bd. dirs. Auraria Higher Edn. Ctr., 1975-79, vice chmn. bd., 1977-78; bd. dirs. Auraria Found., 1992—, treas., 1997—; bd. dirs. Rocky Mountain Hosp., 1979, pres., 1980; chmn. Colo. Postsecondary Edn. Facilities Authority, 1981—; bd. dirs. Denver Civic Ventures, Inc., 1986, chmn., 1987-90; legis. policy com. Colo. Assn. Commerce and Industry, 1986-89; treas. Colo. Pub. Affairs Coun., 1987-89; bd. dirs. Colo. Symphony Orch., 1990—, treas., 1990-96; chmn. The Downtown Denver Partnership, 1991-92. With U.S. Army, 1946-48. Mem. U.S. Savs. and Loan League, Colo. Savs. and Loan League (legis com.), Am. Savs. and Loan Inst. (past pres. Denver chpt.), Contrs. Soc. (past pres. Denver chpt., nat. bd. govs.), Sys. and Procedures Assn. (past pres. Denver chpt.), Adminstrv. Mgmt. Soc. (past pres. Denver chpt.), Greater Denver C. of C. (past chmn. spl. task force studying sch. bond issue, mem. legis. action coun. 1991, pub. affairs coun. 1991—, loaned exec. Nat. Alliance Businessmen's program), Denver Metro C. of C. (pub. affairs coun. 1993—, transp. com. 1992—), Phi Beta Kappa. Democrat.

BUCKENDORFF, ROSEMARY HAUSEMAN, secondary education educator; b. Pottstown, Pa., June 4, 1943; d. Irvin K. and M. Catherine Hauseman; 1 child, Jennifer L. BA, Elizabethtown Coll., 1965; MA, Kutztown U., 1978. Permanent tchg. cert., Pa. Tchr. Elizabethtown (Pa.) Sr. H.S., 1965-66, Boyertown (Pa.) Area Sr. H.S., 1967-72; tchr., dept. chair Exeter Twp. Sr. H.S., Reading, Pa., 1976—; tchr. cons. Pa. Writing Project, West Chester. Mem. NEA, NOW, Pa. State Edn. Assn. Avocations: reading, travel, friends and family. Home: 16 E 34th St Reading PA 19606-3119

BUCKI, CARL L., federal judge; b. 1953. BA, Cornell U., 1974, JD, 1976. Bar: N.Y. 1977. Law clk. to Hon. Matthew J. Jasen, N.Y. Ct. Appeals, 1976-77; assoc. Moot & Sprague, Buffalo, 1977-90; ptnr. Cohen, Swados, Wright, Hanifin, Bradford & Brett, Buffalo, 1990-93; bankruptcy judge for western dist. N.Y., U.S. Bankruptcy Ct., Buffalo, 1993—. Pres., bd. mgrs. Buffalo and Erie County Hist. Soc., 1996—. Office: US Bankruptcy Ct 310 US Courthouse Part 2 300 Pearl St Ste 350 Buffalo NY 14202-3405

BUCKINGHAM, AMYAND DAVID, chemistry educator; b. Sydney, NSW, Australia, Jan. 28, 1930; s. Reginald Joslin and Florence Grace (Elliot) B.; m. Jillian Bowles, July 24, 1965; children: Lucy Elliot, Mark Vincent, Alice Susan. BSc with honors, Sydney U., 1951, MSc, 1953; PhD, Cambridge U., Eng., 1956, ScD, 1985. Cert. chemist; cert. physicist. Lectr., tutor Christ Ch., Oxford, Eng., 1955-65; lectr. Oxford U., 1958-65; prof. theoretical chemistry Bristol (Eng.) U., 1965-69; prof. chemistry Cambridge (Eng.) U., 1969-97, prof. emeritus, 1997—; fellow Pembroke Coll., Cambridge, 1970-97, emeritus fellow, 1997—. Author: Laws and Applications of Thermodynamics, 1964; editor: Organic Liquids, 1978, Principles of Molecular Recognition, 1993; editor Molecular Physics, 1968-72, Internat. Revs. in Phys. Chemistry, 1981-89, Chem. Physics Letters, 1978—. Decorated comdr. Brit. Empire. Fellow Royal Soc. (Hughes medal 1996), Royal Soc. Chemistry, Inst. of Physics, Optical Soc. Am., Am. Phys. Soc., Royal Australian Chem. Inst.; mem. AAAS (hon.), NAS (fgn. assoc.), Am. Chem. Soc., Internat. Acad. Quantum Molecular Sci., Royal Swedish Acad. Scis. (fgn. mem.). Avocations: cricket, tennis, travel. Office: Univ Chem Lab, Lensfield Rd, Cambridge CB2 1EW, England

BUCKINGHAM, EDWIN JOHN, III, lawyer; b. Grand Forks, N.D., Sept. 15, 1947; s. Edwin John and Kathryn Ruth (Aird) B.; m. Cheryl Ann Pantalone, 1971; 1 child, Emma Nicole. AB, Yale U., 1969, JD, 1972. Bar:

N.Y. 1973, Tex. 1978. Assoc. Shea Gould Climenko & Kramer, N.Y.C., 1972-74; assoc. gen. counsel Celanese Corp., N.Y.C., 1974-77; mgr. legal affairs Solvay Polymers, Inc., Houston, 1977-79, dir. legal affairs, 1979-81, gen. counsel, v.p., 1981—; gen. counsel, v.p. Solvay Am., Inc., Houston, 1984—. Sec. Wessex Civic Assn., Houston, 1986-88. Mem. ABA, Am. Corp. Counsel Assn., Tex. Bar Assn., Tex.-Mex. Bar Assn. Avocations: fencing, birding. Office: Solvay Am 3333 Richmond Ave Houston TX 77098-3007

BUCKINGHAM, HAROLD CANUTE, JR., lawyer; b. Wilkes-Barre, Pa., Nov. 3, 1930; s. Harold Canute and Dorothy (Coats) B.; m. Joyce Ethel Chesebro, Sept. 11, 1954; children: Margaret L. Buckingham Eller, Harold Canute III, Janet C. Buckingham Round. BA, Wesleyan U., 1952; JD, U. Va., 1957. Bar: Conn. 1957, U.S. Dist. Ct. Conn. 1961. Assoc. Day, Berry & Howard, Hartford, Conn., 1957-64, ptnr., 1964—; bd. dirs., sec. Anders, Inc., Simsbury, Conn. Conn. decisions editor Trust and Estates mag., 1964-74. Trustee, sec. Wesleyan U., Middletown, Conn., 1967-70; trustee, v.p., N.Y. Ann. Conf. of United Meth. Ch., White Plains, 1972-76; bd. dirs., vice chmn., then chmn. YMCA Met. Hartford, 1978—; trustee, vice chmn. Wyo. Sem., Kingston, Pa., 1983—; trustee Hartford Coll. for Women, 1994—; bd. dirs., sec. Bushnell Park Found., Hartford, 1985-91; bd. dirs. Conn. Cmty. Care, Inc., 1990—, Greater Hartford Architecture Conservancy, Inc., 1991-95; bd. dirs. Capitol Region Conf. of Chs., Hartford, 1989-96. Cpl. U.S. Army, 1952-54, Korea. Recipient Outstanding Scouter award Boy Scouts Am., Hartford, 1963. Fellow Conn. Bar Found., Am. Bar Found.; mem. ABA, Conn. Bar Assn., Hartford County Bar Assn., Am. Judicature Soc., Univ. Club (bd. dirs. Hartford 1982-85), Civitan Club (pres. Hartford 1976-77), 20th Century Club (Hartford). Republican. Office: Day Berry & Howard 2500 City Pl Hartford CT 06103-3499*

BUCKINGHAM, MICHAEL JOHN, oceanography educator; b. Oxford, Eng., Oct. 9, 1943; s. Sidney George and Mary Agnes (Walsh) B.; m. Margaret Penelope Rose Barrowcliff, July 15, 1967. BSc with hons., U. Reading (Eng.), 1967, PhD, 1971. Postdoctoral rsch. fellow U. Reading, 1971-74; sr. sci. officer Royal Aircraft Establishment, Farnborough, Eng., 1974-76; prin. sci. officer Royal Aircraft Establishment, 1976-82; exchange scientist Naval Rsch. Lab., Washington, 1982-84; vis. prof. MIT, Cambridge, 1986-87; sr. prin. sci. officer Royal Aircraft Establishment, 1983-86, 1987-90; prof. oceanography Scripps Instn. of Oceanography, La Jolla, Calif., 1990—; vis. prof. Inst. Sound and Vibration rsch., Southampton, Eng., 1990—; UK nat. rep. Commn. of European Communities, Brussels, Belgium, 1989-92; dir. Arctic rsch. Royal Aerospace Establishment, Farnborough, 1990-94. Author: Noise in Electronic Devices and Systems, 1983; editor: Sea Surface Sound '94, Proceedings of the III Internat. Mtg. on Natural Phys. Processes Related to Sea Surface Sound; editor-in-chief Jour. Computational Acoustics; editor Phys. Acoustics; contbr. articles to profl. jours.; patentee in field. Recipient Clerk Maxwell Premium, Inst. Electronic and Radio Engrs. London, 1972, A.B. Wood Medal, Inst. Acoustics, Bath, Eng., 1982, Alan Burman Pub. award, Naval Rsch. Lab., 1988, Commendation for Disting. Contbns. to ocean acoustics Naval Rsch. Lab., 1986. Fellow Inst. Acoustics (U.K.), Inst. Elec. Engrs. (U.K.), Acoustical Soc. Am. (chmn. acoustical oceanography tech. com. 1991—, Sci. Writing award for profls. in acoustics 1997), Explorers Club; mem. Am. Geophys. Union, N.Y. Acad. Scis., Sigma Xi. Avocations: photography, squash, flying gliders. Home: 7921 Caminito Del Cid La Jolla CA 92037-3404 Office: Scripps Inst Oceanography Marine Phys Lab La Jolla CA 92093-0213

BUCKLAND, BARRY C., chemical engineer; b. London, Jan. 6, 1948. BSc, Manchester (Eng.) U., 1970; MSc, U. Coll. London, 1971, PhD in Biochem. Engring., 1974. Biochem. engr. Abbott Lab., Chgo., 1974-77; sr. engr. Lederle Lab., N.Y., 1977-80; dir. Fermentation Pilot Plant, Merck & Co. Inc., 1980-86, biochem. process R&D, 1986-90, sr. dir., 1990-93, exec. dir., 1993-96; v.p. Bio Process R&D, Merck & Co. Inc., 1996—; vis. prof. Univ. Coll., London, 1989—, Rutgers U., 1990—. Fellow Am. Inst. Med. & Biol. Engring., Internat. Inst. Biotechnology (lectr. 1995); mem. AICE (dir. Food, Pharm. & Bioentring. Divsn. 1993-95), Am. Chem. Soc. (lectr. 1994), Nat. Acad. Engring. Home: 626 Boulevard Westfield NJ 07090-3210 Office: PO Box 2000 RY80Y-370 Rahway NJ 07065-0900

BUCKLAND, MICHAEL KEEBLE, librarian, educator; b. Wantage, Eng., Nov. 23, 1941; came to U.S., 1972; s. Walter Basil and Norah Elaine (Rudd) B.; m. Waltraud Leeb, July 11, 1964; children: Anne Margaret, Anthony Francis. B.A., Oxford U., 1963; postgrad. diploma in librarianship, Sheffield U., 1965, Ph.D., 1972. Grad. trainee Bodleian Library, Oxford, Eng., 1963-64; asst. librarian U. Lancaster (Eng.) Library, 1965-72; asst. dir. for tech. svcs. Purdue U. Libraries, West Lafayette, Ind., 1972-75; assoc. prof. Sch. of Info. Mgmt. and Sys. U. Calif., Berkeley, 1976-79, dean, 1976-84, prof., 1979—, asst. v.p. library plans and policies, 1983-87; v.p. Ind. Coop. Library Svcs. Auth., 1974-75; vis. scholar Western Mich. U., 1979; vis. prof. U. Klagenfurt, Austria, 1980, U. New South Wales, Australia, 1988. Author: Book Availability and the Library User, 1975, (with others) The Use of Gaming in Education for Library Management, 1976, Reader in Operations Research for Libraries, 1976, Library Services in Theory and Context, 1983, 2d edit., 1988, Information and Information Systems, 1991, Redesigning Library Services, 1992. Fulbright Rsch. scholar U. Tech., Graz, Austria, 1989. Mem. ALA, Am. Soc. Info. Sci. (pres. 1998), Assn. Libr. and Info. Sci. Edn., Calif. Libr. Assn. Office: U Calif Sch Info Mgmt and Sys Berkeley CA 94720-4600

BUCKLAND, ROGER BASIL, university dean, educator, vice principal; b. Lower Jemseg, N.B., Can., May 18, 1942; s. Basil John and Nancy (Coates) B.; m. Vicki Nealson, Aug. 7, 1965; children—Kenneth Roger, Adrienne Elise. Diploma, Nova Scotia Agrl. Coll., Truro, 1961; B.Sc., McGill U., 1963, M.Sc., 1965; Ph.D., U. Md., 1968. Assoc. prof. Macdonald Coll., McGill U., Ste. Anne de Bellevue, Que., Can., 1973-80, chmn. prof., 1979-85, vice prin., dean, 1985-95, prof. animal sci., 1995—; sabbatical leave Sta. de Recherche Avicole and Poultry Research Ctr., Nouzilly, France, 1977-78. Bd. dirs. Morgan Arboretum Assn., 1985—, Louis G. Johnson Found., 1989—; mem. hon. bd. West Island Community Radio, 1985-88; mem. bd. govs. RCS-Netherwood, Rothesay, N.B., 1987—. Recipient Scroll award Poultry Sci. Research Assn., 1972; Une Mission France-Quebec, 1977, AIC Fellowship Award, Agricultural Inst. Canada, 1995. Mem. Confederation Can. Faculties Agr. and Vet. Medicine, Poultry Sci. Assn., Centre de Recherche en Zootechnie, Can.-Cuba Joint Poultry Working Group (chmn. 1978—). Office: McGill U Macdonald Campus, 21111 Lakeshore Rd, Sainte Anne de Bellevue, PQ Canada H9X 3V9

BUCKLE, FREDERICK TARIFERO, international holding company executive, political and business intelligence analyst; b. Accra, Ghana, Nov. 17, 1949; s. Festus Kofi Buckle and Clara Anyema Korley; 1 child, Nicole Ohenewa. MBA, PhD in Internat. Relations. Pres., chief exec. officer, chmn. Buckle Internat. Aktiengesellschaft; pres. Tarifero and Tazewell, Inc.; chmn. Lafayette Internat. Bank; bd. dirs. Oxicron Systems Corp., N.J., U.S. Pub. Corp., Chgo., Internat. Investments and Devel. Corp., Transglobal Investment and Devel. Corp., Bermuda, Selwyn Corp., N.Y.C., Richmond Computer Software Corp., Los Angeles. Author: The Logic of Laissez Faire, 1974, Third World and the Economic Supply Process, 1981, Strategic Balance in the Nuclear Age, 1981, Financial Privacy in the World of Computers, 1983, Industrial Espionage, 1984. Named Hon. Consul Gen. Republic of Maldives, 1983-85. Fellow Internat. Strategic Studies Inst.; mem. Chgo. Assn. Commerce, Assn. Internat. Financiers, Mortgage Bankers Assn. Office: Buckle Internat Inc 211 S Clark St PO Box 2522 Chicago IL 60690-2522

BUCKLER, MARILYN LEBOW, school psychologist, educational consultant; b. N.Y.C., Mar. 18, 1933; d. Herman and Gertrude (Abolitz) Lebow; m. Sheldon A. Buckler, June 1, 1952 (div. 1978); children: Julie, Eve, Sarah Buckler Welcome. BS cum laude, NYU, 1954; MEd in Counseling, Northeastern U., 1970. Cert. ednl. psychologist, Mass.; sch. guidance counselor, Mass., sch. psychologist, Mass. Kindergarten tchr. Washington Pub. Schs., 1955-56, Stamford (Conn.) Pub. Schs., 1956-58; guidance counselor Framingham (Mass.) Pub. Schs., 1969-70; sch. psychologist, guidance counselor Carlisle (Mass.) Pub. Schs., 1970-95; parent program cons. Reach out to Schs. program Wellesley Coll.-Stone Ctr., 1993—; tchr. parenting course Middlesex C.C., Bedford, Mass., 1990—, cons. LEAP program, 1992-93; workshop leader, creator parenting courses, various pvt. schs. and orgns., Mass., 1990—; spl. project cons., workshop specialist "Families First" Wheelock Coll., 1995—. Mem. ACA, Mass. Sch. Counselor Assn., Mass. Sch. Psychologists Assn., Pi Lambda Theta. Avocations: films, cooking, traveling, reading.

BUCKLER, SHELDON A., energy company executive; b. N.Y.C., May 18, 1931; s. Morris H. and Mollie M. (Smith) B.; m. Dorothea J. Chandler, June 30, 1978; children: Julie, Eve, Sarah. BA, NYU, 1951; PhD, Columbia U., 1954. Rsch. assoc. U. Md., 1954-56; rsch. group leader Am. Cyanamid Co., Stamford, Conn., 1956-62; mgr. organic unit AMF, Springdale, Conn., 1962-64; with Polaroid Corp., Cambridge, Mass., 1964-94, vice-chmn. bd., 1990-94; chmn. bd. Commonwealth Energy Sys., Cambridge, 1995—; bd. dirs. Lord Corp., ASECO Corp., Nashua Corp., Parlex Corp., Micrologic Corp. Contbr. articles to profl. jours.; patentee in field. Trustee Va. Union U., 1973-75; chmn. Mass. Eye and Ear Infirmary, 1996—. With U.S. Army, 1954-56. Recipient Maurice Holland award Indsl. Rsch. Inst., 1998. Mem. Am. Chem. Soc., Phi Beta Kappa. Office: Commonwealth Energy Sys PO Box 9150 One Main St Cambridge MA 02142-9150

BUCKLES, FREDERICK R., federal judge. Magistrate judge U.S. Dist. Ct. (ea. dist.) Mo., St. Louis. Office: 106 US Courthouse 1114 Market St Fl Ctcl Saint Louis MO 63101-2043

BUCKLES, ROBERT HOWARD, retired investment company executive; b. Champaign, Ill., June 30, 1932; s. Renick Hull and Ethel Maxine (Beach) B.; m. Linda Carol Porter, Dec. 27, 1958; children: Meredith Ann, Christopher John. BA, Stanford U., 1953; MBA, Harvard U., 1957. Security analyst Lehman Corp., N.Y.C., 1957-65, v.p., 1965-69, exec. v.p., 1969-73, pres., 1973-84, also bd. dirs.; pres. Gas Properties, Inc., 1973-84; exec. v.p., dir. Lehman Mgmt. Co., 1973-84; pres., chief investment officer Rothschild Asset Mgmt. Inc., 1984-87; mng. dir. Rothschild, Inc., 1984-87; chief investment officer, sr. mng. dir. Furman Selz Capital Mgmt., 1987-97; dir. One William St. Fund.; bd. dirs. Assn. Publicly Traded Investment Funds. Contbr. articles to profl. publs. With security agy. AUS, 1954-56. Mem. N.Y. Soc. Securities Analysts. Home: 425 E 58th St Apt 35C New York NY 10022

BUCKLES, STEPHEN GARY, economist, educator; b. Kansas City, Mo., June 11, 1943; s. Orland and Leighfern (Emry) B.; m. Mary Parker Harmon, Nov. 28, 1970. AB, Grinnell Coll., 1965; PhD, Vanderbilt U., 1976. Economist Joint Coun. Econ. Edn., N.Y.C., 1970-74; prof. U. Mo., Columbia, 1976-88; pres. Nat Coun. Econ. Edn., N.Y.C., 1989-94; prof. econ. Vanderbilt U., Nashville, 1994—; vis. prof. Vanderbilt U., 1983; tchr. NYU, 1972-74; past chair individual investors adv. com. N.Y. Stock Exch. Recipient teaching awards U. Mo., 1986-87, Student's Choice award Vanderbilt, 1996, William Forbes award for Pub. Awareness, 1998. Mem. Nat. Coun. Econ. Edn. Home: 24 Great Is Darien CT 06820-5932 Office: Vanderbilt U Dept Econs Nashville TN 37235

BUCKLEW, NEIL S., educator, past university president; b. Morgantown, W.Va., Oct. 23, 1940; s. Douglas Earl and Lanah L. (Martin) B.; m. Iona Bucklew; children—Elizabeth, Jennifer, Jeffrey, Gayle, Cara. A.B., U. Mo.; M.S., U. N.C.; Ph.D. (grad. fellow), U. Wis. Dir. personnel Duke U., 1964-66; dir. employee relations U. Wis., 1966-70; prof., v.p. Central Mich. U., Mt. Pleasant, 1970-76; prof., provost Ohio U., Athens, 1976-80; pres. U. Mont., Missoula, 1981-86, W.Va. U., 1986-95; prof. W.Va. U., Morgantown, 1995—; vis. rsch. fellow Pa. State U.; arbitrator in field. Author: Public Sector Collective Bargaining, Planning in Higher Education. Mem. Nat. Assn. State Univs. and Land Grant Colls. Office: West Va U PO Box 6025 Morgantown WV 26506-6025

BUCKLEW, SUSAN CAWTHON, federal judge; b. 1942. BA, Fla. State U., 1964; MA, U. So. Fla., 1968; JD, Stetson U., 1977; LLD (hon.), Stetson Coll. Law, 1994. Tchr. Plant High Sch., 1964-65, 70-72, Seminole High Sch., 1965-67, Chamberlain High Sch., 1969; instr. Hillsborough C.C., 1974-75; corp. legal counsel Jim Walter Corp., 1978-82; county ct. judge Hillsborough County, 1982-86; circuit ct. judge 13th Jud. Circuit, 1986-93; judge U.S. Dist. Ct. (mid. dist.) Fla., 1993—; mem. Gender Bias Study Commn., 1988-90, Fla. Bar Bench Bar Commn., 1990-92; bd. overseers Stetson Coll. Law, 1994—. Recipient award Disting Svc., Fla. Coun. Crime and Delinquincy, 1990, Disting. Alumnus award Stetson Lawyers Assn., 1994. Mem. ABA, Fla. Gar Assn., Fla. Assn. Women Lawyers, Hillsborough Assn. Women Lawyers (award Outstanding Pub. Svc. ADvancing Status Women 1991), Hillsborough County Bar Assn. (Robert W. Patton Outstanding Jursit award young lawyer's sect. 1990), Fla. State U. Alumni Assn., Am. Inns Ct. (LII, William Glenn Terrell chpt.), Athena Soc., Tampa Club, Delta Delta Delta Alumnae. Office: US Dist Ct 611 N Florida Ave Ste 109 Tampa FL 33602-4509*

BUCKLEY, BETTY LYNN, actress; b. Ft. Worth, July 3, 1947; d. Ernest and Betty Bob (Diltz) B.; m. Peter Flood, 1972 (div. 1974). Actress: (Broadway debut) 1776, 1969, (London debut) Promises, Promises (stage prodns.) What's a Nice Country Like You Doing in a State Like This?, Pippin, 1973-75, I'm Getting My Act Together and Taking it on the Road, 1981, Cats, 1982-85 (Antoinette Perry award 1983), Juno's Swans, 1985, The Mystery of Edwin Drood, 1985-86, Song and Dance, 1986, Circle of Sound, Carrie, 1990, (London) Sunset Boulevard, 1994; (feature films) Carrie, 1976, Tender Mercies, 1983, Frantic, 1988, Another Woman, 1988, Rain without Thunder, 1993, Wyatt Earp, 1994, Last Time Out, 1994, Ride for Your Life, 1995, (TV movies) The Ordeal of Bill Carney, 1981, The Three Wishes of Billy Grier, 1984, Roses are For the Rich, 1987, Baby Cakes, 1989, Bonnie and Clyde: The True Story, 1992, The Devil's Work, Betrayal of Trust, 1994, Critical Choices, 1996; (TV mini-series) Evergreen, 1985; regular (TV series) Eight is Enough, 1977-81; also cabaret and club performances; albums include Betty Buckley, 1987, Children will Listen, 1993, With One Look, 1994. Mem. Actors' Equity Assn., Screen Actors Guild, AFTRA. Office: Innovativce Artists care Scott Harris 141 5th Ave., 3rd Fl New York NY 10010

BUCKLEY, CHARLES EDWARD, III, physician, educator; b. Charleston, W.Va., Sept. 2, 1929; s. Charles Edward and Gladys (Kuh) B.; m. Rebecca Anne Hatcher, July 9, 1955; children—Charles Edward, Elizabeth Ann, Rebecca Kathryn, Sarah Margaret. B.S., Va. Poly. Inst., 1950; M.D., Duke U., 1954. Intern Duke U. Med. Ctr., Durham, N.C., 1954-55, resident in medicine, 1958-60, instr., 1960-63, assoc. in medicine, 1963-65, asst. prof. medicine, 1965-68, assoc. prof., 1968-77, prof. medicine, 1977—; fellow Duke Hosp., Durham, 1960-62; mem. adv. council to dir. Nat. Inst. Allergy and Infectious Diseases, 1975-79. Contbr. chpts. to books, articles to med. jours. Served with USNR, 1955-57. USPHS career devel. awardee, 1961-68. Mem. Am. Thoracic Soc. (exec. com. 1979-80), N.C. Thoracic Soc. (pres. 1967-69), Southeastern Allergy Assn. (pres. 1972-73), Am. Acad. Allergy, Am. Assn. Immunologists, So. Soc. Clin. Investigation, A.C.P., Gerontol. Soc., Sigma Xi, Phi Sigma, Tau Kappa Alpha, Alpha Omega Alpha. Republican. Episcopalian. Office: Duke U Med Ctr PO Box 3804 Durham NC 27702-3804

BUCKLEY, CHARLES ROBINSON, III, lawyer; b. Richmond, Va., Oct. 9, 1942; s. Charles Robinson and Eleanor (Small) B.; m. Virginia Lee, Apr. 17, 1971; children: Richard, Rebecca. BS, U. N.C., 1965, JD, 1969. Bars: N.C. 1969, U.S. Supreme Ct., 1979. Asst. city atty. City of Charlotte (N.C.), 1969-78; ptnr. Constangy, Goines, Buckley & Boyd, 1978-81, Taylor & Buckley, Charlotte, 1981-85; ptnr. Buckley McMullen & Buie, P.A., 1994—; town atty. Town of Matthew (N.C.), 1978—; faculty Ctrl. Piedmont C.C., 1970. Bd. dirs. Charlotte City Employees Credit Union, 1974-78; pres. PTA, 1980-82; bd. visitors Luth. Theol. So Sem., 1989-93. Recipient Certificate of Merit, City of Charlotte, 1982. Mem. N.C. Bar Assn., N.C. Assn. Mun. Attys. (dir. 1979-81, 2d v.p. 1995-96, 1st v.p. 1996-97, pres. 1997-98), Phi Alpha Delta. Democrat. Lutheran. Club: Optimist (pres. 1982-83). Home: 6813 Linda Lake Dr Charlotte NC 28215-4019

BUCKLEY, CHRISTOPHER TAYLOR, editor, author; b. N.Y.C, Sept. 28, 1952; s. William F. Jr. and Patricia (Taylor) B.; m. Dec. 8, 1984; children: Caitlin, Conor. BA, Yale U., 1975. Mng. editor Esquire Mag., N.Y.C., 1977; chief speech writer V.P. of U.S., Washington, 1981-83; editor-in-chief Forbes FYI Mag., N.Y.C., 1990—. Author: Steaming to Bamboola, 1982, The White House Mess, 1986, Campion, 1988, Wet Work, 1991, Thank You For Smoking, 1994, Wry Martinis, 1997, God is My Broker, 1998, Little Green Men, 1999. Mem. The Century Assn., Kollegewidgwok Yacht Club, The Yale Club, Mory's Assn., The Brook. Republican. Avocations: sailing, scuba diving, bicycling, the outdoors. Home: 3516 Newark St NW Washington DC 20016-3168 Office: Forbes FYI 60 5th Ave New York NY 10011-8802

BUCKLEY, DEBORAH JEANNE MOREY, manager of process; b. Bethesda, Feb. 26, 1952; d. Robert Earl and Carolyn Ann (Garrity) Morey; m. Robert Gill Buckley, Dec. 2, 1972; 1 child, Leigh Ann. AAS, Trident Tech. Coll., 1978; student, U. N.C., 1982-83. Nuclear chemistry specialist Duke Power Co., Charlotte, N.C., 1978-82; rsch. technician Graphic Arts Tech. Found., Pitts., 1984; sr. process technician U.S. Filter Corp., Warrendale, Pa., 1985-88, applications engr. in tech. svcs. group, 1988-92, market mgr. groundwater systems, sr. application engr., 1993-95, tech. mktg. specialist, 1995-98, mgr. process, 1998—. Sec. Seneca Valley Acad. Games Parents Assn., Harmony, Pa., 1992-93. With USN, 1970-74. Mem. NAFE, Am. Elctroplaters Soc., Hazardous Materials Control Rsch. Inst. Republican. Avocations: weight lifting, jogging, recreational golf. Office: US Filter Corp 181 Thorn Hill Rd Warrendale PA 15086-7527

BUCKLEY, DONALD CHARLES, cardiac thoracic surgeon; b. Mt. Vernon, N.Y., Feb. 24, 1956; s. Charles G. and Marilyn R. B.; m. Genann Esterline, June 16, 1979; children: Michael C., Rachel E., Samantha D. BS, U. Ariz., 1978, MD, 1982. Diplomate Am. Bd. Surgery, Am. Bd. Thoracic Surgery. Intern Ohio State U., Columbus, 1982-83, resident, 1983-88, fellow, 1988-90; surgeon Cinti Cardiac and Thoracic Surgeons, LLC, Cin., 1990—; clin. instr. dept. surgery Ohio State U., Columbus, 1982-90. Mem. com. Boy Scouts Am., Cin., 1993—. Mem. AMA, ACS, Am. Coll. Chest Physicians, Am. Coll. Cardiology, Ohio State Med. Assn., Acad. Medicine, Soc. Thoracic Surgeons. Republican. Presbyterian. Avocations: golfing, snow skiing, reading, traveling. Office: Cinti Cardiac and Thoracic Surgeons 3129 Clifton Ste 130 Cincinnati OH 45220

BUCKLEY, EDWARD T., JR., career officer; b. Chippewa Falls, Wis., Aug. 16, 1945. Commd. U.S. Army, advanced through grades to brig. gen., 1997; dep. chief staff doctrine tng. and doctrine command U.S. Army, Ft. Monroe, Va., 1997—. Office: US Army Tng and Doctrine Command Fort Monroe VA 23651-1067

BUCKLEY, FRANK WILSON, newspaper executive; b. Prentiss, Miss., Oct. 7, 1914; s. Frank Wylie and Otto (Watts) B.; m. Vonnie Verette Crouch, Dec. 22, 1940; children: Charles Ray, Ronald L., Mary Carole. B.A., La. Coll., 1936; LL.B., Vanderbilt U., 1954; M.A., Fla. State U., 1955; Ph.D., So. Ill. U., 1966. Bar: Miss. 1954. Mng. editor Daily News, Mt. Pleasant, Tex., 1936-37; reporter-photographer Daily Town Talk, Alexandria, La., 1937-40; telegraph editor Morning Free Press, Easton, Pa., 1940-41, Mobile Register, 1941; copy editor Buffalo Evening News, 1941-42; editor, pub. Carroll County Democrat, Huntingdon, Tenn., 1945-46; mgr. security brokerage office Alexandria, 1947-49; grad. asst. journalism Fla. State U., 1949-50; copy editor, editor fin. sect. Nashville Tennessean, 1950-55; prof., head dept. journalism U. So. Miss., 1955-64, assoc. prof. journalism, 1966-67; lectr. journalism So. Ill. U., 1964-65; chmn. dept. journalism Southwest Tex. State U., San Marcos, 1967-73, assoc. prof., 1967-70, prof., 1970-80; Pres. Buckley Newspapers, Inc. (pubs. The News-Bay Springs), Miss., The Reformer, Raleigh, Miss., The Weekly Leader, Pearl, Miss., Impact, Hattiesburg and Laurel, Miss., The News, Brandon, Miss. Deacon Bapt. ch. Lt. (s.g.) USNR, 1943-46; lt. Res., 1945-54. Mem. Miss. Bar Assn. Republican. Address: 4 Marseilles St Brandon MS 39047-8452*

BUCKLEY, FREDERICK JEAN, lawyer; b. Wilmington, Ohio, Nov. 5, 1923; s. William Millard and Martha (Bright) B.; m. Josephine K. Buckley, Dec. 4, 1945; children: Daniel J., Fredrica Buckley Elder, Matthew J. Student, Wilmington Coll., 1941-42, Ohio State U., 1942-43; AB, U. Mich., 1948, LLB, 1949. Bar: Ohio 1950, U.S. Dist. Ct. (so. dist.) Ohio 1952, U.S. Supreme Ct. 1978, U.S. Ct. Appeals (6th cir.) 1981, Fla. 1982, U.S. Dist. Ct. (mid. dist.) Fla. 1991; cert. cir. ct. mediator, Fla. Assoc. G.L. Schilling, Sr., Wilmington, 1951-52; ptnr. Schilling & Buckley, Wilmington, 1953-56; sole practice Wilmington, 1956-62; sr. ptnr. Buckley, Miller & Wright, Wilmington, 1962—; chmn., counsel The Wilmington Savs. Bank, 1971—, also dir.; solicitor City of Wilmington, 1954-63. Contbr. articles in field. With AUS, 1943-46, ETO. Joint program Mich. Inst. Pub. Adminstrn. fellow, 1948. Fellow Am. Coll. Trial Lawyers; mem. ABA, Am. Arbitration Assn. (comml. panel), Fed. Bar Assn., Ohio State Bar Assn., Clinton County Bar Assn., Selden Soc., Fla. Bar, Fla. Acad. Profl. Mediators, Soc. Profls. in Dispute Resolution, Collier County Bar Assn., Ohio State Bar Found. Republican. Methodist. Office: 145 N South St Wilmington OH 45177-1646

BUCKLEY, GARY STEVEN, science educator; b. Chgo., May 23, 1953; s. Robert Franklin and Ethel Anna (Stenhouse) B.; m. Molly Santos, Sept. 1, 1984; children: Margaret, Catherine. BS in Chemistry, No. Ill. U., 1975; MS in Chemistry, Tex. A&M U., 1978, PhD, 1982. Tutorial instr. Cameron U., Lawton, Okla., 1977-79; sr. rsch. chemist Dow Chem. Co., Freeport, Tex., 1982-86; prof. phys. sci. Cameron U., 1986—, chmn. dept. phus. sci., 1998—; cons. in field. Contbr. articles to profl. jours. Methodist. Avocations: basketball, racquetball, computers. Office: Cameron U Dept Phys Sci Lawton OK 73505

BUCKLEY, GRETA PAULA, auditor; b. Stanton, Calif., Sept. 8, 1963; d. Joseph Andrew Bertotti and Margarita Ann Marie (Lundgren) Helmut; 1 child, Gianna Marie Dossa; m. Steve Buckley, Nov. 7, 1998. BA, San Diego State U., 1991; Associate degree in Insurance, Insurance Inst. Am., 1997. Supr. Farmers Ins. Group, Carlsbad, Calif., 1991-96; auditor Farmers Ins. Group, Carlsbad, 5, 1996—; mem. com. Children's Hosp. Safe Kids Coalition, San Diego, 1995—. Mem., tchr. Jr. Achievement, Carlsbad H.S., 1996—; mem. speakers bur. March of Dimes, San Diego, 1990—, mem. logistics com., 1995—; team leader Farmers Legis. Action Group, 1997; co-chmn. North County Walk Am., 1998. Mem. Inst. Internal Auditors, Western Ins. Inst. of Speakers. Avocations: camping, travel, biking, skiing, photography. Office: Farmers Ins Group 5815 El Camino Real Carlsbad CA 92008-8801

BUCKLEY, J. STEPHEN, newspaper publisher; b. Pasadena, Calif., Mar. 22, 1942; s. John Stephen and Jane Salyer B.; m. Susannah Marie Smith, Aug. 27, 1965; children: Melissa Lynn, Amy Marie. Student, Dartmouth Coll., 1959-61, Rutgers U., 1963-66. Gen. mgr. Press Enterprise, Inc., Bloomsburg, Pa., 1987-88; pub. The Courier Tribune, Asheboro, N.C., 1989-90, The Times-Reporter, New Phila., Ohio, 1990-92, The Record, Troy, N.Y., 1992-96, The Times-News, Burlington, N.C., 1996—; prof. Bloomsburg U., 1987-88; v.p. cmty. newspaper divsn. Freedom Comm., Inc., 1999—; bd. dirs. Elon Coll. Pres. Indsl. Devel. Authority, Bloomsburg, 1987; commr. N.Y. State Commn. on the Capital Region. Mem. Alamance County C. of C. (vice-chmn. 1999—), Anglers' Club of N.Y., Confrerie de Chevalier de Taste du Vin. Avocations: fishing, hunting, skiing, hockey, golf. Office: Times News 707 S Main St Burlington NC 27215-5844

BUCKLEY, JAMES LANE, federal judge; b. N.Y.C., Mar. 9, 1923; s. William Frank and Aloise Josephine (Steiner) B.; m. Ann Frances Cooley, May 22, 1953; children: Peter P., James F. W., Priscilla L., William F., David L., Andrew T. BA, Yale U., 1943, LLB, 1949. Bar: Conn. 1950, D.C. 1953. Assoc. Wiggin & Dana, New Haven, 1949-53, Reasoner & Davis, Washington, 1953-57; v.p. Catawba Corp., N.Y.C., 1956-70; mem. U.S. Senate from N.Y. State, 1971-77; with Donaldson, Lufkin & Jenrette, N.Y.C., 1977-78; bus. con., 1978-80; undersec. for security assistance U.S. Dept. State, Washington, 1981-82; pres. Radio Free Europe/Radio Liberty, Munich, 1982-85; cir. judge U.S. Ct. Appeals for D.C. Cir., 1985—, now sr. judge; co-chmn. U.S. del. to UN Conf. on Environ., Nairobi, 1982; chmn. U.S. del. UN Conf. on Population, Mexico City, 1984. Author: If Men Were Angels, 1975. Rep. candidate for U.S. Senate, Conn., 1980. Lt. (j.g.) USNR, 1943-46. Office: US Ct Appeals 333 Constitution Ave NW Washington DC 20001-2866

BUCKLEY, JAMES W., librarian; b. Los Angeles, Aug. 16, 1933; s. George W. and Alta L. (Hale) B.; m. Margaret Ann Wall, Aug. 7, 1965; children:

Kathleen Ann, James William, John Whitney. AA, Los Angeles Harbor Coll., 1953; BA, Calif. State U., Long Beach, 1960; MLS, U. So. Calif., 1961, M in Pub. Adminstrn., 1974. Cert. tchr., Calif. Libr. West Gardena br. Los Angeles County Pub. Libr., 1961-62, librarian Carson br., 1962-63; libr. Montebello (Calif.) Regional Libr., 1963-68; regional librarian Orange County (Calif.) Pub. Libr., 1968, dir. pub. services, 1969-74; county librarian San Mateo County (Calif.) Libr., 1974-77, Marin County (Calif.) Libr., 1978; city librarian Torrance (Calif.) Pub. Libr., 1979—; exec. dir. Calif. Nat. Libr. Week, 1970; tchr. pub. svc. Coll. San Mateo, 1975; chmn. Met. Coop. Libr. Sys., 1989-90, Calif. Libr. Assn. Assembly, 1993-95. Served with U.S. Army, 1955-57. Mem. ALA, Am. Soc. Pub. Adminstrn., Calif. Libr. Assn., Rotary. Office: Torrance Pub Libr 3301 Torrance Blvd Torrance CA 90503-5014

BUCKLEY, JANICE MARIE, school administrator; b. Chgo., Apr. 6; d. Charles Lawrence and Yolande Marie (Sarpy) B. BS, So. Ill. U., 1965; MA, Gov.'s State U., 1979, Roosevelt U., 1990; postgrad., Roosevelt U., 1991—, Beijing U., 1994. Cert. adminstr., supt., Ill. 3d-6th grade tchr. Hartigan Sch., Chgo., 1965-75, reading lab. coord., 1975-76, ESEA reading coord., 1976-77, chair English dept., 1977-80, 7th-8th grade tchr., 1980-84, tchr. facilitator, 1984-87, acting prin., 1988-89, acting asst. prin., 1989-93, asst. prin., 1992—; master tchr. Hartigan Sch.; lead tchr. summer sch. Chgo. Bd. Edn., 1984-89, coord. aftersch. reading program, 1985-89, worker coord., 1992. Mem. St. Clotilde Sch. Bd., Chgo., 1987-88; mem. Chatham Cmty. Coun., Chgo., 1990. Mem. ASCD, Am. Fedn. Tchrs., Chgo. Asst. Prins. Assn., Chgo. Tchrs.' Union, Phi Delta Kappa, Alpha Kappa Alpha (chpt. Basileus 1963-65). Democrat. Roman Catholic. Avocations: dancing modern ballet, reading, gourmet cooking, sewing. Office: 8331 S King Dr Chicago IL 60619-5746

BUCKLEY, JEREMIAH STEPHEN, lawyer; b. San Francisco, Oct. 12, 1944; s. Jeremiah Stephen and Flora (Saur) B.; m. Deborah Stanley, Nov. 5, 1983. AB, Fairfield U., 1966; JD, U. Va., 1969. Bar: Conn. 1969, D.C. 1972, U.S. Supreme Ct. 1980. VISTA vol. Wayne County Legal Svcs., Detroit, 1969-70; asst. counsel govt. ops. com. U.S. Ho. of Reps., Washington, 1971-73; minority counsel housing subcom. U.S. Senate, Washington, 1973-77, minority staff dir. banking com., 1977-79; ptnr. Leighton, Lemov, Jacobs & Buckley, Washington, 1979-84, Thacher Proffitt & Wood, Washington, 1984-93, Goodwin, Procter & Hoar, 1994—. Mem. ABA (chair RESPA subcom. of consumer law com.), Fed. Bar Assn., Housing Roundtable, City Tavern Club, Kenwood Golf Club, Millwood Golf Club. Office: 1717 Pennsylvania Ave NW Washington DC 20006-4614

BUCKLEY, JEROME HAMILTON, English language educator; b. Toronto, Ont., Can., Aug. 30, 1917; came to U.S., 1939, naturalized, 1948; s. James Ora and Madeline Isabelle (Morgan) B.; m. Elizabeth Jane Adams, June 19, 1943; children: Nicholas, Victoria, Eleanor. B.A., U. Toronto, 1939; A.M., Harvard U., 1940, Ph.D., 1942; DLitt (hon.), Victoria U., 1997. Successively instr., asst. prof., asso. prof., prof. English U. Wis., 1942-54; Guggenheim fellow, 1946-47; vis. asso. prof. Columbia U., 1952-53, prof., 1954-61; prof. English Harvard U., 1961—, Gurney prof., 1975-87, Gurney prof. emeritus, 1987—; summer vis. prof. various univs.; Neesima lectr. Doshisha U., Japan, 1989. Author: William Ernest Henley, 1945, The Victorian Temper, 1951, Tennyson, the Growth of a Poet, 1960, The Triumph of Time, 1966, Season of Youth, 1974, The Turning Key, 1984; editor: Poems of Tennyson, 1958, Victorian Poets and Prose Writers, 1976, The Pre-Raphaelites, 1968, The Worlds of Victorian Fiction, 1975, David Copperfield, 1990; co-editor: Twelve Hundred Years, 1949, Poetry of the Victorian Period, 1965, Masters of British Literature, 1962. Guggenheim fellow, 1963-64; Recipient Christian Gauss award Phi Beta Kappa, 1952. Mem. MLA, Internat. Assn. U. Profs. English, Tennyson Soc., Am. Acad. Arts and Sci., Phi Beta Kappa (hon.). Episcopalian. Home: 191 Common St Belmont MA 02478-2909

BUCKLEY, JILL, legislative and public affairs administrator; 1 child, Melissa. B in English, U. Oreg., 1962; postgrad., U. Denver, Georgetown U. Founding ptnr. Rothstein/Buckley Inc., 1973-82; pres. J. Buckley and Assocs. Inc., 1983-88; ptnr. FMR Group, 1988-92; pres. Jill Buckley & Assocs., 1993; dir. external affairs U.S. Agy. for Internat. Devel., Washington, 1993-94, asst. adminstr. for legis. and pub. affairs, 1994—; lectr. U. Chgo., Yale U., Harvard U., George Washington U., Am. U. Office: US Agy for Internat Devel Bur Legis and Pub Affairs 1300 Pennsylvania Ave NW Washington DC 20004-3002

BUCKLEY, JOHN JOSEPH, obstetrician, gynecologist; b. Youngstown, Ohio, Jan. 21, 1930; s. John Joseph and Rosalie Catherine (Singler) B.; m. Anne Theresa Finnerty, Apr. 24, 1954; children: John, Joy, Colleen, Mollie. BS in Biology cum laude, Holy Cross Coll., 1952; MD, Ohio State U., 1959. Staff St. Elizabeth Med. Ctr., Youngstown, Ohio, 1963—, chief ob-gyn., 1977-80, chief of staff, 1986—; practice medicine specializing in ob-gyn. Youngstown, Ohio, 1963—; asst. prof. Northeastern Ohio Coll. Medicine, Rootstown, 1980—. co-founder Right to Life, Youngstown, 1970. Served to lt. USN, 1952-55, with res. MC, 1959-63. Fellow Am. Coll. Ob-Gyn; mem. AMA, Ohio Med. Assn., Mahoning County Med. Assn., Youngstown Soc. Ob-Gyns., Alpha Omega Alpha. Democrat. Roman Catholic. Clubs: Youngstown Country, Cotillion. Avocations: skiing, water sports, stamps, travel. Home: 1337 Stonington Dr Youngstown OH 44505-1657 Office: 935 Trailwood Dr Youngstown OH 44512-5008

BUCKLEY, JOHN JOSEPH, JR., health care executive; b. Evanston, Ill., Oct. 5, 1944; s. John Joseph and Mary Ruth (Smith) B.; m. Sarah Amelia Puceloski, May 16, 1970; children—Ruth Mary, Patricia Kimberly, John Joseph III. A.B., Kenyon Coll., 1966; M.B.A., George Washington U., 1969. Asst. adminstr. Maricopa County Gen. Hosp., Phoenix, 1969-71; asst. adminstr. St. Joseph's Hosp. and Med. Ctr., Phoenix, 1971-74, assoc. adminstr., 1974-76, v.p., 1976-79, pres., 1984-88; pres. St. Anthony's Hosp., Amarillo, Tex., 1979-84, St. Anthony's Devel. Corp., Amarillo, 1982-84; chief operating officer Harrington Cancer Ctr., Amarillo, 1982-84; sr. v.p. Mercy Health System, Cin., 1988-91; pres. So. Ill. Healthcare Enterprises, Carbondale, Ill., 1992—; pres. So. Ill. Hosp. Svcs., Health Svcs. of So. Ill., Homebound Infusion Therapy Svcs., So. Ill. Regional Health Plan, So. Ill. Med. Properties, 1992—. Active Amarillo Alliance of Cmty. Svc. Execs., Amarillo Area Acad. Health Ctr. Corp., Amarillo Area Hosp. Home Care, Amarillo Found. Health and Sci., Panhandle chpt. Tex. Soc. to Prevent Blindness, Amarillo Jr. League, Children's Oncology Svcs. of Tex. Panhandle; Amarillo diocesan coord. health affairs; mem. adminstrv. com. Amarillo; pres. Mercy Svcs. Corp., 1984-88; bd. dirs. Greater Phoenix Affordable Health Care Found., 1984-88; trustee Kenyon Coll., Gambier, Ohio, 1991-95; mem. SI Edge, 1995—. Fellow Am. Coll. Healthcare Execs. (regent Ariz. 1984-88, regent So. Ill. 1998—); mem. Tex. Hosp. Assn. (trustee 1983-84), Ill. Hosp. & Health Sys. Assn. (trustee 1995—), Cath. Health Assn. U.S. (bd. dirs., svcs. com., trustee 1985-91), Ariz. Kidney Found., Ariz. Hosp. Assn., Alumni Assn. of George Washington U. Health Svcs. Program and Health Svcs. Mgmt. and Policy (pres. 1995-97), Delta Phi (Phi chpt. Kenyon Coll. chpt., pres. alumni assn. 1988—). Republican. Roman Catholic. Office: So Ill Health Care Enterprises PO Box 3988 Carbondale IL 62902-3988

BUCKLEY, JOHN JOSEPH, JR., lawyer; b. N.Y.C., May 18, 1947; m. Jane Emily Genster, Jan. 12, 1980; children: Emily, Darcy, Claire, Connor. AB, Georgetown U., 1969; JD, U. Chgo., 1972. Bar: N.Y. 1973, D.C. 1977. Law clk. to judge John Minor Wisdom U.S. Ct. Appeals, New Orleans, 1972-73; law clk. to justice Lewis F. Powell Jr. U.S. Supreme Ct., Washington, 1973-74; spl. asst. to atty. gen. U.S. Dept. Justice, Washington, 1975-77; assoc. William & Connolly, Washington, 1977-80, ptnr., 1981—. Mem. ABA, Order of Coif, Phi Beta Kappa. Home: 2955 Newark St NW Washington DC 20008-3339 Office: Williams & Connolly 725 12th St NW Washington DC 20005-5901

BUCKLEY, JOHN WILLIAM, financial company executive; b. Parkersburg, W.Va., Feb. 28, 1932; s. George Brady and Clara Ellen (Humphrey) B.; m. Rena Mae Gaudreau, Aug. 9, 1958; children—Karen Lynn, Jeffrey Scott. Student, Dartmouth Coll., 1950-52; BS, Boston U., 1957; MBA, NYU, 1963. Chartered fin. analyst. Securities analyst Mut. Benefit Life Ins. Co., Newark, 1957-64; securities analyst IDS Fin. Svcs., Mpls., 1964-71, treas., v.p., 1971-89, ret. Treas., Mpls. Soc. for Blind, 1981. Served with U.S. Army, 1952-55. Mem. Twin Cities Soc. Securities Analysts, Lions. Republican. Episcopalian. Home: 710 Brightside Crescent Dr Venice FL 34293-4333

BUCKLEY, JOSEPH PAUL, III, polygraph specialist; b. Chgo., July 6, 1949; s. Joseph Paul and Helen (Lavelle) B.; m. Patricia Nemeth, June 17, 1972; children: Megan, Michael, Patrick, Thomas. B.A., Loyola U., Chgo., 1971; M.S. in Detection of Deception, Reid Coll. Detection of Deception, Chgo., 1973. Lic., Ill. Detection of deception examiner John E. Reid & Assocs., Inc., Chgo., 1971—, chief polygraph examiner, 1978-80, dir. Chgo. office, 1980-82; pres. corp. John E. Reid & Assocs., Inc., Chgo., Milw., 1982—; chmn. Ill. Detection of Deception Examiner Com., 1978-82; mem. adv. com. Office of Tech. Assessment, 1983. Co-author: Criminal Interrogation and Confessions, 3d edit., 1986; contbr. articles to profl. jours. Mem. Am. Polygraph Assn. (v.p. 1979-80, chmn. pub. rels. com. 1979-80, 84-95 awards), Ill. Polygraph Soc. (v.p. 1981, pres. 1982-83), Am. Acad. Forensic Scis., Am. Mgmt. Assn., Am. Soc. Indsl. Security (investigations com. 1983-89), Spl. Agts. Assn., Internat. Pers. Mgmt. Assn., Internat. Assn. Chiefs Policy, Chgo. Crime Commn. Office: 250 S Wacker Dr Ste 1100 Chicago IL 60606-5800

BUCKLEY, KEVIN, magazine editor. Exec. editor Playboy, N.Y.C. Office: Playboy Enterprises, Inc 730 Fifth Ave 3d Fl New York NY 10019-4105*

BUCKLEY, MORTIMER JOSEPH, physician; b. Worcester, Mass., July 1, 1932; s. Mortimer Joseph and Kathleen Josephine (O'Sullivan) B.; m. Marilyn Scully, June 16, 1962; children: Kathleen, Deirdre, Kara, Mortimer. AB, Coll. Holy Cross, 1954; MD, Boston U., 1958; D in Medicine (hon.), Aristotlean U., Salonica, Greece, 1986; DSc, Assumption Coll., Worcester, Mass., 1983; MA (hon.), Harvard U., 1989. Diplomate: Am. Bd. Surgery, Am. Bd. Thoracic Surgery. Intern in surgery Mass. Gen. Hosp., 1958-59, 3d asst. resident in surgery, 1959-60, 2d asst. resident, 1960-62, 1st asst. resident, 1964-65, resident in surgery, 1965-66, asst. in surgery, 1966-67; chief Vascular Clinic, 1967-69, asst. surgeon, 1968-71, assoc. in surgery, 1968-69, chief cardiac surg. unit, 1970—, asso. vis. surgeon, 1972-76, vis. surgeon, 1977—; teaching fellow in anatomy Harvard Med. Sch., Boston, 1960-62, teaching fellow in surgery, 1965-66, instr. surgery, 1966-68, asso. in surgery, 1968-69, asst. prof. surgery, 1969-72, asso. prof. surgery, 1972-76, prof. surgery, 1977—; clin. asso. Clinic of Surgery, Nat. Heart Inst., Bethesda, Md., 1962-64. Decorated Knight Equestrian Order of Holy Sepulchre of Jerusalem, Knight Order of St. John (Knights of Malta). Mem. N.Y. Acad. Sci., AMA, Mass. Med. Soc., Am. Assn. Acad. Surgery, Am. Bd. Thoracic Surgery, Soc. Univ. Surgeons, A.C.S., Internat. Cardiovascular Soc., Soc. for Vascular Surgery, New Eng., Boston surg. socs., Am. Assn. Thoracic Surgeons (chmn. membership com. 1980, pres. 1995-96), Soc. Thoracic Surgeons, Am. Heart Assn. (chmn. cardiovascular surg. council 1980), Mass. Heart Assn. (pres. 1991), Am. Soc. Artificial Internal Organs, Am. Coll. Cardiology, Am. Surg. Assn., Am. Coll. Chest Physicians. Office: Mass Gen Hosp 32 Fruit St Boston MA 02114-2620

BUCKLEY, PAUL RICHARD, insurance executive; b. Brownfield, Maine, Jan. 8, 1935; s. John Joseph and Ruth Ann B.; m. Anita Lucia Lebel, Oct. 11, 1958; children: Lisa, Paul Jr., Scott, Julia. BA, U. Maine, 1957; LLB, U. Maine, Portland, 1961. Bar: Maine 1961. Ptnr. Longley Assocs., Lewiston, Maine, 1958-80; prin. The Buckley Group, Lewiston, 1980—. Contbr. articles to profl. jours. Pres., bd. dirs. St. Mary Hosp., Lewiston, Maine, 1970-77; bd. dirs. Maine Dental Svcs., Portland, 1975-80. Recipient J. Putnham Stephens award, Maine Life Assn., 1987. Mem. ABA, Maine Bar Assn. (bd. dirs. ins. trust 1975-80), Androscoggin Bar Assn., New Eng. Life Lenders Assn. (pres. 1974-75), Am. Coll. LIfe Ins. Underwriters, Advanced Underwriters, Million Dollar Round Table (pres. 1984-85). Avocations: hunting, fishing, tennis, reading. Home: 17 Manning Ave Lewiston ME 04240-5923 Office: The Buckley Group 179 Lisbon St Lewiston ME 04240-7248

BUCKLEY, PRISCILLA LANGFORD, magazine editor; b. N.Y.C., Oct. 17, 1921; d. William Frank and Aloise (Steiner) B. BA, Smith Coll., 1943. Copy girl, sports writer UP, N.Y.C., 1944; radio rewrite staff mem. U.P., 1944-47; corr. U.P., Paris, France, 1953-56; news editor Sta. WACA, Camden, S.C., 1947-48; reports officer CIA, Washington, 1951-53; with Nat. Rev. Mag., N.Y.C., 1956—; mng. editor Nat. Rev. Mag., 1959-86, sr. editor, 1986—; mem. U.S. Adv. Commn. Pub. Diplomacy, 1984-91. Editor: The Joys of National Review, 1995; columnist One Woman's Voice Syndicate, 1976-80. Mem. Cosmopolitan Club, Sharon Country Club (Conn., sec. 1973-77, pres. 1978-80, 94-95). Home: Great Elm Sharon CT 06069 Office: Nat Review 215 Lexington Ave New York NY 10016-6023

BUCKLEY, REBECCA HATCHER, physician, educator; b. Hamlet, N.C., Apr. 1, 1933; d. Martin Armstead and Nora (Langston) Hatcher; m. Charles Edward Buckley III, July 9, 1955; children: Charles Edward IV, Elizabeth Ann, Rebecca Kathryn, Sarah Margaret. BA, Duke U., 1954; MD, U. N.C., 1958. Intern Duke U. Med. Ctr., Durham, N.C., 1958-59, resident, 1959-61; practice medicine, specializing in pediatric allergy and immunology, 1961—; dir. Am. Bd. Allergy and Immunology, Phila., 1971-73, chmn. exam. com., 1971-73, co-chmn. bd. dirs., 1982-84; chmn. Diagnostic Lab. Immunology, 1984-88; mem. staff Duke U. Med. Ctr.; asst. prof. pediatrics and immunology, 1968-72, assoc. prof. pediatrics, 1972-76, prof. pediatrics, 1976-79, assoc. prof. immunology, 1972-79, prof. immunology, 1979—, J. Buren Sidbury prof. pediatrics, 1979—. Contbr. numerous articles to med. publs. Recipient Allergic Diseases Acad. award Nat. Inst. Allergy and Infectious Diseases, 1974-79, Merit Rsch. award NIH, 1987-97, Nat. Bd. award Med. Coll. Pa., 1991, Clemons von Pirquet award Georgetown, 1993, Disting. Tchr. award Duke U. Med. Alumni Assn., 1993, Lifetime Achievement award Immune Deficiency Found., 1994, Disting. Svc. award Am. Acad. Allergy and Immunology, 1996, Disting. Faculty award Duke U. Med. Alumni Assn., 1998. Fellow Am. Acad. Allergy and Immunology (mem. exec. com. 1975-82, pres. 1979-80, hon. fellow award 1999); mem. Am. Assn. Immunologists, Soc. Pediatric Rsch., Am. Acad. Pediatrics (Bret Ratner award 1992), Southeastern Allergy Assn. (pres. 1978-79), Am. Pediatric Soc. (coun. mem. 1991-99, pres.-elect 1999—). Republican. Episcopalian. Home: 3621 Westover Rd Durham NC 27707-5032 Office: Duke U Med Ctr PO Box 2898 Durham NC 27715-2898

BUCKLEY, RICHARD BENNETT, asset management company executive; b. Providence, Nov. 7, 1942; s. Alfred and Helen (Searles) B.; m. Karen Owen, May, 1982; 1 child, Owen Searles. BA, Denison U., 1965; JD, Syracuse U., 1968; Exec. MBA, U. New Haven, 1982. Successively asst. dean, dir. placement, dean admissions, lectr. ins. law, assoc. dean, dir. placement, dir. admissions, asst. prof. law Syracuse (N.Y.) U., 1968-74, assoc. prof., 1974-77; pres. Schiavone Tire & Rubber Reclamation Corp., New Haven, Conn., 1978-80, Schiavone Sports, New Haven, 1978-80; v.p. Cowen Asset Mgmt., N.Y.C., 1980-87, spl. ltd. ptnr., 1986-92, sr. v.p., 1987—, exec. v.p., 1990—; dir., 1992-98, also bd. dirs.; dir. S.G. Cowen, N.Y.C., 1998—; chmn. bd. dirs. Founders Bank, New Haven, 1984-95; mentor Sch. Orgn. and Mgmt. Yale U., New Haven, 1987-89; bd. dirs. Saab Fin. Auto Receivables Corp. Saab Fin. Auto Receivables Corp. II, Saab Fin. Auto Receivables Corp. III, Saab Fin. Svcs. Corp. Author: Handbook on Profl. Ethics and Responsibility, 1973; mng. editor Ins. Counsel Jour., 1971-87; contbr. legal articles to profl. jours. Bd. dirs., mem. fin. com. Shubert Theater; bd. dirs. Yankee coun. Boy Scouts Am.; trustee First Congl. Ch., Guilford, Conn., 1996. Mem. ABA, Order of Coif, Quinnipiack Club (pres. 1992-93), Rotary (pres. 1987-88, Spl. Pers. award 1982-83, Rotarian of Yr. 1985-86). Avocations: sailing, skiing, tennis, fly fishing. Home: 34 Grove Hill Rd Guilford CT 06437-3126 Office: Cowen Investment Counselors 35 Elm St New Haven CT 06510-2023

BUCKLEY, RICK, broadcast executive. Grad., U. Miami. Radio dir. NBC Radio Network, N.Y.C.; music dir. WNEW, N.Y.C.; salesman WHIM, Providence; pres. Buckley Broadcasting Corp. Calif., Buckley Broadcasting Corp., Greenwich, Conn., 1972—. Mem. Radio Operators Caucus, Radio Advt. Bur. (chmn. bd. dirs.). Office: Buckley Radio 166 W Putnam Ave Greenwich CT 06830-5241*

BUCKLEY, STEPHANIE DENISE, health care executive; b. Tulsa, Sept. 19, 1961; d. Richard Harvey and Judith Carol (Holtzinger) Welcher; m. Jeffery Lee Taylor, June 16, 1990 (div. July 1992); m. Dennis Ray Buckley, Oct. 30, 1995 (div. Feb. 1997). BS, Okla. State U., 1983; MA, U. Okla., 1994. News anchor Sta. KOSU-FM, Stillwater, 1981, Sta. KRXO-FM, Stillwater, 1982; asst. producer Sta. KTVY-TV, Oklahoma City, 1983-84; anchor/reporter Sta. KTEN, Ada, Okla., 1985-86; producer Am.'s Shopping Channel, Oklahoma City, 1987; pub. rels. coordinator S.W. Med. Ctr. Okla., Oklahoma City, 1988-89, pub. rels. assoc., 1990-91, mgr. pub. rels. and devel., 1991-93; exec. dir., CEO Neighborhood Alliance, Oklahoma City, 1994-95; cmty. devel. assoc. Integris Health, Oklahoma City, 1995—; cons. on brochure, Woman to Woman, 1990. Mem. comms. com. United Way, Oklahoma City, 1989-90; bd. dirs. Nat. Clown and Laughter Hall of Fame, 1989-97; bd. dirs. HUGS, 1992-94, Firesafe Found., 1994-96, Internat. Ctr. for Humor and Health, 1995-97, Contact, 1996-97; bd. dirs. Youth Build Oklahoma City, 1996; mem. jr. hospitality Xanadu, 1996—, auction chmn., 1998, acquisitions chmn., 1999, bd. dirs., 1999—. Recipient Good Guy award, KTVY-TV, 1988, 89. Mem. Women in Comms. (v.p. 1981-82), Am. Hosp. Assn., Okla. Hosp. Assn., Am. Soc. Health Care Mktg. and Pub. Rels., Pub. Rels Soc. Am., Oklahoma City C. of C., South Oklahoma City C. of C., Lions Internat., Am. Bus. Clubs (bd. dirs.), Rotary Internat. (group study exch. to Queensland, Australia 1995), West Oklahoma City Rotary Club (bd. dirs. 1999—), Oklahoma City Carefree Rose Garden Club. Methodist. Avocations: writing, photography, modeling. Office: Integris Health Ste C-80 3366 NW Expressway St Oklahoma City OK 73112-4416

BUCKLEY, THOMAS HUGH, historian, educator; b. Elkhart, Ind., Sept. 11, 1932; s. Bernard Leroy and Martha B. (Swoveland) B.; m. Julie Griffith; children: Christopher, Kathryn, Elizabeth, Thomas, Barbara. Student, Northwestern U., 1950-53; A.B., Ind. U., 1955, M.A., 1956, Ph.D. (grad. fellow), 1961. From instr. to prof. U. S.D., 1960-69; vis. prof. Ind. U., 1969-71; prof., chmn. dept. U. Tulsa, 1971-81, chmn. humanistic studies, 1975-81, Jay Walker research chair Am. History, 1981—; assoc. dean Grad. Sch., 1995—; cons. on overseas edn. to Nat. Edn. Corp. Author: The United States and the Washington Conference, 1921-1922, 1970 (award as best first book by an historian 1971); co-author: American Foreign and National Security Policies, 1914-1945, 1987; editor: Research and Roster Guide of Soc. Historians of Am. Fgn. Relations, 1980-86; contbr. chpts. in books. Postdoctoral fellow Stanford U., 1968, U. Wis., 1983, Brown U., 1986, U. Tex., 1991; Fulbright fellow, U. Western Australia, 1986. Mem. Orgn. Am. Historians, Soc. Historians of Am. Fgn. Relations, Tulsa Com. Fgn. Relations, Phi Alpha Theta, Lambda Chi Alpha. Republican. Methodist. Home: 2817 E 1st Pl Tulsa OK 74104-1705 Office: Univ Tulsa Dept History Tulsa OK 74104 *Success comes in the race of life not always to the swiftest but to those who keep on running.*

BUCKLEY, VIRGINIA LAURA, editor; b. N.Y.C., May 11, 1929; d. Alfred and Josephine Marie (Manetti) Iacuzzi; m. David Patrick Buckley, July 30, 1960; children: Laura Joyce, Brian Thomas. BA, Wellesley Coll., 1950; MA, Columbia U., 1952. Tchr. English Bennett Coll., Millbrook, N.Y., 1954-56, Berkeley Inst., Bklyn., 1956-58; copy editor World Pub. Co., N.Y.C., 1959-69; children's book editor Thomas Y. Crowell, N.Y.C., 1971-80; editl. dir. Lodestar Books, N.Y.C., 1980-97; contbg. editor Clarion Books, N.Y.C., 1997—. Author: State Birds, 1986; contbr. articles to profl. jours. Mem. ALA. Home: 33 Brook Ter Leonia NJ 07605-1504 Office: Clarion Books 215 Park Ave S New York NY 10003-1603

BUCKLEY, WILLIAM ELMHIRST, publishing consultant; b. Rahway, N.J., Oct. 6, 1913; s. John A. and Margaret Elsie (Elmhirst) B.; m. Virginia Smith, Aug. 2, 1941; children: Carolyn E. Buckley Dreyfoos, William Elmhirst Jr. Student, U. Pa., 1932-34. Jr. exec. Quinn & Boden Co., Inc. (book mfrs.), Rahway, N.J., 1935-42, Doubleday & Co., N.Y.C., 1945-49; with Henry Holt & Co., N.Y.C., 1949-58; v.p., dir. Henry Holt & Co., 1951-58; v.p. sales World Pub. Co., Cleve., 1958-60; v.p. book div. McCall Corp., N.Y.C., 1960-62; v.p. Curtis Pub. Co., N.Y.C., 1962-68; dir. book div. Curtis Pub. Co., 1962-68; asst. to pres. Cowles Communications, Inc., 1968-72; chmn. Cowles Book Co., 1968-72; chmn., pres. Cambridge Book Co. (subsidiaries Cowles Communications Inc.), 1968-72; publishing cons., 1972—. Served to lt. comdr. USNR, 1942-45. Mem. Phi Delta Theta. Clubs: Dutch Treat (N.Y.C.); Soc. Four Arts (Palm Beach, Fla.).

BUCKLEY, WILLIAM FRANK, JR., magazine editor, writer; b. N.Y.C., Nov. 24, 1925; s. William Frank and Aloise (Steiner) B.; m. Patricia Taylor, July 6, 1950; 1 child, Christopher T. Student, U. Mexico, 1943; BA, Yale U., 1950; LHD (hon.), Seton Hall U., 1966, Niagara U., 1967, Mt. St. Mary's Coll., 1969, U. S.C., 1985, Converse Coll., 1988, U. South Fla., 1992, Adelphi U., 1995; LLD (hon.), St. Peter's Coll., Syracuse U., Ursinus Coll., 1969, Lehigh U., 1970, Lafayette Coll., 1972, St. Anselm's Coll., 1973, St. Bonaventure U., 1974, U. Notre Dame, 1978, N.Y. Law Sch., 1981, Colby Coll., 1985; DScO (hon.), Curry Coll, 1970; LittD (hon.), St. Vincent Coll., 1971, Fairleigh Dickinson U., 1973, Alfred U., 1974, Coll. William and Mary, 1981, William Jewell Coll., 1982, Albertus Magnus Coll., Coll. St. Thomas, Bowling Green State U., 1987, Coe Coll., 1989, St. John's U., Minn., 1989, Grove City Coll., 1991. Instr. Spanish lang. Yale U., New Haven, 1947-51; assoc. editor Am. Mercury, N.Y.C., 1952; founder, pres., editor-in-chief Nat. Rev., N.Y.C., 1955-90; editor-at-large Nat. Rev., 1991—; syndicated columnist, 1962—; host weekly TV show Firing Line, 1966—; Froman disting. prof. Russell Sage Coll., 1973; lectr. New Sch. Social Rsch., 1967-68. Author: God and Man at Yale, 1951, (with L. Brent Bozell) McCarthy and His Enemies, 1954, Up from Liberalism, 1959, Rumbles Left and Right, 1963, The Unmaking of a Mayor, 1966, The Jeweler's Eye, 1968, The Governor Listeth, 1970, Cruising Speed, 1971, Inveighing We Will Go, 1972, Four Reforms, 1973, United Nations Journal, 1974, Execution Eve, 1975, Saving the Queen, 1976, Airborne, 1976, Stained Glass, 1978 (Am. Book award best mystery 1980), A Hymnal, 1978, Who's On First, 1980, Marco Polo, If You Can, 1982, Atlantic High, 1982, Overdrive, 1983, The Story of Henri Tod, 1984, The Temptation of Wilfred Malachey, 1985, See You Later Alligator, 1985, Right Reason, 1985, High Jinx, 1986, Racing Through Paradise, 1987, Mongoose, R.I.P., 1988, On The Firing Line, 1989, Gratitude, 1990, Tucker's Last Stand, 1991, WindFall, 1992, In Search of Anti-Semitism, 1992, Happy Days Were Here Again, 1993, A Very Private Plot, 1994, The Blackford Oakes Reader, 1995, Brothers No More, 1995, Buckley: The Right Word, 1996, Nearer, My God, 1997, The Lexicon, 1998; editor: The Committee and Its Critics, 1962, Odyssey of a Friend: Whittaker Chambers' Letters to William F. Buckley, Jr., 1954-1961, 1970, American Conservative Thought in the Twentieth Century, 1970, (with Charles Kesler) Keeping the Tablets, 1988; contbr. to Racing at Sea, 1959, The Intellectuals, 1960, What is Conservatism?, 1964, Dialogues in Americanism, 1964, Violence in The Streets, 1968, The Beatles Book, 1968, Spectrum of Catholic Attitudes, 1969, Great Ideas Today Annual, 1970, Essays on Hayek, 1976; also periodicals. Conservative Party candidate for mayor, N.Y.C., 1965; mem. USIA Adv. Commn., 1969-72; pub. mem. U.S. del. to 28th Gen. Assembly UN, 1973. Served to 2d lt., inf. AUS, 1944-46. Recipient Best Columnist of Yr. award, 1967, Disting. Achievement award in journalism U. So. Calif., 1968, Emmy award for outstanding program achievement NATAS, 1969, Cleveland Amory award for best interviewer/interviewee TV Guide, 1974, Bellarime medal, 1977, Americanism award Young Rep. Nat. Fedn., 1979, Carmel award Am. Friends of Haifa U., 1980, Creative Leadership award NYU, 1981, Lincoln Lit. award Union League, 1985, Shelby Cullom Davis award, 1986, Lowell Thomas Travel Journalism award, 1989, Julius award for outstanding pub. svc. U. So. Calif. Sch. Pub. Adminstrn., 1990, Gold medal award Nat. Inst. Social Scis., 1992, Presdl. Medal of Freedom, 1991, Adam Smith award Hillsdale Coll., 1996. Fellow Soc. Profl. Journalists, Sigma Delta Chi; mem. Council on Fgn. Relations, Mont Pelerin Soc. Clubs: New York Yacht, Century, Phila. Soc., Bohemian. Republican. Roman Catholic. Office: Nat Rev 215 Lexington Ave New York NY 10016-6023

BUCKLIN, LEONARD HERBERT, lawyer; b. Mpls., Apr. 17, 1933; s. Leonard A. and Lilah B. (Norland) B.; m. Charla Lee; children: Karen, Anne, David, Douglas, Lea, Gregory. BS in Law, U. Minn., 1955, JD, 1957. Bar: Minn. 1957, U.S. Dist. Ct. Minn. 1957, N.D. 1960, U.S. Dist. Ct. N.D. 1960, U.S. Ct. Appeals (8th cir.) 1971, U.S. Supreme Ct. 1973, Colo. 1989, U.S. Dist. Ct. Colo. 1989, Tex. 1992, U.S. Dist. Ct. Tex. 1993. Ptnr. Larson, Loevinger, Lindquist, Freeman & Fraser, Mpls., 1957-60, Zuger & Bucklin, Bismark, N.D., 1960-87; gen. counsel Provident Life Ins. Co., 1965-85; pres. Bucklin Trial Lawyers P.C., 1988-95; of counsel Bucklin and Klemine, Bismark, N.D., 1992—, Allison and Huerta, Corpus Christi, 1992-97; owner Bucklin of Counsel Attys., 1997—; lectr. on ins. coverage to various groups, mem. trial procedures com. N.D. Supreme Ct., 1977-92. Author: Civil Practice of North Dakota, 1975, ann. supplements, 1976-92. Fellow Internat. Acad. Trial Lawyers (bd. dirs.); mem. ABA (ins. coverage and ethics coms., Ctr. Profl. Responsibility), UNOS (patient affairs, ethics, profl. stds. com.), ATLA, Tex. Trial Lawyers Assn., Winthrop Soc., Chopin Soc. Tex., Tex. Ctr. for Legal Ethics, Million Dollar Advs. Forum, Rotary (Paul Harris fellow Corpus Christi), Order of Coif, Phi Delta Phi, Delta Sigma Rho, Town Club Corpus Christi. Methodist. Home: 8063 S Michele Ln Tempe AZ 85284-1362

BUCKLIN, LOUIS PIERRE, business educator, consultant; b. N.Y.C., Sept. 20, 1928; s. Louis Lapham and Elja (Barricklow) B.; m. Weylene Edwards, June 11, 1956; children: Randolph E., Rhonda W. Student, Dartmouth Coll., 1950; MBA, Harvard U., 1954; PhD, Northwestern U., 1960. Asst. prof. bus. U. Colo., Boulder, 1954-56; instr. in bus. Northwestern U., Evanston, 1958-59, assoc. dean Grad. Sch. Bus. Adminstrn., 1981-83; prof. bus. adminstrn. U. Calif., Berkeley, 1960-93, prof. emeritus, 1993—; vis. prof. Stockholm Sch. Econs., 1983, INSEAD, Fontainebleau, France, 1984, Erasmus U., Rotterdam, Netherlands, 1993-94, Cath. U. Leuven, Belgium, 1994; prin. Bucklin Assocs., Lafayette, Calif., 1975—;mem. adv. bd. Gemini Cons., San Francisco, 1987-94. Author: A Theory of Distribution Channel Structure, 1966, Competition Evolution in The Distributive Trades, 1972, Productivity in Marketing, 1979; editor: Vertical Marketing Systems, 1971, Channels and Channel Institutions, 1986, Jour. of Retailing, 1996—. Mem. City of Lafayette Planning Commn., 1990-93. Capt. USMC, 1951-53, Korea. Recipient Alpha Kappa Psi Found. award for best paper in Jour. Mktg., 1993. Mem. Inst. for Ops. Rsch. Mgmt. Scis., Am. Mktg. Assn. (Paul D. Converse award 1986), Lafayette-Langeac Soc. (bd. dirs. 1988-92). Democrat. Avocations: travel, microcomputers, photography. Office: U Calif Haas Sch Bus Berkeley CA 94720-1900

BUCKLO, ELAINE EDWARDS, United States district court judge; b. Boston, Oct. 1, 1944; married. AB, St. Louis U., 1966; JD, Northwestern U., 1972. Bar: Calif. 1973, U.S. Dist. Ct. (no. dist.) Calif. 1973, Ill. 1974, U.S. Dist. ct. (no. dist.) Ill. 1974, U.S. Ct. Appeals (7th cir.) 1983. Law clk. U.S. Ct. Appeals (7th cir.), Chgo.; pvt. practice, 1973-85; U.S. magistrate judge U.S. Dist. Ct. (no. dist.) Ill., Chgo., 1985-94, judge, 1994—; spkr. in field. Contbr. articles to profl. jours. Mem. jud. conf. com. on adminstrn. Magistrate Judge Sys., 1998—; mem. vis. com. No. Ill. U. Sch. Law, 1994—; mem. Northwestern U. Law Bd., 1996—. Mem. ABA (standing com. law and literacy 1995—), FBA (v.p. 1990-92, pres. Chgo. chpt. 1992-93), Women's Bar Assn. Ill. (bd. dirs. 1994-96), Chgo. Coun. Lawyers (pres. 1977-78). Office: US Dist Ct No Dist Everett McKinley Dirksen Bldg 219 S Dearborn St Ste 1764 Chicago IL 60604-1706

BUCKMAN, FREDERICK W., gas utility executive. Pres., COO Consumers Power Co., Jackson, Mich., 1988-92; CEO PacificCorp USA, Portland, Oreg. Recipient George Westinghouse Gold medal, ASME, 1993. *

BUCKMAN, JAMES EDWARD, lawyer; b. N.Y.C., Oct. 2, 1944; s. John Burr and Mary Dolores (Ullery) B.; m. Nancy Lee McLaughlin, Aug. 23, 1969; children: Elizabeth Ahern, Anne Tracy, Julia Walsh. AB, Fordham U., 1966; JD, Yale U., 1969. Bar: N.Y. 1969, Ga. 1974, U.S. Dist. Ct. (no. dist.) Ga. 1974. Assoc. Dewey, Ballantine, Bushby, Palmer & Wood, N.Y.C., 1969-72; asst. gen. counsel Gable Industries, Inc., Atlanta, 1972-74; assoc. then ptnr. Troutman, Sanders, Lockerman & Ashmore, Atlanta, 1974-85, ptnr., 1990-92; exec. v.p., gen. counsel Days Inns of Am., Inc., Atlanta, 1985-89, HFS Inc., Parsippany, N.J., 1992—; now vice chmn., gen. counsel Cendant Corp, Parsippany. 1st lt. USAFR, 1969-75. Mem. ABA, Atlanta Bar Assn., State Bar Ga. Roman Catholic. Avocation: running. Office: Cendant Corp 6 Sylvan Way Parsippany NJ 07054-3707*

BUCKMAN, THOMAS RICHARD, foundation executive, educator; b. Reno, May 3, 1923; s. Thomas Eli and Georgia Christina (Damm) B.; m. Gunhild Margareta Malmkjell, May 1, 1948; children: Anne Christina, Carol Erica. BA, U. Pacific, 1947; MA, U. Minn., 1951, B.L.S. (H.W. Wilson scholar), 1953. Clk., Permit Office for Germany, Allied High Commn., Stockholm, 1949-50; sr. clk. U. Minn. Libr., 1952-53; asst. reference libr. Oreg. State U. Libr., 1953-54; King Gustav V fellow in Sweden, Am. Scandinavia Found., 1954-55; asst. libr. Modesto (Calif.) Jr. Coll. Libr., 1955-56; head acquisitions dept. U. Kans. Libr., 1956-60, assoc. dir., 1960-61, dir. libraries, 1961-68, lectr. in Scandinavian, 1958-61; prof. bibliography, univ. libr. Northwestern U., Evanston, Ill., 1968-71; pres. Found. Ctr., N.Y.C., 1971-91, sr. advisor, 1991-93; pres., chmn. Engring. Info. Found., 1995—; past chairperson bd. dirs. Telecom. Coop. Network, E.S.T.C., N.A., Engring. Info., Inc. Editor, translator: Modern Theatre: Seven Plays and an Essay (by Pär Lagerkvist), 1966; editor: Bibliography and Natural History, 1966, University and Research Libraries in Japan and the United States, 1972; contbr. articles to profl. jours. With USNR, 1943-46. Guggenheim fellow, 1964-65, Scandinavian studies fellow U. Minn., 1952, H.W. Wilson scholar, 1953. Mem. ALA (chmn. internat. rels. adv. com. for liaison with Japanese librs. 1967-71, dir. internat. rels. office 1966-67), Soc. for Advancement of Scandinavian Study (sec.-treas. 1959-69), Am. Scandinavian Found. (bd. dirs. 1978-82). Home: 30 Lincoln Plz Apt 30S New York NY 10023-7126 Office: Engring Info Found 180 W 80th St Ste 207 New York NY 10024-6301

BUCK-MOORE, JOANNE ROSE, nursing administrator, educator; b. Cambridge, Mass., Jan. 3, 1939; d. Joseph J. and Louise L. (Buck) Verrochio; m. C. Edwin Buck (dec.); m. Donald P. Moore (dec.); children: Marie-Louise, Victoria, Katrina, Edwin. ASN, Middlesex C.C., Bedford, Mass., 1977; BSN magna cum laude, Worcester (Mass.) State Coll., 1980; MSN, U. R.I., 1983. RN, Mass. Dir. nursing Ctr. for Rehab. at Columbus, East Boston, Mass., Mt. Pleasant Hosp., Lynn, Mass.; nursr mgr. and program dir. Commonwealth of Mass. Dept. of Mental Health, Boston; course instr. Palm Beach C.C., Fla. Atlantic U.; lectr. at schs., clubs, seminars, confs.; legal cons. and expert witness. Author: Management by Objective: A Handbook for Nurses. Mem. ANA (cert. mental health nurse), Sigma Theta Tau. Home: 18 Faulkner Hill Rd Acton MA 01720

BUCKMORE, ALVAH CLARENCE, JR., computer scientist, ballistician; b. Lewiston, Maine, Sept. 11, 1944; s. Alvah Clarence and Mary (Begin) B. Student, Holyoke C.C., Nat. Radio Inst., Famous Writers Sch., U. Mass. Cert. firearms instr.; lic. amateur radio operator. CEO, chief scientist Buckmore Enterprises, Westfield, Mass., 1974—; developer math./engring. software database for microcomputer Calculated Solutions (formerly SC Applied Tech. Inc.), Columbia, S.C.; mgmt. cons. firearms industry; instr. Mass. Mil. NCO Acad., 1976; mem. Mass. State Rifle and Pistol Team, 1976. Contbr. Collier's Ency., articles to profl. jours. Mem. Mass. Rep. Party, Rep. Presdl. Task Force, Mass. Rep. Senate Com., at-large del., 1992—; comm. officer, dir. RACES for Mass. Emergency Mgmt. Agy., Area III, 1996—. Recipient Internat. Recognition award, 1979; NSF fellow, 1978—. Mem. AAAS, Computer Soc. of IEEE, NRA (life), DAV (life), Am. Def. Preparedness Assn., Nat. Assn. Federally Lic. Firearms Dealers (mem. sr. coalition), Assn. for Computer Tng. and Support, Math. Assn. Am., Am. Radio Relay League, Soc. Amateur Radio Astronomers, Amateur Radio Satellite Corp., Vietnam Vets. Am. (mem. vets. coun. Liberty chpt. 219), Am. Fedn. Police, Am. Legion, N.Y. Acad. Scis., Mount Tom Amateur Repeater Assn. Achievements include development of amateur radio satellite communications, of parallel processing techniques, algorithms, and code for ballistic applications; over 38 major discoveries made in ballistics, including the discovery of 3 new sciences: time physics, the study of the physical properties of time; force-fields, the study of the absorption, displacement, projection, or reflection of kinetic energy; and ballistic signatures, the study of the physical characteristics of a bullet in terminal flight. Address: 18 Tannery Rd Westfield MA 01085-4822 *Since the age of 15 years it has been my consistent objective in life to develop a genuine ability to think, talk and use information properly and, over these years—which include the experience of my serving as an illegal POW with only partial official recognition—I have wavered very little, if at all.*

BUCKNAM, MARY OLIVIA CASWELL, artist; b. Modesto, Calif., Feb. 6, 1914; d. Charles Henry and Helen Anne (Cross) Caswell; m. William Nelson Bucknam, June 22, 1946 (dec. 1966); children: William Nelson Jr., Charles Henry. BA, Calif. State U., San Jose, 1936; postgrad., U. Calif., Berkeley, 1938, Calif. State U., Stanislaus, 1968-75, U. San Francisco, 1968-75. Tchr. Stanislaus County (Calif.), 1936-38, Modesto (Calif.) Schs., 1938-43, San Bernardino (Calif.) City, 1943-46; art tchr. Klamath Union Schs., Klamath River, Calif., 1960-61; co-owner Bigfoot Ranch and Resort, Klamath River, 1960-66; art tchr., tchr. Riverbank (Calif.) City Schs., 1966-79; art cons. Riverbank Elem., 1986; gallery artist Cen. Calif. Art League, Modesto, 1986—. Group shows include Siskiyow Artists Assn., 1961-66 (best of show award, first award, other awards), Stanislaus County Shows, 1975-90 (best of show award, first award, other awards); over 150 paintings held by pvt. individuals and pub. orgns., Three Sisters Show Gallery tour, 1991-93, Travels with my Paintbrush Show Tour, 1991-92. Donor with Caswell family of land for Caswell State Park, San Joaquin County, Calif., 1995; pres. Caswell Sch. PTA, Ceres, Calif., 1956-57, Ceres Study Club, 1952-53; v.p. Siskiyou Artists Assn., Yreka, Calif., 1963-65; pres. Modesto Tchrs. Assn., 1940-41; vol. tchr. adult watercolor classes; active Trinity Singers Choirm 1990—. Named Woman of Distinction Soroptimist Internat., Ceres, Calif., 1992, Outstanding Woman of Stanislaus County Stanislaus County Commn. for Women, 1994. Mem. AAUW (Modesto br., fellowships chair 1959-60, historian 1956), Ctrl. Calif. Art League (chmn. bank shows Modesto 1988-94, co-chair young artists show Modesto 1986, 88, 89, 90, head art gallery docent 1994—), Calif. Ret. Tchrs. Assn., Stanislaus County Hist. Soc., Sierra Club, Tuolumne River Lodge, Delta Kappa Gamma (hist.-photography 1985-94, v.p. chpt. 1969-71), Kappa Delta Pi. Republican. Presbyterian. Avocations: painting, world travel, art gallery docent, church service. Home: 2704 La Palma Dr Modesto CA 95354-3229

BUCKNER, ELMER LA MAR, insurance executive; b. Provo, Utah, Apr. 27, 1922; s. Elmer R. and Altis LaVern (Maxfield) B.; m. Melba Hale, Oct. 3, 1945; children: Lynda, Brent, Terry, Kathy, David. BS, Brigham Young U., 1946; HHD (hon.), Weber State U., 1994. CLU. Ptnr. Buckner-Radmall Ins. Counselors, Ogden, Utah, 1947-62, co. inc. pres., 1962-85; mem. Utah Ho. of Reps., 1965-67, Utah Senate, 1967-75, asst. majority leader, 1971-75. Bd. govs. ARC, 1956-62, mem. exec. com., 1961-62; mem. gen. bd. Young Men's Mut. Improvement Assn., LDS Ch., 1957-58, young men's gen. bd., 1980, regional rep., 1981-87; bishop Ogden 55th Ward, 1958-63, pres. Ogden LDS Temple, 1987-90; 2d counselor Weber Heights Stake presidency, 1963-68; pres. Weber State Coll. Stake, 1968-73, Sacramento mission, 1975-78; former dir. Citizens Com. for Hoover Report; mem. Com. on Religion in Am. Life Inc.; former mem. adv. com. FOA; v.p. Lake Bonneville coun. Boy Scouts Am., 1968-69, pres., 1970, program chmn. Western region, 1973-75; mem. alumni bd. Brigham Young U., 1959-63, pres., 1961-62; v.p. Ogden Area United Fund, 1962, pres. No. Utah, 1963; chmn. Utah Cancer Crusade, 1970; v.p. Utah Cancer Soc., 1971, Utah div. Am. Cancer Soc.; del. Rep. Nat. Conv., Chgo., 1960, chmn. Weber County Reps., 1960-64; elector Utah State Reps., 1964; mem. Utah Bd. Regents Higher Edn., 1981-85; bd. dirs. western region bd. Boy Scouts Am., 1986—, pres. area II coun., 1985-87. 1st lt. USAAF, World War II; 23 missions. Recipient Silver Beaver award Boy Scouts Am., 1967, Silver Antelope award, 1983; Disting. Alumni award Weber State Coll., 1983, Alexis de Tocqueville award United Way Am., 1987, Alumni Disting. Svc. award Brigham Young U., 1991; named Utah Ins. Agt. of Yr., 1973. Mem. U.S. C. of C. (bd. dirs. 1955-56), U.S. Jaycees (pres. 1954-55), Utah Jaycees (pres. 1952-53), Ogden C. of C. (bd. dirs. 1980, pres. 1982, Utah Hall of Fame award 1989), Ogden Jaycees (pres. 1950), Jr. Chamber Internat. (treas. 1956), Weber Coll. Alumni Assn. (pres. 1958-59), Kiwanis (pres. Ogden club 1967), Sigma Gamma Chi (internat. pres. 1967-69). Home: 1550 Country Hills Dr Ogden UT 84403-2512

BUCKNER, JENNIE, newspaper editor; m. Steven Landers; 1 child Katie. BS in Journalism with honors, Ohio State Univ. Mng. editor San Jose Mercury News, Calif.; v.p. news Knight-Ridder, Inc., 1989-93; v.p., editor The Charlotte Observer, N.C., 1993—. Bd. visitors Davidson Coll., 1994—. Mem. Am. Soc. Newspaper Editors (bd. dirs. 1998—). Office: The Charlotte Observer PO Box 30308 Charlotte NC 28230-0308

BUCKNER, JOHN HUGH, retired real estate broker, retired construction company executive, retired air force officer; b. Cleburne, Tex., Jan. 11, 1919; s. John Franklin and Eleanor (Wimberly) B.; m. Ann Sonfield, Apr. 24, 1946; children: John Hugh Jr., Ann Lynn, Robert Chantland. AS, John Tarleton Coll., 1938; student, Tex. A. and M. Coll., 1938-39; BS, U.S. Mil. Acad., 1943; MS, Springfield Coll., 1952. Commd. 2d lt. U.S. Army, 1943; advanced through grades to maj. gen. USAF, 1970; assigned Europe, 1943-46, 60-64; assigned U.S. Mil. Acad. and Air U., 1946-53, Korea, 1953-54; assigned Air Tng. Command, 1954-57, Air N.G., 1957-60; assigned Air U., 1964-67, Azores, 1967-69; assigned Tactical Air Command, 1969-70, 7th AF, Vietnam, 1970-71; ret., 1971; pres. Buckner Constrn. Co., Jacksonville, Tex., 1971-84; ret., 1984; real estate broker Gateway Realty, Bullard, Tex., 1980-90. Decorated Legion of Merit, D.F.C., Air medal; Croix de Guerre France; Medal Mil. Merit Portugal). Mem. Assn. Gen. Contractors Am. (pres. Tex. hwy. heavy br. 1981, dir. 1979-82), Air Force Assn., Order Daedalians, Mil. Order World Wars, VFW, Am. Legion, Rotary (pres. Jacksonville club 1986-87), Phi Kappa Phi. Club: Rotary (pres. Jacksonville club 1986-87). Home: Emerald Bay 132 132 Williamsburg Ln Bullard TX 75757-8960

BUCKNER, JOHN KENDRICK, aerospace engineer; b. Indpls., June 13, 1936; s. Roland Kendrick and Lucille (Cave) B.; m. Nancy Ann Smith, June 13, 1974; children: James Kendrick, Bari Kay, Kendrick Ann. BA in Math., DePauw U., 1958; MS in Aero-Engring., Stanford U., 1960. Aerodynamics sr. engr. Gen. Dynamics, Ft. Worth, 1960-69, supr. aerodyns., 1969-75, aircraft project engr., 1975-77, mgr. flight controls, 1977-80, dir. advanced programs, 1980-89, v.p. spl. programs, 1989-95; cons. tech. and strategic aerospace mgmt. Ft. Worth, 1996—; com. mem. Nat. Rsch. Coun./Naval Studies Bd., Washington, 1990, Aeronautics and Space Engring. Bd., 1992-96; mem. aerospace rsch. and tech. subcom. aeronautics adv. com. NASA, Washington, 1988-93. Bd. dirs. Am. Heart Assn., Ft. Worth, 1990—, chmn., 1995-97. Fellow AIAA (chmn. aircraft design tech. com. 1990-92, pub. policy com. 1988—). Achievements include design of high performance jet fighters F-111 and F-16, management of new business strategy, technology development, new aircraft, and special programs including new aircraft, National Aerospace Plane and many advanced technology development projects. Home: 5401 Benbridge Dr Fort Worth TX 76107-3209

BUCKNER, JOHN KNOWLES, pension administrator; b. Springfield, Mo., Sept. 8, 1936; s. Ernest Godfrey and Mary Helen (Knowles) B.; m. Lorraine Catherine Anderson, Sept. 22, 1962; children: John Knowles, Allison. B.A., Williams Coll., 1958; M.S., Mass. Inst. Tech., 1960; Ph.D., nuclear engring., Stanford U., 1965; grad., Advanced Mgmt. Program, Harvard, 1974. Mgr. analysis dept. EG&G Inc., Bedford, Mass., 1966-70; dir. electronic data processing, controller, v.p. financial ops. Eastern Gas & Fuel Assos., Boston, 1970-77; exec. v.p., chief operating officer, dir. Waters Assos., Inc., Milford, Mass., 1977-80; v.p., chief fin. officer Prime Computer, Inc., Natick, Mass., 1980-83; sr. v.p., chief fin. officer EG & G, Inc., Wellesley, Mass., 1983-86; vice chmn., chief fin. officer Control Data Corp., Mpls., 1986-89; chmn. Pensco Pension Svcs. Inc., San Francisco, 1989-98, Bohdan Automation, Inc., Mundelein, Ill., 1994-98. Contbr. articles on engring., data analysis and systems to profl. jours. AEC spl. fellow nuclear sci. and engring., 1959, 62-65. Mem. Phi Beta Kappa, Sigma Xi, Chi Psi. Home: 1824 Green St San Francisco CA 94123-4922 Office: Pensco Pension Svcs Inc 250 Montgomery St San Francisco CA 94104-3406 *My present success, such as it is, has resulted from a willingness and ability to work hard, motivate others, and apply my own training and ideas to the particular task at hand, irrespective of the nature of the field of endeavor. My approach has always been to attain a level of technical and managerial competence necessary to bring about change. Generally, my goal is to make a contribution in as many areas of human conduct as my diligence and native ability will allow.*

BUCKNER, PHILIP FRANKLIN, newspaper publisher; b. Worcester, Mass., Aug. 25, 1930; s. Orello Simmons and Emily Virginia (Siler) B.; m. Ann Haswell Smith, Dec. 21, 1956 (div. Nov. 1993); children: John C., Frederick S., Catherine A.; m. Mary Emily Aird, Dec. 15, 1995. AB, Harvard U., 1952; MA, Columbia U., 1954. With Bay State Abrasive Products Co., 1954-59; Reporter Lowell (Mass.) Sun, 1959-60; pub. East Providence (R.I.) Post, 1960-62; asst. to treas. Scripps League Newspapers, Seattle, 1964-66, divsn. mgr., 1966-71; pres. Buckner News Alliance, Seattle, 1971—; pub. daily newspaper group including Carlsbad (N.Mex.) Current-Argus, 1971-90, Pecos (Tex.) Enterprise, 1971—, Fontana (Calif.) Herald-News, 1971-89, Banning and Beaumont (Calif.) Gazette, 1971-74, Lewistown (Pa.) Sentinel, 1971-93, Tiffin (Ohio) Advertiser-Tribune, 1973-93, York (Pa.) Daily Record, 1978—, Winsted (Conn.) Citizen, 1978, Excelsior Springs (Mo.) Standard, 1978, Oroville (Calif.) Mercury-Register, 1983-89, Corona (Calif.) Independent, 1984-89, Minot (N.D.) News, 1989-93. Avocation: mountain climbing. Office: Buckner News Alliance 2101 4th Ave Ste 2300 Seattle WA 98121-2317*

BUCKNER, WILLIAM CLAIBORNE, real estate broker; b. Ft. Leavenworth, Kans., June 29, 1926; s. Simon Bolivar Jr. and Adele (Blanc) B.; m. Virginia Jordan Lester, Nov. 25, 1955; children: Simon Bolivar IV, Peter Ridenour, Robert Lester. BS in Engring., U.S. Mil. Acad., 1948. Cert. comml. investment mem. Sales engr. Gustin Bacon Mfg., Kansas City, Tulsa, Mo., Okla., 1955-65; exec. v.p. Keystone Chem. Co., North Kansas City, Mo., 1965-66; chmn., CEO Alexander Electronics Inc., Kansas City, 1967-72; broker Jones & Co. Realtors, Kansas City, 1973-81; broker, treas. Kerr & Co. Realtors, Kansas City, 1982-87; owner, operator Buckner Realty, Westwood, Kans., 1988—. Pres. S.W. Area Edn. Coun., Kansas City, 1972-73; active Citizens Assn., Kansas City, 1969-97. Capt. U.S. Army, 1948-54. Mem. Univ. Club, Carriage Club, Kansas City, Mo. chpt. CCIMs (pres. 1982), S.R. Mo. (pres. 1987), Rotary, Comml. Brokers Assn. Kansas City (pres. 1990-92). Republican. Episcopalian. Avocations: firearms, bow hunting deer and turkey. Home: 6526 Pennsylvania Ave Kansas City MO 64113-1819 Office: Buckner Realty 6526 Pennsylvania Ave Kansas City MO 64113-1819

BUCKNER-REITMAN, JOYCE, psychologist, educator; b. Benton, Ark., Sept. 25, 1937; d. Waymond Floyd Pannell and Willie Evelyn (Wright) Whitley; m. John W. Buckner, Aug. 29, 1958 (div. 1970); children: Cheryl, John, Chris; m. Sanford Reitman, Aug. 13, 1994. BA, Ouachita Bapt. Coll., 1959; MS in Edn., Henderson State U., 1964; PhD, North Tex. State U., 1970. Lic. psychologist, Tex., marriage and family therapist; cert. Nat. Registry Health Svc. Providers in Psychology; master trainer in imago relationship therapy. Assoc. prof. U. Tex., Arlington, 1970-80, chmn. dept. edn., 1976-78; pvt. practice psychology, Arlington, 1974—; dir., chief profl. officer Southwest Inst. Relationship Devel., Weatherford, Tex.; author, profl. speaker; appeared on internat. TV shows, including Oprah Winfrey Show. Mem. APA, Nat. Assn. for Imago Relationship Therapy (pres.), Nat. Speakers Assn., Am. Assn. Marital and Family Therapy. Avocations: dancing, travel, art. Home: 2208 Farmer Rd Weatherford TX 76087-6964

BUCKO, JOHN JOSEPH, investment corporation executive; b. N.Y.C., Mar. 19, 1937; s. John Francis and Sophia Helen (Roog) B.; m. Mary Catharine Doyle, Dec. 29, 1962; children: Kathlene, Christopher, Julie Anne. B.S., NYU, 1961. Controller Reynolds Securities, Inc., N.Y.C., 1970-73, v.p., chief fin. officer, 1973-78; first v.p., dir. internal audit Dean Witter Reynolds Inc., N.Y.C., 1978-79, sr. v.p., controller, 1979-84; dir. risk mgmt. Dean Witter Reynolds Inc., 1985-86; sr. v.p., chief fin. officer S.G. Warburg, N.Y.C., 1986-89, ABN AMRO Securities (USA) Inc., N.Y.C., 1989-95; ret., 1995; NASD NYSE arbitrator; fin. compliance cons. Mem. Wall St. Tax Assn., Securities Industry Assn. (fin. mgmt. div.). Home: 438 Manchester Way Wyckoff NJ 07481-2540

BUCKRIDEE, PATRICIA ILONA, international marketing/strategy consultant; b. N.Y.C., Oct. 19, 1960; d. Laszlo Carl and Evelyn Liane (Schauer) Varhegyi; m. Winston D. Buckridee, Dec. 29, 1991; children: Karolyn Liane, Elizabeth Rachel, Zoe Grace. BS, Seton Hall U., 1982; MBA, Rutgers U., Newark, 1987. Statis. analyst UN, Vienna, Austria, 1983-85; cons., tutor, N.J., 1985-87; assoc. mgr. strategy and devel. AT&T, Basking Ridge, N.J., 1987-88; market mgr. microelectronics AT&T, Berkeley Heights, N.J., 1988-89; sr. product mgr. data sys. group AT&T, Morristown, N.J., 1989; sr. fin. analyst Am. Express Travel Related Svcs. Co., N.Y.C., 1989-91; ind. cons. Scotch Plains, N.J., 1991-96; market rsch. mgr. AT&T, Parsippany, N.J., 1996-97, internat. project mgr., 1997—; internat. cons., N.J., 1985-96; interpreter, translator, N.J., 1987-96; pres. PIB Internat. Inc., 1991—. Mem. Am. Mktg. Assn. Avocations: Bible study, fly fishing, skeet shooting, travel. Office: PIB Internat Inc PO Box 965 Scotch Plains NJ 07076 also: AT&T 412 Mount Kemble Ave Morristown NJ 07960-6654

BUCKROTH, MARI BETH, counselor; b. Pontiac, Mich., Oct. 1, 1967; d. Paul W. and Peggy A. Schwimmer; m. Pat Buckroth, Dec. 11, 1993. AA, Valencia C.C., 1988; BA in Criminal Justice, U. Ctrl. Fla., 1993; MPA, U. West Fla., 1999. Pvt. investigator Advanced Investigations, Ft. Walton Beach, Fla., 1993-98; collections clk. Advanced Collections, Ft. Walton Beach, 1994—; aftercare counselor Advanced Aftercare Svcs., Ft. Walton Beach, 1998—. Pres. Eglin/Ft. Walton Beach Student Govt. Assn., 1998-99, rep., 1997-98. Mem. ASPA, Pi Alpha Alpha. Avocation: reading. Fax: (850) 863-6581. E-mail: pmbucks@aol.com. Office: UWF/Advanced Aftercare Svcs 1170 MLK Blvd Fort Walton Beach FL 32547

BUCKS, CHARLES ALAN, airline industry consultant, former executive; b. Lubbock, Tex., Dec. 14, 1927; s. Charles Henry and Nell (Lattimore) B.; m. Joyce Laverne Turner, Aug. 19, 1949; children: Jimmy Charles, David Alan, Robert Doyle, Dawne Alyce. Student, Tex. Technol. Coll., 1947-48, Amarillo Jr. Coll., 1948-49. With Continental Air Lines, Inc., 1948—, gen. sales mgr., 1958-61, v.p. field sales, 1961-65; v.p. sales Continental Air Lines, Inc., Los Angeles, 1965-66; v.p. sales and service Continental Air Lines, Inc., 1966-69, sr. v.p., 1969-75, exec. v.p. mktg., 1975-81, exec. v.p., asst. to pres., 1981-82, also dir.; pres. Charles Bucks & Assocs., Inc., 1982-96; pres., chief exec. officer Philips Airvision, Ltd., 1990-93; pres. Arctic Vending Ltd., Rancho Cucamonga, Calif., 1993—, CEO, 1996—. Pres. One Shot Antelope Hunt, Lander, Wyo., 1968, dir., African First Shotters; pres. Calif. Tourism Council, 1975-77; trustee Continental Found., Denver, 1970-81; bd. dirs. Mustang Sanctuary Found.; trustee Buckley Schs., Sherman Oaks, Calif., 1977-83. Served with USNR, 1945-46, PTO. Recipient Disting. Alumnus award Tex. Tech U., 1970. Mem. Nat. Aeros. Assn. (bd. dirs.), Pacific Area Travel Assn., Conquistadores del Cielo (chmn. bd. dirs., past pres.), So. Calif. Safari Club (bd. dirs.), Calif. Yacht Club (L.A.). Republican. Presbyterian. Office: Arctic Vending Ltd 10700 Jersey Blvd Ste 200-210 Rancho Cucamonga CA 91730-5116

BUCKSBAUM, MATTHEW, real estate investment trust company executive; b. Marshalltown, Iowa, Feb. 20, 1926; s. Louis and Ida (Gerwin) B.; m. Carolyn Swartz, Aug. 3, 1952; children: Ann B. Friedman, John. BA in econ., U. Iowa, 1949. Owner, operator Regional Supermarket Chain, Marshalltown, 1949-54; owner, developer Pvt. Real Estate, Iowa, 1954-64; chmn. Gen. Growth Properties, Des Moines, 1964—. Bd. dir. Iowa Natural Heritage Found., Des Moines; trustee Aspen (Colo.) Music Festival & Sch.; Sgt. USAF, 1944-46, PTO. Mem. Internat. Coun. Shopping Ctrs. (past chmn.), Urban Land Inst., Nat. Assn. Real Estate Investment Trusts. Jewish. Office: General Growth Properties Inc 418 6th Ste 1210 Des Moines IA 50309-1726

BUCKSTEIN, CARYL SUE, writer; b. Denver, Aug. 10, 1954; d. Henry Martin and Hedvig (Neulander) B. BS in Journalism, U. Colo., 1976. Editor Rifle (Colo.) Telegram, 1976; corr. So. Colo. Pueblo (Colo.) Star-Jour. and Chieftain, 1977-84; corr. The Denver Post, 1985; staff editor Nat. Over-the-Counter Stock Jour., Denver, 1985-89; writer Rocky Mountain News, Denver, 1990-92; editor Urban Spectrum, Denver, 1993; contbg. writer Boulder (Colo.) County Bus. Report, 1992—. Bd. mem. Holiday Project, Denver, 1996; mem. exec. bd. Denver Newspaper Guild, 1998. Recipient 1st Place Gen. Assignment Bus. Articles, Colo. Press Women, Denver, 1985, 90, 91. Mem. Colo. Soc. Profl. Journalists (sec.-treas. 1988), Denver Newspaper Guild (bd. dirs. 1998). Avocations: inventing, writing.

BUCKSTEIN, MARK AARON, lawyer, educator; b. N.Y.C., July 1, 1939; s. Henry Al and Minnie Sarah (Russ) B.; m. Rochelle Joan Buchman, Sept. 11, 1960; children: Robin Beth, Michael Alan. BS in Math., CCNY, 1960; JD, NYU, 1963. Bar: N.Y. 1963, U.S. Dist. Ct. (so. and ea. dists.) N.Y. 1965, U.S. Supreme Ct. 1981. Assoc. Russ & Weyl, Massapequa, N.Y., 1963-64; assoc. counsel Mut. Life Ins. Co. N.Y., N.Y.C., 1964-65; assoc. Moses & Singer, N.Y.C., 1965-67, Leinwand, Maron & Hendler, N.Y.C., 1967-68; sr. ptnr. Baer Marks & Upham, N.Y.C., 1968-86; sr. v.p. external affairs, gen. counsel TWA, Inc., N.Y.C., 1986-92; exec. v.p. Am. Arbitration Assn., N.Y.C., N.J., 1992-93; exec. v.p., gen. counsel GAF Corp. and International Specialty Products, Wayne, N.J., 1993-96; counsel Greenberg Traurig, Ft. Lauderdale, Fla., 1996—; spl. prof. law Hofstra U. Law Sch., Hempstead, N.Y., 1981-93; adj. prof. law Rutgers U. Law Sch., Newark, 1994-96; bd. dirs. Bayswater Realty & Capital Corp., N.Y.C., Travel Channel Inc., N.Y.C., TWA; mem. exec. com. Herzfeld & Stern, N.Y.C., 1981-84. Trustee Bronx H.S. Found., 1984—. Mem. ABA, N.Y. Bar Assn., Internat. Bar Assn., KP (past dep. grand chancellor 1978). Democrat. Jewish. Avocations: tennis, music, theater, puzzles. Office: Greenberg Traurig 515 E Las Olas Blvd Fort Lauderdale FL 33301-2296

BUCKWALD, JOEL DAVID, archivist; b. N.Y.C., June 29, 1917; s. Abraham and Yetta (Guzovsky) B. BS in Social Sci., CCNY, 1938; MA, Columbia U., 1969. Jr. archives asst. Nat. Archives, Washington, 1941-42, archivist, 1942, 47-50; archivist Fed. Records Ctr., Gen. Svcs. Adminstrn., N.Y.C., 1950-53, chief disposal sect., 1953-70; chief archives br. Fed. Records Ctr. Nat. Archives and Records Svc., Bayonne, N.J., 1970-85; dir. nat. archives N.Y. br. Nat. Archives and Records Adminstrn., Bayonne, 1985-87; archivist N.E. region Nat. Archives and Records Adminstrn., N.Y.C., 1988—; instr. history L.I. U., Bklyn., 1942; alt. rep. of Soc. Am. Archivists to Coun. Nat. Libr. Assn. and Am. Stds. Assn., N.Y.C., 1963-67; cons. in archives and records mgmt. Ogn. Am. States, Washington, 1963 assigned to tech. asst. Mission to Ministry of Fgn. Affairs, Peru. Contbr.: (book) Handbook of Federal World War Agencies and Their Records, 1917-1921, 1943; author: (pamphlet) Index to Naturalization Petitions of the U.S. District Court for the Eastern District of New York, 1865-1957, 1991. With USNR, 1942-46. N.Y. State vets. scholar, 1957. Mem. Archivists Round Table of Met. N.Y. Office: Nat Archives and Records Adminstrn NE Region 201 Varick St New York NY 10014-4811

BUCKWALTER, JOSEPH ADDISON, orthopedic surgeon, educator; b. Ottumwa, Iowa, June 21, 1947; s. Joseph Addison and Carole Ann (Kelly) B.; m. Kathleen Coen, May 31, 1975; children: Jody, Andrea, Abigail. BS with high distinction, U. Iowa, 1969, MS, 1972, MD, 1974. Diplomate Am. Bd. Orthopaedic Surgery (recert., oral examiner 1988—, dir. 1990—, mem. examinations com. 1992—, chmn. examinations com. 1992-93, chmn. cert. renewal com. 1992—); lic. surgeon Iowa. Intern in internal medicine U. Iowa, Iowa City, 1974-75, resident in orthopaedics, 1975-77, 78-79, Nat. Rsch. Svc. Award rsch. fellow, 1977-78, from asst. prof. to assoc. prof. orthopaedic surgery, 1979-85, prof. orthopaedic surgery, 1985—; mem. R&D devel. com. VA Med. Ctr. Com., 1985-88; mem. orthopaedic tumor therapy group U. Iowa Cancer Ctr., 1981—, cancer edn. subcom., 1982-90; mem. grants and fellowships adv. com. Iowa City Vets. Med. Ctr., 1983-86, chief orthopaedic surgery, 1987-91; mem. Arthritis Found. Rsch. Com., 1985-86; mem. panel NIH Consensus Devel. Confs., Bethesda, Md., 1984, 88; mem. rheumatology rsch. adv. bd. Syntex Corp., 1987-94; mem. adv. bd. WHO Multinational Collaborative Study on Predictors of Osteoarthritis, 1992; mem. sci. adv. com. Specialised Ctr. Rsch. on Osteoarthritis Rush-Presbyn.-St. Luke's Med. Ctr., Chgo., 1993—; mem. Nat. Arthritis and Musculoskeletal and Skin Diseases Adv. Coun., NIH, 1993—; disting. lectr. Hosp. Spl. Surgery, N.Y.C., 1982, Coll. Physicians and Surgeons-N.Y. Orthopaedic Hosp., 1988, U. N.Mex., 1989; guest lectr. Wilford Hall Med. Ctr., San Antonio, 1983, vis. prof., 1984; vis. prof. U. Miami, Fla., 1986, Cath. Med. Colls., Seoul, Republic of Korea, 1989, U. Pitts., 1993, Ohio State U., Columbus, 1994; vis. orthopaedic prof. U. So. Calif., L.A., 1990; Am. Orthopaedic Assn. 1991 Internat. vis. prof. Nuffield Orthopaedic Ctr., Oxford (Eng.) U., 1991, vis. prof. orthopaedics, 1991; vis. prof. orthopaedics, U. N.C., 1991; OREF Hark lectr. and vis. prof. U. Wash., Seattle, 1992; Watson Jones lectr. Royal Coll. Surgeons (Gt. Britain), 1992; A.M. Rechtman lectr. Phila. Orthopaedic Soc., 1993; Predl. guest spkr. 1993 Japanese Orthopaedic Assn. Rsch. Meeting, Matsumoto, Japan, 1993; Kelly Rsch. Award vis. prof. Mayo Clinic, Rochester, Minn., 1993; participant numerous workshops and confs. Cons. reviewer: Jour. Bone and Joint Surgery, 1979—, cons. editor for rsch., 1989—; bd. assoc. editors: Jour. Orthopaedic Rsch., 1982-85, mem. editl. adv. bd., 1985-88, co-editor-in-chief, 1993—; mem. editl. adv. bd. Orthopaedics, 1986-90; reviewer: The Lancet, 1993—; contbr. articles to profl. jours. Student rsch. fellow U. Iowa Coll. Medicine, 1970. Fellow Am. Inst. Med. and Biol. Engring. (founding), Am. Acad. Orthopaedic Surgeons (mem. com. basic scis. 1983-85, chmn. com. evaulation 1985-90, mem. at large, bd. dirs. 1988-89, mem. steering com. for devel. Musculoskeletal Conditions in U.S. 1990-92, chmn. coun. for rsch. and sci. affairs 1990-93, 94—, sec. 1993-94); mem. AAAS, Internat. Soc. Limb Salvage, Brit. Orthopaedic Assn. (companion mem.), Orthopaedic Rsch. Soc. (sec.-treas. 1985-88, bd. dirs. 1985-91, pres. 1989-90), Am. Orthopaedic Assn. (exch. fellowship com. 1989-90, chmn. internat. vis. prof. com. 1993—), Am. Orthopaedic Soc. for Sports Medicine (chmn. rsch. awards com. 1988-90, rsch. com. 1989-91), Internat. Skeletal Soc., Iowa Orthopaedic Soc., Johnson County Med. Soc., Musculoskeletal Tumor Soc., 20th Century Orthopaedic Assn., Girdlestone Orthopaedic Soc., Phi Beta Kappa, Alpha Omega Alpha. Office: U Iowa Hosps Dept Orthopaedics 200 Hawkins Dr Iowa City IA 52242-1009

BUCKWALTER, RONALD LAWRENCE, federal judge; b. Lancaster, Pa., Dec. 11, 1936; s. Noah Denlinger and Carolyn Marie (Lawrence) B.; m. Dollie May Fitting, May 9, 1963; children: Stephen Matthew, Wendy Susan. AB, Franklin and Marshall Coll., 1958; JD, Coll. William and Mary, 1962. Prin. Ronald L. Buckwalter, Esquire, Lancaster, 1963-71; ptnr. Shirk, Reist and Buckwalter, Lancaster, 1971-80; dist. atty. Lancaster County, Lancaster, 1978-80; judge 2nd Jud. Dist. Commonwealth Pa., 1980-90, U.S. Dist. Ct., Phila., 1990—. Sec. City Lancaster Authority, 1970; bd. dirs. Am. Cancer Soc., Lancaster, 1982, Boy Scouts Am., Lancaster, 1984, YMCA, Lancaster, 1990. 1st lt. U.S. Army NG, 1962-68. Recipient Pub. Life and Letter award Phi Sigma Alpha, 1990. Mem. Am. Judicature Soc., Fed. Bar Assn., Fed. Judges Assn., Pa. Bar Assn., Lancaster Bar Assn. (pres. 1988). Office: US Dist Ct 14614 US Courthouse 601 Market St Philadelphia PA 19106-1713

BUCOVE, ARNOLD DAVID, psychiatrist; b. Toronto, Sept. 22, 1934. BA, Columbia U., 1956; MD, NYU, 1961. Diplomate Am. Bd. Psychiatry and Neurology. Intern Lenox Hill Hosp., N.Y.C., 1961-62; resident in psychiatry Bellevue Hosp., N.Y.C., 1962-63, St. Luke's Hosp., N.Y.C., 1963-65; chief psychiatry 36th Tactical Hosp., Bitburg, Germany, 1965-67; pvt. practice psychiatry Pleasant Valley, N.Y., 1967-92, Poughkeepsie, N.Y., 1992-93; pvt. practice Oneonta, N.Y., 1993—; attending staff Craig House, Beacon, N.Y., 1977-93; asst. dir. Dutchess County Mental Health Clinic, Poughkeepsie, N.Y., 1967-68; chief psychiatry Fox Meml. Hosp., Oneonta, 1993—, sec.-treas. med. staff, 1997-98, pres.-elect, 1998-99, pres., 1999—; cons. psychiatrist Greer Children's Cmty., Millbrook, N.Y., 1968-77; mem. courtesy staff Sharon (Conn.) Hosp., 1967-90; cons. IBM, Poughkeepsie, 1968. Contbr. articles to profl. jours. Bd. dirs. Town of Washing Civic Assn., Millbrook, 1986-93, Millbrook Music Assn., 1986-92; mem. vestry Grace Ch., Millbrook, 1971-74, mem. vestry St. Peter's Ch., Millbrook, 1989-92. Capt. USAF, 1965-67. Fellow Am. Psychiat. Assn. (pres. Mid-Hudson chpt. 1977-79); mem. N.Y. State Med. Soc., Otsego County Med. Soc., Millbrook Hunt (bd. govs. 1968-71), Millbrook Golf and Tennis Club, Cooperstown Country Club. Avocations: riding, skiing, tennis. Office: Fox Hosp 1 Norton Ave Oneonta NY 13820-2629

BUCY, RICHARD SNOWDEN, aerospace engineering and mathematics educator, consultant; b. Washington, July 20, 1935; s. Edmond Howard and Marie (Glinke) B.; m. Ofelia Teresa Rivva, Aug. 25, 1961; children: Phillip Gustav, Richard Erwin. B.S. in Math., MIT, 1957; Ph.D. in Math. Stats., U. Calif.-Berkeley, 1963. Researcher in math. Rsch. Inst. Advanced Studies, Towson, Md., 1960-61, 63-64; rsch. asst. U. Calif., Berkeley, 1961-63; asst. prof. math. U. Md., College Park, 1964-65; assoc. prof. aerospace engring. U. Colo., Boulder, 1965-66; prof. aerospace engring. and math. U. So. Calif., Los Angeles, 1966—; professeur associe French Govt., Toulouse, 1973-74, Nice, 1983-84, 90-91; vis. prof. Technische Universität Berlin, 1975-76; co-dir. NATO Advanced Study Inst. on Non-linear Scholastic Problems, Algarve, Portugal; cons. to industry. Author: Filtering for Stochastic Processes, 1968, 2d edit., 1987, Nonlinear Stochastic Problems, 1984, Lectures on Discrete Filtering Theory, 1994; editor Jour. Info. Scis., Jour. Math. Modelling and Sci. Computing; founding editor (jour.) Stochastics, 1971-77; contbr. numerous articles to profl. publs. Recipient Humboldt prize Govt. W. Germany, Berlin, 1975-76; Air Force Office Sci. Sch. grantee, 1965-81, NATO Rsch. grantee, 1979—. Fellow IEEE (del. to Soviet Acad. of Scis. Info. Theory Workshop); mem. Am. Math. Soc. Republican. Home: 420 S Juanita Ave Redondo Beach CA 90277-3824 Office: U So Calif Dept Aerospace Engring Los Angeles CA 90089-1191

BUCZAK, DOUGLAS CHESTER, financial advisor, lawyer; b. Detroit, Feb. 6, 1949; s. Chester and Rose Marie (Czech) B. BA in English, U. Mich., 1971; JD, U. Detroit, 1975. Bar: Mich. 1975. Pvt. practice Lansing, Mich., 1978-80; bus. cons. Dynamic Learning Systems, Farmington Hills, Mich., 1981-82; fin. planner Pacific Fin. Cos., Farmington Hills, 1982-86, Pacific Fin. Group, Birmingham, 1986—; pres. Pacific Adv. Svcs., Inc., 1986—. Fin. columnist Detroit Legal News, 1992-94. Named one of Best 200 Fin. Advisors in Am., Worth Fin. Mag., 1996, 97, 98. Mem. Mich. Bar Assn., Internat. Assn. Fin. Planning (bd. dirs. 1988-91, 96-99, v.p. 1990-91), Optimist Club Farmington Hills (pres. 1984-85), Sigma Phi Epsilon (pres. alumni bd. Ann Arbor, Mich. 1983-93). Home: 6426 Heritage West Bloomfield MI 48322-1336 Office: Pacific Fin Group Ste 126 380 N Old Woodward Birmingham MI 48009-5307

BUDAI, WILLIAM H., music educator; s. James W. and Diane K. Budai. B.Mus.Edn., Ctrl. Mich. U., 1992; M.Music, Bowling Green State U., 1995. Accompanist Interlochen (Mich.) Arts Camp, 1991—; instr. piano Bluffton (Ohio) Coll., 1995-98, Heidelberg Coll., Tiffin, Ohio, 1995-98, Bowling Green State U., 1993-98; pianist Beres/Budai Piano Duo, Bowling Green, 1995—. Mem. Phi Mu Alpha (pres. 1991-92, treas. 1990-91), Kappa Delta Pi (treas. 1991-92), Phi Kappa Phi, Phi Eta Sigma, Pi Kappa Lambda, Golden Key. Home: 750 Ridgecrest Cir #1525 Norman OK 73072

BUDALUR, THYAGARAJAN SUBBANARAYAN, chemistry educator; b. India, July 14, 1929; came to U.S., 1969, naturalized, 1977; s. Subbanarayan Subbuswamy and Parvatham (Gopalakrishnan) B.; children: Chitra, Poorna, Kartik. M.A., U. Madras, 1951, M.Sc., 1954, Ph.D., 1956. Reader organic chemistry U. Madras, 1960-68; prof. chemistry U. Idaho, Moscow, 1968-74; prof. chemistry, dir. div. earth phys. sci. U. Tex., San Antonio, 1974—; lectr. in field. Author: Mechanisms of Molecular Migrations; Selective Organic Transformations; Editorial bd. chem. jours.; contbr. articles to profl. jours.; 3 patents in field. Recipient Intra Sci. Research award, 1966. Fellow Am. Chem. Soc.; mem. Chem. Soc. London, Soc. Cosmetic Chemistry N.Y. Acad. Sci., Am. Inst. Chemists, Sigma Xi, Phi Kappa Phi. Club: Lions. Home: 6119 Amble Trl San Antonio TX 78249-2108 Office: U Tex Loop 1604 NW San Antonio TX 78249

BUDD, BERNADETTE SMITH, newspaper executive, public relations consultant; b. N.Y.C., Feb. 23, 1943; d. Stanley Allen and Toby (Percak) Smith; children: Amanda Rose, Karen Wendy, Paige Elizabeth, Kelly Lyn Budd Tinsley; m. Thomas Witbeck Budd, July 4, 1988. BA in History and English, Bucknell U., 1964; MA in Liberal Studies, SUNY-Stony Brook, 1971; EdM, Columbia U., 1982; JD, Jacob D. Fuchsberg Law Ctr., 1998. Tchr. history N.Y., 1964-69; innovator pre-sch. programs Shoreham, N.Y., 1975-79; editor, pub. Cmty. Jour., Wading River, N.Y., 1978—, advt. mgr., 1978—; editor Shoreham-Wading River Newsletter, 1978-88; assoc. editor Restatement Touro Law Ctr., 1997-98; profl. breeder, shower A.K.C. golden retriever dogs; cons., workshop leader, 1979—; ex. dir. Suffolk County chpt. NYCLU, 1998—. Editor: C. of C. Directory, Shoreham, 1983, 84; contbr. articles N.Y. Times, Reader's Digest, Psychology Today Mag.om., 1979-82. Advisor Teen Recreation Adv. Com., Shoreham-Wading River, 1979-82; mem. Nuclear Emergency Evacuation Com., 1979-82; pres. PTA, Wading River, 1980-83; v.p. Spl. Edn. PTA, Wading River, 1979-80, Am. Civil Liberties Union Student Chpt. Touro Law Ctr.; active Com. Gifted and Talented Children, Wading River, 1979-80, Occupational Edn. Commn., 1979-80; mem. Suffolk County Human Rights Commn. Recipient Disting. Service award Am. Cancer Soc., 1982-83; award of merit N.Y. State Pub. Relations Assn., 1982-83; award of honor Nat. Sch. Pub. Relations Assn., 1981. Mem. Wading River C. of C. (bd. dirs. 1979-80), Suffolk County Bus. and Profl. Women's Assn., Women's Equal Rights Congress, East End Women's Network, N.Y.C. Press Assn., Rocky Point C. of C. (bd. dirs.), Soc. Profl. Journalists, Sigma Delta Chi, Kappa Kappa Gamma. Roman Catholic. Club: L.I. Press. Home and Office: Cmty Jour PO Box 619 Wading River NY 11792-0619

BUDD, EDWARD HEY, retired insurance company executive; b. Zanesville, Ohio, Apr. 30, 1933; s. Curtis Eugene and Mary (Hey) B.; m. Mary Goodrich, Aug. 24, 1957; children: Elizabeth, David, Susan. BS in Physics, Tufts U., 1955. With The Travelers Corp., Hartford, Conn., 1955-94, pres., chief operating officer, 1976-82, chief exec. officer, 1981-93, chmn., 1982-94, pres., 1985-93; bd. dirs. Delta Air Lines, GTE Corp. Fellow Casualty Actuarial Soc., Am. Acad. Actuaries; mem. Bus. Coun. Episcopalian. Office: 270 Chestnut Hill Rd Glastonbury CT 06033

BUDD, ERIC MERRILL, company official, writer, consultant; b. N.Y.C., 1963. BA in Sociology and Anthropology, Oberlin Coll., 1986; cert. in tech. and profl. writing, Framingham (Mass.) State Coll., 1994. User cons. Computer Ctr. Framingham State Coll., 1994; tech. writer Judge Tech. Svcs., Boston, 1994; asst. mgr. customer svc. Julesan, Boston, 1994-98; exec. adminstr. Jodi F. Solomon Spkrs. Bur., Boston, 1998—; writing cons., Boston, 1994—. Author: A Seal Upon My Heart, 1996, Scottish Tartan Weddings: A Pratical Handbook, 1999. Chmn. ethics com. Divsn Humanist Cert., 1992-93, author, editor ethics code and due process, 1993; mem., pub. spkr. Freedom To Marry Coalition Mass., 1996—. Mem. Parents, Family and Friends of Lesbians and Gay, Unitarian Universalist Assn., Mass. Religious Coaltion Freedom to Marry (founder), Scottish Tartans Soc., Clan Gunn Soc. N.Am., St. Andrews Soc. Mass. Avocation: philosophical discussion and study. Office: Freedom To Marry Coalition 325 Huntington Ave Ste 88 Boston MA 02115-4401

BUDD, JIM, communications manager; b. Austin, Minn.; s. Stanley James and Margaret (Deutschman) B. Student, Austin State Jr. Coll. Head of CCTV dept. Northwest Camera Svc., Mpls., 1971-72; head of video svc. dept., engring., TV studio and video svc. dept. ops. Internat. Communications Svcs., Mpls., 1972-73; talent scout coord. and video cons. Wag Arts Prodns.-Talent Agy., Mpls., 1972-75; electronics dept. svc. mgr. Gordon Electric Co., Austin, 1975-78; operational ptnr. in design and mfr. of projection TV consoles with McAllister Trading Co. and ABC Electronics, Austin, 1979-84; video systems specialist The Electronics Warehouse, Inc., Rochester, Minn., 1984-85; engr., video dir., mgr. ABC Electronics & Video, Austin, 1985—; producer, dir. N.W. TV-Prodns., Austin, 1986—; mem. video ops. staff KAAL-TV, Austin, 1997-98; systems design cons. in field. Script author, narrator of documentary videofilm: "Celebration of Hmong New Year"--Laos, 1991; producer: (video) Big Isl. Rendezvous, 1995. Videographer Summerset Theatre Group Austin Cmty. Coll., 1987; prodn. fund vol. PBS Sta. KSMQ-TV, Austin, 1984, 88-98. Mem. Am. Film Inst., Am. Legion, Comm. Computer Club. Roman Catholic. Office: N W TV Prodns/ABC Electronics 1008 5th Ave NW Austin MN 55912-2114

BUDD, LOUIS JOHN, English language educator; b. St. Louis, Aug. 26, 1921; s. Vincent and Sophia (Kajszo) Budrewicz; m. Isabelle Amelia Marx, Mar. 3, 1945; children: Catherine Lou, David Harry. BA, U. Mo., 1941, MA, 1942; PhD, U. Wis., 1949; DLitt, U. Mo., 1988, Elmira Coll., 1995. Instr. U. Mo., Columbia, 1942, 46, U. Ky., Lexington, 1949-52; asst. prof. Duke U., Durham, N.C., 1952-60; assoc. prof. Duke U., 1960-66, prof., 1966-83, James B. Duke prof., 1983-91, chmn. dept. English, 1973-79; mem. vis. faculty Washington U., St. Louis, summer 1954, Northwestern U., Evanston, Ill., summer 1961; lectr. seminar Kraft div. Internat. Paper Co., summer 1959; Fulbright lectr., India, 1967, 72; vis. lectr. U. Damascus, Syria, 1978; chmn. Jay B. Hubbell Ctr. for Am. Lit. Historiography, 1976-87. Author: Mark Twain: Social Philosopher, 1962, Robert Herrick, 1971, Newspaper and Magazine Interviews with Samuel L. Clemens, 1874-1910, 1977, Our Mark Twain: The Making of His Public Personality, 1983; editor: Robert Herrick's The Web of Life and Clark's Field, 1970; (with others) Toward a New American Literary History, 1980, Critical Essays on Mark Twain, 1867-1910, 1982, 1910-80, 1983, New Essays on Adventures of Huckleberry Finn, 1985, On Mark Twain: The Best from American Literature, 1987, Mark Twain's Collected Tales, Sketches, Speeches and Essays (2 vols.), 1992; mem. editorial bd.: A Selected Edition of W.D. Howells, South Atlantic Rev, 1978-81, U. Miss. Studies in English, 1979—, South Atlantic Quar., 1980-87; mng. editor: Am. Lit, 1979-86, chmn. editorial bd., 1986-91, Am. Lit. Realism 1870-1910, 1986—, Studies in Am. Humor, 1974—; contbr. numerous articles to profl. jours. Hon. trustee Mark Twain Meml., 1992—. 2d lt. USAAF, 1942-45. Guggenheim fellow, 1965-66; Am. Philos. Soc. grant, 1956, 70, 73; Nat. Endowment for Humanities sr. fellow, 1979-80; recipient J.H. Fisher award South Atlantic Depts. of English, 1997. Mem. MLA (Hubbell medal 1998), Am. Humor Studies Assn. (pres. 1979, 93), AAUP (pres. Duke chpt. 1971-72), Internat. Humor Studies Assn., Mark Twain Circle of Am. (founding pres. 1986-87, hon. life mem.), Phi Beta Kappa (pres. Duke Chpt. 1963-64). Home: 2753 Mcdowell Rd Durham NC 27705-5715 Office: Duke U Dept English Durham NC 27708-0015

BUDD, RICHARD WADE, university official, communications scientist; b. Henderson, Md., Aug. 24, 1934; s. Bryan William and Dorothea Marie (Fouvy) B.; m. Claudia L. Wolff; children: Kimberly, Richard Wade, Janna, Eric, Gary, Stephanie. B.A., Bowling Green U., 1956; M.A., U. Iowa, 1962, Ph.D., 1964. Reporter, staff writer Dayton (Ohio) Daily News, 1956-57; rsch. assoc., instr., asst. prof., dir. Inst. Comm. Studies, U. Iowa, Iowa City, 1960-71; prof., disting. prof., assoc. dean Rutgers Coll. Rutgers U., New Brunswick, N.J., chmn. dept. human comm., 1971-80, dir. Sch. Comm. Studies, 1980-83, dean. Sch. Comm., Info. and Libr. Studies, 1983-97; v.p. for info. Regent U., Virginia Beach, Va., 1997—; chmn. bd. Newstatements Comm. Cons., 1973-80; cons. in field. Author: Introduction to Content Analysis, 1964, Content Analysis of Communication, 1967, Approaches to Human Communication, 1972, Human Communication Handbook Simulations and Games, 1975, Mass Communication: Dialogue and Alternatives, 1976, Interdisciplinary Approaches to Communication, 1979, Beyond Media, 1988; assoc. editor Human Communication Research, 1974-83, Communication Quar, 1975-83; mem. editorial bd. Jour. Communication, 1976-82, Communication Yearbook, 1977-86, Mass Communications Yearbook, 1979—. Mem. Cmty. Arts Coun. East Brunswick, 1973-80; exec. coun. East Brunswick Youth Baseball Program, 1974; active Boy Scouts Am.; deacon Diocese of N.J. Served to Lt. USNR, 1957-60. Mem. Internat. Comm. Assn. (pres. 1976-77), AAAS, Speech Comm. Assn., Am. Assn. Public Opinion Rsch., Assn. Edn. in Journalism, ALA (com. on accrediting 1995-99), Assn. Libr. Info. Edn. Episcopalian. Home: 120 Cypress Crk Williamsburg VA 23188-7804 Office: Regent U 1000 Regent University Dr Virginia Beach VA 23464-9800

BUDD, THOMAS WITBECK, lawyer; b. Phila., Nov. 1, 1939; s. Reginald Masten and Elizabeth (Charlton) B.; divorced; children—Kelly Lynne, Paige Elizabeth; m. Bernadette Smith Budd, July 4, 1988; stepchildren: Amanda Rose Kronin, Karen Wendy Kronin. B.A., Washington and Lee U., 1961, LL.B., 1964. Bar: Va. 1964, N.Y. 1965, U.S. Supreme Ct. 1982. Assoc., Buell Clifton & Turner, N.Y.C., 1964-69, ptnr., 1969-70; ptnr. Clifton Budd & Burke, N.Y.C., 1970-76, Clifton Budd Burke & Demaria, N.Y.C., 1976-88; ptnr. Clifton, Budd & Demaria, 1988—. Contbg. author, editor to Labor and Employment Law newsletter. Mem. law council Washington and Lee U., 1978-81, 1984-85. Mem. ABA (labor law sect.), N.Y. Bar Assn. (labor law sect.), N.Y.C. Bar Assn. (labor law sect.). Clubs: Princeton (N.Y.C.); St. George's Golf and Country Club (Stony Brook, N.Y.). Home: 3 Colgate Ct Shoreham NY 11786-1221 Office: Clifton Budd & Demaria 420 Lexington Ave New York NY 10170-0002

BUDDE, MITZI MARIE JARRETT, librarian; b. Salisbury, N.C., Aug. 7, 1961; d. James Curtis and Donna Lee (Kluttz) J.; m. John August Budde, Apr. 23, 1994. BA, Lenoir-Rhyne Coll., 1982; MA, Luth. Theol. Sem., 1984; M in Librarianship, U. S.C., 1985. Asst. libr. Luth. Theol. So. Sem., Columbia, S.C., 1985-87, libr. dir., 1987-91; libr. Va. Theol. Sem., Alexandria, 1991—. Sec. Luth./Meth. Campus Ministry, U. S.C., Columbia, 1988-91. Mem. ALA, Am. Theol. Libr. Assn. (bd. dirs. 1992-95), Beta Phi Mu (Beta Omega chpt. pres. 1989-90). Office: Va Theol Sem Bishop Payne Libr 3737 Seminary Rd Alexandria VA 22304-5202*

BUDDE, NEIL FREDERICK, publishing company executive, editor; b. Elmhurst, Ill., June 19, 1956; s. Robert Earl and Phyllis Jean (Plummer) B.; m. Virginia Bowman Edwards, May 22, 1982. BA, Western Ky. U., 1977; MBA, U. Louisville, 1982. Copy editor Richmond (Va.) Times Dispatch, 1977-78; copy editor The Courier-Jour., Louisville, 1978-81, asst. bus. editor, 1984-86; assoc. editor Courier-Jour. Mag., Louisville, 1981-84; reporter, editor USA Today, Rosslyn, Va., 1986-87; assoc. editor Dow Jones Info. Systems, Princeton, N.J., 1987-88, dep. editl. dir., 1988-93; editor The Wall Street Jour. Interactive Edition, N.Y.C., 1993—, editor, exec. dir., 1996-98, v.p., editor, 1998—. Avocations: golf, tennis, photography. Home: 6 Round Top Rd PO Box 75 Oldwick NJ 08858-0075 Office: Dow Jones & Co 200 Liberty St Fl 11 New York NY 10281-1099

BUDERI, ROBERT BRYAN HASSAN, author, journalist; b. Berkeley, Calif., Sept. 26, 1954; s. Fred Fuad and Betty Lou (Krough) B.; m. Nancy Gail Walser, Apr. 11, 1992; children: Kacey, Robert. BA, U. Calif., Davis, 1977; MA, U. Ariz., 1978. Reporter Daily Republic, Fairfield, Calif., 1978-80; non-staff reporter Time-Life News Svc., San Francisco and Boston, 1980-88; contbr. Money Mag., San Francisco and Boston, 1982-90; technology editor Bus. Week, N.Y.C. and Boston, 1990-92; columnist Upside Mag., Cambridge, Mass., 1998—; contbg. writer Tech. Rev. mag., 1998—; advisor Brit. Broadcasting Corp., London, 1997-98; mem. selection com. Knight Fellowships, MIT, Cambridge, 1997-98. Author: The Invention that Changed the World, 1996. Vannevar Bush fellow MIT, 1986-87; Alfred P. Sloan Found. grantee, 1992, 96. Avocations: basketball, chess. Office: 227 Concord Ave Cambridge MA 02138-1334

BUDGE, HAMER HAROLD, mutual fund company executive; b. Pocatello, Idaho, Nov. 21, 1910; m. Jeanne Keithly, Aug. 30, 1941; 1 dau., Kathleen. Student, Coll. of Idaho, 1928-30; AB, Stanford U., 1933; LLB, U. Idaho, 1936. Bar: Idaho 1936. Pvt. practice Boise, 1936-42, 46-51, dist. judge, 1961-64; commr. SEC, 1964-69, chmn., 1969-71; pres., chmn. Investors Mut., Inc., Investors Stock Fund, Inc., Investors Selective Fund, Inc., Investors Variable Payment Fund, Inc., IDS New Dimensions Fund, Inc., IDS Progressive Fund, Inc., IDS Growth Fund, Inc., IDS Bond Fund, Inc., IDS Cash Met Fund Inc., Mpls., 1971-78; also bd. dirs., 1971-86. Mem. Idaho Legislature, 1939, 41, 49, majority floor leader; mem. 82d-86th Congresses from 2d Dist. Idaho, mem. rules, appropriations and interior coms.; Bd. dirs. Salvation Army. Served to lt. comdr. USNR, 1942-45. Mem. Am., Idaho bar assns., Sigma Alpha Epsilon. Republican. Mem. Ch. of Jesus Christ of Latter-day Saints. Clubs: Burning Tree. Home: 12000 N 90th St # 3060 Scottsdale AZ 85260-8632

BUDGE, MARCIA CHARLENE, family nurse practitioner; b. Goodland, Kans., Feb. 10, 1952; d. Edwin J. and Bonnie L. (Walker) Carleton; m. Marc R. Budge, May 7, 1977; 1 child, Steven R. ADN, Barton County Community Coll., 1983; cert. primary care nurse practitioner, U. Kans., 1986. RN, Kans., Tex.; cert. advanced RN practitioner, Kans.; cert. advanced practice nurse, Tex.; cert. pediatric & gerontol. nurse practitioner; cert. family nurse practitioner. Supr. and staff nurse St. John (Kans.) Dist. Hosp., 1983-85; staff nurse spl. care unit and obstetrics Pratt (Kans.) Regional Med. Ctr., 1986; advanced nurse practitioner, family nurse practitioner Med. Ctr. PA, Hutchinson, Kans., 1986-90; advanced nurse and family nurse practitioner Sterling (Kans.) Med. Ctr., 1990-92; advanced nurse practitioner Bapt. Hosp. Rural Health Clinic, Liberty, Tex., 1992-94; clinic dir., maternal & child health specialist, family nurse practitioner U. Tex. Med. Br. Regional Maternal and Child Health Program Walker County Maternal and Child Health Ctr., Huntsville, 1994—; clinic dir. U. Tex. Med. Br.- Crockett Maternal & Child Health Ctr., 1996—; mem. tech. adv. group Study of EACH/RPCH Concept in Kans., 1990-92. Chairperson bd. dirs. St. John Hosp. Dist. No. 1, 1991-92. Mem. Coun. Nurses in Advanced Practice, Am. Acad. Nurse Practitioners (cert. family nurse practitioner), Kans. Nurses Assn. (sec. advanced practice conf. group), Tex. Nurses Assn., Coastal Area Health Edn. Coop. (adv. bd. 1993—, Found. bd. dirs. 1997—). Home: 307 Brenda Ln Conroe TX 77385-9004 Office: Walker County Maternal & Child Health Ctr 1217 Avenue M Huntsville TX 77340-4607

BUDIG, GENE ARTHUR, former chancellor, professional sports executive; b. McCook, Nebr., May 25, 1939; s. Arthur G. and Angela (Schaaf) B.; m. Gretchen VanBloom, Nov. 30, 1963; children: Christopher, Mary Frances, Kathryn Angela. BS, U. Nebr., 1962, MEd, 1963, EdD, 1967; LLD, Ill. State U., 1982; LHD, U. Nebr., 1989, U. Nebr., 1989. Exec. asst. to gov. Nebr., Lincoln, 1964-67; adminstrv. asst. to chancellor, asst. prof. ednl. adminstrn. U. Nebr., Lincoln, 1967-70; asst. vice chancellor acad. affairs, prof. ednl. adminstrn. U. Nebr., 1970, asst. v.p., dir. pub. affairs, 1971; v.p., dean univ. Ill. State U., Normal, 1972; pres. Ill. State U., 1973-77, W.Va. U., Morgantown, 1977-81; chancellor U. Kans., Lawrence, 1981-94; pres. Am. Baseball League, N.Y.C., 1994—. Author: (with Dr. Stanley G. Rives) Academic Quicksand: Expectations of the Administrator, 1973; editor, contbr. chpts. to Perceptions in Public Higher Education, 1970, Dollars and Sense: Budgeting for Today's Campus, 1972, Higher Education - Surviving the 1980s, 1981, A Higher Education Map for the 1990s, 1992; editorial cons. chpts. in Phi Delta Kappan, 1976—; contbr. articles to profl. jours. Mem. Intergovtl. Coun. on Edn., 1980-84; trustee Nelson-Atkins Mus. Art, Kansas City, Mo.; bd. dirs. Truman Libr. Inst., Midwest Rsch. Inst., Univ. Field Staff Internat. Maj. gen. Air N.G., 1985-92; asst. to chief of staff N.G.

Bur., 1990-92. Named One of 10 Outstanding Young Persons, Ill. Jaycees, 1975, One of Top 100 Leaders in Am. Higher Edn., Change mag. and Am. Coun. on Edn., 1979, One of 75 Outstanding Young Men and Women Educators Am., Phi Delta Kappa, 1981; recipient Disting. Svc. award Baker U., 1990. Office: Am Baseball League 245 Park Ave 28 flr New York NY 10167*

BUDINGER, THOMAS FRANCIS, radiologist, educator; b. Evanston, Ill., Oct. 25, 1932; married, 1965; 3 children. BS, Regis Coll., 1954; MS, U. Wash., 1957; MD, U. Calif. Berkeley, 1964, PhD, 1971. Asst. chemist Regis Coll., Colo., 1953-54; analytical chemist Indsl. Labs., 1954; sr. oceanographer U. Wash., 1961-66; physicist Lawrence Livermore Lab., U. Calif., 1966-67; resident physician Donner Lab. and Lawrence Berkeley Lab., 1967-76; H. Miller Prof. med. rsch. and group leader rsch. medicine Donner lab., prof. elec. engring. and computer sci. Donner Lab., U. Calif. Berkeley, 1976—; with Peter Bent Brigham Hosp., Boston, 1964; dir. med. svc. Lawrence Berkeley Lab., 1968-76, sr. staff scientist, 1980—; chmn. study sect. NIH, 1981-84; prof. radiology U. Calif. San Francisco, 1984—. Recipient Special award Am. Nuclear Soc., 1984. Mem. AAAS, Am. Geophysical Union, N.Y. Acad. Sci., Soc. Nuclear Medicine, Soc. Magnetic Rsch. Medicine (pres. 1984-85). Achievements include research in imaging body functions, electrical, magnetic, sound and photon radiation fields, electron microscopy, polar oceanography, nuclear magnetic resonance, reconstruction tomography and instrument development, cardiology. Office: Lawrence Berkeley Lab Ctr for Functional Imaging 1 Cyclotron Rd Mail Stop 55-121 Berkeley CA 94720*

BUDINGTON, WILLIAM STONE, retired librarian; b. Oberlin, Ohio, July 3, 1919; s. Robert Allyn and Mabel (Stone) B.; m. Irma Johnson. B.A., Williams Coll., 1940, L.H.D., 1975; B.S. in L.S. Columbia U., 1941, M.S., 1951; B.S. in Elec. Engring, Va. Poly. Inst., 1946. Reference librarian Norwich U., 1941-42; librarian, engring. and phys. scis. Columbia, 1947-52; asso. librarian John Crerar Library, Chgo., 1952-65; librarian John Crerar Library, 1965-69, exec. dir., librarian, 1969-84; Mem. U.S.-USSR Spl. Libraries Exchange, 1966; bd. dirs. Center for Research Libraries, 1970-72, chmn., 1972; mem. vis. com. on libraries Mass. Inst. Tech., 1972-77. Served with AUS, 1942-46. Fellow AAAS, Med Library Assn.; mem. ALA, Am. Soc. Info. Sci., Spl. Libraries Assn. (pres. 1964-65, Hall of Fame 1984), Am. Soc. Engring. Edn., Assn. Research Libraries (dir. 1970-74, pres. 1973), Assn. Coll. and Research Libraries (Acad. Research Librarian of Year 1982), Phi Beta Kappa, Tau Beta Pi, Eta Kappa Nu. Clubs: Caxton, Arts. Home: 211 Wood Terrace Dr Colorado Springs CO 80903-2337

BUDNIAKIEWICZ, THERESE, author; b. Mons, Belgium, Sept. 28, 1948; came to U.S., 1961; naturalized, 1967; d. Tadeusz Eugeniusz and Janina Antonina (Więckowska) B.; m. Bart S. Ng, July 6, 1972. BA in Math., U. Chgo., 1971; MA in Comparative Lit., U. Mich., 1972, PhD in Comparative Lit., 1986. Lectr. in English Ind. U.-Purdue U., Indpls., 1987-92. Author: Fundamentals of Story Logic, 1992; contbr. Ency. Semiotics, 1998. Recipient 20th Century award for achievement Internat. Biog. Ctr., Cambridge, Eng. Mem. MLA, Semiotic Soc. Am., Can. Semiotic Assn., Internat. Assn. for Semiotics of Law, Internat. Assn. for Semiotic Studies. Avocation: publishing technologies. Home and Office: 5823 Dapple Trace Indianapolis IN 46228-1698

BUDNICK, ERNEST JOSEPH, music industry executive; b. N.Y.C., July 3, 1948; s. Louis and Caroline (Probert) B.; m. Susan Swingle, Sept. 8, 1984. Cert. Data Processing, Comml. Programming Unltd., N.Y.C., 1968; grad., Dale Carnegie Inst., 1988; cert. in pub. rels., NYU, 1991, cert. in real estate sales, 1998. Lic. real estate sales, N.Y. IBM computer operator Seamen's Bank for Savs., 1966-68; programmer/analyst W.T. Grant and Co., 1969-73; owner Underground Records, N.Y.C., 1970; systems analyst Ins. Svcs., N.Y.C., 1973-77; pres., owner Bernard Friedman Video Prodns., N.Y.C., 1973-85, Nat. Digital Diagnostics, N.Y.C., 1973-75; systems analyst Mfrs. Hanover, N.Y.C., 1977-80; mgr. corp. video/media Salomon Bros., Inc., N.Y.C., 1980-92; pres., CEO Consol. Mgmt., Tech. & Comm., N.Y.C., 1993-99; pres. UMO Music, N.Y.C., 1995—; pres., owner Manhattan Real Estate Classified, N.Y.C., 1998—; pres. EJ Budnick Co., 1999—; pres. UMO Music, 1995—. Author: Effectively Leveraging Business Technology, 1993; composer, singer, engr. (single) Keep on Playing, 1980. Conservator N.Y. Pub. Libr., 1990—; mem. Am. Mus. of Moving Image, 1990—. Fellow Mus. of Broadcasting; mem. Am. Film Inst. (mem. coun. 1984—), Nat. Assn. Rec. Arts and Scis., Pub. Rels. Soc. Am., Internat. Assn. Bus. Communicators, Nat. Assn. TV Arts and Scis., Am. Mgmt. Assn., Toastmasters. Avocations: video effects, computer engring., chess, music engring. Office: UMO Music 10 W 15th St Ste 313 New York NY 10011-6819

BUDNICK, LAWRENCE DAVID, physician, medical educator; b. Nov. 17, 1953. BS, CUNY Bklyn. Coll., 1974; MPH, Harvard U., Boston, 1977; MD, SUNY, Bklyn., 1977. Intern Georgetown VA Hosps., Washington, 1977-78; resident Brookdale Hosp., Bklyn., 1978-80; resident in pub. health N.Y.C. Dept. of Health, 1980-81; epidemic intelligence svc. officer Ctrs. for Disease Control, 1982-84; physician, advisor Exxon Corp., East Millstone, N.J., 1989-94; dir. occupl. medicine U. Medicine and Dentistry N.J., Newark, 1995—, assoc. prof. clin. medicine, 1994-98, assoc. prof. medicine, 1998—. With USPHS, 1982-86. E-mail: budnicla@umdnj.edu.

BUDNICK, THOMAS PETER, social worker; b. Ludlow, Mass., Feb. 16, 1947; s. Henry F. and Mildred Mary (Killian) B. BS, Am. Internat. Coll., 1972, MA, 1975. Lic. cert. profl. social worker. Mailhandler U.S. Postal Svc., Springfield, Mass., 1970-72; substitute tchr. Pub. Schs. Dept., Ludlow, Mass., 1973-74; social worker Mass. Dept. Pub. Welfare, Springfield, 1975—; pres. Am.'s Manifest Destiny Soc., Inc., West Harwich, Mass., 1979—; bd. dirs. Mass. Astronomy Club, Boston, 1988—. Contbr. numerous articles to jours. V.p. Local 509, Boston, 1989. Democrat. Home: 19 Harding Ave Ludlow MA 01056-2327

BUDNY, JAMES CHARLES, federal agency administrator; b. Dearborn, Mich., Aug. 11, 1948; s. William B. and Marion Catherine (Jazdzewski) B.; m. Maureen Anne Taylor, July 9, 1970; 1 child, Andrea. BBA, Ea. Mich. U., 1970; JD, Detroit Coll. Law, 1981. Revenue agent IRS, Dearborn, 1972-75; employee plans specialist IRS, Detroit, 1975-79, appeals officer, 1979-87, assoc. chief, 1987-97, sr. assoc. chief, 1997-98, regional appeals employee plans coord., 1990-95; acting chief Cleve. Appeals Office IRS, 1995; chief Mich. appeals IRS, Detroit, 1999—; sec. Cass Plaza Corp., Grosse Ile, Mich., 1980—; v.p. Cass Plaza Corp., Grosse Ile, 1983-90, pres., 1990—; also bd. dirs. Cass Plaza Corp., Grosse Ile, Mich. Sec. Indsl. Park Promotion Com., Grosse Ile, 1986-91; asst. registrar Grosse Ile Youth Recreation Assn. for Football, 1991-92; bd. dirs. Waters Edge C.C., Grosse Ile, 1999—. Mem. Inst. Mgmt. Accts., Ea. Mich. U. Alumni Assn., Detroit Coll. Law Alumni Assn., Metro Detroit Alumni (Senate bd. govs. 1994—), Delta Theta Phi. Roman Catholic. Avocations: racquetball, jogging, walking, music, golf. Office: Mich Appeals Office IRS 477 Michigan Ave Rm 470 Detroit MI 48226-2578 also: Cass Plz Corp PO Box 412 Grosse Ile MI 48138-0412
Personal philosophy: Work hard-play hard....expect to give more than you will receive in any endeavor and enjoy and be proud of what you've attained and don't worry about what you have not attained!.

BUDOFF, PENNY WISE, physician, author, researcher; b. Albany, N.Y., July 7, 1939; d. Louis and Goldene Wise. BA, Syracuse U., 1959; MD, SUNY-Upstate Med. Sch., 1963. Intern St. Luke's Meml. Hosp., Utica, N.Y., 1963-64; practice medicine specializing in family practice, women's health, Woodbury, N.Y., 1964-85; clin. assoc. prof. family medicine SUNY, Stony Brook, 1980—; founder, dir. emeritus Penny Wise Budoff Women's Health Svcs., Bethpage, N.Y., ground-breaking women's health care facility, 1985-97; affiliated with North Shore U. Hosp.; attending dept. ob/gyn. North Shore U. Hosp., 1992-97; asst. prof. ob/gyn. family practice Cornell U. Med. Coll., 1993-96, pres. Bonne Forme Vitamins and Skin Care, divsn. Vitamins for Women, L.I., 1983—; prin. investigator pilot study to determine heavy metals in breast cancer tissue for patients residing on L.I. 10 yrs. or more, North Shore Hosp. and Brookhaven Nat. Lab., 1994; lectr., TV guest on women's medicine and health issues; mem. panel menopause NIH, 1993; clin. rsch. on menstrual pain, premenstrual syndrome, menopause, breast cancer and osteoporosis; med. reviewer JAMA. Author: No More Menstrual Cramps and Other Good News, 1980, No More Hot Flashes and Other Good News, 1983, No More Hot Flashes and Even More Good News, 1998, World Book Health and Medical Annual, 1994; contbr. orig. rsch. articles to profl. jours. Bd. dirs. Coalition Against Domestic Violence. Named one of Women of Yr. C.W. Post Coll., 1981; recipient Nat. Consumers League award, 1983, Max Cheplove award Erie chpt. N.Y. State Acad. Family Physicians, 1983, Women of Distinction award Soroptimist Internat. of Nassau County, L.I., 1990, honoree Nassau County Coalition Against Domestic Violence, 1992. Fellow Nassau County Med. Soc., Am. Acad. Family Physicians (nat. com. on pub. rels.); mem. NOW (Equality award in Health 1988, Unsung Heroine award), Am. Med. Women's Assn. (co-chmn. nat. women's health com., liaison), Nassau Acad. Family Physicians (past pres.).

BUDREVICS, ALEXANDER, landscape architect; b. Riga, Latvia, Jan. 3, 1925; arrived in Can., 1952; s. Alfred and Adele (Martinous) B.; m. Milija Vite, Apr. 8, 1948; children: Valdis, Dace, Arnis. Grad. hort. sch., Latvia, 1944; grad. landscape architect, St. Alban's (Eng.) Sch. Art, 1949, London Coll. Art, 1951. Registered landscape architect, Ont., Can. Practice landscape architecture Latvia, Germany, Belgium, Eng., until 1952; staff various firms, Can., 1952-65; pres. Alexander Budrevics & Assocs. Ltd., Don Mills, Ont., 1965—; ptnr. Golf Course Devel. Assn., 1969—. Designer over 3000 projects including Nat. Home Show, 1958—, CNE hort. shows, Century Sq.; contbr. articles to profl. jours. Trustee Helen M. Kippax Meml. Scholarship Fund; chmn. exec. bd. Latvian Boy Scouts Assn., pres. Latvian Nat. Fedn. Can. Gen. Assembly, 1993-97; pres. Kristus Darz Home for the Aged, 1989; pres. Ont. Swimming Pool Assn., Toronto, 1964. Fellow Can. Soc. Landscape Architects (life), Am. Landscape Architects Soc., Am. Inst. Landscape Architects (internat. pres. 1969-71), Ont. Assn. Landscape Architects (emeritus, pres. 1977-78, Disting. Achievement award 1987), Can. Latvian Bus. and Profl. Assn. (pres. 1971—), Bd. of Trade Club, Empire Club of Can. Mem. Progressive Conservative Party. Lutheran. Avocations: gardening, travel, golf. E-mail: alex@budrevics.com. Fax: 416-444-5208. Office: Alexander Budrevics & Assocs Ltd, 895 Don Mills Rd Ste 212, Don Mills, ON Canada M3C 1W3

BUDZAK, KATHRYN SUE (MRS. ARTHUR BUDZAK), physician; b. Racine, Wis., May 6, 1940; d. Raymond Phillip and Emma Kathryn (Sorensen) Myer; m. Arthur Budzak, Dec. 21, 1961; children: Ann Elizabeth, Lynn Marie. Student, Stephens Coll., 1957-58, Luther Coll., 1958-59; BS with honors, U. Wis., Milw., 1962; MD, U. Wis., 1969. Intern Madison (Wis.) Gen. Hosp., 1969-70; emergency physician emergency ste. St. Mary's Hosp., Madison, 1971-75; urgent care physician Dean Clinic, Madison, 1975-95; contract rsch. Dean Found., Madison, 1991—. Recipient Disting. Alumnae award Stephens Coll., 1979; named to Washington Park H.S. Hall of Fame, 1985. Mem. AMA, Am. Acad. Familiy Physicians, Wis. Acad. Famiily Physicians (pres. south ctrl. chpt. 1979-81), Wis. Med. Soc., Dane County Med. Soc., Am. Med. Women's Assn. (pres. 1989-95), Wis. Med. Alumni Assn. (bd. dirs. 1979-82, pres. 1983-84, sec.-treas. 1994—), Wagon Trail Condo Assn. (dir., treas. 1990—, pres. 1993-95), Sigma Sigma Sigma. Presbyterian. E-mail: Kbudzak@pol.net. Home and Office: 6110 Davenport Dr Madison WI 53711-2446

BUDZINSKI, JAMES EDWARD, interior designer; b. Jan. 4, 1953; s. Edward Michael and Virginia (Caliman) B. Student, U. Cin., 1971-76. Mem. design staff Perkins & Wills Archs., Inc., Chgo., 1973-75, Med. Architectonics, Inc., Chgo., 1975-76; v.p. interior design Interior Environs., Inc., Chgo., 1976-78; pres. Jim Budzinski Design, Inc., Chgo., 1978-80; dir. interior design Robinson, Mills & Williams, San Francisco, 1980-87; dir. design, interior arch. Whisler Patri, San Francisco, 1987-90; v.p. design sales and mktg. Deepa Textiles, 1990-95; v.p. Workplace Studio One Workplace L. Ferrari, San Jose, Calif., 1997—; instr. design Harrington Inst. Design, Chgo.; cons. Chgo. Art Inst., Storwal Internat., Inc.; spkr. profl. confs. Designs include 1st Chgo. Corp. Pvt. Banking Ctr., 1st Nat. Bank Chgo. Monroe and Wabash Banking Ctr., 1978, IBM Corp., San Jose, Deutsche Bank, Frankfort, Crowley Maritime Corp., San Francisco, office for Brobeck, Phleger and Harrison, offices for chmn. bd. Fireman's Fund Ins. Cos., Nob Hill Club, Fairmont Hotel, San Francisco, offices for Cooley, Goodword, Castro, Huddleson, and Tatum, Palo Alto, Calif., offices for Pacific Bell Acctg. divsn., San Francisco, showroom for Knoll Internat., San Francisco, lobby, lounge TransAm. Corp. Hdqs., San Francisco, offices for EDAW, San Francisco, showroom for Steelcase, Inc., Bally of Switzerland, N.Am. Flagship store, San Francisco; corp. Hdqs. Next Inc., Redwood City, Calif., Schafer Furniture Design, Lobby Renovation 601 California, San Francisco, Bennedetti Furniture Inc. Furniture Design. Pres. No. Calif. chpt. Design Industries Found. for AIDS.

BUDZINSKY, ARMIN ALEXANDER, investment banker; b. Steyr, Austria, Nov. 25, 1942; came to U.S., 1951, naturalized, 1957; s. Alexander Wladimir and Maria Gisella B.; m. Pamela Plimmer, Oct. 29, 1978; children: Andrea, Natalie. A.B., John Carroll U., 1964; MA. (NDEA fellow) Fulbright fellow, Rutgers U., 1969. Instr. in English Cleve. State U., 1969-72; corp. fin. cons. Citibank NA, N.Y.C., 1974-76; project fin. Dean Witter & Co., N.Y.C., 1976-77; v.p. oil and gas financing Merrill Lynch Pierce Fenner & Smith, N.Y.C., 1977-83; v.p. corp. fin. Dunoco Corp., Houston, 1983; pres. Porcari Fearnow Capital Markets Group, Inc., Houston, 1985-86, Itec Securities Corp., Houston, 1985-86; v.p., dir. project fin., prin. Eppler, Guerin & Turner, Inc., Dallas, 1984-92; ptnr. Garland Group, 1992-93; sr. v.p., CFO Heard Energy Corp., 1993-98; pres. Archangel Diamond Corp., Vancouver, B.C., 1996-97, pres, CEO, 1997-98, chmn., 1997-98; exec. v.p., dir. United Am. Enterprises Ltd., 1998—. Mem. industry adv. com. N.Am. Security Administrs. Assn, Oil Investment Inst.; dirs. U. Chgo. Grad Sch. Bus. Alumni Assn. Home: 4629 Lorraine Ave Dallas TX 75209-6013 Office: United Am Enterprises Ltd, 595 How St, Vancouver, BC Canada V6C 2T5

BUE, CARL OLAF, JR., retired federal judge; b. Chgo., Mar. 27, 1922; s. Carl Olaf and Mabel Port (Shollar) B.; m. Mary Kathryn Waring, Dec. 27, 1948; children: Kathryn Anne, Richard Charles. AA, U. Chgo., 1942; student, U. Rome, Italy, 1945; PhB, Northwestern U., 1951; D of Jurisprudence, U. Tex., 1954. Bar: Tex. 1954. Assoc. firm Royston, Rayzor & Cook, Houston, 1954-58; mem. firm Royston, Rayzor & Cook, 1958-70; U.S. dist. judge So. Dist. Tex. (Houston div.), 1970-87; lectr. various law schs. and admiralty seminars in Tex. and other states. Contbr. articles to profl. jours. Served to capt., Adj. Gen. Dept. AUS, 1942-46, MTO. Recipient Good Citizenship medal Houston chpt. SAR, 1975, Tex. Supreme Ct. Justice Joe R. Greenhill award as outstanding jurist Mcpl. Cts. Assn., 1977, Northwestern U. Alumni Merit award for disting. profl. svc. in law, 1997; establishment at U. Tex. Sch. of Law of the Judge Carl. O. Bue Jr. Endowed Presdl. scholarship in law, 1988. Mem. Am., Fed., Tex., Houston Bar Assns., Maritime Law Assn. of U.S., Houston Philos. Soc. at Rice U., Alpha Delta Phi, Phi Alpha Delta. Republican. Lutheran. Home: 338 Knipp Rd Houston TX 77024-5044

BUECHE, WENDELL FRANCIS, agricultural products company executive; b. Flushing, Mich., Nov. 7, 1930; s. Paul D. and Catherine (McGraw) B.; m. Virginia M. Smith, June 14, 1952 (dec. May 12, 1992); children: Denise, Barbara, Daniel, Brian; m. Nancy Bird Jacobson, June 24, 1994; children: Meredith, Stuart, Julia. B.S.M.E., U. Notre Dame, 1952. With Allis-Chalmers Corp., 1952-88; dist. mgr. Allis-Chalmers Corp., Detroit, 1961-64, sales and mktg. mgr., 1964-69; group exec. v.p. Allis-Chalmers Corp., West Allis, Wis., 1973-76, exec. v.p. elec. groups, 1976-77, exec. v.p., chief adminstrv. and fin. officer, 1977-80, exec. v.p., head solids process equipment sector and fluids processing group, chief fin. officer, 1980-81, pres., chief operating officer, dir., 1981-83, pres., CEO, dir., 1984-86, chmn., 1986-88, ret., 1988; CEO IMC Global, Northbrook, Ill., 1993-97, chmn. bd. dirs., 1994—; dir. M&I Marshall Illsley Bank., M&I Corp., Wis. Gas Corp., WICOR, Inc. Mem. council Med. Coll. Wis., 1983—, engring. adv. coun., past chmn., U. Notre Dame. Mem. Mid-Atlantic Com. for internat. Bus., Nat. Assn. Mfgrs. (dir.), TFI (past chmn.), Longboat Key Club, Mission Hills Country Club. Clubs: Milwaukee Country, Westmoor Country. Office: IMC Global 2100 Sanders Rd Ste 200 Northbrook IL 60062-6146*

BUECHEL, WILLIAM BENJAMIN, lawyer; b. Wichita, Kans., July 27, 1926; s. Donald William and Bonnie S. (Priddy) B.; m. Theresa Marie Girard, Nov. 3, 1955; children: Sarah Ann, Julia Elaine. Student U. Wichita, 1947-49; BS, U. Kans., 1951, LLB, 1954. Bar: Kans., 1954, U.S. dist. ct. (Kans.), 1954. Sole practice, Concordia, Kans., 1954-56; stockholder Paulsen, Buechel, Swenson, Uri & Brewer, Chartered, and predecessors, Concordia, 1971-75, sec.-treas., 1975-77, pres., 1977-92, of counsel, 1993-95; ret.; bd. dirs. County Bank & Trust, Concordia, 1971-92, Cloud County Community Coll. Found., 1983-89, trust and adminstrn. com. Citizens Nat. Bank, 1992—. Mem. ABA, Kan. Bar Assn. (exec. council 1966-68, chmn. adv. sect. profl. ethics com. 1974-76), Cloud County Bar Assn. (pres. 1984-86). Republican. Methodist. Clubs: Concordia Country, Elks, Moose, Rotary (pres. 1969-70).

BUECHLEIN, DANIEL MARK, archbishop; b. Jasper, Ind., Apr. 20, 1938; s. Carl and Rose (Blessinger) B. BA, St. Meinrad Coll., 1961; student, St. Meinrad Sch. Theology, 1961-64; Licentiate Sacred Theology, Benedictine U. Sant' Anselmo, Rome, 1966. Ordained priest Roman Cath. Ch., 1964, consecrated bishop, 1987, archbishop, 1992. Asst. dean students St. Meinrad Coll., 1966-68, dir. spiritual formation, 1968-71; pres., rector St. Meinrad Sch. Theology, 1971-82, St. Meinrad Sch. Theology and St. Meinrad Coll., 1982-87; bishop Diocese of Memphis, Tenn., 1987-92; installed archbishop of Indpls., 1992—; chmn. divsn. religion St. Meinrad Coll., 1967-71, mem. Archabbey Coun., 1967-87; dir. First Nat. Conf. for Sem. Spiritual Dirs., summer 1971; mem. formation com. Conf. of Major Superiors of Men of USA, 1971-78; mem. nat. steering com. for follow-up of 1983 Nat. Assembly Sem. Rectors and Ordinaries; chmn. com. on proestly formation Nat. Conf. Cath. Bishops, 1990-93, mem. adminstrv. com. 1990-93, com. on marriage and family life, 1987, advisor doctrine com., 1989-93, mem. com. on doctrine, 1989-93, adminstrv. com., 1990-93, budget com., 1990-92, bishop's emergency relief com., 1990-92, chmn. ad hoc com. to oversee use of Catechism of Cath. Ch., 1994—, mem. subcom. on pastoral message in abortion, 1994—; peritus Internat. Synod on Priestly Formation, Rome, 1990; bd. dirs. S.E. Regional Office for Hispanics Afairs and S.E. Pastoral Inst.; co-pres. Disciples of Christ-Roman Cath. Internat. Dialogue, 1995—. Co-author: (with Bleichner and Leavitt) Preparing a Diocesan Priest: The Holistic Experience, 1987; Celibacy for the Kingdom, 1990; Commentary on a Survey of Priests Ordained Five to Nine Years, 1991; contbr. articles to profl. jours. Bd. dirs. Southeast Regional Office for Hispanic Affairs and Southeast Pastoral Inst., 1987—. Hon. chaplain KC, State of Tenn., 1987. Mem. Nat. Assn. Sem. Spiritual Dirs. (founding coord. 1972), Midwest Assn. Sem. Spiritual Dirs. (founding coord. 1971), Midwest Assn. Theol. Schs. (sec.-treas. 1972-74, ptrd. 1974-75), Theol. Edn. Assn. Mid-Am. (sec. 1972-74, 80-82, v.p. 1974-76, pres. 1976-78, 82-84), Nat. Cath. Edn. Assn. (chmn. exec. com. of sem. divsn. 1984-85, 85-86), Nat. Conf. Catholic Bishops (mem. com. on marriage and family life1987-89, com. on priestly formation 1987-89, adminstrv. com. 1988—, bd. dirs. 1988—, budget and fin. com. 1990-92). Office: Archdiocese of Indpls PO Box 1410 1400 N Meridian St Indianapolis IN 46202-2305*

BUECHLER, BRADLEY BRUCE, plastic processing company executive, accountant; b. St. Louis, Dec. 5, 1948; s. Phillip Earl and Mildred M. (Braun) B.; m. Stephanie A. Walker, June 20, 1969; children: Sheila, Lisa, Brian. BSBA, U. Mo., St. Louis, 1971. CPA, Mo. Audit mgr. Arthur Andersen & Co., St. Louis, 1971-81; corp. controller Spartech Corp., St. Louis, 1981-83, exec. v.p., COO, 1984-87, pres., COO, 1987-91, pres., CEO, 1991—, chmn., 1999—. Bd. regents St. Louis U., 1994—; mem. corp. bd. St. Joseph Inst. for the Deaf, 1995—; bd. dirs. Boy Scouts Am., 1998. With Mo. Army N.G., 1969-75. Mem. AICPA, Soc. Plastics Industry (chmn. sheet prodrs. divsn., bd. dirs. 1993-95, mem. exec. com. color and additive compounders divsn.). Methodist. Avocations: golf, baseball. Office: Spartech Corp 120 S Central Ste 1700 Clayton MO 63105-1705

BUECHNER, CARL FREDERICK, minister, author; b. N.Y.C., July 11, 1926; s. Carl Frederick and Katherine (Kuhn) B.; m. Judith Friedrike Merck, Apr. 7, 1956; children: Katherine, Dinah, Sharman. Grad., Lawrenceville Sch., 1943; AB, Princeton U., 1947; BD, Union Theol. Sem., 1958; DD, Va. Episc. Sem., Lafayette U.; LittD, Lehigh U., Cornell Coll.; DD, Yale U., Sewanee U.; LHD, Susquehanna U. Ordained minister United Presbyn. Ch. U.S.A., 1958. Tchr. English Lawrenceville Sch., 1948-53; tchr. creative writing, summer sessions N.Y.U., 1954-55; chmn. dept. religion Phillips Exeter Acad., 1958-67, sch. minister, 1960-67; William Belden Noble lectr. Harvard, 1969; Russell lectr. Tufts, 1971; Lyman Beecher lectr. Yale U., 1977; Harris lector Bangor Sem., 1979; Smyth lectr. Columbia Sem., 1981; lectr. Trinity Inst., 1990. Author: A Long Day's Dying, 1950, The Seasons' Difference, 1952, The Return of Ansel Gibbs, 1958, The Final Beast, 1965, The Magnificent Defeat, 1966, The Hungering Dark, 1969, The Entrance to Porlock, 1970, The Alphabet of Grace, 1970, Lion Country, 1971 (Nat. Book award nominee), Open Heart, 1972, Wishful Thinking, 1973, Love Feast, 1974, The Faces of Jesus, 1974, Treasure Hunt, 1977, Telling the Truth, 1977, Peculiar Treasures, 1979, The Book of Bebb, 1979, Godric, 1980 (Pulitzer Prize nominee), The Sacred Journey, 1982, Now and Then, 1983, A Room Called Remember, 1984, Brendan, 1987, Whistling in the Dark, 1988, The Wizard's Tide, 1990, Telling Secrets, 1991, The Clown in the Belfry, 1992, Listening to Your Life, 1992, The Son of Laughter, 1993, The Longing for Home, 1996, On the Road with the Archangel, 1997, The Storm, 1998, The Eyes of the Heart, 1999. Trustee Barlow Sch., 1965-71. With AUS, 1944-46. Recipient Irene Glascock Meml. intercollegiate poetry award, 1947; O'Henry prize for story The Tiger, 1955; Richard and Hinda Rosenthal award for the Return of Ansel Gibbs, 1958. Mem. Nat. Coun. Churches (com. on lit. 1954-57), Coun. Religion in Ind. Schs. (regional chmn. 1958-63), Presbytery No. New Eng., Century Assn., Univ. Club (N.Y.C.). Home and Office: 3572 State Rte 315 Pawlet VT 05761-9607

BUECHNER, JACK W(ILLIAM), lawyer, government affairs consultant; b. St. Louis, June 4, 1940; s. John Edward and Gertrude Emily (Richardson) B.; children from previous marriage: Patrick John, Terrence J.; m. Nancy Chanitz; 1 child, Charles Chanitz. BA, Benedictine Coll., 1962; JD, St. Louis U., 1965. Bar: Mo. 1965, U.S. Dist. Ct. (ea. dist.) Mo. 1965, U.S. Ct. Appeals (8th cir.) 1965, D.C. 1998. Ptnr. Buechner, McCarthy, Leonard, Kaemmerer, Owen & Laderman, Chesterfield, Mo., 1965-93; mem. 100th-102d U.S. Congresses from 2d Mo. dist., 1987-91; dep. minority whip, 1989-90; vice-chmn. Rep. study group, pres. Internat. Rep. Inst., Washington, 1991-93; prin., dir. internat. svcs. The Hawthorn Group, Arlington, Va., 1993-95; ptnr. Manatt Phelps & Phillips, Washington, 1995—; state rep. 94th dist. Mo. Gen. Assembly, 1972-82, minority leader, 1974-78; mem. state adv. com. U.S. Commn. on Civil Rights, 1975-82. Lay advisor St. Louis Med. Soc., 1989-92; Mo. Tourism Commn., 1976, 82-85. Recipient Meritorious Svc. award St. Louis Globe-Democrat, 1973, Legis. Achievement award St. Louis Police Officers, 1982, Pub. Svc. award Women's Polit. Caucus, Mo., Disting. Svc. award Cardinal Glennon Hosp., Mo., 1982, Nat. Security Leadership award Am. Security Coun. Found., 1988, 89, Family and Freedom award, Golden Bulldog award, 1987, 88, Guardian of Small Bus. award Nat. Fedn. Ind. Bus., 1987, 88, 90, 91, Enterprise award U.S. C. of C., 1988, 89, 90, Sound Dollar award, 1988, Eagle of Freedom award Am. Security Coun. Foun., 1990. Mem. Mo. Bar Assn., D.C. Bar Assn., Met. Bar Assn., Mo. Soc. Washington (pres.), Nat. Conf. State Socs. (1st v.p.), Ctr. Nat. Policy (bd. dirs. 1997—), Assn. Former Mems. of Congress (bd. dirs., sec.), John Marshall Club (Outstanding Atty. award 1986), Lions, Phi Delta Phi. Republican. Episcopalian. Avocations: golf, reading, travel. E-mail: jbuechner@manatt.com. Home: 1303 Altamira Ct Mc Lean VA 22102-2201 Office: Manatt Phelps & Phillips 1501 M St NW Ste 700 Washington DC 20005-1737

BUECHNER, JOHN C., academic administrator. Dir. govtl. rels., then dir. pub. affairs U. Colo. System Office, Denver, until 1989; chancellor U. Colo., Denver, 1988-95, pres., 1996—. Office: U Colo-Denver Office of Pres Campus Box 35 Boulder CO 80309-0035

BUECHNER, MARGARET, composer, music educator; b. Hannover, Germany, May 27, 1922; came to U.S., 1951, U.S. citizenship, 1961; d. Wilhelm and Martha Voss; m. Werner Buechner, 1948 (dvi. 1972). MusM, U. Königsberg and U. Wuerzburg (Germany) and Conservatory, 1943; pvt. studies in composition and orch. with Otto Luening, Columbia U., 1954-55. Ind. composer, 1932—, choir dir., educator, 1946-87; founder, pres. Mich. Composers League, 1960-66; host classical music ednl. radio programs, 1961-64; mem. Composers Conf., Bennington, Vt., 1954, 55. Composer, librettist numerous story ballets including The Key, Phantomgreen, Mayerling, Elizabeth, The Erlking, stageless full-length Princess and the Pea Ballet, stageless Elf-King Ballet, stageless full-length Immensee ballet, stageless Adventures of Easter Bunny ballet; also various symphonies, tone poems, many chamber music works, concert performances; recs. with the

Nürnberger Symphoniker (German Symphony Orch.), including Ballet Suite of Phantomgreen and the complete music of the evening-length ballet Elizabeth and the tone poem The Old Swedes Church, recorded with Royal Scottish Nat. Orch. Essay I and The Flight of the Am. Eagle, Symphonic Poem Erlkönig Symphonic Trilogy The Am. Civil War, Orchestral Choral Reminiscence The Liberty Bell, (ballet music of evening length) La Belle et la Bête (Beauty and the Beast) performances, Bordeaux, France, Genova, Italy; other recs. include Five Symphonic Classics, Symphonic Ballet Music, Sixteen Symphony Orch. Childrens Recital Dances, The Key complete ballet music, Suites and others, also ednl. orchestral CD; many stage performances The Key, Phantomgreen; TV broadcasts The Key; collection of 71 recorded dramatic symphonic concert works. Avocations: gardening. Address: Mgmt Eldo Music Publisher Ste 104 4407 Gladding Ct Midland MI 48640-3383

BUECHNER, ROBERT WILLIAM, lawyer, educator; b. Syracuse, N.Y., Oct. 29, 1947; s. Donald F. and Barbara (Northrup) B.; m. Angela Marian Hoetker, May 28, 1978; children: Julie Marie, Robert William Jr., Leslie Ann, James Bradley. BSE, Princeton U., 1969; JD, U. Mich., 1974. Bar: Ohio, 1974, Fla. 1974, U.S. Dist. Ct. (so. dist.) Ohio 1974, U.S. Tax Ct. 1974. Assoc. Frost & Jacobs, Cin., 1974-79; pres. Buechner, Haffer, O'Connell, Meyers & Healey Co., L.P.A., Cin., 1979—; adj. prof. Salmon P. Chase Coll. Law, No. Ky., 1975-82; instr. Cin. chpt. Chartered Life Underwiters, 1976-96; lectr. Million Dollar Roundtable, Atlanta, 1981. Author: (with others) Why Universal Life, 1982, Prosper Through Tax Planning, 1982, Living Gangbusters, 1986, The 8 Pathways to Financial Success, 1987, 93, 98. Mem. planning divsn. Cin. Cmty. Chest, 1978-84; trustee Cin. Venture Assn., 1994—, pres., 1997-98; trustee Cin. Country Day Sch., 1979-93, pres., 1990-93. Recipient Alumnus of Yr. award Cin. Country Day Sch., 1985, First winner of John Warrington Cmty. Svc. award, 1997. Mem. Cin. Bar Assn. (chmn. taxation sect. 1984-85), S.W. Ohio Tax Inst. (chmn. 1981-82), Cin. Assn. (trustee 1999—), Gyro Club (sec. 1982-83, v.p. 1999-2000), Princeton Club (pres. 1982-84). Republican. Methodist. Avocations: golf, tennis, bridge. Office: Buechner Haffer O'Connell Meyers Healey Co LPA 105 E 4th St Ste #300 Cincinnati OH 45202-4006

BUECHNER, THOMAS SCHARMAN, artist, retired glass manufacturing company executive, museum director; b. Sept. 25, 1926; s. Thomas Scharman and Anne Evans (Lines) B.; m. Mary C. Hawkins, Sept. 15, 1949; children: Barbara Lines, Thomas Scharman, Matthew. Student, Princeton U., 1945, Ecole des Beaux Arts, Fontainebleau, 1946, Paris, 1947, Arts Students League, N.Y.C., 1946, 48, Institut voor Pictologie, Amsterdam, 1947. Designer Compañía de Fomento, San Juan, P.R., 1946; asst. display mgr. Met. Mus. Art, N.Y.C., 1949-51, tchr., 1949-51; dir. Corning Mus. Glass, N.Y., 1951-60, 75-80, pres., 1971-87; v.p., dir. cultural affairs Corning Glass Works, 1985-87, ret., 1987, cons., 1987—; faculty art sch. Bild-Werk, Fravenau, Fed. Republic Germany, 1988—; head dept. art Corning Community Coll., 1958-60; bd. dir. Bklyn. Mus.; chmn. Corning Glass Works Found., 1971-87; v.p. Steuben Glass, Corning, 1971-73, pres., 1973-82, chmn., 1982-85. Author: Glass Vessels in Dutch Painting of the 17th Century, 1952, Life and Work of Frederick Carder, 1952, Guide to the Collections of the Corning Museum of Glass, 1955, Guide to the Collections of the Brooklyn Museum, 1967, Norman Rockwell, Artist Illustrator, 1970, Arts of David Levine, 1979, Ogden Pleissner, 1984; portrait and landscape painter; one-man shows: Adler Gallery, N.Y.C., 1982, 84, Arnot Art Mus., 1985, 95, Heller Gallery, N.Y.c., 1989, Gallery M, Lindau, Germany, 1989, Gallery Nakama, Tokyo, 1990, 93, 96, O.K. Harris Gallery, N.Y.C., Schloss Weissenstein, Regen, Germany, 1996; represented in permanent collections Met. Mus. Art, Nat. Mus. Am. Art, Smithsonian Inst., Bklyn. Mus., Lincoln Ctr., Herbert F. Johnson Mus. Cornell U., Musée des Arts Decoratifs, Lausanne, Switzerland, Renwick Mus., Smithsonian, Washington, Corning Mus. of Glass, Corning, N.Y. Trustee Tiffany Found., Pilchuck Sch., Corning Mus. Glass, Corning Glass Works Found., Rockwell Mus., Arnot Art Mus. Arts of the Southern Finger Lakes; pres. Rockwell Mus. 1982-87, trustee 1987—. Recipient Forsythia award Bklyn. Bot. Garden, 1971, Gari Melchers medal Am. Artist fellows, 1971. Mem. Bklyn. Inst. Arts and Sci. (trustee 1971-72, pres. 1971-72), Nat. Collection Fine Arts. (commr. 1972-91). Episcopalian. Clubs: Century Assn. Studio: 11 North Rd Corning NY 14830-3235

BUEHLER, EVELYN JUDY, poet; b. Chgo.; d. Marzell William and Ida Mae Rubbia (Fields) Regulus; m. Henry Eric Buehler, Aug. 23, 1985; children: Ashley Leonard, Evelyn Judy. Student, Harold Washington Coll., Chgo. Author: Tales of Summer, 1998; contbr. short stories to Daring to Dream, 1995, Tears of Fire, 1995, A Moment to Remember, Wisdom of the Ages, 1997, Mortal Thoughts, 1997, Calm Winds, 1997, To Have and to Hold, 1997, A Writer's Season, 1995, The Best Writers of 1995, Wordly Thoughts and Lyrics of Poetry, 1995; contbr. poetry to Today's Greatest Poems, Our Twentieth Century's Greatest Poems, Our World's Best Loved Poems, Our World's Most Beloved Poems, Night Skies in Winter, Worldly Thoughts, Lyrics of Poetry, Am. Poetry Anthology, Best New Poets of 1987, Poems That Will Live Forever, The Best Poems of the 90's, Whispers in the Wind, Outstanding Poets of 1994, The Songs of Poetry, At Day's End, Calm Fires, 1995, Mortal Words, 1995, Words of the Soul, 1996, Beginning of a New Dawn, 1996, A Time to Remember, 1996, The Best Writers of 1996, Tears of a Soul, 1997, The Isle of View, 1997, The Other Side of Midnight, 1997, Diamonds and Pearls, 1997, Today, Tomorrow and Beyond, 1997, Masquerade of Words, 1997, The Best Writers of 1997, Endless Skies of Blue, 1998, The Best Poems of 1998, 2000 Outstanding People of the 20th Century, 1998, Outstanding Poets of 1998, 1998, others. Elected to Internat. Poetry Hall of Fame; named Internat. Woman of Yr. 197-98, 98-99, Internat. Woman of Millennium; recipient Twentieth Century Achievement award, 1999. Mem. Internat. Soc. Poets (life). Democrat. Baptist. Avocations: gardening, bicycle riding, hiking, art, camping. Home: 5658 S Normal Blvd Chicago IL 60621-2966

BUEHLER, THOMAS, psychotherapist, expressive therapist; b. Zurich, Switzerland, Aug. 9, 1943; came to U.S 1989.; s. Adolf and Margrit (Gredig) B.; m. Marina Schmidheiny, July 27, 1969 (div. 1986); m. Rosemarie Schiller, Apr. 19, 1995. MS, Med. Sch. U. Zurich, 1970. Cert. psychotherapist, Switzerland. Intern Accredited Swiss Hosp., 1969-75; multimedia artist Switzerland, 1973—; psychotherapist and expressive therapist, 1979—; cofounding, training therapist Internat. Sch. of Interdisciplinary Studies, 1982-85, advisory bd. Swiss Assocs. of Psychotherapists, 1984-85; founding chmn. Cardon Found., 1991—, Cirio Found., N.Y., 1993—;. Author: Der Vulkan ist aufgebrochen, 1976; one man performance Roter Stadtkriecher, 1985, Red Broadway Crawler, 1985, one man show, 1999. Mem. Internat. Assoc. of Artist Therapists, Nat. Expressive Therapy Assn., Swiss Assoc. of Psychotherapists. Avocations: piano, guitar, travel, wilderness, foreign cultures. Home: 140 Grand St #3WR New York NY 10013-3127 Office: Cirio Found 853 Broadway Ste 1708 New York NY 10003-4703

BUEL, JEFFREY A., pharmaceutical executive; b. El Paso, Tex., Nov. 22, 1957; s. Charles J. and Nancy L. (Eater) B.; m. Nancy L. Bailes, Sept. 27, 1984; 1 child, J. Alexander Jr. BBA, Tex. A&M U., 1979; BS, Midwestern State U., 1980; MBA, North Tex. State U., 1981. Territory mgr. Bristol-Meyers, N.Y.C., 1982-84; key acct. mgr. Am. Cyanamid, Wayne, N.J., 1984-87; sales dir. Russell-Moss Brokerage, Dallas, 1987-89; sales mgr. Astra USA, Westborough, Mass., 1989—, regional dir., 1995—. Capt. USAR, 1980—. Mem. Am. Mktg. Assn., Nat. Guard Assn. Tex., Nat. Guard Assn. U.S.A. Avocations: running, tennis, golf. Home: 6929 N Hayden Rd # Ckf4-611 Scottsdale AZ 85250-7970

BUEL, RICHARD VAN WYCK, JR., history educator, writer, editor; b. Morristown, N.J., July 22, 1933; s. Richard Van Wyck Sr. and Frances Worthington (Thompson) B.; m. Joy Evelyn Margaret Day, June 5, 1964 (dec. Apr. 1987); m. Marilyn Ellman Frankel, July 18, 1992; 1 child, Margaret Alexandra. A.B., Amherst Coll., 1955; A.M., Harvard U., 1957, Ph.D. in Am. History, 1962. Teaching fellow in history Harvard U., Cambridge, Mass., 1958-62; asst. prof. history Wesleyan U., Middletown, Conn., 1962-69; assoc. prof. Wesleyan U., 1969-75, prof., 1975—, chmn. history dept., 1978-81; Ray A. Billington vis. prof. U.S. history Occidental Coll., 1999-00. Author: Securing the Revolution, 1972, Dear Liberty, 1980 (Round Table of Am. Revolution award 1981), (with Joy D. Buel) The Way of Duty, 1984 (Colonial Dames of Am. Book award 1985), In Irons, 1998; assoc. editor History and Theory, 1970-91; contbr. articles to profl. jours., chpts. to books. Bd. dirs. No. Middlesex United Fund, Middletown, Conn., 1965-68; mem. Bd. Fin., Haddam, Conn., 1972-74. Fellow Charles Warren Ctr., Harvard U., 1966-67, Am. Council Learned Socs., 1966-67, 74-75, NEH, 1985; Guggenheim Found., 1986; jr. humanist fellow NEH, 1971-72; John Carter Brown fellow, 1986. Mem. Conn. Acad. Arts and Scis. (v.p. 1975-81), Am. Hist. Assn., Inst. Early Am. History and Culture, Soc. History of Early Republic, Orgn. Am. Historians, New Eng. Hist. Assn. (v.p. 1991, pres. 1992), Conn. Coordinating Com. for Promotion History, Conn. Humanities Coun., Pettipaug Yacht Club (rear commodore 1984-86, vice commodore 1986-88, commodore 1988-90), Conn. Hist. Commn., Acorn Club, Phi Beta Kappa. Avocation: dinghy racing. Home: 55 N Main St Essex CT 06426-1073 Office: Wesleyan Univ Dept History Middletown CT 06459-0002

BUELL, BRUCE TEMPLE, lawyer; b. Pueblo, Colo., Mar. 18, 1932; s. Jewett C. and Eva Lorraine (Allen) B.; m. Joan Carol Souders, June 20, 1953; children: Alan D., Susan L. Buell, Bonnie L. Iten. AB, Princeton U., 1953; postgrad., Harvard Law Sch., 1953-54, George Washington U. Law Sch., 1955-57; LLB, U. Denver, 1958. Bar: Colo. Asst. trust dept. Cen. Bank & Trust Co., Denver, 1957-58; assoc. Holland & Hart, Denver, 1958-64; ptnr. Holland & Hart, Colorado Springs and Denver, Colo., 1964-96; atty. pvt. practice, Colorado Springs, Colo., 1996—; bd. dirs., counsel Jefferson Bank & Trust, Lakewood, Colo., 1971-76; counsel, sec. Colo. Bus. Devel. Corp., Denver, 1965-83; gen. counsel Colo. Bankers Assn., Denver, 1961-85. Pres. Colo. Lawyer Trust Account Found., Denver, 1982-85, 88-89, Arvada (Colo.) Hist. Soc., 1974-75; chmn. adv. coun. Arvada Ctr. for Arts, 1978-79; dir. North Jeffco Recreation and Pk. Dist., Arvada, 1976-80; trustee, chmn. Presbytery of Denver Trust Fund, 1983-85; trustee, sec.-treas. Viola Vestal Coulter Found., 1964—, pres., 1998—; trustee Edmondson Found., 1996—, Pikes Peak Cmty. Found., 1998—; bd. dirs., v.p. Samaritan Counseling Ctr., Colorado Springs, 1991-96; mem. Colo. Forum, Denver, 1989-93. Served to capt. USNR, 1954-76. Recipient Vol. of Yr. award Denver Bar Assn., 1982, Man of Yr. award Arvada C. of C., 1983, Bruce T. Buell award Colo. Lawyer Trust Acct. Found., 1991, U. Denver Law Sch. Professionalism award, 1995. Fellow Colo. Bar Found.; mem. ABA, Colo. Bar Assn., El Paso County Bar Assn., Colorado Springs Estate Planning Coun., Broadmoor Golf Club, Winter Night Club (pres. 1996-97). Presbyterian. Avocations: tennis, music, prison ministry, church work. Home: 2512 Rigel Dr Colorado Springs CO 80906-1031 Office: Buell Law Firm 118 S Wahsatch Ave Ste 210 Colorado Springs CO 80903-3679

BUELL, DEXTER, artist, sculpture; b. Seattle, 1960. BS in Art magna cum laude, U. Wash., 1984; MFA in Sculpture, Yale U., 1984. Asst. prof. sculpture Coll. of Charleston, S.C., 1989-91; asst. to artists Alice Aycock, Mel Kendrick and Antony Gormley, 1991-93; asst. to artist Chuck Close, 1996-97; artist-in-residence Yale Summer Sch. Music and Art, Norfolk, Conn., 1988; vis. critic art, architecture and ecology Yale U. Sch. Art, New Haven, 1990; lectr. Architecture Ctr., Clemson (S.C.) U., 1991; resident Ucross (Wyo.) Found., 1995; adj. instr. photography Raritan Valley C.C., Somerville, N.J., 1997; vis. critic Cooper Union, N.Y.C., 1997, adj. instr. photography, 1998; lectr. Maine Coll. Art, Portland, 1997, Queens Coll. Grad. Fine Arts, CUNY, 1998. One-man shows include William Halsey Gallery, Coll. of Charleston, 1990, Nexus Contemporary Art Ctr., Atlanta, 1992, A.R.T. inc., N.Y.C., 1998; exhibited in group shows Yale U., 1989, S.C. State U., Columbia, 1992, U. Tenn., Knoxville, 1992, Artists Space, N.Y.C., 1992, Ohio Theater, N.Y.C., 1998, Andrea Rosen Gallery, N.Y.C., 1998, De Chiara/Stewart Gallery, N.Y.C., 1998, A.R.T. inc., 1999, Ex-Teresa Mus., Mexico City, 1999, Art & Idea, Mexico City, 1999; represented i permanent collection Denver Art Mus.; work reviewed in various publs. Recipient award Louis Comfort Tiffany Found., 1997; faculty R&D grantee Coll. of Charleston, 1990-91; fellow in visual arts S.C. Arts Commn., 1991-92, fellow in video art N.Y. Found. for Arts, 1998. Mem. Phi Beta Kappa.

BUELL, DIANA E., nursing administrator, special education professional; b. Herkimer, N.Y., July 18, 1942; d. Harold J. and Edna Arlene (Helmer) Oldick; m. Kenneth L. Buell Jr., Dec. 5, 1961; children: Paula, Gwenda, Carol, Cynthia. Med. sec., Utica (N.Y.) Sch. Commn., 1960; Assoc. Degree, Mohawk Valley Community Coll., Utica, 1988. RN, N.Y.; cert. CPR, standard 1st aid instr., first responder. Med. record tech. New Bern (N.C.) Hosp.; med. sec. Dr. N. Procinio, Schenectady, N.Y.; med. sec. Pathfinder Village, Edmeston, N.Y., nurse supr. Down's syndrome children; head nurse, part-time supr. The Meadows Nursing Home, Cooperstown, N.Y.; RN adminstr. Green Acre Camp for Mentally Retarded Adults. Recipient nursing scholarship. Mem. N.Y. State Nurses Assn. (Dist. 15).

BUELL, EDWARD RICK, II, lawyer; b. Des Moines, Jan. 28, 1948; s. Edward Rick and Betty-Jo (Heffron) B.; B.S. with high honors, Mich. State U., 1969; J.D. magna cum laude, U. Mich., 1972; children—Erica Colleen, Edward Rick III. Bar: D.C. 1973, Calif. 1975; cert. specialist in taxation law, Calif. Assoc. firm Arent, Fox, Kintner, Plotkin & Kahn, Washington, 1972-74, Brobeck, Phlegher & Harrison, San Francisco, 1974-77; ptnr. Winokur, Schoenberg, Maier & Zang, San Francisco, 1977-81; ptnr. Buell & Berner, San Francisco, 1981—. Mem. ABA, San Francisco Bar Assn., Order of Coif. Contbr. articles to legal jours. Home: 50 Stewart Dr Belvedere Tiburon CA 94920

BUELL, FREDERICK HENDERSON, educator; b. Bryn Mawr, Pa., Nov. 17, 1942; s. Clarence Adison and Marjorie (Henderson) B.; married; children: Alexander Silvano, Nicholas Mariano. BA, Yale U., 1964; PhD, Cornell U., 1970. Asst. prof. Queens Coll., Flushing, N.Y., 1970-72, assoc. prof., 1972-78, prof., 1978—. Author: Theseus and Other Poems, 1970, W.H. Anderson as a Social Poet, 1972, Full Summer, 1979, National Culture and The New Global System, 1994. Mem. Warwick (N.Y.) Valley Ctrl. Sch. Dist. Bd. Edn., 1991-97. NEA Writer's fellow, 1972, N.Y. State Coun. on Arts fellow, 1994, Nathan Cummings Contemplative Practice fellow, 1997-98. Avocations: Black Belt in Aikido, camping, hiking. Office: Queens Coll Dept English Flushing NY 11367

BUELL, RODD RUSSELL, lawyer; b. Pitts., Mar. 31, 1946; s. Harold Ellsworth and Jeanne Charlotte (Russell) B. BS, Fla. State U., 1968; JD, U. Fla., 1970; LLM, U. Miami, 1978. Bar: Fla. 1971, U.S. Dist. Ct. (so., mid. and no. dists.) Fla. 1971, U.S. Ct. Appeals (5th and 11th cirs.) 1971. Gen. ptnr. Blackwell & Walker, P.A., Miami, 1970-95; shareholder Fleming, O'Bryan & Fleming, Ft. Lauderdale, Fla., 1995-97; pvt. practice, Coral Gables, Fla., 1997—. Mem. Dade County Def. Bar Assn. (pres. 1985-86), Def. Trial Attys. Assn. (exec. counsel 1986-88), Maritime Law Assn., Am. Bd. Trial Advs., Internat. Assn. Def. Counsel, Bath Club, Riviera Country Club, Miami Club, Univ. Club. Republican. Methodist. Home: 4801 Campo Sano Ct Coral Gables FL 33146-1160 Office: 2355 Salzedo St Ste 202 Coral Gables FL 33134-5035

BUELL, VICTOR PAUL, marketing educator, author, editor; b. McAlester, Okla., Oct. 18, 1914; s. Victor Paul and Genevieve (Keller) B.; m. Virginia Stevens, May 16, 1942; children: Elizabeth Wilson Buell Barrow, Nancy Trimble Buell Tamms, Victor Paul III. A.B., Pa. State U., 1938; grad. advanced tech. tng. bus. adminstn., Harvard U., 1943. Mgr. market research and ops. Real Silk Hosiery Mills, Inc., Indpls., 1938-51; cons. mktg. McKinsey & Co., N.Y.C., 1952-55; mgr. mktg. div. Hoover Co., North Canton, Ohio, 1955-59; v.p. mktg. Archer Daniels Midland Co., Mpls., 1959-64; corp. v.p. mktg. Am. Standard, Inc., N.Y.C., 1964-70; prof. mktg. Sch. Mgmt., U. Mass., Amherst, 1970-83, prof. emeritus, 1983—, vis. prof., 1985; cons. to bus., govt., publs. and assns. Author: Marketing Management in Action, 1966, Changing Practices in Advertising Decision-Making and Control, 1973, Organizing for Marketing/Advertising Success, 1981, Marketing Management: A Strategic Planning Approach, 1984; contbg. author: Effective Marketing Action, 1958, The Marketing Job, 1961, Handbook of Business Administration, 1966, Readings in Marketing Research, 1970, Ency. Profl. Mgmt., 1978, Handbook for Professional Managers, 1985, Dictionary of Marketing Terms, 1988, 2d edit., 1995; contbr. articles to mags., mktg. jours.; editor-in-chief Handbook of Modern Marketing, 1970, 2d edit., 1986; editl. bd. Indsl. Mktg.; spkr. mgmt., mktg. groups and seminars; reporter Fleet Beat newspaper. Bd. dirs. Hennepin County United Fund, vice chmn. indsl. campaign; trustee Grad. Sch. Sales Mgmt. and Marketing, Syracuse U.; mem. Amherst Town Bd. Assessors, 1987-89; bd. dirs. Forum for Humanities; subscription mgr. for resident's mag. Fleet Landing Retirement Cmty. Maj., AUS, 1941-46. Recipient award Alpha Kappa Psi, 1975. Mem. Am. Mktg. Assn. (dir. 1957-59, chmn. nat. co. membership com. 1957-58, nat. v.p. 1960-61, pres. 1968-69, chmn. mktg. fund bd., editorial bd. Jour. Mktg.), Home Mfrs. Assn. (dir.), Am. Mgmt. Assn. (mem. nat. planning council), NAM (mktg. com.), Canton Sales Execs. Club (dir. 1956-58, v.p. 1958-59), Sales and Mktg. Execs. Internat., Sales and Mktg. Execs. Western Mass. (dir. 1980-83), Assn. Nat. Advertisers (dir.), Beta Gamma Sigma, Delta Phi (hon.). Congregationalist. Home: 4104 Fleet Landing Blvd Atlantic Bch FL 32233-7510

BUELOW, GEORGE JOHN, musicologist, educator; b. Chgo., Mar. 31, 1929; s. George J. and Florence (Cook) B. Mus.B., Chgo. Mus. Coll., 1950, Mus.M., 1951; postgrad., U. Hamburg, Germany, 1953-54; Ph.D., N.Y. U., 1961. Instr. music history Chgo. Conservatory, 1959-61; from asst. prof. to asso. prof. musicology U. Calif., Riverside, 1961-68; prof., chmn. dept. music U. Ky., 1968-69; prof., dir. grad. program in music Rutgers U., New Brunswick, N.J., 1969-77; prof. musicology Ind. U., 1977-98; mem. Commn. Mixte Internat. Inventory Musical Sources; co-chmn. Internat. Johann Mattheson Symposium, Wolfenbüttel, Fed. Republic Germany, 1981. Author: Thorough-bass Accompaniment According to J.D. Heinichen, 1966, 3d edit., 1992, Johann Mattheson's Opera, Cleopatra, in Das Erbe deutscher Musik, vol. 69, 1975, The Ariadne auf Naxos by Hofmannsthal and Strauss, 1975, Man and Music: The Late Baroque, vol. 4, 1993; Am. editor: ACTA Musicologica, 1967-86; editor: Coll. Music Soc.'s Symposium, 1970-71; mem. exec. com. The New Grove Dictionary of Music and Musicians, 1971-80; editor: UMI Research Press Studies in Musicology, 1977-89; mem. nat. adv. bd. Die Musik in Geschichte und Gegenwart, 1990-98; contbr. articles profl. jours; co-editor: New Mattheson Studies, 1983, Musicology and Performance Paul Henry Lang, 1997. Mem. German nat. screening com. Fulbright-Hays Program, 1993—. Guggenheim fellow, 1967, Rutgers Rsch. Coun. fellow, 1974-75; Fulbright scholar Germany, 1954-55; Festa musicologica: Essays in Honor of George J. Buelow, 1995. Mem. Am. Musicol. Soc., Internt. Musicol. Socs. (mem. direktorium 1987-97), Royal Mus. Assn., Gesellschaft fur Musikforschung, Am. Bach Soc. (pres. bd. dirs. 1987—), Am. Handel Soc. (v.p., bd. dirs. 1989-94). Home: 2935 N Bankers Dr Bloomington IN 47408-1021

BUENAFLOR, JUDITH LURAY, secondary education educator; b. Phila., Mar. 11, 1949; d. James and Dorothy Tawney (Riley) Arnao; m. Michael Vincent Buenaflor, July 7, 1973 (dec. 1996); children: Amy, Katherine, Ryan. BA, Rosemont Coll., 1971; MA in English, Kutztown U., 1998. Tchr. Ctrl. Cath. High Sch., Allentown, Pa., 1991-97; advisor Odyssey of the Mind, Allentown, 1989-91, Nat. Honor Soc., 1991-97; part-time prof. Allentown Coll. Mem. tower ball com. Sacred Heart Hosp., Allentown, Pa., 1987-89; pres. women's guild, St. Thomas More, Allentown, 1986; mem. bd. assocs. Sacred Heart Hosp. Mem. Nat. Assn. Tchrs. English, Women's Guild, Alpha Epsilon Lambda (hon.). Roman Catholic. Avocation: writing, historical fiction. Home: 1128 Valley View Dr Allentown PA 18103-6042

BUENAVENTURA, MILAGROS PAEZ, psychiatrist; b. Munoz, Nueva Ecija, Philippines, Oct. 28, 1943; came to U.S., 1974; s. Lupo P. and Pilar (Paez) B.; children: Robert, Melani. AA, U. Santo Tomas, Manila, 1962, MD, 1967. Clinic physician Dr. Jose R. Reyes Meml. Hosp., Manila, 1968-71, resident in neurology and psychiatry, 1971-74; resident dept. psychiatry Milton S. Hershey Med. Ctr., Hershey, Pa., 1975-78; staff psychiat. Holy Spirit Hosp., Camp Hill, Pa., 1978-82, Harrisburg (Pa.) State Hosp., 1982—; cons. Psychiatric Ctr., 1994—, Harrisburg, 1984—; mem. courtesy staff Harrisburg Hosp., 1987; med. dir. Helen Stevens Ctr., Carlisle, Pa. Mem. Am. Psychiat. Assn., Pa. Med. Soc., Pa. Psychiat. Soc., Cen. Pa. Psychiat. Soc. Republican. Roman Catholic. Avocations: reading, traveling, swimming.

BUENAVISTA, JOSEPH CONSTANTE, sales manager; b. Sanford, Fla., Mar. 7, 1964; s. Crisostomo Lardizibal and Agnes May (Sears) B.; m. Paula Rachelle Giannini, Apr. 28, 1995; 1 child, Gianna Anastasia Maria. BS in English, U.S. Naval Acad., 1987. Commd. ensign USN, 1982, advanced through grades to lt.; navigation divsn. officer USS Constellation, USN, San Diego, 1987-89, asst. 1st lt. USS Constellation,, 1989-90, staff pub. affairs asst., 1990-92; bus. owner, actor San Diego, 1992-93; ter. mgr. Gillette, San Diego, 1993-95; Midwest regional sales trainer Gillette, Chgo., 1995-96, Midwest retail area mgr., 1996-97; No. Calif. area mgr. Gillette, San Francisco, 1997—. Mem. NCGA Golf Assn., U.S. Naval Acad. Alumni. Republican. Roman Catholic. Avocations: writing/poetry, rugby, golf, sports memorabilia collecting. E-mail: joeübuenavista@Gillette.com. FAX: 925-443-9304. Office: Gillette Duracell Ste 570 19900 MacArthur Blvd Irvine CA 92715

BUENDIA, IMELDA BERNARDO, clinical director, physician; b. Iloilo City, The Philippines, Nov. 12, 1944; d. Carlos P. and Coleta (De la Cruz) Bernardo; m. Arsenio G. Buendia, June 5, 1971; children: Mary Elaine, Joseph Carlo, Adrian Cesar. BS, U. The Philippines, 1964, MD, 1969. Resident in pediats. Philippine Gen. Hosp., Manila, 1969-71; resident in family practice St. Michael's Hosp., Milw., 1971-75; med. officer Talihina (Okla.) Hosp., 1975-78; med. officer Wewoka (Okla.) Indian Clinic, 1978-92, clin. dir., 1992-96; med. officer El Reno Indian Clinic, 1996—, clin. dir., 1997—. Active Phil-Am. Civic Orgn., Oklahoma City, 1978—. Recipient Dir. Excellence award USPHS, 1993. Fellow Am. Acad. Family Physicians; mem. Philippine Med. Assn. Okla. (treas. 1989, sec. 1990, pres.-elect 1994, pres. 1995). Home: 2105 Wyckham Pl Norman OK 73072-3042 Office: 1621A E Highway 66 El Reno OK 73036-5769

BUENO, ANA, healthcare marketing and public relations executive, writer; b. N.Y.C., N.Y., Apr. 27, 1952; m. David M. Kreitzer, June, 1973 (div. Feb. 1979); 1 child, Anatol C. Kreitzer. Sr. writer healthcare Integral Sys., Inc., Walnut Creek, Calif., 1986-88; freelance writer L.A., 1989-92; cons. mktg. Health Net, L.A., 1992-96; pres. Bueno Healthcare Mktg., L.A., 1996-98; dir. mktg. and creative svcs. City of Hope Cancer Ctr., L.A., 1999—. Author: Special Olympics: The First 25 Years, 1994; contbr. articles to profl. jours. Sponsor, vol. Spl. Olympics, Calif., 1988-96. Recipient Disting. Vol. Svc. award Spl. Olympics, 1992. Mem. AAUW, Jewish Bus. and Profl. Women, The Jewish Fedn. Jewish. Avocation: art collector.

BUERGENTHAL, THOMAS, lawyer, educator, international judge; b. Lubochna, Czechoslovakia, May 11, 1934; came to U.S., 1951, naturalized, 1957; s. Mundek and Gerda (Silbergleit) B.; children: Robert, John, Alan; m. Marjorie J. Bell, 1983; stepchildren: Sebastian, Cristina. B.A., Bethany Coll., 1957, LL.D., 1981; J.D., N.Y. U., 1960; LL.M., Harvard U., 1961, S.J.D., 1968; Dr. Jur. (hon.), U. Heidelberg, 1986; Dr.Jur. (hon.), Free U. of Brussels, 1994. Bar: N.Y. State 1961, D.C. 1983, U.S. Supreme Ct. 1982. Instr. law U. Pa., 1961-62; asst. prof. SUNY, Buffalo, 1962-64; assoc. prof. SUNY, 1964-67, prof., 1967-75; vis. prof. U. Tex.-Austin, 1975-76, prof., 1976-77, Fulbright and Jaworski prof., 1977-80; judge Inter-Am. Ct. Human Rights, 1979-91, pres., 1985-87; dean, prof. law Am. U., Washington, 1980-85; disting. prof. law and human rights Emory U. Sch. Law, 1985-86, I.T. Cohen prof. of human rights, 1987-89; Lobinger prof. of comparative law and jurisprudence George Washington U., Washington, 1989—; judge Adminstrv. Tribunal, Inter-Am. Devel. Bank, 1989-94, pres., 1993-94; mem. UN Human Rights Com., 1995—; mem. Claims Resolution Tribunal for Dormant Accts. in Switzerland, 1998—, vice-chmn., 1999—; mem. adv. com. Restatement (3d) of the Fgn. Rels. Law of U.S.; chmn. human rights com. U.S. Nat. Commn. for UNESCO, 1976-79; U.S. rep. UNESCO Human Rights Working Group, 1977-78; U.S. expert UN Interregional Expert Meeting on Crime Prevention and Control, 1978; mem. adv. bd. Pres. Holocaust Commn., 1978-80; v.p. UNESCO Congress on Tchg. of Human Rights, 1978; mem. UN Truth Commn. for El Salvador, 1992-93; mem. U.S. Holocaust Meml. Coun., 1996—, chmn. com. on conscience, 1997—. Author: Law-Making in the International Civil Aviation Organization, 1969, (with L.B. Sohn) International Protection of Human Rights, 1973, (with J.V. Torney) International Law and the Helsinki Accord, 1977, (with R.E. Norris) Human Rights: The Inter-Am. System, 1982, (with Norris and Shelton) Protecting Human Rights in the Americas, 1982, 4th edit., 1995, (with H. Maier) Public International Law in a Nutshell, 1985, 2d edit., 1990, International Human Rights in a Nutshell, 1988, 2d edit., 1995, (with Grossman and Nikken) Manual Internacional de Derechos Humanos, 1990, (with Kiss) La Protection Internationale des Droits de l'Homme, 1991; contbr. articles to profl. jours. Recipient Pro-Humanitas Ring, West-Ost Kulturwerk, Fed. Republic of Germany, 1978, Disting. Svc. in Legal Edn. award NYU Law Sch. Assn., 1987, Wolfgang Friedmann Meml. award Columbia U. Law Sch., 1989. Mem. Am. Law Inst., Am. Soc. Internat. Law (v.p. 1980-82, Goler T.

Butcher medal for excellence in internat. human rights 1997), Coun. Fgn. Affairs, Inter-Am. Inst. Human Rights (pres. 1980-92, hon. pres. 1992—). Office: George Washington U Nat Law Ctr 720 20th St NW Washington DC 20006-4306

BUERKLE, JACK VINCENT, sociologist, educator; b. West Frankfort, Ill., Aug. 9, 1923; s. Henry Adam and Clemence (Henderson) B.; m. Martha Louise Edwards; children: Stephen Vincent, Melanie Lake. B.A., U. Ill., 1948, M.A., 1949; Ph.D., U. Ia., 1954. Asst. prof. Lake Forest Coll., 1954-55; asst. prof. Yale, 1955-60; mem. faculty Temple U., 1960—, prof. sociology, 1963—, chmn. dept., 1963-71; sr. v.p. The French Riviera, Inc., Phila., 1994—; vis. prof. Der Wirtschaftshochschule, Mannheim, West Germany, 1966-67; host Jazz Encounters, Sta. WRTI, Phila., 1987—, Jazz Encounters Today, 1992—. Author: Bourbon Street Black, 1973; assoc. editor: Jour. Marriage and the Family, 1982—; Contbr. articles to profl. publs. Served with AUS, 1943-46. Mem. Am. Sociol. Assn., Am. Psychol. Assn., Eastern Sociol. Soc., Institut International de Sociologie, Sigma Xi. Presbyn. (ruling elder). Club: Corinthian Yacht of Cape May (N.J.) (commodore). Home: 526 Revere Rd Merion Station PA 19066-1033 Office: Temple Univ Dept Sociology Philadelphia PA 19122

BUESCHEL, DAVID ALAN, management consultant; b. Chgo., May 6, 1942; s. Clifford James and Dorothy Jane (Snyder) B.; m. Elizabeth Thorne Conklin, June 20, 1965; children: Andrea Conklin, Lydia Anne, Cynthia Jane. BSME, Cornell U., 1965; MBA, Stanford U., 1967. Mgmt. cons. McKinsey & Co., Inc., Chgo., 1967-75; dir. strategic planning Norlin Music Inc., 1975-76, v.p. bus. devel., 1976-77; pres. MI Fin. Co., Norlin Corp., Chgo., 1977-78; v.p., gen. mgr. Band & Orch. Group, Norlin Corp., Chgo., 1978-79; pres. Moog div. Norlin Corp., Cheektowaga, N.Y., 1979-80; v.p., gen. mgr. Austin Cons., Evanston, Ill., 1981-83; v.p. Lamalie Assocs., Inc., Chgo., 1983-86; pres. Sweeney Shepherd Bueschel Provus Harbert & Mummert, Inc., Chgo., 1986-87; prin. Sweeney Shepherd Bueschel Provus Harbert & Mummert, Inc., 1987-91; pres. Shepherd Bueschel & Provus, Inc., Chgo., 1992—; bd. dirs. Lange Med. Products; pres. Pack It In, Ltd. Cos., 1993-97. Vice chmn., chmn. devel. com., mem. bd. affairs com., trustee Chgo. Theol. Sem., 1987—; bd. dirs., mem. exec. com., chmn. nominating com. and pers. com. Cmty. Renewal Soc., Chgo., 1987-92; rep. Stanford Keystone Fund, Chgo., 1987-89; amb. Cornell U. Alumni, 1988—; mem. nominating com. Ill. Conf. United Ch. of Christ, 1992-95. Mem. Assn. Exec. Search Cons. (bd. dirs. 1994—, govt. affairs com. 1992-95, chmn. membership com. 1995-96, dir. regional affairs, chmn. ann. conf. commn. 1996, bd. vice chmn. 1999—), Stanford U. Bus. Sch. Alumni Assn. (v.p., bd. dirs. Chgo. 1988-91), Econ. Club, Univ. Club. Democrat. Avocations: skiing, sailing, golf. Home: 508 Cherry St Winnetka IL 60093-2613 Office: Shepherd Bueschel & Provus Inc 401 N Michigan Ave Chicago IL 60611-4255

BUESCHEN, ANTON JOSLYN, physician, educator; b. Toledo, June 7, 1940; s. Robert F. and Mary J. (Joslyn) B.; m. Norma Jean McClanahan, Sept. 5, 1964; children—Anton, Elaine. Student, Va. Mil. Inst., 1958-61; M.D., U. Va., 1965. Diplomate: Am. Bd. Urology. Intern in surgery Vanderbilt U., 1965-66, asst. resident in surgery, 1966-67; resident in urology Ind. U., Indpls., 1969-72; practice medicine specializing in urology Birmingham, Ala., 1973—; instr. urology Tulane U. Sch. Medicine, 1972-73; asst. prof. div. urology dept. surgery U. Ala., Birmingham, 1973-75, assoc. prof., 1975-79, prof., 1979—, dir. div. urology, 1975-95, 99—; chief urology sect. Children's Hosp., Birmingham, 1978-86. Contbr. numerous articles on urology to profl. jours. Served with M.C. U.S. Army, 1967-69. Mem. ACS, AMA (Billings Gold medal 1978), AAUP, Am. Urol. Assn. Southeastern Sect. (sec. 1997—), Am. Assn. Clin. Urologists, Soc. Univ. Urologists, Birmingham Urology Club, Jefferson County Med. Soc., Soc. for Pediatric Urology, Soc. Urologic Oncology, So. Med. Assn. (chmn. urology sect. 1987), Soc. Nuc. Medicine, Med. Assn. Ala. Office: U Ala Div Urology University Sta Birmingham AL 35294

BUESCHER, ADOLPH ERNST (DOLPH BUESCHER), aerospace company executive; b. St. Louis, Mo., Oct. 6, 1922; s. Adolph E. Sr. and Eugenie K. (Stroh) B.; m. Ruth L. Fleming, Aug. 21, 1948; children: Timothy Wayne, Philip Clay. BS in Mech. Engring., U. Mo., 1946; MS in Mech. Engring., Stanford U., 1950; postgrad., UCLA, 1950-52, Harvard U., 1958. Registered profl. engr., N.Y., Calif., Mo. Devel. engr. Eastman Kodak Co., Rochester, N.Y., 1946-49; supr. flight test, rsch. engr. Northrop Aircraft Inc., Hawthorne, Calif., 1952-53; mgr. controls and instruments Sverdrup & Parcel, Inc., St. Louis, 1953-56; program mgr. ATLAS, ICBM GE, Valley Forge, Pa., 1956-59, various positions, mktg. mgr., engring. mgr., gen. mgr., 1959-63; mgr. strategic planning, chief staff GE Aerospace Group, Valley Forge, 1963-88; lectr. Franklin Inst., 1965-68. Author: Loran-C, 1990, Radar, 1991; GPS, 1994. V.p. Citizens Coun., Greater Phila., 1958-60; chmn. Planning Commn., Whitemarsh Twp., 1959-68; chmn. Zoning Hearing Bd., Whitemarsh Twp., 1968-74. With USAF/AUS, 1942-45, ETO. Recipient Fellowship Std. Oil of Calif., 1950. Fellow ASME, AIAA (assoc.), The Explorer's Club, Am. Rocket Soc. (chpt. pres. 1942), Inst. Aero. Sci. (assoc.); mem. NSPE, Air Force Assn., U.S. Power Squadron (dist. edn. officer, nat. staff comdr. 1995-96, nat. rear comdr. 1997-98), Am. Def. Preparedness Assn. (bd. dirs. 1964-85), Greater Phila. C. of C. (mem. aviation com. 1963-73, Engr. of Yr. 1966), Sassafras River Yacht Club (commodore 1981), Chesapeake Bay Yacht Clubs Assn. (bd. govs. 1990, vice commodore 1991, commodore 1992), Pi Tau Sigma, Tau Beta Pi. Republican. Lutheran. Achievements include patent for automatic celestial navigation, others in field of aircraft/spacecraft instrumentation; first use of automatic control theory applied to hypersonic fluid flow, and incompressible liquid flow, early, high altitude test flights, in unpressured aircraft. Home: 14 Papermill St Easton MD 21601-2520*

BUESCHER, THOMAS PAUL, labor market analyst; b. Cleve., May 16, 1949; s. Victor Paul and Geraldine Juel (Durkin) B.; m. Pamela Ann Piscitota, Jan. 29, 1977; 1 child, Brittany Beth. BBA, Kent State U., 1975. Guest instr. for exec. MBA program Cleve. State U.; trustee IAPES Found. Corp. Author: (analysis report for nat. league of cities) Demographic Analysis of the Targeted Job Tax Credit program for Cleve., 1985. Mem. allocations panel Fedn. of Cath. Cmty. Svcs., 1987-92; mem. Local Welfare Reform Panel for Congress, 1987, Cleve. area Gov.'s Regional Econ. Adv. Bd., 1992—, Cleve. Area Devel. Corp. Bd., 1994—; mem. consortium to develop a nat. inst. Labor Market Info.; chmn. Initiative V task force, mem. adv. com. Cleve. Pub. Schs., 1988-93; mem. Am.'s Labor Market Info. Sys. Tng. Inst. Consortium. Mem. Internat. Assn. Pers. in Employment Security (Ohio pres. 1988, internat. v.p. 1993-94, award of merit 1989, inducted into Hall of Fame 1990, internat. pres.-elect 1994-95, internat. pres. 1995—), Am. Labor Market Info. Sys. Tng. Inst. Consortium, I.A.P.E.S. (mem. profl. devel. program revision team). Democrat. Avocations: volleyball, softball, golf, tennis. Home: 464 Calverton Pl Brunswick OH 44212-1820 Office: Ohio Bur Employment Svc 5739 Chevrolet Blvd Cleveland OH 44130-1414

BUESSELER, JOHN AURE, ophthalmologist, management consultant; b. Madison, Wis., Sept. 30, 1919; s. John Xavier and Gerda Pernille (Aure) B.; m. Cathryn Anne Hansen, Dec. 26, 1959; 1 child, John McGlone. PhB, U. Wis., 1941, MD, 1944; MBA, U. Mo., 1965. Intern Cleve. City Hosp., 1944-45; resident U. Pa. Hosp., 1948-51; practice medicine specializing in ophthalmology Madison, 1953-59; prof., founding chief ophthalmology U. Mo., Columbia, 1959-66; exec. officer Mo. Crippled Children's Service, 1967-70; exec. dir. Kansas City Gen. Hosp. and Med. Ctr., 1969-70; founding dean Tex. Tech U. Sch. Medicine, Lubbock, 1970-73, v.p. health affairs Univ. Complex, 1970-75, prof. dept. ophthalmology, prof. health orgn. mgmt., 1971-98, chmn. dept. health orgn. mgmt., 1972-75, prof. grad. sch. faculty, 1972-80, chmn. dept. ophthalmology, 1973-75; adj. prof. bus. adminstrn. Coll. Bus. Tex. Tech., Lubbock, 1992-98; Univ. prof. (disting. and multidisciplinary) Univ. Complex, 1973-98; founding v.p. health scis., founding CEO Tex. Tech. Univ. Health Scis. Ctr., 1972-74; pres. Radiol. Testing Lab., Inc., Madison, 1956-59; dir. House of Vision, Inc., Chgo., 1973-82; v.p. Madison Radiation Ctr., Inc., 1956-59; cons. NASA, mem. space medicine adv. group on devel. Orbiting Space Lab., Washington, 1963-66; cons. AEC, mem. Assn. Midwestern Univs.-Argonne (Ill.) Nat. Lab. biology com., 1965-69; cons. to pres. Agronne Univs. Assn., Chgo., 1967-68; comdr. 94th Gen. Hosp., U.S. Army Res., Mesquite, Tex., 1973-75; co-founder, incorporator, bd. dirs., past pres. Joint Commn. on Allied Health Pers. in Ophthalmology, Inc.; mem. Residency Rev. Com. for Ophthalmology, 1974-80, chmn., 1978-80; sr. cons., CEO, founder Health Orgn. Mgmt. Sys. Internat., 1978—; co-founder, chmn. bd. dirs. Tex. Aviation Heritage Found., Inc., 1997—; co-founder, chmn. com. on regional bus., econ. and environ. devel. Lubbock Econs. Coun., 1996-99. Contbr. articles to profl. jours. Served to capt. AUS, World War II, ETO; to maj. USAF, Korea; to col. USAR, Vietnam. Decorated Air medal with cluster, Legion of Merit, Combat Medic badge, Sr. Flight Surgeon badge, Parachutist badge Spl. Forces; recipient Gold Medallion award for disting. achievement in ophthalmology Mo. Ophthal. Soc., 1967, Tex. Tech. U. Bd. Regents Resolution of Congratulations, 1973, Cert. of Citation Tex. Ho. of Reps., 1973, 87, Disting. Alumnus citation U. Wis. Sch. Medicine, 1987. Fellow ACS, Am. Acad. Oththalmology (Disting. Svc. in Edn. award 1969); mem. AMA, Tex. Med. Assn., Mo. Ophthal. Soc. (founder, past sec.-treas., pres., dir.), Alpha Omega Alpha. Home: 3305 59th St Lubbock TX 79413-5517

BUESSER, ANTHONY CARPENTER, lawyer; b. Detroit, Oct. 15, 1929; s. Frederick Gustavis and Lela (Carpenter) B.; m. Carolyn Sue Pickle, Mar. 13, 1954; children: Kent Anderson, Anthony Carpenter, Andrew Clayton; m. Bettina Rieveschl, Dec. 14, 1973. B.A. in English with honors, U. Mich., 1952, M.A., 1953, J.D., 1960. Bar: Mich. 1961. Assoc. Chase, Goodenough & Buesser, Detroit, 1961-66; ptnr. Buesser, Buesser, Snyder & Blank, Detroit and Bloomfield Hills, Mich., 1966-81; sole practice Birmingham, Mich., 1981—. Trustee Detroit Country Day Sch., Beverly Hills, Mich., 1970-94, chmn. bd., 1977-82, 84-87, bd. chmn. emeritus, 1987—, chmn. nominating com., 1987-94. Served with AUS, 1953-55. Recipient Avery Hopwood award major fiction U. Mich., 1953, Outstanding Alumnus award Detroit Country Day Sch., 1988. Mem. ABA, State Bar Mich., Detroit Bar Assn. (pres. 1976-77), Oakland County Bar Assn., Am. Judicature Soc., Thomas M. Cooley Club (pres. 1974-76), Alpha Delta Phi, Phi Delta Phi. Office: 725 S Adams Rd Ste L17 Birmingham MI 48009-6916

BUETOW, DENNIS EDWARD, physiology educator; b. Chgo., June 20, 1932; s. Earl Frank and Helen Anna (Roeske) B.; m. Mary Kathleen Carney, Oct. 29, 1960; children—Katherine, Thomas (dec.), Michael, Ellen. B.A., UCLA, 1954, M.S., 1957, Ph.D., 1959. Biologist NIH, Bethesda, Md., 1959-65; biochemist Balt. City Hosps., 1959-65; asso. prof. physiology U. Ill., Urbana, 1965-70, prof., 1970—, head dept. physiology and biophysics, 1983-88; cons. in field. Contbr. articles to profl. jours. Grantee NIH, NSF, Life Ins. Med. Research Fund, Am. Heart Assn. Fellow Gerontological Soc., AAAS; mem. Am. Soc. Cell Biology, Am. Physiol. Soc., Am. Inst. Biol. Sci., Soc. Protozoologists, Am. Fedn. Aging Research, N.Y. Acad. Sci., Am. Soc. Plant Physiology. Home: 2 Eton Ct Champaign IL 61820-7602 Office: Univ Ill 524 Burrill Hall Urbana IL 61801

BUETTNER, ANNE RAMONA WING-MUI YU, psychologist; b. Apr. 9, 1948; came to U.S., 1968; d. Hing-wan and Sin-wah (Yau) Yu; m. Dennis Vanosdall, Apr. 8, 1989 (div. 1990); m. Patrick E. Buettner, Dec. 1992; 1 child, James. BA in Psychology with honors, Ohio U., 1971; MA, So. Ill. U., 1975. Psychol. examiner Delta Counseling and Guidance Ctr., Monticello, Ark., 1975-76; psychologist Mid-Nebr. Cmty. Mental Health Ctr., Grand Island, 1977—; supr. satellite clinic Loup Valley Mental Health Ctr., Loup City, Nebr., 1978-79; project dir. Protection from Domestic Abuse, 1978-79; pres. Taskforce on Domestic Violence and Sexual Assault, Grand Island, 1980-82; vice chair adv. coun. Nebr. Office of Dispute Resolution, 1999; bd. dirs. Ctrl. Mediation Ctr. of Ctrl. Nebr., 1996, chmn., 1997-98. Mem. Mental Health Bd. Hall County, 1979; mem. fellows Menninger found., 1983-84; commr. Nebr. Commn. on Status of Women, 1990-95, vice chair, 1990-91, sec., 1991-92; bd. dirs. YWCA, 1984-89; bd. examiners Mental Health Practice Nebr., 1992—, sec., 1994-99; mem. adv. coun. Office of Dispute Resolution, Nebr., 1997—, sice-chmn., 1998-99, bd. dirs. 1996—. Ohio U. Psi Chi scholar, 1968-71;. Mem. AAUW (pres. Grand Island chpt. 1984-86, v.p. Nebr. divsn. 1986-90), Nebr. Assn. for Marriage and Family Therapy (v.p. 1981-84, pres. 1985-87, 98, 99, legis. chmn. 1988—), Am. Assn. Sex Educators, Counselors and Therapists, Northam Assn. Masters in Psychology (pres. Nebr. chpt. 1995—), Grand Island Assn. for Child Abuse Prevention (bd. dirs. 1993—, v.p. 1988-90, pres. 1994-95), Internat. Platform Assn., Asian-Am. Psychol. Assn., Assn. Marital and Family Regulatory Bds. (del. Nebr. 1994—, treas. 1997—). Home: 714 S Broadwell Ave Grand Island NE 68803-6243 Office: Mid-Plains Ctr 914 Baumann Dr Grand Island NE 68803-4401

BUFF, MARGARET ANNE, psychiatric nurse; b. Hanover, N.H., Nov. 2, 1955; d. Kenneth Andrew and M. Irene (Pender) Le Clair; m. James Steve Buff, Jan. 2, 1982; children: Jennifer, Steven, J. Thomas. BSN, BA in Psychology, RN, U. N.H., 1979; MA in Counselor Edn., U. N.Mex., 1985; MSN in Psychiatric and Mental Health, Rivier Coll., 1997. RN, N.H. Staff nurse Vista Sandia Hosp., Albuquerque, 1980-81; charge nurse Los Lunas (N.Mex.) Hosp. and Tng. Sch., 1981-82; child devel. specialist Pueblo Infant Parent Edn. Project, Bernalillo, N.Mex., 1985-86; nurse, therapist Heights Psychiat. Hosp., Albuquerque, 1986-87; charge nurse Meml. Hosp., Albuquerque, 1987-88; staff nurse So. N.H. Regional Med. Ctr., Nashua, N.H., 1990-98, Greater Lawrence (Mass.) Mental Health Ctr., 1998—. Roman Catholic. Avocations: swimming, tennis. Home: 28 Hillside Dr Brookline NH 03033-2123

BUFFETT, WARREN EDWARD, entrepreneur; b. Omaha, Aug. 30, 1930; s. Howard Homan and Leila (Stahl) B.; m. Susan Thompson, Apr. 19, 1952; children: Susan, Howard, Peter. Student, U. Pa., 1947-49; B.S., U. Nebr., 1950; M.S., Columbia, 1951. Investment salesman Buffett-Falk & Co., Omaha, 1951-54; security analyst Graham-Newman Corp., N.Y.C., 1954-56; gen. partner Buffett Partnership, Ltd., Omaha, 1956-69; now chmn. Berkshire Hathaway Inc., Omaha, 1970—; chmn. bd. Berkshire Hathaway, Inc., Nat. Indemnity Co., Nat. Fire & Marine Ins. Co., See's Candy Shops, Inc., Columbia Ins. Co., Buffalo Evening News; bd. dirs. Capital Cities/ABC, Salomon, Inc., Coca-Cola Co., Gillette Co., Fechheimer Bros. Co., Associated Retail Stores, Scott and Fetzer Co., Home & Auto Ins. Co., Omaha World Herald, Precision Steel Warehouse, Inc. Life trustee Grinnell Coll., 1968—, Urban Inst. Office: Berkshire Hathaway Inc 1440 Kiewit Plz Omaha NE 68131*

BUFFINGTON, JOHN DOUGLAS, ecologist, researcher; b. Jersey City, Nov. 26, 1941; s. John Franklin and Rosemary Eileen (Snowdy) B.; m. Mary Elizabeth Coughlin, Jan. 23, 1965; children: Jill Anne, John Matthew. BS cum laude, St. Peter's Coll., Jersey City, 1963; MS, U. Ill., 1965, PhD, 1967. Asst. prof. Ill. State U., Normal, 1969-72; scientist, asst. divsn. dir. Argonne (Ill.) Nat. Lab., 1972-77; sr. staff scientist Pres.'s Coun. Environ. Quality, Washington, 1977-80; chief office biol. svcs. U.S. Fish & Wildlife Svc., Washington, 1980-83, dep. reg. dir., 1983-89, regional dir., 1989-93; acting regional dir. Nat. Biol. Survey, Washington, 1993-95; dir. Alaska Sci. Ctr., 1995-97; regional chief biologist U.S. Geol. Survey, Seattle, 1997—; mem. U.S. negotiating delegation Conv. Biol. Diversity, 1990-93. Capt. U.S. Army, 1967-69. Recipient Meritorious Svc. award U.S. Dept. Interior, 1994. Mem. Ecol. Soc. Am. (applied sect. chmn. 1981, Washington chpt. chmn. 1981). Office: US Geol Survey 900 1st Ave Ste 800 Seattle WA 98104

BUFFINGTON, LINDA BRICE, interior designer; b. Long Beach, Calif., June 21, 1936; d. Harry Bryce and Marguerite Leonora (Tucciarone) Van Bellehem; student El Camino Jr. Coll., 1955-58, U. Calif., Irvine, 1973-75; children: Lisa Ann, Phillip Lynn. Cert. interior designer and gen. contractor, Calif.; lic. gen. contractor, Calif. With Pub. Fin., Torrance, Calif., 1954-55, Beneficial Fin., Torrance and Hollywood, Calif., 1955-61; interior designer Vee Nisley Interiors, Newport Beach, Calif., 1964-65, Leon's Interiors, Newport Beach, 1965-69; ptnr. Marlind Interiors, Tustin, Calif., 1969-70; owner, designer Linda Buffington Interiors, Villa Park, Calif., 1970—, LBI, Contractors License, 1993—, cert. interior designer, Calif.; cons. builders, housing developments. Mem. Bldg. Industry Assn. (past pres. Orange County chpt. 1989, 90), Internat. Soc. Interior Designers, Nat. Assn. Home Builders. Republican. Office: 17853 Santiago Blvd Ste 107 Villa Park CA 92861-4113

BUFFKINS, ARCHIE LEE, public television executive; b. Memphis, Mar. 30, 1934; s. John and Ada (Stittians) B.; div.; 1 child, LeRachel Harombe. BS, Jackson State U., 1956; MA, Columbia, 1961, EdD, 1963; postgrad. research, Harvard U., summer 1972; postgrad. study, July 1994; postgrad. research, Oxford U., summer 1972, U. Amsterdam, summer 1972, Tel-Aviv U., 1973-74, U. Maine, 1970-71, Chgo. Conservatory, summer 1956. Instr. div. band music Ft. Ord (Calif.) Mil. Band Sch., 1957-58; instr., chmn. div. humanities Morristown (Tenn.) Coll., 1958-59; asst. prof., dir. freshman studies, div. fine arts Jackson (Miss.) State U., 1960-61; assoc. prof., head dept. music Ky. State U., Frankfort, 1963-66; prof., dir. grad. research in music, dept. music and fine arts Tex. So. U., Houston, 1966-68; prof., chmn. dept. music R.I. Coll., Providence, 1968-70; exec. asst. to chancellor U. Maine Eight-Campus System, Portland, 1970-71; chancellor U. Md., Eastern Shore, Princess Anne, 1971-75; asst. dean grad. studies U. Md. (College Park Campus), 1975-79; pres. Nat. Commn. on Cultural Diversity, Kennedy Center, 1979-85, dir. Office Cultural Diversity, 1985-93; cons. prodr. Kennedy Ctr., 1992-93; sr. v.p. broadcasting Md. Pub. TV, Owings Mills, 1993—, interim pres., CEO, 1995-97, sr. v.p. strategic devel., rsch., 1997—; commr. higher edn. Afro-Am. Edn. Assn. in R.I., 1968-71; dir. Conf. on Black Students and Higher Edn. in R.I., R.I. Coll., 1969, Conf. on Higher Edn. and Urban Setting, Boston, 1969, Md. Pub. Broadcasting Commn., 1986-93; coordinator Conf. on Afro-Am. Studies and High Sch. Curriculum, U. Maine, 1971; chmn. Nat. Black Think Tank, 1976; pres. John F. Kennedy Center Nat. Commn. on Blacks in the Arts; Chief adminstr. Free Urban Edn. Center, Houston, 1966-68; dir. Acad. Tutorial Inst. in Black Community of Houston, 1966-68, Black Fine Arts Festival, 1966; exec. dir. Eastern div. Council on Afro-Am. Studies, Boston, 1968-71; chmn. exptl. curriculum com. Gov.'s Sch. for Gifted in Arts, Providence, 1968, bd. dirs., 1969-70; chmn. ednl. policy com., bd. dirs. Nat. Sch. Vol. Program, Inc., N.Y.C., 1968-70; chmn. edn. task force (Portland Model Cities Project), 1970-71; founder, dir. Center for Exptl. Studies in Higher Edn. Adminstrn., Portland, 1970-71; sr. adviser Nat. Accrediting Assn. for Afro-Am. Programs, N.Y.C., 1968-71; mem. U.S. Nat. Adv. Council on Adult Edn., 1974-79; chmn. Nat. Task Force on Adult Edn. and Urban Policy, 1977, Nat. Black Music Colloquium and Competition, 1978, Md. Black Congress on Higher Edn.; coordinator Black Higher Edn. Caucus of U. Md. System; chmn. Nat. Task Force on Urban Policy and Adult Edn.; chmn. exec. council Regional Research and Clearinghouse Network on Minorities and Grad. Edn.; chmn. Inter-Instnl. Task Force on Pluralism, 1990-95; mem. Gov. Info. Tech. Bd., Md., 1995—; appt. by Md. Gov. to Md. Commn. for Celebration 2000, 1997. Producer: Tribute to Historically Black Colls. and Univs, 1980, White House/Kennedy Center Jazz Salute to Lionel Hampton, White House Phase I, Kennedy Center Concert Hall Phase II, 1981; appeared with, Monterey Symphony Orch., Bach Festival Orch., Columbia U. Orch., Riverside Symphony Orch., Waukegan Community Orch., Tchrs. Coll. Concert Wind Ensemble, Ft. Ord Symphonic Concert Band, San Jose Woodwind Ensemble, Memphis String and Woodwind Chamber Ensemble.; co-producer: television series Tell It Like It Is, Community Service Television Project, Houston, 1967; Author: An Intellectual Approach to Musical Understanding, 1965, Philosophical Thoughts of a University Scholar, 1973, Arts Advocacy: The Economic Impact of the Arts in an Age of Austerity, Parts I and II; mem. bd. advisers, bd. dirs.: Urban Concerns mag; contbr. articles to profl. jours.; Composer: The Night Is Dark, 1967, Trio in A Minor, 1967, Mass, 1967, Integrity: Tone Poem for String Orchestra, 1968, Symphony For Tomorrow, 1969, Melodies For A Soprano, 1969, String Quartet No. 2, 1972, Sonata For Violin and Piano, 1972, Suite For Violin and Piano, 1972, Sonatina for Violin and Piano (for Sanford Allen), 1980, others. Bd. dirs. Eastern Shore Heart Assn., Salisbury, Md., R.I. Council on Arts, R.I. Philharmonic Orch., Internat. Econ. Devel. Corp., 1969-70, Afro-Art Center, Inc., 1968-70, Maine Savs. Bank, Center for Experiments in Higher Edn., Houston, 1967-70; trustee Peninsula Gen. Hosp., Salisbury, Md., 1970-76, Portland Symphony Orch., 1968-70; mem. exec. bd. Afro-Am. Soc., N.Y.C., 1966-70, New Eng. States Coll. Assn. Music Faculties, Plymouth, N.H., 1968-70, Delmarva council Boy Scouts Am., Wilmington, Del., 1970-76; mem. corp. bd. Edn. Devel. Center, Inc., Newton, Mass., 1970-72, Peoples Savs. Bank & Trust, Providence, 1968-70; mem. exec. bd. Nat. Christian Leadership Conf. for Israel, 1970-75; mem. Nat. Arts Evaluation Panel for Minority Programs, 1970-80; bd. dirs. Afro-Am. Museums Assn., Washington, 1980-95; mem. adv. bd. D.C. Youth Chorale Assn., 1981—, Prince George's Performing Arts, 1987-95; mem. nat. task force on anti-Semitic incidents Anti-Defamation League, N.Y.C., 1980-81; mem. nat. steering com. Martin Luther King Holiday, Washington, 1980-95; mem. planning com. Nat. Black Coll. Day, 1981—; mem. Com. for a Free World, N.Y.C., 1981—, The Jazz Philharmonic Orch., 1987—; mem. exec. com. Coalition for Strategic Stability in Middle East, Washington, 1981—; Am. chmn. FUBA: South African Sch. of the Arts, 1986; bd. trustees Md. Citizens for Arts, 1995; bd. dirs. Gordon Ctr. for Performing Arts at Jewish Cmty. Ctr., 1994—; dist. chmn. Balt. Trailblazers-Boy Scouts Am., 1994—. Served with U.S. Army, 1956-58. Recipient Young Classical Musician award Memphis Music Soc., 1952; Black Intellectual Leadership award Houston, 1967; Disting. Alumni award Jackson State U., 1973; Nat. Cultural Recognition award Tuskegee, Ala., 1981; named to Mid-Eastern Athletic Conf. Hall of Fame Durham, N.C., 1981. Mem. Md. Assn. for Higher Edn. (chmn. panel adminstrv. affairs 1973), Mid. States Assn. Colls. and Secondary Schs. (evaluation bd. 1972-96), Am. Coun. on Edn., Nat. Assn. State Univs. and Land-Grant Colls., NAACP (exec. bd. Prince George's chpt. 1979-86, chmn. edn. com. 1980-86, Md. edn. com. 1985-87).

BUFFLER, PATRICIA ANN, epidemiology educator, retired dean; b. Doylestown, Pa., Aug. 1, 1938; d. Edward M. and Evelyn G. (Axenroth) Happ; m. Richard T. Buffler, Jan. 20, 1962; children: Martyn R., Monique L. BSN, Cath. U. Am., 1960; MPH, U. Calif., Berkeley, 1965, PhD in Epidemiology, 1973. Prof. epidemiology sch. pub. health U. Tex. Health Sci. Ctr., Houston, 1979-91; prof. U. Calif., Berkeley, 1991—, dean sch. pub. health, 1991-98, dean emerita, 1998—; mem. expert adv. panel on occupl. health WHO, 1985—; mem. environment, safety and health adv. com. U.S. DOE, 1992-95; mem. bd. on water sci. and tech. Nat. Rsch. Coun., 1992-94; chair, bd. dirs. Mickey Leland Nat. Urban Air Toxics Rsch. Ctr., 1994-97, Societal Inst. of Math. Scis.; mem. Nat. Commn. on Superfund, Keystone Ctr., 1992-94; mem. adv. panel on mng. nuclear materials from warheads U.S. Congress Office Tech. Assessment, 1992-93; bd. scientific counselors Nat. Inst. for Occupl. Safety and Health, 1991-93; mem. sci. adv. bd. radiation adv. com. subcom. on cancer risks associated with electric and magnetic fields U.S. EPA, 1990-93; mem. sci. adv. bd. USEPA, 1996—; mem. Nat. Adv. Coun. on Environ. Health Scis., 1995-98; mem. NAS, Nat. Coun. Radiation Protection. Contbr. articles to profl. jours. Fellow AAS, Am. Coll. Epidemiology (pres.-elect 1990-91, pres. 1991-92), Inst. Medicine; mem. Soc. for Epidemiological Rsch. (pres.-elect, pres., past pres. 1984-88), Am. Pub. Health Assn. (epidemiology sect. 1964—), Am. Epidemiological Soc., Soc. for Occupl. and Environ. Health, Internat. Epidemiological Assn., Internat. Soc. for Environ. Epidemiology (pres.-elect 1989-91, pres. 1992-94), Internat. Soc. for Exposure Assessment (charter, bd. internat. councillors 1993—), Internat. Commn. on Occupl. Health, Collegium Ramazzini, Soc. of Toxicology. Office: U Calif Sch Pub Health 140 Earl Warren Hall Berkeley CA 94720

BUFFMIRE, DONALD K., internist; b. Grand Rapids, Minn., Aug. 18, 1922; m. Jane Enkema, June 11, 1945; 3 children. BS, BM in Zoology, Northwestern U., 1944, MD, 1948. Diplomate Am. Bd. Internal Medicine. Intern Evanston (Ill.) Hosp., 1947-48; resident in internal medicine Mayo Found., Rochester, Minn., 1948-51, U. Minn., Mpls., 1950; founder, past chmn. Phoenix Med. Assocs., Ltd., 1954—; now ret. Elder Orangewood Presbyn. Ch.; Trustee, past chmn. Blood Sys., Inc., Scottsdale, Ariz.; former mem. coord. devel. adv. bd. U. Ariz. Coll. Medicine; trustee Flinn Found., Phoenix, 1965—, pres. bd. trustees 1982-98, chmn., 1984-98, chmn. emeritus, 1998—. Capt. Med. Corps U.S. Army, 1951-53. Recipient Dr. Joseph E. Ehrlich medal Maricopa County Med. Soc., 1992, Dr. Clarence Salsbury award Maricipa County Med. Soc., 1987, Disting. Svc. to Society award Northwestern U., 1998; Donald K. Buffmire Vis. Lectureship in medicine established at U. Ariz. by Flinn Found., 1998; named as one of 25 leaders who helped shape modern-day Phoenix, Phoenix mag., 1991; inducted into Grand Rapids Sports Hall of Fame, 1990. Fellow ACP (Laureate award 1991), Am. Coll. Chest Physicians, Royal Soc. Medicine; mem. AMA, Am. Soc. Internal Medicine, Ariz. Med. Assn. (Pres.' Disting. Svc. award 1998), Ariz. Heart Assn. (pres. 1958-59). Home: 3311 E Valley Vista Ln Paradise Valley AZ 85253 Office: Phoenix Med Assocs Mayo Health System 3600 N 3rd Ave Phoenix AZ 85013

BUFFORD, SAMUEL LAWRENCE, federal judge; b. Phoenix, Ariz., Nov. 19, 1943; s. John Samuel and Evelyn Amelia (Rude) B.; m. Julia Marie Metzger, May 13, 1978. BA in Philosophy, Wheaton Coll., 1964; PhD, U. Tex., 1969; JD magna cum laude, U. Mich., 1973. Bar: Calif., N.Y., Ohio. Instr. philosophy La. State U., Baton Rouge, 1967-68; asst. prof. Ea. Mich. U., Ypsilanti, 1968-74; asst. prof. law Ohio State U., Columbus, 1975-77;

assoc. Gendel, Raskoff, Shapiro & Quittner, L.A., 1982-85; atty. Paul, Weiss, Rifkind, Wharton & Garrison, N.Y.C., 1974-75, Sullivan Jones & Archer, San Francisco, 1977-79, Musick, Peeler & Garrett, L.A., 1979-81, Rifkind & Sterling, Beverly Hills, Calif., 1981-82, Gendel, Raskoff, Shapiro & Quittner, L.A., 1982-85; U.S. bankruptcy judge Ctrl. Dist. Calif., 1985—; bd. dirs. Fin. Lawyers Conf., L.A., 1987-90, Bankruptcy Forum, L.A., 1986-88; lectr. U.S.-Romanian Jud. Delegation, 1991, Internat. Tng. Ctr. for Bankers, Budapest, 1993, Bankruptcy Technical Legal Assistance Workshop, Romania, 1994, Comml. Law Project for Ukraine, 1995-96, Ea. Europe Enterprise Restructuring and Privitization Project, U.S. AID, 1995-96; cons. Calif. State Bar Bd. Examiners, 1989-90; bd. trustees Endowment for Edn.; bd. dirs. nat. Conf. Bankruptcy Judges, 1994—; mem. San Pedro Enterprise Community, 1997—. Editor-in-chief Am. Bankruptcy Law Jour., 1990-94; contbr. articles to profl. jours.; columnist Norton Bankruptcy Advisor, 1988-90. Younger Humanist fellowship NEH. Mem. ABA, L.A. County Bar Assn. (mem. profl. responsibility and ethics com. 1979—, chair profl. responsibility and ethics com. 1985-86, chair ethics 2000 liaison com. 1997—), Order of Coif. Office: US Bankruptcy Ct 255 E Temple St Ste 1582 Los Angeles CA 90012-3334

BUFITHIS, CYNTHIA BILLINGS, media specialist; b. Waterville, Maine, Jan. 7, 1948; d. Richard Whitten and Norma Julia (Taraldsen) Billings; m. Charles Phillip Bufithis, June 21, 1969; children: Katie, Michael, Marcy. BS, Springfield (Mass.) Coll., 1969; MLS, U. R.I., 1981. Cert. media specialist, Maine. Youth dir. YWCA, Springfield, 1969-70, Seattle, 1971-72; media specialist Frisbee Sch., Kittery, Maine, 1982-85, R.W. Traip Acad., Kittery, Maine, 1985-95, Noble H.S., Berwick, Maine, 1995—; chair tech. com., Noble H.S., 1997—. Mem. Maine Ednl. Media Assn. Mem. United Ch. of Christ. Avocation: gardening. Office: Noble High Sch 46 Cranberry Meadow Rd Berwick ME 03901-2408

BUFORD, BILL, editor, writer; b. Baton Rouge, Oct. 6, 1954; s. William H. Buford and Helen Shiel; m. Alicja Kobiernicka, July 6, 1991 (div. Jan. 1996). BA, U. Calif., Berkeley, 1977; MA, King's Coll., U. Cambridge, Eng., 1979. Editor, chmn. Granta Publs. Ltd., London, 1979-95; literary and fiction editor The New Yorker, 1995—. Author: Among the Thugs, 1991, 92; editor: Best of Granta Travel, 1992, Best of Granta Reportage, 1993, The Granta Book of the Family, 1995. Office: The New Yorker 20 W 43d St 17th Fl New York NY 10036-7400

BUFORD, EVELYN CLAUDENE SHILLING, jewelry specialist, merchandising professional; b. Ft. Worth, Sept. 21, 1940; d. Claude and Winnie Evelyn (Mote) Hodges; student Hill Jr. Coll., 1975-76, Tarrant County (Tex.) Jr. Coll., 1992-93; m. William J. Buford, Mar. 1982; children by previous marriage: Vincent Shilling, Kathryn Lynn Shilling La Chappelle. With Imperial Printing Co., Inc., Ft. Worth, 1964-70, 77-79, gen. sales mgr. comml. divsn., 1982-90, corp. sec., 1977-79; with Tarrant County Hosp. Dist., Ft. Worth, 1973-77, asst. to asst. adminstr., 1981-84; merchandising asst. J.C. Penney Co., 1989—. Mem. Exec. Women Internat. (life) (dir., publs. chmn., v.p. 1984, pres. 1985, chmn. adv. com. 1986, 87, scholarship dir. 1988-93, corp. publ. com. 1988-89, dir. South ctrl. region 1993-94). Republican. Methodist. Home: 1025 Kenneth Ln Burleson TX 76028-2246 Office: JC Penney Co Hurst TX 76053

BUFORD, RONETTA MARIE, music educator; b. Kansas City, Mo., Sept. 17, 1946; d. Joseph Ronald and Violet Katheryne (Jennison) Coursey; 1 child, Frederrick Kenyatta. Bachelor of Music Edn., Lincoln U. of Mo., 1968. Cert. vocal and instrumental music tchr., Mo. Chmn. vocal music M.L. King Jr. High Sch., Kansas City, 1968-71; chmn. music dept. Southeast Jr. High Sch., Kansas City, 1971-75; chmn. fine arts Paseo High Sch., Kansas City, 1975-90; vocal music specialist Met. Advanced Tech. H.S., Kansas City, 1990-98, asst. girls basketball coach, asst. cross country coach, 1992-98; owner Buford's Day Care, 1996-97, Buford's Mini Univ.; summer music specialist Horace Mann Elem. Sch., Kansas City, 1972; mentor Students at Risk, Kansas City, 1988; vis. lectr. Lincoln U., Jefferson City, Mo., 1980, 85, 87, NE Mo. State U., Kirksville, 1986; panelist Sta. KPRS, Kansas City, 1987; Title One mentor K.C. Mo. Sch. Dist.; min. music N.W. Mo. Conf. A.M.E. Ch., Kansas City, 1984—, choir dir., 1985—; dir. sr. choir Ward Chapel A.M.E. Ch., KAnsas City, 1985-87; instr. of choir, band and orch. N.E. Law, Pub. Svc. and Mil. Sci. H.S., 1998—; girl's varsity asst. basketball coach, girl's jr. varsity basketball coach, drill mistress N.E. Lady Vikings Drill Team, fine arts dept. chairperson. Author: (curricula) Junior High Learning Task, 1972, Motivating the Unmotivated, 1986. Asst. troop scoutmaster Boy Scouts Am.; spl. cons. music United Meth. Ch. Women; active NAACP; parent chaperone Kansas City Marching Cobras Drill Team, 1993—. Recipient Meritorious Service award Lincoln U. Vocal Ensemble, 1985, Outstanding Tchr. award Black Archives Mid-Am., 1987; named one of Outstanding Young Women of Am., 1983. Mem. NAACP, AAUW, MADD, Am. Choral Dirs. Assn., Am. Fedn. Tchrs., Music Educators Nat. Conf., Nat. Assn. Negro Women, Order Eastern Star, Order Cyrenes, Heroines of Jericho, Tri-M Music Honor Soc., Order Golden Circle, Nat. Coaches Assn., Licoln U. Mo. Alumni Assn., Vocat. Indsl. Clubs Am., "C" Scholarship Club, Alpha Kappa Alpha, Phi Delta Kappa, Sigma Alpha Iota. Avocation: photography. Home: PO Box 301054 Kansas City MO 64130-1054 Office: Kansas City Sch Dist 1211 Mcgee St Kansas City MO 64106-2416

BUFORD-BAILEY, TONJA YEVETTE, track and field Olympic athlete; b. Dayton, Ohio, Dec. 13, 1970; d. Georgianna B.; m. Victor Bailey, Oct. 28, 1995. Grad., U. Ill., 1993. Mem. U.S. Olympic Team, Barcelona, Spain, 1992, Atlanta, 1996. Recipient 16 individual Big Ten championships U. Ill., 9 relay Big Ten championships, conf. title indoor awards for 55 and 200 dashes, 55 hurdles, conf. title outdoor awards for 100, 200, 400 and both hurdles, bronze medal Pan Am. Games, Havana, Cuba, 1991, silver medal Pan Am. Games, Argentina, 1995, silver medal World Championships, Gothenburg, 1995, bronze medal 400 meter hurdles Olympic Games, Atlanta, 1996; participant Olympics, Barcelona, 1992; ranked 7th in world for 400 meter hurdles, 1992, ranked 5th, 1993, ranked 2nd, 1995, ranked 3rd, 1996, ranked 6th, 1997. Office: USA Track and Field PO Box 120 Indianapolis IN 46206-0120

BUGBEE, JOAN BARTHELME, retired corporate communications executive; b. Galveston, Tex., Dec. 31, 1932; d. Donald and Helen (Bechtold) Barthelme; m. George A. Bugbee, Apr. 2, 1966; children: Richard, John. BA in Journalism, U. Colo., 1955. Pub. rels. rep. Philco Corp., Phila., 1957-60; account exec. Jacobs Keeper Newell Assoc., Houston, 1960-63; pub. rels. rep. Tex. Ea. Corp., Houston, 1963-66; assoc. editor Oil and Gas Digest Mag., Houston, 1978-79; mgr. corp. comms. Pennzoil Co., Houston, 1980-87, dir. corp. comms., 1987-90, v.p. corp. comm., 1990-96; ret., 1996, pub. rels. cons. Mem. Blue Ridge Pub. TV Radio Reading Svc. Mem. Pub. Rels. Soc. Am. (Outstanding Presentation award Phila. chpt. 1959), Phi Beta Kappa. Maronite Catholic.

BUGEJA, MICHAEL JOSEPH, educator, writer; b. Hackensack, N.J., May 24, 1952; s. Michael Carl and Josephine (Apap) B.; m. Diane Faye Sears, Sept. 16, 1979; children: Shane Michael, Erin Marie. BA in German, St. Peter's Coll., 1974; MS in Comms., S.D. State U., 1976; PhD in English, Okla. State U., 1985. State editor UPI, Sioux Falls, S.D., 1976-79; prof. Okla. State U., Stillwater, 1979-86; prof. Ohio U., Athens, 1986—, spl. asst. to pres., 1996—; hon. chancellor Nat. Fed. of State Poetry Soc. Author: Art and Craft of Poetry, 1994, Living Ethics, 1996, Guide to Writing Magazine Nonfiction, 1997; mem. adv. bd. Writer's Digest, Cin., 1999. Fellow Nat. Endowment for Arts, 1990, Ohio Arts Coun., 1997; NEH grantee, 1984; recipient Outstanding Tchr. award Amoco, 1985. Lutheran. Avocation: family. Office: Ohio Univ EW Scripps Sch Athens OH 45701

BUGG, CHARLES EDWARD, biochemistry educator, scientist; b. Durham, N.C., June 5, 1941; s. Everett I. and Annie Laurie (Newsom) B.; m. Barbara Bradshaw Bugg, Dec. 23, 1962; 3 children. AB in Chemistry, Duke U., 1962; PhD in Physical Chemistry, Rice U., Houston, 1965. Rsch. chemist E.I. duPont de Nemours & Co., Wilmington, Del., 1966-67; postdoctoral fellow Calif. Inst. Tech., Pasadena, 1965-68; prof. biochemistry, assoc. dir., sr. sci. Comprehensive Cancer Ctr., sr. sci. Rsch. Ctr. in Oral Biol. U. Ala., Birmingham, 1968-93, dir. Ctr. for Macromolecular Crystallography, 1985-93; chmn., CEO BioCryst Pharms., Inc., 1994—; chmn. commn. on jours. Internat. Union of Crystallography, Chester, Eng., 1987-96; chmn. U.S. Nat. Com. Crystallography, Washington, 1994-96. Contbr. articles to profl. jours., 1962—; editor jour. Acta Crystallographica, 1987-96; co-editor Crystallographic & Modelling Methods in Molecular Design, 1990; patentee in crystallography. Mem. AAAS, Am. Crystallographic Assn. (pres. 1987-88), Am. Chem. Soc., Fedn. Am. Socs. for Exptl. Biology, Ala. Acad. Scis., Rotary (v.p. 1990—), Mountain Brook Club, Redstone Club. Avocations: hunting, fishing, traveling. Office: BioCryst Pharms Inc 2190 Parkway Lake Dr Birmingham AL 35244-1803

BUGG, KEITH EDWARD, computer software developer, software company executive; b. Ashland, Ky., Feb. 18, 1952; s. Walter Edward and Sally (Worthington) B. BS in Math., Morehead State U., 1974. Mathematician Goodyear Atomic Corp., Piketon, Ohio, 1981-83; sr. systems analyst Sci. Applications Internat. Corp., Oak Ridge, Tenn., 1983-88, Am. Computer Profls., Columbia, S.C., 1988-90, Analysas Corp., Oak Ridge, 1990-94; pres. Q-Systems, Inc., Oak Ridge, 1993—. Author: The Visual C++ Construction Kit, 1998; contbr. articles to trade mags. Sgt. U.S. Army, 1977-80. Mem. Assn. Computing Machinery. Libertarian. Baptist. Avocations: tennis, hiking and camping, bird hunting, reading, word puzzles. Home and Office: Q Systems Inc 105 Mitchell Rd Oak Ridge TN 37830

BUGG, LEON HAYES, music educator, performer, composer; b. Ft. Smith, Ark., Sept. 22, 1944; s. Lon Hayes and Captola Marie (Beam) B. MusB, Hardin-Simmons U., 1968; MusM, U. Ark., Fayetteville, 1979. Piano instr. U. Mo., Kansas City, 1981—; prof. piano Rockhurst Coll., Kansas City, 1985—. Composer 1st original choral/piano composition premiered in Carnegie Hall, 1997, first original orchestral-choral composition, 1999. Capt. U.S. Army, 1968-71. Office: Rockhurst Coll Dept Comm and Fine Arts 1100 Rockhurst Rd Kansas City MO 64110-2508

BUGG, OWEN BRUCE, state agency administrator; b. Atlanta, Feb. 21, 1961; s. Owen Thomas and Mary Louise (Cobb) B.; m. Cynthia Lynn Symmes, Sept. 29, 1991. BBA in Mgmt., Ga. State U., 1983. Cert. Ga. peace officer and instr., hazardous materials instr. Enforcment officer Ga. Pub. Svc. Commn., Atlanta, 1987-89, sgt., 1989-93, lt., 1993-96, capt., hazardous materials specialist, 1996—; hazardous materials coord. summer olympics, Atlanta, 1993-96, mem. Ga. Title III planning com., 1995—; mem. radioactive waste working group So. Energy Bd., Atlanta, 1990—. Flood relief vol. Amway Relief Team/Salvation Army, Albany, Ga., 1996. Recipient Faithful Svc. award State of Ga., 1996. Mem. Coop. Hazardous Materials Enforcement devel. (chmn. compliance and enforcement 1996—, chair region II 1992-95), N.C. Conf. on HazMat Transp. (bd. regents 1993-94). Avocations: photography, hiking. Office: Ga Pub Svc Commn 1007 Virginia Ave Ste 310 Hapeville GA 30354-1325

BUGGE, LAWRENCE JOHN, lawyer; b. Milw., June 1, 1936; s. Lawrence Anthony and Anita (Westenberg) B.; m. Mary Daly, Nov. 28, 1959 (div.); m. Elaine Andersen, Jan. 29, 1977; children: Kristin, Laura, Jill, David, Carol. AB, Marquette U., 1958; JD, Harvard U., 1963. Bar: Wis. 1963. Assoc. Foley and Lardner, Milw., Madison, Wis., 1963-70; ptnr. Foley and Lardner, Milw., Madison, 1970-96, of counsel, 1996—; pres. Nat. Conf. Commrs. on Uniform State Laws, 1989-91; adj. prof. U. Wis. Law Sch., Madison, 1997—. Mem. Wis. State Bar Assn., Mil. Bar Assn. (pres. 1974-75), Milw. Young Lawyers Assn. (pres. 1969-70). Home: 313 Walnut Grove Dr Madison WI 53717-1228 Office: Foley & Lardner PO Box 1497 150 E Gilman St Madison WI 53701-1497

BUGGEY, LESLEY JOANNE, education educator, consultant; b. Mpls., July 25, 1938; d. Leslie Francis and Blanche (Moore) B. BS, Macalester Coll., 1960; MEd, U. Wash., Seattle, 1968; PhD, U. Wash., 1971. Cert. elem. tchr., Minn. Tchr. elem. Mpls. Pub. Schs., 1960-71; co-dir. Social Studies Svc. Ctr., St. Paul, 1971-73; lectr. in edn. Stanford (Calif.) U., 1973-74; ednl. cons., author, tchr., lectr. in edn. U. Minn., Mpls., 1974—; cons. in field. Speaker various orgns. Mem. ASCD, Nat. Coun. Geographic Edn. (past bd. dirs.), Nat. Coun. Social Studies (nat. com. mem.), Minn. Coun. for Social Studies. Presbyterian. Avocations: sewing, reading, travel. Home: 2800 W 44th St Minneapolis MN 55410-1557 Office: Univ Minn Education Dept Minneapolis MN 55455

BUGGIE, FREDERICK DENMAN, management consultant; b. Toledo, Mar. 27, 1929; s. Horace and Loraine (Denman) B.; m. Betty Jo Chilcote Buggie, Sept. 7, 1951 (div. 1988); children: Martha Louise Buggie Kenney, John Chilcote; m. Debra Hingley, July 15, 1997. BA, Yale U., 1956; MBA, George Washington U., 1961. Sales engr. Alcoa, Balt. and Phila., 1956-66; pres. Gt. Lakes Rsch. Inst., Erie, Pa., 1967-69; mktg. mgr. Technicon Instruments, Tarrytown, N.Y., 1969-71; program mgr. Innotech, Norwalk, Conn., 1971-74; pres. Inomation divsn. Van Dyck Corp., Westport, Conn., 1974-76, Strategic Innovations Internat., Lake Wylie, S.C., 1976—; pres. SII Strategic Innovations A.G., Zurich, Switzerland; founder, chmn. Strategic Innovations Internat. Ltd., Keele, Staffordshire, Eng., Strategic Innovations B.V., Rijswijk, The Netherlands; conf. leader, lectr.; adj. prof. various univs. Author: New Product Development Strategies, 1981; contbr. over 50 articles to profl. jours. With USAF, 1950-54. Mem. Assn. Corp. Growth, Strategic Leadership Forum, Comml. Devel. Assn., Product Devel. Mgmt. Assn., Inst. Dirs., Tower Club, Yale Club (London, Charlotte, N.Y.C.). Home: 8 Sunrise Pt River Hills Lake Wylie SC 29710 Office: Strategic Innovations Internat 12 Executive Ct Lake Wylie SC 29710-9338

BUGGS, ELAINE S., financial analyst; b. Trenton, N.J., Aug. 18, 1954; d. Moses and Hattie (Mitchell) S.; m. Richmond Akumiah, Dec. 1982 (div. Aug. 27, 1987); m. James A. Buggs, Sr., Oct. 2, 1996; 1 child, James A., Jr. BS, Rochester Inst. Technol., 1976; MBA, Atlanta U., 1985. Mktg. rep. Mobil Oil Corp., 1976-77; mfg. analyst Reader's Digest, Pleasantville, N.Y., 1977-80; mgr. fin. instns. Am. Express, N.Y.C., 1980-83; sr. market analyst Ryder Systems Inc., Miami, 1985-86; dir. recruiting Atlanta U., 1986; cons. Consultants & Assocs., Washington, 1987-89; mgr. fin. analysis Blue Cross Blue Shield of Va., Roanoke, 1989-90; dir. group fin. reporting & analysis Blue Cross Blue Shield of Md., Owings Mills, 1990-93; sr. med. group analyst mid-Atlantic states region Kaiser Permanente, Rockville, Md., 1993-95; asst. mgr. Johns Hopkins U., Balt., 1995—. Named IBM scholar, 1983. Mem. NAFE, Md. New Directions (bd. dirs. 1994-96), Internat. Soc. Strategic Planners, Nat. Assn. MBA Execs. Democrat. Methodist. Avocations: tennis, aerobics, antique hunting. Home: 8403 Gold Sunset Way Columbia MD 21045-7407 Office: Johns Hopkins Sch Medicine Reed Hall B-102 1620 Mcelderry St Baltimore MD 21205-1911

BUGHER, ROBERT DEAN, professional society administrator; b. Lafayette, Ind., Oct. 17, 1925; s. Walter Earl and Lillie Victoria (Feldner) B.; m. Patricia Jean McConnell, Sept. 7, 1945; children: Vickie Leigh, Robert James. Student, Millsaps Coll., 1943, Miami U., Oxford, Ohio, 1944; B.S. in Civil Engring, Purdue U., 1948; M.P.A., U. Mich., 1951. Staff engr. Mich. Mcpl. League, 1948-53; mgr. Mcpl. Purchasing Svc., 1951-53; sec.-treas. Mich. Mcpl. Utilities Assn., 1951-53; asst. dir. Am. Pub. Works Assn., 1953-58, exec. dir., 1958-89, exec. dir. emeritus, 1990—; Lectr. Internat. Seminar on Ekistics, Athens, Greece, 1970; chmn. nat. adv. coun. Keep Am. Beautiful, Inc., 1974-75; chmn. Nat. Conf. on Solid Waste Disposal Sites, Washington, 1971; advisor pub. mgmt. program Northwestern U., 1977-82; bd. dirs. Pub. Adminstrn. Svc., Chgo., 1958-73; trustee Nat. Acad. Code Adminstrs.; chmn. Coun. Internat. Urban Liaison, 1982-84; trustee Nat. Tng. and Devel. Svc., Am. Consortium for Internat. Pub. Adminstrn.; adv. com. internat. divsn. GAO, 1979-80. Editor: pub. works sect. Municipal Yearbook Internat. City Mgmt. Assn., 1953-58; cons. editor pub. works sect., Mcpl. Pub. Works Adminstrn., 1957; chmn. adv. bd. Internat. Ctr. Acad. State and Local Govts., 1985-87. Served to 1st lt. USMCR, 1943-45. Mem. ASCE (life), Am. Pub. Works Assn. (hon.), Internat. Pub. Works Fedn. (treas. 1985-89, sec.-gen. 1990), Am. Soc. Assn. Execs., Am. Soc. Pub. Adminstrn., Internat. Union Local Authorities (pres. U.S. sect. 1977-79, v.p. 1968-70, 75-77), Internat. Solid Wastes and Pub. Cleansing Assn. (v.p. 1968-70), Internat. Fedn. Mcpl. Engrs. (treas. 1976-79), Pub. Works Hist. Soc. (hon., treas. 1975-89), Sigma Alpha Epsilon. Baptist. Home: 8238 E Del Cadena Dr Scottsdale AZ 85258-2319 Office: 2345 Grand Blvd Ste 500 Kansas City MO 64108-2641

BUGIELSKI, ROBERT JOSEPH, state legislator; b. Chgo., June 5, 1947; s. Edward Leon and Lottie Regina (Ptak) B.; m. Dona Rosalie Obrzut, Aug. 2, 1980. BS in Bus. Edn., Chgo. State U., 1971. Tchr. Weber High Sch., Chgo., 1971-83; asst. athletic dir., 1973-78; dir. devel. Weber High Sch., Chgo., 1974-83, adminstrv. bd. dirs., 1975-83; rep. Ill. Gen. Assembly, Chgo., 1987—. Named Legislator of Yr. Am. Legis. Exch. Coun., 1991. Democrat. Roman Catholic. Office: 6839 W Belmont Ave Chicago IL 60634-4646

BUGLI, DAVID, conductor, arranger, composer; b. N.Y.C., Apr. 2, 1950. BMus, Ithaca Coll., 1972; MMus, U. Mass., 1978. Founder, musical dir., condr. Carson City Symphony (formerly Carson City Chamber Orch.), Nev., 1984—; pub. sch. music tchr., 1972-77; computer programmer/analyst, 1979—; 1st pres. Carson Access TV Found., 1991. Office: Carson City Symphony PO Box 2001 Carson City NV 89702-2001

BUGLIARELLO, GEORGE, university chancellor; b. Trieste, Italy, May 20, 1927; came to U.S., 1951, naturalized, 1964; s. Federico and Spera (Gefter-Wondrich) B.; m. Virginia Upton Harding, 1960; children: Federico David, Nicholas Luigi. DEng summa cum laude, U. Padua, Italy, 1951; MS in Civil Engring, U. Minn., 1954; DSc, MIT, 1959; LLD (hon.), Carnegie-Mellon U., 1986; MD (hon.), U. Trieste, 1989; EngD (hon.), Milw. Sch. Engring., 1991; LLD (hon.), Ill. Inst. Tech., 1993, Pace U., 1994, Trinity Coll., 1997; LHD (hon.), Ill. Inst. Tech., Pace U. Research engr. U. Padua, 1951; from research asst. to research assoc. MIT, 1956-59; mem. faculty Carnegie-Mellon U., 1959-69, prof. biotech. and civil engring., 1956-69, chmn. biotechnology program, 1964-69; dean engring. U. Ill. at Chgo. Circle, 1969-73; pres. Poly. U., Bklyn., 1973-94; bd. hydraulic cons. U.S. Waterways Exptl. Sta., 1968-74; sci. adv. panel Armed Forces Explosive Safety Bd., 1968-69; biomed. tng. engring. com. NIH, 1966-70; commn. edn. Nat. Acad. Engring., 1970-73, chmn. com. ednl. sys., 1970-73, mem. tech. edn. stds. com.; chmn. bd. sci. and tech. for internat. devel. NAS, 1979-83; U.S. rep. NATO steering com. on sci. for stability program, 1983-97, steering com. on sci. for peace, 1997—; bd. dirs. Lord Corp., Comtech. Corp., Keyspan Energy, Symbol Techs., Inc., Jura Corp., Spectrum Info. Techs.; sci. policy reviewer Portugal OECD, 1983, 91-92, Greece, 1982, Italy, 1991, Portugal, 1992, Turkey, 1995; mem., chair engring. adv. com. Lawrence Livermore Nat. Lab.; mem. U. Chgo. rev. com. for the decision and info. scis. divsn. Argonne Nat. Lab., Los Alamos Nat. Lab. program review com. Civilian and Indsl. Techs. program office; trustee William R. Kenan, Jr. Inst. for Engring. Tech. and Sci., Paul and Daisy Soros Fellowship for New Ams.; mem. Found. Future Bd. Adv. Co-author: Computer Systems and Water Resources, 1974, The Impact of Noise Pollution, 1976, Technology, The Community and the University, 1976; editor: Bioengineering-An Engineering View, 1967, Women in Engineering, 1972, The History and Philosophy of Technology, 1979; co-editor: East-West Technology Transfer, 1996; editor-in-chief: Technology in Society; interim editor-in-chief: The Bridge; contbr. papers in field. Trustee ANSER, Teagle Found., Greenwall Found., Lord Found. N.C., Commn. Ind. Colls. and Universities, 1993—; bd. visitors Duke U. Sch. Engring., 1975—; mem. N.Y. Partnership, 1980—, High Tech. Task Force, 1985-90, chmn., 1988-90, Mayor's Commn. Sci. and Tech., 1984-90, chmn., 1987-88; exec. com. Bd. Trustees Commn. Ind. Colls. and Univs., N.Y., 1986-89; alumni rep. MIT vis. com. for Civil Engring., 1985-91; chair, N.Y.C. Mayor's Task Force on Gramercy Park Steam Pipe Explosion, 1989-90, N.Y.C. Mayor's Adv. Coun. on Devel. of Recycling Markets and Businesses; active Nat. Medal Tech. Nomination Evaluation Com., 1987-92, chmn. 1991-92; chair Nat. Acads. Megacities Project Habitat II Conf.; mem. Nat. Acad. Sci. Com. Human Rights. Recipient Alza prize Biomed. Engring. Soc.; NATO sr. fellow Tech. U. Berlin, 1968; N.Y. Mayor's Awd. Excellence Sci. and Tech., 1994, N.Y. Acad. of Scis. Fellow AAAS (chair com. sci., engring. and pub. policy, 1987-89, chair panel on phys. scis. and engring. 1987-89, project 2061 1985-89), Am. Soc. Engring. Edn., ASCE (chmn. exec. com. engring. mechanics divsn. 1971-72, chmn. interdivisional task com. civil engring. in medicine and health care delivery 1969-73, Huber rsch. prize 1967), Am. Inst. Med. and Biol. Engring. (founding fellow); mem. NAE (coun. 1989-93, adv. com. tech. and the environ. 1989-92, internat. affairs adv. com. 1988-92), Internat. Assn. Hydraulic Rsch. (chmn. task com. computer langs. 1969-72), N.Y. Acad. Medicine, Nat. Assn. for Sci., Tech. and Soc. (trustee 1988—, pres. 1989-90, hon. lifetime mem.), Nat. Rsch. Coun. (bd. engring. edn. 1990—, chair bd. on infrastructure and constructed environ. 1994-97), N.Y. Acad. Scis. (pres'. coun. 1990—, mem. com. human rights 1996—), Italian Soc. Advancement Sci. (hon. mem.), Sigma Xi (disting. lectr. 1996—, past pres., bd. dirs.). Home: 5 Terrace Dr Port Washington NY 11050-3419 Office: Polytechnic U 6 Metrotech Ctr Brooklyn NY 11201-3840

BUHAC, IVO, gastroenterologist; b. Dubrovnik, Croatia, Sept. 4, 1926; s. Ivan and Blazenka (Dulcic) B.; m. Susanne Rossband, Sept. 14, 1963; 1 child, John. MD, U. Med. Sch., Zagreb, Croatia, 1952, ScD, 1963; MD, U. Med. Sch., Erlangen, Germany, 1962. Staff physician Hosp. O. Novosel, Zagreb, 1957-68; resident in gastroenterology VA Hosp., Richmond, Va., 1968-70; asst. prof. medicine Albany (N.Y.) Med. Coll., 1970-74, assoc. prof. medicine, 1974-82, prof. medicine, 1982-88, chief of gastroenterology, 1970-88. Contbr. articles to Gastroenterology, Hepatology, N.Y. State Jour. Medicine, Deutsche Medizinische Wochenschrift. Mem. Am. Gastroenterology Assn., Am. Assn. for Study of Liver Diseases, N.Y. Acad. Scis. Achievements include research on the pathophysiology of ascites formation in liver cirrhosis, diagnosis of disease causing death of Herod the Great. Home: 64 Spruce St Clifton Park NY 12065-1145

BUHAGIAR, MARION, editor, author; b. N.Y.C., Oct. 27, 1932; d. George and Mae (Pietrzak) B.; 1 child, Alexa Ragozin. B.A. cum laude, Hunter Coll., 1953; postgrad., Mt. Holyoke Coll., 1954. Economist U.S. Dept. Commerce, 1954-57; bus. reporter Time mag., 1957-59; assoc. editor Fortune mag., 1960-73, story devel. editor, 1970-73; text editor Time-Life Books, N.Y.C., 1973-76; v.p. Boardroom Inc., 1977-84; editor Boardroom Reports, 1977-84; exec. editor Bottom Line/Personal, 1980-84; pres. Expert Connections, N.Y.C., 1984—; editor Street Smart Investing, 1987-89. Author: How to Build a College Fund for Your Child, 1989, Battle Plan for American Business, 1992, I-Power, 1992; editor: The Book of Secrets, 1989. Adv. bd. Scientists Inst. for Pub. Info., N.Y.C. Office: Expert Connections London Terr Sta PO Box 20100 New York NY 10011-0008

BUHAIN, WILFRIDO JAVIER, medical educator; b. Bacoor, Cavite, Philippines, Oct. 12, 1940; m. Carlota Torres; children: Ronald, Edgar. AA, BS, U. Philippines, 1959, MD, 1964. Diplomate Am. Bd. Internal Medicine, Am. Bd. Pulmonary Diseases. Rsch. fellow in cardiology U. Philippines, Philippine Gen. Hosp., 1964-65; rotating intern Queens Hosp. Ctr., N.Y.C., 1965-66, resident in internal medicine, 1965-68; clin. fellow in pulmonary diseases Hosp. of U. Pa., 1968-69, chief pulmonary function lab. dept. medicine, 1971-72; rsch. fellow in pulmonary diseases Hosp. of U. Pa., VA Hosp., Phila., 1969-71; assoc. in medicine, cardiovascular-pulmonary div. med. dept. U. Pa. Sch. Medicine, 1971-72; assoc. in medicine, dept. medicine Mt. Sinai Sch. Medicine, CUNY, 1972-74; clin. instr. medicine Georgetown U., 1976-95; chief pulmonary function lab. dept. medicine Mt. Sinai Hosp. Svcs./City Hosp. Ctr. at Elmhurst, 1973-74; med. dir. respiratory therapy dept. Mt. Vernon Hosp., 1978—, chmn. dept. medicine, 1987-88, pres. med. staff, 1996-98; mem. exec. com. Alexandria Hosp., 1983; chmn. med. affairs coun. Inova Health System. Contbr. articles to profl. jours. Bd. trustees Inova Health System. Queensborough Soc. grantee; Pa. Thoracic Soc. grantee. Fellow ACP, Am. Coll. Chest Physicians; mem. Am. Soc. Internal Medicine, Alexandria Med. Soc., Va. Med. Soc., Philippine Med. Assn. (exec. dir., past pres. Metro-Washington), Assn. Philippine Physicians in Am. (v.p.). Avocations: tennis, ballroom dancing. Office: 6300 Stevenson Ave Ste B Alexandria VA 22304-3554

BUHLER, LESLIE LYNN, institute administrator. BA with honors in History and Art History, Syracuse U., 1969; postgrad., New Sch. for Social Rsch., 1971, Am. U., 1980. Asst. for cmty. programs Met. Mus. Art, N.Y.C., 1970-72; program coord. resident assoc. program Smithsonian Instn., Washington, 1972-75; instnl. devel. officer Nat. Archives and Records Svc., Washington, 1975-78; ind. cons., 1977-82; dir. membership and mktg. Alban Inst., Inc., Bethesda, Md., 1982-85, dir. devel., membership and mktg., 1985-88, dir. ops., 1988-89, exec. v.p., 1989—, acting pres., 1994-95; grant reviewer Office of Mus. Programs, NEH, Washington, 1973-74. Bd. dirs. Mus. of City of Washington, 1980-84; vol. advisor Nat. Mus. for Bldg. Arts, Washington, 1977-79. Recipient cert. of appreciation Am. Revolution Bicentennial Adminstrn., 1976. Home: 4701 32nd St NW Washington DC

20008-2225 Office: Alban Inst 7315 Wisconsin Ave Ste 1250W Bethesda MD 20814-3240

BUHLER, RICHARD GERHARD, minister; b. Cottonwood, Ariz., July 18, 1946; s. Henry Richard and A. Genevieve (Woodward) B.; m. Linda M. Bates, Dec. 9, 1966; children: Karin, Kristin, Karise, Kenneth, Kevin, Kim, Keith. BA, Biola U., 1968, LLD, 1990; cert., Omega Ctr., Santa Ana, Calif., 1978. Announcer Sta. KBBI-FM, L.A., 1964-68; writer, editor, prodr. Sta. KFWB-AM, L.A., 1968-72, 74-76; writer, editor Sta. KNX-AM Radio, L.A., 1972-74; pres. Branches Comms., Orange, Calif., 1981—; host Tabletalk daily radio program, 1990-96, Talk From the Heart radio show, 1981-90; program dir. Sta. KBRT, L.A., 1984-90. Author: Love...No Strings Attached, 1986, Pain and Pretending, 1988, New Choices, New Boundaries, 1991, Be Good To Yourself, 1993. Recipient Angel award Religion in Media, L.A., 1986. Mem. Writer's Guild Am. Republican. Office: Branches Communications PO Box 6688 Orange CA 92863-6688 *"Let not the wise man boast of his wisdom or the strong boast of his strength or the rich man boast of his riches, but let him who boasts about this: that he understands and knows me, that I am the Lord who exercizes kindness, justice and righteousness on earth, for in these I delight," declares the Lord.' Jeremiah 9:23, 24.*

BUHLER, STEPHEN MICHAEL, English educator; b. Bklyn., Oct. 23, 1954; s. William and Barbara (Birkbeck) B.; m. Carla May Rosenquist, Aug. 27, 1983; 1 child, Teresa. BA, Calif. State U., 1976; MA, UCLA, 1983, PhD, 1989. Tchr. St. Anthony H.S., Long Beach, Calif., 1976-84; tchg. assoc. UCLA, 1986-87; instr. Loyola Marymount U., 1987-88; from asst. prof. to assoc. prof. U. Nebr., Lincoln, 1989—; commentator Nebr. Pub. Radio, 1993—; actor Lincoln Cmty. Playhouse, 1999—. Contbr. articles to profl. jours. including Engish Literary Renaissance, Jour. English and Germanic Philology, others. Literacy vol. Lincoln Pub. Schs., 1996-97. Rsch. fellow Huntington Libr., 1996, dissertation fellow UCLA, 1988-89; grantee NEH. Mem. MLA, Renaissance Soc. Am., Shakespeare Assn. Am., Spenser Soc., Milton Soc. Avocation: music, theatre. Office: U Nebr Dept English Lincoln NE 68588-0333

BUHNER, BYRON BEVIS, health science facility administrator; b. Hammond, Ind., Feb. 19, 1950; s. John Colin and Betty (Bevis) B.; children: Zachery Aaron, Rebecca Bevis. AB in Comm., Ind. U., 1976, MS in Human Resource Devel., 1981. Adminstr. Ind. U., Indpls., 1976-77, instr. evaluator sch. nursing, 1981-82; tng. specialist Ayr-Way, Target Stores, Indpls., 1977-81; assoc. exec. dir. Cen. Ind. Regional Blood Ctr., Indpls., 1984-88, pres., chief exec. officer, 1988—; founding mem. Blood Ctrs. Ins. Exch., Risk Retention Group, 1993, chmn. bd. dirs., 1993-96, dir., 1996—; adminstr. Blood Rsch. and Edn. Foundn. of Ind., Inc., Indpls., 1985-89, bd. mem., 1989-94. Producer: Multi-Image film, Focus on Transition, 1981, A Manager's Perspective, 1981; photographer: Sound, Slide program, Wearable - Arts '81. Trustee Coun. Cmty. Blood Ctrs., 1986—, chmn. purchasing com., 1988-92, chmn. fin. com., treas., 1992-94, v.p., 1994-96, pres., 1997-99, chmn. exec. com., chmn. group svcs. com., chmn. long-range planning com. Mem. Am. Acad. Healthcare Execs. (diplomate), Ind. U. Alumni Assn. (bd. dirs. 1983-88), Am. Assn. Blood Banks, Ind. Assn. Blood Banks (bd. dirs. 1988-91), Kiwanis. Avocations: sailing, jogging, hockey, photography, coaching youth sports. Home: 11362 Bayhill Way Indianapolis IN 46236-9233 Office: Cen Ind Regional Blood Ctr 3450 N Meridian St Indianapolis IN 46208-4437

BUHNER, JAY CAMPBELL, baseball player; b. Louisville, Ky., Aug. 13, 1964; m. Leah Buhner; children: Brielle, Chase, Gunnar. Student, McClennan C.C., Waco, Tex. Player Seattle Mariners. Active Seattle chpt. Cystic Fibrosis Found., Juvenile Diabetes Assn. Named Houston Area Player of Yr. Houston chpt. Baseball Writers Assn. Am., 1993, 95; recipient Gold Glove award, 1996, Breath of Life award Cystic Fibrosis Found., 1997. Office: c/o Seattle Mariners PO Box 4100 83 King St 3rd Fl Seattle WA 98104*

BUHROW, WILLIAM CARL, religious organization administrator; b. Cleve., Jan. 18, 1934; s. Philip John and Edith Rose (Leutz) B.; m. Carole Corinne Craven, Feb. 14, 1959; children: William Carl Jr., David Paul, Peter John, Carole Lynn. Diploma, Phila. Coll. Bible, 1954; B.A., Wheaton (Ill.) Coll., 1956, M.A., 1959. Ordained to ministry Gen. Assn. Regular Bapt. Chs., 1958. Asst. pastor (Hydewood Park Bapt. Ch.), N. Plainfield, N.J., 1959-63; with Continental Fed. Savs. & Loan Assn., Cleve., 1963-81; sr. v.p. Continental Fed. Savs. & Loan Assn., 1971-75, pres., chief exec. officer, dir., 1975-81; chmn. bd. Security Savs. Mortgage Corp., Citizens Service Corp., New Market Corp., CFS Service Corp., 1975-81; trustee Credit Bur. Cleve., 1975-81, Bldg. Expositions, Inc., 1974-84; registered rep. IDS/Am. Express, Cleve., 1982-83; gen. credit mgr. Forest City Enterprises, Inc., Cleve., 1983-85; pres. Forest City Ins. Agy., Inc., Cleve., 1983-85; asst. v.p. Mellon Fin. Services Corp., Cleve., 1985-87; exec. adminstr. The Gospel Ho. Ch. and Evangelistic Ctr., Walton Hills, Ohio, 1988—. Trustee Bapt. Bible Coll. and Theol. Sem., Clarks Summit, Pa., 1977-90; vice chmn. bd. deacons Cedar Hill Bapt. Ch., Cleveland Heights, Ohio, 1981-87; trustee, sec. and treas. Gospel House Prison Ministry Found., 1992—. Mem. Christian Bus. Men's Com. Internat., Nat. Assn. Ch. Bus. Adminstrn. Home: PO Box 24104 Cleveland OH 44124-0104 Office: 14707 Alexander Rd Cleveland OH 44146-4924 *The supreme goal of my life is to please and honor the Lord Jesus Christ in all that I say and do. The standards, goals, and ideals outlined in the Bible, God's Holy Word, are the ones which I have adopted for my life. True happiness for me lies in the accomplishment of God's perfect will in my life and that of my family and in introducing others to Christ so they may know Him as their own personal Saviour, too. Herein lies the key to my success as a Christian administrator.*

BUHYOFF, GREGORY J., forestry specialist, educator; b. Detroit, Sept. 22, 1948; m. Marilyn Brichter; 1 child, Matthew. BS, U. Mich., 1970, M in Forestry, 1972, PhD, 1975. Lectr. U. Mich., Ann Arbor, 1971-74; from asst. prof. to Julian N. Cheatham prof. Forestry Va. Tech. U., Blacksburg, 1974—. Mem. AAAS, Am. Statis. Assn., Soc. Am. Foresters, Environ. Design Rsch. Assn., Xi Sigma Pi, Gamma Sigma Delta. Office: Va Tech Coll Dept Forestry 304 Cheatham Hall Blacksburg VA 24061*

BUI, LONG VAN, church custodian, translator; b. Cao Xa, Vietnam, May 1, 1940; came to U.S., 1985; s. So Van and Ninh Thi (Nguyen) B.; m. Dung Thi Le, May 14, 1970; children: Van Thanh Bui, Long Ba Bui. Student, U. Dalat, Vietnam, 1960; AA, Houston C.C., 1991. H.S. tchr. Vietnam, 1964, mil. svc., 1965-75, detainee, 1975-81; grocery store cashier Houston, 1986; custodian Spring Branch Cmty. Ch., Houston, 1986—. Editor: Holy Family newsletter of Youth Better Found., Houston, 1993—; translator Medjugorie The Message into Vietnamese, 1993, Fatima the Great Sign into Vietnamese, 1994, Testimony of Father Robert DeGrandis, S.S.J., 1998, Healing the Father Relationship, 1998, Failure in Your Life, 1998, The Ten Commandments of Prayer into Vietnamese, 1998, Multiplication des Apparitions de la Vierge Aujourd'hui into Vietnamese, 1998. Capt. Vietnamese Army, 1965-75. Mem. Youth Better Found. Roman Catholic. Avocations: reading, translating. Home: Apt 2303 8801 Hammerly Blvd Houston TX 77080-6507 Office: Youth Better Found 11906 Drummond Park Dr Houston TX 77044-5002

BUI, TY VAN, computer programmer, systems analyst; b. Cai Tau Ha, Sadec, Vietnam, Dec. 7, 1959; came to U.S., 1988; s. Tu Van and Nhung Thi (Ha) B.; m. CamVan Nguyen, Feb. 15, 1986; 1 child, Quoc Trung Dinh. BS in Secondary Edn., Edn. Coll., Vietnam, 1980; BS in Computer Sci. and Applied Math., U. Wis., Oshkosh, 1992. Tchr. math. Cao Lanh (Vietnam) High Sch., 1980-82; tchr. physics Sadec High Sch., 1982-84; chief comm. sect. UN High Commn. for Refugees, The Philippines, 1986-87; computer programmer Wis. Dept. Revenue, Madison, 1990, systems analyst, 1991; cons. computer lab. U. Wis., 1990-92, computer programming cons. English dept., 1992; computer programmer, cons. Kag Labs. Internat., Inc., Oshkosh, 1992; sr. programmer analyst Northwestern Mut. Life Ins., Milw., 1993-96, system analyst, 1995-96; staff analyst CASE Corp., Racine, Wis., 1996-98, bus. system cons., 1998; software engr. Mgmt. Control System, 1991; programmer An Invention or Idea Generating Program, 1992, Case's Unix Standards for Batch Processing, 1997,, Case's Worldwide Infrastructures for Client/Server Environment, 1998. Mem. Assn. for Computing Machinery, Math. Assn. Am., Alpha Lambda Delta. Avocations: tennis, reading, canoeing. Home: 7046 Evans Dr Franklin WI 53132-8908

BUICE, BONNIE CARL, lawyer, priest; b. East Point, Ga., May 20, 1932; s. Bonnie Carl and Mahalia Elizabeth (Ramsey) B.; m. Patterson Nall, Dec. 14, 1957 (div. Apr. 1982); children: Merrianne, Shannon, Samuel, William, Christopher; m. Hulane E. George, Feb. 18, 1984. AB, Mercer U., 1954, JD, 1957; MA in Theology, U. Notre Dame, 1975. Bar: Ga. 1954, U.S. Dist. Ct. (no. dist.) Ga. 1957, U.S. Dist. Ct. (mid. dist.) Ga. 1983, U.S. Ct. Appeals (11th cir.) 1991; ordained priest Episcopal Ch., 1975. Assoc. Nall, Miller, Cadenhead & Dennis, Atlanta, 1957-61; ptnr. Robinson, Buice, Harben & Strickland, Gainesville, Ga., 1961-74; curate Holy Trinity Parish, Decatur, Ga., 1975-79; rector St. Francis Ch., Macon, Ga., 1979-84; ptnr. George & Buice, Milledgeville, Ga., 1984-86, Waddell, Emerson, George & Buice, Milledgeville, 1986-94, Waddell, Emerson & Buice, Milledgeville, 1994—; assoc. priest St. Stephens Episcopal Ch., Milledgeville, 1986-91; rector St. James Episcopal Ch, Macon, 1992—. Mem. Ocmulgee Bar Assn. (pres. 1991-92), Baldwin County Bar Assn. (treas. 1991-92). Home: 115 Maplewood Ave SW Milledgeville GA 31061-3646 Office: Waddell Emerson & Buice PO Box 630 Milledgeville GA 31061-0630

BUICKEROOD, RICHARD W., park and recreation director; b. Plainfield, N.J., Nov. 24, 1942. BA, Rutgers U.; MBA, Golden Gate U. Enlisted USAF, advanced through grades to col.; dir. Dallas Zoo and Aquarium, 1992—. Scholarship selection com. mem. Kimberly-Clarke Found., 1993—. Mem. Dallas Assembly, Oak Cliff C. of C. (bd. dirs.), Ret. Officers Assn., Air Force Assn. (v.p. edn. Austin chpt. 1990-92). Fax: 214 670-7450. Office: Dallas Zoo and Aquarium 621 E Clarendon Dr Dallas TX 75203-2920*

BUIDANG, GEORGE (HADA BUIDANG), educator, administrator, consultant, writer; b. Danang, Vietnam, Dec. 30, 1924; came to U.S., 1981; s. Bui Dang Do and Ha Thi Yen; m. Pham Thi Hong, Feb. 25, 1951; children: Bui Tu Long, Bui Nguyen Khanh, Bui Minh Hoang, Bui Thi Tuong Vi. Grad., Providence Inst., Vietnam, 1944. Tchr. English and French Nhatrang, Vietnam, 1956; head translator USMC, 1956-61; dep. employment officer, personnel specialist Hdqrs. Support Activity Saigon USN, 1962-65; asst. dir. Ctrl. Tng. Inst. U.S. Army, Vietnam, 1966; pers. dir. Foremost Dairies Vietnam of Foremost-McKesson Internat., 1966-79; instr. of French Un Bateau Pour L'Asie Du Sud-Est, Brussels, Belgium, Belgium, 1980; asst. dir. edn. Career Resources Devel. Ctr., Inc., San Francisco, 1981-93; ind. cons. San Francisco, 1993—. Author: George Buidang's Microcomputing Series, including: Using WordPerfect 5.0, 1989, Using Lotus 1-2-3 Release 2.2, 1991, Using WordPerfect 5.1, 1991, Using Microsoft Windows 3.1, 1993, Using WordPerfect 6.0 for DOS, 1994, Using Lotus 1-2-3 for Windows, 1995, Using WordPerfect for Windows, 1996, Using Microsoft Word 97 for Windows 95, 1997, Using Microsoft Access 97 for Windows 95, 1998. Home: 565 Geary St Apt 411 San Francisco CA 94102-1660

BUILDER, J. LINDSAY, JR., lawyer; b. Miami, Fla., Feb. 6, 1943; s. John Lindsay and Majorie (Merrell) L.; m. Jean Fern, Aug. 3, 1968; children Margaret Merrell, John Lindsay III. BE, Vanderbilt U., 1965, JD, 1970. Bar: Fla. 1970, U.S. Dist Ct. (mid. dist.) Fla. 1971, U.S. Supreme Ct. 1976. Assoc., ptnr. Maguire, Voorhis & Wells P.A, Orlando, Fla., 1970-84; ptnr. Godbold, Allen, Brown & Builder P.A., Winter Park, Fla., 1984-88, Allen, Brown & Builder P.A., Winter Park, 1988-90, Honigman Miller Schwartz and Cohn., Detroit, Orlando, 1991-96, Graham, Clark, Jones, Builder, Pratt and Marks, Winter Park, Fla., 1996—. Mem. bd. trust Vanderbilt U., Nashville, 1990-92, Winter Park Mem. Hosp., chmn. 1994-96. Lt. (j.g) USN, 1965-67. Mem. Orange County Bar Assn. (pres. 1983-84), Vanderbilt U. Law Sch. Alumni (bd. dirs. 1985, pres.), Vanderbilt U. Alumni (pres. bd. dirs. 1989-90). Republican. Episcopalian. Avocations: golf, snow skiing, tennis. Office: Graham Clark Jones Builder Pratt and Marks 369 N New York Ave Winter Park FL 32789-3119

BUILER, DOROTHY MARION, business owner; b. Athens, Wis., Apr. 20, 1925; d. Edwin Herman and Katherine Dorothy (Dick) Mueller; m. Donald J. Builer, May 24, 1947; 1 child, Thomas Edwin. Grad. h.s., Athens. Owner, ptnr. Builer's Sport Shop, Wausau, Wis., 1959—, Campers Haven, Heafford Junction, Wis., 1967—. Mem. Internat. Platform Assn., Bus. and Profl. Women Club (pres. Marathon county 1968-69, pres. Northwood dist. 1973-74), Wausau Womans Club (pres.-elect 1988-90, pres. 1990-91), Am. Legion Aux. (pres. local unit 1958-59, pres. 8th dist. 1963-64, chmn. State of Wis. aux. conv. 1964), Valley Garden Club, Wausau Wheelers Bike Club (organizer). Home: 3919 Pine Cone Ln Wausau WI 54403-2384

BUIST, JEAN MACKERLEY, veterinarian; b. Newton, N.J., Dec. 24, 1919; d. Ackerson Jacob and Mary Morris (Morford) Mackerley; m. Richardson Buist, Oct. 2, 1948; children: Peter Richardson, Jean Morford Buist Earle, Mary Elizabeth Buist Lueth. DVM, Cornell U., 1942. Veterinarian Summit (N.J.) Dog and Cat Hosp., 1942-48; pvt. practice Sparta, N.J., 1948—. Mem. Sparta Twp. Bd. Health, 1962-82, chmn., 1972-82; mem., chmn., sec. N.J. State Bd. Vet. Med. Examiners. Recipient Gaines award Newton Kennel Club, 1970, Disting. Svc. award Assn. Women Veterinarians, 1989, Life Achievement award Baldwin Sch., 1992; Paul Harris fellow Newton N.J. Rotary Club, 1995. Mem. Nat. Assn. State Bds. (pres.-elect 1984, pres. 1985-86), Am. Vet. Med. Assn. (nat. bd. exam. com. 1987-91, chmn. 1990-91), N.J. Vet. Med. Assn. (treas. 1982-92), N.J. Acad. Vet. Medicine and Surgery (bd. dirs. 1972-92, sec. 1975-82), Sussex County 4-H Horse Club Leaders Assn. (pres. 1970-76), Sussex County Horse Show Assn. (v.p. 1980-82, pres. 1982-90), Sussex County Farm and Horse Show Assn. (v.p. 1980-94, pres. 1996—). Home: 68 Sand Pond Rd Hamburg NJ 07419-9623 Office: 143 Stanhope Rd Sparta NJ 07871-2118

BUIST, RICHARDSON, corporate executive, retired banker; b. Bklyn., Aug. 8, 1921; s. George Lamb and Adelaide (Richardson) B.; m. Jean Mackerley, Oct. 2, 1948; children: Peter Richardson, Jean Morford Buist Earle, Mary Elizabeth Buist Lueth. Student, Yale U. Advt. copywriter Ecloss Co., Sparta, N.J., 1946-48; advt. mgr. Sussex County Ind., Newton, N.J., 1948-50, Dover (N.J.) Advance, 1950-53; bus. mgr. N.J. Herald, Inc., Newton, 1953-70, dir., v.p., 1958-70, pub., 1967-70; dir. N.J. Press Assn., 1966-70; asst. sec., asst. treas. Morford Conservation Co., Hamburg, 1965-72, pres., 1986-95, v.p., 1995—; trust officer Midlantic Nat. Bank/Sussex & Mchts., Newton, 1971-88, Midlantic Nat. Bank, Edison, N.J., 1972-86, cons. 1986-90, dir. Newton Cemetary Co., 1989—, v.p., 1998. Pres. Sussex County chpt. Am. Cancer Soc., 1956-58, Sussex County Music Found., 1959-61; mem. Morris-Sussex Area Health Facilities Planning Coun., 1965-68; v.p. Sussex County Coun. Arts, 1971-73; chmn. pub. rels. Morris-Sussex Area Coun. Boy Scouts Am., 1986-88; trustee Sussex County Music Found., 1955-75; v.p., chmn. fin. devel. com. Newton Meml. Hosp., 1966-68, bd. govs. 1962-88, 93-95, emeritus 1995—, pres. bd. govs., 1968-71, chmn., 1971-73; founding incorporator, trustee NW Jersey Health Care, 1971-76; trustee, mem. exec. com. regional health planning coun. Health Systems Agy., 1976-83, 1984-87, v.p., 1978-79; trustee United Way of Sussex County, 1984-90, spl. gifts chmn., 1984-88, mem. allocations com. 1990-93; dir. North Jersey Health Care Corp., 1988-95, dir. emeritus, 1995—, asst. treas., 1991-93; dir. Prime Care, Inc., 1989-95, chmn. bd. trustees, 1989-92; mem. Sussex County Arts and Heritage Coun., chmn. hist. house tour, 1993-95; steering com. N.J. Highlands Coalition, 1993—. Mem. N.J. Vet. Med. Soc. Aux. (del. 1979-82, 88-91, 2d v.p. 1990-91), Am. Vet. Med. Soc. Aux. (nat. chmn. legis. com. 1986-88, long-range planning com. 1990-95, chmn. 1992, mem. constitution, by-laws coms. 1993-95), Morristown (N.J.) Club, Rotary (pres. 1967-68, Paul Harris fellow 1988, Svc. Above Self award 1993, Meritorious Svc. award 1998), Vernon Civic Assn. (dir. 1996—, v.p. 1997-98). Home: 68 Sand Pond Rd Hamburg NJ 07419-9623

BUITENHUIS, PETER MARTINUS, language professional, educator; b. London, Eng., Dec. 8, 1925; s. John A. and Irene (Cotton) B. B.A. with honors, Jesus Coll. Oxford (Eng.) U., 1949, M.A., 1954; Ph.D., Yale, 1955. Instr. U. Okla., Norman, 1949-51; instr. Am. studies Yale, 1954-59; assoc. prof. English Victoria Coll. U. Toronto, Ont., Can., 1959-66; vis. prof. U. Calif.-Berkeley, 1966-67; prof. McGill U., Montreal, Que., Can., 1967-75; prof., chmn. dept. English Simon Fraser U., Burnaby, B.C., Can., 1975-82; prof. emeritus English Simon Fraser U., Burnaby, B.C., Can., 1992. Author: Hugh MacLennan, 1968, The Grasping Imagination: the American Writings of Henry James, 1970, The Great War of Words: British, American and Canadian Propaganda and Fiction, 1914-1933, 1987, The House of the Seven Gables: Severing Family and Colonial Ties, 1991; editor: Selected Poems of E. J. Pratt, 1968, (with I. Nadel) George Orwell: A Reassessment, 1988, (with D. Staines) The Canadian Imagination; contbr. articles to profl. jours., popular press. Served to sub-lt. Royal Navy, 1943-46, Eng. Can. Coun. fellow, 1962-63; Am. Coun. Learned Socs. fellow, 1972-73; Social Scis. and Humanities Rsch. Coun. fellow, 1982-83, 91-94. Mem. Am. Studies Assn., Can. Assn. Am. Studies (pres. 1968-70), Can. Assn. Univ. Tchrs., Assn. Can. Studies. Home: 7019 Marine Dr, West Vancouver, BC Canada V7W 2T4 Office: Simon Fraser U, Dept English, Burnaby, BC Canada V5A 1S6

BUJAKE, JOHN EDWARD, JR., beverage company executive; b. N.Y.C., May 23, 1933; s. John E. and Mary (Muzyka) B.; m. Gail E. Cruise, Aug. 1, 1964; children: John Edward III, Laura, Jacquelyn, William. BS, Manhattan Coll., 1954; MS, Holy Cross Coll., 1955; PhD, Columbia U., 1959; MBA, NYU, 1963. Rsch. assoc. Lever Bros., Edgewater, N.J., 1959-68; dir. R & D Foods div. Coca Cola Co., Houston, 1968-72; dir. foods R&D, Quaker Oats Co., Barrington, Ill., 1972-77, dir. R&D, 1977-78; v.p. R&D, Seven Up Co., St. Louis, 1978-87; v.p. R&D Brown-Forman Beverage Co., Louisville, 1987-98; cons., 1998—; indsl. adv. bd. Speed Sch., U. Louisville. Mem. editl. bd. Research Mgmt, 1976-77, 97-98; contbr. articles to profl. jours. Mem. Indsl. Rsch. Inst., Am. Chem. Soc., Inst. Food Technologists, Internat. Life Scis. Inst., Calorie Control Coun. Home: 5805 Round Hill Rd Louisville KY 40222-5954 Office: 5805 Round Hill Rd Louisville KY 40222

BUJOLD, LOIS MCMASTER, science fiction writer; b. Columbus, Ohio, Nov. 2, 1949; d. Robert Charles and Laura Elizabeth (Gerould) McMaster; m. John Fredric Bujold, Oct. 9, 1971 (div. Dec. 1992); children: Anne Elizabeth, Paul Andre. Author: (novels) Shards of Honor, 1986, The Warrior's Apprentice, 1986, Ethan of Athos, 1986, Falling Free, 1988 (Nebula award 1989), Brothers in Arms, 1989, Borders of Infinity, 1989, The Vor Game, 1990 (Hugo award 1991), Barrayar, 1991 (Hugo award 1992, 1st place Locus poll 1992), Mirror Dance, 1994 (Hugo & Locus awards 1995), Cetaganda, 1996, Memory, 1996, Komarr, 1998, A Civil Campaign, 1999, (novellas) The Borders of Infinity, 1987, The Mountains of Mourning, 1989 (Nebula and Hugo awards 1990), Labyrinth, 1989 (Best Novella/Novelette Analytical Lab. 1990), Weatherman, 1990 (Best Novella Analytical Lab. 1991); contbr. short stories to sci. fiction mags., articles to profl. jours. Mem. Sci. Fiction and Fantasy Writers Am., Novelists, Inc. Office: Spectrum Literary Agency 111 8th Ave Ste 1501 New York NY 10011-5296

BUJOLD, TYRONE PATRICK, lawyer; b. Duluth, Minn., Dec. 4, 1937; s. Dewey J. and Lucille C. (Donahue) B.; m. Delia H. Goulet, Sept. 17, 1960; children: Christopher Andrew, Anne Elizabeth, Lara Suzanne. BS, Marquette U., 1959; JD, U. Minn., 1962. Bar: Minn. 1962, U.S. Dist. Ct. Minn. 1963, U.S. Ct. Appeals (8th cir.) 1964, Wis. 1983, U.S. Dist. Ct. (we. dist.) Wis. 1985, N.D. 1987. Assoc. Furuseth & Bujold, International Falls, Minn., 1962-63; assoc. Sullivan, MacMillan, Hanft & Hastings, Duluth, 1963-68, ptnr., 1968-85; ptnr. Robins, Kaplan, Miller & Ciresi, Mpls., 1985—; mem. faculty CLE program, Minn., 1965—, Inst. CLE, Ann Arbor, Mich., 1975—, Nat. Inst. Trial Advocacy, 1983—. Mem. Commn. Fair Housing and Employment Practices, Duluth, 1970-78, City Charter Commn., Duluth, 1983-85, Plymouth, Minn., 1991—. Mem. Am. Coll. Trial Lawyers, Internat. Soc. Barristers, Am. Bd. Trial Advocates. Roman Catholic. Avocations: reading, theatre, guitar, swimming. *

BUKANTZ, SAMUEL CHARLES, physician, educator; b. N.Y.C., Sept. 12, 1911; s. Barnett and Bertha (Stelson) B.; m. A. Jewell Williams, Apr. 5, 1941; children: Jessica, Dorothy. BS, Washington Sq. Coll., N.Y. U., 1930; MD, NYU, 1934. Intern in pathology Mt. Sinai Hosp., N.Y.C., 1934-35; intern in medicine Mt. Sinai Hosp., 1935-36, house physician, resident, 1936-38; assoc. prof. medicine Washington U., St. Louis, 1946-58; fellow in allergy Washington U., 1946-47; assoc. prof. medicine U. Colo., 1958-63; dir. medicine and research Children's Asthma Research Inst. and Hosp., 1958-63; assoc. prof. clin. medicine N.Y. U., 1963-72; prof. medicine U. South Fla., 1972—, head div. allergy and immunology, 1972-82, emeritus dir., 1982—, prof. med. microbiology and immunology, 1996—; pvt. practice medicine specializing in allergy and immunology N.Y.C., 1938-40, 66-72, St. Louis, 1954-58, Tampa, Fla., 1982-97; chief sect. allergy and clin. immunology VA Hosp., Tampa, 1972-82. Editor: Hosp. Practice, 1968—; Contbr. numerous articles on allergy and immunology to profl. jours. Served with AUS, 1941-46. Lucius Littauer and Parmelee fellow in pneumonia research, 1938-41; NIH grantee, 1947-63. Fellow ACP, AAAS; mem. Am. Coll. Chest Physicians, Am. Soc. Clin. Investigation, Cen. Soc. Clin. Rsch., Am. Acad. Allergy, Am. Coll. Allergy, Alpha Omega Alpha. Democrat. Jewish. Home: 4940 W San Rafael St Tampa FL 33629-5404 Office: U South Fla Coll of Medicine Box MDC 19 12901 Bruce B Downs Blvd Tampa FL 33612-4742

BUKER, ROBERT HUTCHINSON, SR., army officer, thoracic surgeon; b. Loi Mwe, Kengtung, Burma, Dec. 6, 1928; came to U.S., 1940; s. Richard S. and Minola (Hutchinson) B.; m. Ethel Hunt, Sept. 25, 1949; children: Robert Hutchinson, Traci, Nina Ruth. A.B., Boston U., 1949; M.S., U. Maine, 1952; M.D., Columbia U., 1956; postgrad., Indsl. Coll. of Armed Forces, 1978-79. Diplomate: Am. Bd. Surgery, Am. Bd. Thoracic Surgeons. Intern Gorgas Hosp, C.Z., 1956-57; gen. surg. residency Gorgas Hosp., C.Z., 1957-60; resident in thoracic surgery Kennedy V.A. Hosp., 1962-64, Tenn. Med. Ctr., 1962-64; capt. U.S. Army, 1964, advanced through grades to maj. gen.; chief surg. cons. Pentagon, Washington, 1973-76; comdr. U.S. Army Hosp., Wuerzburg, Germany, 1976-78; dep. chief staff opns. Health Services Command, Fort Sam Houston, Tex., 1979-80; comdr. Gen. Leonard Wood Army Hosp., Ft. Leonard Wood, Mo., 1980-81; commdr. Acad. Health Scis., Ft. Sam Houston, 1981-83; commdg. gen. Brooke Army Med. Center, Ft. Sam Houston, 1983-85; dep. Surgeon Gen. U.S. Army, Washington, 1985-89; chief surg. svcs. S.E. Kaiser-Permanente Med. Group, Atlanta, 1989-91; chief legal medicine and risk mgmt. Kaiser-Permanente Med. Group, Atlanta, 1991-94; clin. prof. surgery Uniform U. Health Scis., Bethesda, Md., 1981—. Fellow ACS (bd. govs. 1987-89), Am. Coll. Chest Physicians, Am. Coll. Physician Execs.; mem. AMA, Soc. Thoracic Surgeons, So. Thoracic Surg. Assn., Am. Acad. Med. Dirs. Baptist.

BUKONDA, NGOYI K. ZACHARIE, health care management educator; b. Lubumbashi, Shaba, Zaire, Feb. 14, 1951; came to U.S., 1987; s. Munyuka Kalambayi and Tumba (Tshileo) Marie; m. Muyumba Kapinga Agnes, Aug. 29, 1975; children: Munyuka Ngoyi, Muyumba Ngoyi, Kalambayi Ngoyi, Tshileo Ngoyi, Kashala Ngoyi, Ntumba Gloria Ngoyi. BS in Health Systems Mgmt., U. Kinshasa, Zaire, 1981; Diploma in Teaching, U. Zaire, 1983; MPH, U. Minn. Sch. Pub. Health, 1989; PhD, U. Minn., 1994. Hosp. adminstr. Gen. Hosp., Bukavu, Zaire, 1975-76; chief of bur. Ministry of Health Zaire, Kinshasa, 1981-83, chief div., 1983-87; health planner Sanru B.P. 3355 Kinshasa, Kinshasa, 1987; asst. prof. Inst. Superieur de Techniques Medicales, Kinshasa, 1981-87; grad. fellow African Am. Inst., N.Y.C., 1987-94; grad. teaching asst. Grad. Program in Social & Adminstrv. Pharmacy, Mpls., 1991-94; asst. prof. health care mgmt. So. Ill. U., Carbondale, 1994-97; asst. prof. pub. & cmty. health No. Ill. U. Sch. Allied Health Professions, DeKalb, 1997—; acad. sec. Inst. Superieur de Techniques Medicales, Kinshasa, 1983-86. Recipient Afgrad fellowship African Am. Inst., 1987, Melendy Grad. fellowship Coll. of Pharmacy, 1991; grantee Mac Arthur Interdisciplinary Program on Peace Internat., 1991; named Hon. Citizen of Louisville, 1986. Mem. APHA, Am. Pharmacy Assn., Assn. des Adminstrs. Gestionnaires (pres. 1981-87). Roman Catholic. Home: 925 Haish Blvd Dekalb IL 60115-4331 Office: No Ill U Sch Allied Health Profsns Dekalb IL 60115

BUKOVAC, MARTIN JOHN, horticulturist, educator; b. Johnston City, Ill., Nov. 12, 1929; s. John and Sadie (Fak) B.; m. Judith Ann Kelley, Sept. 5, 1956; 1 dau., Janice Louise. BS with honors, Mich. State U., 1951, MS, 1954, PhD, 1957; D honoris causa, U. Bonn, Germany, 1995. Asst. prof. horticulture Mich. State U., East Lansing, 1957-61, assoc. prof., 1961-63, prof., 1963; NSF sr. postdoctoral fellow Oxford U., U. Bristol, Eng., 1965-66; univ. disting. prof., 1992—; vis. lectr. Japan Atomic Energy Rsch. Inst., 1958; adviser IAEA, Vienna, 1961; NAS exch. lectr. Coun. Acads., Yugoslavia, 1971; vis. scholar Va. Poly. Inst., Blacksburg, 1973; guest lectr. Polish Acad. Scis., 1974; disting. vis. prof. N.Mex. State U., 1976; vis. prof. Japan Soc. Promotion Sci., Osaka Prefecture U., 1977; guest lectr. Serbian Sci. Coun., Fruit Rsch. Inst., Cacak, Yugoslavia, 1979; John A. Hannah Disting. lectr. Mich. State Hort. Soc., 1980; vis. prof. U. Guelph, Ont., Can., 1982,

Ohio State U., 1982, U. Zagreb, Yugoslavia, 1983, Ohio State U., 1990; collaborator Agrl. Rsch. Svc. USDA, 1982—; guest rschr. Hort. Rsch. Inst., Budapest, Hungary, 1983, Inst. Obstbau und Gemusebau U. Bonn, Fed. Republic Germany, 1986; Batjer Meml. lectr. Wash. State Hort. Soc., 1985; mem. agrl. rsch. adv. com. Eli Lilly Co., Indpls., 1971-88; cons. Dept. Agr.; disting. lectr. Dept. Sci. and Tech. Peoples Republic China, 1984; commencement spkr. Mich. State U., 1986; mem. internat. adv. bd. divsn. life scis. Ctr. for Nuclear Studies, Atomic Energy Commn., Grenoble, France, 1993—; Monselise Meml. lectr. Hebrew U., 1994; Agrl. Rsch. Svc. B.Y. Morrison Meml. lectr., 1994, Kermit Olson Meml. lectr. Univ. Minn., 1997; pres. Martin J. Bukovac Inc., 1996—; Donald L. Reichard Meml. lectr., Ohio State U., 1999. Mem. exec. adv. bd. Ency. of Agrl. Scis., 1991-96; mem. editl. adv. bd. Ctr. for Agr. and Bioscis. Internat., 1989—; internat. editl. bd. Horticultural Sci., Budapest; mem. editl. bd. Ency. of Agrl. Sci., 1991-96. Pres. Okemos Music Patrons, Mich., 1973-74; bd. dirs. Mich. State U. Press, 1983-92. 1st lt. U.S. Army, 1951-53. Recipient citation meritorious rsch. Am. Hort. Soc., 1970, Disting. Faculty award Mich. State U., 1971, Disting. Svc. award Mich. Hort. Soc., 1974, Disting. Faculty award Mich. Assn. Governing Bds., 1986, Hatch Meml. Medallion award USDA, 1987, Industry Man of Yr. award Nat. Cherry Festival, 1987, Alexander von Humboldt Rsch. prize, 1995, Am. Soc. Agrl. Engring. Outstanding Paper award, 1995; Bukovac Disting. Lectr. established in his honor Mich. State Horticultural Soc., 1995. Fellow AAAS, Am. Soc. Hort. Sci. (hon. life, pres. 1974-75, Joseph Harvey Gourley award 1969, 76, Marion Meadows award 1975, citation of appreciation 1975, Carroll R. Miller award 1980, Outstanding Researcher award 1988, M.A. Blake award for disting. grad. teaching 1975); mem. NAS, Am. Chem. Soc., Am. Soc. Plant Physiologists (Dennis R. Hoagland award 1988), Bot. Soc. Am., Scandinavian Soc. Plant Physiologists, Japanese Soc. Plant Physiologists, Internat. Soc. Hort. Sci., Soc. Exptl. Biology, Sigma Xi (pres. 1978-79 research award Kedzie chpt.), Phi Kappa Phi, Gamma Sigma Delta. Club: Mich. State U. Faculty. Home: 4428 Seneca Dr Okemos MI 48864-2946 Office: Mich State U Dept Horticulture East Lansing MI 48824

BUKOWIECKI, SISTER ANGELINE BERNADETTE, nun; b. Edmonton, Alta., Can., Aug. 24, 1937; came to U.S. 1960; d. Felix Peter and Stella Isabelle (Yagos) B. BA, Marillac Coll., St. Louis, 1969; MA in Dogmatic/Systematic Theology, St. Louis U., 1971. Joined Hosp. Sisters of the Third Order of St. Francis, 1962; co-foundress Franciscan Sisters of New Covenant, Roman Cath. Ch., 1979. Provincial Franciscan Sisters of New Covenant, Denver, 1979—; founder, dir. Cath. Evangelization Tng. Ctr., Denver, 1983-91; internat. dir. Assn. of Coords. of Cath. Schs. Evangelization/2000, Rome, 1991-92, Cath. Evangelizaton Tng. Ctr., Denver, 1991—; adminstrv. bd. Immaculate Heart of Mary Parish Coun., Northglenn, Colo., 1983-85. Author or co-author 16 books, 1983-91. Mem. Nat. Coun. Cath. Evangelization (bd. dirs. 1983-85). Home: 10620 Livingston Dr Denver CO 80234-3732 *I have learned over the years to live in the present moment: the key to peace and joy. It is the only moment we have. The past cannot be changed and the future is as yet unknown. To worry about either leads to a loss of the present moment where true effectiveness is to be found. To walk in the present moment is to walk with God.*

BUKOWINSKI, MARK STEFAN TADEUSZ, geophysics educator; b. Trani, Italy, Oct. 17, 1946; came to U.S., 1962; s. Stanley K. and Jadwiga Teresa (Jezierski) B.; m. Halina V. Mudy, June 20, 1970; children: Katherine, Anne, John, Christopher. BS in Physics, UCLA, 1969, PhD in Physics, 1975. Asst. rsch. geophysicist Inst. Geophysics and Planetary Physics, UCLA, 1975-78; asst. prof. U. Calif., Berkeley, 1978-82, assoc. prof., 1982-89, prof., 1989—, vice chmn. dept. geology and geophysics, 1997—. Assoc. editor Jour. Geophys. Rsch., 1988-91; mem. bd. editors Phys. Earth Planetary Interiors, 1992—; contbr. over 50 articles to sci. jours. NSF grantee, 1976—, Inst. Geophysics and Planetary Physics. Mem. AAAS, Am. Geophys. Union (mem. mineral physics com. 1988-90), Mineralog. Soc. Am. (mem. publs. com. 1988-91, chair 1991-92, elected fellow 1995). Avocations: hiking, photography, computers. Home: 5738 Laurelwood Pl Concord CA 94521-4807 Office: U Calif Berkeley Dept Geology and Geophysics Berkeley CA 94720

BUKOWY, STEPHEN JOSEPH, accounting educator; b. Phila., May 24, 1949; s. Stephen and Ida Teresa (Zigman) B.; m. Joy Coughenour, Oct. 14, 1950; 1 child, Catherine Alexis. BS in Acctg., Pa. State U., 1971; MBA, Coll. William & Mary, 1976; M Forest Resources, U. Ga., 1989, PhD in Acctg., 1993. CPA, Va. Grad. asst. Coll. William and Mary, Williamsburg, Va., 1975-76; acct., auditor GAO, Washington, 1976-82; asst. prof. Emory (Va.) and Henry Coll., 1982-84; grad. asst. U. Ga., Athens, 1984-88; asst. prof. Bradley U., Peoria, Ill., 1988-92; acct. Darts & Pool, Peoria, 1992-93; sr. fin. analyst U.S. Coast Guard, Washington, 1990-94; asst. prof. acctg., MBA dir. U. N.C., Pembroke, 1994—. Comdr. USCGR, 1971-95. Mem. AICPA, Res. Officers Assn. (pres. Peoria chpt. 1991-92), Inst. Mgmt. Accts., Am. Acctg. Assn., Soc. Am. Foresters, Beta Alpha Psi, Beta Gamma Sigma. Avocations: stamp collecting, reading, woodworking. Office: U NC Pembroke PO Box 1510 1 University Dr Pembroke NC 28372

BUKRY, JOHN DAVID, geologist; b. Balt., May 17, 1941; s. Howard Leroy and Irene Evelyn (Davis) Snyder. Student, Colo. Sch. Mines, 1959-60; BA, Johns Hopkins U., 1963; MA, Princeton U., 1965, PhD, 1967; postgrad., U. Ill., 1965-66, De Anza Coll., 1995-96. Geologist U.S. Army Corp Engrs., Balt., 1963; research asst. Mobil Oil Co., Dallas, 1965; geologist U.S. Geol. Survey, La Jolla, Calif., 1967-84, U.S. Minerals Mgmt. Svc., La Jolla, 1984-86, U.S. Geol. Survey, Menlo Park, Calif., 1986-96; scientist emeritus U.S. Geol.Survey, La Jolla, 1996-98, Menlo Park, 1998—; rsch. assoc. geol. rsch. divsn. Scripps Instn. Oceanography-U. Calif., San Diego, 1970—; cons. Deep Sea Drilling Project, La Jolla, 1967-87; lectr. Vetlesen Symposium, Columbia U., N.Y.C., 1968, 3d Internat. Planktonic Conf., Kiel, Fed. Republic Germany, 1974, Brit. Petroleum Exploration Seminar on nannoplankton biostratigraphy, Houston, 1989; shipboard micropaleontologist on D/V Glomar Challenger, 5 Deep Sea Drilling Project cruises, 1968-78; mem. stratigraphic correlations bd. NSF/Joint Oceanographic Instns. for Deep Earth Sampling, 1976-79. Author: Leg I of the Cruises of the Drilling Vessel Glomar Challenger, 1969, Coccoliths from Texas and Europe, 1969, Leg LXIII of the Cruises of the Drilling Vessel Glomar Challenger, 1981; editor: Marine Micropaleontology, 1976-83, mem. editl. bd. Micropaleontology, 1985-90. Mobil Oil, Princeton U. fellow, 1965-67; Am. Chem. Soc., Princeton U. fellow, 1966-67. Fellow AAAS, Geol. Soc. Am., Explorers Club; mem. NSTA, Hawaiian Malacological Soc., Paleontol. Rsch. Inst., Am. Assn. Petroleum Geologists, Soc. Econ. Paleontologists and Mineralogists, Internat. Nannoplankton Assn., Ecol. Soc. Am., European Union Geoscis., Oceanography Soc., U. Calif.-San Diego Ida and Cecil Green Faculty Club, San Diego Shell Club, Princeton Club No. Calif., Sigma Xi. Avocations: basketball, photography, shell and mineral collecting. Achievements include research in stratigraphy, paleoecology and taxonomy for 300 new species of marine nannoplankton used in ocean history studies. Office: US Geol Survey (910) 345 Middlefield Rd Menlo Park CA 94025-3591

BULA, RAYMOND J., agronomist; b. Antigo, Wis., Aug. 3, 1927; s. Stanley and Mary (Klamerus) B.; m. Mary G. Wipperfurth, Aug. 9, 1952; children—R. Gregory, William J., Margaret A., Joseph M., Michael S., Catherine M., Julie C., Carol P. BS, U. Wis., 1949, MS, 1950, PhD, 1952. Asst. prof. N.Y. State Agr. Exptl. Sta., Geneva, N.Y., 1952-53; agronomist Alaska Agr. Expt. Sta., Palmer, 1953-56; agronomist, prof. Purdue U., West Lafayette, Inc., 1956-79; area dir. U.S. Dept. Agr., 1974-79; dir. U.S. Dairy Forage Rsch. Ctr., Madison, Wis., 1979-84.; dir. rsch. Phytofarms Am., Inc., De Kalb, Ill., 1984-86; exec. dir. Wis. Ctr. for Space Automation and Robotics, U. Wis., Madison, 1986-94; dir. Wis. Ctr. for Space Automation and Robotics U. Wis., Madison, 1994-98; prin. Rapigen, LLC, Madison, 1998—. Tech. editor: Agronomy Jour, 1980-83. Served with AUS, 1945-47. Fellow AAAS, Am. Soc. Agronomy; mem. Am. Soc. Gravity and Space Biology, Crop Sci. Soc. Am., Am. Soc. Plant Physiologists, Sigma Xi, Phi Kappa Phi. Roman Catholic. Office: U Wis Ctr Space Automation & Robotics Madison WI 53706

BULCKEN, CAROLYN ANNE BROOKS, retired special education educator; b. Balt., Jan. 10, 1933; d. Roland Bowers and Evelyn Mabel Brooks; m. George W. Bulcken, Nov. 23, 1952 (div. Apr. 1989); children: Cheryl Bulcken Sawyer, Cynthia Bulcken Coker, George W. III, Richard B. BS, Towson State U., 1955; MS, U. Houston, Clear Lake, 1977. Cert. ednl. diagnostician, spl. edn. and elem. tchr., Tex., Md. Tchr. Balt. County Schs., 1955-59; T Friendswood (Tex.) Ind. Sch. Dist., 1965-67; tchr., dept. chair Dickinson (Tex.) Ind. Sch. Dist., 1969-77; ednl. diagnostician Galveston (Tex.) Ind. Sch. Dist., 1977-87, diagnostic learning specialist, 1987-94. Fulbright chmn. Inst. for Internat. Edn., Houston. Recipient cert. of appreciation U.S. Info. Agy. Mem. NEA, Tex. State Tchrs. Assn., Mensa (proctor coord. Gulf Coast chpt.), Tex. Ednl. Diagnosticians Assn., Houston Met. Ednl. Diagnosticians Assn., Order Eastern Star, Phi Kappa Phi, Phi Delta Kappa, Kappa Delta Pi, Beta Sigma Phi. Avocations: travel, gifted children, reading.

BULDRINI, GEORGE JAMES, lawyer; b. N.Y.C.; s. Frederick Paul and Emily Geraldine (Bewick) B. BA, St. Johns U., Jamaica, N.Y., 1969; JD, St. Johns U., 1972; LLM, NYU, 1976. Bar: N.Y. 1973, U.S. Dist. Ct. (no. dist.) N.Y. 1975, U.S. Supreme Ct. 1976. Sr. atty. N.Y. State Dept. Health, Albany, 1974—; shop steward Pub. Employees Fedn., 1982—. Mem. ABA, NRA, N.Y. State Bar Assn., Fed. Bar Assn. Republican. Avocations: golf, chess, reading, gardening, photography. Office: NY Dept Health Legal Affairs Empire State Plz Albany NY 12237

BULGER, BRIAN WEGG, lawyer; b. Chgo., May 27, 1951; s. John Burton and Mary Jane (Wegg) B.; m. Laura Ellen McErlean, Sept. 12, 1981; children: Burton, Kevin. AB cum laude, Georgetown U., 1972, JD, 1977. Bar: Ill. 1977, U.S. Dist. Ct. (no. dist.) Ill. 1977, U.S. Ct. Appeals (4th, 7th and 8th cirs.) 1977, U.S. Supreme Ct. 1980. From assoc. to ptnr. Pope Ballard Shepard & Fowle, Chgo., 1977-87; ptnr., dept. head Katten Muchin & Zavis, Chgo., 1987-94; founding ptnr. Bates, Meckler, Bulger & Tilson, Chgo., 1994—; adj. prof. U. Wis. Mgmt. Inst., Milw., 1980—. Contbr. articles to profl. jours. Bd. dirs. Anixter Ctr., Chgo. Mem. ABA (chair pub. employer labor rels. com. sect. on urban state and govt. law), Ill. State Bar Assn., Georgetown Law Alumni (bd. dirs. 1984-93). Roman Catholic. Avocations: baseball, reading, boating, skeet shooting. Office: Bates Meckler Bulger Tilson 8300 Sears Tower 233 S Wacker Dr Chicago IL 60606-6339*

BULGER, ROGER JAMES, academic health center executive; b. Bklyn., May 18, 1933; s. William Joseph and Florence Dorothy (Poggi) B.; m. Ruth Ellen Grouse, June 8, 1960; children: Faith Anne, Grace Ellen. AB, Harvard U., 1955, MD, 1960; postgrad., Emmanuel Coll., Cambridge (Eng.) U., 1955-56; hon. degree, Thomas Jefferson U., U. Md., Western U. Health Scis., 1998. Intern, then resident in internal medicine U. Wash. Hosps., 1960-62, 64-65; trainee in infectious disease and microbiology U. Wash., 1962-63, 65-66; renal and metabolic diseases Boston U., 1963-64; from asst. prof. to assoc. prof. medicine U. Wash. Med. Sch., Seattle, 1966-70; med. dir. Univ. Hosp., Seattle, 1967-70; prof. cmty. health scis., assoc. dean allied health Duke U. Med. Ctr., 1970-72; exec. officer Inst. Medicine, Nat. Acad. Scis., 1972-76; prof. internal medicine George Washington U. Sch. Medicine, 1972-76; prof. internal medicine, family and community medicine, dean Med. Sch., chancellor Worcester campus U. Mass., 1976-78; pres. U. Tex. Health Sci. Ctr., Houston, 1978-88; pres., CEO Assn. Acad. Health Ctrs, 1988—. Author: Hippocrates Revisited, 1973, In Search of Modern Hippocrates, 1987, Technology, Bureaucracy and Healing, 1988, The Quest for Mercy, 1998; also articles, chpts. in books; mem. editl. bd. various jours. Bd. dirs. Georgetown U., Rsch. Am.!. Lionel de Jersey Harvard fellow, 1955-56. Fellow ACP, Assn. for Health Svcs. Rsch. (disting.); mem. Inst. Medicine, Infectious Disease Soc. Am., Nat. Acad. Social Ins. Office: Assoc Acad Health Ctrs 1400 16th St NW Ste 720 Washington DC 20036-2224*

BULKA, DOUGLAS GLENN, artist; b. Detroit, June 27, 1954; s. Eugene William and Betty Jane (Tripodi) B. Student, U. Mich., 1973-75; BFA, Wayne State U., 1977, MFA, 1986. Instr. Your Heritage House, Detroit, 1977-78, Lawrence Technol. U., Southfield, Mich., 1981-82, Wayne State U., Detroit, 1984-87; conservation program coord. Commn. on Art in Pub. Places, State of Mich., 1990; collection care specialist Detroit Inst. Arts, 1976—; lectr./instr. The Drawing & Print Club, Detroit, 1984, Profl. Picture Framers Assn., Chgo., 1990; vis. artist Wayne State U., 1995, No. Mich. U., Marquette, 1998; curator "Ambient Luminosity" Detroit Artists Mkt., 1997; juror "The Print" Ann Arbor Art Ctr., 1998. Solo shows include Lemberg Gallery, 1992, 95, Cantor/Lemberg Gallery, 1988, Detroit Artists Market, 1993, Muskegon Mus. Art, 1986; group shows include Detroit Inst. of Arts, 1994, 97, Left Bank Gallery, Laguna Beach, Calif., 1997, Eastern Mich. U., 1995, BASF, Dalton, Ga., 1994, New Eng. Fine Art Inst., Boston, 1993, Regiment Armory, N.Y., 1989, U. Mich. Mus. Art, Ann Arbor, 1981. Edn. coord. Cass Corridor Food Coop., Detroit, 1981-82; bd. dirs. Detroit Focus Gallery, 1991-92, chmn. exhbn. com., 1994-95, mem. exhbn. com., 1991-95; mem. exhbn. com., bd. dirs. Detroit Artists Market, 1995—. Recipient Cert. of Merit, Oswego (N.Y.) Civic Art Ctr., 1988; Creative Artists grantee Arts Found. Mich. and Mich. Coun. for Arts and Cultural Affairs, 1992, Purchase award Artworks Fund NEA and Arts Midwest, 1997; Arts Midwest/NEA Reg. Visual Artist fellow, 1996. Home: 1438 Iroquois St Detroit MI 48214-2716

BULKELEY, BROOKE, healthcare administratrator, small business owner; b. Chgo., Feb. 27, 1969. BA in Bus. Admistrn. in Mgmt., Briar Cliff Coll., Sioux City, Iowa, 1991; MBA in Non-Profit Mgmt., U. Nebr., Omaha, 1996. Fin. counselor U. Nebr. Med. Ctr., 1991-94, managed care analyst, 1994-98; contract mgr. U. Utah Hosp., Salt Lake City, 1998—; owner The Vending Connection, Farmington, Utah, 1999—. Mem. ASAP, Hosp. Fin. Mgmt. Assn. Democrat. Roman Catholic. Avocations: golf, fitness, movies, woodwork. Fax: 801-297-4949. E-mail: brooke.bulkeley@hsc.utah.edu. Office: U Utah Hosp 127 South 500 East Ste 310 Salt Lake City UT 84100

BULKLEY, ROBERT DE GROFF, JR., lawyer; b. Toledo, Ohio, June 19, 1943; s. Robert De Groff and Loretta (Coburn) B.; m. Linda Gail Throp, June 20, 1964 (div. May 1982); children: Joanna Eleanor, Katrina Elisabeth; m. Joyce Lorraine MacWilliamson, Feb. 10, 1985. BA, Lewis & Clark Coll., 1964; MA, Princeton U., 1966, PhD, 1971; JD, U. Oreg., 1977. Bar: Oreg. 1977, U.S. Dist. Ct. Oreg. 1978, U.S. Ct. Appeals (9th cir.) 1978, U.S. Supreme Ct. 1990. Instr. history Benedict Coll., Columbia, S.C., 1966-67; asst. prof. history Rocky Mountain Coll., Billings, Mont., 1968-74; law clk. U.S. Ct. Appeals, 9th Cir., Portland, Oreg., 1977-78; asst. atty. gen. Oreg. Dept. Justice, Portland, 1978-83; staff atty. Oreg. Ct. Appeals, Salem, 1983-90, 95—; assoc. Markowitz, Herbold et al, Portland, 1990-92, of counsel, 1992-95. Clk. of session First Presbyn. Ch., Portland, 1986-89, mem. various coms., 1980—; mem. peace and justice com. Presbytery of the Cascades, Portland, 1989-95, mem. higher edn. com., 1998—; mem. cmty. ministries com. Ecumenical Ministries of Oreg., Portland, 1995-97. Woodrow Wilson fellow, 1964. Mem. Oreg. State Bar. Democrat. Avocations: hiking, rail fan, reading. Home: 11585 SW Denfield St Beaverton OR 97005-1580 Office: Oregon Court of Appeals 300 Justice Bldg Salem OR 97310

BULL, BERGEN IRA, retired equipment manufacturing company executive; b. Lansing, Mich., Feb. 28, 1940; s. W. Ira and Thelma (Roof) B.; m. Janet Mary Blachford, Sept. 22, 1961; children: Damon, Lauren. BA, Mich. State U., 1962; MA, Middle Tenn. State U., 1965; JD, Lewis and Clark Coll., 1969. Bar: Oreg. 1969. Acct. Hyster Co., Portland, Oreg., 1965-66, mem. credit dept., 1966-67, asst. to sec., 1967-71, asst. sec., 1971-72, sec., 1972-78, v.p., legal officer, sec., 1978-86, v.p., gen. counsel, sec., 1986-87, v.p. corp. adminstrn., gen. counsel, sec., 1987-89; v.p., gen. counsel, sec. NACCO Materials Handling Group, Inc., 1989-95, ret., 1995; instr. bus. law Portland State U., 1971-72. Loaned exec. United Fund, 1968; bd. dirs. Assoc. Oreg. Industries, 1981-96; bd. dirs. Jr. Achievement, 1980—, vice chmn., 1993, chmn., 1994; bd. dirs. Modern Group, Ltd., 1995—; bd. dirs., treas. Sunriver Music Festival, 1997—; bd. dirs. Sunriver Nature Ctr., 1998—. Lt. USAF, 1963-65. Mem. Oreg. Bar Assn. (inactive), Multnomah Athletic Club, Sunriver Racquet Club, Bend Golf and Country Club, Crosswater Club. Episcopalian.

BULL, BRIAN STANLEY, pathology educator, medical consultant, business executive; b. Watford, Hertfordshire, Eng., Sept. 14, 1937; came to U.S., 1954, naturalized, 1960; s. Stanley and Agnes Mary (Murdoch) B.; m. Maureen Hannah Huse, June 3, 1963; children: Beverly Velda, Beryl Heather. B.S. in Zoology, Walla Walla Coll., 1957; M.D., Loma Linda (Calif.) U., 1961. Diplomate: Am. Bd. Pathology. Intern Yale U., 1961-62, resident in anat. pathology, 1962-63; resident in clin. pathology NIH, Bethesda, Md., 1963-65; fellow in hematology and electron microscopy NIH, 1965-66, staff hematologist, 1966-67; research asst. dept. anatomy Loma Linda U., 1958, dept. microbiology, 1959, asst. prof. pathology, 1968-71, assoc. prof., 1971-73, prof., 1973—, chmn. dept. pathology, 1973—, assoc. dean for acad. affairs sch. medicine, 1993-94, dean sch. medicine, 1994—; cons. to mfrs. of med. testing devices; mem. panel on hematology FDA; mem. Nat. Com. on Clin. Lab. Standards; mem. Internat. Commn. for Standardization in Hematology, pres., 1996-97. Mem. bd. editors Blood Cells, Molecules and Diseases, 1995—; contbr. chpts. to books, articles to med. jours.; patentee in field; editor-in-chief Blood Cells N.Y. Heidelberg, 1985-94. Served with USPHS, 1963-67. Nat. Inst. Arthritis and Metabolic Diseases fellow, 1967-68; recipient Daniel D. Comstock Meml. award Loma Linda U., 1961, Merck Manual award, 1961, Mosby Scholarship Book award, 1961; Ernest B. Cotlove Meml. lectr. Acad. Clin. Lab. Physicians and Scientists, 1972; named Alumnus of Yr., Walla Walla Coll., 1984, Honored Alumnus, Loma Linda U. Sch. Medicine, 1987, Humanitarian award, 1991, Citizen of Yr., C. of C. of Loma Linda, 1997. Fellow Am. Soc. Clin. Pathologists, Am. Soc. Hematology, Coll. Am. Pathologists, FDA Panel on Hematology and Palhology Devices, Nat. Com. on Clin. Lab. Standards, Internat. Commn. for Standards in Hematology (pres.), N.Y. Acad. Scis.; mem. AMA, Calif. Soc. Pathologists, San Berandino County Med. Soc. (William C. Cover Outstanding Contbn. to Medicine award 1994), Acad. Clin. Lab. Physicians and Scientists, Am. Assn. Pathologists, Sigma Xi, Alpha Omega Alpha. Seventh-day Adventist. Achievements include patents in field of blood analysis instrumentation; development of quality control algorithms for blood analyzer calibration; origination of techniques and instrumentation for the measurement of thrombosis risk and for regulation of anti-coagulation during cardiopulmonary bypass. Office: Loma Linda U Sch Medicine 11234 Anderson St Loma Linda CA 92354-2871

BULL, DAVID, fine art conservator; b. Bristol, Eng., Mar. 5, 1934; came to U.S., 1978; s. Andrew John Michael and Betty (Horler) B.; m. Janette Christine Brewer, July 26, 1955 (div. Nov. 1986); children: Victoria, Stephen, Matthew, Nicholas, Sebastian; m. Teresa Jarvis Longyear, June 3, 1989; 1 child, David Douglas John. Nat. diploma, city and guilds diploma, West of Eng. Coll. Art, 1955. Restorer of paintings City Art Gallery, Bristol, 1957-60; restorer Nat. Gallery, London, 1960-65; ptnr. David Bull and Robert Shepherd (art restorers), London, 1965-78; head painting conservation J. Paul Getty Mus., Malibu, Calif., 1978-80; dir. Norton Simon Mus., Pasadena, Calif., 1980-81; pres. Fine Art Conservation and Restoration Inc., Los Angeles, 1981—; head of painting conservation Nat. Gallery Art, Washington, 1984-89, chmn. of painting conservation, 1990—; bd. dirs. Save Venice, Inc., 1996—. Fellow Internat. Inst. Conservation. Home: 173 East 80th St New York NY 10021 Office: c/o REFF STe 202 13107 Ventura Blvd Studio City CA 91604

BULL, GEORGE ALBERT, retired banker; b. Red Lion, Pa., May 28, 1927; s. Mervin E. and Edna May (Gohn) B.; m. Grace Kathryn Rudolph, Nov. 13, 1949; children—Donna Carol, Diana Sue, David Alan. Student Grad. Sch. Banking, Rutgers U., 1961. From teller to cashier Citizens Nat. Bank, Front Royal, Va., 1947-64; asst. v.p., cashier Monticello Nat. Bank, Charlottesville, Va., 1964; asst. cashier Nat. Bank & Trust Co., Charlottesville, 1964-80, asst. to pres., 1980-90, exec. v.p., regional pres., asst. to pres., 1985-88, sr. exec. v.p., asst. to pres., 1988-89; exec. v.p. and treas. Jefferson Bankshares, Inc., Charlottesville, 1979-89; With U.S. Army, 1945-46. Mem. Masons. Home: 2315 Wakefield Rd Charlottesville VA 22901-1843

BULL, HENRIK HELKAND, architect; b. N.Y.C., July 13, 1929; s. Johan and Sonja (Geelmuyden) B.; m. Barbara Alpaugh, June 9, 1956; children: Peter, Nina. B.Arch., Mass. Inst. Tech., 1952. With Mario Corbett, San Francisco, 1954-55; pvt. practice, 1956-68; ptnr. Bull, Field, Volkmann, Stockwell, Calif., 1968-82, Bull, Volkmann, Stockwell, Calif., 1982-90, Bull Stockwell and Allen, Calif., 1990-93, Bull, Stockwell, Allen & Ripley, San Francisco, 1993-96, BSA Architects, San Francisco, 1996—; Vis. lectr. Syracuse U., 1963; Mem. adv. com. San Francisco Urban Design Study, 1970-71. *Recipient of more than 40 major design awards. Best known for timeless designs which fit sensitively into their environments. Regular contributor to Snow Country and Ski Area Management magazines. A recognized authority on the design of buildings in harsh climates. Winner of an invited competition for the planning of the proposed Capital City of Alaska in 1978.* Works include Sunset mag. Discovery House, Tahoe Tavern Condominiums, Lake Tahoe, Calif., Snowmass Villas Condominiums, Aspen, Colo., Northstar Master Plan Village and Condominiums, Moraga Valley Presbyn. Ch., Calif., Spruce Saddle Restaurant and Poste-Montane Hotel, Beaver Creek, Colo., Bear Valley visitor ctr., Point Reyes, Calif., The Inn at Spanish Bay, Pebble Beach, Calif., Taluswood Cmty., Whistler, B.C. Served as 1st lt. USAF, 1952-54. Winner competition for master plan new Alaska capital city, Willow, 1978. Fellow AIA (pres. N. Calif. chpt. 1968, Firm award Calif. chpt. 1989). Democrat. Office: BSA Architects 350 Pacific Ave San Francisco CA 94111-1708

BULL, INEZ STEWART, special education and gifted music educator, coloratura soprano, pianist, editor, author; b. Newark, Apr. 13, 1920; d. Johan Randulf and Aurora (Stewart) B. Diploma in piano, Juilliard, 1946; cert., Chautauqua Inst. Sch. Music, 1940-46; diploma, U. Oslo Grad. Sch., Norway, 1955; MusB, N.Y. Coll. Music, 1965; MA, NYU, 1972, EdD, 1979. Piano tchr. Juilliard Inst. Musical Art, N.Y., 1942-43; chmn. music dept. Casement's Coll., Ormond Beach, Fla., 1949-50; dir. music Essex County Girls Vocat. & Tech. H.S., Newark, 1953-57; dir. music, organist State of N.J. Institution for Retarded Girls North Jersey Tng. Sch., Totowa, N.J., 1953-68; spl. edn. gifted coord. Jefferson Magnet Sch. in Union City (N.J.) Pub. Sch. Sys., 1956-95; dir. Upper Montclair Music Sch., Montclair, N.J., 1945—, Ole Bull Music Sch., Potter County, Pa., 1952-68; adjudicator Lycoming Coll., Williamsport, Pa., 1948—; conductor Whippany Symphony Orch., 1951-52; curator, builder Ole Bull Mus., Carter Camp, Pa., 1968—; dir. youth chorus Jefferson Sch., Union City, 1956-95; dir. Hudson County Elem. Choral Festival, 1971—; artist-in-residence, Union City; guest lectr. Columbia U., N.Y.C., Yale U. Grad. Sch. Music, Hartford, Conn., NYU, Lycoming Coll., Williamsport, Pa., Mansfield U., Pa., Princeton U., N.J., U. Scranton, Pa., Jersey City State Coll. Author 20 books; editor various newsletters and mags.; author (song): Evening Prayer, 1934, I Will Bow and Be Humble, 1954, Voice of America, 1952; recording artist Educo Records; soloist WFMB radio sta. Daytona Beach, Fla., Norsk Rikskringkasting, Oslo, Radio and Television Francaise, Paris; recitals in France, Norway, Eng., Switzerland, South Am., U.S. Choir dir. First Congl. Ch., 1940-43, Holy Trinity Luth. Ch., Nutley Luth. Ch., 1953-55; organist, choir dir. North Jersey Tng. Sch. Chapel, 1952-68; founder, dir. Ole Bull Music Festival, 1952—; dep. gov. and mem. rsch. bd. advisors Am. Biog. Inst., Raleigh; U.S. State Dept amb. of goodwill to Norway by order of Pres. Dwight D. Eisenhower, 1953, Norwegian Goodwill amb. of goodwill to U.S. by order of King Haakon VII, 1953. Decorated knight with St. Olav Cross by King Herald V (Norway), 1999; recipient Freedom medal-Eisenhower medal, 1953, Sterling Silver plaque King Olav V of Norway, 1966, NJEA award, 1970, Performing Arts Prestige award in Edn., 1976, Olympic Gold medal Norwegian Govt., 1992, Silver medal of Honor, 1991, Gold medal of Honor, 1992, Pa. Senate Legis. citation, 1992, Outstanding Tchr. of the Handicapped in the U.S. Nat. Rsch. Coun., 1970, Woman of Distinction honorable mention award Girl Scout Coun. of Greater Essex County, 1996, Artisan award Oakside Bloomfield Cultural Ctr., 1996, 50 Women You Should Know award Internat. YWCA, 1996; Fulbright scholar U. Oslo (Norway) Grad. Sch., 1955; film made in her honor A Child is Waiting, 1963. Mem. Ole Bull Hist. Soc. (pres. 1972—), Phi Delta Kappa (pres. 1984-86, newsletter editor 1984-92), Kappa Delta Pi (pres. 1984—, newsletter editor 1984—, counselor NYU Beta Pi chpt. 1996), Pen & Brush Club, Internat. Percy Grainger Soc. (v.p.), NYU Alumnae Club Inc. (bd. dirs., rec. sec., newsletter editor, 1979—). Republican. Avocations: concert pianist, soprano, writer. Home: 172 Watchung Ave Montclair NJ 07043-1737 Office: Robert Waters Sch 2800 Summit Ave Union City NJ 07087-2329

BULL, JAMES ROBERT, publishing executive; b. Evanston, Ill., Jan. 9, 1956; s. David C. and Mary Louise (Stowers) B.; m. Erin M. Mulligan, Nov. 30, 1991. BA, Colby Coll., 1978. Sponsoring editor Mayfield Pub. Co., Mount View, Calif., 1984-96; pres., pub. Bull Pub. Co., Palo Alto, Calif., 1994—. Office: Bull Pub Co 110 Gilbert Ave Menlo Park CA 94025-2865*

BULL, JOHN P., critical care nurse, electrophysiology nurse; b. Abilene, Tex., Dec. 26, 1963; s. Eddie U. and Phyllis A. (Burkett) B.; m. Dara K. Bull, Dec. 29, 1984. AAS in Nursing, Amarillo Coll., 1986. RN, Tex.; cert. ACLS provider and instr. Charge nurse med. ICU, NW Tex. Hosp., Amarillo, staff nurse med. ICU, staff nurse med.-telemetry floor; staff nurse cardiac catheterization lab. Humana Hosp., Abilene; staff nurse ICU Humana Hosp.; staff electrophysiology nurse Arrhythmia Svcs. Seton Med. Ctr., Austin, Tex.; sales rep. Medtronic, Inc. Mem. AACN, NASPE (AM/AP Testamur cert.). Home: PO Box 1316 Pflugerville TX 78691-1316

BULL, LEONARD S., educational association administrator; b. Westfield, Mass., Jan. 31, 1941. BS in Dairy Sci., Okla. State U., 1963, MS in Animal Nutrition, 1964; PhD in Animal Nutrition, Cornell U., 1969. Pres. Am. Soc. Animal Sci., Savoy, Ill., 1998; v.p. World Assn. Animal Prodn., 1998—; assoc., vice chancellor Internat. Program, 1997—; founding assoc. dir. N.E. Dairy Foods Rsch. Ctr., Vt.-Cornell, 1987-88; guest lectr., spkr. in field; funding devel. activities for various univs., including U. Md., U. Ky., U. Maine, U. Vt., N.C. State U. Editl. bd.: Am. Soc. Animal Sci., 1977-79, 85-87; contbr. articles to profl. jours. Mem. Planning Commn., Fairfax, Vt., 1986-88; asst. den leader Cub Scouts, 1992-94; adminstrv. bd. Benson Meml. Meth. Ch., 1993—, trustees, 1994—, chmn. 1995—. Named Disting. Nutritionist, Distillers Feed Rsch. Coun., 1993, others. Mem. Am. Soc. Animal Sci., Am. Dairy Sci. Assn., Am. Inst. Nutrition, Am. Registry of Profl. Animal Scientists, Am. Forage and Grassland Coun., Registry of Environ. and Agrl. Profls., Coun. for Agr. Sci. and Tech., Sigma Xi, Phi Kappa Phi, Phi Sigma, Alpha Zeta, others. Fax: 919-515-3201. Office: Office of Internat Program NC State Univ Box 7112 Raleigh NC 27695-7112

BULL, LOUIS ANTAL (TONY), sales executive; b. Washington, Pa., Aug. 7, 1961; s. Lawrence M. and Emily J. (Antal) B.; m. Phillis Marie DeVictor, Feb. 7, 1961; children: Haley Marie, Katelyn Elizabeth, Carly Elise. BS in Bus. Adminstrn., Miami U., Oxford, Ohio, 1983. Advt. rep. Procter & Gamble, Cin., 1983-85; ter. mgr. Johnson & Johnson, Raritan, N.J., 1985-87; sales rep. Baxter Healthcare, Deerfield, Ill., 1987-90; regional mgr. Seabrook Med., Cin., 1990-97; nat. sales and mktg. mgr. IHD, Inc., Cin., 1997—. Trustee Highmeadows Civic Assn., Powell, Ohio, 1991—; mem. corp. coun. Soc. Am. Gastrointestinal Endoscopic Surgeons. Mem. Am. Mktg. Assn., Phi Gamma Delta. Avocations: golf, football, history. Home: 5229 Birchwood Farms Dr Mason OH 45040-3625 Office: IHD Inc 4675 Cornell Rd Ste 180 Cincinnati OH 45241-2498

BULL, SANDY (ALEXANDER BENJAMIN BULL), musician, composer; b. N.Y.C., Feb. 25, 1941; s. Harry and Daphne (Bayne) B.; m. Candice Ann Marks, June 20, 1979; children: Cassandra, Jesse, Jackson. Studied banjo with Eric Darling, 1955-57; student in music, Boston U., 1959-61; studied percussion with Billy Higgins, 1961-64, studied oud with Hamza El Din, 1963-68, studied sarod with Ali Akbar Khan, 1976-77. Multi-instrumentalist on guitar, keyboards, bass, banjo, pedal steel, percussion, oud and sarod, also engr., composer, arranger, prodr.; host/prodr. The Music of Man/WNCN-FM, N.Y.C., 1963; compositions include Blend, Gospel Tune, No Deposit No Return Blues, Carnival Jump, Moodswing Salsa, Serious City, Alligator Wrestler, Rain Forest, Sanctified SteelLove is Forever; recordings include The Samplers in Person, 1960, The Folksingers of Washington Square, 1962, Fantasias, 1963, Inventions, 1965, E. Pluribus Unum, 1969, Demolition Derby, 1972, Jukebox Sch. of Music, 1988 (Best Liner Notes award Nat. Assn. Ind. Record distbr. 1989, 20 Best Albums of 1988 Nat. Pub. Radio), Vehicles, 1991, Steel Tears, 1996 (nominated best folk album Nashville Music Awards 1997), Sandy Bull: Re-inventions: The Best of the Vanguard Yrs., 1999; arrangements include L. Bonfa's Manha de Carnival for oud, two movements of Carl Orff's Carmina Burana for 5 string banjo, excerpt from J.S. Bach's Brandenburg Concerto # 5 for Fender guitar, strings and Fender Rhodes; instrumental arrangement of C. Berry's Memphis. Mem. NARAS, ASCAP, Audio Engring. Soc. Avocation: learning Bach chorales on keyboard, skiing, soaring. Office: Timeless Rec Soc PO Box 1177 Franklin TN 37065-1177

BULL, WALTER STEPHEN, police officer; b. Collingswood, N.J., May 17, 1933; s. Walter Stephen and Mabelle (Miller) B.; m. Dolores Ruth Kinkade, June 19, 1954; children: Douglas, Donald, Diana, Daniel, David, Dwayne. AAS, Amarillo Coll., 1977, AS, 1978; BS, Wayland Bapt. U., 1978; MA, West Tex. State U., 1982. Advanced cert. Tex. Commn. Law Enforcement Tng. and Edn. Lt. Amarillo (Tex.) Police Dept., 1957-91; ret. Active Boy Scouts Am. Staff sgt. USAF, 1952-56. Mem. Internat. Assn. Chiefs Police (life), Tex. Police Assn., Air Force Assn., Law Enforcement Lions Club, Am Legion (life, post, dis. and div. comdr.), Gideons Internat., Soc. Mayflower Descs. (mem. coun.). Home: 1915 Manhattan St Amarillo TX 79103-4222

BULLA, CLYDE ROBERT, writer; b. King City, Mo., Jan. 9, 1914; s. Julian W. and Sarah Ann (Henson) B. Columnist Tri-County News, King City, Mo., 1942-47. Author 70 books for young people including White Bird, 1966, Shoeshine Girl, 1975, A Lion to Guard Us, 1981, A Place for Angels, 1995, The Paint Brush Kid, 1999. Recipient Commonwealth Children's Book award Commonwealth Club, Calif., 1970; recipient Christopher award The Christophers, 1972, Sequoyah Book award Okla. Sch. Children, 1978, Charlie May Simon award Ark. Sch. Children, 1976, book award S.C. Sch. Children, 1980, Focal award L.A. Pub. Libr., 1991. Mem. Soc. Children's Book Writers, Authors Guild.

BULLARD, BRUCE LYNN, critical care nurse; b. Canyon, Tex., Nov. 4, 1952; s. Ivan H. and Abbie Nell (Matthews) B. BS in Nursing, West Tex. State U., 1976. Charge, staff nurse High Plains Bapt. Hosp., Amarillo, Tex., 1976-77; supr., head nurse, staff nurse U. Tex. M.D. Anderson Hosp., Houston, 1977-83; dir. home health care Kimberly Nurses, Houston, 1983-84; charge, staff nurse ICU Rosewood Gen. Hosp., Houston, 1984-87; charge, staff nurse Humana Hosp. Met., San Antonio, 1987-91, Health Touch, San Antonio, 1991—; practitioner Rolf-style structural integration, 1993-97, profl. dog handler, field trainer, 1997—. Home and Office: 1125 W Zipp Rd New Braunfels TX 78130-9049

BULLARD, CLAUDE EARL, newspaper, commercial printing and radio and television executive; b. Louisville, July 21, 1920; s. George Adolph and Clara Etta (House) B.; m. Mildred Gambert, July 24, 1943; 1 dau., Susan Earle. Student, U. Louisville, 1946-47. Owner, mgr. C.E. Bullard Printing Co., Louisville, 1938-43; journeyman printer Courier-Jour. and Louisville Times, 1946-65, supt. composing room, 1965-68, dir. ops., 1968-72; v.p., dir. Courier-Jour.; v.p. WHAS Radio/TV, Standard Gravure, Stand Colorprint, Morristown, Tenn., 1972-75, sr. v.p. human resources, dir., 1975-85, ret., 1985. V.p. bd. dirs. Bridgehaven, Louisville, 1980-83, pres. bd. dirs., 1985-88; chmn. admissions com. Met. United Way, Louisville, 1983-92, mem. planning, allocations and rsch. com., 1983-92; bd. dirs. New Directions, Louisville, 1980-82. Mem. Am. Newspaper Pubs. Assn., Am. Newspaper Personnel Assn., Am. Soc. Tng. Dirs., So. Newspaper Pubs. Assn., Louisville Personnel Assn., Soc. Am. Magicians, Louisville Magic Club. Democrat. Clubs: Jefferson, First Tuesday Assocs. Home: 3510 Hughes Rd Louisville KY 40207-4332

BULLARD, EDGAR JOHN, III, museum director; b. L.A., Sept. 15, 1942; s. Edgar John and Katherine Elizabeth (Dreisbach) B. BA, UCLA, 1965, MA, 1968; LHD (hon.), Loyola U., New Orleans, 1987. Asst. to dir., curator spl. projects Nat. Gallery Art, Washington, 1968-73; dir. New Orleans Mus. Art, 1973—; alternate mem. Citizens Stamp Adv. Com., 1969-71; mem. mus. adv. panel Nat. Endowment for Arts, 1974-77. Author: Edgar Degas, 1971, John Sloan 1871-1951, 1971, Mary Cassatt: Oils and Pastels, 1972, A Panorama of American Painting, 1975. Nerdrum: The Drawings, 1994. Bd. dirs. La. Cultural Alliance, 1988-91, New Orleans Jazz and Heritage Found., 1974-78; trustee Ga. Mus. Art, U. Ga., Athens, 1975-80, Kneisel Hall Chamber Music Sch., Blue Hill, Maine, 1986—, La. Soc. for Prevention Cruelty to Animals, 1986-93; mem. New Orleans Commns. for Bicentennial U.S. Constn., 1987. Decorated Order of Republic of Egypt, 1979, Officer Am. Soc. Venerable Order St. John Jerusalem, 1990, chevalier Order of Arts and Lettres of France, 1994; Samuel H. Kress Found. fellow, 1967-68; recipient Mayor's Art award, 1993. Mem. Assn. Art Mus. Dirs., Am. Assn. Mus. (bd. dirs. 1996—), Coll. Art Assn. Democrat. Episcopalian. Home: 1805 Milan St New Orleans LA 70115-5443 also: Greenlea Reach Rd Deer Isle ME 04627 Office: New Orleans Mus Art PO Box 19123 New Orleans LA 70179-0123

BULLARD, GEORGE, newspaper editor; b. Middlesboro, Ky., Feb. 8, 1945; s. George Kibert and Frances Rose (Costanzo) B.; m. Donna DeVoe, Nov. 29, 1980 (div. May 1989); m. Susan Burzynski, Mar. 21, 1992. BA in Journalism, Mich. State U., 1971. Editor-in-chief Mich. State News, East Lansing, 1970-71; reporter The Detroit News, 1971-86, dep. city editor, 1986-87, city editor, 1987-95, asst. mng. editor, 1995-98. Contbr. articles to newspapers and mags., 1975-86. Mem. Leadership Detroit, 1988-89. Sgt. U.S. Army, 1963-66, Korea. Fellow Religious Pub. Rels. Coun. Avocations: flying private plane, ham radio, skiing. Office: Detroit News 615 W Lafayette Blvd Detroit MI 48226-3197*

BULLARD, JOHN KILBURN, university administrator; b. New Bedford, Mass., Aug. 21, 1947; s. John Crapo and Katharine (Kilburn) B.; m. Anne Dunbar, June 27, 1981; children: Elizabeth, Anthony, Matthew. BA magna cum laude, Harvard U., 1969; MArch, M in City Planning, MIT, 1974. Agt. Waterfront Hist. Area League (WHALE), New Bedford, 1974-85; mayor City of New Bedford, 1986-92; dir. fisheries representation New Bedford (Mass.) Seafood Co-op, 1992-93; dir. Office of Sustainable Devel. NOAA, Dept. Commerce, Washington, 1993-98; fellow Harvard Inst. Politics, 1998; dir. Family Bus. Ctr. U. Mass., Dartmouth, 1998—; chmn. urban econ. policy com. U.S. Conf. of Mayors, 1988-92. Photographer 3 covers for Sail mag., 1970-71. Recipient Honor Award Nat. Trust for Hist. Preservation, 1981, Preservation award Mass. Hist. Commn., 1983, Design award Mass. Gov. Michael Dukakis, 1987. Democrat. Unitarian. Avocations: sailing, tennis. Home: 19 Irving St New Bedford MA 02740-3426

BULLARD, JOHN MOORE, religion educator, church musician; b. Winston-Salem, N.C., May 6, 1932; s. Hoke Vogler and May Evangeline (Moore) B. AB, U. N.C., 1953, AM, 1955; MDiv, Yale U., 1957, PhD, 1962. Ordained to ministry United Meth. Ch., 1955. Asst. in instrn. Yale U., New Haven, 1957-61; asst. prof. religion Wofford Coll., Spartanburg, S.C., 1961-65, assoc. prof., 1965-70, Albert C. Outler prof. religion, 1970—, chmn. dept., 1962—, faculty sec., 1988—; minister music (organist-choirmaster) Cen. United Meth. Ch., Spartanburg, 1961-72, Bethel United Meth. Ch., 1972-88, Second Presbyn. Ch., Spartanburg, 1994, Palmetto Moravian Fellowship, 1994—; lectr. Eureka Coll., 1967, Furman U., 1982, Barton Coll., 1992; vis. prof. Biblical Lit. U. N.C., Chapel Hill, 1966, 67, U. N.C. at Charlotte, summer 1974; vis. prof. comparative religion Converse Coll., Spartanburg, S.C., 1984. Contbr. articles to Dictionary of Bibl. Interpretation and profl. jours. With Naval ROTC, 1950-52. Grantee NEH summer seminar Harvard U., 1982, U. Pa., 1986, Yale U., 1987; Fulbright-Hays grantee, Pakistan 1973, Fund for the Study of Gt. Religions in Asia, 1970-71; James fellow Yale U.; NEH/Wofford rsch. grantee U. London, 1975; named to Ky. Cols.; Dana Fellow Emory Univ's. 1992; Grad. Inst. Liberal Arts, 1989-90. Mem. Soc. Bibl. Lit. (pres. so. sect. 1968-69), Am. Acad. Religion, Am. Guild Organists (dean chpt. 1965-67), Organ Hist. Soc., S.C. Acad. Religion (pres. 1974-75), Southeastern Hist. Keyboard Soc., New Bach Soc. (Leipzig), Moravian Music Found., Phi Mu Alpha Sinfonia. Avocation: early keyboard music. Home: 104 Hickman Ct Hillbrook Forest Spartanburg SC 29307 Office: Wofford Coll Dept Religion 429 N Church St Spartanburg SC 29303-3612

BULLARD, MARCIA, publishing executive; b. Springfield, Ill., Aug. 28, 1952; d. Clark Wesley and Eileen (Kloppenburg) B. AA, Springfield (Ill.) Coll., 1972; BS, So. Ill. U., 1974. Reporter Democrat and Chronicle newspaper, Rochester, N.Y., 1974-79, mag. editor, 1979-82; dep. mng. editor Life sect. USA Today, Washington, 1982-85; mng. editor USA WEEKEND mag., Washington, 1985-89, editor, 1989—, pres., CEO, 1997—. Tutor 2 schs. D.C., 1984-89, Literacy Vols., Washington, 1987. Mem. AP Mng. Editors, Newspaper Assn. Am., Am. Soc. Newspaper Editors. Office: USA WEEKEND 1000 Wilson Blvd Arlington VA 22209-3901*

BULLARD, MARY ELLEN, retired religious study center administrator; b. Elkin, N.C., Jan. 12, 1926; d. Roy Brannoch and Mattie Reid (Doughton) H.; m. John Carson Bullard Sr., Apr. 27, 1957; children: John Carson Jr., Roy Harrell. BS, U. N.C., Greensboro, 1947; postgrad., Union Theol. Sem., N.Y.C., 1956; MA, Troy State U., Montgomery, Ala., 1979. Dir. women's and girls' work Gilvin Roth YMCA, Elkin, 1947-49; dir. Christian edn. 1st United Meth. Ch., Salisbury, N.C., 1949-51, Charlotte, N.C., 1951-55; dir. youth ministry United Meth. Ch., Western N.C. Conf., 1956-57; dir. ednl. ministries, div. continuing edn. Huntingdon Coll., 1979-88; dir. U.S. office Bibl. Resources Study Ctr., Inc., Jerusalem, 1988-92; bd. dirs. Ch. Women United Ala., 1970-71; del. World Meth. Coun., 13th World Meth. Conf., Dublin, 1976; mem. 15th World Meth. Conf., Nairobi, Kenya, 1986, 16th World Meth. Conf., Singapore, 1991, exec. com., 1991—, 17th World Meth. Conf., Rio de Janeiro, World Evangelism Inst., 1991—; del. Gen. Conf. United Meth. Ch., St. Louis, 1988, Louisville, 1992; del. Southeastern Jurisdictional Conf., United Meth. Ch., Lake Junaluska, N.C., 1988, 92, 96; mem. gen. coun. fin. and adminstrn. United Meth. Ch., 1992—. Bd. dirs. LWV, Montgomery, 1966-70, Am. Cancer Soc., Montgomery, 1975-81, Ala. Dept. Youth Svcs., Mt. Meigs Campus Chapel, 1984-86; mem. Montgomery Symphony League, 1984—; mem. adv. bd. Resurrection Cath. Mission, 1993—; mem. Nat. Vision 2000 Long-Range Dream Team, United Meth. Ch., 1995; del. Southeastern Jurisdictional Conf., The United Meth. Ch., 1988, 92, 96; bd. trustees Ala. West Fla. Con. The United Meth. Ch., 1995-97. Recipient award of recognition Bd. Edn. We. N.C. Conf. The United Methodist Ch., 1956, Christian Higher Edn., Ala.-West Fla. Conf. United Meth. Ch., 1975, Conf. Coun. on Ministries, Ala. West Fla. Conf., 1987, Candler Sch. of Theology, Emory U., 1990, Alice Lee award Ala. West Fla. Conf. United Meth. Ch., 1994. Mem. Christian Educators Fellowship, Kappa Delta Pi. Home: 3359 Warrenton Rd Montgomery AL 36111-1736

BULLARD, RAY ELVA, JR., retired psychiatrist, hospital administrator; b. Dallas, Jan. 25, 1927; s. Ray Elva and Beatrice (Taylor) B.; children by previous marriage: Suzanne, Ray Elva. BS, U. Wash., 1948; MD (Mead Johnson scholar), U. Tex. Med. Br., Galveston, 1953; BA, U. Tex., 1957. Diplomate Am. Bd. Psychiatry and Neurology. Intern Houston VA Hosp., 1953-54; resident in gen. practice U. Iowa, summer 1954, Nan Travis Meml. Hosp., Jacksonville, Tex., 1954-55; gen. practice medicine Normangee, Blanco and Austin, Tex., 1955-63; resident in psychiatry VA Hosp., Topeka, 1963-66; chief sect. psychiatry VA Hosp., 1966-71, chief svc., 1971-73; asso. prof. psychiatry U. Okla., 1971-73; supt. Hollidaysburg (Pa.) State Hosp., 1973-76, Torrance (Pa.) State Hosp., 1976-94; cons. Allegheny Valley Counseling Ctrs., 1994—; guest lectr. Pa. State U., U. Pitts.; adj. asst. prof. psychiatry U. Pitts. Sch. Medicine, 1978—; adj. asst. prof. St. Francis Coll., 1983-94. Served with U.S. Army, 1944-46. Menninger Found. fellow, 1963-66. Fellow APA (life); mem. AMA (Physicians Recognition award 1997), Am. Psychiat. Assn., Pa. Psychiat. Assn., Pa. Med. Assn., Masons. Episcopalian. Home: RR 1 Box 82A Vandergrift PA 15690-9801

BULLARD, RICKEY HOWARD, podiatric physician, surgeon; b. Corinth, Miss., Aug. 9, 1954; s. Herman A. and Bonnie Ruth (Gurley) B.; m. Carolyn Jean Strickland, June 6, 1981. BS in Biology, Millsaps Coll., Jackson, Miss., 1975; BS in Med. Sci., Ill. Coll. Podiatric Medicine, Chgo., 1980, DPM, 1980. Diplomate Am. Bd. Podiatric Orthops. and Primary Podiatric Medicine. Mem. courtesy med. staff Iuka (Miss.) Hosp., 1980—; pvt. practice Tupelo and Iuka, 1980—; assoc. med. staff North Miss. Med. Ctr., Tupelo, 1992—; cons. Miss. State Bd. Med. Licensure, Jackson, 1982—, Tighomingo Manor Health Ctr., Iuka, 1981—, Cedars Health Ctr., Tupelo, 1983—, Lee Manor Health Ctr., Tupelo, 1984—, Alcorn Care Inn, Corinth, 1985—; bd. dirs. Diabetes Treatment Ctr., Tupelo, 1994—. Watkins scholar Millsaps Coll., 1973. Fellow Am. Assn. Hosp. Podiatrists, Am. Coll. Foot and Ankle Orthops. and Medicine, Internat. Acad. Podiatric Medicine; mem. Am. Podiatric Med. Assn. (del. 1984, 87, 89), Miss. Podiatric Med. Assn. (pres. 1984-86, sec., treas. 1987—), SAR, Christian Med. Soc., Gen. Soc. War of 1812. Methodist. Avocations: golf, fly fishing, military history, gardening. Home: 2381 Amelia Ln Tupelo MS 38801-7203 Office: 1904 W Main St Tupelo MS 38801-3228

BULLARD, ROGER PERRIN, artist; b. N.Y.C., July 2, 1913; s. Roger Harrington and Annie Adams (Sturges) B.; m. Georgie Genevieve Hosford, Nov. 15, 1944; 1 child, Virginia Anne. *Mr. Bullard's wife George G. Hosford was born on August 1, 1921 but did not recover from a heart attack on March 19, 1998. Mr. Bullard is the great-great-great-grandson of Jonathan Harrington, who, at 16 years old, blew a fife in the band and fought alongside the Minute Men in the famous Battle of Lexington, 1775. He was the last survivor of the Battle of Lexington. Howard Fast wrote a novel about the battle, April Morning (1988 TV) with the help of James Lee Barrett. The video recording is a production of the Samuel Goldwyn Co. and Robert Halmi, Inc.* Student, Art Students League, N.Y.C., 1934-37, Universal Photographers Inc., N.Y.C. Freelance artist Fairfield, Conn., 1937-40; machinist Heime Co., Fairfield, 1947-50, Exide Battery, Fairfield, 1950-52, Dictaphone, Bridgeport, Conn., 1952-55; draftsman Aircraft Drafting, Bridgeport, 1955-57, Sikorski Aircraft and Valve Corp., Bridgeport, 1955-56; airbrush artist Poly Photo, Bridgeport, 1957; freelance photographer Fairfield, 1958-77. *At present, Mr. Bullard is trying to complete an innovative Sketch Book Planner-type (format) book with quick reference basic (local color) paint mixtures (A to Z) for most of the common objects artists and students like to paint, and modifications to these mixtures for: intensities, values, temperature, perspective, color values in character, mood, etc.* Contbr. pen and ink drawings to Probosidea Memoirs Nus. Natural History, N.Y.C., 1933-35. With U.S. Army, 1940-45, WWII. Republican. Episcopalian. Avocations: photography, art research, tennis, writing. Home: c/o Mary Rouseau 449 Mill Plain Rd Fairfield CT 06430-5047

BULLARD, SHARON WELCH, librarian; b. San Diego, Nov. 4, 1943; d. Dale L. and Myrtle (Sampson) Welch; m. Donald H. Bullard, Aug. 1, 1969. BS in Edn., U. Ctrl. Ark., 1965; MA, U. Denver, 1967. Tchr. libr. Humphrey pub. schs., Ark., 1965-66, libr., 1966-69; media splst. Adams County Sch. Dist. 12, Denver, 1967-69; catalog libr. Ark. State U., Jonesboro, 1970-75; head documents cataloging Wash. State U., Pullman, 1979-83; head serials cataloging Davidson Libr. U. Calif., Santa Barbara, 1984-88; head ACCESS svcs. Davidson Libr., 1988-99; head adminstrv. svcs., personnel U. N.C., Greensboro, 1998—; cons. Ctr. Robotic Sys. Microelectronics Rsch. Libr., Santa Barbara, 1986, retrospective conversion project Calif. State Libr., 1987, ombudsman's office U. Calif., Santa Barbara, 1988; distributor Amway, 1985-91. Canvasser Citizens for Goleta Valley, 1985-86; adv. bd. Total Interlibr. Exch., 1994-96. Mem. ALA, N.C. Libr. Assn. (mem. planning commn. annual conf. 1998, 99—), Calif. Libr. Assn. (tech. svcs. chpt. so. Calif. sect.), Libr. Assn. U. Calif. Santa Barbara (mem. subcom. on advancement and promotion 1987-91, 95-96, chmn. subcom. advancement and promotin 1996-97), NAFE, So. Calif. Tech. Processes Group (membership com. 1987), Assn. Col. and Rsch. Librs. (intern membership com. 1993-94, extended campus libr. sect. guidelines com. 1995-96), Libr. Adminstrn. and Mgmt. Assn. (mem. circulation/access svcs. sys. and svcs. sect. 1993-97, mem. equipment com. bldgs. for colls. and univs. 1998—, chmn. heads circulation sec. U. Calif. 1997, 98, mem. publs. com. 1998—, mem. equip. 1993-97, mem. bldgs. for colls. and univs. com. 1998—), Notis Users Circulation Interest Group (presenter meeting 1992, mem. CIRC SIG steering com. 1993-97, moderator meeting 1993-95, chair elect 1994-95, chair 1995-96, program com. 1996-97), Pi Lambda Theta (exec. bd., sec. Santa Barbara chpt. 1990-91, hospitality com. 1991-92). Avocations: walking, camping, boogey boarding, swimming.

BULLARD, WILLIS CLARE, JR., state legislator; b. Detroit, July 12, 1943; s. Willis C. and Virginia Katherine (Gilmore) B.; children: Willis C. III, Melissa Ann, Kaila Michelle. AB, U. Mich., 1965; JD, Detroit Coll. Law, 1971. Bar: Mich. 1971. Practice of law Detroit, 1971-77, Troy, Mich., 1977-80, Milford, Mich., 1983—; supr. Highland Twp., Mich., 1980-82; mem. Mich. Ho. of Reps., 1983-96; asst. Rep. caucus chmn., 1983-84, asst. Rep. floor leader, 1985-88, chmn. House Rep. campaign, 1987-90; chmn. House taxation com., 1993-96; chmn. task force Midwe stern Legis. Conf. Coun. State Govts., 1985-86, Mich. Ho. of Reps., 1983-96, Mich. State Senate, 1996—; mediator cir. and dist. cts., 1988—. Bd. dirs. Dunham Lake Property Owners Assn., 1975-78, treas., 1975-76, pres., 1976-78; mem. Dunham Lake Civic Com., 1982-87; trustee Highland Twp., 1978-80, mem. zoning bd. appeals, 1979. Named Legislator of Yr. Mich. Twp. Assn., 1984. Mem. Oakland County Bar Assn., State Bar Mich., Oakland County Assn. Twp. Suprs. (sec.-treas. 1981), Michigamua. Clubs: U. Mich. of Greater Detroit, Highland Republican, Highland Men's (sec. 1979, pres. 1980). Home: 1849 Lakeview Dr Highland MI 48357-4817 Office: State Capitol Lansing MI 48909*

BULLARO, GRACE RUSSO, literature, film and foreign language educator, speaker; b. Salerno, Italy, July 11, 1949; came to the U.S., 1958; d. Salvatore and Carmela (Paciello) Russo; m. Frank John Bullaro, Sept. 19, 1971; children: Christian, Adrian Alexander. BA, CCNY, 1971; MA, SUNY, Stony Brook, 1989, PhD in Comparative Lit., 1993. Grad. tchg. asst. SUNY, Stony Brook, 1988-92; adj. asst. prof. SUNY-Nassau C.C., Garden City, N.Y., 1990—, CUNY-Lehman Coll., Bronx, N.Y., 1991—; asst. prof. CUNY-Lehman Coll., Bronx, 1998; collaborative educator Lincoln Ctr., N.Y.C., 1999—; adj. asst. prof. SUNY-Sannau C.C., Garden City, 1990—; faculty exec. com. Lehman Coll., Bronx, N.Y., 1999—; book reviewer in field. Contbr. chpts. to books and articles to profl. jours. Acad. senate CUNY, Lehman Coll., 1997-99, CUNY, 1998—. Mem. MLA, Nat. Coun. Tchrs. English, Inst. Français, Soc. Profs. Français, Phi Beta Kappa. Avocations: fitness trainer, tennis, travel, swimming. E-mail: gracerbullaro@msn.com. Office: CUNY Lehman Coll English Dept Bedford Park Blvd W Bronx NY 10468

BULLEN, DANIEL BERNARD, mechanical engineering educator; b. Iowa City, July 20, 1956; s. John Bernard and Helen May (Ferguson) B.; m. Elizabeth Ann Clark, Aug. 17, 1979; children: Katherine Andrea, Mark Bernard, Sarah Elizabeth, Rachel Suzanne. BS in Engring. Sci., Iowa State U., 1978; MS in Nuclear Engring., U. Wis., 1979, MS in Material Sci., 1981, PhD in Nuclear Engring., 1984. Registered profl. engr., Calif., N.C., Ga., Iowa. Engr. Lawrence Livermore (Calif.) Nat. Lab., 1984-86; sr. engr. Sci. and Engring. Assocs., Inc., Pleasanton, Calif., 1986-88; pres. DG Engring., Inc., Livermore, 1988-89; asst. prof. nuclear engr. N.C. State U., Raleigh, 1989-90, Ga. Inst. Tech., Atlanta, 1990-92; assoc. prof. mech. engring. Iowa State U., Ames, 1992—, dir. nuclear reactor lab., 1993—, coord. nuclear engring. program, 1993-96; cons. Lawrence Livermore Nat. Lab., 1988-91, Electric Power Rsch. Inst., Palo Alto, Calif., 1989-96, Internat. Lead Zinc Rsch. Orgn., Research Triangle Park, N.C., 1990-98, HDR Engring., Inc., Omaha, 1991—, APA, Inc., Omaha, 1996-97; mem. U.S. Nuclear Waste Tech. Rev. Bd., 1997—. *In January of 1997, Dr. Daniel B. Bullen was appointed by President William Jefferson Clinton to serve a four-year term as a member of the United States Nuclear Waste Technical Review Board (NWTRB). The NWTRB reviews the efforts of the United States Department of Energy to store, transport and dispose of spent nuclear fuel and high-level radioactive waste. The NWTRB is required to report to the S cretary of Energy and the Congress at least two times a year. Dr. Bullen serves as the Chairman of two NWTRB Panels (Performance Assessment and Repository) and is a member of the Waste Management System Panel.* Contbr. 50 articles to profl. jours. Mem. NSPE, ASME, ASM Internat., Mineral, Metals and Materials Soc. AIME, Am. Nuclear Soc., Am. Ceramic Soc. (tech. reviewer 1986—), Materials Rsch. Soc., Am. Soc. Engring. Edn. Roman Catholic. Home: PO Box 1768 Ames IA 50010-1768 Office: Iowa State U 3034 Black Engring Ames IA 50011

BULLEN, RICHARD HATCH, former corporate executive; b. Logan, Utah, May 9, 1919; s. Asa and Georgia Vivian (Hatch) B.; m. Annabelle Smith, June 19, 1942 (div. 1965); children: Richard Hatch, Steven Asa (dec.), Thomas Kenneth; m. Anne-Marie de Leur, Aug. 16, 1965. B.S., Utah State U., 1941, LL.D., 1965; M.B.A., Harvard, 1943. With IBM Corp., 1946-72, treas., 1961-63, v.p., 1963-64, v.p., group exec., 1964- 67, sr. v.p., mgmt. com., 1967-72; pres. Richard H. Bullen Assocs., Inc., 1972-84; gen. ptnr. Bullen Mgmt. Co., 1980-87. Served to 1st lt. Q.M.C. AUS, 1943-46. Mem. Sigma Chi. Home: 1050 5th Ave New York NY 10028-0110

BULLETT, AUDREY KATHRYN, retired public administrator; b. Chgo., Feb. 12, 1937; d. Louis Albert and Eva Belle (Reed) Hill; m. Clark Ricardo Bullett, Sept. 18, 1965 (dec. Oct. 1986); 1 child, Iris J. AA, Ferris State U., 1983, BS in Pub. Adminstrn., 1984. Employee various positions Lake County Mich., Baldwin, 1967-81; twp. supr. Yates Twp., Idlewild, Mich., 1984-92; founder, CEO Dawn's Light Centre, Inc., 1985—; min. Uriel Temple of Spiritual Understanding, Inc., 1994—; stringer, news corr. TV 9/10, Cadillac, Mich., 1973-80; tchr. adult edn. program Mason County Ctrl./

Baldwin Cmty. Schs., Scottville, Mich., 1986-89. Author: Come Colour My Rainbow, 1996. Vol. fire fighter ret. Yates Twp. Fire Dept., 1969-96, tng./planning officer, 1988-93; chairperson Lake County Dem. Party, 1975-78, 85-88, 90-92; vice-chairperson, chairperson Lake County Planning Commn., 1975-80; charter mem., exec. dir. EDC of Yates Twp., 1979-94; lay leader North Ctrl. Coop. Ext. Svc., 1979, 81; apptd. mem. Task Force for Small and Rural Cmtys., 1980, Natural Environment and Pub. Policy Com., MSU, 1983-88, Area Agy. on Aging Western Mich., Inc. Adv. Coun., 1987-90; mem. Mich. Dem. Agrl. Caucus, 1980; mem.-sec. West Ctrl. Mich. Cmty. Growth Alliance, 1987-90; vol. Mich. Quilt Project, 1987; nat. treas. Idlewild Lot Owners Assn., Inc., 1992—; mem. First Bapt. Ch. Idlewild, 1941—, deaconess, 1997; mem. Big Rapids Unity Study Group, 1981-84; assoc. charter mem. Glorious St. Jude Spiritual Ch., 1987; founder Uriel Temple Spiritual Devel., Outreach Ministry, 1994; astarian Astara, Inc., 1997. Avocations: reading, music, crafts. Office: Dawns Light Ctr Inc 6489 Broadway Ave Idlewild MI 49642-9704

BULLETT, VICKY, professional basketball player; b. Oct. 4, 1967. Grad., U. Md., 1989. Forward-center Italy, 1990-93, Cesna, 1993-97; forward-center WNBA - Charlotte (N.C.) Sting, 1997—. Recipient U.S. Olympic Gold medal, 1988, Bronze medal, 1992; named to Italian League All-Star Teams, 1992, 95, 96, 97, Goodwill Games Team, 1989, World Championship Qualifying Team & USA Select Team, 1986, All-ACC Tournament Team, 1989, Kodak All-Am. Team, 1989. Avocations: softball, tennis, tap dancing, keyboard, reading. Office: Charlotte Sting 3308 Oak Lake Blvd Ste B Charlotte NC 28208*

BULLIET, RICHARD WILLIAMS, history educator, novelist; b. Rockford, Ill., Oct. 30, 1940; s. Leander Jackson and Mildred Idell (Williams) B.; m. Lucianne Cherry, June 24, 1962; 1 child, Mark Paul. B.A., Harvard U., 1962, M.A., 1964, Ph.D., 1967. Instr. Harvard U., Cambridge, Mass., 1967-70, asst. prof., 1970-73; lectr. U. Calif.-Berkeley, 1973-75; assoc. prof. history Columbia U., N.Y.C., 1976-79, prof., 1979—. Author: The Patricians of Nishapur, 1972, The Camel and the Wheel, 1977 (Dexter prize), Conversion to Islam in the Medieval Period, 1979, Islam: The View from the Edge, 1993; (novels) Kicked to Death by a Camel, 1973; The Tomb of the Twelfth Imam, 1979, The Gulf Scenario, 1984, The Sufi Fiddle, 1991; co-author: The Earth and Its Peoples, 1997; co-editor: The Encyclopedia of the Modern Middle East, 1996; editor: The Columbia History of the Twentieth Century, 1998; host-narrator: (documentary TV series) The Middle East, 1985; editor Jour. Iranian Studies, 1987-90. Guggenheim fellow, 1975-76. Mem. Mid. East Studies Assn. (exec. sec. 1977-81), Phi Beta Kappa. Avocation: painting. Home: 90 Morningside Dr New York NY 10027-7124 Office: Columbia U Mid East Inst New York NY 10027

BULLINER, P. ALAN, corporate lawyer. BS, Lehigh U., 1965; AM, Princeton U., 1967, PhD, 1970; JD, U. Pa., 1975. Bar: Pa. 1975. V.p. corp. sec. and counsel Bell Atlantic Corp., Phila., 1992-97; assoc. gen. counsel and sec. Bell Atlantic Corp., N.Y.C., 1997—. Office: Bell Atlantic Corp Rm 3876 1095 Avenue Of The Americas New York NY 10036-6797

BULLINGTON, JAMES RICHARD, business educator, former ambassador; b. Chattanooga, Oct. 27, 1940. A.B., Auburn U., 1962; M.P.A., Harvard U., 1969; grad., Fgn. Service Inst., 1971. Asst. desk officer Central Treaty Orgn. Affairs, Dept. State, 1963-65; vice consul Hue, 1965-66; staff aide to ambassador Saigon, 1966-67; dep. province sr. adviser Quang Tri, Vietnam, 1967-68; intellgience analyst Bur. Intelligence and Research, Dept. State, 1969-70; vice consul Chaing Mai, Thailand, 1971-73; polit. officer Vietnam Working Group, Dept. State, 1973-75; consul Mandalay, Burma, 1975-76; polit. and econ. counselor Rangoon, 1976-78; dep. chief mission N'Djamena, Chad, 1979-80; charge d'affaires Cotonou, Benin, 1980-82; sr. adviser African affairs U. S. Del. to UN Gen. Assembly, N.Y.C., 1982; U.S. ambassador to Burundi, 1983-86; coordinator sr. seminar, assoc. dean Sch. Profl. Studies Fgn. Service Inst. Dept. State, 1986-87, dean sr. seminar, 1987-89; dir. internat. affairs City of Dallas, 1989-93; prof., dir. ctr. global bus. Coll. Bus. and Pub. Administrn. Old Dominion U., Norfolk, Va., 1993—. Office: Old Dominion U Constant Hall Rm 125 Norfolk VA 23529

BULLINS, ED, author; b. Phila., July 2, 1935; s. Edward and Bertha Marie (Queen) B. Ed. bus. sch. and various colls.; LittD (hon.), Columbia Coll., Chgo., 1975; BA, Antioch U., San Francisco, 1989; MFA, San Francisco State U., 1994. Instr. playwriting and black theater various univs., colls., workshops, 1971-79; instr. Sch. Continuing Edn. NYU, 1979, instr. Dramatic Writing Dept., 1981; writers' unit coord. N.Y. Shakespeare Festival Pub. Theater, 1975-82; summer playwrights conf. instr. Hofstra U., L.I., N.Y., 1982; playwrights workshop leader People's Sch. Dramatic Arts (San Francisco Sch. Dramatic Arts), 1983; summer drama workshop leader Bay Area Playwrights Festival, Mill Valley, Calif., 1983; instr. drama dept. City Coll. of San Francisco, 1984-88; adminstrv. asst. in pub. info. and admissions recruitment Antioch U., San Francisco, 1986-87; student instr., playwriting Antioch U., San Francisco, San Quentin, 1986-87; lectr. Am. Multicultural Studies Dept. Sonoma State U., Rohnert Pk., Calif., 1988—; lectr. Afro-Am. Studies Dept. U. Calif., Berkeley, 1988—; instr. African Am. humanities/Afri-Am. Theatre Contra Costa Coll., 1989-94; artistic dir. The Bullins/Woodward Theater Workshop, San Francisco; prof. theater Northeastern U., Boston, 1995—; founder, prodr. Black Arts/West, San Francisco, 1965-67; resident playwright, assoc. dir. New Lafayette Theatre, Harlem, 1967-73; writers unit coord., press asst. N.Y. Shakespeare Festival, 1975-82, pub. rels. dir. Berkeley Black Repertory, 1982, promotion dir. (pro tem) The Magic Theatre, San Francisco, 1982-83; group sales coord. Julian Theatre, San Francisco, 1983, prodr., playwright The BMT Theater, Emeryville, Calif., 1988; Mellon lectr. for dramatic lit. Amherst (Mass.) Coll., 1977—; conductor seminar U. Calif. at Berkeley Black Theater, 1988, Workshop Charles Gordone's Theater, Tex. A&M, 1988; lectr. Multicultural Casting Conf., Asian Am. Cultural Ctr., L.A., 1988; participant Foothill Coll. Summer Writers Conf., Los Altos Hills, Calif., 1990; lectr. Calif. State U., Bakersfield, San Jose State U., 1991; acting dir. Northeastern U. Ctr. for Arts, 1996-98; prof. theatre Northeastern U., Boston, 1995, acting dir. Ctr. for Arts, 1996. Author: Five Plays, 1968, New Plays from the Black Theatre, 1969, Including In New England Winter (Obie award), The Fabulous Miss Marie, 1970 (Obie award), The Duplex, 1971, The Hungered One, 1971, Four Dynamite Plays, 1972, The Theme Is Blackness, 1973, The Reluctant Rapist, 1973, The Taking of Miss Janie, 1974 (N.Y. Drama Critics Circle award 1974-75), Salaam, Huey Newton, Salaam, 1990, New/Lost Plays by Ed Bullins, 1994, Boy x Man, 1994, Hot Feet: A Musical Play, 1998; co-author: (play) I Think It's Gonna Turn Out Fine, 1984, American Griot, 1990; producing dir. The Surviving Theatre, N.Y.C., 1974—; instr. English, Elmcor Youth Rehab. Agy., resident playwright, assoc. dir. New Lafayette Theatre, Harlem, N.Y.C., 1968-73; editor The Drama Rev. 1st Black Theater Issue, 1968; prodr. Michael: Two Plays by Ed Bullins, 1989, How Do You Do, Clara's Ole Man, 1989, Bullins Does Bullins, 1988 (all BMT Theater, Emeryville, Calif.), A Sunday Afternoon, City Coll. Theater, San. Francisco, 1987; dir. Bullins Does Bullins, 1988, Savage Wilds, 1988, Boy X Man, 1997, Dr. Grecher and the Blood Junkies, The Peabody House Theater, Somerville, Mass., 1998; actor in Uptown Mrs. Carrie, 1988, The Real Deal, 1988, Tripnology: The Burial of Predjudice; collaborator Raining Down Stars, San Francisco, 1992. Served with USN, 1952-55. Recipient Obie award, 1971, 75, Vernon Rice award, 1968, Audelco award Harlem Theater; Rockefeller grantee, 1968, 70, 73, 83; Guggenheim fellow, 1971, 76; Nat. Endowment for Arts grantee, 1972, 89; CAPS grantee.

BULLIVANT, RUPERT REID, lawyer; b. Portland, Oreg., Nov. 29, 1903; s. Joe and Ethel Cecelia (Rupert) B.; m. Norma Jean Wilson, July 6, 1926 (dissolved); 1 child, Diane Carter; m. Louise S. Storla, Jan. 1980. JD, U. Oreg., 1926. Bar: Oreg. 1926, U.S. Dist. Ct. Oreg. 1926, U.S. Ct. Appeals (9th cir.), U.S. Supreme Ct. 1979. Sole practice Portland, 1926-28; assoc. Clark & Clark, Portland, 1928-37; ptnr. Bullivant, Houser, Bailey and predecessor firms, Portland, 1938—; mem. Oreg. Conf. Uniform Law Comrs., 1948—. Mem. Portland Planning Commn., 1935-45. Mem. Am. Bar Found. (Oreg. chpt.), Oreg. Bar Assn. (pres. 1937-38, bd. govs. 1936-39), Am. Judicature Soc., Phi Beta Kappa. Republican. Clubs: Arlington (v.p.), Waverly, Multnomah Athletic (Portland). Home: 56 Condolea Ter Lake Oswego OR 97035-1008

BULLOCH, JOHN FREDERICK DEVON, foundation administrator; b. Toronto, Ont., Can., Aug. 24, 1933; m. Mary Helen, 1955; 2 children. G-rad. (engring. and bus.), U. Toronto, 1956, MBA, 1964. Chmn., founder Can. Fedn. Independent Bus., 1971—; joined Imperial Oil, 1957; mgr. Baier Fuels, Ltd., Kitchener, Ont., 1959-63; lectr. Ryerson Poly. Inst., Toronto, 1964-69; pres., founder Can. Council Fair Taxation, Toronto, 1970; chmn. steering com. Internat. Small Bus. Congress; founder Virtual U. Small and Medium-Sized Enterprises, 1997. Fellow, Ryerson Poly. Inst., 1981; recipient Disting. Bus. Alumni award U. Toronto, 1987, Wilford L. White fellowship from Internat. Council. for Small Bus., Order of Can., 1996. Mem. Assn. Profl. Engrs. Ont. Office: Canadian Fedn Ind Bus, 4141 Yonge St, Willowdale, ON Canada M2P 2A6

BULLOCH, KATHLEEN LOUISE, educational professional; b. Teaneck, N.J., Feb. 20, 1949; d. Thomas Joseph and Daisy Loretta Oates; m. Clifford Allen Bulloch, June 17, 1972; 1 child, Sean Andrew. BA, William Patterson Coll., 1971; MA, Montclair State Coll., 1972. Cert. speech pathologist Am. Speech/Lang./Hearing Assn. Chief speech pathologist Barnert Speech Clin., Paterson, N.J., 1971-73; speech/lang. pathologist Brick Town, N.J., 1973-79, Riverside (Calif.) County Office of Edn., 1979-98; mentor tchr. Riverside County Office of Edn., 1992-98, curriculum specialist, 1998—; intern program supr. Calif. State U., San Bernardino, 1998—; ednl. cons. Creative Children's Group, N.Y.C., 1995—; C-FASST Sr. Trainer Calif. State Dept. Edn., Sacramento, 1998; book reviewer Am. Speech/Lang. Assn., Washington, 1996—. Scriptwriter: (children's TV) Bloopy's Buddies, 1997; author: Phantom Tollbooth Unit, 1994, Adventures in Space, 1992; co-author: Adult Aphasia Program, 1977. Named to Outstanding Young Women of Am., 1983. Mem. ASCD, Am. Speech/Lang./Hearing Assn., Calif. Speech/Lang./Hearing Assn., Am. Ednl. Rsch. Assn., Coun. for Exceptional Children. Anglican Catholic. Avocations: reading, writing, exercise, music. E-mail: bulloch@earthlink.net. Home: 466 Westridge Cir Anaheim CA 92807 Office: Riverside County Office Edn 3939 13th St Riverside CA 92502

BULLOCK, ANNA MAE See TURNER, TINA

BULLOCK, DONALD WAYNE, elementary education educator, educational computing consultant; b. Tacoma Park, Md., Mar. 24, 1947; s. B.W. and Margaret (Harris) B.; m. Pamela Louise Hatch, Aug. 7, 1971. AA in Music, L.A. Pierce Coll., Woodland Hills, Calif., 1969; BA in Geography, San Fernando Valley State Coll., 1971; Cert. Computer Edn., Calif. Luth. U., 1985, MA in Curriculum-Instrn., 1987. Tchr. music Calvary Luth. Sch., Pacoima, Calif., 1970-71; elem. tchr. 1st Luth. Sch., Northridge, Calif., 1971-73; elem. tchr. Simi Valley (Calif.) Unified Sch. Dist., 1973—, computer insvc. instr., 1982-85, computer mentor tchr., 1985-87, mentor tchr. ednl. tech., 1992-95; lectr. Calif. Luth. U., Thousand Oaks, 1985-92; ednl. computer cons. DISC Ednl. Svcs., Simi Valley, 1985—; speaker profl. confs. Contbr. articles to profl. publs. Pres. Amen Choir, Van Nuys, Calif., 1981-83. Recipient Computer Learning Month grand prize Tom Snyder Prodns., 1988, Computer Learning Found., 1990, Spl. Commendation of Achievement, Learning mag. profl. best tchr. excellence awards, 1990, Impact II Disseminator award Ventura County Supt. of Schs. and Ventura County Econ. Devel. Assn., 1995; grantee Tandy-Radio Shack, Inc., 1985, Calif. Dep. Edn., 1985. Mem. NEA, ASCD, Internat. Soc. Tech. in Edn., Computer Using Educators Calif., Gold Coast Computer Using Educators (bd. dirs. 1988-89, 95-96), Basset Hound Club am., Basset Hound Club So. Calif. (bd. dirs. 1994-95, 98—, pres. 1995-98). Avocations: singing, travel, photography, writing, woodworking. Home: 2805 Wanda Ave Simi Valley CA 93065-1528 Office: Garden Grove Elem Sch 2250 Tracy Ave Simi Valley CA 93063-2753

BULLOCK, ELLIS WAY, JR., architect; b. Birmingham, Ala., Sept. 11, 1928; s. Ellis Way Sr. Bullock and Martha (Foute) Alexander; m. Ann Ardelia Pope, Nov. 28, 1950; children: Ellis Way III, Elbert Pope, John Howard Keith, William Frank. BArch, Auburn U., 1954. Registered architect, Fla., Ala., Ga., Miss., S.C., N.C. Apprentice architect Yonge, Look & Morrison, Pensacola, Fla., 1954-58; owner Ellis Bullock Architect, Pensacola, 1958-73; pres. Bullock-Tice and Assocs., Inc., Pensacola, 1973—; pres. Fla. AIA, 1977, treas. AIA Rsch. Corp., Washington, 1980-81; chmn. Energy in Arch., Washington, 1980-82; mem. faculty adv. com. Auburn U. Sch. Architecture, 1980—, chmn., 1988-89; mem. Nat. Architecture Accrediting Bd., Washington, 1982-86; mem. adv. coun. U. Fla. Coll. Architecture, 1986—. Contbr. articles to profl. jours. Chmn. Pensacola Hist. Commn., 1967; chmn. City of Pensacola Archtl. Review Bd., 1968, Pensacola Bldg. Bd. of Appeals, 1970—; bd. dirs. Pensacola Symphony, 1987-88; mem. Blue Ribbon Task Force on Edn., Escambia County, Fla., 1985-86; mem. adv. coun. U. Fla., 1986—; mem. sesquicentennial commn. State of Fla. 1st lt. U.S. Army, 1950-54. Recipient 1st Honor AIA-Navy, 1977, 78, Award of Merit, 1976; recipient Outstanding Design award for Air Force Systems Command Hdqrs., 1980, Gov.'s Design award, 1982, 84, Merit award for U.S. Air Force Design, 1983, Design Excellence award Air Force Regional Civil Engrs., 1984, award of merit Navy Youth Ctr., 1990, award of merit Navy Bowling Ctr. Complex, 1990; named Profl. of Yr., Pensacola News Jour., 1977. Fellow AIA (bd. dirs. 1979-82, v.p. 1981-82, jury coll. of fellows 1988-91, exec. com. coll. of fellows 1993—, bursar 1993—, vice chancellor 1994-95, chancellor 1995-96, regional rep. Fla. Caribbean 1990—, numerous awards N.W. chpt. 1974—, award of excellence Fla. N.W. chpt. 1980, 82, 86, 89, 90), Am. Archtl. Found. (regent 1995-96, EXCOM 1995-96, task force account and reason 1988, program chmn. nat. conv. com. 1986); mem. Fla. Assn. AIA (pres. 1977, govtl. liaison com. 1984—, Gold medal 1988, gold medal nominating com. 1990-91, balanced curriculum task force 1990, chmn. design awards jur. Ctrl. Fla. chpt. 1990, speaker ann. conf. 1997-98), Fla. Archtl. Found. (trustee 1988—, chmn. 1993), Inst. Bus. Designers (award for contractual interiors 1977), NRA, St. Andrews Soc., Gulf Coast Econs. Club, Rotary (Paul Harris fellow 1994). Home: 2 Hyde Park Rd Pensacola FL 32503-5830 Office: Bullock Tice Assocs 909 E Cervantes St Ste B Pensacola FL 32501-3281

BULLOCK, FRANCIS JEREMIAH, pharmaceutical research executive; b. Brookline, Mass., Jan. 14, 1937; s. Jeremiah Francis and A. Grace (Vitali) B.; m. Lorraine Marie Littig, Aug. 26, 1961; children: Christine, Gregory. BS, Mass. Coll. Pharmacy, 1958; AM, Harvard U., 1961, PhD, 1963. Rsch. assoc. Harvard Med. Sch., Boston, 1963-64, Chem. Biodynamics Lab. U. Calif., Berkeley, 1964-65; sr. project staff Arthur D. Little, Inc., Cambridge, Mass., 1965-72; mgr. medicinal chemistry Abbott Labs., North Chicago, Ill., 1972-79; v.p. new drug discovery Schering-Plough Pharm. Co., Bloomfield, N.J., 1979-81, sr. v.p. rsch. ops., 1981-93; sr. cons. Arthur D. Little, Inc., Cambridge, 1993—; lectr. MIT, Cambridge, 1971-72, Northeastern U., Boston, 1971-72; bd. dirs. TSI Corp., Genzyme Transgenics Corp, Neogenesis, Array BioPharma; bd. govs. Union County Coll., N.J.; mem. com. on young investigators in biol. scis. NRC, 1991-92, com. on nat. needs for biomed. and behavioral rsch. pers., 1993-94. Editor jour. Drug Metabolism and Distbn., 1970-73; contbr. numerous rsch. papers to profl. jours., 1964-75. Fellow NIH, 1961-65. Mem. AAAS, Am. Chem. Soc., Royal Soc. Chemistry, Fedn. Am. Socs. Exptl. Biology, Am. Soc. Pharmacology and Exptl. Therapeutics, Am. Soc. for Microbiology, Assn. Harvard Chemists. Republican. Roman Catholic. Avocation: airplane pilot. Office: Arthur D Little Inc 35 Acorn St Cambridge MA 02139-4722

BULLOCK, FRANK WILLIAM, JR., federal judge; b. Oxford, N.C., Nov. 3, 1938; s. Frank William and Wilma Jackson (Long) B.; m. Frances Dockery Haywood, May 5, 1984; 1 child, Frank William III. B.S. in Bus. Adminstrn., U. N.C., 1961, LL.B., 1963. Bar: N.C. 1963. Assoc. Maupin, Taylor & Ellis, Raleigh, N.C., 1964-68; asst. dir. Adminstrv. Office of Cts. of N.C., Raleigh, 1968-73; ptnr. Douglas, Ravenel, Hardy, Crihfield & Bullock, Greensboro, N.C., 1973-82; judge U.S. Dist. Ct. N.C., Greensboro, 1982—, chief judge, 1992—. Mem. bd. editors N.C. Law Rev., 1962-63; contbr. articles to profl. jours. Mem. N.C. Bar Assn., Greensboro Bar Assn., N.C. Soc. of Cin., Fla. Soc. Colonial Wars. Republican. Presbyterian. Clubs: Greensboro Country. Avocations: golf; tennis; running; history. Office: US Dist Ct PO Box 3223 Greensboro NC 27402-3223*

BULLOCK, GEORGE DANIEL, energy consultant; b. San Francisco, Dec. 19, 1942; s. Joseph Henry and Jane (Cottrell) B.; m. Mary Hopper Brown, Dec. 18, 1969; children: Graham Daniel, Ashley Brown. BA, Portland State Coll., 1964; MA, Stanford U., 1965. Instr. So. Meth. U., Dallas, 1969-70; asst. prof. U. Alaska, Fairbanks, 1970; adminstrv. asst. Office of U.S. Senator Ted Stevens, Washington, 1971; sr. policy advisor Office Econ. Opportunity, Exec. Office of Pres., Washington, 1971-74; dir. Office of State of Wash., Washington, 1974-77; pres. Bullock & Assocs., Washington, 1977-80, 83-91, 1995—; dir. Office of State of Wis., Washington, 1980-83; mgr. state and local rels. Edison Electric Inst., Washington, 1991-95. Pres., various positions Capitol City Little League, Washington, 1986-95. Mem. Soc. for Historians of Am. Fgn. Rels., Soc. Am. Baseball Rschr. Republican. Home and office: 213 S Candler St Decatur GA 30030-3743

BULLOCK, HARVEY READE, screenwriter; b. Oxford, N.C., June 4, 1921; s. Harvey Reade and Vivian Elsie (Murray) B.; m. Betty Jane Folker; children: Kerry, Diana, Courtney, Andrew. AB, Duke U., 1943. Radio, TV, film scriptwriter, producer, 1947—; lectr. creative writing various colls., seminars. Scriptwriter: (radio) The Abe Burrows Show, 1949, (TV shows) Today with Dave Garroway, Robert Q. Lewis Show, numerous prodns. with R. S. Allen including Salute to Baseball (Random House award), Dick and the Dutchess, McKeever and the Colonel, numerous TV show episodes including The Love Boat, Alice, Hogan's Heroes, The Andy Griffith Show, I Spy, The Danny Thomas Show, The Dick Van Dyke Show, My World and Welcome To It, The Jim Nabors Show, (cartoon series) The Flintstones, The Jetsons, (children spl.) The Red Hand Gang, Poppa and Me (Emmy award nomination), (films) Honeymoon Hotel, Girl Happy with Elvis, Who's Minding the Mint, With Six You Get Egg Roll (Box Office Blue Ribbon award), Don't Drink the Water, Going Coconuts, (TV spls. with Everett Greenbaum) Return To Mayberry; author: The Fat Book, How To Cheat On Your Diet. Mem. Writers Guild Am. Home and Office: 32707 Sea Island Dr Dana Point CA 92629-3642

BULLOCK, J(AMES) ROBERT, judge; b. Provo, Utah, Dec. 16, 1916; s. James A. and Norma (Poulton) B.; m. Ethel Hogge, Aug. 29, 1949; children: James Robert Jr., C. Scott, David A., Steven H. BS, Utah State U., 1938; JD with honors, George Washington U., 1942. Bar: U.S. Ct. Appeals (D.C. cir.) 1942, Utah 1946, Colo. 1946, U.S. Supreme Ct. 1969. Ptnr. Aldrich, Bullock & Nelson, Provo, 1950-73; judge 4th Dist. Ct. Utah, 1973-85; sr. judge Dist. Cts. Utah, 1985—, chmn. bd. sr. judges, 1988-92; mem. Utah Jud. Coun., 1973-83, chief judge, 1981-83. Mem. Utah State Ho. of Reps., 1963-67; mem. Utah Constn. Revision Commn., 1969-76, vice chmn., 1974-76. Comdr. USN, 1941-46, ETO, PTO. Mem. ABA, Utah Bar Assn. (pres. 1972-73, Judge of the Yr. 1983), Am. Inns of Ct. (charter), Riverside Country Club, Rotary (pres. 1958-59), Order of Coif, Phi Delta Phi. Avocation: golf. Home and Office: 1584 Willow Ln Provo UT 84604-2802

BULLOCK, JERRY MCKEE, retired military officer, consultant, educator; b. Ralls, Tex., June 2, 1932; s. Arthur Vaughn and Lillian McKee B.; m. Velma Lucille Young, Aug. 30, 1954; children: Ronnie Jay, Randy Ross, Roddy McKee, Kathy L. Bullock Chiero, Kevin L., Kelly L. Bullock Wheeler, Kristie E. Bullock Tumlinson. BA, East Tex. State U., 1954; grad., Indsl. Coll. Armed Forces, 1978, Air War Coll., 1977; MA, Webster U., 1981. Lic. profl. counselor, Tex. Commd. 2d lt. USAF, 1954, advanced through grades to col., 1974, dep. chief security police, ret., 1981; exec. dir. Family and Marriage Counseling, San Marcos, Tex., 1981-83; dir. human resources Tracor Aerospace, Austin, Tex., 1983-90; cons., owner Creative Edn. Inst., San Marcos, 1990-95. Author: Short History of the Air Force Security Police, SP History, Vol. II; staff writer San Marcos Daily Record; contbr. articles toprofl. jours. Active Industry, Edn. Task Force, Austin, 1989—, State Human Resources Com., 1989-91, Bicycle Advocacy Coalition, 1991; pastor, CEO Hill Country Faith Ministries, 1992-98. Decorated Legion of Merit with 3 oak leaf clusters, Bronze Star. Mem. Air Force Security Police Assn. (chmn. bd. dirs. 1986-92, exec. dir. 1992—), Tex. Assn. Bus. (bd. dirs. 1990-92, state exec. com. 1991). Republican. Baptist. Avocation: bicycling (4000 miles per yr.). Home: 818 Willow Creek Cir San Marcos TX 78666-5060

BULLOCK, JOSEPH DANIEL, pediatrician, educator; b. Cin., Jan. 23, 1942; s. Joseph Craven and Emilie (Woide) B.; m. Martha Foss, June 20, 1964; children: Jennifer Zane, Sarah Harrison. BA, Wittenberg U., 1963; MD, Ohio State U., 1967, degree in pediatrics, 1969; degree in immunology, allergy, U. Calif., San Francisco, 1971. Diplomate Am. Bd. Pediatrics, Am. Bd. Allergy and Immunology. Clin. prof. pediatrics Ohio State U., Columbus, 1971—; pres. Midwest Allergy Assocs., Inc., Worthington, Ohio, 1971—. Contbr. articles to profl. jours. Active fund raising Wittenberg U., Springfield, Ohio, 1980-83, Columbus Sch. for Girls, 1977-86. Served to capt. USAF, 1967-71. Recipient Mead Johnson award, 1965. Fellow Am. Acad. Pediatrics, Am. Acad. Allergy, Am. Coll. Allergists (Bd. Regents 1979-82, Clemens von Pirquet award 1968, 69, 70, 71), Am. Thoracic Soc., Interasma, Ohio Soc. Allergy and Immunology (pres. 1985-87). Republican. Lutheran. Clubs: Columbus Country; The Golf (New Albany, Ohio); Indian Creek Country (Miami Beach, Fla.), The Surf (Surfside, Fla.). Home: 189 N Parkview Ave Columbus OH 43209-1435 Office: Midwest Allergy Assocs Inc 85 E Wilson Bridge Rd Columbus OH 43085-2392

BULLOCK, MARK WILLIAM, broadcast journalist; b. Ft. Worth, Aug. 17, 1972; s. William Joseph and Jane Lee (Willson) B. BA in Journalism, U. Ga., 1995. News dir. WRFC/WPUP-Radio, Athens, Ga., 1994-95; reporter WRBL-TV, Columbus, Ga., 1995-97, anchor, reporter, 1997-98; anchor, reporter WSFA-TV, Montgomery, Ala., 1998—; freelance reporter Crain Comms., N.Y.C., 1997. Reporter, prodr. TV news series Bridge to Bosnia, 1996 (award Soc. Profl. Journalists 1997). Bd. dirs. Boy Scouts Am., Columbus, 1997-98; bd. trustees Miss Ga. Pageant, Columbus, 1997-98. Recipient Broadcasting award Ga. AP, 1994, 95, 96; fellow Poynter Inst. for Media Studies, 1995. Mem. Soc. Profl. Journalists, Radio and TV News Dirs. Assn., U. Ga. Alumni Assn., Di Gamma Kappa, Phi Kappa Theta. Methodist. Home: 906-B E Edgemont Ave Montgomery AL 36111 Office: WSFA-TV 12 E Delano Ave Montgomery AL 36105

BULLOCK, MAURICE RANDOLPH, lawyer; b. Colorado City, Tex., Aug. 20, 1913; s. Jesse H. and Georgia (White) B.; m. Wilda Marie Frost, Nov. 25, 1939; children: Dan Randolph, Sara Virginia. LL.B., U. Tex., 1936. Bar: Tex. 1936. Mem. firm Silliman & Bullock, Ft. Stockton, Tex., 1936-39; Pecos County atty., 1939-43; pvt. practice law Ft. Stockton, 1946—; partner firm Bullock, Kerr & Scott, Ft. Stockton, 1963-65; ptnr. Bullock, Scott, Neisig & Owens, Midland, Tex., now shareholder; mem. adv. com. Tex. Supreme Ct., 1975-84. Past chmn. State Securities Bd. Tex.; Texas adv. com. to Civil Rights Commn., 1960-62; mem., past chmn. bd. executors, past exec. com. Permian Basin Petroleum Mus., Library and Hall of Fame; mem. exec. com. Tex. Law Enforcement Found., 1964—; past pres. Midland Symphony Assn., Midland-Odessa Symphony and Chorale, Inc.; Served as chmn. 1958 Tex. Dem. Conv. Served as spl. agt. Security Intelligence Corps AUS, 1943-46. Fellow Am. Bar Found., Tex. Bar Found., Am. Coll. Trust and Estate Counsel; mem. ABA (ho. of dels. 1958-62), Trans-Pecos Bar Assn. (pres. 1964-65), Midland County Bar Assn., State Bar Tex. (pres. 1955-56), Southwestern Legal Found. (trustee 1969-88, exec. com. 1973-88, trustee emeritus 1989—), Tex. Trial Lawyers Assn., Am. Judicature Soc. (past dir.), Permian Basin Petroleum Assn. (past dir.), Ft. Stockton Hist. Soc. (past dir.), Pecos County C. of C. (past pres.), West Tex. C. of C. (past v.p.), Order of Coif. Democrat. Methodist. Lectr. on oil and gas and securities law. Home: 3200 Racquet Club Dr Midland TX 79705-6427 Office: Bullock Scott Neisig & Owens 500 W Texas Ave Ste 700 Midland TX 79701-4270*

BULLOCK, MOLLY, retired elementary education educator; d. Wiley and Annie M. Jordan; m. George Bullock; children: Myra A. Bauman, Dawn M. BS in Edn., No. Ariz. U., 1955, postgrad., 1958; postgrad., LaVerne U., 1962, Claremont Grad. Sch., 1963, Calif. State U. L.A., 1966. Tchr. Bur. Indian Affairs, Kaibeto, Ariz., 1955-56, Crystal, N.Mex., 1956-59; tchr. Covina (Calif.) Valley Unified Sch. Dist., 1961-95, supervising master tchr. for trainees of LaVerne U. and Calif. State U. - L.A., 1961-71, mem. curriculum devel. adv. bd., 1977-79; ret., 1995; mem. voting com. Excellence in Edn. awards Lawry's Foods. Poet: A Tree (Golden Poet 1991), What is Love (Golden medal of honor). Vol., visitor area convalescent hosps. Mini grantee Hughes/Rotary Club/Foothill Ind. Bank, Covina, 1986-90. Mem. Internat. Platform Assn., Internat. Soc. Poets (hon. charter), Covina Unified Edn. Assn. Avocations: poetry, collecting jewelry, dolls, paintings.

BULLOCK, ROBERT D. (BOB BULLOCK), lawyer, lieutenant governor, state legislator; b. Hillsboro, Tex., July 10, 1929; s. Thomas A. and Ruth (Mitchell) B.; m. Jan. Felts Teague; children: Lindy Bullock Ward, Robert Douglas Jr., Kimberly Teague Ader. AA, Hill Coll., 1949; BA, Tex. Tech

U., 1958; JD Baylor U., 1958, D of Humanities in Medicine (hon.), 1992. Bar: Tex. 1958, U.S. Dist. Ct. (so. and ea. dists.) Tex. 1960, U.S. Dist. Ct. (we. dist.) Tex. 1961, U.S. Ct. Appeals (5th cir.) 1972. Sole practice, Hillsboro, Tex., 1957-59, Tyler, Tex., 1960-61, Austin, Tex., 1961-67; asst. atty. gen. State of Tex., Austin, 1967-68, aide to gov., 1969-71, sec. of state, 1971-72, comptr. pub. accounts, 1975-90; lt. gov. State of Tex., 1991—; of counsel Scott, Douglas, Luthon & McConnico, Austin, Dallas, Houston; dir. CAL FED, Calif.; mem. Tex. Hist. Commn., 1963-65; pres. Tex. State Senate. Mem. Tex. Ho. of Reps., 1956-59; mem. Legis. Budget Bd., Legis. Coun., Interstate Oil Compact Commn., Impact 2000; chair Tex. State Dem. Leadership Coun.; mem. Sesquicentennial Coun. of 150 Baylor U. Served with USAF, 1951-54, Korea. Recipient Louisville Gold Medal award Mcpl. Fin. Officers Assn., 1978, Leon Rothenberg Pub. Svc. award Fed. Tax Adminstrs., 1989, Legis. award Clean Water Action and Clean Water Fund, 1991, Pub. Svc. award Common Cause, 1991, Outstanding Legislator of Yr. award Houston Police Patrolman's Union, 1991, Legislator of Yr. award Sportsmen Conservations of Tex., 1991, Champion of Children award Tex. Collation for Juvenile Justice, 1991, Elected Ofcl. award Tex. Human Rights Found., 1991, Leadership award Assn. Retarded Citizens, 1992, Friend Edn. award Tex. Classroom Tchrs. Assn., Elves Smith Meml. award Alcoholic Rehab. Ctr. Bexar County, Pub. Ofcl. award Tex. Pub. Power Assn., 1992, Bill Hobby award Tex. Abortion Rights Action League, 1992, Mirabeau B. Lamar medal Assn. Tex. Colls. and Univs., 1993; named Mr. South Tex., Washington Birthday Celebration Assn., 1993, Better than the Best in 73d Legislature, Tex. Monthly Mag., 1993, Outstanding Legislator of Yr., Tex. Jr. Coll. Tchrs. Assn., 1994, Frank C. Erwin award U. Tex., 1994, Baylor Lawyer of Yr., 1994, Outstanding Svcs. to Librs. award Tex. Libr. Assn., 1994, Legislator of Yr. 1994, Achievement in Suppport of Tort Reform Tex. Civil Justice League, 1995, Hats Off award Tex. Ind. Prodrs. and Royalty Owners Assn., 1995, Gov. Allan Shivers Pub. Svc. award Austin Headliners' Found., 1995, award of excellence Tex. Assn. Symphony Orchs., 1996, Santa Rita award, U. Tex. Bd. of Regents, 1996, Disting. Pub. Servants award, Tex. U. Ctr. for Pub. Svc., 1996, Merit award for 1996, award of Excellence, Nat. Junior Coll. Athletic Assn., and numerous others; honored by People First!, 1993, Exec. Dirs. Tex. Coun. Family Violence, Tex. Family Planning Assn., 1993, honored Bob Bullock Endowed Scholarship Blinn Coll., 1994; named to Nat. Jaycee Hall of Leadership, 1993, others. Mem. ABA, NRA (life), Am. Legion (Post 196), State Bar Tex., Tex. Trial Lawyers Assn., Travis County Bar Assn., Tex. State Hist. Assn., Baylor Law Alumni Assn. (life), Coastal Conservation Assn., Aircraft Owners and Pilots Assn., Tex. Farm Bur., Tex. Vets. of Korea, Tex. and Southwestern Cattle Raisers Assn., Tex. Game Wardens Assn., Tex. State Rifle Assn. (life), Confederate Air Force, Masons (33d degree), Scottish Rite (32nd degree), Century Club Tex. Tech. Ex-Students, Century Club Hill Coll., Baylor Law Alumni Assn. (life), Dallas Safari Club. Democrat. Office: Office of Lt Gov Box 12068 Capitol Station Austin TX 78711-2068

BULLOCK, SANDRA, actress; b. Washington, July 26, 1966; d. John and Helga B. Grad., Washington-Lee H.S., Arlington, Va., 1982. Appearances include (TV movies) Bionic Showdown: The Six-Million Dollar Man and the Bionic Woman, 1989, (TV series) Working Girl, 1990, (feature films) Fire on the Amazon, 1991, Love Potion #9, 1992, The Vanishing, 1993, Demolition Man, 1993, The Thing Called Love, 1993, Wrestling Ernest Hemingway, 1993, Speed, 1994 (Best Female Performance, Most Desirable Female MTV Movie awards), While You Were Sleeping, 1995 (Favorite Actress in a Motion Picture award People Choice Awards 1996), The Net, 1995, Two if by Sea, 1996, A Time to Kill, 1996, In Love and War, 1996, Practical Magic, 1998, Gun Shy, 1999, Forces of Nature, 1999, Exactly 3:30, 1999; actor, prodr. Kate and Leopold, 1996; actor, writer Making Sandwiches, 1996, Speed II, 1997; actor, exec. prodr. Hope Floats, 1998; voice Prince of Egypt, 1998. Recipient Best Actress MTV's Big Picture, 1994-95, Best Actress US Mag., 1995, Favorite Actress in a Comedy/Drama Theatrical and Favorite Actress-Comedy Video awards BlockBuster Entertainment Awards, 1996, Favorite Actress People's Choice award, 1997. Office: UTA 9560 Wilshire Blvd Fl 5 Beverly Hills CA 90212-2401*

BULLOCK, STEVEN CARL, lawyer; b. Anderson, Ind., Jan. 19, 1949; s. Carl Pearson and Dorothy Mae (Colle) B.; m. Miriam E.J. Bullock, May 21, 1982; children: Bradford, Christine. BA, Purdue U., 1971; JD, Detroit Coll., 1985. Bar: Mich. 1985, U.S. Dist. Ct. (ea. dist.) 1985. Pvt. pracitce Inkster, Mich., 1985—. With USAF, 1971-75. Mem. Mich. Bar Assn. (criminal law sect.), Detroit Bar Assn., Detroit Funder's Soc., Recorder's Ct. Bar Assn., Suburban Bar Assn. Avocations: golf, travel. Office: 2228 Inkster Rd Inkster MI 48141-1811

BULLOCK, THEODORE HOLMES, biologist, educator; b. Nanking, China, May 16, 1915; s. Amasa Archibald and Ruth (Beckwith) B.; m. Martha Runquist, May 30, 1937; children—Elsie Christine, Stephen Holmes. Student, Pasadena Jr. Coll., 1932-34; A.B., U. Calif. at Berkeley, 1936, Ph.D., 1940; Sterling fellow zoology, Yale U., 1940-41, Rockefeller fellow exptl. neurology, 1941-42. Research assoc. Yale U. Sch. Medicine, 1942-43, instr. neuroanatomy, 1943-44; instr. Marine Biol. Lab., Woods Hole, Mass., 1944-46; lab. invertebrate zoology Marine Biol. Lab., 1955-57, trustee, 1955-57; asst. prof. anatomy U. Mo., 1944-46; asst. prof. zoology U. Calif. at Los Angeles, 1946, assoc. prof., 1948, prof., 1955-66; Brain Research Inst., U. Calif. at Los Angeles, 1960-66; prof. neuroscis. Med. Sch., U. Calif. at San Diego, 1966-82, prof. emeritus, 1982—; mem. AEC 2d Resurvey of Bikini Expdn., 1948. Author: (with G.A. Horridge) Structure and Function in the Nervous Systems of Invertebrates, 2 vols., 1965; (with others) Introduction to Nervous Systems, 1977; (with W. Heiligenberg) Electroreception, 1986 (with E. Basar) Brain Dynamics, 1989, (with E. Basar) Induced Rhythms in the Brain, 1992, How Do Brains Work?, 1993. Fulbright scholar Stazione Zooologica, Naples, 1950-51; fellow Center Advanced Study in Behavioral Scis., Palo Alto, 1959-60. Fellow AAAS; mem. NAS, Am. Soc. Zoologists (chmn. comparative physiology div. 1961, pres. 1965), Soc. Neurosci. (pres. 1973-74), Internat. Soc. Neuroethology (pres. 1984-86), Am. Physiol. Soc., Soc. Gen. Physiologists, Am. Acad. Arts and Scis., Am. Philos. Soc., Internat. Brain Research Orgn., Phi Beta Kappa, Sigma Xi.

BULLOCK, WELDON KIMBALL, health facility administrator, pathologist, pathology educator; b. Vernal, Utah, Jan. 6, 1908; s. John Kimball and Adelaide (Arnold) B.; m. Dosia Opal Newton, Dec. 26, 1931; children: John, Jim. BA, U. Utah, 1930; MD, Northwestern U., 1934, MSc in Pathology, 1942. Diplomate Am. Bd. Pathology; lic. MD, Calif., Idaho, Utah. Intern Alameda County Hosp., 1933-34; resident in medicine Cook County Hosp., 1940-41; resident in pathology L.A. County-U. So. Calif. Med. Ctr., 1946-47; head surg. pathology LAC-U. So. Calif. Med. Ctr., 1949-69; instr. pathology Sch. Medicine U. So. Calif., 1947-48, asst. prof., 1955-62, clin. prof., 1963-74, clin. prof. emeritus, 1974—; exec. dir. Calif. Tumor Tissue Registry, various locations, 1955-95; dir. emeritus Calif. Tumor Tissue Registry, 1995—; chief pathology svc. Orthop. Hosp., 1956-63; assoc. pathologist St. Luke Hosp., 1963-70, chief pathologist, 1970-77, assoc. pathologist, 1977-81; clin. prof. pathology Sch. Medicine Loma Linda U., 1992—; James Ewing fellow in pathology Meml. Hosp. for Cancer and Allied Disease, 1948-49; cons. Calif. Assn. Cytotechnologists, 1962—, So. Calif. Acad. Oral Pathology, 1963—, Orthop. Hosp., 1963—; mem. Am. Joint Com. Cancer Staging and End Result Reporting, 1963-69, chmn. audio-visual task force, 1966-69, mem. exec. com., 1969; mem. rev. com. clin. cancer tng. grants Nat. Cancer Inst., 1965-68; mem. cancer planning com. Calif. Regional Med. Program, Area V, U. So. Calif., 1967-69; mem. pub. health svc. spl. project rev. com. HEW, State of Calif., 1967-69; meml. lectr. Arthur Purdy Stout Soc. Surg. Pathologists, 1979. Author: Oral Cancer & Tumors of the Jaws, 1956; contbr. articles to profl. jours. Lt. Col. U.S. Army Res., 1941-45, PTO. Decorated Bronze Star. Mem. AMA, Coll. Am. Pathologists (mem. com. cancer 1965-70), Am. Soc. Clin. Pathologists, Soc. Surg. Oncology, Calif. Med. Assn., Calif. Soc. Pathologists (mem. exec. com. 1960-62, sec.-treas. 1962-65, pres.-elect 1965-66, pres. 1966-67), L.A. County Med. Assn. (chmn. com. med. examiner 1968-72), L.A. Soc. Pathologists (past pres. exec. com. 1961-62), Soc. Grad. Pathologists-L.A. County-U. So. Calif. Med. Ctr., Soc. Grad. Surgeons-L.A. County-U. So. Calif. Med. Ctr. E-mail: CTTR@linkline.com. Home: 1460 Vandyke Rd San Marino CA 91108-2747 Office: Calif Tumor Tissue Registry 11021 Campus St # 335 Loma Linda CA 92354

BULLOCK, WILLIAM CLAPP, JR., banker; b. Bronxville, N.Y., June 28, 1936; s. William and Elizabeth (Van Wagnen) B.; m. Edith Swain, June 21, 1958; children: Wendy, Martha, Sarah, Bill. BA, Yale U., 1958; postgrad., NYU, 1958-60. Asst. treas., asst. v.p. nat. divsn. Morgan Guaranty Trust Co., N.Y.C., 1958-69; v.p., sr. loan officer Merrill Trust Co., Bangor, Maine, 1969-71, exec. v.p., 1971-73, pres., 1973—, CEO, 1980-82, also chmn. bd. dirs.; pres. Merrill Bankshares Co., 1973—, CEO, 1980-82; exec. v.p., dir. Fleet Fin. Group, 1986-88; also chmn. bd. dirs. Merrill Bankshares Co.; pvt. practice as fin. cons., 1989—; dir. Fed. Res. Bank of Boston, 1985-88; chmn. Merrill Mchts. Bank, 1992—; bd. dirs. Bangor Hydro-Electric Co., Ea. Maine Health Care. Chmn. Maine Gov.'s Task Force on Indian Land Claims, 1979-80; bd. dirs. Assoc. Industries Maine, 1978-81, Atlantic Salmon Fedn., Miramichi Salmon Assn.; bd. dirs. New England Coun., 1981—, past pres.; past treas., past trustee Maine Maritime Acad.; former trustee Bangor Theol. Sem., Maine State Retirement Sys.; former dir. Bangor & Aroostook R.R. Mem. Maine Bankers Assn. (bd. dirs., past pres.), Am. Bankers Assn., Maine C. of C. (past bd. dirs.), Yale Club, N.Y. Anglers Club. Home: 44 Bald Hill Reach Rd Orrington ME 04474-3630 Office: 201 Main St Bangor ME 04401-6402

BULLOCK, WILLIAM HENRY, bishop; b. Maple Lake, Minn., Apr. 13, 1927; s. Loren W. and Anne C. (Raiche) B. B.A., Notre Dame U., 1948, M.A., 1962; Ed.S., St. Thomas Coll., St. Paul, 1969; HHD (hon.), St. Ambrose U., Davenport, Iowa, 1989. Ordained priest Roman Catholic Ch., 1952, ordained bishop Roman Catholic Ch., 1980. Assoc. pastor Ch. of St. Stephens, Mpls., 1952-55, Ch. of Our Lady of Grace, Edina, Minn., 1955-56, Ch. of Incarnation, Mpls., 1956-57; instr. St. Thomas Acad., Mendota Heights, Minn., 1957-61, headmaster, 1968-71; pastor Ch. of St. John the Baptist, Excelsior, Minn., 1971-80; former pastor Ch. of Our Lady of Perpetual Help, Mpls., from 1980; aux. bishop Archdiocese of St. Paul and Mpls., 1980-87; apptd. bishop Diocese of Des Moines, 1987, installed, 1987-93; apptd. bishop Madison, Wis., 1993—; v.p. Wis. Cath. Conf.; mem. Cath. Relief Svcs. Bd. Trustee St. Francis Sem. Mem. U.S. Bishops-Region II, Nat. Conf. Cath. Bishops (NCCB/USCC com. evangelization), KC (4th degree), Knights of Holy Sepulchre, Cath. Relief Svcs. (exec. com., Africa com., com. overseas programs and ops.). Lodges: KC; Knights of Holy Sepulchre. Office: Diocese of Madison Cath Pastoral Ctr PO Box 44983 Madison WI 53744-4983*

BULLOFF, JACK JOHN, physical chemist, consultant; b. N.Y.C., Dec. 9, 1914; s. John Stevens and Selma (Lyadova) B.; m. Gertrude Scher, Nov. 11, 1942 (dec. Oct. 1951); 1 child, Eric Douglas (dec.); m. Florence Gutin, Oct. 4, 1952 (dec. May 1996); children: Dorie Lee, Aaron Harley, Steven Marc. BS in Chemistry, CUNY, 1939; PhD in Phys. Chemistry, Rensselaer Poly. Inst., 1953. Asst. prof. chemistry Associated Colls. Upper N.Y., Ovid/Plattsburgh, 1946-50; teaching fellow Rensselaer Poly. Inst., Troy, N.Y., 1950-52; project supr. Commonwealth Engrng. Co., Dayton, Ohio, 1953-56; rsch. assoc. Battelle Meml. Inst., Columbus, Ohio, 1956-68; prof., dir. sci. and tech. studies SUNY, Albany, 1968-76; author-revisor Fla. State U., Tallahassee, 1977-78; cons. safety and wastes J.T. Baker Chem. Co., Phillipsburg, N.J., 1978-84; chief cons. scientist N.Y. State Legis. Commn. on Sci. Tech., Albany, 1985-92; prin. J. Bulloff Chem. and Environ. Cons., Schenectady, N.Y., 1968—; jr. scientist Los Alamos Nat. Lab., N.M., 1946; vis. lectr. NSF, 1960-66; Kimberley Clark ann. lectr., 1963; cons., expert witness, Schenectady, N.Y., 1968—. Co-author 18 books in field; co-editor: Semiconductor Abstracts, 1959-62, Foundations of Mathematics, 1969; contbr. over 100 articles to profl. jours. With U.S. Army chem. corps. 1942-44, med. corps. 1944-46, ETOUSA. Recipient Best Paper award Tech. Assn. Graphic Arts, 1961. Fellow AAAS, Am. Inst. Chemists (emeritus, chair safety in the chemists' workplace com., 1993-94, co-chair coms. in chemistry and environ. concerns, govt. activities and safety in the chemists' workplace 1995-96, govt. activities com. 1995—), Am. Chem. Soc. (emeritus 1989—, various positions 1953-78); mem. N.Y. Acad. Scis. (emeritus 1993—), Ohio Acad. Sci. (v.p. 1966). Achievements include 29 patents for volatile compound metals deposition, air odor control, metallic soaps, and dextran chemistry, others; innovation in xerography and lithography, image-wise photopolymerization, technological forecasting and environmental impact and technology assessment. Home and Office: Ste 5220 8140 Township Line Rd Indianapolis IN 46260-5866 *Once you realize that longevity offers opportunity for more than one career and that everything in the universe has been related to every other thing therein for many billions of years, being a polymath is finding that relation.*

BULLOUGH, JOHN FRANK, organist, music educator; b. Washington, Oct. 15, 1928; s. John and Mabel Jean (McCalip) B.; m. Dorothy Baines, Apr. 10, 1950; children: John Frank, Lynn Diane, Patricia Ann. BA, George Washington U., 1954; SMM, Union Theol. Sem., 1958. Organist, asst. prof. music Hartford Theol. Sem. Found., Conn., 1958-64; from asst. prof. music to assoc. prof. to prof. Fairleigh Dickinson U., Teaneck, N.J., 1964-93, chmn. dept. fine arts, 1974-79; music dir. Hartford Ctr. Ch., 1960-64; organist, choirmaster St. Paul's Episcopal Ch., Englewood, N.J., 1973-95; music dir., conductor The Bergen Chorale, Tenafly, N.J., 1987-91. Contbr. articles to profl. jours. V.p. bd. trustees Bergen Philharm. Orch., N.J., 1973-80. Mem. AAUP, Am. Guild Organists (dean Hartford chpt. 1963-64, No. Valley N.J. chpt. 1975-77, chmn. region II 1984-88, convener No. N.J. dist. 1991-92, dean No. N.J. cpth. 1995-97), Coll. Music Soc. Episcopalian. Home: 488 Fairidge Ter Teaneck NJ 07666-2617

BULLOUGH, VERN LEROY, nursing educator, historian, sexologist, researcher; b. Salt Lake City, July 24, 1928; s. D. Vernon Bullough and Augusta Rueckert; m. Bonnie Uckerman, Aug. 2, 1947 (dec. 1996); children: David (dec.), James, Steven, Susan, Michael; m. Gwen Brewer, Aug. 15, 1998. BSN, Calif. State U., Long Beach, 1981; BS, U. Utah, 1951; MA, U. Chgo., 1951, PhD, 1954. Assoc. prof. Youngstown (Ohio) U., 1954-59; prof. Calif. State U., Northridge, 1959-80; dean faculty natural social scis. SUNY Coll., Buffalo, 1980-89, disting. prof., 1988-93, disting. prof. emeritus, 1993—; vis. prof. U. So. Calif., 1994—. Author, co-author of more than 50 books; sr. editor Free Inquiry; mem. editl. bds. 8 jours.; contbr. more than 200 articles to profl. jours. With U.S. Army Security Agy., 1946-48. Named Outstanding Prof. Calif. State U. sys., Disting. Prof., SUNY; recipient Kinsey award, numerous other awards for rsch. into sexuality, history, medicine and nursing. Fellow Am. Acad. Nursing, Soc. Sci. Study Sex (past pres.), Acad. Humanism (laureate); mem. Internat. Humanist and Ethical Union (past pres.). Achievements include discovery of mistakes on historical calculation of menarche; of drop in rates of female anemia in the late medieval period; factors in successful military deterrence; cultural factors in intellectual achievement the early development of medicine as profession; pioneering historical research on sex and gender and on history of sex research.

BULMAN, WILLIAM PATRICK, data processing executive; b. Corona, N.Y., Jan. 11, 1925; s. William T. and Bridget A. (Gibbons) B.; m. Jane G. Jones, June 30, 1952. BS, U. Upper N.Y., 1947; BBA, Syracuse (N.Y.) U., 1949, MBA, 1977. In systems/programming Mohawk Airlines, Utica, N.Y., 1951-55; data processing mgr. Gold Medal Packing, Utica, 1956-59, West End Brewing, Utica, 1960-73; coord. on-line data processing systems Sperry-Univac, Utica, 1973-76, data processing mgr., 1976-77; programmer/analyst MDS, Herkimer, N.Y., 1977-86; sr. programmer, analyst, Momentum Techs., Herkimer, N.Y., 1986-89; ret., 1989; cons. Bilb-Tech, 1989—. With USN, 1941-46. Mem. Data Processing Mgmt. Assn. (v.p., treas.), Assn. Systems Mgmt. Address: 35 Ashwood Ave Whitesboro NY 13492-1701

BULOW, GEORGE MITCHELL, entrepreneur; b. New Rochelle, N.Y., May 26, 1949; s. Harry N. Bulow and Ruth (Silverman) Kaufman; m. Lucienne Carasso, June 22, 1975; children: Harris, Alessandra. BA, Clark U., 1971; MBA, Columbia U., 1974. Asst. v.p. Chase Manhattan Bank, NA, N.Y.C., 1974-87; pres. Interactive Internat. Inc., N.Y.C., 1987—; pres. Bohlen Industries N.Am., Inc., N.Y.C., 1980—, Beaumont Farms, Inc., N.Y.C., 1994—. Office: Interactive Internat Inc 290 W West End Ave New York NY 10023-8106

BULOW, JACK FAYE, library director; b. Elmira, N.Y., June 7, 1942; m. June Burwell, May 22, 1971. Associates degree, Corning (N.Y.) C.C., 1968; BA, U. Ala., Birmingham, 1971; MLS, U. Ala., Tuscaloosa, 1973. Community svcs. libr. Birmingham Pub. Libr., 1973-77, assoc. dir., 1977-93, dir., 1993—. Developer Books-by-Mail program, Birmingham and Jefferson County, 1976; participant exec. in residence program Birmingham-So. Coll., 1987, Leadership Birmingham, 1992; elected as del. White House Conf. on Libr. and Info. Svcs., Washington, 1991; elected as regional rep. White House Conf. on Libr. and Info. Svcs. Task Force, Washington, 1992; bd. dirs. Literacy Coun. Ctrl. Ala., Birmingham, 1993—; mem. Nat. League Cities, Washington, 1993—; mem. long range planning com. Birmingham Mus. Art, 1993—; mem. cultural affairs com. Operation New Birmingham, 1988—; sec. Birmingham Pub. Libr. Found.; patron Cahaba River Soc. Birmingham, 1992—. With USCG, 1960-64. Recipient Forestry Recognition award Ala. Forestry Commn., 1977. Mem. ALA (chair fundraising and fin. devel. sect. 1997), Am. Hist. Print Collectors Soc., Am. Mgmt. Assn., Nat. Soc. Fund Raising Execs., Southeastern Libr. Assn., Ala. Libr. Assn. (pres. 1995), Birmingham-So. Coll. Fine Arts Soc., Birmingham Kiwanis Club. Avocations: reading, golf, travel, fishing. Office: Birmingham Pub Libr 2100 Park Pl Birmingham AL 35203-2744

BULSON, CHRISTINE E., academic librarian; b. Cooperstown, N.Y., Mar. 11, 1942; d. Emmons B. and Edith Krejci Bulson. BA, Hartwick Coll., 1964; MLS, SUNY, Albany, 1967, cert. advanced studies, 1981. Libr. Margaretville Ctrl. Sch., 1964-66, Pleasantville (N.Y.) H.S., 1967-68; asst., sr. asst. libr. SUNY, Oneonta, 1978-91, libr., 1991—, asst. dir. for reference and circulation svcs., 1996—. Author: Current Cookbooks, 1990; author over 130 book revs. Mem. Oneonta Concert Assn. (bd. dirs. 1986—), Beta Phi Mu. Home: 204 Main St Worcester NY 12197 Office: Milne Libr SUNY Oneonta NY 13820

BULTEMA, JANICE KAY, healthcare executive; b. Kalamazoo, Mich., Jan. 18, 1952; d. Henry and Henrietta L. (Kroeze) Sportel; m. Leonard J. Bultema, Sept. 16, 1978. Student, Calvin Coll., 1972; diploma, Mercy Cen. Sch. Nursing, Grand Rapids, Mich., 1974; BSN, U. N.C., 1987; MSN, Duke U., 1989. RN, Ill., Mich.; cert. nurse adminstr. advanced, ANCC; lic. nursing home adminstr., Ill. Staff nurse, psychiat. acute care adult unit Pine Rest Christian Hosp., Grand Rapids, 1974-81; staff nurse, psychiat. nursing div. Duke Univ. Med. Ctr., Durham, N.C., , 1981-83; supplemental staff nurse, med. nursing div. Duke Univ. Med. Ctr., Durham, 1986-90, asst. head nurse, psychiat. nursing div., 1983-89, asst. to dir. psychiat. nursing div., 1989-91; dir. psychiat. nursing Northwestern Meml. Hosp., Chgo., 1991-97, dir. skilled nursing, 1994-97, exec. dir. transition planning, hosp. ops., 1996—; clin. asst. prof. Loyola U., Chgo., 1993—; cons., writer and presenter in field. Mem. Am. Psychiat. Nurses Assn. (bd. mem.-at-large 1994-96), Am. Orgn. Nurse Execs., Ill. Orgn. Nurse Execs. (mem. legis. com. 1993-95), Chgo. Met. Nursing Adminstrs., Sigma Theta Tau (chmn. social com. Beta Epsilon chpt. 1988-90, sec. 1990-91). Home: 18420 Homewood Ave Homewood IL 60430-3346

BULTMANN, WILLIAM ARNOLD, historian; b. Monrovia, Calif., Apr. 10, 1922; s. Paul Gerhardt and Elsa (Johnson) B.; AB, UCLA, 1943, PhD, 1950; m. Phyllis Jane Wetherell, Dec. 28, 1949; 1 child, Janice Jane. Assoc. prof. history Central Ark. U., Conway, 1949-52, prof., 1954-57; assoc. prof. Ohio Wesleyan U., Delaware, 1957-61, prof., 1961-65; prof. Western Wash. U., Bellingham, 1965-87, chmn. dept., 1968-70, dean arts and scis., 1970-72, provost, 1971-73; vis. assoc. prof. U. Tex., Austin, 1952-53; vis. prof. U. N.H., summers 1965, 66; acad. cons. Wash. Commn. for Humanities, 1973-87, Nat. Endowment for Humanities, 1976-87; reader Ednl. Testing Service Princeton, 1973-85. Bd. dirs. Bellingham Maritime Heritage Found., 1980-85; mem. The Nature Conservancy, 1992—, Washington Arboretum Found., 1992-97; adminstrv. officer Bellingham Power Squadron, 1981-82, comdr., 1982-84. Fulbright sr. lectr. Dacca (Bangladesh) U., 1960-61; Ohio Wesleyan U. rsch. fellow, 1964; Fund for Advancement Edn. fellow for fgn. study, 1953-54; recipient rsch. award Social Sci. Rsch. Coun., 1957. Mem. AAUP, Am. Hist. Assn., Nat. Tropical Botanical Garden Soc., Nat. Boating Fedn., Ch. Hist. Soc., Conf. Brit. Studies, Pacific, Pacific N.W. confs. Brit. studies, Mystery Writers of Am., Interclub Boating Assn. Washington, Seattle Power Squadron, Phi Beta Kappa, Phi Delta Kappa, Pi Gamma Mu. Episcopalian. Clubs: Park Athletic Recreation, Bellingham Yacht (chmn. pub. rels. com. 1981-86), Squalicum Yacht (trustee 1979-82), Birch Bay Yacht; Wash. Athletic. Co-author: Border Boating, 1978; co-founder, mem. editorial bd. Albion, 1968-84; mng. editor Brit. Studies Intelligencer, 1973-80; co-editor Current Research in British Studies, 1975; editor Jib Sheet, 1981-86; feature writer, columnist Sea mag., 1974-93; feature writer Venture mag., 1981-85, Poole Publs., 1988-92. Home: 1600 43rd Ave E Apt 101 Seattle WA 98112-3245

BULZACCHELLI, JOHN G., financial executive; b. N.Y.C., July 7, 1939; s. Vito N. and Mary B.; m. Frances R. Rocco, Nov. 30, 1963; children—John F. B.S., CUNY, 1962. Staff acct. Haskins & Sells, N.Y.C., 1962-65; treas., contr. Grumman Allied Ind., Inc., Garden City, N.Y., 1965-69; contr. Wellington Tech. Ind., Inc., Englewood, N.Y., 1969; v.p. fin. Gulf & Western Systems, Inc., N.Y.C., 1970-76; exec. v.p. Kayser-Roth Corp., N.Y.C., 1976-81, Gulf & Western Consumer Products Co., N.Y.C., 1981-82, Gulf & Western Consumer and Indsl. Products Group, N.Y.C., 1983-85, subs. Wickes Cos., Inc., N.Y.C., 1985-86; exec. v.p., chief fin. officer Revlon, Inc., N.Y.C., 1986-88; exec. v.p., bd. dirs. Taren Holdings Inc., N.Y.C., 1989-92; retired pvt. practice cons. Bd. dirs. Cotswold Civic Assn., 1968-69. Served with USMC, 1962. Republican. Roman Catholic. Club: Coveleigh (Rye, N.Y.). Home and Office: 1601 Park Beach Cir Apt 122 Punta Gorda FL 33950-5280

BUMANN, SHARON ANN, sculptor; b. Syracuse, N.Y., June 28, 1953; d. G. Bruce and Erma Jean (Gibbs) Stallknecht; m. George Charles BuMann, Aug. 26, 1972; children: George Bruce, Amy Beth. AAS in Graphic Arts with honors, Onondaga C.C., Syracuse, N.Y., 1975; BFA in Sculpture magna cum laude, Syracuse U., 1984; postgrad., U. Hartford, 1990. Owner, operator BuMann Sculpture Studio, Central Square, N.Y., 1977—; lectr., juror and artist-in-residence, award winning sculptor. Creator bronze monuments, lifesize butter sculptures. Chairperson, bd. Fort Brewerton (N.Y.) Hist. Expansion, 1997-99. Mem. Nat. Sculpture Soc., Internat. Sculpture Ctr., Onondaga C.C. Alumni Assn. (pres., 1992-94). Avocations: equestrian activities, boating. Office: BuMann Sculpture Studio 90 Kellar Rd Central Square NY 13036-2122

BUMAS, E. SHASKAN, writer, educator; b. N.Y.C., Nov. 3, 1962; s. Lester Owen and Janet Marie Bumas. BA, U. Pa., 1982; MFA, Washington U., 1991, PhD, 1998. Vis. prof. U. Mo., Columbia, 1998—. Author: The Price of Tea in China, 1995 (Poets Essayists Novelists West 1996). Recipient Fulbright Rsch. award Fulbright Commn., Chile, 1996-97; Writing fellow Washington U. Writing Program, St. Louis, 1989-90, Univ. fellow Washington U. Comparative Lit., St. Louis, 1993. Mem. MLA, Poets Essayists Novelists, Associated Writing Programs. E-mail: engleb@showme.missouri.edu. Home: 16 E Stewart #2 Columbia MO 65203 Office: Univ Mo 114 Tate Hall Columbia MO 65211

BUMBERY, JOSEPH LAWRENCE, diversified telecommunications company executive; b. St. Louis, May 30, 1929; s. John Andrew and Lillian Belle (DeVinney) B. B.S., St. Louis U., 1951. Asst. comptroller Magic Chef, Inc., St. Louis, 1955-57; dir. audits and systems Bemis Corp., St. Louis, 1957-62; asst. comptroller Studebaker Corp., South Bend, Ind., 1962-65; with ITT, N.Y.C., 1965-86; v.p. ITT, 1979—, asst. comptroller, 1969—. Served to 1st lt. USAF, 1951-53. Decorated Knight Order St. John of Jerusalem; named Mem. Augustinian Order Gen. Curia of Order Rome, 1988, Governor Am. Soc. Order of St. John of Jerusalem, 1990.

BUMBRY, GRACE, soprano; b. St. Louis, Jan. 4, 1937; d. Benjamin and Melzia (Walker) B. Student, Boston U., 1954-55, Northwestern U., 1955-56, also fgn. countries, Music Acad. West, 1956-59; studied with, Lotte Lehmann, 1956-59; HHD (hon.), St. Louis U.; hon. doctorates in humanities, Rust Coll., Holly Spring, Miss., U. St. Louis, U. Mo.; MusD (hon.), Rockhurst Coll. Operatic debut, Paris Opera, 1960; debut Basel Opera, 1960, Bayreuth Festival, 1961, Vienna State Opera, 1963, Royal Opera House, Covent Garden, 1963, Salzburg Festival, 1964, Met. Opera, 1965, La Scala, 1964, Bess in Porgy and Bess, N.Y. Met. Opera, 1985, Les Troyens, Paris, 1990, Turando, Wembley Arena, 1991; has appeared all major opera houses worldwide, S.Am., Japan, U.S.; command performances The White House and London; recs. for Deutsche Grammophon, Angel, London and RCA. Recipient John Hay Whitney award, Richard Wagner medal, 1963, Grammy award, 1979, Royal Opera House medal, 1988, Puccini award, 1990, Commandeur de l'Ordre des Arts et L:ettres, France, 1996. Mem. Zeta Phi Beta, Sigma Alpha Iota. Office: Columbia Artists Mgm Inc 165 W 57th St New York NY 10019-2201*

BUMBULSKY, MAE ALBERTA, medical/surgical nurse; b. Quakake, Pa., June 11, 1944; d. John and Alberta May (Trummel) Whah; m. Peter Anthony Bumbulsky, Dec. 26, 1962 (dec.); children: Peter, Edward, Mark, Dorothy. LPN, Hazleton (Pa.) Area Vocat. Tech., 1978. Cert. EMT; cert. MAST. Staff nurse P.R.N. Profl. Svcs., Hazleton, 1990—; pvt. duty nurse Hazelton St. Joseph's Med. Ctr., 1978—; staff nurse Nurse Staff Builders, 1994—. Mem. Lic. Practical Nurses Assn. Pa., Nat. Assn. Practical Nurses Ednl. Svcs., N.E. Pa. Emergency Med. Svcs., Tri-County Nurses Assn. Home: 65 W Church St Hazleton PA 18201-7909

BUMGARDNER, CLOYD JEFFREY, school principal; b. Lorain, Ohio, Feb. 4, 1964; s. Cloyd Otis and Lois Christina (Todd) B. BS, Eastern Ky. U., 1987, MS, 1990. Cert. sch. adminstr., Ky. Sci. tchr. Pulaski County Schs., Somerset, Ky., 1990-93; asst. prin. Calloway County Schs., Murray, Ky., 1993-94; prin. Calloway County Mid. Sch., Murray, 1994—; adj. faculty U. Ky., 1990-93, Somerset C.C., 1990-93, Ea. Ky. U., Richmond, 1992-93; environ. cons. Am.-Russian Eco-bridge Team, Murray, 1994—; content adv. bd. mem. Ky. Dept. Edn., Frankfort, 1994-96; mem. Beline Sci. Expd., 1996, Nat. Energy Edn. Devel. Project, Washington, 1996—. Contbr. articles to profl. jours. Fundraiser Am. Heart Assn., Murray, 1995-98, Internat. Assn. Lions Clubs, Murray, 1994—; mem. Ky. Col. Commn., Gov. State of Ky., 1995. Named Hon. Capt. of Ky. Lake, Judge Exec. of Calloway County, 1995. Mem. NEA, Nat. Alliance for Restructuring Edn., Nat. Assn. Secondary Sch. Prins., Nat. Sch. Leaders Network, Ky. Assn. Environ. Edn., Internat. Assn. Lions Clubs, Ky. Acad. Scis., Phi Delta Kappa. Republican. Avocations: woodworking, golf. Office: Calloway County Middle School 2108A College Farm Rd Murray KY 42071-8805

BUMGARDNER, JOEL DAVID, biomedical engineer, educator; b. Huntsville, Ala., Apr. 18, 1961; s. Carl L. and Ann (Adams) B. BS in Biology, Fla. State U., 1984; BS in Materials Engring., U. Ala., 1989, MS in Biomed. Engring., 1989, PhD in Biomed. Engring., 1994. Rsch. fellow U. Ala., Birmingham, 1988-93; J. William Fulbright fellow U.S., Sweden, 1993-94; assoc. prof. dept. agrl. and biol. engring. Miss. State U., Starkville, 1994—; dir. 16th So. Biomed. Engring. Conf., Biloxi, Miss., 1996-97. Reviewer Dental Materials Jour., Dallas, 1994—; contbr. articles to profl. jours.; contbr. chpt. to ency., 1995. Co-chmn. Decorative Arts and Preservation Forum-Columbus (Miss.) Historic Found., 1997, mem. steering com., 1995-97; mem. com. Health Choice Am. Heart Walk, Columbus, 1995-97. Biomed. rsch. grantee NIH, Washington, 1992-94, The Whitaker Found., 1999, biomed. equipment grantee NSF, Washington, 1995; named Outstanding Faculty Advisor, Gold Key Soc., 1999; recipient young biomed. engr. investigator award Whitaker Found., 1999—. Mem. ASTM, Soc. Biomaterials (chmn. membership com. 1995-96), Internat. and Am. Assn. Dental Rsch. (mem. constn. com. 1995-98), Biomed. Engring. Soc., Inst. Biol. Engring. Avocations: biking, tennis, reading, antiques. Office: Miss State U Box 9632 Mississippi State MS 39762-9632

BUMGARNER, JAMES MCNABB, judge; b. Peru, Ill., Sept. 13, 1919; s. Joshua Mills and Ethel (McNabb) B.; m. Helen D. Welker, Feb. 7, 1942 (dec. May 1981); children: Barbara Malany, Sally Guth; m. Elizabeth L. Miller, Feb. 12, 1983; step-children: Tad Miller, Brian Miller, Matthew Miller. BS in Psychology with honors, U. Ill., 1941, JD, 1946. Commd. 2nd lt. USAAF, 1942; advanced through grades to col. USAF, 1967, ret., 1974; pvt. practice Rantoul, Ill., 1947, Hannah, Mattoon, Ill.; cir. judge 10th Jud. Cir. of Ill., 1979—. Mem. Rotary Internat., VFW, Am. Legion, Vietnam Vets. Ill., Retired Officers Assn., Retired Judge Advocates Assn., Vietnam Vets. Bar Assn., Ill. Bar Assn., U. Ill. Alumni Assn., Putnam County Bar Assn., Putnam County Hist. Soc., Timber Growers Assn., Judge Advocates Assn., Air War Coll. Alumni Assn., Ill. Coll. Law Deans Club, Phi Alpha Delta. Home: 1010 Market St PO Box 225 Hennepin IL 61327-0225

BUMGARNER, JAMES SCOTT See GARNER, JAMES

BUMP, GERALD JACK, executive recruiter; b. Chgo., June 7, 1927; s. Gerald Chism and Margaret Aline (Raede) B.; m. Jeanne A. Courtney, Sept. 4, 1947 (div. Sept. 1984); children: Jana, Jerry, Jamie, Jeff. BS in Phys. Edn., Purdue U., 1949, MS in Indsl. Sociology, 1950. Staff employment supr. Kimberly-Clark Corp., Neenah, Wis., 1950-60; regional sales mgr. The Trane Co., LaCrosse, Wis., 1960-69; pres. Billington, Fox and Ellis, Chgo., 1969-81; mng. dir. Spencer Stuart, Atlanta, 1981-92; exec. mng. dir. Foster Ptnrs., Atlanta, 1993—; also bd. dirs. Co-author: The Executive Search Collaboration, 1987. Active Leadership Atlanta, 1974. Named One of Top 250 Career Makers in N.Am., 1995. Republican. Episcopalian. Avocations: golf, gourmet cooking, music. Home: 2508 River Green Dr NW Atlanta GA 30327-3083 Office: Foster Ptnrs 303 Peachtree St NE Ste 2000 Atlanta GA 30308-3252

BUMP, KARIN DIANN, animal scientist, educator; b. Peoria, Ill., July 9, 1965; d. David Wayne and Sandra Kay (O'Brien) B. BS, U. Ill., 1987, MS, 1989. Asst. prof. Cazenovia (N.Y.) Coll., 1989-96, assoc. prof., 1996—; dir. equine studies Cazenovia Coll., 1989—, spl. asst. to pres. for quality assurance and assessment, 1995—, acting dean admission, 1996; humane issues coord. N.Y. State Horse Coun., 1994—; bd. dirs. Madison County-Cornell Coop. Extension. Mem. Assn. Registered Profl. Animal Scientists, Equine Nutrition and Physiology Soc., N.Y. State Horse Coun. Office: Cazenovia Coll Cazenovia NY 13035

BUMP, WILBUR NEIL, retired lawyer; b. Peoria, Ill., July 12, 1929; s. Wilbur Earl and Mae (Nelson) B.; m. Elaine Bonneval, Nov. 24, 1951; children: William Earl, Jeffrey Neil, Steven Bonneval. BS, State U. Iowa, 1951, JD, 1958. Bar: Iowa 1958. Solicitor gen. Iowa Atty. Gen.'s Office, Des Moines, 1961-64; pvt. practice law Des Moines, 1964-90; ret., 1990. Served with USAF, 1951-54. Mem. ABA, Iowa Bar Assn. (bd. govs. 1976-81, chmn. agrl. law com. 1982-88), Polk County Bar Assn. (pres. 1976-77), Kiwanis (pres. 1974-75). Presbyterian. Home: 1311 N 2nd St Stuart IA 50250

BUMPAS, STUART MARYMAN, lawyer; b. Little Rock, Oct. 7, 1944; s. Hubert Wayne Bumpas and Martha Conway (Maryman) Gaylord; m. Diane Ellen DeWare, Oct. 1, 1977. BA, Brown U., 1966; JD, U. Tex., 1969; LLM, George Washington U., 1973. Bar: Tex. 1969, D.C. 1972. Atty.-advisor Office of Chief Counsel, Washington, 1969-72; asst. to commr. IRS, Washington, 1973-74; ptnr. Locke, Purnell, Rain, Harrell, Dallas, 1974-98, Locke, Liddell & Sapp, Dallas, 1999—; adj. prof. employee benefits So. Meth. U., Dallas, 1975; lectr. Washington Non-Profit Tax Conf., Am. Law Inst., Ann. Non-Profit Orgns. Inst. Contbr. articles to profl. jours. Mem. exec. com. Meadows Sch. of Arts, So. Meth. U., Dallas; bd. dirs. Callier Ctr. for Comm. Disorders, Dallas, 1984—, Ctr. for Human Nutrition, Southwestern Med. Sch., Goodwill Industries, Dallas; bd. dirs., v.p. Dallas Grand Opera Assn., 1984—; mem. Mayor's Commn. on Internat. Devel. Task Force on Arts and Culture, Dallas, 1988; nat. counsel Am. Heart Assn., Dallas, 1979—; trustee The Lamplighter Sch.; gen. counsel The Hockaday Sch.; gen. counsel, bd. trustees Dallas Mus. Art. Mem. ABA (mem. exempt orgns. com.), Tex. Bar Assn. (chmn. legal aspects of arts com.), Dallas Bar Assn., Bus. Adv. Com., Am. Coun. on Germany. Episcopalian. Clubs: Dallas, Petroleum, Brook Hollow Golf, Idlewild (Dallas); Soc. Cin. (Washington), Coral Beach and Tennis (Bermuda). Home: 5306 Surrey Cir Dallas TX 75209-2427 Office: Locke Purnell Rain Harrell 2200 Ross Ave Ste 2200 Dallas TX 75201-6776*

BUMPERS, DALE L., former senator, former governor; b. Charleston, Ark., Aug. 12, 1925; s. William Rufus and Lattie (Jones) B.; m. Betty Lou Flanagan, Sept. 4, 1949; children: Dale Brent, William Mark, Margaret Brooke. Student, U. Ark., 1943, 46-48; J.D., Northwestern U., 1951. Bar: Ark. 1952. Pres. Charleston Hardware and Furniture Co., 1951-56; pvt. practice Charleston, 1952-70; operator Angus cattle farm, 1966-70; gov. of Ark., 1970-74; U.S. senator from Ark., 1975-98; mem. appropriations com., energy and natural resources com., small bus. com., senate Dem. policy com. Pres. Charleston Sch. Bd., 1969-70. Sgt. USMC, 1943-46. Mem. Charleston C. of C. (pres.). Methodist. Address: 1779 Massachusetts Ave Washington DC 20036*

BUNCE, STANLEY CHALMERS, chemist, educator; b. Bayonne, N.J., Aug. 21, 1917; s. Arthur Chalmers and Elizabeth (Sticht) B.; m. Lillis Adelle Jackson, Oct. 2, 1943; children: Gale Elizabeth Schmidt, Judith Preston Turner, James Arthur. B.S. in Chemistry, Lehigh U., 1938, M.A., 1942; Ph.D. in Chemistry, Rensselaer Poly. Inst., 1951. Secondary sch. tchr. Hershey (Pa.) Indsl. Sch., 1939-41, Bound Brook (N.J.) High Sch., 1941-43; research chemist Johns-Manville Corp., 1943-46; mem. faculty Rensselaer Poly. Inst., Troy, N.Y., 1946—; prof. chemistry Rensselaer Poly. Inst., 1958-84, prof. emeritus, 1984—, asso. chmn. dept., 1972-75. Author: (with others) Principles of Chemistry, 1966, An Approach to Physical Science, 1967; also research publs. Fellow AAAS; mem. Am. Chem. Soc., Sigma Xi, Phi Lambda Upsilon. Home: PO Box 145 Grafton NY 12082-0145 Office: Rensselaer Poly Inst Dept Chemistry Troy NY 12180-3590

BUNCH, ALBERT WILLIAM, minister; b. Eldon, Mo., Feb. 3, 1933; s. Tade W. and Leta Beatrice (Hees) B. AB, William Jewell Coll., 1954; BD, Cen. Bapt. Theol. Sem., Kansas City, Kans., 1958, MDiv, 1972; postgrad., Mo. Valley Coll., 1970-75, U. Mo., 1971. Ordained to ministry So. Bapt. Conv., 1954. Pastor Bethlehem Bapt. Ch., Carrollton, Mo., 1957-61, New Salem Bapt. Ch., Marshall, Mo., 1961—; clk. Saline Bapt. Assn., 1965-67, 75-91, mem. exec. bd., 1961-91, strategy planning com., 1988-90, historian, 1976—; mem. Carroll-Saline Bapt. Assn. Joint Mission Bd., 1966-69, 71-76; Bible tchr. Happy Adult Singles, 1978-90. Author: History of the SBA, 1976. Chmn. student work com. Mo. Valley Coll., Marshall, 1975-80; pres. Friends Libr. Svcs., Marshall, 1984-90. Recipient cert. Saline Bapt. Assn, 1976, Alumnus of Yr. award Cen. Bapt. Theol. Sem., 1983. Mem. ACLU, People for the Am. Way, Nat. Cathedral Assn., So. Bapt. Alliance, Alliance of Bapts., Cooperative Bapt. Fellowship/Mo. Coord. Coun., State Hist. Soc. Mo., S.C. Hist. Soc., Friends of Arrow Rock, Mo. Religion Coalition for Abortion Rights, Saline County Assn. for Mental Health (exec. bd.), Planned Parenthood, Marshall Philharm. Orch., Lyceum Theatre of Arrow Rock. Home: RR 1 Marshall MO 65340-9801 Office: New Salem Bapt Ch Interstate Hwy # 65 Marshall MO 65340

BUNCH, FRANKLIN SWOPE, architect; b. Madison, Ind., Jan. 4, 1913; s. Walker Franklin and Susan Beatrice (Swope) B.; m. Virginia Aurelia Boggs, June 8, 1937; children: Franklin Swope, Dean Boggs. B.S. in Arch, U. Fla., 1934. Draftsman, designer, architect and constrn. supr. various Fla. architects, 1934-41; archtl. engr. U.S. Engrs. Dist. Office, Jacksonville, Fla., 1942-43, Jacksonville Naval Air Sta., 1944-45; partner Kemp, Bunch & Jackson Architects, Inc., Jacksonville, 1946-69; sr. v.p. Kemp, Bunch & Jackson Architects, Inc., 1970-82; Pres. Fla. Bd. Architecture, 1959-61; mem. com. on exams. Nat. Council Archtl. Registration Bds., 1961-62; pres. bldg. code adv. bd., Jacksonville, 1949-68, mem. examining com., from 1949; chmn. bldg. codes adjustment bd. Jacksonville Consol. Govt.; mem. housing com. Jacksonville Council on Aging, 1962. Projects include S. Central Home Office Prudential Ins. Co. Am., gen. offices Seaboard Coast Line R.R., Fla. State Prison, Starke, Hdqrs. Bldg. State Rd. Dept., Tallahassee. Pres. Little Theatre of Jacksonville, 1952-53. Fellow AIA (emeritus); mem. Fla. Assn. Architects (pres. 1947-48, now emeritus), Jacksonville Jr. C. of C. (chmn. luncheon club 1938), Jacksonville Area C. of C. (chmn. city, county, state affairs com. 1963, chmn. fed. assistance 1949-68), Phi Kappa Tau. Baptist.

BUNCH, FRED, newspaper picture editor; b. Leonard, Tex., Sept. 30, 1941; s. Fred A. and Edna A. (Stuteville) B.; m. Frances Ruth Stevens, June 6, 1942 (div.); children: Steven C., David; m. Betty Jane Kraker, Jan. 28, 1947. BS, East Tex. State U., 1965. Staff photographer Galveston (Tex.) News, 1965-67; staff photographer Houston Post, 1967-80, asst. chief photographer, 1980-83, asst. picture editor, 1984-89; picture editor Houston Chronicle, 1989—. Pres. Gulf Coast chpt. Nat. Press Photographers, Houston, 1975-76. Recipient Vigil Honor award Mustang dist. Sam Houston Area coun. Boy Scouts Am., 1977. Mem. Tex Fly Fishers. Avocations: fly fishing, cross country skiing, jogging. Office: Houston Chronicle 801 Texas Ave Houston TX 77002-2996*

BUNCH, JENNINGS BRYAN, JR., electrical engineer; b. Richmond, Va., Feb. 9, 1929; s. Jennings Bryan and Cora Irving (Wilson) B.; m. Dale Metcalf, Feb. 2, 1952 (dec. Nov. 1996); children: Jennifer, Pamela; m. Harriet Walton, Jan. 2, 1999. BSEE with distinction, Va. Mil. Inst., 1950; MSEE, U. Pitts., 1969. Engr. in tng. Va. Electric & Power Co., Alexandria, Richmond, 1950, 53; test engr. and mktg. assignments GE, Schenectady, N.Y., 1956-63, application engr., 1956-63; regional application engr. GE, Pitts., Phila., 1963-73; sr. application engr., project mgr. GE, Phila. and Schenectady, 1973-82, Malvern, Pa., 1982-91; cons. Star Design, Moorestown, N.J., 1992-96. Contbr. articles on electric utility distbn. automation systems to profl. pubs. Exec. dir. Sending Experienced Ret. Vols. Everywhere (SERVE), 1993—. 1st lt. U.S. Army, 1950-52. Fellow IEEE; mem. Tau Beta Pi. Republican. Presbyterian. Avocations: hiking, astronomy.

BUNCH, JOLENE REGINA, educator; b. St. Paul, Oct. 12, 1947; d. Joseph Thomas and Treva Alene (Frasier) Supple; m. Timothy Alan Bunch, Sept. 2, 1972; children: Justin, Julie Anne. BSE, Emporia (Kans.) State U., 1969. Tchr. Louisburg (Kans.) Sch. Dist., 1970-73; tchr., registrar Spring Hill (Kans.) Mid. Sch., 1973-79; substitute tchr. Olathe (Kans.) Sch. Dist., 1981-90; tchr. Olathe Christian Sch., 1990-91; prin. Cornerstone Christian Acad., Olathe, 1992-93; tchr. Maranatha Acad., Shawnee, Kans., 1993—, head spnsor class of 1998, 1995-98. Bd. dirs., sec. Homeowners Assn., Olathe, 1980-82; bd. dirs. Christian Women's Club, Olathe, 1984; vol., pres. PTA, Olathe, 1989-90; leader cub scoutss Boy Scouts Am., Olathe, 1984-86, Camp Fire Girls, Olathe, 1988-90; instr. Jr. Great Books Found. Mem. Nat. Coun. Tchrs. English, Maranatha Acad. Music Advocates (treas. 1995—), Sigma Kappa (nat. sec. 1969-70). Democrat. Presbyterian. Avocations: camping, hiking, reading. Home: 2302 W Sage Cir Olathe KS 66061-5059 Office: 6826 Lackman Rd Shawnee KS 66217

BUNCH, RICHARD ALAN, writer, educator; b. Honolulu, June 1, 1945; s. Thornton Carlisle and DeLores (Veal) B.; m. Rita Anne Glazar, Aug. 11, 1990; children: Katharine, Richard Jr. AA, Napa Coll., 1965; BA in Comms., Stanford U., 1967; MA in History, U. Ariz., 1969, MDiv, 1970, DD, 1971; postgrad. in philosophy, Vanderbilt U., 1972-75; postgrad. in Asian religions, Temple U., 1975-76; JD, U. Memphis, 1980. Tchg. asst. philosophy Vanderbilt U., Nashville, 1973-74; instr. philosophy Belmont U., 1973-74; law clk. Cir. Ct. Shelby County, Tenn., 1979-81; atty. Horne and Peppel, Memphis, 1981-83; law clk. Tenn. Ct. Appeals, 1983; instr. philosophy Chapman U., 1986-87; instr. law Sonoma State U., 1986-87, instr. philosophy, 1990-91; lectr. U. Calif., Berkeley, 1995; adj. humanities faculty Napa Valley Coll., 1985—. Author: Summer Hawk, 1991, Night Blooms, 1992, Wading the Russian River, 1993, Santa Rosa Plums, 1996, A Foggy Moring, 1996, South By Southwest, 1997, Sacred Space, 1998, Rivers of the Sea, 1998; contbr. Hawai'i Rev., Black Mt. Rev., The Plaza, Black Moon, Xavier Rev., European Judaism, The Comstock Rev., Poetry Nottingham, The Alembic, others; assoc. news editor, reporter, feature writer Napa Valley Times, 1985. Mem. staff Nashville Human Rights Forum, 1974-75; chair housing authority-bldg. authority bd. City of Napa, 1985-89. Recipient Grand prize Ina Coolbrith Nat. Poetry Day Contest, 1989, Jessamyn West creative writing prize, 1990. Mem. Acad. Am. Poets, Ina Coolbrith Cir. Home: 248 Sandpiper Dr Davis CA 95616-7546

BUNCH, ROBERT CRAIG, librarian; b. Houston, Mar. 31, 1954; s. Robert Kern and Gretchen Ann (Schopps) B.; m. Delana Ann Roberts, Oct. 30, 1986. BA in Philosophy, U. Houston, 1979, MA in Philosophy, BS in Psychology, 1982, MEd, 1986; MLS, Sam Houston State U., Huntsville, 1992; MLIS, U. Tex., 1994. Cert. tchr., Tex. Psychiat. technician Meth. Hosp., Houston, 1979-83, 84-89; tchg. asst. U. Houston, 1981-82; acad. asst. U. Tex., Austin, 1983-84; tchr. Houston Ind. Sch. Dist., 1986-89, Coldspring-Oakhurst (Tex.) pub. schs., 1989-90; student libr. asst. Sam Houston State U., Huntsville, 1991; dist. libr. Coldspring-Oakhurst Consolidated Ind. Sch. Dist., 1991—. Editl. bd. Ref. Books Bull., Chgo., 1994-98; rev. editor Popular Culture in Librs., 1991-96. Adv. bd. Humanities Exhibits Interactive, Tex. Com. for Humanities, Austin, 1996—. NEH fellow, 1992, 95, 97, Coun. for Basic Edn. fellow, 1996. Mem. ALA, Am. Assn. Sch. Librs. (Frances Henne award 1994), Tex. Libr. Assn., Tex. Assn. Sch. Librs., bd. mem. Libr., Helicon Pub., Oxford, UK, 1997—. Home: PO Box 117 Oakhurst TX 77359-0117 Office: Jones High Sch Libr PO Box 39 Coldspring TX 77331-0039

BUNCHER, CHARLES RALPH, epidemiologist, educator; b. Dover, N.J., Jan. 18, 1938. BS, MIT, 1960; MS, Harvard U., 1964, ScD, 1967. Statistician Atomic Bomb Casualty Comsn., NAS, 1967-70; chief biostatistician Merrell-Nat. Labs., 1970-73, asst. prof. stats., 1970-73; prof. and dir. divsn. epidemiology and biostats. Med. Coll., U. Cin., 1973-96, prof. biostats. and epidemiology, 1973—. Fellow Am. Stats. Assn., Am. Coll. Epidemiology; mem. APHA, Biometrical Assn., Soc. Epidemiol. Rsch., Soc. Med. Decision Making, Soc. Clin. Trials, Tau Beta Pi. Achievements include research in cancer epidemiology; screening, diagnosis and treatment, as well as occupational and environmental epidemiology; risk analysis; statistical research; clinical trials; design of experiments; pharmaceutical research; biostatistical analysis, pharmaceutical statistics, ALS epidemiology. Office: University of Cincinnati Div of Epidemiology & Biostatist PO Box 670183 Cincinnati OH 45267-0183

BUNCHER, JAMES EDWARD, healthcare management executive; b. Moline, Ill., Sept. 19, 1936; s. Ralph Frank and Mae Loretta (Eis) B.; m. Mary Alice Dodge, Sept. 3, 1961; 1 son, Douglas James. BS in Acctg., U. Ill., 1961, M of Acctg. Sci., 1962. CPA, Ill. Staff auditor Peat, Marwick, Mitchell & Co., St. Louis, 1962-63; controller, asst. v.p. Durkee Consumer Foods divsn. SCM Corp., Cleve., 1963-72; controller Hosp. Products div. Abbott Labs., North Chicago, Ill., 1972-74; pres., COO Hosp. Affiliates Internat., Inc., Nashville, 1974-79, 80-81; pres., CEO CIGNA Healthplan, Dallas, 1979-80, 81-82, Republic Health Corp., Dallas, 1982-87; ptnr. Lake Investments, Dallas, 1987-91; chmn., pres., CEO, Cmty. Care Network, Inc., San Diego, 1992-97; pres. Health Plans Group Value Health, Inc., Avon, Conn., 1995-97; pres., CEO Cmty. Dental Svcs./Smile Care, Santa Ana, Calif., 1997-98; healthcare cons., 1992, IWV Healthcare Consulting, 1998—; bd. dirs. Horizon Health Corp., Consensus Health. With USN, 1956-58. Mem. Indian Wells Country Club. Methodist. Home: 45 446 Reina Ct Aliso Viejo CA 92656

BUNDA, STEPHEN MYRON, political advisor, consultant, lawyer, classical philosopher; b. Jersey City, N.J., Oct. 5, 1949; s. Stephen and Anna (Yaschak) B. BA summa cum laude, St. Peter's Coll., Jersey City, 1971; MA with honors, New Sch. Grad. Faculty, N.Y.C., 1976; JD, Rutgers Law Sch., Newark, N.J., 1987. Bar: N.J. Pol. cons. Democratic Party, N.J., 1977-92; pol. adv. Govt. of Ukraine, 1991—; counsellor-at-law Bunda & Co., Lyndhurst, N.J., 1994—; advisor on Ukraine to U.S. Congress, Office of the Pres., Nat. Security Coun., Washington, 1991—. *Stephen Myron Bunda was awarded a rare full scholarship to study Philosophy and Political Theory at the New School Graduate Faculty where he was a seminar student of Hannah Arendt and her last doctoral candidate. He also studied with Aron Gurwitsch, Ernst Vollrath, Reiner Schürmann and Seth Benardete. Since Ukraine's declaration of independence in 1991, Stephen Myron Bunda has acted as a political advisor to the governments of both the United States and Ukraine. His policy recommendations cleared the way for the 1994 Trilateral Agreement among Ukraine, America, and Russia. His policy concept of Ukraine as "the anchor of stability for East-Central Europe" has become the guiding idea regulating the American-Ukrainian strategic partnership he originally conceived and worked to establish.* Mem. Am. Hist. Assn., Am. Philos. Assn., Ukrainian-Am. Bar Assn., N.J. Bar Assn., Soc. for Ukrainian-Jewish Rels., Ukrainian Nat. Assn. Democrat. Mem. Ukrainian Catholic Ch. Avocations: reading philosophy and history, educational travel and sight-seeing, music, art, literature, theatre. Home: 691 Union Ave Lyndhurst NJ 07071-2214 Office: Stephen Myron Bunda Esquire PO Box 461 Lyndhurst NJ 07071-0461

BUNDESEN, CLAUS MOGENS, psychologist, educator; b. Copenhagen, Jan. 26, 1948; s. Marius and Jytte (Kjaer) B.; m. Else Windfeld Jacobsen, Mar. 25, 1971; children: Rune, Jon, Hanna. PhD in Psychology, U. Copenhagen, 1972, Dr. Phil. in Psychology, 1986. Asst. prof. psychology U. Copenhagen, 1973-75, rsch. fellow, 1975-78; vis. scholar Stanford (Calif.) U., 1977-78; assoc. prof. psychology U. Copenhagen, 1978-88, docent prof. psychology, 1988-95, prof. cognitive psychology, 1995—; dir. Ctr. for Visual Cognition, Denmark, 1993—. Mem. editl. bd. European Jour. Cognitive Psychology, 1988—, assoc. editor, 1996—; mem. editl. bd. Psychol. Rsch., 1988—, Visual Cognition, 1993—, Psychol. Rev., 1996-99; contbr. articles to Jour. Exptl. Psychology, Perception & Psychophysics, Psychol. Rev. and other profl. jours. Grantee Human Frontier Sci. Program, 1991-94; invited and keynote speaker in field. Mem. Internat. Assn. for Study Attention and Performance (coun. 1981-88, 92—), European Soc. for Cognitive Psychology (organizer 6th conf. 1993, mem. exec. com. 1990-98). Achievements include measurement of effects of visual size and orientation in pattern recognition and apparent movement; development of mathematical models of selective attention in vision. Home: Ulspilsager 66, 2791 Dragør Denmark Office: U Copenhagen Psychol Lab, Njalsgade 90, 2300 Copenhagen Denmark

BUNDI, RENEE, art director, graphic designer; b. Elmont, N.Y., Apr. 20, 1962; d. Anthony Joseph and Marion Rose (Graziano) B. Student, St. John's U., 1980-84. Creative dir. Coastal Communications, N.Y.C., 1985-86; art and prodn. coord. Cahner's Pub. Co./Datamation mag., N.Y.C., 1986-87; sr. prodn. editor CMP Publs./Var Bus. Computer Sys. News, Manhasset, N.Y., 1987-89, asst. art dir., 1989-91; assoc. art dir. Varbus. CMP Publs., 1991-94; sr. art dir. Info. Week Mag., 1994—. Recipient Print Design award Print mag., 1988, 91, 92, 93, 94, 95, 98, Ozzie Design award Mag. Design and Prodn., 1988, 89, 90, 91, 98. Mem. Graphic Artist Guild, Soc. Publ. Designers (Excellence in Design award 1987, 88, 89, 92, 93, 94), ASBPE (Excellence of Design 1997, 98), MacIntosh User's Group, Soc. Illustrators (Best Spot Illustration). Roman Catholic. Avocations: theatre, bowling, painting, photography.

BUNDICK, WILLIAM ROSS, retired dermatologist; b. Balt., Nov. 22, 1917; s. Percy Ross and Edith Ruth (Smith) B.; m. Katherine Harrison Epps, Apr. 22, 1945 (dec. Nov. 1986); children: Susan Bundick Sukeforth, Karen Lee Bundick Guth, Paul Ross. M.D., U. Md., 1941; postgrad., NYU, 1947-48. Diplomate Am. Bd. Dermatology. Intern Baroness Erlanger Hosp., Chattanooga, 1941-42; resident Ft. Howard (Md.) VA Hosp., 1946-47; practice medicine specializing in dermatology, 1947-96; assoc. dermatologist Mercy Hosp., Balt., 1947-67; assoc. in dermatology U. Md. Sch. Medicine, 1952-58, Johns Hopkins U. Sch. Medicine, 1952-58; asst. dermatologist St. Joseph Hosp., Towson, Md., 1947-69, chief dermatology, 1970-84; pvt. practice medicine, Timonium, Md., 1971-96; ret., 1997. Chess editor: Balt. Sunday Sun, 1963-74; compiler, editor Directory Internat. Assn. Jazz Record Collectors, 1979-88; contbr. articles to med. jours. Served to capt. M.C. AUS, 1942-46. Balt. amateur chess champion, 1973. Fellow Am. Acad. Dermatology; mem. AMA, Md. Dermatol. Soc. (pres. 1975), Med. and Chiurg. Faculty of Md., Md. Chess Assn. (pres. 1964), U.S. Chess Fedn. (del. 1959-64), Assn. Internat. de la Presse Echiqueene, Towson Chess Club (pres. 1959, 65), Timonium Rotary Club (pres. 1961-62). Home: 8800 Walther Blvd Apt 4114 Baltimore MD 21234-9016

BUNDROS, THOMAS ANTHONY, utilities executive; b. Toledo, Aug. 7, 1956; s. Anthony Thomas and Thalia (Collins) B.; m. Lara Sue Seifert, May 7, 1994; 1 child, Anthony. BS in Econs. & Bus. Adminstrn., U. N.C., Greensboro, 1978, MBA in Fin., 1980. Fin. analyst Conoco. Inc., Greensboro, N.C., Houston, 1981-84; with The So. Co., Atlanta & N.Y.C., 1984-97; CFO Dalton (Ga.) Utilities, 1997—. Mem. Rotary, Sigma Tau Gamma. Republican. Greek Orthodox. Avocations: travel, investments, theatre, tennis, gardening. Home: 1918 Chadwell Ct Dalton GA 30720-7126 Office: Dalton Utilities 1200 Parrott Pky Dalton GA 30722-0869

BUNDTZEN, LYNDA KATHRYN, English and women's studies educator; b. Morris, Minn., Nov. 15, 1946; d. Edward Frederick Bundtzen and Alma Emily Ida (Pribbernow) McLearen; m. Dwight Kimball Wells, Oct. 8, 1980; children: Jacob Wells-Bundtzen, Nicholas Wells-Bundtzen. BA, U. Minn., 1968; MA, U. Chgo., 1969, PhD, 1972. Herbert H. Lehman prof. English Williams Coll., Williamstown, Mass., 1972—; participant NEH tchg. seminar, 1995. Author: Plath's Incarnations, 1983 (Hamilton award 1980). Mem. MLA. Office: Williams Coll Stetson Hall Williamstown MA 01267

BUNDY, BLAKELY FETRIDGE, early childhood educator, advocate; b. Chgo., Aug. 31, 1944; d. William Harrison and Bonnie Jean (Clark) Fetridge; m. Harvey Hollister Bundy III, Aug. 20, 1966; children: H. Hollister IV, Clark Harrison, Elizabeth Lowell, Reed Fetridge. BA cum laude, Wheaton Coll., Mass., 1966; MEd, Nat.-Louis U., 1985. Tchr. Norwich (Vt.) Kindergarten, 1966-67, Willow Wood Pre-Sch., Winnetka, Ill., 1983-93, bd. dirs., 1972-81, adv. bd., 1981-83, 93—; bd. dirs. North Ave. Day Nursery,

Chgo., 1970-76, Ill. Family-to-Family Child Care Initiative, 1994-95; exec. dir. Winnetka Alliance for Early Childhood, 1989—; accreditation system validator, mentor Nat. Acad. Early Childhood Programs, Washington, 1986—; mem. pres.'s commn. Wheaton Coll., Norton, Mass., 1987—; trustee Brooks Sch., North Andover, Mass., 1993—; mem. parents exec. com. Colby Coll., Waterville, Maine, 1997—; cons. editor Nat. Assn. Edn. Young Children, 1991-94; editor Winnetka Alliance for Early Childhood Newsletter, 1990—; contbr. articles to Chgo. Tribune, Redbook, Glamour mags., Early Childhood News, Child Care Ctr. Mag., Chgo. Sun-Times, Day Care and Early Education, Young Children, other publs. Mem. Ill. Shore Coun. Girl Scouts U.S., 1981-89, World Found. for Girls Guides and Girl Scouts Friends of Our Cabaña Com., Cuernavaca, Mexico, 1986-94. Mem. Nat. Assn. for the Edn. Young Children (photographer publs.), World Assn. Girl Guides and Girl Scouts, Ill. Soc. Early Childhood Profls. (bd. dirs. 1993-96, editor newsletter), Chgo. Assn. Edn. Young Children (steering com. Near North Suburban chpt. 1986—, commn. on salaries and working conditions, 1988-92, bd. dirs. 1992—, co-chair pub. rels. com. 1992—, chair accreditation project mgmt. com. 1994-98, photography editor Connections 1992—, co-editor News & Views: The Accreditation Project Newsletter 1996-98), Olive Baden-Powell Soc. (London). Episcopalian. Clubs: Indian Hill (Winnetka); Stevensville (Mich.) Yacht; Ocean Reef (Key Largo, Fla.). Avocations: golf, sailing. Office: Winnetka Alliance for Early Childhood 1235 Oak St Winnetka IL 60093-2168

BUNDY, CHARLES ALAN, foundation executive; b. Cheraw, S.C., Jan. 5, 1930; s. Jackson Corbett and Ruby Jones (Hughes) B.; m. Margaret Ellen Jackson, Feb. 27, 1954; children: Charles Alan, Robert Jackson, Dan Hughes. AB, Wofford Coll., 1951; DH (hon.), Charleston So. U. Mgr. prodn. planning J.P. Stevens & Co., Inc., Rockingham, N.C., 1951-54; mgr. Jesup (Ga.) C. of C., 1954-56, Lancaster (S.C.) C. of C., 1956-61; dist. mgr. U.S. C. of C., Birmingham, Ala., 1961-65; exec. v.p. Macon (Ga.) C. of C., 1965-71, Greg Enterprises, Lancaster, 1971-72; pres. Springs Found., Inc. and Close Found., Inc., Lancaster, 1972-97, ret., 1997; pvt. practice cons., 1997—. Chmn. S.C. Parks, Recreation and Tourism Commn., 1983-89; mem. S.C. Coordinating Coun. for Econ. Devel., 1986-89, Coun. on Founds.; past chmn. S.E. Coun. Founds.; trustee Columbia Coll., 1976-88, S.C. Found. Ind. Colls., 1982-93; chmn. bd. 1st Meth. Ch., 1978, 79; chmn. Gov.'s Freshwater Wetlands Forum, 1989; mem. State Govt. Reorgn. Commn., 1991; chmn. Lancaster County Strategic Plan, 1990; bd. dirs. Springs Meml. Hosp.; trustee, treas. J. Marion Sims Found., Inc. Mem. Lancaster County C. of C. (past pres.), Rotary (past pres.). Home: 518 Briarwood Rd Lancaster SC 29720-1802 Office: Springs Found Inc 104 E Springs St PO Box 460 Lancaster SC 29721-0460

BUNDY, DAVID DALE, librarian, educator; b. Longview, Wash., Sept. 27, 1948; s. Cedric Dale and Florence (Prichard) B.; m. Consuelo Ann Briones, Dec. 19, 1969 (div. 1982); children: Keith Dale, Cheryl Ann; m. Melody Lynn Garlock, June 14, 1986; children: Rachel Lynn, Lydia Marie, Joel David. BA, Seattle Pacific U., 1969; MDiv, ThM, Asbury Theol. Sem., Wilmore, Ky., 1973; Licentiate, Cath. U. Louvain, Louvain-la-Neuve, Belgium, 1978. Dean Inst. Univ. Ministry Louvain, 1977-81; rsch. asst. Cath. U. Louvain, 1978-85; assoc. prof. Christian Origins, collection devel. libr. Asbury Theol. Sem., Wilmore, 1985-91; libr., assoc. prof. ch. history Christian Theol. Sem., Indpls., 1991—; dir. Wesleyan Holiness Studies Ctr., Wilmore, 1990-91. Author: Keswick, 1985; editor: Pietist and Wesleyan Studies; contbr. articles to profl. jours. Grantee Fondation Universitaire, Belgium, 1977-84, Pew Charitable Trusts, 1988, Wesleyan/Holiness Studies Ctr., 1992, NEH, 1989—. Mem. N.Am. Patristic Soc., Symposium Syriacum (internat. dir. 1988—), Am. Acad. Religion, Assn. Christian Arabic Studies (editor Mid. Ea. Christian Studies), Wesleyan Theol. Soc. Democrat. Mem. United Meth. Ch. Office: Christian Theol Sem 1000 W 42d St PO Box 88267 Indianapolis IN 46208-0267*

BUNDY, DAVID JOHN, engineering executive; b. Elmhurst, Ill., Jan. 20, 1953; s. David John and Betty Jean (Newgent) B. BSME, Rose Hulman Inst. Tech., 1975; MS in Adminstrn., George Washington U., 1980. Test dir. Materiel Test Directorate, Aberdeen Proving Ground, Md., 1975-79, sr. test dir., 1982-83; chief Test and Evaluation Office U.S. Army Ordnance Ctr. and Sch., Aberdeen Proving Ground, Md., 1983-91; sr. test dir. Materiel Test Directorate, Yuma Proving Ground, Ariz., 1980-81; asst. project mgr. Project Mgr. for Instrumentation Targets and Threat Simul., Orlando, Fla., 1991—. Vol. Make A Wish Found., Ctrl. Fla., 1996-97, Leukemia Soc., Orlando, Fla., 1995-96. Mem. Soc. Automotive Engrs. (chmn. Balt. sect. 1985-86, Outstanding Young Mem. award 1988). Presbyterian. Avocations: golf, walking, stamp collecting, bowling. Home: 1211 Flowers Pointe Ln Orlando FL 32825-5520 Office: PM ITTS 12350 Research Pkwy Orlando FL 32826-3261

BUNDY, HALLIE FLOWERS, biochemist, educator; b. Santa Monica, Calif., Apr. 2, 1925; d. Douglas and Phyllis (Flowers) B. BA in Chemistry, Mt. St. Mary's Coll., L.A., 1947; MS in Biochemistry, U. So. Calif., 1955, PhD in Biochemistry, 1958. Instr. sch. medicine U. So. Calif., L.A., 1959-60; asst. prof. Mt. St. Mary's Coll., 1960-63, assoc. prof., 1963-66, prof. biochemistry, 1966-90, emeritus prof., 1990—; asst. program dir. undergrad. rshc. participation NSF, Washington, 1965-66. Contbr. rsch. articles to profl. jours. USPHS predoctoral fellow, 1955-57; NSF Sci. Faculty fellow, 1969-70; grantee NIH, 1960-66, 86-89, NSF, 1961-78, 87-89, Grad. Women in Sci., 1974. Mem. Am. Chem. Soc., Pacific Slope Biochem. Conf., Sigma Xi. Achievements include research in isolation, characterization and comparison of enzymes from diverse plant and animal species; the use of dyes to monitor protein folding. Avocations: philately, tennis, golf.

BUNDY, MARY LOTHROP, retired clinical social worker; b. Boston, Apr. 9, 1925; d. Francis B. and Eleanor (Abbott) Lothrop; m. McGeorge Bundy, June 10, 1950 (dec. Sept. 1996); children: Stephen M., Andrew L., William L., James A. AB magna cum laude, Radcliffe Coll., 1946; MSW, Hunter Coll., 1980. Assoc. dir. admissions Radcliffe Coll., Cambridge, Mass., 1949-50; clin. social worker Jewish Bd. of Family and Children's Svcs., Bklyn., 1980-84; pvt. practice N.Y.C., 1984-95; ret., 1995; vice-chmn. and trustee Radcliffe Coll., Cambridge, 1962-80, acting v.p., 1978-79 ; overseer Harvard U., Cambridge, 1971-77; bd. dirs. Corning (N.Y.) Inc., 1973-97, Levi Strauss & Co., 1973-85; trustee and chair Edward W. Hazen Found., N.Y.C., 1985-95; bd. dirs. Found. for Child Devel., N.Y.C., 1985-98. Trustee Metropolitan Museum of Art, N.Y.C., 1968-78. Mem. NASW, Acad. Cert. Social Workers, Phi Beta Kappa.

BUNDY, ROBERT CHARLES, prosecutor; b. Long Beach, Calif., June 26, 1946; s. James Kenneth and Kathleen Ilene (Klosterman) B.; m. Virginia Bonnie Lembo, Feb. 3, 1974; 2 children. BA cum laude, U. So. Calif., L.A., 1968; JD, U. Calif., Berkeley, 1971. Bar: Alaska 1972, Calif. 1972. Supervising atty. Alaska Legal Svcs. Corp., Nome, Alaska, 1972-75; dist. atty. Second Jud. Dist., Nome, 1975-78; asst. dist. atty. Alaska Dept. Law, 1978-80, asst. atty. gen. antitrust sect., 1980-82; chief asst. dist. atty. Alaskan Dept. Law, Anchorage, 1982-84; ptnr. Bogle & Gates, Anchorage, Alaska, 1984-94; now U.S. atty. for Alaska dist. U.S. Dept. Justice, Anchorage, 1994—. Mem. Trout Unlimited, Alaska Flyfishers. Office: US Atty for Alaska Rm C-253 222 W 7th Ave Unit 9 Anchorage AK 99513-7504*

BUNDY, WAYNE M., retired geologist, consultant; b. Anderson, Ind., Jan. 10, 1924; s. Ernest Frank and Flossie (Miley) B.; m. Lorraine Vivian Jerabek, May 7, 1945; children: Mark, Janet, Michael. AB, Ind. U., 1950, MA, 1954, PhD, 1957. Geol. technician N. Mex. Bur. of Mines, Socorro, 1951-53; petrographer Ind. Geol. Survey, Bloomington, 1953-57; rsch. dir. Georgia Kaolin Co., Elizabeth, N.J., 1957-75; v.p. tech. Georgia Kaolin Co., Springfield, N.J., 1975-91; cons. Contbr. articles to profl. jours.; author: The Art of Discovery: Fueling Innovation for Company Growth. Sgt. USMC, 1943-45. Mem. Clay Minerals Soc. (pres. 1985), Tech. Pulpaper 12 Industry. Numerous patents in indsl. minerals, including Kaolin Modified for use in various applications. Home: 3026 Chase Ln Bloomington IN 47401-9706

BUNE, KAREN LOUISE, criminal justice official; b. Washington, Mar. 6, 1954; d. Harry and Eleanor Mary (White) B. BA in Am. Studies cum laude, Am. U., 1976, MS in Adminstrn. of Justice with distinction, 1978. Notary pub., Va. Case mgr. Arlington (Va.) Alcohol Safety Action Program, 1979-94; victim specialist Office of Commonwealth's Atty., Arlington, Va., 1994—; case mgr. regional rep. of case mgmt. com. of Dirs. Assn. Commn. on Va. Alcohol Safety Action Program, Richmond, 1980-81, 84-85, 88-89, mem. subcom. studying treatment issues, 1988-94; chair career guidance subcom. alumni adv. com. Sch. Pub. Affairs Am. U., Washington, 1991-94. *Karen Bune has over 20 years of progressively responsible experience as a criminal justice professional in the law enforcement arena. Her areas of expertise include probationary services, victim advocacy and victim's rights, crisis intervention, counseling, interviewing, investigations, evaluations, public speaking, and court testimony. She has written extensively for local newspapers on public safety topics, including law enforcement, victimization, and fire safety issues. She was also featured in a front page story of the local area newspaper for the active role she played in her work with the victim of the Marv Albert trial in Arlington, Va.* Sch. of Justice rep. alumni adv. com. Coll. Pub. Affairs, Am. U. Washington, 1982-86, chmn. student rels., 1982-86, mem. alumni steering com., 1991—. Recipient spl. achievement award Dept. Navy, 1973, merit award Arlington County, 1986, 97, Woman of the Yr. Am. Biog. Inst., 1990, Carl T. Earles meml. cmty. svc. award No. Va. Crime Prevention Assn., 1999; inducted into Hall of Fame for outstanding achievement in case management. Mem. ASPA (No. Va. chpt. coun.), NAFE, APHA, AAUW, Nat. Assn. Chiefs Police (award of merit 1986), Nat. Criminal Justice Assn., Nat. Orgn. Victim Assistance, Am. Police Hall of Fame (cert. of appreciation 1985), Acad. Criminal Justice Scis., So. Criminal Justice Assn., Am. Soc. Criminology, Va. Sherriffs Inst., No. Va. Crime Prevention Assn. (Carl T. Earls meml. cmty. svc. award 1999), No. Va. Fraternal Order Police, Va. Assn. Female Execs., Internat. Platform Assn., Am. U. Alumni Assn. (immediate past pres. sch. pub. affairs chpt. 1994-96), Nat. Ctr. victims of Crime, Women of Washington, Phi Kappa Phi, Phi Alpha Alpha, Phi Delta Gamma (1st v.p. 1981-82). Avocations: aerobics, dancing, travel, theatre, concerts. Home: 926 16th St S Arlington VA 22202-2606 Office: Office of Commonwealth's Atty 1425 N Court House Rd Arlington VA 22201-2659

BUNGARZ, WILLIAM ROBERT, pediatrician; b. N.Y.C., June 21, 1951; s. Robert Charles and Evelyn Mae (Marshall) B.; m. Beverly Ann Blaine, Sept. 30, 1984; children: Katherine, Rebecca. BS, SUNY, Stony Brook, 1974; MD, Autonomous U. Guadalajara, Mexico, 1982. Fifth pathway intern New Rochelle (N.Y.) Hosp. Med. Ctr., 1993; resident North Shore U. Hosp., Manhasset, N.Y., 1994-96, chief resident pediatrics, 1996-97; pediatrician, ptnr. Gould, Elice, Hyman & Bungarz, Great Neck, N.Y., 1987—. Fellow Am. Acad. Pediat.; mem. Great Neck Choral Soc. (pres. 1995—). Republican. Roman Catholic. Avocations: choral singing, skiing. Fax: (516) 829-2713. Home: 178 Rockwood Rd Manhasset NY 11030-2027 Office: Gould Elice Hyman & Bungarz 15 Barstow Rd Great Neck NY 11021-2229

BUNGE, CHARLES ALBERT, library science educator; b. Kimball, Nebr., Mar. 18, 1936; s. Louis Herman and Leona Hazel (Cromwell) B.; m. Joanne C. VonStoeser, Aug. 20, 1960; children: Lorraine A., Jeffrey C. Stephen L. AB, U. Mo., 1959; MSLS, U. Ill., 1960, PhD, 1967. Reference librarian Daniel Boone Regional Library, Columbia, Mo., 1960-62; Ball State Tchrs. Coll., Muncie, Ind., 1962-64; research assoc. Library Research Center, U. Ill., 1964-67; mem. faculty Sch. Library and Info. Studies U. Wis., Madison, 1967-98; prof. emeritus Sch. Library and Info. Studies U. Wis., 1998—. Author: Professional Education and Reference Efficiency, 1967; columnist: Wilson Library Bull, 1972-81. Mem. ALA (pres. ref. and adult svcs. divsn. 1987-88, chair com. on accreditation 1990-92, Mudge award 1983, mem. coun. 1993-96, Beta Phi Mu award 1997), Assn. Libr. and Info. Sci. Edn. (pres. 1980-81, Prof. Contribution award 1997), Wis. Libr. Assn. (pres. 1972-73, Libr. of Yr. 1983), Phi Beta Kappa, Beta Phi Mu. Home: 509 Orchard Dr Madison WI 53711-1316 Office: Univ Wis Sch Libr and Info Studies 600 N Park St Madison WI 53706-1403

BUNGE, RUSSELL KENNETH, writer, poet, editor; b. Long Beach, Calif., Apr. 28, 1947; s. Kenneth Duncan Bunge and Mona Irene (Deleree) Coker; ptnr. Mr. Kelly A. Quiros. BA in Creative Writing, Calif. State U., Long Beach, 1972; MA in Humanities, Calif. State U., Dominguez Hills, 1985. Cert. C.C. tchr., Calif. Spl. svcs. cons. AT&T Comms., San Luis Obispo, Calif., 1973-90; info. cons. Obispo Info. Group, San Luis Obispo, 1990-95; pub. deleree com, San Luis Obispo, Calif., 1996—; mem. adv. bd. Calif. Online Resources for Edn., Long Beach, 1993-94; edn. coord. SLONET Info. Network, 1993-95, dir., 1997-98. Author: Double Lives: Poems 1984-85, 1985; editor: Obispo Web Digest: on the World Wide Web, 1994-96; contbr. poems to profl. publs. Founding mem. AIDS Support Network, San Luis Obispo, 1984. Mem. MLA, Associated Writing Programs, Nat. Coun. Tchrs. English. Office: Deleree Com PO Box 771 San Luis Obispo CA 93406-0771

BUNGER, ROLF, physiology educator; b. Hamburg, Germany, Oct. 19, 1941; came to U.S., 1979; s. Heinz Johannes Albert and Helga (Franz) B.; m. Margriet Akkerman, Dec. 14, 1973; children: Nils, Frank. MD, U. Hamburg, 1969, U. Heidelberg, Germany, 1970; MD habil., U. Munich, 1979. Intern Heidberg Infirmary, Hamburg, 1970; asst. of physiology U. Aachen, Germany, 1970-75, U. Munich, 1975-79; asst. prof. dept. physiology F. E. Hebert Med. Sch., USUHS, Bethesda, Md., 1979-82, assoc. prof., 1983-92; prof. USUHS, Bethesda, Md., 1992—; prof. of molecular and cellular biology US Univ. Health Svc., Bethesda, Md., 1994—; cons. U. Buffalo, 1983, U. Ala., 1986-89, U. Tex., Ft. Worth, 1990—, AAALAC, 1997—; referee, editl. reviewer domestic and fgn. sci. med. rsch. jours. and instns., including NIH, VA, NSF, HFSP, Dutch Heart Found., MRC, 1994—; vis. prof. Erasmus U., Rotterdam, 1992; lectr. in field. Mem. editorial bd. Internat. Jour. Purine and Pyrimidine Rsch., 1989-93, Internat. Jour. Angiology, 1991-95, Am. Jour. Physiology, 1999—; patentee in field. Webelo leader Boy Scouts Am., McLean, Va., 1986-87, packmaster, 1987-89. Capt., German Air Force Med. Corp. Grantee Uniformed Svcs. U. Health Scis., 1979—, NIH, 1982—, Dept. of Def., 1995—. Fellow Am. Heart Assn.; mem. Internat. Study Group for Heart Rsch., Am. Physiol. Soc., Deutsche Physiol. Gesellschaft. Achievements include clarification of adenylate compartments in myocardium; demonstration of energy-linked and work dependence of myocardial pyruvate dehydrogenase flux, of interstitial free AMP in myocardium; research in substrate enhancement of isolated and in-situ preischemic and postischemic heart preparations; metabolic protection of cytosolic phosphorylation potential by pyruvate and adenosine during myocardial reperfusion, adenylate-related theory of metabolic coronary control, energy-linked control of sarcoplasmic reticulum Ca 2+ - ATPase, pyruvate protection against apoptosis and hemorrhagic shock. Home: 1922 Kenbar Ct Mc Lean VA 22101-5321 Office: USUHS Dept Physiology 4301 Jones Bridge Rd Bethesda MD 20814-4799

BUNGEY, MICHAEL, advertising executive; b. 1941. With Nestle, London, 1961-65, Crawford Advt., London, 1965-69, SH Benson, London, 1969-71; founder Michael Bungey & Ptnrs. (sold to Dancer, Fitzgerald & Sample, then Saatchi & Saatchi, then merged into DFS Dorland), 1971; CEO DFS Dorland (name changed to BSB Dorland), 1987-88; regional dir. Europe Backer Spielvogel Bates Worldwide, Inc. (now Bates Worldwide, Inc.), 1988-92; chmn., CEO Cordiant Comm. Group (subs., holding co.) Bates Worldwide Inc., 1993—; bd. dirs. Cordiant plc. Office: Bates Worldwide Inc Chrysler Bldg 498 7th Ave New York NY 10018*

BUNGO, MICHAEL WILLIAM, physician, educator, science administrator; b. Passaic, N.J., July 18, 1950; s. John C. and Mary (Tabachuk) B.; children: Elise Nicole, Jonathan Michael. BS in Chemistry, Rensselaer Poly. Inst., 1971; MD, N.J. Med. Sch., 1975. Diplomate Am. Bd. Internal Medicine, Subsplty. Bd. Cardiovasc. Diseases. Intern in internal medicine New England Deaconess Hosp., Boston, 1975-76, resident, 1976-78; asst. in medicine Peter Bent Brigham Hosp., Boston, 1976-77; cardiology fellow New England Deaconess Hosp., Harvard Med. Sch., Boston, 1978-80; head cardiovascular lab. NASA, Johnson Space Ctr., Houston, 1980-85; mem. Aerospace Medicine Bd., Houston, 1980-91; dir. Space Biomed. Rsch. Inst. NASA, Johnson Space Ctr., Houston, 1986-90; chief scientist med. scis. divsn. NASA, 1990-91; chmn. dept. medicine St. John Hosp., Houston, 1987-89; prof. medicine U. Tex., Galveston, med. dir. heart sta. divsn. cardiology, 1995—, vice chmn. dept. internal medicine, 1999—; fellowship advisor NRC, Washington, 1984-89. Editor: Results of Life Sciences Aboard the Space Shuttle, 1987; contbr. abstracts and articles to jours., chpts. to books; tech. reviewer Circulation, Aviation, Space and environ. Medicine, 1989—; mem. editl. bd. Aviation, Space and Environ. Medicine, 1997—. Recipient medal NASA, 1986. Fellow Am. Coll. Cardiology; mem. Am. Heart Assn., Aerospace Med. Assn. (Louis H. Bauer Founders award 1987), Tex. Med. Assn., Phi Lambda Upsilon. Office: Univ of Tex Med Br Divsn of Cardiology Galveston TX 77555

BUNIAK, RAYMOND, educational professional; b. Sao Paulo, Mar. 21, 1955; came to U.S., 1959; s. Wasyl and Katharina (Kurpita) B.; m. Karen Sue Harbecke, Apr. 28, 1957. BA in Edn., Northeastern Ill. U., Chgo., 1977; MMus, DePaul U., 1981. Cert. tchr. K-12, 6-12 music, Ill. Profl. musician/trombone and euphonium player, condr. Chgo. metro area, 1973—; studio tchr. of brass instruments various, Chgo. metro area, 1979—; band dir. New Trier West High, Northfield, Ill., 1981-82, O.L.P.H. Sch., Glenview, Ill., 1986-94; instrnl. devel. and grants officer/tchr. Kelly H.S., Chgo., 1994—; grant writer for tech., instrnl. program improvements, coord. Internat. Baccaleureate Program, Kelly H.S., 1997—. Author: A 20th Century Treatise on the Trombone, 4 vols., 1984. Recipient Univ. Talent scholarship Northeastern Ill. U., 1974-77. Mem. ACDS, Francis Galpin Soc., Internat. Trombone Assn., Nat. Cath. Bandmaster's Assn., Music Educators Nat. Conf., Chgo. Fedn. of Musicians. Avocations: household renovation, auto repair, Bible tchr. E-mail: rkbuniak@starnetinc.com. Home: 105 N Western Ave Bartlett IL 60103-4030 Office: Thomas Kelly High Sch 4136 S California Ave Chicago IL 60632-1817

BUNIM, MARY-ELLIS, television producer; b. Northampton, Mass., July 9, 1946; d. Frank Roberts and Roslyn Dena (LaMontagne) Paxton; m. Robert Eric Bunim, Jan. 31, 1971; 1 dau., Juliana. Pres. Bunim-Murray Prodns., L.A., 1988—. exec. prodr. daily CBS-TV series Search for Tomorrow, 1976-81, As the World Turns, 1981-84, NBC-TV series Santa Barabara, 1984-86, syndicated Crime Diaries, 198, ABC-TV series Loving, 1989-90, FBC series American Families, 1990; co-creator, exec. prodr. MTV series The Real World, 1992—, Road Rules, 1995—, NBC spl. Friends and Lovers, 1994, NBC Special High School Reunion: Class of '86, 1996, (ABC pilot) Catch Me If You Can, 1998, (ABC pilot) Detroit Receiving, 1999.

BUNIN, JEFFREY HOWARD, manufacturing company executive; b. N.Y.C., July 15, 1948; s. Herbert Bunin and Ruth Bunin Lefkowitz. BS in Engring., CUNY, 1971; MBA, Rutgers U., 1976. Engr. Airco Carbon Graphite, Niagrara Falls, N.Y., 1971-72, Airco Indsl. Gases, Murray Hill, N.J., 1972-76; fin. analyst Great A&P Tea Co., Montvale, N.J., 1976-78; mgr. fin. analysis MRI Div., Am. Can, Clark, N.J., 1978-80; dir. planning Matheson Gas Products Inc., Secaucus, N.J., 1980-99, Matheson Tri-Gas, Inc., 1999—. Mem. Inst. Mgmt. Accts., Alumni Assn. Rutgers U. (trustee Alumni Assn. Sch. Bus. Mgmt. (officer 1995—, pres. 1997—), Masons. E-mail: jbunin@aol.com. Home: 159 Franklin St Bloomfield NJ 07003-4978 Office: Matheson Tri-Gas Inc 959 Route 46 Parsippany NJ 07054-3409

BUNK, GEORGE MARK, civil engineer, consultant; b. Beverly, Mass., June 23, 1952; s. George and Katherine (Montoni) B. BS in Civil Engring., Northeastern U., Boston, 1975; MS in Civil Engring., U. Wyoming, 1976. Commd. officer USPHS, Many Farms, Ariz., 1977-79; civil engr. Hittmann Assocs., Columbia, Md., 1979-80; sr. engr. Morrison-Knudsen Engrs., Norwalk, Conn., 1980-83, dir. water resources, 1987-89; constrn. mgr. Morrison-Knudsen Engrs., Little Falls, N.Y., 1983-87; project mgr. Stetson-Harza, Utica, N.Y., 1989-91, program mgr., 1991-92; pres. George M. Bunk, P.E., P.C., Little Falls, N.Y., 1992—. Commr. Bd. Edn., Little Falls Sch. Dist., 1992—, v.p., 1995-96, pres., 1996-98; dir. The Luth. Home Ctrl. N.Y., Inc., 1996—. Mem. ASCE, Constrn. Specifications Inst., Soc. Am. Mil. Engrs., Am. Water Resource Assn., Water Environment Fedn., Am. Concrete Inst., Little Falls Rotary (group study exec. to Thailand 1983), Patria a Lavoro Soc. Home: 19 Arthur St Little Falls NY 13365-1106 Office: PO Box 308 690 E Main St Little Falls NY 13365-1530

BUNKER, DEBRA J., elementary education educator; b. Oshkosh, Wis., Sept. 19, 1955; d. Donald and Dawn E. (Fischer) B. BSEd, U. Wis., Oshkosh, 1977, MSE in Reading, 1984. Cert. elem. edn. grades 1-6, reading grades K-12, reading tchr., reading specialist. Chpt. 1 reading tchr./specialist Oshkosh (Wis.) Area Sch. Dist.; mem. Citizen Amb. Reading Delegation to Hungary and Russia, 1993; presenter at early childhood and reading confs. Founder, coord. Bookends Reading Club. Mem. ASCD, Internat. Reading Assn. (Community Svc. award), Wis. State Reading Assn. (chair pub. com., reading conf.), Fox Valley Reading Coun. (v.p. elect., v.p., past pres., chair, parents and reading com., pub./memberships com., historian), Bookends Reading Club (founder, coord.), Kappa Delta Pi.

BUNKER, JOHN BIRKBECK, cattle rancher, retired sugar company executive; b. Yonkers, N.Y., Mar. 28, 1926; s. Ellsworth and Harriet (Butler) B.; m. Emma Cadwalader, Feb. 27, 1954; children: Emma, Jeanie, Harriet, John C., Lambert C. BA, Yale U., 1950. With Nat. Sugar Refining Co., 1953-62; pres. Gt. Western Sugar Co., Denver, 1966; pres., CEO Holly Sugar Co., Colorado Springs, Colo., 1967-81, chmn., CEO, 1971-81; pres., CEO Calif. and Hawaiian Sugar Co., San Francisco, 1981-88, vice chmn., 1988-89, ret., 1989; gen. ptnr. Bunker Ranch Co., 1989—; chmn. Wheatland Bankshares and First State Bank of Wheatland, 1992—. Trustee Colo. Coll., 1973-94, Asia Found., 1985-94. Mem. Wyo. Nature Conservancy, Wyo. Stockgrowers Assn., Wyo. Heritage Found., Wyo. Farm Bur., Colo.-Wyo. Nat. Farmers Union. Home: 1451 Cottonwood Ave Wheatland WY 82201-3412

BUNKER, LINDA KAY, dean, physical education educator; b. Kankakee, Ill., Jan. 25, 1947; d. Francis M. and Wilahmine (Kammann) B. BS, U. Ill., 1968, MS, 1969, PhD, 1973. Cert. tchr., Ill. Prof., Parrish chair U. Va., Charlottesville, 1973—, dept. chair, 1976-84, assoc. dean, 1984-98; adv. bd. Melpomene Rsch. Inst., Mpls., 1982—, Women's Sports Found., N.Y.C., 1983—, SHAPE Mag., 1989—; cons. Fed. Exec. Inst., Charlottesville, 1988—, Dept. Motor Vehicles, Richmond, Va., 1990—. Author: Mind Mastery for Winning Golf, 1981, Mind, Set and Match, 1982, Motivating Kids Through Play, 1982, Sport Psychology, 1985, Coaching Golf Effectively, 1989, Golf: Steps to Success, 1995, Steppingstones: A Motor Development Program, 1989, Advanced Golf: Steps to Success, 1992, The Courtside Coach, 1995, Parenting Your Superstar, 1998. Named Outstanding Alumnae, U. Ill., 1981; recipient Honor award Va. Alliance Health, Phys. Edn., Recreation and Dance, 1987, Hall of Fame award, 1996, Billie Jean King award Women's Sports Found., 1998. Fellow Am. Assn. Applied Sport Psychology (cons., cert. sport psychology 1991), Alliance Health, Phys. Edn., Recreation and Dance (pres. Sport Psychology Acad. 1984, Mabel Lee award 1979, R. Tait MacKenzie award 1995), Am. Acad. Kinesiology and Phys. Edn. (Algernon Sydney Sullivan award, Raven Disting. prof. U. Va. 1995, Thomas Jefferson award 1996), Nat. Assn. Sport and Phys. Edn. Avocations: writing, public speaking. Office: U Va Curry Sch Edn 405 Emmet St Charlottesville VA 22903

BUNKER-SOLER, ANTONIO LUIS, physician; b. Caguas, P.R., Oct. 2, 1948. BS, U. P.R., Mayaguez, 1970; MD, U. P.R., San Juan, 1974. Diplomate Am. Bd. Allergy and Immunology, Am. Bd. Pediatrics. Commd. 2d lt. U.S. Army, 1973, advanced through grades to lt. col.; resident in pediatrics Brooke AMC, San Antonio, 1977; with pediatric svc. SHAPE, Belgium, 1977-79; various positions U.S. Army, Ft. Campbell, Ky., 1981-83; chief allergy-immunology svc. U.S. Army, Frankfurt, Germany, 1989-92; various positions U.S. Army, Ft. Hood, Tex., 1988-89; chief allergy-immunology svc. U.S. Army, Frankfurt, Germany, 1989-92; asst. chief allergy-immunology svc. U.S. Army, El Paso, Tex., 1992-94; various positions EAMC, Ga., 1983-88; pediatric pulmonary fellow Tex. Children's Hosp., Houston, 1994-95; pvt. practice Houston, 1995-96, Tampa, 1996—; asst. clin. prof. MCG, Augusta, Ga., 1983-88; allergy cons. southeastern region CONUS, 1984-88, 7th MEDCOM, Europe, 1989-92, allergy cons.; presenter in field. Contbr. articles to profl. jours. Active Asthma and Allergy Support Group, Augusta, 1985-87. Decorated Army Commendation medal with oak leaf cluster, Order of Mil. Med. Merit; Allergy fellow Fitzsimons AMC, 1981. Fellow Am. Coll. Asthma, Allergy and Immunology, Tex. Med. Assn., Mil. Allergists (Dura Pharm. award 1987); mem. AMA, Am. Acad. Pediatrics, Am. Acad. Allergy and Immunology, Am. Thoracic Soc. Office: 14310 N Dale Mabry Hwy Ste 260 Tampa FL 33618-2059

BUNKOWSKE, EUGENE WALTER, religious studies educator; b. Wecota, S.D., July 3, 1935; s. Walter Adolph and Ottille Sophie (Richter) B.; m. Bernice Bock; children: Barbara, Nancy, Walter, Joel. AA, Concordia Acad. and Jr. Coll., St. Paul, 1955; BA, Concordia Seminary, 1958, BD, MDiv,

1960; MA in Linguistics, UCLA, 1964, C Phil in Linguistics, 1968, PhD in Linguistics, 1976; LittD, Concordia Coll., 1983; DD, Christ Coll., 1991; DLitt, Concordia U., St. Paul, 1997. Missionary Luth. Ch.-Mo. Synod, Africa, 1960-82, congl. pastor, pioneer ch. planter, 1960-74, chmn. Nung Udoe dist., 1960-61, builder chs., schs., hosp., 1960-67, medical worker Ogoja Province, 1961-66, justice of peace Ogoja Province, 1962-74, chmn. Ogoja dist., 1964-69, chmn. Evang. Luth. Mission in Nigeria, 1965-67, analyzer Yala lang., orthography devel. & Bible translator, 1967-71, counselor to Yala Paramount Chief, 1969-74; fourth v.p. Luth. Ch.-Mo. Synod, 1989-92, 95-98, third v.p., 1992-95; dir. mission Concordia Theol. Seminary, Ft. Wayne, Ind., 1982-88, mission prof., 1982—, mission chair prof., 1986—, grad. prof. mission, 1990—, chmn. dept. pastoral ministries, 1985-88; chmn. mission dept., 1988-90; supr. D Missiology program, chmn. Mission and Comm. Congress Concordia Theol. Seminary, Ft. Wayne, Ind., 1984—; ling. cons. and adminstr. Luth. Bible Translators, Liberia, Sierra Leone, 1970-74; dir. Vacation Inst. for Tng. in Applied Linguistics and Bible Translation, U. Liberia, Monrovia, 1971-74; cons. United Bible Soc., 1974-80, regional translations coord., 1980-82; cons. Near West Side Cleve. Cluster, St. Paul Internat. Mission Bd. Author: Orede, 1973, Woka yi Ijona, 1974, Topics in Yala Grammar, 1976, God's Mission in Action, 1986, The Body of Christ in Mission, 1987, God's Communicators in Mission, 1988, Receptor Oriented Gospel Communication, 1989, The State of Gospel Communication Today, 1990, Church Growth: A Biblical Perspective, 1991, The Role of the Laity in Gospel Communications, 1992, The Christian Family: Nurture and Outreach, 1993, Multicultural Outreach: Bridging Cultures - Theirs and Ours, 1995; translator Yala Bible, 1967-74; contbr. articles to religious and profl. publs., chpts. to books. Mem. God's Word to Nations Bible Soc. (bd. dirs., trans. and tech. cons.), World Mission Prayer League (bd. dirs.), All Nations Mission (bd. dirs., cons.), Luth. Soc. for Missiology (founding organizer). Republican. Avocations: travel, reading, hiking. Home: 5724 Lancashire Ct Fort Wayne IN 46825-5910 Office: Concordia Theol Seminary 6600 N Clinton St Fort Wayne IN 46825-4916

BUNKŠE, EDMUNDS VALDEMĀRS, geographer, educator, consultant; b. Liepāja, Latvia, July 29, 1935; came to U.S., 1950; s. Jēkabs Bunkše and Anna Leontine Bucholts Birznieks; m. Moira Daly (div.); Elizabeth Murray Sutherland, Feb. 9, 1988 (div.); m. Grizelda Astrida Liepins, Oct. 15, 1995; children: Andrejs, Margarita. AB, Syracuse U., 1962; MA, U. Calif., Berkeley, 1966, PhD, 1973; D honoris causa, U. Latvia, 1991. Tchg. asst. U. Calif., Berkeley, 1963-65; instr. Coll. Holy Names, Oakland, Calif., 1965-67; cartographer Assn. Bay Area Govts., Berkeley, 1965; instr. U. Del., Newark, 1969-73, asst. prof., 1973-80, assoc. prof. dept. geography, 1980—, dir. London program, 1991; vis. Fulbright prof. U. Latvia, Riga, 1990, adj. prof., 1995—; assoc. prodr. Latvian TV, Riga, 1992-95. Co-prodr. TV films/shows; editor GeoJour. Baltic Peoples. . . , 1994; contbr. articles to profl. jours. and book. Mem. com. CIES-Fulbright Selection, Washington, 1992-95, Danish-Latvian Coop., 1990-95; in edn. reform U. Latvia, Riga, 1992—; mem. promotion and Dr. Habilis com. U. Latvia. Fulbright awardee, 1983-84, 90. Mem. Latvian Acad. Sci. (fgn.), Fulbright Alumni Assn., Assn. Am. Geographers, Ea. Hist. Geog. Assn., Assn. Latvian Geographers, Lidums. Mem. Evang. Luth. Ch. Avocations: sailing, skiing, sketching, chess, writing. E-mail: ebunks@udel.edu. Office: U Del Dept Geography Newark DE 19716

BUNN, CHARLES NIXON, strategic business planning consultant; b. Springfield, Ill., Feb. 8, 1926; s. Joseph Forman and Helen Anna Frieda (Link) B.; student U. Ill., 1943-44; BS in Engring., U.S. Mil. Acad., 1949; MBA, Xavier U., Cin., 1958; m. Cecine Cole, Dec. 26, 1951 (div. 1987); children: Sisene, Charles; m. Marjorie Fitzmaurice, Apr. 5, 1988. Flight test engr. Gen. Electric Co., Cin., also Edwards AFB, Calif., 1953-59; sr. missile test engr., space systems div. Lockheed Aircraft Corp., USAF Satellite Test Center, Sunnyvale, Calif., 1959-60, 63-70, economist, advanced planning dept., 1961-63; economic and long-range planning cons., Los Altos, Calif., 1970-73; head systems planning, economist, strategic bus. planning, Western Regional hdqrs. U.S. Postal Service, San Bruno, Calif., 1973-78; strategic bus. planning cons., investment analysis cons., 1978-79; strategic bus. planning Advanced Reactor Systems dept. Gen. Electric Co., Sunnyvale, Calif., 1979-84; strategic planning cons., 1984—. Served with inf. paratroops U.S. Army, 1944-45, with inf. and rangers, 1949-53, Korea. Decorated Battle Star (5). Mem. Nat. Assn. Bus. Economists, World Future Soc., Sigma Nu. Episcopalian. Home and Office: 222 Incline Way San Jose CA 95139-1525

BUNN, JOE MILLARD, retired agricultural engineering educator; b. Wayne County, N.C., Jan. 20, 1932; s. Clarence S. and Zora S. (Woodall) B.; m. F. Marie Baker, June 26, 1955; children: Ronnie Joe, Kenneth Bruce. BS in Agrl. Engring., N.C. State Coll., 1955, MS in Agrl. Engring., 1957; PhD in Agrl. Engring. and Math., Iowa State U., 1960. Registered agrl. engr., Ky. 1963. From asst. prof. to assoc. prof. U. Ky., Lexington, 1960-78; engr. AID-Ky. Team, Khon Kean, Thailand, 1968-70; prof. Clemson (S.C.) U., 1978-97, chair agrl. and biol. engring. dept., 1995-97; ret., 1997. Contbr. tech. papers and chpts. in books in field. mem. Meth. Ch. (Sunday sch. tchr. and bd. deacons), Lexington, Ky., 1965-78., Presbyn. Ch. (Sunday sch. tchr. and elder), Sandy Springs, S.C., 1979—. Grantee various pub. and pvt. agys. $1.5m for rsch. Fellow Am. Soc. Agrl. Engrs. (sec., vice chmn. various nat. state coms.); mem. Coun. Agr. Scis. Tech. Democrat. Presbyterian. Avocations: gardening, bowling. Office: Clemson U Agrl Engring Dept 201 McAdams Hall Clemson SC 29634-0357

BUNN, PAUL A., JR., oncologist, educator; b. N.Y.C., Mar. 16, 1945; s. Paul A. Bunn; m. Camille Ruoff, Aug. 17, 1968; children: Rebecca, Kristen, Paul H. BA cum laude, Amherst Coll., 1967; MD, Cornell U., 1971. Diplomate Nat. Bd. Med. Examiners, Am. Bd. Internal Medicine, Am. Bd. Med. Oncology. Intern U. Calif., H.C. Moffitt Hosp., San Francisco, 1971-72, resident, 1972-73; clin. assoc. medicine br. Nat. Cancer Inst., NIH, Bethesda, Md., 1973-76; sr. investigator med. oncology br. Nat. Cancer Inst., Washington VA Hosp., 1976-81; asst. prof. medicine med. sch. Georgetown U., 1978-81; head cell kinetic sect., Navy med. oncology br. Nat. Cancer Inst., Bethesda, 1981-84; assoc. prof. medicine uniformed svcs. Univ. Health Scis., Bethesda, 1981-84; prof. medicine health scis. ctr. U. Colo., Denver, 1984—, head divsn. med. oncology, 1984-94, dir. cancer ctr., 1987—; mem. instl. rev. bd. NIH, Nat. Cancer Inst., 1982-84; mem. intramural support contract rev. com. Nat. Cancer Inst., 1982-84; cons. Coulter Immunology, 1984-89, Abbott Labs., 1992-94, Seragen, 1993—, others; mem. cancer com. U. Colo., 1984—, mem. faculty senate health scis. ctr., 1985-94, mem. exec. com. sch. medicine, 1987—; mem. fin. com. Univ. Physicians, Inc., 1986-91; mem. med. bd. Univ. Hosp., 1987—; external sci. advisor cancer ctr. U. Miami, 1988-92, U. Ark., 1989-94, U. Va., 1991-94, others; mem. oncology drug adv. com. FDA, 1992—; mem. sci. secretariat 7th World Conf. Lung Cancer, 1994; bd. dirs. Univ. Hosp. Resource Coun.; mem. oncology drug adv. com. FDA, 1993—. Author: Carboplatin (JM-8) Current Perspectives and Future Directions, 1990, Clinical Experiences With Platinum and Etoposide Therapy in Lung Cancer, 1992, (with M.E. Wood) Hematology/Oncology Secrets, 1994; assoc. editor Med. and Pediatric Oncology, 1984—, Jour. Clin. Oncology, 1991—, Cancer Rsch., 1992—, others; contbr. chpts. to books and articles to profl. jours. Bd. dirs. Colo. divsn. Am. Cancer Soc., 1989—, Leukemia Soc. Am., 1991—; bd. dirs. The Cancer Venture, 1993-94, Fair Share Colo., 1993-94; chmn. Solid Tumor Oncology Edn. Found., 1996—. With USPHS, 1973-84. Decorated Medal of Commendation; recipient Sci. of Yr. award Denver chpt. ARCS, 1992; named one of 400 Best Drs. in Am., Good Housekeeping Mag., 1991, 92; grantee Schering Plough, 1988-89, Burroughs Wellcome, 1991—, Bristol-Myers Squibb, 1993—, others. Fellow ACP; mem. AAAS, Am. Soc. Hematology (mem. sci. subcom. neoplasia 1989-92), Am. Assn. Cancer Rsch., Am. Soc. Clin. Oncology (chair program subcom. 1985-86, 90), Am. Fedn. Clin. Rsch., Am. Assn. Cancer Insts. (bd. dirs. 1992—), Internat. Assn. Study Lung Cancer (bd. dirs. 1988—, pres. 1994—), Wesstern Assn. Physicians, S.W. Oncology Group (mem. lung and leukemia com. 1986—, mem. biologic response modifier com. 1987—), Lung Cancer Study Group, Alpha Omega Alpha. Office: U Colo Cancer Ctr Box B188 4200 E 9th Ave Denver CO 80220-3706

BUNN, RONALD FREEZE, political science educator, lawyer; b. Jonesboro, Ark., Aug. 1, 1929; s. S. Neal and Velma (Freeze) B.; m. Rita E. Hess, Mar. 29, 1955; children: Robin Gail, Katharine Sue, Lisabeth Joann. BA, Rhodes Coll., 1951; LLD, Southwestern at Memphis, 1973; MA, Duke U., 1953, PhD, 1956; postgrad., U. Cologne, Fed. Republic Germany, 1954-55; JD, U. Mo., 1989. Bar: Mo. 1990. Instr. U. Tex., Austin, 1956-59; asst. prof. U. Tex., 1960-64; asso. prof. La. State U., Baton Rouge, 1964-67, U Houston, 1967-69; prof., dean U Houston (Grad. Sch.), 1969-74, interim dean arts and scis., 1972-74, asso. dean faculties, 1974-75, acting v.p., dean faculties, 1975-76; v.p. acad. affairs State U. N.Y. at Buffalo, 1976-80; provost U. Mo., Columbia, 1980-86, prof. polit. sci., 1986—; ptnr. Shurtleff, Froeschner, Bunn and Aulgur, Columbia, 1992—; vis. lectr. Ind. U., 1962; cons. Coun. Grad. Schs. Author: Politics and Civil Liberties in Europe, 1967, German Politics and the Spiegel Affair: A Case Study of the Bonn System, 1968; Contbr. articles profl. jours. Bd. dirs. S.W. Center for Urban Research, Houston, chmn. bd., 1975-76. Fulbright predoctoral scholar, 1954-55, Fulbright rsch. scholar, 1963; NATO sr. fellow in sci., 1973. Mem. Mo. Bar Assn. (labor law com.), So. Polit. Sci. Assn. (past mem. exec. coun.), Southwestern Polit. Sci. Assn. (past v.p.), Am. Coun. on Germany, Phi Beta Kappa (pres. Mo. Alpha chpt. 1986-88), Omicron Delta Kappa. Office: U Mo Dept Polit Sci Columbia MO 65211 also: 25 N 9th St Columbia MO 65201-4845

BUNN, TIMOTHY DAVID, newspaper editor; b. Syracuse, N.Y., Sept. 29, 1946; s. John Stewart and Katherine (Smolnycki) B.; m. Nancy Grady, May 27, 1968. B.S. in Journalism, Syracuse U., 1972. Pub. info. officer Central N.Y. Regional Planning Bd., Syracuse, 1972-74; met. editor Rochester Democrat & Chronicle, N.Y., 1974-79; asst. city editor Miami Herald, Fla., 1979-81; mng. editor Syracuse Post-Standard, 1981-82; exec. editor Syracuse Herald Jour., 1982-95; dep. exec. editor Syracuse Post-Std., Herald Jour., Herald Am., 1995—. Bd. dirs. Syracuse Urban League. Served to capt. U.S. Army, 1967-71. Recipient Cmty. Svc. award NAACP, 1984, Cmty. Appreciation award Am.-Arab Anti-Discrimination Com. Mem. Am. Soc. Newspaper Editors. Office: Syracuse Newspapers Clinton Sq PO Box 4915 Syracuse NY 13221-4915

BUNN, WILLIAM BERNICE, III, physician, lawyer, epidemiologist; b. Raleigh, N.C., June 28, 1952; s. William Bernice Jr. and Clara Eva (Ray) B.; m. Shirley Welch, July 31, 1982; children: Ashley Howell, Elizabeth Jordan. AB, Duke U., 1974, MD, JD, 1979; MPH, U. N.C., 1983. Diplomate Am. Bd. Internal and Occupational Medicine. Intern, then resident in internal medicine Duke U. Med. Ctr., 1981-83, fellow in occupational medicine dept. community medicine, 1983; asst. prof. Sch. of Medicine Duke U., Durham, N.C., 1984-86, dir. rsch. in occupational medicine Sch. of Medicine, 1985-86; dir. occupational health and environmental affairs Bristol Myers Co., Wallingford, Conn., 1986-87, sr. dir. occupational health and environ. affairs, 1987-88; asst. clin. prof. Yale U., New Haven, 1986—; clin. asst. prof. U. Colo., Boulder, 1989; assoc. clin. prof. U. Cin., 1989—; corp. med. dir. Manville Sales Corp., Denver, 1988, v.p., corp. med. dir., 1988-89, sr. dir. for health safety and environ., v.p., 1989-92; dir. internat. med. affairs Mobil Corp., Princeton, N.J., 1992—; med. dir., dir. health, workers compensation, health benefits & safety Navistan Internat. Corp., Chgo., v.p. health safety and productivity, 1998—; cons. author, co-editor Dellacorte Publs., N.Y.C., 1984-87; sci. adv. bd. U.S. EPA, Washington, 1991—; chmn. radiation epidemiology com. NAS, Washington, 1991—; assoc. prof. clin. preventive medicine Northwestern Sch. Medicine; bd. sci. counselors Nat. Inst. Occupl. Safety and Health. Author: (with others) Effects of Exposure to Toxic Gases, 1986; author, editor: Poisoning, 1986, Occupational Problems in Clinical Practice; editor: Occupational and Environmental Medicine. Bd. dirs. Colo. Safety Assn., Denver, 1988-90, Gaylord Hosp., Wallingford, 1987-88, Meriden-Wallingford Hosp., 1986-88, Chem. Industry Inst. Toxicology, 1989-91, Am. Coll. Occupational and Environ. Medicine, 1993—. NIOSH scholar, 1980; NIH fellow, 1982-83, Nat. Inst. Occupational Safety and Health fellow, 1983-84. Fellow Am. Occupl. Medicine Assn. (co-chmn. acad. affairs com. and publs. com. 1985-90, nat. affairs com. 1985-86, chmn. pubs. com. 1990, bd. dirs. 1993—, chair internat. coun. 1994, sec. 1995, mem. exec. com. 1995), Am. Coll. Occupl. and Environ. Medicine; mem. ACP, AMA, APHA, Occupl. Medicine Assn. Conn. (sec., pres.-elect 1986-88), Internat. Coll. Occupl. Health, Phi Beta Kappa, Phi Eta Sigma. Office: 455 N Cityfront Plaza Dr Chicago IL 60611-5503 also: Yale U Dept Epidemiology & Pub Health New Haven CT 06520 also: U Colo Sch Pharmacy Dept Toxicology Boulder CO 80309 also: U Cin Dept Occupational Med Cincinnati OH 45267

BUNNEL, CHARLES FRANKLIN, personnel director, lobbyist; b. Bennington, Vt., Mar. 6, 1967; s. Robert Edward and Shirley Keith Bunnel; m. Eva Marie DiFusco, May 14, 1996; stepchildren: Jacinta, Michael, Denise; 1 child, Charles. BA, Trinity Coll., Hartford, Conn. Asst. chief staff Mohegan Tribe, Uncasville, Conn.; personal asst. Sen. Dodd, Washington. Democrat. Office: Mohegan Tribe of Indians PO Box 488 Uncasville CT 06382

BUNNELL, GEORGE ELI, lawyer; b. Miami, Fla., Apr. 28, 1938; s. George A. and Lillian E. (Hurley) B.; m. Dianne Railton, Dec. 1, 1990; children: Kelley, Courtney. BA, U. Fla., 1960, LLB, 1962. Bar: Fla. 1963, U.S. Dist. Ct. (so. dist.) Fla. 1963, U.S. Ct. Appeals (11th cir.) 1982, U.S. Supreme Ct. 1970. Assoc., Nicholson, Howard & Brawner, Miami, 1963-64; assoc. Dean, Adams, George & Wood, Miami, 1964-67, ptnr., 1968-71; officer, dir. Huebner, Shaw & Bunnell, P.A., Fort Lauderdale, Fla., 1972-77; pres., dir. Bunnell, Woulfe, Kirschbaum, Keller Cohen & McIntyre, P.A., Fort Lauderdale, 1977—. Mem. advance staff White House, 1974-76; mem. City of Fort Lauderdale Marine Adv. Bd., 1974-76, City of Fort Lauderdale Civil Svc. Bd., 1977-79; bd. dirs., sec. Ft. Lauderdale Mus. Art, 1990—. Fellow Am. Coll. Trial Lawyers; mem. Internat. Assn. of Def. Counsel, Am. Bd. Trial Advs. (pres. Ft. Lauderdale chpt. 1992), Def. Rsch. Inst., Fla. Def. Lawyers Assn., Broward County Bar Assn., Fla. Acad. of Hosp. Attys., Am. Health Lawyers Assn., Am. Soc. of Law and Medicine, Fla. Med. Malpractice Claims Coun., Inc. Republican. Clubs: Lago Mar Beach, Lauderdale Yacht (Fort Lauderdale). Office: Bunnell Woulfe Kirschbaum Keller Cohen & McIntyre PA 888 E Las Olas Blvd Fl 4 Fort Lauderdale FL 33301-2239

BUNNELL, PETER CURTIS, photography and art educator, museum curator; b. Poughkeepsie, N.Y., Oct. 25, 1937; s. Harold Curtis and Ruth (Buckhout) B. BFA, Rochester Inst. Tech., 1959; MFA, Ohio U., 1961; MA, Yale U., 1965. Curator of photography Mus. Modern Art, N.Y.C., 1966-72; prof. history of photography and modern art Princeton (N.J.) U., 1972—; curator of photography Art Mus. Princeton U., 1972—, dir., 1973-78, 98-99. Author; Clarence H. White, 1987, Minor White: The Eye That Shapes, 1989, Degrees of Guidance, 1993, Thomas Joshua Cooper, 1995, Ruth Bernhard: Photographs, 1996, Aaron Siskind: The Bond and The Free, 1997; editor: A Photographic Vision, 1980, The Art of Pictorial Photography, 1992, Photography at Princeton, 1998. Guggenheim fellow, 1979, Asian Cultural Coun. Rsch. fellow, 1984. Fellow Royal Photographic Soc. (hon.); mem. Soc. for Photog. Edn. (chmn. 1973-76), The Friends of Photography (pres. 1978-87, chmn. 1987-92), Century Assocs. Club. Office: Princeton U Dept Art And Archaelogy Princeton NJ 08544

BUNNER, PATRICIA ANDREA, lawyer; b. Fairmont, W.Va., Sept. 16, 1953; d. Scott Randolph and Virginia Lenore (Keck) B. AB in History & English magna cum laude, W.Va. U., 1975, JD, 1978; postgrad., Trinity Theol. Sem., 1995—, W.Va. U., 1996—. Bar: W.Va. 1978, N.Y. 1981, D.C. 1981, U.S. Dist. Ct. (so. dist.) W.Va. 1978, U.S. Dist. Ct. (no. dist.) W.Va. 1985, U.S. Ct. Claims 1990, U.S. Supreme Ct. 1989; cert. Christian counselor, 1986—. Mem. staff Dem. Nat. Com., Washington, 1978-79; assoc. Gailor, Elias & Matz, Washington, 1979-81, N.Y. State Bankers Assn., N.Y.C., 1981-83; ptnr. Bunner & Bunner, Fairview, W.Va., 1984-94; exec. dir. N.Y. State Consumer Mortgage Rev. Bd.; chmn. dist. VIII Consumer Mortgage Rev. Com., N.Y.C., 1982-83; cons. atty. Energy Cons. Assocs., Spring Harbor, N.Y., 1981; of counsel Monongahela (W.Va.) Soil Conservation Dist., 1985; vis. scholar Pitts. Theol. Sem., 1997—. Author: How Charley Metheney Broke the Four Minute Mile, 1971, Across the Bennefield Prong, 1973, German Anti-Semitism, Bismarck Through Weimar, 1973, N.Y. State Bankers Assn. Legis. Directory, 1983, Through a Glass Darkly, A Compendium of Film Noir, 1996, The Influence of the Seventeenth Century Scientific Revolution on Anglo-American Law, 1996, Rene Descartes, Phenomenologist, 1996, Psychology of Thomas Aquinas, 1997, John Locke's Influence on Modern Science, 1998. Pres. Monongalia County Dem. Women, 1987-89; sec. Monongalia County Devel. Authority, 1984-91; pres. United Taxpayers Assn., Inc., W.Va., 1985-88; bd. dirs. W.Va. U. Morgantown, 1974-75; active W.Va. State Dem. Exec. Com., 1990, 94. Rilla Moran Woods fellow Nat. Fedn. Dem. Women, Washington, 1978. Mem. ATLA, ABA (vice chmn. legal econs. and new lawyers coms. 1986-87, litigation sect., 1st amendment rights and media law com., gen. practice com., corps. and banking com.), W.Va. Bar Assn. (com. econs. of law practice 1987—, com. corps. and banking 1987—), W.Va. Trial Lawyers Assn., N.Y. State Bar Assn., Monongalia County Bar Assn., Marion County Bar Assn., W.Va. Criminal Def. Lawyers Assn., Women's Info. Ctr. (founding), LWV, NAFE, W.Va. Alliance for Women's Studies (founding), Bus. and Profl. Women (bd. dirs.), Climates, Inc., Monongalia County Hist. Soc., W.Va. Brain Injury Assn., Clay-Battelle Alumni Assn., W.Va. Coll. Law Alumni Assn., Nat. Rifle Assn. (life), Nature Conservancy, Nat. Arbor Day Found., World Wildlife Fund, Am. Farmland Trust, AAUW, Sierra Club, Audobon Soc., Young Dems. Club W.Va. (sec. 1976), Phi Alpha Theta (chpt. pres. 1974-75), Phi Beta Kappa, Zeta Phi Eta, Alpha Rho (chpt. pres. 1974), Phi Kappa Phi. Baptist. Club: Woman's (bd. dirs. Morgantown chpt. 1986—). Avocations: clothing design, cooking, creative writing, piano, swimming. Address: Route 2 Box 341 Fairview WV 26570

BUNNER, WILLIAM KECK, lawyer; b. Fairmont, W.Va., Sept. 2, 1949; s. Scott Randolph and Virginia Lenore (Keck) B. BS in Secondary Edn. magna cum laude, W.Va. U., 1970, MA in History, 1973, ABD in History, 1975, JD, 1978, postgrad., 1997. Bar: W.Va. 1978, U.S. Dist. Ct. (so. dist.) W.Va. 1978, U.S. Dist. Ct. (no. dist.) W.Va. 1985. Tchr. Monongalia County Bd. Edn., Morgantown, W.Va., 1970-78; contract lawyer dept. fin. and adminstrn. State of W.Va., Charleston, 1978-79; pvt. practice law Fairview, W.Va., 1979-84; pres. Farm Home Svc., Inc., 1983—; ptnr. Bunner & Bunner, Morgantown and Fairview, 1984-92; pres. Climates, 1988—. Pres. Monongalia County Young Dems., 1974; parliamentarian Monongalia County Dem. Exec. Com., 1982-94; counsel, parliamentarian Young Dem. Clubs W.Va., 1974-77; bd. dirs., supr. Monongahela Soil Conservation Dist., 1982—; advisor West Run Watershed Improvement Dist., 1983—; mem. W.Va. Commn. on Rural Abandoned Mines, Rural Alliance, Monongalia County Solid Waste Auth., 1989—, also chmn., 1990-92. Mem. ABA, Monongalia County Bar Assn., Assn. Rural Conservation, Soil Conservation Soc. Am., United Taxpayers' Assn. (counsel), Monongalia County Hist. Soc., Marion County Hist. Soc., Marion County Bar Assn., W.Va. Trial Lawyers Assn, Phi Alpha Delta, Phi Alpha Theta. Democrat. Avocations: music, politics, farming, videos, regional history and genealogy. Home and Office: 109 LaMesa Village Morgantown WV 26508

BUNNETT, JOSEPH FREDERICK, chemist, educator; b. Portland, Oreg., Nov. 26, 1921; s. Joseph and Louise Helen (Boulan) B.; m. Sara Anne Telfer, Aug. 22, 1942; children—Alfred Boulan, David Telfer, Peter Sylvester (dec. Sept. 1972). BA, Reed Coll., 1942; PhD, U. Rochester, 1945. Mem. faculty Reed Coll., 1946-52, U. N.C., 1952-58; mem. faculty Brown U., 1958-66, prof. chemistry, 1959-66, chmn. dept., 1961-64; prof. chemistry U. Calif., Santa Cruz, 1966-91, prof. emeritus, 1991—; Erskine vis. fellow U. Canterbury, N.Z., 1967; vis. prof. U. Wash., 1956, U. Wurzburg, Germany, 1974, U. Bologna, Italy, 1988; rsch. fellow Japan Soc. for Promotion of Sci., 1979; Lady Davis vis. prof. Hebrew U., Jerusalem, Israel, 1981; mem. adv. coun. dept. chemistry Princeton (N.J.) U., 1985-89; mem. NRC com. on alternative chem. demilitarization techs., 1992-93; mem. Dept. Def. panel on Gulf War Health Effects, 1993-94; co-chmn. peer rev. com. Russian-Am. Joint Evaluation Program, 1995-97; co-chmn. NATO Advanced Rsch. Workshop on Chem. Problems Associated with Old Arsenical and Mustard Munitions, Lodz, Poland, 1996; working group chem. weapons destruction, scientific adv. bd. Orgn. Prohibition Chem. Weapons, 1999—. Co-editor: Arsenic and Old Mustard: Chemical Problems in the Destruction of Old Arsenical and Mustard Munitions, 1998; contbr. articles to profl. jours. Trustee Reed Coll., 1970-97. Fulbright scholar U. Coll., London, 1949-50, U. Munich, 1960-61; Guggenheim fellow U. Munich, 1960-61; recipient James Flack Norris award in phys. organic chemistry Am. Chem. Soc., 1992; named hon. mem. Societa Chimica Italiana. Fellow AAAS; mem. Am. Acad. Arts and Scis., Am. Chem. Soc. (editor jour. Accounts of Chem. Rsch. 1966-86), Royal Soc. Chemistry (London), Internat. Union Pure and Applied Chemistry (chmn. commn. phys. organic chemistry 1978-83, sec. organic chemistry divsn. 1981-83, v.p. 1983-85, pres. 1985-87, chmn. task force on sci. aspects of destruction of chem. warfare agts. 1991-95, chmn. com. on chem. weapon destruction 1995—), Pharm. Soc. Japan (hon.), Acad. Gioenia (U. Catania, hon.), Soc. Argentina de Investigaciones en Quimica Organica (hon.). Home: 608 Arroyo Seco Santa Cruz CA 95060-3148 Office: U Calif Dept Chemistry Santa Cruz CA 95064

BUNNEY, BENJAMIN STEPHENSON, psychiatrist; b. Lansing, Mich., Sept. 27, 1938; s. William E. and Nora Orpha (Null) B.; m. Marjorie Bunney, Oct. 6, 1984; children: Edward Bradshaw, Katherine Stephenson, Elizabeth Janice. BA, NYU, 1960, MD, 1964. Resident in internal medicine Bellevue Hosp. NYU, 1964-66; resident in psychiatry Yale U., New Haven, 1968-71, asst. prof. psychiatry, 1971-74, asst. prof. pharmacology, 1974-75, assoc. prof. psychiatry, 1975-84, assoc. prof. pharmacology, 1976-84, prof. psychiatry, 1984—, prof. pharmacology, 1984—, prof. neurobiology, 1997—; vice chair dept. psychiatry Yale U., 1986-87, acting chair dept. psychiatry, 1987-88, chair dept. psychiatry, 1988—; mem. bd. sci. counselors NIMH, 1987-97, Inst. Medicine NAS, 1993—. Contbr. articles to profl. jours. Capt. USAF, 1966-68. Recipient Daniel H. Efron award for rsch. Am. Coll. Neuropsychopharmacology, 1983, Lieber prize for rsch. Nat. Alliance for Rsch. in Schizophrenia and Depression, 1987, MERIT award NIMH, 1990—. Fellow AAAS, Am. Psychiat. Assn., Am. Coll. Neuropsychopharmacology (past pres. 1997). Office: Yale U Dept Psychiatry 25 Park St New Haven CT 06519-1110

BUNNING, JIM, senator, former professional baseball player; b. Southgate, KY, Oct. 23, 1931. BS, Xavier U., 1953. Profl. baseball player, 1955-71; with Detroit Tigers, 1955-63, Phila. Phillies, 1964-67, Pitts. Pirates, 1968-69, L.A. Dodgers, 1969, Phila. Phillies, 1970-71; ret. profl. baseball, 1971; congressman Ky. State Senate, Frankfort, 1979-83; mem. 100th-104th Congresses from 4th Ky. dist., 1987-98; mem. budget com., mem. ways and means com., U.S. senator from Ky., 1999—; mem. Spl. Com. on Aging, Com. on Energy and Natural Resources, Com. on Banking, Com. Housing and Urban Affairs. Played in eight All-Star Baseball games during career. *

BUNSHAFT, MARILYN JANOSY, community services specialist; b. N.Y.C., July 27, 1935; d. Albert and Fay Janosy; m. Warren Owen Bunshaft, Aug. 28, 1955; children: Albert J., Jess A., Charles E. BA, Queens Coll., 1957; MS, Hofstra U., 1961. Treas. Crawford Pharmacy, Inc., Roslyn, N.Y., 1978-94; tax preparer pvt. practice, East Meadow, N.Y., 1982-90; cmty. info. specialist East Meadow Pub. Libr., 1988—. Mem. Adv. Com. on Environ., Hempstead, N.Y., 1980-84; bd. dirs. Nassau Suffolk Lung Assn., N.Y., 1987-96, N.Y. State Lung Assn., 1991-94; mem. allocations com. United Way of Long Island, N.Y., 1991—. Mem. LWV (bd. dirs. Hempstead E., 1961—, pres. 69-70, 76-78); East Meadow C. of C. (bd. dirs. 1992—), Am. Libr. Assn., Pub. Libr. Assn. Avocations: reading, designing clothes, travel, gardening. Office: East Meadow Pub Libr 1886 Front St East Meadow NY 11554-1700

BUNT, JAMES RICHARD, electric company executive; b. St. Cloud, Minn., Sept. 24, 1941; s. Eberhard Joseph and Christine Frances (Bromberg) B.; children: Gregory, Ashlee. BA, U. S.D., Vermillion, 1967; MA, Claremont Grad. Sch., Calif., 1968. Mgmt. trainee GE, Schenectady, N.Y., 1968-70, corp. auditor, 1970-73; mgr. fin. ops. Nuclear Energy div. GE, San Jose, Calif., 1973-77; cons. fin. planning GE, Fairfield, Conn., 1977-79; mgr. fin. planning and analysis, MABG, Louisville GE, Louisville, 1979-81; v.p., comptr. Gen. Electric Capital Svcs. Inc. Gen. Electric Capital Corp., Stamford, Conn., 1981-87; v.p. corp. exec. office GE, Fairfield, 1987-91, v.p., comptr., 1992-93, v.p., treas., 1994—; bd. dirs. GE Electric Capital Corp., Inc., GE Fin. Svcs., Powerex, Inc., Arkwright Mutual Ins. Co., U. S.D. Found. Fellow NDEA, 1967. Mem. Fin. Acctg. Stds. Adv. Coun., Fin. Execs. Inst., Elfun Soc., U. S.D. Found., Phi Beta Kappa. Republican. Roman Catholic. Home: 6 Imperial Lndg Westport CT 06880-4934 Office: GE 3135 Easton Tpke Fairfield CT 06431-0002

BUNT, RANDOLPH CEDRIC, mechanical engineer; b. Pascagoula, Miss., Dec. 3, 1958; s. Cedric and Linda Lou (McGuire) B.; m. Raechel Amy Ellis, May 15, 1982; children: Ashley Michele, Ryan Christian, Raechel Victoria, Savannah Marie. BME, Auburn U., 1979, MS, 1982. Registered profl. engr., Ala., Ga. Asst. engr. So. Co. Svcs., Birmingham, Ala., 1982-84, engr. II, 1984-86, engr. I, 1986-87, sr. engr., 1987-88; sr. engr. Ga. Power Co., Birmingham, 1988-89; project engr. So. Nuclear Oper. Co., Birmingham, 1989—; project mgr. Ga. Power Co., Atlanta and Birmingham, 1987-89;

chmn. GE Nuclear Turbine Conf., 1993-95, vice-chmn. GE turbine outage optimization com., 1997-99, chmn., 1999—. Trustee Friends of Moody Schs.; chmn., co-founder GE Nuclear Turbine Users Group; vice chmn. Fairbanks Morse Owners Group, 1994-96, chmn. 1996—; stewardship chmn. Moody United Meth. Ch., 1995-96, pres. United Meth. Men; capt. Birmingham Amateur Hockey Assn., 1985. Mem. ASME, NSPE, Am. Nuclear Soc., Ala. Soc. Profl. Engrs. (chmn. student engrng. yr. com. 1987-92, chmn. Math Counts program 1990-95, sec. 1992-93, v.p. 1993-95, pres. 1995-97, co-chmn. 1993 conf., state pres.-elect 1998-99, state pres. 1999—, Young Engr. of Yr. award 1991, Profl. Engr. in Industry award, Engr. of Yr. 1992), Birmingham Engrng. Coun. (chmn. Discover E 1993-95, treas. 1995-96, sec. 1996-97, v.p. 1997-98, pres. 1998-99), So. Nuclear Nat. Mgmt. Assn. (treas. 1991-92, bd. dirs. 1994-95), Terry Turbine Users Group (vice chmn. 1993-99, chmn. 1999—). Republican. Methodist. Home: 1005 Muscadine Cir Leeds AL 35094-1027 Office: So Nuclear Oper Co 42 Inverness Center Pky Birmingham AL 35242-4809

BUNTEN, WILLIAM DANIEL, retired banker; b. Goodland, Kans., Sept. 18, 1931; s. William Livingston and Nelle Elizabeth (Boyle) B.; m. Charlene Sue Riemen, May 23, 1954; children: Jane Denise Bunten Hanisch, Barbara Sue Bunten DeVoe, Patricia Joann Bunten Buckner. AB, Baker U., 1953; LLB, Washburn U., 1956; MBA, U. Pa., 1958. Bar: Kans. 1956, Mich. 1959. From asst. cashier to v.p. Nat. Bank Detroit, 1957-67; v.p., then pres. Mchts. Nat. Bank, Topeka, 1967-79; sr. exec. v.p. United Cen. Bank, Des Moines, 1979-81; sr. v.p., then exec. v.p. United Cen. Bancshares, Des Moines, 1979-82; pres. INTRUST Bank and predecessor firm 1st Nat. Bank, Wichita, Kans., 1982-96; also bd. dirs. INTRUST Bank and predecessor firm 1st Nat. Bank, Wichita; vice chmn. bd. dirs. INTRUST Fin. Corp. and predecessor firm 1st Fin. Corp., Wichita, 1982-96; bd. dirs. Am. Home Life Ins. Co., Topeka; treas., dir. Lakeway Airport, Inc., 1998—. Bd. dirs., v.p. Jayhawk coun. Boy. Scouts Am., Topeka, 1968-78, Mid-Iowa coun., 1980-2; bd. dirs. United Way, Topeka, 1969-77, pres. 1977; bd. dirs. United Way, Des Moines, 1980-82, United Way Wichita, 1983-88, pres. 1987; bd. dirs. Topeka C. of C., 1969-74, pres. 1973; bd. dirs. Wichita C. of C., 1986-88, Greater Downtown Wichita, 1986-88, pres. 1987; bd. dirs. Downtown Action Corp., Wichita, 1988-91; bd. dirs. YMCA, Wichita, 1988-96, pres. 1992-94; sec. bd. dirs. Boys/Girls Clubs S. Cen. Kans., 1990-96; trustee Quivira coun. Boy Scouts Am., 1983-96; trustee Stormont Vail Hosp., Topeka, 1974-79, treas. 1978-79; trustee Baker U., Baldwin City, Kans., 1987-90; bd. dirs. Hospice, Wichita, 1983-84, Wichita State U. Endowment Assn., Wichita, 1984-95, dir. Health Affiliates Inc., Wichita, 1992-96. Mem. Washburn U. Alumni Assn. (bd. dirs. 1989-92, pres. 1991-92), Washburn U. Endowment Assn. (trustee 1990—), Rotary (bd. dirs. Topeka club 1977-78; treas. Wichita club 1988-89, trustee 1999), Masons, Blue Lodge, Shriners. Republican. Ecumenical. Avocations: flying, golf, reading. Home: 5 Cliffbrook Ct Austin TX 78738-1507

BUNTING, CHARLES I., academic administrator; b. New Haven, Conn., Oct. 31, 1942; s. Henry and Mary (Ingraham) B.; m. Ann Doughty, June 28, 1969; children: Matthew, Adam. BA in English, Amherst Coll., 1965; MA in Teaching, Harvard U., 1968, EdD, 1973. Instr. Miles Coll., Birmingham, Ala., 1965-66; tchr., cons. Boston Pub. Schs., 1967-71; adminstr. Fund for Improvement of Postsecondary Edn., Washington, 1973-80; chief of staff U.S. Dept. Edn., Washington, 1980-81; sec. of coll. Vassar Coll., Poughkeepsie, N.Y., 1981-85; chancellor Vt. State Colls., Waterbury, 1985—; bd. dirs. Nat. Sch. Vol. Program, Alexandria, Va., 1981—, New Eng. Bd. Higher Edn., 1987—, United Educators Ins. Co., 1988—; bd. overseers Case Western Res. U., Cleve., 1985—; trustee Coun. for Advancement of Exptl. Edn., 1991—; pres. State Higher Edn. Exec. Officers, 1994-95. Contbr. articles on higher edn. and govt. issues. Mem. alumni council Harvard Grad. Sch. Edn., Cambridge, 1982-85; bd. dirs. Vt. Bus. Roundtable, 1990—. Mem. Am. Assn. Higher Edn. Avocation: canoe poling. Office: Vt State Colls System Office of Chancellor PO Box 359 Waterbury VT 05676-0359

BUNTING, KENNETH FREEMAN, newspaper editor; b. Houston, Dec. 9, 1948; s. Willie Freeman and Sarah Lee (Peterson) B.; m. Juliana Amy Jafvert, July 13, 1989; 1 child, Maxwell Freeman. Student, U. Mo., 1966-67; AA in Journalism, Lee Coll., 1968; BA in Journalism and History, Tex. Christian U., 1970; advanced exec. program, Northwestern U., 1996. Mgmt. trainee, reporter Harte-Hanks Newspapers Inc., Corpus Christi, Tex., 1970-71; reporter, then copy editor San Antonio Express-News, 1971-73; exec. asst. to Hon. G.J. Sutton Tex. Ho. of Reps., San Antonio, 1973-74; reporter Cin. Post, 1974-78, Sacramento Bee, 1978; reporter, asst. city editor, state capitol corr. L.A. Times, 1978-87; capitol bur. chief, city editor, dep. mng. editor, sr. editor Ft. Worth Star-Telegram, 1987-93; mng. editor Seattle Post-Intelligencer, 1993—; journalism instr. Orange Coast Coll., Costa Mesa, Calif., 1981-82; mem. adv. bd. Maynard Inst., Oakland, Calif., 1994—. Bd. dirs. Seattle Symphony, 1995-97; mem. commn. Woodland Park Zoo, Seattle, 1995-96, 98; mem. Leadership Ft. Worth; mem. journalism adv. bd. Tex. Christian U.; former mem. minorities task force Assn. for Edn. in Journalism and Mass Comms.; past pres. Press Club, Orange County, Calif.; past bd. dirs. Covington (Ky.) Cmty. Ctr.; past 1st v.p. Young Dems. of Tex.; past treas., mem. exec. bd. Freedom of Inro. Found. of Tex. Mem. Nat. Assn. Black Journalists, AP Mng. Editors Assn. (mem. ethics com. 1995-96, bd. dirs. 1996-99), Am. Soc. Newspaper Editors (mem. minorities com.), Soc. Profl. Journalists (bd. dirs. western Wash. chpt. 1995-96), Seattle C. of C. (mem. cmty. devel. roundtable 1994—), Alliance for Edn. (bd. dirs.), Tex. Christian U. Alumni Assn. (bd. dirs.), Freedom of Info. Found. Tex., Rainier Club, Washington Athletic Club. Unitarian. Avocations: tennis, bridge, reading. Office: Seattle-Post Intelligencer PO Box 1909 101 Elliott Ave W Seattle WA 98111

BUNTING, ROBERT LOUIS, accounting firm executive, management consultant; b. Sacramento, Oct. 29, 1945; married; 3 children. BS in Acctg., U. Idaho, 1968. With Price Waterhouse & Co., 1968-72; with Moss Adams, L.L.P., Seattle, 1972—, pres., 1981—. Named One of 100 Most Influential Businessmen in Seattle, Seattle Bus. Jour., One of 100 Most Influential Accts. in Am., Acctg. Today. Office: Moss Adams & Co 1001 4th Ave Ste 2830 Seattle WA 98154-1199*

BUNTON, LUCIUS DESHA, III, federal judge; b. Del Rio, Tex., Dec. 1, 1924; s. Lucius Desha and Avis Maurine (Fisher) B.; m. Mary Jane Carsey, June 18, 1947; children: Cathryne Avis Bunton Warner, Lucius Desha. Student, U. Chgo., 1943-44; BA, U. Tex., Austin, 1947, JD, 1950. Bar: Tex. 1949. Individual practice law Uvalde, Tex., 1950; assoc. firm H.O. Metcalfe, Marfa, Tex., 1951-54; dist. atty. 83d Jud. Dist. Tex., 1954-59; mem. firm Shafer, Gilliland, Davis, Bunton & McCollum, Odessa, Tex., 1959-79; judge U.S. Dist. Ct. (we. dist.) Tex., Midland, 1979-87, chief judge, 1987-92, sr. judge, 1989—; mem. jud. resources com., 1989-94. Trustee Ector County (Tex.) Ind. Sch. Dist., 1967-76 . With inf. U.S. Army, 1943-46. Mem. Tex. Bar Found. (charter), Am. Bar Assn., Am. Bar Found., Am. Coll. Probate Counsel, Am. Acad. Matrimonial Lawyers, State Bar Tex. (chmn. 1971-72, v.p. 1973-74, pres.-elect 1979), Masons. Baptist.

BUNTROCK, DEAN LEWIS, waste management company executive; b. Columbia, S.D., June 6, 1931. BA, St. Olaf Coll., Northfield, Minn., 1955. Founder Waste Mgmt. Inc., Oak Brook, Ill., 1968—; chmn. bd., dir. Waste Mgmt. Inc. (changed to WMX Technologies in 1993), Oak Brook, Ill., 1968—; also chmn. bd., bd. dirs. WMI Internat., until 1997; bd. dirs. Wheelabrator Techs., Inc., First Nat. Bank Chgo., Waste Mgmt. Internat., Plc. Trustee Chgo. Symphony Orch.; mem. adv. bd. J.L. Kellogg Grad. Sch. Northwestern U., Evanston, Ill. Named Outstanding CEO, Fin. World Mag., Wall St. Transcript; appointed to Pres.'s Coun. on Environ. Quality. Mem. Am. Pub. Works Assn., Environ. Industries Assn. (co-founder, past pres., sec.-treas., dir.), Bus. Roundtable. Office: Oakbrook Terrace Tower One Tower Ln Ste 2242 Oakbrook Terrace IL 60181-4636

BUNTS, FRANK EMORY, artist; b. Cleve., Mar. 2, 1932; s. Alexander Taylor and Mary (Corbin) B.; m. Norah Jean Grassle, Aug. 1, 1964. Student, Yale U., Cleve. Inst. Art; MA, Case Western Res. U., 1964. Instr. Cleve. Inst. Art, 1963-64, Ark. State U., 1965-67; mem. faculty U. Md., 1967-77, prof., 1973-77, dir. grad. art studio program, 1972-77; pres. VIA Art. One-person shows include Comara Gallery, L.A., 1967, 68, Franz Bader Gallery, Washington, 1969, 73, 75, St. John's Coll., Annapolis, Md., 1972, Deson Zaks Gallery, Chgo., 1972, Gallery 118, Mpls., 1974, Nat. Acad. Scis., Washington, 1976, Cath. U. Am., Washington, 1978, Plum Gallery, Washington, 1979, Flatiron Studio, N.Y.C., 1987, Maryanne McCarthy Fine Art, N.Y.C., 1988-89, Limelight Club, N.Y.C., 1988, Loft Lawyers, N.Y.C., 1990, 91, Roberta Wood Gallery, Syracuse, N.Y., 1993, Effect/Cause Mail Project, 1993-95, others; group shows: San Francisco Mus. Art, 1965, Cleve. Mus. Art, 1961, 62, 63, 65, 66 (2), 67, 68, Cleve. Inst. Art, 1964, Purdue U., Lafayette, Ind., 1964-69, El Paso (Tex.) Mus. Art, 1965, Nat. Arts Club, N.Y.C., 1965, Wittenberg U., Springfield, Ohio, 1966, Pacific Luth. U., Tacoma, Wash., 1966, Scripps Coll., Clairmont, Calif., 1967, U. Detroit, 1967, U. Calif., Long Beach, 1967, Palm Springs Desert Mus., Calif., 1967, Loyola U., L.A., 1968, Salt Lake City Art Ctr., 1968, U. N.H., 1968, Brigham Young U., Provo, Utah, 1968, Ind. State U., Terre Haute, 1968, Brooks Meml. Art Gallery, Memphis, 1968, 73, Cath. U., Washington, 1969, U. Md., 1969, 70, 72, Traveling Show, 1975-76, Fine Arts Gallery San Diego, 1971, Henri Gallery, Washington, 1971, Reicher Gallery, Barat Coll., Lake Forest, Ill., 1972, Corcoran Gallery Art, 1972, Va. Poly. Inst., Blacksburg, 1973, Birmingham (Ala.) Mus. Art, 1973, Indpls. Mus. Art, 1976, Gallery K, Washington, 1978, Studio Gallery, Washington, 1976-77, Modern Mus. Art, Rijeka, Yugoslavia, 1978, Baak Gallery, Cambridge, Mass., 1978, 79, Maryanne McCarthy Fine Art, N.Y.C., 1987, 88, 89, and Southampton, N.Y., 1989, Christie's N.Y.C. Preview and Auction, 1990, Univ. Sch., Cleve., 1990, Guild Hall, East Hampton, N.Y., 1991, 92, Lillian Heidenberg Gallery, N.Y.C., 1991-92, Roberta Wood Gallery, Syracuse, 1993-96, Angel Art Pacific Design Ctr., L.A., 1993, Divine Design 95, L.A., Black and Herron Gallery, N.Y.C., 1996; Intercommunication Ctr., Tokyo Opera City, Tokyo, Japan, 1998, VIA Art Found., New York (one person exhibition), 1999—, represented in collections Mus. Art, Cleve. Mus. Art, Fine Arts Gallery, San Diego, Library of Congress, Corcoran Gallery Art, Washington, Cooperstown Art Assn., N.Y., Chinese Artists Assn., Beijing; artwork in the following videos: The Man from U.N.C.L.E., episode The Pop Art Affair, 1966, Callanetics, M.C.A., 1986, Portrait of an Artist by Konrad Gylfason, 1986, music video Always and Forever, Whistle C.C. Prodns., 1990, documentary video San Francisco Ctr. for Visual Studies, 1990; work reproduced in Cleve. Mus. Art Bull., May 1962, May 1968, Md. Art Gallery Catalog, 1969, 72, Indpl. Mus. Art catalog Painting and Sculpture Today, June 1976, Internat. Exhibition catalog Modern Mus. Art, Rijeka, Yugoslavia, 1978, The Catalog of Am. Drawings, Watercolors, Pastels and Collages Corcoran Gallery Art, Washington, 1983, N.Y. Art Rev., 1988. Office: VIA Art Inc 15 W 24th St New York NY 10010-3214

BUNT SMITH, HELEN MARGUERITE, lawyer; b. L.A., Oct. 8, 1942; d. Alan Verbanks and Nettie Virginia (Crandall) Bunt; m. Charles Robert Smith, Jan. 12, 1974; children: John, Sharon. BS, U. Calif., L.A., 1964; JD, Southwestern U., 1972. Bar: Calif. 1972; cert. secondary tchr., Calif. Tchr. L.A. City Schs., 1965-72; pvt. practice Pasadena, Calif., 1973—; Law Day chmn. Pasadena Bar Assn., 1980, sec., 1981. Editor (newsletter) Lawyer's Club, 1984-85. Sunday sch. tchr. Lake Ave. Congrl. Ch., Pasadena; sec. Pasadena Sister Cities Com., 1994-96. Mem. San Gabriel Bar Assn. (bd. dirs. 1999—). Avocations: jogging, singing, stained glass. Office: 465 E Union St Ste 102 Pasadena CA 91101-1783

BUNYAN, ELLEN LACKEY SPOTZ, chemist, educator; b. Clark Mills, Pa., Aug. 14, 1921; d. Scott Richard and Mary Ellen (Beal) Lackey; children: Mark Stephen Spotz, Leslie Claire Spots, Elizabeth Grace O'Rourke. BS, U. Pitts., 1942; PhD, U. Wis., 1950. Sr. technologist EAstman Kodak Co., Kingsport, Tenn., 1942-44; instr. chemistry U. Wis., Milw., 1946-47; rsch. assoc. dept. chemistry U. Wis., Madison, 1950-52; instr. physics St. Agnes Acad., Houston, 1965; Welch fellow chemistry Rice U, Houston, 1968-69; lectr. Montgomery Coll., Rockville, Md., 1970-72; asst. prof. chem. tech. U. D.C., Washington, 1972-78, assoc. prof., 1978-91, ret., 1991; adj. prof. continuing edn. Walter Reed Army Med. Ctr. U. D.C., 1991-94; adj. prof. U. D.C., 1995-98; guest worker Nat. Bur. Standards, 1976; curriculum developer Allied Health Chemistry. Contbr. articles to profl. jours. Fellow Nat. Urban League Eastman Kodak Co, 1976; bd. dirs. Takoma Park Symphony, 1988—; mem. adv. bd. Cambodian Children's Assn., Inc.; mem. NEA, Am. Chem. Soc., Sigma Xi, Sigma Delta Epsilon. Methodist.

BUNZEL, JOHN HARVEY, political science educator, researcher; b. N.Y.C., Apr. 15, 1924; s. Ernest Everett and Harriett (Harvey) B.; m. Barbara Bovyer, May 11, 1963; children—Cameron, Reed. A.B., Princeton U., 1948; M.A., Columbia U., 1949; Ph.D., U. Calif.-Berkeley, 1954; LL.D., U. Santa Clara, 1976. Mem. faculty San Francisco State U., 1953-56, 63-70, vis. scholar Ctr. Advanced Study in Behavioral Scis., 1969-70; mem. faculty Mich. State U., East Lansing, 1956-57, Stanford U., Calif., 1957-63; pres. San Jose State U., Calif., 1970-78; sr. research fellow Hoover Inst. Stanford U., Calif., 1978—; mem. U.S. Commn. on Civil Rights, 1983-86. Author: The American Small Businessman, 1962; Anti-Politics in America, 1967; Issues of American Public Policy, 1968; New Force on the Left, 1983, Challenge to American Schools: The Case For Standards and Values, 1985, Political Passages: Journeys of Change Through Two Decades 1968-1988, 1988, Race Relations on Campus: Stanford Students Speak, 1992; contbr. articles to profl. jours., popular mags., newspapers. Weekly columnist San Jose Mercury-News. Bd. dirs. No. Calif. Citizenship Clearing House, 1959-61; mem. Calif. Atty. Gen.'s Adv. Com., 1960-61; del. Calif. Democratic Conv., 1968; del. Dem. Nat. Conv., 1968. Recipient Presdl. award No. Calif. Polit. Sci. Assn., 1969, cert. of Honor San Francisco Bd. Suprs., 1974, Hubert Humprey Pub. Policy award Policy Studies Orgn., 1990; grantee Ford Found., Rockefeller Found., Rabinowitz Found. Mem. Am. Polit. Sci. Assn. Home: 1519 Escondido Way Belmont CA 94002-3634 Office: Stanford U Hoover Inst Stanford CA 94305

BUNZL, RUDOLPH HANS, retired diversified manufacturing company executive; b. Vienna, Austria, July 20, 1922; came to U.S., 1940, naturalized, 1944; s. Robert Max and Nellie Margaret (Burian) B.; m. Rema R. Templeton, Apr. 6, 1947; children: Ann Mary Bunzl Kamoe, Carol Elizabeth Bunzl Showker; m. Esther R. Mendelsohn, Nov. 14, 1970. BSChemE, Ga. Inst. Tech., 1943; MA in History, U. Richmond, 1994. With Shell Chem. Co., Calif., 1943-54; v.p. Am. Filtrona Corp., Richmond, Va., 1954-59, pres., 1959-83, CEO, 1983-87, chmn. bd., 1987-95. Trustee Richmond Symphony Found., Greater Richmond Cmty. Found., World Affairs Coun. Greater Richmond, Sci. Mus. Va. Found. With U.S. Army, 1944-46. Mem. AICE. Office: 5516 Falmouth St Ste 205 Richmond VA 23230-1819

BUOCH, WILLIAM THOMAS, corporate executive; b. Atlanta, Mar. 2, 1923; m. Jean Cleste Wright; children: Steven T., David W., William Mark. Student, Ga. State U., 1946-54. Pres. Buoch Enterprises Inc., Atlanta, 1954—. Office: Buoch Enterprises Inc PO Box 90862 Atlanta GA 30364-0862

BUOEN, ROGER, newspaper editor. Nat. news editor Star Tribune. Office: Star Tribune 425 Portland Ave Minneapolis MN 55488-0002*

BUONANNI, BRIAN FRANCIS, health care facility administrator, consultant; b. Pawtucket, R.I., Sept. 2, 1945; s. James and Roselle B.; m. Lynne Buonanni (div. 1982); children: Donna, Karen, Jamie; m. Diane Manenty, Feb. 23, 1985 (div. 1992); m. Gloria Berenguer, Sept. 2, 1995. BA, Providence Coll., 1967; EdM, Boston Coll., 1968; M in Health Adminstrn., St. Louis U., 1973. Lic. nursing home adminstr., N.J. Rehab. counselor, tchr. R.I. Assn. for Blind, Providence, 1968-71; adminstrv. resident Carney Hosp., Boston, 1972; asst. adminstr. Alton (Ill.) Meml. Hosp., 1973-77, Gnaden Huetten Meml. Hosp., Lehighton, Pa., 1977-80; v.p. ops. Burdette Tomlin Hosp., Cape May Ct. House, N.J., 1980-85; COO St. Elizabeth's Hosp., Elizabeth, N.J., 1985—, exec. v.p., 1989—; pres. Health Care Practice Mgmt., Jenkinstown, Pa., 1984—; CEO Cmty. Gen. Hosp. of Sullivan County, Harris, N.Y., 1999, pres., CEO, 1999—; chmn., adv. bd. Shifa, McFaul & Lyons, Morristown, N.J., 1987-95; rev. com. N.J. Health Council, Trenton, 1987—. Fellow Am. Coll. Healthcare Execs.; mem. Nat. Assn. Purchasing Agts., Rotary (past pres.). Home: 950 Lake Shore Dr W Rock Hill NY 12775 Office: Cmty Gen Hosp of Sullivan County Bushville Rd Harris NY 12742

BUONO, FREDERICK JOSEPH, secondary school educator; b. Syracuse, N.J.; s. Albert Buono; m. Nancy Sykes, Aug. 1, 1964. BS, Syracuse U., 1961, MS, 1964, PhD, 1967. Rsch. scientist Rohm & Haas, Bristol, Pa., 1967-72; dir. rsch. Tenneco Chems., Piscataway, N.J., 1972-85; tchr. Lenape Regional H.S., Medford, N.J., 1986—. Contbr. articles to profl. jours. NIH fellow, 1964-67. Mem. Am. Soc. Microbiology, N.J. Edn. Assn. Avocations: reading, gardening. Home: 18 Edgewood Rd Robbinsville NJ 08691-1128

BUOT, FRANCISCO JOSE, industrial engineer; b. Springfield, Va., July 3, 1965; s. Francisco U. and Josefina (Juvida) B. BS in Indsl. Engrng. and Ops. Rsch., Va. Poly. Inst. State U., 1987. Engrng. asst. Casazza, Schultz and Assoc., Arlington, Va., summers 1983-87; quality control inspector Merck and Co., Elkton, Va., 1988-90, mfg. supr., 1990-96, staff engr. validation, 1996—. Fire fighter Harrisonburg (Va.) Fire Dept., 1988—. Mem. Inst. Indsl. Engrs. (sr., sec., treas. local chpt. 1993-94), Parenteral Drug Assn. Home: 317 S Willow St Harrisonburg VA 22801-1958 Office: Merck and Co Rt 340 South PO Box 7 Elkton VA 22827

BUOTE, ROSEMARIE BOSCHEN, special education educator; b. Jamaica, N.Y., Nov. 13, 1939; d. George Frederick and Mary (Bernadich) Boschen; m. Victor Roy Buote, June 27, 1964; children: Kristine, Alissa. BA, Barrington (R.I.) Coll., 1962; MEd, R.I. Coll., Providence, 1985, Fitchburg (Mass.) State Coll., 1991. Cert. spl. edn. and elem. tchr. Elem. tchr. Town of Barrington, 1962-68, 69-70; resource rm. instructional aide Town of Rehoboth (Mass.), 1983-84; spl. edn. tchr., behavior mgmt. specialist dept edn. Dept. of Edn. Tri-County Dist., Ednl. Svcs. in Instnl. Settings, Taunton, Mass., 1985—. Sec. Conservation Commn., Town of Dighton, 1971-74; lay eucharistic minister Pastoral Outreach Commn., Episcopal Diocese Mass.; bd. dirs. Gordon Coll. Alumni Bd., Wenham, Mass., 1989-92; mem. Friends of the Taunton Libr. Bd. Mem. AAUW (Taunton area br. past pres.), Nat. Marine Educators Assn., Mass. Marine Educators, Coun. Exceptional Children, Coun. Children with Behavioral Disorders, Coun. for Children with Learning Disabilities, Mass. Computer Using Educators, Dighton Garden Club (pres. 1979-82), Delta Kappa Gamma. Avocations: reading, writing, gardening, theater. Home: 1690 Wellington St Dighton MA 02715-1000 Office: Dept of Edn-Tri-County Dist 60 Hodges Ave Taunton MA 02780-3034

BURACK, ELMER HOWARD, management educator; b. Chgo., Oct. 21, 1927; s. Charles and Rose (Taerbaum) B.; m. Ruth Goldsmith, Mar. 18, 1930; children—Charles Michael, Robert Jay, Alan Jeffrey. BS, U. Ill., 1950; MS, Ill. Inst. Tech., 1956; PhD, Northwestern U., 1964. Prodn. supt. Richardson Co., Melrose Park, Ill., 1953-55; prodn. control mgr. Fed. Tool Corp., Lincolnwood, Ill., 1955-59; mgmt. cons. Booz, Allen & Hamilton, Chgo, 1959-60; mem. faculty Ill. Inst. Tech., Chgo, 1960-78, prof. mgmt., 1978; prof. mgmt., chair U. Ill.-Chgo., 1978—, head dept., dir. doctoral studies CBA, 1990-96; pres. Ill. Mgmt. Tng. Inst., 1975-77; mem. Ill. Gov. Adv. Coun. Employment and Tng., 1976-83, vice chmn., 1980-83; mem. NSF mission to Russia, 1979. Author: Manpower Planning, 1972, Personnel Management, 1982, Growing-Careers for Women, 1980, Introduction to Management, 1983, Career planning and Management, 1983, Planning for Human Resources, 1983, Creative Human Resource Planning, 1988, Career Management, 1990, Corporate Resurgence and the New Employment Relationships, 1993, Human Resource Planning, 3d edit., 1996. Served with USAAF, 1945-47. Research grantee Dept. Labor, 1965-68; recipient Alumni award for disting. svc. Coll. Bus. U. Ill., Chgo., 1996. Mem. Nat. Acad. Mgmt. (chmn. pers./human resource divsn. 1974-75, health divsn. 1978-79), Human Resource Mgmt. Assn. Chgo. (pres. 1974-75), Soc. Human Resource Mgmt., Pers. Accreditation Inst. (bd. dirs. 1978-89), Midwest Human Resource Planners Group (founding mem., bd. dirs. 1984-95), B'nai B'rith. Office: U Ill MC243 601 S Morgan St Rm 817 Chicago IL 60607-7100

BURACK, MICHAEL LEONARD, lawyer; b. Willimantic, Conn., Oct. 10, 1942; s. Meyer and Rose Ann (Kravitz) B.; m. Maria Gallego, Oct. 20, 1978; children: Victoria Luisa, Cristina Maria. BA summa cum laude, Wesleyan U., Middletown, Conn., 1964; postgrad. in physics, Calif. Inst. Tech., 1965; MS in Applied Physics, Stanford U., 1967, JD, 1970. Bar: Calif. 1971, D.C. 1972. Law clk. to judge U.S. Ct. Appeals for 9th Cir., San Francisco, 1970-71; assoc. Wilmer, Cutler & Pickering, Washington, 1971-77, ptnr., 1978—; mem. staff D.C. Jud. conf. Com. on Adminstrn. of Justice under Emergency Condition, 1972-73; mem. adv. com. govt. applications of ADR of Ctr. for Pub. Resources, 1988; mem. jud. evaluation com. D.C. Bar, 1991-94. Assoc. editor Jour. Pub. Contract Law, 1988-94. Mem. ABA, Order of the Coif, Phi Beta Kappa, Sigma Xi. Office: Wilmer Cutler & Pickering 2445 M St NW Ste 500 Washington DC 20037-1487

BURACK, SYLVIA KAMERMAN, editor, publisher; b. Hartford, Conn., Dec. 16, 1916; d. Abraham and Augusta (Chermak) Kamerman; BA magna cum laude, Smith Coll., 1938, LittD (hon.) Boston U., 1985; m. Abraham S. Burack, Nov. 28, 1940 (dec.); children: Elizabeth Biller Chapman, Susan (Mrs. Chad A. Finer), Ellen J.B. (Mrs. Franklin A. Toker). Editor, pub. Plays, The Drama Mag. for Young People, also The Writer Mag., 1978—. Mem. Brookline Sch. Com., 1949-69, Mass. Bd. Higher Edn., 1973-75; fellow Mass. Hist. Soc. Library; trustee Mass. State Coll. System, 1971-75, chmn., 1974-75; trustee U. Mass., 1975-81, Max C. Rosenfeld Scholarship Fund; mem. PEN Am. Ctr. Recipient Disting. Service award Brookline Rotary Club, 1973, Freedoms Found. award, 1988, Smith Coll. medal, 1995, Raven award Mystery Writers Am., 1998; Sylvia K. Burack Library, Brookline High Sch. named in her honor. Mem. Nat. Book Critics Circle, LWV, Friends of Library at Boston U. (pres. 1981-83, bd. dirs. 1991—), English Speaking Union (bd. dirs. Boston br. 1994-98), Phi Beta Kappa. Editor: Little Plays for Little Players, 1952; Blue Ribbon Plays for Girls, 1955; Blue Ribbon Plays for Graduation, 1957; A Treasury of Christmas Plays, 1958; Children's Plays from Favorite Stories, 1959; Fifty Plays for Junior Actors, 1966; Fifty Plays for Holidays, 1969; Dramatized Folk Tales of the World, 1971; On Stage for Christmas, 1978; Christmas Play Favorites for Young People, 1982; Holiday Plays Round the Year, 1983; Plays of Black Americans, 1987, 88; Patriotic and Historical Plays for Young People, 1987; Plays from Favorite Folk Tales, 1987; The Big Book of Comedies, 1989; The Big Book of Christmas Plays, 1988, The Big Book of Holiday Plays, 1990, The Big Book of Folktale Plays, 1991, Plays of Great Achievers, 1992, The Big Book of Dramatized Classics, 1993, The Big Book of Large-Cast Plays, 1995, The Big Book of Skits, 1996, Great American Events on Stage, 1996, 30 Plays from Favorite Stories, 1997; (adult) Writing the Short Short Story, 1942; Book Reviewing, 1978; The Writer's Handbook, 1999 and annually; Writing and Selling Fillers, Light Verse, and Short Humor, 1982; Writing and Selling the Romance Novel, 1983, Writing Mystery and Crime Fiction, 1985, How to Write and Sell Mystery Fiction, 1990, How to Write and Sell Your Article. Home: 72 Penniman Rd Brookline MA 02445-4137 Office: The Writer Inc 120 Boylston St Boston MA 02116-4615

BURACK, THOMAS S., lawyer; b. Boston, Apr. 2, 1960. AB, Dartmouth Coll., 1982; JD, U. Va., 1988. Legis. asst. U.S. Senator Gordon J. Humphrey, Washington, 1982-84; law clk. Justice David H. Souter, Concord, N.H., 1988-89; ptnr. Sheehan, Phinney, Bass and Green, Manchester, N.H., 1989—; chmn. Waste Cap Rsch. Con. Network, Concord, N.H., 1991—; vice chmn. N.H. Superfund Task Force, Concord, 1992-96. Cons. (book) Brownfields Law and Practice, 1998 (PPA award 1998). Chair N.H. Land and Comty. Heritage Commn., Concord, 1998—; bd. dirs. George C. Marshall Found., Lexington, Va., 1990—; pres., chmn. of bd. Truman Scholars Assn., Del., 1997—. Recipient Young Alumni Disting. Svc. award Dartmouth Alumni Coun., Hanover, 1997, Dartmouth Environ. Network award, 1997. Mem. Audubon Soc. N.H. (chmn. bd. dirs. 1994—). Republican. Avocations: storytelling, skiing, hiking. E-mail: tburack@sheehan.com. Office: Sheehan Phinney Bass & Green 1000 Elm St PO Box 3701 Manchester NH 31053-7010

BURAK, H(OWARD) PAUL, lawyer; b. N.Y.C., July 9, 1934; s. Harry and Bette (Hauer) B.; m. Edna K. Goodman, Oct. 18, 1970; children: Hally Ann., Jason Lewis. BS, Cornell U., 1954; LLB, Columbia U., 1957. Bar: N.Y. 1958, D.C. 1967, U.S. Dist. Ct. (so. and ea. dists.) N.Y. 1967, U.S. Ct. Appeals (2d cir.) 1960, U.S. Supreme Ct. 1964. Assoc. Cadwalader, Wickersham & Taft, N.Y.C., 1957-63; dep. asst., asst. gen. counsel Agy. for Internat. Devel. U.S. State Dept., Washington, 1963-67; assoc. Rosenman Colin Kay Petschek & Freund, N.Y.C., 1967-69; ptnr. Rosenman & Colin, N.Y.C., 1969—; bd. dirs. Sony Corp. Am., N.Y.C., Sony Music Entertainment, Inc., N.Y.C., Sony Pictures Entertainment, Inc., Culver City, Calif., Sony USA Found., N.Y.C. Rev. editor Columbia Law Rev., 1956-57; author pamphlets. Mem. ABA, Assn. of Bar of City of N.Y., Fed. Bar

Coun., N.Y. Bar Assn., Internat. Bar Assn., Univ. Club. Office: Rosenman & Colin 575 Madison Ave New York NY 10022-2585

BURAKOFF, STEVEN JAMES, immunologist, educator; b. N.Y.C., Oct. 13, 1942; s. Jack and Adelene (Van Praag) B.; m. Suzanne Weindling, Sept. 3, 1965; 1 child, Alexis. BA, Lehigh U., 1964; MA, Queens Coll., Flushing, N.Y., 1965; MD, Albany Med. Coll. Union U., 1970; MA (hon.), Harvard U., 1984. Diplomate Am. Bd. Internal Medicine. Intern, resident N.Y. Hosp., Cornell Med. Ctr., 1970-73.; instr. Harvard Med. Sch., Boston, 1976-77, asst. prof., 1977-80, assoc. prof., 1980-83, prof., 1983-98; chief pediat. oncology Dana Farber Cancer Inst., Boston, 1985—; Margaret M. Dyson prof. pediat. Harvard Med. Sch., Boston, 1998—; Ted Williams sr. investigator, Dana Farber Cancer Inst., Harvard Med. Sch., trustee; bd. dirs. The Med. Found. Contbr. over 300 articles to profl. jours. Recipient Sr. Faculty award Am. Cancer Soc., 1980-85. Mem. Am. Soc. Clin. Investigation, Am. Assn. Immunologists (head program com. 1985-86), Assn. Am. Physicians, Transplantation Soc. Office: Dana-Farber Cancer Inst Dept Pediatrics Harvard Med Sch 44 Binney St Boston MA 02115-6084

BURANDT, GARY EDWARD, advertising agency executive; b. Kansas City, Mo., Apr. 13, 1943; s. Herman Edward and Reka Lovice (Harrison) B.; m. Harriet Frances Krumrey, Aug. 12, 1966; children: Heather Lynn, Greta Anne. BJ, U. Mo., 1966. Advt. mgr. GE, Pittsfield, Mass., 1972-74; account supr. Marsteller Inc., Chgo., 1974-76; v.p., mgmt. supr. D'Arcy McManus & Masius, Chgo., 1976-77; sr. v.p. group dir. Marsteller Inc., Chgo., 1977-80; sr. v.p., gen. mgr. Marsteller, Brussels, 1981-84; exec. v.p., mktg. dir. Marsteller Europe, Brussels, 1984-85; exec. v.p., ops. mgr. Havas Conseil Marsteller, Paris, 1985-86; sr. v.p. group dir. Y & R Inc., N.Y.C., 1986-88; CEO Young & Rubicam/Sovero, Moscow, 1989-90; pres., CEO HDM Worldwide, N.Y.C., 1990-92, Dentsu, Young & Rubicam Partnerships, N.Y.C., 1990-96; exec. dir. Internat. Comm. Agy. Network, Rollinsville, Colo., 1998—. With USN, 1968-71. Recipient Disting. Svc. to Journalism medal U. Mo. Avocations: tennis, golf, skiing. Office: PO Box 159 Rollinsville CO 80474-0159

BURANELLI, VINCENT JOHN, writer; b. N.Y.C., Jan. 16, 1919; m. Agnes Wallace Gillespie, Oct. 31, 1952. BA, Nat. U. Ireland, Dublin, 1947, MA, 1948; PhD, Cambridge (Eng.) U., 1951. Writer Lowell Thomas News, N.Y.C., 1952-64, Am. Heritage, N.Y.C., 1965-66; writer, editor Gen. Learning, Time-Life Inc., N.Y.C., 1966-67; freelance writer, editor, book reviewer, 1967—; lectr. U.S. lit. Author: (biographies) Edgar Allan Poe, 1961, 2nd edit., 1977, Josiah Royce, 1964 (Best Biography of 1964, N.J. Authors), Louis XIV, 1966; (history) The Eighth Amendment, 1991; author: (with Nan Buranelli) Spy/Counterspy: An Encyclopedia of Espionage, 1982 (Best History of 1983, N.J. Authors). With U.S. Army, 1941-45. Kaltenborn fellow in journalism, N.Y.C., 1952-53. Mem. Authors Guild, Cambridge Union, Royal Dublin Soc. Home: 866 Denbigh Blvd Apt 302 Newport News VA 23608-4436

BURATTI, DENNIS P., lawyer; b. Madison, Wis., 1949. JD, U. Wis., 1973. Bar: Wis. 1973, Minn. 1973. Gen. counsel Ryan Cos., Mpls. Office: Ryan Companies 700 Internat Ctr 900 2nd Ave S Minneapolis MN 55402-3314*

BURBANK, JANE RICHARDSON, Russian and European studies educator; b. Hartford, Conn., June 11, 1946; d. John and Helen Lee (West) B.; m. Frederick Cooper, Sept. 3, 1985. BA, Reed Coll., 1967; MLS, Simmons Coll., 1969; MA, Harvard U., 1971, PhD, 1981. Asst. prof. Harvard U., Cambridge, Mass., 1981-85; asst. prof. U. Calif., Santa Barbara, 1985-86, assoc. prof., 1986-87; assoc. prof. U. Mich., Ann Arbor, 1987-95; prof., 1995—; reviewer Kritika, 1983, Russian Rev., 1984, 98, Am. Hist. Rev., 1988, 91, 96, Jour. Modern History, 1989, 92, 94, Slavic Rev., 1990, Harvard Ukrainian Studies, 1991; presenter in field; dir. ctr. Russian E. European studies U. Mich., 1992-95. Author: Intelligentsia and Revolution: Russian Views of Bolshevism, 1917-1922, 1986; editor: Perestroika and Soviet Culture, 1989, Imperial Russia, New Historic for the Empire, 1998; editor Kritika, 1978-80; mem. editl. bd. Ind.-Mich. Series in Russian and East European Studies; contbr. articles to profl. jours. Fulbright-Hayes Rsch. award, 1991, Sheldon Traveling fellow Harvard U., 1977-78, Krupp Found. fellow, Ctr. for European Studies, Harvard U., 1977-78, AAUW fellow, 1980-81, Whiting fellow, 1980-81, Am. Coun. Learned Socs. fellow, 1983-84, Hoover Inst. Postdoctoral fellow, 1990-91; grantee NEH, 1984, 97, Harvard U., 1982-84, Internat. Rsch. and Exchs. Bd., Acad. Exch. with the USSR, 1987-88, 91, Fulbright-Hays, 1991, U. Mich., 1990, 91, 93, 94, 97. Mem. Am. Hist. Assn., Am. Assn. for the Advancement of Slavic Studies, Social Sci. Rsch. Coun. (joint com. on Soviet studies 1988-93), Nat. Coun. for Erosion and East European Rsch., Phi Beta Kappa. Office: Dept History U Mich 1029 Tisch Hall Ann Arbor MI 48109

BURBANK, JOHN THORN, entrepreneur; b. St. Paul, Sept. 18, 1939; s. Richard Hart and Rae (Parkins) B.; divorced; children: Jennifer, Leslie, Betsy. Student, U. Minn., 1957-62. V.p. Burbank Burns, Mpls., 1963-65, Twin City Index, Mpls., 1965-68, Pentagon Corp., Mpls., 1968-72, AS Industries, Mpls., 1972-78; pres. Minn. Graphics, Mpls., 1978-84; v.p. Graphics Unltd., Mpls., 1984-87, Perfection Graphics, Mpls., 1987-90; pres. Burbank Svcs., Inc., Edina, Minn., 1990—; mem. adv. bd. Dakota County Votech, Rosemount, Minn., 1982-91. Nation officer YMCA Indian Princess, Bloomington, Minn., 1975; pres. PTA, Bloomington, 1970; coach Traveling Youth Hockey, Bloomington, 1970-84. With USNR, 1961-63. Mem. Internat. Typesetting Assn. (regional pres. 1976-77, program chmn. 1975, 76). Episcopalian. Avocations: tennis, walking, reading, computers, music. Home and Office: 5126 Lincoln Dr # 208 Edina MN 55436

BURBANK, KERSHAW, writer; b. Flushing, N.Y., Jan. 1, 1914; s. Robert Abraham and Lillian Cassels (DuBose) B.; m. Elizabeth E. Hapworth, Mar. 1942 (div.); children: Kershaw Jr., Thorne Burbank Taylor; m. Sally Page Williams Crawford, May 30, 1951 (div.); m. Barbara Bennett, Dec. 16, 1961 (dec. Jan. 1985); 1 child, Bennett. BA, Yale U., 1937. Accredited pub. rels. profl. Unitman MGM Studios, Culver City, Calif., 1937-39; asst. to v.p. 20th Century-Fox Film Corp., N.Y., Calif., 1941-44; dir. nat. promotion Richard Condon Inc., N.Y.C., 1945; sr. ptnr. Burbank Assocs., N.Y.C., 1945-48; dir. pub. info. Colonial Williamsburg (Va.), Inc., 1948-51; advisor pub. affairs Office of the Rockefeller Family, N.Y.C., 1951-61; v.p., sec. Channel 13 Ednl. Broadcasting Corp., N.Y.C., 1961-65; exec. v.p., dir. Infoplan Internat., N.Y.C., 1965-69; mng. dir. Weightman Assocs., Phila., 1969-74; v.p. The Franklin Inst., Phila., 1974-79; cons. Sleepy Hollow Restorations, Tarrytown, N.Y., 1961-64, 69-74, Palisades Interstate Pkwy., N.Y., N.J., 1961-64. Author: A Pleasant Land to See, 1973; contbr. articles to nat. mags. Trustee Elsie Lee Garthwaite Meml. Found., Rosemont, Pa., 1970—, CRC Found., Delray Beach, Fla., 1990-94, Woodhaven Found., Gulf Stream, Fla., 1998—; bd. dirs. Crossroads Club (non-profit orgn.), Delray Beach, 1988-90, Bethesda Hosp. Assn., Delray Beach, 1983-85; chmn. Coalition of Pa. Museums, 1979-80. Episcopalian. Avocations: photography, reading, travel. Home: 125 MacFarlane Dr Delray Beach FL 33483-6803

BURBANK, NELSON STONE, investment banker; b. Winchester, Mass., Sept. 16, 1920; s. Willis H. and Vivian (Casson) B.; m. Rita B. Healey, Feb. 12, 1950; children: Peter N., Nelson Stone, Jane Vivian. Student, Boston U., 1946-47. Registered rep. Vance, Sanders & Co., Inc., Boston, 1946-53; pres. Burbank & Co., Inc., Boston, 1953-83; dir., registered rep. A.G. Edwards and Sons, Inc., 1982-83; pres., bd. dirs. Colonial Investment Services, Inc., 1983-85; bd. dirs. MassBank for Savs., Reading, ret., 1994; bd. govs. Boston Stock Exch., 1965-73, vice chmn., 1968-71, chmn., 1971-73. Vice chmn. ARC, 1963-82; treas., dir. Reading Ice Arena Authority, Inc. With AUS, 1942-45. Decorated D.F.C., Air medals. Mem. Nat. Assn. Securities Dealers (mem. bus. conduct com. 1971-73, gov. 1974-77, cons 1985-88). Home and Office: 24 Juniper Cir Reading MA 01867-1836

BURBANK, ROBINSON DERRY, crystallographer; b. Berlin, N.H., Oct. 3, 1921; s. Paul William and Hazel Louise (Robinson) B.; m. Jeannette Murielle Bisson, July 14, 1945 (div. 1975); children: Paul Robinson, Claudia Olive. BA, Colby Coll., 1942; PhD, MIT, 1950. Rsch. asst. Manhattan Project, MIT, Cambridge, 1942-45, Lab. Insulation Rsch., MIT, 1945-50; sr. physicist Gaseous Diffusion Plant, Oak Ridge, Tenn., 1950-53; group leader, crystallography Olin Industries, New Haven, Conn., 1953-55; tech. staff Bell Telephone Labs., Murray Hill, N.J., 1955-86; U.S. del. Internat. Union Crystallography, Stony Brook, L.I., N.Y., 1969, Amsterdam, 1975; mem. U.S.A. Nat. Com. Crystallography, 1968-76. Contbr. technical papers to profl. jours. Bd. dirs. Chester Twp. Taxpayers Assn., N.J., 1961-65, 70-74, pres. 1973. Mem. AAAS, Am. Crystallographic Assn. (treas. 1965-68, v.p. 1974, pres. 1975), Com. Sci. Soc. Presidents, Phi Beta Kappa, Sigma Xi. Achievements include X-ray crystallography of inorganic compounds, interhalogen compounds, noble gas compounds, phase transformations, thin films. Home: 45 Woodland Ave Summit NJ 07901-2141

BURBANK, STEPHEN BRADNER, law educator; b. N.Y.C., Jan. 8, 1947; s. John Howard and Jean (Gedney) B.; m. Ellen Randolph Coolidge, June 13, 1970; 1 child, Peter Jefferson. AB, Harvard U., 1968, JD, 1973. Bar: Mass. 1973, Pa. 1976, U.S. Supreme Ct. 1977. Law clk. Supreme Jud. Ct. of Mass., Boston, 1973-74, Chief Justice Warren Burger, Washington, 1974-75; gen. counsel U. Pa., Phila., 1975-80, asst. prof. law, 1979-83, assoc. prof. law, 1983-86, prof. law, 1986—, Fuller prof. law, 1991-95; Berger prof. law, 1995—; reporter 3d Cir. Jud. Discipline Rules, Phila., 1981-82, 84, 3d Cir. Task Force on Rule 11, Phila., 1987-89; mem. Nat. Commn. on Jud. Discipline and Removal, 1991-93; mediator, arbitrator Ctr. for Pub. Resources, New York, 1986—; cons. Dechert, Price & Rhoads, Phila., 1986—; mem. CPR Arbitration Commn., 1997—. Mem. Com. to Visit Harvard and Radcliffe Coll., Cambridge, Mass., 1979-85; mem. adv. bd. Inst. Contemporary Art, Phila., 1982—; charter trustee Phillips Acad., Andover, Mass., 1980-97. Mem. Am. Law Inst. (adviser transnational rules of civil procedure 1997—), Am. Arbitration Assn. (panel of arbitrators 1985—), Century Assn., Am. Jud. Soc. (exec. com., v.p. 1997—), Phi Beta Kappa. Avocations: swimming, travel, tennis. Office: U Pa Sch Law 3400 Chestnut St Philadelphia PA 19104-6204

BURBANO, FERNANDO, federal agency administrator. BA in Applied Behavioral Sci., Louis U.; MPA, Am. U., 1995; MS in Info. Resources Mgmt., Syracuse U., 1998. V.p. tech. svcs. Advance Mgmt. inc., 1987-90; dir. office Info. Resources Mgmt. Peace Corps, Washington, 1990-93; dir. computer and comms., dir. info. sys. Nat. Libr. Medicine NIH, Bethesda, Md., 1993-98; chief info. officer Bur. Info. Resource and Mgmt., Dept. State, Washington, 1998—. Recipient Peace Corps Svc. award, 1992, Merit award NIH, 1996, SES award NLM, 1996. Fax: (202) 647-2294. Office: Dept State Office Chief Info Officer 2201 C St NW Rm 6313 Washington DC 20520

BURBICK, JOAN, English educator; b. Chgo., June 20, 1946; d. Michael and Eileen Burbick; 1 child, Claire Burbick Huntsberry. BA, Boston Coll., 1968; MA, Brandeis U., 1969, PhD, 1974; MA, Wesleyan U., Middleton, Conn., 1976. Asst. prof. Wash. State U., Pullman, 1978-83, assoc. prof., 1983-88, prof. English, 1988—, Edward R. Meyer prof., 1996—; vis. prof. U. Colo., Boulder, 1988-89. Author: Thoreau's Alternative History, 1987, Healing the Republic, 1994; mem. adv. bd. Legacy jour., 1985—; mem. editl. bd. ESQ jour., 1978—; contbr. articles, essays, revs. to profl. jours. (Foerster award Am. Lit. 1986). Andrew Mellon fellow Ctr. for Humanities, Wesleyan U., 1976-77, Martha Sutton Weeks fellow Stanford U. Humanities Ctr., 1987-88; recipient Norman Foerster award MLA/Am. Lit. assn., 1986. Mem. Pacific N.W. Am. Studies Assn. (v.p., pres. 1980's). Avocation: photography. Office: Wash State U English Dept Pullman WA 99164-5020

BURBIDGE, E. MARGARET, astronomer, educator; b. Davenport, Eng.; d. Stanley John and Marjorie (Stott) Peachey; m. Geoffrey Burbidge, Apr. 2, 1948; 1 child, Sarah. B.S., Ph.D., U. London; Sc.D. hon., Smith Coll., 1963, U. Sussex, 1970, U. Bristol, 1972, U. Leicester, 1972, City U., 1973, U. Mich., 1978, U. Mass., 1978, Williams Coll., 1979, SUNY, Stony Brook, 1985, Rensselaer Poly. Inst., 1986, U. Notre Dame, 1986, U. Chgo., 1991. Mem. staff U. London Obs., 1948-51; rsch. fellow Yerkes Obs. U. Chgo., 1951-53, Shirley Farr fellow Yerkes obs., 1957-59, assoc. prof. Yerkes Obs., 1959-62; rsch. fellow Calif. Inst. Tech., Pasadena, 1955-57; mem. Enrico Fermi Inst. for Nuclear Studies, 1957-62; prof. astronomy dept. physics U. Calif. San Diego, 1964—; dir. Royal Greenwich Obs. (Herstmonceux Castle), Hailsham, Eng., 1971-73; univ. prof. U. Calif., San Diego, 1984-91, prof. emeritus, 1991—, rsch. prof. dept. physics, 1990—; Lindsay Meml. lectr. Goddard Space Flight Ctr., NASA, 1985; Abby Rockefeller Mauze prof. MIT, 1968; David Elder lectr. U. Strathclyde, 1972; V. Gildersleeve lectr. Barnard Coll., 1974; Jansky lectr. Nat. Radio Astronomy Observatory, 1977; Brode lectr. Whitman Coll., 1986. Author: (with G. Burbidge) Quasi-Stellar Objects, 1967; editor: Observatory mag., 1948-51; mem. editorial bd.: Astronomy and Astrophysics, 1969-85. Recipient (with husband) Warner prize in Astronomy, 1959, Bruce Gold medal Astronomy Soc. Pacific, 1982; hon. fellow Univ. Coll., London, Girton Coll., Lucy Cavendish Coll., Cambridge; U.S. Nat. medal of sci., 1984; Sesquicentennial medal Mt. Holyoke Coll., 1987, Einstein medal World Cultural Coun., 1988. Fellow Royal Soc., Nat. Acad. Scis. (chmn. sect. 12 astronomy 1986), Am. Acad. Arts and Scis., Royal Astron. Soc.; mem. Am. Astron. Soc. (v.p. 1972-74, pres. 1976-78; Henry Norris Russell lectr. 1984), Internat. Astron. Union (pres. commn. 28 1970-73), Grad. Women Sci. (nat. hon. mem.). Office: U Calif-San Diego Ctr Astrophysics Space Scis Mail Code # 0424 La Jolla CA 92093

BURBIDGE, GEOFFREY, astrophysicist, educator; b. Chipping Norton, Oxon, Eng., Sept. 24, 1925; s. Leslie and Eveline Burbidge; m. Margaret Peachey, 1948; 1 dau. B.Sc. with spl. honors in Physics, Bristol U., 1946; Ph.D., U. Coll., London, 1951. Asst. lectr. U. Coll., London, 1950-51; Agassiz fellow Harvard, 1951-52; research fellow U. Chgo., 1952-53, Cavendish Lab., Cambridge, Eng., 1953-55; Carnegie fellow Mt. Wilson and Palomar Obs., Calif. Inst. Tech., 1955-57; asst. prof. dept. astronomy U. Chgo., 1957-58, assoc. prof., 1958-62; assoc. prof. U. Calif. San Diego, La Jolla, 1962-63; prof. physics U. Calif. San Diego, 1963-83, 88—; dir. Kitt Peak Nat. Obs., Tucson, 1978-84; Phillips vis. prof. Harvard U., 1968; bd. dirs. Associated Univs. Research in Astronomy, 1971-74; trustee Associated Univs., Inc., 1973-82. Author: (with Margaret Burbidge) Quasi-Stellar Objects, 1967; editor Ann. Rev. Astronomy and Astrophysics, 1973—; sci. editor Astrophys. Jour., 1996—; contbr. articles to sci. jours. Fellow Royal Soc. London, Am. Acad. Arts and Scis., Royal Astron. Soc., Am. Phys. Soc.; mem. Am. Astron. Soc., Internat. Astron. Union, Astron. Soc. of Pacific (pres. 1974-76). Office: U Calif-San Diego 0424 Ctr Astrophysics Space Scis La Jolla CA 92093

BURBRIDGE, ANN ARNOLD, elementary school educator, music educator; b. Galesburg, Ill., Sept. 13, 1947; d. Adis Michael and Janet Louise (Frymire) Arnold; m. Robert Arthur Burbridge, June 27, 1970; children: Britt, Michael, Mark. BMEd, Augustana Coll., 1969; MMEd, Tex. Tech. U., 1987, postgrad.; Kodaly cert. levels 1, 2 and 3, Silver Lake Coll., 1990; advanced Kodaly cert., U. North Tex., 1993; postgrad., Tex. Tech U.; Choral Music Experience level I cert., London; Choral Music Experience level II cert., No. Ill. U., 1995, Choral Music Experience level III cert., 1996, Choral Music Experience level IV cert., 1997, Choral Music Experience artist-tchr., 1998. Cert. music tchr, MENC. Tchr. Washington Jr. High Sch., Chicago Heights, Ill., 1969-70, Magnolia Sch., Valdosta, Ga., 1970-71; music tchr. Mountain Home AFB (Idaho) Presch. and Kindergarten, 1971-82, Christ the King Cathedral Sch., Lubbock, Tex., 1982-84; tchr. music Nat Williams Elem. Sch. Lubbock Ind. Sch. Dist., 1997—; music instr. Lubbock Christian U., 1997—; mem. campus performance objectives com., author curriculum materials for elem. music; dist. mentor; scorer Tex. Master Tchr. Exam.; fine arts team writer Tex. Edn. Agy., Tex. Essential Knowledge and Skills: Web. Resources & Texas Curriculum, Tex. Edn. Network; founder, artistic dir. Lubbock Children's Choir; clinician/presenter in field; author, cons. Glencoe McGraw Hill Pub. Co. Author: Fundamentals of Music, 1987; author, cons. Silver Burdett Ginn Publ. Co. Bd. mem. Llano Estacado Friends of Piano Found. Recipient Disting. Svc. award Lubbock Jaycees, Innovative Teaching Strategy award, LISD. Mem. Am. Choral Dirs. Assn., Orgn. Am. Kodaly Educators, Music Educators Nat. Conf. (nat. registered and cert.), Kodaly Educators Tex., Tex. Music Educators Assn. (state chair elem. music 1995-97, past region XVI chair), Tex. Classroom Tchrs. Assn. (rep.), Lubbock Elem. Music Tchrs. Assn. (treas.), Choristers Guild, Tex. Music Educators Conf. (state pres. elect), Tex. Coalition Music Advocacy (state pres.), Phi Delta Kappa (past v.p. programs and del. Llano Estacado chpt.).

BURCAT, JOEL ROBIN, lawyer; b. Phila., Oct. 28, 1954; s. David Sidney and Jessie (Goldberg) B.; m. Gail Rene Hartman, May 30, 1982; children: Dina Michelle, Shira Elizabeth. Student, Temple U., 1972-73; BS, Pa. State U., 1976; JD, Vt. Law Sch., 1980. Bar: Pa. 1980, U.S. Dist. Ct. (mid. dist.) Pa. 1980, U.S. Dist. Ct. (we. dist.) Pa. 1988, U.S. Dist. Ct. (ea. dist.) Pa. 1993, U.S. Ct. Appeals (3d cir.) 1981, U.S. Supreme Ct. 1984. Asst. atty. gen. Pa. Dept. Environ. Resources, Harrisburg, 1980-83; assoc. Rhoads & Sinon, Harrisburg, 1983-88; assoc. Kirkpatrick & Lockhart, Harrisburg, 1988-91, ptnr., 1992—; spl. counsel Pa. Senate Com. on Environ. Resources and Energy, Harrisburg, 1986-87; gen. counsel Nat. Wilderness Inst., Washington, 1991-93; mem. rules com. Pa. Environ. Hearing Bd., 1984-88. Author, editor: Pennsylvania Environmental Law and Practice, 1994, 2nd edit., 1999, also supplements; contbr. articles to environ. topics to profl. jours., chpts. to books. Trustee United Jewish Cmty., Harrisburg, 1991-94, v.p., 1996-97; v.p. Yeshiva Acad. Harrisburg, 1986-96, pres., 1996-97; dir. Friends of State of Pa., 1999—. Mem. ABA (mem. standing com. environ. law 1979-80, law student liaison), Pa. Bar Assn. (sec. environ. mineral and natural resource law sect. 1990-91, vice chmn. 1991-92, chmn. 1992-93, ethics com. 1984-97, Spl. Achievement award 1993, cert. of recognition 1994). Republican. Jewish. Avocations: guitar playing, classical music, jogging, hiking, gardening. Office: Kirkpatrick & Lockhart 240 N 3d St Harrisburg PA 17101-1503

BURCH, ANNETTA JANE, writer; b. Valdosta, Ga., Feb. 10, 1947; d. James Louie and Ethel Lucille (Padgett) B.; m. J.D. Barnes. Student, N. Fla. Jr. Coll., Madison, Cen. Fla. C.C., Lecanto. Activity dir. Concordia Manor, Inc., St. Petersburg, Fla., 1983-84; rsch. clk. St. Petersburg Times, 1987; columnist Tampa Tribune, Citrus County, Fla., 1994-96; activity dir. Sugarmill Manor, Inc., Homosassa, Fla., 1990-92; dir. resident svcs. Barrington Place, Lecanto, Fla., 1992-94; office mgr. Boys and Girls Club, Crystal River, Fla., 1995-96; mem. Citrus County Code Enforcment Bd., vice chmn., 1998. Former amb. Citrus County and Homosassa Springs Area Chambers; officer Friends of Beverly Hills Libr., 1994; mem. com. Ctrl. Fla. Symphony, 1994; vol. writer for various clubs and orgns. for local newspapers; active Crystal River United Meth. Ch., Fla.; sec. Nature Coast Rep. Club, 1996, pres. 1997, 99; vol. spl. events; numerous other activities. Recipient Disting. Svc. award Fla. Rep. Party, 1998. Mem. Homosassa Springs Area C. of C. (bd. dirs. 1998—), Manatee Sertoma Club (charter mem., officer), Young Reps. Club of Citrus County (co-founder). Avocations: travel, writing, reading. Home: PO Box 1095 Homosassa Springs FL 34447-1095

BURCH, BARBARA JEAN, special education educator, administrator; b. Seattle, Dec. 16, 1948; d. Robert and Jean Frances (Richards) Griesbach; m. John Mitchell Burch, Aug. 2, 1975; children: Adam John, Joshua Robert. BA, U. Wash., 1973; MEd, Idaho State U., 1978. Cert. tchr., Alaska. Substitute educator Seattle Sch. Dist. 1, 1972-73; edn. educator Butte County Sch. Dist. 111, Arco, Idaho, 1973-76, Pocatello (Idaho) Sch. Dist. 1, 1977-86; educator Fairbanks (Alaska) Northstar Borough Schs., 1986—, dir. spl. edn., 1995-98; prin. Nordale Elem. Sch., Fairbainks, 1998—; instr. in continuing edn. U. Alaska, Fairbanks, 1986-87. Mem. ASCD, Coun. for Exceptional Children (pres. 1987-88, 90-91), Internat. Reading Assn., S.E. Idaho Coun. (treas. 1985-86), Golden Heart Reading Coun. (treas. 1987-91), NEA, Am. Fedn. Tchrs. (pres. Pocatello chpt. 1984-86), Phi Delta Kappa. Avocations: sewing, crafts, cooking. Home: 891 Gold Mine Trl Fairbanks AK 99712-2070 Office: Nordale Elem Sch 20 Eureka Ave Fairbanks AK 99701

BURCH, BRIDGETTE, press secretary City of Rochester, New York. BA, Fisk U., 1981; MS, U. Syracuse, 1982. Pub. rels. mgr. B/L B/S, Rochester, N.Y., 1990-93; press sec. City of Rochester, 1994—. Bd. dirs. Art and Cultural Coun., Rochester, YWCA, Rochester. Mem. Urban League of Rochester, Urban League Guild. Office: Comm Bur City Hall 30 Church St Rm 202A Rochester NY 14614-1290*

BURCH, CLAIRE RITA, writer; b. N.Y.C., Feb. 19, 1925; d. Albert I. and Dorothy (Denhoff) Cohen; m. Bradley A. Burch, Apr. 24, 1944 (dec. 1967); children: Laurie, Emily, Elizabeth. BA, Washington Square Coll., N.Y.C., 1947. Editor, writer N.Y.C., 1947-50; freelance writer, 1950-68; adj. prof. Union of Experimenting Colls., Antioch, N.Y., 1970-73; editor, freelance writer various nat. mags., N.Y.C., 1974-78; contbg. editor No. Calif. Psychiat. Network News, Berkeley, 1978-83; mng. editor No. Calif. Network News, Berkeley, 1983—; exec. dir. Art and Edn. Media Inc., Berkeley; conducted numerous workshops in field. Author: Stranger in the Family, 1972, You Be the Mother Follies, 1985, Goodbye My Coney Island Baby, 1988, Solid Gold Illusion, 1988, Shredded Millions, 1988, Homeless in the Nineties, 1990, Stranger on the Planet: The Small Book of Lauria; filmmaker (documentaries) The James Baldwin Anthology, Entering Oakland (People's Choice award), Alfonia (People's Choice award), Thumbed a Ride to Heaven, Baby Don't Cry, Oracle Rising, People's Park Then and Now, Street Survivors, The Telegraph Ave., Street Calendar Live, Remembering the Summer of Love, Ghost of the S.F. Oracle Meets Tim Leary; author (folk opera) Its' a Blues to Be Called Crazy When Crazy's All There Is; assoc. prodr. (film) Tim Leary's Dead, 1997. Recipient Andrew Carnegie award, 1981; grantee Ctr. for Ind. Living, 1989, City of Berkeley, 1989, 90, 91, Calif. Arts Coun., 1991, 92, 93, Seva Found., 1996. Home: 2747 Regent St Berkeley CA 94705-1212 Office: Art and Edn Media Inc 2747 Regent St Berkeley CA 94705-1212

BURCH, FRANCIS BOUCHER, JR., lawyer; b. Balt., Feb. 27, 1948; s. Francis Boucher and Mary Patricia (Howe) B.; m. Mary Ann Podesta, June 24, 1972; children: Sara E., Francis B. III, Michael F. Student, U. Fribourg, Switzerland, 1968-69; BA, Georgetown U., 1970; JD with honors, U. Md., 1974. Bar: Md. 1974, U.S. Ct. Appeals (4th cir.) 1975, U.S. Supreme Ct. 1994. Assoc. litigation dept. Piper & Marbury LLP, Balt., 1974-81, ptnr. litigation dept., 1981—, mem. policy and mgmt. com., 1986-93, chmn. litigation dept., 1991-94, chmn., 1994—. Contbr. articles to profl. jours. Bd. dirs. Greater Balt. Com., 1996—, vice-chmn., 1998—, mem. Leadership Program, 1990—, bd. dirs., 1993-98, vice-chmn., 1994-96, chmn., 1996-98, chmn. selection com., 1994-95, mem. pub. policy coun.; trustee Calvert Sch., 1989—, exec. com., 1991—, curriculum and pers. com., 1991—, chmn., 1991-95, sec., 1991-95; trustee Western Md. Coll., 1996—, Johns Hopkins Health Sys. Corp., 1994-96, , Johns Hopkins Hosp., 1994-96, Johns Hopkins Medicine, 1996—, Balt. Mus. Art., 1990-96, 98—, mem. exec. com., 1991-96, chmn. ann. giving com., 1991-93, treas., 1992-94, v.p., 1994-96, co-chmn. devel., 1994-96; bd. visitors U. Md. Sch. Law, Balt., 1993—, U. Md., 1995—; fundraising com. Coll. Bound Found., Balt., 1991; bd. dirs. Dome Corp., 1995—; campaign cabinet, chmn. emerging markets United Way Ctrl. Md., 1994; chmn. Leadership Giving, 1999. With U.S. Army N.G., 1970-76. Fellow Am. Bar Found., Am. Coll. Trial Lawyers, Md. Bar Found.; mem. ABA, Am. Law Inst., Md. Bar Assn. (Disting. Svc. award litigation sect. 1981), Balt. City Bar Assn. (chmn. jud. appts. com. 1990-91, exec. coun. 1990-91), 4th Cir. Jud. Conf., Rule Day Club, Lawyers' Round Table Balt., Center Club, Md. Club, Balt. Country Club. Democrat. Roman Catholic. Avocations: skiing, surfing. Office: Piper & Marbury LLP 36 S Charles St Baltimore MD 21201-3020

BURCH, FRANCIS FLOYD, clergyman, English educator; b. Balt., May 15, 1932; s. Thaddeus Joseph and Frances Fidelis (Greenwell) B. BA, Fordham U., 1956, MA, 1958; PhL, Woodstock Coll., 1957, STL, 1964; postgrad., Tronchinnes, Belgium, 1964-65; Docteur, U. Paris, Sorbonne, 1967. Joined Soc. of Jesus, 1950, ordained priest Roman Catholic Ch., 1963. Tchr. Gonzaga H.S., Washington, 1957-60; asst. prof. St. Joseph's U., Phila., 1967-71, assoc. prof., 1971-76, prof. English, 1976—, asst. acad. dean, 1972-74, bd. dirs., 1971-76, sec. bd. dirs., 1971-75; artist-scholar-in-residence Millersville State Coll., Pa., 1978. Author: Tristan Corbiere: l'originalite des "Amours jaunes" et leur influence sur T.S. Eliot, 1970; editor: (with P.O. Walzer) Tristan Corbiere: Oeuvres completes, 1970, Sur Tristan Corbiere: lettres inedites adressees au poete et premieres critiques le concernant, 1975; translator: The Path to Transcendence: From Philosophy to Mysticism in Saint Augustine (Paul Henry), 1981, The Personalist Challenge: Intersubjectivity and Ontology (Maurice Nedoncelle), 1984; contbr. articles to profl. jours. Recipient Merit award St. Joseph's U., 1980, 83. Mem. MLA, Internat. Soc. Neoplatonic Studies, Alpha Epsilon Delta, Alpha Sigma Nu. Home and office: 5600 City Ave Philadelphia PA 19131-1308

BURCH, HAMLIN DOUGHTY, III, retired sheet metal professional; b. Oakland, Calif., June 14, 1939; s. Hamlin D. Burch II and Bernice I. (Ingerski) Bortscheller; m. Zettie A. Honeycutt, Nov. 16, 1957 (div. 1974); children: Paula Christine Grothaus, Victoria Jaylee Alberti, Hamlin D. IV. Grad., Modesto (Calif.) High Sch. Sheet metal worker Fred L. Hill., Modesto, 1960-62, Olson's Plumbing, Turlock, 1962-64, Hansen's Inc., Modesto, 1964-74; Lang's Engerprises, Modesto, 1974-87; sheet metal worker Mendenhall, Sacramento, 1987, South Valley Mech., San Juan Baptiste, 1987-88, Brott Mech., Tulare, 1988; ret. Brott Mech. Mem. Sheet Metal Workers Internat. Assn., Nat. Rifle Assn., Wilderness Soc., Nat. Park and Conservation Assn., Nat. Wildlife Fedn., Calif. State Parks Found. Republican. Mem. LDS Ch. Avocations: metal working, wood working, gardening, fishing, camping.

BURCH, JAMES LEO, science research institute executive; b. San Antonio, Nov. 28, 1942; s. Joseph Leo Jr. and Doris Babette (Hagy) B.; m. Kathleen Marie Dowdy, Dec. 30, 1965; children: Angela Marie, Charles Joseph, Kenneth James. BS in Physics, St. Mary's U., San Antonio, 1964; PhD, Rice U., 1968; MS in Adminstrn., George Washington U., 1973. Space physicist Goddard Space Flight Ctr. NASA, Greenbelt, Md., 1971-74; space physicist Marshall Space Flight Ctr. NASA, Huntsville, Ala., 1974-77; sr. rsch. physicist S.W. Rsch. Inst., San Antonio, 1977-78, sect. mgr., 1978-80, dept. dir., 1980-85, v.p., 1985—; prin. investigator NASA Dynamics Explorer Mission, 1978-92, Nasa Atlas Shuttle Mission, 1989-93, ESA Rosetta Comet orbiter, 1996—, NASA Image Midex mission, 1996—; mem. space sci. and applications adv. com. NASA, 1990-93. Assoc. editor Jour. Geophys. Rsch., 1977-79, 94—, Geophys. Rsch. Letters, 1978-82, editor, 1989-90, editor-in-chief, 1990-93; contbr. numerous articles to profl. jours. Mem. adv. bd. St. Mary's U., 1987—. Capt. U.S. Army, 1968-71. Recipient Disting. Alumnus award St. Mary's U., 1987. Fellow Am. Geophys. Union (pres. space physics and aeronomy sect.), Internat. Acad. Astronautics. Roman Catholic. Avocation: running. Office: SW Rsch Inst 6220 Culebra Rd San Antonio TX 78238-5100

BURCH, JOHN CHRISTOPHER, JR., investment banker; b. Nashville, Jan. 18, 1940; s. John Christopher and Frances Vivian (Harris) B.; m. Susan Marie Klein, Sept. 13, 1969; children: Frances Marie, Christina Polk, John Christopher III. BA, Vanderbilt U., 1966. Credit analyst Bank N.Y., N.Y.C., 1966-70; v.p. instl. sales Loeb Rhoades & Co., N.Y.C., 1970-75, J.C. Bradford & Co., Nashville, 1976-82; mng. dir. SunTrust Equitable Securities Corp., Nashville, 1982—. Active Com. Fgn. Relations, Nashville, 1976, N.C. Soc. Cin., Raleigh, 1979. With U.S. Army, 1962-65. Mem. Nashville Security Dealers Assn., Assn. Investment Mgmt. and Rsch., Securities Industry Assn. (chair syndicate com. 1999, bd. dirs. so. dist.), Belle Meade Country Club, Cumberland Club (Nashville). Episcopalian. Fax: 615-780-4171. E-mail: jburch@equisec.com. Home: 705 Hillwood Blvd Nashville TN 37205-1315 Office: SunTrust Equitable Securities Corp Nashville City Ctr 511 Union St Ste 800 Nashville TN 37219-1743

BURCH, JOHN RUSSELL, JR., technical services librarian; b. Peoria, Ill., Mar. 22, 1968; s. John Russell and Idalia Amparo (Murgas) B.; m. Samantha Jo Bailey, July 1, 1989; children: Morgan Lourrae, Alexandra Christine, Christopher Simpson. BA in History, Berea (Ky.) Coll., 1990; MS in Libr. Sci., U. Ky., 1992. Grad. asst. U. Ky. Agrl. Libr., Lexington, 1991-92; govt. documents libr. So. Ark. U., Magnolia, 1992-93; reference libr. Cumberland Coll., Williamsburg, Ky., 1993-95, pub. svcs. libr., 1995, tech. svcs. libr., 1995—; book reviewer Libr. Jour., Am. Ref. Books Ann., Choice Mag., LIBRES e-jour. Mem. ASCUE, Phi Alpha Theta. Republican. Home: 173 Hutton Dr Williamsburg KY 40769-1620 Office: Cumberland Coll Hagan Libr 821 Walnut St Williamsburg KY 40769-1338

BURCH, JOHN WALTER, mining equipment company executive; b. Balt., July 14, 1925; s. Louis Claude and Constance (Boucher) B. m. Robin Neely Sinkler, Apr. 19, 1952; children: John C., Robert L., Charles C., Anne N. *Great-great-great uncle Francois Boucher was Court Painter for Louis XV; paintings on display at The Louvre and other major galleries. Mother Constance B. Burch was Poet Laureate, Baltimore, Maryland. Brother Francis B. Burch was Attorney General of Maryland for 12 years. Brother Capt. Charles A. Burch, United States Navy, was recipient of Bronze Star and Legion of Merit during World War II. Sons John C. and Robert L. Burch founded major sportswear company Eagle Eye, Inc. Son Charles C. Burch is President and C.O.O. of Burch Materials Company, Inc., supplier of equipment to aggregate and steel industries. Daughter Ann Burch Hayes is humanitarian.* BS in Commerce, U. Va., 1951; postgrad., U.S. Coast Guard Acad., 1951. With Procter & Gamble Co., Phila., 1953-65, sales mgr., 1960-65; v.p. Warner Co., Phila., 1965-73; chmn. bd., CEO S.S. Keely Co., Phila., 1973-75; pres., chmn. bd., CEO Burch Materials Co., Inc., Wayne, Pa., 1975—; ptnr., mgr. Integrated MRO, LLC, 1998—; dir. Eagle's Eye, Inc., Wayne; bd. dirs. Nat. Multiple Sclerosis Soc., 1970-81, v.p., exec. com., 1974-77; bd. dirs. Pa. Sports Hall of Fame, 1974—, v.p., exec. com., 1974-79; chmn. Am. Legion Tennis Tournaments for State of Pa., 1975-82; mem. U.S. Congl. Adv. Bd., 1982, bd. dirs. Eagle's Eye Lacrosse Club, 1982-87. With USN, 1943-46, USCG, 1951-53. Named All-Am. in lacrosse, 1949. Mem. Merion Cricket Club, Merion Golf Club, Newcomen Soc. Club, Willoughby Golf Club. Republican. Roman Catholic. Home: 412 Conestoga Rd Wayne PA 19087-4812 Office: Burch Materials Co Inc 685 Kromer Ave Berwyn PA 19312-1317

BURCH, LORI ANN, obstetrics nurse; b. Charleston, Ill., Jan. 27, 1967; d. Lawrence Lee and Leslie Ann (Biddle) Pedigo; m. Steven Wayne Burch, Oct. 16, 1987 (div. June 1992); 1 child, Colby Steven. Diploma, Bapt. Sch. Nursing, Springdale, Ark., 1992. RN, Ark., Mo. Staff nurse Sprindale Meml. Hosp., 1992-94; agy. RN Healthstaf, Inc., Branson, Mo., 1994-98; sch. nurse Kirbyville (Mo.) Sch. Dist., 1998—; educator, spkr. in field. Avocations: swimming, running, traveling, golfing. Home: PO Box 6634 Branson MO 65615-6634

BURCH, MARY LOU, organization consultant, housing advocate; b. Billings, Mont., Apr. 4, 1930; d. Forrest Scott Sr. and Mary Edna (Hinshaw) Chilcott; m. J. Sheldon Robinson, June 18, 1949 (div. 1956); m. (2) G. Howard Burch, Nov. 27, 1957 (div. 1984); children: Julie Lynne Scully, Donna Eileen, Carol Marie Kimball, Alan Robert, Christine Philips Spruill Enomoto. AA, Grant Tech. Coll., Sacramento, 1949; AB, Sacramento State Coll., 1955; student, U. Alaska, 1976-78, Santa Rosa (Calif.) Jr. Coll., 1987. Diagnostic tchr. Calif. Youth Authority, Perkins, 1955-57; com. chmn. on pub. info. Sequoia Union High Sch. Dist., So. San Mateo County, Calif., 1970-72; exec. dir. Presbyn. Hospitality House, Fairbanks, Alaska, 1979-80; realtor Century 21 Smith/Ring, Renton, Wash., 1980-81; cons. Fairbanks, Alaska, 1981-84; exec. dir. Habitat for Humanity of Sonoma County, Santa Rosa, Calif., 1986-89, Affordable Housing Assoc., Santa Rosa, Calif., 1989-90; pvt. cons. in housing and orgn. Scottsdale, Ariz., 1991-92, Prescott and Dewey, Ariz., 1992—; bd. dirs. Hosp. Chaplainey Svcs, Santa Rosa, Villa Los Alamos Homeowners Assn.; cons. Access Alaska, Anchorage, 1983; contractor Alaka Siding, Fairbanks, 1982-83; founder Let's Get Organized!. Local coord. fgn. exch. student program Acad. Yr. in Am., 1993-94; acad. coord. fgn. exch. student program Cultural Homestay Internat., 1994-97; vol. coms. Habitat for Humanity, exec. asst. long term organizing project, 1997—. Named vol. of the year, Hosp. Chaplaincy Svcs., 1987. Democrat. United Ch. of Christ. Home and Office: 1288 Tapadero Dr #D-PCC Dewey AZ 86327-5823

BURCH, MARY SEELYE QUINN, law librarian, consultant; b. Worcester, Mass., Oct. 16, 1925; d. James Henry and Mary Seelye (O'Donnell) Quinn; m. Walter Douglas Burch, Aug. 18, 1972; children: Cathi, Andrew, David, John, Joan. BS, Suny, 1976; MLS, Pratt Inst., 1979. Law libr. N.Y. Supreme Ct., Troy, 1969-82; chief law libr. Office Ct. Adminstrn., Albany, N.Y., 1982-86; libr. N.Y. State Libr., 1986-89, ret., 1989; owner Mary S. Burch Law Libr. Svc., 1983—; instr. legal rsch. SUNY, 1981; selected to meet with deans of law schs. in China for improvement of legal reference materials in China. Mem. N.Y. State Bar Assn. (lectr. 1980), Ulster County Bar Assn. (cons. 1980), Am. Assn. Law Librs., Assn. Law Librs. Upstate N.Y. (pres. 1971, v.p. 1981). Roman Catholic. Avocations: pilot, swimming, sewing. Home: 946 Hoosick Rd Troy NY 12180-6635

BURCH, MICHAEL IRA, public relations executive, former government official; b. St. Louis, June 20, 1941; s. Horatio and Iona (Anderson) B.; m. Sherilynn J. Hummel, Dec. 26, 1987; children: Paige Anne Engelson, Michelle Hummel. B.A., U. Mo., 1963; postgrad., Boston U., 1965, Am. U., 1972-75. Commd. 2d lt. U.S. Air Force, 1963, advanced through grades to lt. col., 1979, served in tactical air command units, 1963-72, served at Pentagon in offices Air Force and Def. secs., 1972-83, ret., 1983; pres. Washington Communications Corp., 1983; asst. sec. for pub. affairs U.S. Dept. Def., Washington, 1983-85; v.p. communications Aerospace group McDonnell Douglas Corp., Washington, 1985-88; v.p. pub. relations McDonnell Douglas Corp., St. Louis, 1988-92; sr. v.p. Burson-Marsteller, Washington, 1992-95; pres. Civitas Comm. Group, Alexandria, Va., 1995—; mng. dir. Nature Works, Inc., 1997—. Bd. advisors MIT Enterprise Forum. Recipient Disting. Service medal Dept. Def., 1983, Disting. Pub. Service medal Dept. Def., 1985. Mem. Nat. Aviation Club, Def. Orientation Conf. Assn. (bd. dirs.), Air Commando Assn., Am. Legion. Republican. Episcopalian. Avocation: sailing. Office: Civitas Comm Grp 115 S Royal St Ste C-49 Alexandria VA 22314-3327

BURCH, ROBERT DALE, lawyer; b. Washington, Jan. 30, 1928; s. Dallas Stockwell and Hepsy (Berry) B.; m. Joann D. Hansen, Dec. 9, 1966; children—Berkeley, Robert Brett, Barrett Bradley. Student, Va. Mil. Inst., 1945-46; B.S., U. Calif. at Berkeley, 1950, J.D., 1953. Bar: Calif. bar 1954. Since practiced in Los Angeles and Beverly Hills; ptnr. Gibson, Dunn & Crutcher, 1961—; lectr. U. So. Calif. Inst. Fed. Taxation, 1960, 62, 65, 75; guest lectr. U. Calif.-L.A. Law Sch., 1959; lectr. C.E.B. seminars U. Calif.; founder Robert D. Burch Ctr. for Tax Policy and Pub. Fin., U. Calif., Berkeley. Author: Federal Tax Procedures for General Practitioners; Contbr. profl. jours., textbooks. Bd. dirs. charitable founds. With AUS, 1945-47. Mem. Beverly Hills Bar Assn. (bd. govs., chmn. probate and trust com.), Law Trust, Tax and Ins. Council (past czar), Los Angeles World Affairs Council. Home: 1301 Delresto Dr Beverly Hills CA 90210-2100 Office: Gibson Dunn & Crutcher 2029 Century Park E Ste 4000 Los Angeles CA 90067-3032 also: 333 S Grand Ave Los Angeles CA 90071-1504

BURCH, ROBERT EMMETT, retired physician, educator; b. St. Louis, Oct. 9, 1933; s. Robert A. and Virginia J. (Gresham) B.; m. Christina P. Efthim, Sept. 1, 1956; children: Robert M., Paula L. BS, St. Louis U., 1955, MD, 1959. Diplomate Am. Bd. Internal Medicine. Intern Jewish Hosp. St. Louis, 1959-60; resident Firmin Desloge Hosp. of St. Louis U., 1960-62; postdoctoral fellow Case Western Res. U., Cleve., 1962-65; assoc. in medicine to asst. prof. Columbia U., N.Y.C., 1965-71; assoc. prof. to prof. medicine Creighton U., Omaha, 1971-77; prof. and assoc. chmn. dept. medicine Marshall U., Huntington, W.Va., 1977-80; Price Goldsmith prof. medicine Tulane U., New Orleans, 1980-98. Editor: Trace Elements, 1976. Chmn. Mayor's Task Force on Nutrition, New Orleans, 1983-85; mem. Gov.'s Task Force on Sci. and Tech., Baton Rouge, 1985; mem. Office of Tech. Transfer, U. New Orleans, 1988-94; mem. rsch. com. La. br. Am. Heart Assn., 1991-95. Grantee, Nat. Heart Inst., 1965-72, Nat. Inst. Aging, 1977-80. Fellow ACP; mem. Cen. Soc. for Clin. Rsch., Am. Soc. for Clin. Nutrition, Am. Inst. Nutrition, Am. Physiol. Soc.

BURCH, SHARRON LEE STEWART, woman's health nurse; b. Washington, Dec. 19, 1944; d. David A. Jr. and Ruthanna (Craig) Stewart; m. Donald Victor Burch, Aug. 27, 1966; children: Elizabeth Katherine, Craig Donald. BSN, Vanderbilt U., 1966; M in Nursing, U. Miss. Med. Ctr., Jackson, 1975. RN, Miss. Staff nurse Druid City Hosp., Tuscaloosa, Ala., 1966-69; instr. insvc. edn. U. Hosp., Jackson, Miss., 1969-71; specialized nurse cons. Miss. Bd. Health, Jackson, 1972-74; instr. ADN Miss. Gulf Coast Jr. Coll., Biloxi, Miss., 1975-81, Hinds Community Coll., Jackson, 1982-91; staff nurse Rankin Med. Ctr., 1987—. Contbr. articles to profl. jours. Mem. ANA, Advvancement ADN (chmn. ad hoc competency validation com. 1983-91, 1st vice chmn. tech. com. on state of art curricula for vocat. and tech. programs for health and personal svcs. 1991-97), Miss. Nurses Assn., Sigma Theta Tau. Home: 784 Benwick Dr Brandon MS 39047-8112

BURCH, STEPHEN KENNETH, financial services company executive, real estate investor; b. Fairmont, W.Va., Feb. 1, 1945; s. Kenneth Edward and Gloria Lorraine (Wilson) B.; m. Juliana Yuan Yuan, June 17, 1972 (div. Feb. 1985); children: Emily, Adrien. AB in Econs., Washington U., St. Louis, 1969. V.p. TSI Mgmt., Los Angeles, 1970-71; pres. Investors Choice Cattle Co., Los Angeles, 1972-76; v.p. Clayton Brokerage Co., St. Louis, 1976-84; pres. Yuan Med. Lab., St. Louis, 1976-78; v.p. Restaurant Assocs., St. Louis, 1982-83, Am. Capital Equities, St. Louis, 1984-89; pres., owner Burch Properties, Inc., St. Louis, 1984—; owner Clayton-Hanley, Inc., St. Louis, 1987-88; pres., owner Clayton Securities Services, Inc., St. Louis, 1988—; mng. ptnr. 600 S. Ptnrs., St. Louis, 1976-87, Midvale Ptnrs., St. Louis, 1979—; mng. mem. Del Coronado Investment Co., LLC, 1997—. Bd. dirs. AMC Cancer Rsch. Ctr., 1989-91. Mem. Sigma Phi Epsilon (pres. alumni bd. 1981-87). Avocation: wine, movies. Office: Clayton Securities Svcs Inc 112 S Hanley Rd Ste 102 Saint Louis MO 63105-3418

BURCH, VORIS REAGAN, retired lawyer, mediator, arbitrator; b. Liberty, Tex., Feb. 10, 1930; s. Voris Reagan and Jessamae (Coffey) B.; m. Claudia Ramsland, Dec. 30, 1978; children: Melissa Burch Lively, Voris Reagan. BBA, Tex. A&M U., 1952; JD, U. Tex., 1957. Bar: Tex. 1957. Assoc. Baker & Botts, Houston, 1957-69, ptnr., 1969-84, sr. ptnr., 1984-95. Bd. dirs. Clarewood House, 1991—. Served to 1st lt. USAF, 1952-54. Mem. State Bar Tex. (chmn. labor law sect. 1970-71), Houston Bar Assn., Phi Delta Phi. Republican. Presbyterian. Home: 5761 Indian Cir Houston TX 77057-1302 Office: Baker & Botts 1 Shell Plz 1200 Smith St Ste 1200 Houston TX 77002-4592*

BURCHAM, EVA HELEN (PAT BURCHAM), retired electronics technician; b. Bloomfield, Ind., Apr. 11, 1941; d. Paul Harold and Hazel Helen (Buzan) B. Grad., Blackstone Sch. of Law, 1988, Paralegal Inst., Phoenix, 1991; grad. paralegal, So. Career Inst., Boca Raton, Fla., 1991. With Naval Weapons Support Ctr./Crane Div. Naval Surface Warfare, Crane, Ind., 1967-76, 78-80; electronics technician Naval Weapons Support Ctr., Crane, Ind., 1980-97. With U.S. Army, 1976-77, with Res. 1977-81. Named to Am. Women's Hall of Fame. Mem. NAFE (exec. bd. chair), NOW, Am. Soc. Naval Engrs., Soc. Logistics Engrs., Am. Legion, Federally Employed Women, Fed. Women's Program, Profl. Women's Network (pres. 1993, bd. dirs.), Blacks in Govt., Nat. Paralegal Assn. (registered paralegal), Nat. Fedn. Paralegal Assn., Inc., Toastmasters (gov.). Roman Catholic. Home: 200 W Washington St Loogootee IN 47553-2324

BURCHAM, RANDALL PARKS, lawyer, farmer; b. Union City, Tenn., July 20, 1917; s. John Simps and Myrtle Caldwell (Howard) B.; m. Hellon Owens, Sept. 30, 1945; children—Randall Parks Jr., Susan. Student Murray State Coll. (Ky.), 1934-38, U. Miss., 1938-39; LL.B., Cumberland U., Lebanon, Tenn., 1940; J.D., Samford U., Birmingham, 1969. Bar: Tenn. 1941. Sole practice, Union City, 1941; atty. U.S. Govt., Nashville, 1945-49; owner Interstate Oil Co., Fulton, Ky., 1949-53; ptnr. Burcham & Fox, Union City, 1953—. Del., Tenn. Constitutional Conv., Nashville, 1971. Served to comdr. U.S. Navy, 1941-45. Fellow Am. Coll. Probate Counsel; mem. ABA, Tenn. Bar Assn. (bd. govs. 1969-72). Democrat. Methodist.

BURCHARD, JOHN KENNETH, chemical engineer; b. St. Louis, May 12, 1936; s. Kenneth Reginald and Vernora Emma (Angell) B.; m. Elizabeth Lee Suesserott, Aug. 23, 1958; children—John Christopher, Gregory Charles. B.S., Carnegie Mellon U., 1957, M.S., 1959, Ph.D., 1962. Head systems analysis group United Tech. Ctr., Sunnyvale, Calif., 1961-68; chief scientist Combustion Power Co., Menlo Park, Calif., 1968-70; lab. dir. EPA, Research Triangle Park, N.C., 1970-80; dir. chem. engring. div. Research Triangle Inst., Research Triangle Park, 1980-83; pres. Search Assocs., Inc., Chapel Hill, N.C., 1983-85; dir. Office of Research Adminstrn. U. Cen. Ark., Conway, 1985-87; asst. dir. Office Research Devel. Ariz. State U., Tempe, 1987-90; mgr. spl. projects Ariz. Dept. Environ. Quality, Phoenix, 1990—; mem. bd. sci. advisors N.C. Energy Inst. Contbr. articles to profl. jours. Served with AUS, 1963-64. Shell Oil fellow, 1958-59; NSF fellow, 1960-61. Mem. Am. Inst. Chem. Engrs., Soc. Rsch. Adminstrs., Sigma Xi, Tau Beta Pi. Office: Ariz Dept Environ Quality Phoenix AZ 85012

BURCHELL, HOWARD BERTRAM, retired physician, educator; b. Athens, Ont., Can., Nov. 28, 1907; s. James Edward and Edith (Milligan) B.; m. Margaret Helmholz, Aug. 14, 1942; children: Susan Burchell Profeta, Judith Burchell Bush, Cynthia Burchell Patterson, Rebecca Burchell Wilbur. MD, U. Toronto, Can., 1932; PhD., U. Minn., 1939. Intern Toronto Gen. Hosp., 1932-34; rsch. fellow U. Pitts., 1934-36; fellow in medicine Mayo Clinic, Rochester, Minn., 1936-39, cons. in medicine, 1946-68; spl. student London Hosp., 1939-40; prof. medicine U. Minn., Mpls., 1968-85, prof. emeritus, 1985—; mem. adv. com. USAAF, 1947-40, Nat. Heart Coun., NIH, 1955-60; lectr. U.S., Can., The Netherlands, Israel. Contbr. more than 350 articles to profl. jours. Maj. USAAF, 1941-46. Fellow Am. Coll. Cardiology (master tchr. 1969, 74); mem. Am. Heart Assn. (Herrick award 1972), Assn. Am. Physicians, Am. Physiol. Soc. Mem. Unitarian-Universalist Ch. Avocation: history of medicine. Home: 260 Woodlawn Ave Saint Paul MN 55105-1237

BURCHFIEL, BURRELL CLARK, geology educator; b. Stockton, Calif., Mar. 21, 1934; s. Beryl Edward and Agnes (Clark) B.; m. Leigh H. Royden; children: Brian Edward, Brook Evans, Banjamin Clark, Halsey Royden. B.S., Stanford U., 1957, M.S., 1958; Ph.D., Yale U., 1961. Prof. geology Rice U., 1961-76; Prof. geology MIT, 1977-84, Schlumberger prof. geology, 1984—. Served with U.S. Army, 1958-59. Fellow Geol. Soc. Am., Am. Acad. Arts and Scis., Nat. Acad. Scis., Am. Geophys. Union, European Union Geoscis. (hon. fgn.); mem. Geol. Soc. Australia, Am. Assn. Petroleum Geologists, Chinese Acad. Scis. (fgn.). Home: 9 Robinson Park Winchester MA 01890-3717 Office: MIT 77 Massachusetts Ave # 54-1010 Cambridge MA 02139-4307

BURCHFIELD, BOBBY ROY, lawyer; b. Middlesboro, Ky., Oct. 23, 1954; s. Roy and Anna Lee (McCreary) B.; m. Teresa J. Miller, Apr. 6, 1996; 1 child, Taylor Nicole. BA, Wake Forest U., 1976; JD, George Washington U., 1979. Bar: D.C. 1980, U.S. Dist. Ct. D.C. 1982, U.S. Dist. Ct. Md. 1982, U.S. Ct. Appeals (3d cir.) 1981, U.S. Ct. Appeals (D.C. cir.) 1982, U.S. Ct. Appeals (9th cir.) 1985, U.S. Supreme Ct. 1986, U.S. Ct. Appeals (5th cir.) 1989, U.S. Ct. Appeals (6th cir.) 1993. Law clk. to Judge Ruggero J. Aldisert U.S. Ct. Appeals (3d cir.), Pitts., 1979-81; assoc. Covington & Burling, Washington, 1981-87, ptnr., 1987—; gen. counsel Bush-Quayle '92, 1992. Editor in chief George Washington U. Law Rev., 1978-79. Vol. George Bush for Pres., Washington, 1986-88; gen. counsel Rep. Nat. Lawyers Assn., 1991-92; mem. Wake Forest U. Alumni Coun., 1990-93, 97—; chmn. George Washington U. Nat. Law Ctr. Ann Fund, 1990-91. Mem. ABA. Republican. E-mail: BBurchfield@cov.com. Office: Covington & Burling 1201 Pennsylvania Ave NW PO Box 7566 Washington DC 20044-7566

BURCHFIELD, DON R., counselor, youth services administrator; b. Yuba City, Calif., May 24, 1952; s. Ray and Myrtle (Whitecotton) B.; m. Connie L. Hendrix, July 18, 1975; children: Christina, Kailee. BA in Edn., N.N.C., 1975; MA in Counseling, Liberty U., 1996. Youth counselor Peoples Ch., Phoenix, 1976-78, Valley Cathedral, Phoenix, 1978-82; counselor Terros, Phoenix, 1987-92; grad. counselor Grand Canyon, Phoenix, 1992-93; life counselor Life Counseling, Phoenix, 1993-94; counselor Tri City Counseling, Phoenix, 1994—; mem. steering com. Ariz. Adolescent Coalition, Phoenix, 1994-96; charter mem. Ariz. Gun Safety Com., Phoenix, 1994-96; presenter Mothers for Healthy Babies, 1995; chairperson Conf. on Self-Esteem, 1993, 94, 95, 96. Author: Surviving Adolescent City of Phoenix, 1994-95, (prevention program) Give It a Day, 1994-95, (bill) Gun Safety Bill for Safety, 1991, 92, 93, 94, 95. Charter pres. Offering Parents Info. on Needless Suicide; homeless/runaway youth assessor, Phoenix; chairperson Red Ribbon Youth Rally, Phoenix; charter mem. Gov.'s Office Youth Suicide Task Force, 1994-95; mem., chairperson, contact person Hope Coalition, Advocates Against Adolescent Suicide, pres., 1993—; mem. Ch. Alive, pres., 1980—; mem. Ariz. Adolescent Health Coalition, steering com., 1993—. Recipient Gov.'s Office for Children award, Gov. of Ariz., 1993, Cert. Appreciation, Nat. Orgn. Adolescent Pregnancy, 1995, Cert. Appreciation, Dept. Health Svcs., 1996; named Vol. of Yr., Terros Health Ctr., 1987. Democrat. Avocations: workouts, hiking, racquetball. Home and Office: 4547 N 17th Ave Phoenix AZ 85015-3813

BURCHIEL, SUSAN MARGUERITE, nurse educator; b. South Bend, Ind., Dec. 8, 1954; d. Robert Catlett and Josephine (Trygstad) Smith; m. Richard Earl Burchiel, Sept. 30, 1977; 1 child, Stephanie Evelyn. Diploma, U. So. Calif. Med. Ctr., L.A., 1976; BSN, Mount St. Mary's Coll., 1981; MSN, Consortium Calif. State U., 1988. Cert. med.-surg. nurse, ANCC; CNA; ACLS. Pediatric staff nurse St. Johns Hosp., Santa Monica, Calif.; ICU staff nurse UCLA Hosp. and Clinics, 1976-77; staff nurse ICU Valley Presbyn. Hosp., Van Nuys, Calif., 1978-81; staff nurse Sierra Vista Hosp., San Luis Obispo, Calif., 1981-83; staff nurse psychiat. ctr. French Hosp., San Luis Obispo, 1986-93; staff nurse med./surg., DOU staff nurse Twin Cities Cmty. Hosp., Templeton, Calif., 1994—; lectr. Calif. State U. Dominquez Hills; instr., nursing divsn. Cuesta Coll., San Luis Obispo, 1986—, asst. dir., 1988-93; CNA test site coord. San Luis Obispo County, 1992-94; reviewer Addison-Wesley Pub., 1993—. Contbg. author: Addison-Wesley Lab Manual for Nurses, 1996. Spkr. on health careers to teenagers Calif. Youth Authority, 1995—. Kellogg fellow; grantee Fed. Nurse Traineeship. Mem. ANA, Calif. Nurses Assn. (ADN-BSN articulation task force 1989-91), Nat. Coun. Licensing Examination for RNs (item writer 1989, 99), Nightingale Honor Soc.

BURCHMAN, LEONARD, government official; b. N.Y.C., Jan. 30, 1925; s. Hyman John-Hood and Edith (Speede-Cohen) B.; m. Marilyn F. Burchman, June 11, 1950; children—Marc Harris, Corey Andrew. BA, U. Denver, 1949; MA, Columbia U., 1950. Dir. press affairs N.Y. State Eisenhower presdl. campaign, N.Y.C., 1951-52; info. officer-advance sec. labor Dept. Labor, Washington and N.Y.C., 1953-60; pres. Medigard Chem. Corp., N.Y.C., 1961; dir. integovtl. rels. Dept. Labor, Washington, 1971-78; acting asst. sec., gen. dep. asst. sect. pub. affairs HUD, Washington, 1981—; dir. labor rels. to U.S. Senator Kenneth Keating, N.Y., 1964; pub. affairs cons. to Gov. of Conn., 1952; sr. advisor to Coretta Scott King; chmn. Martin Luther King Jr. Fed. Holiday Commn., 1985—, commr., 1989—, treas., 1989-92. Producer Office Mgmt. Budget/NSF film: Strengthening Intergovernmental Relations between Federal and State and Local Governments, 1976. Chmn. bd. Am. Heart Assn., Washinton, 1981-83; pres. Found. for Study U.S. Cabinet, 1985-89; pres. J.R.L.W., Leisure World, Md., 1994-96; chmn. FIIND, Found. to Interrupt Illegal Narcotics and Drugs, 1989—; founding pres. Vote, Voice of the Elderly, 1997—; founder nat. Consumer Watch-Out, to protect sr. citizens, 1988—; mem. Montgomery County (Md.) Commn. on Aging, 1997—. Recipient Disting. Svc. award Sec. HUD. Mem. Am. Legion (comdr. U.S. Dept. Labor).

BURCHUM, JACQUELINE ROSENJACK, family nurse practitioner; b. Corona, Calif., Apr. 17, 1955; d. Richard C. and Jo Ann (Hicks) Rosenjack; m. Charles Tony Burchum, Apr. 17, 1976; 1 child, Charles O. Assoc.'s degree in Nursing, U. Tenn., Martin, 1981; BS in Nursing, Union U., 1985; MSN, U. Tenn., Memphis. Cert. advanced cardiac life support instr., basic cardiac life support instr., EMT, emergency nurse; cert. family nurse practitioner. Faculty U. Memphis Extended Programs, Jackson, Tenn. Mem. Emergency Nurses Assn., Tenn. Nurses Assn., Am. Nurses Assn., Sigma Theta Tau Nursing Honor Soc., West Tenn. Nurse Practitioner Peer Review Orgn. Home: 410 Sand Pit Loop Camden TN 38320-9803

BURCZYK, MARY ELIZABETH, corporate communications executive; b. Racine, Wis., Aug. 19, 1953; d. Raymond and Dolores Cecelia (Swencki) B. BS, U. Wis., 1975; MBA, Northwestern U., 1985. Dir. pub. rels. Indsl. Fabrics Assn. Internat., St. Paul, 1976-80; mgr. pub. info. and audience devel. St. Paul Chamber Orch., 1980-81; dir. pub. rels. Mental Health Assn. Minn., Mpls., 1981-83; sr. v.p. On-Line Communications Corp., Chgo., 1986-90; v.p. corp. communications Catellus Devel. Corp., San Francisco, 1990—; sr. v.p. Am. Classic Voyages, Chgo., 1995-96, CDA/Capital Advisors, Chgo., 1996-97; sr. v.p. corp. rels. Fred Meyer, Inc., Portland, Oreg., 1998—.

BURD, FRANCIS JOHN, packaging executive; b. Dubuque, Iowa, Dec. 27, 1940; s. Francis LaVern and Mary F. (Whalen) B.; m. Sharon Ann Dalsing, Aug. 6, 1966; children: David F., Christine A., Catherine A. BA, Loras Coll., 1964. Tchr. St. Mary's Sch., Kieler, Wis., 1965-68; sales exec. St. Regis Paper Co., Dubuque, 1968-84, Georgia-Pacific Corp., Dubuque, 1984-87; mgr. sales and mfg. John Halper Box Co., Mpls., 1987-88; v.p. sales & mktg. Am. Carton & Polybag, Inc., Mpls., 1988—. V.p. Bd. Edn. Nativity Parish, Dubuque, 1977; vol. Loras Coll. Appeal, 1971, Wahlert High Sch. Appeal, Dubuque, 1984. Recipient Economic Edn. Award Jr. Achievement, Dubuque, 1983, Recognition award Boy Scouts Am., Dubuque, 1984. Mem.

Assn. Ind. Corrugated Converters, TAPPI, Presidents Club, Regent's, Kiwanis (dir. 1983-87). Republican. Roman Catholic. Avocations: philately, numismatics, bridge. Home: 3808 Hazel St Saint Paul MN 55110-4762

BURD, JOHN STEPHEN, academic administrator, music educator; b. Lock Haven, Pa., Apr. 6, 1939; s. John Wilson and Lily (Fye) B.; m. Patricia Ayers, June 3, 1961; children: Catherine Elizabeth, Emily Susanne. B in Music Edn., Greenville Coll., 1962; MS in Sacred Music, Butler U./Christian Theo. Sem., 1964; PhD, Ind. State U., 1971. Adj. music instr. Rose Hulman Inst. Tech., Terre Haute, Ind., 1969-71; assoc. prof. Greenville (Ill.) Coll., 1971-76; prof. edn. Lindenwood Coll., St. Charles, Mo., 1976-80; v.p. acad. affairs Maryville U., St. Louis, Mo., 1980-85; pres. Brenau U., Gainesville, Ga., 1985—; team evaluator Nat. Coun. Accreditation Tchr. Edn., 1979-84; mem. exec. coun. Women's Coll. Coalition, 1989-92, NAICU Commn. on State Rels. Bd., 1991-93, 94—; adv. bd. Wachovia Bank, Gainesville. Editor: New Voices in Education, 1969-71; contbr. articles to profl. jours. Choir dir. Ctr. Presbyn. Ch., St. Louis, 1984-85, Maryville U., St. Louis, 1983-85; v.p. Christian Arts, Inc., N.J., 1965—; mem. adv. bd. N.E. Ga. Med. Ctr.; bd. dirs. Gainesville Symphony, 1991-94, Crawford W. Long Mus.; chair Gainesville Redevel. Authority. Recipient Outstanding Young Alumnus award Greenville Coll., 1982, Disting. Alumnus award, 1991. Mem. Am. Assn. Tchr. Edn., Am. Assn. Higher Edn., So. Assn. Women's Colls. (pres. 1988-89), Ga. Found. Ind. Colls. (exec. bd. 1986—, vice chmn. 1993), Ga. Assn. Colls. (pres. 1989-90), Gainesville C. of C. (bd. dirs. 1985—). Methodist. Avocations: tennis, travel, art. Office: Brenau U 1 Centennial Cir Gainesville GA 30501-3668

BURD, ROBERT MEYER, hematologist, oncologist, educator; b. N.Y.C., Aug. 25, 1937; s. David and Anne (Popkin) B.; m. Alice Stoller, May 30, 1964; children: Russell J., Stephen J. AB, Columbia U., 1959, MD, 1963. Diplomate Am. Bd. Internal Medicine, Am. Bd. Hematology and Oncology. Intern Albert Einstein Med. Sch., N.Y.C., 1963-64, resident in internal medicine, 1964-66; hematology fellow Montefiore Hosp., N.Y.C., 1966-67; pvt. practice medicine, specializing in hematology and oncology, Fairfield, Conn., 1969—; assoc. prof. medicine Yale U., New Haven, 1975; assoc. clin. prof. of medicine, 1975—; chief of hematology/oncology St. Vincent's Med. Ctr., 1980—, chmn. hosp. com. on cancer, mng. ptnr. Med. Specialists of Fairfield, LLC, 1995—; attending physician Yale Hosp., New Haven; mem. staff Bridgeport Hosp; adj. prof. medicine N.Y. Med. Coll. Editorial bd. Conn. Medicine, 1974-78; med. cons. U.S. News and World Report, 1990; dir. oncology fellowship Yale-St. Vincent, 1991-96, N.Y. Med. Coll., St. Vincent's Med. Ctr., Bridgeport. Active Leukemia Soc. Am., Hemophilia Found.; chmn. profl. edn. com. Am. Cancer Soc. Lt. comdr. USN, 1967-69. Ettinger Meml. fellow Am. Cancer Soc., 1982. Fellow ACP; mem. AMA, AAAS, Am. Soc. Hematology, Am. Soc. Internal Medicine, Am. Soc. Clin. Oncology, N.Y. Acad. of Scis., Internat. Soc. Thrombosis and Hemostasis, Conn. Oncology Assn., Soc. Columbia Grads., Columbia U. Alumni Fedn. Coun., Columbia U. Alumni Club (pres. Fairfield County 1983-85, editor newsletter 1982-91), Bridgeport Medical Soc. (Physician of Yr. 1993). Office: 425 Post Rd Fairfield CT 06430-6232

BURD, SHIRLEY FARLEY, clinical specialist, mental health nurse; b. Pluckemin, N.J.; d. Raymond and Katherine Kiser (Horton) Farley; m. Robert L. Burd, Nov. 30, 1957. Diploma, Somerset Hosp. Sch. Nursing, Somerville, N.J.; BS, Rutgers U. Coll. Nursing, 1956, MS, 1958; EdD, Rutgers U. Grad. Sch. Edn., 1966. Asst. prof. Rutgers U. Coll. Nursing, Newark, 1957-63; prof., chair dept., dir. dept. grad. program Vanderbilt U., Nashville, 1967-72; prof., dept. chair U. Tenn. Coll. Nursing, Memphis, 1972-90, prof. emeritus, 1990; pvt. practice, psychiat. Germantown, Tenn., 1972—; prof. emeritus; mem. Tenn. Bd. Examiners, Nursing Home Adminstrs., 1990-96; cons. Health Care Financing Adminstrn., 1991-95. Vol., vice chair appropriations com. United Way Greater Memphis, 1980—; sr. citizen adv. commn. City of Germantown, Tenn., 1996-99. Named Disting. lectr. Sigma Theta Tau; first recipient Pres.'s award ANCC. Fellow Am. Acad. Nursing.

BURD, STEVE, food service executive; b. 1949. BS, Carroll Coll., 1971; MA in Econs., U. Wis., 1973. With fin. and mktg. So. Pacific Transp. Co., San Francisco; with Arthur D. Little, N.Y.C., 1982-87; mgmt. cons., 1986-91; cons. Stop & Shop Cos., Boston, 1988-89, Fred Meyer Inc., Portland, Oreg., 1989-90, Safeway Inc., Oakland, Calif., 1986-87, 91—; pres., CEO Safeway Inc., 1992—, chmn. bd. dirs. Office: Safeway Inc 5918 Stoneridge Mall Rd Pleasanton CA 94588-3229*

BURDE, RONALD MARSHALL, neuro-ophthalmologist; b. N.Y.C., Dec. 24, 1938; s. Eli and Helene B.; m. Sharon Della Kaplan, June 20, 1960; children: Howard, Bradley, Jeffrey. S.B., MIT, 1960; M.D., Jefferson Med. Coll., Phila., 1964. Diplomate Am. Bd. Ophthalmology (bd. dirs. 1984-92, chmn. 1991). Intern Jefferson Med. Coll., 1964-65; resident in ophthalmology Washington U. Med. Center, St. Louis, 1965-68; spl. fellow Nat. Inst. Neurol. Diseases and Blindness, 1968-70; mem. faculty Washington U. Med. Sch., 1970-87, prof. ophthalmology, 1974-87, prof. neurology, 1975-87, prof. neurol. surgery, 1981-87; prof., chmn. dept. ophthalmology and visual sci. Albert Einstein Coll. Medicine/Montefiore Med. Ctr.-U. Hosp., 1988—; prof. neurosurgery Albert Einstein Med. Coll., 1988—; prof. neurology Albert Einstein Coll. Medicine, 1989—; vis. prof. Hebrew U. Med. Sch., Jerusalem, 1977. Editl. bd.: Survey of Ophthalmology, 1980-94, Jour. Clin. Neuro-ophthalmology, 1981-94; editor-in-chief Jour. Neuroophthalmology, 1994—, Ophthalmology, 1984-89, Am. Jour. Ophthalmology, 1985-93. Bd. dirs. Am. Jewish Com., 1984-94 past pres. Traditional Congregation, Creve Coeur, Mo., 1974-76, dir., 1970-88; past mem. ethnic studies adv. bd. Forest park C.C., St. Louis. Fellow ASC, Am. Acad. Ophthalmology (chmn. new techs. task force 1988-94, chmn. OKAP com. 1982-88); mem. AMA, Am. Neurol. Assn., Am. Neurosurgery Soc., Am. Ophthalmol. Soc., Assn. Rsch. in Vision and Ophthalmology, N.Y. Acad. Medicine (chmn. ophthalmology sect. 1991-92), Manhattan Ophthal. Soc., Clin. Soc. N.Y. (membership v.p. 1993, program chair 1994, chmn. 1995, past pres.), Assn. Univ. Profs. Ophthalmology (bd. dirs. 1992-98, chmn. bd. 1998), MIT Alumni Assn. (past treas., bd. dirs. St. Louis chpt. 1972-73). Home: 16 W 77th St Apt 3E New York NY 10024-5126 Office: Albert Einstein Coll Med- Montefiore Med Ctr 111 E 210th St Bronx NY 10467-2401

BURDEN, CEDRIC JEROME, English educator; b. Mobile, Ala., Nov. 6, 1969; s. Andrew O'Neal and Juanita (Coleman) B.; m. Teresa Ballard, Mar. 26, 1995; 1 child, Jasmine Renee. AS, S.D. Bishop State Coll., 1989; BA, Univ. Montevallo, 1991, M, 1992. English prof. Lawson State Cmty. Coll., Birmingham, Ala., 1993—. Editing cons. Writing Voyage, 1996, Fictions, 1997. Sec. Alabaster Parks & Rec. Adv. Bd., 1997—. Mem. Ala. Assn. for Developmental Edn., Nat. Assn. for Devel. Edn., Nat. Coun. of Tchrs. of Eng., Alabaster Lions Club (sec.-treas. 1997-98), Alpha Phi Alpha. Avocations: model car building, pets, playing saxophone. Home: 201 Wildflower Trl Alabaster AL 35007-5280 Office: Lawson State Cmty Coll 3060 Wilson Rd SW Birmingham AL 35221-1717

BURDEN, DONALD WESLEY, publishing executive; b. New Milford, Conn., June 14, 1941; s. Clarence Sanford and Catherine Elvira (Beaton) B.; 1 child, Julie Catherine; m. Mary Lea Heydon; 1 child, James Charles. BA, Gettysburg Coll., 1963. Sales rep., dist. mgr., editor, pub. McGraw-Hill Cos., N.Y.C., 1963-86, dir. mktg. svcs., 1987—; bd. dirs. Pubnet LLC, N.Y.C.; pres. Middle Atlantic Coll. Stores, Inc., N.J., 1997—; pres.-elect Coll. Store Rsch. and Edn. Found. Chmn. Borough of Shrewsbury (N.J.) Shade Tree Commn., 1984—; mem. Shrewsbury Bd. Edn., 1978-80. Mem. Nat. Assn. Coll. Bookstores (mem. com. 1968—), Shrewsbury Hist. Soc. (treas., trustee 1976—). Republican. Presbyterian. Avocations: tennis, biking, reading, gardening. Home: 215 Sycamore Ave Shrewsbury NJ 07702-4512 Office: McGraw-Hill Higher Edn Two Penn Plz New York NY 10121-2298

BURDEN, JAMES EWERS, lawyer; b. Sacramento, Oct. 24, 1939; s. Herbert Spencer and Ida Elizabeth (Brosemer) B.; m. Kathryn Lee Gardner, Aug. 21, 1965; children: Kara Elizabeth, Justin Gardner. BS, U. Calif., Berkeley, 1961; JD, U. Calif., Hastings, 1964; postgrad., U. So. Calif., 1964-65. Bar: Calif. 1965, Tax Ct. U.S. 1969, U.S. Supreme Ct. 1970. Assoc. Elliott and Aune, Santa Ana, Calif., 1965, White, Harbor, Fort & Schei, Sacramento, 1965-67; assoc. Miller, Starr & Regalia, Oakland, Calif., 1967-69, ptnr., 1969-73; ptnr. Burden, Aiken, Mansuy & Stein, San Francisco, 1973-82, James E. Burden, Inc., San Francisco, 1982—; of counsel, Aiken, Kramer & Cummings, Oakland and San Francisco; bd. dirs. IP Floor Products, Inc., San Leandro, Calif., Denver; underwriting mem. Lloyds of London, 1986-93; instr. U. Calif., Berkeley, 1968-74, Merritt Coll.; prin. Dorset Capital LLC. Contbr. articles to profl. jours. Mem. ABA, Lutine Golf Soc. (London), Claremont Country Club, San Francisco Grid Club, Commonwealth of Calif., The Naval Club (London), Inst. Dirs. (London), The Univ. Club. Office: One Maritime Plz 4th Fl San Francisco CA 94111-3407

BURDEN, JEAN (PRUSSING), poet, writer, editor; b. Waukegan, Ill., Sept. 1; d. Harry Frederick and Miriam (Biddlecom) Prussing; m. David Charles Burden, 1940 (div. 1949). BA, U. Chgo., 1936. Sec. John Hancock Mutual Life Ins. Co., Chgo., 1937-39, Young & Rubicam, Inc., Chgo., 1939-41; editor, copywriter Domestic Industries, Inc., Chgo., 1941-45; office mgr. O'Brion Russell & Co., Los Angeles, 1948-55; adminstr. pub. relations Meals for Millions Found., Los Angeles, 1955-65; editor Stanford Research Inst., South Pasadena, Calif., 1965-66; propr. Jean Burden & Assocs., Altadena, Calif., 1966-82; lectr. poetry to numerous colls. and univs., U.S., 1963—; supr. poetry workshop Pasadena City Coll., Calif., 1960-62, 66, U. Calif. at Irvine, 1975; also pvt. poetry workshops. Author: Naked as the Glass, 1963, Journey Toward Poetry, 1966, The Cat You Care For, 1968, The Dog You Care For, 1968, The Bird You Care For, 1970, The Fish You Care For, 1971, A Celebration of Cats, 1974, The Classic Cats, 1975, The Woman's Day Book of Hints for Cat Owners, 1980, 84, Taking Light from Each Other, 1992; poetry editor: Yankee Mag, 1955—; pet editor: Woman's Day Mag, 1973-82; contbr. numerous articles to various jours. and mags. MacDowell Colony fellow, 1973, 74, 76; Recipient Silver Anvil award Pub. Relations Soc. of Am., 1969, 1st prize Borestone Mountain Poetry award, 1963, Gold Crown award for lit. achievement, 1989. Mem. Poetry Soc. Am., Acad. Am. Poets, Authors Guild. Address: 1129 Beverly Way Altadena CA 91001-2517 *I think that man is constantly trying to bring down into the world of time the essences of what he dimly but intuitively feels is timeless. One of the ways in which he tries is through poetry. Without poetry, a certain kind of Reality is speechless. Or to put it a slightly different way, I believe that we inhabit two worlds at once, the world of time and the world of timelessness, and that poetry is a bridge that lets us cross over.*

BURDEN, ORDWAY PARTRIDGE, investment banker; b. N.Y.C., N.Y., Nov. 20, 1944; s. William A. M. and Margaret L. (Partridge) B.; m. Jean Poor Lynch, October 5, 1991. AB magna cum laude, Harvard U., 1966, MBA, 1968; postgrad., Harvard Law Sch., 1969-71. Ltd. ptnr. William A.M. Burden Co., N.Y.C., 1968-86, gen. ptnr., 1986—; cons. on police functions Nat. Commn. for Rev. Fed. and State Laws Relating to Wiretapping and Electronic Surveillance; cons. Commn. on Rev. Nat. Policy Toward Gambling. Former mem. adv. bd. Bur. Justice Stats., Dept. of Justice; mem. nat. sponsoring com. Nat. Law Enforcement Officers Meml. Fund; v.p. Florence V. Burden Found., N.Y.C., 1990—. Mem. Internat. Assn. Chiefs Police (past mem. 5 coms.), Nat. Sheriffs Assn. (former mem. standards-ethics-edn.-devel. com.), Nat. Crime Prevention Coun. (bd. dirs.), Law Enforcement Assistance Found. (founder, pres. 1977—), Nat. Law Enforcement Coun. (founder, chmn. 1979—), Capitol Hill Club, Metropolitan Club.

BURDEN, RHEA ANN, athletic trainer; b. Guymon, Okla., Oct. 16, 1967; d. James Preston and Donna Lynn (Arnold) Thompson; m. Donald R. Burden, Feb. 27, 1993. BS in Edn., U. Tex., El Paso, 1991; MA in Edn., U. Tex., San Antonio, 1992. Grad. asst., athletic trainer U. Tex., San Antonio, 1991-92; athletic trainer, health educator J.M. Hanks H.S., El Paso, 1993-95; athletic trainer Athletic Orthopedics and Knee Ctr., Houston, 1995—; mem. faculty Davis Mountains Sports Medicine Clinic, Ft. Davis, Tex., 1997. Author curriculum guide in field. Mem. Nat. Athletic Trainers Assn. (cert., examiner 1997), Adv. Bd. Athletic Trainers (examiner 1996-97). Avocations: camping, fishing, reading. Office: Athletic Orthops and Knee Ctr 9180 Old Katy Rd Ste 200 Houston TX 77055

BURDESHAW, WILLIAM BROOKSBANK, engineering executive; b. East Orange, N.J., Nov. 20, 1930; s. Thomas Anderson and Margaret (Villecco) B.; m. Monica Dorr, Sept. 27, 1957; children: Leath, Thomas, Anne, Alison. BS, U.S. Mil. Acad., 1953; MSEE, Ga. Inst. of Tech., 1961. Commd. 2d lt. U.S. Army, 1953, advanced through grades to brig. gen., 1975, ret., 1979; CEO, chmn. Burdeshaw Assocs., Ltd., 1979—; cons. Def. Sci. Bd., 1985-87. Engring. mgmt. cons. co. named by INC. mag. as 121st of 500 fastest growing pvt. cos., 1985. Mem. Burning Tree Club, Congl. Country Club, George Town Club (Washington), Cripple Creek Club (Bethany Beach, Del.). Republican. Episcopalian. Office: Burdeshaw Assoc Ltd 4701 Sangamore Rd Bethesda MD 20816-2500

BURDETT, JAMES RICHARD, golf products innovator; b. Oak Park, Ill., Jan. 4, 1934; s. Paul Eswald and Ruth (Woodward) B.; m. Marilyn Carole Stoker, Aug. 29, 1959; children: Deborah Lyn Dodd, Daniel James, Donna Carole Humphress. Student, Grinnell Coll., 1953-54; BS in Econs., U. Ill., 1956. Owner James R. Burdett, Lombard, 1983-92; pres. Burdett's Inc., 1993—, Master of the Links, Lombard, 1988—; speaker conf. Golf Course Superintendent Assn., Anaheim, Calif., 1993. Mem. Golf Course Supts. Assn. Am., Midwest Assn. Golf Course Supts., Ill. Turfgrass Found. (pres. 1965-66). Mem. Christian Sci. Ch. Office: PO Box 1865 Lombard IL 60148-8865

BURDETTE, CAROL JANICE, gerontology nursing administrator; b. Glens Falls, N.Y., Sept. 22, 1936; d. Edward J. Johnson and Daisy M. (Minor) Griffin; m. Edward L. Burdette, Mar. 6, 1981; children: Keith Noseworthy, Scott Noseworthy, Debra Colombo. Student, Bklyn. Meth. Hosp., 1954-57; BS, Coll. of St. Francis, 1990, MS, 1995. Cert. in gerontology. Utilization review coord. Norwich (Conn.) Hosp., 1973-81, med. review nurse I, 1980-81; allergy nurse Drs. Clinic, Vero Beach, Fla., 1981-83; dir. nursing Fla. Bapt. Retirement Ctr., Vero Beach, 1984—; tchr./instr. B.S. Program, Barry U., 1997—. Contbr. articles to profl. jours. Mem. Nat. Assn. Dirs. of Nursing Adminstrn. (cert.), Fla. Assn. Dirs. of Nursing Adminstrn. (cert. CDON/LTC dir. nursing/long term care, pres.), Nat. Gerontol. Nurses Assn., Am. Soc. Long Term Care Dirs. Nursing, Nat. Assn. Gerontological Nursing. Home: 6135 60th Ct Vero Beach FL 32967-5202 Office: Fla Bapt Retirement Ctr P O Box 460 1006 33rd St Vero Beach FL 32960-6910

BURDETTE, JANE ELIZABETH, nonprofit association executive, consultant; b. Huntington, W.Va., Aug. 17, 1955; d. C. Richard and Jewel Kathryn (Wagner) B. AAS, Parkersburg (W.Va.) C.C., 1976; BA, Glenville State Coll., 1978; MA, W.Va. U., 1984. Fund raiser, recruiter Muscular Dystrophy Assn., Charleston, W.Va., 1973, 74, 75; sec., bookkeeper Nationwide Ins. Co., Parkersburg, 1975; v.p. Burdette Funeral Home, Parkersburg, 1976-85; intake and referral specialist Wood County Sheltered Workshop, Parkersburg, 1985-91; cons. in field, 1991—. Bd. dirs. Sheltered Workshop, Parkersburg, 1982-86, Western Dist. Guidance Ctr., Parkersburg, 1984-94; vol. St. Joseph's Hosp., 1991-96; mem. W.Va. Coun. Ind. Living, 1992-94; mem. W.Va. Muscular Dystrophy Assn. task force on disability issues, 1992—; bd. advisors, vice chmn. Parkersburg C.C., 1980-89, Domestic Violence Interdisciplinary Adv. Com., 1987, Just Say No, 1987-91; chmn. Wood County Commn. on Crime, Delinquency and Corrections, Parkersburg, 1985—; chmn. Mid Ohio Valley United Fund Agy., 1986 Heads; v.p. Jr. League of Parkersburg, 1989—; mem. Sanctuary Soc., 1991—, All Saints Guild, 1991-95, St. Margaret Mary Parish Coun., 1992-97; bd. dirs. Cmty. Svc. Coun., 1985—, Parkersburg Transit Authority, 1994-98; mem. W.Va. Statewide Rehab. Adv. Cou., 1998—; liaison Gov. Commn. on Disabled Persons, Charleston, W.Va., 1981-85; mem. Career Adv. Network, 1987-91; treas. W.Va. Women's Conf., 1987, Children's Discovery Ctr. Mus., 1998—; exec. com. W.Va. chpt. Muscular Dystrophy Assn., 1987—; mem. We've Been There Parent Support Group, 1987-90; v.p. A Spl. Wish Found., 1988-98; mem. Parkersburg Consumer Adv. Group; mem. founding com. Banquet of Wealth, 1988-91; bd. dirs. Horizon's Ind. Living Ctr., 1990-98; past transition plan team leader Wood County Bd. Edn.; past liason Internat. Yr. Disabled Persons; past treas., program chmn. Gov.'s Conf.; former pres. Y Teen Club, YWCA; former adv. com. Mountwood Pk. White Oak Village, Organ Donor Com., 1989; mayoral candidate City of Parkersburg, 1997. Named Miss Wheelchair W.Va., 1981, Outstanding Young Woman of Yr. for W.Va., 1981, Outstanding Young Woman of the Yr., 1986; recipient Kenneth Hieges award Muscular Dystrophy Assn., 1982, Outstanding Citizen award Frat. Order of Police, 1984, Cmty. Svc. award Moose Lodge, 1995, Cert. Appreciation, State W.Va., Gov. Jay Rockefeller, Cert. Appreciation, Am. Legion Aux., Trail of New Beginning award Banquet of Wealth Trail Blazer award YWCA/Altrusa, 1989, Personal Achievement award for W.Va., MDA, 1993, 94, 97, Mary Harriman Cmty. Leadership award Jr. League Internat., 1994, Jennings Randolph award W.Va. Rehab. Assn., 1996, Good Neighbor award Supermarket Comm./Big Bear, 1997, Jefferson award Sta. WCHS-TV, 1998; named W.Va.'s Disabled Profl. Woman of Yr. Pilot Internats., 1989, Hometown Hero Sta. WSAZ-TV, 1993, One Who Makes a Difference, Sta. WTAP, 1994, Profl. and Bus. Woman's Internat. Hall of Fame, 1995, Nat. Hall of Fame for Persons with Disabilities, 1998, W.Va. Women Hall of Fame, 1999. Mem. NAFE, Toastmasters (Comm. and Leadership award 1989). Democrat. Roman Catholic. Avocation: designing. Home: 2500 Brooklyn Dr Parkersburg WV 26101-2913

BURDETTE, ROBERT BRUCE, lawyer; b. Cin., Oct. 8, 1945; s. Lumas Carter and Myrtle Margaret (Diesel) B. AB, Columbia Coll., 1967; JD, U. Cin., 1973. Bar: Ohio 1973, U.S. Supreme Ct. 1978. Legis. atty. Libr. Congress, Washington, 1973—. Author: A Step Beyond The Graetz Prepayment Analysis, 1992. Mem. Mensa, St. Andrew Club, Friends of Vieilles Maisons Francaises, W.A.R. Goodwin Soc. Colonial Williamsburg. Methodist. Avocations: gilding and rum collecting. Home: 4337 36th St S Arlington VA 22206-1809 Office: Libr of Congress 1st and Independence Washington DC 20540

BURDETTE, ROBERT SOELBERG, accountant; b. Salt Lake City, Apr. 28, 1955; s. Grant Edward and Jewel Irene (Soelberg) B.; m. Marne Marie Erekson, June 21, 1977 (div. May 1985); children: Aaron Edward, Melissa Marie, Barton Allen; m. Conna Lee Jolley, Feb. 1, 1990; children: Seth Robert, Mark Jacob, Matthew Caleb. BA, U. Utah, 1979; M in Taxation, Wash. Inst. Grad. Studies, 1993. CPA, Utah. Staff acct. Huber & Assocs., Salt Lake City, 1979-80; acctg. mgr. Huntsman-Christensen Corp., Salt Lake City, 1980-81; supervising tax specialist Leverich & Co., Salt Lake City, 1982-83; tax. ptnr. Burdette & Hymas CPAs, Salt Lake City, 1983-93, pres., 1993-94; compt. Art Beats, Inc., Salt Lake City, 1988-90; prof. law in taxation Washington Sch. Law, 1991; tax ptnr. Hansen, Barnett & Maxwell CPA, 1994-97; contr. JT Steel, Inc., West Jordan, Utah, 1997-99; CFO Ind. Funding, Inc., Salt Lake City, 1999—. Conv. del. Salt Lake County Rep. Party, 1980, Utah State Rep. Party, 1992; missionary Ch. Jesus Christ of Latter-Day Saints, 1974-76; basketball coach Salt Lake Boys & Girls Club, 1989; scout master Boy Scouts Am., Sandy, Utah, 1986-87. Mem. AICPA, Utah Assn. CPAs (taxation com. 1983), Intermountain Soc. Practicing CPAs (exec. com.), CPA Law Forum (bd. adv.). Avocations: home remodeling, woodworking, gardening, camping, harmonica. Home: 1750 Countryside Dr Salt Lake City UT 84106-3244 Office: 4885 S 900 E Salt Lake City UT 84117

BURDETTE, WALTER JAMES, surgeon, educator; b. Hillsboro, Tex., Feb. 5, 1915; s. James S. and Ovazene (Weatherred) B.; m. Kathryn Lynch, Apr. 9, 1947; children: Susan, William J. A.B., Baylor U., 1935; A.M., U. Tex., 1936, Ph.D., 1938; M.D., Yale, 1942. Diplomate: Am. Bd. Surgery, Am. Bd. Thoracic and Cardiovascular Surgery. Intern Johns Hopkins Hosp., 1942-43; Harvey Cushing fellow surgery Yale, 1943-44; resident staff surgery New Haven Hosp., 1944-46; instr., asst., assoc. prof. surgery La. State U., 1946-55; vis. surgeon Charity Hosp. of La., 1946-55; cons. Touro Infirmary and So. Baptist Hosp., 1952-55, Oak Ridge Inst. Nuclear Studies Hosp., 1953-59; vis. investigator Chester Beatty Inst. Cancer Research, Brompton, and Royal Cancer Hosp., London, 1953, Max Planck Institut Fuer Biochemie, Tuebingen, Germany, summer 1955; prof., chmn. dept. surgery U. Mo., 1955-56; prof. clin. surgery St. Louis U. Sch. Medicine, 1956-57; prof., head dept. surgery U. Utah, 1957-65; dir. lab. clin. biology, surgeon-in-chief Salt Lake Gen. Hosp., 1957-65; chief surg. cons. VA Hosps., Salt Lake City, 1957-65; prof. surgery, assoc. dir. U. Tex-M.D. Anderson Hosp. and Tumor Inst., Houston, 1965-72; prof. surgery U. Tex. Sch. Medicine at Houston, 1971-79; adj. prof. pharmacology U. Houston, 1975—; chief surgery Univ.Hosp., U. Mo., 1955-56, St. Louis U. Svc., John Cochran VA Hosp., 1956-57; chief thoracic and cardiovascular surgery Park Pla. Hosp., 1990—; pres. Nat. Biomed. Found., 1972—; cons. St. Luke's Hosp., 1975—, Park Plaza Hosp., 1976—, Meth. Hosp., 1976—; Gibson lectr. advanced surgery Oxford U., 1966; vis. prof. U. Oxford, spring 1965; ofcl. U. Congo, summer 1968. Editor, author: Etiology, Treatment of Leukemia, 1958, Methodology in Human Genetics, 1962, Methodology in Mammalian Genetics, 1962, Methodology in Basic Genetics, 1963, Primary Hepatoma, 1965, Carcinoma of the Alimentary Tract, 1965, Viruses Inducing Cancer, 1966, Carcinoma of the Colon and Antecedent Epithelium, 1970, Planning and Analysis of Clinical Studies, 1970, Invertebrate Endocrinology and Hormonal Heterophylly, 1974, Cancer: Etiology, Diagnosis and Treatment, 1997; editl. bd. Surg. Rounds, Yale Jour. Biology and Medicine, Cancer Rsch.; contbr. over 200 articles to med. and sci. jours. Chmn. genetics study sect., mem. morphology study sect. NIH; cons. Nat. Cancer Inst.; mem. Nat. Adv. Cancer Council, Nat. Adv. Heart Council, Surgeon General's Com. on Smoking and Health; chmn. U.S.A. nat. com. Internat. Union Against Cancer; mem. transplantation com. Nat. Acad. Scis.; chmn. working Cadre on cancer large intestine Nat. Cancer Inst.; elder, deacon Christian Ch. Rockefeller travel fellow USSR and Ea. Europe, summer 1957. Fellow ACS; mem. AAAS, Soc. Surgery Alimentary Tract, Am. Assn. Cancer Research (dir., v.p.), Am. Cancer Soc. (chmn. research adv. council, mem. council on analysis and projection), Am. Surg. Assn., Soc. Clin. Surgery (treas.), Soc. U. Surgeons, Soc. Exptl. Biology and Medicine, Genetics Soc. Am., Utah Genetics Soc. (pres.), Western Soc. Clin. Research, Am. Assn. Thoracic Surgery, Transplantation Soc., N.Y. Acad. Sci., Soc. Am. Naturalists, New Orleans, St. Louis, Salt Lake City, Houston surg. socs., Tex. Med. Soc., Harris County Med. Soc., So., Western surg. assns., So. Thoracic Surg. Soc., Peruvian Cancer Soc. (hon.), Am. Soc. Clin. Oncology, Am. Soc. for Cancer Edn., Tex. Surg. Soc., Assn. Yale Alumni in Medicine (exec. com. 1977), Soc. Internat. de Chirurg, Am. Guild Organists, Yale Club of Houston (pres. 1989-91), Phi Beta Kappa, Sigma Xi, Alpha Omega Alpha. Home: 239 Chimney Rock Rd Houston TX 77024-5618

BURDGE, RABEL JAMES, sociology educator; b. Columbus, Ohio, Dec. 14, 1937; s. Alonzo Marshall and Mariam Francis (Prentice) B.; m. Sharon Sue Payne, June 30, 1962 (dec. June 1975); children—Stephanie, Amy, Jill; m. Joyce Loretta Piggush, Aug. 2, 1977. BS, Ohio State U., 1959, MS, 1961; PhD, Pa. State U., 1965. Asst. prof. sociology U.S. Air Force Acad., Colo., 1966-68; lectr. U. Colo., Colorado Springs, 1966-68; asst. prof. sociology U. Ky., Lexington, 1968-72; assoc. prof. U. Ky., 1972-76; assoc. prof. environ. sociology, rural sociology, urban and regional planning and leisure studies; dept. agrl. econs. and leisure studies U. Ill. Inst. Environ. Studies, Urbana, 1976-80; prof. U. Ill. Inst. Environ. Studies, 1980-95; prof. emeritus U. Ill., 1996—; prof. sociology and environ. studies Western Wash. U., Bellingham, 1996—; vis. scholar Sch. of Australian Environ. Studies, Griffith U., Brisbane, 1982, 86, hon. prof., 1991—. Author (books): (with N. Cheek and D. Field) Leisure and Recreation Places, 1976, (with Paul Opryszek) Coping with Change: An Interdisciplinary Assessment of the Lake Shelbyville Reservoir, 1981, (with E.M. Rogers) Social Change in Rural Societies, A Rural Sociology Textbook, 3d edit., 1988, A Community Guide to Social Impact Assessment, 1994, 2d edit., 1999, A Conceptual Approach to Social Impact Assessment, 1994, 2d edit., 1998; editor Jour. Leisure Rsch., 1971-74; co-editor, founder: Leisure Scis., an Interdisciplinary Jour., 1977-82, Society and Nat. Resources: An Internat. Jour., 1988-98; co-editor Longman-Cheshire Internat. Environ. Studies Series, 1990—; contbr. articles to profl. publs. Served to capt. arty. U.S. Army, 1965-68. Recipient George B. Hartzog Jr. award for environ. rsch. Clemson U., 1995. Mem. AAAS, Am. Sociol. Assn., Rural Sociol. Soc. (v.p. 1982-83, treas. 1994—, editor The Rural Sociologist, 1994—, named Disting. Rural Sociologist, 1996), Nat. Recreation and Park Assn. (Theodore/Franklin D. Roosevelt award for outstanding rsch. 1982), Internat. Assn. for Impact Assessment (pres. 1990-91, treas. 1993-96, Rose-Hulman Inst. Tech. award for contbns. to impact assessment), Acad. Leisure Scis., Sigma Xi, Phi Kappa Phi, Gamma Sigma Delta, Alpha Kappa Delta. Democrat. Methodist. Home: PO Box 4056 Bellingham WA 98227-4056 Office: Western Wash U Dept Sociology Bellingham WA 98225-9081

BURDI, ALPHONSE ROCCO, anatomist; b. Chgo., Aug. 28, 1935; s. Alphonse Rocco and Anna (Basilo) B.; m. Sandra Shaw, Mar. 22, 1968; children—Elizabeth Anne, Sarah Lynne. B.S., No. Ill. U., DeKalb, 1957; M.S., U. Ill., 1959, U. Mich., 1961; Ph.D., U. Mich., 1963. Predoctoral fellow physiology U. Ill., 1957-59; NSF summer fellow U. Mich., 1960, NIH trainee, 1960-61, NIH predoctoral research fellow, 1962, mem. faculty, 1962—, prof. anatomyand cell biology, 1974—; rsch. scientist Center for Human Growth and Devel.; dir. integrated pre-med.-med. program U. Mich. Mem. editorial bd.: Cleft Palate Jour. 1972-88 , Am. Jour. Phys. Anthropology, 1971-75, C.C. Thomas Am. Lectr. Series in Anatomy, 1971-88 , Jour. Dental Research, 1977-87 . Grantee NIH. Mem. Internat. Assn. Dental Research, Am. Assn. Dental Research, Am. Cleft Palate Assn., Teratology Soc., Am. Assn. Anatomists, Am. Assn. Phys. Anthropology, Sigma Xi. Home: 2600 Page Ct Ann Arbor MI 48104-6249 Office: U Mich Dept Anatomy & Cell Biology Med Sci Bldg 2 Ann Arbor MI 48109-0616

BURDICK, CLAUDE OWEN, pathologist; b. Oconomowoc, Wis.; s. Lawrence Theodore and Florence (Owens) B.; m. Margaret Huiskamp, June 18, 1955; children: Katherine, Roberta, Lawrence, Jack (dec.). BS in Med. Sci., U. Wis., 1955, MD, 1958. Diplomate Am. Bd. Pathology, Am. Bd. Dermatopathology. Intern Letterman Army Med. Ctr., San Francisco, 1958-59, resident, 1959-63; pathologist, chief hematology Berkshire Med. Ctr., Pittsfield, Mass., 1968-70; pathologist, dir. labs. Valley Care Health Sys., Livermore/Pleasanton, Calif., 1970-98; chmn., bd. dirs. Valley Care Health Sys., 1993-96; med. dir., cons. Spectra Labs., Inc., Fremont, Calif., 1994—; pres. Livermore Alameda Valley Med. Group, 1972-76. Lt. col. U.S. Army, 1957-68. Fellow Am. Soc. Clin. Pathology, Coll. Am. Pathologists; mem. AMA, Calif. Med. Assn., Calif. Soc. Pathologists (bd. dirs. 1983-86), Alameda Contra Costa Med. Soc., Am. Soc. Blood Banks, South Bay Pathology Soc. (pres. 1981). Democrat. Presbyterian. Avocation: choral music (Ohlone College Chamber Singers). Office: Western Labs Med Group 2945 Webster St Oakland CA 94609-3496

BURDICK, DAVID, library director; b. Sacramento, Calif., Nov. 23, 1955; s. Albert and Dorothy (Cline) B.; m. Shelley Sorenson; children: Michael, Stephanie, Ryan. BS in Bus. Mgmt., Brigham Young U., 1989, MLS, 1990; attended, Graceland Coll., Consumnes River Coll. Gen. mgr. Mr. Steak Restaurant, Sacramento; staff microforms & genealogy ref. Lee Library-Brigham Young U., Provo, Utah; extension/outreach librarian Pine Bluff & Jefferson County Library, Ark., dir. Bd. dirs. Literary Coun. of Jefferson County, 1993-97; bishop Pine Bluff ward LDS Ch., 1996—. Mem. ALA, Ark. Libr. Assn. (sec. 1997-98), S.E. Libr. Assn., Assn. Ark. Pub. Librs., West Pine Bluff Rotary (pres. 1996-97), White Hall C. of C. (pres. 1994-95). Republican. Mem. Ch. of Jesus Christ of Latter-day Saints. Avocations: spending time with family, genealogy, golf, photography, travel. Office: Pine Bluff & Jefferson County Libr System 200 E 8th Ave Pine Bluff AR 71601-5006

BURDICK, EUGENE ALLAN, retired judge, lawyer, surrogate judge; b. Williston, N.D., Oct. 15, 1912; s. Usher Lloyd and Emma Cecelia (Robertson) B.; m. May Picard, Feb. 14, 1939; children: William Eugene, Elizabeth Jane Burdick Cantarine. B.A., U. Minn., 1933, J.D., 1935. Bar: N.D. 1935, U.S. Dist. Ct. N.D. Sole practice Williston, 1935-53; state's atty. Williams County, 1939-45; dist. judge, 1953-78; commr. Uniform State Laws for State of N.D., 1959—; draftsman N.D. Rules of Civil Procedure, 1954-57, N.D. Juvenile Ct. Forms, Pattern Jury Instrns. civil and criminal; mem. Juvenile Ct. Judges Adv. Council for Children and Youth, 1959-67, 68-76; draftsman Rules of Ct. for Dist. Cts., 1962-63; pres. Nat. Conf. Commrs. on Uniform State Laws, 1971-73, chmn. com. style, 1975—. Pres. James Meml. Library, Williston, 1948-65; mem. exec. com. N.D. Conf. Social Welfare, 1963-67; chmn. Gov.'s Com. on Children and Youth, 1965-71; mem., vice chmn. exec. com. Gov.'s Council Human Resources. Recipient Outstanding Trustee award ALA, 1956, N.D. Nat. Leadership award of excellence, 1972, Herbert Harley award Am. Judicature Soc., 1985. Fellow Am. Bar Found.; mem. ABA (co-author appellate opinion writing manual), State Bar Assn. N.D. (pres. 1950-51, Disting. Svc. award 1984), Am. Law Inst.(lifemem.), Am. Judicature Soc., Inst. Jud. Adminstrn., Sarasota Yacht Club, Am. Contract Bridge League, Kiwanis (past pres. Williston), Elks (hon. life mem.), Williston Toastmasters (hon. mem.), Hon. Order of Ky. Cols., Order of Coif, Phi Alpha Delta (hon.), Sigma Nu. E-mail: eburdick@gte.net. Home: 1 Ben Franklin Dr # 32 Sarasota FL 34236-1236

BURDICK, LARRY G., school system administrator. Supt. Pryor (Okla.) Pub. Schs. State finalist Nat. Supt. Yr., 1992. Office: Pryor Pub Schs 521 SE 1st St Pryor OK 74361-4600

BURDICK, LOU BRUM, public relations executive; b. Bloomer, Wis., Nov. 4, 1943; s. Francis Albert and Lucille May (Gorton) Peil; m. Robert P. Brum, Dec. 26, 1971 (div. 1977); m. Allan L. Burdick, Feb. 12, 1981; 1 child, Matthew Francis. Adminstr. Bozell & Jacobs, Mpls., 1965-67; pub. rels. mgr. Apache Corp., Mpls., 1967-76; v.p., dir. fin. rels. Edwin Neuger & Assocs., Mpls., 1976-78; chmn. bd., chief exec. officer Brum & Anderson Pub. Relations, Inc., Mpls., 1978-86; pres. Padilla, Speer, Burdick & Beardsley, Inc., Mpls., 1987, Lou Burdick and Assocs., Mpls., 1988—; dir. communications Office of Gov., St. Paul, 1989-91; chmn., bd. dirs. Courage Ctr., Mpls. Bd. dirs. Hennepin County Libr. Found., 1991-97, Minn. Coun. on Founds., 1998—; campaign mgr. Printy for Gov., 1990. Recipient Outstanding Achievement award for Entrepreneurship, Mpls. YWCA, 1985. Mem. Pub. Rels. Soc. Am. (pub. rels. recognition award 1985), Minn. Women's Econ. Roundtable (bd. dirs.), Minnekahda Country Club. Republican. Home and: 6609 Sally Ln Edina MN 55439-1042

BURDICK, ROBERT W., newspaper editor; b. Feb. 11, 1948; m. Patty Burnett; 1 child, David. B in Polit. Sci., Fla. Atl. U., 1969. Reporter Miami Herald, Fla. Today; night city editor Palm Beach (Fla.) Post; mng. editor Palm Beach Daily News; asst. mng. editor Wichita (Kans.) Eagle; city editor/metro editor/asst. to exec. editor San Jose (Calif.) Mercury News, 1978-82; asst. mng. editor Denver Post, 1982-84; asst. mng. editor/mng. editor/editor L.A. Daily News, 1984-94; mng. editor, editor Rocky Mountain News, Denver, 1994-98, pres., 1998—. Mem. Am. Soc. Newspaper Editors, Soc. Profl. Journalists, AP News Execs. Coun. (past bd. mem., past pres. Calif., Nev. chpt., past editor AP Mng. Editors News), Metro Denver C. of C. (bd. dirs.), NCCJ (bd. dirs. Denver chpt.). Avocations: skiing, hiking. Office: Rocky Mountain News 400 W Colfax Ave Denver CO 80204-2694

BURDICK, WILLIAM MACDONALD, biomedical engineer; b. Providence, R.I., Apr. 24, 1952; s. Franklin Pierce and Lola Alice (Cook) B. BS, Ind. U. Pa., 1975; M of Engring., Tex. A&M U., 1981; postgrad., U. Tex., 1982-86. Engring. analyst FDA, Winchester, Mass., 1988-90; reviewer neurological devices FDA, Rockville, Md., 1990-94; reviewer, gen. hosp. and personal use devices FDA, Rockville, 1994—. Inventor in field; contbr. articles to profl. jours.; contbr. poem to: Dance on the Horizon (Editor's Choice award Nat. Libr. Poetry). Active Native Am. Rights Fund. With USAF, 1976-78. Mem. Internat. Platform Assn., Biomed. Engring. Soc., Nature Conservancy, Humane Soc. U.S., Nat. Multiple Sclerosis Soc., World Wildlife Fund. Congregationalist. Avocations: reading, writing (poetry, songs, fiction), gardening, sports. Office: HHS/PHS/FDA/ODE/GHDB 9200 Corporate Blvd Rockville MD 20850-3229

BURDINE, JOHN A., hospital administrator, nuclear medicine educator; b. Austin, Tex., Feb. 7, 1936; married; 3 children. BA, U. Tex., 1959; MD, U. Tex., Galveston, 1961. Diplomate Am. Be. Nuclear Medicine (orgnl. exam. com. 1971, bd. dirs. 1978—, chmn. certifyng exam. com. 1980-81, 81-82, editorial bd. Jour. Nuclear Medicine, 1973-81). Intern Med. Ctr. Ind. U., 1961-62; resident nuclear medicine, internal medicine U. Tex., Galveston, 1962-65; active med. staff St. Luke's Episcopal Hosp.-Tex. Children's Hosp., Houston, 1969-90; chief nuclear medicine svc. St. Luke's Episcopal Hosp.-Tex. Children's Hosp., Tex. Heart Inst., Houston, 1969-85; chief exec. officer, head adminstr. St. Luke's Episcopal Hosp., Houston, 1984-87, pres., chief exec. officer, 1986-91, vice chmn., chief exec. officer, 1991-94; also bd. dirs. St. Luke's Episcopal Hosp., 1991-94; cons. St. Luke's Hosp., 1995—; courtesy staff Tex. Children's Hosp., 1992—; asst. prof. dept. radiology Baylor Coll. Medicine, 1965-68, acting chmn. dept. radiology, 1968-71, chief nuclear medicine dept., 1965-95, assoc. prof. dept. radiology, 1968-74, prof. dept. radiology, 1974—, acting dir. sect. nuclear medicine dept. medicine, 1979-80, prof. dept. medicine, 1979—, mem. exec. faculty com., 1968-71, mem. com. human experimentation, 1969-71, chmn. radiosotope com., 1970-74, mem., 1966-82, other coms.; sec. Tex. Radiation Adv. Bd., 1981-86, exec. com., 1982-86, med. com., 1982-86, radioactive waste com., 1982-86, fee rules com., 1982-83; chmn. radioisotope com. Meth. Hosp., 1979-80, active med. staff, 1979-84, courtesy med. staff, 1984—, acting med. dir. radioisotope lab., 1979-80; chief nuclear medicine sect. Harris County Hosp. Dist., 1965-83; mem. forward planning com. Tex. Med. Ctr., 1986—; trustee Tex. Heart Inst., 1985—. Editorial bd. Cardiovascular Disease, 1974; contbr. book chpts., abstracts, papers. Bd. dirs. Houston Symphony Orch., 1987-88. Fellow Am. Coll. Nuclear Physicians (orgn. com. 1973-74, chmn. radioassay & radiopharmacy com. 1975-76, DOE speaker's bur. 1981-85), mem. AMA (rep. coun. nuclear medicine 1976-77), AAUP, Harris County Med. Assn., Tex. Med. Assn. (vice chmn. com. nuclear medicine 1968-71, chmn. 1971-78, others), Tex. Assn. Physicians in Nuclear Medicine, Soc. Nuclear Medicine (pres. 1982-83, southwestern chpt. trustee 1972-80, mem. numerous coms.), Phi Beta Kappa, Phi Eta Sigma, Alpha Epsilon Delta. Home: 347 Hunters Trail St Houston TX 77024-6900 Office: St Luke's Episcopal Hosp PO Box 20269 Houston TX 77225-0269*

BURDITT, GEORGE MILLER, JR., lawyer; b. Chgo., Sept. 21, 1922; s. George Miller and Flora Winifred (Hardie) B.; m. Barbara Helen Stenger, Feb. 17, 1945; children: Betsey Burditt Blessing, George M., Deborah, Barbara Burditt Perry. BA, Harvard U., 1944, LLB, 1948. Bar: Ill. 1949, D.C. 1981, U.S. Dist. Ct. (no. dist.) Ill. 1952, U.S. Ct. Appeals (7th cir.) 1961, U.S. Ct. Appeals (D.C. cir.) 1962, U.S. Ct. Appeals (4th cir.) 1974, U.S. Supreme Ct. 1974, U.S. Ct. Appeals (2d cir.) 1978, U.S. Ct. Appeals (8th cir.) 1988. With law dept. Swift & Co., Chgo., 1948-54; ptnr. Chadwell & Kayser and predecessors, Chgo., 1955-69, Burditt and Radzius, Chgo., 1969-98, Bell, Boyd and Lloyd, Chgo., 1998—; adj. prof. Northwestern U. Sch. Law, 1967-97; gen. counsel Food and Drug Law Inst.; dir. Gerber Products, 1973-93. Contbr. articles to profl. jours. Active Ill. State Ho. of Reps., 1965-72, asst. majority leader, 1971-72; Rep. candidate U.S. Senate, 1974. 2d lt. USAAF, 1943-45. Named Outstanding Legislator, Better Govt. Assn., 1969, 71; recipient Presdl. award Cook County Bar Assn., 1981, Defender of Justice award Nat. Conf. Christians & Jews, 1992. Mem. ABA, Ill. State Bar Assn., D.C. Bar Assn., Chgo. Bar Assn. (pres. 1980-81), N.Y. Bar Assn., Fed. Bar Assn., Met. Bar Leaders Caucus (pres. 1981-82), Harvard Law Sch. Assn. (pres. 1988-90), Harvard Law Sch. Ill. (pres. 1980-81), Union League Club, Econ. Club, Mid-Day Club, Crystal Downs Country Club, Law Club Chgo. (pres. 1980-81). Office: Bell Boyd and Lloyd 70 W Madison St Chicago IL 60602-4207

BURDSALL, DEBORAH PATTERSON, geriatrics nurse, educator; b. Meadville, Pa., Dec. 9, 1955; d. David B. and Darlene Jacqueline (Shipley) Patterson; m. Richard E. Burdsall, June 28, 1978; children: T. Scott Bentley, Steven David Spencer, James Stuart Taylor. Diploma, Evanston (Ill.) Hosp., 1981; BA in Psychology/Biology, Allegheny Coll., Meadville, 1978. Cert. gerontol. nurse. Oncology staff nurse Evanston Hosp., 1981-82; telemetry staff nurse Glenbrook Hosp., Glenview, Ill., 1982-84; weekend supr. Luth. Home and Svc. for Aged, Arlington Hts., Ill., 1985-90; coord. Omnibus Reconciliation Act 1987 Luth. Home and Svc. for Aged, Arlington Heights, Ill., 1990-91, minimum data set and care plan coord., 1991—, infection control/quality assurance coord., insvc. coord., 1993-96, infection control coord., CPR instr./trainer, 1996—. Office: Luth Home and Svcs for Aged 800 W Oakton St Arlington Heights IL 60004-4602

BURE, PAVEL, professional hockey player; b. Moscow, Mar. 31, 1971. Wing Fla. Panthers, Sunrise. Recipient Calder Meml. trophy, 1991-92; NHL regular season and playoff Top Goal Scorer, 1993-94. Office: Fla Panthers Panthers Pkwy Sunrise FL 33323

BUREAU, MICHEL ANDRÉ, pediatrician, pulmonologist; b. Sherbrooke, Que., Can., Oct. 2, 1943; s. Jean Ernest and Julienne (Couture) B.; m. Renee Louise Bilodeau, May 20, 1967; children: Martin, Anne, Nicolas. MD, Laval (Que.) U., 1968; postgrad., McGill U., 1973. Intern and resident in pediatrics and pulmonology McGill U., Montreal, 1968-73; head newborn medicine Sherbrooke U., 1975-81, dean medicine, 1988-95; head respiratory medicine McGill-Montreal Children's Hosp., 1982-87; pres. Fonds de la recherche en santé du Que., 1995—; pres. R&D CHUS Inc., 1995—; pres. Dean's Conf. Que., 1989, 93; chmn. numerous rsch. coms. Fonds de la recherche en santé du Que./Inst. de recherche en santé et sécurité au travail. Contbr. numerous articles to profl. publs.; external editor Jour. Applied Physiology, Pediatric Rsch., Am. Rev. Respiratory Diseases. Rsch. scholar Med. Rsch. Coun. Can.,1979—, Fonds de la recherche en santé du Que., 1980, Can. Cystic Fibrosis Found., 1981-86. Fellow Royal Coll. Physicians and Surgeons Can., Am. Coll. Chest Physician, Pediatric Rsch. Soc.; mem. Can. Thoracic Soc. (pres. 1987-88, chmn. various rsch. coms.), Can. Assn. Med. Schs. (treas.). Office: U Sherbrooke Faculty Med, 3001 12th Ave N, Sherbrooke, PQ Canada J1H 5N4

BURENGA, KENNETH L., publishing executive; b. Somerville, N.J., May 30, 1944; s. Nicholas Jr. and Louanna (Chamberlin) B.; m. Jean Case, Oct. 29, 1964; children: Kean L., Diene M. BS, Rider Coll., 1970. Budget acct. Dow Jones & Co., South Brunswick, N.J., 1966-67, asst. mgr. data processing control, 1968-69, staff asst. for systems devel., 1970-71, mgr. systems devel. and control, 1972-76, circulation mktg. mgr., 1977-78, circulation sales dir., 1979-80, v.p. circulation, circulation dir., 1980-86; chief fin. officer and adminstrv. officer Dow Jones & Co., N.Y.C., 1986-88, exec. v.p., gen. mgr., 1989-91; pres., chief oper. officer Dow Jones & Co., Inc., 1991—, also bd. dirs.; gen. mgr. Wall Street Jour., 1989—; bd. dirs. Ottaway Newspapers, Inc. Bd. dirs. Better Bus. Bur., N.Y., 1987. Staff sgt. USAR. Avocation: cattle farming. Office: Dow Jones & Co Inc 200 Liberty St Fl 11 New York NY 10281-1099*

BURFEINDT, DOUGLAS GLENN, civilian military official; b. Sioux Falls, S.D., June 10, 1954; s. Raymond Ariel and Tressa Clarine Burfeindt; m. Oriela Victoria Quiros, Apr. 19, 1976; children: Douglas Glenn Jr., O. Melisa. BS, N.Y. Regents Coll., Albany, 1985; MBA, Calif. Coast U., 1996. Enlisted man U.S. Army, 1973, advanced through grades to sgt. sr. grade; intelligence specialist U.S. Army, various locations, 1974-80; resigned, 1981; instr. U.S. Army Intelligency Sch., Ft. Huachuca, Ariz., 1980-83; intellence ops. officer 470th M.I. Brigade, Panama, 1983-94; intelligence prodn. mgr., policy mgr. Dept. Def. IPP, U.S. So. Command, Miami, Fla., 1994—; mem. intelligence prodrs.' coun. Dept. Def., Washington, 1994—; mem. Integrated Air Def. Study Coordinating Group, Washington, 1997—; rep. Joint Intelligence Virual Architecture Com., Washington, 1998—; owner, mgr. timberland. Mem. ASAP, Am. Legion, Fla. Internat. U. Panther Parents. Avocations: fishing, reading, photography, tree farming, conservationism.

BURFORD, ALEXANDER MITCHELL, JR., retired physician; b. Mar. 21, 1929; s. Alexander Mitchell and Mary Young (Tittle) B. BS, Florence (Ala.) State Coll., 1951; MD, U. Tenn., Memphis, 1957. Intern U. Tenn., Knoxville, 1957-58; resident in pathology U. Tenn., Memphis, 1958-62; assoc. pathologist Eliza Coffee Meml. Hosp., Florence, 1962-73, dir. lab., chief pathology, 1973-95, mem. med. staff, 1962-98; practice medicine specializing in pathology, 1958-98, Florence Pathology Svcs., 1983-98; ret., 1998. Active Florence Tree Commn., 1987-92, Am. Chestnut Found., 1985—, Mars Hill Bible Sch. Endowment Assn., 1985—, Nat. Arbor Day Found; trombonist Shoals Symphony and in Southwinds; mem. pres. cabinet U. North Ala., 1992—; mem. alumni coun. Coll. Medicine U. Tenn. Mem. AMA, Ala. Urban Forestry Assn., Ala. Forest Owner's Assn., Tree City USA, Med. Assn. Ala., Ala. Assn. Pathologists (pres. 1974-75), Coll. Am. Pathologists (del. 1972-90), Am. Soc. Clin. Pathologists, Am. Assn. Blood Banks, Am. Forestry Assn., Am. Rifleman Assn., Nat. Wildlife Fedn., Lauderdale County Med. Assn., Shoals Symphony Assn. (bd. dirs. 1993—), Florence C. of C., Friends of Florence-Lauderdale Pub. Libr. (pres. 1993-95), Forest Landowners Assn., Ala. Wildlife Assn., So. Med. Assn., Heritage Found., U. Tenn. Alumni Assn. (Muscle Shoals chpt.), Audubon Soc., Lions Club (past pres. local chpt. 1962-70, dep. dist. gov.), Alpha Kappa Kappa, Kappa Mu Epsilon, Alpha Psi Omega. Republican. Home: 652 Howell St Florence AL 35630-3537

BURFORD, ANNE MCGILL, lawyer; b. Casper, Wyo., Apr. 21, 1942; d. Joseph John and Dorothy Jean (O'Grady) McGill; m. David Gorsuch, June 4, 1964 (div. 1982); children: Neil, Stephanie, J.J.; m. Robert Fitzpatrick Burford, Feb. 20, 1983 (dec. 1993). Student, Nat. U. Mex., 1955-56, 58, Regis Coll., Denver, 1959; BA, U. Colo., 1961, LLB, 1964. Bar: Colo. 1964, D.C., 1985. Asst. trust adminstr. 1st Nat. Bank of Denver, 1966-67; instr. Metro State Coll., 1966-67; asst. dist. atty., Jefferson County, 1968-71; dep. dist. atty., Denver, 1971-73; hearing officer Real Estate Commn., State Bds. Cosmetology, Optometric Examiners, Profl. Nursing and Vet. Medicine, 1974-75; corp. counsel Mountain Bell Telephone Co., Denver, 1975-81; mem. Colo. Ho. of Reps., 1977-81, chmn. state affairs com., 1979-80, chmn. legal svcs. com., 1980; del. Nat. Conf. State Legislators; mem. Nat. Conf. Commrs. on Uniform State Law, 1979, 80; presdl. del. to Kenya's Independence, 1983; loaned exec. mgmt. and efficiency task force Colo. Dept. Regulatory Agys., 1976; adminstr. EPA, Washington, 1981-83; pvt. practice, Denver, 1993—; environ. cons. Author: Are You Tough Enough, 1986. Former bd. dirs. YMCA. Fulbright scholar, Jaipur, India, 1964-65. Mem. Mortar Bd., Phi Alpha Delta, Delta Delta Delta. Republican. Roman Catholic. Home and Office: 3853 S Hudson St Denver CO 80237-1050

BURG, JEROME STUART, financial planning consultant; b. N.Y.C., Aug. 2, 1935; s. Norman and Ruth (Schkurman) B.; m. Janis Elaine Lyon, May 26, 1974; children: Jeffrey Howard, David Matthew, Audree, Harriet, Robert, Stephanie. Student, Temple U., 1953-56; CLU, Am. Coll., 1973, chartered fin. cons., 1984; cert. fin. planner, Coll. Fin. Planning, 1983. Pres., CEO Jerome Burg Assoc., Inc., Cherry Hill, N.J., 1963-79, Contemporary Fin. Planning, Scottsdale, Ariz., 1979-89; sr. acct. mgr. Acacia Group, Phoenix, 1989—; instr. Glendale and Scottdale C.C., 1983-92, Nat. Inst. Fin., N.J., 1984-90. Host (radio program) Money Talks Sta. KFNN, Phoenix, 1993-98. Pres. N.J. Assn. Life Underwriters, Trenton, 1963-65; instr. Jr. Achievement, Scottsdale, 1985-89; bd. dirs. Phoenix Boys Choir, 1997—; 1st v.p. Pres. Cabinet-Acacia Group, Washington, 1991, 93, co-pres., 1992, mem. pres.' cabinet, 1989—. With U.S. Army, 1956-58. Mem. Internat. Assn. Fin. Planning (bd. dirs. Greater Phoenix chpt. 1982—), Inst. Cert. Fin. Planners. Avocations: golf, skiing. Office: Acacia Group 3200 E Camelback Rd Ste 245 Phoenix AZ 85018-2320

BURG, JOHN PARKER, signal processing executive; b. Great Bend, Kans., Dec. 17, 1931; s. Kenneth Edwin and Viola Mae (Parker) B.; m. Ida Elizabeth Groome; children Ida Elizabeth, Clarence Oscar Edwin; m. Shirley Joan Steele, Apr. 10, 1976; children: Nathan Parker, Emily Diane, Paul Andrew. BS in Physics, BA in Math., U. Tex., 1953; MS in Physics, MIT, 1960; PhD in Geophysics, Stanford U., 1975. Asst. engr. Tex. Instruments, Inc., 1956-57; engr. Tex. Instruments, Inc., Dallas, 1960; sr. rsch. geophysicist Geophys. Svc., Inc., Dallas, 1960-73; chmn. bd. dirs. Time and Space Processing, Inc., Santa Clara, Calif., 1973-83; pres. Entropic Processing, Inc., Cupertino, Calif., 1983—, also chmn. bd. dirs.; cons. oil cos., ESL, Inc., Naval Undersea Ctr., 1969-75; cons. Digicon, Inc., Houston, 1982-83; chmn. bd. dirs. Entropic Rsch. Lab., Cupertino, 1984-98, Entropic Speech Inc., 1984—. Inventor patent predictive seismic deconvolution, multichannel filtering. Recipient Rsch. Publication award Naval Rsch. Lab., 1984; named Life Master Am. Contract Bridge League. Fellow IEEE (contbr. to jour.). Avocation: bridge theory. Office: Entropic Processing Inc 20990 Valley Green Dr Apt 703 Cupertino CA 95014-1846

BURG, MAURICE BENJAMIN, renal physiologist, physician; b. Boston, Apr. 9, 1931; s. Charles and Augusta (Green) B.; m. Judith Anne Braverman (dec.); m. Ruth Cooper, Dec. 30, 1967; children: Elizabeth, Laurence, Joan, Robert. AB, Harvard U., 1952, MD, 1955. Investigator Lab. Kidney/Electrolyte Metabolism Nat. Heart Lung and Blood Inst., NIH, Bethesda, Md., 1956—, chief Lab. Kidney/Electrolyte Metabolism, 1975—. Contbr. over 145 articles to profl. jours. Mem. NAS. Office: Nat Heart Lung Blood Inst Bldg 10 Rm 6N260 10 Center Dr MSC-1603 Bethesda MD 20892-1603*

BURG, MICHAEL S., lawyer; b. Chgo., Mar. 12, 1950; s. Sydney M. and Phyliss (Shapiro) B.; m. Deborah Ann White, Aug. 17, 1974 (div. Mar. 1984); children: Scott Edward, Stephen Jonathan; m. Kathryn Anne Bush, May 27, 1988. BA, U. Denver, 1972, JD, 1975. Bar: Colo. 1976, U.S. Dist. Ct. Colo. 1976, U.S. Ct. Appeals (10th cir.) 1979, U.S. Supreme Ct. 1990, U.S. Dist. Ct. Ariz. 1993, Nebr. 1996. Assoc. Atler Zall & Hangman P.C., Denver, 1976-77; ptnr. Dunn, Crane, & Burg P.C., Denver, 1977-80; ptnr., pres. Burg & Aspinwall P.C., Denver, 1980-84, Burg & Eldredge P.C., Denver, 1984-98, Burg, Simpson, Eldredge, Hersh & Houliston, P.C., Englewood, Colo., 1998—; adj. prof. law U. Denver Coll. Law; instr. Metro State Coll., Denver, 1978-82; agt. to profl. athletes, 1988—. Mem. SAG (pres. Denver chpt. 1983-90), Am. Bd. Trial Advocates, Sports Lawyers Assn., Phi Beta Kappa. Jewish. Avocations: acting, lecturing. Office: Burg Simpson Eldredge Hersh & Houliston PC 40 Inverness Dr E Englewood CO 80112-5402 also: 201 3rd St NW Albuquerque NM 87102-5800

BURG, RALPH, art association executive; b. Malden, Mass., Jan. 2, 1914; s. Joseph and Bessie (Meyer) B.; m. Fay E. Pristaw, Jan. 10, 1937; children: Stephen, Harvey. BA, Boston U., 19366. V.p. Beacon Musical Inst. Co., Boston, 1939-70; pres., owner Quisisana Lodge, Center Lovell, Maine, 1946-76; chmn. Edna Hibel Soc., Coral Springs, Fla., 1979-99. Editor: Hibeletter newsletter, 1979-95. Mem. Friends for Life, B'Nai B'rith. Recipient Cultural award Minister of Culture, Flanders, Belgium, 1983. Mem. Kiwanis (various coms. Boston chpt. 1946-70), Synergistic Assn. (pres. Boston chpt. 1962-70), Woodlands Country Club. Avocations: golf, tennis, writing, Bridge, saxophone. Home: 4604 King Palm Dr Tamarac FL 33319-6121 Office: Edna Hibel Soc PO Box 9721 Coral Springs FL 33075-9721

BURG, RANDALL K., federal judge; b. 1951. BA, U. Minn., 1973, JD, 1976. Part-time magistrate judge U.S. Dist. Ct. Minn., Bemidji, 1990—. Office: US Courthouse 207 4th St NW Bemidji MN 56601-3114

BURG, WALTER A., airport terminal executive. Gen. manager, ceo Tucson Airport Authority, Ariz., 1966-79, pres., CEO, 1979—. Office: Tucson Internat Airport 7005 S Plumer Ave Tucson AZ 85706-6926

BURGARD, RALPH, cultural/education planner; b. Buffalo, June 22, 1927; s. Willard Henry and Elise (Waite) B.; m. Cecily Ward, Mar. 17, 1956 (div. Apr. 1985); m. Elaine Johansen Hawk, Apr. 8, 1989 (div. Dec. 1994); children: Christopher, Timothy, Nadia; m. Marjorie Dean Martin, Aug. 8, 1998. BA in Philosophy, Dartmouth Coll., 1949. Mgr. R.I. Philharm. Orch., Providence, 1952-54; assoc. mgr. Buffalo Philharm. Orch., 1954-55; dir. Winston-Salem (N.C.) Arts Coun., 1955-57, St. Paul Coun. Arts and Scis., 1957-65; exec. dir. Am. Coun. for Arts, N.Y.C., 1965-70; pres. Burgard Assocs., N.Y.C., Cambridge, Mass., Kittery Point, Maine, 1970—; founder St. Paul Chamber Orch., 1958, A Schs. Program, 1987, Spectra Schs., 1998. Author: Arts in the City, 1968. former sec. N.Am. Assembly of State and Provincial Arts Agys.; former mem. adv. panel Nat. Endowment for Arts, N.Y. State Coun. on Arts, N.Y.C. Cultural Coun.; mem. Nat. Coun. Amenity Planners. Recipient 10th Yr. Tribute, Hartford Arts Coun., 1981, Merit award Assn. Coll., Univ., Cmty. Arts Adminstrs., 1982, Tribute, Nat. Assembly Cmty. Arts, 1987, Chancellor's award N.C. Sch. Arts, 1997; Ralph Burgard Day, City of St. Paul, 1986. Mem. Century Assn. Avocations: rowing, books, nature, ballooning. Office: Burgard Assocs PO Box 251 Kittery Point ME 03905

BURGARINO, ANTHONY EMANUEL, environmental engineer, consultant; b. Milw., July 20, 1948; s. Joseph Francis Burgarino and Mardelle (Hoeffler) T.; m. Gail Fay DiMatteo, Mar. 13, 1982; children: Paul Anthony, Joanna Lynn. BS, U. Wis., 1970; MS, Ill. Inst. Tech., 1974, PhD, 1980. Registered profl. engr., Ariz. Sales engr. Leeds & Northrup, Phila., 1970-72; rsch. asst. Ill. Inst. Tech., Chgo., 1972-75; chemist City of Chgo., 1975-79; instr. Joliet (Ill.) Jr. Coll., 1978-79; sr. project engr. Carollo Engrs., Walnut Creek, Calif., 1980—; cons. City of Clovis, Calif., 1981-83, City of Fresno, Calif., 1983-96, City of Phoenix, 1981-90, City of Yuma, Ariz., 1989—, City of Santa Maria, Calif., 1991-95, City of Vallejo, Calif., 1991-98, City of Peoria, Ariz., 1996-97, town of Hillsborough, Calif., 1998—, Calif. Water Svcs., 1999—. Contbr. articles to profl. jours. EPA grantee, 1970-72; NSF fellow, 1973, Ill. Inst. Tech. Rsch. Found. fellow, 1974. Mem. Am. Water Works Assn. Roman Catholic. Avocations: mechanical and electronics projects building, stock and real estate investments. Home: 2321 Lafayette Dr Antioch CA 94509-5871 Office: Carollo Engrs 2700 Ygnacio Valley Rd Ste 300 Walnut Creek CA 94598-3466

BURGDOERFER, JERRY, lawyer; b. Jeffersonville, Ind., May 3, 1958; s. Jerry Jack and Barbara Jean (Hofherr) B. BS, Ind. U., 1980, MBA, 1983, JD cum laude, 1983. Bar: Ill. 1984, U.S. Dist. Ct. (no. dist.) Ill. 1984, U.S. Tax Ct. 1984. Assoc. Adams, Fox, Adelstein, Rosen & Bell, Chgo., 1983-88, ptnr., 1988-89; assoc. Jenner & Block, Chgo., 1989-90, ptnr., 1991—; with Mori Sogo Law Offices, Tokyo, 1991-93. Author articles. Vol. United Cerebral Palsy Assn., 1995—, dir., 1999—. Named 2d Benton Nat. Moot Ct. Competition, 1982. Mem. ABA, Internat. Bar Assn., Inter Pacific Bar Assn., Ill. Bar Assn., Chgo. Bar Assn. (chairperson '34 Act Com. 1996-98, reporter, Securities Com. 1997-98, vice chair 1998-99, chair 1999—), Japan Am. Soc. Chgo., Ind. U. Alumni Club Chgo. (vol. 1988-89) , Econ. Club Chgo., Execs. Club Chgo., Chgo. Coun. on Fgn. Rels., Japan-Am. Soc. of Chgo., Phi Eta Sigma, Phi Delta Phi, Phi Delta Theta (sec. chpt. 1977-78, co-founder, steering com. Chgo. alumni club 1988-89). Avocations: bicycling, water skiing, Japanese language. Office: Jenner & Block 1 IBM Plz Fl 4000 Chicago IL 60611-7602

BURGDOERFER, JERRY J., marketing and distribution executive; b. Connersville, Ind., Nov. 20, 1935; s. Louis M. and Edna (Seele) B.; m. Barbara Jean Hofherr, Aug. 15, 1954; children: Steven, Jerry, Jeffrey, Stuart. B.S., Ind. U., 1957. Indsl. engr. Colgate Palmolive Co., Jeffersonville, Ind., 1958-59; mktg. mgr. Colgate Palmolive Co., N.Y.C., 1959-63, Am. Can Co., Green Bay, Wis., 1963-65; dir. sales Am. Can Co., 1966-67; v.p. Am. Can Co., Greenwich, Conn., 1968-70; pres., dir. Am. Garden Products, Inc., Boston, 1970-71; exec. v.p. Facelle Co. div. Internat. Paper Co., N.Y.C., 1971-73; v.p. worldwide mktg. Hertz Corp., N.Y.C., 1973-77; exec. v.p., dir. Hertz Corp., from 1977; pres., chief exec. officer Berkey Inc., N.Y.C., 1979-86, Carysfort Enterprises Inc., Key Largo, Fla., 1987—; v.p. corp. mktg. AT Cross Co., Lincoln, R.I., 1991—, also bd. dirs.; bd. dirs. Avis Inc. Served with arty. U.S. Army, 1957-58. Recipient Torch of Liberty-Man of Yr. award B'nai B'rith. Mem. Acad. Alumni Fellows (Ind. U.), Phi Delta Theta, Barrington Yacht Club (bd. govs.).

BURGE, CHRISTOPHER, auction house executive. Former pres. Christie, Manson & Woods Internat. Inc., N.Y.C., now chmn. Office: Christie Manson & Woods Internat Inc 20 Rockefeller Plz New York NY 10020*

BURGE, DAVID RUSSELL, concert pianist, composer, piano educator; b. Evanston, Ill., Mar. 25, 1930; s. Russell David and Sylvia (Swensen) B.; m. Liliane Choney, 1993; 1 child, Russell David. MusB, Northwestern U., 1951, MusM, 1952; DMus Arts, Eastman Sch. Music, 1956; postgrad., Cherubini Conservatory, Florence, Italy, 1956-57; DFA, Bucknell U., 1980. Instr. piano Northwestern U., 1949-52; assoc. prof. music, composer-pianist in resident Whitman Coll., 1957-62; dir. MacDowell Hall Concert Series at coll., 1959-62; organist Ch. of Christ Scientist, Walla Walla, 1958-62; from asst. prof. music to prof. U. Colo., 1962-75; chmn. piano dept. Eastman Sch. Music, U. Rochester, N.Y., 1975-87, prof., 1975-93, Kilbourn prof., 1978-79; artist-in-residence U. Calif., Davis, 1975; guest prof. piano U. Stockholm, Sweden, 1981, 92, Banff Ctr., Can., 1983-84, 86, U. Auckland, New Zealand, 1988; composer-in-residence San Diego Ballet Co., 1997—; guest prof. piano U. Stockholm, Sweden, 1981, 92, Banff Ctr., Can., 1983-84, 86, U. Auckland, New Zealand, 1988, Odense, Denmark, 1997; guest prof. composition U. Pa., 1977; guest prof. music history U. Gothenberg, Sweden, 1980, 92; feature writer San Diego Reader. Rec. artist, Mercury, Advance, Candide, Nonesuch (grammy nomination 1974), CRI Records, Mus. Heritage Soc. Records, Vox Records, Proviva Records, Wergo, Albany, Capstone Records; composer: opera Intervals, 1961, Trio; trio for violin, cello, piano, 1962; work for piano Eclipse, 1963; for flute-piano Sources I, 1964; for violin-celeste-piano Sources II, 1965; for piano Eclipse II, 1966, Sources IV, 1969; for clarinet-percussion Sources III, 1967; for soprano-piano A Song of Sixpence, 1967, Life Begins at 40, 1998; for flute-clarinet-violin-cello-piano-tape Aeolian Music, 1968; String Quartet, 1969, Twone in Sunshine, an Entertainment for Theater, 1969; for violin-orch. that no one knew, 1969, Songs of Love and Sorrow, 1989, for solo piano Go-Hyang, 1994, Sonata for Violin and Piano, 1994, Liana's Song: A Ballet in Six Parts, 1995, The Dark Journey, 12 Pieces for Dance, 1995, 24 Preludes for Piano, 1996, Luna Lunera, a Ballet in 12 Parts, 1996, Moku (Island) for three percussionists, 1998; La Loteria Ballet, 1998; for piano and orch. Dances of Love and Laughter, 1998; also songs, anthems.; contbr. over 200 articles to periodicals; columnist: Keyboard Mag., Clavier Mag., Piano Quar.; music reviewer: Music Library Assn. Notes; first major postarmistice concert, Seoul, Korea, 1953, New York debut playing all-modern program, 1961; toured, Korea, 1953-54, Europe, 1956-57, U.S.A., annually, 1960—, Eastern Europe, 1974, Far East, Australia, N.Z., 1984, 88; author: Twentieth-Century Piano Music, 1990; Vanishing Spring, 1998. Served with AUS, 1952-54, Korea. Decorated by U.S. Army for cultural relations work in Korea, 1954; recipient Alumni Merit award Northwestern U., 1974, Colo. Gov.'s award, 1975, Distinguished Alumni award Eastman Sch. Music, 1975, Deems Taylor award for mus. journalism ASCAP, 1978-79; Fulbright fellow in Italy, 1956-57; Faculty Research lectr. U. Colo., 1972. Mem. ASCAP, Internat. Webern Soc. (charter), Am. Soc. Univ. Composers (founder, nat. chmn. 1970-74), Pi Kappa Lambda. Address: 5243 Caminito Apartado San Diego CA 92108-4204

BURGE, HEIDI, basketball player; b. Nov. 12, 1971. Grad., U. Va., 1993. Forward ASMontferrand, France, 1993-94, GYSEV=-Sopron, Hungary, 1994-95, Cariparma-Parma, Italy, 1995-96, Panathinaikos, Greece, 1996-97, WNBA - L.A. Sparks, 1997—, USA Women's Nat. Team (World Championship Qualification Tournament), 1997, WNBA, Mystics, Washington, 1998—; f/c for Racing Luxembourg eam. Named to Jr. Nat. Team, 1990, World Univ. Games, 1993. Avocations: sports, volleyball, swimming, surfing, shopping, reading. Home: 2306 Palos Verdes Dr W #101 Palos Verdes Peninsula CA 90274 Office: 601 F Street NW Washington DC 20001

BURGE, JOHN WESLEY, JR., management consultant; b. Mobile, Ala., Sept. 11, 1932; s. John Wesley and Mary Jo (Guest) B.; m. Shirley Paulette Roberts, Mar. 29, 1958; children: John, Delene, Eric, Kurt, Karen. Student, Centenary Coll., San Antonio Coll., UCLA. Various engring. and mgmt. positions ITT Gilfillan, 1954-69; pres., gen. mgr. Rantec, Calabasas, Calif., 1969-71; chmn. bd. Rantec, 1971-89; pres., gen. mgr. electronics and space div. Emerson Electric Co., St. Louis, 1971-80; corp. group v.p. govt., def. Emerson Electric Co., 1977-89; ret.; pvt. practice cons. crisis mgmt. Pensacola, Fla., 1975—. Served with USAF, 1950-54. Decorated Grand Cordon of Order Al-Istiqlal (Jordan). Presbyterian.

BURGE, LARRY BRADY, artist; b. Fayetteville, N.C., Feb. 2, 1948; s. Billie Dixie and Elma Leigh (Westbrook) B.; m. Lori Jo Shepard, June 17, 1995. Student, Coll. of the Albemarle, Elizabeth City, N.C., 1972, Art Instrn. sch., Mpls., 1976. One man shows include Village Smith Galleries, Winston-Salem, N.C., 1982, Kinston (N.C.) Arts Coun., 1983, Ballantyne Art Gallery, New Bern, N.C., 1984, Collector's Gallery, Raleigh, N.C., 1986, N.C. Maritime Mus., Beaufort, N.C., 1986, 91, World Art Gallery, Jacksonville, N.C., 1995, Art Masters Gallery, Beaufort, 1998, Arts and Things, Morehead City, N.C., 1999; group exhibits include Coll. of the Albemarle Art Ctr., Elizabeth City, 1972, Riverside Gallery, New Bern, 1978, Fairfield Harbor Art Exhibit, New Bern, 1978, Weyerhaeuser Art Exhibit, Grifton, N.C., 1981, 7th Ann Realist Invitational Remarque Gallery, High Point, N.C., 1983, Remarque Gallery, High Point, N.C., 1984, Spartanburg (S.C.) Arts Ctr., 1985, Snyder Gallery, Charlotte, N.C., 1987, Wilkes Art Gallery, North Wilkesboro, 1990, Mid-Town Gallery, Winston-Salem, 1993, Hampton House Gallery, Winston-Salem, 1997; works in corp. collections at Wachovia Bank and Trust Co., Winston-Salem, RJR Nabisco, Winston-Salem, Trotman's Gallery, Winston-Salem, Marine Fed. Credit Union, Jacksonville, N.C.; prodr. ltd.-edit. prints of maj. paintings Salem Graphics, Inc., 1990—; listed in Ency. Living Artists, 1990, Am. Artists-A Survey of Leading Contemporaries, 1991. Home and Office: PO Box 623 927 Church St Newport NC 28570-0623

BURGE, WILLIAM LEE, retired business information executive; b. Atlanta, June 27, 1918; s. William Frederick and Leona (Payne) B.; m. Willette Richey, Feb. 27, 1937; children: Judith, William Roger. Ed., Ga. State Coll. Bus. Adminstrn., 1937-42; LL.D. (hon.), Mercer U., 1978. With Equifax Inc. (formerly Retail Credit Co.), 1936-88; br. mgr. Equifax Inc. (formerly Retail Credit Co.), Greensboro, N.C., 1949-51; div. mgr. Equifax Inc. (formerly Retail Credit Co.), Pitts., 1951-58; v.p. Equifax Inc. (formerly Retail Credit Co.), Atlanta, 1959-65; exec. v.p. Equifax Inc. (formerly Retail Credit Co.), 1964-65, pres., 1965—, CEO, 1967-83, chmn. bd., 1976-88; chmn. Equifax Inc. (Equifax Inc. affiliates), 1988, ret., 1988; chmn. emeritus Equifax Inc. (Equifax Services Ltd.), Can.; ret. dir. First Nat. Bank Atlanta Nat. Svc. Industries, Informes de Centrales of Mex.; chmn. Ferntank, Inc., 1951-57. Gen. chmn. United Way, Atlanta, 1961; chmn. United Negro Coll. Fund, 1974-75; regional chmn. Nat. Alliance of Businessmen, 1969-70; chmn. bd. regents Univ. System Ga., 1972-73; mem. coll. accreditation commn. So. Assn. Colls. and Schs.; mem. Commn. Postsecondary Edn.; trustee Atlanta Arts Alliance, YMCA; mem. bd. Central Atlanta Progress; mem. Gov.'s Adv. Council on Job Tng. Coordination, 1985-88 ; bd. dirs. Atlanta chpt. ARC; pres. Mus. Nat. History, 1995-96. Served with AUS, World War II. Named Atlanta's Young Man of Year, 1948, one of Atlanta's Leaders of Tomorrow Time mag., 1952, Alumnus of Yr. Ga. award State U., 1968, 87. Mem. Conf. Bd., Atlanta C. of C. (pres. 1966), Nat. C. of C. (panel on privacy), Jr. C. of C. (pres. 1947-48). Club: Kiwanis (pres. 1965). Office: Equifax Inc 1600 W Peachtree St NE Atlanta GA 30309-2642

BURGEE, JOHN HENRY, architect; b. Chgo., Aug. 28, 1933; s. Joseph Zeno and Helen (Dooley) B.; m. Gwendolyn Mary Henson, June 30, 1956; 1 son, John Gerard. BArch, U. Notre Dame, 1956, DEngr (hon.), 1983. Supt. constrn. Holabird & Root & Burgee, Chgo., 1955-56; project mgr. Naess & Murphy, Chgo., 1958-61; adminstr. design, project architect C. F. Murphy Assos., Chgo., 1961-65; assoc. ptnr. C. F. Murphy Assos., 1965-67, ptnr., 1967; assoc. Philip Johnson (Architects), N.Y.C., 1967-68; ptnr. Johnson/Burgee, N.Y.C., 1968-82, John Burgee Architects, N.Y.C., 1982—, 1986—; Chmn. Archtl. Rev. Bd., Bronxville, N.Y., 1974-75; chmn. Bronxville Planning Commn., 1975-77. Works include, I.D.S. Center, Mpls., Niagara Falls Conv. Center, Pennzoil Place, Houston, Crystal Cathedral, Los Angeles, AT&T Hdqrs., N.Y.C., PPG Hdqrs., Pitts., Transco Tower, Houston, Republic Bank, Houston, Nat. Center for Performing Arts, Bombay, 101 California Street, San Francisco, International Place, Boston, 190 South LaSalle Street, Chicago, IBM Headquarters, Atlanta, Mus. of Broadcasting, New York Canadian Broadcast Ctr., Toronto, Takashamya Dept. Store, N.Y., Capital Holding Ctr., Louisville, Puerto de Europa, Madrid, One Detroit Ctr., Marina Hotel and Shopping Ctr., Singapore, Ch. St. Mary, Lakeville, Conn. Pres. German-Am. Club, Bad Kreuznach, Germany, 1957-58; chmn. bldg. material sect. Met. Crusade of Mercy, Chgo., 1966-67; pres. Chgo. Br. North Montessori Sch. Bd., 1962-63, Lawrence Park Hilltop Assn., 1974-75; chmn. architecture com. Statue of Liberty/Ellis Island Centennial Commn.; mem. adv. coun. Coll. Engring. U. Notre Dame, 1982-88; bd. dirs. Lenox Hill Hosp., 1982-91, Parsons Sch. of Design, 1985-92, U. Notre Dame, 1988—, Chgo. Athenaeum, 1989-92. With AUS, 1956-58. Recipient Reynolds Aluminum prize, 1978, honor award U. Notre Dame, 1981, Chgo. Architecture award. Fellow AIA, Urban Design Inst.; mem. Archtl. League N.Y. (dir.), Inst. Architecture and Urban Studies (dir. 1983, chmn., pres. 1984). Clubs: Saddle Cycle (Chgo.), Arts (Chgo.), University (Chgo.), Shenarock Shore (Rye, N.Y), Am. Yacht, Century Assn. Home: 1592 E Mountain Dr Montecito CA 93108

BURGENER, FRANCIS ANDRÉ, radiology educator; b. Visp, Switzerland, May 21, 1942; came to U.S., 1970; s. Andreas and Dora (Weibel) B.; m. Theres Christen, Aug. 20, 1970; children—Philipp, Michele. M.D., U. Bern, 1967. Cert. diagnostic radiologist Am. Bd. Radiology. Resident in radiology U. Bern, 1967-68, 69-70; fellow in exptl. medicine U. Zürich, Switzerland, 1968-69; instr. U. Mich., Ann Arbor, 1970-71; asst. prof. U. Rochester, N.Y., 1971-76, assoc. prof., 1976-81, prof., 1981—; panelist USPHS, 1975-80. Author: Differential Diagnosis in Conventional Radiology, 1985, 2d edit., 1991, Differential Diganosis in Computed Tomography, 1996, Bone and Joint Disorders, 1997, Differential Diagnosis in Chest X-rays, 1997, Differential Diagnosis in Conventional Gastrointestinal Radiology, 1997; mem. editl. bd. Investigative Radiology, 1977-90, Diagnostic Imaging in Clinical Medicine, 1986-90. Grantee NIH, 1971, 76, 80. Mem. AAAS, Swiss Med. Soc., N.Y. Acad. Scis. Home: 85 Buckland Ave Rochester NY 14618-2107 Office: Univ Rochester 601 Elmwood Ave Rochester NY 14642-0001*

BURGER, AMBROSE WILLIAM, agronomy educator; b. Jasper, Ind., Nov. 27, 1923; s. August and Katherine (Lechner) B.; m. Janice Fay Brandenburg, Aug. 24, 1946; children—Katherine, Marie, Patricia, Carol; m. Phyllis J. Voorhees Jacob, Oct. 25, 1967; stepchildren—Judy, Paul. B.S. in Agronomy, Purdue U., 1947; M.S. in Agronomy, U. Wis., 1948, Ph.D., 1950. Asst. prof. agronomy U. Md., College Park, 1950-53; assoc. prof., then prof. agronomy U. Ill., Urbana, 1953-86, prof. agronomy emeritus, 1987—; researcher in field crop sci.; developer color photographs and descriptions of crop and weed plants. Served with U.S. Army, World War II. Decorated Purple Heart with oak leaf cluster; recipient Paul A. Funk award U. Ill., 1972, Outstanding Freshman Tchr. award Alpha Lambda Delta, 1980, Campus award for excellence in teaching U. Ill., 1980, 82, Sr. Faculty award Coll. Agr., 1986. Fellow Am. Soc. Agronomy (Agronomic Edn. award 1964); mem. Crop Sci. Soc. Am., Nat. Assn. Colls. and Tchrs. Agr. (book rev. editor, Disting. Educator award 1984, Outstanding Tchr. Advisor award 1984, Ensminger-Interstate Disting. Tchr. award 1986), K.C., Moose, Elks, Delta Tau Alpha. Roman Catholic. Home (summer): 2010B Eagle Ridge Ct Urbana IL 61802-8617 Home (winter): 638 Bird Bay Dr E Apt 112 Venice FL 34292-1222

BURGER, CHESTER, retired management consultant; b. Bklyn., Jan. 10, 1921; s. Benjamin W. and Terese (Felleman) B.; m. Hannah Kaufman, Jan. 30, 1948; children: Jeffrey Allen, Todd Oliver, Amy Louise; m. Ninki Hart, Jan. 9, 1959 (dec. Jan. 1969); m. Elisabeth Miller Owen, Sept. 2, 1971. BA, Bklyn. Coll., 1946. With CBS Radio, 1941-42; 1st U.S. TV reporter, visualizer CBS TV News, 1946-48; asst. news editor CBS-TV, 1948-50, news editor, 1950-52, film assignment editor, 1952-53, nat. mgr., 1953; writer-prodr. Omnibus program Ford Found., 1954-55; cons. Life mag., 1955; with pub. rels. dept. AT&T Co. and assoc. cos., 1955-88; pub. rels. counsel, asst. to pres. Ruder and Finn, Inc., 1955-57, v.p. plans, 1957-60; pres. Comm. Counselors (pub. rels. divsn. Interpublic, Inc.), N.Y.C., 1960-62, Echelons Office Temporaries, Inc. (and assoc. cos.), 1963-65; pres. Chester Burger & Co., Inc. (mgmt. cons.), 1964-88, sr. cons., 1988-90; counsel James E. Arnold, Inc., N.Y.C., 1991—; cons. Coca-Cola Export Corp., 1964-65; guest lectr. New Sch. for Social Rsch., 1967, U. Mich. Grad. Sch. Bus. Adminstrn., 1969-72, NYU Divsn. Bus. and Mgmt., 1970-76, Dalhousie U., 1970; cons. Am. Bankers Assn., 1973-85, Alyeska Pipeline Svc. Co., 1974, AARP, 1986; cons. Am. Cancer Soc., 1986-88, ret., 1988; cons. The Carter Ctr., Atlanta, 1994; lectr. pub. rels. role in mgmt. Author: Survival in the Executive Jungle, 1964, Executives Under Fire, 1966, Executive Etiquette, 1969, Walking the Executive Plank (also pub. as Creative Firing), 1972, The Chief Executive, 1978; editor: Inside Public Relations, 1984, 88, also articles; editor: Mike and Screen Press Directory, 1953, 54, 55; contbg. editor Quar. Rev. Pub. Relations (name now Pub. Relations Quar.), 1959-88 , Popular Photography mag, 1967-68; editor monthly newsletter Persuasion, 1972-74; editorial adv. bd. Pub. Relations Jour, 1975-79. Bd. dirs. N.Y. Interracial Coun. for Bus. Opportunity, 1965-68, N.Y. Diabetes Assn., 1964-67, Nat. Comm. Coun. for Human Svcs., 1973-76, Choice in Dying, Inc., 1993-96, treas. 1996, nat. chmn., 1999; bd. dirs. Union Theol. Sem., N.Y.C., 1990-94; sec., exec. com., trustee Nat. Urban League, 1967-76; pub. rels. chmn. Young Pres.' Orgn., 1962-63; adv. com. Black Exec. Exch. Program, 1969-85; 1st v.p. Nat. Urban League Devel. Found., Inc.; mem. pvt. sector adv. commn. U.S. Info. Agy., 1981-86; nat. adv. coun. Conn. Coll., 1982-88; adv. coun. Project Orbis, 1989-94; pres. bd. trustees, elder Ctrl. Presbyn. Ch. City of N.Y., 1984—; mem. White House Health Project Task Force, 1992; adv. bd. Population Commn. Internat., 1993—; bd. advisors Medicare Rights Ctr., 1996—; bd. dirs. Ctr. for Cmty. Leadership, 1996—. With AUS, 1942-46. Recipient Disting. Svc. citation United Negro Coll. Fund, 1974, award for Outstanding Svc., USIA, 1982, 1st Drew Middleton Pub. Affairs award USMC, 1991, medal for Outstanding Svc. to U.S., Govt. of U.S., 1995; named Counselors Counselor and life mem. Counselors Acad., 1988; named to Hall of Fame for Lifetime Contbns. to Profession, Arthur W. Page Soc., 1992. Mem. Telephone Pioneers Am. (hon.), Am. Pub. Rels. Assn. (dir. N.Y. chpt., nat. dir. 1959-60, v.p. ea. chpt. 1960-61), Pub. Rels. Soc. Am. (accredited; dir. 1961-63, John W. Hill award N.Y. chpt. 1980, Gold Anvil award for unusually significant contbns. 1987, chmn. Coll. Fellows 1989-90), Internat. Assn. Bus. Communicators (Spl. award 1995), Am. Arbitration Assn. (nat. panel arbitrators 1972-94), Nat. Assn. Securities Dealers (nat. panel arbitrators 1993—), Assn. Former Intelligence Officers. Home: 33 W 67th St New York NY 10023-6224

BURGER, EDMUND GANES, architect; b. Yerington, Nev., Mar. 28, 1930; s. Edmund Ganes and Rose Catherine (Kobe) B.; m. Shirley May Pratini, Jan. 21, 1968; 1 dau., Jane Lee. B.M.E., U. Santa Clara, 1951; B.Arch., U. Pa., 1959. Engr. Gen. Electric Co., 1951-52; design engr. U. Calif. Radiation Lab., 1952-57; John Stewardson fellow in architecture, 1959; architect Wurster, Bernardi & Emmons, San Francisco, 1960-63; founder Burger & Coplans, Inc. (Architects), San Francisco, 1964; pres. Burger & Coplans, Inc. (Architects), 1964-79; owner Edmund Burger (Architect), 1979—; guest lectr. U. Calif., Berkeley. important works include Acorn Housing Project, Oakland, Calif., Crescent Village Housing Project, Suisun City, Calif., Coplans residence, San Francisco, Betel Housing Project, San Francisco, Grand View Housing Project, San Francisco, Albany (Calif.) Oaks Housing, Grow Homes, San Pablo, Calif., Mariposa Housing, Dunleavy Plaza Housing, Potrero Ct. Housing, San Francisco, Lee residence, Kentfield, Calif., Burger residences, Lafayette, Calif., Oceanside, Oreg., and El Cerrito, Calif., Yamhill Valley Vineyards Winery, McMinneville, Oreg., Portico De Mar, shop and restaurant complex, Barcelona, Spain, Hendrickson residence, Newport Beach, Calif., Hamilton residence, Winters, Calif., Sanders residence, Yuba City, Calif.; author: Geomorphic Architecture, 1986. Recipient citation for excellence in community architecture AIA, 1969, award of merit AIA, award of merit Homes for Better Living, 1970, 79, 1st Honor award, 1973, 81, Holiday award for a beautiful Am., 1970, Honor award 4th Biennial HUD awards for design excellence, 1970, Bay Area awards for design excellence, 1969, 74, 78, Apts. of Year award Archtl. Record, 1972, Houses of Year award, 1973, Calif. Affordable Housing Competition award, 1981, HUD Building Value into Housing award, 1981, Community Design award Calif. Council AIA, 1986; design grant Nat. Endowment for Arts, 1980, HUD, 1980; constrn. grant HUD, 1981. Office: PO Box 10193 Berkeley CA 94709-5193

BURGER, HENRY G., anthropologist, vocabulary scientist, publisher; b. N.Y.C., June 27, 1923; s. B. William and Terese R. (Felleman) B.; m. Barbara G. Smith, Nov. 29, 1991. BA with honors (Pulitzer scholar), Columbia Coll., 1947; MA, Columbia U., 1965, Ph.D. in Cultural Anthropology (State Doctoral fellow), 1967. Indsl. engr. various orgns., 1947-51, Midwest mfrs. rep., 1952-55; social sci. cons. Chgo. and N.Y.C., 1956-67; anthropologist Southwestern Coop. Ednl. Lab., Albuquerque, 1967-69; assoc. prof. anthropology and edn. U. Mo., Kansas City, 1969-73, prof., 1973-93, prof. emeritus, 1994—, founding mem. univ. wide doctoral faculty, 1974-93; founder, pub. The Wordtree, Overland Park, Kans., 1984—; lectr. CUNY, 1957-65; adj. prof. ednl. anthropology U. N.Mex., 1969; anthrop. cons. U.S. VA Hosp., Kansas City, 1971-72; speaker in field. Author: Ethno-Pedagogy, 1968, 2d edit., 1968; editor, compiler: The Wordtree, a Reverse Dictionary for Solving Physical and Social Problems, 1984; selected for exhibit at 3 insts.; selected as a topic in Cambridge Ency. of the English Lang., 1995—; 7-time citee in Oxford English Dictionary; mem. editl. bd. Coun. Anthropology and Edn., 1975-80; author linguistic periodical column New Times, New Verbs, 1988—; contbr. to anthologies; author articles. Capt. AUS, 1943-46. NSF Instl. grantee, 1970. Fellow World Acad. Art and Sci., Am. Anthrop. Assn. (life), Royal Anthrop. Inst. Gt. Britain (life); mem. European Assn. for Lexicography, Internat. Assn. Semiotic Studies, Internat. Soc. for Knowledge Orgn., English-Speaking Union (v.p. Kansas City chpt. 1995-96), Dictionary Soc. N.Am. (life, terminology com.), Assn. Internationale de Terminologie, Academie Europeenne des Scis., Arts et Lettres (corr.), Soc. Conceptual and Content Analysis by Computer, Columbia U. Club, Phi Beta Kappa. Achievements include discovery of the branchability of processes (corresponding, for materials, to the periodic table of elements); research on computerized causality and reasoning. E-mail: burger@cctr.umkc.edu. Office: The Wordtree 10876 Bradshaw St Overland Park KS 66210-1148 *The computer analyzes prose information into tabulation, whence it can be re-formed diversely. Therefore computerization has revolutionized my authorship from textbooks to reference books.*

BURGER, HERBERT FRANCIS, advertising agency executive; b. Ligonier, Pa., Mar. 5, 1930; s. Adolph G. and Elizabeth (Johannsen) B.; m. Jane Coulter, Oct. 1, 1966; children: Matthew F., Jennifer. B.S. in Econs, Thiel Coll., Greenville, Pa., 1952; M.A. in Journalism, Syracuse (N.Y.) U., 1955. C. Mgmt. trainee Joy Mfg. Co., 1955-56; account exec. Ketchum, MacLeod & Grove, Pitts., 1956-58, Marsteller Inc., Pitts., 1958-65; with Creamer Inc., Pitts., 1965-76; pres. Creamer Inc. (Pitts. divsn.), 1976-86; chmn., ptnr. St. George Group, Inc., Pitts., 1986—; bd. dirs. Overly Mfg. Co., Pitts. Offices of Promotion; chmn. Pitts. Media Group, Pitts. Downtown Partnership; pres. Speedwell Enterprises, 1986—. Chmn. Pitts. Downtown Plan. Served with U.S. Army, 1953-55. Mem. Pitts. Advt. Club (dir.), Pitts. Press Club. Republican. Lutheran. Clubs: Duquesne, Longue Vue Country, University. Home: 109 Virginia Ave Pittsburgh PA 15215-3226

BURGER, LESLIE MORTON, physician, army officer; b. Bklyn., Apr. 7, 1940; s. David and Sally (Jacobs) B.; m. Julia J. Usero, Aug. 21, 1960; children: David S., Kenneth A., Joseph A. BS, CCNY, 1963; MD, SUNY Upstate Med. Ctr., 1967. Diplomate Am. Bd. Internal Medicine, Nat. Bd. Med. Examiners. Commd. 2d lt. U.S. Army, 1966, advanced through grades to maj. gen., 1994; resident in internal medicine Tripler Army Med. Ctr., Honolulu, 1967-71; fellow in infectious diseases Southwestern Med. Sch., U. Tex., Dallas, 1971-72; asst. chief dept. medicine Brooke Army Med. Ctr., San Antonio, 1972-75; chief dept. medicine U.S. Army Mil. Acad., West Point, N.Y., 1975-78; cons. in internal medicine to surgeon gen. The Pentagon, Arlington, Va., 1978-80; dep. comdr., then comdr. Nuernberg (Germany) U.S. Army Hosp., 1980-84; dep. comdr. Madigan Army Med. Ctr., Tacoma, 1985-88; comdr. Darnall Army Hosp., Ft. Hood, Tex., 1988-89, Letterman Army Med. Ctr., San Francisco, 1989-92, Madigan Army Med. Ctr., Tacoma, 1992-94; asst. surgeon gen. Hlth. Svcs. Ops. and Log, Falls Church, Va., 1994—. Contbr. articles to profl. jours. Decorated Legion of Merit with 2 oak leaf clusters; recipient recognition awards AMA, 1977, 80, 83, 86, 89, 92, Order of Mil. Med. Merit award U.S. Army Health Svcs. Command, 1983. Fellow ACP (past gov.); mem. Assn. Mil. Surgeons U.S., Assn. U.S. Army, Am. Coll. Physician Execs., Soc. Med. Cons. to Armed Forces. Avocation: sailing.

BURGER, ROBERT EUGENE, author, chess expert; b. Yerington, Nev., June 21, 1931; s. Edmund Ganes and Rose Catherine (Kobe) B.; m. Mary Theresa Dunne, June 26, 1954; children: Eileen, Marlene, Robert, Diane, Elisabeth, Joseph, Daniel, John, Clare, Christopher. BA, U. Calif., Berkeley, 1953, MA, 1955. Founder Ad Agy., San Francisco, 1958, Electronic Navigation Co., 1960; writer Ad Agy., San Francisco, 1968—; lectr. Stanford U., 1964, U. Calif.-Hayward, 1972, various Calif. state colls., 1973, U. Calif.-Berkeley, 1989; U.S. chess master, 1965-73, Internat. chess master, 1973—; internat. problems judge, 1955; U.S. rep. Fedn. Internat. des Echecs, 1981-85; co-founder Quantum Entertainment, 1992; pres. Nutrition Analysts Press; v.p., dir. Integrated Magnetoelectronics, Inc., 1991—. Author: Where They Go to Die, 1968, McCarthy, Words to Remember, 1969, Out From Under, 1970, Twilight Believers, 1971, Pietro on Wine, 1972, The Love Contract, 1972, Ego Speak, 1973, The Simplified Guide to Personal Bankruptcy, 1974, The Chess of Bobby Fischer, 1975, Inside Divorce, 1975, Forbidden Cures, 1976, Jogger's Catalog, 1978, The Polish Prince, 1978, The Jug Wine Book, 1979, A Gift for People, 1979, The Whole Life Diet, 1979, Meganutrition, 1980, The Courage to Believe, 1980, Are you Driving Your Children to Drugs?, 1981, Meganutrition for Women, 1983, The Ford Report, 1983, The Healing Arts, 1985, Earthquake, Fire and Folly, 1988, Design for Disaster, 1989, Brain Loss, Brain Gain, 1991, Eye of Evil, 1993, Profiles in Murder, 1998, Justice Denied, 1999. Trustee Mechanics Inst. Libr., San Francisco, 1980—; pres. Gold Rush Trail Found., 1995—. Fellow Brit. Chess Problem Soc.

BURGER, ROBERT MERCER, semiconductor device research executive; b. Frederick, Md., Feb. 14, 1927; s. William Leslie and Grace Allene (Mercer) B.; m. Marian Elizabeth Abbott, Sept. 10, 1949; children—Sharon A., Lisa A., Robert M. S.B., Coll. William and Mary, 1949; Sc.M., Brown U., 1952, Ph.D., 1955. Br. chief Nat. Security Agy., Fort Meade, Md., 1955-59; fellow engr. Westinghouse Corp., Balt., 1959-62; chief scientist Research Triangle Inst., Research Triangle Park, N.C., 1962-82; v.p., chief scientist Semiconductor Research Corp., Research Triangle Park, 1982-96; cons. in field, 1996—; rsch. assoc. U. Md., College Park, 1955-59; adj. assoc. prof. Duke U., 1962-69; bd. vis. N.C. State U., 1992-98; prof. N.C. State U., 1995—. Author, editor: Fundamentals of Integrated Silicon Devices, 1965. Bd. dirs., v.p. United Fund, Durham, N.C., 1973. Served with U.S. Navy, 1945-46. Fellow IEEE (life); mem. AAAS, Am. Phys. Soc. Republican.

Presbyterian. Avocations: fishing; gardening. Home: 107 Links End Dr Cary NC 27513-5691 Office: Semiconductor Research Corp PO Box 12053 Durham NC 27709-2053

BURGER, TODD OLIVER, management consultant; b. Oyster Bay, N.Y., June 17, 1953; s. Chester Jerome and Hannah Jacqueline (Kaufman) B.; m. Michele Marie Potter, Sept. 22, 1984 (div. Dec. 1986); m. Deborah Susan Fricke Carlisle, Aug. 19, 1990; 1 child, Olivia Susan. BS in Acctg., U. Albany, 1977. CPA, Conn. Acct. Peat Marwick Mitchell & Co., Hartford, Conn., 1977-78, staff acct., 1978-79, sr. acct., 1979; corp. auditor Burlington No., Inc., St. Paul, 1979-80, asst. trainmaster, 1980-81; cons. Arthur D. Little, Inc., Cambridge, Mass., 1981-86, sr. cons., 1986-88, dep. unit mgr., 1988-91, sr. cons. II, dep. unit mgr., 1991-94, dir., 1994-95, dir. and mgr. intermodal group, 1995-96, dir. transport practice, 1996—; dir. N.Am. Consulting, 1997—; project mgr. restructuring Czech Railways, Ministry of Transport, CSFR, Prague, 1991-92; project mgr. Strategic Assessment Report Mass. Aero. Commn., Boston, 1991-93; project dir. on airport sys. integration for SITA, 1998, on safety integration merger planning in ESX/NS/Conrail transaction for U.S. Surface Transp. Bd.; spkr. in field. mem. Mayors Adv. Com. Transp., 1983-84; bd. dirs. Newcomers, Lexington, Mass., 1993-94. Recipient Cert. of Svc., Mayor of City of Newton, Mass., 1984. Mem. Transp. Rsch. Forum (pres. New Eng. chpt. 1990-91). Avocations: carpentry, bicycle touring, gourmet cooking, cross-country skiing. Home: 386 Lincoln St Lexington MA 02421-7417 Office: Arthur D Little Inc Acorn Park 35 # 429 Cambridge MA 02140-2390

BURGER, WERNER CARL, retired art educator; b. Pforzheim, Germany, Dec. 27, 1925; came to U.S., 1926; s. Karl Frederick and Helen Rosalie (Schlaefle) B. BS, NYU, 1950, MA, 1951. Cert. secondary tchr., N.J. Fine arts tchr. Westfield (N.J.) H.S., 1951-56; chmn. art dept. West Morris H.S., Chester, N.J., 1956-60; prof. painting and drawing Kean U., Union, N.J., 1961-92, prof. emeritus, 1993—; cons. Hunterdon Art Mus., Clinton, N.J., 1960—. Exhibited in Newark Mus., 1996, N.J. State Mus., Trenton, 1997. Cpl. U.S. Army, 1944-46. Recipient Grumbacher Outstanding Svc. to Arts award, 1990. Mem. N.J. Watercolor Soc. (bd. dirs. 1970—), Phi Delta Kappa. Avocations: working out, body building, gardening.

BURGESON, JOYCE ANN, travel agency official; b. Jamestown, N.Y., Sept. 10, 1936; d. Walter Edward and Marion (Cree) Van Horn; m. David G. Burgeson, Sept. 10, 1955; children: Kathalene, Donna, Jeffrey, Karen, Christine. AS, Empire State Coll., SUNY, Saratoga Springs, 1990. Bookkeeper Burgeson Wholesale, Jamestown, 1962-88; realtor assoc. Kote Realty, Jamestown, 1982-89; real estate appraiser Goldome Bank, Jamestown, 1986-89; travel saleswoman, tour escort Cert. Travel Tours, Jamestown, 1983-90, 96—, Travelhost of Jamestown, 1990-95; payroll mgr. The Resource Ctr., Jamestown, 1988-95; bd. dirs. Monet Acres Inc.; prin. Burgeson Bus. Seminars, Jamestown, N.Y., 1990—; bd. dirs. Monet Acres, Inc. Mem. bd. Maple Grove H.S., Bemus Point, N.Y., 1979-82; mem. adminstrv. bd. 1st United Meth. Ch., Jamestown, 1985-95; cert. lay spkr. United meth. Ch., 1987—. Mem. Toastmasters, Order of Vikings. Avocations: travel, lay speaking, camping, knitting. Home and Office: 73 Frew Run Rd Frewsburg NY 14738 Address: 622 Monet Acres Palm Beach Gardens FL 33410

BURGESS, ANN WOLBERT, nursing educator. Van Ameringen prof. nursing U. Pa., Phila., prof. of psychiat. and mental health nursing. Mem. NAS. Office: U Pa Sch Nursing Philadelphia PA 19104*

BURGESS, C(HARLES) CONEY, bank executive; b. Brookhaven, Miss., Oct. 2, 1937; s. Coney and Johnnie Margaret (Campbell) B.; m. Cornelia Jane Slemp, Apr. 26, 1964; children: Charles Coney, Cornelius Campbell, Carson Herring, Charlotte Amelia. BS in Geology, Miss. State U., 1960; postgrad., U. Miss., 1964. Geologist Texaco, 1964; ranching, real estate, 1982; pres., bd. dirs., mem. exec. com. Monrch Trust Co., 1982; chmn. bd. Herring Bancorp, Vernon, Tex.; officer, bd. dirs. Zircon, Inc., Amarillo; pres., bd. dirs. Burgess-Herring Ranch Co.; pres. Chain-C & Cattle, Flagg Land & Cattle Co., Castro County, Tex., Rebel Ranches, Brookhaven, Miss.; bd. dirs. Ultra Plating Corp., Green Bay, Wis. Bd. adv. Tex. Tech. U., Lubbock, Tex.; chmn. bd., com. Cal Farley's Boys Ranch and Girlstown, 1986, bd. trustees, Marine Military Acad., Tex., 1992; pres., bd. trustees, Symphony Bd. Amarillo, 1993-94; bd. trustees, Panhandle Plains Historical Soc., bd. trustees, investment com. Panhandle Plains Mus., Canyon, Tex. Mem. Tex. & Southwestern Cattle Raisers (dir., v.p.), Am. Quarter Horse Assn. (chmn. mktg. & pub. info. com., 1992-94), Panhandle Livestock Assn. (past pres., exec. com. dirú, Ranching Heritage Assn. (bd. overseers), Ranching Heritage Assn. (bd. endowment, trustee), Nat. Cattlemens Assn. (dir., com. mem.), Rotary Club (pres., dir. 1992-93), Amarillo C. of C. (com. mem.), Southwestern Pub. Svc.(dir.), Amarillo, Tex. Presbyterian. Avocations: investments, banking, farming and ranching, oil and gas, real estate. Home: 3001 S Lipscomb St Amarillo TX 79109-3533 Office: 1608 S Polk St Amarillo TX 79102-3149

BURGESS, CHARLES ORVILLE, history educator; b. Portland, Oreg., Jan. 18, 1932; s. Rex Orville and Glendora Almanda (Sundrud) B.; m. Cora Cloepfil, June 22, 1952; children: Donna Claire Majer, Jo Dell Nicholls, Robert Charles; m. Patricia Stewart Anderson, Apr. 22, 1976; children: Marc Richard Anderson, Brian Stewart Anderson, Tricia Louise Crozier, Kristen Anne Klein. BA, U. Oreg., 1957; MS (Danforth fellow), U. Wis., 1958, PhD, 1962; Nat. Postdoctoral fellow, Harvard U., 1967-68. Asst. prof. U. Calif., Riverside, 1962-64; asst. prof. history edn. U. Wash., Seattle, 1964-66; assoc. prof. U. Wash., 1966-70, prof., 1970—, chmn. area ednl. policy studies, 1970-92; prof. emeritus, 1992; v.p. div. F Am. Ednl. Research Assn., 1977-79; fgn. expert Peoples Republic of China, 1984-85. Author: The Origins of American Thought (published China as Meiguo Sixiang Yuanyuan); 1988, (with M.L. Borrowman) What Doctrines to Embrace, 1969, Profile of an American Philanthropist (Nettie Fowler McCormick), 1962; co-editor: (with Charles Strickland) G. Stanley Hall on Natural Education, 1965; co-author: (with Y. Yang and G. Zhu) Cultivating the World of Selfhood (published in China as Kaituo Zi Wode Shijie), 1997. Mem. Wash. com. civil rights ACLU, 1965-67; bd. dirs. Seattle Folklore Soc., 1966—. Served in USAF, 1950-54. Mem. Orgn. Am. Historians, Am. Hist. Assn., History Edn. Soc. (pres. 1971-72), Assocs. for Research on Pvt. Edn. (trustee 1982-83), Phi Beta Kappa. Home: 2111 SW 174th St Seattle WA 98166-3259

BURGESS, CHARLOTTE GAYLORD, dean; b. San Diego, Sept. 9, 1947; d. Charles Reid and Virginia (Huck) Gaylord; m. Larry Eugene Burgess, Oct. 7, 1973. BA in Psychology, U. Redlands, 1969, MA in Higher Edn. Adminn. & Counseling, 1970; postgrad., U. Calif., Riverside, 1978-79. Asst. to v.p. for student affairs U. Redlands, Calif., 1970-71; asst. dean, dir. student activities U. Redlands, 1971-79, dean of admissions, 1979-80, dean of students, 1980—. Contbr. articles and essays to profl. publs. Mem. citizens adv. com. LWV, 1981-86; corp. body Redlands Comty. Hosp., 1981-92; bd. dirs. Family Svc. Assn., 1975-81, 82-95, chair nominating com., 1987, counseling com., 1985-89, chair long-range planning com., 1986-95, strategic change com., 1997-98, exec. com., 1994-96; bd. dirs. Redlands YMCA, 1996-98, pres., 1990-92, 94-96, chair women's resource com., 1981-82, chair personnel comm., 1976-77, chair program commn. 1978-81, mem. equip com., 1985-88, exec. evaln. commr., 1987, chair Hometown Home Finder, 1994-99, Y Alliance, 1998—; gala food chair Friends of A. K. Smiley Pub. Libr., 1972—; mem. Redlands Area Hist. Soc., 1972—; mem. citizens adv. com. City of Redlands Open Space, 1986-98; mem. Redlands Street Tree Com., 1987-96; co-chair ann. campaign Redlands United Way, 1979, mem. admissions and allocations com., 1983-86; bd. dirs. Inland Empire World Affairs Coun., 1978-82. Recipient 2d Mile award Redlands Rotary Club, 1996. Mem. Nat. Assn. Student Pers. Adminstrs. (mem.-at-large So. Calif. exec. com. 1994—, Region VI award 1996), Redlands C. of C. (dir. 1998—), , So. Calif. Hist. Soc., Delta Kappa Psi (Redlands Alumni chpt., patroness 1972-89, Woman of Yr. Alumnae award 1978). Episcopalian. Avocations: reading, decorating, antiques, traveling. Home: 923 W Fern Ave Redlands CA 92373 Office: U of Redlands PO Box 3080 Redlands CA 92373-0999

BURGESS, CHESTER FRANCIS, III, journalist, television producer; b. Grand Junction, Colo., Sept. 12, 1946; s. Chester Francis Jr. and Betty (Reigan) B.; m. Bonnie Yates, Nov. 9, 1974; 1 child, Chester F. IV. BA in Journalism, Washington and Lee U., 1974. Reporter The Roanoke (Va.) Times, 1971-74; news dir. WJMA Radio, Orange, Va., 1974-76; news anchor, reporter WTAR-TV and Radio, Norfolk, Va., 1976-80; news editor, anchor CNN, Atlanta, 1980-82, supervising prodr., 1982-91, exec. prodr. environment unit, 1991-95, exec. prodr. interactive programming, 1996-98; tech. project mgr. CNN R&D, Atlanta, 1998—. Exec. prodr. (TV mag.) Network Earth, 1991-93, (documentary) The Big Story, 1991-95, (news program) War in the Gulf, 1990-91; prodr./writer TV documentary: In Nature's Wake, 1993. Merit badge counselor Troop 197, Boy Scouts Am., Atlanta, 1994-95; vol. computer specialist Westminster & Schenck Schs., Atlanta, 1985-91; v.p., bd. dirs. Ardmore/28th Neighborhood Assn., Atlanta, 1986-88; mem. vestry coun. Ch. of Holy Apostles, Virginia Beach, 1978-80. With USN, 1965-69. Recipient Cable Ace award Cable Acad. Arts and Scis., 1990, 93, 95, Environ. Media award Environ. Media Assn., 1992, 94, 95, Gold Cindy award Assn. Visual Communicators, 1993, NEA Award for Advancement of Learning Through Broadcasting, 1993, Worldfest Houston award Houston Internat. Film and Video Festival, 1994 (2), News and Documentary Emmy award TV Acad. Arts and Scis., 1994, Am. Women in Radio and TV award, 1995. Mem. Radio TV News Dirs. Assn. (news in the next century adv. com. 1995—, environment reporting adv. com. 1991-94), Soc. Profl. Journalists (Tidewater chpt. v.p. 1971-82, Outstanding Journalism Grad. 1974), Phi Beta Kappa. Avocations: downhill skiing, reading, computers, running. Office: CNN PO Box 105366 Atlanta GA 30348-5366

BURGESS, CURT, psychologist, computer scientist, educator; b. Phila., June 19, 1953; s. Clarke Jacob and Barbara B.; m. Catherine Helen Decker, May 25, 1991. BGS, Univ. Nebr., 1982, MA, 1985; MA, Univ. Rochester, 1989, PhD, 1991. Asst. prof. psychology Syracuse (N.Y.) Univ., 1989-92; asst. prof. psychology Univ. Calif., Riverside, 1992-97, assoc. prof. psychology, 1997—; faculty computational neurosc. program Syracuse Univ., 1991-92, affiliate prof. dept. computer sci., 1990-92; chair admissions Univ. Calif., Riverside, 1994—, coop. faculty dept. computer sci., 1996—, faculty dept. neurosci. Contbr. over 40 chpts. to books, articles to jours. Presdl. Faculty fellow U.S. Pres./NSF, 1994. Mem. APA, Cognitive Sci. Soc., Psychonomic Soc., Assn. Computational Linguistics, Western Psychol. Assn., Sigma Xi (v.p. 1996-97, pres. 1997—). Avocations: Cornhusker football, skiing, photography. Office: U Calif Dept Psychology 1419 LIfe Sci Bldg Riverside CA 92521

BURGESS, DAVID, lawyer; b. Detroit, Nov. 30, 1948; s. Roger Edward and Claire Theresa (Sullivan) B.; m. Rebecca Culbertson Stuart, 1985 (dec. Dec. 1988); m. Catherine Mounteer, 1993; children: Jalil Riahi, Leila Riahi, Bryan Valentine, Grace Catherine. BS in Fgn. Svc., Georgetown U., 1970, MS in Fgn. Svc., 1978, JD, 1978. Bar: D.C. 1978, U.S. Dist. Ct. D.C. 1979, U.S. Ct. Appeals (D.C. cir.) 1979, U.S. Ct. Appeals (fed. cir.) 1988, U.S. Ct. Internat. Trade 1988. Rsch. asst. Georgetown U. Sch. Bus. Adminstrn., Washington, 1975, asst. to dean, 1975-76; rsch. assoc., prof. Acad. in the Pub. Svc., Washington, 1976-79; asst. editor Securities Regulation Law Report, Washington; legal editor Internat. Trade Reporter Bur. Nat. Affairs, Washington, 1978-79; atty. Cadwalader, Wickersham & Taft, Washington, 1979-81; mng. editor Bur. Nat. Affairs, Washington, 1981-82; dir. U.S. Peace Corps, Niamey, Niger, 1982-84, Rabat, Morocco, 1984-85; dir. policy planning, mgmt. Peace Corps, Washington, 1985-87; dir. Bur. Human Rights and Humanitarian Affairs U.S. Dept. State, Washington, 1987-92; regional dir. Lawyers for Bush-Quayle Re-Election Campaign, 1992; chief party Rwanda Dem. and Governance Project, 1994, Russia NGO Sector Project, Moscow, 1994; dir. democracy and civil soc. program, sr. advisor World Learning, Washington, 1995 (dir. U.S. Democracy Fellows program, Washington, 1995—); spkr. workshops Minority Legis. Edn. Program, Ind. Assn. Cities and Towns, Georgetown U. Continuing Edn. Program, Comms. Workers Am., Colo. State U., U. Wis. Alumni rep. Internat. Sch. Bangkok, 1972-74. Author: Financing Local Government, 1977, 2d edit., 1978, Preparation of the Local Budget, 2 vols., 1976, 2d edit., 1978, Local Government Accounting Fundamentals, 2d edit., 1977, Understanding Federal Assistance Programs, 2d edit., 1978, The POW/MIA Issue: Perspectives on the National League of Families, 1978; contbr. articles to publs. Adv. com. Arlington County Fiscal Affairs, 1993-94; mem. pres. coun. Mary Washington Coll.; mem. Rep. Nat. Com. With USAF, 1970-74. Mem. D.C. Bar Assn., Washington Fgn. Law Soc., Hoyas Unltd. (pres. 1992-94), Federalist Soc., Georgetown U. Alumni Assn. (bd. govs. 1975—, class rep. 1971-91), Rep. Nat. Lawyers Assn., Pachyderm Club No. Va. (pres. 1992-93), Pres.'s Club. Republican. Roman Catholic. Home: 3115 1st Pl N Arlington VA 22201-1037 Office: 1015 15th St NW Ste 750 Washington DC 20005-2605

BURGESS, DAVID LOWRY, artist; b. Phila., Apr. 27, 1940; s. Eric Turner and Ruth Elizabeth (McNees) B.; m. Janet Lucille Levengood, Mar. 25, 1960; children: Kirsten Deidre, Audrey Veronica, Vashti Gabrielle. Grad., Pa. Acad. of Fine Art, U. Pa., 1961. Lectr. Phila. Coll. Art, 1964-66; arts advisor Edn. Devel. Center, 1966-68; mem. faculty Harvard U. Sch. Edn., Cambridge, Mass., 1967-68; instr. Boston U., 1969; prof. Mass. Coll. Art, 1969-89; fellow Center for Advanced Visual Studies M.I.T., 1971-89; dean Carnegie-Mellon U. Coll. Fine Arts, Pitts., 1989-92, A.W. Mellon prof. art, 1992—; dir. SIMLAB, 1995-97; mem. Nat. Humanities faculty, 1968-80; disting. artist ECHO-UQAM, Montreal; fellow Studio for Creative Inquiry, CMU. Author: Fragments, 1967, Looking and Listening, 1969, Memory, Environment, Utopia, 1973, Burgess: The Quiet Axis Trècarré, Montreal, Can., 1987; one-man shows include Inst. Contemporary Art, Boston, 1971, Carpenter Ctr., Harvard U., 1975, MIT, 1978, U. Que., Montreal, 1984, De Cordova Mus., Mass., 1985, 88, Pewna Acad. Fine Arts Mus., 1987-88; group exhbns. include Boston Mus. Fine Arts Elements Exhbn., 1971, Multiple Interaction Team, ten cities, 1972-74, CAYAC, Spain and Latin Am., 1972-74, Documenta 6, Kassel, West Germany, 1977, Vienna Bienal, 1979, Sky Arts Conf., MIT, 1981-83, 86, Ars Electronica, Austria, 1982, 86, Kunst Acad., West Germany, 1982, Artists of Earthwatch, N.Mex., 1984, Monocle, Hamburg Kunsthalle, West Germany, 1985, De Cordova Mus., 1985, Pa. Acad. Fine Arts, 1987-88, Herning Kunst Mus., Denmark, 1989, Kunstverein, Karlsrahe, Germany, 1989, Contemporary Mus., Helsinki, Finland, 1989, Art Transition, 1991, Differentiel, Aix en Provence, France, 1992, Mu Gallery, Boston, 1993, MIT Mus., Cambridge, 1994, Tufts U., Mass., 1995, Pitts. Biennal, 1996, Nagoya City Museum, 1997, Fed. Res. Bank, Boston, 1998; represented in permanent collections Boston Mus. Fine Arts, Houghton Libr., Harvard U., Nat. Collection Fine Arts, Washington, Smithsonian Collection, Washington, Pa. Acad. Fine Arts, Herning Kunstmuseum, Denmark, De Cordova Mus., Lincoln, Mass.; appearances include TV Nat. Broadcasts Nova, Artists in the Lab, 1982, Artists Earthwatch, KNME Albuquerque, 1985, Smithsonian World, 1987, New VR Techs. MSNBC, 1997. Founding mem., exec. bd. Cambridge Arts Council; mem. adv. bd. Art, Edn. and Americans. Recipient Am. Acad. Arts and Letters, Nat. Inst. Arts and Letters award, 1972, Gold award Le Devoir, Montreal, 1989; Guggenheim fellow, 1973-74; Nat. Endowment Arts grantee, 1977-78, 84, 86; Rockefeller Found. grantee, 1979-80, 85-87; Mass. Council on the Arts and Humanities grantee, 1982, 87-88; Mass. Artists Found. grantee, 1983. Address: 185 Spring St Hull MA 02045-1229

BURGESS, DIANE GLENN, real estate broker, paralegal; b. Mar. 5, 1935; d. Howard Glenn and Emma Kathie (Higham) King; m. Raymond H. Symanski, Apr. 23, 1955 (div. 1968); children: Raymond H. Jr., Jeffrey H.; m. L. Michael Burgess, July 19, 1985. Student, Strayer's Coll., Washington. Subrogation supr., paralegal Carr, Jordan, Coyne & Savits, Washington, 1972-82; property mgr. Lewis & Silverman, Fairfax, Va., 1982-87; owner, v.p. Burgess Custom Builders, Inc., Vienna, Va., 1985—; owner, real estate broker, pres. ERA-House of Burgesses, Inc., Vienna, 1988—; tng. and recruiting dir. ERA-House of Burgesses. Chmn. ERA-MDA Ann. Golf Tournament, 1989-90; campaign mgr. Warren Barry for County Court Clerk, Fairfax; vol. Linwood Holton for U.S. Senate, Fairfax, John Warner for U.S. Senate, Fairfax, ARC, 1968-89; vol. Bob Dole for Pres., 1994. Recipient Recognition award Over 500 ARC, 1968-69, 5 gold medals Masters East Coast Championship, 1979. Mem. GMW Broker Coun. (ERA Broker Coun. 1989—), North Va. Assn. Realtors (pub. rels. com.), Colonial Rep. Women's Club (pres. 1994-95, sec./treas. 1997).

BURGESS, DONNA ELAINE, clinical social worker; b. Lancaster, Calif., Apr. 14, 1956; d. Harold Irwin and Phyllis Elaine (Ashby) B. BS, Iowa State U., 1979, 85; MSW, U. Iowa, 1988, cert. in aging studies, 1991. Diplomate Acad. Cert. Social Workers. Family and cmty. counselor Beloit of Iowa, Ames, 1979-82; social worker Luth. Soc. Svcs., Ames, 1982-87; med. social worker Hospice Ctrl. Iowa, Des Moines, 1987-93; clin. social worker Counseling & Assessment Svcs. P.C., Des Moines, 1993—; cons. social worker Calvin Cmty., Des Moines, 1994—, Bishop Drumm Care Ctr., Johnston, Iowa, 1997—. Sec. Ctrl. Iowa AIDS Project, 1988-89, Dreams Can Come True-a Non-Profit AIDS orgn., 1992—. Mem. NASW (pres. 1996-98, sec. 1992-94, grantee 1992).). Office: Counseling & Assessment Svcs PC 2404 Forest Dr Des Moines IA 50312-5400

BURGESS, EDWIN BOND, librarian, archivist; b. Amarillo, Tex., Sept. 21, 1948; s. Edwin Bond and Jean (MacTaggart) B.; m. Cynthia Ann Adelman, June 20, 1970. BA, Macalester Coll., 1970; MA, U. Minn., 1971. Intern Ft. Leonard Wood (Mo.) Libr., 1972-74; dir. SAFEGUARD, Nekoma, N.D., 1974-75; libr. Post Libr., Ft. Riley, Kans., 1975-76, Concepts Analysis Agy., Bethesda, Md., 1976-77; chief pub. svcs. U.S. Army Command and Gen. Staff Coll. Libr., Ft. Leavenworth, Kans., 1978-82; sys. libr. U.S. Army Tng. and Doctrine Command Libr. and Info. Network, Ft. Monroe, Va., 1982-95; archives mgr. Combined Arms Rsch. Libr., Ft. Leavenworth, 1995—; reviewer Libr. Jour., 1976—. Mem. Kans. Libr. Network Bd., Topeka, 1997—. Mem. Spl. Libr. Assn. (chpt. bd. dirs. 1986—), Kansas City Area Archivists. Office: Combined Arms Rsch Libr 250 Gibbon Ave Fort Leavenworth KS 66027-2314

BURGESS, FRANKLIN DOUGLAS, judge; b. 1935. BS in Engring., Gonzaga U., 1961, JD, 1966. Asst. city atty. City of Tacoma (Wash.), 1967-69; judge pro tem Mcpl. Ct. and Pierce County Dist. Ct., 1971-80; ptnr. Tanner & Burgess, Tacoma, Wash., 1971-76, Tanner, McGavick, Felker, Fleming, Burgess & Lazares, Tacoma, Wash., 1976-79, McGavick, Burgess, Heller & Foister, Tacoma, Wash., 1979-80; regional counsel Dept. Housing and Urban Devel., Seattle, 1980-81; U.S. magistrate judge U.S. Dist. Ct. (we. dist.) Wash., Tacoma, 1981-93, 95—; dist. judge U.S. Ct. Appeals (9th cir.), Tacoma, Wash., 1994-95. Resource person annual Nat. Black History Mo., Shiloh Bapt. Ch.; mem. Tacoma Urban League. Named NCAA All Am., 1961, Gonzaga U. Hall of Fame Basketball, 1989. Mem. Wash. State Bar Assn., Pierce County Bar Assn., Loren Miller Bar Assn., Nat. Conf. U.S. Magistrate Judges, NAACP. Office: US Dist Ct Union Station Courthouse 1717 Pacific Ave Ste 3124 Tacoma WA 98402-3234*

BURGESS, GREG, Olympic athlete, swimming; b. Jacksonville, Fla., July 28, 1977. Olympic swimmer Barcelona, Spain, 1992. Recipient 200m Individual Medley Silver medal Olympics, Barcelona, 1992. Office: care US Swimming Inc One Olympic Plz Colorado Springs CO 80909*

BURGESS, HAYDEN FERN (POKA LAENUI), lawyer; b. Honolulu, May 5, 1946; s. Ned E. and Nora (Lee) B.; m. Puanani Sonoda, Aug. 28, 1968. B in Polit. Sci., U. Hawaii, JD, 1976. Bar: Hawaii 1976, U.S. Tax Ct., U.S. Ct. Appeals (9th cir.). Pvt. practice Waianae, Hawaii, 1984—; pres. Hawaii Coun. for 1993 and Beyond, Honolulu, 1991—; exec. dir. Waianae Coast Cmty. Mental Health Ctr., 1997—; v.p. World Coun. Indigenous Peoples before UN, 1984-90; human rights adv., writer, speaker in field; pres. Pacific and Asia Coun. Indigenous Peoples; cons. on indigenous affairs, 1984; indigenous expert to ILO Conv.; expert UN seminar on effects of racism and racial discriminations on social and econ. rels. between indigenous peoples and states, 1989—; del. Native Hawaiian Convention. Trustee Office Hawaiian Affairs, Honolulu, 1982-86; mem. Swedish Nat. Commn. on Mus., 1986; leader Hawaiian Independence Movement; mem. Hawaiian Sovereignty Elections Coun. Mem. Law Assn. Asia and Western Pacific (steering com. on human rights 1988), Union of 3d World Journalists.

BURGESS, J. WESLEY, neuropsychiatrist; b. Mar. 5, 1952. BS, Purdue U., 1974; PhD, N.C. State U., 1979; MD, U. Miami, 1987. Diplomate Am. Bd. Med. Examiners,. Rsch. assoc. N.C. Mental Health Dept., 1975-79; with Caribbean Primate Rsch., La Parquera, P.R., 1976-79; faculty psychology U. Calif., Davis, 1979-81; faculty UCLA, 1981-84, Western Grad. Sch. Psychology, 1989-90; intern Stanford U., 1987-88, resident in psychiatry, 1988-91, staff psychiatrist Alzheimer's Rsch. Inst., 1989-90; dir. psychiat. emergency svc. Palo Alto Veterans Med. Ctr., 1989-90; chief resident Stanford U. Med. Ctr., 1990-91; faculty Pacific Grad. Sch. Psychology, 1990-92; dir. adolescent div. Ctr. Mood Disorders, L.A., 1991-93; faculty Calif. Sch. Profl. Psychology, 1991-92; expert panel Superior Ct., Juvenile Ct., Mcpl. Ct. Calif., L.A.; chief investigator SmithKline Beecham/Chemtrials, 1992-94. Contbr. articles to profl. jours. Neuropsychiatric Inst. fellow UCLA, 1981-83, Stanford fellow, 1990-91; recipient Mead Johnson award Psychiatry, 1991. Mem. AMA (Physicians Recognition award), No. Calif. Psychiat. Soc. (Rsch. award 1991), Los Angeles County Med. Assn., So. Calif. Pediatric Assn., Am. Psychiat. Assn., Calif. Psychiat. Assn., So. Calif. Psychiat. Soc., Am. Assn. Advancement Psychotherapy, Internat. Soc. Adolescent Psychiatry, Am. Soc. Adolescent Psychiatry, Am. Soc. Clin. Psychopharmacology, Calif. Med. Assn., Acad. Magical Arts. Avocations: performing and designing magical illusions, growing orchids, geograical design. Office: 11980 San Vicente Blvd Ste 620 Los Angeles CA 90049-6604

BURGESS, JAMES EDWARD, newspaper publisher, executive; b. LaCrosse, Wis., Apr. 5, 1936; s. William Thomas and Margaret (Forseth) B.; m. Catherine Eleanor, Dec. 20, 1958; children: Karen E. Burgess Hardy, J. Peter, Sydney Ann, R. Curtis. Student, Wayland Acad.; BS, U. Wis. Pub. Ind. Record, Helena, Mont., 1969-71, Tribune, LaCrosse, Wisc., 1971-74; v.p. newspapers Lee Enterprises, Davenport, Iowa, 1974-81; exec. v.p. Lee Enterprises, 1981-84, dir., 1974-85; dir. Madison (Wis.) Newspapers, Inc., 1975-93, pres., 1984-93; pub. Wis. State Jour., Madison, 1984-94. Chmn. Edgewood Coll., Madison, 1984—; founder Future Madison, Inc.; chmn. SAVE Commn. Mem. Wis. Newspaper Assn. (past pres.), Inland Daily Press Assn. (pres., chmn. 1982-84), Wis. Assn. Lakes (bd. dirs., pres.), Madison Community Found. (bd. govs.). Home: 6102 S Highlands Ave Madison WI 53705-1113 Office: PO Box 55060 Madison WI 53705-8860

BURGESS, JAMES HARLAND, physics educator, researcher; b. Portland, Oreg., May 11, 1929; s. Harland F. B. and Marion U. (Burgess); m. Dorothy R. Crosby, June 10, 1951; children: Karen, Donald, Joanne. B.S., Wash. State U., 1949, M.S., 1951; Ph.D., Washington U., St. Louis, 1955. Sr. engr. Sylvania Electric Products, Mountain View, Calif., 1955-56; research assoc. Stanford U., Palo Al to, Calif., 1956-57; asst. prof. physics Stanford U., Palo Alto, Calif., 1958-62; assoc. prof. physics Washington U., St. Louis, 1962-73, prof., 1973-98, prof. emeritus, 1998—; cons. in field, 1956-66. Mem. Am. Phys. Soc., Am. Assn. Physics Tchrs., Phi Beta Kappa, Sigma Xi. Office: Washington U Physics Dept 1 Brookings Dr Saint Louis MO 63130-4899

BURGESS, JOHN ALLEN, lawyer; b. Waltham, Mass., Feb. 6, 1951; s. William A. and Joyce E. (Finkle) B.; m. Nancy S. Adams; children: Rachel, Eleanor. BA, Yale U., 1973; JD, Harvard U., 1976. With Hale and Dorr, Boston, 1976—; adj. prof. Fletcher Sch. Law and Diplomacy. Coun. fellow U.S. State Dept., 1987. Mem. Coun. on Fgn. Rels. Office: Hale and Dorr LLP 60 State St Ste 25 Boston MA 02109-1816

BURGESS, JOHN FRANK, management consultant, former utility executive, former army officer; b. Lanett, Ala., Nov. 18, 1917; s. John Frank and Mary Catherine (Heard) B.; m. Helen Hamby, Aug. 26, 1939; children: Beverly, Barbara, Frank. BS, Auburn U.; MA, George Washington U. Commd. 2d lt. U.S. Army, 1941, advanced through grades to col., ret., 1969; regional v.p. Consol. Edison Co. of N.Y., Inc., N.Y.C., 1969-83; cons. mgmt. Melville, N.Y., 1983-85; assoc. cons. Power Mgmt. Assocs., Inc., Groton, Conn., 1985-87; Columbia, Md., 1985-89. Active bds. various civic and profl. orgns., Queens, N.Y., 1969-83. Decorated Legion of Merit with 2 oak leaf clusters; named Man of Yr. Queens County Bldg and Contractors Assn., 1977. Episcopalian. Home: 9860 Terrace Lake Pt Roswell GA 30076-3742

BURGESS, JOHN HERBERT, physician, educator; b. Montreal, Que., Can., May 24, 1933; s. John Frederick and Willa Reta (McGinness) B.; m. Andrea Clouston Rutherford, May 30, 1958; children: Willa, Cynthia, Lynn, John. BSc, McGill U., Montreal, 1954, MD, CM, 1958. Med. resident Montreal Gen. Hosp., 1958-60, 62-64, dir. div. cardiology, 1973-94; Nuffield rsch. fellow U. Birmingham, Eng., 1960-62; McLaughlin rsch. fellow Cardiovascular Rsch. Inst., San Francisco, 1964-66; asst. prof. medicine McGill U., 1966-69, assoc. prof., 1969-75, prof., 1975—. Contbr. articles to profl. jours. Decorated Order of Can.; hon. fellow Coll. Medicine, South Africa. Master ACP; fellow Am. Coll. Cardiology, Royal Coll. Physicians and Surgeons Can. (pres. 1990-92), Royal Coll. Physicians (Edinburgh), Royal Australasian Coll. Physicians (hon.), Royal Coll. Physicians (London); mem. Can. Soc. Clin. Investigation. Avocations: cross country skiing, photography. Home: 639 Murray Hill, Westmount, PQ Canada H3Y 2W8 Office: Montreal Gen Hospital, 1650 Cedar Ave, Montreal, PQ Canada H3G 1A4

BURGESS, LARRY EUGENE, library director, history educator; b. Montrose, Colo., July 18, 1945; s. Eugene Floyd and Edyth Eleanor (Faussone) B.; m. Charlotte Reid Gaylord, Oct. 7, 1973. BA, U. Redlands, 1967; MA, Claremont Grad. U., 1969, PhD, 1972. Cert. Acad. Archivists. Archivist A.K. Smiley Pub. Libr., Redlands, Calif., 1972-85; libr. dir. A.K. Smiley Pub. Libr., Redlands, 1986—; adj. prof. history U. Redlands, 1972—, U. Calif., Riverside, 1979—; book reviewer Lincoln Herald, 1988—. Author: Mohonk: Its People and Spirit, 1980; (with others) A Day with Mr. Lincoln, 1994; co-author: The Hunt for Willie Boy, 1994. Vice-chmn. Calif. Heritage Preservation Commn., 1977-84; dir. Hist. Soc. So. Calif., L.A., 1984—; bd. dirs. U. Redlands, 1987-95. Recipient Archival award of excellence Calif. Heritage Preservation Commn., 1991, Preservation Merit award Calif. Hist. Soc., 1992, Cmty. Enrichment award Hist. Soc. So. Calif., 1994. Mem. Soc. Am. Archivists, So. Calif. Archivists (past pres.), Zamorano Club (bd. dirs. 1994—, pres. 1999), Rotary (bd. dirs. Redlands, pres. 1999—). Avocations: travel, book collecting, gardening. Home: 923 W Fern Ave Redlands CA 92373-5877 Office: AK Smiley Pub Libr 125 W Vine St Redlands CA 92373-4728

BURGESS, LEONARD RANDOLPH, business administration and economics educator, writer; b. Washington, Mar. 8, 1919; s. W. Randolph and May Ayres B.; m. Virginia Frost, May 26, 1946 (dec. Feb. 1978); m. Marga Minnick, Dec. 26, 1979 (div. 1983); m. Hyon Suk Kim, Dec. 30, 1983. BA, Brown U., 1947; MBA, Harvard U., 1947; PhD, Columbia U., 1961; grad. officer course, U.S. Army Cmd. and Gen. Staff, 1968. Chief statistician W.Va. Pulp and Paper Co., N.Y.C., 1947-52; sr. staff assoc. Nat. Indsl. Conf. Bd., N.Y.C., 1952-57; lectr., instr. CCNY, N.Y.C., 1958-59; asst. prof. N. Tex. State U., Denton, 1961-64; assoc. prof. Tex. A&M U., College Station, 1964-68, prof., 1968-73; vis. prof. Temple U., Phila., 1973-74; part-time prof. U. Del., Wilmington, 1974-75; from lectr. to assoc. prof. San Francisco State U., 1975-78; prof. Lincoln U., San Francisco, 1978-87, head dept. bus. adminstrn. and econs., 1981-87; trustee Lincoln U., 1991—; prof. Bus. Adminstrn. Lincoln U., San Francisco, 1994—; mem. Lang. Rsch. Inc., Cambridge, Mass., 1961-76; substitute tchr. San Mateo County Sch. Dist., 1991-93. Author: Five Operations with a Tank Destroyer Platoon, 1945, Top Executive Pay Package, 1963, Wage and Salary Administration in a Dynamic Economy, 1968, Wage and Salary Administration: Pay and Benefits, 1984, Compensation Administration, 1989, An Open Letter to the President-Elect: Recommendations for a New U.S. Medical System, 1992; co-author: (with Malcolm C. Neuhoff) Managing Company Airplanes, 1954. Staff asst. Brazos County Cmty. Action Com., Tex., 1966-72, Brazos Valley Cmty. Action Program, 1972-73; chmn. Hastings-on-Hudson (N.Y.) Citizens for Eisenhower campaign, 1952. 1st lt., U.S. Army, 1941-45, ETO; ret. lt. col. USAR. Decorated 5 Battle Stars. Mem. AAUP, NOW, Acad. Mgmt., Acad. Polit. Sci., Harvard Bus. Sch. Assn., Nat. Writers Union/UAW, 893d Tank Destroyer Bn. Veterans Orgn., Am. Legion, Delta Upsilon. Home: 899 Crestview Dr San Carlos CA 94070-3458 Office: Lincoln U Dept Bus Adminstrn & Econs 281 Masonic Ave San Francisco CA 94118-4498

BURGESS, LINDA, basketball player; b. July 27, 1969. Student, U. Ala., 1992. Basketball player Belinzona, Switzerland, 1992-93, Ramat HaSharon, Israel, 1992-93, Beni-Yeuda, Israel, 1993-94, S.P.O. Rouen, France, 1995-96; basketball player Los Angeles Sparks, Women's NBA, Inglewood, Calif., 1997-98; basketball player Sacramento Monarchs, Women's NBA, 1998—. Office: Sacramento Monarchs Arco Arena 1 Sports Pky Sacramento CA 95834*

BURGESS, MARJORIE LAURA, protective services official; b. Whitakers, N.C., Nov. 24, 1928; d. Benjamin and Laura Lenora (Ford) Harrison; m. Bonus David Dixon, July 24, 1948 (div. Apr. 1970); children: David Kingsley (dec.), Terence David, Michael Jerome; m. William A. Burgess, June 6, 1970 (div. July 1976). AS in Correction Adminstrn., John Jay Coll. Criminal Justice, N.Y.C., 1971; BA in Social Scis., John Jay Coll Criminal Justice, N.Y.C., 1972, postgrad., 1973-75. Correction officer N.Y. State Dept. Correction, Bedford Hills, N.Y., 1959-67, correction sgt., 1967-73, correction lt., 1973-82, 86-90, capt., 1982-86; ret., 1990; adv. coun. divsn. sr. svcs. Bergen County, 1997. Author: (poetry) Walking on the Road of Life, 1997. Vol. intergenerational program Martin Luther King Srs. Ctr. Mem. AAUW, Am. Correctional Assn., Alumni Assn. John Jay Coll., The Smithsonian Assocs., Retired Pub. Employees Assn., AARP. Democrat. Baptist. Avocations: writing, singing, playing Scrabble, reading.

BURGESS, MARVIN FRANKLIN, human resources, management specialist, consultant; b. Heathsville, Va., Mar. 18, 1932; s. Marvin Judson and Emma Elizabeth (Bradberry) B.; m. Beatrice Ione Hildahl, Feb. 7, 1932; children: Michael Marvin, Linda Ione. BA in Math. and Physics, U. Richmond, 1953; postgrad., Va. Tech., 1953-54; MA in Sociology and Psychology, Duke U., 1962. Commd. USCGR, 1956, advanced through grades to capt., dist. insp., port security, adminstr., ret., 1992; NASA engr., admin., mgmt., tech. pub. Langley Rsch. Ctr., Hampton, Va., 1954-84; cons. outplacement Career Dynamics II, Virginia Beach, Va., 1984—; adj. prof. sociology Christopher Newport Coll., Newport News, 1970-72; mgmt. tng., human resources orgn. analyst, efficiency and planning cons. U.S. Dept. Transp., Washington, 1972-80; funding, human resources mgmt., productivity cons. NASA, 1965-84; spkr., rschr. in field. Author: Rebuilding Downtrodden Job Market and Madhouse Society, 1996. Post comdr. Am. Legion, Yorktown, Va., 1978-82; chmn., pres. PTA Yorkshire Acad., York County, Va., 1968-69; mgr. Little League and Am. Leagion Baseball, York County, 1970-80; player Chesapeake League semi-pro baseball, Northern Neck, Va., 1951-56; mem. govt. com. Kiwanis, Yorktown, 1966-68. Methodist. Avocations: politics, writing, speaking, restoring old houses, sports. Home: 130 Mill Ln Yorktown VA 23692-3214 Office: Career Dynamics II 1 Columbus Ctr Ste 673 Virginia Beach VA 23462-6722 Address: 130 Mill Ln Yorktown VA 23692-3214

BURGESS, MICHAEL, library science educator, publisher; b. Fukuoka, Kyushu, Japan, Feb. 11, 1948; came to U.S., 1949; s. Roy Walter and Betty Jane (Kapel) B.; m. Mary Alice Wickizer, Oct. 15, 1976; stepchildren: Richard Albert Rogers, Mary Louise Reynnells. AB with honors, Gonzaga U., 1969; MLS, U. So. Calif., 1970. Periodicals librarian Calif. State U., San Bernardino, 1970-81, chief cataloger, 1981-94, prof., 1984—, head tech. svcs. and collection devel., 1994—; editor Newcastle Pub. Co., North Hollywood, Calif., 1971-92; pub. Borgo Press, San Bernardino, 1991—, Brownstone Books, San Bernardino, 1991—, Sidewinder Press, San Bernardino, 1991—, Unicorn & Son, San Bernardino, 1991—, Burgess & Wickizer, San Bernardino, 1991—, Emeritus Enterprises, 1993—, Starmont House, 1993—; assoc. editor SFRA Rev., 1993-94. Author 89 books under pen names Michael Burgess, R(obert) Reginald, Boden Clarke, and others, with occasional co-authors, including: Stella Nova, 1970, Cumulative Paperback Index, 1939-1959, 1973, Contemporary Science Fiction Authors, 1975, The Attempted Assassination of John F. Kennedy, 1976, Things to Come, 1977, Up Your Asteroid!, 1977, Science Fiction and Fantasy Literature, a Checklist, 1700-1974, 1979, The Paperback Price Guide, 1980, 2d edit., 1983, Science Fiction & Fantasy Awards, 1981, If J.F.K. Had Lived, 1982, The House of Burgesses, 1983, 2nd edit., 1994, The Wickizer Annals, 1983, Tempest in a Teapot, 1983, A Guide to Science Fiction & Fantasy in the Library of Congress Classification Scheme, 1984, 2nd edit., 1988, The Work of Jeffrey M. Elliot, 1984, Futurevisions, 1985, Lords Temperal & Lords Spiritual, 1985, 2nd edit., 1995, The Work of Julian May, 1985, The Work of R. Reginald, 1985, The Work of George Zebrowski, 1986, 2nd edit., 1990, 3rd edit., 1996, Mystery and Detective Fiction in the Library of Congress Classification Scheme, 1988, The Work of William F. Nolan, 1988, The Arms Control, Disarmament, and Military Security Dictionary, 1989, Hancer's Price Guide to Paperback Books, 3d edit., 1990, Reginald's Science Fiction and Fantasy Awards, 2nd edit., 1991, 3d edit., 1993, Reference Guide to Science Fiction, Fantasy, and Horror, 1992, Science Fiction and Fantasy Literature, 1975-1991, 1992, The Work of Robert Reginald, 2nd edit., 1992, The State and Province Vital Records Guide, 1993, The Work of Katherine Kurtz, 1993, St. James Guide to Science Fiction Writers, 1996, CSUSB Faculty Authors, Composers and Playwrights, 1996, rev. edit., 1996, BP 250, 1996, Xenograffiti, 1996; editor: Ancestral Voices, 1975, Alistair MacLean, 1976, Ancient Hauntings, 1976, Phantasmagoria, 1976, R.I.P., 1976, The Spectre Bridegroom and Other Horrors, 1976, John D. MacDonald and the Colorful World of Travis McGee, 1977, Dreamers of Dreams, 1978, King Solomon's Children, 1978, They, 1978, Worlds of Never, 1978, Science Fiction & Fantasy Book Review, 1980, Candle for Poland, 1982, The Holy Grail Revealed, 1982, The Work of Bruce McAllister, 1985, rev. edit., 1986, George Orwell's Guide Through Hell, 1986, 2nd edit., 1994, The Work of Charles Beaumont, 1986, 2nd edit., 1990, California Ranchos, 1988, The Work of Chad Oliver, 1989, The Work of Colin Wilson, 1989, The Work of Ian Watson, The Work of Reginald Bretnor, 1989, The Work of Ross Rocklynne, 1989, To Kill or Not To Kill, 1990, The Work of Dean Ing, 1990, The Work of Jack Dann, 1990, The Work of Pamela Sargent, 1990, 2nd edit., 1996, The Trilemma of World Oil Politics, 1991, The Work of Louis L'Amour, 1991, The Work of Brian W. Aldiss, 1992, Geo. Alec Effinger, 1993, Polemical Pulps, 1993, Sermons in Science Fiction, 1994, The Work of Elizabeth Chater, 1994, The Work of Jack Vance, 1994, The Work of William Eastlake, 1994, The Work of William F. Temple, 1994, The Work of Gary Brandner, 1995, The Work of Stephen King, 1996, Running From The Hunter, 1996; author of 150 essays; editor of 650 books. Recipient MPPP award, 1987, Lifetime Collectors award for Contbn. to Bibliography, 1993, Pilgrim award, 1993; named title II fellow U. So. Calif., 1969-70. Mem. NEA, AAUP, ALA, Sci. Fiction and Fantasy Writers Am., Calif. Tchrs. Assn., Kent Hist. Soc., Sci. Fiction Writers Am., Calif. Faculty Assn. (statewide librs. task force 1986-89, 93—, editor newsletter 1987-89), Calif. Libr. Assn., San Bernardino Hist. and Pioneer Soc., Internat. Assn. for Fantastic in Arts, Internat. Geneal. Soc., Internat. PEN, U.S.A. Ctr. West, Ky. Hist. Soc., Nat. Geneal. Soc. Sci. Fiction Rsch. Assn., Horror Writers Am., Upper Cumberland Valley Geneal. Assn., ACLU, World SF. Office: Borgo Press PO Box 2845 San Bernardino CA 92406-2845 also: Calif State U Libr 5500 University Pkwy San Bernardino CA 92407-7500*

BURGESS, MICHAEL H., management consultant; b. Jacksonville, Fla., Aug. 25, 1956; s. Robert H. and Margaret (Raulerson) B.; m. Patricia Ferguson, Sept. 8, 1979; children: Daniel H., Thomas B. BSBA, Stamford U., 1978; MBA, Ga. State U., 1989. Credit mgr. GE Capital, Gainesville, Fla., 1978-79; br. mgr. GE Capital, Tallahassee, 1979-91; mktg. svcs. rep. GE Capital, Jacksonville, 1981-82, mgr. mktg. svcs., 1982-85, mgr. inventory financing, 1985-86; new bus. devel. mgr. GE Capital, Atlanta, 1986-94; dir. of mktg./Mexico GE Capital, Mexico City, 1994-95, client svc. mgr., 1995-97; pres. Burgess Cons., Inc., Atlanta, 1997—. Republican. Presbyterian. Avocations: water skiing, camping, hunting.

BURGESS, NORMA J., sociology educator; b. Stanton, Tenn., May 24, 1954; d. John A. and Alvis M. (Jones) Bond; m. Charlie Burgess, Sept. 3, 1976; children: Wesley, Sherron. BA, U. Tenn., Martin, 1975; MPA, N.C. State U., 1980, PhD, 1986. Asst. prof. Miss. State U., 1986-93; rsch. fellow U. Memphis, 1990-93; assoc. prof., dept. chair Syracuse (N.Y.) U., 1993—, prof., 1999—. Contbr. articles to profl. jours. Mem. Nat. Coun. Family Rels. (bd. dirs. student rep. 1988-90, sect. chair bd. dirs. 1994-96, pres.-elect assn. couns. 1997—). Avocation: international travel. Office: Syracuse U 201 Slocum Hall Syracuse NY 13244

BURGESS, PAULA LASHENSKE, health facility administrator; b. Athol, Mass., Mar. 22, 1955; d. John Joseph and Lotta Catherine (Maroni) Lashenske; m. Jack Leland Burgess Jr., May 15, 1982; children: Jack Leland III, Brian Lane. AAS in Paralegal Studies, Durham (N.C.) Tech. C.C., 1988; Assoc. Risk Mgmt., Ins. Inst. Am., 1990; BSN, St. Anselm's Coll., 1977; MHA, Duke U., 1983. RN, N.C.; lic. real estate agt., N.C. Staff nurse Morton Plant Hosp., Clearwater, Fla., 1977-78; staff nurse Duke U. Med. Ctr., Durham, 1978-86, risk mgr., 1984—; adminstrv. intern Durham County Gen. Hosp., 1982; dir. utilization rev. High Point (N.C.) Meml. Hosp., 1983-84. Co-author: Mapping Your Risk Management Course in Stand-Alone Hospitals, 1996; co-contbr.: Liability Issues in Perinatal Nursing, 1997; co-author newsletter N.C. Soc. for Healthcare, 1990. Mem. Durham County Rep. Women's Club, 1996—; vol. Duke Children's Classic, Durham; mem. N-Vestment Inc., Durham, 1996—. Mem. Am. Soc. Healthcare Risk Mgmt. (spl. projects com. 1994, nominating com. 1996), Risk and Ins. Mgmt. Soc. (Piedmont chpt. society dir. 1994-96, pres. 1990-91, Southeastern regional conf. com. 1990, 94, co-chair golf tournament 1992-93). Republican. Roman Catholic. Avocations: golf, tennis, basketball, investments, croquet. Home: 2013 Sprunt Ave Durham NC 27705-3251 Office: Duke U Med Ctr PO Box 3811 Durham NC 27702-3811

BURGESS, RICHARD RAY, oncology educator, molecular biology researcher, biotechnology consultant; b. Mt. Vernon, Wash., Sept. 8, 1942; s. Robert Carl and Irene Marjorie (Wegner) B.; m. Ann Baker, June 17, 1967; children—Kristin, Andreas. B.S. in Chemistry, Calif. Inst. Tech., 1964; Ph.D. in Biochemistry and Molecular Biology, Harvard U., 1969. Helen Hay Whitney fellow Inst. Molecular Biology, Geneva, Switzerland, 1969-71; asst. prof. oncology McArdle Lab. Cancer Research U. Wis., Madison, 1971-77, assoc. prof., 1977-82, prof., 1982—, dir. Biotech. Ctr., 1984-96; cons. in field; mem. NSF study sect. in biochemistry, 1979-84; chmn. bd. Consortium for Plant Biotech. Rsch., Inc., 1992-96. Series editor U. Wis. Biotech. Ctr. Resource Manuals; editor-in chief Jour. Protein Expression and Purification; contbr. articles to profl. jours. Bd. dirs. Coun. Biotech. Ctrs., 1991-93; mem. Gov.'s Coun. on Biotech. Grantee NSF, 1978-80, 85-90, NIH, 1980—, Nat. Cancer Inst., 1971—; Guggenheim fellow, 1983-84. Mem. Am. Soc. Biochemistry and Molecular Biology, Am. Chem. Soc. (Pfizer award 1982), Am. Assn. Cancer Research, Am. Soc. Microbiology, Protein Soc. Home: 10 Knollwood Ct Madison WI 53713-3479 Office: U Wis McArdle Lab Cancer Rsch 1400 University Ave Madison WI 53706-1526

BURGESS, ROBERT, software company executive; married; three children. B in commerce, McMaster Univ. Pres. Silicon Graphics Can., Inc., 1984-90, v.p. applications, 1990, v.p. mktg., applications and bus. devel., 1991; CEO, COO, dir. Alias Rsch., 1992-95; pres. Macromedia, Inc., 1996—. Office: Macromedia 600 Townsend St Ste 310 San Francisco CA 94103-4945*

BURGESS, ROBERT LEWIS, ecologist, educator; b. Kalamazoo, Mich., Sept. 12, 1931; s. James Lewis and Hazel Lira Mae (Warren) B.; m. Vera Ballegoin, July 30, 1955; children: Karen, Steven, Susan, Ellen, Jonathan. BS, U. Wis., Milw., 1957; MS, U. Wis., Madison, 1959; PhD, U. Wis., 1961. From tchg. asst. to rsch. asst. U. Wis., 1957-60; asst. prof. Ariz. State U., 1960-63; dir. Summer Inst. in Desert Biology, 1963; from asst. to assoc. prof. N.D. State U., 1963-70; dep. dir. ea deciduous forest biome Oak Ridge Nat. Lab., 1970-77, sect. head, 1975-79, sr. rsch. staff, 1980-81; prof. ecology U. Tenn., 1974-81; prof., chmn. dept. environ. and forest biology SUNY Coll. Environ. Sci. Forestry, Syracuse, 1981—, dir. divsn. forest resources, 1988-91, 94—; vis. prof. Pahlavi U., Shiraz, Iran, 1965-66; rsch. collaborator Nat. Park Svc., 1961-64; traveling lectr. Ariz. Acad. Sci., 1962-63, Am. Inst. Biol. Scis., 1968-70, Oak Ridge Assoc. Univs., 1973-75. Rev. editor Ecology, 1971-78; mem. editl. bd. Arid Lands Abstracts, 1979-84, Ecology and Ecological Monographs, 1971-78, Forest Ecology and Mgmt., 1985-88; contbr. articles to profl. jours. Active N.D. Wildlife Adv. Com., 1967-72; adv. panel RANN program NSF, 1974-75; co-chmn. IV Internat. Congress Ecology, 1986. With AUS, 1953-55, Korea. Recipient N.D. Conservationist of Yr. award Nat. Wildlife Fedn., 1969, N.D. Cons. of Yr. award Safari Club Internat., 1970, Distinction award Soc. for Tech. Comm., 1978, Disting. Svc. citation Ecological Soc. Am., 1988. Fellow AAAS; mem. Am. Inst. Biol. Scis. (governing bd. 1981-84, membership chmn. 1981-82, nominating com. 1984-86, bd. dirs. 1990-92), Ecol. Soc. Am. (membership com. 1965-73, com. on professionalism 1971-81, governing coun. 1971-80, 83-88, com. on hist. records 1976—, chmn. 1982-88, program chmn. 1977-80, awards com. 1990-93), Internat. Assn. for Ecology, Internat. Soc. for Tropical Ecology, N.D. Natural Sci. Soc. (pres. 1967-68), Forest History Soc., Botanical Soc. Am., N.D. Acad. Sci. (pres. 1970-71), S.W. Assn. Naturalists, Nature Conservancy (bd. dirs. Tenn. chpt. 1975-81, chmn, 1976-77, bd. dirs. N.Y. chpt. 1987-93), Wilderness Soc., Sigma Xi. Democrat. Methodist. Home: 4049 Lafayette Rd Jamesville NY 13078-8765 Office: SUNY Dept Environ & Forest Biology Coll Environ Sci & Forestry Syracuse NY 13210

BURGESS, RUTH LENORA VASSAR, speech and language educator; b. Pune, India, Aug. 6, 1939; d. Theodore R. and F. Estelle (Barnett) Vassar; m. Stanley Milton Burgess, Feb. 26, 1960; children: John Bradley, Stanley Matthew, Scott Vassar, Heidi Amanda Elizabeth, Justin David. BS in Edn., Tex. Tech. U., 1960; MA, U. Mo., 1968, PhD, 1979. Speech therapist Inkster (Mich.) Pub. Schs., 1961-62; mid. sch. tchr. Strafford (Mo.) Pub. Schs., 1962-63; speech therapist Fulton (Mo.) Pub. Schs., 1967-68; speech-lang. clinician Springfield (Mo.) Pub. Schs., 1963-66; asst. prof. Evangel Coll., Springfield, 1968-76; prof. dept. reading, spl. edn. and tech. S.W. Mo. State U., Springfield, 1976—, dir. Ctr. Rsch. and Svc., 1990-97; mem. sci. adv. bd. Internat. Ctr. Enhancement of Jerusalem, Israel, 1993-96; field reviewer Dept. Edn., Washington, 1993-96, U.S. Vocat. Rehab., Washington, 1993, 94, 96,99; mem. evaluation team Title I Springfield Schs., 1994. Author: The Status of the Educational Resource Teacher, 1981; editor The Learner in the Process, 1978-80; contbr. articles to profl. jours. Ex-officio bd. dirs. Orphanage Assn., Pune, 1968—; mem. Kodaikanal-Woodstock Alumni Assn., Atlanta, 1956—; mem. Women Issues Network, Springfield, 1993—. Grantee Dept. Edn., 1978-83, 90-92, Dept. Elem. and Secondary Edn., 96, Mellon Found., 1988-90. Mem. AAUW, ASCD, Am. Speech, Lang. and Hearing Assn. (cert.), Internat. Assn. for Cognitive Edn. (field editor 1990-94). Avocations: literary group, hiking, creative writing, travel, advocacy. Office: SW Mo State U 901 S National Ave Springfield MO 65804-0088

BURGET, DEAN EDWIN, JR., plastic surgeon; b. Toledo, June 29, 1936; s. Dean E. Sr. and Marie E. (Alwine) B.; m. A. Undine Ehrman, Mar. 16, 1957 (div. Mar. 1993); children: Mark A.E., Kevin Phillips, Undine Peeples; m. Gabriella Morocz, May 14, 1993. BS, U. Toledo, 1958; MD, Yale U., 1962. Diplomate Am. Bd. Plastic Surgery; lic. physician, Ohio, Pa., N.Y., Ill. Intern surgery U. Hosps., Cleve., 1962, resident in anesthesiology, 1963; resident in gen. surg. Hahnemann Med. Coll. and Hosp., Phila., 1966-68; resident in plastic surg. Temple U. Hosp., Phila., 1968-70, U.S. Govt. fellow in rehab. surgery, 1970-71, instr. plastic surgery, 1970-71; instr. plastic surgery Med. Coll. Pa., Phila., 1970-71, assoc. clin. prof., 1979-81; asst. prof., dir. divsn. plastic surgery Hahnemann Med. Coll. and Hosp., Phila., 1972-75; staff surgeon, cons. surgeon various cmty. hosps., 1975-85; pvt. practice Devon, Pa., 1985—. Fellow ACS; mem. Am. Soc. Plastic and Reconstructive Surgeons, Pickering Hunt Club (Phila.), Ausable Club/Adirondack Mountain Res. (St. Huberts, N.Y.), Yale Club (N.Y.C.), Rittenhouse Club (Phila.), Penn Club, St. Nicholas Soc. City N.Y., Pa. Soc. Sons Revolution, Colonial Soc. Pa., Soc. Colonial Wars Pa., Nat. Huguenot Soc., Soc. War 1812, Phila. Soc. Promoting Agr. Office: 176 E Conestoga Rd Devon PA 19333

BURGGRAF, FRANK BERNARD, JR., landscape architect, retired educator; b. N.Y.C., Nov. 13, 1932; s. Frank Bernard and Johanna (Verbaan) B.; m. Jane Martin Rannenberg, June 25, 1955 (div. 1997); children: Helen Marguerite, Frank Bernard, John Christian; m. Margaret Goff, Oct. 31, 1998. BS, SUNY-Syracuse, 1954; MLA, U. Pa., 1958. Registered landscape architect, Ark., N.Y. Asst. prof. U. Ga., Athens, 1958-63; assoc. prof., dir. regional planning grad. program Pa. State U., University Park, 1963-70; chief planning analyst N.Y. State Pub. Service Commn., Albany, 1970-80; cons. landscape architect, planner Delmar, N.Y., 1980-84; prof. landscape architecture U. Ark., Fayetteville, 1984-97, dir. program in landscape architecture, 1984-87, emeritus prof. landscape architecture, 1997—; mem. N.Y. State Bd. Landscape Architecture, 1977-84, chmn., 1979-81. Contbr. articles to profl. jours. Served to lt. col. USAFR, 1954-81. Fellow Am. Soc. Landscape Architects; mem. Am. Planning Assn., Elks (exalted ruler local lodge, 1990), Delta Upsilon (chpt. faculty advisor 1984-90). Democrat. Avocations: sailing; handball. Home: 18665 Brentwood Mountain Rd Winslow AR 72959 Office: U Ark Sch Architecture 230 Memorial Hall Fayetteville AR 72701

BURGHARDT, LINDA F., writer; b. Nov. 11, 1946. BA, CUNY, 1968, MA, 1998. Writer, editor N.Y. Daily News, N.Y.C., 1972-75; editor JCPenney Co., N.Y.C., 1975-81; owner Burghardt Comms., Great Neck, N.Y., 1981—; contbg. writer N.Y. Times, N.Y.C., 1989—. E-mail: burgcomm@aol.com. Home: 11 Stoner Ave Great Neck NY 11021-2150

BURGHARDT, WALTER FRANCIS, JR., veterinarian; b. Columbus, Ohio, Sept. 18, 1952; s. Walter Francis and Helen Wanda (Watrobinski) B.; m. Charleen S. Horkott, July 24, 1993; stepchildren: Joel Webster, Christopher Webster; 1 child, Kurt. BA, Fla. Atlantic U., 1974, MA, 1975; DVM, U. Fla., 1980; PhD in Biopsychology, U. Md., 1988. Prin. investigator, dept. exec. officer Armed Forces Radiobiology Research Inst., Bethesda, Md., 1980-84; animal behavior cons. Behavior Clin. for Animals, Washington, 1985-95; assoc. veterinarian Colonial Animal Hosp., Boynton Beach, Fla., 1985; chief mil. pub. health 482d Med. Squadron, Homestead AFB, Fla., 1984-95; hosp. dir. Abacus Animal Hosp., Coral Springs, Fla., 1985-95; chief pub. health 433 Med. Squadron, Kelly AFB, Tex., 1995-97; hosp. admin. 433 Med. Squadron, Kelly AFB, 1998—; chief behavioral medicine and mil. working dog studies Mil. Working Dog Vet. Svc., Lackland AFB, Tex., 1995—; cons. Whittle Communications (Purina), Am. Vet. Med. Assn., Reader's Digest. Contbg. writer Pet Supplies Mktg.; contbr. articles and papers in field. Capt. USAF, 1980-84, Res. maj. 1989-97, Lt.C. 1997—. Research fellow U. Fla. Coll. Vet. Medicine, 1977. Mem. AVMA, APA, Am. Vet. Soc. Animal Behavior (sec.-treas. 1984-88, pres. 1989-92), Animal Behavior Soc., Bexar County Vet. Med. Assn., Assn. Mil. Surgeons U.S., Res. Officers Assn., Mensa, Blue Key. Republican. Presbyterian. Avocations: bicycling, boating, scuba diving. Office: 341 TRS/SGV 1219 Knight St Lackland AFB TX 78236-5631

BURGHART, JAMES HENRY, electrical engineer, educator; b. Erie, Pa., July 18, 1938; s. Chester Albert and Mary Virginia (Burke) B.; m. Judith Ann Hoff, July 8, 1961; children—Jill Kathryn, Mark Alan. B.S. in Elec. Engring, Case Inst. Tech., 1960, M.S. (U.S. Steel Found. fellow 1961-63), 1962, Ph.D., 1965. Asst. prof., then assoc. prof. elec. engring. SUNY, Buffalo, 1969-75; prof. elec. engring. Cleve. State U., 1975—, chmn. dept., 1975-85, 89-97. Served as officer USAF, 1965-68. Mem. IEEE (chmn. Cleve. sect. 1980-81, sec. region 2, 1989-96, profl. activities coord., region 2, 1997—), Am. Soc. Engring. Edn., Sigma Xi, Eta Kappa Nu. Home: 5501 Strathaven Dr Cleveland OH 44143-1970 Office: 1983 E 24th St Cleveland OH 44115-2403

BURGHDUFF, JOHN BRIAN, mathematics educator; b. Augusta, Ga., July 16, 1958; s. Richard Dean and Betty Kay (Hebeler) B. BS in Applied Maths., Tex. A&M U., 1980; MS in Maths., Ohio State U., 1982; PhD in Math., U. Houston, 1994. Teaching asst. Tex. A&M U., College Station, 1978-80, Ohio State U., Columbus, 1980-82; instr. San Jacinto Coll., Houston, 1982-88, U. Houston, 1988-92; prof. Kingwood Coll., 1992—. Vol. youth dir. League City (Tex.) Ch. of Christ, 1982-86; faculty sponsor San Jacinto Coll. Bapt. Student Union, Houston, 1982-86; vol. Magnificat House Homeless Shelter, Houston, 1989—. Mem. Math. Assn. Am., Am. Math. Soc., Inst. for Combinatorics and its Applications. Democrat. Episcopalian. Achievements include research in spectra of graphs and permanents of matrices. Home: 2600 Westridge St Apt 364 Houston TX 77054-1545 Office: Kingwood Coll Dept Math Kingwood TX 77339

BURGHEIM, RICHARD, magazine editor; b. St. Louis, July 5, 1933; s. Nathaniel H. and Mary (Rudman) B. BA, Harvard U., 1955. Show bus. writer Time Mag., N.Y.C., 1960-71; dir. cable TV programming Time Inc., N.Y.C., 1972-73; editor People Mag., N.Y.C., 1974-81, 89-92; mng. editor TV-Cable Week, White Plains, N.Y., 1982-83; editor Money Mag., N.Y.C., 1986-89; cons. editor Time Inc., N.Y.C., 1993—; cons. community cable programming Ford Found., N.Y.C., 1972; lectr. Harvard Inst. Telecommunications and Pub. Policy, Cambridge, 1972. Contbg. editor mags. Variety, Harper's, numerous others. Bd. dirs. Children's Express, N.Y.C., 1994-97, Doe Fund, N.Y.C., 1999—, Goddard Riverside Comty. Ctr., N.Y.C., 1999—. Avocations: running, reading. Home: 230 Central Park W Apt 16D New York NY 10024-6040 Office: Time Inc Time And Life Bldg New York NY 10020

BURGIN, CHARLES E., lawyer; b. Marion, N.C., Dec. 16, 1938; m. Ellen Salsbury Burgin; children: Ellen, Lucy. BA, U. N.C., 1961; LLB, Duke U., 1964. Bar: N.C.; U.S. Supreme Ct. Law clk. to Hon. J. Braxton Craven Jr. U.S. Dist. Ct., U.S. Ct. Appeals, 1964-66; prosecuting atty. McDowell County Criminal Ct., 1966-68; sr. ptnr. Dameron, Burgin & Parker, P.A., Marion, N.C., 1968—; bd. dirs. Shadowline, Inc.; lectr. in field. Contbr. articles to profl. jours. Bd. dirs. McDowell County Recreation Commn. 1977-87, First Union Nat. Bank 1975—; McDowell County Mountain

Rescue Team 1980—; McDowell Arts and Crafts Assn. 1980—. Fellow Am. Coll. Trial Lawyers (state chmn. 1996-98), Internat. Soc. Barristers, Am. Bar Found.; mem. ABA, N.C. Bar Assn. (pres. 1993-94), Defense Rsch. Inst., Am. Soc. Hosp. Attys., N.C. Assn. Defense Lawyers, U.S. Supreme Ct. Bar Assn. Office: Dameron Burgin & Parker PA PO Drawer 1049 14 W Court St Marion NC 28752-3900

BURGIN, GEORGE HANS, computer scientist, educator; b. Liestal, Switzerland, Feb. 13, 1930; s. Jakob and Fanny B.; m. Ulrike Franziska, July 8, 1960; children: Bernard, Claudia, Paul. Diplom ingenieur, Swiss Fed. Inst. Tech., Zurich, 1953, PhD, 1961. Registered profl. engr., Calif. Design specialist Gen. Dynamics Corp., San Diego, 1962-64; sr. scientist Decision Sci., San Diego, 1964-82; chief scientist Titan Systems, San Diego, 1982-94; prin. staff engr. Titan Info. Systems, 1994-96, chief engr., 1996-98; staff engr. CommQuest Techs., 1998—; lectr. San Diego State U., 1979-89. Contbg. author: Simulation, 1968, 2d edit., 1989; author, inventor air combat simulation program Adaptive Maneuvering Logic; contbr. articles to profl. jours. Served to 1st lt. Swiss Army. Mem. IEEE. Achievements include invention of adaptive maneuvering logic air combat simulation program. Home: 6284 Avenida Cresta La Jolla CA 92037-6505 Office: CommQuest 527 Encinitas Blvd Encinitas CA 92024-3740

BURGIN, KAREN JEAN, special education educator; b. Conway, Ark., Jan. 18, 1957; d. Romie F. and Bonnie J. Tindall; m. Hinson K. Burgin, Oct. 20, 1956; childre: Jay D., Natalie K. BS in Edn., U. Ctrl. Ark., 1979. Tchr. Mt. Vernon (Ark.) Schs., 1979-82, Greenbrier (Ark.) Schs., 1982—. Mem. Greenbrier Edn. Assn. (pres. 1998-99), Greenbrier Alumni Assn. (Tchr. of Yr. 1997), Delta Kappa Gamma. Baptist. Avocations: water sports, computers, sports. Office: Greenbrier Pub Schs 10 School Dr Greenbrier AR 72058

BURGIN, MAX EDWARD, minister, farmer; b. Forest City, N.C., Feb. 26, 1934; s. Robert Cheek and Nannie Bell (Harris) B.; m. Mickie Jean Kelly, June 30, 1962; children: Kelli Lynn, Edward Lee. BA, Wake Forest U., 1959; BD, Southwestern Bapt. Theol. Sem., 1962; MA, L.I. U., 1974; D Ministry, N.Y. Theol. Sem., 1976. Ordained to ministry Bapt. Ch., 1962. Pastor Union Bapt. Ch., Shelby, N.C., 1963-65; commd. 1st lt. U.S. Army, 1963, advanced through grades to col., 1985; dir. dept. ministry and pastoral care Walter Reed Army Med. Ctr., Washington, 1986-91; ret., 1991; dir. clin. pastoral edn. program VA Med. Ctr., Asheville, N.C., 1992-96; pastor Lattimore (N.C.) Bapt. Ch., 1992—; owner, operator cow/calf operation Burgin Farms. Contbr. articles to profl. jours. Chmn. personnel com. Sch. Bd., Fort Benning, Ga., 1978-81. Decorated Bronze Star, Nat. Def. Ribbon, 2 Legion of Merit, 5 Meritorious Svc. medals, 5 Army Commendations. Fellow Coll. of Chaplains. Home: 167 Stroud Rd Ellenboro NC 28040-5798

BURGIN, RICHARD WESTON, writer, educator, editor; b. Brookline, Mass., Mar. 30, 1947; s. Richard and Ruth (Posselt) B.; m. Linda Kinnard Harris, Sept. 7, 1991 (div.); 1 child, Richard Daniel. BA with honors, Brandeis U., 1968; MA with highest honors, Columbia U., 1969, MPhil in Modern Am. Lit., 1980. Instr. English Tufts U., Medford, Mass., 1970-74; editor N.Y. Arts Jour., N.Y.C., 1975-80; assoc. prof. Drexel U., Phila., 1984-96, St. Louis U., 1996—; vis. lectr. U. Calif., Santa Barbara, 1981-83. Author: Ghost Quartet, 1999, (collections) Man Without Memory, 1989, Private Fame, 1991, Fear of Blue Skies, 1998, Conversations with Jorge Luis Borges, 1969, Conversations with Isaac Bashevis Singer, 1985; editor: Jorge Luis Borges: Conversations, 1998; editor Blvd. Mag., 1985—; contbr. articles to mags. Recipient Pushcart Press prize, 1982, 86, 98. Mem. Nat. Book Critics Cir., St. Louis Writers Workshop. Avocations: composing, piano, sports. Home: 18 S Kings Hwy Apt 10JK Saint Louis MO 63108 Office: Blvd 4579 LaClede Ave #332 Saint Louis MO 63108

BURGIN, WALTER HOTCHKISS, JR., educational administrator; b. Harrisburg, Pa., Apr. 14, 1935; s. Walter Hotchkiss and Wilhelmina (Buntin) B.; m. Barbara Isabelle Waddell, June 15, 1957; children: Christine, Jennifer. AB, Dartmouth Coll., 1957; postgrad., Princeton U., 1957-59; EdM, Harvard U., 1964. Tchr. math. Phillips Exeter (N.H.) Acad., 1964-72; tchr. math. Mercersburg (Pa.) Acad., 1959-64, chmn. dept., 1961-64, headmaster, 1972-97; tchr. math. Sidwell Friends Sch., Washington, 1997-98; exec. dir. Edward E. Ford Found., Washington, 1998—; mem. Pa. Bd. for Pvt. Acad. Schs., 1973-94. NSF fellow, 1957-59, Shell fellow, 1964. Mem. Math. Assn. Am., Nat. Assn. Prins. Sch. for Girls, Headmasters Assn. (treas. 1993-96, v.p. 1996-97), Nat. Coun. Tchrs. Math., Nat. Assn. Ind. Schs. (bd. dirs. 1989-96, sec. 1992-96), Pa. Assn. Ind. Schs. (exec. com. 1980-90). Democrat. Mem. United Ch. of Christ. Home: 2153 California St NW Apt 402 Washington DC 20008-1845

BURGIN, WILLIAM LYLE, architect; b. Colorado Springs, Colo., Apr. 30, 1946; s. William Herman and Lorraine (Beeson) B.; m. Virginia Margaret Wojtul, Sept. 23, 1967; 1 child, Desdemona. BA, R.I. Sch. Design, 1972, BArch, 1973. Ptnr. Estes/Burgin Partnership, Providence, 1980-89; pres. William L. Burgin Architects, Newport, R.I., 1989—. Trustee Jamestown Hist. Soc., 1994; mem. Newport Hosp. Assn. Recipient Preservation award Nat. Trust for Hist. Preservation, 1986, Custom Housing Selection award Builder mag., Nat. Assn. Home Builders, 1989, Design and Planning Merit award Builder's Choice, 1993, Mayor's award City of Newport, 1988-90, People's Choice award for affordable housing design R.I. Housing and Fin. Corp., 1990, AID honor award, 1995-96, Gold medal for best new house, 1995, Housing award Fine Homebuilding mag., 1997; Rhode Island AIA Honor award Capt. Roger Wheeler Stage Beach Pavilion, 1998, Custom Home Mag. merit award Black Point House, 1999. Mem. AIA (citation 1993, Spl. citation for care 1987, honor award 1988, 93), Conanicut Yacht Club (commodore 1996—), Nat. Tennis Club (bd. govs. Newport, R.I.). Avocations: court tennis, skiing, yachting, astronomy. Office: William L Burgin Architects Inc 150 Bellevue Ave Newport RI 02840-3230

BURGOS, NORMA, secretary of state. BA in Econs. with hons., U. P.R., 1978, MPA, 1982; postgrad., Ga. Inst. Tech.; D in Polit. Sci. (hon.), Caribbean U. Cert. housing mgr. Nat. Ctr. Housing Mgmt., profl. planner. With Govt. P.R., 1976—; assoc. mem., chair, sec. of state P.R. Planning Bd., 1992—; pres., exec. dir. Old San Juan Devel. Corp., 1986-90; cons. dept. transp. pub. works, P.R.; spl. project Puerto Rico 2005, 1992; exec. dir. Gov.'s Coun. Econ. Productivity; bd. dirs. So. Growth Policy. Co-author: Transnationalization in the Decade of the 80's: An Opportunity to Export Knowledge, 1984, Public Administration in Puerto Rico and the New Century: The Experts' Opinion; contbr. articles to profl. jours. Recipient Eagle award Nat. Hispanic Heritage Leadership Conf.;named 1996 Disting. Citizen P.R., Pub. Servant of Yr., Encuantro Found. Office: State Dept Office of Gov PO Box 9023271 San Juan PR 00902-3271

BURGOS-SASSCER, RUTH, chancellor; b. N.Y.C., Sept. 5, 1931; m. Donald Sasscer, June 14, 1958; children: Timothy, James, Julie, David. BA, Maryville (Tenn.) Coll., 1953; MA, Columbia U., 1956; PhD, Fla. State U., 1987. Mem. faculty Inter-Am. U., P.R., 1968-71; dept. chair U. P.R., Aguadilla, 1972-76; dir. non-traditional programs Cen. Adminstrn. Regional Coll. U. P.R., 1976-81; dir., dean, chief exec. officer U. P.R., Aguadilla, 1981-85; v.p. faculty and instrn. Harry S. Truman Coll., Chgo., 1988-93; pres. San Antonio Coll., 1993-96; chancellor Houston C.C. Sys., 1996—; bd. dirs. Nat. Hispanic Coun. C.C.s. Bd. dirs. Greater Houston Partnership, Houston Read Commn., City of Houston Ethics Com., Am. Assn. C.C., Internat. Consortium for Ednl. and Econ. Devel., Laredo Nat. Bank, Houston. Mem. Am. Assn. C.C., Internat. Consortium for Ednl. and Econ. Devel. Presbyterian. Home: 530 Bolton Pl Houston TX 77024-4601 Office: Houston CC Sys 22 Waugh Dr Houston TX 77007-5813

BURGOYNE, DAVID SIDNEY, psychiatrist; b. Montpelier, Idaho, Mar. 28, 1923; s. Sidney Eynon and Beatrice (Holmes) B.; m. Helen Louise Seewer, Nov. 15, 1945; children: David Sidney II, Rhoda Lee, James Carl (dec.), Steven John. Student, Utah State U., 1941-42, 46-47; MD, Cornell U., 1951. Med. intern LDS Hosp., Salt Lake City, 1951-52; gen. practice medicine Coolidge, Ariz., 1952-59; commd. ens. USN, 1960, advanced through grades to comdr.; resident in psychiat. medicine U.S. Naval Hosp., Oakland, Calif., 1960-62; chief neuropsychiatry USN-Pearl Harbor (Hawaii) Shipyard, 1963-65; chief of psychiatry U.S. Naval Hosp., Camp Pendleton, Calif., 1965-66; resigned USN, 1966; pvt. practice psychiatry Phoenix, 1966—; chief of staff Camelback Hosp., Phoenix, 1975-76, Scottsdale, Ariz., 1989. Author: Psychiatric Disorders - Identification and Emergency Care Aboard Submarines, 1964; contbr. articles to profl. jours. Lt. USN, 1942-46, PTO. Fellow Am. Psychiat. Assn. (life, Ariz. rep. 1972-77, dep. regional rep. area 7, 1977-79); mem. Ariz. Psychiat. Soc. (pres. 1971-72), Pinal County Med. Assn. (pres. 1958). Avocations: downhill skiing, tennis, running. Home: 4523 E Orange Dr Phoenix AZ 85018-1714 Office: 4630 E Indian School Rd Phoenix AZ 85018-5416

BURGOYNE, MOJIE ADLER, clinical social worker; b. Abilene, Tex., Apr. 26, 1942; d. Leonard A. and Mojie W. (Jennings) Adler; m. Wallace Carr Burgoyne, June 27, 1964 (div. Dec. 1974); children: Kristina, Pamela, Carr. BA, Tex. Woman's U., 1964; MSW, U. Houston, 1979. Lic. master social worker-advanced clin. practitioner, Tex.; diplomae Am. Bd. Cert. Managed Care Providers, Am. Bd. Examiners. in Clin. Social Work. Clin. social worker Post Oak Psychiatry & Assocs., Tomball, Tex., 1986-90, Raul R Gomez & Assocs., Tomball, 1990-91; owner, clin. social worker Affiliated Mental Health Svcs., Tomball, 1991—; pres. Home Health Adv. Bd., Tomball, 1979-84. Contbg. author: Social Work Treatment with Abused and Neglected Children, 1985. Polit. activist Child Welfare Bd., Montgomery County, Tex., 1974-77. Named Woman of Yr., Montgomery County (Tex.) YWCA, 1981. Mem. NASW (diplomate in clin. social work). Avocations: reading, restoring an antique barn in farm country of south central Texas. Office: Affiliated Mental Health Svcs 607 Mason St Ste 1 Tomball TX 77375-4451

BURGWALD, BERYLE ALAN, political science educator; b. Michigan City, Ind., Nov. 13, 1945; s. George R. and Lillian H. (Brown) B. BA in Govt. and Polit. Sci., Valparaiso U., 1968, MA in Govt., 1970. U.S. congl. asst. 2nd Dist. Ind., Valparaiso, 1970; assoc., rsch. writing asst. Law Office of Luis Kutner, Esq., Chgo., 1971-91; prof. polit. sci. Purdue U., Westville, Ind., 1991—. Contbr. articles to profl. jours. City coun. mem. Michigan City Common Coun., 1971-83, 88-91, pres. city coun., 1975, chmn. judiciary and rules com., 1972-83, 88-91, chmn. coun. ethics commn., 1989-91; county coun. mem. Laporte County (Ind.) Coun., 1994—. Mem. Pi Sigma Alpha. Republican. Congregationalist. Avocation: collecting campaign memorabilia. Home: 1914 Greenwood Ave Michigan City IN 46360-5636

BURGWEGER, FRANCIS JOSEPH DEWES, JR., lawyer; b. Evanston, Ill., July 5, 1942; s. Francis Dewes and Helen Theodosia (Chancellor) B.; m. Kathleen Marie Wessel, Sept. 3, 1978; children: Lauren Elizabeth, Francis Joseph Dewes III, Sherman Ward Chancellor. BA, Yale U., 1964; JD, U. Pa., 1970. Bar: Calif. 1971, N.Y. 1988, U.S. Ct. Appeals (9th cir.) 1971, U.S. Dist. Ct. (cen. dist.) Calif. 1971. Law clk. to Hon. Shirley M. Hufstedler U.S. Ct. Appeals 9th Cir., L.A., 1970-71; assoc. O'Melveny & Myers, L.A., 1971-78, ptnr., 1978-85; ptnr. O'Melveny & Myers LLP, N.Y.C., 1985-97, sr. counsel, 1997—. Contbr. articles on environ. law. Capt. U.S. Army, 1964-67, Vietnam. Mem. Assn. of Bar of City of N.Y., N.Y. State Bar Assn., L.A. County Bar Assn. (exec. com. R.P. sect.). Avocations: books, wine, agriculture. Office: O'Melveny & Myers LLP 153 E 53rd St Fl 54 New York NY 10022-4611

BURHOE, BRIAN WALTER, automotive service executive; b. Worcester, Mass., Apr. 9, 1941; s. Walter De Forest and Dorothy Merrium (Gould) B.; m. Lynda Clayton, May 28, 1960 (div. May 1972); children: Mark S., Ty C., Scott M.; m. Joan Elaine Bredenberg, Oct. 21, 1989. Arts Baccalaureate, Clark U., Worcester, 1963, MA in History, Internat. Relations, 1971; cert. advanced mgmt. program, Northwestern U., 1985. Tchr. Orleans (Mass.) Sch. System, 1965-67; mgr. labor rels. Ill. Central R.R., Chgo., 1967-74, exec. asst., 1974-77; dir. human resources Midas Internat. Corp., Chgo., 1977-79, v.p. human resources, 1979-89, sr. v.p. human resources, 1989-98; pres. The Old Bookseller, Inc., 1998—. Mem. Ill. Safety Coun. (chmn. 1992-94). Avocation: collecting out of print books. Home: 325 Nebraska St Frankfort IL 60423 Office: The Old Bookseller Inc 808 Harrison St Oak Park IL 60304-1101

BURI, CHARLES EDWARD, lawyer; b. Lancaster, Pa., Jan. 20, 1950; s. Karl Emerson and Verna Irene (Linville) B.; m. Susan Louise Camou, May 8, 1971; 1 child, Charles David. BS, U. Ariz., 1971, JD, 1973. Bar: Ariz. 1974, U.S. Dist. Ct. Ariz., 1974, U.S. Ct. Appeals (9th cir.) 1977, U.S. Supreme Ct. 1980. Asst. atty Gen. Office Atty. Gen., Phoenix, 1974-83; exec. dir. Ariz. State Lottery, Phoenix, 1983-87; ptnr. Friedl, Richter & Buri, Phoenix, 1987—. Life mem. Fiesta Bown com., Phoenix, 1984—, Luke's Men, Phoenix, 1985—, Gov.'s Cabinet, Phoenix, 1983-87; trustee St. Luke's Hosp., Phoenix, 1990-91. Mem. ABA, Nat. Trial Lawyers Assn., Ariz. Trial Lawyers Assn., Ariz. Bar Assn., Maricopa County Bar Assn., Phoenix-East Rotary. Democrat. Avocations: tennis, skiing, jogging. Home: 6002 E Lafayette Blvd Scottsdale AZ 85251-3040 Office: Friedl Richter & Buri Ste 200 6909 E Greenway Pkwy Scottsdale AZ 85254

BURICK, LAWRENCE T., lawyer; b. Dayton, Ohio, May 15, 1943; s. Lee and Doris (Brenner) B.; m. Cynthia Joy Rosen, Aug. 31, 1969; children: Carrie R., Samuel J. BA, Miami U., 1965; JD, Northwestern U., 1968. Bar: Ohio 1968. Assoc. Smith & Schnacke, Dayton, 1969-78, ptnr., 1978-89; ptnr. Thompson Hine & Flory LLP, Dayton, 1989—. Chmn. Dayton Jewish Ctr., 1982-83, Jewish Cmty. Rels. Coun., 1980-81; pres. Jewish Fedn. Greater Dayton, 1989-93, bd. dirs., 1977—; chmn. United Jewish Campaign, 1997-99; bd. dirs. Jewish Edn. in Svc. to N.Am., 1994—, v.p., 1997—, bd. dirs. nat. conf., 1997—, treas. 1998—, v.p., 1999—; bd. dirs. Beth Abraham Synagogue, 1997—. Recipient Wasserman Leadership award, Jewish Fedn. Greater Dayton, 1978. Mem. ABA, Ohio State Bar Assn., Dayton Bar Assn., Am. Bankruptcy Law Forum, Am. Bankruptcy Inst. Office: Thompson Hine & Flory PO Box 8801 2000 Courthouse Plz NE Dayton OH 45401-8801

BURINI, SONIA MONTES DE OCA, apparel manufacturing and public relations executive; b. Havana, Cuba, Apr. 28, 1935; d. Francisco and Nilda (Diaz) Montes de Oca; m. Franco Burini, Apr. 5, 1959. Student, U. Havana, 1954-57, Georgetown U., 1958; BA in History cum laude, U. Miami, Coral Gables, Fla., 1971. Adminstr. Roma Fashions, Inc. D/B/A Franco B., Coral Gables, 1976-95; entrepreneur, pub. rels. exec., 1995—. Founder Nat. Parkinson Found., 1986—; v.p. Vizcayans Fund Raising Orgn., 1990—, chmn. fine arts events, 1993-95; co-chmn. 1st annual fund raising event Am. Cancer Soc. Winn-Dixie Hope Lodge Ctr.; mem. women with heart group Heart Assn. Greater Miami, Fla., 1981—; founder, bd. dirs. Cancer Link program U. Miami Comprehensive Cancer Ctr., 1987; chmn. spring fantasy luncheon Am. Cancer Soc., 1988; founding chmn. Rose Group, Am. Lung Assn., chmn. Rose Ball, 1989; amb. Mercy Hosp. Found., 1987-95; bd. dirs. Newborn program U. Miami, 1978, bd. dirs., 1982-87, amb. category years; vol. guide Viscaya Mus., Dade County, Fla., 1972-79, chmn. various coms., 1979—, found. bd. dirs., steering com., mem. com. of 100; bd. dir., Young Patroness of the Opera, 1979-87; grand patron Greater Miami Opera, 1986-95, bd. dirs., 1978—, chmn. opera gala, 1987, mem. opera guild, 1988; founding bd. mem. Ears Dears U. Miami, 1986—, chmn. 1990 gala; mem. Dade County Performing Art Ctr. Trust, 1993—; spl. chmn. fine arts events Vizcayans, 1993—; mem. sister cities com. Cities of Miami, Fla. and Nice, France, 1994—, Nat. Trust Hist. Preservation, 1997—. Named Oustanding Woman of Yr. Mayor of Dade County, 1986, Woman of Yr. Heart Assn. Greater Miami, 1986, named to Miss Charity Biscayne Bay Marriott Hotel and Marina, 1987. Mem. NAt. Trust Historic Preservation, Ballet Soc. Miami (bd. dirs. 1979-80, named one of Miami's Oustanding Women 1986), Confrerie de la Chaine des Rotisseurs. Home: 700 Coral Way Coral Gables FL 33134-4880 Office: Roma Fashions Inc 3311 Ponce De Leon Blvd Coral Gables FL 33134-7210 also: Corregidor Aguirre 21, Las Palmas de Canaria Spain also: Burini Enterprises, Inc PO Box 347374 Coral Gables FL 33234-7374

BURISH, THOMAS GERARD, psychology educator; b. Peshtigo, Wis., May 4, 1950; s. Bennie Charles and Donna Mae (Willkom) B.; m. Pamela Jean Zebrasky, June 19, 1976; children: Mark Joseph, Brent Christopher. AB summa cum laude, U. Notre Dame, 1972; MA, U. Kans., 1975, PhD, 1976. Lic. psychologist, Tenn. Asst. prof. psychology Vanderbilt U., Nashville, 1976-80, assoc. prof., 1980-86, prof., 1986-88, dir. clin. tng., 1980-84, chair dept. psychology, 1984-86, assoc. provost, 1986-93, provost, 1993—; cons. VA Hosp., Tenn., 1978—; mem. cancer rsch. manpower rev. com. Nat. Cancer Inst., 1991-96; co-chair Bridge task force com. Am. Cancer Soc., 1994-96; mem. breast cancer rsch. panel U.S. Army Med. Rsch., 1995—. Co-editor: Coping with Chronic Disease, 1983, Cancer, Nutrition and Eating Behavior, 1985; co-author: Behavior Therapy, 1987, Health Psychology, 1991. Chmn. St. Mary's Sch. Bd., Nashville, 1982-83; participant Leadership Nashville, 1989-90; bd. dirs. Am. Cancer Soc. Fellow Am. Psychol. Assn., Am. Psychol. Soc.; mem. Acad. Behavioral Medicine Rsch., Phi Beta Kappa. Roman Catholic. Office: Vanderbilt Univ 221 Kirkland Hall Nashville TN 37240

BURK, JAMES STEVEN, sociologist; b. Balt., Oct. 9, 1948; s. John Franklin and Peggy Gladys B.; m. Patricia Andrea Garcia, Oct. 21, 1967; children: Jacqueline Lee, Theodore Michael. BS, Towson U., 1975; AM, U. Chgo., 1978, PhD, 1982. Lectr. U. Chgo., 1980-81; asst. prof. Tex. A&M U., College Station, 1984-90, assoc. prof., 1990-97, prof., 1997—; vis. asst. prof. McGill U., Montreal, Que., Can., 1981-83, Tex. A&M U., 1983-84. Author: Values in the Marketplace, 1988; editor: On Social Organization and Social Control, 1991, The Military on New times, 1994, The Adaptive Military, 1998. Exec. coun. Inter-Univ. Sem. Armed Forces & Soc., 1981—. NSF grantee, 1980-81; Nat. Inst. Mental Health fellow, 1978-79. Mem. Am. Sociol. Assn. Democrat. Presbyterian. Avocations: racquetball, watercolors. Office: Tex A&M U Dept Sociology College Station TX 77843-4351

BURK, RAYMOND FRANKLIN, JR., physician, educator, researcher; b. Kosciusko, Miss., Dec. 9, 1942; s. Raymond Franklin and Florence Annie (Davis) B.; m. Enikoe Vikor, June 17, 1967; children: Teresa Marie, Stephen Morrison. BA, U. Miss., 1963; MD, Vanderbilt U., 1968. Diplomate Am. Bd. Internal Medicine. Intern, Vanderbilt Hosp., Nashville, 1968-69, resident in medicine, 1969-70; asst. prof. medicine and biochemistry U. Tex. S.W. Med. Sch., Dallas, 1975-78; assoc. prof. medicine and biochemistry La. State U. Sch. Medicine, Shreveport, 1978-80; assoc. prof. medicine U. Tex. Health Sci. Ctr., San Antonio, 1980-82, prof., 1982-87; prof. medicine Vanderbilt U., 1987—; researcher in field; mem. staff Vanderbilt U. Hosp., Nashville. Served to maj. U.S. Army, 1970-73. NIH grantee, 1974—. Mem. Am. Soc. Biol. Chemists, Am. Soc. Clin. Investigation, Am. Inst. Nutrition. Contbr. articles to profl. jours. Office: Vanderbilt U Med Sch Div Gastroenterology Med Ctr N Nashville TN 37232

BURK, ROBERT S., lawyer; b. Mpls., Jan. 13, 1937; s. Harvey and Mayme (Cottle) B.; m. Eunice L. Silverman, Mar. 22, 1959; children: Bryan, Pam, Matt. BBA in Indsl. Rels., U. Minn., 1959; LLB, William Mitchell Coll. Law, 1965. Bar: Minn. 1966; qualified neutral under Rule 114 of the Minn. Gen. Rules of Practice, 1995—. Labor rels. cons. St. Paul Employers Assn., 1959-66; labor rels. mgr. Koch Refining Co., St. Paul, 1966-72, mgr. indsl. rels., 1972-75, mgr. indsl. rels., environ. affairs, 1975-77; sr. atty. Popham, Haik, Schnobrich & Kaufman, Ltd., Mpls., 1977-95, pres., CEO, 1986-90; ptnr. Burk & Seaton, P.A., Edina, Minn., 1995—. Chair bd. trustees William Mitchell Coll. Law, St. Paul, 1994-96, sec. 1991. Recipient Hon. Ronald E. Hachey Outstanding Alumnus award William Mitchell Coll. Law Alumni Assn., 1993. Mem. ABA (labor sect.), Minn. Bar Assn. (labor sect.). Office: Burk & Seaton PA 7301 Ohms Ln Ste 320 Edina MN 55439-2336 *Credibility is the only trait that marks your existence.*

BURKA, ROBERT ALAN, lawyer; b. Washington, Dec. 25, 1944; s. Fred and Louise S. (Lehmann) B.; m. Maria Eva Karpati, Dec. 22, 1968; children: Jacqueline A., Michael S., Jennifer L. AB, Dartmouth Coll., 1966; MSc in Econs., U. London, 1967; JD, Harvard U., 1970. Bar: N.Y. 1971, D.C. 1975, U.S. Supreme Ct. 1978. Law clk. to Hon. Judge Milton Pollack U.S. Dist. Ct. (so. dist.) N.Y., N.Y.C., 1971; assoc. Kaye Scholer Fierman Hays & Handler, N.Y.C., 1971-74, Bergson, Borkland, Morgolis & Adler, Washington, 1974-79; dep., then acting asst. dir. Bur. of Competition FTC, Washington, 1979-82; ptnr. LaRoe Winn & Moerman, Washington, 1982-84; pvt. practice Washington, 1984-87; ptnr. Knopf & Burka, Washington, 1987-92, Foley & Lardner, Washington, 1992—. Fulbright and Reynolds scholars, 1966-67. Mem. Phi Beta Kappa. Office: Foley & Lardner 3000 K St NW # 500 Washington DC 20007-5109

BURKART, BURKE, geology educator, researcher; b. Dallas, Feb. 23, 1933; s. Herman Frederick and Velma Viola (Ball) B.; m. Marilyn Caskey; children—Patrick Caskey, Michael David. B.S. in Geology, U. Tex., 1954, M.A. in Geology, 1960; Ph.D. in Geology, Rice U., Houston, 1965. Asst. prof. geology Temple U., Phila., 1965-70; asst. prof. U. Tex.-Arlington, 1970-73, assoc. prof. geology, 1973-82, prof., 1982—; cons. in field. Contbr. articles, maps. to profl. publs. Served to 1st. lt. USAF, 1955-58. Fulbright fellow, 1972. Fellow Geol. Soc. Am.; mem. Am. Geophys. Union, Am. Assn. Petroleum Geologists, Am. Inst. Profl. Geologists (registered), Sigma Xi. Research in tectonics of Central America and Southern Mexico: strike slip faults; environmental geochemistry. Home: 1818 Kenwood Ter Arlington TX 76013-6403 Office: U Tex Dept Geology PO Box 19049 Arlington TX 76019

BURKART, FRANCIS WILLIAM, III, lawyer; b. Flushing, N.Y., May 28, 1953; s. Francis William and Virginia E. B.; m. Crystal G.; children: Lauren, John. BA in History, William and Mary, 1975; JD, Washington and Lee, 1978. Bar: Va. 1978. Mem. Salem/Roanoke County Bar Assn., Va. Assn. Commonwealth Attys. Republican. Roman Catholic. Avocations: hunting, fishing, reading. Office: Roanoke County Commonwealth Atty 305 E Main St Salem VA 24153-4347

BURKART, JEFFREY EDWARD, communications educator; b. Chgo., Sept. 12, 1948; s. Irwin John and Florence Henrietta (Drzich) B.; m. Martha Louise Gaertner, Aug. 13, 1972; children: Jonathan, David, Andrew. BA, Concordia Tchrs. Coll., 1971; MA, U. Nebr., 1977; PhD, U. Minn., 1988. Cert. elem. and secondary sch. tchr., Ind., Mo. Wis., Nebr. Organist, choral dir., youth dir. St. John's Luth. Ch., Bingen, Ind., 1969-70; tchr. Wyneken Meml. Luth. Sch., Decatur, Ind., 1969-70; residence counselor Concordia Coll., River Forest, Ill., 1970-71; instr. Luth. High Sch. North, St. Louis, 1971-72, Martin Luther High Sch., Greendale, Wis., 1972-75; tchr. St. John's Luth. Sch., Seward, Nebr., 1975-77; prof. ednl. communications/media, dir. audiovisual svcs. Concordia U., St. Paul, 1977-97, media cons., 1997—, assoc. dean for Christian ministry, 1999—; cons. Luth. Ch.-Mo. Synod, St. Louis; ednl. cons. St. Paul Pub. Schs., 1989, Elk River (Minn.) Sch. Dist., 1988-89; dir. European study Am. Inst. Fgn. Study, Greenwich, Conn.; editor-at-large Concordia Pub. Ho., 1996. Author: The Sonday School Book, 1995, Sure You Can Use a Little Good News!, 1996, Creative Worship, 1996, The Seeds That Grew and Grew, 1997, The Man Who Couldn't Speak, 1998; composer contemporary ch. music; author articles on children's lit. and early childhood edn.; author religious video, filmstrip series; presenter in field; author, composer: (musical) Man Overboard, 1995. Mem. Assn. for Supervision and Curriculum Devel., Luth. Edn. Assn., Phi Delta Kappa. Avocations: music, photography, reading, astronomy, travel. Office: Concordia Univ 275 Syndicate St N Saint Paul MN 55104-5494

BURKART, PETER THOMAS, hematologist; b. Albany, N.Y., Aug. 6, 1942. BS, St. Bernardine Siena, Loudonville, N.Y., 1964; MD, Albany Med. Coll., 1968. Lic., N.Y. Attending hematologist St. Peter's Hosp., Albany, N.Y., 1975-84; chief divsn. hematology Albany Med. Coll., 1984-96, chief divsn. hematology/oncology, 1996—; lab. dir. hematology Albany Med. Coll., 1984-96, dir. spl. hematology & diagnostic lab., 1984—, dir. outpatient transfusion apheresis area, 1984—. Bd. dirs. ARC, Albany; bd. trustees, chmn. Leukemia Soc. Am., Albany, 1983-91. Recipient Citation for Exceptional Vol. Svc., ARC, 1984, Robert deVilliers Med. award Upstate N.Y. chpt. Leukemia Soc. Am., 1987. Fellow ACP; mem. Am. Soc. Hematology, Alumni Assn. Albany Med. Coll. (pres. 1996-98). Office: Albany Med Coll Cancer Ctr 43 New Scotland Ave Albany NY 12208-3412*

BURKART, WALTER MARK, manufacturing company executive; b. Ferndale, Mich., Sept. 29, 1921; s. Michael A. and Beatrice (Pominville) B.; m. Mary Jane Hilts, Apr. 22, 1942; children: Michael Robert, Michele Sue. Student, Lawrence Inst. Tech., 1941-43. Supr. Ex-Cello Corp., Detroit, 1940-51; v.p. machine tool div. Ex-Cello Corp., 1965-69; chief process engr. Wright Aero Co., Detroit, 1951-55; mgr. Machine Tool div. Sheffield Corp. div. Bendix, Dayton, Ohio, 1956-65; chmn. bd. Kingsbury Machine Tool Corp., Keene, N.H., 1969—; pres. Am. Machine Tool Consortum, Tehran, 1976-77; mem. industry sector adv. com. on capital goods for U.S.A. trade policy matters, Dept. Commerce. Active Boy Scouts Am., 1958—; mem. N.H. Gov.'s Mgmt. Rev. Bd., 1981-82. Served with USNR, 1944-46. Mem.

Keene C. of C. (dir. 1971), Bus. and Industry Assn. N.H. (dir. 1980-81), Am. Mgmt. Assn., Soc. Mfg. Engrs., Nat. Machine Tool Builders Assn. Republican. Presbyterian. Clubs: Orchard Lake (Mich.); Keene Country (N.H.); Piper's Landing Country (Fla.). Office: Kingsbury Machine Tool Corp 80 Laurel St Keene NH 03431-4278 *It has been my managerial philosophy to give people a goal and let them choose which road to take in reaching that goal. This allows people to utilize their strengths while becoming more committed and involved. Through this participation the individual can get a greater sense of personal accomplishment. Rarely will two people go about solving a problem in the same way. While some problems do require a group solution, most simply require a solution and I believe the method is not as important as the result.*

BURKE, ARTHUR THOMAS, engineering consultant; b. Pueblo, Colo., Nov. 26, 1919; s. Daniel Michael and Naomi Edith (Brashear) B.; BS, U.S. Naval Acad., 1941; postgrad. UCLA; m. Regina Ahlgren Malone, June 15, 1972 (dec. July 1996); children: Arthur Thomas, Craig Timothy. With USN Electronics Lab. Center, San Diego, 1947-72, sr. satellite communications cons., 1964-72, satellite communications engring. cons., 1974—. Sweepstakes judge, San Diego Sci. Fair, 1960—. With USN, 1938-46; comdr. Res., ret. Recipient Presdl. Unit citation, 1942, Superior Performance award USN Electronics Lab. Center, 1967. Mem. IEEE (mem. San Diego membership com. 1958-68), AAAS, San Diego Astronomy Assn., San Diego Computer Assn., Am. Radio Relay League. Patentee electronic bathythermograph. Home and Office: 4011 College Ave San Diego CA 92115-6704

BURKE, ARTHUR WADE, retired physician; b. Richmond, Va., Jan. 15, 1927; s. Arthur Wade Burke and Lillian Earl Moran. BA in Biology, U. Va., 1947, MA in Biology, 1948; PhD in Biophysics, St. Louis U., 1957; MD, Med. Coll. of Va., 1960. Rsch. asst. in biology Oak Ridge (Tenn.) Nat. Lab., 1950-52; grad. fellow in biophysics St. Louis U., 1952-56; intern in internal medicine Med. Coll. Va., Richmond, 1960-61; rsch. assoc. in cancer R.I. Hosp., Providence, 1961-64; asst. prof. pharmacology Med. Coll. Va., Richmond, 1964-72; coord. bio rsch. Am. Tobacco Co., Richmond, 1965-72; asst. prof. radiology Med. Coll. Va., Richmond, 1975-80; dir. radiation oncology Cancer Ctr. of Va., Fredericksburg, 1985-90; dir. radiation therapy Henrico Drs. Hosp., Richmond, 1990-96, ret., 1996. Fellow Va. Acad. Sci. (pres. 1975-76, exec. sec.-treas. 1996—, Ivy F. Lewis Disting. Svc. awrd 1985); mem. AAAS, Am. Coll. Radiology, Med. Soc. Va., Am. Soc. Radiology Therapy and Oncology, Richmond Acad. Medicine, Va. Orchid Soc. (pres.) Eastern Orchid Congress (pres.), Richmond Jr. Club, Clin. Club (pres. 1983). Avocations: orchids, travel. Home: 9070 Shady Grove Rd Mechanicsville VA 23116-2838 Office: Va Acad Sci 2500 W Broad St Richmond VA 23220-2057

BURKE, BERNARD FLOOD, physicist, educator; b. Boston, June 7, 1928; s. Vincent Paul and Clare (Brine) B.; m. Jane Chapin Pann, May 30, 1953 (dec. Aug. 1993); children—Geoffrey Damian, Elizabeth Chapin, Mark Vincent, Matthew Brine; m. Elizabeth King Platt, Oct. 28, 1998. SB, MIT, 1950, PhD, 1953. Staff mem. terrestrial magnetism Carnegie Instn. of Washington, 1953-65, chmn. radio astronomy sect., 1962-65; prof. physics, Burden prof. astrophysics MIT, 1965—; vis. prof. U. Leiden, Netherlands, 1971-72, U. Manchester, Eng., 1992-93; trustee N.E. Radio Obs. Corp., 1973-95, vice chmn., 1975-82, chmn., 1982-95; cons. NSF, NASA, Dept. Transp.; Oort lectr. U. Leiden, 1993; Karl Jansky lectr. NAt. Radio Astronomy Obs., 1998. Trustee Associated Univs., Inc., 1972-90; mem. Nat. Sci. Bd., 1990-96. Recipient Helen Warner prize Am. Astron. Soc., 1963; Rumford prize Am. Acad. Arts and Scis., 1971; Sherman Fairchild scholar Calif. Inst. Tech., 1984, Smithsonian Regents fellow, 1985; sr. fellow Carnegie Instn. of Washington, 1997. Fellow AAAS; mem. NAS, Am. Acad. Arts and Scis., Am. Phys. Soc., Am. Astron. Soc., Royal Astron. Soc., Internat. Astron. Union, Internat. Astron. Fedn. (Pecek lectr. 1993), Internat. Sci. Radio Union, Merle Tuve Sr. fellow Carnegie Instn. of Washington. Research on microwave spectroscopy, radio astronomy, galactic structure, antenna design, cosmology. Office: MIT Dept Physics Cambridge MA 02139

BURKE, BILL, art educator; b. N.Y.C., Mar. 26, 1948; s. Edward Richard and Eileen (O'Keefe) B. BS in Ceramics, U. Ga., 1972; MFA, SUNY, New Paltz, 1974. Grad. teaching asst. SUNY, New Paltz, N.Y., 1973-74; instr. design State U. Coll. N.Y., New Paltz, N.Y., 1974; asst. prof. Fla. Internat. U., Miami, 1974-78, assoc. prof., 1978-94, prof., 1994—; vis. artistSkidmore Coll. Saratoga Springs, N.Y., 1973, others; lectr. in field. Represented in permanent collections at North Miami Mus. Contemporary Art, The Art Mus., Fla. Internat. U., Miami, Appalachian Ctr. for Crafts, Smithville, Tenn., Art in Pub. Places, Miami, Xerox Corp., Rochester, N.Y., Art in State Bldgs., Miami, Dayton Beach (Fla.) Visual Arts Gallery, Lockhaven (Pa.) State Coll., Purdue I., West Lafayette, Ind., Richard and Ruth Shack Art Collection, Miami, SUNY, U. N.D., Fargo, Valencia C.C., ORlando, Fla., Hollywood Art & Cultural Ctr., Hollywood, Fla. Mem. Am. Crafts Coun., Nat. Coun. Edn. for the Ceramic Arts, Fla. Craftsmen, Inc., Southeastern Coll. Art Conf., Coll. Art Assn. *

BURKE, BRIAN B., state senator, lawyer; b. Milw., Apr. 19, 1958; s. Thomas Joseph and Mary White (Higgins) B.; m. Patricia J. Coorough, Aug. 7, 1982; children: Colleen Marie, Kathleen Clare, Erin Elizabeth. BA magna cum laude, Marquette U., 1978; JD, Georgetown U., 1981. Bar: Wis. 1981, U.S. Dist. Ct. (ea. and we. dists.) Wis. 1981, U.S. Ct. Appeals (7th cir.) 1983, U.S. Supreme Ct. 1984. Asst. dist. atty. Milwaukee County, Milw., 1981-84; alderman Milw. Common Coun., 1984-88; mem. Wis. Senate, Madison, 1988—. Mem. editl. bd. Georgetown Internat Law Jour.; contbr.: Wisconsin Lawyer, 1992, 94, 98. Trustee Milw. Pub. Libr., 1984-88, Pabst Theatre Bd., Milw., 1984-88, Milw. County Federated Libr. Sys., 1997—; commr. Milw. Met. Sewerage Dist., 1990—, Milw. Redevel. Authority, 1985-88, Wis. Ctr. Dist. Bd., 1996—, Hist. Preservation Commn., Milw., 1987-88; exec. bd. Wis. Pub. Utility Inst., 1993—; mem. State Capitol and Exec. Residence Bd., 1996—, Wis. Trust for Hist. Preservation, 1992—; mem. Dem. Leadership Coun., Nat. Conf. State Legis. Environ. Com.; mem. Wis. Environ. Edn. Bd., 1995—; mem. U. Wis. Hosps. and Clinics Authority, 1996—. Recipient Legislator of Yr. award Wis. Urban Transit Assn., 1997, Wis.'s Environ. Decade Clean 16 award, 1989-98, Bridge Builder's award Nature Conservancy, 1994, Cesar Chavez Humanitarian award Hispanic Leadership Coun., 1994, Friend of Wis. Jewish Cmty. award Wis. Jewish Conf., 1994, Friend of Hispanic Cmty. award United Cmty. Ctr., 1994, Hon. Riverkeeper award Friends of the Menomonee River, 1996, Disting. Svc. award Wis. Alliance of Cities, 1992-98. Mem. Washington Heights Neighborhood Assn., State Hist. Soc., Hispanic C. of C., Greater Mitchell Street Assn., Shamrock Club of Wis., Phi Beta Kappa. Democrat. Roman Catholic. Avocation: tennis. Office: Wis Senate PO Box 7882 Madison WI 53707-7882

BURKE, BRUCE LOWELL, consumer products company executive; b. Brklyn., May 13, 1936; s. Jack and Gertrude (Gardner) B.; children: Abby Muhlfelder, Jeffrey Allen, Florie Michelle. BS, Fairleigh Dickinson U., 1960, MBA (cum laude), 1965. Packaging exec. Chgo., 1959-74; food svc. exec. N.Y.C., 1974-87; priv. practice cons. Clifton, N.J., 1987—; sales and mgmt. cons. Tourneau, Inc., N.Y.C., 1993—. Judge Am. Inst. at the City of N.Y., 1962. With N.J. Nat. Guard, 1957-60. Jewish. Avocations: computers and technology. Home & Office: 45C Sycamore Rd Clifton NJ 07012-1317

BURKE, CHARLES MICHAEL, military officer; b. Denver, June 28, 1944; s. Charles Martin and Gwendolyn Rae (Smith) B.; m. Mary Kathleen Flanagan, Feb. 17, 1968; children: Michael Kevin, Marueen Catherine, Shannon Colleen. BS in Bus., U. Tampa, 1974. Commd. 2d lt. U.S. Army, 1967, advanced through grades to brig. gen., 1990; comdr. 228th attack helicopter bn. U.S. Army, Ft. Hood, Tex., 1983-85, dep. comdr. 6th cavalry brigade, 1985-87; chief concepts and doctrine divsn. hdqs. Dept. of Army-Pentagon, Washington, 1988-90; comdr. combat aviation brigade 3d armored divsn. U.S. Army, Hanau, Fed. Republic Germany, 1990-92; dep. asst. comdt. U.S. Army Aviation Sch., Ft. Rucker, Ala., 1992-93; asst. chief of staff G-3 and chief of staff III U.S. Army Corps., Fort Hood, Tex., 1993-95; dep. chief of staff for support HQ Landsouth, Verona, Italy, 1996—. Contbr. articles to profl. jours. Decorated Silver Star, Legion of Merit, Bronze Star, Air Medal, Meritorious Svc. medal U.S. Army. Mem. Army Aviation Assn. Am. (chpt. pres. 1968-94). Republican. Roman Catholic. Avocations: golf, sailing. Home: Cmr 428 Box 1344 APO AE 09628-1200 Office: US Army III Corps Hdqs Fort Hood TX 76544

BURKE, DELTA, actress; b. Orlando, Fla., July 30, 1956; m. Gerald McRaney, May 28, 1989. Educated, London Acad. Music & Dramatic Arts. Appeared in TV movies Charleston, A Last Cry for Help, Mickey Spillane's Mike Hammer: Murder Me, Murder You, A Bunny's Tale, Where the Hell's That Gold?!!?, A Promise to Carolyn, 1996, Melanie Darrow, 1997; appeared in TV series Filthy Rich, The Chisholms, First and Ten; guest appearance on series Simon & Simon; regular role on series Designing Women, 1986-91; star own series Delta, 1992-93, The Women of the House, 1995; (film) Maternal Instincts, 1996. Named Miss Fla., later competed in Miss Am. Pageant. Office: Martin Hurwitz Assn Inc 427 N Canon Dr Ste 215 Beverly Hills CA 90210-4840*

BURKE, DOUG, author, director, producer, inventor; b. July 25, 1963; s. Robert Louis and Joan Mary (Rowbotham) B. BS, U. Calif., Irvine, 1986, MS, 1987, PhD in Physics, 1990; D of Sci. of Drama (hon.), Case Western Res. U., 1991. Co-author: (novel) The Dark Prophet, 1995; author: (textbook) Psychophysics and Drama, 1991, (play) Rebel King, 1995, (screenplay) Gull, 1995; actor, dir., prodr. (movie) Gull, 1998; patentee in the field of three-dimensional image creation and display systems.

BURKE, EDMOND WAYNE, retired judge, lawyer; b. Ukiah, Calif., Sept. 7, 1935; s. Wayne P. and Opal K. B.; children from previous marriage: Kathleen R., Jennifer E.; m. Anna M. Hubbard, Dec. 29, 1990. A.B., Humboldt State Coll., 1957, M.A., 1958; J.D., U. Calif., 1964. Bar: Calif., Alaska, Mont. Individual practice law Calif. and Alaska, 1965-67; asst. atty. gen. State of Alaska, 1967; asst. dist. atty. Anchorage, Alaska, 1968-69; judge Superior Ct., Alaska, 1970-75; justice Supreme Ct. State of Alaska, Anchorage, 1975-93, chief justice, 1981-84; of coun. Bogle & Gates, 1994-95; mem. Burke Bauermeister, Anchorage, 1996—. Republican. Presbyterian. *

BURKE, EDWARD M., alderman; b. Chgo., Dec. 29, 1943; s. Joseph and Ann (Dolan) B.; m. Anne Marie McGlone, 1968; children: Jennifer, Edward, Emmett, Sarah. BA, DePaul U., 1965, JD, 1968. Atty. Klafter & Burke; underwriter Lloyd's of London, 1980—; alderman Chgo. City Coun.; former chmn. Dem. com. and alderman 14th ward, Chgo.; chmn. police, fire, civil svc., schs., fin. and mcpl. instns. coms., former chmn. fin. com. Chgo. City Coun. Commr. Chgo. and Cook County Criminal Justice Commn., 1975; counsel Ill. Mcpl. Problems Commn., 1975. 1st lt. U.S. Army Res. Recipient Man of Yr. award Chgo. Police Capts. Assn., 1975. Mem. ABA, Ill. Bar Assn., Chgo. Bar Assn., Moose, K of C (4th degree, Leo XIII coun.), Celtic Lawyers' Assn. Am., Order of Holy Sepulchre, Irish Fellowship Club (chmn. bd. dirs.). Roman Catholic. Office: 2650 W 51st St Chicago IL 60632-1560*

BURKE, EDWARD NEWELL, radiologist; b. Wakefield, Mass., Apr. 28, 1916; s. Charles Edward and Laura Cecelia (Doherty) B.; BS, Holy Cross Coll., 1938; MD, CM, McGill U., 1942; postgrad. Brit. Postgrad. Med. Sch., 1946, Johns Hopkins Sch. Public Health, 1943; m. Mary A. Bryon, Nov. 26, 1949; children: Laureen, Martha, Newell, Laurence. Resident in pathology Mallory Inst., Boston City Hosp., 1942-43; intern Salem (Mass.) Hosp., 1946-47, resident in radiology, 1947-50; resident in supervoltage Therapy Lahey Clinic and MIT, 1949; assoc. radiologist Mass. Meml. Hosp., Boston, 1951-56; lectr. radiologic tech. Northeastern U., 1953-65; radiologist Lawrence Meml. Hosp., Medford, Mass., also Charles Choate Hosp., Woburn, Mass., 1956—; individual practice medicine specializing in radiology Medford, 1956—; radiologist St. Joseph's Hosp., Lowell, Mass., 1956-64, Hooper Infirmary, Tufts Coll., Medford, 1971-80; chmn., chief depts. radiology Lawrence Meml. Hosp., 1961-85, assoc. chief radiology, 1985—; chief dept. Charles Choate Meml. Hosp., 1963-82; assoc. prof. radiology Boston U., 1951-56; asst. clin. prof. radiology Tufts U., 1971-81, assoc. clin. prof., 1981—; pres. Charles Choate Hosp. med. staff, 1974-76, incorporator, trustee, 1974-81; incorporator Lawrence Meml. Hosp., 1972-96, pres. med. staff, 1980-82; dir. Carroll Ctr. for the Blind. Served to maj. M.C., U.S. Army, 1943-46. Diplomate Am. Coll. Radiology. Radiology wing dedicated in his honor Choate Hosp., 1982. Decorated Sovereign Mil. Order Malta. Fellow Am. Coll. Radiology; mem. AMA, Am. Roentgen Ray Soc., New Eng. Roentgen Ray Soc., Radiol. Soc. N.Am., N.Y. Acad. Scis., Mass. Radiol. Soc., Soc. Nuclear Medicine, Am. Inst. Ultrasound Medicine, New Eng. Ultrasound Soc., Mass. Med. Soc. Roman Catholic. Clubs: Clover Boston, Winchester Country. Contbr. articles to med. publs. Home: 40 Pine Ridge Rd Medford MA 02155-2135 Office: 170 Governors Ave Medford MA 02155-1643

BURKE, FRANK GERARD, archivist; b. N.Y.C., Apr. 22, 1927; s. James Francis and Eleanor Josephine (Thomas) B.; m. Hildegard Waltraud Arndt, Aug. 1, 1959; children: Margaret Eleanor, Catherine Elizabeth, Christina Hildegard, Thomas Francis, Elisabeth Maria. MA, U. Chgo., 1959, PhD, 1969. Radio operator Trans World Airlines, Washington, 1948-51; communicator CAA, Fairbanks, Alaska and Oklahoma City, 1952-54; announcer, engr. Alaska Broadcasting Co., Fairbanks, 1955, Northwest Airlines, 1955-60; librarian U. Chgo., 1959-60, bookkeeper, 1960-61, manuscript curator, 1962-64; instr. Chgo. Tchrs. Coll., 1961-62; manuscript curator Library of Congress, Washington, 1964-67; spl. asst. for info. retrieval Nat. Archives and Records Service, Washington, 1967-68, asst. archivist for ednl. programs, 1968-74; asst. to archivist U.S. Nat. Archives, Washington, 1974-75; exec. dir. Nat. Hist. Publs. and Records Commn., Nat. Archives, Washington, 1975-84, acting asst. archivist Office of Nat. Archives, 1984-85; acting archivist, dep. archivist U.S. Nat. Archives and Records Administration, Washington, 1985-87; prof. U. Md. Coll. Libr. and Info. Svcs., College Park, 1988-96, prof. emeritus, 1996—, instr. Coll. Libr. and Info. Sci., 1974-88; instr. history NYU, 1981-85, Western Archives Inst., Palo Alto, Calif., 1997, 99. Author: Research and the Manuscript Tradition, 1997; contbr. articles to profl. jours. Radarman 3d class USN, 1945-46. Fellow Soc. Am. Archivists (v.p., pres. 1990-92); mem. Am. Hist. Assn., Assn. for Documentary Editing (v.p., pres. 1989-91), Soc. for History in Fed. Govt., Manuscript Soc., Cosmos Club (Washington), Potomac River Jazz Club (Va., bd. dirs. 1990—, pres. 1991-92—). Avocations: carpentry, cabinet making, photography. Office: U Md Coll Libr & Info Svcs College Park MD 20742-4345

BURKE, GERARD PATRICK, business executive, lawyer; b. Darby, Pa., Apr. 3, 1930; s. Patrick Joseph and Mary Elizabeth (Breslin) B.; m. Ann Marie Burke, Nov. 12, 1955; children: Gerard P. Jr., Maura Anne, Christine Marie. AB, Holy Cross Coll., 1952; JD, Georgetown U., 1958; postgrad., U. Paris, 1960-61. Bar: U.S. Dist. Ct. (D.C.) 1958, U.S. Ct. Appeals (D.C. cir.) 1968, U.S. Ct. Internat. Trade 1984, U.S. Supreme Ct. 1973. Asst. dir. legal and legis. affairs, spl. counsel Nat. Security Agy., Ft. Meade, Md., 1954-69; pres. fgn. intelligence adv. bd., exec. dir. White House, Washington, 1969-73; pvt. practice Washington, 1978-84; chmn., CEO The Parvus Co., Silver Spring, Md., 1984—, Jerico Internat. Ltd., Hamilton, Bermuda, 1986—; chmn. ZAO Parvus Dzheriko, Moscow, 1995—, Parvus Brasil Ltda., Rio de Janeiro, 1996-98, Parvus Andes C.A., Caracas, 1996-98. Lt. comdr. USNR, 1952-57. Recipient U.S. govt. and fgn. govt. awards. Mem. D.C. Bar Assn., FBA, Inter-Am. Bar Assn., Phi Delta Phi. Roman Catholic. Office: The Parvus Co 8403 Colesville Rd Ste 610 Silver Spring MD 20910-3368

BURKE, JAMES DONALD, museum administrator; b. Salem, Oreg., Feb. 22, 1939; s. Donald J. and Ellin (Adams) B.; m. Diane E. Davies, May 17, 1980. B.A., Brown U., 1961; M.A., U. Pa., 1966; Ph.D., Harvard U., 1972. Curator Yale U. Art Gallery, New Haven, 1972-78; asst. dir. St. Louis Art Mus., 1978-80, dir., chief exec. officer, 1980-99, dir. emeritus, 1999—; cons., panel mem. IRS, Washington, 1980—. Author: Jan Both, 1974, Charles Meyron, 1974; contbr. articles to profl. jours.; organizer in field. Pres. St. Louis Art Mus. Found., 1985—, Gateway Found., 1986—. Fulbright fellow, 1968-69. Mem. Coll. Art Assn., Print Council Am., Am. Assn. Mus., Assn. Art Mus. Dirs. Office: Saint Louis Art Mus One Fine Arts Dr Forest Park Saint Louis MO 63110*

BURKE, JAMES EDWARD, consumer products company executive; b. Feb. 28, 1925; s. James Francis and Mary (Barnett) B.; m. Alice Eubank, Apr. 27, 1957 (dec.); children: Mary Clotilde, James Charles; m. Diane W. Burke, Nov. 7, 1981. BS in Econs., Holy Cross Coll., 1947; MBA, Harvard U., 1949. Sales rep., then asst. brand mgr., brand mgr. Procter & Gamble, 1949-52; product dir. Johnson & Johnson, 1953-54, dir. new products, 1954-57, dir. advt. and merchandising, 1958-62, gen. mgr. Baby Products Co. divsn., 1962-64, exec. v.p. mktg., 1964-65, gen. mgr. Johnson & Johnson Products Co. divsn., 1965-66, pres., 1966-70, chmn. bd., 1970-71, corp. dir., mem. exec. com., 1973-76, dir., mem. exec. com. parent co., 1965-89, former vice-chmn. exec. com., from 1971, CEO, chmn. bd. parent co., 1976-89; bd. dirs. Washington Post Co.; chmn. bd. dirs. Bus. Enterprise Trust. Chmn. Partnership for Drug-Free Am.; bd. trustees Robert Wood Johnson Found. Ensign USN, WWII, PTO. Office: Johnson & Johnson 100 Albany St Ste 200 New Brunswick NJ 08901-1227

BURKE, JAMES JOSEPH, JR., investment banker; b. Wilmington, Del., Dec. 19, 1951; s. James Joseph and Kathleen Gertrude (Nauss) B.; m. Jeanne Elizabeth Burke, Aug. 6, 1977; children: James III, Jennifer, Brian. AB in Psychology, Brown U., 1973; MBA with distinction, Harvard U., 1979. 2d v.p. Chase Manhattan Bank, N.Y.C., 1973-77; assoc. Merrill Lynch, N.Y.C., 1979-83, v.p., 1983-85, mng. dir., 1985-94; pres., CEO Merrill Lynch Capital Ptnrs., N.Y.C., 1987-94; mng. ptnr. First Capital Ptnrs., N.Y.C., 1994—, Stonington Ptnrs., Inc. (formerly First Capital Ptnrs.), N.Y.C., 1995—; chmn. Chapel Mortgage Co., Rancocas, N.J.; bd. dirs. Borg-Warner Security Corp., Chgo., Ann Taylor Stores Corp., N.Y.C., Pathmark Stores, Inc., Woodbridge, N.J., United Artists Theatre Circuit Inc., Englewood, Colo., Brown U. Third Century Fund, Edn. Mgmt. Corp., Pitts. Trustee Seton Hall Prep. Sch., West Orange, N.J., Boy Scouts Am., N.Y.C.; chmn. Eerie Entertainment, LLC, N.Y.C. Office: Stonington Ptnrs 767 5th Ave New York NY 10153-0023

BURKE, JAN HELENE, author; b. Houston, Aug. 1, 1953; d. John Francis and Velda Marie Fischer; m. Timothy Edward Burke, May 28, 1988. BA, Calif. State U., Long Beach, 1978. Author: (novels) Goodnight, Irene, 1993, Hocus, 1997, Harm, 1999. Recipient readers award and Macavity award for short story Ellery Queen Mystery Mag., 1994. Mem. Mystery Writers Am., Am. Crime Writers League, Internat. Crime Writers Assn., Sisters in Crime. Fax: 562-429-1811. E-mail: jan@janburke.com. Office: PO Box 1128 Los Alamitos CA 90740-1128

BURKE, JOHN, science technology company executive; b. L.A., Oct. 14, 1947; s. Robert J. and Virginia Lee (Albany) B.; m. Myriah Lennox, May 25, 1990. BS in Engring., UCLA, 1969, MS in Engring., 1973; postgrad., Calif. State U., San Diego, 1974-78. Sect. mgr. Logicon, Inc., San Pedro, Calif., 1970-73; program mgr. Sci. Applications Inc., La Jolla, Calif., 1973-75; div. mgr. SAI Comsystems Corp., San Diego, 1975-77, v.p., 1977-81; v.p. Sci. Applications Internat. Corp., San Diego, 1981-87, corp. v.p., 1987-88, group sr. v.p., 1988-89, sector v.p., 1989-90; pres. SAIC Tech. Svcs. Co., San Diego, 1990-92, sector v.p., 1992—. Democrat. Avocations: travel, wine collecting. Home: 939 Coast Blvd Unit 14H La Jolla CA 92037-4119 Office: Sci Applications Internat 10260 Campus Point Dr San Diego CA 92121-1522

BURKE, JOHN, priest; b. Washington, Sept. 15, 1928; s. William Francis and Grace Allison (Logan) B. AB, Cath. U. Am., 1950, MA, 1965, STD, 1969. Joined Order Preachers, ordained priest Roman Cath. Ch., 1960. Prof. homiletics St. Stephen's Coll., Dover, Mass., 1961-64, Immaculate Conception faculty, 1964-67, 90, asst. prof., summers 1964-69, asst. prof. drama, 1968-72, dir. Preaching Workshop, 1965-67, dir. Preachers Inst., 1967-72; mem. faculty Washington Theol. Coalition, 1968-69; coord. Nat. Congress for the Word of God, 1972; founder, exec. dir. Nat. Inst. for the Word of God, Washington, 1972—; prof. Dominican Hosue of Studies, Washington, 1990—. Author: Bible Sharing Youth Retreat Manual, 1983, Beginners' Guide to Bible Sharing, Vol. I, II, 1984, The Homilist's Guide to Scripture, Theology and Canon Law, 1987; editor: Gospel Power: Toward the Revitalization of Preaching, 1978, Bible Sharing: How to Grow in the Mystery of Christ, 1979, A New Look at Preaching, 1983; contbr. articles to profl. jours.; producer TV film Chimbote, 1964. Mem. Radio-TV Dirs. Guild of AFTRA, Phi Beta Kappa. Address: 487 Michigan Ave NE Washington DC 20017-1584 *For lasting happiness in life, one needs to experience the active presence of God.*

BURKE, JOHN FRANCIS, JR., economist; b. Bath, Maine, Mar. 25, 1937; s. Ruth; m. Lynda Scheer, Sept. 15, 1962 (div.); children: Colleen, George, Maureen, John; m. Nancy A. Fuerst, Aug. 16, 1986; children: Ruth, Patrick. BS, Boston Coll., 1961; MA, U. Notre Dame, 1963, PhD, 1967. Teaching asst. U. Notre Dame, South Bend, Ind., 1963-65; instr. Ind. U., South Bend, 1963-65; asst. prof. Ea. Ill. U., 1965-67; asst. prof. Cleve. State U., 1967-69, assoc. prof. econs., 1970-93, prof. emeritus, 1994; ptnr. Burke, Rosen & Assocs., Cleve., 1973—; invited lectr. U. Ljubljiana, Yugoslavia, 1989, Brazil, 1979, 86, Mex., 1995, Jamaica, 1995, Grand Cayman, 1995, Bahamas, 1983, French Guiana, 1986; host Cleve. State U. Forum, 1989—; econ. advisor to atty. gen. State of Ohio, 1983-85; staff economist WKYC-TV and NBC, Cleve., 1981-84; host radio talk show WERE Radio, 1983-84; mem. Coll. Entrance Exam. Bd., 1978-81; ad hoc TV commentator Sta. WJW (CBS), Cleve.; expert forensic econ. witness in over 2000 cases; econ. advisor in field. Contbr. numerous articles to profl. jours.; reviewer Rev. of Social Economy, 1971-81. Mem. AAUP, Am. Econ. Assn., Am. Statis. Assn., Assn. for Social Econs., Nat. Assn. Bus. Economists, Atlantic Econ. Assn., Ea. Econ. Assn., Midwest Econ. Assn., Nat. Tax Assn., nat. Acad. Econ. Arbitrators. Office: Burke Rosen & Assocs 2800 Euclid Ave Ste 300 Cleveland OH 44115-2418

BURKE, JOHN JAMES, utility executive; b. Butte, Mont., July 25, 1928; m. Nancy M. Calvert, July 12, 1952; children: Cheryl Burke Harris, Mary Burke Orizotti, Kathleen Novak, John James, III, Elisabeth Orizotti. BS in Bus., BA in Law, U. Mont., 1950, JD, 1952. Bar: Mont. 1952, U.S. Supreme Ct. 1957. Ptnr. Weir, Gough, Booth and Burke, Helena, 1954-59; atty. Mont. Power Co., Butte, 1959-67, v.p., 1967-78, exec. v.p., 1979-84, vice chmn. bd. dirs., 1984-93; dir. Lazard Funds Inc., Pacific Steel & Recycling, Sletten Constrn. Co. Trustee U. Mont. Found., Carroll Coll., Mont., Mont. Hist. Soc., 1988—, B.K. Wheeler Found.; co-chmn. Mont. Renaissance Fund Bus. Coun.; past pres. City County Planning Bd., 1966-78; past dir. Vigilante coun. Boy Scouts Am., Shining Mountains coun. Girl Scouts U.S.A.; vice chmn. Gov. Task Force/Renew Mont. Govt. Capt. JAGC, USAF, 1952-54, with Res., 1954-61. Mem. ABA (mem. coun. pub. utility law sect.), State Bar Mont., Silver Bow County Bar Assn., Mountain States Legal Found. (past bd. dirs.), Nat. Assn. Mfrs. (past bd. dirs.), Edison Electric Inst. (exec. adv. com. on planning), Butte C. of C. (v.p. 1965-72), U. Mont. Alumni Assn. (past bd. dirs.), Phi Delta Phi. Roman Catholic. Clubs: Montana, Butte Country, Elks, Rotary (sec. Helena 1955-58); 116 (Washington). Home and Office: 50 Burning Tree Ln Butte MT 59701-3904

BURKE, JOHN K(IRKLAND), JR., lawyer; b. Richmond, Va., Jan. 26, 1952; s. John Kirkland and Archer (Christian) B.; m. Miriam Smith, July 23, 1977; children: John K. III, Ruth H., B. Smith. BA in History with distinction, U. Va., 1974, JD, 1977. Bar: Va. 1977, U.S. Dist. Ct. (ea. and we. dists.) Va. 1977, U.S. Ct. Appeals (4th cir.) 1977. Law clk. to Justice George M. Cochran Supreme Ct. Va., Staunton, 1977-78; assoc. Mays and Valentine, Richmond, Va., 1978-84, ptnr., 1984—. Mem. City of Richmond's Human Rels. Comm., 1991-97. Mem. ABA, Va. Bar Assn., Bar Assn. of City of Richmond (bd. dirs. 1994-98), Soc. of the Cin. for State of Va. (standing com. 1992-95), Va. State Bar, Country Club Va. (bd. dirs.). Avocations: sports, reading, music. Office: Mays and Valentine PO Box 1122 Richmond VA 23218-1122

BURKE, JOHN P., state agency administrator; m. N. Patricia Yarborough; 2 children. BS in Econs., Coll. of Holy Cross, 1953. With IBM Corp., Centerbank, 1964-90; pres., CEO Security Savs. and Loan Assn., 1990-92, Bristol Savs. Bank, 1992-94; commr. Conn. Dept. Banking, Hartford, 1994—. Chmn. Waterbury Hosp.; chmn., pres. United Way Waterbury; bd. dirs. Teikyo Post Coll. Found. With U.S. Army. Mem. Conf. State Bank Suprs. (chmn. bd. dirs.). Office: Conn Dept Banking 260 Constitution Plz Hartford CT 06103-1811*

BURKE, JOSEPH C., former university official; b. New Albany, Ind., Mar. 20, 1932; s. Dennis F. and Beatrice V. (McDevitt) B.; m. Joan Thompson, Sept. 1, 1956; children: Maura, Colleen. BA, Bellarmine Coll., Louisville, 1954; MA, Ind. U., 1958, PhD, 1965. Instr. Ohio Wesleyan U., Delaware, 1960-62; asst. prof. to prof. history Duquesne U., Pitts., 1962-70; prof.

history Loyola of Montreal, 1970-73, acad. v.p., 1970-73; acad. v.p. SUNY Coll., Plattsburgh, 1973-74, pres., 1974-85; provost, vice chancellor for acad. affairs SUNY Sys., Albany, 1985-95; pres. Rsch. Found. SUNY, Albany, 1990-95, interim chancellor, 1994; sr. fellow, dir. ctr. for effective higher edn. prog. Nelson A. Rockefeller Inst. Govt., Albany, 1956; cons. leadership adn planning for colls. and univs.; resident scholar Rockefeller Found. Study Ctr. Contbr. books, monographs, chpts. and articles to profl. jours., chpts. to books on higher edn. Trustee Miner Found. Rsch.; chmn. bd. Miner Agrl. Inst. Grantee Pew Charitable Trusts and Luce Found., 1996-99.

BURKE, JOSEPH ELDRID, materials scientist; b. Berkeley, Calif., Sept. 1, 1914; s. Charles Eldrid and Ruth (Hadcock) B.; m. Kathleen Mary Wilson, Sept. 16, 1939(dec.); children: Charles Robert, Margaret VanDecar; m. Marjorie Ridgway, Dec. 14, 1997. BA, McMaster U., Hamilton, Ont., 1935; PhD in Chemistry, Cornell U., 1940. Metallurgist Internat. Nickel Co., Bayonne, N.J., 1940-41; chemist Norton Co., Worcester, Mass., 1941-43; group leader Manhattan Dist. Project, Los Alamos, N.Mex., 1943-46; assoc. prof. U. Chgo., 1946-49; mgr. metallurgy Knolls Atomic Power Lab., Schenectady, 1949-54; mgr. ceramics GE Corp. Rsch. & Devel. Ctr., Schenectady, 1954-79; cons. in matls. sci. Burnt Hills, N.Y., 1979—; adj. prof. Rensselaer Poly. Inst., Troy, 1980-85; cons. Gillette Co., Boston, 1980-92. Author (with A. Seybolt) Procedures in Experimental Metallurgy, 1955; editor rev. vols. Progress in Ceramic Science, Vols. 1-4, 1961, 62, 64, 66; contbr. articles to profl. jours. Chmn. Zoning Bd. Appeals, Ballston, N.Y., 1970-74. Recipient Frenkel Prize, Internat. Inst. of Sintering, Belgrade, 1981. Fellow ASM, Am. Nuclear Soc., Am. Ceramic Soc. (pres. 1974-75, Jeppson award 1981, Kingery award 1999); mem. Acad. of Ceramics (Italy), Nat. Acad. Engring. Achievements include development of first pore-free ceramic, which made possible modern high-pressure sodium vapor lamp for outdoor lighting; research in uranium metal, uranium dioxide and nuclear materials. Home and Office: 2463 Nott St E Niskayuna NY 12309-4385

BURKE, KATHLEEN B., lawyer; b. Bklyn., Sept. 2, 1948. BA, St. John's U., 1969, JD, 1973. Bar: Ohio 1973. Ptnr. Jones, Day, Reavis & Pogue, Cleve. Mem. Ohio State Bar Assn. (pres. 1993-94). Office: Jones Day Reavis & Pogue North Point 901 Lakeside Ave E Cleveland OH 44114-1116*

BURKE, KELLY HOWARD, former air force officer, business executive; b. Mobile, Ala., June 7, 1929; s. Kelly Howard and Vesta (Trussell) B.; m. Denny Ray Hosey, Dec. 30, 1951; children: Bethany, Patricia, Kelly Howard, III. BS in History, Auburn U., 1952; MS in Internat. Rels., George Washington U., 1968; postgrad., Naval War Coll., 1967-68, RAF Staff Coll., 1969-71, Indsl. Coll. Armed Forces, 1964-65. Commd. 2d lt. U.S. Air Force, 1953, advanced through grades to lt. gen., 1979; comdr. 379th Bomb Wing Wurtsmith AFB, Mich., 1973-74; comdr. 2d Bomb Wing Barksdale AFB, La., 1974-75; dep. chief of staff/plans SAC, 1975-78; dir. operational requirements Hdqrs. U.S. Air Force, Washington, 1978-79; dep. chief of staff/research, devel. and acquisition Hdqrs. U.S. Air Force, 1979-82; ret., 1982; chmn. bd. Stafford, Burke and Hecker, Inc., Alexandria, VA, 1982; bd. dirs. Singer Co., Tiger Internat. Inc., Flying Tigers Line Inc., Orbital Scis. Corp., Phoenix Numerics Inc.; cons. White House Sci. Office, NRC, Def. Sci. Bd., Sci. Adv. Bd., others; frequent lectr. Chmn. editorial bd. Aerospace Am.; contbr. numerous articles on nat. security issues to publs. Decorated D.S.M. with oak leaf cluster, Legion of Merit, D.F.C., Meritorious Svc. medal, Air medal with oak leaf clusters; established Burke Scholarship Endowment for 12 4-yr. coll. scholarships annually to needy students; named Fla. Benefactor of Yr. for this and other charitable activities, 1995. Mem. Nat. Space Club, Nat. Aviation Club. Episcopalian. Home: 803 Choctaw Ln Shalimar FL 32579-2248 Office: Stafford Burke and Hecker 1006 Cameron St Alexandria VA 22314-2427

BURKE, KENNETH ANDREW, advertising executive; b. Cleve., Sept. 9, 1943; s. Frank Francis and Margret Anne (Tomé) B.; BSBA in Mktg., Bowling Green (Ohio) State U., 1965; m. Karen Lee Burley, July 1, 1968; children: Allison Leigh, Aric Jason. Mem. Green Bay Packers, NFL football team; account exec. Lang, Fisher, Stashower, Cleve., 1967-69; v.p., account supr. Tracy-Locke, Dallas, 1969-72; v.p. Grey Advt., N.Y.C., 1972-76; v.p. Griswold Eshleman, Cleve., 1976-79; sr. v.p., gen. mgr. Simpson Mktg., Columbus, Ohio, 1979-81; pres., chief exec. officer, chmn. bd. Martcom Inc., Columbus, 1981-91; chmn. ret. Ad Factory, Inc., Ad Factory Outlets, 1991-98; exec. v.p. Berkshire Product Inc., Tampa, Fla., 1983-89. Author: Bordini and the Black Knight, 1975. Mem. adv. bd. Columbus chpt. Am. Cancer Soc., 1980-88. Recipient USN Achievement in Advt. award, 1975. Mem. Am. Mktg. Assn., Columbus Advt. Fedn., NFL Alumni Assn., Cleve. Advt. Club (Merit award 1968), Columbus C. of C., Upper Arlington C. of C., Theta Chi. Republican. Roman Catholic. Home: 1753 Bedford Rd Columbus OH 43212-2004 Office: Ad Factory Corp Offices 274 Third St Columbus OH 43215

BURKE, KENNETH JOHN, lawyer; b. Washington, Aug. 23, 1939; s. John Lawrence and Edna Catherine B.; m. Judith Ann Blass (div. July 1979); children: Jill Shannon, Corey Edmund, Erin Elisabeth; m. Gay Ann Crosier, June 4, 1983; 1 child, John Tynan. BS in Physics, Coll. Holy Cross, 1961; JD, U. Denver, 1969. Bar: Colo. 1969, U.S. Dist. Ct. Colo. 1969, U.S. Ct. Appeals (10th cir.) 1969, U.S. Supreme Ct. 1977. Assoc. Fuller & Evans, Denver, 1969-71; trial atty. U.S. Dept. Justice, Denver, 1971-74; ptnr. Bermingham, White, Burke & Ipsen, Denver, 1974-77, Holme, Roberts & Owen, Denver, 1977-86, Burke & Burke, 1986-88, Massey, Burke & Showalter, 1988-90, Baker & Hostetler, Denver, 1990—. Contbr. numerous articles to legal jours. 1st lt. USAF, 1962-66. Mem. ABA (vice chmn. water resources com. 1987-92, energy and natural resources litigation com. 1986-87), Colo. Bar Assn. Republican. Avocations: astronomy, fly fishing. Office: Baker & Hostetler 303 E 17th Ave Ste 1100 Denver CO 80203-1264*

BURKE, KEVIN CHARLES ANTONY, geologist; b. London, Nov. 13, 1929; came to U.S., 1973; s. Charles Henry and Kathleen (Daly) B.; m. Angela Marion Phipps, Jan. 23, 1960; children: Nicholas, Matthew, Jane. B.Sc., Univ. Coll., London, 1951, Ph.D., 1953. Lectr. U. Ghana, 1953-56; geologist Brit. Geol. Survey, 1956-61; head geology dept. U. West Indies, Kingston, Jamaica, 1961-65; prof. geology U. Ibadan, Nigeria, 1963-71, SUNY-Albany, 1973-83; prof. U. Houston, 1983—; dir. Lunar and Planetary Inst., 1983-88; scholar in residence NRC, Washington, 1989-92; vis. prof. U. Toronto, 1971-73, Calif. Inst. Tech., 1976, U. Minn., 1977, U. Calgary, 1979; cons. in field. NSF grantee, 1976—. Fellow Geol. Soc. Am.; mem. Am. Geophys. Union, Nigerian Mining, Geol. and Metall. Soc. (pres. internat. com. on the lithosphere 1992-95, Du Toit meml. lectr. 1995). Research in plate tectonics. Office: U Houston Dept Geoscis Houston TX 77204-5503 *There is much luck in a scientific career. I could not have known when I chose to become a geologist in 1948 that understanding of the problems I studied would be revolutionized by Plate Tectonics in 1965. To make the most of such an opportunity in geology a breadth of experience, both geographically and in different branches of geology, has proved vital.*

BURKE, LEAH WEYERTS, physician; b. Richland, Wash., Jan. 29, 1954; d. Alfred Cornelius and Phyllis (Nietfeld) Weyerts; m. David Lew Burke, Oct. 15, 1994. BA, U. N.C., Chapel Hill, 1975; MAT, Duke U., Durham, N.C., 1978; MD, U. N.C., Chapel Hill, 1987. Diplomate Am. Bd. Med. Genetics, Am. Bd. Pediatrics. Asst. prof. East Carolina U., Greenville, N.C., 1992-94, Allegheny U. Health Scis., Pitts., 1994—. Vol. Safe Summer Program, Pitts., 1995; vol. physician Little People of Am., Denver, 1995, Indpls., 1996. Recipient Resident Tchg. award UCSD Pediatric Residency, 1990, WSPR Travel award Ross Lab. and Geneteck, 1993. Fellow Am. Coll. Med. Genetics, Am. Acad. Pediatrics; mem. Am. Cleft Palate-Craniofacial Assn., Am. Soc. for Human Genetics, Allegheny County Med. Soc., Pitts. Pediatrics Soc. Office: Allegheny Univ Health Scis Allegheny Campus 320 E North Ave Pittsburgh PA 15212-4756

BURKE, LEE HALL, administrative assistant; b. Logan, Utah, Mar. 1, 1940; s. Vern L. and Elsie H. (Hall) B. BS in Polit. Sci., Utah State U., 1965, MS in Polit. Sci., 1967; PhD in Polit. Sci., U. Md., 1971. Asst. to U.S. senator U.S. Senate, Washington, 1970; asst. to U.S. congressman U.S. Ho. of Reps., Washington, 1971; pub. affairs staff U.S. Dept. State, Washington, 1971-77; asst. to pres., sec. bd. trustees Utah State U., Logan, 1977—; grad. asst. Utah State U., Logan, 1965-66, instr., 1969; grad. asst. U. Md., College Park, 1966-69. Author: Ambassador at Large, 1972, Homes of Department of State, 1977, Secretaries of State, 1978, History of Washington Ward, 1990; contbr. articles to profl. jours. Bd. dirs. ARC-Cache County Chpt., Logan, 1983-88; mem. Dist. Ct. Nominating Com., Logan, 1983-85, Logan City Recreation Com., 1990. With USAR, 1958-66. Md. fellow U. Md., College Park, 1969-71. Mem. Am. Polit. Sci. Assn., Internat. Studies Assn., Soc. for Historians of Am. Fgn. Rels., Cache C. of C. (bd. dirs. 1981-84, chmn. com. on legis. affairs 1984-86), Logan Golf and Country Club (pres., bd. dirs. 1988-89), Pi Sigma Alpha (v.p. U. Md. chpt., pres. Utah State U. chpt.), Blue Key (pres. 1964-65), Alpha Sigma Nu, Pi Kappa Alpha. Mem. LDS Ch. Avocations: golf, tennis, travel, music, sports. Home: 1471 Maple Dr Logan UT 84321-3627 Office: Utah State Univ UMC 1425 Logan UT 84322

BURKE, LILLIAN WALKER, retired judge; b. Thomaston, Ga., Aug. 2, 1917; d. George P. and Ozella (Daviston) Walker; m. Ralph Livingston Burke, July 8, 1948 (dec.); 1 son, R. Bruce. BS, Ohio State U., 1947; LLB, Cleve. State U., 1951, postgrad., 1963-64; grad., Nat. Coll. State Judiciary, U. Nev., 1974. Bar: Ohio 1951. Gen. practice law Cleve., 1952-62; asst. atty. gen. Ohio, 1962-66; mem., vice chmn. Ohio Indsl. Commn., 1966-69; judge Cleve. Mcpl. Ct., 1969-87, chief judge, 1981, 85, vis. judge, 1988-97; ret., 1997; guest lectr. Heidelburg Coll., Tiffin, Ohio, 1971; cons. Bur. Higher Edn., HEW, 1972. Pres. Cleve. chpt. Nat. Council Negro Women, 1955-57, recipient certificate of award, 1969; sec. East dist. Family Service Assn., 1959-60; mem. council human relations Cleve. Citizens League, 1959-79; mem. Gov.'s Com. on Status of Women, 1966-67; pres. Cleve. chpt. Jack and Jill of Am., Inc., 1960-61; v.p.-at-large Greater Cleve. Safety Council, 1969-79; mem. Cleve. Landmarks Commn., 1990-97; woman ward leader 24th Ward Republican Club, 1957-67; mem. Cuyahoga County Central Com., 1958-68; sec. Cuyahoga County Exec. Com., 1962-63; alt. del. Rep. Nat. Conv., Chgo., 1960; bd. dirs., chmn. minority div. Nat. Fedn. Rep. Women, 1966-68; life mem., past bd. dirs. Cleve. chpt. NAACP; bd. dirs. Greater Cleve. Neighborhood Centers Assn., Catholic Youth Counselling Services; trustee Ohio Commn. on Status of Women, 1966-70, Consumers League Ohio, 1969-75, Cleve. Music Sch. Settlement; bd. mgmt. Glenville YWCA, 1960-70; mem. project com. Cleve. Orch.; apptd. mem. City Planning Comm. Cleve., 1997—. Recipient achievement award Parkwood Christian Meth. Episcopal Ch., 1968, Martin Luther King Citizen's award, 1969, outstanding achievement award Ta-Wa-Si Scholarship Club, 1969, Outstanding Svc. award Morning Star Grand chpt., Cleve., 1970, award of honor Cleve. Bus. League, 1970, svc. award St. Paul AME Ch., Lima, Ohio, 1972, Woman of Achievement award Inner Club Coun., Cleve., 1973, cert. of award Nat. Coun. Negro Women, 1969, Goff Leadership award Clemson Found., 1997, Philanthropic Leadership award Cleve. Found., 1998; named Career Woman of Yr., Cleve. Women's Career Clubs, 1969. Mem. ABA, Nat. Assn. Investment Clubs (pres. Dynasty Investors Club 1992-96, bd. dirs. N.E. Ohio Coun. 1993—), Nat. Bar Assn., Ohio Bar Assn., Cuyahoga County Bar Assn., Cleve. Bar Assn., Am. Judicature Soc., Am. Judges Assn. (bd. govs. 1982-86, chmn. conv. agenda com. 1981-83), Phillis Wheatley Assn., Women Lawyers Assn. (hon. adviser), Ohio State U. Alumni Assn. (life), Cleve. Marshall Law Sch. (life), Am. Bridge Assn. (life), Women's City Club (Cleve.), Altrusa, Alpha Kappa Alpha. Episcopalian. Home: 1357 East Blvd Cleveland OH 44106-4018

BURKE, LINDA BEERBOWER, lawyer, aluminum manufacturing company executive, mining executive; b. Huntington, W.Va., June 19, 1948; d. William Bert and Betty Jane (Weddle) Beerbower; m. Timothy F. Burke, Jr., Aug. 26, 1972; children: Ryan Timothy, Hannah Elizabeth. BA in Govt., Coll. of William and Mary, 1970; JD, U. Pitts., 1973. Bar: Pa. 1973. Tax atty. legal dept. Aluminum Co. Am., Pitts., 1973-77, gen. tax atty. tax dept., 1977-80, mgr. legal and planning taxes, 1980-86, tax counsel, 1987—, asst. officer, 1992—, dir. taxes, 1993—; now v.p. Suriname Aluminum Co., Pitts., Alcoa Minerals of Jamaica, Inc., Pitts., Alcoa Steamship Co., Inc., Pitts.; with Alcoa Svc. Corp., Pitts.; now v.p. Northwest Alloys, Inc., Pitts.; v.p. various Alcoa subs.; presenter on fields internat. and employee benefits taxation, IRS audit procedures, atty.-client privilege. Note editor U. Pitts. Law Rev., 1972-73. Bd. dirs. YWCA Greater Pitts., 1987-95, 97—, v.p., 1989-92, pres., 1993-94; Alcoa co-chmn. Taylor Allderdice-Alcoa Partnership in Edn., 1982-84, chmn., 1985-88; mem. law fellows com. U. Pitts. Law Sch., 1988—, chmn. class ann. giving fund for law sch. class, 1982-94, chmn. law fellows, 1998—; mem. rev. com. United Way, 1987-94; bd. dirs. Vol. Action Ctr., 1982-85; mem. pers. com. Woman's Ctr. and Shelter Greater Pitts., 1986-94; trustee St. Edmund's Acad., 1986-94, sec., 1989-90, treas., 1990-92, mem. fin. com., 1986-93, chmn. enrollment com., 1988-90, co-chmn. ann. giving, 1986-87; mem. Leadership Pitts., 1990-91, bd. dirs., 1997—; bd. trustees Am. Tax Policy Inst., 1996—; mem. program com. Tax Found., 1996—; mem. adv. group to commr. Internal Revenue, 1996-98. Recipient tribute in corp. tax Triangle Corner, 1982, Asst. Commr.'s award IRS, 1992. Mem. ABA, Allegheny County Bar Assn., Am. Corp. Counsel Assn., Pitts. Internat. Tax Soc. (program com. 1988-94), Tax Execs. Inst. (bd. dirs. Pitts. chpt. 1981-86, pres. 1985-86, nat. bd. dirs., nat. exec. com. 1988-89, 90-91, 92-95, nat. chmn. IRS adminstrv. affairs com. 1989-90, 91-92, nat. sec. 1992-93, nat. sr. v.p. 1993-94, v.p. region VI 1990-91, internat. pres. 1994-95), Pitts. Tax Club (bd. dirs. 1989-95, pres. 1993-94), Duquesne Club. Democrat. Avocations: snow skiing, bridge, cooking, golf. Office: ALCOA Corp Ctr 201 Isabella St Pittsburgh PA 15212-5858

BURKE, LINDA JUDITH, real estate broker; b. Norristown, Pa., Jan. 28, 1958; d. Eugene Joseph and Dorothy Mae (Levering) Forrest; m. Joseph Anthony Burke, Dec. 6, 1980 (div. May 1994); children: Shawn Michael, Kimberly Ann. Cert. of completion, Lyons Tech. Inst., Cherry Hill, N.J., 1978; student, Camden County Coll., Blackwood, N.J., 1981-84, U. Pa., 1997—. Lic. real estate broker, N.J. Field svc. engr. MKD Corp., Cherry Hill, 1978-79; sys. technician 3M Corp., Mt. Laurel, N.J., 1979-82; bio-med. field svc. engr. Allied Chem. Co., Lexington, Mass., 1982-86; real estate sales assoc. Bleakly Agy.-Century 21, Cherry Hill, 1985-87; real estate broker Re/Max of Cherry Hill, 1987—. Vol. Children's Miracle Network, Cherry Hill, 1992—, Burlington County Meml. Hosp., Mt. Holly, N.J., 1971-77, Luth. Home, Moorestown, N.J., 1972-76, St. Theresa's Elem. Sch., Runnemede, N.J., 1991-95, Jaggard Elem. Sch., Marlton, N.J., 1995—. Mem. Re/Max Exec. Club, Camden County Bd. of Realtors (Million Dollar Sales Club), Re/Max Pres. Club. Roman Catholic. Avocations: reading, writing, sewing, gardening, traveling. Office: Re/Max of Cherry Hill 1736 Route 70 E Cherry Hill NJ 08003-2307

BURKE, MARGUERITE JODI LARCOMBE, writer, computer consultant; b. Pasadena, Calif.; d. Richard Albert and Marguerite (Colella) L.; m. M. Theodore Jockers; children: Richard Larcombe, Sir Blair; m. Roger Eugene Burke. BA, Columbia U., 1949. Model Ford Agy., N.Y.C., 1949-54; freelance writer Savannah, Ga., 1969-80; pres. Jodi Larcombe Assocs., Murfreesboro, N.C., 1970—; freelance computer programmer Murfreesboro, 1981—; exec. asst. Resinall Corp., Severn, N.C., 1981—, computer programmer, 1981-89. Author: Sailing Cookbook, 1979, others; contbr. numerous articles to mags.; dir. Shotgun Theater Prodns., 1995. Dir. Shotgun Theater Prodns., N.Y., 1996—. Mem. Met. Opera Oncore Soc., Am. Film Soc., Met Opera Patron Assn. (2d century cir.), Met. Opera Nat. Coun., N.Y.C. Opera. Avocations: sailing, reading, sewing, traveling. Home and Office: Jodi Larcombe Assocs 306 Holly Hill Rd Murfreesboro NC 27855-2110

BURKE, MARIANNE KING, state agency administrator, financial executive; b. Douglasville, Ga., May 30, 1938; d. William Horace and Evora (Morris) King; divorced; 1 child, Kelly Page. Student, Ga. Inst. Tech., 1956-59, Anchorage C.C., 1964-66, Portland State U., 1968-69; BBA, U. Alaska, 1976. CPA, Alaska. Sr. audit mgr. Price Waterhouse, 1982-90; v.p. fin., asst. sec. NANA Regional Corp., Inc., Anchorage, 1990-95; v.p. fin. NANA Devel. Corp., Inc., Anchorage, 1990-95; sec.-treas. Vanguard Industries, J.V., Anchorage, 1990-95, Alaska United Drilling, Inc., Anchorage, 1990-95; treas. NANA/Marriott Joint Venture, Anchorage, 1990-95; v.p. fin. Arctic Utilities, Inc., Anchorage, 1990-95, Tour Arctic, Inc., Anchorage, 1990-95, Purcell Svcs., Ltd., Anchorage, 1990-95, Arctic Caribou Inn, Anchorage, 1990-95, NANA Oilfield Svcs., Inc., Anchorage, 1990-95, NANA Corp. Svcs., Inc., Anchorage, 1992-95; dir. divsn. ins. State of Alaska, 1995—; mem. State of Alaska Medicaid Rate Commn., 1985-88, State of Alaska Bd. Accountancy, 1984-87; bd. dirs. Nat. Assn. Ins. Commrs. Edn. and Rsch. Found. Bd. dirs. Alaska Treatment Ctr., Anchorage, 1978, Alaska Hwy. Cruises; treas. Alaska Feminist Credit Union, Anchorage, 1979-80; mem. fund raising com. Anchorage Symphony, 1981. Mem. AICPA, Internat. Assn. Ins. Suprs. (funded mem.), Alaska Soc. CPAs, Govtl. Fin. Officers U.S. and Can., Fin. Execs. Inst. (bd. dirs.), Nat. Assn. Ins. Commrs. (bd. dirs.). Avocations: travel, reading. Home: 3818 Helvetia Dr Anchorage AK 99508-5016 Office: State Office Bldg PO Box 110805 333 Willoughby Ave Juneau AK 99801 also: 3601 C St Ste 1324 Anchorage AK 99503-5948

BURKE, MARTIN J., United States marshall; b. Bronx, Dec. 21, 1942. BS, Mercy Coll., 1973. U.S. marshall N.Y. So. dist. U.S. Marshalls Svc., 1995—. Office: 500 Pearl St Ste 400 New York NY 10007

BURKE, MARTIN NICHOLAS, lawyer; b. Green Bay, Wis., Dec. 27, 1936; s. Martin Nicholas and Jacqueline Marjorie (Morris) B.; m. Barbara Louise Forster, Sept. 11, 1957 (div. 1967); children—M. Nicholas, Forrest G., Jacqueline Louise. B.A., Yale U., 1959; J.D., U. Chgo., 1962. Bar: Minn. 1962. Assoc. Faegre & Benson, Mpls., 1962-70, ptnr., 1970—, chair gen. litigation group. Contbr. articles to Grapevine Mag. Bd. dirs. Twin Cities Marathon, Mpls., 1982—, pres., 1984—. Mem. Fedn. Ins. Counsel, Minn. Def. Lawyers Assn. (bd. dirs. 1976-81, pres. 1979-80). Republican. Clubs: Mpls. Athletic; Madeline Island Yacht (LaPointe, Wis.). Avocations: running; skiing; writing. Home: 1770 Humboldt Ave S Minneapolis MN 55403-2811 Office: Faegre & Benson 2200 Norwest Crt 90 S 7th St Ste 2200 Minneapolis MN 55402-3901*

BURKE, MARY GRIGGS (MRS. JACKSON BURKE), art collector; b. St. Paul. BA, Sarah Lawrence Coll.; MA in Clin. Psychology, Columbia U.; postgrad., New Sch. for Social Rsch. Pvt. collector Japanese art, St. Paul, 1966—; founder The Mary & Jackson Burke Found., N.Y.C., 1972—; mem. vis. com. Freer Gallery Art, Smithsonian Instn.; mem. Met. Mus. Art; pres. The Mary and Jackson Burke Found. Mem. nominating com., mem. membership com., mem. exec. com., mem. activities com. The Japan Soc., 1959-77, chmn. student and visitors com., 1957-63, chmn. art gallery adv. com., 1970-73, bd. dirs., 1968-77, also hon. life trustee; chmn. friend mem. Japan House Gallery, 1969-75, 87—; bd. dirs. The Cable (Wis.) Natural History Mus., 1968-92, also hon. life trustee, Sarah Lawrence Coll., Bronxville, N.Y., 1968-78, also hon. life trustee, The Internat. Crane Found., Baraboo, Wis., 1978-90, The Hobe Sound (Fla.) Nature Ctr., 1987—; mem. adv. coun. dept. art history and archeology Columbia U., N.Y.C., 1970—; mem. internat. coun. Mus. Modern Art, N.Y.C., 1970—; mem. vis. com. Freer Gallery of Art, Smithsonian Instn., Washington, 1971—, vice chmn., 1989-92; mem. vis. com. dept. Asiatic art Mus. Fine Arts, Boston, 1972-90, also friend, 1972-90; mem. vis. com. dept. Islamic art, mem. vis. com. dept. Asian art, mem. edn. com., mem. acquisitions com., bd. dirs. Met. Mus. Art, N.Y.C., 1976—, also friend Far Ea. dept., 1984—; mem. Smithsonian Assocs. nat. bd. Smithsonian Instn., Washington, 1977-83; mem. art gallery adv. com., mem. exec. com., mem. devel. com., bd. dirs. The Asia Soc., 1978-88, also hon. life trustee; friend Bklyn. Mus. Art, 1982—, Friends of Asian Art, Freer and Sackler Galleries, 1991—; William Beene fellows N.Y. Zool. Soc., 1986—. Decorated Order of The Sacred Treasure (Japan), Second Leve Gold and Silver Star (Japan). Home: 3 E 77th St #6A New York NY 10021-1732*

BURKE, MARY THOMAS, university administrator, educator; b. Westport, County Mayo, Ireland, Nov. 28, 1928; d. Thomas J. and Anne (McGuire) B. BA, Belmont (N.C.) Abbey Coll., 1958; MA, Georgetown U., 1965; PhD, U. N.C., Chapel Hill, 1968. Elem. tchr. St Patrick's Sch., Charlotte, N.C., 1950-51, St Agnes Sch., Greenport, N.Y., 1951-54; tchr. Charlotte (N.C.) Cath. High Sch., 1954-64; academic dean Sacred Heart Coll., Belmont, N.C., 1967-70; assoc. prof. U. N.C., Charlotte, 1970-75, prof., chmn. human svcs. dept., 1975—, prof., coord. grad. counseling program, 1996—; chmn. State Adv. Coun. on Pupil Pers. Svcs., 1972-76. Co-editor: (with Judith Miranti) Ethical and Value Issues in Counseling, 1992, Counseling: The Spiritual Dimension, 1995. Bd. dirs. McKlenburg chpt. and state divsn. Am. Cancer Soc., 1977-83, treas., 1983-86, crusade chmn., 1986; chairperson United Way, U. N.C., Charlotte, 1974; bd. dirs. St. Joseph Hosp. and St. Joseph's Health Svcs., Asheville, Selwyn Life Ctr., Charlotte, 1986-90; bd. dirs. Nat. Bus. Forms, Greeneville, Tenn., 1973—, asst. sec., treas. bd. dirs., 1975-92, sec., treas., 1992—; mem. bd. trustees Belmont Abbey Coll., 1994—, chair acad. com., mem. exec. com., 1996—. Recipient Anti-Defamation award B'nai B'rith Women, 1978, Ray Thompson Human Rels. award N.C. Assn. for Non-White Concerns, 1978, WBT Woman of Yr. award, 1979, Ella Stephen Barret Leadership award, 1983, AWO Good of Soc. award Am. Cancer Soc., 1981, Leadership award Am. Cancer Soc., 1988, Faculty Svc. award Gen. Alumni Assn. U. N.C., 1994, Silver Medalian Humanitarian award Nat. Conf. Christians and Jews, 1995, Meritorious award Assn. for Spiritual Ethical and Religious Values in Counseling, 1995; named Excellence in Teaching award finalist Nations Bank, 1995, Tchr. Excellence award, 1996, Cal Francis Beatty Humanitarian award, 1997; named Counselor of Yr., ACA, 1998. Mem. AACD (human rights com. 1992-93), N.C. Pers. and Guidance Assn. (exec. com. 1973-90, edtl. bd. jours. 1975-78, pres. Metrolina chpt. 1973-74, state pres.-elect 1980-81, pres. 1981-82, leadership award 1983), N.C. Guidance Assn. (program com. 1974-75), Nat. Cath. Guidance Assn. (state rep. 1974-79), N.C. Assn. Religious and Value Issues in Counseling (chairperson 1974—, pres. 1985-86, 93-94, bd. dirs. 1986-94), N.C. Assn. Counselors Educators and Suprs. (pres. 1997—), Am. Pers. and Guidance Assn., Am. Counselor Educators and Suprs. Assn., Assn. Religious Values in Counseling, N.C. Assn. Group Work, N.C. Mental Health Assn., N.C. Sch. Counselors Assn. (Counselor Educator of Yr. award 1975), So. Assn. Counselor Educators and Suprs., Assn. for Religious Values in Counseling (bd. dirs. Metrolina AIDS Project 1989-90, pres. bd., 1990-92, pres.-elect 1989-90, pres. 1990-91, Pres.' award 1992), Coun. Accreditation of Counseling and Related Edn. Programs (bd. dirs. 1993—, vice chair 1994-96, chairperson 1996—, ACA liaison to Nat. Bd. Cert. Counselors 1994-97), Phi Delta Kappa, Delta Kappa Gamma, Chi Sigma Iota (pres. 1997-98, Leadership award 1998), Mu Tau Beta (Devoted Svc. award 1994). Office: U NC Dept Counseling/Child Devel Charlotte NC 28223 *Life is a journey. Each moment is sacred. We need to live in the present and respond to the sacredness of the moment, always being sensitive to the needs of others, particularly those whom we serve. We must use power as a gift and not impose our values on others. The way we live and treat others is much more poignant than anything we may say.*

BURKE, MICHAEL AUGUSTUS, miliatary officer; b. San Diego, July 27, 1951; s. Edwin Joseph and Dorothy (Lewis) B.; m. Mary Ann Hagan, Feb. 23, 1980; 1 child, Emilie. BA with honors, Va. Mil. Inst., 1973; MA, U. N.C., 1983. Commd. 2d lt. U.S. Army, 1973, advanced through grades to lt. col.; logistics officer U.S. Army Transp. Ctr., Ft. Eustis, Va., 1973-76; unit comdr. U.S. Army Combat Equipment Group, West Germany, 1976-80; asst. prof. English U.S. Mil. Acad., West Point, N.Y., 1983-86, assoc. prof. English, 1995—; supply and svcs. officer U.S. Army Signal Sch., Fort Gordon, 1986-88; logistics officer 1st Armored Divsn., Nürnberg, Germany and Middle East, 1988-92; compensation policy officer Hdqr. Dept. of the Army, Washington, 1992-95. Editor: Reengineering DOD Travel, 1994, (catalog) The Art of the Warners, 1986. Demcorated Legion of Merit. Mem. Nat. Coun. Tchrs. of English, U.S. Naval Inst., Phi Kappa Phi. Democrat. Roman Catholic. Office: Dept of English US Mil Acad West Point NY 10996

BURKE, MICHAEL DESMOND, pathologist; b. Galway, Ireland, May 25, 1935; came to U.S., 1959; s. James and Margaret (McKee) B.; m. Joan Long, June, 1960 (div. Apr. 1966); children: James Niall, Richard Joseph; m. Maria Sperazi, June 19, 1966: children: Marina, Claudia. MB, BCh., BAO, Nat. U. of Ireland, Galway, 1959. Diplomate Am. Bd. of Pathology in Clin., Chem. and Anatomical Pathology. Assoc. pathologist Mt. Sinai Hosp., Mpls., 1969-81; from asst. prof. to prof. pathology U. Minn., Mpls., 1971-81; prof. pathology and dir. clin. pathology U. Hosp. SUNY, Stony Brook, N.Y., 1981-95; prof. pathology, vice chmn. lab. medicine, dir. clin. labs. The N.Y. Hosp. Cornell Med. Ctr., N.Y.C., 1996—; Faculty of Pathology fellow Royal Coll. Physicians of Ireland, 1993; trustee Am. Bd. Pathology, Tampa, Fla., 1997; edtl. cons. clin. pathology Stedman's Med. Dictionary 25th edit., 1990. Editor Clinical Decisions and Laboratory Use, U. Minn. Press, 1982; adv. editor Lab. Medicine, 1985; assoc. editor Am. Jour. of Clin. Pathology, 1990. Capt. USAR, 1961-63. Fellow Am. Soc. Clin. Pathologists (pres. 1995-96, Disting. Svc. award 1984, Ward Burdick award 1998), Coll. of Am. Pathologists; mem. AMA, Am. Assn. for Clin. Chemistry (Outstanding Speaker award 1991), Acad. Clin. Lab. Physicians and Scientists (pres. 1993-

94, Gerald T. Evans award 1997, Cotlove Lectureship award 1998). Office: NY Hosp Cornell Med Ctr 525 E 68th St New York NY 10021-4885

BURKE, MICHAEL DONALD, oil and gas company executive; b. Salem, Oreg., Feb. 27, 1944; s. James Michael Burke and Mary Jane (Farrington) Gage; m. Louise Mennow, June 3, 1972; children: Kendra Anne, Michael John. BSChemE, Tex. A&M U., 1966; MBA in Fin. and Mktg., U. Tex., Austin, 1970. Chem. and process engr., mktg., product mgr. Houston Chem. Co. subs. PPG Industries, Pitts., 1966-76; cons. PACE Cons., Houston, 1976-78; mktg. mgr. ICI Americas (CCPC), Houston, 1978-80, dir. tri-states synfuel project, 1980-81; v.p. synfuels Tex. Ea. Corp., 1981-82; v.p. mfg. and refining La Gloria Oil & Gas Co. subs. Tex. Ea. Corp., Houston, 1982-84, pres., 1984-86; pres. Tex. Eastern Products Pipeline Co. subs. Tex. Eastern Corp., Houston, 1986-90; group v.p. Tex. Ea. Corp., 1986-90; pres., CEO, Tex. Ea. Products Pipeline Ltd., Houston, 1990-92, Tesoro Petroleum Corp., San Antonio, 1992-95, EOTT Energy Corp., Houston, 1998—; pres., CEO M.D. Burke and Co., 1995—, Personal Devel. Forum, Houston, 1982-85; nat. fellow Am. Leadership Forum, 1985. Chmn. Tex. Ea. Polit. Action Com., Houston, 1985-86, United Way Campaign Effectiveness Coun., Houston, 1986, Houston chpt. Am. Leadership Forum, 1987-89; bd. dirs. Houston Mental Health Assocs., 1987-91, Gulf Coast chpt. ARC, 1987-92, vice chmn., 1989-92, mem. bd. and exec. com., 1990-92, chmn. elect, 1992; bd. dirs., mem. exec. com. Sam Houston Coun. Boy Scouts Am., 1987-92, vice chmn. exploring, 1989-92; mem. adv. bd. U. Houston, 1990-92; Alamo area coun. Boy Scout Am., exec. com., 1994-96; chmn. Alamadoma Task Forces, 1994; bd. dirs., exec. com. San Antonio Bexar County United Way, 1994—, Our Lady of Lake U., 1995—, World Affairs Coun., 1994-97, San Antonio Via Met. Transit Bd., 1996-98, South Tex. YMCA, 1994—, Free Trade Alliance San Antonio, 1996—, Tex. Pub. Policy Found., 1996—, Mind Sci. Found., 1996—; mem. San Antonio Mayor's Commn. on Brooks AFB Redevel., Econ. Vitality and Workforce Edn. Mem. Nat. Petroleum Refiners Assn. (bd. dirs. 1984—), Am. Petroleum Inst. (gen. refining com. 1982-84, pipeline transp. com. 1986-92), Nat. Petroleum Coun., Tex. Ea. Toastmasters (pres. 1984), Houston C. of C. (chmn. Houston Bus. Group 1986-88, founder Innovate Houston 1986), Corpus Christi Jaycees (past. dir.), Southbriar Community Assn. (past pres.), Assn. Oil Pipelines (bd. dirs. 1986-92), Mt. Belvieu Industry Assn. (chmn. 1987-89), San Antonio C. of C. (bd. dirs., exec. com., 1994-97), Petroleum Club. Republican. Roman Catholic. Office: EOTT Energy Corp 1330 Post Oak Blvd Ste 2700 Houston TX 77056-3017 *Life committment to lead others to achieve a common vision and outstanding service for others by building self-esteem and promoting trust, cooperation and teamwork. Strongly believe we should become all we are capable of becoming...and have fun in the process.**

BURKE, MICHAEL HENRY, lawyer; b. Washington, Oct. 28, 1952; s. John Joseph and Mary Catherine (Gaul) B.; m. Ann McFarland, Jan. 31, 1981; children: Allison M., Andrew M. BA magna cum laude, Tufts U., 1974; JD, Georgetown U., 1977. Bar: Mass. 1977, U.S. Dist. Ct. Mass. 1979. Assoc. Bulkley, Richardson and Gelinas L.L.P., Springfield, Mass., 1977-83; ptnr. Bulkley, Richardson and Gelinas L.L.P., 1983—. Pub. adminstr. Commonwealth of Mass., 1980-90. Mem. ABA, Mass. Bar Assn., Hampden County Bar Assn. Roman Catholic. Home: 50 Meadowbrook Rd Longmeadow MA 01106-1341 Office: Bulkley Richardson and Gelinas LLP 1500 Main St Springfield MA 01115-0001

BURKE, PAUL E., JR., governmental relations consultant; b. Kansas City, Mo., Jan. 4, 1934; s. Paul E. and Virginia (Moling) B.; m. Debbie Weihe; children: Anne Elizabeth, Kelly Patricia, A. Catherine, Jennifer Marie. B.S. in Bus. Adminstrn., U. Kans., 1956. Mem. Kans. Ho. of Reps., 1972-74; mem. Kans. State Senate, 1975-97, pres., 1989-97, majority leader, 1985-89; chmn. Legislative Coordinating Coun., 1995; pres.-elect Nat. Conf. State Legislatures, 1990-91, pres., 1992; pres. Nat. Conf. State Legislatures Found., 1994; mem. Fed. Adv. Commn. Intergovtl. Rels., 1993-96; pres. Issues Mgmt. Group, Inc., 1996—. Councilman, City of Prairie Village (Kans.), 1959-63; mem. Kans. Turnpike Authority, 1965-69, chmn., 1969; mem. adv. bd. Sec. of Corrections, 1973-78. Capt. USAF, 1956-59; capt. USNR, 1963-88. Mem. Kans. Assn. Commerce and Industry. Republican. Episcopalian. Lodges: Masons, Shriners, Rotary. Address: 26391 W Cedar Niles Cir Olathe KS 66061-7478 *Personal philosophy: The responsibility for serving in an elected capacity is one of the greatest privileges extended by one's constituents. Understanding how to convert that responsiblity to the highest level of benefit for them is our greatest challenge. Service to others--rather than self-- is the key.*

BURKE, RAYMOND L., bishop. ordained June 29, 1975. Bishop Diocese of La Crosse, 1994—. Office: PO Box 4004 La Crosse WI 54602-4004*

BURKE, RICHARD A., manufacturing executive. CEO Trek Corp., Waterloo, Wis. Office: Trek Corp 801 W Madison St Waterloo WI 53594-1243*

BURKE, RICHARD KITCHENS, lawyer, educator; b. Helena, Ark., Aug. 21, 1922; s. James Graham and Myrtie May (Kitchens) B.; m. Bonnie Beth Byler, Jan. 21, 1946; children: Charles, Bonnie Louise. Student, U. Va., 1939-40; BA, U. Ark., 1942, LLB, 1947; PhD, Vanderbilt U., 1957. Bar: Ark. 1947, Ariz. 1959, S.D. 1974. Ptnr. Burke, Moore & Burke, Helena, 1947-52; asst. prof. polit. sci. U. Ariz., 1957-60; ptnr. Robertson, Childers, Burke & Drachman, Tucson, 1960-67; prof. polit. sci. U. Southwestern La., 1967-69; U.S. atty. Dist. Ariz., Dept. Justice, 1969-72; dep. asst. atty. gen. U.S. Dept. Justice, Washington, 1972-73; prof. law U. S.D. Sch. Law, 1973-84, dean, 1974-80; prof. law U. Ark., 1984-86, prof. emeritus, 1986—. Mem. Ariz. Rep. State Com., 1963-67; Rep. congl. candidate So. Dist. Ariz., 1962; chmn. citizen's adv. com. Ampitheater Sch. Dist., Tucson, 1964-66. With USN, 1942-45, 53-54. Decorated Air medal; Ford fellow Vanderbilt U., 1957. Mem. Am. Bar Assn., State Bar S.D., State Bar Ariz., Ark. Bar Assn. Republican. Mem. Christian Ch. Home: 11390 E Janan Dr Scottsdale AZ 85259

BURKE, ROBERT BERTRAM, lawyer, political consultant, lobbyist; b. Cleve., July 9, 1942; s. Max and Eve (Miller) B.; m. Helen Choate Hall, May 5, 1979 (div. Oct. 1983). B.A., UCLA, 1963, J.D., 1966; LL.M., London Sch. Econs., 1967. Bar: D.C. 1972, Calif. 1978, U.S. Supreme Ct. 1977. Exec. dir. Lawyer's Com. Civil Rts. under Law, Washington, 1968-69; ptnr. Fisk, Wolfe & Burke, Paris, 1969-71; assoc. O'Connor & Hannan, Washington, 1972-74; sole practice, Washington, 1974-79, Los Angeles, 1978-93; cons. Commonwealth Pa., Harrisburg, 1973. Chmn. So. Calif. Hollings for Pres., 1984; pres. Bldg. and Appeals Bd. City of Los Angeles; bd. dirs. Vols. of Am.; mem. exec. com. State Bar of Calif. pub. law sect. Mem. ABA, Am. Inst. Architects (profl. affiliate), UCLA Law Alumni Assn. (pres.). Jewish. Home: 277 S Irving Blvd Los Angeles CA 90004-3809

BURKE, ROBERT HARRY, surgeon, educator; b. Cambridge, Mass., Dec. 22, 1945; s. Harry Clearfield and Joan Rosalyn (Spire) B.; m. Margaret Cauldwell Fisher, May 4, 1968; children: Christopher David, Catherine Cauldwell. Student, U. Mich. Coll. Pharmacy, 1964-67; DDS, U. Mich., 1971, MS, 1976; MD, Mich. State U., 1980. Diplomate Am. Bd. Oral and Maxillofacial Surgery, Am. Bd. Cosmetic Surgery. Pvt. practice cosmetic and reconstructive surgery Ann Arbor, Mich.; house officer oral and maxillofacial surgery U. Mich. Sch. Dentistry, U. Mich. Hosp., Ann Arbor, 1973-76; clin. asst. prof. dept. oral surgery U. Detroit Sch. Dentistry, 1976-77; adj. asst. rsch. scientist Ctr. Human Growth and Devel. U. Mich., 1976-77, adj. rsch. investigator, 1982-85; clin. asst. prof. Mich. State U., East Lansing, 1978-80, 1987—; house officer surg. emphasis St. Joseph Mercy Hosp., Ann Arbor, 1980-81; adj. rsch. investigator dept. anatomy U. Mich. Med. Sch., 1982-85; clin. asst. prof. oral and maxillofacial surgery U. Mich., 1984-86; lectr. U. Detroit Sch. Dentistry, 1986, assoc. clin. prof. oral and maxillofacial surgery, 1987-90; cons., lectr. dept. occlusion U. Mich. Sch. Dentistry, 1986; head sect. dentistry and oral surgery dept. gen. surgery St. Joseph Mercy Hosp., 1982-87, mem. exec. com. dept. gen. surgery, 1984-87; chmn. com. emergency care rev. Beyer Meml. Hosp., Ypsilanti, Mich., 1986, also active, 1987, 1990—; active staff St. Joseph Meml. Hosp.; courtesy staff Saline (Mich.) Cmty. Hosp., 1978-88; Chelsea (Mich.) Med. Ctr., 1978-88, 90-92, McPherson Cmty. Hosp., Howell, Mich., 1984-87, Herrick Meml. Hosp., 1998—, Bixby Hosp., 1998—; dir. Mich. Ctr. Cosmetic Surgery. Mem. editl. bd. Topics in Pain Mgmt., 1985—; contbg. editor Am. Jours. Cosmetic Surgery, 1990-91; sect. editor Internat. Jour. Aesthetic and Restorative Surgery, 1992-95, 96—. Campaign chmn. med. and dental sects. United Way Washtenaw County, Ann Arbor, 1982, dental sect. 1983; profl. adv. com. March of Dimes Genesee County Valley Chpt., Flint, 1979; pres. Huron Pkwy. Pla. Condominium, 1984—. Fellow ACS, Internat. Coll. Surgeons (bd. dirs. Mich. chpt., vice regent), Am. Coll. Oral and Maxillofacial Surgeons (v.p. 1987-88, pres.-elect 1989-90, pres. 1991-93), Am. Acad. Aesthetic and Restorative Surgery (trustee 1997—); mem. AMA, Am. Assn. Cosmetic Maxillofacial Surgeons (chmn. bd. dirs. 1997—), Am. Assn. Craniomaxillofacial Surgeons (pres. 1992—, chmn. bd. dirs. 1997—), Internat. Soc. Cosmetic Laser Surgeons (trustee 1992-93, sec. 1992), British Soc. for Oral and Maxillofacial Surgeons (assoc.), European Soc. Aesthetic Surgery and Liposuction, Chalmers Lyons Acad. Oral Surgery, European Assn. for Cranio-Maxillofacial Surgery (assoc.), Washtenaw County Med. Soc. (exec.com. sec. 1987-88, pres. 1990), Inst. Study Profl. Risk (bd. dirs. 1985-90), Victor's Club, Pres.'s Club, Omicron Kappa Upsilon. Congregationalist. Avocations: triathlon, chang moo kwan, tae kwon do. Home: 5207 Red Fox Run Ann Arbor MI 48105-9364 Office: 2260 S Huron Pky Ann Arbor MI 48104-5151

BURKE, ROBERT LAWRENCE, consultant; b. Elmira, N.Y., Dec. 30, 1928; s. Edmund and Gertrude Landin B.; m. Dorothy Ann Halvorsen, June 4, 1952; children: Randi Ann, Karen, Robert L. Jr., Elizabeth. BS, U.S. Mil. Acad., 1952; MA in Journalism, U. Ala., 1964. Commd. 2d lt. U.S. Army, 1952, advanced through grades to col., 1972, retired, 1977; mgr. Am. Newspaper Pubs. Assn., 1977-82, sr. v.p., 1982-91; cons. Orange, Va., 1991—; lectr. in field. Contbr. articles to profl. jours. Pres. Civic Assn., Fairfax, Va., 1979-80; chmn. Orange County (Va.) Rep. Party, 1997—; treas 30th Legis. Dist. Rep. Com., Va., 1997—; mem. 17 Sen. Dist. Com., 1997—, 7th Congrl. Dist. Com., 1997—, Piedmont Environ. Coun., Va., 1998—. Decorated Vietnam Cross of Gallantry with gold palm, Army Commendation medal, Joint Svc. Commendation medal, Legion of Merit with (2) oak leaf clusters, Def. Superior Svc. medal; recipient Disting. Grad. award Def. Lang. Inst., 1966, Outstanding Alumnus Journalism award U. Ala., 1980. Mem. Nat. Press Club, Nat. War Coll. Alumni Assn., U.S. Mil. Acad. Assn. Grads., U. Ala. Alumni Assn. Roman Catholic. Home: 13506 Conway Ln Orange VA 22960

BURKE, RUTH, writer; b. L.A., Jan. 16, 1933; d. Thomas Arthur and Bertha Morgan King; children: D. Julian Montelbano, Alan D., Carol Burke Ward, Michael L., Laurel, Abram D. AA, East L.A. Coll., 1957; AB, San Diego State U., 1967; postgrad., Western N.Mex. U., 1996—. Cert. tchr., Ariz. English instr. Reed Christian Coll., Compton, Calif., 1985; writing instr. Cochise Coll., Benson, Ariz., 1996; book reviewer Interrace Mag., Atlanta, 1993, Lambda Book Report, Washington, 1996—. Mem. editl. staff True Romance, True Experience; columnist Ariz. Range News, Willcox, 1995-99; contbr. numerous works to profl. publs. Mem. sch. coun. Bowie (Ariz.) Schs., 1996. Libertarian. Roman Catholic. Avocations: study of the desert, Black history, study of the Great Depression. Home: PO Box 247 Bowie AZ 85605-0247

BURKE, SABRINA NELSON, sales and marketing professional; b. Albany, Ga., Nov. 3, 1969; d. Wiley Frederick Nelson II and Eve-Anne (Duke) Wall. BS in Mktg., U. Cen. Fla., 1992. Lic. real estate broker, Fla. Realtor, assoc. Duke Properties, Maitland, Fla., 1990-92; property acquisition specialist Post, Buckley, Schuh and Jernigan, Inc., Winter Park, Fla., 1992-96; v.p., dir. sales and mktg. Wall Travel, Granbury, Tex., 1996-98; tobacco prevention coord. Gulf County Health Dept., Port St. Joe, Fla., 1999—. Mem. NAFE, Internat. Right of Way Assn., Am. Mktg. Assn., Phi Theta Kappa, Mu Kappa Tau, Phi Kappa. Republican. Baptist. Avocations: creative writing, horseback riding, travel, dancing. Office: Gulf County Health Dept 9621 Monticello Dr Port Saint Joe FL 32456

BURKE, SHEILA P., legislative staff member; b. San Francisco, Jan. 10, 1951; d. George Abbott and Mary Joan (Winfield) B.; m. David Chew, Jan. 1983; children: Daniel, Kathleen, Sarah. BSN, U. San Francisco, 1973; MA in Pub. Adminstrn., Harvard U., 1982. Staff nurse Alta Bates Hosp., Berkeley, Calif., 1973-74; dir. student affairs Nat. Student Nurses Assn., N.Y., 1974-75; dir. program and field svcs. Nat. Student Nurses Assn., 1975-77; legis. asst. Senator Bob Dole, 1977-78; profl. staff mem. for Senator Bob Dole Senate Com. Fin., U.S. Senate, 1979-82, dep. staff dir. for Senator Bob Dole, 1982-85; dep. chief of staff Senate Majority Leader Bob Dole, U.S. Senate, 1985-86; chief of staff Senator Bob Dole, 1986-96; sec. U.S. Senate, Washington, 1995; adj. nursing faculty Georgetown U.; rsch. asst J.F. Kennedy Sch. Govt., Harvard U., 1980-81, advisor to dean, 1996, exec. dean, lectr. pub. policy, 1996—. Address: 1323 Merrie Ridge Rd Mc Lean VA 22101-1826

BURKE, STEVEN CHARLES, healthcare administration executive; b. Atlanta, May 23, 1951; s. Charles Hulett and Carole Ruth (Mason) B.; m. Margaret Hudgins, Aug. 9, 1975; 1 child, David. BA, U. So. Sewanee, 1973; MHA, Duke U., 1975. Planning analyst Greenville Hosp. Sys., S.C., 1975-78, asst. dir. facility devel. and constrn., 1978-79, asst. v.p. planning, 1979-83; dir. planning and mktg. Youngstown Hosp. Assn., Ohio, 1983-84, v.p. planning and mktg. Western Res. Care System, Youngstown, 1984-86; v.p. mktg. Richland Meml. Hosp., Columbia, S.C., 1986-91; v.p. corp. svcs. Gaston Health Care, 1992-98; exec. dir. Preferred Care Network, Charlotte, N.C., 1998-99; sr. v.p. physician enterprise svcs. Presbyn. Healthcare, Charlotte, 1999—. Fellow Am. Coll. Healthcare Adminstrs., Am. Soc. Hosp. Planning and Mktg., Carolinas Soc. Hosp. Planning and Mktg. Episcopalian. Avocations: choral singing, woodworking, bicycling. Home: 201 Timberlane Dr Belmont NC 28012-7726 Office: Presbyn Healthcare 200 Hawthorne Ln Charlotte NC 28233-3549

BURKE, TAMARA LYNN, marketing professional; b. Appleton, Minn., July 4, 1960; d. Merlyn Eugene and Patricia Yvonne (Johnson) Munsterman; m. James Warren Burke, Jr., Mar. 26, 1983 (div. June 1993); 1 child, Madelyn Amanda. BA, U. Minn., 1982; postgrad., Calif. Luth. U., 1999. Asst. acct. exec. Sheggeby Advt., Mpls., 1982-83, BBDO, Inc., L.A., 1983-84; program mgr. Cable Music Channel, Hollywood, Calif., 1984-85; acct. exec. Ogilvy & Mather, L.A., 1985-88; mktg. mgr. Teleflora, L.A., 1988-93; asst. mgr. mktg. & merchandising Jafra Cosmetics Internat. Inc. (A Gillette Co.), Westlake Village, Calif., 1993-97, mgr. product mktg., 1997-98; mgr. mktg. Jafra Cosmetics Internat. Inc., Westlake Village, Calif., 1998-99; group mktg. mgr. Sebastian Internat., Inc., Woodland Hills, Calif., 1999—. Recipient Silver Clio award, 1986, N.Y. Internat. Film and TV Festival bronze award, 1986, Ogilvy & Mather Creative Excellence award, 1986, Disting. Scholar award Calif. Luth. U., 1998. Mem. Rho Lambda Hon. Soc. Office: Sebastian Internat Inc 6109 DeSoto Ave Woodland Hills CA 91367

BURKE, THOMAS JOSEPH, accountant; b. Washington, Dec. 27, 1959; s. Thomas Gervase and Carol Marie (Lysaght) B.; m. Diane Carole Foster, Dec. 27, 1986; children: Thomas J., Shannon Carole. BA in Acctg., Benedictine Coll., 1982. CPA, VA. Acct. U.S. Navy, Virginia Beach, Va., 1983—. Fellow Va. Soc. CPAs; mem. Am. Inst. CPA, Inst. Mgmt. Accts. (cert. mgmt. acct., cert. fin. mgmt.). Roman Catholic. Home: 5725 Brandon Blvd Virginia Beach VA 23464-6530 Office: Nexcom 3280 Virginia Beach Blvd Virginia Beach VA 23452-5724

BURKE, THOMAS JOSEPH, JR., lawyer; b. Chgo., Oct. 23, 1941; s. Thomas Joseph and Violet (Green) B.; m. Sharon Lynne Forke, Aug. 29, 1964; children: Lisa Lynne, Heather Ann. BA, Elmhurst Coll., 1963; JD, Chgo.-Kent Coll. Law, 1966. Bar: Ill. 1966, U.S. Dist. Ct. (no. dist.) Ill. 1967, U.S. Ct. Appeals (7th cir.) 1972, U.S. Supreme Ct. 1972, U.S. Ct. Appeals (11th cir.) 1994, U.S. Ct. Appeals (6th cir.), 1995. Assoc., Lord, Bissell & Brook, Chgo., 1966-74, ptnr., 1974—. Dir. and pres. Buffalo Prairie Gang Camp. Fellow Am. Coll. Trial Lawyers; mem. ABA, ATLA, Chgo. Bar Assn., Soc. Trial Lawyers, Trial Lawyers Club Chgo., Def. Rsch. Inst., Ill. Assn. Def. Trial Counsel, Product Liability Adv. Coun., Soc. Automotive Engrs., Assn. Advancement Automotive Medicine, Internat. Coun. Motorsport Scis., Mid-Day Club, Pi Kappa Delta, Phi Delta Phi. Republican. Roman Catholic. Office: Lord Bissell & Brook 115 S La Salle St Ste 3200 Chicago IL 60603-3972

BURKE, THOMAS MICHAEL, lawyer; b. Summit, N.J., Feb. 10, 1956; s. Robert William and Eleanor Mary (Kelley) B.; m. Nancy Robin Mogab, Sept. 24, 1983; children: Colleen Margaret, Michael Thomas, Brendan Robert. BA, Notre Dame U., 1978; JD, St. Louis U., 1981. Bar: Mo. 1981, Ill. 1982, U.S. Dist. Ct. (ea. dist.) 1981. Assoc. Moser, Marsalek, Carpenter, Cleary & Jaeckel, St. Louis, 1981-86; ptnr. Noonan & Burke, St. Louis, 1986-92; prin. Thomas M. Burke, PC, St. Louis, 1992—; bd. dirs. Legal Svcs. Ea. Mo., 1995-97. Active Vol. Lawyers program, St. Louis, St. Louis Hills Homeowner's Assn., 1984-94. Mem. Mo. Bar Assn., Ill. (bd. govs., 1998—), Bar Assn., Interest On Lawyers' Trust Accounts (bd. dirs. 1997—), Bar Assn. Met. St. Louis (trial sect. asst. chmn. 1987-89, chmn. bylaws and election com. 1989—, treas. 1992-93, sec. 1993-94, v.p. 1994-95, pres.-elect 1995-96, pres. 1996-97), St. Louis Bar Found. (sec. 1993-94, treas. 1995-96), Lawyers Assn. St. Louis (exec. com. 1987-92, sec. 1992-93). Office: 701 Market St Ste 1075 Saint Louis MO 63101-1886

BURKE, TIMOTHY FRANCIS, JR., lawyer. AB in Classics, Holy Cross Coll., 1970; JD, U. Pitts., 1973. Former estate tax atty. IRS; past capt. USAFR; assoc. Berkman Ruslander Pohl Lieber & Engel, ptnr.; ptnr. Klett Lieber Rooney & Scholring; now with Tener, Van Kirk, Wolf & Moore, Pitts.; adj. prof. estate planning sch. law U. Pitts.; lectr. Pa. Inst. CPAs, Pa. Bar. Inst., Pitts. Tax Conf. Past bd. dirs. Shady Lane Sch., Louis Child Care Ctr., Pitts. Dynamo Youth Soccer Assn.; mem. lawyers com. Pitts. Found.; mem. Desert Storm Meml. Fund Com., Greensburg Found.; lector St. Bede's Ch. Fellow Am. Coll. of Trust and Estate Counsel; mem. ABA (tax and real property, probate and trust law sect.), Pa. Bar Assn., Allegheny County Bar Assn. (probate and trust law sect. 1978—, coun. 1983—, vice chair 1990-92, chair 1992-94, jud. com., exec. com. 1996—, sec.-treas. 1997—), Pitts. Tax Club. Office: Tener Van Kirk Wolf & Moore 407 Oliver Ave Pittsburgh PA 15219-1806*

BURKE, TIMOTHY JOHN, lawyer; b. Syracuse, N.Y., June 5, 1946; s. Francis Joseph and Alice Marie Burke; m. Denise Kay Blied, Mar. 18, 1978; 1 child, Aimee Noel; 1 child from a previous marriage, Ryan Alexander. BA with distinction, Ariz. State U., 1967, JD cum laude, 1970. Bar: Ariz. 1970, U.S. Dist. Ct. Ariz. 1970, U.S. Ct. Appeals (9th cir.) 1974. Trial atty. Antitrust divsn. U.S. Dept. Justice, Washington, 1970-72, asst. to dir. ops., 1972-74; assoc. Fennemore Craig, Phoenix, 1974—, dir., 1978—; part-time instr. legal writing Ariz. State U., 1974-75. Mem. pabel rev. bd. Phoenix United Way, 1975-76; bd. dirs. Florence Crittenton Svcs., Phoenix, 1980-88, pres., 1985-87; bd. dirs. Law Soc. Ariz. State U. Coll. Law, 1991-97, Valley of Sn Cmtys. in Schs., 1995—. Recipient spl. commendation U.s. Dept. Justice, 1973. Fellow Am. Bar Found., Ariz. Bar Found.; m3m. ABA (antitrust and litigation sects., vice chmn. bus. torts and unfair competition com. 1996-98, chair 1998—, editor Bus. Torts and Unfair Competition Newsletter 1996—), FBA, Assn. Profl. Responsibility Lawyers (bd. dirs. 1993-98, pres. 1993-97), State Bar Ariz. (coun. antitrust sect., chmn. 1985-88, chmn. advt. com. 1992-94, ethics com. 1994—, chmn. 1995—), Maricopa County Bar Assn. Office: Fennemore Craig 3003 N Central Ave Ste 2600 Phoenix AZ 85012-2913

BURKE, WILLIAM A., broadcast executive. Pres. Turner Broadcasting Sys., Atlanta. Office: Turner Broadcasting Sys 1050 Techwood Dr NW Atlanta GA 30318-5604*

BURKE, WILLIAM TEMPLE, JR., lawyer; b. San Antonio, Oct. 30, 1935; s. William Temple and Adelaide H. (Raba) B.; m. Mary Sue Johnson, June 8, 1957; children: William Patrick, Michael Edmond, Karen Elizabeth. BBA, St. Mary's U., San Antonio, JD, 1961. Bar: Tex. 1961. Practice law Dallas; founder, pres. Burke Wright & Keiffer, P.C., 1985-98; of counsel Hance/Scarborough/Wright, 1998—. Pres., founder Greater Dallas Assn. KC, 1968-69; v.p., co-founder, dir. Tex. Cath. Credit Union, 1966-69, vice-chmn. bd. dirs., 1990-91 (Man of Yr., 1969-70); grand knight, trustee Dallas Coun. City 799 KC, 1964-69; v.p., dir. Dallas Optimists Club, 1965-66 (Mem. of Yr., 1966, Pres.'s award, 1968); dist. exemplar 4th degree KC, 1968-89; pres., dir. Dallas County Small Bus. Devel. Ctr., 1965-66; v.p. Dallas County Hist. Survey Com., 1966; pres. Dallas Mil. Govt. Assn., 1962-63; pres. men's club St. Patrick's Parish Roman Cath. Ch., 1963, prin. jr. H.S. Christian devel. program, 1970, chmn. scout troop com., 1976-78, chmn. fin. com., 1984-87, mem. bldg. com., 1978-87, chmn. bd. consultors, 1978-81; bd. dirs. Dallas County War on Poverty, 1965-66; trustee Montserrat Jesuit Retreat House, 1995—, treas., 1996-97; bd. dirs. The Montserrat Found., 1999—; vice-chmn. Cath. Commn. Appeal Diocese of Dallas, 1993-97. Served to 1st lt. AUS, 1958-60; capt. Res. ret. Fellow Tex. Bar Found., Coll. of State Bar Tex.; mem. ABA, Tex. Bar Assn., Dallas Bar Assn. (chmn. bankruptcy and comml. law sect. 1976-77, 86-87, courthouse liaison com. 1985—, lectr. 1985—), Am. Bankruptcy Inst., Dallas C. of C., Serra Internat. Met. Club (pres. Met. Dallas 1997-98, Outstanding Mem. award 1995), Internat. Order Alhambra (exemplar 1978-95), Phi Delta Phi (life), Tau Delta Sigma. Home: 9751 Larchcrest Dr Dallas TX 75238-2112 Office: 2900 Renaissance Cir Dallas TX 75287-5943

BURKE, WILLIAM THOMAS, law educator, lawyer; b. Brazil, Ind., Aug. 17, 1926. JD, U. Ind., 1953; JSD, Yale U., 1959. Bar: Ind. 1953. Rsch. assoc. and lectr. Yale U., 1956-62; assoc. prof. Ohio State U., 1962-64, prof., 1964-68; prof. U. Wash. Sch. Law, Seattle, 1968—; mem. adv. com. Law of Sea Task Force, Dept. State; mem. A217 Ocean Policy Com., Nat. Acad. Scis. Author: (with M. S.McDougal) The Public Order of the Oceans, 1962; Contemporary Legal Problems in Ocean Development, 1969; (with Legatski and Woodhead) National and International Law Enforcement in the Ocean, 1975, The New International Law of Fisheries, 1994, International Law of the Sea-Documents and Notes, 1997. Office: U Wash Sch Law Condon Hall Seattle WA 98105

BURKEE, IRVIN, artist; b. Kenosha, Wis., Feb. 6, 1918; s. Omar Lars and Emily (Quardokas) B.; diploma Sch. of Art Inst. Chgo., 1945; m. Bonnie May Ness, Apr. 12, 1945; children: Brynn, Jill, Peter (dec.), Ian (dec.). Owner, silversmith, goldsmith Burkee Jewelry, Blackhawk, Colo., 1950-57; painter, sculptor, Aspen, Colo., 1957-78, Cottonwood, Ariz., Pietrasanta, Italy, 1978—; instr. art U. Colo., 1946, 50-53, Stephens Coll., Columbia, Mo., 1947-49. John Quincy Adams travel fellow, Mex., 1945. Executed copper mural of human history of Colo. for First Nat. Bank, Englewood, Colo., 1970, copper mural of wild birds of Kans. for Ranchmart State Bank, Overland Park, Kans., 1974; exhibited Art Inst. Chgo., Smithsonian Instn. (award 1957), Milw. Art Inst., Krannert Mus., William Rockhill Nelson Gallery, St. Louis Art Mus., Denver Art Mus.; represented in southwestern galleries, also pvt. collections throughout U.S.; work illustrated in books Design and Creation of Jewelry, Design through Discovery, Walls. Mem. Nat. Sculpture Soc., Sedona Chamber Music Soc.; printer, pub. White Tanks Press. Address: PO Box 5361 Lake Montezuma AZ 86342-5361

BURKE-FANNING, MADELEINE, artist; b. New Orleans, Feb. 12, 1941; d. Henry Raymond Burke Sr. and Ella Mae Falgout-Burke; children: Denise Angele Duizend-Glenn, Michele Renee Duizend-Meyer, Jeanne Monet Duizend-Fillman; m. Joel Cornell Fanning, Mar. 28, 1981. Student, Pensacola (Fla.) Jr. Coll., 1988-96. coord. New Orleans World Trade Ctr., Pensacola Cultural Ctr.; adj. prof. advanced watercolor Pensacola Jr. Coll.; tchr., workshops. One-woman shows include Michele Dion Gallery, 1994, Soho Gallery, 1994, Wise Choice Gallery, 1996, The Wright Place, 1997, Awakenings, Gulf Breeze, Fla., 1997-98, The Shoppe Gallery, 1998, Pensacola Mus. Art, 1998, Adams Street Gallery, 1998, Ducks Unltd., Pensacola, 1998, Right Angles Gallery, Pensacola, 1999, Kate Holmes-Branton Gallery, Pensacola, 1999; exhibited in group shows including Pensacola Jr. Coll., 1988-96, Gnu Zoo, 1995, 96, Pensacola Regional Airport, 1996, World Trade Ctr., 1996, Schmidt's Gallery, 1996, Pensacola Cultural Ctr., 1997, Adams Street Gallery, 1998, Artel Gallery, 1999, Right Angles Gallery, Pensacola, 1999, ARTEL, Inc., Art with an Edge; host TV show Art and Healing, 1997. Art judge Just Say No Program, 1996-97, PTA Reflective Program, 1997-98; art chairwoman Pensacola chpt. Ducks Unltd., 1998; instr. Ctr. Ind. Living, Pensacoloa, 1998-99. Recipient Rockport Pubs. award of distinction for inclusion in Best of Watercolor: Painting Texture, 1997. Mem. Am. Soc. Portrait Artists, Nat. Mus. Women in Arts, Fla. Watercolor Soc., La. Watercolor Soc., Tallahassee Watercolor Soc., Pensacola Mus. Art, Woodbine Figure Painters, Bay Cliff Watercolor Soc. (founder), Artel.Art with an Edge. Avocations: gardening, reading, travel, sailing, photography. Home and Studio: Palm Cottage Studio 4160 Rommitch Ln Pensacola FL 32504-4490

BURKERT, ROBERT RANDALL, artist; b. Racine, Wis., Aug. 20, 1930; s. Clarence George and Margaret Ann (Sorenson) B.; m. Nancy Ekholm, Aug. 29, 1953; children: Claire, Rand. BS., U. Wis., 1952, M.S., 1955. Instr. art Denison U., 1955-56; prof. drawing, printmaking, painting U. Wis., Milw., 1956-92, prof. emeritus, 1993—. One-man shows include Bradley Galleries, Milw. (8 shows), 1972-86, Rubiner Galleries, Milw. (6 shows), 1973-85, Posner Galler, Milw., 1990, 93, Retrospective, U. of Wis., Milw., 1994, others; group shows include Pratt Graphic Ctr., 1972, U.S. Cultural Ctr., Tel Aviv, 1973, Milw. Art Mus., 1975, 30 Yr. Retrospective, Wustum Mus., Racine, Wis., 1985; represented in permanent collections Tate Gallery, London, Boston Mus. Fine Arts, Met. Mus. Art, Phila. Mus., numerous others; wall mural Road to Country, 1972, wall mural Butterflies, 1986; work reproduced in Artist Proof, 1971, Compleat Printmaker, 1973, Art of the Print, 1976, 100 Years of American Printmaking, 1983, 150 Years of Wis. Printmaking, 1998; directed and produces "Colors of Change" documentary video, 1994. Former trustee Milw. Art Mus. Recipient numerous awards for prints, drawings and paintings; U. Wis. research grantee, 1969, 71, 73, 75, 77; Knapp grantee for ednl. research, 1973, Wis. Arts grantee, 1977; Fromkin grantee, 1980; recipient Gov.'s Print Commn., 1985. Home: PO Box 858 East Orleans MA 02643-0858

BURKET, GEORGE EDWARD, JR., retired family physician; b. Kingman, Kans., Dec. 10, 1912; s. George Edward and Jessie May (Talbert) B.; m. Mary Elizabeth Wallace, Nov. 12, 1938; children: George Edward III, Carol Sue, Elizabeth Christine. Student, Wichita State U., 1930-33; MD, U. Kans., 1937. Diplomate Am. Bd. Family Practice (pres. 1975-77). Intern Santa Barbara (Calif.) Gen. Hosp., 1937-38, resident, 1938-39; grad. asst. in surgery Mass. Gen. Hosp., Boston, 1955-56; practice medicine Kingman, 1939-73; preceptor in medicine U. Kans. Med. Sch., 1950-73, assoc. prof., 1973-78, clin. prof., 1978-84; bd. dirs. Kingman Savings and Loan Assn. Contbr. articles to profl. jours. Mem. Kingman Bd. Edn., 1946-58; mem. Kans. State Bd. Health, 1960-66. Mem. AMA, Kans. Med. Soc. (pres. 1966-67), Am. Acad. Family Physicians (pres. 1967-68, John Walsh Founders award 1979), Inst. Medicine (sr.), Assn. Am. Med. Colls., Soc. Tchrs. Family Medicine, Alpha Omega Alpha. Republican. Episcopalian. Clubs: Garden of Gods (Colorado Springs, Colo.); Wichita Country, Wichita. Lodges: Masons, Shriners. Home: Larksfield Pl V-208 7373 E 29th St N Wichita KS 67226-3405

BURKETT, GERALD ARTHUR, lawyer, musician; b. Oklahoma City, Apr. 23, 1939; s. Francis Gerald and Leta Carey (Weaver) B.; m. Carolyn Ruth Hicks, Aug. 7, 1960; 1 child, Debora Lynne Burkett Nutt. BA, David Lipscomb U., 1962; MA, Peabody Coll., 1967; JD, Nashville Sch. of Law, 1974. Bar: Tenn. 1975, U.S. Dist. Ct. (mid. dist.) Tenn., 1976, U.S. Ct. Appeals (6th cir.), 1977, U.S. Tax Ct., 1981, U.S. Supreme Ct. 1993. Leader Fritz's German Band, Nashville, 1972-97; pvt. practice law office Nashville, 1975—; adj. instr. Vol. State Community Coll., Gallatin, Tenn., 1979-93, Nashville State Tech. Inst., 1984-89; band leader Strohaus, 1982 World's Fair, Knoxville, 1982. Conductor of German band for commls. and concerts including Monday Night Football, 1994, Super Bowl, 1995, Oktoberfest Concert, Soldier Field, Chgo., 1995. Accordionist Charlie Rich's Bi-Centennial Album, 1976, film soundtrack Sweet Dreams, 1983. Mem. Nashville Assn. Musicians, Alliance Francaise (treas. 1985-86), Nashville Bar Assn., Tenn. Assn. of Spanish Spkg. Attys., Phi Delta Kappa (treas. 1967-68). Mem. Ch. of Christ. Avocations: travel, foreign languages. Office: Ste 610 Stahlman Bldg 211 Union St Nashville TN 37201

BURKETT, HELEN, artist; b. Washington, Feb. 15, 1942; d. Harding Theodore and Helen Louise (Torris) B.; m. J.D. Collins, Sept. 1, 1961 (Apr. 16, 1975); children: Mark W. Collins, Donna L. Collins; m. Charles Talbot Marshall, Dec. 24, 1975; 1 child, Gabrielle T. Marshall. Student, Strayer Sch. of Bus., 1960-61, Corcoran Sch. of Art, 1968-69, Md. U., 1970-73, Hilton Leech Studio-Gallery, 1976-80, Ringling Sch. Art, 1980-81. Asst. to dir. Hilton Leech Studio, Sarasota, Fla., 1975-80, workshop organizer, figure study coord., 1978-80; demonstrator, tchr., artist, owner/operator Helen Burkett Studios, Sarasota, Fla., 1975—; juror Ann Arbor St. Art Fair, 1998. One person show at Manatee Jr. Coll., 1984, Ctrl. Fla. C.C., Ocala, 1987, State Capitol, Tallahassee, Fla., Divsn. Cultural Affairs, Sec. State Offices, 1997; exhibited in group show at Watercolor Soc. Show, Thousand Oaks, Calif., 1999; permanent exhibits include Ctrl. Fla. C.C., Ocala, Epsom Clinic, Orlando, Fla., Orlando Sentinel, Winter Park (Fla.) Meml. Hosp., Polk Mus., Lakeland, Fla., The Disney Corp., The Ford Motor Co., The Amoco Corp., Fla. Dept. State; exhibitor numerous art festivals, 1987—; subject of periodical The Artist Mag., 1992, The Am. Artist Mag., 1996, also newspaper article Ann Arbor News, 1998. Tchr. Vis. Artist Program, Coconut Grove, Fla., 1990—; artist, tchr. Donne Bitner Studio, Cocoa Beach, Fla., 1996. Recipient 2d prize in watercolor U. Tampa, 1991, 93, 1st prize in watercolor Lowe Art Mus./U. Miami, 1992, Purchase award Festival of the Masters-Disney Corp., 1995, Purchase award Wayne State U.-Ford Motor Co., 1995. Mem. ACLU, NOW, Am. Watercolor Soc. (assoc.), Nat. Watercolor Soc. (assoc.), Nat. Assn. Ind. Artists, Sarasota Art Assn. (bd. dirs. 1980-82), Fla. Watercolor Soc. (life, Award of Distinction 1985, 92), So. Watercolor Soc., Mich. Guild Artists. Avocations: photography, reading, hiking, bicycling. Home and Studio: Helen Burkett Studio 2988 Oak St Sarasota FL 34237-7346

BURKETT, JOHN DAVID, professional baseball player; b. New Brighton, Pa., Nov. 28, 1964. With San Francisco Giants, 1987-94, Fla. Marlins, 1995-96, Tex. Rangers, 1996—. Mem. Nat. League All-Star Team, 1993. Office: Tex Rangers 1000 Ballpark Way Arlington TX 76011-5168

BURKETT, LAWRENCE V., insurance company executive. BA, U. Va., 1967, JD, 1973. Bar: Mass. 1974. V.p., assoc. gen. counsel Mass. Mut. Life Ins. Co., Springfield, 1984-88, sr. v.p., assoc. gen. counsel, 1988-92, exec. v.p., gen. counsel, 1993—. Office: Mass Mutual Life Ins Co 1295 State St Springfield MA 01111-0002

BURKETT, NEWTON JONES, III, broadcast journalist; b. Orange, N.J., May 6, 1962; s. Newton Jones Jr. and Barbara R. (Alley) B.; m. Margaret Mary Rice, Aug. 27, 1988; 1 child, Newton Jones IV. BA, Columbia Coll., 1984, MA, 1985. Newswriter WNEW-TV News, N.Y.C., 1983-85; reporter WFSB-TV News, Hartford, Conn., 1986-89, WABC-TV News, N.Y.C., 1989—. Recipient Emmy nomination, 1997, 98; recipient Outstanding Achievement award N.Y. State Broadcasters Assn., 1991. Mem. NATAS, N.Y. Yacht Club, Seawanhaka Corinthian Yacht Club. Avocation: sailing, yacht racing. Office: WABC-TV News 7 Lincoln Square New York NY 10023

BURKETT, RANDY JAMES, lighting designer; b. DuBois, Pa., Nov. 12, 1955; s. Lloyd John and Helen Louise (North) B.; m. Carol Jeanne Collins, Aug. 22, 1981; 1 child, Meredith. B in Archtl. Engring., Pa. State U., 1978. Application engr. Johns-Manville, Denver, 1978-80; lighting designer HOK, St. Louis, 1980-82, assoc., 1982-85, v.p., 1986-88; pres. Randy Burkett Lighting Design, Inc., St. Louis, 1988—. Contbr. articles to profl. jours. Recipient Internat. Illumination Design Award of Excellence, 1987, 89, 93, 96, Edison award, 1993. Mem. Illuminating Engring. Soc., Internat. Assn. Lighting Designers (pres. 1996-97). Home: 5334 Chapelford Ln Saint Louis MO 63119-5017 Office: Randy Burkett Lighting Design Inc 127 Kenrick Plz Ste 207 Saint Louis MO 63119-4416

BURKETT, ROBERT L., investment company executive; b. Sept. 8, 1945. BA, NYU, 1968; JD, Boston U. Law Sch., 1971. V.p. pub. affairs Embassy Comms., L.A., 1984-86; sr. v.p. corp. affairs Interscope Comms., L.A., 1986-92; pres. The Burkett Group, L.A., 1992—; pres. strategic devel. Gilman Investment Co., N.Y.C., 1995—. E-mail: bburkett@gilman.com.

BURKETT, THOMAS O., manufacturing executive. Pres. Goodman Mfg. Co., Houston, 1995—. *

BURKETT, WILLIAM ANDREW, banker; b. nr. Herman, Nebr., July 1, 1913; s. William H. and Mary (Dill) B.; m. Juliet Ruth Johnson, Oct. 5, 1940 (dec. Mar. 1976); children: Juliet Ann Burkett Hooker, Katherine C. Burkett Congdon, William Cleveland; m. Nancy Schallert Morrow, June 20, 1992. Student, U. Nebr., 1931-32, Creighton U. Law Sch., 1932-33; LL.B., U. Omaha, 1936. Exec. trainee Bank Am., 1937-38; Sr. spl. agt., intelligence unit Treasury Dept., 1945-50; exec. v.p. Calif. Employers Assn. Group, Sacramento, 1950-53; dir. Calif. Dept. Employment, 1953-55; chmn. Calif. Employment Stabilization Commn., 1953-55; supt. banks, chmn. Dept. Investments Calif., 1955-59; dir. Liquidation Yokohama Specie Bank; also Sumitomo Bank, San Francisco, 1955-59; cons. Western Bancorp, San Francisco, 1959-61; chmn. bd., pres. Security Nat. Bank Monterey County, Monterey-Carmel, Calif., 1961-66, Burkett Land Co., Monterey, 1966—; chmn. bd. Securities Properties Corp., Monterey; witness Calif. Crime Com., U.S. Senate Kefauver Crime Com., 1950-52, U.S. Congress Banking Com., 1991; nat. chmn., founder Bank Savs. & Loan Depositor's League, 1991. Author: Mount Rushmore National Memorial's History of America, 1776-1904, 1971. Elected nominee Nebr. Sec. State, 1936; witness Calif. Crime Commn. and U.S. Senate Kefauver Crime Commn., 1950-52, U.S. Congress Banking Com., 1991; dir. banking and investments, cabinet gov., Calif., 1953-59; dir. Calif. Emergency Manpower Commn., 1953-55; chmn. Gov. Calif. Com. Refugee Relief, 1953-55; mem. Calif. Securities Commn., 1955-59; mem. financial bd. Pine Manor Jr. Coll., Chestnut Hill, Mass., 1967—; mem. Monterey County Hist. Commn., Nat. Trust Found., Royal Oak Found.; bd. dirs. Monterey Symphony Assn.; chmn. bd. trustees Nat. Hist. Found.; trustee Monterey Mus. Art, Bishop Kip Sch., Carmel Valley, Calif.; co-chmn., trustee Mt. Rushmore Hall of Records Commn., 1987; mem. adv. bd. Robert Louis Stevenson Sch., Pebble Beach, Calif., 1971-74, candidate for gov. Calif., 1978 . Served as officer USCGR, 1943-45. Mem. Am., Calif., Ind. bankers assns., Nat. Assn. Supts. State Banks (pres. 1958-59), Monterey History and Art Assn., Mt. Rushmore Nat. Meml. Soc. (life mem., trustee), Amvets (dept. comdr. Calif. 1947, nat. vice comdr. 1948), Soc. Calif. Pioneers, Bank and Savs. and Loan Depositor's League (nat. chmn. 1991—), Monterey Peninsula Mus. Art, Mt. Rushmore Hall of Records Commn. Inc. (nat. co-chmn.1990—). Episcopalian. Clubs: Monterey Peninsula Golf and Country (Pebble Beach), Beach and Tennis (Pebble Beach), Stillwater Yacht (Pebble Beach); Carmel Valley Golf and Tennis; Commonwealth (San Francisco), Rotary (San Francisco); Sutter Lawn (Sacramento). Home: PO Box 726 Pebble Beach CA 93953-0726 Office: Viscaino Rd Pebble Beach CA 93953

BURKEY, FREDERICK D., lawyer. BS, Fla. State U., 1985; JD, Mercer U. Law clk. Hon. Bryant Huff Gwinnett County Superior Ct., Lawrenceville, Ga., 1990-92; asst. county atty. Gwinnett county Law Dept., Lawrenceville, Ga., 1992-94; ptnr. Burkey & Burkey, Roswell, Ga., 1994—. Mem. Assn. Trial Lawyers Am., Ga. Trial Lawyers Assn., Atlanta Bar Assn., North Fulton Bar Assn. (bd. dirs. 1994-99). Office: Burkey & Burkey 770 Old Roswell Pl Ste B100 Roswell GA 30076

BURKEY, LEE MELVILLE, lawyer; b. Beach, N.D., Mar. 21, 1914; s. Levi Melville and Mina Lou (Horner) B.; m. Lorraine Lillian Burghardt, June 11, 1938; 1 child, Lee Melville, III. B.A., U. Ill., 1936, M.A., 1938; J.D. with honor, John Marshall Law Sch., 1943. Bar: Ill., 1944, U.S. Dist. Ct., 1947, U.S. Ct. Appeals, 1954, U.S. Supreme Ct.; 1983; cert. secondary tchr., Ill. Tchr. Princeton Twp. High Sch., Princeton, Ill., 1937-38, Thornton Twp. High Sch., Harvey, Ill., 1938-43; atty. Office of Solicitor, U.S. Dept. Labor, Chgo., 1944-51; ptnr. Asher, Gubbins & Segall and successor firms, Chgo., 1951-94; of counsel, 1995—; lectr. bus. law Roosevelt Coll., 1949-52; chmn. bd. dirs., pres. West Suburban Fin. Corp., 1975-94. Contbr. numerous articles on lie detector evidence. Trustee, Village of La Grange, Ill., 1962-68, mayor, 1968-73, village atty., 1973-87; commr., pres. Northeastern Ill. Planning Commn., Chgo., 1969-73; mem. bd. dirs. United Ch. Christ, Bd. of Homeland Ministries, 1981-87; mem. exec. com. Cook County Coun. Govts., 1968-70; life mem. La Grange Area Hist. Soc.; bd. dirs. Better Bus. Bur. Met. Chgo., Inc., 1975-82, Plymouth Place, Inc., 1973-82; mem. exec. bd., v.p. S.W. Suburban Ctr. on Aging, 1993—. Brevet 2nd Lt. Ill. Nat. Guard, 1932. Recipient Disting. Alumnus award John Marshall Law Sch., 1973, Good Citizenship medal S.A.R., 1973, Patriot medal S.A.R., 1977, meritorious Service award Am. Legion Post 1941, 1974, Honor award LaGrange Area Hist. Soc., 1987; col. Ky., 1989. Fellow Coll. Labor and Employment Lawyers (charter); mem. ABA (coun., sect. labor and employment law 1982-86, governance officer 1986-96), Ill. Bar Assn., Chgo. Bar Assn., SAR (state pres. 1977), S.R., La Grange Country Club, Masons, Order of John Marshall, Theta Delta Chi. Mem. United Ch. of Christ. Office: 125 S Wacker Dr Chicago IL 60606-4402

BURKHALTER, SUSAN SHIVELY, music educator, organist; b. Washington, Apr. 16, 1946; d. William Mays and Thelma Louise (Kanatzer) B.; m. Curtis Allen Shively, Feb. 5, 1977; children: Rachel Mirabel, Stuart William. MusB, Coll. Wooster, 1970. Organist, choir dir. Olivet Episcopal Ch., Springfield, Va., 1976-77; children's choir dir. Our Savior Lutheran Ch. and Sch., Arlington, Va., 1997-1998; pvt. piano tchr., freelance organist, 1976—; advisor music majs. Coll. Wooster, Ohio, 1995—. Contbr. mags. and newspapers including Washington Post, American Organist, Psychology Today, and more; performer in various concerts. Vol. Carderock Springs Elem. Sch., Bethesda, Md., 1989-95, Pyle Middle Sch., 1995—; mem. Sierra Club, ASPCA, World Wildlife Fund, African Wildlife Fund. Mem. Music Tchrs. Nat. Assn., Carderock Springs Swim and Tennis Club. Democrat. Presbyterian, Episcopalian. Avocations: cats, sewing, gardening, art, writing poetry. Home: 7504 Hamilton Spring Rd Bethesda MD 20817-4542

BURKHARDT, ANN, occupational therapist, clinical educator; b. Providence, Dec. 21, 1954; d. Kenneth Ralph and Betty Jane (Neale) B. BA in Psychobiology, Wheaton Coll., 1976; MA in Occupl. Therapy, NYU, 1979. Lic. occupl. therapist, N.Y., R.I., Mass. Staff therapist Charlton Meml. Hosp., Fall River, Mass., 1979; staff therapist, sr. therapist Columbia U.-Harlem Hosp., N.Y.C., 1979-84; staff therapist, burn specialist Cornell Med. Ctr.-N.Y. Hosp., N.Y.C., 1984-86; dir. occupl. therapy Greater Harlem Nursing Home, N.Y.C., 1986-87; chief occupl. therapist Meml. Sloan-Kettering Cancer Ctr., N.Y.C., 1987-92; asst. dir. occupl. therapy Columbia-Presbyn. Med. Ctr., N.Y.C., 1992—; clin. instr. Columbia U., N.Y.C., 1993—; pvt. practice N.Y.C., 1984—; del. Coll. of Occupl. Therapists, Edinburgh, Scotland, 1995, World Fedn. Occupl. Therapists, London, 1994, Montreal, Can., 1998; spkr. in field. Co-author: Occupational Therapy Intervention in Recreational Settings in Acute Care, 1993, Stroke Rehabilitaton: A Junction Based Approach, 1997; (pamphlet) Lymphedema: Self-Care and Treatment, 1992; co-author: A Therapists Guide to Oncology, 1996; contbr. articles to profl. jours.; columnist O.T. Week, The Sacred Fire Newsletter. Svc. award Touro Coll., N.Y., 1996. Mem. Am. Occupl. Therapy Assn. (cert., alt. rep. to rep. assembly 1992-94, polit. action com. 1994, Recognition of Achievement award 1997, Svc. award 1997), N.Y. State Occupl. Therapy Assn. (alt. rep. 1992-94, pres.-elect. 1994-95, pres. 1995—, Merit award 1990, Svc. award), Metro N.Y. Dist. Occupl. Therapy Assn. (bd. dirs., sec. 1990-96, Abren award 1998), Am. Congress Rehab. Medicine, N. Am. Soc. Lymphology, Internat. Soc. Lymphology, Am. Phys. Medicine, Am. Soc. Assn. Execs., Am. Med. Writers Assn., Am. Burn Assn., Congress of Rehab. Medicine. Avocations: kyacking, singing, theater going, traveling, writing. Home: 160 E 91st St Apt 4B New York NY 10128-2458 Office: Milstein Hosp Bldg 8 Garden North 405 177 Fort Washington Ave New York NY 10032-3713

BURKHARDT, CHARLES HENRY, professional society executive, author, lecturer, consultant; b. Bklyn., June 17, 1915; s. Adolph Michael and Mildred (Herman) B.; m. Lillian Sanders, Jan. 31, 1942; children: Gregory Charles, Christopher Michael. BS, St. John's U., 1938; postgrad., Pratt Inst., 1947-48. Svc. mgr., asst. sales mgr. Concord Oil Corp., N.Y.C., 1939-43; instr. heat engring. Walter Hervey Jr. Coll., N.Y.C., 1947-49; dir. edn. Perfex Corp., Milw., 1949-51; gen. mgr. Paragon Maintenance Co., Mineola, N.Y., 1951-55; mng. dir., sec.-treas. Oil Heat Inst. Am., N.Y.C., 1955-60; v.p. Nat. Oil Fuel Inst., N.Y.C., 1960-62; exec. v.p. New England Fuel Inst., Boston, 1962-81, pres., 1981-86; cons. Std. Oil Co. N.J., 1957-58, Bacharach Instrument Co., 1947, Richfield Mfg. Co., 1948, Arthur D. Little Inc., Global Petroleum Inc., Centennial and Atlantic Mutual Ins. Cos., Scully Signal Co., Nutter, McClennan & Fish, Boston, Rich, May, Bilodeau & Flaherty, Boston, Hinshaw, Culbertson, Moelmann, Hoban & Fuller, Chgo., CNA Ins. Co., New London (Conn.) Mut. Ins. Co., Sentry Ins. Co., Liberty Mut. Ins. Co., Robins, Kaplan, Miller and Ciresi, Minn., Morrison, Mahoney and Miller; mem. fuel oil mktg. adv. com. U.S. Dept. Energy, residential conservation task force; del. New England Energy Congress, 1978, White House Conf. on Small Bus.; chmn. fuel oil marketers' fin. viability task force SBA; mem. Mass. state residential conservation adv. com. Author: Residential and Commercial Air Conditioning, 1959, Baseboard Heating, 1952, Domestic and Commercial Oil Burners, 1969. The Oil Heating Technician, 1957. Trustee St. Elizabeth's Hosp., Brighton, Mass., 1985-89; nat. coord. Oil Heat Centennial Celebration, 1985; pres. New Eng. Fuel Inst. Edn. Found., 1983-86, cons., 1987-90; chmn. Prudential Ctr. Residents Assn., 1989-91; chmn. Ea. Region Enablement Coun., Dominican Sisters, Louisville, 1992-94; established Charles H. Burkhardt $500,000 Rsch. Fund for Macular Degeneration Rsch., Mass. Eye & Ear Infirmary, Boston, 1999. Capt. AUS, 1943-46. Decorated knight Equestrian Order Holy Sepulchre, Jerusalem, 1986; recipient Disting. Achievement award New Eng. Oil Heat Industry, 1972, certs. of commendation Conn. Petroleum Assn., 1974, 80, Oil Man of New Eng. award Better Home Heat Coun. N.H., 1975, cert. of appreciation Soc. Mfg. Engrs., 1976, 15th Anniversary commendation New Eng. Fuel Isnt., 1977, Man of Yr. award Met. Energy Coun., 1984; commd. hon. Ky. Col., 1994. Mem. ASHRAE (life), ASTM, Am. Soc. Assn. Execs., Nat. Soc. Bus. Economists, Mass. Oil Heat Coun. (hon. life). Republican. Roman Catholic. Home: 770 Boylston St Apt 23B Boston MA 02199-7720

BURKHARDT, DOLORES ANN, library consultant; b. Meriden, Conn., July 28, 1932; d. Frederick Christian and Emily (Detels) Burkhardt; B.A., U. Conn., 1955; M.S., So. Conn. State Coll., 1960; postgrad. Cen. Wash. State Coll., 1962, Columbia, 1964—; 6th yr. diploma U. Conn., 1972. Asst. librarian So. Conn. State Coll. Library, summers 1960, 62; sch. library tchr. Farmington High Sch., Unionville, Conn., 1955-65; library cons.; media specialist East Farms Sch., Farmington, Conn., 1967-70; sch. library coordinator K-12, Durham-Middlefield, Conn., 1970-72; media specialist regional dist. 10, Burlington-Harwinton, Conn., 1972-78; ednl. media cons., 1978—. Instr. Boston U. Media Inst. Spl. cons. Conn. Dept. Edn., 1965—. Mem. AAUW (sec. 1956-58), NEA, Conn. Edn. Assn., New Eng. (pres. 1969-70), Conn. (2d v.p. 1965—, chmn. sch. library devel.; chmn. standards com. 1970-72, chmn. instructional materials selection policy com. Region 10) sch. library assns., Am. Assn. Sch. Librarians, New Eng. Sch. Devel. Council, Phi Delta Kappa. Lutheran. Home and Office: 812 Savage St Southington CT 06489-4629

BURKHARDT, EDWARD ARNOLD, transportation company executive; b. N.Y.C., July 23, 1938; s. Edward Arnold Burkhardt Sr. and Kathryn C. (Pfister) Dow; m. Sandra Kay Schwaegel, June 9, 1967; 1 child, Cynthia Kay. BS Indsl. Adminstrn., Yale U., 1960. Various operating positions Wabash R.R., St. Louis, 1960-64, Norfolk and Western Rlwy., St. Louis, 1964-67; asst. to gen. mgr. Chgo. Northwestern Transp. Co., 1967-68, gen. supt. transp., 1968-70, asst. v.p. transp., 1970-76, v.p. mktg., 1976-79, v.p. transp., 1979-87; bd. dirs., chmn., pres., CEO Wis. Ctrl. Transp. Corp., Chgo., 1987—, also bd. dirs.; chmn. Tranz Rail Ltd., 1993—; pres. Algoma Ctrl. Rlwy. Inc., 1995—, also bd. dirs.; chmn., CEO English, Welsh & Scottish Railway Ltd., 1995—; bd. dirs., chmn. Australian Transport Network, 1997—. Trustee Village of Kenilworth, Ill., 1984-93; bd. dirs. Wheeling & Lake Erie Rlwy. Co., Nat. Transport Mus., York, England, Lake Superior Mus. Transp., Duluth, Minn., John W. Barringer R.R. Libr., St. Louis, U.S./New Zealand Coun., Washington. Hon. consul New Zealand, Chgo. Mem. Am. Assn. R.R. Supts., Nat. Freight Transp. Assn., Western Ry. Club , Kenilworth Club, Union League Club. Republican. Episcopalian. Home: 573 Earlston Rd Kenilworth IL 60043-1014 Office: Wis Cen Transp Corp PO Box 5062 Rosemont IL 60017-5062

BURKHARDT, FREDERICK HENRY, editor; b. Bklyn., Sept. 13, 1912. BA, Columbia U., 1933; B of Litt., Oxford U., 1935; PhD, Columbia U., 1940, LLD (hon.); LLD (hon.), Mich. U., Ball State U. Instr., asst. prof. philosophy U. Wis., Madison, 1937-43, assoc. prof. philosophy, 1946-47; pres. Bennington (Vt.) Coll., 1947-57, Am. Coun. Learned Socs., N.Y.C., 1957-74; gen. editor The Works of William James, 19 vols. Harvard Press, 1975-88; editor The Corr. of Charles Darwin, 11 vols. sponsored by ACLS and Cambridge U. Libr., 1985—; rsch. analyst Office of Strategic Svcs., 1943-45; acting chief Divsn. Rsch. for Europe, Dept. State, 1945-46; dep. dir. Office Pub. Affairs, U.S. High Commr. for Germany, 1950-51; mem. N.Y.C. Bd. Higher Edn., 1966-73, chmn., 1969-71; trustee N.Y. Pub. Libr., 1970-71, chmn., 1974; chmn. Nat. Commn. on Librs. and Info. Svcs., 1971-78. Editor, translator: God, Some Conversation on Spinoza's System, 1940, 62; editor: Cleavage in Our Culture, 1952; contbr., editor: The Comparative Reception of Darwinism, 1975. Lt. USNR, 1944-46. Recipient Alumni award for excellence Columbia U., 1987, Morton N. Cohen award for disting. edition of letters MLA, 1991. Mem. Am. Philos. Soc., Am. Acad. Arts and Scis., Century Assn. E-mail:fhb@sover.net. Home and Office: 137 Monument Ave Ext Bennington VT 05201

BURKHARDT, RONALD ROBERT, advertising executive; b. Jackson, Mich., July 25, 1948; s. Robert Edward and Lois Jeane (Ordway) B. AA, Jackson C.C., 1968; BBA in Advt., Western Mich. U., 1970. Copywriter, producer Campbell-Ewald Co., Detroit, 1973-75; sr. writer Cargill-Wilson & Acree/DDB, Atlanta, 1976-78; sr. v.p., creative dir. Flemister & Burkhardt, Atlanta, 1978-80; sr. writer Bozell & Jacobs, N.Y.C., 1980-81, Young & Rubicam, N.Y.C., 1981-84; v.p., creative group head Lowe-Marschalk, N.Y.C., 1984-86; chmn., CEO, exec. creative dir., ptnr. Burkhardt & Christy Advt., Inc., N.Y.C., 1986-95; CEO, creative dir., ptnr. Burkhardt & Hillman, Ltd., N.Y.C., 1995—; pro bono cons. mayor's office N.Y.C.; judge Clios, Internat. TV and Film Festival N.Y., CEBA Awards, Andy Awards, Stephen Kelly Awards, Addy Awards, Mercury Radio Awards, N.Y. Festivals. Contbr. articles to profl. jours. including Adweek, AdAge. Mem. exec. com. N.Y. Korean Vets. Meml. Commn. Recipient more than 200 awards including Andy award Advt. Club, 1978, 79-93, 85-89, Clio award, 1983, 85, 87-88, 90-91, 92-93, award Art Dirs. Club, 1983, 85, 87-89, 94, N.Y. Internat. Festivals, 1989-95, Gold Addy award, 1983, 89, 91, Creativity award 1988-94, 96, 97, Graphics Ann. award, 1992, Mobius Gold, 1991, 95, 96, Black Book award, 1993, Telly statue, 1990-91, 92-93, 94-95. Mem. One Club for Art and Copy (award 1976, 78, 80, 82,84, 86, 89, 93, Comm. Arts Advt. Ann. award 1995, Effie Silver award 1997, Effie Gold award 1998). Republican. Avocations: skiing, tennis, motorcycling, baseball, karate. Office: Burkhardt & Hillman Ltd 145 E 57th St New York NY 10022-2141 *Intensity of purpose is the force that fuels energy, and makes life a relentless series of powerful achievements.*

BURKHART, DENNIS LLOYD, artist, illustrator; b. Lancaster, Pa., July 20, 1952; s. Lloyd Henry and Anna Laura (Lefevre) B.; m. Joan Rachel Harbison, Apr. 18, 1980; 1 child, Charity Leigh. Student, York Acad. Art. Tchr., instr. Pa. Sch. Art and Design, Lancaster, 1984-98; owner, mgr. D.L. Burkhart/Illustrations. Illustrator over 1000 postage stamp designs for 22 fgn. countries, 1992—, giftware illustrations for world-wide marketed designs, 1992-98. Democrat. Avocations: hunting, fishing. Office: 55 Wood Duck Ln Wrightsville PA 17368

BURKHART, GLENN RANDALL, corporate internal auditor; b. Reading, Pa., May 31, 1947; s. V. Russel and Dorothy (Heist) B.; m. Linda Marie Kanas, Sept. 1, 1978; children: Christopher S. Heffner, Melissa L. Heffner, Tiffany Anne Burkhart. BA in Econs., Muhlenberg Coll., 1973. Cert. Bank Auditor, Cert. Fin. Svcs. Auditor, Pa. Asst. EDP auditor Merchants Nat. Bank, N.A., Allentown, Pa., 1973-75, audit mgr., 1975-79; auditor Cement Nat. Bank, Northampton, Pa., 1979-80; audit mgr. First Nat. Bank of Allentown, 1980-84; regional audit mgr. Meridian Bancorp, Reading, Pa., 1984-85; corp. auditor Vista Bancorp, Phillipsburg, N.J., 1985—, compliance officer, 1987-93. With U.S. Army, 1966-68. Mem. Nat. Soc. Cert. Fin. Svcs. Auditors (cert.), Lehigh Valley Amateur Astron. Soc., Inst. Internal Auditors, Nat. Soc. Cert. Bank Auditors, Am. Bankers Assn., N.J. Bankers Assn. (compliance com.), Bank Adminstrn. Inst. (auditor PennJersey chpt. 1990-91, bd. dirs. 1991-92, v.p. 1992, pres. 1994-96), Pa. Jersey Fin. Instns. Assn. (bd. dirs. 1998—), Penn Jersey Instns. Assn. (bd. dirs. 1998—). Republican. Roman Catholic. Avocations: photography, astronomy. Home: 4833 S Cypress Dr Walnutport PA 18088-9459 Office: Vista Bancorp 61 N 3d St Easton PA 18042

BURKHART, HAROLD EUGENE, forestry educator; b. Wellington, Kans., Feb. 29, 1944; s. Walter F. and Zelma (Lutz) B.; m. Katherine West, June 12, 1971; 1 child, Anna Katherine. BS, Okla. State U., 1965; MS, U. Ga., 1967, PhD, 1969. Asst. prof. Va. Poly. Inst. and State U., Blacksburg, 1969-73, assoc. prof., 1973-78, prof., 1978-81, Thomas M. Brooks prof., 1981—. Author: Forest Measurements, 1983, 94; contbr. sci. articles to profl. jours. Sr. Rsch. fellow NRC, 1976-77; recipient Sci. Achievement award Internat. Union Forestry Rsch. Orgns., 1981, J. Shelton Horsley

Rsch. award Va. Acad. Sci., 1983, Outstanding Faculty award State Coun. for Higher Edn. in Va., 1988, Disting. Agr. Alumnus award Okla. State U., 1993. Fellow AAAS, Soc. Am. Foresters (Barrington Moore Meml. award 1991); mem. Biometric Soc., Am. Forestry Assn., Sigma Xi, Phi Kappa Phi, Xi Sigma Pi. Presbyterian. Avocations: gardening, running. Home: 1481 Mt Tabor Rd Blacksburg VA 24060-8601 Office: Va Poly Inst and State U Dept Forestry Blacksburg VA 24061

BURKHART, JOHN, manufacturing company executive; b. Tipton, Ind., July 25, 1908; s. John Burkhart and Edna Clark; m. Lorene McCormich, Mar. 23, 1985; children: John III, Gay. AB, DePauw U., 1928, LLD (hon.), 1959; LLD (hon.), U. Indpls., 1971, Vincennes U., 1992. Chmn. VitaChlor Corp., 1984—; founder Coll. Life Ins. Am., Indpls., Univ. Life Ins., Indpls. Bus. Jour. of Similar Bus. Newspapers. State fin. chmn. Rep. Party. Mem. U.S. C. of C. (past bd. dirs.), Indpls. C. of C. (past pres., life dir.), Nat. Assn. Mfrs. Republican. Methodist. Home: 775 Williams Cove Dr Indianapolis IN 46260-5342

BURKHART, JOHN ERNEST, minister, religion educator; b. Riverside, Calif., Oct. 25, 1927; s. Joseph Ernest and Lockie Louisa (Dryden) B.; m. Virginia Bell French, Sept. 16, 1951; children: David Aaron, Audrey Elizabeth, Deborah Ann. BA, Occidental Coll., 1949; BD, Union Theol. Sem., 1952; PhD, U. So. Calif., 1959; DD, Occidental Coll., 1964. Ordained to ministry United Presbyn. Ch., 1952. Pastor Presbyn. U. U. So. Calif., L.A., 1953-59, from instr. to prof. of Theology, 1959-1990; prof. Systematic Theology McCormick Theol. Sem., Chgo., 1990-93, prof. emeritus, 1993—; vis. prof. Garrett Theol. Sem. Evanston, Ill., 1966, DePaul U., Chgo., 1970. Author: Kingdom, Church, and Baptism, 1959, Understanding the Word of God, 1964, Worship, 1982; contbr. articles to profl. jours. 1st lt., chaplain USAF, 1952-53. Fellow Royal Anthrop. Inst., Soc. for Values in Higher Edn.; mem. Am. Acad. Religion, Cath. Theol. Soc. of Am., N.Am. Acad. Liturgy, Am. Theol. Soc. (pres. 1969-70), Midwest Alumni Club (v.p. 1985-90), Quadrangle Club, Blue Key, Rotary, Phi Beta Kappa. Democrat. Presbyterian. Home: 15 Sundance Trl Galena IL 61036-8729

BURKHART, JOHN HENRY, retired physician; b. Knoxville, Tenn., May 14, 1920; s. Fred McKinley and Stella Bogle (Henry) B.; m. Marjorie Nell Blaylock, Nov. 20, 1943; children: John McLain, Patrick Henry, William Lindsey. BA, U. Tenn., Knoxville, 1941; MD, U. Tenn., Memphis, 1945. Intern Knoxville Gen. Hosp., 1945-46, resident internal medicine, 1948-49; pvt. practice, Knoxville, 1949-94; chief staff St. Mary's Hosp., Knoxville, 1965; retired, 1994. Mem. Knoxville Bd. edn., 1958-59, chmn., 1959-65; ruling elder Presbyn. Ch. Capt. M.C., USAAF, 1946-48. Recipient Outstanding Alumnus award U. Tenn. Coll. Medicine, 1990. Mem. AMA (Disting. Svc. award 1991), Tenn. Med. Assn. (pres. 1965, Disting. Svc. award 1975, Outstanding Physician of Yr. award 1984), Knoxville Acad. Medicine (pres. 1964), Kiwanis (pres. Knoxville 1959), Omicron Delta Kappa, Alpha Omega Alpha, Kappa Sigma, Phi Chi. Home: 1905 Emoriland Blvd Knoxville TN 37917-3115 Office: 108 Midlake Dr Knoxville TN 37918-3038

BURKHART, WILLIAM HENRY, lawyer; b. Chgo., Jan. 3, 1931; s. Claude Albert and Mary Vern (Hall) B.; m. Rosemary Purcell, Apr. 28, 1973; 1 child, Aaron. BS Bus., Northwestern U., 1953; JD, U. Mich., 1958, MBA, 1959; LLM Taxation, NYU, 1963. Bar: Mich. 1958, N.Y. 1964, Washington 1975; CPA, Mich. Tax supr. Coopers & Lybrand, Detroit, 1960-62; assoc. atty. Cahill Gordon & Reindel, N.Y.C., 1963-72; tax ptnr. Preston, Gates & Ellis, Seattle, 1974—; chmn. Seattle Tax Group, 1986, Seattle Internat. Tax Roundtable, 1983-85; bd. dirs. Atty. CPA Tax Clinic, Seattle. Lt. (j.g.) USN, 1953-55. Mem. Washington Athletic Club. Home: 10554 Riviera Pl NE Seattle WA 98125-6937 Office: Preston Gates & Ellis 5000 Columbia Seafirst Ctr 701 5th Ave Seattle WA 98104-7078

BURKHEAD, VIRGINIA RUTH, rehabilitation nurse; b. Marlow, Okla., Apr. 11, 1937; d. Norvin Woodrow Whitehead and Harriet Louise (Pittman) Mayes; m. Marvin Vern Foster, Oct. 16, 1956 (div. 1964); children: Deborah, Marcia, Marva, Laurie, Sheila; m. Robert Burdett Burkhead, Apr. 11, 1987. ADN, Casper Coll., 1971; BSN, Wash. State U., 1994. RN, Wash. Staff nurse, house supr., enterostomal therapy nurse Meml. Hosp. Natrona County, Casper, Wyo., 1971-79; enterostomal therapy nurse, coord. ostomy program Holy Family Hosp., Spokane, 1979—, coord. neurol. rehab. program, 1985—. Deaconess 1st Christian Ch., Spokane, 1986—. Mem. Assn. Rehab. Nurses, Wound, Ostomy and Contence Nurses Soc., Jacks and Jennys Square Dance Club (coun. del. 1992), Sigma Theta Tau. Mem. Christian Ch. (Disciples of Christ). Avocations: square dancing, bird watching, reading, travel. Home: 2116 E Lincoln Rd Spokane WA 99217-7723 Office: Holy Family Hosp 5633 N Lidgerwood St Spokane WA 99207-1295

BURKHOLDER, DONALD LYMAN, mathematician, educator; b. Octavia, Nebr., Jan. 19, 1927; s. Elmer and Susie (Rothrock) B.; m. Jean Annette Fox, June 17, 1950; children: Kathleen, Peter, William. BA, Earlham Coll., 1950; MS, U. Wis., 1953; PhD, U. N.C., 1955. Asst. prof. math. U. Ill., Urbana, 1955-60, assoc. prof., 1960-64, prof., 1964-98, prof. Ctr. for Advanced Study, 1978-98, prof. emeritus, 1998—; sabbatical leaves U. Calif., Berkeley, 1961-62, Westfield Coll., U. London, 1969-70; vis. prof. Rutgers U., 1972-73; researcher Stanford U., 1961, Hebrew U., 1969, Mittag-Leffler Inst., Sweden, 1971, 82, U. Paris, 1975, Institut des Hautes Études Scientifiques, 1986, U. Edinburgh, 1986, Tel Aviv U., 1989, U. New South Wales, 1991; Mordell lectr. Cambridge U., 1986; Zygmund lectr. U. Chgo., 1988; trustee Math. Scis. Rsch. Inst., 1981-84; bd. govs. Inst. Math. and Its Applications, 1983-85, chmn., 1985. Editor: Annals Math. Statistics, 1964-67. Fellow Inst. Math. Statistics (Wald lectr. 1971, pres. 1975-76); mem. NAS, Am. Math. Soc. (mem. editorial bd. Trans. 1983-85), London Math. Soc., Am. Acad. Arts and Scis. Achievements include research in probability theory and its applications to other branches of analysis. Home: 506 W Oregon St Urbana IL 61801-4044

BURKHOLDER, MARK ALAN, historian, educator; b. Chgo., Sept. 3, 1943; s. M.M. Burkholder and Agnes V. Neuenschwander; children: Kristen, Jennifer. BA, Muskingum Coll., 1965; MA, U. Oreg., 1967; PhD, Duke U., 1970. Asst. prof. history U. Mo., St. Louis, 1970-76, 1976-81, prof. history, 1981—, asst. dean arts and scis., 1977-80, assoc. dean arts and scis., 1980-83, chair dept. history, 1995—; acad. assoc. to v.p. acad. affairs U. Mo. Sys., Columbia, 1983-84, assoc. v.p. acad. affairs, 1989-91. Author: Biographical Dictionary of Councilors of the Indies, 1717-1808, 1986, Politics of a Colonial Career, 1982; co-author: Biographical Dictionary of Audiencia Ministers in the Americas, 1687-1821, 1982, From Impotence to Authority: The Spanish Crown and the American Audiencias, 1687-1808, 1977, Colonial Latin America, 1990, 3d edit., 1998 (Edwin Lieuwin award for promotion of excellence in tchg. of Latin America, 1990). Bd. dirs. Citizens for Modern Transit, St. Louis, 1997—. Fax: (314) 516-5680. E-mail: hismburk@umslvma.umsl.edu. Office: 14 N Kingshighway 3B Saint Louis MO 63108 Office: U Mo 8001 Natural Bridge Rd Saint Louis MO 83121

BURKHOLDER, OWEN EUGENE, religious organization administrator; b. Bluesky, Alta., Can., Oct. 28, 1949; s. Paul and Doris Burkholder; m. Ruth Ann Augsburger; children: Minnette, Marla, Michelle. Grad., Ont. Mennonite Bible Inst., Kitchener, 1967; BA, U. Alta., Edmonton, 1970; MDiv, Eastern Mennonite Sem., Harrisonburg, Va., 1975. Assoc. pastor Bluesky Mennonite Ch., summer 1972; congl. coord., pastor Cmty. Mennonite Ch., Harrisonburg, Va., 1972-80; Campus Life Club dir. Shenandoah Valley Youth for Christ, Harrisonburg, 1973-80; pastor Park View Mennonite Ch., Harrisonburg, 1981-95; moderator Va. Mennonite Conf., Harrisonburg, 1982-84, conf. min., 1995—; rep. Va. Mennonite Conf. Mennonite Ch. Gen. Bd., Elkhart, Ind., 1985-93, moderator, 1995-97. Office: Va Mennonite Conf 901 Parkwood Dr Harrisonburg VA 22802-2418

BURKHOLDER, ROGER GLENN, artist, author; b. Omaha, Feb. 5, 1944; s. Christian Kenneth and Beverley Pierce (Manning) B. BA, Harvard U., 1967. Owner Mosaic, Denver, 1970-78, L.A., 1979-80; owner Formers' Understandings, Omaha, 1982—. Mem. Peace Action, Washington, 1997—, Lawyers' Com. on Nuclear Policy, N.Y.C., 1997—, Nat. Interreligious Svc. Bd. for Conscientious Objectors, Washington, 1997—, Fellowship of Reconciliation, 1998. Mem. Internat. Soc. for Krishna Consciousness. Avocation: pets, singing, guitar. Home: 5624 Burdette St Omaha NE 68104-4902 Office: Formers' Understandings PO Box 4406 Omaha NE 68104-0406

BURKHOLDER, TIMOTHY JAMES, religious organization administrator; b. Athabasca, AB, Canada, Aug. 25, 1948; s. Paul Leonard and Doris Wilma (Stalter) B.; m. Sharon Rose Sitler, Aug. 2, 1969; three children. B in Commerce, U. Alberta, 1970. Computer project mgr. Govt. Alberta, Edmonton, Canada, 1970-80; gen. mgr. Burkholder Bldg. Supplies Ltd., Bluesky, AB, 1980-84; exec. sec. N.W. Conf. Mennonite Ch., Edmonton, AB, 1984-93; v.p. Mennonite Bd. Edn., Elkhart, Ind., 1993—; ind. travel agt. Inteletravel Internat., Ft. Lauderdale, Fla., 1997—. Bd. dirs. Hesston (Kans.) Coll., 1977-85, Mennonite Reporter, Waterloo, Ont., 1988-93, Mennonite Ch. Gen. Bd., Elkhart, Ind., 1985-93. Recipient medal of bravery Gov. Gen. of Can., 1981. Mem. Am. Mktg. Assn., Am. Assn. Higher Edn., Mennonite Econ. Devel. Assn., Canadian Info. Processing Soc.

BURKHOLDER, WENDELL EUGENE, retired entomology educator, researcher; b. Octavia, Nebr., June 24, 1928; s. Elmer and Susie (Rothrock) B.; m. Leona Rose Flory, Aug. 18, 1951; children: Paul Charles, Anne Carolyn, Joseph Kern, Stephen James. A.B., McPherson Coll., 1950; M.Sc., U. Nebr., 1956; Ph.D., U. Wis., 1967. Rsch. entomologist U.S. Dept. Agr., 1956—, Madison, Wis., 1965—; asst. prof. U. Wis.-Madison, 1967-70, asso. prof., 1970-75, prof. entomology, 1975-96; prof. emeritus, 1996; lectr. in field. Mem. editorial bd.: Jour. Chem. Ecology, 1980—, Jour. Stored Products Rsch., 1992—; contbr. chpts. to books and articles to profl. jours. Served with U.S. Army, 1951-53. NSF grantee, 1972-75, 79; Rockefeller Found. grantee, 1974-77; Nat. Inst. Occupational Safety and Health grantee, 1977-79. Mem. AAAS, Entomol. Soc. Am., Wis. Entomol. Soc., Wis. Acad. Sci. Arts, and Letters, Internat. Soc. Chem. Ecology, Sigma Xi. Patentee in field. Home: 1726 Chadbourne Ave Madison WI 53705-4108 Office: U Wis Entomology Dept 537 Russell Lab Madison WI 53706-1598

BURKI, FRED ALBERT, labor union official; b. Chgo., Apr. 8, 1926; s. John and Helen (Kramer) B.; children—Bill, Ken, Scott. Student, Northwestern U., U.Ill. Started as grocery clk., 1947; pres. local 470 United Retail Workers Union, Westchester, Ill., 1951-53; rep. 470 United Retail Workers Union, 1953-62, field supr., 1963-65, nat. v.p., 1966-71, nat. exec. dir., 1971-81; internat. v.p. United Food and Comml. Workers Union, AFL-CIO, 1981—; pres. local 881, 1981—; guest lectr. labor edn., advisor U. Ill. Circle Campus, Chgo.; labor edn. adv. U. Ind., 1967—, Loyola U., 1978—; mem. Midwest Com. Labor Study in Europe; labor adv. com. Senator Charles Percy, 1977—; chmn. Westchester Bldg. Corp., 1971-83. Bd. dirs. Chgo. Regional Blood Bank/Blood Services, Blood Ctr. of No. Ill., 1983—, Midwest Assn. for Sickle Cell Anemia, 1986—; trustee United Retail Workers Union-Super-Valu Trust Fund.; mem. Ill. Detection of Deception Com., 1982—; pres. Human Services Ltd., 1984—. Served with AUS, 1943-47; battalion exec. officer, maj. Res., 1947-67, ret. Decorated Bronze Star medal; named Man of Year Combined Counties Police Assn., 1977. Mem. V.F.W. (past officer), Mil. Police Assn., Res. Officers Assn.

BURKI, SHAHID JAVED, bank executive; b. Simla, British India, Sept. 14, 1938; m. Jahanara Burki; children: Emaad, Sairah. Student, Oxford U., Harvard U. Chief economist West Pakistan; sr. fellow Devel. Adv. Svc., Harvard U.; sr. economist World Bank, 1974-76, divsn. chief policy planning and program review dept., 1976-81, sr. econ. and policy advisor Office of V.P. External Rels.,, 1981-83, dir. internat. rels. dept. Office of V.P. External Rels.,, 1983-87, dir. for China and Mongolia,, 1987-93, v.p. Latin Am. and Caribbean region, 1994—. Author: A Study of Chinese Communes, 1969, Pakistan: Development Choices for the Future, 1986, Pakistan: Continuing Search for Nationhood, 1991, Pakistan: A Historical Dictionary, 1998; co-author (with Paul Streeten and others): First Things First, 1981. Rhodes scholar Oxford U.; Masons fellow Harvard U. FAX: 202-477-6391. Office: The World Bank Group Hdqrs Washington DC 20433

BURKLE, RONALD W., food service executive; b. 1953. Pvt. practice, 1975-88; pres. Jurgensen's, Pasadena, Calif., 1986-88; prin. Yucaipa Mgmt. Co., Claremont, Calif., 1986—; chmn. Food 4 Less Supermarkets, La Habra, Calif., 1989—, Dominick's Finer Foods, Northlake, Ill., until 1998; chmn., mem. exec. com. Kroger's Foods, Inc.; CEO Smith's Food & Drug Ctrs., Inc., Salt Lake City; chmn. Fred Meyer. Office: Smith's Food & Drug Ctrs Inc 1550 S Redwood Rd Salt Lake City UT 84104*

BURKMAN, ERNEST, JR., education educator; b. Detroit, Oct. 4, 1929; s. Ernest and Rose (Emmehizer) B.; m. Nancy Barron, Mar. 11, 1953; children: Laura, Linda, Jan, Patricia. BS, Ea. Mich U., 1952; MS, U. Mich., 1955, MA, 1958, EdD, 1961. Sci. tchr. Edsel Ford High Sch., Dearborn, Mich., 1955-60; from asst. prof. to prof. Fla. State U., Tallahassee, 1960—; co-dir. Turkish Nat. Sci. Lise Project, Ankara, 1961-66; dir. Intermediate Sci. Curriculum Study, 1966-72, U.S. and nationwide, Individualized Sci. Instruction System Project, U.S. and nationwide, 1972-81; cons. over 35 agys., U.S. and 15 countries, 1961—. Author: Current Trends in Science Education, 1966, The Natural World, 1975-88; co-author, editor: Individualized Science Instructional System, (25 vol. book series), 1981-88; contbr. articles to profl. jours. Fellow AAAS; mem. Nat. Sci. Tchr. Assn., Am. Ednl. Rsch. Assn. Office: Fla State U Coll Edn Tallahassee FL 32306

BURKS, BRIAN SCOTT, veterinarian; b. Fresno, Calif., Aug. 12, 1968; s. Marlton Maurice and Cynthia Gail (Dick) B. Student, Calif. State U., Fresno, 1986-90, U. Liverpool, Eng., 1990-92; DVM, Okla. State U., 1995. Intern in veterinary medicine Equine Med. Assocs., Glencoe, Mo., 1995-96; resident in veterinary medicine U. Ga., Athens, 1996-97; veterinarian Reed Equine Assocs., Grantville, Pa., 1997-98; assoc. veterinarian Fox Run Equine Ctr., Apollo, Pa., 1998—. Contbr. articles to profl. jours. Mem. Am. Vet. Med. Assn., Am. Assn. Equine Practitioners, Alpha Psi. Republican. Baptist. Avocations: piano, hiking, leathercraft, tennis, country music. Home: 3120 Leechburg Rd Lower Burrell PA 15068-2746 Office: Fox Run Equine Ctr 798 Fox Rd Apollo PA 15613

BURKS, DAVID BASIL, academic administrator, educator; b. Ava, Mo., May 13, 1943; m. Leah Ann Gentry; children: Bryan, Stephen, Marleah. BA, Harding Coll., 1965; MBA, U. Tex., 1966; PhD, Fla. State U., 1974. CPA, Tex. Mem. internal audit staff Exxon Inc., Houston, 1966-67; dir. placement, bus. instr. Harding Coll., Searcy, Ark., 1967-71, dean sch. bus., 1974-87, dir. Am. Studies program, 1982, pres., 1987—. Deacon Coll. Ch. of Christ, Searcy, 1985, elder, 1996, chmn. bd. dirs. Camp Wildwood, Searcy, 1975-79. Author: The Christian Alternative for Business, 1978; creator computerized bus. game Strategic Management Simulation, 1974. Mem. Kiwanis, Searcy Club. Republican. Office: Harding U Office of Pres 900 E Center Ave Stop 12256 Searcy AR 72149-0002*

BURKS, JACK D., investment executive; b. San Antonio, Apr. 1, 1951; s. D.C. and Inez M. (Lyons) B.; m. Pamela Kay Bowen. BA, Ind. U., 1972, MBA, 1979. V.p. Pitts. Nat. Bank, 1973-84; mgr. dir. Offitbank, N.Y.C., 1984—. Bd. dirs. Alzheimers Assn., N.Y.C., 1994-98. Avocations: travel, military history, wine.

BURKS, ROBERT EDWARD, minister, educator; b. Washington, Aug. 20, 1930; s. Jesse Audie and Elizabeth (Morton) B.; m. Norma Jean Banner, Sept. 5, 1953 (div. Oct. 1984); children: Jennifer Burks Dawson, Kari Beth Trent, Robert Tucker; m. Elizabeth Steadman, Oct. 23, 1987. BA, Mercer U., 1951; BD, So. Bapt. Theol. Sem., 1954, ThM, 1955, PhD, 1961. Ordained to ministry So. Bapt. Conv., 1953. Pastor Bethel Bapt. Ch., Scottsburg, Ind., 1955-60; assoc. pastor 1st Bapt. Ch., Anderson, S.C., 1961-65; prof., chmn. dept. religion Anderson Coll., 1965-90, prof., 1965—, faculty chmn., 1973-74, 89-90. Former chmn. bd. dirs. ARC; bd. dirs. Anderson Scholastic Loan Fund, 1963—, past pres.; bd. dirs. Anderson Sch. Theology for Lay Persons, 1962—, also past pres. Recipient Svc. to Community award Kiwanis, 1965. Mem. Soc. Bibl. Lit., Nat. Assn. Bapt. Profs. Religion (mem. editorial bd. 1980-85, sec. S.E. region 1984-89), Rotary (past pres., Paul Harris fellow). Democrat. Home: 504 Squire Cir Clemson SC 29631-2137 Office: Anderson Coll 316 Boulevard Anderson SC 29621-4002

BURKS, ROCKY ALAN, independent living center executive, consultant; b. San Bernardino, Calif., June 12, 1952; s. Lloyd Jackson and Vivian Elnora B.; m. Nikki Ann Stone (div. 1974); 1 child, Gannon LeRoy; m. Lydia Ann Deatherage, Aug. 20, 1983. BA in Social Welfare, Calif. State U., Chico, 1979, BA in Sociology, 1979. Instrument flight instr. USAF, Del Rio, Tex., 1971-75; dir. outreach and recruitment, Office of Vets. Affairs Calif. State U., Chico, 1976-81; exec. dir. Easter Seal Soc. of Butte County, Chico, 1981-82, No. Calif. Ind. Living Program, Chico, 1982-85; soc. worker Butte County (Calif.) Welfare Dept., 1985-87; exec. dir. Ind. Living Svcs. of N. Calif., Inc., Chico, 1988—; bd. dirs. Calif. Coalition of Ind. Living Ctrs., Sacramento, Calif., pres., 1991-94; bd. dirs. Pub. Interest Ctr. on Long-term Care, Sacramento, treas., 1994-98; mem. disability access adv. bd. Divsn. of the State Arch., Sacramento, 1995—, Disabled Access Bd. of Appeals, Butte County Building Divsn., Oroville, 1994—. Editor: (newsletter) Independent Life, 1988—, Voice, 1976-81. Mem. Transp. Adv. Commn., Butte County Assn. Govts., Oroville, 1992—; mem. Californians for Disability Rights. Recipient Cert. of Congl. Recognition, Congressman Wally Herger, Chico, 1993, 96, Disability Advocate award Calif. Assn. Persons with Handicaps, 1994, Region IX Disability Advocate award Nat. Coun. Ind. Living, 1998, Master Instr. award Air Tng. Command, USAF, 1975; named citizen Chickasaw Indian Nation. Mem. Am. Legion, Vietnam Vets. Am., Masons, Shriners, Scottish Rite, Chico Breakfast Lions (pres. 1991-92, Lion of Yr. award 1990, Melvin Jones fellow), Lions Eye Found. Calif. and Nev. (life). Avocations: scuba diving, boating, reading, art. Home: 4135 Keefer Rd Chico CA 95973-8956 Office: Ind Living Svcs No Calif 555 Rio Lindo Ave Ste B Chico CA 95926-1847

BURLACU, CONSTANTIN, journalist, educator; b. Botosani, Romania, Jan. 20, 1949; came to U.S., 1980; s. Petru and Elena (Matei) B.; m. Elisabeta Busaga, Apr. 4, 1974; children: Monica, Johnny. BS, U. Nicolas Doubloway, Santiago, Chile, 1994; MA, Pacific Western U., 1996; D (hon.), U. Nicolas Doubloway, 1994. Chmn. The League of Nat. Def., N.Y.C., 1985—; pub. The New Right Mag., N.Y.C., 1985—; dep. mem. assembly Internat. Parliament for Safety and Peace, Sicily, Italy, 1993—; consul gen. Oceanus Govt., Miami, Fla., 1996—; prof. U. Nicolas Doublaway, 1996—. Author: The History of Nationalism in Eastern Europe: A Study of Its Origins and Background in Romania, 1996, History of Moldova and its Connection with Political and Social Circumstances from the Earlist Time to the Present Day, 1998. Mem. Rep. Nat. Com., Washington, 1985—, Rep. Presdl. Legion of Merit, Washington, 1993—, Rep. Presdl. Task Force, Washington, 1989—, Am. Fedn. Police, Miami, 1990—, N.Y. State Fraternal Order Police, N.Y.C., 1998—. Named Knight, Sovereign Noble Religious Order of St. Tatjana, Belgium, 1994; recipient Presdl. Order of Merit, Nat. Rep. Senatorial Com., 1991, Citizen of Yr. award Principality of Hutt River Province, Australia, 1995, Polish Patriotic Eagle Freedom award, Salem, Mass., 1989; diplomate of honor The League of Romanian Freedom Fighters, Brasov, Romania, 1989, diploma of honor Anticomunist Revolutionary Movement, Brasov, 1997. Mem. NRA, Nat. Rep. Senatorial Com., Nat. Rep. Congl. Com., Freedom Army, Amnesty Internat. USA, Am. Defense Com., Am. Security Coun., Liberty Lobby, Reform Party, Populist Action Com., New Iron Guard. Avocations: reading, swimming, hunting, keeping up with current events. Home: 464 Woodward Ave Ridgewood NY 11385-1533 Office: League of Nat Def PO Box 292 Brooklyn NY 11237-0292

BURLEIGH, A. PETER, ambassador; b. L.A., Mar. 7, 1942; s. Ralph Wendell and Margaret (McKenney) B. AB, Colgate U., 1963; postgrad., U. Pa., 1965-66. Vol. Peace Corps, Nepal, 1963-65; joined Fgn. Svc., 1967; various positions Dept. State, Washington, 1967-85, dir. No. Gulf Affairs, 1985-87, dep. asst. sec. for Near Eastern and South Asian Affairs, 1987-89, dep. asst. sec. for intelligence and rsch., 1989-91, coord. for counter-terrorism, amb., 1991-92, dep. asst. sec. for pers., 1992-95; amb. Dem. Socialist Republic Sri Lanka, Republic Maldives, 1995-97; dep. U.S. rep. to UN, 1997—. Recipient Presdl. Svc. award U.S. Govt., 1990, 93. Home and Office: US Mission to UN 799 UN Plz New York NY 10017 also: 985 Fifth Ave Apt 19B New York NY 10021-0142

BURLEIGH, LEWIS ALBERT, lawyer; b. Augusta, Maine, May 15, 1940; s. Lewis A. and Ursula (Maher) B.; m. Rinda H. Burleigh, June 22, 1963; children: Lewis A. IV, Jennifer, Erica. AB cum laude, Harvard U., 1962, JD, 1965. Bar: N.Y. 1966, Mass. 1973,Calif. 1982, Pa. 1985. Assoc. Dewey Ballantine Bushby Palmer & Wood, N.Y.C., 1965-72; ptnr. Csaplar & Bok (name changed to Gaston & Snow), Boston and San Francisco, 1973-91, Day Berry & Howard, Boston, 1991—. Fellow Am. Coll. Investment Counsel; mem. ABA, N.Y. State Bar Assn., Calif. Bar Assn., Am. Soc. Internat. Law, Harvard Club. Avocation: flying. Office: Day Berry & Howard 260 Franklin St Ste 2150 Boston MA 02110-3179

BURLEIGH, WILLIAM ROBERT, newspaper executive; b. Evansville, Ind., Sept. 6, 1935; s. Joseph Charles and Emma Bertha (Wittgen) B.; m. Catherine Anne Husted, Nov. 28, 1964; children: David William, Catherine Anne, Margaret Walden. BS, Marquette U., Milw., 1957; LLD (hon.), U. So. Ind., 1979. From reporter to editor and pres. Evansville Press, 1951-77; editor Cin. Post, 1977-83; v.p., gen. editorial mgr. Scripps-Howard Newspapers, 1984-86, sr. v.p. newspapers and publs., 1986-90, exec. v.p., 1990-94; pres., COO, 1994-96, pres., CEO, 1996—. Served with AUS, 1957-58. Mem. Am. Soc. Newspaper Editors, Alpha Sigma Nu. Roman Catholic. Clubs: Queen City, Cincinnati Lit, Cincinnati Country, Cincinnati Commercial. Office: E W Scripps Howard 312 Walnut St Cincinnati OH 45202-4024

BURLESKI, JOSEPH ANTHONY, JR., information technology executive; b. Poughkeepsie, N.Y., June 30, 1960; s. Joseph Anthony Burleski Sr. and Fredeline Cyr; m. Judith Ann Lezon, June 10, 1989; children: Joseph Anthony III, Jessica Ann. BSBA, Marist Coll., 1982; MBA Mktg., U. Phoenix, 1992; grad. in human rels. and effective speaking, Dale Carnegie, 1990. Cert. project mgmt. profl. Project Mgmt. Inst. Computer operator IBM, Poughkeepsie, 1982-83, lead/sr. computer operator, 1983-84, systems programmer, 1984-85, assoc. systems programmer, 1985-86, mgr. offshift computer ops., 1986-87; mgr. info. processing IBM, Boulder, Colo., 1987-88, mgr. MVS systems programming, 1988-91; mgr. location and field svcs. devel. Integrated Systems Solutions Corp. subs. IBM, Boulder, 1991-93, mgr. location and field svc. devel. ind. test, 1992-93; mgr. VM/VSE svcs. Integrated Sys. Solutions Corp. subs. IBM, Boulder, 1993-94, account mgr., 1994-96; delivery project exec. IBM Global Svcs., Boulder, 1997-98; delivery exec. IBM Global Svcs., St. Louis, 1998—; mentor IBM, 1987—; mem. IBM Data Processing Ops. Coun., Poughkeepsie, 1983-92, Project Mgmt. Inst., 1995—; grad. asst. Dale Carnegie Inst., Boulder, 1990-98. Coach Spl. Olympics, 1987-98; mem. Order of the Arrow Hon. Soc., chpt. sec., editor, 1976-77, chpt. pres. 1977-78, chpt. treas. 1980-81. Mem. Am. Mgmt. Assn., Am. Assn. Individual Investors, Marist Coll. Alumni Assn. (contbr.), Vigil Nat. Honor Soc. Roman Catholic. Avocations: running, reading, camping, hiking, raising tropical fish. Office: 800 Lindbergh Blvd Saint Louis MO 63167

BURLESON, HUGH LATIMER, II, retired foreign service officer, translator; b. Springfield, S.D., Jan. 2, 1927; s. John Keble Sr. and Gwendolen English Burleson; m. Kimie Ina Burleson, Aug. 21, 1947; children: Ritsuko B. Geoghegan, Hugh L. III. BA with highest honors, U. Calif., Berkeley, 1954, MA, 1956; cert., U.S. Army War Coll., 1973. Fgn. svc. officer U.S. Info. Agy., Washington, 1956-87; adj. prof. Spokane (Wash.) Falls C.C., 1991-92, Gonzaga U., Spokane, 1992-93; pres. Spokane-Nishinomiya Sister City Soc., 1992-95. Coord. relief for Kobe earthquake victims in Nishinomiya, Spokane Sister Cities Assn., 1995. Cpl. U.S. Army, 1945-46. Mem. Bellevue Sister City Assn. (v.p. 1997—), Japanese-Am. Citizens's League (v.p. Lake Washington chpt. 1996—), Japan Am. Soc. Wash. State, World Affairs Coun. Seattle (exec. dir. 1981-82). Unitarian-Universalist. Avocations: reading, music appreciation, writing, gardening, family activities. E-mail: hburleson@att.net. Home and Office: 1332 183rd Ave NE Bellevue WA 98808

BURLINGAME, ALMA LYMAN, chemist, educator; b. Cranston, R.I., Apr. 29, 1937; s. Herman Follett Jr. and Rose Irene (Kohler) B.; children: Mark, Walter; m. Marilyn F. Schwartz, Feb. 14, 1993; 1 stepchild, Corey Schwartz. BS, U. R.I., 1959; PhD, MIT, 1962. Asst. prof. U. Calif., Berkeley, 1963-68, assoc. chemist, 1968-72, rsch. chemist, 1972-78; prof. U. Calif., San Francisco, 1978—, Univ. Coll., London, 1996—; vis. prof. Ludwig Inst. for Cancer Rsch., London, 1993-94. Editor: Topics in Organic Mass Spectrometry, 1970, Mass Spectrometry in Health and Life Science, 1985, Biological Mass Spectrometry, 1990, Mass Spectrometry in the Biological Sciences, 1995; contbr. articles to profl. jours. With USAR, 1954-62. Guggenheim Found. fellow, 1970. Fellow AAAS. Office: U Calif Dept Pharm Chemistry San Francisco CA 94143-0446

BURLINGAME, ANSON HOLLYDAY, retired engineer; b. Chilhowee, Mo., Apr. 29, 1942; s. Anson Hollyday Burlingame; m. Sally Weber Adamson, 1965; children: John, Paul. BS, U.S. Naval Acad., 1965; MA in Internat. Rels., Salve Regina Coll., 1986; MA in Strategic Studies, Naval War Coll., 1986. Commd. ensign USN, 1965, advanced through grades to capt.; comdr. officer U.S.S. Bluefish USN, Norfolk, Va., 1981-84; capt., staff chief naval ops. USN, Washington, 1986-88; ret. USN, 1988; dir. support sys. EG&G Rocky Flats, Golden, Colo., 1990-92, pres., 1994-95; dep. gen. mgr. REECO, Las Vegas, 1992-94; v.p. DOE programs Jacobs Engring., Pasadena, Calif., 1995-97. Decorated Legion of Merit, Meritorious Svc. medals. Mem. Elks. Republican. Avocations: woodworking, teaching. E-mail: anson65@earthlink.net.

BURLINGAME, EDWARD LIVERMORE, book publisher; b. N.Y.C., Jan. 21, 1935; s. Anson and Elizabeth Harlow (Hussey) B.; m. Perdita Remony Plowden, May 18, 1963; children: Remony Elizabeth, Phyllida Anne, Roger Anson. BA, Harvard U., 1957; AMP, Harvard Bus. Sch., 1982. Editor MacGibbon & Kee, Ltd., London, 1959-61; sr. editor New Am. Library, N.Y.C., 1961-65; v.p., editor in chief Walker & Co., N.Y.C., 1965-68; sr. v.p., editor-in-chief trade div. J.B. Lippincott Co., Phila. and N.Y.C., 1968-78; dir. J.B. Lippincott Co., 1970-78; v.p., pub. Lippincott & Crowell, N.Y.C., 1979-80; v.p., editor-in-chief, pub. trade group Harper & Row, Pubs., Inc., N.Y.C., 1980-87; pub. Edward Burlingame Books (an imprint of HarperCollins Pubs.), 1987-93; pres. The Adventure Libr., 1993—. Mem. Eastern regional panel Pres.'s Commn. on White House Fellowships, 1982-84; mem. vis. com. New Sch. for Social Rsch., 1991-95. Served to lt. (j.g.) USNR, 1957-59. Mem. Coun. Fgn. Rels., Assn. Am. Pubs. (copyright com. 1976-77, internat. freedom to publish com. 1977-80, exec. council gen. pub. div. 1981-88, vice chmn. 1984-85, chmn. 1985-86), PEN (treas., exec. bd. 1970-73). Clubs: Century Assn. Home: 79 Nash Rd North Salem NY 10560-3710

BURLINGAME, JOHN HUNTER, lawyer; b. Milw., Apr. 27, 1933; s. Leroy James and Mary Janet (Burchard) B.; m. Carolyn Elizabeth Beachley, Aug. 27, 1960 (div. Feb. 1981); children: Carolyn, Janet, Amy, Alexander; m. Dorcas Hodges, June 5, 1982. BS, U. Wis., 1960, LLB, 1963. Bar: Ohio 1964. From assoc. to ptnr. Baker & Hostetler, Cleve., 1963-82, exec. ptnr., 1982-97, ptnr., 1998—; bd. dirs. The E. W. Scripps Co. Lt. USN, 1955-59. Mem. ABA, Cleve. Bar Assn., Union Club, Shoreby Club. Republican. Presbyterian. Avocations: skiing, outdoor life.

BURLINGAME, LLOYD LAMSON, retired design instructor; b. Washington, Dec. 31, 1934; s. Harry Lamson and Estelle (Embry) B. BFA, Carnegie Inst. Tech., Pitts., 1956. Head design dept. Tisch Sch. Arts, N.Y.C., 1972-97, chair emeritus design dept., 1997—. Designer scenery, lighting, costumes: (Broadway plays) including Marat/Sade, A Midsummer Night's Dream, Philadelphia, Here I Come, Hadrian VII, (opera cos.) including San Francisco Opera Co., Boston Opera Group, Peabody Art Theatre, Chautauqua Opera, Manhattan Sch. Music, Repertory Theatre New Orleans, Arena Stage, Washington, Detroit Repertory Theatre, Pitts. Playhouse, Am. Shakespeare Festival, (TV stas.) ABC, CBS, NET; one man show in N.Y.C., 1984, Wadsworth Atheneum, Hartford, Conn., 1988; retrospective show scene designs and touchable art, N.Y.C., 1985; also regional group shows. Served with U.S. Army, 1958-59. Recipient 1st prize Nat. Juried Show, 1986; Fulbright scholar, 1959-60, 93, Disting. Tchg. medal NYU, 1997; rsch. grantee Fulbright, 1993. Mem. United Scenic Artists.

BURLINGAME, MICHAEL ASHTON, historian, educator; b. Washington, Sept. 13, 1941; s. Harry Lamson and Estelle Boughton (Embry) B.; m. S.L. Silberman, Aug. 22, 1968 (div. Mar. 15, 1980); children: Rebecca, Jessica. Student, Phillips Acad., Andover, Mass., 1956-60; BA, Princeton (N.J.) U., 1964; PhD, Johns Hopkins U., Balt., 1971; Lincoln diploma of honor, Lincoln Meml. U., 1998. May Buckley Sadowski prof. history Conn. Coll., New London, 1968—. Author: The Inner World of Abraham Lincoln, 1994, An Oral History of Abraham Lincoln, 1996, Inside Lincoln's White House, 1997, Lincoln Observed, 1998, A Reporter's Lincoln, 1998, Lincoln's Journalist, 1998. Recipient Abraham Lincoln Assn. prize, Springfield, Ill., 1995, Lincoln Diploma Honor Lincoln Meml. U., 1998. Mem. Orgn. Am. Historians, Am. Hist. Assn., Abraham Lincoln Assn., Nat. Assn. Scholars, Conn. Assn. Scholars, Abraham Lincoln Inst. Mid-Atlantic. Avocations: concerts, opera, hockey, tennis, lacrosse. Home: 8 Winchester Rd New London CT 06320-4135 Office: History Dept Connecticut College 270 Mohegan Ave New London CT 06320-4125

BURMAN, DIANE BERGER, organization development consultant; b. Pitts., Dec. 7, 1936; d. Morris Milton and Dorothy June (Barkin) Berger; m. Sheldon Oscar Burman, Dec. 15, 1926; children: Allison Beth, Jocelyn Holly, Harrison Emory Guy. BA, Vassar Coll., 1958; MA, Middlebury Coll., 1961. Tchr. of French Allderdice High Sch., Pitts., 1960-61, Mamaroneck (N.Y.) High Sch., 1961-64; personnel specialist G.D. Searle & Co., Skokie, Ill., 1972-77, orgn. devel. tng. cons., 1977-78; personnel and orgn. devel. cons. Abbott Labs., North Chgo., 1978-82; orgn. devel. cons., v.p., mgr. career devel. Harris Bank, Chgo., 1982-97; ind. mgmt. cons. in orgn. devel., career devel., 1997—; pres. Dee Burman & Assoc., Highland Park, Ill., 1997—. Mem. edit. bd. Orgn. Devel. Jour., 1987. Bd. advisors Grad. Sch. Bus. No. Ill. U. Mem. ASTD (bd. dirs. Chgo. career devel. profl. practice area 1987—), Orgn. Devel. Network (exec. dir. Chgo. chpt. 1986-89), Assn. Psychol. Type-Nat. Conf., Orgn. Devel. Inst. (adv. bd. 1987-91, chmn. nat. conf. 1990), Nat. Assn. Bank Women, Internat. Assn. Career Mgmt. Profls. (bd. dirs. Chgo. chpt. 1999—, co-chair pub. com. 1999), Vassar Club (bd. dirs. 1975-80, 95—, chair career assistance com. 1997—). Jewish. Avocations: biking, playing flute, traveling. Home and Office: 247 Prospect Ave Highland Park IL 60035-3357

BURMAN, MARSHA LINKWALD, lighting manufacturing executive, manpower development professional; b. Balt., Jan. 9, 1949; d. William and Lena (Ronin) Linkwald; m. Robert Schlosser, July 2, 1972 (div. 1980); children: Melanie, David. BS in Edn. cum laude, Kent State U., 1970, MA in Sociology summa cum laude, 1971. Cert. in secondary edn., Ohio. Spl. project dir. tng. and rsch. ctr. Planned Parenthood, Chgo., 1978; with mgmt. edn. ctr. Gould, Inc., Chgo., 1979, program adminstr., 1979-80; sys. trainer Lithonia Lighting, 1981, mgr. tng. and edn., 1981-86; dir. mktg., tng. and devel., corp. tng., mgr. Lithonia Lighting Ctr., Atlanta, 1986-97, dir. human resources planning and devel., 1998—. Author: (booklet) Putting Your Best Foot Forward (award Am. Soc. Tng. and Devel.), 1982; author, editor: Dictionary of Lighting Industry Terminology, 1989, 3d edit., 1990; editor ED.50 Lighting, 1999. Bd. dirs. Rockdale County Boys and Girls Club, 1999—; mem. adv. coun. DeKalb Tech.; mem. archtl. engring. adv. bd. U. Kans. Sch. Architecture. U.S. Office Edn. grantee, 1971. Mem. ASTD (bd. dirs. 1982, spl. projects dir. Atlanta chpt. 1982, Vol. of Yr., Cmty. Leader Am. 1987, 89, 92), Tng. Dirs. Roundtable (founding mem.), Lithonia Lighting Mgmt. Club (v.p. 1982-83, sponsor 1998—), Toastmasters. Avocations: reading, botanical gardening. Email: mburman@lithonia.com. Office: Lithonia Lighting Div Nat Svc Industries 1400 Lester Rd Conyers GA 30012-3908

BURMAN, SHEILA FLEXER ZOLA, special education educator; b. N.Y.C., May 1, 1935; d. Jack and Edna (Eagle) Flexer; m. Eugene Lee Zola, July 7, 1957 (div. Aug. 1973); children: Leslie Sheldon, Sharon Joanne; m. Milton Burman, Mar. 19, 1978. Student, Hunter Coll., 1952-55; BA in Edn., BS, UCLA, 1957, 85, spl. edn. cert. for learning handicapped, 1985; and severely handicapped; MS in Counseling, U. LaVerne, 1983; resource specialist cert., Calif. Luth. U., 1988. Cert. tchr., spl. edn. tchr., resource specialist, pupil pers. credential. Tchr. L.A. Unified Sch. Dist., 1957-81, spl. edn. tchr., 1981-88, resource specialist jr. H.S., 1988-89, resource specialist elem. sch., 1989-96, resource specialist mid. sch., 1997—, commr. spl. edn. commn.; Cert. tchr., spl. edn. tchr., resource specialist, pupil pers. credential. Grantee CTIP 1988, Computer 1989. Mem. Coun. for Exceptional Children, Assn. Ednl. Therapists, United Tchrs. L.A., Calif. Tchrs. Assn., UCLA Alumni Assn., UCLA Grad. Sch. Edn. Alumni Assn., Hunter Coll. Alumni Assn., Pi Lambda Theta. Avocations: swimming, reading, needlepoint. Home: 15455 Hamner Dr Los Angeles CA 90077-1802

BURMAN, SONDRA, social work educator; b. Bklyn., Sept. 16, 1935; d. William and Marie (Alpern) B.; m. Philip L. Gildenberg, June 10, 1955 (div. Feb. 1986); children: Susan, Steven, Ronald, Laura. BS, U. Pa., 1957; MSW, U. Houston, 1979; PhD, U. Ill., 1993. Lic. clin. social worker, N.J., lic. master social worker, Tex. Phys. therapist Grad. Hosp. U. Pa., Phila., 1957-59, Northeast Hosp., Phila., 1963-64; social worker, psychotherapist Med. Arts Hosp., Houston, 1979-83, 85-86, Pasadena (Tex.) Gen. Hosp., 1986-87, Orchard Greek Hosp., Rosenberg, Tex., 1987-88, Houston Internat. Hosp., 1988-89; editl. asst. Rehab. Edn. Jour., Champaign, Ill., 1990-93; asst. prof. Rutgers U., New Brunswick, N.J., 1993—. Contbr. articles to profl. jours. Mem. Rutgers AIDS Task Force, N.J., 1994-96. Univ. coun. rsch. grantee, Rutgers U., 1995; recipient Lois & Samuel Silberman Fund award, N.Y.C., 1995. Mem. NASW (N.J. chpt. alcohol, tobacco, and other drugs), Nat. Assn. Alcoholism and Drug Abuse Counselors, Tex. Assn. Alcoholism and Drug Abuse Counselors, Coun. Social Work Edn. Avocations: reading, writing, travel, walking. Office: Rutgers U Sch Social Work 536 George St New Brunswick NJ 08901-1167

BURMEISTER, EDWIN, economics educator; b. Chgo., Nov. 30, 1939; s. Edwin Carl and Dorothy (Braithwaite) B. BA, Cornell U., 1961, MA, 1962; PhD, MIT, 1965. Asst. prof. econs. Wharton Sch., U. Pa., Phila., 1965-68, assoc. prof., 1968-71; vis. prof. econs. Duke U., 1971-72, vis. prof. econs. Fuqua Sch. Bus. and dept. econs., 1981-82; vis. prof. econs. Sch. Gen. Studies and vis. fellow dept. econs. Research Sch. Social Sci. Australian Nat. U., 1974-75; prof. econs. U. Pa., Phila., 1972-76; prof. econs., mem. Ctr. for Advanced Studies U. Va., Charlottesville, 1976-79, Commonwealth prof. econs., 1979-90; rsch. prof. econs. Duke U., 1990—; vis. prof. econs. U. Chgo., 1980; prof. econs. and fin. U. Ill., 1982. Author: (with A. Rodney Dobell) Mathematical Theories of Economic Growth, 1970, Capital Theory and Dynamics, 1980, (others); contbr. articles to profl. jours. NSF grantee, 1964-81, 83-89; FTC contractee, 1979-80; Guggenheim fellow, 1974-76, NSF grad. fellow, 1962-65, NSF summer fellow, 1962, hon. Woodrow Wilson fellow, 1961-62. Fellow Econometric Soc. Address: Duke University Dept Econs DPC 90097 Durham NC 27708-0097

BURMEISTER, JOHN LUTHER, chemistry educator, consultant; b. Fountain Springs, Pa., Feb. 20, 1938; s. Luther John and Frieda May (Tielmann) B.; m. Doris Aileen Crawford, June 25, 1960; children: Lisa Anne, Jeffrey Scott. B.S. in Chemistry, Franklin and Marshall Coll., 1959; Ph.D. in Chemistry, Northwestern U., 1964; Instr. chemistry U. Ill., Urbana, 1963-64; asst. prof. chemistry U. Del., Newark, 1964-69, assoc. prof., 1969-73, prof., 1973-93, assoc. chmn. dept. chemistry, 1974—, alumni disting. prof., 1993—, NCAA faculty athletic rep., 1982—; chmn. chemistry editorial review bd. Control Data Corp., Mpls., 1981-85. Mem. editorial bd. Inorganica Chimica Acta, Padua, Italy, 1967-88, Synthesis and Reactivity in Inorganic and Metal-Organic Chemistry, N.Y.C., 1970-98; contbr. numerous articles to profl. jours. Ruling elder Head of Christiana Presbyn. Ch., Newark, 1969—; pres. Covered Bridge Farms Maintenance Corp., Newark, 1977-79. Recipient Excellence in Teaching award Lindback Found. Del. Alumni Assn., 1968, 1979; award for Excellence in Chemistry Teaching, Chem. Mfrs. Assn., Washington, 1981; Mortar Board faculty recognition award, 1984; Coll. Arts and Sci. Prof. of Yr. award, 1985; State of Del. Prof. of Yr award Carnegie Found. for Advancement Teaching/Coun. for Advancement and Support Edn., 1994, Disting. Del. Scientist award Del. Acad. Sci., 1994, Excellence-in-Tchg. award Alpha Lambda Delta, 1997. Mem. Am. Chem. Soc. (inorganic div. sec.-treas. 1975-77, alt. councillor, 1977-79, assoc. nat. com. on chem. edn. 1983-84, Del. sect. councillor 1987-89), Sigma Xi, Phi Lambda Upsilon, Phi Kappa Phi (Del. chpt. v.p. 1979-80, pres. 1980-81), Omicron Delta Kappa. Republican. Office: U Del Dept Chemistry & Biochemistry Newark DE 19716

BURMEISTER, PAUL FREDERICK, farmer; b. Great Bend, Kans., June 11, 1938; s. Ferdinand Frederick Adam and Gertrude Nellie (Hanson) B. BA in Chemistry and Agr., Ft. Hays State U., 1960; postgrad., U. Kans., 1961. Farmer Claflin, Kans., 1952-61, 64—; farmer coop. Kans. Agrl. Experiment Sta., Ft. Hays Br. Sta., Hays, Kans., 1970, Kans. Rural Ctr., Whiting, 1991, 92; panel mem. Kans. Sustainable Agr. Conf., Great Bend and Salina, 1991, 92; mem. Kans. Natural Resource Coun., Topeka, 1975—, Nat. Resources Def. Coun., N.Y.C., 1975—; participant,U. Akron Nat. Energy Forum, 1976, Nat. Low-Level Radioactive Waste Mgmt. Strategy Rev. Workshop, Washington, 1981; participant pub. forum on radioactive wastes Office Radiation Programs, EPA, Denver, 1978; guest speaker, Rapid City, S.D., 1993. Contbr. articles to environ. and agrl. jours. Vol. Am. Peace Corps, Ludhiana, India, 1961-63; local organizer campaign Union of Concerned Scientists, Cambridge, Mass.; lobbyist on environ. protection and conservation issues, Topeka, 1976-80; mem. Renew Am., Washington, 1980—; mem. The Menninger Found., Topeka, 1989—, Environ. Action, 1982—; lay mem. ad hoc task force on ecology Christian lifestyle United Ch. of Christ, 1977-78, commn. on outreach Kans.-Okla. conf., 1988-96, 98-99, network environ. and econ. responsibility; participant Kans. Citizens Forum Com. for Humanities, Topeka, 1987; mem. farmer adv. com. Sunshine Farm Project, Land Inst., Salina, Kans., 1995—. With USNG, 1963-69. Recipient Bankers award Banks of Barton County, Kans. and U.S. Soil Conservation Svc., 1990. Mem. Nat. Wildlife Fedn. (life), Nat. Coun. Returned Peace Corps Vols., Nat. Arbor Day Found., World Wildlife Fund (charter), Am. Wind Energy Assn., Am. Solar Energy Soc. (life), Midwest Renewable Energy Assn., 1998—, Kans. Assn. Wheat Growers, Kans. Farmers Union, Kans. Organic Prodrs., Inc., Friends of the Earth, Cousteau Soc. (founding yr. mem.), Kans. State Hist. Soc. (life), Kans. Wildlife Fedn., Sierra Club (life), Native Forest Coun., Ducks Unlimited Inc., Environ. Def. Fund, Wilderness Soc., Friends of India, Tau Kappa Epsilon (sec. 1958-59, scholar 1959), Nature Conservancy, Phi Eta Sigma (historian 1958-59), Phi Kappa Phi, Delta Epsilon. Avocations: photography, hiking, exploring. Home: RR 1 Box 168 Claflin KS 67525-9219

BURNESS, JAMES HUBERT, chemistry educator; b. Phila., Nov. 20, 1949; s. James Hubert and Josephine Elizabeth Burness; m. Mary Regel, Dec. 11, 1971; children: Monika Leigh, Allison Nicole. BA in Chemistry, Rutgers U., 1971; PhD in Inorganic Chemistry, Va. Poly. Inst. & State U., 1975. Quality control chemist Harshaw Chem. Co., Gloucester, N.J., 1969-71; quality control supr. GAF Corp., Gloucester, 1971; instr. Lansing (Mich.) Community Coll., 1976; postdoctoral fellow Mich. State U., East Lansing, 1975-76; instr. U. Md., Munich, 1983-85; asst. prof. chemistry Pa. State U., York, 1976-92, assoc. prof. chemistry, 1992-98, prof. chemistry, 1998—; computer cons., York, 1985—; software reviewer DC Heath and Co., 1990. Referee Jour. of Chem. Edn., 1989—; contbr. articles to profl. jours. Recipient J. Shelton Horsley award Va. Acad. Sci., 1973, Student Appreciation award York Campus, 1979, York Campus Annual Teaching award Pa. State U., 1986, 99, George W. Atherton award for Excellence in Teaching, 1990. Mem. Am. Chem. Soc. (chmn. southeastern Pa. sect. 1991), Sigma Xi (rsch. award 1975). Avocations: personal computing, pvt. pilot, photography, fgn. langs., sports. Office: Pa State U 1031 Edgecomb Ave York PA 17403-3326

BURNETT, ARTHUR LOUIS, SR., judge; b. Spotsylvania County, Va., Mar. 15, 1935; s. Robert Louis and Lena Victoria (Bumbry) B.; m. Ann Lloyd, May 14, 1960; children: Darnellena, Arthur Louis II, Darryl, Darlisa, Dionne. B.A. summa cum laude, Howard U., 1957; LL.B., NYU, 1958; grad., Fed. Exec. Inst., 1978. Bar: D.C. 1958, U.S. Dist. Ct. Md. 1963, U.S. Supreme Ct. 1964. Atty. Gen.'s Honor Program atty. fraud sect. criminal div. U.S. Dept. Justice, Washington, 1958; atty. to acting dep. chief gen. crimes sect. U.S. Dept. Justice, 1960-65; spl. asst. U.S. atty., Balt. and East St. Louis, Ill., 1961-63; asst. U.S. atty. D.C., 1965-68; legal adviser, gen. counsel D.C. Dept. Met. Police, 1968-69; U.S. magistrate U.S. Dist. Ct., Washington, 1969-75; asst. gen. counsel legal adv. div. U.S. CSC, 1975-78; assoc. gen. counsel Office of Personnel Mgmt., 1979-80; U.S. magistrate U.S. Dist. Ct. D.C., 1980-87; judge Superior Ct. D.C., 1987-98, sr. judge, 1998—; faculty Fed. Jud. Center, 1970—, Nat. Jud. Coll., 1974—; judge-in-residence Children's Def. Fund, 1998—; program chmn. ann. meeting Nat. Conf. Spl. Ct. Judges, Washington, 1973, chmn. elect, acting chmn., 1974-75, chmn., 1975; program chmn. ann. meeting Nat. Council U.S. Magistrates, Williamsburg, Va., 1974, pres., 1983-84; program participant D.C. Circuit Jud. Conf., 1974, U.S. Ct. Claims Jud. Conf., 1979; adj. prof. Columbus Sch. Law, Cath. U. Am., 1997—, Cath. U., 1997—, Sch. Law Harvard U., 1998—. Mem. NYU Law Rev., 1957-58. Recipient Founders Day award NYU, 1958; Army Commendation medal, 1960; Sustained Superior Performance award U.S. Atty. Gen., 1963; Disting. Service award CSC, 1978; Meritorious Service award U.S. Office of Personnel Mgmt., 1980, Jud. award of excellence Washington Met. Trial Lawyers Assn., 1999, award of excellence Nat. Conf. State Trial Judges, 1999; Outstanding Disting. Service award Fed. Bar Assn., 1983. Mem. ABA (Franklin N. Flashner jud. award as outstanding judge on ct. of spl. jurisdiction 1985, coun. adminstrv. law and regulatory practice sect. 1987-90, liaison rep. of adminstrv. law and regulatory practice sect. to adminstrv. conf. of U.S. 1990-94, mem. JAD task force on improving opportunities for minorities 1988-97, 98—, judge Edward R. Finch Law Day USA speech award 1991, asst. sec. 1991-93, chair civil right and employment discrimination com. 1992-95, sec. adminstrv. law and regulatory practice 1993-95, chair CJS com. on criminal rules and evidence 1993-97, standing com. on substance abuse 1995—, co-chair editl. bd. Criminal Justice Mag.), Fed. Bar Assn. (sect. coord. 1987-88, chmn. fed. litigation sect. 1984-85, chmn. standing com. on U.S. magistrates, dep. chmn. sect. adminstrn. of justice 1983-84, chmn. standing com. on U.S. magistrate, chmn. sect. adminstrn. of justice 1983-84, 95-97, pres. D.C. chpt. 1984-85, chair profl. ethics com. 1991-93, Disting. Svc. award 1978, The Pres.'s award 1994), Washington Bar Assn. (Ollie Mae Cooper award 1997), Nat. Bar Assn. (chair cmty. and youth action com. jud. coun. 1995—, chair profl. ethics com., jud. coun. asst. sec., The Pres.'s award 1996), Bar Assn. D.C., D.C. Unified Bar, Am. Judicature Soc., Am. Judges Assn. (sec-treas. Pretyman-Leventhal Inn of Ct. Washington 1991-92, 1993-94, pres. 1994-95), Phi Beta Kappa, Omega Psi Phi. Office: Superior Ct DC 500 Indiana Ave NW Ste 5520 Washington DC 20001-5520

BURNETT, CAROL, actress, comedienne, singer; b. San Antonio, Apr. 26, 1933; d. Jody and Louise (Creighton) B.; m. Joseph Hamilton, 1963 (div.); children: Carrie Louise, Jody Ann, Erin Kate. Student, UCLA, 1952-54. Introduced comedy song I Made a Fool of Myself Over John Foster Dulles, 1957; Broadway debut in Once Upon a Mattress, 1959; regular performer in Garry Moore TV show, 1959-62; appeared several CBS-TV spls., 1962-63; star Carol Burnett Show, CBS-TV, 1966-77, Carol & Co., 1990-91; appeared on Broadway, play Once Upon a Mattress, 1960, play Plaza Suite, 1970, musical play I Do, I Do, 1973, Same Time Next Year, 1977, TV miniseries Fresno, 1986, play Moon Over Buffalo, 1995 (Tony nomination); films include Who's Been Sleeping in My Bed, 1963, Pete 'n' Tillie, 1972, Front Page, 1974, A Wedding, 1977, Health, 1979, Four Seasons, 1981, Chu Chu and the Philly Flash, 1981, Annie, 1982, Noises Off, 1992, Moon Over Broadway, 1997, The Marriage Fool, 1998, Get Bruce, 1999; TV movies Friendly Fire, 1978, The Grass is Always Greener Over the Septic Tank, 1979, The Tenth Month, 1979, Life of the Party, 1982, Between Friends, 1983, Hostage, 1988, Men, Movies & Carol, 1994, Seasons of the Heart, 1994, Happy Birthday Elizabeth: A Celebration of Life, 1997, Grace, 1998; club engagements, Harrah's Club, The Sands, Caesar's Palace, MGM Grand; TV Men, Movies, and Carol, 1994, Seasons of the Heart, 1994, Happy Birthday Elizabeth: A Celebration of Life, 1997; TV series Mad About You, 1996—; dir., writer The Universal Story, 1995, also prodr. Southern Star: Portrait of Atlanta, 1996; prodr. Fred Astaire: Puttin' On His Top Hat, 1980, Fred Astaire: Change Partners and Dance, 1980, Bacall on Bogart, 1988, Fred Astaire Songbook, 1991, Southern Star: A Portrait of Atlanta, 1996, others. Recipient outstanding comedienne award Am. Guild Variety Artists, 5 times; Emmy award for outstanding variety performance Acad. TV Arts and Scis., 5 times; Emmy award for best supporting actress in a comedy series for Mad About You, 1997; TV Guide award for outstanding female performer, 1961, 62, 63; Peabody award, 1963; Golden Globe award for outstanding comedienne of year Fgn. Press Assn., 8 times; Woman of Year award Acad. TV Arts and Scis.; 12 People's Choice awards ; 1st ann. Nat. TV Critics Circle award for outstanding performance, 1977; San Sebastian Film Festival award for best actress for A Wedding, 1978; 1st Ace award Best Actress Between Friends, 1983, Horatio Alger award Horatio Alger Assn. Disting. Ams., 1988; named One of 20 Most Admired Women Gallup Poll, 1977. Address: ICM 8942 Wilshire Blvd Fl 2 Beverly Hills CA 90211-1934*

BURNETT, CASSIE WAGNON, middle school educator; b. Atlanta, Aug. 31, 1950; d. Lovic Pierce and Virginia (Slaughter) Wagnon; m. Irvin D. Burnett, Sept. 26, 1970; children: Bryan, Brittany. BA, Oglethorpe U., 1971; MEd, Ga. State U., 1975. Tchr. elem. sch. Dekalb County Bd. Edn., Decatur, Ga., 1971-81; tchr. jr. high sch. Greater Atlanta Christian Sch., Norcross, Ga., 1982—; 6th grade sponsor History Club, 1992-94; co-sponsor Joy Club, 1990-92. Home: 5071 Hodgkins Pl SW Lilburn GA 30047-7313 Office: Greater Atlanta Christian Sch PO Box 4277 Norcross GA 30091-4277

BURNETT, CHARLES, film director; b. Vicksburg, Miss., 1944; m. Gaye Shannon; children: Johnathan, Steven. BA, UCLA, MFA. Prodr. films, including Killer of Sheep, 1978, My Brother's Wedding, 1983, To Sleep with Anger, 1990, (TV documentary) American Becoming, 1991, The Glass shield, 1995, (screenplay) Bless Their Little Hearts, 1984. MacArthur Found. grantee, 1988-93. Office: Broder Kurland Webb Offner 9242 Beverly Blvd Ste 200 Beverly Hills CA 90210-3731*

BURNETT, CRYSTAL BLYTHE, marketing professional; b. Moundridge, Kans., Nov. 12, 1965; d. John Milford and Judy Carlene (Stucky) S.; married, 1993. Student, Wichita State U., 1984-87; BS in Journalism, U. Kans., 1989. Dispatcher, sec. Digital Computing Ctr., Wichita, Kans., 1985-86; production asst. Stephan Advt. Agy., Wichita, 1986-87; asst. to exec. sec. Kans. Scholastic Press Assn., Lawrence, 1987-89; recreation leader Boston Recreation Ctr., Wichita, 1987; profl. intern The Clay Ctr. Dispatch, Clay Center, Kans., 1988; photography stringer AP, 1988; profl. intern Stephan Advt. Agy., Wichita, 1989; retail exec. trainee Dillard Dept. Stores, Inc., Wichita, 1989-90, area sales mgr., 1990-91; asst. mktg. dir. West Ridge Mall, Topeka, 1991-92, The Forum Shops at Caesers, Las Vegas, Nev., 1992; mktg. dir. Machesney Park (Ill.) Mall, 1992-94, West Ridge Mall, Topeka, Kans., 1994-98; regional mktg. dir. Simon Property Group, Little Rock, Ark., 1998—. Mem. steering com. Topeka Breast Cancer Coalition; bd. dirs. Honor A Student Incentive Program, 1995-98. Recipient U.S. Nat. Leadership Merit award, 1984; Frances E. Taylor scholar, U. Kans., 1988. Mem. NAFE, Internat. Coun. Shopping Ctrs., Women in Comms., Inc., Topeka C. of C. (Honor A bd. dirs.), Order of Omega, Alpha Phi (promotions chmn. and philanthropy chmn. Gamma Xi chpt. 1984—). Home: # 1004 11810 Pleasant Ridge Rd Little Rock AR 72223-2262 Office: University Mall 300 S University Ave Little Rock AR 72205-5209

BURNETT, E. C., III, state supreme court justice; b. Spartanburg, S.C., Jan. 26, 1942; s. E.C. Jr. and Lucy (Byars) B.; m. Jami Grant, 1963; children: Curry, Sharon, Jeffrey. AB, Wofford Coll., 1964; JD, U. S.C., 1969. Bar: S.C. 1969. Mem. S.C. Ho. of Reps., 1973-74; probate judge Spartanburg County, 1976-80; judge family ct., 1980-81, Seventh Jud. Cir., 1981-95; assoc. justice S.C. Supreme Ct., 1995—. Elder Mt. Calvary Presbyn. Ch. Mem. ABA, S.C. Bar Assn. Home: 200 Burnett Rd Pauline SC 29374-2610 Office: PO Box 1742 180 Magnolia St Spartanburg SC 29304-1742*

BURNETT, ERIC STEPHEN, environmental consultant; b. Manchester, Eng., Apr. 5, 1924; s. William Louis and Edith Winifred (Gates) B.; came to U.S., 1963; naturalized, 1974; BSc in Physics (with honors), London U., 1954; MS in Environ. Studies, Calif. State, Dominguez Hills, 1976; PhD in Environ. Engring., Calif. Coast U., 1982. children: Diana, Ian, Brenda, Keith. Program mgr. Brit. Aircraft Corp., Stevenage, Eng., 1953-63; sr. systems engr. RCA, Princeton, N.J., 1963-66; project mgr. Gen. Electric Co., Valley Forge, Pa., 1966-67; dept. head TRW systems Group, Redondo Beach, Calif., 1967-72; dir. energy and pollution control ARATEX Svcs., Inc., Calif., 1974-81, dir. tech. devel., 1981-83, staff cons., 1983-91, retired, 1992; cons., lectr. in spacecraft sensor tech., energy conservation, environ. and contamination controls. With Royal Air Force, 1942-47. Assoc. fellow AIAA; mem. Inst. Environ. Scis. (sr.). Contbr. articles in field to profl. jours. Home and Office: 3423 Excalibar Rd Placerville CA 95667-5418

BURNETT, FRANCES, concert painist, teacher of piano; b. Centralia, Ill., Dec. 3, 1920; d. Bernard Baumheuter and Ollie Dee Burnett; m. Hinton Joseph Baker, June 24, 1943 (div. 1956); children: Eve Baker Street, Celeste Baker Simonds. MMus, Cin. Conservatory Music, 1942; studied with David Saperton,; Gina Bachaeur, Ilona Kabos, N.Y.C., London, Switzerland; studied with Guido Agosti, Siena and Rome; diploma di merito, Acad. Musicale Chigiana, Siena. Piano faculty Longy Sch. Music, Cambridge, Mass., 1955-64; piano faculty Coll. Mus. Arts Bowling Green (Ohio) State

U., 1964-91, mem. piano staff Coll. Mus. Arts, tchr. creative arts dept., 1991—. Appeared as recitalist, ensemble artist and soloist with orchs. throughout U.S., Europe and Mex.; pub. appearances include concerts at Town Hall and Merkin Hall in N.Y.C., Jordan Hall and the Gardner Mus., Boston, Abraham Goodman House, N.Y.C., Carnegie Recital Hall, N.Y.C., Phillips Gallery and Nat. Gallery, Washington, Toledo Mus. Art, Cleve. Inst., Wigmore Hall, London, Broadcast BBC, London, Musikrerein, Vienna, Hamburg, Berlin, Amsterdam; played on 3 CDs, 1994; recording of a concerto written for her by William Thomas McKinley with Seattle Symphony, 1999; contbr. articles to Clavier Mag. Mem. Toledo Piano Tchrs., Monday Musicale, Ohio Music Tchrs. Assn., Music Tchrs. Nat. Assn. Democrat. Roman Catholic. Avocation: swimming. Home: 23 Georgetown Dr Bowling Green OH 43402-9373

BURNETT, GARY MAIN, social work administrator, crisis counselor; b. Pontiac, Mich., Sept. 14, 1951; s. Kenneth Almeron Burnett and Thalia Ann (Main) Cather; m. Gail Susan Hewitt, Sept. 21, 1974; children: Alexander Main, Adam Tyler. BS in Psychology, No. Mich. U., Marquette, 1973; MA in Counseling, Oakland U., Rochester, Mich., 1977. Lic. profl. counselor, Mich.; cert. social worker, Mich. Asst. mgr. K-Mart Corp., Mt. Morris, Mich., 1974-75; coord. residence hall Oakland U., Rochester, 1975-78, adminstrv. asst., 1978-80, asst. dir. student affairs, 1980; exec. dir. Threshold Counseling Svcs., Royal Oak, Mich., 1980-84; client svcs. mgr. Cmty. Placement Program, Mt. Clemens, Mich., 1984-86; dir. Macomb County Crisis Ctr., Mt. Clemens, 1986—. Chmn. bd. dirs. Common Ground, Birmingham, Mich., 1978-81; mem. adv. bd. Sq. Lake Mental Health, Pontiac, Mich., 1988-89; chmn. adv. coun. Macomb County Substance Abuse Svcs., Mt. Clemens, 1990—; clin. coord. Macomb Emergency Response Group, Mt. Clemens, 1991—. Recipient Vol. Svc. award Gov. William Milliken, Birmingham, 1977, Plaque of Appreciation, Common Ground Bd. Dirs., Birmingham, 1981. Mem. Mich. Crisis Response Assn., Internat. Critical Incident Stress Found., Warren Hist. Soc., The Planetary Soc., Maple Leaf Club, House of Burnett, Inc. Avocations: piano, genealogy, astronomy, computers. Home: 3829 Dawson Ave Warren MI 48092-3209 Office: Macomb County Crisis Ctr 46360 Gratiot Ave Chesterfield MI 48051

BURNETT, GLENDA MORRIS, community health nurse; b. Chgo., Nov. 2, 1953; d. Booker T. and Alfreida (Knight) Morris; m. Rick Burnett, Dec. 18, 1981; children: Dana Marie, Diana Ashley. BSN, Rush U., Chgo., 1978; M in Urban Planning and Policy, U. Ill., Chgo., 1991. RN, Ill. Staff nurse Cook County Hosp., Chgo., 1978-79; nurse specialist staff devel. Mansfield (Ohio) Gen. Hosp., 1979-80; pub. health nurse City of Chgo., 1981; project coord., project reach futures U. Ill. Hosp., Chgo., 1989-94; project dir. teens, educating, learning and leading (TELL) U. Ill. Med. Ctr., Chgo., 1995—. Mem. ANA, Ill. Nurses Assn. (pres. dist. 21 1982-87).

BURNETT, HENRY, lawyer; b. N.Y.C., Feb. 24, 1927; s. Lucien Dallam and Ruth (Hinkle) B.; m. Florence Stewart, July 19, 1952; children: Marian Starr, Betsy Callaway, Henry Stewart. BA, U. Va., 1947, LLB, 1950. Bar: Va. bar 1950, Fla. bar 1951. Ptnr. Fowler, White, Burnett, Hurley, Banick & Strickroot, Miami, Fla., 1957-93, pres., 1957-93, ptnr., 1993—. Bd. dirs. Dade County Citizens Safety Council, Travelers Aid, United Family and Children's Services. Served with USNR, 1945-46. Fellow Am. Coll. Trial Lawyers; mem. Am., Fla., Dade County bar assns., Fla. Def. Lawyers Assn. (pres. 1967-68), Dade County Def. Bar Assn. (pres. 1966-67), Internat. Assn. Def. Counsel (exec. com. 1972-74, pres. 1976-77). Episcopalian. Clubs: Riviera Country. Home: 4720 SW 85th St Miami FL 33143-8632 Office: Nations Bank Tower 100 SE 2nd St Fl 13 Miami FL 33131-2195

BURNETT, HOWARD JEROME, college president; b. Holyoke, Mass., Oct. 14, 1929; s. William and Bridget (Breck) B.; m. Barbara J. Ransohoff, June 12, 1954 (dec. Mar. 1991); children: Lee Ann, Sue Allison, Mark Howard; m. Maryann de Palma, May 28, 1994. B.A., Amherst Coll., 1952, Oxford U., 1954; M.A. (Rhodes scholar), Oxford U., 1958; LL.D., Ithaca Coll., 1965; Ph.D., N.Y. U., 1965; DHL, Washington and Jefferson Coll., 1998. Cons. Booz, Allen & Hamilton, 1958; sec. A.L. Ransohoff Co., Inc., N.Y.C., 1958-60; mem. internatl. econs. staff Texaco, Inc., N.Y.C., 1960-62; asst. to pres. Corning (N.Y.) Community Coll., 1962-64; pres. Coll. Center of the Finger Lakes, Corning, 1964-70, Washington and Jefferson Coll., Washington, Pa., 1970-99; civilian aide to Sec. of the Army for Western Pa., 1978-80; mem. Nat. Adv. Bd. on Internat. Edn. Programs, U.S. Dept. Edn., 1987-88. Served to lt. USNR, 1955-58. Mem. Assn. Am. Rhodes Scholars, Pa. Assn. Colls. and Univs., Duquesne Club, Rolling Rock Club, Phi Beta Kappa, Delta Kappa Epsilon. Office: Washington & Jefferson Coll Office of Pres Washington PA 15301

BURNETT, JEAN BULLARD (MRS. JAMES R. BURNETT), biochemist; b. Flint, Mich., Feb. 19, 1924; d. Chester M. and Katheryn (Krasser) Bullard; B.S., Mich. State U., 1944, M.S., 1945, Ph.D. (Council fellow), 1952; m. James R. Burnett, June 8, 1947. Research assoc. dept. zoology Mich. State U., East Lansing, 1954-59, dept. biochemistry, 1959-61, acting dir. research biochem. genetics, dept. biochemistry, 1961-62, assoc. prof., asst. chmn. dept. biomechanics, 1973-82, prof. dept. anatomy, 1982-84, prof. dept. zoology, Coll. Natural Sci. and Coll. Osteo. Medicine, 1984—; assoc. biochemist Mass. Gen. Hosp., Boston, 1964-73; prin. research assoc. dermatology Harvard, 1962-73, faculty medicine, 1964-73, also spl. lectr., cons., tutor Med. Sch.; vis. prof. dept. biology U. Ariz., 1979-80. USPHS, NIH grantee, 1965-68; Gen. Research Support grantee Mass. Gen. Hosp., 1968-72; Ford Found. travel grantee, 1973; Am. Cancer Soc. grantee, 1971-73; Internat. Pigment Cell Conf. travel grantee, 1980; recipient Med. Found. award, 1970. Mem. AAAS, Am. Chem. Soc., Am. Inst. Biol. Sci., Genetics Soc. Am., Soc. Investigative Dermatology, N.Y. Acad. Scis., Sigma Xi (Research award 1971), Pi Kappa Delta, Kappa Delta Pi, Pi Mu Epsilon, Sigma Delta Epsilon. Home: PO Box 805 Okemos MI 48805-0805 Office: Mich State Univ Dept Zoology Natural Sci Bldg East Lansing MI 48824

BURNETT, JOHN NICHOLAS, retired chemistry educator; b. Atlanta, Aug. 19, 1939; s. Joseph Nicholas and Maurine (Morris) B. AB in Chemistry, Emory U., 1961, MS in Analytical Chemistry, 1963, PhD in Analytical Chemistry, 1965. Rsch. chemist organic chems. dept. DuPont Co., Wilmington, Del., 1965-66; rsch. assoc. chemistry dept. U. N.C., Chapel Hill, 1966-68; asst. prof. chemistry Davidson (N.C.) Coll., 1968-72, assoc. prof., 1972-80, prof., 1980-81, Maxwell Chambers prof., 1981-98, Maxwell Chambers prof. emeritus, 1998—, asst. to the pres., 1977-79, chmn. chemistry dept., 1972-85, assoc. dean faculty, 1980-85; vis. fellow dept. civil engring. Princeton (N.J.) U., 1983, 85-87; vis. prof. dept. chemistry, Ind. U., Bloomington, 1983; sec./treas. Internat. Ctr. for Disarmament and Conversion, Washington, 1993—. Contbr. articles to profl. jours. A.P. Sloan Found. Sabbatical fellow Princeton U., 1985-86. Mem. AAUP, AIChE, Am. Chem. Soc., Royal Soc. Chemistry, Soc. Hist. Tech., Hist. Sci. Soc. Republican. Episcopalian. Home: 727 Virginia Rd PO Box 238 Davidson NC 28036-0238 also: ICDC PO Box 592 Davidson NC 28036-0592

BURNETT, KEITHA DENISE, social studies educator; b. Tarboro, N.C., July 26, 1961; d. Allen and Roxie (Hinton) L.; m. Michael David Burnett, Nov. 9, 1996; 1 child, Melanie. BA, U. N.C., 1982; MPA, U. N.D., 1985; PhD, Fla. Internat., 1995. Tchr. Miami-Dade Pub. Schs., 1985—; evaluation com. State of Fla., Daytona, 1996-97. Mem. PTA, Miami, 1991—. Named Social Studies Tchr. of Yr. Dade County Coun. for Social Studies, 1996, Outstanding Svc. award Alumni at Bethune Cookman Coll., 1997. Mem. NAACP, Nat. Writer's Assn., Local Coun. for Social Studies, Nat. Coun. for Social Studies, Alpha Kappa Alpha. Democrat. Baptist. Avocations: reading, writing, traveling, family gathering/reunions. E-mail: mkbur293@aol.com. Office: Coral Reef Sr High 10101 SW 152nd St Miami FL 33157

BURNETT, LONNIE SHELDON, obstetrics and gynecology educator; b. Saratoga, Tex., Aug. 2, 1927; s. Lonnie and Lois (Swift) B.; m. Betty Pearle Scruggs, Dec. 22, 1950; children: Anne Julian, Michael Julian. BS, U. Tex., 1948; MD, U. Tex., Galveston, 1953. Diplomate Am. Coll. Obstetricians and Gynecologists (chmn. Tenn. sect. 1988-91, mem. com. on sci. program, 1988-91). Intern Henry Ford Hosp., Detroit, 1953-54; resident in internal medicine Mayo Clinic, Rochester, Minn., 1954-55; resident in ob-gyn Johns Hopkins Hosp., Balt., 1957-62, fellow in microbiology, 1962-64; asst. prof. microbiology Johns Hopkins U., Balt., 1964-67, asst. prof. ob-gyn., 1964-70, assoc. prof., 1970-76; chmn. dept. ob-gyn. Vanderbilt U., Nashville, 1976-95, prof. ob-gyn., 1976—; mem. ob-gyn. text com. Nat. Bd. Med. Examiners, 1988-91. Co-author: Novak's Textbook of Gynecology, 11th edit., 1988; contbr. articles to profl. jours. Capt. USAF, 1955-57. Macy scholar Josiah Macy Jr. Found., 1965-70. Mem. Tenn. Ob-Gyn. Soc. (pres. 1988-90), Nashville Acad. Medicine (pres. 1999—). Republican. Episcopalian. Avocation: photography. Home: 78 Concord Park W Nashville TN 37205-4707 Office: Vanderbilt Med Ctr N Dept Ob-Gyn 1611 21st Ave S Nashville TN 37212-3103

BURNETT, LYNN BARKLEY, health science educator; b. Reedley, Calif., Oct. 20, 1948; s. Charles Erbin and Ruth Clarice (Erickson) B. BS, Columbia Pacific U., MSc; diploma in nat. security mgmt. Nat. Def. U. of U.S.; PhD in Physiology and Psychology, Columbia Pacific U.; EdD in Higher Edn. Nova Southeastern U.; Faculty of Laws, U. London. Cert. c.c. tchr., Calif., instr. in emergency care, basic CPR, ACLS, Pediatric ALS. Med. advisor Fresno County Sheriff's Depart., 1972—, assoc. dir. Cen. Valley Emergency Med. Svcs. System, Fresno, Calif., 1974-75; faculty Fresno City Coll., 1978—, prof. health sci., 1981-87, dir. continuing edn. in health, Calif. State U. Fresno, 1981—, adj. faculty West Coast Christian Coll., 1989-92, med. and health commentator Sta. KVPR-FM Valley Pub. Radio, 1990—; lectr., cons. in field; cons. emergency med. svcs., 1975—, bioethics, 1992—, clin. and path. ogforensic scis., 1992—; co-dir. conjoint rsch. program of Stanford U. Sch. Medicine and Dept. Health Sci. Calif. State U., Fresno, 1986; established pilot paramedic program Fresno County, 1974-75; dir. Cent. Valley's Inaugural Paramedic Tng. Program, 1975; established CPR tng. Programs Fresno Fire Dept., 1968, Fresno Police Dept., 1972, Fresno County Sheriff's Dept., 1973. Chmn. Fresno County steering com. The Chem. People, 1983-86, Generation at Risk, 1987; mem. Emergency Med. Care Com. Fresno County, 1979-85, vice chmn., 1984-85; mem. Calif. State Commn. Emergency Med. Services, 1974-75; mem. Fresno County Adv. Bd. on Drug Abuse, 1984-92, chmn. drug adv. bd., 1985-88; bd. mgrs. First Bapt. Ch. Fresno, 1994—, vice chmn., 1995—, chmn., 1996, pres. corp., 1996; chmn. pub. edn. Fresno County unit Am. Cancer Soc., 1984-87, 90-92, bd. dirs. 1984—, v.p., 1985-87, pres. elect 1987-88, pres. 1988-90, past. pres., 1990-92, chmn. nominations and leadership devel. Fresno County unit, 1990-92, task force cancer and underserved populations Fresno County unit, 1992—, youth and cancer, Calif. Divsn. Am. Cancer Soc., 1992-94; com. mem. Early Detection and Treatment, Prevention and Risk Reduction, Fresno County Unit Am. Cancer Soc., 1993;; chmn. Alcohol, Drug adv bd. Fresno County, 1992—; pres. Fresno County Safety Coun., 1985—; mem. steering com. Fresno Health Promotion Coalition, chmn. com. on crime, violence and safety, 1987-89; chmn. bd. Fresno County Drug and Alcohol Prevention Coalition, Inc., 1991-92; mem. med. staff, steering com. All-Star Football Game. 1965—; emergency med. cons. Dept. Intercollegiate Athletics Calif. State U., Fresno, 1982—; mem. Community Collaborative of Fresno Tomorrow, Inc., com. Juvenile Crime Benchmarks, 1990-91; mem. core com. Student Assistance Program for Substance Abuse and Related Problems Fresno City Coll., 1989—; mem. coms. on bus. and industry and govt. Fresno County Master Plan Adv. Body for Comprehensive Coordination of Substance Abuse Svcs.; faculty advanced trauma life support and trauma nurse tactics Valley Med. Ctr., 1982—; bd. dirs. Calif. div. Am. Cancer Soc., 1990-92; chmn. com. pub. policy Fresno County Drug, Alcohol Prevention Coalition, Inc., 1992—; mem. cancer svcs. adv. bd., Calif. Cancer Ctr., 1992-94; mem. com. biomed. ethics Fresno Community Hosp. and Med. Ctr., 1992—; subcom. mem. Resuscitation Status, Advance Directives, and Organ Donation, Protocol for Consultations and Med. Records, Intramural and Extramural Bioethics Edn., 1993; mem. com. emergency cardiac care, Central Valley Divsn. of Am. Heart Assn., 1992—; mem. steering com., subcom. neighborhood revitalization and svc. coord., Oper. "Weed and Seed", office of U.S. attorney gen. eastern dist. Calif., 1992-93; chmn. master plan adv. body to reduce alcohol and other drug abuse in Fresno County. Recipient State Service medal Calif. Mil. Dept., 1980; Bronze medal Am. Heart Assn., 1974, Appreciation award Am. Cancer Soc., 1985, Outstanding Svc. award Fresno County Drug & Alcohol Prevention Coalition, Inc. Mem. AAAS, Am. Coll. Preventive Medicine, Am. Acad. Forensic Scis. (alt. del. People's Republic of China, citizen ambassador program People to People Internat. 1986), Am. Assn. Suicidology, N.Y. Acad. Scis., Internat. Platform Assn., Fresno County Bar Assn. Republican. Baptist. Avocations: reading, musical conducting, writing screenplays. Co-author: manuscript for motion picture Quarantine. Home: PO Box 4512 Fresno CA 93744-4512

BURNETT, PATRICIA HILL, artist, author, sculptor, lecturer; b. Bklyn., Sept. 5, 1920; d. William Burr and Mimi (Uline) Hill; m. William Anding Lange, 1944 (div. 1947); 1 child, William Hill; m. Harry Albert Burnett, Oct. 9, 1948 (dec. 1979); children: Harry Burnett III, Terrill Hill, Hillary Hill; m. Robert L. Siler, 1989. Student, U. Toledo, 1937-38, Goucher Coll., 1939-41, MA program Inst. D'Allende, Mex., 1967, Wayne State U., 1972; pvt. studies with, John Carroll, Detroit, 1941-44, Sarkis Sarkisian, Detroit, 1956-60, Wallace Bassford, Provincetown, Mass., 1968-72, Walter Midener, Detroit, 1960-63. Actress Long Ranger and Green Hornet prgrams, Radio Blue Network, 1941-46; tchr. painting and sculpture U. Mich. Extension, Ann Arbor, 1965—; lectr. N.Y. Speakers Bur., 1971—; propr. Burnett Studios, Detroit, 1962-88, mgr., 1962—. Numerous one-woman shows of paintings and sculptures include Scarab Club, Detroit, 1971, Midland (Mich.) Art Ctr., Wayne State U., Detroit, The Gallery, Ft. Lauderdale, Fla., Agra Gallery, Washington, Salon des Artes, Paris; numerous group shows include: Palazzo Pruili Gallery, Venice, 1971, Detroit Inst. of Arts, 1967, Butler Mus., North Cleveland, 1972, Windsor (Ont., Can.) Art Ctr., 1973, Weisbaden (Germany) Gallery, 1976, Retrospective Show: Birmingham Bloomfield Art Assn., 1997; represented in permanent collections: Detroit Inst. Arts, Wayne State U., Wooster (Ohio) Coll., Ford Motor Co., Detroit, Bloomfield Art Assn., Bloomfield Hills, Mich., Henry Ford Hosp. Collection, Fed. Ct. Appeals in Washington, City-County Bldg., Detroit, Mich. State Capitol Bldg., Royal Acad. of Art, London, Royal Palace of India, New Delhi, Palace of The Philippines, Manila, Mansion of Prime Minister, Greece; also pvt. collections: numerous portrait paintings including Indira Ghandi, Benson Ford, Joyce Carol Oates, Mrs. Edsel Ford, Betty Ford, Roman Gribbs, Princess Olga Mrivani, Lord John Mackintosh, Marlo Thomas, Viveca Lindfois, Betty Freidan, Gloria Steinem, Congresswoman Martha Griffiths, Margaret Papandreou, Valentina Tereshkova, Barbara Walters, Margaret Thatcher, Corazon Aquino, Violetta Chamarra, Jackie Joyner Kersee, Mayor Dennis Archer, Wayne U. pres. David Adamany, author Kate Millett, Michele Engler and triplets, Patricia Ireland, Rosa Parks, others; mem. editl. bd. Am. Portrait Soc.; author: True Colors: An Artist's Journey from Beauty Queen to Feminist. Chairwoman of Mich. Women's Commn., 1972—; pres. Detroit House of Correction Commn., 1975—; treas. Rep. Dist. 1 of Mich., 1973—; mem. Issues com., Rep. State Ctrl. Com., 1975-76; sec. Rep. State Ways and Means com., 1975—, Detroit Libr. Commn., 1980-85, Detroit Human Rights Commn., 1976-80, Detroit City Planning Commn., 1985-90; mem. Mich. State Adv. Coun. vocat. Edn.; mem. Mich. Arts in Edn. Coun., 1978—; mem. New Detroit Arts Com., 1979—; chmn. World Feminist Commn., 1974—; life mem. NAACP. Recipient Silver Salute award Mich. State U., 1976, Most Popular award San Diego Sculpture Show, 1971, First prize award Cape Cod Artists Show, 1968, State of Mich. award for creativity Gov. John Engler, 1999; named Disting. Woman of Mich., Bus. and Profl. Women's Orgn., 1974, Disting. Woman Northwood Inst., 1977, Artist of Yr., Mich. Art Train, 1989, Disting. Woman award Mich. Bus. and Profl. Women Internat.; named to Ohio Hall of Fame, 1987, Mich. Women's Hall of Fame, 1988, one of Most Outstanding Women in Mich., Women in Advt., 1998, one of 10 People with Most Clout Outside of County, Detroit Free Press, 1998. Mem. Mich. Women's Forum (founder 1989, bd. dirs. 1989-99, internat. women's forum), Detroit Inst. Arts (dir. membership com. 1958—), Nat. Assn. Commns. for Women (pres. 1976-78), Mich. Acad. of Arts, Detroit Soc. Women Painters and Sculptprs, Women in the Arts, Scrab Club (dir. 1962-63), Ibex Club (pres. 1951), NOW (nat. bd. 1971-75, del. UN conf. Mex., 1975, Feminist of Yr.), Coun. Leading portrait Painters (elect), Women's Econ. Club, N.Y. Portrain Club (nat. adv. bd. 1977—), French-Am. C.of C. (v.p.), Alpha Phi, Zonta, Detroit Econ. Club (bd. dirs.). Episcopalian. Home and Studio: 13 Oaks Ct Bloomfield Hills MI 48304

BURNETT, PAUL DAVID, small business owner; b. Arlington, Tex., Sept. 19, 1963; s. Paul W. and Joyce (Childers) B.; m. Jeri Dee Walker, June 23, 1989; children: Kayli Danielle, Brayden Paul, Makenzie Dee. BBA, Tex. Christian U., 1985, MBA, 1989. Pres. Burnett's Staffing, Arlington, Tex., 1985—. Dir. Vol. Adv. Com., Arlington, 1991-92. Mem. Tex. Assn. Pers. Cons. (bd. dirs. 1991), Metroplex Assn. Pers. Cons. (bd. dirs. 1991-93), Nat. Assn. Pers. Cons., Nat. Assn. Temporary Cons. Avocations: golf, football, basketball, baseball, softball. Home: 1303 Burgandy Ct Southlake TX 76092-7819 Office: Burnetts Staffing 2710 Avenue E Arlington TX 76011-5206

BURNETT, ROBERT A., retired publisher; b. Joplin, Mo., June 4, 1927; s. Lee Worth and Gladys (Plummer) B.; m. Gloria M. Cowden, Dec. 25, 1948; children: Robert A., Stephen, Gregory, Douglas, David, Penelope. AB, U. Mo., 1948. Salesman Cowden Motor Co., Guthrie Center, Iowa; then Equitable Life Assurance Soc., Joplin, Mo.; retired chmn., CEO Meredith Corp.; ret., 1991; bd. dirs. Whirlpool corp., Hartford Fin. Svcs., ITT Industries. Served with AUS, 1945-46. Congregationalist. Home: 2942 Sioux Ct Des Moines IA 50321-1446 Office: Regency West 6 Ste 115 4600 Westown Pkwy West Des Moines IA 50266-1042

BURNETT, ROBERT ADAIR, university administrator, history educator; b. Spartanburg, S.C., Jan. 25, 1934; s. Wendell and Curtiss Catherine (Adair) B.; m. Mary Maude Vaughan, July 26, 1958; children: Dorothy Catherine Autin, Wendy Jo. AB in Econs., Wofford Coll., 1956; MA in History, U. N.C., 1959, PhD in History, 1968. Asst. prof. Pfeiffer Coll., Misenheimer, N.C., 1960-63; instr. U. N.C., Chapel Hill, 1963-66; asst. prof. U. Louisville, 1966-69, assoc. prof., 1969-74, prof., 1974-78, chmn. history dept., 1968-71, univ. ombudsman, 1974-76; prof. Armstrong State Coll., Savannah, Ga., 1978—, dean arts and scis., 1978-80, acad. v.p., 1980-82, acting pres., 1982-84, pres., 1984—. Editor: Marshall's World War II Encyclopedia, 1979; contbr. articles to profl. jours. Mem. Savannah Arts Commn., 1985-90; trustee Ga. Coun. on Econ. Edn., Atlanta, 1984—, Candler Gen. Hosp., Savannah, 1985—; bd. dirs. Boy Scouts Am., Savannah, 1982—; mem. bd. Savannah Econ. Devel. Authority, 1987—. 1st lt. U.S. Army, 1956-58. Mem. Am. Assn. State Colls. and Univs. (various coms.), So. Assn. Colls. and Schs. (cons. 1983—), NCAA (Pres.' commn.), Phi Beta Kappa, Phi Alpha Theta. Episcopalian. Office: Armstrong Atlantic State U Office of Pres 11935 Abercorn St Savannah GA 31419-1989*

BURNETT, ROBERT BARRY, professional football player; b. Livingston, N.J., Aug. 27, 1967. Student, Syracuse U. Defensive end Cleve. Browns, 1990-96, Balt. Ravens (formerly Cleve. Browns), 1996—. Selected to Pro Bowl, 1994. Office: Balt Ravens 11001 Owings Mills Blvd Owings Mills MD 21117-2857*

BURNETT, WALTER, JR., city official. Alderman Chgo., 1996—. Office: 2009 W Grand Ave Chicago IL 60612-1501 also: 1336 N Sedgwick St Chicago IL 60610-1828*

BURNETTE, ADA M. PURYEAR, educational administrator; b. Darlington, S.C., Oct. 24; d. Theodore and Floia (King) Peoples; m. Paul Lionel Puryear, Sr., Mar. 27, 1954 (div. 1975); children: Paul Lionel Puryear, Jr., Paula Lynn Puryear; m. Thomas Carlos Burnette, Sr., Aug. 25, 1984; stepchildren: Diane Burnette Day, Thomas Carlos Burnette, Jr., Anita Burnette Houser. BA in Math., Talladega Coll., 1953; postgrad., Chgo. State U., 1954-56; MA in Reading, U. Chgo., 1958; PhD, Fla. State U., 1986; postgrad., Fla. A&M U., 1994. High sch. math. tchr. Winston-Salem, N.C., 1953-54; elem. tchr. Chgo. Pub. Schs., 1954-58; reading clinician U. Chgo., 1958; dir. reading clinic, asst. prof. Norfolk State U., 1958-61, Tuskegee Inst., 1961-66; coord. freshman math., asst. prof. math., Fisk U., 1966-70; adminstr. early childhood basic skills and elem. edn. State of Fla. Dept. Edn., Tallahassee, 1973-88; assoc. prof., program dir., grad. studies dir. Bethune-Cookman Coll., Daytona Beach, Fla., 1988-90; dir., supt. Fla. A&M Univ. Devel. Rsch. Pub. Sch. Dist., Tallahassee, 1990-93; coord., prof., dept. chmn., dir. PhD program devel. Fla. A&M Univ., 1993-98, coord., prof., 1998—; hostess radio talk show, 1977-79; sec.-treas. Afro-Am. Rsch. Assocs., 1968-74; tutor, diagnostician, lectr., cons., planner, 1958—; cons. Job Corps, Alpha Kappa Alpha, N.C. Advancement Sch., pub. co.; lectr. univ. classes. Pres., PTA, 1975-76, v.p., 1983-84; del. state Dem. women's meeting, Fla., 1978, 79; mem. Dem. Exec. Com. Leon County, 1981-88, 91-93; edn. commentator WFSU radio, 1993-94; mem. NAACP, United Fund com., Leon County 4C Bd.; pres. Norfolk Women's Interracial Coun., 1960; mem. Urban League. Mem. Fla. Assn. Suprs. and Adminstrs., Fla. Coun. on Elem. Edn., Fla. State Reading Assn., Assn. State Cons. on Early Childhood Edn., Alliance of Black Sch. Educators, Fla. Assn. for Supervision and Curriculum Devel. (regional dir. policy rev. jour. editl. bd. 1995—), Internat. Reading Assn. (nat. early childhood com., nat. textbook com. nat. awards com., nat. media com., pres. Concerned Educators Black Students, 1983-86, nat. med. com., library/media com.), Nat. Assn. Elem. Sch. Prins., Fla. Assn. Elem. Sch. Prins., Nat. Assn. Edn. Young Children, Fla. Assn. Children Under Six, So. Assn. Children Under Six, Leon Assn. Children Under Six (pres. 1977), Assn. Childhood Edn. Internat., So. Assn. Colls. and Schs. (elem. and mid. sch. commn.), Socs. Docta Inc. (sec. 1987-93), Phi Delta Kappa, Phi Kappa Phi (pres. 1985-86, v.p. pub. rels. chair), Pi Lambda Theta, Alpha Kappa Alpha (treas., summer sch. dir., undergrad. adv., parliamentarian sec.), Drifters (pres., nat. membership chmn. 1977-79, historian, reporter 1992-94, pres. 1994—, Nat. Now Black Woman 1984), The Holidays (pres., v.p., nat. sec. fin. 1993-97, v.p. 1997—), Am. Assn. Sch. Adminstrs., FAMU Ladies Art and Social Club (pres.), Fla. Soc. Cert. Pub. Mgrs. (newsletter bd.). Regular columnist profl. jours., 1974—; writer grants proposals; weekly columnist Capital Outlook, 1991-97; contbr. articles to profl. publs. Presbyterian (deacon). Home: PO Box 7432 Tallahassee FL 32314-7432 Office: Fla A&M U Gore Edn Ctr B-308 Tallahassee FL 32307 *Never do anything illegal or immoral as you strive for excellence and do your best in all you do in your journey to make this world a better place.*

BURNETTE, JAMES THOMAS, lawyer; b. Stuart, Va., Apr. 7, 1959; s. Edwin Lee and Marye Joanne (Minter) B.; m. Sarah Katherine Kelly, Dec. 2, 1989; children: Sarah Elizabeth, Thomas Pullen. BS, Campbell U., 1981; JD, Wake Forest U., 1984. Bar: N.C. 1985. Atty. Womble Carlyle Sandridge & Rice, Winston-Salem, N.C., 1985-86; ptnr. Edmundson & Burnette, Oxford, N.C., 1986—; atty. City of Oxford, 1995—; pres. 9th Jud. Dist. Bar Assn., 1998-99. Mem. ATLA, Ninth Jud. Dist. Bar Assn. (pres. 1999), N.C. Acad. Trial Lawyers, N.C. State Bar, N.C. Bar Assn., South Granville Country Club (bd. dirs.), Thorndale Country Club, Capital City Club. Episcopalian. Avocations: golf, traveling, reading. Home: 4129 Salem Farm Rd Oxford NC 27565-9199 Office: Edmundson & Burnette 106 Main St # 108 Oxford NC 27565-3319

BURNETTE, RALPH EDWIN, JR., lawyer; b. Lynchburg, Va., Sept. 25, 1953; s. Ralph Edwin and Carlease (Samuels) B. BA, Coll. William & Mary, 1975, JD, 1978. Bar: Va. 1978, U.S. Dist. Ct. (we. dist.) Va., U.S. Ct. Appeals (4th cir.). Assoc. Edmunds & Williams, Lynchburg, 1978-83, ptnr., 1983—; adj. prof. law Coll. William and Mary, 1996—. Deacon Peakland Bapt. Ch., Lynchburg, 1983-86; pres. Kaleidoscope Festival, Lynchburg, 1985, Lynchburg Symphony Orch., 1989-91; bd. dirs. Centra Health, Inc., 1987-97, United Way Cen. Va., 1989-90, Amazement Sq. Children's Mus. Mem. Va. Bar Assn., Va. State Bar (pres. 1993-94, pres. young lawyers conf. 1985, chmn. com. on alternative dispute resolution 1985-89, mem. bar coun., 1986-95, vice chmn. standing com. on legal ethics 1986-88, chmn. com. on long range planning 1988-91, mem. exec. com. 1990-95), Lynchburg Bar Assn. (pres. 1991-92), Va. Trial Lawyers Assn., Va. Assn. Def. Attys., Def. Rsch. Inst. Avocations: golf, music, boating. Home: PO Box 958 Lynchburg VA 24505-0958 Office: Edmunds & Williams 800 Main St Ste 400 Lynchburg VA 24504-1533

BURNETTE, THOMAS N., career officer; b. Oct. 23, 1944. Commd. U.S. Army, advanced through grades to lt. gen., 1997. Office: US Army 400 Army Pentagon Washington DC 20310-0400

BURNEY, VICTORIA KALGAARD, corporate business executive, consultant, civic worker; b. Los Angeles, Apr. 12, 1943; d. Oscar Albert and Dorothy Elizabeth (Peterson) Kalgaard; children: Kim Elizabeth, J. Hewett. BA with honors, U. Mont., 1965; MA, U. No. Colo., 1980; postgrad. Webster U., St. Louis, 1983-84. Exec. dir. Hill County Community Action, Havre, Mont., 1966-67; community orgn. specialist ACCESS, Escondido, Calif., 1967-68; program devel. and community orgn. specialist Community Action Programs, Inc., Pensacola, Fla., 1968-69; cons. Escambia County Sch. Bd., Fla., 1969-71; pres. Kal Kreations, Kailua, Hawaii, 1974-77; instr., dir. office human resources devel. Palomar Coll., San Marcos, Calif., 1978-

81; chief exec. officer IDET Corp., San Marcos, 1981-87; dir. United Syss. Inst., 1998—; cons. County of Riverside, Calif., 1983. Mem. San Diego County Com. on Handicapped, San Diego, 1979; cons. tribal resource devel., Escondido, Calif., 1979; mem. exec. com. Social Services Coordinating Council, San Diego, 1982-83; mem. pvt. sector com. and planning and rev. com. Calif. Employment and Tng. Adv. Council, Sacramento, 1982-83; bd. mgrs. Santa Margarita Family YMCA, Vista, Calif., 1984-86; bd. dirs. North County Community Action Program, Escondido, 1978, Casa de Amparo, San Luis Rey, Calif., 1980-83; mem. San Diego County Pub. Welfare Adv. Bd., 1979-83, chairperson, 1981; mem. Calif. Rep. Cen. Com., Sacramento, 1989—; ofcl. San Diego County Rep. Cen. Com., 1985-93, exec. com., 1987-92, 2nd vice-chmn. 1991-92; chmn. 74th Assembly Dist. Rep. Caucus, 1989-90; chmn. Working Ptnrs., 1987-90; trustee Rancho Santa Fe Community Ctr., 1991-92; active Nat. Assistance League, 1993—; bd. dirs. Assistance League North Coast, 1994—, mem. 1993-96. Mem. Nat. Assn. County Employment and Tng. Adminstrs. (chairperson econ. resources com. 1982-85), Calif. Assn. Local Econ. Devel., San Diego Econ. Devel. Corp., Oceanside Econ. devel. Council (bd. dirs. 1983-87), Oceanside C. of C., San Marcos C. of C. (bd. dirs. 1982-85), Carlsbad C. of C. (indsl. council 1982-85), Escondido C. of C. (comml. and indsl. devel. council 1982-87), Vista C. of C. (vice chairperson econ. devel. com. 1982-83), Vista Econ. Devel. Assn., Nat. Job Tng. Partnership, San Diego County Golden Eagle Club. Home: 2010 Valley Rd Oceanside CA 92056-3111

BURNHAM, BRYSON PAINE, retired lawyer; b. Chgo., Oct. 11, 1917; s. Raymond and Patti (Paine) B.; m. Frances Katherine Burns, Feb. 8, 1941; children: Janice Young, Stephanie Paine. B.A., U. Chgo., 1938, J.D., 1940. Bar: Ill. 1940, Colo. 1983. Assoc., then ptnr. Mayer, Brown & Platt, Chgo., 1940-83; of counsel Shand, McLachlan and Newbold, Durango, Colo., 1985-93. Bd. dirs. Fort Lewis Coll. Found., 1986—. Home: 315 Highland Hill Dr Timberline View Estates Durango CO 81301

BURNHAM, CHARLES WILSON, mineralogy educator; b. Detroit, Apr. 6, 1933; s. Charles Hubbard and Anne (Wilson) B.; m. Mary Sue Morgan, June 21, 1958; children—Jeffrey Wentworth, David Wilson. S.B., Mass. Inst. Tech., 1954, Ph.D., 1961; A.M., Harvard, 1966. adj. prof. geology Ft. Lewis Coll., 1997—. Postdoctoral fellow Geophys. Lab. Carnegie Instn., Washington, 1961-63; staff scientist Geophys. Lab. Carnegie Instn., 1963-66; assoc. prof. mineralogy Harvard, 1966-69; prof. Harvard U., 1969-96, chmn. dept. geol. scis., 1983-84, prof. mineralogy emeritus, 1996—. Assoc. editor: Am. Mineralogist, 1974-77. Mem. Acton (Mass.) Planning Bd., 1974-78, chmn., 1976-77; trustee Mt. Washington Obs., 1981—, v.p., 1983-95; lic. tech. del., ofcl. FIS Alpine Ski Racing, 1994—. Served as 1st lt. USAF, 1955-57. Fellow Mineral. Soc. Am. (councillor 1980-83, v.p. 1988, pres. 1989); mem. AAAS, Am. Crystallographic Assn., Am. Geophys. Union, N.H. Alpine Racing Assn. (pres. 1991-94), Sigma Xi, Phi Gamma Delta. Episcopalian. Club: Appalachian Mountain (Boston) (pres. 1979-81). Home: 522 Cottonwood Creek Rd Durango CO 81301-6183 Office: 20 Oxford St Cambridge MA 02138-2902

BURNHAM, DANIEL PATRICK, manufacturing company executive; b. Birmingham, Mich., Nov. 28, 1946; s. Edward Francis and Helen Cecilia (Keane) B.; m. Mary Margaret Cavanaugh, June 8, 1968; children—Daniel, Amy, Peter, Ellen. B.S. in Econs., Xavier U., 1968; M.B.A. in Fin., U. N.H., 1970. Corp. controller Carborundum Corp., Niagara Falls, N.Y., 1976-78, dir. strategy devel., 1979-80, dir. abrasives mktg., 1980-81, gen. mgr. insulation div., 1981-82; v.p., controller Allied Corp., Morristown, N.J., 1982-84, v.p., gen. mgr. engineered plastics, 1984-86; pres. Plastics and Performance Matls. div. Allied-Signal Inc., Morristown, N.J., 1986-88, pres. fibers div., 1988-90; pres. AiResearch Group, Torrance, Calif., 1990-91, Allied-Signal Aerospace Co., Torrance, Calif., 1991—; chmn. Internat. Turbine Engine Co.; bd. dirs. Light Helicopter Turbines Engring. Co.., Normalair Garrett Ltd. (U.K.); bd. govs. Aerospace Ind. Assn. Served to capt. U.S. Army, 1970. Republican. Roman Catholic. Home: 66 Charles St # 541 Boston MA 02114-4604 Office: Allied-Signal Aerospace Co PO Box 2960 Torrance CA 90509-2960

BURNHAM, DAVID BRIGHT, writer, educator; b. Boston, Jan. 24, 1933; s. Addison Center and Dorothy (Moore) B.; m. Sophy Tayloe Doub, Mar. 12, 1960 (div. 1984); children: Sarah Tayloe, Molly Bright; m. Joanne Omang, 1985. BA, Harvard, 1955. Reporter UPI, Washington, 1959-61, Newsweek mag., Washington, 1961-63; writer CBS, N.Y.C., 1963-65; asst. dir. Pres.'s Commn. Law Enforcement and Adminstrn. of Justice, Washington, 1965-67; reporter N.Y. Times, 1967-86; journalist/writer Aspen Inst. Humanistic Studies, 1980-82; co-dir. Transactional Records Access Clearinghouse, 1989—; assoc. rsch. prof. S.I. Newhouse Sch. Pub. Communications, Syracuse U. Author: The Rise of the Computer State, 1988, A Law Unto Itself: Power, Politics and the IRS, 1989 (Best Investigative Book Investigative Editors and Reporters 1990), Above The Law: Secret Deals, Political Fixes, and other Misadventures of the U.S. Dept. of Justice, 1996,. Recipient George K. Polk award, L.I. U. , 1968, Silurians award, 1968; N.Y. New spaper Guild award, 1968; Gold Typewriter award for investigative reporting N.Y. Reporters Assn., 1972; named fellow Alicia Patterson Found., 1987, Rockefeller Found. scholar, Bellagio, Italy, 1992. Home: 524 6th St SE Washington DC 20003-2705

BURNHAM, DAVID HENDERSON, management consultant; b. Quincy, Mass., Mar. 4, 1942; s. Roger Appleton and Phyllis Katherine (Kline) B.; m. Frances Margarita Parry, Feb. 15, 1964; children: Amery Appleton, Hugh Tebault Ramseyer. BA, Northeastern U., 1964; MBA, Harvard U., 1969. Assoc. Sterling Inst., Boston, 1969; v.p., treas. McBer & Co., Boston, 1970-72, pres., 1972-77; pres. David H. Burnham and Assocs., orgn. devel. cons., Boston, Singapore, Sydney, London, 1977-91; dir. strategic planning Interaction Assocs., Cambridge, Mass., 1992-94; ptnr. Burnham Rosen Group, Boston, 1994—. Producer film Motives Moving Business (Am. Film Festival award 1975); contbr. articles to profl. jours. Treas., v.p. Children's Mus., Boston, 1972-81, pres., CEO, 1981-83, chmn., 1984-86, hon. trustee, 1988—; pres. Cavalier King Charles Spaniel Club, Louisville, 1972-78; bd. dirs. Children's Mus., London, 1984-86, Mental Health Found., U.K., 1987-88, Drive for Youth Programme, U.K., 1986-91; mem. com. Derby Acad. Coun., Hingham, Mass., 1974-81; active strategic leadership forum ASTD, OD Network, Harvard Bus. Sch. Assn. Mem. Inst. Tng. and Devel. (Eng.), Inst. Pers. Mgmt. (Eng.), Assn. Mgmt. Edn. and Devel. (Eng.), New England Hist. and Genealogical Soc. (dir. 1999—), Greater Boston Assn. Tng. and Devel. (dir. 1997—), Somerset Club (Boston), Harvard Club (Boston), Harvard Club (Boston), Cohasset Golf Club, Cohasset Yacht Club. Home: 30 Atlantic Ave Cohasset MA 02025-1803 Office: Burnham Rosen Group 199 State St Boston MA 02109-2648

BURNHAM, DONALD CLEMENS, manufacturing company executive; b. Athol, Mass., Jan. 28, 1915; s. Charles Richardson and Freda (Clemens) B.; m. Virginia Gobble, May 29, 1937; children: David Charles, Joan (Mrs. Robert Graham), John Carl, William Lawrence (dec. 1994), Mary Barbara (Mrs. F. David Throop). B.S. in Mech. Engring, Purdue U., 1936, D.Eng. (hon.), 1959; D.Eng. (hon.), Ind. Inst. Tech., 1963, Drexel Inst. Tech., 1964, Poly. Inst. Bklyn., 1967. With Gen. Motors Corp., 1936-54, asst. chief engr. Oldsmobile div., 1953-54; with Westinghouse Electric Corp., 1954-80, group v.p., 1962-63, pres., chief exec. officer, 1963-68, chmn., chief exec. officer, 1969-75, dir.-officer, 1975-80. Mem. The Bus. Coun.; emeritus trustee Carnegi Inst., Am. Wind Symphony Orch., Pitts. Theol. Sem. Maj. AUS, WWII. Recipient Outstanding Achievement in Mgmt. award Am. Inst. Indsl. Engrs., 1964. Mem. ASME, Soc. Mfg. Engr. (Hoover Medal award 1978), Soc. Automotive Engrs., IEEE, Nat. Acad. Engring., Am. Assn. Engring. Socs. (Nat. Engring. award 1981). Club: Duquesne (Pitts.). Home: 1290 Boyce Rd Apt C233 Pittsburgh PA 15241-3912

BURNHAM, DUANE LEE, retired pharmaceutical company executive; b. Excelsior, Minn., Jan. 22, 1942; s. Harold Lee and Hazel Evelyn (Johnson) B.; m. Susan Elizabeth Klinner, June 22, 1963; children—David Lee, Matthew Beckwith. BS, U. Minn., 1963, MBA, 1972. CPA, Wis. Sr. v.p. fin., chief financial officer Abbott Labs., North Chgo., 1982-84, exec. v.p., chief financial officer, dir., 1985-87, vice chmn., chief fin. officer, 1987-89, chmn., CEO, 1990-98; chmn. Abbott Labs., Lake Forest, Ill., 1999—; bd. dirs. Sara Lee Corp., No. Trust Corp. Bd. dirs. Lyric Opera; trustee Northwestern U., chmn. med. affairs com. of med. sch.; mem . adv. bd. J.L. Kellogg Grad. Sch. Mgmt.; chmn. The Chgo. Coun. on Fgn. Rels.; life trustee Mus. Sci. and Industry, Chgo. Office: Abbott Labs 150 Field Dr Ste 160 Lake Forest IL 60045-2500

BURNHAM, GILBERT MIRACLE, physician, educator. MD, Loma Linda U., 1968; PhD, U. London, 1988. Dep. hosp. comdr. Noble Army Hosp., Ft. McClellan, Ala., 1974-75; med. supt. Malamulo Hosp., Makwasa, Malawi, Africa, 1977-91; assoc. prof. Johns Hopkins Sch. Pub. Health, Balt., 1991—; dir. Ctr. for Refugee and Disaster Studies Johns Hopkins U., Balt., 1998—; dir. Shire Valley (Malawi) Leprosy Ctr. Program, 1980-91, Malamuio Sch. Health Scis., 1982-91. Dir. Thyolo Dist. River Blindness Control Program, Malawi, 1980-91. E-mail: Gburnham@jhsph.edu. Office: 615 N Wolfe St # E8132 Baltimore MD 21205-2103

BURNHAM, HAROLD ARTHUR, pharmaceutical company executive, physician; b. Boston, Nov. 6, 1929; s. Howard Rowland and Edna Adelaide (Teachout) B.; m. Lucienne Jeanne Seas, June 28, 1952; children: Philippe Henri, Isabelle Jeanne. BS, Union Coll., 1951; MA, Middlebury Coll., 1952; postgrad., Albany State Tchrs. Coll., 1953-54, Adelphi U., 1958-59, Nassau Community Coll., 1961-62; MD, U. Md., 1966. Diplomate Am. Bd. Med. Examiners, Am. Bd. Family Practice (charter). Tchr. sci., French and track team coach South Glens Falls Cen. High Sch., N.Y., 1952-54; med. rep., hosp. salesman Upjohn Co., Bklyn., 1956-62; intern South Baltimore Gen. Hosp., 1966-67; resident Glen Cove Community Hosp., N.Y., 1967-69; practice family medicine Glen Cove, 1969-75; assoc. med. dir. Winthrop Labs. div. Sterling Drug Inc., N.Y.C., 1975-76, med. dir. Glenbrook Labs. div., 1977, v.p. med. affairs, sr. v.p. Winthrop Product Inc., 1977-80; v.p. med. affairs, sr. v.p. Winthrop Product Inc. Sterling Drug Inc., N.J., 1977-80, Sydney Ross Co. and Sterling Products Internat., N.Y.C., 1977-80; v.p., med. dir. Glenbrook Labs. div. Sterling Drugs, Inc., N.Y.C., 1980; med. dir. Choay Labs. Inc., N.Y.C., 1980-82; asst. med. dir. L.I. State Vets. Home, Stony Brook, 1993-94; primary care physician ambulatory care clinics Nassau County Dept. Health, Mineola, N.Y., 1995-96; spl. cons. Labs. Choay, S.A., Paris, 1982—; asst. med dir. United Presbyn. Residence, Woodbury, N.Y., 1983-93; instr. Sch. Practical Nursing, Glen Cove Community Hosp., 1970-75; instr. geriatrics in coop. with Glen Cove Community Hosp. Family Practice Residency Program, 1983-93; cons., clinician in medicine Nassau County Pub. Health Dept., 1975-76, mem. long term health care com., 1989-96; med. cons. Webb Inst. Naval Architecture and Marine Design, Glen Cove, N.Y., 1970—; clin. asst. prof., SUNY, 1993; attending physician infectious diseases HIV Clinic, Nassau County Med. Ctr., East Meadow, N.Y., 1995-96. N.Am. corr. weekly Internet French med. publ. Expression Médicale, 1998—. Scoutmaster Boy Scouts Am., Glens Falls, N.Y., 1953-54, com. mem., 1968—, merit badge counsellor for first aid, pub. health emergency care, chemistry and mammals for Sagamore dist., 1968—; mem. Clan Gordon, 1983—, bagpiper Highlanders Pipes and Drums Band, Locust Valley, N.Y., 1982—, chmn., 1986—; lay reader St. John's of Lattingtown Episcopal Ch., N.Y , 1968—, vestryman, 1983—, clk. of vestry, 1986—, mem. search com. for new rector, 1993—; trustee Hawley Found., 1984—, v.p. bd., 1991—; del. to 120th conf. Episcopal Diocese of L.I.; vol. primary care physician Project U.S.A., Rural Indian Health Svc. Ctrs., Oneida (N.Y.) Iroquois Reservation and Owyhee (Nev.) Indian Hosp., 1995—. Fellow Am. Acad. Family Physicians (charter); mem. AMA (14 continuing edn. awards), Pan Am. Med. Soc., N.Y. State Med. Soc. (life), Nassau County Med. Soc. (life), L.I. Scottish Clans Assn. (trustee 1984—, piper to chief 1986—), Nu Sigma Nu. Episcopalian. Office: 18 Purdue Rd Glen Cove NY 11542-2009

BURNHAM, J. V., sales executive; b. Pascagoula, Miss., May 23, 1923; s. George Luther and Eli Vashti (Hough) B.; m. Patti Lauri Latham, May 18, 1946; children: James Steven, Jon Douglas, Richard Scott, Bruce Edward, Vernon Alan. AA, Jones County (Miss.) Jr. Coll., 1946; AS, Rochester Inst. Tech., 1948; BS, U. Houston, 1951, MEd, 1953. Mgr. The Progress-Item, Ellisville, Miss., 1948-50; asst. prof., asst. mgr. U. Houston Journalism and Printing Plant, 1950-57; estimator, product supt. purchasing Chas. P. Young Co., Houston, 1957-67, asst. sec.-treas., 1967-69, v.p. sales, 1969-91, sr. v.p., 1991—. Assoc. editor Am. Oceanography, 1968-71; southwest corr. Inland Printer and Nat. Lithographer, 1952-60. Pres. Printing Industries of Gulf Coast, Houston, 1971-73; chmn. emeritus, bd. dirs. Tex. Printing Edn. Found., Houston; treas./bd. dirs. Mus. of Printing History, Houston; mem. Rep. Presdl. Task Force, Nat. Rep. Senatorial Com. Order of Merit, Nat. Rep. Congl. Com., Rep. Nat. Com. (life, chmn.'s adv. bd.), Rep. Party of Tex., Rep. Nat. Candidate Trust, The Heritage Found., Gramm Senate Club, The Concord Coalition; active Houston Mus. Natural Sci., Adm. Nimitz Found., Am. Air Mus., Am. Farmland Trust, Nat. Wildflower Rsch. Ctr. Lt. USNR, 1943-46. Recipient Scouters award Boy Scouts Am., 1960, Scouters Key award, 1965, Wood Badge award, 1964; named Man of Yr., Houston Graphics Soc., 1968, Printing Industry of Gulf Coast, 1970. Mem. NRA (life), Am. Fedn. Police, Gun Owners Am., Second Amendment Found. (charter), Second Amend Task Force, USS Constitution Mus. Found., Pres's. Club of Chas. P. Young Co. (charter, Outstanding Sales Achievement award), Houston Lithographic Club, U.S. Hist. Soc. (life), Nat. Eagle Scout Assn. (life), Tex. State Rifle Assn. (life), Tex. Police Officers Assn., Naval Airship. Assn., Rep.-Presdl. Legion of Merit, Am. Legion (life), U. Houston Alumni (life), Jones County Jr. Coll. Alumni (life), Rochester Inst. Tech. Alumni Assn., U.S. Golf Assn., Houston Golf Assn., 100 Club Houston, Braeburn Country Club, Hummel Collecters Club (Houston), The Landing at Seven Coves (Conroe, Tex.), NRA Whittington Ctr. Founders Club, Santa Fe Trail Gun Club (life), Houston Craftsmens Club (hon. life., past pres., Ben Franklin award 1971), Crime Stoppers of Houston (gold cir. mem.), Pinto Horse Assn. Am., Ducks Unltd., U.S. Navy Meml. Found., Naval Aviation Mus. Found., U.S. Navy Pub. Affairs Alumni Assn. (life), VFW (life), Houston Public TV, United Srs. Assn., WWII Meml. Found., Claremont Inst., BAMPAC, High Frontier, Citizens Against Govt. Waste, Nat. Arbor Day Found., Am. Kidney Fund, PGA Ptnrs. Club (charter, life), Nab Home Gardening Club. Republican. Methodist.

BURNHAM, JOHN CHYNOWETH, historian, educator; b. Boulder, Colo., July 14, 1929; s. William Allds and Florence (Hasbrouck) B.; m. Marjorie Ann Spencer, Aug. 31, 1957; children: Leonard, Abigail, Peter, Melissa. BA, Stanford U., 1951, PhD, 1958; MA, U. Wis., 1952. Lectr. Claremont Men's Coll., Calif., 1956-57; mem. faculty Stanford U., 1956, 57-58; postdoctoral fellow Founds. Fund for Research in Psychiatry, New Haven, 1958-61; asst. prof. San Francisco State Coll., 1961-63; mem. faculty Ohio State U., Columbus, 1963—, prof. history, 1969—; sr. Fulbright lectr. U. Melbourne, Australia, 1967, U. Tasmania, Australia, 1973, U. New Eng., Australia, 1973; Tallman vis. prof. history and psychology Bowdoin Coll., Brunswick, Maine, 1982; cons. panelist NEH, 1974—, dir. nat. seminar for professions, 1975, 76, 79; assoc. area adv. Coun. on Internat. Exch. of Scholars, 1975-78; mem. spl. study sect. NIH, 1978-79, 84-85, 92. Author: Psychoanalysis and American Medicine 1894-1918, 1967, Jelliffe: American Physician and Psychoanalyst, 1983, How Superstition Won and Science Lost: Popularizing Science in the United States, 1987, Paths into American Culture: Psychology, Medicine, and Morals, 1988, Bad Habits: Drinking, Smoking, Taking Drugs, Gambling, Sexual Misbehavior, and Swearing in American History, 1993, How the Idea of Profession Changed the Writing of Medical History, 1998; (with Buenker and Crunden) Progressivism, 1977; editor: Science in America-Historical Selections, 1971; editor Jour. of History of Behavioral Scis., 1997—. Recipient Publ. award Ohio Acad. History, 1993. Fellow AAAS; mem. Am. Assn. for History of Medicine (v.p. 1988-90, pres. 1990-92), Orgn. Am. Historians, Am. Hist. Assn., History of Sci. Soc., Midwest History of Sci. Junto (pres. 1982-83), Cheiron Internat. Soc. for History of Behavioral and Social Scis. (presiding officer 1977-78), Am. Psychol. Assn. (recognition mem.). Home: 4158 Kendale Rd Columbus OH 43220-4136 Office: Ohio State U Dept History 230 W 17th Ave Columbus OH 43210-1361

BURNHAM, JOHN LUDWIG, agent; b. L.A., Mar. 1, 1953; s. Jerome Ludwig and Linda (Benjamin) B.; m. Andrea Buckland Feldstein, Aug. 12, 1989; 1 child, Daisy. BA, UCLA, 1976, JD, 1980. Agt. Kohnner Levy, L.A., 1979-81, ICM, L.A., 1981-84; agt. William Morris Agy., Beverly Hills, Calif., 1984—, co-head, sr. v.p. movie dept., 1991—. Office: William Morris Agy Inc 151 S El Camino Dr Beverly Hills CA 90212-2775*

BURNHAM, LEM, psychologist; b. Winter Haven, Fla., Aug. 30, 1947; s. John L. and Lillie Belle B.; m. Barbara J. Mackin, Sept. 8, 1981; children: Shannon LeeAnne, Lewis, Kara, Bryan. Diploma, N.Am. Sch. Conservation, Irvine, Calif., 1969; BA in Psychology, U.S. Internat. U., 1974; MS in Counseling Psychology, Minn. State U., 1978; PhD in Psychoednl. Processes, Temple U., 1984. Diplomate Am. Bd. Forensic Examiners, Am. Bd. Psychol. Specialties; cert. forensic clin. psychology, psychol. assessment, evaluation and testing, substance abuse psychology, psychotherapist Am. Psychotherapy Assn. Profl. football player World Football League, Honolulu, 1974-75, Can. Football League, Winnipeg, Can., 1976, NFL Phila. Eagles, 1977-80; cross-cultural community planner City and County of Honolulu, 1975; sr. counselor Pa. Prison Soc., Phila., 1982; pres. bd. Career Transition Inst., Inc., Phila., 1981-83; psychologist, health care adminstr. West Jersey Health System, 1984-87; pvt. practice cons., 1988—; pres., chief exec. officer Athletic Motivation, Inc., 1989-92; team psychologist for Balt. Orioles, 1989-94, Phila. Eagles, 1988-92, Phila. 76ers, 1986-92; lectr. in field; dir. player programs NFL, 1992-97, v.p. employee and player devel., 1997—. Mem. Nat. Adv. Coun. on Violence Against Women, chmn. sports subcom., 1995—; bd. dirs. Corp. Alliance to End Ptnr. Violence, 1995—. Served with USMC, 1965-69, Vietnam. Decorated Vietnamese Service award, Vietnamese Commendation award; recipient cert. of appreciation Kiwanis Club, Ramon, Calif., 1979, Del. Valley Med. Ctr., Phila., 1980, Community Service award Com. on Alcohol and Drug Abuse Crozer Chester Hosp., 1981. Mem. Am. Psychol. Assn., Am. Psychotherapy Assn., N.Y. Acad. Scis., Am. Coll. Forensic Examiners, World Fedn. Mental Health, NFL Alumni Assn. (bd. dirs. Phila. Eagles chpt. 1986-98), Maxwell Football Club (life, v.p. community rels. 1990—, bd. govs.). Office: NFL Hdqs 280 Park Ave New York NY 10017-1216

BURNHAM, PATRICIA WHITE, consultant advocate, writer on aging, business executive, author; b. Omaha, July 30, 1933; d. William Max and Berniece Irene (Shockey) Orr; m. William L. White, June 18, 1955 (div. Nov. 1979); children: Lucinda, Christopher, Duncan; m. Robert A. Burnham, Feb. 23, 1980. BA in English, DePauw U., Greencastle, Ind., 1955; MA in English, Ill. State U., 1966, PhD in Adminstrn., 1977. Tchr. Morton Grove (Ill.) and Evansville (Ind.) pub. schs., 1955-60; instr. Ill. State U., Normal, 1963-71, dir. Nat. Student Exchange, 1971-74, dir. continuing edn., 1974-76, asst. dean, 1976-79; assoc. dir. Ill. Bd. Higher Edn., Springfield, 1979-80; assoc. vice provost Ohio State U., Columbus, 1980-81; specialist bus. ins. Nationwide Ins. Co., Columbus, 1981-83; v.p. pvt. banking Chase Manhattan Bank, N.A., N.Y.C., 1983-88; pres. Transitions Group, Inc., East Burke, Vt., 1986—; adj. prof. U. Vt., 1997—. Author: Life's Third Act, 1994; contbr. articles to publs. and seminars on successful aging, adult policies and programs. Bd. dirs. No. Vt. Hosp., St. Johnsbury, 1995—, Vt. Cmty. Loan Fund, Vt. Coun. on Humanities, 1998—; pres. Coun. Vt. Elders, 1994—. Mem. Gerontol. Assn., Phi Beta Kappa, Phi Delta Kappa. Congregationalist. Avocations: hiking, literature, computers. Office: Transitions Group Inc PO Box 239 East Burke VT 05832-0239

BURNHAM, ROBERT ALAN, educator, academic administrator; b. Rochester, N.Y., July 4, 1928; s. J. Robert and Susan (Mason) B.; m. Shirley Semingson, Feb. 12, 1953 (div.); children: Teya, Jessica; m. Patricia Orr White, Feb. 23, 1980; 1 stepchild, Duncan. BA magna cum laude, U. Wash., 1955; PhD, Stanford U., 1972. Assoc. prof., assoc. dean Coll. of Edn. U. Ill., Urbana, 1969-76; research dir. Ill. Sch. Problems Commn., Springfield, 1974-77; prof., dean. Coll. Edn. Ill. State U., Normal, 1976-79; prof., dean. Coll. Edn. Ohio State U., Columbus, 1979-83, acting v.p. for communications and devel., 1982-83; prof., dean Sch. Edn., Health, Nursing and Arts Professions NYU, N.Y.C., 1983-89, prof., dir. Ctr. for Ednl. Tech. and Econ. Productivity, 1989-96, mem. adv. bd. Ctr. for Global Bus. Mgmt.Sch. Edn., 1993-95, prof. emeritus, 1996—; v.p. Transitions Group, Inc., East Burke, Vt., 1989—; interim pres. Lyndon State Coll., 1997-98; cons. Vt. State Colls., 1998—; resident cons. Belarus Ministry of Edn., Minsk, 1995; pres. Educator's Distance Learning Consortium, Inc., 1990-93; coord. N.Y. Ednl. Policy Fellowship Program Inst. Ednl. Leadership, N.Y.C., 1986-94; mem. nat. edn. adv. com. Statue of Liberty-Ellis Island Commn., 1985-90, tech. adv. bd. H.S. of Telecom. Arts and Tech., Bklyn., 1985-91; frequent workshop presenter, lectr. Contbr. articles to profl. jours. Trustee, chair adminstrv. com. Ctr. for Pub. Edn., Columbus, 1980-83; bd. dirs. reparative bd. Vt. Dept. Corrections, 1997—. With U.S. Army, 1948-52. Grantee U.S. Office Edn., 1966. Mem. Am. Assn. Colls. of Tchr. Edn. (instnl. rep., bd. dirs. 1981-85), Tchr. Edn. Conf. Bd. (pres. Albany, N.Y. 1984-89), Kingdom Trail Assn. Inc. (bd. dirs. 1996—), Phi Beta Kappa. Presbyterian. Avocations: hiking, skiing, technology. Home: Box 239 Victory Rd East Burke VT 05832-0239

BURNHAM, TOM, state school system administrator; b. Jackson, Miss., May 5, 1946; 1 child, Cassandra Burnham Vanderford. BSBA, Miss. Coll., Clinton, 1969, MEd, 1975; EdS, Delta State U., Cleveland, Miss., 1983, EdD, 1985. Cert. in social studies adminstrn., Miss., sch. adminstrn., Miss. Tchr., dept. chair Pearl (Miss.) High Sch., 1969-72; asst. prin. McLuarin Jr. High, Pearl, 1973-81; asst. dean cont. edn. Delta State U., Cleve., Miss., 1981-86; prin. Solomon Jr. High, Greenville, Miss., 1986-87; supt. Biloxi (Miss.) Pub. Schs., 1987-92; state supt. edn. Miss. Dept. Edn., Jackson, 1992-97; exec. dir. Gulf Coast Edn. Consortium, Long Beach, Miss., 1998—. Mem. Am. Assn. Sch. Adminstrs., Miss. Profl. Educators, Miss. Assn. Sch. Supts., Phi Delta Kappa. Baptist. Office: Gulf Coast Edn Initiative U So Miss 730 E Beach Blvd Long Beach MS 39560-6259*

BURNHAM, WALTER DEAN, political science educator; b. Columbus, Ohio, June 15, 1930; s. Alfred Huntington Jr. and Gertrude Elinor (Hamburger) B.; m. Patricia Ann Mullan, June 7, 1958; children: John Patrick, Anne More. BA, Johns Hopkins U., 1951; AM, Harvard U., 1958, PhD, 1962; LittD (hon.), Rutgers U., 1982. Instr. polit. sci. Boston Coll., 1958-61; asst. prof. Kenyon Coll., Gambier, Ohio, 1961-64, Haverford (Pa.) Coll., 1964-66; from assoc. to full prof. Washington U., St. Louis, 1966-71; prof. MIT, Cambridge, Mass., 1971-88, Ruth and Arthur Sloan prof. polit. sci., 1984-88; Frank C. Erwin Jr. Centennial prof. govt. U. Tex., Austin, 1988—; vis. scholar Phi Beta Kappa, 1995—. Author: Presidential Ballots, 1955, 2d. edit., 1976, Critical Elections, 1970, The Current Crisis in Am. Politics, 1982, Democracy in the Making, 1983, 2d edit., 1986. With U.S. Army, 1953-56. Fellow Social Sci. Rsch. Coun., 1963, Guggenheim Found., 1974, Ctr. Advanced Study in Behavioral Sci., 1979. Fellow Am. Acad. Arts and Scis.; mem. Am. Polit. Sci. Assn. (mem. coun. 1984-86, pres. organized sect. on politics and history 1993-94), Phi Beta Kappa (vis. scholar 1995-96). Avocation: opera. Home: 4207 N Hills Dr Austin TX 78731-2827 Office: U Tex Dept Govt Burdine Hall # 536 Austin TX 78712*

BURNIM, KALMAN AARON, theatre educator emeritus; b. Malden, Mass., Mar. 7, 1928; s. Jack K. and Sadie (Levy) B.; m. Verna Ruth Lesser, June 6, 1928; children: Ira, Judith, Esther Burnim Ouray. BA in Drama magna cum laude, Tufts U., 1950; MA in Theater, Ind. U., 1951; PhD, Yale U., 1958. Mng. exec. New England Adding Machine Co., Boston, 1951-55; asst. prof. Valparaiso (Ind.) U., 1958-59, U. Pitts., 1959-60; asst. prof. Tufts U., Medford, Mass., 1960-61, assoc. prof., dir. theater, 1961-65, prof. drama, 1965, chmn. dept. drama, exec. dir. theater, 1966-75, Fletcher prof. oratory and drama, 1971-87, emeritus prof., 1987—; rsch. prof. English George Washington U., Washington, 1975-76, 85-86; mem. nat. screening com. for theater Fulbright Commn., Washington, 1985-89; mem. exec. com. Internat. Fedn. for Theatre Rsch., 1979-83, 91-95; panelist, del. various confs. Author: David Garrick, Director, 1961; co-author: The Prompter, An Eighteenth Century Theatrical Paper, 1966, The Biographical Dictionary of Actors, Actresses, Dancers, Managers, and Other Stage Personnel in London Stage, 1660-1800, 16 vols., 1973-93, (George Freedley Meml. award Theatre Library Assn. 1979, 94), Pictures in the Garrick Club. A Catalogue, 1997, (with P.H. Highfill Jr.) John Bell, Patron of Theatrical Portraiture, 1998; editor (anthology) The Complete Plays of George Colman the Elder, 6 vols., 1983, (monograph) The Letters of Sarah and William Siddons to Hester Lynch Thrale Piozzi, 1969; assoc. editor Ednl. Theatre Jour., 1968-70; contbr. articles to profl. jours. Guggenheim fellow, 1964-65, Folger Library fellow, 1957-58, 69, 71; Sterling fellow Yale U., 1957-58; Am. Council for Learned Socs. grantee, 1966, 71; NEH grantee, 1967-68, 70, 74-76, 85-86; Tufts faculty research grantee, 1960-81. Mem. Am. Soc. for Theatre Rsch. (pres. 1985-91, mem. exec. com. 1960-63, 64-69, 72-75, 83-86, program chmn. 1963-65, 76, chmn. publs. com. 1975-76, 79-82, del. to Am. Coun. Learned Socs. 1976-82, spl. citation 1994), Brit. Soc. for Theatre Rsch., Am. Soc. for Eighteenth-Century Studies, IREX (chmn. commn. on Am.-Soviet theatre exchs. 1988-91), Coll. Fellows Am. Theatre, Phi Beta Kappa (pres. Tufts chpt. 1983-85). Home: 2633 Imperial Pine Dr Spring Hill FL 34606-3417 also: 22 Cranmore Ln Melrose MA 02176-1507

BURNINGHAM, KIM RICHARD, former state legislator; b. Salt Lake City, Sept. 14, 1936; s. Rulon and Margie (Stringham) Burningham; m. Susan Ball Clarke, Dec. 19, 1968; children: Christian, Tyler David. BS, U. Utah, 1960; MA, U. Ariz., 1967; MFA, U. So. Calif., 1977. Cert. secondary tchr., Utah. Tchr. Bountiful (Utah) High Sch., 1960-88; mem. Utah Ho. of Reps., Salt Lake City, 1979-94; cons. Shipley Assocs., Bountiful, 1989-94, Franklin Covey, 1994—; gubernatorial appointee as exec. dir. Utah Statehood Centennial Commn., 1994-96, mem. Utah State Bd. Edn., 1999—. Author dramas for stage and film, also articles. Mem. state strategic planning com. Utah Tomorrow, 1989—. Mem. NEA, PTA (life), Utah Edn. Assn., Davis Edn. Assn., Nat. Forensic League. Republican. Mem. LDS Ch. Avocations: gardening, history. Home: 932 Canyon Crest Rd Bountiful UT 84010-2002

BURNISON, BOYD EDWARD, lawyer; b. Arnolds Park, Iowa, Dec. 12, 1934; s. Boyd William and Lucile (Harnden) B.; m. Mari Amaral; children: Erica Lafore, Alison Katherine. BS, Iowa State U., 1957; JD, U. Calif., Berkeley, 1961. Bar: Calif. 1962, U.S. Supreme Ct. 1971, U.S. Dist. Ct. (no. dist.) Calif. 1962, U.S. Ct. Appeals (9th cir.) 1962, U.S. Dist. Ct. (ea. dist.) Calif. 1970, U.S. Dist. Ct. (ctrl. dist.) Calif., 1992. Dep. counsel Yolo County, Calif., 1962-65; of counsel Davis and Woodland (Calif.) Unified Sch. Dists., 1962-65; assoc. Steel & Arostegui, Marysville, Calif., 1965-66, St. Sure, Moore & Hoyt, Oakland, 1966-70; ptnr. St. Sure, Moore, Hoyt & Sizoo, Oakland and San Francisco, 1970-75; v.p. Crosby, Heafey, Roach & May, P.C., Oakland, 1975—, also bd. dirs. Adviser Berkeley YMCA, 1971—; adviser Yolo County YMCA, 1962-65, bd. dirs. 1965; bd. dirs. Easter Seal Soc. Crippled Children and Adults of Alameda County, Calif., 1972-75, Moot Ct. Bd., U. Calif., 1960-61; trustee, sec., legal counsel Easter Seal Found., Alameda County, 1974-79, hon. trustee, 1979—; bd. dirs. East Bay Conservation Corps, 1997—. Fellow ABA Found. (life); mem. ABA (labor rels. and employment law sect., equal employment law com. 1972—), Nat. Conf. Bar Pres.'s, State Bar Calif. (spl. labor counsel 1981-84, labor and employment law sect. 1982—), Alameda County Bar Assn. (chmn. memberships and directory com. 1973-74, 80, chmn. law office econs. com. 1975-77, assn. dir. 1981-85, pres., 1984, vice chmn. bench bar liaison com. 1983, chmn. 1984, Disting. Svc. award 1987), Alameda County Bar Found. (bd. dirs. 1993-95), Yolo County Bar Assn. (sec. 1965), Yuba Sutter Bar Assn., Bar Assn. San Francisco (labor law sect.), Indsl. Rels. Rsch. Assn., Sproul Assoc. Boalt Hall Law Sch. U. Calif. Berkeley, Iowa State Alumni Assn., Order Knoll, Round Hill Country Club, Rotary (Paul Harris fellow), Pi Kappa Alpha, Phi Delta Phi. Democrat. Home: PO Box 743 2300 Caballo Ranchero Dr Diablo CA 94528 Office: Crosby Heafey Roach & May 1999 Harrison St Ste 2300 Oakland CA 94612-3520

BURNLEY, KENNETH STEPHEN, school system administrator; m. Eileen Burnley; children: Traci, Trevor. BS, U. Mich., MA, PhD. Tchr. various schs. Mich.; asst. track coach U. Mich.; tchr., coord., asst. prin., prin., dir. Ypsilanti Bd. Edn.; instr. Ea. Mich. U.; asst. supt. instrn. Waverly Bd. Edn.; supt./CEO Fairbanks (Alaska) North Star Borough Sch. Dist.; supt. schs. Colorado Springs (Colo.) Sch. Dist. 11, 1987—; speaker in field. Bd. dirs. Colo. Nat. Bank Exch. Named Supt. of Year, Am. Assn. Sch. Adminstrs., 1993. Mem. Colo. Springs C. of C. (bd. dirs.). Avocations: exercising, weight training, boxing, reading, chess. Office: Colorado Springs Sch Dist #11 1115 N El Paso St Colorado Springs CO 80903-2519*

BURNS, ALEXANDRA DARROW (SANDRA BURNS), health program administrator; b. West Point, Ky., Mar. 28, 1946; d. Eugene Alexander and Phyllis Anna (Kedroski) Darrow; m. Maurice Edward Burns Jr., Sept. 8, 1966 (div. May 1985); 1 child, Megan Alexandra. BS in Journalism, U. Colo., 1967, MA in Guidance and Counseling, 1974. Cert. rehab. counselor. Probation and parole officer Office of Probation and Parole, Olympia, Wash., 1969-70; employment counselor Div. Employment, Denver, 1971-73; rehab. counselor Colo. Div. Rehab.-Blind Svcs., Denver, 1973-77; rehab. supr. Colo. Div. Rehab., Denver, 1978-81, program supr. rehab. ins. svcs. for employment, 1981-91; program adminstr. Americans With Disabilities Act, Denver, 1991-94; supr. mktg. and resource acquisition Colo. Div. Rehab., Denver, 1994-95, tng. adminstr., 1995-98, adminstr. pers. devel., 1998—; affiliate faculty rehab. counseling program U. No. Colo., 1998—. Vice chmn. Juvenile Parole Bd., Denver, 1982-91, acting chmn., 1987, chmn., 1988-91; del. Dem. County Caucus, Aurora, Colo., 1986; coun. del. Girl Scouts U.S.A., 1988-90, co-leader Brownie troop, 1988-9-, mem. area svc. team, 1989-90; mem. adv. bd. Indsl. Commn., 1983-86; mem. Jr. Symphony Guild, 1986-87; sec., bd. dirs. Mission Viejo Homeowners Assn., 1989-90; vol. mediator Colo. State Employees Mediation Program, 1992—. Mem. Nat. Rehab. Assn., Nat. Rehab. Adminstrn. Assn., Colo. Rehab. Adminstrn. Assn. (bd. dirs. 1988—, pres.-elect pvt. sector div. 1989, pres. 1990-91), Zonta (corr. sec. 1984-86). Mem. Ch. of Religious Science. Avocations: skiing, hiking, writing, do-it-yourself projects. Home: 15770 E Mercer Pl Aurora CO 80013-2559 Office: Colo Div Rehab 110 16th St Fl 2 Denver CO 80202-5204

BURNS, ARNOLD IRWIN, lawyer; b. N.Y.C., Apr. 14, 1930; s. Herman Leon and Rose (Lauterstein) B.; m. Felice Bernstein, June 17, 1951; children: Linda Susan, Douglas Todd. A.B., Union Coll., Schenectady, 1950; LL.B., Cornell U., 1953; postgrad., Parker Sch. Internat. Law, 1960; JD, Hofstra U., 1986. Bar: N.Y. 1953, D.C. 1977. Ptnr. Burns Summit Rovins & Feldesman (and predecessors), N.Y.C., 1960-86; assoc. atty. gen. U.S. Govt., Washington, 1986; dep. atty. gen. U.S. Dept. Justice, Washington, 1986-88; mem. Proskauer Rose LLP, N.Y.C., 1988—. Note editor: Cornell Law Quar, 1952-53. Former chmn., life trustee Union Coll., Schenectady, former chmn., now vice chmn. bd. dirs. Freedom Found., Valley Forge, Pa.; vice chmn. nat. bd. dirs. Boys and Girls Clubs Am.; mem. adv. com., co-chmn. nat. capital campaign Cornell Law Sch., Ithaca, N.Y., former nat. chmn. Cornell Law Sch. Fund; mem. adv. coun. Hofstra U. Sch. Law; former chmn. N.Y.C. Commn. on Youth Empowerment Svcs.; former mem. N.Y.C. Commn. to Monitor Police Corruption; bd. dirs. Nat. Victim Ctr., Nat. Ctr. Missing and Exploited Children, Vis. Nurse Svc., N.Y.; mem. adv. bd. Century Coun.; active Nat. Prison Indsl. Task Force. Capt. U.S. Army, 1953-57. Mem. Am. Israeli Polit. Action Com. (nat. exec. bd.), Anti-Defamation League (assoc. nat. com.), Fed. Bar Assn., N.Y. State Bar Assn., Fed. Bar Coun., Cornell Law Inst., Am. Arbitration Assn. (nat. panel arbitrators), Army Navy Club, N.Y. Athletic Club, Friars Club, Order of Coif, Phi Kappa Phi, Kappa Nu, Alpha Phi Omega. Republican. Jewish. Home: 25 Sutton Pl S Apt 11F New York NY 10022-2462 Office: Proskauer Rose LLP 1585 Broadway New York NY 10036-8200*

BURNS, ARTHUR LEE, architect; b. Indpls., July 5, 1924; s. Charles Raymond and Dorothy Frances (Young) B.; m. Dorothy Maxine Kingsland, Oct. 26, 1946 (dec.); children—Stephen Robert (dec.), Melody Lee; m. Frances C. Mathers, Jan. 12, 1988. B.S. in Architecture, U. Cin., 1949. Archtl. draftsman Foster Engring. Co., Ltd., Indpls., 1941-42; archtl. draftsman Albert V. Walters (Architect), Cin., 1946-48; chief draftsman Arend & Arend (Architects), Cin., 1948-49; architect The McGuire & Shook Corp., Indpls., 1949-84, v.p., 1964-71, sec.-treas., 1972-73, pres., 1974-75, exec. v.p., 1976-77, v.p., 1978-79, sec.-treas., 1980-84; archtl. cons., 1984—. Bd. dirs. Friends of Winter Haven Pub. Libr., 1995—, pres., 1997-98. Served with USAAF, 1943-46. Fellow AIA (sec.-treas. Indpls. chpt. 1965-66, v.p. 1967, pres. 1968, mem. documents bd. 1973-85, chmn. 1978-79); mem. Ind. Soc. Architects (bd. dirs. 1968-69, v.p. 1971, pres. 1972, Edward D. Pierre medal 1972), Constrn. Specifications Inst. (v.p. Indpls. chpt. 1966-67, pres. 1967-68), Broad Ripple Sertoma Club Indpls. (v.p. 1973-74, pres. 1974-75, Gold Honor Club), Cypress Gardens Sertoma Club Winter Haven (bd. dirs. 1991-93). Republican. Methodist. Home: 2987 Plantation Rd Winter Haven FL 33884-1235

BURNS, B. THOMAS, broadcasting executive; b. East St. Louis, Ill., Jan. 10, 1936; s. Thomas Stephen Burns and Anita Marguerite (Sale) Piot; m. Mary Ellen Christgau, Dec. 29, 1957; children: Anna Lee Burns Fine, Jeannine Charlotte Burns Dvorak. BS in Broadcast Journalism, U. Ill., 1957; MBA, U. Chgo., 1974; postgrad., Harvard U., 1980. News dir. Sta. WSDR Radio, Sterling, Ill., 1957; news editor Sta. WLS Radio, Chgo., 1958; mktg. writer ITT, Chgo., 1959-61; pub. rels. mgr. GTE, Northlake, Ill., 1961-69; pres., gen. mgr. Sta. WEFM Radio, Michigan City, Ind., 1969—; pres., gen. mgr. Sta. WLLT Radio, Sterling-Rock Falls-Dixon, Ill., 1989—; prin., gen. mgr. Sta. WDKR Radio, Decatur, Ill., 1996—; cons. Sta. WXFM Radio and others, Mt. Zion, Ill., 1984—; assoc. prof. Valparaiso (Ind.) U. Coll. Bus., 1974-77. Ind. dir. Nat. Assn. FM Broadcasters, 1972-73; bd. dirs. Blackhawk Waterways Conv. and Vis. Bur., Polo, Ill., 1993—, Michigan City (Ind.) Main St. Assn., 1992-96, Downtowns of Ill. Associated, 1996—, v.p., 1997-98, pres. 1999; pres. N.W. Ill. MBA Roundtable, Sterling, 1997—; active Downtown Econ. Devel. Com., Decatur, 1997; bd. dirs. Decatur Small Bus. Coun., 1986-87; mem. Sterling Sister City Com., 1995—. Mem. U. Chgo. Mgmt. Roundtable, Mt. Zion C. of C. (bd. dirs. 1987-88), Rock Falls C. of C. (bd. dirs. 1996—), Rotary. Methodist. Avocations: sailing, amateur radio, travel, photography, motorcycling. Home: 602 Woodland Ct Mount Zion IL 62549-1440

BURNS, BARBARA, lawyer; b. Jersey City, May 12, 1951; d. Thomas Jr. and Regina (Trzanowska) Gangemi; m. Damon Williams, Jan. 4, 1977 (div. 1986); 1 child, Jacob Williams; m. Matthew Burns, Feb. 7, 1987; 1 child, Olivia Burns. BA, Newton Coll., 1973; JD cum laude, New Eng. Sch. Law, 1976. Bar: Mass. 1977, N.J., 1984, U.S. Dist. Ct. Mass. 1977, U.S. Dist. Ct. N.J. 1984, U.S. Supreme Ct. 1988. Corporate counsel Acton (Mass.) Corp., 1977-79; asst. gen. counsel Greater Media, Inc., East Brunswick, N.J., 1984-88, assoc. gen. counsel, 1988-93, v.p., gen. counsel, 1993—. Mem. Am. Corporate Counsel Assn., Fed. Comm. Bar Assn., N.J. Bar Assn. Office: Greater Media Inc Two Kennedy Blvd East Brunswick NJ 08816

BURNS, BEBE LYN, journalist; b. Baytown, Tex., Nov. 2, 1952; d. L.L. and Edith Elizabeth (Smith) B.; m. George Frederick Rhodes Jr., Nov. 30, 1980; 1 child, Elizabeth Kathleen. BA, U. Houston, 1974; MS in Journalism, Northwestern U., 1975. Reporter, anchor Sta. WSPA-TV, Spartanburg, S.C., 1975-76, Sta. KHOU-TV, Houston, 1976-79; reporter Sta. KTVI-TV, St. Louis, 1979-82; bus. reporter Sta. KPRC-TV, Houston, 1982-95; prin. Burns Kopatic, Houston, 1996-97, Bebe Burns Comm., Houston, 1997—; adj. prof. U. Houston Sch. Comm., 1998—. Bd. dirs. Presbyn. Sch., 1996—, Houston Area Parkinson's Soc., 1991-95, CanCare of Houston, Inc., 1995-97; founding mem. Greater Houston Women's Found.; active Friends of Fleming Park, Boulevard Oaks Civic Assn.; mem. adminstrv. bd. St. Paul's United Meth. Ch., 1998—. Recipient awards Headliners Club Tex. 1988, Tex. AP Broadcasters, 1988, Am. Women in Radio & TV, 1988, Press Club Houston, 1987, 88, Press Club Dallas, 1981, 93, Employee award for help to jobless Tex. Employment Commn., 1993, Bus. Advocacy award North Harris-Montgomery C.C. Dist. & Bus. & Industry Coun., 1993; named one of Women on the Move Houston Post and Tex. Exec. Women, 1988, Small Bus. Media Adv. of Yr. SBA, 1992. Mem. Soc. Profl. Journalists.

BURNS, BERNARD JOHN, III, public defender; b. Alexandria, Va., Apr. 28, 1956; s. Bernard John and Mary Theresa (O'Malley) B.; m. Pamela Sue Endres, June 9, 1990; 1 child, Kristie Keener. BA in Journalism, U. Iowa, 1982, JD, 1984. Bar: Iowa 1985, U.S. Dist. Ct. (so. dist.) Iowa 1987, U.S. Supreme Ct. 1989, U.S. Ct. Appeals (8th cir.) 1992. Asst. appellate defender Iowa Appellate Defender, Des Moines, 1985-94; asst. pub. defender Des Moines Adult Pub. Defender, 1994-99; asst. fed. defender Office of Fed. Defender, Des Moines, 1999—. Bd. mem. Met. Arts Alliance Greater Des Moines, 1996—, pres.-elect, 1999; chmn. Jazz in July Planning Com., Des Moines, 1997; keyboard player Goodnight Dallas. Mem. Iowa Pub. Defenders Assn. (pres. 1991—), Iowa Criminal and Juvenile Justice Planning Commn., Phi Beta Kappa. Avocations: composer, actor, writer, Tae Kwon Do instructor, musician. Office: Fed Defender 300 Walnut St Ste 295 Des Moines IA 50309

BURNS, BERNARD O., county legislator; b. Utica, N.Y., Oct. 11, 1923; s. James Leonard and Alice Kathryn (Larkin) B.; m. Carol Ann Davies, Aug. 21, 1954; children: Nancy, Elizabeth, Stephen, Paul. BA, Hamilton Coll., 1948; MA, Syracuse U., 1951. Tchr. Punahou Sch., Honolulu, 1948-50, Chadwicks (N.Y.) H.S., 1951-55; tchr., coach Clinton (N.Y.) H.S., 1955-88; county legislator Oneida County, Utica, 1985—; hockey coach Clinton H.S., 1955-84. 1st Lt. USAAF, 1942-45, Italy. Democrat. Roman Catholic. Avocations: libraries, golf, skiing. Home: 21 Hamilton Pl Clinton NY 13323-1317

BURNS, BETH, women's collegiate basketball coach; b. Chatham, N.J., Oct. 7, 1957. BS in Phys. & Health Edn., Ohio Wesleyan U., 1979; MS in Edn., Ohio State U., 1981. Grad. asst. coach Ohio State U., Columbus, 1980-81; asst. coach East Carolina State U., 1981-83, U. Colo., 1983-88; head coach San Diego State U., 1988-97, Ohio State U., 1997—. Inducted Hall of Fame Ohio Wesleyan U.; named coach of yr. Western Athletic Conf., 1994, 95, 97, Co-Sida Dist. 7, 1995. Avocation: long distance running. Office: Ohio State U Athletic Comms 1 Basketball Office 555 Arena Dr Columbus OH 43210-1104*

BURNS, B(ILLYE) JANE, museum director; b. Yeager, Okla., Nov. 1, 1940; d. William O. and Berniece (Floyd) French; m. Richard D. Burns, June 12, 1960 (div. 1990); children: Jennifer, Richard, Timothy, Daniel. AS, Okla. State U., 1960; BA in Bus., Goshen Coll., 1988. Treas. Woodlawn Nature Coun., Inc., Elkhart, Ind., 1975-82; cons. Am. art Midwest Mus. Am. Art, Elkhart, 1978-81, founding trustee, 1978—, dir., 1980-91; cons. Heritage Fine Arts, Elkhart; bd. dirs. Key Bank. Mem. Woodlaw Nature Coun., Inc., Elkhart, 4-Arts Club, Elkhart, Ind. Advs. for Art, Elkhart County Symphony. Mem. LWV (bd. dirs. 1985-99, v.p. 1990-99), Michiana Arts and Scis. Coun., Concert Club. Democrat. Methodist. Avocations: collecting art, antiques, skiing, curling, traveling. Home: 2413 Greenleaf Blvd Elkhart IN 46514-4055 Office: MW Mus Am Art 429 S Main St Elkhart IN 46516-3210

BURNS, BRENDA CAROLYN, retired special education administrator; b. Scalf, Ky., July 22, 1947; d. Lindberg and Ina Jean (Mills) B.; m. Michael Burns (div. 1985). BA in English, Wright State U., Dayton, OH, 1968, BA in Spanish, 1971, MEd in Spanish, English and Edn., 1973; MEd in Counseling, Cleve. State U., Cleve., 1985; MAEd in Sch. Psychology, U. Akron, 1985. Cert. in Spanish, English, counseling, sch. psychology, sch. social work, pupil pers., Ohio. Tchr. Spanish Centerville (Ohio) City Sch., 1971-73; tchr. Spanish and English Rocky River (Ohio) City Sch., 1973-78; sch. counselor Brooklyn (Ohio) City Sch., 1978-84; intern sch. psychologist Westlake (Ohio) City Sch., 1984-85; sch. psychologist Brooklyn City Sch., 1985-87, sch. psychologist, coord. student svcs., 1987-97, dir. pupil svcs., 1997-99; ret., 1999; adv. coun., chair Cuyahoga Spl. Edn. Svc. Ctr., Cleve., 1991-92. Mem. Nat. Assn. Sch. Psychologists, Ohio Sch. Psychologists Assn., Cleve. Assn. Sch. Psychologists, Cleve. Psychol. Assn., Coun. for Exceptional Children, Ohio Assn. Pupil Svcs. Adminstrs. Avocations: reading, traveling, walking, music, movies. Office: Brooklyn City Schs 9200 Biddulph Rd Brooklyn OH 44144-2614

BURNS, BRENT EMIL, electrical engineer; b. Wynnewood, Okla., Dec. 3, 1952; s. Frank Brent and Dorothy Esther (Westberg) B. BSEE, U. Okla., 1978, MSEE, 1979; PhD of Elec. Engring., Stanford U., 1987. Mgr. Northrop Grumman Integrated Micro Sensors Group, Palos Verdes, Calif., 1985-98; prod. R and D mgr. Integrated Micromachines Inc., Pasadena, Calif., 1998—. Patentee on micro-electro-mechanical systems/silicon micromachining. With U.S. Army, 1972-74. Scholarship NSF 1979-82. Mem. IEEE, Electrochem. Soc., Tau Beta Pi, Eta Kappa Nu. Achievements include 4 U.S. patents in micro-electro-mechanical sys., silicon micromachining. Avocations: racquetball, bicycling, outrigger canoeing. Home: 26566 Basswood Ave Rancho Palos Verdes CA 90275-2269 Office: Northrop Grumman ESID PO Box 5032 Hawthorne CA 90251-5032

BURNS, BRIAN PATRICK, lawyer, business executive; b. Cambridge, Mass., July 12, 1936; s. John Joseph and Alice (Blake) B.; m. Sheila Ann O'Connor, June 23, 1962; children: Sheila Ann, Brian Patrick, Sean Richard, Roderick O'Connor. BA, Holy Cross Coll., 1957; LLB, Harvard U., 1960. Bar: Mass. 1960, N.Y. 1961, Calif. 1965. Law clk., spl. asst. to regional adminstr. New York Regional Office, SEC, 1958-59; assoc. Webster, Sheffield, Fleischmann, Hitchcock & Brookfield, N.Y.C., 1960-64; ptnr. Cullinan, Hancock, Rothert & Burns, San Francisco, 1965-74; sr. ptnr. Cullinan, Burns & Helmer, San Francisco, 1975-78; firm Burns & Whitehead, San Francisco, 1978-86; chmn., chief exec. officer, chmn. exec. com. Boothe Fin. Corp., San Francisco, 1981-87, also bd. dirs.; chmn. Robert Half Internat. Inc., 1987-88; chmn., CEO BF Enterprises Inc., 1987—; dir. U.S. Banknote Corp., N.Y.C., from 1967, chmn. exec. and fin. coms., 1973-76; dir. Coca Cola Bottling Co., N.Y., 1974-86, chmn. exec. com., 1979-86; dir. Kellogg Co., 1979-89, chmn. fin. com. 1984-89; dir. Calif. Jockey, 1980-89; dir., chmn. audit com. Flexi-Van Corp., N.Y.C., 1984-85; dir., chmn. exec. com. Pinnacle Petroleum Corp., The Woodlands, Tex., 1983-85; dir., chmn. ops. review com. Brink's Inc., Chgo., 1976-78; dir., chmn. acquisition com. Pacific Holding Corp., Los Angeles, 1972-78; dir., mem. exec. com. Beverly Wilshire Hotel, Beverly Hills, Calif., Calif., 1967-86; dir., chmn. exec. com. USR Industries, The Woodlands, 1980-83; dir., chmn. audit com. ROCOR Internat., Palo Alto, Calif., 1976-82; underwriting mem. Lloyds of London, 1978-89; lectr. continuing edn. of bar U. Calif., 1969, 74, 76, advanced bus. seminar, 1971; seminar on investment opportunities in wine industry McGraw Hill Coll., N.Y., 1973, Legal Edn. Inst., 1976. Bd. dirs. Boys Club of San Francisco, 1971-80, Am. Irish Found., 1978-87, Am. Ireland Fund, 1987—; trustee Holy Cross Coll., 1978-89. Mem. ABA (mem. small bus. com. corp. bus. and banking sect. 1972-76), State Bar Cal. (vice chmn. com. on corps. 1971-75), Bar Assn. San Francisco (chmn. com. on corp. banking and bus. law 1968-69), Calif. Jockey Club (dir. San Mateo, Calif. 1988-89). Roman Catholic. Clubs: Royal Dublin Soc.; Bohemian, Burlingame Country, Family, Olympic, Sky, N.Y. Athletic, Les Ambassadeurs, Mil. and Hospitaller Order St. Lazarus of Jerusalem (comdr. companion). Office: BF Enterprises Inc 100 Bush St Ste 1700 San Francisco CA 94104-3914*

BURNS, CAROL J., architect, educator; b. Cedar Rapids, Iowa, Nov. 24, 1954; d. Robert Joseph and Alice T. (Neuhaus) B. Student, Bryn Mawr Coll., 1973-75; BA, Yale Coll., 1980, MArch, 1983. Asst. prof. U. Cin., 1984-86; adj. prof. R.I. Sch. Design, Providence, 1986-87; assoc. prof., asst. chair archtl. dept. Harvard U., Cambridge, Mass., 1987—; prin. C. Burns, Architect, Guilford, Conn., 1986-93, Taylor MacDougall Burns Architects, Boston, 1993—; mem. Rotch Travelling Scholarship Com.; bd. dirs. Jour. Archtl. Edn. Author: (with others) Drawing/Building/Text, 1990; author, editor (with others): Thinking the Present, 1990; editor Yale Sch. Architecture Perspecta 21, 1984; designer Greybirch House (Conn. AIA award 1992); designer bank br. (Soc. Am. Registered Architects award 1988); group shows include Robert Lehman Gallery, N.Y.C., 1996, Erector Sq. Gallery, New Haven, 1987—, Norfolk 4 Plus 4: Architects and Sculptors, Norfolk, Conn., 1983; curator A Few Bldgs. and Some Chairs, Am. Architectur of the 1950's exhibit, 1991; contbr. articles to profl. and acad. jours. Active Mass. Dept. Housing and Comty. Devel. Recipient Edn. Honors award AIA, 1996. Mem. Boston Soc. Archs. (bd. dirs., commr. edn. and rsch.), Yale Club. Office: Harvard U Dept of Architecture 48 Quincy St Cambridge MA 02138-3000

BURNS, CARROLL DEAN, insurance company executive; b. Chattanooga, Dec. 22, 1932; s. William Thomas and Lillis (Gill) B.; m. Jean Baird, Aug. 29, 1954; children: Randy, Lori. B.S., U. Tenn., 1954. C.P.A., Tenn., Ohio. With Provident Life and Accident Ins. Co., Chattanooga, 1957-63; mgr. data processing Provident Life and Accident Ins. Co., 1960-63; with Union Central Life Ins. Co., Cin., 1963-79; exec. v.p., comptr., bd. dirs. Union Central Life Ins. Co., 1974-79; pres., CEO Life Ins. Co. Ga., Atlanta, 1979-94; exec. v.p. Georgia US Corp., Atlanta, 1989-94; ret., 1995; pres., COO Southland Life Ins. Co.; bd. dirs. Union Cen. Life Assurance Corp., Life Ins. Co. Ga., First of Ga. Ins. Group, Assoc. Drs. Ins. Co., Southland Ins. Co.; former chmn. Civil Svc. Bd., Fairfield, Ohio. Former trustee Better Bus. Bur. Cin. Served with USAF, 1955-57. Mem. BEta Alpha Psi, Atlanta Country Club, Georgian Club, Sugarloaf Country Club. Baptist. Home: 2075 Sugarloaf Club Dr Duluth GA 30097-4098

BURNS, C(HARLES) PATRICK, hematologist-oncologist; b. Kansas City, Mo., Oct. 8, 1937; s. Charles Edgar and Ruth (Eastham) B.; m. Janet Sue Walsh, June 15, 1968; children—Charles Geoffrey, Scott Patrick. BA, U. Kans., 1959, MD, 1963. Diplomate Am. Bd. Internal Medicine, subsplty. bds. hematology, med. oncology. Intern Cleve. Met. Gen. Hosp., 1963-64; asst. resident in internal medicine Univ. Hosps., Cleve., 1966-68, sr. resident in hematology, 1968-69; instr. medicine Case Western Res. U., Cleve., 1970-71; asst. chief hematology Cleve. VA Hosp., 1970-71; asst. prof. medicine U. Iowa Hosps., Iowa City, 1971-75, assoc. prof. medicine, 1975-80, prof., 1980—, dir. sect. med. oncology, co-dir. divsn. hematatol./oncology, 1980-85, dir. div. hematology-oncology, 1985-99; vis. scientist Imperial Cancer Rsch. Fund Labs., London, 1982-83; cons. U.S. VA Hosp.; mem. study sect. on exptl. therapeutics NIH, Cancer Ctr. Support Rev. Commn. Nat. Cancer Inst., NIH, NIH Cancer Clin. Investigation Rev. Com., VA Med. Rsch. Svc. Career Devel. Com.; mem. external adv. com. U. Oreg. Cancer Ctr., 1994—. Mem. bd. assoc. editors Cancer Rsch., 1988—; rsch. and publs. on hematologic malignancies, tumor lipid biochemistry, leukemia and oncology. Served to capt. M.C., AUS, 1964-66. Am. Cancer Soc. fellow in hematology-oncology, 1968-69, USPHS fellow in medicine, 1969-70; USPHS career awardee, 1978. Fellow ACP; mem. AAAS, Am. Bd. Internal Medicine (Subsplty. bd. hematology 1992-98), Am. Soc. Hematology, Am. Assn. Cancer Rsch., Internat. Soc. Hematology, Ctrl. Soc. Clin. Rsch., Am. Soc. Clin. Oncology, Soc. Exptl. Biology and Medicine, Oxygen Soc., Royal Soc. Medicine, Am. Fedn. Clin. Rsch., Internat. Soc. for the Study of Fatty Acids and Lipids, Phi Beta Pi, Lambda Chi Alpha, Alpha Omega Alpha. Home: 2046 Rochester Ct Iowa City IA 52245-3246 Office: U Iowa Univ Hosps Dept Medicine Iowa City IA 52242

BURNS, CHESTER RAY, medical history educator; b. Nashville, Dec. 5, 1937; s. Leslie Andrew and Margaret (Drake) B.; m. Ann Christine Griffey, Aug. 31, 1962; children: Christine, Derek. BA, Vanderbilt U., 1959, MD, 1963; PhD, Johns Hopkins U., 1969. Asst. prof. history medicine U. Tex. Med. Br., Galveston, 1969-71, James Wade Rockwell asst. prof. history medicine, 1971-75, James Wade Rockwell assoc. prof., 1975-79, James Wade Rockwell prof., 1979—; cons. Nat. Ctr. for Health Svcs. Rsch., Washington, 1976-78; mem. nat. bd. cons. NEH, Washington, 1978-83. Editor: Humanism in Medicine, 1973, Legacies in Ethics and Medicine, 1977, Legacies in Law and Medicine, 1977; co-editor: Philosophy of Medicine and Bioethics: A Twenty Year Retrospective and Critical Appraisal, 1997; author numerous essays. Bd. dirs. The Grand 1894 Opera House, Galveston, 1986-88. Mem. Am. Assn. for History of Medicine (exec. coun. 1972-75), Soc. for Health and Human Values (pres. 1975-76), Am. Osler Soc. (bd. govs. 1984-87), Internat. Soc. for History of Medicine (treas. 1991—), Tex. State Hist. Assn. (exec. coun. 1993-97), Rotary (pres. Galveston club 1980-81, gov. Dist. 5910, 1993-94). Democrat. Methodist. Avocations: swimming, photography. Office: U Tex Med Br Rm 2 208 Ashbel Smith Bldg Galveston TX 77555-1311

BURNS, CONRAD RAY, senator; b. Gallatin, Mo., Jan. 25, 1935; s. Russell and Mary Frances (Knight) B.; m. Phyllis Jean Kuhlmann; children: Keely Lynn, Garrett Russell. Student, U. Mo., 1952-54. Field rep. Polled Hereford World Mag., Kansas City, Mo., 1963-69; pub. rels. Billings (Mont.) Livestock Com., 1969-73; farm dir. KULR TV, Billings, 1974; pres., founder No. Ag-Network, Billings, 1975-86; commissioner Yellowstone County, Billings, 1987-89; U.S. Senator from Montana, 1989—; Mem. Aging Com., Small Bus. Com., chmn. Appropriations Subcom. of Mil. Constrn., chmn. Com. Sci. and Transp. Subcom. of Comms., chmn. Energy and Nat. Resources. With USMC, 1955-57. Mem. Nat. Assn. Farm Broadcasters, Am. Legion, Rotary, Masons, Shriners. Republican. Lutheran. Avocation: football officiating. Office: US Senate 187 Dirksen Senate Office Washington DC 20510

BURNS, DAN W., manufacturing company executive; b. Auburn, Calif., Sept. 10, 1925; s. William and Edith Lynn (Johnston) B.; 1 child, Dan Jr. Dir. materials Menasco Mfg. Co., 1951-56; v.p., gen. mgr. Hufford Corp., 1956-58; pres. Hufford div. Siegler Corp., 1958-61; v.p. Siegler Corp., 1961-62, Lear Siegler, Inc., 1962-64; pres., dir. Electrada Corp., Culver City, Calif., 1964; pres., chief exec. officer Sargent Industries, Inc., L.A., 1964-85, chmn. bd. dirs., 1985-88; now chmn. bd. dirs., CEO Arlington Industries, Inc.; bd. dirs. Gen. Automotive Corp., Dover Tech. Internat., Inc., Kistler Aerospace Corp. Bd. dirs. San Diego Aerospace Mus., Smithsonian Inst., The Pres.'s Cir., Nat. Acad. Scis., Atlantic Coun. of U.S., George C. Marshall Found. Capt. U.S. Army, 1941-47; prisoner of war Japan; asst. mil. attache 1946, China; adc to Gen. George C. Marshall 1946-47. Mem. OAS Sports Com. (dir.), L.A. Country Club, St. Francis Yacht Club, Calif. Club, Conquistador del Cielo, Cosmos Club Washington. Home: 7400 Bryan Canyon Rd Carson City NV 89704-9588

BURNS, DAVID MITCHELL, writer, musician, former diplomat; b. Pineville, Ky., Dec. 1, 1928; s. Judge and Louise (Cooke) B.; m. Sandra

Dunlop, June 8, 1955; children: David A., Patrick C. BA, Princeton U., 1953; student, Sch. Advanced Internat. Studies, Johns Hopkins U., 1957, 60, Howard U., 1957, 60, Fgn. Service Inst., Tangier, Morocco, 1967-69. Advt. trainee Gen. Electric Co., 1953; instr. English U. Kans., 1954-55; asst. cultural affairs officer Am. embassy, Damascus, Syria, 1955-56, Beirut, Lebanon, 1956; dir. Iran-Am. Soc., Isfahan, 1957; information officer Am. consulate general Salisbury, Fedn. Rhodesia and Nyasaland, 1957-59; pub. affairs officer Am. embassy, Bamako, Mali, 1960-62; cultural affairs officer Tunis, Tunisia, 1962-63; cultural policy officer Africa, USIA, Agy., 1963-67; pub. affairs officer Am. interests sect. embassy of, Switzerland, Algiers, Algeria, 1969-72; dir. sci. and tech. programs USIA, 1972-77; dir. climate project AAAS, Washington, 1978-90. CD's as leader of Hot Mustard Quintet include Swing Song, Don't Postpone Joy, Nothing Loved Is Ever Lost, 1975—; contbr. articles to newspapers and mags., 1953—. Served with USAF, 1946-49. Fulbright grant l'Universite de Lille and Salzburg Seminar in Am. Studies, 1953-54. Mem. Nat. Assn. Sci. Writers, Nat. Book Critics Cir., Jazz Journalists Assn. Clubs: Cosmos, Dacor (Washington). Office: 1712 19th St NW Washington DC 20009-1606 *Constant course correction--see plans contingent.*

BURNS, DENVER P., forestry research administrator; b. Bryan, Ohio, Oct. 27, 1940; married; 1 child. BS, Ohio State U., 1962, MS, 1964, PhD in Entomology, 1967; MPA, Harvard U., 1981. Asst. entomologist So. Forest Experiment Sta., 1962-68, rsch. entomologist, 1968-72, asst. dir., 1972-74; staff asst. to dep. chief for rsch. U.S. Forest Svc., 1974-76; dep. dir. North Ctrl. Experiment Sta., 1976-81; dir. Northeastern Forest Experiment Sta., Radnor, Pa., 1981-92, Rocky Mountain Sta., 1992—. Mem. AAAS. Office: US Forest Service 240 W Prospect Rd Fort Collins CO 80526-2002

BURNS, DONALD SNOW, registered investment advisor, financial and business consultant; b. Cambridge, Mass., July 31, 1925; s. Jules Ian and Ruth (Snow) B.; m. Lucy Lee Keating, July 15, 1947 (div.); children: Julie Ann Wrigley, Patti B. Boyd, Laurie Bidegain, Wendi Collins, Loni Monahan, Robin Alden; m. Bettye Geurin, July 31, 1997. Student, Williams Coll., 1943-44; M in Baking, Am. Inst. of Baking, 1947. Baker O'Rourke Baking Co., Buffalo, 1946-49; gen. mgr. Glaco Co. of So. Calif., L.A., 1949-51; regional mgr. Glaco Div. of Ekco Prodn. Co., Chgo., 1951-53, gen. mgr., 1953-56; pres. McClintock Mfg. Div. Ekco Prodn. Co., Chgo., 1956-61; v.p. Ekco Products Co., Chgo., 1961-67; pres., chmn. Prestige Automotive Group, Garden Grove, Calif., 1967-78; chmn. Prestige Holdings Ltd., Newport Beach, Calif., 1978—; chmn. bd. Newport Nat. Bank, Newport Beach, 1961-67; bd. dir. Securitas Trust, Monte Carlo, Monaco, Am. Safety Equipment Co., Glendale, Calif., Internat. Tech. Corp., Torrance, Calif., Escorp, San Luis Obispo, Calif.; dir. Internat. Rectifier, El Segundo. Author: (short story) The Goose that Neighed, 1967, (books) Two and a Half Nickels, 1970, Light My Fire, 1979. Mem. Calif. State U. Adv. Bd., Fullerton, 1973-76; bd. dirs. Santiago Coll. Found., Santa Ana, Calif., 1989-90, Orange County Sheriff's Adv. Coun., Calif., 1978—, pres., 1987-88; chmn. bd. trustees Orme Sch. Mayer Ariz., 1976-78. With USNR, 1943-46. Mem. Jonathan Club. Avocations: sailing, scuba diving, flying, auto racing, fishing.

BURNS, DUFFY, women's basketball coach university level; b. 1960. BS in Phys. Edn., Ball State U., 1985. Asst. head basketball coach Wapahani H.S., Muncie, Ind., 1981-84; asst. coach men's basketball Ball State U., Muncie, 1984-85, Ill. State U., Normal, 1985-86, U. Pitts., 1986-87, U. Mass., Amherst, 1987-88; asst. coach men's basketball Ctrl. Conn. State Coll., New Britain, 1988-90, asst. coach men's basketball and recruitment coord., 1990-94; head coach women's basketball Cleve. State U., 1995—. Office: Cleve State U Athletics Dept 2000 Prospect Ave Cleveland OH 44115-2408*

BURNS, EDWARD CHARLES, infosystems specialist; b. Newark, Sept. 22, 1942; s. Edward Joseph and Anna Marie (Grim) B.; divorced; children: Anneliese, Edward. BS, St. Peter's Coll., 1964; MBA cum laude, Fairleigh Dickinson U., 1973. Assoc. programmer IBM, Cranford, N.J., 1969-70; tech. support mgr. Beneficial Data Processing Corp., Morristown, N.J., 1970-75; mgr. computer performance planning group Warner-Lambert Co., Morris Plains, N.J., 1975-82; mgr. tech. devel. Internat. Paper Co., Denville, N.J., 1982-83; v.p. data ctr. svcs. The CIT Group, Livingston, N.J., 1983—; adj. assoc. prof. computer tech. County Coll. of Morris, Randolph, N.J., 1973-87; assessment cons. Thomas Edison State Coll., Trenton, N.J., 1978—, mem. bus. degree adv. com., 1979-94; evaluator Am. Coun. on Edn., Washington, 1980—; mentor Distance Independent Adult Learning, 1995—. Capt. AUS, 1960-68. Decorated Bronze Star. Mem. Civil Air Patrol, Am. Assn. Collegiate Independent Study. Roman Catholic. Avocation: flying. Home: 23 Molly Stark Dr Morristown NJ 07960-5140 Office: The CIT Group Inc 650 Cit Dr Livingston NJ 07039-5703

BURNS, EDWARD J., JR., actor, director; b. Valley Stream, N.Y., Jan. 29, 1968. Motion picture director, writer, prodr., motion picture actor. Actor, dir., writer films The Brothers McMullen, 1995 (Jury Spl. prize Deauville Film Festival 1995, Ind. Spirit award 1995, Nova award 1995, Grand Jury prize Sundance Film Festival 1995), She's the One, 1996, No Looking Back, 1998; film appearances include Saving Pvt. Ryan, 1998, 15 Mins., 1999, Any Given Sunday, 1999. Recipient ShoWest award for Screenwriter of Yr., 1996. Office: c/o ICM 8942 Wilshire Blvd Beverly Hills CA 90211*

BURNS, SISTER ELIZABETH MARY, hospital administrator; b. Estherville, Iowa, Mar. 3, 1927; d. Bernard Aloysius and Viola Caroline (Brennan) B. Diploma in Nursing, St. Joseph Mercy Sch. Nursing, Sioux City, Iowa, 1952; B.S. in Nursing Edn, Mercy Coll., Detroit, 1957; M.Sc. in Nursing, Wayne State U., 1958; Ed.D., Columbia U., 1969. Joined Sisters of Mercy, Roman Cath. Ch., 1946; nursing supr. Mercy Med. Center, Dubuque, Iowa, 1952-55; supr. orthopedics and urology St. Joseph Mercy Hosp., Sioux City, 1955-56; dir. Sch. Nursing, 1958-63; chmn. dept. nursing Mercy Coll. of Detroit, 1963-73; dir. health services Sisters of Mercy, Province of Detroit, 1973-77; pres., chief exec. officer Marian Health Center, Sioux City, 1977-87; sabbatical leave, 1988; coord. life planning Sisters of Mercy, 1989-90, mem. province adminstrv. team, 1990-98. Bd. dirs. Mercy Sch. Nursing of Detroit, 1968-77; mem. exec. com. Greater Detroit Area Hosp. Council, 1973-77; trustee St. Mary Coll., Omaha, 1981-82, Briar Cliff Coll., Sioux City, 1981-87; chmn. Mercy Health Adv. Council, 1978-80. Mem. Western Iowa League for Nursing (pres. 1960-62), Nat. League for Nursing, Sisters of Mercy Shared Svcs. Coordinating Com., Cath. Hosp. Assn. (trustee 1977-80), Sisters of Mercy Health Corp. (trustee 1988-90, governance coord. 1998—), Mercy Health Svcs. (chair bd. 1990-95, membership bd. 1995-98, historian 1998—). Office: 34605 Twelve Mile Rd Farmington Hills MI 48331

BURNS, ELIZABETH MURPHY, media executive; b. Superior, Wis., Dec. 4, 1945; d. Morgan and Elizabeth (Beck) Murphy; m. Richard Ramsey Burns, June 24, 1984. Student U. Ariz., 1963-67. Promotion and programming sec. Sta. KGUN-TV, Tucson, 1967-68; programming and traffic sec. Sta. KFMB-TV, San Diego, 1968-69; owner, operator Sta. KKAR, Pomona, Calif., 1970-73; co-owner Evening Telegram Co. (parent co. Murphy Stas.); pres. Morgan Murphy Stas., Madison, Wis., 1976—; dir. Nat. Guardian Life Ins. Co., various media stas. and corps. Trustee Coll. St. Scholastica; bd. dirs. Republic Bank. Mem. Nat. Assn. Broadcasters, Wis. Broadcasters Assn. Republican. Roman Catholic. Clubs: Madison, Nakoma Country; Northland Country (Duluth), Boulders Country (Carefree, Ariz.). Avocations: golf, travel. Home: 180 Paine Farm Rd Duluth MN 55804-2609 Office: Sta WISC-TV 7025 Raymond Rd Madison WI 53719-5053

BURNS, ELLEN BREE, federal judge; b. New Haven, Conn., Dec. 13, 1923; d. Vincent Thomas and Mildred Bridget (Bannon) Bree; m. Joseph Patrick Burns, Oct. 8, 1955 (dec.); children: Mary Ellen, Joseph Bree, Kevin James. BA, Albertus Magnus Coll., 1944, LLD (hon.), 1974; LLB, Yale U., 1947; LLD (hon.), U. New Haven, 1981, Sacred Heart U., 1986, Fairfield U., 1991. Bar: Conn. 1947. Dir. legis. legal svcs. State of Conn., 1949-73; judge Conn. Cir. Ct., 1973-74, Conn. Ct. of Common Pleas, 1974-76, Conn. Superior Ct., 1976-78; judge U.S. Dist. Ct. Conn., New Haven, 1978—, chief judge, 1988-92, sr. judge, 1992—. Trustee Fairfield U., 1978-85, Albertus Magnus Coll., 1985—. Recipient John Carroll of Carrollton award John Barry Council K.C., 1973, Judiciary award Conn. Trial Lawyers Assn., 1978, Cross Pro Ecclesia et Pontifice, 1981, Law Rev. award U. Conn. Law Rev., 1987, Judiciary award Conn. Bar Assn., 1987, Raymond E. Baldwin Pub. Svc. award Bridgeport Law Sch., 1992. Mem. ABA, Am. Bar Found., New Haven County Bar Assn. Roman Catholic. Office: US Dist Ct 141 Church St New Haven CT 06510-2030*

BURNS, ELLEN JEAN, arts educator; b. Memphis, Sept. 1, 1953; d. Eugene Harold and Elizabeth Josephine Burns; m. Daniel Bruce Eisenberg, July 25, 1987. BM, U. Memphis, 1976, BME, 1976; MSLS, U. Tenn., 1977; MM, Fla. State U., 1982, PhD, 1994. Asst. prof. Ala. State U., Montgomery, 1991-92; instr. Fla. State U., London, 1994; asst. prof. Fla. State U., Tallahassee, Fla., 1994-95; instr., asst. prof. Northern Ariz. U., Flagstaff, 1996-98. Editor: Texts on Texts and Textuality, 1999; editor H-Net, 1993—; clarinet soloist Germantown Symphony Orch., 1979; clarinet recitalist Ballet South, 1981, La Camara transatlantica, 1995. Recipient Young Artist award Beethoven Club, 1980. Mem. Am. Musicol. Soc., Am. Soc. of Aesthetics, Lyrica Soc. for Word-Music Rels. (v.p. 1996-98, pres. 1998—, assoc. editor 1984-94), Lyrica Soc. (assoc. editor 1989-94, v.p. 1996-98, pres. 1998—), Phi Eta Sigma (hon.), Pi Kappa Lambda. Avocation: Taoist Tai Chi.

BURNS, GLENN RICHARD, dentist; b. Marietta, Ohio, Mar. 23, 1951; s. Alphas Gale Burns and Elma June (Sayres) George; m. Linda Edith Bailey, June 10, 1978; children: Geoffrey William, Katharine May. BS in Zoology, Ohio U., 1973; DDS, Ohio State U., 1980. Gen. practice dentistry Lancaster, Ohio, 1980—. Bd. dirs. Lancaster YMCA, Fairfield County, 1985-91; Presbyn. elder. Served to sgt. U.S. Army, 1973-77. Fellow Acad. Gen. Dentistry, 1991. Fellow Pierre Fauchard Acad.; mem. ADA, Ohio Dental Assn., Hocking Valley Dental Soc. (chmn. children's dental health month 1983-86, v.p. 1991, pres. 1993), Acad. Gen. Dentistry, Christian Dental Soc., Aircraft Owners and Pilots Assn., Flying Dentist Assn., Am. Bonanza Soc., Pilots for Christ Internat., Lifeline Pilots, Kiwanis (v.p. 1988, 1st v.p. 1989, pres. 1990), Xi Psi Phi (v.p. 1984-88, pres. 1988-92). Republican. Avocations: golf, reading, flying, photography. Home: 3931 Mudhouse Rd NE Lancaster OH 43130-8716 Office: 208 N Columbus St Lancaster OH 43130-3005

BURNS, GLORIA M., judge. Bankruptcy judge U.S. Bankruptcy Ct. N.J., Camden, 1994—. Office: US Bankruptcy Court 15 N 7th St Camden NJ 08102-1104

BURNS, H(ERBERT) MICHAEL, corporate director; b. Toronto, Ont., Can., June 19, 1937; s. Charles Folwer Williams and Janet Mary (Wilson) B.; m. Susan P. Cathers, Dec. 23, 1980; children: Charles F.M., Janet Michelle. Student, Cornell U., Trinity Coll. Sch., Port Hope, Can. With Nesbitt Burns (and predecessor cos.), 1958-77; dep. chmn., bd. dirs. Extendicare Inc.; pres., treas. Kingfield Investments Ldt. and assoc. subs.; bd. dirs. Crown Life Ins. Co., Algoma Ctrl. Corp., Denison Mines Ltd., Derby Internat. SA, Landmark Techs. Inc., Lateral Victor, MinRoc Ltd. Bd. dirs., past pres. Royal Agrl. Winter Fair; bd. govs. Trinity Coll. Sch., Olympic Trust Can.; bd. dirs. McMichael Can. Art Found., Can. Fedn. for AIDS Rsch. Mem. Toronto Club, York Club, Kappa Alpha. Avocations: recreation, farming. Home: Kingswood, 1314 King Vaughan Rd, Maple, ON Canada L6A 2A5 Office: Extendicare Inc, 3000 Steeles Ave E Ste 300, Markham, ON Canada L3R 9W2

BURNS, IVAN ALFRED, grocery products and industrial company executive; b. Leamington Spa, England, Jan. 18, 1935; s. Cecil Ivan and Dorothy Constance (Mote) B.; m. Angela Loeffel, May 16, 1959; children: Pauline Cecile, Charla Cheyney, Claudine. BS, Coventry Coll., 1958. Various positions Deere & Co., Moline, Ill., 1960-69; dir. internat. ACF Industries Inc., N.Y.C., 1972-75, v.p., 1975-81, pres., COO, 1981-83, chmn., CEO, 1983-90; dir. CPC Internat. Inc., Englewood Cliffs, N.J., 1983-90, pres. corn refining div., 1985-87, exec. v.p. adminstrn., 1987-90; pres., dir. Picca Enterprises, Inc., New Canaan, Conn., 1984-96; bd. dirs. Continental Corp., N.Y.C. Patentee valve, 1980. Bd. dirs. United Way, New York, 1984-85; mem. bus. adv. bd. Northwestern U., 1983—. Mem. Conf. Bd. Republican. Mem. Ch. of England. Avocations: horse breeding, collecting netsukes. Home and Office: Deer Park Rd New Canaan CT 06840

BURNS, JACQUELINE MARY, laboratory administrator; b. N.Y.C., Sept. 18, 1938; d. Charles Francis and Kathryn Teresa Peknic; m. Gerard Joseph Burns, July 22, 1967; children: Mary, Elizabeth, Katharine, Agnes (dec.). RN, Columbus Hosp., Chgo., 1963; BS, Marymount Manhattan Coll., 1978; PhD, Cornell U., 1984. Cert. clin. cytogeneticist, PhD med. geneticst, Am. Bd. Med. Genetics. Staff nurse emergency rm. St. Johns Queens Hosp., N.Y.C., 1965-68; predoctoral, postdoctoral fellow Meml. Sloan Kettering, N.Y.C., 1978-88; dir. cytogenetics Danbury (Conn.) Hosp., 1988—. Fellow Am. Coll. Med. Genetics (founding); mem. Am. Soc. Med. Genetics, Internat. Soc. Nurses Genetics. Roman Catholic. Office: Danbury Hosp 24 Hospital Ave Danbury CT 06810-6099

BURNS, JAMES B., prosecutor; b. Quincy, Ill., Sept. 21, 1945; married; 3 children. BA in History, Northwestern U., 1967, JD, 1971. Former profl. basketball player Chgo. Bulls, Dallas Chaparrals; asst. U.S. atty., then dep. chief and chief criminal litigation divsn. U.S. Dept. Justice, Chgo., 1971-78; assoc. Isham, Lincoln & Beale, Chgo., 1978-80, ptnr., 1980-88; ptnr. Keck, Mahin & Cate, Chgo., 1988-93; U.S. atty. for no. dist. Ill. U.S. Dept. Justice, Chgo., 1993-97; pvt. practice Sibley & Austin, Chgo., 1997—. Bd. trustees Northwestern U., Evanston, Ill., 1981-83; Dem. candidate for lt. gov. State of Ill., 1990. Office: Sibley & Austin 1 1st National Plz Ste 4700 Chicago IL 60603*

BURNS, JAMES MACGREGOR, political scientist, historian; b. Melrose, Mass., Aug. 3, 1918; s. Robert Arthur and Mildred Curry (Bunce) B.; m. Janet Rose Dismorr Thompson, May 23, 1942; children: David MacGregor, Timothy Stewart, Deborah Edwards, Margaret Rebecca Antonia; m. Joan Simpson Meyers, Sept. 7, 1969 (div.). B.A. Williams Coll, 1939; postgrad., Nat. Inst. Pub. Affairs, 1939-40; M.A., Ph.D., Harvard, 1947; postgrad., London Sch. Econs., 1949. Exec. sec. non ferrous metals commn. NWLB, 1942-43; faculty polit. sci. Williams Coll., Williamstown, Mass., 1941-88, prof., 1953-88, prof. emeritus, 1988—; sr. scholar Jepson Sch. Leadership, U. Richmond, 1990-93, co-chmn., 1976-87; sr. scholar James MacGregor Burns Acad. Leadership, U. Md., College Park, 1997—; mem. staff Hoover Commn., 1948; faculty Salzburg Seminar in Am. Studies, 1954, 61; history cons. TV programs ABC, CBS, 1980—; sr. scholar The Acd. of Leadership, U. Md. Author: Guam: Operations of the 77th Infantry Div, 1944, Okinawa: The Last Battle, (with others), 1947, Congress on Trial, 1949, Government by the People, (with Jack W. Peltason and Thomas E. Cronin), 1981, Roosevelt: The Lion and the Fox, 1956, John Kennedy: A Political Profile, 1960, The Deadlock of Democracy: Four Party Politics in America, 1963, Presidential Government: The Crucible of Leadership, 1966, Roosevelt: The Soldier of Freedom, 1970, Uncommon Sense, 1972, Edward Kennedy and the Camelot Legacy, 1976, Leadership, 1978, The Vineyard of Liberty, 1982, The Power to Lead, 1984, The Workshop of Democracy, 1985, The Crosswinds of Freedom, 1989, Cobblestone Leadership, 1990, (with Stewart Burns) A People's Charter, 1991; contbr. to periodicals. Mem. Mass. delegation Democratic Nat. Conv., 1952, 56, 60, 64, Dem. Charter Conv., 1974; mem. Mass. Dem. Party Charter Commn., 1977-79, Mass. Dem. Charter Conv., 1979, Berkshire County delegation Mass. state conv., 1954; Dem. candidate for Congress, 1st Dist. Mass., 1958; Former trustee Stockbridge Sch., Woodrow Wilson Internat. Center for Scholars. Served with AUS, 1943-45; combat historian Guam, Saipan, Okinawa. Recipient Tamiment Inst. award for best biography, 1956, Woodrow Wilson prize, 1957, Pulitzer prize in history, 1971, Nat. Book award, 1971, Francis Parkman prize, 1971, Christopher award, 1983, 90, Harold D. Lasswell award, 1984, Robert F. Kennedy Book award for cumulative writing on freedom, 1990, Rollo May award forHumanistic Studies, 1994. Mem. Am. Polit. Sci. Assn. (pres. 1975-76), New Eng. Polit. Sci. Assn. (pres. 1960-61), Internat. Soc. Polit. Psychology (pres. 1982-83), Am. Hist. Assn., Am. Philos. Soc., ACLU, Am. Legion, Phi Beta Kappa, Delta Sigma Rho. Home: Highgate Barn High Mowing Bee Hill Williamstown MA 01267 Office: U Md James MacGregor Burns Acad 1107 Taliaferro Hall College Park MD 20742-7715

BURNS, JAMES MILTON, retired educator; b. Coal City, Ind., Feb. 22, 1922; s. Ray L. and N. Eugenie (Pickett) B.; m. Thomasina Ciofalo, Aug. 22, 1970. MusB, Manhattan Sch. Music, 1949, MusM, 1953; EdD, Fairleigh Dickinson U., 1984. Tchr. music Atlantic City Bd. Edn., 1968-92; researcher acoustics of band instruments. With USAAF, 1942-46. Mem. over 20 profl. assns.

BURNS, JAMES WILLIAM, business executive; b. Winnipeg, Man., Can., Dec. 27, 1929; s. Charles William and Helen Gladys (Mackay) B.; m. Barbara Mary Copeland ; children: James F.C., Martha J., Alan W. B in Commerce, U. Man., 1951; MBA, Harvard U., 1953, LLD (hon.), 1988. With Great-West Life Assurance Co., 1953—, dir., 1970, pres., CEO, 1971-79; pres. Power Corp. Can., 1979-86, dep. chmn., 1986; chmn., CEO Power Fin. Corp., 1986-90; chmn. bd. dirs. Gt. West Life Assurance Co., Gt. West Lifeco, Inc., London Life Ins. Co., London Ins. Group, Inc.; bd. dirs. Power Corp. Can., Power Fin. Corp., IBM Can. Ltd., Investors Group, Inc. Hon. chmn. Man. Mus. Man and Nature; past chmn. Conf. Bd. Can.; mem. Gov.'s Coun., Shaw Festival. Decorated Officer of the Order of Can.; Hon. col. Queen's Own Cameron Highlanders of Can. Mem. St. Charles Country Club, Man. Club, Toronto Club, Mount-Royal Club, The Landings Club. Office: Power Corp Can, 751 Victoria Sq, Montreal, PQ Canada H2Y 2J3

BURNS, JOAN SIMPSON, writer, editor; b. Boulder, Colo., 1927; d. George Gaylord Simpson and Anne Roe (stepmother); m. Alfred Lee Meyers, 1952 (div.); m. James MacGregor Burns, 1969 (div. 1989); children by previous marriage: Trienah Meyers, Peter Alexander Meyers. BA, U. Mich., 1950. Editor CBS/Columbia Records, Harcourt Brace, N.Y.C., 1960s; mng. editor Reader's Subscription Book Club, N.Y.C., 1961-63. Author: The Awkward Embrace, 1975; (with George Whitaker) Dinosaur Hunt, 1965; editor, memoirist: The Dechronization of Sam Magruder, 1996; editor: John F. Kennedy as We Remember Him, 1965 (Grammy award 1966). Mng. dir. Highgate Art Trust, Williamstown, Mass., 1980s; mem. Bd. Selectmen, Williamstown, 1997—, Zoning Bd. Appeals, Williamstown, 1995-97. Mem. Authors Guild. Home and Office: 600 Bee Hill Rd Williamstown MA 01267-2714

BURNS, JOHN F., reporter; b. 1944. Fgn. corr., New Delhi bur. chief N.Y. Times, 1975—, spl. corr. Islamic affairs, 1999—; bur. chief N.Y. Times, Johannesburg, Moscow, Peking, Toronto, Sarajevo, New Delhi. Recipient Pulitzer Prize for internat. reporting, 1993, 97, George Polk award for Fgn. Corr., 1979, 97. Office: NY Times 229 W 43rd St New York NY 10036-3959

BURNS, JOHN FRANCIS, state official, educator; b. Joliet, Ill., Sept. 13, 1945; s. Francis J. and Agnes A. (Vidmar) B.; m. Melinda A. Peak, 1995; 1 child, Alyssa Marie. BA in History, Lewis Coll., 1967; MA in History, Wash. State U., 1972; cert., Western Wash. U., 1977, Acad. Cert. Archivists, 1989. Instr. Skagit Valley Coll., Mt. Vernon, Wash., 1972-75; Pace prof. Chapman Coll., Orange, Calif., 1975-76; instr. Western Wash. U., Bellingham, 1976; project adminstr. Wash. State Records Bd., Olympia, 1977-81; chief of archives State of Calif., Sacramento, 1981-95; dir. Calif. State Archives and Golden State Mus., 1995-97; history and social sci. cons. Calif. Dept. Edn., 1997—; cons. and lectr. in field; adj. prof. history Calif. State U., Sacramento, 1987—. Author: Approaching the Millenium: Prospects and Perils in California's Archival Future, 1992; editor: Historical Records of Washington State, 3 vols., 1980-81, Guide to the Los Angeles Police Department Records of the Robert F. Kennedy Assassination Investigation, 1993, Social Studies Review, 1999, History of Sacramento, 1999; co-editor Washington State Guide to Governor's Papers, 1977; contbr. articles to profl. jours. Sec. Calif. Heritage Preservation Commn., Sacramento, 1981-97; coord. Calif. Hist. Records Adv. Bd., Sacramento, 1981-97; chmn. Nat. Steering Com. of State Records Coord., Sacramento, 1983-85; mem. Calif. Hist. State Capitol Commn., Sacramento, 1984-97, exec. dir. Calif. State Archives Found., 1987-97; commr. Sacramento Comm. History and Sci., 1993-99. Lt. USN, 1967-70, Vietnam. Recipient Calif. State Govt. Mgmt. award, 1986, 89, Calif. Mil. History Medal award, 1997; grantee Nat. Hist. Publ. and Records Commn., Washington, 1977-86, U.S. Dept. Edn., 1998—. Mem. Nat. Assn. Govt. Archives and Records Adminstrs. (v.p. 1986-88, bd. dirs. 1983-85, pres. 1988-90), Soc. Am. Archivists (chmn. com. goals and priorities 1987-90), Calif. Com. for Promotion of History (award of merit 1989, steering com. 1984-87), Spindex Users Network (chmn. 1979-81), Orgn. Am. Historians, Soc. Calif. Archivists (cert. recognition 1989), Calif. Coun. for the Social Studies (dept. rep. 1998—), Nat. Coun. for the Social Studies, Am. Assn. for State and Local History (host com. chair 1998), Nat. Coun. for History Edn. Office: Calif Dept Edn Stds and Assessment 721 Capitol Mall Fl 6 Sacramento CA 95814-4702

BURNS, JOHN JOSEPH, pharmacology educator; b. Flushing, N.Y., Oct. 8, 1920; s. Thomas F. and Katherine (Kane) B. BS, Queens Coll., 1942; MA, Columbia U., 1948, PhD, 1950. With lab. chem. pharmacology Nat. Heart Inst., 1950-60, dep. chief lab., 1957-60; head sec. clin. pharmacology, also adj. asst. prof. biochemistry NYU research service Goldwater Meml. Hosp., Welfare Island, N.Y., 1950-57; dir. research pharmacodynamics div. Wellcome Research Labs., Burroughs Wellcome & Co. (U.S.A.) Inc., Tuckahoe, N.Y., 1960-66; v.p. for research Hoffmann-LaRoche Inc., Nutley, N.J., 1967-84; vis. prof. pharmacology Albert Einstein Coll. Medicine, 1966-68, Cornell U. Med. Coll., 1996—; adj. prof. Cornell U. Med. Coll., 1969-84, Rockefeller U., 1984-94; adj. mem. Roche Inst. Molecular Biology, 1984-96; cons. pharmacology and toxicology programs NIH; chmn. com. problems drug safety Drug Rsch. Bd., 1965-72. Author articles metabolism drugs, vitamins and carbohydrates. Served with AUS, 1944-46. Fellow Am. Inst. Chemists; mem. Inst. Medicine, Nat. Acad. Scis., N.Y. Acad. Scis. (v.p. 1964-65), Am. Soc. Pharmacology and Exptl. Therapeutics (pres. 1972-73), Am. Soc. Biol. Chemists, Am. Inst. Nutrition, Am. Coll. Neuropsychopharmacology, Internat. Union Pharmacology (pres. 1975-78). Home: 331 Lansdowne Westport CT 06880-5651

BURNS, JOHN JOSEPH, JR., financial and insurance holding company executive; b. Cambridge, Mass., June 27, 1931; s. John Joseph and Alice (Blake) B.; m. Barbara Ann Miller, Oct. 18, 1958; children: John J. III, Christine, Gregory, Timothy, Jennifer. BS in Fin., Boston Coll., 1953; MBA, Harvard U., 1955. Asso. buying dept. and arbitrage dept. Goldman Sachs & Co., N.Y.C., 1957-63; assoc. N.Y. Securities, N.Y.C., 1963-67, gen. ptnr., 1968; v.p. fin., dir. Alleghany Corp., N.Y.C., 1968-77, pres., dir., 1977—, mem. exec. com., 1977—, CEO, 1992—; bd. dirs. Chgo. Title Corp., World Minerals Inc., Underwriters Reins Co., Woodland Hills, Calif., Burlington No. Santa Fe. Corp., Dallas. With USN, 1955-57. Mem. Links Club. Roman Catholic. Office: Alleghany Corp 375 Park Ave Ste 3201 New York NY 10152-3297

BURNS, JOHN MITCHELL, academic administrator. BS in Edn. and Chemistry, N.Mex. State U., 1963, MS in Biology and Microbiology, 1966; PhD in Zoology and Endocrinology, Ind. U., 1969. Endocrinology rsch. fellow Mayo Med. Sch., Rochester, Minn., 1976-77; chmn. dept. biol. scis. Tex. Tech U., Lubbock, 1987-95, vice provost acad. affairs, 1995-97, interim provost, 1996-97, provost, 1997—; spkr. in field. Contbr. articles to profl. jours. Recipient Disting. Tchg. award Amoco, 1977, Outstanding Tchg. and Svc. award Arts and Scis. Coun., 1980, Omicron Delta Kappa, 1991, Outstanding Tchg. award Jr. Panhellenic Assn., 1975, Mortar Bd., 1981, Pres.' Excellence in Tchg. award, 1986; named Outstanding Centennial Alumnus Coll. Arts and Scis. N.Mex. State U., 1988. Fellow Endocrine Soc. Address: Box 42019 Lubbock TX 79409-4349

BURNS, JOSEPH ARTHUR, planetary science educator; b. N.Y.C., Mar. 22, 1941; s. John Driscoll and Genevieve Mary (McCarthy) B.; m. Judith Ann Klein, July 1, 1967; children: Patrick M., Caitlin M. BS, Webb Inst., Glen Cove, N.Y., 1962; PhD, Cornell U., 1966. Asst. prof. Cornell U., Ithaca, N.Y., 1966-67, 68-74, assoc. prof., 1974-81, prof., 1981-94; Irving Porter Church prof. engring., prof. astronomy, 1994—; chmn. theoretical and applied mechs. Cornell U., Ithaca, N.Y., 1987-93; NRC rsch. assoc. NASA Goddard Space Ctr., Greenbelt, Md., 1967-68; NAS exch. fellow Inst. Geophysics, Moscow, 1973; sr. scientist NASA Ames Rsch. Ctr., Mountain View, Calif., 1975-76, 82-83; astronome titulaire Observatoire de Paris, France, 1979, 84; vis. prof. astronomy U. Calif., Berkeley, 1982-83; vis. prof. planetary sci. U. Ariz., Tucson, 1989-90; mem. space and earth scis. adv. com. NASA, 1983-87, solar sys. exploration com., 1988-92, NAS space studies bd., 1989-95, chair NAS com. planet exploration, 1992-95. Author 160 rsch. articles, 1966—; editor: Planetary Satellites, 1977, Satellites, 1986; editor Icarus-Internat. Jour. of Solar Sys. Studies, 1979-97. Recipient various rsch. awards and grants NSF, 1976-86, 97, NASA, 1976—, N.Y. Coun. Arts, 1972, NASA Sci. Achievement awards, 1997, 98. Fellow AAAS (councilor, astronomy), Am. Geophys. Union; mem. Internat. Acad. Astronautics, Russian Acad. Sci., Am. Astron. Soc. (chmn. planetary scis. 1983-84, vice chmn. com. on dynamical astronomy 1999—, Masursky Prize 1994), Internat. Astron. Union (mem. solar sys. com. 1986-89, v.p. solar system 1996—). Office: Cornell U Kimball Hall Dept Astronomy Ithaca NY 14853

BURNS, JULIAN H(ALL), JR., military officer; b. Camden, S.C., Dec. 6, 1947; s. Julian Hall and Helen Northrop (Wall) B.; m. Ruth Ann Schumacher, May 17, 1978; children: Joan, Julia, Jacqueline. BS, U.S. Mil. Acad., 1970; MS, U. So. Calif., L.A., 1976; postgrad., Army War Coll., 1989. Commd. 2d lt. U.S. Army, 1970, advanced through grades to lt. col., 1985; co. comdr. Armor Ctr., Ft. Knox, Ky., 1974-76, 1st Inf. Div. U.S. Army, Ft. Riley, Kans., 1976-78; ops. officer 8th Inf. Div. U.S. Army, Fed. Republic of Germany, 1978-81; staff officer Army Staff, Pentagon, Washington, 1981-83; spl. asst. to chmn. Joint Chiefs Staff, Washington, 1983-86; tank bn. comdr. 8th Inf. Div. U.S. Army, Fed. Republic of Germany, 1986-88; dir. Ops. Group Nat. Tng. Ctr., Ft. Irwin, Calif., 1989—. Contbr. articles to mil. jours. Bd. dirs. Boy Scouts Am., Bad Hersfeld, Fed. Republic Germany, 1971-74; sponsor Cub Scouts Am., Baumholder, Fed. Republic Germany, 1986-88. Decorated Legion of Merit. Mem. Assn. U.S. Army, Soc. of Cin., Armor, 1st Inf. and 8th Inf. assn., U.S. Mil. Acad. Alumni Assn. Episcopalian. Avocations: racquet sports, fishing, hunting, skiing, military history. Office: Ops Group Nat Tng Ctr Fort Irwin CA 92310

BURNS, KENNETH JONES, JR., lawyer, consultant; b. Cleve., Oct. 3, 1926; s. Kenneth Jones and Isabel (Nanson) B.; m. Edith Louise Mitten, June 23, 1949; children: Deborah, Kenneth Jones III, Sarah, Elizabeth, Nancy, Andrew. B.S., Northwestern U., 1948, J.D., 1951. Bar: Ill. 1951, Ohio 1972. Asso. Jenner & Block, Chgo., 1951-60; partner Jenner & Block, 1961-72; sr. v.p., gen. counsel, sec. Anchor Hocking Corp., Lancaster, Ohio, 1972-79; v.p., gen. counsel, sec. IMCERA Group, Inc. (formerly Internat. Minerals & Chem. Corp.), Northbrook, Ill., 1979-93; exec. legal cons. Mallinckrodt Group Inc. (formerly IMCERA Group, Inc.), Northbrook, 1993-98; legal counsel Chgo. Jr. Assn. Commerce and Industry, 1955-58; lectr. Northwestern U. Sch. Law, 1955. Pres. Wilmette Civic Improvement Assn., 1958-62; v.p., dir. Citizens of Greater Chgo., 1961-64; bd. dirs. Am. Bar Endowment, 1975-90, v.p., 1981-83, pres., 1983-85. With USNR, 1945-46, 51-52. Recipient Key award Chgo. Jr. Assn. Commerce, 1956. Fellow Am. Bar Found. (dir. 1983-85, 90—, treas. 1993-96, v.p. 1996-98, pres. 1998—); mem. ABA (chmn. jr. bar conf. 1961-62, ho. of dels. 1962-64, 71—, asst. sec. 1967-71, sec., gov. 1971-75), Ill. Bar Assn., Chgo. Bar Assn. (bd. mgrs. 1961-63), Am. Bar Retirement Assn. (bd. dirs. 1982-86), Assn. Gen. Counsel, Am. Law Inst., Ill. Bar Found., Chgo. Barrister Inn (pres. 1966-67), Legal Club Chgo. (exec. com. 1981-82), Law Club Chgo., Order of Coif, Sigma Chi, Phi Delta Phi. Club: Skokie (Ill.) Country. Home and Office: 15 Warrington Dr Lake Bluff IL 60044-1322

BURNS, KENNETH LAUREN, filmmaker, historian; b. Bklyn., July 29, 1953; s. Robert Kyle and Lyla Smith (Tupper) B.; children: Sarah, Lilly. BA, Hampshire Coll., 1975; LHD (hon.), Bowdoin Coll., 1991; LittD (hon.), Amherst Coll., 1991; LHD (hon.), U. N.H.; DFA, Franklin Pierce Coll.; LittD (hon.), Notre Dame Coll., Manchester, N.H.; HHD (hon.), Coll. of St. Joseph, Rutland, Vt.; LHD (hon.), Springfield Coll. Ill., Pace U.; PhD (hon.), CUNY. Pres., owner Florentine Films, Walpole, N.H., 1975—. films include Brooklyn Bridge, 1981 Christopher award 1963, Erik Barnouw prize Hist. Films), The Shakers: Hands to Work, Hearts to God, 1984 (CINE Golden Eagle award 1984), Huey Long, 1985 (Silver Baton award Dupont-Columbia Journalism 1988), The Statue of Liberty, 1985 (Christopher award 1987, CINE Golden Eagle award, Acad. award nomination 1986), Thomas Hart Benton, 1988 (CINE Golden Eagle award 1988, Golden Apple award Nat. Ednl. Film Festival 1989), The Congress, 1988 (CINE Golden Eagle award 11989, Red Ribbon Am. Film Festival 1989), The Civil War, 1990 (Emmy award for outstanding information series 1991, for outstanding individual achievement, writing 1991, CINE Gold Eagle award, Lincoln prize Gettysburg Coll. 1991, Dartmouth Film award 1990, Bell I. Wiley award Civil War Round Table, N.Y., 1991, D.W. Griffiths award, Christopher award, Peabody award 1990, Gabriel award 1991, People's Choice award 1991, Humanitas award 1991, Charles Frankel prize NEH 1991, Grammy award (2) 1992, numerous others), Radio Pioneers, Baseball (Outstanding Informational Series Emmy award), The West, 1996 (Erik Barnouw prize 1997), Thomas Jefferson, 1997, Lewis and Clark: The Journey of the Corps of Discovery, 1997, Frank Lloyd Wright, 1998; author: (with others Centennial, 1986, (with Amy Stechler Burns) The Shakers: Hands to Work, Hearts to God, 1987, (with Geoffrey Ward and Ric Burns) The Civil War: An Illustrated History, 1990, Empire of the Air, 1992: retrospectives Smithsonian Instn., 1991, WAalker Arts Ctr., Mpls., 1991, Pub. Broadcasting Svc., 1991-92. Trustee Hampshire Coll., Amherst, Mass., 1992—, N.H. Humanities Coun.; bd. dirs. MacDowell Colony, Peterborough, N.H. Mem. Acad. Motion Picture, Arts and Scis., Soc. Am. Historians, N.H. Humanities Coun. (trustee), Mass. Hist. Soc. (corr.). Home and Office: Maple Grove Rd Walpole NH 03608

BURNS, KITTY, playwright; b. Chgo., Feb. 1, 1951; d. Joseph Lewis and Evelyn Marian (Smith) B. CNA, Bay City Coll., San Francisco, 1971. Adminstrv. asst. Syntex, Palo Alto, Calif., 1984-94. Author: (plays) Terminal Terror, 1991 (Silver award San Mateo Playwriting Contest 1991), Psycho Night at the Paradise Lounge, 1994, If God Wanted Us to Fly He Would Have Given Us Wings!, 1996. Treas. Hillbarn Theatre, Foster City, 1986, social chmn., 1987-89, 96-98, bd. dirs. Mem. Dramatists Guild. Democrat. Avocations: writing children's books, poetry, short stories, acting, horseback riding.

BURNS, KRISTI J., school counselor; b. Webb City, Mo., May 16, 1955; d. James Fletcher and Joanne (Cole) Evered; m. Richard Francis Burns, Nov. 19, 1988 (div. Mar. 1992). BS, North Tex. State U., Denton, 1976, MEd, 1981; MEd, U North Tex., Denton, 1999. Cert. tchr., counselor, Tex. Social studies tchr., chmn. dept. Plano (Tex.) Ind. Sch. Dist., 1978-88, acad. specialist, 1988-98, acad. counselor, 1998—. Vol. Plano Police Dept.-Christmas Cops, 1995-97. Mem. Delta Kappa Gamma (pres. Mu Beta chpt. 1996-98, scholarship 1996, 97), Phi Delta Kappa. Republican. Methodist. Avocations: hiking, snowskiing, fishing, singing, listening to jazz. Home: 2809 Lemmontree Ln Plano TX 75074-4863 Office: Spl Programs Ctr 2221 Legacy Dr Plano TX 75023-2156

BURNS, LESLIE KAYE, documentary video producer and director; b. Columbus, Miss., Sept. 21, 1953; d. Fayette Charles Jr. and Mary Theo (Wright) B. BFA in Printmaking/Advt. Art cum laude, Miss. U. for Women, 1975; MFA in Photography/Printmaking, U. Ala., 1978. Multi-image prodr., photographer Pitluk Group Advt. Agy., San Antonio, 1981-87; dir. media prodn. Inst. Texan Cultures U. Tex., San Antonio, 1987—. Producer, dir., writer/co-writer numerous documentaries and ednl. videos including From the Ground Up: Theirs to Tell, Ours to Share, 1989, Panna Maria; The Heart of Polish Texans, 1990 (San Antonio Conservation Soc. citation), Circle of Life: The Alabama-Coushattas, 1991 (San Antonio Conservation Assn. citation, 41st Ann. Columbus Internat. Film and Video Festival honoree), Tex. Folklife Festival 1991-95 :30 Pub. Svc. Announcement (1st Pl. Internat. Festivals Assn. Media Competition 1991, Mktg. award Tex. Festivals Assn. 1991, 92), Train Your Brain: A Science, Engineering, and Mathematics Video, 1991, "I Remember...": The Impact of World War II on Children in Texas, 1991, The Day of the Dead, 1991 (San Antonio Conservation Soc. citation 1992, 41st Ann. Columbus Internat. Film and Video Festival honoree, Am. Assn. Mus. Muse award 3rd place cultural studies divsn. 1993), Big City Trail: The Urban Indians of Texas, 1992 (42d Annual Columbus Internat. Film and Video Festival honoree), Texas Children's Festival Promotional Video, 1992, People of the Sun: The Tiguas of Ysleta, 1992 (Soc. Visual Anthropology Film and Video Festival honoree 1993, 42d Annual Columbus Internat. Film and Video Festival honoree), Tejanos: Quiénes somos?, 1993, Noki Pematedieni (To Have a New Life), 1993, Scientists Are Everywhere!, 1994, Tex. Folklife Festival Promotional Video, 1995, Tex. Folklife Festival 1995 Pub. Svc. Announcement (1st place Pinnacle award Internat. Festivals and Events Assn. 1995), Workin' From Can't to Can't: African-American Cowboys in Texas, 1995 (Am. Assn. Mus. Muse award 2d place cultural studies divsn. 1996, Women in Comms., Inc. San Antonio profl. chpt. award of excellence TV documentary program, 1996, 44th Ann. Columbus Internat. Film and Video Festival Bronze plaque), American Indians in Texas Today, an Interactive Multimedia Exhibit, 1996 (Multimedia Prodr. mag. Top 100 of 1996), Tex. Folklife Festival 1996 pub. svc. announcement (Silver Pinnacle award Best T.V. Pub. Svc. Announcment Internat. Festivals and Events Assn., 1996), 1997 pub. svc. announcement (Silver Spur/Best of Tex. award Tex. Pub. Rels. Assn. 1998). Recipient mktg. award Tex. Festivals and Events Assn., 1997, Silver Spur-Best of Tex. award Tex. Pub. Rels. Assn., 1998. Mem. Am. Assn. Museums. Avocation: collecting Mexican folk art. Office: U Tex Inst Texan Cultures 801 S Bowie St San Antonio TX 78205-3209

BURNS, M. ANTHONY, transportation services company executive; b. Las Vegas, Nev., Nov. 1, 1942; s. Mitchel and Zella (Pulsipher) B.; m. Joyce Jordan, Nov. 14, 1962; children: Jill, Mitchel, Shauna. BS in Bus. Mgmt, Brigham Young U., 1964; MBA in Fin., U. Calif., Berkeley, 1965; hon. doctorate, Fla. Internat. U., 1989. With Mobil Oil Corp., N.Y.C., 1965-74, controller, 1970-72, cost-of-living coordinator, 1973, fin. analysis mgr., 1973-74; with Ryder System, Inc., Miami, Fla., 1974—, exec. v.p., chief fin. officer, 1978-79, pres., chief ops. officer, 1979-83, pres., chief exec. officer, 1983-85, chmn., pres., chief exec. officer, 1985—, also bd. dirs.; exec. v.p., CFO, pres. Ryder Truck Rental, Inc., 1980-81; bd. dirs. J.C. Penney Co., Inc., Pfizer Inc., The Chase Manhattan Corp., The Chase Manhattan Bank, N.A.; mem. nat. adv. coun. sch. mgmt. Brigham Young U., 1981—. mem. bd. visitors Grad. Sch. Bus. Adminstrn., U. N.C., Chapel Hill, 1988-93; mem. bd. overseers Wharton Sch., 1989-94; assoc. trustee U. Pa., 1989-94; bd. dirs., trustee United Way Dade County, Fla., 1981—, chmn., 1991-93, Dade County campaign, 1988, bd. govs., 1989-92, chmn. S.E. region United Way of Am., 1989-92; trustee Nat. Urban League, 1984-94, chmn., 1987-89, vice chmn., 1989-94, hon. trustee, 1994—. Named Marketer of Yr. Acad. Mktg. Sci., 1983, Americanism award Anti-Defamation League, 1984, Bus. Leader of Yr. The Miami News, 1985, Ricks Coll. Bus. Leader of the Century, 1989, Fin. World CEO of Decade in Transp., Freight & Leasing, 1989, CEO of Yr., 1984, 85, 87, Bus. Leadership Hall of Fame, 1987; recipient Boneh Yisroel award Greater Miami Jewish Fedn., 1989, Silver medallion award Nat. Conf. Christians & Jews, 1988, Community Svc. award Advt. Fedn. Gt. Miami, 1987, Joseph Wharton Bus. Statesman award Wharton Sch. Club, 1987, Jesse Knight Indsl. Citizenship award Brigham Young U., 1988, Robert W. Laidlaw Humanitarian award Epilepsy Found. South Fla., 1989, Good Scout award Boy Scouts Am., 1990., Sand in my Shoes award Greater Miami C. of C., 1991, Equal Opportunity award Nat. Urban League, 1992, Humanitarian of Yr. award ARC, 1993. Mem. Bus. Coun., Bus. Roundtable (policy com.), Bus.-Higher Edn. Forum. Office: Ryder System Inc 3600 NW 82nd Ave Miami FL 33166-6623*

BURNS, MARIE T., retired secondary education educator; b. Nashua, N.H.; d. Charles Henry and Eleanor Agnes (Martin) O'Neil; m. Thomas M. Burns; children: Ann Burns Pelletier, Mary Burns Powlowsky, Catherine Burns Patten. BA, Regis Coll.; postgrad., Rivier Coll. Cert. tchr., N.H. Tchr. English Pelham (N.H.) Sch. Dept., City of Nashua. Former trustee, chmn. of house com., sec. bd. dirs. Mary A. Sweeney Home; judge, participant River Coll. Literacy Festival. Mem. Nashua Tchrs. Union (mem. secondary grouping practices com. Nashua Sch. Dist.), N.H. Ret. Tchrs., Nashua Ret. Tchrs.

BURNS, MARSHALL SHELBY, retired judge, lawyer, arbitrator; b. Cleve., Jan. 29, 1931; s. Marshall Shelby and Fairybelle (Moses) B.; m. Blanche Marie Coleman, Jan. 28, 1953; children: William M., Brian M. AA, Flint (Mich.) Jr. Coll., 1957; BA, U. Mich., Flint, 1972; JD, Thomas M. Cooley Law Sch., 1979; LLM, Wayne State U., 1984; grad., Nat. Jud. Coll., 1985. Bar: Mich. 1980, U.S. Dist. Ct. (ea. and we. dists.) Mich. 1980, U.S. Tax Ct. 1980, U.S. Supreme Ct. 1980. Tax supr. City of Flint, 1965-69; indsl. recreation adminstr. IMA, Flint, 1969-75; dir. personnel and labor relations Flint Gen. Hosp., 1975-76; asst. dir. personnel dept. pub. health State of Mich., Lansing, 1976-78, judge adminstrv. law, 1978-96; gen. counsel Greater Lansing Urban League, 1983—; arbitrator Fed. Mediation and Conciliation Svc., Washington, 1983—, Better Bus. Bur., 1983—, Am. Arbitration Assn., 1983—; faculty advisor Nat. Jud. Coll., 1986. Mem. exec. bd. Tall Pine Counsel Boy Scouts Am., Flint, 1970-75; bd. dirs. Greater Lansing Urban League, 1982-84, Vol. Action Ctr. of Greater Lansing, 1982-84. Served to pvt. 1st class U.S. Army, 1953-55. Mem. NAACP, Am. Arbitration Assn. (arbitrator), Nat. Bar Assn., Indsl. Rels. Rsch. Assn., Rotary (v.p. East Lansing club 1990-91), Masons, Phi Alpha Delta (justice, treas. 1978-80), Alpha Phi Alpha (chpt. pres. 1989). Office: 417 N Pine St Lansing MI 48933-1025

BURNS, MARVIN GERALD, lawyer; b. Los Angeles, July 3, 1930; s. Milton and Belle (Cytron) B.; m. Barbara Irene Fisher, Aug. 23, 1953; children: Scott Douglas, Jody Lynn, Bradley Frederick. BA, U. Ariz., 1951; JD, Harvard U., 1954. Bar: Calif. 1955. Bd. dirs. Inner City Arts for Inner City Children. With AUS, 1955-56. Clubs: Beverly Hills Tennis, Sycamore Park Tennis. Home: 10350 Wilshire Blvd Ph 4 Los Angeles CA 90024-4734 Office: 4th Fl 10390 Santa Monica Blvd Los Angeles CA 90025-5058 *I believe that hard work in its time and place, play in its time and place, love, understanding and practice of the golden rule at all times, in all places, a firm belief in truth and honesty and that there is no better land, no better system, no better life than our imperfect, necessary to improve, America, leads to personal fulfillment and a better life for all.*

BURNS, MARYANN MARGARET, elementary education educator; b. Portland, Maine, Mar. 4, 1944; d. William and Emma (Greco) B. Finishing sch. grad., Chandler Sch. for Women, Boston, 1963; BS in Edn. and English summa cum laude, U. Maine, 1974. Cert. elem. tchr., Maine. Pvt. sec. IBM, L.A., 1968-70; learning lab. tchr. Sch. Adminstrv. Dist. # 6, Bar Mills, Maine, 1974—, Frank Jewett Sch., W. Buxton, Maine. Mem. NEA, Maine Tchrs. Assn., U. Maine Alumni Assn., Polit. Action Com. Democrat. Roman Catholic. Home: 17 Wild Rose Ave S Portland ME 04106-6619 Office: Sch Adminstrv Dist 6 PO Box 38 Bar Mills ME 04004-0038

BURNS, MICHAEL JOSEPH, operations and sales-marketing executive; b. Passaic, N.J., Feb. 18, 1943; s. Michael Joseph and Ellen Kathryn (Warman) B.; m. Emma Anne, Dec. 19, 1964; children: Michael, Jeffrey, Tricia, Stephen. B.A. in English, William Paterson Coll., Wayne, N.J., 1964; J.D., Seton Hall U., Newark, 1975. Bar: N.J. 1975. Purchasing analyst Am. Brands Co., 1972-75; div. purchasing mgr. Dutch Boy Paints, NL Industries, 1975-76; v.p. purchasing Dutch Boy, Inc., 1977-78; pres., gen. mgr. Dutch Boy, Inc. (Dutch Boy coatings div.), 1978-80; pres., CEO Kroehler Mfg. Co., Naperville, Ill., 1980-88; pres., COO Rymer Co., Rolling Meadows, Ill., 1983-88; pres. Emerald Group, Lake Forest, Ill., 1989-90; pres., CEO Designer Foods, Inc., Wilmington, Del., 1990-91; chmn., pres., CEO SeaWatch Internat., Ltd., Easton, Md., 1991-99; pres., CEO Pioneer Human Svcs., Seattle, 1999—. Served to capt. USMCR, 1964-67, Vietnam. N.J. State scholar; recipient Disting. Alumni award Wm. Paterson Coll. Mem. ABA, Am. Arbitration Assn. Presbyterian. Office: 8978 Glebe Park Dr Easton MD 21601-7004

BURNS, NED HAMILTON, civil engineering educator; b. Magnolia, Ark., Nov. 25, 1932; s. Andrew Louis and Ila Mae (Martin) B.; m. Martha Ann Fontaine, June 11, 1955; children: Kathryn Jane, Stephanie Ann, Michael Everett. B.S., U. Tex., 1954, M.S., 1958; Ph.D., U. Ill., 1962. Registered profl. engr., Tex. Instr. U. Tex., Austin, 1957-59, asst. prof., 1962-65, assoc. prof., 1965-70, prof. civil engring., 1970-83, Zarrow Centennial prof. engring., 1983—; assoc. dean engring. for acad. affairs, 1989-93, dir. Ferguson Structural Engring. Lab., 1994-97; research asst. U. Ill., Urbana, 1959-62. Author: (with T. Y. Lin) Design of Prestressed Concrete Structures, 1981 (McGraw Hill Book of Month 1982), S.I. Version—Design of Prestressed Concrete Structures, 1982; contbr. tech. papers, reports on structural engring. to profl. publs. Served with U.S. Army, 1955-57. Recipient Gen. Dynamics Tchg. award U. Tex. Coll. Engring., 1965, AMOCO Tchg. award, 1983, Kartin P. Korn award for Outstanding Jour. paper, 1993, Blunk Meml. Professorship tchg. award U. Tex., 1996-97. Fellow Prestressed Concrete Inst. (com. mem. 1968—, Martin Korn award for best paper in PCI Jour. 193),; mem. NSPE (chpt. pres. 1970), ASCE (com. chmn. 1975—, T. Y. Lin award 1994), Am. Concrete Inst. (bd. dirs. 1983—, Joe Kelley award for contbns. to engring. edn. 1990), Post-Tensioning Inst. (bd. dirs. 1975), Tex. Soc. Profl. Engring. (Young Engr. of Yr. award 1970, Travis chpt. Engr. of Yr. award 1987). Democrat. Baptist. Home: 3917 Rockledge Dr Austin TX 78731-2921 Office: U Tex Dept Civil Engring Austin TX 78712

BURNS, PAT, professional hockey coach; b. Montreal, Que., Can., Apr. 4, 1952. Coach Les Olympiques de Hull, Montreal, 1983-87; head coach affiliate club Montreal Canadiens, Sherbrooke, Que., Can., 1987-88; head coach Montreal Canadiens, Que., Can., 1988-92, Toronto Maple Leafs, 1992-97, Boston Bruins, 1997—; asst. coach Can. Jr. Team, 1986. Named Coach of Yr. NHL's Broadcasters Assn., 1989, Sporting News, 1989 Hockey News, 1989. Office: Boston Bruins One FleetCenter, Ste 250 Boston MA 02114-1303*

BURNS, PAT ACKERMAN GONIA, information systems specialist, software engineer; b. Birmingham, Ala., July 16, 1938; d. Richard Lee and Hattie Eugenia (Bragg) Ackerman; m. Robert Edward Gonia, June 4, 1957 (div. Jan. 1973); children: Deborah Hayes, Junita Grantham, Ronald Gonia; m. James Clayton Burns, June 23, 1984 (dec. Dec. 1989). BS in Math., U. Ala., 1970, postgrad., 1971-77. Cert. secondary tchr., Ala. Missionary United Meth. Bd. of Missions, Sumatra, Indonesia, 1961-64; homebound tchr. Huntsville (Ala.) City Schs., 1970-75; mem. tech. staff Gen. Rsch. Corp., Huntsville, 1975-79; rsch. scientist Nichols Rsch. Corp., Huntsville, 1979-84, mgr. personnel div., 1984-87, mgmt. info. systems dept. head, 1987-90, dir. info. systems div., 1990-95; program mgr. MIS and tech. MIS U.S. Army Space and Strategic Defense Systems, 1990-93; dir. info. sys. Trinity United Meth. Ch., Huntsville, 1996-98; exec. dir. Trinity Personal Growth Ctr., Huntsville, 1999—; mem. adv. com. Drake Tech. Sch., Huntsville, 1988-94; program mgr. USASDC MIS//TMIS, 1990-94. Mem. PTA, Huntsville, 1994, Ch. Women United, Huntsville, Cmty. Chorus, Huntsville. Mem. IEEE, NAFE, Data Processing Mgmt. Assn., Assn. Pers. Adminstrs., Am. Computer Soc., Huntsville C. of C. (spkr. 1986-95). Democrat. Methodist. Avocations: travel, music, old movies. Office: Trinity United Meth Ch 607 Airport Rd Huntsville AL 35802

BURNS, PATRICK OWEN, venture capital company executive; b. Yonkers, N.Y., Aug. 6, 1937; s. Edward Dermott and Anne L. (Gallagher) B.; AB (Class of '26 fellow), Dartmouth Coll., 1959; LLB cum laude, Harvard U., 1962; m. Barbara Hope Van Riper, Nov. 4, 1967; children: Patrick Owen, Elizabeth Willett. Bar: N.Y. 1964, U.S. Dist. Ct. (so. dist.) N.Y. 1965; legal advisor Dept. Coops., Lesotho, 1962-63; assoc. Milbank, Tweed, Hadley & McCloy, N.Y.C., 1963-69; nat. dep. dir. Interracial Coun. for Bus. Opportunity, N.Y.C., 1969-75, acting nat. exec. dir., 1972-74; exec. v.p. Minority Equity Capital Co., Inc., N.Y.C., 1971-78, dir., 1974-85, pres., 1978-85; ptnr. Consumer Venture Group, 1985; v.p. R&D Funding Corp., 1986-97, bd. dirs., 1989-92; v.p., 1st v.p., sr. v.p. Prudential Securities, 1986-1997; sr. advisor Early Stage Enterprises, 1997—; bd. dirs. Symbiotics Corp., Euclid Sys. Corp., Bearsden Bio, Inc.; Progen Industries, Ltd; cons. Warren Commn., 1964; mem. exec. com. SEC Govt.-Bus. Forum on Small Bus. Capital Formation, 1983-85, chmn. Task Force State Capital Formation, 1984. Bd. dirs. Cobble Hill Nursing Home, 1976—; regent L.I. Coll. Hosp., 1976—, vice chmn. bd., 1981-97; dir. Resources for Children with Spl. Needs, Inc., 1990—, pres., 1994—; trustee New Cmty. Found., 1998—; dir. Nat. Ctr. Social Entrepreneurs, 1985—; candidate for N.Y.C. City Coun., 1969. Mem. Am. Assn. Minority Enterprise Small Bus. Investment Cos. (dir. 1979-85, chmn. bd. 1983-85), Coun. Fgn. Rels., N.Y. Venture Capital Forum, Nat. Assn. Small Bus. Investment Cos. (gov. 1983-85). Democrat. Contbr. articles to profl. publs. Home: 22 Sidney Pl Brooklyn NY 11201-4607 Office: 995 Route 518 Skillman NJ 08558

BURNS, PAUL YODER, forester, educator; b. Tulsa, Okla., July 4, 1920; s. Paul Patchin and Mary Emily (Knowles) B.; m. Kathleen Iola Chase, Dec. 4, 1942; children: Virginia B. Belland, Margaret B. Feierabend, Nancy B. McNeill. BS, U. Tulsa, 1941; M in Forestry, Yale U., 1946, PhD, 1949. Asst., assoc. prof. U. Mo., Columbia, 1948-55; prof. forestry La. State U., Baton Rouge, 1955-86, prof. emeritus of forestry, 1986-96; dir. sch. forestry La. State U., Baton Rouge, 1955-76; commr. La. Forestry Commn., Baton Rouge, 1955-76. Editor: Forest Management in Plan & Practice, 1956, Southern Forest Soils, 1959; co-editor: Southern Forestry in Practice, 1977, Christmas Tree Production & Marketing, 1983. Pres. bd. dirs. La. State U. YMCA-YWCA, Baton Rouge, 1957-59; mem. La. Conf. Ch. Bd., Baton Rouge, 1967-73; pres. La. Coun. Human Rels., Baton Rouge, 1987-89; chair bd. dirs. The FISH Good Samaritans, Baton Rouge, 1996. Recipient Disting. Alumnus award U. Tulsa, 1974, Humanitarian award Baton Rouge Coun. Human Rels., 1984, Peacemaking award, Bienville House Ctr. for Peace, Baton Rouge, 1991, Brotherhood award Baton Rouge chpt. NCCJ, 1995. Fellow Soc. Am. Foresters, La. Soc. Am. Foresters (chmn. 1990, Disting Svc. to Forestry 1989), Phi Kappa Phi, Sigma Xi, Xi Sigma, Pi. Presbyterian. Avocations: tennis, piano. Home: 2137 Cedardale Ave Baton Rouge LA 70808-2810 Office: Sch Forestry Wildlife and Fisheries La State Univ Baton Rouge LA 70803

BURNS, R. NICHOLAS, federal official; b. Buffalo, Jan. 28, 1956. BA in European History summa cum laude, Boston Coll., 1978; MA in Internat. Econs. and Am. Fgn. Policy with distinction, Johns Hopkins Sch. Advanced Internat. Studies, 1980. Intern U.S. Embassy Nouakchott, Mauritania, 1980-81; program officer A.T. Internat., 1981-82; vice counsul and staff asst. to the Amb. in Cairo, Egypt, 1983-85; polit. officer Am. Consulate Gen., Jerusalem, 1985-87; staff officer dept. ops. ctr. and secretariat Dept. of State, 1987-88, spl. asst. to the counselor of the dept. for Soviet and Ea. European Affairs, 1989-90, dir. Soviet affairs, 1990-93, sr. dir. for Russian, Ukraine and Eurasia affairs and spl. asst. to the pres., 1993-95, sr. fgn. svc. officer, nat. security coun. staff at the White House, 1991—. Mem. Phi Beta Kappa. Office: Dept of State 2201 C St NW Washington DC 20520-0001

BURNS, RALPH, conductor, orchestrator. Jazz pianist, orchestrator Woody Herman. Arranger, condr. recordings for Aretha Franklin, Ray Charles, Tony Bennett, Natalie Cole, many others; orchestrator Broadway shows and movies including: Chicago, Sweet Charity, Dancin', Little Me, Pippin, Big Deal, Cabaret (Academy Award), All That Jazz (Academy Award), Lenny, Star 80. Office: American Fedn of Musicians 1501 Broadway New York NY 10036*

BURNS, REBECCA ANN, educator, librarian; b. Waynesboro, Pa., Dec. 28, 1946; d. John Albert and Betty Jane (Mason) Castelluccio; m. Terry Lee Burns, 1966; children: Todd Darin, Derick Jason. BS, Shippensburg U., 1968, postgrad., 1969, 70, 75; postgrad., Pa. State U., 1973-74, 87, 89, U. Wyo., 1989. Cert. elem. tchr., library sci. tchr., Pa. Migrant educator Waynesboro (Pa.) Sch. Dist., 1971-72, elem. tchr., 1968-71, 74-79; elem. tchr. Mifflin County Sch. Dist., Lewistown, Pa., 1972-74; test examiner Office Personnel Mgmt. U.S. Govt., State College, Pa., 1982-83; instr. Adult Basic Edn.- Gen. Edn. Devel. and Career Tng. Mifflin County Job Tng. Partnership Act, Lewistown, 1985-86; libr. State Correctional Inst.-Rockview, Bellefonte, Pa., 1983-85, Midd-West Sch. Dist., Middleburg, Pa., 1986-89; edn. adminstrn. assoc., pupil transp. specialist Pa. Dept. Edn., Harrisburg, 1989-90, edn. adminstrn. specialist, coord. non pub. sch. svcs., 1990-93, basic edn. assoc., youth edn. and employment coord., 1993-97, basic edn. assoc., work-based learning coord., 1997—. Lobbyist for stamp commemorating adult edn.; educator for women's rights, devel. and implementation of regis. apprenticeships for youth in Penn. Mem. Am. Fedn. Tchrs., Am. Assn. Retired People, Pa. Fedn. Tchrs., Apprenticeship Assn., Fedn. of State Cultural and Ednl. Profl., Aux. to Pa. Retired State Police. Roman Catholic. Avocations: reading, collecting antique prints, travel. Home: 4422 Saybrook Ln Harrisburg PA 17110-3477 Office: Pa Dept Edn 333 Market St Fl 5 Harrisburg PA 17101-2215

BURNS, RICHARD DEAN, history educator, publisher, author; b. Des Moines, June 16, 1929; s. Richard B. and Luella (Everling) B.; m. Frances R. Sullivan, Jan. 14, 1950 (dec. July 1993); 1 son, Richard Dean; m. Glenda F. Burns, Sept. 21, 1996; stepchildren: Scott E. Burns, Kent C. Burns, Dana Burns Mayadag. B.S. with honors, U. Ill., 1957, M.A., 1958, Ph.D., 1960. Prof. emeritus Calif. State U., L.A., 1960-92, prof., 1970-92, chmn. dept., 1969-72, 86-92; pubr./pres. Regina Books, 1980—; vis. lectr. L.A. City Coll., Whittier Coll., U. Minn., Mpls., 1964-65, UCLA, U. So. Calif.; program cons., lectr. Western Ctr., NEH, 1973-75. Author: (with W. Fisher) Armament and Disarmament, 1964, (with D. Urquidi) Disarmament in Historical Perspective, 4 vols, 1969, (with E. Bennett) Diplomats in Crisis, 1975; editor:

An Arms Control and Disarmament Bibliography, 1977, Guide to American Foreign Relations Since 1700, 1982, (with M. Leitenberg) The Wars in Vietnam, Cambodia, and Laos, 1945-82, 1984, Harry S. Truman: A Bibliography of His Times and Presidency, 1984, Herbert Hoover: A Bibliography of His Times and Presidency, 1991, Encyclopedia of Arms Control and Disarmament, 3 vols., 1993; bibliographer, series editor: War/Peace Bibliographies, 1973—; pub. Regina Books, 1981—; contbr. articles to profl. jours. Served with USAF, 1947-56. Named Univ. Outstanding Prof., 1978-79; Social Sci. Rsch. Coun. fellow, 1959-60; grantee NEH, 1978-79, U.S. Inst. Peace, 1991-92. Mem. Conf. on Peace Rsch. (nat. coun. 1970-72), Soc. Historians Am. Fgn. Rels. (nat. coun. 1986-89), Phi Kappa Phi, Phi Alpha Theta. Office: Regina Books PO Box 280 Claremont CA 91711-0280

BURNS, RICHARD FRANCIS, mechanical engineer; b. Detroit, May 21, 1931; s. John Adgidius and Mary Teresa (Lockman) B.; m. Mary Kathryn McAlister, May 23, 1959; children: Richard Francis Jr., Christopher Joseph, Moira Elizabeth, Colleen Siobhan. BS, U.S. Naval Acad., 1954; MS in Marine Engring., MIT, 1962. Registered profl. engr., Va. Commd. ens. USN, 1954, advanced through grades to comdr.; ops. officer, navigator USS Shark, Norfolk, Va., 1962-64; submarine repair supt. Norfolk Naval Shipyard, Portsmouth, Va.; project officer Planning, Estimating, Repairs and Alterations to Submarines, Portsmouth, N.H., 1967-69; sr. advisor Joint U.S. Mil. Mission Aid to Turkey, Gö, Turkey, 1970-72; navigation project officer Trident Strategic System project Office, Washington, 1973-76; sr. engr. Vitro Corp., Silver Spring, Md., 1976-88, Scientex Corp., Washington, 1989-90; assoc. editor Sea Tech. Mag., Compass Publs., Arlington, Va., 1990—. Mem. Soc. Naval Arch. and Marine Engrs., Nat. Def. Indsl. Assn., MIT Club Washington, Sigma Xi. Avocations: triathletics, biathletics, skiing.

BURNS, RICHARD GORDON, retired lawyer, writer, consultant; b. Stockton, Calif., May 15, 1925; s. Earl Gordon and Alberta Viola (Whale) B.; m. Eloise Estelle Beil, June 23, 1951 (div. May 25, 1985); children: Kenneth Charles, Donald Gordon. AA, U. Calif., Berkeley, 1948; AB, Stanford U., 1949, JD, 1951. Atty. Clausen & Burns, San Francisco, 1951-61; pvt. practice Corte Madera, Calif., 1961-86; cons. Wyo. Pacific Oil Co., L.A., 1986—; pub. Good Book Pub., Kihei, Hawaii, 1991—. Author (As Dick B.): New Light on Alcoholism: God, Sam Shoemaker and A.A., 1999, The Akron Genesis of Alcoholics Anonymous, 1998, (with Bill Pittman) Courage To Change, 1998, Anne Smith's Journal, 1998, Dr. Bob and His Library, 1998, The Good Book and The Big Book: AA's Roots in the Bible, 1998, The Oxford Group and Alcoholics Anonymous, 1998, That Amazing Grace, 1996, The Books Early AAs Read for Spiritual Growth, 1998, Good Morning! Quiet Time, Morning Watch, Meditation, and Early A.A., 1998; Turning Point: A History of Early A.A.'s Spiritual Roots and Successes, 1997, Hope!: The Story of Geraldine D., 1998, Utilizing A.A.'s Spiritual Roots for Recovery Today, 1999, The Golden Text of A.A., 1999; case editor Stanford Law Rev., 1950. Dir. Almonte Sanitary Bd., Marin County, Calif., 1962-64; v.p./sec. Lions Club, Corte Madera, 1961-64; pres. Almonte Improvement Club, Mill Valley, Calif., 1960, Cmty. Ch., Mill Valley, 1971, C. of C., Corte Madera, 1972, Corte Madera Ctr. Merchant Co., 1975, Redwoods Retirement Ctr., Mill Valley, 1980. Sgt. U.S. Army, 1943-46. Mem. Am. Hist. Assn., Authors Guild, Maui Writers Guild, Christian Assn. for Psychol. Studies, Phi Beta Kappa. Avocations: travel, Bible study, swimming. Office: PO Box 837 Kihei HI 96753-0837

BURNS, RICHARD OWEN, lawyer; b. Bklyn., Nov. 16, 1942; s. James I. and Ida (Shore) B.; m. Lynda Gail Birnbaum, Dec. 24, 1967; children: Marc Adam, Lisa Ann, Susan Danielle. BS, Wilkes Coll., 1964; JD, Bklyn. Law Sch., 1967. Bar: N.Y. 1967, U.S. Dist. Ct. (so. dist.) N.Y. 1969, U.S. Dist. Ct. (ea. dist.) N.Y. 1979. Assoc. Clune & O'Brien, Mineola, N.Y., 1967-73, Clune, Burns, White & Nelson, Harrison, N.Y., 1973-78; ptnr. Schurr & Burns, P.C., Spring Valley, N.Y., 1978-98; pvt. practice, 1998—. Bd. dirs. Rockland County unit Am. Cancer Soc., West Nyack, N.Y., 1979-85, 86-92, pres., 1981-83; bd. dirs. Hudson Valley Health System Agy., Sterling Park, N.Y., 1979, Vets. Meml. Assn., Congers, N.Y., 1980-86; mem. Wilkes U. Coun., Wilkes-Barre, Pa., 1995—. Recipient Reese D. Jones award Wilkes Coll. Jr. C. of C., 1964. Mem. Rockland County Bar Assn., N.Y. State Bar Assn., N.Y. State Trial Lawyers Assn. Democrat. Jewish. Home: 140 Waters Edge Congers NY 10920-2622 Office: 500 Chestnut Ridge Rd Chestnut Ridge NY 10977-5622

BURNS, RICHARD RAMSEY, lawyer; b. Duluth, Minn., May 3, 1946; s. Herbert Morgan and Janet (Strobel) B.; Jennifer, Brian; m. Elizabeth Murphy, June 15, 1984. BA with distinction, U. Mich., 1968, JD magna cum laude, 1971. Bar: Calif. 1972, U.S. Dist. Ct. (no. dist.) Calif. 1972, U.S. Ct. Appeals (9th cir.) 1972, Minn. 1976, U.S. Dist. Ct. Minn. 1976, Wis. 1983, U.S. Tax. Ct. 1983. Assoc. Orrick, Herrington, Rowley & Sutcliffe, San Francisco, 1971-76; ptnr. Hanft, Fride, O'Brien, Harries, Swelbar & Burns P.A., Duluth, 1976—; gen. counsel Evening Telegram Co., Superior, Wis., 1982—, Murphy TV Stas., Madison, Wis., 1982—. Chmn. Duluth-Superior Area Comty. Found., 1988-90; chair United Way of Greater Duluth, Inc., 1998—; bd. dirs. Miller Dwan Found., Duluth Airport Authority. Fellow Am. Coll. Trust and Estate Counsel; mem. Calif. Bar Assn., Wis. Bar Assn., Minn. Bar Assn. (bd. govs., past chmn. probate and trust coun.), 11th Dist. Bar Assn. (past pres., past chmn. ethics com.), Arrowhead Estate Planning Coun. (pres. 1980), Northland Country Club (pres. 1982), Boulders Club, Kitchi Gammi Club, Mpls. Athletic Club. Republican. Avocations: travel, golf, tennis, fishing. Home: 180 Paine Farm Rd Duluth MN 55804-2609 Office: Hanft Fride O'Brien Harries Swelbar & Burns PA 1000 First Bank Pl 130 W Superior St Ste 1000 Duluth MN 55802-2094

BURNS, RICHARD ROBERT, chemicals executive; b. Litchfield, Ill., July 7, 1947; s. Martin E. and Virginia M. (Prange) B.; m. Sandra R. Meadows, Oct. 13, 1973; children: Kevin M., Sean T., Paul A., Lara M. BSChE, U. Tex., 1970. Prodn. engr. Union Carbide Corp., Tex., W.Va, 1970-78; dept. head Union Carbide Corp., Tex., W.Va, Fla., 1978-85; asst. plant mgr. Union Carbide Corp., Tex., W.Va, 1986-97; process cons. Union Carbide Corp., Tex., La., 1997—. Lutheran. Avocations: boy scout activities, golf, family activities. Home: 4502 Masters Dr League City TX 77573-5805

BURNS, ROBERT ARTHUR, lawyer; b. Independence, Iowa, 1944. BS, Iowa State U., 1966; JD, U. Iowa, 1972. Bar: Minn. 1972, Iowa 1972. Ptnr. Dorsey & Whitney L.L.P., Mpls., 1978—. Office: Dorsey & Whitney LLP 220 S 6th St Ste 2200 Minneapolis MN 55402-1498

BURNS, ROBERT E., bank executive. BS in Acctg., Fairleigh Dickinson U., 1972. CPA Eisner Lubin, N.Y.C., 1972-73; auditor Auburn Savs. (N.Y.) Bank, 1974-75, v.p., controller, 1976-83; sr. v.p. Norstar Bank, Syracuse, N.Y., 1983-90; sr. v.p., treas., controller Fleet Bank New Hampshire, N.H., 1990-92; sr. v.p., controller Fleet Bank of Maine, Portland, Maine, 1992-94; sr. v.p. corp. acctg. ops. Fleet Svc. Corp., Providence, 1994—. Office: Fleet Svc Corp 125 Dupont Dr Providence RI 02907-3105*

BURNS, ROBERT EDWARD, editor, publisher; b. Chgo., May 14, 1919; s. William Joseph and Sara (Foy) B.; m. Brenda Coleman, May 15, 1948; children: Maddy F., Martin J. Student, De Paul U., 1937-39; Ph.B., Loyola U., Chgo., 1941; PhD (hon.), Rosary Coll., 1983. Pub. relations dir. Cath. Youth Orgn., Chgo., 1943-45, 47-49; exec. dir. No. Ind. region Nat. Conf. Christians and Jews, 1946; exec. editor U.S. Cath. mag.; gen. mgr. Claretian Publs., Chgo., 1949-84. Author: The Examined Life, 1980, Catholics on the Cutting Edge, 1983. Bd. dirs. Thomas More Assn. Recipient St. Francis de Sales award Cath. Press Assn., 1973, Proecclesia et Pontifice award Pope John Paul II, 1984. Home: N 4590 19th Ave Montello WI 53949-7926

BURNS, ROBERT EDWARD, lawyer; b. Bedford, Ohio, June 18, 1953; s. Robert Joseph and Barbara (Charvat) B.; m. Patricia Bosler, Oct. 15, 1983. BA in Polit. Sci. magna cum laude, Marietta Coll., 1975; JD, Ohio State U., 1978. Bar: Ohio 1978. Research asst. Program for Energy Research, Edn. and Pub. Service Ohio State U., Columbus, 1978-80, research assoc. Nat. Regulatory Research Inst., 1980-81, sr. research assoc., 1981-90, sr. rsch. specialist, 1990—. Author, co-author numerous monographs, articles, speeches, presentations, papers and reports to profl. orgns. and journals. Mem. ABA (vice chmn. energy com. 1984—, adminstrv., antitrust and pub. utility law sects.), Nat. Assn. Regulatory Utility Commrs. (subcom. adminstrv. law judges 1985—, subcom. law 1980—, coord. info. conf. 1986-87), Sertoma (pres. University club 1984-85, dist. gov. 1992-94, Internat. Community Svc. award 1984-85, outstanding dist. gov. 1994). Democrat. Methodist. Avocation: reading. Home: 3180 Bowdoin Ct Columbus OH 43204-2167 Office: Ohio State U Nat Regulatory Rsch Inst 1080 Carmack Rd Columbus OH 43210-1002

BURNS, ROBERT IGNATIUS, historian, educator, clergyman; b. San Francisco, Aug. 16, 1921; s. Harry and Viola Marie (Whearty) B. B.A., Gonzaga U., 1945, M.A., 1947; M.A., Fordham U., 1949; Phil.B., Jesuit Pontifical Faculty, Spokane, Wash., 1946, Phil.Lic., 1947; S.Th.B., Jesuit Pontifical Faculty, Alma, Calif., 1951, S.Th.Lic., 1953; postgrad., Columbia U., 1949, Oxford (Eng.) U., 1956-57; Ph.D. summa cum laude, Johns Hopkins U., 1958; Doc.ès Sc.Hist., Fribourg (Switzerland) U. (double summa cum laude), 1961; hon. doctorates, Gonzaga U., 1968, Marquette U., 1977, Loyola U., Chgo., 1978, Boston Coll., 1982, Georgetown U., 1982, U. San Francisco, 1983, Fordham U., 1984, U. Valencia, 1985. Mem. Jesuit order; ordained priest Roman Catholic Ch., 1952. Asst. archivist Jesuit and Indian Archives Pacific N.W., Province, Spokane, 1945-47; instr. history dept. U. San Francisco, 1947-48, asst. prof., 1958-62, assoc. prof., 1963-66, prof., 1967-76; sr. prof. dept. history UCLA, 1976—, named overscale (chair), 1987—; dir. Inst. Medieval Mediterranean Spain, 1976—; prof. methodology, faculty history Gregorian U., Rome, 1955-56; guest lectr. humanities honors program Stanford U., 1960; vis. prof. Coll. of Notre Dame, Belmont, Calif., 1963; James chair Brown U., Providence, 1970; faculty mem. Inst. Advanced Study, Princeton, N.J., 1972; Levi della Vida lectr. UCLA, 1973; vis. prof., Hispanic lectr. U. Calif. at Santa Barbara, 1976; staff UCLA Near Eastern Center, 1979—, UCLA Center Medieval-Renaissance Studies, 1977—; Humanities Coun. lectr. NYU, 1992; Columbus Quincentennial Commn. of Calif. State Legislature, 1992. Author: The Jesuits and the Indian Wars of the Northwest, 1966, reprinted 1985, The Crusader Kingdom of Valencia: Reconstruction on a Thirteenth-Century Frontier, 1967, Islam Under the Crusaders: Colonial Survival in the Thirteenth-Century Kingdom of Valencia, 1973, Medieval Colonialism: Post-Crusade Exploitation of Islamic Valencia, 1975, Moors and Crusaders in Mediterranean Spain, 1978, Jaume I i els Valencians del segle XIII, 1981, Muslims, Christians and Jews in the Crusader Kingdom of Valencia, 1983, El reino de Valencia en el siglo XIII, 1983, Society and Documentation in Crusader Valencia, 1985, The Worlds of Alfonso the Learned and James the Conqueror, 1985, Emperor of Culture: Alfonso X, 1990, Foundations of Crusader Valencia, 1991, rev. transl. Els fonaments del regne croat de València, 1995, El Regne Croat de Valencia, 1994, Jews in the Notarial Culture, 1996; bd. editors: Trends in History, 1979—, Anuario de Estudios Medievales (Spain), 1985—, Bull. of the Cantigueiros, 1986—, Catalan Rev., 1986—, Medieval Encounters, 1998—; co-editor: Viator, 1980-93; assoc. editor Ency. of Medieval Iberia; mem. editl. bd. U. Calif. Press, 1985-88, chair, 1987-88, mem. bd. of control, 1987-88; contbr. articles to profl. jours. Trustee Hill Monastic Manuscript Library, 1977-81; mem. adv. bd. Am. Bibliog. Center, 1982—. Recipient Book award Am. Hist. Assn. Pacific Coast Br., 1968, Am. Assn. State Local History, 1967, Am. Cath. Hist. Assn., 1967, 68, Book award Inst. Mission Studies, 1966, Am. Cath. Press Assn., 1975, Phi Alpha Theta, 1976; Haskins medal Medieval Acad. Am., 1976; Premi de la Critica, 1982; Premi Catalonia, 1982, Premi Internacional Llull, 1988; Cross of St. George Catalan Govt., 1989; Guggenheim fellow, 1963-64; Ford Found. and Guggenheim grantee, 1980; NEH fellow, 1971, 73, 75-83, 88, Am. Coun. Learned Socs. fellow, 1972; travel grantee, 1975; Robb Publ. Grantee, 1974; Darrow Publ. grantee, 1975; Consejo Superior de Investigaciones Cientificas (Spain) travel grantee, 1975, 82; Valencia province and Catalan region publ. grantee, 1981; Del Amo Grantee, 1983; U.S.-Spain treaty grantee, 1983-85; grantee Consejo Superior de Investigaciones Cientificas (Spain), 1985; Mellon Publ. grantee, 1985. Fellow Medieval Acad. Am. (trustee 1975-77, prize com. 1980-82, scribe 1987—), Accio Cultural del Pais Valencia; mem. Hispanic Soc. Am. (hon.), Am. Cath. Hist. Assn. (pres. 1975, coun. 1976—), Soc. Spanish Portuguese Hist. Studies (exec. coun. 1974-77), Am. Hist. Assn. (del. Internat. Congress Hist. Scis. 1975, 80, pres. Pacific Coast br. 1979-80, exec. coun. 1981-83), Medieval Assn. Pacific (exec. coun. 1975-77), Acad. Rsch. Historians Medieval Spain (pres. 1976), N.Am. Catalan Soc., Tex. Medieval, Inst. Catalan Studies, Barcelona (elected). Office: UCLA History Dept Los Angeles CA 90095

BURNS, ROBERT PASCHAL, architect, educator; b. Roxboro, N.C., Dec. 7, 1933; s. Robert Paschal and Majorie Dearing (Lacy) B.; m. Norma DeCamp, Dec. 4, 1973; children—Emily Carter, Robert Adam, Linda Paige. B. Arch., N.C. State U., 1957; M.Arch., MIT, 1962; postgrad., Ecole Des Beaux Arts, France, 1957-58. Archtl. designer Eduardo Catalano, Architect, Cambridge, Mass., 1962-65; asst. prof. architecture N.C. State U., Raleigh, 1965-67, assoc. prof., 1967-70, prof., 1970—, head dept., 1967-74, 83-91, assoc. dean Sch. of Design, 1984-90; prin. Envirotek, Inc., Raleigh, 1972-74, Burnstudio Architects, Raleigh, 1978—; exhbn. curator Matthew Nowicki: Sketches and Visions, N.C. State U. Visual Arts Ctr., 1993. Author, editor: 100 Courthouses, 1978; prin. works include Chatham County Law Enforcment Ctr., Lenoir County Courthouse. Bd. dirs. The Cinema, Raleigh, 1966-79. Served with U.S. Army, 1959. Recipient Paris prize Nat. Inst. for Archtl. Edn., 1957, AIA Sch. medal N.C. State U., 1957, Book award, 1957, Alexander Quarles Holloday medal for excellence, 1995, cert. N.C. State Bar, 1979, various awards for archtl. design; Graham Found. grantee, 1994. Fellow AIA; mem. Assn. Collegiate Schs. Architecture (pres. 1979-80, Disting. Prof. award 1995), Phi Kappa Phi (Nat. Artist award 1998—). Democrat. Avocations: book collecting; cooking. Home: 750 Washington St Raleigh NC 27605-3241 Office: NC State U Sch of Design Box 7701 Raleigh NC 27695

BURNS, ROBIN C(AROL), mathematics theoretician, accountant; b. L.A., Mar. 18, 1948; d. Kenneth and Jeanne C. (Murray) B.; m. Philip L. Benedict, Aug. 25, 1966 (dec. 1968); m. Terrance R. Fuchek, Sept. 5, 1969 (div. 1988); children: Tracy, Bryan, Conni, Loren, Allan; m. William E. Pavone, July 6, 1991 (div. June 1993). Owner Math Pro Bus. Svcs., Tacoma, Wash., 1992—. Creator/producer pub. TV series: 9 Patch Palace, 1979-83, Robin's Nest, 1983-86; creator/owner WWW.MOMWIZ.COM; writer/producer songs: Cry on My Shoulder, Nothin' Average About Him, 1992-93; inventor in field; contbr. articles to profl. jours. Mem. Math. Assn. Am., Am. Assn. Profl. Bookkeepers, Alpha Sigma Lambda. Avocations: ethnic dance choreography, camping, songwriting, internet publishing. Home and Office: 2522 N Proctor Ste 33 Tacoma WA 98406

BURNS, ROSALIE ANNETTE, neurologist, educator; b. Phila., July 29, 1932; married. BA, Smith Coll., 1953; MD, Yale U., 1956. Intern in medicine Cornell Med. divsn. Bellevue Hosp., N.Y.C., 1956-57; resident in neurology Neurol. Inst. N.Y.-Columbia-Presbyn. Med. Ctr., 1957-60; asst. in neurology, fellow Nat. Cerebral Palsy Study, 1959-60; fellow in cerebral vascular disease NIH-dept. neurology Tufts U.-New Eng. Ctr. Hosp., Boston, 1960-61; asst. dir. 2d neurology divsn. Bellevue Hosp., N.Y.C., 1962-64; instr. neurology dept. medicine Cornell U. Sch. Medicine, 1962-64; asst. neurologist to outpatients N.Y. Hosp., N.Y.C., 1962-64; electroencephalographer The Inst. of Pa. Hosp., 1964-65; instr. in neurology Med. Coll. Pa., 1964-65, dir. neurology clinics, 1965-74, assoc. in neurology, 1965-66, head sect. neurology, dept. psychiatry and neurology, 1965-71, asst. prof. neurology, 1966-70, assoc. prof. neurology, 1970-74, acting chmn. dept. neurology, 1971-74, prof. neurology, 1974-95, chmn. dept. neurology, 1975-95; univ. prof., exec. dir. Ctr. for Clin. Neurosci. Med. Coll. Pa./Hahnemann Univ., 1995-98; clin. prof. neurology Thomas Jefferson U. Sch. Medicine, 1998—; program dir. NIH Devel. Grant Med. Coll. Pa., 1966-73; consulting physician in neurology Ea. Pa. Psychiat. Inst., 1965-76, Pathway Sch. for Learning Disorders, 1978-81, Phila. VA Med. Ctr., part-time staff, 1975-77, attending physician in neurology, 1967-68; cons. staff Inglis House, 1967-93, Phila. Geriatric Ctr., 1985; half-time rsch. asst. neuropathology lab. Walter E. Fernald State Sch. Mental Retardation, Waverly, Mass., 1961-62; adj. attending neurologist dept. neurology Sloan-Kettering Cancer Ctr., 1986; presenter in field. Contbr. chpts. to books, articles to profl. jours. Nat. Found. fellow, 1955. Fellow Am. Acad. Neurology (edn. com. 1975-78, practice com. 1990-92, del. to Coun. of Acad. Socs. 1987-91, nominating com. 1993, 2d v.p. 1983-85, women's liaison officer 1991); mem. Am. Bd. Med. Specialties, Am. Bd. Psychiatry and Neurology (bd. dirs. 1993-2001, nominating com. 1993, rev. appeals com. 1992, credential com. 1992 and many other coms.), Am. Neurol. Assn. (annals of neurology oversight com. 1993), Assn. Univ. Profs. Neurology (sec.-treas. 1983-88, pres.-elect 1988-90, pres. 1990-92), Phila. Neurol. Soc. (1st v.p. 1971, 2nd v.p. 1977, pres. 1979-80, chmn. nominating com. 1981, and other coms.), Smith Coll. Club Phila., Alumnae Assn. Woman's Med. Coll. (assoc., Delaware Valley chpt.), Phi Beta Kappa, Sigma Xi, Alpha Omega Alpha (Delta chpt., chmn. membership com. 1980-81). Office: Thomas Jefferson Univ Hosp Ste 8130 111 S 11th St Philadelphia PA 19107

BURNS, SANDRA, lawyer, educator; b. Bryan, Tex., Aug. 9, 1949; d. Clyde W. and Bert (Rychlik) B.; 1 son, Scott. BS, U. Houston, 1970; MA, U. Tex.-Austin, 1972, PhD, 1975; JD, St. Mary's U., 1978. Bar: Tex. 1978; cert. tchr., adminstr., supr. instrn., Tex. Tchr. Austin (Tex.) Ind. Sch. Dist., 1970-71; prof. child devel./family life and home econs. edn. Coll. Nutrition, Textiles and Human Devel. Tex. Woman's U., Denton, 1974-75; instrnl. devel. asst. Office of Ednl. Resources div. instrnl. devel. U. Tex. Health Sci. San Antonio, 1976-77; legis. aide William T. Moore, Tex. Senate, Austin, fall, 1978, com. clk.-counsel, spring, 1979; legal cons. Colombotti & Assocs., Aberdeen, Scotland, 1980; corp. counsel 1st Internat. Oil and Gas, Inc., 1983; contracted atty. Humble Exploration Co., Inc., Dallas, 1984; assoc. Smith, Underwood, Dallas, 1986-88; pvt. practice, Dallas, 1988—; atty. contracted to Republic Energy Inc., Bryan, Tex., 1981-82, ARCO, Dallas, 1985; vis. lectr. Tex. A&M U., fall 1981, summer, 1981; lectr. home econ. Our Lady of the Lake Coll., San Antonio, fall, 1975. Mem. ABA, State Bar of Tex., Phi Delta Kappa. Contbr. articles on law and edn. to profl. jours. Office: 8300 Douglas Ave Ste 800 Dallas TX 75225-5826

BURNS, SCOTT, columnist; b. Cambridge, Mass., Nov. 9, 1940; s. Robert Milton Clark Burns and Joanne (Mahoney) Blasius; m. Allegra Wendy Eames, Dec. 11, 1965 (div. Sept. 1990); children: Jasper Bayard, Oliver Byron; m. Carolyn Jo Schroeder, Jan. 2, 1995. BS, MIT, 1962. Columnist, editor Boston (Mass.) Herald Am., 1977-83; columnist Dallas (Tex.) Morning News, 1985—; syndicated columnist, 1980—; contbg. editor Worth; bd. dirs. Nat. Taxpayers Union, Washington, Brain Behavior Ctr., Dallas. Author: Squeeze It Til The Eagle Grins, 1972, Home, Inc., 1975. Office: Dallas Morning News Communications Ctr PO Box 655237 Dallas TX 75265-5237

BURNS, STEPHEN GILBERT, lawyer; b. N.Y.C., Apr. 29, 1953; s. Gilbert Leo and Ellen (Scully) B.; m. Joan Louise Wallace, Aug. 6, 1977; children: Christopher, Allison. Student, U. Vienna, Austria, 1974; BA, Colgate U., 1975; JD, George Washington U., 1978. Bar: D.C. 1978, U.S. Dist. Ct. D.C. 1979, U.S. Ct. Appeals (D.C. cir.) 1980. Atty. Nuclear Regulatory Commn., Washington, 1978-83, dep. chief counsel regional ops. and enforcement, 1983-86, legal asst. to commr., 1986-89, exec. asst. to chmn., 1989-91, dir. Office of Commn. Appellate Adjudication, 1991-94, assoc. gen. counsel, 1994-98, dep. gen. counsel, 1998—. Mem. ABA, Fed. Bar Assn. Presbyterian. Office: US Nuclear Regulatory Commn Office of Gen Counsel MS 15B18 Washington DC 20555

BURNS, STEPHEN REDDING, golf course architect; b. Troy, Ohio, Nov. 6, 1958; s. John Vernon and Nancy (Caroline Natalie) (Grimm) B.; m. Laraine (Dorothy Laraine) Brazell, July 25, 1987. BS in Landscape Architecture, Ohio State U., 1981. Registered landscape architect, Fla., S.C., Wash., nationally cert. Golf course architect Charles F. Ankrom, Inc., Stuart, Fla., 1981, Fazio Golf Course Designers, Inc., Jupiter, Fla., 1981-88; owner, golf course architect Burns Golf Design, Fernandina Beach, Fla., 1988—; golf course designer Club de Golf, Malinalco, 1992, Hawks Nest Golf Club, 1993, Fox Meadow Golf and Country Club, 1994, Laura S. Walker State Park Golf Course, 1995, Cobblestone Golf Course, 1997, Legion Meml. Golf Course, 1997. Mem. Nat. Golf Found., Donald Ross Soc. Presbyterian. Avocations: skiing, golf, tennis. Home and Office: Burns Golf Design 5449 Marshview Ln Fernandina Beach FL 32034-5445

BURNS, TERRENCE MICHAEL, lawyer; b. Evergreen Park, Ill., Mar. 2, 1954; s. Jerome Joseph Burns and Eileen Beatrice (Collins) Neary; m. Therese Porucznik, Mar. 24, 1979; children: David, Steven, Theresa, Daniel. BA, Loyola U., Chgo., 1975; JD, DePaul U., 1978. Bar: Ill. 1978, U.S. Dist. Ct. (no. dist.) Ill. 1978, U.S. Ct. Appeals (7th cir.) 1979, U.S. Supreme Ct. 1985, U.S. Dist. Ct. (no. dist.) Ind. 1989. Asst. state's atty. Cook County, Chgo., 1979-85; ptnr. Rooks, Pitts & Poust, Chgo., 1985—. Commr. inquiry bd. Ill. Supreme Ct. Atty. Registration and Disciplinary Commn., Chgo., 1986-90, commr. hearing bd., 1990—. Mem. ABA, Chgo. Bar Assn. (treas. 1997—, bd. mgrs. 1995-97, chair fin. com. 1997—, criminal law com. 1979-83, jud. candidate evaluation com. 1981-86, 87-95, chmn. investigation divsn. evaluation com. 1991-92, chmn. hearing divsn. evaluation com. 1992-93, gen. chmn. 1993-95, ct. liaison com. 1993-95, tort reform subcom. 1997). Roman Catholic. Office: Rooks Pitts & Poust 10 S Wacker Dr Ste 2300 Chicago IL 60606-7407

BURNS, THAGRUS ASHER, manufacturing company executive, former life insurance company executive; b. Columbia City, Ind., Feb. 19, 1917; s. Harlow A. and Hazlette (Wise) B.; m. Dorothy Kimble, May 1, 1942; children: Steven L., Gerald A. A.B., Wabash Coll., 1939. With Lincoln Nat. Life Ins. Co., Ft. Wayne, Ind., 1939-80; treas. Lincoln Nat. Life Ins. Co., 1967-80, Lincoln Nat. Life Co., 1967-80, Lincoln Nat. Corp., 1968-80; pres. Burns Mfg. Inc., Ft. Wayne, 1980—; Treas., dir. Lincoln Nat. Life Found. Served to lt. USNR, 1942- 45. Mem. Financial Execs. Inst., Phi Beta Kappa. Inventor automatic feeder for typewriter, inserting machine and clipping catcher for hedge trimmer. Home and Office: 5611 Roaring Fork Run Fort Wayne IN 46825-5928

BURNS, THOMAS DAVID, lawyer; b. Andover, Mass., Apr. 4, 1921; s. Joseph Lawrence and Catherine (Horne) B.; m. Sylvia Lansing, Sept. 14, 1946 (div. 1982); children—Wendy Tilghman, Lansing, Diane Longley, Lisa; m. Marjorie Andrew Brown, Mar. 12, 1983. Student, Phillips Andover Acad., 1938, Brown U., 1938-41; LLB, Boston U., 1943. Bar: Mass. 1944, U.S. Dist. Ct. 1948, U.S. Ct. Appeals 1951, U.S. Supreme Ct. 1957. Assoc. Friedman, Atherton, King & Turner, Boston, 1946-50, ptnr., 1950-60; sr. and founding ptnr. Burns & Levinson, Boston, 1960—; mem. Jud. Coun. Com. of Mass., 1973-77, mem. Mass. Jud. Nominating Commn., 1979-83; mem. Mass. Spl. Legis. Commn. on Malpractice, 1975—; chmn. Joint Com. Boston and Mass. Bar Com. on Jud. Selection, 1970-75; spl. counsel to Boston City Coun., 1981. Contbr. articles to profl. jours. Chmn. Planning Bd. Appeals, Andover, 1956-57; trustee Stratton Mountain Vt. Civic Assn., Mus. Am. Textile History, 1992—; v.p., bd. dirs. Birch Hill Corp., Stratton, Vt.; chmn. Andover Rep. Fin. Com., 1953-57; trustee, clk. Pike Sch., Andover; mem. alumni coun. and devel. com. Phillips Andover Acad., Boston U. Law Sch.; mem. Mass. Hist. Soc., Western Front Assn.; mem. adv. bd. PBS channel WGBH, Boston. Lt. USNR, 1943-46, PTO, ETO. Fellow Am. Coll. Trial Lawyers, (state chmn. 1968, bd. regents 1970-76, treas. 1974-77), Am. Coll. Trial Lawyers Found. (dir.), Mass. Bar Found. (trustee), Mass. Bar Assn. (mem. exec. com.), Am. Bar Found., ABA, Boston Bar Assn. (exec. coun.), Boston Bar Found., Fed. Ins. and Corp. Counsel, Internat. Assn. Def. Counsel, Nat. Assn. R.R. Trial Counsel, Mass. Def. Lawyers Assn. (dir.), Delta Kappa Epsilon, North Andover Country Club, The Country Club (Brookline), Coral Beach Club (Bermuda), Duxbury Yacht Club, Boston City Club, Boston U. Law Sch. (alumni award, Disting. profl. svc. award 1996). Republican. Home: 5 Union Wharf Boston MA 02109-1202 Office: Burns & Levinson 125 Summer St Ste 602 Boston MA 02110-1624

BURNS, THOMAS SAMUEL, history educator; b. Michigan City, Ind., June 7, 1945; m. Carol Ann Morris, June 29, 1968; 1 child, Catherine Elizabeth. AB, Wabash Coll., 1967; postgrad., Am. Sch. Classical Studies, Athens, summer 1967; MA, U. Mich., 1968, PhD, 1974. Asst. prof. history Emory U., Atlanta, 1974-80, assoc. prof., 1980-85, Samuel Candler Dobbs prof. history, 1985—, chmn. dept. history, 1989-92; dir. summer seminar for sch. tchrs. NEH, 1985, 88; adj. prof. U. Windsor, Ont., summer 1978, 79; vis. research prof. Kommission für alte Geschichte und Epigraphik des deutschen archäologischen Instituts in München, spring 1982; vis. research prof. Römisch-Germanische Kommission des deut. arch. Instituts, Frankfurt, spring 1982; Gastprof. Universität Augsburg, 1986. Author: The Ostrogoths: Kingship and Society, 1980, A History of the Ostrogoths, 1984 (History Book Club selection 1984), (with B.H. Overbeck) Rome and the Germans as Seen in Coinage, 1987, Barbarians within the Gates of Rome, 1994 (History Book Club selection 1995); co-dir. of Archaeological excavations in Passau, Ger78-79, Manching, Germany, 1985, Pecs, Hungary, 1998; contbr. articles to profl. jours. With U.S. Army, 1969-71. Fulbright fellow Fed. Republic Germany, 1986; Boak fellow in ancient history U. Mich.,

1971-74; recipient Emory Williams Disting. Teaching award Emory U., 1982. Mem. Medieval Acad. Am. (nominating com. 1987-88), Am. Hist. Assn., Am. Inst. Archaeology, So. Hist. Assn., Ga. Classical Assn., AAUP (pres. Emory U. chpt. 1983-84), Phi Beta Kappa, Omicron Delta Kappa. Club: Am. Canoeing Assn. Avocations: camping, fishing, wilderness canoeing, travel. Home: 268 Woodview Dr Decatur GA 30030-1037 Office: Emory U Dept History Atlanta GA 30322

BURNS, TONI ANTHONY, artist; b. L.A., Sept. 6, 1937; d. Earle Francis and LaVerne Myrtle (Holmberg) Anthony; m. George Orin Burns, May 14, 1965; children: Robert Anthony, James Randolph. BA in Fine Arts, Calif. State U., Long Beach, 1959, postgrad., 1960. Cert. secondary tchr., Calif. Interior decorator Ruth Connor Interiors, Downey, Calif., 1960-62; tech. illustrator N.Am. Rockwell Corp., Downey, 1962-64, McDonnell-Douglas Aircraft, Long Beach, Calif., 1964-65; graphic layout artist Beckman Instruments, Fullerton, Calif., 1968-70; owner, creator original art Rock Owls, San Juan Capistrano, Calif., 1970-78; custom jewelry designer Jewelry by Toni Burns, San Juan Capistrano, 1979-98; jewelry designer, ptnr. SuperNatural Art, San Juan Capistrano, 1999—; wholesale exhibitor L.A. Gift Show, 1971-78, Beckman Handcrafts, L.A., 1982. Juried shows include Village West Gallery, Laguna Beach, Calif., summers 1971-75, Art-A-Fair Festival, Laguna Beach, 1984-86, Downey Art Mus., 1992, Fine Arts Pavilion, 1993. Recipient 1st pl. San Clemente Art Gallery, 1984. Mem. Am. Craft Coun., Metal Arts Soc. So. Calif. Avocations: family genealogy, travel, photography. Office: SuperNatural Art 31412 Windsong Dr San Juan Capistrano CA 92675-2788

BURNS, VICKI LYNN, writer, poet; b. Lancaster, Ohio, May 28, 1961; d. Thomas Lee and Jerie Rae (Shepard) Hendrickson; m. Judge K. Burns, May 4, 1985; 1 child, Hannah Faye. Student, Cumberland Coll., 1983-85. Receptionist Canal Winchester, Ohio, 1979-80; ins. rep. Midland Mut., Columbus, Ohio, 1980-81; word processor Gates McDonald, Columbus, 1982-83; small bus. owner Baskets N Berries, Bridgeville, Del., 1996—; author, 1996—. Author: The Lamb That Returned Home, 1996, The King Who Was Blessed, 1996; author (poetry) If Only You Knew, A Flower Pleads; composer (musical recording) Fear Ye Not Little Child!, 1994. Activities coord. Boys'/Girls' Club of Am., Dayton, Ohio, 1988; children's Ch. coord., Eastview Baptist Ch., Dayton, 1989-90, Del Paso Baptist Ch., Sacramento, Calif., 1992-93. Avocations: calligraphy, birdwatching, clarinet. Home: RR No 2 Box 195C Bridgeville DE 19933 Office: Baskets N Berries RR No 2 Box 195C Bridgeville DE 19933

BURNS, WARD, textile company executive; b. New Bedford, Mass., May 31, 1928; s. Frederick Lloyd and Pauline (Ward) B.; m. Cynthia A. Butterworth, Dec. 19, 1964; children: Helen Abby, David Ward, Walton Lloyd. B.A., Amherst Coll., 1950; M.B.A., Harvard U., 1952; spl. student, NYU, 1955-57; LLD (hon.), Phila. Coll. Textiles and Sci., 1984. CPA, N.Y. Mgr. Price Waterhouse & Co. (C.P.A.s), N.Y.C., 1954-62; assoc. Laurence S. and David Rockefeller, Brussels, Belgium, 1962-65; with J.P. Stevens & Co., Inc., N.Y.C., 1965-88, controller, 1969-78, group v.p., 1978-80, pres., 1980-86, vice chmn., 1987-88; also dir., mem. exec. com.; bd. dirs. Stevens Graphics, Inc., Atlanta, 1972-92; cons. ARS, Milan, Italy, HVL, Brussels, ARCO, Florence and Milan, 1963-65. *Founded in 1965 in Nashua, New Hampshire, Daniel Webster College maintains a commitment to both regional and national constituencies, currently serving 1,200 students from 29 states and 10 countries, 42% of whom are traditional undergraduates. The College educates purposeful men and women for professional entry, advancement, and advanced studies in the fields of aviation, computer science, management and engineering. Students prepare through residential and continuing studies programs which emphasize the integration of theory and practice through interactive teaching and learning in the professional and liberal studies. The College is accredited by the New England Association of Schools and Colleges, Inc.* Mem. editorial adv. bd.: Jour. Accountancy, 1969-72. Treas., dir. Internat. Sch. Brussels, 1963-65; bd. dirs. Internat. Sch. Brussels Found., N.Y.C., 1965—, pres. 1967-97; pres. Friends New Cavell Hosp. Inc.; bd. dirs., 1972-78; trustee Daniel Webster Coll., Nashua, N.H., 1995—, chmn., bd. trustees, 1997—; vice chmn. Friends of the Amherst Coll. Libr., 1978—. Served as capt. USAF, 1952-53. Mem. AICPA, N.Y. State Soc. CPAs, Fin. Execs. Inst., St. Andrews Soc., Univ. Club, Links Club, Econs. Club N.Y.C., The Pilgrims, Sky Club, Chappaquiddick Beach Club, Edgartown Yacht Club, Clove Valley Rod and Gun Club, Amherst Club (N.Y.), Harvard Club (Boston), Phi Alpha Psi, Phi Kappa Psi.

BURNS, WILLIAM STUART, legislative administrator; b. Macon, Ga., June 28, 1965. BA, King Coll., Tenn., 1988. Legis. dir. to Rep. Dave Weldon U.S. Ho. of Reps., Washington, 1995—. Office: US Ho of Reps 332 CHOB Washington DC 20515

BURNSHAW, STANLEY, writer; b. N.Y.C., June 20, 1906; s. Ludwig Behr and Sophia (Kievmann) B.; m. Lydia Powsner (dec.); children: Sandra Bonnie, Valerie, Amy, David. B.A., U. Pitts., 1925; M.A., Cornell U., 1933; L.H.D. honoris causa, Hebrew Union Coll.-Jewish Inst. Religion, 1983; DL, CUNY, 1996. Advt. bus. Pitts., 1925-27, N.Y.C., 1928-32; drama critic, coeditor New Masses, N.Y.C., 1933-36; pubs. The Cordon Co., Inc., N.Y.C., 1936-39; pres., gen. mgr. Dryden Press, Inc., N.Y.C., 1939-58; v.p. Holt, Rinehart & Winston, Inc., N.Y.C., 1958-65; adviser to pres. Holt, Rinehart & Winston, Inc., 1965-67; Regents lectr. U. Calif., winter 1980; disting. vis. prof. English U. Miami, 1989; Mem. organizing group, then lectr., dir. studies in World lit. Grad. Inst. of Book Publishing, N.Y. U., 1958-62; Bd. judges Nat. Book Award, 1967, 72; awards adv. com. Nat. Book Com., 1967—; Mem. organizing bd. editors, then cons. editor Adult Leadership (mag. supported by Fund for Adult Edn., Ford Found.), 1953-55; bd. dirs. Nat. Translation Ctr., Columbia U. Author: The Wheel Age, 1928, Andre Spire and His Poetry, 1933, The Iron Land, 1936, The Bridge, 1945, The Revolt of the Cats in Paradise, 1945, The Sunless Sea, 1947, Early and Late Testament, 1952, Caged in an Animal's Mind, 1963, The Seamless Web, 1970, 2d edit., 1991, In the Terrified Radiance, 1972, Mirages: Travel Notes in the Promised Land, 1977, The Refusers, 1981, My Friend, My Father, 1986, Robert Frost Himself, 1986, A Stanley Burnshaw Reader, 1990; editor: Two New Yorkers, 1938, The Poem Itself, 1960, 1995, Varieties of Literary Experience, 1962, The Modern Hebrew Poem Itself, 1965, rev. edit., 1989; editor Poetry Folio mag., 1926-28; contbg. editor Modern Quar., 1932-33, Theatre Workshop, 1935-38; contbr. to Columbia U. Dictionary Modern European Literature, 1947, Dictionary World Literature; L'Approdo Letterario, Italy, Delphica Tetradia, Greece, Nouvelle Revue Francaise, N.Y. Times Book Rev., Poetry, Atlantic Monthly, Sewanee Rev., Saturday Rev.; Stanley Burnshaw Spl. Issue pub. by Agenda, Brit. mag., 1984. Recipient award for lit. Nat. Inst. Arts and Letters, 1971; ann. Stanley Burnshaw Lectr. in Poetics established in his name at U. Tex., Austin, 1997, CUNY, 1998. Mem. Am. Inst. Graphic Arts (dir. 1960-61), Coll. Pubs. Group; mem. emeritus MLA. Home: 250 W 89th St New York NY 10024-1700

BURNSIDE, JOHN WAYNE, medical educator, university official; b. Bryn Mawr, Pa., Jan. 15, 1941; s. Wayne D. and Catherine (Neamand) B.; m. Lynda Deanne Haskins, Mar. 21, 1964; children: Andrew, Matthew, Paul. M.D., U. Ill., 1966. Resident Mass. Gen. Hosp., Boston, 1966-72; instr. Harvard U., Cambridge, Mass., 1969-72; asst. prof. Hershey Med. Ctr., Pa. State U., 1972-74, prof. medicine, 1980-87, assoc. provost and dean for health affairs, 1982-84, assoc. sr. v.p. for health affairs, vice dean, 1984-87; prof. internal medicine, assoc. dean for profl. edn. U. Tex. Southwestern Med. Ctr., Dallas, 1987—. Author: Physical Diagnosis, 1972, Physical Diagnosis, 2d edit., 1978, Health and Human Values, 1982, Burnside's Medical Examination Review, 1985. Pres. Greater Dallas Coun. on Alcohol and Drug Abuse, 1995; bd. dirs. Ctrl. Pa. Arthritis Found., 1974-79, Health Sys. Agy., Camp Hill, 1978-80, Blue Shield, 1982-87; co-dir. Ctr. for Humanistic Medicine, 1979-87; legis. asst. to senator, Washington, 1979, to congressman, 1980. With USNR, 1968-74. Recipient Senear award U. Ill., 1968; Health Policy fellow Robert Wood Johnson Found., 1979-80. Fellow ACP; mem. AMA (del. 1994), Am. Soc. Internal Medicine, Tex. Med. Assn. (chmn. coun. sci. affairs 1993—), Soc. Health and Human Values, Dauphin County Med. Soc. (pres. 1982), Rotary, Alpha Omega Alpha. Republican. Episcopalian. Office: Southwestern Med Sch 5323 Harry Hines Blvd Dallas TX 75235-7208

BURNSIDE, MARY BETH, biology educator, researcher; b. San Antonio, Apr. 23, 1943; d. Neil Delmont and Luella Nixon (Kenley) B. BA, U. Tex., 1965, MA, 1967, PhD in Zoology, 1968. Instr. med. sch. Harvard U., Boston, 1970-73; asst. prof. U. Pa., Phila., 1973-76; asst. prof. U. Calif., Berkeley, 1976-77, assoc. prof., 1977-82, prof., 1982—, dean biol. scis., 1984-90, chancellor prof., 1996—; mem. nat. adv. eye coun. NIH, 1990-94; mem. sci. adv. bd. Lawrence Hall of Sci., Berkeley, 1983—, Whitney Labs., St. Augustine, Fla., 1993-97; mem. bd. sci. councillors Nat. Eye Inst., 1994—. Mem. editl. bd. Invest. Ophthalmol. Vis. Sci., 1992-94; contbr. numerous articles to profl. jours. Mem. sci. adv. bd. Mills Coll., Oakland, Calif., 1986-90; trustee Bermuda Biol. Sta., St. George's, 1978-83; dir. Miller Inst., Berkeley, Calif., 1995—. Recipient Merit award NIH, 1989—, Outstanding Alumna award U. Tex., 1999; rsch. grantee, NIH, 1972, NSF. Fellow AAAS; mem. Am. Soc. Cell Biology (coun. 1980-84). Avocations: hiking, deserts, mountains, Great Danes. Office: U Calif Dept Molecular & Cell Biology 335 Life Scis Addn Berkeley CA 94720-3200

BURNSIDE, ORVIN CHARLES, agronomy educator, researcher; b. Hawley, Minn., June 9, 1932; s. John J. and Sena (Dwyre) B.; m. Delores Schattschneider, Dec. 22, 1954 (dec. 1990); 2 children; m. B.D. Clarice Hanson, Aug. 10, 1991. BS, N.D. State U., 1954; MS, U. Minn., 1958, PhD, 1959. Rsch. asst. U. Minn., St. Paul, 1956-59; prof. dept. agronomy U. Nebr., Lincoln, 1959-85; prof. weed sci., dept. agronomy and plant genetics U. Minn., St. Paul, 1985-98, ret., 1998; cons. weed sci. Contbr. chpts. to textbooks, articles to jours.; patentee. 1st lt. M.I., Counter Intelligence Corp, U.S. Army, 1954-56. Named Outstanding Spokesman for Agr., Nebr. Agrl. Chem. Assn., 1970; recipient CIBA-Geigy award, 1979, Rsch. award Gamma Sigma Delta, 1980, 97. Fellow Am. Soc. Agronomy, Weed Sci. Soc. Am. (rsch. award 1979); mem. Internat. Weed Sci. Soc., North Cen. Weed Sci. Soc. (hon.), Am. Legion, Toastmasters, Kiwanis. Republican. Lutheran.

BURNSTEIN, DANIEL, lawyer; b. Hartford, Conn., Oct. 12, 1946; s. Lawrence J. and Margaret (Le Vien) B. AB, U. Calif., Berkeley, 1968; JD cum laude, New Eng. Sch. Law, 1975. Bar: Mass. 1975, U.S. Dist. Ct. Mass. 1976, U.S. Ct. Appeals (1st cir.) 1976. Pres. Beacon Expert Systems, Inc., 1989—; adj. prof. Clark U.; dir. Interactive Video Project Harvard Law Sch., Cambridge, 1985-89, clin. instr.; lectr. Clark U., 1997—; pres. Ctr. for Atomic Radiation Studies, Acton, Mass., 1982—; advisor Am. Mgmt. Assn. for Negotiation Curriculum to Mgrs., 1993; pres. BuzzIT.com, 1999—. Editor: The Digital MBA, 1995. Mem. ABA, Mass. Adv. Coun. on Radiation Protection, The Mgmt. Software. Office: 35 Gardner Rd Brookline MA 02445-4512

BURNWORTH, RANDY JAMES, video company executive; b. Portland, Oreg., Aug. 1, 1949; s. Arliegh Clifton and Virginia May (Bobbit) B.; m. Carolyn Ruth Bowers, Apr. 18, 1967; children: James Randy, Deanna Michelle, Darrin Daniel. AA in Machine Technology, Bates Coll., 1969; postgrad., Pierce Coll., 1974, San Jose State U. CEO Video Ventures, Inc. and Showtime Video Ventures, Tillamook, Oreg., 1978—; sr. sci. and tech. officer Rave Engring. Corp., San Diego; founder, tech. provider NuWave Techs. Corp.; designer show booths for 33 internat. trade shows, also featured spkr.; product designer for RCA, Philips, Magnavox, DBX, BSR, Naritsu, GE, and numerous others. Contbr. tech. articles to profl. jours. Elder Mormon Ch.; mem. Republican Presdl. Task Force. Recipient Merit medal Rep. Presdl. Task Force, 1982; named Man of Decade Audio Video Digest, 1982; Entrepreneur of Yr. Video Entertainment, 1982; Best Products of Yr. awards, 1980, 81, 82, Video Rev., 1982; Internat. EIA Design and Engring. awards (11); 2 awards for innovative engring. and design video and audio products omni Mag., 17 internat. design and engring. awards for video, computer, audio and personal electronics; Acad. Award nominee for tech. achievement Motion Picture Acad. Arts and Scis.; seal and cert. of product excellence Soc. Audio Video Cons. Mem. U.s. Senatorial Club, Elks. Avocations: fishing, automobile racing, collecting fine art, machine technology. Inventor 1st phone TV sys., auto phaser, picture placer, smart bd., hyper graphics video computer, also others. Home: 13444 Turlock Ct San Diego CA 92129-2171 Office: Rave Engring Corp 12300 Stowe Dr Bldg A&B Poway CA 92064

BURR, BROOKS MILO, zoology educator; b. Toledo, Aug. 15, 1949; s. Lawrence E. and Beverly Joy (Herald) B.; m. Patti Ann Grubb, Mar. 5, 1977 (div. July 1987); 1 child, Jordan Brooks. BA, Greenville Coll., 1971; MS, U. Ill., 1974, PhD, 1977. Cert. scuba diver, Nat. Assn. Underwater Instrs. Lab. instr. dept. biology Greenville (Ill.) Coll., 1971-72; rsch. asst. Ill. Natural History Survey, Champaign, 1972-77; affiliate scientist Ctr. for Biodiversity Ill. Natural History Survey, Urbana, 1989—; from asst. prof. to prof. dept. zoology So. Ill. U., Carbondale, 1977—; mem. adv. panel U.S. Fish and Wildlife Svc., 1990—; adj. prof. dept. biology U. N.Mex., Albuquerque, 1991—; adj. prof. dept. ecology, ethology and evolution U. Ill., 1993—. Co-author: A Distributional Atlas of Kentucky Fishes, 1986, A Field Guide to Fishes, North America North of Mexico, 1991 (selected as one of Outstanding Acad. Books of 1992 by Choice Mag.); contbr. more than 90 articles to profl. jours. Recipient Paper of Yr. award Ohio Jour. Sci., 1986. Mem. AAAS, Am. Soc. Ichthyologists and Herpetologists (sec., mem. exec. com. 1990-94), Soc. Systematic Zoology, Biol. Soc. Washington, Assn. Systematic Collections, Sigma Xi (Leo M. Kaplan award 1990). Achievements include the discovery and description of 7 species of fish new to science from North American fresh waters. Home: 203 S Wedgewood Ln Carbondale IL 62901-2147 Office: So Ill Univ Dept Zoology Carbondale IL 62901-6501

BURR, DAVID BENTLEY, anatomy educator; b. Findlay, Ohio, June 28, 1951; s. Willard Bentley and Dorothy Eleanor (Beiler) B.; m. Lisa Marie Pedigo; children: Kathryn Lise, Michael David. BA, Beloit Coll., 1973; MA, U. Colo., 1974, PhD, 1977. Instr. anatomy U. Kans. Med. Ctr., Kansas City, 1977-78, asst. prof. anatomy, 1978-80; asst. prof. anatomy and orthop. surgery W.Va. U., Morgantown, 1980-83, assoc. prof., 1983-86, prof., 1986-90; chmn. dept. anatomy, prof. anatomy and orthopedic surgery Ind. U., Indpls., 1990—; mem. adv. bd. dirs. Primate Found. Am., Tempe, Ariz., 1978—; cons. County Med. Examiner, Morgantown, 1983-89; mem. Adv. Group for the Treatment Human Remains, USDA, Monongahela Nat. Forest Svc., 1989; cons. NASA, 1990-91, Am. Inst. Biol. Sci., NAS, 1990—, U.S. Congress Office Tech. Assessment, 1990; mem. biochemistry study sect. Arthritis found., 1992-95; spl. grants rev. com. NIH, 1996—. Author: Structure, Function & Adaptation of Compact Bone, 1989, Skeletal Tissue Mechanics, 1998; mem. editl. bd. Bone, 1993—, Jour. Bone and Mineral Metabolism, 1994—; contbr. articles to profl. jours. Pres. First Ward Sch. PTA, Morgantown, 1987-88; sec. Cub Scout Pack Com., Morgantown, 1989; chmn. troop com. Boy Scouts Am., 1993-95; mem. adminstrv. bd. Epworth United Meth. Ch., Indpls., 1992-93; linesman Morgantown Soccer League, 1988; sec. Classic Ragtime Soc. Rsch. grantee NIH, 1988—, Orthopedic Rsch. and Edn. Found., 1985-86. Mem. Orthop. Rsch. Assn., Am. Anatomy Assn. (exec. com.), Assn. Anatomy, Cell Biology and Neurobiology Chairpersons, Classic Ragtime Soc. (sec. 1997-98), Sigma Xi. Avocations: piano, softball, racquetball, stamps, reading. Office: Ind U Sch Medicine 635 Barnhill Dr Dept Anatomy Indianapolis IN 46202-5126

BURR, EDWARD BENJAMIN, life insurance company executive, financial executive; b. Worcester, Mass., Dec. 19, 1923; s. Guy Weatherbee and Bertha Mary (Clark) B.; m. Mary Elizabeth Hayes, Sept. 2, 1944 (div. Sept. 1970); children—Susan Jean Burr Williams, Nancy Carol Burr Montanaro; m. Kay Frances Flanagan, Nov. 1, 1970 (div. 1992); children—Kristine Kay (deceased), Kelly Anne. B.A., Bowdoin Coll., 1945; M.B.A., U. Pa., 1948; grad., Am. Coll. Life Underwriters, 1951. C.L.U. Dir. Inst. Life Ins., N.Y.C., 1948-54; exec. dir. Investment Co. Inst., N.Y.C., 1954-58; exec. v.p., dir. One William Street Fund, N.Y.C., 1958-62; pres., dir. William Street Sales, Inc., N.Y.C., 1958-62; pres., vice chmn. Anchor Corp., Elizabeth, N.J., 1964-78; chmn. bd. Anchor Nat. Life, Phoenix, 1965-85, hon. chmn., 1985—; chmn. bd. Anchor Nat. Fin. Services, Phoenix, 1971-85, hon. chmn. 1986—; pres. United Planners Fin. Services Am., 1987-95. Trustee Scottsdale Meml. Hosp., Ariz., 1985-95, chmn., 1990-91; dir. Ariz. Cmty. Found., 1985-93. With U.S. Army, 1943-46, ETO. Decorated Bronze Star, Silver Star. Mem. Am. Soc. CLUs, Nat. Assn. Life Underwriters, Phoenix Met. C. of C. (bd. dirs. 1982-88), Scottsdale Club at Gainey Ranch, Camelback Golf Club. Home: 7331 E Griswold Rd Scottsdale AZ 85258-2731 Office: United Planners Group 7333 E Doubletree Ranch Rd Scottsdale AZ 85258-2042

BURR, FRANCIS HARDON, lawyer; b. Nahant, Mass., July 21, 1914. A.B. cum laude, Harvard U., 1935, LL.B, 1938, LL.D., 1982. Bar: Mass. 1938. Assoc. Ropes & Gray, Boston, 1938-47, ptnr., 1947-87, of counsel, 1988—; dir. emeritus AMR Corp., Corning Inc., State St. Investment Trust; Raytheon Co. Hon. trustee Mass. Gen. Hosp., Spaulding Rehab. Hosp., McLean Hosp.; pres. Humane Soc., Commonweath of Mass.; dir emeritus Cotting Sch. Fellow Harvard Coll., 1954-82; sr. fellow Harvard Coll., 1971-82. Fellow AAAS, Am. Bar Found; mem. ABA, Boston Bar Assn., Am. Law Inst. Office: Ropes & Gray One International Pl Boston MA 02110 *No one will remember very long what you do for yourself. With a bit of luck they may remember what you do for others.*

BURR, GRAY, poet, educator; b. Omaha, Mar. 20, 1919; s. Alfred Earnest and Geraldine Gray Burr; m. Carol Taber, June 15, 1943 (div. Jan. 1960); children: Elizabeth, Rebecca, Katherine; m. Ellen Jean Krohn, Aug. 5, 1960; 1 child, Martha. AB, Harvard U., 1943, AM, 1948. Instr. Philips Exeter (N.H.) Acad., 1948-49, Tufts U., Medford, Mass., 1949-53; asst. prof. Wheaton Coll., Norton, Mass., 1953-60; assoc. prof. SUNY, New Paltz, 1960-81, assoc. prof. emeritus, 1981—. Author: A Choice of Attitudes, 1969, the Moon by Day, 1984, Leaving the House, 1993, Afterlives, 1996. Lt. USN, 1943-45, PTO. Grantee Ingram Merrill Found., 1976, State of N.Y., 1978, 79. Home: 7 Snows Rd Box 575 Truro MA 02666

BURR, HIRAM HALE, JR., retired air force officer; b. Kingsville, Tex., May 10, 1943; m. Barbara Roberts; children: Lara, Lesa. BA in Econ., Tex. A&M U., 1965; MA in Internat. Rels., U. Ark., 1973; postgrad., U.S. Army Command and Gen. Staff Coll., 1975, Air War Coll., 1977, Nat. War Coll., 1980. Commd. 2d lt. USAF, 1965, advanced through grades to maj. gen., 1991; F-4 pilot 45th Tactical Fighter Squadron, MacDill AFB, Fla., 1966-67, 557th Tactical Fighter Squadron, Cam Ranh Bay Air Base, South Vietnam, 1967-68; 0-2 forward air contr. 20th Tactical Air Support Squadron, Da Nang Air Base, South Vietnam, 1968, 82d Airborne Divsn., Phu Bai Air Base, South Vietnam, 1968; F-4 aircraft comdr. 45th Tactical Fighter Squadron, MacDill AFB, 1968-69; F-4 squadron scheduler 81st Tactical Fighter Squadron, Hahn Air Base, West Germany, 1970-73; F-4 flight examiner 86th Tactical Fighter Wing, Zweibruken Air Base, West Germany, 1970-73; F-4 flight examiner, dir. standardization and evaluation Hdqrs. USAF Europe, Ramstein Air Base, West Germany, 1973-74; staff officer, dir. plans Hdqrs. USAF, Washington, 1975-78; rsch. assoc. Ctr. for Advanced Internat. Studies U. Miami, Fla., 1978-79; F-15 pilot 94th Tactical Fighter Squadron, Langley AFB, Va., 1980-81; comdr. 71st Tactical Fighter Squadron, Langley AFB, Va., 1981-82; chief ops. divsn., insp. gen. Hdqrs. Tactical Air Command, Langley AFB, Va., 1982-83; asst. dep. comdr. ops. 49th Tactical Fighter Wing, Holloman AFB, N.Mex., 1983-85; vice comdr., then comdr. 325th Tactical Tng. Wing, Tyndall AFB, Fla., 1985-86; comdr. 31st Tactical Fighter Wing, Homestead AFB, Fla., 1986-88; dep. for security assistance, logistics and security assistance directorate Hdqs. U.S. Ctrl. Command, MacDill AFB, Fla., 1988-89; dep. comdr. Joint Task Force Mid. East, Persian Gulf, 1989-90; dep. dir. ops. Nat. Mil. Command Ctr., Joint Staff, Washington, 1990-91; comdr. 13th Air Force, Andersen AFB, Guam, 1991-94; asst. dep. under sec., internat. affairs USAF, Washington, 1994-97, ret., 1997. Decorated D.F.C. with four oak leaf clusters, D.S.M. with one oak leaf cluster, Legion of Merit, Def. Superior Svc. medal, Def. Meritorious Svc. medal, Meritorious Svc. medal with two oak leaf clusters, Air medal with 31 oak leaf clusters, Air Force Commendation medal. Home: 6720 Myrtle Beach Dr Plano TX 75093-6324

BURR, JEAN MARIE, university women's basketball coach; m. Peter Burr; children: Judee Lee, Jessica Marie, Joanna Christine, Jenna Rose. BSBA, U. N.H., 1977; MS in Sports Mgmt., U. Mass., 1982. Asst. coach Davidson Coll.; asst. basketball coach, head volleyball coach Amherst Coll.; women's athletic dir., head basketball and volleyball coach Bethany Coll., W.Va.; head coach Fairfield U., Brown U.; lectr. in field. Named to Athletic Hall of Honor U. N.H. Mem. Women's Basketball Coaches Assn. (bd. dirs.), Nat. Assn. of Basketball Coaches, Women's Sports Found. Office: Brown Univ Womens Athletic Dept Pizzitola Sports Ctr PO Box 1932 Providence RI 02902*

BURR, LAURIE DIANE, information technology consultant; b. Bath, N.Y., Jan. 29, 1953; d. Jonathan Williams and Dorothy Evelyn (Daines) B.; m. Jeffrey Howard Halpern. AB, Vassar Coll., 1974; MBA, U. Va., 1983. Fin. planner Burlington, Vt., 1975-76; mktg. rep. IBM, Burlington, 1976-80; fin. planner IBM/Lab.-Mfg., Poughkeepsie, N.Y., 1983-84; marketer, analyst IBM/Regional & Br. Offices, Balt., 1984-86; proposal mgr. IBM/Pub. Sector Group, Balt., 1986-88; cons. pub. sector industry IBM, Bethesda, Md., 1988-93; pres. Renaissance Consulting Co., Inc., Annapolis, Md., 1993-96; dir. fin. vertical market Oracle Corp., Bethesda, 1996-98; sr. prin. Am. Mgmt. Systems, Fairfax, Va., 1998—. Mem. Eastport Yacht Club.

BURR, RICHARD M., congressman; b. Charlottesville, Va., Nov. 30, 1955; m. Brooke Burr; children: Tyler, William. BA in Comm., Wake Forest U., 1978. Nat. sales mgr. Carswell Distributing, 1978-94; state co-chmn. N.C. Taxpayers United, 1993—; mem. 104th-106th Congress from 5th N.C. dist., 1995—; commerce com. 105th Congress; mem. energy & power, health & environ., oversight & investigations coms., internat. relations com., internat. economic policy and trade subcom. Republican. Office: US House Reps 1513 Longworth HOB Washington DC 20515-3305*

BURR, ROBERT LYNDON, information services specialist; b. Boonville, N.Y., May 9, 1944; s. James Isaac and Virginia Ellen (Davidson) B.; m. Angela Delores Tucci, June 26, 1965; 1 son, Robert Anthony. Student, U. Rochester, 1962-65; A.B., Canisius Coll., 1972; M.S. in L.S, Case-Western Res. U., 1973; Ed.D., Gonzaga U., 1981. Asst. prodn. mgr., purchasing mgr. Carleton Controls Corp., Buffalo, 1966-71; asst. to pres. Audn Corp., Buffalo, 1971-72; circulation services librarian Coll. William and Mary, Williamsburg, Va., 1973-77; dean libr. svcs. Gonzaga U., Spokane, 1977—, adj. asso. prof. edn., 1979—, assoc. acad. v.p., 1996—; library cons. Contbr. articles to profl. jours. Trustee Mus. Native Am. Cultures, 1979—. Served with AUS, 1967-69. Mem. ALA (nat. research award 1974), Nat. Libraries Assn., Wash. Library Assn., Pacific N.W. Library Assn., AAUP, Mensa, Moses Lake Golf and Country Club. Office: Gonzaga U Foley Ctr 502 E Boone Ave Spokane WA 99258-0001

BURR, TIMOTHY FULLER, lawyer; b. New Bedford, Mass., Oct. 18, 1952; s. John Thayer and Joan (Ames) B.; AB, Harvard U., 1975; JD, U. Miami, 1979; m. Marguerite Conti, Feb. 28, 1981; children: Emily Ames, Lisa Conti, David Thayer. Bar: La. 1979, Tex. 1993, Fla. 1996, U.S. Supreme Ct., U.S. Cir. Ct., U.S. Dist. Ct.; mng. dir. firm Galloway, Johnson, Tompkins & Burr, New Orleans, 1987—, admiralty and litigation atty., 1979—. Past chmn. St. Tammary Parish Zoning Bd. Mem. La. Bar Assn., Tex. Bar Assn., Fla. Bar Assn., Maritime Law Assn. U.S., Tammany Yacht Club, Pensacola Yacht Club. Republican. Home: 208 Pinetree Dr Gulf Breeze FL 32561-4050 Office: Galloway Johnson Tompkins and Burr 4040 1 Shell Sq Ste 4040 New Orleans LA 70139 also: 55 Bay Bridge Dr Gulf Breeze FL 32561-4468

BURRAGE, BILLY MICHAEL, judge, federal. JD, U. Okla., 1974. Pvt. practice Antlers, Okla., 1974-94; judge U.S. Dist. Ct. (ea. no. and we. dists.) Okla., Muskogee, 1994-96; chief judge U.S. Dist. Ct. (ea. dist.) Okla., Muskogee, 1996—. Fellow Am. Bar Found.; mem. ABA, Am. Coll. Trial Lawyers, Pushmataha County Bar Assn., Order of Coif. Office: US Dist Ct PO Box 2999 Muskogee OK 74402-2999*

BURRELL, CALVIN ARCHIE, minister; b. Fairview, Okla., June 22, 1943; s. Lawrence Lester and Lottie Edna (Davison) B.; m. Barbara Ann Mann, May 29, 1966; children: Debra, Darla, Donna. BS, Northwestern State U., 1965; MA, So. Nazarene U., Bethany, Okla., 1978. Ordained to ministry Ch. of God, 1966. Tchr., prin., dean boys Spring Vale Acad., Owosso, Mich., 1964-76; pastor Ch. of God (Seventh Day), Ft. Smith, Ark., 1970-73, Shawnee, Okla., 1976-78, Denver, 1978-88; pastor Ch. of God, Galena Park, Tex., 1996—; pres. gen. conf. Ch. of God, Denver, 1987-97; editor Bible Advocate mag., Denver, 1997—; instr. Summit Sch. Theology, Denver, 1978-95; officer Bible Sabath Assn., 1983-96. Editor: Bible Advocate, 1997—. Office: Ch of God 330 W 152d Ave PO Box 33677 Denver CO 80233-0677

BURRELL, CAROL ANN, trade association executive; b. Toronto, Ont., Can., Jan. 7, 1963; d. Sidney Thomas and Margaret Beveridge (Brown)

Haynes; m. Glen Stuart Burrell, May 18, 1985; 1 child, Shevaun Haynes Stuart. BA, U. Toronto, 1986; pub. rels. cert., Humber Coll., Toronto, 1988. Fundraiser Salvation Army, Toronto, 1988-89; coord. memberships Can. Assn. Expn. Mgrs., Toronto, 1989-91, gen. mgr., 1991-93, exec. dir., 1993—. Lt. Can. Naval Res., 1982—. Mem. Can. Soc. Assn. Execs., Am. Soc. Assn. Execs. Avocations: hiking, camping, crafts. Office: Can Assn Expn Mgrs 6900 Airport Rd Ste 239A Box 82 Mississauga ON Canada L4V 1E8*

BURRELL, GARLAND E., JR., federal judge; b. L.A., July 4, 1947. BA in Sociology, Calif. State U., 1972; MSW, Washington U., Mo., 1976; JD, Calif. Wes. Sch. Law, 1976. Bar: Calif. 1976, U.S. Dist. Ct. (ea. dist.) Calif. 1976, U.S. Ct. Appeals (9th cir.) 1981. Dep. dist. atty. Sacramento County, Calif., 1976-78; dep city atty. Sacramento, 1978-79; asst. U.S. atty., dep. chief civil divsn. Office of U.S. Atty. for Ea. Dist. Calif., 1979-85, asst. U.S. atty., chief civil divsn., 1990-92; litigation atty. Stockman Law Corp., Sacramento, Calif., 1985-86; sr. dep. city atty. Office of City Atty., Sacramento, 1986-90; judge U.S. Dist. Ct. (ea. dist.) Calif., Sacramento, 1992—. With USMC, 1966-68. Office: Dist Ct 501 I St Sacramento CA 95814-4708

BURRELL, JOEL BRION, neurologist, researcher, clinician; b. Orange, N.J., Nov. 27, 1959; s. Robert and Barbara (Miller) B. BS in Biology, Rutgers U., 1982, grad. student, 1983; MD, Temple U., 1987. Diplomate Am. Bd. Med. Examiners. Intern Abington (Pa.) Meml. Hosp., 1987-88; neurology resident The Mt. Sinai Med. Ctr., N.Y.C., 1988-91; neuroimmunology fellow Cleve. Clin. Found., 1991-93; attending physician with pvt. clin. practice, 1993—; asst. clin. prof. Med. Coll. Ohio, 1993-98. Presenter in field. Recipient Pinnacle award Being Single Mag., 1995; named to Outstanding Young Men of Am., 1998. Fellow Stroke Coun. of Am. Heart Assn., Internat. Biog. Assn. (named one of 2000 outstanding people of 20th century); mem. AMA (Physician's Recognition award 1992—), Am. Acad. Clin. Neurophysiology, Internat. Cerebral Hemodynamics Soc., Am. Acad. Neurology, Nat. Med. Assn., Acad. Medicine Cleve., Cleve. Med. Assn., Ohio Acad. Sci., Ohio State Med. Assn. (named one of top 8 young physicians 1995), Med. Alumni Assn. Temple U., Temple U. Gen. Alumni Assn., Assoc. Alumni of Mt. Sinai Med. Ctr. of N.Y.C.; Huron County Medical Soc. (treas./sec. 1996-97), New York Academy of Science. Avocations: tennis, skiing, ice skating, golf, travel. Office: Ste C 511 S Abbe Rd Elyria OH 44035

BURRELL, LEROY RUSSEL, track and field athlete; b. Phila., Feb. 21, 1967. Grad. h.s., Lansdowne, Pa. Track and field profl. Ranked No. 5 in the world in the 100 m. race and 7th among U.S. long jumpers by Track and Field News, 1989; ranked No. 1 in the world in the 100m, No. 5 at 200m, 1990; world record USA/Mobile victory at N.Y.'s Randalls Island, 1990; winner Olympic gold medal in the 4x100 relay. Office: USA Track and Field One RCA Dome 1 Rca Dome Ste 140 Indianapolis IN 46225-1023*

BURRELL, ORVILLE RICHARD, popular musician. Albums include Boombastic, 1995 (Best Reggae Album Grammy award 1996). Address: Virgin Records 1790 Broadway Fl 20 New York NY 10019-1412*

BURRELL, SIDNEY ALEXANDER, history educator; b. Choteau, Mont., Feb. 24, 1917; s. Sidney Harris and Frances (Timmis) B.; m. Ann Theresa Gibbons, Sept. 2, 1945; children: John A., Sidney Antony, Andrew J. Student, DePauw U., 1934-35; A.B., U. Chgo., 1938; Ph.D., Columbia, 1953. Mem. faculty seamanship and navigation U.S. Naval Acad., 1945-46; instr. history Columbia, 1948-50, Barnard Coll., 1950-52; mem. research staff Center Research on World Polit. Instns., Princeton, 1952-53; mem. faculty Barnard Coll., 1953-66; prof., chmn. dept. history Boston U., 1966-79, prof. emeritus, 1982—; resident dir. study abroad programs Boston U., London and Oxford, Eng., 1986. Author: (with others) Political Community in the North Atlantic Area, 1957; Editor: (with others) Amiable Renegade: Memoirs of Capt. Peter Drake, 1671-1753, 1960; Editor, compiler: (with others) Role of Religion in Modern European History, 1964; Contbr. to: (with others) Some Modern Historians of Britain, 1951, The Protestant Ethic and Modernization (S.N. Eisenstadt, ed.), 1968; Contbr. (with others) articles profl. jours. Served with USNR, 1942-46, PTO. Recipient Metcalf cup and prize for Disting. Teaching Boston U., 1981; Univ. lectr. Boston U., 1982; Guggenheim fellow, 1961-62. Mem. Am. Hist. Assn., New Eng. Hist. Assn. (pres. 1972-73), Conf. Brit. Studies, Colonial Soc. Mass., Phi Beta Kappa, Phi Delta Theta. Home: 10 Longwood Dr Apt 210 Westwood MA 02090-1139

BURRELL, VICTOR GREGORY, JR., marine scientist; b. Wilmington, N.C., Sept. 12, 1925; s. Victor Gregory and Agnes Mildred (Townsend) B.; m. Katherine Stackley; Jan. 7, 1956; children: Cheri, Cathey, Charlene, Sarah. BS, Coll. Charleston, 1949; MA, Coll. William and Mary, 1968, PhD, 1972. Rsch. assoc. Va. Inst. Marine Sci., Gloucester Point, 1966-68, asst. marine scientist, 1968-70, assoc. marine scientist, 1970-72; assoc. marine scientist S.C. Marine Resources Rsch. Inst., Charleston, 1972-73, assoc. marine scientist, asst. dir., 1973-74, sr. marine scientist, dir., 1974-91, dir. emeritus, 1991—. Contbr. numerous articles to profl. jours. With USN, 1943-46, PTO. Mem. Nat. Shell Fisheries Assn. (pres. 1982-83, hon. life mem. 1992), Estuarine Rsch. Fedn. (sec. 1975-77), Gulf and Caribbean Fisheries Inst., Southeastern Estuarine Rsch. Soc. (pres. 1986-88, hon. mem. 1990). Episcopalian. Office: SC Marine Resources Rsch Inst PO Box 12559 Charleston SC 29422-2559

BURRES, CARLA ANNE, medical technologist; b. Lawrence, Kans., Feb. 18, 1938; d. Emil Bowen Robison and Emma Annabelle (Boots) R.; m. Kenneth Lee Burres, Aug. 24, 1956; children: Cara L., Katrina Burres Heinzen, Heather Burres Petry. BA, Ctrl. Meth. Coll., 1972; BS, U. Mo., 1982. Tchr. biology and chemistry Glasgow (Mo.) H.S., 1977-80; rsch. specialist Cytogenetics Lab., U. Mo. Hosp., Columbia, 1980; med. technologist Cooper County Hosp., Boonville, Mo., 1982-89, ARC, Columbia, 1989—. Editor: Preachers, Pioneers, Professors, Printers, 1997. Mem. Soc. for Better Fayette (Mo.) Cmty., 1995—, Cmty. Task Force, Fayette, 1997; sec. bd. dirs. Wesley Found., Fayette, 1995—. Mem. Am. Soc. Clin. Pathologists (assoc., cert. med. technologist). Democrat. Methodist. Avocations: gardening, photography, hiking, travel, reading. Home: 320 S Main St Fayette MO 65248-1269

BURRIDGE, MICHAEL JOHN, veterinarian, educator, research administrator; b. St. Albans, Eng., Apr. 27, 1942; came to U.S., 1973; s. Arthur Wilfred Bailey and Georgina Augusta (Davis) Burridge; m. Desree Margaret Wiggins, Aug. 13, 1973 (div. Sept. 1981); m. Karen Maureen Bengtsson, Jan. 1, 1983; 1 child, Christina Michelle. BVM&S, U. Edinburgh, Scotland, 1966; MPVM, U. Calif., Davis, 1974, PhD, 1976. Rsch. asst. East African Trypanosomiasis Rsch. Orgn., Tororo, Uganda, 1966; vet. practitioner Grant and Arnold, Woking, Eng., 1967-68; animal health officer Food & Agr. Orgn., Kabete, Kenya, 1968-73; grad. rsch. asst. U. Calif., Davis, 1973-76; assoc. prof. U. Fla., Gainesville, 1976-82, prof., 1982—, chmn. dept., 1984-93; mem. com. on animal health NAS, Washington, 1980-83; cons. World Bank, Zaire, 1982, USAID, India, 1987, 91; cons. vet. medicine Williams & Wilkins, Balt., 1982—; bd. dirs. Internat. Laveran Found., Annecy, France, 1991-94. Editor: Impact of Diseases on Livestock Production in the Tropics, 1984. Grantee U.S. AID, 1985—. Mem. AVMA. Achievements include co-invention of attractant decoy for tick control and self-medicating applicators for parasite control. Home: 10021 SW 67th Dr Gainesville FL 32608-6304 Office: U Fla Dept Pathobiology PO Box 110880 Gainesville FL 32611-0880

BURRIER, GAIL WARREN, physician; b. Newark, Ohio, Apr. 6, 1927; s. Harold I. and Esther M. (Simpson) B.; m. Mary Lou Miller, June 12, 1948 (dec. 1982); children: Dale, Marie. BS, Ohio State U., 1950, MS, 1952, MD, 1956. Diplomate Am. Bd. Family Practice; cert. geriatrist. Intern Grant Hosp., Columbus, Ohio, 1956-57; pvt. practice Canal Winchester, Ohio, 1957-73; dir. family practice Grant Med. Ctr., Columbus, 1973-88; med. dir. Alum Crest Nursing Home, Columbus, 1988—; clin. instr. Ohio State U., Columbus, 1969-74, clin. asst. prof., 1974-81, clin. assoc. prof., 1981—; med. dir. Winchester Place Nursing Home, Canal Winchester, 1983—; med. tech. asst. State of Ohio, Columbus, 1988—. Trustee Columbus Area Mental Health, 1974-81; bd. dirs. Meth. Ch., Canal Winchester, 1959-63; team physician high sch. tournaments, Columbus, 1957—. Fellow Am. Acad. Family Physicians (local pres. 1973); mem. Am. Coll. Physician Execs., AMA, Am. Geriatric Soc., Am. Soc. on Aging, Ohio State U. Alumni Club (pres. Columbus chpt. 1985-86). Republican. Home and Office: 45 Trine St Canal Winchester OH 43110

BURRILL, KATHLEEN R. F. (KATHLEEN R. F. GRIFFIN-BURRILL), Turkologist, educator; b. Canterbury, U.K., Mar. 8, 1924; d. William Henry and Ruby Amy (Webber) Griffin; children: Anne Ruth, Jane Ruth. A.M., Columbia U., 1957; cert. Middle East Inst., 1959, Ph.D., 1964. Officer of Brit. Council, Ankara, Turkey and U.K., 1947-55; lectr. to prof. Middle East and Asian langs. and cultures, dir. Ctr. of Turkish Studies, Columbia U., N.Y.C., 1957—. Author: The Quatrains of Nesimi, Fourteenth-Century Turkic Hurufi Poet; co-editor Archivum Ottomanicum, 1984-95; contbr. articles to profl. jours. and encyclopedias. Fellow Columbia U., 1957-59, Ford Found., 1959-60, Am. Research Inst. in Turkey, summers 1967, 75; recipient research and fellowship travel award Council for Research in the Humanities, 1966-67, Fellow Middle East Studies Assn. (founding fellow, dir. 1974-76); mem. Am. Oriental Soc., Turkish Studies Assn. (dir. 1974-76), Inst. Turkish Studies (founding assoc., governing bd. 1995—), Brit. Soc. for Middle East Studies, Middle East Inst. (Washington), Am. Turkish Soc. (N.Y.C., dir.), Am. Assn. Tchrs. of Turkic Langs. (pres. 1986—). Office: Columbia U Dept Mid-East & Asian Langs & Cultures New York NY 10027

BURRIS, BOYD LEE, psychiatrist, psychoanalyst, physician, educator; b. Knoxville, Tenn., Jan. 28, 1930; s. Fred Roosevelt and Mildred Blanche Burris. BS, U. Tenn., Knoxville, 1951; MD, U. Tenn., Memphis, 1952. Diplomate in psychiatry Am. Bd. Psychiatry and Neurology; cert. in psychoanalysis. Co-dir. Balt.-Washington Inst. for Psychoanalysis, Washington, 1980-86; clin. prof. psychiatry and behavioral scis. George Washington U. Sch. Medicine, Washington, 1983—; clin. prof. psychiatry Georgetown U. Sch. Medicine, Washington, 1990—; dir., pres. bd. trustees Ctr. for Advanced Psychoanalytic Studies, Princeton, N.J., Aspen, Colo., 1994—; pvt. practice psychiatry and psychoanalysis Washington, 1960—; active staff George Washington U. Hosp., 1963-96; cons. Potomac Found. for Mental Health, Bethesda, Md., 1969-78, St. Elizabeth's Hosp., Washington, 1969-88. Contbr. chpt. to book, articles to profl. jours. Lt. comdr. M.C., USN, 1954-56. Mem. Am. Psychiat. Assn. (chair tellers com. 1987-88), Am. Psychoanalytic Assn. (bd. on profl. standards 1982-86), Balt./Washington Soc. for Psychoanalysis (pres. 1978-79). Home: 3100 Rolling Rd Chevy Chase MD 20815-4038 Office: 4545 42nd St NW Ste 310 Washington DC 20016-4623

BURRIS, CRAVEN ALLEN, retired education administrator, educator; b. Wingate, N.C., Sept. 11, 1929; s. Craven Cullom and Virginia Neulin (Currie) B.; m. Jane Russell Burris, June 19, 1955; children: Christa Cullom, David Allen. AA, Wingate Coll., 1949; BS, Wake Forest U., 1951; BDiv, Southeastern Bapt. Sem., Wake Forest, N.C., 1958; MA, Duke U., 1959, PhD, 1964. Prof. history and govt. Gardner-Webb Coll., Boiling Springs, N.C., 1958-66; prof. history, govt. and interdisciplinary studies St. Andrews Presbyn. Coll., Laurinburg, N.C., 1966-69; v.p., dean of coll., prof. history and politics Meredith Coll., Raleigh, N.C., 1969-98, ret., 1998, acting pres., 1971. Contbr. articles to profl. jours. Precinct ofcr. State Conv. del., N.C. Dem. Party, 1969, 71; pres., dir. Tammy Lynn Found./Retarded Children, Raleigh, 1980—. Lt. USNR, 1951-55, Italy. Recipient Disting. Alumni award Wingate Coll., 1983, Fulbright Study Trip, U.S. Govt., Pakistan, 1973. Mem. Civitan Internat. (v.p. bd. dirs. 1970—), Lions Club (editor 1965), Masons. Baptist. Avocations: choral singing, tennis, racquetball, golf, sailing. Home: 1322 Duplin Rd Raleigh NC 27607-3721 Office: Meredith Coll 3800 Hillsborough St Raleigh NC 27607-5237

BURRIS, FRANCES WHITE, retired state official; b. Cuero, Tex., Oct. 18, 1933; d. Marian Cecil and Dorothy Christine (Pruetz) White; m. Berlie Burris Jr, Mar. 8, 1958 (div. 1982); children: William Alan, Joel Maurice. BA, Mary Hardin Baylor Coll., Belton, Tex., 1955; M in Eng., Trinity U., San Antonio, 1959. Cert. tchr., Tex. Elem. tchr. East and Mt. Houston Independent Sch. Dist., 1956, Edgewood Ind. Sch. Dist., San Antonio, 1956-57, 58-59; tchr. Edna (Tex.) Ind. Sch. Dist., 1957-58; elem. tchr. Northside Ind. Sch. Dist., San Antonio, 1960-62, Southside Schs., San Antonio, 1962-63; mgr. Michael's Dept. Store, Houston, 1980-81; eligibility worker Tex. Dept. Human Resources, Houston, 1981-99; ret., 1999. Mem. Meridith Manor Civic Club, Houston, 1966-78, Settlers Valley Civic Club, Katy, Tex., 1979-81, Catalina North Civic Club, Alief, Tex., 1992—. Mem. Tex. State Employees Union (exec. bd. 1984—, del. gen. assembly 1984-98, lobbyist 1985—), Bridge Club (Houston). Democrat. Baptist. Avocations: creative writing, stitchery, reading, swimming.

BURRIS, HARRIET LOUISE, emergency physician; b. Alexandria Bay, N.Y., Apr. 7, 1949; d. Robert Barker and Harriet Louise (Dorman) Burtch; m. John Samuel Burris Jr., Nov. 30, 1974; children: Elizabeth Jane, Katherine Ann. SB, MIT, 1972; MD, SUNY, Syracuse, 1976. Diplomate Am. Bd. Family Practice, Am. Bd. Emergency Medicine, Nat. Bd. Med. Examiners; cert. added qualification in geriatrics. Resident in family practice St. Joseph's Hosp. Health Ctr., Syracuse, 1976-79; pvt. practice Cazenovia, N.Y., 1979-81; staff MD emergency dept. Middlesex Hosp., Middletown, Conn., 1982-83; staff MD family practice Cmty. Health Care Plan, Wallingford, Conn., 1983-84; staff MD emergency dept. Middlesex Med. Ctr.-Shoreline divsn. Middlesex Hosp., Essex, Conn., 1984—, acting med. dir., 1994. Fellow Am. Acad. Family Physicians, Am. Coll. Emergency Physicians; mem. Handweavers Guild Conn. (libr.). Avocations: knitting, handweaving, needle arts. Home: 422 Westland Ave Cheshire CT 06410-3142 Office: Middlesex Med Ctr-Shoreline 260 Westbrook Rd Essex CT 06426-1513

BURRIS, JAMES FREDERICK, federal research administrator, educator; b. Mauston, Wis., Apr. 15, 1947; s. James Duane and Margaret Katherine (Jones) B.; m. Christine Tuve, July 3, 1971; 1 child, Cameron William Tuve. AB, Brown U., 1970, ScB, 1970; MD, Columbia U., 1974. Diplomate Am. Bd. Internal Medicine, Subspecialty Bd. Geriatrics, Am. Bd. Clin. Pharmacology. Intern Roosevelt Hosp., N.Y.C., 1974-75; resident in internal medicine Georgetown U. Med. Ctr., Washington, 1977-79; fellow in hypertension VA Med. Ctr., Washington, 1979-81; asst. prof. Sch. Medicine, Georgetown U., Washington, 1981-86, assoc. prof., 1986-91, coord. MD/PhD program, 1988-94, prof., 1991-97; clin. prof., 1997—; asst. dean Sch. Medicine, Georgetown U., Washington, 1987-90; assoc. dean Sch. Medicine Georgetown U., 1990-97, dir. continuing profl. edn., 1994-97; dep. chief R&D officer Vets. Health Adminstrn., U.S. Dept. Vets Affairs, Washington, 1997—; bd. dirs. Inst. for Clin. Rsch., Washington, 1989-92; bd. regents Am. Bd. Clin. Pharmacology, 1992-98, rsch. adminstr. cert. coun.; rsch. assoc. hypertension unit VA Med. Ctr., Washington, 1981-92; vis. investigator Centre Hospitalier, U. Vaudois, Lausanne, Switzerland, 1982-83; dir. clin. rsch. Cardiovasc. Ctr. No. Va., Falls Church, 1988-92. Mem. editl. bd. Jour. Clin. Pharmacology, Jour. Am. Geriat. Soc., Clin. Pharmacology and Therapeutics; contbr. over 200 articles to profl. jours. Cubmaster Boy Scouts Am., 1995-98, asst. scoutmaster, 1998—. Lt. comdr. USPHS, 1975-77. Recipient svc. award ARC, 1970, outstanding svc. citation DAV, 1987, meritorious svc. award Am. Heart Assn., 1994, Cubmasters award Boy Scouts Am., 1998, James E. West award 1997; commd. officer student tng. and extern program scholar USPHS, 1973-74; rsch. fellow Found. for Rsch. of Cardiovascular Diseases, Lausanne, 1983. Fellow ACP, Am. Geriatrics Soc., Am. Coll. Preventive Medicine, Am. Coll. Clin. Pharmacology (bd. regents 1990-95, 98—, Disting. Svc. award 1992), Am. Coll. Cardiology; mem. AMA (physician's recognition award 1982, 85, 88, 91, 94, 97), Am. Heart Assn. (fellow couns. on high blood pressure rsch., circulation, epidemiology, clin. cardiology, bd. dirs. Nation's Capital affiliate 1994-97, chmn. rsch. peer rev. com. 1992-94, rsch. com. 1994-96, v.p. 1995-96), Sigma Xi. Achievements include education and research in hypertension, hyperlipidemia, preventive cardiology and clinical pharmacology; grants and contracts management and regulatory affairs and technology transfer administration; direction of continuing professional education programs; federal research policy development and program implementation. Office: Vets Health Adminstrn (12A) Dept VA 810 Vermont Ave NW Rm 775 Washington DC 20420-0001

BURRIS, JOHN EDWARD, biologist, educator, administrator; b. Feb. 1, 1949; s. Robert Harza and Katherine (Brusse) B.; m. Sally Ann Sandermann, Dec. 21, 1974; children: Jennifer, Margaret, Mary. AB, Harvard U., 1971; postgrad., U. Wis., 1971-72; PhD, U. Calif., San Diego, 1976. Asst. prof. biology Pa. State U., University Park, 1976-83, assoc. prof., 1983-85, adj. assoc. prof., 1985-89, adj. prof., 1989—; dir. bd. biology NRC, Washington, 1984-89, exec. dir. Commn. Life Scis., 1988-92, mem., 1993-97; dir., CEO Marine Biology Lab., Woods Hole, Mass., 1992—; pres.-elect Am. Inst. Biol. Scis., 1995, pres., 1996; chmn. adv. com. student sci. enrichment program Burroughs Wellcome Fund, 1995—; mem. NASA Life and Microgravity Scis. and Applications Adv. Com., 1997—; bd. trustees Krasnow Inst., 1999—. Mem. Consiglio Sci., Naples Stazione Zoologica, Phi Beta Kappa. Home: 65 Clowes Dr Falmouth MA 02540-2333 Office: 7 MBL St Woods Hole MA 02543

BURRIS, JOSEPH STEPHEN, agronomy educator; b. Cleve., Apr. 18, 1942; s. Charles Richard and Catherine T. (Pravica) B.; children: Jeffery S., John C., Jennifer K., Jason R. B.S., Iowa State U., 1964; M.S., Va. Poly. Inst., 1965, Ph.D., 1967. Research asst., Nat. Def. fellow Va. Poly. Inst., Blacksburg, 1964-67, dir. tobacco analysis lab., 1967; asst. prof. Iowa State U., Ames, 1968-72, assoc. prof., 1972-76, prof. agronomy and seed sci., 1976-99, prof. emeritus, 1999—; pres. Burris Cons., Ames, 1999—; internat. cons. on seed prodn. FAO/UN Devel. Program, World Bank. Contbr. articles to profl. publs. Pres. PTA, Ames, 1980-81. Mem. Am. Soc. Agronomy, Crop Sci. Soc. Am. (Seed Sci. award 1998), Assn. Ofcl. Seed Analysts. Presbyterian. Office: Burris Cons 1707 Burnett Ave Ames IA 50010

BURRIS, KENNETH WAYNE, biologist, educator; b. Salisbury, N.C., Nov. 22, 1941; s. Ira J.B. and Dorothy Virginia (Rodgers) B.; m. Peggy Rogister Whitt, June 7, 1964; children: Kenneth Wayne Jr., Susan M. BS, High Point U., 1964; MA, East Carolina U., 1968; postgrad., N.C. State U., 1973-75. Specialist environ. health Moore County Health Dept., Carthage, N.C., 1964-65; instr. biology Mitchell Coll., Statesville, N.C., 1967-68; assoc. prof. biology Louisburg (N.C.) Coll., 1968-75; prof. biology Sandhills C.C., Pinehurst, N.C., 1975—. Author: Laboratory Exercises for Microbiology, 1985; co-author: Diseases of Fish, 1974; contbr. articles to profl. jours. Grantee NSF, 1969, 71. Mem. AAUP, Human Anatomy and Physiology Soc., Phi Theta Kappa (Horizon award 1995, advisor 1991—). Democrat. Avocations: sailing, sailboat racing, gardening. Home: 530 North Seven Lakes NC 27376 Office: Sandhills Cmty Coll 2200 Airport Rd Pinehurst NC 28374-8283

BURRIS, ROBERT HARZA, biochemist, educator; b. Brookings, S.D., Apr. 13, 1914; s. Edward T. and Mable C. (Harza) B.; m. Katherine Irene Brusse, Sept. 12, 1945; children: Jean Carol, John Edward, Ellen Louise. B.S., S.D. State Coll., 1936, D.Sc., 1966; M.S., U. Wis., 1938, Ph.D., 1940. NRC fellow Columbia U., 1940-41; faculty U. Wis., Madison, 1941—; prof. U. Wis., 1951-84; chmn. biochemistry Coll. Agr., 1958-70, W.H. Peterson prof. biochemistry, 1976-84, prof. emeritus, 1984—. Recipient Charles Thom award Soc. Indsl. Microbiology, 1977; Nat. Medal of Sci., 1980; Carty award Nat. Acad. Scis., 1984; Wolf award in Agr., 1985; Guggenheim fellow Cambridge U., 1954. Mem. Am. Chem. Soc. (Spencer award 1990), Am. Soc. Biochemistry and Molecular Biology, Am. Philos. Soc., Am. Soc. Plant Physiologists (Stephen Hales award 1968, Charles Reid Barnes award 1977, pres. 1960), Biochem. Soc., AAAS, Am. Soc. Microbiology, NAS, Indian Nat. Sci. Acad. (fgn. assoc.). Home: 1015 University Bay Dr Madison WI 53705-2250

BURRIS, VALLON LEON, JR., sociologist, educator; b. Beeville, Tex., May 8, 1947; s. Vallon Leon, Sr. and Phyllis Bertha (Tatro) B.; m. Beverly Lynn Hudeck, Mar. 8, 1969 (div. 1978). BA, Rice Univ., 1969; MA, Princeton Univ., 1972, PhD, 1976. Asst. prof. CUNY, N.Y.C., 1976-77; from asst. prof. to prof. Univ. Oreg., Eugene, 1977-92, prof., 1992—. Editor Critical Sociology, 1991—; assoc. editor Social Sci. Quar., 1983-93, Am. Sociol. Rev. 1992-95; contbr. over 30 articles to profl. jours. Mem. Am. Sociol. Assn., Phi Beta Kappa. Office: U Oreg Dept Sociology Eugene OR 97403

BURRIS-SCHNUR, CATHERINE, medical/surgical nurse, educator, minister, pastoral psychologist; b. Ft. Lee, Va., Nov. 22, 1961; d. Charlie Franklin and Geneva Mae (Melton) B. ADN, Elizabethtown Community Coll., 1981; BSN, U. Ky., 1984; postgrad., So. Bapt. Theol. Sem., Louisville, 1986-90; MDiv, Garrett Evang. Theol. Sem., Evanston, Ill., 1994. RN, Ill.; ordained to ministry Am. Bapt. Ch., 1997. Staff nurse Cen. Bapt. Hosp., Lexington, Ky.; rehab. specialist Intacorp, Louisville; nurse mgr. St. Anthony Med. Ctr., Louisville, nurse mgr., med.-surg. educator, continuing edn. adminstr., dir. edn. svcs., 1991-92; clin. fellow pastoral psychotherapy tng. program Ctr. for Religion and Psychotherapy, Chgo., 1992-94; assoc. dir. admissions Garrett Evang. Theol. Sem., 1995—; pastoral psychotherapist The Ctr. for Religion and Psychotherapy, Chgo., 1997—. Recipient various nursing scholarships; named to Outstanding Young Women of Am., 1991. Mem. ANA, NAFE.

BURROUGHS, CHARLES EDWARD, lawyer; b. Milw., June 9, 1939; s. Edward Albert and Ann Monica (Bussman) B.; m. Kathleen Walton, Jan. 30, 1965; children—James, Michael, Lauri, Stephanie. B.S., U. Wis.-Madison, 1962, LL.B., 1965; LL.M., George Washington U., 1968. Bar: Wis. 1965, U.S. Dist. Ct. (ea. and we. dists.) Wis. 1965, U.S. Ct. Clms. 1967, U.S. Ct. Mil. Apls. 1967, U.S. Ct. Apls. (7th cir.) 1969, U.S. Supreme Ct. 1968. Assoc., Porter & Porter, Milw., 1969-71, Purtell, Purcell, Wilmot & Burroughs, 1971-86; ptnr. VonBriesen & Purtell, 1986-91, Hinshaw & Culbertson, Milw. Served to capt. U.S. Army, 1965-69. Mem. ABA, AHLA, HFMA, State Bar Wis. (pres. health law sect.). Roman Catholic. Club: Milw. Athletic. Home: 10937 N Hedgewood Ln Mequon WI 53092-4907

BURROUGHS, GARY L., city official; b. Independence, Kans., Apr. 9, 1943. Auditor City of Long Beach, 1992—. Office: Office of City Auditor Civic Center Plz 333 W Ocean Blvd Fl 8 Long Beach CA 90802-4604*

BURROUGHS, JACK EUGENE, dentist, management consultant; b. Harlingen, Tex., Nov. 24, 1946; s. Jack Eugene and Virginia (Ayoub) B.; children by previous marriage: Brian A., Brad A.; m. Laura Burroughs; children: Kyle, Tiffany. BS, U. Tex., Arlington, 1969; DDS, U. Tex. Dental Br., Houston, 1973. Practice dentistry Houston, 1973—; seminar leader, cons. Quest, Dallas, 1983—. Contbr. articles to profl. jours. Recipient Spkr. awards Aspen Med.-Dental Conf., 1982, 83, 84, N.Am. Med.-Dental Assn., 1984, Am. Internat. Seminars, 1984. Fellow Acad. Gen. Dentistry; mem. ADA, Tex. Dental Assn., Houston Dist. Dental Soc., Houston N.W. C. of C. (bd. dirs.), Exchange Club (bd. dirs.), Toastmasters (officer). Republican. Mem. Christian Ch. Office: 17200 Red Oak Dr Houston TX 77090-2642

BURROUGHS, PAMELA GAYLE, information systems specialist; b. Dayton, Ohio, July 31, 1957; d. Dale Davis and Anita Madge (Allen) Hallsted; m. Donald W. Burroughs, Oct. 7, 1978; children: Kristin Rene, Kevin Wayne. Diploma, Jewish Hosp. Sch. Nursing, 1977. RN, Ohio. Staff nurse Epp Meml. Hosp., Cin., 1977-78; relief charge nurse ICU, Clermont Mercy Hosp., Batavia, Ohio, 1978-90, supr. patient care, 1990-95, coord. nursing edn., 1991-92, staff nurse ICU, 1993-94, edn. instr., 1992-94, info. svcs. nursing coord., 1994-96, clin. info. sys. specialist, 1996—.

BURROW, DAVID MICHAEL, mathematics educator, academic administrator; b. Moline, Ill., Oct. 11, 1962; s. George Irving and Elizabeth Zane (Miller) B. BA with high honors, No. Iowa U., 1983; MEd with highest honors, So. Miss. U., 1992; TAG Cert., Morningside Coll., 1995. Cert. tchr., Iowa. Tchr., broadcasting sponsor, speech dir., student coun. moderator, quiz bowl coach Bishop Garrigan H.S., Algona, Iowa, 1983—; gifted/talented coord., 1993—; instr. Iowa Lakes C.C., Emmetsburg, 1993—; evaluator North Ctrl. Assn. Schs., Iowa City, 1990—; pvt. tutor, 1990—. Bd. dirs. First Congl. Ch., Algona, 1988—. Finalist Iowa Tchr. of Yr., 1993. Mem. Math. Assn. Am., Nat. Coun. Tchrs. Math., Iowa Coun. Tchrs. Math., Nat. Cath. Edn. Assn., Nat. Fedn. Interscholastic Activities, Phi Delta Kappa. Democrat. Avocations: internet, travel, reading, hiking, music. Office: Garrigan High Sch 1224 N Mccoy St Algona IA 50511-1299

BURROW, GERARD NOEL, physician, educator; b. Boston, Jan. 9, 1933; s. William and Noelle Elvira (Money) B.; m. Ann Huntington Rademacher, June 22, 1956; children: Peter Noel, Elisabeth Huntington, Sarah Rogers. BA, Brown U., 1954; MD, Yale U., 1958. Diplomate Am. Bd. Internal Medicine. Resident in internal medicine Yale-New Haven Med. Ctr., 1965-66; from asst. prof. to prof. Yale U. Sch. Medicine, New Haven,

1966-76; prof. dept. medicine U. Toronto, Ont., Can., 1976-81, Sir John and Lady Eaton prof. medicine, 1981-88, chmn. dept., 1981-88; physician-in-chief Toronto Gen. Hosp., 1981-88; vice-chancellor for health scis., dean U. Calif. Sch. Medicine, San Diego, 1988-92; prof. dept. medicine U. Calif., San Diego, 1988-92; dean Yale U. Sch. Medicine, New Haven, 1992-97; prof. dept. medicine Yale U., New Haven, 1992-97, David Paige Smith prof. medicine, 1997—. Author: The Thyroid Gland in Pregnancy, 1972; editor: (with Ferris) Medical Complications During Pregnancy, 1975, 82, 88, 94, 99 (with Duffy). Bd. dirs. Nat. Med. Fellowships, Sea Rsch. Found., Gaylord Hosp. Fellow ACP, Royal Coll. Physicians (Can.); mem. Am. Soc. Clin. Investigation, Assn. Am. Physicians, Am. Thyroid Assn. (pres. 1986), Inst. Medicine of NAS. Office: Yale U Sch Medicine 333 Cedar St New Haven CT 06510-3289

BURROW, PAUL IRVING, educator; b. Iowa City, Iowa, Aug. 16, 1955; s. George Irving and Elizabeth Zane (Miller) B.; m. Nancy Kay Rader, Sept. 8, 1979; children: Rachel, Timothy. BA, Drake U., 1976, MA, 1981. Tchr. Spanish, social studies Adair (Iowa) -Casey Schs., 1977-78, Oskaloosa (Iowa) Sr. H.S., 1978—. Mem. exec. bd. Crisis Intervention Svcs., Oskaloosa, 1996—; mem. coun. Boy Scouts Am., Oskaloosa, 1988-95. Mem. ACTFL, Iowa Fgn. Lang. Assn. (pres. 1985-87), Iowa State Edn. Assn. (mem. exec. bd. 1997—), Oskaloosa Edn. Assn. (spokesperson 1985-98, Tchr of Yr. 1992). Democrat. Methodist. Avocations: computers, genealogy, camping, travel. Home: 2212 Lynndale Rd Oskaloosa IA 52577-9129

BURROW, WILLIAM HOLLIS, II, dermatologist; b. Walla Walla, Wash., Nov. 19, 1945; s. William Hollis and Patricia (Hoke) B.; m. Lafon Walcott, Jan. 29, 1967; children: William H. III, Kristina, Jamey. BA in Chemistry, Vanderbilt U., 1967; MD, U. Miss., 1973. Bd. cert. in dermatology. Dermatology resident U. Ala., Birmingham, 1974-77; pvt. practice Jackson, Miss., 1977—; clin. assoc. prof. medicine U. Miss. Med. Ctr., Jackson, 1977—. V.p. Young Life, Jackson, 1990, Downtown YMCA Bd., Jackson, 1991. Fellow AMA, Am. Acad. Dermatology, So. Med. Assn.; mem. Alpha Omega Alpha. Avocations: golf, gardening, being a grandfather. Office: # 303 850 E River Pl Jackson MS 39202-3443

BURROWS, BENJAMIN, retired physician, educator; b. N.Y.C., Dec. 16, 1927; s. Samuel and Theresa Helen (Handelsman) B.; m. Nancy Kreiter, June 14, 1949; children—Jan C., Susan K., Lynn A., Steven M. MD, Johns Hopkins, 1949. Intern Johns Hopkins Hosp., 1949-50; resident King County Hosp., Seattle, 1950-51; resident U. Chgo., 1953-55, instr. to asso. prof. medicine, 1955-68; prof. internal medicine U. Ariz. Coll. Medicine, Tucson, 1968—, dir. Respiratory Sci. Ctr., 1987-96, Chalfant-Moore prof. of medicine, 1987-96, ret., emeritus prof. medicine, 1996; cons. Tucson VA Hosp.; dir. Respiratory Scis. Ctr., Nat. Heart Lung and Blood Inst. Specialized Ctr. Research in Pulmonary Diseases, U. Ariz. Coll. Medicine, 1971-95. Mem. editl. bd. Am. Rev. Respiratory Diseases, 1967-71, 74-80, Chest, 1971-76, Annals Internal Medicine, 1973-76, Archives of Environ. Health, 1976-93, Jour. of allergy and clin. Immunology, 1992-95; contbr. articles to profl. jours., chpts. to books. Served to capt. USAF, 1951-53. Rsch. grantee USPHS, 1958-95. Fellow Am. Coll. Chest Physicians (regent dist. 11 1970-75), A.C.P.; mem. Assn. Am. Physicians, Am. Soc. Clin. Investigation (emeritus), Am. Physiol. Soc. Home: 6840 N Table Mountain Rd Tucson AZ 85718-1329

BURROWS, BRIAN WILLIAM, research and development manufacturing executive; b. Burnie, Tasmania, Australia, Nov. 15, 1939; came to U.S., 1966; s. William Henry and Jean Elizabeth (Ling) B.; 1 child, Karin; m. Penny Nathan Kahan, 1998. BSc, U. Tasmania, 1960, BSc with honors, 1962; PhD, Southampton U., 1966. Staff scientist Tyco Labs., Inc., Waltham, Mass., 1966-68; lectr. Macquarie U., Sydney, Australia, 1969-71; chef de sect. Battelle-Geneva, Switzerland, 1971-75; group leader Inco, Ltd., Mississauga, Ont., Can., 1976-77; program mgr., lab. dir. Gould, Inc., Rolling Meadows, Ill., 1977-86; v.p. rsch. and tech. USG Corp., Chgo., 1986—; co. rep., Indsl. Rsch. Inst., Washington. Contbr. articles to tech. jours.; patentee in field. Fellow AAAS; mem. IEEE, Am. Chem. Soc., Materials Rsch. Soc., Union League Club. Home: 927 Longmeadow Ct Barrington IL 60010-9391 Office: USG Rsch Ctr 700 N Us Highway 45 Libertyville IL 60048-1268

BURROWS, DONALD ALBERT, college dean, artist, painter,; b. Chgo., June 26, 1937; s. Charles Fredrick and Bertha Lillian (Olesen) B.; m. Philomena Durkin, Mar. 3, 1962 (div. 1983); children: Jennifer Maria, Charles Fredrick, Quentin Connor; m. Charlyn Butterfield, Apr. 2, 1995. BFA, Sch. of the Art Inst. of Chgo., 1961, MFA, 1963. Dir. Mobile (Ala.) Art Mus., 1964-66, Ft. Worth Mus., 1966-67, Ctr. for Creative Studies, Detroit, 1967-68; prof. humanities City Colls. of Chgo., 1968-83; assoc. dean Harrington Inst., Chgo., 1974-84; acad. dean Ray Coll. of Design, Chgo., 1986-93; prin. artist, designer Misaine, Inc., Torrance, Calif., 1990—; pres., CEO ChyCogo and Co., Ltd., Willowbrook, Ill., 1987—. One-man shows include Hansen Gallery, Chgo., Sept.-Oct. 1986, Elmhurst (Ill.) Coll., Mar.-Apr., 1986, Galleria Renata, Chgo., Mar.-Apr. 1988. Mem. Am. Soc. Interior Designers, Alumni Assn. Sch. of Art Inst. Chgo., Alumni Assn. U. Chgo., Art Inst. Chgo. (Ryerson Fgn. Traveling fellow, 1961-63). Democrat. Home and Studio: 717 Maplewood Ct Unit D Hinsdale IL 60521-7539

BURROWS, E. MICHAEL, art educator, artist; b. Denver, Oct. 18, 1952; s. Edwin Harry and Beverly Mae (Hopley) B.; m. Leilani Haubner, Nov. 1977 (div. Mar. 1983); children: Ian, Leila; m. Jann Bell Simpson, Oct. 15, 1983; children: Kristan, Erika. BFA, U. Colo., Denver, 1974, postgrad., 1985-86; MFA, U. Colo., Boulder, 1977. Tchr. U. Colo., Boulder, 1976-77; artist Boulder Art Assn., 1978-79; picture framer Montgomery House, Boulder, 1979-81; tchr. Kent Denver Sch., Englewood, Colo., 1981-97; substitute tchr. U. Colo., Denver, 1981-97; sec. Media Svcs. Inc., Denver, 1989—; instr. No. N.Mex. C.C. Exhibited in shows at Greenwood Village, 1988-91, Arvada Ctr., Aspen Mus., 1989, Lake Oswego Festival of Arts, 1994, Stable Gallery, Taos, N.Mex., 1996. Recipient 2d prize Boulder Art Assn., 1975, 1st pl., Jurors Choice award Colo. Inst. Art, 1989, Merit award Northwestern Colo. Art Mus., 1995, 2d prize, 1996. Mem. Assn. Colo. Ind. Schs., Am. Numis. Assn., Colored Pencil Soc., Spark Gallery (assoc.; historian). Avocation: numismatics.

BURROWS, EDWIN GLADDING, retired broadcaster, writer, poet; b. Dallas, July 23, 1917; s. Millar and Irene (Gladding) B.; m. Gwenyth Lemon, 1940 (div. 1971); children: Edwin Gwynne, Daniel William, David John; m. Beth Elpern, Dec. 7, 1973. BA, Yale U., 1938; MA, U. Mich., 1940. Program dir. Sta. WWJ-FM, Detroit, 1940-43, Sta. WPAG, Ann Arbor, Mich., 1946-48; program dir., mgr. Stas. WUOM-WVGR, U. Mich., Ann Arbor, 1948-70, exec. prodr., 1973-82; dir. Nat. Ctr. for Audio Experimentation, U. Wis., Madison, 1970-73; ret., 1982; condr. poetry readings through Mich., 1965-82, State of Wash., 1986—; helped charter radio divsn. Nat. Ednl. Radio of Nat. Assn. Ednl. Broadcasters, former region III dir., chmn. bd., 1965; also chmn. network adv. com. and mem. bd. Nat. Assn. Ednl. Broadcasters; a lobbyist for inclusion of radio in Pub. Broadcasting Act of 1967. Author: (poetry) The Arctic Tern and Other Poems, 1957, Man Fishing, 1970, Kiva, 1976, Properties: A Play for Voices, 1979, The House of August, 1985, (chapbooks) The Crossings, 1976, On the Road to Bailey's, 1979, Handsigns for Rain, 1989, The Birds Under the Earth, 1997; contbr. poetry to anthologies, including Anthology of Magazine Verse, 1984, A Centennial Sampler of Edmonds Writing, 1989, ORL 50th Anniversary Anthology, 1993, The Age of Koestler: Practices of the Wind, 1994, The Sumac Reader, 1997, Wild Song: Poems of the Natural World, 1998; contbr. poems to over 150 jours., including Atlantic Monthly, Ascent, Am. Poetry, Black Warrior, Blue Mesa, Chariton, Cream City, Gettysburg, Hawaii, Mass., Mich. Quar., Paris, Seattle, and Va. Quar. revs., Confluence, Epoch, Fine Madness, Poetry, Zone 3; Gotham: History of New York City, to 1898., 1999. Lt. USN, 1943-46. Recipient Ohio State awards, 1953, 54, 55, 56, 71, 74, Borestone Mountain poetry award, 1964, 1st ann. poetry award Ascent, 1987; fellow Yaddo Found., 1963, 66; donated his papers to U. Md. at College Park Librs., 1991; Pulitzer Prize, History, 1999.

BURROWS, EMILY ANN, nurse; b. Spokane, Wash., June 30, 1960; d. James Aaron and Agnes Cecilia (Wilke) McKenzie; m. Carl Douglas Burrows, Feb. 7, 1981; children: Cassandra Lynn, Timothy Carl. ADN, Amarillo Coll., 1982. RN, Tex.; cert. neonatal cardiac life support. Staff nurse Upjohn Co., Amarillo, Tex., 1986-87, High Plains Bapt. Hosp., Amarillo, 1987-88; nurse infant care specialist Tex. Tech U Health Sci. Ctr., Amarillo, 1988-90; staff nurse N.W. Tex. Hosp., Amarillo, 1982-96, Bapt. St. Anthonies, Amarillo, 1997—. Roman Catholic. Avocations: reading, walking, doll collecting. Home: 1000 Mulberry Trl Amarillo TX 79124-3760

BURROWS, HENRY PETER, III, secondary education educator; b. Selma, Ala., Jan. 26, 1944; s. Henry Peter Jr. and Josepine (Porter) B.; m. Dinah Shore, Aug. 26, 1983. BA in English, U. Del., 1967; BS in Edn., Auburn U., Montgomery, Ala., 1996; MA in History, U. Ala., 1986. Cert. tchr., Ala.; cert. airline trasnport pilot, command pilot. Commd. 2d lt. USAF, 1967, advanced through grades to lt. col., 1986; fighter pilot/staff officer USAF, worldwide, 1967-88; ret. USAF, 1988; airline pilot Pan Am. World Airways, Miami, Fla., 1989-91; tchr. math. Autauga County Bd. Edn., Prattville, Ala., 1996—. Contbr. articles and short stories to mags.; mem. editl. bd. Ala. Jour. Math., Montgomery, 1996—. Decorated DFC, Air medal; Chancellor's scholar Auburn U., 1996. Mem. NEA, Ala. Edn. Assn., Math. Assn. Am., Phi Kappa Phi, Kappa Delta Pi, Phi Alpha Theta. Avocations: coin collecting, photography, jogging, reading. Home: 1671 Rambling Brook Ln Prattville AL 36066-3601 Office: Prattville Jr HS 1135 N Chestnut St Prattville AL 36067

BURROWS, JAMES, television and motion picture director, producer; b. L.A., Dec. 30, 1940; s. Abe Burrows. BA, Oberlin Coll.; MFA, Yale U. Off-Broadway prodns.: dir. (motion picture) Partners, 1982, (TV film) More Than Friends, 1978, (TV series episodes) Mary Tyler Moore Show, Bob Newhart, Taxi, Lou Grant, Dear John, Night Court (pilot), Wings (pilot), Roc (pilot), Frasier (pilot), Friends (pilot), Newsradio (pilot), Third Rock from the Sun (pilot), Caroline in the City (pilot); co-creator, co-exec. producer, dir. (TV series) Cheers. Recipient Dirs. Guild Am. award for comedy direction, 1984, 91, 94, Emmy awards NATAS for dir. in comedy series Taxi, 1979-80, 81-82 seasons, Cheers, 1982-83, 90-91 seasons; Emmy award as co-producer Cheers, 1982-83, 83-84, 89-90, 90-91 seasons; Emmy award as director of a Comedy Series for Fraiser, 1994. Office: care Paramount TV Prodns 5555 Melrose Ave Los Angeles CA 90038-3112

BURROWS, JOHN EDWARD, communications company executive; b. Englewood, N.J., Aug. 6, 1950; s. Laurence McCallum and Pauline Hannah (McClave) B. BA in Journalism, Rutgers U., 1972. From staff asst. to account exec. Ogilvy & Mather Inc., N.Y.C., 1977-80; mgr. sales devel. CBS Radio Spot Sales, N.Y.C., 1980-81; dist. dir. affiliate relations CBS Radio Network, N.Y.C., 1981-84, dir. affiliate relations, 1984-86, v.p. affiliate relations, 1986-87; v.p. news and sports affiliate relations CBS Radio Networks, N.Y.C., 1987-89; broadcast cons. Hackensack, N.J., 1989-91; broadcast cons., classical piano instr. Norfolk, Conn., 1991—. Author: A Country Heart, 1983. Episcopalian. Avocations: golf, writing, cross-country skiing, genealogy. Home: PO Box 623 10 Laurel Ln Norfolk CT 06058-1135

BURROWS, MICHAEL DONALD, lawyer; b. Oak Park, Ill., May 23, 1944; s. Milford Denton and Helen Jean (Spitali) B.; m. Sandi Miller, Feb. 6, 1982; 1 child, Matthew Denton. BA, Williams Coll., 1967; JD, N.Y. Law Sch., 1973. Bar: N.Y. 1974, U.S. Dist. Ct. (ea. and so. dists.) N.Y. 1974, U.S. Ct. Appeals (2d cir.) 1978, U.S. Supreme Ct. 1981. Assoc. Baker & McKenzie, N.Y.C., 1973-80, ptnr., 1980-95, of counsel, 1995-99, mem. internat. exec. com., 1986-88; of counsel Winston & Strawn, N.Y.C., 1999—. Co-author: The Practice of International Litigation, 1992; co-author monthly column N.Y. Law Jour., 1981—. Served with USMC, 1968-70. Mem. ABA, Assn. Bar City N.Y. Office: Winston & Strawn 200 Park Ave New York NY 10166-4193

BURROWS, ROBERT PAUL, optometrist; b. Chehalis, Wash.; s. Fremont O. and Pauline A. (Kostick) B.; m. Marilyn Burrows. BS in Visual Sci., Pacific U., 1979, OD, 1981. Assoc. optometric physician L.E. Hedgen, O.D. & Assocs., Chehalis, 1981-86; ptnr. Lewis County Eye & Vision Assocs., Chehalis, 1986—. Mem. United Way, 1981—. PTU Rsch. grantee, 1980. Mem. Am. Optometric Assn. (charter contact lens sect., recognition award 1984-99), Wash. Assn. Optometric Physicians, Kiwanis (dir. 1984-85, 89-90), Twin City C. of C., Omega Epsilon Phi. Methodist. Office: 1179 S Market Blvd Chehalis WA 98532-3427

BURROWS, WILLIAM CLAUDE, aerospace executive, retired air force officer; b. Washington, Aug. 13, 1925; s. Paul Edmund and Lynna (Cary) B.; m. Patricia Dawn Huntley, Sept. 6, 1952; children: William Claude, Barry Huntley. Student, Cornell U., 1943-44; B.S., U.S. Mil. Acad., 1948; M.A., Columbia, 1953; student, Nat. War Coll., 1965-66. Commd. 2d lt. USAAF, 1948; advanced through grades to maj. gen. USAF; polit. sci. instr. U.S. Mil. Acad., 1953-56, asst. prof. geography, 1955-56; chief staff U.S. Taiwan Defense Command, Taipei, Taiwan, 1972-74; dep. dir. plans Hdqrs. USAF; mem. (Mil. Liaison Com. to AEC), Washington, 1974-76; dep. chief staff plans and programs NORAD/ADCOM, Colo., 1976-77; vice comdr. in chief ADCOM, Colo., 1977-79; ret., 1979; program mgr. Boeing Aerospace and Boeing Electronics Cos., Seattle, 1979-88; ret., 1988. Active Boy Scouts Am. Decorated D.S.M., Legion of Merit with 2 oak leaf clusters, Bronze Star, Air medal; Order of Cloud and Banner (Republic of China). Mem. Air Force Assn., Order Daedaleans. Home: 45 Greenhaven Circle East Lake Woodlands Oldsmar FL 34677

BURRUS, CHARLES ANDREW, JR., research physicist; b. Shelby, N.C., July 16, 1927; s. Charles Andrew and Velma (Martin) B.; m. Barbara Ione Dunlevy, May 4, 1957; children—Charles Andrew III, Barbara Jean, John Alan. B.S. cum laude in Physics, Davidson Coll., 1950; M.S. in Physics, Emory U., 1951; Ph.D. in Physics (Tex. Co. fellow, Shell Co. fellow), Duke U., 1955. Research assoc. dept. physics Duke U., Durham, N.C., 1954-55; mem. tech. staff AT&T Bell Labs., Holmdel, N.J., 1955-96; cons. Lucent Technologies Bell Labs., 1996—. Contbr. articles on millimeter and submillimeter-wave spectroscopy, techniques and semicondr. devices for lightwave communications, long-wavelength photoemitters and high-speed photodetectors, quantum-well devices, and optical fibers for lightwave communications to tech. jours. Served with USNR, 1945-46. Named Disting. Mem. Tech. Staff AT&T Bell Labs., 1982, fellow, 1988. Fellow AAAS, Am. Phys. Soc., IEEE (life), Optical Soc. Am. (David Richardson medal 1982). Methodist. Home: 62 Highland Ave Fair Haven NJ 07704-3641 Office: Lucent Technologies Bell Labs Crawford Hill Lab 791 Holmdel Keyport Rd Holmdel NJ 07733-0400

BURRUS, DANIEL ALLEN, research company executive, consultant; b. Portland, Oreg., Aug. 22, 1947; s. Joe Howard and Mary Kathleen (Boelk) B. BS, U. Wis., Oshkosh. Founder, pres. Burrus Media Prodns., Brookfield, Wis., 1978-80, Burrus Powered Gliders, Waukesha, Wis., 1980-82, Midwest Skynasaurs, Waukesha, 1982-84, Ultrasports Inc., Waukesha, 1982-84, Burrus Research Assocs., Inc., Milw., 1983—; cons. various corps., assns. and univs.; speaker in field. Author, editor Tech. Futures Newsletter, 1985-93, Technotrends Newsletter, 1993—; author: (audio tape learning sys.) The Future of Educatiaon, 1985, Beyond Megatrends, 1985, Teaching Creativity, 1986, Futureview: A Look Ahead, 1986, 88, Maximimizing your Creativity, 1989, Reengineering Yourself, 1995; co-author: The New Tools of Technology, 1990, Medical Advances, 1990, Environmental Solutions, 1990, Advances in Agriculture, 1990, Insights into Excellence, 1992, Technotrends, 1993; editor Applied Sci. Rev., 1985, 88; writer, dir., prodr. films Deja Vu, 1972, Phantasmagoria, 1972, The New Adventures of Superman, 1972; contbr. articles to profl. publs. Mem. AAAS, Internat. Personal Robot Assn. (founding), Internat. Ctr. Profl. Speaking (founding, bd. dirs.), Nat. Speakers Assn. (bd. dirs. 1991-96, cert. speaking profl., Profl. Speakers Hall of Fame 1992). Avocations: film making, photography, mountain climbing, flying, scuba diving. Office: Burrus Rsch Assocs PO Box 47 Hartland WI 53029-0047

BURRUS, JOHN N(EWELL), sociology educator; b. Gilmer, Tex., Jan. 23, 1920; s. Herman Clifford and Beulah (Blalack) B.; m. Sarah Gray. A.B., U. Miss., 1942; M.A., La. State U., 1944, Ph.D., 1950; postgrad., U. Minn., 1945-47, Vanderbilt U., 1947-48. Asst. prof. sociology U. Miss., Oxford, 1943-45; instr. Vanderbilt U., Nashville, 1947-48; rsch. assoc. rural sociology La. State U., Baton Rouge, 1948-50; asst. prof. U. Fla., Gainesville, 1950-51, U. So. Miss., Hattiesburg, 1951-52; asso. prof. U. So. Miss., 1952-57, prof., 1957-70, Disting. Univ. prof. sociology, 1970-83, Disting. Univ. prof. sociology emeritus, 1982—, chmn. dept. sociology, 1951-70, chmn. dept. sociology and anthropology, 1978-80; disting. univ. prof. emeritus Sociology and Anthropology, U. So. Miss., 1982—. Author: monographs Differential Mortality in Mississippi, 1951, (with M. King, H. Pedersen) Mississippi's People, 1955, Mississippi Life Tables, 1950-51, 54, Composition of Population of the Coastal Counties; books (with T.L. Smith) Social Problems, 1955, (with others) A Legacy of Knowledge: Sociological Contributions of T. Lynn Smith, 1980; contbr. chpts., articles and revs. to profl. jours, books including History of Mississippi (2 vols.), 1973, Ency. Brit., 15th edit. Bd. dirs. Hattiesburg Area Hist. Soc., 1971-73, S. Central Miss. chpt. A.R.C., 1961-71. Miss.-Ala. Sea Grant Consortium grantee, 1973-74. Mem. So. Sociol. Soc. (mem. exec. com. 1955-58), Rural Sociol. Soc., Population Reference Bur., Sigma Chi, Phi Kappa Phi, Alpha Kappa Delta, Pi Gamma Mu, Omicron Delta Kappa. Club: Kiwanian (dir. Hattiesburg 1975-76). Home: 1305 Windsor Dr Hattiesburg MS 39402-2852

BURRUS, ROBERT LEWIS, JR., lawyer; b. Richmond, Va., Sept. 16, 1934; s. Robert Lewis and Bessie (Hart) B.; m. Ann Williams, Aug. 1, 1964; children: David Curran, Peter Tandy, Lewis Graves. BA, U. Richmond, 1955; LLB, Duke U., 1958. Bar: Va. 1958. Assoc. McGuire, Woods, Battle & Boothe, LLP, Richmond, Va., 1959-63; ptnr. McGuire, Woods, Battle & Boothe, Richmond, Va., 1963—, chmn., 1990—; bd. dirs. CSX Corp., Richmond, Smithfield Foods, Norfolk, Va., Heilig-Meyers Co., Richmond, S&K Famous Brands, Richmond, O'Sullivan Corp., Winchester, Va., Riverton Investment Corp., Winchester, Capitol Cement Corp., Martinsburg, W.Va., Concepts Direct, Longmont, Colo.; sec. Genicom Corp., McLean; trustee Circuit City Found., Richmond. Trustee, rector U. Richmond; trustee Va. Mus. Fine Arts, Va. Hist. Soc.; bd. visitors Duke U. Law Sch., Durham, N.C.; past chmn. State Coun. Higher Edn. for Va.; past dir., chmn. exec. com. Richmond Renaissance; past bd. dirs. Richmond Children's Mus.; active Govs. Commn. Intercollegiate Athletics, 1991-92; past pres. St. Christopher's Sch. Found., Richmond. Fellow Am. Bar Found., Va. Bar Found.; mem. ABA, Va. Bar Assn. (chmn. corp. law com. 1975-77, chmn. bus. sect. 1976-77), Richmond Bar Assn., Commonwealth Club, Country Club Va., Bull and Bear Club, Forum Club, Omicron Delta Kappa. Episcopalian. Home: 220 Ampthill Rd Richmond VA 23226-2235 Office: McGuire Woods Battle & Boothe LLP One James Ctr Richmond VA 23219*

BURRUSS, TERRY GENE, architect; b. Little Rock, Dec. 30, 1950; s. Alvin Eugene and Fern (Pelton) B.; m. Merilyn Kloss, Dec. 20, 1981; children: Mamie Christine, Gracie Aline. BArch, BA, U. Ark., 1973. Registered architect, Ark. Intern architect firm Robinson and Wassell, Inc., Little Rock, 1973-75; practice architecture Evo-Tech Prodn., Little Rock, and I.D.E.A., Eureka Springs, Ark., 1976-78; architect Store Planning Assos., San Francisco, 1978; asso. Design 3, Architects, Little Rock, Ark., 1979; v.p., div. mgr. Mehlburger, Tanner, Renshaw and Assocs., Little Rock, 1980-84; v.p. Mehlburger, Tanner, Robinson & Assocs., 1984-87; pres. Terry Burruss, Architects, 1987—; instr. Hatha Yoga Community Edn. Program, 1976-77, St. Francis House, Little Rock, 1978, Parapsychology Ctr., 1978-79. Mem. Ark. Environ. Barriers Coun.; chmn. ministerial rels. Unity Ch. of Little Rock, 1986-87, pres. bd. dirs., 1987; pres. Montessori Children's Ctr. Parent Tchrs. Orgn., 1986-87; pres. Unity Ch., 1987, Ctrl. High Neighborhood Assn., 1989-90; chmn. Gov's. Mansion Area, 1998—. Mem. AIA (state chmn. 1981), U. Ark. Alumni Assn., Little Rock Jaycees (dir. 1981-83, sec. 1982-83), chmn. TV auction 1982). Alpha Phi Omega, Pi Kappa Alpha. Author: Flow Gently Sweet Alpha, 1972, Inflatables, An Alternative to the Deflated Classroom, 1973, Accessibility Guidelines for Meeting and Lodging Facilities, 1981, "Housing for the Developmental Disabled", 1986. Home: 12 Tallyho Ln Little Rock AR 72227-2416 Office: 1202 Main St Ste 230 Little Rock AR 72202-5057

BURSEY, MAURICE M., chemistry educator; b. Balt., July 27, 1939; s. Reginald Price and Edna Frances (Moyer) B.; m. Joan Marie Tesarek, Dec. 28, 1970; children—John Thomas Kieran, Sara Helen Moyer. BA, Johns Hopkins U., 1959, MA, 1960, PhD, 1963. Lectr. Johns Hopkins U., Balt., 1963-64; asst. prof. Purdue U., Lafayette, Ind., 1964-66; asst. prof. chemistry U. N.C., Chapel Hill, 1966-69, assoc. prof., 1969-74, prof., 1974-96, prof. emeritus, 1996—. Editor Mass Spectrometry Revs., 1990-93; contbr. articles to profl. jours. Recipient various research grants. Fellow Am. Inst. Chemists, Royal Soc. Chemistry (assoc.); mem. Am. Chem. Soc. (bd. dirs. 1993—), Am. Soc. Mass Spectrometry, Alpha Chi Sigma (Grand Master Alchemist nat. pres. 1986-88). Democrat. Roman Catholic. Home: 101 Longwood Pl Chapel Hill NC 27514-9584 Office: U NC Dept Chemistry CB#3290 Chapel Hill NC 27599-3290

BURSHTAN, JOHN WILLIS, television producer; b. Cedar Rapids, Iowa, July 4, 1958; s. Alvin and Ann Carol (Lichtenstein) B.; m. Audrey Elling, Apr. 1, 1989; children: Eduard (Erik), Marina. BS in Mass. Comm., Miami U., Oxford, Ohio, 1980. Prodr./dir. WKEF TV, Dayton, Ohio, 1978-81; prodr./dir. QUBE Interactive TV/Warner Cable Comm., Cin., 1981-85, promotions mgr., 1985-87; prodr., dir., writer Paradise Prodrs. Group, Inc., L.A., 1987-91; prodr./dir. mktg. and devel. Rocky Mountain PBS, Denver, 1991-95, exec. prodr. sta. and cultural affairs, 1995—. Recipient Nat. Cable TV Assn. Ace award for Swordquest, 1983, Emmy award Gov.'s Trophy for Vietnam: We Remember, 1984, Heartland Emmy awards, 1992, 93, 94, 95, 96, 97, 98, NEA award for Really Short Shows, 1994, Gold plaque, Chgo. Internat. Film Festival, 1994,CINE Golden Eagle award for Klondike and Snow: A Tale of Twin Polar Bears, 1997, others. Mem. Writers Guild of Am. West,. Office: Rocky Mountain PBS KRMA TV 6 1089 Bannock St Denver CO 80204-4066

BURSK, CHRISTOPHER I., educator; b. Cambridge, Mass., Apr. 23, 1943; s. Edward C. and Catherine (Irwin) B.; m. Mary Ann Bursk, June 19, 1966; children: Christian, Nora, Justin. PhD, Boston U., 1970; MBA, Warren Wilson Coll., Swannanoa, N.C., 1987. Prof. in english Bucks County C.C., Newtown, Pa., 1970—; facilitator VITA, Doylestown, Pa., 1973—. Author: Places of Comfort, 1987, The Way Water Rubs Stone, 1997, The One True Religion, 1997, Cell Count, 1997. Fundraiser, A Woman's Place. Named Pa. Tchr. of Yr., Coun. for Advancement of Edn., 1989; Guggenheim fellow, 1984; NEA fellow, 1987; PEW Found. fellow, 1997. Home: 704 Hulmeville Ave Langhorne PA 19047 Office: Bucks County CC Swamp Rd Newtown PA 18940

BURSKY, HERMAN AARON, lawyer; b. Bklyn., Jan. 16, 1938; s. Abraham S. and Anna R. (Polstein) B.; m. Dolores Kelner, Sept. 3, 1961; children: Daniel Jay, Jennifer Dina. BA, B in Hebrew Lit., Yeshiva U., 1959; LLB, Cornell U., 1962. Bar: N.Y. 1963. Assoc. Levin & Weintraub, N.Y.C., 1963-69; atty. CIT Fin. Corp., N.Y.C., 1969-70; assoc. Otterbourg, Steindler, Houston & Rosen, P.C., N.Y.C., 1970-71; ptnr. Shea & Gould, N.Y.C., 1971-91, Rosenman & Colin, N.Y.C., 1991—. Contbg. author: Practical Guide to Bankruptcy and Debtor Relief, 1964. Served as pvt. U.S. Army, 1962-63. Mem. ABA, N.Y. State Bar Assn., Fed. Bar Council, Assn. Comml. Fin. Attys., N.Y. County Lawyers Assn. (bankruptcy com. 1973-80). Jewish. Club: Inwood Country (N.Y.). Home: 25 Muriel Ave Lawrence NY 11559-1810 Office: Rosenman & Colin 575 Madison Ave Fl 26 New York NY 10022-2585

BURSMA, ALBERT, JR., publishing company executive; b. Holland, Mich., May 19, 1937; s. Albert and Jessica (Van Wieren) B.; m. Phyllis Joan Brink, June 27, 1959; children—Jane Elizabeth, James Mark. B.A., Hope Coll., 1959; M.A., U. Redlands, 1961; postgrad. U. Wis.-Madison, 1963. Tchr. pub. schs., Long Beach, Calif., 1960-61, Madison, 1961-63; salesman McGraw-Hill, N.Y.C., 1963-70; dir. mktg. D.C. Heath, Lexington, Mass., 1970-79, sr. v.p., gen. mgr., 1979-86; pres. sch. pub. div., 1986-95; exec. v.p. Houghton Mifflin Co., 1995—. Mem. Assn. Am. Pubs. (chmn. sch. div. exec. com. 1984-85, 93-94). Home: 258 Willis Rd Sudbury MA 01776-1330 Office: Houghton Mifflin Co 222 Berkeley St Fl 7 Boston MA 02116-3764

BURSON, BETSY LEE, librarian; b. Olney, Tex., Dec. 16, 1942; d. James Hollis and Lora Elizabeth (Talbott) B.; m. Winston Rabb Henderson, June 26, 1976. BS in Edn., Kans. State Tchrs. Coll., 1964; MLS, Tex. Woman's U., 1967, PhD in Libr. Info. Studies, 1987. With Phoenix Pub. Libr., 1967-74; libr. dir. Glendale (Ariz.) Pub. Libr., 1974-75; project archivist Phoenix History Project, 1975-77; adj. faculty U. Ariz., Tucson, 1979, Tex. Woman's U., Denton, 1980; libr. cons. La. State Libr., Baton Rouge, 1982-85; libr. dir. El Paso (Tex.) Pub. Libr., 1987-90, Arlington (Tex.) Pub. Libr., 1990—.

Named Librarian of the Yr. Tex. Library Assn., 1995. Office: Arlington Pub Libr 101 E Abram St Arlington TX 76010-1183

BURSON, CHARLES W., federal official, former state attorney general; b. Memphis, TN; m. Marion 1971; children: Clare, Kate. BA, U. Mich., 1966; MA, Cambridge U., England, 1968; JD, Harvard U., 1970. Assoc. Burson & Burson and Burson & Walkup, Memphis; ptnr. Wildman, Harrold, Allen, Dixon, & McDonnell, Memphis, 1981-88; atty. gen. State of Tenn., Nashville; counsel to v.p. Office of V.P., Washington, 1993—. Del. Tenn. Constl. Conv., 1977, (chmn. State Spending Limitation Com.). Mem. Nat. Assn. Attys. Gen. (pres. 1994-95, chair FTC working group, mem. exec. com. securities group, chair consumer protection com. 1990-91, vice chair securities working group, Wyman award 1994), Tenn. Bd. Law Examiners (past pres.). Office: Exec Office of VP Old Exec Office Bldg NW Washington DC 20501*

BURSON, HAROLD, public relations executive; b. Memphis, Feb. 15, 1921; s. Maurice and Esther (Bach) B.; m. Bette Ann Foster, Oct. 30, 1947; children: Scott, Mark. BA, U. Miss., 1940; DHL (hon.), Boston U., 1988. Corr., reporter Memphis Comml. Appeal, 1938-40; dir. Ole Miss News Bur., Oxford, Miss., 1939-40; dir. pub. rels. H.K. Ferguson Co., N.Y.C., 1941-43; chmn. Burson-Marsteller, N.Y.C., 1953—; bd. dirs., mem. exec. com. Young & Rubicam, N.Y.C.; pub. affairs adviser to Pres. Ronald W. Reagan, 1989-94; mem. adv. coun. Emory U. Bus. Sch., Medill Sch. Journalism Northwestern U., U. So. Calif. Sch. Journalism, trustee, Abe Fortas Meml. Fund, Kennedy Ctr.; hon. prof. Fudan U., Shanghai, 1999. Chmn. bd., mem. exec. com. Nat. Coun. on Econ. Edn.; bd. dirs., exec. com., v.p. pub. info. Nat. Safety Coun., 1968-76; bd. dirs. Kennedy Ctr. Prodns., Washington, Catalyst Inc., 1978-89; former trustee World Wildlife Fund, 1979-81, Found. for Pub. Rels. Rsch. and Edn.; trustee Hackley Sch., Tarrytown, N.Y., 1968-76; chmn. pvt. sector pub. rels. com. USIA; mem. Fine Arts Commn., 1981-85, exec. com. Young Astronauts Coun., 1984-88, adv. bd. Bus. Coun. for Internat. Understanding, pres. coun. N.Y. Acad. Sci.; trustee World Environ. Ctr. Named Public Rels. Profl. of Year Public Rels. News, 1977, 89; recipient Gold Anvil award Public Rels. Soc. Am., 1980, Horatio Alger award, 1986, Arthur Page award, 1990, Life Achievement award Inside PR, 1993; named to U. Miss. Hall of Fame, 1980. Mem. Am. Pub. Relations Assn., Internat. Pub. Rels. Assn., N.Y. Soc. Security Analysts, Am. Philatelic Soc., N.Y. Acad. Medicine, Horatio Alger Assn., Overseas Press Club, Mid-Am. Club, Scarsdale Golf Club, Econ. Club N.Y. (exec. com.), Blue Key, Omicron Delta Kappa. Office: Burson-Marsteller 230 Park Ave S New York NY 10003-1513

BURSTEIN, BEATRICE S., judicial administrator, retired judge; b. Bklyn., May 18, 1915; d. Joseph and Tillie (Star) Sobel; m. Herbert Burstein, June 17, 1937; children: Karen, Patricia, Ellen, Jessica, John, Judd. Bar: N.Y. 1940, U.S. Supreme Ct. 1957. LLB, St. John's U.; LLD (hon.), Hofstra U., 1983. Assoc. Zelby & Burstein, N.Y.C.; ptnr. Burstein & Agata, Mineola, N.Y.; commr. corrections State N.Y., 1956-61; dist. ct. judge, N.Y., 1962-68; family ct. judge, N.Y., 1968-73; justice N.Y. Supreme Ct., Mineola, 1974-92; judicial hearing officer appellate divsn. 2nd judicial dept. N.Y. Supreme Ct., Mineola, 1992—. Mem. N.Y. State Permanent Jud. Commn. on Justice for Children; former bd. dirs. Mental Health Assn. Nassau County, Nassau coun. Girl Scouts U.S.A., NCCJ, Rehab. Inst., Tempo, Health and Welfare Coun. Nassau County, LWV, Nat. Coun. Crime and Delinquency, Nat. Coun. Jewish Women; hon. life mem. Dist. 15 PTA; mem. N.Y. State Commn. on Bicentennial of U.S. Constitution. Named Woman of Yr., Horizon chpt. B'nai B'rith, 1965, Assn. for Help Retarded Children, 1965; recipient Judge Norman Lent award Nassau County Criminal Cts. Bar Assn., 1968, Americanism award Jewish War Vets., 1971, Meritorious Svc. cert. N.E. region Nat. Rehab. Assn., 1972, Human Relations award Am. Jewish Congress, 1973, Outstanding Woman of Year award N.Y. Inst. Tech., 1973, Boss of Year award L.I. chpt. Nat. Secs. Assn., 1975, Myrtle Wreath Achievement award Hadassah, 1975, Disting. Svc. award C.W. Post Ctr. Dept. Criminal Justice, L.I. U., 1979, J.L.E. award Exemplifying the Essence of Justice Women' Bar of State of N.Y., 1987, many others. Mem. ABA, ATLA, Am. Judicature Soc., Internat. Fedn. Women Lawyers (past v.p. for U.S., rep. to UN Social Commn. 1953, 55, 56, 61), Assn. Justices Sup. Ct. State N.Y., Bar Assn. Nassau County (Disting. Svc. medallion 1989), Nat. Assn. Women Judges, Assn. Women Judges of State N.Y., Nassau Women's Bar Assn. (pres., past chmn. legal clinic), Nat. Assn. Women Lawyers, Nat. Conf. State Trial Judges, N.Y. State Permanent Commn. on Juvenile Justice, N.Y. State Bar Assn., Iota Tau Tau. Contbr. articles to profl. lit. Office: NY State Supreme Ct Mineola NY 11501

BURSTEIN, ELIAS, physicist, educator; b. N.Y.C., Sept. 30, 1917; s. Samuel and Sarah (Plotkin) B.; m. Rena Ruth Benson, Sept. 19, 1943; children—Joanna Bliss, Sandra Joy, Miriam Stephanie. AB, Bklyn. Coll., 1938; A.M., U. Kans., 1941; postgrad., MIT, 1941-43, Cath. U., 1946-48; DTech (hon.), Chalmers U. Tech., Göteborg, Sweden, 1982; DSc (hon.), Bklyn. Coll., 1985, Emory U., 1994, Ohio State U., 1999. Physicist Crystal br. U.S. Naval Research Lab., 1945-58, head semiconductor br., 1958; prof. physics U. Pa., Phila., 1958-82, Mary Amanda Wood prof. physics, 1982-88, emeritus, 1988—; Jubilee vis. prof. physics Chalmers U. Tech., Goteborg, 1981; mem. solid state scis. adv. panel NRC-NAS, 1971-80, chmn., 1977-79, condensed matter physics adv. com. Internat. Ctr. for Theoretical Physics, 1990-96, Trieste; com. on sci. and the arts, Franklin Inst., 1994—; Miller Inst. vis. rsch. prof. physics U. Calif., Berkeley, 1996. Founding editor Solid State Comms., 1963, sec. bd. editors, 1963-69, editor emeritus, 1992—; co-editor Comments on Solid State Physics, 1971—. Recipient Navy Civilian Meritorious Service award, 1957; John Price Wetherill medal Franklin Inst., 1979; Guggenheim fellow, 1980; Alexander Von Humboldt Sr. U.S. Scientist award, 1988-90, 92-93. Fellow Am. Phys. Soc. (sec.-treas. div. solid state physics 1956-61, Isakson prize 1986), Optical Soc. Am.; mem. Nat. Acad. Scis., AAAS, Phi Beta Kappa, Sigma Xi. Club: Internat. House Japan (Tokyo). Patentee in field. Office: U Pa Dept Physics Philadelphia PA 19104

BURSTEIN, RICHARD JOEL, lawyer; b. Detroit, Feb. 9, 1945; s. Harry Seymour and Florence (Rosen) B.; m. Gayle Lee Handmaker, Dec. 21, 1969; children: Stephanie Faith, Melissa Amy. Grad., U. Mich., 1966; JD, Wayne State U., 1969. Bar: Mich. 1969, U.S. Ct. Appeals (ea. dist.) Mich. 1969. Ptnr. Smith Miro Hirsch & Brody, Detroit, 1969-81, Honigman Miller Schwartz & Cohn, Detroit, 1981-96; bd. dirs. Sandy Corp., Troy, Mich.; bd. dirs. Met. Affairs Corp., Detroit; co-chmn. Artrain. Mem. Am. Coll. Real Estate Lawyers. Office: Honigman Miller Schwartz & Cohn 2290 1st Nat Bldg Detroit MI 48226

BURSTEIN, STEPHEN DAVID, neurosurgeon; b. Bklyn., Apr. 10, 1934; s. Moe and Anna (Bloch) B.; m. Ronnie Sue Deutsch, Oct. 8, 1972; 1 dau., Alissa Aimee. B.A. with distinction, U. Mich., 1954; M.D., SUNY-Bklyn., 1958; M.S. in Neurosurgery, U. Minn.-Rochester, 1965. Diplomate Am. Bd. Neurol. Surgery Surg. intern Johns Hopkins Hosp., Balt., 1958-59; neurosurgery fellow Mayo Clinic, Rochester, 1961-65; chief dept. neurosurgery South Nassau Community Hosp., Oceanside, N.Y., 1980—, pres. med. staff, 1980-82; chief dept. neurosurgery Franklin Gen. Hosp., Valley Stream, N.Y., 1980—; prin. Neurol. Surgery & Neurology, P.C., Freeport, N.Y., 1965—. Contbr. articles to med. jours. Bd. dirs. South Nassau Community Hosp., 1978—. Served to lt. USNR, 1959-61. Recipient Neurosurg. Travel award Mayo Found., 1966. Fellow ACS; mem. L.I. Hearing and Speech Soc. (bd. dirs.), N.Y. State Neurosurgeons Soc. (bd. dirs.), N.Y. State Neurosurg. Soc. (pres. 1981-82), Sigma Xi, Alpha Omega Alpha. Hebrew. Avocations: theatre; travel. Home: 19 Bridle Path Roslyn NY 11576-3115 Office: Neurol Surgery & Neurology 88 S Bergen Pl Freeport NY 11520-3510

BURSTON, DANIEL, psychology educator; b. Naharia, Israel, Dec. 12, 1954; arrived in Can., 1955; s. Benedict (Baruch) and Margaret (Diamond) B.; m. Sharna Olfman, Jan. 14, 1990; children: Adam, Gavriela. MA in Social and Polit. Thought, York U., Ont., Can., 1980, PhD in Social and Polit. Thought, 1985, PhD in Psychology, 1989. Asst. prof. psychology Duquesne U., Pitts., 1992-97, assoc. prof. psychology, 1998—; adj. faculty C.J. Jung Analyst Tng. Program Pitts., 1994-98. Author: The Legacy of Erich Fromm, 1991, The Wing of Madness: The Life and Work of R.D. Laing, 1996; mem. editl. bd. Jour. Soc. Existential Analysis. Mem. U. Pitts. Ctr. Philosophy of Sci. (assoc. mem.). Office: Duquesne U 600 Forbes Ave Pittsburgh PA 15219-3002

BURSTON, RICHARD MERVIN, business executive; b. Brookline, Mass., Oct. 31, 1924; s. Mark and Anita (Andrews) B.; m. Phoebe Harvey Hopkins, Aug. 29, 1958; children: Abby Lyn, Seth Hopkins, Joshua Craig, Mark Andrews, Amanda Lee. BA, Bowdoin Coll., 1949; MBA, Harvard U., 1952. Mgr. beauty dept. Kendall Co., Boston, 1953-58; regional sales mgr. M. Pier Co., Ft. Lauderdale, Fla., 1958-59; nat. sales mgr. Ozon Products, Inc., Bklyn., 1959-63; v.p., co-founder Burston/Larkin Assocs., Stamford, Conn., 1964-88; pres., chief exec. officer Excalibur, Inc., Stamford, 1981-88; founder, pres. Burston Inc., Stamford, 1987—; dir. Nat. Beauty and Barber Reps. Assn., N.Y.C., 1973-74, Louv Yacht Yard, Norwalk, Conn., 1969-73; cons. Ruckel Mfg., Inc., N.Y.C., 1969-87. Dir. Roxbury Babe Ruth, Stamford, 1969-85; pres., dir. Roxbury-Riverbank Little League, Stamford, 1971-82; trustee, pres. Miramichi Rod & Gun Club, Lyttleton, New Brunswick, Can., 1980—; fund raiser Bowdoin Coll., Brunswick, Maine, 1984-90, mem. alumni coun., 1994—, pres., 1997-98. Served to lt. USNR, 1943-46, PTO. Recipient Man of Yr. award United Beauty Supply Corp., Bridgeport, Conn., 1983. Mem. Beauty and Barber Supply Inst., Am. Beauty Assn., Kents Hill Sch. Alumni Assn. (bd. dirs., bd. trustees 1994—), Miramichi Rod & Gun Club, Bowdoin Club (Southwest Conn.), High Head Yacht Club (dir. 1997—). Republican. Jewish. Avocation: fly fishing. Home: 27A High Head Rd RR 2 Harpswell ME 04079-9802 Office: Burston Inc 45 Church St Stamford CT 06906-1740

BURSTYN, ELLEN (EDNA RAE GILLOOLY), actress; b. Detroit, Dec. 7, 1932; m. Paul Roberts; m. Neil Burstyn; 1 child, Jefferson. LHD (hon.), Dowling Coll.; DFA (hon.), Sch. Visual Arts. Artistic dir. The Actor's Studio, N.Y.C., 1982-88. Actress: films include Resurrection, 1980, Silence of the North, 1981, In Our Hands, 1984, The Ambassador, 1984, Twice in a Lifetime, 1985, Hanna's War, 1988, Grand Isle, 1991, Dying Young, 1991, The Cemetery Club, 1993, The Color of Evening, 1994, Choosing One's Way: Resistance in Auschwitz/Birkenau (narrator, presenter), 1994, When a Man Loves a Woman, 1994, Roommates, 1995, The Baby-Sitters Club, 1995, How to Make an American Quilt, 1995, The Spitfire Grill, 1996, Deceiver, 1997, You Can Thank Me Later, 1998, Playing by Heart, 1998, Walking Across Egypt, 1999, Requiem for a Dream, 1999, The Yards, 1999, numerous others; tv movies include: The People vs. Jean Harris, 1981, Acting: Lee Strasberg and the Actos Studio, 1981, Surviving, 1985, Into Thin Air, 1985, Something in Common, 1986, Act of Vengeance, 1986, The Ellen Burstyn Show, 1986, Hellow Actors Studio, 1987, Dear America: Letters Home from Vietnam, 1987, Pack of Lies, 1987, When You Remember Me, 1990, Mrs. Lambers Remembers Love, 1991, Taking Back My Life: The nacy Ziegenmeyer Story, 1992, Shattered Trust: The Shary Karney Story, 1993, Getting Out, 1994, Getting Gotti, 1994, Trick of the Eye, 1994, My Brother's Keeper, 1995, Follow the River, 1995, Timepiece, 1995, Our Son, The Matchmaker, 1996, Murder in the Mind, 1996, A Deadly Vision, 1997, Flash, 1998, The Patron Saint of Liars, 1998, (mini-series) A Will of Thir Own, 1998, Night Ride Home, 1999; tv appearances include Cheyenne, 1955, Gunsmoke, 1955, Maverick, 1957, The Big Valley, 1965, The Time Tunnel, 1966, The Bold Ones: The Lawyers, 1969. Mem. individual artists grants and policy overview panels Nat. Endowment for the Arts, Theater Adv. Council City of New York. Mem. Actors Equity Assn. (pres. 1982-85). Office: CAA care Steve Tellez 9830 Wilshire Blvd Beverly Hills CA 90212-1804*

BURT, ALVIN MILLER, III, anatomist, cell biologist, educator, writer; b. Bridgeport, Conn., Aug. 14, 1935; s. Alvin Miller and Esther Louise (Carey) B.; m. Dorothy Hanlin, July 15, 1961 (div.); children: Constance Walker, Carolyn Marie; m. Judith Nath, July 13, 1991; 1 stepchild, Stephen Jacob Nath. B.A., Amherst Coll., 1957; Ph.D. (USPHS fellow 1960-61), U. Kans., 1962. Asst. prof. anatomy Med. Coll. Va., Richmond, 1962-63; instr. Yale U. Med. Sch., 1963-66; mem. faculty Vanderbilt U. Med. Sch., 1966—, prof. anatomy, 1974-85, prof. cell biology, 1985—; prof cell biology Nursing Sch. Vanderbilt U., Nashville, 1994—; vis. scientist Agrl. Research Council, Inst. Animal Physiology, Babraham, Cambridge, Eng., 1972-73. Author: Textbook of Neuroanatomy, 1993; contbr. articles to profl. jours. Vestryman Episcopal Ch. of Advent, Brentwood, Tenn., 1977-81, sr. warden, 1979-81, lay reader, chalice bearer, 1975-87, tchr. adult classes, mem. diocesan lay ministry com., 1981-85; lay reader, chalice bearer St. Philips Episcopal Ch., Donelson, Tenn., 1989-92, vestryman, 1991-92, mem. diocesan total ministry com., 1990-93; mem. Stephen Ministry Diocese of Tenn., 1991—; dir. pastoral care St. Ann's Episcopal Ch., Nashville, 1993-96, lay reader, 1994—, chalice bearer, 1996—; mem. steering com. Interfaith AIDS Ministry, 1994-96. Recipient Research Career Devel. award USPHS, 1968-73. Mem. Am. Assn. Anatomists, Am. Soc. Neurochemistry, Human Anatomy & Physiology Soc., Internat. Soc. Neurochemistry, Internat. Brain Rsch. Orgn., Soc. Neurosci., Tenn. Outdoor Writers Assn. (v.p. 1985-86, pres.-elect 1986-87, pres. 1987-88, chmn. bd. dirs. 1988-89), Southeastern Outdoor Press Assn., Bass Anglers Sportsmens Soc., Tenn. Spoonplugging Club (bd. dirs. 1980-88, editor newsletter 1980-85), Sigma Xi. Home: 317 Mccoin Dr Goodlettsville TN 37072-1568 Office: Vanderbilt U Dept Cell Biology Nashville TN 37232-0275

BURT, ALVIN VICTOR, JR., journalist; b. Oglethorpe County, Ga., Sept. 11, 1927; s. Alvin Victor and Mabel (Sorrow) B.; m. Gloria White. BA in Edn, U. Fla., 1949. With U.P., 1949-50, Atlanta Jour., 1950-51, Jacksonville (Fla.) Jour., 1951-55; with Miami (Fla.) Herald, 1955-66, Latin Am. editor, 1962-66; assigned Miami (Fla.) Herald, Washington, 1962; editorial writer Miami (Fla.) Herald, 1967-73, columnist, 1973-96; editor Hartwell (Ga.) Sun, 1966-67. Co-author: Papa Doc, 1969; author: Florida A Place in the Sun, 1974, Becalmed in the Mullet Latitudes, 1983, Al Burt's Florida, 1997, The Tropic of Cracker, 1999. Recipient Ernie Pyle award for newspaper writing, 1961, State award A.P. for feature writing, 1964, citation Fla. Legislature, 1965, Scripps-Howard award for best interviews in nation, 1966, Editorial Writing award Fla. Soc. Newspaper Editors-Fla. Press Assn., 1973, Overseas Press award, 1974, J.C. Penney spl. award U. Mo., 1980, Outstanding Journalist award Fla. Audubon Soc., 1984, First Ann. AL Burt award for extraordinary lifelong commitment 1000 Friends of Fla., 1989, Commentator of Yr. award Fla. Wildlife Fedn., 1990, Patrick Smith Lit. award Fla. Hist. Soc., 1998; inducted into Ind. Alligator Hall of Fame, 1998; named Alumnus of Distinction U. Fla. Coll. of Journalism and Comms., 1999. Office: PO Box 17 Melrose FL 32666-0017

BURT, BILLY GEORGE, oil company professional; b. New Orleans, Feb. 19, 1954; s. James Henry and Irene Mary Burt; m. Katherine Wilson, July 23, 1972 (div. Oct. 1980); children: Keith, Raymond; m. Deborah Gaye Gibson, Apr. 15, 1983 (div. Nov. 1985); children: Billy Jr., Brandon; m. Samantha Hile, Oct. 12, 1989; children: Stephanie, Justin. Student, Lamar U., 1988-92, Tex. A&M U., 1992-99. Operator Crown Cen. Petroleum, Pasadena, Tex., 1978-86, Montell USA Inc., Pasadena, 1988—. Mem., capt. fire brigade Montell USA Inc., Pasadena, 1988—. Sgt. USAF, 1975-77. Republican. Roman Catholic. Avocations: art, music, sports. E-mail: b.g.burt@worldnet.att.net. Home: 3009 Wagon Trail Rd # 2 Pearland TX 77584-9082 Office: Montell USA Inc 12001 Bay Area Blvd Pasadena TX 77507-1309

BURT, CHRISTOPHER CLINTON, publisher; b. N.Y.C., Oct. 12, 1954; s. Nathaniel and Margaret Brooks (Clinton) B.; m. Jeernen Songsaeng, Aug. 9, 1992. BA Econs., U. Wis., 1981. Pub., mng. dir. Pacific Rim Press, Inc., Bangkok, 1985—; pub. Compass Am. Guides, Inc., Oakland, Calif., 1990-92; exec. editor, creative dir. Compass Am. Guides, Inc./Random House, Inc., Oakland, 1992—; bd. dirs. Moon Handbooks, Inc., Chico, Calif. Bd. dirs. Jaquelin Found., Princeton, N.J., 1980—. Mem. Soc. of The Cincinatus. Office: Compass Am Guides 5332 College Ave Ste 201 Oakland CA 94618-2805

BURT, DIANE MAE, women's health nurse; b. Camden, N.J., Jan. 1, 1960; d. Charles Richard and Dolores Joan (Kienzle) Cooke; m. Richard A. Burt, Feb. 14, 1987; children: Brandon Charles, Justin Bryan. LPN, Corps Sch., 1979; ASN, Cumberland Community Coll., Vineland, N.J., 1990; BSN, Thomas Edison State Coll., Trenton, N.J., 1997; MSN, Wilmington (Del.) Coll., 1999. RN, N.J.; cert. advanced cardiac life support, critical care. Charge nurse pediatrics unit H.I.P. of N.J., Cherry Hill; week-end charge nurse Meridian Nursing Home, Voorhees, N.J.; nurse emergency rm. and labor/delivery Newcomb Hosp., Vineland. With USN, 1978-84. Home: 177 Cedar Rd Pittsgrove NJ 08318-3830

BURT, GWEN BEHRENS, elementary school administrator; b. Clinton, Ind., Nov. 6, 1946; d. Henry Milum Allbright and Marjorie Evelyn (Muir) Wiot; m. Kurt Fredric Behrens, Mar. 28, 1970 (div. June 1984); m. Gary Orren Burt (dec. Sept. 1998), Sept. 5, 1996; 1 child, Amy Lynn. BS, Ind. State U., 1969, MS, 1974. Tchr. Center Grove Cmty. Schs., Greenwood, Ind., 1969-71; tchr. reading Vigo County Sch. Corp., Terre Haute, Ind., 1971-77; summer adminstr. Maercker Sch. Dist., Clarendon Hills, Ill., 1991-98, Title I dir., 1977-98; prin. Sauk Sch., Matteson (Ill.) Dist. 162, 1998—; adj. lectr. Lewis U., Romeoville, Ill., 1996; presenter workshops and lectures, 1987—. Coord. single adult program, Grace United Meth. Ch., Naperville, Ill., 1992-95, coord. youth ministry program, 1985-87; vol. numerous charitable orgns. including Am. Cancer Soc., Am. Heart Assn., etc. Mem. NEA (various offices Ill. and Ind. chpts.), AAUW, Internat. Reading Assn. (various offices Ill. and Ind. chpts.), Nat. Assn. Elem. Schs. Prins., AAUW, ASCD, Ill. Prins. Assn., Ill. Reading Coun., Ill. Women Adminstr., Ill. Title I coords., Adminstrs. and Reading Spl. Interest Coun., Delta Kappa Gamma. Republican. Avocations: power boating, golf, antiques, geneology, lighthouses. Home: 1245 Baythorne Dr Flossmoor IL 60422-2057 Office: Sauk Sch 4435 S Churchill Dr Richton Park IL 60471-1101

BURT, JEFFREY AMSTERDAM, lawyer; b. Phila., Apr. 27, 1944; s. Samuel Matthew and Esther (Amsterdam) B.; m. Sandra Cass, Dec. 17, 1967; children: Stephen, Daniel, Jonathan, Andrew. BA, Princeton U., 1966; LLB, Yale U., 1970, MA in Econs., 1970. Bar: Md. 1971, D.C. 1971. Law clk. to judge U.S. Ct. Appeals (4th cir.), Balt., 1970-71; assoc. firm Arnold & Porter, Washington, 1971-77, ptnr., 1978—; adj. prof. law Georgetown U., 1987-95; frequent lectr. Pres., Green Acres, Inc., Ind. Sch., Rockville, Md., 1984-86. Author: (with others) International Joint Ventures, 1986, 2d edit., 1992; co-editor Joint Ventures with Internat. Ptnrs., 1997. Mem. ABA (co-chairperson NIS Law Com. Sect. of Internat. Law and Practice), Russian Am. C. of C. (dir., sec.). Office: Arnold & Porter 555 12th St NW Washington DC 20004-1206

BURT, JOHN HARRIS, bishop; b. Marquette, Mich., Apr. 11, 1918; s. Bates G. and Emily May (Bailey) B.; m. Martha M. Miller, Feb. 16, 1946; children: Susan, Emily, Sarah, Mary. B.A., Amherst Coll., 1940, D.D. (hon.), 1960; B.A., Va. Theol. Sem., 1943, B.D., 1967; D.D., Youngstown U., 1958, Kenyon Coll., 1967. Boys worker Christodora House, N.Y.C., 1940-41; ordained to ministry Episcopal Ch., 1943; canon (Christ Ch. Cathedral); rector (St. Paul's Ch.), St. Louis, 1943-44; chaplain to Episc. students U. Mich., 1946-50; rector St. John's Ch., Youngstown, Ohio, 1950-57, All Saints Ch., Pasadena, Calif., 1957-67; bishop coadjutor Ohio, 1967-68, Episc. bishop of, 1968-84; pres. So. Calif. Council Chs., 1962-65; mem. bd. Ch. Soc. Coll. Work, 1964-71; chmn. clergy deployment bd. Episc. Ch., 1971-73. Co-author: World Religions and World Peace, 1969, Joy in the Struggle - Memoirs of Ecumenical Dialogue, 1993; author: Economic Justice and the Christian Conscience, 1987. Pres. Youngstown Coordinating Coun., 1953-56, Pasadena Cmty. Coun., 1964-66; trustee Pomona Coll., 1963-66, Va. Theol. Sem., 1967-72, Colgate-Rochester Div. Sch., 1968-84, Kenyon Coll., 1967-84; bd. dirs. United Way L.A., 1964-67, Cleve. Urban Coalition, 1968-70, Ams. for Energy Independence, 1975-85; bd. dirs. Nat. Com. Against Censorship, 1974—; chmn. bd. dirs. St. John's Home for Girls, Painesville, Ohio, 1968-84; governing bd. Nat. Coun. Chs., 1970-81; mem. Com. on Ch. Order, Consultation of Ch. Union, 1980-88; chmn. com. on theology Episc. Ch. House Bishops, 1973-80; chmn. Urban Bishops Coalition, 1977-93, Faith and Order Commn. Ohio Coun. Chs., 1970-74; bd. dirs. Episcopal Ch. Pub. Co., 1985-92, pres., 1990-92; chmn. commn. ecumenical rels. Episc. Ch., 1973-79, also chmn. commn. mid. judicatories, cons. on ch. union, 1975-79; chmn. com. human affairs and health Episc. Ch., 1982-85; chmn. Bishops Com. Nat. and Internat. Affairs, 1982-85; chmn. Ecumenical Gt. Lakes Project on Econ. Crisis, 1983-89; chmn. Presiding Bishop's Com. Christian-Jewish Rels., 1986-91; pres. Nat. Christian Leadership Conf. on Israel, 1988-99; mem. ch. rels. com. U.S. Holocaust Meml. Coun., 1989-96; mem. Ecumenical Consultation on New Religions Movements, 1985-87; bd. dirs. Ams. for Med. Progress, Inc., 1992-95. Chaplain USNR, 1943-46. Recipient Arvona Lynch Human Relations award Youngstown, 1956; Rissica Human Relations award Jewish War Vets., 1966; Pasadena Community Relations award, 1967; Cleve.'s Simon Bolivar award, 1972; Pitts.'s Thomas Merton award, 1978; Human Rights award Ohio br. ACLU, 1980; Ecumenical Leadership award Christian Ch. (Disciples of Christ), 1986, Am. Jewish Com. award, 1991. Mem. Phi Gamma Delta. Home: Middle Island Point Rd # 25 Marquette MI 49855-9726

BURT, MARVIN ROGER, financial advisor, investment manager; b. L.A., Mar. 5, 1937; s. Henry Howard Burt and Iris Faith (Green) Welton; m. Joy Lee Rougk, July 20, 1958; children: Sandra Marie, Scott Marvin. BA, UCLA, 1958; MPA, George Washington U., 1965, D in Pub. Adminstrn., 1969. Cert. fin. planner. Mgmt. trainee Bank Am., L.A., 1961-62; program analyst Dept. Def., Washington, 1962-65, Exec. Office Pres., Washington, 1965-66; mem. sr. rsch. staff Resource Mgmt. Corp., Bethesda, Md., 1966-67; sr. cons. Peat Marwick Mitchell, Washington, 1967-68; cons. Potomac, Md., 1968-69; mem. sr. staff Urban Inst., Washington, 1969-72; pres. Burt Assocs., Inc., Bethesda, 1972—, Inst. Human Resources Rsch., Bethesda, 1973-82; asst. v.p. Sci. Applications Internat., McLean, Va., 1982-85; cons. govt. agys., Washington, 1965-82. Author: (books) Options for Improving the Care of Neglected and Dependent Children, 1971, Policy Analysis, 1974, A Comprehensive Emergency Services System for Neglected and Abused Children, 1977, Drug Abuse, 1979, Children of Heroin Addicts, 1980 ; contbr. articles to profl. jours. Mem. Community Coordinated Child Care, Bethesda, 1976-77, Montgomery County Drug Abuse Adv. Coun., 1990-92; chmn. coun. on ministries North Bethesda (Md.) United Meth. Ch., 1975-76, 81-82, chmn. bd. dirs., 1977-78, bd. dirs., 1986-92, lay del. to ann. conf., 1989, chmn. staff-parish rels. com., 1990-92. USPHS grantee, 1977-82. Fellow AAAS; mem. Ops. Rsch. Soc. Am. (chmn. tech. sect. 1979-80), Internat. Assn. Fin. Planning (v.p. nat. capital chpt. 1987-89), Inst. Cert. Fin. Planners (dean mid-atlantic conf. 1995), Registry Fin. Planning Practitioners, Potomac Rotary (pres. 1991-92, bd. dirs. 1987-93, pres. Potomac Rotary Charities, Inc. 1992), Bethesda/Chevy Chase C. of C. (chmn. small bus. com. 1990-91, v.p. small bus., bd. dirs. 1991-93), Avenel Commn. Assn. (pres. 1998-99, bd. dirs. 1996-99). Avocations: hiking, backpacking, tennis, golf, skiing. Home: 5 Willow Gate Ct Bethesda MD 20817-4110 Office: Burt Assocs Inc 7910 Woodmont Ave Ste 1055 Bethesda MD 20814-3081

BURT, ROBERT AMSTERDAM, lawyer, educator; b. Phila., Feb. 3, 1939; s. Samuel Matthew and Esther (Amsterdam) B.; m. Linda Gordon Rose, June 14, 1964; children: Anne Elizabeth, Jessica Ellen. AB, Princeton U., 1960; BA in Jurisprudence, Oxford (Eng.) U., 1962, MA, 1968; JD, Yale U., 1964, MA (hon.), 1976. Bar: D.C. 1966, Mich. 1973, U.S. Supreme Ct. 1971. Law clk. to chief judge U.S. Ct. Appeals D.C., 1964-65; asst. gen. counsel Office President's Spl. Rep. Trade Negotiations, 1965-66; senatorial legis. asst., 1966-68; assoc. prof. law U. Chgo. Law Sch., 1968-70; assoc. prof., then prof. law U. Mich. Law Sch., 1970-76; prof. law in psychiatry U. Mich. Med. Sch., 1973-76; Southmayd prof. Yale U. Law Sch., 1976-93, Alexander M. Bickel prof., 1993—; spl. master U.S. Dist. Ct. Conn., 1987-92, 95. Bd. dirs. Benhaven Sch. Autistic Persons, New Haven, 1977—, chmn., 1983-96; bd. dirs. Judge David L. Bazelon Ctr. for Mental Health Law, 1985—, chmn., 1990—; mem. adv. bd. Project on Death in Am., Open Soc. Inst., 1994—; bd. dirs. Yale Hillel Found., 1996—. Rockefeller fellow, 1976, John Simon Guggenheim fellow, 1997-98. Mem. Inst. Medicine (coun. 1992-94). Democrat. Jewish. Home: 66 Dogwood Cir Woodbridge CT 06525-1254 Office: Yale U Sch Law PO Box 208215 127 Wall St New Haven CT 06511-6636

BURT, ROBERT NORCROSS, diversified manufacturing company executive; b. Lakewood, Ohio, May 24, 1937; s. Vernon Robert and Mary (Norcross) B.; m. Lynn Chilton, Apr. 19, 1969; children: Tracy, Randy, Charlie. BSChemE, Princeton U., 1959; MBA, Harvard U., 1964. With Mobil Oil Corp., N.Y.C. and Tokyo, 1964-68; dir. corp. planning and acquisitions Chemetron Corp., Chgo., 1968-70, mgr. internat. div., 1970-73; dir. corp. planning FMC Corp., Chgo., 1973-76; v.p. agrl. chems. group FMC Corp., Phila., 1976-83; v.p. def. group FMC Corp., San Jose, Calif., 1983-88; exec. v.p. FMC Corp., Chgo., 1988-90, pres., 1990-91, chmn., CEO, 1991—; bd. dirs. Phelps Dodge, 1993—, Warner-Lambert, 1995—. Bd. dirs. Rehab.

Inst. Chgo., 1991—, Evanston (Ill.) Hosp., 1995—, exec. com.; trustee Orchestral Assn. of Chgo. Symphony Orch., 1992—, vice chmn., 1995—. Lt. USMC, 1959-62. Mem. Mfrs. Alliance Productivity and Innovation (trustee 1990—), Bus. Roundtable (policy com., chmn. environ. task force), Ill. Bus. Roundtable. Avocations: reading, golfing, spectator sports. Home: 5 Kent Rd Winnetka IL 60093-1815 Office: FMC Corp 200 E Randolph St Ste 6700 Chicago IL 60601-6436

BURT, WALLACE JOSEPH, JR., insurance company executive; b. Burlington, Iowa, Apr. 1, 1924; s. Wallace Joseph and Lela (Catlow) B.; m. Alice Olmsted, June 22, 1946; children: Lockwood, David, Virginia. student Iowa State Coll., 1942, U. Wis., 1945. V.p., dir. 1st Ins. Fin. Co., Des Moines, 1946-50, Northeastern Ins. Co., Hartford, Conn., 1950-59; pres., owner Hail Reinsurance Mgmt., Inc., Ormond Beach, Fla., 1960-89; chmn. Burt & Scheld, Inc., Ormond Beach, 1961-89; chmn. U.S. br. Hamburg Internat. Reins. Co., 1976-81; chmn. First N.Y. Syndicate Corp., 1979-89, W.J. Burt Mgmt., Inc., N.Y.C., 1979-89; pres. Ormond Reins. Co., 1976-92, Oceanside RE Group, Inc., 1989; dir., v.p. Barnett Bank, Ormond Beach; underwriting mem. Lloyd's of London; dir. N.Y. Ins. Exchange, 1983-84. Trustee, pres. Ormond Beach Meml. Hosp. Served to 1st lt. USAAF, World War II. Decorated D.F.C., Purple Heart, Air medal with 5 oak leaf clusters. Home: 222 Riverside Dr Ormond Beach FL 32176-6504 Office: 140 S Atlantic Ave Ormond Beach FL 32176-6689

BURT-BRADLEY, DELLA ANN, English educator, consultant; b. Kosciusko, Miss., July 7; d. Milton Luther and Gladys Burt; m. Hilbert Bradley; 1 child, April Letitia. BA, Jackson State U., 1965; MA, Mich. State U., 1967; PhD, Ind. U., 1979. Tchg. asst. Mich. State U., East Lansing, 1965-67; tchr. Gary Cmty. Sch. Corp., 1967-69; lectr. Ind. U. N.W., Gary, 1967-74; assoc. instr. Ind. U., Bloomington, 1976-79; interim pres., provost Malcolm X Coll., Chgo., 1987-88; assoc. vice chancellor City Colls. Chgo., 1986-87, 89-90; exec. dean Ivy Tech State Coll., Gary, 1990-92; prof. English Harold Washington Coll., Chgo., 1969-86, 92—; mem. editl. adv. bd. Collegiate Press, Alta Loma, Calif., 1997; book reviewer Simon & Schuster, Saddle River, N.J., 1996, 98; cons., evaluator North Ctrl. Assn., Chgo., 1989—, accreditation rev. coun., 1995—; cons. Lakeshore Employment and Tng., Gary, 1992; book reviewer Bedford/St. Martin's, 1999. Contbr. articles to profl. jours.; contbr. author: (poetry book) Black Sister, 1981. Chairperson Gary Accord Ednl. Partnership, 1987—; mem. N.W. Ind. Arts & Humanities Consortium, Gary, 1990-96, Hist. and Cultural Soc., Gary, 1985-93, Ind. Lawyers Aux., 1992; trustee Gary Sch. Bd., 1980-88. Recipient Ednl. Leadership award Phi Delta Kappa, 1987, Outstanding Citizen award Phi Beta Sigma and INFO Newspaper, 1983, 86, 87, numerous cmty. svc. and leadership awards. Mem. AAUW, Am. Assn. Higher Edn., Am. Assn. Women in Cmty. Colls., Cook County Coll. Tchrs. Union, Writers Ctr. Indpls., Links, Delta Sigma Theta Sorority (numerous cmty. svc. and leadership awards). Avocations: writing poetry and short stories, reading, swimming, biking. Office: Harold Washington Coll 30 E Lake St Chicago IL 60601-2403

BURTI, CHRISTOPHER LOUIS, lawyer; b. Muroc, Calif., Oct. 15, 1950; s. Louis Burti and Johanna Renate (Schmidt) Landa; m. Linda Carol Pipkin, Sept. 15, 1973; children: Christopher Louis Jr., Erika Pipkin. BSBA, East Carolina U., 1975; JD, U. N.C., 1979. Bar: N.C. 1979, U.S. Dist. Ct. (ea. dist.) N.C. 1983. Assoc. Lewis, Lewis & Lewis, Farmville, N.C., 1979-82; ptnr. Lewis & Burti, Farmville, 1982-94; v.p., legal counsel Statewide Title, Inc., Greenville, N.C., 1994—; atty. Town of Farmville, N.C., 1982-94, Town of Falkland, 1989—. Bd. dirs. Farmville Child Devel. Ctr., 1983-84, Farmville Cmty. Arts Coun., 1983-84, Farmville Charitable Svcs., 1987-89; cubmaster Farmville Troop 25 Boy Scouts Am. With U.S. Army, 1970-72. Mem. N.C. Bar Assn., N.C. Mcpl. Attys. Assn. (bd. dirs. 1988-89, chmn. cable communications com. 1991), Pitt County Bar Assn., Nat. Inst. Mcpl. Law Officers (mcpl. utilities com.), Farmville C. of C. (bd. dirs. 1982-83), Farmville Country Club, Masons (past master, past dist. dep. grand master), Phi Kappa Phi, Beta Gamma Sigma, Phi Sigma Pi. Democrat. Episcopalian. Avocations: sailing, skiing, woodworking, photography. Office: Statewide Title Inc 110 E Arlington Blvd Greenville NC 27858-5019

BURTLE, DEBRA ANN, needlework and gift shop owner; b. Decatur, Ill., Oct. 24, 1953; d. Albert Eugene and Barbara Ann (Watson) Naab; m. Paul Walter Burtle, July 22, 1978; 1 child, Laura Rose. AA, Lincoln Land C.C., 1973; BS, Ea. Ill. U., 1975; cert., Martha Pullen Sch. Fashion, 1986, Margaret Boyle Sch. Needlework, 1989. Cert. tchr., Ill. Tchr. home econs. Athens (Ill.) Cmty. Unit Sch. Dist., 1977-78, Waverly (Ill.) Cmty. Unit Sch. Dist., 1978-80; instr. adult edn. Sew with Flo, Springfield, Ill., 1980-83, The Quilting Bee, Rochester, Ill., 1980-83, Springfield Crafts and Ceramics Club, 1987—; owner, mgr. Ruffles, Flourishes, and Satin Bows, Auburn, Ill., 1985—; textile judge Christian County Fair, Taylorville, Ill., 1972-94, Ill. State Fair Springfield, 1992, 93, 94, 95, 97; demonstrator wool spinning Clayville Rural Life Ctr., Pleasant Plains, Ill., 1967-74, Ill. State Fair, Springfield, 1974-75; instr. wool spinning Lincoln's New Salem State Park, Petersburg, Ill., 1969; needlework demonstrator Winter Folk Fest, Blackburn Coll., Carlinville, Ill., 1992. Artisan exhibitor Springfield Art Assn. Fine Art Fair, 1989, others. Winner textile and garment awards Sangamon County Fair, New Berlin, Ill., 1971, Ill. State Fair, 1988, 89, 91, 92, 93, 94, 95, 97; recipient Outstanding Farm Family award Ill. Farmers Union, 1993. Mem. Auburn Jr. Women's Club (sec. 1985), Elegant Stitchers Needlework Guild (v.p. 1986, pres. 1987-89). Avocations: reading, gardening, antique restoration. Home: 5435 Snell Rd Auburn IL 62615-9252 Office: Ruffles Flourishes and Satin Bows 115 N 4th St Auburn IL 62615-1451

BURTLE, PAUL WALTER, farmer; b. Springfield, Ill., May 31, 1950; Walter Jerome and Esther (Bodnar) B.; m. Debra Ann Naab, July 22, 1978; 1 child, Laura Rose. BS in Agriculture, U. Ill., 1972. Farm mgr., operator Burtle Farm, Auburn, Ill., 1972—; chmn. Sangamon County Exec. Extension Coun., Springfield, 1975-76, Sangamon County Agrl. Coun., Springfield, 1983-84, dir. Farm Credit Svcs. of West Cen. Ill., Springfield, 1990, vice chmn. Fed. Land Bank Assn. of West Cen. Ill., Champaign, 1988-90, chm. bd. Farm Credit Svcs. of Cen. Ill. 1995-98, Fed. Land Credit Assn., Champaign, 1991; pres. Sangamon County Farmers Union, 1993; dir. exec. bd. Ill. Farmers Union, 1994; dir. leadership inst. task force U.S. Farm Credit Coun., 1998. Squadman Champaign County Rescue Squad, Urbana, Ill., 1970-72. Recipient Svc. award Champaign County Civil Def., 1972, 4-H Alumni award Sangamon County 4-H Leaders, 1975, Ill. Farmers Union Outstanding Farm Family award, 1993; named Nat. Corn Yield Contest winner Seedtec, Internat., 1985. Mem. Ill. Farm Bur. Fedn., Ill. Farmers Union (exec. bd. 1994), Sangamon County Farmers Union (pres. 1993). Democrat. Roman Catholic. Avocations: beekeeping, woodworking, birdwatching, flute playing, reading. Home: 5435 Snell Rd Auburn IL 62615-9252

BURTLESS, GARY THOMAS, economist, consultant; b. Cayuga County, N.Y., Apr. 11, 1950; s. Charles Bernie and Patricia Ann (MacCone) B.; m. Elise Kathe Bruml, Nov. 27, 1976; children: Andrew B., Matthew B. BA, Yale U., 1972; PhD, MIT, 1977. Economist Office Sec., HEW, Washington, 1977-79, U.S. Dept. Labor, Washington, 1979-81; sr. fellow Brookings Instn., Washington, 1981—; vis. prof. pub. affairs U. Md., College Park, 1993; cons. various orgns., 1981—, U.S. Dept. Lab., 1985—, World Bank, Washington, 1990—. Author: Can America Afford To Grow Old, 1989, Growth With Equity: Economic Policymaking for the Next Century, 1993, Globaphobia: Confronting Fears about Open Trade, 1998; editor Jour. Human Resources, 1988-96, A Future of Lousy Jobs?, 1990, Does Money Matter? Effect of School Resources, 1996, Aging Societies: The Global Dimension, 1998; contbr. articles to profl. jours. Commn. mem. panel on fin. adequacy Trustees Social Security, 1989; mem. tech. panel Adv. Coun. on Social Security, 1994-95. Recipient Leontief prize Ea. Econ. Assn., 1978. Mem. Am. Econ. Assn., Nat. Acad. Social Ins. (commn. mem. panel on Social Security notch 1988, panel on privatizing Social Security 1997-98). Avocations: history, hiking. Office: Brookings Instn 1775 Massachusetts Ave NW Washington DC 20036-2188

BURTNICK, RONALD, sales executive; b. Stuttgart, Germany, Nov. 9, 1946; came to U.S., 1947.; s. Robert Brennan and Ellen (Wondratchek) B.; m. Alice Galofaro, June 21, 1975; children: Katherine, Megan, Michael. AAS, Middlesex County Coll., Edison, N.J., 1970; BA, Montclair State U., 1972, MA, 1973; EdS, Rutgers U., 1982. Cert. mgr. Inst. Cert. Profl. Mgrs. Asst. dir. student ctr. Montclair State U., 1972-73; from coord. reg. vet. tng. ctr. to dir. N.J. vet. edn. Kean Coll. (now Kean U.), Union, N.J., 1973-76; assoc. dir. ctr. adult devel. Rutgers U. Grad. Sch. Edn., 1976-79; coord. mgmt. inst. Adelphi U., Garden City, N.Y., 1979-80; mgmt. trainer Thomas J. Lipton, Inc., Englewood Cliffs, N.J., 1980-83; mgr. computer auditing tng. Deloitte, Touche, N.Y.C., 1983-88; adjunct prof. Raritan Valley Community Coll., Somerville, N.J., 1989-94, Northampton Community Coll., Bethlehem, Pa., 1989-94; dir. training tech. KBI Systems, Mountainside, N.J., 1990-93; cons. Clinton, N.J., 1993-94; trng. dir. Hertz Corp., Park Ridge, N.J., 1994-96; sales engr. TALX Corp., Clark, N.J., 1996-98; cons. SAP Am., Parsippany, N.J., 1998—; cons. U.S. Office of Edn., Washington, 1975-76. Active mem. Clinton (N.J.) Pub. Sch. PTA, 1990-91; exec. com. Middlesex County Coll. Alumni Assn., Edison, N.J., 1989—, Rutgers U. Grad. Sch. Edn. Alumni Assn., New Brunswick, N.J., 1988—. With U.S. Army, 1966. Mem. ASTD (chair career counseling com. 1979-94), Inst. Cert. Profl. Mgrs. Avocations: computers, fooseball, volleyball. Home: 23 Marudy Dr Clinton NJ 08809-1220 Office: 60 Walnut Ave Ste 100 Clark NJ 07066-1647

BURTON, AL, producer, director, writer; b. Chgo.; s. D. Chester and Isabelle (Olenick) G.; m. Sally Lou Lewis, Jan. 8, 1956; 1 dau., Jennifer. BS cum laude, Northwestern U. Exec. v.p. creative affairs Norman Lear-Embassy Communications, Inc., 1973-83; exec. producer-cons. Universal TV, 1983-92; exec. prodr., v.p. syndication Castle Rock Entertainment, 1992-95; pres. Al Burton Prodns., Beverly Hills, Calif., 1995—; bd. dirs. Pilgrim Group Funds; adv. bd. Samantha Smith Found. Producer Johnny Mercer's Mus. Chairs, 1952-55, Oscar Levant Show, 1955-61; creative producer Teen-Age Fair, 1962-72; exec. producer Charles in Charge, CBS-TV, 1984-85, Tribune Entertainment, 1986-91, Together We Stand, CBS-TV, 1986-87, Nothing Is Easy, 1987-88, The New Lassie, The Family Channel, 1989-92 (Outstanding Family Classic award Youth in Film 1994), Out of the Blue, Tribune Entertainment, 1995-96, Win Ben Stein's Money, Disney, Comedy Ctrl., 1997— (Cable Ace nomination, 3 Emmy nomination 1998, shared 2 Emmys, 1998); creative supr. Mary Hartman, Mary Hartman, Fernwood 2Night, America 2Night; prodn. supr. One Day At a Time, Facts of Life, Silver Spoons, The Jeffersons, Square Pegs, Different Strokes; composer-lyricist theme songs for Facts of Life, Different Strokes, Charles in Charge, The New Lassie (Genesis award, 1992), Together We Stand, Nothing Is Easy; cons. Domestic Life CBS-TV, 1983-84, Alan King Show, 1986. Shared Emmy award for outstanding comedy series All in the Family, 1978-89, Producers award Nat. Coun. for Families and TV, 1984, Jackie Coogan award for Oustanding Contbn. to Youth through Entertainment, 1991; honored for Different Strokes, NCCH, 1979-80; honored by Calif. Gov.'s Com. for employment of the handicapped for Facts of Life, 1981-82, for Charles in Charge, 1988; recipient Youth in Film award Charles in Charge, 1990, The New Lassie, 1994, Genesis award for portrayal animal issues The New Lassie, 1992; spl. commendation Entertainment Industries Coun. for The New Lassie and Charles in Charge, 1990. Mem. AFTRA, Chmn.'s Coun. of Caucus for Producers, Writers and Dirs., Dirs. Guild Am., Writers Guild Am., Acad. TV Arts and Scis., Acad. Magical Arts. *I believe that, in order to achieve success, one should make an occupation of his or her hobby.*

BURTON, ALAN HARVEY, city official; b. Chgo., Mar. 26, 1952; s. Harvey C. and Lois (Fitzpatrick) B.; (div. Oct. 1987); children: Douglas Alan, Marla Joy. Bs, Western Ill. U., 1974, MS, 1986. Recreation supr. Park Ridge (Ill.) Park Dist., 1974-75; dir. parks and recreation York Ctr. Park Dist., Lombard, Ill., 1975-78; dir. parks and recreation City of Berwyn, Ill., 1978-82, adminstr., 1982-86; dir. parks and recreation Norridge (Ill.) Park Dist., 1986-93; recreation bur. chief City of Orlando, Fla., 1993-96; dir. leisure svcs. City of Ormond Beach, Fla., 1996—; chmn. Berwyn Bus. Commn., 1984-86; cons. Berwyn Devel. Corp., 1986-88. Mem. Suburban Cook County Spl. Olympics, Franklin Park, Ill., 1983; hon. EMT Ill. Dept. Pub. Health, 1984; mem. at large Boy Scouts Am., La Grange, Ill., 1986, chmn. dist. nominating com.; rep. West Cen. Mcpl. Conf., Western Springs, Ill., 1987; pres. United Way of Harwood Heights (Ill.)/Norridge, 1990; active Fla. Conservation Corps., 1994; bd. dirs. Ormond Art Mus. Recipient Arbor Day award Ill. Assn. Park Dists., 1977, Individual Merit award, 1986, Gold Medal finalist Nat. Sporting Goods Found., 1991, 92, 93. Mem. Nat. Park and Recreation Assn. (U.S. del. to Japan, youth at risk sect., so. rep.), Nat. Soc. Fundraising Execs., Fla. Recreation and Park Assn., Ill. Park and Recreation Assn. (issues com., long-range planning com., Meritorious Svc. award 1990), Northeastern Ill. Planning Commn. (open space com. 1991-92), Fla. Park and Recreation Assn., West Suburban Spl. Recreation Assn. (bd. dirs. 1991), Berwyn Hist. Soc., Kiwanis Club of Ormond Beach. Lutheran. Avocations: backpacking, theater, genealogy, biking, science fiction. Home: 915 Ocean Shore Blvd Apt 707 Ormond Beach FL 32176-8307

BURTON, ANNA MARJORIE, nurse; b. Pontiac, Mich., May 1, 1931; d. Harold Vale and Sophia (Eaton) Kelly; children: Julie A. Burton Stone, William A., Rory R., Kenneth G. Student Mich. State U., 1949-51; A.A. in Bus. Mgmt., Fla. Keys Community Coll., 1976, A.S. in Nursing, 1983; R.N., Fla., Calif., N.Y. Orthodontic technician Birmingham, Mich., 1960-67; ofcl. rep. Social Security Adminstrn., Lexington, Ky., 1967-71, Key West, Fla., 1972-79; pvt. duty nurse specializing in internat. travel for persons with med. and phys. challenges, 1979—. Recipient Appreciation award Vets. Council, 1974; hon. Conch and Key, City of Key West, 1974, 100 Countdry award, Trod the 24 award for having stepped on land in all 24 time zones Internat. Travel News. Mem. U.S. Coast Guard Aux. (permanent) (1st female comdr. 1976), U.S. Power Squadron, Key West Power Squadron (safe boating instr., sec. 1984-85), Am. Nurses Assn., Fla. Nurses Assn., Dist. 25 Nurses Assn., Bus. and Profl. Women (treas. 1988-93), Handicapped Boaters Assn., Boat Owners Assn. of U.S., U.S. Yacht Racing Union, Key West Art and Hist. Soc. (life), Am. Cancer Soc., Am. Diabetes Assn., Juvenile Diabetes Assn., Am. Heart Assn., Travelers Century Club (life), Key West Yacht Club (hon.). Home: PO Box 1084 Key West FL 33041-1084

BURTON, ANTHONY JOHN, bishop; b. Ottawa, Ont., Can., Aug. 11, 1959; s. Peter Michael and Rachel Harragin Wood (Greaves) B.; m. Anna Kristine Erickson, Apr. 8, 1989; children: Caroline Rachel Georgina, Peter Charles Hugh. BA with honors, Trinity Coll. U. Toronto, 1982, U. Oxford, 1987; MA, U. Oxford, 1992; DD, U. King's Coll., 1994. Ordained priest, 1988; consecrated bishop, 1993. Curate St. John the Bapt. Ch., North Sydney, N.S., 1987-88; rector Trinity Ch., Sydney Mines, N.S., 1988-91; rector, canon residentiary Cath. Ch. St. Alban the Martyr, Prince Albert, Sask., 1991-93; dean Diocese of Saskatchewan, Prince Albert, 1991-94, bishop, 1993—. Contbg. author: Anglican Essentials: Reclaiming Faith Within the Anglican Church of Canada, 1995; contbr. articles and columns to profl. jours. Anglican. Avocation: walking. Office: Diocese of Sask Synod, 1308 5th Ave E, Prince Albert, SK Canada S6V 2H7

BURTON, ARTHUR HENRY, JR., insurance company executive; b. Phila., Jan. 24, 1934; s. Arthur H. and Gertrude May (Williams) B.; m. Gail M. LaBonte, Sept. 6, 1955; children: Bradford, Steven, Robert, John. AB, Princeton U., 1955; grad. Exec. Program, Columbia U., 1967. C.L.U. With Prudential Ins. Co. Am., 1968—; assoc. dir. group ins. Newark, 1968-70; dir. group ins. Chgo., 1970-75; v.p. group ins. Mpls., 1975-78; v.p. Newark, 1978-80, Parsippany, N.J., 1980-81; pres. Cen. Atlantic ops. Ft Washington, Pa., 1981-83; pres. North Cen. ops. Mpls., 1983-88; asst. to chmn. Prudential-Bache Securities, N.Y.C., 1988; sr. v.p. human resources Prudential, Newark, 1988-89; ret., 1992; vice chmn. Prudential Securities, 1990-92; bd. dirs. Options Clearing Corp., 1991-92; sr. advisor Seabridge Investment Advisors, LLC, 1997. Trustee United Way SE Pa., Phila., 1982-83; bd. dirs. World Affairs Council, 1982-83, Chgo. Area Council, 1983-86, United Way Mpls., 1987—; counties chmn. United Way S.E. Pa., 1982-83. Served to 1st lt. U.S. Army, 1956-57. Mem. Ins. Fedn. Pa. (bd. dirs., chmn. 1981-83), Ins. Fedn. Minn. (exec. com. 1983—), Mpls. C. of C. (bd. dirs. 1983-87), Pa. Economy League (bd. govs. 1981-83), First Inf. Corp. (bd. dirs. 1990—). Republican. Episcopalian. Clubs: Princeton of N.Y., Merion Cricket (Phila.), Windsor (Vero Beach, Fla.). Home: 3425 Windsor Blvd Vero Beach FL 32963-4714 *Honesty, fair dealing and respect for others ultimately spawn success.*

BURTON, BARBARA ABLE, psychotherapist; b. Columbia, S.C.; d. Eugene Walter Able and Mary Louise (Chadwick) Cantelou; 1 child, Stacia Louise. BA in Psychology, Ga. State U.; MSW, U. Ala., 1970. Diplomate Am. Bd. Examiners in Clin. Social Work, Internat. Acad. Behavioral Medicine, Counseling and Psychotherapy; cert. Am. Acad. Cert. Social Workers, NASW, diplomate clin. social work. Assoc. exec. dir. Positive Maturity, Inc., Birmingham, Ala., 1970-72; comm. org. planner Community Svc. Council, INc., Birmingham, Ala., 1972-75; adj. faculty U. Ala., Tuscaloosa, Ala., 1975-77; dir. Ensley Outpatient Drug Abuse Clinic, Birmingham, Ala., 1975-77, Sch. of Social Work, Miles Coll., Birmingham, Ala., 1977-78; prog. mgr. and clin. cons. Goodwill Industries of Ala., Birmingham, Ala., 1977-81; pvt. practice New Orleans, 1983--; cons. Omega Internat. Inst., New Orleans, 1988--. Author: Love Me, Love Me Not, and Other Matters That Matter, 1990. Past chmn. Policy and Program Com. Birmingham Urban League; Ala. Adv. Com. on Social Svcs.; Ala. Com. for the Dev. of Higher Ed.; Ala. Conf. of Social Work. NIMH fellow Inst. on Human Sexuality, U. Hawaii, 1976. Mem. Am. Assn. Sex Educators, Counselors and Therapists, Nat. Assn. Social Workers, Pvt. Practitioners Unit of New Orleans, Acad. Cert. Social Workers, Internat. Platform Com., Psi Chi. Avocations: creative writing, reading, interior design. Office: 1631 Constantinople St New Orleans LA 70115-4707

BURTON, BARRY ALAN, county official; b. Georgetown, Ohio, July 20, 1964; s. Charles D. B. and Wanda Faye Sehier; m. Janet Elaine, June 6, 1987; children: Michael, Christopher. BS in Urban Adminstrn., U. Cin., 1987; MPA in Pub. Adminstrn., No. Ky. U., 1995. Budget analyst Hamilton County, Cin., 1988-93, dir. environ. svc., 1993-96; county adminstr. Allegheny County, Cumberland, Md., 1996-98; deputy county adminstr. Franklin County, Columbus, Ohio, 1998—. Mem. Bishop Walsj H.S. Bd., Cumberland, 1997-98. Maj. U.S. Army res., 1982—. Named Pub. Arminstr. of Yr. Am. Soc. Pub. Adminstrs., 1997. Mem. Md. County Adminstrs. Assn. (pres. 1998), County Adminstrs. Assn. Ohio, Internat. City/County Mgrs. Assn., Rotary. Avocation: running. Home: 6328 Conleth Cir Dublin OH 43017 Office: Franklin County Commrs 373 S High St Columbus OH 43215

BURTON, BRANDIE, professional golfer; b. San Benardino, CA, Jan. 8, 1972. Student, Ariz. State U. 5th ranked woman LPGA Tour, 1992; mem. U.S. Solheim Cup Team, 1992, 94, 96, 98; mem. U.S. Curtis Cup Team. Named LPGA Rookie of Yr., 1991, Female Player of Yr., Golf World, 1993; winner San Diego Jr. World Championships, 1987, 89, PGA Nat. Champion, 1988, USGA Jr. Champion, 1989, North and South Championship, 1990, Broadmoor Championship, 1990, PING Welch's Championship, 1992, Jamie Farr Toledo Classic, 1993, du Maurier Ltd. Classic, 1993, SAFECO Classic, 1993, du Maurier Classic, 1998. Avocations: fishing, softball. Address: care LPGA 100 International Golf Dr Daytona Beach FL 32124-1082*

BURTON, CHARLES HENNING, lawyer; b. Washington, Nov. 25, 1915; s. Charles Henry and Bessie R. (Harrell) B.; m. Mary Sheppard, Sept. 6, 1941; children: Nancy Leigh Burton Wysling, Susan C. Burton Roberts, Mary Ellen Burton Graves, Charles S. Attended, George Washington U., 1937-41; LLB, Am. U., 1936, LLM, 1937. Bar: D.C. 1936, Md. 1957. Gen. counsel D.C. Unemployment Compensation Bd., 1938-42; mem. firm MacCracken & O'Rourke, Washington, 1946-50; mem. Law Offices Robert Ash, Washington, 1950-56; gen. partner Bauersfeld, Burton, Hendricks and Vanderhoff, Bethesda, Md., 1956—; ltd. ptnr. A.W.S. Assocs., S & H Assocs.; pres., dir. North Shore Corp., Links, Inc., Charles H. Burton, P.A.; dir. Mattos, Inc., Sisk Mailing Svc. Inc., Sisk Fulfillment, Inc.; gen. counsel Bapt. World Alliance, McLean, Va., 1958, Calvary Bapt. Ch., 1950. Bd. dirs. Jovius Found., Mustard Seed Found., F.W. Harris Found. for Personal Evangelism; trustee Kendall Mission Fund; v.p. Cen. Union Mission; nat. chmn. World Peace Through Law of World Jurist Assn. Comdr. USNR, 1942-46. Fellow Am. Bar Found.; mem. Am. Bar Assn. (editor Young Lawyer 1946-48, nat. sec. Jr. Bar 1949, nat. vice-chmn. 1950, nat. chmn. 1951, ho. of dels. 1952-59), Sigma Chi, Sigma Nu Phi. Club: Montgomery County Country. Home: 21600 Davis Mill Rd Germantown MD 20876-4418 Office: Bauersfeld Burton Hendricks & Vanderhoff 7101 Wisconsin Ave Ste 1011 Bethesda MD 20814-4805

BURTON, CHARLES VICTOR, physician, surgeon, inventor; b. N.Y.C., Jan. 2, 1935; s. Norman Howard and Ruth Esther (Putziger) B.; m. Joy Burton; children—Matthew, Timothy, Andrew, Dawn, Stacy, Chad. Student, Johns Hopkins U., Balt., 1952-56; MD, N.Y. Med. Coll., 1960. Diplomate Am. Bd. Neurol. Surgery, Nat. Bd. Med. Examiners, Am. Bd. Forensic Medicine, Am Bd. Spinal Surgery. Intern surgery Yale U. Med. Ctr., 1961-62; asst. resident neurol. surgery Johns Hopkins Hosp., Balt., 1962-66, chief resident, 1966-67; assoc. chief surgery, chief neurosurgery USPHS Hosp., Seattle, 1967-69; vis. research affiliate Primate Ctr., U. Wash., 1967-69; asst. prof. neurosurgery Temple U. Health Scis. Ctr., Phila., 1970-73, assoc. prof., 1973-74; neurol. research coordinator Temple U. Health Scis. Ctr., 1970-74; dir. dept. neuroaugmentive surgery Sister Kenny Inst., Mpls., 1974-81, med. dir. Low Back Clinic, 1978-81; med. dir. Inst. for Low Back Care, Mpls., 1981-96; sr. med. dir. Inst. Low Back and Neck Care, Mpls., 1996—; Biomed. Instrumentations Internat., Ltd., 1988-92; co-chmn. Joint Neurosurg. Com. on Devices and Drugs, 1973-77; chmn. adv. panel on neurologic devices FDA, 1974-77, Internat. Standards Orgn., 1974-76; mem. U.S. Biomed. Instrumentation Del. to Soviet Union, 1974. Editor Neuroorthopedics jour., 1987—. Patentee surgical devices, operating room fiberophic headlights, clin. therapy systems and techniques. Research fellow Nat. Polio Found., 1956, HEW, 1958; neurosurg. fellow Johns Hopkins Hosp., 1960-61, 62-67, 69-70. Fellow ACS (exec. com. Minn. chpt. 1989-92); mem. Congress Neurol. Surgeons (chmn. com. materials and devices 1972-79), Am. Assn. Neurol. Surgeons, Minn. Neurosurg. Soc., AAAS, ASTM (chmn. com. materials 1973-78), Internat. Soc. Study of Lumbar Spine (exec. com. 1986-89), N.Am. Spine Soc. (exec. com. 1987-91, chmn. com. on profl. conduct 1991-92, dir. coun. mem. affairs 1992-94, bd. dirs. 1990-94), Am. Nat. Standards Inst. (med. device tech. adv. bd. 1973-78), Am. Bd. Spine Surgery (bd. dirs. 1997—, chair ethics com. 1998—), Philadelphia County Med. Soc. (med.-legal com. 1970-74), Minn. Med. Assn. (Gold medal award for best sci. presentation at 1975 meeting, subcom. on med. testimony 1978—), Hennepin County Med. Soc. (med.-legal com. 1975—), Mpls. Acad. Medicine, Cor et Manus Soc., Profl. Assn. Diving Instrs. (underwater photography splty. diver), Am. Back Soc., Twin Cities Spine Soc. (pres. 1994-95), Back Pain Assn. Am. (hon. chmn. 1995—), bd. dirs. Am. Bd. Sinal Surgery, 1997, Chmn. Com. on Ethics, Am. Bd. of Spinal Surgery, 1998, Johns Hopkins U. Alumni Assn. (pres. Minn. chpt. 1988-92), Yale Surg. Soc., Alpha Epsilon Delta. Home: 148 W Lake St Excelsior MN 55331-1744 Office: Inst Low Back and Neck Care 2800 Chicago Ave Minneapolis MN 55407-1318

BURTON, DAN L., congressman; b. Indpls., June 21, 1938; m. Barbara Jean Logan, 1959; children: Kelly, Danielle Lee, Danny Lee II. Mem. Ind. Ho. Reps., Indpls., 1967-68, 77-80, Ind. State Senate, 1969-70, 81-82; owner ins. and real estate firm, 1968—; mem. 98th-105th Congresses from 6th Ind. dist., 1983—; mem. internat. rels. com.; chmn. govt. reform and oversight com. Pres. Vols. of Am.; pres. Ind. Christian Benevolent Assn., Com. for Constl. Govt., Family Support Ctr. Served with U.S. Army, 1957-58. Republican. Office: US Ho of Reps 2185 Rayburn Ofc Bldg Washington DC 20515-1406*

BURTON, DANIEL G., insurance executive; b. N.Y.C., Mar. 12, 1935; s. Herbert Edward and Leabelle (Bigelman) Goodstein; m. Roberta Rosenbaum, Dec. 25, 1957 (div. Mar. 1980); children: Marc, Lisa, Paul; m. Anita Jurrist, Nov. 28, 1982. BSBA, NYU, 1960; D of Commerce Sci., London Inst. Applied Sci., 1973; CFP cert., Adelphi U., 1982. Registered investment adviser; cert. fin. planner. Nat. sales mgr. Bernardi Originals, NYU, 1958-68; agt. New Eng. Life Ins. Co., 1968-77; gen. agt. U.S. Life Ins. Co., 1978—; pres., CEO Innovative Monetary Designs Group, Rockville Centre, N.Y., 1979-98, Burton Security and Investigation, 1986—; mem. Nassau County Police Res., 1990—; lectr. in field. Contr. articles to profl. jours. Pres. bd. mgrs. Lido Beach (N.Y.) Towers Condominium, 1990-98. Sgt. U.S. Army, 1954-56. Mem. Inst. CFPs, Nassau Life Underwriters Assn. (bd. dirs. 1987-88), Soc. Fin. Planners Adelphi U. (pres. 1983-85), Million Dollar Round Table (life), Shriners, Masons. Avocation: fishing. Home: 5058 Windsor Parke Dr Boca Raton FL 33496-1637 Office: 100 Merrick Rd Rockville Centre NY 11570-4800 also: 5030 Champion Blvd Ste G6 Boca Raton FL 33496-2496

BURTON, DARRELL IRVIN, engineering executive; b. Ashtabula, Ohio, Sept. 21, 1926; s. George Irvin and Barbara Elizabeth (Streyle) B.; m. Lois

Carol Warkentien, Apr. 14, 1951; children: Linda Jean Burton Clinton, Lisa Ann Burton Watts, Lori Elizabeth Burton Admokom. BS in Radio Engring., Chgo. Tech. Coll., 1954. R&D engr. Motorola, Inc., Chgo., 1951-60; devel. engr. Hallicrafters, Chgo., 1960-62; chief engr. TRW, Inc., Des Plaines, Ill., 1962-65; devel. engr. Warwick, Niles, Ill., 1965-68; systems mgr. Admiral Corp., Chgo., 1968-76; elec.-electronics lab. mgr. Montgomery Ward & Co., Chgo., 1976-82; staff engr. Wells-Gardner Electronics Corp., Chgo., 1982-85; sr. engr. Zenith Electronics Corp., Chgo., 1985-91, ret., 1991; pres. Burton Electronics Co., Elmhurst, Ill., 1992—; tchr. electronics and math. Pres. Addison Homeowners Assn., 1958-60, v.p., 1960-62; mem. Addison Plan Commn., 1960-63; mem. bd. edn. Immanuel Luth. Sch., 1985-87, dir. sound/tape ministry, 1973-98, ret., 1998, v.p., 1997, pres., 1998. Home: 112 Lawndale Ave Elmhurst IL 60126-3522

BURTON, DONALD JOSEPH, chemistry educator; b. Balt., July 16, 1934; s. Lawrence Andrew and Dorothy Wilhelmina (Koehler) B.; m. Margaret Anna Billing, June 21, 1958; children—Andrew, Jennifer, David, Julie, Elizabeth. B.S., Loyola Coll., Balt., 1956; Ph.D., Cornell U., 1961; post-grad., Purdue U., 1961-62. Asst. prof. chemistry dept. U. Iowa, Iowa City, 1962-67; assoc. prof. U. Iowa, 1967-70, prof., 1970—, Roy Carver/Ralph Shriner prof. chemistry, 1989—. Recipient Gov.'s Sci. Medal for Sci. Achievement, 1988; Japanese Soc. for Promotion Sci. fellow, 1979. Mem. Am. Chem. Soc. (chmn. fluorine div. 1978, award for creative work in fluorine chemistry 1984, Midwest Chemistry award 1990), Chem. Soc. London, Sigma Xi, Alpha Chi Sigma. Home: 4304 Oakridge Trl NE Iowa City IA 52240-7735 Office: U Iowa Dept Chemistry Iowa City IA 52242

BURTON, DOUGLAS GRAY, magazine editor; b. Midland, Tex., Apr. 15, 1951; s. Horace N. and Helen G. (Greer) B.; m. Keiko Demachi, May 10, 1979; children: Daniel, Michele, George. Student, Inst. for European Studies, Vienna, Austria, 1971-72; BA, Washington & Lee U., 1973. Assoc. sr. editor The World & I Mag., Washington, 1985-93; assoc. editor Insight on the News, Washington, 1993—. Essayist: (book revs.) The World & I, 1985-93; column writer: (opinion essays) Insight Mag., 1995-99; contbr. The Washington Times. Polit. activist Md. Rep. Party, Prince Georges County, 1996; contbg. mem. Prince Georges Civic Fedn., Upper Marlborough, Md., 1992-97; active Citizens for Greenbelt, 1994-97. Mem. Nat. Press Club (mem. com. 1995-96). Republican. Avocations: long-distance running, white-water rafting. Home: 2 Laurel Hill Rd # M Greenbelt MD 20770-1702 Office: Insight 3600 New York Ave NE Washington DC 20002-1947

BURTON, EDWARD LEWIS, retired industrial procedures and training consultant, educator; b. Colfax, Iowa, Dec. 8, 1935; s. Lewis Harrison and Mary Burton; m. Janet Jean Allan, July 29, 1956; children: Mary, Cynthia, Katherine, Daniel. BA in Indsl. Edn., U. No. Iowa, 1958; MS in Indsl. Edn., U. Wis.-Stout, 1969; postgrad., Ariz. State U., 1971-76. Tchr. apprentice program S.E. Iowa Community Coll., Burlington, 1965-68; tchr. indsl. edn. Keokuk (Iowa) Sr. H.S., 1965-68, Oak Park (Ill.)-River Forest High Sch., 1968-70; tchr. Rio Salado Community Coll., Phoenix, 1972-82; tchr. indsl. edn. Buckeye (Ariz.) Union High Sch., 1970-72; cons. curriculum Westside Area Career Opportunities Program - Ariz. Dept. Edn.; instr. vocat. automotive Dysart High Sch., Peoria, Ariz., 1979-81; tng. adminstr. Ariz. Pub. Service Co., Phoenix, 1981-90; tng. devel. cons. NUS Corp., 1991-95; tchr. vocat. automobile Holbrook (Ariz.) H.S., 1995-96, Gila Bend (Ariz.) H.S., 1996—; mem. dispatcher tng. com. Western Systems Coord. Coun., Salt Lake City, 1986-90; owner Aptitude Analysis Co., 1987—; mem. IEEE Dispatcher Tng. Work Group, 1988-91. Editor: Bright Ideas for Career Education, 1974, More Bright Ideas for Career Education, 1975. Mem. Citizens Planning Com., Buckeye, 1987-90, Town Governing Coun., Buckeye, 1990-91. NDEA grantee, 1967. Mem. NEA (life), NRA (life, endowment), Ariz. Rifle and Pistol Assn., Ariz. Indsl. Edn. Assn. (life), Mensa (test proctor 1987—), Masons. Republican. Methodist. Avocations: shooting, photography, camping, boating, travel. Home and Office: 19845 W Van Buren St Buckeye AZ 85326-5676

BURTON, GARY, musician; b. Anderson, Ind., Jan. 23, 1943; s. Wayne and Bernice B.; m. Catherine Goldwyn, July 12, 1975; children: Stephanie Clare, Samuel John. Ed., Berklee Coll. Music, Boston Conservatory Music. Vibraphone player, leader jazz group, 1967—; instr. Berklee Coll. Music, 1972-84, dean, 1985—. Rec. artist, including: Alone At Last, 1972 (Grammy award 1972), Artist's Choice, 1988. Named Jazzman of Yr. Downbeat Mag., 1968; winner Downbeat Mag. Poll, 1968-86; recipient Grammy award 1972, 78, 79, 99. Office: care Ted Kurland Assos 173 Brighton Ave Allston MA 02134-2003*

BURTON, HERBERT, composer; b. Berlin, 1918; m. Marianne Kortner; children: Michael, Stefan. Student piano composition with, Stefan Wolpe, Eli Friedmann, Frank Pelleg, Tel-Aviv; student piano composition, Jerusalem Conservatory Music, Columbia U. Prof. composition U. Ill. Sch. Music, Urbana, 1963—. Composer: Mobile for Orch., Sonoriferous Loops, Gestures for Eleven, Non-Sequitur VI, Gesto for Piccolo and Piano, Trio for Flute, Double Bass and Percussion, Trio for Trumpet, Trombone and Percussion, Futility 1964, Mutatis Mutandis: Computer Graphics for Interpreters, Infraudibles, Nonet, Piece of Prose, Three String Quartets, "at loose ends:, In and...and Out, Dust, More Dust, Dustiny, A Mere Ripple, U-Turn-To, I Told You So, Twice Upon Three Times, SNOW 1984, Six for Five by Two in Pieces; per contra: serenata: bassa; just seven for drum; The Laughing Third for Piano, 1993, Come, Scenario and Go for 13 Players, 1994, On Stilts Among Ducks for viola and tape, 1995, Floating Hierarchies for various small ensembles, 1995, for double-bass solo...yet with a heart of gold!, 1997; also scores for theatre; author: Über Musik und zum Computer, 1971, My Words and Where I Want Them, 1986, 2d edit., 1990, Drawing Distinctions Links Contradictions, 1997; contr. articles to profl. jours. Founder The Performers' Workshop, 1974, The Performers' Workshop Ensemble, 1978. Recipient Norbert Wiener medal Am. Soc. for Cybernetics, 1993. Research in computer composition, designer computer project SAWDUST. Office: U Ill Sch Music Urbana IL 61801*

BURTON, IAN, environmentalist, consultant, scholar, writer; b. Derby, Eng., June 24, 1935; came to U.S., 1957; s. Frank and Elsie Victoria (Barnes) B. BA, U. Birmingham, Eng., 1956, MA, 1957; PhD, U. Chgo., 1962. From asst. prof. to prof. U. Toronto, Ont., Can., 1961-90, dir. Environment Inst., 1979-84; vice chmn., bd. dirs. Internat. Fedn. Insts. for Advanced Study, Toronto, 1986-90; spl. advisor Corp. Policy Group, Environment Can., 1989-90; dir. Can. Climate Ctr. Environment Can., Ottawa, 1990-94; dir. Environ. Adaptation Rsch. Group, Toronto, 1994-96; sr. cons. Ford Found., Calcutta, India. 1964-66, Internat. Devel. Research Centre, Ottawa, 1972-75; bd. dirs. Internat. Fedn. Inst. for Advanced Study, Toronto, Maastricht, The Netherlands, 1984-90, Found. Intrnat. Tng.; adj. prof. U. Toronto, 1990—; juror St. Francis Environ. Prize, Assisi, Italy; cons. UNESCO, WHO, UN Environment Program, Global Environment Facility, Rockefeller Found., World Bank, Lead Inst., 1994, European Commn., 1997, World Resources Inst., 1996—. Author: (with others) Environment as Hazard, 1978, 2d edit. 1993; co-editor: Environmental Risk Assessment, 1980, Geography Resources and Environment. Fulbright scholar Oberlin Coll., 1957-58; Sr. Connaught fellow, 1984-86. Fellow Royal Soc. Can., World Acad. Arts and Sci.; mem. Internat. Soc. Biometeorology (v.p. 1996—). Home: 72 Coolmine Rd, Toronto, ON Canada M6J 3E9 Office: Atmospheric Environ Svc, 4905 Dufferin St, Downsview, ON Canada M3H 5T4 *Say to yourself once every day, "I am not my job, my job is not me". Believe and work passionately according to your own values. Your job should reflect your values, not your values reflect your job. Do not let where you stand depend on where you sit.*

BURTON, JAMES SAMUEL, physical chemist; b. Richmond, Ky., Aug. 1, 1936; s. Albert and Callie (Brooks) B.; m. Ophelia L. Weaver, July 16, 1959; 1 child, Traci Michele. AB in Chemistry, Berea Coll., 1958; MS in Phys. Chemistry, Howard U., 1962, PhD in Phys. Chemistry, 1964. Dir. D.C. Water Resources Ctr., Washington, 1974-75; asst. dir. rsch. Office of Water Rsch. and Tech., Washington, 1975-79, acting dir., 1977; staff asst. Dept. Interior, Washington, 1979-81; spl. asst. rsch. program Bur. Reclamation, Washington, 1981-83; spl. asst. water rsch. program Office of Water Policy, Washington, 1983; spl. asst. water rsch. program U.S. Geol. Survey, Reston, Va., 1983-85, mem. water rsch. program mgmt. staff, 1985-89; chief Nat. Water Data Exch. U.S. Geol. Survey, Reston, 1989—; program mgr.; lectr. chemistry No. Va. C.C., Alexandria, 1971-72, George Mason U., Fairfax U., 1987-88. Contbr. articles to profl. jours. Recipient Disting. Alumnus award Berea Coll., 1980. Mem. ASTM, Am. Chem. Soc., Am. Water Resources Assn., Sigma Xi. Avocations: singing, martial arts. Office: US Geol Survey 440 National Ctr Reston VA 20192

BURTON, JEFF, professional race car driver; b. June 29, 1967; m. Kim Burton; 1 child, Kimberle Paige. Orange County Speedway champion, 1987; 21-time winner NASCAR Winston Racing Series; 4-time NASCAR Busch Grand Nat. Divsn. Series winner, 1989-92; qualified 6th NASCAR Winston Cup, Loudon, N.H., 1993, 3 top-10 finishes, 1994, 2 top-10 finishes 1995, 6 top-5 finishes 1996, 3 Winston Cup victories 1997, including Tex., Loudon, Martinsville, Va.; 2 wins, 13 top-10 finishes, 18 top-5 finishes, 1998; 2d in points lead Winston Cup 1999; winner DuraLube/KMart 500, 1999. Named South Boston (Va.) Most Popular Driver, 1988, NASCAR Rookie of Yr., 1994. Avocations: basketball, boating. *

BURTON, JOHN BRYAN, music educator; b. Lubbock, Tex., Nov. 10, 1948; s. John Clark and Geraldine (Wolf) B. B in Music Edn., West Tex. State U., 1970; MA, Western State Coll. Colo., 1973; D in Music Edn., U. So. Miss., 1986. Dir. bands, humanities Jal (N.Mex.) Schs., 1978-79; dir. bands, gen. music Bronte (Tex.) Schs., 1979-80; dir. bands Comfort (Tex.) Schs., 1980-82; dir. high sch. band, music coord. Kirbyville (Tex.) Ind. Schs., 1982-84; grad. asst. U. So. Miss., Hattiesburg, 1984-86; asst. prof. music, dir. bands, music theatre dir. Frostburg (Md.) State U., 1986-91; prof. music edn. West Chester (Pa.) Univ., 1991—, coord. grad. studies, 1997—; panelist Symposium on Native Am. Musics, Coll. Music Soc. 33d Nat. Meeting, Washington, 1990; curriculum cons. Prince Georges County Schs., Upper Marlboro, Md., 1991, other Mid-Atlantic schs.; guest condr. Allegany County Honor Band, Tri-State Honor Band, 1986-87, Allegany County Band, Bedford County Band, Mineral County Band, 1987-88, Allegany Solo and Ensemble Festival Harford County Intermediate Bands Festival, 1990-91; presenter conf. Ea. divsn. Music Educators Nat. Conf., 1993, 95, 97, So. divsn., 1994, Internat. Kodaly Soc. Conf., Am. Orff-Schulwerk Assn., Orff 100 Internat. Conf. on Music and Dance, Melbourne, Australia, 1995, Internat. Soc. for Music Edn., Amsterdam, 1996, Internat. Soc. for Music Edn. Commn. on Cmty. Music Making, Liverpool, 1996, many others; lectr. nat. meeting Music Educators Nat. Conf., 1992, 94, 96; cons. Native Am. music, 1993, 94, nat. chair, editor Social Scis. Rsch. Group Soc. for Rsch. in Music Edn., 1994-96; edit. adv. bd. mem. Tchg. Music, 1996-98; keynote lectr. World Conf. Internat. Soc. Music Edn., 1994, 96, 98; mem. ISME Commn. on cmty. music activity, Durban, South Africa, 1998; mem. exec. bd. Soc. for More Tchr. Edn. (ea. rep.), 1998—; presenter and lectr. in field; vis. prof. U. Washington, 1995, Ga. State U., 1995, Trenton State Coll., 1996, U. Okla., 1996, U. Nebr., 1997, U. Sioux Falls, 1997, Rider U., 1998. Assoc. editor: Scholars, 1994—; author: moving Within the Circle: Contemporary Native American Music and Dance, 1993, Global Experiences in Music, 1992, Fundamentals of Music Made Easy, 1990, Music of the Minority Nationalities of the People's Republic of China, 1989, When the Earth Was Like New: Songs and Stories of the Western Apache, 1994, Songs of A Living Apache Tradition: The Musical Life of Chesley Goseyun Wilson, 1994, (with Maria P. Kreiter) Give Voice to the Sound of the Wind: Native American Flute Music, 1997; contbg. author: Multicultural Perspectives in Music Education, 2d edit., 1996, Getting Started with Teaching Multicultural Music, 1996, Making Connections: Multicultural Traditions and the National Standards in Music Education, 1996, Strategies for Teaching: General Music K-4, 1996, Strategies for Teaching: General Music 5-8, 1996, Strategies for Teaching: General Music 9-12, 1996, Strategies for Teaching: Beginning and Middle Level Band Grades 5-8, 1996, Strategies for Teaching: High School Band, 1996, Strategies for Teaching: College Methods Class, 1996, Strategies for Teaching: High School Chorus, 1996, Many Seeds, Different Flowers--The Music Education Legacy of Carl Orff, 1997, On the Sociology of Music Education, 1997; contbr. songs to World of Children's Song, 1993, lessons and photographs to The Music Connection, 1995, songs and lessons to Share the Music, 1995, song transcriptions to OAKE Multicultural Songs, Dances and Games, 1995, articles to profl. jours. Mem. Nat. Band Assn., Music Educators Nat. Conf. (presenter nat. meeting 1992, 94, 96), Pa. Music Educators Assn., Coll. Band Dirs. Nat. Assn., Coll. Music Soc., Soc. for Ethnomusicology, Associated Photographers Internat., Audubon Soc., Amnesty Internat., Phi Mu Alpha, Alpha Chi, Kappa Delta Pi, Kappa Kappa Psi. Avocations: photography, travel, gardening. Home: 39 Webb Rd Chadds Ford PA 19317-9125 Office: West Chester U Sch Music West Chester PA 19383

BURTON, JOHN CAMPBELL, university dean, educator, consultant; b. N.Y.C., Sept. 17, 1932; s. James Campbell and Barbara (French) B.; m. Jane Garnjost, Apr. 6, 1957; children: Eve Bradley, Bruce Campbell. B.A., Haverford Coll., 1954; M.B.A., Columbia U., 1956, Ph.D., 1962. C.P.A., N.Y. Staff acct. Arthur Young & Co., N.Y.C., 1956-60; prof. acctg. and fin. Grad. Sch. Bus. Columbia U., N.Y.C., 1962-72, Ernst & Young prof. acctg. and fin., 1978—, dean Grad. Sch. Bus., 1982-88; chief acct. SEC, Washington, 1972-76; dep. mayor fin. City of N.Y., 1976-77; bd. dirs. Scholastic Inc.; dir., chmn. audit com. Commerce Clearing House Inc., 1979-95, First Pa. Corp.-First Pa. Bank, 1982-85; mem. adv. and valuation com. Warburg-Pincus Venture Capital Funds; mem. U.S. Comptroller Gen. Cons. Panel, 1978-95; bd. dirs. Accts. for Pub. Interest, 1978-85. Editor: Corporate Financial Reporting: Conflicts and Challenges, 1969, Corporate Financial Reporting: Ethical and Other Problems, 1972, (with Russell Palmer and Robert Kay) Handbook of Accounting and Auditing, 1981, The International World of Accounting: Challenges and Opportunities, 1981; co-mng. editor Acctg. Horizons, 1989-91; author: Accounting for Business Combinations, 1970, (with W.T. Porter) Auditing: A Conceptual Approach, 1971, and others; contbr. articles to profl. jours. Pres., trustee Millbrook Sch. (N.Y.), 1958-88; trustee ex officio Am. Assembly, 1982-88. Recipient Disting. Scholar award Hofstra U., 1975; Ford Found. fellow, 1961-62. Mem. AICPA (coun. 1980-83), Am. Acctg. Assn. (acad. v.p. 1980-82), Am. Fin. Assn., Am. Econ. Assn., Fin. Execs. Inst., Assn. Govtl. Accts., Nat. Assn. Securities Dealers (pub. gov. 1990-94), Met. Club (N.Y.C.), Lake Sunapee Yacht Club (N.H.). Clubs: Metropolitan (N.Y.C.); Lake Sunapee Yacht (N.H.). Home: 130 E End Ave Apt 12A New York NY 10028-7553 Office: Columbia U Uris Hall New York NY 10027

BURTON, JOHN LEE, SR., banker; b. Blaine, Ky., Mar. 30, 1927; s. H.G. and Gladys Marie (Gambill) B.; student Morehead State U., 1943-44; m. Guinola Hill Oct. 3, 1945; children: John Lee, Joseph Edward. Mcht., farmer, 1944-46; banker, 1946—. With Peoples Security Bank, Louisa, Ky., 1946—, pres., 1964—; pres., dir. Grayson Rural Electric Coop. (Ky.), 1950-95; pres., dir. Foothills Rural Telephone Coop., Staffordsville, Ky., 1966—; vice chmn., dir. East Ky. Power Corp., Winchester. Advisor, Ky. Gov.'s Econ. Devel. Commn., 1976; past agrl. chmn. Lawrence County; past mem. jury com. and election com. of Lawrence Co. Named hon. clk. Ct. Appeals Ky., 1976; hon. treas. State of Ky., 1978, hon. sec. state, 1980. Mem. Ky. Bankers Assn. (past sec., v.p., pres. group 9), Ind. Community Bankers Ky., Ky. Hist. Soc. Mem. Ch. of Christ. Office: PO Box 60 Louisa KY 41230-0060

BURTON, JOSEPH ALFRED, state legislator; b. Atlanta, Aug. 30, 1923; s. Louis Albert and Lillian Catherine (Stroupe) B.; m. Bessie Lucille Walraven, Apr. 15, 1950; children: Virginia, Patricia, Carolyn, Lewis. BS in Indsl. Mgmt., Ga. Tech. U., 1949. Clerical worker Nat. Biscuit Co., Atlanta, 1941; clerical and civil svc. worker U.S. Army Signal Corps, Ft. McPherson, Ga., 1941-42; sales assoc. U.S. Envelope Co., Doraville, Ga., 1949-51, 52-56; sales assoc., mgr. dist. and regional divsn. Tectum Corp., Atlanta, 1956-63; pres. Joe Burton Co., Tucker, Ga., 1963-88; mem. Ga. Ho. Reps., Atlanta, 1973-83, Ga. Senate, Atlanta, 1983—; bd. dirs., mem. adv. bd. SPEC needs students DeKalb Coll., 1990—. Bd. dirs. Goodwill Industries, Atlanta, 1988—; mem. adv. bd. Salvation Army, Atlanta; chair adv. bd. Peachcrest Corps, 1990—; mem. adv. bd. Friends Disabled Adults; mem. Nat. Adv. Bd. Birthright. 1st lt. U.S. Army Air Corp, 1942-45, ETO, 1951-52, Korea.

BURTON, KAY FOX, retired secondary education educator, guidance counselor; b. Ottawa, Ill., Jan. 4, 1938; d. Andrew Owen and Hattie L. (Rasmusson) Fox; m. Edward John Burton, Dec. 26, 1966. BA, St. Xavier U., Chgo., 1960; MEd, Loyola U., Chgo., 1967. Instr. math. Coll. of St. Benedict, St. Joseph, Minn., 1960-61; tchr. math. Gage Park High Sch., Chgo., 1962-74; tchr., coord. math. dept. Westmont (Ill.) High Sch., 1974-94, coll. counselor, 1980-90, ret., 1994; counselor Coll. of DuPage, Glen Ellen, Ill., 1982-83. Contbg. author Elementary Mathematics Series, 1964-68. Mem. NEA, Nat. Coun. Tchrs. Math., Ill. Coun. Tchrs. Math., Ill. Assn. Coll. Admissions Counselors, Ill. Edn. Assn. (chpt. treas. 1986-90), Delta Kappa Gamma (v.p. Beta Phi chpt. 1990-92). Roman Catholic. Avocations: collecting advertising rulers and antique mathematics books, travel. Home: 5S 517 Allison Ln Naperville IL 60540

BURTON, LAWRENCE DEVERE, agriculturist, educator; b. Afton, Wyo., May 27, 1943; s. Lawrence VanOrden and Maybell (Hoopes) B.; m. Arva Merrill, Nov. 20, 1967; children: LauraLee, Paul, Shawn, Renee, Kaylyn, Kelly, Brett. BS, Utah State U., 1968; MS, Brigham Young U., 1972; PhD, Iowa State U., 1987. Agr. tchr. Box Elder County Sch. Dist., Brigham City, Utah, 1967-68, Morgan County Sch. Dist., Morgan, Utah, 1968-70, Minidoka County Sch. Dist., Rupert, Idaho, 1972-79, Cassia County Sch. Dist., Declo, Idaho, 1979-84; instr. Iowa State U., Ames, 1984-87; area vocat. edn. coord. Idaho State Div. Vocat. Edn., Pocatello, 1987-88; state supr. agrl. sci. and tech. Idaho State Div. Vocat. Edn., Boise, 1988-97; dir. rsch. Idaho State Divsn. Vocat. Edn., Boise, 1997—; mem. telecomm. coun. Idaho State Bd. Edn., 1997-98, mem. coun. acad. affairs and programs, 1997—; biochem. cons. rep. Ctr. for Occupational Rsch. and Devel., Waco, Tex., 1989-94; chmn. Nat. Task Force, Agrl. Edn. Ind. Study Honors program, 1993; mem. Nat. Task Force, Environ. Edn., 1996. Author: Agriscience and Technology, 1991, 97, Ecology of Fish and Wildlife, 1995, Introduction to Forestry Science, 1998; contbr. articles to profl. jours. Vice-chmn. Minidoka County Fair Bd., Rupert, Idaho, 1977-80. Mem. Am. Vocat. Assn., Am. Vocat. Info. Assn., Nat. Vocat. Agrl. Tchrs. Assn., Idaho Vocat. Agrl. Tchrs. Assn. (pres. 1981-82, Adminstr. of Yr. 1989), Am. Vocat. Info. Assn., Nat. Assn. Suprs. Agrl. Edn. (western v.p. 1990-91, nat. pres. 1993-94), Gamma Sigma Delta, Alpha Zeta. Mem. LDS Ch. Home: 10966 Highlander Rd Boise ID 83709-5243 Office: State Div Vocat Edn PO Box 83720 Boise ID 83720-3720

BURTON, MARY LOUISE HIMES, computer specialist; b. Altoona, Pa., Oct. 4, 1948; d. Paul Silas and Clara Marie (Bettwy) Himes; m. Carl Hansel Burton, Aug. 28, 1983; children: Michael, Edward, Carla. AA, Mt. Aloysius Jr. Coll., 1968; BS in Edn., Slippery Rock U., 1970; MLS magna cum laude, U. Pitts., 1982. Cataloguer Slipper Rock (Pa.) U., 1968-70; cataloguer, children's librn. Altoona Area Pub. Libr., 1970-71; dir. libr. svcs. Altoona Hosp., 1971-83; project coord. Coll. of Physician of Phila., 1983-84; med. libr. VAMC, Coatesville, Pa., 1984-85; acting chief libr. svc. VAMC, Coatesville, 1985-86, chief libr. svc., 1986-94; asst. chief IRM, 1994-96, instr., 1996—; mem. Nat. Adv. Group for Info. Security, 1991—, vice chmn., 1996-98; security officer Automated Info. Sys., 1988—; local resource libr. Mideastern Regional Med. Libr. Program, Phila., 1976-82, Greater Northeastern Regional Med. Libr. Program, N.Y.C., 1983-93. Mem. United Ch. of Christ. Mem. Spl. Librs. Assn., Pa. Libr. Assn. (chmn. spl. librs. divsn. and bd. dirs. 1980-82, 85-86, 89-90), Med. Libr. Assn., Acad. Health Info. Profls. (sec. DV-MUG 1996), VFW Aux., Assn. Health Info. Profls., Consortium Health Info. (pres. 1990-93). Avocations: vocalist, organist, pianist. E-mail: marylou.burton@med.va.gov. Home: 5495 Highview Dr Gap PA 17527-9553 Office: VAMC C10 1400 Blackhorse Hill Rd Coatesville PA 19320-2040

BURTON, MICHAEL LADD, anthropology educator; b. Long Beach, Calif., June 6, 1942; s. Warren Nathan Burton and Dorothy Brent (Braden) Asquith; children: Melissa, Christopher; m. Ellen Greenberger, Aug. 26, 1979. BS in Econs., MIT, 1964; PhD in Anthropology, Stanford U., 1968. Rsch. fellow Harvard U., 1968-69; asst. prof. U. Calif., Irvine, 1969-76; rsch. fellow U. Nairobi, Kenya, 1973-74; assoc. prof. U. Calif., Irvine, 1976-83, prof., 1983—, chmn., dept. anthropology, 1986-91. Contbr. articles to profl. jours. NSF grantee, 1981-89, 91-93. Mem. Am. Anthropol. Assn., Soc. for Cross-Cultural Rsch., Soc. Econ. Anthropology, Soc. Applied Anthropology, Assn. Social Anthropology of Oceania. Democrat. Avocation: hiking. Home: 6 Angell St Irvine CA 92612-2121 Office: U Calif Dept Anthropology Irvine CA 92697-5100

BURTON, MIKE, regional government officer. Mem. Oregon Ho. Reps.; chmn. bus. mgmt. dept. Marylhurst Coll.; exec. officer Metro, Portland, Oreg., 1995—. Mem. N.W. Coun. of Pres. Clinton's Coun. on Sustainable Devel., Transatlantic Policy Coun. for Clean Air and Transp., Oregon Gov.'s Growth Task Force, Gov.'s Salmon Strategy Group. Office: Metro 600 NE Grand Ave Portland OR 97232-2799

BURTON, ORVILLE VERNON, history educator; b. Royston, Ga., Apr. 15, 1947; s. Orville Verner and Vera Beatrice (Human) B.; m. Anne Johnson (div.); 1 child, Vera Joanna; m. Georganne Butler, Nov. 6, 1980; children: Beatrice Georgia, Carrah Alice-Anne. BA, Furman U., 1969; MA, Princeton U., 1971, PhD, 1976. Instr. Mercer C.C., Trenton, N.J., 1971-72; asst. master Princeton (N.J.) U., 1972-74; from instr. to asst. prof. to assoc. prof. U. Ill., Urbana, 1974-89; univ. scholar, 1988; prof. history and sociology U. Ill., Urbana, 1989—; disting. tchr. scholar, 1999; cons. U.S. Dept. Justice, NAACP, ACLU, MALDEF, CLRA, Washington, Balt., Atlanta, San Francisco, Mex. Am. Legal Def. Edn. Found., Calif. Legal Rural Assn., 1980—; participant Am. studies program USIA, Washington, 1989-93. Author: (books) In My Father's House Are Many Mansions, 1985, A Gentleman and an Officer, 1996; editor: (book) Class, Conflict, and Consensus, 1982, (book) Multimedia Renaissance in Social Science Computing, 1999, (book) Toward a New South?, 1982 (CD) Wayfarer: Charting Advances in Social Science Computing. Mem. steering com. Bread for the World, Chgo., 1978-80, Edcom Computer Literacy Project, Washington, 1969, 74; chair, del. Mex./Am. Commn. Cultural Coop., Mexico City, 1990; mentor So. Regional Coun., Atlanta, 1991-94. Fellow Rockefeller Found., 1977-78, Woodrow Wilson Ctr., 1988-89, Nat. Humanities Ctr., 1994-95, PEW, 1996. Mem. So. Hist. Assn. (nominating com. 1999-2000, com. on women 1992-95, program com. 1987, 98), Agrl. History Soc. (exec. com. 1997-2000, chmn. nominating com. 1991-94), Social Sci. Hist. Assn. (nominating com. 1990-91), Am. Hist. Orgn. (AFL-CIO award com. 1997-99), H-Net (exec. com. 1993-94). Democrat. Presbyterian. Avocations: tennis, fishing. Home: 605 W Washington St Urbana IL 61801 Office: U Ill History Dept 810 S Wright St Urbana IL 61801

BURTON, PAUL FLOYD, social worker; b. Seattle, May 24, 1939; s. Floyd James and Mary Teresa (Chovanak) B.; BA, U. Wash., 1961, MSW, 1967; m. Roxanne Maude Johnson, July 21, 1961; children: Russell Floyd, Joan Teresa. Juvenile parole counselor Div. Juvenile Rehab. State of Wash., 1961-66; social worker VA, Seattle, 1967-72, social worker, cons. Work Release program King County, Wash., 1967-72; supr., chief psychiatry sect. Social Work Svc. VA, Topeka, Kans., 1972-73; pvt. practice, Topeka and L.A., 1972—; chief social work svc. VA, Sepulveda, Calif., 1973—, EEO coord. Med. ctr., 1974-77. Mem. NASW (newsletter editor Puget Sound chpt. 1970-71), Acad. Cert. Social Workers, Ctr. for Studies in Social Functioning, Am. Hosp. Assn., Soc. Social Work Adminstrs. in Health Care, Assn. VA Social Work Chiefs (founder 1979, charter mem. and pres. 1980-81, newsletter editor 1982-83, 89-91, pres. elect 1993-95, pres. 1995-97). Home: 14063 Remington St Arleta CA 91331-5359 Office: 16111 Plummer St Sepulveda CA 91343-2036

BURTON, PEGGY, advertising executive; b. N.Y.C.; B.S.B.A., 1957, NYU, 1960. Freelance TV producer, N.Y.C., 1964-67; TV producer Young & Rubicam, N.Y.C., 1967-69; sr. acct. exec. Daniel & Charles, N.Y.C., 1969-74; ptnr., v.p. Bruderer Hartnett Advt. Agy., N.Y.C., 1974-76; dir. Communications Am. Express Co., N.Y.C., 1976-83; pres. advt. Dreyfus Corp., N.Y.C., 1983-95; pres. Burton Comms. Multi Media, N.Y.C., 1995—. Mem. Internat. Advt. Assn., Advt. Women of N.Y., N.Y. New Media Assn., Fin. Women's Assn., Bus. Execs. for Nat. Security, NYU Gallatin Arts com. Address: 220 Central Park S New York NY 10019-1417

BURTON, PHILIP WARD, advertising executive, educator; b. Chgo., May 23, 1910; s. Carl Marshall and Gladys (Mann) B.; m. Ellen Schell Garber, Dec. 21, 1941; children: Elisabeth, Philip Ward and Bruce Garber (twins). A.B. summa cum laude, Stanford U., 1944, A.M., 1945. With advt. dept. Colgate-Palmolive Co., 1929-31; sales promotion adminstr. Bird & Son, Inc., 1932-34; mgr. med. promotion Bell & Howell Co., 1935-37; copy editor Procter & Gamble Co., 1938-41; asst. prof. Syracuse U. Sch. Journalism, 1945-46, prof., head advt. dept., 1949-55, chmn. advt. dept., after 1956; J. Stewart Riley prof. journalism Ind. U., Bloomington, 1976—; assoc. prof.

journalism and bus. adminstrn. State U. Iowa, 1946, prof., head dept., 1947-49; creative dir. Bruce B. Brewer Advt. Agy., Mpls., 1955-57; dir. marketing and research Barlow Advt. Agy., 1956—; copy chief T.A. Best Co.; dir. Auburn Pub. Co.; book rev. editor Skaneateles (N.Y.) Press; editor Internat. Corr. Schs.; also editor-cons. internat. textbook div.; vis. prof., Riley prof. Sch. Journalism, Ind. U. Author: Advertising Copywriting, 1949, 4th edit., 1978, 5th edit., 1983, 7th edit., 1997, Retail Advertising for Small Stores, 1951, Putting Advertising to Work, 1953, Principles of Advertising, 1955, Making Media Work, 1958, Which Ad Pulled Best, rev. edit, 1971, 6th edit., 1990, 8th edit., 1996, Advertising Fundamentals, 3d edit, 1980, Account Management for General Learning Corporation, 1976, Casebook of Advertising Management, 1981; contbg. author: Marketing Managers Handbook for Dartnell Corporation, 1976, 2d edit., 1983; also articles in mags. Named Advt. Educator in U.S., 1961; recipient Disting. Prof. award , Ind. U. Alumni Assn., 1976, Disting. Prof. award Newhouse Communications Sch. Syracuse U, 1977, Disting. Tchr. award Ind. U., 1986, Disting. Prof. award, Syracuse U. Alumni Assn., 1987, Disting. Tchr. award Ind. Assn. Advt. Agys., 1992. Fellow Am. Acad. Advt. (regional dean); mem. Advt. Fedn. Am. (dir. 1953-57, 1st recipient Disting. Advt. Prof. award 1987), Nat. Indsl. Advertisers Assn., Alpha Delta Sigma (nat. pres. 1953-57, chmn. nat. council 1957-59, recipient citation for contbns. to frat.), Sigma Delta Chi, Delta Upsilon. Home: 500 Ballantine Rd Bloomington IN 47401-5018 Office: Ind U Sch Journalism Bloomington IN 47401

BURTON, RANDALL JAMES, lawyer; b. Sacramento, Feb. 4, 1950; s. Edward Jay and Bernice Mae (Overton) B.; children: Kelly Jacquelyn, Andrew Jameson; m. Kimberly D. Rogers, Apr. 29, 1989. BA, Rutgers U., 1972; JD, Southwestern U., 1975. Bar: Calif. 1976, U.S. Dist. Ct. (ea. dist.) Calif. 1976, U.S. Dist. Ct. (no. dist.) Calif., 1990, U.S. Supreme Ct, 1991. Assoc. Brekke & Mathews, Citrus Heights, Calif., 1976; pvt. practice, Sacramento, 1976-93; ptnr. Burton & White, Sacramento, 1993—; judge pro tem Sacramento Small Claims Ct., 1982—. Bd. dirs. North Highlands Recreation and Park Dist., 1978-86, Family Svc. Agy. of Sacramento, 1991-96; active Local Bd. 22, Selective Svc., 1982—, Active 20-30 Club of Sacramento, 1979-90, pres., 1987. Recipient Disting. Citizen award, Golden Empire Council, Boy Scouts Am. Mem. Sacramento Bar Assn., Sacramento Young Lawyers Assn. Presbyterian. Lodge: Rotary (pres. Foothill-Highlands club 1980-81). Office: 1540 River Park Dr Ste 224 Sacramento CA 95815-4609

BURTON, RAYMOND CHARLES, JR., transportation company executive; b. Phila., Aug. 29, 1938; s. Raymond Charles and Phyllis (Clifford) B.; m. Madeline Ann Starmann, Feb. 13, 1999; children: Carolyn Starmann, Raymond Starmann. BA, Cornell U., 1960; MBA, U. Pa., 1963. Various operating positions Santa Fe Ry. Co., 1963-68, asst. controller, 1968-69; asst. treas. Santa Fe Industries, Chgo., 1969-74; asst. v.p. planning, treas. Burlington No., Inc., 1974-79; v.p. and treas. Burlington No., Inc., St. Paul and Seattle, 1979-82; v.p. planning Internat. Harvester Co., Chgo., 1982; pres., chief exec. officer TTX Co., Chgo., 1982—, Railbox Co., Railgon Co., Chgo., 1982—. 1st lt. U.S. Army, 1960-61. Mem. Met. Club, Chgo. Club, Execs. Club Chgo., Canal Corridor Assn., Econ. Club Chgo., Tower Club. Republican. Presbyterian. Office: TTX Co 101 N Wacker Dr Chicago IL 60606-1718

BURTON, RICHARD GREENE, retired marketing executive; b. Pawtucket, R.I., Jan. 4, 1936; s. Fred Marsden and Winifred Congdon (Greene) B.; m. Nancy Jane Fairgrieve, June 27, 1959; children: Jeffrey Greene, Janet Lynn, Steven Richard. AB, Duke U., 1958. Salesman Riegel Paper Corp., Chgo., 1958-66; sales mgr. publ. papers Mead Corp., Chgo., 1966-75, regional sales mgr., N.Y.C., 1976-79, v.p. sales, Dayton, Ohio, 1979-82; v.p. mktg. Paper Corp. Am., Valley Forge, Pa., 1982-92; exec. v.p. Paper Corp. Internat. (name now Unisource Internat.), 1992-97, ret., 1997. Past mktg. com., bd. dirs. Phila. divsn. Am. Cancer Soc. Mem. Sales Assn. Paper Industry (program chmn. 1964-65, v.p. Chgo. region 1965-66, Man of Yr. award 1966). Republican. Clubs: Naperville (Ill.) Country; Waynesborough Country (Paoli, Pa.), Landfall Club (Wilmington, N.C.). Home: 2220 Deepwood Dr Wilmington NC 28405-4290

BURTON, RICHARD IRVING, orthopedist, educator; b. Providence, Sept. 18, 1936; s. Kenneth Gould and Edith Irving (Vayro) B.; m. Margaret Ann Leaman, Apr. 5, 1961; children: Thomas Kenneth, Douglas Leaman. BA, Amherst Coll., 1958; MD, Harvard U., 1962. Diplomate Am. Bd. Orthopaedic Surgery (examiner 1980—, bd. dirs. 1989-98). Intern U. Rochester, N.Y., 1962-63, resident in surgery, 1963-64; resident in orthopedic surgery Harvard U., 1966-70; fellow in hand surgery Roosevelt Hosp., N.Y.C., 1970-71; asst. prof. Cleve. Clinic Found., 1971-72, head sect. surgery of hand, 1971-74, assoc. prof., 1973-74; mem. faculty U. Rochester Med. Sch., 1974—, head sect. surgery of hand, 1974—, prof. orthopedics, 1979—, Marjorie Strong Wehle prof. orthopedics, 1995—, assoc. chmn. dept. orthopedics, 1981-88, chmn., 1988—; sr. assoc. orthopedist Strong Meml. Hosp., Rochester, 1974-79, orthopedist, 1979—; Chmn. Cert. of Added Qualifications com., Am. Bd. Orthopaedic Surgery, 1994-98. Assoc. editor Jour. Hand Surgery, 1980-84; contbr. articles to profl. jours., chpts. to books. Mem. exec. com. Monroe County chpt. Am. Arthritis Found., 1983-86; elder Presbyn. Ch. Buswell Disting. Svc. fellow, U. rochester, 1980-81. Recipient Exec. of Yr. award Profl. Secs. Internat., Flower City chpt., 1981. Mem. ACS, AAAS, Am. Acad. Orthopedic Surgeons (chmn. hand and wrist com. 1986-89, orthopedic resources com. 1989-91), Am. Bd. Med. Specialties (voting rep. 1995-98), Am. Soc. Surgery of the Hand (coord. divsn. edn. 1982-85, coun. 1985-89, chmn. membership com. 1991, v.p. 1990, pres.-elect 1991, pres. 1992), Am. Bd. Orthopedic Surgery, Am. Orthopedic Assn. (exec. com. 1986, resident rsch. conf. com. 1987-89, chair 1989, membership com. 1989-92, chmn. 1992, exec. com. 1992, forward planning com. 1996—), Interurban Orthopedic Soc., Am. Rheumatism Assn., Eastern Orthopedic Assn., Monroe County Med. Soc., N.Y. State Med. Soc., Rochester Acad. Medicine, Rochester Orthopedic Soc., Soc. N.Y. State Orthopedic Surgeons, J. William Littler Soc., Amherst Alumni Assn., Harvard U. Med. Sch. Alumni Assn. Home: 7869 Hidden Oak Pittsford NY 14534-9607 Office: U Rochester Med Ctr Dept Orthopedics 601 Elmwood Ave Rochester NY 14642-0001

BURTON, ROBERT GENE, printing and publishing executive; b. Pontiac, Mich., Apr. 4, 1938; s. Earl R. and Verna L. Burton; m. Paula M. Suwanski, May 26, 1972; children: Robert Gene, Jr., Michael, Joseph. BS, Murray (Ky.) State U., 1962; MA, U. Tenn., 1964; postgrad., U. Chgo., U. Ala.; D (hon.), Murray State U. From salesman to nat. sales dir. SRA/IBM Corp., Dallas and Chgo., 1967-76; Midwest dir., then mktg. dir. CBS, Chgo. and N.Y.C., 1976-78, v.p. mktg., 1978-79; v.p. ops. CBS, N.Y.C., 1978-79; v.p. pub. ABC, N.Y.C., 1980, pres. leisure mags., 1980-81, group v.p. spl. interest pub., 1981, pres., 1981-91; v.p. Capital Cities/ABC, Inc., 1991; chmn. bd., pres., CEO World Color Press Inc., N.Y.C., 191—; mem. adv. bd. NYU Bus. Press; chmn., CEO World Color Press, Inc., Greenwich, Conn., 1991. Trustee Eagle Hill Sch., Greenwich, conn.; mem. bd. overseers U. Conn. Sch. Bus. Adminstrn.; mem. corp. adv. coun. Syracuse U. Sch. Mgmt.; bd. dirs. Cancer Care of Conn.; mem. bd. advisors Breast Cancer Alliance; bd. dirs. Kentuckians of N.Y., Burton Charitable Found.; former chmn. Nat. Bible Week/Laymen's Nat. Bible Assn.; former pub. industry chmn. Juvenile Diabetes Found.; bd. dirs. N.Y.U., former mem. press adv. bd.; bd. dirs. Murray State U. Coll. bus. and Pub. Affairs, former mem. dean's adv. coun.; past trustee Murray State U., Boy Scouts Am. Nat. Mus., Murray. Recipient award Spl. Achievement Soc. and Athletic Hall of Fame, West Frankfort, Ill., Oak award Ky. Advocates for Higher Edn.; inductee Murray State Football Hall of Fame. Mem. Assn. Bus. Pubs. (past chmn.), Washington Nat. Press Club, Greenwich (Conn.) Country Club. Republican. Baptist. Office: World Color Press Inc The Mill 340 Pemberwick Rd Greenwich CT 06831-4240

BURTON, ROBERT LYLE, accounting firm executive; m. Lee Sanders; 2 children. Diploma, Kinman Bus. U. CPA. With LeMaster & Daniels, Spokane, Wash., 1963-86; mng. ptnr. LeMaster & Daniels, 1986-97, sr. advisor, 1997—; mem. adv. bd. acctg. dept. U. Wash.; chmn. The Am. Group of CPA Firms. Trustee Econ. Devel. Coun.; past chmn. Samaritan Hosp. Found., Moses Lake, Wash. Mem. AICPA (agri-bus. com., adv. group B), Washington Soc. CPAs (former dir., v.p., com. chmn., legis. com.), Spokane Club, Inland Empire Fly Fishermen, Moses Lake Golf and Country Club, Rotary. Office: LeMaster & Daniels 8817 E Mission Spokane WA 99212

BURTON, ROBERT WILLIAM, retired office products executive; b. Seymour, Conn., Aug. 1, 1927; s. Loren Nelson and Christina Marguerite (Duff) B.; m. Virginia Bigelow Kernochan, Nov. 19, 1955; children: Robert Mark, Jeffrey James, Virginia Lee Burton Fowler. B.A., Western Res. U., 1951. Floor dir. WEWS-TV, Cleve., 1951-52; v.p. Spero & Burton, Inc., Cleve., 1952-53; asst. to dir. sales promotion Anaconda-Am. Brass Co., Waterbury, Conn., 1953-58; sales mgr. Times Wire & Cable Co., Wallingford, Conn., 1958-66; v.p. sales Times Wire & Cable Co., 1966-68, v.p., gen. mgr., 1968-69, pres., 1969-77; pres., chief exec. officer Rolodex Corp., Secaucus, N.J., 1977-89, ret.; pres., CEO Rolodex de P.R., Moca, 1977-89; pres. New Generation Oil and Chem. Products Inc., Stamford, Conn., 1991-94; bd. dirs. Okay Industries, Inc., New Britain, Conn. Pub. relations chmn. ARC, Waterbury, 1954-58, United Fund, Waterbury, 1954-58; bd. dirs. Cheshire Community Theatre, 1959-70; corporator Meriden-Wallingford Hosp., bd. dirs., 1975-77. Served with USNR, 1944-47. Mem. Wholesale Stationers Assn. (dir. 1981-84), Nat. Office Products Assn., Meadowlands C. of C. (dir. 1977-89), Phi Gamma Delta, Club at Ocean Edge, Brewster, Mass., The Club at Jacaranda West, Venice, Fla. Republican. Congregationalist. Home: 505 Wood Hill Rd Cheshire CT 06410-4334

BURTON, RUSSELL ROHAN, aerospace scientist, researcher; b. Chico, Calif., Jan. 15, 1932; s. Russell Huntt and Merle (Rohan) B.; m. M. Ruth Ferguson, Nov. 8, 1958 (div. Dec. 1979); children: Robert Paul, Russell Patrick Douglas; m. Sharon Lea Milton, Aug. 8, 1983; children: Jennifer Paige, Heather Lea. BS, U. Calif., Davis, 1954, DVM, 1956, MS, 1965, PhD, 1970. Pvt. practice Grover City, Calif., 1956-62; rsch. physiologist U. Calif., Davis, 1962-71, Brooks AFB, Tex., 1971-80; chief aerospace rsch. br. USAF Sch. of Aerospace Medicine, Brooks AFB, Tex., 1980-88, chief scientist, 1988-91, chief scientist crew systems directorate, 1991-96; chief scientist Armstrong Lab., Brooks AFB, 1995-97; sr. scientist human effectiveness directorate Air Force Rsch. Lab., Brooks AFB, 1997-99, ret., 1999; cons. NASA, Johnson Space Ctr., Ames Rsch. Ctr., 1980—, cons. adv. group Aerospace R&D, Paris, 1987-92, mem. panel, 1992-97; com. chair, project officer, custodian Air Standardization Coord. Com., Washington, 1984-91. Co-author: High G Physiological Protection Tng. (AGARD-AG-322), 1990, Adaptation to Acceleration Environments, 1996; contbr. chpts. to books, articles to profl. jours. Recipient Sci. Achievment award RTO/NATO, 1998, Outstanding Civilian Svc. medal USAF, 1999, Examplary Civilian Svc., 1998. Fellow Aerospace Med. Assn. (Tuttle award 1976, Environ. Sci. award 1980, Liliencrantz award 1988, USAF Basic Rsch. award 1988); mem. AAAS, Am. Physiol. Soc. (editorial bd. 1976-78), Aerospace Physiol. Soc. (pres. 1982), Safety and Flight Equipment (editor jour. 1993-98), Sigma Xi (pres. local chpt. 1988). Avocations: stained glass, sailing, jogging, cooking. Home: 128 Shalimar Dr San Antonio TX 78213-2605

BURTON, TIM, film director; b. Burbank, Aug. 25, 1958. Student Calif. Inst. Arts (Disney Fellowship). Cartoon artist Disney Prodn., apprentice animator. Film dir. Pee-Wee's Big Adventure, 1984, Beetlejuice, 1988, Batman, 1989, Edward Scissorhands, 1990, Batman Returns, 1992, Ed Wood, 1994, Mars Attacks, 1996; others include: Frankenweenie, Vincent; prodr. The Nightmare Before Christmas, 1993, Cabin Boy, 1994, Batman Forever, 1995, James and the Giant Peach, 1996; dir. TV film Aladdin, Faerie Tale Theatre series; appeared in film Singles, 1992; author: My Art & Films, 1993, The Melancholy Death of Oyster Boy and Other Stories, 1997. Office: Chapman Bird & Grey 1990 S Bundy Dr Ste 200 Los Angeles CA 90025-5240*

BURTON, WARD, professional race car driver; b. South Boston, Va., Oct. 25, 1961; m. Tabitha Burton; children: Sarah, Jeb. Student, Elon Coll. Race car driver NASCAR Busch Series Grand Nat. Divsn., 1990, Bill Davis Racing, High Point, N.C. Winner Winston Cup, 1995. Achievements include 23 top 5 career starts, 37 top 10 stars in 148 races; career finishes include 5 top 5 finishes and 24 top 10 finishes in 146 races; winner N.C. Motor Speedway, 1995. Avocations: wildlife conservation, hunting. Office: c/o Bill Davis Racing 301 Old Thomasville Rd High Point NC 27260*

BURTON, WILLIAM JOSEPH, engineering executive; b. Gaffney, S.C., Mar. 22, 1931; s. Emory Goss and Olivia (Copeland) B.; m. Joan Holland Burton, Sept. 26, 1987. BSME, U. S.C., 1957, MSME, 1964; PhDME, Tex. A&M U., 1970. Registered profl. engr., Tenn., Fla. Sr. dynamics engr. Lockheed-Ga. Co., Marietta, 1957-62; sr. project engr. Allison div. GM Corp., Indpls., 1964-67; asst. prof., researcher Tex. A&M U., College Station, 1968-70; asst. prof. U. Tenn., Knoxville, 1970-74; projects mgr. Tenn. Valley Authority, Chattanooga, 1974-79; program mgr. Dept. Navy, Washington, 1979-94; cons. engr. Ocean and Power Applications, Lakeland, Fla., 1993—; chmn. equal employment opportunity com. Chesapeake div. Naval Facilities Engring. Command, Washington, 1982-83. Author: On the Heating Surface Effects of Nucleate Boiling Data Correlation, 1964, The Effects of Surface Roughness on the Wave Forces on a Circular Cylindrical Pile, 1970; author more than 50 articles on ocean engring., power and propulsion, aircraft structures, planning and economics, ethics. Secretary, mem. hospitality com. Exch. Club, Knoxville, 1975, bd. dirs., 1976; coord. charitable campaign Naval Facilities Engring. Com., Washington, 1981. With U.S. Army, 1951-53. Recipient Occupation medal and Nat. Def. Svc. medal U.S. Army, Antarctic Svc. medal U.S. Dept. of Navy, 1962. Fellow ASME (chmn. exec. com. ocean engring. divsn. 1985, mem.-at-large energy resources bd. 1986-92, chmn. com. honors & awards energy resources bd. 1992-98, com. on tech. planning coun. on engring. 1992-94, fellow peer rev. bd. 1992-97, rep. energy resources bd. to nat. nominating com. 1998—, Golden Cert. ocean engring. divsn. 1989), Va. Soc. Profl. Engrs. (no. Va. regional coun. 1988); mem. AAAS, NSPE (pres.-elect Fairfax chpt. 1988), Soc. Mfg. Engrs., Soc. Naval Architects and Marine Engrs., S.C. Hist. Soc., Nat. Trust for Historic Preservation, VFW, Marine Tech. Soc., The Univ. South Caroliniana Soc., Sigma Xi. Baptist. Avocations: travel, bicycling, classic guitar, golf, tennis. E-mail: wmburton@hotmail.com. Home: 307 Miramar Dr Lakeland FL 33803-2633 Office: Naval Facilities Engring Svc Ctr East Coast Detachment 901 M St SE Bldg 218 Washington Navy Yd Washington DC 20374-5063

BURTT, JAMES, humanities educator; b. Freehold, N.J., Oct. 24, 1948; s. Howard and Mary (Layton) B.; m. Anne Marie Dampman, Aug. 5, 1972. BSEd, Duquesne U., 1971, MEd, 1974; cert. English, La Salle U., 1986, cert. Latin, 1987; cert. supervisory social studies, Beaver Coll., 1998. Cert. Tchr. Pa. Tchr. Columbus Mid. Sch., Pitts., 1976-77, Dynamic Springs Preparatory Sch., Newtown Square, Pa., 1977-79; tchr Springfield (Pa.) Sch. Dist., 1979-84; tchr. humanities Bensalem (Pa.) Sch. Dist., 1984—. Contbr. articles to profl. jours. Dem. comitteemen, Upper Moreland Pa., 1978-87; mem. local PTO. Govt. fellow African Studies, 1972-74. Mem. Nat. Talented and Gifted Assn., Coun. Exceptional Child, Pa. Gifted Edn. Orgn., Pa. State Edn. Assn., Bensalem Gifted Adv. Coun. Home: 131 Maple Ave Willow Grove PA 19090-2902 Office: Bensalem Sch Dist 3000 Donallen Dr Bensalem PA 19020-1829

BURTT, LARICE A.R., artist; b. Phila., June 22, 1928; d. Milo A.J. Roseman and Anna Sterling; m. James C. Burtt, June 25, 1960; childen, James M., Kyleann S. *Mr. Burtt taught Chinese, Russian, and African History, and was a Dean at Neshaminy High School from 1968-72. Her son James, operates Burtt Construction Company. He is married to Cynthia Marx Burtt, their children are Justine and Nadine. Daughter Kyleann is a musical director for the Spirit of New York Lines. She has performed in the past at Whaler Bar and at Top of the Sixes, As well as being a composer, pianist, and vocalist, she graduated Magna Cum Laude from Shenandoah University and Conservatory in Virginia. Jennie Brownscimbe, a distant relative was the painter of "The First Thanksgiving".* BS in Biology, Bucknell U., 1950; MS in Nursing, Yale U., 1955; studied art with Dr. Selma Burke, studied with William A. Smith; cert., Katherine Gibbs Sec. Sch., 1951. Med. clinical instr. Jefferson Hosp., Phila., 1956-57; med. surgical instr. Rowan Meml. Hosp., Salisbury, N.C., 1958-59; workshop leader Yale, New Haven Hosp. Pain Mgmt. Ctrs., New Haven, Ct., 1996, Attleboro Nursing Home, Langhorne, Pa., Chandler Hall, Newtown, Pa.; instr. Delaware Valley Schs., Pa., 1979—. Painter (three-dimensional stone painting), many locations, 1976-96; one person exhbns. at Arnot Art Mus., Elmira, N.Y., 1987, Grand Canyon Nat. Park Mus., Utah, 1991, Cannon Bldg., Washington, 1995, Yale Sch. Nursing Immaculate Col Group Exhibitions, New Haven, 1996. Mem. AAUW, Heritage Conservatory Bucks County, Northhampton Hist. Soc., Middletown Grange, Childrens Cultural Ctr., Pa. & Bucks County Guild Craftsman (exhbn. at Franklin and Marshall Coll. 1988-96), James Michener Art Mus., Doylestown (Pa.) Art League, Ctrl. Bucks C. of C., Arts Bridge. Avocations: tennis, piano, visual/performing arts. Home: 31 Beth Dr Richboro PA 18954-1901

BURWELL, DAVID GATES, transportation executive. Pres. Rails-to-Trails Conservancy, Washington; mem. exec. com. Transp. Rsch. Bd., also other bds.; chmn. Surface Transp. Policy Project; bd. dirs. Green Seal. Mem. Gt. Am. Train Sta. Found. Office: Rails-to-Trails Conservancy 1100 17th St NW Fl 10 Washington DC 20036-4601*

BURWEN, BARBARA R., painter; b. Mass., Aug. 30, 1934; d. Barnet and Martha Y. (Gordon) Wallace; m. Richard S. Burwen, May 27, 1956; children: Diane S., Dale R., Russell W. BS, Boston U., 1956, EdM, 1958. mem. Depot Square Gallery, Lexington, Mass., 1993-96. One-woman shows include West Tisbury (Mass.) Field Gallery, 1988, 89, Martha's Vineyard Nat. Bank, Chilmark, Mass., 1990, Nineteen Marsh Street Gallery, Stamford, Conn., 1992, Piper Gallery, Lexington, Mass., 1995, Depot Square Gallery, Lexington, 1995, 96; group shows include N.Am. Open Show, 1990, 92, 94, Doshi Ctr. for Contemporary Art, Harrisburg, 1995, Copley Soc. of Boston Juried Show, 1995, 25th Internat. Exhbn. of the La. Watercolor Soc., 1995, Rocky Mountain Nat. Show 1994, 1996, Ky. Watercolor Soc. Nat. Show 1993, 95, others.; published in "Best of Watercolor, 1995, Best of Watercolor 2, 1997, Abstracts in Watercolor, 1995, Creative Expressions, 1997; radio guest Sonja Tonkajoy Show, 1995. Recipient First award N.Am. Open Show, 1992, award of honor Niagara Frontier Watercolor Soc., 1992, Windsor Newton award and Silver Brush Ltd. award Ky. Watercolor Soc., 1995, Forstall award 25th Internat. Exhbn. of the La. Watercolor Soc., 1995, Vance Kirkland award Rocky Mountain Nat., 1996. Mem. New Eng. Watercolor Soc. (Guild of Boston Artists award 1993, 2d prize 1994, North Shore Art Assn. award 1995, Gold medal 1996), Concord Art Assn., Cambridge Art Assn. Avocations: skiing, bicycling, tennis. Home: 12 Holmes Rd Lexington MA 02420-1917

BURZYNSKI, NORMAN STEPHEN, editor; b. Pitts., Nov. 21, 1928; s. Ladislaus and Eleanor Marie B.; m. Ann Louise Adams, June 11, 1951; children: Michael Derek, Stephanie Ann, Eric Adams, Karen Ruth, John Kerstan, Joan Lorraine. B.A. in Journalism, U. Pitts., 1953; M.S. in Bus. Adminstrn., George Washington U., 1971; A. Applied Sci. summa cum laude in Aviation Tech.—Airport Mgmt., No. Va. Community Coll., Manassas, 1977, A. Applied Sci. summa cum laude in Aviation Tech.—Air Traffic Control, A. Applied Sci. magna cum laude in Comml. Art, 1982. Editor corporate publs. PPG Industries, Pitts., 1958-72; pub. relations rep. PPG Industries, 1972-73; air res. forces liaison officer Office of Info., U.S. Air Force, Washington, 1968-72; chief Office of Info., U.S. Air Force Res., 1973-76; editor The Officer, Res. Officers Assn. U.S., Washington, 1976-95. Editor Civil War Camera, Luray, Va., 1998—. Served to lt. U.S. Army, 1951-52; to col. USAF, 1968-76. Mem. Res. Officers Assn., Air Force Assn., Aircraft Owners and Pilots Assn., Exptl. Aircraft Assn., Aviation and Space Writers Assn. Home: 4 Jackson Dr Luray VA 22835-9606

BURZYNSKI, STANISLAW RAJMUND, internist; b. Lublin, Poland, Jan. 23, 1943; s. Grzegorz and Zofia Miroslawa (Radzikowski) B.; came to U.S., 1970; M.D. with distinction, Med. Acad., Lublin, 1967, Ph.D., 1968. Teaching asst. Med. Acad. Lublin, 1962-67; intern, resident in internal medicine, Med. Acad., 1967-70; research assoc. Baylor U., 1970-72, asst. prof., 1972-77; pvt. practice specializing in internal medicine, Houston, 1977—; dir. Burzynski Research Lab., 1977-83; pres. Burzynski Research Inst., Inc., 1983—. Nat. Cancer Inst. grantee, 1974 West Found. grantee, 1975. Mem. AAAS, Am. Assn. Cancer Research, AMA, Harris County Med. Soc., Polish Nat. Alliance (pres. Houston chpt. 1974-75), Soc. Neurosci., Tex. Med. Assn., Sigma Xi. Roman Catholic. Contbr. articles profl. jours. Discoverer of antineoplastons components of biochem. def. system against cancer; described structure of Ameletin, 1st substance known to be responsible for remembering sound in animal's brain; invented new treatment for cancer, AIDS, viral infections, autoimmune diseases, neurofibromatosis, and Parkinson's disease. Home: 20 W Rivercrest Dr Houston TX 77042-2127 Office: 12000 Richmond Ave Houston TX 77082-2431

BURZYNSKI, SUSAN MARIE, newspaper editor; b. Jackson, Mich., Jan. 1, 1953; d. Leon Walter and Claudia (Kulpinski) B.; m. James W. Bush, May 22, 1976 (div. 1989); children: Lisa M., Kevin J.; m. George K. Bullard, Jr., Mar. 21, 1992. AA, Jackson C.C., 1972; BA, Mich. State, 1974. Reporter Saratogian, Saratoga Springs, N.Y., 1974, Gongwer News Svc., Lansing, Mich., 1975, The State Jour., Lansing, 1975-79; Metro editor Port Huron (Mich.) Times Herald, 1979-82, mng. editor, 1982-86; asst. city editor Detroit News, 1986-87, Sunday news editor, 1987, news editor, 1988-91, asst. mng. editor/news, 1991-96, asst. mng. editor, recruiting and tng., 1996-98, asst. mng. editor, adminstr., 1998—. Roman Catholic. Avocations: swimming, skiing, tennis, biking. Office: Detroit News 615 W Lafayette Blvd Detroit MI 48226-3197

BUS, JAMES STANLEY, toxicologist; b. Kalamazoo, June 27, 1949; s. Charles J. and Sena (Wolthuis) B.; m. Gerda W. Hekman, Apr. 20, 1974; children: Sara E., Timothy J., Brian M. BS in Medicinal Chemistry, U. Mich., 1971; PhD in Pharmacology, Mich. State U., 1975. Diplomate Am. Bd. Toxicology (v.p., pres. 1985-87). NIH predoctoral trainee Dept. Pharmacology, Mich. State U., East Lansing, 1971-75; asst. prof. environ. health U. Cin., 1975-76; scientist I (biochem. toxicologist) Chem. Industry Inst. Toxicology, Research Triangle Park, N.C., 1977-84, scientist II (biochem. toxicologist), 1984-86; assoc. dir. pathology/toxicology, dir. drug metabolism rsch. The Upjohn Co., Kalamazoo, 1986-89; toxicology rsch. lab. Dow Chem. Co., Midland, Mich., 1989-91, project mgr., 1992-93, rsch. mgr., tech. dir., 1994—; adj. assoc. prof. curriculum in toxicology U. N.C., Chapel Hill, 1984-88; adj. prof. pharmacology/toxicology Mich. State U. East Lansing, 1987—; toxicology expert Am. Conf. for Govtl. Indsl. Hygienists, Cin., 1993—; mem. safety assessment bd. advisors Merck, Sharp & Dohme Lab., West Point, Pa., 1985-86; mem. bd. sci. counselors EPA, 1996—; mem. bd. sci. counselors NTP, 1997—; bd. dirs. CIIT, 1997—. Co-editor: Patty's Industrial Hygiene and Toxicology, Vol. 3B, 1995; assoc. editor Toxicology and Applied Pharmacology, 1989-92; editl. bd. Reproductive Toxicology, 1986-96; contbr. articles to profl. jours. Bd. trustees Covenant Coll., Lookout Mountain,. Ga., 1984-87. Recipient Robert A. Scala award Environ. Occupl. Health Sci. Inst., Rutgers U., 1999. Mem. Soc. Toxicology (pres. 1996-97, Achievement award 1987), Am. Soc. for Pharmacology and Exptl. Therapeutics, Teratology Soc., Am. Conf. Govt. Indsl. Hygiene. Republican. Achievements include research dealing with mechanisms of chemical toxicity, including oxidant and glutathione mediated toxicities. E-mail: jbus@dow.com. Office: Dow Chemical Co Toxicology Rsch Lab 1803 Bldg Midland MI 48674

BUSBEE, KLINE DANIEL, JR., law educator, lawyer; b. Macon, Ga., Mar. 14, 1933; s. Kline Daniel and Bernice (Anderson) B.; children: Rodgers Christopher, Jon Edward. BBA, So. Meth. U., 1961, JD 1962. Bar: Tex. 1962. Ptnr. Worsham, Forsythe, Sampels & Busbee, Dallas, 1962-70, Locke, Purnell, Rain & Harrell, P.C., Dallas, 1970-98, Gibson, Dunn & Crutcher, Dallas, 1998—; adj. prof. law So. Meth. U. Sch. Law, 1974-83, 92; adj. prof. pub. internat. law U. Tex. Grad. Sch. Mgmt., Dallas; bd. dirs. Atmos Energy Corp. Mem. ABA, Tex. Bar Assn., Dallas Country Club, Dallas Com. on Fgn. Rels., Snowmass Club, Petroleum Club. Home: 4360 San Carlos St Dallas TX 75205-2052 Office: 1717 Main St Ste 5400 Dallas TX 75201-7367

BUSBY, DAVID, lawyer; b. Ada, Okla., Jan. 29, 1926; s. Orel and Hope (Threlkeld) B.; m. Mary Beth Baker, June 9, 1962; children: Helen Hope Busby Burleigh, Alison Sears Busby Vareika, David, John Orel. BA; LLB, Yale U., 1948; LL.B., Okla. U., 1951. Bar: Okla. 1950, D.C. 1959, N.Y. 1959, U.S. Supreme Ct. 1959. Assoc. Busby, Harrell & Trice, Ada, 1951-55; counsel Subcom. on Automobile Mktg. Practices, Com. on Interstate and Fgn. Commerce, U.S. Senate, Washington, 1955-58, Subcom. Fgn. Commerce, 1958; ptnr. Hays, Busby & Rivkin, N.Y.C., 1958-77, Busby, Rehm & Leonard, 1977-87, Dorsey & Whitney, Washington, 1988—; trade advisor Ministry of Fin., Republic of Latvia, 1996; lectr., Moscow, Kiev, Chisinev,

Kampala, 1995-98; mem. accountability rev. bd. terrorist attack on U.S. Embassy, Dar Es Salaam, 1998-99. Mem. Nat. Motor Vehicle Safety Adv. Coun., 1966-68; pres. League Young Dems. of Okla., 1951; city judge, Ada, 1952-53; bd. dirs. Legal Aid Soc. D.C.; mem. Washington Nat. Cathedral chpt., 1984-91. Served with USNR, 1944-46. Mem. ABA (chmn. standing com. on customs law 1973-76), Fed. Cir. Bar Assn. (bd. dirs.), D.C. Bar Assn., Customs and Internat. Trade Bar Assn. (bd. dirs.), Nat. Cathedral Assn. (bd. trustees 1992-96), Nat. Legal Ctr. for Pub. Interest (adv. coun. 1990-96), Met. Club, Phi Delta Phi. Episcopalian. Office: Dorsey & Whitney 1330 Connecticut Ave NW Washington DC 20036-1704

BUSBY, EDWARD OLIVER, retired dean; b. Macomb, Ill., June 22, 1926; s. Lynn John and Pauline (Hoebel) B.; m. Lois E. Tehan, June 17, 1950; children: Thomas L., John E., Paula L. BS, U. Wis., 1950, MS, 1962, PhD, 1971. Resident engr. Wis. Hwy. Commn., 1950-51; asst. city engr. City of LaCrosse, Wis., 1951-53; sales engr. Wis. Culvert Co., 1953-59; lectr. civil engring. U. Wis., Madison, 1959-66; dean Coll. Engring. U. Wis.-Platteville, 1966-84, dean emeritus, 1985—; mem. Wis. Examining Bd. for Profl. Engrs., 1981-84; v.p. Platteville Area Indsl. Devel. Corp., 1977-80; vis. prof. U. Tenn., 1984-85; treas. U. Wis.-Platteville Found., 1989-95. Contbr. articles in field to profl. jours. Served with U.S. Navy, 1944-46. NSF fellow, 1970-71. Fellow ASCE (chmn. profl. registration com. 1985-86); mem. Wis. Soc. Profl. Engrs. (pres. 1972-73), Nat. Soc. Profl. Engrs. (nat. dir. 1976-81, vice chmn. engrs. edn. 1971-73). Republican. Home: 7628 Widgeon Way Madison WI 53717-1805

BUSBY, MARJORIE JEAN (MARJEAN BUSBY), journalist; b. Kansas City, Mo., Jan. 31, 1931; d. Vivian Eric and Stella Mae (Lindley) Phillips; m. Robert Jackson Busby, Apr. 11, 1969 (dec. Feb. 1989). BJ., U. Mo., 1952. With Kansas City Star Co. (Knight Ridder purchased 1997), 1952—, editor women's news, 1969-73, assoc. Sunday editor, People Sect. editor, 1973-77, fashion editor, 1978-81, feature and home writer, 1981—. Mem. Fashion Group (1st recipient Kansas City appreciation award 1978), LSV, Mortar Board, Soc. Profl. Journalists, Friends of Art, Belle of Am. Royal Orgn., Kappa Alpha Theta (pres. Alpha Mu chpt. 1951-52). Presbyterian. Home: 9804 Mercier St Kansas City MO 64114-3860 Office: 1729 Grand Blvd Kansas City MO 64108-1413

BUSBY, MORRIS D., ambassador; b. Memphis; married; 2 children. BA, Marshall U.; MS, George Washington U.; postgrad., U.S. Naval Destroyer Sch., Def. Intelligence Sch., Naval War Coll. With USN, various locations including Vietnam, 1971-73; mem. staff Office of Coord. of Ocean Affairs, dir. Office Oceans and Polar Affairs, dep. asst. sec. ocean affairs, amb. oceans and fisheries affairs Dept. of State, 1973-81; alt. rep. to conf. on disarmament Dept. of State, Geneva, Switzerland, 1981-83; dep. chief of mission Dept. of State, Mexico City, 1984-87; founder, office head assistance program for Nicaraguan resistance Dept. of State, 1987-88, prin. dep. asst. sec. inter-Am. affairs, 1987-88, spl. envoy to C.Am., sr. dep., 1988-89; head counter-terrorism Dept. State, 1989-91; amb. to Colombia Dept. of State, Bogota, 1991-94; pres. BGI, Inc., 1994—; dir. Invision Tech., Newark, CA, 1998—; bd. dirs. InVision Techs., Newark, Calif. Decorated Bronze Star; recipient 3 Presdl. Meritorious Svc. awards Govt. Colombia Gran Cruz de Boyaca. Office: BGI Inc 1800 K St NW Ste 716 Washington DC 20006-2202

BUSBY, SHANNON NIXON, special education educator; b. Gainesville, Tex., Nov. 30, 1955; d. James H. and Helen M. (Ross) Nixon; m. Larry W. Busby, Apr. 3, 1982; 1 child, James Ross. BS in Home Econs. Edn., Tex. Tech U., 1977; MEd, Sul Ross State U., Alpine, Tex., 1982. Cert. profl. ednl. diagnostian, tchr. of lang. and/or learning disabilities, tchr. of vocat. homemaking. Home econ. tchr. Pecos (Tex.)-Barstow-Toyah Ind. Sch. Dist., 1978-83, ednl. diagnostian spl. edn. dept., 1983—; exec. dir. West of the Pecos Guild, Inc., 1995—; interior design cons. L.W. Busby and Co., Pecos, 1989—; bd. dirs. Dept. Mental Health and Mental Retardation, Pecos, 1980-83. Chairperson Tex. War on Drugs, Pecos, 1980-83. Mem. AAUW (local pres. 1982-86, local v.p. 1978-81, Tex. state bd. dirs. 1982-83), Tex. Ednl. Diagnosticians Assn. (sec. region 18), Tex. Soc. for Autistic Citizens. Home: 1519 S Mary St Pecos TX 79772-5615

BUSCEMI, PETER, lawyer; b. Bklyn., Sept. 25, 1950; s. Vincent and Ilse (Griesser) B.; m. Judith Ann Miller, June 27, 1981. BA, Columbia U., 1969, JD, 1976; MA, Princeton U., 1971. Bar: N.Y. 1977, D.C. 1979, U.S. Supreme Ct. 1980, U.S. Dist. Ct. (D.C. dist) 1981, U.S. Dist. Ct. (so. dist.) N.Y. 1982, U.S. Ct. Appeals (D.C. cir.) 1981, U.S. Ct. Appeals (5th and 11th cirs.) 1982, U.S. Ct. Appeals (2d cir.) 1985, U.S. Ct. Appeals (fed. cir.) 1986, U.S. Ct. Appeals (3d and 4th cirs.) 1990, U.S. Ct. Appeals (6th cir.) 1993, U.S. Ct. Appeals (1st cir.) 1994, U.S. Ct. Appeals (7th cir.) 1995, U.S. Ct. Appeals (10th cir.) 1998. Law clk. to Hon. Carl McGowan U.S. Ct. Appeals (D.C. cir.), Washington, 1976-77; asst. to solicitor gen. U.S. Dept. Justice, Washington, 1977-81; spl. asst. U.S. atty. U.S. Atty.'s Office, Alexandria, Va., 1980; assoc. Paul, Weiss, Rifkind, Wharton & Garrison, Washington, 1981-86; assoc. Morgan, Lewis & Bockius, LLP, Washington, 1986-87, ptnr., 1987—. Home: 5215 Chamberlin Ave Chevy Chase MD 20815-6646 Office: Morgan Lewis & Bockius LLP 1800 M St NW Washington DC 20036-5802

BUSCEMI, STEVE, actor; b. Bklyn., Dec. 13, 1957; m. Jo Andres; 1 child, Lucian. Student, Lee Strasberg Inst., N.Y.C. Fireman; stand-up comedian N.Y.C. Appeared in films Parting Glances, 1986, Sleepwalk, 1986, Kiss Daddy Good Night, 1987, Vibes, 1988, Heart of Midnight, 1989, Slaves of New York, 1989, Mystery Train, 1989, The Grifters, 1990, Miller's Crossing, 1990, King of New York, 1990, Zandalee, 1991, Barton Fink, 1991, Billy Bathgate, 1991, Criscross, 1992, In the Soup, 1992, Reservoir Dogs, 1992, Me and the Mob, 1992, Twenty Bucks, 1993, The Hudsucker Proxy, 1994, Airheads, 1994, Pulp Fiction, 1994, Floundering, 1994, Desperado, 1995, Things to Do in Denver When You're Dead, 1995, Fargo, 1996, Black Kites, 1996, Kansas City, 1996, Search for One-Eye Kimmy, 1996, Escape from LA., 1996, The Real Blonde, 1997, Divine Trash, 1997, Con Air, 1997, The Big Lebowski, 1998, The Wedding Singer, 1998, Louis et Frank, 1998, Armageddon, 1998, The Impostors, 1998; producer, dir. films What Happened to Pete?, 1993; dir. film Tress Lounge, 1996; appeared in Tales from the Crypt, 1993, also Miami Vice, L.A. Law; other TV appearances include Lonesome Dove, The Last Outlaw. Office: William Morris Agy care Lee Stollman 151 S El Camino Dr Beverly Hills CA 90212-2704*

BÜSCH, ANNEMARIE, retired mental health nurse; d. Jurgen Julius and Anna (Stark) B. RN, Anschar Sch. Nursing, Kiel, Fed. Republic Germany, 1954; student, Traverse City State Hosp., Mich., 1959, Wayne State U., 1962, Colby-Sawyer Coll., New London, N.H., 1981. Lic. nurse, N.H., Vt., Fed. Republic Germany. Asst. head nurse Univ. Eye Inst., Kiel, 1954-56; nurse aide, grad. nurse Ontario Hosp., London, Can.; staff nurse, charge nurse Grace Hosp., Receiving Hosp., Detroit, 1962-67; coll. health nurse Wayne St. U., Detroit, 1967-70; staff nurse Mary Hitchcock Meml. Hosp., Hanover, 1970-71, nurse mental health dept., 1978-82; charge nurse Dartmouth Coll. Health Svc., Hanover, N.H., 1971-77; staff nurse, charge nurse Hanover Health Terrace; staff nurse Temporary Nurses, Inc., Hanover, Vis. Nurse Alliance of Vt. and N.H., White River Junction, Vt.; ret., 1997; camp nurse Nat. Music Camp InterLochen, Mich.

BUSCH, ANNIE, library director; b. Joplin, Mo., Jan. 6, 1947; d. George Lee and Margaret Eleanor (Williams) Chancellor; 1 child, William Andrew Keller. BA, Mo. U., 1969, MA, 1976. Br. mgr. St. Charles (Mo.) City Coun. Libr., 1977-84; br. mgr. Springfield/Greene County (Mo.) Libr., 1985-89, exec. dir., 1989—; exec. bd. Mo. Libr. Network Corp., St. Louis, 1991-96. Adv. bd. Springfield Pub. Sch. Found., 1992-94; pres. Ozarks Regional Info. On-Line Network, Springfield, 1993—; mem. Gov.'s Commn. on Informational Tech.; exec. bd. Mo. Rsch. and Edn. Network, pres., 1996-97; bd. dirs. Ozarks Pub. TV, 1994—; mem. task force Mo. Goals 2000, 1995; coord. com. Springfield Vision 20/20; mem. Cmty. Task Force, Springfield, 1993-98, Cmty. Partnership of the Ozarks, 1998; adv. bd. St. John's Health Sys., Boys & Girls Town. Mem. ALA, Mo. Libr. Assn. (pres. 1993-94, exec. bd. 1990-94), Pub. Libr. Assn., Springfield Rotary (pres. 1998—). Office: Springfield-Greene Cty Libr 620 W Republic Rd Springfield MO 65807-5818

BUSCH, AUGUST ADOLPHUS, III, brewery executive; b. St. Louis, June 16, 1937; s. August Anheuser and Elizabeth (Overton) B.; m. Susan Marie Hornibrook, Aug. 17, 1963 (div. 1969); children: August Adolphus IV, Susan Marie II; m. Virginia L. Wiley, Dec. 28, 1974; children: Steven August, Virginia Marie. Student, U. Ariz., 1957-58, Siebel Inst. Tech., 1960-61. With Anheuser-Busch, Inc., St. Louis, 1957—, pres., 1974-75; chmn. bd., pres. Anheuser Busch Cos., Inc., St. Louis, 1979—, chmn. bd., pres., CEO; bd. dirs. Southwestern Bell Corp., Gen. Am. Life Ins. Co., Emerson Electric Co. Exec. bd. St. Louis Boy Scouts Am.; bd. dirs. United Way Greater St. Louis. Mem. St. Louis Country Club, Log Cabin Club. Office: Anheuser-Busch Cos Inc 1 Busch Pl Saint Louis MO 63118-1852

BUSCH, BRITON COOPER, historian, educator; b. Los Angeles, Sept. 5, 1936; s. Niven and Phyllis (Cooper) B.; m. Deborah B. Stone, Aug. 16, 1958 (div. 1984); children: Philip Briton, Leslie Cooper; m. S. Jill Harsin, June 4, 1985. A.B., Stanford U., 1958; M.A., U. Calif. at Berkeley, 1960, Ph.D., 1965. Instr. Colgate U., 1963-65, asst. prof. history, 1965-68, assoc. prof. history, 1968-73, prof., 1973-78, William R. Kenan, Jr. prof., 1978—, dept. chmn., 1980-85, dir. div. social scis., 1985-91; mem. coun. Internat. Commn. of Maritime History, 1996-2000. Author: Britain and the Persian Gulf, 1894-1914, 1967, Britain, India and the Arabs 1914-1921, 1971, Mudros to Lausanne: Britains Frontier in West Asia 1918-1923, 1976, Master of Desolation: The Reminiscences of Capt. Joseph J. Fuller, 1980, Hardinge of Penshurst: A Study in The Old Diplomacy, 1980, Alta California 1840-1842: The Journal and Observations of William Dane Phelps, Master of the Ship Alert, 1983; The War Against the Seals: A History of the North American Seal Fishery, 1985; Fremont's Private Navy: the 1846 Journal of Capt. W.D. Phelps, 1987, Whaling Will Never Do For Me: The American Whaleman in the 19th Century, 1994, (with B.M. Gough) Fur Traders From New England: The Boston Men, 1787-1800, 1996; book rev. editor Am. Neptune, 1991—. Woodrow Wilson fellow, 1963; Nat. Endowment for the Humanities fellow, 1967-68; Social Sci. Research Council fellow, 1968-69. Mem. Am. Hist. Assn., Royal Soc. Asian Affairs, Mid. East Inst., Mid. East Studies Assn., Western Front Assn., Soc. Mil. History (book prize com. 1996-98, chair 1998-2000), N.Am. Soc. Oceanic History (exec. coun. 1983-88, v.p. 1988-91, pres. 1991-92, 95-98, chmn. book award com. 1987-92, book prize 1984, 86, 94, 97). Home: PO Box 154 Hamilton NY 13346-0154 Office: Colgate U Dept History 13 Oak Dr Hamilton NY 13346

BUSCH, FREDERICK MATTHEW, writer, literature educator; b. N.Y.C., Aug. 1, 1941; s. Benjamin and Phyllis (Schnell) B.; m. Judith Burroughs, Nov. 29, 1963; children: Benjamin, Nicholas. BA, Muhlenberg Coll., Allentown, Pa., 1962, LittD (hon.), 1980; MA, Columbia U., 1967. Writer for mags. N.Y.C., and Greenwich, Conn., 1966—; from instr. to prof. Colgate U., Hamilton, N.Y., 1966-87, Fairchild prof. lit., 1987—; acting dir. Program in Creative Writing U. Iowa, Iowa City, 1978-79; vis. lectr. Creative Writing Program Columbia U., 1979. Author 23 books including Sometimes I Live in the Country, 1986, Absent Friends, 1989, Harry and Catherine, 1990, Closing Arguments, 1991, Long Way From Home, 1993, The Children in the Woods: New and Selected Stories, 1994 (PEN/Faulkner award nomination 1995). Girls, 1997; (essays) A Dangerous Profession, 1998, (novel) The Night Inspector, 1999; editor: (anthology) Letters to a Fiction Writer, 1997; numerous other essays and short stories. Recipient Nat. Jewish Book award for fiction Jewish Book Coun., 1985, Fiction award AAAL, 1986, PEN/Malamud award, 1991; fellow Guggenheim Found., 1981-82, Ingram Merrill Found., 1981-82. Mem. PEN, Writers Guild Am., Authors Guild Am. Home: 839 Turnpike Rd Sherburne NY 13460-3507 Office: Colgate U Dept English Hamilton NY 13346

BUSCH, HARRIS, medical educator; b. Chgo., May 23, 1923; s. Maurice Ralph and Rose Lillian (Feigenholtz) B.; m. Rose Klora, June 16, 1945; children: Daniel Avery, Laura Anne Busch Smolkin, Gerald Irwin, Fredric Neal. BS, U. Ill., 1944, MD with honors, 1946; MS, U. Wis., 1950, PhD, 1952. Intern Cook County Hosp., Chgo., 1946-47; asst. surgeon, sr. asst. surgeon USPHS, 1947-49; postdoctoral fellow Nat. Cancer Inst., 1950-52; asst. prof. biochemistry, internal medicine Yale U., 1952-55; assoc. prof., prof. pharmacology U. Ill., 1955-60; prof. biochemistry, chmn. dept. Baylor U. Coll. Medicine, 1960-62, prof. pharmacology, chmn. dept., 1960-98, Michael E. DeBakey disting. svc. prof. and chmn., 1995—, chmn. student promotions com., 1969-72, mem. pres.'s coun., 1972-93, dir. Cancer Rsch. Ctr.; vis. prof. U. Chgo., 1968, 71, Northwestern U., 1968, Ga. Med. Coll., 1971, Washington U., St. Louis, 1972, U. Ala., Birmingham, 1972, Ind. U., Indpls., 1972, U. Nev., Reno, 1978, U. Colo., Denver, 1980; cons. lectr. U. Tenn., U. Tex., San Antonio, 1971; Disting. lectr. SUNY, Buffalo, 1977; Centennial lectr. U. Ill. Coll. Medicine, 1981; Disting. lectr. Tohoku Med. Sch., Japan, 1990, Japan Chemotherapy Soc., 1990, Taiwan, 1992; invited lectr. Vienna, Austria, 1992, George Washington U., 1992, Naples, Italy, 1994, Wilhelm Bernard Workshop, Spa (Liege), Belgium, 1995; mem. adv. com. cell and devel. biology Am. Cancer Soc., 1978-82; cancer chemotherapy study sect. USPHS; mem. Nat. Cancer Planning Com., 1971; mem. bd. sci. counselors to div. cancer treatment Nat. Cancer Inst., 1975. Author: Chemistry of Pancreatic Diseases, 1959, An Introduction to the Biochemistry of the Cancer Cell, 1962, Histones and Other Nuclear Proteins, 1965; co-author: Chemotherapy, 1966, The Nucleolus, 1970; editor: Frontiers in Medical Biochemistry, 1962, The Nucleus of the Cancer Cell, 1963, Jour. Phys. Chemistry and Physics, Methods in Cancer Research, vol. I, 1966, vols. II and III, 1967, vol. IV, 1968, Methods in Cancer Research, vol. V, 1970, vol.VI, 1971, vols. VII-IX, 1973, vol. X, 1973, Methods in Cancer Research, vol. XI, 1975, vols. XII and XIII, 1976, Methods in Cancer Research, vols. XIV, XV, 1978, Molecular Biology of Cancer, 1974, Cell Nucleus, Vols. I-III, 1974, IV-VII, 1978, VIII-IX, 1980; editorial bd.: Jour. Cancer Research and Clin. Oncology, Jour. Biol. Chemistry, Cancer Investigation, New Drugs, Physiol. Chemistry, Phys. Life Scis. Recipient Outstanding Alumnus award for svc. to edn. and rsch. U. Ill., 1977, Disting. Faculty award Baylor Coll. Medicine, 1982, Maimonides award, 1996; Baldwin scholar oncology Yale U. Sch. Medicine, 1952-55; scholar cancer rsch. Am. Cancer Soc., 1955. Mem. Am. Soc. Biol. Chemists and Molecular Biologists, Am. Assn. Cancer Rsch. (pres. elect 1988-89, pres. 1989-90, bd. dirs., sci. and public affairs com. 1987), Am. Chem. Soc., Soc. Pharmacology and Exptl. Therapeutics, Soc. Exptl. Biology and Medicine, Internat. Acad. of Tumor Marker Oncology, Sigma Xi, Alpha Omega Alpha. Home: 4966 Dumfries Dr Houston TX 77096-4230

BUSCH, JOHN ARTHUR, lawyer; b. Indpls., Mar. 23, 1951; s. John L. and Betty (Thomas) B.; m. Barbara Ann Holt, June 23, 1973; children: Abigail, Elizabeth, Amanda, Rachel. BA, Wabash Coll., 1973; JD, Duke U., 1976. Bar: Wis. 1976, U.S. Dist. Ct. (ea. we. dists.) Wis., U.S. Ct. Appeals (5th and 7th cirs.) 1976. Assoc. Michael, Best & Friedrich, Milw., 1976-83, ptnr., 1983—; chmn. litigation dept. Michael Best & Friedrich, Milw., 1990-95, chmn. mgmt. com.; mem. ad hoc com. on alternative dispute resolution Milw. Cir. ct. Treas. North Shore Rep. Club, Milw., 1984-85, vice chmn., 1985-86, chmn., 1987-89; del. Rep. State Conv., Milw., 1986; mem. local rules adv. com. Ea. dist., Wis. Master Am. Inns of Ct.; mem. ABA, Wis. Bar Assn., Milw. Bar Assn. Home: 122 E Trillium Rd Mequon WI 53092-6175 Office: Michael Best & Friedrich 100 E Wisconsin Ave Ste 3300 Milwaukee WI 53202-4108

BUSCH, JOYCE IDA, small business owner; b. Madera, Calif., Jan. 24, 1934; d. Bruno Harry and Ella Fae (Absher) Toschi; m. Fred O. Busch, Dec. 14, 1956; children: Karen, Kathryn, Kurt. BA in Indsl. Arts & Interior Design, Calif. State U., Fresno, 1991. Cert. interior designer, Calif. Stewardess United Air Lines, San Francisco, 1955-57; prin. Art Coordinates, Fresno, 1982—, Busch Interior Design, Fresno, 1982—; art cons. Fresno Community Hosp., 1981-83; docent Fresno Met. Mus., 1981-84. Treas. Valley Children's Hosp. Guidance Clinic, 1975-79, Lone Star PTA, 1965-84; mem. Mothers Guild San Joaquin Mem. H.S., 1984-88. Mem. Am. Soc. Interior Designers. Republican. Roman Catholic. Club: Sunnyside Garden (pres. 1987-88). Avocations: gardening, art history.

BUSCH, MARC LAWRENCE, government educator; b. Madison, Wis., Mar. 30, 1966; s. Peter Alan and Ruth (Weiss) B.; m. Xenia Kuris, June 2, 1990; children: Zachary Nicolas, Lelia Ellena. BA with honors, Queen's U., 1988; MA, U. Toronto, Ont., Can., 1989; MPhil, Columbia U., 1993, PhD, 1994. Rsch. cons. Can. Cons./Boston Cons. Group, Toronto, 1989-90; asst. prof. of govt. and social studies Harvard U., Cambridge, Mass., 1994-98; assoc. prof. Harvard U., Cambridge, 1998—; dir. grad. student programs, WCFIA, mem. adv. com. Harvard-MIT Data Ctr., Cambridge, 1998—. Author: Trade Warriors; contbr. articles to profl. jours. and books. Recipient Thomas P. Hoopes Tchg. prize Harvard Coll., 1996; Philip E. Mosely fellow dept. polit. sci. Columbia U., 1991-92, fellow in Internat. Peace and Security, MacArthur Found., N.Y.C., 1992-93, Gillian Lindt fellow Grad. Sch. of Arts and Scis., Columbia U., N.Y.C., 1993-94, fellow Inst. for the Study of World Politics, 1993-94, John M. Olin Nat. Faculty fellow, 1996-97. Mem. Am. Polit. Sci. Assn., Internat. Studies Assn. Avocations: ice hockey, roller blading. Office: Harvard U CFIA-1737 Cambridge St Cambridge MA 02138

BUSCH, NOEL HENRY, banker; b. Jordan, Minn., Dec. 9, 1940; s. Albert Meinrad and Hildegarde Sophie (Bauer) B.; m. Bertina Nancy Lee Helgeson, July 9, 1966; children: Maria Renee, Lavinia Christine, Owen Martin, Mark Allen, Amineh Adrienne. BA, U. Minn., 1965. Legis. and bus. devel. counsel various trade assns., 1966-71; CEO Ind. Bankers Minn., Mpls., 1972-75; prin. organizer, founding dir., CEO Ind. State Bank Minn., Mpls., 1975-81; chmn. bd. Ind. Bankers Credit Corp., Mpls., 1980-82; pres. Ind. Bancservices Exch., Mpls., 1981-82; founding dir., pres., CEO, chmn. exec. com. Ind. Bankers Bank Fla., Orlando, 1982-94; chmn., treas. Busch & Co. Resource Strategies, Inc., 1994—; chmn. Bankers Bank Coun.; founding dir., pres. Bankers' Bancorp of Fla., 1989-94; prin. organizer, founding exec. officer bankers bank movement; publ. Pine Hills Press, 1995—; Fla. rep. Apt. Home Equity Program, Inc., 1994—; exec. v.p. Svejda and Co. Inc., 1997—. Named Banker Advocate of Yr. Orlando C. of C., 1985, Fin. Services Advocate of Yr. U.S. Small Bus. Adminstrn., Jacksonville, Fla., 1985. Republican. Avocations: wood sculpture, philosophical research.

BUSCH, PAUL L., engineering executive. BS in Humanities and Engring., MIT, BSCE, MS in Sanitary Engring. Registered profl. engr. N.Y. vis. prof. U. N.C.; mentor to M Engring. program Cornell U.; mem. adv. coun. Sch. of Civil and Environ. Engring., U. Cornell, others; mem. NRC Water Sci. and Tch. Bd., NRC com. to rev. Met. Washington Water Supply Study; provider expert testimony USEPA hearings and to Ho. of Reps. Com. on Pub. Works; mem. NRC Bd. Environ. Studies and Toxicology; mem. EPA's Nat. Adv. Coun. for Environ. Policy and Technology; trustee-at-large Bd. of Control of the Water Environment Fedn.; mem. Constrn. Industry Round Table; mem. sci. adv. bd. Strategic Environ. R&D Program, 1998—. Past pres. Am. Acad. Environ. Engrs. Designated AAEE Kappe Disting. Lectr., 1990; recipient Gordon Maskew Fair award 1991. Mem. AAAS, ASCE (Freese prize 1998), Am. Water Works Assn., Water Environ. Fedn., Am. Chem. Soc., N.Y. Acad. Sci., Nat. Acad. Engring. Fax: 914-641-2410. Office: Malcolm Pirnie Inc 104 Corporate Park Dr White Plains NY 10602-0751

BUSCH, SHARON LYNNE, elementary and secondary education educator; b. Beavercreek, Ohio, Nov. 16, 1952; d. James Earl and Lena Mae (Brown) B.; m. John Robert Busch, Oct. 8, 1977; 1 child, Brian Alexander. MusB, Miami U., Oxford, Ohio, 1976; postgrad., Wright State U., Fairborn, Ohio, 1981. Tchr. piano Hoffman Studios, Fairfield, 1970-72; desk clk. YMCA, Fairfield, 1972-73; choir dir., accompanist Ch. of the Nazarene, Fairfield, 1972-74; tchr. music Albert Kirocofe Jr. High and Elem. Sch., Gratis, Ohio, 1976-77, Ankeney Jr. High Sch., Beavercreek, Ohio, 1977-98, Beavercreek High Sch., Beavercreek, 1978-98; dir. Friends showchoir, Beavercreek, 1977-95, Guys and Dolls showchoir, Beavercreek, 1979—, dir. a capella choir and concert choir, 1977-98, dir. Nothing But Men group, 1997-98; dir. Beavercreek High. Sch. musicals, 1977-85; soloist Coventry Green Madrigal Group, Dayton, Ohio, 1982-85. Singer Dayton Philharm. Chorus, 1988—; chmn. North Cen. Vis. Team, Edgewood High Sch., Hamilton, 1989, Middletown High Sch., 1991, mem. North Cen. Vis. Team, Stebbins High Sch., Dayton, 1988. Named Outstanding Tchr. of Yr. Beavercreek Sch. Dist., 1991. Mem. Ohio Music Edn. Assn. (hon. choir dir. dist. 12), Am. Choral Dirs. Assn., Ohio Choral Dirs. Assn., Music Educators Nat. Conf., Ohio Music Educators Assn., U. Dayton Music Dept. (guest clinician, 1998). Republican. Avocations: composing music, swimming, bowling, singing. Home: 1363 Meadow Bridge Dr Beavercreek OH 45432-2602

BUSCHA, RALPH VICTOR, security firm executive; b. Houston. AA, Phoenix Coll., 1973. Undercover investigator, 1968-70, gen. investigator, 1970-75, from br. mgr. to dist. mgr., 1978-91; v.p. ESS Inc., Phoenix, 1991-97; investigator Pinkerton's Inc.; v.p., COO Excel Protective Ssvcs., Inc., Phoenix, 1997—. With USAF, 1964-68. Mem. Am. Soc. Indsl. Security. Republican. Lutheran. Avocations: golf, travel, tennis. Office: Excel Protective Svcs Inc PO Box 51507 Phoenix AZ 85076-1507

BUSCHBACH, THOMAS CHARLES, geologist, consultant; b. Cicero, Ill., May 12, 1923; s. Thomas Dominick and Vivian (Smiley) B.; m. Mildred Merle Fletcher, Nov. 26, 1947; children—Thomas Richard, Susan Kay, Deborah Lynn. B.S., U. Ill., 1950, M.S., 1951, Ph.D., 1959. Geologist, structural geology, stratigraphy, underground storage of natural gas Ill. Geol. Survey, 1951-78; coordinator New Madrid Seismotectonic Study, U.S. Nuclear Regulatory Commn., 1976-85; research prof. geology St. Louis U., 1978-85; geologic cons. Champaign, Ill., 1985—. Served to lt. comdr. USNR, 1942-47. Fellow Geol. Soc. Am. Home: 604 Park Lane Dr Champaign IL 61820-7631 Office: PO Box 1608 Champaign IL 61824-1608

BUSCHE, ROBERT MARION, chemical engineer, consultant; b. St. Louis, June 14, 1926; s. Ferdinand and Irma (Seim) B.; m. Norma Jean Nickles, Sept. 17, 1950 (div. Mar. 1978); children: Robert Eric, David Clay, Kristin Anne, Amy Ellen; m. Emma Elizabeth Ruch, June 21, 1980. BSChE, Washington U., St. Louis, 1948, MSChE, 1949, DSc in Chem. Engring., 1952. Project engr. coal-to-oil demonstration br. U.S. Bur. Mines, Louisiana, Mo., 1950-53; rsch. supr. plastics dept. rsch. div. E.I. DuPont de Nemours & Co. Inc., 1953-62; tech. svcs. supr. plastics dept. mktg. div. E.I. DuPont de Nemours & Co. Inc., Wilmington, Del., 1962-64, tech. mgr. devel. dept. heat transfer products div., 1964-68, staff cons. devel. dept. mgmt. svcs. div., 1968-74, planning cons. cen. rsch. dept. life scis. div., 1974-85; pres. Bio En-Gene-Er Assocs. Inc., Wilmington, 1985—; adj. prof. chem. engring. U. Pa., Phila., 1983—; mem. adv. bd. Nat. Solar Energy Plan, Mitre Corp., Washington, 1980-85; mem. adv. bd. liaison com. Forest Products Lab., Madison, Wis.; mem. adv. bd. NSF cellulose hydrolysis program N.C. State U., Raleigh, 1980-82. Contbr. numerous articles to profl. jours. Deacon, elder Presbyn. ch., Wilmington and Orange, Tex., 1957—; dist. and coun. mem. Delmarva coun. Boy Scouts Am., Wilmington, 1959—; bd. dirs. New Castle Cotillion, Wilmington, 1989-91. Heerman's fellow Washington U., 1948, Honor scholar, 1943; recipient Order of Merit award Del-Mar-Va coun. Boy Scouts Am., 1970, Silver Beaver award, 1974, Wood Badge award, 1974, God and Svc. award, 1998. Mem. AIChE, Am. Chem. Soc., Am. Mensa, Intertel, Tau Beta Pi, Tau Kappa Epsilon, Alpha Chi Sigma, Alpha Phi Omega. Republican. Home and Office: 533 Rothbury Rd Wilmington DE 19803-2439

BUSCHERT, JASON LEE, accountant; b. Topeka, Oct. 10, 1971; s. Murray Ralph and Barbara Faye (Classen) B.; m. Jennifer Ann McCord, Sept. 30, 1995. BS in Acctg. summa cum laude, S.W. Bapt. U., 1994. CPA, Mo. Staff acct. Baird Kurtz and Dobson, Springfield, Mo., 1994-96, sr. acct., 1996-98, supr., 1998—. Mem. AICPA, Mo. Soc. CPAs. Republican. Baptist. Avocations: stamp collecting, golf, basketball, music. Office: Baird Kurtz and Dobson 901 E Saint Louis St Fl 10 Springfield MO 65806-2537

BUSCHKE, HERMAN, neurologist; b. Berlin, Oct. 15, 1932; came to U.S., 1934, naturalized, 1945; s. Franz Julius and Ruth Helen (Minkowski) B.; children: Thomas, Katherine; m. Bertelle Selig, 1993. B.A., Reed Coll., 1954; M.D., Western Res. U., 1958. Diplomate: Am. Bd. Psychiatry and Neurology. Intern Bronx (N.Y.) Mcpl. Hosp. Center, 1958-59, resident in neurology, 1959-62; asst. instr. neurology Albert Einstein Coll. Medicine, Bronx, N.Y., 1961-62; asso. prof. Albert Einstein Coll. Medicine, 1969-74, prof., 1974—, prof. neurosci., 1974—; practice medicine specializing in neurology Bronx, N.Y., 1969—; staff mem., attending neurologist Hosp. of Albert Einstein Coll. of Medicine; instr. medicine Stanford U., 1962-63, asst. prof., 1963-69. Named Lena and Joseph Gluck Disting. Scholar in Neurology, 1973. Home: 50 E 89th St New York NY 10128-1225 Office: Albert Einstein Coll Medicine Saul R Korey Dept Neurology 1300 Morris Park Ave Bronx NY 10461-1926

BUSCHMANN, SIEGFRIED, manufacturing executive; b. Essen, Germany, July 12, 1937; s. Walter and Frieda Maria (von. Stamm) B.; m. Rita Renate Moch, May 7, 1965; children: Verena, Mark. Diploma, Wilhelms U. Various exec. positions Thyssen AG, Duesseldorf, Germany, 1964-82; pres. Thyssen Holding Corp., Troy, Mich., 1982—; sr. v.p. Budd Co., Troy, 1982-

83, sr. v.p., CFO, 1983-86, vice chmn., CFO, 1986-89, chmn., CEO, 1989—; chmn. exec. bd. Thyssen Budd Automotive GmbH, Essen, Germany, 1997—. Avocation: golf. Office: The Budd Co PO Box 2601 3155 W Big Beaver Rd Troy MI 48007-2601

BUSDICKER, GORDON G., lawyer; b. Winona, Minn., Oct. 12, 1933; s. Harry John and Edna Mae (Rogers) B.; m. Noreen Decker; children—Karla E., Pamela J., Alison G., Neal A. B.A., Hamline U., St. Paul, 1955; J.D., Harvard U., 1958. Bar: Minn. Atty. Aluminum Co. of Am., Pitts., 1958-61; assoc. Faegre & Benson, Mpls., 1961-67, ptnr., 1967—. Trustee Hamline U., St. Paul, 1973—. Mem. Minn. Bar Assn., ABA. Republican. Congregationalist. Club: Minneapolis. Avocations: boating, geanealogy; Clubs: Mpsl. Club, Interlachen Golf Club. Home: 3833 Abbott Ave S Minneapolis MN 55410-1036 Office: Faegre & Benson 2200 Norwest Ctr 90 S 7th St Ste 2200 Minneapolis MN 55402-3901

BUSECK, PETER ROBERT, geochemistry educator; s. Paul M. and Edith G. (Stern) B.; m. Alice E. Bien, June 20, 1960; children: Lori, David, Susan, Paul. AB, Antioch Coll., 1957; MA, Columbia U., 1959, PhD, 1962. Fellow Geophys. Lab. Carnegie Inst., Washington, 1961-63; mem. faculty depts. chemistry and geology Ariz. State U., Tempe, 1963—, Regents' prof., 1989—; vis. prof. geology Oxford (Eng.) U., 1970-71, Stanford (Calif.) U., 1979-80, U. Paris, 1986-87; spl. asst. to dir. NSF, 1994-95; mem. sci. staff Office of Sci. and Tech. Policy, White House, 1994-95. Contbr. articles to profl. jours. NSF fellow, 1970-71. Fellow AAAS, Geol. Soc. Am., Meteorite Soc., Mineral Soc. Am., Soc. Econ. Geologists; mem. Am. Geophys. Union, Geochem. Soc., Microbeam Soc., Can. Mineral Soc., Microscope Soc. Am., Am. Crystallographic Assn. Office: Ariz State U Dept Geology Tempe AZ 85287

BUSELMEIER, BERNARD JOSEPH, insurance company executive; b. Detroit, Feb. 10, 1956; s. Bernard August and Rita Mathilda (Cook) B.; m. Sharon Lynette Hoffman, Nov. 28, 1975; 1 child, Andrew Joseph. BBA in Acctg., U. Detroit, 1980, MBA, 1990. Various fin. positions ins. group Auto Club Mich., Dearborn, Mich., 1974-81; various fin. positions Motors Ins. Corp., Detroit, 1981-89, treas., 1989-98, v.p., treas., 1993-98; exec. v.p., CFO, Integon Corp., Winston-Salem, N.C., 1998—. Office: Integon Corp 500 W 5th St # 1802 Winston Salem NC 27101-2728

BUSELT, CLARA IRENE, religious organization administrator; b. Detroit, Jan. 30, 1921; d. Andrew and Bernice (Marcian) Kochanowski; m. Michael Leo Buselt, Apr. 18, 1940; children: Edwin, Nancy, Robert, John, Jane. Student, MacGregor Beauty Coll., Kansas City, 1939. Cosmetician various beauty shops, Leavenworth, 1940-45; surp. dir. Sch. Lunch Program Sacred Heart Cafeteria, Immaculata High, Leavenworth, 1957-68; dietetic worker VA Med. Ctr., Leavenworth, 1968-81; office clk. Storage Box Inc., Leavenworth, 1987—; sr. Times corr., photographer Leavenworth Times, 1990—. Photographer (contest) Congress Americas, 1986. Mem. Sr. Coun. Park and Recreation, Leavenworth, 1988, Sr. Citizen Inc. Kitchen Band, 1993—. Recipient Gov. and First Lady Vol. award Gov. of Kans., 1990, Sr. Citizen of Yr. award Leavenworth County Coun. on Aging, 1994, Sr. Citizen award Am. Assn. Ret. Persons, 1995; named Silver Haired Legislator Leavenworth County, 1993. Mem. Am. Assn. Ret. Persons (recording sec. 1995-96), Women's Div. C. of C., Parish Council Sacred Heart Ch., Sacred Heart Alter Soc. (pres. 1977-87), Am. War Mothers (state pres. 1983-85, nat. color bearer 1985-87, nat. chaplain 1987-89), Cath. Literary Club (pres. 1983-85), Sch. Food Svc. Assn. (charter pres. 1958), St. John Hosp. Guild (pres. 1975-76), Loyal Christian Benefit Assn. (br. pres. 1977-88, nat. trustee 1981—), Daughters Isabella, Arch Diocese Coun. (pres. 1981-83), Nat. Assn. Ret. Fed. Employees, Loyal Christian Benefit Assn. (br. pres. 1977—), Leavenworth County Coun. Aging (chair adv. coun. aging), Ret. Eagles Activity Club (v.p. 1991-93, pres. 1993—). Avocations: volunteer work, sewing, photography, tap dancing, ballroom dancing. Home: 1413 S 16th St Leavenworth KS 66048-2914 *In my lifetime I have found that you must place your trust in God, and have a positive attitude; there is good in every person, but sometimes someone has to bring it out.*

BUSER, CAROLYN ELIZABETH, correctional education administrator; b. St. Paul, June 14, 1946; d. Jerome Alfred and Ella Caroline (Anderson) B.; m. Richard John Ward, Sept. 17, 1977; children: John Jerome Buser Ward, Carl Alfred Buser Ward. BA in English, Carleton Coll., 1968; MS in Spl. Edn., U. Md., 1985, PhD in Ednl. Policy and Adminstrn., 1996. Correctional tchr. Md. Div. Correction, Hughesville, 1970-74, Balt., 1974-76; correctional edn. supr. Md. Dept. Edn. Md. Penitentiary, Balt., 1976-80, Md. Correctional Instn., Jessup, 1980-88; correctional edn. supr. Md. Dept. Edn., Md. correctional pre-release program Md. Correctional Instn. for Women, Jessup, 1988-94; field coord. correctional edn. Md. Dept. Edn., 1994—; cons. Am. Correctional Assn., Laurel, Md., 1980; Md. state dir. Correctional Edn. Assn., Laurel, 1988-90; program supr. Prison Literacy, Nat. Inst. Corrections, Washington (designated exemplary program, 1986). Active Ft. Washington (Md.) Recreational Coun., 1985—. Fellow Edn. Behaviorally Disordered Students, U. Md., 1985. Mem. ASCD, Coun. Exceptional Children, Coun. Adminstrs. Spl. Edn., Correctional Edn. Assn. (sec. 1986), Md. Assn. Adult Cmty. and Continuing Edn., Phi Kappa Phi. Office: Md State Dept Edn 200 W Baltimore St Ste 1 Baltimore MD 21201-2595

BUSEY, GARY, actor, musician; b. Goose Creek, Tex., June 29, 1944; s. Delmer Lloyd and Virginia (Arnett) B.; m. Judy Lynn Helkenberg, Dec. 30, 1968; 1 child, William Jacob. AA, Coffeyville Jr. Coll., 1963; student, Okla. State U., Kans. State Coll. Played drums with The Rubber Band, 1963-70; played drums as Teddy Jack Eddy with Leon Russell, Kris Kristofferson, Willie Nelson; actor, 1972—; made film debut in Angels Hard as They Come, 1971; films include Dirty Little Billy, 1972, The Magnificent Seven Ride, 1972, Lolly Madonna XXX, 1973, Hex, 1973, Thunderbolt and Lightfoot, 1974, The Gumball Rally, 1976, A Star is Born, 1976, Straight Time, 1978, Big Wednesday, 1978, Buddy Holly Story, 1978, Carny, 1980, Foolin' Around, 1980, Barbarosa, 1982, D.C. Cab, Let's Get Harry, 1986, Eye of the Tiger, 1986, Lethal Weapon, 1987, Bulletproof, 1988, Act of Piracy, 1990, Predator II, 1990, My Heroes Have Always Been Cowboys, 1990, Hider in the House, Point Break, 1991, The Player, 1992, Under Siege, 1992, The Firm, 1993, Rookie of the Year, 1993, Surviving the Game, 1994, Drop Zone, 1994, Chasers, 1994, Livers Aint Cheap, 1995, Stick's and Stones, 1996, The Rage, 1996, Man with a Gun, 1996, Lost Highway, 1996, The Chain, 1996, Carried Away, 1996, Black Sheep, 1996, Rough Draft, 1997, Plato's Run, 1997, Lethal Tender, 1997; TV films include Blood Sport, Hitchiker, 1/2 A Lifetime, A Dangerous Life (for HBO), Neon Empire (for Showtime), 1989, The Big T, 1991, Wild Texas Wind, 1991; appeared in TV series The Texas Wheelers, 1974-75; other TV appearances include Saturday Night Live. Office: care ICM 8942 Wilshire Blvd Beverly Hills CA 90211-1934

BUSEY, ROXANE C., lawyer; b. Chgo., June 15, 1949. BA cum laude, Miami U., 1970; MAT, Northwestern U., 1971, JD, 1975. Bar: Ill. 1975. Ptnr. Gardner, Carton & Douglas, Chgo. Mem. ABA (chair health com., antitrust sect. 1989-92, antitrust sect. coun. 1992-95, antitrust sect. vice-chair 1995-96, 98-99, fin. office 1996-98), Ill. State Bar Assn. (chair antitrust coun. 1984-85), Chgo. Bar Assn. (chair antitrust sect. 1990-91). Office: Gardner Carton & Douglas 321 N Clark St Ste 3000 Chicago IL 60610-4762*

BUSFIELD, ROGER MELVIL, JR., retired trade association executive, educator; b. Ft. Worth, Feb. 4, 1926; s. Roger Melvil and Julia Mabel (Clark) B.; m. Jean Wilson, Mar. 26, 1948 (div. Oct. 1960); children: Terry Jean, Roger Melvil III, Timothy Clark; m. Virginia Bailey, Dec. 1, 1962 (dec. July 1991); 1 child, Julia Lucille; m. Addie Howard Davis, June 17, 1995. Student, U. Tex., 1943, 46; BA, Southwestern U., 1947, MA, 1948; PhD, Fla. State U., 1954. Asst. prof. Southwestern U., 1947-49; instr. U. Ala., 1949-50, Fla. State U., 1950-54; asst. prof. speech Mich. State U., 1954-60; editl. svcs. specialist Oldsmobile divsn. Gen. Motors Corp., Lansing, Mich., 1960; gen. publs. supr. Consumers Power Co., Jackson, Mich., 1960-61; assoc. dir. Mich. Hosp. Assn., Lansing, 1961-73; exec. dir. Ark. Hosp. Assn., Little Rock, 1973-81, pres., 1981-94, pres. emeritus, 1994—; adj. prof. health svcs. mgmt. Webster U., 1979-97. Trustee, Ctrl. Mich. U., 1967-73, chmn., 1970; mem. Mich. Gov.'s Commn. on Higher Edn., 1972-74; mem. Ark. Gov.'s Emergency Med. Svcs. Adv. Coun., 1975-94, chmn., 1978-84; mem. Ark. Gov.'s Task Force on Rural Hosps., 1988-89, Ark. Dept. of Health Long Range Planning Com., 1988-89; chmn. AIDS adv. com. Ark. Dept. Health, 1990-97; mem. Ark. Gov.'s Task Force Health Care Reform, 1993-96; chmn. Health Data Task Force, Ark. Resources Comm., 1994-95; mem. adv. bd. Ark. Pediat. Facility, 1995-96. Served with USMC, 1943-46. Named Tex. Outstanding Author, Theta Sigma Phi, 1958; recipient Disting. Alumnus award Southwestern U., 1971; Senate-House Concurrent Resolution of Tribute, Mich. Legis., 1973; Bd. Trustees award Am. Hosp. Assn., 1994; Merit award Ark. Hosp. Assn., 1994. Mem. Am. Soc. Assn. Execs., Ark. Soc. Assn. Execs. (pres. 1981-82), Pub. Rels. Assn. Mich. (pres. 1966), Speech Comm. Assn., Am. Coll. Health Care Execs., State Hosp. Assn. Exec. Forum (sec., treas. 1989, pres. 1991), Am. Hosp. Assn. (coun. legis. 1975-77, coun. allied and govtl. rels. 1983-86), Rotary (Little Rock). Methodist. Author: The Playwright's Art, 1958, Arabic transl., 1964; (with others) The Children's Theatre, 1960; editor Theatre Arts Bibliography, 1964; contbr. articles to profl. jours.; author profl. motion picture scenarios. Home: PO Box 2267 Georgetown TX 78627-2267

BUSFIELD, TIMOTHY, actor; b. Lansing, Mich., June 12, 1957; divorced; 1 child, Willy; m. Jennifer; children, Daisy and Samuel. From apprentice to mem. Actors Theatre of Louisville; mem. Circle Repertory Co., N.Y.C.; founder Fantasy Theatre, Sacramento. Appeared in theater prodns. including Robin Goodfellow (children's version of A Midsummer Night's Dream), Getting Out, Actors Theatre, A Life, Long Wharf Theatre, Broadway prodn. Brighton Beach Memoirs (understudy), TV prodns. Reggie, After M.A.S.H., Paper Chase; TV series include Trapper John, M.D. (role as J.T.), thirtysomething (role as Elliot)(Emmy award as Outstanding Supporting Actor in a Drama Series, 1991), Byrds of Paradise (role as Sam Byrd), 1994, In the Line of Duty Kidnapped, 1995, In the Shadow of Evil, 1995, Champs, 1996, The Unspeakable, 1996; television movies include Strays, 1991, Calendar Girl, Cop Killer?, The Bambi Bembrenek Story, 1992, When Secrets Kill, 1997, Trucks 1997, When Secrets Kill, 1997, Buffalo Soldiers, 1997, The Darklings, 1999; films include Stripes, 1981, Revenge of the Nerds, 1984, Revenge of the Nerds II: Nerds in Paradise, 1987, Field of Dreams, 1989, Sneakers, 1992, Little Big League, 1994, Quiz Show, 1994, First Kid, 1996, Wanted, 1999, Time at the Top, 1999. Address: care William Morris Agency 151 S El Camino Dr Beverly Hills CA 90212-2704*

BUSH, BARBARA PIERCE, volunteer, wife of former President of the United States; b. Rye, N.Y., June 8, 1925; d. Marvin and Pauline (Robinson) Pierce; m. George Herbert Walker Bush, Jan. 6, 1945; children: George Walker, John Ellis, Neil Mallon, Marvin Pierce, Dorothy Walker. Student, Smith Coll., 1943-44; hon. degrees, Stritch Coll., Milw., 1981, Mt. Vernon Coll., Washington, 1981, Hood Coll., Frederick, Md., 1983, Howard U., Washington, 1987, Judson Coll., Marion, Ala., 1988, Bennett Coll., Greensboro, N.C., 1989, Smith Coll., 1989, Morehouse Sch. Medicine, 1989. Oper. & facilities div. Dept. Administration, Washington, 1992; with Office of George Bush, Washington, 1992—. Author: C. Fred Story; Millie's Book; Barbara Bush: A Memoir, 1994. Hon. chair adv. bd. Reading is Fundamental; hon. mem. Bus. Coun. for Effective Literacy; mem. adv. coun. Soc. of Meml. Sloan-Kettering Cancer Ctr.; hon. mem. bd. dirs. Children's Oncology Svcs. of Met. Washington, The Washington Home, The Kingsbury Ctr.; hon. chmn. nat. adv. coun. Literacy Vols. of Am., Nat. Sch. Vols. Program; sponsor Laubach Literacy Internat.; nat. hon. chmn. Leukemia Soc. of Am.; hon. mem. bd. trustees Morehouse Sch. of Medicine; hon. nat. chmn. Nat. Organ Donor Awareness Week, 1982-86; pres. Ladies of the Senate, 1981-88; mem. women's com. Smithsonian Assocs., Tex. Fedn. of Rep. Women, life mem., hon. mem.; hon. chairperson for the Nat. Com. on Literacy and Edn. United Way, Barbara Bush Found. for Family Literacy, Washington Parent Group Fund, Girls Clubs of Am., 10th anniversary Harvest Nat. Food Bank Network; hon. chmn. Nat. Com. for the Prevention of Child Abuse and Childhelp U.S.A.; hon. pres. Girl Scouts U.S; hon. chair Nat. Com. for Adoption; mem. bd. trustees Mayo Clinic Found.; hon. chair Read Am., Boarder Baby Project; mem. bd. visitors M. D. Anderson Cancer Ctr.; hon. chair Leukemia Soc. Am., Children's Literacy Initiative; hon. mem. Reading is Fundamental; ambassador at large Americares; honorary mem. Barbara Bush Found. for Family Literacy. Recipient Nat. Outstanding Mother of Yr. award, 1984, Woman of Yr. award USO, 1986, Disting. Leadership award United Negro Coll. Fund 1986, Disting. Am. Woman award Coll. Mt. St. Joseph, 1987, Free Spirit award Freedom Forum, 1995. Mem. Tex. Fedn. Rep. Women (life), Internat. II Club (Washington), Magic Circle Rep. Women's Club (Houston), YWCA. Episcopalian.

BUSH, CRYSTAL REED, lawyer; b. Chgo., Dec. 14, 1957; d. Alonzo and Elmethra (Luster) Reed. BA in History, Roosevelt U., 1979; JD, DePaul U., 1995. Tchr. Chgo. Bd. Edn., 1979-90; pvt. practice Chgo., 1990—; pres. Buree Assocs., Chgo., 1991-96. Fin. editor The Leguenet, 1991; contbr. articles to jours. Treas., chair program com. Women's Entrepreneur Network, Chgo., 1990-91; treas. League of Black Women, Chgo., 1991-92. Recipient Exceptional Contbn. award to Afro-Am. Cmty. AT&T, 1991-93. Mem. ABA, Nat. Assn. Women Bus. Owners (Chgo. chpt.), Chgo. Bar Assn. (dir. young lawyers sect., past co-chair client devel. and firm econs. com., past legislation liaison estate planning com.), Young Execs. Club. Home: 8644 S Kenwood Ave Chicago IL 60619-6416 Office: Buree Assocs 22 N Morgan St Apt 114 Chicago IL 60607-2608

BUSH, DAVID H., management consultant; b. St. Louis Park, Minn., Mar. 19, 1964; s. Mel B. and Carol (Steinberg) B.; married. B Mech. Engring., U. Minn., 1987, MS Indsl. Engring., 1990, PhD Indsl. Engring., 1997. Cert. quality engr. Quality systems engr. SCIMED Life Systems, Inc., Maple Grove, Minn., 1993-97; improvement and innovation specialist Northwest Airlines, St. Paul, Minn., 1991-92; sr. engr. Rosemount, Inc. (Aerospace Divsn.), Burnsville, 1988-91; cons. Mpls., 1997—; adv. Ideation/TRIZ, Detroit, 1996—; examiner Minn. Quality Award, Mpls., 1992; adj. prof. U. Minn., 1997—; cons. Minn., 1997—. Contbr. articles to profl. jours. Dir. No. DKE Scholastic Found., Mpls., 1987-89. Mem. ASME. Home: 5315 York Ave S Minneapolis MN 55410-2134 Office: Excel Instrn Inc 1313 5th St SE Minneapolis MN 55414-4504

BUSH, DENNIS, radio personality; b. Birmingham, Ala., Sept. 8, 1962; s. William H. and Willadean (McCarver) B.; m. Donna Michola Bush, May 20; 1 child, Sabrina Nicole. BS in Mass. Comm., U. Montevallo, Ala., 1985; M.Vocat. Edn., Athens (Ala.) State U., 1996. Cert. tchr., Ala. Promotion dir. prodn. External Word TV Network, Birmingham, 1984-89; prodr./dir. TV Birmingham, 1989-94; talk show host Drag Racing USA Radio/WAPI Radio, Birmingham, 1990-99, Drag Racing USA/WJOX Radio, Birmingham, 1991-96, 99—; TV prodn. instr. Clay-Chalkville H.S., Jefferson County, Ala., 1994—. Photojournalist Mo. Racing Newspaper, Behind the Wheel, 1991-94. Adv. bd. Jefferson County TV Prodn. Bd., Birmingham, 1994—. Mem. Ad Coun. Birmingham, Radio Announcers Guild, Am. Fedn. Tchrs., Alpha Epsilon Rho. Avocations: drag racing, videography, motorcycles, golf, outdoors. Home and Office: 600 Newton Dr Midfield AL 35228-2032

BUSH, EUGENE NYLE, pharmacologist, research scientist; b. McKeesport, Pa., Apr. 14, 1952; s. Nyle E. and Rosalia M. (Merlino) B.; m. Janet Rosemary Ruscitto, May 7, 1977; children: Stephen Michael, Rebecca Renee, Timothy George. BS in Pharmacy, U. Pitts., 1977, PhD in Pharmacology, 1981. Registered pharmacist, Pa., Ill. Tchg. asst. U. Pitts., 1978-81; staff pharmacist Western Pa. Hosp., Pitts., 1977-81; pharmacologist II Abbott Labs., 1981-84, pharmacologist I, 1984-87; sr. rsch. sci. Abbott Labs., Abbott Park, Ill., 1986-88, rsch. investigator, 1988-89, group leader, endocrine pharmacol., 1989-91; sr. group leader endocrine pharmacol. Abbott Labs., 1991-97, assoc. Volwiler rsch. fellow, 1996—. Co-author numerous publs.; contbr. articles to profl. jours. Mem. Endocrine Soc., Am. Pharm. Assn., Am. Diabetes Assn., Nat. Eagle Scout Assn., Sigma Xi. Republican, Roman Catholic. Avocations: gardening, photography, computers, bicycling. Home: 816 Bedford Ct Libertyville IL 60048-3002 Office: Abbott Labs Bldg Ap 9A Dept 47H 100 Abbott Park Rd Abbott Park IL 60064-6115

BUSH, FRED MARSHALL, JR., lawyer; b. Newhebron, Miss., Jan. 25, 1917; s. Frederick Marshall Sr. and Elizabeth Stewart (Buck) B.; m. Katie Ruth Field, May 8, 1942; children: Frederick Marshall III, Carl J., Richard S. AA, Hinds Jr. Coll., 1935; BS, U.S. Naval Acad., 1939; LLB, U. Miss., 1950. Bar: Miss. 1948, U.S. Dist. Ct. Miss. 1948, U.S. Ct. Appeals (5th and 11th cirs.) 1948, U.S. Supreme Ct. 1965. Commd. ensign USN, 1939, advanced through grades to capt., resigned, 1948, with Res., 1948-60; ptnr. Fant & Bush, Holly Springs, Miss., 1950-60, Mitchell, McNutt, Bush, Lagrone & Sams, Tupelo, Miss., 1962-89, Phelps Dunbar, Tupelo, Miss., 1989—. Bd. dirs. Miss. Bd. Econ. Devel., Jackson, Miss., 1960-68, Tenn.-Tombigbee Waterway Devel. Authority, Columbus, Miss., 1980-84. Fellow Miss. Bar Found. (chmn. 1978); mem. ABA (ho. of dels. 1986-87, 89-90), Miss. Bar Assn. (pres. 1986-87, various coms. and offices), Miss. Def. Lawyers Assn. (pres. 1973-74). Episcopalian. Lodge: Rotary (pres. local club 1954-55). Office: Phelps Dunbar PO Box 1220 Tupelo MS 38802-1220

BUSH, FREDERICK MORRIS, federal official; b. Newport News, Va., Feb. 6, 1949; s. Morris and Dorothy Montony B.; m. Catherine Marie Murphy, Sept. 10, 1977; children—Alexander Murphy Morris, Taylor McGrath, Channing Barbara and Margaret Montony (twins). BA, U. Colo., 1971; MA in Internat. Studies, Am. U., 1974. Clk. Republican policy com. U.S. Senate, 1971-73; legis. asst. Ho. of Reps., 1973; asst. to fin. chmn. Rep. Nat. Com., 1973-74; dep. fin. dir. Pres. Ford Com., 1975-77; nat. fin. dir. George Bush for Pres., 1979-80; asst. sec. commerce for tourism, dep. Chief of Staff to v.p.; pres. Bush & Co.; commr. gen. U.S.A. Universal Expn., Seville, Spain, 1991-92; U.S. amb., commr. gen. Expo 92, Seville, 1992—; dir. devel. Woodrow Wilson Internat. Ctr. for Scholars, Washington. Founder Rep. Assocs. Chgo.; trustee Am. Ctr. Internat. Leadership; dep. fin. chmn. for George Bush for Pres.; fin. chmn. San Diego host com. Rep. Nat. Conv.; fin. chmn. Reps. Abroad; fin. chmn. Washington bdi. com. 2012 Olympic Games, 1998—; devel. dir. Woodrow Wilson Internat. Ctr. for Scholars, 1998—. Home: 8208 Kerry Rd Chevy Chase MD 20815-4808

BUSH, GEORGE HERBERT WALKER, former President of the United States; b. Milton, Mass., June 12, 1924; s. Prescott Sheldon and Dorothy (Walker) B.; m. Barbara Pierce, Jan. 6, 1945; children: George W., John E., Neil M., Marvin P., Dorothy W. Koch. BA in Econs., Yale U., 1948; numerous other hon. degrees. Co-founder Bush-Overbey Oil Devel. Co., 1951; Co-founder, dir. Zapata Petroleum Corp., Midland, 1953-59; pres. Zapata Off Shore Co., Houston, 1956-64; chmn. bd. Zapata Off Shore Co., 1964-66; mem. 90th-91st Congresses from 7th Dist. Tex., 1967-71, Ways and Means com.; U.S. amb. to UN, 1971-73; chmn. Rep. Nat. Com., 1973-74; chief U.S. Liaison Office Peking, People's Republic China, 1974-75; dir. CIA, 1976-77; adj. prof. adminstrv. sci. Rice U., Houston, 1978; V.P. of U.S., 1981-89, Pres. of U.S., 1989-93; chmn. Eisenhower Exch. Fellowships; bd. visitors M.D. Anderson Cancer Ctr., Houston. Del. Rep. Nat. Conv., 1964, 69; Rep. candidate U.S. senator from Tex., 1964, 70. Lt. (j.g.), pilot USN, WWII. Decorated D.F.C., Air medals (3). Office: 10000 Memorial Dr Houston TX 77024-3422

BUSH, GEORGE W., governor; b. July 6, 1946; s. George Herbert and Barbara (Pierce) B.; m. Laura; children: Barbara and Jenna (twins). BA in History, Yale U., 1968; MBA, Harvard U., 1975. Founder, mgr. Spectrum 7 Energy Corp. (merger with Harken Energy Corp. 1986), Midland, Tex.; dir. Harken Energy Corp.; gov. State of Tex., 1994—. With Tex. Air N.G. Recipient Big D award Dallas All Sports Assn., 1989. Office: Office Gov State Capitol PO Box 12428 Austin TX 78711-2428*

BUSH, HAROLD EHRIG, computer consultant; b. Pottsville, Pa., Jan. 21, 1943; s. William Griffith and Mildred Marie (Kissawetter) B. AS with honors, Triton Coll., 1972; BA with honors, Northeastern Ill. U., 1974; cert. specialized electronics tng., Gen. Motors, Moorestown, N.J., 1987. Sr. electronics technician Motorola, Inc., Chgo., 1967-70, Beckman Instruments, Chgo., 1970-74; freelance writer Wordsearch Puzzles by H.E., Carlsbad, Calif., 1975-76; tech. writer Info. Internat., Inc., Culver City, Calif., 1976-77; engring. writer Pertec Computer Corps., Chatsworth, Calif., 1977-80; mktg. engring. writer Litton Energy Control Systems, Chatsworth, 1980; cons. Computer Concepts, Bristol, Pa., 1978—; sr. ptnr. Premier Internat., Bristol, Pa., 1994—; computer cons. North City Congress, Phila., 1990—, DELCO Blind/Sight Ctr., Chester, Pa., 1990—. Author: (series of pocket reference manuals) Disk Extended Basic, COBOL '80, CP/M Basic, 1979-80. Mentor CommpuMentor, San Francisco, 1990—; pub. rels. com. North City Congress, Phila., 1991-96; Shrine clown Crescent Temple-AAONMS, Trenton, N.J., 1992—. Named Melvin Jones fellow Lions Club Internat. Found., 1991; recipient Letter of Commendation, Commanding Officer USS Northampton, FPO N.Y., 1962, Achievement award Soc. for Tech. Comms., Western Region, 1979, Appreciation award Pa. Lions Hearing Rsch. Found., Hershey, Pa., 1989-90, Legion of Honor, Chapel of the Four Chaplains, 1991. Mem. IEEE, Assn. Computing Machinery, N.Y. Acad. Scis., Newtown Lodge #427 F&AM, Ancient Accepted Scottish Rite Valley of Trenton, Crescent Shrine Temple. Avocations: auto racing, power boating, antique cars. Home: 9071 Mill Creek Rd Apt 722 Levittown PA 19054-4217 Office: Computer Concepts PO Box 2224 Bristol PA 19007-8224 also: Computer Concepts 97-B Wood St Bristol PA 19007-4816 also: Premier Internat 97 Wood St Bristol PA 19007-4816 *Idealism, integrity, diligence, trust, faith, confidence, loyalty, charity, forgiveness, humility. These ten principles when incorporated into the foundations of one's life, may not guarantee success or prosperity; but will positively lead to a full and satisfying life.*

BUSH, HARRY LEONARD, JR., surgery educator; b. Auburn, Ala., July 11, 1942; m. Ellen Parker; children: Alexander, Charles, Scott. BS, Princeton U., 1964; MD, Columbia U., 1968. Diplomate Am. Bd. Surgery; cert. gen. vascular surgeon. Surgical intern Presbyn. Hosp., N.Y.C., 1968-69, fellow, dept. surgery, 1969-70, resident gen. surgery, 1973-76; instr. surgery Columbia U., N.Y.C., 1975-76, Boston U. Sch. Medicine, 1976-77; asst. prof. surgery Tufts U. Sch. Medicine, Boston, 1979-86, assoc. prof. surgery, 1986-87; assoc. prof. surgery Cornell U. Med. Coll., N.Y.C., 1987—; dir. surg. ICU Boston VA Med. Ctr, 1983-84, staff surgeon 1979-87, asst. dir. transplant svc. 1979-87, chmn. animal studies subcommittee 1980-85, chmn. R & D com. 1983-84; assoc. staff surgeon New Eng. Med. Ctr., Boston, 1979-83, staff surgeon 1983-87; asst. dir. organ preservation lab. New Eng. Organ Bank, Boston, 1979-87, trustee 1984-87; chief div. vascular surgery N.Y. Hosp., 1988—, assoc. attending surgeon 1987—, dir. non-invasive vascular lab 1987—, chief divsn. vascular surgery, 1988-97; asst. dir. transplant svc. Tufts New Eng. Med. Ctr., Boston, 1979-87; chief surg. svc. Lemuel Shattuck Hosp., Boston, 1984-87; cons. med. rsch. svc. Va. Cen. Office, Washington, 1985-86; vice-chmn. dept. surgery Presbyn. Hosp., 1997—. Author (with others): Complications of Thoracic and Cardiovascular Surgery, 1979, Peripheral Vascular Diseases, 1987, Common Problems in Vascular Surgery, 1989, Aortic Surgery, 1989, Current Critical Problems in Vascular Surgery, 1989, Current Therapy in Vascular Surgery, 1991; contbr. over 70 articles to profl. jours. Mem. Am. Heart Assn., 1976—. With U.S. Navy, 1970-73. Westchester Heart Assn. Rsch. fellow, 1969-70; co-prin. investigator VA Merit Rev. Program, 1980-82; prin. investigator, VA Merit Rev. Program, 1983-86, 86-89; co-investigator NIH, 1982-84; prin. investigator NIH, 1988-91, Wyeth-Ayerst Labs., 1989-90. Fellow Am. Coll. Surgeons; mem. Internat. Cardiovascular Soc., Internat. Soc. for Applied Cardiovascular Biology, New Eng. Soc. for Vascular Surgery, New Eng. Surg. Soc., N.Y. Soc. for Cardiovascular Surgery, N.Y. Surg. Soc., N.Y. Clin. Soc., Boston Surg. Soc., Ea. Vascular Soc., Assn. for Acad. Surgery, Soc. Critical Care Medicine, Soc. for Vascular Surgery, Coun. on Cardiovascular Surgery, Soc. Univ. Surgeons, Stroke Coun., Sigma Xi. Achievements include research in arterial blockage, cardiology, drug and surgical treatment for arterial and cardiological therapy, limb salvage, vein grafts, kidney transplantation, renal transplantation. Office: NY Hosp Cornell Med Ctr Dept Surgery 525 E 68th St # 2003 New York NY 10021-4885

BUSH, JOANNE TADEO, financial consultant, corporate executive; b. Norristown, Pa., May 17, 1947; d. I.C. and Anne (DeJohn) Arena; 1 child, Ryan J. Tadeo; m. David F. Bush, Oct. 15, 1989. BS in Acctg. cum laude, Villanova U., 1979; MBA in Taxation, Drexel U., 1982. Lic. investment advisor, securities broker. Adminstrv. asst. Cen. Montgomery Mental Health and Mental Retardation Ctr., Norristown, 1970-80; grad. teaching asst. Drexel U., Phila., 1981-82; lectr. Pa. State U., Abington, 1982-83; asst. prof. Ursinus Coll., Collegeville, Pa., 1883-84; v.p., fin. cons. Merrill Lynch, Exton, Pa., 1984—. bd. dirs. Chester County Estate Planning Coun., 1988—, Chester County Chamber for Bus. and Industry; West Chester charity ball com. Mem. Rotary, Alpha Sigma Lambda, Beta Gamma Sigma, Phi Kappa Phi. Avocations: tennis, sailing. Office: Merrill Lynch Oaklands Corp Ctr 101 Arrandale Blvd Exton PA 19341-2564

BUSH, JOHN ELLIS, governor; b. Midland, Tex., Feb. 11, 1953; m. Columba Bush; children: George, Noelle, Jeb. B.Latin Am. Affairs, U. Tex. Co-founder Codina Group, Miami, Fla., 1981—, pres., COO; gov. State of Fla., Tallahassee, 1998—. Sec. of commerce State of Fla.; vol. Miami Children's Hosp., United Way of Dade County, Dade County Homeless Trust; founder Found. for Fla.'s Future, 1995, chmn.; co-founder Liberty City Charter Sch. Roman Catholic. E-mail: flágovernor@eog.state.fl.us. Office: Office of the Governor The Capitol Tallahassee FL 32399-0001*

BUSH, JOHN KENDALL, management consultant; b. Lancaster, Eng., Apr. 21, 1952; came to U.S., 1996; s. John and Gladys (Kendall) B.; m. Catriona Mary Clay, Apr. 30, 1983. BA, Cambridge (Eng.) U., 1973, MA (hon.), 1977; C.A.S.O.R., Brunel U., Uxbridge, Eng., 1975. Sr. cons. Nat. Coal Bd., London, 1974-83; sr. cons. Price Waterhouse, London, 1984-90, ptnr., 1990—, ops. dir. govt. practice, 1992-95; change integration leader utilities practice Price Waterhouse, Atlanta, 1996-98; new energy practice leader Price Waterhouse Coopers, Atlanta, 1998; utilities advisor U.K. Govt. Author: Stock Control in Hospital Pharmacies, 1980. Chair Newtimber Parish Meeting, Sussex, Eng., 1992-96. St. John's Coll. scholar, 1970. Mem. OR Soc., Inst. Chartered Accts. Mem. Ch. of Eng. Avocations: walking, rugby, music, food, company. Office: Price Waterhouse Coopers 3200 Windy Hill Rd SE Ste 900 Atlanta GA 30339-5650

BUSH, JOHN WILLIAM, federal transportation official; b. Columbus, Ohio, Sept. 17, 1909; s. William Hayden and Esther (Brushart) B.; m. Mary Elizabeth Van Doren, June 4, 1932 (dec. 1958); children: Jan Hayden (Mrs. Richard L. Jennings), Emily Van Doren Bush; m. Dorothy Vredenburgh, Jan. 13, 1962 (dec. 1991). BSBA, Va. Poly. Inst., 1931. With Standard Oil Co. La., 1932-37, T.K. Brushart Oil Co., Portsmouth, Ohio, 1937-49; pres. Ohio System Inc., 1946—, dir. purchasing Ohio,, 1949-57; dir. commerce, 1959-61; commr. ICC, 1961-71, chmn., 1966; spl. transp. adviser Senate Commerce Com., 1971—; mem. gov.'s adv. coun. Fla., 1957-59; v.p. Coastal Petroleum Co., 1972-89; bd. dirs. Can. So. Petroleum Ltd., 1972-89, R.C. Williams & Co., Inc., N.Y.C.; chmn. bd. Old Judge Foods Corp., St. Louis, 1988-91. Mem. Ohio Small Bus. Commn., 1954-56, Ohio Water Pollution Control Bd., 1954-56; mem. Fla. Gov.'s adv. coun., 1989-90; councilman, Portsmouth, 1941-44; Dem. nominee for Congress, 1974; dir. Ohio Vietnam Vets. Bonus Commn., 1973-74. Mem. Nat. Assn. State Purchasing Ofcls. (pres. 1954). Address: Box C104 106 Moorings Park Dr Naples FL 34105-2157

BUSH, JUNE LEE, real estate executive; b. Philippi, W.Va., Sept. 20, 1942; d. Leland C. and Dolly Mary (Costello) Robinson; m. Jerry Lee Coffman, June 15, 1963 (div. 1970); 1 child, Jason Lance; m. Richard Alfred Bush, May 20, 1972. Grad., Fairmont State Coll., 1962, Dale Carnegie, Anaheim, Calif., 1988. Exec. sec. McDonnell Douglas, Huntington Beach, Calif., 1965-72; adminstrv. asst. Mgmt. Resources, Inc., Fullerton, Calif., 1978-80; bldg. mgr. Alfred Gobar Assocs., Brea, Calif., 1980-95; treas. Craig Park East, Fullerton, 1982, bd. dirs., 1982-84. Author instrn. manual Quality Assurance Secretarial Manual, 1971. Sec. PTA, La Palma, 1974. Mem. Gamma Chi Chi. Avocations: golf, sailing, reading. Home: 12553 Crystal Ranch Rd Moorpark CA 93021

BUSH, LARRY, sportswriter; b. Wellsboro, Pa., Dec. 5, 1933; s. Neal and Elizabeth (Howe) B.; m. Meredith Jane Wood, Dec. 5, 1959; children: Elizabeth, Linda. Grad., Acad. H.S., Erie, Pa. Staff writer, announcer Delray Beach (Fla.) News/WDBF, 1955-56; staff writer Palm Beach Post Times, West Palm Beach, Fla., 1958; sports editor News Tribune, Ft. Pierce, Fla., 1958-60, 62-68; sports writer Tampa (Fla.) Tribune, 1960-62, Today Newspaper, Cocoa, Fla., 1968-69; asst. sports editor, sports editor Evening Times, West Palm Beach, 1969-81; freelance sports writer West Palm Beach, 1981—; mem. adv. bd. Fla. PGA, South Fla. PGA, 1973-83. Mem. com. Palm Beach County Sports Hall of Fame, West Palm Beach, 1976—, treas., 1976-86, media rep., 1986—. With U.S. Army, 1956-58. Recipient Sports Column award Fla. Press Assn., 1991, 93, John Hervey award U.S. Harness Writers Assn., 1975, 84. Mem. Internat. Network of Golf, Golf Writers Assn. Am. (Sports Column award 1977), Fla. Freelance Writers Assn., Fla. Golf Writers Assn. Baptist. Avocations: golf, walking.

BUSH, MARJORIE EVELYNN TOWER-TOOKER, educator, media specialist, librarian; b. Atkinson, Nebr., Mar. 12, 1925; d. Albert Ralph and Vera Marie (Rickover) Tower-Tooker; m. Louis T. Genung, Feb. 2, 1944 (dec. Jan. 1982); 1 son, Louis Thompson; m. Laurence Scott Bush, Sept. 22, 1984; 1 stepson, Roger A. Bush. Student U. Nebr.,1951, Wayne State Coll., 1942-47; BA Colo. State Coll., 1966, U. No. Colo., 1970; postgrad. Doane Coll., 1967-68, U. Utah, 1973-74, PhD (hon.), 1973. Elem. tchr. Atkinson Public Schs., 1958-69; adminstr. libraries and audiovisual communications Clay County Dist. I-C, Fairfield, Nebr., 1972-81; media specialist Albion (Nebr.) City Schs., 1981—; mem. Neb. Gov.'s White House Conf. on Libraries. Chmn. edn. adminstrv. bd. Park Hill United Meth. Ch., Denver, also pres.; sec. Denver Symphony Guild, Colo. Symphony Guild, 1990-96. Mem. NEA (life), Nebr., Colo. edn. assns., Assn. Childhood Edn. Internat., ALA, Nebr., Mountain Plains library assns., Nat. Council Tchrs. English, AAUW, Nebr. Ednl. Media Assn., Assn. Supervision and Curriculum Devel., Assn. Ednl. Communications and Tech., Internat. Visual Literacy Assn., Nat. Council Exceptional Children, Alumni Assn. U. No. Colo. (life charter), Women Educators Nebr., United Meth. Women (pres.), Am. Legion Aux., Nebr. Lay Citizens Edn. Assn. (exec.), Am. Nat. Cowbelles, Nebr. Cowbelles, Internat. Platform Assn., LWV, Women's Soc. Christian Service, Ak-Sar-Ben. Club: Windsor Gardens (Denver). Lodges: Opti-Mrs. (pres.), Optimists Internat., Columbine Optimists (pres. 1987-88), Eastern Star. Address: 1003 E 9th St Hastings NE 68901-4140

BUSH, MARK ROBERT, physician; b. San Mateo, Calif., July 4, 1962; s. Paul Robert and Roberta Sue (Penninsten) B.; m. Christine Stephanie Smith, Aug. 6, 1988; children: Cameron Michael, Alexis Victoria. BA in Biology, U. Calif., Berkeley, 1985; MD, Georgetown U., 1991. Diplomate Nat. Bd. Med. Examiners. Resident in ob-gyn William Beaumont AMC, El Paso, Tex., 1991-95; assoc., attending faculty dept. ob-gyn Duke U. Med. Ctr., Durham, N.C., 1995-98; chief divsn. reproductive endocrinology and infertility Madigan AMC, Tacoma, 1998—; clin. asst. prof. dept. ob-gyn. U. Wash. Sch. Medicine, Seattle, 1998—; guest rschr. LMC, NIEHS, NIH, Research Triangle Park, N.C., 1997—. Contbr. articles to profl. jours. Maj. Med. Corps., U.S. Army. Mem. AMA (Physician's Recognition award 1994-97, 97-2000), ACOG (Oustanding Scientific Paper award 1993, Best Scientific Paper award 1996), Am. Soc. Reproductive Medicine, Soc. for Gynecol. Investigation (assoc.), Soc. Reproductive Endocrinology and Infertility (assoc.). E-mail: MAJúMarkúBush@smtplink.mamc.amedd.army.mil. Home: 5219 77th Ave Ct W University Place WA 98467 Office: U Wash Sch Medicine Seattle WA

BUSH, MICHAEL KEVIN, lawyer; b. Davenport, Iowa, May 23, 1952; s. Roy Alvin and A. Carmelita (Gilroy) B.; m. Kathleen M. Grace, Nov. 26, 1977; children: Kelly Anne, Daniel Stephen, Brendan Michael. BA, U. Notre Dame, South Bend, Ind., 1974; JD, Valparaiso (Ind.) U., 1977. Bar: Iowa 1977, U.S. Dist. Ct. (no. dist.) Iowa 1980, U.S. Ct. Appeals (7th cir.) 1980, U.S. Dist. Ct. (ctrl. dist.) Ill. 1983, U.S. Ct. Appeals (8th cir.) 1996, U.S. Supreme Ct. 1990. Mem. Wells, McNally & Bowman, Davenport, 1977-80; prosecutor Scott County Atty.'s Office, Davenport, 1980-82; mem. Henninger & Henninger, Davenport, 1979-82; founding ptnr. Walton, Creen & Bush, Davenport, 1982-86; ptnr. Carlin, Hellstrom & Bittner, Davenport, 1987—. Mem. ATLA (sustaining mem.), Am. Bd. Trial Advocates (assoc.), Iowa Assn. Trial Lawyers (bd. govs.), Million Dollar Advocates Forum, Iowa Bar Assn., Scott County Bar Assn. Roman Catholic. Avocation: tennis. Home: 2806 E 42nd Ct Davenport IA 52807-1576 Office: Carlin Hellstrom & Bittner 201 W 2nd St Ste 1000 Davenport IA 52801-1817

BUSH, MITCHELL LESTER, JR., retired federal agency administrator; b. Syracuse, N.Y., Feb. 1, 1936; s. Mitchell Bush and Sarah (Skenandore) Gonyea. Grad. H.S., Lawrence, Kans. Tribal enrollment specialist Bur. Indian Affairs, Washington, 1962, 66; area tribal enrollment officer Bur. Indian Affairs, Anadarko, Okla., 1964-65; acting chief Bur. Tribal Enrollment Svcs., Washington, 1982, chief, 1983, ret., 1991. Co-editor: American Indian Society Cookbook, 1974, 2d edit., 1984. Vice-chmn. Va. Coun. on Indians, Richmond, 1989-95. With U.S. Army, 1958-61. Recipient Points of Light cert., award for Outstanding Pub. Svc. to U.S.A., U.S. Sec. of Interior, Washington, 1990, Maharishi award Maharishi U., Washington, 1985. Mem. Am. Indian Soc. (founder, pres. 1966-91, editor newsletter 1991—, Disting. Svc. award 1971, 90, Outstanding Elder/Advisor award 1996). Methodist. Avocations: raising ornamental fowl, collecting Native American artwork, travel, collecting coins. Home: 22230 Cool Water Dr Ruther Glen VA 22546-3309 Office: AIS Newsletter 22258 Cool Water Dr Ruther Glen VA 22546-3309

BUSH, NORMAN, research and development executive; b. N.Y.C., Dec. 10, 1929; s. Louis and Ida (Trembola) B.; m. Audrey Faith Blumberg, Dec. 28, 1952; children: Stewart Alan, I. Jeffrey, Ellen Gail Dash. BBA, CUNY, 1951, MBA, 1952; PhD, N.C. State U., 1962. Statistician Army Chem. Ctr., Edgewood, Md., 1952-56, RCA Svc. Co., Patrick AFB, Fla., 1956-58, DBA and ICF, Melbourne, Fla., 1962-64, Pan Am Airlines, Patrick AFB, Fla., 1964-72; div. mgr. ENSCO Inc., Melbourne, Fla., 1972-83; pres., chief oper. officer ENSCO Inc., Springfield, Va., 1983-94, chmn. bd., 1989-95;, 1989-95. Contbr. articles to statis. jours. With U.S. Army, 1952-54. Mem. Am. Statis. Assn. Republican. Avocation: travel. Office: PO Box 410279 Melbourne FL 32941-0279

BUSH, PATRICIA EILEEN, education educator; b. Butler, Pa., Nov. 29, 1938; d. Ralph Henry and Helen Marie (Elliott) B.; 1 child, Kathleen McHugh. BS in Edn., Indiana U. of Pa., 1960, MEd, 1968; EdD, U. Ctrl. Fla., 1994. Cert. tchr., Fla. Elem. tchr. Leslie (Mich.) Schs., 1977-79, Brevard County Schs., Mims, Fla., 1979-80; tchr. alternative edn. Brevard County Schs., Titusville, Fla., 1980-85; reading specialist, tchr. Brevard County Schs., Cocoa, Fla., 1985-86, Titusville, 1986-90; prekindergarten tchr., dir. Child Care Assn., Titusville, 1990-91; health educator Brevard County Health Dept., Titusville, 1991-92; edn. coord. Eckerd Family Youth Alternative Edn., Clearwater, Fla., 1992-96; asst. prof. Sping Hill Coll., Mobile, Ala., 1996-98, Rollins Coll., 1998—; judge spelling bee Archidiocese of Mobile, 1996-97, judge speech contest, 1996, instr. tchr. aides, 1996. Contbr. articles to profl. jours. Chair Project Hope/Luth. Ministries, Mobile, 1997. Mem. ASCD, Internat. Reading Assn. (proposal reviewer 1996-98), Ala. Reading Assn., Kappa Delta Pi (fac. adv. Rollins Coll.). Democrat. Lutheran. Avocations: reading, travel. Home: 1659 Saratoga Dr Titusville FL 32796-4207

BUSH, RAYMOND T., accountant, corporate professional; b. Providence, R.I., Sept. 7, 1939; s. Raymond F. and Regina C. (Pearl) B.; m. Barbara Ann Cormier, May 31, 1962; children: Laura Jean, Raymond F., Matthew T., James J., Michael. BS in Acctg. and Fin., Bryant Coll., 1960. CPA, R.I. Auditor USDA, Providence, 1960-66; audit supr. KPMG Peak Marwick LLP, Providence, 1966-69; mgr. system and audit Ludlow Corp., Needham Heights, Mass., 1969-71, asst. treas., 1971-73, v.p., gen. mgr., 1973-80; pres. Recticel Foam Corp., Needham Heights, 1980-83; sr. v.p. fin. and adminstrn. Maguire Group Inc., Providence, 1983—; treas. Ocean State Bus. Devel.; pres. East Atlantic Casualty Co. Ltd.; cons. Bryant Coll. Small Bus. Devel. Ctr. Mem. R.I. Indsl. Recreational Bldg. Authority; trustee Providence Pub. Libr. Fellow R.I. Soc. CPA's; mem. Am. Inst. CPA's. Roman Catholic. Home: 3 Hayfield Ln Cumberland RI 02864-4114 Office: Maguire Group Inc 225 Foxborough Blvd Foxboro MA 02035-2885*

BUSH, REX CURTIS, lawyer; b. Longview, Wash., Oct. 21, 1953; s. Rex Cole Bush and Arline (Quanstrom) Fitzgerald; m. Joy Ann Pallas, July 22, 1977 (div.); children: Alicia, Angela, Carrie; m. Janet Rae Hicks July 2, 1988; children: Jeni, Mykal. BA cum laude, Brigham Young U., 1980; JD, U. Utah, 1983. Bar: Utah 1983, U.S. Dist. Ct. (no. dist.) Utah 1983, U.S. Tax Ct. 1985. Tax atty. Arthur Andersen & Co., Houston, 1983-84; assoc. Mortensen & Neider, Midvale, Utah, 1984-85; in-house counsel Fin. Futures, Salt Lake City, 1985-87; registrar Hollander Cons., Portland, Oreg., 1987-88; in-house counsel Bennett Leasing, Salt Lake City, 1987-88; pres. Bush Law Firm, Sandy, Utah, 1988—; judge pro tempore 3d Cir. Ct., Salt Lake City, 1985-87. Author: (booklet) What To Do in Case of an Automobile Accident, 1994. Mayor University Village, U. Utah, 1981-82; Rep. candidate Utah state senate, 1992; Rep. voting dist. sec., treas., 1992. Recipient Meritorious Leadership award, Nat. Com. for Employer Support of Guard and Reserve, 1990. Mem. ATLA, Utah Trial Lawyers Assn., Utah State Bar (chmn. small firm and solo practitioners com. 1994-96, honored for outstanding svc. to legal profession 1996). Office: Bush Law Firm 9615 S 700 E Sandy UT 84070-3557

BUSH, RICHARD CLARENCE, III, federal government executive; b. Chgo., Nov. 21, 1947; s. Richard Clarence Jr. and Mary Ethlyn (Ball) B.; m. Martha Virginia Hodge, June 21, 1969; children: Sharmon Melissa, Andrew Milton. BA, Lawrence U., Appleton, Wis., 1969; MA, Columbia U., 1973, M Philosophy, 1975, PhD, 1978. Program assoc. China Coun., Asia Soc., N.Y.C., 1977-79, Washington, 1979-81; staff cons. fgn. affairs com. U.S. Ho. of Reps., Washington, 1983-95; nat. intelligence officer East Asia, Washington, 1995-97; chmn., mng. dir. Am. Inst. in Taiwan, Rosslyn, Va., 1997—. Author: The Politics of Cotton Textiles in Khomintang China, 1927-37, 1982; co-compiler The People's Republic of China: A Basic Handbook, 1979, 81, 82. Sgt. U.S. Army, 1970-72. Mem. Cheverly Swim and Racquet Club. Democrat.

BUSH, RICHARD JAMES, engineering executive, lay worker; b. Bronx, N.Y., Aug. 19, 1921; s. Hanford James and Margaret Sophie (Mall) B.; m. Margaret Evelyn Kemmerer, Apr. 28, 1946 (dec. 1997). BME magna cum laude, Poly. Univ., Bklyn., 1953. Various engring. positions with numerous firms N.Y.C., 1939-42; design group leader Edo Aircraft Corp., College Point, N.Y., 1944-46; with Abbott, Merkt & Co., Inc., N.Y.C., 1946-74, v.p., 1960-74; v.p. engring. and ops. Conn. Resources Recovery Authority, Hartford, 1974-81; dir. archtl. and engring. svcs. Yale U., New Haven, 1981-83; active with Gideons Internat. With AUS, 1942-43. Mem. ASME (life), Am. Inst. Cons. Engrs., Am. Soc. Heating, Refrigerating and Air conditioning Engrs. (life), Pi Tau Sigma. Home (summer): 506 Long Pond Dr Harwich MA 02645-1216 also (winter): 2502 SW Natura Blvd Deerfield Beach FL 33441-3289

BUSH, ROBERT G., food service executive; b. 1926; s. Merlin G. B.; married. Grad., U. Wis., 1950. Exec. Schreiber Foods, Inc. and predecessor co., Green Bay, Wis., 1948-62, officer, 1962-77, v.p., 1977-78, pres., COO, 1978-85, chmn., CEO, 1985-89, chmn., 1989—. Office: Schreiber Foods Inc 425 Pine St Green Bay WI 54301-5179*

BUSH, ROBERT THOMAS, shipping company executive; b. Newbury, Berkshire, Eng., May 18, 1928; came to U.S., 1968; s. Randolph George and Catherine Ellen (Benger) B.; m. Haydee Ojeda, Jan. 23, 1966; children: Allan David, Linda Martha, Grace Katherine. Master Mariner, Southampton (Eng.) U., 1953. Shipmaster Burmah Oil Co., Rangoon, Burma, 1955-60; marine surveyor Sydney, Australia, 1960-68; terminal supt. Exportadora De Sal, Cedros Island, Mex., 1968-70; marine mgr. Balfour Williamson, London, 1970-73; sr. marine advisor Aramco, Saudi Arabia, 1974-76; ops. mgr. Mercantile & Marine (Tex.) Inc., Houston, 1976-80; sr. marine advisor Phillips Petroleum Co., Bartlesville, Okla., 1980-86; gen. mgr. Universe Tankships (Del.) Inc., N.Y.C., 1986-94; pres. Neptune Marine Consultants (Ams.) Inc., Dickinson, Tex., 1994—. Contbr. numerous articles to profl. jours. Charter mem. Better World Soc., Washington, 1988; tutor Literacy Vols. Am., Edison, N.J., 1988—; founder Friends of the Sea, N.Y., 1991. Mem. N.Y. Acad. Sci., Nautical Inst. of London. Avocations: reading, history, walking. Home: 427 Sunset Dr Apt 1 Dickinson TX 77539-4272

BUSH, SARAH LILLIAN, historian; b. Kansas City, Mo., Sept. 17, 1920; d. William Adam and Lettie Evelyn (Burrill) Lewis; m. Walter Nelson Bush, June 7, 1946 (dec.); children: William Read, Robert Nelson. *Ms. Bush's son, Bill, is a researcher at Sun Microsystems Laboratories, where hehas worked on various implementations of the Java programming language. His research interests include programming language design and implementation, program analysis, computer-aided design, computer architecture and software engineering, in which areas he has published papers. Before joining Sun, Bill was a founder and principal scientist of Intrinsa Corporation. Her son, Bob, is a summa cum laude graduate of Harvard College with a master from Stanford. He is currently a geologist who works in Houston, Texas applying and developing computer applications to geological problems.* AB, U. Kans., 1941; BS, U. Ill., 1943. Clk. circulation dept. Kansas City Pub. Library, 1941-42, asst. librarian Paseo br., 1943-44; librarian Kansas City Jr. Coll., 1944-46; substitute librarian San Mateo County Library, Woodside amd Portola Valley, Calif., 1975-77; various temporary positions, 1979-87; owner Metriguide, Palo Alto, Calif., 1975-78. Author: Atherton Lands, 1979, rev. edition 1987. Editor: Atherton Recollections, 1973. Pres., v.p. Jr. Librarians, Kansas City, 1944-46; courtesy, yearbook & historian AAUW, Menlo- Atherton branch (Calif.) Br.; asst. Sunday sch. tchr., vol. Holy Trinity Ch., Menlo Park, 1955-78; v.p., membership com., libr. chairperson, English reading program, parent edn. chairperson Menlo Atherton High Sch. PTA, 1964-73; founder, bd. dirs. Friends of Atherton Community Library, 1967—, oral historian, 1968—, chair Bicentennial event, 1976; bd. dirs. Menlo Park Hist. Assn., 1979-82, oral historian, 1973—; bd. dirs. Civic Interest League, Atherton, 1978-81; mem. hist. county commn. Town of Atherton, 1980-87; vol. Allied Arts Palo Alto Aux. to Children's Hosp. at Stanford, 1967—, oral historian, 1978—, historian, 1980—; vol. United Crusade, Garfield Sch., Redwood City, 1957-61, 74-88, Encinal Sch., Menlo Park, Calif., 1961-73, program dir., chmn. summer recreation, historian, sec.; vol. Stanford Mothers Club, 1977-81, others; historian, awards chairperson Cub Scouts Boy Scouts Am.; founder Atherton Heritage Assn. 1989, bd. dirs., 1989—, dir., 1989-94; mem. Guild Gourmet, 1971—, Mid Peninsula History Consortium, 1993-95. Recipient Good Neighbor award Civic Interest League, 1992. Mem. PTA (life). Episcopalian. Avocations: gourmet cooking, entertaining, reading.

BUSH, SPENCER HARRISON, metallurgist; b. Flint, Mich., Apr. 4, 1920; s. Edward Charles and Rachel Beatrice (Roser) B.; m. Roberta Lee Warren, Aug. 28, 1948; children: David Spencer, Carl Edward. Student, Flint Jr. Coll., 1938-40, Ohio State U., 1943-44, U. Mich., 1946-53. Registered profl. engr., Calif. Asst. chemist Dow Chem. Co., 1940-42, 46; assoc. Engring. Rsch. Inst., U. Mich., 1947-53; research asst. Office Naval Rsch., 1950-53, instr. dental materials, 1951-53; metallurgist Hanford Atomic Products Operation, Gen. Electric Co., 1953-54, supr. phys. metallurgy, 1954-57, supr. fuels fabrication devel., 1957-60, metall. specialist, 1960-63, cons. metallurgist, 1963-65; cons. to dir. Battelle Pacific N.W. Labs., Richland, Wash., 1965-70, sr. staff cons., 1970-83, sr. staff scientist, 1985—; pres. Rev. & Synthesis Assocs., cons., 1983—; lectr. metall. engring. Ctr. for Grad. Study U. Wash., 1953-67, affiliate prof., 1967-78; chmn., mem. com. study group on pressure vessel materials Electric Power Rsch. Inst., 1974-78; cons. U. Calif. Lawrence Livermore Labs., 1975-79, Integral Fast Reactor U. Chgo., 1984-94; chmn. com. on reactor safeguards U.S. AEC, 1971; mem. Wash. Bd. Boiler Rules, 1972-85; mem. Bd. Nuclear Codes and Stds., 1983— mem. spec. adv. com. for Argonne Nuc. Tech. Pgm., U Chgo. 1994—; chmn. piping design com. Joint NRC/Pressure Vessel Rsch. Coun., 1982-90, PVRC Peer Rev. on ASME Code Simplification, exec. com., 1982—, mem. steering com. on fatigue, 1992—, hon. emeritus mem., 1999; mem. nuclear safety rsch. rev. com. NRC, 1988-94; mem. high level waste structural integrity panel Dept. Energy Brookhaven Nat. Lab., 1992-97. Contbr. tech. articles to profl. jours. Served with U.S. Army, 1942-46. Recipient Silver Beaver award Boy Scouts Am.; Am. Foundrymens Soc. fellow, 1948-50; Regents prof. U. Calif., Berkeley, 1973-74. Fellow ASME (chmn. sec. XI 1985-90, exec. bd. NDE divsn. 1984-90, chmn. 1987-88, nat. nominating com. 1988-90, Langer award 1983, Melvin R. Green Codes & Stds. medal 1997), ASM (life, chmn. program coun. 1966-67, trustee 1967-69, chmn. fellow com. 1968), Am. Nuc. Soc. (adv. editl. bd. nuc. applications 1965-77, bd. dirs. 1984-87, Thompson award 1987); mem. AIME (chmn. ann. seminar com. 1967-68), ASTM (Gillette lectr. 1975), Am. Soc. Nondestructive Testing (Mehl lectr.), Nat. Acad. Engring., Sigma Xi, Tau Beta Pi, Phi Kappa Phi. Home: 630 Cedar Ave Richland WA 99352-3632 Office: Battelle Pacific NW Labs PO Box 999 Richland WA 99352-0999

BUSH, STANLEY GILTNER, secondary school educator; b. Kansas City, Mo., Nov. 4, 1928; s. Dean Thomas and Sallie Giltner (Hoagland) B.; m. Barbara Snow Adams, May 23, 1975 (dec. Mar. 1994); stepchildren: Deborah Gayle Duclon, Douglas Bruce Adams. BA, U. Colo., 1949, MA, 1959, postgrad., 1971; postgrad., U. Denver, 1980, 85, 90. Tchr. Gering (Nebr.) Pub. Schs., 1949-51, 54-57, Littleton (Colo.) Pub. Schs., 1957-91; emergency plan dir. City of Littleton, 1961—; safety officer Littleton Pub. Schs., 1968—; founder, chief Arapahoe Rescue Patrol, Inc., Littleton, 1957-92, search mission coord., 1975—; pres. Arapahoe Rescue Patrol, Inc., 1957—, Expedition, Inc., Littleton, 1973—; owner Emergency Rsch. Cons., 1990—. Contbr. chpts. to Boy Scout Field Book, 1984; co-author: Managing Search Function, 1987; contbr. articles to profl. jours. Safety advisor South Suburban Parks Dist., Littleton, 1985—; advisor ARC, Littleton, 1987—, Emergency Planning Com., Arapahoe County, Colo., 1987—; coord. search and rescue Office of Gov., Colo., 1978-82; state judge Odyssey of the Mind, 1996-97. Sgt. U.S. Army, 1951-54. Shell Oil Co. fellow, 1964; recipient Silver Beaver award Boy Scouts Am., 1966, Vigil-Order of Arrow, 1966, Award of Excellence Masons, 1990, Service to Mankind award Arapahoe Sertoma, 1999. Mem. Nat. Assn. for Search and Rescue (life, Hall Foss award 1978), Colo. Search and Rescue Bd., NEA (life). Methodist. Avocations: mountaineering, wilderness emergency care, emergency services. Home: 2415 E Maplewood Ave Littleton CO 80121-2817 Office: Littleton Ctr 2255 W Berry Ave Littleton CO 80165

BUSH, THOMAS NORMAN, lawyer; b. Lancaster County, Va., Nov. 13, 1947; s. T. Edwin and Willie Ann (Landman) B.; m. Carolyn Sue Brown; children: Jason, Jennifer. BS in Acctg., Va. Tech, 1970; JD, U. Richmond, 1977. Bar: Va.; CPA, Va. Staff acct. KPMG Peat Marwick, Richmond, Va., 1970-71; sr. auditor U.S. Army, Frankfurt, Germany, 1972-74; pvt. practice acctg. Richmond, 1974-77; tax mgr. PricewaterhouseCoopers, Richmond, 1977-81; v.p., tax counsel Fort James Corp., Richmond, 1981—. V.p. James River Found., 1993—; chmn. corp. matching gift U. Richmond Annual Fund steering com., 1996-97; mem. dept. acctg. adv. bd. Va. Tech., 1991—; mem. steering com. Ctr. for Leadership, Govt. and Global Econs., 1995—. Mem. ABA, AICPA, Va. State Bar, Internat. Fiscal Assn., Am. Forest and Paper Assn. (tax com. 1986-94), Tax Execs. Inst. (pres. Va. chpt. 1989-90, regional v.p. 1995-96, bd. dirs. 1993-96, nominating com. 1996-97, vice chair IRS adminstrv. affairs com. 1997-99, mem. IRS customer satisfaction task force 1998-99), Tax Found. (program com. 1996—), Va. Soc. CPAs, Va. Mfrs. Assn. (tax com. 1988—), Civitan (pres. West End Richmond 1982). Methodist. Avocations: coaching, baseball, travel. Home: 10007 Ashbridge Pl Richmond VA 23233-5402 Office: Fort James Corp PO Box 2218 6802 Paragon Pl Ste 400 Richmond VA 23230

BUSH-COUNTS, CHRISTINE GAY, dental hygienist; b. Toledo, Dec. 31, 1951; d. Jack G. and Virginia Aileen (Doyle) Tornga; m. John Howard Mosher, May 11, 1974 (div. July 1990); children: Heather Kristen, Andrew Jacob; m. Robert Milton Counts, July 5, 1991 (dec. Mar. 1993); m. Charles T. Bush II, June 16, 1998. BS in Dental Hygiene, U. Mich., 1974. Registered dental hygienist, Nat. Bd. Dental Examiners, Ind. State Bd. Dentistry, Fla. State Bd. Dentistry, Mich. State Bd. Dentistry. Asst. supr. dental hygiene Ind. U., South Bend, Ind., 1974-75; expanded functions hygienist South Bend Dental Ctr., 1975; periodental hygienist Dr. John B. Lehman, South Bend, 1976-82, Dr. Cristene Maas, Longwood, Fla., 1983-84; periodontal hygienist Dr. Richard Altman, Orlando, Fla., 1984-85; dental hygienist Dr. H. Raymund Barcus, Winter Park, Fla., 1984—; adj. instr. So. Coll., Orlando, 1984. Med./dental mission Wekiva Presbyn. Ch., Honduras, 1987, 89, Diocese of Orlando, Dominican Republic, 1994, 95, Fla. Hosp. Found., Jamaica, 1997; deacon Presbyn. Ch., 1992. Mem. Greater Orlando Dental Hygiene Assn. (sec. 1986-87), U. Mich. Club Orlando (treas. 1998—), Alpha Chi Omega (chpt. pres. 1995-97, Lyre editor 1997-98, pres. Gamma Upsilon Gamma chpt. 1998—). Republican. Roman Catholic. Avocations: cross-stitch, playing piano, reading. Office: Dr H Raymund Barcus Office 271 W Canton Ave Winter Park FL 32789-3188

BUSHEY, ALAN SCOTT, retired insurance holding company executive; b. Peoria, Ill., Apr. 16, 1930; s. Leo James and Luella Frederica (Brunnenmeyer) B. B.A., Augustana Coll., Rock Island, Ill., 1952; M.B.A., Stanford U., 1954. Asst. prof. mktg. and stats. San Jose State Coll., Calif., 1958-59; dir. econ. and mktg. rsch. Continental Casualty Co., Chgo., 1959-68; asst. v.p. CNA/Ins., Chgo., 1968-72; v.p. CNA Fin. Corp., Chgo., 1972-74; v.p. USLIFE Corp., N.Y.C., 1974-84, sr. v.p., 1984-88, exec. v.p., 1988—. Bd. dirs. Ecumenical Inst., Chgo., 1963-74. Served to lt. (j.g.) USNR, 1954-57. Mem. Nat. Assn. Bus. Economists (coun. 1973-76), Life Ins. Mktg. Rsch. Assn. (chmn. mkt. rsch. com. 1985-87, vice chmn. rsch. coun. 1994, chmn. adv. svcs. coun. 1995), Am. Statis. Assn. (bd. dirs. Chgo. chpt. 1965-67), LOMA (strategic mgmt. com. 1987-93), Brit. Schs. and

Univs. Found. (bd. dirs. 1993—, hon. sec. 1995-97, pres. 1997—). Republican. Lutheran. Home: 340 S Palm Ave # 122 Sarasota FL 34236-6741

BUSHEY, RICHARD KENNETH, utility executive; b. Alhambra, Calif., May 1, 1940; s. Kenneth H. and Dale E. (Wheeler) B.; m. Janeil Deane Anderson, Feb. 23, 1963; 1 child, Michael. BS, UCLA, 1963; postgrad., U. So. Calif., 1965; grad. Pub. Utility Execs. program, U. Mich., 1973; grad. fin. program, Stanford U., 1976. Acct., supr., mgr. So. Calif. Edison Co., Rosemead, 1963-74, asst. treas., 1974-75, asst. contr., 1975-84, v.p., contr., 1984—; v.p., contr. Edison Internat., Rosemead, 1988—. lst lt. U.S. Air N.G., 1963-70. Mem. L.A. C. of C., UCLA Alumni Assn., Phi Kappa Psi. Office: So Calif Edison Co 2244 Walnut Grove Ave Rosemead CA 91770-3714

BUSHINSKY, DAVID ALLEN, nephrologist, educator, researcher; b. Elizabeth, N.J., Mar. 16, 1949; s. Morris and Frieda (Price) B.; m. Nancy Sue Krieger, Aug. 29, 1976; children: Joshua Mark, Seth Michael. BSChemE magna cum laude, Lehigh U., 1971; MD, Tufts U., 1975. Instr. medicine Tufts U., Boston, 1979-80; asst. prof. medicine U. Chgo., 1980-87, assoc. prof. medicine, 1987-89, attending physician hosps., 1982-89; assoc. prof. physiology, assoc. prof. medicine U. Rochester, N.Y., 1989-92, prof. medicine, physiology, pharmacology, 1992—, assoc. chair acad. affairs, 1997—; attending physician Michael Reese Hosp. & Med. Ctr., Chgo., 1980-82; chief nephrology Strong Meml. Hosp., Rochester, 1989—, attending physician, 1989—. Contbr. 35 chpts. to books; contbr. over 85 articles to profl. jours. on calcium, protons and bone; editor: Renal Osteodystrophy; mem. editl. bd. Am. Jour. Physiology (Renal), Kidney, Jour. Bone and Mineral Rsch., Kidney Internat. Pres. region 1 Nat. Kidney Found.; pres. med. adv. bd. Kidney Found. Upstate N.Y. Andrew Mellon fellow; grantee NIH, Am. Heart Assn., NSF, Michael Reese Rsch. Inst., Nat. Kidney Found. Mem. Am. Soc. Nephrology, Am. Heart Assn., Am. Fed. Clin. Rsch., Am. Soc. Bone and Mineral Rsch., Am. Soc. Clin. Investigation, Am. Physiol. Soc., Internat. Soc. Nephrology, Cen. Soc. Clin. Rsch. Achievements include advanced research on the effect of protons on bone and the pathophysiology of renal stone formation. Home: 123 Heatherstone Ln Rochester NY 14618-4864 Office: U Rochester 601 Elmwood Ave Rochester NY 14642-0001

BUSHINSKY, JAY (JOSEPH MASON), journalist, radio/TV correspondent, columnist; b. Buffalo, N.Y., Dec. 8, 1932; s. Joshua M. and Malka (Coralnik) B.; m. Dvora Apte, Dec. 30, 1952; children: Jesse, Aviv, Dahlia. BA, Queens Coll., 1955; MS in Edn., Yeshiva U., N.Y.C., 1959; MS in Journalism, Columbia U., 1963. Mcpl. reporter Times Herald/Record, Middletown, N.Y., 1963-64; copy editor Miami (Fla.) Herald, 1964-66; spl. corr. Chgo. Daily News Fgn. Svc., Middle East, 1966-78; corr. Sta. WINS and KYW (CBS Radio), 1967-69; Tel Aviv bur. chief Westinghouse Broadcasting Co., 1969—; corr. Chgo. Sun-Times, Tel Aviv, 1978-85; Middle East bur. chief, columnist Chgo. Sun-Times, 1986-96; Jerusalem bur. chief Cable News Network, 1980-85; corr. Independent News Network, 1985-87, WWOR-TV, N.Y.C., 1987, Sta. WPIX-TV, N.Y.C., 1991-94, Global TV Network (Can.), 1993-95, Fox TV Network, 1995-96, 1993-95, Toronto Sun, 1994—, Boston Herald, 1998—; diplomatic corr. The Jerusalem Post, 1997-98; tchr. social studies L.I. City (N.Y.) High Sch., 1958-59, William C. Bryant High Sch., N.Y.C., 1959-62; lectr. journalism Tel Aviv U., 1966-70, 94—, Bar Ilan U., 1993—; asst. prof. journalism U. Mo., 1978—. Corr., columnist The Daily Herald, 1996—, Toronto Sun. Served with AUS, 1955-57. Chgo. Newspaper Guild award for investigative reporting for expose of Nazi war criminals in U.S., 1978; co-recipient Media award for econ. understanding Amos Tuck Sch. Bus. Adminstrn., Dartmouth Coll., 1979. Mem. Fgn. Press Assn. in Israel (chmn. 1968-71), Overseas Press Club Am. (award for Best Radio Spot News Reporting from Abroad to Group W Foreign News Service for coverage of Oct. War in Mideast, Joint citation 1974). Home and Office: Rehov Hatsafon 5, Savyon Israel 56540

BUSHMAN, EDWIN FRANCIS ARTHUR, engineer, plastics consultant, rancher; b. Aurora, Ill., Mar. 16, 1919; s. George J. and Emma (Gengler) B.; B.S., U. Ill., 1941, postgrad., 1941-42, Calif. Inst. Tech., 1941; m. Louise Kathryn Peterson, Jan. 3, 1946; children: Bruce Edwin, Gary Robert, Joan Louise, Karen Rose, Mary Elisabeth, Paul George. Jr. engr, Gulf Refining Co. Gulf Oil Corp., Mattoon, Ill., 1940-41; engr. radio and sound lab. war rsch. div. U. Calif. at Navy Electronics Lab., Pt. Loma, San Diego, 1942-45; project engr. Bell and Howell Co., Lincolnwood, Ill., 1945-46; research cons., Scholl Mfg. Co., Inc., Chgo., 1946-48; project engr. deepfreeze div. Motor Products Corp., North Chicago, Ill., 1948-50; research and product design engr. Bushman Co., Aurora, Ill. also Mundelein, Ill., 1946-55; with Plastics div. Gen. Am. Transp. Corp., Chgo., 1950-68, tech. dir., 1950-55, mgr. sales and sales engring. Western states, Compton, Calif., 1955-68, sales and sales engring. research and devel. div., 1962-64; with USS Chems., 1968-70; plastics cons. E.F. Bushman Co., 1970—, Tech. Conf. Assocs., 1974-80. Program mgr. Agriplastics Symposium Nat. Agrl. Plastics Conf., 1966; program mgr. Plastics in Hydrospace, 1967; originator Huisman Plastics awards, 1970, Un-Carbon Polymer prize and Polymer Pool Preserve Plan, 1975, Polymer Independence award, 1977, 78. Bd. dirs. Coastal Area Protective League, 1958-66, Lagunita Community Assn., 1959-66 (pres. 1964-65), Calif. Marine Parks and Harbors Assn., 1959-69. Sr. editor Plastic Trends mag., 1985-90. Recipient Western Plastics Man of Yr. award, 1972. Mem. Soc. Plastics Industry Inc. (chpt. pres. 1971-72), Soc. Plastic Engrs. (Lundberg award 1981), Western Plastics Pioneers, Western Plastics Mus. and Pioneers, Plastics Pioneers Assn., Sunkist Growers, Cal. Citrus Nurserymen's Soc., Calif. Farm Bur. Fedn. U. Ill. Alumni Assn., Soc. for Advancement Materials and Process Engring., Geopolymers Inst. Roman Catholic. Author various profl. and strategic resource papers. Patentee in field of plastics, carbon and colored glass fibers, process, and applications. Home: 19 Lagunita Ln Laguna Beach CA 92651-4237 Office: PO Box 581 Laguna Beach CA 92652-0581

BUSHMAN, MARY LAURA JONES, developer, fundraiser; b. Mpls., 1946; d. William Ray and Emily Mary H. Jones; m. Donald Otto Bushman, Dec. 5, 1971; children: Donald Aaron, Justin David, Mark Joseph. BA in English, U. S.C., 1968. Assoc. dir. Funding & Devel., Chgo., 1971-75, The Inst. of Cultural Affairs, Chgo.; dir. Cleve. Region, 1975-79, Pacific, Oceania Region, Apia, Western Samoa, 1979-83. Co-creator Human Devel. Tng. Curriculum, 1984-85. Dir. pilot project for Uptown Community Resource Ctr. Inst. of Cult. Affairs, Chgo., 1986-99. Mem. Uptown C. of C. (pres.), Internat. Women Entrepreneurs. Lutheran. Home and Office: Inst Cultural Affairs 4750 N Sheridan Rd Chicago IL 60640-5042

BUSHNELL, GEORGE EDWARD, JR., lawyer; b. Detroit, Nov. 15, 1924; s. George E. and Ida Mary (Bland) B.; children: George Edward III, Christopher Gilbert Whelden, Robina McLeod Bushnell Hogan. Mil. student, U. Kans., 1943; BA, Amherst Coll., 1948; LLB, U. Mich., 1951; LLD, Detroit Coll. Law, 1995. Bar: Mich. 1951, D.C. 1980, U.S. Dist. Ct. (ea. dist.) Mich. 1951, U.S. Dist. Ct. (we. dist.) Mich. 1971, U.S. Ct. Appeals (6th cir.) 1955, U.S. Ct. Appeals (fed. cir.) 1995, U.S. Ct. Appeals for the Armed Forces 1995, U.S. Supreme Ct. 1971, U.S. Ct. Internat. Trade 1995. From assoc. to sr. ptnr. Miller, Canfield, Paddock and Stone, Detroit, 1953-77, of counsel, 1989—; sr. ptnr. Bushnell, Gage, Doctoroff & Reizen, Southfield, Mich., 1977-89; commr. Mich. Jud. Tenure Commn., 1969-83, chmn., 1978-80; pres. State Bar Mich., 1975-76; bd. dirs. Nat. Jud. Coll., 1985-89; mem. Mich. Atty. Discipline Bd., 1990-96; lectr. in field. Elder Grosse Pointe Meml. Ch.; moderator Detroit Presbytery, United Presbyn. Ch. U.S.A., 1972, pres. program agy. bd., 1972-76; bd. dirs. Econ. Devel. Corp. of Detroit, 1976—, Econ. Growth Corp. of Detroit, 1978-96, Tax Increment Fin. Authority, Detroit, 1984—, Econ. Devel. Authority, Detroit, 1988-98; bd. trustees New Detroit, Inc., 1972—, chmn., 1974-75. Served with USAR, 1942-56. Decorated Bronze Star, Army Commendation medal. Mem. NAACP (life, co-chmn. fight for freedom fund dinner 1968), ABA (ho. of dels. 1976—, chmn. ho. of dels. 1988-90. pres.-elect 1993-94, pres. 1994-95, past pres. 1995-96, others, Trial Attys. of Am. (pres. 1971-89), State Bar Mich. . bd. of bar commrs. 1970-76, pres. 1975-76, John Hensel award for svcs. to the arts 1990, Roberts P. Hudson award for spl. svcs. to the bar and the people of Mich., 1979, 85, Cooley Law Sch. Louis A. Smith disting. jurist award 1995), Detroit Bar Assn. (bd. dirs. 1958-65, pres. 1964-65, past pres. com. 1980—, bench & bar award for svc. to the judicial sys., the legal profession and the cmty. 1989), Nat. Conf. of Bar Pres. (pres. 1984-85), 6th Jud. Cir. Conf. (life), Am. Law Inst., Am. Arbitration Assn. (bd. dirs. 1970-82), Am. Coll. Trial Lawyers, Am. Bar Found. (life), Am. Judicature Soc. (bd. dirs. 1977-82), Can. Bar Assn. (hon.), Internat. Soc. Barristers, Fed. Bar Assn., Masons (33 deg.), Met. Club (N.Y.C.) Psi Delta Phi, Psi Upsilon. Democrat. Office: Miller Canfield Paddock & Stone 150 W Jefferson Ave Ste 2500 Detroit MI 48226-4429

BUSHNELL, GEORGE EDWARD, III, lawyer; b. Detroit, Feb. 18, 1952; s. George Edward Jr. and Elizabeth (Whelden) B.; m. Eileen Mary Maguire, Sept. 16, 1989; children: Ann-Elizabeth, Emily Spears, George Edward. BA, Bucknell U., 1974; JD, Emory U., 1981. Bar: Ga. 1981, D.C. 1983, N.Y. 1986. Vol. U.S. Peace Corps, Burkina Faso, 1974-76, tng. dir., 1976-77; staff asst. to hon. Lucien Nedzi U.S. Ho. of Reps., Washington, 1977-78; assoc. Duncan, Allen and Mitchell, Washington, Ivory Coast, Congo, 1981-85, Shearman & Sterling, N.Y.C., 1985-91; corp. counsel Joseph E. Seagram & Sons, Inc., N.Y.C., 1991—. Mem. ABA, N.Y. State Bar Assn. Home: 410 E 57th St New York NY 10022-3059 Office: Joseph E Seagram & Sons Inc 800 3rd Ave New York NY 10022-7604

BUSHNELL, PRUDENCE, former diplomat, management consultant, trainer; b. Washington, Nov. 26, 1946; d. Gerald Sherman and Bernice Edna (Duflo) B.; m. Richard Alan Buckley, Oct. 26, 1979. BA, U. Md., 1969; MS, Russell Sage Coll., 1980. Bi-lingual sec. Embassy of Morocco, Washington, 1969-70; chief sec. U. Md., College Park, 1970-72; tng. mgr. Legal Svcs. Tng. Program, Washington, 1972-76; dir. Cultural Learning Concepts, Dallas, 1976-81; mgr. adminstrv. ops. U.S. Consulate Bombay, U.S. Embassy, Dakar, 1982-86; dir. exec. devel. Fgn. Svc. Inst., Washington, 1986-89; dep. chief mission U.S. Embassy Dakar, Dept. State, Washington, 1989-92; dep. asst. sec. for African affairs Dept. State, Washington, 1993-95; amb. to Kenya U.S. Embassy, Nairobi, 1996—; mem. policy adv. coun. Una Chapman Cox Found., Washington, 1993-96. Avocations: gardening, walking, writing. *

BUSHNELL, RODERICK PAUL, lawyer; b. Buffalo, Mar. 6, 1944; s. Paul Hazen and Martha Atlee B.; m. Suzann Yvonne Kaiser, Aug. 27, 1966; 1 child, Arlo Phillip. BA, Rutgers U., 1966; JD, Georgetown U., 1969. Bar: Calif. 1970, U.S. Supreme Ct. 1980; cert. civil trial specialist. Atty. dept. water resources Sacramento, 1969-71; ptnr. Bushnell, Caplan & Fielding, San Francisco, 1971—; adv. bd. dirs. Bread & Roses, Inc., Mill Valley, Calif. Bd. dirs. Calif. Lawyers for the Arts, Ft. Mason, San Francisco, 1985—. Mem. ATLA, San Francisco Bar Assn. (arbitrator), San Francisco Superior Ct. (arbitrator), Fed. Ct. Early Neutral Evaluator, Calif. Bar Assn., Consumer Attys. Calif., San Francisco Trial Lawyers Assn., No. Calif. Criminal Trial Lawyers Assn., Nat. Employment Lawyers Assn., Calif. Employment Lawyers Assn., Consumer Attys. L.A. Fax: 415-217-3820. Office: Bushnell Caplan & Fielding 221 Pine St Ste 600 San Francisco CA 94104-2715

BUSHRE, PETER ALVIN, investment company executive; b. Ketchikan, Alaska, Dec. 14, 1943; s. Robert Almon and Violet Orene (Neal) B. BS, U. Ariz., 1967, MA in Acctg., 1971. Staff auditor Peat Marwick Mitchell & Co., Honolulu, 1971-72; sr. auditor Touche Ross & Co., Anchorage, 1972-73; sr. legis. auditor State of Alaska, Juneau, 1973-76, comptroller, 1976-78, treas., 1978-83; comptroller Alaska Permanent Fund Corp., Juneau, 1983-93, CFO, 1993—; pres. Bushre Trading and Investment Co., Douglas, Alaska, 1980—. Republican. Baptist. Avocations: investing, art, history. Home: PO Box 240028 Douglas AK 99824-0028 Office: Alaska Permanent Fund Corp 801 W 10th St Ste 302 Juneau AK 99801-1878

BUSHRUI, SUHEIL BADI, educator; b. Nazareth, Israel, Sept. 14, 1929; m. Mary Ellul, Sept. 19, 1954. BA, Alexandria (Egypt) U., 1954; PhD, Southhampton (Eng.) U., 1962. Prof. The Am. U., Beirut, Lebanon, 1968-86, U. Md., College Park, Md., 1989—; cultural adv. Pres. of Lebanon, 1982-88. Recipient Una Ellis-Fermor Literary prize U. London, 1963, Lebanese Order of Merit award Rep. Lebanon, 1987, Military Order of Constantine and St. George award The Vatican, 1990. Fellow Temenos Acad.; mem. Temple of Understanding (bd. dirs.), Club of Budapest (creative mem.). Fax: 301-314-9256. E-mail: bushrui@bss1.umd.edu. Office: Univ Maryland 0145 Tydings Hall College Park MD 20742

BUSICK, DENZEL REX, lawyer; b. Council Bluffs, Iowa, Oct. 16, 1945; s. Guy Henry and Selma Ardith (Woods) B.; m. Cheryl Ann Callahan, June 17, 1967; children: Elizabeth Colleen, Guy William. BS in Bus. Adminstrn., U. Nebr.-Omaha, 1969; JD, Creighton U., 1971. Bar: Nebr. 1971, U.S. Dist. Ct. Nebr. 1971, U.S. Ct. Appeals (8th cir.) 1975, U.S. Supreme Ct. 1974; Law clk., U.S. Dist. Ct. Nebr., 1970-72; mem. Fraser, Stryker, Veach, Vaughn, Meusey, Olsen & Boyer, Omaha, 1972-78; assoc. Kay & Satterfield, North Platte, Nebr., 1979-80; ptnr. Luebs, Leininger, Smith, Busick & Johnson, Grand Island, Nebr., 1980—. Fellow Am. Coll. Trial Lawyers, Nebr. Bar Found. (bd. dirs.), Am. Coll. Legal Medicine (law); mem. ABA, ATLA, Am. Bd. Trial Advocates (assoc. diplomate), Nat. Bd. Trial Advocacy (civil diplomate), Am. Bd. Profl Liability Attys. (diplomate), Am. Judicature Soc., Nebr. Bar Assn. (past mem. ho. of dels., exec. coun., past chmn. ins. com.), Nebr. Assn. Trial Attys. (bd. dirs., 1991-98), Nebr. Lawyers Trust Account Found. (past pres., bd. dirs.), Nebr. Bar Commn., Grand Island Area C. of C. (past vice-chair, bd. dirs.), Kiwanis (past pres. Grand Island), Phi Alpha Delta. Republican. Contbr. to publs. in field. Home: 3027 Brentwood Pl Grand Island NE 68801-7222 Office: PO Box 790 Wheeler at 1st St Grand Island NE 68802-0790

BUSIG, RICK HAROLD, mining executive; b. Vancouver, Wash., June 21, 1952; s. Harold Wayne and Ramona (Riley) B. AA, Clark Coll., Vancouver, 1972; BA in Econs., U. Wash., 1974. CPA, Wash. Acct., Universal Svcs., Seattle, 1975-78; acct., acctg. mgr., controller Landura Corp., Woodburn, Oreg., 1978-80; asst. controller Pulte Home Corp., Laramie, Wyo., 1980-81; treas., controller Orcal Cable, Inc., Sparks, Nev., 1981-82; controller Saga Exploration Co., Reno, Nev., 1982—; acct. Sterling Mine Joint Venture, Beatty, Nev., 1982-95. Del. Nev. State Dem. Conv., Reno, 1984, 94, Las Vegas, 1988. Recipient Spaatz award CAP. Mem. AICPA, Wash. Soc. CPA's, Oreg. Soc. CPA's. Home: 2735 Lakeside Dr # A Reno NV 89509-4203 Office: Saga Exploration Co 2660 Tyner Way Reno NV 89503-4926

BUSKIRK, ELSWORTH ROBERT, physiologist, educator; b. Beloit, Wis., Aug. 11, 1925; s. Ellsworth Fred and Laura Ellen (Parman) B.; m. Mable Heen, Aug. 28, 1948; children: Laurel Ann Buskirk Wiegand, Kristine Janet Buskirk Hallett. Student, U. Wis., 1943; BA, St. Olaf Coll., Northfield, Minn., 1950; MA, U. Minn., 1951, PhD, 1954. Lab. and tchg. asst. Lab. Physiol. Hygiene, U. Minn., 1951-53; rsch. fellow Life Inst. Med. Rsch. Fund, 1953-54; physiologist Environ. Rsch. Ctr., Natick, Mass., 1954-57, Nat. Inst. for Arthritis, Metabolic and Digestive Diseases, NIH, Bethesda, Md., 1957-63; prof. applied physiology Pa. State U., University Park, 1963-92, dir. Lab. Human Performance Rsch., 1963-92; Marie Underhill Noll prof. Human Performance Pa. State U., 1988-92, emeritus, 1992—; mem. sci. adv. com. Pres.' Coun. on Phys. Fitness, 1959-61; mem. applied physiology study sect. divsn. rsch. grantes NIH, 1964-68, 76-80; mem. com. on interplay of engring. with biology and medicine NAS-NAE, 1968-74, 82-88; mem. rsch. com. Pa. Heart Assn., 1970-73, 82-86, 87-89, 90-95; mem. Pa. Gov.'s Coun. on Phys. Fitness and Sports, 1978-82; mem. com. on mil. nutrition rsch. NAS/NRC, 1982-90; mem. clin. scis. study sect. divsn. rsch. grants NIH, 1989-92; mem. Def. Women's Rsch. Com. IOM, NAS-NRC, 1995. Sect. editor Jour. Applied Physiology, 1974-78, assoc. editor, 1978-84; co-editor Sci. and Medicine in Sports and Exercise, 1974, editor, 1973-75; editor-in-chief, 1984-88, cons., editor, 1989—; mem. editl. bd. Physician and Sports Medicine, 1974-85, Jour. Cardiopulmonary Rehab., 1980—, Underseas and Hyperbaric Medicine, 1988-95, Am. Jour. Clin. Nutrition, 1982-92, Jour. Gerontology, 1982-92, Exptl. Gerontology, 1989-98; also over 235 articles on physiology, revs. to sci. jours. Bd. visitors Sargent Coll., Boston U., 1976-92; bd. dirs. Ctr. Cmty. Hosp., Pa., 1966-70, sec., 1971-72, v.p., 1973, pres., 1974-75. Served with U.S. Army, ETO. Recipient Disting. Alumni award St. Olaf Coll., 1969; rsch. grantee NIH, 1963-92, U.S. Olympic Com., 1965-68, USAF, 1965-69, Pa. Dept. Health, 1966-67, Pa. Heart Assn., 1966, 76-80, NSF, 1968-70, Nat. Inst. Occupl. Safety and Health, 1969-74; NATO sr. fellow in sci., 1977. Mem. AAAS, AAPHERD, ASHRAE, Aerospace Med. Assn., Am. Acad. Phys. Edn., Am. Coll. Sports Medicine (citations 1973, 75, Honor award 1984, editl. award 1989, 93, Mid-Atlantic regional chpt. Svc. award 1991), Am. Inst. Nutrition, Am. Physiol. Soc. (pres. environ. and exercise sect. 1987-91, com. on coms. 1988-92, Honor award environ. exercise physiology sect. 1993), Am. Heart Assn. (coun. on epidemiology), N.Y. Acad. Scis., NIH Alumni Assn., Pa. Heart Assn. (rsch. com. 1988-94), Am. Diabetes Assn., Coun. Biology Editors (Healthy Am. Fitness Leaders award 1992). Lutheran. Club: Centre Hills Country. Home: 216 Hunter Ave State College PA 16801-6947 Office: Pa State U 119 Noll Lab University Park PA 16802-6900

BUSNAINA, AHMED ALI, mechanical engineering educator; b. Benghazi, Sept. 2, 1953; s. Ali A. Busnaina and Fathia H. Belrassali; m. Zainab A. Shwaihdi; children: Wedad, Ibrahim, Ali. BS with honors, Tripoli U., 1976; MS in Mech. Engring., Okla. State U., 1979, PhD in Mech. Engring., 1983. Maintenance engr. GE, Benghazi, 1976, Esso Oil Co., Briga, 1977; teaching and rsch. asst. Okla. State U., Stillwater, Okla., 1978-79; teaching and rsch. assoc. Okla. State U., Stillwater, 1980-83; visiting asst. prof. San Diego State U., 1983-84; asst. prof. Clarkson U., Potsdam, N.Y., 1984-88; assoc. prof. Clarkson U., Potsdam, 1988-96, prof., 1996—; dir. Ctr. for Particulate Control in Process Equipment, Potsdam, 1990—; cons. IBM Corp., Burlington Vt., 1985—, Du Pont Co., Wilmington, Del., 1988; pres. Advanced Computational Scis., Potsdam, N.Y., 1986—; dir. Microcontamination Rsch. Lab., Potsdam, 1988—. Developer (software) General Flow, 1984, Clean Room Modeling, 1986, Swirl Flow, 1987; contbr. articles to profl. jours. Recipient Ralph R. Teetor award Soc. Automotive Engrs., 1986, Fulbright Sr. scholar, Egypt, 1993-94; Robert L. Patrick fellow, 1999. Fellow ASME; Mem. AIAA (spl. svc. award 1986, faculty advisor award 1988), Am. Soc. Engring. Edn. (outstanding faculty 1988), Inst. Environ. Scis. (sr. mem.), Fine Particle Soc. Avocations: reading, soccer, travel, classical music. Office: Clarkson U MIE Dept Potsdam NY 13676

BUSNER, PHILIP H., retired lawyer; b. Bklyn., Mar. 26, 1927; s. Joseph and Ray (Grajewer) B.; m. Naomi Marcia Greenfield, June 24, 1951; children: Joan Alexandra, Carey Elizabeth. BA cum laude, NYU, 1949; LLB, Harvard U., 1952. Bar: N.Y. 1953, U.S. Dist. Ct. (so. dist.) N.Y. 1956, U.S. Dist. Ct. (ea. dist.) N.Y. 1958, U.S. Ct. Appeals (2d dir.) 1956, U.S. Supreme Ct. 1974. Assoc. Rein, Mound & Cotton, N.Y.C., 1953, Hess, Mela, Segall, Popkin & Guterman, N.Y.C., 1954-55, Carroad & Carroad, N.Y.C., 1955-72; ptnr. Young, Sonnenfeld & Busner, N.Y.C., 1972-75, Sonnenfeld & Busner, N.Y.C., 1976-78, Sonnenfeld, Busner & Weinstein, N.Y.C., 1986-88; pvt. practice Great Neck, N.Y., 1989-97; ret., 1998. Trustee Asthmatic Children's Found. N.Y., 1978-87; adminstrv. judge N.Y.C. Dept. Transp., 1989-93; arbitrator N.Y.C. Civil Ct., 1990-92, Nassau County Dist. Co., 1990-95, Suffolk County Dist. Ct., 1990-93. With USAAF, 1945-47. Mem. ABA, Am. Arbitration Assn. (arbitrator 1990-92), N.Y. State Bar Assn., Nassau County Bar Assn., Phi Beta Kappa. Home: One Todd Dr Sands Point NY 11050

BUSS, DANIEL FRANK, environmental scientist; b. Milw., Jan. 13, 1943; s. Lynn Charles and Pearl Elizabeth (Ward) B.; m. Ann Makal, Jan. 22, 1977. B.S., Carroll Coll., 1965; M.S. in Biology, U. Wis., 1972, M.S. in Environ. Engring., 1977, P.D.D. in Environ. Engring., 1985. Registered profl. engr., Wis. Dir. limnological studies Aqua-Tech, Inc., Waukesha, Wis., 1969-72; project mgr. environ. studies Point Beach Nuclear Plant, Two Creeks, Wis., 1972-76; assoc., dir. aquatic studies environ. sci. div. Camp Dresser & McKee, Inc., Milw., 1977—; dir. indsl. service Camp Dresser & McKee, Inc., 1978-90; office mgr., coord. for environ. assesments Camp Dresser & McKee, Inc., Milw., 1990—; lectr. on nuclear power and environ., environ. auditing; mgr. hazardous waste superfund projects, dredge disposal planning projects; asbestos insp., mgmt. planner EPA, 1988, also nat. accounts mgr. for performance of environ. site assessments for property trans. Author: An Environmental Study of the Ecological Effects on Lake Michigan of the Thermal Discharge from the Point Beach Nuclear Plant, 1976, Environmental Auditing-- A Systematic Approach, 1984; contbr. articles to profl. jours, chpts. to books and environmental site investigation protocols for ASTM, ASCE and other soc. guidance documents. Mem. ASCE (chmn. site constrn. and remediation implementation manual task com.),Am. Nuclear Soc. (sec.-treas. Wis. sect., program mgr. waste disposal studies, program mgr. for remedial programs involving jet fuel and deicer contamination at Gen. Mitchell Internat. Airport), Midwest Soc. Electron Microscopists, Internat. Soc. Theoretical and Applied Limnology and Oceanography, Internat. Assn. Gt. Lakes Rsch., Am. Indsl. Hygiene Soc., Nat. Assn. Environ. Profls., Fed. Water Pollution Control Adminstrn., Cons. Engrs. Coun. (chmn. liaison com. Ill. and Chgo. Bar Assn., mem. com. for devel. site investigation manual ASCE, sec. ASCE com. to develop remedial design, feasibility study manual), Am. Assn. Environ. Engrs. (diplomate 1990, cert. hazardous materials mgr. 1988, hazard control mgr. 1988), Program mgr. design, construction mgmt., oper. UV/Oxidation system (used for treating herbicide contaminated ground water in Wisconsin), Am. Acad. Environ. Engrs. (Wis. state rep.), Glendale Wis. Econ. Devel. Com. and Bus. Coun., Sigma Xi. Home: 5543 N Shasta Dr Milwaukee WI 53209-4924 Office: Camp Dresser & McKee Inc The Sears Tower 233 S Wacker Dr Ste 450 Chicago IL 60606-6418 also: 312 E Wisconsin Ave Ste 500 Milwaukee WI 53202-4305

BUSS, EDWARD GEORGE, geneticist; b. Concordia, Kans., Aug. 28, 1921; s. George E. and Kathryn (Luginsland) B.; m. Dorothy Ruth Arvidson, May 7, 1949; children: Ellen, Norman. BS, Kans. State Coll., 1943; MS, Purdue U., 1949, PhD, 1956. Grad. rsch. teaching asst. Purdue U., West Lafayette, Ind., 1946-49; asst. prof. Colo. A&M Coll., Ft. Collins, 1949-55; instr. Purdue U., 1955-56; assoc. prof., prof. Pa. State U., University Park, 1956-86; prof. emeritus Pa. State U., 1987—; cons. P.T. Anputraco Ltd., Surabaya Indonesia, 1987-94; sr. scientist Biopore Inc., State College, Pa., 1987-94; Fulbright lectr., Sierra Leone, West Africa, 1988. Co-author: Meat Production in Turkeys, 1990; contbr. articles to profl. jours. Vol. Internat. Exec. Svc. Corps., Egypt, 1995. Mem. Am. Genetic Assn. (coun. mem.), Am. Inst. Biological Scis. (gov. bd., exec. com.), AAAS (fellow 1962); Poultry Sci. Assn. (fellow 1988), World's Poultry Sci. Assn. Democrat. Home: 1420 S Garner St State College PA 16801-6330 Office: Pa State U Dept Poultry Sci 213 Henning Bldg University Park PA 16802-3501

BUSS, LEO WILLIAM, biologist, educator; b. Alexandria, Va., Sept. 27, 1953; s. Leo Alfred and Margaret (Nyhan) B.; m. Jane Moore, June 12, 1982; children: Evan Daniel, Blake William. BA, Johns Hopkins U., 1975, MA, 1977, PhD, 1979; MA (hon.), Yale U., 1990. Asst. prof. dept. biology Yale U., New Haven, 1979-84, assoc. prof., 1984-90, assoc. prof. dept. geology and geophysics, 1988-90, prof. dept. biology, 1990-96, prof. dept. ecology and evolutionary biology, 1996—, chmn. program in organismal biology, 1990-95, dir. Inst. Biospheric Studies, 1991-96; curator Peabody Mus. Nat. History, New Haven, 1979—; dir. Sears Found. Marine Rsch., 1992—. Author: The Evolution of Individuality, 1987; co-editor: Population Biology and Evolution of Clonal Organisms, 1985. John Simon Guggenheim fellow, 1984, Prize fellow John D. and Catherine MacArthur Found., 1989. Office: Dept Ecology & Environ Biology Yale Univ New Haven CT 06511

BUSS, PATRICIA ARNOLD, plastic surgeon; b. Albany, N.Y., May 11, 1956; d. Edward Henry and Marion Gray (Griffing) Arnold; m. Donald Anderson Buss, May 21, 1983; children: Alison, Lindsey, Colin. ScB, Brown U., 1978, MD, 1981. Diplomate Am. Bd. Plastic Surgery. Commd. ens. USN, 1977, advanced through grades to capt., 1997; intern U. Rochester, N.Y., 1981-82, resident in gen. surgery, 1981-83; gen. med. officer U.S. Naval Hosp., Phila., 1983-84; resident in gen. surgery Brown U., Providence, 1984-85, resident in plastic surgery, 1985-87; plastic surgeon U.S. Naval Hosp., Oakland, Calif., 1987-90; head dept. surgery U.S. Naval Hosp., Charleston, S.C., 1990-93; managed care analyst Navy Bur. Medicine and Surgery, Washington, 1993-97; dir. clin. mgmt. and plans Navy Bur. Medicine and Surgery, Washington, Va., 1997—; plastic surgeon DeWitt Army Cmty. Hosp., Ft. Belvoir, Va., 1994—, Nat. Naval Med. Ctr., Bethesda, Md., 1994—; bd. dirs. My Image After Breast Cancer, Charleston, 1991-93. Fellow ACS; mem. Am. Assn. Plastic and Reconstructive Surgeons, Assn. Women Surgeons, Am. Coll. Physician Execs. Presbyterian. Office: Bur Medicine and Surgery Med-323 2300 E St NW Washington DC 20372-0001

BUSSARD, ROBERT WILLIAM, physicist; b. Washington, Aug. 11, 1928; s. Marcel Julian and Elsa Mathilda (Griesser) B.; m. Dolly H. Gray, 1981; children: Elise Marie Bussard Chisholm, William Julian, Robert Lee, Virginia Lesley Bussard Barausky. BS in Engring., UCLA, 1950, MS in Engring., 1952; MS in Physics, Princeton U., 1959, PhD in Physics, 1961. Design engr. Falcon program Hughes Aircraft Co., 1949-51; mech. engr.

aircraft nuclear propulsion project Oak Ridge Nat. Lab., 1952-55; alt. group leader nuclear rocket program Los Alamos Sci. Lab., 1955-62, alt. leader laser div., 1971-73; dir. nuclear systems staff, asst. dir. mechanics div. Space Tech. Labs., TRW Inc., Redondo Beach, Calif., 1962-64; assoc. mgr. research and engring., corp. chief scientist Electro-Optical Systems div. Xerox Corp., Pasadena, Calif., 1964-69; with CSI Corp., Los Angeles, 1969-70; mgr. Cherokee Assocs., Pasadena, Calif., 1970-72; asst. dir. div. controlled thermonuclear research U.S. AEC, Washington, 1973-74; founder, pres., chmn. Energy Resources Group (ERG), Inc., Arlington, Va., 1974-86, Internat. Nuclear Energy Systems Co. (INESCO), Inc., La Jolla, Calif. and McLean, Va., 1976-84; sr. scientist PSR Corp., Arlington, Va., 1985-89; founder, tech. dir. Energy/Matter Conversion Corp. (EMC2), San Diego, 1984—; cons. NATO, 1960-64, U.S. Dept. Energy, 1974-78, Los Alamos Sci. Lab., 1973-88, dir. ctrl. intelligence, 1971-78; lectr. UCLA, 1960-69, U. Fla., 1962-64. Author: (with R.D. DeLauer) Nuclear Rocket Propulsion, 1958, Fundamentals of Nuclear Flight, 1965; editor: Nuclear Thermal and Electric Rocket Propulsion, 1967; contbr. articles to profl. jours. Fellow AIAA; mem. Am. Phys. Soc., Internat. Acad. Astronautics. Clubs: Princeton (N.Y.C.); Cosmos (Washington), Capitol Hill (Washington). Patentee space nuclear propulsion, power generation, fusion and fission power, solar power systems. Office: Ste 103 9705 Carroll Ctr Rd San Diego CA 92126 *The future is constructed in a fashion and to a scale envisioned by those who perceive what it might be, and who work to make these visions happen. At any one time, only a few thousand people are working to shape the world of tomorrow from the tools, techniques, and ideas of today. I hope with God's grace to help this work, to improve the lot of man and ensure the survival and growth of humankind in such a way that the freedom of all people might be preserved and extended for future generations.*

BUSSE, EWALD WILLIAM, psychiatrist, educator; b. St. Louis, Aug. 18, 1917; s. Frederick Ewald and Emily Louise (Stroh) B.; m. Ortrude Helen Schnaedelbach, July 18, 1941; children: Ortrude Susan Busse White, Barbara Ann, Ewald Richard, Deborah Emily Busse Bragg. AB, Westminster Coll., 1938, ScD (hon.), 1960; MD, Washington U., St. Louis, 1942. Diplomate Am. Bd. Psychiatry and Neurology, Am. Bd. Qualification in Clin. Neurophysiology. Intern St. Louis City Hosp., 1942; resident in neuropsychiatry and psychiatry McCloskey Gen. Hosp., Temple, Tex., 1943-46, Colo. Psychiat. Hosp., Denver, 1946-48; faculty, head dept. psychosomatic medicine U. Colo., Denver, 1950-53; prof. Duke U. Med. Ctr., Durham, N.C., 1953-65, J.P. Gibbons prof. psychiatry, 1965-87, chmn. dept., 1953-74, dir. Ctr. for Study Aging, 1957-70, assoc. provost, dean Sch. Medicine, 1974-82, dean emeritus, 1982—; pres., CEO N.C. Inst. Medicine, 1987-94, pres. emeritus, 1994—; mem. council Nat. Inst. on Aging, Bethesda, Md., 1979-83; chmn. geriatrics and gerontology adv. com. VA, 1981-86. Author, editor: Behavior and Adaptation in Late Life, 1969, 2d edit., 1977, Handbook of Geriatric Psychiatry, 1980, 2d edit., 1994, Part II, Vol. II-Psychiatry Update, 1983, The Duke Longitudinal Studies, 1985, Aging: The Universal Human Experience, 1987, Geriatric Psychiatry, 1989, (textbook) Geriatric Psychiatry, 1996; author: Cerebral Manifestations of Cardiac Dysrhythmias, 1979. Mem. N.C. State Commn. on Care of Elderly, Raleigh, 1968-73; mem. Durham County Commn. in Mental Health, 1971-74; pres. biomed. rsch. panel White Ho. Conf. on Aging, 1975-76, sect. chmn. del., 1978-81; mem. sci. adv. bd. Alliance for Aging Rsch., 1986—; bd. dirs. Greater Durham United Way, 1987-92. Maj. U.S. Army, 1943-46. Recipient Brookdale Found. award, 1982, Alumni Achievement award Westminster Coll., 1984, Disting. Alumni award Washington U., 1992, Pioneer award Govs. Commn. on Reduction of Infant Mortality, 1993; Busse Bldg. named in his honor Duke U., 1985; Busse Internat. Rsch. award endowed, 1990; Ewald Busse award created in his honor N.C. Dept. Human Resources, 1990; Busse Lecture endowment, 1995. Fellow Am. Psychiat. Assn. (pres. 1971-72, chmn. ethics com. 1981-85, Jack Weinberg Meml. award, Warren Williams award 1987, Disting. Service award 1988), Am. Geriatrics Soc. (pres. 1975-76 Allen Thewlis award), Gerontol. Soc. Am. (pres. 1967-68 Freeman award), ACP (Menninger award 1971), Southeastern Med. Dental Soc. (pres. 1978-80); mem. Internat. Assn. Gerontology (pres. 1983-89, Sandoz prize1983), World Psychiat. Assn. (ethics com.), N.Y. Acad. Medicine (Salmon award 1980). Clubs: Hope Valley; Beech Mountain (N.C.). Lodges: Rotary/Durham; Masons. Home: 25 Old Oak Ct Durham NC 27705-5644 Office: Duke U Med Ctr PO Box 2948 Durham NC 27715-2948

BUSSE, LEONARD WAYNE, banker, financial consultant; b. Chgo., June 29, 1938; s. Edwald William and Elsie Helen (Weidner) B.; m. Gretchen Guam Beal, Sept. 7, 1963; children: Whitney Lee, Carter Douglas. BS, Purdue U., 1960; postgrad., Northwestern U., 1964-67. CPA, Ill. With Continental Ill. Corp., Chgo., 1963-88, v.p., 1973-81, sr. v.p., 1981-85, head internat. banking dept., 1985; exec. v.p. Continental Bank, Chgo., 1985-88; cons. The Busse Group, Vail, Colo., 1989-93; pres., CEO The Pacific Bank, San Francisco, 1993-94, also bd. dirs., 1994; CEO, bd. dirs. First Citizen Bank Ltd., Port of Spain, Trinidad, 1994-96; CFO Worldbridge Broadband Svcs., Denver, 1998—. Bd. dirs. McGraw Wildlife Found., Elgin, Ill., 1982-92, Vectra Banking Corp., Denver, 1993-94. Mem. AICPA. Republican. Lutheran. Avocations: skiing, hunting, biking, fishing.

BUSSELEN, STEVEN CARROLL, journalist, editor; b. Midland, Mich., Aug. 14, 1971; s. Harry Julius Jr. and Carroll (Kincaid) B. BA in English, Santa Clara U., 1993; postgrad., Scripps Coll., 1997-99. Reporter, photographer The Daily Press, Paso Robles, Calif., 1993-94; reporter The Bus. Jour., Fresno, Calif., 1994, copy editor, 1994-96, asst. editor, 1996-97; spl. projects editor The Bus. Jour., Fresno, 1997. Mem. Soc. Am. Bus. Editors and Writers. Avocations: backpacking, nordic skiing, tennis, reading. Office: 807 Skyline Dr San Luis Obispo CA 93405-1053

BUSSELLE, JAMES A., educational administrator. PhD, U Va. Exec. dir. Postsecondary Edn. Com.; mem. State Higher Edn. Exec. Officers. Office: Postsecondary Edn Com 2 Industrial Park Dr Concord NH 03301-8520

BUSSEY, GEORGE DAVIS, psychiatrist; b. Salta, Argentina, Apr. 14, 1949; s. William Harold and Helen (Wygant) B.; m. Moira Savage, July 26, 1975; children: Andrew Davis, Megan Elizabeth. BS, U. Denver, 1969; MD, Ea. Va. Med. Sch., 1977; JD, U. Hawaii, 1993. Diplomate in psychiatry, forensic psychiatry and addiction psychiatry Am. Bd. Psychiatry and Neurology. Intern Eastern Va. Grad. Sch. Medicine, 1977-78; resident Ea. Va. Grad. Sch. Medicine, 1978-79, Vanderbilt U. Hosp., Nashville, 1979-81; staff psychiatrist Hawaii State Hosp., Kaneohe, 1981-82; asst. prof. dept. psychiatry U. Hawaii, Honolulu, 1982-84; dir. adult svcs. Kahi Mohala Hosp., Ewa Beach, Hawaii, 1983-89; assoc. med. dir. Queens Healthcare Plan, Honolulu, 1988-94, v.p., 1997—; med. dir. Queen's Health Mgmt., Honolulu, 1994—; clin. assoc. prof. Dept. Psychiatry U. Hawaii, Honolulu, 1990—. Mem. U. Hawaii Law Rev., 1991-93; contbr. articles to profl. jours. Fellow Am. Psychiat. Assn., Hawaii Psychiat. Soc. (treas. 1982-83, pres. 1985-87).; mem. Am. Coll. Physician Execs. (cert.).

BUSSEY, JOHN W., III, lawyer; b. Miami, Fla., Oct. 25, 1943. BA, Fla. State U., 1965; JD with honors, Stetson U., 1968. Bar: Fla. 1968; U.S. Dist. Ct. (mid. dist., no. dist.), U.S. Supreme Ct. Ptnr. Johnson & Bussey P.A. (now John W. Bussey III & Assoc.), Orlando, Fla. Mem. ABA, Am. BD. Trial Advs., The Fla. Bar Assn. (trial lawyers sect., bd. cert. civil trial law), Fla. Defense Lawyers Assn., Orange County Bar Assn., Phi Delta Phi. Office: John W Bussey III & Assoc 105 E Robinson St 4th Fl PO Box 531086 Orlando FL 32801*

BUSSGANG, JULIAN JAKOB, electronics engineer; b. Lwow, Poland, Mar. 26, 1925; came to U.S., 1949, naturalized, 1954; s. Joseph and Stephanie (Philipp) B.; m. Fay Rita Vogel, Aug. 14, 1960; children: Jessica Edith, Julia Claire, Jeffrey Joseph. B.Sc., U. London, 1949; S.M. in Elec. Engring., MIT, 1951; Ph.D. in Applied Physics, Harvard U., 1955. Mem. tech. staff Lincoln Lab., MIT, Lexington, 1951-55; mgr. applied research RCA, Burlington, Mass., 1955-62; pres. Signatron, Inc., Lexington, 1962-87; pvt. practice cons. Lexington, 1988—; vis. lectr. Harvard U., 1964; lectr. Northeastern U., Boston, 1962-65; mem. Mass. del. White House Conf. on Small Bus., 1980. Assoc. editor: Radio Sci., 1976-78; translator: The Last Eyewitnesses: Children of the Holocaust Speak, 1998; contbr. chpts. to books, also articles. Mem. Town Mtg., Lexington, 1975-93; mem. alumni coun. MIT, 1965-72; bd. overseers Mus. of Sci., Boston, 1989-95; vol. exec. Internat. Exec. Svcs. Corps., 1993, 94, 95. Served with Free Polish Forces, 1942-46. Fellow IEEE (life fellow, chmn. Boston sect. 1994-95). Patentee in field. *I was a child-refugee, an adolescent-soldier, a student-immigrant, a young engineer and an adult entrepreneur. In every phase of my life I was blessed with the friendship and support of many wonderful people from various walks of life. Even in the darkest moments I had faith that each of us could improve the world a little.*

BUSSLER, ROBERT BRUCE, management consultant; b. Ramey, Pa., Apr. 7, 1925; s. Arthur and Mary Eleanor (McCrossin) B.; m. Evelyn Louise Murrell, June 28, 1952; children: Mary Louise, Janice Lynn. BEE, George Washington U., 1950. Electronics engr. Melpar, Inc., Falls Church, Va., 1953-55; elec. engr. Bur. of Ships, Washington, 1955-59; value engr. Bur. Naval Weapons, Washington, 1959-66; br. head Naval Air Systems Command, Washington, 1966-80; dir. engring., v.p. Nat. Systems Mgmt. Corp., Arlington, Va., 1980-89; pres., chmn. bd. dirs. REMAR, Inc., Alexandria, Va., 1990—. Lt. comdr. USNR, 1943-52, PTO. Mem. Free and Accepted Masons (Worshipful Master 1975), Royal Arch Masons Internat. (com. chmn., Bronze medal 1975, Grand High Priest 1980). Republican. Methodist. Avocations: golf, squash, theater, travel. Home and Office: 2515 Page Ter Alexandria VA 22302-2714

BUSSMAN, CHARLES HAINES, publisher; b. Pitts., Mar. 9, 1924; s. Amos George and Ann (Haines) B. Student, Colgate U., 1946. With Pitt & Quarry Publs., Inc., 1946-63, v.p., 1957-63, dir., 1960-63; pres., dir., publisher Compass Publs., Inc., Arlington, Va., 1963—. Bd. dirs. trustee Branch Oceanographic Instn., Inc., Harbor Branch Instn., Inc. Served with USAFF, 1942-43. Fellow Marine Tech. Soc. (hon.); mem. Indsl. Marketers Cleve. (past bd. dirs.), Am. Bus. Press, Marine Tech. Soc., Am. Oceanographic Orgn., Advt. Club Cleve., T.F. Club Cleve. (past pres.), Theta Chi. Office: 1117 19th St N Ste 1000 Arlington VA 22209-1790*

BUSSMAN, DONALD HERBERT, lawyer; b. Lakewood, Ohio, July 15, 1925; s. Herbert L. and Hilda L. (Henrichs) B. PhB, U. of Chgo., 1947, JD, 1951. Bar: Ill. 1951. Atty. Swift & Co., Chgo., 1950-84; pvt. practice Chgo., 1985—. With U.S. Army, 1944-46. Mem. ABA, Chgo. Bar Assn., Am. Assn. of Individual Investors, Club Internat. (Chgo.). Office: Ste 2102 860 N Dewitt Pl Chicago IL 60611-5780

BUSSMAN, JOHN WOOD, physician, health care administrator; b. Mankato, Minn., July 4, 1924; s. A.M. and Myrtle E. (Wood) B.; m. Muriel J. Koenck, June 17, 1950; children: David, John, Sarah, James, Rebecca, Penelope. BSc, U. Minn., 1946, MB, 1947, MD, 1948. Diplomate Am. Bd. Pediatrics, Am. Bd. Pediatric Cardiology. Intern Sioux Valley Hosp., Sioux Falls, S.D., 1948; residency in pediatrics U. Minn. Hosp., Mpls., 1949-50, pediatric cardiology fellow, 1951; gen. practice medicine The Children's Clinic-Sylvan Med. Svcs., Inc., Portland, Oreg., 1953-91; med. dir. Oreg. Med. Profl. Rev. Orgn., 1988—; clin. prof. pediatrics U. Oreg. Md. Sch.; cons. in pediatric cardiology; chief pediatrics Emanuel Hosp., 1966-69, health maintenance orgn. com. 1972; bd. dirs. Health Choice, Inc., 1983-86; chmn. Physicians' Health Network, 1982-83; med. dir. Oreg. Med. Peer Rev., 1989—, Oreg. Med. Assistance Program, 1991—; bd. dirs. Am. Med. Peer Rev. Assn. Chmn. health services adv. com. Multnomah County Commrs., 1973-77; mem. Multnomah County Health Care Commn. 1977-82. Fellow Am. Acad. Pediatrics, Am. Coll. Chest Physicians (sec. com. myopathy in childhood 1976), Am. Coll. Cardiology (Oreg. gov. 1974-77); mem. Nat. Acad. Sci. (Inst. of Medicine), Portland Acad. Pediatrics (pres. 1963), Portland Acad. Medicine, Portland Heart Club, Oreg. Heart Assn. (chmn. 1976-77, exec. com., bd. dirs. 1960-81,89-92, chmn. community service com. 1972-74, chmn. rheumatic fever commn. 1954-77, del. Am. Heart Assn. regional heart com. 1973-80, budget com., chmn. program rev. council, 1985), Oreg. Thoracic Soc. (chmn. research com. 1966), Multnomah Found. Med. Care (pres. 1970-80, med. dir. 1972-83, treas. 1980-83), Multnomah County Med. Soc. (pres. 1970, trustee 1963-71, treas .1965, sec. 1966, v.p. 1967, pres.-elect 1969, chmn. bd. censors 1971, chmn. peer rev. commn. 1971, chmn. Portland Council Hosps. liaison com. 1971), Oreg. Med. Assn. (v.p. 1972, chmn. health manpower 1972, ad hoc com. peer rev. 1972, long-range planning com. 1972, trustee 1969-80), Oreg. Found. Med. Care (bd. dirs. 1972-77), Oreg. Comprehensive Health Planning Authority (health manpower com.), Comprehensive Health Planning Assn. (chmn. project rev. com., chmn. profl. health service com., bd. dirs. 1970-77, exec. com. 1970-74), N.W. Oreg. Health Systems (health planning com. 1978-80, diagnosis and treatment subcom. 1978-80, chmn. health care tech. assessment com. 1983), HEW (Exptl. Med. Care Rev. Orgns. 1972-73), Am. Assn. Profl. Standards Rev. Orgns. (pres. 1974-77), Nat. Prof. Standards Rev. Council (chmn. 1978-80), and others. Clubs: Portland City, Multnomah Athletic. Lodge: Rotary.

BUSSMANN, CHARLES HAINES, publisher; b. Pitts., Mar. 9, 1924; s. Amos George and Ann (Haines) B. Student, Colgate U., 1946. With Pit & Quarry Publs., Inc., 1946-63, v.p., 1957-63, dir., 1960-63; pres. dir. Compass Publs., Inc., Arlington, Va., 1963—. Bd. dirs., trustee Harbor Branch Oceanographic Instn., Inc., Harbor Branch Instn., Inc. Served with USAAF, 1942-43. Fellow Marine Tech. Soc. (hon.); Mem. Indsl. Marketers Cleve. (past bd. dirs.), Am. Bus. Press, Marine Tech. Soc., Am. Oceanographic Orgn., Advt. Club Cleve., T.F. Club Cleve. (past pres.), Theta Chi. Office: 1117 19th St N Ste 1000 Arlington VA 22209-1755

BUSSONE, FRANK JOSEPH, foundation executive, television broadcaster; b. Pontiac, Ill.; s. Joseph Dominick and Olma Francis (DesCarpentrie) B.; m. Karen Marie Watson, May 27, 1972; 1 child, R.J. BS, Bradley U., 1964, MA, 1966; PhD, U. So. Calif., 1968. Adminstr. Bradley U., Peoria, Ill., 1969-77; v.p., COO Dirksen Congl. Ctr., Pekin and Washington, 1977-80; pres., CEO Sta. WEEK-TV, Peoria, 1980-86; exec. v.p. Eagle Broadcasting Co., N.Y.C., 1985-86; pres., CEO The Proctor Found., Peoria, 1986—; TV broadcaster ESPN SportsChannel, Chgo., 1972—; anchor TV broadcaster Ill. State Basketball Tournament, 1980-91; bd. dirs. BankPlus, Ill., St. Jude, Memphis; motivational speaker, 1970—. Author: The Tag Line, 1975; editor: Surprising Peoria, 1990; columnist for various newspapers, 1982—. Bd. dirs. Am. Heart Assn., Springfield, Ill., 1991—; TV host St. Jude Telethons, Ill., 1980-86; mem. Presdl. Task Force, Washington, 1988; speaker Bush for Pred. Campaign, Ill., 1988, Edgar for Gov. Campaign, Ill., 1990; mem. Bradley U. Community Bd., 1982—. Recipient Love a Child award Neighborhood House, Peoria, 1987, Citation of Hon. City of L.A., 1968; named to Bradley U. Hall of Fame, 1989, Ill. Basketball Hall of Fame Ill. Coaches Assn., 1983, One of Outstanding Young Men in Am. Mem. Ill. Hosp. Assn., The Dirksen Soc., Creve Coeur Club, Mt. Hawley Country Club, Downtown Rotary Club. Roman Catholic. Avocations: tennis, jogging, reading, cooking, writing. Home: 53 Hyde Park Dr Morton IL 61550-9534 Office: The Proctor Found 5409 N Knoxville Ave Peoria IL 61614-5016

BUSTAMANTE, CRUZ M., state official; b. Dinuba, Calif., 1953; s. Cruz and Dominga Bustamante Jr.; m. Arcelia De La Pena; children: Leticia, Sonia, Marisa. Student, Fresno City Coll., Fresno State U. Past intern for Congressman B.F. Sisk Washington; formerly with Fresno employment and tng. commn. City of Fresno, past program dir. summer youth employment tng. program; past dist. rep. Congressman Rick Lehman and Assemblyman Bruce Bronzan State of Calif.; mem. Calif. State Assembly, 1993, spkr. of assembly, 1996-98; lt. gov. State of Calif., 1998—. Trustee Calif. State U. Named Legislator of Yr. Faculty Assn. Cmty. Colls., Assn. Mexican Am. Educators, U. Calif. Alumni Assn., True Am. Role Model Mexican Am. Polit. Assn.; recipient Lifetime award Golden State Mobilehome Owners League, Friend of Labor award Mexican Am. Polit. Assn. Office: State Capitol Rm 1114 Sacramento CA 95814

BUSTAMANTE, NESTOR, lawyer; b. Havana, Cuba, Apr. 20, 1960; came to the U.S., 1961; s. Nestor and Clara Rosa (Sanchez) B.; m. Marilyn Gonzalez, Sept. 20, 1986; children: Tiffany Alexandra, Nestor C. AA, U. Fla., 1980, BS in Journalism, 1982, JD, 1985. Bar: Fla. 1986, U.S. Dist. Ct. (so. dist.) Fla. 1989, U.S. Supreme Ct. 1991. Asst. state atty. State Atty.'s Office 11th Cir., Miami, 1986-88; juvenile serious offender prosecutor State Atty.'s Office, Miami, 1987-88, spl. prosecutor, gang prosecutor, 1987-88; asst. divsn. chief State Atty.'s Office-11th Jud. Cir., Miami, 1987-88; of counsel Fernandez-Caubi, Fernandez & Aguilar et al., Miami, 1988-89; atty. Ferencik, Libanoff, Brandt and Bustamante PA, Ft. Lauderdale, Fla., 1989—, ptnr., 1996—; mem. code and rules of evidence com. The Fla. Bar, 1989-90. Contbr. articles to newsletters. Named Hon. mem. Quien es Quien Publs., Inc., N.Y.C., 1990. Mem. ATLA (scoring judge nat. finals student trial advocacy competition 1994, 95), Fed. Bar Assn., Dade County Bar Assn. (mem. juvenile divsn. com. 1988-92, mem. media and pub. rels. com. 1989-91, mem. constrn. law com. 1990-91), Phi Delta Phi, U. Fla. Alumni Assn. Office: Ferencik Libanoff Brandt & Bustamante PA 150 S Pine Island Rd Ste 400 Fort Lauderdale FL 33324-2667

BUSTARD, CLARKE, music critic, newswriter, radio producer; b. Richmond, Va., May 16, 1950; s. C.A. and Mamie (Patterson) B. BA, U. Richmond, 1971. Staff writer Richmond Times-Dispatch, 1974—, music critic, 1979—; producer, host Sta. WRFK-FM, Richmond, 1976-83, Concertmasters Sta. WCVE-FM, Richmond, 1989—. With U.S. Army, 1972-73. Recipient award for column writing Va. Press Assn., 1987, award for reporting, 1995, award for reporting, 1996; award for commentary Am. Soc. Feature and Sunday Editors, 1991. Mem. Music Critics Assn., Va. Writers Club, Va. Folklore Soc., Sigma Delta Chi. Office: Richmond Times-Dispatch 333 E Grace St Richmond VA 23293-1000

BUSTER, ALAN ADAIR, control engineer; b. Houston, May 30, 1918; s. Edwin Crozier and Eva Lea (Shelby) B.; m. Virginia Anne Clarkson, Oct. 1, 1945; children: Anne Shelby Windsor, Alan A. Jr. BSChE, Rice U., 1949; postgrad., Washington U., St. Louis, 1951, U. Houston, 1958-59; dipl., Army Command/Gen. Staff Coll., Ft. Leavenworth, Kans., 1960. Registered profl. engr., Calif., Tex. Artilleryman, flying cadet, air photo officer U.S. Army, 1936-47, res. instr.; lt. col. Army Corps Engrs., Houston, Paris, Germany, 1947-78; rsch. lab. technician Shell Oil Co., Deer Park, Tex., 1946-47; refining technologist Shell Oil Co., Wood River, Ill., 1949-52; chem. engr. Crown Ctrl. Petroleum Corp., Pasadena, Tex., 1952-60; process analyst, computer control Thompson-Ramo-Wooldridge, L.A., 1960-63; chef de projet Feyzin, Cie des Machines Bull, Paris, 1963-65; engr. computer control GE, Houston, 1965-74; engr. consulting control Honeywell, Houston, 1974-86; ret., 1986. Contbr. articles to profl. jours. Leader Boy Scouts Am., 1938-58; hon. life mem. Oxford U. Rover Crew, 1945. Mem. AIChE, Am. Chem. Soc., Instrument Soc. Am., 7th Photo Group Assn. Achievements include leading teams that accomplished computer control of a petroleum crude unit (first in the world), computer model predictive control of styrene-butadiene polymerization train (second in the world), of the second fluid catalytic cracking unit, first direct digital control of dye becks (a batchwise process), first real-time on-line simultaneous optimization of refinery steam and electricity generation and distribution, other pioneer projects. Home: 3502 Elk Cliff Pass San Antonio TX 78247-4463

BUSTER, JOHN EDMOND, gynecologist, medical researcher; b. Oxnard, Calif., July 18, 1941; s. Edmound B. and Beatrice (Keller) B.; m. Frances Bunn (dec.). Student, Stanford U., 1959-62; MD, UCLA, 1966. Diplomate Am. Bd. Gynecology. Intern., Harbor UCLA Med. Ctr., Torrance, 1966-67, resident, 1967-71, research fellow, 1971-73, faculty, 1975—; prof. obstetrics and gynecology UCLA Sch. Medicine, 1983, dir. divsn. reproductive endocrinology; prof. obstetrics and gynecology U. Tenn., Memphis, 1987-94; prof. ob-gyn., dir. divsn. reproductive edn. Baylor Coll. Medicine, Houston, 1994—; examiner Am. Bd. Obstetrics and Gynecology. Contbr. articles to profl. jours. Served to lt. col., U.S. Army, 1973-75. Mem. Am. Gynecologic & Obstetrics Soc., Soc. for Gynecologic Investigation. Presbyterian. Office: Baylor Coll Medicine 6550 Fannin St Ste 801 Houston TX 77030-2739

BUSTER, KENDALL, art educator. BFA, Corcoran Sch. Art, Washington, 1981; MFA, Yale U., 1987. One-man shows include Rockville (Md.) Arts Place, 1992, McLean (Va.) project for Arts, 1993, Portland (Oreg.) State U., 1994, Anderson Gallery, Richmond, Va., 1996, Baumgartner Galleries, Washington, 1996; group shows include Sculpture Ctr., N.Y.C., 1993, U. Md., Balt., 1994, Corcoran Gallery Art, Washington, 1994, Baumgartner Galleries, Washington, 1995. Office: The Corcoran Sch Art 500 17th St NW Washington DC 20006

BUSTIN, EDOUARD JEAN, political scientist, educator; b. Hollogne aux Pierres, Belgium, Apr. 9, 1933; came to U.S., 1961; s. Maurice and Mariette (De Graeve) B.; m. Francine Lekeu, Apr. 13, 1957 (dec. 1984); children: Denis, Olivier; m. Marisol Maura, Nov. 16, 1991. Cand.Phil., U. Liege, 1953, D. en Droit, 1956, Lic.Sc. Diplomat., 1957. Asst. in pub. law and adminstrn. U. Liege, 1956-59; atty. in Liege, 1956-59; sr. lectr., then vis. prof. U. Officielle du Congo, 1959-71; vis. lectr. polit. sci. UCLA, 1961-63; mem. faculty Boston U., 1963—, prof. polit. sci., 1970—, chmn. dept., 1977-82, 86-87, assoc. African Studies Ctr., 1963—; dir. Francophone Africa Rsch. Group, 1993—; vis. prof. U. de Bordeaux, 1996-97. Author: Lunda Under Belgian Rule: The Politics of Ethnicity, 1975; co-author: Five African States: Responses to Diversity, 1963. Decorated officer Palmes Académiques (France). Mem. African Studies Assn., Centre d'Etudes d'Afrique Noire, Inst. Africain. Home: 57 Columbine Rd Milton MA 02186-1724 Office: 270 Bay State Rd Boston MA 02215-1403

BUSTIN, GEORGE LEO, lawyer; b. Perth Amboy, N.J., Feb. 10, 1948; s. George and Agnes W. (Bulvanoski) B.; m. Halina Orestovna Kaniuka, July 9, 1979; children: Michael G., Alexander G. AB summa cum laude, Princeton U., 1970; JD magna cum laude, Harvard U., 1973. Bar: N.Y. 1973, U.S. Dist. Ct. (so. dist.), U.S. Ct. Appeals ((2nd cir.), 1974. Assoc. Cleary, Gottlieb, Steen & Hamilton, N.Y.C., 1973-81, ptnr., 1982-84; vis. prof. Princeton (N.J.) U., 1991; ptnr. Cleary, Gottlieb, Steen & Hamilton, Brussels, 1984-90, 1992—; chair Brussels chpt. Internat. divsn. N.Y. State Bar Assn., 1996—; mem. Ctr. for European Policy, Brussels, 1988—, European Cmty. Studies Assn., N.Y.C., 1991—; dir. Sabre Found. (Europe) S.p.r.l. Author: Business Transactions with the USSR, 1975, International Business Transactions, 1980, International Financial Law Review, 1990, Insights, 1990. Mem. Cercle Gaulois Artistique et Litteraire, Harvard Law Sch. Assn. (sec. Brussels 1989-92), Am. European Union Assn. (pres.'s group), Am. and Common Market Club, N.Y. State Bar Assn., Ordre Francais du barreau de Bruxelles, Brussels Sports Assn. (bd. dirs. 1996-98). Home: 39 Rue de La Gendarmerie, 1380 Lasne Belgium Office: Cleary Gottlieb Steen & Hamilton, 23 Rue de La Loi, 1040 Brussels Belgium

BUSWELL, ARTHUR WILCOX, physician, surgeon; b. Oklahoma City, Jan. 6, 1926; s. Albert Currier and Enid May (Scott) B.; B.Sc., U. Okla., 1950, M.D., 1952; m. Loleta JoAnn Sherrill, June 11, 1950; children—Arthur Lee, Robert Joseph, Barbara JoAnn, Brian A., Gayla, Richard; m. 2d, Jane Marie Fuksa, Mar. 1, 1969. Intern. Fitzsimons Army Hosp. Aurora, Colo., 1952-53; surg. resident Wesley Hosp., Oklahoma City, 1954-55; practice medicine and surgery, Hennessey, Okla., 1955-63; dep. surgeon, Fort Wainwright and Yukon Command, 1963-65; chief staff Kingfisher (Okla.) Community Hosp., 1956-57; supt. health Kingfisher County, 1960-61; chief profl. service Bassett Army Hosp., 1963-65; div. surgeon 1st Armored Div., Ft. Hood, Tex., 1965-67, 1st Inf. Div., Republic of Vietnam, 1967-68; med. project officer U.S. Army Combat Devels. Command, Experimentation Command, Ft. Ord, Calif., 1968-72, also chief human factors div. and chief experimentation div. of experimentation command; chief profl. services Reynolds Army Hosp., Ft. Sill, Okla., 1972-73; comdr. med. dept. activities Ft. Stewart, Ga., 1973-77; chief profl. services Kenner Army Hosp., Ft. Lee, Va., 1977-78; comdr. med. dept. activities, Alaska, 1979-83; adj. asst. prof. med. scis. Baylor U., 1973—. Pres., Ft. Stewart Sch. Bd., 1977; bd. dirs. Ft. Stewart Fed. Credit Union, 1977, Chisholm Trail Mus., 1986—, Friends of Librs. in Okla., 1987—; mem. Kingfisher Meml. Libr. Bd.; pres. Friends of Libr. for Kingfisher County, 1984-88. Served with AUS, 1944-46, 1st lt. U.S. Army, 1952-54, maj. to col., 1961-83. Decorated Legion of Merit with 2 oak leaf cluster, Soldier's medal, Bronze Star for Valor with oak leaf cluster, Meritorious Service medal, Air medal with 3 oak leaf clusters, Army Commendation medal; Gallantry cross with palm, Honor medal 1st class (both Vietnam); named to Kingfisher High Sch. Hall of Fame, 1987, Citizen of the Yr. Kingfisher C. of C., 1988. Fellow Royal Soc. Health; mem. Am., Okla. State (mem. no. dels.), Aerospace, Army Aviation (charter) med. assns., Assn. Mil. Surgeons U.S., Garfield-Kingfisher County Med. Soc. Home: PO Box 703 Kingfisher OK 73750-0703

BUSWELL, DEBRA SUE, small business owner, programmer, analyst; b. Salt Lake City, Apr. 8, 1957; d. John Edward Ross and Marilyn Sue (Patterson) Potter; m. Randy James Buswell, AUg. 17, 1985; 1 child, Trevor Ryan. BA, U. Colo., Denver, 1978. Programmer, analyst Trail Blazer Systems, Palo Alto, Calif., 1980-83; data processing mgr. Innovative Concepts, Inc., San Jose, Calif., 1983-86; owner Egret Software, Milpitas, Calif.,

1986—. Mem. IEEE, No. Calif. Pick Users. Home and Office: 49701 Vineyard Ave Fremont CA 94539

BUTALA, ANTHONY FRANCIS, vocalist, entertainer, small business owner; b. Sharon, Pa., Nov. 20, 1938; s. John George and Mary Ann (Ference) B.; m. Judith Ann Blaskovich, Mar. 8, 1969 (div. 1984); children: Anthony John, Rebecca Ann, Lisa Marie, Regina Mary; m. Julia Anne Twichell, June 17, 1995. AA, L.A. City Coll., 1956-58. Started vocal group with Connie Stevens Fourmost, 1954-57; solo and group singer Bill Norvas and Upstarts, Eddie Lawrence and the Whatnotts, Las Vegas, Nev., 1957-58, The Lettermen, Las Vegas, 1958—; pres. Butala Vinyards, Napa Valley, Calif., 1989—; bd. dirs. Soc. of Singers, Beverly Hills; co-founder Vocal Group Hall of Fame & Mus., Sharon, Pa., 1998. Composer songs Lettermen In Concert album, 1963. Founding participant Children's Miracle Network TV Telethon, Salt Lake City, 1982—; spokesperson Am. Lupus Soc.. Recipient numerous Gold Albums and rec. industry awards in U.S.A., Japan, Europe and the Philippines. Mem. Nat. Assn. Recording Arts and Scis., SAG, AGVA, Am. Guild Mus. Artists, AFTRA, Am. Fedn. Musicians. Democrat. Roman Catholic. Avocations: coin and stamp collecting, hiking, camping, fishing. Office: The Lettermen 1004 11th St McKees Rocks PA 15136

BUTCHER, AMANDA KAY, retired university administrator; b. Lansing, Mich., Oct. 25, 1936; d. Foster Eli and Mayme Lenore (Taft) Stuart; m. Claude J. Butcher, Aug. 24, 1957; 1 child, Mary Beth. BS in Bus., Cen. Mich. U., 1981. Office asst. Dept. Dairy Sci., East Lansing, Mich., 1966-76; bus. mgr. dept. pathology Coll. Vet. Medicine Mich. State U., East Lansing, 1976-96. Mem. Adminstrv. Profl. Suprs. Assn. (v.p. 1982), Adminstrv. Profl. Assn. East Lansing (pres. 1976-80). Democrat. Avocations: photography, antiques, bowling. Home: 610 Emily Ave Lansing MI 48910-5404

BUTCHER, BOBBY GENE, retired military officer; b. Mineral Wells, W.Va., Apr. 30, 1936; s. John Franklin and Anna Pearl (Hersman) B.; m. Patricia Maureen O'Keefe, Dec. 15, 1961 (dec. Dec. 1996); 1 child, Lisa Lee Butcher Clardy. BS, W.Va. U., 1958; grad., USN Flight Sch., 1960; post-grad., USMC Amphibious Warfare Sch., 1966-67, USMC Command and Staff Coll., 1973-74. Commd. 2d lt. USMC, 1959, advanced through grades to maj. gen., 1989; officer in charge USMC Officer Selection Office, Phila., 1971-73; ops. officer Marine Attack Tng. Squadron 102, Yuma, Ariz., 1974, exec. officer, 1974-76, comdg. officer, 1976-77; ops. officer Marine Corps Air Sta., Yuma, 1977-79; ops. plans officer 3d Marine Div., Camp Courtney, Okinawa, 1979-80; comdg. officer Marine Aviation Weapons and Tactics Squadron One, Yuma, 1980-82; participant Dept. State Sr. Seminar, Arlington, Va., 1982-83; asst. chief staff, plans and policy, comdr. Naval Striking and Support Forces, So. Europe, Naples, Italy, 1983-86; asst. wing comdr. 3d Marine Aircraft Wing, El Toro, Calif., 1986-87; comdg. gen. 6th Marine Expeditionary Brigade, Camp Lejeune, N.C., 1987-89; dir. ops. U.S. Pacific Command, Honolulu, 1989-91; comdg. gen. Landing Force Command, Coronado, Calif., 1991-92; cons. specializing in Marine Corps and joint mil. matters. Decorated Def. D.S.M., D.S.M., Def. Superior Svc. medal, Legion of Merit, DFC, Bronze Star with combat V, Air medals (15); recipient various other unit and personal medals and ribbons. Mem. The Ret. Officers Assn. (pres. Silver Strand chpt., nat. bd. dirs.), Flying Leatherneck Mus. Soc. (chmn. bd. dirs.), USS Midway Mus. (bd. dirs.). Republican. Methodist. Home: 110 Carob Way Coronado CA 92118-2433

BUTCHER, BRUCE CAMERON, lawyer; b. N.Y.C., Feb. 17, 1947; s. John Richard and Dorothy Helen (Wehner) B.; m. Kathryn Ann Fiddler, Oct. 12, 1979; 1 child, Kristen Ann. BS, Belknap Coll., 1969; JD, St. John's U., N.Y.C., 1972. Bar: N.Y. 1973, U.S. Dist. Ct. (so. dist.) N.Y. 1974, La. 1980, U.S. Dist. Ct. (ea. dist.) La. 1980, U.S. Ct. Appeals (5th and 11th cirs.) 1981, Tex. 1993. Assoc. Laporte and Meyers, N.Y.C., 1972-73; asst. chief contract div. Corp. Counsel's Office City of N.Y., 1973-79; ptnr. Chaffe, McCall, Phillips, Toler & Sarpy, New Orleans, 1980-84; prin. Bruce C. Butcher, P.C., Metairie, La., 1985-93; of counsel Smith Martin & Schneider, New Orleans, 1993-94; gen. coun. The Vulcan Group, Birmingham, Ala., 1994-95, Favalora Constructors, Inc., 1995—; pres., gen. counsel Tailgators Restaurant, LLC, New Orleans, LA, 1994—. Mem. ABA (regional chmn. pub. report 1975, state chmn. pub. contracts sect. 1984-95, cert. of performance 1975), La. Bar Assn., Am. Arbitration Assn., New Orleans Country Club (pres. 1994), New Orleans Squash Club, Crescent Club. Home: 344 Homestead Ave Metairie LA 70005-3707 Office: 933 Metairie Rd Metairie LA 70005-4037

BUTCHER, DUANE CLEMENS, economist, consultant; b. Okla. City, Sept. 12, 1939; s. Cecil E. and Helen Louise (Clemens) B.; m. Barbara Needham, Feb. 2, 1963; children: Duane C. Jr., Christopher N. BA in Polit. Sci., Okla. State U., 1961; MA in Econs., Princeton U., 1970. Various positions foreign svc. U.S. Dept. State, Washington, 1962-74; econs. officer U.S. Embassy, Jidda, Saudi Arabia, 1974-76, Stockholm, Sweden, 1976-80; counselor for econ. affairs U.S. Embassy, Nairobi, Kenya, 1980-83; spl. asst. to gov. Office of the Gov., Denver, 1983-84; econ. counselor U.S. Embassy, Bonn, Germany, 1984-86, New Delhi, India, 1986-89; sr. fellow Ctr. Study Fgn. Affairs, Washington, 1989-91; coord. Kuwait Task Force, 1990; cons. Global Bus. Assocs., Grand Junction, Colo., 1991—. Author (booklet) Campaign for Quality, 1984; (with others) Computer Integrated Manufacturing, 1992. Democrat. Avocations: running, scuba diving. Home and Office: 408 1/2 Ridgeway Dr Grand Junction CO 81503-1652

BUTCHER, FRED R., biochemistry educator, university administrator; b. Rochester, Pa., Aug. 11, 1943; s. Goble S. and Monnie (Gibson) B.; m. Letty Jean Lytton, June 19, 1965; children: Allen Ray, Amy Jo. B.S., Ohio State U., 1965, Ph.D., 1969. Postdoctorial fellow U. Wis., Madison, 1969-71; asst. prof. Brown U., Providence, 1971-76; assoc. prof. Brown U., 1976-78; prof. W.Va. U., Morgantown, 1978—; chmn. dept. biochemistry W.Va. U., 1981-84, assoc. dean Sch. Medicine, 1984-89, dir. MBR Cancer Ctr., 1989—, sr. assoc. v.p., 1993—. Mem. Am. Soc. Biol. Chemists. Home: RD 1 Box 242 Independence WV 26374 Office: WVa U Mary Babb Randolph Cancer Ctr PO Box 9300 Morgantown WV 26506-9300

BUTCHER, JACK ROBERT (JACK RISIN), manufacturing executive; b. Akron, Ohio, Dec. 10, 1941; s. William Hobart and Marguerite Bell (Dalton) B.; m. Gloria Jean Hartman, June 1, 1963 (dec. July 1995); children: Jack R. II, William H. (dec. 1970), Charlotte Jean. BA in Math., Jacksonville U., 1964; cert. mgmt. consulting, Akron U., 1979; cert. paralegal, CCT Inst., 1990; cert. radio broadcasting, Chaffey Coll., 1994. Pres. Portableacher Corp., Hesperia, Calif., 1977—; v.p. Nice Day Products, Hesperia, 1980-85; pres. The Mark of Profl. Mgmt. and Design Co., Hesperia, 1983—, Nice Day Products, Hesperia, 1985—; owner The Movie Funding Without Risk Co., 1996—; bd. govs. Internat. Platform Assn., 1996—; co-owner JB Scale Co., Hesperia, Calif., 1991—; acting, voice-overs and commls. Film Industry Workshop Sch. of Acting, 1995—. Author: (poems) Something Good, 1978, Forever My Valentine, 1996; patentee in field. Mem. Internat. Platform Assn. (bd. govs. 1996—, Silver Bowl award 1995), Screen Actors Guild, Masons, Shriners, Royal Order of Jesters. Avocations: hunting, travel, designing, acting, commercial voice-overs. Office: PO Box 402540 Hesperia CA 92340-2540

BUTCHER, RUSSELL DEVEREUX, author, photographer; b. Bryn Mawr, Pa., Feb. 8, 1938; s. Devereux and Mary Frances (Taft) B.; student Colo. State U., 1957-58; BA, U. Colo., 1960; postgrad. U. Mich. Law Sch., 1960-61; m. Pamela Richards, Apr. 12, 1967 (div. 1993); children: Pamela Marie (dec.), Neill Devereux, Wendy Nan; m. Karen T. Black, Nov. 29, 1997. Rsch. editor Sierra Club, San Francisco, 1961-65; editl. writer N.Y. Times, 1963-79; publicity writer Save-the-Redwoods League, San Francisco, 1963-65; conservation specialist Nat. Audubon Soc., N.Y.C., 1965-66, also mem. editl. bd. Audubon mag.; chief of pub. rels. and publs. Mus. of N.Mex., Santa Fe, 1967-69; free-lance writer, photographer and author, 1969-80; conservation zoning cons. Town of Mount Desert (Maine), 1978-79, SW and Calif. rep. Nat. Parks and Conservation Assn., 1980-90, Pacific S.W. regional dir., 1990-93, NPCA fellow, 1993-99; manuscript editor KC Publs., 1985-88. Mem. Ariz. Strip Dist. adv. coun. U.S. Bur. Land Mgmt., 1983-90, Phoenix Dist. adv. coun. U.S. Bureau Land Mgmt., 1991-94; bd. dirs. Friends Saguaro Nat. Pk., 1997—. Mem. Save-the-Redwoods League (life), Nat. Parks and Conservation Assn., Maine Audubon Soc. (pres. Down East chpt. 1978-80, trustee 1979-80), Nat. Trust for Scotland, Friends of Lake Dist. Eng. (life), Sierra Club (life). Episcopalian (vestryman 1978-81). Author: Maine Paradise, 1973, New Mexico: Gift of the Earth, 1975, The Desert, 1976, Field Guide to Acadia National Park, Maine, 1977, Exploring Our National Parks and Monuments, 9th edit., 1995, Exploring Our National Historic Parks and Sites, 1997, National Park Discovery Guides, revised edit., 1999; contbr. articles to environ. jours. Address: 5948 N Misty Ridge Dr Tucson AZ 85718-3438

BUTCHER, VANESSA JEAN, critical care nurse; b. Norfolk, Va., Apr. 10, 1953; d. Conrad W. and Mary (Oreskovich) Stolman; m. Joseph Butcher, June 7, 1975; 1 child, Erin. AD, Purdue U. Calumet, Hammond, Ind., 1974, BS, 1978, MS, 1986. RN, Ill., Ind. Staff nurse CCU/IMCU St. Margaret Hosp. and Health Ctr., Hammond, 1974-82, coord. critical care edn., 1982-89; clin. specialist in critical care Palos Community Hosp., Palos Heights, Ill., 1989—; guest lectr. Purdue U.-Calumet, 1988—. Mem. AACN, Sigma Theta Tau Internat.

BUTCHKES, SYDNEY, artist; b. Covington, Ky., Oct. 13, 1922; s. Isadore and Bertha (Gussis) B. Student, Cin. Art Acad., 1936-40, Art Students League, N.Y.C., 1940-42, New Sch., N.Y.C., 1957-59. Exhibited one-man shows, Amel Gallery, N.Y.C., 1966, Bertha Schaefer Gallery, N.Y.C., 1969, 71, 73, Benson Gallery, Bridgehampton, N.Y., 1971, 76, 80, 91, Alonzo Gallery, N.Y.C., 1978, Touchstone Gallery, N.Y.C., 1982, Benson Gallery, Bridgehampton N.Y., 1986, 89, 98, Bace Gallery, Southampton, 1993; Bujese Gallery, E. Hampton, 1998; group shows Mus. Modern Art, N.Y.C., 1964, San Francisco Mus., 1967, Inst. Contemporary Art, Boston, 1969, Robert Elkon Gallery, N.Y.C., 1974, 76; pub. collections: Bklyn. Mus., Cin. Mus. Art, Wadsworth Atheneum, Hartford, Conn., Met. Mus. Art, N.Y.C., Nat. Collection of Smithsonian Inst., Washington, Newark Mus. Served with U.S. Army, 1942-45. Hon. fellow Am. Craft Council; mem. Abstract Am. Artists. Home: Sagg Main St Sagaponack NY 11962-9999

BUTCHVAROV, PANAYOT KRUSTEV, philosophy educator; b. Sofia, Bulgaria, Apr. 2, 1933; s. Krustyu Panayotov and Vanya (Tsaneva) B.; m. Sue Graham, Sept. 28, 1954; children: Vanya, Christopher. BA, Robert Coll., Istanbul, 1952; MA, U. Va., 1954, PhD, 1955. Instr. philosophy U. Balt., 1955-56; asst. prof. U. S.C., 1956-59; asso. prof. Syracuse U., 1959-66, prof., 1966-68; vis. prof. U. Iowa, 1967-68, prof., 1968—, chmn. dept. philosophy, 1970-77; univ. found. disting. prof., 1995—; vis. prof. U. Miami, Coral Gables, Fla., 1979-80; Simon lectr. U. Toronto, 1984; guest prof. Akad. für Philosophie, Liechtenstein, 1997. Author: The Concept of Knowledge, 1970, Resemblance and Identity, 1966, Being Qua Being, 1979, Skepticism in Ethics, 1989, Skepticism About the External World, 1998; editor: Jour. Philosophical Rsch., 1993—; mem. editl. bd.: Midwest Studies in Philosophy, Philos. Monographs; contbr. numerous articles and revs. to profl. jours. Mem. Am. Philos. Assn. (chmn. program com. 1971, 75, nominating com. 1978, chmn. 1993-94, pres. ctrl. div. 1992-93), Ctrl. States Philos. Assn. (v.p. 1987-88, pres. 1988-89), Phi Beta Kappa. Home: 2507 Princeton Rd Iowa City IA 52245-3721

BUTEL, JANET SUSAN, virology educator; b. Overbrook, Kans., May 24, 1941; d. Floyd Charles and Berniece (Humbert) B.; m. David Yates Graham, Mar. 31, 1967; children: Susan Kathleen, David Peter. BS summa cum laude, Kans. State U., 1963; PhD with honors, Baylor U., 1966. Postdoctoral fellow Baylor Coll. Medicine, Houston, 1966-68; asst. prof. Houston, 1968-72; assoc. prof. Baylor U. Coll. Medicine, Houston, 1972-76, prof., 1976-95, head div. of molecular virology, 1989—; disting. svc. prof. Baylor Coll. Coll. Medicine, Houston, 1995—; Joseph L. Melnick prof. virology Houston, 1986; study sect. mem. NIH, Bethesda, Md., 1980-84; bd. sci. counselors Nat. Cancer Inst., Bethesda, 1985-89; mem. NIAID Coun., 1994—. Contbg. editor: Lange Med. Microbiology, 1987—; contbr. sci. articles to profl. jours. Grad. fellow NSF, 1963-66; rsch. grantee NIH, 1973—. Mem. AAAS, Am. Assn. for Cancer Rsch., Am. Soc. for Cell Biology, Am. Soc. for Microbiology (div. chair 1990-91, group IV rep. 1993-95), Am. Soc. for Virology, Internat. Assn. Breast Cancer Rsch. (bd. govs. Lakewood, Colo. 1987-91), Sigma Xi. Office: Baylor Coll Medicine One Baylor Pla Houston TX 77030*

BUTENHOFF, SUSAN, public relations executive; b. N.Y.C., Jan. 13, 1960. BA in Internat. Rels. with hons., Sussex U., Eng.; MPhil, Wolfson Coll., Cambridge U., Eng. Account exec. Ellen Farmer Prodns., 1984-85; account exec. Ketchum Pub. Rels., N.Y.C., 1988-90, v.p., account supr., 1990-91; prin., CEO Access Pub. Rels., San Francisco, 1991—. Mem. Pub. Rels. Soc. Am. Office: Access Comm 101 Howard St San Francisco CA 94105-1629*

BUTERA, ANN MICHELE, consulting company executive; b. Bayside, N.Y., Apr. 27, 1958; d. Gaetano Thomas and Josephine (Inserro) B. BA, L.I. U., 1979; MBA, Adelphi U., 1982. Dept. mgr. Abraham & Straus Stores, Huntington, N.Y., 1978-80; mgmt. cons. Chase Manhattan Bank N.A., Lake Success, N.Y., 1980-83, Nat. Bankcard Corp., Melville, N.Y., 1983-84; pres. Whole Person Project, Inc., Elmont, N.Y., 1984—. Bd. dirs. Nassau County coun. Girl Scouts U.S., 1985-95. Recipient Bus. Achievement award Women on the Job, 1990. Mem. NAFE, ASTD, Fin. Women Internat., L.I. Networking Entrepreneurs (pres. 1984-91), Inst. Internal Auditors, Assn. Govt. Auditors, L.I. Ctr. for Bus. and Profl. Women, World Futurists Soc. Republican. Roman Catholic. Avocations: tennis, dancing, gardening. Home and Office: Whole Person Project Inc 82 Cerenzia Blvd Elmont NY 11003-3631

BUTH, CARL EUGENE, civil engineer; b. Gatesville, Tex., June 17, 1940; married; three children. BS, Tex. A&M U., 1963, ME, 1964, PhD in Civil Engring., 1972. Rsch. asst. Tex. Transp. Inst., 1963-66, engr. rsch. assoc., 1966-68, 74-79, asst. rsch. engr., 1968-74, head, safety divsn., 1978—, rsch. engr., 1979—; head fabrication and testing sect. Tech. Support Svcs., 1969-70; head engring. and constrn. Proving Ground Rsch. Program, 1970-73, head, 1973-78; from instr. to asst. prof. civil engring. Tex. A&M U., 1974-79, assoc. prof. civil engring., 1977-82. Mem. NSPE, Am. Soc. Civil Engrs., Am. Soc. Engring. Edn., Sigma Xi. Office: Tex Transp Inst Tex A&M Univ MS 3135 College Station TX 77843-3135

BUTHMAN, NANCY SMITH, nurse practitioner, critical care nurse; b. Chgo.; d. Robertson and Ruth (Metcalf) Smith; m. G.B. Bostock, Aug. 1955 (dec. 1964); m. A.J. Buthman, Sept. 18, 1965 (div. 1977); children; David, Daniel, Mark, John, Jay, Lisa, Jim. BA in Psychology, Drew U., 1956; BSN, Rush U., 1977; MS in Mgmt. and Orgnl. Behavior, Ill. Benedictine Coll., 1988; MSN, Fla. Internat. U., 1996. RN, Ill., Fla; cert. instr. BLS and ACLS, Am. Heart Assn. Staff nurse surg. floor Rush Presbyn. St. Luke's Hosp., Chgo., 1977-78, staff nurse surg. ICU, 1978-80, asst. head nurse surg. ICU, 1980-81; clin. care instr. Edgewater Hosp., Chgo., 1981-82; unit mgr. ICU/critical care unit Luth. Gen. Hosp., Chgo., 1982-89; staff nurse cath. lab. Sarasota (Fla.) Meml. Hosp., 1989-90; dir. ICU and cardiac care unit Cape Coral (Fla.) Hosp., 1990-95; clin. coord. subacute care unit Integrated Health Svcs., Ft. Myers, Fla., 1995-96; nurse practitioner Family Health Ctrs., Ft. Myers, Fla., 1997—. Author, dir. video and teaching booklet: Mock Code, 1984 (Hon. Mention Critical Care award), Mock Code II, 1986. Mem. BLS affiliate faculty; mem. disaster med. assistance team U.S. Dept. Emergency Preparedness. Mem. AACN (cert. RN), Sigma Theta Tau. Avocations: family, reading, guitar, water sports. Home: 2534 SW 39th Ter Cape Coral FL 33914-5409

BUTHOD, MARY CLARE, school administrator; b. Tulsa, Aug. 20, 1945; d. Arthur Paul and Mary Rudelle (Dougherty) B. MA in Teaching, Tulsa U., 1969; M Christian Spirituality, Creighton U., 1981. Joined Order of St. Benedict. Asst. tchr. HeadStart, Tulsa, 1966; tchr. Madalene Parish Sch., Tulsa, 1968-69, Monte Cassino Pvt. Sch., Tulsa, 1969-79; prin. Monte Cassino Elem. Sch., Tulsa, 1979-86; dir. Monte Cassino Sch., Tulsa, 1986—; mem. convent coun. Benedictine Sisters, Tulsa, 1975-88, dir. formation programa, 1983—. Mem. State Congl. Ednl. Com., Tulsa, 1989-90; co-chair for edn. and human devel. Tulsa Coalition Against Illegal Use of Drugs, 1990-91; mem. adv. com. Schs. Attuned, U. N.C. Recognized for Excellence in Edn. U.S. Dept. Edn., 1993-94. Mem. Tulsa Reading Coun. (sec. 1975-77), Nat. Cath. Edn. Assn., Delta Kappa Gamma. Home: 2200 S Lewis Tulsa OK 74114-3117 Office: Monte Cassino Sch 2206 S Lewis Ave Tulsa OK 74114-3109

BUTKIN, ROBERT, state treasurer. Treas. State of Okla., Oklahoma City. Office: State of Okla Treas Office 217 State Capitol 2300 N Lincoln Blvd Oklahoma City OK 73105-4895*

BUTLAND, JEFFREY H., former state senator, retail company official; b. Portland, Dec. 7, 1950; m. Nancy Butland; children: Jenna, Meghan, Jeff. BA in Polit. Sci., Bates Coll. Vice chair Cumberland Town Coun., 1985-88; mem. Maine Ho. of Reps., Augusta, 1988-92; mem. Maine Senate, Augusta, 1992-95, pres., 1994-96; customer svc. rep. L.L. Bean, Inc., Freeport, Maine. former pres. Cumberland Hist. Soc.; former pres., bd. mem. People's Regional Opportunity Program; mem. MSAD # 51 Enrollment and Facilities Study Com., Maine Turnpike Authority Northern Corridor Com., Cumberland Mainland and Island Land Trust, Prince Meml. Libr. Bldg. Com. Maj. USMR ret. Republican. Address: PO Box 431 Cumberland Center ME 04021-0431*

BUTLER, ALAN M., retired physical education educator; b. Troy, N.Y., Feb. 28, 1934; s. Leonard and Anna (Kulick) B.; m. Millicent M., Apr. 14, 1957; children: Susan, Leonard. BS in Phys. Edn., SUNY, Cortland; MS in Phys. Edn., Springfield (Mass.) Coll. Phys. edn. tchr. Guilderland (N.Y.) Cen. Schs., 1957; phys. edn. tchr. Herricks Jr. High Sch., New Hyde Park, N.Y., 1957-64, coach various sports, 1986-87, dir. athletics, chmn. phys. edn. dept., 1987-89; dist. dir. phys. edn. and athletics Southold Schs., New Hyde Park, 1997-98; dean Southold Athletics, 1997-98; owner Prostar Promotions, 1996—; adj. prof. St John's U., 1993-94; dir. Nassau County Vol. Coaches' Inst., 1988; creator first area Summer Sports Acad., New Hyde Park, 1987; owner, dir. Whizzer Sports Camp, others. Mem. prog. com. for drug edn., 1985; mem. ednl. com. for coaches of pre-adolescents, N.Y. State Sports Authority, Nassau Community Coll., 1975-81, others; mgr. U.S. Macabee Wrestling Team, 1969. Recipient R.T. French award, 1981; Nassau County Lacrosse Coach of Yr., 1968; named All North Soccer Goalie, All N.Y. State Goalie in Lacrosse, others. Mem. NEA, N.Y. State Tchrs. Assn., N.Y. State Coaches Assn., N.Y. State Assn. for Health, Phys. Edn. and Recreation (pres. 1984-86, Amazing Phys. Educator award 1985), AAHPERD (Merit award 1986), Nat. Soc. Sports Edn. Avocations: tennis, golf. Home: 29 Myron Rd Plainview NY 11803-6434

BUTLER, ALICE CLAIRE, rehabilitation nurse; b. Lander, Wyo., Sept. 9, 1925; d. Donald A. and Violet C. (Carney) Sherlock; m. Harry Wallace Butler, July 25, 1948 (dec. Feb. 1994); children: Gladys Norene, Linda Marie, Janet Christine, Mary Alice, David Paul, Anna Louise, Rebecca Ruth, Philip Clyde, John Glenn, James Sheldon. ADN, Penn Valley C.C., 1976; AA, Kansas City (Mo.) Jr. Coll., 1949; BA in Elem. Edn., U. Mo., Kansas City, 1986. RN, Mo. Charge nurse Rehab. Inst., Kansas City; asst. dir. nursing Children's Mercy Hosp., Kansas City, 1977-81; staff relief nurse Clara Manor Nursing Home, Kansas City; part-time nursing coord. Park Lane Med. Ctr., Kansas City. Mem. Assn. Rehab. Nurses (cert.), Mo. League for Nursing, Nat. League for Nursing. Home: 4311 Campbell St Kansas City MO 64110-1621

BUTLER, BRETT, comedian, actress; b. Montgomery, AL, 1958; d. Roland Decatur Anderson, Jr. and Carol; adoptive parent Bob Butler; m. Charles Wilson, 1978 (div. 1981); m. Ken Ziegler, 1987. Waitress Houston, TX, 1981-82; stand-up comedian, 1982—. Star, exec. prodr. TV series Grace Under Fire, 1993-98; appeared on TV in It's Just A Ride, 1994; in film Bruno, 1999; TV film It's Just a Ride, 1994. Office: ABC 9100 Wilshire Blvd Ste 401 Beverly Hills CA 90212-3415*

BUTLER, BYRON CLINTON, obstetrician, gynecologist; b. Carroll, Iowa, Aug. 10, 1918; 1; s. Clinton John and Blance (Prall) B.; m. Jo Ann Nicolls; children: Marilyn, John Byron, Barbara, Denise; 1 stepdau., Marrianne. MD, Columbia Coll. Physicians and Surgeons, 1943; ScD, Columbia U., 1952; G.G. grad. gemologist, Gemol. Inst. Am., 1986. Diplomate Am. Bd. Ob/Gyn. Intern Columbia Presbyn. Med. Ctr.; resident Sloane Hosp. for Women; instr. Columbia Coll. Physicians and Surgeons, 1950-53; dir. Butler Rsch. Found., Phoenix, 1953-86, pres., 1970—; ret. as gyn. surgeon, 1989; pres. World Gems/G.S.G., Scottsdale, Ariz., 1979—, World Gems Software, 1988, World Gems Jewelry, 1990—; cosmologist, jewelry designer Extra-Terrestrial-Alien Jewelry & Powerful Personal Talismans, 1992—, 3rd Millineum Line of Tektite Jewelry, 1994—; cons. in diagnosis, treatment, prognosis of HIV, AIDS, sexually transmitted diseases, 1975. Patentee in field. Bd. dirs. Heard Mus., Phoenix, 1965-74; founder Dr. Byron C. Butler, G.G., Fund for Inclusion Research, Gemol. Inst. Am., Carlsbad, Calif., 1987. Served to capt. M.C. AUS, 1944-46. Grantee Am. Cancer Soc., 1946-50, NIH, 1946-50, 50-53. Fellow Mufon, Mutual UFO Networks. Featured in Life; patentee in field; discovery of cause of acute fibrinolysis in humans; research on use hypnosis for relief of pain in cancer patients, use of tPA (tissue plaminogen activator) in acute coronary occlusion treatment, research in indochinite tektite origins, chemical analysis, radioactive ingredients, psychic powers; designer jewelry using polished tektite, finder tplasminogen as cause of incoaguable blood during premature separation of placenta in pregnancy. Home and Office: 77 E Missouri Ave Unit 20 Phoenix AZ 85012-1380

BUTLER, CAROL KING, advertising executive; b. Charlotte, N.C., May 29, 1952; d. Charles Snowden Watts and Marion (Thomas) King; m. James Rodney Butler, Aug. 12, 1972 (div. 1975). Student U. N.C., Greensboro, 1970-72, U. N.C., Charlotte, 1997—. Sales rep. Sta.-WKIX, Raleigh, N.C., 1978-82, N.C. Box, Inc., Raleigh, 1982-84; radio sales account exec. WRAL-FM, Raleigh, 1984-88, team sales mgr., 1989; prin. Butler-Smith Assocs., Raleigh, 1988-89; ind. programming and video producer, Raleigh, 1989-90; prin., freelance presentation/video script writer, producer and sales person, Carol Butler Sales Writer/Photographer, 1991—; sales mgr. BW Territory of Lifetouch, 1996; creative cons. Creative Comms., 1997-98. Democrat. Mem. Unity Ch. Avocations: water skiing, golf, tennis, boating, bicycling. Home: 1600 Blue Moss Point Dr Charlotte NC 28214

BUTLER, CHARLES RANDOLPH, JR., federal judge; b. 1940. BA, Washington and Lee U., 1962; LLB, U. Ala., 1966. Assoc. Hamilton Butler Riddick and LaTour, Mobile, Alal., 1966-69; asst. pub. defender Mobile County, 1969-70, dist. atty., 1971-75; ptnr. Butler and Sullivan, Mobile, 1975-84, Hamilton Butler Riddick Tarlton and Sullivan P.C., Mobile, 1984-88; dist. judge U.S. Dist. Ct. (so. dist.) Ala., Mobile, 1988-94, chief dist. judge, 1994—; adj. prof. criminal justice program U. So. Ala., 1972-76. Active UMS Prep. Sch. Alumni Assn. Ist lt. USAR, 1962-64. Named One of Outstanding Young Men of Am., Mobile County Jaycees, 1971. Mem. Ala. Bar Assn., Mobile County Bar Assn. (jud. coun. 11th cir., jud. conf. com. on criminal law, jud. conf. com. 1999—). Office: US Dist Ct 113 Saint Joseph St Mobile AL 36602-3683

BUTLER, CHARLES THOMAS, museum director, curator; b. Pearisburg, Va., Apr. 20, 1951; s. John Thomas Butler and Luenette (Evans) Hughes; m. Marilyn Laufer, Oct. 28, 1979. BA cum laude, U. Del., 1976; postgrad., U. N.Mex., Albuquerque, 1976-78. Asst. dir. Sioux City (Iowa) Art Ctr., 1979-85; exec. dir. Mitchell Mus., Mt. Vernon, Ill., 1985-88, Huntington (W.Va.) Mus. Art, 1988-94, Columbus (Ga.) Mus., 1994—. Author: New Talent/New York, 1984, Gary Bowling Paintings, 1987, Recent Graphics from American Print Shops, 1986, Out of the Mainstream: Photographs by Dick Arentz, 1991, Close to the Surface: Expressionist Prints of Edvard Munch and Richard Bosman, 1996. Bd. dirs. Southea. Mus. Conf., 1990—. Mem. Southea. Mus. Assn., Assn. Art Mus. Dirs., Mus. Trustee Assn. (chair adv. coun. 1998—), Am. Assn. Mus., Rotary. Office: Columbus Mus 1251 Wynnton Rd Columbus GA 31906-2899

BUTLER, DAREL ANTHONY, neurologist; b. Holly Springs, Miss., Apr. 5, 1961. BA in Biology cum laude, Harvard U., 1983; MD, U. Calif., San Francisco, 1989. Diplomate Am. Bd. Psychiatry and Neurology. Intern in medicine Pacific Presbyn. Med. Ctr. (now Calif. Pacific Med. Ctr.), San Francisco, 1989-90; resident in neurology U. Calif., San Francisco, 1991-94, clin. instr. neurology, 1994-96; clin. asst. prof. U. Tenn. Ctr. Health Scis., 1996—; neurologist Wesley Neurology Clinic, P.C., Memphis, Tenn., 1996—; dir. We CARE!, 1996—. Contbr. articles to profl. jours. Advisor U. Calif., San Francisco Student Nat. Med. Assn., 1993-96, Black Students Health Alliance, 1993-96, mem. Med. Student Mentor Program, 1994-96. Recipient Rsch. award U. Calif. San Francisco/San Francisco Found., 1986, Alpha Kappa Alpha Cmty. Svc. award, 1998, Living Legend award Tenn. Black

Caucus State Legis., 1998; Nat. Med. fellow, 1983, 84; Rsch. fellow Alpha Omega Alpha, 1988; Med. Rsch. fellow Commonwealth Fund, 1988; Fondation pour la Recherche Medicale, 1990; Bourse Chateaubriand, Ambassade France aux Etas-Unis, 1990; Robert Derzon-Darel Butler Fund established in his honor by U. Calif. San Francisco, 1993; Clin. Investigator Devel. grantee NIH/NINDS, 1994-96. Mem. AMA, AAAS, Nat. Med. Assn., Am. Acad. Neurology. Fax: 901-725-8934. Office: Wesley Neurology Clinic 1211 Union Ave Ste 400 Memphis TN 38104

BUTLER, DARTHA JEAN, middle school educator; b. Hickory Flat, Miss., Jan. 27, 1940; d. Alvie Vernan and Lera (Knox) Robbins; m. Robert Eugene Butler, June 9, 1963; children: Susan, Robin, Nina. BA, Blue Mountain Coll., 1961; postgrad., Tulane U., 1962; MEd, Henderson State U., 1978. Cert. English, social studies and higher edn. tchr., Ark. Social worker Miss. State Dept. Welfare, 1961-63, Kern County Welfare-Adoptions, Bakersfield, Calif., 1963-65, Alexandria (La.) Dept. Child Svcs., 1966-67; tchr. Arkadelphia (Ark.) Sch. Dist., 1979—. Stephens min. First Meth. Ch., Arkadelphia, 1995—. Ross Found./Arkadelphia C. of C. grantee, 1990-98. Mem. Am. Fedn. Tchrs. (sec.), Ark. Fedn. Tchrs. (sec.). Democrat. Methodist. Avocations: gardening, sewing, reading, crocheting. Home: 2817 Sylvia St Arkadelphia AR 71923-5326 Office: Goza Jr HS 1305 Caddo St Arkadelphia AR 71923-5705

BUTLER, DAVID, lawyer; b. St. Paul, June 11, 1930; s. Francis David and Alida (Bigelow) B.; m. Diana Dodge Duffy, Aug. 29, 1952 (div. 1957); children: Anne, Lawrence David; m. Barbara Williams Clark, July 12, 1958; children: Molly Elizabeth, Peter, Katherine. BA, Princeton U., 1952; LLB, Harvard U., 1957. Bar. Colo. 1958, U.S. Dist. Ct. Colo. 1958. Assoc. Holland & Hart, Denver, 1957-63, ptnr., 1963-95, chmn. mgmt. com., 1990-95; of counsel, 1996—; gen. counsel 1st Interstate Bank Denver, 1984-86; bd. dirs. UMB Bank Colo., Denver. Mem. bd. editors Harvard Law Rev., 1955-57. Chmn. lawyers adv. com. United Way, Denver, 1989-94; bd. dirs. Met. Denver Legal Aid Soc., 1971-74; trustee Graland Country Day Sch., Denver, 1971-79, Legal Aid Found. Colo., 1991-97, chmn., 1993-97; chmn. Colo. Planning Group for Legal Svcs. to the Poor. 1st lt. U.S. Army, 1952-54. Mem. ABA, Colo. Bar Assn. (chmn. tax sect. 1970), Denver Bar Assn. Office: Holland & Hart 555 17th St Ste 2900 Denver CO 80202-3979

BUTLER, DENA LOUISE, mathematics educator; b. Las Cruces, N.Mex., July 7, 1951; d. Alfred August and Auda Frances Schoolcraft; m. Ronald Wayne Butler, Mar. 28, 1972; children: Amy Myriah, Jason Wayne. BA in Math. and English, Ea. N.Mex. U., 1973; MA in Computers, Lesley Coll., 1986; MA in Edn. Adminstrn., U. Denver, 1994. Self-employed Tool Mender, Evergreen, Colo., 1975-82; math. tchr. Littleton (Colo.) Pub. Schs., 1982—. Leader Girl Scouts U.S.A., Evergreen, 1982-86; coach asst. Stingers Soccer, Evergreen, 1985-90. Avocations: needlework, knitting. Office: Goddard Mid Sch 3800 W Berry Ave Littleton CO 80123

BUTLER, ETHEL VIEIRA, utilization review nurse; b. New Bedford, Mass., Aug. 14, 1923; d. Antonio C. and Marianna (Cieto) Vieira; m. Donald P. Butler, May 30, 1964; children: Marianna Margaret, Ramona Louise. RN, St. Luke's Hosp., 1945; student, Boston Coll., 1950. RN, Mass., R.I. Head nurse Truesdale Hosp., Fall Rivers, Mass.; office nurse Dr. William E. Kenney, Fall Rivers; utilization rev. coord. St. Anne's Hosp., Fall Rivers; dir. quality assurance, utilization rev. and risk mgmt. St. Luke's Hosp., Middleboro, Mass.; utilization rev. coord. Morton Hosp., Taunto, Mass. Past. mem. Libr. Trustees, Swansea; past chair Swansea Cancer Crusade, Heart Fund.; vol. Jarabek Ctr., Charleston, Meml. Hosp., Fall River, Mass. With U.S. mil., 1942-45. Mem. ANA, Mass. Nurses Assn., Mass. Assn. Quality Assurance Profl., Cath. Nurse's Guild (past pres.), St. Luke's Hosp. Alumni Assn. Home: 21 Coleman St Swansea MA 02777-2101

BUTLER, FREDERICK GEORGE, retired drug company executive; b. Greenwich, Conn., Mar. 25, 1919; s. Harold Nassau and Rosa (Rhinhart) B.; m. Sarah Lou Allred, Sept. 23, 1945; children: Pamela Sue, Frederick Houston. AB, Middlebury (Vt.) Coll., 1941; MBA, Columbia U., 1947. CPA, N.Y. With Price Waterhouse & Co. (C.P.A.'s), 1941-42, 47-49; with McKesson & Robbins, Inc., N.Y.C., 1949-63; asst. comptroller McKesson & Robbins, Inc., 1952-61, comptroller, 1961-63; controller Bristol-Myers Co., N.Y.C., 1963-66; v.p., controller Bristol-Myers Co., 1966-69, v.p. ops., 1970-76. Pioneered developement of bar code (compatible universal product code and nat. drug code) for supermarket automated checkout scanning and inventory control. Village mayor, Briarcliff Manor, N.Y., 1969-71. Served to comdr. USNR, 1942-46, 51-52. Mem. Fin. Execs. Inst., Fairfield Mountains Club (Bald Mountain and Apple Valley, N.C.), Pres.'s Club, Hillsdale (Mich.) Coll., Chi Psi. Methodist. Home: 58 N Collier Blvd Apt 2103 Marco Island FL 34145-3754

BUTLER, GEOFFREY SCOTT, systems engineer, educator, consultant; b. Jacksonville, Fla., July 19, 1958; s. George Lauritzen and Mary Elizabeth (Cox) B.; m. Diana Lynn Martin, Aug. 29, 1987. BS in Aerospace Engring., U. Fla., 1981; MS in Aerospace Engring., San Diego State U., 1986; MS in Aerospace Systems, West Coast U., 1988. Engr. Lockheed Missiles & Space Co., Sunnyvale, Calif., 1981-83; engring. specialist Convair div. Gen. Dynamics, San Diego, 1983-92; project mgr. Horizons Tech., Inc., San Diego, 1992-95, Marconi Integrated Sys., Inc., 1995—; tech. program chmn. 13th Applied Aerodynamics Conf.; cons. WEB Engring., San Diego, 1992—. Contbr. articles to profl. publs. Speaker Scott's Valley Homeowners Assn., Encinitas, Calif., 1992. Mem. AIAA (sr. mem., tech. com. mem. 1992—). Republican. Roman Catholic. Achievements include conception and direction of first tests of store separation at hypersonic speeds within a ballistic range, specialized software development activities. Avocations: surfing, skiing, model aircraft. Office: Marconi Integrated Sys Inc PO Box 509008 San Diego CA 92150-9008

BUTLER, GEORGE FRANK, editor, literary historian; b. Bridgeport, Conn., 1962; s. Stanley M. and Wanda F. Butler. AB, Lafayette Coll., 1984; MA, U. Conn., 1985, PhD, 1988. Cert. Inst. for Effective Teaching, Conn. Teaching asst. U. Conn., Storrs, 1984-88; acquisitions editor Greenwood Pub. Group, Westport, Conn., 1990-93, assoc. editor acquisitions, 1993-99, sr. editor, 1999—; invited spkr. mid-winter conv. ALA, Denver, 1993, panelist, Phila., 1995, San Antonio, 1996. Contbr. articles and revs. to profl. jours. Predoctoral fellow U. Conn., 1984; State of Conn. scholar, 1980; Francis A. March fellow Lafayette Coll., 1984. Mem. MLA, Renaissance Soc. Am., Milton Soc. Am. (life). Roman Catholic.

BUTLER, GRACE CAROLINE, medical administrator; b. Lima, Peru, Dec. 19, 1937; (parents Am. citizens); d. Everett Lyle and Mary Isabella (Sloatman) Gage; m. William Langdon Butler, Dec. 28, 1961; children: Mary Dyer, William Langdon Jr. AA, Stephens Coll., 1957; BS in Nursing, Columbia U., 1960; postgrad., Union County Coll., 1984. Head nurse N.Y. State Psychiat. Inst., N.Y.C., 1960-61; clin. instr. Columbia U., N.Y.C., 1960-61; staff nurse, educator Vis. Nurse Service, Summit, N.J., 1962-63; health adminstr. Eagle Island Girl Scout Camp, Tupper Lake, N.Y., 1964; evening supr. Ashbrook Nursing Home, Scotch Plains, N.J., 1968-72; teaching asst. Scotch Plains-Fanwood (N.J.) Sch. System, 1975-78; staff nurse Westfield (N.J.) Med. Group, 1980-82, head nurse, 1982-83, supr., 1983-84; office adminstr. Harris S. Vernick, MD, PA, Westfield, 1984-86, corp. v.p., office adminstr., 1986-88; corp. v.p., office adminstr. Assocs. in Medicine, Westfield, 1988-90; pvt. researcher, 1990—; diabetes educator Boehringer Manneheim Diagnostics, 1984—, Eli Lilly and Co., Indpls., 1984—; microbiologist tester Med. Technol. Corp., Somerset, N.J., 1984—; computer advisor Cordis Corp., Miami, 1985—. Asst. leader Girl Scouts U.S., Fanwood, N.J., 1970-73; religious educator All Saints Episcopal Ch., Scotch Plains, 1967-82; bd. dirs. PTA, Scotch Plains and Fanwood, 1973-79; mem. altar guild All Saints Episcopal Ch., Scotch Plains, 1994—, mem. vestry, 1999—. Mem. League For Ednl. Advancement for Registered Nurses, Am. Soc. of Notaries, Columbia U./Presbyn. Hosp. Sch. of Nursing Alumni Assn. Republican. Episcopalian. Avocations: sewing, water sports, gardening, wood refinishing. Home: 125 Russell Rd Fanwood NJ 07023-1063

BUTLER, HENRY JAMES, academic administrator, consultant; b. Ft. Belvoir, Va., Dec. 29, 1956; s. Arthur George and Marie Louise (DeVos) B. BA in Creating Writing for Lit. and Performing Arts, U. Fla., 1980. Reporter Ind. Fla. Alligator, Gainesville, 1976-79, Ind. Profl., Gainesville, 1980-83, Bus. Jour., Gainesville, 1983-85; news editor North Fla. Bus. Jour., Gainesville, 1985-87; editor-in-chief Gainesville Voice, 1986-89; freelance writer Gainesville, 1977—; computer cons. Ergonomic Sys. Integration, Gainesville, 1984—; chair gen. edn. dept. City Coll., Gainesville, 1990—. Contbr. articles to profl. jours. Trustee Libr. Internet Resource Network. Mem. MLA, North Fla. Motion Picture and TV Arts. Democrat. Roman Catholic. Avocations: scuba, sailing. Office: City Coll 2400 SW 13th St Gainesville FL 32605

BUTLER, IAN JOHN, neurologist; b. Adelaide, Australia, Sept. 19, 1941; came to U.S., 1972; s. John Alfred and Susan Pearl (Matters) B.; m. Patricia Mary Gordon, Feb. 28, 1969; children: Sarah, Katherine, Philip. MBBS, U. Adelaide, 1964. Diplomate Am. Bd. Psychiatry and Neurology. Resident Adelaide (Australia) Childrens Hosp., 1966-67; med. registrar Royal Childrens Hosp., Victoria, Australia, 1968; fellow neurology U. Melbourne, Victoria, 1969; sr. house officer Hosp. for Sick Children, London, 1970; registrar U. Wales Hosp., Cardiff, 1971; resident neurology, asst. prof. Johns Hopkins Univ. Hosp., Balt., 1972-76; assoc. prof. neurology U. Tex., Houston, 1976-79, prof. neurology and pediatrics, 1979—; prof. pediatrics dept. M.D. Anderson Cancer Ctr., Houston, 1980—; assoc. prof. Grad. Sch. Biomed. Scis., U. Tex. Health Sci. Ctr., Houston, 1978—; cons., dir. neuromuscular clinic Shrine Hosp., Houston; lectr. in field. Mem. editl. bd. Jour. Child Neurology, 1987—, assoc. editor, 1990—; contbr. articles to profl. jours. Chmn. prof. adv. com. Ctr. for Retarded, Inc., 1981—, bd. govs. mem., 1981—. Grantee Huntington Chorea Found., 1977-79, NSF, 1978, March of Dimes, 1978-80, Am. Parkinson Disease Assn., 1980-83, Epilepsy Ctr. Baylor Coll. Medicine, 1984-86, 88-93, Brandt Family Found., 1986, Meadows Found., 1986-91, Muscular Dystrophy Assn., 1988-90, 90-91, 91-93, NIH, 1989-94, 91-94, Shriner Hosp. for Crippled Children, 1990-93, 93-94, 95-97, 96-99, NASA, 1991-93. Fellow Royal Soc. Medicine, Royal Australasian Coll. Physicians; mem. AAAS, Am. Neurol. Assn., Assn. Rsch. in Nervous and Mental Disease, Am. Acad. Neurology, Soc. Neurosci., Internat. Child Neurology Assn., Child Neurology Soc., N.Y. Acad. Scis., Tex. Med. Assn., Harris County Med. Soc., Houston Pediatric Soc., Houston Neurol. Soc., Alpha Omega Alpha. Episcopalian. Avocations: music, reading, tennis. Home: 2200 Glen Haven Blvd Houston TX 77030-3606 Office: Univ Tex Dept Neurology 6431 Fannin St Ste 7044 Houston TX 77030-1501

BUTLER, J. BRADWAY, lawyer; b. Orange, N.J., Feb. 10, 1941. BA, Harvard U., 1963; LLB, U. Minn., 1966; LLM, George Washington U., 1968. Bar: D.C. 1969, U.S. Ct. Appeals (D.C. cir.) 1974. Mem. Arnold & Porter, Washington. Office: Arnold & Porter Thurman Arnold Bldg 555 12th St NW Washington DC 20004-1206*

BUTLER, JACK FAIRCHILD, semiconductors company executive; b. El Centro, Calif., July 18, 1933; s. Jack Orval and Dorothy (Marsh) B.; m. Colette Alice Guerard, Sept. 6, 1959; children—Alice, Jack, Michael, Patricia. Student, San Jose State Coll., 1951-54; B.S., U. Calif., Berkeley, 1959, M.S., 1960, Ph.D., 1962. Research staff mem. Mass. Inst. Tech., Lincoln Lab., Lexington, Mass., 1962-68; staff scientist Gen. Dynamics Corp., Pomona, Calif., 1968-71; sr. staff mem. Arthur D. Little, Inc., Cambridge, Mass., 1971-74; co-founder, co-owner, dir., pres. Laser Analytics, Inc., Lexington, 1974-81; founder, owner, dir., pres. Butler Research and Engring., Inc., 1981-85; co-founder, co-owner, dir., pres. San Diego Semicondrs., Inc., 1985-91, Aurora Techs. Corp., 1991-95; co-founder, co-owner, pres. Digirad (formerly Aurora Techs. Corp.), 1995—. Contbr. articles to sci. jours. Served with USMC, 1954-57. Mem. IEEE, Am. Inst. Physics, AAAS, Gen. Soc. Mayflower Descendants.

BUTLER, JAMES NEWTON, chemist, educator; b. Cleveland, Ohio, Mar. 27, 1934; s. Clyde Henry and Margaret (Manor) B.; m. Nancy Elizabeth Close, Aug. 31, 1957 (div.); 1 son, Christopher J.; m. Rosamond Hatch Bee, Dec. 10, 1966; stepchildren: Alden G. Bee, Kenneth M. Bee. BS, Rensselaer Poly. Inst., 1955; PhD, Harvard U., 1959. Staff scientist NACA Lewis Lab., Cleve., summers 1952-57, MIT Lincoln Lab., summer 1958; instr. U. B.C., Vancouver, 1959-61, asst. prof., 1961-63; sr. scientist Tyco Labs., Inc., Waltham, Mass., 1963-66, dept. head, 1966-71, cons., 1962-63, 71-73; lectr. Harvard U., 1970-71, Gordon McKay prof. applied chemistry, 1971—, mem. faculty geol. scis., 1972-86, mem. com. on oceanography, 1972-90, mem. faculty earth and planetary scis., 1986—; mem. steering com. co-author report Petroleum in the Marine Environment, Nat. Acad. Scis.—NRC, 1973-75, 80-82; mem. tech. panel, report drafting com. Com. on Environ. Decision-Making, 1975-77; chmn. com. on effectiveness of oil spill dispersants, NRC, 1985-89; cons. EPA, 1978— , NOAA, 1981—. Author: Ionic Equilibrium, 1964, rev. edit., 1998, Solubility and pH Calculations, 1964, The Calculus of Chemistry, 1965, Problems for Introductory University Chemistry, 1967, Pelagic Tar from Bermuda and the Sargasso Sea, 1973, Carbon Dioxide Equilibria and Their Applications, 1982, reprinted, 1991, Studies of Sargassum and the Sargassum Community, 1983, Using Oil Spill Dispersants on the Sea, 1989, The Exxon Valdez Oil Spill: Fate and Effects in Alaskan Waters, 1995; also articles. Trustee Bermuda Biol. Sta., 1972—, v.p., 1985-86, 89-93, pres., 1986-89. NSF Faculty Sci. fellow, 1977; Alumni scholar Relsselaer Poly. Inst., 1955, NSF fellow, GE fellow Harvard U., 1959. Mem. Am. Chem. Soc., AAAS, Am. Soc. Limnology and Oceanography, Internat. Soc. Electrochemistry, Electrochem. Soc. N.Y. (chmn. Boston sect.), Gordon Research Conf. on Electrochemistry (chmn.), Assn. Harvard Chemists (pres.), Sigma Xi, Phi Lambda Upsilon. Office: Harvard U Div Applied Scis Pierce Hall 29 Oxford St Cambridge MA 02138-2901

BUTLER, JAVED, internist; b. Karachi, Sindh, Pakistan, Oct. 4, 1965; came to U.S., 1991; s. Abdur Rehman and Sharifa (Banu) B. Higher secondary cert. in Biology, Adamjee Sci. Coll., Karachi, Pakistan, 1983; MBBS in Medicine, Aga Khan U., Karachi, Pakistan, 1990; MPH, Harvard U., 1999. Diplomate Am. Bd. Internal Medicine; lic. MD, Conn. Intern dept. internal medicine/primary care Yale U. Sch. Medicine, New Haven, 1991-92, jr. asst. resident, 1992-93, sr. asst. resident, 1993-94, chief med. resident, instr. medicine, 1994-95; fellow in cardiovascular scis. Vanderbilt U., Nashville, 1995-98, asst. prof. cardiology, 1999—; mem. residence rev. com. Yale Internal Medicine/Primary Care Residency, 1992-95. Recipient Pres.'s scholarship for Outstanding Performance in Med. Sch., 1989, Second award for Rsch. Presentation, Aga Khan U., 1990, Second award for Poster Presentations at Spring Sci. Session of Conn. Chpt. Am. Coll. Physician, 1993, First award for Assoc. Rsch., 1993. Mem. AMA, Am. Coll. Physicians (First award for assoc. rsch. Conn. chpt. 1994, chmn. Conn. chpt. scientific com. 1994-95). Avocations: music, theater. Home: 734 Shadowood Dr Nashville TN 37205-4613

BUTLER, JAY, women's basketball coach; b. North Bergen, N.J., 1961. BS, Castleton (Vt.) State Coll., 1983; MA, U. Md., 1986. Head coach women's basketball Davis and Elkins Coll., Elkins, W.Va., 1986-89; asst. head coach women's basketball Brown U., Providence, 1980-94; head coach women's basketball St. Marys Coll., 1994-96, Columbia U., N.Y.C., 1996—. Named to Castleton State Coll. Hall of Fame, 1997. Office: Columbia U Women's Athletic Dept Dodge Phys Fitness Ctr New York NY 10027

BUTLER, JODY TALLEY, gifted education educator; b. Columbus, Ga., Mar. 14, 1958; d. Bill Ray and Jacqueline (Hay) T.; m. Danny Butler. BS in Edn., West Ga. Coll., 1979, MEd, 1982; EdD, Auburn U., 1988. Cert. tchr., Ga. Tchr. Cen. Primary Sch., Carrollton, 1979-88; tchr. gifted student program QUEST Cen. Middle School, Carrollton, 1988-98; co-owner Hay's Mill Antiques, Ga., 1994—; QUEST tchr. Roopville Elem., Mt. Zion Elem., 1998—; Co-owner Hay's Nill Antiques. Coach Acad. Bowl Team; mem. handball choir Carrollton Presbyn. Ch. Mem. Internat. Reading Assn., Profl. Assn. Ga. Educators, Carroll County Cmty. Chorus, Phi Delta Kappa (Dissertation of Yr. award 1989), Phi Kappa Phi, Alpha Gamma Delta. Presbyterian. Avocations: antiques, travel, music, writing children's fiction and non-fiction. Office: Roopville Elementary School 60 Carrollton Rd Roopville GA 30170

BUTLER, JOHN, professional sports team executive; b. Chgo., Aug. 13, 1946; m. Alice Butler; 1 child, Andrea. Student, San Bernadino Jr. Coll.; BA in Parks and Recreation, U. Ill. Coach under Randy Rogers U. Evansville, N.J., 1979-81; dir. pro scouting Chgo. Blitz, 1981-85; staff scout San Diego Chargers, 1985-86; dir. coll. scouting Buffalo Bills, 1987-89, dir. player personnel, overseerer scouting ops., 1989-93, exec. v.p., gen. mgr., 1993—; played football San Bernardino Jr. Coll., U. Ill. Sgt. USMC, Vietnam. Office: Buffalo Bills 1 Bills Dr Orchard Park NY 14127-2296*

BUTLER, JOHN MUSGRAVE, business financial consultant; b. Bklyn., Dec. 6, 1928; s. John Joseph and Sabina Catherine (Musgrave) B.; m. Ann Elizabeth Kelly, July 9, 1955; children: Maureen, John, Ellen, Suzanne. BA cum laude, St. John's U., 1950; MBA, NYU, 1951. CPA, N.Y., Ill. Sr. acct. Lybrand, Ross Bros. & Montgomery (CPAs), N.Y.C., 1953-59; sr. auditor ITT Corp., N.Y.C., 1959-62; asst. to contr. Dictaphone Corp., Bridgeport, Conn., 1962-63; contr. Dictaphone Corp., Bridgeport, Rye, N.Y., 1964-68; v.p. acctg. Chgo. & North Western Ry. Co., Chgo., 1968-69; v.p. fin. and acctg. Chgo. & North Western Ry. Co., 1969-72, Chgo. and North Western Transp. Co., Chgo., 1972-79; sr. v.p. fin. and acctg. Chgo. and North Western Transp. Co., 1979-89, dir., 1976-89, trustee, 1978-82; sr. v.p. fin. and acctg., dir. CNW Corp., 1985-89; cons. in fin. and acctg. for bus., 1989—; acting sr. v.p. fin. and acctg. Chgo. and North Western Transp. Co., 1994; instr. fin. DePaul U., Chgo., 1989—. Served with USCGR, 1951-53. Mem. Fin. Execs. Inst. Roman Catholic. Office: 119 E Palatine Rd Ste 206 Palatine IL 60067-5132

BUTLER, JOHN PAUL, sales professional; b. Lexington, S.C., Sept. 6, 1935; s. Albert G. and Alma J. (Braswell) B.; m. Clare Vestal, Nov. 8, 1958 (div. 1978); children: Cathy, Tom, Frank. BSME (NROTC scholar), U. S.C., 1957; MBA, U. Conn., 1965. Sr. engr. Pratt & Whitney Aircraft, East Hartford, Conn., 1960-65; engring. supr. Westinghouse Electric Corp., Pitts., 1966-70, mktg. supr., 1971-76; dir. sales and mktg. Morgan div. Amca, Alliance, Ohio, 1977-78; sales dir. Mid-East, Westinghouse Electric Corp., Orlando, Fla., 1979-84; pres. Butler Assocs., Orlando, 1984-86; mgr. Tandy Corp., Tampa, Fla., 1987-94. Pres., Butler Enterprises, 1995—. Committeeman Rep. Com. Lt. USN, 1957-60. Mem. ASME. Methodist. Contbr. articles to profl. jours.; patentee in field. Home: 4712 Olive Branch Rd Apt 415 Orlando FL 32811-7247 Office: 5924 S Orange Ave Orlando FL 32802

BUTLER, JON TERRY, computer engineering educator, researcher; b. Balt., Dec. 26, 1943; s. Herbert Harriss and Vera Esse (Buck) B.; m. Susan Beth Wood, Feb. 24, 1968 (d iv. Aug. 1996); 1 child, Anne Elizabeth; m. Fujiko Sakaguchi, Jan. 31, 1998. BEE, Rensselaer Poly. Inst., 1966, M in Engring., 1967; PhD, Ohio State U., 1973. Registered profl. engr., Ohio. NRC postdoctoral assoc. Air Force Avionics Lab., Wright-Patterson AFB, Ohio, 1973-74; sr. postdoctoral assoc. Naval Postgrad. Sch., Wright-Patterson AFB, Ohio, 1980-81; assoc. prof. Northwestern U., Evanston, Ill., 1974-87; prof. Naval Postgrad. Sch., Monterey, Calif., 1987—, Navalex Chair prof., 1985-87. Editor: Multi-Valued Logic in VLSI, 1991; contbr. articles to profl. jours. Capt. USAF, 1967-70. Recipient Faculty Performance award Naval Postgrad. Sch., 1990-93. Fellow IEEE; mem. IEEE Computer Soc. (chmn. multiple-valued logic com. 1980-81, Disting. vis. 1982-86, press editor 1986-90, editor-in-chief Computer mag. 1991-92, editor-in-chief Computer Soc. Press 1993-97, chmn. Computer Soc. fellows evaluation com. 1999, chmn. Computer Soc. transactions ops. com. 1998-99, Meritorious Svc. award 1988, 92, TAB Pioneer award 1989, cert. appreciation 1982, 89, 91, 95, 96, Disting. Svc. award 1995, bd. govs. 1991-97). Presbyterian. Avocation: jogging. Office: Naval Postgrad Sch Dept Elec Computer Engring Code EC-BU Monterey CA 93943-5121

BUTLER, JONATHAN PUTNAM, architect; b. Portchester, N.Y., June 6, 1940; s. Jonathan Fairchild and Mary Elizabeth (Putnam) B.; BA, Princeton U., 1962, MFA, 1965; MArch, Columbia U., 1966; m. Deborah Day Rogers, Mar. 18, 1967; children: Jonathan Rogers, Pauline Washburn, Benjamin Putnam, Cynthia Day. Designer, programmer, planner Skidmore Owings & Merrill, Architects, N.Y.C., 1966-68; assoc. Rogers, Butler & Burgun, N.Y.C., 1968-71; ptnr. Rogers, Butler, Burgun & Shahine, N.Y.C., 1971-79; pres. Butler, Rogers, Baskett, N.Y.C., 1979—. Trustee N.Y.C. Mission Soc.; bd. dirs. Woodlawn Cemetary, Bronx, N.Y., Search & Care. Mem. AIA, N.Y. Soc. Architects, N.Y. State Assn. Architects, Columbia Archtl. Alumni Assn., Nat. Council Archtl. Registration Bds. (cert.). Presbyterian. Clubs: Union, Princeton. Home: 1642 York Ave New York NY 10028-6569 Office: Butler Rogers & Baskett 381 Park Ave S New York NY 10016-8806

BUTLER, KEITH ARNOLD, psychologist, software researcher; b. L.A., Dec. 22, 1945; s. John Harold and Phyllis Alder (Falke) B.; m. Janis Lynn Mowry, Dec. 23, 1972 (div. Jan. 1981); children: Iraj, Reza, Leila, John Keith. BA, Calif. State U., Long Beach, 1972; PhD in Exptl. Psychology, Tufts U., Medford, Mass., 1980. Lectr. Emmanual Coll., Boston, 1975-77; mem. tech. staff Bell Telephone Labs., Piscataway, N.J., 1978-81; sr. prin. scientist The Boeing Co., Bellevue, Wash., 1981—; tutorial lectr. SIGCHI Conf., 1989—, gen. co-chair, New Orleans, 1991; sr. prin. scientist Boeing Tech. Fellowship, Seattle, 1991. Contbr. articles to profl. jours. Founding bd. mem. Citizens for Better Schs., Snoqualmie, Wash., 1989-91. With U.S. Army, 1967-69. Mem. Assn. Computing Machinery. Congregationalist. Achievements include development of an engineering method for the design of usable human-computer interfaces; organized industry-wide initiative for usability criteria in software product selection; design of the experiment which revealed the role of beta-estradiol in male reproductive behavior. Avocations: endurance sports, operatic singing, coaching youth sports. Office: Boeing Phantom Works M&CT PO Box 3707 MS 7L-40 Seattle WA 98124-2207

BUTLER, LESLIE ANN, advertising agency owner, artist, writer, editor; b. Salem, Oreg., Nov. 19, 1945; d. Marlow Dole and Lala Ann (Erlandson) Butler. Student, Lewis and Clark Coll., 1963-64; BS, U. Oreg., 1969; postgrad., Portland State U., 1972-73, Lewis and Clark Coll., 1991. Creative trainee Ketchum Advt., San Francisco, 1970-71; asst. advt. dir. Mktg. Systems, Inc., Portland, Oreg., 1971-74; prodn. mgr., art dir., copywriter Finzer-Smith, Portland, 1974-76; copywriter Gerber Advt., Portland, 1976-78; freelance copywriter Portland, 1983-84, 83-85; copywriter McCann-Erickson, Portland, 1980-81; copy chief Brookstone Co., Peterborough, N.H., 1981-83; creative dir. Whitman Advt., Portland, 1984-87; prin. L.A. Advt., 1987—; advertising agency owner, artist, writer, editor; b. Salem, Oreg., Nov. 19, 1945; d. Marlow Dole and Lala Ann (Erlandson) Butler. Student Lewis and Clark Coll., 1963-64; BS, U. Oreg, 1969; postgrad. Portland State U. 1972-73, Lewis & Clark Coll., 1991. Creative trainee Ketchum Advt., San Francisco, 1970-71; asst. advt. dir. Mktg. Systems, Inc., Portland, Oreg., 1971-74; prodn. mgr., art dir., copywriter Finzer-Smith, Portland, 1974-76; copywriter Gerber Advt., Portland, 1976-78; freelance copywriter, Portland, 1983-84, 83-85; copywriter McCann-Erickson, Portland, 1980-81; copy chief Brookstone Co., Peterborough, N.H., 1981-83; creative dir. Whitman Advt., Portland, 1984-87; prin. L.A. Advt., 1987—. Author: The Dream Road and Other Tales From Hidden Hills, 1997; arts and antiques editor Portland Living mag. Co-founder, v.p., newsletter editor Animal Rescue and Care Fund, 1972-81; mem. Friends of One Performing Arts Ctr., Portland Art Mus., Oreg. Humane Soc. Recipient Internat. Film and TV Festival N.Y. Finalist award, 1985, 86, 87, 88, Internat. Radio Festival of N.Y. award, 1984, 85, 88, Hollywood Radio and TV Soc. Internat. Broadcasting award, 1981, TV Comml. Festival Silver Telly award, 1985, TV Comml. Festival Bronze Telly, 1986, AVC Silver Cindy, 1986, Los Angeles Advt. Women LULU, 1986, 87, 88, 89 Ad Week What's New Portfolio, 1986, N.W. Addy award Seattle Advt. Fedn., 1984, Best of N.W. award, 1985, Nat. winner Silver Microphone award, 1987, 88, 89. Mem. ASPCA, Portland Advt. Fedn. (Rosey Finalist award 1986), People for Ethical Treatment of Animals. Author: The Dream Road and Other Tales From Hidden Hills, 1997; arts and antiques editor Portland Living mag. Co-founder, v.p., newsletter editor Animal Rescue and Care Fund, 1972-81; mem. Friends of One Performing Arts Ctr., Portland Art Mus., Oreg. Humane Soc. Recipient Internat. Film and TV Festival N.Y. Finalist award, 1985, 86, 87, 88, Internat. Radio Festival of N.Y. award, 1984, 85, 88, Hollywood Radio and TV Soc. Internat. Broadcasting award, 1981, TV Comml. Festival Silver Telly award, 1985, TV Comml. Festival Bronze Telly, 1986, AVC Silver Cindy, 1986, Los Angeles Advt. Women LULU, 1986, 87, 88, 89 Ad Week What's New Portfolio, 1986, N.W. Addy award Seattle Advt. Fedn., 1984, Best of N.W. award, 1985, Nat. winner Silver Microphone award, 1987, 88, 89. Mem. ASPCA, Portland Advt. Fedn. (Rosey Finalist award 1986), People for Ethical Treatment of Animals. Home and Office: 1475 SW Cardinell Dr Portland OR 97201

BUTLER, MANLEY CALDWELL, retired lawyer; b. Roanoke, Va., June 2, 1925; s. W.W.S. Butler Jr.; m. June Nolde, June 26, 1950; children:

Manley, Henry, James, Marshall. AB, U. Richmond, 1948; JD, U. Va., 1950; LLD (hon.), Washington & Lee U., 1978. Bar: Va. 1950. Mem. Va. Ho. Dels., 1962-72, minority leader; mem. 92d-97th Congresses from 6th Va. dist., Judiciary Com., Com. on Govt. Ops., Woods, Rogers & Hazlegrove, P.L.C., 1983-99; ret.; mem. Nat. Bankruptcy Rev. Commn., 1995-97. Lt. USNR, 1943-46. Fellow Am. Bar Found., Am. Coll. Bankruptcy, Va. Law Found.; mem. ABA, Va. State Bar Assn., Roanoke Bar Assn., Am. Bankruptcy Inst., Raven Soc. Order of Coif, Phi Beta Kappa, Tau Kappa Alpha, Omicron Delta Kappa, Phi Gamma Delta. Episcopalian. Home: 5624 Village Way Roanoke VA 24014-4952

BUTLER, MARGARET KAMPSCHAEFER, retired computer scientist; b. Evansville, Ind., Mar. 7, 1924; d. Otto Louis and Lou Etta (Rehsteiner) Kampschaefer; m. James W. Butler, Sept. 30, 1951; 1 child, Jay. AB, Ind. U., 1944; postgrad., U.S. Dept. Agr. Grad. Sch., 1945, U. Chgo., 1949, U. Minn., 1950. Statistician U.S. Bur. Labor Statistics, Washington, 1945-46, U.S. Air Forces in Europe, Erlangen and Wiesbaden, Germany, 1946-48, U.S. Bur. Labor Statistics, St. Paul, 1949-51; mathematician Argonne (Ill.) Nat. Lab., 1948-49, 51-80, sr. computer scientist, 1980-92; dir. Argonne Code Ctr. and Nat. Energy Software Ctr. Dept. Energy Computer Program Exch., 1960-91; spl. term appointee Indsl. Tech. Devel. Ctr. Argonne Nat. Lab., 1993—; cons. AMF Corp., 1956-57, OECD, 1964, Poole Bros., 1967. Author: Careers for Women in Nuclear Science and Technology, 1992; editor Computer Physics Communications, 1969-80; contbr. (chpt.) The Application of Digital Computers to Problems in Reactor Physics, 1968, Advances in Nuclear Sci. and Technology, 1976; contbr. articles to profl. publs. Treas. Timberlake Civic Assn., 1958; rep. mem. nomination com. Hinsdale (Ill.) Caucus, 1961-62; coord. 6th dist. ERA, 1973-80; del. Rep. Nat. Conv., 1980; bd. mgr. DuPage dist. YWCA Met. Chgo., 1987-90; mem. computer and info. sys. adv. bd. Coll. DuPage, 1987-95; mem. industry adv. bd. computer sci. dept. Bradley U., 1988-91; vice-chair Ill. Women's Polit. Caucus, 1987-90; chair voter's svc. LWV, Burr-Ridge-Willowbrook, 1991-93. Recipient Cert. Leadership, Met. YWCA, Chgo., 1985, Merit award Chgo. Assn. Technol. Socs., 1988; named to Fed. 100, 1991; named Outstanding Woman Leader of DuPage County Sci., Tech. and Health Care, 1992; recipient spl. award Am. Nuclear Soc. Math and Comp. divsn., 1992. Fellow Am. Nuclear Soc. (mem. publs. com. 1965-71, bd. dirs. 1976-79, exec. com. 1977-78, chmn. bylaws and rules com., 1979-82, profl. women in ANS com. 1991-93, reviewer for publs.); mem. Assn. Computing Machinery (exec. com., sec. Chgo. chpt. 1963-65, publs. chmn. nat. conf. 1968, reviewer for publs.), Assn. Women in Sci. (pres. Chgo. area chpt. 1982, nat. exec. bd. 1985-87), Nat. Computer Conf. (chmn. Pioneer Day com. 1985, tech. program chmn. 1987). Republican. Home: 17W139 Hillside Ln Hinsdale IL 60521-6062 *My goal is the removal of barriers restricting individuals from achieving their full potential and the furtherance of individual rights.*

BUTLER, MARK SHERMAN, controller; b. Fremont, Mich., Apr. 12, 1960; s. Roger Sherman and Frances Irene (Frickle) B. AAS, Davenport Coll., 1982; BS in Acctg., Ferris State U., 1984; MBA magna cum laude, Grand Valley State U., 1997. Cert. mgmt. acct., in Prodn. and inventory mgmt. Cost analyst II Westinghouse Furniture Systems, Grand Rapids, Mich., 1984-87; mgr. fin. and cost acctg. Grumman Corp., Sturgis, Mich., 1987-92; mgr. cost acctg. and planning Toyota U.S.A., Battle Creek, Mich., 1992; mgr. cost acctg. and pricing Bussell, Inc., Grand Rapids, Mich., 1992-95; mgr. cost acctg. and budgeting Textron Automotive Co., Muskegon, Mich., 1995-99; contr. Campbell Grinder Co., Muskegon, 1999—. Vol. mentor Big Bros., Grand Rapids, 1993-95; co-chair United Way, Grand Rapids, 1985. Mem. Am. Prodn. and Inventory Control Soc., Inst. Mgmt. Accts., Delta Mu Delta, Beta Gamma Sigma. Republican. Avocations: golf, basketball, softball, reading, skiing. Home: 18217 W Spring Lake Rd Spring Lake MI 49456-1063 Office: Campbell Grinder Co 1974 E Sherman Blvd Muskegon MI 49444

BUTLER, MERLIN GENE, physician, medical geneticist, educator; b. Atkinson, Nebr., Aug. 2, 1952; s. Garold Melvin and Berdena June (Sandall) B.; m. Ranae Ilene Kisker, Oct. 2, 1976; children: Michelle Ranae, Brian Gene. BA with very high distinction, Chadron State Coll., 1974, BS with very high distinction, 1975; MD, U. Nebr., Omaha, 1978; MS, U. Nebr., Lincoln, 1980; PhD, Ind. U., Indpls., 1984. Supervising physician Med. Info. Svcs., Omaha, 1978-80; rsch. assoc. dept. biology U. Notre Dame, South Bend, Ind., 1983-84; med. dir. North Ctrl. Ind. Regional Genetics Ctr., South Bend, 1983-84; dir. cytogenetics Meml. Hosp., South Bend, 1983-84; NIH postdoctoral fellow dept. med. genetics Sch. Medicine Ind. U., Indpls., 1980-83, adj. asst. prof. dept. med. genetics Sch. Medicine, 1984; asst. prof. dept. pediatrics Sch. Medicine Vanderbilt U., Nashville, 1984-90, dir. regional genetics program Sch. Medicine, 1984-98, dir. Cytogenetics Lab. dept. pediatrics Sch. Medicine, 1989-98, assoc. prof. dept. pediatrics, 1990-98, assoc. prof. dept. pathology, 1991-98, investigator John F. Kennedy Ctr. Rsch. on Edn. and Human Devel., Peabody Coll., 1987-98; assoc. dir. Inst. Behavior and Genetics; assoc. prof. dept. orthopedics Vanderbilt U., 1994-98; chief sect. med. genetics and molecular medicine Children's Mercy Hosp./U. Mo. Kansas City Sch. Medicine, 1998—, William R. Brown prof., chmn., 1998—; adj. assoc. prof. dept. pediatrics Meharry Med. Coll., Nashville, 1988-98; genetics cons. Baptist Hosp., Nashville, 1985-98, Westside Hosp., Nashville, 1985-98, Nashville Gen. Hosp., 1985-98, chief, section of Med. Genetics and Molecular Medicine, Children's Mercy Hosp., Kansas City, Mo., 1998—, prof. dept. pediats., U. Mo.-Kansas City Sch. Medicine; mem. epidemiology genetic diseases subcom. Ind. State Bd. Health, 1983-84; faculty interviewer Vanderbilt U., 1987; peer reviewer Am. Jour. Human Genetics, Am. Jour. Med. Genetics, Clin. Genetics, Am. Jour. Diseases of Children, Dysmorphology and Clin. Genetics, Am. Jour. Mental Retardation, Jour. Pediatrics, So. Med. Jour., Human Mutations, Cancer Genetics and Cytogenetics, Pediatrics, Genomics, Prader-Willi Perspectives; mem. adhoc grant review com. NIH, 1990—, craniofacial assessment team Vanderbilt U., 1992-98; lectr., presenter in field. Author: Fragile X Syndrome: A Major Cause of X-Linked Mental Retardation, 1988, 1989; author: (with others) Genetics for the Medically Oriented, 1983, Novak's Textbook of Gynecology, 11th edit., 1988, Birth Defects Encyclopedia, 1990, Prader-Willi Syndrome and Other Chromosome 15q Deletion Disorders, 1992, Human Genetics: New Perspectives, 1994, 1992 International Fragile X Conference Proceedings, 1992, Prader-Willi and Angelman Syndromes Examples of Genetic Imprinting in Man, 1994; mem. editorial bd. Prader-Willi Perspectives, 1992—; contbr. numerous articles to profl. jours. including Nature and New England Jour. Medicine. Grant reviewer March of Dimes Birth Defects Found., 1985—. Recipient Disting. Svc. award Chadron State Coll., 1986, Teaching award Osler Inst., 1989; grantee Univ. Rsch. Coun., 1985, 92-93, Tenn. Dept. Mental Health and Mental Retardation, 1986-91, Clin. Nutrition Rsch. Unit, 1986-88, Joseph P. Kennedy, Jr. Found., 1988, Clin. Rsch. Ctr. Meharry Med. Coll., 1989-98, Dept. Pathology, 1992-93, Orthopedic Rsch. Edn. Found., 1993-95, NIH, 1995—; Cancer Rsch. grantee Ind. U. Med. Ctr., 1980, Biomed. Rsch. Support grantee, 1985, 88, 89—, Clin. Rsch. grantee March of Dimes Birth Defects Found., 1987, 88, 90-92, Lyle V. Andrews Meml. scholar, 1974. Fellow Am. Coll. Med. Genetics (founder, diplomate, lab. practice subcom. 1993); mem. AMA (Physician Recognition award 1984, 87), AAAS, Am. Bd. Med. Genetics (cert. clin. genetics and clin. cytogenetics), Am. Genetics Assn., Am. Soc. Human Genetics (cytogenetics resource com. 1992-97), Am. Fedn. Clin. Rsch., Coll. Am. Pathologists (cytogenetics resource com. 1992-97, molecular pathology resource com. 1993-97), So. Med. Assn., Davidson County Pediatric Soc., Prader-Willi Syndrome Assn. (med. rsch. task force 1985—, diagnostic task force 1991—), N.Y. Acad. Scis., Sigma Xi, Phi Chi. Avocations: gardening, camping, fishing, collecting sports memorabilia. Home: 6410 Hillside St Shawnee KS 66218-9070 Office: Children's Mercy Hosp 2401 Gillham Rd Kansas City MO 64108-4698

BUTLER, MICHAEL FRANCIS, lawyer; b. Pitts., Aug. 17, 1935; s. Frank J. and Mary M. (Montgomery) B. BA magna cum laude, Harvard U., 1957; LLB, Yale U., 1960. Bar: Pa., D.C. Mem. Kirkpatrick & Lockhart, Pitts., 1960-69; asst. gen. counsel for domestic and internat. bus., then dep. gen. counsel U.S. Dept. Commerce, Washington, 1969-73; v.p., gen. counsel Overseas Pvt. Investment Corp., Washington, 1973-75; gen. counsel Fed. Energy Adminstrn., Washington, 1975-77; ptnr. Andrews & Kurth, Washington, 1977-92; bd. dirs. U.S. Bancorp, U.S. Nat. Bank; mem. adv. com. Fagan & Co.; mem. panel of arbitrators Dispute Settlement Ctr., Internat. Energy Agy., Paris; mem. adv. com. on fgn. investment Office of Spl. Trade of U.S.; past mem. or chmn. U.S. dels. to OECD coms., Berne Union, Adminstrv. Conf. of U.S. Contbr. articles to profl. publs. Vice chmn. class spl. gifts com. Harvard Coll. and Yale Law Sch.; past bd. dirs., sec. Three Rivers Arts Festival, Pitts.; bd. dirs. Bryce Harlow Found. Fellow Am. Bar Found. (life); mem. ABA (chmn. com. on fgn. investment in U.S. internat. law sect.), Am. Arbitration Assn. (mem. comml. panel of arbitrators), U.S. C. of C. (mem. internat. policy com.), Pa. Bar Assn., D.C. Bar Assn., Allegheny County Bar Assn., Am. Law Inst., Am. Judicature Soc., Am. Soc. Internat. Law, Internat. Bar Assn., Washington Fgn. Law Soc., Inter-Am. Bar Assn., Supreme Ct. Hist. Soc., Harvard Club West Pa. (past sec.), Harvard Club of D.C. (past bd. dirs.), Met. Club, Rolling Rock Club (Ligonier, Pa.), Harvard-Yale-Princeton Club (Pitts.), Pa. Soc. Republican. Presbyterian. Home and Office: 2214 Massachusetts Ave NW Washington DC 20008-2812

BUTLER, NANCY TAYLOR, gender equity specialist, program director; b. Newport, R.I., Oct. 31, 1942; d. Robert Lee and Roberta Claire (Brown) Taylor; m. Edward M. Butler, Aug. 22, 1964; children: Jeffrey, Gregory, Katherine. AB, Cornell U., 1964. Asst. dir. Career Equity Assistance Ctr. for Tng. Coll. of N.J., 1990-98; owner Equity Resources, Tinton Falls, N.J., 1993—; mem. N.J. Gender Equity Adv. Comm., 1995-98, sec., 1996-98. Editor Equity Exch., 1991—. Mem. Monmouth County dist. ethics com. Supreme Ct. N.J., 1987-91; pres. Vol. Ctr. Monmouth County, Red Bank, 1985-89; mem. Cornell U. Coun., Ithaca, N.Y., 1987-91, 94—, adminstrv. bd., 1996—; dir. Cornell Assn. Class Officers, 1991-97; chmn. Cornell Alumni Trustee Nominating Com., 1994. Recipient Woman of Achievement award Commn. on Status of Women, 1988, Women's History Tribute NOW-N.J., 1995, Woman Leader award N.J. Assn. Women Bus. Owners, 1996. Mem. AAUW (life; pres. N.J. chpt. 1988-90, Edn. Found. Named Gift 1982, 83, 84, 86, 87, 89, 91), Nat. Coalition for Sex Equity in Edn. Home: 20 Cedar Pl Tinton Falls NJ 07724-2807

BUTLER, OCTAVIA ESTELLE, free-lance writer; b. Pasadena, Calif., June 22, 1947; d. Laurice and Octavia Margaret (Guy) B. AA, Pasadena City Coll., 1968; student, Calif. State U., Los Angeles, 1969—. Free-lance writer Los Angeles, 1975—; MacArthur fellow, 1995. Author: Patternmaster, 1976, Mind of My Mind, 1977, Survivor, 1978, Kindred, 1979, Wild Seed, 1980, Clay's Ark, 1984, Dawn, 1987, Adulthood Rites, 1988, Imago, 1989, Parable of the Sower, 1993, Bloodchild, 1995, Parable of the Talents, 1998; also sci. fiction short stories. Recipient fifth prize Writer's Digest Short Story Contest, 1967, Creative Arts Achievement award L.A. YWCA, 1980, Sci. Fiction (Hugo) Best Novelette award World Sci. Fiction Conf., 1985, Best Short Story award World Sci. Fiction Conv., 1984, Nebula Best Novelette award Sci. Fiction Writers Am., 1985, Locus Best Novelette award, 1985, Best Novelette award Sci. Fiction Chronicle Reader, 1985; fellow John D. and Catherine T. MacArthur Found., 1995. Mem. Sci. Fiction Writers Am. Address: PO Box 60725 Pasadena CA 91116-6725

BUTLER, PATRICIA, protective services official; b. Salem, Mass., Aug. 13, 1958; d. Frank Arthur and Ruth Elizabeth (Bartlett) B. Paramedic degree, Davenport Coll., 1984, AA in Mgmt. of Emergency Med. Svcs., 1987; Mich. Law Enforcement Officers Tng. Coun. cert., Grand Valley State U., 1988; BA in MHR, Spring Arbor Coll., 1994. CEO Whispering Winds, Inc., L'Anse, Mich., 1985—; firefighter Grand Rapids (Mich.) Fire Dept., 1985; security, data entry clerk Lacks Industries, Grand Rapids, 1985-88; loss prevention officer Woodland Mall Security, Kentwood, Mich., 1988-89, Butterworth Hosp., Grand Rapids, 1989; police officer Lakeview Police Dept., 1989, Edmore (Mich.)-Home Mcpl. Police Dept., 1989-90, Coopersville (Mich.) Police Dept., 1989-90; chief police Lakeview Village Police Dept., 1990-94, Mich. State Police, 1994—; mem. Mich. Paramedic, 1986-98. Mem. NAFE, Nat. Assn. Chiefs, Mich. Chief's Assn. (v.p. 1991-94), Internat. Assn. Women Police, Mich. Assn. Chief of Police, Women Police Mich. Avocations: freelance artist. Office: Mich State Police L'Anse Post 88 PO Box 100 Lanse MI 49946-0100

BUTLER, PATRICIA LACKY, mental health nurse, educator, consultant; b. Galesburg, Ill., Aug. 31, 1943; d. Allen Dale and Mary Lacky; m. Glen William Butler, Mar. 14, 1964 (div. Apr. 1974); children: Scott Lewis, Andrew William, Suzanne Elizabeth; m. Keith Warren Turner, Oct. 13, 1992. AA in Nursing/Journalism, Sacramento City Coll., 1965; BS in Sociology/Psychology, SUNY, Albany, 1992. Clin. nurse Mercy Gen. Hosp., Sacramento, Sacramento Med. Ctr.; Davis (Calif.) Cmty. Hosp.; clin. nurse Woodland (Calif.) Meml. Hosp., 1965-74; dir. nurses Woodland Skilled Nursing, 1978-79; head nurse/psychiatry St. Croix Mental Health, Christiansted, U.S. V.I., 1974-79; clin. program coord. Yolo County Mental Health, Woodland, 1980—; instr. Yuba C.C., Marysville, Calif., 1988—. Author curriculum; mem. editl. adv. bd. Daily Democrat. Bd. dirs. Concilio of Yolo County, Woodland, 1984-87; mem. Red Cross Nat. Disaster Mental Health, 1996—. Recipient Bell award Mental Health Assn. Yolo County, 1993; NIMH grantee, 1989-90. Mem. LWV (recording sec. 1997, 98, copres. 1999—), Calif. Elected Women's Assn. Edn. & Rsch., Virgin Islands Nurses Assn., Forensic Mental Health Assn. Calif. (sec. 1991-93, conf. planning 1990-91, dir. edn. and tng. 1996-98, West award 1999), Rotary Internat. Democrat. Roman Catholic. Avocations: diving, boating, travel, golf. Home: McKinney-Rubicon Rd Homewood CA 96141 Office: Yolo County Mental Health 213 W Beamer St Woodland CA 95695-2510

BUTLER, PAUL BASCOMB, JR., lawyer; b. Charleston, S.C., Nov. 27, 1947; s. Paul B. and Mary Anna (Tisdale) B.; m. Virginia Eldridge, June 14, 1969; children: Jeffrey Bryan, Robert Paul. BA, Emory U., 1969, MDiv cum laude, 1972, JD with distinction, 1976. Bar: Ga. 1976, Fla. 1977; ordained to ministry United Meth. Ch., 1970. United Meth. Ch., 1970—; Assoc. min. First United Meth. Ch., Phoenix, 1972-73; assoc. Swift, Currie, McGhee and Hiers, Atlanta, 1976-79; ptnr. Butler, Burnette & Pappas, Tampa, Fla., 1979-97, of counsel, 1998—; Chancellor Fla. Ann. Conf. United Meth. Ch., 1997—. Contbr. articles to profl. jours. Chair com. on new church devel. Fla. annual conf. United Meth. Ch., 1996—, chair bd. missions and ch. ext. Tampa dist. Uited Meth. Ch., Inc., 1992-96; p astor Temple Terrace United Meth., Tampa, 1998—. Mem. ABA (chmn. Nat. Inst. sect. of tort and ins. practice 1987-89, ho. of dels. 1993-95, coun. mem. sect. of tort and ins. practice 1990-93, chmn. task force on civil justice reform, chmn. property ins. law com. 1985-86, editor So. Region Annotated Homeowner's Policy), Fedn. of Ins. and Corp. Counsel (dean Litigation Mgmt. Coll. 1996-98, chair litigation mgmt. coll. adv. coun. 1998—), Def. Rsch. Inst. (chmn. ins. law com. 1989-92, chmn. Amcus com. 1994-97, bd. dirs. 1995-98, vice chair law inst. 1998—), Fla. Def. Lawyers Assn., Hillsborough County Bar Assn., Internat. Assn. Def. Counsel (vice chair property ins. com. 1993-96), Assn. Def. Trial Attys. Democrat. Clubs: Temple Terr. (Fla.) Golf and Country. Avocations: golf, tennis. Office: Butler Burnette & Pappas Ste 1100 6200 W Courtney Campbell Cswy Tampa FL 33607-5946

BUTLER, PAUL THURMAN, retired religious studies educator; b. Springfield, Mo., Nov. 17, 1928; s. Willard Drew and Verna Lois (Thurman) B.; m. Gale Jynne Kinnard, Nov. 20, 1948; children: Sherry Lynne, Mark Stephen. ThB, Ozark Bible Coll., 1961, M Bibl. Lit., 1973; ThD, Theol. U. Am., 1990. Oradined to ministry Christian Ch. (Disciples of Christ), 1958. Noncommd. officer USN, 1946-56; mem. staff Amphibious Forces Pacific, 1947-51; mem. guided missile unit 41 Guided Missile Unit 41, Port Mugu, Calif., 1951-56; ret., 1956; min. Washington Christian Ch., Lebanon, Mo., 1958-60; registrar Ozark Christian Coll., Joplin, Mo., 1960-92, prof. Bible and philosophy, 1960-98; ret., 1998; min. Westside Christian Ch., 1960-63, North Joplin Christian Ch., 1969-71. Author: The Gospel of John, 1961, The Minor Prophets, 1968, Daniel, 1976, Isaiah, 3 vols., 1978, Esther, 1979, The Gospel of Luke, 1981 (transl. into Korean, French, Portuguese, East Indian-Tamil), Revelation, 1982, I Corinthians, 1984, II Corinthians, 1986, What the Bible Says about Civil Government, 1990, Approaching the New Millennium—An Amillennial Look at A.D. 2000, 1997; also author 7 geneal. family histories: Butlers, Thurmans, Ganns, Alleys, Painters, Kinnard, Driefuses. Bd. dirs. Jasper County chpt. Am. Heart Assn., 1992. Mem. SAR (nat. chaplain gen. 1991-92, pres., sec. Mo. Soc. chpt., pres. Sgt. Ariel Nims chpt.), Nat. Soc. Sons. Colonial New Eng., Nat. Soc. Sons and Daus. Pilgrims, Ret. Officers Assn. (hon.), Am. Legion, Mo. Territorial Pioneers, Mo. Geneal. Soc., Tenn. Geneal Soc., Tenn. Pioneer Ancestors, Joplin Hist. Soc., Gann Family Hist. Soc. (pres. 1993-95). Republican. Home: 2502 Utica St Joplin MO 64801-1246

BUTLER, R. W., engineering company executive; b. 1942. BS, Auburn U., 1965; MS, U. Tenn., 1967. With Sverdrup Tech Inc., Tullahoma, Tenn., 1967—, pres., 1984—. Office: Sverdrup Tech Inc 600 William Northern Blvd Tullahoma TN 37388-4729*

BUTLER, REX LAMONT, lawyer; b. New Brunswick, N.J., Mar. 24, 1951; s. Ekker and Beatrice (Curry) B.; m. Stephanie Butler; children: Nijel Jaibrun, Vikteria Lamontra, Octavia Reneè Lamontra, Synclaire Lamontra. AA with honors, Fla. Jr. Coll., 1975; BA, U. North Fla., 1977; JD, Howard U., 1983. Bar: Alaska 1983, U.S. Dist. Ct. Alaska 1983, U.S. Ct. Appeals (9th cir.) 1984, U.S. Ct. Appeals (D.C. cir.) 1984, U.S. Supreme Ct. 1996. Assoc. M. Ashley Dickerson, Inc., Anchorage, 1983-84; profl. legis. asst. State of Alaska, Juneau, 1984; asst. atty. gen. State of Alaska, Anchorage, 1984-85; pvt. practice Anchorage, 1985—; adj. prof. law Anchorage C.C., 1985; adj. prof. U. Alaska, Anchorage, 1990—; mem. State Ct. Criminal Pattern Jury Instructions Com., 1997; chmn. lawyer rep. com. Alaska 9th Cir. Judicial Conf., 1997-98. Pres. Alaska Black Caucus, Anchorage, 1986, bd. dirs., 1987-88; gen. counsel NAACP, Anchorage, 1985-87, life mem.; commr. Anchorage Telephone Utility, 1985-87; trustee Anchorage Sr. Ctr., Inc., 1985-87, Shiloh Missionary Bapt. Ch., Anchorage, 1985—; bd. dirs. Ctr. Drug Problems, Anchorage, 1985-86, Alaska Civil Liberties Union, 1987-88; active fin. com. Dem. Cen. Com. Alaska. With USN, 1969-73. Named one of Outstanding Young Men Am., 1984; recipient Cert. Appreciation, African Relief Campaign, 1985. Mem. ABA, Nat. Bar Assn., Nat. Assn. Criminal Defense Lawyers, Alaska Bar Assn., Assn. Trial Lawyers Am., Anchorage Bar Assn., Alaska Trial Lawyers Assn., Lions Internat., Omega Psi Phi (dist. counselor 1995-96, 98—). Democrat. Fax: (907) 276-3306. E-mail: rexb@pobox.alaska.net. Home: PO Box 200025 Anchorage AK 99520-0025 Office: 745 W 4th Ave Ste 300 Anchorage AK 99501-2136

BUTLER, RICHARD COLBURN, banker, lawyer; b. Little Rock, Jan. 1, 1910; s. R. Colburn and Edna (Clok) B.; m. Gertrude Remmel, Mar. 7, 1936; 1 son, Richard Colburn. Student, Little Rock Jr. Coll., 1929; AB, U. Ark., 1931, LLD (hon.), 1986; LLD (hon.), Hendrix Coll., 1981. Bar: Ark. 1933, U.S. Supreme Ct. 1943. Gen. practice law Little Rock, 1933-63; partner firm House, Holmes, Butler & Jewell, 1941-63; pres., chmn. bd. Comml. Nat. Bank Little Rock, 1963-80, sr. chmn., 1980-81; pres., dir. Ark. Nat. Stockyards Co., 1958-78, First Ark. Devel. Fin. Corp.; chmn., dir. Little Rock Abstract Co., 1971-81; chmn. Peoples Savs. & Loan Assn., Little Rock, 1980-84; dir. Kin-Ark Corp., Tulsa, 1972-91, 94—. Bd. dirs., treas. Heifer Project Internat., 1986-91; pres. Maumelle Gardens, Inc., 1968—; mem. United Meth. Found., 1964—, chmn. bd. dirs., 1981-84; pres. bd. trustees Little Rock U., 1961-63; bd. dirs. Little Rock Boys Club, pres., 1960; bd. dirs. Heifer Internat. Found., 1991—; nat. assoc. for Ark. Boys Clubs America, 1964-74; mem. Pillars Club, United Way Pulaski County; trustee Hendrix Coll., Conway, Ark., 1969-81; trustee Heifer Internat. Found., 1993—; founder Butler Arboretum, Little Rock, Butler Ctr. at Little Rock public library. Maj. USAAF, 1942-46, CBI. Decorated Bronze Star. Mem. ABA, Ark. Bar Assn., Am. Judicature Soc., Am. Hemerocallis Soc., Am. Iris Soc. Found. (life, regional v.p. 1960-61), Iris Found. (pres. 1995—, bd. dirs.), Bookfellows (pres. 1961), Little Rock C. of C. (pres. 1952), Am. Daffodil Soc. (bd. dirs. 1987-90), Nat. Trust for Historic Preservation, U. Ark.-Little Rock Heritage Assn. (founding mem.), Little Rock Country Club, Little Rock XV Club, U. Ark. Chancellor's Club, Union League (Chgo.), Kiwanis. Methodist (chmn. bd. trustees 1960-82). Office: 5300 Evergreen Little Rock AR 72205 *To some, the acquisition of great material wealth, or appearing in "Who's Who" is "success." Fortunately, there are many who still believe that a person is successful if he has "lived well, laughed often and loved much," and who recognize that "success is in the silences, though fame is in the song.".*

BUTLER, RICHARD JOHN, business educator; b. Watertown, N.Y., Aug. 28, 1942; s. William Francis and Carol Gertrude (Sheley) B.; m. Linda Mary Hurd, June 27, 1964; children: Eric, Kristi. BS, Clarkson U., 1964, MS, 1972; MBA, Ind. U., 1979. Mgr. AT&T, N.Y.C., 1964-70; lectr. Clarkson U., Potsdam, N.Y., 1970-72; grad. asst. Ind. U., Bloomington, 1972-75; asst. prof. Rochester (N.Y.) Inst. Tech., 1975-85; exec. dir. RIT Employees Fed. Credit Union, Rochester, 1984-85; mentor, assoc. prof. SUNY Empire State Coll., Syracuse, 1985—; convenor Bus., Mgmt. and Econs. Area of Study, Saratoga Springs, N.Y., 1989-90. Contbr. articles to profl. publs. Area rep., vol. Youth for Understanding, Washington, 1994—; dir., past pres., conf. chair Coalition for Adult and Continuing Edn., Syracuse, 1992—; trustee Jamesville (N.Y.) Cmty. Ch., 1996—. Capt. U.S. Army Signal Corp., 1965-68. Mem. Acad. Mgmt., Informs, Rotary. Republican. Methodist. Avocations: reading, photography. Office: Empire State Coll 219 Walton St Syracuse NY 13202-1226

BUTLER, ROBERT ALLAN, psychologist, educator; b. Pittsfield, Mass., Mar. 29, 1923; s. Thomas Arthur and Beulah Adeline (Combs) B.; m. Caroline Laura Emery, Jan. 19, 1952; children—Amy, Ann, Catherine, Elizabeth. B.A., U. Fla., 1947; Ph.D., U. Chgo., 1951. Instr. dept. psychology U. Wis., Madison, 1951-53; rsch. psychologist Walter Reed Army Hosp., Washington, 1953-57, rsch. assoc. dept. surgery, 1957-65; assoc. prof. depts. behavioral scis. and surgery U. Chgo., 1965-72, prof., 1972-93, prof. emeritus depts. psychology and surgery, 1993—, divsnl. fellow, chmn. dept. behavioral scis., 1979-82, acting chmn. sect. otolaryngology dept. surgery, 1983-84, chmn. bd. sch. athletics and recreational sports, 1988-89, divisional fellow, 1993—; vis. prof. Erlangen (West Germany) U., 1966-68; mem. deafness and other comm. disorders programs adv. com. Nat. Inst. Deafness and other Comm. Disorders, 1991-94; farmer. Contbr. articles to profl. jours. Served with USN, 1943-46. Fellow Acoustical Soc. Am.; mem. Assn. for Rsch. in Otolaryngology (past pres.), Am. Otol. Soc. Office: 5848 S University Ave Chicago IL 60637-1515

BUTLER, ROBERT ANDREWS, clinical psychologist; b. Lancaster, Calif., June 19, 1955; s. Robert Andrews and Ines Gertrude (Ottaviano) B.; m. Nadine Suzanne Pastor, Dec. 27, 1975; 1 child, Alex Robert. BA, Long Beach (Calif.) State U., 1977; MA, Dominguez Hills State U., 1979; PhD, Washington State U., 1983. Cert. Am Bd. Med. Psychotherapy; lic. psychologist, Wis. Dir. psychology Brown County Mental Health, Green Bay, Wis., 1983-89; pvt. practice psychology Green Bay, 1984-90; clin. dir. anxiety and affective disorders Fox Valley Hosp., Green Bay, 1989-90; dir. divsn. psychology Bellin Psychiat. Ctr., Green Bay, 1991-93; adj. prof. psychology U. Wis., Green Bay, 1983-86; cons. Family Violence Ctr., Green Bay, 1984, Whitman County (Wash.) Mental Health, 1981, St. Vincent Hosp. Sleep Disorders Ctr., 1989—. Contbr. articles to profl. jours. Fulbright fellow. Mem. Am. Psychol. Assn., Wis. Psychol. Assn.. Avocations: skiing, tae kwon do, scuba diving. Home: 3963 Presque Isle Ct Green Bay WI 54301-1086 Office: Jefferson Ct Bldg 125 S Jefferson St Ste 306 Green Bay WI 54301-4500

BUTLER, ROBERT LEONARD, sales executive; b. West Warwick, R.I., Aug. 8, 1931; s. Leonard Thomas and Henrietta Marie (Theroux) B.; m. Rosemarie Ann D'Ambra, Nov. 5, 1955; children: Robert Arthur, David Paul. MS in Fin. Svcs., Am. Coll., 1982, MS in Mgmt., 1985. ChFC, CLU. With sales and dept. mgmt. Sears Roebuck & Co., Worcester, Mass., 1956-67; dir. investment, prodn., sales State Mut. Am., Worcester, 1976-86; asst. sec. SMA Life Assurance Co., Worcester, 1974-86; v.p. SMA Equities Inc., Worcester, 1976-86; sr. v.p. sales Phoenix Equity Planning Corp., Hartford, Conn., 1986-92; spkr., workshop leader conf. Life Office Mgmt. Assn. Contbr. articles to ins. mags. Mem. Am. Soc. Life Underwriters, Am. Abritration Assn. (comml. arbitrator 1993), Internat. Assn. Fin. Planners, Ins. Affiliated Broker-Dealer Forum (chmn. 1978-81), Nat. Assn. Securities Dealers (mem. dist. bus. com., mem. ins. affiliated broker/dealer com. 1991-92), Limra Fin. Products and Svcs., KC. Roman Catholic. Avocations: golf, jogging, swimming, photography, sports cars.

BUTLER, ROBERT MOORE, JR., podiatrist; b. Camp Lejeune, N.C., Mar. 21, 1949; s. Robert Moore and Virginia Lee (Keen) B. BA in Anthropology, U. Calif., Santa Barbara, 1971; BS in Med. Scis., Calif. Coll. Podiatric Medicin, San Francisco, 1975; DPM, Calif. Coll. Podiatric Medicin, 1976. Diplomate Am. Bd. Podiatric Surgery, Am. Bd. Podiatric Orthop. and Primary Podiatric Medicine (examinations com. 1993-95). Pvt. practice San Diego, 1977-78, U.S. Army Reynolds Army Med. Ctr., Ft. Sill, Okla., 1978-80, U.S. Army 97th Gen. Hosp., Frankfurt, Germany, 1980-83; cons. in podiatry to commdg. gen. 7th Med. Command, 1980-83; with U.S. Army Walter Reed Army Med. Ctr., Washington, 1984-85, VA Med. Ctr.,

Alexandria, La., 1985—; clin. instr. Calif. Coll. Podiatric Medicine, San Francisco, 1978-80. Maj. USAR, ret. Decorated Army Commendation medal, 1981; recipient Expert Field Med. badge 3d Bat., U.S. Army, 1984. Fellow Am. Coll. Foot and Ankle Surgeons, Am. Coll. Foot and Ankle Orthop. and Medicine, Am. Acad. Pain Mgmt. (diplomate, bd. cert., Am. Podiatric Med. Assn. (del. ho. of dels. 1985-96, budget com. 1994-96). Avocation: snow skiing. Office: VA Med Ctr Alexandria LA 71306

BUTLER, ROBERT NEIL, gerontologist, psychiatrist, writer, educator; b. N.Y.C., Jan. 21, 1927; s. Fred and Easter (Dikeman) B.; m. Diane McLaughlin, Sept. 2, 1950; children: Ann Christine, Carole Melissa, Cynthia Lee; m. Myrna I. Lewis, May 17, 1975; 1 dau., Alexandra Nicole. BA, Columbia U., 1949, MD, 1953; hon. degree, U. So. Calif., U. Gothenburg, Sweden. Intern St. Lukes Hosp., N.Y.C., 1953-54; resident U. Calif. Langley Porter Clinic, 1954-55; resident NIMH, 1955-56, research psychiatrist, 1955-62; founder geriatric unit Chestnut Lodge, 1958, adminstr., 1958-59; research psychiatrist Washington Sch. Psychiatry, 1962-76; dir. Nat. Inst. on Aging, NIH, 1976-82; prof. geriatrics and adult devel. Mt. Sinai Sch. Medicine, N.Y.C., 1982—; dir. Internat. Longevity Ctr., 1990—, pres., CEO, 1998—; mem. faculty George Washington U. Med. Sch., Washington, 1962-82, Howard U. Sch. Medicine; cons. NIMH, 1967-76, U.S. Senate Spl. Com. on Aging. Author: (with others) Human Aging, 1963, (with Myrna I. Lewis) Aging and Mental Health, 1973, 5th edit., 1998, Why Survive? Being Old in America, 1975, Sex After Sixty, 1976, (with A. Bearn) The Aging Process, 1985, (with Herbert Gleason) Productive Aging, 1985, (with Myrna I. Lewis) Love and Sex After Forty, 1986, Modern Biological Theories of Aging, 1987, Human Aging Research, 1988, The Promise of Productive Aging, 1990, Who is Responsible for My Old Age?, 1993, (with Myrna I. Lewis) Love and Sex After Sixty, 3d edit., 1993, (with Jacob Brody) Delaying the Onset of Late-Life Dysfunction, 1995, (with Howard Fillit) Cognitive Decline, Strategies for Prevention, 1997; editor: Geriatrics; mem. editl. bd. Jour. Geriatric Psychiatry. Sec. Nat. Ballet of Washington, 1962-75; chmn. D.C. Advisory Commn. on Aging, 1969-72; bd. dirs. Nat. Council on Aging, Mildred and Claude Pepper Found. Served with U.S. Maritime Service, 1945-47. Recipient Pulitzer prize for gen. nonfiction, 1976, Leo Laks award, 1976; McIntyre award, 1977, Allied-Signal award, Gustav O. Lienhard award Inst. Medicine NAS, 1996; others. Fellow Am. Psychiat. Assn., Am. Geriatrics Soc. (founding mem.); mem. Group for Advancement Psychiatry (trustee 1974-76), Gerontol. Soc., Forum for Profls. and Execs. (founding). Clubs: Cosmos (Washington); Century (N.Y.C.). Office: Internat Longevity Ctr 60 East 86th St New York NY 10028 *To always stretch the limits of the possible through personal relationships, scholarship, science, writing, action and political activism. To work toward making life a work of art. To do no harm.*

BUTLER, ROBERT OLEN, writer, educator; b. Granite City, Ill., Jan. 20, 1945; s. Robert Olen Sr. and Lucille Frances (Hall) B.; m. Carol Supplee, Aug. 10, 1968 (div. Jan. 1972); m. Marylin Geller, July 1, 1972 (div. July 1987); 1 child, Joshua Robert; m. Maureen Donlan, July 21, 1987 (div. Mar. 1995); m. Elizabeth Dewberry, Apr. 23, 1995. BS summa cum laude in Oral Interpretation, Northwestern U., 1967; MA in Playwriting, U. Iowa, 1969; postgrad., New Sch. Social Rsch., 1979-81; LHD, McNeese State U., 1994. Editor-in-chief Energy User News, N.Y.C., 1975-85; assoc. prof., then prof. fiction writing McNeese State U., Lake Charles, La., 1985—; prof. McNeese State U., 1993—; summer faculty Iowa Summer Writing Festival U. Iowa, Port Townsend (Wash.) Writers Conf., New Orleans Writers' Conf., Southampton Writers' Conf., Long Island U., N.Y., Hofstra U. Summer Writing Conf., Hempstead, N.Y., others 1988—. Author: The Alleys of Eden, 1981 (also wrote screenplay 1991-92), Sun Dogs, 1982, Countrymen of Bones, 1983, On Distant Ground, 1985, Wabash, 1987, The Deuce, 1989, (short story collection) A Good Scent from a Strange Mountain, 1992 (Pulitzer Prize for fiction 1993, Richard and Hinda Rosenthal Found. award Am. Acad. Arts & Letters 1993, nominee PEN/Faulkner award 1993, Notable Book 1993 Notable Books Coun. Am. Libr. Assn.), They Whisper, 1994, Tabloid Dreams, 1996, The Deep Green Sea, 1998; author numerous short stories; works translated to 12 langs.; contbr. articles, book reviews to jours., newspapers, screenplays. Sgt. U.S. Army, 1969-72, Vietnam. Recipient Emily Clark Balch award best work fiction, 1990 Va. Quar. Rev., 1991, TuDo Chinh Kien award outstanding contbns. Am. culture by Vietnam vet. Vietnam Vets. Am., 1987, Medal of Merit, Lotos Club, 1996; grantee NEA, 1994; fellow John Simon Guggenheim Found., 1993. Mem. PEN, WGAWest. Office: Dept of Lang Arts McNeese State U PO Box 92655 Lake Charles LA 70609*

BUTLER, ROBERT THOMAS, retired advertising executive; b. Westmont, N.J., Feb. 22, 1925; s. John T. and Kathryn M. (Donehower) B.; m. Eleanore MacIndoe, May 4, 1950; children—R. Mark, Kathryn J., Elizabeth Anne. B.S., Temple U., Phila., 1951. Market research mgr. James Lees Carpet Co., 1951-53; v.p. N.W. Ayer, Phila., 1953-74; pres. Gray & Rogers, Phila., 1975-90. Served with USCG, 1943-46. Republican. Episcopalian. Clubs: St. David's (Pa.) Golf, Merion Cricket (Haverford, Pa.).

BUTLER, ROBIN ERWIN, retired vocational technical educator, consultant; b. St. Louis, May 16, 1929; s. Erwin and Florence Katherine Butler; m. Marie Day, Aug. 22, 1947; children: Lawrence Robin, Nicki Ruth; m. Linda Koenig, June 12, 1993. BA, Alma Coll., 1960; MDiv., U. Dubuque, 1964; postgrad., U. Wis., 1981—, Pacific Western U., Los Angeles, 1986—. Cert. vocat., tech. and adult edn. tchr. Printer, journalist various corps., Ohio, Ky., Ind., Iowa, 1945-64; asst. pastor presby. Ch., Manitowoc, Wis., 1964-67; program dir. YMCA, Manitowoc, 1968-69; owner operator Butler & Son Contractors, Manitowoc, 1969-72; supr. Mirro Corp., Manitowoc, 1972-81; adult educator Lakeshore Tech. Inst., Cleve., 1981-97, lead instr. mgmt. tech., 1985-86; ednl. cons. Rebcon, Manitowoc, Wis., 1997—; adj. prof. mgmt. Cardinal Stritch Coll., Milw., 1985—, Silver Lake Coll. Manitowoc, 1999—; cons. accelerated adult edn., consensus building, human rels. skills, 1986—. Author: Andragogical Guidelines, 1985; columnist: The Midwest Flyer, 1981-85. Mem. Gov's. Task Force on Aero. Revenues, Madison, 1981. Served to sgt. U.S. Army, 1948-49. Mem. Am. Mgmt. Assn., Internat. Alliance for Learning, Wis. Regional Writers Assn. Roman Catholic. E-mail: rbutler@lsol.net. Home and Office: Rebcon 1408 Columbus St Manitowoc WI 54220-5602

BUTLER, SAMUEL COLES, lawyer; b. Logansport, Ind., Mar. 10, 1930; s. Melvin Linwood and Jane Lavina (Flynn) B.; m. Sally Eugenia Thackston, June 28, 1952; children: Samuel Coles, Leigh F., Elizabeth J. AB magna cum laude, Harvard U., 1951, LLB magna cum laude, 1954. Bar: D.C. 1954, Ind. 1954, N.Y. 1957. Law clk. to Justice Minton U.S. Supreme Ct., 1954; assoc. Cravath, Swaine & Moore, N.Y.C., 1956-60, ptnr., 1961—; dir. Ashland Inc., Millipore Corp., U.S. Trust Corp. Trustee Vassar Coll., 1969-77, N.Y. Pub. Libr., 1979—, Am. Mus. Natural History, 1989-93; chmn. Harvard Coll. Fund, 1977-85; bd. overseers Harvard U., 1982-88, pres. bd., 1986-88; bd. dirs. Culver Ednl. Found., 1981—. With U.S. Army, 1954-56. Mem. Coun. Fgn. Rels. Home: 1220 Park Ave New York NY 10128-1733 Office: Cravath Swaine & Moore 825 8th Ave New York NY 10019-7475

BUTLER, SCOT, economist, researcher; b. Washington, Jan. 6, 1923; s. Ovid McOuat and Adele Steenrod (McMaster) B.; m. Joan Mary Collet, Aug. 28, 1948; children: Scot III, Susan. BA, Swarthmore Coll., 1946; MA, Columbia U., 1951. Econs. intelligence officer U.S. Govt., Washington, 1948-80; cons., 1982-98. Editor Boxwood Bull., 1982-87. Mem. Citizen Assns., McLean, Va., 1960-80, Bluemont, Va., 1982-90. Cpl. U.S. Army, 1943-46, ETO. Recipient Hist. Preservation/Restoration citation Preservation Soc. Loudoun County, 1980, 82. Mem. Shenandoah Astron. Soc., Cosmos Club (com. chmn. 1982), City Tavern Club. Episcopalian. Avocations: gardening, conservation/preservation, astronomy, music, hiking. Home: 107 Cottage Dr Winchester VA 22603-4273

BUTLER, SHEILA MORRIS, occupational health nurse; b. Paducah, Ky., Sept. 12, 1944; d. Edwin Morris and Beatrice Aileen (Hobbs) Word; m. Benjamin Edward Butler, Dec. 4, 1976; 1 child, Michelle Renee. ADN, Paducah Jr. Coll., 1966. Cert. occupational health nurse, Am. Bd. Occupational Health, occupational hearing conservationist. Staff nurse Marshall County Hosp., Benton, Ky., 1966-67; shift nursing supr. Parkview Hosp., Dyersburg, Tenn., 1967-69, obstet. nursing supr., 1969-72; clin. nursing instr. State of Tenn. Dept. of Edn., Nashville, 1968-69; charge nurse Dravo-Groves-NEwberg, Hamlettsburg, Ill., 1972-74; surg. nurse Western Bapt.

Hosp., Paducah, Ky., 1974-76; ophthalmic asst. Dr. Harry Abell, Jr., Paducah, Ky., 1976-83; occupational health cons. self-employed, Paducah, Ky., 1983-86; plant nurse Air Products & Chemicals, Inc., Calvert City, Ky., 1986—; bd. dirs. Nat. Nurses Soc. on Addiction, 1983-84; bd. dirs. Am. Bd. Occupational Health Nurses, 1994—, treas., 1997—; sec. Jackson Purchase Oper. Nurses, Paducah, 1975-76; cmty. asst. panel Agy. for Toxic Substance and Disease Registry of CDC, Atlanta, 1991—; pres. Jackson Purchase Occupational Health Nurse, 1993—. Mem. Nat. Arbor Day Found. Named Student Nurse of Yr., Circle K-Paducah Jr. Coll., 1966, Ky. Col., Gov. Louie B. Nunn, 1971—; recipient Chem. Group Recognition award Air Products & Chems., 1990, 91. Mem. NAFE, Am. Assn. Occupational Health Nurses (pres. Jackson Purchase sect. 1993-95, assoc. bd. dirs. 1994—, treas. 1997—), Civil Def. of McCracken County, Order of Ea. Star, Esther # 5 Ruth, Daus. of the Nile Neith Temple, Chinese Shar-Pei Club of Am. Democrat. Baptist. Avocations: bicycling, swimming, gardening, needle work. Home: 248 Hayes St Benton KY 42025-6649 Office: Air Products & Chemicals PO Box 97 Calvert City KY 42029-0097

BUTLER, SHIRLEY ANN, social worker; b. New Orleans, Apr. 18, 1951; d. John and Will A. (Powell) Cain; children: Chander Lynn, Twann Gerald-Lynn. BSW, So. U. New Orleans, 1980, MSW, 1991. Lic. practical nurse; cert. phlebologist; qualified mental retardation profl. Social worker intern Comty. Svc. Ctr., New Orleans, 1979, VA Hosp. New Orleans, 1979-80; social worker Hope Haven/Madonna Manor, Marrero, La., 1980-81; tchr. Orleans Parish Sch. Bd., New Orleans, 1981-87; psychiat. technician River Oaks Mental Hosp., West Harahan, La., 1981-82; counselor Vols. of Am. of New Orleans, 1987-89; mental retardation profl. Met. Developmental Ctr., Belle Chase, La., 1989-92; case mgr. No AIDS Task Force, New Orleans, 1992-93; nurse St. Anna Nursing Home, New Orleans, 1993-94, Meds Force, 1994—, St. Charles Manor, 1994—; social worker intern Carrollton Hollgrove Comty. Ctr., New Orleans, 1977. Contbr. rsch. articles to profl. jours. Active People's Inst. for Survival and Beyond, New Orleans, 1990—. Mem. NASW, Acad. Cert. Baccalaureate Social Workers. Democrat. Baptist. Home: 9412 Fig St New Orleans LA 70118-1723

BUTLER, STEPHEN GREGORY, accountant; b. Kansas City, Mo.. BBA cum laude, U. Mo. Columbia, 1969. CPA. With KPMG Peat Marwick LLP, Kansas City, 1969-79, ptnr. fin. svcs., 1979-84; mng. ptnr. KPMG Peat Marwick LLP, Memphis, 1984-88, Jacksonville, Fla., 1988-89, Amsterdam, The Netherlands, 1989-92; mng. ptnr. internat. KPMG Peat Marwick LLP, 1992-94; mng. ptnr. KPMG Peat Marwick LLP, N.Y.C., 1994-96, chmn., chief exec., 1996—. Bd. govs. United Way Tri-State; trustee U.S. Coun. Internat. Bus.; mem. adv. bd. European Inst. Bus. Adminstrn. France. Mem. AICPA, N.Y.C. Partnership. Office: KPMG Peat Marwick LLP 345 Park Ave Fl 40 New York NY 10154-0102

BUTLER, STEVEN BAILEY, journalist; b. Berlin, N.H., Mar. 3, 1951; s. John Bailey and Barbara (Buitekan) B.; m. Rose Eng Lee, Aug. 11, 1979; 1 child, Lanya Lee. BA, Sarah Lawrence Coll., 1973; MA, Columbia U., 1976, PhD polit. sci., 1980. Vis. asst. prof. Cornell U., Ithaca, N.Y., 1981-82; fellow Inst. of Current World Affairs, Seoul, 1983-86; Seoul corr. Fin. Times, 1984-86; southeast Asia corr. Fin. Times, Singapore, 1986-87; energy corr. Fin. Times, London, 1988-90; Tokyo corr. Fin. Times, 1991-92; Tokyo bur. chief U.S. News & World Report, 1993—. Mem. Foreign Corr. Club of Japan. Office: U S News & World Report 2400 N St NW Washington DC 20037-1153*

BUTLER, THOMAS WILLIAM, retired health and social services administrator; b. Aiken, S.C., Aug. 29, 1931; s. Eddie and Lillie Mae B.; BA, Adelphi U., 1958; MS in Social Work, Columbia U., 1964; MPA, NYU, 1970; children: Kathi Susan, Thomas William, Michael David. Case supr. Nassau County (N.Y.) Dept. Social Svcs., 1959-67; exec. asst. Joint Legis. Com. on Problems of Public Health Svcs., Medicare, Medicaid and Compulsory Health Ins., N.Y. State, 1967-69; dir. cmty. affairs N.Y.C. Health and Hosps. Corp., 1969-72; with div. alcohol, drug abuse and mental health Public Health Service, Dept. Health and Human Svc., N.Y.C., 1972-95, regional cons. for mental health, 1972-79, regional supr. substance abuse and mental health, 1979-81, co-acting dir. Region II, N.Y.C., 1981, chief health services, 1981-85, chief primary care health services, 1985-86, chief planning, evaluation and data mgmt. services, 1986-95, acting dir. grants mgmt., 1987-88, dep. dir., Divsn. of Health Svcs. Delivery, 1992-95, ret., 1995; guest lectr. NYU, 1977, Grad. Sch. Mgmt. and Urban Professions, New Sch. for Social Rsch., 1977-95. Mem. alumni bd. Columbia U., 1964-67, 76-78, 81-84, Columbia U. Sch. of Social Work rep. Alumni Fedn., 1975-78; bd. dirs. NCCJ, N.Y.C., 1978-80, 80—. Served with U.S. Army, 1954-56; ETO. Recipient Internat. Service award Salvation Army, 1978; univ. athletic scholar, 1952-54, 56-58, univ. acad. scholar, 1952-54. Mem. N.Y. U. Alumni, Adelphi Alumni, Acad. Cert. Social Workers, Nat. Assn. Social Workers, Child Welfare League Am., Am. Legion. Author: Community Organization: A Case Study, 1970; contbr. articles to profl. publs.; inventor in field. Home and Office: 14 N Ferndale Pl Montauk NY 11954 also: 52 Udall Dr Great Neck NY 11020-1530

BUTLER, TYRONE G., records manager; b. Morehead, Ky., Jan. 15, 1948; s. Robert T. and Mercedes (Roncallo) Hance; m. Anne P. Taylor, May 17, 1988; children: Tina, Kean, Nfatal. BA, Xavier U., 1970; MA, Boston Coll., 1972. Cert. records mgr., archivist. Archivist State of Tenn., Nashville, 1977-79, Salvation Army, N.Y.C., 1979-81; coll. archivist Medgar Evers Coll., Bklyn., 1981-82; dep. dir. records mgmt. N.Y.C. Dept. Records, 1982-90, dep. commr., 1990-92; records mgr. N.Y.C. Sch. Constrn. Authoridy, Long Island City, N.Y., 1992-94; cons., CEO Transnational, Staten Island, N.Y., 1995—. Dem. candidate for U.S. Congress, 1994, 96; mem. Dem. County Com., Staten Island, 1990—; mem. Dem. Pub. Policy Com., Staten Island, 1994—; mem. Staten Island Dem. Assn., 1988—, Dem. State Com. Mem. Nat. Assn. Govt. Archives (sec. bd. dirs. 1985-92), Assn. Records Mgrs. and Adminstrs. (pres. 1992-95), N.Y.C. Assn. Records Mgrs. and Adminstrs. (pres. 1988-89, Mem. of Yr. 1988), N.Y. Assn. Govt. Records Adminstrs. (bd. dirs. 1986-90), Mud Ln. Soc. (historian 1997, award 1997, pres. 1999—), Staten Island Inst. for Arts, Snug Harbor. Home and Office: 489 Saint Pauls Ave Staten Island NY 10304-2101

BUTLER, VINCENT PAUL, JR., physician, educator; b. Jersey City, Feb. 16, 1929; s. Vincent Paul and Ruth Eilene (Lynch) B.. A.B., St. Peter's Coll., 1949; M.D., Columbia U., 1954. Intern Presbyn. Hosp., N.Y.C., 1954-55; resident Presbyn. Hosp., 1955-56, 58-59, asst. physician, 1963-68, asst. attending physician, 1968-71, asso. attending physician, 1971-74, attending physician, 1974—; trainee clin. immunology U. Rochester Med. Center, 1959-61; research fellow immunochemistry dept. microbiology Columbia U., 1961-63, asst. prof. medicine, 1963-70, assoc. prof., 1970-74, prof., 1974-98, prof. emeritus, 1999—, spl. lectr., 1999—; asst. vis. physician 1st med. div. Bellevue Hosp., N.Y.C., 1963-68, Harlem Hosp., N.Y.C., 1968-88; mem. VA Merit Rev. Bd. in Immunology, 1974-77, chmn., 1976-77; mem. immunol. sci. study sect. NIH, 1979-83, chmn., 1980-83. Mem. rsch. com. Arthritis Found., 1986-91, chmn., 1989-91; bd. trustees St. Peter's Prep. Sch., Jersey City, 1985-93, chmn., 1991-93. Lt. M.C. USN, 1956-58. Helen Hay Whitney Found. fellow, 1960-63; Arthritis Found. investigator, 1963-68; Josiah Macy, Jr. Found. scholar dept. zoology Univ. Coll., London, 1979-80; recipient Research Career Devel. award NIH, 1968-73; Joseph Mather Smith prize Columbia U. Coll. Physicians and Surgeons, 1973; Irma T. Hirschl Charitable Trust Career Scientist, 1973-78. Fellow AAAS; mem. Assn. Am. Physicians, Am. Soc. Clin. Investigation, Am. Assn. Immunologists, Am. Soc. Pharmacology and Exptl. Therapeutics, Am. Heart Assn., N.Y. Heart Assn., Am. Fedn. Med. Research, Harvey Soc. Roman Catholic. Home: 301 E 66th St Apt 6B New York NY 10021-6215 Office: 630 W 168th St New York NY 10032-3702

BUTLER, WILLIAM H., military officer; b. Cranston, R.I., Nov. 28, 1946; m. Eileen Butler; children: Emily, Meredith. Student, Vanderbilt U. Commd. ensign USN, 1968, CIC/electronic officer USS Forster, 1968-70; naval advisor, logistics officer USN, Vietnam, 1970-72; ret. USN, 1972; with USNR, 1972—, comdr. mil. sealift command Pacific/Far East, dep. comdr. na, 1994—; v.p. prin. Montgomery Watson Ams., Inc.; program mgr. Met. Wastewater Dept. City of San Diego; commdg. officer MIUWU 107, CINCPAC WWMCCS ADP DET 199, COMNAVSURFGRU Long Beach, CINCPACFLT DET 219, comdr. Naval Inshore Undersea Warfare Group 1. Decorated Legion of Merit, Bronze Star with Combat V, Navy Com-

mendation Medal, RVN Gallantry Cross. Mem. Soc. Am. Mil. Engrs. (pres. San Diego post), San Diego C. of C. (mil. affairs com.), Water Environment Fedn. Office: USNR 960 North Harbor Drv San Diego CA 92132-5108*

BUTLER, WILLIAM JOSEPH, lawyer; b. Brighton, Mass., Mar. 22, 1924; s. Patrick Lawrence and Delia (Conley) B.; m. Jane Hays, Dec. 22, 1945; children: Arthur Hays, Patricia. Student, Harvard U., 1946, N.Y. U. Sch. Law, 1949; DHL (hon.), U. Cin., 1988. Bar: N.Y. 1950. Assoc. firm Hays, St. John, Abramson & Schulman, N.Y.C., 1949-53; partner firm Butler, Jablow & Geller, N.Y.C., 1953—; spl. counsel ACLU; lectr. Practising Law Inst., 1966; sec., dir., gen. counsel Walco Nat. Corp., FAO Schwarz, N.Y.C., 1961-85; internat. legal observer to South African Elections, 1994. Author: Human Rights and the Legal System in Iran, 1976, The Decline of Democracy in the Phillipines, 1977, Human Rights in United States and United Kingdom Foreign Policy, Guatemala, a New Beginning, 1987, Palau: A Challenge to the Rule of Law in Micronesia, 1988, The New South Africa - The Dawn of Democracy, 1994; contbr. articles to profl. jours. Mem. commn. urban affairs Am. Jewish Congress, 1965-70; dir. emeritus N.Y. Civil Liberties Union, Internat. League for Human Rights; exec. com. League to Abolish Capital Punishment; standing com. human rights World Peace Through Law Ctr., Geneva; chmn. adv. com. Morgan Inst. Human Rights, U. Cin. Sch. Law; internat. legal observer Internat. Human Rights Orgn., Internat. Criminal Tribunal for Former Yugoslavia in the Hague, The Netherlands, 1996—, various confs. and seminars; mem. faculty Salzburg (Austria) Seminar, 1989; UN Devel. Prog. (UNDP) to Poland, 1992. With U.S. Mcht. Maritime Svc., 1942-45. Recipient spl. citation for contbn. to cause of religious freedom, 1962. Mem. Internat. Commn. Jurists (Geneva) (chmn. exec. com., dir., pres. Am. Assn., UN rep.), Coun. on Fgn. Rels., ABA, Assn. Bar City N.Y. (bd. dirs. ctr. internat. policy, chmn. com. internat. human rights), Inter-Am. Assn. Democracy and Freedom, Internat. Law Assn. (Am. br.), Am. Soc. Internat. Law, HArvard Club (N.Y.C.) (Boston). Home: 24 E 10th St New York NY 10003-5965 Office: 400 Madison Ave New York NY 10017-1909

BUTLER, WILLIAM LANGDON, manufacturing company representative; b. Indpls., Jan. 26, 1939; s. Edward Morris Jr. and Louise Hughes (Dyer) B.; m. Grace Caroline Gage, Dec. 28, 1961; children: Mary Dyer, William Langdon Jr. BA, Middlebury Coll., 1962. With J.J. Newberry Co., N.Y.C., 1961-63; owner Butler Sales Assocs., Summit, N.J., 1965-66; regional mgr. Hi-Fashion Inc., Atlanta, 1966-67; chief exec. officer, owner Butler Sales & Mktg. Inc., Summit, 1967-80; regional sales mgr. Trina Inc., Fall River, Mass., 1980-82, v.p. sales, 1982-87, v.p. gen. mdse. divsn., 1987-97; pres., owner Butler Sales Assocs., 1998—. Coach Jr. Raider Football League, Fanwood, N.J., 1968; trustee Summit Jaycee Found., 1970. Served to 1st lt. U.S. Army, 1963-65. Named One of Outstanding Young Man of Am. Jaycees, 1971. Mem. N.J. NG Assn., Summit Jaycees (Outstanding Dir. award 1970, Key Man award 1970), Soc. for Preservation Barbershop Quartet Singing in Am. (bd. dirs. Westfield 1972-74), Sigma Phi Epsilon. Republican. Presbyterian. Avocations: barbershop quartet singing, philately, spectator sports. Home: 125 Russell Rd Fanwood NJ 07023-1063

BUTLER, WILLIAM THOMAS, college chancellor, physician, educator; b. Boston, Aug. 10, 1932; s. Albert Quigg and Elizabeth West (Viskniskki) B.; m. Marilou Beutel, Apr. 26, 1957; children: Marilyn West, Thomas Charles, Robin Eileen; m. Carol Ann Pike, Nov. 23, 1977. A.B., Oberlin Coll., 1954; M.D., Western Res. U., 1958; grad. program for health systems mgmt., Harvard U., 1974, A.M.P., 1979. Intern and asst. resident in internal medicine Mass. Gen. Hosp., Boston, 1958-61; clin. fellow in medicine Mass. Gen. Hosp. 1960-61, resident in internal medicine, 1964-65; research fellow in bacteriology and immunology Harvard Med. Sch., 1960-61; clin. assoc. Lab. Clin. Investigations, Nat. Inst. Allergy and Infectious Diseases, NIH, Bethesda, Md., 1961-62; chief clin. assoc. Lab. Clin. Investigations, Nat. Inst. Allergy and Infectious Diseases, NIH, 1962-63, clin. investigator, 1963-64, acting head clin. immunology sect., 1965-66; asst. prof. Baylor Coll. Medicine, Houston, 1966-68; assoc. prof. Baylor Coll. Medicine, 1968-71, prof. microbiology and immunology, prof. internal medicine, 1971—, asso. dean, 1973-74, dean admissions, 1974-77, acting exec. v.p., 1976-77, exec. v.p., dean, 1977-79, pres., 1979-96, chancellor, 1996—; mem. spl. med. adv. group VA, 1981-91, chmn., 1984-91; bd. dirs. C.R. Bard Inc., Browning-Ferris Industries, Lyondell Chem. Co., chmn. bd., 1997—; mem. Am. Quality and Productivity Ctr., 1991—, chmn. S.W. CEO Coun., 1997-98, mem., 1994—. Mem. forward planning com. Tex. Med. Ctr., 1981-96; bd. dirs. South Main Ctr. Assn., exec. com., 1980-94, chmn., 1989-91, coun. advisors, 1995—; past assoc. chmn. key group United Way Campaign, Flagship Divsn., group chmn., 1990; mem. Houston Econ. Summit Host Com., 1990; bd. dirs. Blvd. Oaks Civic Assn., 1982-85, Sci. Engring. Fair of Houston, United Way Tex. Gulf Coast, trustee, 1993—, exec. com. 1998—; nat. bd. dirs. Points of Light Found., 1995—; mem. coordinating bd. Tex. Coll. and Univ. System, Health Professions Edn. Adv. Com., 1984-95, chmn., 1988-95; mem. The Houston Forum, 1981—, bd. govs., 1983-92, 96—; mem. Tex. Sesquicentennial Celebration Com., 1984-86; mem. bd. edn. blue ribbon com. Houston Ind. Sch. Dist., 1986; adv. bd. Covenant House Tex., 1987-90; HISD City-Wide Com., 1987; vice-chmn. health svcs. U.S. Savs. Bond Program. Mem. AMA, Am. Assn. Immunologists, Am. Soc. Clin. Investigation, N.Y. Acad. Scis., Infectious Diseases Soc. Am., Inst. Medicine, Nat. Acad. Scis. (membership com. 1992-96, sect. 12 1992—, vice chmn., 1992-94, chmn. 1994-96, com. on prevention and control of sexually transmitted diseases 1995-96, chmn. 1995-96), Assn. Acad. Health Ctrs., Assn. Am. Med. Colls. (chmn. coun. deans 1987-89, adminstrv. bd. 1983-90, exec. coun. 1984-92, mgmt. edn. programs planning com. 1986-96, chmn.-elect 1989-90, chmn. 1990-91, project 3000x2000 implementation com. 1991—, nominating com. chmn. 1992), Royal Soc. Medicine, Harris County Med. Soc., Houston Acad. Medicine, Tex. Med. Assn. (adv. coun. med. edn.), Houston C. of C. (bd. dirs. 1981-82, 83-89), Greater Houston Partnership, Inc. (bd. dirs. 1989, 92-97, co-chair healthcare task force 1994-97, bus. issues adv. com. 1994-98, govtl. rels. adv. com. 1994-97), Points of Light Found. (nat. bd. dirs. 1995—), Houston Ptnrs. Com. (co-chmn. 1991-92), Houston Mus. Nat. Sci. (ex officio 1989-94), River Oaks Country Club, Doctors' Club (bd. govs. 1980-84, pres. 1982), Harvard Bus. Sch. of Houston Club, Sigma Xi, Alpha Omega Alpha. Methodist. Research, numerous publs. on infectious disease and immunology. Office: Baylor College of Medicine One Baylor Pl Houston TX 77030

BUTMAN, BRADFORD, oceanographer; b. Medford, Mass., Oct. 4, 1947; s. Robert Charles and Olive (Coolidge) T.; m. Cheryl Ann Butman, Aug. 18, 1984; children: Dylan, Campbell. BS, Cornell U., 1969; PhD, MIT, 1975. Oceanographer U.S. Geol. Survey, Woods Hole, Mass., 1975—, br. chief, 1989-96. Co-editor: Georges Bank, 1987; contbr. articles to profl. jours. Mem. AAAS, Am. Geophys. Union, Am. Meterol. Soc., Oceanography Soc. Office: US Geol Survey Woods Hole Field Ctr 384 Woods Hole Rd Woods Hole MA 02543-1523

BUTMAN, HARRY RAYMOND, clergyman, author; b. Beverly, Mass., Mar. 20, 1904; s. John Choate and Elsie Louise (Raymond) B.; m. Jennette Alice Stott, Jan. 5, 1929; children: Beverly, Raymond, Jack, Jennette. BD, Bangor Sem., 1928; postgrad., U. Vt., 1933; DD (hon.), Piedmont Coll., 1955. Ordained to ministry Congregational Ch., 1932. Minister Federated Ch., Edgartown, Mass., 1932-37, Congl. Ch., Randolph, Mass., 1937-45, Allin Congl. Ch., Dedham, Mass., 1945-53, Ch. of the Messiah, L.A., 1953-78; interim minister First Congl. Ch., L.A., 1978-81, cons., 1982—; moderator Nat. Assn. Congl. Christian Chs., 1963, chmn. exec. com., 1958, 59, 74; editor, The Congregationalist, 1967-68; chmn. Internat. Congl. Fellowship, London, 1977-81. Author: History of Randolph, 1942, Far Islands, 1949, Preamble to Articles of Assn. for Nat. Assn. Congl. Christian Chs., 1956, The Measure of the Immeasurable, 1967, The Lord's Free People, 1968, Serve with Gladness, 1971, The Theology of Congregationalism, 1975, The Chislehurst Thanksgiving, 1976, The Argent Year, 1980, World Book Ency., Manuscript of Nat. Assn. Congl. Christian Chs., 1981, The Desert Face of God, 1985, Brown Boy, 1987, The Good Beasts, 1991, The Soul's Country, 1994, Symbols of Our Way, 1994, A Quiet and Durable Joy, 1996; contbr. articles to profl. jours. Named for Best Patriotic Sermon Freedoms Found., 1972; honoree of the Harry R. Butman Endowed Chair of Religion and Philosphy Piedmont Coll., Demorest, Ga., 1994; prelate The Soc. of Descendants of Knights of the Most Noble Order of the Garter, 1972—. Republican. Avocations: boating, desert driving. Home: 2451 Soledad Canyon Rd Acton CA 93510-2416*

BUTNER, FRED WASHINGTON, JR., architect; b. Winston-Salem, N.C., Dec. 15, 1927; s. Fred Washington and Katharine Elizabeth (Pritchard) B.; m. Sarah Martha Hinkle, Mar. 25, 1950; children—Fred Raymond, Blain Byerly, David Eugene. B. in Archtl. Engring., N.C. State U., 1949. Draftsman, architect Macklin-Stinson Architects, Winston-Salem, 1949-52; prin. Fred W. Butner, Jr., Assocs., Winston-Salem, 1952—; mem. N.C. Bd. Architecture, 1962-77, pres. 1971-72. Fellow AIA (pres. N.C. chpt. 1971). Democrat. Methodist. Lodge: Lions (pres. 1961-62). Avocations: golf; card games; travel. Home: 100 Westhaven Cir Winston Salem NC 27104-1855 Office: Fred W Butner Jr Assocs 847 W 5th St Winston Salem NC 27101-2505

BUTORAC, FRANK GEORGE, librarian, educator; b. Crosby, Minn., Feb. 12, 1927; s. Frank and Mary (Paun) B.; AB, U. Mich., 1950, AM, 1956, AMLS, 1958; postgrad. Cornell Law Sch., 1950-51, Harvard U., 1953; postgrad. in philosophy U. Notre Dame, 1959, 60-62; postgrad. in theology Holy Cross Coll., 1962-66; postgrad. Cath. U., 1963, Georgetown U., 1965, Cambridge U., 1975, Oxford U., 1989, 95, Trinity Coll., Dublin, 1990; Ph.D. candidate, NYU, 1970; m. Mary Regis McGowan Ratigan, Apr. 8, 1972; stepchildren: Helen Elizabeth, Nicholas. With exec. tng. program U.S. Rubber, Mishawaka, Ind., 1952-53; tchr. 6th grade Jefferson Sch., Wayne, Mich., 1953-54; tchr. social studies Slauson Jr. H.S., Ann Arbor, Mich., 1954-55; supervising tchr. social studies Lincoln Consol. H.S. Eastern Mich. U., Ypsilanti, 1955-57; circulation librarian, engring. libr. U. Mich., Ann Arbor, 1958-59; joined Congregation of Holy Cross, 1959; postulant U. Notre Dame, 1959; seminarian and temporary profession, 1959-66; novice Sacred Heart Novitiate, Jordan, Minn., 1959-60; registrar Mercer C.C., Trenton, N.J., 1966-68, asst. dir. cmty. and extension services, 1968-70, dir. evening and extension ops., 1970-71, dir. spl. programs, 1971-74, dir. libr. svcs., 1974-84, , chmn. libr. tech. program, 1974-84, dir. libr. devel., 1984-87, libr., 1987—; cons. libr. edn., libr. mgmt. Pres. U. Mich. Clubs Coun. 2d Dist., 1991-93; chmn. U. Mich. Newman Ctr. Fund Drive, 1958; professed Secular Franciscan Order Monastery of St. Clare, Bordentown, N.J., 1984. Bd. dirs. U. Mich. Alumni Assn., 1995-98; chmn. Anna B. Stokes Found., Trenton, 1972; dean's adv. com. Cornell Law Sch., 1972-73; mem. N.J. State Adv. Com. on Aging, 1971; mem. Mich. State. Ctrl. Com. Young Democrats, 1949-50. Served with USN, 1944-47. Recipient Tall Cedars of Lebanon award for Cmty. Svc., Trenton, 1974. Mem. ALA, N.J. Libr. Assn. (exec. bd. 1977-78), Purnell Sch. Parents Assn., Cornell Law Assn., Bennington Coll. Parents Assn., Pine Manor Coll. Parents Assn., U. Mich. Cen. N.J. (pres. 1987-91), Mensa, English Speaking Union, Nassau Club (Princeton, N.J.), Princeton Club (N.Y.C.), Trenton Lions Club (pres. 1972), Trenton Torch Club (pres. 1972), Cornell Club of Central N.J. (pres. 1977-78), Marines' Meml. Club (San Francisco), Cath. Alumni Club Trenton (pres. 1968), Theta Delta Chi, Phi Delta Phi, Phi Delta Kappa, Kappa Delta Pi, Alpha Phi Omega. Republican. Roman Catholic. Home: 6 Mercer St Princeton NJ 08540-6808 Office: 1200 Old Trenton Rd Trenton NJ 08690-1004

BUTOW, ROBERT JOSEPH CHARLES, history educator; b. San Mateo, Calif., Mar. 19, 1924; s. Frederick W.C. and Louise Marie B.; m. Irene Elkeles; 1 child, Stephanie Cecile. BA magna cum laude, Stanford U., 1947, MA, 1948, PhD, 1953. Instr. history Princeton U., 1954-59, asst. prof., 1959-60, rsch. assoc. Ctr. of Internat. Studies, 1954-60; assoc. prof. East Asian history and internat. studies U. Wash., Seattle, 1960-66, prof., 1966-90, prof. emeritus, 1990—; mem. Inst. for Advanced Study, 1962-63. Author: Japan's Decision to Surrender, 1954, 67, Tojo and the Coming of the War, 1961, 69, The John Doe Associates: Backdoor Diplomacy for Peace, 1941, 1974. 2d lt. U.S. Army, 1943-46. Grantee Social Sci. Rsch. Coun., 1956-57, Rockefeller Found., 1956-57, Eleanor Roosevelt Inst., 1977-78; Guggenheim fellow, 1965-66, 78-79, fellow Woodrow Wilson Ctr., 1987-88, Japan Found., 1987-88. Mem. Assn. Mems. of Inst. Advanced Study, Soc. Historians of Am. Fgn. Rels., World War Two Studies Assn. Office: U Wash Box 353650 Seattle WA 98195-3650

BUTOWSKY, DAVID MARTIN, lawyer; b. Phila., Aug. 14, 1936; s. Hyman and Pearl (Berks) B.; children: Michael, Ellen, Edward, Erica; m. Fredda Butowsky. A.B., Temple U., 1958; LL.B., George Washington U., 1962. Bar: Md. 1962, N.Y. 1971. Practice law N.Y.C., 1971—; chief enforcement atty. SEC, Washington, 1962-70; assoc. Breed Abbott & Morgan, N.Y.C., 1970-71; ptnr. Butowsky Schwenke & Devine, N.Y.C., 1971-75, Gordon Altman Butowsky Weitzen Shalov & Wein, N.Y.C., 1975—; lectr. to orgns. Contbr. articles to profl. publs. Mem. Am., Fed., N.Y. County bar assns., City Bar Assn. N.Y. Home: 360 E 72nd St Apt C-3202 New York NY 10021-4766 Office: 114 W 47th St New York NY 10036-1510

BUTRIMOVITZ, GERALD PAUL, financial planner, securities analyst, investment advisor; b. Detroit. BA, Wayne State U., 1969; MSc, Ohio State U., 1973; PhD, U. Md., 1977; postgrad. U. Wash., 1978, Inst. for Legis. Assts., Nat. Def. U., 1978, Golden Gate U., 1985. CFP, registered prin., NASD. AAAS congl. sci. fellow, cons. to U.S. Congress, Washington, 1978-80, writer bills on fiscal budgets and health, 1979; asst. prof., affiliate in health policy U. Calif.-San Francisco, 1980-82, biotechnology analyst, cons. 1982-84, Mt. Zion Hosp., San Francisco, 1984; pres. Gerald Butrimovitz and Assocs. Adv. Svcs. Author: Hospital Cost Containment, 1979. Developed NIH Clin. Nutrition Insts. Program, 1977-80; dir. polit mobilization Am.-Israel Pub. Affairs Com. Leadership Coun., San Francisco; fin., investment and endowment coms. Jewish Children and Family Svcs.; former bd. dirs. Jewish Community Ctr., Jewish Community Relations Coun., bd. mem. Hebrew Free Loan of San Fransisco. Fellow Nat. Acad. Clin. Biochemists; mem. Internat. Assn. Fin. Planners, Internat. Fedn. Tech. Analysts, Am. Assn. Individual Investors (bd. dirs., founder fin. planning 1983-88), Tech. Securities Analysts Assn. (pres. 1990, co-dir. mentor program 1991-92, dir. long range planning com. 1992-93, chmn. 1994-97, chmn. emeritus 1998), Internat Fedn. of Tech. Analysts (bd. dir. 1999), Nat. Assn. Securities Dealers (registered prin.), Coll. for Fin. Planning, Inst. Cert. Fin. Planners, Internat. Bd. Standards Practices for Certified Fin. Planners, Internat. Fedn. Tech. Analysts, Sigma Xi (Dalbar seal for fin. profls. 1998).

BUTT, CHARLES CLARENCE, food service executive; b. Houston, Tex., 1938. BS in Econs., U. Pa., 1959; grad. advanced mgmt. program, Harvard U. Pres. H.E.B. Grocery Co., San Antonio, 1971-84, chmn., CEO, 1984—, dir. Tex. Commerce Bancshares, 1974-89. Mem. bd. overseers The Wharton Sch.; mem. bd. dirs. of the assocs, Harvard Bus. Sch.; chmn. adv. coun. U. Tex. Marine Sci. Inst., 1976-86; chmn. M.D. Anderson Cancer Hosp. ann. campaign, 1981; mem. coord. bd. Tex. Coll. and Univ. Sys., 1978-83, chmn. faculty salaries com.; mem. Harvard Bus. Sch.'s Bd. Dirs. of Assocs.; dir. Tex. Commerce Bancshares, 1974-89. Recipient Conservation award Winedale Hist. Ctr., U. Tex., Amanda Cartwright Taylor award San Antonio Conservation Soc., Mr. South Tex. award Washington's Birthday Celebration Assn., 1996. Mem. Order of the Alamo, San Antonio German Club, Argyle Club, Corpus Christi Yacht Club, Nantucket Yacht Club, N.Y. Yacht Club. Avocations: sailing, historical preservation, photography. Office: H E Butt Grocery Co 646 S Main Ave San Antonio TX 78204-1210*

BUTT, EDWARD THOMAS, JR., lawyer; b. Chgo., Oct. 27, 1947; s. Edward T. and Helen Kathryn (Guy) B.; m. Leslie Laidlaw Hilton, Oct. 20, 1972; children: Julie Guy, Andrew McNaughton. BA, Lawrence U., 1968; JD, U. Mich., 1971. Bar: Ill. 1971, U.S. Dist. Ct. (no. dist.) Ill. 1971, Wis. 1975, U.S. Dist. Ct. (ea. dist.) Wis. 1978, U.S. Ct. Appeals (7th cir.) 1978, U.S. Ct. Claims 1982, U.S. Ct. Appeals (6th cir.) 1986, U.S. Ct. Appeals (6th cir.) 1987, Mich. 1997. Assoc. Wildman, Harrold, Allen & Dixon, Chgo., 1971-75, 76-78, ptnr., 1979-94; ptnr. Lund & Butt, S.C., Minocqua, Wis., 1975-76; of counsel Swanson, Martin & Bell, Chgo. and Wheaton, Ill., 1994—. Bd. dirs. Constl. Rights Found., Chgo. Mem. ABA, State Bar Wis., 7th Cir. Bar Assn., Def. Rsch. Inst., Crystal Lake Yacht Club, Crystal Downs Country Club. Avocations: distance running, sailing, golf. Home: Michabou Shores 1006 Tiba Rd Frankfort MI 49635 also: 3903 Forest Ave Western Springs IL 60558-1049 Office: Swanson Martin & Bell 2100 Manchester Rd Ste 1420 Wheaton IL 60187-4534

BUTT, JOHN BAECHER, chemical engineering educator; b. Norfolk, Va., Sept. 10, 1935; s. Willoughby Joseph and Mary Angela (Baecher) B.; m. Regina Elizabeth Roche, June 29, 1963; 1 son, John Baecher (dec.). B.S., Clemson U., 1956; M.Engring., Yale, 1958, D.Engring., 1960. Registered profl. engr., Conn. Instr. chem. engring. Yale, 1959-60, asst. prof., 1960-63, asst. prof. engring. and applied sci., 1963-64, assoc. prof., 1964-69; prof. chem. engring. Northwestern U., Evanston, Ill., 1969—; Walter P. Murphy Prof. Northwestern U., 1981—; vis. prof. U. Tex., summer 1961, U. Calif. at Davis, spring 1967; Solvay vis. prof. U. Libre, Brussels, Belgium, 1971; chmn. Gordon Conf. on Catalysis, 1979; chmn. Internat. Symposium on Catalyst Deactivation, 1991. Assoc. editor: Catalysis Reviews, Chem. Engring. Jour.; contbr. articles to profl. jours. Alexander von Humboldt sr. U.S. scientist award, 1985. Fellow Am. Inst. Chem. Engrs. (A.P. Colburn award 1968, Profl. Progress award 1978, dir. 1975-77); mem. Am. Chem. Soc. (petroleum research fund adv. bd. 1973), AAAS, Catalysis Soc. (E.B. Maxted award 1997), Va. Hist. Soc. Patentee applied chemistry. Home: 2614 Marian Ln Wilmette IL 60091-2208 Office: Dept Chem Engring Northwestern U Evanston IL 60208

BUTTARS, GERALD ANDERSON, librarian; b. Logan, Utah, Oct. 12, 1939; s. Thomas James and Mary (Anderson) B.; m. Jeannie Webb, June 3, 1966; children: Brian Gerald, Angela. BS, Utah State U., 1967; MLS, Brigham Young U., 1970. Dir. libr. for blind and phys. handicapped Utah State Libr., Salt Lake City, 1965—. Recipient Disting. Svc. awards Utah Coun. for Blind, 1979, Brigham Young U., 1986, Francis Joseph Campbell award and citation ALA, 1998. Mem. AIA, Utah Libr. Assn. (exec. sec. 1972-87), Nat. Fedn. Blind, Am. Coun. for Blind. Democrat. Mem. LDS Ch. Home: 4749 W 3280 S Salt Lake City UT 84120-1566 Office: Utah State Libr Blind & Physically Handicapped Program 250 N 1950 W Ste A Salt Lake City UT 84116-7901*

BUTTE, ANTHONY JEFFREY, healthcare executive; b. Greenwich, Conn., June 19, 1951; s. Anthony D. and Lucie R. B.; m. Joan M. McGratty, June 13, 1981; children: Kevin, Erin, Kathleen. BA, Northwestern U., 1973; MBA, Kellogg Grad. Sch. Mgmt., Evanston, Ill., 1975. CPA, Ill. Pres., CEO Westgate Holdings Inc., West Palm Beach/Orlando, 1984-90, Nations Healthcare, Inc., Atlanta, 1990-95; chmn., CEO MedAscend, Inc., Atlanta, 1995—. Mem. Dunwoody C. of C., Isleworth Golf and Country Club, Golf Club Ga. Republican. Roman Catholic. Avocations: golf, running, hiking, reading. Home: 535 Old Cobblestone Dr Atlanta GA 30350-3529

BUTTE, KENNETH MICHAEL, executive; b. N.Y.C., Sept. 5, 1958; s. Henry G. and Jeanne E. B.; m. Carrie Carter, Aug. 28, 1982 (div. Feb. 1983); m. Michele An Chintala, Apr. 24, 1987; children: Jaron Michael, Kyle William, Nicole Lynn. BS in Engring. Mgmt., Ariz. State U., 1980; MBA in High Tech., San Jose State U., 1985. Tech. sales rep. GE, Schenectady, N.Y., 1980-83; mgr. area tech. sales GE, Coshocton, Ohio, 1983-84; mgr. western regional sales Allied Signal, LaCorsse, Wis., 1984-86; sr. process engr. Hughes Aircraft, Fullerton, Calif., 1986-89, mgr. mfg. engring., 1989-90, sr. state mgr. quality, 1990-91; mgr. divsn. quality Hughes Identification Devel., Rancho Santa Margarita, Calif., 1991-93, ops. dir., 1993-95; ops. cons. Westhinghouse Security Elec., Santa Clara, Calif., 1995-97; pres., ptnr. BasIQ Systems, Boulder, Colo., 1997-98, ISONAS Inc., Boulder, Colo., 1998—. Counselor Jr. Achievement, Atlanta, 1980. Wine Street scholar Mid. Country Sch. Dist., Centerbeach, N.Y., 1976. Mem. Am. Soc. Quality Control, Calif. Circuits Assn., Ariz. State U. Alumni Assn., Phi Sigma Kappa (v.p. 1978-80, scholar 1979). Republican. Avocations: golf, skiing. Home: 13 Via Encaro Rancho Santa Margarita CA 92688

BUTTENHEIM, EDGAR MARION, publishing executive; b. Yonkers, N.Y., Dec. 23, 1922; s. Edgar J. and Marian R. (Voorhees) B.; m. Mary Elizabeth Robertson, Aug. 22, 1947; children: Margaret Collier, Anne Robertson, Elizabeth Gay, Martha Bradford. A.B. magna cum laude, Princeton U., 1943; M.B.A., NYU, 1955. Instr. Hotchkiss Sch., Lakeville, Conn., 1946-47; with Buttenheim Pub. Corp., Pittsfield, Mass., 1947-74; exec. v.p. Buttenheim Pub. Corp., Pittsfield, 1963-68, pres., 1969-75; pres. Morgan-Grampian Pub. Co. subs. Morgan-Grampian Ltd., 1975-76, Buttenheim Assocs., Pittsfield, 1976-79; exec. v.p. Springhouse (Pa.) Corp., 1979-87; mgmt. cons. Nat. Exec. Svc. Corps, N.Y.C., 1987—; advisor to pres. William Patterson Coll., Wayne, N.J., 1990-91; adj. prof. mgmt. Union Coll., Schenectady, Rider Coll., Lawrenceville, N.J., autumn, 1987; adj. lectr. MS in pub. degree program Pace U., N.Y.C., 1986-94. Mem., Westchester County Rep. Com., 1957-61; candidate for Mass. Legislature, 1978. 1st lt., F.A. AUS, 1943-46, 51-52. Decorated Bronze Star; McAllister fellow Medill Sch. Journalism Northwestern U., Evanston, Ill., 1984. Mem. UN Assn., Phi Beta Kappa. Home and Office: 186 Lambert Dr Princeton NJ 08540-2307

BUTTENWIESER, LAWRENCE BENJAMIN, lawyer; b. N.Y.C., Jan. 11, 1932; s. Benjamin Joseph and Helen (Lehman) B.; m. Ann Harriet Lubin, July 13, 1956; children—William Lawrence, Carol Helen Sharp, Jill Ann Schloss, Peter Lubin. BA, U. Chgo., 1951, MA, 1955; JD, Yale U., 1956; DHL (hon.), Yeshiva U., 1974. Bar: N.Y. 1956. Assoc. Rosenman & Colin, N.Y.C., 1956-66, ptnr., 1966—; chmn., bd. dirs. Gen. Am. Investors Co., Inc., N.Y.C. Past pres., trustee Associated YM-YWHAs of Greater N.Y.; past v.p., dir. Citizens Housing and Planning Coun. of N.Y.; past treas., dir. City Ctr. of Music and Drama, Inc.; past dir. Coun. on Social Work. Edn.; past trustee Dalton Sch. ; past. hon. chmn. bd., trustee, past pres. Fedn. Jewish Philanthropies N.Y.; past chmn. bd., trustee Montefiore Med. Ctr.; past gen. campaign chmn. United Neighborhood Houses N.Y.; past trustee UJA/Fed. Joint Campaign; past chmn., past trustee Am. Jewish World Svc.; past chmn., trustee Citizens Budget Commn.; dir. Playwrights Horizons Inc., N.Y. Acad. Sci.; trustee U. Chgo. Mem. Assn. Bar City of N.Y. Office: Rosenman & Colin Fl 21 575 Madison Ave New York NY 10022-2585

BUTTER, TOM, sculptor, educator; b. Amityville, N.Y., Oct. 19, 1952; s. George August and Joan (Lund) B. BFA, U. of Arts, Phila., 1975; MFA, Washington U., St. Louis, 1977. Asst. prof. Yale Sch. Art, New Haven, 1986-87, Tyler Sch. Art, Elkins Park, Pa., 1993-94; adj. faculty New Sch./Parsons, N.Y.C., 1988-98; assoc. prof. R.I. Sch. Design, Providence, 1996-97. One-person shows at Curt Marcus Gallery, 1997, two-prson show E.S. Vandam Gallery, 1996; curator group sculpture show E.S. Vandam Gallery, 1995. Vol. firefighter Hankins (N.Y.) Vol. Fire Co., 1992-98. Emerging artist grantee Nat. Endowment for Arts, Washington, 1980, 82, 86, grantee N.Y. Found. for Arts, N.Y.C., 1987, 97. Democrat. Avocation: beekeeping. Home: PO Box 20 Fremont Center NY 12736-0020

BUTTERBRODT, JOHN ERVIN, real estate executive; b. Beaver Dam, Wis., Feb. 14, 1929; s. Ervin E. and Josephine M. (O'Mare) B.; m. June Rose Bohalter, Sept. 27, 1952; children—Claire, Daniel, Larry. U. Agriculture short course, 1946-47. Cert. tchr. real estate, rental weatherization inspector, real estate appraiser, sr. profl. appraiser; internat. cert. farm appraiser; cert. gen., lic. appraiser, Wis. Vice-pres. Pure Milk Assn., 1967-69; pres. Asso. Milk Producers, Inc. Chgo., 1969-75, State Brand Creameries, Madison, Wis., 1970—, Wis. Real Estate Co., Wis. Real Estate of Burnett Inc., 1978—, Sunset Hills Golf & Supper Club Inc., 1979—; chmn. bd. Realty World-Wis. Real Estate, Inc., 1985—; treas. Real Estate Cons., 1983—; dir. Town Mut. Ins. Co., Central Milk Sales, Central Milk Producers Coop. Pres. Sch. Bd., 1968; Bd. dirs. Nat. Milk Producers Fedn., Central Am. Coop. Fedn., World Dairy Expo. Recipient Am. Farmer degree Future Farmers of Am., 1949, hon. degree, 1973; Outstanding Wis. Farmer award, 1965; Outstanding Wis. 4-H Alumni award, 1973; named Realtor of Yr., 1979. Mem. United Dairy Industry Assn. Republican. Office: 1708 N Spring St Beaver Dam WI 53916-1106

BUTTERFIELD, BRUCE SCOTT, publishing, communications and education executive, consultant; b. N.Y.C., Feb. 4, 1949; s. Richard Julian and Mary (Hart) B.; m. Karin Lynn Wittlinger, June 20, 1986; children: Elizabeth Holly, Timothy Hart. BA cum laude, Amherst Coll., 1971; MA, Harvard U., 1972; MBA, U. Conn., 1977; advanced cert. in journalism and creative fiction, Newspaper Inst. Am, 1981. Mng. editor, adminstr. Golden Press/Western Pub. Co., N.Y.C., 1972-77; v.p., pub. Scholastic Inc., N.Y.C., 1978-83; pres. Longman Pub. Group/Pearson PLC, White Plains, N.Y., 1984-93; CEO Prentice Hall Regents/Simon & Schuster/Viacom Inc., Upper Saddle River, N.J., 1993-97; ptnr. Butterwood Venture and Jersey Star, 1998—. Author: Fantasy and the Free School Thought: E.B. White and His Literature for Children, A Plea for Fantasy; Our Real Work Can't Be Drudgery; editor various books including: ABC's Wide World of Sports, Buccaneers; Book of the Mysteries, Chroma-Schema, Calculator Games; Children's Bible Stories, Oh Heavenly Dog, The Watcher in the Woods. Named Most Valuable Pitcher, Bergen Highlanders, 1969, All New Eng. Baseball Pitcher, 1971, All Am. Baseball Pitcher, 1971, named to U. Conn. Bus. Sch. Hall of Fame, 1998; recipient Wall St. Jour. Achievement award; Nat. Fedn. Music award; J.F. Kennedy Brotherhood Essay award; Gardener Fletcher fellow; St. Clair Meml. fellow; Amherst Coll. fellow. Mem. Am. Acad. Arts and Scis., Am. Acad. Polit. and Social Scis., Assn. Am. Pubs., Children's Book Council, M.B.A. Execs., Internat. Platform Assn., Beta Gamma Sigma, Phi Delta Kappa, Phi Delta Sigma. Clubs: Forum, Harvard (N.Y.C.). Home: 752 Charnwood Dr Wyckoff NJ 07481-1085

BUTTERFIELD, CHARLES EDWARD, JR., educational consultant; b. Urbana, Ill., Mar. 31, 1928; s. Charles E. and Bessie J. (Winters) B.; m. Gayle Coberley, Jan. 27, 1952; children: Jeffrey M., Carey J. BS in Biology, Chemistry, Physics, U. Ill., 1951, MS, 1953; postgrad., Duke U., 1958, No. Ill. U., 1958-59, Mich. State U., 1959, 64-65, 72, Knox Coll., 1962, Fla. State U., 1969, U. Colo., 1970. Field exec. Nottawa Trails coun. Boy Scouts Am., Battle Creek, Mich., 1953-54; instr. sci. Gardner (Ill.)-South Wilmington Twp. H.S., 1954-59, Lake Park H.S., Medinah, Ill., 1959-65; sr. sci. project editor Singer/Random House Pub. Co., 1965-68; sci. supr. Ramsey (N.J.) Pub. Schs., 1968-82; sci. edn. cons., 1981—; cons. Rand McNally Pubs., 1972-80; mem. sci. adv. bd. Raintree Publs., Milw., 1981-86; assoc. Thomas A. Edison Found., 1981-88; condr. various workshops for sci. tchg., 1965—. Contbg. author: NSSA Sourcebook for Science Supervisors, 2nd edit., 1976, 3rd edit., 1988. Pres. Bd. Edn., Gardner, 1956-57, Foxwood Village FMO, 1988-90; co-project dir., fin. officer suprs. programs NSF/NSSA/PEEC, 1979-83; treas., bd. dirs. Highland Fairways POA, 1993-96; judge Seiko Youth Challenge, 1994, 95. With USN and USMC, 1946-48. Recipient Allendale (N.J.) Cmty. Lifesaving award, 1976; NSF/AAAS fellow Mich. State U., 1964-65, fellow 1st Southeastern NASA Aerospace Conf., 1961. Fellow AAAS; mem. NEA, Nat. Sci. Suprs. Assn. (mem. exec. com. 1974-80, pres. 1977-78, sr. staff mem. various other confs. U. Calif. at San Diego, 1979, U. Iowa 1979-80, supr. nat. elections 1982—, mem. editl. adv. bd. 1986-91, Outstanding Svc. award 1990), Nat. Sci. Tchrs. Assn. (exec. bd. 1977-78, Disting. Svc. Sci. Edn. citatioin 1981), N.J. Sci. Tchrs. Assn., N.J. Sci. Suprs. Assn. (Disting. Svc. award 1982), Ramsey Suprs. Assn. (founding pres. 1980-81), Bergen County Sci. Suprs. Assn. (pres. 1971-73, Outstanding Svc. award 1974, 78), Sch. Sci. and Math. Assn., Am. Inst. Biol. Scis., Nat. Assn. Biol. Tchrs., Coun. Elem. Sci. Internat., Assn. Edn. Tchrs. Sci., N.J. Prins. and Suprs. Assn., Am. Assn. Notaries, Nat. Notary Assn., U. Ill. Alumni Assn., Cmty. Assns. Inst., 1st Marine Divsn. Assn., Fleet Marine Force Combat Med. Pers. Assn., Am. Legion, USN Meml. Found., Mensa, Masons, DeMolay Internat. (chevalier), Order of Ea. Star, Humanist Assn. West Ctrl. Fla. (charter), Psi Chi. Office: 22 Spring Ave Oakland NJ 07436

BUTTERFIELD, DEBORAH KAY, sculptor; b. San Diego, May 7, 1949. BA, U. Calif., Davis, 1971, MFA, 1973. Asst. prof. sculpture U. Wis., Madison, 1975-76; asst. prof. sculpture Mont. State U., Bozeman, 1979-81, adj. prof., 1981-84. One-man shows include Lowe Mus. Art U. Miami, Coral Gables, Fla., 1992, San Diego Mus. Art, 1996; exhibited in groups shows U. Mus. Berkeley, Calif., 1974, Whitney Mus. Am. Art, N.Y., 1979, Albright-Knox Gallery, Buffalo, 1979, Israel Mus., Jerusalem, 1980, Arco Ctr. Visual Art, 1981, Walker Art Ctr., Mpls., 1982, Dallas Mus. Fine Arts, 1982, Oakland, 1983, Chgo., 1985, Contemporary Art Ctr., Honolulu, 1986, Whitney Mus., 1988, Contemporary Art Mus., Honolulu, 1993, Seattle Mus. Art, 1994, The White House, Washington, Yale U., New Haven, Conn., 1997; represented in permanent collections Whitney Mus. Am. Art, N.Y., San Francisco Mus. Contemporary Art, Israel Mus., Jerusalem, Walker Art Ctr., Mpls., Met. Mus. Art, N.Y., Hirshhorn Mus., Washington, Seattle Art Mus., UCLA Sculpture Garden; commd. Copley Square, Boston, Portland (Oreg.) Airport, Denver Art Mus., Kansas City (Mo.) Zoo. Nat. Endowment Arts grantee, 1977, 80, Guggenheim grantee, 1980; Commission Portland Internat. Airport.

BUTTERFIELD, JAMES T., small business owner; b. Galion, Ohio, July 9, 1951; s. Carlos and Ethel Louise (Miller) B.; m. Mary Anne Shaffo, May 17, 1986; children: Jacob Alan, Emily Lauren. Cert. plumbing insp., backflow insp., cert. pipe welder, EPA cert. refrigerant handling technician, lic. low pressure steam operator, cert. automatic sprinkler installer, cert. plumbing contractor, Ohio. Apprentice Don Barnett Plumbing, Galion, Ohio, 1968-69, Rinehart Plumbing and Heating, Galion, 1969-71; owner Butterfield Plumbing and Heating, Galion, 1972—, Galion Sheet Metal, 1982—. Mem. Am. Soc. Sanitary Engrs., Ohio Assn. Plumbing Insps. Home: 375 W Atwood St Galion OH 44833-2553 Office: Butterfield Plumbing and Heating PO Box 33 Galion OH 44833-0033

BUTTERFIELD, SAMUEL HALE, former government official and educator; b. Moscow, Idaho, Nov. 8, 1924; s. Rolston Samuel and Leone (Hamilton) B.; m. Lois Herrington, Feb. 10, 1948; children: Charles Oliver, Stephen Crandall, Susan Hale (Mrs. Charles P. Waite, Jr.). Student, U. Idaho, 1942-43, 46-47; B.S. in Fgn. Service, Georgetown U., 1949, M.A. in Am. History, 1953. Retail salesman, 1949-50; labor economist Dept. Labor, 1950-53; examiner, fiscal economist, internat. div. Bur. Budget, 1953-58; with AID and predecessors, 1958-80; dir. Office East and So. Africa, 1960-62; dep. dir. Mission to Tanganyika, 1962-64, Mission to Sudan, 1964-65; dir. Mission to Tanzania, 1966-68; mem. sr. seminar in fgn. policy Dept. State, 1968-69; assoc. asst. adminstr. for tech. assistance AID, 1969-76; dir. Mission to Nepal, 1976-80; affiliate prof. U. Idaho, Moscow, 1981-89; sr. advisor on nat. conservation strategy Internat. Union Conservation Nature (IUCN), Govt. Botswana, 1985-87; environ. planning cons. Nepal, 1990. Contbr. articles profl. jours. Pres. Wash.-Idaho Symphony Assn., 1992-95. With USAAF, 1943-46. Recipient Superior Honor award U.S. AID, 1974, Outstanding Career Achievement award, 1981; named disting. vol. Wash.-Idaho Symphony, 1996; named to alumni Hall of Fame U. Idaho, 1999. Mem. Soc. for Internat. Devel. (pres. Palouse chpt. 1982-83), Kalahari Conservation Soc., Wash. Idaho Symphony Assn., Sr. Seminar Alumni Assn., Beta Theta Pi. Office: 328 N Polk St Moscow ID 83843-2747

BUTTERFIELD, STEPHEN ALAN, education educator; b. Middlebury, Vt., Sept. 10, 1948; s. Stewart Ellsworth and Mary Elizabeth (Coursey) B.; m. Jeanne Allison Zong, June 20, 1970; children: Sarah, Jason, Scott. BS, Springfield (Mass.) Coll., 1971; MEd, Keene State Coll., 1980; PhD, Ohio State U., 1984. Tchr. 4th grade Whitingham Sch., Jacksonville, Vt., 1971-72; prin., tchr. Halifax Sch., West Halifax, Vt., 1972-73; tchr. phys. edn. Austine Sch. for the Deaf, Brattleboro, Vt., 1973-81; prof. edn. and spl. edn. U. Maine, Orono, 1984—; project dir. Nat. Youth Sports Program, state coord.; chmn., mem. Maine Task Force on Adapted Phys. Edn.; mem. Maine Comprehensive Sys. Pers. Devel. Editor Maine Jour. Health, Phys. Edn., Recreation and Dance, 1988-96; contbr. articles to profl. jours. Bd. dirs. Bangor (Maine) YMCA, 1990-92, Maine Adapted Sports and Recreation, 1994-98; mem. Gov.'s Coun. Phys. Fitness and Sports; mem. nat. stds. com. Adapted Phys. Edn.; mem. adv. bd. U.S. Sports and Fitness Ctr. for Disabled. Recipient Meritorious award for Exceptional Project Performance, Nat. Youth Sports Program; state, fedn. found. grantee. Mem. AAHPERD (ea. dist. merit award for phys. edn. 1989), Maine Assn. Health, Phys. Edn., Recreation and Dance (pres. 1986-87, Honor award for disting. leadership 1989), Nat. Consortium Phys. Edn. Recreation for Individuals with Disabilities (bd. dirs. 1997—, editor The Advocate 1994-96). Republican. Avocation: military history. Home: 277 14th St Bangor ME 04401-4454 Office: U Maine 5740 Lengyel Hall College Ave Orono ME 04469-5740

BUTTERKLEE, NEIL HOWARD, lawyer; b. Bklyn., Mar. 17, 1958; s. Samuel and Edith (Uday) B.; m. Arlene Marie Eberle, July 5, 1982. BA, SUNY, Stony Brook, 1980, MS, 1982; MBA, Adelphi U., Garden City, N.Y., 1987; JD, N.Y. Law Sch., 1992. Bar: Conn. 1992, N.Y. 1993, D.C. 1994, U.S. Dist. Ct. (ea. and so. dists.) N.Y. 1993, U.S. Ct. Appeals (D.C. cir.) 1997, U.S. Supreme Ct., 1997. Tech. writer Consolidated Edison Co. N.Y. Inc., N.Y.C., 1982-83, analyst, 1983-89, sr. analyst, 1989-93, atty., 1993-95, staff atty., 1995-99, sr. staff atty., 1999—. Editor: Law Review. Recipient Scholarship N.Y. Law Sch., N.Y.C., 1988-92; nationally ranked fencer U.S. Fencing Assn., 1984-88. Mem. ABA, N.Y. State Bar Assn., Conn. Bar Assn., Assn. Bar City N.Y. Avocations: golf, writing. Office: Consolidated Edison Co NY 4 Irving Pl Rm 1815 New York NY 10003-3598

BUTTERS, JOHN PATRICK, educator, tour director; b. Janesville, Wis., Jan. 11, 1933; s. John William and Mary Helen (Tracey) B.; m. Collette

Helen Jung, Apr. 20, 1963; children: Blair John, Laura Lisbeth. BA, U. Wis., 1955. cert. travel counselor. Traffic supr., field training Pan Am. Airways, Chgo., 1958-64; ops. mgr. incentives Lerios/E.F. MacDonald, San Francisco, 1964-67; retail agy. mgr. Bungey Travel, Palo Alto, Calif., 1967-68; dist. sales mgr. Lissonne Lindeman, San Francisco, 1968-71; group travel mgr., Wis. div. Am. Automobile Assn., Madison, 1971-75; owner, v.p., sec. Travel/ease Inc., Madison, 1975-88; owner, pres. Travel Learn, Ltd., Madison, 1981-90; sr. curriculum specialist Inst. Cert. Travel Agts., Wellesley, Mass., 1989-93; free lance tour coord., tour escort Gretchen Petersen Tours, Inc., Madison, Wis., 1993—, Van Galder Tour and Travel, Janesville, Wis., 1996—; cons. Madison Area Tech. Coll., 1982-88, Rockford (Ill.) Bus. Coll., 1988-90; treas. Capital Area Travel Soc., Madison, 1973-77. Editor: Travel Industry Mktg., 1990, Travel Industry Bus. Mgmt., 1992, U.S.A.-Can., 1992, Pacific Rim, 1993, Latin Am., 1994; contbr. articles to profl. jours. Program chmn. The Travel Club, Madison, 1973-77; bd. trustees St. Andrew's Soc., Madison, 1976-88 (treas. 1975-79); chmn. mus. svc. coun. Rock County Hist. Soc., Janesville, Wis., 1985-89; trustee Schumacher Farm Conservancy, Waunakee, Wis., 1984—. Mem. Inst. Cert. Travel Agts. (life), U. Wis. Alumni, Madison Club. Avocations: travel, reading, geneology, history, geography. Home: 1328 Oakland Ave Janesville WI 53545-4243 Office: Van Galder Tour and Travel 20 S Main St Janesville WI 53545-3959

BUTTERS, RONALD RICHARD, English language educator; b. Cedar Rapids, Iowa, Feb. 12, 1940; s. Richard Orton and Dorothy Mae B.; children: Rebecca, Catherine, Rachel. BA, U. Iowa, 1962, PhD, 1967. Asst. prof. English Duke U., Durham, N.C., 1967-74, assoc. prof. English, 1974-90, prof. English, 1990—; editor Am. Speech Jour. of the Am. Dialect Soc., 1981-95; vis. scholar Ctr. for Applied Linguistics, Washington, 1988-89. Author: The Death of Black English, 1989; co-author: Displacing Hompohobia, 1989 (CEW best spl. issue award 1989); chief editor Am. Dialect Soc. publs., 1996—. Recipient Rsch. grant NEH, 1973-74. Mem. Am. Dialect Soc. (v.p. 1997-98), Internat. Assn. Forensic Linguists, Linguistic Soc. Am., Southeastern Conf. on Linguistics (pres. 1983), Law and Soc. Assn., Dictionary Soc. of N.Am. Home: 1002 Lamond Ave Durham NC 27701-2021 Office: Duke U PO Box 90018 Durham NC 27708-0018

BUTTERWORTH, DANIEL DREW, humanities educator, consultant; b. Mountain View, Calif., Aug. 3, 1968; s. Ralph Drew Butterworth and Kathryn Louise (Muehsam) Gallagher; m. Rose Marie Woerdeman, May 27, 1989. BA in Psychology, Bethany Coll., Scotts Valley, Calif., 1993; MA in English and Creative Writing, Tex. Tech U., 1997. Tchg. asst. psychology Tex. Tech U., Lubbock, 1993-94, tchg. asst. Stats. Lab., 1994-95, instr. dept. English,, 1995—, cons. writing, 1996—. Author poems (Editor's Choice award 1995). Fundraiser South Plains AIDS Resource Ctr., Lubbock, 1997. With U.S. Army, Germany, 1986-90. Chancellor's fellow Tex. Tech U., 1997-2000, Incentive scholar dept. English, 1995, Locke scholar dept. psychology, 1994, acad. scholar Bethany Coll., 1991-93. Mem. Acad. Am. Poets, Grad. English Soc., The Poet's Circle. Avocations: oral poetry readings, writing poetry, reading. Office: Tex Tech U English Dept MS 43091 Lubbock TX 79409

BUTTERWORTH, RITAJEAN HARTUNG, broadcast executive; b. 1931; m. Fred R. Butterworth; 5 children. Bd. dirs. Corp. Pub. Broadcasting, Washington, 1992—; chmn. bd. Corp. Pub. Broadcasting, 1995-96; treas., bd. dirs. Discovery Inst., 1990—. Bd. trustees Western Wash. U., Bellingham, 1969-77, sec., vice chmn., chmn. bd.; mem. NPR Bd., 1977-85, sec., vice chmn.; mem. adv. bd. Sta. KUOW-FM, Seattle, 1985-88, KCTS, Seattle, 1989—; mem. coun. Annenberg/CPB Project; Wash. state dir. Senator Slade Gorton, 1981-86, 88-90; active Children's Orthop. Hosp., Child Ryther Ctr., Seattle, 1989-91; mem. merit selection panel eastern dist. U.S. Dist. Ct., Wash. Office: Corp Pub Broadcasting 901 E St NW Washington DC 20004-2012*

BUTTERWORTH, ROBERT A., state attorney general; b. Passaic, N.J., Aug. 20, 1942; m. Marta Prado. BA, BS, U. Fla.; JD, U. Miami. Prosecutor Fla., 1970-74; circuit and county judge, 1974-78; sheriff Broward County Sheriff's Office, 1978-82; head Fla. Dept. Hwy. Safety and Motor Vehicles, Tallahassee, 1982-84; mayor City of Sunrise, 1984-87; atty. gen. State of Fla., Tallahassee, 1987—. Office: Capital PL01 Dept Legal Affairs Tallahassee FL 32399-1050*

BUTTERWORTH, ROBERT ROMAN, psychologist, researcher, media therapist; b. Pittsfield, Mass., June 24, 1946; s. John Leon and Martha Helen (Roman) B. BA, SUNY, 1972; MA, Marist Coll., 1975; PhD in Clin. Psychology, Calif. Grad. Inst., 1983. Asst. clin. psychologist N.Y. State Dept. Mental Hygiene, Wassaic, 1972-75; pres. Internat. Trauma Assocs., L.A. and Downey, Calif., 1976—; cons. L.a. County Dept. Health Svc.; staff clinician San Bernardino County Dept. Mental Health, 1983-85; staff psychologist State of Calif. Dept. Mental Health, 1985—; media interviews include PA, L.A. Times, N.Y. Times, USA Today, Wall St Jour., Washington Post, Redbook mag., London Daily Mail and many others; TV and radio interviews include Larry King Live, CBA, NBA and ABC networks, Oprah Winfrey Show, CNN Newsnight, Can. Radio Network, Mut. Radio Network and many others. Served with USAF, 1965-69. Mem. Am. Psychol. Assn. for Media Psychology, Calif. Psychol. Assn., Nat. Accreditation Assn. Psychoanalysis. Office: PO Box 76477 Los Angeles CA 90076-0477

BUTTLAR, RUDOLPH OTTO, retired college dean; b. Chgo., Dec. 31, 1934; s. Otto Robert and Lucille Ann (Blasnig) B.; m. Lois Jacqueline Mercier, June 5, 1955; children—Michael Robert, Andrew Scott, John David. B.S. in Chemistry, Wheaton (Ill.) Coll., 1956; Ph.D. in Inorganic Chemistry, Ind. U., 1962. Mem. faculty Kent (Ohio) State U., 1962-96, asso. prof. chemistry, 1971-96; dean Kent (Ohio) State U. (Coll. Arts and Scis.), 1975-96; adminstrv. cons., 1996—. Mem. Am. Chem. Soc., Am. Sci. Affiliation. Baptist. Home: 5936 Horning Rd Kent OH 44240-4140

BUTTNER, JEAN BERNHARD, publishing company executive; b. New Rochelle, N.Y., Nov. 3, 1934; d. Arnold and Janet (Kinghorn) Bernhard; m. Edgar Buttner, Sept. 13, 1958 (div.); children: Janet, Edgar Arnold, Marianne. BA, Vassar Coll., 1957; cert. bus. adminstrn., Harvard-Radcliffe program, 1958; Montessori diploma, Coll. Notre Dame, Belmont, Calif., 1967; D Bus. Adminstrn. (hon.), U. Bridgeport, 1994. Past v.p. Buttner Cos., Oakland, Calif.; pres., COO Value Line Inc. (subs. Arnold Bernhard & Co.), N.Y.C., 1985-87, chmn., pres., CEO, 1988—; chmn., CEO, pres. Arnold Bernhard & Co., Inc., 1988; chmn., pres. Compupower, 1998—, Vanderbilt Advertising, 1998—; chmn., pres. Value Line Mutual Funds. Editor-in-chief The Value Line Investment Survey, The Value Line Mut. Fund Survey, The Value Line No-Load Fund Advisor, The Value Line Options Survey, The Value Line Convertible Survey, The Value Line OTC Spl. Situations Survey, Value Line Investment Survey for Windows, Value Line Mut. Fund Survey for Windows, Value Line No-Load Analyser for Windows, Value Line on Compuserve, Value Line Daily Options, Convertible DataFile, Mut. Fund DataFile, DataFile and DataFile II, Estimates and Projections, Value Line and Microfiche, Value Screen III, Value Line Select, others. Trustee Radcliffe Coll.; past pres. Piedmont Sch. Bd.; past dir. Berkeley Montessori Sch.; mem. N.Y.C. Partnership, Com. of 200; past mem. adv. coun. Stanford Bus. Sch.; past mem. The Presdl. Roundtable; past vis. com. for bd. overseers Harvard Bus. Sch.; past bd. dirs. Harvard Bus. Sch. Club Greater N.Y.; past west coast admissions rep. Vassar Coll., Harvard U., Harvard Bus. Sch; past trustee, Williams Coll., Emma Willard School, Coll. Prep. School, comm. for econ. devel.sss. Named one of N.Y.'s 75 Most Influential Women in Business, Crain's, 1996; recipient Alumni Achievement award, Harvard U. Grad. Sch. Bus. Adminstrn., 1995, Alumnae award Choate Rosemary Hall, Wallingford, Conn., 1995, Emma Lazarus award Associated Builders and Owners of N.Y., Inc., 1996; Life Achievement Award, 1998. Mem. Com. 200, Harvard Bus. Sch. Club Greater N.Y., Inc., N.Y. Partnership; trustee, Radcliffe Coll.; mem. NYC partnership, comm. of 200, Harvard Bus. School Club of Greater New York. Republican. Congregationalist. Avocations: reading, swimming, biking, tennis, skiing. Office: Value Line Inc 220 E 42nd St Fl 6 New York NY 10017-5891

BUTTOLPH, JOHN, company executive; b. Dec. 24, 1928. Pres. Sholodge Franchise Sys., Inc., Hendersonville, Tenn., 1993—; v.p. Sholodge, Inc., Hendersonville, 1993—. Office: Sholodge Franchise Sys. Inc and Sholodge Inc 130 Maple Dr N Hendersonville TN 37075

BUTTON, JERRY EDWARD, biologist; b. Coos Bay, Oreg., Dec. 8, 1946; s. George Deward and Gladys Wilhelmina (Lunden) B.; m. Dorothy P. Steele, June 17, 1977 (div. Aug. 1991). BS summa cum laude, Lewis & Clark Coll., 1969; MS with honors, U. Oreg., 1974; EdD, Portland State U., 1991. Grad. tchg. fellow dept. biology U. Oreg., Eugene, 1971-73; prof. biology Portland C.C., 1973—; cons. in field. Vol. numerous orgns. NSF grant, 1998; named Outstanding Instr., Heart Inst., 1994, Great Tchr., Great Tchrs. Assn. Mem. AAAS, Human Anatomy & Physiology Soc., Union of Concerned Scientists, N.W. Biology Assn., Oreg. Acad. Sci., N.Y. Acad. Sci. Democrat. Unitarian. Avocations: flower gardening, photography, physical fitness, travel, reading. Office: Portland CC 12000 SW 49th Ave Portland OR 97219-7132

BUTTON, KENNETH JOHN, physicist; b. Rochester, N.Y., Oct. 11, 1922; s. Kenneth Paul and Ruth Caroline (Wagner) B.; m. Margaret Jane Wells, Dec. 22, 1952 (div. 1971); m. Susan Madeleine Wood, Apr. 6, 1997. B.S., U. Rochester, 1950, M.S. in Physics, 1952; Sc.D., Tokyo Inst. Tech., 1985. Research physicist MIT, Cambridge, Mass., 1952-62, research group leader, 1962-72, sr. scientist, 1972-87, vis. sr. scientist, 1988—; organizer, program chmn. Ann. Internat. Conf. on Infrared and Millimeter Waves, 1974—. Author: Microwave Ferrites & Ferrimagnetics, 1962; editor: Infrared and Millimeter Waves, Vol. 1-16, 1979-86, Internat. Jour. Infrared and Millimeter Waves, Vol. 1-20, 1980—, Topics in Guided Wave Propagation, Vol. 1-2, 1988. Served with U.S. Army, 1942-46. Decorated Bronze Star with oak leaf cluster; recipient Ann. K.J. Button award in far infrared physics Inst. Physics (London), 1990. Fellow IEEE (Disting. Svc. award Microwave Soc. 1980, Cert. of Merit 1981), Am. Inst. Physics, Am. Phys. Soc. Republican. Episcopalian. Office: 2095 N Highway A1A Indialantic FL 32903-2514

BUTTON, LUELLA MARY WATKINS (LUE), retired physicist, dog trainer, coach rescue team; b. Fargo, N.D., Jan. 17, 1929; d. F. Leland and Luella Audrey (Cowen) Watkins; m. Thomas W. Hall, July 7, 1954 (div. Feb., 1965); m. Donald Marshall Button, Sept. 18, 1972; stepchildren: Marie, James, Roger (dec.), Frank. BA in English, Speech, Hamline U., 1950; MA in Speech, U. Minn., 1951; BS in Physics, U. N. Mex., 1967, MS in Physics, 1974. Office mgr. Brooks-Feeger Assocs., Albuquerque, N. Mex., 1953-57; acct., office mgr. Data Tech., Inc., Albuquerque, N. Mex., 1957-64; contract adminstr. Sparton SW, Albuquerque, N. Mex., 1965-66; instr. Draughtons Coll., Albuquerque, 1953-67; failure rate analyst U.S. Navy Ship Missile System Engring. Sta., Port Heuneme, Calif., 1967-68; physics writer Los Alamos (N. Mex.) Nat. Lab., 1968-90; co-owner, mgr. Von Knopf Weimaraners & K-9 Kindergarten, Albuquerque, 1990—. Author: (book) Practical Scent Dog Training, 1990 (Best Tng. Book of Yr. Dog Writers Am., 1990); contbr. articles and fiction to Am. Kennel Club Gazette (winner 1st ann. fiction contest). Recipient Founder award for disting. svc. Mountain Canine Corps, Los Alamos, N. Mex., 1995, 97. Mem. Weimaraner Club Am., Weimaraner Club Albuquerque (pres. 1982—, show, field chair), Los Alamos Dog Obedience Club (instr., trial chair, sec.-treas 1969), Sangre de Cristo Kennel Club (sec. 1994, treas., 1005-97). Avocations: riding, hiking, gardening, reading, inventing. Office: K-9 Kindergarten Von Knopf Weims PO Box 39 Albuquerque NM 87510

BUTTON, RENA PRITSKER, public affairs executive; b. Providence, Feb. 15, 1925; d. Isadore and Esther (Kay) Pritsker; m. Daniel E. Button, Aug. 16, 1969; children by previous marriage: Joshua, Bruce, David Posner. Student, Pembroke Coll., 1942-45; BS, Simmons Coll., 1948; postgrad., Union U., 1968-69. Spl. asst. to U.S. Rep., 1967-69; spl. projects coord. United Jewish Appeal, 1971-74; exec. dir. Nat. Coun. Jewish Women, Inc., N.Y.C., 1974-76; pres. Button Assos., N.Y.C., 1976—; exec. v.p. Catalyst, N.Y.C., 1980-82; pres. Button & Button, Albany, N.Y., 1982—; mem. adv. coun. N.Y. State Senate Minority, 1980—; exec. dir. N.Y. State Coun. on Alcoholism and Other Drug Addictions, 1990-93; pres. Two Together, A Pilot Reading Program for Young People. Co-producer, moderator: TV pub. affairs program Speak For Yourself, Albany, N.Y., 1963-66. chmn. pub. affairs com. Marymount Manhattan Coll.; past bd. dirs. Albany YWCA, Albany Coun. Chs. Devel. Corp., World Affairs Coun., Planned Parenthood Assn. Albany; trustee Jerusalem Women's Seminar, Citizens for Family Planning, N.Y. Com. Integrated Housing, Hist. Albany Found. Ctr. for Counseling; pres. Sr. Svc. Ctr. Albany Area, Two Together, 1997; bd. dirs. Com. Modern Cts.; exec. dir. N.Y. Head Injury Assn., 1993-96; candidate N.Y. Stae Assembly 102d Dist., 1996. Mem. Siasconset Casino Club, Univ. Club. Clubs: Siasconset Casino (Siasconset, Mass.), Univ. (Albany). Home and Office: 16 Spruce Ct Delmar NY 12054-2614

BUTTON, RICHARD TOTTEN, television and stage producer, former figure skating champion; b. Englewood, N.J., July 18, 1929; s. George and Evelyn Bunn (Totten) B.; children: Edward Totten, Emily Rada. BA, Harvard U., 1952, LLB, 1956; LHD (hon.), Buena Vista Coll., 1988. Founder, pres. Candid Prodns., Inc., N.Y.C., 1959—; dir. Decorative Arts Trust, 1979-80; commentator ABC Sports; creator, owner The Superstars sports competitions, The World Profl. Figure Skating Championships, ABC World Challenge of Champions figure skating competitions; producer Broadway shows: Sweet Sue, 1987, Artist Descending a Staircase, 1989. Author: Dick Button on Skates, 1955, Instant Skating, 1964; contbr. articles to various mags. Pres. Richmondtown Restoration, Inc., 1968-77. U.S. figure skating champion, 1946-52; world figure skating champion, 1948-52; European figure skating champion, 1948; Olympic gold medalist, 1948, 52; recipient James E. Sullivan award, 1949, Emmy award for outstanding sports personality-analyst, 1980-81; named to U.S. Olympic Hall of Fame. Mem. Bar Assn. D.C., Skating Club N.Y., Skating Club Boston, Phila. Skating Club. Office: Candid Prodns Inc 250 W 57th St Ste 1818 New York NY 10107-1899

BUTTRAM, DEBRA DORIS, dog trainer, apparel executive; b. Port St. Joe, Fla., Aug. 22, 1954; d. Wayne Morrison Sr. and Doris Mae (Amos) B.; m. David Cheuk Kun Kong, Dec. 29, 1979 (div. 1989); m. Marcello Galimberti, June 12, 1993. BS in Early Childhood Edn., Fla. State U., 1978. English tchr. Metta Found. for Refugees, Sydney, Australia, 1979; exec. asst. East West Freight Ltd., Hong Kong, 1981-82; boutique dir. Diane Fries Ltd., Hong Kong, 1985; buyer, boutique dir. Joyce Boutique Ltd., Hong Kong, 1985-87; mktg., sales exec. Icarus Ltd. (Chanel), Hong Kong, 1988-90; freelance wholesale fashion vendor Milan, Italy, 1991—; sales mgr. New York Industrie, Milan, Italy, 1997-98; showroom mgr. Staff Internat., Milan, 1998—; trainer, sec. Italian Assn. for use of Assistance Dogs, Bsisio Parini, 1992—. Avocations: mountain walking, reading, dog training, travel. Home and Office: Via IV Novembre 26, 23842 Bosisio Parini Italy

BUTTREY, DONALD WAYNE, lawyer; b. Terre Haute, Ind., Feb. 6, 1935; s. William Edgar and Nellie (Vaughn) B.; children: Greg, Alan, Jason; m. Karen Lake, Mar. 23, 1985. BS, Ind. State U., 1956; JD, Ind. U., 1961. Bar: Ind. 1961, U.S. Dist. Ct. 1961, U.S. Ct. Appeals (7th cir.) 1972, U.S. Tax Ct. 1972, U.S. Supreme Ct. 1972. Law clk. to chief judge Steckler, U.S. Dist. Ct. So. Dist. Ind., 1961-63; mem. McHale, Cook & Welch, P.C., Indpls., 1963—, pres., 1986-93, chmn., 1993—; chmn. Ctrl. Region IRS-Bar Liaison Com., 1984; mem. jud. nominating com. marion County Mcpl. Ct., 1993-96; mem. Estate Planning Coun. Indpls. Note editor Ind. Law Jour., 1960-61. Trustee Ind. State U., 1992—, v.p. bd., 1997—; bd. dirs. Ind. State U. Found., 1991—. With AUS, 1956-58, Korea. Fellow Am. Coll. Tax Counsel, Am. Bar Found., Ind. State Bar Found., Indpls. Bar Found. (pres. 1993-96); mem. ABA (taxation, real property, probate and trust sect., liaison IRS-Bar Liaison com., taxation sect. 1995-96), Ind. State Bar Assn. (bd. govs. 1994-96, taxation, real property, probate and trust sect., chmn. taxation sect. 1982-83), Indpls. Bar Assn. (pres. 1990, mem. probate, taxation sects.), Ind. Soc. Chgo., Highland Golf and Country Club, Indpls. Athletic Club (bd. dirs. 1982-88), Skyline Club, Univ. Club (bd. dirs. 1997—). Presbyterian. Office: McHale Cook & Welch PC 1100 C of C Bldg 320 N Meridian St Ste 1100 Indianapolis IN 46204-1781

BUTTRICK, HAROLD, architect; b. Bryn Mawr, Pa., Jan. 2, 1931; s. Charles Edgar and Constance (La Boiteaux) B.; m. Ann Octavia White, Sept. 3, 1955; children: John Ward, Jerome Chanler, Mary Constance, Sarah Elizabeth, Catherine. Student, The Sorbonne, Paris, 1950-51; AB, Harvard U., 1953, MArch, 1959. Cert. NCRB. Prin. Harold Buttrick & Assocs., N.Y.C., 1963-75, Smotrich Platt & Buttrick, N.Y.C., 1975-76, Buttrick White & Burtis, N.Y.C., 1976-97, Murphy Burnham & Buttrick, N.Y.C., 1998—. Prin archtl. works include Corpus Christi Monastery, Nairobi, Kenya, 1967, Green Vale Sch., Iselin Ctr., Glen Head, N.Y., 1971, Trans World Airlines 747 Hangar, John F. Kennedy Airport, 1971, Carter Giraffe House, Bronx Zoo, 1981, 42 Tower Records Stores, 1982—, St. Thomas Choir Sch., N.Y.C., 1987, Central Park projects, Loeb Boathouse, 1986, Ballplayers Refreshment Stand, 1990, Outdoor Performance State in Bushnell Park, Hartford, Conn., restoration of the Pulitzer Fountain and Grand Army Plz., 1990, The Charles A. Dana Discovery Ctr., 1993, Battery Park City Authority Offices, 1996, Trinity Mid. Sch., N.Y.C., 1998. Bd. dirs. N.Y. Soc. Libr., 1989-93. Recipient Preservation League of N.Y. State awards, 1990-91, 96, City Club of N.Y. Bard awards Loeb Boathouse, 1986, St. Thomas Choir Sch., 1990, Ballplayers Refreshment Stand, 1992. Fellow AIA (Honor award 1972, Brick in Architecture award 1991-95), N.Y. State Assn. Architects; mem. Century Assn., Harvard Club of N.Y.C.

BUTTS, CAROL HENDERSON, personnel consultant; b. Anniston, Ala., Feb. 11, 1946; d. William Edward and Mary (Hill) Henderson; m. Robert Russell Butts, Feb. 12, 1976 (div. Mar. 1989); 1 child, Jabe Bowden. BA, Jacksonville State U., 1970. Cert. pers. cons. Fellow Am. Biographical Inst. From pers. counselor to tng. dir. Norrell, Inc., Atlanta, 1971-77; creative dir. TV Tempo Stevens County, Toccoa, Ga., 1978-82; gen. mgr. Niermann Pers. Svcs., Atlanta, 1983-87; dir. tng. and continuing edn. KOT Pers., Atlanta, 1987-90; gen. mgr., v.p. med. divsn. Prestige Pers. Svcs., Norcross, Ga., 1990-94; dir. med. divsn. MedPro Pers., Atlanta, 1994-95; pres. MedStat, Inc., Alpharetta, Ga., 1995—. Pres. Habitat for Humanity, 1996-97. Fellow Nat. Assn. Pers. Cons.; mem. NAFE (pres. 1996-97), NAUW (pres 1996-97), NOW, Ga. Assn. Pers. Cons. (chair, Disting. Cons. of Yr. 1978), Jacksonville State U. Alumni Assn. (Alumni of Yr. nominee 1997), Alpha Xi Delta, Sigma Tau Alpha. Avocations: reading, writing, poetry, fishing, water sports. Office: MedStat Inc 551 N Main St Alpharetta GA 30004-1325

BUTTS, DAVID PHILLIP, science educator; b. Rochester, N.Y., May 9, 1932; s. George Albert and Susie Bertha (Hicks) B.; m. Velma M. Walton, Aug. 2, 1958; children—Carol Sue, Douglas Paul. B.S., Butler U., 1954; M.S., U. Ill., 1960, Ph.D., 1962. Asst. prof. Olivet Nazarene Coll., Kankakee, Ill., 1961-62; prof. U. Tex., Austin, 1962-74; prof., chmn. dept. sci. edn. U. Ga., 1974-85, Aderhold Disting. prof., 1985-92, ret., prof. emeritus, 1996—; ednl. cons., writer AAAS. Author: (with A. Lee) Vanilla, 1964, Chocolate, 1965, Watermellon, 1966, The Teaching of Science A Self Directed Guide, 1973, Teaching Science in the Elementary School, 1973, (with Hall) Science and Children, 1976; Editor: Designs for Progress in Science Education, 1970, (with others) Science and Society, 1985, Research-Development in Science Education, 1971, Jour. of Research in Sci. Teaching, 1974-79. Served to capt. USAF, 1954-57. Fellow A.A.A.S., Tex. Acad. Sci.; mem. Assn. for Edn. Tchrs. Sci. (regional v.p. 1966-68, pres. 1973-75), Nat. Sci. Tchrs. Assn. (dir. 1970-72), Council Elementary Sci. Internat., Nat. Assn. Research in Sci. Teaching (pres. 1984-87), Am. Ednl. Research Assn., Am. Sci. Affiliation. Home: 145 Deerfield Rd Bogart GA 30622-1737

BUTTS, EDWARD PERRY, civil engineer, environmental consultant; b. Ukiah, Calif., July 29, 1958; s. Edward Oren Butts and Orvilla June (Daily) Hutcheson; m. JoAnne Catherine Zellner, Aug. 14, 1978; children: Brooke C., Adam E. Cert. continuing studies in Irrigation Theory and Practices, U. Nebr., 1980. Registered profl. civil and environ. engr., Oreg., Wash.; cert. water rights examiner, Oreg.; registered control sys. engr., Oreg.; cert. sprinkler irrigation designer; cert. pump installer. Technician Ace Pump Sales, Salem, Oreg., 1976; technician Stettler Supply Co., Salem, 1976-78, assoc. engr., 1978-86, chief engr., 1986-90, v.p. engring., 1990-97, pres., 1997—; profl. engr. exam. question reviewer Nat. Coun. Engring. Examiners, Clemson, S.C., 1989—; profl. engr. exam. supr. Oreg. State Bd. Engring. Examiners, Salem, 1986—; lectr. various water works profl. groups; mem. Marion County Water Mgmt. Coun., 1993—, Oreg. Drinking Water Adv. Com., 1999—. Contbr. articles to Jour. Pub. Works Mag., AWWA Opflow, Water Well Jour. Coach Little League Cascade Basketball Leage, Turner, Oreg., 1990-94; vol. Jr. Achievement. Recipient Merit award Am. City and County Mag., 1990, Cmty. Vol. citation City of Keizer, Oreg., 1993, Cert. of appreciation Oreg. State Bd. Engring. Examiners, 1996, Letter of Commendation for flood assistance City of Salem, 1996, Application Design award Spraying Systems Co., 1996. Mem. ASCE, NSPE, IEEE, Am. Pub. Works Assn., Assn. Groundwater Scientists and Engrs., Nat. Ground Water Assn., Profl. Engrs. Oreg. (mid-Willamette chpt. v.p. 1990-91, pres. 1992-93, state v.p. 1993-95, state pres.-elect 1995-96, state pres. 1996-97, nat. dir. 1999—, Young Engr. of Yr. award 1993-94), Am. Water Works Assn., Oreg. Assn. Water Utilities (bd. dirs. 1998—). Republican. Achievements include devel. of system used to install multiple pumps in water wells. Office: 1810 Lana Ave NE Salem OR 97303-3116

BUTTS, HERBERT CLELL, dentist, educator; b. Dover, Tenn., Aug. 24, 1924; s. Sidney Lewis and Georgia (Sawyer) B.; m. Quay Coker; children: Marla Lyce, April Chyrese, Dawn Denise, Sidney Coker. Student, U. Tenn. Jr. Coll., 1942-43, Memphis State U., 1946-47; DDS, U. Tenn., 1950; MS, U. Iowa, 1966. Pvt. practice dentistry Memphis, 1950-58; mem. faculty Coll. Dentistry, U. Tenn., Memphis, part-time 1950-58, 58-60, assoc. dean acad. affairs, 1978-81, spl. advisor to dean, 1986—; fgn. svc. officer, dental edn. advisor State Dept. Fgn. Aid program, San Salvador, El Salvador, 1960-64; assoc. prof. St. Louis U. Sch. Dentistry, 1966-67; prof., chmn. dept. operative dentistry Coll. Dental Medicine, Med. U. S.C., Charleston, 1967-70, asst. dean for admissions and student affairs, 1970, 72-74, acting dean, 1971; editor-in-chief ADA, Chgo., 1974-77; dean Sch. Dental Medicine So. Ill. U., Alton, 1981-86. Editor U. Tenn. Coll. Dentistry Bull., 1990—. With USNR, 1943-46. Recipient Outstanding Alumnus award U. Tenn. Coll. Dentistry, 1975. Mem. ADA, Tenn. Dental Assn. (fellowship award 1993), Memphis Dental Soc., Am. Coll. Dentists (pres. Tenn. sect. 1994, sec.-treas. Tenn. sect. 1995-98), Internat. Coll. Dentists, Am. Assn. Dental Schs., Ala. Dental Assn. (hon.), Am. Assn. Women Dentists (hon.), Omicron Kappa Upsilon. Home: 1360 Peabody Ave Memphis TN 38104-3636 Office: U Tenn Coll Dentistry 875 Union Ave Memphis TN 38103-3513

BUTTS, VIRGINIA, corporate public relations executive; b. Chgo.. BA, U. Chgo. Writer Dave Garroway radio show NBC, N.Y.C., 1953; writer, producer, talent Sta. WBBM-TV, Chgo.; midwest dir. pub. relations for mags. Time, Fortune, Life and Sports Illustrated, Time Inc., 1956-63; dir. pub. relations Chgo. Sun-Times and Chgo. Daily News, 1963-74; v.p. pub. relations Field Enterprises Inc., Chgo., 1974-84; v.p. pub. rels. The Field Corp., 1984-90; pub. rels. counsel Marshall Field V, Chgo., 1991—; pub. affairs com. Art Inst. Chgo., exec. prodn. assoc., 1985; instr. TV Columbia Coll. Contbr. Lesly's Public Relations Handbook, 1978, 83, World Book Ency. Recipient Clarion award Women in Communications, Inc., 1975-76, Businesswoman of the Yr. award Lewis U., 1976. Mem. Pub. Rels. Soc. Am. (nat. bd. ethics 1987-93), Publicity Club Chgo. (Golden Trumpet award 1968-69, 75-76, 80), Nat. Acad. TV Arts and Scis., The Chgo. Network. Lion at Lincoln Park Zoo named for her public relations work; late Milton Caniff's character in Steve Canyon Comic Strip named for her.

BUTZ, GENEVA MAE, pastor; b. Emmaus, Pa., May 11, 1944; d. Edwin F. and Arlene E. (Engler) B. BA, Hood Coll., 1966; MRE, Union Theol. Sem., 1968; D Divinity (hon.), Ursinus Coll., 1994. Ordained clergywoman United Ch. of Christ, 1972. Dir. Christian edn. United Ch. of Christ, Palos Verdes, Calif., 1968-72; mng. editor Youth mag., United Ch. Bd. for Homeland Ministries, Phila., 1972-75; affiliate rep. Ecumenical Community of Taizé, France, New Zealand, Australia, Indonesia, India and others, 1975-77; parish worker Temple Presbyn. Ch., Phila., 1978-83; pastor Old First Reformed Ch., United Ch. of Christ, Phila., 1984—; bd. dirs. Met. Christian Coun. of Phila., 1985-96, 98—; chair Ch. and Ministry Com., Phila. Assn. United Ch. Christ, 1983-86; cons. Auburn Theol. Sem., N.Y.,, 1988-89; coord. 5-Day urban seminar for incoming students Lancaster Theol. Sem., 1986-93, The Small Ch. and Cultural Change, Bangor Theol. Sem., 1988; mem. adv. com. on evangelism and membership growth priority United Ch. Christ, 1989=90; team chair Toward the 21st Century, A Church-wide Planning Process for the United Ch. Christ, 1990-93; spkr. Faith Journey, consultation XVI in Parish Ministry for United Ch. Christ Clergy, Orlando, Fla., 1991; guest preacher Nat. Cathedral, Washington, 1993; commencement spkr. Lancaster Theol. Sem., 1996. Author: Color Me Well, 1986,

Christmas Comes Alive, 1988, Christmas in All Seasons, 1995; contbr. Women Pray, Karen Roller, Ed, 1986. Bd. dirs. Bethesda Project, Inc., Phila., 1986-98; del. Gen. Synod-United Ch. of Christ, Cleve., Ft. Worth, Providence, 1987-89, 99-2001; ecumenical del. Gen. Assembly Presbyn. Ch. (U.S.A.), 1989; bd. dirs. Phila. Religious Leadership Devel. Fund, 1988-98; adv. bd. Seamen's Ch. Inst., Phila., 1992—; trustee Lancaster Theol. Sem., 1992—. Recipient Numan Rels. award NCCJ, Phila., 1985; named One of 85 People to Watch, Phila., amg., 1985, One of 7 Clergy Leading U.S. Constl. Bicentennial Parade, 1987, Valiant Woman of Yr., Ch. Women United, 1991; Merrill fellow Harvard Div. Sch., 1993. Mem. Nat. Orgn. of Women, Ch. Women United of Greater Phila., Old Phila. Clergy, Assn. United Arts and Religion, Phila. Assn. (ministrial standing). Democrat. Office: Old First Reformed Ch 153 N 4th St Philadelphia PA 19106-1515 *Being religious is so simple that as adults we find it hard to achieve. Children do it easily. We need to work with children so we don't destroy their natural religious inclination. The future of the faith lies in our ability to evoke the innate religious sensitivity in all people.*

BUTZ, OTTO WILLIAM, political science educator; b. Floesti, Romania, May 2, 1923; came to U.S., 1949, naturalized, 1959; s. Otto E. and Charlotte (Engelmann) B.; m. Velia DeAngelis, Sept. 13, 1961. B.A., Victoria Coll., U. Toronto, 1947; Ph.D., Princeton, 1953. Asst. prof. polit. sci. Swarthmore Coll., 1954-55; asst. prof. politics Princeton U., 1955-60; asso. editor Random House, N.Y.C., 1960-61; prof. social sci. San Francisco State Coll., 1961-67; academic v.p. Sacramento State Coll., 1967-69, acting pres., 1969-70; pres. Golden Gate U., 1970-92; pres. emeritus, 1992—. Author: German Political Theory, 1955, The Unsilent Generation, 1958, Of Man and Politics, 1960, To Make a Difference—A Student Look at America, 1967. Recipient Calif. State Colls. Outstanding Tchr. award, 1966. Mem. Am. Polit. Sci. Assn. Home: Wolfback Rdg Sausalito CA 94965 Office: 536 Mission St San Francisco CA 94105-2921

BUTZNER, JOHN DECKER, JR., federal judge; b. Scranton, Pa., Oct. 2, 1917. B.A., U. Scranton, 1939; LL.B., U. Va., 1941. Bar: Va. bar 1941. Pvt. practice law Fredericksburg, 1941-58; judge 15th and 39th Jud. Cir. of Va., 1958-62; U.S. judge Ea. Dist. Va., 1962-67; cir. judge U.S. Ct. Appeals (4th cir.), Richmond, Va., 1967—; judge for appointment of ind. counsel U.S. Ct. Appeals for D.C. Cir., 1988-98. Served with USAAF, 1942-45.

BUUM, MARY KAY, dialysis nurse; b. Rapid City, S.D., Oct. 2, 1953; d. Ralph Charles and Aleatha Annetta Pesek; m. Dennis Alan Buum, Aug. 24, 1974; children: Jessica Lynn, Christopher Alan. Diploma, Rapid City Regional Hosp., 1976. RN, S.D.; CNN. Staff nurse med. Rapid City Regional Hosp., 1976-77, staff nurse hemodialysis, 1977-89, staff nurse peritoneal dialysis, 1989—. Mem. Am. Nephrology Nurses Assn. Democrat. Lutheran. Avocations: cross country skiing, mountain biking, hiking. Office: Rapid City Regional hosp 353 Fairmont Blvd Rapid City SD 57701-7375

BUVINGER, JAN, library director; b. Lampasas, Tex., Oct. 4, 1943; d. Orville Layne and Myriam (Hamer) Rogers; m. Robert C. Ward. BS, Coll. Charleston, S.C., 1965; MLS, Emory U., 1970. Childrens asst. libr. Charleston (S.C.) County Libr., 1970-71, reference libr., 1972-75, head reference dept., 1976-77, dep. dir., 1977-79, dir., 1979—. Mem. Am. Libr. Assn., S.C. Libr. Assn., S.E. Libr. Assn. Office: Charleston County Pub Libr 68 Calhoun St Charleston SC 29401-3508*

BUX, WILLIAM JOHN, lawyer; b. Wadsworth, Ohio, Nov. 10, 1946; s. William J. and Helen M. (Sybelnik) B.; m. Linda Alice Zenar, Feb. 13, 1971. BSME, Ohio State U., 1969, MS, 1970; JD, So. Meth. U., 1977. Bar: Tex. 1977, U.S. Dist. Ct. (so. dist.) Tex. 1978, U.S. Ct. Appeals (5th cir.) 1978, U.S. Dist. Ct. (no. dist.) Tex. 1980, U.S. Dist. Ct. (ea. and we. dists.) Tex. 1981, U.S. Ct. Appeals (11th cir.) 1981, U.S. Supreme Ct. 1982; cert. Labor & Employment Law Tex. Bd. Legal Specialization. Assoc. Vinson & Elkins, Houston, 1977-85; ptnr. Hughes & Luce, Dallas, 1985-93; shareholder Locke Purnell Rain Harrell, Dallas, 1994-97; ptnr. Liddell, Sapp, Zivley, Hill & La Boon, Houston, 1997-98, Locke, Liddell & Sapp, Houston, 1999—. Author: Developing and Enforcing Drug and Alcohol Abuse Work Rules: A Primer for Texas Employers, 1984. Sec. So. Meth. U. Law Sch. Alumni Council, Dallas, 1986-88. Capt. USAF, 1971-74. Mem. ABA, Tex. Bar Assn. (chmn. labor and employment law sect. 1992-93), Houston Bar Assn., Dallas Bar Assn., 5th Cir. Bar Assn. Republican. Roman Catholic. Home: 2511 Westgate St Houston TX 77019-6609 Office: Locke Liddell & Sapp 600 Travis St 3400 Chase Twr Houston TX 77002-3095

BUXBAUM, RICHARD M., law educator, lawyer; b. 1930. A.B., Cornell U., 1950, LL.B., 1952; LL.M., U. Calif.-Berkeley, 1953; Dr. (hon.) U. Osnabrück, 1992, Eötvös Lorand U., Budapest, 1993. Bar: Calif. 1953, N.Y. 1953. Practice law, pvt. firm, Rochester, N.Y., 1957-61; prof. U. Calif.-Berkeley, 1961—, dean internat. and area studies; hon. prof. U. Peking, 1998. Editor-in-chief Am. Jour. Comparative Law. Recipient Humboldt prize, 1991, German Order of Merit, 1992, Officier Arts et Lettres, France, 1997, Order of Rio Brauco, Brazil, 1998. Mem. German Soc. Comparative Law (corr.), Coun. on Fgn. Rels. Office: U Calif Internat & Area Studies 260 Stephens Hall Berkeley CA 94720-2300

BUXBAUM, ROBERT C(OURTNEY), internist; b. Milw., Dec. 16, 1930; s. Edwin C. and Lillian (Tousman) B.; m. Ann S. Shocket, Dec. 26, 1955; children: Laura, Carl, Paula, Margaret. AB, Harvard U., 1952; MD, U. Pa., 1956. Diplomate Am. Bd. Internal Medicine, Am. Bd. Hospice and Palliative Medicine. Intern Henry Ford Hosp., Detroit, 1956-57; officer USPHS, San Carlos Apache Res., Ariz., 1957-59; resident, rsch. fellow U. Wis. Hosp., Madison, 1959-63; from rsch. assoc. to instr. Harvard Med. Sch., Boston, 1963-69; asst. prof. medicine Harvard Med. Sch., 1969—; internist Harvard Cmty. Health Plan, Boston, 1969—; cons. health policy. Author: Sports for Life, 1979; contbr. articles to profl. jours. Chmn. Gov.'s Com. on Fitness, Mass., 1975-80. Fellow Am. Coll. Physicians. Avocations: playing oboe, swimming, skiing. Office: Harvard Vanguard Med Assocs 140 Brookline Ave Boston MA 02215-3907

BUXTON, WINSLOW HURLBERT, manufacturing company executive. Degree in Chem. Engring., U. Washington, 1961. Pres. Niagara of Wisc. Paper Corp., 1986-89; with Pentair Inc., St. Paul, 1986—, v.p. paper group, 1989-90, pres., COO, 1990—, also dir.; pres., COO, 1990-92; chmn., pres., CEO Pentair, 1993—.

BUYALOS, RICHARD PAUL, JR., physician; b. Ashland, Ky., Sept. 13, 1956. BS, U. Md., 1979; MD, Thomas Jefferson U., 1983. Diplomate Nat. Bd. Med. Examiners; diplomate in ob-gyn. and reproductive endocrinology Am. Bd. Ob-Gyn. Intern Georgetown U. Hosps., Washington, 1983-84, resident in ob-gyn., 1984-87; clin. rsch. fellow divsn. reproductive endocrinology UCLA, 1987-89, asst. prof. dept. ob-gyn., 1989-96; assoc. prof. ob-gyn. U. Ky., Lexington, 1996—, chief divsn. reproductive endocrinology and infertility, 1996—. Contbr. articles to profl. jours. Grantee UCLA, 1989-90, NIH, 1989-93, U. Ky., 1996—, Rsch. MRI Ctr., 1997-98. Fellow Am. Coll. Ob-Gyn.; mem. AMA, Am. Soc. for Reproductive Medicine, Soc. Reproductive Endocrinologists, Pacific Coast Fertility Soc., Endocrine Soc., Soc. for Study of Reprodn., Ky. Med. Assn., Fayette County Med. Assn., Soc. Reproductive Surgeons, Phi Kappa Phi, Psi Chi, Phi Eta Sigma, Delta Tau Delta. Avocations: running, golf, fly fishing, writing, tennis, theater. Home: 1158 26th St # 532 Santa Monica CA 90403-4698 Office: U Ky Sch medicine Dept Ob-Gyn 325 Rolling Oaks Dr Ste 110 Thousand Oaks CA 91360

BUYER, STEVE EARLE, congressman, lawyer; b. 1958; m. Joni Buyer; children: Colleen, Ryan. BS in Bus. Adminstrn., The Citadel, 1980; JD, Valparaiso U., 1984. Officer Med. Svc. Corps U.S. Army, 1980; spl. att to U.S. Atty. U.S. Army, Va., 1984-87; atty., 1988—; dep. atty. gen. Ind., 1987-88; legal counsel 22nd Theater Army, Saudi Arabia, 1990-91; legal advisor U.S Armed Forces/Western Enemy Prisoner of War Camps/War Crimes Interrogations, Saudi Arabia, 1991; mem. 103d Congress from 5th Ind. Dist., 1993—; com. mem. mil. forces and personnel, vets. affairs, judiciary. Decorated Bronze Star. Republican. Office: US Ho Reps 227 Cannon Washington DC 20515-1405

BUYERS, JOHN WILLIAM AMERMAN, agribusiness and specialty foods company executive; b. Coatesville, Pa., July 17, 1928; s. William Buchanan and Rebecca (Watson) B.; m. Elizabeth Lindsey, July 17, 1999; children: Elsie Buyers Viehman, Rebecca Watson Buyers-Basso, Jane Palmer Buyers-Russo. B.A. cum laude in History, Princeton U., 1952; M.S. in Indsl. Mgmt., MIT, 1963. Div. ops. mgr. Bell Telephone Co. Pa., 1953-66; dir. ops. and personnel Gen. Waterworks Corp., Phila., 1966-68; pres., chief exec. officer Gen. Waterworks Corp., Phila, 1971-75; v.p. adminstrn. Internat. Utilities Corp., Phila., 1968-71; pres., chief exec. officer, dir. C. Brewer and Co., Ltd., Honolulu, 1975—, chmn. bd., 1982—; chmn. Calif. and Hawaiian Sugar Co., 1982-84, 86-90; pres. Buyco, Inc., 1986—; mem. Hawaii Joint Coun. Econ. Edn., Japan-Hawaii Econ. Coun.; bd. dirs. 1st Hawaiian Inc., John B. Sanfilippo & Sons, Inc., Outrigger Hotels and Restors; chmn. bd. C. Brewer Homes, Inc.; vice chmn. Pacific Internat. Ctr. for High Tech. Rsch., 1976—. Trustee U. Hawaii Found., Hawaii Prep. Acad., 1986—; chmn. bd. dirs. Hawaii Visitors Bur., 1990-91; mem. Gov.'s Blue Ribbon Panel on the Future of Healthcare in Hawaii; bd. dirs. Hawaii Sports Found., 1990—; mem. adv. group to U.S. Dist. Ctr. With USMC, 1946-48. Sloan fellow, 1963. Mem. Hawaiian Sugar Planters Assn. (chmn. bd. dirs. 1980-82, dir.), c. of C. Hawaii (chmn. bd. dirs. 1981-82), Nat. Alliance Bus. (chmn. Hawaii Pacific Metro chpt. 1978), Cap and Gown Club (Princeton), Hilo Yacht Club, Oahu County Club, Pacific Club, Waialae county Club, Prouts Neck (Maine) County Club, U.S. C. of C. (mem. food and gr. com. 1991—), Beretania Tennis Club. Presbyterian. Clubs: Cap and Gown (Princeton); Hilo Yacht, Oahu Country, Pacific, Waialae Country; Prouts Neck (Maine) Country. Office: C Brewer & Co Ltd PO Box 1826 Papaikou HI 96781-1826

BUYNY, MARIANNE JO, eating disorders therapist, addictions counselor; b. Connellsville, Pa., Mar. 19, 1949; d. Marion Alyowich and Stella Louise (Sowinski) Marchewka; m. Jerome Michael Buyny, Oct. 21, 1972; children: Janean Estell, Jared Michael, Allison Victoria. BA in Psychology and Sociology, Alliance Coll., Cambridge Springs, Pa., 1971; MA in Psychology, Marywood Coll., Scranton, Pa., 1976; postgrad., C.C. Allegheny County, Pitts., 1985. Cert. allied addictions practitioner; cert. clin. criminal justice specialist, masters addictions counselors. Med. social worker Schneider Home Health Care Agy., Inc., Pitts., 1985-87; mental health specialist Intercare, Hillside Psychiat. Ctr., McKeesport, Pa., 1987-91, Intercare, Lakewood Psychiat. Hosp., Canonsburg, Pa., 1991-95; psychol. specialist counselor II Med. Ctr. U. Pitts., 1995—, clin. cmty. instr., 1998—; sr. rsch. assoc. Western Psychiat. Inst. and Clinic, Pitts., 1990—; therapist Willough at Naples, Naples, Fla., 1994-97; asst. dir. in tng. of Group Psychotherapy and Psychodrama, Pitts., 1991-96; reconstrn. therapist, Pitts., 1991-93; ednl. conf. cons., 1998—. Mem. Dance Therapy Assn., Pi Gamma Mu, Lambda Alpha. Home: 2624 Wyncote Rd Bethel Park PA 15102-1708

BUYSE, EMILE JULES, film company executive; b. Brussels, Apr. 16, 1927; came to U.S., 1976; s. Omer J. and Flore G. (Copain) B.; m. Evelyne Mulpas, June 26, 1964. M.A., Ecole Normale Charles Buls, Brussels, 1947. Dir. advt. and publicity for continental Europe and Middle East United Artists Corp., Paris, 1962-66; dir. advt. and publicity 20th Century-Fox Film Corp., 1966-70, v.p. internat. distbn., 1970-76; pres. 20th Century-Fox Internat. Corp., Los Angeles, 1976-81, EBE Internat., Beverly Hills, Calif., 1981—. Mem. Acad. Motion Picture Arts and Scis. Home: 101 Ocean Ave Unit E 302 Santa Monica CA 90402-1427 Office: BROOKSFILMS Culver Studios Culver City CA 90232

BUYSE, LEONE KARENA, orchestral musician, educator; b. Oneida, N.Y, Feb. 7, 1947; d. Leonard Cornelius and Ione Esther (Hinman) B.; m. Michael Fanning Webster, Sept. 7, 1987. MusB, Eastman Sch. Music, Rochester, N.Y., 1968; MusM, Emporia (Kans.) State U., 1980; cert., Paris Conservatory, 1971. 2d flute and piccolo Rochester Philharm. Orch., 1971-78; asst. prin. flute San Francisco Symphony, 1978-83; asst. prin. flute Boston Symphony Orch., 1983-90, acting prin., 1990-93; prin. flute Boston Pops Orch., 1983-90; prof. flute U. Mich., Ann Arbor, 1993-97; prof. flute and chamber music Shepherd Sch. Music, Rice U., Houston, 1997—; mem. faculty Boston U., 1983-93, Tanglewood Inst. of Boston U., Lenox, Mass., 1984-94, New Eng. Conservatory, 1988-93. Fulbright grantee, Paris, 1968-69. Mem. Nat. Flute Assn. (bd. dirs. 1985-86, conv. program chmn. 1987), Greater Boston Flute Assn. (founder, pres. 1992-93), Mu Phi Epsilon (winner internat. competition 1970), Pi Kappa Lambda. Avocations: physical fitness, gardening, vegetarian cuisine. Office: Rice University Shepherd Sch of Music PO Box 1892 Houston TX 77251-1892

BUZACOTT, JOHN ALAN, engineering educator; b. Sydney, N.S.W., Australia, May 21, 1937; emigrated to Can., 1967; s. Alan Ernest and Jean Elizabeth (Bingle) B.; m. Ursula Schulmerich, Sept. 7, 1963; children: Alan J., Kimberly A. BSc, U. Sydney, 1957, BE, 1959; MSc, U. Birmingham, Eng., 1962, PhD, 1967. Engr. Associated Elec. Industries, Rugby, Eng., 1959-61; ops. research systems officer A.E.I. Hotpoint Ltd., London, 1963-64; asst. prof. U. Toronto, 1967-71, assoc. prof., 1971-77, prof., 1977-83; prof. U. Waterloo, Ont., Can., 1984-91, York U., North York, Ont., 1991—. Author: Scale in Production Systems, 1982, Stochastic Models of Manufacturing Systems, 1993; corr. editor: Canadian Jour. Info. Processing and Ops. Research, 1974-78. Mem. Can. Operational Rsch. Soc. (pres. 1983-84), Inst. for Ops. Rsch. and Mgmt. Sci., Prodn. and Ops. Mgmt. Soc. (pres. 1999). Home: 68 Divadale Dr, Toronto, ON Canada M4G 2P2 Office: York U, Schulich Sch Bus, North York, ON Canada M3J 1P3

BUZARD, JAMES ALBERT, healthcare management consultant; b. Warren, Ohio, Nov. 2, 1927; s. Milton Vogan and Mary Cora (Matthews) B.; m. Caroline L. Jansen, July 28, 1951; children: Catherine A. Sazdanoff, James M. BS, Kent (Ohio) State U., 1949; MA, U. Buffalo, 1951, PhD, 1954. Rsch. biochemist, then dir. R & D Norwich (N.Y.) Pharmacal Co., 1954-68; dir. devel., then exec. v.p. G.D. Searle & Co., Skokie, Ill., 1968-79, also bd. dirs.; exec. v.p. Merrell Internat./Richardson Merrell Inc., Wilton, Conn., 1979-81, Merrell Dow Pharm., Inc., Cin., 1981-89; v.p. corp. affairs, mergers & acquisitions Marion Merrell Dow Inc., 1989-90; ret., 1990, mgmt.-health care cons., 1990—; bd. dirs. Meridian Diagnostics Inc., Cin.; chmn. bd. trustees Biostart, Cin.; vice chmn. Edison Biotech. Ctr., Cleve.; dir. Bioconcepts, Cin. Contbr. 40 articles to profl. jours. With USNR, 1945-46, 51-55. Republican. Roman Catholic. Avocations: woodworking, golf, gardening, painting.

BUZAS, JOHN WILLIAM, hospital administrator, surgical nurse; b. Elyria, Ohio, Feb. 4, 1955; s. Robert Thomas and Dorothy Elizabeth (Batcha) B.; m. Susan Lee Koch, Feb. 19, 1977; children: Andrea Nicole, Morgan Kristen. AAS, Lorain County C.C., 1978, 82; BSN, Bowling Green State U., 1994. Cert. surg. tech. Lorain (Ohio) Cmty. Hosp., 1978-82, staff nurse oper. rm., 1982-88, asst. nurse mgr., 1988-94, nurse mgr. oper. rm., 1994-95; dir. surg. svcs. Cmty. Health Ptnrs., 1995—; mem. surg. assisting adv. bd. Lorain County C.C., Elyria, 1992—. Fellow Assn. Oper. Rm. Nurses. Avocations: reading, movies, ti-chi, family. Office: Cmty Health Ptnrs 3700 Kolbe Rd Lorain OH 44053-1611*

BUZBEE, JOHN DUFFIE, JR., sales executive; b. Jonesboro, Ark., Dec. 19, 1958; s. John D. and Louise (Tice) B.; m. Jana Denise Brown, Jan. 26, 1991; children: Jillian, Caitlin. BS, BA in Mgmt. and Gen. Bus., U. Ark., 1981. Acct. mgr. Consolidated Holding Co., Tulsa, Okla., 1981-83; sls. rep. Davis and Geck, Tulsa, Okla., 1983-86, Jobst Inst., Inc., Tulsa, Okla., 1986-88; dist. sls. mgr. Jobst Inst., Inc., L.A., 1989-90, regional sls. mgr., 1990-93, regional bus. mgr., 1994-95; nat. acct. mgr. Beiersdorf-Jobst, Inc., L.A., 1996—. Republican. Avocations: golf, basketball, football, running, tennis. Home: 32315 Via Cordoba Temecula CA 92592-1614 Office: Beiersdorf-Jobst Inc 32315 Via Cordoba Temecula CA 92592-1614

BUZBEE, RICHARD EDGAR, newspaper editor; b. Fordyce, Ark., Aug. 16, 1931; s. Edgar Andrew and Helen Koester (Darling) B.; m. Marie Palmer, Apr. 16, 1955; children: Robert Edgar, William Bruce, James Palmer, John Richard. B.J., B.A., U. Mo., 1954. Mgmt. intern Harris Newspaper Group, Chanute (Kans.) Tribune, Burlington (Iowa) Hawk-Eye, also Olathe (Kans.) News, 1957-63; editor, pub. Olathe News, 1963-79, Hutchinson (Kans.) News, 1979-93; hon. chmn. bd. dirs. Hutchinson Pub. Co., 1993—; partner Radine Enterprises, Olathe. Pres. Olathe C. of C., 1969, Olathe United Way, 1968, Johnson County chpt. ARC, 1978-79; chmn. Johnson County Scholarship Found., 1968; mem. Olathe Public Bldg. Commn. 1, 1964-65, 2, 1978-79; co-chmn. Olathe Home-for-Christmas from Vietnam Project, 1969-72; mem. bd. Hutchinson Public Library, 1980-87, chmn., 1982-83; bd. dirs. Hutchinson Symphony Assn., 1980-88, pres. 1987. Served to lt. (j.g.) USNR, 1954-57. Mem. Am. Soc. Newspaper Editors, William Allen White Found., Greater Hutchinson C. of C. (chmn. 1988), Rotary (bd. dirs. 1981-83), Phi Beta Kappa. Republican. Methodist. Club: Rotary. (dir. 1981-83). Home: 4 Crescent Blvd Hutchinson KS 67502-5541

BUZICK, WILLIAM ALONSON, JR., investor, lawyer, educator; b. Sylvan Grove, Kans., Nov. 4, 1920; s. William Alonson and Mildred (Hickman) B.; m. Mary Lee Emerson, Nov. 18, 1954; children: William Alonson III, Bonnie Lee. AB, Kans. U., 1942; JD, Washburn U., 1950. Bar: Kans. bar 1950. Vice pres., dir. Sylvan State Bank, Sylvan Grove, 1946-48; 1st sec. Alcoholic Beverage Bd., Kans., 1948-50; pres. Shasta Water Co., San Francisco, 1950-60, Shasta div. Consol. Foods Corp., Chgo., 1960- 66; dir., v.p. Sara Lee Corp., 1964, exec. v.p., 1966-68, pres., chmn. bd., chief exec. officer, 1968-75; dean Sch. Bus. and Adminstrv. Sci., Calif. State U., Fresno, 1975-78; pvt. investor. Served to lt. USNR, 1942-46. Recipient Disting. Service citation Kans. U., 1972. Mem. ABA, Kans. Bar Assn., Ret. Officers Assn., Navy League, Beta Sigma Pi. Home: 6533 N Van Ness Blvd Fresno CA 93711-1247

BUZUNIS, CONSTANTINE DINO, lawyer; b. Winnipeg, Man., Can., Feb. 3, 1958; came to U.S., 1982; s. Peter and Anastasia (Ginakes) B. BA, U. Man., 1980; JD, Thomas M. Cooley Law Sch., 1985. Bar: Mich. 1986, U.S. Dist. Ct. (ea. and we. dists.) Mich. 1986, Calif. 1986, U.S. Dist. Ct. (so. dist.) Calif. 1987, U.S. Supreme Ct. 1993. Assoc. Church, Kritselis, Wyble & Robinson, Lansing, Mich., 1986; assoc. Neil, Dymott, Perkins, Brown & Frank, San Diego, 1987-94, ptnr., 1994—; arbitrator San Diego County Mcpl. and Superior Cts.; judge pro tem San Diego Mcpl. Ct. Sec., treas. Sixty Plus Law Ctr., Lansing, 1985; active Vols. in Parole, San Diego, 1988—; bd. dirs. Hellenic Cultural Soc., 1993-98. Mem. ABA, FBA, ATLA, Mich. Bar Assn., Calif. Bar Assn., San Diego County Bar Assn., Desert Bar Assn., San Diego Trial Lawyers Assn., So. Calif. Def. Coun., State Bar Calif. (gov. 9th dist. young lawyers divsn. 1991-94, 1st v.p. 1993-94, pres. 1994-95, bd. govs. 1995-96) San Diego Barristers Soc. (bd. dirs. 1991-92), Pan Arcadian Fedn., Order of Ahepa (chpt. bd. dirs., v.p. 1995-98), Phi Alpha Delta. Home: 3419 Overpark Rd San Diego CA 92130-1865 Office: Neil Dymott Perkins Brown & Frank 1010 2nd Ave Ste 2500 San Diego CA 92101-4913

BUZZARD, SIR ANTHONY FARQUHAR, religion educator; b. Godalming, Surrey, Eng., June 28, 1935; came to U.S., 1981; s. Anthony W. and Margaret E. (Knapp) B.; m. Barbara Jean Arnold, July 21, 1970; children: Sarah J., Claire J., Heather E. MA in Modern Langs., Oxford U., 1960; ThM, Bethany Theol. Coll., 1990. Tchr. fgn. langs. Am. Sch., London, 1974-81; lectr. in Bible Oregon (Ill.) Bible Coll. (now Atlanta Bible Coll.), Morrow, Ga., 1982—; coord. Restoration Fellowship, Oregon, 1981—. Author: The Coming Kingdom of the Messiah: A Solution to the Riddle of the New Testament, 1988, The Doctrine of the Trinity: Christianity's Self-Inflicted Wound, 1994, Our Fathers Who Aren't in Heaven: The Forgotten Christianity of Jesus the Jew, 1995; spkr. on radio program Focus on the Kingdom. Home: 185 Summerville Dr Brooks GA 30205-1533 *The most remarkable fact of church history is that the churches bearing the name 'Christian' have never clearly announced Jesus' Gospel about the Kingdom of God.*

BUZZARD, STEVEN RAY, lawyer; b. Centralia, Wash., May 22, 1946; s. Richard James and Phylis Margaret (Bevington) B.; m. Joan Elizabeth Merrow, Nov. 11, 1967; children: Elizabeth Jane, Richard Wolcott, James Merrow. BA, Cen. Wash. State Coll., 1971; postgrad., U. Wash., 1973; JD, U. Puget Sound, 1975. Bar: Wash. 1975, U.S. Dist. Ct. (we. dist.) Wash. 1975, U.S. Supreme Ct. 1979, U.S. Tax Ct. 1983. Assoc. Shires, Kruse, Wallace, Roper & Kamps, Port Orchard, Wash., 1975-77; ptnr. Buzzard & O'Connell, Centralia, 1978-80, Buzzard & Tripp, Centralia, 1980-94, Buzzard & Assoc., Centralia, 1994—; city atty. Mossyrock, Wash., 1979-94, Vader, Wash., 1989-96, Bucoda, Wash., 1989-99; judge Centralia, 1979-80, Winlock, Wash., 1982—; sec. Consolidated Enterprizes Inc., Centralia, 1986-88; judge Clehalis (Wash.) Mcpl. Ct., 1998—. Chmn. bd. dirs. Lewis County Cmty. Svcs., Chehalis, Wash., 1981-84; bd. dirs. Lewis County United Way, 1993-95; mem. adv. bd. Centralia Sch. Dist., 1995—; trustee Dollars for Scholars, Scholarship Found., 1997—. Mem. ABA (rural judges com. 1986), Wash. State Bar Assn. (ct. rules com. 1992—), Lewis County Bar Assn. (past pres.), Assn. Trial Lawyers Am., Wash. State Trial Lawyers Assn., Wash. State Govt. Lawyers Bar Assn. (trustee, dist. and mcpl. rural judges com.), Dist. & Mcpl. Judges Assn. (ct. improvement com., long range planning com.), Kiwanis (pres.-elect 1991, pres. 1992-93, Disting. Past Pres. 1994), Elks (trustee Centralia chpt. 1981—). Avocations: running, boating, hiking, biking, fishing. Fax: (360) 330-2078. Office: Buzzard & Assoc 314 Harrison Ave Centralia WA 98531-1326

BUZZELL, ROBERT DOW, management educator; b. Lincoln, Nebr., Apr. 18, 1933; s. Dow Alan and Grace (Blomquist) B.; m. Edith F. Moser, June 5, 1953; children: Susan, Robert Dow, Barbara, William. A.B., George Washington U., 1953; M.S., U. Ill., 1954; Ph.D., Ohio State U., 1957. Grad. asst. Ohio State U., Columbus, 1953-54, instr., 1955-57, asst. prof., 1957-59, assoc. prof., 1960-61; asst. prof. bus. Harvard U., Boston, 1961-63, assoc. prof., 1963-67, prof., 1967-93; Disting. prof. George Mason U., Fairfax, Va., 1993-98; Disting. vis. prof. Georgetown U., 1998—; vis. prof. Inst. European d'Administrn. des Affaires, 1967; exec. dir. Mktg. Sci. Inst., 1968-72, trustee, 1968-81; trustee Strategic Planning Inst.; mem. nat. mktg. adv. com. U.S. Dept. Commerce, 1969-71; bd. dirs. VF Corp., Harleysville Ins. Co.; cons. in field, 1960—. Author or co-author: Wholesaling, 1959, Mathematical Models and Marketing Management, 1964, Marketing: An Introductory Analysis, 1964, rev. edit., 1972, Marketing Research, 1969, Marketing in an Electronic Age, 1985, Strategic Marketing, 1986, The PIMS Principles: Linking Strategy to Performance, 1987, Global Marketing Management: Cases and Readings, 1994, The Marketing Challenge of 1992, 1990. Mem. Am. Mktg. Assn., Strategic Mgmt. Soc., Phi Beta Kappa. Republican. Congregationalist. E-mail: buzzrd@erols.com. Office: McDonough Sch of Bus Georgetown U Washington DC 20057

BUZZELLI, CHARLOTTE GRACE, educator; b. Mar. 21, 1947; d. Edmund Albert and Sarah Agnes (Russo) Buzzelli. BS, U. Akron, 1969, MS in Edn., 1976. Tchr. St. Anthony Sch., Akron, 1969-76; program coord., tchr. Akron Montessori Sch. Continuing Edn. Program, Eastwood Ctr., Akron, 1976-77; dir. edn. Fallsview Psychiat. Hosp., Cuyahoga Falls, Ohio, 1977-92, developer job tng. partnership grant program and spl. needs handicapped grant program, 1992-97; tng. coord. N.E. regional & program educator children svcs. Ohio Dept. Mental Health State Operated Svcs., 1997—; spl. edn. svcs. developer and educator cmty svcs. div. North Coast Behavioral Healthcare Sys., 1997—; part-time tchr. adult basic edn. program Akron City Sch. Dist., 1992—; cons. in field; pioneered first spl. edn. program in Ohio for adult state psychiat. hosp.; developed 1st community-based adult basic edn. program in state instn. in Ohio; program cons. state operated svcs. State of Ohio. Gospel Meets Symphony choral mem. Akron Symphony Gospel Choir, 1996-99. Named Ohio Tchr. of Yr., 1979; recipient A Key award U. Akron. Mem. CEC (coun. pres.), ASCD, Assn. Children with Learning Disabilities, Internat. Reading Assn., U. Akron Alumni Assn., Univ. Club, Akron Women's City Club, Pi Lambda Theta (pres.), Phi Delta Kappa, Delta Kappa Gamma, Gamma Beta (pres.). Home: 662 Dayton St Akron OH 44310-2301 Office: Ohio Dept Mental Health NorthCoast Behav HealthCare 1756 Sagamore Rd Northfield OH 44067

BUZZELLI, LAURENCE FRANCIS, lawyer; b. Cleve., Jan. 24, 1943; s. Frank Vincent and Viola J. (Piccolino) B.; m. Judith Louise Shope, July 16, 1966; children: Christopher Laurence, Lauren Marie. BS in Edn., Ohio U., 1965; JD, Cleve. State U., 1973. Bar: Ohio, 1973; cert. secondary tchr., Ohio; lic. comml. pilot. Claims supr., regional analyst Allstate Ins. Co., Cleve. and Hudson, Ohio, 1969-74; atty., mng. atty. Continental Ins. Co./ Buckeye Union Ins. Co., Cleve. and Cin., 1977-94; ptnr., prin. Quandt, Giffels & Buck Co., L.P.A., Cleve., 1994—; arbitrator Cuyahoga County Common Pleas Ct., Cleve., 1974, Hamilton and Clermont County Pleas Ct., Cin. and Batavia, Ohio, 1978-83. Served to capt. U.S. Army, 1965-68, Vietnam. Mem. Def. Research Inst., Ohio Bar Assn., Bar Assn. Greater Cleve., Ohio Assn. Civil Trial Attys., Am. Arbitration Assn. (arbitrator),

DAV (life). Office: Quandt Giffels & Buck Co LPA 800 Leader Bldg 526 Superior Ave # 526 Cleveland OH 44114-1900

BUZZELLI, MICHAEL JOHN, critical care nurse; b. Hibbing, Minn., Aug. 5, 1954; s. Evarist A. and Beverly A. Buzzelli; m. Janice Buzzelli; children: Kimberly, Laura, Beverly. BSN, U. N.D., 1976; MA, Webster U., 1993. Staff nurse ICU U.S. Army, Washington, 1978-81; asst. head nurse ICU U.S. Army, Seoul, Korea, 1981-82, Ft. Ord, Calif., 1982-86; instr. practical nurses U.S. Army, Ft. Sam Houston, Tex., 1986-90; head nurse surg. ICU Brooke Army Med. Ctr., 1990-91; chief nurse 41st Combat Support Hosp., Ft. Sam Houston, 1991-94; chief mobilization edn. tng. & security Ft. Wainwright, Ark., 1994-98; ret. U.S. Army, 1998; unit mgr. Harborside Healthcare, Broadview Heights, Ohio, 1998—. Contbr. articles to profl. jours. Lt. Col. U.S. Army, 1977-98. Recipient Expert Field Med. Badge, Meritorious Svc. Medal. Mem. AACN, 38th Parallel Nurses Assn., Nat. League Nursing. Home: 3625 Southern Rd Richfield OH 44286-9554

BUZZETTI, GEORGE HOWARD, small business owner, chemical miller; b. July 17, 1947. Owner, mgr. George Buzzetti, Pacoima, Calif., 1980—. Mem. Assn. for Accountability and Equitable Edn. (chmn. 1997-99). Office: 12424 Montague St Ste 120 Pacoima CA 91331

BUZZETTI, LORI EBBERS, obstetrician and gynecologist; b. Spencer, Iowa, Apr. 23, 1964; d. Larry Harold and Barbara Ellen (Smith) Ebbers; m. Anthony Romaine Buzzetti, Dec. 26, 1987; 1 child, Tessa Ellen. BS, Iowa State U., 1986; MD, U. Iowa, 1991. Resident Ind. U. Med. Ctr., Indpls., 1991-95; ob-gyn Southside Ob-gyn P.C., Indpls., 1995—; mem. patient care com. St. Francis, Indpls., 1996—. Fellow ACOG; mem. AMA, Indpls. Med. Soc. Republican. Lutheran. Avocations: travel, reading, aerobics, attending professional basketball games. Office: Southside Ob-gyn PC 8051 S Emerson Ste 400 Indianapolis IN 46237

BY, ANDRE BERNARD, engineering executive, research scientist; b. Detroit, May 19, 1955; s. Bernard Joseph and Margaret (Voytish) By. BS in Aerospace Engring., U. Mich., 1977, BS in Mech. Engring., 1977; MS in Mech. Engring., MIT, 1979, postgrad., 1985. Mech./chem. engr. Motor Vehicle Emissions Lab. EPA, Ann Arbor, Mich., 1977; teaching asst., rsch. asst. MIT, Cambridge, 1977-79; engr., sr. engr., sr. project engr. Computer Aided Engring. Group, No. Rsch. and Engring. Corp., Woburn, Mass., 1979-84; mgr. automated sytems group No. Rsch. and Engring. Corp., Woburn, Mass., 1984-90; rsch. assoc., lectr. mech. engring. dept. Tufts U., Medford, Mass., 1990-96; pres., tech. dir. Automation Engring. Inc., Woburn, Mass., 1990—; seminar lectr., panel mem. Cell Contr. Seminar, Soc. Mfg. Engrs., Detroit, 1989. Contbr. articles to profl. jours. Mem. AIAA, ASME, Soc. Mfg. Engrs., Soc. Automotive Engrs. Avocations: music, contemporary literature, impressionist art, skiing, electronics. Office: Automation Engring Inc 2 Gill St Woburn MA 01801-1721

BYAL, NANCY LOUISE, food editor; b. Plainfield, N.J., Mar. 12, 1944; d. Albert William and Anna Marie (Goering) Zeiner; m. Wayne Ole Byal, May 2, 1967; 1 child, Jason David. BS, Iowa State U., 1965. Cert. home economist; cert. culinary profl. Product counselor Gen. Mills, Inc., Mpls., 1965-67; assoc. food editor Better Homes & Gardens Books Meredith Corp., Des Moines, 1968-72, assoc. food editor Better Homes & Gardens, 1972-74, sr. food editor, 1974-83, sr. dept. head Food and Nutrition, 1983-86, exec. food editor Better Homes and Gardens, 1986—; chair, com. mem. Iowa State U. Coll. Family and Consumer Scis. Adv. Com., Ames; chmn., exec. mem. Julia Child Cookbook Awards Com. Editor, author: Better Home and Gardens Fondue Cook Book, 1970, Better Home and Gardens Salad Book, 1969. Named Home Economist in Bus. of Yr., Iowa Home Economists in Bus., 1992. Mem. Internat. Assn. Culinary Profls., Am. Inst. Food and Wine (mem. tast and health com.), Am. Assn. Family and Consumer Scis., Luth. Women's Missionary League. Avocations: gardening, crafting, reading. Office: Meredith Corp 1716 Locust St Des Moines IA 50309-3023

BYALICK, MARCIA, author, columnist, reporter, educator; b. Apr. 9, 1947. BA in Edn., CUNY, 1970, MA in English. Tchr. memoir writing Hofstra U., Hempstead, N.Y., 1993—, L.I. U. C.W. Post Ctr., N.Y., 1993—; freelance reporter for L.I., N.Y. Times, N.Y.C., 1996—; columnist Distinction mag., Melville, N.Y., 1996—. Author 3 young adult novels, 2 self-help books. Homee: 22 Lydia Ct Searington NY 11507

BYARD, VICKI FAYE, English educator; b. Evansville, Ind., Apr. 11, 1961; d. Richard Ray and Frances Faye (O'Daniel) B.; 1 child, Alex Benjamin. BA, Towson State U., 1983; MA, Purdue U., 1985, PhD, 1993. Assoc. prof. English, Northeastern Ill. U., Chgo., 1991—, mem. women's studies core faculty, 1993—. Author: Instructor's Resource Manual for The Allyn and Bacon Guide to Writing, 1997, 2d edit., 1999.

BYARS, BETSY (CROMER), author; b. Charlotte, Aug. 7, 1928; d. George Guy and Nan (Rugheimer) Cromer; m. Edward Ford Byars, June 24, 1950; children: Laurie, Betsy Ann, Nan, Guy. Author: Clementine, 1962, The Dancing Camel, 1965, Rama, the Gypsy Cat, 1966, The Groober, 1967, The Midnight Fox, 1968 (Am. Book of Yr. selection Child Study Assn. 1968, Lewis Carroll Shelf award 1970), Trouble River, 1969 (Am. Book of Yr. selection Child Study Assn. 1969), The Summer of the Swans, 1970 (Am. Book of Yr. selection Child Study Assn. 1970, John Newbery medal 1971), Go and Hush the Baby, 1971, The House of Wings, 1972 (Am. Book of Yr. selection Child Study Assn. 1972, Nat. Book award nomination 1973), The 18th Emergency, 1973 (Am. Book of Yr. selection Child Study Assn. 1973, New York Times Outstanding Book of Yr. 1973, Dorothy Canfield Fisher Meml. Book award Vt. Conress of Parents and Teachers 1975), The Winged Colt of Casa Mia, 1973 (Am. Book of Yr. selection Child Study Assn. 1973, New York Times Outstanding Book of Yr. 1973), After the Goat Man, 1974 (Am. Book of Yr. selection Child Study Assn. 1974), The Lace Snail, 1975 (Am. Book of Yr. selection Child Study Assn. 1975), The TV Kid, 1976 (Am. Book of Yr. selection Child Study Assn. 1976), The Pinballs, 1977 (Woodward Park School Annual Book award 1977, Child Study Children's Book award Child Study Children's Book Com. at Bank Street Coll. of Edn. 1977, Ga. Children's Book award 1979, Charlie May Simon Book award Ark. Elem. School Coun. 1980, Surrey School Book of Yr. award Surrey School Librs. of Surrey 1980, Mark Twain award Mo. Assn. of School Librs. 1980, William Allen White Children's Book award Emporia State Univ. 1980, Young Reader medal Calif. Reading Assn. 1980, Golden Archer award Dept. Libr. Sci. Univ. of Wis.-Oskosh 1982), The Cartoonist, 1978, Goodbye Chicken Little, 1979 (New York Times Outstanding Book of Yr. 1979), The Night Swimmers, 1980 (Am. Book of Yr. selection Child Study Assn. 1980, Best Book of Yr. School Libr. Jour. 1980, Am. Book award for Children's Fiction 1981), The Cybil War, 1981 (Tenn. Children's Choice Book award Tenn. Libr. Assn. 1983, Sequoyah Children's Book award 1984), The Animal, the Vegetable, and John D. Jones, 1982 (Parents' Choice award for Lit. Parents' Choice Found. 1982, Best Children's Book Sch. Libr. Jour. 1982, CRABbery award Oxon Hill Br. of Prince George's County Libr. 1983, Mark Twain award Mo. Assn. of School Librs. 1985), The Two-Thousand-Pound Goldfish, 1982 (New York Times Outstanding Book of Yr. 1982), The Glory Girl, 1983, The Computer Nut, 1984 (Charlie May Simon award 1987), Cracker Jackson, 1985 (S.C. Children's Book award 1988, Md. Children's Book award 1988), The Not-Just-Anbody Family, 1986, The Golly Sisters Go West, 1986, The Blossoms Meet the Vulture Lady, 1986, The Blossoms and the Green Phantom, 1987, A Blossom Promise, 1987, Beans on the Roof, 1988, The Burning Questions of Bingo Brown, 1988, Bingo Brown and the Language of Love, 1989, Hooray for the Golly Sisters, 1990, Bingo Brown, Gypsy Lover, 1990, Seven Treasure Hunts, 1991, Wanted...Mud Blossom, 1991, The Moon & I, 1992, Bingo Brown's Guide to Romance, 1992, McMummy, 1993, The Golly Sisters Ride Again, 1994, The Dark Stairs: A Herculeah Jones Mystery, 1994, Coast to Coast, 1994, My Brother, Ant., 1996, Tornado, 1996, Dead Letter: A Herculeah Jones Mystery, 1996; editor: Growing Up Stories, 1995, Death's Door, 1997, Ant plays Bear, 1997, Disappearing Acts, 1998. Recipient Regina medal Catholic Libr. Assn., 1987. Home: 126 Riverpoint Dr Clemson SC 29631-1049*

BYARS, WALTER RYLAND, JR., lawyer; b. Birmingham, Ala., Oct. 5, 1928; s. Walter Ryland and Essie (Hopper) B.; m. Mildred Lucile Rhodes, Dec. 22, 1950; children: Debra Leigh Byars Patterson, Walter Ryland III, Rebecca Lynn Byars Pradat, John Baxter. BS, U. Ala., 1948, LLB, 1952, JD, 1969. Bar: Ala. 1952, U.S. Ct. Appeals (5th and 11th cirs.), U.S. Dist. Ct. (no., mid. and so. dists.) Ala., U.S. Supreme Ct. Pvt. practice Troy, Ala., 1953-57; atty. legal dept. So. Bell. Tel. & Tel. Co., Atlanta, 1957-59; gen. atty. So. Bell. Tel. & Tel. Co., Birmingham, 1959-68; ptnr. Steiner, Crum & Baker, 1968—. Bd. editors Ala. Law Rev., 1951-52. Lt. (j.g.) USNR, 1952-53. Fellow Am. Bar Found., Internat. Soc. Barristers (gov. 1977-83, sec.-treas. 1979-80, 2d v.p. 1980-81, 1st v.p. 1981-82, pres. 1982-83), Am. Coll. Trial Lawyers; mem. ABA (Young Lawyers past mem. exec. council, com. chmn.), Ala. Bar Assn. (pres.-elect 1983-84, pres. 1984-85, past pres. Young Lawyers, past sect. chmn., past com. chmn.), Pike County Bar Assn. (past pres.), Birmingham Bar Assn. (past com. chmn.), Montgomery County Bar Assn. (past com. chmn., bd. dirs. 1976-79, v.p. 1978, pres. 1979), Nat. Assn. R.R. Trial Counsel, Ala. Law Inst. (council), Montgomery Area Com. of 100, Masons, Sigma Chi, Phi Alpha Delta. Methodist. Home: 1744 Fairforest Dr Montgomery AL 36106-2602 Office: Regions Bank Bldg PO Box 668 Montgomery AL 36101-0668

BYARSE, ANTHONY, artist; b. Tucson, Mar. 28, 1939; s. Willie and Anna Mae (Wynn) Walker; m. Jean Dewberry (div. May 1959); 1 child, Anthony; m. Ingeborg M. Schorr, Dec. 18, 1962; children: Frank, John, Ilone, Roberta, Anita, Ilena. Grad., high sch., Cleve., 1956. Sgt. U.S. Army, 1956-62, 70-84; served in U.S., Germany, Japan, Korea; instr. art Ariz. Children's Home, Tucson, 1998. Artist, illustrator: The Animals Came Too, 1995, Free As the Wind, 1998, Potpourri, 1998. Mem. NAACP, DAV, Tucson Black C. of C. Home: 1655 W Ajo Way Unit 523 Tucson AZ 85713-6654 Office: Inks by Tony Art 'N More 1003 Wesley Dr Broken Arrow OK 74012-4215

BYBEE, CHARLES FORREST, writer, poet; b. Davis County, Iowa, May 28, 1920. Student, Capitol Radio Engring. Inst., Washington, 1946-48. Engr. CIA, Washington; freelance writer, poet Winter Haven, Fla. Author: One Man's Family, 1995; contbr. poetry to nat. anthologies and newspapers. Home: 200 Chaucer Ln Winter Haven FL 33884

BYBEE, JAY SCOTT, lawyer, educator; b. Oakland, Calif., Oct. 27, 1953; s. Rowan Scott and Joan (Hickman) B.; m. Dianna Jean Greer, Feb. 15, 1986; children: Scott, David, Alyssa, Ryan. BA, Brigham Young U., 1977, JD, 1980. Bar: D.C. 1981, U.S. Ct. Appeals (4th cir.) 1983, U.S. Supreme Ct. 1985, U.S. Ct. Appeals (5th cir.) 1986, U.S. Ct. Appeals (2d, 9th, 10th and D.C. cirs.) 1987. Law clk. to judge U.S. Ct. Appeals (4th cir.), 1980-81; assoc. Sidley & Austin, Washington, 1981-84; atty., advisor U.S. Dept. Justice, Washington, 1984-89; assoc. counsel to Pres. of U.S. The White House, 1989-91; prof. law La. State U., Baton Rouge, 1991-98, U. Nev., Las Vegas, 1999—. Contbr. articles to profl. jours. Missionary Mormon Ch., Santiago, Chile, 1973-75. Edwin S. Hinckley scholar, Brigham Young U., 1976-77. Mem. Phi Kappa Phi. Avocations: piano, all sports, reading. Home: 739 Sandy Hook Ter Henderson NV 89012-5207

BYBEE, RODGER WAYNE, science education administrator; b. San Francisco, Feb. 21, 1942; s. Wayne and Mary Genevieve (Mungon) B.; m. Patricia Ann Brovsky, May 28, 1966. BA, Colo. State Coll., 1966; MA, U. No. Colo., 1969; PhD, NYU, 1975. Tchr. sci. Greeley (Colo.) Pub. Schs., 1965-66; instr. sci. U. No. Colo., Greeley, 1966-70; teaching fellow NYU, N.Y.C., 1970-72; instr. edn. Carleton Coll., Northfield, Minn., 1972-75, asst. prof., 1975-81, assoc. prof., chmn. dept., 1981-85; assoc. dir. Biol. Scis. Curriculum Study, Colorado Springs, 1986-95, acting dir., 1992-93; exec. dir. Ctr. Sci., Math. and Engring. Edn. NRC, Washington, 1995-99; exec. dir. BSCS, Colorado Springs, Colo., 1999—; mem. adv. bd. for sci. assessment Nat. Assessment Ednl. Progress, Princeton, N.J., 1987-89, 92-93, 95-96; mem. adv. bd. Social Sci. Edn. Consortu=ium, Boulder, Colo., 1987-90; chairperson working group on curriculum NRC project on Nat. Sci. Ednl. Stds., 1993-95. Author: numerous books; contbr. numerous articles to profl. jours. NSF grantee, 1986—. Fellow AAAS (mem.-at-large 1987-90, chair sect. Q 1993-94, coun. del.), Nat. Assn. Rsch. Sci. Teaching (rsch. coord. 1986-89). Home: PO Box 563 Frisco CO 80443-0563 Office: BSCS 5415 Mark Darling Blvd Colorado Springs CO 80918-3842

BYCK, ROBERT SAMUEL, psychiatrist, educator; b. Newark, Apr. 26, 1933; s. Louis and Lucy Ruth Byck; children of former marriage: Carl, Gillian, Lucas; m. Susan Elizabeth Wheeler, Aug. 19, 1976; 1 child, John Ivey. A.B., U. Pa., 1954, M.D., 1959; M.A. hon., Yale U., 1978. Intern U. Calif.-San Francisco, 1959-60; asst. prof. pharmacology and rehab. medicine Albert Einstein Coll. Medicine, Bronx, N.Y., 1964-69; resident in psychiatry Yale U., New Haven, 1969-72, lectr. in pharmacology, 1969-72, assoc. prof. psychiatry and pharmacology, 1972-77, prof. psychiatry and pharmacology, 1977—; dir. psychiat. cons. Yale New Haven Hosp., 1987-94; cons. N.Y. Zool. Soc., Bronx, 1968—, Nat. Inst. Drug Abuse, Bethesda, Md., 1976-80, West Haven VA Hosp., 1972-98, Med. Letter on Drugs and Therapeutics, 1970-90. Editor: Cocaine Papers: Sigmund Freud, 1974; contbr. (articles to sci. publs.). Recipient Career Devel. award NIH, 1967, H.L. Mencken award Free Press Assn., Apple Valley, Calif., 1988; Burroughs-Wellcome scholar in clin. pharmacology, Triangle Park, N.C., 1972-77. Mem. Am. Soc. Pharmacology and Exptl. Therapeutics, Am. Soc. Clin. Pharmacology and Therapeutics, Am. Coll. Neuropsychopharmacology, Sherlock Holmes Soc. Office: Yale U Sch Medicine 333 Cedar St New Haven CT 06510-3289

BYCZKOWSKI, JANUSZ ZBIGNIEW, toxicologist; b. Gdansk, Poland, May 29, 1947; came to U.S., 1979; s. Stanislaw and Halina (Osterczy) B.; m. Janina K. Slosarska, Aug. 6, 1977; children: Ian S., L. Peter. MSc in Toxicology, Acad. Medicine, Gdansk, 1970, PhD in Pharmacology, 1975, DSc in Biochem. Pharmacology, 1979. Diplomate Am. Bd. Toxicology. Cancer rsch. scientist dept. exptl. therapeutics Roswell Park Meml. Inst., Buffalo, 1979-80, 1985-87; adj. ast. prof. pharmacology Acad. Medicine Gdansk, 1980-83; pharmacologist and dir. of pharmacy Internat. Red Cross and Red Crescent, Tobruk, Libya, 1983-84; asst. prof. and rsch. scientist Coll. Pub. Health U. South Fla., Tampa, 1987-91; project scientist and study dir. ManTech. Environ. Tech., Inc., Dayton, Ohio, 1991-98; sr. toxicologist TN&A Inc., Cin., 1998—; editorial reviewer Bull. Environ. Contamination and Toxicology, Reno, Nev., 1989—, Free Radical Biology and Medicine, Baton Rouge, 1989—, Placenta, Manchester, Eng., 1991—. Contbr. articles to profl. publs., chpts. to books. Active mem. Solidarity, Poland, 1980-83. Recipient Rsch. award 1st degree Sci. Soc. Gdansk, 1975, Polish Pharmacol. Soc., 1977, Ministry Health and Social Welfare of Poland, 1977. Mem. AAAS, Soc. for Rsch. on Polyunsaturated Fatty Acids (pres. 6th sci. meeting 1992—, travel grantee 1992), N.Y. Acad. Scis., Oxygen Soc., Soc. Toxicology, Soc. for Risk Analysis (councilor Ohio chpt. 1994—). Achievements include finding mechanism of action of DDT on mitochondrial respiration; discovery of NAD-Dependent mode of action of vanadium, cooxygenation of benzopyrene by lipoxygenase; developing physiologically-based pharmacokinetic model for lactational transfer of chemicals. Home: 212 N Central Ave Fairborn OH 45324-5006

BYCZYNSKI, EDWARD FRANK, lawyer, financial executive; b. Chgo., Mar. 17, 1946; s. Edward James and Ann (Ruskey) B.; children—Stefan, Suzanne. B.A., U. Wis., 1968; J.D., U. Ill., 1972; Certificat de Droit, U. Caen, France, 1971. Bar: Ill. 1972, U.S. Dist. Ct. (no. dist.) Ill. 1972, U.S. Supreme Ct. 1976. Title officer Chgo. Title Ins. Co., 1972-73; asst. regional counsel SBA, Chgo., 1973-76; pres. Alderstreet Investments, Portland, Oreg., 1976-82; pres. Nat. Tenant Network, Portland, 1981—, Bay Venture Corp., Portland, 1984—; ptnr. Haley, Pirok, Byczynski. Chgo., 1973-76. Contbr. articles to profl. jours. Mem. ABA, Ill. Bar Assn. Democrat. Home: PO Box 2377 Lake Oswego OR 97035-0614 Office: 525 SW 1st Ste 105 Lake Oswego OR 97034

BYE, ARTHUR EDWIN, JR., landscape architect; b. Arnhem, Holland, Aug. 25, 1919; came to U.S., 1920; s. Arthur Edwin and Mary Catherine (Heldring) B. B.S. in Landscape Architecture, Pa. State U., 1942. Registered landscape architect, N.Y., Pa., Conn., Mass. Prin. landscape architect A.E. Bye, Ridgefield, Conn., 1951—; Vis. design critic, lectr. numerous schs. architecture at univs.; adj. prof. Sch. Architecture, Columbia U., 1952-74, Pratt Isnt., 1978-81, Cooper Union, 1951—; vis. prof. in landscape archl. design dept. landscape architecture and regional planning Grad. Sch. Fine Arts, U. Pa., 1981-88; lectr. in field. Work exhibited at Univ. of Guelph, Guelph, Can., Pa. State U., Columbia U., N.C. State U., Syracuse U., Cooper Union, Archtl. League N.Y., Pratt Inst., U. Constrn. Fund Office, Albany, Wave Hill Bot. Garden, Bronx, N.Y., The Port of History Mus., Phila., The Octagon hdqrs. Am. Inst. Architects, Washington D.C., U. Penn., Phila., U. Vir., Charlottesville, Harvard U., Cambridge, Mass., U. Toronto and U. Guelph, Can., Iowa State U., Ames, Andrews U., Mich., Ball State U., Ind.; prin. works include renovation of planting for campus Barnard Coll., Columbia U., County Coll. of Morris, Randolph Twp., N.J., Monmouth Coll., N.J., U. Bridgeport, Conn., Wagner Coll., S.I., N.Y., numerous colls. and univs., landscaping for housing devels. including Coney Island West Housing Project, Bklyn., Dartmouth West, N. Dartmouth, Mass., Lambert Houses, Bronx, N.Y., Beechwood Condominiums, Scarborough, N.Y., religious instns. including Agudath Sholom Temple, Stamford, Conn., Christian and Missionary Alliance, Nyack, N.Y., St. Francis Episcopal Ch., Stamford, indls. and comml. bldgs. and landscaping including Bloomingdale's Dept. Store, White Plains, N.Y., Estee Lauder, Melville, N.Y., Harlem Savs. Bank, Massapequa, N.Y., Gainesway Farm, Lexington, Ky., Blue Cross Bldg., Wilkes-Barre, Pa., Lincoln Meml., Washington, Jefferson Meml., Washington, numerous others; author: Art into Lanscape-Landscape into Art, 1983; also exhbn. catalogues; contbr. articles to profl. jours. Recipient award for Outstanding Design, Boston Arts Festival, HUD Merit award for Design Excellence, 1968, Cert. of Merit, Am. Assn. Nurserymen, 1970, Nat. Landscape Assn., 1971, Nat. awards Am. Assn. Nurserymen for Indsl. and Indsl. Planning, Cert. Merit for Excellence in Design, N.Y. State Assn. Architects, 1972, Cert. Merit and Excellence in Design N.Y. State Assn. Architects, 1978, Cert. Appreciation for Design Excellence, East Ky. chpt. AIA, 1981, Alumni Achievement award Sch. Art and Architecture, Pa. State U., 1982, Nat. award Am. Assn. Nurserymen for Indsl. Planning, 1974; John R. Bracken fellow Dept. Landscape Architecture, Pa. State U., 1990; Alumni fellow Pa. State U., 1990. Fellow Am. Soc. Landscape Architects (honor award 1970, nat. jury for profl. and student exhibit 1968, award of merit 1974, world honor award 1993, the medal award, 1993). Avocations: photography; reading; travel. Home: PO Box 224 Ridgefield CT 06877-0224 Office: A E Bye 158 Danbury Rd Ridgefield CT 06877-3200

BYE, JAMES EDWARD, lawyer; b. Thief River Falls, Minn., May 2, 1930; s. Morris and Ida Mathilda (Dahl) B.; m. Patricia Ann Nadolski, Dec. 27, 1952; children: David Stanley, Anne Elizabeth. BBA with distinction, U. Minn., 1951; LLB cum laude, Harvard U., 1956. Bar: Colo. 1957, U.S. Tax Ct., U.S. Ct. Appeals (10th cir.), U.S. Supreme Ct. 1992. Assoc. Holme Roberts & Owen, Denver, 1957-61; ptnr. Holme, Roberts & Owen LLP, Denver, 1961—. Editor Harvard U. Law Rev. Chmn. continuing legal and jud. edn. Colo. Supreme Ct., Denver, 1977-78; chmn. Alexis de Tocqueville Soc. Met. Denver, 1986-89, Met. Denver GIVES, 1986-91; trustee Loretto Hts. Coll., Denver, 1977-88, Regis. Coll., 1988-92, U. Colo. Found., The Two Percent Club, 1991, Children's Hosp., 1993-95; chmn. urban emphasis program, Denver Area coun. Boy Scouts Am., 1992—, The Spot, 1996—; bd. dirs. Mex. Cultural Ctr. & Ctr. Affordable Housing. Recipient Silver Beaver award, 1996, Disting. Svc. to Humanity award Vols. of Am., 1996, Pub. Svc. award U. Colo. Grad. Sch. Pub. Affairs, 1996, Alex de Tocqueville Soc. award United Way, Reconocimiento Ohtli award Sec. of Fgn. Rels. of Mex., 1998, William Funk award Colo. Assn. Nonprofit Orgns., 1998. Fellow Am. Bar Found. (life), Colo. Bar Found.; mem. ABA (natural resources com. tax sect.), Colo. Bar Assn., Denver Bar Assn., Am. Coll. Tax Counsel, Denver Estate Planning Coun., Greater Denver Tax Counsel Assn. Avocation: golfing. Office: Holme Roberts & Owen LLP 1700 Lincoln St Ste 4100 Denver CO 80203-4541

BYE, LYNN ELLEN, social work educator; b. Jersey City, Nov. 23, 1950; d. Harry and Phyllis (Paxton) Horgen; m. Douglas Bye. BA, U. Minn., 1972, MSW, 1975; PhD, Rutgers U., 1994. Lic. ind. social worker, Minn. Sch. social worker Dist. 742, St. Cloud, Minn., 1975-95; asst. prof. social work Coll. St. Benedict, St. Joseph, Minn., 1995—. Author publs. in field. Clk. Dist. 912 Sch. Bd., Milaca, Minn., 1978-84; bd. dirs. Cmty. Edn. Adv., Milaca, 1978-81; chair Milaca Vocat. Bd., 1979-80. Recipient Sch. Bd. award Milaca Sch. Bd., 1984. Mem. NASW, Minn. Sch. Social Workers Assn. (pres. 1985, Sch. Social Worker of Yr. 1986), Coun. on Social Work Edn. (treas.). Avocations: reading, swimming. Office: Coll St Benedict 37 College Ave S Saint Joseph MN 56374-2001

BYE, RANULPH DEBAYEUX, artist, author; b. Princeton, N.J., June 17, 1916; s. Arthur Edwin and Mary C. (Heldring) B.; m. Mary DuBois McCarty, May 24, 1941 (div. 1981); children: Dennis L., Barbara D., Stephen G., Catherine M.; m. Glenna C. Lange, Oct. 16, 1983. Diploma, Phila. Mus. Sch. Indsl. Art, 1938; student, Art Students League, N.Y.C., 1940-41; D Pub. Svc. (hon.), Bucks County C.C., Newtown, Pa., 1994. Assoc. prof. painting Moore Coll. Art, Phila., 1949-79; condr. watercolor workshop in Eng. and Ireland, 1987, Maine Coast Art Workshop, 1990. One-man shows Newman Galleries, Phila, Hahn Gallery, Phila.; group shows Am. Watercolor Soc. ann., 30 yrs., Allied Artists anns., N.Y.C., NAD, 10 yrs., Phila. Waercolor Club, 40 yrs.; represented in permanent collections Smithsonian Instn., Davenport, Iowa, Mcpl. Art Gallery, Reading, Pa., James A. Michener Art Mus. , Doylestown, Pa., Pub. Mus., Temple U. Sch. Pharmacy, Phila., Munson, Williams Proctor Inst., Utica, N.Y., Mus. of Fine Arts, Boston, William Penn Mus., Harrisburg, Pa.; author, illustrator: The Vanishing Depot, 1973, rev. edit., 1983, 3d edit., 1994, Ranulph Bye's Bucks County, 1989; author: (with Margaret Bye Richie) Victorian Sketchbook, Painting Buildings in Watercolor, 1994. Served with U.S. Army, 1942-45. Recipient numerous awards various art orgns.including Gold medal Nat. Arts Club, 1963, Nat. Arts Club Award, 1988, Newman Galleries award, Mems.' Show award N.J. Water Color Soc., 1991, 3d award with merit Pa. Watercolor Soc., Keystone medal and award, 1996, Patrons Purchase award Watercolor U.A.S., Springfield, Mo., 1997. Mem. NAD (nat. academician 1994, cert. of merit, Adolph and Clara Obrig prize 1993), Am. Watercolor Soc. (6 awards 1964-92, Dolphin fellow 1985), Phila. Watercolor Club (Franklin Mint award 1988, 90, Savoir Faire prize 1993), Allied Artists Am. (Strathmore award 1986, Henry Gasser Meml. award 1989), Salmagundi Club (34 awards 1958—). Mem. Soc. of Friends. Home: PO Box 362 Mechanicsville PA 18934 *I felt fortunate in being able to pursue a career of my own choice; painting and interpreting my envioronment in landscape and genre subjects. I am a watercolorist in the tradition of American realism—the impressionist school of Sargent and Homer. My concern for architectural preservation caused me to publish two books on this theme. One with illustrations of bygone railroad stations and another on Victorian structures, hoping to enlighten the public's awareness of our architectural heritage.*

BYE, RAYMOND ERWIN, JR., academic administrator; b. Mobile, Ala., Feb. 22, 1944; s. Raymond Erwin and Frances (Bain) B.; m. Katherine Jackson, Dec. 28, 1971; children: Philip Jackson, Eleanor Ashley. BA, Rhodes Coll., Memphis, 1966; MA, Kent State U., 1968, PhD, 1972. Resident dir., 1966-68; area residence dir. Kent (Ohio) State U., 1968-69, asst. to pres., 1969-71, asst. to vice pres. student affairs, 1971-72; asst. to dir., deputy head, head congl. affairs NSF, Washington, 1973-83, dir. office of legis. and pub. affairs, 1983-94; assoc. v.p. rsch. Fla. State U., 1994-98, interim v.p. rsch., 1999—. Bd. dirs. Tallahassee Chamber, 1995—, Econ. Devel. Comm., 1995-98, Coun. on Gov. A ffairs, D.C., (pres. 1998—), FSU Rsch. Foun., 1995—; bd. dirs. TMN Hosp., 199. Recipient Disting. Svc. award NSF, 1989, Pres. Meritorious Exec. award, 1991. Mem. AAAS, So. Polit. Sci. Assn., Acad. Mgmt. Avocations: tennis, antiques. Office: Fla State U Westcott Bldg Tallahassee FL 32306-1330

BYEARS, LATASHA, professional basketball player; b. Aug. 12, 1973. Student, N.E. Okla. A&M Jr. Coll., 1992-94; grad., DePaul U., 1996. Basketball player Faenza, Italy, 1996-97, Beskijas, Turkey, 1996-97; basketball player Sacramento Monarchs Women's NBA, 1997—. Vol. Meals on Wheels. Office: Sacramento Monarchs One Sports Pky Sacramento CA 95834*

BYER, DIANA, performing arts company executive; b. Trenton, N.J., Aug. 31, 1946; d. Fred and Norma (Handis) B. Grad. high sch., Trenton. Soloist Manhattan Festival Ballet, N.Y.C., 1972, Les Grands Ballet Canadiens, Montreal, Can., 1975; dir. Ballet Sch. of N.Y., N.Y.C., 1978—, N.Y. Theatre Ballet, 1978—; dir., founder Project LIFT scholarship program for children living N.Y.C. homeless shelters, 1989—. Helen Weiselberg scholar Nat. Arts Club, 1988, 90, 93. Subject of Lincoln Ctr. presentation Dreams on a Shoestring, 1992. Office: NY Theatre Ballet 30 E 31st St New York NY 10016-6825

BYER, HAROLD GEORGE, environmental engineer; b. Phila., May 23, 1943; s. Harold G. and Estelle (Mirtz) B.; m. Susan C. Buchter, Apr. 24, 1976. AS in Engring., Cmty. Coll. Phila., 1972; BS in Civil Engring., Drexel U., 1975; MS, U. Pa., 1997. Sect. chief, engr. U.S EPA, Phila., 1975-87; project dir., mgr. R.F. Weston, Inc., West Chester, Pa., 1987-95; project dir. DuPont Environ. Remediation, Wilmington, Del., 1995-96; ind. environ. cons. Phila., 1997—; policy adviser U.S. EPA, 1984-86. Adv. coun. Frankford Hosp., Phila., 1987-97; dir. Northwood Civic Assn., Phila., 1986-89; pres. Pa. State Ch. Youth Orgn., 1980-81. Served in U.S. Army, 1965-69, PTO, Korea, Japan. Mem. ASCE (bd. dirs. 1977-81), Am. Water Works Assn., Masons. Presbyn. Avocations: skiing, sailing, fishing, backpacking, geology. Home: 1129 Allengrove St Philadelphia PA 19124-2901

BYER, THEODORE SCOTT, accountant; b. Trenton, N.J., Oct. 2, 1957; s. Fred and Norma (Handis) B.; m. Marcy Pam Steier, Aug. 8, 1981; children: Sarah, Tara, Hallie. BA, Muhlenberg Coll., 1979; MBA, Rider Coll., 1986. CPA. Auditor State of N.J., Trenton, 1979-80; staff acct. Louis H. Linowitz and Co., Trenton, 1980-82; supr. Amper, Politzner & Mattia, Flemington, N.J., 1982-88; tax mgr. Price Waterhouse, N.Y.C., 1988-90; sr. mgr. Salomon & Co., P.C., N.Y.C., 1990-94; ptnr. Mintz, Rosenfeld & Co., Fairfield, N.J., 1994—. Co-author: Taxation of Foreign Nationals in the United States, 1990; editor: Selecting and Installing Medical Practice Computer Software, 1996. Fellow N.J. State Soc. CPAs (co-founder Hunterdon-Warren chpt.); mem. AICPA, N.Y. State Soc. CPAs. Avocations: avid reader, music, computers. Home: 87 Cedar Ln Berkeley Heights NJ 07922-2400 Office: Mintz Rosenfeld & Co 60 Route 46 E Fairfield NJ 07004-3007

BYERLY, RADFORD, JR., science policy official; b. Houston, May 22, 1936; s. Radford and Garvis N. (Cook) B.; m. Kathryn Jester, May 13, 1960 (div. 1980), children: Laura, Hamilton, Charles; m. Carol Ann Ries, Apr. 10, 1987. BA, Williams Coll., 1958, MA, 1960; PhD, Rice U., 1967. Sr. engr. No. Rsch. & Engring. Co., Cambridge, Mass., 1961-63; postdoctoral fellow U. Colo., Boulder, 1967-69, dir. Ctr. for Space and Geoscis. Policy, 1987-91; physicist, mgr. Nat. Bur. Standards, Washington, 1969-75; mem. profl. staff com. on sci. and tech. U.S. Ho. of Reps., Washington, 1975-87, chief of staff, com. on sci. and tech., 1991-93; v.p. pub.policy U. Corp. for Atmosphere Rsch., Boulder, 1993-94; dir. Roberts Inst., Boulder, 1993-94; mem. space sta. adv. com. NASA, 1988-91, space sci. adv. com., 1987-91, 93-98; mem. adv. com. on space launch industry OTA, 1993-95; mem. bd. assessment NIST NAS, 1993—, mem. NAS com. on DOE peer rev. 1997-98; hon. lectr. Mid-Am. State Univs. Assn., 1988-89. Editor Space Policy Reconsidered, 1989, Space Policy Alternatives, 1991, Westview Press; contbr. articles to profl. jours. NSF fellow, 1963-67. Mem. AAAS (com. on sci. engring. and pub. policy 1998—), AIAA (chmn. civil space subcom. 1988-89), Assn. Univs. Rsch. in Astronomy (bd. dirs. 1998—), Am. Phys. Soc., Phi Beta Kappa, Sigma Xi (pres. U. Colo. chpt. 1995-97). Avocations: skiing, hiking, gardening. Home: 3870 Birchwood Dr Boulder CO 80304-1419

BYERRUM, RICHARD UGLOW, college dean; b. Aurora, Ill., Sept. 22, 1920; s. Earl Edward and Florence (Uglow) B.; m. Claire Somers, Apr. 3, 1945; children: Elizabeth, Mary, Carey. A.B., Wabash Coll., 1942, D.Sc. (hon.), 1967; Ph.D., U. Ill., 1947. Teaching asst. U. Ill., 1942-44; research asso. U.S. Chem. Corps, toxicity dept. U. Chgo., 1944-47; faculty Mich. State U., East Lansing, 1947—; prof. biochemistry Mich. State U., 1957-91, prof. emeritus, 1991—; acting dir. Mich. State U. (Inst. Biology and Medicine), 1961-62; dean Mich. State U. (Coll. Natural Sci.), 1962-86. Author: (with others) Experimental Biochemistry, 1956; Editorial bd.: (with others) Phytochemistry, 1961-81; Contbr. (with others) numerous articles to profl. jours. Mem. Project Hope, 1961—; Trustee Mich. Health Council, 1961—, pres., 1966. Travel grantee Internat. Congress Biochemistry, Vienna, 1958; Travel grantee Internat. Congress Biochemistry, Montreal, 1959. Mem. Am. Chem. Soc. (lectr. vis. scientist program, awards com., visitor for com. profl. tng.), N. Central Assn. Colls. and Secondary Schs., A.A.A.S., Am. Soc. Plant Physiologists (trustee, exec. com.), Am. Soc. Biol. Chemists, Soc. Exptl. Biology and Medicine, Mich. Acad. Arts, Sci. and Letters, Phi Beta Kappa (pres. local chpt. 1962), Sigma Xi (awards com., Jr. Research award Mich. State U. chpt. 1958), Phi Kappa Phi (pres. 1968-69), Phi Lambda Upsilon, Alpha Chi Sigma, Beta Theta Pi. Patentee cancer tumor inhibiting material. Home: 602 Wildwood Dr East Lansing MI 48823-3209

BYERS, ALBERT SAMUEL, aerospace education specialist; b. Washington, Sept. 30, 1962; s. Lawrence Leon and Carole Ann Byers; m. Julie Ann Thomas, Sept. 7, 1996. BS, Va. Poly. Inst. and State U., 1985, MA, 1995; postgrad., Va. Tech. Mortgage loan officer Lomas & Nettleton Mortgage Corp., Springfield, Va., 1986-90; asst. v.p. mortgage loan office Investors Savs. Bank, Richmond, Va., 1990-93; acct. rep. GMAC, Richmond, 1993; educator Chesterfield (Va.) County Pub. Schs., 1991-94; aerospace edn. specialist NASA Goddard Space Flight Ctr., Greenbelt, Md., 1995—; cons. Maine Dept. Edn., Augusta, Conn. NASA Edn. Collaborative. Contbg. author: (curriculum guide) Beyond the Looking Glass, 1993; author NASA web site Hubble Second Servicing Mission: Related Education Links, 1997. Recipient Citation of Appreciation Conn. Sci. Suprs. Assn., 1997; grantee NASA Langley Rsch. Ctr., 1997, Va. Dept. Edn., 1984. Mem. ASCD, Nat. Sci. Tchrs. Assn., Nat. Coun. Tchrs. Math., Internat. Tech. Edn. Assn. Republican. Baptist. Avocations: snow skiing, water skiing, rocketry, web design. E-mail: al@specialts.net. Home: 2812 Wellesley Ct Blacksburg VA 24060-4127

BYERS, GARLAND FRANKLIN, JR., private investigator, security firm executive; b. Rutherfordton, N.C., Jan. 11, 1968; s. Garland Franklin Sr. and Helen Kathryn (Cannon) B.; m. Heather Kristina Emory, June 5, 1987; children: Amber Dianna, Jonathan Wesley. AAS in Criminal Justice, Isothermal C.C., Spindale, N.C., 1991; BS in Criminal Justice, U. S.C., Spartanburg, 1993; postgrad., N.C. Ctrl. Sch. Law, 1996—. Chief of police Alexander Mills Police Dept., Forest City, N.C., 1988; police officer Rutherfordton Police Dept., 1988-90; cpl., dep. sheriff Rutherfordton County Sheriff's Dept., 1990-91; roving technician The New Cherokee Corp., Spindale, 1992-93; pvt. practice ins./loan agt. Primerica Fin. Svcs., Spindale, 1994-95; criminal justice instr. Isothermal C.C., Spindale, 1994-95; chief investigator N.C. State Dist. Attys. Office 29th Prosecutorial Dist., Rutherfordton, 1995-96; owner, pvt. investigator, counterintelligence specialist Byers Investigations, Hillsborough, N.C., 1997—. Mem. ABA (student). Avocations: reading, martial arts, swimming. Office: 1512 S Alston Ave Durham NC 27707

BYERS, GEORGE WILLIAM, retired entomology educator; b. Washington, May 16, 1923; s. George and Helen (Kessler) B.; m. Martha Esther Sparks, Feb. 25, 1945 (div. 1953); children: George William, Carolyn Sylvia; m. Gloria B. Wong, Dec. 16, 1955; children: Bruce Alan, Brian William, Douglas Eric. BS, Purdue U., 1947; MS, U. Mich., 1948, PhD, 1952. Asst. prof. dept. entomology U. Kans., Lawrence, 1956-60, curator Snow Entomol. Mus., 1956-83, dir., sr. curator, 1983-88, assoc. prof., 1960-65, prof. entomology, 1965-88, ret., prof. dept. systematics and ecology, 1969-88, chmn. dept. entomology, 1969-72, 84-87, ret., 1988; vis. prof. Mountain Lake Biol. Sta. U. Va., alt. summers, 1961-92, U. Minn., 1970. Author: several book chpts.; contbr. articles to profl. jours. With U.S. Army, 1942-46, 53-56, WWII and Korea; lt. col. M.S.C., USAR, ret. Rackham fellow U. Mich., 1952-53; NSF grantee, 1958-87, 97-99. Mem. Entomol. Soc. Am. (editl. bd. Annals 1967-72, chmn. 1971-72), Entomol. Soc. Can., Ctrl. States Entomol. Soc. (pres. 1958-59), Entomol. Soc. Washington, Soc. Systematic Biology (editor Syst. Zool. jour. 1963-66), Phi Beta Kappa, Phi Kappa Phi, Sigma Xi. Avocations: invertebrate paleontology; photography; ornithology. Home: 909 Holiday Dr Lawrence KS 66049-3006 Office: U Kans Dept Entomology Lawrence KS 66045

BYERS, KENNETH VERNON, insurance company executive; b. Logan, Ohio, Apr. 6, 1940; s. Kenneth Vernon and Ruth Elizabeth (Klingel) B.; m. Diane Petty, Aug. 21, 1972; children: Juli, Kimberly, Jeffrey, Matthew, Kristine, Brandon. BA in Edn., U. Cin., 1962. CLU (pres. Cin. chpt. 1989); ChFC. Football player N.Y. Giants then Minn. Vikings, 1962-67; pres. Ken Byers and Assocs., Cin., 1968—; chmn. adv. coun. Gen. Am. Life Ins. Co., St. Louis, 1987—. Mem. NFL Alumni Assn. (bd. dirs. 1983-96), Cin. Assn. Life Underwriters (pres. 1978), CLU/ChFC (past pres. Cin. chpt. 1989-90), Gen. Agts. and Mgrs. Assn. (pres. 1976), Internat. Assn. Fin. Planners, Nat. Assn. Life Underwriters, Internat. Forum (bd. dirs. 1996—), Cin. C. of C. (mem. sports council 1987—), Coldstream Country Club. Republican. Episcopalian. Avocations: golf, tennis, squash. Home: 4650 Willow Hills Ln Cincinnati OH 45243-4228 Office: Ken Byers & Assocs 7710 Shawnee Run Rd Cincinnati OH 45243

BYERS, NINA, physics educator; b. Los Angeles, Jan. 19, 1930; d. Irving M. and Eva (Gertzoff) B.; m. Arthur A. Milhaupt, Jr., Sept. 8, 1974. BA in Physics with highest honors, U. Calif., Berkeley, 1950; MS in Physics, U. Chgo., 1953, PhD, 1956; MA, U. Oxford, Eng., 1967. Research fellow dept. math. physics U. Birmingham, Eng., 1956-58; research assoc., asst. prof. Inst. Theoretical Physics and dept. physics Stanford, 1958-61; asst. then assoc. prof. physics UCLA, 1961-67, prof. physics, 1967—; mem. Sch. Math., Inst. Advanced Studies, Princeton, N.J., 1964-65; ofcl. fellow Somerville Coll., Oxford, 1967-68, Janet Watson vis. fellow, 1968-74; faculty lectr., mem. dept. theoretical physics Oxford U., 1967-74, sr. vis. scientist, 1973-74; official fellow and tutor in physics, Somerville Coll. John Simon Guggenheim Meml. fellow, 1964-65, Sci. Rsch. Coun. fellow Oxford U., 1978, 85. Fellow AAAS (mem-at-large physics sect., com. on freedom and responsibility 1983—), Am. Phys. Soc. (councillor-at-large 1977-81, panel pub. affairs 1980-83, vice-chmn. forum on physics and soc. 1981-82, chmn. 1982-83); mem. Fedn. Am. Scientist (nat. coun. 1972-76, 78-80, exec. com. 1974-76, 78-80). Achievements include research in theory of particle physics and superconductivit y; history of physics; contributions of 20th century women to physics. Office: U Calif Dept Physics Los Angeles CA 90095

BYERS, PAUL HEED, television news producer, consultant; b. Balt., Mar. 6, 1943; s. Paul Horatio and Corinne May (Gardner) B.; m. Frances Regina Barbour, June 10, 1967. BA, Am. U., 1966; MS with honors, Columbia U., 1967. Reporter, cameraman Sta. WTOP-TV, Washington, 1961-65; assignment editor, producer Post-Newsweek Stas., Washington, 1969-74; asst. assignment editor CBS News, Washington, 1974-75; dep. fgn. editor CBS News, N.Y.C., 1975-78; bur. mgr. CBS News, Hong Kong, 1978-83; producer CBS News, Washington, 1983-85; coordinating producer NBC News, Washington, 1985-87; pres. Gateway Video Svcs. Inc., Washington, 1987—; asst. prof. communications Marymount U., Arlington, Va., 1988—; dir. Health Vols. Overseas, Washington, 1986-89. With U.S. Army, 1967-69. Columbia U. internat. fellow, 1966-67. Mem. Nat. Press Club, Sigma Delta Chi, Kappa Tau Alpha. Episcopalian. Avocations: camping, photography, sailing. Office: Gateway Video Svcs Inc 5418 Hawthorne Pl NW Washington DC 20016-2667

BYERS, PETER H., geneticist; b. N.Y.C., May 31, 1943. MD, Case Western Reserve U., 1969. Diplomate Am. Bd. Internal Medicine, Am. Bd. Molecular Genetics, clin. geneticist. Intern U. Calif., San Francisco, 1969, resident, 1969-70; fellow U. Wash., Seattle, 1974-77, asst. prof. pathology and medicine, 1979-82, assoc. prof., 1982-86, prof., 1986—. Editor Am. Jour. Human Genetics, 1994—. Fellow AAAS, Am. Soc. Human Genetics, Am. Soc. for Clin. Investigation; mem. Am. Bd. Med. Genetics (pres. 1997). Office: U Wash Dept Pathology Box 357470 Seattle WA 98195-0001*

BYERS, THOMAS WILLIAM, optometrist; b. Syracuse, N.Y., July 10, 1951; m. Suzanne Marie Perry, Nov. 3, 1979; children: Anna, Abigail. BS, U. Ctrl. Fla., 1974; BS in Visual Scis., Ill. Coll. Optometry, 1974, OD, 1976. Lic. optometrist, Ill., Mo.; cert. therapeutic pharmaceutic agt. Pvt. practice Springfield, Mo., 1976-86. Lt. USN, 1986-93. Mem. Armed Forces Optometric Soc., Optimist Club. Avocation: amateur radio. Home: 605 E Glendale St Aurora MO 65605-2609 Office: Payless Optical Outlet 2346 S Campbell Ave Springfield MO 65807

BYERS, WALTER, athletic association executive; b. Kansas City, Mo., Mar. 13, 1922; s. Ward and Lucille (Hebard) B.; children: Ward, Ellen, Frederick. Student, Rice U., 1939-40, U. Iowa, 1940-43. News reporter United Press Assn. (later U.P.I.), St. Louis, 1944, U.P.I., Madison, Wis., 1945; sports editor U.P.I., Chgo., 1945; asst. sports editor U.P.I., N.Y.C., 1946-47; also fgn. sports editor; dir. Big Ten Conf. Service Bur., Chgo., 1947-51; exec. asst. NCAA, Chgo., 1947-51, exec. dir., 1951-52; exec. dir. NCAA, Kansas City, Mo., 1952-73; exec. dir. NCAA, Shawnee Mission, Kans., 1973-87, exec. dir. emeritus, 1988-90; pres. Byers Seven Cross Ranch, Inc., Emmett, Kans., 1974—, Ironwood Seven Cross Ranch, Inc., Hatfield, Mo., 1992—, Byers Land and Cattle Co., Mission, Kans., 1996—; mgr. Byers Ranches, Limited Liability Co., 1997. With M.C. AUS, 1944. Home: PO Box 6412 Leawood KS 66206-0412

BYFORD, EMMA, rancher; b. Marlin, Tex., Jan. 30, 1918; d. Joseph and Emma (Conner) Watkins; m. Ray Homan Byford, Sept. 2, 1937 (dec. 1980). Stenographer, sec. Waco (Tex.)-McLennan County Health Unit, 1944-50; sec. to plant mgr. Owens-Illinois Glass Co., Waco, 1950-54; co-owner, office mgr. Byford Machine & Tool, Waco, 1956-76; owner Byford Ranch, Clifton, Tex., 1963—. Methodist.

BYINGTON, WILLIAM W., JR., federal judge; b. 1951. JD, U. Ga., 1976. Atty. Jones, Byington, Durham & Payne; part-time magistrate judge U.S. Dist. Ct. (no. dist.) Ga., Atlanta, 1990—. Office: 75 Spring St SW Atlanta GA 30303-3309

BYKOFSKY, STUART DEBS, newspaper columnist; b. N.Y.C., Sept. 24, 1941; s. Sydney Bernard and Jeanette (Rose) B.; m. Joanne Rothman, May 31, 1962 (div. Feb. 1972); children: Shaw Thomas, Sonya Sue; m. Maria Merlino, July 22, 1990. AA, CUNY, 1964. Editor Chilton Pub., Radnor, Pa., 1966-72; columnist Phila. Daily News, 1972—. Author: Stu Bykofsky's Little Black Book: A Gentlemen's Guide to Philadelphia, 1995. Nominated for Pulitzer Prize, 1995. Mem. Soc. Profl. Journalists, Pen and Pencil Club, Variety Club (bd. dirs.), Infamous Club (pres. 1989-95). Avocations: travel, photography, dog training. Office: Phila Daily News 400 N Broad St Philadelphia PA 19130-4015

BYLER, VICKIE LYNNE JENNIFER, educator, athletic director; b. Riddle, Pa., Apr. 4, 1959; d. Walter Blake and Irene Virginia (Homan) Huddell; married, July 2, 1995. BS in Phys. Edn., The King's Coll., 1981; MS in Sports Mgmt., U.S. Sports Acad., 1993, postgrad., 1997—. Tchr., athletic dir. Atlantic Christian Sch., Ocean City, N.J., 1981-85, Annapolis (Md.) Area Christian Sch., 1985-90; athletic dir., fin. aid Washington Bible Coll., Lanham, Md., 1990-94; athletic dir., prof. Lancaster (Pa.) Bible Coll., 1994—; instr. Am. sport edn. program, coach, instr. sport first aid, 1996—; mem. editl adv. bd. Collegiate Press, Alta Loma, Calif., 1996-97; presenter in field. Instr. ARC, Lancaster, 1996—m Am. Sport Edn. Program, Champaing, Ill., 1996—. Fellow Nat. Christian Conf. Athletic Assn. (dist. chair 1993-95), Am. Alliance Health Phys. Edn. Avocations: athletics, hiking, camping, restoring old home. Office: Lancaster Bible Coll 901 Eden Rd Lancaster PA 17601-5036

BYLES, ROBERT VALMORE, manufacturing company executive; b. Robeline, La., Dec. 7, 1937; s. Robert S. and Ann (Murray) B.; m. Mary E. Hornsby, Sept. 14, 1954; children: Robert V. Jr., Rebecca Kay, Raymond Gale, Aaron Blake. Student, Northwestern State U., Natchitoches, La., 1955-57, La. Tech. U., 1957-58. Ptnr. Byles Bros. Welding and Tractor Co., Many, La., 1960-72; owner, pres. R.V. Byles Industries, Many, 1972-80, R.V. Byles Enterprises, Inc., Many, 1980—; ptnr. Byles Internat., Shreveport, La., 1984-92; pres. West La. Hot Mix Asphalt, Inc., Many, 1986-96; bd. dirs. Sabine Med. Ctr. Hosp. Bd., 1994—, chair, 1997, 98, 99. Chmn. Sabine Parish Dem. Exec. Com., 1968-79; mem. Repub. State Cen. Com., 1979-94; chief Many Fire Dept., 1965-69. Served with USN, 1959-60. Named one of Outstanding Young Men Am., 1970. Mem. La. Assn. Bus. and Industry, Am. Soc. Concrete Constrn., Nat. Fedn. Bus. and Industry, Sabine Parish C. of C. (bd. dirs. 1966—, pres. 1969-70), Many Jaycees (pres. 1970-71, Outstanding Young Men of Am. 1970). Republican. Methodist. Lodge: Shriners (pres. 1988). Avocations: flying, swimming, scuba diving, tennis. Office: RV Byles Enterprises Inc 1751 Robby St Many LA 71449-3361

BYLES, TORREY KOPPE, communications technolgy specialist; b. Los Angeles, June 12, 1957; s. Howard Douglas and Dorothy (Wardwell). BA, U. Calif., San Diego, 1979; postgrad., Calif. State U., L.A., 1981-83. Secondart tchr. Alhambra (Calif.) Sch. Dist., 1981-82, 83-84; editor Internat. Bus. Svcs., Inc., Taipei, Taiwan, 1982-83; interpreter Mandarin Chinese L.A. Olympic Organizing Com., 1984; freelance contract writer Pasadena, Calif., 1984-85; staff writer IEEE Computer Soc., Los Alamitos, Calif., 1985-87; journalist, writer Long Beach, Calif., 1987—; cons. Amtrade Internat., Los Alamitos, 1987—. Spl. correspondent, Jour. of Commerce; contbr. articles to profl. jours. Mem. Chinese Interagency Coun., Los Angeles, 1983, 84, 85, 87. Democrat. Unitarian. Avocations: swimming, sailing, surfing, hiking, camping. Office: 366 Redondo Ave Apt 7 Long Beach CA 90814-4663

BYLINSKY, GENE MICHAEL, magazine editor; b. Belgrade, Yugoslavia, Dec. 30, 1930; s. Michael Ivan and Dora (Shadan) B.; m. Gwen Gallegos, Aug. 14, 1955; children: Tanya, Gregory. B.A. in Journalism, La. State U., 1955. Staff reporter Wall St. Jour., Dallas, 1957-59, San Francisco, 1959-61, N.Y.C., 1961; sci. writer Nat. Observer, Washington, 1961-62, Newhouse Newspapers, Washington, 1962-66; bd. editors Fortune Mag., N.Y.C., 1966—. Author: The Innovation Millionaires, 1976, Mood Control, 1978, Life in Darwin's Universe, 1981, Silicon Valley, High Tech Window on the Future, 1985. Served with AUS, 1956. Recipient 21st Ann. Albert Lasker Med. Journalism award, 1970, Deadline award Sigma Delta Chi, 1970, 72, 79, spl. commendation AMA, 1967, 68, 72, Journalism award, 1974, Claude Bernard Sci. Journalism award Nat. Soc. Med. Rsch., 1973, 74, James T. Grady award for interpreting chemistry to pub. Am. Chem. Soc., 1976, Am. Space Writers Assn. award, 1976-79, Bus. Journalism award U. Mo.-Columbia, 1984, Journalism award Am. Assn. Engring. Socs./Engring. Found., 1995, hon. mention award, 1970, 71, hon. mention award AAAS-Westinghouse Corp., 1975, 76, 77, hon. mention award Overseas Press Club, 1988. Mem. Nat. Assn. Sci. Writers, N.Y. Acad. Scis. Mem. Russian Orthodox Ch. Office: Fortune Magazine Time and Life Bldg Rockefeller Ctr New York NY 10020

BYNES, FRANK HOWARD, JR., physician; b. Savannah, Ga., Dec. 3, 1950; s. Frank Howard and Frenchye (Mason) B.; m. Janice Ratta, July 24, 1987; children: Patricia, Frenchye. BS, Savannah State Coll., 1972; MD, Meharry Med. Coll. Resident gen. surgery Staten Island (N.Y.) Hosp., 1978-82; resident internal medicine N.Y. infirmary Beekam Downtown Hosp., N.Y.C., 1983-86; dir. medicine USAF Sheppard Regional Hosp., Sheppard AFB, Tex., 1986-87; pvt. practice internal medicine N.Y.C., 1987-90; attending physician Bronx (N.Y.) Lebanon Hosp., 1990-93; pvt. practice intenral medicine Savannah, Ga., 1994—. Maj. USAF, 1986-87. Mem. AMA, AAAS, ACP, N.Y. Acad. Scis., Assn. Mil. Surgeons of U.S., Alpha Phi Alpha.

BYNOE, PETER CHARLES BERNARD, real estate developer, lawyer; b. Boston, Mar. 20, 1951; s. Victor Cameron Sr. and Ethel May (Stewart) B.; m. Linda Jean Walker, Nov. 20, 1987. BA, Harvard U., 1972, JD, 1976, MBA, 1976. Bar: Ill. 1982; cert. real estate broker, Ill. Exec. v.p. James H. Lowry & Assocs., Chgo., 1977-82; chmn., chief exec. officer Telemat Ltd., Chgo., 1982—; mng. dir. Howard Ecker & Co. Real Estate, Chgo., 1986-87; of counsel Davis, Barnhill & Galland, Chgo., 1987-88; exec. dir. Ill. Sports Facilities Authority, Chgo., 1988-92; mng. gen. ptnr. Denver Nuggets, 1989-92; ptnr. Rudnick & Wolfe, Chgo., 1995—; bd. dirs. Uniroyal Tech. Corp., Jaycor Comms., Ind., TransAfrica Forum. Chmn. Chgo. Landmarks Commn., 1985; vice chmn. Goodman Theater; dir. Chgo. Econ. Club, Ill. Sports Facilities Authority; trustee Rush-Presbyn. St. Luke's Med. Ctr.; bd. overseers Harvard U. Mem. East Bank Club. Democrat. Avocations: squash, tennis, racquetball, skiing, travel, golf. Office: Rudnick & Wolfe 203 N La Salle St Ste 1850 Chicago IL 60601-1225*

BYNUM, ANN BAILEY, medical educator; b. Siloam Springs, Ark.; d. Robert Carl and Francis Sue (West) Bailey; m. William Pickens, Aug. 12, 1963 (div. 1972); children: Holly Ann Pickens Bowles, Susan Heather Pickens Fritz; m. Preston Conrad Bynum, May 31, 1987. BS, U. Ark., 1961, MEd, 1976; EdD, Nova Southeastern U., 1983. Health edn. dir. Dept. Def., Tokyo, 1968-70; instr. chemistry Heritage Sch., Gainesville, Fla., 1971-74; clin. coord./staff U. Fla. Shands tchg. Hosp., Gainesville, 1976-80; chmn. dept. sci. Pinellas County Sch. Dist., Palm Harbor, Fla., 1980-86; edn. dir. Bapt. Hosp. Chem. Dependency Program, Little Rock, 1987-89; pres. ABCO Physician Registry ABCO Inc., Little Rock, 1987-91; assoc. dir. AHEC Program U. Ark. for Med. Sci., Little Rock, 1991—, dir. UAMS Rural Hosp. Program, 1991—. Contbr. articles to profl. jours. Treas. St. Margaret's Episc. Ch., Little Rock, 1994; supt. youth summer program Holy Trinity Episc. Ch., Gainesville, Fla.; bd. dirs., pres., Affordable Housing Preservation Found., Little Rock, 1989-92; bd. dirs. U. Ark. Deans Devel. Coun., 1991—; chmn. Gov.'s Breast Cancer Control adv. Bd., Little Rock, 1997; mem. task force on telemedicine So. Govs. Assn. Office of Reg. Health Policy, HRSA grantee, 1997; recipient Outstanding Achievement in Drug Edn. Curriculum Devel., Dept. of Def., 1970. Mem. Am. Telemedicine Assn., Soc. Pub. Health Edn., Soc. Tchrs. Family Medicine, Assn. Health Svcs. Rsch. Episcopalian. Office: Univ of Arkansas for Med Sci 1123 S University Ave Ste 400 Little Rock AR 72204-1611

BYNUM, HENRI SUE, education and French educator; b. Columbia, Miss., Feb. 7, 1944; d. George Milton and Lois Marie (Newsom) Dearing; m. James Lamar Bynum Jr., Feb. 28, 1965; children: James Wesley, Charles Drew. BA, U. So. Miss., 1967, MEd, 1977, PhD, 1979. Cert. tchr., Fla. Tchr. French, Spanish, modern dance Natchez (Miss.) Adams Pub. Schs., 1972-76; tchr. ESL U. So. Miss., Hattiesburg, 1977-79, coord. academic programs English Lang. Inst., 1979-81, adj. prof., 1980-81; dir. internat. edn. So. Ctr. for Rsch. and Innovation, Hattiesburg, 1981-82; chmn., asst. prof. dept. ESL U. So. Ala., Mobile, 1982-85; tchr. French, Spanish Moss Point (Miss.) High Sch., 1985-86; tchr. French Vero Beach (Fla.) Jr. High, 1986-87; prof. edn., French, chair edn. dept. Indian River Community Coll., Ft. Pierce, Fla., 1987—; adj. prof. Mobile Coll., 1986; cons. for curriculum devel. Colegio LaCruz, Puerto LaCruz, Venezuela, Escuela Anaco (Venezuela); co-dir. ESL curriculum Workshop, Assn. Venezuelan Am. Schs., Anaco. Cons. Safe Space, Inc., Vero Beach, 1989—; mem. bd. dirs. Fla. Fund for Minority Tchrs., Inc., 1998—. Mem. Phi Delta Kappa, Kappa Delta Pi. Republican. Avocations: reading, gourmet cooking, cross stitching. Office: Indian River Community Coll 3209 Virginia Ave Fort Pierce FL 34981-5541

BYNUM, JUDITH LANE, special education educator; b. Forrest City, Ark., Jan. 21, 1948; d. Herbert Sydney and Corine (Traweek) Lane; m. Barton Alan Bynum; children: Judith Ann, Alan Woodrow. BSE, Ark. A&M Coll., 1969; MEd, U. Ark., Little Rock, 1991. Cert. tchr. sec. math., English, gifted and talented, Ark. Tchr. Monticello (Ark.) Pub. Sch., 1969-70, Dermott (Ark.) Sch. Dist., 1970-71, Montrose (Ark.) Acad., 1972-75, 80-87; tchr. gifted and talented Fountain Hill (Ark.) Sch. Dist., 1987-88; tchr., coord, gifted and talented Drew Ctrl. Sch. Dist., Monticello, 1988—, curriculum coord., 1993—; insvc. presenter Mid-Mapping Multiple Intelligences, 1992—. Illustrator: Catch Them Learning, 1993, The Pre-Adolescent, 1997; artist calendars, 1995, 96. Mem. parsonage com. First United Meth. Ch., Dermott, 1990—; coord. Pride of Dermott Festival, 1989. Named Ark. Oldsmobile Tchr. of the Yr., Ark. Oldsmobile Assn., 1990; recipient Disting. Leadership award Ark. Leadership Acad., 1995, Master Educator award Union Bank, Monticello, 1997. Mem. Agate Gifted and Talented Educators (nomination com. 1996-98). Avocations: writing, reading, artwork, music. Home: PO Box 341 Dermott AR 71638-0341

BYRD, ANDREW WAYNE, investment company executive; b. Nashville, Apr. 16, 1954; s. Benjamin F. and Allison (Caldwell) B.; m. Marianne Menefee; children: Marianne, Valere, Andrew Jr. BA, Vanderbilt U., 1976, JD, 1979; LLM, Georgetown U., 1981. Bar: Tenn., 1979, U.S. Dist. Ct. (mid. dist.) Tenn. 1979. Atty. Stokes & Bartholomew, Nashville, 1981-84; exec. v.p. Gen. Cap Am. Inc., 1987-94; exec. v.p. Gen. Capital Corp., Nashville, 1984-89, pres., 1989-94; pres. Andrew W. Byrd & Co., LLC, 1994—. Mem. Leadership Nashville, 1984-85; deacon 1st Presbyn. Ch., 1982-92; bd. dirs. Tenn. divsn. Am. Cancer Soc., 1982-88, 92-97, Cheekwood, 1987-93; bd. dirs. Boy Scouts of Am., Mid. Tenn. Coun., 1995—; bd. dirs. Vanderbilt Children's Hosp., 1987-93, chmn., 1991-93. Mem. ABA, Tenn. Bar Assn., Nashville Bar Assn., Nashville C. of C., Cumberland Club Nashville, Exch. Club (pres. 1993-94). Democrat. Avocations: tennis, gardening, travel. Home: 4419 Harding Pl Nashville TN 37205-4530 Office: Andrew W Byrd & Co LLC 201 4th Ave N Ste 1250 Nashville TN 37219-2092

BYRD, BARBARA A., professional society administrator; b. Martinsburg, W.Va., Aug. 31, 1952; d. James Leonard and Elizabeth (Somerfield) Byrd; 1 child, Marjorie Lynn. BS, Old Dominion U., 1973, MS, 1975; postgrad., U.

Maryland, 1976. Cert. assn. exec. Instr. Old Dominion U., Norfolk, Va., 1972-75; asst. prof. U. Maryland, Balt., 1975-76; assoc. dir. Am. Dental Hygienists Assn., Chgo., 1976-79; dir. edn. Am. Coll. Preventive Medicine, Washington, 1979-81; dir. profl. affairs Tex. Pharm. Assn., Austin, 1981-83; dir. edn. and research Tex. Med. Assn., Austin, 1983-86; exec. v.p. Internat. Assn. Hospitality Accts., Austin, 1986-90; exec. v.p. Community Assns. Inst., Alexandria, Va., 1990-99, pres., 1999—; chair Assns. Advance Am. Com., 1994—. Bd. dirs. Nat. Bd. Cardiopulmonary Credentialing, Gaitersburg, N.D., 1981-82, mem. exec. com. 1982; bd. dirs. South Tex. Arthritis Found., San Antonio, 1987-89, Capital Area Arthritis Found., Austin, 1986-89; founding chmn. Travis County Adult Literacy Coun., Austin, 1984-90, chmn. emeritus 1990—; bd. dirs. Am. Hotel and Motel Assn. Research Found., 1988-90. Recipient award Internat. Assn. Bus. Communicators, 1988; named one of Outstanding Young Women Am., 1981, Top 10 Bus. Women of Yr., Am. Bus. Women's Assn., 1986. Fellow Am. Soc. Assn. Execs. (charter, vice chmn. 1991-92, planning com. 1985-88, 91-92, chair Assn. Advance Am. com. 1994, bd. dirs. 1985-86, 88—, chmn. ednl. sect. 1985-86, chmn. task force on social responsibility 1989—, chair fellows 1989-90, Excellence award 1985, 88, 94, CAE commr. 1991-93, sec.-treas. 1993-94, gov. task force 1992-93, chair rsch. com. 1996-97, Mgmt. Achievement award 1983, Key award 1996, award of excellence in edn. 1997); mem. Town Lake Bus. Women's Assn. (Woman of Yr. 1986), Tex. Soc. Assn. Execs. (com. chair 1981—), Greater Washington Soc. Assn. Execs. (CAE cert. com., instr. and tutor 1991-92, cmty. svc. com. 1996-97, bd. dirs. 1997—, Monument award in edn. 1992), Leadership Austin, Leadership Tex. (bd. dirs., tng. group 1987—), Internat. Assn. Hosp. Accts. (hon. 1990), U.S. C. of C. (mem. Com. of 100). Home: 1630 Duke St # 3rd-fl Alexandria VA 22314-3426 Office: Community Assns Inst 1630 Duke St Alexandria VA 22314-3426*

BYRD, BENJAMIN FRANKLIN, JR., surgeon, educator; b. Nashvillle, May 18, 1918; s. Benjamin Franklin and Ida (Brister) B.; m. Allison Caldwell, Feb. 6, 1950; children: Benjamin Franklin, Barney Duncan, Damon Winston, Andrew Wayne, Evelyn Hope, John W. Thomas. A.B., Vanderbilt U., 1938, M.D., 1941. Intern, Nashville Gen. Hosp., 1941-42, asst. resident, 1942; asst. resident Vanderbilt U. Hosp., 1945-47, resident, 1947-48; practice medicine, specializing in surgery Nashville, 1948—; chief surgery St. Thomas Hosp., 1964-70, pres. staff, 1977-79; mem. staff Baptist Hosp.; instr. surgery Vanderbilt U., Nashville, 1947-54; assoc. clin. prof. surgery Vanderbilt U., 1954-71, clin. prof. surgery, 1971-99; chmn. bd. of overseers Vanderbilt U. Cancer Ctr., 1993—; assoc. clin. prof. surgery Meharry Med. Coll., Nashville, 1951-69; prof. clin. surgery Meharry Med. Coll., 1969—, clin. prof. surgery emeritus, 1999—; dir., mem. trust bd. Commerce Union Bank, 1974-80, 82-91; dir. NLT Corp. Pres. Tenn. divsn. Am. Cancer Soc., 1963, nat. bd. dirs., 1965—, nat. exec. com., 1970-80, chmn. med. and sci. exec. com., 1973—&, nat. pres., 1975-76; pres., mem. exec. bd. Tenn. Bot. Gardens and Fine Arts Ctr., 1971-73; trustee Sr. Citizens, Hermitage Assn.; bd. dirs. Cumberland Mus., Univ. Sch., 1985-91. Lt. col. M.C., AUS, 1941-45. Decorated Bronze Star with 2 oak leaf clusters, Silver Star, Purple Heart; named Nashvillian of Yr., Nashville Kiwanis, 1986; recipient Human Rels. award Nat. Fellow ACS (gov. 1973-79, chmn. commn. on cancer); mem. Am. Surg. Assn., So. Surg. Assn., Nashville Surg. Soc. (pres. 1962-63), Soc. Surg. Oncology, Tenn. Med. Assn. (mem. council, Disting. Service award, Physician of Yr. 1986), So. Med. Assn. (mem. council), Société International de Chirurgie, Southeastern Surg. Congress (mem. council, pres. 1968-69, Disting. Service award 1977), Nashville Acad. Medicine (pres. 1980, chmn. 1981), Nashville C. of C. (bd. govs. 1967-70, 82—, pres. 1985), Vanderbilt U. Med. Alumni (pres. 1979-81), Sigma Xi. Club: Nashville Exchange. Home: 400 Ellendale Ave Nashville TN 37205-3402 Office: PO BOx 380 4220 Harding Rd Nashville TN 37202

BYRD, CHARLES EVERETT, clergyman; b. Brinkerhoff, N.Y., Mar. 19, 1909; s. James Edward and Mamie (Lovelle) B.; m. Violetta Eleanor Price. AB, Howard U., 1932; MDiv, Union Theol. Sem., 1935; MA, Columbia U., 1947; D of Ministry, Drew U., 1978. Pastor Cen. Bapt. Ch., Salt Point, N.Y., 1939-47, Mt. Zion Bapt. Ch., Green Haven, N.Y., 1936-52, Ebenezer Bapt. Ch., Poughkeepsie, N.Y., 1947-52; program rep. Am. Bapt. Svc. Corp., Valley Forge, Pa., 1969-74; chaplain Dutchess County Jail, Poughkeepsie, 1974-89. Author: Review of the Policies of the Baptist Home in Light of the Theology of Service, 1978. Bd. dirs. Bapt. Home, Rhinebeck, N.Y., 1976-94, Dutchess County Office Aging, Poughkeepsie, 1976-94, The Rural and Migrant Ministry, New Paltz, N.Y., 1980-94, Dutchess County Mental Health Assn., Poughkeepsie, 1981—. With USAAF, 1943-46; lt. col. USAF, 1952-68. Decorated Commendation medal with oak leaf cluster; recipient Marist Coll. Pres. award, 1997. Mem. Dutchess Interfaith Coun. (Disting svc. medal 1987), Rotary (sr. active mem.). Home: 3030 Park Ave # 5E-15 Bridgeport CT 06604-1138 *During the time of my prayers prior to very high risk cancer surgery, the third with 2 in 1987, my courage and faith grew as I reached the point that nothing could change or diminish the goodness of God to me over the past 78 years.*

BYRD, CHRIS, amateur boxer; b. Flint, Mich., Aug. 15, 1970. Olympic boxer, middleweight divsn. Barcelona, Spain, 1992. Recipient Silver medal middleweight boxing divsn. Olympics, Barcelona, 1992. Office: USA Boxing One Olympic Plz Colorado Springs CO 80909 Address: NJ Sports Prodn Inc d/b/a Main Events 811 Totowa Rd Ste 100 Totowa NJ 07152*

BYRD, CHRISTINE WATERMAN SWENT, lawyer; b. Oakland, Calif., Apr. 11, 1951; d. Langan Waterman and Eleanor (Herz) Swent; m. Gary Lee Byrd, June 20, 1981; children: Amy, George. BA, Stanford U., 1972; JD, U. Va., 1975. Bar: Calif. 1976, U.S. Dist. Ct. (ctrl., so. no., ea. dists.) Calif., U.S. Ct. appeals (9th cir.). Law clk. to Hon. William P. Gray, U.S. Dist. Ct., L.A., 1975-76; assoc. Jones, Day, Reavis & Pogue, L.A., 1976-82, ptnr., 1987-96; asst. U.S. atty. criminal divsn. U.S. Atty.'s Office-Cen. Dist. Calif., L.A., 1982-87; ptnr. Irell & Manella, L.A., 1996—; mem. Calif. Law Revision Commn., 1992-97. Author: The Future of the U.S. Multinational Corporation, 1975; contbr. articles to profl. jours. Mem. Calif. State Bar (com. fed. cts. 1985-88), Los Angeles County Bar Assn., Women Lawyers Assn. Los Angeles County, Am. Arbitration Assn. (large and complex case panel 1992—, nat. energy panel 1998—, bd. dirs. 1999—), Stanford Profl. Women Los Angeles County, Stanford U. Alumni Assn., 9th Jud. Cir. Hist. Soc. (bd. dirs. 1986—, pres. 1997—), Assn. Bus. Trial Lawyers (bd. govs. 1996—). Republican. Office: Irell & Manella LLP 1800 Ave Of Stars Ste 900 Los Angeles CA 90067-4276

BYRD, ELLEN STOESSER, dermatology nurse; b. Dayton, Tex., Dec. 10, 1941; d. Edward Joseph and Nina Mae (Cannon) Stoesser; m. C. Robert Byrd, June 6, 1964; children: Byron, Preston, Aaron, Robyn. BSN, Baylor U., 1964. RN, Tex. Nurse Parkland Hosp., Dallas, 1964-65; nurse gyn. svcs. Baylor U. Med. Ctr., Dallas, 1965-66; charge nurse med./surg. Collin Meml. Hosp., McKinney, Tex., 1967-68; nurse newborn nursery St. Paul Hosp., Dallas, 1972; pvt. duty nurse Dist. 4 Tex. Nurse Assn., Dallas, 1976; sch. nurse Dallas Ind. Sch. Dist., 1989-90; home health nurse Rehab Home Care, DeSoto, Tex., 1994-98; dermatology nurse, 1999—; mem. adv. bd. Baylor U. Sch. Nursing, Dallas, 1994—, chmn. adv. bd. 1999—; advisor Baylor U. Woman's Coun., Dallas, 1995—, pres., 1994-95. Author: History of Dallas CPA Wives, 1983, Biography of Mae Stoesser, 1988, Byrd Family 25 Years, 1990. Program chmn. Freedom Found. Valley Forge, Dallas, 1986-89; centennial circle chmn. Dallas County Heritage Soc., Dallas; deacon Cliff Temple Bapt. Ch., 1988; v.p. DeSoto Svc. League, 1990; pres. Dallas CPAs Wives Club, 1984-85; mem. Richardson Jr. League. Recipient W.T. White Meritorious Svcs. award Baylor U. Alumni Assn., 1996. Mem. Richardson Jr. League, Richardson Newcomers Club. Repubican. Baptist. Avocations: European travel, grandchildren. Fax: 972-234-1122. E-mail: EllenByrd@aol.com. Home: 304 Prince Albert Ct Richardson TX 75081-5059

BYRD, EVA WILSON, communications executive. Dir. media Girgenti, Hughes, Butler & McDowell, New York, NY, 1994—. Office: Girgenti Hughes Butler & McDowell Fl 8 100 Ave of the Americas New York NY 10013-1687*

BYRD, GARY ELLIS, lawyer; b. Dothan, Ala., Mar. 8, 1957; m. Emily Marie Reid; children: Elizabeth, Virginia and Victoria (twins). BS in Pre-Law and Am. History summa cum laude, Troy State U., 1979; JD, U. Ala., 1982. Bar: Ga. (no. and middle dists.) 1983, U.S. Dist. Ct. (no. and so. dists), Ga., U.S. Ct. Appeals. Pntr. Bishoff & Byrd, Talbotton, Ga., 1982—; assoc. Bunn & Kirby, Hamilton, Ga., 1993—; ptnr. Bunn & Byrd, Hamilton, Ga., 1996—; city atty. Woodland, Ga., 1986—, Geneva, Ga., 1988—, Shiloh, Ga., 1994—; chmn. bd. dirs. Talbot County Law Libr., Talbotton, 1992-99; bd. dirs. Harris County Law Libr., Hamilton. Contbr. numerous articles to newspapers and profl. jours., chpt. to book; author City of Woodland city code, 1986. Bd. dirs. Chattahoochie-Flint RESA, Americus, Ga., 1986-87, Pine Mountain Regional Arts Coun., Manchester, Ga., 1986-88; pres., chmn. exec. com. Talbot County 2000 Group, Talbotton, 1987-88; coach debate team dept. social studies Manchester (Ga.) H.S., 1982; chmn. appropriations com. Harris County YMCA, Hamilton, 1994, 95, 96, 97, 98, 99, bd. dirs. 1994, 95, 96, 97, 98, 99; mem. budget com. City of Talbotton, 1989-92, councilman, 1985-92, mem. policy adv. com., 1986-92, vol. fireman, 1982-93; ct. apptd. adminstr. City of Geneva, Ga., 1992; mem. adv. com. Am. Security Coun., Washington, 1976-82. Recipient Outstanding Svc. award Talbot County Jaycees, 1983,. Mem. Ga. Bar Assn., Ga. Mcpl. Assn. (atty.'s sect.), Talbot County C. of C. (chmn. membership com. 1992-93, bd. dirs. 1993), Harris County C. of C., Troy State U. Alumni Assn. (membership com. East Ala./West Ctrl. Ga. chpt. 1993-99, Phi Kappa Phi, Phi Alpha Theta (State Hist. Rsch. award 1979). Avocations: model trains, stock car racing, antique car restoration. Home: PO Box 119 Hamilton GA 31811-0119 Office: 103 N College St PO Box 489 Hamilton GA 31811-0489

BYRD, HARRY FLOOD, JR., newspaper executive, former senator; b. Winchester, Va., Dec. 20, 1914; s. Harry Flood and Anne Douglas (Beverley) B.; m. Gretchen B. Thomson, Aug. 9, 1941 (dec. Oct. 1989); children: Harry, Thomas Thomson, Beverley. Student, Va. Mil. Inst., 1931-33, U. Va., 1933-35; hon. LL.D., L.H.D., D. Internat. Service. Editor Winchester Evening Star, from 1935; pub. Harrisonburg (Va.) Daily News-Record, 1937—; Pres., dir. Rockingham Pub. Co., from 1946; dir. A.P., 1950-66; v.p., mem. exec. com.; mem. Va. Senate, 1947-65; mem. U.S. Senate from Va., 1965-83. Author state automatic tax reduction law. Mem. Va. Democratic Central Com., 1940-66. Served to lt. comdr. USNR, 1942-46. Recipient Honor medal Freedoms Found. Mem. VFW, Va. Press Assn. (Man of Yr.), Am. Legion, Masons (33 degree, insp. gen. hon.). Clubs: Rotarian, National Press, Army-Navy. Office: Rockingham Pub Co Inc 2 N Kent St Winchester VA 22601-5038

BYRD, HARVEY CLIFFORD, III, information management company executive; b. Durham, N.C., July 4, 1947; s. Harvey Clifford and Sarah Elizabeth (Morgan) B.; m. Mary Elizabeth Bell, Dec. 27, 1969; children: Harvey Clifford, IV, Kevin Michael. BS in Psychology, Old Dominion U., 1969; MA in Urban Planning, Morgan St. U., 1976. Chief program devel. planning Exec. Dept. St. Md., Towson, 1972-80; mgmt. analyst-Nat. Criminal Justice Reference Service, Aspen Systems Corp., Rockville, Md., 1980-81, dir., 1981-86, dir. govt. ops., 1983-85, v.p. govt. ops., 1985-86; v.p. and gen. mgr. Cons. Group, 1986-89; v.p., gen. mgr. Applied Mgmt. Scis., 1989-95; pres. Eagle Mgmt. Sys., Inc., 1995—; pub. Educating for Citizenship curriculum guides, 1983. Pres. Towson Loch Raven Cmty. Coun., 1980; pres. Loch Raven Community Assn., Towson, 1978-80. Mem. Info. Industry Assn., Am. Soc. Assn. Execs., Md. Bar Assn. (law edn. com.). Democrat. Episcopalian. Home and Office: 12894 Eagles View Rd Ste B Phoenix MD 21131-2313*

BYRD, ISAAC BURLIN, fishery biologist, fisheries administrator; b. Canoe, Ala., Mar. 14, 1925; s. Isaac Britt and Mary Adline (Wright) B.; m. Marjorie Fé Elmore, Sept. 24, 1949; children—Cathy Ann, Teresa Carol, Gary Curtis. B.S., Auburn U., 1948, M.S., 1950. Chief fisheries sect. Ala. Dept. Conservation, 1951-65; fed. aid coordinator fisheries research and devel. Bur. Comml. Fisheries, Dept. Interior, 1965-70; chief div. state-fed. relationships, fisheries research, devel. and mgmt. Nat. Marine Fisheries Service, St. Petersburg, Fla., 1970-85; asst. regional dir. S.E. Region Nat. Marine Fisheries Service, 1985-91, ret., 1991; adminstr. Internat. Fisheries Agreement (for U.S. shrimp fishermen to fish Brazilian coastal waters), 1975-76; mem. adv. com. to organize 1st fishery mgmt. councils and to develop initial fed. policies under Fisheries Conservation and Mgmt. Act 1976 (for marine fisheries in fisheries conservation zone of U.S.); chmn. Gulf of Mexico State/Fed. Fisheries Mgmt. Bd., 1985-86, 88-89; chmn. South Atlantic State/Fed. Fisheries Mgmt. Bd., 1990-91. Contbg. author: McCanes Standard Fishing Ency., Internat. Angling Guide, 1965; contbr. articles to sci. jours. Served with USAAF, 1943-46. Recipient Gov. Ala. award outstanding tech. accomplishments conservation, 1964. Fellow Am. Inst. Fishery Research Biologists; mem. Am. Fisheries Soc. (pres. So. div. 1958, pres. 1965-66, asso. editor trans. 1955-58), World Mariculture Soc. (dir. 1972-73), Internat. Assn. Fish and Wildlife Agys., Gulf and Caribbean Fisheries Inst., Inland Comml. Fisheries Assn., Phi Kappa Phi, Omicron Delta Kappa, Gamma Sigma Delta, Alpha Zeta, Alpha Gamma Rho. Methodist. Initiated 1st fisheries mgmt. and fisheries research program in state for Ala. Dept. Conservation. Home: 11105 7th St E Treasure Island Saint Petersburg FL 33706

BYRD, JAMES EVERETT, lawyer; b. Cin., Aug. 1, 1958. BS, U. Dayton, Ohio, 1980, JD cum laude, 1984. Law clk. U.S. Dist Ct. (so. dist.), Ohio, 1983; assoc. Smith & Schnacke, Dayton, 1984-89; v.p., gen. counsel Internat. Cargo Svcs., Virginia Beach, Va., 1989-91; assoc. Beale, Balfour et al., Richmond, Va., 1991-92; corp. counsel Huffy Corp., Dayton, 1992-94; ind. corp. legal cons., 1994-95; assoc. gen. counsel LEXIS-NEXIS divsn. Reed Elsevier, Inc., Dayton, 1995—. Pres. Condominium Owners Assn., Dayton, 1995-99. Mem. ABA, Ohio Bar Assn., Va. Bar Assn. Office: Lexis-Nexis 9443 Springboro Pike Miamisburg OH 45342-4425

BYRD, JOAN EDA, film librarian; b. May 12, 1942. BFA, Howard U., 1965; MLS, Cath. U. Am., 1976; MA, New Sch. for Social Rsch. Reference librarian Bklyn. Pub. Libr., 1985-87, sr. librarian, 1987-89; sr. film librarian N.Y. Pub. Libr., N.Y.C., 1989-93, supervising librarian, 1993—. E-mail: jbyrd@nypl.org.

BYRD, LARRY DONALD, behavioral pharmacologist; b. Salisbury, N.C., July 14, 1936; s. Donald Thomas and Mildred (Gardner) B.; m. Corrinne Williams, Dec. 23, 1961; children: Kay, Lynn, Renee, Andrew. AB, E. Carolina U., Greenville, N.C., 1962; MA, E. Carolina U., 1964; PhD, U. N.C., 1968; postgrad., Harvard U., 1967-70. Faculty E. Carolina U., 1962-64; tchg. and rsch. asst. exptl. psychology U. N.C., Chapel Hill, 1964-67; rsch. fellow pharmacology, instr. psychobiology Harvard Med. Sch., 1967-70; assoc. scientist Lab. Psychobiology New Eng. Reg. Primate Rsch. Ctr., 1969-74; psychobiologist, chmn. divsn. primate behavior Yerkes Primate Rsch. Ctr., Emory U., Atlanta, 1974-79, assoc. rsch. prof., chmn. divsn. primate behavior, 1979-80, lectr. dept. psychology, 1974-81, assoc. rsch. prof., chief divsn. behavioral biology, 1980-82, prof., chief divsn. behavioral biology, 1982-97, prof. dept. pharmacology, 1995-97; prof. emeritus, 1998; adj. prof. dept. psychology Emory U., 1981-97; cons. Dept. Pharmacological and Physiol. Scis. U. Chgo., 1973, MIT Press, Cambridge, 1975, Nat. Ctr. for Toxicological Rsch. FDA, Jefferson, Ark., 1976-77, S.W. Found. for Rsch. and Edn., San Antonio, 1977, Naval Aerospace Med. Rsch. Lab. U.S. Naval Air Sta., Pensacola, Fla., 1977, G.D. Searle and Co., Skokie, Ill., 1986, Battelle Meml. Inst., Columbus, Ohio, 1989-94; mem. spl. rev. com. Contract Rev. Unit Nat. Inst. on Drug Abuse, Lexington, Ky., 1979-81, mem. spl. rev. com. biomed. rsch. rev. com., 1981-82, spl. rev. cons. clin., behavioral and psychosocial rsch. rev. com., 1981-82, mem., 1982-85, chmn., 1984-85, others; spl. rev. cons. dept. medicine and surgery VA, Washington, 1983, NSF, Washington, 1984, div. of rsch. resources NIH, Washington, 1983, mem. spl. study sect. div. rsch. grants, 1984, panel mem. Workshop on Implemenation of Pub. Health Svc. Policy on Humane Care and Use of Lab. Animals, 1989, others; panel mem. USPHS Animal Welfare Forum Alcohol, Drug Abuse and Mental Health Adminstrn., 1985; active numerous other career related orgns. Editorial bd. Jour. Exptl. Analysis of Behavior, 1969-79, 87-91; assoc. editor Jour. Exptl. Analysis of Behavior, 1970-76; cons. editor Am. Jour. Primatology, 1980-83; editor Psychopharmacology Newsletter, 1976-82; editorial advisor Jour. Pharmacology and Exptl. Therapeutics, Jour. Exptl. Analysis of Behavior, others; contbr. numerous articles to profl. jours. Mem. sci. adv. com. Nat. Families in Action, 1991-95. Recipient Outstanding Alumnus award, E. Carolina U., 1977, Disting. Alumnus award, U. N.C., 1987. Fellow AAAS, Am. Psychol. Assn. (exec. com. psychopharmacology divsn. 1976-95, neurobehavioral toxicity test standards com. 1980-97, coord. Young Psychopharmacologist award 1985-95, bd. sci. affairs com. on animals in rsch. and ethics 1990-93); mem. Assn. for Assessment and Accreditation Lab. Animal Care (trustee 1990-98, exec. com. 1991-98, sec. 1993, vice chmn. 1994-96, chmn. 1996-98), Am. Soc. Pharmacology and Exptl. Therapeutics, Nat. Families in Action (sci. adv. com. 1991-95), Am. Soc. Primatologist, Behavioral Pharmacology Soc. (pres. 1984-86), Soc. Exptl. Analysis of Behavior (v.p. 1975-76, bd. dirs. 1970-78), European Behavioral Pharmacology Soc., Southeastern Pharmacology Soc., Am Pub. Health Assn., Behavioral Toxicology Soc., Southeastern Assn. for Behavior Analysis, Internat. Study Group Investigating Drugs as Reinforcers, Emory Neurosci. Group, Phi Sigma Pi. Home: 2730 Camp Branch Rd Buford GA 30519-4455

BYRD, LINWARD TONNETT, lawyer, rancher; b. Hamburg, Ark., June 25, 1921; s. Charley E. and Arrie (Montgomery) B.; m. Reba Ann Rowe, Dec. 22, 1965; 1 child, Jana Lynn. LLB, U. Tex., 1950. Bar: Tex. 1950, U.S. Dist. Ct. (we. dist.) Tex. 1956, U.S. Ct. Appeals (5th cir.) 1965, U.S. Ct. Appeals (11th cir.) 1981. Sr. ptnr. Byrd, Davis & Eisenberg, Austin, Tex., 1959—. With USN, 1942-43. Fellow Am. Trial Lawyers Found., Tex. Bar Found., Am. Coll. Trial Lawyers; mem. Assn. Trial Lawyers Am., Am. Bd. Trial Advs. (adv.), Tex. Trial Lawyers Assn., State Bar Tex., Travis County Bar Assn. (lifetime disting. achievement award), Travis County Young Lawyers Assn. (lifetime disting. achievement award). Baptist. Home: 2400 Vista Ln Apt A Austin TX 78703-2344 Office: Byrd Davis & Eisenberg 707 W 34th St Austin TX 78705-1204

BYRD, LLOYD GARLAND, civil engineer; b. Atlanta, May 6, 1923; s. Lloyd Porter and Gladys Ardee (Daniell) B.; m. Jeanne Mae Parkhurst, Jan. 23, 1943; children: Gary Daniell, Donna Jeanne, Jeffrey Alan, Julie Anne. BCE, Ohio State U., 1950. Staff engr. Ohio Dept. Hwys., Columbus, 1949-52; maintenence engr. Ohio Turnpike Commn., Berea, 1952-60; assoc. editor Pub. Works Publs., Ridgewood, N.J., 1960-63; ptnr. Byrd, Tallamy, MacDonald & Lewis, Falls Church, Va., 1963-72; sr. v.p., mgr. Byrd, Tallamy, MacDonald & Lewis div. Wilbur Smith & Assocs., Falls Church, 1972-84; interim dir. Strategic Hwy. Rsch. Program, Washington, 1984-86; pvt. practice Washington, 1986—; chmn. group 3 coun. Transp. Rsch. Bd., Washington, 1972-76, chmn. overview com.; ex-officio governing bd. NRC, Washington, 1989-95; mem. bd. cons. Eno Found., Westport, Conn., 1986-89. Co-author: Street and Highway Maintenance Manual: American Public Works Association, 1985; assoc. editor: Handbook of Highway Engring., 1975; chmn. pub. affairs coun. Am. Assn. Engring. Socs., 1992. Chmn. Fairfax County (Va.) Human Rights Commn., 1978-79; pres. Fairfax County C. of C., 1975-76. Recipient Disting. Alumnus award Ohio State U. Coll. Engring., 1978, Roy W. Crum award Transp. Rsch. Bd., Washington, 1986, P.D. McLean Meml. award Road Gang, Washington, 1989, Disting. Lectr. award, 1998, Transp. Rsch Bd. Fellow ASCE (pres. nat. capital sect. Washington 1976-77, nat. bd. dirs. N.Y.C. 1979-82, Wilbur S. Smith award 1985, Francis C. Turner Lecture award 1995); mem. NAE, Am. Pub. Works Assn., Univ. Club (Washington), Mt. Vernon (Va.) Country Club. Republican. Methodist. Avocations: golf, bridge.

BYRD, LORENDA SUE, nursing administrator; b. Eureka, Ill., Jan. 31, 1941; d. Denver C. and Sadie M. (Van Sickle) Aucutt; m. Larry L. Byrd, Jan. 2, 1984; children: Scott, Ellen, Leslie, Brian. Diploma, Meth. Hosp. Cen. Ill. Sch., Peoria, 1962; BSN, McKendree Coll., 1981; MSN, So. Ill. U., Edwardsville, 1990. RN, Ill., Mo.; cert. nursing adminstr. ANCC. Staff nurse Charleston Community Hosp., 1962-65; mem. faculty Mennonite Hosp. Sch. Nursing, Bloomington, Ill., 1965-76; head nurse emergency rm. Belleville (Ill.) Meml. Hosp., 1976-80; nurse mgr. med.-surg. oncology dept. St. Elizabeth Med. Ctr., Granite City, Ill., 1980-87; assoc. dir. patient svcs. Alexian Bros. Hosp., St. Louis, 1988-91; dir. nursing St. Joseph Hosp.-West, Lake St. Louis, Mo., 1991-96, v.p. patient svcs., 1996-97; chief nursing officer Lucy Lee Healthcare Sys, Poplar Bluffs, Mo., 1998—. Mem. "We Can 2000" Cmty. Orgn., Wentzville, Mo., 1992-95, Bus. and Profl. Women, Wentzville, 1993-94. Mem. Am. Orgn. Nurse Execs., Mo. Orgn. Nurse Execs., St. Louis Coun. Nurse Execs. (pres.-elect 1993, pres. 1994), O'Fallen (Mo.) Rotary (sec. 1995, pres.-elect 1996), C. of C. Lake St. Louis (sec. 1994—, bd. dirs. 1994, 96), Sigma Theta Tau.

BYRD, MALCOLM TODD, public health administrator; b. Phila., Mar. 22, 1956; s. Joseph Edward and Kathleen Jean (Quarterman) B. BA, Antioch U., Phila., 1984, MEd, 1986; cert. drug and alcohol counselor, Villanova U., 1991; M in Govtl. Adminstrn., U. Pa., 1993; grad. Phila. Urban League, Leadershp Inst., Phila., 1993; grad., Leadership Inc., 1994. Cert. indsl. and labor rels. specialist. Cmty. organizer Local Cmty. Based Orgn., 1976-82; educator, counselor Local Health Facility, 1982-84; behavioral health specialist, 1984-88; coord. II mental health emergency svcs. Phila. Dept. Pub. Health, 1988-94, exec. asst., 1997—. Hon. degree com. U. Pa., 1992-94; preceptor to grad. human svcs. program Lincoln U., 1991-92, 94—; mem. Juv. Justice Alliance, 1993—; bd. dirs. Phila. Tribune Charities, 1996; chmn. bd. dirs. Philabundance, 1998; cmty. devel. fund allocation com. United Way, 1996; adv. coun. Thomas Jefferson U. Hosp. Cancer Ctr., 1996; mem. Health Promotions coun. Southeastern Pa., 1996; adv. bd. physicians asst. grad. program Phila. Coll. Osteo. Medicine; bd. dirs. Utility Emergency Svcs. Fund, Utility Emergency Svcs. Fund. Mem. Nat. Black MBA Assn., 100 Black Men of the Phila. Region, Inc. Democrat. Baptist. Avocations: reading, gospel music, chess. Home: 435 N 66th St Philadelphia PA 19151-4007 Office: City of Philadelphia Dept Pub Health 10th Fl ARA Towers 1101 Market St Philadelphia PA 19107

BYRD, MARC ROBERT, florist; b. Flint, Mich., May 14, 1954; s. Robert Lee and Cynthia Ann (Poland) B.; m. Bonnie Jill Berlin, Nov. 25, 1975 (div. June 1977). Student, Ea. Mich. U., 1972-75; grad., Am. Floral Sch., Chgo., 1978. Gen. mgr., dir. flowers shop; designer Olive Tree Florist, Palm Desert, Calif., 1978-79, Kayo's Flower Fashions, Palm Springs, 1979-80; owner, designer Village Florist, Inc., Palm Springs, 1980-85; pres. Mon Ami Florist, Inc., Beverly Hills, 1986-87; gen. mgr. Silverio's, Santa Monica, 1987; gen. mgr., hotel florist, creative dir. Four Seasons Hotel, Beverly Hills, 1988-90; pres. Marc Fredericks, Inc., Beverly Hills, 1990-97; event florist Marc Byrd of Floral Works, L.A., 1997—. Author: Celebrity Flowers, 1989. Del., Dem. County Conv., 1972, Dem. County Conv., 1972, Dem. State Conv., 1972, Dem. Nat. Conv., 1972. Mem. Soc. Am. Florists, So. Calif. Floral Assn., Desert Mus., Robinson's Gardens. Republican. Mem. Dutch Reformed Ch. Avocations: skiing, tennis, community service. Fax: (323) 962-9275. Home: 2415 Creston Dr Los Angeles CA 90068-2203 Office: Floral Works 2415 Creston Dr Los Angeles CA 90068-2203

BYRD, MARY JANE, education educator; b. Topeka, Apr. 21, 1946; d. Vernon Thomas and Mary Elizabeth (Caldwell) Wharton; m. Gerald David Byrd, June 24, 1965; children: Kari, Juli, Cori. BS, U. So. Ala., 1980, MBA, 1984; D of Bus. Adminstrn., Nova Southeastern U., 1991. Dental asst. Gerald E. Berger, DMD, Mobile, Ala., 1963-65; dental hygenist Robert P. Hall, DMD, Mobile, Ala., 1965-66; teller Am. Nat. Bank, Mobile, Ala., 1972-75; office mgr. Byrd Surveying, Inc., Mobile, Ala., 1975-80; div. acct. cafeteria Morrison, Inc., Mobile, Ala., 1980-82; mgmt. cons. pvt. practice Mobile, Ala., 1982-84; lectr. acctg. U. South Ala., Mobile, Ala., 1984; asst. prof. acctg. & mgmt. Univ. Mobile, Mobile, Ala., 1984-89; assoc. prof. acctg. and mgmt. Mobile Coll., 1989-95; prof. mgmt., 1995—; reviewer Internat. Jour. Pub. Adminstrn., 1991—; dir. Nat. Assn. Accts., Mobile, 1986-89. Author: Supervisory Management Study Guide/Southwestern, 1993, 97, Small Business Management; An Entrepreneur's Guide to Success/Irwin, 1994, 2d edit. 1996, Human Resource Management, Dame, 1995; contbr. articles to profl. jours. Named Assoc. of the Month, Home Builders Assn., 1986, Charles S. Dismukes Outstanding Mem., Nat. Assn. Accts. Mem. AAUW, Acad. Mgmt., Am. Bus. Women Assn., Assn. for Bus. Grad. Dirs., Mortgage Lenders Assn., So. Acad. Mgmt. Office: Univ Mobile PO Box 13220 Mobile AL 36663-0220

BYRD, MILTON BRUCE, college president, former business executive; b. Boston, Jan. 29, 1922; s. Max Joseph and Rebecca (Malkiel) B.; m. Susanne J. Schwerin, Aug. 30, 1953; children: Deborah, Leslie, David. A.B. cum laude, Boston U., 1948, M.A., 1949; Ph.D., U. Wis., 1953; postgrad. (fellow), U. Mich., 1961-62. Teaching asst. English U. Wis., 1949-53; instr., asst. prof. English Ind. U., 1953-58; asst. prof., asso. prof. humanities So. Ill. U., 1958-62, head div. humanities, 1958-60, supr. acad. advisement, 1959-60, asso. dean, 1960- 62; v.p. acad. affairs No. Mich. U., 1962-66; pres. Chgo. State U., 1966-74; provost Fla. Internat. U., 1974-78; pres. Adams State Coll., Alamosa, Colo., 1978-81; v.p. corp. devel. Frontier Cos., Anchorage, 1981-85; pres. Charter Coll., 1985—; bd. dirs Chgo. Council for Urban Edn.,

Union for Experimenting Colls. and Univs., Am. Assn. State Colls. and Univs., Resource Devel. Council Alaska, Alaska Commn. Econ. Edn.; v.p. Common Sense for Alaska, Inc.; former pres. Alaska Support Industry Alliance. Author: (with Arnold L. Goldsmith) Publication Guide for Literary and Linguistic Scholars, 1958; contbr. to profl. jours. Commr. Alaska Commn. on Postsecondary Edn. Served with USAAF, 1943-46. Mem. MLA, Nat. Council Tchrs. English, Coll. English Assn., Am. Studies Assn., AAUP, Fla. Assn. Univ. Adminstrs. (former pres.), Rocky Mountain Athletic Conf. (former pres.), Assn. for Higher Edn., Pub. Relations Soc. Am., NEA, Alaska Press Club, Mich. Edn. Assn., Phi Beta Kappa, Phi Delta Kappa. Club: Rotary. Office: # 120 2221 E Northern Lights Blvd Anchorage AK 99508-4143

BYRD, ROBERT CARLYLE, senator; b. North Wilkesboro, N.C., Nov. 20, 1917; s. Cornelius Sale and Ada (Kirby) B.; m. Erma Ora James, May 29, 1937; children: Mona Carole (Mrs. Mohammad Fatemi), Marjorie Ellen (Mrs. John Moore). Student, Beckley Coll., Concord Coll., Morris Harvey Coll., 1950-51, Marshall U., 1951-52; JD cum laude, Am. U., 1963. Mem. W.Va. Ho. of Reps., 1947-50, 83d-85th Congresses from 6th W.Va. dist., W.Va. Senate, 1951-52; U.S. senator from W.Va., 1959—, senate majority leader, 1977-80, 87-88, senate minority leader, 1981-86; mem. appropriations com., armed svcs. com., rules and adminstrn. com., senate Dem. steering and coord. com. Recipient Disting. Svc award Radio and TV News Dirs. Assn. 1986; named Most Influential Mem. U.S. Senate, U.S. News and World Report Poll, 1979, Legislator of Yr. Nat. Coal Assn., 1986. Mem. Country Music Assn. (hon.). Democrat. Baptist. Lodge: Masons (33 degree). Office: US Senate 311 Hart Bldg Washington DC 20510-0009*

BYRD, RONALD DICKY, lawyer; b. Balt., Aug. 19, 1953; s. Charles Merriken and Agnes Marie (Lauriet) B. BA, Bethany Coll., 1975; JD, U. Balt., 1979. Bar: Md. 1980, U.S. Ct. Appeals (4th cir.) 1989. Law clk. to presiding justice Cir. Ct. for Balt. City, Balt., 1979-80; asst. states atty. State of Md., Balt., 1980-82; from litigation atty. to environ. regulatory atty. Balt. Gas and Electric, 1982-97, assoc. gen. counsel litigation, 1997—, assoc. gen. counsel comml., 1999. Mem. Am. Corp. Counsel Assn., Balt. Claimsmens Assn., Balt. Def. Trial Counsel, Balt. Jr. Assn. of Commerce. Republican. Roman Catholic. Avocations: golf, travel. Home: 2030 Snapdragon Dr Finksburg MD 21048-2137 Office: Balt Gas And Electric PO Box 1475 Baltimore MD 21203-1475

BYRD, STEPHEN FRED, human resource consultant; b. Charleston, S.C., June 12, 1928; s. Paul Fred and Dorothy B.; m. Margaret A. McAulay, Apr. 15, 1955; children: Owen, Susan. Student, CCNY, 1945-48; LLB, N.Y. Law Sch., 1951. Bar: N.Y. 1951. Corp. indsl. rels. rep. Pan Am. Airways, 1957-62, Sinclair Oil Corp., 1962-64; v.p. employee rels. indsl. chems. div. Allied Chem. Corp., 1964-68; v.p. indsl. rels. and pers. Internat. Nickel Co., Ltd., 1968-72; sr. v.p. human resources Schering-Plough Corp., Madison, N.J., 1973-88; cons. Right Assocs., Parsippany, N.J., 1988-90. Author: Front Line Supervisors Labor Relations Handbook, 1962, Management Strategy in Collective Bargaining, 1964. Bd. dirs. United Fund Morris County, N.J., Big Bros. Morris County, Morristown YMCA, 1962-63; chmn. Madison council Boy Scouts Am., 1975-76; trustee Drew U., Madison, N.J., 1976-80. With AUS, 1952-53, Korea. Mem. Indsl. Relations Research Assn., N.Y. Law Sch. Alumni Assn. Home and Office: 23 Academy Rd Madison NJ 07940-2001

BYRD, SWETTIE LEE, minister; b. Montgomery County, Ala., Mar. 22, 1939; d. N.D. and Lucille Effie (Gambles) Williams; m. Norman Byrd, Sept. 23, 1962; children: Norman David, Brenda Rachelle, Lionel Scott. Student, Youngstown State U., 1963-66. Cert. cmty. counselor. Sales clk. G.M. McKelvey Dept. Store, Youngstown, Ohio, 1957-66; choir dir., musician World Fellowship Ch., Youngstown, 1963-69, Oak Bapt. Ch., Youngstown, 1970-79; asst. pastor Good Shepherd Ministry, Youngstown, 1983-89, sr. pastor, 1989—; sec., bd. overseers Greater Youngstown Coalition of Christians, 1995—; dir. Family Week, Concerned Christians for the Family, Youngstown, 1990—. Producer: (radio broadcast) Joy of the Morning, 1993-96. Chairperson Ward 2, Am. Cancer Soc., Youngstown, 1980s. Recipient Barnabas award Women's Aglow, Youngstown, 1995; Rev. Swettie L. Byrd Day named in her honor City of Youngstown, 1994. Mem. Flame Fellowship Internat. (pres. 1983-88, chaplain Ohio chpt. 1989—), NAACP. Avocations: reading, writing, playing piano. Office: Good Shepherd Ministry 1902 Woodcrest Ave Youngstown OH 44505-3721

BYRD, WARREN EDGAR, II, lawyer; b. Bogalusa, La., Dec. 28, 1950; s. H. Warren and Martha Helen (Conner) B.; m. Arlene Dianne Calcote, June 16, 1974; children: Lauren Elizabeth, Matthew Warren. BS, La. State U., 1973, JD, 1978. Bar: La. 1978, U.S. Dist. Ct. (mid., ea. and we. dists.) La. 1978, U.S. Ct. Appeals (5th cir.) 1978. Law clk. Judge E. Gordon West U.S. Dist. Judge, Baton Rouge, La., 1978-80; assoc. Due, Dodson & de Gravelles, Baton Rouge, 1980-81, Wray, Robinson & Kracht, Baton Rouge, 1981-83; asst. atty. gen. La. Dept. Justice, Baton Rouge, 1983-88; assoc. Adams and Reese, Baton Rouge, 1988—, ptnr., 1992—; speaker Nat. Bus. Inst., Baton Rouge, 1991-92, Fed. Publs. Seminar, New Orleans, 1993, Exec. Enterpriser Seminar, New Orleans, 1994, environ. law seminar La. State U., Baton Rouge, 1997. Bd. dirs. Audubon Coun. Girl Scouts, Baton Rouge, 1986-94, 3d v.p. 1990-91 (Thanks Badge 1990, honor award 1990, Vol. award 1997); soccer referee FIFA, LHSAA. Mem. Fed. Bar Assn. (Baton Rouge chpt. treas. 1980-86), La. State Bar Assn. (environ. law sect. coun. 1997), Baton Rouge Bar Assn. (ADR com. 1990—, chmn. com. 1993-95), La. State U. Track and Field Ofcls. Assn., Greater Baton Rouge C. of C. (govtl. fiscal affairs com.). Avocations: running, soccer referee, baseball, track. Office: Adams and Reese Bank One Ctr N Twr 19th Fl 451 Florida St Baton Rouge LA 70801-1700

BYRNE, C. WILLIAM, JR., athletics program director; b. Boston; m. Marilyn Kent; children: Bill, Greg. BBA, Idaho State U, 1967, MBA, 1970. Exec. dir. Lobo Club, U. N.Mex., Albuquerque, 1976-79; asst. athletic dir. San Diego State U., 1980-82; assoc. dir., adminstr. Duck Athletic Fund, U. Oreg., Eugene, 1983-84, dir. athletic dept., 1984-92; dir. athletic dept. U. Nebr., Lincoln, 1992—. Mem. Nat. Assn. Collegiate Dirs. of Athletics (exec. com., pres.), U.S. Collegiate Sports Coun. (v.p., bd. dirs.), All-Am. Football Found. (v.p.), Football Assn. (bd. dirs.), NCAA (spl. events com., mktg. com., cert. com.). Office: U Nebr Dir Athletics 103 South Stadium Lincoln NE 68588-0120

BYRNE, CATHERINE, swimmer. BS in Kinesiology, U. Tenn., 1992; M in Physical Therapy, Emory U., 1995. 14 time winner All-America swimmer. Named Woman of the Yr. NCAA, 1992.

BYRNE, DANIEL WILLIAM, biomedical research consultant, biostatistician, computer specialist, educator; b. Bklyn., Jan. 21, 1958; s. Thomas Edward and L.M. (Collins) B.; m. Loretta Marie May, June 22, 1985; children: Michael, Virginia. BA in Biology, SUNY, Albany, 1983; MS in Biostatistics, N.Y. Med. Coll., 1991. Programmer, med. software Dept. Surgery N.Y. Med. Coll., Valhalla, 1983-84; computer/data analyst N.Y. Med. Coll., Westchester County Med. Ctr. and affiliate hosps., 1984-87; rsch. asst. prof. Dept. Surgery N.Y. Med. Coll., Valhalla, 1988-98, rsch. asst. prof. dept. cmty. and preventive medicine, 1996—; founder, med. rsch. cons. Byrne Research, Ridgefield, Conn., 1989—. Author: Publishing Your Medical Research Paper: What They Don't Teach in Medical School, 1997; author/programmer various software including Trauma Management System, 1990, Occupational Stress Database, 1990, Nuclear Disaster Evacuation Plan Database, 1990; contbr. numerous articles to med. jours. Mem. Am. Statis. Assn., Am. Med. Writers Assn., Inst. Math. Stats., Biometric Soc. Roman Catholic. Home and Office: 17 Dogwood Dr Ridgefield CT 06877-2707

BYRNE, DAVID, musician, composer, artist, director; b. Dumbarton, Scotland, May 14, 1952; came to U.S., 1958; s. Thomas and Emily Anderson (Brown) B.; m. Adelle Lutz, 1987, 1 child, Malu Abeni Valentine. Student, R.I. Sch. Design, 1970-71, MD Inst. Coll. of Art, 1971-72. Performer Talking Heads, N.Y.C., 1975-1992. Musician, composer, producer, 1980—; dir., producer Index Video, N.Y.C., 1983—; songwriter Talking Heads, 1976-1992; albums include: (with Talking Heads) Talking Heads: 77, 1977, More Songs About Buildings and Food, 1978, Fear of Music, 1979, Remain in Light, 1980, The Name of This Band Is Talking Heads, 1982, Speaking in Tongues, 1983, Stop Making Sense, 1984, Little Creatures, 1985, True Stories, 1986, Naked, 1988, Popular Favorites 1976-1991/Sand in the Vaseline, 1992, (solo albums) My Life in the Bush of Ghosts (with Brian Eno), 1981, The Complete Score from "The Catherine Wheel", 1982, The Knee Plays, 1985, Songs from True Stories, 1986, Rei Momo, 1989, The Forest, 1991, Uh Oh, 1992, david byrne, 1994, Feelings, 1997; film appearances include Stop Making Sense, 1984, True Stories (aso dir., co-screenwriter) 1986, Checking Out, 1988, Ile Aiyé (also dir.), 1989, Between the Teeth (also co-dir.), 1993; dir. videotapes, 1981—; artist stage design, lighting, LP covers and posters, 1977—; author Stay Up Late, 1987, What the Songs Look Like: The Illustrated Talking Heads, 1987, Strange Ritual, 1995; film scores include Married to the Mob, 1988, (with Rhuichi Sakamoto and Cong Su) The Last Emperor (Academy, Grammy, Golden Globe and Hollywood Foreign Press Awards for Best Original Score), 1987; TV host Sessions at West 54th, 1998. *

BYRNE, DONN ERWIN, psychologist, educator; b. Austin, Tex., Dec. 19, 1931; s. Bernard Divine and Rebecca (Singleton) B.; m. Lois Ann Pugsley, Sept. 12, 1953 (div. 1978); children: Keven Singleton, Robin Lynn; m. Kathryn Kelley, Aug. 17, 1979 (div. 1996); children: Lindsey Kelley, Rebecka Byrne Kelley. BA, Calif. State U., Fresno, 1953, MA, 1956; PhD, Stanford U., 1958. Instr. psychology Calif. State U., San Francisco, 1957-59; asst. to assoc. prof. psychology U. Tex., Austin, 1959-66, prof. psychology, 1966-69, dir. exptl. personality program, 1963-69, asst. dept. chmn., 1964-66; prof. psychology Purdue U., West Lafayette, Ind., 1969-79, chmn. social personality program, 1972-78; prof. psychology SUNY, Albany, 1979-91, disting. prof., 1991—, chmn. social-personality program, 1980-84, 90-99, chmn. dept., 1984-89; vis. prof. psychology Stanford U., Palo Alto, Calif., 1966-67, U. Hawaii, Honolulu, 1968; panel mem. NSF grad. fellowship program NRC, 1972; NIH participant Inst. Sex Research Summer Program, 1974; G. Stanley Hall lectr. Am. Psychol. Assn., 1981. Author: (with H.C. Lindgren) Psychology: An Introduction to the Study of Human Behavior, 1961, 4th edit., 1975, (with P. Worchel) Personality Change, 1964, An Introduction to Personality: A Research Approach, 1966, 3d edit., 1981, (with M.L. Hamilton) Personality Research: A Book of Readings, 1966, The Attraction Paradigm, 1971, (with R.A. Baron and W. Griffitt) Social Psychology, 1974, (with R.A. Baron) 8th edit., 1997, (with R.A. Baron, B.H. Kantowitz) Psychology: Understanding Behavior, 1977, 2d edit., 1980, (with L.A. Byrne) Exploring Human Sexuality, 1977, (with W.A. Fisher) Adolescents, Sex, and Contraception, 1983, (with K. Kelley) Alternative Approaches to the Study of Sexual Behavior, 1986, (with K. Kelley) Exploring Human Sexuality, 1992; contbr. numerous articles to psychol. jours. and chpts. to anthologies. Grantee NSF, NIMH, U. Tex. Rsch. Inst., USAF, others; recipient Disting Sci. Achievement award Soc. for Scientific Study of Sexuality, 1989. Mem. Midwestern Psychol. Assn. (pres. 1979-80), Soc. for Sci. Study Sexuality (pres. 1990-93). Home: 15 Indian Hill Rd Feura Bush NY 12067-2602 *All of us are seeking the ultimately impossible aims of happiness and self-satisfaction. The former is achieved, however fleetingly, by sensual pleasures and by reaching a series of challenging but attainable goals. Satisfaction depends not only on attaining such goals, but also on the unoriginal but golden ideal of treating other individuals with the same measure of fairness and kindness that we desire from them.*

BYRNE, FRANK LOYOLA, history educator; b. Hackensack, N.J., May 12, 1928; s. Francis Loyola and Betty Louise (Widman) B.; m. Marilyn Lou Sobraske, June 9, 1962; children—Anne, Frank. BS, Trenton State Coll., 1950; MS in History, U. Wis., 1951, PhD in History, 1957. Instr. La. State U., Baton Rouge, 1957-58; from asst. prof. to assoc. prof. Creighton U., Omaha, 1958-66; from assoc. prof. to prof. history Kent (Ohio) State U., Ohio, 1966-95, chmn. grad. program in history, 1969-72, prof. emeritus, 1995—. Author: Prophet of Prohibition: Neal Dow and His Crusade, 1961; editor: The View From Headquarters Civil War Letters of Harvey Reid, 1965, (with others) Haskell of Gettysburg: His Life and Civil War Papers, 1970, 2d edit., 1989, Your True Marcus: The Civil War Letters of a Jewish Colonel, 1985, reprinted as a Jewish Colonel in the Civil War: Marcus M. Spiegel of the Ohio Volunteers, 1995; project editor Taft Papers, 1987-98, editor emeritus, 1998—; series editor Voices of the Civil War, U. Tenn. Pres., 1992—; contbr. articles to profl. jours. Mem. Nebr. Civil War Centennial Commn., 1960-65, Franklin Twp. Bd. Zoning Appeals, 1980—. With U.S. Army, 1954-56. Wis. Civil War Centennial Commn. research grantee, 1962-63; Am. Philos. Soc. research grantee, 1965; Kent State U. Faculty research grantee, 1967, 69, 72, 83. Mem. Am. Hist. Assn., Orgn. Am. Historians, So. Hist. Assn. (exec. coun. 1991-94), Ohio Hist. Soc., Ohio Soc. Mil. History (bd. dirs. 1985-96), Western Res. Hist. Soc. (exhibits com. 1988—), Wis. Hist. Soc., Ancient Order Hibernians. Democrat. Roman Catholic. Home: 5800 Horning Rd Kent OH 44240-4223 Office: Kent State U Dept History Kent OH 44242 *Time is a divine gift to humans. History, the study of past time, really embodies all knowledge; hence, we each do well to devote part of our own time to its study.*

BYRNE, GABRIEL, actor; b. Dublin, Ireland, 1950; m. Ellen Barkin, 1988 (separated); children: Jack, Romy. Actor: (films) On a Paving Stone Mounted, 1978, The Outsider, 1979, Excalibur, 1981, The Keep, 1983, Hannah K., 1983, Defence of the Realm, 1985, Gothic, 1985, Lionheart, 1987, Hello, Again, 1987, Siesta, 1987, Julia and Julia, 1988, A Soldier's Tale, 1988, The Courier, 1988, Miller's Crossing, 1990, Shipwrecked, 1991, Dark Obsession, 1991, Cool World, 1992, Point of No Return, 1993, A Dangerous Woman, 1993, A Simple Twist of Fate, 1994, Trial by Jury, 1994, Little Women, 1994, The Usual Suspects, 1995, Frankie Starlight, 1995, Past into Present, 1996, Mad Dog Time, 1996, Dr. Hagard's Disease, 1996, Somebody is Waiting, 1996, The End of Violence, 1997, Polish Wedding, 1998, Enemy of the State, 1998, This Is the Sean, 1998, Quest for Camelot (voice), 1998, The Brylcreem Boys, 1998, Stigmata, 1999, End of Days, 1999; (TV movies) Wagner, 1983, Reflections, 1983, Mussolini: The Untold Story, 1985, Christopher Columbus, 1985, Buffalo Girls, 1995, (TV series) The Riordan's, Bracken; actor, assoc. prodr.: (films) Into the West, 1993; co-exec. prodr.: (films) In the Name of the Father, 1993; actor, exec. prodr. Last of the High Kings, 1996, Smilla's Sense of Snow, 1997, Weapons of Mass Destruction, 1996, Toby's Story, 1998, Polish Wedding, 1998, This is the Sea, 1998, The Man in the Iron Mask, 1998, (voice) Quest for Camelot, 1998, An Ideal Husband, 1999; dir. End of Violence, 1996; actor, writer Draiocht, 1996; narrator Irish Cinema: Ourselves Alone?, 1997. Office: ICM 8942 Wilshire Blvd Los Angeles CA 90211*

BYRNE, GERARD ANTHONY, publishing company executive, marketing consultant; b. N.Y.C., Apr. 27, 1944; s. Thomas Edward and Eileen (Reilly) B.; m. Elizabeth Julia Daly, Dec. 6, 1969; children: Megan, Gavin. BA in Econs., Fordham U., 1966. Advt. sales rep. N.Y. Daily News, N.Y.C., 1969-73, Advt. Age, N.Y.C., 1973-77; internat. sales dir. Advt. Age, 1977-80; ea. sales mgr. Advt. Age, N.Y.C., 1980-82; pub., v.p. Electronic Media, N.Y.C., 1982-84; v.p./pub. Crain's N.Y. Bus., N.Y.C., 1984-87; v.p., dir. corp. communications Crain Communications, N.Y.C., 1987-88; sr. v.p. corp. planning and internat. devel. Act III Pub., N.Y.C., 1988-89; pub. Variety, N.Y.C., 1990-92, v.p., dir. pub. ops., 1993-95; group v.p., pub. Daily Variety and Weekly Variety, N.Y.C., 1996-97; v.p., group pub. Variety, Inc., N.Y.C., 1997—. Bd. dirs. African Med. Relief Found., Environ. Media Assn., Operation Smile Internat., Cath. Youth Orgn., N.Y.C., Mus. Moving Image, The Intrepid Mus., The Westhampton Performing Arts Ctr. Capt. USMC, 1966-69, Vietnam. Recipient combat action ribbon, Navy achievement medal, Show East Salah Hassanein Humanitarian award, 1996; named Pub. of Yr., East Midtown C. of C., 1986. Mem. Internat. Radio and TV Soc., N.Y. Athletic Club, VFW, Friendly Sons of St. Patrick, Greater Miami C. of C. (co-chair long-range planning com. entertainment task force). Roman Catholic. Avocations: fishing, tennis, photography, skiing, golf. Home: 10 Wintergreen Way Quogue NY 11959 Office: Cahners Pub Co Divsn Reed Elsevier 5700 Wilshire Blvd Ste 120 Los Angeles CA 90036-3659

BYRNE, GRANVILLE BLAND, III, lawyer; b. San Antonio, Jan. 26, 1952; s. Granville Bland and Mary (Dowling) B.; divorced; children: Peyton Smith, Fulton Buckner; m. Monique Renée Wise, 1999. AB, U. N.C., Chapel Hill, 1974; JD, Harvard U., 1978. Bar: Ga. 1978, U.S. Dist. Ct. (no. dist.) Ga. 1978, U.S. Ct. Appeals (5th cir.) 1978, U.S. Ct. Appeals (11th cir.) 1981. Assoc. Swift, Currie, McGhee & Hiers, Atlanta, 1978-84, ptnr., 1984-94; prin. Byrne, Eldridge, Moore & Davis, P.C., Atlanta, 1994—; bd. dirs. Compeer Atlanta, Inc., chmn., 1996—; bd. dirs. Cagle's, Inc. Elder, mem. session 1st Presbyn. Ch. Atlanta, 1993-96, 99—. Mem. ABA, Ga. Bar Assn., Atlanta Bar Assn. Democrat. Presbyterian. Home: 2664 Birchwood Dr NE Atlanta GA 30305-3822 Office: Byrne Eldridge Moore & Davis PC 3340 Peachtree Rd NE Atlanta GA 30326-1000

BYRNE, JAMES EDWARD, international banking expert; b. Detroit, Dec. 6, 1945; s. John F. and Grace Byrne; m. Maria, Nov. 24, 1973; children: John M., Michael P., Mary C., James E. Sr. BA, U. Notre Dame, 1968; JD, Stetson U., 1977; LLM, U. Pa., 1978. Bar: Fla. 1977, Md. 1982. Faculty George Mason U. Sch. Law, Arlington, Va., 1982—; dir. Inst. Internat. Banking Law & Practice, Gaithersburg, Md., 1992—; head U.S. delegation UN Commn. on Internat. Trade Law, Vienna, N.Y., 1988-95; advisor UCC Article 5 Drafting Com., 1990-95; dir. Internat. Ctr. LC Arbitration, Gaithersburg, 1995—; chair, reporter Internat. Stand Practices, Gaithersburg, 1995—. Contbr. articles to profl. jours. Mem. Internat. Acad. Comml. and Consumer Law, Am. Bankers Assn. (chair letter credit subcom. 1996—). Office: Inst Internat Banking Law & Practice PO Box 2235 Montgomery Village MD 20886-2235

BYRNE, JAMES FREDERICK, banker; b. Fairmont, N.C., July 30, 1931; m. Daphne Martin, July 22, 1955; children—Paula Jean, Daphne Ann, Laura. BS, Wake Forest U., 1953; MBA, U. N.C., 1959. Ptnr. Byrne-Floyd Realty, Fairmont, N.C., 1961-80; v.p., city exec. So. Nat. Bank, Fairmont, 1963-69; mgr. master charge So. Nat. Bank, Lumberton, N.C., 1969-71; v.p., dir. mktg. So. Nat. Bank, 1971-77, sr. v.p., dir. customer services, 1977-83, exec. v.p., 1983, exec. v.p., dir. retail banking, 1985-89, sr. exec. v.p., chief adminstrv. officer, 1989-94; mem. endowment bd. Pembroke State U., N.C., 1985-87, chmn. libr. bd., 1995-96. Pres. Am. Lung Assn. of N.C., Wilmington, 1971, Raleigh, 1972, N.C. rep. dir., N.Y., 1977-89; nat. v.p. Am. Lung Assn., 1989. Recipient Vol. of Yr. award Am. Lung Assn. of N.C., 1972-90, Nat. Humanitarian award, 1993. Mem. Bank Mktg. Assn., N.C. Bankers Assn., Shrine Club (pres. 1996-97), Rotary (pres. 1968), Shriners (pres. 1996-97), Masons. Home: 905 Dogwood Dr Fairmont NC 28340-2115

BYRNE, JAMIE MARIA, communications educator; b. Belleville, Ill., July 31, 1961; d. Charles Henry III and Betty Jean (Stokes) Doerge ; m. Charles Alan Byrne, Oct. 10, 1987. BS in English and Journalism, Murray (Ky.) State U., 1983, MS in Comm., 1985; PhD in Mass Comm., Pa. State U., 1998. Sys. mgr. Murray State News, 1983-84; asst. prof. U. Wis., Platteville, 1984-88, Elizabethtown Coll., 1988-91, Millersville U. of Pa., Millersville, 1991—; dir. regional studies ctr. Millersville U. of Pa., 1999—; adj. prof. Millersville U. of Pa., 1989-91; primary instr. degree completion program Eastern Coll., 1996—; bd. dirs. Internat. Radio and TV Soc. Found., 1999—. Active Big Sister Grant County (Wis.) Dept. Family Svcs., 1985-88; dir. Platteville Community Players, 1986; pub. rels. specialist Theatre of the Seventh Sister, Lancaster, Pa., 1990-91; chairperson Relay for Life, nat. adv. com., 1999—, nat. mktg. com., 1999—, Lancaster County Unit, Am. Cancer Soc., 1996—, pub. rels. com., 1996—, Pa. divsn. task force chair, 1999—; publicity com. mem. Jamison Mus. Assn., Platteville, 1987-88; bd. dirs. Lancaster County unit Am. Cancer Soc., 1995—, 2nd v.p., 1998—. Faculty Devel. grantee Pa. State Sys. Higher Edn., 1992, Journalism Edn. grantee Gannett Found., 1990, grantee U. Wis., 1986-87, Social Equity grantee Pa. State System Higher Edn., 1998, Spl. Projects grantee State Sys. Higher Edn., 1999; Jesse Stuart fellow Murray State U., 1983; recipient Vol. of Yr. award Lancaster County unit Am. Cancer Soc., 1997, Income Devel. award, 1997. Mem. NAFE, Pub. Rels. Soc. Am. (sec. Ctrl. Pa. chpt. 1990-91, pres. 1993, bd. dirs. 1990-91, 94-95), Nat. Broadcasting Soc. (nat. v.p. regional devel. 1986-92, nat. pres. 1993—, Outstanding Profl. mem. U. Wis., Platteville chpt. 1987), Coll. Media Advisors, Am. Culture Assn. Roman Catholic. Avocations: theatre, walking, singing, painting, reading.

BYRNE, JEFFREY EDWARD, pharmacology researcher, educator, consultant; b. Mpls., July 15, 1939; s. Maurice Charles and Edna F. (Kinney) B.; m. Janice Grove, Feb. 1, 1960 (dec. Apr., 1976); children: Christopher, Maura; m. Margaret Ann Kaiser, June 17, 1978, 1 child, Jason. BA, U. N.D., 1962; MA, U. S.D., 1964, PhD, 1966. Sr. rsch. assoc. Bristol-Myers Co., Evansville, Ind., 1969-81, prin. rsch. scientist, 1981-87; sr. rsch. scientist II Bristol-Myers Squibb Co., Wallingford, Conn., 1987-91, Princeton, N.J., 1991-94; cons. in field, 1994—; adj. faculty Ind. U. Sch. Medicine, Evansville, 1972-81, Evansville U. Sch. Nursing, 1972-81. Contbr. articles to profl. jours.; author (with others) books. Mem. Am. Soc. for Pharmacology and Exptl. Therapeutics, Am. Heart Assn., Internat. Soc. for Heart Rsch., AAAS. Lutheran. Achievements include discovery of Encainide, an antiarrythmic drug. Home: 590 Atkinson Ln Langhorne PA 19047-1462

BYRNE, JEROME CAMILLUS, lawyer; b. Grand Rapids, Mich., Oct. 3, 1925; s. Camillus Abraham and Katherine Blanche (Kelly) B. BA, Aquinas Coll., 1948; JD magna cum laude, Harvard U., 1951. Bar: Calif. 1952. Assoc. Gibson Dunn & Crutcher, L.A., 1952-59, ptnr., 1960-93; adv. counsel Gibson Dunn & Crutcher, 1993—; spl. counsel to regents U. Calif., 1965. Bd. dirs. Constl. Rights Found., 1967—, pres., 1971-72; bd. regents Mt. St. Mary's Coll., 1979—; trustee Aquinas Coll., 1983-95, trustee emeritus, 1995—; dir., sec. Kolb Found., 1984—. Office: Gibson Dunn & Crutcher 2029 Century Park E Ste 4000 Los Angeles CA 90067-3032

BYRNE, JOHN EDWARD (JEB BYRNE), writer, retired government official; b. N.Y.C., Jan. 15, 1925; s. Harry Theodore and Mary Elizabeth (Whelen) B.; m. Beverly Ann McKinley, Mar. 31, 1951; children—Peter J., David F., John P., Michael T. BA, Marquette U., 1949; MA, George Washington U., 1973, PhD, 1987. News service corr. UPI, Milw., 1949-50, Albany, N.Y., 1951, Portland, Maine, 1951-56, Augusta, Maine, 1956-58; gov.'s press sec., state promotion ofcl. State of Maine, Augusta, 1959-60; exec. GSA, Washington, 1961-80; dir. fed. register Nat. Archives and Records Adminstrn., Washington, 1980-88; Fulbright scholar Alexander Turnbull Libr., Wellington, New Zealand, 1989. Served to 2d lt. USAAF, 1943-45. Roman Catholic. Home: 2104 Marthas Rd Alexandria VA 22307-1823

BYRNE, JOHN MICHAEL, energy and environmental policy educator, researcher; b. Chgo., Nov. 2, 1949; s. Michael Thomas and Mabel Victoria (Cranford) B.; m. Elizabeth Maria Garey, Aug. 9, 1975; children: Brian, Tara. BA in Econs., U. Del., 1971, MA, 1973, PhD in Urban Affairs and Pub. Policy, 1980. Asst. prof. Coll. Urban Affairs and Pub. Policy, U. Del., Newark, 1982-86, assoc. prof., 1986-92, prof., 1992—, dir. Energy Policy Rsch. Group, 1981-84, dir. Ctr. for Energy and Environ. Policy, 1984—, chair Urban Affairs and Pub. Policy grad. program, 1992-96. Co-editor: Energy and Cities, 1985, The Politics of Energy R&D, 1986, Energy and Environment: The Policy Challenge, 1992, Governing the Atom: The Politics of Risk, 1996; mem. editorial bd. Bull. of Sci. and Tech. Soc., 1995—. Bd. dirs. Urban Environ. Ctr., 1997—. Grantee ESMAP/World Bank, 1990-91, U.S. Dept. Energy/Nat. Renewable Energy Lab., 1991—, UNIDEL Found., 1992, U.S. EPA, 1994, 97—, Asia Found., 1995, Inst. Internat. Edn., 1996-97, W. Alton Jones Found., 1997—; recipient Fulbright Sr. Lectr./Rschr. award, 1995. Mem. IEEE Social Implications of Tech. Affiliate, Nat. Assn. Sci., Tech. and Society (adv. bd. 1991—). Avocations: music, woodworking, hiking. Office: U Del Ctr Energy & Environ Policy Newark DE 19716-7301

BYRNE, JOHN VINCENT, higher education consultant; b. Hempstead, N.Y., May 9, 1928; s. Frank E. and Kathleen (Barry) B.; m. Shirley O'Connor, Nov. 26, 1954; children: Donna, Lisa, Karen, Steven. AB, Hamilton Coll., 1951, JD (hon.), 1994; MA, Columbia U., 1953; PhD, U. So. Calif., 1957. Research geologist Humble Oil & Refinery Co., Houston, 1957-60; assoc. prof. Oreg. State U., Corvallis, 1960-66, prof. oceanography, 1966—, chmn. dept., 1968-72, dean Sch. Oceanography, 1972-76, acting dean research, 1976-77, dean research, 1977-80, v.p. for research and grad. studies, 1980-81, pres., 1984-95; adminstr. NOAA, Washington, 1981-84; pres. Oreg. State U., 1984-95; higher edn. cons. Corvallis, 1996—; program dir. oceanography NSF, 1966-67; exec. dir. Kellogg Commn. on Future of State and Land Grant Univs., 1996—; dir. Oreg. Coast Aquarium, Harbor Br. Ocean Inst. Recipient Carter teaching award Oreg. State U., 1964. Fellow AAAS, Geol. Soc. Am., Am. Meteorol. Soc.; mem. Am. Assn. Petroleum Geologists, Am. Geophys. Union, Sigma Xi, Chi Psi. Home: 3190 NW Deer Run St Corvallis OR 97330-3107 Office: Autzen House 811 SW Jefferson Ave Corvallis OR 97333-4506

BYRNE, LESLIE LARKIN, former federal agency administrator, former congresswoman; b. Salt Lake City, Oct. 27, 1946; m. Larry Earl Byrne; children: Alexis S., Jason D.,. Student, U. Utah. Former del. 38th Dist.

Fairfax County State of Va., 1986-92; mem. 103rd Congress from 11th Va. dist., Washington, D.C., 1993-95; former pres. Quintech Assoc., Inc., 1985-92; now dir. consumer affairs HHS, Washington, 1996-98; candidate Va. State Senate, 1999—. Mem. LWV. Home: PO Box 2612 Falls Church VA 22042-0612 Office: Consumer Affairs 808 17th St NW Washington DC 20006-3910*

BYRNE, MICHAEL JOSEPH, business executive; b. Chgo., Apr. 3, 1928; s. Michael Joseph and Edith (Lueken) B.; B.Sc. in Mktg., Loyola U., Chgo., 1952; m. Eileen Kelly, June 27, 1953; children—Michael Joseph, Nancy, James, Thomas, Patrick, Terrence. Sales engr. Emery Industries, Inc., Cin., 1952-59; with Pennsalt Chem. Corp., Phila., 1959-60; with Oakton Cleaners, Inc., Skokie, Ill., 1960-70, pres., 1960-70; pres. Datatax Inc., Skokie, 1970-74, Midwest Synthetic Lubrication Products, 1978—, Pure Water Systems, 1984—, Superior Tax Service, 1984—. Served with ordnance U.S. Army, 1946-48. Mem. A.I.M., VFW, Alpha Kappa Psi. Club: Toastmasters Internat. Home: PO Box 916 Prospect Heights IL 60070-0916

BYRNE, NOEL THOMAS, sociologist, educator; b. San Francisco, May 11, 1943; s. Joseph Joshua and Naomi Pearl (Denison) B.; m. Dale W. Elrod, Aug. 6, 1989. BA in Sociology, Sonoma State Coll., 1971; MA in Sociology, Rutgers U., 1975, PhD in Sociology, 1987. Instr. sociology Douglass Coll., Rutgers U., New Brunswick, N.J., 1974-76, Hartnell Coll., Salinas, Calif., 1977-78; from lectr. to assoc. prof. dept. mgmt. Sonoma State U., Rohnert Park, Calif., 1978-94, chmn. dept. of mgmt., 1990-91, from. assoc. prof. to prof. sociology dept., 1994—, chmn. dept. sociology, 1997—; cons. prof. Emile Durkheim Inst. for Advanced Study, Grand Cayman, B.W.I., 1990-93. Contbr. articles and revs. to profl. lit. Recipient Dell Pub. award Rutgers U. Grad. Sociology Program, 1976, Louis Bevier fellow, 1977-78. Mem. AAAS, Am. Sociol. Assn., Pacific Sociol. Assn., N.Y. Acad. Sci., Soc. for Study Symbolic Interaction (rev. editor Jour. 1980-83), Soc. for Study Social Problems, Commonwealth Club. Democrat. Home: PO Box 660 Cotati CA 94931-0660 Office: Sonoma State U Dept Sociology Rohnert Park CA 94928

BYRNE, OLIVIA SHERRILL, lawyer; b. Trenton, N.J., Aug. 14, 1957; d. Stewart and Elizabeth (Sherrill) B. Student, Vanderbilt U., 1975-76; BA, Bowdoin Coll., 1979; JD, U. Toledo, 1982; LLM in Taxation, Georgetown U., 1987. Bar: Tex. 1982, Ohio 1984, Md. 1985. Assoc. Whiteford, Taylor & Preston, Balt., 1984-87, Linowes & Blocher, Silver Spring, Md., 1987-90; ptnr. Weinberg & Jacobs, Rockville, Md., 1990-96, Shulman Rogers Gandal Pordy & Ecker, Rockville, 1996—. Author: The At-Risk Rules Under the Tax Reform Act of 1986, The Door Closes on Tax Motivated Investments, IRS Issues New Guidelines for Management Contracts Used for Facilities Financed with Tax Exempt Bonds, 1993, RRA '93 Loosens Real Estate Rules for Exempt Organizations, 1993; contbr. articles to profl. jours. Mem. Tax Coun. for State of Md., Leadership Montgomery, 1996; bd. dirs. Bethesda Acad. Performing Arts, Inst. for In Vitro Scis., Inc.; chair GULC Nat. Tax Exempt Bond Conf., 1997. Mem. ABA (exempt orgn. com. taxation sect. 1991—), Md. Bar Assn. (coun. taxation sect.), Balt. City Bar Assn. (chmn. speakers bur. young lawyers sect.), Lawyers for Arts Washington, Comml. Real Estate Woman (bd. dirs., pres.), Profls. for Strathmore Hall (co-chmn.), D.C. Bowdoin Coll. Alumni Assn. (pres. 1992—), Howard County C. of C. (legis. com. 1989), Rotary. Home: 1811 Brentridge St Vienna VA 22182-2579 Office: Shulman Rogers et al 11921 Rockville Pike Rockville MD 20852-2737

BYRNE, RAYMOND HARRY, electrical engineer; b. Baton Rouge, La., Dec. 12, 1965; s. Harry C. Jr. and Judite K. (Kamarauskas) B. BSEE, U. Va., 1987; MSEE, U. Colo., 1989; PhD, U. N.Mex., 1995. Mem. tech. staff Sandia Nat. Labs., Albuquerque, 1989—; adj. prof. U. N.Mex., Albuquerque, 1996—. Named N.M. qualifier mid-amateur USGA, 1996, 98. Mem. IEEE (chmn., vice chmn., sec., treas. Albuquerque sect. 1992—), Four Hills Country Club (golf com. chmn. 1997), Sandia Golf League (A-League Dir. 1992-95), North Eubank Ski Club (pres., v.p., winter trips treas. 1989—), Tau Beta Pi, Eta Kappa Nu, Sigma Xi. Avocations: golf, skiing, mountain biking, roller-blading. Office: Sandia Nat Labs MS 1003 PO Box 5800 Albuquerque NM 87185-0100

BYRNE, RICHARD HILL, counselor, educator; b. Lancaster, Pa., Aug. 3, 1915; s. Jacob Hill and Mary Deborah (Allwein) B.; m. Magdalene Antoinette Wardell, June 12, 1954; children—Christopher, Mary, Matthew, Peter. A.B., Franklin and Marshall Coll., 1938; M.A., Columbia U., 1947, Ed.D., 1952. Tchr. several sch. systems, Lancaster County, Pa., 1939-42; counselor Allegany County Schs., Cumberland, Md., 1949-50; state guidance supr. State of N.H., Concord, 1950-51; assoc., then prof., chmn. counseling dept. U. Md., College Park, 1951-82, prof. emeritus, 1983—; resident grad. prof. counseling dept. U. Md., Upper Heyford, Eng., 1982-84, Boston U., Germany, 1984-86; cons. U.S. Dept. Labor, Washington, 1964-68; cons. in guidance numerous sch. systems, Md., Pa., Va., 1951-82; dir. interprofl. research ctr. on pupil services, College Park, Md., 1963-68. Author: The School Counselor, 1963, Guidance: A Behavioral Approach, 1977, Becoming a Master Counselor, 1994. Served to capt. U.S. Army, 1942-46, ETO. Mem. Am. Psychol. Assn., Md. Personnel and Guidance Assn. (1st pres. 1957-58). Home: 1390 Ventnor Ave Tarpon Springs FL 34689-2731

BYRNE, ROBERT EUGENE, chess columnist; b. N.Y.C., Apr. 20, 1928; s. Frank and Elizabeth Eleanor (Cattelier) B.; m. Florence Mary Dolley, Sept. 8, 1954 (div. Feb. 1971); children: Benjamin (dec.), Thomas Edward; m. Ursula Maria von Krebs, Sept. 11, 1971. BA, Yale U., 1952; postgrad., Ind. U., 1952-60. Chess reporter N.Y. Daily News, N.Y.C., 1971-72; chess columnist N.Y. Times, 1972—; mem. U.S. Olympiad teams U.S. Chess Fedn., New Windsor, N.Y., 1952-84, capt., 1984, U.S. chess champion, 1972, quarter finalist world chess championship; world chess champion Internat. Chess Fedn., Geneva, 1974; U.S. Open champion U.S. Chess Fedn., New Windsor, 1960, 63, 66; cons. for IBM on Deep Blue chess computer project. Author: Beginning Chess, 1972, Both Sides of the Chessboard, 1972, The Road to the World Championship, 1976, (calendar) The Chess Calendar, 1998, 99, N.Y. Times Book of Great Chess Victories and Defeats, 1990. Mem. U.S. Chess Fedn., Manhattan Chess Club (hon. bd. dirs. 1980—). Avocations: opera, ballet, archaeology, tennis. Home and Office: 16 Rockledge Ave Scarborough NY 10518

BYRNE, ROBERT WILLIAM, lawyer; b. Frankfurt, Germany, Dec. 12, 1958; s. Robert Patrick and Anne Lise (Brondelsbo) B. BA, Rutgers U., 1981; JD, Seton Hall U., 1984; postgrad., Colo. State U. Bar: N.J. 1984, U.S. Dist. Ct. N.J. 1984, D.C. 1986, U.S. Ct. Appeals (3d cir.) 1987, U.S. Ct. Appeals (D.C. and fed. cirs.) 1988, (11th cir.), 1993, U.S. Dist. Ct. D.C. 1989, U.S. Supreme Ct. 1989, N.Y. 1991, U.S. Dist. Ct. (so. and ea. dists.) N.Y. 1991, Fla. 1992, U.S. Dist. Ct. (no. and mid. dists.) Fla. 1992. Law clk. to presiding judge Superior Ct. Passaic County N.J., 1984-85; asst. prosecutor Bergen County, N.J., 1985-88; assoc. Harwood Lloyd Esqs., Hackensack, N.J., 1988-90, Mudge Rose Guthrie Alexander & Ferdon, N.Y.C., 1990-91; sr. assoc. O'Connor, Reddy & Jensen, N.Y.C., 1991-92; pvt. practice Panama City, Fla., 1992-94; v.p./gen. counsel Bay Bank & Trust Co., Panama City, Fla., 1994—. Contbr. Seton Hall Legislative Jour., 1983-84. Henry Rutgers scholar, 1981. Mem. D.C. Bar, Fla. Bar, Bay County (Fla.) Bar Assn., Assn. Bar City N.Y., St. Andrew Am. Inns Ct. (barrister), Phi Alpha Delta, Pi Sigma Alpha. Democrat. Lutheran. Home: PO Box 18889 Panama City FL 32417-8889 Office: 509 Harrison Ave Panama City FL 32401-2621

BYRNE, SHAUN PATRICK, law enforcement officer; b. Atlantic City, Aug. 22, 1963; s. Warren Patrick and Donna Mae (Curlott) B. Student, Nat. Acad. Paralegals, Egg Harbor, N.J., 1991; AS, Cumberland County Coll., Vineland, N.J., 1994; BA in Criminal Justice, Stockton State Coll., Pomona, N.J., 1995; postgrad., Widener U. Sch. Law, 1997—. Police officer Atlantic City Police Dept., 1984-85; with trade union, 1986-91; sr. detective Jamesway Corp., Secaucus, N.J., 1991-95; security advisor P.S.I., Inc.; paralegal, 1991-92; mediation counselor Criminal Justice Inst., 1995—. Martial arts trainer/demonstrator Fighting Dragons Dojo, Atlantic City, 1980—; high sch. presentations on violence/drugs, Vineland, 1995. Republican. Roman Catholic. Avocations: martial arts, kick boxing, scuba diving, weight training. Home: PO Box 1081 Absecon NJ 08201-5081

BYRNE, THOMAS J., lawyer; b. Rochester, N.Y., June 17, 1944; m. Brenda C. Byrne, June 4, 1994; children: Thomas, David, Heather. AB, U. Rochester, 1967; JD, U. Denver, 1976. Bar: Colo. 1977, Calif. 1977, U.S. Ct. Appeals (10th cir.) 1977, U.S. Dist. Ct. Colo. 1977, U.S. Dist. Ct. (so. dist.) Tex. 1990, N.Y. 1990, U.S. Ct. Appeals (3d cir.) 1992, U.S. Dist. Ct. (ea. dist.) Pa. 1992, U.S. Dist. Ct. (ea. dist.) Va. 1992, U.S. Ct. Appeals (4th cir.) 1993, U.S. Dist. Ct. (no. dist.) Ill. 1993, U.S. Dist. Ct. Ariz. 1993, U.S. Dist. Ct. Utah 1996, U.S. Dist. Ct. (so. dist.) N.Y. 1997. Law clk. Dist. Ct. Colo., Denver, 1976-77; assoc. Ullstrom Law Offices, Denver, 1978-83; ptnr., Denver mgr. Conklin & Adler, Ltd., Denver and Chgo., 1983-86; mng. ptnr. Byrne, Kiely & White LLP, Denver, 1986—. Mem. fin. com. Citizens for Romer, Denver, 1990—. Capt. USAF, 1967-73. Mem. ABA (tort and ins. practice sect., vice chair aviation and space law com., litigation sect., forum on air and space law), Internat. Bar Assn., Colo. Bar Assn., Denver Bar Assn., State Bar Calif., N.Y. State Bar Assn., Def. Rsch. Inst., Colo. Def. Lawyers Assn., Nat. Bus. Aircraft Assn., Lawyer-Pilot Bar Assn., Aviation Ins. Assn. Avocations: flying, travel, sports. Office: Byrne Kiely & White LLP 1120 Lincoln St Ste 1300 Denver CO 80203-2140

BYRNE, WILLIAM MATTHEW, JR., federal judge; b. L.A., Sept. 3, 1930; s. William Matthew Sr. and Julia Ann (Lamb) B. BS, U. So. Calif., 1953, LLB, 1956; LLD, Loyola U., 1971. Bar: Calif. 1956. Ptnr. Dryden, Harrington & Schwartz, 1960-67; asst. atty U.S. Dist. Ct. (so. dist.) Calif., 1958-60; atty. U.S. Dist. Ct. (cen. dist.) Calif., Los Angeles, 1967-70, judge, 1971—; now sr. judge U.S. Dist. Ct. (cen. dist.) Calif.; exec. dir. Pres. Nixon's Commn. Campus Unrest, 1970; instr. Loyola Law Sch., Harvard U., Whittier Coll. Served with USAF, 1956-58. Mem. ABA, Fed. Bar Assn., Calif. Bar Assn., Los Angeles County Bar Assn. (vice chmn. human rights sect.), Am. Judicature Soc. Office: US Dist Ct Ste 110 312 N Spring St Los Angeles CA 90012-4703*

BYRNE-DEMPSEY, CECELIA (CECELIA DEMPSEY), journalist; b. L.A., Aug. 7, 1925; d. John Joseph and Margaret Agnes (Frakell) B.; m. John Dempsey, Mar. 25, 1951 (dec. June 1981); children: Margaret, Elizabeth, John, Cecelia, Cathrine, Patricia, Bridget, Charles, Mary Teresa. *Cecelia's Great Grandmother Hannah Payne Loftus' father, Sea Captain Robert Payne witnessed and wrote about the Boston Tea Party. Three years prior, her Uncle Edward Payne, Esq., observed the Boston Massacre from his shop doorway and was wounded. Also in Boston, 1770, her Grandfather, Sir Ralph Payne,later Baron, became the Royal Appointed Governor of the Leeward Islands in the Caribbean Sea. During 35 years of stewardship, he was instrumental in the English Parliamentary process of the Emancipation of Slavery in the Islands. In 1790, Hannah's family, her father Robert Payne, wife Honora, Hannah's mother, and her four brothers were listed in the first American census, in Albany, New York. John Adams granted her father a presidential pardon for his loyalist activities during the War of Independence.* Student, Immaculate Heart Coll., 1944; BA in Psychology, Calif. State U., Northridge, 1975, BA in Journalism, 1978, MA in Mass Communication, 1992. Staff Lockheed Aircraft Corp., Burbank, Calif., 1943—, Office Naval Rsch., San Francisco, 1947—; with Sisters of Mercy, Burlingame, Calif., 1945—, Sisters of Presentation, San Francisco, 1949—; mem. staff Calif. State U., Calif., 1976—; rschr., journalism historian early Am. newspapers, 1978—. Mentor 4-H Club; past mem. Urban Corp., L.A. Mem. Mensa, Kappa Gamma Delta. Republican. Jewish. Avocations: poetry, gardening, philosophical meditation.

BYRNES, CHRISTOPHER IAN, academic dean, researcher; b. N.Y.C., June 28, 1949; s. Richard Francis and Jeanne (Orchard) B.; m. Catherine Morris, June 24, 1984; children: Kathleen, Alison, Christopher. BS, Manhattan Coll., 1971; MS, U. Mass., 1973, PhD, 1975; D (hon.) of Tech., Royal Inst. Tech., Stockholm, 1998. Instr. U. Utah, Salt Lake City, 1975-78; asst. prof. Harvard U., Cambridge, Mass., 1978-81, assoc. prof., 1981-85; rsch. prof. Ariz. State U., Tempe, 1985-89; prof., chmn. dept. systems sci. and math. Washington U., St. Louis, 1989-91, dean engring. and applied sci., 1991—; adj. prof. Royal Inst. Tech., Stockholm, 1985-90; cons. Sci. Sys., Inc., Cambridge, 1980-84, Sys. Engring., Inc., Greenbelt, Md., 1986; sci. advisor Sherwood Davis & Geck, 1996-98; mem. NRC; bd. dirs. Belden Inc., Mih-Max, Inc.; chmn. bd. dirs. Ctr. for Emerging Techs.; pres., bd. dirs. WUTA, Inc. Editor: (book series) Progress in Systems Control, 1988—, Foundations of Systems and Control, 1989—; Nonlinear Synthesis, 1991, 10 other books; contbr. numerous articles to profl. jours., book revs. Recipient Best Paper award, IFAC, 1993. Fellow IEEE (George Axelby award 1991), Japan Soc. for Promotion Sci., Acad. Sci. St. Louis; mem. AAAS, Soc. for Indsl. Applied Math. (program com. 1986-89), Am. Math. Soc., Sigma Xi., Tau Beta Pi. Avocations: cooking, fishing, travel. Office: Washington U Sch Engring and Applied Sci 1 Brookings Dr Saint Louis MO 63130-4899

BYRNES, JAMES BERNARD, museum director emeritus; b. N.Y.C., Feb. 19, 1917; s. Patrick J.A. and Janet E. (Geiger) B.; m. Barbara A. Cecil, June 10, 1946; 1 son, Ronald L. Student, N.A.D., 1936-38, Am. Artist Sch., 1938-40, Art Students League, 1940-42, U. Perugia, Italy, 1951, Inst. Meschini, Rome, 1952. Art tchr. mus. activity program N.Y.C. Bd. Edn., 1936-40; indsl. designer Michael Saphier Assos., N.Y.C., 1940-42; docent L.A. County Mus., 1946-47, assoc. curator modern contemporary art, 1947-48, curator, asst. to dir., 1948-53; dir. Colorado Springs Fine Arts Center, 1954-55; from assoc. dir. to dir. N.C. Mus. Art, 1956-60; dir. New Orleans Mus. Art, 1961-71, dir. emeritus, 1989—; dir. Newport Harbor Art Mus., Newport Beach, Calif., 1972-75; vis. lectr. U. Fla., 1961, Newcomb Coll., Tulane U., 1963; art cons. Author: Masterpieces of Art, W.R. Valentiner Memorial, 1959, Tobacco and Smoking in Art, 1960, Fetes de la Palette, 1963, Edgar Degas, His Family and Friends in New Orleans, 1965, Odyssey of an Art Collector, 1966, Art of Ancient and Modern Latin America, 1968, The Artist as Collector of Primitive Art, 1975, also numerous mus. catalogs. Decorated Knight Order Leopold II, Belgium; recipient Isaac Delgado Meml. award New Orleans Mus. of Art, 1988. Mem. Am. Soc. Interior Design (hon. life), Am. Soc. Appraisers (sr., internat. examining bd.), Appraisers Assn. Am. Office: James B Byrnes and Assocs 7820 Mulholland Dr Hollywood CA 90046-1223

BYRNES, KEVIN P., military officer. BA in Econs. and Bus. Adminstrn., Park Coll.; MA in Mgmt., Webster U.; student, U.S. Army Command/Gen. Staff, U.S. Army War Coll. Commd. 2d lt. U.S. Army, 1969, advanced through grades to maj. gen., 1997; comdr. Battery C 1st bn. 39th field arty. U.S. Army, Ft. Bragg, N.C., 1972-74; asst. prof. mil. sci. Rose-Hulman Inst. Tech., Terre Haute, Ind., 1975-78; exec. officer 2d bn. 3d field arty. 3d armored divsn. U.S. Army Europe, Germany, 1980-81; team ops. officer, then team chief Office Inspector Gen. U.S. Army Europe, 1985-87, comdr. 4th bn. 3d field arty. 2d armored divsn., 1987-89; strategic rsch. analyst U.S. Army War Coll., Carlisle Barracks, Pa., 1990-91; comdr. divsn. arty. 1st cavalry divsn. Ft. Hood, Tex., 1991-93; chief of staff 1st cavalry divsn. Ft. Hood, 1993; comdg. gen. joint task force 6 U.S. Forces Command, Ft. Bliss, Tex., 1994-95; asst. divsn. comdr. 1st cavalry divsn. Ft. Hood, 1995-96; dir. force programs integration Office Dep. Chief of Staff for Ops. & Plans, U.S. Army, Washington, 1996-97; comdr. gen. 1st Cavalry Divsn., 1997-99, Multi-Nat. Divsn., North Bosnia, 1998-99. Office: 1st Cavalry Divsn Bldg 2800 Fort Hood TX 76545

BYRNES, PAUL DAVID, software engineer, consultant; b. Mpls., Jan. 27, 1962; s. Ferdinand F. and Rosemary (Abrams) B.; m. Laurie S., May 20, 1989. BS in Engring., USAF Acad., 1984; MBA in Fin., Bentley Coll., 1988; postgrad., Air Force Inst. Tech., 1989. Commd. 2d lt. USAF, 1984, ret. capt., 1990; mgr. software engring. program Carnegie Mellon U., Pitts., 1990-94, project mgr. Software Engring. Inst., 1992-94; prin., mng. dir. Integrated System Diagnostics, Inc., Pocasset, Mass., 1994—; presenter in field. Contbr. articles to profl. jours. Vol. Meals on Wheels, Boston, 1984-88, Northland Pub. Libr., McCandless, Pa., 1990—, WQED Pub. Rels., Pitts., 1994—. Capt. USAFR, 1990—. Mem. IEEE, Am. Assn. Individual Investors, Assn. Computing Machinery, Tech. Transfer Soc., USAF Acad. Assn. Grads. Democrat. Roman Catholic. Avocations: sports, weight-lifting, music, investing. Home: 9351 Timber Trl Pittsburgh PA 15237-4272 Office: Ste 230 Two Chatham Ctr Pittsburgh PA 15219

BYRNES, ROBERT WILLIAM, secondary school educator; b. Morristown, N.J., July 30, 1948; s. Robert Sinon and Mary Loraine (Benz) B.; m. Sherri Lynn Ackerman. BA in Secondary English, Newark State Coll., 1970; MA in English, Fairleigh Dickinson U., 1995. Cert. tchr. English 7-12, N.J. Tchr. Deptford Twp. (N.J.) Bd. Edn., 1971-72; tchr. English Dover (N.J.) Bd. Edn., 1972—. Mem. sewer Ban Relief Com., Denville, N.J., 1980, Zeek Rd. Recreation Planning Commn., Denville, 1980; girl's sch. rep. N.J. Cath. track Conf., Kearny, 1983-89, treas., 1990—. Recipient Svc. award N.J. Cath. Track Conf., 1988, Morris County Track Coaches Assn., 1997. Mem. Dover Edn. Assn. (v.p. 1999—). Avocations: track and field, golf, reading, art. Home: 5 Snyder Ave Denville NJ 07834-2135 Office: Dover High Sch 100 Grace St Dover NJ 07801-2697

BYRNES, WILLIAM JOSEPH, lawyer; b. Bklyn., Apr. 11, 1940; s. William James and Margaret Mary (English) B.; m. Catherine Belle Rollings, Aug. 15, 1970; children: Jennifer, Suzanne. BS, Fordham U., 1961; JD, Yale U., 1964. Bar: N.Y. 1965, D.C. 1970, Va. 1992. Atty. AEC, Washington, 1964-68; internat. mgr. Comm. Satellite Corp., Washington, 1968-70; ptnr. Haley, Bader & Potts, Arlington, Va., 1970-95; of counsel Irwin Campbell & Tannenwald, Washington, 1995-96; pvt. practice, McLean, Va., 1997—. Co-author: The Common Carrier Provisions--A Product of Evolutionary Development in A Legislative History of the Communications Act, 1989, Decency Redux: The Curious History of the New FCC Broadcast Indecency Policy, 1989, A New Telecommunications Paradigm, 1993; mem. Great Falls Players, Elden Street Players, Castaways Repertory Theatre, Rockville Little Theatre, Cedar Lane Stage, Sterling Playmakers. Candidate Fairfax County Bd. Suprs., 1995; bd. dirs. McLean Comm. Ctr.; v.p. McLean Citizens Found.; active Castaways Repertory Theatre, Rockville Little Theatre. Recipient cert. U.S. Atomic Energy Commn., 1967. Mem. Fed. Comms. Bar Assn., Va. State Bar, D.C. Bar Assn., McLean Citizens Assn. (ex-pres.), Fairfax Com. 100. Avocations: acting, videography. Office: 7921 Old Falls Rd Mc Lean VA 22102

BYRNSIDE, OSCAR JEHU, JR., professional society administrator; b. Huntington, W.Va., June 2, 1935; s. Oscar Jehu and Eula (Bayliss) B.; m. Patricia Ann Oxley, Aug. 1, 1954; children: Barbara Ann, Brenda Gail, Bethany Lynne. B.S., Concord Coll., Athens, W.Va., 1960; M.S., Va. Poly. Inst. and State U., Blacksburg, 1961; Ph.D., Ohio State U., Columbus, 1968. Tchr. bus. Kanawha County schs., Charleston, W.Va., 1960; coordinator vocat. edn. Danville (Va.) public schs., 1961-63; asst. prof. bus., dir. data processing Longwood Coll., Farmville, Va., 1963-65; state dir. bus. edn. W.Va. Bd. Edn., 1965-66; research assoc., cons. Ohio State U., 1966-68; exec. dir. Nat. Bus. Edn. Assn., Reston, Va., 1968-89, Future Bus. Leaders Am.-Phi Beta Lambda, Inc., 1968-73; vis. prof. Va. Poly. Inst. and State U., 1969-70, Catholic U. Am., 1969-82, U. Wyo., 1988—; pres. Center Ednl. Assns., Reston, 1976-77, 83-84; treas., bd. dirs. Alliance Assns. Advancement Edn., 1973-74; bd. dirs., exec. v.p. Found. for Teaching Free Enterprise, 1979-86; pres. Assn. Data Mgmt., Inc., Reston, Va.; chmn. Trust for Insuring Educators, 1981-89; dir. fin. and adminstrn. Am. Sch. Food Svc. Assn., Alexandria, Va., 1989—; mem. nat. task force edn. and tng. minority bus. enterprise HEW, 1971-74; trustee Joint Coun. on Econ. Edn., 1985-88. Editor: Bus. Edn. Forum, 1968-79, pub. 1979-89. Bd. dirs. Reston Soccer Assn., 1979-81, commr. girls travel divsn., 1979-82; exec. bd. Washington Area Girls Soccer League, 1978-81; co-dir. Reston Internat. Soccer Festival, 1979; bd. dirs. Bus. Edn. Hall of Fame, 1978-89; mem. Policies Commn. for Bus. and Econ. Edn., 1968-89. With USMC, 1953-56. Recipient Centennial award Ohio State U., 1970. Mem. Nat. Bus. Edn. Assn., Am. Vocat. Assn. (life), NEA (life), Internat. Council Small Bus., Am. Soc. Assn. Execs., Nat. Assn. Secondary Sch. Prins., Am. Assn. Sch. Adminstrs., Assn. Supervision and Curriculum Devel., Internat. Soc. Bus. Edn., Phi Kappa Phi, Phi Delta Kappa, Pi Omega Pi, Delta Pi Epsilon, Kappa Delta Pi. Baptist. Home: 2053 Eakins Ct Reston VA 20191-1313 Office: Am Sch Food Svc Assn 1600 Duke St Fl 7 Alexandria VA 22314-3421

BYROM, FLETCHER LAUMAN, chemical manufacturing company executive; b. Cleve., July 13, 1918; s. Fletcher L. and Elizabeth (Collins) B.; m. Marie L. McIntyre, Feb. 17, 1945; children: Fletcher Lauman, Carol A. Byrom Conrad, Susan J. Byrom Evans. BS in Metallurgy, Pa. State U., 1940. Sales engr. Am. Steel & Wire Co., Cleve., 1940-42; procurement and adminstrv. coord. Naval Ordnance Lab., also Bur. Ordnance and Research Planning Bd., Navy Dept., 1942-47; from asst. to gen. mgr. Tar Products divsn. Koppers Co., Inc., Pitts., 1947-82, pres., chmn., 1970-82; mem. Pitts. br. Fed. Res. Bd. Cleve., 1962-68, chmn., 1966-68, N.Y. Stock Exch., 1980-86; mem. bd. govs. Com. Devel. Am. Capital; bd. dirs. Purecycle Corp., Globe Bldg. Materials, Inc., Mid-West Spring Mfg. Co., Pathe Techs., Inc., TCW Americas Devel., Inc., Adience, Inc., Standard Brands Paint Co.; pres., bd. dirs. Micasu Corp. Bd. dirs. Allegheny Conf. on Community Devel., v.p., 1970-83; chmn. Hershey Med. Ctr., 1970-73; chmn. Pres.'s Export Council, 1974-79, Pub. Edn. Fund, 1980-85; chmn. bd. trustees Presbyn.-Univ. Hosp., 1972-83, Kiskiminetas Springs Sch., 1971-82; trustee Carnegie Mellon U., 1975-81, Allegheny Coll., 1969-79, Pa. State U., 1970-73; former trustee, Inst. Advanced Study, Inst. for Future Mem., Hudson Inst., Keystone Ctr.; trustee Conf. Bd., 1962-82, lifetime chancellor, 1968—; mem. president's circle NAS; trustee Com. for Econ. Devel., chmn. bd. dirs., 1978-84. Recipient Disting. Civilian Service award U.S. Navy Dept., Disting. Alumnus Pa. State U., David Ford McFarland award Pa. State U., 1979, Alumni Achievement award Harvard U. Bus. Sch., 1981, William Metcalf award West Pa. Engring. Soc., 1985; Woodrow Wilson Edn. Found. vis. fellow, Pa. State U. fellow. Mem. Bus. Coun., Pa. State U. Alumni Assn. (pres. 1965-66), Desert Forest Golf (Carefree, Ariz.) Club, Duquesne (Pitts.) Club, Links (N.Y.C.) Club, Phi Kappa Psi. Presbyterian. Home: PO Box 1055 7822 Stagecoach Pass Carefree AZ 85377

BYRON, BEVERLY BUTCHER, congresswoman; b. Balt., July 27, 1932; d. Harry C. and Ruth Butcher; m. Goodloe E. Byron, 1952 (dec.); children: Goodloe E. Jr., Barton Kimball, Mary McComas; m. B. Kirk Walsh, 1986. Student, Hood Coll., 1962-64. Mem. 96th-102nd Congresses from 6th Md. dist., 1979-93; Presdl. appt. to base closing and realignment commn., 1993; bd. dirs. McDonnell Douglas, Balt. Gas and Electric, Blue Cross/Blue Shield, UNC Corp., Farm and Mech. Nat. Bank, Def. Adv. Commn. on Women in the Mil., 1961-?; exec. panel Chief of Naval Ops.; adv. bd. NASA. State treas. Md. Young Dems., 1962, 65; bd. assocs. Hood Coll.; bd. visitors USAF Acad., 1980-87; trustee Mt. St. Mary's Coll.; bd. dirs. Frederick County chpt. ARC; sec. Frederick Heart Assn., 1974-79; mem. Frederick Phys. Fitness Commn.; chmn. Md. Phys. Fitness Commn., 1979-89; mem. Frederick County Landmarks Found.; bd. dirs. Am. Hiking Soc.; bd. dirs. Adventure Sports Inst., 1992—; bd. advisors Internat. Studies Frostburg State U., 1990—, Am. Volkssport Assn., 1991—; mem. bd. vis. U.S. Naval Acad., 1995—, chair, 1997-98. Episcopalian. Recipient Pres.'s medal John Hopkins U. Home: 306 Grove Blvd Frederick MD 21701-4813

BYRON, E. LEE, real estate broker; b. Gt. Falls, Mont., Oct. 1, 1945; d. Chase and Mary Lee (Evans) Kimball; m. H. Thomas Byron Jr., May 18, 1966; children: H. Thomas Byron III, Chase K., Lee-Hayes. AB, Smith Coll., 1967; MA, Monterey Inst. Fgn. Studies, 1971; Montessori cert., St. Nicholas. Ctr., London, 1971. Lic. real estate broker, Fla. Lectr. Monterey (Calif.) Inst. Fgn. Studies, 1971-72; founder, dir., owner Children's Sch. and Summer Dynamics, Auburn, Ala., 1975-79; instr. Child Study Ctr. Auburn U., 1973-79; hosp. dir. Fruitville Vet. Clinic, Sarasota, Fla., 1980-93; broker assoc. Michael Saunders & Co., Sarasota, 1993—; founder, adv. bd. mem. Guaranty Bank, North Port, Fla., 1987—; owner, ptnr. Lee Ventures Real Estate Partnership, Sarasota, 1984—; presenter in field, organizer various discussion panels. Co-author: Preschool Theme Lesson Plans, 1975. Bd. dirs. Jr. League, Sarasota, 1981-90; bd. dirs. Pine View Assn. PTA, 1981-90, chmn., 1984-85; bd. dirs. Teen Ct., Sarasota, 1990—, Fla. Sch. Bd. Assn., cert., 1993; bd. dirs. Taxpayers Assn. Sarasota County, 1995—, pres., 1996-97; bd. dirs. Civic League Sarasota, 1995—, 2nd v.p., 1997-98, 1st v.p., 1998-99, pres., 1999—; chmn. Sarasota County Exceptional Student Edn. Sch. Adv. Bd., 1984-90; mem. Pine View Sch. Adv. Com., 1994-98, chmn., 1994-97; bd. dirs. Consortium for Children and Youth, Sarasota, 1986—, pres., 1993-97; vice chair Action Task Force Venice (Fla.) 20/20, 1995-97, Children and Youth Svcs. Adv. Com., 1993—, chair, 1996-98, vice chair, 1999—; co-chmn. Pres.'s Spl. Com. Exceptional Edn. Fla. Sch. Bd. Assn., 1992-93; mem. Bishop's Com. Sexual Misconduct Cath. Diocese, Venice, 1994-95, Multi-Stakeholder's Group (Future Land Planning East Sarasota County), 1995—; mem. adv. com. Fla. House Inst., 1998—; mem. Sarasota County Sch. Bd., 1990-94; bd. govs. Big Bros./Big Sisters of the Suncoast, 1998—, Fla. Women's Alliance, 1994—. Recipient Sustainer of Yr. award Sarasota Jr. League, 1993, Cmty. Svc. award, 1995; Women of Power award Nat. Coun. Jewish Women, 1997; named One of 100 Vols. for 100th birthday, Internat. Assn. Jr. Leagues, 1996. Mem. Sarasota Assn. of Realtors (program com. 1995—), Nat. Assn. Realtors (Grad. Realtor Inst. 1996). Republican. Roman Catholic. Avocations: reading, swimming, skiing.

Home: 653 Sinclair Dr Sarasota FL 34240-9367 Office: Michael Saunders & Co 5100 Ocean Blvd Sarasota FL 34242-1693

BYRON, ERIC HOWARD, sculptor, museum researcher and administrator; b. N.Y.C., Jan. 14, 1948; s. Melville and Ruth (Levine) Byron. BA, Beloit Coll., 1970; postgrad., Hunter Coll., 1972-75, YIVO Inst./Columbia U., 1972-76; MA, Goddard Coll., 1979; postgrad, NYU, 1985. Founder, dir. The Synagogue Rescue Project, Inc., N.Y.C., 1974-85; mus. technician South St. Seaport Mus., N.Y.C., 1992-93, Statue of Liberty Nat. Monument/Ellis Island Immigration Mus, N.Y.C., 1993—; lectr. sr. citizens N.Y. Tech. Inst., 1982; coord. oral history project Brookdale Ctr. on Aging, Hunter Coll., N.Y.C., 1982. Exhibited in group shows at Ward-Nasse Gallery, 1975-76, Detail, N.Y.C., 1989, Nathaniel's Music Box, N.Y.C., 1989, Civilization, 1989, Am. Craftsman, 1989-90, Dinosaur Hill, N.Y.C., 1990, Mus. Am. Folk Art, N.Y.C., 1990, Mark Milliken Gallery, N.Y.C., 1990, Faith Nightengale Gallery, San Diego, 1991-92, Whitney Mus., N.Y.C., 1992; sculpture, performer Washington Sq. Pk., 1989—; featured on PBS Channel 13' City Arts, 1998. Fellow Brookdale Ctr. on Aging, N.Y.C., 1985; recipient archeology award Profl. Archeologists N.Y.C., 1997. Mem. Indsl. Archeologists, N.Y. Archeol. Assn., Smithsonian Instn., Nat. Trust Historic Preservation, Antique Telephone Collections Assn. Home: 411 E 10th St Apt 15F New York NY 10009-4212 Office: Statue of Liberty Nat Mus Liberty Is New York NY 10004-1467

BYRON, FREDERICK WILLIAM, JR., physicist, educator, university vice chancellor; b. Manchester, N.H., July 8, 1938; s. Frederick William and Anna (Muir) B.; m. Edith Iselin, June 23, 1961; children: Kenniston, Alexander deNeufville. A.B., Harvard U., 1959; Ph.D., Columbia U., 1963. Acting asst. prof. U. Calif., Berkeley, 1963-65; asst. prof. U. Calif., 1965-66; asst. prof. U. Mass., Amherst, 1966-69, assoc. prof., 1969-74, prof., 1974—, head dept. physics and astronomy, 1975-79; dean U. Mass. (Faculty Natural Scis. and Math.), Amherst, 1979-93; coordinating dean U. Mass. (Coll. of Arts and Scis.), Amherst, 1989-91; vice chancellor rsch. and econ. devel. U. Mass., Amherst, 1994—; bd. dirs. Mfg. Partnership We. Mass.; bd. dirs. Mass. Ventures Corp., chmn., 1995-97. Author: (with Robert W. Fuller) The Mathematics of Classical and Quantum Physics, 1970; contbr. articles to profl. jours. Alfred P. Sloan Found. fellow, 1965-67; Fulbright research scholar, 1973-74. Fellow Am. Phys. Soc. Office: U Mass Dept Physics Amherst MA 01003

BYRON, H. THOMAS, JR., veterinarian, educator; b. Troy, N.Y., Feb. 13, 1944; s. Henry Thomas and Mary Katherine (Hayes) B.; m. E. Lee Kimball, May 18, 1966; children: H. Thomas III, Chase Kimball, Lee Hayes. *Mr. Byron's wife, Lee, is a Real Estate broker with Michael Saunders, who's firmproduces over $10 million a year. His son Tom, is an attorney with the Justice Department trying cases for the U.S. at the Federal and Supreme Court level. Son, Chase is an independent businessman doing software consulting throughout the state of Florida. His company, Bison Consulting, helps small businesses blossom to large companies. His daughter, Lee Hayes Byron, is a recent Stanford University graduate. She now does policy planning for environmental protection and permitting for Sarasota and Alachua county Florida.* BS, Stonehill Coll., 1965; MS, U. Fla., 1973; DVM, Auburn U., 1977. Intern Animal Med. Clinic, Lakeland, Fla., 1977; resident in radiology, instr. Auburn (Ala.) U., 1977-79; chief staff Ctrl. Animal Hosp., Tampa, Fla., 1979-80; founder Fruitville Vet. Clinic, Sarasota, Fla., 1980-94; chief vet., dir. animal programs Circus World, Haines City, Fla., 1981-83; pvt. practice Bus. Resource Group, Sarasota, Fla., 1994—; liasion S.W. Fla. Vet. Med. Assn., Humane Soc., 1984-92; cons. Ringling Bros., Barnum and Bailey Circus, Venice, Fla., 1986—, Busch Gardens, TAmpa, 1984—, Roberts Bros. Circus, Hanneford Circus, Coronas Circus, Hoxie Bros. Circus, Sarasota, 1979—, Circus Vargas Internat., L.A., 1984—, Parc Safari, Hemingford, Que., Can., 1993; lectr. U. Fla. Vet. Sch., 1989—, mem. adv. coun. Coll. Vet. Medicine, 1991—. Contbr. articles to profl. jours. Troop leader Boy Scouts Am., Auburn, Sarasota, 1977-81, scoutmaster, packmaster; vet. chmn. Sarasota United Way, 1980—; lectr., vol. Sarasota County Schs., 1980—; mem. Sarasota County rabies control com. Pub. Health Dept., 1980-92; founding mem. Sarasota County Animal Welfare Adv. Com., 1992; bd. dirs. Sarasota Girls' Choir, 1987-89, Pine View Sch. Parents' Assn. Bd., 1990—; bd. dirs., pres. Sunset Royale Condominium Assn., Siesta Key, Fla., 1988-89, 91-93. Lt. USNR. Recipient Aux. award AVMA, 1977, recognition award Sarasota County Commrs., 1993; Alexander Hamilton scholar Stonehill Coll., 1964-65; fellow NAS, 1972-73, Geraldine Page wildlife fellow, 1987. Mem. Fla. Pub. Health Assn., Fla. Vet. Medicine Assn. (fin. com. 1982-86, bd. dirs. 1986-92, chmn. legis. com. 1982-90, Gold Star award 1988), S.W. Fla. Vet. Med. Assn. (bd. dirs., sec.-treas., v.p., pres. 1980-85), Aquatic Animal Vet. Assn., Zoo Animal Vet. Assn., Sarasota C. of C. (legis. com. 1986-91), Phi Zeta. Republican. Roman Catholic. Avocations: water skiing, fishing, scuba diving. Home and Office: 653 Sinclair Dr Sarasota FL 34240-9367

BYRON, KIM, artist; b. La Jolla, Calif., 1961. BA, Yale U., 1983; student, Kowhegan Sch. Painting & Sculp, 1986. One-woman shows include Baumgartner Galleries, Washington, 1993, Wadsworth Athenaeum, Hartford, Conn., 1994, Korea Arts Found. Am., L.A., 1995, Hirshhorn Mus. and Sculpture Garden, Washington, 1996, Max Protetch Gallery, N.Y.C., 1997, Mus. Contemporary Art, Chgo., 1998, others; exhibited in group shows at Max Protetch Gallery, 1994, Ottawa Art Gallery, 1994, Neuberger Mus. Art, 1995, Todd Gallery, 1995, Galerie Sfeir-Semler, 1995, Parrish Art Mus., 1995, Milw. Art Mus., 1995, Inst. Contemporary Art, 1995, High Mus., 1995, Mus. Am. Art, 1995, Newlyn Art Gallery, 1996, Friedreich Peitzel Gallery, 1996, Wexner Ctr., 1996, List Visual Arts Ctr., 1996, Randolph St. Gallery, 1997, Snug Harbor Cultural Ctr., 1997, U. Mich. Mus. Art, 1998, David and Alfred Smart Mus. Art, 1998, Montclair Art Mus., 1999, others; represented in permanent collections Mus. Contemporary Art, Norton Family Collection, Wadsworth Athenaeum, Walker Art Ctr., Whitney Mus. Am. Art; featured in numerous articles in mags. and newspapers. Office: Max Protetch 511 W 22nd St New York NY 10011-1109

BYRON, MICHAEL J., career officer; b. Albany, N.Y., Oct. 1, 1941; m. Kathleen Hannegan; children: Patrick, Bridget Mary, Megan. BA in Latin Am. Studies, U. Miami, 1963; grad., Greek Airborne Course, USMC Amphibious Warfare Sch., Armed Forces Staff Coll., InterAm. Def. Coll. Commd. 2nd lt. USMC, 1963; co. comdr. 3rd Marine Divsn.; comdg. gen. 9th Marine Expeditionary Brigade, 3rd Marine Expeditionary Force; unit comdr. 3rd Marine Divsn.; dir. InterAm. Region Office of Def.; asst. to under sec. of def. for policy Office of the Sec. of Def.; dir. for plans and policy U.S. Atlantic Command; vice dir. for strategic plans and policy Joint Staff; U.S. mil. rep. to NATO Mil. Com., 1997—. Decorated D.S.M. with oak leaf cluster, Legion of Merit, Purple Heart, Bronze Star with Combat V and Gold Star, Silver Star, Republic of Vietnam Honor medal 1st class. Avocations: parachuting, scuba diving, skiing. Office: J-5 Strategic Plans and Policy Directorate JCS/5000 Pentagon Washington DC 20318-5000 also: Hdqs Marine Corps Divsn Pub Affairs Washington DC 20380-1775*

BYRON, RITA ELLEN COONEY, travel executive, publisher, real estate agent, photojournalist, writer; b. Cleve.; d. Harry James and Marie (Hakey) Cooney; m. Carl James Byron Jr., Nov. 27, 1954 (dec.); children: Carey Lewis, Carl James, Bradford William. Student Cleve. Coll., 1954, Western Res. U., 1955, John Carroll U., 1956; PhD (hon.), Colo. State Christian Coll., 1972. Mgr. European Immigration dept. U.S. Steamship Lines, Cleve., 1956; real estate agt. W.I. White Realtor Inc., Shaker Heights, Ohio, 1965-67, J.P. Malone Realtors Inc., Shaker Heights, 1967-70, Thomas Murray & Assocs., 1971-76, Mary Anderson Realty, Shaker Heights, 1978-79, Barth Brad & Andrews Realtors Inc., Shaker Heights, 1979—, Heights Realty, 1986—; v.p., co-owner Your Connection To Travel, Kent, Ohio, 1980—; v.p., gen. mgr. World Class Travel Agy., 1985—; dir. Travel One div. Quaker Sq., Akron, Travel Trends for Singles, 1985, Playhouse Sq. Travel, 1986, World Class Internat., 1986. Mem. U.S. Figure Skating Assn., 1960—, Wightman Cup Women's Com., 1965—; mem. women's com. Cleve. Mus. of Art, 1969—, Friendship Force Ohio, 1986 ; co-chmn. Cleve. Invitational Figure Skating Competition, 1972—; chmn. Gold Rush Rush, U.S. Ski Team, 1982, Cleve. benefit U.S. Olympic Teams, Midas Touch, 1983, Gran Apres-Ski Prix, 1981, blue ribbon ball Hunt Club for Handicapped; patron Cleve. 500, 1983; originator Benefits Unltd., Exceptional Single Person's, Connections Unltd., 1983; founder, coordinator Singled Out Club, 1983; co-ptnr., adv. bd. The Service Service, 1984; benefit chmn., patroness various balls and fund-raising events; vol. Foster Parents Inc., 1983; vol. Council on World Affairs, 1983, Bellefaire Home for Spl. Children, 1983, Big Sisters Greater Cleve., 1983, Camp Cheerful, 1983, Chisholm Ctr., 1983, Children's Diabetic Camp Ho Mita Koda, 1984, Young Audiences, 1985; adv. trustee Friends of Fairmount Theatre of the Deaf, 1983; mem. Greater Cleve. Growth Assn., 1983. Mem. Western Res. Hist. Soc., Garden Ctr. Greater Cleve., Friends Cleve. Pub. Library, UN Assn. of U.S., Cleve. Council World Affairs, U.S. Ski Ednl. Fund (chmn. benefits), English Speaking Union (jr. bd.), Travel Age Exchange, Globetrotters Internat. Fedn. Women's Travel Orgns., North Coast Exec. Women's Network, Growth Assn., Council on Small Enterprises. Cleve. Real Estate Bd., Cleve. Photographic Soc. (bd. dirs. 1989—), Camera Guild (exec. bd. trustees 1989), Associated Photographers, Photographic Soc. Am. Clubs: Cleve. Skating, Broadmoor World Arena Figure Skating, Colony Beach and Racquet, Suburban Ski, Cleve. Advertising, Communicator's, Towne Hall, Women's City, Gilmour Acad. Women's, Mid-Day, Cleve. Wellesley, Arctic Circle, Intrepid Traveler, Tibet, Mongolia and China Explorers', Himalaya Yeti (1987 Nepal Expdn.), Internat. Chagrin Valley Camera, Nat. Hist. Mus. Photo Soc., Kodochrome Adventure Soc., Nature Artists Soc., Cleve. Astronomical Soc., Archeol. Soc., Holden Aborteum Soc., East Berlin Photo Club, Chagrin Valley Photo Club, Shaker Lakes Nature Club, Met. Parks, Photography Club, Photocrafters, Sanctuary Marsh Photo, Cuyahoga Valley Nat. Pk. Photo Club (assoc. photographer, various photography awards). Co-pub., exec. editor The Single Register (pub. documentary book The Fall of the Wall 1989), other publs.; featured in numerous publs. Home: 18126 Lomond Blvd Cleveland OH 44122-5012 Office: World Class Travel 3520 Ingleside Rd Cleveland OH 44122-5002 also: Es Turo Edificio, Kontiki, Majorica Balearic Islands Spain

BYRON, WILLIAM JAMES, management educator, former university president; b. Pitts., May 25, 1927; s. Harold J. and Mary I. (Langton) B. A.B. in Philosophy, St. Louis U., 1955, Ph.L., 1956, M.A. in Econs, 1959; S.T.B., Woodstock Coll., 1960, S.T.L., 1962; Ph.D. in Econs, U. Md., 1969; cert., Harvard U. Inst. Ednl. Mgmt., 1974. Joined S.J., 1950, ordained priest Roman Cath. Ch., 1961. Tchr. math. Scranton (Pa.) Prep. Sch., 1956-58; manpower rsch. fellow Dept. Labor, 1965-66; asst. prof. econs. Loyola Coll., Balt., 1967-69; assoc. prof. social ethics, rector Woodstock Coll., Woodstock Jesuit Community, 1967-73; dean Coll. Arts and Scis. Loyola U., New Orleans, 1973-75; pres. U. Scranton, 1975-82, Cath. U. Am., Washington, 1982-92; rsch. assoc. Georgetown U., 1992-93; Disting. prof. mgmt. Sch. of Bus. Georgetown U., Washington, 1993—. Author: Toward Stewardship: An Interim Ethic of Poverty, Pollution and Power, 1975, Quadrangle Considerations, 1989, Take Your Diploma and Run, 1992, Finding Work Without Losing Heart, 1995, The 365 Days of Christmas, 1996, Answers from Within, 1998; editor: Causes of World Hunger, 1982; contbr. numerous articles to profl. jurs. Bd. dirs. Fed. City Coun., Joint Commn. on Accreditation Healthcare Orgns., U. San Francisco, Loyola Coll. in Md., Balt. With U.S. Army, 1945-56. Mem. Am. Econs. Assn., Am. Soc. Christian Ethics, Assn. Cath. Colls. and Univs., Phi Beta Kappa, Alpha Sigma Nu. Home: Georgetown U Jesuit Cmty Washington DC 20057-1200 Office: Georgetown U Sch Bus Adminstrn Washington DC 20057-1019

BYRUM, JUDITH MIRIAM, accountant; b. Bismarck, N.D., Sept. 24, 1943; d. Adolph Mathew and Gertrude Cecelia (Lechner) H.; m. Richard W. Byrum, July 30, 1965 (div. Oct. 1984); children: Thomasin Jane, Toby Oliver; m. Danny D. Jansen, Oct. 21, 1989 (dec. Nov. 1989); m. Jack N. Sutton, June 26, 1993. BS in Acctg., Ariz. State U., 1967. CPA, Ariz., Kans. Underwriter Gt. SW Fire Ins. Co., Mesa, Ariz., 1963-65; staff auditor Touche Ross & Co., London, 1967-69, Arthur Andersen & Co., Kansas City, Mo., 1970-71; treas. John J. Peterson Real Estate, Overland Park, Kans., 1971-75; internal auditor Bus. Men's Assurance Co., Kansas City, 1975-78; owner Judith H. Byrum, CPA, Chartered, 1978—; ptnr. G.R. Starbuck & Co. P.A., Leawood, Kans., 1996—. Contbr. articles to newsletter. Mem. adv. bd. Rockhurst Coll. Women's Ctr., Kansas City, 1977; mem. Congressman Larry Winn II Small Bus. Com., Washington, 1977-80; treas. Trinity Luth. Ch., Mission, Kans., 1990-94. Mem. AICPA (legis. liaison), Am. Woman's Soc. CPAs (treas., v.p. Chgo. 1977-83), Am. Soc. Women Accts. (pres. Kansas City 1980-81), Kans. Soc. CPAs (com. mem. 1977—, pres., v.p., treas. Metro chpt. 1989—, bd. dirs. 1994-97), Kansas City Women's C. of C. (v.p. 1980), Beta Alpha Psi. Avocations: skiing, golf, reading, gardening, hunting. Office: 4601 College Blvd Ste 160 Leawood KS 66211-1678

BYSIEWICZ, SUSAN, state official; b. New Haven, Conn.. BA magna cum laude, Yale Coll., 1983; JD, Duke U., 1986. Corp. atty. White & Case, N.Y., 1986-88; campaign mgr., issues dir. Robinson & Cole, Hartford, Conn., 1988-92; mem. staff law dept. Aetna Life and Casualty, 1992-94; mem. Middletown Dem. Com., 1989—; state rep. 100th dist. judiciary com. State of Conn., 1992-98, chair govt. adminstrn. and elections com., 1995-98, Sec. of State, 1998—. Author: Ella: A Biography of Governor Ella T. Grasso, 1984; contbr. chpt. to book. Conn. Bar Assn., N.Y. Bar Assn. Democrat. Address: Rm 104 State Capitol Hartford CT 06106

BYSTRYN, JEAN-CLAUDE, dermatologist, educator; b. Paris, May 8, 1938; came to U.S., 1949, naturalized, 1958; s. Iser and Sara Bystryn; m. Marcia Hammill, May 14, 1972; children: Anne, Alexander. BS, U. Chgo., 1958; MD, NYU, 1962. Diplomate Am. Bd. Dermatology, Am. Bd. Immunodermatopathology. Intern Montefiore Hosp., N.Y.C., 1962-63, resident in medicine, 1963-64; resident in dermatology NYU Sch. Medicine, N.Y.C., 1966-69, USPHS postgrad. tng. fellow in immunology, 1968-72, asst. prof. clin. dermatology, 1971-72, assoc. prof., 1976-84, prof., 1984—; asst. dispensary physician Albany Med. Coll., 1964-66; asst. attending physician Univ. Hosp., N.Y.C., 1969—; asst. vis. dermatologist Bellevue Hosp. Ctr., N.Y.C., 1969—; dir. Melanoma Program and Melanoma Immunotherapy Clinic, NYU Kaplan Cancer Ctr., dir. Bullous Disease Clinic and Immunofluorescence Lab. NYU Med. Sch.; mem. adv. bd. Skin Cancer found., Vitiligo Found., Nat. Alepecia Areata Found.; presenter Am. Skin Assn., Nat. Pemphigus Found. Contbr. articles to profl. jours. Lt. comdr. USPHS, 1964-66. Recipient Husik Prize, NYU Sch. Medicine, 1968; Irma T. Hirschl research career award AOA; Ford. Found. fellow, 1954-58; NIH grantee, 1970—. Mem. Am. Dermatology Assn., Am. Acad. Dermatology, Am. Assn. Immunologists, Am. Assn. Cancer Rsch., Soc. Investigative Dermatology, N.Y. Dermatol. Soc. (dir.), Am. Soc. Cell Biology. Office: NYU Med Ctr U Hosp 530 1st Ave New York NY 10016-6481

BYSTRYN, MARCIA HAMMILL, city program administrator; b. Louisville, Dec. 17, 1947; d. William Arthur and Jane Lind (Krieger) Hammill; m. Jean-Claude Bystryn, May 14, 1972; children: Anne, Alexander. BA, NYU, 1969, PhD, 1977. Asst. prof. sociology Northeastern U., Boston, 1977-81; program officer The Twentieth Century Fund, N.Y.C., 1981-84, asst. dir., 1984-88, acting dir., 1988-89; exec. dir. N.Y. State Moreland Act Commn. on the Returnable Container, N.Y.C., 1989-90; asst. commr. Bur. of Waste Prevention, Reuse and Recycling N.Y.C. Dept. Sanitation, 1990-94; chief environ. officer Port Authority of N.Y. and N.J., N.Y.C., 1994-99; exec. dir. N.Y. League of Conservation Voters, N.Y.C., 1999—. Contbr. articles to Social Rsch., Am. Jour. Sociology, Sociol. Quar. NEH fellow, 1979-80. Mem. Mcpl. Waste Mgmt. Assn. (exec. com. 1992-93). Office: NY League Conservation Voters 130 William St Ste 801 New York NY 10038

BYUN, HANG S., neurosurgeon, educator; b. Korea, Nov. 14, 1940. MD, Korea U. Med. Sch., Seoul, 1965. Diplomate Am. Bd. Neurosurgey. Rotating internship Mt. Sinai Svcs. City Hosp. Ctr., Elmhurst, N.Y., 1965-66; attending neurosurgeon Elmhurst Hosp. Ctr., 1985—; resident in general surgery Mt. Sinai Hosp., N.Y.C., 1966-69, resident in neurosurgery, 1969-73; asst. prof. neurosurgery Mt. Sinai Sch. Medicine, N.Y.C., 1986—; asst. attending neurosurgeon Mt. Sinai Hosp., N.Y.C., 1993—. Mem. Am. Congress of Neurol. Surgeons, Am. Assn. Neurol. Surgeons. Office: Elmhurst Hosp Ctr 79-91 Broadway Elmhurst NY 11373-1329

BZOCH, KENNETH RUDOLPH, speech and language educator, department chairman; b. Chgo., Nov. 6, 1927; s. Rudolph and Mildred (Novotney) B.; m. Lorrayne M. Cali, Oct. 29, 1950; children: Kathleen Marie, Kevin Jude. BA, DePaul U., Chgo., 1951; MA, Northwestern U., 1952, PhD, 1956. Cert. clin. competence-speech pathology, CCC-audiology; lic. speech pathologist, Fla. Asst. prof. Loyola U., Chgo., 1953-57, Northwestern U., Chgo., 1957-59; assoc. prof. U. Fla., Gainesville, 1960-64, prof., chair, 1964-96; program dir. Communicative Disorders and Craniofacial Ctr., Shands Hosp., U. Fla.; researcher in field. Author: Communicative Disorders Related to Cleft Lip and Palate, 4th edit., Emergent Language Development Craniofacial Disorders. Cpl. USMC, 1946-47. Fellow Am. Cleft Palate Assn. (past pres.), Fla. Cleft Palate Assn. (hon., past pres.), Fla. Speech Lang. and Hearing Assn. (hon., past pres.). Home: 640 NW 57th St Gainesville FL 32607-6103 Office: U Fla PO Box 100174 Gainesville FL 32610-0174

BZOSKIE, JAMES STEVEN, minister; b. Owatonna, Minn., Sept. 18, 1949; s. Lawrence Justin and Margret Lucille (James) B.; m. Charlotte Anne Carroll, Mar. 2, 1971; children: James Steven Jr., Sarah Anne, Isaiah John. BA, Kingsway Bible Coll., 1986; ThM, Kingsway Sem., 1987, ThD, 1987. Ordained to ministry Pentecostal Ch., 1978. Pastor Jesus Believers Ch., Hastings, Minn., 1978-79; co-pastor Assemblies of God, Hastings, 1979-83; pastor Cornerstone Bible Ch., Hastings, 1983—; pres. Cornerstone Bible Coll., 1984; chaplain Dakota County Sheriff Dept. (Jail), Hastings, 1979, also adult skills asst. tchr., 1993-98, Hastings (Minn.) Police Dept., 1993—. Author: The Book of Revelation, 1983. Cmty. edn. advisor Adv. Coun., Hastings, 1989-94; bd. regents Kingsway Coll., Des Moines, 1984-98; rep. Salvation Army, Dakota County, 1992—; bd. dirs. Damascus Way, 1995—; bd. regents Kingsway Coll., 1984-98. Home: 311 State St Hastings MN 55033-1038 *A successful person is one who puts his faith in Jesus Christ and recognize his need of God in every area of his life.*

CAAMANO, KATHLEEN ANN FOLZ, gifted education professional; b. Rozellville, Wis., Dec. 20, 1944; d. Joseph and Isabel Ann (Brost) Folz; m. Gerald J. Caamano, Aug. 10, 1968; children: Michelle, David. BS, U. Wis., Stevens Point; MA, Cen. Mich. U. Cert. tchr., Ill. Tchr. Midland (Mich.) Pub. Schs., 1968-74, Newark (Ohio) City Schs., 1974-77; tchr. Minooka (Ill.) Sch. Dist., 1986—, coord. gifted edn., 1986—. Pres. Camelot Homeowners Assn., Joliet, Ill.; tutor Big Bros./Big Sisters Assn. Will County; voter registrar Will County, Joliet. Recipient Those Who Excel award Ill State Bd. Edn. Mem. Internat. Reading Assn., Ill. Edn. Assn. (tchr. rep), Gifted Edn. Coun., Ill. Assn. Ednl. Rsch. and Evaluation, Will County Reading Coun., Delta Kappa Gamma (v.p.), Beta Sigma Phi (pres.). Roman Catholic. Avocations: travel, reading, golf, bridge. Home: 22257 S Galahad Dr Joliet IL 60431-7611

CAAN, JAMES, actor, director; b. N.Y.C., Mar. 26, 1940; m. Linda O'Gara, 1995; children: James Arthur, Jacob Arthur; children from previous marriage: Tara, Scott, Alexander. Student, Hofstra Coll., Mich. State U. Appeared in off-Broadway play La Ronde, 1961; film appearances include Lady in a Cage, 1964, The Glory Guys, 1965, Red Line 7000, 1965, Eldorado, 1967, Games, 1967, Journey to Shiloh, 1968, Submarine X-1, 1969, Rain People, 1969, Rabbit, Run, 1970, The Godfather, 1972, Slither, 1973, Freebie and the Bean, 1973, Cinderella Liberty, 1974, The Gambler, 1974, Funny Lady, 1975, Rollerball, 1975, The Godfather-Part II, 1974, The Killer Elite, 1975, Harry and Walter Go to New York, 1976, Silent Movie, 1976, A Bridge Too Far, 1977, Another Man, Another Chance, 1977, Comes a Horseman, 1978, Chapter Two, 1979, Thief, 1981, Kiss Me Goodbye, 1983, Bolero, 1983, Gardens of Stone, 1987, Alien Nation, 1988, Misery, 1990, For The Boys, 1991, Honeymoon in Vegas, 1992, The Program, 1993, Flesh and Bone, 1993, A Boy Called Hate, 1994, North Star, 1995, Bottlerocket, 1995, Eraser, 1996, Bulletproof, 1996, This is My Father, 1998, Mickey Blue Eyes, 1998, The Yards, 1999; dir. Hide in Plain Sight, 1980; appeared in TV film Brian's Song, 1971, Poodle Springs, 1998; numerous TV appearances. Office: Creative Artists Agy care Fred Specktor 9830 Wilshire Blvd Beverly Hills CA 90212*

CABAL, THEODORE JAMES, dean, religious studies educator; b. Whittier, Calif., Dec. 24, 1952; s. Theodore Joseph Cabal and Maxine H. Cabal-Shcrader; m. Cheryl Ann Bush, May 20, 1977; children: Daniel, David, John. BA, Dallas Bapt. U., 1988, MA, 1989; MDiv, Southwestern Bapt. Theol. Sem., 1990, PhD, 1995. Pastor Green Oaks Cmty. Ch., Arlington, Tex., 1979-95, Christ Cmty. Ch., Graham, Tex., 1985-88, Greenwood (Tex.) Bapt. Ch., 1989-93; asst. prof. religion and philosophy Dallas Bapt. U., 1993-95; asst. prof. philosophy of religion Southwestern Bapt. Theol. Sem., Ft. Worth, 1995-98, dean, assoc. prof. Christian philosophy, 1998—. Contbr. articles to profl. jours. Pres. scholar Southwestern Bapt. Theol. Sem., Ft. Worth, 1989. Mem. Am. Acad. Religion, Am. Philos. Assn., Soc. Bibl. Lit., Evang. Theol. Sem. Baptist. Avocations: reading, golfing, hiking. E-mail: tcabal@sbts.edu. Fax: 502-897-4799. Office: So Bapt Theol Sem 2825 Lexington Rd Louisville KY 40280

CABALLERO, BERTHA LUCIO, gifted and talented education educator; b. Brownsville, Tex., Feb. 9, 1947; d. Eduardo Andres Sr. and Josefa (Liendo) L.; m. Ruben Jaime Caballero Sr., Dec. 27, 1969; children: Claudia Christina, Ruben Jaime Jr., Jason Ryan Caballero. Student, Tex. Southmost Coll., 1967-68; BA in Elem. Edn. and English, Pan Am. Coll., 1969; M of English, U. Conn., 1974. Tchr. 6th grade Ctr. Jr. H.S., Brownsville, Tex., 1967-69; tchr. 3d grade Stokes Elem. Sch., Rome, N.Y., 1972-73; tchr. 5th, 6th grades St. Aloysius Pvt. Sch., New Canaan, 1974-75; tchr. 6th grade Northeast Elem. Sch., Stamford, Conn., 1975-80; tchr. 7th grade English Oliveira Mid. Sch., Brownsville, 1980—, chair dept. English, UIL co-coord., 1983-97, site-based decision making co-chair, 1997-98. Feature writer Newspapers in Education, 1996-97. Active VFW Ladies Aux., Good Neighbor Settlement House. Recipient Brownsville Endowment for Tchg. Excellence award Rotary Club, 1991; named Brownsville Ind. Sch. Dist. Tchr. of Yr., 1991, Gifted and Talented Tchr. of Yr. for Region 1, 1992, Newspapers in Edn. Tchr. of Yr., 1998. Mem. NEA, Nat. Coun. Tchrs. English, Tex. Assn. Gifted and Talented, Assn. Brownsville Educators, Tex. State Tchrs. Assn., Ft. Brown Geneal. Soc., Alpha Delta Kappa (dist. sec. 1988—), Phi Lamba Theta. Democrat. Roman Catholic. Avocations: genealogy, running. Home: 205 Virtudes Ct Brownsville TX 78526-1878

CABALLERO, MARIO GUSTAVO, investment company executive, gaming executive; b. Trujillo, Peru, Mar. 24, 1959; came to U.S., 1969; s. Flavio Virgilio and Maria Isabel (Torres) C. BS Biology, U. Ill., Chgo., 1981; BA Fin., Loyola U., Chgo., 1987. Account exec., trader Brooks Securities, Chgo., 1982-84; ptnr., v.p. Ill. Corp. Investments, Rosemont, 1985—; chmn. Plastisys, Inc., Elgin, Ill., 1990—; owner CGOH, Inc. and HDC, Inc. Casinos, The Caribbean, 1997—; ptnr. Hanasco, Inc., Port-au-Prince, Haiti. Bd. mem. Mexican Am. Legal Def. Fund, Chgo., 1989. Mem. Coun. Fgn. Rels., Art Inst. Chgo., Elgin C. of C. Republican. Roman Catholic. Avocations: basketball, jogging, mountain climbing. E-mail: marioc@ziplink.net. Home: 1217 Frontage Rd Wilmette IL 60091-1067 Office: Ill Corp Investments Inc 175 Olde Half Day Rd Lincolnshire IL 60069-3061

CABALQUINTO, LUIS CARRAZCAL, free-lance writer; b. Magarao, Camarines, Sur, Philippines, Jan. 31, 1935; came to U.S., 1968; s. Geminiano and Irene (Carrazcal) C. BA in Journalism, U. Philippines, 1967; postgrad., Cornell U., 1968-71, NYU, 1982-84. Editor Office Philippine Pres., Manila, 1960-66; editor, instr. U. Phillipines, Los Baños, 1966-75; customer svc. rep. Pfizer Inc., N.Y.C., 1980-90; pvt. practice N.Y.C., 1990—. Author: The Dog-eater and Other Poems, 1989, The Ibalon Collection, 1991, Dreamwanderer, 1992. Recipient Dylan Thomas Poetry award New Sch. Social Rsch., 1979, Poetry prize Acad. Am. Poets, 1985, fiction prize Philippine Graphic Mag., 1992; fellow N.Y. Found. Arts, 1989. Mem. Poetry Soc. Am., Poets Writers, Writers Cmty. Avocations: fishing, movies, gardening, sports, travel. Home and Office: 1 Stuyvesant Oval New York NY 10009-2101

CABANAS, ELIZABETH ANN, nutritionist; b. Port Arthur, Tex., Oct. 27, 1948; d. William Rosser and Frances Merle (Block) Thornton. BS, U. Tex., 1971; MPH, U. Hawaii, 1973; postgrad., Tex. Woman's U., 1991—. Registered dietitian. Clin. nutritionist Family Planning Inst. Kapiolani Hosp., Honolulu, 1972-74; dietitian Kauikeolani Children's Hosp.-Pacific Inst. Rehab. Medicine, Honolulu, 1974-75; asst. food service administr. San Antonio Ind. Schs., 1975-89; coord. equipment and facilities Dallas Ind. Sch., 1990-91; nutritionist SureQuest Solutions in Software, Richardson, Tex., 1990-91; nutritionist div. endocrinology, metabolism and hypertension, clin. studies unit rsch. nutritionist, asst. prof. dept. health promotion & gerontology U. Tex. Med. Br., Galveston, 1991—; lectr. nutrition U. Hawaii, Honolulu, 1974-75, St. Mary's U., San Antonio Coll., 1984-90; adj. faculty

Tex. Woman's U., 1994—; cons. nutritionist, 1980—; presenter in field. Contbr. papers to profl. jours. Recipient diabetes educator recognition Eli Lilly & Co., 1994. Mem. Am. Dietetic Assn., Am. Assn. Diabetes Educators (chair holistic care specialty practice group 1997—), Assn. Sch. Bus. Ofcls. Internat., Nutrition and Food Svc. Mgmt. Com., Am. Diabetes Assn. (adv. com. U. Tex. Med. Br. children's diabetes mgmt. program 1993—, mem. Galveston County diabetes support group 1991—, Disting. Svc. award 1995, mem. Galveston County Outreach adv. com., UTMB rep. 1996—), Coun. Nutritional Scis. and Metabolism (profl. sect., non-peer rev. com. 1993-94), Tex. Sch. Food Svc. Assn. (dist. bd. dirs. 1977-78), Tex. Nutrition Coun. (nominating com. 1996-97, 2d v.p. 1997-99, sports and cardiovasc. nutritionists practice group, Tex. gerontol. nutritionists practice group), Houston Area Dietetic Assn. (legis. network com. 1995—), San Antonio Sch. Food Svc. Assn. (com. chmn. 1975-89), Tex. Assn. Sch. Bus. Ofcls., Tex. Restaurant Assn., San Antonio Area Food Svc. Adminstrs. Assn. (pres. 1989-90), Assn. Profls. in Positions of Leadership in Edn., Dallas Dietetic Assn. (cons. nutritionists practice group, chmn. 1990-91), Harris County Biofeedback Soc., San Antonio Mus. Assn., Randolph C. of C., Grand Opera House, Galveston (patron), Galveston Hist. Found., Phi Kappa Phi. Avocations: perpetuation of Hawaiian culture, Nordic skiing, equestrian sports, painting, Dixieland jazz. Home: 711 Holiday Dr Apt 75 Galveston TX 77550-5579 Office: U Tex Med Br Rte 1188 301 University Blvd Galveston TX 77555-1188

CABANISS, CHARLOTTE JONES, library services director; b. Jefferson County, Ala., Apr. 13, 1951; d. Laurens Whipple Sr. and Sally Riddell Jones; m. Thomas Willard Cabaniss, Sept. 14, 1971 (div. Nov. 1998); children: Lauren Cabaniss Sellers, Amanda May, Willard Matthew. BA, Auburn U., 1973. English tchr. Rogers (Ark.) City Schs., 1984-92; libr. svcs. dir. Bay Minette (Ala.) Pub. Libr., 1994—. Dir. North Baldwin Cmty. Concerts, Inc., Bay Minette, 1995-98; mem. Baldwin County United, 1996—; chmn. bd. North Baldwin Literacy Coun., Bay Minette, 1995—. Recipient Outstanding Svc. award Area Action Women's Group, 1998. Mem. ALA, C. of C. (youth task force chair 1996-98, tourism com. chair, 1998), North Baldwin C. of C. (dir. 1996-99), Baldwin County Libr. Cooperative, Kappa Delta Pi, Phi Kappa Phi. Methodist. Avocations: reading, community volunteerism. Office: Bay Minette Pub Libr 205 W 2nd St Bay Minette AL 36507

CABANSAG, VICENTE DACANAY, JR., medical association administrator; b. Solano, Neuva Vizcaya, Philippines, Jan. 20, 1942; Arrived in U.S., June 1968.; s. Vicente Pascua and Marcelina Espero (Dacanay) C.; m. Nieves Lalas, Dec. 6, 1970; children: Sharon Rose, Karen Mae, Vincent Walter. Student, Philippine Union Coll., Baesa, Caloocan City, 1962; postgrad., U. of the East RMMMC, Quezon City, Philippines, 1968. Surg. intern Christ Hosp., Cin., 1968-69; surg. resident Bapt. Hosp., Nashville, 1969-70, St. John's Hosp., Detroit, 1970-73; pvt. practice Sturgis, Mich., 1974—; chief of surgery Sturgis Hosp., 1976-86, v.p. med. staff, 1987—; pres. med. staff, trustee Sturgis Hosp., 1988-89; cons. gen. surgery LaGrance County Hosp., Ind., 1979-85; med. dir. Southwestern Mich. Laser Clinic, Sturgis, 1987—. Fellow Am. Soc. Abdominal Surgeons, Soc. Philippine Surgeons in Am., Am. Soc. Laser Medicine and Surgery; mem. AMA, Mich. Med. Soc., St. Joseph Med. Soc., Mich. Soc. Gen. Surgeons, N.Am. Soc. of Phlebology. Avocations: fishing, hunting, bicycling. Home: 439 Liberty Rd Sturgis MI 49091-9583

CABANTING, JUDY BAYUCA, elementary educator; b. Lihue, Hawaii, Aug. 29, 1955; d. Fausto Domingo and Lucina Dizon (Bayuca) C. MA in Edn., Tex. Christian U., 1980, BS in Edn., 1977. Cert. ednl. diagnostician, Tex., cert. spl. edn. tchr. educable mentally retarded, learning disabled, Tex., Hawaii, elem. tchr. Tex., Hawaii. Spl. edn. educator Mineral Wells (Tex.) Ind. Sch. Dist., Elem. Level, 1977-79, Castleberry Ind. Sch. Dist., Fort Worth, Tex., 1979-81, Leander (Tex.) H.S., 1981-83; educator K, 1st, 4th Yello Corner Sch., Cedar Park, Tex., 1983-86; spl. edn. educator Dept. of Edn., Elsie H. Wilcox Elem. Sch., Lihue, Hawaii, 1986—. Sch. rep. Strategic Planning Com. Complex, Lihue, 1998—; treas. Bishop's Bd. of Persons with Disabilities, Honolulu, 1997—; leader, advisor, educator Holy Cross Parish Youth Ministry, Kalaheo, Hawaii, 1988—. Mem. Hawaii State Tchrs. Assn. (bd. dirs. 1998—), Delta Kappa Gamma (pres. 1998—, treas. 1994-98). Avocations: needlecraft, reading, music, travel, cooking. E-mail: judyúcabanting@notes.kiz.hi.us. Office: Elsie H Wilcox Elem Sch 4319 Hardy St Lihue HI 96766

CABBABE, EDMOND BECHIR, plastic and hand surgeon; b. Aleppo, Syria, Feb. 21, 1947; Came to U.S., 1973; s. Bechir Wahid and Samia (Hamoui) C.; m. Rima Gorab, Apr. 22, 1973; children: Nabil, Samer, Monica. BS in Physics, Chemistry Biology, Damascus U. Sch. Scis., 1967, MD, 1972. Diplomate Am. Bd. Surgery, Am Bd. Plastic Surgery, cert hand surgery. Surg. intern St. Mary of Nazareth Hosp., Chgo., 1973-74; surg. resident U. Tenn., Chattanooga, 1974-78; resident in plastic surgery St. Louis U., 1978-80, asst. prof., 1980-86, asst. clin. prof., 1986-98, assoc. clin. prof., 1998—; practice medicine specializing in plastic surgery Plastic Surgery Cons., St. Louis, 1986—, pres., 1994-95, 97—; chief plastic surgery St. Anthony Med. Ctr., St. Louis, 1990-95, De Paul Health Ctr., St. Louis, 1991—; chief plastic surgery John Cochran VA Hosp., St. Louis, 1981-86; dir. cleft palate clinic Cardinal Glennon Children's Hosp., St. Louis, 1984-86; mem. adv. com. Healthlink CompMgmt., asst. med. dir., 1997-99, vice chmn., 1999—; mem. adv. bd. to Senator Christopher Bond, chmn. small bus. com. U.S. Senate, 1995—. Editor: St. Louis Met. Medicine, 1991-93; contbr. articles to profl. jours. Mem. Arab Am. Anti Discrimination Com., Washington, 1982—. Fellow ACS; mem. AMA, Am. Soc. Maxillofacial Surgeons (socioeconomic com.), Am. Soc. Plastic and Reconstructive Surgeons (sci. program com.), Am. Assn. Hand Surgery (sci. program com.), St. Louis Arab Am. Med. Assn. (pres. 1985-86), Nat. Arab Am. Med. Assn. (pres. 1995), Nat. Arab Am. Med. Assn. Found. (chmn. 1999), Mo. Med. Assn. (treas. 1996-99, councilor 1999—), Mo. Assn. Plastic Surgeons (sec. 1995-96, treas. 1997-98, v.p. 1998—), St. Louis Met. Med. Soc. (pres. 1995), St. Louis Soc. for Med. and Sci. Edn. (trustee 1991-93, pres. 1995), St. Louis Area Soc. Plastic Surgeons (pres. 1993-95). Roman Catholic. Avocations: writing, fitness exercises, antiques, photography. Home: 1249 Takara Ct Saint Louis MO 63131-1013 Office: Plastic Surgery Cons Ltd 10004 Kennerly Rd Ste 200 Saint Louis MO 63128-2174

CABELLO, J. DAVID, lawyer; b. 1951. BS, Tex. A&M U.; JD, South Tex. Coll. Bar: Tex. 1983. Mng. atty. Compaq Computer Corp, Houston, sr. v.p., v.p., asst. gen. counsel bus. group. Mem. ABA. Office: Compaq Computer Corp PO Box 123 20555 SH 249 Houston TX 77070*

CABEY, ALFRED ARTHUR, JR., business owner, publisher; b. N.Y.C., Nov. 23, 1935; s. Alfred Arthur Sr. and Consuelo Louise (Wynns) C.; m. Loretta Arline Summers, June 1, 1957 (div. Feb. 1974); children: Dawn, Jihad, Khadijah, Lateefah; m. Sally Willie Street, May 1, 1974 (div. 1993); m. Clara H. Page, Sept. 25, 1993. Student, Kennesaw Jr. Coll., 1973, DeKalb Community Coll., 1974. Owner Holiday Limousine Svc., Atlanta, 1978—, Alfred's Photographers, Atlanta, 1978—, Holiday Pubs., Atlanta, 1988—; motivatioal speaker DeKalb County Schs., 1987—, John F. Kennedy Mid. Sch., Atlanta, 1988—, Grad. Sch. learning disabilities program Ga. State U.; conv. speaker Ga. Coun. of the Blind, 1989; cons. on adult literacy State of Ga.; mem. Study of Adult Literacy panel Ga. State U., adv. bd. Howard Schs., Inc. and Project Read, 1991; panelist Ga. Family Literacy Symposium, 1991. Author: Spirit of the Heart, 1987. Active DeKalb (Ga.) Coun. for the Arts, 1988—; mem. focus com., rep. computer tech. and instructional resource material Ga. Dept. Tech. and Adult Edn., 1990-91; advisor to trainers IBM's Principles of the Alphabet Literacy System. Portraiture, N.Y. Inst. Photography, 1965. Mem. Internat. Platform Speakers Assn., Internat. Soc. Poets, Golden Poets Soc. of the World of Poetry (award 1991). Democrat. Islam. Avocations: horticulture, writing. Home: 1747 Fayetteville Ct SE Atlanta GA 30316-2908

CABEZAS-GIL, ROSA M., lawyer; b. Santa Cruz, Spain, Oct. 26, 1959; came to U.S., 1973; d. Alejandro and Maria Rosa (Darias) Cabezas; m. Jose D. Gil, July 10, 1982 (div. May 1997); children: Debby F. Gil, Lani Angelina Gil. AA in Humanities, Gavilan Coll., Gilroy, Calif., 1978; BA in Internat. Rels., San Francisco State U., 1980; JD, St. Mary's U., 1987. Bar: Tex. 1987, U.S. Dist. Ct. (we. dist.) Tex. 1989, U.S. Ct. Appeals (5th cir.) 1989, U.S. Supreme Ct. 1991. News anchor, reporter Sta. KDTV-Channel 14, San Francisco, 1980-81; reporter, weather anchor Sta. KWEX-TV Channel 41, San Antonio, 1981-82; atty. Bexar County Legal Aid, San Antonio, 1988-91; pvt. practice San Antonio, 1991—; rep./liaison Canary Islands Govt., San Antonio, 1989-91; spkr. on probate and family law to various orgns., San Antonio. Treas. La Casa de España, San Antonio, 1984—. Named Vol. Beyond Excellence McAulife Mid. Sch., 1994; recipient Cert. of Recognition Leadership, Club Mentor Tafoya Mid. Sch., 1992-93. Fellow San Antonio Bar Found. (bd. dirs. 1996—); mem. State Bar Tex. (bd. dirs. women in the law sect. 1995—, bd. dirs. local bar com. 1994—, bd. dirs. Dist. 10C grievance com. 1996—), Tex. Women Lawyers (charter bd. dirs., founding mem. 1994—), Bexar County Women's Bar Assn. (pres. 1994), San Antonio Mex. Am. Bar Assn. (pres. 1993), Bexar County Legal Aid Assn. (bd. dirs. 1995—), St. Mary's Univ. Law Sch. Alumni Assn. (bd. dirs. 1992-97). Roman Catholic. Avocations: travel, reading. Office: 111 Soledad St Ste 1230 San Antonio TX 78205-2296

CABLE, CHARLES ALLEN, mathematician; b. Akeley, Pa., Jan. 15, 1932; s. Elton Thomas and Margaret (Fox) C.; m. Mabel Elizabeth Yeck, Dec. 19, 1955; children: Christopher A., Carolyn E. B.S., Edinboro State Coll., 1954; M.Ed., U. N.C., 1959; Ph.D. in Math., Pa. State U., 1969. Instr. math. Interlaken High Sch., N.Y., 1954-55, Tidioute High Sch., Pa., 1957-58; asst. prof. math Juniata Coll., Huntingdon, Pa., 1959-67; assoc. prof. dept. math. Allegheny Coll., Meadville, Pa., 1969-75, prof. dept. math., 1975-96, chmn. dept., 1970-90. Editorial reviewer: Math. Mag., 1975-80; assoc. editor: Focus, 1981-85. Served with AUS, 1955-57. Gen. Elec. fellow, 1958; NSF fellow, 1959, 61, 68, 73; NDEA fellow, 1969. Mem. Am. Math. Soc., Math. Assn. Am. (chmn. Allegheny Mountain chpt. 1973-75, bd. govs. 1981-84, mem. newsletter editorial com. 1981-85, com. on student chpts. 1987-93, publs. com. 1983-86), AAUP. Republican. Presbyterian. Home: 199 Jefferson St Meadville PA 16335-1108 Office: Allegheny Coll N Main St Meadville PA 16335

CABLE, JOHN FRANKLIN, lawyer; b. Hannibal, Mo., Dec. 22, 1941; s. John William and Dorothy (Stanley) C.; m. Leslie Gibbs, Apr. 5, 1965; child ren: Coventry, Tory, John. AB, Stanford U., 1964; LLB, Harvard U., 1967. Bar: Oreg. 1967. Assoc. Miller, Nash, Wiener, Hager & Carlsen, Portland, Oreg., 1967-73, ptnr., 1973—. Office: Miller Nash Wiener Hager & Carlsen 111 SW 5th Ave Fl 35 Portland OR 97204-3604

CABLE, MABEL ELIZABETH, urban planner, artist; b. Sewickley, Pa., May 23, 1935; d. Andrew Lee and Josephine (James) Yeck; m. Charles Allen Cable, Dec. 19, 1955; children: Christopher A., Carolyn E. BS, Edinboro U., 1958; M in Urban-Regional Planning, U. Pitts., 1982. Tchr. Mount Union (Pa.) Jr.-Sr. High Sch., 1964-69; graphics illustrator Crawford County Planning Commn., Meadville, Pa., 1974-79, planner, 1979-86; asst. dir. planning Crawford County Planning Commn., Meadville, 1987-94; ret., 1994. Exhibitor Foothills Art Gallery, Golden, Colo., 1986-87, Pastimes Gallery, Meadville, Pa., 1987-99. Bd. dirs. Penn Lakes coun. Girl Scouts U.S.A., Meadville, 1974-79; pres. John Brown Heritage Assn., Meadville, 1985-88; mem. adv. coun. Pa. Community Devel. Block Grant Com., Harrisburg, 1987-94, chmn., 1990-94. Mem. Am. Inst. of Cert. Planners, Am. Planning Assn., Pa. Planning Assn. Home: 199 Jefferson St Meadville PA 16335-1108

CABOT, CHARLES CODMAN, JR., lawyer; b. Boston, June 11, 1930; s. Charles C. and Ellen Phelps (White) C.; m. Dale Pirie, Jan. 3, 1953; children: Elisa C. Dooley, Charles C. III, Emily C. Chamblin. AB, Harvard U., 1952, LLB, 1957. Bar: Mass. 1957, U.S. Supreme Ct., 1961. Assoc. Herrick, Smith, Donald, Farley & Ketchum, Boston, 1957-59, 61-66; asst. gen. counsel U.S. Info. Agy., Washington, 1959-61; ptnr. Sullivan & Worcester, Boston, 1966—; bd. dirs. 6 Boston-based Merrill Lynch investment cos. Selectman Dover, Mass., 1974-80; chmn. or pres. Conservation Law Found., Dare Family Svcs., Inc., Fed. Dorchester Neighborhood Houses, Inc. and Neighborhood House Charter Sch.; dir., trustee or mem. several other human svc., civic and med. orgns. Mem. ABA, Mass. State Bar Assn., Boston Bar Assn. Office: Sullivan & Worcester 1 Post Office Sq Ste 2300 Boston MA 02109-2129

CABOT, DIANA MARIE, marketing professional, travel and transportation executive; b. Phila., July 22, 1961; d. Walter Leon Cinkowski and Doris Irene Wojtkowiak. AS, Lab. Inst. Mdse., 1981; BS, Rowan U., 1983; postgrad., Purdue U., 1999. Asst. mgr. Jean Nicole, Cherry Hill, N.J., 1981-82; asst. buyer Hamrahn, Cresskill, N.J., 1984; fashion cons. Le Meilleur, Phila., 1984-86; reservation sales agt. Amtrak, Ft. Washington, Pa., 1986-87; sales cons. Amtrak, Ctrl. N.J., 1987-94; area sales mgr. Amtrak, N.Y.C., 1994; mktg. mgr. Amtrak, Phila., 1994—. Mem. Evesham (N.J.) Twinning com., 1988; bd. dirs. Evesham Tri-Centennial com., 1988; mem. Greater Boston Conv. and Visitors Bur., Providence Conv. and Visitors Bur., N.Y. Conv. and Visitors Bur. Mem. NAFE, Am. Soc. Travel Agts., N.Y. Soc. Assn. Execs., Greater Washington Soc. Assn. Execs., Am. Bus. Assn., Am. Soc. Assn. Execs., Am. Travel Mktg. Execs., Vt. C. of C., Evesham Hist. Soc., Evesham Twinning Soc. Avocations: antique collecting, skiing, biking. Home: 23 Fairway Ct Marlton NJ 08053-3718 Office: Amtrak 30th St Sta 5S Philadelphia PA 19104

CABOT, LEWIS PICKERING, manufacturing company executive, art consultant; b. Hague, Netherlands, Sept. 6, 1937; s. John Moors and Elizabeth (Lewis) C.; m. Judith Ogden, July 1, 1960 (div. 1974); children: Elizabeth Lewis, Edward Ogden, Timothy Pickering; m. Susan Knight, July 15, 1978; children: James Eliot, Alexander Lee. AB, Harvard U., 1961, MBA, 1964. Trainee F.S. Moseley & Co., Boston, 1961-62; analyst John P. Chase, Inc., Boston, 1964-68; prin. Gardner & Preston Moss, Boston, 1968-73; chmn., pres. Artcounsel, Inc., Portland, Maine, 1973—; chmn., CEO Southworth Internat. Group, Inc., 1977—; pres. ZY-AX Realty, 1977—; chmn. Shellback Corp., 1984-93; pres., chmn. Maine Art Leasing, 1988—; bd. dirs. Material Handling Roundtable; trustee NE Pooled Common Fund, Princeton, N.J., 1972-94. Trustee, pres. Soc. Arts and Crafts, Boston, 1962-66; trustee Phila. Maritime Mus., 1963-68, Mus. Fine Arts, Boston, 1966-90, Mus. Am. Folk Art, N.Y.C., 1973-77, Maine Coll. Art, 1982-91, Portland (Maine) Mus. Art, 1994—, Storm King Art Ctr., Mountainville, N.Y., 1961-72, Maine Maritime Mus., 1997—; mem. com. Harvard U. Art Mus., Cambridge, Mass., 1982-88; bd. dirs. Maine State Music Theater, 1996—. Mem. Met. Club (Washington), Somerset Club (Boston), N.Y. Yacht Club (N.Y.C.), Portland Yacht Club. Office: Southworth Internat Group 11 Gray Rd Falmouth ME 04105-2027

CABOT, LOUIS WELLINGTON, foundation trustee; b. Boston, Aug. 3, 1921; s. Thomas Dudley and Virginia (Wellington) C.; m. Mabel Hobart Brandon, 1997. AB, Harvard U., 1943, MBA, 1948; LLD (hon.), Norwich U., 1961. With Cabot Corp., 1948-96, pres., 1960-69, chmn. bd., 1969-86; chmn. Brookings Instn., Washington, 1986-92, chmn. emeritus; chmn. Cabot Wellington, LLC; trustee Cabot Family Trust, VWC Found.; bd. dirs. Owens-Corning Fiberglas Corp., 1961-91, Wang Labs Inc., 1982-91, New Eng. Tel. & Tel., 1965-82, R.R. Donnelley & Sons Co., 1965-91; bd. dirs. Fed. Res. Bank Boston, 1970-78, chmn., 1975-78; U.S. rep. 15th Plenary Session UN Econ. Commn. for Europe, 1960; mem. bus. ethics adv. coun. Dept. Commerce, 1961-63; dir., New Eng. chmn. Nat. Alliance Businessmen, 1970-72, Boston chmn., 1968-69; chmn. Sloan Commn. on Govt. and Higher Edn., 1977-80; mem. Pres.'s Blue Ribbon Commn. on Def. Mgmt., 1985-86; mem. Def. Sec.'s Commn. on Base Realignment and Closure, 1988; dir. Nat. Coun. for U.S.-China Trade, 1978-82. Mem. bd. overseers Harvard U., 1970-76; chmn. Harvard Coll. Fund Coun., 1963-65; pres. Beverly (Mass.) Hosp., 1958-61; chmn. Com. Corp. Support Pvt. Univs., 1977-83; trustee Norwich U., 1952-77, Mus. of Sci., Boston; corp. mem. MIT; trustee Northeastern U Conservation Internat. Fellow NAS (co-chmn. Pres.'s Cir. 1992-95), Am. Acad. Arts and Scis.; mem. Bus. Coun., Coun. Fgn. Rels., Somerset Club, Comml. Club (Boston, pres. 1970-72), Harvard Club, Met. Club, N.Y. Yacht Club, Phi Beta Kappa, Sigma Xi. Office: Cabot-Wellington LLC One Post Office Sq Boston MA 02109 also: Brookings Instn 1775 Massachusetts Ave NW Washington DC 20036-2188

CABOT, STEPHEN JAY, lawyer; b. Phila., Nov. 21, 1942; s. Charles and Roslyn (Levin) C.; m. Patti D. Gilberg, June 26, 1966 (div. Dec. 1996); children: Michele, Jennifer; m. Anna M. Farmer, Dec. 21, 1996. BS in Econ., Villanova U., 1964; JD, U. Pa., 1967. Bar: Pa. 1967. Field atty. Nat. Labor Rels. Bd., Pitts., 1967-69; labor atty. Obermayer, Rebmann, et al, Phila., 1970-72, Summit Rovens, N.Y.C., Phila., 1990; sr. ptnr., chmn. labor rels. and employment law Pechner, Dorfman et al, Phila., 1973-76, Myerson & Kuhn, N.Y.C., Phila., 1987-89; sr. ptnr., chmn. labor rels. and employment law Harvey, Pennington, Herting & Renneisen, Phila., 1991—, chmn. labor rels. and employment law dept.; cons. Bottom Line Bus., N.Y.C., 1980—; mem. labor rels. com. U.S. C. of C., Washington, 1982-86; lectr. in field. Author: Labor Management Relations Act Manual: A Guide to Effective Labor Relations, 1978, Everybody Wins!, 1986, Labor Relations Guidebook: Practical Techniques for Managing Workplace Issues, 1988; contbg. editor The Developing Labor Law for the ABA, 1980—, Phila. Bus. Jour., 1995—; contbr. numerous articles to profl. publs. Mem. ABA, Fed. Bar Assn., Soc. Human Resource Mgmt., Am. Coll. Health Care Admintrs. (Educator of Yr. 1985), Pa. Bar. Assn., Phila. Bar Assn. Avocations: golf, jogging, hiking, biking, weight lifting. Office: Harvey Pennington et al 1835 Market St Fl 29 Philadelphia PA 19103-2968

CABRANES, JOSÉ ALBERTO, federal judge; b. Mayaguez, P.R., Dec. 22, 1940; s. Manuel and Carmen (López) C.; children: Jennifer Ann, Amy Alexandra; m. Kate Stith, Sept. 15, 1984; children: Alejo, Benjamin Josè. AB, Columbia U., 1961; JD, Yale U., 1965; MLitt in Internat. Law, Cambridge (Eng.) U., 1967; LLD (hon.), Colgate U., 1988, Trinity Coll., Hartford, Conn., 1990; LHD (hon.), U. New Haven, 1990; LLD (hon.), Williams Coll., 1993, Valparaiso U., 1994, Hofstra U., 1995, N.Y. Law Sch., 1995, Quinnipiac Coll., 1996, U. Conn., 1998. Bar: N.Y. 1968, D.C. 1975, U.S. Dist. Ct. Conn. 1976. Assoc. Casey, Lane & Mittendorf, N.Y.C., 1967-71; assoc. prof. law sch. Rutgers U., Newark, 1971-73; spl. counsel to gov. P.R., head Office Commonwealth P.R., Washington, 1973-75; gen. counsel Yale U., New Haven, 1975-79; judge U.S. Dist. Ct. Conn., New Haven, 1979-94, chief judge, 1992-94; judge U.S. Ct. Appeals for 2d Cir., 1994—; mem. Pres.'s Commn. White House Fellowships, 1993-96, Pres.'s Commn. Mental Health, 1977-78, U.S. del. Conf. Security and Coop. in Europe, Belgrade, 1977-78; mem. James Madison Meml. Fellowship Found., 1995—; founding mem. P.R. Legal Def. and Edn. Fund, 1972, chmn. bd., 1977-80; counsel Internat. League for Human Rights, 1971-77, v.p., 1977-80; cons. to sec. Dept. State, 1978; mem. Fed. Cts. Study Com., 1988-90; instr. history P.R. Colegio San Ignacio de Loyola, Rio Piedras, 1962; supr. in internat. law Queens' Coll., Cambridge U., 1966-67. Author: Citizenship and the American Empire, 1979; co-author: (with Kate Stith) Fear of the Judging: Sentencing Guidelines in the Federal Courts, 1998, (with Kate Stith) Fear of Judging: Sentencing Guidelines in the Federal Courts, 1998; also articles on law and internat. affairs. Trustee Yale U., 1987-99, Yale-New Haven Hosp., 1978-80, 84-87, Colgate U., 1981-90, 20th Century Fund, 1983—, Fed. Jud. Ctr., 1986-90; bd. dirs. Aspira of N.Y. (Puerto Rican edn. agy.), 1970-74, chmn., 1971-73; mem. Coun. on Fgn. Rels. Recipient life achievement award Nat. P.R. Coalition, 1987, John Jay award Columbia Coll., 1991, life achievement award student divsn. Nat. Hispanic Bar Assn., 1991; Kellett rsch. fellow Columbia Coll., Cambridge U., 1965-67. Fellow Am. Bar Found., Mex.-Am. Lawyers Assn. (spl. recognition award 1994); mem. ABA, Conn. Bar Assn., Assn. of Bar of City of N.Y., Am. Law Inst. Roman Catholic. Office: US Ct of Appeals US Courthouse 141 Church St New Haven CT 06510-2030

CABRERA, ALBERTO F., education educator; b. L.A.; married. BS in Pub. Adminstrn. and Polit. Sci., Nat. U. of Mex., 1979; diploma with honors, U. Colo., 1980; MS in Indsl. Rels., U. Wis., Madison, 1982, PhD in Edn. Adminstrn., 1987. Asst. prof. edn. and human svc. Ariz. State U., 1989-91; assoc. prof. dept. ednl. adminstrn. and policy studies U. Albany, 1991-97; assoc. prof., rsch. assoc. Ctr. for Study of Higher Edn. Pa. State U., 1997—. Editl. bd. Jour. of Higher Edn., 1993—, Rsch. in Higher Edn., 1993—, Rev. of Higher Edn.; contbr. numerous articles to profl. publs. Grantee SUNY, Albany, 1993, 95, U.S. Dept. of Edn., 1992. Mem. Am. Ednl. Rsch. Assn., Assn. for the Study of Higher Edn., Indsl. Rels. Rsch. Assn., Wis. Indsl. Rels. Alumni Assn., Assn. for Institutional Rsch. E-mail: afc4@psu.edu. Office: Ctr for the Study of Higher Edn Pa State U 403 South Allen St Ste 104 State College PA 16803

CABRERA, CARMEN, secondary education educator; b. Havana, Cuba, Dec. 31, 1948; came to U.S., 1962; d. Armando and Carmen (Gomez) C. AA, East L.A. Coll., 1970; BA, Calif. State U., L.A., 1972; MA, Calif. State U., 1975. Cert. tchr., Calif. Tchr. Sacred Heart of Mary H.S., Montebello, Calif., 1973-91, acad. dean, 1989-91; tchr., curriculum dir. Cantwell Sacred Heart of Mary H.S., Montebello, 1991—; instr. East L.A. Coll., Monterey Park, Calif., 1974-77; chairperson dept. fgn. lang. Sacred Heart of Mary H.S., 1980-91, Cantwell Sacred Heart of Mary H.S., 1991-93, 95—. Assoc. Beverly Hosp. Found., Montebello, 1990-93. Mem. ASCD, Am. Assn. Tchrs. Spanish and Portuguese (contest dir. 1987-89), Am. Coun. on Tchg. Fgn. Langs., Nat. Cath. Ednl. Assn., Phi Kappa Phi. Office: Cantwell Sacred Heart Mary 329 N Garfield Ave Montebello CA 90640-3803

CACCAMISE, ALFRED EDWARD, real estate executive; b. LeRoy, N.Y., June 9, 1919; s. Joseph Peter and Rose Marie (Petrella) C.; m. Louise Ball, July 7, 1974. Student, Officers' Candidate Sch., Camp Davis, N.C., 1943, Cen. Calif. Comml. Coll., 1946-47. Lumber co. and hardware store owner Chili, N.Y., 1956-65; motel owner DeLand, Fla., 1965-71; real estate salesman DeLand, 1974-75, real estate investments co. owner, 1972—; real estate broker Alliance Realty, DeLand, 1976—. Served with U.S. Army, 1940-46. Recipient John McCready award Community Outreach Services, DeLand, 1979, 81. Mem. Nat. Assn. Realtors, Fla. Assn. Realtors, DeLand and West Volusia Bd. Realtors (bd. dirs. 1978-79, grievance com. chmn. 1983, bldg. com. chmn. 1985-87), Alhambra Villas Home Owners' Assn. (pres. 1979-80), DeLand C. of C., DeLand Com. of 100. Democrat. Roman Catholic. Lodge: Kiwanis (Sav-a-Life chmn. 1977, membership chmn. 1979), Lions (charter). Avocations: golf, traveling, reading. Home: PO Box 241 Deland FL 32721-0241 Office: Alliance Realty 1122 N Woodland Blvd Deland FL 32720-2250

CACCAMISE, GENEVRA LOUISE BALL (MRS. ALFRED E. CACCAMISE), retired librarian; b. July 22, 1934; d. Herbert Oscar and Genevra (Green) Ball; m. Alfred E. Caccamise, July 7, 1974. BA, Stetson U., 1956; MLS, Syracuse U., 1967. Tchr. grammar sch. Sanford, Fla., 1956-57; tchr. elem. sch. Longwood, Fla., 1957-58; tchr., libr. Enterprise (Fla.) Sch., 1958-63; libr. media specialist Boston Ave. Sch., DeLand, Fla., 1963-83; head media specialist Blue Lake Sch., DeLand, 1983-87; ret., 1987. Author: Volusia County manual Instructing the Library Assistant, 1965, Echoes of Yesterday: A History of the DeLand Area Public Library, 1912-1995, 1995, A Quest for Beauty: A History of the Garden Club of DeLand, Florida, 1927-97. Charter mem. West Volusia Meml. Hosp. Aux., DeLand, 1962-81; leader Girl Scouts U.S., 1955-56; area dir. Fla. Edn. Assn., Volusia County, 1963-65; bd. dirs. Alhambra Villas Home Owners Assn., 1972-75; trustee DeLand Pub. Libr., 1977-86, sec., 1978-80, v.p., 1980-82, pres., 1982-84; v.p. Friends of DeLand Pub. Libr., 1987-88, 98—, bd. dirs., 1987—, pres., 1989-90, 95-97, newsletter editor 1992-95, 99—; charter mem. Guild of the DeLand Mus. Art, 1988—, v.p., 1990, pres., 1991-92, mem. Guild of bd. dirs., 1991-98, mus. bd. dirs., 1991-95, co-rec. sec., 1997-98; co-orgn. chmn. Friends DeLand Mus. Art, 1993. Mem. AAUW (2d v.p. chpt. 1965-67, rec. sec. 1961-65, 78-80, pres. 1980-82, parliamentarian 1982-84), Assn. Childhood Edn. (1st v.p, 1965-66, corr. sec. 1963-65), DAR (chpt. registrar 1969-80, asst. chief page Continental Congress, Washington 1962-65), Fla. Libr. Assn., Bus. and Profl. Women's Club (corr. sec. DeLand 1968-71, 2d v.p. 1969-70), Stetson U. Alumni Assn. (class chmn. for ann. fund dr. 1968), Volusia County Assn. Media in Edn. (treas. 1977), Volusia County Ret. Educators Assn. (pres. Unit II 1988-90, scholarship chmn. 1992-95), Soc. of Mayflower Descendants (lt. gov. Francis Cook Colony 1988-90), Pilgrim John Howland Soc., Colonial Dames XVII Century, Magna Carta Dames, Nat. Soc. New Eng. Women (v.p. Daytona Beach Colony 1990-91), Nat. League Am. Pen Women (corr. sec. 1996-98, pres. 1998—), Hibiscus Garden Cir. (treas. 1988-89, v.p. 1990-93, 96-97, pres. 1997-99), Nat. Soc. U.S. Daus. of 1812 (rec. sec. Peacock chpt. 1989-90), West Volusia Hist. Soc. (sec. 1996, libr. 1993—, bd. dirs.), Fla. Hist. Soc., DeLand Garden Club (corr. sec. 1993-95, editor newsletter 1993-95, v.p. 1997-99), Delta Kappa Gamma (pres. Beta Psi chpt. 1982-84). Address: PO Box 241 DeLand FL 32721-0241

CACCAMO, ALDO M., oil industry executive. BS in Civil Engring., N.J. Inst. Tech., 1960; MBA, Harvard U., 1964. With Chevron Corp., 1964—, fin. analyst, 1964; asst. area mgr. aviation sales Chevron International Oil Co., London, 1967; aviation fuels mgr. Chevron International Oil Co., San Francisco, 1971; pres. Chevron International Oil Co., 1993; mgr. pricing and evaluation Chevron U.S.A. Mktg., 1979, mktg. mgr. west ctrl. divsn., 1982; gen. mgr. eastern region supply and distbn. Chevron U.S.A. Products Co., 1986, gen. mgr. mktg. sales, 1988; v.p. pub. affairs Chevron Corp., 1996—; dir. Caltex Petroleum Corp., 1996—. Bd. dirs. Global Climate Coalition, San Francisco Friends Urban Forest, San Francisco Acad. Mem. San Francisco C. of C. (bd. dirs.). Office: Chevron Corp 575 Market St San Francisco CA 94105-2856*

CACCIATORE, S. SAMMY, JR., lawyer; b. Tampa, Fla., Aug. 2, 1942; s. Sam and Margarita C.; m. Carolyn Michels, Aug. 10, 1963; children: Elaine Michel, Sammy Michel. BA, JD, Stetson U., DeLand, Fla., 1966. Bar: Fla. 1966, U.S. Ct. Appeals (5th cir.) 1967, U.S. Supreme Ct. 1971, U.S. Ct. Appeals (11th cir.) 1981, U.S. Dist. Ct. (mid. dist. 1966) Fla. Asst. public defender 9th jud. cir. State of Fla., State of Fla., 1966; assoc. firm Orlando, Fla., 1966-67; pvt. practice Melbourne, Fla., 1967—; ptnr. Nance, Cacciatore & Hamilton, Melbourne, Fla., 1970—; mem. 5th Dist. Appellate Nomination Commn., 1979-83; mem. Fla. Med. Malpractice Adv. Com., 1982; mem. Fla. Supreme Ct. Jud. Nominating Commn., 1986-90; bd. overseers Stetson U. Coll. Law, 1995—; lectr. in field. Contbr. articles to profl. jours., chpts. to books. Trustee A. Max Brewer Meml. Law Libr., Brevard County, Fla., 1972-76, chmn., 1972-75. Mem. ABA, ATLA, Am. Law Inst., Internat. Acad. Trial Lawyers, Am. Bd. Profl. Liability Lawyers, Am. Bd. Trial Advocates, Nat. Bd. Trial Advocacy, Acad. Fla. Trial Lawyers (bd. dirs. 1970—, pres. 1984-85, Pres.'s award 1983), Internat. Acad. Trial Lawyers Assn. (adminstrn. of justice com. 1989), Fla. Bar (bd. govs. 1994-99, exec. com. 1995-99, vice chmn. advt. task force 1995-97, budget com. 1994-97, chmn. 1996, mem. exec. com. trial lawyer sect. 1975, chmn. constl. revision com. 1997—, mem. legis. com. 1995-99, chmn. 1998-99), Stetson Lawyers Assn. (1st v.p. 1992-93, pres.-elect 1994-95, pres. 1995-96), Brevard County Bar Assn. (bd. dirs., Pres.'s award 1975), Eau Gallie Yacht Club (gov., vice commodore 1981-82, commodore 1983-84). Democrat. Roman Catholic. Office: 525 N Harbor City Blvd Melbourne FL 32935-6837 *The law is a living, growing institution of our lives. Lawyers need to remember this and nurture its development as one would a child. It should grow straight and strong for the benefit of the people.*

CACCIAVILLAN, AGOSTINO, archbishop; b. Vicenza, Italy, Aug. 14, 1926. JCD, Pontifical Lateran U.; JD, State U., Rome. Ordained priest Roman Cath. Ch., 1949, archbishop, 1976. Joined diplomatic svc. Holy See, Rome, 1959; served The Philippines, Spain, Portugal in Vatican Secretariat of State, until 1976; apostolic pro-nuncio Kenya, 1976-81, India, 1981-90; joint appointment to Nepal, 1985-90, apptd. apostolic pro-nuncio to U.S., 1990—, permanent observer of the Holy See to OAS. Home and Office: 3339 Massachusetts Ave NW Washington DC 20008-3610

CACHERIS, JAMES C., federal judge; b. Pittsburgh, Pa., Mar. 30, 1933. BS in Econs., U. Pa., 1955; JD cum laude, George Washington U., 1960. Bar: D.C. 1960, Va. 1962. Asst. corp. counsel Washington, 1960-62; assoc. Miller Brown & Gildenhorn, Washington, 1962-64; pvt. practice Washington and Alexandria, Va., 1964-70; ptnr. Howard. Stevens, Lynch, Cake & Cacheris, Alexandria, Va., 1970-71; judge 19th Jud. Cir. Ct. Va., Fairfax, 1971-81; judge U.S. Dist. Ct. (ea. dist.) Va., Alexandria, 1981—, now sr. judge. Mem. Va. Bar Assn., Fairfax County Bar Assn. Office: US Dist Ct 401 Courthouse Sq Alexandria VA 22314-5704*

CACHIA, PIERRE JACQUES, Middle East languages and culture educator, researcher; b. Fayoum, Egypt, Apr. 30, 1921; came to U.S., 1975; s. François and Anna Rachel (Axler) C.; m. Phyllis Barbara Oyston, Mar. 20, 1953; children: Susan Margaret, Philip Greville, Helen Frances; m. Merle McNeill Dalziel, Sept. 26, 1992. B.A., Am. U., Cairo, 1942; Ph.D., U. Edinburgh, 1951. Mem. faculty Am. U., Cairo, 1946-48, U. Edinburgh, Scotland, 1949-75; prof. Middle East langs. and cultures Columbia U., N.Y.C., 1975-91, chmn. dept. Middle East langs. and cultures, 1980-83, prof. emeritus, 1991—. Author: Taha Husayn, 1956, Popular Egyptian Narrative Ballads, 1989, An Overview of Modern Arabic Literature, 1990, The Arch Rhetorician: A Handbook of Late Arabic Badi', 1998; co-author: History of Islamic Spain, 1965, 77, 92, 96; translator: (by Tawfiq al-Hakim) The Prison of Life, 1992, (by Yahya Haqqi) Blood and Mud, 1999; compiler: The Monitor-Arabic Grammatical Terms, 1973; editor: The Book of the Demonstration by Eutychius, Vol. 1, 1960, The Book of the Demonstration by Eutychius, Vol. 2, 1961; joint editor: Islam: Past Influence and Present Challenge, 1979; joint editor Jour. Arabic Lit., 1970-96; contbr. to encys., Orientalist jours., Great Lit. of Eastern World, African Writers. Grantee NEH, 1977; grantee Smithsonian Instn., 1979; fellow Am. Research Ctr. in Egypt, Cairo, 1982; fellow Woodrow Wilson Ctr., Washington, 1991-92. Mem. Am. Oriental Soc., Middle East Studies Assn., Am. Assn. Tchrs. Arabic, Union Européenne d'Arabisants et d'Islamisants.

CACHOLA, ROMY MUNOZ, state representative; b. Vigan, Ilocos Sur, Philippines, Mar. 8, 1938; m. Erlinda M. Cachola; children: Lyla, Earl. LLB, M.L. Quezon U., The Philippines, 1961. Mem. State Ho. of Reps., 1984—; chair com. on water and land use Ho. of Reps., past chair house tourism com., 1987-98. Bd. govs. Kalihi YMCA; bd. dirs. Susannah Wesley Cmty. Ctr.; hon. chmn. Statewide Sakada Com.; pres. St. Anthony's Sch. Bd. Recipient Pub. Servant of Yr. Community Advocate Mag., 1990, Disting. Legislator award Dem. State Legis. Leaders Assn., 1990. Mem. Filipino C. of C., Ilocos Surian Assn. of Hawaii, St. Anthony's Filipino Cath. Club, Waipahu Bus. Assn. (past. pres.), Kalakaua Lions Club, Kalihi Bus. Assn. (bd. dirs.). Office: House of Representatives State of Hawaii State Capitol Rm 402 Honolulu HI 96813

CACIOPPO, JOHN TERRANCE, psychology educator, researcher; b. Marshall, Tex., June 12, 1951; s. Cyrus Joseph and Mary Katherine (Kazimour) C.; m. Barbara Lee Andersen, May 17, 1981 (div. 1998); children: Christina Elizabeth, Anthony Cyrus. BS in Econs., U. Mo., Columbia, 1973; MA in Psychology, Ohio State U., 1975, PhD in Psychology, 1977. Asst. prof. psychology U. Notre Dame (Ind.), 1977-79; asst. prof. psychology U. Iowa, Iowa City, 1979-81, assoc. prof., 1981-85, prof. psychology, 1985-89; prof. psychology Ohio State U., 1989-98, Univ. chaired prof. psychology, 1998—; prof. U. Chgo., 1999—; vis. faculty U. Hawaii, 1990; vis. faculty U. Chgo., 1998—; bd. dirs. Ohio State U. Rsch. Found., 1993-98, NIMH Social Psychology tng. grant dir., 1993—. Author, editor 6 books; editor Psychophysiology, 1994-97; assoc. and cons. editor various profl. jours.; contbr. more than 200 articles to profl. jours. Mem. John D. and Catherine T. MacArthur Found. Network on Mid-Body Integrations, 1995-98. Recipient Early Career Contbn. award Psychophysiology, 1981, Troland Rsch. award NAS, 1989, Disting. Scholar award Ohio State U., 1996; NSF grantee, 1979&. Mem. AMA, APA (past pres. 2 divsns.), Am. Psychol. Soc., Acad. Behavioral Medicine Rsch., Internat. Orgn. Psychophysiology; mem. Soc. Exptl. Social Psychology, Soc. Psychophysiol. Rsch. (bd. dirs. 1985-88, officer 1991-94, pres. 1992-93), Soc. Personality and Social Psychology (pres. 1995), Sigma Xi (nat. lectr. 1996-98). Office: U Chgo Dept Psychology Ohio State U Dept Psychology Chicago IL 60637

CADDELL, JOHN A., lawyer; b. Tuscumbia, Ala., Apr. 23, 1910; s. Thomas Arthur and Florence Lee (Huff) C.; m. Lucy Bowen Harris, Sept. 1, 1935; children—Thomas A., Lucinda Lee, Henry Harris and John A. (twins). AB, U. Ala., 1931, LLB, 1933, LLD (hon.), 1982. Bar: Ala. bar 1933. Since practiced in Decatur.; Sec., dir. Southeastern Metals Co., Inc., Birmingham, 1946-68; chmn. bd. First Nat. Bank Decatur, 1976-81; City atty., Decatur, 1936-59; counsel com. investigating campaign expenditures U.S. Ho. of Reps., 1944; bd. commrs. Ala. State Bar, 1939-54, Jud. Council Ala., 1946-58; mem. bd. Bar Examiners Ala., 1949, 50. Mem. Ala. Democratic Exec. Com., 1938-50; Trustee U. Ala., 1954-79, also pres. pro tem, 1974-78. Fellow Am. Coll. Trust and Estate Counsel, Am. Coll. Trial Lawyers, Am. Bar Found.; mem. ABA, Ala. Bar Assn. (pres. 1951-52), Morgan County Bar Assn., U. Ala. Alumni Assn. (pres. 1953), Decatur C. of C. (pres. 1943-44), Ala. Acad. Honor, Pi Kappa Alpha, Omicron Delta Kappa, Phi Delta Phi. Democrat (mem. Ala. exec. com. 1938-50). Presbyn. (elder). Clubs: Athletic, U. Alabama, Decatur Kiwanis (pres. 1939). Home: PO Box 2688 Decatur AL 35602-2688 Office: 214 Johnston St SE Decatur AL 35601-2516

CADDELL, JOHN ALLEN, construction and engineering company executive; b. Montgomery, Ala., Mar. 13, 1930; s. Martin Lesser and Vivian (Deel) C.; m. Lowell Joyce Kirby, Sept. 8, 1951; children: Cathy, Michael, John Kirby, Jeffery, Christopher. B.S., Ga. Inst. Tech., 1952; grad., U.S. Air Force Officer Engr. Sch., 1953; advanced mgmt. program, Harvard U., 1968; postgrad. in basic advanced mgmt., U. Va., 1959. Estimator Blount Bros. Constrn. Co., 1952-55, chief estimator, 1955-61; project mgr. Blount Bros. Corp., Cape Canaveral, Fla., 1961-63, v.p., mgr. constrn. div., 1963-69, pres., chief exec. officer, 1969-78; pres. and chief exec. officer Blount Internat., Ltd., Montgomery, 1978-80, chmn. bd. and chief exec. officer, 1980-83; pres. Caddell Constrn. Co., Montgomery, 1983—, now chmn. CEO; dir. Delchamps, Inc. Bd. dirs. YMCA, Montgomery, Bapt. Med. Center, Bapt. Found. Ala. Served with USAF, 1952-54. Mem. Associated Gen. Contractors Am., Moles, Beavers. Clubs: Montgomery Country, Capital City. Office: Caddell Constrn Co 2700 Lagoon Park Dr Montgomery AL 36109-1100*

CADDEO, MARIA ELIZABETH, critical care nurse; b. San Pedro, Calif., Oct. 26, 1967; d. Frank Paul Sr. and Lois Lee (Johnson) Caddeo. BSN, U. Md., 1989. Primary nurse I R.A. Cowley Shock Trauma Ctr., Balt., 1989—; staff nurse, coord. labor & delivery nursing edn. 67th CSH, Würzburg, Germany, 1992; staff nurse, unit orientation coord. North Arundel Hosp., 1995; dir. staff devel. and infection control Genesis Eldercare, Spa Creek, Annapolis, Md., 1996—; lectr. SNIT (Student Nurse in Tng.) program, trauma theory classes Md. Inst. for Emergency Med. Svcs. Sys.; instr. trauma prevention for high-risk adolescents; cert. instr. geriatric nurse's aide courses.

CADDIGAN, MARY, health facility administrator; b. N.Y.C., June 25, 1943; d. John S. and Loretta (Zabicki) Budzinski; m. John F. Caddigan II, Sept. 5, 1964; children: Lisa Marie, Jacqueline Ann. Diploma, St. Clare's Hosp. Sch., N.Y.C., 1963; student, William Patterson Coll. RN, N.J.; Certified Rehab. RN. Nursing adminstr. Gen. Hosp., Passaic, N.J., head nurse, CCU; cardiac nurse practitioner pvt. office, Rutherford, N.J.; staff nurse Kessler Rehab. Hosp., Chester, N.J., 1990-91, unit coord., 1991—; pastoral minister in hospice program. Recipient recognition Passaic County Heart Assn., 1990. Home: 19 Rhone Rd Hopatcong NJ 07843-1822

CADDY, EDMUND H.H., JR., architect; b. N.Y.C., Apr. 17, 1928; s. Edmund Harrington Homer and Glenna Corinne (Garratt) C.; m. Mary Audrey Ortiz, Dec. 22, 1951; children—Edmund Harrington Homer III, Mary Elizabeth. B.A., Princeton, 1952, M.F.A. (grad. sch. fellow), 1955. With Louis E. Jallade, N.Y.C., 1949-53, Eggers & Higgins, N.Y.C., 1953-55; dir. design Dalton-Dalton Assocs., Cleve., 1955-60; assoc. Raymond & Rado, N.Y.C., 1960-68; gen. ptnr. Raymond & Rado and Ptnrs., N.Y.C., 1968-72, Raymond, Rado, Caddy & Bonington, P.C., N.Y.C., 1972-80; pres. Raymond, Rado, Caddy & Bonington, P.C., 1980-83; project mgr. Robinson, Mills & Williams, San Francisco, 1983-87, McCue, Boone, Tomsick, San Francisco, 1987-88, O'Brien-Kreitzberg, San Francisco, 1988-90; Sverdrup Corp., 1990-94; archtl. design cons., 1994—; apptd. by Pres. John F. Kennedy to adv. com. arts John F. Kennedy Ctr. Performing Arts, 1963-70; mem. archtl. adv. commn. N.Y.C. C.C., CUNY, 1979-83. Works include Suburban Hosp, Cleve., 1957, J.M. Smucker Co, Salinas, Cal., 1957, Brookpark (Ohio) City Hall, 1959; Cleve. Transit System addition, 1959, adminstrn. bldg., Met. Water Treatment System, Saigon, 1960, Franklin D. Roosevelt High Sch, N.Y.C., 1963, Crown Heights Intermediate Sch, N.Y.C., 1966, engring. complex, Stony Brook Campus, State U. N.Y., 1970, Sibley's dept. stores, Syracuse, N.Y., 1973, Rochester Downtown Devel. Study, 1975, R.H. Macy & Co. dept. store, Stamford, Conn., 1979; project mgr. Main Postal Facility, San Francisco, 1985, Univ. Ctr., U. Calif., Irvine, 1987, Santa Clara (Calif.) County CourtHouse, Ft. Mojave Resort Devel., 1991-94. Pres. bd. trustees Montclair (N.J.) Cmty. Hosp., 1973-80. Served with USMC, 1946-48, USMCR, 1948-53. Mem. AIA, NCARB, Calif., N.J., Ohio, N.Y. State architects Assns., Tower Club (Princeton), Racquet and Tennis Club (N.Y.C.). Home: 1999 Baldwin Way Bolingbrook IL 60490-6551

CADDY, MICHAEL DOUGLAS, lawyer; b. Long Beach, Calif., Mar. 23, 1938; s. Frank Edward and Tabitha (Miles) C.; BS in Fgn. Svc., Georgetown U., 1960; JD, NYU, 1966. Bar: D.C. 1970, Tex. 1979. Practice in Washington and Tex.; exec. dir. Com. on Public Affairs, McGraw-Edison Co., N.Y.C., 1960-61; asst. to lt. gov. N.Y., 1962-65; asst. to exec. v.p. NAM, N.Y.C., 1966-67; Washington liaison Gen. Foods Corp., 1968-70; asso. Gall, Lane, Powell & Kilcullen, 1970-74; legis. counsel Nat. Assn. Realtors, Washington, 1975-76; atty. Office Tex. Sec. of State, 1980-81. Mem. Republican County Com., N.Y.C., 1965-66; nat. dir. Young Ams. for Freedom, 1960-62. Scholar, Intercollegiate Studies Inst., 1957-59. Mem. ABA, ATLA, ACLU, D.C. Bar, Fed. Bar Assn., Tex. Bar, Houston Bar Assn., Houston Bar Assn. for Human Rights, Federalist Soc., Am. Conservative Union, Am. Judicature Soc., Assn. of Former Intelligence Officers, Am. Econ. Assn., Am. Acad. Polit. and Social Sci., Internat. Platform Assn., Nat. Coun. Crime and Delinquency, Supreme Ct. Hist. Soc., People for the Am. Way, Nat. Trust for Historic Preservation. Author: The Hundred Million Dollar Payoff, 1974; How They Rig Our Elections, 1975; Understanding Insurance, 1984; Legislative Trends in Insurance Regulation, 1985; Exploring America's Future, 1987. Home: 745 W Creekside Dr Houston TX 77024-3234

CADEGAN, JAIME B., educational administrator; b. Austintown, Ohio, Apr. 9, 1962; m. Liam J. Cadegan, June 22, 1985; children: Shannon Elyse, Emily Sarah. BFA cum laude, Bowling Green State U., 1984. Asst. to dir. Ctr. for Tech. and Policy, Boston U., 1985-86; mktg. asst. Haley & Aldrich, Inc., Cambridge, Mass., 1986-87; writer, editor, coms. cons. Owens-Corning Fiberglas Corp., Toledo, Ohio, 1987-91; pvt. practice graphic design, 1992—; mktg. and pub. coord. Nichols Edn. Corp., Perrysburg, Ohio, 1993-95; devel. dir. The Montessori Sch. of Bowling Green, Ohio, 1995-99. One woman show Mileti Alumni Ctr., Bowling Green (Ohio) State U., 1984. Recipient Award of Merit Toledo Chpt. Women in Comm., 1988. Office: Montessori Sch 630 S Maple St Bowling Green OH 43402-3700

CADELLO, JAMES PETER, philosopher, educator; b. Westfield, Mass., June 29, 1958; s. Peter Michael and Madelyn (Jeglewicz) C. BA, Westfield State Coll., 1982; MA, Purdue U., 1984, PhD, 1990. Vis. prof. Purdue U.-Calumet, Hammond, Ind., 1988-89; asst. prof. Regis U., Denver, 1989-95; assoc. prof. philosophy Ctrl. Wash. U., Ellensburg, 1995—; mem. summer seminar for coll. tchrs. NEH, 1991; sec. Philosophy in Context, 1994—, Social Philosophy Rsch. Inst., 1987—. Mng. editor Social Philosophy Rsch. Inst. book series, 1990—; contbr. articles to profl. publs. Grantee Ctrl. Wash. U., 1996. Mem. Am. Philos. Assn., N.Am. Soc. Social Philosophy, N.Am. Nietzsche Soc., Am. Assn. Philosophy Tchrs. (program chair 1994-96). Home: 600 S Ruby St Trlr 20 Ellensburg WA 98926-3790 Office: Ctrl Wash U Dept Philosophy Ellensburg WA 98926-7555

CADEN, JOHN L., federal judge; b. 1943. BS, St. Peter's Coll., 1964; LLB, Bklyn. law Sch., 1967; LLM, NYU, 1973. Bar: N.Y. Asst. U.S. atty. criminal divsn. for ea. dist. N.Y., U.S. Dept. Justice, Bklyn., 1972-77; magistrate judge for ea. dist. N.Y. U.S. Magistrate Ct., Bklyn., 1977—. Capt. JAGC, U.S. Army, 1968-72; officer USAR, 1973—. Decorated Bronze Star with oak leaf cluster. Office: 225 Cadman Plz E Brooklyn NY 11201-1818

CADENHEAD, ALFRED PAUL, lawyer; b. LaGrange, Ga., Oct. 14, 1926; s. Roy E. and Omie (Bishop) C.; m. Sara Davenport, Oct. 14, 1945; children: Steven Paul, David James. Jr. coll. certificate, W. Ga. Coll., 1944; LL.B., Emory U., 1949. Bar: Ga. 1949. Sr. counsel, ptnr. Hurt, Richardson, Garner, Todd & Cadenhead, Atlanta; with Hurt, Richardson, 1977-92; now of counsel Fellows, Johnson & La Briola, Atlanta, 1993—; pres. Atlanta Legal Aid Soc., 1958. Pres. Met. Atlanta Mental Health Assn., 1964-65, Ga. Assn. Mental Health, 1968; past trustee Queens Coll., Charlotte, N.C. Served with paratroops U.S. Army, 1944-46. Recipient West Ga. Coll. Disting. Svc.award, 1993, Emory U. Law Sch. Disting. Alumnus award, 1996, Ben F. Johnson Pub. Svc. award Ga. State U., 1999. Fellow ABA, Am. Acad. Matrimonial Lawyers, Am. Coll. Trial Lawyers, Internat Soc. Barristers; mem. State Bar Ga. (past bd. govs.), Atlanta Bar Assn. (pres. 1970-71, Charles E. Watkins award for disting. and sustained svc. 1992), Atlanta Estate Planning Coun. (pres. 1976). Presbyterian. Home: 6305 Riverside Dr NW Atlanta GA 30328-3646 Office: South Tower Peachtre Ctr Ste 2300 225 Peachtree St NE Atlanta GA 30303-1731

CADES, STEWART RUSSELL, lawyer, communications company executive; b. Phila., Jan. 16, 1942; s. Ralph E. and Lillian G. (Mann) C. BS in Econs., U. Pa., 1964, LLB, 1967; MEd, Temple U., 1971. Bar: Pa. 1971. Sole practice Phila. and Bala-Cynwyd, Pa., 1971—; chmn. bd. Porcupine Communications Co., Phila., 1971—; pres. Nairn U.S. Holdings divsn. Stewart Nairn Group P.L.C., 1980-86; bd. dirs. Cloche Assocs., Inc., Andrews & Leith, Ltd., ACM Worldwide, Ltd.; mng. dir. Overseas Strategic Consulting; chmn. bd. dirs. Towne Met., Inc., 1985-92, pres. Election judge Montgomery County, Pa., 1975-77; ct. vol. probation dept. Ct. Common Pleas of Phila. County; vice chmn. Montgomery County Planning Commn., 1980-95; bd. dirs. pension fund, trustee, mem. pension com., chmn. real estate com. Southeastern Pa. Transp. Authority, 1991-97; adv. bd. City of Phila. Airport; sec., sch. chmn. alumni undergrad. admissions U. Pa., alumni pres. Class of '64, 1975-90; bd. dirs. Friends of Phila. Mus. Art, 1985-91, Juvenile Law Ctr., Septa Transit Mus.; trustee Pa. Acad. Fine Arts; v.p. Fabric Workshop. Mem. ABA, Pa. Bar Assn., Phila. Bar Assn., Montgomery County Bar Assn., Print Club (bd. govs.), Racquet Club Phila. Office: 191 Presidential Blvd Bala Cynwyd PA 19004-1207

CADGE, WILLIAM FLEMING, gallery owner, photographer; b. Phila., May 5, 1924; s. Arthur and Janet (Fleming) C.; m. Anne Marie English, Feb. 5, 1949; children: Stephen Anthony, Jeffrey John, Catherine Anne. Student, Phila. Coll. Art, 1945-49. Free-lance designer Phila., 1949-50; asst. art dir. Eve. Bull., Phila., 1950-52, Woman's Home Companion, 1952-56; art dir. Doyle, Dane & Bernbach (advt.), N.Y.C., 1956-57; asso. art dir. McCall's mag., 1959-61; art dir. Redbook mag., 1961-75; owner, mgr. Jeff and Bill Cadge Photography; owner Pinwheel Studio and Gallery, Cape May, N.J., 1989—; cons. art dir. Think Mag. Photog. covers nat. and European mags., also editorial and advt. illustration. Served with RAF, 1941-43; with USAAF, 1943-45. Recipient 2 gold medals, 8 award distinctive merit Art Director's Club N.Y.; 1 gold medal; 1 award distinctive merit Art Director's Club Phila.; 1 award excellence Art Director's Club N.J.; also N.J. 2 awards of excellence.; 1 award outstanding achievement for 1966 Soc. Illustrators; 1 gold medal, 1971, 72; 5 awards excellence Type Director's Club N.Y.; 1 award excellence for 3 consecutive issues of Redbook in 1966, 1969; 1 award excellence for 3 consecutive issues of Redbook in 1966 Soc. Publ. Designers; also 1 award excellence best typography in 1966, and award distinctive merit for 3 consecutive issues Redbook, 1970; awards excellence CA Mag. Show, 1967, 68; awards excellence Soc. Publ. Designers, 1968; awards excellence Soc. Illustrators, 1968, 1977; gold medal Art Dirs. Club Show, 1977. Mem. Soc. Illustrators, Art Dirs. Club N.Y. (exec. bd. 1966-68). Home and Office: 222 N Broadway West Cape May NJ 08204

CADIEUX, CHESTER, gas industry executive; b. 1932. BBA, U. Okla., 1954. Salesman Maneke-Kinzie Printing Co., Tulsa, Okla., 1954-58; CEO QuikTrip, Tulsa, Okla., 1958—. Office: QuikTrip Corp PO Box 3475 Tulsa OK 74101-3475*

CADIEUX, DENNIS BARRY, religious organization administrator, minister; b. Chicago Heights, Ill., Jan. 2, 1936; s. Lawrence C. and Leone E. (Parks) C.; m. Louise E. Mehlhorn, Oct. 26, 1955 (dec. July 1996); children: Catherine, Jennifer, Michael, Joshua; m. Bette Buras, Aug. 29, 1998. Grad. high sch., Aurora, Ill. Ordained to ministry Evangelistic Messengers Assn., 1977; ministerial lic. for pastoral office Evang. Covenant Ch., 1989—. Regional dir. Christian Action Coun., Chgo., 1984—; min. Jesus People USA Covenant Ch., Chgo., 1975—, also bd. dirs. Editor newsletters Action/Alert, 1984, View From the Towers, 1990. Sec. Cornerstone Community Outreach, Chgo., 1990—; tchr., adminstr. Cornerstone Festival, Chgo., 1985—; mem. adv. bd. Harry S. Truman Coll., Chgo., 1985-91; em. Task Force Against Displacement of Poor, Chgo., 1987—; active Aldermn's Community Svc., Chgo.; activities dir. Sr. Citizens at Friendly Towers. Commd. Ky. Col., Gov. Paul E. Patton, 1997—. Mem. Am. Assn. Christian Counselors (charter), Northside Evang. Fellowship (exec. bd. 1980—), Fellowship of Christian Peace Officers (charter), Kiwanis (chair spiritual aims Lake View club, bd. dirs. 1985-91). Home and Office: Ste 436 920 W Wilson Ave Chicago IL 60640-5707

CADIEUX, ROGER JOSEPH, physician, mental health care executive; b. Bay Shore, N.Y., Feb. 7, 1945; m. Kathryn Cadieux; children: Kevin, Kristin. BS, Northwestern State U., 1973; MD, La. State U., 1977. Cert. geriatric psychiatrist, RN anesthetist. Intern, then resident in psychiatry Coll. Medicine Pa. State U., Hershey, 1977-81, psychogeriatric fellow, instr. Coll. Medicine Milton S. Hershey Med. ctr., 1980-81, asst. prof. dept. psychiatry, 1981-93; assoc. prof. psychiatry, 1993—; dir. geriatric assessment program Pa. State U. Coll. Medicine, 1992-98; psychiat. cons. Jewish Home of Harrisburg, 1985—, Homeland Ctr. of Harrisburg, 1993—; program dir. Pa. Dept. Aging, 1986—, physician cons., 1987—; pres. Commonwealth Affiliates, P.C., 1992—. Contbr. articles to profl. jours. Fellow Am. Bd. Psychiatry and Neurology (diplomate); mem. Am. Psychiat. Assn., Am. Geriatric Soc., Am. Assn. for Geriatric Psychiatry, Acad. Sleep Disorders Medicine, Alpha Omega Alpha. Office: 2215 Forest Hills Dr Harrisburg PA 17112-1099

CADIGAN, ELISE, social worker; b. Topeka, Mar. 8, 1947; d. Grattan C. Huckabee and Virginia (Ross) Huckabee Specht; m. Glenn Koski, 1989; children: Kent, Matthew, Drew. BS, Washburn U., 1972; MSW, Kans. U., 1977. Bd. cert. diplomate clin. social work; lic. clin. social worker, Ill. Adj. prof. social work Ottawa (Kans.) U., 1977-78; social worker Lawrence (Kans.) Sch. Dist., 1978-79, Harlem Sch. Dist., Loves Park, Ill., 1979-82; pvt. practice Glenwood Evaluation and Treatment Ctr., Rockford, Ill., 1980—; mgr. adolescent svcs. Swedish Am. Hosp., Rockford, 1984-88; adj. faculty U. Ill., Rockford. Bd. dirs. Big Bros./Big Sisters, Rockford, 1980-85, Rock River Valley United Way, 1997—; bd. dirs. Children's Devel. Ctr., 1986-94, pres., 1992-93; mem. bd. counselors Rockford Coll.; sr. warden St. Anskars Episcopalian Ch., 1996-98. Mem. NASW (dist. chair 1983-85, Social Worker of Yr. award 1985), Rockford Area Substance Abuse Coun. (Cmty. Vol. of Yr. award 1988), Rockford Jr. League, Rockford Womans Club (dept. pres. 1997-98), Rotary (bd. dirs. Rockford club 1994-96, 97—, pres. 1999—), Phi Delta Kappa. Avocations: downhill skiing, travel. Fax: 815-968-4656. Office: Glenwood Ctr 2823 Glenwood Ave Rockford IL 61101-3599

CADLE, FARRIS WILLIAM, land title abstractor; b. Millen, Ga., Aug. 12, 1952; s. William Eden and Johnnie Lorys (Overstreet) C. BS in forest resources, Univ. Ga., 1974; MA in geography, San Diego State Univ., 1997. Land surveyor's asst. Ga. Land Surveying Co., Atlanta, 1975, Delta Engrs. & Surveyors, Smyrna, Ga., 1976-78, Donaldson Surveys, Metter, Ga., 1979-81; land surveyor Helmly & Assocs., Savannah, Ga., 1982-89; title abstractor Belford Land Title Co., Savannah, Ga., 1990-91, 1996—. Author: Georgia Land Surveying History and Law, 1991. Founding mem., bd. dirs. Clean Coast, Savannah, 1990-91. Avocations: legal history, environmental activities. E-mail: fcadle@sysconn.com. Home: 21 Colonial Trl #10 Garden City GA 31408 Office: Belford Land Title Co PO Box 22455 Savannah GA 31403-2455

CADMAN, EDWIN CLARENCE, health facility administrator, medical educator; b. Bandon, Oreg., May 14, 1945; s. Edwin Herbert Cadman and Gloria (Ranellie) Wilson; m. Mary Ellen Ross, June 22, 1968; children: Tim, Kevin, Brian. AB, Stanford U., 1967; MD, U. Oreg., 1971. Intern in internal medicine Stanford (Calif.) U. Hosp., 1971-74; fellow in oncology Yale U., New Haven, 1974-76, asst. prof. medicine, 1976-79, assoc. prof. medicine, 1979-83, prof., chmn. medicine, 1987-94, prof., 1994—; prof. medicine, dir. Cancer Rsch. Inst. U. Calif., San Francisco, 1983-87, vice chmn. dept. medicine, 1985-87; chief of staff, sr. v.p. med. affairs Yale New Haven Hosp., 1994—; pror. Am. Cancer Soc., 1985-87. Contbr. over 300 articles to profl. jours. Basketball coach Novato (Calif.) Park and Recreation, 1985. Capt. USNG, 1972-78. Recipient Gold Headed Cane award U. Oreg. Med. Sch., 1971. Fellow AAAS, ACP; mem. AFCR (pres. 1984-86), ASCI, AAP, ASCO/AACR, AOA. Avocations: running, fishing, reading. Home: 41 Ridgewood Ter North Haven CT 06473-1256 Office: Yale New Haven Hosp 1063CB 20 York St New Haven CT 06511-8900

CADMAN, WILSON KENNEDY, retired utility company executive; b. Wichita, Kans., Sept. 7, 1927; s. Wilson K. and Ethel Louise (Wheeler) C.; m. Mary Roslyn Rowley, Nov. 22, 1950; children: Elizabeth Louise, Cadman Jarrett, Robert Wilson. AB, Wichita State U., 1951, postgrad., 1953; postgrad., Okla. State U., 1965. With Kans. Gas & Electric Co., Wichita, 1951-92, mgr. Wichita divsn., 1967-70, v.p., 1970-79, pres., 1979-92, chief exec. officer, 1981-92, also chmn. bd. dirs.; ret., 1992; sr. advisor Barr Devlin & Assocs. Investment Bankers, N.Y.C.; bd. dirs. Bank IV of Wichita, El Paso (Tex.) Electric Co., Columbia Energy Group, Herndon, Va., Clark/Bardes Inc., Dallas. Bd. govs. Wichita State U. Endowment Assn.; bd. dirs. Wichita State U. Athletic Scholarship Orgn.; mem. Gov.'s Task Force on High Tech. Devel., Mayor's Econ. Adv. Council, Kans. Water Resources Council. Served with USN, 1945-46. Mem. Edison Electric Inst., Wichita Area Devel. (exec. com.), Wichita State U. Endowment Assn., Wichita Club, Wichita Country Club, Univ. Club, Kiwanis, Phi Lambda Psi. Home: The Cloisters 8905 E Douglas Wichita KS 67207 also: PO Box 160-583 33 Hidden Village Big Sky MT 59716

CADMUS, PAUL, artist, etcher; b. N.Y.C., Dec. 17, 1904; s. Egbert and Maria (Latasa) C. Student, N.A.D., N.Y.C., 1919-26, Art Students League of N.Y., 1926-27; DFA (hon.), SUNY, Oswego, 1994. Advt. work, 1928-31; lived and painted in Europe, 1931-33. First one-man show, N.Y.C., 1937; represented in Met. Mus. Art, Whitney Mus. Am. Art, Library of Congress, Chgo. Art Inst., Balt. Mus., N.Y. Pub. Library, Seattle Mus., Milw. Mus., Sara Roby Found., Smithsonian Inst.; works include Coney Island, 1934, Gilding the Acrobats, 1935, Sailors and Floosies, 1938, Hinky Dinky Parley Voo, 1939, The Seven Deadly Sins, 1945-49, Bar Italia, 1952-55, Subway Symphony, 1975-76; subject of books: Paul Cadmus/Prints and Drawings, 1922-67, Paul Cadmus Yesterday and Today (by Philip Eliasoph), 1981, Paul Cadmus (Lincoln Kirstein), 1984, rev. edit., 1992, The Drawings of Paul Cadmus, 1989, The Photographs of Paul Cadmus, Margaret French and Jared French, 1992; subject of film Paul Cadmus: Enfant Terrible at 80 (David Sutherland), 1984. Recipient Purchase award Norfolk Mus. Arts and Scis., 1964, Benjamin West Clinedinst Meml. medal Artist's Fellowship, 1989, Gerard Manley Hopkins award for visual arts Fairfield U., 1990, Salmagundi Honor award, 1995; grantee Am. Acad. and Isnt. Arts and Letters, 1961. Mem. Nat. Acad. (academician 1980), Soc. Am. Graphic Artists, Am. Acad. of Arts and Letters. Home: PO Box 1255 Weston CT 06883-0255

CADNEY, CAROLYN, secondary education educator; b. Port Gibson, Miss., Jan. 27, 1952; d. Norman and Mary Viola (Rogers) C. BS, Alcorn State U., 1972; MEd, U. So. Miss., 1978. Cert. adult edn. Tchr. Fernwood Jr. H.S., Biloxi, Miss., 1972-73, Nichols Jr. H.S., Biloxi, Miss., 1973-80, Biloxi H.S., Miss., 1980—; adj. instr. Jefferson Davis Jr. Coll. Miss. Gulf Coast C.C., Biloxi, 1988—; tchr. adv. com. Southeastern Regional Vision for Edn., Greensboro, N.C., 1993—. Recipient Enhancement award Biloxi Bay Chamber, Miss., 1995; named Outstanding Educator Biloxi Rotary Club, Miss., 1993, Miss. State Tchr. of Yr. State of Miss., 1994, Outstanding Woman of Yr. New Horizons, Gulfport, Miss., 1995. Mem. Miss. Profl. Educator (outstanding mem. award 1994), Delta Sigma Theta (v.p. 1990-92, woman of yr. 1993). Baptist. Avocation: tennis. Office: Biloxi High Sch 1424 Father Ryan Ave Biloxi MS 39530-3598*

CADORETTE, LISA ROBERTS, medical, surgical nurse; b. Johnson City, N.Y., June 12, 1966; d. John Lawrence and Dorothy Ellen (Ace) Roberts; m. Jeffrey Cadorette, May 31,1991; children: Jessica Renee, Jacqueline Elyse, Joshua Ryan. BSN magna cum laude, Neumann Coll., 1989. RN, Pa.; cert. ACLS Am. Heart Assn. Commd. lt. USAF Nurse Corps., 1989; staff nurse USAF Nurse Corps., Andrews AFB, Md., 1989-90, Dover AFB, Del., 1990-91; asst. to chair divsn. nursing and health scis. Neumann Coll., Aston, Pa., 1992-99; vol. emergency med. technician Lima (Pa.) Fire Co., 1988-91, Media (Pa.) Fire Co., 1988-91. Mem. Nightingale Soc., Sigma Theta Tau (pres. Delta Tau chpt. 1997-99), Delta Epsilon Sigma. Avocations: piano, singing, volleyball, gardening, needlework. Office: Neumann Coll Divsn Nursing and Hlth Scis Aston PA 19014

CADY, EDWIN HARRISON, English language educator, author; b. Old Tappan, N.J., Nov. 9, 1917; s. Edwin Laird and Ethel Sprague (Harrison) C.; m. Norma Woodard, Aug. 31, 1939; children: Frances (Mrs. Edward Hitchcock), Elizabeth (Mrs. Larry Saler). AB, Ohio Wesleyan U., 1939, LittD (hon.), 1964; MA, U. Cin., 1940; PhD, U. Wis., 1943; LittD (hon.), Oklahoma City U., 1967; LHD (hon.), Georgetown U., 1989. Instr. English U. Wis., 1945, Ohio State U., 1946; from asst. prof. to prof. Syracuse U., 1946-59; Rudy prof. English Ind. U., 1959-73; prof. English Duke U., 1973-87, Andrew W. Mellon prof. humanities, 1975-87, prof. emeritus, 1987—; vis. prof. Am. lit., Uppsala and Stockholm, Sweden, 1951-52. Author: The Gentleman in America, 1949, The Road to Realism: The Early Years, 1837-1885, of William Dean Howells, 1956, The Realist at War: The Mature Years, 1885-1920, of William Dean Howells, 1958, Stephen Crane, 1962, rev. edit., 1980, John Woolman: The Mind of the Quaker Saint, 1965, The Light of Common Day, 1971, The Big Game: College Sports and American Life, 1979, Young Howells and John Brown, 1985. Editor: (with H.H. Clark) Whittier on Writers and Writing, 1950, Literature of the Early Republic, 1950, rev. edit, 1969, (with L. Ahnebrink) An Anthology of American Literature, 1953, (with L.G. Wells) Stephen Crane's Love Letters to Nellie Crouse, 1954, (with F.J. Hoffman and R.H. Pearce) The Growth of American Literature, 1956, W.D. Howells, The Rise of Silas Lapham, 1957, Corwin K. Linson, My Stephen Crane, 1958, (with D.L. Frazier) The War of the Critics Over William Dean Howells, 1962, W.D. Howells, The Shadow of a Dream and An Imperative Duty, 1962, William Cooper Howells, Recollections of Life in Ohio, 1963, The American Poets, 1800-1900, 1966, (with D.F. Hiatt) W.D. Howells, Literary Friends and Acquaintance, 1968, Nathaniel Hawthorne, The Scarlet Letter, 1969, W.D. Howells as Critic, 1973, (with C. Anderson and L. Budd) Toward a New American Literary History: Essays in Honor of Arlin Turner, 1980, (with N.W. Cady) Critical Essays on W.D. Howells, 1866-1920, 1983, A Modern Instance, 1984; (with Louis J. Budd) On Whitman: The Best from American Literature, On Mark Twain: The Best from American Literature, 1987, On Emerson: The Best from American Literature, On Melville: The Best from American Literature, 1988, On Faulkner: The Best from American Literature, 1989, On Dickinson: The Best from American Literature, 1989, On Hawthorne: The Best from American Literature, 1990, On Henry James: The Best from American Literature, 1990, On Robert Frost: The Best from American Literature, 1991, On Humor: The Best from American Literature, 1991, On Howells: The Best From American Literature, 1993, On Poe: The Best From American Literature, 1993; gen. editor: A Selected Edition of W.D. Howells, 1966-68; assoc. editor: Am. Lit. mag, 1973—; chmn. bd. editors, 1979-86, mng. editor, 1986-87. Mem. exec. com. Center Am. Editions, 1964-68; mem. U.S. Nat. Commn. for UNESCO, 1969-71. Served with Am. Field Service, 1943-44, Italy; with USNR, 1945. Recipient citation Ohio Wesleyan U., 1991; Guggenheim fellow, 1953-54, 75-76. Mem. MLA (chmn. Am. lit. sect. 1979, Jay B. Hubbell medal Am. lit. sect. 1990), Guild Scholars, Am. Antiquarian Soc., Phi Beta Kappa, Omicron Delta Kappa, Phi Gamma Delta. Episcopalian. Home: 2701 Pickett Rd Apt 2045 Durham NC 27705-5649

CADY, ELWYN LOOMIS, JR., medicolegal consultant, educator; b. Ames, Iowa, Feb. 21, 1926; s. Elwyn Loomis Sr. and Annabel (Lacey) C.; m. Jane Carolyn Elliott, Jan. 27, 1964 (dec. Dec. 1989); children: James Anson, Kathryn Anne; stepchildren: Martin Norman Jensen III, Paul Elliott Jensen. BS in Medicine, U. Mo., 1955; JD, Tulane U., 1951. Bar: Mo. 1951, U.S. Supreme Ct., 1965. Sci. comml. tchr., athletic dir. and coach Vermillion (Kans.) Rural High Sch., 1948-49; pvt. practice Kansas City, St. Louis, Independence, Mo., 1951—; dir. law-medicine program U. Kansas City, 1951-56; asst. dir. Law-Sci. Inst. U. Tex., Austin, 1956-57, sec. Law-Sci. Acad. Am., 1956-57; of counsel Koenig & Dietz, St. Louis, 1959-74; gen. counsel Elliott Oil, Inc., Independence, 1966—, Overland Park Dry Cleaners, Inc.; mem. com. on mgmt. Ea. Jackson County Planned Parenthood Clinics, Independence, 1970-75. Author: (book) Law and Contemporary Nursing, 1961, 1st. rev. edit., 1963; Author: (with others) Immediate Care of the Acutely Ill and Injured, 1974, Cardiac Arrest and Resuscitation, 1958, 4th rev. edit., 1974, West's Federal Practice Manual, 1960, rev. 2nd edit., 1989, Gradwohl's Legal Medicine, 1954; book reviewer: sci. books and films. Legal Counsel Friends of the Truman Campus, U. Mo.-Kansas City, Independence, 19 87-97, Cmty. Assn. for the Arts, Independence, 1991—; charter mem. Friends of Nat. Frontier Trails Ctr., Independence, 1990—, Independence Hist. Trails City Com., 1991—. With U.S. Army, 1944-45, ETO. Fellow Harry S. Truman Libr. Inst. for Nat. and Internat. Affairs (hon.), Am. Acad. Forensic Sci. (ret.); mem. AAAS (life), Nat. Geog. Soc. (life), Am. Legion (past comdr., judge adv., chaplain, chmn. state blood donor program, chmn. dist. oratorical contest), Mo. Writers' Guild (past pres., historian), Soc. Mayflower Descs., Phi Alpha Delta (life), Phi Beta Pi, Tau Kappa Epsilon. Home and Office: 1919 Drumm Ave Independence MO 64055-1836

CADZOW, JAMES ARCHIE, engineering educator, researcher; b. Niagara Falls, N.Y., Jan. 3, 1936; s. John Francis and Mildred Lois (Lankis) C.; m. Alice Ruby Bissell, June 21, 1958; children: Gregory C., Patricia A., Robert J., Debra L., James C. BSEE, U. Buffalo, 1958; MSEE, SUNY, Buffalo, 1963; PhDEE, Cornell U., 1964. Engr. U.S. Army R&D Labs., Ft. Monmouth, N.J., 1958-59; design engr. Bell Aerosystems, Wheatfield, N.Y., 1959-61; rsch. asst. Cornell Aeronautical Labs., Cheektowaga, N.Y., 1961-62; prof. SUNY, Buffalo, 1964-77, Va. Poly. Inst., Blacksburg, 1977-81; rsch. prof. Ariz. State U., Tempe, 1981-88; Centennial prof. Vanderbilt U., Nashville, 1988—. Author: Discrete-Time and Computer Control, 1970, Discrete-Time Systems, 1973, Signals, Systems and Transforms, 1985, Foundation of Digital Signal Processing, 1987; contbr. articles to profl. jours. Recipient Spectral Estimation Disting. award Rome (N.Y.) Air Devel. Ctr., 1978, 79; Joshua Gibbs fellow Cornell U., 1962-64; NIH fellow, 1972-73. Fellow IEEE; mem. IEEE Signal Processing Soc. (Sr. award 1990), Sigma Xi, Phi Kappa Phi. Roman Catholic. Avocations: basketball, reading, crossword puzzles, tennis. Office: Vanderbilt U Dept Elec Engring Nashville TN 37235

CAESAR, HENRY A., II, sculptor; b. N.Y.C., Oct. 20, 1914; m. Allison Garver, Mar. 15, 1941; children: Sanderson, Porter Dean, Austin Brewster, John Garver. AB, Princeton U., 1937; LLB, Yale U., 1940. Ptnr. H.A. Caesar & Co., N.Y.C., 1946-69; pres., dir. H.A. Caesar & Co., Inc., 1969-73, chmn. bd., 1973-74; chmn. bd., former dir. Bank of Manhattan (later Chase Manhattan), First Union Bank of N.C. Sculptor in bronze: shows include Lever House, N.Y.C., 1991, 92, 93, Heidi Neuhoff Gallery, N.Y.C., 1992, 93, Elaine Benson Gallery, Bridgehampton , N.Y., 1993, 94, 95, Shidoni Gallery, Santa Fe, others; work represented in 10 corp. hdqs.. more than 300 pvt. collections. Trustee, chmn. bd. trustees N.Y. Inst. Credit, 1971-74; pres., trustee New Canaan Nature Center, 1978-80. Lt. USNR, World War II. Clubs: New Canaan Country. Home: 50 Hemlock Hill Rd New Canaan CT 06840-3001

CAESAR, SHIRLEY, gospel singer, evangelist; b. Durham, N.C., 1938; d. James and Hallie Caesar; m. Harold Williams, 1983. BSBA, Shaw U., 1984; DHL (hon.), Southeastern U., 1980, Shaw U., 1989. Mem. gospel group Caravan, until 1966; formed gospel group The Caesar Singers, 1968; founder Shirley Caesar Outreach Ministries, Durham, 1968—. Albums include Rejoice, 1980, go, 1981, Jesus, I Love Calling Your Name, 1982, Sailin, 1994, Christmasing, 1986, Celebration, 1986, Her Very Best, 1987, Live...In Chicago, 1988, I Remember Mama, 1989, He's Working It Out For You, 1991, Stand Still, 1993, He Will Come, 1995, Faded Rose, 1996; RIAA Gold Records include I'll Go, Stranger, Don't Drive Your Mama Away; video Hold My Mule. Coun. mem. City of Durham, from 1987. Recipient Grammy awards NARAS, 1971, 80, 84, 85, for Best Traditional Soul Gospel Album, 1994, Image Achievement award NAACP, 1985, 87; named to Gospel Hall of Fame. Office: Shirley Caesar Outreach Mins PO Box 3336 Durham NC 27702-3336*

CAESAR, SID, actor, comedian; b. Yonkers, N.Y., Sept. 8, 1922; s. Max and Ida (Raphael) C.; m. Florence Levy, June 17, 1943; children: Michele, Richard, Karen. Grad., Yonkers High Sch., 1939; studied saxophone and clarinet, N.Y.C. Played in small bands, later orchs. of Charlie Spivak, Shep Fields and Claude Thornhill following World War II; toured leading theatres and night clubs as comedian; appeared in film version Tars and Spars Revue; in Broadway musical prodns. of Make Mine Manhattan, 1948, Admiral Broadway Revue, 1948, Your Show of Shows, 1950-54; star of own show Caesar's Hour, 1954-57; star and producer own show Sid Caesar Invites You, 1958, As Caesar Sees It, 1962-63; TV guest appearances include Robert Morse Show; star of Broadway musical Little Me, 1962-63; film appearances include It's a Mad, Mad, Mad, Mad World, 1963, The Spirit is Willing, 1967, Ten from Your Show of Shows, 1973, Silent Movie, 1975, Fire Sale, 1977, The Cheap Detective, 1978, Grease, 1978, History of the World, Part I, 1981, Over the Brooklyn Bridge, 1984, Cannonball Run III, 1984, Grease 2, 1984, The Emperor's New Clothes, 1987, The Life and Times of Charlie Putz, 1991, Vegas Vacation, 1997, The Wonderful Ice Cream Suit, 1998; TV film appearances include Side by Side, 1988, Nothing's Impossible, 1988, Freedom Fighter, 1988, The Great Mom Swap, 1995; appeared in opera Die Fledermaus, 1987; author autobiography: Where Have I Been?, 1982. Recipient Best Comedian on TV award Look mag., 1951, 56; recipient Emmy award, best comedian, 1956, Sylvania award best comedy-variety show, 1958; named to U.S. Hall of Fame, 1967. Club: Old Falls Rod and Gun (Fallsburgh, N.Y.). *

CAESAR, VANCE ROY, newspaper executive; b. New Kensington, Pa., Dec. 22, 1944; s. Jack Raymond and Norma Norine (Wiles) C.; m. Carol Ann Richards, Apr. 22, 1967; 1 son, Eric Roy. BSBA, The Citadel, 1966; MBA, Fla. Atlantic U., 1969; grad., Stanford U. Exec. Program, 1982; PhD in Organizational Psychology Mgmt., Walden U., 1994. From asst. to gen. mgr. to consumer mktg. dir. Miami Herald, Fla., 1970-77; assoc. editor Detroit Free Press, 1977-78; sr. v.p., gen. mgr. Long Beach Press-Telegram, Calif., 1978-88; pres. P.C.H. Publs., 1989-93, Treasure Coast Newspapers Inc., 1992-93; chmn. The Vance Caesar Group, 1994—. Bd. dirs. Meml. Med. Ctr., Silverado Sr. Living Inc., Am. Women Econ. Devel., Rancho Los Alamitos; chmn. Sch. Bus. Adminstrn. Calif. State U., Long Beach; vice-chmn. adv. bd. Bus. Roundtable; exec. com. mem. Boy Scouts Am., Long Beach, Internat. Forum for Corp. Dirs.; chmn. Long Beach Bus. Devel. Group, So. Calif. Profl. Assocs.; pres., bd. dirs. Profl. Coaches & Mentors Assn.; bd. dirs. Orange County Venture Network, Accelerate Bus. Devel. Corp. Mem. Long Beach Area C. of C., Am. Newspaper Pubs. Assn., Stanford Bus. Sch. Alumni Assn., The Citadel Alumni Assn., World Trade Ctr. Assn., Assn at Long Beach, Long Beach Yacht Club, Old Ranch Country Club, Rotary. Home: 110 Ocean Ave Seal Beach CA 90740-6027

CAETANO, RAUL, psychiatrist, educator; b. São Paulo, Brazil, May 5, 1945; came to U.S., 1978; s. Silvestre Vieira and Vera Vieira (Barbosa) C.; m. Patrice Vaeth, Sept. 30, 1995; children: Izabel, Lauren, Helena. MD, U. Rio de Janeiro, 1969, diploma in psychiatry, 1971; MPH, U. Calif., Berkeley, 1979, PhD, 1983. Psychiatrist Pine Hosp., Rio de Janeiro, 1969-73; asst. prof. State U., Rio de Janeiro, 1969-73; rsch. psychiatrist Inst. Psychiatry U. London, 1973-76; asst. prof. Inst. Psychiatry, Rio de Janeiro, 1976-78; vis. scholar Alcohol Rsch. Group, Berkeley, 1978-83, assoc. scientist to sr. scientist, 1983-94, dir., 1992—; adj. prof. Sch. Pub. Health, U. Calif., Berkeley, 1991-98; assoc. dir. Calif. Pacific Med. Ctr. Rsch. Inst., San Francisco, 1992-93; prof., asst. dean Sch. Pub. Health, U. Tex., 1998—. Contbr. numerous sci. papers to profl. jours. WHO fellow, 1973-76; rsch. grantee Nat. Inst. Alcohol Abuse and Alcoholism, 1985—. Mem. APHA, Am. Coll. Epidemiology, Rsch. Soc. Alcoholism. Roman Catholic. Office: Rm U8112 5323 Harry Hines Blvd Dallas TX 75235-9128

CAFFEE, LORREN DALE, judge; b. Decatur, Ind., Oct. 22, 1947; s. Howard Dale and Maxine Faye (Smith) C.; m. Mary Katherine Hostetler, May 25, 1968 (div. Apr. 1982); children: Liesl Katherine, Evan Dale, Colin Dale (dec.); m. Mary Jannice Dyer, June 14, 1986. BA, Bluffton Coll., 1969; JD, Georgetown U., 1972. Bar: Ind. 1972, U.S. V.I. 1994, U.S. Dist. Ct. (no. dist.) Ind. 1974. Pvt. practice, Decatur, 1972-73, 74-76; assoc. DeVoss & DeVoss Law Offices, Decatur, 1973-74; judge Adams County Ct., Decatur, 1976-84, Adams Superior Ct., Decatur, 1985-90, Adams Cir. Ct., Decatur, 1991-99; assoc. A.J. Weiss & Assoc. Law Office, 1999—; mem. county ct. com. Ind. Jud. Ctr., 1978-88, chmn., 1983-86; mem. juvenile benchbook com. Jud. Conf. of Ind., 1991-99, bd. dirs., 1995-99. Bd. dirs. Ind. Right to Life, 1974-76; mem. constn. and by-laws com. Ind. Young Reps. Fedn., 1974, of counsel, 1975-76; chmn. Adams County Young Reps., 1973-76. Mem. Ind. State Bar Assn., Adams County Bar Assn. (pres. 1975-76), Ind. Judges' Assn., Am. Judges Assn., Nat. Coun. Juvenile and Family Ct. Judges, Federalist Soc. Lutheran. Avocations: jazz music, aviation, sports cars, art, reading. Home: PO Box 11479 Saint Thomas VI 00801 Office: AJ Weiss and Assoc PO Box 1612 Saint Thomas VI 00804

CAFFEE, MARCUS PAT, publishing company executive; b. Tulsa, Feb. 23, 1948; s. Malcolm Wesley and Martha Marjorie (Deming) C.; m. Virginia Maureen Gladden, May 31, 1975; 1 child, Katheryn Elizabeth. Student, Tulsa U., 1965-66, Okla. State U., 1966-67, 77-78. Pres. Computer Sales & Svc., Tulsa, 1972-75; owner Data Mgmt. Systems, Tulsa and Houston, 1975-77; staff analyst Okla. State U., Stillwater, 1977-78; project leader Ranger Ins. Cos., Houston, 1979-80; group mgr. corp. and fin. svcs. Am. Gen. Life Ins., Houston, 1980-82; mgr. systems devel. U. Tex. Health Sci. Ctr., Houston, 1982-84; owner Marcus Caffee, Cons., Conroe, Tex., 1984-89; pres., chief exec. officer Emcee Systems, Inc., 1989-90; dir. ops. I.C. Svcs., St. Petersburg, Fla., 1989-91; pvt. practice computer consulting Largo, Fla., 1991-95; pres., chmn. bd. Web Pub. Assocs., Inc., Ft. Worth, 1995—; dir. ops. AIM Am., Fort Worth, 1996-98; ind. computer cons., 1998—; spkr. in field. Author: Time Scaled Real Time Simulators, U.S. Navy, 1970, Satelite Data Communication Criteria Between Mainframe Computer Sites, Am. General 1981, Evaluation, Justification and Purchasing Guidelines for MicroComputers and Word Processors, U. Texas Health Science Ctr. at Houston 1982; copyright computer operaing system IBOL, 1972, integrated bus. software Office Master!, 1988, 89; author, editor bus. newsletter Read Me, 1986, 89, 91. Mem. Montgomery County Econ. Devel. Team, 1987; mem. adminstrv. bd. First United Meth. Ch., Conroe, 1987, instr. computer literacy, 1985-87. With USN, 1967-71. Mem. Airman's Aero Club, Rotary (Conroe chpt., guest speaker 1988). Republican. Avocations: chess (Okla. regional champion), sailing (Master's lic.), bridge, flying.

CAFFEE, VIRGINIA MAUREEN, executive administrative associate; b. Kansas City, Mo., Feb. 25, 1948; d. Frederick Arthur Gladden and Ethel Elizabeth (Keithly) Courier; m. Marcus Pat Caffee, May 31, 1975; 1 child, Katheryn Elizabeth. Student, Ctrl. Mo. State U., 1966-73, Okla. State U., 1977-78; BBA in Bus. Edn., Sam Houston State U., 1985. Cert. profl. sec., 1975. Land abstractor Johnson County Title Co., Warrensburg, Mo., 1967-68; dept. sec., bus. placement office Ctrl. Mo. State U., Warrensburg, 1968-69; exec. sec. European Exchange System, Giessen, Germany, 1969-70; confidential sec. Consolidated Freightways, Kansas City, 1972-73; exec. sec. Behring Internat., Houston, 1974-75; sr. sec. Tenneco Oil Co.-E&P, Houston, 1979-84; exec. sec. St. Petersburg (Fla.) Hilton & Towers, 1989-90; adminstrv. mgr. Tampa Bay Engring., Clearwater, Fla., 1990-92; office mgr., WP trainer Marcus Caffee, Consulting, Largo, Fla., 1992-95; sr. adminstrv. asst. BMH Inc., Dallas, 1995-97; exec. sec. GTE Comms. Corp., Irving, Tex., 1997—; ad hoc instr. St. Petersburg (Fla.) Jr. Coll., 1993, Profl. Secs. Internat. chpt. liaison for CPS rev. course, 1993-94; presenter in field. Editor (performance programs) Suncoast Singers, 1991-94 (Cmty. Svc. award Arts Coun. Co-op 1993), Clearwater Cmty. Chorus, 1993-95, Ft. Worth Civic Chorus, Fall 1995, (newsletters) Clearwater Sparkler, 1992-93 (1st pl. award 1993), Fla. Divsn. The Secretariat, 1993-94; editor: Livin, Lovin, Laughin, 1995, Texana Newsletter, 1997-98; webmaster T-L Divsn., 1997—. Sec. Montgomery County Choral Soc., Conroe, Tex., 1986-88, publicity co-chmn., 1987-89; pres. Anona Meth. Ch. Choir, Largo, 1990-91; mem. adv. bd. Mountain View C.C., Dallas, 1999. Named Sec. of Yr. Profl. Secs. Internat. Inc. Clearwater chpt., 1994; recipient Mo. State Tchrs. scholarship Mo. Congress Parents and Tchrs., 1966. Mem. NAFE, CPS Acad., Profl. Secs. Internat. (chmn. secs. week, sec. Clearwater chpt. 1992-93, pres. 1994, chmn. seminar and v.p. Clearwater chpt. 1992-93, workshop spkr. Fla. divsn. 1993, program spkr. St. Petersburg chpt. 1993, alt. del. to internat. conv. 1993, 96, 98, del. to internat. conv. 1999, alt. del. to divsn. meeting 1993, 94, del. dist. conv. 1994, 98, Sec. of Yr. 1994-95, del. Fla. divsn. meeting 1995, program spkr. Trinity chpt. 1996, del. Tex.-La. meeting 1996, 97, 98, 99, divsn. treas. Tex.-La. divsn. 1996, v.p. 1997-98, pres.-elect 1998-99, pres. 1999—), CPS Soc. Tex. (roster chmn. 1983-85). Republican. Methodist. Avocations: choral singing, sewing, movies, ensemble singing performances. Home: 218 Oakmont Dr Trophy Club TX 76262-5472

CAFFERY, LISA KAYE, nurse; b. Davenport, Iowa, Sept. 6, 1960; d. John P. and Genevieve Ann (Hart) C.; m. Eric Shofroth, Oct. 4, 1986. ADN, Scott Community Coll., Bettendorf, Iowa, 1982; BSN, Marycrest Coll., Davenport, 1992. RN, Iowa; cert. med. and surg. nurse, nurse case mgr. AANC. Clin. nurse III Mercy Hosp., Davenport, 1985-93, adminstrv. nurse, 1993-94; case mgr. Genesis Med. Ctr., Davenport, 1995—. Mem. ANA, Iowa Nurses Assn., Soc. Gastroenterology Nurses and Assocs. (cert. clinician), Case Mgmt. Soc. Am., Midwest Soc. Gastroenterology Nurses and Assocs. (past pres.). Home: 4310 Christie Ct Davenport IA 52807-1105

CAFFEY, H. DAVID, music educator; b. Austin, Tex., June 2, 1950; s. Howard Lee and Dorthy May (Mangum) C.; m. Linda Kay Larson, June 13, 1970; children: Heather Leigh, Sean Efraim. BMus, U. Tex., 1972, MMus, 1974; postgrad., Calif. State U., Northridge, 1973. Asst. prof. music So. Oreg. State Coll., Ashland, 1974-76; dir. jazz studies, instr. Sam Houston State U., Huntsville, Tex., 1976-79; asst. prof. music U. Denver, 1979-83, assoc. prof., 1983-84; asst. prof. music Calif. State U., L.A., 1984-86, assoc. prof., 1986-91, prof., 1991—, chmn. dept., 1993—; mem. adv. bd. Luckman Fine Arts Ctr., L.A., 1993-96; bd. dirs. Friends of Music, Calif. State U., L.A., 1993—; mem. adv. bd. L.A. County H.S. of Arts, 1993-98; mem. bd. advisors Calif. Inst. for Preservation Jazz, Calif. State U., Long Beach, 1996—; mem. adv. bd. cultural arts coun. Mt. San Antonio Coll., 1996-98. Composer over 40 compositions, 1975—; prodr. 9 record albums, 1979-90; contbr. articles to profl. jours. Com. chair Troop 448 Boy Scouts Am., Covina, Calif., 1991-92. Mem. ASCAP (award for composition 1981-85), Internat. Assn. Jazz Educators (Calif. state pres. 1991-96, U.S. rep. internat. exec. bd. 1998-2000, winner composition contest 1978), Comml. Music Educators (nat. bd. 1992-96), Music Educators Nat. Conf., Am. Fedn. Musicians, Nat. Assn. Schs. Music (region vice chair, instn. rep. 1995-97). Avocations: golf, reading, travel. Office: Calif State U Music Dept 5151 State University Dr Los Angeles CA 90032-4226

CAFFEY, H(ORACE) ROUSE, university official, agricultural consultant; b. Grenada, Miss., Mar. 24, 1929; s. C. Horace and Anna Belle (James) C.; children: Brenda, Jerry, Belle, Rex. B.S., Miss. State U., 1951, M.S., 1955; Ph.D., La State U., 1959. Agronomist in charge rice project Miss. Agrl. Exptl. Sta., Stoneville, 1958-62; supt. La. State U. Rice Sta., La. Agrl. Exptl. Sta., Crowley, 1962-70; assoc. dir., prof. La. State U., La. Agrl. Exptl. Sta., Baton Rouge, 1970-79; vice-chancellor adminstrn. La. State U. Agrl. Ctr., 1979-80, vice-chancellor internat. programs, 1980-81; chancellor La. State U., Alexandria, 1981-84, La. State U. Agr. Ctr., 1984-97; pres., CEO Caffey Internat. Inc., 1997—; internat. rice cons. AID, World Bank, other orgns., 1965—; mem. pub. health study team Nat. Acad. Sci., Washington, 1973-74; mem. adv. bd. Bd. Regents Masters Plan Higher Edn., Baton Rouge, 1977; Nat. co-chair joint coun. for Food and Agr., 1989-94, Internat. Sci. and Edn. Coun., 1986-90; chmn. Nat. Assn. State Univs. and Land Grant Colls. divsn. Agr. Budget Com., 1989. Contbr. chpts. to books, articles to profl. jours. Pres. Internat. Rice Festival, Crowley, 1968; bd. dirs. Boy Scouts U.S.A., United Way, others. Served to 1st lt. U.S. Army, 1951-54. Recipient Internat. award of Merit Gamma Sigma Delta, 1970, 81; honoree Internat. Rice Festival, 1974; named Man of Yr. Crowley C. of C., 1969-70, Progressive Farmer Man of Yr. in Svc. to La. Agr., 1986, Outstanding Alumnus Coll. Agr. of La. State U., 1992, Alumnus of Yr., La. State U., 1993, Outstanding Alumnus of Yr., Coll. Agr., Miss. State U., 1993. Mem. Sigma Xi, Gamma Sigma Delta, Phi Delta Kappa, Omicron Delta Kappa, Phi Delta Phi, Phi Zeta. Democrat. Baptist. Club: . Lodges: Masons; Rotary. Home: 10471 Barry Dr Baton Rouge LA 70809-3265 Office: Chancellor Emeritus LSU Agrl Ctr 4560 Essen Ln Baton Rouge LA 70809-3424

CAFRITZ, ROBERT CONRAD, art historian, critic, consultant; b. July 5, 1953; s. Conrad B. Cafritz and Jennifer (Stats) Phillips; 1 child, Nicholas H. BA, Columbia U., 1977, MA, 1978. Asst. curator Phillips Collection, Washington, 1978-82, assoc. curator, 1982-87, curator 19th Century Art, 1987-88; fine arts advisor, critic and historian, 1989—. Author: Georges Braque, 1981; contbg. author: Master Paintings from the Phillips Collection, 1981; co-author: Places of Delight: The Pastoral Landscape, 1988; editor exhbn. catalogs Three Pioneers of Japanese Painting, 1979, Leon Spilliaert, 1980, Sam Francis, 1980, Georges Braque: Late Paintings, 1982, Howard Hodgkin, 1984, Odilon Redon: The Ian Woodner Collection, 1988; contbr. to scholarly jours. Home and Office: 3044 O St NW Washington DC 20007

CAGE, BOBBY NYLE, research and statistics educator; b. Runnells, Iowa, Apr. 27, 1937; s. H. Nyle and Pauline G. (Thomas) C.; m. Dorothy J. Van Houweling, June 24, 1960; children: Marla Socha, Jill Nance, Jeffrey R., Bryan A., Denise Robinson. BS, Central Coll., Pella, Iowa, 1959; MSE, Drake U., 1965; PhD, Iowa State U., 1968. Cert. tchr., prin., supt., Iowa. Tchr. math Valley High Sch. and various other schs., West Des Moines,

1959-66; asst. prof. U. Fla., Gainsville, 1968-73; prof., asst. dean U. Miss., 1973-86; dean edn. N.E. La. U., Monroe, 1986-95, prof., sch. facilities planner, 1995—; assoc. dir. Nat. Jr. Coll. Fin. Project, Gainsville, 1970-72; dir. bur. U. Miss., 1973-85; bd. dirs. Fla. Migrant Edn. Evaluation Project, U. Fla., 1968-73. Author: Statistical Analyses for Educational Research, 1980; (with others) More Money for More Opportunity: Financial Support of Community College Systems, 1974; also articles in profl. field. Named Outstanding Tchr., Kappa Delta Pi, U. Miss., 1975. Mem. Am. Edn. Research Assn., La. Assn. Sch. Execs., Assn. La. Evaluators, Kappa Delta Pi, Phi Delta Kappa (chpt. pres.). Presbyterian. Club: Exchange (Oxford, Miss. dist. dir. 1984-86). Avocation: golf. Office: NE La U 117 Strauss Hall Monroe LA 71209

CAGE, NICOLAS (NICOLAS COPPOLA), actor; b. Long Beach, Calif., Jan. 7, 1964. Actor: (feature films) Fast Times At Ridgemont High, 1982, Valley Girl, 1983, Rumble Fish, 1983, Racing with the Moon, 1984, Birdy, 1984, The Boy in Blue, 1986, The Cotton Club, 1984, Peggy Sue Got Married, 1986, Raising Arizona, 1986, Moonstruck, 1988, Vampire's Kiss, 1989, Never on a Tuesday, 1989, Tempo di Uccidere, 1989, Fire Birds, 1990, Wild at Heart, 1990, Zandalee, 1991, Honeymoon in Vegas, 1992, Time to Kill, 1992, Amos & Andrew, 1993, Red Rock West, 1993, Deadfall, 1993, Guarding Tess, 1994, It Could Happen to You, 1994, Trapped in Paradise, 1994, Kiss of Death, 1995, Leaving Las Vegas, 1995 (Best Actor award L.A. Film Critics 1995, Best Actor award N.Y. Film Critics 1995, Golden Globe award for best actor 1996, Acad. award for best actor 1996), The Rock, 1996, The Funeral, 1996, Con Air, 1997, Face Off, 1997, Welcome to Hollywood, 1998, Snake Eyes, 1998, City of Angels, 1998, 8MM, 1999, Bringing Out the Dead, 1999. Office: Saturn Films 9000 W Sunset Blvd Ste 911 West Hollywood CA 90069-5809 Office: CAA 9830 Wilshire Blvd Beverly Hills CA 90212*

CAGE-BIBBS, PATRICIA, coach; b. Monroe, La., Aug. 28, 1950. BS, MS, Grambling State U., 1972. Coach Ruston H.S., Dubach H.S.; head coach Grambling State U., 1984-97; head women's basketball coach Hampton (Va.) U., 1997—. Named La. H.S. Coach of Year, 1981, 83, Coach of Yr. Southwestern Athletic Conf. Office: Hampton U Womens Athletics Dept Holland Hall Rm 121 Hampton VA 23668*

CAGEN, EDWARD LESLIE, surgeon, physician; b. Bklyn., May 12, 1962; s. George and Elaine (Thurer) C.; m. Deborah Ann Bzdick, Apr. 2, 1989; 1 child, Lauren Jennifer. BS in Biomedicine, CCNY, 1984; MD, SUNY, N.Y.C., 1986. ACLS, ATLS. Intern, resident Jackson Meml. Hosp. U. Miami, Fla., 1986-88; resident in family practice Cmty. Hosp., N.Y., 1988-89; med. examiner Examination Mgmt. Svc., Inc., Miami, 1989; group practice assoc. Tower Med. Group, Inc., Homestead, Fla., 1989-91; family practice physician, occpl. medicine Sunshine Med. Ctr., Miami, Fla., 1991; pvt. practice Miami, 1991—; attending physician Coral Gables (Fla.) Hosp., Columbia Deering Hosp., Bapt. Healthsystems, Health South Hosp.; primary care physician health and rehab. svcs. Dade County Pub. Health Unit, Perrine, Fla., 1992; emergency physician spl. operation response team FEMA Mobile Emergency Hosp., Homestead, 1992; emergency dept. physician Homestead AFB Hosp., 1992; asst. prof. U. Miami Sch. Medicine. Capt. U.S. Army, 1986-96. Mem. Am. Acad. Family Physicians, Am. Assn. Physician Specialists, Am. Bd. Cert. in Family Practice, Am. Bd. Clin. Medicine and Surgery, Am. Bd. Clin. Cmty. Medicine and Family Practice, AMA, Am. Bd. Internal Medicine, Dade County Med. Assn. (bd. dirs., del. to Fla. Med. Assn.), Fla. Med. Assn. (coun. mem., del. to FMA Young Physicians section), Fla. Acad. Family Physicians, Fla. Ind. Physicians Assn. (bd. dirs., founding, mem. credentials com.), South Miami Hosp. Physician Hosp. Orgn. (mem. utilization com.), Am. Med. Informatics Assn., Aircraft Owners and Pilots Assn., Classic Jet Aircraft Assn., Exptl. Aircraft Assn., Greater South Dade-South Miami C. of C., Rotary (sgt.-at-arms Perrine-Cutler Ridge club 1994-95), VFW (life), Tau Epsilon Phi. Avocations: jet aircraft, linguistics, computer science, martial arts. Office: 8277 SW 124th St Miami FL 33156-5957

CAGGIANO, JOSEPH, advertising executive; b. N.Y.C., Oct. 22, 1925; s. Daniel Joseph and Lucia (Gaudiosi) C.; m. Catherine Marie Gilmore, Aug. 28, 1948; children—Cathleen, Mary Yvonne. B.B.A., Pace Coll., 1953. Chief accountant Criterion Advt. Co., N.Y.C., 1947-57; treas. Emerson Foote, Inc., N.Y.C., 1957-67; became sr. v.p. Bozell & Jacobs, Inc. (now Bozell, Jacobs, Kenyon & Eckhardt Inc.), N.Y.C., 1967; exec. v.p. finance and adminstrn. Bozell & Jacobs Inc. (now Bozell, Jacobs, Kenyon & Eckhardt Inc.), Omaha, 1971-91; vice chmn. bd., chief financial officer Bozell & Jacobs, Inc. (now Bozell, Jacobs, Kenyon & Eckhardt Inc.), 1991-97; vice chmn. bd. dirs. emeritus Bozell, Jacobs, Kenyon & Eckhart Inc., 1991—, ret., 1998; dir. Emerson Foote Inc. Bd. dirs. St. Mary's Coll., Omaha Zool. Soc. Served with USNR, 1943-46, ETO, PTO. Mem. N.Y. Credit and Financial Mgmt. Assn., Omaha Zool. Soc. (dir.). Home: 9731 Fieldcrest Dr Omaha NE 68114-4932 Office: Bozell Jacobs Kenyon & Eckhardt 40 W 23rd St New York NY 10010-5215 *Luck in business is best defined as preparation meeting opportunity while always keeping a positive attitude. Dedication and fairness to a cause is mandatory. There are few short cuts to success in business or meaningful relationships with family and friends; and still fewer gray areas. It would have been impossible to achieve any degree of success without the help and understanding of my wife and family.*

CAGINALP, AYDIN S., lawyer; b. Ankara, Turkey, Aug. 2, 1950. AB, Ind. U., 1972; JD, Tulane U., 1974; LLM in Taxation, NYU, 1975. Bar: N.Y. 1976, U.S. Dist. Ct. (so. and ea. dists.) N.Y. 1976, U.S. Tax Ct. 1976. Atty. Walter, Conston, Alexander & Green, P.C., N.Y.C., chmn. mgmt. com. Bd. editors Tulane U. Law Rev., 1973-74. Mem. ABA (taxation sect.). Address: Walter Conston Alexander & Green PC 90 Park Ave New York NY 10016-1301*

CAGINALP, GUNDUZ, mathematician, educator, researcher; b. Ankara, Turkey, July 20, 1952; came to U.S., 1959; s. Nejat Tahsin and Munire Feyma (Deniz) C; m. Eva Keller, Aug. 14, 1992; children: Carey Allen, Reginald Jarrett. AB cum laude with distinction, Cornell U., 1973, MA, 1976, PhD, 1978. Postdoctoral fellow Cornell U., Ithaca, N.Y., 1978; rsch. assoc. Rockefeller U., N.Y.C., 1978-80; Zeev Nehari rsch. asst. prof. Carnegie-Mellon U., Pitts., 1980-83, vis. asst. prof., 1983-84; asst. prof. math. U. Pitts., 1984-85, assoc. prof., 1985-90, prof., 1990—, group leader applied math., 1988-90; reviewer Math. Revs., Ann Arbor, Mich., 1981-90. Mem. editl. bd. Applied Math. Fin.; contbr. articles to profl. jours. Cornell U. grad. fellow, 1973; grantee NSF, 1980—, NIST, 1990-92, Disting. Found., 1997—; disting. vis. rsch. scholar Internat. Found. for Rsch. in Exptl. Econs., 1999. Mem. Am. Math. Soc., Am. Phys. Soc., Soc. for Indsl. and Applied Math., Econs. Scis. Assn., Phi Beta Kappa. Achievements include proof of theorems on existence and properties of surface free energy; studied connections between statistical mechanics and quantum field theory; developed phase field methods for studying free boundary problems; research on applying renormalization group methods to differential equations; analyzed experimental economics using differential equations and time series; established that price patterns in financial markets have predictive value. Home: 12 Rosemont Ln Pittsburgh PA 15217-3161 Office: U Pitts Dept Math Pittsburgh PA 15260

CAGLE, PAULETTE BERNICE, mental health administrator and psychologist; b. Ft. Worth, July 14, 1944; d. James Frank and Cordelia Pauline (Bourke) C. BS, North Tex. State U., 1972; MA, So. Meth. U., 1976. Lic. chem. dependency counselor; cert. diagnostic and evaluation psychologist; qualified mental health profl. Part-time psychometrist Jack Waxler, Psychologist, Richardson, Tex., 1973-77; social worker Vernon (Tex.) State Hosp., 1977-78, psychologist, 1978-88; adminstr. tech. programs Wichita Falls (Tex.) State Hosp., 1988-91, assoc. dir. cmty. svcs., 1991-96; dir. mgmt. and support Rolling Plains Socs., Tex., 1996—; cons. mem. quality improvement coun. Vernon State Hosp., 1992-96. Co-founder, mem. Cmty. Svcs. Quality Assurance Dirs. Tex., 1993—; designated contact Mental Health Disaster Assistance, Austin, 1994-97; mem. Wichita County Mental Health, 1992-96. Named Sister of the Yr. Sisterhood of Freedom, 1991. Mem. Am. Counseling Assn., Am. Mental Health Counselors Assn., Tex. Assn. Alcoholism and Drug Abuse Counselors, Internat. Assn. of Marriage and Family Counselors. Avocations: reading, boating, animal wildlife observation. Office: Texas Dept MH-MR Rolling Plains Socs 1720 4th St Graham TX 76450-2926

CAGLE, TERRY DEE, clergyman; b. Charlotte, N.C., June 7, 1955; s. James Clarence and Jean (Belk) C.; m. Julia Ann Conner, June 30, 1979; children: Julia Lynn, Christopher Terry, Benjamin Conner. BA, Gardner-Webb U., 1979; MDiv, Southeastern Bapt. Theol. Sem., 1982. Ordained to ministry So. Bapt. Conv., 1982. Pastor Mountain Creek Bapt. Ch., Oxford, N.C., 1982-85, Southside Bapt. Ch., Gaffney, S.C., 1985-88, Pleasant Ridge Bapt. Ch., Boiling Springs, N.C., 1988—; adj. prof. O.T. Gardner-Webb U., Boiling Springs, 1989—; mem. Christian Life com. King Mountain Bapt. Assn., Shelby, N.C.; v.p. Greater Gaffney Ministerial Fellowship, 1987-88. Mem. Boiling Springs Area Rotary Club (v.p. elect, club svc. chmn. 1989-94), Shelby Amateur Radio Club (repeater com. 1994—). Home: 203 Gordon Ave # 1084 Boiling Springs NC 28017 Office: Pleasant Ridge Bapt Ch 198 Pleasant Ridge Church Rd Shelby NC 28152-9022 *Adam and Eve dismissed the consequences of their decision. We are reminded that every deed is followed by its own consequence. Today should be lived in full, knowing full well that tomorrow's consequences are the results of today's decisions.*

CAGLE, THOMAS M., electronics engineer; b. Chillicothe, Tex., Apr. 26, 1927; s. William Robert and B. Clyde (White) C.; m. Jane E. De Bute, May 16, 1964; children: Kent, Thomas. BS, U. So. Calif., 1968. Engr. N.Am. Rockwell Corp., L.A., 1950-71; engring. cons. Scottsdale, Ariz., 1971-77; elecs. engr. Dept. Defense, L.A., 1977—. Past pres., dir. Inglewood Jaycees; pres. YMCA, Ingelwood Youth Counseling Orgn. With USN, 1945-46. Mem. IEEE. Home: 10461 Greenbrier Rd Santa Ana CA 92705

CAGLE, WILLIAM REA, librarian; b. Hollywood, Calif., Nov. 15, 1933; s. Howard Clinton and Eunice (Colcord Althouse) C.; m. Terry Lucinda Conrad, Jan. 17, 1975; children by previous marriage: Michael Stewart, Chantal Gabrielle, Mark Christopher, Monique Antoinette. AB in English, UCLA, 1956, MLS, 1962; postgrad., Oxford U., 1959-60. Asst. to librarian Henry E. Huntington Library and Art Gallery, San Marino, Calif., 1960-62; librarian for English Ind. U. Libraries, Bloomington, 1962-67, asst. Lilly librarian, 1967-75; acting Lilly librarian Ind. U. Libraries, Bloomington, 1975-77; Lilly librarian Ind. U. Libraries, Bloomington, 1977-97; dir.'s acad. adv. com. Harry Ransom Humanities Rsch. Ctr. U. Tex. Author: A Matter of Taste, 1990, revised and enlarged, 1999, Two Hundred and Fifty Years of the British Novel: 1740-1989, 1990, American Books on Food and Drink, 1998, 150 Years of the American Short Story, 1998; contbr. to Printing and the Mind of Man, 1967; editor Ind. U. Bookman, 1966-89; mem. adv. bd. Dictionary Lit. Biography, Cambridge edit. Joseph Conrad, Bibliography of United States Literature, Chadwyck-Healey American Poetry Full-Text Database; mem. editl. bd. Pitts. Series in Bibliography; contbr. articles to profl. jours. Trustee Carver Meml. Libr., Searsport, Maine; mem. collection adv. bd. Kinsey Inst. Sex, Gender and Reprodn. With U.S. Army, 1956-59. Mem. Benjamin Franklin Guild (bd. govs.), Assn. Internationale de Biliophilie, Lincoln Soc. Clubs: Century, Grolier (N.Y.C.); Caxton (Chgo.). Home: PO Box 837 Searsport ME 04974-0837

CAGNEY, MICHAEL JOSEPH, foundation adminstrator; b. N.Y.C., Aug. 3, 1945; s. Joseph and Rita Mary (Koelln) C.; m. Jane Ware Goforth, Apr. 4, 1974 (div. Sept. 1985); children: Aislin Seay, Joshua Conor. AAS, No. Va. Cmty., Annandale, 1972; BA, Marshall U., Huntington, W.Va., 1976; MA, U. Ill., Chgo., 1979. Cert. fund raising exec. Exec. dir. Jesuit Program, Wilmette, Ill., 1979-85; v.p. Glenwood (Ill.) Sch., 1985-87; sr. fund raising counsel Ketchum, Inc., Pitts., 1987-91; chief devel. officer Pan Am. Devel. Found., Washington, 1991-96; pres., CEO Environ. Rsch. & Edn. Found., Washington, 1996—. Bd. dirs. Internat. Svc. Agys., 1991-96; trustee Evanston (Ill.) Art Ctr., 1982-84. Mem. Nat. Assn. Fund Raising Execs., Nat. Potomac Yacht Club, Dist. Yacht Club. Republican. Roman Catholic. Avocations: boating, golf, softball, running. Office: Environ Rsch & Edn Found 4301 Connecticut Ave NW Washington DC 20008-2304

CAGUIAT, CARLOS JOSE, health care administrator, episcopal priest; b. N.Y.C., Jan. 23, 1937; s. Carlos C. and Carmen (Rovira) C.; m. Julianna Skomsky, Aug. 29, 1958; children: Stephen D., Jonathan J., Sarah E. Caguiat Borthwick. BA, CCNY, 1958; MDiv, Gen. Theol. Sem., 1965; MPA, NYU, 1976. Ordained priest Episcopal Ch., 1965. Vicar St. Christopher's Chapel, N.Y.C., 1965-71; exec. dir. project for human comm. Episcopal Diocese of N.Y.; N.Y.C., 1971-73; project mgr. ambulatory care/cmty. rels. N.Y.C. Health and Hosps. Corp., 1973-76, regional coord. for adminstrn./ops., 1975-76; assoc. dir. adminstrn./ops. Morrisania Neighborhood Family Care Ctr., Bronx, N.Y., 1976-78, adminstr., 1978-81; adminstrv. dir. Clin. Ctr., Mich. State U., East Lansing, 1981-90; v.p., strategic planning St. Francis Acad., Lake Placid, N.Y., Pa., 1990-99; ventures v.p. St. Francis Acad., Saranac Lake, N.Y., 1999—; chair decentralized unit of several parishes, N.Y.C.; mem. Diocese of N.Y. Pension Bd., Ecumenical Commn., Budget Com.; vice chairperson North Country Behavioral Health Devel. Corp., 1997—. Chair Two Bridges Settlement Housing Corp.; bd. dirs. Settlement Housing Fund.; pres. Mid-Mich. South Health Sys. Agy. Served with Infantry and Intelligence Office, U.S. Army. Fellow Am. Coll. Health Care Execs., Am. Hosp. Assn., Lake Placid Rotary. Home: 29 Oakwood Pl Saranac Lake NY 12983 Office: St Franics Acad 29 Oakwood Pl Saranac Lake NY 12983

CAHAL, MAC FULLERTON, lawyer, publisher; b. Kiowa, Kans., Mar. 28, 1907; s. Frank Bastian and Carrie (Fullerton) C.; m. Wilma Marshall, June 1, 1935; children: Carolyn Holder, William Marshall. A.B., U. Kans., 1931; postgrad., Northwestern U., 1937; J.D., De Paul U., 1942. Bar: Ill. 1942, Mo. Newspaper reporter, feature writer Wichita (Kans.) Beacon, 1928; pub. relations dept. Grigsby-Grunow, Kansas City, 1929; 1st exec. sec. Sedgwick Co. (Kans.) Med. Soc., 1931-37; exec. dir. Am. Coll. Radiology, Chgo., 1937-48; exec. v.p. Southwestern Med. Found., Dallas, 1943-44; exec. v.p., gen. counsel Am. Acad. Family Physicians (pub. Am. Family Physician), Kansas City, 1948-73; now pres. Med. Book Club, Inc.; publisher Continuing Edn.; lectr. legal and social medicine U. Kans. Med. Sch.; Cons. Med. Task Force of Hoover Commn. for Orgn. Exec. Br. Govt., 1953-55; founder Med. Soc. Execs. Assn., pres., 1947-48. Author monographs on legal, social and econ. aspects of medicine.; Pres., pub.: Continuing Edn. Jour; Contbr. articles to med. and legal publs. Recipient Gold medal German Inst. Medicine, 1972, Founders award Am. Acad. Family Physicians, 1997; named to Hall of Leaders, Nat. Conv. Ctr., Washington, 1985, Hon. fellow Am. Coll. Radiology, 1974. Mem. AMA (Distinguished Service award 1972), Mo., Kansas City, Chgo. bar assns., U.S. C. of C. (bd. regents Inst. for Assn. Mgmt., mem. tax council), Am. Soc. Assn. Execs. (dir.), Profl. Conv. Mgrs. Assn. (founder, Disting. Service award 1979), Chartered Assn. Execs. (trustee), Kansas City Soc. Western Art (pres.), C. of C., Acad. Health Profls. (trustee). Episcopalian. Clubs: Indian Hills Country, Kansas City (Kansas City); Internat. Wine and Food (pres. 1972); Lawyers (Washington); Bohemian (San Francisco); Mission Valley Hunt, Saddle and Sirloin. Home: 8101 Mission Rd # 328 Shawnee Mission KS 66208-5248

CAHALEN, SHIRLEY LEANORE, retired secondary education educator; b. LaHarpe, Kans., Aug. 20, 1933; d. Hugh E. and Irma Eunonia (Russell) Pearman; m. Keith E. Cahalen, Sept. 2, 1953; 1 child: Keith P. Student, Iola Jr. Coll., 1951-52, McPherson Coll., 1952-53, Pratt C.C., 1963-64; BS, Northwestern State U., Alva, Okla., 1966; MS, Kans. State U., 1981; postgrad., Emporia State U., 1982-86. Cert. spl. edn. tchr., Kans. With Kans. Power & Light Co., McPherson, 1952-53, State Farm Ins. Co., Jacksonville, Fla., 1957-59, Kans. Fish and Game Commn., Pratt, 1960-62; tchr. home econs. Kirby-Smith Jr. H.S., Jacksonville, Fla., 1966-67, Unified Sch. Dist. 254, Medicine Lodge, Kans., 1968-71, Sch. Dist. 259, Wichita East, Wichita, Kans., 1971-73, Dist. 490, El Dorado, Kans., 1975-82; tchr. spl. edn. Augusta (Kans.) Sr. H.S., 1982-93; ret., 1993; sec. IDP Unified Sch. Dist. 490, 1986-88, dirs. coun., 1987-93, effective sch. track com., 1990-93; mem. abuse intervention team Unified Sch. Dist. 402, 1989-91. Mem. edn. com. First United Meth. Ch., 1981-87. Mem. Walnut Valley Edn. Assn., Kans. Edn. Assn. (state rep.), NEA (El Dorado chpt.), Butler County Spl. Edn. Assn., ADK, AAUW (pres. 1979-81), Coun. for Exceptional Children, Am. Legion Aux., Kappa Delta Pi. Methodist. Home: 205 N Main #6 El Dorado KS 67042

CAHAN, WILLIAM GEORGE, surgeon, educator; b. N.Y.C., Aug. 2, 1914; s. Samuel George and Flora (Gomperts) C.; m. Mary Arnold Sykes, Dec. 26, 1952 (div.); children: Christopher, Anthony; m. Grace Mirabella, Nov. 24, 1974. BS, Harvard U., 1935; MD, Columbia U., 1939. Diplomate Am. Bd. Surgery. Surg. pathology Presbyn. Hosp., N.Y.C., 1939; intern, house surgeon Hosp. Joint Diseases, N.Y.C., 1940-41; fellow cancer surgery Meml. Hosp., N.Y.C., 1942-48; thoracic cons. Strang Clinic, 1949-53, attending surg. staff thoracic svc., 1949-85, cons. thoracic svc., 1985—; asst. attending surgeon Manhattan Eye, Ear and Throat Hosp., 1950-58, cons. gen. surgeon, 1964—; assoc. vis. surgeon James Ewing Hosp., N.Y.C., 1959-68; cons. tumor svc. Newark Beth Israel Hosp., 1968; instr. surgery Cornell U. Med. Coll., 1950-56, mem. faculty, 1956—, assoc. prof. surgery, 1966-74, prof., 1974-84, prof. emeritus, 1984—; asst. clinician Sloan-Kettering Inst., 1953-68; co-chmn. Internat. Workshop on Multiple Primary Cancers, Meml. Sloan-Kettering Cancer Ctr., co-chmn. smoke free Am. awards, 1996; vis. scholar U. Ctr. Va., Richmond, 1967; mem. Lasker Award Jury, 1980-84; mem. nat. adv. bd. Look Good Feel Better Program, 1988—; bd. advisors Am. Coun. Sci. and Health; bd. dirs. Am.-Italian Found. Cancer Rsch. Author: No Stranger to Tears, 1992, (with Hans von Leden) Cryogenics in Surgery, 1971; editl. bd. (with Hans von Leden) Jour. Cryosurgery; contbr. numerous articles to med. jours. Pres. Treadwell Farm Hist. Dist., N.Y.C., 1966-69;; mem. overseers vis. com. music Harvard U., 1968-69, bd. advisors Sch. Pub. Health, 1995; chmn. People for a Smoke Free Indoors; adv. bd. Leeds Castle Found.; co-chair Smoke-Free Am. Awards, 1996. Maj. M.C. USAAF, 1943-46. Recipient Disting. Svc. award Am. Cancer Soc., 1982, Life and Breath award N.Y. Lung Assn., 1990, Dynamic Duo Am. Cancer Soc., N.Y.C., 1994, 1st Pub. Svc. award Cancer Care, 1995. Fellow ACS; mem. Am. Assn. Thoracic Surgery, Am. Cancer Soc., Am. Coll. Chest Physicians, AMA, Am. Radium Soc., Internat. Congress Smoking and Health (adv. bd.), N.Y. Cancer Soc. (sec. 1955-58), N.Y. County, N.Y. State med. socs., N.Y. Surg. Soc., N.Y. Soc. Thoracic Surgeons, Royal Soc. Medicine (affiliate), Soc. Cryobiology, Soc. Thoracic Surgeons. Office: 1275 York Ave New York NY 10021-6007

CAHILL, ANNE PICKFORD, economist, demographer; b. Dayton, Ohio, Oct. 11, 1953; d. James H. and Margaret J. Pickford; m. Francis Patrick Cahill, Feb. 18, 1984; 1 child, Emily J. BS with honors in spl. edn., Va. Commonwealth U., 1975; MA in Econs., Va. Poly. Inst. and State U., 1983. Spl. edn. tchr. Nelson County Pub. Schs./Chelsea Sch., 1976-79; assoc. Robert R. Nathan Assocs., Washington, 1982-86; analyst Fairfax County Office of Rsch. and Stats., Fairfax, Va., 1986-88; br. chief Fairfax County Office of rsch. and Stats., Fairfax, Va., 1989-94; econ. and demographic rsch. supr. Fairfax County Office Mgmt. and Budget, 1994—. Troop cookie sales coord. Girl Scouts U.S.A., Fairfax, 1996-97, 98-99, troop svc. project coord., 1998-99; mem. PTA, Fairfax, 1995—, sch. budget com., 1997-98; bd. dirs., treas. Fairfax Plaza Civic Assn., 1983-85. Recipient Nat. Assn. Counties Achievement award, 1996. Mem. NAFE, Fairfax LWV (unit chair 86, budget chair 1995-96), Sierra Club (group chair, treas. 1987-90), Phi Kappa Phi. Avocations: reading, art. Home: 9353 Tartan View Dr Fairfax VA 22032-1207

CAHILL, CATHERINE M., orchestra executive. Gen. mgr. N.Y. Philharmonic, N.Y.C., 1994-98; exec. dir. Toronto Symphony, Can., 1998—. Office: Toronto Symphony, 212 Kings St West, Toronto, ON Canada M5H1K5*

CAHILL, CHARLES L., university administrator, chemistry educator; b. El Reno, Okla., Feb. 23, 1933; m. Dorotha Ann Creek, Feb. 14, 1954; children: Steven Charles, Terri Ann, Susan Beth. AB in Chemistry, Okla. Bapt. U., 1955; MS in Biochemistry, U. Okla., 1957, PhD in Biochemistry, 1961. Rsch. asst., biochemist Vets. Hosp., Sch. Medicine, U. Okla., Oklahoma City, 1955-57; NIH predoctoral fellow Sch. Medicine, U. Okla., Oklahoma City, 1957-60; clin. chemist med. arts labs. Oklahoma City U., 1960-61, asst. prof. chemistry, 1961-63, asst. prof., chmn. dept., 1963-67, assoc. prof., chmn. dept., assoc. dean Coll. Arts and Sci., 1967-69, prof. chemistry, assoc. dean, dir. rsch., 1970-71; vice chancellor for acad. affairs U. N.C., Wilmington, 1971-85, provost, vice chancellor for acad. affairs, 1985-92, prof. chemistry, 1992—. Mem. Rotary. Avocations: bass fishing, hunting, golf. Office: UNC 601 S College Rd Wilmington NC 28403-3297

CAHILL, CHRIS J., hotel executive. BS, U. Ottawa, 1975, BEd, 1976; MBA, U. Toronto, 1990. With Delta Hotels & Resorts, v.p. ops. Ea. Can.; with Can. Pacific Hotels, exec. v.p., v.p. sales, pres., COO, 1998—. Office: Can Pacific Hotels, 1 University Ave Ste 1400, Toronto, ON Canada M5J 2P1

CAHILL, CLYDE S., retired federal judge; b. St. Louis, Apr. 9, 1923; s. Clyde and Effie (Taylor) C.; m. Thelma Newsom, Apr. 29, 1951; children: Linda Diggs, Marina, Valerian, Randall, Kevin, Myron. BS, St. Louis U., 1949, JD, 1951, JD (hon.), 1990. Bar: Mo. Sole practice, 1951-56; asst. circuit atty. City of St. Louis, 1956-64; regional atty. OEO, Kansas City, 1966-68; gen. mgr. Human Devel. Corp., 1968-72; gen. counsel, exec. dir. Legal Aid Soc., St. Louis, 1972-75; circuit judge State of Mo., 1975-80; U.S. dist. sr. judge Eastern Dist. Mo., 1980—; lectr. St. Louis U. Law Sch., 1974-79; counsel to Mo. NAACP, 1958-65. Bd. dirs. St. Louis Urban League, 1974, Met. YMCA, St. Louis, 1975—, Comprehensive Health Center, 1975, Cardinal Ritter High Sch., 1978. Served with USAAF, World War II. Recipient NAACP Disting. Svc. award, St. Louis Argus award, Civil Liberties award ACLU, 1992, Award of Honor Lawyers Assn. St. Louis, 1993. Mem. ABA, Nat. Bar Assn. (Judge William Hastie award 1992), Am. Judicature Soc., Mo. Bar Assn., Met. St. Louis Bar Assn., St. Louis Lawyers Assn., Mound City Bar Assn. Home: 3218 Sullivan Ave Saint Louis MO 63107-2620*

CAHILL, GERARD ALBIN, university educator; b. N.Y.C., Dec. 21, 1936; s. Albin G. and Susan E. (Maschenic) C.; m. Lea D. Chandler, Jan. 29, 1993. BS in Elec. Engring., Manhattan Coll., 1958; MBA, CCNY, 1962; PhD, NYU, 1973. Registered profl. engr., N.Y. With Lucent Tech., N.Y.C., 1959-67; divsn. contr. Gen. Dynamics Corp., Orlando, Fla., 1967-68; corp. contr. Liberty Equities corp., Washington, 1968-69; v.p. HETRA Co., Melbourne, fla., 1969-71, CODI Corp., Fairlawn, N.J., 1971-73; v.p. fin., treas. Cablecom-Gen. Inc., Denver, 1973-81; sr.v.p. Capital Cities Cable Inc., Bloomfield Hills, Mich., 1981-82; sr. v.p. Simmons Comm., Inc., Stamford, Conn., 1982-85; prof. Westfield (Mass.) State Coll., 1986-87, Fla. Inst. Tech., 1987—; cons. in field. Ford Found. fellow, 1965. Mem. NSPE, Nat. Assn. Forensic Economists, Am. Mgmt. Assn., Suntree Country Club. Office: 575 Dawson Dr Melbourne FL 32940-1974

CAHILL, HARRY AMORY, diplomat, educator; b. N.Y.C., Jan. 10, 1930; s. Harry Amory and Elaine Olga (Loumena) C.; m. Angelica Margarita Ravazzoli, Dec. 12, 1956; children—Alan, Daniel, Sylvia, Irene, Madeleine, Steven. BA, Manhattan Coll., N.Y.C., 1951; postgrad., Johns Hopkins U., 1964-65; MS, George Washington U., Washington, 1972. Sales exec. Johns Manville Corp., N.Y., 1954-56; fgn. service officer U.S. Dept. of State, Washington, 1956-59, Oslo, Norway, 1959-61, Warsaw, Poland, 1961-64, Belgrade, Yugoslavia, 1965-68, Montevideo, Uruguay, 1968-71, Lagos, Nigeria, 1975-78, Colombo, Sri Lanka, 1979-81; dir. comml. service U.S. Dept. Commerce, 1982-83; U.S. consul gen. Dept. of State, Bombay, India, 1983-87; U.S. Mission to UN, dep. U.S. rep. UN Econ. and Social Coun., N.Y.C., 1987-89; cons. U.S. Dept. State, 1991-99; pres. Amory Assoc., Inc., McLean, Va., 1990—, World of Film Found., N.Y.C., 1990—; prof. George Mason U., 1982, Pepperdine U., 1992-99, Georgetown U., 1995. Author: The China Trade and U.S. Tariffs, 1973. Pres. Hinduja Found., N.Y.C., 1993—. Woodrow Wilson Nat. Fellowship found. fellow, 1990-93. Mem. Am. Fgn. Svc. Assn. Roman Catholic. Avocation: photography. Office: 1240 Daleview Dr Mc Lean VA 22102-1539

CAHILL, JAMES FRANCIS, retired art history educator; b. Ft. Bragg, Calif., Aug. 13, 1926; s. James Francis and Mae (Bond) C.; m. Dorothy Dunlap, July 15, 1951; children: Nicholas, Sarah; m. Tsao Hsingyuan, Mar. 28, 1988; children: Benedict and Julian (twins). BA, U. Calif., Berkeley, 1950; MA, U. Mich., 1952, PhD, 1958. Curator Chinese art Freer Gallery Art, Smithsonian Instn., Washington, 1957-65; prof. history of art, curator Oriental art U. Calif., Berkeley, 1965-94; ret., 1994; Charles Eliot Norton prof. poetry Harvard U., 1978-79. Author: Chinese Painting, 1960, Scholar Painters of Japan: The Nanga School, 1972, Hills Beyond a River: Chinese Painting of the Yuan Dynasty, 1976, The Compelling Image: Nature and Style in 17th Century Chinese Painting, 1982. Guggenheim fellow, 1972-73. Mem. Am. Acad. Arts and Scis., Assn. Asian Studies, Coll. Art Assn. Home: 94 Einstein Dr Princeton NJ 08540-4946

CAHILL, KATHLEEN, broadcast executive. Gen. mgr. Sta. WLIT-FM, Chgo. Office: Sta WLIT-FM 150 N Michigan Ave Chicago IL 60601-7524

CAHILL, MARION FRANCES, nursing and psychology educator; b. New Haven; d. Thomas J. Sr. and Ruth (Curley) C. BSN, Johns Hopkins U., 1958; MA, Columbia U., 1963, MEd, 1976, EdD, 1977. Asst. prof. nursing U. Conn., Storrs, 1965-67; assoc. prof. human devel. U. Bridgeport (Conn.), 1968-87; researcher Yale U., New Haven, 1988-89; chair, prof. Barton Coll., Wilson, N.C., 1989-90; prof. nursing U. Southwestern La., 1990-92, Our Lady of the Lake Coll., Baton Rouge, 1993—; participant Internat. Conf. on Family and Children, Athens, Greece, 1984; mem. U.S. Health Delegation to Japan and Mainland China, 1985; mem. Internat. Cong. Psychologists, Australia, 1988. Contbr. articles to profl. publs. WHO fellow, 1986. Mem. ANA, APA, Am. Psychol. Soc., Nat. League Nursing, World Fedn. Mental Health, Phi Theta Kappa, Phi Lambda Theta, Kappa Delta Pi, Sigma Theta Tau. Home: 5112 Claycut Rd Baton Rouge LA 70806-7123

CAHILL, RICHARD FREDERIC, city planner; b. Bath, Maine, Mar. 31, 1931; s. Andrew Russell and Mabel Olive (Mitchell) C.; m. Vivian Rose Eastman, May 1958; children: Tammy, Penny, Karen. BA in Town and City Mgmt., U. Maine, 1956; MPA in Urban and Regional Devel., U. Pitts., 1961. Cert. planner. Chief programs assistance Maine Dept. Econ. Devel., Augusta, 1962-68; planning and urban devel. dir. Auburn, Maine, 1968-77; planing dir. Town of Gray, Maine, 1989—. Chmn. planning bd. City of Hallowell, Maine, 1958-60; chmn. citizens adv. com. City of Gardiner,Maine, 1965-66; chmn. So. Kennebee Valley Regional Planning Commn., Augusta, 1965-66. With U.S. Army, 1950-52. Mem. Maine Assn. Planners (pres. 1966, 67, 68), Nat. Assn. Housing and Redevel. Ofcls. (pres. 1966, 67, 68). Avocation: marathon running. Home: 18 Greenwood Rd Auburn ME 04210-8969 Office: Town of Gray 6 Shaker Rd Gray ME 04039-9501

CAHILL, RICHARD FREDERICK, lawyer; b. Columbus, Nebr., June 18, 1953; s. Donald Francis and Hazel Fredeline (Garbers) C.; m. Helen Marie Girard, Dec. 4, 1982; children: Jacqueline Michelle, Catherine Elizabeth, Marc Alexander. Student, Worcester Coll., Oxford, 1973; BA with highest honors, UCLA, 1975; JD, U. Notre Dame, 1978. Bar: Calif. 1978, U.S. Dist. Ct. (ea. dist.) Calif. 1978, U.S. Dist. Ct. (cen. dist.) Calif. 1983, U.S. Dist. Ct. (so. dist.) Calif. 1992, U.S. Ct. Appeals (9th cir.) 1992. Dep. dist. atty. Tulare County Dist. Atty., Visalia, Calif., 1978-81; staff atty. Supreme Ct. of Nev., Carson City, 1981-83; assoc. Acret & Perochet, Brentwood, Calif., 1983-84, Thelen, Marrin, Johnson & Bridges, L.A., 1984-89; ptnr. Hammond Zuetel & Cahill, Pasadena, Calif., 1989-98, Pivo & Halbreich, Irvine, Calif., 1999—. Mem. Pasadena Bar Assn., Los Angeles County Bar Assn., Assn. So. Calif. Defense Counsel, Notre Dame Legal Aid and Defender Assn. (assoc. dir.), Phi Beta Kappa, Phi Alpha Delta (charter, v.p. 1977-78), Pi Gamma Mu, Phi Alpha Theta (charter pres. 1973-74), Phi Eta Sigma, Sigma Chi. Republican. Roman Catholic. Avocation: tennis. Home: 201 Windwood Ln Sierra Madre CA 91024-2677 Office: Pivo Halbreich Cahill & Yim 1920 Main St Ste 800 Irvine CA 92614-7227

CAHILL, THOMAS ANDREW, physicist, educator; b. Paterson, N.J., Mar. 4, 1937; s. Thomas Vincent and Margery (Groesbeck) C.; m. Virginia Ann Arnoldy, June 26, 1965; children: Catherine Frances, Thomas Michael. B.A., Holy Cross Coll., Worcester, Mass., 1959; Ph.D. in Physics; NDEA fellow, U. Calif., Los Angeles, 1965. Asst. prof. in residence U. Calif., Los Angeles, 1965-66; NATO fellow, research physicist Centre d'Etudes Nucleaires de Saclay, France, 1966-67; prof. physics U. Calif., Davis, 1967—; acting dir. Crocker Nuclear Lab., 1972, dir., 1980-89; dir. Inst. Ecology, 1972-75; cons. NRC of Can., Louvre Mus. UN Global Atmospheric Watch, 1990—; mem. Internat. Com. on PIXE and Its Application, Calif. Atty. Gen., Nat. Audubon Soc., Mono Lake Com. Author: (with J. McCray) Electronic Circuit Analysis for Scientists, 1973; editor Internat. Jour. Pixe, 1989—; contbr. articles to profl. jours. on physics, applied physics, hist. analyses and air pollution. Prin. investigator IMPROVE Nat. Air Pollution Network., 1987-97; co-dir. Crocker Hist. and Archeol. Projects.; mem. internat. com. Ion Beam Analysis. OAS fellow, 1968, Japanese Nat. Rsch. fellow, Kyoto, 1992. Mem. Am. Phys. Soc., Air Pollution Control Assn., Am. Assn. Aerosol Rsch., Sigma Xi. Democrat. Roman Catholic. Club: Sierra. Home: 1813 Amador Ave Davis CA 95616-3104 Office: U Calif Dept Physics Crocker Nuclear Laboratories Davis CA 95616

CAHILLANE, JAMES FRANCIS, writer; b. Northampton, Mass., Jan. 3, 1933; s. James and Imogene (Smith) C.; m. Maureen Patricia Stone, Sept. 10, 1955; children: Richard J., Daniel E., Christopher P., Matthew J., Maria T. BA, U. Mass., 1989, MA, 1997. Pres. Cahillane Motors, Inc., Northampton, Mass., 1963-93. Columnist The Daily Hampshire Gazette, 1993—. Chair Northampton Redevel. Authority, 1970-75. Staff sgt. USAF, 1951-54. Mem. Nat. Writers Union. Democrat. Roman Catholic. Avocations: hiking, gardening, travel. Home and Office: 9 Judd Ln Williamsburg MA 01096-9729

CAHINHINAN, NELIA AGBADA, retired public health nurse, administrator; b. Laguna, Philippines, Sept. 20, 1939; d. Manuel Navarro and Milagros Agbay (Adea) Agbada; m. Rodolfo DeGuia Cahinhinan, Jan. 29, 1967; children: Rodney Paul, Roel James, Renee Ann, Nelie Rose. Diploma, U. Philippines, 1961; BSN, U. Guam, 1985. RN; cert. in nursing adminstrn. Pub. health nurse Dept. Health, Laguna, 1962-67, Dept. Pub. Health and Social Svc., Agana, Guam, 1967-73; pub. health nurse supr., home care Dept. PHSS, Mangilao, Guam, 1974-82; cmty. health nurse supr. Regional Pub. Health Ctr., Dept. PHSS, Tamuning, Guam, 1982-86; nursing and program supr. maternal child health Family Planning Program, Dept. PHSS, Mangilao, 1986-89; asst. nursing adminstr. Bur. Family Health and Nursing Svcs., Dept. PHSS, Mangilao, 1990-94; mem. adv. coun. Coll. Nursing, U. Guam, Mangilao, 1994-95; mem. nursing asst. program adv. coun. Guam C.C., Mangilao, 1995-96; mem. profl. adv. bd. Clarke Home Nursing Svcs., Tamuhning, 1995-97. Bd. dirs. Am. Cancer Soc., Agana, 1976-78; mem., sec., chair nursing and health svcs. com. ARC, Agana, 1980-83; mem. com. chair So. Tagalog Assn., Agana, 1980-99. Recipient Centennial Leadership award Nat. League of Nursing, 1993, Outstanding Woman of Yr. award Govt. of Guam, 1996; named Guam Top Ten Suprs., Gov. of Guam, 1990. Mem. Guam Nurses Assn. (pres. 1994-95, treas., dir. 1980, com. chair 1993-99, Svc. award 1983, Guam Nurse of Yr. 1985, Most Disting. Mem. award 1996), U. Philippines Alumni Assn. (pres. 1991-93, adviser 1994-99, treas., dir., Outstanding Svc. award 1993), Guam Meml. Hosp. Vol. Assn. (com. chair 1998-99), Cath. Daughters of Ams. Roman Catholic. Avocations: decorating, gardening, flower arrangement. Home: PO Box 11234 Tamuning GU 96931-1234

CAHIR, JOHN JOSEPH, meteorologist, educational administrator; b. Scituate, Mass., Oct. 8, 1933; s. Jeremiah Francis and Mary Eleanor (Duggan) C.; m. Mary Anne Louise Schrott, Dec. 1, 1962; children: Ellen, William, Kathryn, Barton. BS in Meteorology, Pa. State U., 1961, PhD, 1971. Meteorologist trainee, meteorologist U.S. Weather Bur., 1956-64; instr. meteorology Pa. State U., University Park, 1965-70, asst. prof., 1971-74, assoc. prof., 1975-79, prof., 1980—; assoc. dean Coll. Earth and Mineral Scis., Pa. State U., University Park, 1980-93; vice provost, dean for undergrad. edn. Pa. State U., University Park, 1993—; vis. prof. St. Augustine's Coll., Va. State Coll.; cons. in field; mem. Commn. for Atmospheric Scis., World Meteorol. Orgn. (UN), 1986-97, alt. prin. U.S. del. to 9th session, Sofia, Bulgaria, 1986, del. to 10th session, Offenbach, Fed. Republic Germany, 1990, 11th session, Geneva, 1994; mem. com. on info. sys. for ports and harbors Marine Bd., NRC, 1985; Earth Sci. Adv. com. U. Space Rsch. Assn., 1987-93, convenor, 1992-93; mem. policy adv. com. Coop. Program for Meteorol. Edn. and Tng. (COMET), U. Corp. for Atmospheric Rsch., 1988-96, chair, 1996—; instnl. mem. The Coll. Bd., 1993—. Co-author: Principles of Climatology, 1969, The Atmosphere, 1975, 78 81; editor: Monthly Weather Rev., 1977-80; contbr. papers, research reports to profl. publs. Served with USN, 1958-60. Fellow Nat. Ctr. Atmospheric Research, 1974. Fellow Am. Meteorol. Soc. (chmn. com. on weather forecasting and analysis 1979-89, 20th seal of approval for TV weathercasting, nat. councillor 1986-89, chmn. com. on undergrad. awards 1986, nominating com. 1990-91, chmn. 1991, investment com. 1997—, chair 1999—); mem. Royal Meteorol. Soc., Am. Geophys. Union, Nat. Weather Assn. (pres. 1981-82, Svc. award 1979), Am. Assn. Univ. Commn. on Undergrad. Edn., Sigma Xi. Home: 952 Robin Rd State College PA 16801-4138 Office: 417 Old Main University Park PA 16802-1505

CAHN, DAVID STEPHEN, cement company executive; b. Los Angeles, Jan. 12, 1940; s. Edward Lincoln and Monya (Schuchett) C.; m. Mary Constance Maschio, June 18, 1960 (div. 1972); children: Elizabeth Suzanne, Deborah Michelle; m. Sharon Ann Marting, Sept. 8, 1972; 1 child, Melissa Jacquiline. BS with honors, U. Calif.-Berkeley, 1962, MS, 1964, DEng, 1966. Engr. Bethlehem Steel Corp., 1966-68; research engr. Amcord, Inc., Riverside, Calif., 1968-71; dir. environ. matters Amcord, Inc., Newport Beach, Calif., 1971-77, v.p., 1977-80; dir. environ. affairs Calif. Portland Cement Co., Los Angeles, 1980-82, v.p. regulatory matters, 1982-84; v.p. regulatory matters CalMat Co., 1984-90; sr. v.p. corp. svcs. Calif. Portland Cement Co., Glendora, 1990—. Recipient Rossiter W. Raymond award Soc. Mining Engrs., 1972. Mem. AIME, ASTM, AIChE, Air and Waste Mgmt. Assn., Calif. Mining Assn. (past pres.), Calif. Mfrs. Assn. (dep. vice chair). Republican. Office: Calif Portland Cement Co 2025 E Financial Way Glendora CA 91741-4692

CAHN, EDWARD N., retired federal judge; b. Allentown, Pa., June 29, 1933; s. Norman A. and Miriam H. C.; m. Alice W.; Dec. 7, 1963; children: Melissa, Jessica. BA magna cum laude, Lehigh U., 1955; LLB, Yale U., 1958. Bar: Pa. 1959. Atty. Cahn & Roberts, 1971-75; judge U.S. Dist. Ct. (ea. dist.) Pa., 1974-98, chief judge, 1993-98; assoc. Blank Rome Comisky & McCauley LLP, Allentown, Pa., 1998—. Corporal USMCR, 1958-64. Mem. Pa. Bar Assn., Lehigh County Bar Assn. Republican. Avocations: golf, tennis, classical guitar. Fax: 610-706-4343; email: cahn@blankrome.com. Office: 1620 Pond Rd Ste 200 Allentown PA 18104-2255

CAHN, JEFFREY BARTON, lawyer; b. N.Y.C., Jan. 1, 1943; s. Harold Leon and Vivian (Loewy) C.; m. Miriam Epstein, Jan. 22, 1965; children: Lauren Samantha, Vanessa Shari. BA, Ind. U., 1964; JD, Rutgers U., 1967. Bar: N.J. 1967, U.S. Dist. Ct. N.J. 1967, U.S. Ct. Appeals (3d cir.) 1971, U.S. Supreme Ct. 1971, U.S. Tax Ct. 1973, U.S. Ct. Appeals (D.C. cir.), 1979, N.Y. 1980, U.S. Ct. Appeals (9th cir.) 1981, U.S. Claims Ct. 1981, U.S. Dist. Ct. (so. dist.) N.Y. 1992, U.S. Dist. Ct. (ea. dist.) N.Y. 1994, U.S. Ct. Appeals (2nd cir.) 1998. Law clk. to sr. presiding judge Appellate Div. N.J. Superior Ct., Trenton, N.J., 1967-68; assoc. Schapira, Steiner & Walder, Newark, 1968-72; ptnr. Sills, Cummis, Radin, Tischman, Epstein & Gross, Newark, 1972—. Author: (with others) New Jersey Transaction Guide, Vol. 12, 1993, The Use of Another's Trademark: A Review of the Law in The United States, Canada, and Western Europe, 1997; rsch. editor: Rutgers Law Rev., 1966-67; contbr. articles to profl. jours. Mem. ATLA, ABA, N.J. State Bar Assn., Essex County Bar Assn., Internat. Trademark Assn., N.Y. State Bar Assn. (sect. intellectual property), Am. Intellectual Property Law Assn., N.J. Intellectual Property Law Assn., Phi Delta Phi (Outstanding Grad. 1967). Jewish. Home: 34 Underwood Dr West Orange NJ 07052-1322 Office: Sills Cummis Radin Tischman Epstein & Gross Legal Ctr 1 Riverfront Plz Fl 13 Newark NJ 07102-5400*

CAHN, JOHN WERNER, metallurgist, educator; b. Germany, Jan. 9, 1928; came to U.S., 1939, naturalized, 1945; s. Felix H. and Lucie (Schwarz) C.; m. Anne Hessing, Aug. 20, 1950; children: Martin Charles, Andrew Blender, Lorie Selma. BS, U. Mich., 1949; PhD, U. Calif. at Berkeley, 1953; DSc (hon.), Northwestern U., 1990, U. d'Evry, France, 1996. Instr. U. Chgo., 1952-54; with research lab. Gen. Electric Co., 1954-64; prof. metallurgy MIT, 1964-78; ctr. scientist Nat. Inst. Standards and Tech. (formerly Nat. Bur. Standards), 1978—, sr. fellow, 1984—; vis. prof. Israeli Inst. Tech., Haifa, 1971-72, 80; cons. in field, 1963—; chmn. Gordon conf. Phys. Metallurgy, 1964; vis. scientist Nat. Bur. Standards, Gaithersburg, Md., 1977; affiliate prof. physics U. Wash., Seattle, 1984—. Rsch. and articles on surfaces and interfaces, thermodynamics, phase changes, quasicrystals. Recipient Dickson prize Carnegie Mellon U., 1981, Gold medal U.S. Dept. Commerce, 1982, Von Hippel award Materials Rsch. Soc., 1985, Stratton award Nat. Bur. Standards, 1986, Michelson-Morley prize Case Western Res. U., 1991, William Hume-Rothery award Minerals, Metals and Materials Soc., 1993, Harvey prize Israel Inst. Tech., 1995, Nat. Medal of Sci., 1998, Bakhuis-Roozeboom medal Netherlands Acad. Sci., 1999; Guggenheim fellow, 1960; Japan Soc. for Promotion of Sci. rsch. fellow, 1981-82. Fellow Am. Acad. Arts and Scis., Am. Inst. Metall. Engrs., Am. Soc. Metals Internat. (Saveur award 1989); mem. NAS, NAE, Japan Inst. Metals (gold medal 1994), Indian Materials Rsch. Soc. (hon.). Home: 6610 Pyle Rd Bethesda MD 20817-5454 Office: Nat Inst Standards and Tech Gaithersburg MD 20899-8555

CAHN, ROBERT NATHAN, physicist; b. N.Y.C., Dec. 20, 1944; s. Alan L. and Beatrice (Geballe) C.; m. Frances C. Miller, Aug. 22, 1965; children: Deborah, Sarah. BA, Harvard U., 1966; PhD, U. Calif., Berkeley, 1972. Rsch. assoc. Stanford (Calif.) Linear Accelerator Ctr., 1972-73; rsch. asst. prof. U. Wash., Seattle, 1973-76; asst. prof. U. Mich., Ann Arbor, 1976-78; assoc. rsch. prof. U. Calif., Davis, 1978-79; sr. staff physicist Lawrence Berkeley Nat. Lab, 1979-91; div. dir. Lawrence Berkeley Lab., 1991-96, sr. scientist, 1996—. Author: Semi Simple Lie Algebras and Their Representations, 1984; co-author: Experimental Foundations of Particle Physics, 1989. Fellow Am. Phys. Soc. (sec.-treas. divsn. particles and fields 1992-94).

CAHN, STEVEN MARK, philosopher, educator; b. Springfield, Mass., Aug. 6, 1942; s. Judah and Evelyn (Baum) C.; m. Marilyn Ross, May 4, 1974. AB, Columbia U., 1963, PhD, 1966. Vis. instr. Dartmouth Coll., Hanover, N.H., 1966; vis. prof. U. Rochester, N.Y., 1967; asst. prof. philosophy Vassar Coll., Poughkeepsie, N.Y., 1966-68, NYU, N.Y.C., 1968-71; assoc. prof. NYU, 1971-73, dir. grad. studies, 1972, dir. undergrad. studies, 1971-73; prof., chmn. dept. philosophy U. Vt., Burlington, 1973-80, adj. prof. philosophy, 1980-83; dean grad. studies, prof. philosophy Grad. Sch. and Univ. Ctr., CUNY, 1983-84, provost, v.p. for acad. affairs, 1984-92, acting pres., 1991; program officer Exxon Edn. Found., N.Y.C., 1978-79; assoc. dir. Rockefeller Found., N.Y.C., 1979-81, acting dir. humanities, 1981-82; dir. div. gen. programs NEH, Washington, 1982-83; pres. John Dewey Found., 1983—; cons., panelist NEH, 1975-82. Author: Fate, Logic, and Time, 1967, 82, A New Introduction to Philosophy, 1971, The Eclipse of Excellence: A Critique of American Higher Education, 1973, Education and the Democratic Ideal, 1979, Saints and Scamps: Ethics in Academia, 1986, rev. 1994, Philosophical Explorations: Freedom, God and Goodness, 1989; editor: (with Frank A. Tillman) Philosophy of Art and Aesthetics: From Plato to Wittgenstein, 1969, The Philosophical Foundations of Education, 1970, Philosophy of Religion, 1970, Classics of Western Philosophy, 1977, 4th edit., 1995, New Studies in the Philosophy of John Dewey, 1977, Scholars Who Teach: The Art of College Teaching, 1978, (with David Shatz) Contemporary Philosophy of Religion, 1982, (with Patricia Kitcher and George Sher) Reason at Work: Introductory Readings in Philosophy, 1984, 3d edit., 1996, Morality, Responsibility and the University: Studies in Academic Ethics, 1990, Affirmative Action and the University: A Philosophical Inquiry, 1993, (with Joram G. Haber) Twentieth Century Ethical Theory, 1995, The Affirmative Action Debate, 1995, Classic and Contemporary Readings in the Philosophy of Education, 1997, Classics of Modern Political Theory: Machiavelli to Mill, 1997, (with Peter Markie) Ethics: History, Theory, and Contemporary Issues, 1998; gen. editor Issues in Acad. Ethics, 1994—, Critical Essays on the Classics, 1997—. Chmn. standing com. on teaching philosophy Am. Philos. Assn., 1985-90, del. Am. Coun. Learned Societies, 1998—. Mem. Phi Beta Kappa. Home: 100 W 57th St New York NY 10019-3327 Office: CUNY Grad Sch U Ctr 33 W 42nd St New York NY 10036-8099

CAHOUET, FRANK VONDELL, banking executive; b. Cohasset, Mass., May 25, 1932; s. Ralph Hubert and Mary Claire (Jordan) C.; m. Ann Pleasonton Walsh, July 14, 1956; children: Ann P., Mary G., Frank V., David R. BA, Harvard U., 1954; MBA, U. Pa., 1959. Corp. loan asst. Security Pacific Nat. Bank, L.A., 1960-66, v.p., 1966-69; sr. loan adminstr. Security Pacific Nat. Bank, Europe, Middle East, Africa, 1969-73; exec. v.p. Security Pacific Nat. Bank, 1978-80, vice chmn., 1980-84; exec. v.p. Security Pacific Corp., L.A., 1973-80, vice chmn., 1980-84; chmn., pres., CEO Crocker Nat. Bank, San Francisco, 1984-86; pres., COO Fed. Nat. Mortgage Assn., 1986-87; chmn., CEO Mellon Bank, Corp., Pitts., 1987-99, pres., 1990-92, ret., 1999; bd. dirs. Avery Internat. Corp., Los Angeles. Trustee Carnegie-Mellon U., Pitts., U. Pitts., Pa's. S.W.Assn., Pitts.; mem. bd. overseers Wharton Sch., U. Pa. Mem. Newcomen Soc. Clubs: Duquesne, Edgeworth, Laurel Valley Golf (Pitts.); California (Los Angeles); Pacific Union (San Francisco). Office: Mellon Bank Corp One Mellon Bank Center 500 Grant Street Ste 4840 Pittsburgh PA 15258-0001 also: Pitts Pirates 600 Stadium Cir Pittsburgh PA 15212-5731*

CAI, KHIEM VAN, technologist, researcher, administrator; b. Phu Cat, Binh Dinh, Viet Nam, Sept. 10, 1954; s. Trang Van and Chi Thi (tran) C.; m. Thuy T. Ha (div. Dec. 1988); children: Kim Thien, Dan Van; m. Tuyet Hong Bui-Tran. BEE, Viet Nam Poly. U., 1975; MEE, Purdue U., 1978, PhD, 1981. Rsch. asst. Radar Lab. Purdue U., West Lafayette, Ind., 1976-81; sr. staff engr., head advanced data link and analysis group Hughes Aircraft Co., Fullerton, Calif., 1982—; divsn. chief scientist, mgr. sys. engrng. operation Raytheon Sys. Co., Torrance, Calif., 1996—; mem. adv. com. Tay Son Binh Dinh Assocs., So. Calif., 1990—. Contbr. tech. papers to profl. jours.; patents in communications and signal processing. Co-founder Vietnamese Student Assn., 1981, Vol. Svc. Group, 1981; instr. Vietnamese Youth Ctr., Garden Grove, Calif., 1982. Recipient Disting. Patent award in comms. Hughes Aircraft Co., 1990; David Ross scholar Purdue U., 1978. Mem. IEEE, N.Y. Acad. Sci., Tau Beta Pi, Eta Kappa Na, Sigma Xi. Avocations: photography, skiing, volleyball, writing. Home: 2151 Clear Springs Rd Brea CA 92821-4390 Office: Hughes Aircraft Co NS 231/2011 3100 Lomita Blvd Torrance CA 90505-5177

CAI, YONG, chemist; b. Pingdu, Shandong, China, Oct. 22, 1961; s. Deke Cai and Xiangting Li; m. Yin Chen, Feb. 1, 1988; 1 child, Yincheng. BSc, Ocean U. of Quindao, China, 1982; MS, Nankai U., Tianjin, China, 1986, PhD, 1989. Technician Pingdu Bur. Environ. Protection, Shandong, China, 1982-83; lectr. Nankai U., 1986-89; postdoctoral fellow Max-Planck-Inst. Chemistry, Mainz, Germany, 1989-93; rsch. assoc. Centro de Investigación y Desarrollo Consejo Superior de Investigaciones Científicas, Barcelona, 1993-95; rsch. assoc. Fla. Internat. U., Miami, 1995-97, asst. prof. dept. chemistry, 1997—. Contbr. articles to profl. jours. Fellow Max-Planck-Gesellschaft, 1989, Ministry of Edn. and Scis., Madrid, 1993. Mem. AAAS, Am. Chem. Soc., Am. Geophys. Union. Home: 10621 SW 113th St Miami FL 33176-4032 Office: Fla Internat U SERP University Park Campus Miami FL 33199

CAIAZZA, FRANCIS X., federal judge; b. 1935. BA, Duquesne U., 1958; LLB, U. Pitts., 1961. Bar: Pa. Judge Pa. Ct. Common Pleas for 53d Dist., New Castle, 1982-94, U.S. Magistrate Ct., Pitts., 1994—. With U.S. Army, 1961-63. Office: US Magistrate Ct 1036 US PO and Courthouse 700 Grant St Pittsburgh PA 15219-1906

CAILLÉ, ANDRÉ, public service company executive; b. Saint-Luc, Que., Can., Sept. 11, 1943; s. Jean-Paul C.; m. Lyse Senécal; children: Daniel, Guillaume, Marc-Vincent. BSc, U. Montreal, Que., Can., 1965, MSc, 1966, PhD, 1968, D in Phys. Chemistry, 1969. Dir. Fed./Provincial Com. on St. Lawrence River, Quebec, 1975-76, Environ. Protection Services, Quebec, 1977-79; dep. minister Dept. Environ., Quebec, 1980-82; sr. v.p. adminstrn. and pub. affairs Gaz Metro., Montreal, 1983-85, exec. v.p., 1985-87; pres., CEO Hydro-Que, Montreal, 1996—; chmn. bd. Noverco Inc.; bd. dirs. Hydro-Que. Internat., Montreal Internat., Conseil Des Gouverneurs De La Federation Quebecoise Du Saumonatlantique and Fonds de recherche de l'Institut de cardiologie de Montreal, Sears Can. Inc., Enbridge Energy; mem. Conf. Bd. Can. Avocations: reading, theatre, tennis, golf. Home: 345 Bloomfield, Outremont, PQ Canada H2V 3R7 Office: Hycro-Que, 75 René-Levesque Blvd W, Montreal, PQ Canada H2Z 1A4

CAILLOUETTE, JAMES CLYDE, physician; b. L.A., June 2, 1927; s. Albert F. and Vera Helen C.; m. Joanne Thompson, Dec. 17, 1950; children: Laure, James Thompson, Anne. AB, Coll. Puget Sound, 1950; MD, U. Wash., 1954. Diplomate: Am. Bd. Ob-Gyn. Intern Los Angeles Gen. Hosp., 1954-56, resident in Ob-Gyn, 1956-59; instr. U. So. Calif. Sch. Medicine, 1959-64, asst. clin. prof., 1964-69, asso. clin. prof., 1969-78, clin. prof., 1978—; mem. sr. attending staff Los Angeles County-U. So. Calif. Med. Center; sec. med. staff Huntington Meml. Hosp., Pasadena, Calif., 1973—. Contbr. articles to profl. jours.; inventor med. products. Bd. dirs. Pasadena Physicians United Crusade, 1961-63, chmn., 1964; v.p. Oak Knoll Property Owners Assn., 1965-75; chmn. ann. drive Nat. Found. March of Dimes, Pasadena, 1966, mem. med. adv. bd. 1966-76; bd. dirs., chmn. med. adv. bd. Pasadena Planned Parenthood World Population, 1970-75; trustee Poly. Sch. Pasadena, 1969-78, chmn. devel. com., 1970-76; bd. councilors U. So. Calif. Sch. Medicine, 1978-92; bd. dirs. Scripps Home, 1980-83, 88-94, Friends of Huntington Libr., 1996—. With USNR, 1945-46. Fellow ACS, Am. Coll. Ob-Gyn. (mem. primary care task force 1991-92); mem. AMA, N.Y. Acad. Scis., Calif. Med. Assn. (past sec., chmn. ob-gyn. sect.), Pasadena Med. Soc., Pacific Coast Ob-Gyn. Soc. (bd. dirs. 1978—, pres. 1996-97), L.A. Ob-Gyn. Soc. (pres. 1977-78), Ob-Gyn. Assembly So. Calif. (chmn. 1981-82), Los Angeles County-U. So. Calif. Med. Ctr. Profl. and Attending Staff Assn. (pres. 1988-90), Valley Hunt Club (bd. dirs. 1980-87, v.p. 10983-84, pres. 1984-85), Calif. Club, Alpha Omega Alpha, Nu Sigma Nu, Phi Sigma, Sigma Chi. Office: 50 Bellefontaine St Ste 401 Pasadena CA 91105-3132

CAIN, ALBERT CLIFFORD, psychology educator; b. Chgo., July 19, 1933; s. Edward Arthur and Fae Anita (Shafton) C.; m. Barbara Strean, Nov. 15, 1959; children: Steven, Kenneth. BA, U. Mich., 1954, PhD, 1962. From asst. prof. to assoc. prof. depts. psychology and psychiatry U. Mich., Ann Arbor, 1962-69, prof. dept. psychology, 1969—, chmn. dept. psychology, 1981-91; chief psychologist Childrens Psychiatric Hosp., Ann Arbor, 1964-69; mem. rev. com. Ctr. for Studies of Suicide Prevention NIMH, 1969-72. Editor: Survivors of Suicide, 1972; contbr. articles to profl. jours. Recipient Young Contributor award Am. Assn. Suicidology, 1973. Fellow APA, Am. Orthopsychiatric Assn. (bd. dirs. 1978-81, editor jour. 1983-88); mem. Phi Beta Kappa. Home: 1927 Hampton Ct Ann Arbor MI 48103-4521 Office: U Mich Dept Psychology 2251 East Hall 525 E University Ann Arbor MI 48104-2649

CAIN, BEVERLY LYNN, library director; b. Barberton, Ohio, Aug. 5, 1959; d. Norwood Wayne and Mildred Marie Cain. MusB, U. Akron, 1981; MLS, Kent State U., 1986. Reference libr. Medina County Libr., Medina, Ohio, 1986-88, reference mgr., 1988-92; br. mgr. Upper Arlington (Ohio) Libr., 1992-97; dir. Portsmouth (Ohio) Pub. Libr., 1997—. Mem. Portsmouth Cmty. Orch., 1997—. Libr. Svcs. Constrn. Act grantee State Libr. Ohio, 1989, 90. Mem. ALA, Ohio Libr. Coun. (asst. coord. N.E. chpt. 1999—, Diana Vescelius Meml. award 1992), Portsmouth C. of C., Rotary (bd. dirs. 1999—). Avocations: music, antiques, animal welfare. E-mail: cainbe@oplin.lib.oh.us. Office: Portsmouth Pub Libr 1220 Gallia St Portsmouth OH 45662

CAIN, DAVID, state senator, lawyer; b. Pampa, Tex., Nov. 13, 1947; s. Don and Betty Anne C.; m. Sally Anne Haenelt; children: David, Jennifer. BA in History, McMurry Coll., 1970; JD, U. Tex., 1973. Bar: Tex. 1973. Assoc. Crowder & Mattox, Dallas, 1973-78; ptnr. Bennett & Cain, Dallas, 1979-82; pvt. practice Dallas, 1982-86; assoc. Burleson, Pate, and Gibson, Dallas, 1986—; mem. Tex. Ho. of Reps., Austin, 1977-95, chmn. transp. com., 1983-95; mem. Tex. Senate, Austin, 1995—, vice chmn. econ. devel. com., 1997-99, chmn. Senate subcom. on infrastructure, 1999—, vice chmn. spl. com. on electric utility restructuring, 1999—; chair Tex. Sunset Adv. Commn., 1991-93, transp. com. So. Legis. Conf., 1991-93. Founder Clean Dallas East; mem. Parents as First Tchrs. Recipient Friend of Bus. award Tex. C. of C., 1993; named Outstanding Young Man of Am. by Jaycees, 1978, 81, Legis. Crime Fighter of Yr. by Greater Dallas Crime Commn., 1993, One of Ten Best Legislators by Tex. Monthly Mag., 1993. Mem. State Bar of Tex., Dallas Bar Assn., East Dallas Bar Assn., Nat. Conf. State Legislatures, Greater Dallas C. of C. Democrat. Methodist. Avocations: running, travel. Office: 6301 Gaston Ave Ste 355 Dallas TX 75214-6202

CAIN, DAVID LEE, corporate executive; b. Morgantown, W.Va., Oct. 14, 1941; s. David Melvin and Dorothy Eleanor (Burchinal) C.; m. Dawn Marie Parker, July 2, 1983; children: Diana Jo, Michael Allen, Mark Aaron. BSME, W.Va. U., 1965. Adminstrn. mgr. Value Engrng. Co., Alexandria, Va., 1966-72; gen. mgr. Walker Iron Works, Woodbridge, Va., 1972-75; owner, mgr. Dyna Products, Richmond, Va., 1975-78; adminstrn. mgr. VSE Corp., Alexandria, 1978-83; sr. v.p. The Orkand Corp., Falls Church, Va., 1983—. Vol. youth progs., various orgns., 1965—; head coach freshman wrestling team, W.Va., U., Morgantown, 1965, asst. coach varsity wrestling team, 1965; judge various pageants in Va., N.C., S.C., Md., Del., Pa., 1984—; mem. Rep. Nat. Com., 1990—. Capt. U.S. Army, 1965-68. Recipient scholarship W.Va. U., 1961-64, Disting. Student grant, ROTC, 1963-64, Disting. Mil. Grad., 1964-65. Mem. Nat. Contracts Mgmt. Assn., Wellington Civic Assn. Methodist. Avocations: gardening, sports, collections. Office: The Orkand Corp 7799 Leesburg Pike Falls Church VA 22043-2499

CAIN, DONALD EZELL, judge; b. San Marcos, Tex., Oct. 8, 1921; s. Erie Montclair and Betty Belle (Howell) C.; m. Betty Anne Culberson, June 14, 1952; children: David, Dale Cain Husen, Donald Ezell, Randolph. A.S., North Tex. Agrl. Coll., 1941; B.B.A., U. Tex., 1943, LL.B., 1948; postgrad., Nat. Jud. Coll., Reno, 1974, 78, 82. Bar: Tex. 1948. With contracts dept. Convair, Ft. Worth, 1948-50; pvt. practice law Pampa, Tex., 1951-76; county atty. Gray County, Tex., 1955-68, county judge, 1971-77; dist. judge 223rd Dist. Ct. Tex., 1977-91; sr. dist. judge State of Tex., 1991—. Pres. Adobe Walls coun. Boy Scouts Am., 1957-59; bd. dirs. Pampa United Fund, 1956-60. Served from ensign to lt. USNR, 1943-46; as lt., 1950-51. Recipient Silver Beaver award Boy Scouts Am., 1958. Fellow Tex. Bar Found.; mem. ABA, Tex. Bar Assn., Gray County Bar Assn. (pres. 1968), Am. Judicature Soc., Tex. Judges and Commrs. Assn., Panhandle County Judges and Commrs. Assn. (pres. 1975), Pampa C. of C. (dir. 1959-60), Phi Alpha Delta. Democrat. Baptist. Clubs: Masons, Rotary (pres. 1958-59), Pampa Country. Home: 2321 Chestnut Dr Pampa TX 79065-2910

CAIN, DOUGLAS MYLCHREEST, lawyer; b. Chgo., Sept. 8, 1938; s. Douglas M. Jr. and Louise C. (Coleman) C.; m. Constance Alexis Adams Moffit, Apr. 18, 1970; children: Victoria Elizabeth Moffit, Alexandra Catherine Moffit. A.B., Harvard U., 1960; J.D. with distinction, U. Mich., 1966; LL.M., N.Y. U., 1970. Bar: Colo. 1966, U.S. Ct. Appeals (10th cir.) 1972, U.S. Supreme Ct. 1972. Assoc. Sherman & Howard, L.L.C., Denver, 1966-72, ptnr., 1972-93; equity mem., 1993—; chmn. policy council Sherman & Howard, Denver, 1984-87; adj. prof. law U. Denver, 1972-78; mem. Rocky Mountain Estate Planning Council, pres., 1976-77. Assoc. editor: Mich. Law Rev, 1964-66; contbr. articles to profl. jours. Bd. dirs. Craig Hosp. Found., 1980-86, v.p., 1984-85, pres., 1986-87, 88-89; bd. dirs. Colo. Jud. Inst., 1990-96, chmn., 1992-93; bd. dirs. Colo. chpt. Am. Diabetes Assn., 1993; mem. Estate Planning Seminar Group; bd. dirs. Colo. Coun. Econ. Edn., 1996-98. With USN, 1960-63. Fellow Am. Coll. Tax Coun., Am. Coll. Trust and Estate Counsel; mem. ABA, Colo. Bar Assn. (gov. 1980-82), Greater Denver Tax Coun. Assn. (v.p. 1987, pres. 1988), Assn. Harvard Alumni (regional dir. 1978-81), Rocky Mountain Harvard Club (pres. 1977-78, 92-93), Denver Country Club, Mile High Club, Rotary. Home: 1960 Hudson St Denver CO 80220-1459 Office: Sherman & Howard LLC 633 17th St Ste 3000 Denver CO 80202-3665

CAIN, EDDIE, army officer; b. Apr. 1, 1948. BS in Chemistry, Jackson State U. Commd. 2d lt. U.S. Army, 1971, advanced through grades to brig. gen., 1998; chem. officer 1st Cavalry Divsn., Ft. Hood, Tex., 1987-88; polit.-mil. affairs officer Office of Sec. of State, Washington, 1988-90; comdr. 23d Chem. Bn., 9th U.S. Army, Korea, 1990-92; detailed to U.S. Army War Coll., Carlisle Barracks, Pa., 1992-93; dep. comdr. U.S. Army Chem. Materiel Destruction Agy., Aberdeen Proving Ground, Md., 1993-94; comdr. U.S. Army Chem. Activity Pacific, Johnston Island, 1994-95; chem. officer III Corps, Ft. Hood, 1995-98; joing program mgr. Biol. Def., Falls Church, Va., 1998—. Decorated Legion of Merit, Army Commendation medal, others. Office: Biol Def Ste 1200 Sky 3 5201 Leesburg Pike Falls Church VA 22041

CAIN, GEORGE HARVEY, lawyer, business executive; b. Washington, Aug. 3, 1920; s. J. Harvey and Madeleine (McGettigan) C.; m. Patricia J. Campbell, Apr. 23, 1946 (div.); children: George Harvey, James C., John P., Paul J.; m. Constance S. Collins, Aug. 10, 1985. BS, Georgetown U., 1942; JD, Harvard U., 1948. Bar: N.Y. 1949, Ohio 1972, Conn. 1977, U.S. Supreme Ct. 1995. Practiced law N.Y. State, 1949-71, 73-76; pvt. practice Ohio, 1972-73; sec., gen. counsel Nat. Carloading Corp., 1949-54; mem. firm Spence & Hotchkiss, 1954-55; gen. atty., asst. sec. Cerro Corp., 1955-68, sec., gen. atty., 1968-72; v.p., gen. counsel Pickands Mather Co., Cleve., 1971-73; v.p., sec., gen. counsel Flintkote Co., White Plains, N.Y., 1973-76, Stamford, Conn., 1976-80; spl. counsel Day, Berry & Howard, Hartford and Stamford, Conn., 1980-82; ptnr. Day, Berry & Howard, Stamford, 1983-90, of counsel, 1991—; sec. Cerro Sales Corp., 1955-71; bd. dirs., sec. Leadership Housing Sys., Inc., 1970-71; bd. dirs., gen. counsel Atlantic Cement Co., Inc., 1962-71; bd. dirs. Hajoca Corp., 1975-79, Polymer Bldg. Sys., Inc.; adj. prof. U. Bridgeport Law Sch., 1983-86. Author: Turning Points: New Paths and Second Careers for Lawyers, 1994, Law Firm Partnership: Its Rights and Responsibilities, 1995, 2nd edit., 1999. Served to 1st lt. USAAF, 1942-46; to capt. USAF, 1951-52. Fellow Am. Bar Found.; mem. ABA, N.Y. State Bar Assn., N.Y.C. Bar Assn., Ohio Bar Assn., Conn. Bar Assn., Am. Law Inst., Am. Soc. Corp. Secs., Georgetown U. Alumni Assn. (mem. alumni senate), Harvard Club N.Y., Dutch Treat Club. Home: 14 Burnt Hill Rd Farmington CT 06032-2039 Office: Day Berry & Howard City Place I Hartford CT 06103-3499

CAIN, JAMES NELSON, arts school and concert administrator; b. Arcadia, Ohio, Jan. 6, 1930; s. Alfred Ray and Gladys Eliza (Cruikshank) C.; m. Marthellen Jones, June 12, 1950; children—Nelson, Jennifer, Richard, Elizabeth. A.B., Ohio State U., Columbus, 1955. Dir. Prestige Concerts, Inc., Columbus, 1948-62; exec. dir. Music Assos. Aspen, Inc., Colo., 1962-68; from asst. mgr. to mgr. St. Louis Symphony Orch., 1968-80; v.p. St. Louis Conservatory and Schs. Arts, 1980-94. Home: 2 Nantucket Ln Saint Louis MO 63132-4111

CAIN, JOHN L., city councilman; b. Oct. 1, 1939. City councilman 1st dist. Balt., 1991—. With U.S. Army, 1961-64. Mem. Am. Legion. Lutheran. Office: Balt City Hall Rm 423 100 N Holiday St Baltimore MD 21202

CAIN, KAREN MIRINDA, musician, educator; b. Anna, Ill., Feb. 25, 1944; d. James Paul and Margaret Camilla (Sinks) C. MusB, So. Ill. U., 1966, MusM in Voice and Choral Conducting, 1967; postgrad., Trinity Coll., Washington, 1985. Cert. music tchr., Md. Choral music tchr. Prince George's County, Md., 1969-71; music tchr. class piano Montgomery County, Md., 1972-89; music tchr., founder of studio Rockville, Md., 1972—; co-founder, dir., arranger, profl. madrigal ensemble The Renaissance Revelers, 1985—; choral music dir. and soloist various chs. and synagogues, Rockville, Md., 1972-92; singer Paul Hill Chorale, Washington, 1982-90, mem. choral staff, music theory instr., 1984-90; contbr. minstrel and history guilds, performer, mem., Md. Renaissance Festival, 1987—. Dir., editor: (CD) Renaissance Romance, 1994; arranger choral works featured on Renaissance Romance; dir.: performances at The Lutheran Reformation Svc. held at The Washington Nat. Cathedral, 1995, The White House, Kennedy Ctr.; co-author (with John Sinks): Sinks: A Family History, 1980. Mem. AAUW, Md. Music Tchrs. Assn., Montgomery County Class Piano Tchrs. Assn., Mu Phi Epsilon. Home and Office: 862 College Pkwy # T-1 Rockville MD 20850-1938

CAIN, LEO FRANCIS, retired special education educator; b. Chico, Calif., July 30, 1909; s. Edmund Joseph and Myrtle (Perdue) C.; m. Margaret Brennan, Aug. 17, 1940; children: Barbara (Mrs. Richard Miller), Nancy, Caroline (Mrs. Peter Detwiler). A.B., Chico State Coll., 1931; M.A., Stanford U., 1935, Ph.D., 1939. Tchr., prin. pub. schs. Calif., 1929-40; research assoc. Am. Council on Edn., 1939; asst. prof. U. Md., 1940-43; dir. edn. Dept. Justice, 1940-43; prof. U. Okla., 1946-47; dir. spl. edn. San Francisco State Coll., 1947-51, dean ednl. services and summer session, 1951-57, v.p., 1957-62; pres. Calif. State U., Dominguez Hills, 1962-76; pres. emeritus Calif. State U., 1976—; assoc. dir. sr. accrediting commn. Western Assn. Schs. and Colls., 1976-78; dir. Inst. for Rsch. on Exceptionality, San Francisco State U., 1976-84, prof. spl. edn., coord. joint doctoral program, 1980—; spl. cons. on youth problems, West Germany, 1953, chief of party, ednl. project, Liberia, 1961; mem. Gov.'s Commn. on Mental Retardation, 1963-64; chmn. mental health council Western Interstate Commn. for Higher Edn., 1969-72; cons. Pres.'s Commn. on Mental Retardation, 1970-73, HEW Evaluation Team, Saudi Arabia, 1975, U.S. Office Edn., 1978, U. Riyadh, 1981; mem. task force on handicapped children's edn. project Edn. Commn. of States, 1972-76; mem. Calif. Commn. on Tchr. Preparation and Licensing, 1972-77; mem. accreditation commn. for sr. colls. and univs. Western Assn. Schs. and Colls., 1972-76; mem. bd. Protection and Advocacy (handicapped) State of Calif., 1978-83; mem. adv. com. Coll. Notre Dame, Calif., 1997—. Contbr. articles to profl. jours.; author: Cain-Levine Social Competency Scale. Mem. spl. ednl. adv. com. United Cerebral Palsy Assn., 1961; planning coun. United Way, 1972; bd. dirs. Nat. Easter Seal Soc., 1979-85; trustee Easter Seal Rsch. Found., 1981-84; chmn. bd. Inst. Human and Social Devel., San Mateo, 1985—; bd. dirs., v.p. Alcoholism Coun. Calif., 1984-90; bd. dirs. No. Calif. Grad. U. Lt. USNR, 1944-46. Fellow Am. Assn. Mental Deficiency (Nat. Leadership award 1977); mem. Coun. for Exceptional Children (nat. pres. 1961-62, pres.-elect pioneers div. 1990-91, pres. 1991-92, Wallin award 1972, CEC Mackie award 1999), Western Assn. Schs. and Colls. (sr. commn. rep., dir.), Phi Delta Kappa, Kappa Delta Pi. Home: 1 Baldwin Ave San Mateo CA 94401-3846 Office: San Francisco State U 1600 Holloway Ave San Francisco CA 94132-1722

CAIN, MICHAEL DEAN, research forester; b. Pascagoula, Miss., Nov. 9, 1946; s. Thomas R. and Bennie (Gleghorn) C. AS, Perkinston (Miss.) Jr. Coll., 1966; BS, Miss. State U., 1969; MS, La. State U., 1973. Registered forester, Miss. Rsch. forester So. Rsch. Sta., Pineville, La., 1975-78, Crossett, Ark., 1978-87, Monticello, Ark., 1987—. Contbr. articles to Forest Sci., So. Jour. Applied Forestry, Forest Ecology and Mgmt., Internat. Jour. Wildland Fire, New Forests, Nat. Areas Jour., Can. Jour. Forest Rsch., Am. Midland Naturalist, Jour. of the Torrey Bot. Soc., Wildlife Soc. Bull., The Cons., Tree Planters Notes, Fire Mgmt. Notes, Soc. Am. Foresters Conf. Procs., Procs. of the So. Weed Sci. Soc., univ. rsch. publs., USDA Forest Svc. rsch. publs., Ont. Forest Rsch. Inst. publ. With U.S. Army, 1969-71. Mem. Soc. Am. Foresters, Weed Sci. Soc. Am., So. Weed Sci. Soc., Ecol. Soc. Am., Internat. Assn. Wildland Fire, Soc. for Conservation Biology, Torrey Bot. Soc. Office: So Rsch Sta PO Box 3516 Monticello AR 71656-3516

CAIN, PATRICIA JEAN, accountant; b. Decatur, Ill., Sept. 28, 1931; d. Paul George and Jean Margaret (Horne) Jacka; m. Dan Louis Cain, July 12, 1952; children: Mary Ann, Timothy George, Paul Louis. Student, U. Mich., 1949-52, Pasadena (Calif.) City Coll., 1975-76; BS in Acctg., Calif. State U., L.A., 1977, MBA, 1978; M in Taxation, Golden Gate U., Los Angeles, 1988; Diploma in Pastry, Hotel Ritz, France, 1991. CPA, Calif.; cert. personal fin. planner; cert. advanced fin. planner. Tax supr. Stonefield & Josephson, L.A., 1979-87; CFO Loubella Extendables, Inc., L.A., 1987-96; pvt. practice Pasadena, Calif., 1996—; participant program in bus. ethics U. So. Calif., L.A., 1986; trainer for A-Plus in house tax Arthur Andersen & Co., 1989-90; instr. Becker CPA Rev. Course, 1989-93. Bd. dirs. Sierra Madre coun. Girl Scouts U.S.A., 1968-73, treas., 1973-75, nat. del., 1975; mem. Town Hall, L.A., 1987—, L.A. Bus. Forum, 1991—. Listed as one of top six tax experts in L.A. by Money mag., 1987. Mem. AICPA (chair nat. tax teleconf. 1988, taxation com./forms subcom. 1994—), Am. Women's Soc. CPAs (bd. dirs. 1986-87, v.p. 1987-90), Calif. Soc. CPAs (chair free tax assistance program 1983-85, high road com. 1985-86, chair pub. rels. com. 1985-89, microcomputer users discussion group taxation com., fin. com./speaker computer show and conf. 1987-93, planning com. and speaker San Francisco Tax and Microcomputer show 1988, state com. on taxation 1991—, speaker Tax Update 1992, dir. L.A. chpt. 1993-95, v.p. 1995-96), Internat. Arabian Horse Assn., Wrightwood Country Club, Beta Alpha Psi. Democrat. Episcopalian. Avocations: gourmet cooking, hiking, fishing, rug making, Arabian horses.

CAIN, R. WAYNE, sales, finance and leasing company executive; b. 1937. BA, Wayne State U., 1959; LLB, N.Y.U., 1962. Lawyer Cleary, Gottlieb, Steen & Hamilton, 1962-63; with Chrysler Corp., Chrysler Fin. Corp., 1965-81; asst. treas. Navistar Internat. Corp., 1981-85; v.p., treas. Navistar Fin. Corp., 1985—, Harco Leasing Co., Inc. Del.; treas. Harco Nat. Ins. Co. With USAF, 1963-65. Office: Navistar Fin Corp 2850 W Golf Rd Rolling Meadows IL 60008-4050*

CAIN, RAYMOND FREDERICK, landscape architect, planning company executive; b. Harrisburg, Ill., Sept. 13, 1937; s. Raymond Ransome and Edna (Kirkham) C.; m. Galen S. Short, Sept. 13, 1965 (div. 1971); m. Lois A. Kiehl, Dec. 27, 1981. B.A., U. Ill., 1959, M.A., 1962. Cert. profl. landscape architect, Md., Hawaii. Landscape architect W.J. Spear & Assoc., Houston, 1962-66; landscape architect Belt, Collins & Assoc., Honolulu, 1966-76, dir. landscape architecture, 1976—, v.p., 1981—; speaker Urban Devel. Seminar, Singapore, 1980, Fiji Hotel Assn., Nandi, Fiji, 1981; lectr. Tourist Mgmt. Sch., Honolulu, 1978. Mem. Hawaii Year 2000, Honolulu, 1971; advisor Outdoor Cir., Honolulu, 1976; mem. Waikiki Improvement Assn., Honolulu, 1973. Recipient Nat. Landscape award Mauna Kea Beach Hotel, Hawaii, 1976; Nat. Design award Kona Surf Hotel, Hawaii, 1980, Mauna Lani Golf course, 1982, Aga Khan award Tanjong Jara Hotel, Malaysia, 1983. Fellow Am. Soc. Landscape Architects (treas. 1975-76); mem. Am. Planning Assn. (assoc.). Clubs: Outrigger (ground chmn. 1976-77), Honolulu, Oahu Country (ground chmn. 1972-73). Office: Belt Collins & Assocs 1st Fl 680 Ala Moana Blvd Honolulu HI 96813-5406

CAIN, RICHARD DUANE, small business owner; b. Sullivan, Ill., Mar. 18, 1941; s. Bert and Wilma Ellen (Rhodes) C.; m. Sue Ann Price, May 20, 1967; children: J. Douglas, Ryan M., Bradley P. BS, Ea. Ill. U., 1964; postgrad., U. Ill., Champaign, 1964-66. Mktg. rep. IBM Corp., Springfield, Ill., 1966-75; owner Tom's Grill, Decatur, Ill., 1975—; co-owner Lock, Stock & Barrel, Decatur, 1977-78; tchr. Richland C.C., Decatur, 1984-88. Pres. Decatur Area Convention and Vis. Bur., 1981-83. Sgt. USAR, 1960-66. Recipient Glen Hesler award Ea. Ill. U., 1989, Alumni Svc. award Ea. Ill. U., 1996; named to Ea. Ill. U. Athletic Hall of Fame, 1997. Mem. Ea. Ill. U. Panther Club (pres. 1987), Southside Country Club (pres. 1989-90), Chgo. Dist. Golf Assn. (assoc. dir. 1997—), Elks, Jaycees (pres. Decatur club 1973), Rotary (pres. Decatur club 1990). Republican. Avocations: golf, piano, poetry. Home: 4 Montgomery Pl Decatur IL 62522-2654 Office: Toms Grill 1856 N Main St Decatur IL 62526-4332

CAIN, ROBERT JOSEPH, elementary school educator; b. Floral Park, N.Y., June 18, 1947; s. Edwin Thomas and Cecilia Marie (Dunn) C. BA in English, Hofstra U., 1972; BA in Edn., Ariz. State U., 1978, MEd, 1988. Cert. elem. tchr. Auditor Williamsburgh Savs. Bank, Bklyn., 1973-74; skip tracer, adjuster Ariz. Bank, Phoenix, 1974-75; tchr. 1st & 2d grade Paradise Valley Unified Sch. Dist. #69, Phoenix, 1979—. Actor City of Phoenix Shakespeare, 1978, Janus Theatre, Phoenix, 1980-81; actor, dir. Glendale Little Theatre, 1974-80; cantor St. Joseph's Ch., 1974—; benefactor Ariz. Opera, 1989—; supporter Met. Opera, 1980—; mem. Titanic Hist. Soc., 1980—. With U.S. Army, 1968-69. Republican. Roman Catholic. Avocations: singing, acting, antique record players and 78 rpm records, Titanic memorabilia and history, Maria Callas bibliography and discography. Home: 11012 N 45th St Phoenix AZ 85028-3013 Office: Quail Run Elem Sch 3303 E Utopia Rd Phoenix AZ 85050-3900

CAIN, SHANNON MARGARET, fundraising executive; b. Denver, June 3, 1964; d. Kathleen Margaret (Day) Day-Cain; 1 child, Brennan Margaret Cain-Nuccio. BA, U. Ariz., 1988. Mgr. special projects Fgn. Policy Assn., N.Y.C., 1989-91; fundraising assoc. Shakin, Lichty & Boreyko, N.Y.C., 1991-92; exec. dir. Women's Health Edn. Project, N.Y.C., 1992-94; pres. Cain & Co. Fundraising, Tucson, 1994—; program officer Amazon Found., 1999—. Bd. dirs. Primavera Found., Tucson, 1995-97, Rose F. Kennedy Family Ctr., New York, 1993-95; active WHAM! Women's Health Action and Mobilization, New York, 1991-94. Mem. Women's Found. So. Ariz. (bd. dirs. 1997—). Office: Ste 1102 100 North Stone Ave Tucson AZ 85701

CAIN, VERNON, information services executive; b. Bisbee, Ariz., Jan. 5, 1947. BA, No. Ariz. U., 1969; MA with honors, Roosevelt U., 1983. Pres. U.S. holdings Dawson Holdings PLC, Westwood, Mass., 1985-96; CEO, mng. dir. info. svcs. group Dawson Holdings PLC, Oregon, Ill., 1996—. Mem. Am. Libr. Assn. Office: Dawson Holdings PLC 1001 W Pines Rd Oregon IL 61061-9599*

CAIN, WILLIAM STANLEY, psychologist, educator; b. N.Y.C., Sept. 7, 1941; s. William Henry and June Rose (Stanley) C.; m. Claire Murphy, Oct. 30, 1993; children: Justin, Alison, Michael, Jennifer, Courtney. BS, Fordham U., 1963; MSc, Brown U., 1966, PhD, 1968. From asst. fellow to fellow John B. Pierce Lab., New Haven, 1967-94; from instr. to assoc. prof. depts. Epidemiology, Pub. Health, and Psychology Yale U., New Haven, 1967-84, prof. dept. epidemiology, pub. health, psychology, 1984-94; prof. surgery (otolaryngology) U. Calif., San Diego, 1994—; mem. sensory disorders study sect. NIH, Bethesda, Md., 1991-95; mem. sci. adv. bd. Ctr. Indoor Air Rsch., Linthicum, Md., 1991—. Mem. editl. bd. Chem. Senses, 1985-94; editl. adv. bd. Indoor Air, 1990—, Physiology and Behavior, 1995-96; editor 5 books, 1971—; contbr. over 200 articles to profl. jours. Recipient Crosby Field award ASHRAE, 1984, Jacob Javits/Claude Pepper award NIH, 1984, Sense of Smell award, Fragrance Rsch. Fund, 1986. Fellow APA, ASHRAE, Am. Psychol. Soc., Acad. Indoor Air Rsch.; mem. Assn. Chemoreception Scis. (exec. chmn. 1983-84), N.Y. Acad. Scis. (pres. 1986). Home: 4459 Nabal Dr La Mesa CA 91941-7168 Office: U Calif Dept Surgery 9500 Gilman Dr # Mc0957 La Jolla CA 92093-5003

CAINE, MICHAEL, actor; b. London, Mar. 14, 1933; s. Maurice and Ellen Frances Marie Micklewhite; m. Patricia Haines, 1954; children: Dominique, Natasha; m. Shakira Baksh, 1973. Asst. stage mgr. Westminster Repertory, Horsham, Sussex, England, 1953; actor Lowestoft Repertory, 1953-55, Theatre Workshop, London, 1955. Author: What's It All About?: An Autobiography, 1993; numerous TV appearances, 1957-63; appeared in play Next Time I'll Sing for You, 1963; films include A Hill in Korea, 1956, How to Murder a Rich Uncle, 1958, Zulu, 1964, The Ipcress File, 1965, Alfie, The Wrong Box, Gambit, 1966, Hurry Sundown, Woman Times Seven, Deadfall, 1967, The Magus, Battle of Britain, Play Dirty, 1968, The Italian Job, 1969, Too Late the Hero, 1970, The Last Valley, Get Carter, 1971, Zee & Co., Kidnapped, Pulp, 1972, Sleuth, 1973, The Black Windmill, Marseilles Contract, The Wilby Conspiracy, 1974, Fat Chance, The Romantic Englishwoman, The Man Who Would Be King, Harry and Walter Go to New York, 1975, The Eagle Has Landed, A Bridge Too Far, Silver Bears, 1976, The Swarm, 1977, California Suite, 1978, Beyond the Poseidon Adventure, 1979, Dressed to Kill, The Island, 1980, The Hand, Victory, 1981, Deathtrap, 1982, Educating Rita, 1983, Beyond the Limit, 1983, The Jigsaw Man, The Holcroft Covenant, Blame It On Rio, 1984, The Whistle Blower, 1985, Hannah and Her Sisters, 1986 (recipient Acad. award for best supporting actor, 1987), Water, Sweet Liberty, Mona Lisa, Half Moon Street, 1986, Jaws The Revenge, Surrender, The Fourth Protocol (also co-exec. prodr.), 1987, Without a Clue, Dirty Rotten Scoundrels, 1988, Shock to the System, 1989, Bullseye!, Jekyll and Hyde, Mr. Destiny, 1990, Noises Off, 1991, The Muppets Christmas Carol, 1992, On Deadly Ground, 1994, Bullet to Beijing, 1995, Blood and Wine, 1996, Curtain Call, 1997; (TV miniseries) Jack the Ripper, 1988, World War II: When Lions Roared, 1994 (Emmy nominee for Lead Actor in a Miniseries, 1994), (TV movie) Blue Ice, 1993, Midnite in St. Petersburg, 1995, Mandela and Deklerk, 1996, (ABC-TV) 20,000 Leagues Under the Sea, 1996, Curtain Call, 1997, Shadow Run, 1997, Little Voice, 1998, Debtors, 1999, Cider House Rules, 1999, Quills, 1999. Office: care Pam PR Inc 6290 W Sunset Blvd Fl 12 Hollywood CA 90028-8702 also: Chelsea Harbour, London England

CAINE, RAYMOND WILLIAM, JR., retired public relations executive; b. Fall River, Mass., June 30, 1932; s. Raymond W. and Emma (Gardella) C.; m. Sharon G. Henry, Nov. 10, 1956; children: Karen, Kimberly, Patrick, Peter. BS, Providence Coll., 1956. Sr. v.p. advt., pub. relations Creamer, Dickson, Basford, N.Y.C. and Providence, 1966-74; v.p. pub. rels. Blue Cross (Blue Shield), Providence, 1974-80; v.p. corp. communications Textron, Inc., Providence, 1980-94. Contbr. articles to profl. jours. Bd. dirs. R.I. Commodores, 1987—, Newport Preservation Soc., Newport Hist. Soc.; trustee The Miriam Hosp. Recipient Bell Ringer award Publicity Club Boston, 1971, 72. Mem. Pub. Rels. Soc. Am. (bd. dir. 1971-73), Machinery and Allied Products Inst. (pub. rels. coun.). Club: Turks Head (bd. dirs. Providence 1987-89). Avocations: golf, skiing, home remodeling.

CAINE, STANLEY PAUL, college administrator; b. Huron, S.D., Feb. 11, 1940; s. Louis Vernon and Elizabeth (Holland) C.; m. Karen Anne Mickelson, July 11, 1964; children: Rebecca, Kathryn, David. BA, Macalester Coll., 1962; MS, U. Wis., 1964, PhD, 1967. Asst. prof. history Lindenwood Coll., St. Charles, Mo., 1967-71; from asst. to assoc. prof. history DePauw U., Greencastle, Ind., 1971-77; prof. history, v.p. for acad. affairs Hanover (Ind.) Coll., 1977-89; pres. Adrian (Mich.) Coll., 1989—; bd. dirs. NCAA Coun., 1995-96, vice chair mgmt. coun. divsn. III, 1997-99; cons., evaluator North Ctrl. Assn., 1984—. Author: The Myth of a Political Reform, 1970; contbr. to book The Progressive Era, 1974; co-editor: Political Reform in Wisconsin, 1973. Bd. dirs. Nat. Assn. Schs., Colls. and Univs. of United Meth. Ch., 1994-97; mem. Lenawee Tomorrow, Adrian, 1989—. Recipient D.C. Everest prize Wis. State Hist. Soc., 1968; Woodrow Wilson fellow, 1962-63, Nat. Presbyn. fellow Presbyn. Ch. U.S., 1963-65. Mem. Orgn. Am. Historians, Nat. Assn. Ind. Colls. Univs. (bd. dirs. 1997—), Rotary. Methodist. Avocations: sports, reading. Office: Adrian Coll Office of Pres 110 S Madison St Adrian MI 49221-2518

CAINE, STEPHEN HOWARD, data processing executive; b. Washington, Feb. 11, 1941; s. Walter E. and Jeanette (Wenborne) C. Student Calif. Inst. Tech., 1958-62. Sr. programmer Calif. Inst. Tech., Pasadena, 1962-65, mgr. sys. programming, 1965-69, mgr. programming, 1969-70; pres. Caine, Farber & Gordon, Inc., Pasadena, 1970—; gen. mgr. Gatekeeper Systems, Pasadena, 1995—; lectr. applied sci. Calif. Inst. Tech., Pasadena, 1965-71, vis. assoc. elec. engring., 1976, vis. assoc. computer sci., 1976-84. Dir. San Gabriel Valley Learning Ctrs., 1992-95. Mem. Pasadena Tournament of Roses Assn., 1976—. Mem. AAAS, Nat. Assn. Corrosion Engrs., Am. Ordnance Assn., Assn. Computing Machinery, Athanaeum Club (Pasadena), Houston Club. Home: 77 Patrician Way Pasadena CA 91105-1039

CAIRE, WILLIAM, biologist, educator; b. Savannah, Ga., Nov. 3, 1946; s. James Andrew and Anna Elizabeth (Rahn) C.; children: William James, Jacob Wooldridge, Samuel Rahn. AA, Howard Coll., Big Spring, Tex., 1966; BS, Tex. Tech. U., 1969; MS, U. North Tex., 1972; PhD, U. N.Mex., 1978. Tchr. math. and sci. J.L. Long Jr. High Sch., Dallas, 1969-70; biologist U.S. Fish and Wildlife Svc., Ft. Collins, Colo., 1974; rsch. assoc. U. Mo., Sullivan, 1975-76; prof. biology U. Cen. Okla., Edmond, 1976—, asst. dean Coll. Math. and Sci., 1992-96; cons. on bats and rodents to various state and nat. orgns.; speaker ednl. instns. and civic orgns. Author: Mammals of Oklahoma, 1989; reviewer jour. articles; contbr. articles to profl. jours. NSF grantee U. Cen. Okla. Mem. Southwestern Assn. Naturalists, Am. Soc. Mammalogists, Okla. Acad. Sci. Avocations: golf, woodworking, gardening. Home: 10774 Coyote Cir Arcadia OK 73007-9206 Office: U Cen Okla Dept Biology Edmond OK 73034

CAIRNS, ANNEMARIE, public relations executive. Pres. Cairns & Assocs., Inc., N.Y.C., 1982—. Office: Cairns & Assocs Inc 3 Park Ave New York NY 10016*

CAIRNS, DIANE PATRICIA, motion picture executive; b. Fairbanks, Alaska, Mar. 2, 1957; d. Dion Melvin and Marsha Lala (Andrews) C. BBA, U. So. Calif., 1980. Literary agt. Sy Fischer Agy., L.A., 1980-85; sr. v.p. Internat. Creative Mgmt., L.A., 1985-96; sr. v.p. prodn. Universal Pictures, L.A., 1996-97. Mem. NOW, Acad. Motion Picture Arts and Scis., Women in Film, Amnesty Internat., L.A. County Mus. of Art, Mus. of Contemporary Art (L.A.).

CAIRNS, DONALD FREDRICK, engineering educator, management consultant; b. Coulterville, Ill., Sept. 9, 1924; s. Fred Barton and Elsie Loretta (Barbary) C.; B.S., U. Ill., 1950; M.B.A., St. Louis U., 1966, Ph.D., 1972; m. Marion Grace Huey, Sept. 2, 1950; 1 son, Douglas Scott. Asst. engr. Mo. Pacific R.R. Co., St. Louis, 1950-56; project engr., plant engr., asst. to pres., v.p. Granite City Steel Co. (Ill.), 1956-79; pres. Nat. Inter-Tech, Inc., subs. Nat. Intergroup, Inc., St. Louis, 1979-84; chmn. bd. Nat. Engrs. and Assocs. Inc., 1984-90; prof. engring. retired, Washington U., St. Louis, 1990-95, dean Sch. Tech. and Info. Mgmt. 1992-93; pres., chmn. bd. Indsl. Waste Control Council; mem. Mo. Bd. Architects, Profl. Engrs. and Land Surveyors, 1983; former guest lectr. Washington U. Grad. Sch. Bus.; adj. prof. mgmt., U. Mo., St. Louis, 1989-91; faculty Wash. U.; consulting engr. Chmn. Webster Groves (Mo.) City Planning Commn., 1958; mem. St. Louis County Traffic Commn., 1960-61, Webster Groves Bus. Devel. Commn., 1962, St. Louis County Charter Commn., 1979; mem., chmn. St. Louis County Planning Commn., 1968-76; pres., dir. Edgewood Children's Center, 1963-72; program dir. two grad. engring. degrees, mem. exec. com. Sch. Engring.; chmn. finance com. Webster Groves, 1989-90; dir. Thompson Ctr., St. Louis,

1996—, dir., treas. Webster Oaks Place, 1999; v.p. bd. trustees Webster Groves Presbyterian Ch., 1999. Served with AUS, 1943-46. Decorated Bronze Star; recipient recognition for control of air pollution Pres.'s Johnson and Nixon, 1970; registered profl. engr., Mo., Ill., Md. Mem. Am. Iron and Steel Inst., ASCE (life), Air Pollution Control Assn., Assn. Iron and Steel Engrs. (life), Southwestern Ill. Indsl. Assn. (chmn. bd.). Club: Algonquin Golf (dir.) Whitemore House, Washington U. Home: 1115 Webster Oaks Ln Saint Louis MO 63119-4661

CAIRNS, ELTON JAMES, chemical engineering educator; b. Chgo., Nov. 7, 1932; s. James Edward and Claire Angele (Larzelere) C.; m. Miriam Esther Citron, Dec. 26, 1974; 1 dau., Valerie Helen; stepchildren: Benjamin David, Joshua Aaron. B.S. in Chemistry, Mich. Tech. U., Houghton, 1955; B.S. in Chem. Engring, 1955; Ph.D. in Chem. Engring. (Dow Chem. Co. fellow, univ. fellow, Standard Oil Co. Calif. grantee, NSF fellow), U. Calif., Berkeley, 1959. Phys. chemist GE Rsch. Lab., Schenectady, 1959-66; group leader, then sect. head chem. engring. div. Argonne (Ill.) Nat. Lab., 1966-73; asst. head electrochemistry dept. GM Rsch. Labs., 1973-78; assoc. lab. dir., dir. energy and environment divsn. Lawrence Berkeley Nat. Lab., Calif., 1978-96, C.D. Hollowell meml. lectr., 1996, head, Energy Conversion and Storage Program, 1982—; prof. chem. engring. U. Calif., Berkeley, 1978—; cons. in field; mem. numerous govt. panels; Croft lectr. U. Mo., 1979. Author: (with H.A. Liebhafsky) Fuel Cells and Fuel Batteries, 1968; mem. editor bd. Advances in Electrochemistry and Electrochm. Engring., 1974—; div. editor Jour. Electrochem. Soc., 1968-91; regional editor Electrochimica Acta, 1984—; contbr. articles to profl. jours. Recipient IR-100 award, 1968, Centennial medal Case Western Res. U., 1980, R&D 100 award, 1992, Melvin Calvin medal of distinction Mich. Technol. U., 1998; named McCabe lectr. U. N.C., 1993; grantee DuPont Co., 1956. Fellow Am. Insts. Chemists, Electrochem. Soc. (chmn. phys. electrochem. divsn. 1981-84, v.p. 1986-89, pres. 1989-90, Francis Mills Turner award 1963); mem. AIChE (chmn. energy conversion com. 1970-94), AAAS, Am. Chem. Soc., Internat. Soc. Electrochemistry (chmn. electrochem. energy conversion divsn. 1977-85, U.S. nat. sec. 1983-89, v.p. 1984-88, pres. 1999—), Intersoc. Energy Conversion Engring. Conf. (steering com. 1970—, gen. chmn. 1976, 90, 97, program chmn. 1983). Patentee in field. Home: 239 Langlie Ct Walnut Creek CA 94598-3615 Office: Lawrence Berkeley Nat Lab 1 Cyclotron Rd Berkeley CA 94720

CAIRNS, JAMES DONALD, lawyer; b. Chelsea, Mass., Aug. 7, 1931; s. Stewart Scott and Kathleen (Hand) C.; m. Alice Crout Cairns, June 18, 1988; children from previous marriage: Douglas S., Timothy H., Pamela S., Heather M. AB, Harvard U., 1952; JD, Ohio State U., 1958. Bar: Fla. 1974, Ohio 1958, U.S. Dist. Ct. (no. dist.) Ohio 1975, U.S. Tax Ct. 1963. Ptnr. Squire, Sanders & Dempsey, Cleve., 1958-95, Spieth, Bell, McCurdy & Newell, Cleve., 1995—. Served to lt. (j.g.) USNR, 1952-55. Mem. ABA, Fla. Bar Assn., Ohio State Bar Assn., Bar Assn. Greater Cleve., Union Club, Edgewater Yacht Club, Shoreby Club. Democrat. Episcopalian. Office: Spieth Bell McCurdy Newell 2000 Huntington Bldg 925 Euclid Ave Cleveland OH 44115-1408*

CAIRNS, JAMES ROBERT, mechanical engineering educator; b. Indpls., Feb. 4, 1930; s. John Joseph and Agatha Bertha (Krebs) C.; m. Catherine I. DiCicco, Feb. 6, 1954; children: James Robert, Steven J., Michael P., Daniel F., Timothy E., Robert B. B.S. in Mech. Engring, U. Detroit, 1954; M.S. in Engring, U. Mich., 1959, Ph.D., 1963. Registered profl. engr., Mich. cert. energy mgr. Instr. U. Detroit, 1954-57, U. Mich., Ann Arbor, 1957-63; asst. prof. U. Mich., Dearborn, 1963-65; asso. prof. U. Mich., 1965-68, prof. mech. engring., 1968—, chmn. engring. div., 1964-73, acting dean, 1973-75, dean, 1975-81; cons. and expert witness in product liability litigation. Contbr. articles to profl. jours. Ford Faculty fellow, 1960-63. Mem. ASME, ASHRAE, Assn. Energy Engrs., Am. Soc. Engring. Edn., Common Cause, Tau Beta Pi, Pi Tau Sigma. Roman Catholic. Home: 836 Dover Dr Dearborn Heights MI 48127-4144 Office: 4901 Evergreen Rd Dearborn MI 48128-2406

CAIRNS, JOHN, JR., environmental science educator, researcher; b. Conshohocken, Pa., May 8, 1923; s. John and Eunice S. (Fesmire) C.; m. Jean Ogden, Aug. 5, 1944; children: Karen Jean, Stefan Hugh, Duncan Jay, Heather. AB, Swarthmore Coll., 1947; MS, U. Pa., 1949, PhD, 1953; DSc, SUNY, Binghamton, 1994. Curator limnology Acad. Natural Scis., Phila., 1948-66; prof. zoology U. Kans., Lawrence, 1966-68; univ. disting. prof. Va. Poly. Inst. and State U., Blacksburg, 1968-95, prof. emeritus, 1995—, dir. Univ. Ctr. Environ. and Hazardous Materials Studies. Author: Testing for Effects of Chemicals on Ecosystems, 1981, Artificial Substrates, 1982, Biological Monitoring, 1982, Modeling the Fate of Chemicals in the Aquatic Environment, 1982, Multispecies Toxicity Testing, 1985, EcoAccidents, 1985, Community Toxicity Testing, 1986, Environmental Regeneration II: Managing Water Resources, 1986, Rehabilitating Damaged Ecosystems, 1988, 2d edit., 1995, Functional Testing for Hazard Estimation, 1989, Integrated Environmental Management, 1991, Predicting Ecosystem Risk, 1992, Restoration of Aquatic Ecosystems, 1992, Environmental Literacy and Beyond, 1993, Ecological Toxicity Testing: Scale, Complexity, and Relevance, 1995, Implementing Integrated Environmental Management, 1994, Handbook of Ecotoxicology, 1995; contbr. chpts. to books, articles to profl. jours. Served with USN, 1942-46. Recipient Presdl. Commendation, 1971, Dudley award for Outstanding Publ. ASTM, 1978, Superior Achievement award U.S. EPA, 1980, Founders award Soc. Environ. Toxicology and Chemistry, 1981, Morrison medal for Outstanding Accomplishments in Environ. Scis., 1984, Environ. Program medal UN, 1988, Excellence award Am. Fisheries Soc., 1989, Life Achievement award in sci. Commonwealth Va. and Sci. Mus. Va., 1991, Disting. Svc. award Am. Inst. Biol. Scis., 1995. Fellow AAAS, Am. Acad. Arts and Scis., Women in Sci., Linnean Soc. of London, Va. Acad. Sci.; mem. NAS, Am. Microscopical Soc. (pres. 1980), Am. Water Resources Assn. (editorial bd. 1975-81, Icko Iben award 1984), Inst. Ecology (founder), Acad. Natural Scis. (rsch. assoc.), Phi Beta Kappa. Unitarian. Office: Va Poly Inst and State U Dept Biology 1020 Derring Hall Blacksburg VA 24061

CAIRNS, SARA ALBERTSON, physical education educator; b. Bloomsburg, Pa., July 18, 1939; d. Robert Wilson and Sara (Porter) Albertson; m. Thomas Cairns, Apr. 13, 1968. BS in Edn., Pa. State U., 1961; MS in Edn., West Chester U., 1965. Cert. tchr., Pa., Del., prin., Del.; adaptive p.e. specialist. Phys. edn. tchr., coach Cen. Columbia County High Sch., Bloomsburg, Pa., 1961-64; phys. edn. tchr. Christina Sch. Dist., Newark, Del., 1964—; cons. U. Del., Newark, 1984—, coop. tchr., 1965—; area coord. New Castle (Del.) County Parks and Recreation, 1973—; presenter in field. Contbr. articles to profl. publs. Chair Leasure Elem. Sch. campaign United Fund, 1987-91. Recipient Outstanding Svc. award New CAstle County Parks and Recreation, 1985. Mem. NEA, AAUW, AAHPERD, Del. Assn. Health, Phys. Edn., Recreation and Dance (v.p. dance 1991-94, exec. bd.), Del. State Edn. Assn. Democrat. Presbyterian. Avocations: toy poodles, beach, walking. Home: 40 Vansant Rd Newark DE 19711-4839 Office: Leasure Elem Sch 925 Bear Corbitt Rd Bear DE 19701-1323

CAJORI, CHARLES FLORIAN, artist, educator; b. Palo Alto, Calif., Mar. 9, 1921; s. Florian Anton and Marion (Haines) C.; m. Barbara Grossman, June 23, 1967; children: Marion, Nicole. Student, Colo. Coll., 1939-40, Cleve. Art Sch., 1940-42, Columbia, 1946-48, Skowhegan Sch., 1947, 48. Instr. Notre Dame of Md., Balt., 1950-56, Cooper Union, N.Y.C., 1956-59, 60-65; vis. artist U. Calif., Berkeley, 1959; instr. N.Y. Studio Sch., N.Y.C., 1964-69, 85—, Yale U., Hew Haven, 1989; prof. Queens Coll., N.Y.C., 1965-86. Co-founder Tanager Gallery, N.Y.C., 1952, N.Y. Studio Sch., N.Y.C., 1964; one-man shows include Howard Wise Gallery, N.Y.C., 1963, Bennington (Vt.) Coll., 1969, Landmark Gallery, N.Y.C., 1974, 81, Ingber Gallery Ltd., N.Y.C., 1976, Am. U., Washington, 1977, 88, Gross McCleaf Gallery, Phila., 1983, 85, N.Y. Studio Sch., N.Y.C., 1988, Cen. Conn. State U., New Britain, Conn., 1992, Dartmouth Coll., N.H., 1996; exhibited in numerous group shows including Chgo. Art Inst., 1964, Whitney Mus., N.Y.C., 1965, Artists Choice, 1977, 3-man show, Loeb Ctr., NYU, N.Y.C., 1970, Wadsworth Atheneum, Hartford, Conn., 1983, Bruce Mus., Greenwich, Conn., 1989, New Britain Mus., 1990; represented in permanent collections including Am. U., Washington, Del. Art Ctr., Wilmington, Met. Mus. Art, N.Y.C., Mitchner Collection, Austin, Tex., NYU, N.Y.C., U. N.Mex., Albuquerque, Walker Art Ctr., Mpls., Whitney Mus., Geigy Chem. Corp. Ardsley, N.Y., Snite Mus., U. Notre Dame, Ind., Honolulu Art Acad., Hirshhorn Mus., Washington. Served with USAAF, 1942-46. Recipient Distinction in Arts award Yale U., 1959; purchase awards Longview Found., 1962; purchase awards Ford Found., 1963; purchase awards Childe-Hassam, 1975, 76, 80; award for painting Inst. Arts and Letters, N.Y.C., 1970; Louis Comfort Tiffany award, 1979; Altman Figure prize Nat. Acad., 1983, 87, 94; Fulbright grantee, 1952-53; Nat. Endowment Arts grantee, 1981. Mem. NAD, Coll. Art Assn. Home: Litchfield Rd Watertown CT 06795 Office: NY Studio Sch 8 W 8th St New York NY 10011-9002

CAKEBREAD, STEVEN ROBERT, minister, chef; b. Pittsburg, Calif., June 19, 1946; s. Robert Harold Cakebread and Mildred Irene (McQeen) Cowing; m. Margaret Anne Spandall, July 16, 1967; children: Robert, Scott, Andrew. ABS, Nazarene Bible Coll., Colorado Springs, Colo., 1977; BA, Mid. Am. Nazarene Coll., 1979; MDiv, Am. Bapt. Sem. of the West, Berkeley, Calif., 1983; grad., Calif. Culinary Acad., San Francisco, 1996. Ordained to ministry Ch. of the Nazarene, 1980, Am. Bapt. Ch., 1984. Pastor Ch. of the Nazarene, Brookfield, Md., 1978-80; hosp. chaplain VA Hosp., San Francisco, 1988—, Oakland (Calif.) Naval Hosp./Operation Desert Storm, 1990-91, Naval Res./Naval Base, San Francisco, 1985—; pastor 21st Ave Bapt. Ch., San Francisco, 1984-92, Yountville (Calif.) Cmty. Ch., 1992—; ret. Naval Res. Chaplain Corps, 1994; chef, 1994—; coun. mem. Coun. of Chs., San Francisco, 1988; owner Paddy Cakes Home Cookin, 1999—. E-5 USN, 1966-70, Vietnam. Decorated Humanitarian Svc. medal USN, Navy Achievement medal (Desert Storm). Mem. Naval Res. Assn., ABA/USA Chaplains Coun., Am. Legion. Avocations: profl. chef, caterer, movies, walking a foggy beach. Office: Am Baptist Personnel Svc 35 E 19th St Antioch CA 94509-2643

CAKMAK, AHMET SEFIK, civil engineering educator; b. Izmir, Turkey, Feb. 14, 1934; came to U.S., 1957; s. Sefik and Nigar Cakmak; m. Norik Nagafuji, Mar. 26, 1971; children: Erika, Lisa. BS in Engring., Robert Coll., Istanbul, Turkey, 1957; MS in Engring., Princeton U., 1958, MA, 1960, PhD, 1962. Research assoc. civil engring. dept. Columbia U., N.Y.C., 1960-62; research assoc. civil engring. dept. Princeton (N.J.) U., 1962-63, asst. prof. civil engring., 1963-69, assoc. prof., 1969-71, prof., 1972—, chmn. dept. civil engring., 1971-80, 94-97, assoc. dean sch. engring., 1981-87; vis. prof. Kyoto (Japan) U., 1970-71, U. Southampton, Eng., 1981—; vis. fellow Calif. Inst. Tech., Pasadena, 1980-81; organizer conf. Soil Dynamics and Earthquake Engring., 1983, 85, 87, 89, 93, 95, 97. Co-author: Computational and Applied Mathematics for Engineering Analysis, 1987; editor Conf. Proc. Internat. Conf. Soil Dynamics and Earthquake Engring., 1983, 85, 87, 89, 93, 95; founding editor Internat. Jour. Soil Dynamics and Earthquake Engring.; contbr. articles to profl. jours. Mem. ASME, ASCE, Soc. Rheology, N.J. Soc. Profl. Engrs. Office: Princeton Univ Dept Civil Engring & Ops Rsch Princeton NJ 08544

CALABI, EUGENIO, mathematician, educator; b. Milan, May 11, 1923; Naturalized, U.S.; married, 1952; two children. BS, MIT, 1946; AM, U. Ill., 1947; PhD in Math., Princeton U., 1950. Asst. and instr. Princeton (N.J.) U., 1947-51; asst. prof. math. La. State U., 1951-55; from asst. prof. to prof. U. Minn., 1955-64, prof., 1964-69, chmn. dept., 1973-76; Thomas A. Scott Prof. math. U. Pa., Phila., 1969-93, emeritus prof., 1993—; adj. prof. U. Pa., 1993—; with Inst. Advanced Study, 1958-59, fellow, 1962-63. Mem. NAS, Am. Math. Soc. (Leroy P. Steele prize 1991). Achievements include rsch. on differential geometry and on complex manifolds. Office: U Pa Dept Math David Rittenhouse Lab 209 S 33rd St Philadelphia PA 19104-6395*

CALABRESE, ANTHONY, marine biologist; b. Providence, Feb. 25, 1937. BS, U. R.I., 1959; MS, Auburn U., 1962; PhD in Zoology, Ecology, U. Conn., 1969. Fishery biologist Nat. Oceanic & Atmospheric Adminstrn., Nat. Marine Fisheries Svc., 1962—. Mem. Am. Fisheries Soc., Nat. Shellfisheries Assn. (sec.-tres. 1974-76, v.p. 1976-77, pres. elect 1977-78, pres. 1978-79), Estuarine Rsch. Fedn., World Aquaculture Soc. Achievements include research on aquaculture and the development of biological information concerning the effect of pollutants on marine organisms, including shellfish, finfish and crustaceans, to provide a basis for environmental management. Office: Nat Marine Fisheries Svc NE Fisheries Sci Ctr Milford Lab 212 Rogers Ave Milford CT 06460-6435

CALABRESE, ANTHONY JOSEPH, gastroenterologist; b. Newark, Dec. 1, 1946; s. Arnold J. and Anna T. (Cicalese) C.; m. Nancy A. Meier, Aug. 8, 1970; children: Christopher, Michael. BS in Biology, St. Peter's Coll., 1968; MD cum laude, Jefferson Med. Coll., 1972. Intern and resident in internal medicine Temple U. Hosp., Phila.; fellow gastroenterology Thomas Jefferson U. Hosp., Phila.; chief gastroenterology svc. Andrews AFB, Washington, 1977-79; gastroenterology cons. Calvert Meml. Hosp., Prince Frederick, Md., 1979-81; staff gastroenterologist Anne Arundel Med. Ctr., Annapolis, Md., 1979—; staff No. Arundel Hosp., 1996—; pres. med. staff Anne Arundel Med. Ctr., 1993-95, trustee, 1993-98. Bd. trustees Archbishop H.S., Severn, Md., 1991-93. Maj. USAF, 1977-79. Fellow Am. Coll. Gastroenterology; mem. AMA, Am. Gastroenterological Assn., Am. Liver Found., Crohn's & Colitis Found. Am., Ocean City Light Tackle Club, Alpha Omega Alpha. Republican. Roman Catholic. Avocations: saxophone, clarinet, fishing, cooking. Office: Anne Arundel Gastroenterology Assocs 171 Defense Hwy Annapolis MD 21401-7004

CALABRESE, ARNOLD JOSEPH, lawyer; b. Summit, N.J., Nov. 18, 1960; s. Jack and Valentine (Pannullo) C.; m. Kathryn DeRosa, Aug. 16, 1986. BS in Econs. and Fin., Fairleigh Dickinson U., 1983; JD, U. Bridgeport, 1986. Bar: N.J. 1986, U.S. Dist. Ct. N.J. 1986. Law clk. intern to judge U.S. Dist. Ct. Conn., Hartford, 1985; assoc. Robert J. Hueston (merged with E. Richard Kennedy 1987), Florham Park, Montville, N.J., 1986-88, Rosenberg & Rosenberg, Florham Park, 1988-89; ptnr. Rosenberg, Rosenberg & Calabrese, Florham Park, 1990-96; pvt. practice, 1996—; lectr. N.J. chpt. Community Assn. Inst., Pennington, 1987—. Mem. ABA, N.J. Bar Assn., Morris County Bar Assn., Phi Delta Phi. Home: 4 Jolen Ct Florham Park NJ 07932-2519 Office: 171 Ridgedale Ave Ste A Florham Park NJ 07932-1764

CALABRESE, KAREN ANN, artist, educator; b. N.Y.C., May 27, 1952; d. Daniel Alexander McKnight and Janet Russell Anderson-McKnight; m. Joseph Salvatore Calabrese, Apr. 27, 1974; children: Joseph S. Jr., Brian Patrick. Art cert., Ridgewood Sch. Art, 1973. Paste-up artist, designer Ridge Type Svc., Ridgewood, N.J., 1973-77; artist, prodn. mgr. Ea. Art, Garfield, N.J., 1977-81; various jobs, freelance artist, 1981-98; art tchr. Highland Lakes, N.J., 1995—, Phoenix Sch. Art, Vernon, N.J., 1998—. Exhibited in group shows at Highland Lakes Country Club, 1994 (1st Pl. award), 95 (Hon. mention), Pub. Gallery, 1995 (Juried Show award), 98 (Juried Show award), Lake Mohawk Country Club, Sparta, N.J., 1995 (Juried Show award), Skylands Assn., Ringwood, N.J., 1997 (Juried Show award), Drue Chryst Gallery, Sparta, 1999, Perona Farms, Andover, N.J., 1999, The Pub. Glalery, Newton, Mass., 1999. Recipient 1st pl. award Decorative Artist's Workbook Mag., 1998. Avocations: photography, hiking, hunting, fishing, physical fitness.

CALABRESE, LEONARD M., social services administrator; b. Cleve., Nov. 22, 1946; s. Anthony O. and Mary M. (Buzzelli) C. BA magna cum laude, John Carroll U., 1968; MA summa cum laude, Northwestern U., Evanston, Ill., 1974; postgrad., Northwestern U., 1974-78. Cons. in neighborhood devel. Cuyahoga C.C., 1977; assoc. prof. U. Akron (Ohio), 1977-88; cons. in human resources City of Cleve., 1978; exec. dir. Commn. on Cath. Community Action, Cleve., 1987—; ofcl. election observer Nicaragua Elections, 1990; Segundo Montes lectr. John Carroll U., 1993; presenter Internat. Thomas Merton Soc. Conf., 1995; mem. interfaith civic and religious leaders del. to Israel, 1996. Co-author: Multicultural Diversity Training Manual, 1989; prodr. TV videos, 1985, 88. Active Witness for Peace, 1984, 86; chmn. Consumer Adv. Panel, Cleve., 1989-92; commr. Cleve. Poverty Commn., 1990-93; mem. Nat. Urban Ministry Bd., 1993—; bd. dirs. Greater Cleve. Interreligious Task Force on Ctrl. Am., 1991-95, Wings of Hope, Cleve., 1991-95; trustee Collinwood Art Coun., 1990-95, trustee Greater Cleve. Substance Abuse Initiative, 1995—; trustee, chair program com., exec. com. Cleve. City Club, 1996-99; mem. Cuyahoga County Welfare Reform Coun., 1997-98; chmn. Clergy and Laity Concerned, Cleve., 1984-85; nat. bd. Roundtable Action Dirs., 1995—; mem. Cleve. Workers Rights Bd., 1994—; trustee Bridge Found., 1998, RTA Dowtown Adv. Com.; mem. St. Cecilia Parish, Intercultural Cmty. Coun.; trustee, mem. exec. com. Greater Cleveland Roundtable; co-founder Small Bus. Support Ctr., 1989. Named Consumer of Year, Ohio Consumers Coun., Columbus, 1990; recipient William Evans New Frontier award, 1991, Civic Svc. award Citizens League Greater Cleve., 1996; Leadership Study grantee Louisville Inst., 1998. Mem. United Nations Assn. of USA (Greater Cleve. chpt.), Greater Cleve. Coun. on World Affairs. Avocations: music, movies, reading, poetry. Office: Commn Cath Community Action 1027 Superior Ave E Cleveland OH 44114-2503

CALABRESE, ROSALIE SUE, arts management consultant, writer; b. N.Y.C., Feb. 17, 1938; d. Julius and Florence (Tuck) Hochman; m. Anthony J. Calabrese, June 15, 1960 (div.); 1 child, Christopher. BA in Journalism, CCNY, 1959. Asst. news editor Electronic News, N.Y.C., 1960; asst. to publicist Abner Klipstein, N.Y.C., 1963; asst. to producer Leonard Field, N.Y.C., 1964; mgr. Am. Composers Alliance, N.Y.C., 1969-85, exec. dir., gen. mgr., 1985-94; dir. Rosalie Calabrese Mgmt., N.Y.C., 1983—; music advisor Phyllis Rose Dance Co., N.Y.C., 1987—, also bd. dirs.; sec. bd. dirs. Am. Composers Orch., N.Y.C., 1987-93; pres., bd. dirs. 1st Ave. Ensemble, 1993—, Golden Fleece Ltd., 1994—; bd. dirs. Friends Am. Composers, treas., 1991-94; mem. adv. bd. Downtown Music Prodns., 1991—, Joan Miller's Dance Players, N.Y.C., 1991-94; mem. adv. bd. Copland House, 1996-97. Author, lyricist: (musicals) A Hell of An Angel, Simone, Not in Earnest, Murdering MacBeth, Pop Life, Does Anyone Here Speak Arabic?, Friends and Relations, Double-Play; assoc. producer, treas. box office: (play) Courtyard, 1959, The Mime and Me; co-producer: various plays at White Lake (N.Y.) Playhouse, also packaged tours for Prodn. Assocs.; dir. night club acts for Florence Hayle; lyricist with various composers; contbr. short stories and poetry to lit. and nat. mags. Mem. Dramatists Guild, Broadcast Music Inc., Am. Music Ctr., Poets and Writers, Poetry Soc. Am. Office: Rosalie Calabrese Mgmt PO Box 20580 New York NY 10025-1521

CALABRESI, GUIDO, federal judge, law educator; b. Milan, Oct. 19, 1932; s. Massimo and Bianca Maria (Finzi Contini) C.; m. Anne Gordon Audubon Tyler, May 20, 1961; children: Bianca Finzi Contini, Anne Gordon Audubon, Massimo Franklin Tyler. BS in Analytical Econs., Yale U., 1953, LLB, 1958, MA (hon.), 1962; BA in Politics, Philosophy and Econs., Oxford U., 1955, MA in Politics, Philosophy and Econs., 1959; LLD (hon.), Notre Dame U., 1979, Villanova U., 1984, U. Toronto, 1985, Boston Coll., 1986, Cath. U. Am., 1986, U. Chgo., 1988, Conn. Coll., 1988, Chgo.-Kent-I.T.T., 1989, William Mitchell Coll. Law, 1992, Princeton U., 1992, Detroit Mercy Sch. Law, 1994, Seton Hall U., 1995, Albertus Magnus Coll., 1995, Lewis and Clark Coll., 1996, St. John's U., 1997, Pace U., 1998, Iona Coll., 1998, Roger Williams U., 1999, Hofstra U., 1999, N.Y. Law Sch., 1999; Dott. Ius SD (hon.), U. Turin, Italy, 1982; JD (hon.), U. Pavia, Italy, 1987, U. Stockholm, 1993; PhD (hon.), U. Haifa, Israel, 1988; DPhil, U. Tel Aviv, 1998; LHD (hon.), U. New Haven, 1989, Williams Coll., 1991, Roger Williams U., 1999, Hofstra U., 1999, Quinnipiac Coll., 1993; DSc in Politics (hon.), U. Padua, Italy, 1990; Dott. Jur. (hon.), U. Bologna, Italy, 1991, U. Milan, 1998. Bar: Conn. 1958. Asst. instr. dept. econs. Yale U., New Haven, Conn., 1955-56; law clk. to Justice Hugo Black U.S. Supreme Ct., Washington, 1958-59; asst. prof. Yale U. Law Sch., 1959-61, assoc. prof., 1961-62, prof., 1962-70, John Thomas Smith prof. law, 1970-78, Sterling prof. law, 1978-95; prof. emeritus, lectr. Yale U., 1995—; dean Yale U. Law Sch., 1985-94; Sterling prof. law emeritus, lectr. Yale U. Law Sch., New Haven, 1995—; judge U.S. Ct. Appeals 2d cir., New Haven, 1994—; fellow Timothy Dwight Coll., 1960—; vis. prof. Harvard U. Law Sch., 1969-70, Japan Am. Studies Seminar, Kyoto-Doshisha Univs., summer 1972, European U. Inst., Florence, Italy, 1979; Arthur L. Goodhart prof. legal sci. Cambridge U., also fellow St. John's Coll., 1980-81. Author: The Costs of Accidents: A Legal and Economic Analysis, 1970; (with P. Bobbitt) Tragic Choices, 1978; A Common Law for the Age of Statutes, 1983 (ABA citation of merit, Order of Coif Triennial Book award); Ideals, Beliefs, Attitudes and the Law: Private Law Perspectives on a Public Law Problem (Silver Gavel award ABA), 1985; contbr. articles to legal jours. Hon. trustee Hopkins Grammar Sch., pres. 1976-80; trustee St. Thomas More Chapel, Yale U.; vice chmn. bd. trustees Carolyn Found., Minn. Rhodes scholar, 1953; named one of Ten Outstanding Young Men Am., U.S. Jaycees, 1962; recipient Laetare Medal, U. Notre Dame, 1985, Marshall-Wythe medal Coll. William and Mary, 1985. Fellow Am. Acad. Arts & Scis., Associazione Italiana di Diritto Comparato, Brit. Acad. (corr.), Royal Swedish Acad. Scis. (fgn.), Accademia Nazionale dei Lincei (fgn.), Accademia delle Scienze di Torino (fgn.); mem. Conn. Bar Assn., Assn. Am. Law Schs. (exec. com. 1986-89), Am. Philos. Soc. Home: 639 Amity Rd Woodbridge CT 06525-1206 Office: US Ct Appeals 2d Cir 157 Church St New Haven CT 06510-2100

CALABRESI, PAUL, oncologist, educator, pharmacologist; b. Milan, Apr. 5, 1930; U.S. citizen; married; three children. BA, Yale U., 1951, MD, 1955; MD (hon.), U. Genova (Italy), 1996. Diplomate Am. Bd. Internal Medicine. Intern Harvard Med. Svc., Boston City Hosp., 1955-56, asst. resident, 1958-59; project assoc. U. Wis., 1956-58; from instr. to assoc. prof. medicine and pharmacology Yale U., 1960-68; prof. med. sci. Brown U., 1968-83, chmn. dept. medicine, 1974-93, Emer chmn. dept. medicine, 1993—; clin. prof. pharmacology Coll. Pharmacy, U. R.I., Kingston, 1977—; prof. pharmacology R.I. Hosp, 1981—; field investigator Nat. Cancer Inst., NIH, 1956-60, mem. cancer chemotherapy collaborative program rev. com., 1965-66, bd. sci. counselors, 1983-88; mem. Pharmacol.-Toxicol. Rev. Com., Nat. Inst. Genetic Med. Sci., 1967-70, exptl. therapeutic study sect., 1972-76, chmn., 1975-76; rsch. fellow dept. medicine Yale U., 1959-60, head divsn. clin. pharmacology and chemotherapy, dir. clin. pharmacol. rsch. ctr., 1965-67; vis. scientist U. Lausanne, Switzerland, 1966-67; physician-in-chief, chmn. dept. medicine Roger Williams Gen. Hosp., Providence, 1968-91, v.p. acad. affairs, 1977-91; mem. rsch. coun. and drug rsch. bd. NAS, 1968-75; mem. sci. group on evaluation and testing of drugs for mutagenicity, principles and problems WHO, 1971; cons. Study Group Hycanthone, 1971; counselor Environ. Mutagen Soc., 1971-74; chief medicine Women and Infants Hosp. R.I., 1974-80; cons. Miriam Hosp., Meml. Hosp., Providence VA MEd. Ctr., R.I. Hosp., St. Joseph's Hos., 1974—; mem. Sci. and Pub. Affairs Com., Am. Assn. Cancer Rsch., 1983—; mem. Nat. Cancer Adv. Bd., Nat. Cancer Inst., 1991—, chmn., 1991-94, mem. pres.'s cancer panel, 1995—; dir. divsn. clin. pharmacology R.I. Hosp., 1994—; dir. Brown-Tufts Cancer Ctr., 1997—; vis. prof. numerous univs. Burroughs Wellcome scholar clin. pharmacology, 1964-68; Eleanor Roosevelt Internat. Cancer fellow Am. Cancer Soc., 1966-67. Master ACP (mem. sci. program com. 1975-78, clin. pharmacol. com. 1977-82, chmn. 1978-82); mem. Inst. Medicine-NAS, Am. Soc. Hematology, Am. Soc. Pharmacology and Exptl. Therapeutics, Am. Soc. Clin. Oncology (pres. 1969-70), Am. Fedn. Clin. Rsch., Am. Assn. Clin. Rsch., Am. Bd. Internal Medicine (sec.-treas. 1982-84), Am. Cancer Soc. (St. George medal 1996), Am. Soc. Clin. Pharmacology and Therapeutics (38th Oscar B. Hunter Meml. award 1995). Office: Rhode Island Hosp Aldrich Bldg Rm 124 593 Eddy St Providence RI 02903-4923

CALABRIA, DEB FLANAGAN, playwright, director; b. N.Y.C., Jan. 11, 1957; d. Gerald Bernard Flanagan and Audrey Elaine (Noell) Calabria. BS in Comm., Fla. State U., 1981; MA in Comm., Ga.. State U., 1997. Ordained minister Universal Life Ch., 1998. Mental health specialist Peachford Charter Psychiat. Hosp., Dunwoody, Ga., 1981-83; dir. sales/mktg. Top of the Line Distbrs., Atlanta, 1984-86; grad. asst. Ga. State U., Atlanta, 1992-97; exec. v.p. Chapter 2 Pub., Atlanta, 1993-95; co-leader Resolutions Inc./Fulton County Jail, 1995—; dir./instr. Shepherd Ctr.'s One Step Beyond Comedy Troup, Atlanta, 1992—; founder, artistic and mng. dir. Funny...That Way Theatre Co., Atlanta, 1989—. Playwright/dir.: The Wars With In, 1999, Skits-o-Frenzy, 1998, Roadtrips Revisited, 1998, Outcasts of the Sea Swishbucklers and Dykeneers, 1997, Bones and Mae, 1997, Homo on the Range, 1996, Hetside Story, 1996, Out into The Woods, 1995, Suicidal Tendencies, 1994, Snow White & The 6 Dykes, COMEALOT, 1992, Sleepin' Baby, 1992. Mem. Human Rights campaign, Atlanta, 1997; vol. instr. Detention Ctr., Tallahassee, 1976-81. Recipient Cert. of Appreciation, Office of the Gov., State of Fla., 1980, Trispro Scholarship Fund award, 1997. Mem. Global Relationship Ctr. Democrat. Avocations: movies, travel, bungy junping, reading. Home and Office: Studio B 731 Highland Ave NE Atlanta GA 30312-1400

CALABRO, JOANNA JOAN SONDRA, artist; b. Waterbury, Conn., Dec. 2, 1938; d. Theodore Gruwien and Madeleine Elizabeth (Raynor) Reinhard; m. John Paul Calabro, Oct. 15, 1960; 1 child, Victor Theodore. Student, Paier Sch. Art, 1965-66, Mus. of Fine Arts Sch., 1976, Rice U., 1977; student of sculpture with, Bruno Lucchesi, Pietrasanta, Italy, 1982. Art instr. at gallery workshops Houston, 1975-78; co-owner Archway Gallery, Houston,

1975-78, Fine Arts of Rockport, Mass., 1989—. One woman shows include Five Star Gallery, Houston, 1974-75, Roberts Gallery, Houston, 1977, Dayton (Ohio) Soc. of Painters, 1983, Wilmington (Ohio) Coll., 1983, Rockport Art Assn., 1989, 92; represented in permanent collections at Am. Embassy, Bratislava, Slovak Republic. Sculpture instr. for merit badge Sam Houston Area coun. Boy Scouts Am., Houston, 1978; juror for scholastic art shows, Tex., 1975, Ohio, 1982, numerous other art shows, Conn., Tex., Ohio, Mass., 1970—; mem. art coun. Bd. Selectmen, Rockport, 1994. Recipient numerous awards including 1st Place award Champions Art, 1974, Am. Pen & Brush Women, 1975, Conn. Classic Art, 1978, Martha Moore Meml. award, 1989, Richard Ricchia Meml. award, 1990, R.V. T. Steeves award, 1990, William N. Ryan award, 1991. Mem. Am. Artist Profl. League, Rockport Art Assn. (bd. dirs. 1992-93), Guild Boston Artists, The Copley Soc. of Boston, Am. Medallic Sculpture Assn., Federation Internat. de la Me'daille. Avocations: foreign travel, study of the arts. Studio: 32 Main St Rockport MA 01966-1532

CALADO, MIGUEL MARIA, food company executive; b. Lisbon, Portugal, July 25, 1955; came to U.S., 1994; d. Jose Maria and Maria Rosario (Oliveira) C.; m. Maria Da Gama, Apr. 15, 1980; children: Maria Gama, Filipa Gama, Andre Gama. BS in Acctg., Cath. U., Brazil, 1979, BS in Bus. Adminstrn., 1981. Asst. contr. Samarco SA, Belo Horizonte, Brazil, 1976-81; contr. Renz-Zanini, Sao Paulo, Brazil, 1981-82, fin. dir., CFO, 1982-83; v.p. fin., CFO Pepsi Cola do Brazil, Rio de Janeiro, 1983-87, Pepsi Cola Far East, Singapore, 1987-90, Pepsi Cola Asia, Hong Kong, 1990-92, Gamesa SA, Monterrey, Mexico, 1992-94; v.p. fin. Pepsico Foods Internat., N.Y.C., 1994-95; sr. v.p. fin., CFO Frito-Lay Internat., Dallas, 1996-98; exec. v.p., pres. Internat. Suiza Foods Corp., Dallas, 1998—. Home: 3600 Amherst Ave Dallas TX 75225-7421 Office: Suiza Foods Corp 2575 McKinney Ave # 1200 Dallas TX 75201

CALAHAN, DONALD ALBERT, electrical engineering educator; b. Cin., Feb. 23, 1935; s. Joseph Dexter and Loretta Margaret (Reichling) C.; m. Martha Meyer, Aug. 22, 1959; children: Donald Theodore, Patricia Susan, Mary Susan, Judith Lynn. B.S., U. Notre Dame, 1957; M.S., U. Ill., 1958, Ph.D., 1960. Asst. prof. elec. engring. U. Ill., 1961-65; prof. elec. engring. U. Ky., 1965-66; prof. computer engring. U. Mich., Ann Arbor, 1966—; indsl. cons. in high speed computation, 1976—. Author: Modern Network Synthesis, 1964, Computer-Aided Network Design, 1967, rev. edit., 1972, Introduction to Modern Circuit Analysis, 1974. Served to 1st lt. U.S. Army, 1961-62. Fellow IEEE. Roman Catholic. Home: 3139 Lexington Dr Ann Arbor MI 48105-1461 Office: U Mich Dept Elec Engring & Computer Sci Ann Arbor MI 48109

CALAMAR, GLORIA, artist; b. N.Y.C., Sept. 7, 1921; d. Louis B. and Dina (Cotter) Calamar; m. R.L. Redgate, Aug. 22, 1950 (div. 1972); children: Chris James, Steven Clay, Michael Cotter. Cert., Otis Art Inst., L.A., 1943; student, Art Students League, N.Y.C., 1944-45; BA in Art History, State Univ. Coll. N.Y. at New Paltz, 1970. Instr. art history and painting Orange County (N.Y.) Community Coll., 1964-69; instr. art history Mt. St. Mary Coll., Newburgh, N.Y., 1968-69; instr. painting Santa Barbara City Coll., 1975-80; judge Hallmark Art Contest, N.Y., 1968; lectr. Woodstock (N.Y.) Sch. Art, 1994; color slide lectr. throughout world. Artist in water color, oil, pen and ink, 1946—; onw woman shows include Georgetown U., 1974, Portland (Oreg.) C.C., 1973, Willamette U., 1972, U. Oreg., 1971-72, U. Calif. at Berkeley, 1969, Santa Barbara (Calif.) Mus. Art, 1950, Musée d'Art Moderne de la Ville de Paris, 1967, Galérie de la Madeleine, Brussels, Belgium, 1964, Landau Gallery, Beverly Hills, Calif., 1953, Parnassus Sq., Woodstock, N.Y., 1978, Ibiza, Balearic Islands, Spain, 1978, Santorini, Greece, 1980, Beaux Arts Ctr., Tunis, Tunisia, 1981, Alkamal Gallery, Jerusalem, Israel, 1981, Jaisalmer, India, 1984, Women's Cmty. Bldg., Santa Barbara, 1986, Jewish Cmty. Ctr., San Francisco, 1986; group shows include Delgado Mus., New Orleans, 1950, San Francisco Art Assn., 1953, L.A. County Mus. Art, 1954, Bertrand Russell Centenary Invitational, London, 1972-73, Woodstock Art Assn., 1978, Faulkner Gallery Santa Barbara, 1992, 93; curated Santa Barbara Visual Art League Exhbn., 1993, 94; book, video Tar Pits Park Landmark Proposal, Portola Sycamore Tree Landmark Proposal, Carpinteria Airport Landmark Proposal, Juarez-Hosmer Adobe Landmark Proposal, Leaping Greyhound Bridge Landmark Proposal, Los Clavelitos Landmark Proposal, Los Cruces Adobe Landmark Proposal, De la Cuesta Adobe Landmark Proposal; author: Traveling Artist, 1995; contbr. articles to publs; prodr. (video) The Traveling Artist, 1996—. Curator Visual Artists League Exhbn., Santa Barbara, 1992, 93, 94, 95; mem. Santa Barbara County Hist. Landmark Adv. Commn. Nat. Endowment for Arts grantee, 1980-81. Mem. Woodstock (N.Y.) Art Assn. (life), Alumni Assn. Otis Art Inst. (L.A.), Art Students League N.Y. (life), Santa Barbara Visual Artists League. Web site: http://www.comtv.com/air/prg/ptart.html. Studio: PO Box 844 Summerland CA 93067-0844 *Many people have told me that I am a strong painter and add in the same breath—like a man. Others have asked me which comes first—my work or my children. I wonder how many male artists have been evaluated or interrogated in the same way. To the former I say thank you for the evaluation of strength but to be a woman artist does not preclude this ingredient. To the latter (I say) one interest supports the other and each is given priority at different times. Much in the same way that food and drink are necessary to the whole person and each is given priority at different times.*

CALAMARI, ANDREW M., lawyer; b. N.Y.C., Jan. 23, 1918; s. Frank and Caterina Calamari; m. Madeline Redmond, Aug. 1, 1959; children: Andrew, Michael, Joseph, David. BA, CCNY, 1939; JD cum laude, Fordham U., 1942. Bar: N.Y. 1942, U.S. Dist. Ct. (so. dist.) N.Y. 1948, U.S. Dist. Ct. (ea. dist.) N.Y. 1950, U.S. Ct. Appeals (2d cir.) 1964, U.S. Supreme Ct. 1973. Assoc. McLanahan, Merritt & Ingraham, N.Y.C., 1946-59, Buell, Clifton & Turner, N.Y.C., 1959-68; ptnr. Manning, Nakasian & Carey, N.Y.C., 1968-83, Calamari & Calamari, N.Y.C., 1983—. Sgt. U.S. Army, 1943-46. Mem. ABA, N.Y. State Bar Assn., Am. Arbitration Assn. (nat. panel arbitrators 1957—), Fordham Law Rev. Assn. (editorial bd. 1941-42), KC. Democrat. Roman Catholic. Office: Calamari & Calamari 2429 Hering Ave Bronx NY 10469-5425

CALAMARO, RAYMOND STUART, lawyer; b. Cairo, May 28, 1944; came to U.S., 1947, naturalized, 1960; s. Albert and Charlotte (Golub) C.; m. Jaana Pirinen; 1 child, Alexander M. AB, Cornell U., 1966; JD, NYU, 1969. Bar: N.Y. State 1970, U.S. Supreme Ct. 1975, D.C. 1976. Legis. dir. Sen.Gaylord Nelson, Washington, 1973-75; exec. dir. Com. for Pub. Justice, N.Y.C., 1975-76; adj. faculty New Sch. Social Rsch., N.Y.C., 1976; staff profl. Carter/Mondale Transition Team, Washington, 1976-77; dep. asst. atty. gen. Office Legis. Affairs, Dept. Justice, Washington, 1977-79; pvt. practice Washington and Brussels, 1979-85; team leader Clinton-Gore Transition Team, 1992-93; ptnr. Hogan & Hartson, Washington, 1995—; U.S. vice-chmn. U.S.-Korea Com. on Bus. Coop., 1997—. Recipient Royal Order of Polar Star King Carl XVI Gustav, Sweden, 1989. Mem. Met. Club (Washington), St. Albans Tennis Club (Washington). Home: 5073 Lowell St NW Washington DC 20016-2616 Office: Hogan & Hartson 555 13th St NW Washington DC 20004-1109 also: Ave des Arts 41, 1040 Brussels Belgium

CALAME, BYRON EDWARD, journalist; b. Appleton City, Mo., Apr. 14, 1939; s. Harry Franklin and Gladys Verl (Neal) C.; m. Kathryn Lee Boehm, June 9, 1962; children: Christine Lee, Jonathan David. B.J., U. Mo., 1961; M.A. in Polit. Sci, U. Md., 1966. Staff reporter Wall St. Jour., 1965-74, bur. mgr., 1974-87, asst. mng. editor, 1985-87, sr. editor, 1987-92, dep. mng. editor, 1992—; Thomas Jefferson disting. vis. lectr. U. Mo., Columbia, 1997. Served to lt. USN, 1961-65. Recipient Faculty-Alumni award U. Mo., Columbia, 1996. Mem. Am. Soc. Newspaper Editors, Soc. Am. Bus. Editors and Writers (bd. govs.). Office: Wall Street Journal 200 Liberty St New York NY 10281-0083

CALAME, KATHRYN LEE, microbiologist, educator; b. Leavenworth, Kans., Apr. 23, 1940; d. Jay O. and Marjorie B.; m. Byron Edward Calame, June 9, 1962; children: Christine Lee, Jonathan David. BS, U. Mo., 1962; MS, George Washington U., 1965, PhD, 1975. Asst. prof. biol. chemisty UCLA, 1980-85, assoc. prof., 1985-88, prof., 1988; prof. microbiology Coll. Physicians and Surgeons Columbia U., N.Y.C., 1988—. Exec. editor: Nucleic Acids Rsch., 1992-98; mem. bd. rev. editors: Sci. Mag., 1988—; contbr. articles to profl. jours. Bd. trustees Leukemia Soc. Am., N.Y.C., 1992—, chair grant rev. com., 1992-96. Recipient Stohlman award Leukemia Soc. Am., 1989, Faculty Alumni award U. Mo., Columbia, 1996; disting. lecture in basic sci., Columbia Physicians and Surgeons, 1998. Fellow AAAS; mem. Am. Assn. Biochemistry and Molecular Biology (chair pub. com. 1992-93). Democrat. Avocations: cooking, gardening, reading, antiques. Office: Columbia U Dept Microbiology 701 W 168th St New York NY 10032-2704

CALARCO, N. JOSEPH, theater educator; b. N.Y.C., Mar. 19, 1938; s. Charles and Vincenza (Marrara) C.; m. Margot Demarais, Mar. 1964 (div. 1981); children: Deidre L., Joseph V. AB, Columbia U., 1959, MA, 1962; PhD, U. Minn., 1966. Instr. U. Minn., Mpls., 1964-66; asst. prof. U. Calif., Berkeley, 1966-68; from asst. prof. to prof. theatre Wayne State U., Detroit, 1968—; artistic dir. Wayne State Playwrights' Workshop, 1992-94; pres. TransArt Prodns., N.Y.C., 1982-86; cons. in field. Author: Tragic Being: Apollo and Dionysus in Western Drama, 1968; (play) Telephone: A Play in Three Calls, 1990, The Tragedy of Ajax, 1992, Beethoven, 1996; prin. theorist of tragedy: Tragedy and Tragic Theory: An Analytical Guide, 1992; contbr. articles to profl. jours.; dir. 50 theatrical prodns. (Best Play of Decade award 1970-80). Bd. dirs. City of Troy (Mich.) Bicentennial Ethnic Festival, 1976. Recipient Theatre Achievement award Detroit Free Press, 1996. Mem. Dramatists Guild, AAUP, Soc. Stage Dirs. and Choreographers, Assn. Theatre in Higher Edn. Avocations: weight training, photography, music. Home: 1826 Eastport Dr Troy MI 48083-1719 Office: Wayne State U Dept Theatre Detroit MI 48202

CALARCO, VINCENT ANTHONY, specialty chemicals company executive; b. N.Y.C., May 29, 1942; s. George Michael and Madeline C.; m. Linda Joyce Maniscalco, Apr. 10, 1971; children: David V., Christopher G. B.S., Poly. Inst., Bklyn., 1963; M.B.A., Harvard U., 1970. With Crompton & Knowles Corp; pres., CEO Crompton & Knowles Corp, N.Y.C., 1985—; chmn. bd. Crompton & Knowles Corp, 1986—. Trustee Poly. U. Served with U.S. Army, 1966-68. Mem. Am. Chem. Soc., Soc. Chem. Industry (pres. 1998—, chmn. Am. sect. 1998-99), Harvard Bus. Sch. Club, Chem. Mfrs. Assn. (chmn. bd. internat. com., chmn. Office of Chem. Industry Trade Advisor, mem. fin. com.), Nat. Foun. for History of Chemistry (trustee), Rhodia (bd. dirs.), ASARCO (bd. dirs.). Office: Crompton & Knowles Corp Metro Ctr 1 Station Pl Stamford CT 06902-6800

CALATO, DAMIAN, television executive; b. New Orleans, Oct. 9, 1956. BA in Media & TV, U. Southwestern La., 1978. Sales rep. KLFY-TV, Lafayette, La., 1989-91; gen. mgr. WGMB-TV, Baton Rouge, 1991—. Mem. Sales & Mktg. Execs. Internat., Nat. Assn. Broadcasting, TV Broadcasters. Office: WGMB-TV 5220 Essen Ln Ste B Baton Rouge LA 70809-3542*

CALAWAY, DENNIS LOUIS, insurance company executive, real estate broker, financial execuitce; b. Helena, Ark., Dec. 10, 1960; s. Carl Jr. and Mary Jean (Taylor) C.; m. Elizabeth Anne Suiter, July 16, 1988; children: Sean Joseph, Katherine Elizabeth, Bridget Marie, Sarah Anne. BS in Bus. Adminstrn., Ark. State U., 1983, MBA, 1988, grad. leaders program, 1999. Registered health underwriter; life underwriter tng. coun. fellow; lic. real estate broker, Ark.; registered employee benefit cons.; cert. profl. in human resources. Ops. mgr. Churchill Truck Lines, Jonesboro and Litte Rock, Ark., 1983-85; rep. Mut. of Omaha Cos., Jonesboro, 1985-88; pres. Profl. Ins. Svcs., Inc., 1988—; gen. agt. State Life Ins. Co. of Ind., Time Ins. Co. and United Am. Ins. Co., 1988—, Security Gen. Life Ins. Co., 1989—, GPM Life Ins. Co., 1991—; prin. broker Calaway Realty Co., 1992—; pres. Profl. Fin. Svcs., Inc., 1993—; CFO, Davis Electric Motors, Inc., 1993-94; co-founder TDI Bearing & Supply, Inc., 1994; account exec., indsl. benefit cons. Health Choice of Jonesboro, Inc./Meth. Hosp. of Jonesboro, 1995-98; with First American Group, 1998; CFO, Davis Electric Motors, Inc., 1993-94; benefit cons. Health Choice of Jonesboro, 1995, bus. instr. Ark. State U., 1995, 98, 99, Sterling Coll., 1997, S.W. Baptist U., 1997-99. Chief counsellor Columbian Squire Cir., 1988-93; mem. pastoral coun. Blessed Sacrament Cath. Ch., 1990-92, founder, pres. Soc. St. Therese, 1975—; mem. fin. com. Blessed Sacrament Cath. Sch., 1994-95; asst. cubmaster Boy Scouts Am., 1998—. Fellow Life Underwriters Tng. Coun. (instr. 1990-91, moderator 1991, 1998, chmn. 1991-92, Amb. Club, Silver Club); mem. Nat. Assn. Health Underwriters, Nat. Soc. Human Resource Mgmt., N.E. Ark. Soc. Human Resource Mgmt. (v.p. legis. affairs 1997-98, v.p. programs, pres. elect 1999), Gen. Agts. and Mgrs. Conf., Nat. Assn. Life Underwriters, Ark. State Assn. Life Underwriters (state health chmn. 1997-98), Jonesboro Assn. Life Underwriters (sec.-treas. 1986-88, pres.-elect 1988-89, pres. 1989-91, health chmn. 1992—), Govs. Partnership for Chldn's and Families (bd. dirs. 1997—), Assn. Health Ins. Agts., World Safety Orgn. (v.p. membership 1996-97), KC (treas. 1982-83, 84-87, faithful scribe 1983-84, faithful navigator 1986-88, grand knight 1981-83, faithful adm. 1989-90, faithful trustee 1991—, Ark. youth dir. 1989-92, chmn. Ark. squires 1989-92, Knight of Yr. award 1982, 88), Lions, Jerry Suiter Found. (bd. dirs. 1998—), Beta Gamma Sigma, Omicron Delta Epsilon, Gamma Iota Sigma. Home: PO Box 1 State University AR 72467-0001 Office: Profl Ins Fin Svcs Inc PO Box 419 Jonesboro AR 72403-0419 also: CSA Mktg Inc PO Box 2700 State University AR 72467-2700

CALAWAY, JAMES, elementary education educator. Secondary tchr. conservation sci. MacArthur Jr. High Sch., Lawton, Okla. Recipient Conservation Tchr. award (South Central, Nat. Assn. Conservation Dist., ICI Americas, 1992. Office: MacArthur Jr High Sch 510 NE 45th St Lawton OK 73507-6199*

CALCAGNO, ANNE, writer, educator; b. San Diego, Nov. 14, 1957; d. Louis and Kathryn Smoke Calcagno; m. Leo Michael Fitzpatrick, Sept. 7, 1986; children: Jessamyn Claire, Lucien Gabriel. BA, Williams Coll., 1979; MFA, U. Mont., 1984. Lectr. Sch. Art Inst., Chgo., 1990-93; assoc. prof. DePaul U., Chgo., 1993—; program coord. Ill. Arts Coun., Chgo., 1991. Author: Pray for Yourself, 1993; editor: Travelers Tales Italy, 1998. Nat. Endowment for Arts fellow, 1989, Ill. Arts Coun. fellow, 1991. Mem. Poets and Writers, Authors Guild. E-mail: acalcagn@wppost.depaul.edu. Office: DePaul Univ English Dept 802 W Belden Chicago IL 60614

CALCATERRA, EDWARD LEE, construction company executive; b. St. Louis, Mar. 26, 1930; s. Frank John and Rose Theresa (Ruggeri) C.; m. Patricia Jean Marlow, July 4, 1953; children—Christine, Curtis, David, Richard, Tracy. B.S.C.E., U. Mo., Rollo, 1952. Registered profl. engr., Mo. Estimator J.S. Alberici Constrn. Co., St. Louis, 1955-57, mgr. project, 1957-63, v.p. ops., 1963-71, sr. v.p., 1971-76, exec. v.p., 1976-91, pres., 1991-96; exec. dir. J.S. Albenci Constrn. Co., St. Louis, 1996—. Bd. dirs. Cardinal Ritter Inst., St. Louis, 1980-83; bd. regents Rockhurst Coll., Kansas City, Mo., 1983—. Served with U.S. Army, 1953-55. Mem. Assoc. Gen. Contractors St. Louis (pres. 1980). Roman Catholic. *

CALCAVECCHIA, MARK, professional golfer; b. Laurel, NE, June 12, 1960. Profl. golfer, 1981—. Winner S.W. Classic, 1986, Honda Classic, 1987, Bank of Boston Classic, 1988, L.A. Open, 1989, Phoenix Open, 1989, 90, 92, Austrailian Open, 1988; British Open, 1989; Argentine Open, 1993, 95; BellSouth Classic, 1995; Greater Vancouver Open, 1997; Subaru Sarazen World Open, 1997; Honda Classic, 1998. Office: IMG c/o David Yates 1360 E 9th St Cleveland OH 44114*

CALCE, BRENDA V., airport executive; b. Sault Ste Marie, Ont., Canada, Sept. 5, 1954. Resource mgr. Sault Ste Marie Airport, mgr. ops. and maintenance, mgr., 1996—. Mem. Am. Assn. Airport Execs., Internat. Assn. Airport Execs. Canada. Office: Sault Ste Marie Airport, PO Box 1 RR 1, Sault Sainte Marie, ON Canada P6A 5K6*

CALDER, IAIN WILSON, publishing company executive; b. Scotland, Feb. 27, 1939; came to U.S., 1967; s. William and Charlotte G. (West) C.; m. Jane Brownlea Bell, Apr. 17, 1965; children—Douglas William, Glen Robert Bell. Student pub. schs., Falkirk, Scotland. Reporter Falkirk Sentinel, 1955-56, Stirling Jour., 1956, Falkirk Mail, 1956-60, Glasgow Daily Record, 1960-64; London bur. chief Nat. Enquirer, 1964-67, articles editor, 1967-73, exec. editor, 1973-75, editor, 1975-91; pres. Nat. Enquirer, Lantana, Fla., 1976-95, editor-in-chief, 1991-95; editor emeritus Nat. Enquirer, Lantana, 1995-97; exec. v.p. pub. Am. Media Inc., 1994-97; dir. Am. Media, Inc./Nat. Enquirer, Inc.; Disting. lectr. Fla. Atlantic U. Bd. dirs. Bethesda Hosp. Assn., 1997—. *

CALDER, KENT EYRING, political science educator, diplomat; b. Salt Lake City, Apr. 18, 1948; s. Grant H. and Rose (Eyring) C.; m. Toshiko Matsuura; children: Mari, Ryan. BA with honors, U. Utah, 1970; AM, Harvard U., 1972, PhD, 1979. Staff mem. U.S. Ho. of Reps., Washington, 1968-69; teaching fellow Harvard U. Dept. of Govt., Cambridge, Mass., 1972-74; rsch. economist U.S. Fed. Trade Commn., Washington, 1974-78; visiting fellow U. Tokyo, Japan, 1977-78; exec. dir. U.S.-Japan Program Harvard U., Cambridge, 1979-80, lectr., 1979-83; asst. prof. Woodrow Wilson Sch. Princeton (N.J.) U., 1983-89, assoc. prof., 1989—, dir. U.S.-Japan program, 1990—; internat. adv. bd. Japanese Ministry of Fin., Inst. of Fiscal and Monetary Policy, Tokyo, 1987-96; Japan chair Ctr. for Strategic and Internat. Studies, Washington, 1989-91, 96; spl. advisor to U.S. Amb. to Japan, 1996—. Author: Crisis and Compensation, 1988 (Ohira and Arisawa Meml. prizes 1990), Japan's Changing Role in Asia, 1992, Strategic Capitalism, 1993, Pacific Defense, 1996 (Mainichi Asia-Pacific Grand prize 1997); co-author: The Eastasia Edge, 1982. Instr. Japan Soc. U.S.-Japan Leadership Program, N.Y.C., 1988-91, U. Pa. Wharton Sch. Internat. Forum, 1990—; trustee Princeton in Asia, 1987—; mem. Coun. on Fgn. Rels., 1990—, internat. adv. bd. Waseda U. Sch. Asia-Pacific Studies, 1998—. 1st lt. U.S. Army, 1975-76. Named Fulbright Faculty Fellow and Doctoral Fellow, 1985-86, 75-76, Faculty Research Fellow The Japan Found., 1984, Graduate Prize Fellow Harvard U., 1970-74. Mem. Am. Polit. Sci. Assn., Assn. for Asian Studies, Phi Beta Kappa, Phi Kappa Phi (Sparks Fellow 1970-71, Gibbs Fellow 1970), OECD Tide 2000 Club. Avocations: stamp collecting, collecting classic African musical instruments, tennis. Home: 197 Shadybrook Ln Princeton NJ 08540-4135 Office: US Embassy Tokyo Unit 45004 Box 200 APO AP 96337-5004

CALDERA, LOUIS EDWARD, federal official; b. El Paso, Tex., Apr. 1, 1956; s. Benjamin Luis and Soledad (Siqueiros) C.; m. Eva Orlebeke Caldera. BS, U.S. Mil. Acad., 1978; JD, MBA, Harvard U., 1987. Bar: Calif. 1987. Commd. 2nd lt. U.S. Army, 1978, advanced through ranks to capt., 1982, resigned commn., 1983; assoc. O'Melveny & Myers, L.A., 1987-89, Buchalter, Nemer, Fields & Younger, L.A., 1990-91; deputy county counsel County of L.A., 1991-92; mem. Calif. State Assembly, 46th Dist., L.A., 1992-97, chmn. banking and fin. com.; mng. dir., COO Corp. for Nat. Svc., Washington, 1997-98; Sec. of the Army Washington, 1998—. Democrat. Roman Catholic. Home: 5605 York Ln Bethesda MD 20814-1150 Office: Secretary of the Army 101 Army Pentagon Washington DC 20310-0101*

CALDERON, MARK A., artist, sculptor; b. Bakersfield, Calif., Oct. 31, 1955; s. Julian Paul and Patricia Ruth Calderon. BA with distinction, San Jose (Calif.) State U., 1978. Artist and sculptor. Recipient Betty Bowen Meml. award Seattle Art Mus., 1986, Seattle Artists award Seattle Arts Commn., 1997; WESTAF/NEA regional fellow for visual arts, Santa Fe, 1993; Art Matters Inc. fellow, 1989, 95. Democrat. Avocations: yoga, hiking, camping. Home: 924 26th Ave Seattle WA 98122

CALDERWOOD, JAMES LEE, former English literature educator, writer; b. Corvallis, Oreg., Apr. 7, 1930; s. George P. and Ruby (Williamson) C.; m. Cleo Xeniades, Aug. 14, 1955; children: Stuart P., Ian G. BS, U. Oreg., 1952; PhD, U. Wash., 1963. Instr. English Mich. State U., East Lansing, 1961-63; asst. prof. UCLA, 1963-66; prof. U. Calif., Irvine, 1966-94, vice chair dept., 1968-74, assoc. dean Sch. Humanities, 1974-94. Author: Shakespearean Metadrama, 1971, Metadrama in Shakespeare's Henriad, 1979, To Be and Not To Be: Negation and Metadrama in Hamlet, 1983, If It Were Done: Tragic Action in Macbeth, 1986, Shakespeare and the Denial of Death, 1987, The Properties of Othello, 1989, A Midsummer Night's Dream, 1992; editor: Shakespeare's Love's Labour's Lost; (with H. E. Toliver) Forms of Poetry, 1968, Perspectives on Drama, 1968, Perspectives on Poetry, 1968, Perspectives on Fiction, 1968, Forms of Drama, 1969, Essays in Shakespearean Criticism, 1969, Forms of Prose Fiction, 1972, Forms of Tragedy, 1972; contbr. articles to profl. jours. 1st lt. U.S. Army, 1952-54. Recipient Alumni Achievement award Coll. of Arts & Sci., U. Oreg., 1991. Democrat. Avocation: tennis. Home: 1323 Terrace Way Laguna Beach CA 92651-2829 *Anyone who appears in Who's Who and does not feel in some degree an impostor is an impostor.*

CALDERWOOD, STANFORD MATSON, investment management executive; b. Scottsbluff, Nebr., Nov. 6, 1920; s. Herbert Merle and Hazel Emjore (Matson) C.; m. Norma Jean Smith, Mar. 17, 1942. B.A., U. Colo., 1942. Reporter-photographer Manchester (N.H.) Union-Leader, 1946-48; staff corr. U.P.I., 1948-51, bus. rep., 1951-52; pub. relations writer Eastern Gas & Fuel Assos., Boston, 1952-53; with Polaroid Corp., Cambridge, Mass., 1953-70; v.p. advt. Polaroid Corp., 1960-62, v.p. sales and advt., 1962-66, v.p. marketing, 1966-69, exec. v.p., 1969-70; pres., dir. Polaroid of Japan, 1962-70, Polaroid Overseas, 1962-70, Polaroid Can., 1962-70, Polaroid France, 1965-70; pres. Polaroid GmbH, 1965-70, Polaroid (Italia) S.p.A., 1965-70; gen. mgr. dir. Polaroid (Nederlands), N.V., 1962-70; gen. mgr. Polaroid (Internat.) N.V., 1965-70; pres. WGBH Ednl. Found., Boston, 1970-71; cons. Corp. Pub. Broadcasting, 1971-72; vice chmn., dir. Endowment Mgmt. & Research Corp., Boston, 1972-77; pres. Trinity Investment Mgmt. Corp., Boston, 1978-85, chmn., chief exec. officer, 1985—; lectr. econs. Wellesley Coll., 1972-73, vis. prof., 1974—; trustee Ea. Enterprises, 1977-93. Bd. dirs. Internat. Student Assn., 1965-69; bd. dirs. MacDowell Colony, also treas., 1973-78; bd. overseers Old Sturbridge (Mass.) Village; trustee Radcliff Coll., 1960-72, Boston Inst. Contemporary Art; corporator Boston Mus. Sci.; vis. com. Center for Internat. Affairs, Harvard, 1976-83. Served to lt. USNR, 1942-46. Recipient Norlin award for Disting. Achievement U. Colo., 1986. Mem. Pi Gamma Mu. Home: 136 Fletcher Rd Belmont MA 02478-2019 Office: 75 Park Plz Boston MA 02116-3934

CALDERWOOD, WILLIAM ARTHUR, physician; b. Wichita, Kans., Feb. 3, 1941; s. Ralph Bailey and Janet Denise (Christ) C.; m. Nancy Jo Crawford, Mar. 31, 1979; children: Lisa Beth, William Arthur II. MD, U. Kans., 1968. Diplomate Am. Bd. Family Practice. Intern Wesley Med. Ctr., Wichita, 1968-69; gen. practice family medicine Salina, Kans., 1972-80, Peoria, Ariz., 1980—; med. dir. First Am. Home Care, 1994-96, First Am. Homecare, 1995—; pres. staff St. John's Hosp., Salina, 1976; 28th jud. dist. coroner State of Kans., Wichita, 1978-80; cons. in addiction medicine VA Hosp., 1989-94; bd. dirs. Pelms House; assoc. prof. Midwestern U., Phoenix AZ, 1998—. Inventor, patentee lighter-than-air-furniture. Bd. dirs. Pelms House (For Chem. Dependence), 1995—, Gen. Health Medcare, 1995—. Fellow Am. Acad. Family Physicians; mem. AMA, Ariz. Med. Soc. (physicians med. health com., exec. com. 1988-92), Maricopa County Med. Soc., Ariz. Acad. Family Practice (med. dir. N.W. Orgn. Vol. alternatives 1988-91), Am. Med. Soc. on Alcoholism and Other Drug Dependencies (cert.), Shriners. Home: 7015 W Calavar Rd Peoria AZ 85381-4706 Office: 14300 W Granite Valley Dr Sun City West AZ 85375-5783

CALDWELL, ANN WICKINS, academic administrator; b. Rochester, N.Y., Dec. 3, 1943; d. Ralph Everett and Constance Ann (McCoy) Wickins; m. Herbert Cline Caldwell, Sept. 17, 1966; children: Constance Haley, Robert James. BA in English Lit., U. Mich., 1965. Reporter Democrat & Chronicle, Rochester, 1961-64; asst. to dean Harvard Grad. Sch. of Edn., Cambridge, Mass., 1965-70; editor alumni quarterly Harvard Grad. Sch. of Edn., Cambridge, 1968-71; freelance editor, writer Harvard U. and Radcliffe, Cambridge, 1971-73; assoc. sec. Philips Acad., Andover, Mass., 1973-80; v.p. for planning and resources Wheaton Coll., Norton, Mass., 1980-90; assoc. dir. Mus. Fine Arts, Boston, 1990-91; v.p. for devel. Brown U., Providence, 1991-97; interim pres. Mass. Gen. Hosp. Inst. Health Professions, Boston, 1997—; trustee Women's Edn. and Indsl. Union, Boston, 1989-91, John Hope Settlement House, Providence, 1997—. Contbr. chpt. to book. Chair Bicentennial Com., Newburyport, Mass., 1974-76, Citizens Adv. Com./Pub. Sch., Newburyport, 1979-80; bd. dirs. Am. Laryngological Voice Rsch. & Edn. Found., 1997—. Mem. Coun. for Advancement and Support of Edn. (trustee, sec. dist. 1 1985-87, trustee, sec. nat. 1987-89), Women in Devel. Boston (founder, pres. 1984-86), Chilton Club, Phi Delta Kappa. Avocations: skiing, sailing, traveling, reading. Office: MGH Inst Health Professions 101 Merrimac St Boston MA 02114-4724

CALDWELL, BILLY RAY, geologist; b. Newellton, La., Apr. 20, 1932; s. Leslie Richardson and Helen Merle (Clark) C.; m. Carolyn Marie Heath;

children: Caryn, Jeana, Craig. *Wife Caroline Caldwell, Baylor University graduate, retired as secretary for Texas Utilities after 29 years of service. Daughter Caryn Weaver, is assistant physical education teacher at Plano Independent School District. Son-in-law Steve is electrical engineering graduate from Texas A&M University, and sales engineer for FUJITSU, Richardson, Texas. Their children are Stephanie, Christopher and Lindsay. Daughter Jeana Braley, University of North Texas graduate, Interdisciplinary Studies, is fifth grade teacher for Denton Independent School District. Son-in-law Tracy is foreman for Huffines Dodge, Lewisville, Texas. Son Craig Caldwell is project Engineer at NORTEL, Richardson, Texas. Daughter-in-law Lisa is marketing coordinator for Micrografx, Garland, Texas.* BA, Tex. Christian U., 1954, MA, 1970. Cert. petroleum geologist, cert. profl. geologist. Geologist Geol. Engring. Svc. Co., Ft. Worth, Tex., 1954-60; sci. tchr. Ft. Worth and Lake Worth Sch. Dists., 1960-63; mgr. Outdoor Living, 1963-71; instr. geology Tarrant County Coll., Ft. Worth, 1971—; petroleum and environ. geologist cons., Ft. Worth, 1971—. Bd. dirs. Ft. Worth and Tarrant County Homebuilders Assn., 1973; co-chmn. Ft. Worth Environ. Coun. Named Dir. of Yr. Ft. Worth Jaycees, 1966-67. Mem. Am. Inst. Profl. Geologists, Am. Assn. Petroleum Geologists, Geol. Sco. Am., Ft. Worth Geol. Soc., Soc. Profl. Well Log Analysts. Republican. Baptist. Avocations: traveling, church work. Home: 305 Bodart Ln Fort Worth TX 76108-3804 Office: PO Box 150989 Fort Worth TX 76108-0989

CALDWELL, CHARLES M., federal judge; b. 1954. BS, Evansville U., 1976; JD, Northwestern U., 1979. Asst. U.S. trustee U.S. Dist. Ct. (so. dist.) Ohio, 1988-93; staff atty. bankruptcy divsn. Adminstrv. Office U.S. Cts., Washington, 1986-88; bankruptcy judge U.S. Dist. Ct. (so. dist.) Ohio, Columbus, 1993—. Fax: (614) 469-2478. Office: US Dist Ct So Dist Ohio 170 N High St Columbus OH 43215

CALDWELL, CORRINNE ALEXIS, academic administrator; b. Vancouver, B.C., Can., May 16, 1942; d. Alex and Auriol (Jewell) Forst; m. Elio Amadeus Azzara, May 20, 1966 (div. June 1977); children: Alexander Azzara, Benjamin Azzara; m. Lawrence Caldwell, Jan. 2, 1981. BA in Psychology and English, U. British Columbia, 1963, MSW, 1966; PhD, U. Pa., 1985. Supr. Child Welfare, Mental Health and Hosp. Social Work, 1966-75; dir. career programs Fraser Valley Coll., Abbotsford, B.C., Can., 1975-80; rsch. asst. U. Pa. Grad. Sch. Edn., Phila., 1980-81; dean. math., phys. scis., engring. technologies Community Coll. of Phila., 1981-87; campus exec. dir. Penn State Mont Alto, 1987—; affiliate asst. prof. Coll. of Edn. Pa. State U., University Park, 1989; presenter in field. Contbr. articles in profl. jours. Named Tri-State Women on Move Herld-Mail Co., 1989. Mem. Pa. Assn. Colls. and Univs., Am. Coun. Edn., Nat. Identification Program for Women in Higher Edn., Pa. Hosp. Trustees Assn., Am. Assn. for Higher Edn., Am. Assn. Community and Jr. Colls., Am. Assn. Women Community and Jr. Colls., Waynesboro Rotary, Franklin County Area Devel. Corp. Edn. Com., Easter Seal Soc. Franklin and Adams Counties Task Force. Avocations: tennis, horseback riding, sailing, travel. Office: Pa State U Mont Alto Campus Campus Dr Mont Alto PA 17237-9799

CALDWELL, COURTNEY LYNN, lawyer, real estate consultant; b. Washington, Mar. 5, 1948; d. Joseph Morton and Moselle (Smith) C. Student, Duke U., 1966-68, U. Calif., Berkeley, 1967, 1968-69; BA, U. Calif., Santa Barbara, 1970, MA, 1975; JD with highest honors, George Washington U., 1982. Bar: D.C. 1984, Wash. 1986, Calif. 1989. Jud. clk. U.S. Ct. Appeals for 9th Cir., Seattle, 1982-83; assoc. Arnold & Porter, Washington, 1983-85, Perkins Coie, Seattle, 1985-88; dir. western ops. Edn. Real Estate Svcs., Inc., Irvine, Calif., 1988-91, sr. v.p., 1991-98; ind. cons., Orange County, Calif., 1998—. Bd. dirs. Univ. Town Ctr. Assn., 1994; bd. dirs. Habitat for Humanity, Orange County, 1993-94, chair legal com., 1994. Named Nat. Law Ctr. Law Rev. Scholar, 1981-82. Mem. Calif. Bar Assn. Avocation: foreign languages. Home and Office: 140 Cabrillo St Apt 15 Costa Mesa CA 92627-3038

CALDWELL, CURTIS IRVIN, acoustical engineer; b. Columbus, Ohio, Mar. 4, 1947; s. Elmer Irvin and May Alice (Wing) C.; m. Susan Marion Belcher, Dec. 22, 1972; 1 child, Joshua Benjamin Lee. BS, U. S.C., 1972; MA, U. North Fla., 1983; PhD, Pa. State U., 1994. Sr. analyst Analysis and Tech., Inc., North Stonington, Conn., 1973-81, cons., 1981-84; instr. U. North Fla., Jacksonville, 1984; grad. rsch. asst. Pa. State U., State College, 1984-91; servant Coll. Engring. Office Continuing and Distance Edn. Pa. State U., 1995; asst. prof. U.S. Naval Acad., Annapolis, Md., 1997—; v.p., editor Pa. State U. Engring. Grad. Student Coun.; mem. NOISECON 87 com. Inst. Noise Control Engring.; mem. organizing com. E. Coast Multi-REDCOM Tech. Tng. Meeting, 1993; chmn. Session Info. Mgmt. Issues; lectr. on stats. of complex variables with applications to sonar signal processing. Rep. precinct chmn., 1995-97; vol. Clinger for Congress Campaign, State College, 1988, 90, 92, 94, Clinger's Thornburg for Senate Campaign, State College, 1991, Conway for Congress primary campaign, 1996, Peterson for Congress Campaign, 1996; majority insp. of elections Patton Twp. Primary Elections, 1997; mem. com. to combat prejudice St. Andrew's Episcopal Ch., State Coll., 1996-97; Trinity Episcopal Sch. for Ministry network rep. Diocese of Ctrl. Pa., 1994-97. With USN, 1968-70, 73, 97-99. Mem. Acoustical Soc. Am. (conf. com. 1989-90, 97, sec. local chpt. 1985-86), Inst. Math. Statistics, Am. Math. Soc., Am. Statis. Assn., Math. Assn. Am., Sons of Am. Revolution. Republican. Episcopalian. Achievements include research in development of general multivariate exponential family maximum likelihood detector as an estimator-subtractor, adaptive beamforming, multivariate statistics of complex variables, Jacobians of transformations of complex variables, trigonometry of complex matrices and zonal polynomials of two complex matrix arguments. Home: 1147 Skyway Dr Annapolis MD 21401-4902

CALDWELL, DAVID BRUCE, music store executive; b. N.Y.C., Mar. 19, 1956; s. John M. and Faye (DeFalco) C. BA in Creative Writing, Queens Coll., 1976. Mgr. Halco Music, Massapequa, N.Y., 1974-80; pres. Caldwell Connection, Whitestone, N.Y., 1980—; cons. in field; music instr. in field. Author: (poetry) Night Drinks, 1976; songwriter for music group Thirst (Most Promising Band, 1984); appeared in music video Prysmid, 1984. Mem. Whitestone Civic Orgn., 1985—. Recipient High Honors Creative Writing Queens Coll., 1976, Regents scholarship N.Y. State Regents, 1972; winner Writers Digest Poetry Contest, 1976. Mem. Internat. Soc. Musical Instrument Repairmen, Audio Engring. Soc., Soc. Profl. Audio Recording Svcs. Avocations: paddleball, walking, reading, carpentry, local politics. Office: Caldwell Connection 14-20 150th St Whitestone NY 11357-1750

CALDWELL, DELMAR RAY, ophthalmologist, educator; b. Putnam, Okla., Oct. 29, 1935; children: Delmar Ray Jr., William Mark, Samantha Ann. MD, U. Okla., 1961. Lic. physician, Okla., Tex., Miss., La. Intern U. Tex., Galveston, 1961-62; pvt. practice Richmond, Tex., 1962-69; resident in ophthalmology Baylor Coll. Medicine, Baylor U., 1969-72, fellow in anterior segment surgery and external disease, 1972-73; assoc. prof. ophthalmology Sch. Medicine, U. Miss., 1973-78; chief ophthalmology svc., mem. exec. com. Tulane Med. Ctr. Hosp. and Clinic, New Orleans, 1978; prof., chmn. dept. ophthalmology Sch. Medicine, Tulane U., New Orleans, 1978—; dir. sect., mem. dean's com. VA Hosp., New Orleans, 1978—, Alexandria, La., 1978—; chief ophthalmology Charity Hosp.-Tulane, New Orleans, 1978-86, Huey P. Long Charity Hosp., Alexandria, 1978-82; dir. sect., mem. dean's com. VA Hosp., Biloxi, Miss., 1980—; assoc. examiner Am. Bd. Ophthalmology, 1980-83; mem. sci. adv. bd. Genetic Labs., Inc.; mem. internat. med. adv. bd. Project Orbis; cons. Touro Infirmary, New Orleans, 1978—, Lafayette (La.) Gen. Hosp., 1978—; cons. to editorial bd. Jour. La. State Med. Soc.; mem. med. adv. bd. Eye Bank Assn. Am., 1984—; med. dir. So. Eye Bank, New Orleans, 1980—, also bd. dirs.; med. dir. Miss. Lions Eye Bank, 1973-78; acting med. dir. Lions Eyes of Tex. Eye Bank, Houston, 1971-73; presenter profl. confs.; mem. internat. med. adv. bd. Project ORBIS. Editor: Medi-Guide to Ophthalmology, 1980-82; contbr. numerous articles and revs. to profl. and sci. jours., 1970—; author/co-author poster presentations for profl. orgns. With Tex. Army N.G. Recipient Mosby Scholastic Book award; named La. State Thoroughbred Breeder of Yr., 1996; rsch. grantee numerous orgns., including Burroughs Wellcome & Co., 1975, Stella Butler Rsch. Fund, 1978—, Tulane Med. Aux., 1979, 80, Alcon Labs., Inc., 1986, 87, 88, 89, Merck Sharp & Dohme, 1987, 88, 89, 90, Dupont Pharms., 1988, Optical Radiation Corp., 1990, CryoOptics, Inc., 1990. Fellow ACS, Am. Acad. Ophthalmology (mem. pub. and profl. educating com., mem. pub. edn. resource group); mem. AMA, ARVO, Am. Ophthalmol. Soc. (assoc.), Am. Soc. Cataract & Refractive Surgery, Assn. Univ. Profs. of Ophthalmology, Assn. Rsch. in Vision and Ophthalmology, Internat. Eye Surgeons Assocs., Soc. for Prevention of Blindness (bd. dirs. Miss. chpt. 1978), La.-Miss. Ophthalmol. and Otolaryngology Soc. (program chmn. 1981, councilor for La. 1982-83), Internat. Glaucoma Congress, Jackson Ophthalmol. Soc. (pres. 1978), Baylor Eye Resident Assn., New Orleans Acad. Ophthalmology (treas. 1986, chmn. transactions com. 1981—, mem. exec. com. 1984), Tulane Eye Alumni, La. Ophthalmology Assn., Ocular Microbiology and Immunology Soc., County Med. Soc. (pres. 1969), Orleans Parish Med. Soc., Castroviejo Soc. (assoc.), Phi Eta Sigma. Office: Tulane Univ Med Ctr 1430 Tulane Ave New Orleans LA 70112-2699*

CALDWELL, DOUGLAS W., clergyman; b. Charlotte, N.C., May 7, 1943; s. David Franklin and Margaret (Ashburn) C.; m. Barbara Ann Brautigam, June 4, 1966; children: Douglas, Ashley. BA, Moravian Coll., Bethlehem, Pa., 1966; MDiv, Moravian Theol. Sem., Bethlehem, 1969; DMin, Drew U., 1985. Ordained to ministry Moravian Ch., 1969. Pastor Reading (Pa.) Moravian Ch., 1969-75, College Hill Moravian Ch., Bethlehem, 1975-83; sr. pastor Ctrl. Moravian Ch., Bethlehem, 1983—; mem., v.p. ea. dist. exec. bd. Moravian Ch., 1974-86; mem., sec. bd. trustees Moravian Coll., 1990—; mem., vice chmn. bd. trustees St. Luke's Hosp., 1985—. Author newspaper column Bethlehem Globe Times, 1989-91. Bd. dris. Lehigh Valley Cmty. Found., 1996—, Bethlehem Area Moravians, 1996, AAA East Penn, 1997. Mem. Moravian Theol. Sem. Alumni Assn. (founding mem., pres. 1974-78), The Bethlehem Club, Saucon Valley Country Club. Avocations: golf, tennis, skiing. Home: 63 W Church St Bethlehem PA 18018

CALDWELL, ELWOOD FLEMING, food scientist; b. Gladstone, Man., Can., Apr. 3, 1923; s. Charles Fleming and Frances Marion (Ridd) C.; m. Irene Margaret Sebille, June 13, 1949; children: John Fleming, Keith Allan; m. Florence Annette Zar, June 23, 1979. BS, U. Man., 1943; MA in Food Chemistry, U. Toronto, 1949, PhD in Nutrition, 1953; MBA, U. Chgo., 1956. Chemist Lake of the Woods Milling Co., Can., 1943-47; research chemist Can. Breweries Ltd., Toronto, Ont., 1948-49; chief chemist Christie, Brown & Co. div. Nabisco, Toronto, 1949-51; research assoc. in nutrition U. Toronto, 1951-53; with Quaker Oats Co., Barrington, Ill., 1953-72, dir. research and devel., 1969-72; prof., head dept. food sci. and nutrition U. Minn., St. Paul, 1972-86, exec. assoc. to dean Coll. Agr., 1986-88; dir. sci. svcs. Am. Assn. Cereal Chemists, 1988-94, analysis svcs. coord., 1994-98; exec. editor Cereal Foods World, 1986-91; chmn. bd. Dairy Quality Control Inst., Inc., St. Paul, 1972-88, R. & D. Assocs. for Mil. Food & Packaging, Inc., San Antonio, 1970-71; chmn. evening program in food sci. Ill. Inst. Tech., Chgo., 1965-69. Contbr. articles to sci. jours. Chmn. North Barrington (Ill.) Bd. Appeals, 1966-69, mayor, 1969-72; vice-chmn. Barrington Area Council Govts., 1972; bd. dirs. Family Guidance Barrington, 1971-72. Recipient cert. of appreciation for civilian service U.S. Army Materiel Command, 1970. Fellow Am. Assn. Cereal Chemists (Geddes Meml. award 1996), Inst. Food Technologists (Chmn.'s Svc. award Chgo. sect. 1975, Chmn.'s award Minn. sect. 1977, Calvert L. Willey Disting. Svc. award 1991); mem. Am. Assn. Family and Consumer Scis., Kiwanis, Phi Tau Sigma (nat. pres. 1980-81), Gamma Sigma Delta (award of merit 1988), Phi Upsilon Omicron. Republican. Lutheran.

CALDWELL, GAIL, book critic; b. Amarillo, Tex., Jan. 20, 1951; d. Bill M. and Ruby C. BA, U. Tex., 1978, MA in Am. Studies, 1980. Instr. U. Tex., Austin, to 1981; book critic, book editor Boston Globe, 1985—; judge Radcliffe Bunting Fiction Fellowship; nominator Irish-Times/Aer Lingus Internat. Fiction Prize; mem. Pulitzer jury fiction, 1991. Mem. PEN New Eng. (bd. dirs.), Nat. Book Critics Circle. Office: The Boston Globe PO Box 2378 135 Morrissey Blvd Boston MA 02125-3338

CALDWELL, GARNETT ERNEST, lawyer; b. Houston, July 2, 1934; s. William Ernest and Ethel Leona (Jones) C. B.A., U. Houston, 1957, J.D., 1959. Bar: Tex. 1958. Pvt. practice law Houston, 1959-64; ptnr. Ginther, Erwin, Dillard & Caldwell, Houston, 1964-65, Prappas, Caldwell & Moncure, Houston, 1965-77, Caldwell & Baggott, Houston, 1977-82, Caldwell, Wallis, Pruitt & Baggott, Houston, 1982; pvt. practice Houston, 1982-85, 87-90, Houston and Galveston, 1990—; ptnr. Caldwell & Lareau, 1985-87; lectr. govt. U. Houston, 1961-62. 2d lt. U.S. Army, 1957, lt. col. Res., 1977—. Decorated knight and knight comdr. Royal Yugoslavian Order St. John of Jerusalem. Mem. Galveston County Bar Assn., Houston Bar Assn., Houston Bankruptcy Conf., Res. Officers Assn., Houston Early Music Soc., Delta Theta Phi. Roman Catholic. Home: 1619 Post Office St Galveston TX 77550-4813 Office: 1619 Post Office St Galveston TX 77550-4813

CALDWELL, HOWARD CLAY, retired broadcast journalist, writer; b. Indpls., July 18, 1925; s. Howard Clay and Elsie Rebecca (Felt) C.; m. Helen Lynn Gruenholz, Mar. 20, 1955; children: Tracy Lynn Caldwell Reidy, Virginia Ellen Caldwell Hingst, Susan Caldwell. Diploma in journalism, Butler U., 1950, M in Polit. Sci., 1968, PhD (hon.), 1984; PhD (hon.), Ind. U., Kokomo, 1992. Reporter, editor Hagerstown (Ind.) Exponent, 1950-51; reporter WTHI Radio, Terre Haute, Ind., 1952-54; news anchor, news dir. WTHI-TV, Terre Haute, 1954-59; asst. news dir., anchor, reporter WRTV-TV, Indpls., 1959-94, commentator, 1994-95; tchr. Ind. U.-Purdue U., Indpls., 1987. Author: Coach of All Seasons, 1984, pictorial book of Indpls., 1984, History of Circle Theatre, 1984. Mem. Ind. Journalism Hall of Fame Selection Com., Greencastle, 1975—; pres. Svc. Club of Indpls., 1985-86; chmn. pub. rels. com. Goodwill Industries, Indpls., 1963-76; chmn. student affairs com. Butler U. Bd. Trustees, 1979-82; bd. dirs. Ctrl. Ind. Reading for Blind. Served with USN, 1944-46, 51-52. Named to Ind. Broadcasters Hall of Fame, Ind. Broadcasters Assn., Indpls., 1991; recipient Casper awards Cmty. Svc. Coun., Indpls., 1989, 94. Mem. Soc. Profl. Journalists (pres. Indpls. chpt. 1966, named to Ind. Journalism Hall of Fame 1991), Radio-TV News Dirs. Assn. (assoc.), Ind. Broadcaster Pioneers (co-chmn. adv. com. 1996—), Svc. Club Indpls. (historian 1995—), Indpls. Press Club (pres. 1973, scholarship com. 1985—). Republican. Methodist. Avocations: tennis, walking, local theater history, literature, music. Home: 6742 Lowanna Ct Indianapolis IN 46220-4361

CALDWELL, JAMES D., hospitality company executive; married; 3 children. BBA in Acctg. with highest honors, U. Tex., 1977, JD with honors. Acct. Peat Marwick, Houston, Corpus Christi; ptnr. law firm; v.p., gen. counsel TRT Holdings, Inc., 1991-96; pres. Omni Hotels, 1996. Office: Omni Hotels 420 Decker Dr Irving TX 75062

CALDWELL, JOHN ALVIS, JR., experimental psychologist; b. New Orleans, June 16, 1955; s. John Alvis and Patsy Ruth (Richardson) C.; m. Jo Lynn Woodard, July 18, 1981. BA cum laude, Troy State U., 1976; MS in Psychology, U. South Ala., 1979; PhD in Psychology, U. So. Miss., 1984. Psychologist II Eufaula (Ala.) Adolescent Adjustment Ctr., 1979-80, coord. drug-free clinic, 1980-81; asst. dir. behavioral med. lab. Children's Hosp. Nat. Med. Ctr., Washington, 1984-86; rsch. psychologist U.S. Army Aeromed. Rsch. Lab., Ft. Rucker, Ala., 1986—; sec., chief edn. working group 19 NATO Adv. Group R&D, 1991-94; math. and sci. adv. com. mem. Troy State U., 1992—; adj. faculty U.S. Army Sch. Aerospace Medicine, 1996—; mem. spkrs. bur. Nat. Sleep Found., 1996—, mem. scientific coun., 1999—; instr. Army Flight Surgeon's course, Ft. Rucker, Ala., 1996—; instr. Army Aviation Psychology course, Ft. Rucker, 1998—; instr. U.S. Army Aviation Pre-Command Course, 1997—; chmn. sci. rev. com. U.S. Army Aero. Rsch. Lab., 1996—; prepared and distributed unique ednl. brochures on aviator fatigue; sleep expert USA Today/Nat. Sleep Found. 1999 Hotline. Spl. guest editor Biol. Psychology, Amsterdam, 1994; jour. referee Aviation Space and Environ. Med., 1992—; referee Jour. Exptl. Psychology, 1998—; contbr. articles to profl. jours. Dir. ch. choir St. John Cath. Ch., Enterprise, Ala., 1991-97; vol. counselor Wiregrass Emergency Pregnancy Svc., Daleville, Ala., 1992; mem. Enterprise cmty. choir, 1991, St. Luke's Meth. Ch. Christmas choir, Enterprise, 1995-97, U.S. Army Aeromed. Rsch. Lab., Ft. Rucker, 1992-93; mem. spl. choir Enterprise Ch. Latter Day Saints 1993-94; mem. ch. choir St. Columba Cath. Ch., Dothan, Ala., 1998—. Named Outstanding Young Man in Am., 1981; recipient Writing award U.S. Army Aviation Med. Assn., 1996. Mem. AAAS, Soc. for Psychophysiol. Rsch., Psi Chi (v.p. 1976, Achievement award 1976), Sigma Xi. Republican. Roman Catholic. Achievements include conducting the first aviator performance study of the new stimulant modafinil, the first controlled study of performance sustaining effects of dextroamphetamine in helicopter pilots, first in-flight helicopter pilot evaluation of the chem. def. antidote atropine sulfate, first studies on the feasibility of monitoring helicopter pilot brain activity during actual flight conditions. Home: 100 Stonehaven Ct Dothan AL 36305-6962 Office: US Army Aeromed Rsch Lab PO Box 620577 Fort Rucker AL 36362-0577

CALDWELL, JOHN L., international company executive; b. Algiers, Algeria, Mar. 5, 1940; m. Nina C. McClain; 1 child, Ian. BA, U. Md., 1965; MA, George Washington U., 1966. Liaison to comdr.-in-chief NATO Fontainebleau, France, 1960-64; exec. sec., staff dir. Task Force World Shortages, Mex.-U.S. Com., East-West Trade Task Force, 1966-73; exec. sec. European Community-U.S. Bus. Council, 1972-75, Adv. Council Japan-U.S. Econ. Relations, 1970-73; dir. Center for Internat. Bus. Relations, 1973-77; mgr. internat. div. U.S. C. of C., 1977-78, v.p. internat., 1978-81; sr. v.p. Carl Byoir & Assocs., Washington, 1981-83; mng. dir. U.S. Trading Co., 1983-87; pres. U.S. Trading & Investment Co., Washington, 1987—; mem. bd. advisors Landegger Internat. Bus. Diplomacy Program Georgetown U.; bd. dirs. Bus. Basics, Shook Electronics USA, Inc.; past chmn. bd. dirs. Taipei-Washington Coord. Coun.; past chmn. internat. com. Greater Washington Bd. Trade; bd. dirs., chmn. Nat. Ctr. Therapeutic Riding, Citizens Network for Fgn. Affairs; councillor Atlantic Coun. U.S. Bus. Basics; adj. prof. George Mason U.; lectr. George Washington U. Mem. U.S. C. of C. (internat. policy com.). Office: US Trading & Investment Co 3050 K St NW Washington DC 20007-5108

CALDWELL, JOHN S., career officer; b. Nov. 16, 1944. Commd. U.S. Army, advanced through grades to maj. gen., 1998. Office: 5001 Eisenhower Ave Alexandria VA 22333-0001

CALDWELL, JOHN THOMAS, JR., communications executive; b. Sewickley, Pa., July 30, 1932; s. John Thomas and Helen Olive (Sheats) C.; m. Margery Eleanor Hill, Dec. 31, 1971. A.B., U. Pitts., 1955; postgrad., Mich. State U., U. Mich., Harvard U. Sch. Bus. Mem. prodn. staff Sta. WKAR-TV, East Lansing, Mich., 1955-56; dir. Sta. WKAR-TV, 1957, producer, 1958, prodn. mgr., 1959-62; distbn. mgr. Nat. Ednl. TV, Inc., Ann Arbor, Mich., 1962-64; v.p. distbn. and ops., 1964-66; ops. mgr. Sta. WGBH, Boston, 1966-70; gen. mgr. Sta. WGBY-TV, Springfield, Mass., 1971-79; pres., gen. mgr. Sta. WTVS-TV, Detroit, 1979-83; dir. electronic communication, corp. pub. affairs Ford Motor Co., Dearborn, Mich., 1983-86, dir. internal communications, pub. affairs, 1986-94; v.p. bus. comm. planning Convergent Media Systems, 1995-98; pres. The Caldwell Co., Grosse Pointe, Mich., 1998—; bd. dirs. Public Broadcasting Service, 1977-81, Sta. WTVS-TV, 1979-92. Bd. dirs. Detroit Symphony Orch., 1979-87, Mich. Cancer Found., 1980-96, Boys and Girls Clubs Mich., 1981-84, Springfield (Mass.) Symphony Orch., 1975-79; mem. U. Mich. Cmty. Adv. Bd., 1979-88, Mich. State Film, TV and Rec. Arts Adv. Coun., 1984-86; exec. com., bd. dirs. Karmanus Cancer Inst., 1996—; bd. dirs. Mich. Info. Tech. Network, 1995—. Woodrow Wilson fellow, 1981. Mem. Nat. Acad. TV Arts and Sci., Mich. Corp. Public Broadcasting (dir. 1979-83), Internat. TV Assn., Economic (Detroit) Club, Grosse Pointe Yacht Club, Skyline Club. Home: 874 Lake Shore Rd Grosse Pointe MI 48236-1273*

CALDWELL, JOHN WALTER, United States marshal. AA in Criminal Justice, South Ga. Coll., 1973; BS in Criminal Justice, Ga. So. U., 1975. Patrolman Demarest (N.J.) Police Dept., 1969-70; state trooper Ga. State Patrol, 1970-76; sr. instr. Fed. Law Enforcement Tng. Ctr., 1976-94; deputy sheriff Camden County (Ga.) Sheriff's Dept., 1994—. Sgt. U.S. Army, military police, 1966-68. Recipient Spl. Achievement award U.S. Treasury, 1980, 89. Mem. FOP, Fed. Criminal Investigators Assn., Peace Officers Assn. Ga., Ducks Unltd. Avocations: hunting, fishing, motorcycle riding. Office: US Marshal's Svc 125 Bull St Savannah GA 31401

CALDWELL, JOHN WILLIAM, pastor; b. Springfield, Mo., Aug. 26, 1943; s. Manville Olen and Ella Francis (Larimore) C.; m. Janis Thelma Stenzinger, Aug. 15, 1965; children: John Shannon, Jennifer Noel. BTh, Ozark Christian Coll., Joplin, Mo., 1967, M of Ministry, 1974; MDiv, Cin. Christian Sem., 1985; D of Ministry, Trinity Evang. Div. Sch., Deerfield, Ill., 1989. Ordained to ministry Ind. Christian Ch., 1967. Student min. Louisburg (Mo.) Christian Ch., 1964-68; evangelist, 1968-74; pastor Kingsway Christian Ch., Indpls., 1974—; adj. prof. Cin. Bible Sem., 1986—; mem. continuation com. N.Am. Christian Conv., nat. prayer chmn., 1991-92, pres., 1996. Author: Growing Up in Christ, 1974, Reaching the Lost, 1975, Intimacy with God, 1992, Top Priority, 1996; contbr. articles to profl. jours. Recipient Seth Wilson Disting. Alumnus award Ozark Christian Coll., 1991. Mem. Ind. Christian Men's Fellowship (pres. 1981). Republican. Office: Kingsway Christian Ch PO Box 34560 Indianapolis IN 46234-0560

CALDWELL, JONI, psychology educator, small business owner; b. Chgo., Aug. 8, 1948; d. Bruce Wilber and Eloise Ethel (Ijams) C. BS in Home Econs. Edn., Mich. State U., 1970; MA in Psychology, U. San Francisco, 1978. Cert. high sch. and coll. tchr., Mich. Instr. Northwestern Mich. Coll., Traverse City, 1972-78, Mott Community Coll., Flint, Mich., 1974-78; tchr. Grand Blanc (Mich.) High Sch., 1970-73, Clio (Mich.) High Sch., 1974-78; parent educator, vol. coord. Family Resource Ctr., Monterey, Calif., 1981-82; owner, gen. mgr. Futons & Such, Monterey, 1982—; instr. psychology Hartnell Coll., Salinas, Calif., 1993-96; spl. project dir. YWCA, 1996-97; instr. women's studies Monterey Peninsula Coll., 1997—. Bd. dirs., v.p., pres. Ch. Religious Sci., Monterey, 1984-87; mem. bd. stewards Pacific Coast Ch., Monterey, 1988-92, v.p.; bd. dirs. YWCA, Monterey, 1986-88, mem. nominating com., 1995-98, pers. comm., 1996—; vol., fund raiser Buddy Program, 1992—; membership com. Profl. Womens Network, 1989—. Mem. AAUW (state del., 1997, co-chair equity comm., 1998—), New Monterey Bus. Assn. (past pres., bd. dirs. 1984-95, v.p. 1993-97), Monterey C. of C. (cons. workshop com. 1985-87, Small Bus. Excellence award 1990), del. First Women's Conv., 1998. Avocations: skiing, sailing, skin diving, remodeling houses, travel. Home: 29 Portola Ave Monterey CA 93940-3731 Office: Futons & Such 475 Alvarado St Monterey CA 93940-2722

CALDWELL, JUDITH, horticultural educator. Prof. Clemson U., S.C. Recipient Outstanding Undergrad. Educator award, 1992. Office: Dept of Horticulture Rm E142 Pool EGG Ctr Clemson U Clemson SC 29631*

CALDWELL, JUDY CAROL, advertising executive, public relations executive; b. Nashville, Dec. 28, 1946; d. Thomas and Sarah Elizabeth Carter; 1 child, Jessica. BS, Wayne State U., 1969. Tchr. Bailey Mid. Sch., West Haven, Conn., 1969-72; editorial asst. Vanderbilt U., Nashville, 1973-74; editor, graphics designer, field researcher Urban Observatory of Met. Nashville, 1974-77; account exec. Holden and Co., Nashville, 1977-79; bus. tchr. Federated States of Micronesia, 1979-80; dir. advt. Am. Assn. for State and Local History, Nashville, 1980-81; dir. prodn. Mktg. Communications Co., Nashville, 1981-83; ptnr. Victory Images of Tenn., Inc., Nashville, 1990-92; owner, pres. Ridge Hill Corp., Nashville, 1983—.

CALDWELL, KARIN D., biochemist educator. PhD in Biochemistry, U. Uppsala, Sweden, 1968, FilDr, 1976. Assoc. prof. biochem. rsch. U. Utah, Salt Lake City, 1985-98, adj. assoc. prof. chemistry, 1986-96, assoc. prof. dept. bioengring., 1986-97, dir. Ctr. Biopolymers & Interfaces, 1986-98, now acting chair, 1998. *

CALDWELL, NAOMI RACHEL, library media specialist; b. Providence, Mar. 31, 1958; d. Atwood Alexander II and Juanita (Johnson) Caldwell; 1 child, William Earl Wood. BS, Clarion State Coll., 1980; MSLS, Clarion U. Pa., 1982; postgrad., Tex. A&M U., 1986-87, Providence Coll., 1990-92, U. Pitts., 1992—. Cert. tchg. libr.; cert. libr. media specialist. Asst. dir., adult svcs. libr. Oil City (Pa.) Pub. Libr., 1984-85; microtext reference libr. Sterling C. Evans Libr., Tex. A&M U., College Station, 1985-87; libr. media specialist Nathan Bishop Mid. Sch., Providence, 1987-92; libr. sci. doctoral fellow dept. libr. sci. Sch. Libr. and Info. Sci. U. Pitts., 1992-94; sch. library media specialist Feinstein H.S. for Pub. Svc., Providence, 1994—; mem. discovery award com. U.S. Bd. on Books for Young People, 1994; mem. com. R.I. Children's Book Award, 1990-92, R.I. Read-Aloud, 1990-92; participant Native Am. and Alaskan Native Pre-Conf. to White House Conf. on Librs. and Info. Scis., Washington, 1991, George Washington U. Nat. Indian Policy Ctr. Forum on Native Am. Librs. and Info. Svcs., Washington, 1991; hon. del. White House Conf. on Libr. and Info. Svcs., Washington, 1991; bd.

dirs. Ocean State Freenet; mem. exec. bd. R.I. Ednl. Media Assn., 1996-97; cons. Am. Coll. Testing, 1995—; presenter in field. Mem. editorial adv. bd., reviewer Multicultural Rev., 1991—; mem. adv. bd. Native Ams. Info. Dir., 1992, OYATE, 1992—, Gale Ency. Multicultural Am.. Native N.Am. Ref. Libr.; reviewer Clarion Books, Greenwood Press, Random House, Harcourt Brace Trade Divsn., Browndeer Press, Oryx Press; contbr. articles to profl. jours. Mem. State of R.I. Libr. Bd., 1996-97, Spl. Presdl. Adv. Com. on Libr. of Congress, 1996-97; mem. nominating com. R.I. chpt. Girl Scouts of Am., 1998—. Mem. ALA (chmn. com. on status of women in librarianship 1995-97, councilor-at-large 1992-96, 96—, nominating com. 1996-97, legis. assembly 1996-98, assembly on planning and budget 1998—, presdl. task force spectrum program), Am. Indian Libr. Assn. (pres. 1990-94, sec. 1994-96, new mems. round table publicity com. 1986, new mems. round table minority recruitment com. 1986-88, OLOS libr. svcs. for Am. Indian people subcom. 1986-88, 90-91, chmn. 1992-94, sec. 1994-96, ALCTS micropub. com. 1988-90, mem. coun. com. on minority concerns 1991-92, 94-96), Am. Assn. Sch. Librs., Spl. Librs. Assn., Libr. Adminstrn. Mgmt. Assn., Windwalker Coalition, Worcraft Cir. Native Writers and Storytellers. Home: 475 Sowams Rd Barrington RI 02806-2745 Office: Feinstein HS for Pub Svc 544 Elmwood Ave Providence RI 02907-1820

CALDWELL, PHILIP, retired automobile manufacturing company executive, retired financial services company executive; b. Bourneville, Ohio, Jan. 27, 1920; s. Robert Clyde and Wilhelmina (Hemphill) C.; m. Betsey Chinn Clark, Oct. 27, 1945; children: Lawrence Clark, Lucy Hemphill Caldwell-Stair (Mrs. Thomas O. Stair), Désirée Caldwell Armitage (Mrs. William F. Armitage, Jr.). BA in Econs., Muskingum Coll., 1940, HHD (hon.), 1974; MBA, Harvard U., 1942; DBA (hon.), Upper Iowa U., 1978; LLD (hon.), Boston U., 1979, Ea. Mich. U., 1979, Miami U., 1980, Davidson Coll., 1982, Ohio U., 1984, U. Mich., 1984, Lawrence Inst. Tech., 1984. Served to lt. USNR, 1942-46; civilian Navy Dept., 1946-53, dir. procurement policy div., 1948-53; with Ford Motor Co., 1953-90, v.p., gen. mgr. truck ops., 1968-70; pres., dir. Philco-Ford Corp. subs., 1970-71, v.p. mfg. group N.Am. automotive ops., 1971-72; chmn., CEO Ford of Europe, Inc., 1972-73, exec. v.p. internat. automotive ops., 1973-77; dir. Ford of Europe Inc., Ford Latin Am., Ford Mideast and Africa, Ford Asia Pacific, 1973-85; vice chmn. bd. Ford Motor Co., 1977-79, dep. CEO, 1978-79, pres., 1978-80, CEO, 1979-85, chmn. bd. dirs., 1980-85, dir., 1973-90; dir. Ford Motor Credit Co., Ford of Can., 1977-85; mem. Ford European Adv. Coun., 1976-88, chmn., 1987-88; sr. mng. dir. Lehman Bros. Inc., N.Y.C., 1985-98; chmn. bd. dirs. Mettler-Toledo, Inc., 1996-98; bd. dirs. Russell Reynolds Assoc., Inc., The Mex. Fund, Am. Guarantee and Liability Ins. Co., Zurich Am. Ins. Group, Mettler-Toledo, Inc., Waters Corp.; Castech Aluminum Group, Inc., 1994-96; Chase Manhattan Corp., Chase Manhattan Bank NA, 1982-85; Digital Equipment Corp., 1980-95; Federated Dept. Stores Inc., 1984-88; The Kellogg Company, 1985-92; Shearson Lehman Bros. Holdings, 1985-93; Specialty Coatings Grp. Inc., 1991-93; Zurich Reinsurance Ctr. Holdings, 1993-97; mem. policy com. The Bus. Roundtable, 1980-85, Bus. Coun., 1980—, Com. for Econ. Devel., 1979—, Conf. Bd., 1979—, Trilateral Commn., 1979-86; mem. U.S. Trade Rep. Adv. Com. for Trade Negotiations, 1983-85; mem. Pres.'s Export Coun., 1985-89; mem. Mex.-U.S. Bus. Com., 1985—; adv. coun. Japan-U.S. Econ. Rels., 1981-85; dir. Japan Soc., 1983-89, vice chmn., chmn. exec. com. 1987-89; mem. motor truck com. Automobile Mfg. Assn., 1964-70; mem. transp. com. U.S. C. of C., 1968-77; mem. U.S. coun. Internat. C. of C., 1973-77, U.S. Coun. for Internat. Bus., 1977-85; mem. internat. adv. com. Chase Manhattan Bank, 1979-85; mem. Coun. Fgn. Rels., 1985—. Trustee Muskingum Coll., 1967—, Winterthur Mus. and Gardens, 1986—; dir. Harvard Bus. Sch. Assocs., 1977-93; dir. Inst. Europeen de Adminstrn. des Affaires (INSEAD), 1978-81, chmn. U.S. adv. bd., 1979-84, mem. internat. coun., 1983—; bd. advisors The Jerome Levy Econs. Inst., 1988—; bus. adv. coun. Kent State U., 1968-70; mem. Merrill-Palmer Inst., 1971-81, New Detroit, Inc., vice-chair, 1977-85, Detroit Renaissance, 1979-85, dir. Detroit Symphony Orch., 1974-85; charter mem. Bus. Higher Edn. Forum, 1979-84; dir. Citizens Rsch. Coun. of Mich., 1980-85; hon. bd. mem. Plan Internat. USA, 1989—; dir. Econ. Club of Detroit, 1977-86. Recipient 1st William A. Jump Meml. award, 1950, Meritorious Civilian Svc. awardUS Navy Dept., 1953, Disting. Svc. Alumni award Muskingum Coll., 1978, Internat.Exec. of Yr. award Sch. Mgmt. Brigham Young U., 1983, Bus. Statesman of Yr. award Harvard Bus. Sch. Club Greater N.Y., 1984, Businessman of Yr. award Harvard Bus. Sch. Club Columbus, Ohio, 1984, Alumni Achievement award Harvard Bus. Sch.,1985; named Automotive Industry Leader of Yr. Automotive Hall of Fame, 1984; elected to Automotive Hall of Fame. 1990; Harvard Bus. Sch. Philip Caldwell Professorship of Bus. Adminstrn. named in his honor, 1989; named Statesman of Yr. Harvard Bus. Sch. Club Detroit, 1991; elected laureate Nat. Bus. Hall of Fame, 1995. Mem. The Links, River Club (N.Y.C.). Fax: 203-357-8241. Office: Ford Motor Co W Bldg 225 High Ridge Rd Ste 180 Stamford CT 06905-3000

CALDWELL, RODNEY KENT, lawyer; b. Washington, Feb. 19, 1937; s. Rodney Huntington and Marion Elisabeth (Sasher) C.; m. Marjorie Lee Zink, Apr. 15, 1965 (div. 1975); children: Dana Kent, Susan Ashley; m. Yolanda Silva, June 22, 1979; 1 child, David Huntington. BChemE, U. Va., 1959; JD, U. Houston, 1969. Bar: Tex. 1969, U.S. Supreme Ct. 1975. With Arnold, White & Durkee, Houston, 1970—. Author: Patent Litigation: Procedure & Tactics, 1978-84. Lt. USAF, 1959-62. Fellow Tex. Bar Found., Houston Bar Found.; mem. ABA, Am. Intellectual Property Law Assn., Internat. Bar Assn., Internat. Intellectual Property Assn., Univ. Club., Army and Navy Club. Methodist. Home: 4021 Ella Lee Ln Houston TX 77027-3910 Office: Arnold White & Durkee 750 Bering Dr Houston TX 77057-2198

CALDWELL, RONALD DEWITT, SR., industrial engineer, consultant; b. Dayton, Ohio, Dec. 9, 1958; s. James Edward Jr. and Mary Alice (Watson) C.; m. Yvonne Denise Brown, Mar. 21, 1981; children: Ronald DeWitt, Danielle Nicole, Nia Denise. BS in Indsl. Engring., U. Cin., 1982; MS in Engring., Wright State U., 1996. Material pricing analyst McDonnell Douglas Corp., St. Lois, 1983-85; advanced mfg. engring. supr. B.F. Goodrich Co., Troy, Ohio, 1985-91; assoc. prof. Sinclair C.C., Dayton, Ohio, 1988-98; pres., CEO Future Systems Internat. Corp., Trotwood, Ohio, 1994—; pres., co-owner, founder Superior Cuts of Trotwood Barber Shop, 1997—; mem. drafting adv. com. Patterson Co-op H.S., Dayton, 1992-95; mem. adv. coun. Broadmoor Acad. Elem., Dayton, 1992-95. Contbr. tech. articles to profl. jours. Pres. Gifted Child Assn., Trotwood-Madison Sch. Dist., 1994-95; v.p. Trotwood Wee Rams Football, 1994; team mgr. YMCA Youth Basketball Program, Trotwood, 1992-94. Mem. Inst. Indsl. Engrs. (sr. mem.; bd. dirs. Dayton chpt. 1996), Human Factors and Ergonomics Soc., Soc. Mfg. Engrs. (sr. mem.), Avraham Y. Goldratt Inst. (Acad. Jonah). Achievements include invention of an innovative automatic U.S. postal box. Avocations: physical fitness through weight lifting, youth coaching of softball and track. Office: Future Systems Internat Corp PO Box 26043 Trotwood OH 45426-0043

CALDWELL, ROSSIE JUANITA BROWER, retired library service educator; b. Columbia, S.C., Nov. 4, 1917; d. Rossie Lee and Henrietta Olivia (Irby) Brower; m. Harlowe Evans Caldwell, Aug. 6, 1943 (dec. 1983); 1 adopted dau., Rossie Laverne Caldwell Jenkins. BA magna cum laude, Claflin U., 1937; MS, S.C. State Coll., 1952; MSLS, U. Ill., 1959. Tchr. libr. Reed St. H.S., Anderson, S.C., 1937-39, Emmett Scott H.S., Rock Hill, S.C., 1939-42; tchr. libr. Wilkinson H.S., Orangeburg, S.C., 1942-43, libr., 1945-57; civilian pers. War Dept., Tuskegee Army Air Field, 1943-45; asst. prof., then assoc. prof. libr. svc. dept. S.C. State U., Orangeburg, 1957-83. Contbg. author book in field; author articles. Life mem. NAACP; trustee, Christian advocate United Meth. Ch. in S.C., 1978-86; assoc. mem. Orangeburg Regional Hosp. Aux,; coord. comms. Trinity United Meth. Ch. Recipient Presdl. citation Claflin Coll., 1989, Links award for cmty. achievement, 1998, numerous ann. vol. work citations; Founders Day honoree, 1994; named to Scroll of Honor, Omega Lambda Sigma, 1988, Claflin Coll. Hall of Fame, 1997. Mem. ALA (continuing life mem.), ALA Black Caucus (emeritus), AAUP (emeritus), VFW Aux. (life), S.C. Libr. Assn. (hon.), AAUW (editor Orangeburg br. bull.), Friends of the Libr. (Orangeburg County), Palmetto Med. Dental Pharm. Assn. Aux. (historian, state pres., Woman of Yr. 1972), Internat. Libr. Sci. Hon. Soc., Links Club (archivist, historian), As You Like It Bridge Club, Daus. of Isis, Claflin Coll. Forerunners Club (coord., founder), Golden Scholarship Club (co-founder), Sigma Pi Phi (archousa, Chaflin queen emeritus 1935-37), Phi Delta Kappa, Alpha Kappa Alpha, Psi Phi (Lambda Sigma chpt.). Home: 1320 Ward Ln NE Orangeburg SC 29118-1342

CALDWELL, ROYCE S., communications executive. Pres. Southwestern Bell Ops., San Antonio. Office: Southwestern Bell Ops 175 E Houston St Ste 1307 San Antonio TX 78205-2233*

CALDWELL, SARAH, opera producer, conductor, stage director and administrator; b. Maryville, Mo., Mar. 6, 1924. Student, U. Ark., Hendrix Coll., New Eng. Conservatory, Berkshire Music Ctr., Tanglewood, Mass.; D. Mus. (hon.), Harvard U., Simmons Coll., Bates Coll., Bowdoin Coll. Mem. faculty Berkshire Music Ctr.; dir. Boston U. Opera Workshop, 1953-57; created dept. music theater Boston U.; founded Boston Opera Group (later became Opera Co. of Boston), 1957, sinced served as artistic dir. and condr., 1968—. Asst. to Boris Goldovsky in direction of New Eng. Opera Co.; operatic directorial debut with Rake's Progress, Opera Workshop, 1953; operatic debut as condr. with Opera Group of Boston, 1957, Carnegie Hall debut with Am. Symphony Orch., 1974; condr. and/or dir. maj. opera cos. in U.S., including N.Y. Met. Opera, Dallas Civic Opera, Houston Grand Opera, N.Y.C. Opera; condr. with maj. orchs. including: Indpls. Symphony, Milw. Symphony, Am. Symphony, N.Y. Philharmonic; condr. at Ravinia Festival, 1976. Recipient Rogers and Hammerstein award. 1st woman to appear as conductor with the Met. Opera, N.Y.C., 1976.

CALDWELL, THOMAS HOWELL, JR., accountant, financial management consultant; b. Wichita Falls, Tex., Feb. 5, 1934; s. Thomas Howell and LaVerne Louise C.; m. Bernell Irons, Apr. 12, 1968 (div. Jan. 1979); 1 child, Thomas Howell III (dec.). BA in Religion, Baylor U., 1956; postgrad., Tex. Christian U., 1958-63, North Tex. State U., 1973-75; LLD (hon.), London Inst. Applied Rsch., 1994. Cert. internal auditor. Tech. writer Gen. Dynamics, Ft. Worth, 1956-60; asst. dir. pers. Harris Hosp., Ft. Worth, 1960-62; with fiduciary tax sect. 1st Nat. Bank, Ft. Worth, 1962-64; jr. acct. various CPA's, Dallas, 1964-65; auditor Def. Contract Audit Agy., Dallas, 1965-74; tax appraiser, mcpl. acct. City of McKinney, Tex., 1974-75; systems acct. USDA, Dallas, 1975-83; auditor U.S. Army C.E., Dallas, 1983-86; acct. rep. IRS, Dallas, 1986-87; systems acct. Def. Fin. & Acctg. Svc., Dallas, 1987-93; fin. mgmt. cons. Caldwell Fin. Mgmt. Cons., Dallas, 1993—. Mem. jr. bd. 1st Bapt. Ch., Dallas. With USAFR, 1957-63. Mem. Descs. Vets. Mexican War, (bd. dirs., treas.), Baylor U. Ex-Students Assn., Masons, Shriners, Scottish Rite. Republican. Avocations: flying, dogs, watching football, church. Home and Office: 10822 Pagewood Dr Dallas TX 75230-4468

CALDWELL, TOM O., pediatric physician; b. Birmingham, Ala., May 16, 1926; s. Sam W. and Anna D. (S.) C.; m. Betty J. Baker, June 3, 1950; children: Cathryn Lynn, Anna Claire, Mary Kyle. AB, U. Ala., Tuscaloosa, 1946; MD, Med. Coll. Ala., Birmingham, 1949. Diplomate Am. Bd. Pediatrics. Pediatrican, 1954-95, ret., 1995; Mem. hosp. com. Children's Hosp. Ala., Bapt. Med. Ctr. Montclair, St. Vincent's Hosp. Contbr. numerous articles to jours. Mem. exec. com. Alumni Assn. Med. Coll. Ala. Capt. M.C., U.S. Army, 1949-51. Mem. AMA, Am. Acad. Pediatrics, Jefferson County Med. Soc., Ala. Geneal. Soc. (bd. dirs.), Birmingham Geneal. Soc. (bd. dirs.), The Shelby County Hist. Soc. (bd. dirs.), Birmingham-Jefferson Hist. Soc. (bd. dirs.), The Caduceus Club (bd. dirs.). Methodist. Avocations: genealogy, history, quilting, gardening. Home: 3760 Locksley Dr Birmingham AL 35223-2757

CALDWELL, TONI L., court official, charitable organization executive; b. Chambersburg, Pa., June 25, 1963; d. Herbert Leroy Waters and Ruth Virginia (Webb) Richardson; children: D. Marquis Henry, Sharif Q. Caldwell. Student, Am. U., 1973-74, Rutgers U., Newark, 1981-83, Caldwell Coll., 1998—. Legal sec. Kleinfield, Kaplan & Becker, Washington, 1974-76, Budd Larner Gross Rosenbaum Greerberg & Sade, Short Hills, N.J., 1988-93; office mgr. Smith & Howard Assocs., Washington, 1976-78; adminstrv. mgr., corp. treas. Common Bros. USA, N.Y.C., 1978-79; adminstrv. asst. to exec. dir.-supr. automobile equipment N.J. Transit Corp., Newark, 1980-85; ind. contractor, 1985-88; campaign mgr. Com. To Elect Corinna Kay Williams, East Orange, N.J., 1993; jud. sec. U.S. Dist. Ct. for N.J., Newark, 1993—, mediation adminstr., 1993-96; pres., CEO, InHim Charities, Inc., East Orange, 1997—; exec. v.p. N.J. chpt. Conf. Minority Transp. Ofcls., 1982-85. Pres. East Orange H.S. PTA, 1991-95, sec.-tras., 1995—; chmn. East Orange Unified Coun. PTAs and PTOs, 1992—; sec. bd. dirs. East Orange Police Athletic League, 1993-96; chmn. bd. mgmt. East Orange YMCA, 1993-97, chmn. minority achievers bd. govs., 1993-97; bd. dirs. Met. YMCA of Oranges, 1996-97; sec.-acting treas. Essex County Coun. PTAs, 1996—; bd. dirs. Tri-City Peoples Corp., 1997—. Recipient Mayor's Adult Vol. Cmty. Svc. award City of East Orange, 1987, Cmty. Svc. award Essex County Bd. Chosen Freeholders, 1998, also numerous PTA and East Orange Sch. Dist. awards, including supt.'s award; named 2d Ward Woman of Yr. East Orange City Coun., 1993, 2d Ward Unsung Hero, 1997. Democrat. Avocations: reading, listening to music, basketball. Home: 141 S Burnett St East Orange NJ 07018-3034 Office: InHim Charities Inc PO Box 28041 Newark NJ 07101-2482

CALDWELL, WALTER EDWARD, editor, small business owner; b. L.A., Dec. 29, 1941; s. Harold Elmer and Esther Ann (Fuller) C.; m. Donna Edith Davis, June 27, 1964; 1 child, Arnie-Jo. AA, Riverside City Coll., 1968. Sales and stock professional Sears Roebuck & Co., Riverside, Calif., 1963-65; dispatcher Rohr Corp., Riverside, Calif., 1965-67; trainee Aetna Fin., Riverside, 1967-68; mgr. Aetna Fin., San Bruno, Cal., 1968-70, Amfac Thrift & Loan, Oakland, Calif., 1970-74; free lance writer San Jose, Calif., 1974-76; news dir. Sta. KAVA Radio, Burney, Cal., 1977-79; editor-pub. Mountain Echo, Fall River Mills, Calif., 1979—. Contbg. author Yearbook of Modern Poetry, 1976. Del. Farmers and Ranchers Congress, St. Louis, 1985; participant Am. Leadership Conf., San Diego, 1989; pres. United Way, Burney, 1979, co-chmn., 1977, chmn., 1979; disaster relief worker ARC, Redding, Calif., 1988-91, disaster action team leader, 1991-95; bd. dirs. Shasta County Women's Refuge, Redding, 1988-91, Shasta County Econ. Devel. Corp., 1986-90, Crossroads, 1985; bd. dirs. Shasta County Econ. Devel. Task Force, 1985-86, exec. bd. dirs., 1988; pres. Intermountain Devel. Corp., 1989; leader Girl Scouts U.S.A., San Jose, 1973-76; announcer various local parades; trustee Mosquito Abatement Dist., Burney, 1978-87, 89—, chmn., 1990—; commr. Burney Fire Protection Dist., 1987-91, v.p., 1990, pres., 1991; chmn. Burney Basin Days Com., 1984-95, Hay Days Com., 1995-96; candidate for Shasta County Bd. Suprs., 1992; alt. commr. Local Agy. Formation Commn. Shasta County, 1995—. With USMC, 1959-63. Mem. Burney Basin C. of C. (advt. chmn. 1982, Cmty. Action award 1990, 93), Fall River Valley C. of C. (bd. dirs. 1991, pres. 1995), Am. Legion (citation of recognition 1987, Cmty. Action award 1989, 93), Calif. Newspaper Pubs. Assn., Rotary (pres. 1977-78, chmn. bike race 1981-85), Lions (student spkr. chmn. Fall River 1983—, 1st v.p. 1991, pres. 1992, co-chmn. disaster com., newsletter chmn. dist. 4-C1 1989-91), Moose, Masons (master 1995), Shriners (sec.-treas. 1992-94). Republican. Avocations: photography, painting, archeology. Office: Mountain Echo Main St Fall River Mills CA 96028 also: PO Box 224 Fall River Mills CA 96028-0224

CALDWELL, WESLEY STUART, III, lawyer, lobbyist; b. Teaneck, N.J., June 3, 1946; s. Wesley S. Jr. and Helen Skrek C.; m. Theresa Hale, Apr. 20, 1970 (div. Jan. 1988); children: Ashley Hale, Ferris Elena; m. J.R. Dillenback, May 27, 1988. BA in Liberal Arts, Fairleigh Dickinson U., 1968; JD, Rutgers U., 1975. Bar: N.J. 1975, U.S. Dist. Ct. N.J. 1975, U.S. Supreme Ct. 1992. Dep. atty. gen. N.J. Atty. Gen.'s Office, Trenton, 1975-78; assoc. gen. counsel Prudential Reins. Co., Newark, 1978-79; v.p. Am. Ins. Assn., N.Y.C., 1979-86; ptnr. LeBoeuf, Lamb, Greene & MacRae, Newark, 1986-95, Caldwell Megna & Brewster, Trenton, 1995-97, Caldwell Megna, Trenton, 1997—; legis. counsel Liberty Mut. Ins. Co., Boston, 1987—, Am. Family Life Assurance Co., Columbus, Ga., 1991—, also others. With U.S. Army, 1969-72. Mem. N.J. Bar Assn. (past chmn. ins. law sect.), Mercer County Bar Assn. Avocations: golf, pocket billiards. Home: 1266 River Rd Titusville NJ 08560-1603 Office: Caldwell Megna 224 W State St Trenton NJ 08608-1002

CALDWELL, WILEY NORTH, retired distribution company executive; b. L.A., Apr. 24, 1927; s. Wiley North and Jean (Clarke) C.; m. Joanne Humphrey, Mar. 25, 1950; children: David, Wendy, Charles, Thomas. BSME, Stanford U., 1950; MBA, Harvard U., 1952. Mgr. prodn. control Waste King Corp., L.A., 1952-54; v.p., co-founder Poroloy Equipment, Inc., Van Nuys, Calif., 1954-58, dir. sales and mktg. Bendix Filter div., 1958-60; v.p. Jamieson Labs., Inc., Van Nuys, 1960-61; v.p. mktg., exec. v.p. McGaw Labs., Am. Hosp. Supply Corp., L.A., Chgo., 1961-69; v.p. internat. Am. Hosp. Supply Corp., Chgo., 1969-72, pres. Midwest Dental div., 1972-77; v.p. ops. distbn. group W.W. Grainger, Inc., Skokie, Ill., 1977-78, pres. distbn. group, 1978-81, exec. v.p., 1981-84, pres., 1984-92; ret., 1993; also bd. dirs. W.W. Grainger, Inc., Skokie, Ill., 1979-93; ret., 1993; bd. dirs. Kewaunee Sci. Corp., Statesville, N.C., Consol. Papers, Inc., Wisconsin Rapids, Wis., Evanston Northwestern Healthcare, Inc., Ill., The Presbyn. Home, Evanston, Ill., Chgo. Found. for Edn. Mem. adv. bd. J.L. Kellogg Grad. Sch., Northwestern U., mem. Northwestern U. Assocs. With USN, 1945-46. Mem. Indian Hill Club, Chgo. Club, Old Elm Club, The Econ. Club Chgo., The Chgo. Com. Home: 125 Woodstock Ave Kenilworth IL 60043-1231 Office: 5215 Old Orchard Rd Ste 440 Skokie IL 60077-1047

CALDWELL, WILLARD E., psychologist, educator; b. Flushing L.I., N.Y., July 10, 1920; s. Howard Eugene and Lillian (Warner) C. AB in Psychology, U. Fla., 1940, MA in Psychology, 1941; PhD in Psychology, Cornell U., 1946; postgrad., Washington Sch. Psychiatry, 1948-53. Lic. psychologist, D.C. Grad. asst. psychology U. Fla., Gainesville, 1940-41; teaching asst. Psychology Dept. Cornell (N.Y.) U., 1943-46; prof. psychology, dept. chmn. Mary Baldwin Coll., Staunton, Va., 1947-48; asst. prof., assoc. prof., prof. psychology The George Washington U., Washington, 1948-85, prof. emeritus psychology, 1985—; psychotherapist. Editor, contbg. author: Principles of Comparative Psychology, 1960; contbr. over 50 articles to profl. jours. Pvt. U.S. Army, 1941-42. Mem. APA, Am. Psychol. Soc., D.C. Psychology Assn., Internat. Soc. Biometerology. Republican. Episcopalian. Avocations: swimming, gardening, traveling. Home: Apt 316 1101 New Hampshire Ave NW Washington DC 20037-1509

CALDWELL, WILLIAM EDWARD, educational administration educator, arbitrator; b. Providence, Aug. 18, 1928; s. James E. and Eva E. (Barker) C.; m. Doris E. Parlee, June 17, 1950; children: William E., Donna E., Allen E. BA in Math., Ea. Nazarene Coll., 1950; MEd in Secondary Edn., U. N.H., 1957; PhD in Ednl. Adminstrn., NYU, 1968. Cert. prin., supt., arbitrator. Tchr. math., dir. music, coach pub. schs. Berwick, Maine, 1950-54; tchr. math., supr. pub. schs. Valley Stream, N.Y., 1954-61; guidance counselor, prin. pub. schs. Manchester, Conn., 1961-67; dir. secondary tchr. tng. U. Hartford, Conn., 1967-69; exec. dir. Pa. Sch. Study Coun., University Park, 1970-78; prof. ednl. adminstrn. Pa. State U., University Park, 1969—, pres. faculty coun., 1985-86, ombudsman Coll. Edn., 1986-90, chmn. edn. adminstrn. program, 1987-90, chmn. adminstrn., policy, founds. and internat. edn., 1990-93, prof. emeritus, 1993—; state dir. mediation Commonwealth of Pa., Harrisburg, 1979-80; conciliator, fact finder Pa. Labor Rels. Bd., Harrisburg, 1971—; arbitrator AAA, FMCS, Pa. Labor Rels. Bd., 1971—. Author: Collective Negotiation in Public Education, 1970, Agreement, Policy for Principal/Supervisor, 1983; mem. editl. bd. Jour. Individual Employment Rights, 1993—; contbr. articles to profl. jours., chpts. to books, author reports. Nat. del. Am. Assn. Sch. Adminstrs., Washington, 1976, 77, 79; bd. dirs. Fed. Credit Union, Manchester, Conn., 1963-67, Appalachian Ednl. Lab., Charleston, W.Va., 1970-78; examiner Pa. Civil Svc. Commn., Harrisburg, 1972-79. Lt. col. USMCR, ret. 1988. Recipient Commendation award Pa. Sch. Bds. Assn., 1980, Acad. Achievement award NYU, 1969, Outstanding Svc. award Commonwealth Pa., 1973, Outstanding Svc. award Pa. Dept. Labor, 1987, Excellence in Instrn. award Pa. Sch. Study Coun., 1994, William E. Caldwell Excellence in Adminstrn. award Pa. Sch. Study Coun., 1997—. Mem. Am. Edn. Rsch. Assn. (presenter), Pa. Assn. Secondary Sch. Prins. (rsch. chmn., Commendation award 1983, Excellence in Edn. award 1986).

CALDWELL, WILLIAM MACKAY, III, business executive; b. L.A., Apr. 6, 1922; s. William Mackay II and Edit Ann (Richards) C.; m. Mary Louise Edwards, Jan. 16, 1946 (dec. 1980); children: William Mackay IV, Craig Edwards, Candace Louise; m. Jean Bledsoe, Apr. 27, 1985. BS, U. So. Calif., 1943; MBA, Harvard U., 1948. Sec.-treas., dir. Drewry Photocolor Corp., 1957-60, Adcolor Photo Corp., 1957-60; treas., dir. Drewry Bennetts Corp., 1959-60; sr. v.p., CFO Am. Cement Corp., 1960-67, sr. v.p. corp., 1967-70; pres., chmn. bd., CEO Vorst Corp., Washington, 1969; pres. Van Vorst Corp., Washington, 1969-77; chmn. bd., pres. So. Cross Industries, U.S. Bedding Co., 1979-84, St. Croix Mfg. Co., 1979-81, Hawaiian Cement Corp.; pres. Englander Co., 1979-84; v.p., dir. Am. Cement Internat. Corp., Am. Cement Properties; chmn. Kyco Industries Inc., 1982—; pres. BHI Inc., 1984-96; chmn. King Koil Licensing Co., 1982—; cons. prof. U. So. Calif.; mem. men's com. L.A. Med. Ctr.; bd. dirs. Commerce Assocs., Calif. Mus. Sci. and Industry, U. So. Calif. Assocs., Pres.'s Cir., Am. Cement Found. Mem. Friends Huntington Libr. Served to lt. USNR, 1943-46. Mem. Newcomen Soc., Harvard Bus. Sch. So. Calif. (dir. 1960-63), Kappa Alpha, Alpha Delta Sigma. Clubs: L.A. Country Club, Town Hall Club, Calif. Club (L.A.), Trojan Club, Annandale Golf Club, Eldorado Country Club, Chaparral Golf Club. Office: PO Box 1151 Pasadena CA 91102-1151

CALDWELL, WILLIAM MCNEILLY, insurance agent; b. Kingston, Pa., Dec. 31, 1953; s. William Parks and Lois Elizabeth (McNeilly) C.; m. Paula Teresa Harvey; 1 child, William Harvey. BS in Econs., U. Pa., 1976. CLU, ChFC. Rep. Equitable Life, Austin, Tex., 1976-78, agt., registered rep., 1983-90; agt. Southland Life, Austin, 1978; dir. mktg. div. ins. trust Automotive Svc. Assn., Bedford, Tex., 1978-83; mng. rep. Covenant Life, Austin, 1990-94; Sibley & Assocs. Fin. Group; ptnr. Sibley Fin. Group, Austin, 1994—; moderator Life Underwriter Tng. Coun., Austin, 1987-97. Deacon 1st Presbyn. Ch. Austin, 1989-92. Fellow Life Underwriter Tng. Coun.; mem. Am. Soc. CLU and ChFC (bd. dirs. Austin chpt. 1988), Exch. Club Austin (past pres. 1989-90). Avocations: camping, reading, stamp collecting, model railroading. Office: 3921 Steck Dr Ste A-117 Austin TX 78759-8647

CALDWELL, WILLIAM WILSON, federal judge; b. Harrisburg, Pa., Nov. 10, 1925; s. Thomas D. and Martha B. C.; m. Janet W. Garber. A.B., Dickinson Coll., 1948, LL.B., 1951. Ptnr. Caldwell, Fox & Stoner, Harrisburg, 1951-70; 1st asst. dist. Atty. Dauphin County, 1960-62; counsel, chmn. Bd. Arbitration of Claims State of Pa., 1963-70; judge Common Pleas Ct., Dauphin County, 1970-82; judge U.S. Dist. Ct. (mid. dist.) Pa., 1982-94, sr. judge, 1994—. Office: Fed Bldg PO Box 11877 Harrisburg PA 17108-1877*

CALE, CHARLES GRIFFIN, lawyer; b. St. Louis, Aug. 19, 1940; s. Julian Dutro and Judith Hadley (Griffin) C.; BA, Principia Coll., Elsah, Ill., 1961; LLB, Stanford U., 1964; LLM, U. So. Calif., 1966; m. Jessie Leete Rawn, Dec. 30, 1978; children: Whitney Rawn, Walter Griffin, Elizabeth Judith. Bar: Calif. 1965. Pvt. practice L.A., 1965-90; ptnr. firm Adams, Duque & Hazeltine, 1970-81, Morgan, Lewis & Bockius, L.A., 1981-91; bd. dirs., co-chmn., CEO World Cup USA 1994, Inc., L.A., 1991. Group v.p. sports L.A. Olympic Organizing Com., 1982-84; assoc. counselor U.S. Olympic Com., 1985, spl. asst. to pres., 1985-89, asst. to pres, dir. olympic del., 1989-92; bd. dirs. Century 21 Real Estate-Can. Ltd., 1995-97; trustee St. John's Hosp. and Med. Ctr., Santa Monica, Marymount H.S.; asst. Chef de Mission, U.S. Olympic Team, 1988; bd. dirs. Hallum Prevention of Child Abuse Fund, 1976-96. Recipient Gold medal of Youth and Sports, France, 1984. Mem. State Bar Calif., Calif. Club, L.A. Country Club, The Beach Club, Ind. Order Foresters (bd. dirs.), Eagle Springs Golf Club, Country Club of the Rockies. Office: PO Box 688 Pacific Palisades CA 90272-0688

CALEGARI, MARIA, ballerina; b. N.Y.C., Mar. 30, 1957; d. Richard A. and Marion (Gentile) C. Student, DuPons Dance Sch., Queens., 5 yrs., Ballet Acad., Queens, 6 yrs., Sch. Am. Ballet, 3 yrs. Mem. corps de ballet N.Y.C. Ballet, 1974-81, soloist, 1981-83, prin., 1983-94; guest artist Richmond Ballet, 1996—; artist-in-residence Richmond Ballet, Richmond Ctr. for Dance, State Ballet of Va., 1997-98. Dancer in N.Y.C. Ballet's Balanchine Celebration, 1993, Celebrating Balanchine, Kennedy Ctr., 1995. Répétiteur George Balanchine Trust. Recipient Alumni award Profl. Children's Sch., 1986.

CALENGAS, LEONARDO, writer; b. Distomon, Greece, Jan. 16, 1916; came to U.S., 1946; s. Peter John and Vasiliki Kelermenos C.; m. Margaret Nicholas Herianteris, Feb. 18, 1944. B of Edn., Pedagogiki Acad., Athens, Greece, 1944. Tchr. Greek Greek Orthodox Cmty., Newark, N.J., 1948, Gary, Ind., 1947; owner Jim's Sandwich Shop, Valparaiso, Ind., 1952-54,

Humpty Humpty, Chesterton, Ind., 1953-64, Famous Grill, Gary, 1957-64, Leonards Restaurant, Chesterton, 1964-75; retired, 1976—. Author: Blue Diamonds in the Sun, 1996, Shooting Star (in Greek), 1997; contbg. editor Omogeneia, Chgo., 1975—. With Greek Army, 1939-41. Mem. Image Makers, Masons. Greek Orthodox. Avocation: photography. Home: 801 W US 20 Chesterton IN 46304

CALENOFF, LEONID, radiologist; b. Vienna, Austria, Aug. 24, 1923; came to U.S., 1957, naturalized, 1962; s. Albert and Anna (Prover) C.; m. Miriam Arnon, Oct. 30, 1955; children—Jean Zucker, Deborah Lipoff. M.D., U. Paris, 1955. Diplomate: Am. Bd. Radiology. Intern Jewish Hosp., Cin., 1958; resident in radiology U. Ill. Med. Center, Chgo., 1959-61; asst. radiologist Ill. Research and Ednl. Hosp., Chgo., 1961-64; chief radiology Chgo. State Hosp., 1963-68; dir. radiology Sheridan Gen. Hosp., Chgo., 1964-68; attending radiologist West Side VA Hosp., Chgo., 1963-68; attending radiologist Rehab. Inst. Chgo., 1974-89, chief diagnostic radiology, 1974-86; attending radiologist Northwestern Meml. Hosp., Chgo., 1968—; chief outpatient diagnostic radiology Northwestern Meml. Hosp., 1979—, vice chmn. dept. radiology, 1991-96; chief diagnostic radiology Passavant Pavillion of Northwestern Meml. Hosp., 1972-79; asst. prof. radiology Northwestern U. Med. Sch., 1970-73, asso. prof., 1973-78, prof., 1978—. Author articles in field, chpts. in books.; Editor: Radiology of Spinal Cord Injury, 1981. Fellow Am. Coll. Radiology, Am. Coll. Chest Physicians; mem. Radiol. Soc. N.Am., Am. Roentgen Ray Soc., AMA, Soc. Univ. Radiologists. Home: 1515 N Astor St Chicago IL 60610-1627 Office: 250 E Superior St Chicago IL 60611-2958

CALEVAS, HARRY POWELL, management consultant; b. Williamsburg, Va., Nov. 18, 1918; s. Gus and Elizabeth (Powell) C.; m. Betty Nicoolette Chronaker, July 4, 1939 (wid. Nov. 1989); children: Phillip H., Stanley P.; m. Lillian Ida Satrum. Diploma in mech. engring., Case Sch. Applied Scis., Cleve., 1939; MBA, Pacific Western U., 1980, DBA, 1985. Lic. real estate broker, real estate property mgr., Fla. Real Estate Commn. V.p., gen. mgr. Radisson Hotel, Mpls., 1949-53; v.p. Banker Life & Casualty, Chgo., 1953-63; pres. Fla. Bd. Trade, Ft. Lauderdale, 1963-95. Author: Condominium Management Handbook, 1985, The Wandering Moon, 1994, Positive Way to Profit, 1965; author twelve cookbooks/internat. food recipes. Capt. Merchant Marines, ATO. Mem. Am. Legion, SAR, Decendants George Washington, Optimist Club (bd. dirs. 1990-96). Republican. Baptist. Avocations: writing, golf, travel, tennis. Fax: 954-782-2023. Home: 1010 S Ocean Blvd Apt 803 Pompano Beach FL 33062-6630

CALFEE, JOHN BEVERLY, retired lawyer; b. Cleve., May 2, 1913; s. Robert M. and Alwine (Haas) C.; m. Nancy Leighton, Feb. 8, 1944; children: John Beverly Jr., David L., Peter H., Mark E. Grad., Hotchkiss Sch., 1931; BA, Yale U., 1935; LLB, Western Res. U., 1938. Bar: Ohio 1939. Sr. ptnr. Calfee, Halter & Griswold, Cleve., 1939-86; ret., Calfee, Halter & Griswold, 1987. Dir. civil def., Cleveland Hgts., 1951; chmn. Cuyohoga County Rep. Fin. Com., 1978-81; mem. Ohio N.W. Ordinance Bicentennial Commn., 1986. Maj. AUS, 1942-46. Mem. ABA, Ohio Bar Assn., Cleve. Bar Assn., Ohio Hist. Soc. (trustee 1988-97. Presbyterian. Home: 4892 Clubside Rd Cleveland OH 44124-2539 *A person has many guiding principles, but if I am limited to the main one, it would be the motto of Hawken School, my first preparatory institution in Cleveland—"Fair Play." This is a term which for me has become translated into a game goal to be ambitiously sought and achieved by hard work. The effort applied must be honest in thought as well as deed and in achieving it a firm purpose is the motivating concept, tempered by respect for the other person's viewpoint.*

CALFEE, WILLIAM LEWIS, lawyer; b. Cleveland Heights, Ohio, July 12, 1917; s. Robert Martin and Alwine (Haas) C.; m. Eleanor Elizabeth Bliss, Dec. 6, 1941; children: William R., Bruce K., Cynthia B. B.A., Harvard Coll., 1939; LL.D., Yale U., 1946. Bar: Ohio 1946. Assoc. Baker & Hostetler, Cleve., 1946-56, ptnr., 1957-90, of counsel, 1990-92. Bd. dirs. Growth Assn. Greater Cleve., 1979-92; trustee Greater Cleve. United Appeal; pres. Health Fund Greater Cleve. Served to lt. col. M.I., U.S. Army, 1941-45. Decorated Legion of Merit; decorated Order of Brit. Empire. Mem. ABA (ho. of dels. 1980-93), Ohio Bar Assn., Bar Assn. Greater Cleve. (trustee 1980-93, pres. 1979-80), Nat. Conf. Bar Pres. (exec. coun. 1982-85), Ohio C. of C. (bd. dirs. 1993), Mayfield Country Club (pres.), Union Club, Pepper Pike Club, Sanctuary Golf Club. Republican. Episcopalian. Home: 21200 Claythorne Rd Shaker Heights OH 44122-1962 Office: Baker & Hostetler 3200 Nat City Ctr 1900 E 9th St Ste 3200 Cleveland OH 44114-3475

CALHAMER, ALLAN BRIAN, retired postal worker; b. Hinsdale, Ill., Dec. 7, 1931; s. Timothy Michael and Helen Augusta (Morton) C.; m. Hilda Camelia Morales, Sept. 1, 1967; children: Tatiana, Selenne. AB, Harvard U., 1953. lectr. on game of diplomacy and diplomatic history Keio U., 1997. Contbr. articles to profl. jours.; inventor Game of Diplomacy (named to Prod. Hall of Fame, Acad. of Adventure Game Design 1993; named to Hall of Fame by Games Mag.; Diplomacy named Game of Yr. by Games & Puzzles 1977). Avocations: strategic games, reading, writing. Home: 501 N Stone Ave La Grange Park IL 60526-5523

CALHOUN, DEBORAH LYNN, emergency room nurse, consultant; b. Tulsa, Aug. 6, 1958; d. Charles Cooper Calhoun and Delores Susan (Deardorf) Metzger. BSN, Clemson U., 1982. RN, S.C.; cert. emergency nurse, ACLS instr., TNCC instr. Staff nurse, clin. nurse III Roper Hosp., Charleston, S.C., 1982-99; owner Charleston Med.-Lega. Cons., 1994—; dept. mgr. CareAlliance Health Svcs. Emergency Svcs., Hyperbaric Med., Charleston, 1999—; clin. coord. emergency svcs. and hyperbaric medicine Roper Hosp. Instr. ENCARE, 1993. Mem. ENA, TNCC, S.C. Emergency Nurses Assn. (pres. 1994, ann. symposium chair 1996), Low Country Emergency Nurses Assn. (pres. 1991-92). Republican. Episcopalian. Avocations: reading, needlework, photography, aerobics. Home: 1212 Gilmore Rd Charleston SC 29407-5333 Office: Roper Hosp 316 Calhoun St Charleston SC 29401-1125

CALHOUN, DONALD EUGENE, JR., federal judge; b. Columbus, Ohio, May 15, 1926; s. Donald Eugene and Esther (Cope) C.; m. Shirley Claggett, Aug. 28, 1948; children: Catherine C., Donald Eugene III, Elizabeth C. BA in Polit. Sci., Ohio State U., 1949, JD, 1951. Bar: Ohio 1951. Pvt. practice, 1951-68; ptnr. Folkerth, Calhoun, Webster, Maurer & O'Brien, 1968-82, Guren, Merritt, Feibel, Sogg & Cohen, 1982-84; of counsel Lane, Alton, Horst, 1984-85; U.S. bankruptcy judge Columbus, 1985—; gen. counsel Ohio Conf. United Ch. of Christ, 1964-85. Chmn. City-wide Citizens Com. for Neighborhood Seminars on Sch. Program and Fin., 1963; mem. Columbus Bd. Edn., 1963-71, pres., 1966, 70. With USNR, 1944-46. Mem. Columbus Bar Assn. (pres. 1967-68, Community Svc. award 1972), Nat. Conf. Bar Pres., Am. Arbitration Assn., Columbus Jaycees (life), Univ. Club, Masons. Congregationalist. Office: US Bankruptcy Ct 170 N High St Columbus OH 43215-2421

CALHOUN, EMILY MITCHELL, elementary education educator; b. Hawkinsville, Ga., July 30, 1939; d. Glenn Lewis Sr. and Evelyn (Athon) Mitchell; m. Frank Marion Calhoun, Aug. 5, 1961 (div. Feb. 1979); children: Craig Mitchell, Wade Morgan. BA in Social Sci., elem. tchg. cert., LaGrange Coll., 1961; MS in Reading Edn., Nova U., 1982. Cert. in elem. edn. and reading edn., Fla. Tchr. Rockway Elem. Sch., Miami, Fla., 1961-62, 63-64, Kate Sullivan Elem. Sch., Tallahassee, Fla., 1964-65, Hazelwood Elem. Sch., Waynesville, N.C., 1969-70; tchr. kindergarten 1st United Meth. Ch., Waynesville, 1972-76, Ctrl. Elem. Sch., Waynesville, 1977; tchr. Fern Creek Elem. Sch., Orlando, Fla., 1977-83, title I reading tchr., 1983-94, reading recovery tchr., 1994-97; testing resource tchr. Pineloch Elem. Sch., Orlando, 1997-98; literacy tchr. Dream Lake Elem. Sch., Apopka, Fla., 1998—; field tester math. series Harcourt, Brace, Jovanovich, Orlando, 1982; grade chmn. Fern Creek Elem., Orlando, 1980-82. Team author: (math. mgmt. sys.) Pre-Tests and Post-Tests, 1978, Stepping Stones Handbook, 1979, (implementation module) Implementing PREP Team, 1980. Mem. membership class Aloma United Meth. Ch., Winter Park, Fla., 1990-93, mem. homeless coalition, 1996-99, leader STAR team, 1999—; mem. reading del. People to People Internat., Hungary and Russia, 1993. Mem. NEA, PEO (chpt. D.J. Orlando, meeting com. 1993—), Internat. Reading Assn. (conv. hostess 1983, 98), Fla. Edn. Assn., Orange County Classroom Tchrs. Assn., N.Am. Coun. Reading Recovery. Republican. United Methodist. Avocations: reading, traveling, tennis. Office: Dream Lake Elem Sch 500 N Park Ave Apopka FL 32712-3599

CALHOUN, FRANK WAYNE, lawyer, former state legislator; b. Houston, Apr. 15, 1933; s. Wilmer Cecil and Ruby Edith (Willis) C.; m. Suzanne Paden Davis, Dec. 14, 1985; children: Michael Lee, Frank David. B.A. in History, Tex. Tech U., 1956; J.D., U. Tex., 1959. Bar: Tex. 1959, U.S. Supreme Ct. 1965, U.S. Dist. Ct. (no. and western dists.) Tex., U.S. Ct. Appeals (5th cir.). Ptnr. Byrd, Shaw, Weeks & Calhoun, Abilene, Tex., 1959-73, Locke Liddell & Sapp, LLP, Houston, 1974—; mem. Tex. Ho. of Reps., 1966-75; del. Tex. Constl. Conv., 1974; mem. exec. com. Tex. Film Commn., 1979-83. Contbg. editor Tex. Lawyers Weekly Letter, 1964. Bd. dirs. Tex. Assn. Bank Counsel, 1982-85; chmn. San Jacinto Hist. Adv. Bd., 1984—; trustee Colo. Outward Bound Sch., 1982-92, San Jacinto Mus. History, 1988—, Tex. Hist. Found., 1988-90; trustee, fellow Tex. Tech. U. Law Sch. Found., 1975-87; chmn. bd. dirs. Inst. Texan Cultures, 1989—; past bd. dirs. Abilene YMCA; mem. Houston Fine Arts Mus.; adv. coun. Harry Ransom Humanities Rsch. Ctr. With USN, 1951-53. Named Outstanding Young Man Abilene Jaycees, 1968; recipient Disting. Service award Tex. Bar Assn., 1969, 71, 73. Mem. ABA, Tex. Bar Assn., Travis County Bar Assn., Tex. Tech. U. Ex-Students Assn. (past pres.), Tex. Archeol. Soc., Nat. Aubudon Soc., Sierra Club, Nat. Trust for Hist. Preservation, Tex. State Hist. Assn., Sons of Confederate Vets., Sons of the Republic of Tex., St. Andrews Soc. Tex., Rotary (past pres), Houston Club, Austin Club, Sigma Alpha Epsilon, Alpha Kappa Psi. Democrat. Methodist. Clubs: Houston, Austin. Lodge: Rotary (past pres.). Home: 6001 Little Bull Cove Austin TX 78731-6532 Office: Liddell Sapp Zivley Hill & LaBoon 700 Lavaca St Ste 800 Austin TX 78701-3102

CALHOUN, HAROLD, architect; b. Mineral Springs, Ark., Oct. 11, 1906; s. Albert Sidney and Willie (Reeder) C.; m. Annie Louise Robertson, Dec. 3, 1932; 1 child, Nancy Ann (dec.). BA, Rice U., 1932. Freelance delineator and archtl. draftsman, 1925-29; founder Wirtz & Calhoun (architects), 1932; with Robert & Co. (architects and engrs. on design of Corpus Christi Naval Air Center), Corpus Christi, Tex., 1940-43; vis. critic, grad. students archtl. dept. Rice U., 1946; with Wirtz, Calhoun, Tungate & Jackson, Houston, 1947-66, Calhoun, Tungate & Jackson, Houston, 1966-75, Calhoun, Tungate, Jackson & Dill, Houston, 1975—. Lt. (s.g.) USNR, 1943-46. Recipient First Hon. mention House Beautiful competition, 1946; 3d prize Georgia Builds competition, 1947; hon. mention, 1953. Fellow AIA (Cert. of award Houston chpt. 1947); mem. Tex. Soc. Architects (past pres., Merit award 1954, Arch. Merit award 1960), Soc. Arch. Mexicanos (hon.), Masons, Lions. Baptist (deacon). Home: 1 Concord Cir Houston TX 77024-6309 Office: CTJ&D Architects 2323 S Voss Rd Ste 440 Houston TX 77057-3812*

CALHOUN, JIM, college basketball coach; m. Patricia McDevitt; children: James, Jeffrey. BA in Sociology, Am. Internat. Coll., 1968. Asst. basketball coach Am. Internat. Coll., 1966-68; head coach basketball Old Lyme H.S., Conn., 1969, Westport (Mass.) H.S., 1970, Dedham H.S., Mass., 1971-72; head coach Northeastern U., U. Conn., 1986—; rep. Big East Conf. Yugoslavia, 1988; head coach Big East Conf. All-Star Team which toured Finland, Soviet Union; mem. selection com. U.S. Pan-Am. Basketball Team U.S.A. Basketball, 1991; numerous others. past chair Ronald McDonald Houses, We. New England; hon. chmn. Conn. chpt. Am. Cancer Soc.; hon. chmn. New Haven Pub. Edn. Fund; mem. adv. staff we. region Big. Bros./Big Sisters; mem. adv. bd. Hartford Whalers Hockey Club NHL; mem. nat. adv. bd. Ctr. for the Study of Sports in Soc.; hon. chmn. Conn. Sports Mus. and Hall of Fame, greater Hartford chpt. Juvenile Diabetes Found. Named Coach of the Yr., Big East Coach of the Yr.; winner NCAA Big East Title, 1999; NCAA Divsn. I champs. Mem. Nat. Assn. Basketball Coaches (mem. nom. com. Hall of Fame), Big East Conf. Coaches Assn. (pres.). Office: Univ of Connecticut 2095 Hillside Rd Storrs Mansfield CT 06269-9017*

CALHOUN, JOHN ALFRED, social services administrator; b. Phila., Dec. 1, 1939; s. John Alfred and Helen Fordham (Webster) C.; m. Ottilia Klenota, May 29, 1971; children: Byron, Hollis. BA, Brown U., 1962; M in Div., Episcopal Div. Sch., Cambridge, Mass., 1965; MPA, Harvard U., 1986. Tchr. Phila. pub. schs., 1965-66; program adminstr. Action for Boston Community Devel., 1966-70; v.p. Tech. Devel. Corp., Boston, 1970-73; exec. dir. Justice Resource Inst., Boston, 1973-76; commr. Mass. Dept. of Youth Svcs., Boston, 1976-79, U.S. Adminstrn. for Children, Youth and Families, Washington, 1979-81; dir. Ctr. for Govtl. Affairs Child Welfare League, Washington, 1981-83; exec. dir. Nat. Crime Prevention Coun., Washington, 1983—; pres. bd. dirs. Nat. Ctr. for Youth as Resources; pres. Internat. Ctr. for the Prevention of Crime; bd. dirs. Nat. Funding Collaborative on Violence Prevention, Ctr. for Internat. Leadership, D.C.; bd. dirs. Pacific Ctr. for Violence Prevention, The Nat. Assembly of Voluntary Health and Social Welfare Ags., Childrens Trust Neighborhood Initiative; assoc. in edn. Harvard U., 1978; moderator Aspen Inst., 1980—; founder Pre-trial Diversion Programs, Mass., Urban Ct. Mediation Cmty. Sentencing, Mass., Cmty. Responses to Drug Abuce, 10 Sites Across the U.S.; mem. U.S. Atty. Gen.'s Coordinating Coun. on Juvenile Justice; founder Youth as Resources, Mass. and Ind. Author: What, Me Evaluate?, 1986; editor: Crime in Urban Communities, 1986, Making a Difference, 1985, Reaching Out: School-based Community Service Programs, Teen Crime and the Community, National Service and Public Safety: Partnerships for Safer Communities, Taking the Offensive: How Seven Cities Did It; contbr. articles to profl. jours. Coach McLean (Va.) Youth; tchr. confirmation class Louisville Presbyn. Ch., McLean; state chmn. Mass. Adolescent Task Force, 1978; chmn. Mass. State of the Family Task Force, 1979; pres. Franklin Flaschner Found., 1978; treas. Met. Beaverbrook Area Mental Health Bd.; bd. advisors U. Mass. Coll. Cmty. Pub. Svc., 1979; bd. dirs. Edna Stein Acad., Boston, Pekinese Island Sch., Woods Hole, Mass. Littauer fellow Harvard U. Kennedy Sch. of Govt., 1986; recipient award of Recognition Am. Arbitration Assn., 1978, award of Recognition, U.S. Office Juvenile Justice and Delinquency Prevention. Mem. Am. Probation/ Parole Assn. (project planning commn. 1986-88, prevention com.). Democrat. Episcopalian. Avocations: photography, tennis, gardening, coaching, skiing. Home: 921 Mackall Ave Mc Lean VA 22101-1617 Office: Nat Crime Prevention Coun Office of Exec Dir 1700 K St NW Fl 2D Washington DC 20006-3817

CALHOUN, JOHN C., JR., academic administrator; b. Betula, Pa., Mar. 21, 1917; s. John C. and Martha (Rowe) C.; m. Ruth Elizabeth Huston, June 10, 1941; children: John, Emily, Mary Beth, Ruth Ellen. BS in Petroleum and Natural Gas Engring., Pa. State U., 1937, MS, 1941, PhD, 1946; DSc (hon.), Ripon Coll., 1975. Research asst., instr. petroleum and natural gas engring. Pa. State U., 1937-46, prof., head dept. petroleum and natural gas engring., 1950-55; assoc. prof., then prof. Sch. Petroleum Engring., U. Okla., 1946-50, chmn., 1948-50; dean Sch. Engring. Tex. Agrl. and Mech. Coll., College Station, 1955-57; dir. Engring. Expt. Sta., Engring. Ext. Service Tex. Agrl. and Mech. U., College Station, 1955-57, v.p. engring., 1957-59, vice chancellor for engring., 1959-60, vice chancellor for devel., 1960-63, v.p. programs, 1965-71, Disting. prof. petroleum engring., 1965-83, dir. Office Sea Grant Programs, 1968-72, dean geoscis., 1969-71, v.p. acad. affairs, 1971-77, exec. vice chancellor for programs Tex. A&M U. System, 1977-80, dep. chancellor for engring., 1980-83; dir. Crisman Inst. Petroleum Reservoir Mgmt., 1984-87; dep. chancellor for engring. emeritus Tex. A&M U. Sys., College Station, 1983—; asst., sci. advisor to sec. Dept. Interior, Washington, 1963-65; vice chmn. Engring. Coll. Rsch. Coun., 1959-62; mem. Fed. Coun. for Sci. and Tech., 1963-65, Presdl. Task Force on Oceanography, 1969, Nat. Adv. Coun. on Oceans and Atmosphere, 1971-72, Tex. Coastal and Marine Coun., 1972-83; acting dir. Office Water Resources Rsch., 1964; mem. environ. pollution panel Pres.'s Sci. Adv. Com., 1964-66; chmn. com. on oceanography NAS, 1967-70, chmn. ocean sci. affairs bd., 1970-72; chmn. Pres.'s Santa Barbara Oil Spill Panel and Panel on Union Oil Lease, 1969; mem. adv. panel Internat. Decade Ocean Exploration, NSF, 1970-72; mem. nat. adv. coun. on minorities in engring. Nat. Acad. Engring., 1973-74; mem. naval studies bd. Nat. Acad. Scis., 1974-79; bd. dirs. Inst. Nautical Archeology, 1976-86; dir. Tex. Petroleum Rsch. Com., 1978-82; cons. So. Regional Edn. Bd., 1953-54, Pa. Dept. Forests & Waters, 1955, World Bank, 1978-85, Coun. Internat. Edn. Exch., 1988-92; mem. rsch. coordination panel Gas Rsch. Inst., 1977-82; mem. adv. com. on mining and mineral resources rsch. Dept. Interior, 1987-94. Author: Fundamentals of Reservoir Engineering, 1953; contbr. articles to profl. jours. Chmn. Coll. Sta. United Fund, 1961; trustee U. Corp. for Atmospheric Rsch., 1969-71, chmn. bd., 1968-71; trustee Tex. Agrl. and Mech. Rsch. Found., 1961-82, Tex. Inst. for Rehab. and Rsch., 1981-82; bd. dirs. EDUCOM, 1966-69, Houston Area Rsch. Ctr., 1982-83; exec. dir., pres. Gulf Univs. Rsch. Corp., 1966-69. Recipient 15th Sea Grant award Sea Grant Assn., 1984; alumni fellow Pa. State U., 1976. Fellow AAAS, Marine Tech. Soc. (pres. 1975-76), Am. Soc. Engring. Edn. (v.p., dir. 1968-72, pres. 1974, Centennial medallion 1993, Collins award 1996); mem. Nat. Acad. Engring., Engrs. Coun. Profl. Devel. (bd. dirs. 1964-67), Engrs. Joint Coun. (bd. dirs. 1972-77), AIME (hon.), Soc. Petroleum Engrs. (pres. 1964, DeGolyer medal 1982, Anthony F. Lucas Gold medal 1997), Am. Assn. Engring. Socs. (mem. exec. com. internat. affairs coun. 1980-81), Sigma Xi, Tau Beta Pi, Sigma Gamma Epsilon, Phi Kappa Phi, Tau Kappa Epsilon. Presbyterian. Home: 1106 Ashburn Ave College Station TX 77840-2502

CALHOUN, JOHN R., lawyer; b. Fairfield, Iowa, Nov. 22, 1933; m. Elizabeth Calhoun; four children. BA in Polit. Sci., U. Iowa, 1956, JD, 1958. Bar: Iowa, 1958, Calif. 1960, U.S. Ct. Appeals (9th cir.) 1987, U.S. Ct. Appeals (fed. cir.) 1997, U.S. Dist. Ct. (cen. dist.) Calif. 1960, U.S. Supreme Ct. 1963, U.S. Ct. Mil. Appeals 1963. Commd. 2d lt. U.S. Army Res., 1958, advanced through grades to col., JAG Corp., ret., 1988; atty. U.S. Securities and Exch. Commn., 1960, Automobile Club of So. Calif., 1960-61; dep. dist. atty. L.A. Dist. Atty.'s Office, 1961-62; dep. city prosecutor Long Beach (Calif.) City Prosecutor's Office, 1962-67; dep. city atty. Long Beach City Atty.'s Office, 1967-78, asst. city atty., 1978-85, city atty., 1985-98. Decorated Legion of Merit, Meritorious Svc. medal. Mem. Calif. Bar Assn., Long Beach Bar Assn. (bd. govs. 1974-75, 87-88), Rotary, Res. Officers Assn., Long Beach Area C. of C., Phi Delta Phi, Phi Delta Theta. Office: 4011 Chestnut Ave Long Beach CA 90807-3207

CALHOUN, MILBURN, publishing executive, rare book dealer, physician; b. West Monroe, La., Jan. 15, 1930; s. Darrell L. and Mary Elizabeth (Crowell) C.; m. Nancy Kathryn Harris, July 14, 1956; children: Kathleen, David. BS, La. State U., Baton Rouge, 1951; MD, La. State U., New Orleans, 1955. Intern Charity Hosp., New Orleans, 1955-56; physician Buras, La., 1956-57, Buras Clinic, Buras, La., 1959-65; pres., founder Bayou Books, Gretna, La., 1961—; physician Nicholson Baehr Calhoun Marrero, L.A., La., 1965-97; pub. Pelican Pub. Co., Gretna, La., 1970—; gen. mgr. Nancy Enterprise LLC, Gretna, 1998—; mem. staff West Jefferson Gen. Hosp., Marrero, La., past chief staff; mem. staff Meadowcrest Hosp., physician Columbia HCA, 1996-97. Editor La. Almanac, 1988, 92, 95, 97. Fellow Am. Acad. Family Practice; mem. Am. Mktg. Assn., La. Acad. Family Practice, La. Assn. Bus. and Industry, New Orleans C. of C. Democrat. Baptist. Office: Pelican Pub Co Inc PO Box 3110 Gretna LA 70054-3110

CALHOUN, NOAH ROBERT, oral maxillofacial surgeon, educator; b. Clarendon, Ark., Mar. 23, 1921; s. Noah and Della (Sherman) C.; m. Cecelia Christopher, Oct. 19, 1950; children: Stephen Marc, Cecelia Noel. D.D.S., Dental Sch., Howard U., 1948; M.Dental Sci., Tufts Med. and Dental Sch., 1955. Oral surgeon VA Hosp., Tuskegee, Ala., 1950-52, Kessler AFB, Biloxi, Miss., 1952-53; chief dental service VA Hosp., Tuskegee, Ala., 1955-57; oral surgeon, asst. chief dental surgeon VA Hosp., Washington, 1964-74; chief dental service, oral surgeon VA Med. Center, Washington, 1974—; prof. oral surgery Dental Sch., Howard U., Washington, 1966-92, Georgetown U., Washington, 1975-93; prof. emeritus Dental Coll. Howard U., 1992—; Dir. Tuskegee (Ala.) Red Cross, 1962-64; chmn. Nat. Concerned VA Dentists, 1975, Inst. Medicine/Acad. Sci., 1975. Sect. editor Current Lit. in Internat. Oral/Maxillofacial Surgery, 1986; mem. editorial bd. Jour. Oral and Maxillo-facial Surveys, 1993; contbr. articles to profl. jours. Mem. ADA, NAACP (trustee D.C. chpt.), Am. Soc. Oral and Maxillofacial Surgeons (Audio Visual award 1978), Internat. Coll. Dentistry, Am. Coll. Dentistry, Inst. Medicine, Omicron Kappa Upsilon. Roman Catholic. Office: Dental Coll Howard U Washington DC 20001

CALHOUN, PEGGY JOAN, fundraising executive; b. La Salle, Ill., Sept. 14, 1957; d. Floyd Anthony and Sophia (Regula) Sarwinski; m. James R. Calhoun, Apr. 19, 1989; children: (twins) Robert Blair and Christina Sophia. Student, Ill. Valley C.C., Oglesby, 1975, So. Ill. U., 1976, 77; MA, St. Mary's Coll., Minn., 1994. Assoc. dir. United Way, Sarasota, Fla., 1979-85; devel. dir. Boy Scouts Am., Sarasota, 1985-86; assoc. campaign dir. United Way, Ft. Lauderdale, Fla., 1986-87; dir. devel. YMCA, Sarasota, 1987-88, Salvation Army, Ft. Lauderdale, 1988-91, Diabetes Rsch. Inst. Found., U. Miami Sch. Medicine, 1992-93; pres. Calhoun & Co., Inc., Ft. Lauderdale, 1993—; prin. Miller, Calhoun & Co., Inc.; instr. Nova U., Ft. Lauderdale, Barry U., 1996—. Com. mem. United Way, 1988-91. Mem. Nat. Soc. Fund Raising Execs. (advanced cert. fund raising exec., pres. bd. dirs. 1985, Outstanding Profl. Fund Raiser 1991, bd. dirs. 1990—, pres. 1996), Women's Exec. Com. (mentor), Broward Planned Giving Coun. (bd. dirs. 1991), Pub. Rels. Soc. Am. (pres. 1993, bd. dirs. 1991-93), Jr. League, Mothers of Twins. Republican. Avocations: water sports, reading, travel. Home and Office: 2741 NE 57th Ct Fort Lauderdale FL 33308-2723

CALHOUN-SENGHOR, KEITH, lawyer; b. Richmond, Va., June 14, 1955; s. Clarence Calhoun Jr. and Senegal Senghor; m. Sharon White. AB with honors, Stanford U., 1977; JD, Harvard U., 1981. Bar: D.C. 1981, U.S. Ct. Appeals (4th cir.) 1982. Law clk. to judge U.S. Ct. Appeals for 4th Cir., Richmond, 1981-82; assoc. Gibson, Dunn & Crutcher, L.A. and Washington, 1983-85; fgn. legal fellow Kreuz, Niebler & Mittl, Munich, 1986; v.p., gen. counsel Tech. Applications, Inc., Alexandria, Va., 1986-90; pres. Noma Internat. Enterprises, Inc., Washington, 1990-93; of counsel Wood, Williams, Rafalsky & Harris, Washington, 1991-93; dir. Office of Space Commercialization U.S. Dept. Commerce, Washington, 1993—. Fulbright scholar U. Bonn., 1977-78; German Acad. Exch. Svc. Fgn. fellow, 1985-86. Mem. ABA, D.C. Bar Assn. Office: US Dept Commerce Office Space Commercializtn 15th & Constitution Ave NW Washington DC 20230

CALIANDRO, ARTHUR, minister; b. Portland, Maine, 1933; m. Gloria Brown (div.); m. Lea Weeks; children: Charles, Paul. BA, Ohio Wesleyan U., 1955; MDiv, Union Theol. Sem., N.Y.C., 1958; postgrad., Bellevue Hosp., N.Y.C., 1958, Tex. Med. Ctr., Houston, 1959-62. Pastor Union Meth. Ch., Bklyn., 1962-67; minister Marble Collegiate Ch., N.Y.C., 1967-84, sr. minister, 1984—; founder MarbleVision ministry, 1987; spkr. in field. Author: Make Your Life Count, 1990, Simple Steps, 1999; contbr. articles to mags., jours. Bd. dirs. Religion in Am. Life, Trinity-Pawling Sch., Blanton-Peale Inst., A Partnership of Faith in N.Y.C., A Fellowship in Prayer. Named Clergyman of Yr., Religious Heritage Am., 1991, Religion Am. Life, 1995. Address: 1 W 29th St New York NY 10001-4501

CALI-ASCANI, MARY ANN, oncology nurse; b. Bethlehem, Pa., Aug. 12, 1959; d. John and Mae Rita (Dikeman) Cali; m. Donald Roger Ascani, Sept. 8, 1984. Diploma, St. Luke's Sch. of Nursing, Bethlehem, 1979; BSN, Cedar Crest Coll., 1984; MSN in Oncology, clinical nurse specialist, U. Pa., 1989. RN, Pa.; cert. oncology nursing, med. surg. nurse. Nurse mgr. oncology unit Easton (Pa.) Hosp. Mem. ANA, Pa. Nurses Assn., Oncology Nursing Soc., Sigma Theta Tau (nat. nursing honor soc.). Home: 220 Church Rd Pen Argyl PA 18072-1314

CALIENDO, G. D. (JERRY CALIENDO), public utility executive; b. Bklyn., Feb. 17, 1941; s. Philip and Antoinette (Zacarro) Caliendo; m. Barbara Joyce Bonkiewicz, June 30, 1962; children: Barbara Jean, Steven. BA, NYU, 1962; JD, Fordham U., 1965. Bar: N.Y. 1966, D.C. 1966, Pa. 1969. Atty. FCC, Washington, 1965; pvt. practice Washington, 1966-68; atty. Pa. Power & Light Co., Allentown, 1968-75, asst. counsel, 1975-78, chief counsel regulatory affairs, 1978-81, v.p., chief counsel regulatory affairs, 1981-85, v.p., gen. counsel, 1985-89, sr. v.p., gen. counsel and sec., 1989-95; sr. v.p., gen. counsel, sec. Orange and Rockland Utilities, Inc., Pearl River, N.Y., 1995—. Mem. ABA, Pa. Bar Assn. Office: Orange & Rockland Utilities One Blue Hill Plz Pearl River NY 10965

CALIFANO, JOSEPH ANTHONY, JR., lawyer, public health policy educator, writer; b. Bklyn., May 15, 1931; s. Joseph Anthony and Katherine (Gill) C.; m. Hilary Paley Byers, 1983; children by previous marriage: Mark Gerard, Joseph Anthony III, Claudia Frances; stepchildren: Brooke A. Byers, John Fredric Byers IV. BA, Holy Cross Coll., 1952; LLB, Harvard U., 1955. Bar: N.Y. 1955, U.S. Supreme Ct. 1966, D.C. 1969. With firm Dewey Ballantine, N.Y.C., 1958-61; spl. asst. to gen. counsel Dept. Def., 1961-62; spl. asst. to sec. Army, 1962-63; gen. counsel Dept. Army, 1963-64;

spl. asst. to sec. and dep. sec. Def., 1964-65, spl. asst. to Pres. of U.S., 1965-69; ptnr. Arnold & Porter, Washington, 1969-71, Williams, Connolly & Califano, Washington, 1971-77; sec. HEW, 1977-79; ptnr. Califano, Ross & Heineman, Washington, 1980-82; sr. ptnr. Dewey Ballantine, Washington, 1983-92; prof. pub. health policy Columbia U. Schs. Medicine and Pub. Health, N.Y.C., 1992—; chmn., pres. Nat. Ctr. on Addiction and Substance Abuse at Columbia U., N.Y.C., 1992—; bd. dirs. Authentic Fitness Corp., ADP, Inc., Chrysler Corp., HealthPlan Svcs. , Inc., Kmart Corp., Travelers Group Inc., Warnaco Inc.; gen. counsel Dem. Nat. Com., 1971-72. Author: The Student Revolution: A Global Confrontation, 1969, A Presidential Nation, 1975, Governing America: An Insiders Report from the White House and the Cabinet, 1981, The 1982 Report on Drug Abuse and Alcoholism, America's Health Care Revolution, 1986, The Triumph and Tragedy of Lyndon Johnson, 1991, Radical Surgery: What's Next for America's Health Care, 1995, (with Howard Simons) The Media and the Law, 1976, The Media and Business, 1978. Trustee Urban Inst., NYU, Am. Ditchley Found., 20th Century Fund; bd. govs. N.Y. and Presbyn. Hosp. Inc.; chmn. Inst. Social and Econ. Policy in Middle East, Harvard U., 1983-98. Recipient Distinguished Civilian Svc. award Dept. Army, 1964; Man of Year award Justinian Soc. Lawyers, 1966; Disting. Pub. Svc. medal Dept. Def., 1965; named One of Ten Outstanding Young Men of America, 1966. Mem. N.Y. State Bar Assn., D.C. Bar Assn., Met. Club (Washington), Century Assn., Univ. Club. *

CALIGIURI, JOSEPH FRANK, retired engineering executive; b. Columbus, Ohio, Feb. 13, 1928; s. Frank and Angeline Josephine (Gentile) C.; m. Barbara Jane Delaney, June 15, 1948 (dec. 1996); children: Mark, Timothy, Jeffrey, Andrew; m. Tanya Alberta Condon, June 24, 1998. BSEE, Ohio State U., 1949, MSEE, 1951. Chief engr. Sperry Gyroscope Co., Great Neck, N.Y., 1966-69; v.p. engring. Guidance and Control Systems div. Litton Industries, Inc., Woodland Hills, Calif., 1969-71, pres., 1971-77; v.p. Litton Industries, Inc., Woodland Hills, 1974-77, sr. v.p., group head, Beverly Hills, 1977-81, exec. v.p., advanced electronics group head, 1981-93; ret., 1993; bd. dirs. Avnet Inc., Titan Corp., Intracel Corp. Home: 1353 Oak Grove Pl Westlake Village CA 91362-4248

CALINESCU, ADRIANA GABRIELA, museum curator, art historian; b. Bucharest, Romania, Dec. 30, 1941; came to U.S., 1973; d. Nicolae and Tamara Gane; m. Matei Alexe Calinescu, Apr. 29, 1963; children: Irena, Matthew. BA, Cen. Lyceé, Bucharest, 1959; MA in English, U. Bucharest, 1964; MLS, Ind. U., 1976, MA in Art History, 1983. Asst. prof. Inst. Theater and Cinema, Bucharest, 1967-73; rsch. assoc. Ind. U. Art Mus., Bloomington, 1979-83, Thomas T. Solley curator ancient art, assoc. scholar, 1992—; vis. assoc. mem. Am. Sch. Classical Studies, Athens, Greece, 1984. Author: The Art of Ancient Jewelry, 1994; author, co-editor: Ancient Art from the V. G. Simkhovitch Collection, 1988; editor: Ancient Jewelry and Archaeology, 1996. NEA fellow, 1984; grantee Salzburg Seminar, 1970, NEA, 1987, 93, Kress Found., 1991, Internat. Rsch. and Exchanges Bd., 1991. Mem. Am. Inst. Archaeology, Classical Art Soc., Beta Phi Mu. Office: Ind U Art Mus E 7th St Bloomington IN 47405

CALINESCU, MATEI ALEXE, literature educator; b. Bucharest, June 15, 1934; came to U.S., 1973, naturalized, 1981; s. Radu and Dora Maria (Vulcanescu) C.; m. Adriana Gane, Apr. 29, 1964; children: Irena, A. Matthew. MA in English, U. Bucharest, 1957; PhD in Comparative Lit., U. Cluj, Romania, 1972. Asst. prof. comparative lit. U. Bucharest, 1963-65, assoc. prof. comparative lit., 1965-72; vis. assoc. prof. comparative lit. Ind. U., Bloomington, 1973-75, assoc. prof. comparative lit. and west European studies, 1976-79, prof. comparative lit., 1979—, chair dept. comparative lit., 1996-98; vis. fellow U. Chgo., 1988, Yale U., 1989. Author: Faces of Modernity: Avant-Garde, Decadence, Kitsch, 1977, Five Faces of Modernity: Modernism, Avant-Garde, Decadence, Kitsch, Postmodernism, 1987, Rereading, 1993, (with Ion Vianu) Amintiri in dialog, 1994, (with D.W. Fokkema) Exploring Postmodernism, 1990; contbr. numerous articles to profl. jours. Guggenheim fellowship, 1975-76, NEH Summer fellowship, 1991, Woodrow wilson Internat. Ctr. for Scholars fellowship, 1994-95. Home: 1028 E Wylie St Bloomington IN 47401-5082 Office: Comparative Lit Ind U Bloomington IN 47405 Office: 1028 E Wylie St Bloomington IN 47401-5082

CALINGAERT, MICHAEL, nonprofit organization executive; b. Detroit, Sept. 17, 1933; s. George and Dorothy C.; m. Efrem Funghi, June 20, 1962; children: Alexander, Daniel, Nicholas. BA, Swarthmore Coll., 1955; postgrad., U. Cologne, Fed. Republic Germany, 1955-56, U. Calif., Berkeley, 1963-64. Commd. fgn. svc. officer Dept. State, 1956; intelligence rsch. specialist Dept. State, Washington, 1957-58; vice consul Am. consulate gen. Mogadiscio, Somalia, 1959-61; econ. officer Am. consulate gen. Bremen, Fed. Republic Germany, 1961-63; econ. officer Am. Embassy, Colombo, Sri Lanka, 1964-68; chief food policy div. Dept. State, Washington, 1968-72; econ. counselor Am. Embassy, Tokyo, 1972-75; econ./comml. min. Am. Embassy, Rome, 1975-79; dep. asst. sec. for internat. resources and food policy Dept. State, 1979-83; econ. min. Am. Embassy, London, 1983-87; vis. sr. fellow Nat. Planning Assn., Washington, 1987-89, sr. fellow, 1993-97; non-resident sr. fellow Atlantic Coun. U.S., 1989; dir. of European ops. Pharm. Mfrs. Assn., Belgium, 1989-93; dir. The Monnet-Madison Inst., Brussels, 1994-97; rsch. fellow Inst. for European Studies, Free U. Brussels, 1994-98, mem. polit. sect., 1998—; guest scholar The Brookings Inst., 1996—. Author: The 1992 Challenge from Europe: Development of the European Community's Internal Market, 1988, European Integration Revisited: Progress, Prospects, and U.S. Interests, 1996; contbr. numerous articles to profl. jours. Exec. dir. Coun. for U.S. and Italy, 1997—. Recipient Meritorious Honor award Dept. State, 1971, Superior Honor award, 1981. Mem. Am. Fgn. Svc. Assn., Royal Inst. Internat. Affairs, Inst. Affari Internat. Office: The Brookings Inst 1775 Massachusetts Ave NW Washington DC 20036-2188

CALINGER, RONALD STEVE, historian; b. Aliquippa, Pa., Apr. 6, 1942; s. Thomas H. and Mary (Blicha) C.; m. Betty Jeanne Mikulecky, Dec. 21, 1974; children: John Michael, Anne. A.B. summa cum laude, Ohio U., 1963; M.A., U. Pitts., 1964; Ph.D., U. Chgo., 1971. Assoc. editor scis. A.N. Marquis Publ. Co., Chgo., 1966-68; mem. faculty Rensselaer Poly. Inst., Troy, N.Y., 1969-85, assoc. prof. history, 1975-85, chmn. dept. history and polit. sci., 1977-82, dean Undergrad. Coll., 1982-85; dean sch. arts scis. The Cath. U. Am., Washington, 1985-87, mem. faculty dept. history, 1987—. Author: Gottfried Wilhelm Leibniz, 1976, A Contextual History of Mathematics: Up to Euler, 1999; co-author: Dictionary of Twentieth Century World Politics, 1993; editor: Classics of Mathematics, 1982, rev. edit., 1995, Vita Mathematica, 1996; contbr. Dictionary Sci. Biography, 1971-74, Dictionary Am. Biography, 1977; sect. editor History and Pedagogy of math. newsletter, 1989—; contbr. articles and revs. to scholarly jours. German Marshall Fund grantee, summer, 1987, 89, NSF, 1995, 96, 98, Hitachi grant Internat. Virtual Inst. for Hist. Studies of Math., 1998—; recipient Austrian Cross Scis. & Arts 1st Class, 1996. Mem. Am. Hist. Assn., History of Sci. Soc. (Washington rep. 1991—), Am. Soc. 18th Century Studies, Atlantic Coun. (acad. assoc.), Math. Assn. Am. (hist. maths. com.), Phi Beta Kappa. Roman Catholic. Achievements include research in the history of mathematics, science biographies (Leonhard Euler and Gottfried Leibniz), development of Newtonian science and competing Leibniz-Wolffian thought in 18th century Prussia and Russia, the University Berlin Mathematics Seminar under Kummer-Weierstrass, and Imperial Austria. Home: 12806 Lacy Dr Silver Spring MD 20904-2916

CALIO, ANTHONY JOHN, scientist, business executive; b. Phila., Oct. 27, 1929; s. Antonio and Mary Emma (Cappuccio) C.; divorced. BA, U. Pa., 1953, postgrad., 1953; postgrad., Carnegie Inst. Tech., 1959; ScD (hon.), Washington U., St. Louis, 1974; postgrad. (Sloan fellow), Stanford U., 1974-75. With Westinghouse Electric Corp., Pitts., 1956-59; chief nuclear physics sect. Am. Machine & Foundry Co., Alexandria, Va., 1959-61; v.p. Mt. Vernon Rsch. Co., 1961-63; electronic rsch. task group NASA Hdqrs., Washington, 1963-64; chief rsch. engring. NASA (Electronics Rsch. Ctr.), Boston, 1964-65; chief instrumentation and systems integration br. NASA Hdqrs., Washington, 1965-67; asst. dir. planetary exploration NASA Hdqrs., 1967-68; dir. sci. and applications NASA Johnson Space Ctr., Houston, 1969-75; dep. assoc. adminstr. office space scis. NASA Hdqrs., Washington, 1975-77, assoc. adminstr. Office of Space and Terrestrial Applications, 1977-81; dep. adminstrn. NOAA Dept. Commerce, 1981-84, under sec. for oceans and atmosphere, 1984-87; sr. v.p. Planning Rsch. Corp., McLean, Va., 1987-90; from exec. v.p. to sr. v.p. Hughes Info. Tech. Corp., Reston, Va., 1991-97; sr. v.p. Hughes Info. Tech. Sys., 1996-97; pres. Space Sys., 1996-97, Hughes Info. Tech. Sys., 1997-99; ret., 1999. With U.S. Army, 1954-56. Recipient Group Achievement award (2) NASA, 1969, Exceptional Service medal, 1969, Apollo Achievement award, 1970, Exceptional Sci. Achievement medal, 1971, Lunar Sci. Team award, 1973, Disting. Service medal, 1973, 81, presdl. rank of Disting. Exec., 1980. Fellow AIAA, Am. Astron. Soc.; mem. Am. Geophys. Union. Home: 1174 Randolph Rd Mc Lean VA 22101-2929

CALIO, VINCENT S., public relations executive. BFA, Pratt Inst. Creative dir. Revlon, Lippincott and Margulies; prin., creative dir. Lefkowith Inc.; mng. ptnr., dir. creative svcs. KCSA Pub. Rels., N.Y.C., 1992—. Office: KCSA Public Relations 800 2nd Ave 5th Fl New York NY 10017-4709*

CALISE, ANTHONY JOHN, aerospace engineering educator; b. Chester, Pa., Feb. 27, 1943; m. Alice A. Boyle; children: John V., Linda M., Jean K., Anthony W. BSEE, Villanova U., 1964; MSEE, U. Pa., 1966, PhD, 1968. Asst. prof. Widner U., Chester, 1967-68; rsch. engr. Raytheon Missile Systems, Lexington, Mass., 1968-69; sr. rsch. engr. Dynamic Rsch. Corp., Wilmington, Mass., 1969-78; assoc. prof. Mech. Engring. Drexel U., Phila., 1978-85, prof. Mech. Engring., 1985-86; prof. Aerospace Engring. Ga. Inst. Tech., Atlanta, 1986—; cons., 1978—. Assoc. editor: AIAA, Washington, 1988-90, IEEE, Washington, 1987-91; over 150 pub. articles and rsch. reports. Recipient Tech. Achievement award USAF Systems Command, 1973. Fellow AIAA (Mechanics and Control of Flight award 1992); mem. IEEE (sr.). Achievements include theory and application of singular perturbation methods for near optimal real time guidance of aerospace vehicles, neural network based adaptive flight control. Office: Ga Inst Tech Aerospace Engring Atlanta GA 30332

CALISE, WILLIAM JOSEPH, JR., lawyer; b. N.Y.C., May 22, 1938; s. William Joseph and Adeline (Rota) C.; m. Elizabeth Mae Gagne, Apr. 16, 1966; children: Kimberly Elizabeth, Andrea Elizabeth. BA, Bucknell U., 1960; MBA, JD, Columbia U., 1963. Bar: N.Y. 1963, D.C. 1981. Assoc. then ptnr. Chadbourne & Parke, N.Y.C., 1967-94; sr. v.p., gen. counsel, sec. Rockwell Internat. Corp., Costa Mesa, Calif., 1994—. Dir. Henry St. Settlement, N.Y.C., 1977-94; mem. Allendale (N.J.) Sch. Bd., 1977-80. Capt. U.S. Army, 1964-66. Mem. Assn. Bar N.Y.C., Duquesne Club (Pitts.). Roman Catholic. Office: Rockwell Internat Corp 600 Anton Blvd Costa Mesa CA 92626-7147

CALISHER, HORTENSE (MRS. CURTIS HARNACK), writer; b. N.Y.C., Dec. 20, 1911; d. Joseph Henry and Hedvig (Lichtstern) C.; m. Curtis Harnack, Mar. 23, 1959; children by previous marriage: Bennet Hughes, Peter Heffelfinger. A.B., Barnard Coll., 1932; LittD (hon.), Skidmore Coll., 1980, Grinnell Coll., 1986; LittD, Adelphi U., 1988. Adj. prof. English Barnard Coll., N.Y.C., 1956-57; vis. lectr. State U. Iowa, 1957, 59-60, Stanford U., 1958, Sarah Lawrence Coll., Bronxville, N.Y., 1962, 67; adj. prof. Columbia U., N.Y.C., 1968-70, CCNY, 1969; vis. prof. lit. SUNY, Purchase, 1971-72, Brandeis U., 1963-64, U. Pa., 1965; Regent's prof. U. Calif., 1976; vis. prof. Bennington Coll., 1978, Washington U., St. Louis, 1979, Brown U., spring 1986; lectr., Fed. Republic of Germany, Yugoslavia, Rumania, Hungary, 1978; guest lectr. U.S./China Arts Exch., Republic of China, 1986. Author: (novels) False Entry, 1961, Textures of Life, 1962, The New Yorkers, 1969, Journal from Ellipsia, 1965, Queenie, 1971, Standard Dreaming, 1972, Eagle Eye, 1973, On Keeping Women, 1977, Mysteries of Motion, 1984, The Bobby-Soxer, 1986 (Kafka prize U. Rochester 1987), Age, 1987, (under pseudonym Jack Fenno) The Small Bang, 1992, In the Palace of the Movie-King, 1994, In the Slammer with Carol Smith, 1997; (novellas) The Railway Police, 1966, The Last Trolley Ride, 1966; short stories include In The Absence of Angels, 1951, Tale for the Mirror, 1962, Extreme Magic, 1963, Collected Stories, 1975, Saratoga Hot, 1985; autobiography: Herself, 1972; memoir: Kissing Cousins, 1988; contbr. short stories, articles, revs. to Am. Scholar, N.Y. Times, Harpers, Yale Rev., New Criterion, others. Guggenheim fellow, 1952, 55; Dept. of State Am. Specialists's grantee to S.E. Asia, 1958; recipient Acad. of Arts and Letters award, 1967, Nat. Council Arts award, 1967, Lifetime Achievement award Nat. Endowment for the Arts, 1989. Mem. Am. Acad. Arts and Letters (pres. 1987-90), PEN (pres. 1986-87). Office: care Marion Boyars Publishers 237 E 39th St New York NY 10016-2110 *Going back over one's work, one can see from earliest times certain para-forms emerging. If one is crazy, these are idées fixes: if one is sane these are systemic views. A mind is not given but makes itself, out of whatever is at hand and sticking-tape—and is not a private possession but an offering . . . I had always had to write everything, no matter the subject, as if my life depended upon it. Of course—it does. (from— Herself: An Autobiographical Work.).**

CALKIN, JOY DURFÉE, healthcare executive, consultant, educator; b. Wolfville, N.S., Can., Apr. 7, 1938; came to U.S., 1970; d. Garth Longworth and Rena Coffin (Cox) C. BSN, U. Toronto, 1960; MSN, U. Wis., 1968, PhD, 1980; DSc (hon.), U. N.B., Can., 1997. Nurse various hosps., Toronto, N.S.and Aberdeen, Scotland, 1960-63; instr. U. N.B., Fredericton, Can., 1963-66, asst. prof., 1968-70; from asst. to assoc. to prof. Sch. Nursing U. Wis., Madison, 1970-85; from asst. to assoc. to full prof. nursing Faculty Medicine, Dept. Preventive Medicine, 1980-85; dean, prof. sch. nursing U. Calgary, Alta., Can., 1985-89, assoc. acad. v.p., 1989-90, acad. v.p., provost, 1990-97; pres., CEO Extendicare Inc., Markham, Ont., Can., 1997—; vis. prof. health scis. U. Oreg., Portland, 1980; cons. Troll Assocs., Madison, 1976-80, Thorne, Stevenson & Kellogg, Edmonton, 1985-86; mem. Premier's commn. on future health care for Alberta. Mem. editorial bd. Recent Advances in Nursing, U.K.; reviewer various nursing jours.; contbr. articles to profl. jours. Bd. dirs. Alberta Found. Nursing Rsch., 1988-91, Alberta Family Life and Substance Abuse Found., 1992-93; v.p. Muttart Found., 1993—, v.p., 1996-99, pres., 1999—; bd. dirs. Extendicare, 1995—. Grantee in field. Mem. Am. Nurses Assn., Can. Nurses Assn. (various coms.). Office: Extendicare Inc 3000 Steeles Ave E Markham, ON Canada L3R 9W2

CALKINS, BRUCE EDGAR, computer company executive; b. Sacramento, Mar. 9, 1952; s. Dixon H. and Kathyrn L. Calkins; m. Nancy Greig, Jan. 11, 1976; 1 child, Matthew Ryan. AA in Drafting Tech., Am. River Coll., Sacramento, 1978; BS, U. San Francisco, 1983. Drafter, CAD operator Lawrence Livermore (Calif.) Nat. Lab., 1978-81; CAD designer Bechtel Petroleum, San Francisco, 1981-84; CAD support mgr. USN, Mare Island, Calif., 1984-93; sr. mgr., fed. SIG chmn. Intergraph Corp., Bellevue, Wash., 1993-95; exec. mgr. vehicle design dept. Intergraph Corp., Huntsville, Ala., 1995—; chmn. architecture, engring. and constrn. group Comutervision U.G., Mare Island, 1985-87; mem. initial graphics exch. std. Navy Industry Digital Data Exch. Stds. Com., Mare Island, 1987-90. With U.S. Army, 1972-75. Avocations: reading, wood working, science fiction. Home: 5013 Laura St SE Olympia WA 98501-4715

CALKINS, CHRISTOPHER MILES, historian; b. Detroit, Mar. 3, 1951; s. Eugene Albert and Longena Marie (Kapecki) C.; m. Sarah Elizabeth Brown, Oct. 2, 1976. BS in History and Geography, Longwood Coll., 1981. Historian/interpretation Petersburg (Va.) Nat. Battlefield, 1981—. Author: Thirty-Six Hours Before Appomattox, 1980, From Petersburg to Appomattox April 2-9, 1865: A Tour Guide, 1983, (with Edwin Bearss) The Battle of Five Forks, 1985, The Battle of Appomattox, vol. 1, 1987, The Final Bivouac: The Surrender Parade at Appomattox and the Disbanding of the Armies, April 10-May 20, 1865, vol. 2, 1988; contbr. Civil War Battlefield Guide, 1990, Ency. So. Confederacy, 1991; contbr. articles to profl. jours. and newspapers. Chmn. tourism adv. bd., City of Petersburg, 1988-98. Rsch. grantee U.S. Army History Inst., Ea. Nat. Park and Monument Assn. Mem. Assn. Preservation Civil War Sites (bd. dirs.), Hist. High St. Assn. (pres. 1987), Hist. Blandford Cemetery Assn., Lynchburg Civil War Roundtable (hon. mem., pres. 1980—), Mich. Regimental Civil War Roundtable (hon.). Avocations: white-water rafting, collecting antiques, archaeology. Office: Petersburg Nat Battlefield 1539 Hickory Hill Rd Petersburg VA 23803-4721*

CALKINS, DAVID ROSS, physician, medical educator; b. Kansas City, Kans., May 27, 1948; s. Leroy Adelbert and Emily Virginia (Kyger) C.; m. Susan Spalding Rice, Sept. 22, 1989; 1 child, Christopher Ross. AB, Princeton (N.J.) U., 1970; MD, MPP, Harvard U., 1975. Diplomate Am. Bd. Internal Medicine. Intern U. Wash., Seattle, 1975-76; resident in medicine Beth Israel Hosp., Boston, 1976-78, from asst. to assoc. in medicine, 1981-96; fellow The White House, Washington, 1978-79; spl. asst., dep. exec. sec. HHS, Washington, 1979-81; from instr. to asst. prof. dept. medicine Harvard U. Med. Sch., Boston, 1981-96; from instr. to asst. prof. Harvard Sch. Pub. Health, Boston, 1985-96, dir. profl. programs dept. health policy and mgmt., 1985-96; chief div. gen. internal medicine, med. dir. ambulatory svc. New Eng. Deaconess Hosp., Boston, 1991-96; assoc. dean for primary care U. Kans. Sch. Medicine, Kansas City, 1996-98, from assoc. prof. to prof. internal and preventive medicine, 1996—, sr. assoc. dean for edn., 1998—. W.K. Kellogg Found. fellow, 1987. Office: 3901 Rainbow Blvd Kansas City KS 66160-7830

CALKINS, EVAN, physician, educator; b. Newton, Mass., July 15, 1920; s. Grosvenor and Patty (Phillips) C.; m. Virginia McC. Brady, Sept. 9, 1946; children: Sarah Calkins Oxnard, Stephen, Lucy McCormick, Joan, Benjamin, Hugh, Ellen Rountree, Geoffrey, Timothy. Grad., Milton Acad., 1939; AB, Harvard U., 1942, MD, 1945. Intern, asst. resident medicine Johns Hopkins, 1946-47, 48-50; chief resident physician Mass. Gen. Hosp., 1951-52, mem. arthritis unit, 1952-61; NRC fellow med. scis. Harvard, 1950-51, instr., asst. prof. medicine, 1952-61; practice medicine, specializing in rheumatology Boston, 1951-61, Buffalo, 1961—; prof. medicine SUNY, Buffalo, 1961-94, prof. emeritus, 1994—; chmn. dept. SUNY, 1965-77; head dept. medicine Buffalo Gen. Hosp., 1961-68; dir. medicine E.J. Meyer Meml. Hosp., 1968-78; head gerontology sect. Buffalo VA Med. Ctr., 1978-90; head div. geriatrics/gerontology SUNY-Buffalo, 1978-90; founder, pres. Network in Aging of Western N.Y., Inc., 1980-83; cons. Nat. Inst. Arthritis and Metabolic Diseases Tng. Grants Com., 1958-62, Program Project Com., 1964-68, Nat. Instn. Spl. Study Sect. for Health Manpower, 1969-77, for Behavioral Medicine, 1978-79; mem. acad. awards com. Nat. Inst. on Aging, 1979-80, mem. nat. adv. coun., 1985-88; dir. Western N.Y. Geriatric Edn. Ctr., 1983-88, co-dir., 1988-90; dir. Multidisciplinary Ctr. on Aging SUNY-Buffalo, 1989-90, prof. family medicine, 1987-94; sr. physician and coord. geriatric programs Health Care Plan, 1990-97; ptnr. Promedicus Health Group, 1998—, chmn. med. edn. com.; chmn. steering com. WNT/Rochester Osteopsrosis Ednl. Resource Ctr., 1999. Editor: Handbook of Medical Emergencies, 1945, Geriatric Medicine, 1983, Practice of Geriatrics, 1986, 2d edit., 1991, New Ways to Care for Older People: Building Systems Based on Evidence, 1998; contbr. articles to profl. jours. Pres. Nat. Assn. Geriatric Edn. Ctrs., 1992-93. Capt. M.C. AUS, 1943-45, 46-48. Recipient Presdl. citation for Community Service, 1983. Fellow ACP (master 1989, Laureate award N.Y. Upstate chpt. 1998), Am. Coll. Rheumatology (founder, pres. 1967-68, master 1986), Gerontol. Soc. Am. (chair clin. med. sect. 1989, Freeman award 1991), Am. Geriatrics Soc. (Milo D. Leavitt award 1986); mem. Am. Clin. and Climatological Assn. (v.p. 1987), Am. Soc. Clin. Investigation, Assn. Am. Physicians, Soc. Medicine Argentina (hon.), Argentine Soc. Gerontology and Geriatrics (hon.), Soc. Fellows John Hopkins U., Alpha Omega Alpha. Home: 3799 Windover Dr Hamburg NY 14075-6338 Office: Mosher Med Bldg 899 Main St Buffalo NY 14203-1109

CALKINS, GARY NATHAN, lawyer, retired; b. N.Y.C., Mar. 1, 1911; s. Gary Nathan and Helen R. (Williston) C.; m. Constantia H. Hommann, June 22, 1940 (div. Dec. 1948); m. Susannah Eby, Nov. 19, 1949; children: Helen (dec.), Margaret Calkins Van Auken, Sarah, Abigail. Student, Ecole Internationale, Geneva, Switzerland, 1926-27, Storm King Sch., 1927-29; A.B., Columbia U., 1933; LL.B., Harvard U., 1936. Bar: N.Y. 1936, D.C. 1955, U.S. Supreme Ct. 1965, Va. 1982. Assoc. Beekman & Bogue, N.Y.C., 1936-41; staff CAB, 1941-56, chief internat. and rules div., 1947-56; mem. Galland, Kharasch, Calkins & Morse, P.C. and predecessors, Washington, 1956-81, mng. ptnr., 1969-80, pres., 1980-81, of counsel, 1981-90; pvt. practice, Washington, 1981-86; of counsel to county atty. Fairfax County (Va.), 1982-87, practice as assigned by Fairfax County Juvenile Ct., 1987-89; mem. U.S. sect. Comité Internat. Tecnique d' Experts Juridiques Aériens, 1946-47; mem. U.S. dels. legal com. Internat. Civil Aviation Orgn., 1947-55; delegation chmn. 1st, 3d, 5th, 9th and 10th meetings; chief U.S. negotiator and draftsman Mortgage Conv., Geneva, Switzerland, 1948, mem. drafting com. Rome Conv. on Surface Damage, 1952; chmn. U.S. delegation internat. Diplomatic Conf. for Revision of Warsaw Conv., The Hague, 1955; chmn. legal div. U.S. Air Coordinating Com., 1955-56; industry observer U.S.-U.K. bilateral air transport talks, London, 1956; asst. sec. Philippine Airlines, 1974-86.; draftsman rules and regulations U.S. Adv. Commn. on Intergovtl. Relations, 1986; vol. atty. Legal Counsel for the Elderly, AARP, Washington, 1988-96. Asso. editor: United States and Canadian Aviation Reports, 1956-61; asso. editor: Jour. Air Law and Commerce, 1956-58; editor-in-chief, 1958-63; Contbr. articles to profl. jours. Served as lt. USNR, 1943-45. Mem. ABA, D.C., Va., Fairfax County Bar Assns., Am. Judicature Soc., Soc. Quiet Birdmen, Lincoln's Inn Soc., Soc. Sr. Aero. Execs., Cosmos Club, Georgetown Club (Washington), Nacoms (Columbia Univ.), Psi Upsilon. Home and Office: 6504 Dearborn Dr Falls Church VA 22044-1115

CALKINS, HUGH, foundation executive; b. Newton, Mass., Feb. 20, 1924; s. Grosvenor and Patty (Phillips) C.; m. Ann Clark, June 14, 1955; children: Peter, Andrew, Margaret, Elizabeth. AB, LLB, Harvard U., 1949, D in Law (hon.), 1985. Bar: Ohio 1950. Law clk. to presiding judge U.S. Ct. Appeals (2d cir.), N.Y.C., 1949-50; law clk. to justice Felix Frankfurter U.S. Supreme Ct., Washington, 1950-51; from assoc. to ptnr. Jones, Day, Reavis & Pogue, Cleve., 1951-90; tchr. elem. schs. Cleve. City Sch. Dist., 1991-94. Contbr. articles on fed. income tax to profl. jours. Mem. Cleve. Bd. Edn., 1965-69; assoc. dir. Pres.'s Commn. on Nat. Goals, Washington, 1960; mem., pres., fellow Harvard U., 1968-85; mem. task forces Cleve. Summit on Edn., 1990-94; pres., trustee Initiatives in Urban Edn., 1991—. Capt. USAF, 1943-46. Mem. ABA (chmn. tax sect. 1985-86, chair Cityen's Acad. 1998—), Am. Law Inst. (coun.), City Club, Cleve. Skating Club, Phi Beta Kappa. Democrat. Unitarian. Home and Office: 3345 N Park Blvd Cleveland OH 44118-4258

CALKINS, JERRY MILAN, anesthesiologist, educator, administrator, biomedical engineer; b. Benkelman, Nebr., Sept. 10, 1942; s. Robert Thomas and Mildred Rachel (Stamm) C.; m. Connie Mae Satterfield, Oct. 17, 1964; children: Julie Lynn, Jenifer Ellan. BSChemE, U. Wyo., 1964, MSChemE, 1966; PhD in Chem. Engring., U. Md., 1971; MD, U. Ariz., 1976. Diplomate Am. Bd. Anesthesiology. Lectr. engring. U. Md., College Park, 1970-71; asst. prof. engring. Ariz. State U., Tempe, 1971-73; asst. prof. anesthesiology U. Ariz., Tucson, 1979-84, assoc. prof., 1984; assoc. prof., vice chmn. dept. U. N.C., Chapel Hill, 1984-86; clin. assoc. U. N.Mex., Albuquerque, 1986-88, chmn. dept. anesthesiology Lovelace Med. Ctr., 1986-88; chmn. dept. anesthesiology Maricopa Med. Ctr., Phoenix, 1988-98; clin. prof. anesthesiology U. Ariz., 1988—; v.p. med. affairs Metasensors, Inc., 1998—; adj. assoc. prof. indsl. engring. N.C. State U., 1984-86; dir. med. engring. lab. Harry Diamond Labs., Washington, 1968-71; cons. Bur. Med. Devel., FDA, Washington, 1977-86; asst. prof. engring., bd. dir. advanced biotech. Lab. Ariz. Health Sci. Ctr., Tucson, 1979-84. Co-author: Future Anesthesia Delivery Systems, 1984, High Frequency Ventilation, 1986; editor Annals Biomed. Engring., 1979, Clin. Monitoring, 1984—; contbr. numerous articles to profl. jours., chpts. to books. Bd. dirs. Gladys Taylor McGary Found., 1999—. Recipient Outstanding Tchr. award Upjohn Co., 1979; spl. fellow NIH, 1970. Mem. AMA, AICE, Am. Soc. Anesthesiologists, Am. Soc. Artificial Internal Organs, Closed and Lowflow Anesthesia Systems Soc. (pres. 1986-88), Soc. Tech. Anesthesia (pres. 1993—), Ariz. Med. Assn., Ariz. Soc. Anesthesiology (v.p. 1998), Am. Found. Med. Acupuncture (pres. 1992), Maricopa County Med. Assn., Masons, Sigma Xi. Republican. Avocations: swimming; skiing; tennis; golf; model railroading. Office: Metasensors Inc 358 Hungerford Dr Rockville MD 20850

CALKINS, LOREN GENE, church executive, clergyman; b. Walla Walla, Wash., Feb. 6, 1942; s. Albert T. and Verna M. (Smith) C.; m. Lorena L. Tittle, Apr. 19, 1962; children: Lance E., Lonny G., LaRae L. BS, George Fox Coll., Newburg, Oreg., 1967; MDiv, We. Evangel. Sem., Portland, Oreg., 1970; DMin, San Francisco Theol. Sem., 1980. Ordained to ministry Free Methodist Ch., 1970. Sr. pastor Free Meth. Ch., Carlton, Oreg., 1965-68, West Linn, Oreg., 1968-69, Eugene, Oreg., 1970-72; sr. pastor Christian and Missionary Alliance, Bainbridge Island, Wash., 1972-74, Memphis, 1975-79, Spokane, 1979-84; sr. pastor Dallas (Oreg.) Alliance Ch., 1995—; dist. dir. ext. Christian and Missionary Alliance, Canby, Oreg., 1984-89; dist. supt. Christian and Missionary Alliance, Ft. Worth, 1989-95; ch. growth cons. Christian and Missionary Alliance, 1984—, stewardship cons., 1985—. Trustee Crown Coll., St. Bonifacius, Minn., 1989—, LeTourneau U., Longview, Tex., 1991—. Mem. Nat. Assn. Evangelicals (local pres. 1970-72, 80-84), Kiwanis. Republican. Office: Dallas Alliance Ch 775 E Ellendale Ave Dallas OR 97338-3007

CALKINS, RICHARD W., college president; b. June 3, 1939. BA in Music, Albion Coll., 1960; MA in Edn., Mich. State U., 1966, MA, 1971, postgrad., 1972—; Doctorate (hon.), Ferris State U., 1992. Vocal music tchr. Ridgeview Jr. High Sch., 1961-64; vocal music tchr. Creston High Sch., 1964-68, asst. dir. pers., 1968-71, gen. assoc. supt., 1971-74, asst. supt. pers. and community svcs., 1974-75; pres. Grand Rapids (Mich.) C.C., 1975—. Bd. dirs. religious activities Epworth Assembly, Ludington, Mich., 1960-82; mins. music Eastminster Presbyn. ch., Grand Rapids, 1964-93; v.p. planning, mem. exec. com. Downtown Mgmt. Bd., 1985-91; pres. Grand Rapids C.C. Found., 1978—; bd. dirs. Mich. Info. Tech. Network, 1988—; mem. Mid Am. Training Group, 1989—, Downtown Planning Com., 1991, Nat. Modernization Forum, 1990-91, Nat. Coalition Advance Tech. Ctrs., 1990—, Alliance for Mfg. Productivity, 1990—, IBM CIM Higher Edn., 1990—; bd. dirs., mem. pub. policy and pers. coms. YMCA, 1989-92; chair edn. div. United Way Kent County, chair major accounts, 1992; founding bd. dirs. Noorthoek Acad., 1989—; bd. dirs. edn. and summer facility coms. Grand Rapids Symphony, 1989—;. Mem. Indsl. Tech. Inst., Am. Assn. Community and Colls., Assn. C.C. Trustees, Assn. Tchr. Educators, Mich. Assn. Sch. Adminstrs., Mich. Assn. Pub. Adult Continuing Educators, Mich. Assn. Tchr. Educators, Mich. C.C. Assn. (chair polit. action com. 1983—, exec. com. 1987-90, v.p. 1987-88, past pres. 1989-90, treas. 1990-91), C.C. Assn. for Tech. Transfer, Grand Rapids Dunkers Club, Peninsular Club Grand Rapids, Phi Delta Kappa. Home: 2519 Riveredge Dr SE Grand Rapids MI 49546-7450 Office: Grand Rapids Community Coll 143 Bostwick Ave NE Grand Rapids MI 49503-3201

CALKINS, ROBERT BRUCE, aerospace engineer; b. Pasadena, Calif., Apr. 10, 1942; s. Bruce and Florence May (Bennit) C.; m. Dana B. Ericson. BS in Aerospace Engring., Calif. State Polytech., 1965; BA in Applied Math., San Diego State U., 1970; MS in Computer Sci., Wright State U., 1984. Project engr. U.S. Air Force Flight Test Ctr., El Centro, Calif., 1965-75; sr. engr. U.S. Air Force Aero. Systems Divsn., Dayton, Ohio, 1975-85; prin. engr. Douglas Aircraft Co., Long Beach, Calif., 1985-90, McDonnell Douglas Aerospace, Long Beach, 1990-97, Boeing Co., Seattle, 1997—. Recipient U.S. Presidential citation, Fed. Govt., 1967. Fellow AIAA (Disting. Svc. award 1992, assoc., chmn. tech. standards com.); mem. SAFE Assn. (sec. chpt. 1 1991, pres. 1992). Achievements include 2 patents. Home: 13418 Issaquah Hobart Rd SE Issaquah WA 98027-8582 Office: Boeing Co PO Box 3707 MS 45-89 Seattle WA 98124-2207

CALKINS, SUSANNAH EBY, retired economist; b. Bucyrus, Ohio, Jan. 16, 1924; d. Samuel L. and Mae (McClure) Eby; m. G. Nathan Calkins, Nov. 19, 1949; children: Helen E. (dec.), Margaret S. Van Auken, Sarah A., Abigail Calkins Aguirre. AB, Goucher Coll., 1945; MS in Econs. (Univ. scholar 1946-47), U. Wis., 1947. Fiscal analyst U.S. Bur. Budget, 1945-50; economist U.S. Council Econ. Advisors, 1950-51, U.S. Office Price Stabilization, 1951-53, U.S. Bur. Budget, 1953-55; cons. U.S. Adv. Commn. on Intergovtl. Rels., Washington, 1972-73, 74-75, cons. on counter-cyclical aid programs, 1977-78, sr. analyst, 1979-87, exec. asst. to dir., 1987-89; cons. revenue sharing Brookings Instn., Washington, 1973-74. Author: (with R. Nathan and A. Manvel) Monitoring Revenue Sharing, 1975. Sponsor S.S. Goucher Victory, Balt., 1945; bd. dirs. Bread for the City-Zacchaeus Free Clinic, 1994—. Mem. Am. Econs. Assn., Woman's Nat. Dem. Club (bd. govs. 1995-98), George Towne Club (Washington), Phi Beta Kappa. Presbyterian. Home: 6504 Dearborn Dr Falls Church VA 22044-1115

CALL, CARY C., transportation specialist; b. Lewiston, Idaho, Oct. 5, 1940; s. Charles Clayton and Edna Alice Call; m. Venita Marie Rabideau, July 11, 1964; children: Craig, Michelle, Brad, Brenda. AA, Kankakee (Ill.) C.C., 1979; BA in Social Sci., Gov.'s State U., University Park, Ill., 1992. Lab. technician Henkel Corp., Kankakee, 1966-74, technician trainer, 1974-77, adminstrv. asst., 1977, supt. IC, 1977-79, supt. FC, 1979-84, supt. mfg. reg. compliance, 1984-86, supt. reg. affairs, 1986-97, transp. specialist, 1997—. with USAF, 1962-66. Avocations: golf, fishing, reading, travel. Office: Henkel Corp S Kensington Rd Kankakee IL 60901

CALL, ELIZABETH ANN, mental health counselor; b. New Brunswick, N.J., May 31, 1966; d. Lawrence Michael and Patricia Elizabeth (Popp) C. BA in Humanities, Georgian Court Coll., 1991; MA in Cmty. Counseling, Loyola U., Chgo., 1997. Dist. sales mgr. Agy. Rent-A-Car, Lakewood, N.J., 1992-93; family therapist intern Alternatives, Inc., Chgo., 1995-96; mental health counselor Washington State Prison, Davisboro, Ga., 1997—. Mem. APA, ACA. Avocations: hiking, biking, outdoor photography, reading, golf.

CALL, JOSEPH RUDD, accountant; b. Pensacola, Fla., Oct. 18, 1950; s. Melvin Eliason and Doris Mae (Rudd) C.; m. Nola Jean Pack, Dec. 20, 1973; children: Benjamin, Jeremy, Joshua, Rebecca, Jacob, James. BS, Brigham Young U., 1974. CPA, Calif., Idaho, Wy.; cert. fin. planner 1986, personal fin. specialist 1998. Small bus. specialist Deloitte, Haskins & Sells, L.A., 1974-78; audit mgr. Rudd, DaBell & Hill, Rexburg, Idaho, 1978-80, audit ptnr. Rudd & Co., 1980-82, ptnr. in charge Idaho Falls office, 1982-90, founder, pres. Spinnaker Fin. Advs. PLLC, 1998. Mem. task force Small Bus. High Tech. Devel. State of Idaho, 1983; pres. Bonneville-Idaho Falls Crimestoppers, Inc., 1984-85; bd. dirs. Idaho Falls symphony Soc., 1988-91. Mem. Am. Inst. CPAs (hon. mention on CPA exam 1975, exec. coms. pvt. cos. 1989-92, continuing profl. edn. exec. com. 1992-97), Calif. Soc. CPAs., Idaho Soc. CPAs (pres. S.E. Idaho chpt. 1983-84, state bd. dirs. 1984-89, pres.-elect 1987, pres. 1988-89), Idaho Falls C. of C. (bd. dirs. 1984-90, chmn. bd. dirs. 1986-87), Rexburg C. of C. (dir. 1981-82), Eastern Idaho Sailing Assn. (rear commodore 1983-89). Mormon. Office: Rudd & Co PLLC 725 S Woodruff Ave Idaho Falls ID 83401-5286

CALL, M. DOUGLAS, university administrator; m. Patty Call; 1 child, Mark Douglas. BA in Bus. Adminstrn., Marshall U., 1967; MS in Reading Edn. and Ednl. Psychology, Ind. U., 1968; EdD in Higher Edn. Adminstrn., W.Va. U., 1973. Lab technician Internat. Nickel Co., Huntington, W.Va., 1963-67; dir. admissions Morris Harvey Coll., U. Charleston, W.Va., 1968-73; dir. student svcs. W.Va. Coll. Grad. Studies, 1973-75; pres. Parkersburg (W.Va.) C.C., 1977-78; dir. planning and mgmt. info. sys. W.Va. Bd. Regents, 1975-80, chancelor, 1980, exec. asst. for internal affairs, 1987-98, dir. C.C. and vocat. edn., 1981-89; interim chancellor W.Va. State Coll. Sys., 1989-90, vice chancellor for C.C.s, 1990-93; spl. asst. to pres. W.Va. State Coll., 1993-95; pres. State Tech. Inst., Memphis, 1996—; spkr. in field. Contbr. articles to profl. publs. Sunday sch. tchr., coach h.s. boys basketball, mem. pulpit com. 1st Bapt. Ch. of St. Albans. Avocations: reading, golf, fishing, playing/coaching basketball, baseball and softball. Office: State Tech Inst Memphis 5983 Macon Cove Memphis TN 38134-7693

CALL, NEIL JUDSON, corporate executive; b. Detroit, June 15, 1933; s. Judson Francis and Glennys Jean (Amluxen) C.; m. Jane E. Rathslag, Feb. 4, 1956; children: Laura, Keith; m. Eleanor Ann King, Nov. 23, 1978. B.B.A., U. Mich., 1955, M.B.A., 1956. C.P.A., Mich. With Hogan Juengel & Harding (C.P.A.'s), Detroit, 1956-61, Ford Motor Co., Dearborn, Mich., 1961-65; with Ford Motor Credit Co., Dearborn, 1965-67, Gulf & Western Industries Inc., N.Y.C., 1968-86; v.p. Gulf & Western Industries Inc., 1970-79, sr. v.p., 1979-83, exec. v.p., 1983-84; exec. v.p. D.F. King & Co., Inc., N.Y.C., 1986-89, Dewe Rogerson Inc., N.Y.C., 1990-92, Mackenzie Ptnrs., Inc., N.Y.C., 1992—. Served with U.S. Army, 1956-58. Home: Unit 307 1500 Atlantic Blvd Apt 307 Key West FL 33040-5071 Office: Mackenzie Ptnrs Inc 156 5th Ave New York NY 10010-7002

CALLAGHAN, GEORGANN MARY, management consultant; b. Bklyn., June 25, 1944; d. George Louis and Jean (Russo) Carpenito; m. Matthew John Callaghan, June 7, 1969; children: Matthew, Michael, Christian. BS in Hist. Studies, SUNY Empire State Coll., 1994; JD, Pace U., 1999. Asst. to dir. pers. Kemper Ins., N.Y.C., 1962-65, asst., sec. to assoc. gen. counsel, 1965; sec. to pres. Kalvin Miller, Meyer & Sacks, N.Y.C., 1969-70; asst. to ptnr. Dewey, Ballantine Bushby Palmer & Wood, N.Y.C., 1970-74; fashion cons. Bonwit Teller, Scarsdale, N.Y., 1979-91; self-employed office mgmt. cons. Scarsdale, 1980-85; legal asst., office adminstr. Wood & Scher, 1986—. Den mother, exec. com. Boy Scouts Am. Mem. Maroon & White Athletic Assn. (bd. dirs.), Scarsdale PTA, Town and Village Club. Home and Office: 49 Carman Rd Scarsdale NY 10583-6328

CALLAGHAN, SHEILA, playwright, graphic designer; b. Queens, N.Y., Jan. 24, 1973; d. John Augustine and Eileen Callaghan. BA, Coll. N.J., 1995; MFA, UCLA, 1998. Nicholl Screenwriting fellow Acad. Motion Pictures Assn., L.A., 1998. literary assoc. Ask Theatre Projects, L.A., 1996. Author (plays) Two Weeks, 1995, Smog, 1996, New Shoes, 1997, The Hunger Waltz, 1998, No Returns, 1998, Needle, 1999, Scab, 1999, (screenplays) Killing Sarah, 1997, Caroline Gets a Man, 1998. Home: 1435 N Curson #9 Los Angeles CA 90046

CALLAHAN, ALSTON, physician, author; b. Vicksburg, Miss., Mar. 16, 1911; s. Neil and Effie (Alston) C.; m. Eivor Holst, Feb. 23, 1941; children: Kristina Alice, Patrick Alston, Michael Alston, Timothy Alston, Karin Eivor, Kevin (dec. 1961). AB, Miss. Coll., 1929; MD, Tulane U., 1933, MS in Ophthalmology, 1936; RSM, Tulane U., London, 1990. Diplomate Am. Bd. Ophthalmology. Intern Charity Hosp., New Orleans, 1933-35, resident in ophthalmology, 1936-37; hon. mem. emeritus Eye Found. Univ. Hosps., Birmingham, Ala., 1959—; also founder Eye Found. Hosp., Birmingham, Ala., 1964; co-developer Rsch. and Profl. Office Bldg. E.F. Hosp., 1985-87; founder The Internat. Retinal Rsch Found., Inc., Birmingham, 1997. Author: Surgery of the Eye, Injuries, 1950, Surgery of the Eye, Diseases, 1956, Reconstructive Surgery of the Eyelids and Ocular Adnexa, 1966, (with M. Callahan) Ophthalmic Plastic Surgery, 1979; contbr. articles to profl. jours. Served to capt. M.C., AUS, 1944-46. Recipient award Ala. Acad. Honor, 1996; named Tulane Alumnus of Yr., 1997, to Ala. Healthcare Hall of Fame, 1998. Fellow ACS; mem. Am. Acad. Ophthalmology, So. Med. Assn. (emeritus), Am. Soc. Ophthal. Plastic Surgery, Alpha Omega Alpha, Sigma Alpha Epsilon. Clubs: Mountain Brook, The Club, Metropolitan, Explorers. Home: 2020 Warwick Dr Birmingham AL 35209-1360 Office: 711 29th St S Birmingham AL 35233-2809 also: Internat Retinal Rsch Found Inc 700 18th St South Ste 511 Birmingham AL 35233

CALLAHAN, DANIEL JOHN, biomedical researcher; b. Washington, July 19, 1930; s. Vincent Francis and Anita (Hawkins) C.; m. Sidney Cornelia de Shazo, June 5, 1954; children: Mark Sidney, Stephen Daniel, John Vincent, Peter Thorn, Sarah Elisabeth, David Lee. B.A., Yale U., 1952; M.A., Georgetown U., 1957; Ph.D., Harvard U., 1965; D.Sc. (hon.), U. Medicine and Dentistry of N.J., 1981; DHL (hon.), U. Colo., 1990, Williams Coll., 1992, Oreg. State U., 1997. Exec. editor The Commonweal, N.Y.C., 1961-68; staff assoc. Population Council, 1969-70; co-founder, pres. The Hastings Ctr., 1969-96, dir. internat. programs, 1997—; resident scholar Aspen Inst. Humanistic Studies, 1975; vis. asst. prof. religion Temple U., 1064; vis. asst. prof. religious stuies Brown U., 1965; vis. prof. theology Marymount Coll., 1966; vis. prof. U. Pa., 1970; sr. fellow Harvard Ctr. for Population and Devel. Studies, 1996; cons. med. ethics, jud. coun. AMA, 1972-82, ACP, 1979—; spl. cons. Commn. on Population Growth and Am. Future, 1970-71, NEH, 1979; hon. prof. Charles U. Med. Sch., Prague, 1997—; vis. scholar Harvard Med. Sch., 1998—. Author: The Mind of the Catholic Layman, 1963, Honesty in the Church, 1965, The New Church, 1966, Abortion: Law, Choice and Morality, 1970, Ethics and Population Limitation, 1971, The Tyranny of Survival, 1973, The Teaching of Ethics in the Military, 1982, Setting Limits: Medical Goals in an Aging Society, 1987, What Kind of Life: The Limits of Medical Progress, 1990, The Troubled Dream of Life: Living with Mortality, 1993, False Hopes: Why America's Quest for Perfect Health is a Recipe for Failure, 1998; also essays, articles; co-editor: Christianity Divided: Protestant and Roman Catholic Theological Issues, 1961, Ethical Issues in Human Genetics, 1973; editor: Federal Aid and Catholic Schools, 1964, Secular City Debate, 1966, The Catholic Case for Contraception, 1969, The American Population Debate, 1971, Science, Ethics and Medicine, 1976, Knowledge, Value and Belief, 1977, Morals, Science and Sociality, 1978, Knowing and Valuing, 1979, Ethics Teaching in Higher Education, 1980, Ethical Issues in Population Aid, 1980, The Roots of Ethics, 1981, Ethics in Hard Times, 1981, Ethics, the Social Sciences and Policy Analysis, 1983, Abortion: Understanding Differences, 1984, Applying the Humanities, 1985, Representation and Responsibility, 1985, A World Growing Old, 1995, What Price Mental Health?, 1995; mem. editl. adv. bd. Tech. in Soc., 1981—; mem. adv. bd. Ency. of Life Scis., 1982, Sci., Tech. and Human Values, 1979—, Bus. and Profl. Ethics, 1981, Criminal Justice Ethics, 1982, Environ. Ethics, 1982, Jour. Bioethics, 1985-96. Mem. N.Y. Coun. for Humanities, 1975-79; mem. Nat. Book Award Com., 1975, N.Y. State Health Adv. Coun., 1975-76; selection com. Ford-Rockefeller Program in Population Policy, 1975-78, Rockefeller Found. Program in Humanities, 1980; elector Nat. Medal for Lit., 1979-83; pub. mem. Am. Bd. Med. Specialties, 1982-87, N.Y. Sci. Policy Assn., 1985-91; mem. N.Y. Task Force on Life and Law, 1985-87; mem. nat. adv. bd. Health Promotion Program, Henry J. Kaiser Family Found., 1987-91, N.Y. Panel and HIV Screening, 1987; trustee U. Pa. Med. Ctr., 1987-91; mem. adv. com. on sci. integrity HHS, 1991-93; adv. com. to dir. Ctr. for Disease Control, DHHS. Recipient Thomas More medal, 1970, Daryl J. Mase Disting. Leadership award, 1987, Book of Yr. award Am. Jour. Nursing, 1987, Henry Knowles Beecher award The Hastings Ctr., 1989, James H. Hamilton Book award Am. Coll. Health Care Execs., 1990, Pres. Cabinet award U. Tex., 1995, Scientific Freedom and Responsibility award AAAS, 1995; named one of 200 Outstanding Young Men Leaders Time mag., 1974, Tekolste scholar Ind. Hosp. Assn., 1986; nat. fellowship Bus. Enterprise Trust, 1989-95. Fellow AAAS (Sci. Freedom and Responsibility award 1996); mem. Am. Assn. for Advancement Humanities, Inst. Medicine of NAS, Soc. for Study Social Biology (bd. dirs. 1987-95), Harvard Grad. Soc. (coun. 1989-92). Home: PO Box 260 Ardsley On Hudson NY 10503-0260 Office: The Hastings Ctr Rt 9D Garrison NY 10524-5555

CALLAHAN, DEBRA JEAN, environmental organization executive; b. Burbank, Calif., June 4, 1958; d. Robert Bascom and Betty Jean (Park) C. Student, Calif. State Poly. U., San Luis Obispo, 1976-79; BA magna cum laude, U. Calif., Santa Barbara, 1981. Legal asst. Loo, Merideth & McMillan, L.A., 1982-83; field staff Mondale for Pres., Washington, 1984; dep. campaign mgr. Mondale-Ferraro Com., Kansas City, Mo., 1984; regional polit. dir. League of Conservation Voters, Portsmouth, N.H., 1985-86; dep. campaign mgr. Kent Conrad for U.S. Senate, Bismarck, N.D., 1986; exec. asst. to Senator Kent Conrad, Washington, 1986-87; dep. nat. polit. dir. Gore for Pres., Washington, 1987-88; exec. dir. Ams. for the Environment, Washington, 1988-90; campaign mgr. Re-election Rep. Howard Wople (D-Md.), 1990-92; dir. W. Alton Jones Found., 1992-95; exec. dir. Brainard Found., Seattle, 1995-96; pres. League of Conservation Voters, Washington, 1996—; polit. cons. League of Conservation Voters, 1988. Editor: The Rising Tide: Public Opinion, Policy and Politics, 1989. Field dir. Hands Across Am., St. Louis, 1986. U. Calif. Dept. Environ. Studies scholar, Santa Barbara, 1981, Alumni award, 1998. Avocations: travel, reading, scuba, cycling. Office: League of Conservation Voters 1707 L St NW Ste 750 Washington DC 20036-4210

CALLAHAN, EDWARD WILLIAM, chemical engineer, retired manufacturing executive; b. N.Y.C., July 17, 1930; s. William Patrick and Clara (Schultz) C.; m. Barbara Jane Willmarth, Nov. 23, 1985; children: Susan Lynne, Kevin Foster. B.Ch.E., Cornell U., 1953. Engr. Solvay div. Allied Chem. Corp., Syracuse, N.Y., 1953-65, dir. comml. devel., 1965-66; asst. to pres. Allied Signal Corp., N.Y.C., 1966-70; gen. mgr. environ. services Allied Signal Corp., Morristown, N.J., 1970-78; v.p. health, safety and environ. scis. Allied Signal Corp., Morristown, 1978-95; ret. Bd. dirs. Am. Cancer Soc., Morristown, 1982-84; trustee Ind. Coll. Fund. of N.J., 1988-94. Mem. Internat. Environ. Forum (chmn. 1986-94), Chem. Industry Inst. Toxicology (dir. 1974-91, Conf. Bd. environ. com. chmn. 1994-95), Am. Indsl. Health Coun. (dir. 1978-91), Chem. Mfrs. Assn. (chmn. environ. mgmt. com. 1978-82), World Environ. Ctr. (bd. dirs. 1992-98), Union Club, Cornell Club (N.Y.C.), Shinnecock Yacht Club, Jonathan's Landing Golf Club, Quogue Field Club, Quantuck Beach Club. Home: 16940 Bay St Apt 207 N Jupiter FL 33477-1207

CALLAHAN, FRANCIS JOSEPH, manufacturing company executive; b. Lima, Ohio, July 8, 1923; s. Francis J. and Bertha E. (Falk) C.; m. Mary Elizabeth Krouse, June 30, 1945; children: Francis Joseph III, Cornelia S. Callahan Richards, Timothy J. Student, U. Dayton, 1941; BS, U.S. Naval Acad., 1945; B.S.E.E., MIT, 1948; MS in Nuclear Engring., 1953. Commd. ensign USN, 1945; project officer USS Nautilus, USS Sea Wolf, 1954-58; pres. Nupro Co., Willoughby, Ohio, 1958—; v.p. Crawford Fitting Co., Solon, Ohio, 1959-81; pres., 1981—, Whitey Co., Cleveland Heights, Ohio, 1960—; dir. Midwest Bank & Trust Co., 1969—, Midwestern Nat. Life Ins. Co., 1970—, Tappan Co., 1977-80, Invacare Co., 1980—, Environ. Growth Control Co., 1970—, Royal Appliance Co., 1984—, Applied Concrete Tech., 1984—. Patentee for valves, fittings. Chmn. bd. trustees Gilmoor Acad., 1973-79; chmn. bd. dirs. Marymoutn Hosp., 1983; trustee cleve. Boys Clubs, 1970—; bd. dirs. Jr. Achievement, 1963—. Capt. USNR, 1976. Recipient Man of Yr. award Gilmoor Acad., 1973. Mem. NAM, ASME, Atomic Indsl. Forum, Kirtland Country, Pepper Pike, Union, Hillbrook (Cleve.), Quail Creek Country (Naples, Fla.). Roman Catholic. Home: 3195 Roundwood Rd Chagrin Falls OH 44022-6635*

CALLAHAN, HARRY LESLIE, civil engineer; b. Kansas City, Mo., Jan. 11, 1923; s. B. Frank and Myrtle Lou (Anderson) C.; m. V. June Yohn, Dec. 16, 1944; children: Michael Thomas, Maureen Lynn, Kevin Leslie. BSCE, U. Kans., 1944. Exec. ptnr. Black & Veatch Co., Kansas City, Mo., 1946-89; ret. Black & Veatch Co., 1989; chmn. B & V Waste Sci. & Tech. Corp., 1987-88, also bd. dirs.; chmn. CCL Constrn. Cons., Overland Pk., Kans. Contbr. articles to profl. jours. 1st lt., inf. AUS, 1944-46, Japan. Recipient Mo. Design Excellence award 1st pl., 1972. Fellow ASCE, Am. Cons. Engrs. Council; mem. Am. Nuclear Soc., Nat. Soc. Profl. Engrs., Soc. Mil. Engrs., Am. Concrete Inst., Water Pollution Control Fedn., Combustion Inst., Kappa Sigma. Congregationalist. Clubs: Kansas City, Leawood South Country, Chancellor, U. Kans., Sadelle & Sirloin, Rancho Viejo. Office: CCL Constrn Cons 7219 Metcalf #202 Overland Park KS 66204-1974

CALLAHAN, HARRY MOREY, photographer; b. Detroit, Oct. 22, 1912; s. Harry Arthur and Hazel (Mills) C.; m. Eleanor Knapp, Nov., 1936; children: Barbara, Mary. DFA (hon.), RISD, 1979; DFA (hon., Atlanta Coll. Art, 1990, Corcoran Gallery Art, 1996. Mem. faculty Inst. Design, Ill. Inst. Tech., Chgo., 1946-61, head dept. photography, 1949-61; prof., head dept. RISD, 1971-76. One-man shows Mus. Modern Art, N.Y.C., 1976, Seibu Mus. Art, Japan, 1983, Art Inst. Chgo., 1984, San Francisco Mus. Modern Art, 1984, Nat. Gallery Victoria, Australia, 1986, Centre Georges Pompidou, France, 1990; retrospective Nat. Gallery Art, Washington, 1996; U.S. rep. Venice Biennial, 1978. Recipient award Gov. R.I., 1969, Citation NASA, 1972, Knight Purchase award Akron Mus. Art, 1991, Ill. Acad. Arts award, 1992, Edward MacDowell medal, 1993, Brandeis Creative medal 1985, Arles honored photographer medal Arles Recontres Internat. de la Photographie, 1977, Nat. Medal of the Arts, Pres. Clinton, 1996; named Master Photographer ICP, 1991; fellow Graham Found., 1956, Guggenheim Found., 1972; grantee Nat. Endowment Arts, 1976, R.I. Sch. Design Svc. award for Photography, 1998. Studio: 145 15th St NE Ste 421 Atlanta GA 30309-3557 *Died Mar. 15, 1999.*

CALLAHAN, JAMES K., fire chief. BA in Social Sci., U. South Fla.; M in Pub. Adminstrn., Troy State U., 1994; grad., Nat. Fire Acad. With Fire Dept., St. Petersburg, Fla., 1970-81, lt., 1981-83, capt., 1983-85, fire marshall, 1985-87, asst. chief, 1987-90, chief, 1996—; chief Hillsborough County (Fla.) Fire Dept., 1990-96; mem. steering com. State of Fla. Fire Rescue Disaster Response Com. Chief St. Petersburg Fire and Rescue, 1996—. With USMC, Vietnam. Mem. Internat. Fire Chiefs Assn., Fla. Fire Chiefs Assn., Fla. Fire Marshal's Assn., Pinellas County Fire Chiefs Assn. Office: 400 Ml King St S Saint Petersburg FL 33701-4419*

CALLAHAN, JOHN J., federal official; b. Quincy, Mass., 1944; m. Susan Doherty; children: Kathleen, Erin, Sean. BA in Polit. Sci., Fordham U., 1965; MA in Regional Planning, Syracuse U., 1971, PhD in Social Sci., 1972. Staff mem. N.Y. Joint Legis. Com. to Revise & Simplify Edn. Law, 1968-69; cons. Syracuse Univ. Policy Rsch. Corp., 1969-70; sr. analyst U.S. Adv. Commn. Intergovtl. Rels., 1969-74; asst. prof. edn. & planning U. Va., 1971-72; exec. dir. Legislators' Edn. Action Project Nat. Conf. State Legislatures, 1974-77, dir. Fed.-State rels., 1977-79; staff dir. U.S. Senate Govtl. Affairs subcom. Intergovtl. Rels., Washington, 1979-83, minority staff dir., 1981-83; chief of staff U.S. Senator Jim Sasser, Washington, 1983-86, 93-95; dep. staff dir. U.S. Senate Budget com., Washington, 1987-93; asst. sec. mgmt. & budget HHS, Washington, 1995—; acting commr. Social Security Adminstrn., 1997—; fellow Nat. Acad. of Pub. Adminstrn., 1997—. Office: HHS 200 Independence Ave SW Rm 514G Washington DC 20201-0004*

CALLAHAN, JOSEPH PATRICK, lawyer; b. N.Y.C., Mar. 19, 1945; s. Parnell J.T. and Jane M. (Tubridy) C.; m. Nancy K. Jones; children: Timothy P., Jane K., Clare E., Hannah M. BA, Columbia U., 1966; JD, Albany (N.Y.) Law Sch., Union U., 1969. Bar: N.Y. 1969, S.C. 1992, U.S. Supreme Ct. 1993. Ptnr. Callahan & Wolkoff, N.Y.C., 1972-99; counsel McCanliss & Early, N.Y.C., 1999—; Chmn., pres. Mackran Assocs., Inc., mortgage brokers, N.Y.C., 1973—. Mem. Am. Irish Hist. Soc., N.Y. Athletic Club. Roman Catholic. Office: McCanliss 7 Early 98 Pine St New York NY 10005

CALLAHAN, LEEANN LUCILLE, psychologist; b. San Diego, Calif., Dec. 7, 1950; d. Charlie A. Olsen and Delores A. (Libke) Turner; m. Chuck Callahan, Oct. 31, 1970; children: Clint, Devin, Chet. BS/MS in Psychology, San Diego State U., 1983; PhD in Psychology, USIU, San Diego, 1990. Lic. clin. psychologist. Clin. dir. Sharp Cabrillo Hosp., San Diego, 1989-91, Charter Hosp., San Diego, 1991-93; psychologist San Diego, 1989—; preferred provider Charter Hosp., San Diego, 1990—, speakers bur., 1990—; staff psychologist Sharp Cabrillo Hosp., San Diego, 1989-92. Editor Parentteen Mag.; contbr. articles to profl. jours. Pres. PTA, San Diego, 1985; citizen adv./city coun. City of San Diego, 1987; vol. Poway Unified Sch. Dist., San Diego, 1975—; speaker Rotary, San Diego, 1994. Recipient Citizen of Yr. award, Sigma Chi, 1997. Mem. APA, Calif. State Psychol. Assn. Office: 9320 Carmel Mountain Rd Ste D San Diego CA 92129-2159

CALLAHAN, MARILYN JOY, social worker; b. Portland, Oreg., Oct. 11, 1934; d. Douglas Q. and Anona Helen Maynard; m. Lynn J. Callahan, Feb. 27, 1960 (dec.); children: Barbara Callahan Baer, Susan Callahan Sewell, Jeffrey Lynn. BA, Mills Coll., 1955; MSW, Portland State U., 1971, secondary teaching cert., 1963. Bd. cert. diplomate in clin. social work. Developer, adminstr. ednl. program Oreg. Women's Correctional Ctr., Oreg. State Prison, Salem, 1966-67; mental health counselor Benton County Mental Health, Corvallis, Oreg., 1970-71; inst. tchr. Hillcrest Sch., Salem, Oreg., 1975-81; social worker protective svcs. Mid Willamette Valley Sr. Svcs. Agy., Salem, 1981-88; psychiat. social worker dept. forensics Oreg. State Hosp., 1988-93; pvt. practice treatment of adult male and female sexual offenders Salem, 1987—; pvt. practice in care/mgmt. of elderly, 1987—; panel mem. Surgeon Gen.'s N.W. Regional Conf. on Interpersonal Violence, 1987; speaker in field; planner, organizer Seminar on Age Discrimination, 1985. Mem. NASW (past mem. bd. dirs. Oreg. chpt.), Nat. Org. Forensic Social Work, Am. Acad. Forensic Scis., Acad. Cert. Social Workers (lic. clin. social worker), Assn. for Treatment Sex Abusers, Oreg. Gerontol. Assn., Catalina 27 Nat. Sailing Assn. E-mail: marilynC@teleport.com. Office: Ste 304 780 Commercial St SE Salem OR 97301-3455

CALLAHAN, MICHAEL J., chemicals and manufacturing company executive; b. Detroit, Feb. 12, 1939; s. John William and Virginia (Allair) C.; m. Clare Breuer, Jan. 16, 1971; children—James Blair, Susan Allair. B.A., U. Mich., 1962, M.B.A. with distinction, 1967. Various positions Esso Ea., Inc., Tokyo, N.Y.C., Sydney, Australia, 1969-78; treas. Esso Ea., Inc., Houston, 1978-81; asst. gen. mgr. Exxon Co. U.S.A., Houston, 1981-82; chief fin. officer, sr. v.p. Quaker Oats Co., Chgo., 1982-88, exec. v.p. groceries specialties div., 1988-89, exec. v.p. Internat. Grocery Products div., 1989-91, also bd. dirs.; exec. v.p., CFO Whirlpool Corp., Benton Harbor, Mich., 1991-94, FMC Corp., Chgo., 1994—; bd. dirs. Brunswick Corp. Pres., trustee Leukemia Soc. Ill., Chgo., 1985-88, nat. trustee; bd. dirs. Met. Family Svcs., 1984-91, 95—. Mem. Chgo. Commonwealth Club, Point O' Woods Country Club, Chgo. Club, Exmoor Country Club (Chgo.), Phi Kappa Phi, Beta Gamma Sigma. Roman Catholic. Home: 82 Locust Rd Winnetka IL 60093-3750 Office: FMC Corp 200 E Randolph St Ste 5200 Chicago IL 60601-6662

CALLAHAN, MICHAEL THOMAS, construction consultant, lawyer; b. Kansas City, Mo., Oct. 7, 1948; s. Harry Leslie and Venita June (Yohn) C.;

m. Stella Sue Paffenbach, Mar. 21, 1970; children: Molly Leigh, Michael Kroh. BA, U. Kans., 1970; JD, U. Mo., 1973, LLM, 1979; postgrad., Temple U., 1976-77. Bar: Kans. 1973, N.J. 1975, Mo. 1977. V.p. T.J. Constrn., Inc., Lenexa, Kans., 1973-74; sr. cons. Wagner-Hohns-Inglis, Inc., Mt. Holly, N.J., 1974-77; v.p. Wagner-Hohns-Inglis, Inc., Kansas City, Mo., 1977-86; exec. v.p. CCL Constrn. Cons., Overland Park, Kans., 1986-88, pres., 1988—; adj. prof. U. Kans., Iowa State U.; arbitrator, lectr. in field, author; chmn. CCL Pacific Corp.; pres. Handcrafted Wines Kans., Inc. Home: 9011 Delmar St Shawnee Mission KS 66207-2343 Office: CCL Constrn Cons 7219 Metcalf Ave Ste 202 Overland Park KS 66204-1974

CALLAHAN, NORTH, author, educator; b. near Sweetwater, Tenn., Aug. 7, 1908; s. Robert B. and Naomi (North) C.; m. Jennie Waugh, Sept. 27, 1939 (div. 1970); m. Helen Pemberton Jones, July 5, 1974; children: Mary Alice, North. AB cum laude, U. Chattanooga, 1930, LHD, 1964; postgrad., U. Tenn., 1930-32; MA, Columbia U., 1950; PhD, NYU, 1955. Educator, 1930-34; ednl. pub. relations counselor TVA-Civilian Conservation Corps., 1934-37; reporter, columnist, spl. writer, editor Chattanooga Times, Chattanooga News, Knoxville Jour., Tyler (Tex.) Courier-Times, Morning Telegraph; N.Y.C. corr. Dallas News, 1939-44; writer syndicated column So This is New York, 1943-68; pub. relations cons. various firms and orgns., N.Y.C., 1954-55; prof. Am. hist., head soc. sci. dept. Finch Coll., N.Y.C., 1956-57; assoc. prof. NYU, 1957-62, prof. history, 1962-73, prof. emeritus, 1973—; vis. lectr. Brit. univs., 1965; vis. prof. U. Tenn., 1973. Author: The Army, 1941, The Armed Forces as a Career, 1947, Smoky Mountain Country, 1952, Henry Knox: General Washington's General, 1958, Daniel Morgan, Ranger of the Revolution, 1961, Royal Raiders: the Tories of the American Revolution, 1963, Flight from the Republic (Vol. II), 1967, Carl Sandburg, a Biography, 1970, 2d edit., 1987, George Washington: Soldier and Man, 1972, TVA: Bridge Over Troubled Waters, 1980; (novels) Peggy, 1983, Daybreak, 1985, Thanks Mr. President: The Trail-Blazing Second Term of George Washington, 1991, (play) George Washington Visits Chattanooga, 1994; editor Army Life mag., 1943-46, Europe's View of America, 1954; contbg. editor So. Observer mag.; composer (with Norman Cloutier) Voice of the Army, adopted by War Dept. as ofcl. song Army Recruiting Service; editor-in-chg. History of Mountain City Club, Chattanooga, 1998. Mem. N.Y.C. Bicentennial Hist. Commn.; supr. army radio show Voice of Army; chmn. U. Tenn. Lupton Libr. Friends, 1992-94, U. Tenn. Commemoration Ceremonies George Washington, 1998; Served from 1st Lieut. to Lieut. Col. AUS, 1940-46. Penfield fellow NYU, 1954-55; recipient NYU Founders Day Honors award, 1956, Am. Revolution Round Table placque Henry Knox, 1958; vis. scholar Huntington Library, 1960; named Disting. Alumnus U. Tenn., 1983. Fellow Am. Studies Assn.; mem. Am. Hist. Assn., Soc. Hist. Assn., Am. Acad. Polit. and Social Sci., So. Soc. (historian), Civil War Round Table N.Y. (pres. 1954-55), Tenn. Soc. N.Y. (historian), Conf. Brit. Studies, Tenn. Hist. Soc., Am. Revolution Round Table (chmn.), Writer's Group, Princeton Club (founder, chmn.), Chattanooga Golf and Country Club, Mountain City Club, Delta Sigma Phi, Kappa Tau Alpha, Theta Alpha Phi, Delta Theta Phi,Kappa Tau Alpha, Theta Alpha Phi, Delta Theta Phi, Sigma Delta Phi. Home: 600 Pine St Chattanooga TN 37402-1712

CALLAHAN, PATRICK MICHAEL, lawyer; b. Trenton, N.J., Aug. 1, 1947; s. Aloysius Walter and Doris Beatrice (Schwing) C.; m. Elizabeth R. Cohen, May 6, 1984; children: Andrew Lawrence, Samantha Devon; children by previous marriage: Erin Kathleen, Patrick Michael Jr. AA, Rider Coll., 1977, BA summa cum laude, 1978, MA, 1980; JD, Seton Hall. U., 1984. Bar: N.J. 1984, U.S. Dist. Ct. N.J. 1984; cert. civil trial atty. Supreme Ct. of N.J. bd. on trial atty. cert. Trooper N.J. State Police, 1970-84; assoc. Shanley & Fisher, P.C., Morristown, N.J., 1984-93; ptnr. Tompkins, McGuire & Wachenfeld, Newark, N.J., 1993-98, Tompkins, McGuire, Wachenfeld & Barry, LLP, Newark, 1998—; dir. Appellate Moot Ct., 1983-84; mem. N.J. Supreme Ct. Dist. Ethics Com., Dist. V-A (Newark), 1994-96, chair, 1996-97; master Seton Hall U. Law Sch. Inn of Ct., 1994—. Mem. Somerset County Dem. Com., 1988—. With USNR, 1965-72. Andrew J. Rider scholar, 1976, Oscar W. Rittenhouse scholar, 1982. Mem. ABA, N.J. State Bar Assn. (vice-chmn. malpractice ins. com. 1998-99, chair 1999—), Somerset County Bar Assn. (trustee 1997—), Essex County Bar Assn. (chair civil litigation practice com. 1999—), Trial Attys. of N.J. (trustee 1996—). Unitarian Universalist. Avocation: photography. Home: 211 Daval Rd Neshanic Station NJ 08853-3019 Office: Tompkins McGuire & Wachenfeld & Barry Four Gateway Ctr 100 Mulberry St Newark NJ 07102-4070

CALLAHAN, RICKEY DON, business owner; b. Dallas, Mar. 17, 1956; s. Dayton Easton and Alice Jane (Holloway) C. AA, Eastfield Coll., 1976; BA in Polit. Sci., U. Tex.-Dallas, 1978; MBA in Gen. Mgmt., Amber U., 1986. Cert. secondary tchr., Tex. Real estate assoc. ERA Sage Realty, Inc., Dallas, 1979-80, First Mark Real Estate, Dallas, 1980-81; adminstrv. asst. Dallas Precious Metal Plating, Inc., Garland, Tex., 1981-84; legis. asst. to state rep. Alvin R. Granoff, Dallas, 1984-87; owner, broker Callahan Properties, Dallas, 1987—. Pres. Dallas County East Dem. Orgn., 1986-88, Clean Dallas-S.E., Inc., 1987-88, Tex. Jr. C. of C. Found.; bd. dirs. Dallas Conv. and Visitors Bur., 1995-98; mem. Dallas Bond Campaign Com., 1995; bd. dirs. S.E. Emergency Food Ctr., 1996—, v.p. 1998—; mem. Cotton Bowl Dome found. organizing com. Mem. Nat. Assn.Realtors, Tex. Assn. Realtors, North Tex. Comml. Assn. of Realtors (arbitration panel), S.E. Dallas C. of C. (bd. dirs. 1987—, vice chmn. econ. devel. 1991-92, chmn. 1994-95), U. Tex. Dallas Alumni Assn., Amber U. Alumni Assn., Tex. Jaycees (dist. dir. 1981-82, Prestigious J.C.I. Senator award #38931, pres. Mesquite chpt. 1980-81, 82-83, bd. dirs. Dallas 1990-91), N. Tex. Comml. Assn. Realtors, Phi Theta Kappa. Democrat. Baptist. Avocations: scuba diving, guitar, genealogy, reading, softball. Office: Callahan Properties 8344 E R L Thornton Fwy Ste 308 Dallas TX 75228-7134

CALLAHAN, ROBERT F., JR., radio executive; m. Janice Callahan; children: Elizabeth, Claire, Helen. B.S. in Journalism, Univ. of Kansas. Media planner Young & Rubicam advt., from 1976; then positions in acct. mgmt. with McCann-Erickson and Wells, Rich, Greene, Inc.; Eastern Sales Mgr. Fairchild Pubs., from 1981, various sales and pub. positions; then sr. v.p., group pub. Fairchild Pubs. Capital Cities/ABC Pub., sr. v.p. diversified pub. group, 1990; pres. ABC Radio Divsn., N.Y.C., 1990-99; pres. broadcasting ABC Inc., N.Y.C., 1999—. Office: ABC Inc 77 W 66th St Fl 17 New York NY 10023-6201

CALLAHAN, ROBERT JEREMIAH, state supreme court justice; b. Norwalk, Conn., June 3, 1930; s. Jeremiah J. and Elizabeth A. (Connolly) C.; m. Dorothy B. Trudel, Jan. 24, 1959; children: Sheila, Kerry, Denise, Janine, Patrick, Megan, Jane, Robert Jr. BS in History and Govt., Boston Coll., 1952; JD, Fordham U., 1955. Judge Cir. Ct. Conn., 1970-75, Ct. Common Pleas, Conn., 1975-76, Conn. Superior Ct., 1976-85; assoc. justice Conn. Supreme Ct., 1985-96, chief justice, 1996; mem. Bd. Pardons, Conn., 1985-87. Served with U.S. Army, 1956-58. Recipient Fordham U. Sch. Law Dean's medal of recognition, 1986, Fordham Law Alumni Assn. medal of excellence, 1997, Fordham Disting. Alumnus award, 1998, U. Conn. Alumni Assn. Disting. Svc. award, 1998. Roman Catholic. Office: Conn Supreme Ct Drawer N Sta A 231 Capitol Ave Hartford CT 06106-1548

CALLAHAN, RONALD, federal investigator, historian; b. San Francisco, Jan. 8, 1947; s. Raymond Edward and Camille (Masucci) C.; m. Delores Leona Cody Callahan, Nov. 15, 1986; children: Randell James Stowe, Miranda Dawn Stowe, Christopher Ronald Callahan, Kimberly Ann Callahan. BS, Calif. State U., 1973, student, 1987-91. Cert. spl. agt. Air traffic controller USAF, Davis-Monthan AFB, Ariz., 1967-68; air traffic controller USAF, Kadena AB, Japan, 1968-70; clk. Franchise Tax Bd., Sacramento, 1973; acct. clk. Employment Devel. Dept., Sacramento, 1973-74; air cargo specialist 82nd Aerial Port Squadron, Travis AFB, Calif., 1978-80; adjudicator VA, San Francisco, 1974-82; historian 349th Mil. Airlift Wing, Travis AFB, Calif., 1980-82, Fourth Air Force, McClellan AFB, Calif., 1986-90; sr. investigator Def. Security Svc., Sacramento, 1982—. Author: Annual Histories of McClellan and Travis Air Bases, 1980-82, 86-90, Airpower Journal, 1991-93. Vol. El Dorado County Juvenile Svc. Coun., Placerville, Calif., 1992, Calvary Refuge, Sacramento, Marysville, Calif., 1992-97, Calvary Chapel of Placerville, 1997—; mem. Grace Cmty. Ch., Pleasant Valley, Calif., 1993—; adult literacy tutor El Dorado County Literacy Action Coun., Placerville, 1994—; mem. bd. elders Calvary Refuge, 1996-97. Sgt. USAF, 1966-70. Named Dean's Honors list Calif. State U., Sacramento, 1971, 72; recipient Spl. Act award Def. Investigative Svc., Sacramento, 1983, Air Force Commendation medal USAF, McClellan AFB, Calif., 1989. Mem. Air Force Assn., Orgn. Am. Historians, Am. Christian History Inst., Friends of Libr., Grace Cmty. Ch., Calvary Refuge, Phi Alpha Theta. Republican. Avocations: writing, collecting rare books and memorabilia, tutoring, teaching history. Home: 1640 Glen Dr Placerville CA 95667-9302 Office: Def Security Svc 801 I St Rm 488 Sacramento CA 95814-2510

CALLAHAN, SONNY (H.L. CALLAHAN), congressman; b. Mobile, Ala., Sept. 11, 1932; m. Karen Reed; children: Scott, Patrick, Shawn Cushing, Chris, Cameron (dec.), Kelly. Grad., McGill Inst. Pres., chmn. bd., chief exec. officer Finch Cos., Mobile and Montgomery, Ala., 1964-84; mem. Ala. Ho. of Reps., 1970-78, chmn. Mobile County delegation; mem. Ala. Senate, 1978-82, 99th-104th Congresses from 1st Ala. dist.; mem. appropriations com., chmn. subcom. on fgn. ops. Served with USN, 1952-54. Mem. Mobile Area C. of C., Ala. Movers Assn., Ala. Trucking Assn., Kiwanis, Optimists. Office: 2970 Cottage Hill Rd Ste 126 Mobile AL 36606-4795 also: US Ho of Reps 2418 Rayburn House Offc Bldg Washington DC 20515-0101

CALLAHAN, VINCENT FRANCIS, JR., publisher, state legislator; b. Washington, Oct. 30, 1931; s. Vincent Francis and Anita (Hawkins) C.; B.S. in Fgn. Service, Georgetown U., 1957, Degree in Humane Letters (hon.) No. Va. C.C., 1997; m. Dorothy Helen Budge, Aug. 27, 1960; children—Vincent Francis III, Elizabeth Lauren, Anita Marie, Cynthia Helen, Robert Bruce. Became partner Callahan Publs., 1957; past pres. Ind. Newsletters Assn., Washington; mem. Va. Ho. of Dels., 1968—, minority leader, 1982-85. Candidate for lt. gov. Va., 1965; state fin. chmn. Rep. Party of Va., 1966-68; candidate for U.S. Congress, 1976; past dir. Washington Met. Council Govts. Served with USMC, 1950-53; as lt. USCGR, 1959-63; chmn. No. Va. Community Found. Mem. U.S. Naval Inst., Marine Tech. Soc., Am. Def. Preparedness Assn. Republican. Roman Catholic. Clubs: Nat. Press; Kiwanis (past pres.) (McLean, Va.). Author eight books including; Missile Contracts Guide, 1958; Space Guide, 1959; Underwater Defense Handbook, 1963; Military Research Handbook, 1963. Office: PO Box 1173 Mc Lean VA 22101-1173

CALLAHAN, WILLIAM E., JR., federal judge; b. 1948. BA, Marquette U., 1970, JD, 1973. Atty. Goldberg, Previant and Uelman, 1973-75; asst. U.S. atty. Eastern Dist. Wis., 1975-82, 1st asst. U.S. atty., 1982-84; atty. Davis & Kuelthau, S.C., 1984-95; magistrate judge U.S. Dist. Ct. (ea. dist.) Wis., Milw., 1995—. Office: 449 US Courthouse 517 E Wisconsin Ave Milwaukee WI 53202-4500

CALLAIS, ELAINE DENISE ROGERS, accountant; b. Cleveland, Tenn., Dec. 30, 1962; d. Eddie L. and Dennie Jo (Richards) R.; m. Edwin T. Callais Jr.; 1 child, Rachel Savannah. BS cum laude, Tenn. Wesleyan Coll., 1985. CPA, Ga. Asst. contr. Luesing Group, Inc., Atlanta, 1985-90; acct. Life Care Ctrs. Am., Cleveland, Tenn., 1990-98, McKenzie Cos., Cleveland, 1998—. Co-author: (manual) Policies and Procedures of the Luesing Group, Inc., 1988, Life Care Centers of America Accounts Receivable Financial Manual, 1993; author: McKenzie Companies Home Office Policies and Procedures Manual, 1998. Vol. United Way, Cleveland, 1991, ARC, Cleveland, 1978-82. Mem. AICPA, Tenn. Wesleyan Coll. Bd. Alumni, Beta Sigma Phi, Sigma Kappa (pres. 1984-85). Republican. Presbyterian. Avocations: ballet, travel, movies. Home: 1111 Cookdale Trl NW Cleveland TN 37312-3610 Office: McKenzie Cos PO Box 1479 Cleveland TN 37364-1479

CALLAN, EDWARD THOMAS, English educator; b. Ballina, Ireland, Dec. 3, 1917; s. Owen and Ellen (O'Connor) C.; m. R. Claire Wegner, Aug. 6, 1955; children: Joseph Mark, Ruth Ann. BA, Witwatersrand U., 1947; MA, Fordham U., 1953; DPhil, U. South Africa, 1959. Instr. in English Fordham U., N.Y.C., 1952-54, Loyola U., Chgo., 1954-57; assoc. prof. English Western Mich. U., Kalamazoo, 1957-63, prof. English, 1964-83, Disting univ. prof., 1982-83, Disting. univ. prof. emeritus, 1983—; vis. prof. English U. Mich., Ann Arbor, 1968; nat. panel of spkrs. Ministry for Info., London, 1950-52; external examiner Rhodes U., South Africa, 1968-72, U. Toronto, 1975-76; lectr. Oxford U., 1974. Author: Auden, 1983, Yeats on Yeats, 1981, Alan Paton, 1968, 2d edit., 1982, (play) I Am of Ireland, 1988. Bd. dirs. New Vic Theatre, Kalamazoo, 1974-79. With South African Artillery, 1941-46. Carnegie grant Oxford U., 1960-61. Mem. MLA (life), Oxford Soc. Roman Catholic. Avocation: tennis. Home: 2012 Quail Cove Dr Kalamazoo MI 49009-1868

CALLAN, JOHN GARLING, management executive, marketing consultant; b. N.Y.C., Oct. 12, 1946; s. Andrew Thomas and Virginia Garling (Wheatley) C.; m. Linda Ferguson Adkinson, Aug. 28, 1978. B.A. in Russian Lang., U. N.C., 1969. Pres., Alex Nichols Agy., Inc., L.A., 1971-73; pres., founder Calico Air Courier Svc., L.A., 1973-79; v.p. mktg. DHL Worldwide Express, Burlingame, Calif., 1979-82; pres. TNT Skypak Inc., Burlingame, 1982-83; sr. v.p. mktg. and sales Purolator Courier Corp., Basking Ridge, N.J., 1983-84, sr. v.p. internat., 1984-85; pres. Callan Assocs., Mendham, N.J., 1985-87; dir. entertainment imaging Polaroid Corp., Cambridge, Mass., 1987-93, dir. new bus. devel., 1993-95; COO Milestone Sys. Inc., Lexington, Mass., 1995-97; founder, owner E-Picture.com, Weston, Mass., 1998—; prin. John G. Callan, Cons., 1997—; contract cons., thought leader PriceWaterhouseCoopers postal practice, Arlington, Va., 1997—; dir. Video Guide, Inc., Bedford, Mass., 1993-96. V.p. Washington Valley Cmty. Assn., Mendham, N.J., 1986; bd. govs. The Gore Pl. Soc., Waltham, Mass., 1993-96; lay Eucharistic min. St. Peter's Episcopal Ch., Weston, 1995—. Morehead scholar, U. N.C., Chapel Hill, 1965-69. Mem. Air Courier Conf. Am., Inc. (sec. 1981-82, dir. 1979-82), Travel Industry Assn. Am. (dir. 1987-92).

CALLAN, JOSEPH PATRICK, social service administrator; b. Washington, July 29, 1944; s. G. Christopher and Mary Jane (Gorsuch) C.; m. Judith Marie Bell, June 14, 1980; children: Kimberly Jane, Kathleen Marie. AA, St. Petersburg (Fla.) Jr. Coll., 1964; BA, U. So. Fla., 1972, MSW, 1985; MS, Nova U., 1985. Group work supr. Eckerd Found., Clearwater, Fla., 1968-72, dir. tng., 1977-83; coord. Collier County Mental Health, Naples, Fla., 1972-76; pvt. practice psychotherapy Tampa, Fla., 1985—; dir., owner Univ. Psychotherapy Group, P.A., Tampa, 1987—; psychotherapist Employee Assistance Programs and Sex Therapy, Tampa, 1987—; vis. faculty U. So. Fla., Tampa, 1987—; clin. dir. Traverse Equestrian Therapy Program for traumatized youth, Tampa, 1995—; pres. Tng. and Edn. Ctr., Naples, 1972-77, Immokalee (Fla.) Adult Refuge, 1972-77; cons. social svcs. agys. Tampa area, 1987—. Sgt. U.S. Army, 1966-71. Mem. NASW, Am. Acad. Clin. Sexologists, Fla. Soc. Clin. Social Work, Collier County Assn. Retarded Citizens (charter), U. So. Fla. Social Work Alumni Assn. (pres. 1986-88), N. Am. Handicapped Riding Assn., Phi Kappa Phi, Pi Gamma Mu. Avocation: horseback riding. Home: 3450 Lake Padgett Dr Land O'Lakes FL 34639-6514 Office: Univ Psychotherapy Group PA 12210 N 56th St Tampa FL 33617-1531

CALLAN, JOSI IRENE, museum director; b. Yorkshire, Eng., Jan. 30, 1946; came to U.S., 1953; d. Roger Bradshaw and Irene (Newbury) Winstanley; children: James, Heather, Brett Jack; m. Patrick Marc Callan, June 26, 1984. BA in Art History summa cum laude, Calif. State U., Dominguez Hills, 1978, MA in Behavioral Scis., 1981. Dir. community rels./alumni affairs Calif. State U., Dominguez Hills; adminstrv. fellow office chancellor Calif. State U., Long Beach, assoc. dir. univ. svcs. office chancellor, 1979-85; dir. capital campaign, assoc. dir. devel. Sta. KVIE-TV, Sacramento, 1985-86; dir. project devel. Pacific Mountain Network, Denver, 1986-87; dir. mktg. and devel. Denver Symphony Orch., 1988-89; assoc. dir. San Jose (Calif.) Mus. Art, 1989-91, dir., 1991—; asst. prof. sch. social and behavioral scis. Calif. State U., Dominguez Hills, 1981—; mem. adv. com. Issues Facing Mus. in 1990s JKF U., 1990-91. Mem. com. arts policy Santa Clara Arts Coun., 1990-92; chair San Jose Arts Roundtable, 1992-93; active ArtTable, 1992—, Community Leadership San Jose, 1992-93, Am. Leadership Forum, 1994; mem. adv. bd. Bay Area Rsch. Project, 1992—; mem. Calif. Arts Coun., Visual Arts Panel, 1993-95, Santa Clara Arts Coun. Visual Arts Panel, 1993; bd. dirs. YWCA, 1993—. Recipient Leadership award Knight Found., 1995; Women of Vision honoree Career Action Ctr., 1998; fellow Calif. State U., 1982-83. Mem. AAUW, Am. Assn. Mus., Nat. Soc. Fund Raising Execs. (bd. dirs. 1991), Colo. Assn. Fund Raisers, Art Mus. Devel. Assn., Assn. Art Mus. Dirs., We. Mus. Assn., Calif. State U. Alumni Coun. (pres. 1981-83), Rotary Internat. Office: San Jose Mus Art 110 S Market St San Jose CA 95113-2383

CALLANAN, LAURA PATRICE, foundation manager; b. St. Louis, June 25, 1965; d. James Carson and Mary Ann (Plati) C.; m. Romulus Zachariah Linney, Mar. 8, 1996. BA, Barnard Coll., 1987; MPA, Columbia U., 1991. Devel. assoc. Lincoln Ctr. Theater, N.Y.C., 1987-88; devel. mgr. Am. Ballet Theatre, N.Y.C., 1988-89; assoc. Lehman Bros., N.Y.C., 1990-94, JP Morgan Securities Inc., N.Y.C., 1994-95; asst. v.p. Moody's Investors Svc., N.Y.C., 1995-96; assoc. treas. Lila Wallace-Reader's Digest Fund, N.Y.C., 1996-98, DeWitt Wallace-Reader's Digest Fund, N.Y.C., 1996-98; mgr. investments Rockefeller Found., N.Y.C., 1998—; treas. bd. dirs. Signature Theatre Co., N.Y.C., 1993-98; cons. Alliance for the Arts, N.Y.C., 1996. Home: 289 Dales Bridge Rd Germantown NY 12526-5222

CALLANDER, BRUCE DOUGLAS, journalist, free-lance writer; b. Malone, N.Y., Dec. 23, 1923; s. Douglas Newton and Blanche Keller (Redfield) C.; m. Imogene A. O'Malley, Nov. 23, 1979; children by previous marriage—Richard Scott, John Byron. A.B. with cert. in Journalism, U. Mich., Ann Arbor, 1948. Indsl. editor Kaiser Frazer Co., Willow Run, Mich., 1948-50; pub. relations officer U.S. Air Force, Ohio, Md., 1951-52; assoc. editor Air Force Times, Washington, 1952-67, mng. editor, 1967-72; editor Air Force Times, Springfield, Va., 1972-85; freelance writer, mil. historian Mullett Lake, Mich., 1986—. Served to capt. USAF, 1942-45, 51-52; Italy. Recipient Hopwood awards U. Mich., 1945, 48; Freedom Found. award, 1982. Club: St. Andrews Soc. (Washington). Avocations: painting; sculpting; woodworking; playing the flute.

CALLANDER, KAY EILEEN PAISLEY, business owner, retired gifted talented education educator, writer; b. Coshocton, Ohio, Oct. 15, 1938; d. Dalton Olas and Dorothy Pauline (Davis) Paisley; m. Don Larry Callander, Nov. 18, 1977. BSE, Muskingum Coll., 1960; MA in Speech Edn., Ohio State U., 1964, postgrad., 1964-84. Cert. elem., gifted, drama, theater tchr., Ohio. Tchr. Columbus (Ohio) Pub. Schs., 1960-70, 80-88, drama specialist, 1970-80, classroom, gifted/talented tchr., 1986-90, ret., 1990; sole prop. The Ali Group, Kay Kards, 1992—; coord. Artists-in-the Schs., 1977-88; cons., presenter numerous ednl. confs. and sems., 1971—; mem., ednl. cons. Innovation Alliance Youth Adv. Coun., 1992—. producer-dir., Shady Lane Music Festival, 1980-88; dir. tchr. (nat. distbr. video) The Trial of Gold E. Locks, 1983-84; rep., media pub. relations liason Sch. News., 1983-88; author, creator Trivia Game About Black Americans (TGABA), exhibitor of TGABA game at L.A. County Office Edn. Conf., 1990; presenter for workshop by Human Svc. Group and Creative Edn. Coop., Columbus, Ohio, 1989. Benefactor, Columbus Jazz Arts Group; v.p., bd. dirs. Neoteric Dance and Theater Co., Columbus, 1985-87; tchr., participant Future Stars sculpture exhibit, Ft. Hayes Ctr., Columbus Pub. Schs., 1988; tchr. advisor Columbus Coun. PTAs, 1983-86, co-chmn. reflections com., 1984-87; mem. Columbus Mus. Art, Citizens for Humane Action, Inc.; mem. supt.'s adv. coun. Columbus Pub. Schs., 1967-68; presenter Young Author Seminar, Ohio Dept. Edn., 1988, Illustrating Methods for Young Authors' Books, 1986-87; cons. and workshop leader seminar/workshop Tchg. About the Constitution in Elem. Schs., Franklin County Ednl. Coun., 1988; sponsor Minority Youth Recognition Awards, 1994. Named Educator of Yr., Shady Lane PTA, 1982, Columbus Coun. PTAs, 1989, winner Colour Columbus Landscape Design Competition, 1990; Sch. Excellence grantee Columbus Pub. Schs.; Commendation Columbus Bd. Edn. and Ohio Ho. of Reps. for Child Assault Prevention project, 1986-87; first place winner statewide photo contest Ohio Vet. Assn., 1991; recipient Muskingum Coll. Alumni Disting. Svc. award, 1995. Mem. ASCD, AAUW, Assn. for Childhood Edn. Internat., Ohio Coun. for Social Studies, Franklin County Ret. Tchrs. Assn., Nat. Mus. Women in the Arts, Ohio State U. Alumni Assn., U.S. Army Officers Club, Navy League, Liturgical Art Guild Ohio, Columbus Jazz Arts Group, Columbus Mus. Art, Nat. Coun. for Social Studies, Columbus Art League, Columbus Maennerchor (Damen sect.). Republican. Avocations: painting, photography, swimming, golfing, playing piano and organ. Home: 2323 Colts Neck Rd Blacklick OH 43004-9648 Office: The Ali Group Kay Kards PO Box 13093 Columbus OH 43213-0093

CALLARD, DAVID JACOBUS, private equity investor; b. Boston, July 14, 1938; s. Henry Hadden and Clarissa Cooley (Jacobus) C.; m. Deborah Winston, 1960 (div. 1982); children: Owen Winston, Francis Jacobus, Anne Lloyd, Elizabeth Hadden, Samuel Porter; m. Mary R. Morgan, July 14, 1990. AB, Princeton U., 1959; postgrad., Union Theol. Sem., 1964-65; JD, NYU, 1969. With Morgan Guaranty Trust Co., N.Y.C., 1959-61, asst. v.p., 1965-69, v.p., 1970-72; gen. ptnr. Alex Brown & Sons, Balt., 1972-84; mng. dir., 1984-89; bd. dirs. Alex Brown Inc., Balt., 1984-89; pres. Wand Ptnrs. Inc., N.Y.C., 1991—; bd. dirs. Chartwell Re. Corp., Info. Mgmt. Assocs. Bd. dirs. Union Theol. Sem., N.Y.C., Episcopal Charities of Diocese of N.Y.; trustee Rockefeller Bros. Fund, Panorama Trust; dep. exec. dir. Pres.'s Commn. on All Vol. Armed Forces, 1969-70. Lt. USMC, 1961-64. Boothe Ferris fellow, 1964-65. Mem. Union Club, Knickerbocker Club, Elkridge (Balt.). Democrat. Episcopalian.

CALLAWAY, BEN ANDERSON, journalist; b. Oakland, Calif., Mar. 16, 1927; s. Owen M. and Aulis (Anderson) C.; m. Patricia Hurd, Apr. 7, 1951; children: Randall Owen, Karen Anne Franks. Student, Stanford, 1946-47; BA, Denison U., 1950. Sports writer, wildlife editor Denver Post, 1950-57; with Phila. Daily News, 1957-80, sports editor, 1961-70, outdoor columnist, 1961-80; outdoor editor Phila. Inquirer, 1980-91, editor fishing reports, 1992—; outdoor columnist Courier-Post, 1992—; exec. editor Metro East Outdoor News, 1973-77; co-editor Penn-Jersey Outdoor Sportsman, 1976-77; free-lance mag. writer-photographer; commentator Sta. KYW, 1972-95. Sports chmn. Phila. United Fund, 1966-70; active local Boy Scouts Am., Eagle, 1942. Served with USNR, 1945-46. Recipient Henshall award Am. Fishing Tackle Mfrs. Assn., 1964, Old Salt award N.J. Resort Assn., 1967, Johnson Deep Woods award, 1977; gold medal Pa. Fish and Game Protective Assn., 1978; McCulloch Outdoor Writing award, 1978. Mem. Phila. Sports Writers Assn. (pres. 1968-70), Denver Sports Writers and Broadcasters Assn. (pres. 1957), Outdoor Writers Am. (dir. 1976-79, 89—92, Pa. Outdoor Writers, Boating Writers Internat. (dir. 1976-85), Met. N.Y. Rod and Gun Editors, N.J. Outdoor Writers Assn. (v.p. 1982-86, pres. 1988-91), Blue Key, Beta Theta Pi, Pi Delta Epsilon, Omicron Delta Kappa. Presbyn. (elder). Home and Office: 420 Kingston Dr Cherry Hill NJ 08034-1630 *The only true measure of success is that the world is, and will be, a better place because of his or her presence. As an outdoor writer, I fulfill an important function, in helping others understand and enjoy the great outdoors.*

CALLAWAY, CLIFFORD WAYNE, physician; b. Easton, Md., May 28, 1941; s. Charles Herschel and Anna Agnes (Stradley) C.; 1 child, David Wayne; m. Jackie Chalkley. BA, U. Del., 1963; MD, Northwestern U., 1967. Diplomate Am. Bd. Internal Medicine, Am. Bd. Endocrinology, Diabetes and Metabolism, Am. Bd. Nutrition. Resident internal medicine Northwestern U. Med. Ctr., Chgo., 1967-69, Mayo Grad. Sch. Medicine, Rochester, Minn., 1971-73; advanced clin. resident endocrinology Mayo Grad. Sch. Medicine, 1973-75; assoc. cons. Mayo Clin., Rochester, 1975-78; cons. endocriminology Mayo Clin., 1978-85, dir. nutrition and lipid clins., 1980-85; rsch. assoc. Harvard Med. Sch., Boston, 1976-78; dir. ctr. clin. nutrition George Washington U., Washington, 1986-88; sr. sci. cons. Food & Ntrition Bd., NRC/NAS, Washington, 1987-88; pvt. practice Washington, 1988—. Author 4 books; contbr. articles to profl. jours. Acting exec. sec. nutrition coordinating office HHS, Washington, 1980. Mayo Found. scholar, 1976-78. Mem. Am. Soc. Clin. Nutrition (treas. 1988), Am. Bd. Nutrition (mem. bd. dirs. 1983-89, 95-98, sec.-treas. 1984-86, v.p. 1986-88), Am. Inst. Nutrition (chair and various coms.), Am. Osler Soc. (bd. dirs.), Am. Assn. Clin. Endocrinologists (bd. dirs. 1992-95), Cen. European Ctr. for Health and Environment (bd. dirs. 1993—). Achievements include development and writing of dietary guidelines for Americans(USDA/DHHS); member advisory committee which defined concept of healthy weights. Office: 2311 M St NW Ste 301 Washington DC 20037-1445

CALLAWAY, HOWARD HOLLIS, business executive; b. La Grange, Ga., Apr. 2, 1927; s. Cason Jewell and Virginia (Hand) C.; m. Elizabeth Walton, June 11, 1949; children: Elizabeth Callaway Considine, Howard Hollis Jr., Edward Cason, Virginia Callaway Martin, Ralph Walton. Student, Ga. Inst. Tech., 1944-45; BS, U.S. Mil. Acad., 1949. Commd. 2d lt. AUS, 1949, advanced through grades to 1st. lt., 1952; resigned, 1952; mem. 89th Congress from 3d Ga. dist.; U.S. sec. Army Washington, 1973-75; campaign mgr. Pres. Ford Com., 1975-76; CEO Crested Butte (Colo.) Mountain Resort, 1975—; bd. dirs. SCI systems, Inc., Hunstville, Ala. Pres. Nat. 4-H, mem. svc. com., 1957-73; chmn. bd. trustees Ida Cason Callaway Found., Pine Mountain, Ga., Freedoms Found. at Valley Forge; former mem. bd. regents Univ. Sys. Ga.; Rep. candidate for gov. of Ga., 1966; candidate Rep. primary for U.S. Senate from Colo., 1980; chmn. Colo. Rep. Com., 1981-87, chmn. GOPAC, 1987-93; mem. Def. Base Realignment and Closure Commn., 1992. 1st lt. inf. U.S. Army, 1949-52. Mem. World Pres.' Orgn. (past pres.), Young Pres.' Orgn. (past pres.), Chief Execs. Orgn., Capital City Club (Atlanta), Piedmont Driving Club (Atlanta), Bohemian Club (San Francisco), Phi Delta Theta. Episcopalian. Home: Callaway Gardens Pine Mountain GA 31822

CALLAWAY, KAREN A(LICE), journalist; b. Daytona Beach, Fla., Sept. 5, 1946; d. Robert Clayton III and Alice Johnston (Webb) C. (deceased). BS in Journalism, Northwestern U., 1968. Copy editor Detroit Free Press, 1968-69; asst. woman's editor, features copy editor, news copy editor, asst. makeup editor Chgo. Am. and Chgo. Today, 1969-74; asst. makeup editor Chgo. Tribune, 1974-76, asst. news editor, 1976-81, assoc. news editor spl. sect., 1981—, assoc. news editor vertical publs., 1993—; adviser Jr. Achievement Tribune sponsored co., Chgo., 1976-77; editor Infant Mortality sect., 1989; vis. prof. student chpt. Soc. Profl. Journalists, Northwestern U., 1989. Chmn. class of 1968 20th reunion Northwestern U., 1989, mem. seminar day com., 1989-90, chmn., 1991, mem. alumni bd. dirs. Medill Sch. Journalism, Northwestern U., Evanston, Ill., 1991—; vol. Northwestern U. Settlement House. Mem. Soc. of Profl. Journalists, Sigma Delta Chi, Kappa Delta. Methodist. Avocations: scuba diving; swimming; cooking; traveling. Office: Chicago Tribune 435 N Michigan Ave Ste 500 Chicago IL 60611-4066

CALLAWAY, STEPHEN V., federal judge; b. 1947. BA, La. State U., 1970, JD, 1973. Ptnr. Burnett, Sutton, Walker & Callaway, 1973-86; bankruptcy judge U.S. Dist. Ct. (we. dist.) La., Shreveport, 1986—. With USMCR. Fax: (318) 676-4241. Office: US Dist Ct (we dist) La. Rm 4400 300 Fannin St Shreveport LA 71101-3088

CALLAWAY, TROWBRIDGE, banker. Chmn. bd. dirs., CEO U.S. Trust Co. Fla. Savings Bank. Office: U S Trust Co FL Savings Bank 132 Royal Palm Way Palm Beach FL 33480-4254*

CALLÉ, CRAIG R.L., packaging executive; b. Greenwich, Conn., Dec. 17, 1959; s. Hans Martin Erich and Mary Ann (Sadtler) C.; m. Catherine Maechling, June 18, 1993. BA, BS in Econ., U. Pa., 1981; MBA, Harvard U., 1985. Fin. analyst Salomon Bros. Inc., N.Y.C., 1981-83, assoc., 1985-88, v.p., 1988-91; treas. Crown Cork & Seal Co., Inc., 1991, v.p. & treas., 1991-95, sr. v.p. fin., treas., 1995—. Mem. St. Anthony Club, Harvard Club, Phila. Cricket Club. Republican. Office: Crown Cork & Seal Co One Crown Way Philadelphia PA 19154

CALLEAR, MILDRED O., federal agency administrator; b. Herrin, Ill., July 15, 1955. Bachelor Degree summa cum laude, U. Ill., 1976; JD cum laude, Georgetown U., 1979. With Reid and Priest, Washington; sr. legal counsel Overseas Pvt. Investment Corp., Washington, 1982-88, dep. treas., 1988, v.p., treas., CFO, 1988—, acting pres., CEO, 1993, 97, acting v.p. investment devel. dept., 1996. Office: Internat Devel Coop Agy 1100 New York Ave NW Washington DC 20527

CALLEN, DAVID H., hotel executive. Pres., chmn. bd. H.I. Devel. Corp., Tampa, Fla., 1980—. Office: HI Devel Corp 111 W Fortune St Tampa FL 33602-3206*

CALLEN, JAMES DONALD, nuclear engineer, plasma physicist, educator; b. Wichita, Kans., Jan. 31, 1941; s. Donald Dewitt and Bonnie Jean (Walton) C.; m. Judith Carolyn Chinn, Aug. 26, 1961; children: Jeffrey Scott, Sandra Jean. BS in Nuclear Engring., Kans. State U., 1962, MS in Nuclear Engring., 1964; PhD in Nuclear Engring., MIT, 1968. Postdoctoral fellow Inst. for Advanced Study, Princeton, N.J., 1968-69; asst. prof. aeros. and astronautics MIT, Cambridge, 1969-72; mem. rsch. staff fusion energy div. Oak Ridge (Tenn.) Nat. Lab., 1972-74, group leader, 1974-75, head plasma theory sect., 1975-79; prof. nuclear engring. and physics U. Wis., Madison, 1979-86, D.W. Kerst prof. engring. physics, and physics, 1986—. Mem. editor. bd. Nuclear Fusion Jour., 1978-97; assoc. editor divsn. plasma physics Phys. Rev. Letters Jour., 1980-85; contbr. over 150 articles to profl. jours. Fulbright fellow Tech. Hogesch. to Eindhoven, Netherlands, 1962-63; recipient Dept. of Energy Disting. Assoc. award, 1988; named to Coll. Engring. Hall of Fame, Kans. State U., 1991; Guggenheim fellow, 1986. Fellow Am. Phys. Soc. (chmn. div. plasma physics 1986), Am. Nuclear Soc.; mem. NAE, AAAS. Office: U Wis 1500 Engineering Dr Madison WI 53706-1687

CALLEN, JEFFREY PHILLIP, dermatologist, educator; b. May 30, 1947; s. Irwin R. and Rose P. (Cohen) C.; m. Susan B. Manis, Dec. 21, 1968; children: Amy, David. BS, U. Wis., 1969; MD, U. Mich., 1972. Diplomate Am. Bd. Internal Medicine, Am. Bd. Dermatology. Intern, resident in internal medicine U. Mich., Ann Arbor, 1972-75, intern, resident in dermatology, 1975-77; from asst. clin. prof. to dir. residency tng. program U. Louisville Sch. Medicine, 1977-84, dir. residency tng. program, 1984-88; chief dermatology svc. Louisville VA Hosp., 1984-93, prof., chief dermatology divsn., 1988—. Author: Manual of Dermatology, 1980, Cutaneous Aspects of Internal Disease, 1981, Neurology Clinics North America, 1987, Dermatologic Signs of Systemic Disease, 1988, 2nd edit., 1994, Color Atlas of Dermatology, 1993, Current Practice of Dermatology, 1995; editor: Clinics in Rheumatic Disease, 1982, Dermatologic Clinics, 1985, 89, Medical Clinics of North America, 1982, 84, 86, 89; editor-in-chief Dermavision video program; mem. editl. bd. Internat. Jour. Dermatology, 1990-95; asst. editor Internat. Jour. Dermatology, 1993-95; editor spl. issues of jours. in field. Bd. dirs. Actor's Theater of Louisville, 1982-91, 92-98, sec., 1986-97, Ky. Arts and Crafts Found., 1991-97; bd. govs. JB Speed Art Mus., 1995—. Fellow ACP, Am. Acad. Dermatology (chmn. audio/visual edn. com., task force therapeutic agts., internal med. symposium 1978-83, chmn. sci. and tech. exhibits 1986-89, dir. various symposiums, mem. coun. sci. assembly 1993-98, chair 1997-98, chair com. to evaluate annual meeting, 1999—, bd. dirs. 1995-99, mem. exec. com. 1997-99), Am. Coll. Rheumatology (founder); mem. AMA, Am. Fedn. Clin. Rsch., Am. Dermatol. Assn., Dermatology Found. (trustee 1984-90). Achievements include research on condition in which systemic disease has cutaneous manifestations, lupus erythematosus, psoriasis, dermatomyositus. Office: U Louisville Dept Dermatology 310 E Broadway Ste 200 Louisville KY 40202-1745

CALLEN, LON EDWARD, county official; b. Kingman, Kans., Mar. 31, 1929; s. Cleo Paul and Josephine Nell (Mease) C.; BA in Math. and Physics, U. Wichita (Kans.), 1951; m. Barbara Jean Sallee, Oct. 12, 1954; children: Lon Edward, Lynnette J. Commd. 2d lt. USAF, 1951, advanced through grades to lt. col., 1968; comdr. Tuslog Detachment 93, Erhac, Turkey, 1966-67; sr. scientist Def. Atomic Support Agy., Washington, 1967-71; ret., 1971; dir. emergency preparedness City-County of Boulder, Colo., 1976—; bd. dirs. Boulder County Emergency Med. Svcs. Coun., 1977, Boulder County Amateur Radio Emergency Svcs., 1978—. Mem. hon. awards com. Nat. Capital Area council Boy Scouts Am., 1971; chmn. Boulder County United Fund, 1976-82; mem. asst. staff Indian Princesses and Trailblazer programs Boulder YMCA, 1974-78. Decorated Joint Svc. Commendation medal; recipient cert. achievement Def. Atomic Support Agy., 1970. Mem. AAAS, Am. Ordnance Soc., Am. Soc. Cybernetics, Planetary Soc., Math. Assn. Am., N.Y. Acad. Scis., Fedn. Am. Scientists, Nat. Assn. Atomic Vets., Union Concerned Scientists, Boulder County Fire Fighters Assn., Colo. Emergency Mgmt. Assn., Ret. Officers Assn., Colo. Front Range Protective Assn., Mensa, Sigma Xi, Pi Alpha Pi. Clubs: Boulder Knife and Fork, Boulder Gunbarrel Optimists, Denver Matrix, U. Colo. Ski, U. Wichita. Author articles in field. Home: 4739 Berkshire Ct Boulder CO 80301-4055 Office: County Courthouse PO Box 471 Boulder CO 80306-0471

CALLEN, TARQUIN M., hotel executive. V.p. H.I. Devel. Corp., San Juan, P.R. Office: HI Devel Corp PO Box 38079 San Juan PR 00937-1079

CALLENBACH, ERNEST, writer, editor; b. Williamsport, Pa., Apr. 3, 1929; m. Christine Leefeldt, May 19, 1978; children: Joanna, Hans. Ph.B., U. Chgo., 1949, M.A., 1953. Editor Film Quar., U. Calif. Press, Berkeley, 1958-91, editor books, 1958-91. Author: Living Poor With Style, 1971, rev. as Living Cheaply With Style, 1993, Ecotopia, 1975, Ecotopian Ency. for the Eighties, 1981, Ecotopia Emerging, 1981, Publisher's Lunch, 1989, Earth's Ten Commandments, 1990, Bring Back the Buffalo!, 1995, Ecology: A Pocket Guide, 1998; co-author: The Art of Friendship, 1979, Citizen Legislature, 1985, Humphrey the Wayward Whale, 1986, EcoManagement, 1993. Mem. Nat. Writers Union. Address: care Banyan Tree Books 1963 El Dorado Ave Berkeley CA 94707-2441

CALLENDER, CLIVE ORVILLE, surgeon; b. N.Y.C., Nov. 16, 1936; s. Joseph and Ida (Burke) C.; m. Fern Irene Marshall, May 25, 1968; children: Joseph, Ealena, Arianne. AB, Hunter Coll., 1959, DSc (hon.), 1998; MD, Meharry Med. Coll., 1963. Diplomate Am. Bd. Surgery, 1970. Intern U. Cin., 1963-64; asst. resident Harlem Hosp., N.Y.C., 1964-65, Howard U. and Freedmans Hosp., Washington, 1965-66, 67-68; chief resident Howard U. and Freedmans Hosp., 1968-69, instr. dept. surgery, 1969-71; asst. resident Meml. Hosp. for Cancer and Allied Diseases, N.Y.C., 1966-67; cons. surgery Port Harcourt Gen. Hosp., Nigeria, 1970, 71; med. officer D.C. Gen. Hosp., 1970-71; NIH postdoctoral rsch. and clin. transplant fellow U. Minn., 1971-73; asst. prof. surgery Howard U. Med. Coll., Washington, 1973-76; assoc. prof. Howard U. Med. Coll., 1976-81, prof. surgery, 1981—, vice-chmn. dept. surgery, 1980-95, chmn. dept. surgery, 1996—, LaSalle D. Leffall, Jr. prof. surgery, 1996—, dir. transplant ctr., 1973—; transplantation cons., Bermuda, 1977, V.I., 1978, 82-86; cons. Ethiopian Surg., Amenity Med. Sch., 1984; G.P.A. Ford Meml. lectr., 1978; mem. task force on organ procurement and transplantation HEW, 1984; testifier com. on labor and human resources U.S. Senate, 1983; mem. end stage renal disease study com. Inst. Medicine, 1989-90, com. on xenograft transplantation: ethical issues and pub. policy Inst. of Medicine, 1995-96 , to the Sec. Health, 1990-94; mem. Inst. of Medicine Com. on Non-Heart-Beating ORgan Transplantation II, 1999; fellowship in liver transplantation Pitts. U., 1986-87; founder, prin. investigator Nat. Minority Organ and Tissue Transplant Edn. Program, 1991—. Mem. editl. adv. bd. New Directions, 1974-91, Contemporary Dialysis and Nephrology Jour., 1993-95; contbr. articles to med. jours. Testifier for Ho. of Reps. Com. on Appropriation, U.S. Congress, 1992, others; councilor Soc. Organ Sharing, 1993, sec., 1995; chmn. tissue com. D.C. chpt. ARC, 1993-95. Recipient Hoffman LaRoche award, 1961, Charles Nelson Gold medal, 1963, Hudson Meadows award, 1963, Charles R. Drew Rsch. award, 1969, Daniel Hale Williams award, 1969, William Alonzo Warfield award, 1977, Howard U. Faculty Outstanding Unit award, 1982, 1st Humanitarian award Cmty. of Caring Ctr., 1990, Disting. Svc. award Surg. Sect. Nat. Med. Assn., 1990, Howard U. Health Affairs Disting. Svc. award, 1984, Outstanding Svc. award Dialysis and Transplant Support, Inc., 1993, Howard U. Legacy of Leadership in Health award, 1995, 11th ann. Minds in Motion award Sci. Skills Ctr., 1993, Edler Garnet Hawkins Humanitarian award Bronx Urban League, 1993; appreciation plaque for 1st renal transplant in V.I., Gov. St. Thomas, 1983, plaque for outstanding contbns. V.I. Legislature, 1984; named to Hunter Coll. Hall of Fame, 1989, Practitioner of Yr., Nat. Med. Assn., 1989, 1 of 10 Outstanding African Am. Male, WHMM-TV, Washington, 1994, 1 of 133 Gifts to the World Alumni Achievers, CUNY, 1995, Pearl Watson Meml. award for excellence in health care delivery Carribbean Am. Intercultural Orgn., Inc., 1995, Pioneer in Edn. award Inst. for Ind. Edn., 1995, Kidney Patients medal of Excellence 2nd Am. Assn., 1997. Fellow ACS (LaSalle D. Leffall, Jr. award 1998), Am. Cancer Soc.; mem. D.C. Med. Soc. (past vice chmn., chmn. surg. sect. 1994—, bd. trustees 1995), Soc. Acad. Surgeons Transplantation Soc., Am. Soc. Transplantation Surgeons (chmn. membership com. 1986, organ placement com. 1991, mem. ethics com. 1995-97), N.Y. Acad. Medicine, Am. Assn. Kidney Patients (bd. dirs. 1998), Nat. Assn. Former Foster Care Children Am. (bd. dirs. 1998-99), Nat. Kidney Found. (nat. bd. dirs. 1991-94, nat. capital area 1977-90), Am. Surg. Assn., Am. Coun. on Transplantation (bd. dirs.), Nat. Med. Assn., Alpha Omega Alpha, Alpha Phi Omega, Alpha Phi Alpha. Home: 509 Kimblewick Dr Silver Spring MD 20904-6341 Office: 2041 Georgia Ave NW Washington DC 20060-0001

CALLENDER, DAVID L., medical educator, administrator. MD, Baylor U., 1984; MBA, U. Houston, 1995. Asst. prof. U. Tex. M.D. Anderson Cancer Ctr., Houston, 1992-97, assoc. prof., 1997-98, v.p. for clin. programs, 1998, sr. v.p., chief med. officer, 1999, dir. M.D. Anderson Outreach Corp., 1998—, dir. M.D. Anderson Physicians Network Corp., 1998—. Mem. AMA, Am. Head and Neck Soc., Am. Acad. Otolaryngology, Head and Neck Surgery, Tex. Med. Assn. Avocations: outdoor sports, travel. E-mail: dcallender@mdanderson.org. Office: U Tex MD Anderson Cancer Ctr 1515 Holcombe Houston TX 77030

CALLENDER, JONATHAN FERRIS, environmental geologist, consultant; b. L.A., Nov. 7, 1944; s. Robert Ford and Ruth Merigold (Ferris) C.; m. Cynthia E. Bennett, Aug. 16, 1967 (div. Apr. 1982); children: Katherine Snowden, Elizabeth, Jennifer, Sarah. BS, Calif. Inst. Tech., 1966; AM, Harvard U., 1968, PhD in Geology, 1975. Asst. prof. U. N.Mex., Albuquerque, 1972-77, assoc. prof., 1977-84, asst. chmn. geology dept., 1979-81, adj. prof. geology, 1985-90; chief sci. programs N.Mex. Mus. Natural History, Albuquerque, 1983-84, dir., 1984-90, also bd. dirs.; v.p., prin. Adrian Brown Cons., Denver, 1990-96; sr. project engr. Kennecott Utah Copper Corp., Magna, 1996—; adj. prof. geology N.Mex. Inst. Mining and Tech., Socorro, 1985-90. Editor numerous books on N.Mex. geology; author numerous tech. papers in field. Active N.Mex. First, 1986-90, Hispanic Cultural Found., Albuquerque, 1986-90; bd. dirs. N.Mex. Mus. Found., 1984-90. Nat. Sci. Found. fellow, 1971-72; recipient Presdl. Recognition award U. N.Mex., 1982. Fellow Geol. Soc. Am.; mem. Am. Assn. Petroleum Geologists, Am. Geophys. Union (chmn. transl. bd. 1985-96), N.Mex. Geol. Soc. (hon., pres. 1977). Avocations: photography, writing. E-mail: JCalle2525@aol.com. Home: 9300 Redwood Rd Apt 5-9 West Jordan UT 84088-6607 Office: Kennecott Utah Copper Corp PO Box 112 Bingham Canyon UT 84006-0112

CALLENDER, NORMA ANNE, psychology educator, counselor; b. Huntsville, Tex., May 10, 1933; d. C. W. Carswell and Nell Ruth (Collard) Hughes Bost; m. B.G. Callender, 1951 (div. 1964); remarried 1967 (div. 1973); children: Teresa Elizabeth, Leslie Gemey, Shannah Hughes, Kelly Mari; m. E. Purfurst, June 1965 (div. Aug. 1965). BS, U. Houston, 1969; MA, U. Houston at Clear Lake, 1977; postgrad. U. Houston, 1970, Lamar U., 1972-73, Tex. So. U., 1971, St. Thomas U., 1985, 86, U. Houston-Clear Lake, 1979, 87, 89-93, summer 98, San Jacinto Coll., 1988, 89, 94, PhD, Cornerstone U., 1998. Aerospace Inst., NASA, Johnson Space Ctr., 1986. Cert. profl. reading specialist, Tex.; lic. profl. counselor. Tchr., Houston Ind. Schs., 1969-70; co-counselor and instr. Ellington AFB, Houston, 1971; tchr. Clear Creek Schs., League City, Tex., 1970-86; cons., LPC intern Guidance Ctr., Pasadena (Tex.) Ind. Sch. Dist., 1993-95; part-time instr. San Jacinto Coll., Pasadena, Tex., 1980-81, 91-93; univ. adj., U. Houston, Clear Lake, 1986-91; owner, dir. Bay Area Tutoring and Reading Clinic, Clear Lake City, Tex., 1970—, Bay Area Tng. Assocs., 1982-98, Bay Area Family Counseling, 1995—; founder, editor BATA Books Pub., 1997—; cons. in field, 1994—. Contbr. poetry to profl. jours. State advisor U.S. Congl. Adv. Bd., 1985-87; vol. bd. dirs. Family Outreach Ctr., 1989-92; vol. Bay Area Coun. on Drugs and Alcohol, Nassau Bay, Tex., 1993-94; bd. dirs. Ballet San Jacinto, 1985-87; adv. bd. Cmty. Ednl. TV, 1990-92. Recipient Franklin award U. Houston, 1965-67; Delta Kappa Gamma/Beta Omicron scholar, 1967-68; PTA scholar, 1973; Berwin scholar, 1976; Mary Gibbs Jones scholar, 1976-77; Found. Econ. Edn. scholar, 1976; Insts. Achievement Human Potential scholar, Phila., 1987. Mem. ACA, Clear Creek Educators Assn. (past, honorarium 1976, 77, 85), Internat. Reading Assn., U. Houston Alumni Assn. (life), Leadership Clear Lake Alumni Assn. (charter, program and projects com mem. 1986-87, edn. com. 1985), Houston Psychol. Assn., Clear Lake Toastmasters, Kappa Delta Pi, Phi Delta Kappa, Phi Kappa Phi (life), Psi Chi (life). Mem. Life Tabernacle Ch. Office: 1234 Bay Area Blvd Ste R Houston TX 77058-2538

CALLENS, CHARLOTTE, psychology educator; b. Boston, July 24, 1931; d. John Joseph and Dorothy Francis (Taylor) Losero; m. George W. White, Oct. 9, 1951 (div. 1963); children: Susan Victoria White, Johann Robert White; m. Ramon F. Callens, July 25, 1965 (dec. Oct. 1986); 1 child, Laura Charlene Callens; m. Peter Frederick Loschialpo. BA in Psychology, U. Md., 1965, PhD in Edn., 1977; MA in Psychology, George Washington U., 1968. Lic. psychologist, Md. Sch. psychologist D.C. Pub. Schs., 1966-67; prof. psychology Prince Georges C.C., Largo, Md., 1968—. Contbr. articles to profl. jours. Judge sci. projects, Largo, 1984-87. Fellow Md. Psychol. Assn. (mem. legis. com. 1990—); mem. APA, Ea. Psychol. Assn, Am. Psychol. Soc., Internat. Coun. Psychology (area chair State of Md. 1990—). Democrat. Episcopalian. Avocations: scuba diving, weight training, tennis, piano, bridge. Home: 11001 Belton St Upper Marlboro MD 20774-1401 Office: Prince Georges CC 301 Largo Rd Upper Marlboro MD 20774-2109

CALLEO, DAVID PATRICK, political science educator; b. Binghamton, N.Y., July 19, 1934; s. Patrick and Gertrude (Crowe) C.; m. Avis Thayer Bohlen. BA, Yale U., 1955, MA, 1957, PhD, 1959. Instr. polit. sci. Brown U., Providence, 1959-60; from instr. to asst. prof. polit. sci. Yale U., New Haven, 1961-67; cons. to undersec. for polit. affairs U.S. Dept. of State, Washington, 1967-68; sr. Fulbright lectr. Fed. Republic Germany, 1975; assoc. fellow Jonathan Edwards Coll, Yale U., New Haven, 1972—; v.p. Lehrman Inst., N.Y.C., 1972-87; project dir. The Twentieth Century Fund, N.Y.C., 1981-85; pres. and trustee Washington Found. for European Studies, Washington, 1987—; prof., dir. European studies Nitze Sch. Advanced Internat. Studies, Johns Hopkins U., Washington, 1968—; project dir. The 20th Century Fund, N.Y.C., 1993-99; assoc. Centre d'Etudes et de Recherches Internationales, 1993-94; enseignant invité Institut d'Etudes Politiques de Paris, 1993-94; Dean Acheson chair Nitze Sch. Advanced Internat. Studies, Washington, 1988—. Author: America and the World Political Economy, 1973 (Gladys M. Kammerer award Best Book Analyzing Am. Nat. Policy, Am. Polit. Sci. Assn. 1973), The German Problem Reconsidered, 1978, The Imperious Economy, 1982, Beyond American Hegemony, 1987, The Bankrupting of America, 1992. Trustee, Jonathan Edwards Trust. Rsch. fellow Nuffield Coll., Oxford U., 1966-67. Mem. Am. Polit. Sci. Assn., Coun. on Fgn. Rels., Internat. Inst. for Strategic Studies, Brooks' (London), Met. Club Washington, Century Assn. (N.Y.C.), The Literary Soc. (Washington). Avocations: gardening, squash, opera.

CALLETON, THEODORE EDWARD, lawyer; b. Newark, Dec. 13, 1934; s. Edward James and Dorothy (Dewey) C.; m. Elizabeth Bennett Brown, Feb. 4, 1961; children: Susan Bennett, Pamela Barritt, Christopher Dewey.; m. Kathy E'Beth Conkle, Feb. 22, 1983; 1 child, James Frederick. BA, Yale U., 1956; LLB, Columbia U., 1962. Bar: Calif. 1963, U.S. Dist. Ct. (so. dist.) Calif. 1963, U.S. Tax Ct. 1977. Assoc. O'Melveny & Myers, L.A., 1962-69; assoc. Agnew, Miller & Carlson, L.A., 1969, ptnr., 1970-79; pvt. practice L.A., 1979-83; ptnr. Kindel & Anderson, L.A., 1983-92, Calleton & Merritt, Pasadena, Calif., 1992-99, Calleton & Trytten, Pasadena, Calif., 1999—; academician Internat. Acad. Estate and Trust Law, 1974—; lectr. Calif. Continuing Edn. Bar, 1970-96, U. So. Calif. Tax Inst., 1972, 76, 91, Calif. State U., L.A., 1974-93, Practicing Law Inst., 1976-86, Am. Law Inst., 1985; bd. dirs. UCLA/Continuing Edn. of Bar Estate Planning Inst., 1979—; adj. prof. Golden Gate U. Law Sch., 1997—. Author: The Short Term Trust, 1977, A Life Insurance Primer, 1978, Calleton's Wills and Trusts, 1992-99; co-author: California Will Drafting Practice, 1982, Tax Planning for Professionals, 1985; contbr. articles to legal jours. Chmn. Arroyo Seco Master Planning Commn., Pasadena, Calif., 1970-71; bd. dirs. Montessori Sch., Inc., 1964-68, chmn., 1966-68, Am. Montessori Soc., N.Y.C., 1967-72, chmn., 1969-72; trustee Walden Sch. of Calif., 1970-86, 90-94, chmn., 1980-86; trustee Episc. Children's Home of L.A., 1971-75; bd. dirs. L.A. Master Chorale Assn., 1989-94. Lt. USMC, 1956-59. Fellow Am. Coll. Trust and Estate Counsel; mem. L.A. County Bar Assn. (chmn. taxation sect. 1980-81, chmn. probate and trust law sect. 1981-82, Dana Latham Meml. award 1996), Aurelian Honor Soc., Elihu, Beta Theta Pi, Phi Delta Phi. Home: 301 Churchill Rd Sierra Madre CA 91024-1354 Office: Calleton & Trytten Ste 678 200 S Los Robles Ave Pasadena CA 91101-4600

CALLEY, JOHN, motion picture company executive, film producer; b. N.J., 1930; m. Olinka Schoberova, 1972 (div.) m. Meg Tilly, 1995; 4 stepchildren, Emily, David, Will, Sabrina. Dir. nighttime programming, dir. programming sales NBC, 1951-57; prodn. exec. and TV producer Henry Jaffe Enterprises, 1957; v.p. radio and TV Ted Bates Advt. Agy., 1958; exec. v.p., film producer Filmways, Inc., 1960-69; with Warner Bros., Inc., Burbank, Calif., 1969-87, exec. v.p. world-wide prodn., 1969-75, pres., 1975-80, vice chmn. bd., 1977-80, cons., 1980-87; film prodr., 1987—; pres., COO, United Artists Pictures, 1993-96; pres., CEO, Sony Pictures Entertainment, Inc., Culver City, Calif., 1996—, now chmn., CEO. Office: care Sony Pictures Entertainment Inc 10202 Washington Blvd Culver City CA 90232-3119*

CALLIER, MARIA CECILE, writer, actress. BA in English Edn., U. No. Colo., 1979. Cert. secondary tchr. English. Broadcast journalist and prodr. various TV and pub. radio sta. programs, Colo., 1983—; freelance writer Colo., 1993—; pub. rels. dir. and grantwriter Grand River Hosp. Dist., Rifle, Colo., 1997-98; pub. rels. writer Colo. Mountain Coll., Glenwood Spring, Colo., 1997—; tchr. various schs. in Denver area and Roaring Fork Valley, 1979-96; sales and mktg. rep. various radio stas. Colo., 1986—; local coord. and cmty. counselor, Acad. Yr. Am., Am. Inst. Foreign Study, 1991—, Au Pair in Am., 1992-97; local coord. Multiple Sclerosis Walk, Glenwood Springs, Colo., 1998. Appeared in (films) Christmas Vacation '95, Murder in High Places, He's Still There, Endangered Species; (TV shows) Unsolved Mysteries, Sky Merchant Home Shopping Program; provides voiceover and narration for various TV and radio commls. Mem. SAG, NAFE, Nat. Writer's Union. Home and Office: 610 Cowdin Ave Unit B Glenwood Springs CO 81601

CALLIES, DAVID LEE, lawyer, educator; b. Chgo., Apr. 21, 1943; s. Gustav E. and Ann D. Callies; m. Laurie Breeden, Dec. 28, 1996; 1 child, Sarah Anne. AB, DePauw U., 1965; JD, U. Mich., 1968; LLM, U. Nottingham, England, 1969. Bar: Ill. 1969, Hawaii 1978. Spl. asst. states atty. McHenry County, Ill., 1969; assoc. firm Ross, Hardies, O'Keefe, Babcock & Parsons, Chgo., 1969-75; ptnr. Ross, Hardies, O'Keefe, Babcock & Parsons, 1975-78; prof. law Richardson Sch. Law, U. Hawaii, Honolulu, 1978—; Benjamin A. Kudo prof. law U. Hawaii, Honolulu, 1995—; mem. adv. com. on planning and growth mgmt. City and County of Honolulu Coun., 1978-88, mem. citizens adv. com. on State Functional Plan for Conservation Lands, 1979-93. Author: (with Fred P. Bosselman) the Quiet Revolution in Land Use Control, 1971 (with Fred P. Bosselman and John S. Banta) The Taking Issue, 1973, Regulating Paradise: Land Use Controls in Hawaii, 1984, (with Robert Freilich and Tom Roberts) Cases and Materials on Land Use, 1986, 3d edit., 1999, Preserving Paradise: Why Regulation Won't Work, 1994 (in Japanese 1994, in Chinese 1999), Land Use Law in the United States, 1994; editor: After Lucas: Land Use Regulation and the Taking of Property Without Compensation, 1993, Takings! Land Development Conditions and Regulatory Takings: After Dolan and Lucas, 1995, (with Hylton, Moudelker and Franzese) Property Law and the Public Interest, 1998. Life Fell., Clare Hall, Cambridge Univ. Named Best Prof., U. Hawaii Law Sch., 1990-91, 91-92; Mich. Ford Found. fellow U. Nottingham (Eng.), 1969, fgn. rsch. fellow Clare Hall, Cambridge U., 1999. Mem. ABA (chmn. com. on land use, planning and zoning 1980-82, coun. sect. on state and local govt. 1981-85, 95—, exec. com. 1986-90, sec. 1986-87, chmn. 1989-90), Am. Law Inst., Am. Inst. Cert. Planners, Am. Planning Assn., Hawaii State Bar Assn. (chair, real property and fin. svc. sect., 1997), Am. Bar Found., Ill. Bar Assn., Internat. Bar Assn. (coun. Asia Pacific Forum 1993-96, co-chair Acads. Forum 1994-96, chair 1996-98), Nat. Trust for Hist. Preservation, Royal Oak Soc., Sierra Club, Lambda Alpha Internat. (pres. Aloha chpt. 1989-90, Internat. Mem. of Yr. 1994). Home: 1532 Kamole St Honolulu HI 96821-1424 Office: U Hawaii Richardson Sch Law 2515 Dole St Honolulu HI 96822-2328

CALLIGAN, WILLIAM DENNIS, retired life insurance company executive; b. Hibbing, Minn., Mar. 21, 1925; s. Raymond George and Ann Matilda (Olson) C.; m. Aletha E. Cornelius, Dec. 21, 1949; children—Ann M., Timothy M. B.A., Yankton (S.D.) Coll., 1949. With N.Y. Life Ins. Co., 1953—; dir. mass market products N.Y. Life Ins. Co., N.Y.C., 1963-77; v.p. pensions N.Y. Life Ins. Co., 1977-87; mem. Internat. Found. Employee Benefit Plans, Inc. Served with USMC, World War II. Home: 66 Noe Ave Madison NJ 07940-2835

CALLIS, BRUCE, insurance company executive; b. Sedalia, Mo., Dec. 4, 1939; s. George Elgin and Jo (Trigg) C.; m. Nancy Williams, Nov. 14, 1959; children: Cheryl, Kevin, Kimberly. B.S., U. Mo., 1961. Plant mgr. Boonslick Mfg. Co., Boonville, Mo., 1961-62; field claim rep. State Farm Mut.

Automobile Ins. Co., Rolla, Mo., 1963; asst. personnel mgr. State Farm Mut. Automobile Ins. Co., Columbia, Mo., 1964-66; various personnel, sales positions State Farm Mut. Automobile Ins. Co., Bloomington, Ill., 1966-76, v.p., 1976-83; sr. v.p. Office of Pres., 1983-98, exec. v.p., 1998—; bd. dirs. State Farm Life & Accident Assurance Co., State Farm Life & Annuity Co. and State Farm Internat. Svcs., State Farm Found., State Farm Rail Classic-LPGA Tour, NCAA Women's Basketball Hall of Fame. Mem. McLean County (Ill.) Bd., 1958-74; chmn. McLean County Rep. Com., Bloomington, 1978-91; bd. dirs. Brokaw Hosp., Normal, Ill., 1979-82; trustee Ill. Wesleyan U. Recipient appreciation award Am. Compensation Soc., 1969. Mem. Am. Soc. Pers. Adminstrn. (chmn. adv. com. 1976-83), Ins. Inst. for Hwy. Safety (chmn. pers. com. 1977-83), McLean County Assn. Commerce, Westminster Coll. Alumni Assn. (award 1986). Home: 4 Tami Ct Bloomington IL 61701-2018 Office: State Farm Mut Automobile Ins Co 1 State Farm Plz Bloomington IL 61701-4300

CALLIS, CLAYTON FOWLER, research chemist; b. Sedalia, Mo., Sept. 25, 1923; s. Edward J. and Mary L. (Fowler) C.; m. Sara R. Steele, Apr. 9, 1949 (dec.); children: Joanne, Judy. BA, Ctrl. Meth. Coll., Fayette, Mo., 1944; MS, U. Ill., 1946, PhD, 1948. Rsch. chemist Gen. Electric Co., Richland, Wash., 1948-51; rsch. chemist Monsanto Co., Anniston, Ala., 1951-52, Dayton, Ohio, 1952-57, St. Louis, 1957-85; dir. R & D inorganic div., St. Louis, 1969-70; dir. R & D detergents and phosphates div. Monsanto Co., St. Louis, 1971-75; dir. environ. ops. and tech. planning Monsanto Indsl. Chems. Co., St. Louis, 1975-83; dir. environ. ops. Monsanto Fibers & Intermediate Co. Monsanto Co., St. Louis, 1983-85; ret., 1985; v.p. Chelan Assocs., 1985-89, pres., 1990-91; dir. ad interim Chem. Abstracts Svc. div. Am. Chem. Soc., 1991-92, cons., 1992—; mem. exec. com. sci. adv. bd. EPA, 1984-86. Mem. editorial bd. Jour. Am. Chem. Soc., 1963-72; author: (with Ray R. Irani) Particle Size, Measurement, Interpretation and Application, 1963; contbr. articles to profl. jours.; patentee. Trustee Mt. Mercy Coll., 1979—; bd. curators Ctrl. Meth. Coll., 1983-91, 92—. Recipient Disting. Alumni award Central Meth. Coll., 1970, U. Ill. Alumni Achievement award, 1997. Mem. Am. Chem. Soc. (dir.-at-large 1977-81, chmn. bd. 1982, 83, pres.-elect 1988, pres. 1989, St. Louis award 1971, Henry A. Hill award 1990, Heroes of Chemistry award 1997), Soap and Detergent Assn. (steering com. 1975), Am. Inst. Chemists (mems. and fellows award 1984), Sigma Xi, Alpha Chi Sigma, Phi Kappa Phi, Phi Lambda Upsilon, Sigma Epsilon Pi. Republican. Presbyterian. Home: 2 Holiday Ln Saint Louis MO 63131-3238

CALLIS, JERRY JACKSON, veterinarian; b. Parrot, Ga., July 28, 1926; s. Samuel Clayton and Sue (Glover) C.; m. Loisanne Roon, July 23, 1964 (dec. Aug. 1996); 1 child, Fredrick Alan. Student, North Ga. Coll., 1943-44; D.V.M., Auburn U., 1947; M.S., Purdue U., 1949, D.Sc. (hon.), 1979; D.Sc. (hon.), Southampton Coll., 1980. With U.S. Dept. Agr., 1948-88; veterinarian-in-charge of research Plum Island Animal Ctr., 1953-56; asst. dir. Plum Island Rsch. Ctr., 1956-63, dir., 1963-87; sr. rsch. advisor Agrl. Rsch. Svc., 1987-88; cons. on animal health, 1988—; cons. Pan Am. Health Orgn., 1968—. Mem. AAAS, AVMA. Home: PO Box 537 Southold NY 11971-0537

CALLISON, CHARLES STUART, retired foreign service officer, development economist; b. Boonville, Mo., July 11, 1939; s. Charles Hugh Callison and Ruth Marie (Ecord) Woolsey; m.m Michelle My-Dung Pham, Sept. 29, 1965; children: Cynthia Thuy-Tien, Patricia Mong-Tuyen, Clarissa Thien-Huong. BS in Fgn. Svc., U. Md., 1961; cert. Vietnamese lang. course, Defense Lang. Inst., 1964; MA in S.E. Asian Studies, Yale U., 1969; PhD in Devel. Econs., Cornell U., 1976. Asst. prof. econs. Ohio U., Athens, 1973-74; econ. advisor Office of Vietnam Affairs Agy. for Internat. Devel. (AID), Washington, 1974-76; econ. advisor Bicol River Basin Devel. program AID, Naga City, Philippines, 1976-79; program economist AID, Manila, 1979-82; program economist regional office AID, Nairobi, Kenya, 1982-84, chief analysis div., 1984-87; dep. assoc. asst. adminstr. Office Policy Devel. AID, Washington, 1987-90; counselor Sr. Fgn. Svc. AID, 1987; dep. exec. dir. bd. for internat. food and agrl. devel. (BIFAD) AID, Washington, 1990-91, dep. exec. dir. Agy. Ctr. for Univ. Coop. in Devel., 1991-93; dir. Office of Econs. and Enterprise AID, Dhaka, Bangladesh, 1993-95; ret., 1995; chief of party, devel. econs policy reform analysis team Nathan Assocs. Inc., Cairo, 1996—; bd. govs. Mgrs. Network, AID, Washington, 1990-92. Author: Land-to-the-Tiller in the Mekong Delta, 1983; editor-in-chief 1960 Terrapin Yearbook, 1959-60; editl. bd. Fgn. Svc. Jour., 1990-93. Bd. dirs. Internat. Sch., Makati, Manila, 1980-82, Am. Internat. Sch., Dhaka, 1993-95. Capt. USAF, 1961-67, Vietnam. Decorated Bronze Star, Air Force Commendation medal; Vietnamese Air Force Honor medal; recipient fellowships Yale U., 1967-69, Cornell U., 1969-71 73, Ford Found., South Vietnam, 1971-73, Meritorious Honor award AID, 1993. Mem. Am. Econ. Assn., Am. Fgn. Svc. Assn. (v.p. for AID 1993), Phi Kappa Phi, Omicron Delta Kappa, Scabbard & Blade, Phi Eta Sigma, Sigma Alpha Epsilon (chpt. corres. sec. 1958-61). Democrat. Christian Ch. (Disciples of Christ). Avocations: photography, genealogy, jogging. Home: 53 Trumbull St West Haven CT 06516-7029 Office: DEPRA Project Ministry of Economy, PO Box 49/11521, Cairo Egypt

CALLISON, JAMES W., former lawyer, consultant, airline executive; b. Jamestown, N.Y., Sept. 8, 1928; s. J. Waldo and Gladys A. C.; m. Gladys I. Robinson, Oct. 3, 1959; children: Sharon Elizabeth, Maria Judith, Christopher James. AB with honors, U. Mich., 1950, JD with honors (Overbeck award 1952, Jerome S. Freud Meml. award 1953), 1953. Bar: D.C. 1954, Ga. 1960. Atty. Pogue & Neal, Washington, 1953-57; with Delta Air Lines, Inc., Atlanta, 1957-93, v.p. law and regulatory affairs, 1974-78, sr. v.p., gen. counsel, 1978-81, sr. v.p. gen. counsel, corp. sec., 1981-88; sr. v.p. legal and corp. affairs, sec. Delta Air Lines Inc., 1988-90; sr. v.p. corp. and external affairs Delta Air Lines, Inc., 1990-91, sr. v.p. corp. affairs, 1991-93; ret., 1993; cons. Inman Deming Internat., Washington. Contbr. articles to legal jours.; asst. editor: Mich. Law Rev, 1952-53. Bd. dirs. Atlanta Union Mission, sec. and chmn. pers. com., 1993—, bd. dirs. Atlanta Hist. Soc., St. Joseph's Mercy Found.; adv. bd. mem. Village St. Joseph. Recipient Papal Pro Ecclesia Et Pontifice award, 1966. Mem. ABA (vice chmn. internat. law sect. 1980-81, corp. law depts. com. 1983—), State Bar Ga. (chmn. corp. counsel sect. 1989-90), Atlanta Bar Assn. (life), Atlanta Athletic Club, Order of Coif. Home: 2034 Dunwoody Club Way Dunwoody GA 30338-3024

CALLISON, NANCY FOWLER, nurse administrator; b. Milw., July 16, 1931; d. George Fenwick and Irma Esther (Wenzel) Fowler; m. B.G. Callison, Sept. 25, 1954 (dec. Feb. 1964); children: Robert, Leslie, Linda. Diploma, Evanston Hosp. Sch. Nursing, 1952; BS, Northwestern U., 1954. RN, Calif.; cert. case mgr. Staff nurse, psychiat. dept. Downey VA Hosp., 1954-55; staff nurse Camp Lejeune Naval Hosp., 1955, 59-61; obstet. supr. Tri-City Hosp., Oceanside, Calif., 1961-62; pub. health nurse San Diego County, 1962-66; sch. nurse Rich-Mar Union Sch. Dist., San Marcos, Calif., 1966-68; head nurse San Diego County Community Mental Health, 1968-73; dir. patient care services Southwood Mental Health Ctr., Chula Vista, Calif., 1973-75; program cons. Comprehensive Care Corp., Newport Beach, Calif., 1975-79; dir. Manpower Health Care, Culver City, Calif., 1979-80; dir. nursing services Peninsula Rehab. Ctr., Lomita, Calif., 1980-81; clinic supr., coordinator utilization and authorizations, acting dir. provider relations Hawthorne (Calif.) Community Med. Group, 1981-86; mgr. Health Care Delivery Physicians of Greater Long Beach, Calif., 1986-87; cons. Quality Rev. Assocs., West L.A., 1988-93; case mgr. Mercy Physicians Med. Group, 1992-93; med. mgmt. specialist The Zenith Ins., 1993—; mem. Rehab. Nurse Coord. Network, 1992-97, treas. 1997-98; clin. coord., translator Flying Samaritans, 1965—, mem. internat. bd. dirs., 1975-77, 79-86, 89—, dir. San Quentin project, 1991-93, dir. univ. program, 1996—, pres. South Bay chpt., 1975-81, v.p., 1982-85, bd. dirs. San Diego chpt., 1987-90, pres. San Diego chpt. 1991-92, adminstr. Clinica Esperanza de Infantil Rosarito Beach 1990-93. Mem. Rehab. Nurse Coord. Network (bd. dirs., treas. 1997-98), U.S.-Mex. Border Health Assn., Cruz Roja Mexicana (Delegacion Rosarito 1986-92).

CALLISON, RUSSELL JAMES, lawyer; b. Redding, Calif., Sept. 4, 1954; s. Walter M. and Norma A. (Bruce) C. BA in Polit. Sci., U. of Pacific, 1977, JD cum laude, 1980. Bar: Calif. 1980, U.S. Dist. Ct. (ea. dist.) Calif. 1981, U.S. Dist. Ct. (no. dist.) Calif. 1986, U.S. Ct. Appeals (9th cir.) 1989. Assoc. Memering & DeMers, Sacramento, Calif., 1980-85; pres. DeMers, Callison & Donovan, P.C., Sacramento, 1985-95; ptnr. Lewis, D'Amato, Brisbois & Bisgaard, San Francisco, 1995—; spl. master Calif. State Bar, 1991—; arbitrator, judge pro tem Sacramento County Superior Ct., 1986—. Co-author: Premises Liability in California, 1996. Mem. ABA (litigation sect.), SAR (chpt. pres. 1992-93), Am. Arbitration Assn. (panel of arbitrators), Assn. Def. Counsel No. Calif., Commonwealth Club, Natomas Racquet Club, Order of Coif, Phi Alpha Delta. Republican. Episcopalian. Avocations: golf, hunting, fishing, antique restoration. Home: 3889 20th St San Francisco CA 94114 Office: Lewis D'Amato Brisbois & Bisgaard One Sansome St Ste 1400 San Francisco CA 94104-4431

CALLNER, BRUCE WARREN, lawyer; b. Camden, N.J., Sept. 20, 1948; s. Phillip David and Miriam June (Caplan) C.; m. Janet Adams, Apr. 25, 1970 (div. Dec. 1982); children: David, Michelle; m. Kathy Lynne Portnoy, Mar. 9, 1983; 1 child, Samantha. BS in Psychology, Western Mich. U., 1970; JD, U. Notre Dame, 1974. Bar: Ga. 1974, U.S. Dist. Ct. (no. dist.) Ga. 1975, U.S. Ct. Appeals (5th cir.) 1975, U.S. Ct. Appeals (11th cir.) 1981. Ptnr. Nall & Miller, Atlanta, 1974-81, Alembik, Fine & Callner, P.A., Atlanta, 1981—; lectr. law Emory U., Atlanta. Author: Georgia Domestic Relations Casefinder, 1990, 2d edit., 1996. Vol. numerous legal orgns. Mem. ABA (family law and litigation sects.). Ga. Bar Assn. (family law and litigation sects.), Atlanta Bar Assn. (family law, litigation and sects., speaker's bur.); fellow Am. Acad. Matrimonial Lawyers, Nat. Council Family Relations, Southeastern Council Family Relations, NOW, Assn. Family Conciliation Cts. Democrat. Jewish. E-mail: bcallner@afclaw.com. Home: 956 Heritage Hls Decatur GA 30033-4146 Office: Alembik Fine & Callner PA 4th Fl Marquis One Tower 245 Peachtree Center Ave NE Atlanta GA 30303-1222

CALLOW, ALLAN DANA, surgeon; b. W. Somerville, Mass., Apr. 9, 1916; s. Edward Rol and Carrie (Fowles) C.; m. Eleanor Magee (dec. 1986); children: Beverly Ann Callow Nelson, Susan Diane Callow Moseley, Allan Dana Jr.; m. Una Scully Ryan, May 26, 1989; stepchildren: Tamsin Smith, Amy Ryan. BS, Tufts U., 1938, MS, 1948, PhD in Physiology, 1952; MD, Harvard, 1942, DSc (hon.), 1987. Intern Boston City Hosp., 1942-43; rsch. fellow, resident in gen. and vascular surgery Tufts New Eng. Med. Ctr., Boston, 1947-51; vice chmn. dept. surgery Tufts New Eng. Med. Ctr., 1966-82; cons. vascular surgery, dir. Vascular Surgery Rsch. Group, TNEMC, 1982-90; prof. surgery vascular div. Washington Univ Sch Medicine, St. Louis, 1990-94; rsch. prof. medicine, surgery Boston U. Med. Ctr., 1995—; mem. Whitaker Inst. Advanced Cardiovascular Rsch.; spl. fellow vascular diseases Mayo Clinic, Rochester, Minn., 1948-49; instr. to prof. surgery Tufts U. Sch. Medicine, Boston, 1948-64; cons. to surgeon gen. Med. Corps, U.S. Navy, also civilian community hosps.; mem. study com. div. med. scis. NRC, 1969-72. Author: Carotid Surgery, 1996; editor: Vascular Surgery, 1995; assoc. editor Jour. Vasc. Surgery, 1969—; contbr. articles on vascular surgery, gen. surgery, med. edn. to profl. jours. Trustee Tufts U., 1971—, chmn. bd., 1977-87; trustee Civic Edn. Found., Lincoln Filene Center; chmn. bd. deacons Wellesley Congl. Ch., 1962-66. With M.C. USNR, 1943-46, PTO; rear adm. Res. (ret.). Decorated Legion of Merit; recipient award Hellenic Internat. Red Cross, Predl. medal Tufts U. Mem. Internat. Cardiovascular Soc. (sec.-gen. 1967-77, pres. 1977-79, pres. N.Am. chpt. 1974-75), A.C.S. (gov. 1974—, pres. Mass. chpt. 1973), New Eng. Surg. Soc., AMA (ho. dels. 1966-70), New Eng. Soc. Vascular Surgery (pres. 1977-78), Soc. Vascular Surgery (pres. 1986), Soc. Biomaterials (Clemson award 1988), Boston Surg. Soc. (pres. 1978), Mass. Med. Soc., Mass. Soc. Med. Rsch. (pres. 1988—), Am. Surg. Assn., European Soc. Vascular Surgery, So. Vascular Assn., Assn. Med. Consultants to Armed Forces, Navy Inst., Navy League, Navy Res. Officers Assn., Phi Beta Kappa, Sigma Xi, Delta Upsilon, Alpha Omega Alpha; hon. mem. Hellenic, Mexican, Argentine socs. angiology, Italian, Belgian surg. socs., European Soc. Cardiovascular Surgery. Clubs: Union (Boston), Wardroom (Boston). Home: 329 Hammond St Chestnut Hill MA 02467-1207 Office: Boston U Med Ctr 80 E Concord St Boston MA 02118-2307

CALLOW, KEITH MCLEAN, judge; b. Seattle, Jan. 11, 1925; s. Russell Stanley and Dollie (McLean) C.; m. Evelyn Case, July 9, 1949; children: Andrea, Douglas, Kerry. Student, Alfred U., 1943, CCNY, 1944, Biarritz Am. U., 1945; BA, U. Wash., 1949, JD, 1952. Bar: Wash. 1952, D.C. 1974. Asst. atty. gen. Wash., 1952; law clk. to justice Supreme Ct. Wash., 1953; dep. pros. atty. King County, 1954-56; ptnr. Little, LeSourd, Palmer, Scott & Slemmons, Seattle, 1957-62, Barker, Day, Callow & Taylor, 1964-68; judge King County Superior Ct., 1969-71, Ct. of Appeals Wash., Seattle, 1972-84; presiding chief judge Ct. of Appeals Wash., 1985-90; justice State Supreme Ct. Wash., Olympia, 1985-90, chief justice, 1989-90; 2d v.p. Conf. of Chief Justices; Booneville Power Admin. Rate Hearings Officer, 1995-96; lectr. bus. law U. Wash., 1956-62, Shefelman Disting. lectr., 1991; faculty Nat. Jud. Coll., 1980, Seattle U. Environ. Law, 1992, 94-95; co-organizer, sec. Coun. of Chief Judges of Cts. of Appeals; Rep. of Estonia, 1993-96, advisor Nat. Ct. and Ministry of Justice; advisor Kyrgyzstan, Kazakhstan, Georgia, Armenia, 1997; presenter in field. Editor-in-chief Commercial Law Desk Book, 1992-95; editor works in field. Chief Seattle coun. Boy Scouts Am.; adviser Gov. Health Care Commn. State of Washington, 1991-92; pres. Young Men's Rep. Club, 1957. With AUS, 1943-46. Decorated Purple Heart; recipient Brandeis award Wash. State Trial Lawyers Assn., 1981, Douglas award, 1990. Fellow Am. Bar Found.; mem. ABA (chmn. com. on judiciary 1984-90), Wash. State Bar Assn. (mem. exec. com., appellate Judges Conf.), D.C. Bar Assn., Seattle-King County Bar Assn., Estate Planning Coun., Navy League, Rainier Club (sec. 1978, trustee 1989-92), Forty Nine Club (pres. 1972), Masons, Rotary, Psi Upsilon, Phi Delta Phi.

CALLOW, WILLIAM GRANT, retired state supreme court justice; b. Waukesha, Wis., Apr. 9, 1921; s. Curtis Grant and Mildred G. C.; m. Jean A. Zilavy, Apr. 15, 1950; children: William G., Christine S., Katherine H. PhB in Econs, U. Wis., 1943, JD, 1948. Bar: Wis. Asst. city atty. Waukesha, 1948-52; city atty., 1952-60; county judge Waukesha, 1961-77; justice Supreme Ct. Wis., Madison, 1978-92; asst. prof. U. Minn., 1951-52; mem. faculty Wis. Jud. Coll., 1968-75; Wis. commr. Nat. Conf. Commrs. on Uniform State Laws, 1967—; arbitrator Wis. Employment Rel. Commn.; arbitrator-mediator bus. disputes; arbitration and mediation nat. and internat. res. judge, 1992—. With USMC, 1943-45; with USAF, 1951-52, Korea. Recipient Outstanding Alumnus award U. Wis., 1973. Fellow Am. Bar Found.; mem. ABA, Dane County Bar Assn., Waukesha County Bar Assn. Episcopalian.

CALLOWAY, DORIS HOWES, nutrition educator; b. Canton, Ohio, Feb. 14, 1923; d. Earl John and Lillian Ann (Roberts) Howes; m. Nathaniel O. Calloway, Feb. 14, 1946 (div. 1956); children: David Karl, Candace; m. Robert O. Nesheim, July 4, 1981. BS, Ohio State U., 1943; PhD, U. Chgo., 1947; DSc (hon.), Tufts U., 1992. Head metabolism lab., nutritionist, chief div. QM Food and Container Inst., Chgo., 1951-61; chmn. dept. food sci. and nutrition Stanford Rsch. Inst., Menlo Park, Calif., 1961-63; prof. U. Calif., Berkeley, 1963-91, provost prof. schs. and colls., 1981-87, prof. and provost emeritus, 1987—; mem. expert adv. panel on nutrition WHO, Geneva, 1972-92, tech. adv. com. Consultative Group on Internat. Agrl. Rsch., 1989-93, Internat. Commn. on Health Rsch. for Devel., 1987-90, adv. coun. Nat. Inst. Arthritis, Metabolic and Digestive Diseases, Nat. Inst. Aging, NIH, Bethesda, Md., 1974-77, 78-82; trustee Internat. Maize and Wheat Improvement Ctr., 1983-88; trustee, bd. dirs. Winrock Internat. Inst.; cons. FAO, UN, Rome, 1971, 74-75, 81-83; lectr. Cooper Meml., 1983, Roberts Meml., 1985. Author: Nutrition and Health, 1981, Nutrition and Physical Fitness 11th edit., 1984; mem. editorial bd. Am. Dietetic Assn. Jour., 1974-77, Environmental Biology and Medicine, 1969-79. Recipient Meritorious Civilian Svc. Dept. Army, 1959, Disting. Achievement in Nutrition Rsch. award Bristol-Myers Squibb, 1994, Edna and Robert Langholtz Internat. Nutrition award Am. Dietetic Assn., 1997; named Disting. Alumna Ohio State U., 1974, Wellcome vis. prof. Fedn. Am. Soc. Exptl. Biol., U. Mo., 1980. Fellow Internat. Union of Nutritional Scis., Am. Inst. Nutrition (pres. 1982-83, sec. 1969-72, editorial bd. 1967-72, Conrad A. Elvehjem award 1986); mem. Inst. Medicine NAS, Sigma Xi. Office: U Calif Morgan Hall Berkeley CA 94720

CALLOWAY, JEAN MITCHENER, mathematician, educator; b. Indianola, Miss., Dec. 18, 1923; s. James Earl and Mittie Lou (Mitchener) C.; m. Anne Marie Whitney, June 21, 1952; children—Nancy Lou, Catherine Anne. BA with high honors, Millsaps Coll., 1944; AM, U. Pa., 1949, PhD, 1952. With Millsaps Coll., 1944, McCallie Sch., Chattanooga, 1944-47; with U. Pa., 1947-52; asst. prof. Carleton Coll., 1952-58, assoc. prof., 1958-60, acting chmn., 1958-59; Olney prof. math. Kalamazoo Coll., 1960-91, prof. emeritus, 1991—, chmn. dept., 1960-73; mem. study group Sch. Math., Inst. Advanced Study, 1959; writer math. workshop Ednl. Svcs., Inc., Mombasa, Kenya, 1965. Author: Fundamentals of Modern Mathematics, 1964. Vol. coord. Irving S. Gilmore Internat. Keyboard Festival, 1990-91. Mem. AAUP (pres. Kalamazoo Coll. chpt. 1964-65), Am. Math. Soc., Math. Assn. Am. (chmn. Mich. sect. 1963-64, mem. com. on undergrad. program in math. 1986-88, Disting. Svc. award Mich. sect. 1994), Sigma Xi. Home: 1341 Bunkerhill Dr Kalamazoo MI 49009-8049

CALLOWAY, LARRY, columnist; b. Lovell, Wyo., Nov. 21, 1937; s. Joseph Charles and Frances (Linda) C.; children: Lara, Maia. BA, U. Colo., 1962. Staff writer United Press Internat., 1963-69; gov. and polit. writer The Associated Press, Santa Fe, 1969-79; bureau chief, zoned-edition editor The Albuquerque Jour., 1980-88, featured columnist, 1988—. Stanford U. fellow, 1979-80. Home: 12 Reno Rd Santa Fe NM 87505-2133 Office: Albuquerque Jour 328 Galisteo St Santa Fe NM 87501-2606

CALLOWAY, MARK T., prosecutor; married. Grad. in Polit. Sci., N.C. State U., 1980, JD, 1983. Bar: N.C. 1983, U.S. Dist. Ct. (we., mid., ea. dists.) N.C., U.S. Ct. Appeals (4th cir.), U.S. Supreme Ct. Rsch. asst. to Hon. Jack L. Cozort N.C. Ct. Appeals; law clk. to Hon. Robert D. Potter U.S. Dist. Ct. (we. dist.) N.C.; assoc., then ptnr./shareholder James, McElroy & Diehl, P.A., Charlotte, N.C., 1987-94; U.S. atty. for we. dist. N.C. U.S. Dept. Justice, Charlotte, 1994—. Office: US Atty We Dist NC 227 W Trade St Charlotte NC 28202-1675

CALLSEN, CHRISTIAN EDWARD, medical device company executive; b. 1938; married. AB, Miami U., 1959; MBA, Harvard U., 1966. With Cole Nat. Corp., Cleve., 1966-87, various mgmt. and v.p. positions, 1966-87, exec. v.p., 1983-87; pres. Hyatt Legal Svcs., Cleve., 1987-90, Profl. Vet. Hosps., Detroit, 1991, Profl. Med. Mgmt., Cleve., 1992—, Applied Med. Tech., Cleve., 1993-96; chmn., CEO Allen Med. Sys., Cleve., 1995—; pres. Polymer Concepts, Inc., 1999; dir. Sight Resources Corp. Lt. USN, 1959-64. Home: 235 College St Hudson OH 44236-2908 Office: 15637 Neo Pkwy Cleveland OH 44128-3150

CALLUM, MYLES, magazine editor, writer; b. Lynn, Mass., Apr. 4, 1934; s. Abraham Edward and Ann Edith (Caswell) C.; m. Suzanne Connellis, Apr. 22, 1967 (div. 1974); children—Deborah, Jennifer. Student, U. Conn., 1951-53, N.Y. U., 1958-61. Pvt. investigator Stamford, Conn., 1958-59; assoc. editor Leisure mag., N.Y.C., 1959-60; asst. editor Good Housekeeping mag., N.Y.C., 1961-63; asso. editor Good Housekeeping mag., 1963-69, dir. spl. publs. div., 1969-70; mng. editor Better Homes and Gardens, Des Moines, 1971-75; assoc. editor TV Guide, Radnor, Pa., 1977-86; sr. editor. TV Guide, Radnor, 1986-91; sr. writer TV Guide, N.Y.C., 1991-96, contbg. editor, 1996-97; White House cons., writer Fed. health programs, 1968. Author: Body-Building and Self-Defense, 1961, Body Talk, 1972, also articles. Served with CIC AUS, 1955-57. Mem. Mensa, U.S. Chess Fedn., Greater Phila. Search and Rescue. Home: 2367 Julio Ln Santa Rosa CA 95401-5725

CALMAN, CRAIG DAVID, writer, actor, director; b. Riverside, Calif., June 11, 1953. Student, Pacific U., Forest Grove, Oreg., 1971-72, U. de Querétaro, Mex., 1972-73; BA in Motion Picture/TV, UCLA, 1975. Sr. admitting worker UCLA Med. Ctr., 1974-76; actor/playwright Old Globe Theatre, San Diego, 1977-78, Off Broadway and regional, N.Y.C. and East Coast, 1979-86; exec. asst. various film/TV studios and law firms, L.A., 1986-89, Orion Pictures Corp., L.A., 1989-90; dir. staged readings L.A., 1991—; Actor with starring roles (TV and film) ADP Industrial, Teamwork, Macbeth, Flesteron in Amazonia, co-starring/lead roles in Commercial Break, Sullivan's Travels; actor with co-starring/lead roles (theatre) in Book of the Dead, Dark Lady of the Sonnets, Hamlet, Rosencrantz and Guildenstern are Dead, Much Ado About Nothing, Too True to be Good, Henry V, The Counterfeit Rose, Richard III, The Rivals, Merchant of Venice, A Day for Surprises, The Tavern, Madame De..., and others; columnist World Wide Web mag. FilmZone, 1995-97. Author play/screenplays: The Turn of the Century, Strangled Nocturne, Skidoo Ruins; author novel: The Turn of the Century; author one-act plays, screenplays, full-length plays, poetry; writer asst. Hal Roach, Bel Air, Calif., 1987-88. Vol. book reader Recording for the Blind, L.A., 1991—. Recipient Old Globe Theatre Atlas award for best actor in a comedy role for Too True to be Good, 1977-78; Helene Wurlitzer Found. of N.Mex. Writers Residency grantee, 1988; finalist Walt Disney fellowship program, 1992, Chesterfield Film Writers Project, 1997. Mem. SAG, Actors Equity Assn. Office: 6632 Lexington Ave Ste 77 Los Angeles CA 90038-1306

CALMAN, ROBERT FREDERICK, mining executive; b. Mineola, N.Y., May 14, 1932; s. William Arthur and Ida (Albersworth) C.; m. Susan Jean Raphael, June 20, 1959 (div. 1978); children: Andrew Frederick, Camille, Matthew Alexander; m. Doris Sumerson, June 9, 1979. B.A., Yale U., 1954; M.S., MIT, 1967. With Chase Manhattan Bank, N.Y.C., 1954-61; asst. treas. Chase Manhattan Bank, 1961; with Mobil Oil Corp., N.Y.C., 1961-70; treas. N.Am. div. Mobil Oil Corp., 1964-68, treas. Internat. div., 1968-69; v.p. finance, treas. IU Internat. Corp., Phila., 1970-72; group v.p. devel. IU Internat. Corp., 1972-74, exec. v.p., 1974-78, vice chmn., 1978-85, chmn. fin. com., dir., 1986-88; chmn., dir. Echo Bay Mines Ltd., Edmonton, Alta., Can., 1981-96; bd. dirs. Corp. Cons. Group, Ltd., Bank of N.Y. Trust Co. of Fla., The Gold Inst., Am. Mining Congress; lectr. NYU, 1968-69. Author: Linear Programming and Cash Management/Cash Alpha, 1968. Pres., Phila. chpt. Nat. Found. for Ileitis and Colitis, Inc., 1974-75; pres., mem. bd. govs. Soc. Alfred P. Sloan Fellows; dir. alumni fund, mem. corp. devel. com. Mass. Inst. Tech. Served to 1st lt., arty. AUS, 1955-57. Recipient E.P. Brooks prize Mass. Inst. Tech., 1967. Mem. Phi Beta Kappa, Phi Gamma Delta. Republican. Christian Scientist. Office: 241 S 6th St Apt 2302 Philadelphia PA 19106-3736

CALNAN, ARTHUR FRANCIS, ophthalmologist; b. Boston, Mar. 11, 1926; s. Augustine Francis and Mary Ellen (Callahan) C.; m. Jeanne Elizabeth Faber, Nov. 27, 1954; children: Kathleen, Diane, Barbara, Jeffrey, Douglas, David. BS, Tufts U., 1946, MD, 1950; MS, U. Pa., 1954. Diplomate Am. Bd. Ophthalmology, Am. Bd. Med. Examiners. Rotating intern St. Louis City Hosp., 1950-51; resident ophthalmology, rsch. fellow Wills Eye Hosp., Phila., 1954-55, resident, 1955-57; preceptorship Trygye Gundersen MD, Boston, 1957-65; chair ophthamology dept. Lahey Clinic, Boston, 1965-70; sr. mem. South Suburban Ophthalmology, Hingham, Mass., 1970—; clin. instr. ophthalmology Tufts U. Sch. Medicine, 1958; mem. active staff ophthalmology South Shore Hosp., Weymouth, Mass., 1960—; jr. assisting surgeon ophthalmology Carney Hosp., Dorchester, Mass., 1963—; asst. ophthalmology Milton (Mass.) Hosp., 1973—. Mem. Plymouth County Rep. Club. Served to capt. USAF, 1950-53. Recipient Humanitarian of Yr. award Vis. Nurse Assn., 1992. Mem. AMA, Internat. Assn. Ocular Surgeons, Am. Acad. Ophthalmology, Am. Intra-Ocular Implant Soc., New Eng. Ophthalmol. Soc., Mass. Soc. Ophthalmic Physicians and Surgeons, Mass. Med. Soc., Norfolk-South Med. Soc., Am. Soc. Cataract and Refractive Surgeons, Am. Soc. Contemporary Ophthalmology, Contact Lens Assn. Ophthalmologists, Mass. Eye and Ear Infirmary Alumni Assn., Wills Eye Hosp. Alumni Assn., Erie Soc., Clan Gillean Assn., South Shore C. of C., Air Force Assn., Guild St. Luke. Roman Catholic. Avocations: travel, gardening, music. Home: 170 Old Oaken Bucket Rd Scituate MA 02066-4435 Office: S Suburban Ophthalmology 31 Derby St Hingham MA 02043-3706

CALNEK, BRUCE WIXSON, veterinary virologist; b. Manchester, N.Y., Jan. 29, 1932; married, 1954; 2 children. DVM, Cornell U., 1955, MS, 1956. Diplomate Am. Coll. Vet. Microbiology, Am. Coll. Poultry Vets. Acting asst. prof. poultry disease Cornell U., 1956-57; assoc. prof. vet. sci. U. Mass., 1957-61; prof. avian disease Cornell U., Ithaca, N.Y., 1961-95, chmn. dept. avian and aquatic animal medicine, 1977-95, Steffen prof. vet. medicine emeritus, 1995—; Nat. Cancer Inst. fellow virology U. Calif., Berkeley, 1967-68; vis. scientist oncology Houghton Poultry Rsch. Sta., Eng., 1974-75; cancer rsch. fellow Internat. Union Against Cancer, 1974-75; cons. virology study sect. NIH, 1975-79; vis. scientist CSIRO, Melbourne, Australia, 1983-84. Mem. AVMA, Am. Assn. Avian Pathologists, World Vet Poultry Assn. Achievements include research in viral oncology, with particular emphasis on pathogenesis of avian neoplastic diseases of chickens induced by DNA-containing viruses, known as Marek's disease. Office: Cornell U Coll Vet

Medicine Dept Microbiology/Immunolog Unit Avian Medicine Ithaca NY 14853*

CALOGERO, PASCAL FRANK, JR., state supreme court chief justice; b. New Orleans, Nov. 9, 1931; s. Pascal Frank and Louise (Moore) C.; children—Deborah Ann Calogero Applebaum, David, Pascal III, Elizabeth, Thomas, Michael, Stephen, Gerald, Katherine, Christine. Student, Loyola U., New Orleans, 1949-51, J.D., 1954; ML in the Jud. Process, U. Va., 1992; DLL (hon.), Loyola U., New Orleans. Bar: La. Ptnr. Landrieu, Calogero & Kronlage, 1958-69, Calogero & Kronlage, 1969-73; gen. counsel La. Stadium and Expn. Dist., 1970-73; assoc. justice Supreme Ct. La., New Orleans, 1973-90, chief justice, 1990—. Mem. La. Democratic State Central Com., 1963-71; mem. subcom. on del. selection La. Dem. Party, 1971; del. Dem. Nat. Conv., 1968. Served to capt. JAGC U.S. Army, 1954-57. Recipient Disting. Jurist award La. Bar Founds., 1991; Judge Bob Jones Meml. award, Am. Judges Assn., 1995. Mem. ABA, La. Bar Assn., New Orleans Bar Assn., Greater New Orleans Trial Lawyers Assn. (v.p. 1967-69), Order of the Coif. Office: Supreme Ct La 301 Loyola Ave New Orleans LA 70112-1814*

CALOVSKI, NASTE, diplomat. Macedonia rep. to UN, N.Y.C. Office: UN 866 U N Plz Rm 517-518 New York NY 10017-1822

CALTER, PAUL ARTHUR, mathematics educator, mechanical engineer; b. N.Y.C., June 18, 1934; s. Arthur and Frances (Bankowitz) Calcaterra; m. Margaret Jolind Carey, May 13, 1959; children: Amy, Michael. BS in Engring., The Cooper Union, N.Y., 1962; MS in Mech. Engring., Columbia U., 1966; MFA in Sculpture, Norwich U., 1993. Lab. technician Columbia U., 1952-60; devel. engr. Kollsman Instrument Corp., 1960-65; sr. project engr. Intertype Co., Bklyn., 1965-68; prof. math. Vt. Tech. Coll., 1968-89, prof. emeritus, 1990—, dir. Summer Math. Insts., 1989—; vis. prof. math. Dartmouth Coll., 1997. Author: Problem Solving with Computers, 1973, Magic Squares, 1977, Schaum's Outline of Technical Mathematics, 1979, Technical Mathematics, 1983, 3d edit., 1995, Practical Math Handbook for the Building Trades, 1983, Mathematics for Electricity and Electronics, 1984, Mathematics for Computer Technology, 1986, Technical Calculus, 1988, 2d edit., 1999, Technical Mathematics with Calculus, 1984, 3d edit., 1995, Introductory Algebra and Trigonometry, 1997. With U.S. Army, 1957-59. Recipient Ralph Horton Meml. award in Sci., 1952; vis. scholar Dartmouth Coll., 1995. Mem. ASME, Am. Math. Assn. 2-Year Colls., Math. Assn. Am., Nat. Coun. Tchrs. Math., Vols. Tech. Assistance, Coll. Art Assn., New Eng. Math. Assn. 2-Year Colls., Internat. Sculpture Soc., Leonardo-The Internat. Soc. for the Arts, Scis. and Tech. Avocations: sculpture, painting, mountaineering. Home: 33 S Pleasant St Randolph VT 05060-1318

CALTON, SANDRA JEANE, accountant; b. Portales, N.Mex., Feb. 3, 1945; d. Lloyd Paul and Nana Mae (Parris) Grant; m. Gary Jim Calton, Nov. 26, 1964; children: Deborah, April, Craig. BS, Ea. N.Mex. U., 1967, U. Md., 1984. CPA, Md. Comptr. Purification Engring. Inc., Columbia, Md., 1981-85, IBF Biotechnics Inc., Savage, Md., 1987-88; pres. Srchem, Inc., Elkridge, Md., 1988—; acct. Calton Rsch. Assocs., Elkridge, 1974—; v.p. Calwood Chem. Industries, Inc., Elkridge, 1991—, AuRx, Inc., Elkridge, 1996—. Treas. Howard Coun. Extension Homemakers Coun., Ellicott City, Md., 1984. Mem. AICPA, Nat. Soc. Tax Profls., Md. Assn. CPAs. Home: 5331 Landing Rd Elkridge MD 21075-5717

CALVANI, TERRY, lawyer, former government official, law educator; b. Carlsbad, N.Mex., Jan. 29, 1947; s. Torello Howard and Mary Virginia (Hawkins) C.; m. Mary Virginia Anderson, May 3, 1969; m. 2d, Judith Thompson, Aug. 28, 1980; children: Dominic Mario, Torello Howard. BA, U. N.Mex., 1969; JD with distinction, Cornell U., 1972. Bar: N.Mex. 1972, Calif. 1972, Tenn. 1978, D.C. 1992, U.S. Dist. Ct. N.Mex. 1972, U.S. Dist. Ct. (no. dist.) Calif. 1972, U.S. Dist. Ct. (mid. dist.) Tenn. 1978, U.S. Dist. Ct. D.C. 1994—, U.S. Ct. Appeals (9th cir.) 1972, U.S. Ct. Appeals (6th cir.) 1977, U.S. Ct. Appeals (5th cir.) 1981, U.S. Ct. Appeals (11th cir.) 1981, U.S. Ct. Appeals (D.C. cir.) 1994, U.S. Supreme Ct. 1985. Teaching fellow Stanford U. Law Sch., 1972-73; assoc. Pillsbury, Madison & Sutro, San Francisco, 1973-74, ptnr., 1990—; asst. prof. law Vanderbilt U. Sch. Law, Nashville, 1974-77, assoc. prof., 1977-80, prof., 1980-83; vis. prof. law U. Va., Charlottesville, 1981-82; of counsel Haskell Slaughter & Young, Birmingham, Ala., 1980-83; commr. U.S. FTC, 1983-90; acting chmn., 1985-86; lectr. law Sch. Law Harvard U., 1998—. Author: (with John Siegfried) Economic Analysis and Antitrust Law, 1979, 2d edit., 1988; bd. editors Antitrust Bull., 1982—, Bur. Nat. Affairs RICO Report, 1986-96. Mem. Am. Law Inst., ABA (chmn. spl. com. to study antitrust penalties and damages Antitrust Sect. 1979-82, chmn. Robinson-Patman com. antitrust sect. 1981-83, council mem. 1985-86, 90-93), 6th Cir. Jud. Conf. (life), Adminstrv. Conf. U.S. 1985-90, Newcomen Soc. N.Am., Order of Coif. Republican. Roman Catholic. Clubs: The Club (Birmingham), The G.C. of Tenn. (Nashville), Olympic (San Francisco), Pacific Union (San Francisco), Riverside Country Club (Carlsbad, N.Mex.). The Harvard Faculty Club (Cambridge, MA); The Colonnade Club (Charlottesville, VA). Office: Pillbury Madison & Sutro 1100 New York Ave NW Lbby 9 Washington DC 20005-6178 also: 235 Montgomery St San Francisco CA 94104-2902

CALVANICO, JOSEPH JAMES, financial company executive; b. Burlington, Vt., Mar. 22, 1961; s. Nickolas Joseph and Rose Marie (Hlobil) C.; m. Susan Ann Calvanico, May 20, 1989. BA in Econs., U. Wis., 1987. Appraiser JM Cleminshaw Co., Waukesha, Wis., 1982-83; v.p. Tysen & Assoc. Appraisal, Milw., 1983-87; staff appraiser Valuation Rsch. Corp., Milw., 1986-87; mgr. property tax Morton Thiokol Inc., Chgo., 1988-91; mgr. Price Waterhouse, Chgo., 1991-92; sr. mgr. KPMG Peat Marwick, Chgo., 1992-97, ptnr., 1997—; textbook and edn. com. Inst. of Property Tax, 1993—; tech. advisor State Taxation Inst., 1995—. Editl. bd. Internat. Assn. of Assessing Officers, 1988—; article reviewer Appraisal Inst., 1989-94; contbr. articles to profl. jours. Bd. dirs. YMCA Camp Duncan, Ingleside, Ill., 1988-91; vol. Homework Hotline, Chgo., 1988-91, Chgo. Crime Commn., 1998—. Mem. Inst. of Property Taxation, Am. Soc. of Appraisers, The Appraisal Inst. Avocation: golf. Office: KPMG Peat Marwick 303 E Wacker Dr Chicago IL 60601-5212

CALVANO, LINDA SUE LEY, insurance company executive; b. Franklin, Ind., Nov. 27, 1949; d. Jiles Rex and Naomi Katherine (Van Horn) Riggs; m. Thomas Alan Ley Calvano, Feb. 28, 1987. BS in Edn. with distinction, Ind. U.-Purdue U., 1971, MS in Edn. with highest distinction, 1975. Cert. paralegal; lic. life, accident, health, property and casualty ins. agt., Ind.; cert. total quality mgmt. Elem. tchr. Indpls. Pub. Schs., 1972-74, Center Grove Community Schs., Greenwood, Ind., 1974-81; dir. adminstrn. Brougher Agy., Inc., Greenwood, 1981-84; mgr. claims/customer svc. The Associated Group, Inc., Indpls., 1984-89; v.p. team ops. Key Benefit Adminstrs., Inc., Indpls., 1989-92; regional mgr. ops. & rev. projects Anthem Blue Cross Blue Shield, Indpls., 1992-97, quality assurance dir., 1997—. Mem. cotillion com. Humane Soc. Indpls., 1991; vol. Riley Run for Children, Indpls., 1985-92. Recipient Good Girl Citizenship award Women's Aux. of Am. Legion, 1968. Mem. Am. Mgmt. Assn., Nat. Assn. Life Underwriters, Nat. Assn. Health Underwriters, Inst. Internal Auditors, Indpls. Paralegal Assn., Project Mgmt. Inst., Toastmasters Internat. Republican. Episcopalian. Home: 6358 Bluff Acres Dr Greenwood IN 46143-9037 Office: Anthem Blue Cross Blue Shield 65 Airport Pkwy Greenwood IN 46143-1439

CALVANO-SMITH, RITA, journalist, small business owner; b. Pasadena, Calif., Jan. 11, 1948; d. Alfred Augustus and Rose Lucille (DeFazio) Calvano; m. Clifford R. Smith, Nov. 6, 1992. BA in Journalism, San Diego State U., 1972, MA in Am. Studies, 1976. Reporter The Daily Californian, El Cajon, Calif., 1972-76, San Diego Tribune, 1977-92; instr. Fashion Careers of Calif., San Diego, 1993-97, Fashion Inst. Design & Merchandising, San Diego, 1993, Mira Costa C.C., Oceanside, Calif., 1992-93; pres., owner Make Mine Petite, San Diego, 1992—; vol. instr. San Diego Journalism Project, 1996; mem. fashion prodn. com. Crawford H.S., 1994—. Editor/writer PS Features, San Diego, 1996—. Recipient Cmty. Svc. award AAUW, LaMesa, Calif., 1970's, Feature Writing award AP, 1970's, Ring of Truth award Copley Press, 1980's. Democrat. Avocations: travel nationally and internationally.

CALVERA, JORGE, artist; b. Barcelona; m. Elizabeth Cure, July 20, 1968. Exhibited works in shows at Galeria Michelena, Caracas, Venezuela, 1977, 78, Gallery 3, Roanoke, Va., 1985, Veerhoff Galleries, Washington, 1991, White House Galleries, Roanoke, 1988, 89, 91, 92, 93, 95, 96, Blacksburg (Va.) Regional Arts Assn. shows, 1988, 95, 96, 97. Mem. Blacksburg Regional Arts Assn. Home: 2816 Wellesley Ct Blacksburg VA 24060-4127

CALVERLEY, JOHN ROBERT, physician, educator; b. Hot Springs, Ark., Jan. 14, 1932; s. John A. and Della (O'Neill) C.; m. Alice Mae Feller, Dec. 27, 1953; children: Mark (dec.), David. B.S., U. Oreg., 1953, M.D., 1955. Diplomate: neurology Am. Bd. Psychiatry and Neurology (dir. 1977-84, sec. 1981-83, v.p. 1983-84). Intern U. Iowa, Iowa City, 1955-56; resident in neurology U. Iowa, 1956; resident in internal medicine Mayo Found., Rochester, Minn., 1957; neurology resident Mayo Found., 1957-59; mem. faculty dept. neurology med. br. U. Tex., Galveston, 1964—; assoc. prof. med. br. U. Tex., 1966-70, prof. med. br., 1970—, chief div. neurology med. br., 1967-73, chmn. dept. neurology med. br., 1973—; interim chmn. dept. psychiatry U. Tex., Galveston, 1989-90; cons. neurology USAF, 1965-94, nat. cons. to surgeon gen., 1976-94. Capt. M.C. USAF, 1957-64. Served to capt. M.C. USAF, 1957-64. Mem. AMA (chmn. sect. coun. on neurology 1974-76), Tex. Med. Assn., Am. Acad. Neurology (exec. bd. 1983-86), Am. Neurol. Assn., Assn. Univ. Profs. of Neurology (pres. 1993-94). Home: 733 N Shore Dr Clear Lake Shores TX 77565 Office: U Tex Med Br Dept Neurology 301 University Blvd Galveston TX 77555-5302

CALVERT, C(LYDE) EMMETT, state agency adminstrator, retired; b. Lexington, Ky., Feb. 24, 1937; s. Emmett I. and Minnie (Hall) C.; m. Violet Stafford, Sept. 22, 1962; children: Emmett Bradford, Eric Brandon. BS in Commerce and Acctg., U. Ky., 1959. Rsch. asst. U. Ky., Lexington, 1959; from auditor to audit mgr. Ky. Revenue Cabinet, Lexington, 1959-87; sec. Ky. Revenue Cabinet, Frankfort, 1987-91; bd. dirs. Ky. Housing Corp., Frankfort, Ky. Workers Compensation Funding Commn., Frankfort, State Property and Bldg. Commn., Frankfort, Commonwealth Venture Fund, Ky. Employees Deferred Compensation System, Frankfort, 1991-94. Mem. tax com. Ky. Farm Bur., Louisville, 1991; vol. non-profit schs., Lexington; coach, league ofcl. various sport orgns., Lexington, 1975-86. Recipient Cert. of merit Office Vocat. Rehab., 1990. Mem. Southeastern Assn. Tax Adminstrs., Fedn. Tax Adminstrs., Lexington Yacht Club. Democrat. Presbyterian. Avocations: boating, woodworking, brick laying. Home: 3536 Castlegate Wynd Lexington KY 40502-7701

CALVERT, DAVID VICTOR, soil science educator; b. Chaplin, Ky., Feb. 26, 1934; s. Stanford Byron and Willia Neal Calvert; m. Joyce Faye LeMay, July 27, 1957; children: Victor Neal, Yvonne Carole Calvert Lee. BS, U. Ky., 1956, MS, 1958; PhD, Iowa State U., 1962. Cert. profl. soil scientist, Am. Registry of Cert Profls. in Agronomy, Crops and Soils, Ltd. Grad. rsch. asst. U. Ky., Lexington, 1956-58, Iowa State U., Ames, 1958-62; asst. prof. soil sci. U. Fla., Ft. Pierce, 1962-68, assoc. prof., 1968-76, prof., 1976—, acting dir. Indian River Rsch. & Edn. Ctr., 1978-79, dir. Indian River Rsch. & Edn. Ctr., 1979-94; ofcl. collaborator S.E. region USDA, Athens, Ga., 1965-79; cons. World Bank, Jamaican Sch. Agr., Kingston, 1970-71; cons. soil sci. Coun. for Agrl. Sci. and Tech., St. Louis. Contbr. over 175 articles to profl. jours. including Soil Sci. Soc. Am. Proceedings, Jour. Agrl., Food Chem., Jour. Environ. Quality, Soil Sci., Proceedings Internat. Soc. Citriculture. Recipient Soil-Water-Air-Plant grant USDA Agrl. Rsch. Svc., Fla., 1968-80; grantee EPA, 1970-73, Water Quality Rsch. City of Okeechobee, Fla., 1990-93, St. Johns and South Fla. Water Mgmt. Dists., Palatka and West Palm Beach, 1993-96; award Fla. Dept. Agr. and Consumer Svcs., Tallahassee, 1996—; recipient Rsch. Achievement award Fla. Fruit and Vegetable Assn., 1979, Agrl. Hall of Fame award Saint Lucie County Farm Bur., 1997; U. Ky. fellow; named Outstanding Conservationist of Yr., Soil Conservation Svc. USDA, Fla., 1983, Disting. Out-of-State Alumnus for the U. Kys. Coll. of Agrl., 1997. Mem. Soil Sci. Soc. Am., Internat. Soc. Soil Sci., Am. Soc. for Hort. Sci., Coun. of Agrl. Sci. and Tech., Soil and Crop Sci. Soc. Fla., Fla. State Hort. Soc. (hon. membership award 1997), Internat. Soc. Citriculture, Rsch. Ctr. Adminstrs. Soc., Am. Soc. Agronomy, Farmhouse Fraternity, Scovell Soc. U. Ky. (charter mem.), Sigma Xi, Gamma Sigma Delta, Alpha Zeta. Achievements include contbns. to devel. and deployment of working water quality stds. to guide growers using low-volume sprinkler and micro irrigation systems and devel. of a soil and water mgmt. strategy for control of nitrates leaching from citrus groves into surface water and ground water. Home: 1007 Grandview Blvd Fort Pierce FL 34982-4323 Office: U Fla IFAS Indian River Rsch & Edn Ctr 2199 South Rock Rd Fort Pierce FL 34945-3138

CALVERT, DELBERT WILLIAM, chemical company executive; b. Bosworth, Mo., Jan. 29, 1927; s. William McKinley and Ruby Leona (Berrier) C.; m. Mary Lee Brown, Feb. 10, 1947 (div. Mar. 1971); children: Gary D., Danial L.; m. Melva Allen Hurst, Sept. 4, 1971; stepchildren: Holly Hurst, Allen Hurst. BSCE, U. Mo., 1952. Asst. mgr. supply and transp. divsn. Phillips Petroleum Co., Bartlesville, Okla., 1952-63; asst. to v.p. Tex. Ea. Transmission Corp., Houston, 1963-65; mgr. diversification dept. No. Natural Gas Co., Omaha, 1965-68; pres. Williams Bros. Pipe Line Co., Tulsa, 1968-71; exec. v.p. The Williams Cos., Tulsa, 1971-85, also bd. dirs.; chmn. bd. Williams Energy Co., 1975-79, also bd. dirs.; chmn., CEO, Agrico Chem. Co., Tulsa, 1977-85, also bd. dirs.; pres. Williams Techs., Inc., 1992-97; chmn. of bd. Black Mesa Pipeline Co., 1996-97, adv. dir., 1997-98. Appointed to gov.'s agroindustry policy commn., 1987—; mem. exec. bd. Indian Nations council Boy Scouts Am., 1969—, pres., 1974-76; bd. dirs. Goodwill Industries Tulsa; mem. U. Mo. Devel. Fund, 1969—, chmn., 1972-73. Served with AUS, 1945-47. Mem. Okla. Petroleum Coun. (dir. 1968—, pres. 1977-78), Am. Petroleum Inst. (gen. com. div. transp. 1971), Fertilizer Industry Assn. (chmn. bd.), Potash and Phosphate Inst. (dir. 1982-85), Tulsa C. of C., Southern Hills Country (Tulsa), University (Columbia, Mo.), Waikoloa (Hawaii) Village Golf Club, Garden of Gods (Colorado Springs, Colo.), Tau Beta Pi, Chi Epsilon, Pi Mu Epsilon. Republican. Home: 7240 S Gary Ave Tulsa OK 74136

CALVERT, GORDON LEE, retired legal association executive; b. Wardensville, W.Va., Sept. 2, 1921; s. Aaron Lee and Ada (Brill) C.; m. Margaret James, June 9, 1945; children—Gordon R., Roger L., Walter R. B.A. with distinction, George Washington U., 1943, J.D. with distinction, 1945. Bar: D.C. 1946. Assoc. firm Covington & Burling, Washington, 1944-46; with Investment Bankers Assn. Am., Washington, 1946-71; exec. dir., gen. counsel Investment Bankers Assn. Am., 1966-71; exec. v.p., gen. counsel Securities Industry Assn., 1972; v.p., gen. counsel N.Y. Stock Exchange, Washington, 1973-76; exec. dir. comml. collection agy. sect. Comml. Law League Am., Washington, 1976-92. Author: Fundamentals of Municipal Bonds, 1959, Digest of Investments of State Pension Funds, 1960, Digest of State Laws Regulating Debt Collection Agencies, 1977, 81. Mem. ABA, Order of Coif, Pi Kappa Alpha, Phi Delta Phi, Omicron Delta Kappa, Met. Club (Washington), Columbia Country Club (Chevy Chase, Md.). Presbyterian. Home: 6712 Michaels Dr Bethesda MD 20817-2220

CALVERT, JACK GEORGE, atmospheric chemist, educator; b. Inglewood, Calif., May 9, 1923; s. John George and Emma (Eschstruth) C.; m. Doris Arlene Breimon, Nov. 8, 1946; children: Richard John, Mark Steven. BS in Chemistry, UCLA, 1944, PhD, 1949. Mem. faculty Ohio State U., 1950-81, prof. chemistry, 1960-81, Kimberly prof. chemistry, 1974-81, prof. emeritus, 1981—, chmn. dept., 1964-68; sr. scientist Nat. Ctr. Atmospheric Rsch., Boulder, Colo., 1982-94, sr. rsch. assoc., 1994—; cons. air pollution tng. com. USPHS, 1964-66; mem. Nat. Air Pollution Control Manpower Devel. Com., 1966-69, chmn., 1968-69; bd. dirs. Gordon Rsch. Confs., 1969-71; mem. air pollution control rsch. grants com. EPA, 1970-72, chmn., 1971-72, mem. chemistry and physics adv. com., 1973-75; chmn. air pollution com. Conservation Found., 1968-70; mem. air conservation commn. Am. Lung Assn., 1973-75; chmn. EPA environ. chemistry/physics grants rev. panel, 1979-83; mem. State of Colo. Air Quality Control Commn., 1987-90, Disting. Acad. Adv. Group of Auto/Oil Air Quality Improvement Rsch. Program, 1989-96; mem. panel on atmospheric effects of aviation NRC/NAS, 1995-98, mem. com. on ozone potential of reformulated gasoline, 1997-99; atmospheric chemistry tech. implementation panel Chem. Mfrs. Assn., 1998—. Author: (with J. N. Pitts, Jr.) Photochemistry, 1966, Graduate School in the Sciences, 1972; also articles. Ensign USNR, 1944-46. Named Honor Prof. of Year Coll. Arts and Scis., Ohio State U., 1957; recipient Alumni award for disting. tchg., 1961, Disting. Rsch. award, 1981; fellow NRC Can., 1949; Guggenheim fellow, 1977-78. Fellow Ohio Acad. Sci., Am. Inst. Chemists, Am. Geophys. Union; mem. AAUP, Am. Chem. Soc. (award for creative rsch. in environ. sci. and tech. 1981, Columbus sect. award 1981), Air Pollution Control Assn. (Chambers award 1986), Phi Beta Kappa, Sigma Xi, Pi Mu Epsilon, Phi Lambda Upsilon, Alpha Chi Sigma. Achievements include research on photochemistry, reaction kinetics, atmospheric chemistry, mechanisms free radical reactions. Office: NCAR Atmospheric Chemistry Divsn PO Box 3000 Boulder CO 80307-3000

CALVERT, JAMES FRANCIS, manufacturing company executive, retired admiral; b. Cleve., Sept. 8, 1920; s. Charles Spence and Grace (Gholson) C.; m. Nancy Ridgeway King, Aug. 9, 1942 (dec. Dec. 1965); children: James, Margaret (dec.), Charles; m. Margaretta Sergeant Harrison, Apr. 8, 1968. Student, Oberlin Coll., 1937-39, D.Sc. (hon.), 1960; B.S. in Elec. Engring., U.S. Naval Acad., 1942. Commnd. ensign U.S. Navy, 1942, advanced through grades to vice-adm., 1970; served in submarines PTO, World War II; comdr. diesel submarine U.S.S. Trigger, 1952-55; comdr. nuclear power submarine U.S.S. Skate, 1958-59, engaged in polar ops., 1958, 59; (1st submarine to break through ice and surface in Arctic Ocean), 1958, (1st ship to surface at North Pole), 1959; dir. politico-mil. policy Navy Dept., 1965-67; comdr. Cruiser-Destroyer Flotilla Eight, 1967-68; supt. U.S. Naval Acad., Annapolis, Md., 1968-72; comdr. U.S. First Fleet, 1972-73; ret., 1973; asst. to chmn. bd. Texaco Inc., N.Y.C., 1973-74; v.p. Combustion Engring., Inc., Stamford, Conn., 1974-75; v.p. ops. Combustion Engring., Inc., 1975-84, dir., 1975-84; chmn. bd. Aqua-Chem. Inc., Milw., 1989-93; corp. mem. Woods Hole Oceanographic Inst. Author: Surface at the Pole, 1960 (paperback edit. 1996), A Promise to Your Country, 1961, The Naval Profession, 1965, Silent Running, 1995. Decorated D.S.M. (2), Silver Star (2), Bronze Star (2), Legion of Merit (4), Navy Commendation ribbon, Dept. Def. Commendation medal; French Govt. Merite Maritime; recipient Presdl. Unit citation. Mem. U.S. Naval Acad. Alumni Assn., U.S. Naval Inst., Univ. Club (N.Y.C.), N.Y. Yacht Club, Chesapeake Bay Yacht Club (Easton, Md.), Cruising Club Am.

CALVERT, JAY H., JR., lawyer; b. Charleston, S.C., Mar. 19, 1945; m. Ann E., June 14, 1969; children: Amanda, Emily, Sarah. BA, Amherst (Mass.) Coll., 1967; JD, U. Va., 1970. Bar: Pa. 1970, U.S. Dist. Ct. (ea. dist.) Pa. 1970, U.S. Ct. Appeals (3d cir.) 1971, U.S. Dist. Ct. (mid. dist.) Pa. 1973, U.S. Ct. Appeals (2d cir.) 1980, U.S. Ct. Appeals (8th cir.) 1987, U.S. Supreme Ct. 1989, U.S. Dist. Ct. Ariz. 1994. Assoc. Morgan, Lewis & Bockius LLP, Phila., 1970-78, ptnr., 1978—, exec. ptnr., 1987-90, mng. ptnr., 1990-94; mem. litigation sect., firm governing bd. Morgan Lewis & Bockius LLP, Phila., 1990-98, mem. exec. com., 1997-98. Trustee Agnes Irwin Sch., Rosemont, Pa., 1988-94, Leukemia Soc. Am., Phila., 1982—; bd. dirs. St. David's Nursery Sch., Wayne, Pa., 1980-94; chmn. devel. com. Phila. Zool. Soc., 1993-96, chmn. facilities, exhibits and safety com., 1997—, bd. dirs., 1992—, vice-chmn. bd. dirs., 1994-96. Mem. ABA, Pa. Bar Assn., Phila. Bar Assn., Lawyers Club of Phila. Avocations: biking, gardening, hiking, horseback riding, animal husbandry. Fax: 215-963-5299. Office: Morgan Lewis & Bockius LLP 1701 Market St Philadelphia PA 19103-2921

CALVERT, JON CHANNING, family practice physician; b. Sonora, Calif., May 17, 1941; s. Floyd Raymond and Aloha Jean (Fernandes) C.; m. Lynnette Laurene Jacobson, June 6, 1970; children: Joshua and Stephen (twins). AB, Stanford U., 1963; MS, Baylor U., 1968, MD, 1968, PhD in Anatomy and Cell Biology, 1970, postdoctoral fellow in anatomy, 1970. Diplomate Am. Bd. Family Practice, Am. Bd. Ob-gyn. Intern Meth. Hosp., Houston, 1970-71; pvt. practice medicine Houston, 1971-73; asst. prof. anatomy and cell biology Baylor U., 1970-73; asst. prof. family practice Med. Coll. Ga., Augusta, 1973-75, assoc. prof., 1975-77, prof., 1977-82, chmn. dept., 1976-81; prof. family medicine Oral Roberts U. Sch. Medicine, Tulsa, 1982-88, chmn. dept., 1982-87, prof. dept. anatomy, 1982-88, assoc. dean clin. scis., 1984-87; chief dept. cmty. and family medicine City of Faith Med. and Rsch. Ctr., Tulsa, 1982-87; prof., chmn. dept. family medicine U. Okla. Coll. Medicine, Tulsa, 1988-92; resident in ob-gyn. U. Okla. Coll. Med., Tulsa, 1992-95; prof. family medicine, ob-gyn. U. Okla. Coll. Medicine, Tulsa, 1995—; mem. Gov.'s Joint Bd. Family Practice, 1976-81; chmn. Ga. Fedn. Family Practice Residency Programs, 1976-77; mem. Ga. Dept. Human Resources Adv. Coun. on Phys. Health Needs of Children and Youth, 1977-78; med. dir. Tri-County Health System, Inc., 1981-82, HMO of Okla., 1985-86; mem. family medicine del. to China, 1983. Mem. bd. deacons Covenant Presbyn. Ch., 1979-81; chmn. bd. govs., COO, City of Faith Med. and Rsch. Ctr., Inc., 1987-88. Fellow ACOG, Am. Acad. Family Physicians; mem. AMA, AAAS, Am. Assn. Med. Colls., So. Soc. Anatomists, So. Med. Assn. (chmn. family practice sect. 1977-78), Ga. Acad. Family Physicians (Disting. Svc. award 1975), Soc. Tchrs. Family Medicine, Sci. Rsch. Soc. N.Am., Christian Med. Soc., Tulsa County Med. Soc. Office: U Oklahoma Coll of Medicine Tulsa OK 74129

CALVERT, KEN, congressman; b. Corona, Calif., June 8, 1953. AA, Chaffey Coll., 1973; BA Econs., San Diego State U., 1975. Corona/ Norco youth chmn. for Nixon, 1968, 82; county youth chmn. rep. Vesey's Dist., 1970, 43d dist., 1972; congl. aide to rep. Vesey, Calif., 1975-79; gen. mgr. Jolly Fox Restaurant, Corona, Calif., 1975-79, Marcus W. Meairs Co., Corona, Calif., 1979-81; pres., gen. mgr. Ken Calvert Real Properties, Corona, Calif., 1981—; Reagan-Bush campaign worker, 1980; co chmn. Wilson for Senate Campaign, 1982, George Deukmejian election, 1978, 82, 86, George Bush election, 1988, Pete Wilson senate elections, 1982, 88, Pete Wilson for Gov. election, 1990; mem. 104th Congress (now 106th Congress) from 43rd Calif. dist., 1993—; mem. natural resources com., sci., space and tech. com., 1993—, also mem. ag. com.; former v.p. Corona/ Norco Rep. Assembly; chmn. Riverside Rep. Party, 1984-88, County Riverside Asset Leasing; bd. realtors Corono/ Norco. Exec. bd. Corona Community Hosp. Corp. 200 Club; mem. Corona Airport adv. commn.; adv. com. Temescal/ El Cerrito Community Plan. Mem. Riverside County Rep. Winners Circle (charter), Lincoln Club (co-chmn., charter, 1986-90), Corona Rotary Club (pres. 1991), Elks, Navy League Corona Norco, Corona C. of C. (pres. 1990), Noroco C. of C., Monday Morning Group, Corona Group (past chmn.), Econ. Devel. Ptnrship., Silver Eagles (March AFB support group, charter). Office: US Ho of Reps 1034 Longworth HOB Washington DC 20515-0543

CALVERT, LEONARD JAMES, editor, writer; b. Eugene, Oreg., Aug. 14, 1933; s. Ross Mark Calvert and Florence A. (Brooks) Ball; m. Janet K. Lohrenz, Nov. 19, 1960; children: Timothy Leonard, Douglas Jacob. BA, U. Oreg., 1955, MA, 1976. News editor Valley Sentinel, Coquille, Oreg., 1955-58; editor Argus-Observer, Ontario, Oreg., 1958-60, Headlight-Herald, Tillamook, Oreg., 1960-61; comm. specialist ext. svc. Oreg. State U., Corvallis, 1961-65, 69-95; pub. affairs officer U. Oreg., Eugene, 1967-69; editor Jour. of Ext., Eugene, 1996-99. Recipient Writing Award of Excellence, Agrl. Communicators in Edn., 1995. Mem. Soc. Profl. Journalists, Lions, Epsilon Sigma Phi (chpt. pres. 1997, Regional Disting. Svc. award 1995). Episcopalian. Avocations: gardening, music. Home and Office: 1062 Woodside Dr Eugene OR 97401-6412

CALVERT, LOIS WILSON, civic worker; b. Hartford, Conn., Sept. 12, 1924; d. Royal Wouldhave and Evelyn Charlotte (Danielson) Wilson; m. Wallace Erdix Calvert, Mar. 29, 1947; children: Pamela, Gary, Craig and David (twins). Grad., Bryant Coll., 1943. Registrar of voters Town of Simsbury, Conn., 1982—. Bd. dirs. Simsbury Hist. Soc., 1978-86, mng. dir., 1978-98; mem. Simsbury Com. on Aging, 1980-89, Friends of Simsbury Libr.; trustee Simsbury Cemetery Assn., 1987—, Simsbury Land Trust, 1984-88; del. 6th dist. Dem. Conv., Bristol, Conn., 1984-86; justice of the peace Town of Simsbury, 1985—, mem. design rev. bd., 1989-93; mem. constl. conv. bicentennial commn. Hometown Hero, 1986, awards selection com., 1996, 99; alt. Conn. Dem. Conv. for Gov., Hartford, 1986; del. State Dem. Conv., 1990, 92; mem. tourism com. Town of Simsbury, 1994-96, 96-98, ann. report com. 1994, 95, 325th ann. com., 1995; judge Regional History Day, 1993-96, 97-98, 99; vol. Hartford Symphony Talcott Mountain Music Festival, 1996-97, 99; mem. Bridge of Flowers Com., 1997—; coord. Simsbury Visitors Ctr., 1998. Named a Simsbury Woman Hartford Woman mag., 1987. Mem. Registrar of Voters Assn. Conn., Soc. of Mary and John, Simsbury Geneal. Soc. Congregationalist. Avocations: knitting, needlepoint, travel. Home: 28 Riverside Rd Simsbury CT 06070-2517

CALVERT, WILLIAM PRESTON, radiologist; b. Warrensburg, Mo., July 2, 1934; s. William Geery and Elizabeth (Spaulding) C.; m. Mary Kay Kersh, Apr. 4, 1976. BS, MIT, 1956; MD, U. Pa., 1960. Diplomate Am. Bd. Nuclear Medicine, Am. Bd. Radiology. Intern Pa. Hosp., Phila., 1960-61, resident in medicine, 1961-62, 64-66, chief med. resident, chief resident physician, 1965-66; resident in gastroenterology U. Miami, 1966-67, NIH fellow in gastroenterology, 1967-68, resident in radiology, 1968-71; radiologist Meml. Hosp., Hollywood, Fla., 1971-72; chief dept. radiology Larkin Gen. Hosp., South Miami, Fla., 1972-80, radiologist, 1980-89; radiologist Jackson Meml. Hosp., U. Miami, 1989-93, Univ. Hosp., Tammarac, Fla., 1993-95; part-time radiologist Northern Navajo Med. Ctr., Shiprock, N.Mex., 1995—; clin. instr. radiology U. Miami Sch. Medicine, 1971-76, clin. asst. prof. radiology, 1984-88, clin. assoc. prof. radiology, 1988-94. Bd. dirs. Wediko Farms Children's Svcs., Carbondale, Ill. Served with M.C., USAF, 1962-64. Mem. AMA, Fla. Med. Assn., Fla., Greater Miami radiol. socs., Soc. Nuclear Medicine, Radiol. Soc. N.Am., Explorers Club.

CALVIELLO, JOSEPH ANTHONY, research electrophysicist, consultant; b. Genzano, Potenza, Italy, Nov. 29, 1933; came to U.S., 1952; s. Nicola and Grazia (Lomuto) C.; m. Carmela M. Ciaramella, Dec. 26, 1959; 1 child, Joseph John. BSEE, Poly. Inst. Bklyn., 1962, MS in Electrophysics, 1966, postgrad., 1966-72. Engr. asst. Microwave Rsch. Inst., Bklyn., 1956-61; engr. AIL System Inc., Melville, N.Y., 1961-73, rsch. scientist, 1973-78, sr. rsch. scientist, 1978-91; cons. on advanced solid state tech. and application, 1991—. Author tech. publs.; contbr. chpt. to book; patentee in field. Bd. dirs. Poly. Inst. Bklyn., 1980—. Fellow IEEE (Charles J. Hirsch Meml. award 1985); mem. Electron Devices Soc., IEEE, N.Y. Acad. Scis., Sigma Xi. Roman Catholic. Avocations: boating, soccer, baseball. Home: 2117 Platinum Dr Sun City Center FL 33573-6487

CALVILLO, RICARDO C., communications executive. Chmn., CEO Veritas, N.Y.C., 1994—. Office: Veritas 250 Park Ave S New York NY 10003-1402

CALVIN, DOROTHY VER STRATE, computer company executive; b. Grand Rapids, Mich., Dec. 22, 1929; d. Herman and Christina (Plakmyer) Ver Strate; m. Allen D. Calvin, Oct. 5, 1953; children: Jamie, Kris, Bufo, Scott. BS magna cum laude, Mich. State U., 1951; MA, U. San Francisco, 1988; EdD, U. San Francisco, 1991. Mgr. data processing. Behavioral Rsch. Labs., Menlo Park, Calif., 1972-75; dir. Mgmt. Info. Systems Inst. for Prof. Devel., San Jose, Calif. 1975-76; systems analyst, programmer Pacific Bell Info. Systems, San Francisco, 1976-81; staff mgr., 1981-84; mgr. applications devel. Data Architects Inc., San Francisco, 1984-86; pres. Ver Strate Press, San Francisco, 1986—. Instr., Downtown C.C., San Francisco, 1980-84, Cañada C.C., 1986-92, Skyline Coll., 1988-92, City Coll. of San Francisco, 1992—; mem. computer curriculum adv. coun. San Francisco City Coll., 1982-84. V.p. LWV, Roanoke, Va., 1956-58; pres. Bulliss Purissima Parents Group, Los Altos, Calif., 1962-64; bd. dirs. Vols. for Israel, 1986-87. Mem. NAFE, Assn. Computing Machinery, IEEE Computer Soc., Assn. Systems Mgmt., Assn. Women in Computing, Phi Delta Kappa. Democrat. Avocations: computing, gardening, jogging, reading. Office: Ver Strate Press 1645 15th Ave San Francisco CA 94122-3523

CALVIN, JAMES WILLARD, thoracic and vascular surgeon; b. Oakland, Calif., Dec. 7, 1929; s. George Fairchild and Mary Morris Calvin; m. Claudine Depris (div. 1971); m. Carrie Carman, 1973; children: Carolyne, Frances, Sophie. BA, Stanford U., 1951; MD, McGill U., 1955. Diplomate Nat. Bd. Med. Examiners, Am. Bd. Surgery, Am. Bd. Thoracic Surgery. Intern Stanford (Calif.) U., 1955-56, resident dept. surgery, 1959-63, chief resident dept. surgery, 1963-64; group practice Sansum Med. Clinic, Santa Barbara, Calif., 1964-66; pvt. practice Thoracic and Cardiovascular Med. Group, Inc., Ventura, Calif., 1966-95; bd. dirs. Rehab. Inst. of Santa Barbara, bd. trustees; scientific adv. coun. Ramus Med. Technologies, Carpinteria, Calif., 1996—; hosp. staff Cmty. Meml. Hosp., Ventura. Contbr. articles to profl. jours. With USAF, 1956-58. Fellow ACS (rep. hosps. of ventura county 1980-87), Am. Coll. of Chest Physicians; mem. AAAS, AMA, Am. Cancer Soc. (Ventura county chpt., bd. dirs. 1969-72), Am. Heart Assn. (coun. on cardiovascular diseases), Am. Lung Assn., Am. Thoracic Soc., Calif. Med. Assn., Internat. Cardiovascular Soc. (N.Am. chpt.), N.Am. Soc. for Pacing and Electrophysiology, Samson Thoracic Surg., Soc. for Clin. Vascular Surgery, Soc. for Thoracic Surgeons, So. Calif. Vascular Surg. Soc., Ventura County Heart Assn. (pres. 1970-71), Ventura County Med. Soc. (pres. 1979, bd. govs. 1975-81). Fax: 760-564-4840. Home: 47-515 Via Florence LaQuinta CA 92253

CALVIN, ROCHELLE ANN, development association administrator; b. St. Paul, Feb. 28, 1936; d. Peter Herbert and Leah (Noun) Schaffer; m. Arnold Orloff, 1957 (div. 1984); children: Robin, Nadine, Steven; m. Stafford R. Calvin, Nov. 25, 1988. BA, U. Minn., 1958. Dir. woman's divsn. United Jewish Fund, St. Paul, 1979-91, devel. dir., 1991—. Pres. Hadassah, St. Paul, 1977. Jewish. Avocations: performing arts, biking. Office: United Jewish Fund 790 Cleveland Ave S Ste 201 Saint Paul MN 55116-1989

CALVIN, STAFFORD RICHARD, academic administrator; b. St. Paul, Apr. 6, 1931; s. Carl and Zelda Ida (Engelson) C.; m. Nancy Goldbert (div. 1984); m. Rochelle Ann Schaffer, Nov. 26, 1988; children: Lawrence, Carlton, Loran. BA, U. Minn., 1952; MFA, U. Mexico City, 1954. Pres. Sibley Co., St. Paul, 1953-58, Dealers Distbrs., St. Paul, 1958-65; v.p. Internat. Sys. Assn., N.Y.C., 1965-70, Carlson Cos., Mpls., 1970-74; CEO Calstar, Mpls., 1974-85; v.p. Acad. Learning Ctrs., Inc., St. Paul, 1988-90; pres. Calvin Acad., St. Paul, 1991—; Founder Inst. Essential Edn. Author: Save Your Child, 1989. Democrat. Jewish. Avocations: performing arts, biking, rafting. Office: Calvin Acad 2574 Hwy 10 Mounds View MN 55112

CALVO, ROQUE JOHN, professional society administrator; b. Allentown, Pa., Sept. 26, 1958; s. Rocco John and Ruth Hattie (Zimpfer) C.; m. Marianne Willever, Feb. 27, 1982; children: Amy Elizabeth, Roque John. BS, Lebanon Valley Coll., 1980; MBA, Rider U., 1986. Acctg. supv. The Electrochemical Soc., Inc., Pennington, N.J., 1980-82, asst. exec. dir., 1982-91, exec. dir., 1991—; mem. adv. bd. Fedn. Materials Socs., Washington, 1991—; mem. meeting adv. bd. Starwood Hotels and Resorts Worldwide. Mem. Am. Soc. Assn. Execs., Coun. Engring. & Sci. Soc. Execs. (mem. task force in mem. satisfaction 1992-94, bd. dirs. 1995—), N.J. Soc. Assn. Execs. Avocations: golf, basketball, tennis, reading. Office: Electrochemical Soc Inc 10 S Main St Pennington NJ 08534-2817

CAMACCI, MICHAEL A., commercial real estate broker, development consultant; b. Youngstown, Ohio, Feb. 6, 1951; s. Martin B. and Viola F. (Conti) C.; m. Susan Hawkins, Oct. 18, 1985; 1 child, Michael Philip. BBA, Youngstown Coll., 1974. Cert. bus. analyst. Acct. U.S. Steel Corp., Youngstown, 1969-80; mgr. sales Soc. Realty, Boardman, Ohio, 1980-81; dir. sales Pop-ins Maid Services, Columbiana, Ohio, 1981-82; bus. broker Eranco Assocs., Girard, Ohio, 1982-86; pres. JMC Realty, Inc., Youngstown, 1986-99; pres., broker Camacci Real Estate, 1986—; pres. Hillview Nursing Home, 1988-99, Valley View Nursing Home, 1990-99, Pyramid Printing, Inc., 1991-99; dir. Crestview Nursing & Rehab. Facility, 1999—; pres. Wedgewood Property Mgmt., Inc., 4682 North, LLC, 55 West, LLC, 1997—, 19th Hole Investments, 1997—; pres. CRE Holding Corp., 1996; pres. 20 West, LLC, 1998—, v.p., 1997-98; pres. 4682 North, LLC. Mem. Youngstown-Warren Regional Growth Alliance; v.p. Austintown Growth Found., 1994-96. Served with U.S. Army, 1971-77. Mem. Am. Health Care Assn., Ohio Health Care Assn., Nat. Assn. Printers and Lithographers, Internat. Coun. Shopping Ctrs., Youngstown-Warren Area C. of C., Columbiana Area C. of C., Mahoning County Home Builders Assn. Democrat. Roman Catholic. Office: Camacci Real Estate Inc 5533 Mahoning Ave Youngstown OH 44515-2316

CAMACHO, ALFREDO, accountant; b. Havana, Cuba, Sept. 18, 1951; came to U.S., 1961; s. Alberto and Silvia Maria (San Pedro) C.; m. Maria Rodriguez, June 24, 1972; 1 child, Jorge Alfredo. BBA, Fla. Internat. U., 1975, MS in Taxation, 1984. CPA, Fla. Acct., auditor Oppenheim, Appel, Dixon & Co., Miami, Fla., 1973-79; sr. auditor Aristar, Inc., Coral Gables, Fla., 1979-80; controller Wynne Bldg. Corp., Miami, 1980—; tchr. Mercy Coll., Miami, 1979. Mem. Am. Inst. CPA's, Fla. Inst. CPA's. Democrat. Roman Catholic. Office: Wynne Bldg Corp 12804 SW 122nd Ave Miami FL 33186-6203

CAMACHO, HECTOR, boxer. Lightweight champion, 1983, WBO Jr. Welterweight title, 1991, middleweight champion, 1996. *

CAMACHO, TOMAS AGUON, bishop; b. Chalon Kanoa, Saipon, Sept. 18, 1933. Ed., St. Patrick's Sem., Menlo Park, Calif. Ordained priest Roman Cath. Ch., 1961, ordained first bishop of Chalon Kanoa, 1985. Bishop Roman Cath. Ch., Chalon Kanoa, Northern Marianas, U.S. trust territory, 1985—. Address: PO Box 745 Saipan MN 96950-0745*

CAMARA, JORGE DE GUZMAN, ophthalmologist, humanitarian, educator; b. Ann Arbor, Mich., May 21, 1950; s. Augusto A. and Feliciana (de Guzman) C.; m. Virginia Valdes, June 23, 1977; 1 child, Augusto Carlos. BS in Pre-Medicine, U. Philippines, 1972, MD cum laude, 1976. Diplomate Am. Bd. Ophthalmology. Surg. intern U. Tex, Houston, 1977-78; resident in ophthalmology Baylor Coll. Medicine, Houston, 1978-81, fell in ophthalmic plastic and reconstructive surgery, 1981-82; ophthalmologist Straub Clinic and Hosp., Honolulu, 1982-88; pvt. practice Honolulu, 1988—; assoc. prof. U. Hawaii Sch. Medicine, Honolulu, 1982—; cons. Tripler Army Hosp., Honolulu, 1982—; chmn. dept. ophthalmology and otorhinolaryngology, bd. dirs. St. Francis Healthcare Systems; bd. dirs. Am. Savs. Bank, Hawaiian Electric Industries. Bd. dirs. Aloha Med. Mission, Honolulu, 1988—. Fellow Am. Acad. Ophthalmology, Am. Soc. Ophthalmic Plastic and Reconstructive Surgery; mem. AMA, Hawaii Ophthal. Soc. (pub. rels. officer 1984-85, pres. 1992, chmn. com. for indigent svcs. 1994—), Philippine Med. Assn. Hawaii (pres. 1988—). Roman Catholic. Avocations: tennis, piano. Office: 2228 Liliha St Ste 106 Honolulu HI 96817-1651

CAMARA, PAULINE FRANCOEUR, secondary school educator; b. Somerset, Mass., May 3, 1962; d. Rene L. and Anita E. (Cadoret) Francoeur; m. Robert P. Camara, Aug. 9, 1986; children: Kalyn E., Kyle R. AS in Bus. Adminstrn., Bristol C.C., Fall River, Mass., 1982; student, Bryant Coll., Smithfield, R.I., 1982-84; BS in Acctg., U. Mass., Dartmouth, 1987; M.Ednl. Leadership Adminstrn., Bridgewater State Coll., 1997. Cert. tchr. bus. edn., 5-12, prin. 9-12, info. tech. specialist K-12. Sr. acct., acct., mgr. Elbe-Cesco Inc., Fall River, Mass., Bank of Boston; tchr. Our Lady of Fatima H.S., Warren, R.I., 1994; acad. coord., instr. Westport (Mass.) H.S., 1994-98; tchr. Somerset H.S., 1998—; part-time tchr. bus. and tech. Bristol C.C., 1997—; coach Providence Coll., 1996—; site coord. Schs. That Work, 1998—. Vice pres. Somerset Chace Stret Sch. PTO, 1996-97; bd. dirs. Town of Somerset Spectrum Program, 1996-99; mem. schools-That-Work, 1994—; mem. PALMS, 1995—. Mem. Nat. bus. Educators Assn., New Eng. Bus. Educators Assn., Mass. Bus. Educators Assn. (pres. 1999—, v.p. 1997-99, bd. dirs. 1995—), Mass. Cheer Coaches Assn. (treas. 1987-89). Office: Somerset HS Grandview Ave Somerset MA 02726

CAMARDA, EDITH, nurse educator; b. N.Y.C., Sept. 21, 1928; d. Bedford and Jennie (Ranucci) Bruno; m. Frank Camarda, Apr. 30, 1950; children: Robert, Karen Jennie. RN, AAS, Coll. of Staten Island, N.Y., 1983, BSN, 1986; MS, Wagner Coll., 1994. RN, N.Y., cert. diabetes educator. Staff nurse surg. fl. Bayley Seton Hosp., S.I., N.Y., 1983; asst. supr. Staten Island Med. Group, 1986-97; program coord. diabetes edn. program S.I. Med. Group,; Diabetes nurse educator, 1986—. Recipient Spl. Recognition award Borough of Staten Island. Mem. Sigma Theta Tau-Epsilon Mu, Mu Epsilon (exec. com., by-laws com.). Home: 304 Vineland Ave Staten Island NY 10312-2924

CAMAYD-FREIXAS, YOEL, management, strategy & planning consultant; b. Holguin, Oriente, Cuba, Nov. 27, 1948; came to U.S., 1962; s. Alberto and Olga (Freixas) Camayd; m. Ana Maria Perez, Jan. 2, 1982; 1 child, Cristina Camayd. BA summa cum laude, U. Mundial, San Juan, P.R., 1970; MEd, Northeastern U., 1972; MA, Boston Coll., 1978, PhD, 1982. Planner Multi-Svc. Ctr., New Bedford, Mass., 1971-74; psychologist Jamaica Plain Outreach Program, Boston, 1975-78, program dir., 1978-80, exec. dir., 1980-81; asst. prof. grad. sch. urban studies and planning MIT, Cambridge, 1982-86; sr. officer Office R & D Boston Pub. Schs., 1985-87; pres. Boston R & D, 1987-90; bd. chmn. Pavers & Tiles of Fla., Inc., Miami, 1987-91; exec. v.p. Health & Hosps. Corp., N.Y.C., 1990-91; bd. chmn., mng. dir. Nurse Referrals, Inc., N.Y.C., 1990-91; mng. ptnr. Camayd Cons., Miami, Fla., 1992—. Author: The Costs of Opportunity, 1983 (award Psi Chi 1983), Hispanics in Massachusetts, 1987, Effective Dropout Prevention, 1987, Crisis in Miami, 1988, Latino Health in New York City, 1992, Affordability Controls in Affordable Housing and Disaster Relief, 1995. Mem., co-chmn. Mass. Legislature Commn. on Hispanic Affairs, Boston, 1984-88; co-chmn. add-ons com. Mass. Dem. Com., Boston, 1985-90; bd. dirs. United Way Massachusetts Bay, Boston, 1986-90; pres. Mass. Coalition for Electoral Reform, Boston, 1987-90; pres. Coral Way Elem. Sch. PTA, 1997—. Recipient nat. community svc. award Coalition Hispanic Human Svc. Orgns., 1980, gubernatorial citation State of Mass., 1988, 90, commendation Boston City Coun., 1990, legis. citation Mass. Ho. of Reps., 1990, recognition Miami Design Preservation League, 1995. Avocations: computers, film.

CAMBERS, PHILIP WILLIAM, pastor, music minister, music educator; b. Kansas City, Mo., May 5, 1957; s. William Hammond Cambers and Mary Elisabeth (Sharp) Kehrer; m. Sharon Kay Thompson, Apr. 28, 1984; children: Ashley Carmen, Jeffrey Philip, Scott William. B of Music Edn., Cen. Mo. State U., 1979, BA of Sci. Edn., 1979. Lic. to preach Assemblies of God, 1987; cert. tchr. music and French. Youth min. First Assembly of God, St. Joseph, Mo., 1982; min. of music Calvary Assembly of God, Toledo, 1982-85, First Assembly of God, Mobile, Ala., 1985, N. Highland Assembly of God, Columbus, Ga., 1985-86, Southside Assembly of God, Jackson, Miss., 1986-92; with First Assembly of God, Honolulu, 1992-94, 1st Assembly of God Ch., East Lansing, Mich., 1994-95; sr. pastor New Life Assembly of God Ch., Ann Arbor, Mich., 1995—; tchr. music Truman Mid. Sch., St. Joseph, Mo., 1979-82, Calvary Christian Sch., Columbus, Ga., 1982-85, Briarcrest Christian Sch., Columbus, 1985-86, Southside Christian Sch., Jackson, Miss., 1986-92; dist. music dir. Miss. Dist. Coun., Assembly of God, Jackson, 1986-92; host Miss. Dist. Coun. Choral Workshop, Jackson, 1987; adjudicator Nat. Fine Arts Festival Assembly of God, Springfield, Mo., 1988; choral clinician Evangel Assembly of God, Columbus, Miss., 1988-90; prodr. Melody on Ice, Ann Arbor Figure Skating Club, 1998; sec.-treas. Metro South sect. Assemblies of God, 1999—. Contbr. articles to profl. jours. Choir dir. Children's Choir & Handbell Choir (for nursing homes), Jackson, 1989-90; handbell choir dir. TV comml. Sta. WAPT-TV, Jackson, 1990. Recipient First Place Nat. Assn. Tchrs. Singing, 1979. Mem. Am. Guild English Handbell, Am. Choral Dir.'s Assn. Home: 2112 Ann Arbor Saline Rd Ann Arbor MI 48103-9710 Office: New Life Assembly of God Ch 2118 Ann Arbor Saline Rd Ann Arbor MI 48103-9710 *Through all my life's toils, the only things that really matter are the ones that glorify God.*

CAMBIO, BAMBILYN BREECE, state legislator; b. Johnston, R.I., Dec. 14, 1956; m. James V. Cambio. Cert. Am. Inst. Paralegal Studies. Mem. R.I. Ho. of Reps., Providence, mem. HEW com., joint com. on environ. and energy, vice chmn. ho. edn. welfare com.; commr. Exec. Dept. on Deaf and Hard of Hearing; sec. State Govt. Intern Commn.; freelance paralegal, title examiner. Chair North Providence Citizen's Environ. Com.; mem. North Providence Preservation Com., North Providence Women's Dem. Caucus, North Providence Dem. Town Com. Mem. Am. Polit. Item Collectors, R.I. Caucus Women Legislators, Nat. Order Women Legislators. Office: RI Ho of Reps State Capitol Providence RI 02903*

CAMBIO, IRMA DARLENE, nursing consultant; b. Belleville, Kans., July 23, 1936; d. James and Agnes Marie (Morehead) Dooley; m. Anderson Cambio (div.); children: Jim, Connie Rae. AA, East L.A. Coll., 1960; student continuing ednl. courses, UCLA, 1966-69; student Coll. Nursing, U. Md., 1985. RN, Calif., Colo., Washington, N.Mex., Wyo. Nurse oper. rm. Beverly Cmty. Hosp., Montebello, Calif., 1960-63; DON Pico Rivera (Calif.) Cmty. Hosp., 1963-64, Burbank (Calif.) Convalescent Hosp., 1964-66; staff nurse oper. rm., then head nurse, insvc. instr. Huntington Meml. Hosp., Pasadena, Calif., 1966-68; staff nurse oper. rm. Sunrise Hosp., Las Vegas, Nev., 1969-71; supr. oper. rm. Valley Hosp., Las Vegas, 1971-72; head nurse med./surg. fl. Chino (Calif.) Gen. Hosp., 1972-73; staff nurse emergency rm. Dr.'s Hosp. Montclair, Calif., 1972-73; head nurse med. fl. Boulder (Nev.) Cmty. Hosp., 1973; staff nurse recovery rm. Holy Cross Hosp., Ft. Lauderdale, Fla., 1973; float nurse, then house shift supr. Imperial Point Hosp., Ft. Lauderdale, 1973-74; staff nurse oper. rm. Lauderdale Lakes (Fla.) Hosp., 1973-74; patient care coord. oper. rm., recovery rm. Imperial Point Hosp., Ft. Lauderdale, 1974-78; asst. head nurse level IV open heart surgery/transplant surgery dept. and transplant divsn. St. Anthony's Hosp., Denver, 1978-80; oper. rm. cons., equipment planner internat. divsn. Nat. Med. Enterprises, 1980-85; mem. oper. rm. staff, float nurse Rocky Mountain Hosp., Denver, 1985; mem. oper. rm. staff St. Joseph Hosp., Denver, 1985-86; head nurse level IV oper. rm. King Faisal Splty. Hosp., Riyadh, Saudi Arabia, 1986-93; cons. oper. rm., recovery rm. and cntrl. sterile supply mgmt. Denver, 1993—; cons. Gortex Graft Co., 1978-80; on-call staff nurse Nursefinders Nurses' Registry, L.A., 1984-85, Olsten Nurses' Registry, Denver, 1985—; travel nurse oper. rm. Georgetown U. Hosp., Washington, 1994, Penrose/St. Francis Hosp., Colorado Springs, Colo., 1994-95; past mem. commissioning team for start-up ops. of 5 new acute care hosps. Taif, Dhahran and Riyadh, Saudi Arabia, 1 acute care hosp. Kuala Lumpur, Malaysia; compiler book for new hosps. detailing equipment, instrumentation and supplies necessary for oper. suite and recovery rm., 1982; rschr./developer policy and procedure manuals for nursing svcs. several hosps., Saudi Arabia, 1983; cons. commd. hosps. and Royal Family Pvt. Med. Clinics, Saudi Arabia, 1986-87; cons. equipment purchase for expansion, cons. materials flow and mgmt. svs. various hosps., Saudi Arabia, 1986-91, NME New Hosp., Malaysia, 1991—, mem. commn. team., Oxford U., England, 1997; pvt. practice, 1999—. Contbr. articles to profl. publs. Participant Health Vols. Overseas, Washington. Mem. Assn. Oper. Rm. Nurses (pres. Las Vegas chpt. 1978-79, mem. mgmt. splty. assembly/divsn. 1994—, rschr. new products, developer plan for presentation and integration to hosps.). Republican. Methodist. Avocations: skiing, hiking, knitting, photography. Home and Office: 439 Wright St Apt 26 Lakewood CO 80228-1152

CAMBRAY-NÚÑEZ, RODRIGO, mathematics educator, translator; b. La Reforma, Guerrero, Mex., Mar. 13, 1963; came to U.S., 1996; s. Felipe Cambray-Urquiza and Alberta Leopolda Núñez-Estrada. Grad. in Math., Nacional U. Autonoma de Mex., 1988; MS in Math. Edn., Cinvestav Instituto Politecnic, Mex., 1993; MA in Math., Ball State U., 1997, postgrad. in Ednl. Leadership, 1997—. Part-time prof. math. Instituto Politecnico Nacional, Mexico, 1988-91; tech. editor, coord. Mathesis, Mexico, 1992-95; part-time prof. math. Instituto Tecnologico Autonomo de Mexico, 1992-95; grad. asst. dept. math. scis. Ball State U., Muncie, Ind., 1996-98, doctoral asst. dept. ednl. leadership, 1998—. Translator: (from French into Spanish) Analisis de los infinitamente pequenos para el estudio de las lineas curvas, 1998. E-mail: OOrOcambray@bsuvc.bsu.edu. FAX: 765-285-2166. Home: Apt 19 3480 N Tillotson Ave Muncie IN 47304-1610 Office: Ball State Univ TC-915 Dept Ednl Leadership Muncie IN 47304-0590

CAMBRIDGE, WILLIAM G., federal judge; b. 1931. BS, U. Nebr., 1953, JD, 1955. With Madgett, Hunter and Cambridge, 1957-63; pvt. practice law Hastings, Nebr., 1964-81; judge 10th Jud. Dist. Nebr., 1981-88; judge U.S. Dist. Ct. Nebr., Omaha, 1988-94, chief judge, 1994—. Hon. trustee Hastings (Nebr.) Coll. 1st lt. U.S. Army, 1955-57, USAR, 1957-65. Mem. ABA, Nebr. Bar Assn., Omaha Bar Assn., 10th Jud. Dist. Bar Assn., Adams County Bar Assn. Office: US Dist Ct PO Box 1076-dts Omaha NE 68101-1076

CAMDEN, VERA JEAN, psychoanalyst; b. Cleve., Aug. 10, 1953; d. John E. and Vera E. (Sheldon) C.; m. Kevin M. Cahill, Feb. 13, 1993; children: Emily, Beatrice. BA, Ariz. State U., 1976; MA, U. Chgo., 1977; PhD, U. Va., 1986. Assoc. prof. Kent (Ohio) State U., 1984—; psychoanalyst Cleve. Psychoanalytic Inst., 1986—. Editor: Compromise Formations, 1988, Narrative of Agnes Beaumont, 1992, (jour.) Bunyan Studies; contbr. numerous articles to profl. jours. Grantee NEH, Dupont, 1984, Rsch. Challenge State of Ohio, 1986-95. Mem. MLA, APA (com. on rsch. spl. tng. 1995—), Cleve. Skating Club. Avocations: scuba diving, running, gardening, sailing. Office: Cleve Psychoanalytic Inst 11328 Euclid Ave Ste 202 Cleveland OH 44106-3959

CAMDESSUS, MICHEL (JEAN), federal agency administrator, international organization executive; b. Bayonne, France, May 1, 1933; s. Alfred and Madeleine (Cassembon) Camdessus; m. Brigitte d'Arcy, Dec. 7, 1957; children: Francois, Marie-Odile, Christine, Thibaut, Claire, Marie-Genevieve. Licencie en Droit, U. Paris; Diplome d'etudes superieures d'economie politique et de sciences economiques, Diplome de l'Institut d'etudes politiques, Ancien eleve de l'Ecole Nationale d'Administration (promotion Alexis de Tocqueville). Civil servant Treasury French Ministry Fin., 1960-66; chief bur. indsl. affairs Treasury, French Ministry Econs. and Fin., 1969-70, dep. dir. treasury, 1974-82, dir. Treasury, 1982-84, gov. Bank of France, Paris, 1984-87; fin. attache Permanent Representation, EEC, Brussels, 1966-68, mem. monetary com. EEC, 1978-84, pres. monetary com., 1982-84; mng. dir. Internat. Monetary Fund, Washington, 1987—. Chmn. Paris Club, 1978-84. Decorated chevalier Nat., chevalier Légion d'Honneur, Order Merit, Cross of Mil. Valor. *

CAMEL, MARK HOWARD, neurological surgeon; b. St. Louis, May 30, 1955; s. H. Marvin and Greta (Hahn) C.; m. Linda J. Chisnick, May 3, 1987; 1 child, Andrew. BA, U. Rochester, 1977; MD, Washington U., St. Louis, 1981. Diplomate Am. Bd. Neurol. Surgery. Intern in gen. surgery Barnes Hosp., 1981-82; resident in neurol. surgery Barnes Hosp., St. Louis, 1982-86; fellow in neurol. surgery Washington U., 1986-87; pvt. practice, Greenwich, Conn., 1987—. Mem. Congress Neurol. Surgeons (exec. com. 1993—, v.p. 1995), New Eng. Neurol. Soc. (bd. dirs.), Belle Haven Club. Office: Orthopaedic and Neurol Surgery Specialists 6 Greenwich Office Pk Greenwich CT 06831

CAMERINO, PAT W., medical college official; b. Niles, Ohio, May 25, 1935; m. Karen J. Swank, June 22, 1958; children: Deborah, Kenneth, Christopher. BS, Kent State U., 1957, BS in Edn., 1957; PhD, Cornell U., 1961. Postdoctoral fellow Dartmouth Med. Sch., Hanover, N.H., 1961-63; asst. prof. Oreg. State U., Corvallis, 1963-65; scientist adminstr. NIH, Bethesda, Md., 1965-71; assoc. grad. dean for rsch. U. Mass., Amherst, 1971-78; dir. faculty resources Baylor Coll. Medicine, Houston, 1978—; permanent deacon Diocese of Galveston-Houston, 1984. Office: Baylor Coll Medicine One Baylor Plz Houston TX 77030

CAMERON, ALASTAIR DUNCAN, engineering consultant; b. Fredericton, N.B., Can., Oct. 28, 1920; s. Adam and Dora Isabel C.; m. Audrey Charlton, May 17, 1951; children: Duncan, Harry, Sheila, Janet. BSc in Civil Engring., U. N.B., 1942; Diploma in Mgmt., McGill U., 1970. Design engr. Dominion Bridge Co. Ltd., Montreal, 1946-47; with Montreal Engring. Co. Ltd., 1947-56, supervising engr., 1949-56; gen. mgr. Maritime Electric Co. Ltd., Charlottetown, P.E.I., Can., 1957-63; with Montreal Engring. Co. (now AGRA Monenco Inc.), 1963-71; mgr. econs. and valuation div. Montreal Engring. Co., 1969-71; v.p., mgr. mgmt. cons. div. Montreal Engring. Co. (now Monenco AGRA Inc.), 1972-75; v.p. Utility Mgmt., 1976-83, sr. cons., 1984—. Served with Can. Army, 1942-45. Decorated mem. Order Brit. Empire. Mem. Order of Engrs. Que., Can. Soc. Civil Engrs., Engring. Inst. Can., Energy Coun. Can., World Energy Coun. (constituent mem.). Clubs: Mt. Stephen, Montreal Amateur Athletic Assn. Office: 2045 Stanley St 11th Fl, Montreal, PQ Canada H3A 2V4

CAMERON, ALASTAIR GRAHAM WALTER, astrophysicist, educator; b. Winnipeg, Man., Can., June 21, 1925; came to U.S., 1959, naturalized, 1963; s. Alexander Thomas and Airdrie Edna (Bell) C.; m. Elizabeth Aston MacMillan, June 11, 1955. B.Sc., U. Man., 1947; Ph.D., U. Sask., 1952, D.Sc. (hon.), 1977; A.M. (hon.), Harvard U., 1973. Asst. prof. physics Iowa State Coll., Ames, 1952-54; asst., assoc. and sr. research officer Atomic Energy Can., Ltd., Chalk River, Ont., 1954-61; sr. research fellow Calif. Inst. Tech., Pasadena, 1959-60; sr. scientist Goddard Inst. Space Studies, N.Y., 1961-66; prof. space physics Yeshiva U., 1966-73; prof. astronomy Harvard U., Cambridge, Mass., 1973-97, Donald H. Menzel prof. astrophysics, 1997—; chmn. Space Sci. Bd., 1976-82, Nat. Acad. Scis. Contbr. articles to profl. jours. Recipient J. Lawrence Smith medal NAS, 1988, Disting. Pub. Service medal NASA, 1983. Mem. NAS, AAAS, Am. Phys. Soc., Am. Geophys. Union (Harry H. Hess medal 1989), Am. Astron. Soc. (Russell lectr. 1997), Internat. Astron. Union, Meteoritical Soc. (Leonard medal 1994). Office: Harvard U 60 Garden St Cambridge MA 02138-1516

CAMERON, CHARLES HENRY, petroleum engineer; b. Greeley, Colo., Oct. 21, 1947; s. Leo Leslie and Naomi Tryphena (Phillips) C.; m. Cheryl Christine Debelock, Aug. 30, 1969; 1 child, Ericka Dawn. AS, Mesa State Coll., 1968; BS in Geology, Mesa Coll., 1978; AS in Hazardous Materials

Tech., Front Range C.C., Wesminister, Colo., 1990. Cert. info. resource mgmt. approving ofcl. (CIAO), 1998. Retardation technician Colo. State Home and Tng. Sch., Grand Junction, 1967-69; journeyman carpenter Brotherhood of Carpenters and Joiners, Grand Junction, 1969-76; hydrocompaction mgr. Colo. Dept. Hwys., Grand Junction, 1975-77; rsch. geologist Occidental Oil Shale, Inc., Grand Junction, 1977-78; geol. engr. Cleveland Cliffs Iron Co., Morgantown, W.Va., 1978-81; tech. advisor Ute Indian Tribe, Ft. Duchesne, Utah, 1981-86; ops. mgr. Charging Ute Corp., Golden, Colo., 1986-87; cons. Golden, 1987-90; petroleum engr. U.S. Dept. Interior/Bur. of Indian Affairs, Ft. Duchesne, 1990—, hazardous material mgr., freedom of info./privacy act coord., 1990—, natural resources officer, 1996—, ADP com. chmn., LAN adminstr., PL 93-638 com. chmn. grants/loan mgr., 1990—; minerals specialist Phoenix area Bur. Indian Affairs, Y2K coord. U&O Agency computer systems upgrade project, 1998. Contbr. articles to profl. jours. Mem. Colo. Oil Field Investigators Assn., Vernal (Utah) C. of C., Internat. Platform Assn. Avocations: motorcycle touring, antiques, photography, hunting, fishing. Home: 255 East 200 North Vernal UT 84078-1713 Office: BIA Uintah Ouray Agy 988 S 7500 E PO Box 130 Fort Duchesne UT 84026-0130

CAMERON, CHRISTIE SPEIR, lawyer; b. Bethel, N.C., Feb. 12, 1954; d. David Ordway and Betty Maude (Smith) Speir; children: David Craig Price, John Harvey Price. BS, U. N.C., 1976, JD, 1979. Bar: N.C. 1981. Research asst. N.C. Ct. Appeals, Raleigh, 1979-81; asst. reporter appellate div. N.C. Supreme Ct., Raleigh, 1981-84; assoc. Wyrick, Robbins, Yates and Ponton, Raleigh, 1984-91, head real estate sect., 1986-91; clk. of ct. N.C. Supreme Ct., Raleigh, 1991—. Mem. N.C. Bd. Corrections, 1977-84, N.C. Legis. study commn. on neurologically-impaired infants, 1989-91, N.C. legis. study commn. on railroads and pub. transp., 1991—; treas. Wake County Dem. Women, 1985-87, pres., 1987-89; v.p. N.C. Dem. Women, 1984-86; chmn. adv. bd. YWCA, 1988-90; chmn. task force on excellence in secondary edn. Parents Study Panel, 1989-90; treas. Triangle Transit Authority, 1990-91, sec. 1992, vice chair, 1993-94, chair, 1994-95; bd. dirs. N.C. Mus. Natural Scis., 1990-92; bd. dirs. N.C. Child Advocacy Inst., 1991—, chmn., 1995-97; trustee Edenton St. United Meth. Ch., 1990-95; bd. dirs. Kids Voting of Wake County, 1996-98. Coun. of States Toll fellow, 1993. Mem. ABA, N.C. Bar Assn., Wake County Bar Assn. Methodist. Home: 1905 Sturbridge Ct Raleigh NC 27612-4929 Office: NC Supreme Ct PO Box 2170 Raleigh NC 27602-2170

CAMERON, CHRISTINA STUART, government official; b. Toronto, Can., Mar. 15, 1945; d. Donald Stuart Forsyth and Bertah Millar (Roy) C.; m. Hugh Fraser Townsend, Dec. 29, 1988. BA, U. Toronto, 1967; MA, Brown U., 1970; PhD, Laval U., 1983. Rsch. asst. Indian and No. Affairs Parks Can., Quebec City, Que., 1970-74; archtl. analyst Can. Inventory Historic Bldgs. Parks Can., Environ. Can., Quebec City, Que., 1974-76, head archtl. analysis, 1976-81, dir. archtl. history, 1982-86; dir. gen. Nat. Historic Sites dept. Parks Can., Quebec City, Que., 1986—; guest lectr. archtl. history dept. fine arts Concordia U., 1975-78; sec. Historic Sites and Monuments Bd. Can.; adj. prof. art history Carleton U., 1991; local archtl. conservation adv. com. City of Ottawa, 1977-79; sec. Rockcliffe Park Local Archtl. Conservation Adv. Com., 1978-86, vice-chair, 1986-91; mem. adv. bd. Can. Centre Architecture, 1978-90; cons. architecture Can. Ency., 1981-84; mem. rsch. tools com. Social Scis. and Humanities Coun. Can., 1985-86; rapporteur World Heritage Com., 1989-90, chmn., 1990-91; gov. Heritage Can. Found., 1990-95; mem. Can. Commn. of UNESCO, Sub-Comm. on Culture, 1992—; dir. gen. UNESCO Sci. Adv. Com. on Angkor World Heritage Site, 1993—. Mem. editl. bd. Jour. Can. Art History, 1981—; author: The Portrait Bust: Renaissance to Enlightenment, 1969; (with Geneviève G. Bastien and Doris D. Dubé) Inventaire des marchés de construction des archives civiles de Québec 1800-1870, 3 vols. in History and Archaeology/Histoire et archéologie, 1975; (with Jean Trudel) The Drawings of James Cockburn: A Visit Through Quebec's Past, 1976, Québec au temps de James Patterson Cockburn, 1976; (with Francoise Beaudin and Ginette Noel) C. Baillairgé, arct. ing., dessins architecturaux, 1979; (with Janet Wright) Second Empire Style in Canadian Architecture, in Canadian Historic Sites, Occasional Papers in Archaeology and History, 1980, Le Style Second Empire en architecture canadienne, in Lieux historiques canadiens, cahiers d'archéologie et d'histoire, 1980; Domestic Architecture of Old Quebec/L'Architecture domestique du Vieux-Québec, 1980, Index of Houses Featured in Canadian Homes and Gardens from 1925 to 1944, 1980, Walking in the Village of Rockcliffe Park, 1982; (with Monique Trépanier) Vieux-Québec: son architecture intérieure, 1986; Charles Baillairgé, Architect, 1989; (with Loren R. Lerner and Mary F. Williamson) Art and Architecture in Canada: A Bibliography and Guide to Literature to 1981; contbr. articles to profl. jours. Fellow Royal Can. Geog. Soc. (gov. 1994—); mem. Ont. Assn. Architects (hon.), Soc. Study Architecture in Can. (treas. 1976-80, pres. 1984-86), Assn. for Preservation Tech., Soc. Archtl. Historians, Com. for Devel. of Ecclesiastical Block, Can. Conf. Hist. Resources, Heritage Interpretation Internat., Getty Inst. Arch. Conservation Grants. Avocations: skiing, tennis, Scottish country dancing, sailing, bicycling. Home: 419 Hinton Ave, Ottawa, ON Canada K1Y 1B2

CAMERON, DANIEL FORREST, communications executive; b. Santa Monica, Calif., Mar. 8, 1944; s. Dan W. and Bonnie (Forrest) C.; m. Sharon Tompos, June 1, 1968; children: Daniel Christian, Stephen Forrest. BSBA, U. Tulsa, 1974; MBA, Morehead (Ky.) State U., 1978, MA, 1981; PhD, U. Ky., 1989. Editor Appalachian News-Express, Pikeville, Ky., 1976-77; coord. mining tech. program Pikeville (Ky.) Coll., 1977-78, Morehead State U., 1978-85; dir. devel. and pub. rels. Monte Cassino Sch., Tulsa, 1986-89; exec. dir. coll. advancement Coll. Osteo. Medicine Okla. State U., Tulsa, 1989-92; pres. D. Forrest Cameron and Assocs., Tulsa, 1992—. Editor: Kentucky Underground Coal Mine Guidebook, 1985; editor, pub. Greater Tulsa Reporter Newspapers (Union Boundary, Jenks Gazette, Owasso Rambler, Broken Arrow Express and Tulsa Free Press), 1993—. Pres. Comet Jr. Athletic Assn., Tulsa, 1989; co-founder Collegiate Assn. for Mining Edn., Lexington, Ky., 1983; bd. dirs. U. Tulsa Golden Hurricane Club, 1993-99, Camp Fire Boys and Girls of Green Country Coun., Inc., 1999—. Mem. U. Tulsa Alumni Assn., U. Ky. Alumni Assn., Tulsa Green Country Rotary Club (pres. 1994-95).

CAMERON, DAVID BRIAN, health service administrator; b. Detroit, Feb. 17, 1953; s. John Gray and Helen Jane (Schueler) C.; m. Sharon Sue Pruss, Nov. 28, 1980; children: David Brian, Calvin Alexander. BA, Albion Coll., Mich., 1975; MS, Ohio State U., 1977. Adminstrv. asst. Harper Hosp., Det., 1977-79; cons. Arthur Young & Co., Detroit, 1979-81; advanced cons. Ernst & Whinney, Detroit, 1981, sr. cons., 1981-83; asst. adminstr. Detroit Receiving Hosp., 1983-87; asst. dir. med. staff affairs Det. Receiving Hosp., 1987-93; adminstrv. dir. med. affairs Harris Meth. S.W., 1994-96, dir. profl. svcs., 1997; acct. exec. MSI, Dallas, 1997, HPR Health Staff, Arlington, Tex., 1997—; adj. prof. U. Detroit, 1984; adj. instr. Mercy Coll., Detroit, 1987, 88. Contbr. articles to profl. jours. Active Harsens Island-St. Clair Flats Assn., Mich., 1981—. Fellow Am. Coll. Healthcare Execs. Republican. Episcopalian. Avocations: golfing, boating, water skiing, biking. *

CAMERON, DON R., educational association administrator; b. Detroit, Oct. 15, 1937; s. Joseph Roland and Helen (Freeman) C.; m. Ida Jane Arcand, Aug. 16, 1958 (dec. 1989); children: Amanda Marie, Benjamin David. BA, Eastern Mich. U., 1961, MA, 1962, Doctor of Edn., 1985. Tchr. Birmingham (Mich.) Pub. Schs., 1962-66; exec. dir. Birmingham Edn. Assn., 1966-69; comm. specialist Mich. Edn. Assn., East Lansing, 1969-75, dir. comm., 1975-76; exec. dir. Fla. Teaching Profession Nat. Edn. Assn., Tallahassee, 1976-79; asst. exec. dir. Nat. Edn. Assn., Washington, 1979-83; exec. dir. NEA, Washington, 1983—. contbr. articles to mags. Bd. dirs. People for the Am. Way, Washington, 1983—, Am. Arbitration Assn., N.Y.C., 1983—, UN Assn., N.Y.C., 1982—; bd. dirs., treas. Nat. Found. for the Improvement Edn., Washington, 1981—. Mem. Americans for Democratic Action, Forum Edn. Leaders, Edn. Commn. States (bd. dirs.), Econ. Policy Inst. (bd. dirs.), Nat. Ctr. Policy Alternatives (bd. dirs.), Home and Sch. Inst. (bd. dirs.). Democrat. Avocations: sailing. Office: NEA 1201 16th St NW Washington DC 20036-3290*

CAMERON, DORT, electronics executive; b. 1945. With Drexel Burnham Comml. Paper, Inc., Dallas, 1966-84; pres. Drexel Burnham Comml. Paper, Inc.; with Investment Limited Partnership, Greenwich, Conn., 1984—, mng. gen. ptnr.; chmn. Entex Info. Svcs., Rye Brook, N.Y., 1993—. Office: Airlie Group 115 E Putnam Ave Greenwich CT 06830-5643*

CAMERON, DUKE EDWARD, cardiac surgeon, educator; b. Miami, Fla., Mar. 9, 1952; s. Edward John and Joanne (Abbott) C.; m. Claudia Oppenheim; children: Danielle, Nicole. AB, Harvard Coll., 1974; MD, Yale U., 1978. Resident gen. surgery Yale-New Haven Hosp., 1978-84, resident cardiothoracic surgery, 1984-87; assoc. prof. surgery, dir. pediatric cardiac surgery Johns Hopkins Hosp., Balt. Fellow ACS; mem. Soc. Thoracic Surgeons, So. Thoracic Surg. Assn., Am. Assn. Thorac Surg. Home: 2209 South Rd Baltimore MD 21209-4437 Office: Johns Hopkins Hosp Blalock 618 600 N Wolfe St Baltimore MD 21287-0005

CAMERON, DUNCAN HUME, lawyer; b. Brandon, Man., Can., May 26, 1934; s. Donald Ewen and Jean Carruthers (Rankine) C.; m. Caroline I. Gilbert, 1975; children: Sarah, Anne. BA cum laude, Harvard U., 1956; LLB, Columbia U., 1959, PhD, 1965. Bar: N.Y. 1959, D.C. 1967, U.S. Supreme Ct. 1970. Assoc. Paul, Weiss, Rifkind, Wharton & Garrison, 1959-62; atty. office gen. counsel AID U.S. Dept. State, 1963-67, legal advisor mission to Dominican Republic, 1966; ptnr. Appleton, Rice & Perrin, 1967-71; mng. ptnr. Cameron & Hornbostel, Washington, 1972—; adj. prof. law Georgetown U. Law Ctr., 1970-80, 89—; vis. prof. law Victoria U., New Zealand, 1986; adj. prof. Sch. Fgn. Svc. Georgetown U., 1973-88. Contbr. articles to profl. jours. Chmn. bd. Pan Am. Sch. Agr., 1991-97, bd. dirs., 1986—; bd. dirs. Washington Hist. Soc., 1998—, Washington Tennis Found., 1995-99. Mem. ABA, Fed. Bar Assn., Internat. Bar Assn., Washington Fgn. Law Soc. (bd. govs. 1988-90), Chilean-Am. C. of C. of Washington (pres. 1991-96, chmn. bd. 1997—), Cosmos Club. Home: 3532 Chesapeake St NW Washington DC 20008-2957 Office: Cameron & Hornbostel 818 Connecticut Ave NW Washington DC 20006-2702

CAMERON, ELEANOR CRANSTON FOWLE, author; b. Palo Alto, Calif., Nov. 22, 1909; d. William McGregor and Carol Edith (Dixon) Cranston; m. John Miller Fowle, June 19, 1929 (dec. Apr. 1983); children: Michael, Linda Fowle Burke; m. Donald Churchill Cameron, Aug. 25, 1984 (dec. Nov. 1996). Student, Stanford U., 1928-31. Author: Cranston, The Senator from California, 1980. Chmn. Dem. State Women, Calif., 1966-80; officer Dem. State Ctrl. Com., 1966-80; pres. Foothill-De Anza C.C. Found., 1980-90, bd. dirs., 1996-98; bd. dirs. Stanford U. Founding Grant Soc., 1980—; trustee Hidden Villa, Los Altos Hills, Calif., 1996—. Congregationalist. Avocations: travel, tennis, politics, community activist. Home: 27060 Old Trace Ln Los Altos Hills CA 94022

CAMERON, GLENDA FAYE, secondary education educator; b. Brownfield, Tex., Apr. 24, 1948; d. Jesse Thomas and Belva Blanch (Durham) C. BS in Edn., Tex. Tech. U., 1970, MA, 1975. Tchg. cert. Tchr. English Advanced Placement and gifted and talented Brownfield (Tex.) Consol. Ind. Sch. dist., 1970—; mgr. Rapunzel, Lubbock, Tex., 1990-96; exec. dir. R.A.D.A.R. Tower, Brownfield, 1991-99. Author (ednl. lessons) Rapunzel Anti-Drug Units, 1991-92, (pamphlets) Rapunzel, 1996-97, Rave On With Peggy Sue, 1997—. Mem. NEA, Tex. Tchrs. Assn., Terry County Tchrs. Assn. Mem. Church of the Living God. Avocations: guitar. Home: 912 E Oak St Brownfield TX 79316-3814

CAMERON, GLENN NILSSON, loan executive; b. Orange, N.J., Apr. 20, 1956; s. John Richardson and Alma (Nilsson) C. BA in History, Wheaton (Ill.) Coll., 1978; ThM in Biblical Studies, Dallas Theol. Sem., 1983. Lic. real estate broker, Tex. Real estate developer shopping ctrs. and apts. Hunsicker & Assocs., Dallas, 1983-85; dir. comml. investment brokerage Donald Kinney & Assocs., Dallas, 1985-86; dir. sales So. Classical Homes/Northtown Sq., Dallas, 1986-87, Glenn Cameron & Co., Residential Real Estate Brokerage, Dallas, 1987-90; broker assoc. Realty Execs., Residential Real Estate Brokerage, Plano & Dallas, Tex., 1990-95; dir. sales Martin Raymond Homes Inc., 1995-97; broker assoc. Remax, Dallas, 1997-98; sr. mortgage fin. officer Consumer Direct Mortgage, Dallas, 1998—. Mem. So. Meth. U. Internat. Friendship Program, 1985-87, Lone Star Masters Swim Team, 1983-89, North Dallas Aquatics, 1989-93; vol. Lifewalk, Contact Counseling Line, Black Tie Dinner; mem. Tex. Human Rights Found., Human Rights Campaign Fund; vol. AIDS Svcs. Denton County, HIV counselor. Named to Outstanding Young Men of Am., 1983-87. Mem. Nat. Assn. Realtors, Tex. Assn. Realtors, Greater Dallas Assn. Realtors, Human Rights Found., Collin County Assn. Realtors, Dallas Songwriters Assn., Dallas Dance Assn., Realty Execs. Internat., Exec. Club., Fed. Club (mem. exec. com.), DRW Fed. Club (mem. exec. com.). Avocations: industrial, transpersonal and counseling psychology, sports, volunteer committees, writing non-fiction, playing piano. Home: 5335 Bent Tree Forest Dr Dallas TX 75248-3483 Office: Consumer Direct Mortgage 8333 Douglas Ave Ste 1320 Dallas TX 75225-5820

CAMERON, HUGH C., career officer. BA in Bus. Adminstrn. and Mgmt., E. Carolina U., 1972; student pilot tng., Reese AFB, Tex., 1972-73; student, 474th Tactical Fighter Wing, Nellis AFB, Nev., 1976-77; MA in Mgmt., U. No. Colo., 1977; student, Squadron Officer Sch., 1978, Armed Forces Staff Coll., 1984, 56th Tactical Tng. Wing, MacDill AFB, Fla., 1984, Nat. War Coll., 1989. Commd. 2d lt. USAF, 1972, advanced through grades to brig. gen., 1996; T-38 instr. pilot Reese AFB, 1973-76; F-111E aircraft comdr. and instr. pilot 20th Tactical Fighter Wing, Royal Air Force, Upper Heyford, Eng., 1977-80; F-111E instr. pilot and wing exec. officer 27th Tactical Fighter Wing, Cannon AFB, N.Mex., 1980-82; aide to comdr. 12th Air Force, Bergstrom AFB, Tex., 1982-83; ops. officer 35th Tactical Fighter Squadron, Kunsan Air Base, S. Korea, 1984-85; stationed at Nellis AFB, 1985-88; plans officer Hdqs. U.S. Ctrl. Command, MacDill AFB, 1989-91; comdr. 51st Ops. Group, Osan Air Base, S. Korea, 1991-93; insp. gen Hdqs. Pacific Air Forces, Hickam AFB, Hawaii, 1993-94; comdr. 8th Fighter Wing, Kunsan Air Base, 1994-95, 3rd Wing, Elmendorf AFB, Alaska, 1995-96, Air Force Ctr. Quality and Mgmt. Innovation, Randolph AFB, Tex., 1996-98; vice comdr. 9th Air Force, dep comdr. U.S. Ctrl. Command Air Forces, Shaw AFB, S.C., 1998—. Decorated Legion of Merit with oak leaf cluster, Bronze Star. Office: 9 AF/CV 524 Shaw Dr Ste 200 Shaw A F B SC 29152

CAMERON, J. ELLIOT, retired parochial educational system administrator; b. Panguitch, Utah, Feb. 9, 1923; s. B.A. and Leonia (Sargent) C.; m. Maxine Petty, Dec. 23, 1942; children—Bruce, Kim, Kerry Lynn, Preston. BS, MA, Brigham Young U., 1946-49; EdD, 1966. High sch. prin., supt. schs. Duchesne, Sevier, Utah, 1949-56; later pres. Snow Coll., Ephraim, Utah, 1956-58; dean students Utah State U., 1958-62; dean of student life, prof. edn., v.p. student svcs. Brigham Young U., Provo, Utah, 1962-80; pres. Hawaii campus Brigham Young U., 1980-86; commr. ch. ednl. system LDS Ch., 1986-89, ret., 1989. Served with AUS, World War II. Mem. NEA, Nat. Assn. Student Personnel Adminstrs., Phi Delta. Kappa. Mem. Ch. of Jesus Christ of Latter-day Saints.

CAMERON, JAMES, film director, screenwriter, producer; b. Kapuskasing, Ont., Can., Aug. 16, 1954; m. Gale Ann Hurd (div.); m. Katheryn Bigelow (div.); 1 child with Linda Hamilton, Josephine Archer. Grad. in Physics, Calif. State U., Fullerton. Head Lightstorm Entertainment, Burbank, Calif., 1992—; CEO Digital Domain, 1993—. Film industry experience includes art dir.: Battle Beyond the Stars, 1980; prodn. designer: Galaxy of Terror, 1981; creator spl. effects: Escape from New York, 1981; film dir.: Piranha II: The Spawning, 1981; dir., screenwriter: The Terminator, 1984, Aliens, 1986, The Abyss, 1989; screenwriter: Rambo: First Blood Part II, 1985; dir., prodr., screenwriter: Terminator II: Judgement Day, 1991, True Lies, 1994; exec. prodr.: Point Break, 1991; dir., Terminator 2 3-D, 1996, Titanic, 1997. Office: Lightstorm Entertainment 919 Santa Monica Blvd Santa Monica CA 90401-2704*

CAMERON, JANICE CAROL, executive assistant; b. Pitcairn, N.Y., Feb. 16, 1940; d. Lawrence Baird and Alice Irene (Manchester) Morgan; m. Albert A. Cameron, III, June 11, 1960 (div. Oct. 26, 1967); children: Albert A. IV, Richard D. AA, Jefferson C.C., Watertown, 1978; BA in Mgmt., St. Mary's Coll., Moraga, Calif., 1984. Nat. dir. Howard Ruff cmty. forums Target, Inc., 1982-86; sr. mktg. adminstr. IPF divsn. The Pacific Bank N.A./Providian Bancorp, San Francisco, 1989-96; with legal dept. Nat. IPF, Mesa, Ariz., 1996-97; exec. asst. to pres. and v.p. Smith-Southwestern, Inc., Mesa, Ariz., 1997—; notary public. Contbr. articles to profl. jours. Founder, chair First Support Group for Parents of Gay Mormons LDS, Social Svcs. Divsn., Fremont, Calif., 1986-94, Utah Gen. Authorities for Soc. Svcs. Program; 1st chpt. dir. Parents, Families and Friends of Lesbians and Gays, Danville-San Ramon chpt., Calif., 1993-94. Democrat. Home: 2400 E Baseline Ave Lot 147 Apache Junction AZ 85219-5712

CAMERON, JOANNA, actress, director; b. Greeley, Colo.; d. Harold and Erna (Borgens) C. Student, U. Calif., 1967-68, Pasadena Playhouse, 1968; A in Mktg., Monterey Peninsula Coll., 1996. media cons. to Cath. Bishops on Papal Visit of Pope John Paul II, Calif., 1987. Starred in: weekly TV series The Shazam-ISIS hour, CBS, 1976-78; host, dir.: for TV equipped ships USN Closed Circuit Network Program, 1977, 78, 79, 80; guest star: numerous network TV shows, including Merv Griffin Show, The Survivors, Love American Style, Mission Impossible, The Tonight Show; appeared in numerous commls.; network prime time shows including Name of the Game, Medical Center, Bob Hope Special, The Bold Ones, Marcus Welby, Columbo, High Risk, Switch; motion picture debut in How to Commit Marriage, 1969; other film appearances include The Amazing Spiderman; dir. various commls., CBS Preview Spl.; producer, dir. documentaries include Razor Sharp, 1981, El Camino Real, 1987; discovered by Walt Disney while spl. tour guide at Disneyland; named in Guiness Book of Records for most nat. network programmed commls. Mem. Dirs. Guild Am., Acad. TV Arts and Scis., AFTRA, Screen Actors Guild, Delta Delta Delta. Club: Los Angeles Athletic.

CAMERON, JOHN CLIFFORD, lawyer, health science facility administrator; b. Phila., Sept. 17, 1946; m. Eileen Duffy, July 12, 1975; children: Christopher, Meghan. BA, U. Pitts., 1969; MBA, Temple U., 1972; JD, Widener U., 1976; LLM, NYU, 1980. Bar: Pa. 1977, N.J. 1977, Md. 1995. Asst. adminstr. Phila. Psychiatric Ctr., 1972-76; jud. clk. to presiding justice N.J. Superior Ct., Newark, 1976-77; asst. adminstr. St. Elizabeth Hosp., Elizabeth, N.J., 1977; v.p. corp. legal affairs Methodist Hosp., Phila., 1978-94; solicitor, 1988-94; legal cons. North Penn Hosp, Lansdale, Pa., 1994-95; counsel, legal adminstr. Hodes, Ulman, Pessin & Katz, P.A., Towson, Md., 1995-96; asst. to pres. Temple U. Health Sys., Phila., 1996—; asst. sec. Neumann Med. Ctr., Phila., 1997—, Temple U. Children's Med. Ctr., Phila., 1997—, Jeanes Hosp., Phila., 1997—, Northwood Nursing Home, Phila., 1997—, Temple Physicians, Inc., Phila., 1997—, Temple Univ. Hosp., Phila., 1997—, Lower Bucks Hosp., Bristol, Pa., 1997—, Episcopal Hosp., Phila., 1997—, Temple U. Children's Med. Ctr., Phila., 1997—; sec. Suthbrelt Properties, Ltd., Phila., 1981-94, Asbury Corp., Wilmington, Del., 1982-94, Healthmark, Inc., Moorestown, N.J., 1982-94, Meth. Hosp. Nursing Ctr., Phila., 1983-94; asst. sec. various hosps. and nursing homes, 1997—, instr. Grad. Sch. Mgmt., Pa. State U., 1991—; instr. mgmt. dept. Neumann Coll., 1991-96; instr. bus. divsn. Rosemont Coll., 1995-96. Contbr. articles to profl. jours. Mem. campaign United Way, Phila., 1979-94; mem. health and welfare com. United Meth. Eastern Pa. Conf., 1978-94; advisor Explorer Post, Boy Scouts Am., 1988-94; mem. steering com. Golden Cross, Phila., 1984-94; sec. Tredyffrin Twp. Park and Recreation Bd., 1987-95; alumni rep. Widener U.; mem. environ. adv. com. and open space task force Tredyffrin Twp., 1991-95. Fellow Am. Coll. Healthcare Execs. (chmn. bylaws com. 1995-96); mem. ABA, N.J. Bar Assn., Pa. Bar Assn., Phila. Bar Assn., Am. Hosp. Assn., Hosp. Assn. Pa., Swedish Colonial Soc. (bd dirs. 1992—, gov. 1993-95), Sons of Union Vets. of Civil War, SAR. Avocations: swimming, music. Home: 1410 Church Rd Malvern PA 19355-9714

CAMERON, JOHN M., nuclear scientist, educator, science administrator; b. Aug. 9, 1940. BSc, Queens U., Ireland, 1962; MSc, UCLA, 1965, PhD, 1967. Tech. asst. U.K. Atomic Energy Authority, Eng., 1962-63; asst. prof. UCLA, 1967-68; rsch. assoc. U. Wash., Seattle, 1968-70; asst. prof. to prof. U. Alta., 1970-87; dir. Cyclotron Facility, prof. dept. physics Ind. U., Bloomington, 1987—; asst. dir. initial ops. TRIUMF, Vancouver, 1973-74; vis scientist U. Paris, SIN Switzerland, 1977-78; staff scientist Nat. Saturne Lab., France, 1971-82; dir. Nuclear Rsch. Ctr., U. Alta., 1985-87. Fellow Am. Phys. Soc. Office: IN Univ Bloomington Cyclotron Facility 2401 Milo Sampson Ln Bloomington IN 47408-1368*

CAMERON, JUDITH LYNNE, secondary education educator, hypnotherapist; b. Oakland, Calif., Apr. 29, 1945; d. Alfred Joseph and June Estelle (Faul) Moe; m. Richard Irwin Cameron, Dec. 17, 1967; 1 child, Kevin Dale. AA in Psychol., Sacramento City Coll., 1965; BA in Psychol., German, Calif. State U., 1967; MA in Reading Specialization, San Francisco State U., 1972; postgrad., Chapman Coll.; PhD, Am. Inst. Hypnotherapy, 1987. Cert. tchr., Calif. Tchr. St. Vincent's Cath. Sch., San Jose, Calif., 1969-70, Fremont (Calif.) Elem. Sch., 1970-72, LeRoy Boys Home, LaVerne, Calif., 1972-73; tchr. Grace Miller Elem. Sch., LaVerne, Calif., 1973-80, resource specialist, 1980-84; owner, mgr. Pioneer Take-out Franchises, Alhambra and San Gabriel, Calif., 1979-85; resource specialist, dept. chmn. Bonita H.S., LaVerne, Calif., 1984—; mentor tchr. in space sci. Bonita Unified Sch. Dist., 1988—, rep. LVTV; owner, therapist So. Calif. Clin. Hypnotherapy, Claremont, Calif., 1988—; bd. dirs., recommending tchr., asst. dir. Project Turnabout, Claremont, Calif.; Teacher-in-Space cons. Bonita Unified Sch. Dist., LaVerne, 1987—; advisor Peer Counseling Program, Bonita High Sch., 1987—; advisor Air Explorers/Edwards Test Pilot Sch., LaVerne, 1987—; mem. Civil Air Patrol, Squadron 68, Aerospace Office, 1988—; selected amb. U.S. Space Acad.-U.S. Space Camp Acad., Huntsville, Ala., 1990; named to national (now internat.) teaching faculty challenger Ctr. for Space Edn., Alexandria, Va., 1990; regional coord. East San Gabiel Valley Future Scientists and Engrs. of Am.; amb. to U.S. Space Camp, 1990; mem. adj. faculty challenger learning ctr. Calif. State U., Dominguez Hills, 1994; rep. ceremony to honor astronauts Apollo 11, White House, 1994. Vol. advisor Children's Home Soc., Santa Ana, 1980-81; dist. rep. LVTV Channel 29, 1991; regional coord. East San Gabriel Valley chpt. Future Scientists and Engrs. of Am., 1992; mem. internat. investigation Commn. UFOs, 1991; field mem. Ctr. for Search for Extraterrestrial Intelligence, 1996. Recipient Tchr. of Yr., Bonita H.S., 1989, continuing svc. award, 1992; named Toyolaa Tchr. of Yr., 1994. Mem. NEA, AAUW, Internat. Investigations Com. on UFOs, Coun. Exceptional Children, Calif. Assn. Resource Specialists, Calif. Elem. Edn. Assn., Calif. Tchrs. Assn., Calif. Assn. Marriage and Family Therapists, Planetary Soc., Mutual UFO Network, Com. Sci. Investigation L5 Soc., Challenger Ctr. Space Edn., Calif. Challenger Ctr. Crew for Space Edn., Orange County Astronomers, Chinese Shar-Pei Am., Concord Club, Rare Breed Dog Club (L.A.). Republican. Avocations: skiing, surfing, guitar, flying, astrophotography. Home: 3257 La Travesia Dr Fullerton CA 92835-1455 Office: Bonita High Sch 115 W Allen Ave San Dimas CA 91773-1437

CAMERON, KAY, conductor, music director, arranger; b. Robbins, N.C.; d. Joe and Gladys (Hussey) C. MusB, U. N.C., 1972, MusM, 1973. Music dir. Kennedy Ctr. For the Performing Arts, Washington, 1994—; tchr. Richmond Pub. Schs., Va., 1973-77; music dir., condr. broadway and nat. tours, N.Y., 1978—; arranger, orchestrator musicals and TV, N.Y., 1979—; vis. lectr. U. N.C., Wilmington, 1997-98. Music dir., condr. State Fair, The Will Rogers Follies, Phantom, The King and I, On The 20th Century, Sugar Babies, Showboat, The Sound of Music, Salute To The Broadway Composer, The Sound Of Rodgers And Hammerstein, New Moon, La Cage Aux Folles (opera) Amelia Goes To The Ball, Candide, Die Fledermaus, Hansel and Gretel, The Medium, Madama Butterfly, The Telephone, others; arranger, orchestrator Show Boat on PBS, United Nations 40th Anniversary, Herman & Soundheim Together, (compositions) A Christmas Carol, Heroes, others. Mem. Am. Fedn. Musicians. Home: 2909 Caliber Ct Wilmington NC 28405-8802

CAMERON, KIRK MACGREGOR DRUMMOND, statistician; b. Glendale, Calif., Oct. 27, 1962; s. Paul Drummond and Virginia May (Rusthoi) C.; m. Kelly Mitchell, May 21, 1994; chilre: Kaitlyn Gray, Kit MacGregor. BS in Math., U. Nebr., 1984; MS in Statis., Stanford U., 1989, PhD in Statis., 1990. Statis. cons. Family Rsch. Inst., Colorado Springs, Colo., 1983—; sr. statis. Sci. Applications Internat. Corp., McLean, Va., 1990-95; pres., statis. cons. Macstat Cons., Colorado Springs, 1995—; bd. dirs. Family Rsch. Inst., editor, 1995—. Contbr. articles to profl. jours. Youth counselor McLean Bible Ch., 1991-94; Sunday sch. leader Village Seven Presbyn., Colorado Springs, 1995—; county del. El Paso County Rep. Conv., Colorado Springs, 1998. NSF Grad. fellow, 1984, Pew Found. Teaching fellow, 1990. Mem. Phi Beta Kappa. Avocations: rock collecting, guitar, hiking, camping, tennis.

CAMERON, KRISTEN ELLEN SCHMIDT, nurse, construction company executive, educator, writer; b. Waterbury, Conn., Mar. 11, 1953; d. William Thomas and Shirley Ellen (Peck) Schmidt; m. Roderick P. Cameron, Feb. 12, 1972; children: Sara Ellen, James Ryan. Diploma in practical nursing, Eli Whitney Tech., 1973; ASN, Pasco Hernando C.C., Brooksville, Fla., 1987; BSN, Fla. So. Coll., Lakeland, 1992; MS, U. So. Fla., 1994. RN, Fla. Office nurse J.B. Forman, MD, New Haven, 1973-74; staff nurse Hewitt Meml. Hosp., Shelton, Conn., 1979-80; medication nurse Zephyr Haven Nursing Home, Zephyrhills, Fla., 1982-85; utilization rev. coordinator East Pasco Med. Ctr., Zephyrhills, 1985-86; staff nurse East Pasco Med. Ctr., Zephyrhills, Fla., 1987—; sec., treas. Sunscape Builders Inc., Ridge Manor, Fla., 1986—; clin. coord. med.-surg. East Pasco Med. Ctr., Zephyrhills, 1988-90, adminstrv. asst., 1990; field RN Gulf Coast Home Health Svc., 1990-91; lab. facilitator RN program Pasco Hernando C.C., Brooksville, Fla., 1991, instr. RN program, faculty advisor student nurse's orgn., 1992-98, asst. prof. nursing, 1998—; mem. nursing celebration com. East Pasco Med. Ctr., 1987-90, chmn., 1989, sec. nursing guild, 1990; participant APHA Nat. Conv., Washington, 1994. Contbr. articles to profl. nursing jours. Mem. Ridge Manor Fla. Blood Bank, 1986—, Ridge Manor Property Assn., 1985—, East Pasco Adventist Ednl. Ctr. Home and Sch. Assn., Dade City, Fla. 1987-88; editor Dade City Seventh Day Adventist Ch. newsletter; bd. dirs. East Pasco Adventist Ednl. Ctr., Dade City, 1983—, newsletter editor 1986, 87. Mem. APHA, Nat. League Nurses (chmn. mission governance faculty and students com. 1998—), Fla. Nurses Assn., Greater Hernando County C. of C., Hernando County Builders Assn., Alumni Assn. Fla. So. Coll., Alumni Assn. U. So. Fla., Sigma Theta Tau, Phi Kappa Phi. Republican. Avocations: raising roses and African violets, boating, fishing, writing. Home: 33408 Pennsylvania Ave Ridge Manor FL 33523-9044

CAMERON, LUCILLE WILSON, retired dean of libraries; b. Nashua, N.H., Dec. 21, 1932; d. Hugh Alexander and Louise Perham (Baldwin) C.; m. James Robert Doris, Aug. 19, 1976; children: Glenn A. Browning, Gail W. Browning, Valerie B. Cruickshank. BA, U. R.I., 1964, MLS, 1972. Social case worker R.I. Dept. Pub. Assistance, Providence, 1964-70; asst. circulation libr. U. R.I. Libr., Kingston, 1970-72, reserve libr., 1972-73, reference/bibliographer, 1973-88, head reference unit, 1983-86, chair pub. svcs., 1988-89, interim dean, 1989-90, dean, 1990-92, dean emerita; bd. trustees North Scituate (R.I.) Pub. Libr., 1995, pres., 1996. Co-author: Labor and Industrial Relations Journals and Serials, 1989; contbr. articles to profl. jours. Bd. trustees North Scituate (R.I.) Pub. Libr., 1995—, pres., 1996—. Recipient Computerized Intergrated Libr. System award Champlin Founds., Providence, 1989, 90, 91, Coll. Tech. Libr. Program award U.S. Dept. Edn., Washington, 1990, Disting. Alumna award Grad. Sch. Libr. and Info. Studies, U. R.I., Kingston, 1991. Mem. ALA, Assn. Coll. and Rsch. Librs., Consortium R.I. Acad. and Rsch. Librs., Higher Edn. Libr. Info. Network (chair), Univ. Press New England (gov.), North Scituate (R.I.) Pub. Libr. Assn. (bd. trustees 1995—, pres. 1996—), Alpha Kappa Delta.

CAMERON, MARYELLEN, science association administrator, geologist, educator; b. New Orleans, Nov. 15, 1943; m. Kevin D. Crowley. BS in Geology, U. Houston, 1965, MS, 1969; PhD, Va. Poly. Inst. and State U., 1972. Rsch. and teaching asst. Va. Poly. Inst. and State U., Blacksburg, 1968-70; fellow geophysical lab. Carnegie Inst. Washington, 1971; rschr. SUNY, Stony Brook, 1971-73; rsch. assoc., asst. rsch. earth scientist U. Calif., Santa Cruz, 1973-81; assoc. prof. U. Okla., Norman, 1981-87; prof., chair geology dept. Miami U., Oxford, Ohio, 1987-92; program. dir. NSF, Arlington, Va., 1992-97, from acting exec. officer to exec. officer, 1997—; proposal review panel NSF, 1985-88, adv. com. for earth scis., 1992; disting. vis. scientist facility for high resolution electron microscopy Ariz. State U., Tempe, 1990; vis. scientist dept. earth and planetary scis. U. N.Mex., Albuquerque, 1991; Donnay lectr. Carnegie Inst. Washington, 1993. Contbr. numerous articles and abstracts to profl. jours. Grantee NSF, 1977-92. Fellow Geol. Soc. Am. (councilor 1995-97), Mineral. Soc. Am. (lectr. short course 1980, assoc. editor Am. Mineralogist 1980-83, sec. 1987-91, Inaugural lectr. 1989-90); mem. AAAS, Am. Geophys. Union, Geochem. Soc., Am. Chem. Soc., Materials Rsch. Soc., Geol. Soc. Washington, Sigma Xi. Achievements include rsch. in structural variations in silicate and phosphate minerals, thermal annealing systematics and radiation damage of apatites, igneous petrology and geochemistry of Tertiary igneous rocks of the southwestern U.S. and Mexico; development of NSF's environmental geochemistry and biogeochemistry research activity. Home: 6408 Recreation Ln Falls Church VA 22041-1217 Office: NSF Polar Programs Office Rm 755 4201 Wilson Blvd Arlington VA 22230-0001

CAMERON, NICHOLAS ALLEN, diversified corporation executive; b. Phila., Jan. 6, 1939; s. Nicholas Guyot and Katherine (Rogers) C.; m. Leslie Wood, Dec. 14, 1974; children: Christopher Wilson, Pamela Wilson. BS, Yale U., 1960. Treas. Allied Corp., Morristown, N.J., 1979-81, v.p. and treas., 1981-82, v.p. fin., 1982-83, v.p. planning and devel., 1983-85; sr. v.p. planning, devel. and adminstrn. Allied-Signal Inc., Morristown, N.J., 1985-86; sr. v.p. tech. and bus. devel. Bendix Aerospace-Allied-Signal, Inc., Arlington, Va., 1986-87; group pres. Allied-Signal Aerospace, 1988; sr. v.p. ops. svcs. Allied-Signal, Inc., Morristown, N.J., 1988-90, sr. v.p., gen. mgr. chem. intermediates, 1990-95. Bd. dirs. Morristown Meml. Health Found., 1996—, United Way of Morris County, Morristown, N.J., 1980-86, 90-98, campaign chmn., 1991, chief vol. officer, 1993-95, bd. chmn., 1996-98; bd. dirs. Morris 2000, 1990, chmn., 1993-96; mem. adv. bd. Morristown Hosp., 1998—; commr. Morris County Park Commn., 1999-2004. Mem. Morris County C. of C. (bd. dirs. 1975-86, 1990-98), Tau Beta Pi. Republican. Episcopalian. Clubs: St. Elmo Soc. (New Haven); Morris County Golf. Home and Office: 37 Barkman Way Chester NJ 07930

CAMERON, OLIVER GENE, psychiatrist, educator, psychobiology researcher; b. Evanston, Ill., Aug. 28, 1946; s. Gene Oliver and Elizabeth Marie (Burns) C.; m. Susan Linda Friedman, June 22, 1972; children—Leah Victoria, Peter Sean. B.A., U. Notre Dame, 1968; Ph.D., U. Chgo., 1972, M.D., 1974. Diplomate Am. Bd. psychiatry and Neurology. Med. intern U. Mich., Ann Arbor, 1974-75, psychiatry resident, 1975-78, psychiatry fellow, 1978-79, asst. prof. psychiatry, 1979-86, assoc. prof., 1986-92, prof., 1992—; dir. anxiety disorders program, dept. psychiatry, 1984-85, dir. adult psychiatry outpatient program, dept. psychiatry, 1985-90, Combined Mood & Anxiety Program, 1994—. Contbr. articles to profl. jours. Mem. Am. Psychiatric Assn., Am. Psychosomatic Soc., AAAS, Sigma Xi. Avocations: photography; travel; golf. Home: 1215 Southwood Ct Ann Arbor MI 48103-9735 Office: U Mich 1500 E Medical Center Dr Ann Arbor MI 48109-0005

CAMERON, PAUL DRUMMOND, research facility administrator; b. Pitts., Nov. 9, 1939; s. Nelson Drummond and Veronica (Witco) C.; m. Virginia May Rusthoi. BA, L.A. Pacific Coll., 1961; MA, Calif. State U., L.A., 1962; PhD, U. Colo., 1966. Asst. prof. psychology Stout State U., Menomonie, Wis., 1966-67, Wayne State U., Detroit, 1967-69; assoc. prof. psychology U. Louisville, 1970-73, Fuller Grad. Sch. Psychology, Pasadena, Calif., 1976-79; assoc. prof. marriage and family U. Nebr., Lincoln, 1979-80; pvt. practice psychologist Lincoln, 1980-83; chmn. Family Rsch. Inst., Washington, 1982-95, Colo. Springs, 1995—; reviewer Am. Psychologist, Jour. Gerontology, Psychol. Reports; presenter, witness, cons. in field. Author: Exposing the AIDS Scandal, 1988, The Gay 90's, 1993; contbr. articles to profl. jours. Mem. Ea. Psychol. Assn., Nat. Assn. for Rsch. and Treatment of Homosexuality. Republican. Lutheran. Achievements include investigation of health effects of second-hand tobacco smoke; investigation of first comprehensive national random sample of sexuality; documented abbreviated lifespan of homosexuals. Office: Family Rsch Inst PO Box 62640 Colorado Springs CO 80962-2640

CAMERON, RITA GIOVANNETTI, writer, publisher; b. Washington; d. Joseph Angelo and Adeline Katherine (Fochett) C. BS with honors, U. Md., 1957; MEd, Am. U., Washington, 1962; DEd, Nova U., 1978. Tchr. D.C. pub. schs., Washington, 1959-64; prin. Prince George's County (Md.) Pub. Schs., 1964-73, 76-84; supr. instrn. K-12 Prince George's County pub. schs., 1973-76; free-lance writer ednl. materials Media, Materials Inc., Balt., 1965-75; Learning Well, Balt., 1995; free-lance writer travel articles AAA, Washington, 1978-83; owner, pub. Sch. House Global Enterprises, Fort Washington, Md., 1980—; presenter, cons. to sch. systems and ednl. orgns., 1985—. Author: Let's Learn About Maryland and Prince George's County, 1970, Let's Learn About Maryland, 1972, 95, Super Sub! Or How to Substitute Teach in Elementary School, 1974, AAA Travel articles and Traffic Safety Teacher Guide Grades 4-6, 1982, 83; author, pub.: The Master Teacher's Plan and Record Book, 1985, The School House Encyclopedia of Educational Programs and Activities, 1991; author, publisher and nat. marketer of 80 social studies and sci. ednl. materials for students grades 4-10; developer/owner School House Global Enterprises Pub. Co. Food preparer So Others Might Eat, Washington, 1985—, food preparer for Missions of Charity Home for AIDS Victims, Washington, 1992—, child sponsor Christian Found. for Children and Aging. Recipient Outstanding Citizenship award DAR, 1954, Nat. Tchr. award Expedition Nat. Tchr. Awards Program, 1960-61, Outstanding Tchr. Sci. award D.C. Coun. Engring. and Archtl. Soc. and Washington Acad. Scis., 1964, Outstanding Educator of Yr. award Prince George's County Bd. Edn., 1982-83, Am. Hist. award DAR, 1987, Outstanding Contbn. to Bicentennial Leadership Project award Couns. for Advancement of Citizenship, 1989. Mem. Md., Fla., N.C., N.Y., Pa. N.J., Va., Tex., Ga., Gt. Lakes, Mid. States, S.E., and N.E. Regional Coun. for Studies, U. Md. Alumni Assn., Am. U. Alumni Assn., Nova U. Alumni Assn., Nat. Press Club, Phi Kappa Phi. Roman Catholic. Avocations: art, music, theater, antiques, travel. Office: Sch House Global Enterprises PO Box 441028 Fort Washington MD 20749-1028 *In one form or another, I have been a teacher all my life. It's been an enormous responsibility, matched only by enormous satisfaction. The knowledge, skills, love for learning, and feelings of self-worth given to students are among the finest gifts they will ever receive.*

CAMERON, RONDO, economic history educator; b. Linden, Tex., Feb. 20, 1925; s. Burr S. and Annie Mae (Dalrymple) C.; m. Claydean Zumbrunnen, July 26, 1946; children: Alan, Cindia. A.B., Yale U., 1948, A.M., 1949; Ph.D., U. Chgo., 1952. Instr. Yale, 1951-52; asst. prof. U. Wis. at Madison, 1952-56, assoc. prof., 1957-61, prof. econs. and history, dir. grad. program econ. history, 1961-69; William Rand Kenan Univ. prof. Emory U., 1969-93, emeritus, 1993—; vis. prof. U. Chgo., 1956-57, U. Glasgow, 1962-63, U. Chile, 1965-67, Keio U., Tokyo, 1987, U. Augsburg, Fed. Republic Germany, 1988-89, Fed. U. Rio de Janeiro, 1990; spl. field rep. Rockefeller Found., S.A., 1965-67. Author: France and the Economic Development of Europe, rev. edit., 1966, trans. to French and Spanish, 1971, Banking in the Early Stages of Industrialization, 1967, trans. to Japanese, 1973, Spanish, Italian, The European World, 2d edit., 1970, Civilizations: Western and World, 1975, A Concise Economic History of the World from Paleolithic Times to the Present, 3d rev. edit., 1997, trans. into Spanish, French, German, Dutch, Italian, Polish, Finnish, Hungarian, Czech, Japanese, Korean and Chinese; editor: Essays in French Economic History, 1970, Civilization Since Waterloo, 1971, Banking and Economic Development, 1972, International Banking, 1870-1914, 1991, Financing Industrialization, 1992; Am. rev. editor jour. Econ. History, 1968-69, editor, 1975-81; Econ. History Rev., 1960-65, rev. editor; contbr. articles to profl. jours. Chmn. Council Research Econ. History, 1967-69; bd. dirs. Albert Schweitzer Fellowship. Fulbright scholar France, 1950-51; Guggenheim fellow Europe, 1954-55, 70-71; fellow Center Advanced Study Behavioral Scis., 1958-59; Fulbright prof. U. Glasgow, 1962-63, Fed. U. Rio de Janeiro, 1990; Fellow Woodrow Wilson Internat. Center for Scholars, 1974-75. Mem. Am. Hist. Assn. (co-chmn. program com. 1983), Internat. Econ. Hist. Assn. (exec. com., v.p. 1986-90), Am. Econ. Hist. Assn. (pres. 1974-75), Brit. Econ. Hist. Assn., French Econ. Hist. Assn. Home: 1088 Clifton Rd NE Atlanta GA 30307-1228

CAMERON, THOMAS WILLIAM LANE, investment company executive; b. Newton, Mass., Feb. 19, 1927; s. Percy G. and Mary W.D. (Mitchell) C.; m. Carol Louise Soliday, June 17, 1950; children: Helen Delone, Thomas Mitchell (dec.). A.B. cum laude, Harvard, 1948, M.B.A., 1951. With sales dept. Procter & Gamble, Boston, 1951-53; with Hopper, Soliday, & Co., Inc., Phila., 1953-66; ptnr. Hopper, Soliday, & Co., Inc., 1961—, pres., 1966-72, chmn., 1972-83; dir. Hopper, Soliday & Co., Inc., 1983-86; sr. v.p. Interstate/Johnson Lane, Johns Island, S.C., 1986—; chmn. Sovereign Investors Inc., 1979-91; vice chmn. John Hancock Sovereign Investors, 1991-96; chmn. Phila.-Balt.-Washington Stock Exch., 1970-74, bd. govs., 1963-75. Bd. mgrs. Franklin Inst., 1970-90, chmn., 1978-81; bd. dirs. Holling Cancer Ctr., Med. U. S.C., 1992—. Served with USNR, 1944-46. Clubs: Waynesborough Country (Paoli, Pa.) (pres. 1965-67); Harvard (Phila.) (pres. 1965-66), Harvard Bus. Sch. (Phila.) (pres. 1962-64). Home: 332 Catbrier Ct Johns Island SC 29455-5618 Office: Interstate/Johnson Lane 1892 Andell Bluff Blvd Johns Island SC 29455-6301

CAMERON, WILLIAM DUNCAN, plastics company executive; b. Harrell, N.C., June 14, 1925; s. Paul Archiebald and Atwood (Herring) C.; m. Betty Gibson, Oct. 3, 1953; children: Phillip MacDonald, Colleen Kay. Student Duke U., 1945-49. Chmn. emeritus Reef Industries Inc., Houston. Pres. bd. trustees Trinity Episcopal Sch., Galveston, Tex., 1981-82; trustee William Temple Found., 1987-90. Served with U.S. Army, 1943-45. Mem. Houston C. of C. (chmn. mfg. com. 1967), Rotary, Galveston Artillery, Bob Smith Yacht. Home: PO Box 310 Smith Ranch Rd Cuero TX 77954-0310 Office: Reef Industries Inc 9209 Almeda Genoa Rd Houston TX 77075-2339

CAMERY, JOHN WILLIAM, computer engineer; b. Cin., Feb. 5, 1951; s. Donald Otis and Mary Lynne (Edgington) C. *In July, 1997, using his frequent flyer miles, he organized the family vacation. His parents, well known in amateur radio and Army MARS, his Aunt Emily Leslie, his sisters, Amy Sue and Marianne, their husbands, Moussa Abdallah and John Meyer, and their children, Kristen, Matthew, John and Mary Elizabeth flew to Hawaii, staying at Puamana, Maui and the Imperial. They traversed the islands, up Haleakela and Diamond Head and even underseas courtesy of his friend Maily Schara at Atlantis Submarines. Kristen and Matthew snorkeled at Hanauma Bay and learned to train dolphins at Sea Life Park. Matthew learned to surf.* BA, U. Cin., 1972; MS, Carnegie-Mellon U., 1974. Mathematician U.S. Army Material Systems Analysis Agy., Aberdeen Proving Grounds, Md., 1973; student asst. engring. spectrum analysis task force Fed. Comms. Commn., Park Ridge, Ill., 1974; mathematician U.S. Army Comms. Electronics-Engring. Agy., Washington, 1975-83; computer specialist U.S. Army Mgmt. Systems Analysis Agy., Washington, 1983; mathematician Def. Comms. Agy., Washington, 1983-86; programmer, analyst Gen. Scis. Corp., Laurel, Md., 1986-87; software engr. Sygnetron Protection Systems, Timonium, Md., 1987-88, Automation Cons., Inc., Balt., 1988-89, RDA Logicon, Leavenworth, Kans., 1989—; cons. Martin Marietta Ocean Systems Ops., Glen Burnie, Md., 1988—. *He was instrumental in designing the system to consolidate the "genser" message traffic centers for the Pentagon. During the pre-INF Treaty period, he supported the software maintenance effort on the Theater Mission Planning System and Mission Data Preparation System for TLAM-N and GLCM. He has collected data for the FCC to evaluate their Automated Frequency Assignment Model, enhanced the Data Systems Dynamic Simulator for NASA at Goddard Space Flight Center, developed the communication software for the Global Telemetered Seismograph Network and provided technical support for the "Corps Battle Simulation" warfighter exercises world-wide for the Battle Command Training Program.* Carnegie-Mellon U. fellow, 1972-73. Mem. Am. Math. Soc., Societe Mathematique de France, Soc. for Indsl. and Applied Math., European Math. Soc., Internat. Platform Assn., Imperial Hawaii Vacation Club, Greater Cin. Amateur Radio Club. Republican. Mem. Christian Ch. Avocations: music, dancing, swimming, electronics, travel. Home: 655 Sheridan Ct Leavenworth KS 66048-4449 Office: RDA Logicon PO Box 681 Leavenworth KS 66048-1098

CAMFIELD, WILLIAM ARNETT, art educator; b. San Angelo, Tex., Oct. 29, 1934; s. William Augustus and Frances Maurine (Arnett) C.; m. Virginia Anne Kindig, June 1, 1958; children: Lynn Alexia, Paul Justin, Mark Arnett. BA, Princeton U., 1957; MA, Yale U., 1961, PhD, 1964. Asst. to assoc. prof. U. St. Thomas, Houston, 1964-69; assoc. prof. to prof. Rice U., Houston, 1969—, Joseph and Joanna Nazro Mullen prof., 1980; mem. art adv. coun. Princeton (N.J.) U., 1975-91; advisor Archives Am. Art, Tex. area, Houston, 1980-85. Author: Francis Picabia, 1979; author/curator exhbns. Francis Picabia at Guggenheim Mus., 1970, Tabu Dada, Kunsthalle Berne, 1983, Marcel Duchamp: Fountain, Menil Coll., Houston, 1989, Max Ernst: Dada and the Dawn of Surrealism, MOMA, 1993, The Paintings of Frank Freed, Museum of Fine Arts, Houston, 1996. Bd. dirs. Citizens for Good Schs., Houston, 1966-68; deacon, elder St. Phillip Presbyn. Ch., Houston, 1974-80; juror/advisor various civic art projects, Houston; trustee Mus. Fine Arts, Houston, 1979-88, The Eleanor and Frank Freed Found. Capt. arty. U.S. Army, 1957-59. Fellow Am. Coun. Learned Socs., 1973-74, NEH, 1981, John Simon Guggenheim Found., 1988-89; Am. Philos. Soc. grantee, 1965. Mem. Coll. Art Assn., Tex. Conf. Art Historians (co-founder 1978-79). Democrat. Avocations: jogging, reading, travel. Office: Rice U 6100 Main St Houston TX 77005-1892

CAMHY, SHERRY WALLERSTEIN, painter; b. N.Y.C., Nov. 12, 1940; d. Abraham and Irene Kronen Wallerstein; children: Abraham, Caroline. M of Art Edn., Columbia U., 1970; postgrad., NYU. Med. sch. tchr. anatomy Montclair Art Mus., Montclair, N.J., 1987, 88; tchr. painting and drawing Rockland Ctr. for the Arts, N.Y., 1989-93; tchr. Tisch Sch. Arts N.Y. Univ., 1998—; tchr. anatomy Sch. of Visual Arts, N.Y.C., 1999—; tchr. anatomy and life drawing Art Students League, N.Y.C., 1999—. Author: The Art of the Pencil, 1997; one-person shows Pace U., N.Y.C., 1993, Nat. Arts Club, N.Y.C., West Hampton Beach Libr., L.I.; groups shows include Santa Barbara Mus. of Natural History, 1990, Frank Caro Gallery, Santa Barbara, Calif., 1992, Nat. Art Club, 1996, Faculty Sch. of Visual Arts and Art Students League, 1994-97, Prince Street Gallery, 1994, Hammond Mus., 1993, So. Alleghenies Mus. Art, Aldrich Mus. Ridgefield, 1999, numerous others; work collected at Isreal Mus., The Internat. Fin. Group, Atlantic Levenson Internat., Inc., Art Student's League, others. Mem. Nat. Arts Club. Office: Studio 819 West Chelsea Art Ctr 526 W 26th St # W New York NY 10001-5517

CAMIC, DAVID EDWARD, lawyer; b. Indpls., June 11, 1954; s. Edward Franklin Camic and Carolyn (Hooker) Camic-Longland. BA, Aurora U., 1982; postgrad., DePaul U., 1982-83; JD cum laude, John Marshall Law Sch., 1987. Bar: Ill. 1987, U.S. Dist. Ct. (no. dist.) Ill. 1990, N.Y. 1996. Ptnr. Camic, Johnson, Wilson & McCulloch P.C., Aurora, Ill., 1987—; mem. faculty, lectr. Aurora U.; lectr. in criminal law Regional Police Tng., Aurora, 1987—. Contbr. articles to profl. jours. Chmn. Rape Def. Seminar, Aurora, 1986. Named Man of Yr. Todays Orgn. Youth, 1987. Mem. ABA, Ill. Bar Assn. (past-chair criminal justice sect.), Kane County Bar Assn. (past chair criminal law com.), Assn. Trial Lawyers Am., Nat. Assn. Criminal Lawyers, Phi Delta Phi. Office: Camic Johnson Wilson & McCulloch PC 546 W Galena Blvd Aurora IL 60506-3855

CAMILLERI, MICHAEL, lawyer, educator; b. N.Y.C., July 16, 1953; s. Joseph and Lena (Calatozzo) C.; m. Debralyn Fisher, Aug. 5, 1989; children: Bryan, Brandon, Brooke. BA, L.I. U., 1974; JD, Fordham U., 1977. Bar: N.Y. 1978. Sr. v.p., gen. counsel Nat. Coun. Compensation Ins., N.Y.C., 1978-91; ptnr. Adorno & Zeder, Miami, 1991—; pres. Ins. Data Resources, 1997—; cons. Family Counseling Ctr., Bklyn., 1980-85; adj. prof. law Coll. Ins., N.Y.C., 1981-91; arbitrator civil ct., N.Y.C., 1983-91. Author: Matthew Bender's Accident and Health Law, 1989; editor: Werbel's N.Y. Worker's Compensation Law, 1986-94. Mem. ABA, N.Y. State Bar Assn., D.C. Bar Assn., Profl. Bowlers Assn. Office: IDR 5200 Town Center Cir Ste 500 Boca Raton FL 33486-1012 also: 888 SE 3rd Ave Ste 500 Fort Lauderdale FL 33316-1159

CAMINITI, DONALD ANGELO, lawyer. BA magna cum laude, Rutgers U., 1973, JD, 1976. Bar: N.J. 1976, D.C. 1977, N.Y. 1980; cert. civil trial atty. N.J. Supreme Ct., cert. trial lawyer Nat. Bd. Trial Advocacy. Ptnr. Breslin & Breslin, P.A., Hackensack, N.J., 1977—; counsel Housing Authority of Bergen County, 1977—; asst. counsel Twp. of River Vale, 1977-80; counsel Housing Devel. Corp. Bergen County, 1978—, North Bergen Rent Leveling Bd., 1980—, North Bergen Housing Authority, 1980-84, Englewood Housing Authority, 1991—, Fort Lee Housing Authority, 1993—; spl. counsel Dept. Housing and Urban Devel., N.J., 1990—; counsel Guttenberg Housing Authority, 1995—; Master Morris Pashman Inns Ct., 1998—; speaker in field. Author: (with others) Products Liability Practice Guide, 1988. With USAF, 1966-70. Mem. ABA, N.J. Bar Assn., D.C. Bar Assn., N.Y. Bar Assn., Bergen County Bar Assn., Assn. Trial Lawyers Am. (bd. govs. N.J. chpt. parliamentarian N.J. chpt. 1984-85, seminar com. chmn. 1984-87, chmn. edn. com. 1990-91, v.p. 1990-91, 2d v.p. 1991-92, 1st v.p. 1992-93, pres.-elect 1993-94, pres. 1994-95), Nat. Bd. Trial Adv., Phi Beta Kappa. Home: 48 Union Ave Saddle River NJ 07458-2020 Office: Breslin and Breslin PA 41 Main St Hackensack NJ 07601-7087

CAMINITI, KENNETH GENE, professional baseball player; b. Harford, Calif., Apr. 21, 1963. Grad. high sch., San Jose, Calif. With Houston Astros, 1987-94 98-; 3d baseman San Diego Padres, 1995-98. Named "The Sporting News" Coll. All-Am. Team, 1984, Nat. League All-Star Team, 1994; recipient Nat. League's Most Valuable Player award Baseball Writers' Assn. Am., 1996. *

CAMINS, MARTIN B., neurosurgeon; b. Feb. 14, 1943. MD, Chgo. Med. Sch., 1969. Diplomate Am. Bd. Neurol. Surgeons. Asst. clinician Memoria Hosp., N.Y.C., 1975-76; attending physician Lenox Hill Hosp., N.Y.C., 1978—, Hosp. for Joint Diseases, N.Y.C., 1979—, Mt. Sinai Hosp., N.Y.C., 1989—; clin. prof. neurol. surgery; For what organization, and during which year(s), are you/have you been clin. prof. neurol. surgery (CAR/career section)?. Office: 205 E 68th St New York NY 10021-5735

CAMISHION, RUDOLPH CARMEN, physician; b. Riverside, N.J., July 16, 1927; m. Nancy Muzzarelli, June 28, 1952; children: Germain, Sandra, Lisa, Nancy, Janice. BS, St. Joseph's Coll., 1950; MD, Jefferson Med. Coll. of Phila., 1954. Cert. Am. Bd. Surgery, 1960, Bd. of Thoracic Surgery, 1961, Bd. Gen. Vascular Surgery, 1983. USNR Petty Officer, 1944-46; intern Cooper Hosp., Camden, N.J., 1954-55; resident in surgery Jefferson Med. Coll. Hosp., Phila., 1955-59; trainee Nat. Cancer Inst., 1958-59, 1959-62; asst. in surgery Jefferson Med. Coll., 1959-60, instr. in surgery, 1960-62, asst. prof. surgery, 1963-64; cons. thoracic surgery VA Hosp., Phila., 1963-66; assoc. prof. surgery Jefferson Med. Coll., 1964-67, prof. surgery, 1967-73; prof., head dept. surgery Robert Wood Johnson Med. Sch., Camden, 1973-91, prof. surgery, 1991—. Numerous medical presentations. Recipient Surgical Excellence award, 1991, rev. Clarence E. Shaffrey, S.J., award, 1991. Mem. Acad. Surgical Rsch., Am. Assn. Advancement of Sci., Am. Assn. for Thoracic Surgery, AAUP, Am. Coll. Chest Physicians, ACS, AHA, AMA, Am. Thoracic Soc., Am. Surgical Assn., Pa. Assn. for Thoracic Surgery, Phila. Acad. of Surgery, Camden County Med. Soc., Soc. of Univ. Surgeons, Soc. for Vascular Surgery, Vascular Soc. N.J., Eastern Vascular Soc., Soc. Clin. Vascular Surgery, Southeastern Surgical Cong., N.J. Chpt. Am. Coll. Surgeons, Alpha Omega Alpha. Office: R Wood Johnson Med Sch 3 Cooper Plz Rm 411 Camden NJ 08103-1438

CAMLIBEL, DIZDAR, marketing professional, advertising consultant; b. Ankara, Turkey, July 9, 1950; came to U.S., 1996; s. Nuri and Mubahat (Acikgoz) C.; m. A. Canan Ucer, June 6, 1981; children: Zeynep, Nazli. BA, Schiller Coll., Heidelberg, Germany, 1978; BS, San Diego State U., 1980. Specialist in fgn. banking Pamukbank, Istanbul, Turkey, 1981-83; dep. gen. mgr. Gama Mktg., Ankara, 1983-86; mng. dir., owner C&D Mktg. Ltd., Ankara, 1986—, Scala Advt. Co., Ankara, 1991-95, C&D World Mktg., Chevy Chase, Md., 1996—. Mem. Ankara Coll. Sports Club (pres. 1994-96). Avocations: skiing, travel, soccer. Home: 5610 Wisconsin Ave Apt 18C Chevy Chase MD 20815-4415 Office: C ve D 1C Dis Ticaret, Nenehatun Caddesi 81/3, Ankara Turkey

CAMM, GERTRUDE ELIZABETH, physician, writer; b. Enid, Okla., Aug. 21, 1930; d. John Palmer and Gertrude (Hollis) C. AB, Duke U., 1951, postgrad., 1951-53; postgrad., Sarah Lawrence Coll., 1962-63, Columbia U., 1963-64, U. Okla, 1964-66; MD, U. Pa., 1968. Rschr. in biochem. and biophys. Duke U. Sch. Medicine, Durham, N.C., 1953-55; intern, resident in internal medicine Royal Victoria Hosp., Montreal, Que., Can., 1968-70; resident in pediat. U. Ill. Hosp., Chgo., 1970-71, Emory U. Affiliated Hosps., Atlanta, 1971-72; pvt. practice in pediat. and family medicine Fla., 1973-75, Ala., 1975-76; pvt. practice in emergency medicine Chgo., 1976-84, Cen. Fla., Ala., Ga., 1984-89; practice in pub. health Fla., 1987-90; practice internal/family med., pediat. & pub. health svcs., 1990—; instr. pediat. U. Ill., Chgo., 1970-71, ACLS, 1982-90, med. dir. clinic, 1991-96; med. dir. Epilepsy Assn. Ctrl. Fla., 1994—; lectr. med. topics for cmty. groups, 1984-96; dir. hosp. emergency depts., 1976-78, 84-87, cmty. emergency med. sys., 1976-78, 84-86; chmn. profl. adv. bd. Epilepsy Assn. Ctr. Fla., 1995—; assoc. trustee Epilepsy Assn. Ctrl. Fla., 1995-97, trustee, 1997—; med. cons. disaster health svcs. com. Orlando chpt. ARC, 1998—; mem. cmty. adv. coun., mem. profl. adv. bd. two home health orgns., 1994—. Author: Atlanta Constitution, 1956-59, In the Deep Blue Sea, 1961; contbr. articles to profl. and popular jours.; sci. and med. writer, 1960-64;

co-editor The Second Decade, Atlantic Ctr. for the Arts, 1996. Musician amateur cmty. symphony orchs., chamber ensembles and choral groups, 1947—, Seminole Coll. Cmty. Orch., 1996—, Orch. of Maitland First Presbyn. Ch., 1997—; trustee, mem. disability project residency Atlantic Ctr. for Arts, 1996—, sec., 1997—; sec. Fla. Symphony Orch. affiliate bd. Lake County, 1985-86; patron, mem. of Friends of Orlando Philharm. Orch., 1995—, pres., 1999—; bd. dirs. Orlando Philharm. Orch., 1996—; patron Festival de Musica de Camara, San Miguel de Allende, Mex., 1995—; mem. adv. coun. and facilitator Sr. Outreach Arts Resource of Orlando Mus. of Art, 1998—; bd. of Friends of Cornell Fine Arts Mus., 1999—; active environ. groups: Orlando and Ormond Beach, 1984—, Friends of Spruce Creek Preserve, 1997—; hon. bd. mem. Found. New Smyrna Beach (Fla.) Hist. Mus., 1998—; active John F. Lindsey for Mayor campaign, N.Y.C., 1960; resident physician Grenfell Mission, St. Anthony, Nfld.-Labrador, Can., 1970; vol. physician for Vietnam, AMA, 1972; vol. physician Boggy Creek Gang Camp for chronically ill, 1996-97. Chemistry fellow Dept. Army Chem. Warfare Duke U. Grad. Sch., 1951-53, clin. fellow U. Pa. Sch. Medicine, 1967-68, NIH student fellow, 1964-66; preceptorship Columbia-Presbyn. Hosp., 1966. Mem. AAAS, AAUW (pres. Ormond Beach chpt. 1974-75), So. Med. Assn., Ctrl. Fla. Pediatric Soc., Flying Physicians Assn., Alliance of Artists' Cmtys., Le Salon, Arts for Complete Edn., Orlando Mus. Art, Cornell Fine Arts Mus., Atlantic Ctr. for Arts (life, founders cir., Able Trust grantee for disability project residency), Aircraft Owners and Pilots Assn., Fox Meadow Tennis Club, Penn Club, University Club Winter Park, Phi Beta Kappa. Presbyterian. Avocations: arts, water sports, travel, flying, photography.

CAMMA, ALBERT JOHN, neurosurgeon; b. Cleve., Dec. 27, 1940; s. August and Amelia (Catalioti) C.; m. Sheryl Virginia Doptis, Aug. 27, 1966 (div. Jan. 1986); children: August Leon, Albert David; m. Rebecca Ann Wenzel July 27, 1996; children: Joshua Wenzel, Nicholas Wenzel, Jaime Wenzel. BS cum laude, John Carroll U., 1963; MD, Western Res. U., 1967. Diplomate Am. Acad. of Pain and Mgmt., Am. Bd. Neurol. Surgeons, Nat. Bd. Med. Examiners. Intern, surg. resident U. Pitts., 1967-69, resident in neurosurgery, 1971-75; pvt. practice in neurosurgery Zanesville, Ohio, 1975—. Trustee Zanesville YMCA, 1976-82; bd. dirs. Ohio Rails-to-Trails; pres. bd. dirs. Muskingum Recreational Trail, 1994—. With M.C., USN, 1969-71. Mem. AMA, AAAS, Ohio State Med. Assn., Am. Pain Soc., Am. Acad. Pain Medicine, Am. Back Soc., Am. Assn. Advance Sci., Am. Coll. Angiology, N.Y. Acad. Scis., Muskingum County Acad. Medicine (pres. 1996-97), Congress Neurol. Surgeons, Am. Acad. Thermology, Midwest Pain Soc., Soc. Behavioral Medicine, ACS, Am. Assn. Neurol. Surgeons, Ohio State Neurosurg. Soc. (bd. dirs. 1985-87, treas. 1987-89, v.p. 1989-91, pres. 1991-92), Mid-Atlantic Neurosurg. Soc., Am. Pain Soc., Am. Acad. Scis., Am. Soc. Neuroimaging. Office: 855 Bethesda Dr Zanesville OH 43701-1894

CAMMACK, TRANK EMERSON, retired university dean; b. Columbus, Kans., July 11, 1919; s. Levi Jackson and Ida Maud (Hull) C. Student, N.E. Okla. Jr. Coll., 1936-37; B.S., U. Okla., 1940, M.A., 1941; Huebner fellow in ins. edn., U. Pa., 1941-43. Fin. statistician SEC, Phila., 1943-48, Washington, 1948-49; prof. fin. U. Ill., Urbana, 1949-90, assoc. dean charge undergrad. program Coll. Commerce and Bus. Adminstrn., 1968-90. Author: (with Robert I. Mehr) The Insurance Contract and Its Analysis, 1950, Principles of Insurance, 1952. Mem. Champaign County Democratic Central Com., 1962-78; chmn. Champaign Dem. Orgn., 1966-68. Mem. AAUP, Am. Risk and Ins. Assn., Royal Econ. Soc. Methodist. Home: 1704 W Green St Champaign IL 61821-3721

CAMMALLERI, JOSEPH ANTHONY, financial planner, retired air force officer; b. Bronx, N.Y., Feb. 2, 1935; s. Leo Anthony and Angela Marie (Mirandi) C.; BS, Manhattan Coll., 1956; M.S., Okla. State U., 1966; postgrad. Golden Gate U., 1974; children: Anthony R., Aaron L., Thomas K., Jeffrey A. Cert. life ins. instr., Calif. Commd. 2d lt. USAF, 1956, advanced through grades to lt. col., 1973; trainee flight crew, 1956-58; crew mem. B-52, 1958-64; behavioral scientist Aerospace Med. Rsch. Labs., Wright-Patterson AFB, Ohio, 1966-68; EB-66 crew mem. Tahkli AFB, Thailand, 1968-69; faculty mem. dept. life and behavioral scis. USAF Acad. (Colo.), 1969-74, assoc. prof., dir. operational psychology div., 1972-74, B-1 human factors engring. mgr. Air Force Flight Test Center, Edwards AFB, Calif., 1974-76, chief handbook devel., 1976-77; ret., 1977; account exec. Merrill Lynch, Pierce, Fenner & Smith, Sherman Oaks, Calif., 1977-80; acad. program rep. U. Redlands (Calif.), 1980-84, regional dir. admissions, 1984-86, mem. faculty Whitehead Coll., 1979—, assoc. dean admissions, 1986-89; faculty Golden Gate U., 1975-80; account exec. Humanomics Ins., 1989-90; corp. dir. tng. and edn. Fin. West Group, 1990-92, prin. CEO Spectrum Securities, Inc., Westlake Village, Calif., 1992-95; assoc. dean admission Alfred North Whitehead Coll. U. of Redlands, 1996; registered gen. securities prin. Thomas F. White & Co., Inc., 1996—; CFO, registered prin. PLC Securities Corp., Ventura, Calif., 1996-98; adj. faculty Calif. Luth. U., 1990—, Antioch U., 1992—; sec., 7th Ann. Narrow Gauge Conv. Com., Pasadena, Calif., 1986. Contbr. articles to profl. jours. Sec. com. centennial celebration Rio Grande So. Ry., Dolores, Colo., 1991; USAF Acad. Liason Officer, North Los Angeles County, 1992—. Decorated D.F.C., Air medal (5), Meritorious Service medal. Mem. Nat. Ry. Hist. Soc., Ry. and Locomotive Hist. Soc., Rocky Mountain R.R. Club, L.A. Live Steamers, Nat. Model R.R. Assn., Colo. R.R. Hist. Found. (life), Alpine Tunnel Hist. Soc. (life), Disting. Am. Vets. (life), Santa Fe Ry. Hist. Soc., USAF Acad. Athletic Assn. (life), DAV, Psi Chi. Home: 601 Hampshire Rd Apt 550 Westlake Village CA 91361-2303

CAMMARATA, BERNARD, retail company executive; b. 1940. Mdse. mgr. J. W. Mays, N.Y.C., 1962-67, Wilmington (Del.) Dry Goods, 1967-70; v.p., gen. mdse. mgr. Marshalls Dept. Store, Woburn, Mass., 1976; pres., CEO TJX Operating Cos., 1976-89, TJX Cos., Inc., Framingham, Mass., 1989—. With U.S. Army, 1959-62. Office: TJX 770 Cochituate Rd Framingham MA 01701-4672*

CAMMARATA, RICHARD JOHN, financial advisor; b. Boston, June 29, 1950; s. Dominic Joseph and Anna Mary (Masone) C. BA, Stonehill Coll., 1972. Mgr. Ace Fence Co., South Boston, 1972-83; fin. advisor, investor self-employed Randolph, Mass., 1983—; mem. Am. Security Coun., Nat. Adv. Bd., Boston, Va., 1988—. Mem. Rep. Presdl. Task Force, Washington, 1987—, Rep. Nat. Com., Washington, 1984—, GOPAC, Washington, 1984—. Mem. N.Y. Acad. Scis., AAAS. Republican. Roman Catholic. Home and Office: 47 Eugenia St Randolph MA 02368-1950

CAMMAROTA, MARIE ELIZABETH, nursing administrator, nursing educator; b. Phila., Oct. 12, 1943; d. Angelo J. Cardile and Angeline M. Cardile; m. Charles C. Cammarota, Aug. 14, 1965; 1 child, Sharon Marie. AS, Orange County Coll., Middletown, N.Y., 1963; BA, Glassboro State Coll., 1977, MA, 1981; EdD, Nova Southeastern U., 1995. Cert. sch. social worker, sch. nurse, pupil personal svcs., supr., FNP, sch. nurse practitioner, N.J.; RN, N.J., N.Y., Pa. Staff nurse to asst. head nurse Thomas Jefferson U. Hosp., Phila., 1963-65; instr. St. Joseph's Hosp., Sch. Nursing, 1965-66; sch. nurse Gloucester County Vocat. Tech. Sch., Sewell, N.J., 1974-88; asst. prof. Rowan U., Glassboro, N.J., 1988—; adj. prof. Gloucester County Coll., Sewell, 1985-95, Glassboro (N.J.) State Coll., 1986-88; cons. com. on sch. health N.J. Acad. Pediatrics, Trenton, 1986—; cons. Edn., Info. and Resource Ctr., Sewell, 1989—; spkr. in field; state advisor N.J. Health Occupations Am. Recipient Golden Apple award Edn., Info. & Resource Ctr., Sewell, 1991. Mem. ANA, Am. Acad. Pediatrics (affiliate sect. sch. health), Am. fedn. Tchrs., Gloucester County Sch. Nurse Assn. (pres. 1983-85), Phi Delta Kappa (Zeta Nu chpt. v.p. membership 1993-96, historian 1996—, Outstanding Leadership award 1984). Avocations: traveling, reading, arts and crafts. Home: 44 Bryant Rd Turnersville NJ 08012-1447

CAMMISA, FRANK P., JR., surgeon, educator; b. Waterbury, Conn., Jan. 18, 1956; m. Gail McGovern; children: Anne Katherine, Frank P. III, John Patrick. BS summa cum laude, Tufts U., 1978; MD, Columbia U., 1982. Diplomate Nat. Bd. Med. Examiners, Am. Bd. Orthopaedic Surgery. Resident in gen. surgery The Presbyn. Hosp., Columbia-Presbyn. Med. Ctr., N.Y.C., 1982-83; resident in orthopaedic surgery The Hosp. for Spl. Surgery, N.Y.C., 1983-87; fellow in spinal surgery U. Miami (Fla.)-Jackson Meml. Med. Ctr., 1987-88; asst. scientist rsch. divsn. The Hosp. for Spl. Surgery, N.Y.C., 1988—, asst. attending surgeon, 1988—, chief spine svc., 1995—; vis. clin. fellow surgery Coll. of Physicians and Surgeons, Columbia U., N.Y.C., 1982-83; clin. assoc. surgery Cornell U. Med. Coll., N.Y.C., 1983-87, instr. orthopaedic surgery, 1988-89, asst. prof. orthopaedic surgery, 1990—; attending surgeon VA Hosp., Miami, 1987-88; asst. attending surgeon The N.Y. Hosp., N.Y.C., 1988—; attending surgeon spinal cord injury svc. Burke Rehab. Ctr., White Plains, N.Y., 1988—; attending surgeon VA Hosp., Bronx, N.Y., 1988—; presenter in field; cons. Meml. Sloan Kettering Cancer Ctr., N.Y.C., 1988—; spinal cons. St. John's U. Athletic Teams, 1988—, N.Y. Knights World League of Am. Football, 1991-92, Phoenix Alliance, 1993, N.Y. Racing Assn., 1993. Editorial bd.: Orthopaedic Product News, 1990-91; contbr. chpts. to books and articles to profl. jours. Grantee The Hosp. for Spl. Surgery, 1986, Acromed Corp., 1988, Orthopaedic Rsch. and Edn. Found., 1991-92; recipient Harvard Book prize Harvard Club So. Conn., 1974, Tufts Psychology Soc. Rsch. award Tufts U., 1978, Resident award N.Y. Acad. Medicine, Sect. Orthopaedic Surgery, 1986, 87, Lewis Clark Wagner award Hosp. for Spl. Surgery, N.Y.C., 1986; N.Am. Traveling fellowship Am. Orthopaedic Assn., 1989; Ofcl. citation Gen. Assembly State of Conn., 1992. Mem. ACS, ACP, Am. Acad. Orthopaedic Surgeons, Internat. Coll. Surgeons, Am. Coll. Spine Surgery; mem. AMA, N.Am. Spine Soc., Am. Spinal Injury Assn., Internat. Soc. for Study of Lumbar Spine, Cervical Spine Rsch. Soc., Scoliosis Rsch. Soc., Med. Soc. State N.Y., N.Y. State Soc. Orthop. Surgeons, N.Y. County Med. Soc., Alumni Assn. The Hosp. for Spl. Surgery, Assn. of the Alumni, Coll. Physicians and Surgeons, Columbia U., The Irish-Am. Orthop. Soc., Ea. Orthop. Assn. (Fellow scholar award 1988, Spinal Rsch. award 1989), Groupe Internat. Cotrel-Dubousset, N.Y. Athletic Club, Winged Foot Golf Club, Phi Beta Kappa, Psi Chi, Alpha Omega Alpha, Delta Tau Delta. Office: Hosp for Spl Surgery 535 E 70th St New York NY 10021-4892

CAMNER, HOWARD, author, poet; b. Miami, Fla., Jan. 14, 1957; s. Edward I. and Ida (Puldy) C. BA in English, Fla. Internat. U., 1982; LittD (hon.), London Sch. Applied Rsch., 1995. Cert. English tchr., Fla. Editor Southwind Mag., Miami, Fla., 1976-78; performance poet Writers' Exch., N.Y.C., 1979-81; freelance writer various publications, Miami, 1982-84; screenwriter Harris Prodns., L.A., 1985-89; TV prodr., host Century Cable, L.A., 1986-88; writing instr. Dade County Schs., Miami, 1990—. *Howard Camner's works have been placed in the most distinguished literary collections in the world. These include historical, international, university, and royal archives. He has published over 1300 works in various anthologies and literary journals throughout the U.S. and Great Britain. He also has the distinction of having been one of the youngest poets ever nominated for Poet Laureate of a state (Florida, 1980). He has performed his poetry at major literary events, including: Miami Book Fair International, the Cross-Bron-Cross Arts Festival, the Saint Marks Restoration Readings, Literary Outlaws at Barnard, and the First Planetary Congress.* Author: (poems) Notes from the Eye of a Hurricane, 1979, Transitions, 1980, Scattered Shadows, 1980, Road Note Elegy, 1980, A Work in Progress, 1981, Poetry from Hell to Breakfast, 1981, Midnight at the Laundromat, 1983, Hard Times on Easy Street, 1987, Madman in the Alley, 1989, Stray Dog Wail, 1991, Banned in Babylon, 1993, Jammed Zipper, 1994, Bed of Nails, 1995, Brutal Delicacies, 1996; contbr. to anthology: Florida in Poetry, 1995, also over 100 lit. collections. Mem. Nat. Writers Assn., Acad. of Am. Poets, Poets and Writers, Inc., Poetry Soc. of Am., So. Fla. Poetry Inst., Authors Guild. Home: 10440 SW 76th St Miami FL 33173-2903

CAMOUGIS, GEORGE, health, safety and environmental consultant; b. Concord, Mass., May 10, 1930; s. Charles George and Angeliki (Georgekopoulou) C.; BS magna cum laude (Olmstead fellow), Tufts U., 1952; MA, Harvard U., 1957, PhD, 1958; m. Irene Andreson, Nov. 18, 1961; children—Caroline A., Elizabeth M., Sarah A. Asst. prof. physiology Clark U., 1958-62, assoc. prof., 1962-64, affiliate prof., 1964-79; sr. neurophysiologist Astra Pharm. Products, Inc., Worcester, Mass., 1964-66, head sect. neuropharmacology, 1966-68; pres., research dir., dir. New Eng. Research, Inc., Worcester, 1968-88; sr. cons. New Eng. Indsl. Waste, Inc., 1988-89; v.p., compliance officer Am. Reclamation Corp., 1989-96; cons. Bd. Radioactive Waste Mgmt. NAS, 1987-92, numerous state and fed. agys. including Army C.E., Fed. Hwy. Adminstrn., U.S. Dept. Interior, EPA; cons. Mass. Dept. Mental Health, 1997—; affiliate prof. Worcester Poly. Inst., 1970-82; adj. prof. toxicology Tufts U. Sch. Vet. Medicine, 1981-84; panelist NSF; mem. corp. Bermuda Biol. Sta. for Research, 1968-85; lectr. in field, U.S., Can.; mem. Worcester Sci. Center Planning Com., 1963. Bd. dirs. Worcester Children's Friend Soc., 1968-92, v.p., 1978-84, pres., 1984-87. Served with USNR, 1952-54; Korea. Virginia B. Gibbs scholar, 1954-55; E.L. Mark fellow, 1956; USPHS fellow, 1957-58; NIH grantee, 1962-64; Office Naval Research grantee, 1963-64; recipient Sci. Achievement award Worcester Engring. Soc., 1985 . Mem. AAAS, Biophys. Soc., Am. Physiol. Soc., N.Y. Acad. Scis., ASTM, Soc. Environ. Toxicology and Chemistry, Phi Beta Kappa, Sigma Xi. Republican. Greek Orthodox. Clubs: Tatnuck Country (Worcester); Harvard (Boston). Author: Nerves, Muscles and Electricity, 1970; Environmental Biology for Engineers, 1981; contbr. numerous articles to profl. jours., 1959—; patentee drug; cons. editor Acad. Press, Inc., 1978; mem. editorial adv. bd. Hazardous Waste Mgmt., 1983-90. Home and Office: 7 Wheeler Ave Worcester MA 01609-1707

CAMOUS, LOUISE MICHELLE, secondary education educator, sister; b. San Francisco, Oct. 21, 1954; d. Eugene Paul and Anna Elizabeth (Shay) C. BA, San Francisco State Univ., 1975. Cert. tchr., Calif. Tchr. Santa Barbara Sch., Dededo, Guam, 1975-76, Our Lady Mt. Carmel Sch., Agat, Guam, 1976-77, Our Lady of Visitacion, San Francisco, 1977-80, St. Vincent de Paul Sch., Phoenix, 1982-85, Marian Sch., Montebello, Calif., 1985-87, Notre Dame Regional Sch., Price, Utah, 1987-96, St. Vincent de Paul Sch., Phoenix, 1997—. Founding bd. dirs. Habitat for Humanity of Castle Country, Price, 1989-92. Recipient Dedication to Youth Carbon County award Nat. Honor Soc. Carbon H.S. Chpt., Price, 1994, Notre Damean award from Notre Dame Regional Sch., 1995, Golden Gator award Xavier Coll. Prep., Phoenix, 1998. Mem. Nat. Cath. Edn. Assn., Nat. Coun. Tchrs. Math. Democrat. Avocations: liturgical music, youth ministry, quilling, guitar, reading. Home: 3130 N 51st Ave Phoenix AZ 85031

CAMP, ALETHEA TAYLOR, executive and organizational design consultant; b. Wingo, Ky., Nov. 12, 1938; d. Wayne Thomas and Ethel Virginia (Austin) Taylor; children: Donna Paul, Sean Richard. BA, Murray State U., 1961; MA, So. Ill. U., 1975. Tchr. McLean and Hopkins (Ky.) County Schs., 1961-64; instr. homebound Harrisburg (Ill.) Community Sch. Dist., 1971-73; counselor evaluation Coleman Rehab. Ctr., Shawneetown, Ill., 1974-75; counselor corrections and parole Dept. Corrections, State Ill., Springfield, 1975-77, supr. casework, 1977, supr. parole, 1977-80; asst. warden programs Dept. Corrections, State Ill., Hillsboro, 1980-84, warden, 1984-91; correctional program specialist Nat. Inst. Corrections, Washington, 1991-95; exec. and orgnl. cons. Camp-Blair Consulting, Inc., 1995-99; exec. dir. Women Execs., 1998. Mem. NAFE, Assn. Exec. Women in Corrections, Am. Correctional Assn., N. Am. Wardens Assn., Bus. and Profl. Women, Del Ray Artisans, Potomac West Bus. Assn. Avocations: gardening, sailing, traveling, extensive walking.

CAMP, CLIFTON DURRETT, JR., newspaper consultant, rancher; b. Trenton, Ky., Aug. 2, 1927; s. Clifton Durrett and Virginia (McElwain) C.; m. Mary Jane Peters, June 9, 1950; children: Daniel Durrett, Thomas Clifton, Pamela Jane, Emily Ann. BS, U. Ky., 1950. Sr. acct. Sheldon, Curry and Masterson, St. Petersburg, Fla., 1950-54; asst. contr. Times Pub. Co., St. Petersburg, 1954-57, contr., 1957-71, treas., 1960-73, v.p. adminstrn., 1967-73, sec., 1969-85, bus. mgr., 1974-82, sr. v.p., 1982-88, also bd. dirs.; owner, pub. Sumter County Times, Bushnell, Fla., 1973-76, Wildwood Herald Express, Bushnell, 1973-76; owner Oakwood Ranch, Bushnell, 1981-88; bd. dir. Poynter Inst. for Media Studies, St. Petersburg; sec. Mod. Graphic Arts, St. Petersburg, 1976-87, also bd. dirs.; pres. Fla. Trend, Inc., St. Petersburg, 1984-87; bd. dirs. Fla. Press Ctr., Tallahassee, 1980-87, pres., 1984; bd. dirs. Congl. Quar., Inc., Washington, 1986-88; bd. dir. Poynter Libr. U. South Fla. Treas. United Way, St. Petersburg, 1965-68; bd. dirs. Salvation Army Adv. Bd., 1970-78, Bayfront Med. Ctr., 1981-87, St. James United Meth. Ch., Tampa, 1995—. With USN, 1945-46. Mem. Fla. Press Assn. (bd. dirs. 1982-87), Internat. Newspaper Fin. Execs. (bd. dirs. 1964-70), Hunters Green Country Club (Tampa).

CAMP, CYNTHIA M., writer, consultant; b. Hammond, La., Mar. 23, 1973; d. Warren Joseph and Dorothy O. (Fonchuberta) Carver. BA, Southeastern La. U., 1995. Freelance writer The Adv., Baton Rouge, 1996—; owner Tangipahoa Pub. Rels., 1998—; co-owner Action Media, 1998—. Campaign cons., 1996—. Dem. Roman Catholic. Avocations: exercise, writing creative works, traveling. Office: Action Media/TPR PO Box 1450 Independence LA 70443

CAMP, DAVE, congressman; b. Midland, Mich., July 9, 1953; m. Nancy Keil, Sept. 10, 1994; children: Andrew David, Lauren. BA, Albion (Mich.) Coll., 1975; JD, U. San Diego, 1978. Bar: Mich., Calif., D.C., U.S. Supreme Ct., U.S. Dist. Ct. (ea. dist.) Mich., U.S. Dist. Ct. (so. dist.) Calif. With Riecker, Van Dam, Looby & Barker, 1978-90; spl. asst. atty. gen., 1980-84, adminstrv. asst. to Congressman Bill Schuette, 1985-87; state rep. 102nd Dist. Mich., 1989-91; mem. 102d-105th Congresses from 10th (now 4th) Mich. dist. 102nd-103rd Congresses from 10th (now 4th) Mich. dist., 1991—; mem. ways and means com.; chmn. Spkrs. Correction Day Com. Mem. ABA, Midland County Bar Assn. Republican. Office: US Ho of Reps 137 Cannon Bldg Washington DC 20515-2204

CAMP, DELPHA JEANNE, counselor; b. Yakima, Wash., Apr. 20, 1937; d. George Emerson and Emilie Loraine (Rivard) Stevens; m. George Ernest Mills, Aug. 13, 1960 (dec. 1975); children: Adriene Phillips, Stacey Harcus, Ryan, Tiffany; m. James Clell Camp, June 24, 1978; children: Catherine Thompson (dec.), Wayne (dec.), Darla Coolman, John, Janna Barnes. BEd, Gonzaga Univ., 1959; MS, Univ. Oreg., 1977. Lic. profl. counselor; cert. grief counselor and death educator. Tchr. Riverside Sch. Dist., Milan, Wash., 1959-61, Cheney (Wash.) Sch. Dist., 1968-70; asst. prof. Univ. Oreg., Eugene, 1979-92; pvt. practice Eugene, 1992—; mem. faculty Marylhurst (Oreg.) U., 1992—. Mem. Assn. for Death Edn. and Counseling (bd. dirs. 1990-93, co-chair conf. 1994, 1st v.p. 1998-99, pres. 1999-00, Svc. award 1990), Am. Mental Health Counselors Assn., Oreg. Counseling Assn., Oreg. Mental Health Counselors Assn. Avocations: reading, classical music. Home: 440 E 39th Ave Eugene OR 97405-4722 Office: 317 W Broadway Ste 217 Eugene OR 97401-2890

CAMP, DONALD EUGENE, experimental photographer, educator; b. Meadville, Pa., July 28, 1940; s. Ira Guy and Martha Gladys (Irving) C.; m. Marie Josephé Dumont, Nov. 26, 1966; children: Stephanie Martha Helené, Dorothea Rae. BFA, Tyler Sch. Art, Phila., 1987; MFA, Tyler Sch. Art, 1989. Staff photographer Phila. Bulletin, 1972-81; asst. prof. Tyler Sch. of Art, Phila., 1989-91, Slippery Rock (Pa.) U., 1992—; dir. Future Faculty Fellowship Program Temple U., Phila., 1990-91. Photographs have appeared in many popular magazines including Ebony, News Week, People; represented in numerous pub. collections including ARCO collection, Phila. Mus. Art, and Schaumberg Ctr. for Black Culture, N.Y.C., Pa. Conv. Ctr., U. Mich. Mus. of Art; appeared in Face to Face Exhbn. Nat, Jewish Am. Mus. in Phila., U. Mich. Mus. Art, 1998, Inst. Contemporary Art, U. Pa., 1999. Mem. Spiritual Assembly of Bahais of Phila., 1981—, Interfaith Support Group, Phila., 1989-92. Recipient Future Faculty fellowship Temple U., Phila., 1988, Eugene Feldman award The Print Club, 1983; named Pa. Visual Artist fellow, 1990, Smithsonian Am. Artist Oral History, 1991, PEW Charitable Trust resident artist to the Am. Acad. in Rome, 1994; John Simon Guggenheim Found. fellow, 1995-96, NAE fellow, Pew Charitable Trust fellow, Pa. Coun. for the Arts fellow. Mem. Soc. Photographic Educators (bd. dirs. 1990-94, chmn., founder multicultural caucus, 1990-93), Recherche. Avocations: Baha'i promotion, magic. Home: 4511 Spruce St Philadelphia PA 19139-4526

CAMP, JACK TARPLEY, JR., federal judge; b. Newnan, Ga., Oct. 30, 1943; s. Jack Tarpley and Sophia (Stephens) C.; m. Elizabeth Thomas, Apr. 24, 1976; children: Thomas Henry, Sophia Rose. BA, The Citadel, Charleston, S.C., 1965; MA, U. Va., 1967, JD, 1973. Bar: Ala. 1973, Ga. 1975. Atty. Cabaniss, Johnston, Dumas & O'Neal, Birmingham, Ala., 1973-75, Glover & Davis, P.A., Newnan, 1975-88; U.S. dist. judge Atlanta, 1988—; mgr. family timber land holdings. Mem. Newnan Hist. Soc., 1975—, Ga. Trust for Hist. Preservation, Atlanta, 1975—. Capt. U.S. Army, 1967-70, Vietnam. Decorated Bronze Star; Ford Found. fellow, 1965-66. Mem. Ga. State Bar (bd. govs. 1987-89), Newnan-Coweta Bar Assn. (pres. 1978), Fed. Judges Assn., Kiwanis. Presbyterian. Office: US Dist Ct 2142 US Courthouse 75 Spring St SW Atlanta GA 30303-3309

CAMP, JOSEPH SHELTON, JR., film producer, director, writer; b. St. Louis, Apr. 20, 1939; s. Joseph Shelton and Ruth Wilhelmena (McLaulin) C.; m. Andrea Carolyn Hopkins, Aug. 7, 1960; children: Joseph Shelton III, Brandon Andrew. BBA, U. Miss., 1961. Jr. account exec. McCann-Erickson Advt., Houston, 1961-62; owner Joe Camp Real Estate, Houston, 1962-64; account exec. Norsworthy-Mercer, Dallas, 1964-69; dir. TV comls. Jamieson Film Co., Dallas, 1969-71; founder, pres., writer, producer, dir. feature films Mulberry Square Prodns., Inc., Dallas, 1971-90, Gulfport, Miss., 1991-94, Chapel Hill, N.C., 1994—. Producer, dir., writer films including Benji, 1974, Hawmps, 1976, For the Love of Benji, 1977, The Double McGuffin, 1979, Oh Heavenly Dog, 1980, Benji The Hunted, 1987; TV spls. The Phenomenon of Benji, 1978, Benji's Very Own Christmas Story, 1978, Benji at Work, 1980, Benji (Takes a Dive) at Marineland, 1981; TV series Benji, Zax and the Alien Prince, 1983; author: Underdog, 1993. Bd. trustees Piney Woods Country Life Sch., Warren Wilson Coll.; adv. bd. N.C. Sch. of Arts, Sch. of Film Making. Mem. Dir.'s Guild Am., Writer's Guild Am. Home: 31322 Monterey St Laguna Beach CA 92651 *I hope that I have been able to help people in a troubled time to lose themselves for a moment in a piece of entertainment and, when it's over, to feel better for having done so, to have a new respect for persistence in achieving objectives and a new feeling of hope and happiness in their lives. I hope to inspire others to follow their dreams with passion and persistence, to reach further than they might have otherwise.*

CAMP, KIMBERLY N., museum administrator, artist; b. Camden, N.J., Sept. 11, 1956; d. Hubert E. and Marie (Dimery) C.m. Seydou Coulibaly, Apr. 1997. BA, U. Pitts., 1978; MS, Drexel U., 1986. Dir. artistic design project City Camden, 1984-86; program dir. Pa. Coun. on Arts, Harrisburg, 1986-89; dir. exptl. gallery Smithsonian Instn., Washington, 1989-94; pres. Mus. African Am. History, Detroit, 1994-98; exec. dir., CEO Barnes Found., Merion, Pa., 1998—; evaluator Am. Assn. Mus., Washington, 1994—; panel chair Nat. Endowment for Arts, Washington, 1991-92; vice chair, bd. dirs. Assn. Am. Cultures, Washington, 1987-89. One-woman shows include Glouchester County Coll., Deptford Township, N.J., Passaic Count C.C., Paterson, N.J., Diggs Gallery, Winston-Salem, N.C., Galerie Francois, Washington, Banneker Douglass Mus., Annapolis, Md., 3d Bienniel Nat. Black Arts Festival, Atlanta, Manchester Craftsmen's Guilde, Pitts., Caribbean Cultural Ctr., N.Y.C., Jr. Black Acad. Arts and Letters, Dallas, Walt Whitman Ctr. Arts and Humanities, Camden, Longwood Gardens, Kennett Square, Pa., Art Mus. Western Va., Raonoke, Harrison Mus. African Am. Culture, Roanoke, 1994; represented in permanent collections J.B Speed Art Mus., Manchester Craftsmen's Guild, Reader's Digest, Camden Hist. Soc.; mng. editor Nat. Conf. Artists Phila. Chpt. newsletter, 1980-84. Bd. dirs. Bus. Vols. for Arts, 1994—. Recipient Nat. Svc. award Nat. Conf. Artists, 1984, Arts Achievement award City of Camden, 1984, Cmty. Svc. award Assn/ Negro Bus. and Profl. Women, 1985, Builders of Cmty. award Camden County Cultural and Heritage Commn., 1986, Purchase award J.B. Speed Art Mus., 1988, Spirit of Detroit award Detroit City Coun., 1994; Arts Internat. grantee Ctr. Internat. Exch. Scholars, 1994; fellow Kellogg Nat. Leadership Program. Mem. Assn. Am. cultures (bd. dirs. 1995—), Am. Assn. Muss. (bd. dirs.), Links, Inc., N.J. Coun. on Arts. Office: The Barnes Found 300 N Latch's Ln Merion Station PA 19066-1729

CAMP, KRISTIN MARY, primary school educator; b. Urbana, Ill., Dec. 6, 1957; d. Eldred Jansen and Janet Nell (Duitsman) Cornelius; m. Michael Alan Camp, Feb. 17, 1978; children: Wendy, Ashley. BE, Ea. Ill. U., 1988; ME, U. Ill., 1998. Cert. elem. tchr., Ill. Tchr. North Ridge Mid. Sch., Danville, Ill., 1988-92, Liberty Elem. Sch., Danville, Ill., 1992—; coord. Sci. Olympiad North Ridge Mid. Sch., 1990-92, track coach, 1993; mem. dist. curriculum com. Danville Sch. Dist., 1992-95; coach Scholastic Bowl Liberty Elem. Sch., 1994—, coord. staff devel., 1994—. Re-enactment mem. Illiana Civil War Hist. Soc., Danville, 1980-86; mem. and com. chair Psi Iota Xi Sorority, Armstrong, Ill., 1984-88; mem. Youth Coun. Adv. Group Vermilion County Ext. 4-H Programs, 1987-89; leader Collison (Ill.) Country Clovers 4-H Club, 1992-93; mem. Potomac (Ill.) Libr. Adv. Com., 1995; mem. Lincoln Trail Libr. System Regional Planning Panel, Vermilion County, 1996-97. Mary Miller scholar Danville Area C.C., 1987. Mem.

Outdoor Heritage Found. (bd. dirs. 1996—), Delta Kappa Gamma (Edn. scholar 1987), Alpha Sigma Lambda, Kappa Delta Pi. Avocations: gardening, walking, horseback riding, travelling.

CAMP, RONALD STEPHEN, educational technologist, television producer, educator; b. Joplin, Mo., Oct. 22, 1941; s. Arthur Benson and Willetta M. (Exendine) C.; m. Dulcie Maryann Creasy, June 28, 1965; 1 child, Jason. AA, Joplin Jr. Coll., 1961; BA, U. Mo., 1963, MA, 1967. Ednl. TV producer, dir. U. Mo., Columbia, 1964-66, acting TV prodn. mgr., 1966-67; project dir. M.E.T.R.I.L. S.W. Mo. State Coll., Springfield, 1967-68; instr. radio, TV and dir. radio, TV dept. Colo. State Coll., Greeley, 1968-70; gen. mgr. KUNC Radio U. No. Colo., Greeley, 1970-78, dir. media prodn., 1970-76, asst. prof. mass comm., 1975-81, dir. ednl. media svc., 1976-93, assoc. prof. telecom., 1981-98, dir. acad. tech. svcs., 1993-98, emeritus assoc. prof. journalism and mass comm., 1998—; tech. advisor Western Inst. Distance Edn., Greeley, 1989—; chmn. TV Adv. com., Greeley, 1987—; cons. Wind River Reservation, Wyoming, 1977, U. Denver, 1977; v.p. Coll. Credit Union, 1998—. Dir. video documentary When Will Our Turn Come, 1981, Vela, 1985; writer, producer, dir. Pelota Mixteca, 1986, Oigame, 1990. Mem. adv. com. Civic Ctr., Greeley, 1990—, Com. Cmty. Devel., Greeley, 1980-84; chmn. No. Colo. Press Club Scholarship Com., Greeley, 1985. Recipient TV Facilities grant Dept. Edn., 1978-80, Pub. Svc. grant Corp. Pub. Broadcasting, 1971-78, Best Pub. Rels. Video award No. Colo. Press Club, 1989, Best Radio Pub. Svc. Announcement award Colo. Broadcasters Assn., 1977. Mem. Consortium Coll. & Univ. Media Ctrs., Internat. TV Assn., Colo. Edn. Media Assn., High Plains Film Coop. (pres. 1979-82), North Colo. Media Profls., Assn. Edn. Communications & Tech. (evaluator 1986). Avocations: climbing, fishing, backpacking, skiing, biking. Home: 1014 22d St Greeley CO 80631-6931

CAMP, STEVEN JOHN, civil engineer; b. Spokane, Wash., Nov. 20, 1961; s. David William and Janet Lois (Gotthart) C.; m. Theresa Sue Sween, Dec. 31, 1985; children: Ashley M., Christina L., Catherine M., David J., John S., Briana S., Erica S., Bryan W. BSCE, USAF Acad., 1984. Registered profl. engr., Calif., Iowa. 2d lt., civil engr. USAF, George AFB, Calif., 1984-86; asst. civil engr. City of Victorville, Calif., 1986-89; assoc. civil engr. City Galt, Calif., 1989-95; county engr. Pocahontas (Iowa) County, 1995—. Mem. Nat. Assn. County Engrs., Rotary. Republican. Avocations: camping, parenting. Office: Pocahontas County 1 Court Sq Pocahontas IA 50574-1621

CAMP, THOMAS HARLEY, economist; b. Charlotte, N.C., Aug. 13, 1929; s. Thomas Franklin and Agnes Mae (Davis) C.; m. Frances Ann Rogers, Mar. 20, 1953 (dec. Feb. 1998); children: Thomas Harley Jr., Landon G. BSc, U. N.C., 1956; postgrad, Am. U., 1965-67. Industry econ. USDA, Washington, 1959-70; location leader USDA, Austin, Tex., 1970-74; rsch. leader USDA, College Station, Tex., 1974-86; program leader USDA, Weslaco, Tex., 1986-88; agrl. mktg. specialist USDA, Lane, Okla., 1988-90; cons. Georgetown, Tex., 1990—. Author, co-author 44 sci. publs.; contbr. articles to profl. jours. Cubmaster Boy Scouts Am., Springfield, Va., 1965-69, asst. scoutmaster, 1966-70, scoutmaster, Round Rock, Tex., 1970-72, asst. scoutmaster, Austin, 1972-74. With USN, 1946-51, Korea. Mem. Am. Soc. Agrl. Engrs., Animal Air Transp. Assn., Food Distbn. Rsch. Soc., Transp. Rsch. Forum, Masons. Presbyn. Avocations: photography, boating. Home and Office: 230 Mesa Dr Georgetown TX 78628-1529

CAMP, VIRGINIA ANN, medical/surgical nurse; b. Chgo., Dec. 25, 1946; d. Victor S. and Annabelle (Todd) Rakow; m. Carey D. Camp, Dec. 28, 1974; children: Kimberly Ann, Alison Marie. RN, St. Paul Sch. Nursing, Dallas, 1967; BS, Incarnate Word Coll., San Antonio, 1975. Commd. 2d lt. U.S. Army, 1969—, advanced through grades to lt. col., 1980; staff nurse Walter Reed, Washington, 1986, Newborn Nursery, 1969-70; staff nurse med./surg. Martin Army Hosp., Ft. Benning, Ga., 1970-71; head nurse operating rm. U.S. Army, Ireland Army Hosp., Ft. Knox, Ky., 1979-84; staff nurse oper. rm. U.S. Army Hosp., Ft. Campbell, Ky., 1971-73, Brook Army Med. Ctr., Ft. Sam Houston, Tex., 1975-76; head nurse oper. rm. 2d Gen. Hosp., Landstuhl, Fed. Republic Germany, 1977-79; chief operating rm./CMS nursing sect. Bayne-Jones Army Hosp., Ft. Polk, La., 1984-86, 97th Gen. Hosp., Frankfurt, Fed. Republic Germany, 1986-89, Ireland Army Hosp.; ret., 1990; nurse mgr. operating room Humana Hosp. Med. Cities Dallas, 1990-91; staff nurse oper. rm. Dallas, 1992-95; asst. nurse mgr. OR/CSS Medical City, Dallas, 1995—. Mem. Tex. Soc. Healthcare Sterile Processing Personnel, Assn. Operating Rm. Nurses (cert.), Assn. Mil. Surgeons, Ret. Officers Assn., Nat. Assn. Uniformed Svcs.

CAMPAGNA, TIMOTHY NICHOLAS, institute executive; b. Chgo., June 8, 1957; s. Nicholas and Dorothy (Hoffmeister) C.; m. Diana Lynn Czarny, Aug. 1, 1981; children: Maria, Joseph. BA, Lewis U., Romeoville, Ill., 1980, MA, 1985. Basketball referee NCAA and Ill. High Sch. Assn., 1976-88; asst. dir. housing Lewis U., 1978-80; tchr. Fairmont Jr. High Sch., Lockport, Ill., 1979-80; tchr., therapist Guardian Angel Home, Joliet, Ill., 1980-82; assoc. dean students DeVry Inst. Tech., Lombard, Ill., 1982-84, dean students, 1984-87; dean adminstrv. svcs. DeVry Inst. Tech., Irving, Tex., 1987-93, dean evening coll., dir. Ctr. Bus. and Industry Ednl. Svcs., 1993-95, dean enrollment mgmt. and mktg., 1994-95; v.p. Am. Inst. Commerce, Davenport, Iowa, 1995-97; pres. Westwood Coll. Tech., 1997—; mem. sch. bd. Holy Family Nazareth; mem. nominating bd. Outstanding Men and women of Am. Coach Nativity of Our Lord Basketball Team. Named Tchr. of Yr., Fairmont Jr. High Sch., 1980, Adminstr. of Yr., DeVry Inst. Tech., 1984. Mem. Nat. Assn. Student Pers. Adminstrs., Am. Assn. Coll. Registrars and Admissions Officers, Nat. Assn. Fgn. Student Advisors, Nat. Assn. Coll. and Univ. Bus. Officers, Denver C. of C., CEO Network. Roman Catholic. Avocations: golf, travel. Office: Westwood College of Tech 7350 Broadway Denver CO 80221-3610

CAMPANA, PHILLIP JOSEPH, German language educator; b. Jersey City, Apr. 10, 1941; s. Ralph Joseph and Alberta Alphonsine (Lepis) C.; m. Paulette Monique Beauregard, Apr. 20, 1968 (div. Apr. 19, 1978); children: Lisa Marie, Michael Phillip. BA in German magna cum laude, St. Peters Coll., Jersey City, 1962; postgrad. (Fulbright scholar), U. Saarbrücken, Germany, 1962-63; PhD, Brown U., 1970. Instr. German St. Peter's Coll., Jersey City, summer 1964; grad. asst. in German Brown U., Providence, 1965-67; assoc. prof. German Tenn. Tech. U., Cookeville, 1970-74, prof. German, 1974—; chmn. dept. fgn. langs., 1970—; founder and 1st dir. English Lang. Inst. Tenn. Tech. U., Cookeville, 1977, dir. Interactive Videodisc Project, 1984-94; state chmn. So. Conf. on Lang. Tchg., 1981-85; reviewer grant proposals (EESA, Title II) Tex. Coord. Bd. for Higher Edn., 1986, U.S. Dept. Edn., 1987; evaluator Nat. Tchrs. Exam in German for Ednl. testing Svc., 1990; lectr., presenter in field. Assoc. editor Schatzkammer, 1980-89, cons. editor, 1990-93, editl. bd., 1993—; evaluator: the materials Ctr. of Am. Assn. Tchrs. German, 1980-81, Modern Lang. Jour., Fgn. Lang. Annals, Seminar; contbr. numerous articles and revs. to profl. jours. Mem. faculty adv. group on master plan for higher edn. Tenn. Higher Edn. Comm., 1973, steering com. on tchr. edn., 1983-84; chmn. Tenn. Bd. Regents Task Force on Improvement of Quality in Tchr. Edn., 1982; mem. Com. on Bus. and Fiscal Affairs, Tenn. Bd. Regents, 1975-76. Recipient Outstanding Faculty award in Tchg., Tenn. Tech. U., 1976, Goethe-Inst. award, 1977, 84, 99, Nat. Endowment for the Humanities, 1981, Meritorious Svc. award Nat. Coun. State Suprs. of Fgn. Langs., 1981, Svc. award Rural Educators Alliance for Lang., 1993, Outstanding Faculty award for Profl. Svcs., Tenn. Tech. U., 1995; Fulbright scholar, 1962-63, 80, 88; Woodrow Wilson fellow, 1962-64, NDEA fellow, 1963-66; grantee Tenn. Tech., 1984, 86-87, 87-88, 88-89, 90, Govt. of Germany, 1983, Tenn. Higher Edn. Commn., 1986-87, 88, 89, 97, 98, 99, Tenn. Bd. Regents, 1989, Tenn. Humanities Coun., 1990. Mem. AAUP, MLA, Am. Assn. Tchrs. German (Tenn. chpt. pres. 1975-77, treas. 1980-92, cert. of Merit award 1982), Tenn. Fgn. Lang. Tchg. Assn. (bd. dirs. 1974-77, 80-81, 82-85, 98-2001, pres. 1977-80, mem. com. 1990-96, rep. Ctrl. States Conf. bd. 1990-93, Jacqueline C. Elliott award 1984), Ctrl. States Conf. on Tchg. Fgn. Langs. (chmn. 1984-87, bd. dirs. 1979-80, 81-84, 91-94, adv. coun. 1978—, co-editor annual volume 1995, co-chair Leadership CSC, 1995-96), Am. Coun. on Tchg. Fgn. Langs. (exec. coun. 1985-86, 91-94, chmn. pub. com. 1993-94, Florence Steiner award 1987), Tenn. Fgn. Lang. Inst. (bd. govs. 1986—, v.p., sec.-treas.), Tenn. Coun. Internat. Edn. (bd. dirs. 1976-78), Ill. Fgn. Lang. Tchrs. Assn. (mem. adv. bd. 1986-88, nominating com. 1987-88, Land of Lincoln Svc. award 1986, 87), Consortium for German in S.E. (founding mem., treas. 1991-96), Omicron Delta Kappa. Roman Catholic. E-mail: pcampana@TNTECH.edu. Home: 1135 Meadow Rd Cookeville TN 38501-2035 Office: Tenn Tech U Dept Fgn Langs Box 5061 Cookeville TN 38505

CAMPANA, RICHARD JOHN, retired plant pathology educator, writer, consultant; b. Everett, Mass., Dec. 5, 1918; s. Joseph and Sarah A. (Shea) C.; m. Jean Marie MacKenzie, July 2, 1945; children: Jane Helen Campana Earley, Mark Robert. BS in Forestry, U. Idaho, 1943; M in Forestry, Yale U., 1947, PhD, 1952. Rsch. asst. Harvard U., Petersham, Mass., summer 1946; instr. Pa. State U., Mont Alto, 1947; asst. prof. botany N.C. State U., Raleigh, 1947-49; asst. plant pathologist, divsn. forest pathology USDA, New Haven, 1949-52; resident plant pathologist Ill. Natural History Survey, Urbana, 1952-58; prof. botany and plant pathology U. Maine, Orono, 1958-85, prof. emeritus, 1985—, head dept., 1958-68, 82-83; cons. Invitation Only, 1956—; Gov. appointee Maine Arborist Exam. Bd., 1965-85; chmn. Orono Conservation Commn., 1970-75; pres. Maine Assn. Conservation Commn., 1974. Editor Dutch Elm Disease 60 Yr. Rev., 1978, Compendium of Elm Diseases, 1981; contbr. over 150 articles to profl. jours., chpts. to books. Mem. Orono Planning Bd., 1970-75. With U.S. Army, WWII; POW in Germany. Decorated Bronze Star; recipient Merit award Conservation Com. Orono, 1975, Disting. Achievement award for Dutch Elm Disease Rsch., Mich. State U., 1992, Merit award Am. Assn. Cons. Arborists, 1993; named to U. Idaho Alumni Hall of Fame, 1998. Fellow Am. Phytopathol. Soc. (news editor 1970-76, councilor 1979-82, 85); mem. Internat. Soc. Arboriculture (pres. 1966-67, Citation 1975), New Eng. chpt. Internat. Soc. Arboriculture (pres. 1964-66, Merit award 1966), N.E. Divsn. Am. Phytopathol. Soc. (pres. 1974-75, Merit award 1984), N.E. Forest Pathologists Soc. (merit 1984), Ea. Maine Yale Alumni Assn. (pres. 1986-89), Sigma Xi, Phi Kappa Phi, Xi Sigma Pi. Unitarian. Avocations: reading, travel, hiking, tennis, golf. Home: 25 Sunrise Ter Orono ME 04473-1449 Office: U Maine Dept Biol Sci 5722 Deering Hall Orono ME 04469-5722

CAMPANELLI, PAULINE EBLE, artist; b. N.Y.C., Jan. 25, 1943; d. Joseph and Dorothy Eble; m. Dan Campanelli, May 24, 1969. Grad., Ridgewood Sch. of Art, 1964; student, Art Students League, 1965-67. fine arts pub. N.Y. Graphic Soc. Exhibited in group shows including Am. Art Gallery, Greenwich, Conn., Temple U., Lever House; represented in pub., corp. and pvt. collections throughout U.S.; author: Wheel of the Year, 1989, Ancient Ways, 1991, Circles, Groves and Sanctuaries, 1992, Rites of Passage, 1994, Halloween Collectibles, 1995, Art of Pauline and Dan Campanelli, 1995, Romantic Valentines, 1996, Holiday Collectibles, 1997; art work and home featured in Colonial Homes, Country Living, Country Almanac, Country Collectibles. Avocations: artist, historian, naturalist.

CAMPAS, ANNA PENELOPE, civil engineer, architect; b. Balt., Nov. 21, 1949; d. William and Katy (Hondros) Campas; children: Thomas William, Scott Stratton. BArch, Rensselaer Polytech. Inst., 1972; BSCE, Union Coll., 1977. Registered profl. engr., architect, N.Y.; cert. asbestos designer, N.Y. Staff architect-engr. GE Co., Schenectady, N.Y., 1972-73; architectural designer Fay Evans, P.C., Troy, N.Y., 1974-75, Golub Corp., Schenectady, 1975-77, Einhorn, Yaffee, Prescott, P.C., Albany, N.Y., 1979-80; jr. engr. N.Y. State Office Gen. Svc., Design and Constrn. Group, Albany, 1980-82, asst. bldg. structural engr., 1982-87, sr. bldg. structural engr., 1987—; bd. dirs. Montessori Sch. of Albany, 1990-92. Mem. Bethlehem Music Assn. (treas.). Home: 41 Darroch Rd Delmar NY 12054-3916

CAMPASINO, ELLEN MARIE, elementary education educator; b. Titusville, Pa., Aug. 30, 1950; d. Frank and Helen (Lowicki) C. BS in Elem. and Early Childhood Edn., Edinboro U., 1972, cert. elem. and early childhood edn., 1978. 1st grade tchr. St. Titus Sch., Titusville, 1975-76, 4th grade tchr., 1976-77, 3rd grade tchr., 1977—; coaching tchr. St. Titus Tchr. Induction Program, 1989-90, asst. to prin., 1993.. Mem. ministry tng. program Diocese of Erie Award for Participation in Levil I CORE; minister hospitality St. Walburga Parish, Roman Cath. Ch., Titusville, pa. Recipient Svc. awards, Diocese of Erie, 1988, 1990, 96. Avocations: reading, doll collecting, embroidery. Office: St Titus Sch 528 W Main St Titusville PA 16354-1598

CAMPAZZI, EARL JAMES, physician; b. N.Y.C., Mar. 25, 1962; s. Earl James and Betty Elvira (Carlson) C. BA in Natural Sci., Johns Hopkins U., 1984, M of Health Sci., Immunology and Infectious Disease, 1986, M of Pub. Health, Health Care Fin. and Mgmt., 1991; MD, U. Pitts., 1989; postgrad. in MBA program, Duke U., 1999. Diplomate Am. Bd. Preventive Medicine. Resident physician in internal medicine Mercy Hosp. Pitts., 1989-90; resident in preventive medicine sch. hygiene and pub. health Johns Hopkins U., Balt., 1990-92, chief resident, 1992-93; pres. Campazzi & Associates, Inc., Balt., 1993—; cons. managed care planning sch. medicine Johns Hopkins U., 1992-93; cons. occupl. health Cons. Epidemiology and Occupl. Health, Washington, 1992-93; occupl. medicine physician Bethlehem Steel, Balt., 1992-95; treas. Md. Coll. Occupl. and Environ. Medicine; occupl. medicine physician CMC Occupl. Health, Balt., 1993-95; site med. dir. Worksite Ptnrs., Charleston, S.C., 1996-97. Scholar Mercyhurst Coll., scholar N.Y.C. Police Dept. Lt.'s Assn. Mem. AMA, APHA, Am. Coll. Physician Execs., Am. Coll. Occupl. and Environ. Medicine, Johns Hopkins U. Alumni Coun. (exec. com.), Johns Hopkins U. Sch. Pub. Health Soc. Alumni (treas.), Am. Mensa, Ltd. Office: Campazzi & Assocs Inc 5973 SE Oakmont Pl Stuart FL 34997-8637

CAMPBELL, ADDISON JAMES, JR., writer; b. Dilliner, Pa., Dec. 16, 1933; s. Addison James Campbell and Nora Lee (Marshall) Reynolds; m. Fumie Murashige, Oct. 13, 1962; 1 child, Gary Clark Campbell. Pres. Action Bolt Corp., Houston, 1965-72. Author: Nanci's World, Ukelele Lil of Lihue, The Object; co-author: Fumie Murashige Campbell, 1994; contbr. numerous articles and research papers to profl. jours. Sgt. USMC, 1952-55. Recipient recognition award for Adult Correction Officer for Island of Kauai, State of Hawaii, 1987, 88.

CAMPBELL, ALLAN MCCULLOCH, bacteriology educator; b. Berkeley, Calif., Apr. 27, 1929; s. Lindsay and Virginia Margaret (Henning) C.; m. Alice Del Campillo, Sept. 5, 1958; children—Wendy, Joseph. B.S. in Chemistry, U. Calif. at Berkeley, 1950; M.S. in Bacteriology, U. Ill., 1951; Ph.D., 1953; Ph.D. hon. degree, U. Chgo., 1978, U. Rochester, 1981. Instr. bacteriology U. Mich., 1953-57; research assoc. Carnegie Inst., Cold Spring Harbor, N.Y., 1957-58; asst. prof. biology U. Rochester, N.Y., 1958-61, assoc. prof., 1961-63, prof., 1963-68; prof. biol. sci. Stanford (Calif.) U., 1968—, Barbara Kimball Browning prof. humanities and scis., 1992—; Author: Episomes, 1969; co-author: General Virology, 1978; editor Gene, 1980-90, mem. editl. bd., 1990—; assoc. editor Virology, 1963-69; assoc. editor Ann. Rev. Genetics, 1969-84, editor, 1984—; spl. editor Evolution, 1985-88; editl. bd. Jour. Bacteriology, 1966-72, Jour. Virology, 1967-75, New Biologist, 1989-92. Served with AUS, 1953-55. Recipient Research Career award USPHS, 1962-68. Mem. Nat. Acad. Scis., Am. Acad. Arts and Scis., Am. Soc. Microbiology, Soc. Am. Naturalists, Genetics Soc. Am., AAAS, Am. Acad. Microbiology. Democrat. Home: 947 Mears Ct Palo Alto CA 94305-1041 Office: Stanford U Dept Biol Scis Stanford CA 94305 *I've always thought that each individual has some contribution to human knowledge that he is uniquely suited to make. So I try to be organized and to avoid doing things that I expect will get done, anyway, by others. And, of course, everything worthwhile requires hard work.*

CAMPBELL, ALMA JACQUELINE PORTER, elementary education educator; b. Savannah, Ga., Jan. 5, 1948; d. William W. and Gladys B. Porter. BS in Elem. Edn., Savannah State Coll., 1969; MEd, SUNY, Brockport, 1971, cert. advanced study in adminstrn. magna cum laude, 1988. Cert. permanent elem. tchr., N.Y. Elem. tchr. Savannah, 1969-70, 71-74; tchr. intern project unique Rochester (N.Y.) City Sch. Dist., 1970-71, tchr., 1974-88, adminstrv. intern chpt. 1 office, 1988; mem. student progress task force, 1994, mem. coun. elem. leadership, mem. instrnl. com.; basic skills cadre Francis Parker Sch., Rochester, 1988—, lead tchr. mentor, 1991—; lead tchr., mentor tchr., basic skills cadre John Walton Spencer Elem. Sch. No. 16, 1992—; vice prin. Theodore Roosevelt Sch # 43, 1993-94, prin., 1994-99; apptd. mem. Profl. Devel. Acad. Adv. Bd., 1999; Distar demonstration tchr. Rochester City Sch. Dist., 1976-78, curriculum writer, 1987, 88, tchr. rsch. linker, demonstration tchr., 1987-88; active Effective Parenting Info. and Children program, 1987-89; active coop. tchr. program Nazareth Coll. and Rochester City Sch. Dist., 1987; mem. policy bd. Rochester Tchr. Ctr., 1994, adminstrv. rep. to policy bd., 1995-97; adv. com. N.Y. State Systemic Iniative, 1994, sch. quality reviewer; coord., presenter ednl. workshops; apptd. mem. Student Progress Task Force, 1995; asst. WXXI Broadcasting Partnership and Sch. Number 43; coord. Sch. Quality Rev. Initiative, 1996-97; establisher partnership with Urban Schs. Inst. in conjunction with U. Rochester, 1996-97; mem. Supt. Janey's Profl. Devel. Focus Group, 1997. Author: (with McGriff) Quick Reference Manual for Teachers, 1989-90; co-author: A Quick Reference Manual for Teachers and Absolutely Jam-Packed With Super Teaching Tips, 1991-92. Mem. Martin Luther King Commn. on Edn., Rochester, 1988-89, Francis Parker Sch. PTA, 1988—; mental health asst. Curriculum Task Force, Rochester City Sch. Dist., 1991, coop. learning tchr., trainer, 1990, 91-92; asst. dir. Meml. A.M.E. Zion Ch., 1979-82, dir. summer camp, 1982-85, asst. sec. bd. Christian edn., 1987-89; bd. dirs. Hamm House, Jefferson Area Child Devel. Ctr., 1990-91; active United Way; mem steering com. African Am. Devel. Program. Mem. ASCD (assoc.), NAFE (sub-adv. com. Strong Mus. sch. programs), Am. Assn. Sch. Adminstrs., Internat. Reading Assn., Rochester Coun. Elem. Leadership, Phi Delta Kappa (treas. 1996-97), Alpha Kappa Alpha (chair nominating com. 1988-89, Ivy Leaf reporter 1992—, Cert. of Achievement 1988). Democrat. Avocations: reading, travel, collecting mugs, visiting amusement parks. Home: 40 Menlo Pl Rochester NY 14620-2718 also: Meml AME Zion Ch Clarissa St Rochester NY 14604 Office: Theodore Rossevelt Sch 1305 Lyell Ave Rochester NY 14606-2119

CAMPBELL, ANDREW WILLIAM, immunotoxicology physician; b. Beirut, Apr. 3, 1948; s. William Alexander and Gisela (Landes) C.; children: Denia Giselle, Michelle Elise, Colin Alexander, Ian William. BA in Pre-med., Psychology, Franklin Piere Coll., Rindge, N.H., 1970; MD, U. Autonoma de Guadalajara, Mex., 1974. Diplomate Am. Bd. Family Practice, Am. Bd. Forensic Examiners, Am. Bd. Forensic Medicine. Intern Pediat. Hosp. Infantil, Ob-gyn., Clin. Santa Monica, Guadalajara, Mex., 1974-75, Pub. Health Dept., Guadalajara, Mex., 1975-76; resident gen. surgery Orlando (Fla.) Regional Med. Ctr., 1977-78; resident family practice Med. Coll. Ga., Augusta, 1978-81; pvt. practice family physician Two Physician Practice, Sarasota, Fla., 1981, with former chief surgeon Eisenhower Med. Ctr., Augusta, Ga.; pvt. practice Augusta, Wrens and Louisvlle, Ga., 1983-84, Houston, Tex., 1985—; med. dir. Ctr. for Immune, Environ. and Toxic Disorders, Houston, 1993—; staff mem. Meml. City Med. Ctr., West Houston Med. Ctr., Spring Branch Med. Ctr.; chmn. dept. family practice Sam Houston Meml.. Hosp., Houston, 1987, chmn. credentials com. 1988, mem. exec. com. 1987-89; internat. cons. and med. expert on artifical implants, toxic exposure and occupational medicine; lectr. and speaker at Artificial Implants and Toxic Exposure Symposia; mem. faculty U. Tex. Sch. Medicine, 1993—. Contbr. numerous articles to profl. jours.; made numerous presentations to sci. meetings; author: (with others) Health Effects of Toxic Chemicals, 1994, Textbook of Nephrology (2 vols.), 1995; co-editor Internat. Jour. Occupl. Medicine and Toxicology, 1992-95; mem. editl. bd. Toxicology and Indsl. Health, 1994-95. Founder Clinic for the Indigent, St. John Vianney Ch., Houston, 1987; trustee Sam Houston Meml. Hosp., 1987-93. Recipient Consumer's Choice award Am. Nurses in Bus. Assn., Houston, 1994. Fellow Am. Acad. Family Physicians; mem. AAAS, Tex. Acad. Family Physicians, Am. Coll. of Occupational and Environ. Medicine, The Chronic Fatigue and Immune Dysfunction Syndrome Assn., Inc., Internat. Soc. Neuroimmunology, Soc. Mucosal Immunology, So. Med. Assn., Pan Am. Allergy Soc., Houston Med.-Legal Soc., Tex. Med. Assn., Tex. Med. Found., Harris County Med. Soc., Am. Bd. Forensic Examiners, Tex. Physicians Resource Coun. Republican. Avocations: golf, collecting pipes, collecting pens. Office: Ctr Immune Environ & Toxic Disorders 14441 Memorial Dr Houston TX 77079-6744

CAMPBELL, ANITA JOYCE, computer company executive; b. Jefferson City, Mo., Sept. 24, 1953; d. George Rigsby and Betty Jean (Heade) Sanders; m. Michael Joseph Campbell (div. 1986); children: Kim Erik Seaver, Daniel Joseph Campbell. AAS in Computer Sci., Lincoln U., Mo., 1985; BA in Psychology, Maryville U., 1998. Student lab. mgr. Lincoln U., 1985; integrated systems analyst Xerox Corp., St. Louis, 1988-89, ins. industry project mgr., western region ops. mgmt. staff, 1990-91, advanced product specialist, western regions ops. mgmt., 1991, advanced solutions tech. mgr., western region ops. mgmt., 1992-93, tech. market project mgr., rsch. & engring, integrated systems orgn., 1993-94, tech. mktg. mgr. integrated solutions, systems sales and support, 1994-95; tech. con., integrated document solutions Integrated Document Solutions, 1995-96; project mgr. state and local govt. Xerox Profl. Document Svcs., Bridgeton, Mo., 1996-97; project mgr. govt. practice Xerox Profl. Svcs., 1997-99, opportunity mgr. cons. and sys. integration, 1999—. Co-developer Delta Plan, 1988. Office staff campaign mgr. for Carter-Mondale Reelection Com., Washington, 1989-90; waterfront dir. Spl. Olympics, Lake of the Ozarks, Mo., 1987; bd. dirs. ARC, Jefferson City, 1986. Avocations: reading, swimming. Home: 912 Leawood Dr Saint Louis MO 63126-1114 Office: Xerox Corp 3221 Mckelvey Rd Bridgeton MO 63044-2551

CAMPBELL, ANN MARIE, artist; b. Burbank, Calif., June 14, 1956; d. Stephen and Ann Marie (Luis) C.; children: Richard Arthur, Robert Campbell, Victoria Ann. BA in Painting, Sculpture, Graphic Arts, UCLA, 1980. spkr. Mural Art Seminar, ASID Student Career Forum, 1995. Artist: (murals) The Pickle Barrel, 1992, Old World Sky with Angels, 1996, Cottage Garden, 1995, Two Street Window, 1996, Heather's Jazz Band, 1996, California Groaning Board, 1997, History of Virgin Records, 1997, numerous others throughout U.S. and Can., San Francisco, N.Y., L.A., Las Vegas, Orlando, Dallas, Phoenix, New Orleans, Denver, Chgo., Miami, and Vancouver, B.C. Mem. Nat. Soc. Mural Painters, Am. Soc. Portrait Artists, Alpha Lambda Delta. Roman Catholic. Office: PO Box 581 Folsom CA 95763-0581

CAMPBELL, ARTHUR ANDREWS, retired government official; b. Bklyn., Feb. 8, 1924; s. Arthur Monroe and Jo Ethel (Andrews) C.; m. Nancy Elizabeth Pyle, Jan. 28, 1961; children—Julia, Tay. A.B., Antioch Coll., 1948; postgrad., Columbia U., 1947-50. Editorial clk. Met. Life Ins. Co., N.Y.C., 1950-52; statistician U.S. Bur. of Census, Washington, 1952-56; asso. research prof. Scripps Found. for Research in Population Problems, Miami U., Oxford, Ohio, 1956-64; chief natality stats. br. Nat. Center for Health Stats., Washington, 1964-68; dep. dir. Center for Population Research, NIH, Bethesda, Md., 1968-94; ret., 1994. Co-author: Family Planning, Sterility, and Population Growth, 1959, Fertility and Family Planning in the U.S, 1966, Trends and Variations in Fertility in the U.S, 1968, Manual of Fertility Analysis, 1983. Served with USN, 1943-46. Recipient Meritorious Service award U.S. Dept. Commerce, 1957; Dir.'s award NIH, 1976. Fellow Am. Statis. Assn.; mem. Population Assn. Am. (pres. 1973-74), Internat. Union for Sci. Study Population.

CAMPBELL, ARTHUR C., federal agency adminstrator; b. Waugh, Ala.; married; 3 children. BS in Architecture, Tuskegee Inst.; M in City Planning, Ga. Inst. Tech. Cons. planning and devel. Chattanooga, Tenn., 1986-95; dep. under sec. policy and planning USDA, Washington, 1995—. Mem. transition team Pres.-elect Bill Clinton and V.P.-elect Al Gore, 1992-93; mem. bd. commrs. Hamilton County, Tenn., 1993; chmn. bd. dirs. Ho. Appropriations Com. Office: Policy and Planning 1400 Independence Ave SW Washington DC 20250-0002

CAMPBELL, BARTH LYNN, theology educator; b. Aug. 23, 1952. BA, Calif. State Coll., Stanislaus, 1975; MA, Simpson Coll., 1982; PhD, Fuller Theol. Sem., 1995. H.S. dir. First Bapt. Ch., Modesto, Calif., 1974-75; asst. prof. Bible and theology Simpson Coll., Redding, Calif., 1996—; min. of youth First Bapt. Ch., Mesa, Ariz., 1975-76; min. youth edn. First Bapt. Ch., Ukiah, Calif., 1976-84; pastor youth ministry Elim Chapel, Winnipeg, Man., Can., 1984-87; asst. prof. Bible and theology Simpson Coll., Redding, Calif., 1996—. Office: Simpson Coll 2211 College View Dr Redding CA 96003

CAMPBELL, BEN NIGHTHORSE, senator; b. Auburn, Calif., Apr. 13, 1933; m. Linda Price; children: Colin, Shanan. BA, Calif. U., San Jose, 1957. Educator Sacramento Law Enforcement Agy.; mem. Colo. Gen. Assembly, 1983-86, U.S. Ho. Reps., 1987-93; U.S. Senator from Colorado, 1993—; rancher, jewelry designer, Ignacio, Colo. Chief No. Cheyenne Tribe. Named Outstanding Legislator Colo. Bankers Assn., 1984, Man of Yr. LaPlata Farm Bur., Durango, Colo., 1984; named one of Ten Best Legislators Denver Post/Channel 4, 1986. Mem. Am. Quarter Horse Assn., Am.

Brangus Assn., Am. Indian Edn. Assn. Republican. Office: US Senate 380 Russell Senate Office Bldg Washington DC 20510-0605

CAMPBELL, BERT LOUIS, lawyer, mediator, arbitrator; b. Tyler, Tex., Aug. 11, 1939; s. Bert M. and Jocelyn M. (Day) C.; m. Mary Ann Suatoni, July 17, 1965; children: Stephen, Brian, Rebecca. BA, U. Tex., 1961, B in Journalism, 1970, JD, 1970. Ptnr. Vinson & Elkins, Houston, 1970—; writer, lectr. in field. Trustee Cullen Found. Lt. (j.g.) USN, 1963-66. Mem. ABA, Tex. Bar Assn., Houston Bar Assn., Am. Health Lawyers Assn. (atty.-mediators mediation panel), Am. Arbitration Assn., Atty.-Mediators Assn. Office: Vinson & Elkins 1001 Fannin St Ste 2500 Houston TX 77002-6706

CAMPBELL, BILL, mayor; b. Raleigh, N.C., 1954; s. Ralph and June C.; m. Sharon Tapscott, 1978; children: Billy, Christina. BA in History, Polit. Sci., Sociology cum laude, Vanderbilt U., 1974; JD, Duke U., 1977. Atty. Kilpatrick & Cody, Atlanta, 1978-80; prosecutor U.S. Dept. Justice, Atlanta, 1980-81; ptnr. Ellis, Funk, Goldberg, Labovitz, Campbell, Atlanta; mayor City of Atlanta, 1994—. Mem. Atlanta City Coun., 1981-93. Office: Office of the Mayor 55 Trinity Ave SW Ste 2400 Atlanta GA 30303-3531

CAMPBELL, B(OBBY) JACK, university official; b. Fort Worth, Oct. 12, 1929; s. Jack Bryan and Ruby Opal (Lamberth) C.; m. Frances Carol Alexander, Aug. 24, 1957; children: Carol Stuart Davis, John William Campbell. BA, Tex. Christian U., 1951, MA, 1953; PhD, U. N.C., 1960. Asst. dir. U. N.C. Inst. of Govt., Chapel Hill, 1957-59; chief accident rsch. br. Cornell U. Aero. Lab., Buffalo, 1959-66; dir. U. N.C. Hwy. Safety Rsch. Ctr., Chapel Hill, 1966-91, sr. investigator, dir. emeritus, 1992—; chmn. com. accident stats. Nat. Safety Coun., 1964-68; chmn. nat. motor vehicle safety adv. coun. U.S. Dept. Transp., 1975-76, mem., 1987-89, chmn. nat. driver register adv. com., 1983-86; chmn. panel on automotive assessment into 21st century U.S. Congress Office Tech. Assessment, 1976-77; chmn. com. to study CB radios on buses NRC, 1983-84, mem. com. to identify measures to improve safety of sch. bus transp., 1987-88; chmn. Global Traffic Safety Trust, Melbourne, Australia, 1988-92; lectr. or cons. in Australia, Azerbaijan, Brazil, Can., China, Denmark, Dominica, France, India, Hong Kong, Japan, Republic of Korea, Malawi, Malaysia, New Zealand, Russia, Saudi Arabia, Spain, Switzerland, Uruguay. Author: Driver Improvement: The Point System, 1958, Reducing Traffic Injury: A Global Challenge, 1988; (with others) Reflections on the Transfer of Highway Safety to Developing Nations, 1998, Collier's Encyclopedia, 1962, Human Factors in Technology, 1963, Trauma and the Automobile, 1966, Traffic Safety: A National Problem, 1967, Key Issues in Highway Loss Reducation, 1970, Restraint Technologies: Rear Seat Occupant Protection, 1987; contbr. numerous articles to profl. jours. SFC. U.S. Army, 1948-49. Recipient Gerin Medal for Rsch. Internat. Assn. for Accident and Traffic Medicine, 1992, Gustafson Leadership award Hwy. Users Fedn., 1989, Volvo Internat. Traffic Safety award, 1988, Volvo Pub. Safety award 1984, Disting. Svc. award Am. Assn. for Automotive Medicine, 1978, N.C. Pub. Health Assn., 1972, Alvah Lauer award Human Factors Soc., 1976, Met. Rsch. award Commendation Nat. Safety Coun., 1971, 60. Avocations: astronomy, flying, tennis, classical music, opera/drama. Home: 502 Belmont St Chapel Hill NC 27514-3000*

CAMPBELL, BRIAN SCOTT, army officer; b. Union City, Pa., Mar. 14, 1959; s. Paul Ralph and Beverly Jean (Allen) C.; m. Susan Carol Palone, Nov. 26, 1988. BS, Edinboro U. Pa., 1980; postgrad., U. Scranton, 1980-81; DO, Phila. Coll. Osteo. Medicine, 1985; MPH, U. Tenn., 1992, U.S. Army Command & Gen. Staff Coll., 1996. Diplomate Am. Bd. Preventative Medicine, Am. Osteo. Bd. Preventive Medicine, Nat. Bd. Examiners for Osteo. Physicians and Surgeons, Pa. State Bd. Examiners. Enlisted USMC, 1976; commd. 2d lt. U.S. Army, 1981, advanced through grades to lt. col., 1996; specialist in occupational, environ. and aerospace medicine U.S. Ctrl. Command, McDill AFB, Fla., 1996—; asst. adj. prof. preventive medicine and biometrics Uniformed Svcs. U. Health Scis., Bethesda, Md. Author: University of Tennessee Wellness Handbook; contbr. articles to profl. jours. Instr. Baize Sch. Karate, Clarksville, Tenn., 1988-96; res. dep. sheriff Hillsborough County, Fla., 1997—. Health Professions scholar, 1981; decorated Bronze Star. Mem. NRA (life), Aerospace Med. Assn., Am. Osteo. Coll. Preventive Medicine, Wilderness Med. Soc., Soc. U.S. Army Flight Surgeons (life), Am. Osteo. Assn., Assn. Mil. Osteo. Physicians and Surgeons, U.S. Judo Assn. (Black Belt, patron life), United Bujutsu Fedn. (black belt), N. Am. Hunting Club (life), Beta Beta Beta. Republican. Avocations: martial arts, science fiction, knife making, shooting.

CAMPBELL, BRUCE ALAN, market research consultant; b. Washington, Jan. 19, 1944; s. Albert Angus and Jean Lorraine (Winter) C.; m. Jennifer Lee Drew, May 3, 1968 (div. Dec. 1986); children: Kirsten, Robert; m. Lorna Marion Wise Ekholm, Aug. 21, 1993. BA, Oberlin Coll., 1966; MA, U. Mich., 1968, PhD, 1971. From asst. prof. to assoc. prof. U. Ga., Athens, 1971-83, dir. survey rsch. ctr., 1981-83; v.p. Marktrend Mkt. Rsch., Vancouver, B.C., Can., 1983-84; pres., CEO Campbell Goodell Traynor Consul, Vancouver, B.C., Can., 1984—; v.p. Corp. Insights, Inc., Vancouver, B.C., Can., 1992-96. Dir. Downtown Vancouver Assn., 1989-96, pres., 1994-96, mem. adv. bd., 1996—; dir. Parking Corp. of Vancouver, 1992—, v.p., 1994-96, chmn. bd., 1996-98; bd. dirs. Downtown Vancouver Bus. Improvement Assn., 1994-96; mem. Vancouver Econ. Devel. Commn., 1996. Author: The American Electorate, 1979, profl. jours. Mem. Am. Assn. Pub. Opinion Rsch., Profl. Mktg. Rsch. Assn. Avocations: musical theatre, minor hockey officiating. E-mail: bcampbell@cgtnet.com. Office: Campbell Goodell Traynor Cons, 675 W Hastings St Ste 1100, Vancouver, BC Canada V6B 1N2

CAMPBELL, BRUCE CRICHTON, hospital administrator; b. Balt., July 21, 1947; s. James Allen and Elda Shaffer (Crichton) C.; m. Linda Page Cottrell, June 28, 1969; children: Molly Shaffer, Andrew Crichton. B.A., Lake Forest Coll., 1969; M.H.A., Washington U., St. Louis, 1973; D.P.H., U. Ill., 1979. Adminstrv. asst. Passavant Meml. Hosp., Chgo., 1970-71; adminstrv. resident Albany (N.Y.) Med. Center Hosp., 1972-73; adminstrv. asst. Rush-Presbyn.-St. Luke's Med. Center, Chgo., 1973-75; asst. adminstr. Rush-Presbyn.-St. Luke's Med. Center, 1975-77, asst. v.p., 1977-79, v.p. adminstrv. affairs, 1979-83; chmn. dept. health systems mgmt. Rush U., Chgo., 1977-81, dean Coll. Health Scis., 1981-83; exec. dir. U. Chgo. Hosps. and Clinics, 1983-85; lectr. Grad. Sch. Bus., U. Chgo., 1983-85; pres. Campbell Assocs., Chgo., 1985-92; exec. v.p. Ill. Masonic Med. Ctr., Chgo., 1993, pres., 1993—. W.K. Kellogg Found. fellow, 1977; Leadership Greater Chgo. fellow, 1984-85. Fellow Am. Coll. Healthcare Execs.; mem. Young Adminstrs. Chgo. (pres. 1977), Assn. Univ. Programs in Health Adminstrn., Am. Hosp. Assn., Ill. Hosp. Assn., Chgo. Hosp. Council. Office: Ill Masonic Med Ctr 836 W Wellington Ave Chicago IL 60657-9224

CAMPBELL, BRUCE IRVING, lawyer; b. Mason City, Iowa, July 7, 1947; s. E. Riley Jr. and Donna Mae (Andresen) C.; children: Anne, John; m. Beverly J. Evans. BA, Upper Iowa U., 1969; JD, Harvard U., 1973. Bar: Iowa 1973, U.S. Dist. Ct. (so. dist.) Iowa 1973, U.S. Dist. Ct. (no. dist.) Iowa 1974, U.S. Tax Ct. 1976, U.S. Ct. Appeals (8th cir.) 1977, U.S. Ct. Claims 1982. Shareholder Davis, Brown, Koehn, Shors & Roberts, P.C., Des Moines, 1973—; adj. prof. law Drake U., Des Moines, 1974-90. Trustee Upper Iowa U., Fayette, 1978—, chair bd. trustees, 1992—. Mem. ABA, Iowa State Bar Assn., Polk County Bar Assn. Republican. Home: 62 Meadowbrook Cir Cumming IA 50061-1014 Office: Davis Brown Koehn Shors & Roberts PC 666 Walnut St Ste 2500 Des Moines IA 50309-3904

CAMPBELL, BRUCE JAMES, . BS in Indsl. Mgmt., Pa. State U., 1962; MS in Tech. Mgmt., Am. U., 1971; PhD, Harvard U., 1976. Mgr. office plans and ops. Office Nat. Comm. System Ops., Washington; dir. office info. resources mgmt. Fed. Emergency Mgmt. Agency, Washington, 1981-92, acting regional dir. region II, 1993, divsn. dir. resources support divsn. response and recovery, assoc. dir. ops. support, 1994—. Capt. USMC, 1962-68, Vietnam. Recipient Meritorious Civilian Svc. Medal Sec. of Def., 1982, Meritorious Exec. award Pres. Bush, 1989. Office: Fed Emergency Mgmt Agency Ops Support Directorate 500 C St SW Washington DC 20472-0001

CAMPBELL, BYRON CHESSER, publishing company executive; b. Evanston, Ill., Feb. 6, 1934; s. Chesser Milburn and Hallie (Calhoun) C.; m. Barbara Mace, Aug. 16, 1958 (div. Apr. 1982); children: Evan, Aimee Campbell Grey; m. Meta Pierce, Aug. 13, 1983; stepchildren: Marc Wise, Meier Wise, Matthew Wise, Miles Wise. BA, Yale U., 1955; MBA, Harvard U., 1959. Various positions Burlington (Vt.) Free Press, 1959-61; prodn. engr., asst. labor rels. mgr. Chicago Tribune, 1961-68, prodn. mgr., 1970-73; bus. mgr. Chicago Today, 1968-70; asst. to pres. Tribune Co., 1973-75; pres., gen. mgr. Area Publs. Corp., Merrill Printing Co., Chgo., 1975-77; pres., chief exec. officer News and Sun-Sentinel Co., Ft. Lauderdale, Fla., 1977-83; pres., pub. L.A. Daily News; pres., chief exec. officer Tribune Newspapers West, Inc., L.A., 1983-87; pres., pub. The Record, Hackensack, N.J.; v.p. Macromedia Inc., Hackensack, 1988-91; bd. dirs. Home News Pub. Co., New Brunswick, N.J., Newspapers of New Eng., Concord, N.H., George W. Prescott Pub. Co., Quincy, Mass., Journal-Star Printing Co., Lincoln, Nebr. Bd. dirs. Lyric Opera Chgo., Newberry Libr. Chgo., Sta. WPBT, Miami, Fla., Rush-Presbyn.-St. Luke's Med. Ctr., Chgo.; bd. dirs., campaign chmn. United Way of Bergen County, 1989-91; adv. bd. Bergen 2000; bd. dirs., pres., campaign chmn. United Way of Broward County, Fla.; bd. dirs., chmn. San Fernando Valley Cultural Found., L.A.; bd. dirs., pres. Chgo. Youth Ctrs., Broward Community Blood Ctr.; bd. dirs., exec. com. Broward Workshop; bd. dirs. United Way, L.A., campaign chmn. San Fernando Valley; bd. dirs., 1st v.p. Ft. Lauderdale Symphony. Lt. USN, 1955-57. Mem. AP (nominating com.), Am. Newspaper Pubs. Assn. (govt. affairs com., newsprint com. 1989-92), Am. Press Inst. (bd. dirs. 1984-93), Inland Press Assn. (pres., bd. dirs.), Greater L.A.C. of C. (bd. dirs.), Econ. Club (Chgo.), Yale Club (Chgo., bd. dirs., pres.), Lotos Club (N.Y.C.), Univ. Club (Chgo., bd. dirs., admissions com.), Saddle and Cycle Club (Chgo., bd. dirs., admissions com.), Lauderdale Yacht Club (Ft. Lauderdale, Fla.). Avocations: tennis, wine, fly fishing, travel, golf.

CAMPBELL, CARL DAVID, oil industry executive; b. Oklahoma City, July 4, 1959; s. David Gwynne and Janet Gay (Newland) C. B in Bus. Adminstrn., U. Okla., 1982. Cert. profl. landman. Land cons. Leede Exploration, Okla. City, 1978, 79; lease broker W.M. Bryan, Inc., Okla. City, 1980, 81; corp. sec., land mgr. Earth Hawk Exploration, Inc., Okla. City, 1980-96, v.p., 1996—; landman PetroCorp, Okla. City, 1983-87, mid-continent divsn. landman, 1987-91; Gulf Coast divsn. landman PetroCorp, Houston, 1991-92, Gulf, Rockies, Can. divsn. landman, 1993—. Mem. Cherokee Nation Okla., Tahlequah, 1979—. Mem. Am. Assn. Petroleum Landmen, Houston Assn. Petroleum Landmen, Canadian Assn. Petroleum Landmen, Okla. Ind. Petroleum Assn., Okla. City Assn. Petroleum Landmen, Houston Soc., U. Okla. Found. Assocs., First Families East Tenn. (charter), Clan Campbell of N.Am., Cherokee Nation of Okla., First Families of the Cherokee Nation (charter), First Families of the Twin Territories, Cherokee Hist. Soc. (charter mem. heritage coun. 1982—), Houston Mus. Fine Arts, Aircraft Owners and Pilots Assn., Phi Gamma Delta. Republican. Presbyterian. Avocations: biking, flying (lic. pilot), travel, scuba diving (cert.). Home: 1701 Hermann Dr Unit 2702 Houston TX 77004-7330 Office: PetroCorp Ste 300 N Atrium 160800 Greenspoint Park Dr Houston TX 77060-2391

CAMPBELL, CARL LESTER, banker; b. Sunbury, Pa., Apr. 10, 1943; s. Claude L. and Viola W. (Voneida) C.; m. Mary E. Bingaman, June 5, 1965; children: Carla L., Craig L. B.S., Susquehanna U., 1965; postgrad., Stonier Grad. Sch. Banking, 1978. Br. mgr. asst. v.p. Tri-County Nat. Bank, Middleburg, Pa., 1965-72; asst. v.p. adminstrn. Pa. Nat. Bank, Pottsville, 1972-74, adminstrv. v.p., 1974-80, sr. v.p., 1980-81, exec. v.p., 1981-82, pres. chief exec. officer, 1982-86; pres., chief exec. officer Keystone Fin., Inc., Harrisburg, Pa., 1986-98; chmn., CEO Keystone Fin., Inc., Harrisburg, 1998—. Office: Keystone Fin Inc PO Box 3660 Harrisburg PA 17105-3660

CAMPBELL, CATHERINE ELLEN, French language educator; b. Cleve., Jan. 7, 1948; d. Malcolm Freeman and Ruth (Kingsley) C. AB, Mt. Holyoke Coll., 1969; MA, Colgate U., 1970; PhD, U. Mo., Columbia, 1982. Tchr. Whitesboro (N.Y.) H.S., 1970, Poland (N.Y.) Ctrl. Sch., 1970-73; tchg. asst. U. Mo., Columbia, 1974-82; prof. French Cottey Coll., Nevada, Mo., 1982—. Author: The French Procuress, 1984; editor/translator: The Widow (La Veuve), 1993; reviewer scholarly jours. Mem. Am. Assn. Tchrs. of French, Renaissance Soc. Am., Assn. of Literary Scholars and Critics, 16th Century Studies Conf., Alpha Mu Gamma (reg. v.p. 1997—). Home: 412 Main St Nevada MO 64772 Office: Cottey Coll 1000 W Austin Nevada MO 64772

CAMPBELL, CATHERINE LYNN, elementary and middle school educator; b. Lynchburg, Va., Mar. 16, 1961; d. Tomie Eawell Campbell and Barbara (Arthur) McCraw. BA, Sweet Briar Coll., 1983; postgrad., U. Va. Cert. elem. tchr., NK-8 tchr., Va. Tchr. Amherst (Va.) County Pub. Schs., 1984—. Mem. Nat. Honor Soc. Avocations: horseback riding, raising quarter horses. Home: 139 Cedar Crest Dr Ste 107 Madison Heights VA 24572-2366 Office: Amherst County Pub Schs Amherst VA 24521

CAMPBELL, CHARLES ALTON, manufacturing corporate executive; b. Brunswick, Ga., Mar. 10, 1944; s. Rayford Monroe and Cecelia Elizabeth (Camilla) C.; B Indsl. Engring., Ga. Inst. Tech., 1966; MBA, Harvard U., 1973; m. Mary Alla Traber, Aug. 15, 1970; children—Christine Beensen, Elizabeth Traber, Charles Traber. Mgr. ops. projects Camak Lumber Ops., ITT Rayonier, Thomson, Ga., 1974-75, mgr. ops. projects Wood Products Group, N.Y.C., 1975-77, dir. chems. devel. parent co., 1977-79, dir. operational planning and control, Seattle, 1979-80; pres. Fox Mfg. Co., Rome, Ga., 1980-81, Camtec, Inc., Rome, 1981-88; chmn. bd. Universal Ceramics, Inc., Adairsville, Ga., 1984-87; exec. v.p. Saunders, Inc., Birmingham, Ala., 1987-88, pres., chief oper. officer, 1988-90; pres. N.Am. Tech. Corp., Birmingham, 1990—. Lt. C.E., USNR, 1967-69. Episcopalian. Club: Mountain Brook (Ala.) Swim and Tennis. Lodge: Rotary (Birmingham). Home: 3725 Briar Oak Cir Birmingham AL 35223-2826 Office: NAm Tech Corp PO Box 43462 Birmingham AL 35243-0462

CAMPBELL, C(HARLES) ROBERT, architect. BS in Archtl. Engring., U. N.Mex., 1958. Registered architect, N.Mex., Tex., Ariz., Colo., Okla. With SMPC Architects, Albuquerque, 1955—, prin., 1969—, pres., CEO, 1991—; mem. State Bd. Examiners Architects, 1992-93, vice chmn., 1994, chmn., 1995-96; mem. adv. com. sch. architecture U. N.Mex.; vis. critic U. N.Mex. Profl. mem. Bernalillo County Bd. Appeals; bd. dirs. Presbyn. Healthcare Found. Mem. AIA (corp., pres., v.p., sec. Albuquerque chpt., mem. joint practice com. 1989—), Am. Arbitration Assn., Nat. Coun. Archtl. Registration Bd. (cert., juror/grader architecture registration exam, mem. architecture registration exam com. 1993-94, 94-95, 95-96), N.Mex. Soc. Architects (sec. 1974, pres. 1975-76). Office: 115 Amherst Dr SE Albuquerque NM 87106-1425

CAMPBELL, CLARENCE BOWEN, retired educator, real estate developer, columnist; b. Minotola, N.J., May 26, 1913; s. Edward B. and Rebecca White (Paris) C.; m. Clara Stelzer, Aug. 12, 1941 (div. Feb. 1973); children: Robert Bruce, Raymond Kent; m. Edna Mae Monahan, Feb. 23, 1974. BA, Temple U., 1937; MA, Lehigh U., 1947. Cert. secondary sch. tchr., guidance counselor, adminstr., Pa. Minister Meth. Ch., Eldora, N.J., 1934-37, Camden, N.J., 1937-40; tchr. Sch. Dist., Pleasant Valley, Pa., 1941-43, 46-47; admissions officer Lehigh U., Bethlehem, Pa., 1947-52; dir. fin. aid Lehigh U., Bethlehem, 1955-57, prof., dean of residence, 1957-74; v.p. pers. Edward Campbell Co., Vineland, N.J., 1952-55; real estate developer Ft. Myers Beach, Fla., 1977-89; columnist Shoppers Guide, Ft. Myers Beach, 1997—. Author: (poetry) The Promise of Shily, 1968, My Share of Pot, 1970; composer: Love You Like Roses, 1973, Kiss Me and Make Me Forget, 1973; mem. editl. bd. Jour. Coll and Univ. Housing, Bethlehem, 1957-74. Bd. dirs. Confront, Bethlehem, 1972-74, Pa. Assn. for the Blind, Bethlehem, 1972-74; pres. Estero Island Soc. Preservation Barbershop Quartet Singing in Am., Ft. Myers Beach, 1979-83; mem. coun. Moravian Coll., Bethlehem, 1971-74. Capt. USMCR, 1943-46, PTO. Named Barbershopper of Yr., Estero Island Soc. Preservation Barbershop Quartet Singing in Am., 1981, 86. Mem. AARP (coord. tax aide vol. 1982—), Lions (pres. Bethlehem 1957-74). Avocations: writing, sports, music, gardening.

CAMPBELL, CLYDE DEL, academic administrator; b. Wheeling, W.Va., Apr. 1, 1930; s. Clyde William and Vera (Speidel) C.; m. Joan Luhan, Aug. 25, 1956; 1 child, Leslie Ann Campbell. BS, BA, West Liberty Coll., 1953; MS, N.C. State U., 1955; PhD, W.Va. U., 1958. Instr. chemistry West Liberty (W.Va.) State Coll., 1958-61; sr. research chemist Mobay Chem. Co., New Martinsville, W.Va., 1961-67; prof. chemistry, chmn. sch. natural sci. West Liberty State Coll., 1967-70, assoc. acad. dean, 1970-73, dean adminstrn., 1973-82, acad. dean, 1982-84, pres., 1984-95; interim pres. Jefferson C.C., Steubenville, Ohio, 1998—. Patentee in field; contbr. articles to profl. jours. Mem., pres. Ohio County Bd. Edn., W.Va., 1966-72, W.Va. Intercollegiate Athletic Conf., 1986-95; bd. dirs. Oglebay Inst., Wheeling, 1985—. Mem. Am. Chem. Soc., W.Va. Acad. Sci., Phi Lambda Upsilon, Alpha Chi Sigma, Sigma Xi. Club: Blue Pencil (Wheeling). Lodge: Rotary. Avocations: jogging, golf, numismatics, music. Home: 199 Clearview Ave Wheeling WV 26003-6755

CAMPBELL, COLE C., journalist, educator; b. Roanoke, Va.. BA in English, U. N.C.; postgrad., Poynter Inst. Media Studies. Obituary writer The News and Observer, Raleigh, reporter city hall news; reporter Chapel Hill News; editor The Tar Heel mag., Norfolk, Va.; reporter city hall news Greensboro (N.C.) News & Record, asst. city editor, metro editor, asst. mng. editor; asst. mng. editor Va. Pilot and the Ledger-Star, Norfolk, 1990-91, mng. editor, 1991-93, editor, 1993-97; editor St. Louis Post Dispatch; instr. journalism Guilford Coll., U. N.C., Greensboro; journalism adv. bd. Norfolk State U. Bd. dirs. Goodwill Industries South Hampton Roads, United Way; alumni Leadership Hampton Roads. John S. Knight Journalism fellow, 1989-90. Office: St Louis Post Dispatch 900 N Tucker Blvd Saint Louis MO 63101-1099*

CAMPBELL, COLIN, obstetrician, gynecologist, school dean; b. Washington, June 24, 1927; s. Colin and Margaret (Kingsland) Masters C.; m. Catherine Marian Hayden, Aug. 20, 1952; children: Catherine, Janet, Philip. AB, Stanford U., 1949; MD, CM, McGill U., 1953; EdM, Temple U., 1967; DHL, U. Akron, 1991. Diplomate Am. Bd. Ob-Gyn. Intern George Washington Hosp., Washington, 1953-54; asst. resident in pathology U.S. VA Hosp., Coral Gables, Fla., 1954; gen. practice resident Dade County Hosp., Kendall, Fla., 1955; gen. practice medicine Perrine, Fla., 1955-57; asst. resident, resident in ob-gyn. Hosp. for the Women of Md., Balt., 1957-60; practice medicine specializing in ob-gyn. Balt., 1960-61; instr. ob-gyn. Temple U., Phila., 1961-64; asst. prof. ob-gyn. U. Mich., Ann Arbor, 1964-67, assoc. prof., 1967-71, prof., 1971-78, asst. dean Med. Sch., 1972-76, assoc. dean, 1976-78; prof. ob-gyn., dean U. Ala. Sch. Primary Med. Care, Huntsville, 1978-83; prof. ob-gyn., pres., dean Northeastern Ohio Univs. Coll. Medicine, Rootstown, 1983-92, pres., dean emeritus, 1992—. Contbr. numerous articles to profl. jours. Fellow ACOG. Home: 265 Hampshire Rd Akron OH 44313-4303 Office: Northeastern Ohio Us Coll Medicine 4209 State Route 44 Rootstown OH 44272-9698

CAMPBELL, COLIN GOETZE, foundation president; b. N.Y.C., Nov. 3, 1935; s. Joseph and Marjorie (Goetze) C.; m. Nancy Nash, June 20, 1959; children: Elizabeth, Jennifer, Colin, Blair. AB, Cornell U., 1957; JD, Columbia U., 1960; LLD (hon.), Amherst Coll., 1972, Williams Coll., 1973, Dickinson Coll., 1982, U. Hartford, 1983, Wesleyan U., 1989, Conn. Coll., 1990; DHL (hon.), Trinity Coll., 1981, Georgetown U., 1984; PhD (hon.) in Pub. Sci., Cedar Crest Coll., 1997. Bar: Conn. 1961. Atty. Cummings & Lockwood, Stamford, Conn., 1960-62; asst. to pres. Am. Stock Exchange, N.Y.C., 1962-63, sec., 1963-64, v.p., 1964-67; adminstrv. v.p. Wesleyan U., Middletown, Conn., 1967-69, exec. v.p., 1969-70, pres., 1970-88, pres. emeritus, 1988—; pres. Rockefeller Bros. Fund; bd. dirs. Pitney Bowes, HSB Group, Sysco Corp., Rockefeller Fin. Svcs. Bd. dirs. Winrock Internat. Inst. Agrl. Devel., PBS; trustee Charles E. Culpeper Found., Colonial Williamsburg Found., Ctrl. European U., N.Y. Hist. Soc. Mem. Am. Acad. Arts and Scis., Coun. on Fgn. Rels., Century Assn., Psi Upsilon, Phi Delta Phi. Episcopalian. Home: 66 E 79th St Apt 12N New York NY 10021-0217 Office: Rockefeller Bros Fund 437 Madison Ave New York NY 10022-7001

CAMPBELL, COLIN HERALD, former mayor; b. Winnipeg, Man., Can., Jan. 18, 1911; s. Colin Charles and Aimee Florence (Herald) C.; m. Virginia Paris, July 20, 1935; children: Susanna Herald, Corinna Buford, Virginia Wallace. BA, Reed Coll., 1933. Exec. sec. City Club of Portland, 1934-39; alumni sec., dir. endowment adminstrn. Reed Coll., 1939-42; exec. sec. N.W. Inst. Internat. Rels., 1940-42; contract supr., engr. Kaiser Co., Inc., 1942-45; asst. pers. dir. Portland Gas & Coke Co., 1945-48; dir. indsl. rels. Pacific Power & Light Co., Portland, 1948-76. Mem. Oreg. Adv. Com. on Fair Employment Practices Act, 1949-55; trustee, chmn., pres. Portland Symphonic Choir, 1950-54; trustee Portland Civic Theater, 1941-54; bd. dirs. Portland Symphony Soc., 1957-60, Cmty. Child Guidance Clinic, 1966-68; active United Way, 1945-75; bd. drs. Contemporary Crafts Assn., 1972-76, treas., 1975-76; bd. dirs. Lake Oswego Corp., 1961-65, 71-73, 74-76, corp. sec., 1964, pres., 1973-74, treas., 1975-76; mem. Com. on Citizen Involvement, City of Lake Oswego, 1975-77; chmn. Bicentennial Com., Lake Oswego; sec.-treas. Met. Area Comms. Commn., 1980-85; treas. Clackamas County Cmty. Action Agy., 1980-82, chmn., 1982-85; mem. fin. adv. com. West Clackamas County LWV, 1974-76, 78-80; councilman City of Lake Oswego, 1977-78, mayor, 1979-85, chmn. libr. growth task force, 1987-89, chmn. hist. rev. bd., 1990-92; chmn. energy adv. com. League Oreg. Cities, 1982-84; mem. adv. bd., chmn. fin. com. Lake Oswego Adult Cmty. Ctr., 1985-88; pres. Oswego Heritage coun., 192-95, sec., 1995-96, treas., 1997—; mem. County Blue Ribbon Com. on Law Enforcement, 1987-89; mem. fee arbitration panel Oreg. State Bar Assn., 1995—. Mem. Edison Electric Inst. (exec. com.), N.W. Electric Light and Power Assn., Lake Oswego C. of C. (v.p. 1986-87, chmn. land use com. 1990-91), Nat. Trust for Hist. Preservation, Hist. Prreservation League Oreg., Pacific N.W. Pers. Mgmt. Assn. (past regional v.p.), St. Andrews Soc., Oreg. Hist. Soc., Rotary (treas. Lake Oswego chpt. 1990-93). Republican. Presbyterian. Home: 398 Furnace St Lake Oswego OR 97034-3917

CAMPBELL, COLIN KYDD, electrical and computer engineering educator, researcher; b. St. Andrews, Fife, Scotland, May 3, 1927; s. David Walker and Jean (Hutchison) C.; m. Vivian Gwyn Norval, Apr. 17, 1954; children—Barry, Gwyn, Ian. B.Sc. in Engring. with honors, St. Andrews U., 1952; S.M., MIT, 1953; Ph.D., St. Andrews U., 1960; D.Sc., U. Dundee, 1984. Registered profl. engr., Ont. Communications engr. Fgn. Office and Diplomatic Wireless Service, London, Eng., 1946-47; communications engr. Brit. Embassy, Washington, 1947-48; electronics engr. Atomic Instrument Co., Cambridge, Mass., 1954-57; asst. prof. elec. and computer engring. McMaster U., Hamilton, Ont., Can., 1960-63, assoc. prof. elec. and computer engring., 1963-67, prof. elec. engring., 1967-89, prof. elec. and computer engring., 1989—, prof. emeritus. Author: Surface Acoustic Wave Devices and Their Signal Processing Applications, 1989, Surface Acoustic Wave Devices for Mobile and Wireless Communication, 1998; contbr. numerous articles to profl. jours. Served with Brit. Army, 1944-46. Recipient The Inventor insignia Can. Patents and Devel. Ltd., 1973, invitation fellowship Japan Soc. for Promotion of Sci., 1995; Rsch. fellow Rand Afrikaans U., South Africa, 1995. Fellow Royal Soc. Can. (Thomas Eadie medal 1983), Engring. Inst. Can., Royal Soc. Arts London, IEEE (life); mem. Sigma Xi. Mem. Ch. of England. Club: Royal Canadian Mil. Inst. (Toronto). Avocation: fishing. Home: 160 Parkview Dr, Ancaster, ON Canada L9G 1Z5 Office: McMaster U Elec Computer Engring, 1280 Main St W, Hamilton, ON Canada L8S 4L7

CAMPBELL, COLIN MCLEOD, journalist; b. Boston, Nov. 25, 1945; s. Peter Archibald and Elizabeth Blalock (Black) C.; m. Caroline P. Bethea, Aug. 25, 1973 (div. 1991); 1 child, Colin Gray; m. Deborah L. Scroggins, Feb. 20, 1993; 2 children, Anna Barrington, Elizabeth Baker. BA, U. Calif, Berkeley. Assoc. editor Psychology Today mag., 1973-77; mng. editor Sports Afield mag., 1977; sr. editor Human Nature mag., 1978, mng. editor, 1979; editorial writer The N.Y. Times, 1979-81, reporter, 1981, 84-86, Bangkok bur. chief, 1982-84; fgn. corr. The Atlanta Jour. & Constn., 1987-90, columnist, 1990—. Recipient Human Rights Reporting award Overseas Press Club, 1988, Robert F. Kennedy Journalism award, 1988; Yale U. assoc. fellow, 1986—. Mem. The Johnsonians Club. Office: The Atlanta Jour & Constn 72 Marietta St NW Atlanta GA 30303-2804

CAMPBELL, DAVID GEORGE, ecologist, researcher, author; b. Decatur, Ill., Jan. 28, 1949; s. George Robert and Jean Blossom C.; m. Karen S. Lowell; 1 child, Tatiana Claire. BA, Kalamazoo Coll., 1971; MS, U. Mich., 1973; PhD, Johns Hopkins U., 1984. Exec. dir. Bahamas Nat. Trust, Nassau, 1974-77; ecologist N.Y. Bot. Garden, Bronx, 1984-88, leader Amazon Expdns., 1974-92, research fellow, 1989—; prof. biology, Henry R. Luce prof. nations-global environ. Grinnell (Iowa) Coll., 1991—; adj. prof. U. Nanjing, China; prof. Semester at Sea, 1997; cons. Internat. Union for Conservation of Nature, 1978-79, leader Maya forest project, Belize, 1993-96; biologist and lectr. M.V. World Discoverer in Amazon and Antarctic, 1981-

87, I.B. Yamal to North Pole, 1995; biologist Brazilian Antarctic Expdn., 1987-88. Author: The Ephemeral Islands, 1978, The Crystal Desert, 1992, Islands in Space and Time, 1996; editor: Floristic Inventory of Tropical Countries, 1989; contbr. articles to profl. jours. Recipient Fulling award Soc. Econ. Botany, 1987, Houghton Mifflin Lit. fellow, 1992, Pen/Martha Albrand award for nonfiction, 1993, John Burroughs medal, 1994; Guggenheim fellow, 1989. Fellow Linnean Soc. London. Office: Grinnell Coll Dept Biology Grinnell IA 50112

CAMPBELL, DAVID GWYNNE, petroleum executive, geologist; b. May 2, 1930; s. Lois Raymond Henager and La Vada (Ray) Henager Campbell; m. Janet Gay Newland, March 1, 1958; 1 child, Carl David. BS, Tulsa U., 1953; MS, U. Okla., 1957. Geologist Lone Star Producing Co., Okla. City, 1957-65; dist. geologist, geol. cons. Tenneco Oil Co., Okla. City, 1965-77; exploration mgr. Leede Exploration, Okla. City, 1977-80; pres. Earth Hawke Exploration, Inc., Okla. City, 1980—; divsn. exploration mgr. PetroCorp., Inc., Okla. City, 1983-92, divsn. gen. mgr. 1992-96; cons. Jr. Achievement, Okla. City, 1996—; adv. coun. U. Okla. Sch. Geology and Geophysics Alumni 1988-90; Donald R. Reichard meml. lectr. Ohio State U., 1999. Contbr. articles to Jour. Cherokee Studies. Active Last Frontier Coun. Boy Scouts Am., 1960-73 (edn. chmn. Eagle Dist. 1963-67, asst. scoutmaster Wiley Post dist. 1971-73). Recipient Certificate of Appreciation award Nat. Exchange Club, Okla. City, 1999. Mem. AAAS, Internat. Assn. Energy Economists, Soc. Ind. Prof. Earth Scientists (pres. Okla. chpt. 1988, chmn. 1989, chmn. polit. affairs com. 1991), Soc. Profl. Well Log Analysts, Am. Assn. Petroleum Geologists (hon. mem., adv. coun. 1984-87, astrogeology com. 1984-97, nat. v.p. 1990-91, mid-continent coun. energy minerals divsn. 1992-94, chmn. com. of coms. 1992-98, others), Okla. City Geol. Soc. (hon. life mem., Tulsa chpt.), Okla. City Geol. Found. (pres. 1993-98), Ind. Petroleum Assn. Am. (Okla. chpt. regulatory affairs com. 1991-93), Okla. City Assn. Petroleum Landmen, Houston Geol. Soc., Okla. City Petroleum Club (bd. dirs. 1987-90, 1995-98, sec. 1989, 2d v.p. 1990, chmn. membership com. 1988-90), Geol. Soc. Moscow, N.Y. Acad. Scis., Okla. City C. of C., Okla. Hist. Soc., Cherokee Nat. Hist. Soc. (devel. com. 1987-95, bd. trustees nat. soc. 1983-96), Ctr. Am. Indian (bd. dirs. 1988-92), Red Earth Indian Ctr. (bd. dirs. 1992—, chmn. auction 1993, v.p. 1994-97, pres. 1997-98), Nat. Mus. Am. Indian, Am. Indian Cultural Soc., Houston Mus. Fine Arts, Okla. Pilots Assn., Exptl. Aircraft Assn., Aircraft Owners and Pilots Assn., First Families of Twin Territories, Clan Campbell of N. Am., Sigma Xi, Pi Kappa Alpha. Home: 6109 Woodbridge Rd Oklahoma City OK 73162-3220 Office: Earth Hawk Exploration Inc 210 Park Ave Ste 2100 Oklahoma City OK 73102-5605

CAMPBELL, DAVID NED, retired electric utility executive, business consultant; b. Lodi, Ohio, Feb. 20, 1929; s. Carl David and Mary Eleanor (McDaniel) C.; m. Helen Margaret Beck, June 8, 1952; children—Philip, Catherine, Allison. BA, Ashland U., 1951; postgrad., U. Mich., 1974. With Dairypak, Inc., Cleve., 1954-59; with Sealtest Foods Div., Kraft, Inc., Phila., 1959-73; asst. to div. personnel mgr. Phila., 1959-60; dist. personnel mgr. Washington, 1960-63; div. personnel dir. N.Y.C., 1963-64, gen. mgr. city plants, 1964-65, corp. personnel dir., 1965-73; employee rels. dir Tampa (Fla.) Electric Co., 1973-76, v.p. adminstrn., 1976-80, sr. v.p., adminstrn., 1980-87; v.p. Teco Energy, Inc., Tampa, 1982-87, sr. v.p. staff svcs., 1987-89, ret.; pvt. bus. cons. Tampa, 1989—; adj. instr. mgmt. U. South Fla., Tampa, 1977; past bd. dirs. TECO Transport and Trade Corp., Tampa, TECO Coal Corp., Tampa, TECO Techs. Inc., Tampa, Ideal Mut. Ins. Co., N.Y.C., Pharmacy Mgmt. Svcs., Inc., Tampa; past chmn., rep. Southeastern Electric exch., Employee Rels. and Pers. sect. Edison Electric Inst.; mem. exec. adv. com. Human Resources Mgmt.; ret. chmn. bd. dirs. Employers Purchasing Alliance, Inc., Tampa. Contbr. articles to profl. jours., chpt. in book. Chmn. Supt.'s Com. for Ednl. Excellence, Tallahassee, Fla., 1984; vice chmn. Fla. Coun. Ednl. Mgmt., 1981-84; mem. Sr. Mgmt. Adv. Com., Tallahassee. Served with USN, 1951-53. Recipient Silver Knight of Mgmt. award Nat. Mgmt. Assn., 1979, Emblem award Fla. Assn. Sch. Adminstrs., 1984, Disting. Achievement award Ashland U., 1967, Pres.'s award Greater Tampa C. of C., 1990. Mem. Exch. Club, St. Andrews Soc. (pres. 1986-87). Republican. Office: 2502 W Morrison Ave Tampa FL 33629-5329

CAMPBELL, DAVID NEIL, physician, educator; b. Peoria, Ill., Dec. 1, 1944; s. William Neil and Lillian May (Hunter) C.; m. Charlyn Harris, Nov. 16, 1968; children: Scott, Chris, Brad. BA, Northwestern U., 1966; MD, Rush Med. Sch., 1974. Resident in gen. and cardiothoracic surgery U. Colo. Health Sci. Ctr., Denver, from asst. prof. to prof. surgery, 1988-95, prof. surgery, 1995—; cons., Denver, Colo., 1986—. Lt. U.S. Army, 1966-67, Korea. Office: U Colo Health Sci Ctr 4200 E 9th Ave # C310 Denver CO 80220-3706

CAMPBELL, DAVID ROGERS, engineer; b. St. Mary's, Ohio, Sept. 3, 1962; s. Rogers Hornsby C. Student, Cen. Ohio Tech. Coll., 1996. FCC radio telephone operator. Svc. tech. Warren County TV, Lebanon, Ohio, 1979-84, Sears & Roebuck, Cin., 1985-90; analog engr. Control Brain, Newark, Ohio, 1995-96; electro-mech. technician Vertex Tech., Cin., 1997-99; rschr. Campbell's Electronics, St. Mary's, Ohio, 1990—. Contbr. articles to profl. jours. Recipient Editor's award Am. Goldwing Assn., Disaster Svc. award Ross County Ohio Civil Def., 1977. Mem. Am. Goldwing Assn. (former nat. dir.), Goldwing Road Riders Assn., Soc. Automotive Engrs., Warren County Conservation, Elks. Mem. Seventh Day Adventist. Avocations: skiing, motorcycling, martial arts, guitar. Home: 439 Morrow Rd Trlr 191 South Lebanon OH 45065-1459

CAMPBELL, DEBRA LYNN, marketing and new venture consultant; b. Phoenix, Apr. 8, 1954; d. Joseph David and Elaine Lucinda (Krueger) C.; m. J. Frederick Stillman III, Oct. 26, 1985; 1 child, J. Frederick Stillman IV. BS, U. Ariz., 1975; MBA, Harvard U., 1980. Brand mgr. Procter & Gamble Co., Cin., 1975-78; project mgr. Dunham & Marcus, N.Y.C., 1980-81; v.p. Cox, Lloyd Assocs., N.Y.C., 1981-83; cons. Am. Cons. Corp., N.Y.C., 1983-85, dir., 1985-87, dir., CFO, 1987-88, pres., COO, 1988-90; pres. DCA, 1990—. Treas. Cathedral Guild, St. John the Divine; pres. 173-175 Tenants Corp. Recipient Reggie award Promotion Mktg. Assn. Am. (Reggie award 1986, 87, 90). Mem. Nat. Sculpture Soc. (treas.), Cathedral Guild. Avocations: travel, collecting American Indian art, golf, tennis. Office: DCA 175 Riverside Dr New York NY 10024-1616

CAMPBELL, DEMAREST LINDSAY, artist, designer, writer; b. N.Y.C.; d. Peter Stephen III and Mary Elizabeth (Edwards) C.; m. Dale Gordon Haugo, 1978. BFA in Art History, MFA in S.E. Asian Art History, MFA in Theatre Design. Art dir., designer murals and residential interiors Campbell and Haugo Design Consultants, San Francisco, 1975—; chargeman scenic artist Am. Conservatory Theatre, 1976—. Designed, painted and sculpted over 200 prodns. for Broadway, internat. opera, motion pictures. Mem. NOW, Asian Art Mus. Soc., San Francisco. Mem. United Scenic Artists, Scenic & Title Artists and Theatrical Stage Designers., Sherlock Holmes Soc. London, Amnesty Internat., Nat. Trust for Hist. Preservation (Gt. Brit. and U.S.A. chpt.), Shavian Malthus Soc. (charter Gt. Brit. chpt.). Avocations: medical history, pre-Twentieth Century military history.

CAMPBELL, DENNIS MARION, educator, university administrator, theologian; b. Dalhart, Tex., Aug. 23, 1945; s. Francis Marion and Margaret (Osterberg) C.; m. Leesa Heydenreich, June 13, 1970; children: Margaret Heyden, Robert Trevor. AB, Duke U., 1967, PhD, 1973; BD, Yale U., 1970; DD (hon.), Fla. So. U., 1986. Ordained to ministry United Meth. Ch., 1974. Min. Trinity United Meth. Ch., Durham, N.C., 1973-74; chmn. dept. religion Converse Coll., Spartanburg, S.C., 1974-79; dir. continuing edn. Div. Sch. Duke U., Durham, 1979-82, prof. theology, 1982—, dean. Div. Sch., 1982-97; headmaster Woodberry Forest (Va.) Sch., 1997—; mem. Oxford (Eng.) Inst. Theol. Studies, 1982, 87, 92, Denver, 1996; gen. conf. United Meth. Ch., Balt., 1984, St. Louis, 1988, Louisville, 1992; del. World Meth. Coun., Nairobi, Kenya, 1987, World Coun. Chs. 7th Assembly, Canberra, Australia, 1991. Author: Authority and the Renewal of American Theology, 1976, Doctors, Lawyers, Ministers: Christian Ethics in Professional Practice, 1982, The Yoke of Obedience: The Meaning of Ordination in Methodism, 1988, Who Will Go For Us?, 1994. Chmn. Protection of Human Subjects Com.; bd. dirs. Family Health Internat., Research Triangle Park, 1986—; bd. visitors Perkins Sch. Theology So. Meth. U., Dallas, 1987—; overseers com. Harvard U., 1992—. Mem. Am. Theol. Soc., Am. Acad. Religion, Soc. Christian Ethics, Assn. Theol. Schs. (accrediting com. 1986—), Phi Beta Kappa, Omicron Delta Kappa. Home: PO Box 48 Woodberry Forest VA 22989 Office: The Residence Woodberry Forest VA 22989-0048

CAMPBELL, DONAL, state official; b. Lewisburg, Tenn., May 1, 1951. B of Criminal Justice, Tenn. State U., 1981. Youth dormitory attendant, supr. Mid. Tenn. Reception and Guidance Ctr.; psychiat. technician State of Tenn. Mental Health Dept.; correctional officer, local warden of security, adminstr. Deberry Correctional; commr. Corrections Dept., State of Tenn., Nashville, 1995—. Mem. Am. Corrections Assn. (bd. commn. for accreditation), Tenn. Corrections Assn., Assn. State Correctional Adminstrs., So. State Correctional Assn. Office: Dept Corrections State of Tenn 320 6th Ave N 4th Fl Nashville TN 37243-0465

CAMPBELL, DONALD ACHESON, nuclear engineer, consultant; b. Glendale, Ohio, Jan. 7, 1919; s. Acheson Meacham and Helen Gertrude (Boyle) C.; m. Ruth Marian Cory, Sept. 15, 1945 (div. June 1966); children: Bruce Hawick, Kathleen Cory; m. Tomiko Sugahara, June 1, 1968. Degree in mech. engring., U. Cin., 1940. Machine-design engr. Alvey Ferguson Co., Cin., 1940-41; heating and air-conditioning engr. Wright Field, Ohio, 1941-44; pres. Airco Inc., St. Bernard, Ohio, 1945-56; application engr. Westinghouse Electric, Pitts., 1956-66; nuclear-plant dir. Westinghouse of Japan, 1966-67; prin. engr. Westinghouse, 1967-84; nuclear-standards cons. Internat. Atomic Energy Agy., Vienna, Austria, 1988; standards coord. Westinghouse Electric Corp., Pitts., 1969-84. Contbr. nat. standards on nuclear power plants. Chmn. youth program com. YMCA, Dayton, Ohio, 1944-45, chmn. duplicate bridge club, gen.-program com., Cin., 1948-49, leader tng. series, 1991-98, chmn. bldg.-addn. com. Monroeville Sr. Citizen Ctr., 1992-98; bd. dirs. Suburban YMCA, Wyoming, Ohio, 1946-49; pres. Monroe Heights Civic Assn., Monroeville, Pa., 1961-62; 1st pres. Gateway Heights Recreation Club, Monroeville, 1963-64; mgr. Gateway Heights Softball Team, Monroeville, 1985-86; pres. Circle Eight Sq. Dance Club, North Versailles, Pa., 1985-86; pres. Prime Timers Club, 1987-88. Ohio Dept. Edn. scholar, 1935. Mem. Am. Nuclear Soc., Pi Tau Sigma, Tau Beta Pi. Achievements include patents for methodology to provide accurately ongoing measures of total amounts of leakage of all water and steam from pressure retaining systems within the reactor-containment enclosure of a nuclear-power plant and provide for discrimination of the proportion of leakage attributable to systems with radioactivity in contained fluids. Home: 2439 Saunders Station Rd Monroeville PA 15146-4451

CAMPBELL, DONALD ALFRED, retired government official; b. St. Louis, Mar. 31, 1928; s. Clarence Alfred and Dorothy Ethyl (Eggeman) C.; m. Mary Kathryn McKay, June 17, 1951; children: Cynthia Kathleen Campbell Knupp, Jean Elizabeth Campbell DiBlasio. Student, Mercer U., 1945, Ga. Inst. Tech., 1945-46; J.D., George Washington U., 1949. Bar: U.S. Dist. Ct. D.C. 1949, U.S. Ct. Appeals (D.C. cir.) 1951, U.S. Supreme Ct. 1955. Atty. Office Gen. Counsel USDA, Washington, 1949-62, asst. to asst. gen. counsel, 1959-62, dir. packers and stockyards div. Consumer and Mktg. Svc., 1962-67, adminstr. Packers and Stockyards Adminstrn., 1967-71, judicial officer, 1971-96; mem. Adminstrv. Conf. U.S., Washington, 1973-76. Contbr. articles to legal jours.; contbg. author Agricultural Law, 1981. Deacon, elder Presbyn. Ch. U.S., Fairfax County, Va. Served with USNR, World War II; lt. comdr. Res. ret. Mem. Fed. Bar Assn., Order of Coif. Avocations: travel, hiking, swimming, fishing.

CAMPBELL, DOUGLAS J., legislative staff member. Student, U. St. Andrews, Scotland, 1987-88; BA in Polit. Sci., U. Calif., Berkeley, 1989; MA in Internat. Rels., Yale U., 1992. Fellow Office Munitions Control U.S. Dept. State, Washington, 1989; fellow Office for Rsch. and the Collection of Info. UN, N.Y.C., 1991; campaign staff Clinton/Gore '92 Com., Washington, 1992; adminstrv. asst. econs./trade cluster Presdl. Transition Team, Washington, 1992-93; internat. trade analyst U.S. Dept. Commerce, Washington, 1993; legis. dir. Congressman Howard L. Berman, Washington, 1993—. Office: Congressman Howard L Berman 2330 Rayburn Ho Office Bldg Washington DC 20515

CAMPBELL, DOUGLASS, banker; b. N.Y.C., Aug. 31, 1919; s. William Lyman and Helene (Underwood) C.; m. Marion Danielson Strachan, Jan. 13, 1962 (dec. Nov. 1998); step-children: Richard and Stephen Strachan. A.B., Yale U., 1941. With N.Y. Central System, 1939-67, timekeeper, traveling car agt., asst. train master, train master, asst. supt. asst. to freight traffic mgr., asst. to pres., supt. exec. rep., 1939-58; v.p. N.Y.C. R.R. (and subs.), 1958-67; also in charge pub. relations and advt. dept. N.Y.C. R.R. (and subsidiaries), 1960-67; also dir. N.Y.C. R.R. (affiliates and subsidiaries); chmn. pres. Bowater Paper Co., Inc., 1967-68; pres. Argyle Rsch. Corp. (cons.), N.Y.C., 1968-83; v.p. Hambro Am., Inc., 1983-85; sr. v.p. Resource Holdings Ltd., N.Y.C., 1986-98. Served as maj. AUS, 1942-46. Episcopalian. Clubs: Down Town Assn., River, Yale (N.Y.C.); Chagrin Valley Hunt (Cleve.); Saturn (Buffalo); Racquet (Chgo.), Chgo. Club. Home: 3 E 71st St New York NY 10021-4154 *Deceased.*

CAMPBELL, EDWARD ADOLPH, judge, electrical engineer; b. Boonville, Ind., Jan. 16, 1936; s.Revis Allen and Sarah Gertrude (Hunsaker) C.; m. Nancy Colleen Keys, July 26, 1957; children: Susan Elizabeth Campbell Frisse, Stephen Edward, Sara Lynne. BEE, U. Evansville, 1959; JD, Ind. U., 1965; grad. Nat. Coll. Dist. Attys., U. Houston, 1972; grad. Nat. Jud. Coll., U. Nev., 1978; grad. Am. Acad. Jud. Edn., U. Va., 1979; grad. Ind. Grad. Program for Judges, Ind. Jud. Ctr., 1999. Bar: Ind. 1965, U.S. Dist. Ct. (so. dist.) Ind. 1965, U.S. Supreme Customs and Patent Appeals 1967, U.S. Supreme Ct. 1973, U.S. Ct. Appeals (fed. cir.) 1982. Patent examiner U.S. Patent Office, Washington, 1959-60; patent adv. U.S. Naval Avionics, Indpls., 1960-65; patent atty. Gen. Elec. Co., Ft. Wayne, Ind., 1965-66; ptnr. Weyerbacher & Campbell, attys., Boonville, Ind., 1966-71; pros. atty. 2nd Jud. Cir., Warrick County, Ind., 1971-77; judge Warrick Superior Ct. No. 1, 1977—. Fellow Ind. Bar Found.; mem. IEEE, Ind.State Bar Assn., Evansville Bar Assn., Warick County Bar Assn., Ind. Judges Assn., Nat. Coun. Juvenile and Family Ct. Judges, Ind. Coun. Juvenile and Family Ct. Judges, Warrick County C. of C. (bd. dirs. 1978-84, 97—), Lions Club, Kiwanis Club, Sigma Pi Sigma, Phi Delta Phi. Democrat. Methodist. Home: 911 Julian Dr Boonville IN 47601-9556 Office: Warrick Superior Ct No 1 PO Box 666 Boonville IN 47601-0666

CAMPBELL, EDWARD JOSEPH, retired machinery company executive; b. Boston, Feb. 21, 1928; s. Edward and Mary (Doherty) C.; divorced; children: Gary, Kevin, Diane. BSME, Northwestern U., 1952, MBA, 1959. With Am. Brakeshoe Co., 1952-58, Whirlpool Corp., 1958-65; gen. mgr. Joy Mfg. Co., 1965-67; exec. v.p. J.I. Case Co. subs. Tenneco, Inc., 1968-78; pres., chief exec. officer Newport News Shipbuilding & Dry Dock Co. subs. Tenneco, Inc., Va., 1979-91; pres. J.I. Case Co. subs. Tenneco Inc., Racine, Wis., 1992-94; bd. dirs. Global Marine Co., Titan Wheel, ABS Group; chmn. Campbell Enterprises. Mem. adv. coun. Northwestern U., William & Mary Coll. Served with USNR, 1945-48. Home: 1A Deepwood Dr Racine WI 53402-2868 Office: PO Box 8 Racine WI 53401-0008

CAMPBELL, EDWIN DENTON, consultant; b. Boston, June 25, 1927; s. William Edwin and Mildred (Altmiller) C.; m. Crystal Cousins, 1973; children: Geraldine, Linda, David, Sean, Jennifer. Grad., Bentley Coll., Boston, 1948; CAS, Harvard U., 1971; EdD, 1975. CPA, Mass. Mgr. Arthur Andersen & Co. (C.P.A.s), Boston, 1948-53; v.p. Lab. for Electronics, Inc., Boston, 1953-62, also dir.; exec. v.p. Itek Corp., Lexington, Mass., 1962-70, dir., 1962-83; pres. Edn. Devel. Ctr., Newton, Mass., 1971-76, trustee, 1971—; pres. Gulf Mgmt. Inst. div. Gulf Oil Corp., Boston, 1976-83; on loan as exec. v.p. Nat. Alliance of Bus., Washington, 1983-86; dean sch. bus. Adelphi U., Garden City, N.Y., 1986-87; trustee Ednl. Testing Svc., Princeton, N.J., 1983-87, v.p., 1987-89; exec. dir. Coalition of Essential Schs., Annenberg Inst. for Sch. Reform, Brown U., Providence, 1990-96; prin. Padanaram Assocs., Inc., 1996—; interim exec. dir. Plimoth Plantation, 1997; bd. dirs. Keystone Funds, Padanaram Assocs., Inc., Nat. Alliance Bus., CAST, Inc., ARtworks!; mem. faculty Bentley Coll., Boston, 1956-58. Cons. editor: Change, 1980—. Trustee Bentley Coll., 1963—, New Bedford Whaling Mus., 1996—, Friends Acad., 1996—, Ptnrs. in Edn., Inc., 1997—; v.p. Mass. Assn. Mental Health, 1965-68, bd. dirs., 1962-73; mem. Mass Commn. Vocat. Rehab., 1966-68, Coll. Bd. Commn. on Pre-coll. Counseling, 1984-86; mem. vis. com. Harvard Sch. Edn., 1977-83; mem. fin. com. Town of Carlisle, Mass., 1965-68; trustee Boston Urban Found., 1969-75, Mass. Taxpayers Found., 1962-68, Fenn Sch., 1970-75, OSTI, Inc., 1971-76, Lesley Coll., 1972-76, Mass. Advocacy Ctr., 1975-76. Served with USMC, 1943-45. Mem. Assn. Industries Mass. (pres. 1967-69, now dir.), Harvard Club Boston, Cosmos Club Washington, New Bedford Yacht Club.

CAMPBELL, ELAINE JOSEPHINE, educational director, writer, critic, educator; b. Phila., Aug. 6, 1932; d. William Maxwell and Anna Marie (Roller) Bauer; m. John Bruce Campbell, Dec. 21, 1957; children: Jennifer Ann, Rebecca Ellen, Sabrina Frances. BA with maj. honors (Univ. scholar), U. Pa., 1954; MA, Simmons Coll., 1973; PhD (Univ. scholar), Brandeis U., 1981; MEd, Boston U., 1993. Tchg. fellow dept. English and Am. lit. Brandeis U., 1974-80; lectr. English Regis Coll., Weston, Mass., 1980-81; asst. prof. English, dir. freshman writing program Regis Coll., Weston, 1981-84; writer-editor The MITRE Corp., Bedford, Mass., 1984-86; staff devel. specialist MITRE Inst., 1986-88, inst. affairs staff, 1988-91, dir. spl. programs, 1992-94; ptnr. Campbell Consulting, 1995-98; lectr. English, Boston U., 1985-86; lectr. writing MIT, 1986—; mem. task force Nat. Acad. Sci. Edn. Standards. Author: ESL Resourcebook for Engineers and Scientists, 1995, (introduction) The Orchid House (P. Allfrey), 1982; editor: The Whistling Bird: Writing by Caribbean Women, 1998; contbr.; Studies in Modern Commonwealth Literature, Subjects Worthy Fame, Fifty Caribbean Writers, Studies in Commonwealth Literature, A Double Colonization: Colonial and Post-Colonial Women's Writing, Dictionary of Literary Biography; book reviewer World Literature Written in English, Kunapipi; adv. bd. Jean Rhys REv.; contbr. articles, revs., reports to profl. jours., U.S., Can., Jamaica, Denmark, India, Eng., S.Am.; panelist at profl. meetings, convs. Mem. MLA, Caribbean Studies Assn., European Assn. Commonwealth Lit. and Lang. Studies, Assn. Caribbean Women Writers and Scholars, Kappa Delta, Pi Lambda Theta. Home: 63 Puritan Ln Sudbury MA 01776-2424 also: PO Box 1703 Cruz Bay VI 00831-1703

CAMPBELL, ELIZABETH TODD, judge; b. Russellville, Ala., Mar. 5, 1952; d. A. W. and Robbie L. (Smith) Todd; m. Andrew P. Campbell, Nov. 25, 1978; 3 children. BA, Auburn Univ., 1974; JD, Univ. of Ala. Law Sch., 1977. Bar: Ala. 1977. Clk. Ala. Legis., 1974; law clk. Ala. Atty. Gen.'s Office, 1975, Jefferson County Dist. Atty.'s Office, 1976; law clk. to Judge Inzer B. Wyatt U.S. Dist. Ct. (so. dist.) N.Y., 1977-78; asst. U.S. atty., 1978-85; magistrate judge U.S. Dist. Ct. (no. dist.) Ala., Birmingham, 1985—. Recipient John Morrisette Constitutional Law award, M. Leigh Harrison award. Mem. Birmingham Bar Assn., Fed. Bar Assn., Birmingham Women's Network, League of Women Voters. Office: Hugo L Black US Courthouse 1729 5th Ave N Ste 274 Birmingham AL 35203-2050

CAMPBELL, F(ENTON) GREGORY, college administrator, historian; b. Columbia, Tenn., Dec. 16, 1939; s. Fenton G. and Ruth (Hayes) C.; m. Barbara D. Kuhn, Aug. 29, 1970; children: Fenton H., Matthew W., Charles H. AB, Baylor U., 1960; postgrad., Philipps U., Marburg/Lahn, Fed. Republic of Germany, 1960-61; MA, Emory U., 1962; postgrad., Charles U., Prague, Czechoslovakia, 1965-66; PhD, Yale U., 1967; postgrad. in ednl. mgmt., Harvard U., 1981. Rsch. staff historian Yale U., New Haven, 1966-68, spl. asst. to acting pres., 1977-78; asst. prof. history U. Wis., Milw., 1968-69; asst. prof. European history U. Chgo., 1969-76, spl. asst. to pres., 1978-69, sec. bd. trustees, 1979-87, sr. lectr., 1985-87; pres., prof. history Carthage Coll., 1987—; fellow Woodrow Wilson Internat. Ctr. for Scholars, Smithsonian Instn., Washington, 1976-77; participant Japan Study Program for Internat. Execs., 1987. Author: Confrontation in Central Europe, 1975; joint editor: Akten zur deutschen auswartigen Politik, 1918-1945, 1966-95; contbr. articles and revs. to profl. jours. Bd. dirs. AAL Mutual Funds, Johnson Mut. Funds, Prairie Sch., Kenosha Hosp. and Med. Ctr., Wis. Fulbright grantee, 1960-61, 1973-74; Woodrow Wilson fellow, 1961-62, U.S.A.-Czechoslovakia exchange fellow, 1965-66, 73-74, 85. Mem. Mid-Day Club (Chgo.), Kenosha (Wis.) Country Club, Phi Beta Kappa, Omicron Delta Kappa. Home: 623 17th Pl Kenosha WI 53140-1360 Office: Carthage Coll Kenosha WI 53140-1360

CAMPBELL, FINLEY ALEXANDER, geologist; b. Kenora, Ont., Can., Jan. 5, 1927; s. Finley McLeod and Vivian (Delve) C.; m. Barbara Elizabeth Cromarty, Oct. 17, 1953; children—Robert Finley, Glen David, Cheryl Ann. B.Sc., Brandon Coll., U. Man., Can., 1950; M.A., Queen's U., Kingston, Ont., 1956; Ph.D., Princeton U., 1958. Exploration and mining geologist Prospectors Airways, Toronto, 1950-58; asst. and asso. prof. geology U. Alta., Can., Edmonton, 1958-65; prof., head dept. geology U. Calgary, Alta., 1965-69, v.p. capital resources, 1969-71, v.p. acad., 1971-76, prof. geology, 1976-84, v.p. priorities and planning, 1984-88, prof. emeritus, 1988—; geol. cons., 1988—; bd. dirs., vice chmn. Can Energy Research Inst. Contbr. articles on geol. topics to profl. jours. Bd. dirs. Calgary Olympic Devel. Assn.; mem. minister's adv. bd. Tyrrell Mus. Palaeontology. Decorated Queen's Jubilee Medal Can.; recipient Commemorative medal for 125th Anniversary of Can., Geology medal Brandon U. Honor Soc.; Sir James Dunne fellow, 1955-56; Princeton Alumni fellow, 1957-58. Fellow Royal Soc. Can.; mem. Assn. The Univ. of Calgary (pres. emeritus), Geol. Assn. Can., Mineral Assn. Can., Soc. Econ. Geologists, Assn. Profl. Geologists Alta., Am. Mineral Soc. Royal Soc. Can., Can. Inst. Mining and Metallurgy, Brandon Univ. Alumni Assn. (reg. dir., Disting. Svc. award Hockey Hall of Fame 1994), Glenmore Yacht Club, Silver Springs Golf and Country Club, Clearwater Bay Yacht Club. Home: 3408 Benton Dr NW, Calgary, AB Canada T2L 1W8 Office: U Calgary, Dept Geology and Geophysics, Calgary, AB Canada T2N 1N4

CAMPBELL, FRANCIS JAMES, retired chemist; b. Toledo, Ohio, July 29, 1924; s. Herbert J. and Florence E. (Kelch) C.; m. Elizabeth P. Savage, Aug. 21, 1948; children: Nancy, MaryLou, Joan, Kathryn, Janice, James, Daniel. B.S. in Chem. Engring., U. Toledo, 1948. Cert. profl. chemist. Chemist Dow Chem. Co., Midland, Mich., 1948-53; chemist Dow Corning Corp., Midland, 1953-58, Naval Rsch. Lab., Washington, 1958-93; retired, 1993; Chmn. radiation effects on elec. insulation com. Internat. Electrotech. Commn., Geneva, 1974-85. House com. mem. Ind. Living for Handicapped, Inc., Washington, 1983-92; No. Va. chmn. Joint Bd. on Sci. and Engring. Edn., Washington, 1965-92. With U.S. Army, 1943-45. Recipient Research Publs. award Naval Research Lab., 1982, USN Meritorious Civilian Svc. award, 1997; decorated D.F.C., Air medal with 2 oak leaf clusters, Asiatic-Pacific Theater ribbon, WWII victory medal; inducted into Edward Drummond Libbey High Sch. Hall of Fame, 1996. Fellow IEEE (life); mem. IEEE Dielectrics and Elec. Insulation Soc. (Eric O. Forster award for Disting. Svc. 1992), Am. Chem. Soc., Sigma Xi. Achievements include patents on thermal control coatings and battery packaging to prolong satellite life; research in thermal aging and multi-factor effects on reliability of electrical insulation of wire and cable, radiation curing of polymer matrix composites and adhesives, and in radiation damage in organic materials; in identifying the failure mechanisms in Kapton insulated wires that were responsible for a high number of electrical fires in Naval aircraft. Home: 2412 Crest St Alexandria VA 22302-2715

CAMPBELL, FREDERICK HOLLISTER, retired lawyer, historian; b. Somerville, Mass., June 14, 1923; s. George Murray and Irene Ivers (Smith) C.; A.B., Dartmouth, 1944; J.D., Northwestern U., 1949; postgrad. Indsl. Coll. Armed Forces, 1961-62; M.A. in History, U. Colo., 1984, PhD in History, 1993; m. Amy Holding Strohm, Apr. 14, 1951; 1 dau., Susan Hollister. Served with USMCR, 1943-46, 50-53; joined USMC, 1953, advanced through grades to lt. col., 1962; admitted to Ill. bar, 1950, U.S. Supreme Ct. bar, 1967, Colo. bar, 1968; judge adv. USMC, Camp Lejeune, N.C., Korea, Parris Island, S.C., El Toro, Calif., Vietnam, Washington, 1950-67; asso. editor Callaghan and Co., Chgo., 1949-50; practiced law, Colorado Springs, Colo., 1968-88; ptnr. firm Gibson, Gerdes and Campbell, 1969-79; pvt. practice law, 1980-88; gen. counsel 1st Fin. Mortgage Corp., 1988-96, vice chmn., corp. sec., 1993-96; hon. instr. history U. Colo., Colorado Springs, 1986—; vis. instr., Colo. Coll., 1993-95, asst. prof., 1996—. Mem. Estate Planning Coun., Colorado Springs, 1971-81, v.p., 1977-78. Rep. precinct committeeman, 1971-86; del. Colo. Rep. State Conv., 1972, 74, 76, 80, alt., 1978; trustee Frontier Village Found., 1971-77; bd. dirs. Rocky Mountain Nature Assn., 1975—, pres., 1979-92; dir. Rocky Mountain Nat. Park Assocs. 1986—, v.p. 1986-92, sec. 1992-95. Mem. Colo. Bar Assn., El Paso County Bar Assn., Am. Arbitration Assn., Marines Meml. Club, Phi Alpha Theta. Congregationalist. Author: John's American Notary and Commissioner of Deeds Manual, 1950. Contbr. articles to profl. jours. Home and Office: 2707 Holiday Ln Colorado Springs CO 80909-1217

CAMPBELL, GAVIN ELLIOTT, real estate investor and developer; b. Alton, Ill., Feb. 29, 1960; s. Colin Chandler and Mariana Nicholas (Hardwick) C.; m. Diana Aixala, May 31, 1997; 1 child, Tara Alyssa. BA in Polit. Philosophy magna cum laude, Yale U., 1982; MBA in Fin., U. Chgo., 1989. Analyst internat. trade Ill. Dept. Agr., Springfield, 1982-83; asst. to gov. State of Ill., Springfield, 1983-85; dep. dir. Civic Com., Chgo., 1985-90; assoc. acquisitions LaSalle Advisors Ltd., Chgo., 1990-92, v.p. acquisitions, 1992-93, exec. v.p. acquisitions, 1994-95, prin., acquisitions, 1996-98, mng. dir., aquisitions, 1999—; COO Fla. Office Property Co., 1998—; pres. Restoration Capital, 1986—. Pres. Latino Chgo. Theater Co., Chgo., 1990-96, Leadership Fellows Assn., Chgo., 1996-98; dir. Yale Coll. Alumni Schs. Com., Chgo., 1991-95; com. rep. A.N. Pritzker Local Sch. Coun., 1993-98; co-founder, mem. exec. com. Young Leader's Fund, 1994-96. Gov.'s fellow, Springfield, 1982, fellow Leadership Greater Chgo., 1987. Avocation: historic building restoration. Home: 1930 N Honore St Chicago IL 60622-1043 Office: LaSalle Advisors Ltd 200 E Randolph St Chicago IL 60601-6436

CAMPBELL, GEORGE, JR., physicist, administrator; s. George Washington and Lillian (Britt) C.; m. Mary Schmidt, Aug. 24, 1968; children: Garikai, Sekou, Britt. BS, Drexel U., 1968; PhD, Syracuse U., 1977; postgrad., Yale U., 1988. Sr. faculty Nkumbi Internat. Coll., Kabwe, Zambia, 1969-71; staff scientist AT&T Bell Labs., Holmdel, N.J., 1977-83; third level mgr. AT&T Bell Labs., Holmdel, 1983-89; pres., CEO Nat. Action Coun. for Minorities in Engring., Inc., N.Y.C., 1989—; Porth disting. lectr. U. Mo.-Rolla, 1993; adv. bd. U.S. Sec. of Energy, Washington, 1990-93, NRC Com. on Women in Sci. and Engring., 1991-95, Coll. Engring. Cooper Union, Sta. WGBH-TV Discovering Women series, 1993-94, Merck Inst. Sci. Edn., 1993-99; mem. nat. commn. Ill. Inst. Tech., 1994; pres. Coalition for Equity and Access to Sci., Tech., Engring. and Math., 1996-97. Contbr. chpts. to books, articles to profl. jours. including Phys. Rev. D, Jour. Math. Physics, Issues in Sci. and Tech., Procs. IEEE Globecom, Black Issues in Higher Edn., Black Collegian, Chronicle of Higher Edn., NACME Rsch. Letter, AAAS Sci. and Tech. Policy Yearbook, 1995; commentator Nightly Bus. Report, 1993—. Bd. dirs. N.Y. Hall of Sci., 1994—, Oak Ridge Assoc. Univs., 1993-99, Crossroads Theater Co., 1990-95; mem. NSF adv. bd. Comprehensive Regional Ctr. for Minorities, N.Y. chmn., 1990-93; trustee, mem. exec. com. Rensselaer Poly. Inst., Troy, N.Y., 1991—; chmn. N.Y.C. Chancellor's Task Force on Sci. Edn., 1992-93; task force on minorities in sci. Nat. Inst. Environ. Health Scis./AAAS, 1994; bd. govs. All Nations Alliance for Minority Participation in Sci. and Engring., 1995—; trustee Poly. U., Bklyn., 1997—; mem. Pres.' Info. Tech. Adv. Com. Socio-Econ. and Workforce Panel, 1998—; mem. Congl. Commn. on Advancement of Women and Minorities in Sci. and Tech., 1999—. Recipient George Arents Pioneer medal in physics Syracuse U., 1993, Drexel U. Centennial medal, 1992, Presdl. award for excellence in math., sci. and engring. mentoring, 1996, EPIC award U.S. Dept. Labor, 1998; named Black Achiever in Industry, YMCA, N.Y.C., 1987; Simon Guggenheim scholar Guggenheim Found., Phila., 1963-67. Fellow AAAS (com. on sci., engring. and pub. policy 1990-96), N.Y. Acad. Scis. (pres. coun. 1991—), ; mem. Am. Phys. Soc. (pres. cir. 1997—), Nat. Acad. Scis., Nat. Acad. Engring. and Inst. Medicine, Sigma Pi Sigma. Achievements include extending bootstrap model to SU(4)-symmetric strong interaction physics; responsible for third generation satellite 3 power system development. Home: 457 W 144th St New York NY 10031-4733 Office: Nat Action Coun for Minorities Empire State Bldg 350 5th Ave Ste 2212 New York NY 10118-2212

CAMPBELL, GEORGE EMERSON, lawyer; b. Piggott, Ark., Sept. 23, 1932; s. Sid and Mae (Harris) C.; m. Anna Claire Janes, June 22, 1960 (dec. Mar. 1971); children: Dianne, Carole; m. Joan Stafford Rule, Apr. 7, 1973. J.D., U. Ark., Fayetteville, 1955. Bar: Ark. 1955, U.S. Supreme Ct. 1971. Law clk. to judge Ark. Supreme Ct., 1959-60; mem. Rose Law Firm, P.A., Little Rock, 1960—; Del. 7th Ark. Constl. Conv., 1969-70; regional v.p. Nat. Mcpl. League, 1974-86; mem. Ark. Ednl. TV Commn., 1976-92, chmn., 1980-82, 88-91; bd. dirs. Ark. Ednl. TV Found., 1984-92, chmn., 1988-91. Chmn. bd. Pulaski County Law Libr., 1980—; bd. dirs. Ark. Arts Ctr., 1991-95, sec. 1992-93), Ark. Symphony Orch. Soc., 1982-87, Ark. Capital Corp., Ark. Cert. Devel. Corp., Downtown Partnership; bd. dirs. Youth Home Inc., 1986-92, pres., 1991-92. With USNR, 1955-77, ret.. Fellow Am. Bar Found.; mem. ABA, Ark. Bar Assn., Pulaski County Bar Assn., Am. Law Inst., Am. Judicature Soc., Nat. Assn. Bond Lawyers. Office: Rose Law Firm PA 120 E 4th St Little Rock AR 72201-2893

CAMPBELL, GILBERT SADLER, surgery educator, surgeon; b. Toronto, Ont., Can., Jan. 4, 1924; s. Gilbert S. and Ellen (Thorson) C.; m. Dorothy Jean Nugent, Sept. 18, 1947 (div. 1960); children: Kathryn Ellen, Rebecca Sadler, Thomas Kim, William Riley; m. Joan Louise Hancock, Sept. 28, 1961; children: Susan Muffin, John Gilbert. Student, Hampden Sydney Coll., 1939-40; B.A., U. Va., 1943, M.D., 1946; M.S., U. Minn., 1949, Ph.D., 1954. Intern U. Minn. Hosps., Mpls., 1946-47, tchg. asst., 1947-49, researcher Am. Cancer Soc., 1951-53, sr. surgery resident, 1953-54; instr. physiology U. Minn., Mpls., 1948-49, instr. surgery, 1954-55, asst. prof., 1955-58; prof. surgery U. Okla., Oklahoma City, 1958-65; prof. surgery and thoracic surgery U. Okla. Med. Ctr., Oklahoma City, 1958-65; prof. surgery, chief thoracic surgery U. Ark. for Med. Scis., Little Rock, 1965-90; cons. surgery Little Rock VA Hosp, 1965-90, Ark. Children's Hosp., Little Rock, 1973-90; mem. courtesy staff Ark. Bapt. Med. Ctr., Little Rock, 1972-90; prof. emeritus, 1990—. Contbr. articles in field to med. jours. Served to capt. U.S. Army, 1949-51. Decorated Purple Heart, Bronze Star with oak leaf cluster, Silver Star with oak leaf cluster U.S. Army; Mary R. Markle scholar, 1954-59; recipient Horsley prize U. Va., 1954; named Surgery Alumnus of Yr. U. Minn., 1983. Mem. Am. Assn. Thoracic Surgery, AMA (ho. of dels. 1976-82), Am. Physiol. Soc., Am. Surg. Assn., Halsted Soc. (pres. 1978), Internat. Cardiovascular Soc. (v.p. N. Am. Chpt. 1973), Societe Internationale de Chirurgie, Soc. Thoracic Surgeons, Soc. Univ. Surgeons, Soc. Vascular Surgery, So. Surg. Assn. (1st v.p. 1981), Western Surg. Assn., S.W. Surg. Congress (pres. 1980), Raven Soc., Alpha Omega Alpha. Home: 66 River Ridge Rd Little Rock AR 72227-1526

CAMPBELL, GROVER STOLLENWERCK, university official; b. Dallas, May 6, 1954; s. Frank Whitney and Elizabeth Ann (Stollenwerck) C.; m. Nancy L. Bauerle, Dec. 5, 1981; children: Logan Bauerle, Lee Hillman. BJ, U. Tex., 1977, MBA, 1986. Asst. sgt. at arms Tex. House Reps., Austin, 1973-74; adminstrv. asst. State Rep. Herman Adams, Austin, 1974-78; spl. asst. govtl. rels. U. Tex. Sys., Austin, 1978-84; vice chancellor U. Houston Sys., 1984-97, vice chancellor, v.p., 1997—. Exec. prodr. The Capitol Report, Sta. KUHT. Mem. Austin Heritage Soc., 1982-86, Sta. KLRU Action Com., Austin, 1982-84, Les Patrons of the Paramount, Austin, 1982-85, Symphony Sq. Com., Austin; mem. William P. Hobby adv. bd. pub. svc. S.W. Tex. State U. Named Outstanding Young Man in Am. U.S. Jaycess, 1980. Mem. Am. Assn. Univ. Adminstrs., Nat. Assn. State Univs. and Land-Grant Colls., Coun. for Advancement and Support of Edn., Pub. Affairs Assocs., Houston C. of C., Beta Gamma Sigma. Home: 1510 Westover Rd Austin TX 78703-1912 Office: U Houston System 1005 Congress Ave Ste 820 Austin TX 78701-2415

CAMPBELL, HARRY WOODSON, geologist, mining engineer; b. Carthage, Mo., Jan. 14, 1946; s. William Hampton and Elizabeth Verle (LeGrand) C. BSEE, Kans. State U., 1969; MBA, U. Oreg., 1973, BS in Geology, 1975; MS in Geology, Brown U., 1978. Registered profl. engr., Wash.; cert. profl. geologist, Va. Geologist, mining engr. and phys. scientist U.S. Bur. Mines, Spokane, 1980-96; geologist U.S. Geol. Survey, Spokane, 1996—. Served with U.S. Army, 1969-71. Recipient Spl. Achievement award U.S. Bur. Mines, 1983, 86, 88. Mem. Geol. Soc. Am., Soc. Mining Engrs. Avocation: genealogy. Office: US Bur Mines 4257 E 26th Ave Spokane WA 99223-5623

CAMPBELL, HENRY CUMMINGS, librarian; b. Vancouver, C., Can., Apr. 22, 1919; s. Henry and Margaret (Cummings) C.; m. Sylvia Woodsworth, Sept. 13, 1943; children—Shiela (Mrs. David Macrae), Bonnie, Robin. BA, U. B.C., 1940; BLS, U. Toronto, 1941; MA, Columbia U., 1949. Librarian, film producer Nat. Film Bd., Can., Ottawa, 1941-46; with Secretariat UN, N.Y., 1946-48, UNESCO, Paris, 1949-56; chief librarian Toronto (Can.) Pub. Library, 1956-78; gen. mgr. Cinfolink Svcs., Toronto, 1994—; lectr. U. Toronto Sch. Libr. Sci., 1970-71; cons. on info. systems and libr. svcs. Canadian Govt. Social Sci. Rsch. Coun. Can., UNESCO; active State Sci. and Tech. Commn., Beijing, China, 1991—, China Internet Info. Svcs., 1997—. Author: How To Find Out About Canada, 1967, Canadian Libraries, 1972, rev. edit., Early Days on the Great Lakes, 1971, The Public Library in the Urban Metropolitan Setting, 1973, Development of Public Library Systems and Services, 1982, Computer Information Systems in the People's Republic of China, Cinfolink Directory of Information Services in China and Hong Kong, 1993-94, 1993, Cinfolink Annual Review of Information Services in China, 1995-96, 1996, Looking for Harrison, 1993, Cinfolink China Internet Directory, 1998. Recipient Prof. Kawla award for Library and Info. Sci., 1984. Fellow IFLA (hon.); mem. Internat. Assn. Met. City Libraries (pres. 1971-74), Canadian Library Assn. (pres. 1973-74), Ont. Continuing Edn. Assn. (pres. 1966), Fedn. Can.-China Friendship Socs. (pres. 1985-88).

CAMPBELL, HUGH BROWN, JR., lawyer; b. Charlotte, N.C., Feb. 19, 1937; s. Hugh Brown and Thelma Louise (Welles) C.; m. Mary Irving Carlyle, Nov. 3, 1962; children: Hugh B. III, Irving Carlyle, Thomas Lenoir. AB, Davidson Coll., 1959; JD, Harvard U., 1962. Atty. Craighill, Rendleman, Charlotte, 1964-77, Weinstein & Sturges, Charlotte, 1977-94, Cansler Lockhart Campbell Evans Bryant & Garlitz; chmn. Jury Commn., Mecklenburg County, N.C., 1985-97; exec. com. County Bar Assn., Mecklenburg County, 1989-92, civil cts. com. chair, 1990-92. Rep. N.C. House, Raleigh, 1969-71; legis. liaison Charlotte/Mecklenburg County, Raleigh, 1971-72; state chmn. N.C. Zoo Bond Campaign, 1972; chmn. Carolinas Med. Ctr. Bond Campaign, 1976. Col. JAG U.S. Army, 1962-64, Res., 1964-92. Decorated Legion of Merit, Meritorious Svc. medal (2); Honored Order of Hornet, Mecklenburg County, 1976. Mem. N.C. Bar Coun. (exec. com., chair ethics 1981-90), Planned Parenthood Charlotte (bd. dirs., chmn. 1980-81), YMCA Charlotte (adv. bd. 1992—), Rotary Club E. Charlotte (pres. 1976-77). Democrat. Episcopalian. Avocations: tennis, swimming, hiking, reading, politics. Home: 1428 Scotland Ave Charlotte NC 28207-2561 Office: Cansler Lockhart Campbell Evans Bryant & Garlitz 227 W Trade St Charlotte NC 28202-1675

CAMPBELL, IAN DAVID, opera company director; b. Brisbane, Australia, Dec. 21, 1945; came to U.S., 1982; m. Ann Spira; children: Benjamin, David. BA, U. Sydney, Australia, 1967. Prin. tenor singer The Australian Opera, Sydney, 1967-74; sr. music officer The Australia Council, Sydney, 1974-76; gen. mgr., stage dir. The State Opera of South Australia, Adelaide, 1976-82; asst. artistic adminstr. Met. Opera, N.Y.C., 1982-83; gen. dir. San Diego Opera, 1983—; guest lectr. U. Adelaide, 1978; guest prof. San Diego State U., 1986—; cons. Lyric Opera Queensland, Australia, 1980-81; bd. dirs. Opera Am., Washington, 1986-95, 97—; chmn. judges Met. Opera Auditions, Sydney, 1989, Masterclasses, Music Acad. of the West, 1993-96. Producer, host San Diego Opera Radio Program, 1984—, At the Opera with Ian Campbell, 1984—; stage director La Boheme, 1981, The Tales of Hoffmann, 1982 (both in South Australia), Falstaff (San Diego Opera), 1999, Cavalleria Rusticna/Pagliacci (Santa Barbara Grand Opera), 1999. Mem., bd. dirs. San Diego Conv. and Visitors Bur., 1997—. Recipient Peri award Opera Guild So. Calif., 1984; named Headliner of Yr., San Diego Press Club, 1991, Father of Yr., San Diego, 1997. Fellow Australian Inst. Mgmt.; mem. Kona Kai Club, Rotary, San Diego Pres Club (Headliner award 1991). Avocations: squash, golf, tennis. Office: San Diego Opera 1200 3rd Ave Fl 18 San Diego CA 92101

CAMPBELL, JACK JAMES RAMSAY, microbiology educator; b. Vancouver, C., Can., Mar. 29, 1918; s. Murdoch and Margaret (Campbell) C.; m. Emily Ann Fraser, Sept. 4, 1942; children: Sheila, Merle, Ann, Ross. B.S.A., U. B.C., Vancouver, 1939; Ph.D., Cornell U., 1944. Research assoc. chem. warfare Dept. Def., Kingston, Ont., Can., 1944-46; mem. dairying dept. U. B.C., 1946-65, prof., head microbiology dept., 1965-82. Fellow Royal Soc. Can., AAAS; mem. Am., Can. socs. microbiology, Sigma Xi, Phi Kappa Phi, Alpha Delta, Sigma Tau Upsilon. Home: 3949 W 37th St, Vancouver, BC Canada V6N 2W4

CAMPBELL, JAMES ALBERT BARTON, association executive, retired marketing executive; b. Chattanooga, Tenn., Nov. 2, 1940; s. James Harry and Elizabeth Tipton (Johnson) C.; m. Julia Madge Clark, Sept. 12, 1964; children: Richard Barton, Julia Clark. BS, Princeton U., 1962; grad., U.S. Army Command Gen. Staff Coll., 1975, U.S. Army War Coll., 1985. Devel. engr. DuPont Co., Wilmington, Del., 1964-66; mktg. specialist Formex Co., Greeneville, Tenn., 1966-67; field sales engr. Reynolds Metals Co., Richmond, Va., 1967-70; regional sales rep. Reynolds Metals Co., Charlotte, N.C., 1970-74; mktg. mgr. Reynolds Metals Co., Richmond, 1975-81, mgr. market planning, 1982-84, market group mgr., 1984-86, mktg. svcs. mgr., 1986-93, mgr. sales and mktg. svcs., 1994-96, mem. pres.'s task force on corp. definition, 1996, mem. process definition team, 1996; ret., 1996; dir. membership and ROTC affairs Res. Officer Assn., Washington, 1997—; founder, owner Priceless Pages Christian Bookstore, Richmond, 1983-90; light postal vehicle task force Aluminum Assn., N.Y.C., 1978-79; advisor Marine Pleasure Boat Assn., Chgo., 1984. Pres. Res. Officers Assn., Richmond, 1987, area 3 dir., 1988, state v.p. Army, 1992-93; exec. com. Assn. U.S. Army, Richmond, 1988-90; mil. advisor State of Va. Com. Employer Support Guard and Res.; mem. exec. com. Young Life, 1988-92; bd. dirs. Encounter Ministries; elder local Presbyn. Ch. Col. USAR ret. Decorated Legion of Merit, Meritorious Svc. medal with three oak leaf clusters, Army Commendation medal, Army Achievement medal with oak leaf cluster. Mem. SCV (Ga. comdr. 1969-70, Va. lt. comdr. 1992-96, chmn. nat. strategy planning com. 1994-96, chmn. centennial nat. conv. 1996), Gideons Internat. (local pres., v.p., sec. 1969-90), Jeb Stuart Camp (comdr. 1991-92), Res. Officers Assn., mem. com., The Mus. of the Conferderacy, 1996—. Avocations: history lectr., strategy gaming. Home: 2211 Heathland Dr Midlothian VA 23113-4183 Office: Res Officers Assn 1 Constitution Ave NE Washington DC 20002-5655

CAMPBELL, JAMES L., military career officer; b. Ft. Benning, Ga., Aug. 16, 1949; m. Carol Anderson; children: Scott, Casey. Grad., U. Mo.; BS in Phys. Edn., 1971; MS in Phys. Edn., U. Ill.; MA in Nat. Security & Strategic Studies, Naval War Coll.; grad., U.S. Army Command & Gen. Staff, Naval War Coll. Commd. 2nd lt. U.S. Army, advanced through grades to brig. gen.; dir. instrn. dept. phys. edn. U.S. Mil. Acad.; with 15th Battalion, 4th combat support tng. brigade U.S. Army, Ft. Jackson, S.C.; co. comdr. 1st Battalion, 32d Infantry, 2nd Infantry Divsn. U.S. Army, Camp Casey, Korea; rifle platoon leader, reconnaissance platoon leader U.S. Army; comdr. 4th Bn., 27th Inf., 25th Inf. Divsn. (Light) U.S. Army, Schofield Barracks, Hawaii; ACofS, G3, 9th Inf. Divsn. (Motorized) U.S. Army, Ft. Lewis, Wash.; dep. chief staff I Corps U.S. Army, Ft. Lewis; chief of staff, comdr. 1st Brigade, 10th Mountain Divsn. U.S. Army, exec. officer to the chief of staff, comdr. Joint Task Force-Full Acctg., asst. divsn. comdr., 25th Inf. Divsn. (Light), asst. divsn. comdr. (ops.), 25th Inf. Divsn. (Light), 1998—. Decorated Def. Superior Svc. medal with oak leaf cluster, Legion of Merit with 2 oak leaf clusters, Bronze star, Meritorious Svc. medal with 3 oak leaf clusters, Army Commendation medal, Army Achievement medal. Office: 25th Infantry Divsn Light Schofield Barracks HI 96857

CAMPBELL, JAMES R., transportation executive; b. July 16, 1941; s. Ray E. and Anne Louise (Wooten) C.; B.S., U. Houston, 1965; postgrad. in behavioral sci. Case Western Res. U., 1967-68; postgrad. cert. in Leadership and Decision Making, Yale U., 1990. Personnel asst. The Standard Oil Co., Cleve., 1966-68; dir. equal opportunity programs Turner Constrn. Co., Cleve., 1968-73; employment project dir. Nat. Assn. on Drug Abuse Problems, N.Y.C., 1973-74; exec. dir. The Cuyahoga Plan Ohio, Cleve., 1974-77; dir. EEO compliance and community activities The Continental Group, Inc., Stamford, Conn., 1978-85; cons. human resources James Campbell & Assocs., Inc., 1985-88; asst. v.p. strategic human resource planning MTA N.Y.C. Transit, Bklyn., 1988-96, acting dep. v.p. employee resources, 1993-96; asst. v.p. employee resources, 1988-90; v.p. human resources and adminstrn. MTA L.I. Bus, 1996—; expert witness HUD, 1970, U.S. Ho. of Reps. subcom., 1972. Task force chmn., mem. steering com. Cleve. Fedn. Community Devel. Manpower Planning and Devel. Commn., 1971-73; mem. community adv. bd. Cleve. Press, 1972; mem. Pres.'s Com. Employment of People with Disabilities, 1985-91. Served with USAF, 1958-62; Japan. Recipient key to city Cleve., 1970; Outstanding Community Service award Urban League Cleve., 1972. Mem. ASTD, am. soc. Tng. and Devel., Human Resource Assn. N.Y., 1974—, N.Y. Caledonian Club, Inc. (chieftan, 1999), The Clan Campbell Soc. (N.Am. chpt., convenor N.Y.), Soc. Human Resources Mgmt. (life-time profl. cert. advanced level), Personnel Accreditation Inst., N.Y. Human Resources Planning Soc., N.Y. Caledonian Club, Inc., Clan Campbell Soc., North Am., Omicron Delta Kappa (circle v.p. 1965, Gold Key 1965). Author profl. publs. Home: 504 W 110th St Apt 8-d New York NY 10025-2008 Office: MTA LI Bus 700 Commercial Ave Garden City NY 11530-6410

CAMPBELL, JAMES ROBERT, banker; b. Rochester, Minn., May 24, 1942; s. Donald William and Alice Marie (Gray) C.; m. Carmen Dawn Starkson, July 11, 1964; children: Peter Ian, Kathryn Ann. B.S. in Bus, U. Minn., 1964. Comml. banking officer Norwest. Nat. Bank Mpls., 1964-67, asst. v.p., 1967-71, sr. v.p. nat. dept., 1976-79, pres., chief operating officer, 1984-86; pres., dir. Lease Northwest, Inc., Mpls., 1971-75, Norwest Bank Omaha N.A., Omaha, 1979-82; regional pres. Norwest Corp.-Norwest Banks, 1982-84; pres., chief exec. officer Norwest Bank Minn. N.A., Mpls., 1986-95, chmn. bd. dirs., 1995—, chmn. bd., 1995-98; group exec. v.p. Wells Fargo Corp., 1998—; group exec. v.p. Wells Fargo Corp., 1998—; exec. v.p. Norest Corp.; bd. dirs. Merrill Corp., Allianz U.S.A. Bd. dirs. Mpls. Inst. Arts, U. Minn. Found., Abbott-Northwestern Hosp., Viking coun. Boy Scouts Am., United Way Mpls. Mem. Minn. Exec. Orgn., World Press Orgn., Minikahda Club, Mpls. Club, Bankers Round Table, Spring Hill Golf Club, Bay Colony Golf Club. Republican. Presbyterian. Home: 5521 Woodcrest Dr Minneapolis MN 55424-1651

CAMPBELL, JAMES SARGENT, lawyer; b. Chgo., Sept. 19, 1938; m. Mary Tydings Eager, Sept. 3, 1960; children: Catherine, Julia, John. BA summa cum laude, Yale U., 1960; LLB, Stanford U., 1964. Bar: D.C. 1966. Carnegie teaching fellow Yale U., 1960-61; law clk. Justice William O. Douglas, U.S. Supreme Ct., 1964-65; spl. asst. antitrust div. Dept. Justice, 1967-68; gen. counsel Nat. Commn. Causes and Prevention Violence, 1968-69; assoc. Wilmer, Cutler & Pickering, Washington, 1965-67, 70-71, ptnr., 1972—, chair internat. practice, 1988-95, mem. mgmt. com., 1990-92; cons. Office Sec. HUD, 1977-78, HHS, 1979. Author, editor: Law and Order Reconsidered, 1970, Doctor Faustus: Archetypal Subtext at the Millenium, 1999. Mem. ABA, Internat. Bar Assn., Internat. Aviation Club, Elizabethan Club, Order of Coif, Phi Beta Kappa. Office: Wilmer Cutler & Pickering 2445 M St NW Washington DC 20037-1420

CAMPBELL, JANE TURNER, former educator and realtor; b. Macon, Mo., July 8, 1931; d. Thomas Freeman and Rena Ellen (Vandiver) Turner; m. Duard Ray McDonald, Aug. 25, 1952 (div. 1955)); m. Ian MacCallum Campbell, Mar. 28, 1958; children; Colin Turner, Clay Ian. BS in Edn., U. Mo., 1953; postgrad., San Diego State Coll., 1955-57, UCLA, 1958. Cert. secondary sch. tchr., Calif., Ill., N.J.; lic. real estate salesperson, broker, N.J., lic. real estate salesperson, Pa., N.J. Tchr. Hallsville (Mo.) High Sch., 1953-54; co-owner McDonalds' Clothiers, Wewoka, Okla., 1954-55; tchr., class advisor Imperial (Calif.) High Sch., 1955-58, Temple City (Calif.) High Sch., 1958-59; prof. Coll. San Mateo, Calif., 1965-70, McHenry County Coll., Crystal Lake, Ill., 1972-76, Waubonsee Coll., Aurora, Ill., 1976-79; tchr., adminstr. Purnell Sch., Pottersville, N.J., 1980-86; realtor Sig Kuhne Realtors, Milford, N.J., 1986-89, Burgdorff Realtors, Inc., Pittstown, N.J., 1989-94; ret., 1994; co-founder Audio, Verbal, & Tutorial Ctr. McHenry County Coll., 1975-77. Author: Shorthand I, Shorthand II, Shorthand III, Office Procedures I, Bookkeeping I, Bookkeeping II, Bookkeeping III, Medical Sec., Legal Sec., Office Procedures II, Bus. Materials, Bus. Law, Office Machines I, Office Machines II. Chairperson Del. Valley Autumn Antique Show, Holland Twp., N.J., 1988-93; chair Holland Twp. Hist. Preservation Commn., 1989-95, Christmas Project, Hunterdon County, N.J., 1988—. Mem. Hunterdon County Bd. Realtors (Community Svc. award 1988), N.J. Assn. Realtors, Holland Twp. Women's Club (chairperson Clarence Carter Night 1988), Golden Talents (pres., v.p., trustee 1988-91), Pi Beta Phi (province pres.). Republican. Episcopalian. Avocations: swimming, boating, antique collecting. Home: 606 Summit Ridge Dr Tahlequah OK 74464-9259

CAMPBELL, JEAN, retired human services organization administrator; b. Fairhaven, Mass., Mar. 4, 1925; d. Elwyn Gilbert and Marion Hicks (Dexter) C. AA, Lasell Coll., Auburndale, Mass., 1944; BA, Brown U., 1946; MEd, U. Hartford, 1963. Field dir. Waterbury (Conn.) Area Coun. Girl Scouts, Inc., 1946-52; exec. dir. Manchester (Conn.) Girl Scouts, Inc., 1952-60; dist. dir. Conn. Valley Girl Scout Coun., Inc., Hartford, 1961-63; dir. field svcs. Plymouth Bay Girl Scout Coun., Taunton, Mass., 1963-64, exec. dir., 1964-68; exec. dir. New Bedford (Mass.) YWCA, 1968-87. Trustee Millicent Libr., Fairhaven, 1970—, pres. 1998—; corporator Compass Bank for Savs., 1976-98, St. Luke's Health Found., 1986-96, Lasell Coll., 1997—; bd. dirs. Greater New Bedford Concert Series, 1978—; com. mem., past pres. Interchurch Coun. of Greater New Bedford, 1969-97; bd. dirs., former treas. ICC Svcs. Corp., 1970-97; bd. dirs. ICC Congregate Housing, Inc., 1991-97, Fairhaven Improvement Assn., 1990-93; mem. 1st Congl. Ch. Fairhaven, chair history com., 1990-94; mem. Fairhaven/New Bedford—Tosashimizu (Japan) Sister City Com., 1991-94; asst. treas. Ladies Br. of the N.B. Port Soc., 1990-94, treas., 1994—. Recipient Thanks badge Girl Scouts U.S., 1956, Sidney Adams Cmty. Svc award Interch. Coun. of Greater New Bedford, 1984, AAUW Achievement award, 1987; named Woman of Yr., Internat. Women's Day Com., 1987; Annual Jean Campbell Svc. award established by YWCA of Southeastern Mass., 1995, Fairhaven Improvement assn. Testimonial, 1998. Mem. AAUW (3d v.p. New Bedford br. 1991-93), Fairhaven Hist. Soc. (investment com. 1992-96), Lasell Coll. Alumnae Inc. (bd. mgmt. 1994-97), Delta Kappa Gamma (pres. Eta chpt. 1986-88, chair family lit. project 1991-98, state lit. coun. mem. 1991-96, Alpha Upsilon State Area Achievement award 1992). Avocations: travel, photography, crafts, music, writing.

CAMPBELL, JILL FROST, university official; b. Buffalo, July 29, 1948; d. Jack and Elaine Mary (Hamilton) Frost; m. Gregory H. Campbell, May 31, 1969; children: Geoffrey, Kimberly, Kristina. BS, SUNY, Brockport, 1970, MSED, 1981; PhD, U. Buffalo, 1997. Acct. clk. bursar's office SUNY, Brockport, 1974-75, sr. acct. clk., 1975-78, instl. rsch. asst., 1978-82, asst. dir. instl. rsch. office, 1982-86, acting pers. assoc., pers. office, 1986-87, dir. contract and grant adminstrn. Rsch. Found., 1987-97, adminstrv. svcs. coord. for profl. devel., 1995-96, admissions liaison/acad. advisement, 1997—, mem. enrollment ops. group, campus jud. officer, 1997—; sDm. enrollment ops. group SUNY, Brockport, 1997-99, mem. metroctr. com. for student svcs., 1997—, chair campus com. on profls.' roles and rewards, 1997-98, campus jud. officer, 1997-99, mem. coll. rev. panel, 1995—, coll. com. profl. evaluation, 1995—, strategic planning com., 1995-97, mem. retention com., 1998—, mem. presdl. scholars com., 1998—, mem. strategic planning implementation com. on retention, 1999—, mem. strategic planning implementation com. on systemic change, 1999—. Mem. exec. com. Nativity Home Sch. Assn., Nativity Blessed Virgin Sch., Brockport, 1985-87, mem. sch. pub. rels. and mktg. com., 1985-88; mem. Friends of Brockport Athletics, 1985—; coach Brockport Youth Summer Soccer, 1988-91; host family Assn. for Teen-Age Diplomats, 1995-96; mem. com. Chancellor's Award for Excellence in Profl. Svc., Brockport, 1989-90; liaison Brockport Child Care Ctr., 1995-96. Grantee United Univ. Professions, 1985, 90, 93, 94. Mem. NAFE, Nat. Assn. Instl. Rsch. (mem. exec. com., co-originator and discussion leader books and current issues 1985-87, co-author profl. file, presenter papers, presenter panels 1979-87), SUNY Assn. Instl. Rsch. and Planning Officers (mem. exec. com., presenter papers, presenter panels 1984-87), Nat. Coun. Univ. Rsch. Adminstrs., 1988-96, North East Assn. Instl. Rsch. (mem. exec. com., sec. 1985-87, presenter papers, presenter panels 1978-87), Internat. Conf. for Women in Higher Edn. (presenter 1992), SUNY Brockport Alumni Assn., Brockport Profl. Women's Group, Rsch. Found. Cen. Office (users group 1987-90, sponsored program comm. com. 1990-97, 4-yr. rsch. coun. 1988-93, vice chmn. 1991, chmn. 1992, univ. colls. rsch. coun. 1993-97), N.Y. State Transfer Articulation Assn. (workshop presenter 1998), N.Y. State/United Univ. Professions (Excellence award 1990). Home: 5129 Redman Rd Brockport NY 14420-9601 Office: SUNY Acad Advisement 350 New Campus Dr Brockport NY 14420-2935

CAMPBELL, JOAN VIRGINIA LOWEKE, secondary school educator, language educator; b. Detroit, Nov. 8, 1942; d. George Paul and Lolamae (Weians) L.; m. James Bachelder Campbell, July 26, 1975; 1 child, James Bachelder Loweke. BA in German, French, Hope Coll., 1965; student, U. Cologne (Germany), 1964, U. Salzburg (Austria), 1968, U. Stuttgart (Germany), 1970-71, Sampere Inst., Madrid, 1982, Millersville (Pa.) State U., 1983, 84, 90, Va. Poly. Inst. and State U., 1976-77, 80-84, U. Va., 1996-97,

98-99. Cert. secondary tchr., Mich., Kans., Va. Tchr. French and German I, II Grand Haven (Mich.) Jr. H.S., 1965-69; asst. instr. elementary and intermediate German U. Kans., Lawrence, 1969-70, 71-72; tchr. German I, II Ctrl. Jr. H.S., Lawrence, Kans., 1972-74; tchr. French I, II, sr. English Oskaloosa (Kans.) H.S., 1974-75; tchr. German I-IV Highland Park H.S., Topeka, 1975-76; tchr. French I-V, Spanish I and II Blacksburg (Va.) H.S., 1977—; tchr. French, Spanish YMCS, YMCA evening courses, Blacksburg, Va., 1976-80; mem. audio visual com. Montgomery County Fgn. Lang. Collaborative Group, Blacksburg, 1984-87; chaperone Am. Inst. Fgn. Study, Germany, France, Spain, 1968-82, area adminstr. summer and winter programs abroad, We. Mich., 1968-69; chaperone Ednl. Adventures, Quebec City, Montreal, 1984, 90-91, 93-94, 98, Montgomery County Schs.; presenter in field. Author: The Gothic Cathedral, 1995. Mem. Internat. Host Family Orgn. Va. Poly. Inst. and State U., Blacksburg, 1977—;. Fulbright exch. fellow U. Kans., 1970-71, Fulbright fellow Goethe Insts., 1976, Rockefeller fellow Rockefeller Assn. and Nat. Endowment Humanities, 1986, NDEA fellow, 1966; recognized as Va. Gov.'s Sch. Outstanding Educator, 1990. Mem. Am. Assn. Tchrs. French (state and region IV U.S. Recognition effort, dedication and high scores on nat. French exams, 1988, 96, 97, founder La Soc. Hon. de Français for Outstanding Students in French Blacksburg chpt. 1977, state com., dist. adminstr. Le Grand Concours-Nat. French Exams 1980—), Am. Assn. Tchrs. Spanish and Portuguese, Am. Assn. Tchrs. German (Va. exec. com. sec. 1977-83, co-chmn. nat. German exams Va. chpt. 1984-87, state nominating com. 1984-87, chmn. 1984-85), Nat. Assn. Edn. (Blacksburg H.S. rep. 1980-82), Va. Assn. Edn., Montgomery County Assn. Edn., Assn. Supervision and Curriculum Devel., Fgn. Lang. Assn. Va. (life). Republican. Presbyterian. Avocations: flower gardening, hiking, mountain climbing, violin, art history. Home: 3003 Mclean Ct Blacksburg VA 24060-8110 Office: Blacksburg HS 520 Patrick Henry Dr Blacksburg VA 24060-3106

CAMPBELL, JOHN COERT, political scientist, author; b. N.Y.C., Oct. 8, 1911; s. Allan Reuben and Gertrude Helen (DuBois) C.; m. Mary Elizabeth Hillis, Aug. 1, 1936; childrenAllan Reuben II, Alexander Bruce. A.B., Harvard, 1933, M.A., 1936, Ph.D., 1940. Instr. polit. sci. U. Louisville, 1940-41; specialist Eastern Europe State Dept., 1942-46; sec. U.S. delegation, polit. adviser Coun. Fgn. Ministers, also; Paris Peace Conf., 1946; polit. adviser U.S. delegation Danube Conf., 1948; officer charge Balkan affairs, mem. policy planning staff State Dept., 1949-55; editor, sr. rsch. fellow, dir. studies Coun. Fgn. Rels., 1946-69, 55-78, sr. fellow emeritus, 1988—; cons. and adv. State Dept., 1963-80, mem. policy planning council, 1967-68. Author: The United States in World Affairs, 3 vols, 1947-49, Defense of the Middle East, Problems of American Policy, rev. edit, 1960, American Policy Toward Communist Eastern Europe, The Choices Ahead, 1965, Tito's Separate Road, America and Yugoslavia in World Politics, 1967; Editor: Successful Negotiation; Trieste, 1954, 1976; mem. editorial bd.: Slavic Rev, 1969-76. V.p. Middle East Inst., 1967-78, bd. govs., 1963-79, mem. emeritus; mem. joint com. Slavic studies Am. Council Learned Soc. Fellow Middle East Studies Assn.; mem. Council Fgn. Relations, Am. Hist. Assn., Am. Assn. Advancement Slavic Studies (award for disting. contbn. to Slavic studies 1980). Home: 100 Pond St Unit 14 Cohasset MA 02025-1945

CAMPBELL, JOHN CREIGHTON, political science educator, association administrator; b. N.Y.C., June 12, 1941; s. Charles Edward and Ruth (Creighton) C.; m. Ruth Zimring, Sept. 21, 1962; children: David Riggs, Robert Charles, Judy Fredericka. BA, Columbia Coll., 1965; Cert. East Asian Inst., Columbia U., 1973, PhD in Polit. Sci., 1973; postgrad., Interuniv. Ctr. Japanese Lang., Tokyo, 1965-66. Staff assoc. Social Sci. Rsch. Coun., N.Y.C., 1970-73; asst. prof. polit. sci. U. Mich., Ann Arbor, 1973-80, assoc. prof., 1980-91, prof., 1991—, dir. Ctr. Japanese Studies and East Asia Nat. Resource Ctr., 1982-87, dir. East Asia Bus. Program, 1984-88, 90—, dir. Japan Tech. Mgmt. Program, 1991-93, co-dir., 1993—; fellow Woodrow Wilson Internat. Ctr. for Scholars, Washington, 1980-81; vis. prof. law Keio U., Tokyo, 1989-90, vis. prof. medicine, 1997—; sec., treas. Assn. for Asian Studies, 1994—. Author: Contemporary Japanese Budget Politics, 1977, How Policies Change: The Japanese Government and the Aging Society, 1992; (with Naoki Ikegami) The Art of Balance in Health Policy, 1997; editor: (with Naoki Ikegami) Containing Health Care Costs in Japan, 1996, Long-Term Care for Frail Older People: Reaching for the Ideal System, 1999; contbr. articles to profl. jours., chpts. to books. With U.S. Army, 1959-62, Japan. Ford Found. travel and study fellow, 1972, Fulbright-Hayes fellow U.S. Dept. State, Japan, 1976-77, 89-90, Japan Found. fellow, 1980, Abe fellow, 1997-98; recipient Masayoshi Ohira Meml. prize, 1993. Mem. Assn. Asian Studies (bd. dirs. 1994—, Disting. Lectr. 1994), Am. Polit. Sci. Assn., Internat. House of Japan. Democrat. Avocations: reading novels, listening to music. Home: 916 Miner St Ann Arbor MI 48103-3122 Office: Univ Mich Dept Polit Sci Corner House 202 S Thayer St Ann Arbor MI 48104-1608

CAMPBELL, JOHN DEE, retired insurance executive; b. Lincoln, Nebr., Dec. 21, 1928; s. John D. and Alice (Heldt) C.; m. Sally Holmes, Mar. 26, 1951; children: John Daniel, Amy Campbell Lamphere, Peter J. BSBA with distinction, U. Nebr., 1950. Bank loan officer First Nat. Bank, Lincoln, 1950-52; agt. Mass Mut. Life Ins. Co., Lincoln, 1954-65, gen. asst., 1965-92, gen. agt. emeritus, 1992—; pres., CEO Compensation Programs Inc., Lincoln, 1986—; dir. Cooper Found., Lincoln, 1965—, NBC Bank, Lincoln, 1972-82, Norwest Bank Lincoln, 1988-98. Chmn. Nebr. Libr. Commn., 1982-83, Contact Inc., Lincoln, 1980-97; pres. Nebrs. Humanities Found., 1993-96. Mem. Am. Soc. CLU/ChFC (nat. pres. 1992-93), Shriners, Elks, Lincoln Country Club. Republican. Episcopalian. Avocations: golf, fishing, travel, gardening. Home: 2901 Bonacum Dr Lincoln NE 68502-5725 Office: Compensation Programs Inc 5539 S 27th # 206 Lincoln NE 68502-1002

CAMPBELL, JOHN HYDE, laser materials researcher, consultant; b. Ithaca, N.Y., Dec. 2, 1947. BS in Chemistry, Rochester Inst. of Tech., 1970; PhD in Phys. Chemistry, U. Ill., 1975. Rsch. chemist Lawrence Livermore (Calif.) Lab., 1975-77, nuclear waste project leader, 1977-80, laser material rsch. leader, 1980-88, BEAMLET project leader, 1989-94, laser glass project leader, 1994—. Patentee in field; contbr. over 50 articles to profl. jours. Recipient R&D-100 award R&D Mag., 1987, 88, Otto Schott internat. rsch. award, Ernst Abbe Fund, 1999. Home: 2136 Westbrook Ln Livermore CA 94550-6429 Office: Lawrence Livermore Nat Lab PO Box 808 Livermore CA 94551-0808

CAMPBELL, JOHN MORGAN, retired chemical engineer; b. Virden, Ill., Mar. 24, 1922; S. John M. and Ione Marie (Whittler) C.; m. Gwendolyn Thompson, Aug. 27, 1945; children: John Morgan, Robert, Charles. B.S. in Chem. Engring, Iowa State U., 1943; M.S., U. Okla., 1948, Ph.D., 1951. Devel. engr. and supr. E.I. duPont de Nemours & Co., Inc., 1943-46; spl. instr. chem. engring. U. Okla., 1946-50; tech. adviser to v.p. Black Sivalls and Bryson, Oklahoma City, 1951-54; mem. faculty U. Okla. Sch. Petroleum Engring., 1954-69, chmn. dept., 1956-63, Erle P. Halliburton prof., 1963-69, dir., 1969; dir. Petroleum Research Center, 1964-69; pres. John M. Campbell & Co. (engring. counselors, mgmt. consultants), 1968-82; chmn. bd. Petrotech Ltd., Petroleum Learning Programs Ltd. Author: Oil Property Evaluation, 1959, Effective Technical Communications, 1969, Decision Methods For Petroleum Investments, 1969, Gas Conditioning and Processing, 2 vols., 1970, 6th edit., 1984, The Professional - From Puberty to Senility, 1970, Effective Communication for the Technical Man, 1972, Petroleum Reservoir Property Evaluation, 1973, Mineral Property Economics (3 vols.), 1978, Petroleum Evaluation for Financial Disclosures, 1983, Analysis and Management of Petroleum Investments, 1987; also numerous articles, chpts. in books. Recipient Hanlon award Gas Processors Assn., 1987, Disting. Achievement award Iowa State U., 1988. Mem. NAE, AIME (hon. mem. 1994, exec. com. coun. edn., mineral industries econs. award 1989), Soc. Petroleum Engrs. (hon. mem. 1994, J.F. Caril award 1978, Arps award 1989), Am. Arbitration Assn. (arbitration panel), Internat. Petroleum Inst. (pres. 1968-82), Sigma Alpha Epsilon, Phi Lambda Upsilon, Pi Epsilon Tau. Club: Lion. Home: 6 Rustic Hills St Norman OK 73072-7411

CAMPBELL, JOHN RICHARD, pediatric surgeon; b. Pratt, Kans., Jan. 16, 1932; s. John Ross and Laura (Harkrader) C.; m. Susan Charlotte Baker, June 9, 1962; children: Kathryn, John Richard, George Ridgway. B.A., U. Kans., 1954, M.D., 1958. Diplomate Am. Bd. Surgery with cert. of spl. qualifications in pediatric surgery. Rotating intern Hosp. U. Pa., 1958-59; resident in gen. surgery U. Kans. Hosp., 1959-63; resident in pediatric surgery Children's Hosp. of Phila., 1965-67; asst. instr. U. Pa. Med. Sch., 1965-67; mem. faculty U. Oreg. Health Scis. Ctr., Portland, 1967-99, prof. surgery and pediat., 1972-99, chief pediatric surgery; surgeon-in-chief Doernbecher Children's Hosp., Portland, 1967-99; cons. VA, Shriners Crippled Children's hosps., Alaska Native Med. Ctr., Anchorage. Served to lt. comdr. M.C. USNR, 1963-65. Mem. A.C.S., Soc. Acad. Surgeons, Am. Acad. Pediatrics, Am. Pediatric Surg. Assn., Pacific Assn. Pediatric Surgeons, North Pacific Pediatric Soc., North Pacific Surg. Assn., Pacific Coast Surg. Assn., Portland Acad. Pediatrics, Portland Surg. Soc. Presbyterian. Office: Oreg Health Scis Univ 745 SW GAnes Rd CDW7 Portland OR 97201-2984

CAMPBELL, JOHN ROY, animal scientist educator, academic administrator; b. Goodman, Mo., June 14, 1933; s. Carl J. and Helen (Nicoletti) C.; m. Eunice Vieten, Aug. 7, 1954; children: Karen L., Kathy L., Keith L. BS, U. Mo., 1955; MS, U. Mo., Columbia, 1956, PhD, 1960. Instr. dairy sci. U. Mo., Columbia, 1960-61, asst. prof., 1961-65, assoc. prof., 1965-68, prof., from 1968; assoc. dean, dir. resident instrn. Coll. Agr., U. Ill., Urbana-Champaign, 1977-83; dean Coll. Agr. U. Ill., Urbana, 1983-88; pres. Okla. State U., Stillwater, 1988-93. Author: (with J.F. Lasley) The Science of Animals That Serve Humanity, 1969, 3d edit., 1985, In Touch with Students, 1972; (with R.T. Marshall) The Science of Providing Milk for Man, 1975; Reclaiming A Lost Heritage...Land-Grant and Other Higher Education Initiatives for the Twenty-First Century, 1995. Recipient Superior Tchg. award Gamma Sigma Delta, 1967, Internat. award for disting. svc. to agrl., 1985, Disting. Svc. award Coll. Osteo. Medicine Okla. State U., 1992. Fellow Am. Dairy Sci. Assn. (dir. 1975-78, 80-86, pres. 1980-81, Ralston Purina Disting. Tchg. award 1973, Award of Honor 1987); mem. Nat. Assn. Coll. Tchrs. Agr. (Ensminger Interstate Disting. Tchr. award 1973, Teaching fellow 1973, Disting. Educator award 1990, Nat. Assn. State and Univ. and Land-Grant Colls. (commns. on home econs. and vet. medicine, com. on water resources, coun. of presidents), Okla. Futures, Gamma Sigma Delta. Office: Okla State U 105 Citd Stillwater OK 74078-8080

CAMPBELL, JONATHAN WESLEY, astrophysicist, aerospace engineer; b. Alexander City, Ala., Sept. 1, 1950; s. Harry Underwood and Sarah Ruth Campbell; children: Jason Jonathan, Christopher Sanders, Benjamin Robert. BS distinguished grad., Auburn U., 1972, MS, 1974; MS, U. Ala., 1988, PhD, 1992. Cert. flight instr. Coop. engr. Pratt & Whitney Aircraft, West Palm Beach, Fla., 1968-70; instr. physics Auburn U., 1972-74; astrophysicist, aerospace engr. Missile and Space Intelligence Ctr., Huntsville, Ala., 1978-80; space scientist, supervisory aerospace engr. propulsion, exec. asst. to dir., lead engr. space telescope fine guidance sensor NASA/Marshall Space Flight Ctr., Huntsville, Ala., 1980—; pres. Redstone Aerospace Inc.; cons. Starflight Assocs. Served to capt. AUS, 1975-78. Col. USAFR. Recipient Eagle Scout award. Mem. AIAA, Air Force Assn., Res. Officer Assn., Aircraft Owners and Pilots Assn., Scabbard and Blade, Tau Beta Pi, Sigma Gamma Tau, Sigma Pi Sigma. Methodist. Home: PO Box 295 Harvest AL 35749-0295 Office: NASA E51 Marshall Space Flight Ctr Huntsville AL 35812

CAMPBELL, JOSEPH LEONARD, trade association executive; b. Independence, Mo., 1938. BS in Acctg., U. Kans., 1960, MS in Acctg., 1963. CPA, Mo. Audit mgr. Arthur Young & Co., Kansas City, Mo., 1962-75; v.p., sec., treas. Assoc. Wholesale Grocers, Kansas City, Kans., 1975—. Active Boy Scouts Am., Overland Park, Kans., 1983-93. Mem. AICPA. Office: Associated Wholesale Grocers Inc PO Box 2932 Kansas City KS 66110-2932

CAMPBELL, JUDITH LOWE, child psychiatrist; b. Indpls., Jan. 21, 1946; d. Albert St. Clair and Adele V. (Lobraico) Lowe; m. Robert Frank Campbell, Nov. 30, 1968; children: Christiaan Robert, Kevin Lowe, Geoffrey Ford. BS in Zoology, Butler U., 1967; MD, Ind. U., 1971. Resident psychiatry Ind. U. Sch. Medicine, 1971-73, fellow child psychiatry, 1973-75; asst. dir. Riley Child Guidance Clinic, Indpls., 1975-79, dir. child psychiatry consultation, liaison svc. to pediat., 1975-79; dir. child psychiatry svcs. Riley Hosp. for Children, Indpls., 1979-85; pvt. practice child psychiatry Indpls., 1985—; instr. Ind. U. Sch. Medicine, Indpls., 1974-75, asst. prof. dept. psychiatry, 1975-89, clin. assoc. prof., 1989—; child psychiatry cons. Luth. Child Welfare Assn., Indpls., 1974—, Lutherwood Children's Home, Indpls., 1974—, Ctr. for Mental Health Madison County, Anderson, Ind., 1975-77, Jewish Family and Children's Svcs., 1983-84; child and adolescent psychiat. svcs. Cmty. Hosps. Indpls., Inc., 1989-90; med. dir. outreach svcs. Arbor Hosp. Greater Indpls., 1990, med. dir. children's unit, 1990-92, pres. med. staff, 1990-92; med. dir. Arbor Hosp., 1992-94; child psychiatry cons. Charter Behavioral Health Sys., Lafayette, Ind., 1995-97; cons. Gallahue Mental Health Ctr., 1996—. Contbr. article on child psychiatry to profl. jours. Mem. parent's adv. coun. Butler U., 1989-93, pres., 1990-93; vice-precinct committeeman Rep. Party, 1990-94; team mem. Chaucie's Place Child Adv. Ctr., 1998—; bd. mem., v.p. Hamilton County Vesta Found. for Children, Inc., 1998—. Recipient Helen McQuiston award in sci., 1967, Physician's Recognition award in continuing edn. AMA, 1974, 77. Fellow Am. Psychiat. Assn., Ind. Psychiat. Soc. (councilor 1978-80, 90-91, sec. 1981-83, editor newsletter 1981-83, chmn. com. women 1983-92, mem. ethics com. 1992—), Am. Acad. Child and Adolescent Psychiatry, Nat. Alliance for the Mentally Ill, Ind. Coun. Child and Adolescent Psychiatry (sec. 1986-87, pres.-elect 1987-88, pres. 1988-89), Ind. Med. Women's Assn., Smithsonian Assocs., Indpls. Mus. Art, Indpls. Zool. Soc., Ea. Star, Woodland Country Club, Pi Beta Phi. Achievements include research on emotional aspects of burns in children, craniofacial anomalies in children, also sex differences in child and adolescent population groups. Office: 1525 N Ritter Ave Indianapolis IN 46219-3026

CAMPBELL, JUDITH MAY, physical education educator; b. Terre Haute, Ind., May 13, 1938; d. O.H. and D. Juanita C. B.S. in Phys. Edn., Ind. State U., 1960, M.S., 1963; D.Phys. Edn., Ind. U., 1978. Recreational dir. Terre Haute Park Dept., summers 1958-60; tchr. St. Louis pub. schs., 1960-61; instr. dept. phys. edn. Ind. State U., Terre Haute, 1961-66, asst. prof., 1966-75, assoc. prof., 1975-79, prof., 1979—, dir. undergrad. preparation; coach volleyball and basketball teams Univ. Sch., 1970-74, girl sports dir., 1974-78; founder Ind. Spl. Olympics, Inc., 1970; chmn. basketball Wabash Valley Bd. Women Ofcls., 1963-65, 68-74; nat. adv. bd. Spl. Olympics, Inc.; mem. nat. adv. bd. Joseph P. Kennedy, Jr. Found., 1972-74, chmn. Contbr. articles to profl. publs.; developer phys. edn. program in sch. curriculums. Bd. dirs. Ind. Spl. Olympics, 1968-74, state co-dir., 1970-74; bd. dirs. State Girls Sports Adv. Bd., 1975-77, Leadership Terre Haute, 1989—; mem. Air Pollution Bd. Vigo County, 1987-90; trustee Vigo County Sch. Bd., 1986-94. Recipient Lambert award Ind. State U., 1960; recipient Outstanding Phys. Fitness Leadership award Vigo County Jaycees, 1968, Service award Vigo County Assn. for Retarded Citizens, 1971, Community Service award Vigo County Jaycees, 1974, Eleanor St. John Disting. Alumni award, 1977, Katherine Hamilton Vol. award, 1989; Lilly Found. grantee, 1974; Chismar Found. grantee, 1972; Internat. Leadership Scholar; selected grand marshall Homecoming Parade Ind. State U., 1985. Mem. AAUP (pres. 1981—), Ind. Assn. Health, Phys. Edn. & Recreation (program devel. leadership award 1972, leadership award 1974), Mental Health Assn. Vigo County (bd. dirs. 1985-93), LWV (bd. dirs. Vigo County chpt. 1987-89), Delta Kappa Gamma (pres. 1980-82, grantee 1978), Phi Delta Kappa, Delta Psi Kappa. Home: 6745 E Manor Dr Terre Haute IN 47802-9019

CAMPBELL, KARLYN KOHRS, speech and communication educator; b. Blomkest, Minn., Apr. 16, 1937; d. Meinhard and Dorothy (Siegers) Kohrs; m. Paul Newell Campbell, Sept. 16, 1967 (dec. Mar. 1999). BA, Macalester Coll., 1958; MA, U. Minn., 1959, PhD, 1968. Asst. prof. SUNY, Brockport, 1959-63; with The Brit. Coll., Palermo, Italy, 1964; asst. prof. Calif. State U., L.A., 1966-71; assoc. prof. SUNY, Binghamton, 1971-72, CUNY, 1973-74; prof. communication studies U. Kans., Lawrence, 1974-86, dir. women's studies, 1983-86; prof. speech-communication U. Minn., Mpls., 1986—, dept. chair, 1993-96; inaugural Gladys Borchers lectr. U. Wis., Madison, 1974. Author: Critiques of Contemporary Rhetoric, 1972, rev. edit., 1997, Form and Genre, 1978, The Rhetorical Act, 1982, rev. edit. 1996, The Interplay of Influence, 1983, rev. edits., 1987, 92, 96, Man Cannot Speak for Her, 2 Vols., 1989, Deeds Done in Words, 1990, Women Public Speakers in the United States, 1800-1925: A Bio-Critical Sourcebook, 1993, Women Public Speakers in the United States, 1925—: A Bio-Critical Sourcebook, 1994; co-editor: Guilford Revisioning Rhetoric series, 1995—; mem. editl. bd. Communication Monographs, 1977-80, Quar. Jour. Speech, 1981-86, 92-94, Critical Studies in Mass Commn., 1993—, Rhetoric and Pub. Affairs, 1997—, Philosophy and Rhetoric, 1988-93; contbr. articles to profl. jours. Recipient Woolbert Rsch. award, 1987, Winans-Wichelns book award, 1990, Ehninger Rsch. award, 1991; Tozer scholar Macalester Coll., 1958, Tozer fellow, 1959; Fellow Shorenstein Barone Ctr., JFK Sch. of Govt., Harvard, 1992; Disting. Scholar award Human Communications, 1992. Mem. Nat. Comm. Assn. (disting. scholar award, Francine Merritt award for significant contbns. to the lives of women in comm. 1996 Women's Caucus), Ctrl. States Speech Comm. Assn., Ctr. Study of the Presidency, Phi Beta Kappa, Pi Phi Epsilon. Office: U Minn Dept Speech Commn 460 Folwell 9 Pleasant St SE Minneapolis MN 55455

CAMPBELL, KATHLEEN CHARLOTTE MURPHEY, audiology educator, administrator, researcher; b. Sioux Falls, S.D., Mar. 20, 1952; d. Chester Humphrey and Ruth Maxine (Thompson) Murphey; m. Craig Anthony Campbell, Nov. 15, 1975. BA, S.D. State U., 1973; MA, U. S.D., 1977; PhD, U. Iowa, 1989. Cert. audiologist. Clin. grad. asst. dept. communication U. S.D., Vermillion, 1976-77; regional audiologist II British Columbia Ministry Health, Cranbrook, 1977-82; audiologist II dept. otolaryngology head and neck U. Iowa, Iowa City, 1983-88, rsch. asst. dept. speech, pathology and audiology, 1985; doctoral fellow Health Svcs. R&D, VA, Iowa City, 1987-88; prof. div. otolaryngology dept. surgery So. Ill. U. Sch. Medicine, 1989—, prof., 1996—; cons. Packer Engring., Naperville, Ill., 1992—. Editorial cons. Am. Jour. Audiology, 1992; reviewer Annals of Otolaryngology, 1992; contbr. articles to profl. jours. Mem. Midamerica Playwrights Theatre, Springfield, Ill., 1989—, Sierra Club, Springfield, 1989—. Recipient Clin. Investigator Devel. Award grant NIH, 1990, Small Bus. Innovative Rsch. grant NIH, 1990, Ctrl. Rsch. Coun. grant So. Ill. U., 1991, Children's Miracle Network award So. Ill. U., 1991, 92, Alzheimer Disease Ctr. grant So. Ill. U. Sch. Medicine, 1992, James A. Shannon Dir.'s award NIH, 1997-99. Mem. Am. Speech-Lang.-Hearing Assn., Am. Acad. Audiology, Assn. Rsch. in Otolaryngology, Am. Acad. Otolaryngology-Head/Neck Surgery (assoc.), Mensa. Achievements include development of a device for treatment of Meniere's disease; research in electrocochleography and perilymphatic fistual; in ototoxicity. Office: SIU Sch Medicine PO Box 19629 Springfield IL 62794-9629 also: SIU Sch Medicine PO Box 19230 Springfield IL 62794-9230

CAMPBELL, KENNETH EUGENE, JR., vertebrate paleontologist; b. Jackson, Mich., Nov. 4, 1943; s. Kenneth Eugene and Betty Louise (Duffey) C. BS, U. Mich., 1966, M.S., 1967; Ph.D., U. Fla., 1973. Research asso. Fla. State Mus., Gainesville, 1972-74; asst. prof. zoology U. Fla., Gainesville, 1974-77; asst. prof. geology U. Fla., 1975-77; curator vertebrate paleontology/ornithology Natural History Mus. Los Angeles County, L.A., 1977—; acting dir. George C. Page Mus., 1995-96. Contbr. articles to sci. publs. Mem. AAAS, Am. Ornithologists' Union, Assn. Tropical Biology, Cooper Ornithol. Soc., Soc. Vertebrate Paleontology, Wilson Ornithol. Soc., Sigma Xi. Office: Natural History Mus 900 Exposition Blvd Los Angeles CA 90007-4057

CAMPBELL, KEVIN T., military officer; b. Worcester, Mass., Dec. 31, 1950; m. Kathleen Ash; chidlren: Scott, Erin. BS in Geography, Worcester State Coll., 1973; M Pers. Mgmt., U. N.H., 1982. Commd. 2d lt. U.S. Army, 1973, advanced through grades to col.; asst. dep. chief of staff combat devel. U.S. Army Tng. and Doctrine Command, Ft. Monroe, Va.; comdr. 94th Air Def. Arty. Brigade, Darmstadt, Germany; polit.-mil. planner Joint Staff, Washington; exec. officer 3d Battallion Air Def. Arty., Hanau, Germany, Ft. Bliss, Tex.; ROTC instr. U. N.H.; adjutant 1st Battalion 2nd Air Def. Arty., Korea; asst. ops. officer 38th Air Def. Arty. Brigade, Korea; comdr. Nike Hercules Battery, Homestead, Fla.; arty. team comdr. Datteln, Germany; dep. comdr. gen. U.S. Army Air Def. Arty. Ctr., Ft. Bliss; asst. commandant U.S. Army Air Def. Arty. Sch., Ft. Bliss. Office: US Army Air Def Arty Ctr Fort Bliss TX 79916

CAMPBELL, KRISTINE KOETTING, academic administrator; b. Arcadia, Wis., Feb. 22, 1952; d. John Joseph and Dorothy Ann (Vogel) Koetting; m. Douglas William Campbell, Feb. 1, 1980; children: Colin William, Ryan Joseph. BSN, Viterbo Coll., La Crosse, Wis., 1974; MSN, Ohio State U., 1983; postgrad., Oregon Health Scis. U., Portland, 1988—. RN Oreg., Wash.; TNCC, Emergency Nurses Assn. Staff nurse Natal ICU Madigan Army Med. Ctr., Tacoma, Wash., 1974-76; head nurse nursery US Army Hosp., Augsburg, Germany, 1976-79; head nurse pediatrics US Army Hosp., Ft. Campbell, Ky., 1979-81; instr. pediatric and nursey nurses Columbus (Ohio) Tech. Inst., 1983-84; instr. pediatric nursing Ohio State U., Columbus, 1984-87; grad. rsch. asst. Oreg. Health Scis. U., Portland, 1988-97; nursing supr. Landstuhl (Germany) Army Med. Ctr., 1990-91; chief nurse 396th Combat Support Hosp., Vancouver, Wash., 1995-97; comdr. 396th Combat Support Hosp., Bosnia, 1997-98, 6250th U.S. Army Hosp., Ft. Lewis, Wash., 1998-99; asst. chief nurse for mobilization and res. affairs The Office of the Surgeon Gen., Falls Church, Va., 1999—; child educator tng. adults in positive parenting, Longview, Wash., 1992-95. Co-author: (computer simulation) Lucy Web a four year old with Down's Syndrome undergoing a tonsillectomy. Mem. PTO, Longview, Wash., 1988—. Capt. U.S. Army, 1974-81; col. USAR. Recipient Instnl. Nat. Rsch. Svc. award, Oreg. Health Scis. U., 1990. Mem. ANa, Nat. Coun. on Family Rels., Res. Officers Assn., Assn. Mil. Surgeons U.S., Sigma Theta Tau. Democrat. Avocations: jogging, reading, family and friends. Home: 3 Country Club Dr Longview WA 98632-5424

CAMPBELL, LEONARD MARTIN, lawyer; b. Denver, Apr. 12, 1918; s. Bernard Francis and May (Moran) C.; m. Dot J. Baker, Sept. 23, 1944; children: Brian T., Teri Pat, Thomas P. A.B., U. Colo., 1941, LL.B., 1943. Bar: Colo. 1943. Since practiced in Denver; of counsel Gorsuch, Kirgis, LLC and predecessor firm, 1946—; cons. pub. utility matters Colo. Mcpl. League; city atty. Denver, 1951-53. Mem. Denver Charter Com., 1947; mgr. Safety and Excise for Denver, 1947-48; chmn. Denver Com. Human Relations, 1954; mem. Denver Planning Bd., 1950-51; mem. Bd. Water Commrs., Denver, 1965-70, pres., 1968-69; mem. Gov.'s Com. on Jud. Compensation, 1972; chmn. U. Colo. Law Alumni Devel. Fund, 1962. Served with USAAF, 1943-46. Mem. ABA, Colo. Bar Assn. (pres. 1978-79, Award of Merit 1967), Denver Bar Assn. (pres. 1969), Am. Coll. Trial Lawyers, Cath. Lawyers Guild Denver (pres. 1962, St. Thomas More award 1978), Nat. Inst. Mcpl. Law Officers (v.p. 1952), Colo. Judicial Inst. (Chancellor Chester Alter award 1987). Democrat. Roman Catholic. Clubs: Denver Athletic (Denver) (sec. 1960-61, pres. 1962), Cherry Hills Country (Denver). Home: 3447 S Birch St Denver CO 80222-7212 Office: Gorsuch Kirgis LLC 1515 Arapahoe St Ste 1000 Denver CO 80202-2120

CAMPBELL, LEVIN HICKS, federal judge; b. Summit, N.J., Jan. 2, 1927; s. Worthington and Louise (Hooper) C.; m. Eleanor Saltonstall Lewis, June 1, 1957; children: Eleanor S., Levin H., Sarah H. AB cum laude, Harvard U., 1948, LLB, 1951; postgrad., Nat. Coll. State Judiciary, 1970; LLD (hon.), Suffolk U., 1975. Bar: D.C. 1951, Mass. 1954. Assoc. firm Ropes & Gray, Boston, 1954-64; mem. Mass. Ho. of Reps., 1963-64; asst. atty. gen. State of Mass., 1965-66, spl. asst. atty. gen., 1966-67, 1st asst. atty. gen., 1967-68; assoc. justice Superior Ct. of Mass., 1969-72; judge U.S. Dist. Ct. Mass., Boston, 1972; judge U.S. Ct. Appeals (1st cir.), Boston, 1972—, chief judge, 1983-90, sr. judge, 1992—; fellow Inst. of Politics J.F. Kennedy Sch. Govt. Harvard U., 1968-69, study group leader 1980; faculty chmn. law session Salzburg Seminar in Am. Studies, 1981. Pres. Cambridge 9 Neighborhood Assn., 1960-62; treas. Cambridge Ctr. for Adult Edn., 1961-64; campaign chmn. Cambridge United Fund, 1965; mem. bd. overseers Boston Symphony Orch., 1969-75, 77-80; pres. bd. overseers Shady Hill Sch., 1969-70; mem. vis. com. Harvard U. Press, 1958-64; v.p. Cambridge Community Svcs.; corp. mem. SEA Ednl. Assn., 1982—; trustee Colby Coll., Waterville, Maine 1981-90, 91-99, Asheville (N.C.) Sch.; overseer U.S. Constitution Mus. 1st lt. (j.g.) U.S. Army, 1951-54, Korea. Mem. ABA, Am. Law Inst., Am. Bar Found., Mass. Bar Found., Boston Bar Assn., U.S. Jud. Conf. (ct. adminstrn. com. 1975-83, chmn. subcom. on supporting pers. 1980-83, exec. com. 1985-90, chmn. com. to rev. cir. coun. conduct and disability orders 1989-94, ad hoc com. study jud. conf. 1987, fed. ct. study com. 1988-90, nat. commn. on jud. discipline and removal 1991-93), Mass. Hist. Soc. (coun. 1993-96, v.p. 1996—, long range planning com. 1999—). Office: US Ct of Appeals US Courthouse 1 Courthouse Way Rm 6720 Boston MA 02210

CAMPBELL, LINDA SUE, guidance counselor; b. Carbondale, Pa., Oct. 9, 1960; d. Charles Frederick and Grace Elizabeth (Mackle) Koehler; m. Terrance Lee Campbell, May 5, 1984. BS in Social Work, Mansfield U., 1982; postgrad., U. Scranton, 1988-93. Student caseworker Children's Svcs. Tioga County, 1981; live-in resident advisor Dauphin Residences, Inc., Harrisburg, Pa., 1982-83; live-in resident mgr. Human Resources Ctr., Inc., 1983-84, evaluator, placement officer, 1984-86, program specialist, 1986-93; guidance counselor Veritas Therapeutic Community Inc., Barryville, N.Y., 1993—. Mem. adminstrv. coun. Bethany United Meth. Ch., Honesdale, Pa., 1993-95, 95—. Mem. ACA, Am. Sch. Counselor Assn., Pa. Counseling Assn., Social Work/Anthropol./Sociol. Club (v.p. 1981). Republican. Avocations: walking, biking, swimming, ice-skating, cross-country skiing. Home: RR 3 Box 760 Honesdale PA 18431-9521

CAMPBELL, LINZY LEON, molecular biology researcher, educator; b. Panhandle, Tex., Feb. 10, 1927; s. Linzy Leon and Eula Irene (McSpadden) C.; m. Alice P. Dauksa, Feb. 7, 1953. B.A. in Bacteriology and Chemistry, U. Tex., 1949, M.A., 1950, Ph.D., 1952. Rsch. scientist U. Tex., 1947-51; predoctoral rsch. fellow NIH, 1951-52; postdoctoral rsch. fellow Nat. Microbiol. Inst., U. Calif. at Berkeley, 1952-54; asst. prof., then assoc. prof. Wash. State U., 1954-59; assoc. prof. Western Res. U. Sch. Medicine, 1959-62; sr. rsch. fellow USPHS, 1959-62; prof. microbiology U. Ill. at Urbana, 1962-72, head dept., 1963-71, dir. Sch. Life Scis., 1971-72; prof. microbiology, provost and v.p. acad. affairs U. Del., Newark, 1972-88, univ. rsch. prof. molecular bioscis., 1988-89, Hugh M. Morris rsch. prof. molecular bioscis., 1989—. Editorial bd.: Jour. Bacteriology, 1961-65; editor, 1964-65, editor-in-chief, 1965-77; Contbr. articles to profl. jours. Served with USNR, 1944-46. Fellow AAAS; mem. Am. Soc. Microbiology (chmn. publ. bd. 1965-80, councilor at large 1962-64, v.p. 1972-73, pres. 1973-74), Am. Soc. Biochemistry and Molecular Biology. Office: U Delaware Dept Biology 400 Morris Library Newark DE 19717

CAMPBELL, L(OUIS) LORNE, mathematics educator; b. Winnipeg, Man., Can., Oct. 20, 1928; s. Elgin Smith and Jonina Solveig (Johnson) C.; m. Eha Johanson, June 12, 1954; children: Ian, Barry, Barbara. BSc, U. Man., 1950; MS, Iowa State U., 1951; PhD, U. Toronto., 1955. Def. sci. officer Def. Rsch. Bd., Ottawa, Ont., Can., 1954-58; asst. prof., then assoc. prof. U. Windsor, Ont., Can., 1958-63; assoc. prof., then prof. Queen's U., Kingston, Ont., Can., 1963-96, prof. emeritus, 1996—, head dept. math and stats., 1980-90. Contbr. articles to profl. pubis. Fellow IEEE; mem. Can. Math. Soc. (treas. 1982-85), Can. Statis. Soc., Am. Math. Soc., Soc. for Indsl. and Applied Math., Assn. Profl. Engrs. of Ont. Home: 153 Byron Crescent, Kingston, ON Canada K7M 1J2 Office: Queens U, Dept Math and Stats, Kingston, ON Canada K7L 3N6

CAMPBELL, MARGARET M., retired social work educator; b. New Orleans, Dec. 1, 1928; d. Walter and Caroline Louise (Seither) C. BA, St. Mary's Dominican Coll., 1950; MSW, Boston Coll., 1952; 3d yr. cert. clin. practice, N.Y. Sch. Social Work, 1959; DSW, Columbia U., 1970. Caseworker Charity Hosp., New Orleans, 1951-53, Cath. Social Services, San Francisco, 1953-55; supr. Spl. Service Club sect. U.S. Army Europe, 1956-58; caseworker Children's Bur., New Orleans, 1959-60, Associated Cath. Charities, New Orleans, 1960-63; lectr. Dominican Coll., New Orleans, 1961-66; spl. projects worker Associated Cath. Charities, New Orleans, 1964-65; dir. Fla. Family Ctr., New Orleans, 1965-67; asst. prof. Tulane U. Sch. Social Work, New Orleans, 1968, assoc. prof., 1971; dir. continuing edn. programs Tulane U., New Orleans, 1976-80; dir. Child Welfare Svcs. Tng. Ctr. Region VI, New Orleans, 1979-82; dean Tulane U. Sch. Social Work, New Orleans, 1982-94, prof., 1986—; dir. Ctr. on Aging, 1993-96, ret., 1996; chmn. various coms. sch. social work including Advanced Programs Continuing Edn., Ednl. Policy, NASW Student Liaison, Priorities Com. Author numerous publications and articles in profl. jours. in field. Mem. Kingsley House Bd., 1985, Area Agy. on Aging, 1988; bd. dirs. Tulane Ctr. Aging Rsch. and Svcs., 1993. Recipient Alumnae award Dominican Coll., 1970, Dominican Coll. Torchbearer award, 1985. Mem. NASW (chpt. pres. 1973-75, bd. dirs., treas., program dir., membership com., 1955-85; social worker of yr. Southeastern La. chpt. 1976; La. chpt. award 1978, La. chpt. Lifetime Achievement award 1992), Acad. Cert. Social Workers, Internat. Conf. on Social Welfare, New Orleans Children's Council, Child Welfare Info. Exchange Panel for La., Task Force on Adolescent Treatment Ctr., New Orleans Collaborative Tng. Program, Child Welfare League (chmn. southeastern conf. 1980-83), Council on Social Work Edn. (steering com. 1980-81, coordinator 1985), La. State Med. Soc. (geriatrics subcom. 1985-86), Nat. Council on Aging, Gerontological Soc. Am. (conf. com. 1985), Southern Gerontology Soc., Adult Protection Services Network, Coun. on Social Work Edn. (planning com. ann. meeting 1990-91), Am. Pub. Welfare Assn. (regional conf. com. 1989-90), Nat. Assn. Deans and Dirs. Schs. Social Work (chair 1991 meeting).

CAMPBELL, MARGARETTE MONJOA, interpreter, translator; b. Lagos, Nigeria, Feb. 3, 1940; d. Emilea Lyengu (Esame) Campbell; 1 child, Joke Malafa. Bilingual Degree, U. Cameroon, Laounde, 1970; Translators Diploma, U. Geneva, 1974; postgrad. diploma in Interpretation, Poly. Ctrl. London, 1976. Translator, interpreter Nat. Assembly Cameroon, Laounde, chief linguistic svc., sub dir. translation and interpretation, dep. dir. linguistics and legislation, dir., tech. advisor; dep. head interpretation and translation UN, Ruanda, Angola, 1995—; external examiner MA Bula (Cameroon) U. Ctr. Mem. Internat. Assn. Conf. Interpreters, Am. Biog. Inst. (leadership award). Roman Catholic. Avocations: crosswords, dressmaking, reading, music. Office: Monua UN Angola PO Box 5860 New York NY 10163-5860

CAMPBELL, MARIA BOUCHELLE, lawyer, church executive; b. Mullins, S.C., Jan. 23, 1944; d. Colin Reid and Margaret Minor (Perry) C. Student, Agnes Scott Coll., 1961-63; AB, U. Ga., 1965, JD, 1967. Bar: Ga. 1967, Fla. 1968, Ala. 1969. Pvt. practice law Birmingham, Ala., 1968-94; law clk. U.S. Cir. Ct. Appeals, Miami, Fla., 1967-68; assoc. Cabaniss, Johnston and Gardner, 1968-73; sec., counsel Ala. Bancorp., Birmingham, 1973-79; sr. v.p., sec., gen. counsel AmSouth Bancorp., 1979-84, exec. v.p., gen. counsel, 1984-94; exec. v.p., gen. counsel AmSouth Bank, 1984-94; exec. asst. to rector Parish of Trinity Ch., N.Y.C., 1994—; bd. trustees Ptnrship for Women's Health Columbia U., 1996—; bd. dirs. Leake and Watts Childrens Svcs., Inc., 1997—; lectr. continuing legal edn. programs; cons. to charitable orgns. Exec. editor Ga. Law Rev, 1966-67. Bd. dirs. St. Anne's Home, Birmingham, 1969-74, chancellor, 1969-74; bd. dirs. Children's Aid Soc., Birmingham, 1970-94, 1st v.p., 1988-90, pres., 1990-92; trustee Canterbury Cathedral Trust in Am., 1992—, Discovery 2000 Children's Mus., 1991-94, Soc. for Propagation of Christian Knowledge, 1991-93; bd. dirs. NCCJ, 1985-94, state chair, 1990-93; bd. dirs. Positive Maturity, 1976-78, Mental Health Assn., 1978-81, YWCA, 1979-80, Op. New Birmingham, 1985-87, pers. com., 1987-90, v.p., 1990-94; bd. dirs. Soc. for the Fine Arts U. Ala., 1986-89, Baptist Hospital Found. of Birmingham Inc., 1994-95, Alliance for Downtown N.Y., 1995—; commr. Housing Authority, Birmingham Dist., 1980-85, Birmingham Partnership, 1985-86, Leadership Birmingham, 1986—, program com., 1989-90, co-chair program com., 1990-91; mem. pres. adv. coun. Birmingham So. Coll, 1988-92, chair bd. overseers Masters Program, 1990-94; mem. pres.'s cabinet U. Ala., 1990-95; trustee Ala. Diocese Episcopal Ch., 1971-72, 74-75, mem. canonical revision com., 1973-75, 89-91, liturg. commn., 1976-78, treas., chmn. dept. fin., 1979-83, mem. coun., 1983-87, chancellor, 1987-91, cons. on stewardship edn., 1981-94, dep. to gen. conv., 1985, 88, 91; mem. Standing Commn. on Constn. and Canons, 1988-94; vestryman St. Luke's Episcopal Ch., 1991-94; bd. advisors So. region of Am. Soc. Corp. Secs., pres., 1992-94; community advisor Jr. League Birmingham, 1992-93; mem. adv. bd. Cahaba River Soc., 1991-94; trustee St. Andrew's Sewanee Sch., 1998—. Named One of Top 10 Women in Birmingham, 1989, One of Top 5 Women in Bus., 1993. Mem. ABA, State Bar Ga., Fla. Bar, Ala. Bar Assn., Birmingham Bar Assn., Am. Corp. Counsel Assn. (bd. dirs. Ala. 1984-89), Assn. Bank Holding Cos. (chmn. lawyers com. 1986-87), Greater Birmingham C. of C. (bd. dirs. 1988-94, exec. com. 1992-94, vice chmn., gen. counsel 1993-94), India House, Kiwanis, The Ch. Club N.Y., Order of St. John of Jerusalem. Home: PO Box 3290 Sewanee TN 37375-3290 Office: Parish of Trinity Ch 74 Trinity Pl New York NY 10006-2003

CAMPBELL, MARTIN, film director, producer, writer; b. Wellington, New Zealand, Oct. 16, 1958. Dir.: The Sex Thief, 1973, Three for All, 1974, Eskimo Nell, 1975, Handful of Diamonds/Her Family Jewels, 1976, Criminal Law, 1988, Defenseless, 1990, No Escape/Escape from Absolom, 1994, GoldenEye, 1995, The Mask of Zorro, 1998; dir. (TV series): The Professionals, 1977, Minder, 1979, Charlie, 1984, Edge of Darkness, 1986, Cast a Deadly Spell, 1991, Homicide: Life on the Street, 1993; assoc. prodr.: Scum, 1979; prodr.: Black Joy, 1977. Office: c/o DGA 7920 Sunset Blvd Los Angeles CA 90046*

CAMPBELL, MARY KATHRYN, chemistry educator; b. Phila., Jan. 20, 1939; d. Henry Charles and Mary Kathryn (Horan) C. A.B. in Chemistry, Rosemont Coll., 1960; Ph.D., Ind. U., 1965. Instr. Johns Hopkins U., 1965-68; asst. prof. chemistry Mt. Holyoke Coll., South Hadley, Mass., 1968-74; assoc. prof. Mt. Holyoke Coll., 1974-81, prof., 1981—; vis. scholar U. Paris VII, 1974-75; vis. prof. U. Ariz., 1981-82, 88-89; mem. panel on grad. fellowships NSF, 1979-81. Author: Biochemistry, 1991, 3d edit., 1998; co-author: Understand! Biochemistry, 1999; contbr. articles to profl. jours. Fellow Woodrow Wilson Found., 1960, NSF, 1960-64, NIH, 1964-65; grantee in field. Mem. Am. Chem. Soc., AAAS, AAUP, Sigma Xi. Office: Mt Holyoke Coll Carr Lab Dept Chemistry South Hadley MA 01075

CAMPBELL, MARY SCHMIDT, dean art school; b. Phila., Oct. 21, 1947; d. Harvey Nathaniel and Elaine Juanita (Harris) S.; m. George Campbell, Jr., Aug. 24, 1968; children: Garikai, Sekou, Britt Jackson. BA in Eng. Lit., Swarthmore Coll., 1969; MA in Art Hist., Syracuse U., 1973, PhD Humanities, 1982; ArtsD (hon.), Pace U., 1991; DFA (hon.), CCNY, 1992; PhD (hon), Colgate U., 1994. Art ed. Syracuse New Times, N.Y., 1973-77; guest curator, curator Everson mus., Syracuse, 1974-76; exec. dir. Studio mus. in Harlem, N.Y.C., 1977-87; commr. cultural affairs city of N.Y., 1987-91; dean Tisch Sch. Arts, NYU, N.Y.C., 1991—; bd. mgrs. Swarthmore (Pa.) Coll., 1987—; mem. fine arts vis. com. bd. overseers, Harvard Coll., Harvard U., Cambridge, Mass., 1991-95; mem. Tony nominating com., 1996-98. Co-author: Harlem Renaissance: Art of Black America, 1987, Memory & Metaphor, 1991; prodr. (film) Sembene: A Biography, 1994. Mem. N.Y.C. Mayor's Adv. Commn. on Culture, 1991—; co-chmn. subcom. on culture Dem. Nat. Conf., N.Y.C., 1992; bd. dirs. N.Y. Shakespeare Festival, 1993—, Jazz at Lincoln Ctr., Upper Manhattan Empowerment Zone, Harlem Sch. Arts, 1997. Recipient George Arents award Syracuse U., 1993, Project of Yr. award N.Y. Coun. on Humanities, Tisch Sch., NYU and Black Filmakers Found., 1995. Mem. Century Assn. Democrat. Baptist. Avocations: jogging, writing. Office: NYU Tisch Sch of the Arts 721 Broadway Fl 12 New York NY 10003-6862*

CAMPBELL, SISTER MAURA, religious studies and philosophy educator; b. Bayonne, N.J.; d. Patrick John and Helena Marie (Collins) C. BS, Seton Hall U., 1940, MA, 1945; MA, Providence Coll., 1953, D in Religious Edn. (hon.), 1985; PhD, St. Mary's Sch. Theology, Notre Dame, Ind., 1955; postgrad., Marquette U., Ottawa U., 1969, Cath. U. Am., 1970-71. Joined Dominican Order, Roman Cath. Ch., 1927. Tchr. elem. and secondary schs., 1930-42; dir. postulants Mt. St. Dominic, Caldwell, N.J., 1955-59; dir. scholastics Mt. St. Dominic, Caldwell, 1959-69; mem. faculty Caldwell Coll., 1955—, prof. religious studies, 1957-86, prof. emerita, 1986—, chmn. dept., 1969-86; permanent rep. internat. Cath. edn. office UN Non-Govtl. Orgns., 1969—; cons. Thomas Edison State Coll., 1982—; v.p. internat. Cath. orgns. N.Y. Info. Ctr., 1978, pres., 1987-87; permanent rep. World Assembly Internat. Cath. Edn. Office, Bangkok, 1982; participant Women's Forum, Nairobi, Kenya, 1985, Mexico City, 1986, Madrid, 1993, Rome, 1994; participant World Congress of Office of Cath. Internat. Edn., Rome, 1994; del. Fourth Internat. UN Conf. Women, Beijing, 1995. Mem. editl. bd. The Cath. Adv. Mem. Ecumenical/Interfaith Commn. Archdiocese of Newark, 1986-90; elected mem. exec. bd. Non-Govtl. Orgn./Dept. Pub. Info. at UN, 1988-90. Recipient Recognition award for outstanding achievement in higher edn. State of N.J., 1989, Jubilee medal Archdiocese of Newark, 1994, Disting. Svc. award Sacred Heart Inst., 1994, Peace Initiative award First Dominican Sisters, 1995, Jubilee Medal Pro Meritis, Archdiocese of Newark, 1995, Office of Cath. Internat. Edn. award for representation at UN, 1998. Mem. Dominican Edn. Assn. (past pres.), Coll. Theology Soc. (past v.p., sec.), Am. Acad. Religion, Religious Edn. Assn., Cath. Theology Soc., Coun. Religion and World Affairs, Theta Alpha Kappa (hon. mem. alumnus 1989, Veritas award 1989, Outstanding Prof. award 1989). Home: St Catherine Convent 7 Ryerson Ave Caldwell NJ 07006-6199 Office: Caldwell Coll 9 Ryerson Ave Caldwell NJ 07006-6195

CAMPBELL, MILDRED CORUM, business owner, nurse; b. Warfield, Va., Feb. 24, 1934; d. Oliver Lee and Hazel King (Young) Corum; m. Hugh Stuart Campbell, Dec. 2, 1972. BSN, U. Va., 1956; operating rm. mgr. cert., U.S. Army Med. Svcs. Sch., San Antonio, 1967; gen. mgr. cert., Cedars of Lebanon Med. Ctr., L.A., 1968. Head nurse plastic surgery U. Va. Med. Ctr., Charlottesville, 1956-58, head nurse cardio-surg., 1958-61; staff nurs operating rm. NIH Heart Inst., Bethesda, Md., 1961-62; supr. operating and recovery rms. Med. Univ. of S.C., Charleston, 1962-64; head nurse cardio operating rms. Meth. Hosp., Tex. Med. Ctr., Houston, 1964-67; supr. operating and recovery rms. Cedars of Lebanon Med. Ctr., L.A., 1967-68; product-nurse cons. Ethicon, Inc., Somerville, N.J., 1968-69; nurse cons. Johnson & Johnson, New Brunswick, N.J., 1969-70; gen. mgr. Ariz. Heart Inst., Phoenix, 1970-72; owner, pres., bd. dirs. Highland Packaging Labs., Inc., Somerville, 1983—. Mem., moderator Nat. Ass. Operating Rm. Nurses, Denver, 1963-76; pres. Aux. Orgn., Muhlenberg Hosp., Plainfield, N.J., 1979-80; chmn. Assn. for Retarded Citizens Fund Raising Ball, Somerset County, N.J., 1982. Mem. Inst. Packaging Profls. Home: 29 Lambert Dr Princeton NJ 08540-2304 Office: Highland Packaging Labs Inc 1181 Us Highway 202 Somerville NJ 08876-3909

CAMPBELL, NEAL FRANKLIN, musician, educator; b. Pittsboro, N.C., Jan. 27, 1953; s. Owen Riley and Aline Grey (Mangum) C.; m. Gwynn McLaurine Callis, May 13, 1996. MusB, Manhattan Sch. Music, 1983, MusM, 1985, D of Mus. Arts, 1996. Asst. organist All Saints' Ch., Chevy Chase, Md., 1973-76; organist, choirmaster St. Peter's Ch., Phila., 1976-77, St. George's By the River, Rumson, N.J., 1977-80, Christ Ch., Bloomfield, N.J., 1980-85, St. Stephen's Ch., Richmond, Va., 1985—; adj. asst. prof. music U. Richmond, 1997—. Author: Music and Life of Harold Friedell, 1996; performer recordings, radio and TV. Recipient Bronson Ragan award Manhattan Sch. Music, 1983. Mem. Am. Guild Organists (dean 1989-90, chair recital com. 1995-96), Assn. Anglican Musicians, Organ Hist. Soc. Democrat. Episcopalian. Office: 6000 Grove Ave Richmond VA 23226-2730

CAMPBELL, NEVE, actress; b. Guelph, Ont., Can., Oct. 3, 1973; m. Jeffrey Colt, Apr. 1995 (div. 1997). Student, Nat. Ballet Sch. Can. Appeared in film Scream, 1996 (Saturn award for Best Actress, MTV Movie award nomination, MTV Movie award for Best Female Performance), Scream 2, 1997 (Blockbuster Entertainment award for Favorite Actress-Horror, MTV Movie award for Best Female Performance). Named one of 50 Most Beautiful People, People mag., 1998. Office: Creative Artists Agy 9830 Wilshire Blvd Beverly Hills CA 90212-1825

CAMPBELL, PATTON, stage designer, educator; b. Omaha, Sept. 10, 1926; s. Ralph Harold and Frances Lorraine (Patton) C. BA, Yale U., 1950, MFA, 1952. Instr. costume design and history Barnard Coll., 1955-57; instr. scenery, costume design and history NYU, 1962-67; assoc. prof. Columbia U., 1967-91, SUNY, Purchase, 1975-76, 86—; vis. lectr. Bklyn. Coll., 1973-74, 80, 86-89, Brandeis U., 1975-76, 82-83; faculty New Sch., 1985; vis. prof. So. Methodist U., 1986, SUNY, Stony Brook, 1987; lectr. O'Neill Ctr., Suffolk Community Colls., 1987, Ohio U., 1996, So. Meth. U., Dallas, 1996, 97, Easton, Conn. Libr., 1997. Designer: costumes for plays and operas including 27 Wagons Full of Cotton, Playhouse Theatre, 1955, Trouble in Tahiti, 1955, Fallen Angels, 1956, A Hole in the Head, Plymouth Theatre, 1957, All American, Winter Garden Theatre, 1962, Wuthering Heights, N.Y.C. Opera, 1959, The Mikado, 1959, The Inspector General, 1960, Natalia Petrovna, 1964, Katya Kabonova, 1964, Capriccio, 1965, Lizzie Borden, 1965, La Traviata, 1966, The Pirates of Penzance, 1968, Carry Nation, 1969, Susannah, 1971, The Ballad of Baby Doe, 1988 (PBS), La Belle Helene, 1976, The Student Prince, 1980, La Traviata, 1981, Il Tabarro, Gianni Schicchi, Juilliard Opera Theatre, N.Y.C., The Lady from Colorado, 1964, Madame Butterfly, Central City (Colo.) Opera, 1964, After The Fall, Nat. Co., Wilmington, Del., 1964, Oliver!, 1964, Man of La Mancha, ANTA Washington Square, 1965 (Tony award nominee), On A Clear Day You Can See Forever, Nat. Co. Cleve., 1966, Loot, Biltmore Theatre, 1968, Der Rosenkavalier, Santa Fe Opera, 1968, Tosca, Santa Fe Opera, 1969, Cosi Fan Tutte, 1969, The Fisherman and His Wife, Opera Co. of Boston, 1970, Scarlett, Imperial Theatre, Tokyo, 1970, Between Time and Timbuktu (on PBS), 1972, Gone With The Wind, Drury Lane Theatre, London, 1972, Regina, Houston Grand Opera, 1980, Merry Wives of Windsor, So. Meth. U., The Mighty Casey and Gianni Schicchi, Glimmer Glass Opera Theatre, Cooperstown, N.Y., 1986, Teddy and Alice, Omaha Playhouse, 1990; costumes and scenery The Rake's Progress, Santa Fe Opera, 1957, Ariadne auf Naxos, 1957, La Boheme, 1958, Capriccio, 1958, Falstaff, 1958, Fledermaus, 1959, The Abduction From The Seraglio, 1959, The Makropoulos Affair, N.Y.C. Opera, 1970, H.M.S. Pinafore, 1975; exhibited in shows at Wright Hepburn Gallery, 1969, Praha Quedrennial, 1985, 89, Omaha Playhouse, 1986, Gone with the Wind Mus., 1993. Served with USN, 1944-46. Mem. United Scenic Artists. Episcopalian.

CAMPBELL, PAUL, III, lawyer; b. Chattanooga, Feb. 1, 1946; children: Paul IV, Kolter M. BA, Vanderbilt U., 1968; MA, Middlebury Coll., 1972; postgrad., So. Meth. U., 1971-72, Emory U., 1972-73; JD, U. Tenn., 1975. Bar: Tenn. 1976, Ga. 1977. Tchr. English St. Mark's Sch., Dallas, 1968-72; ptnr. Campbell & Campbell, Chattanooga, 1976-98; mem. Witt, Gaither & Whitaker, Chattanooga, 1998—; adj. prof. English, U. Tenn., Chattanooga, 1976, adj. prof. law, 1979-81, adj. prof. pre-trial litigation, Knoxville, 1996; mem. Tenn. Ct. of Judiciary, 1995—; mem. Tenn. Jud. Evaluation Guidelines Commn., 1994-95. Author: Tennessee Admissibility of Evidence in Civil Cases, 1987; co-author: Tennessee Automobile Liability Insurance, 1986, 95, 96, 99; editor-in-chief Tenn. Law Rev., 1975; contbr. articles to profl. jours. Bd. mgrs. YMCA Youth Residential Ctr., 1977-80; mem. McCallie Sch. Alumni Coun., 1987-93, U. Tenn. Dean's Alumni adv. coun. law coll., 1979—; trustee, Harbison Found., 1994-96. Recipient Am. Jurisprudence award U. Tenn., 1974, U. Ten. Coll. Law Pub. Svc. award, 1995; Alumni Achievement award McCallie Sch., 1994. Mem. ABA, Am. Bar Found., Tenn. Bar Assn. (bd. govs. 1985-94, pres. 1992-93), Tenn. Bar Found., Chattanooga Bar Found., Chattanooga Bar Assn. (bd. govs. 1983-85), State Bar Ga., Fed. Bar Assn. (dir. chpt. 1983-88), Fed. Ins. and Corp. Counsel, Def. Rsch. Inst., Internat. Assn. Def. Counsel, Order of Coif, Phi Kappa Phi. Office: Witt Gaither & Whitaker 736 Market St Chattanooga TN 37402-4807

CAMPBELL, PAUL BARTON, retired lawyer; b. Owosso, Mich., Feb. 24, 1930; s. George Wiley and Louise Marian (Pletke) C.; m. Joan Louise Brown, June 21, 1952 (div. 1974); children: Jane Louise, Paul Barton, James Wiley; m. Carol Marie Horning, Apr. 29, 1977 (dec. Oct. 1993); m. Beverly Bierbusse, May 26, 1994. BBA, U. Mich., 1951, MBA, 1954, JD, 1954. Bar: Ohio 1955, Mich 1955, Fla. 1978. Assoc. Squire, Sanders & Dempsey, Cleve., 1954-66, ptnr., 1966-96, counsel, 1996; sec. Ferro Corp., Cleve., 1970-95, bd. dirs., 1991-94; sec., bd. dirs. Shelby Paper Box, Cleve., 1980-93. Democrat. Home: 12700 Lake Ave Apt 1312 Cleveland OH 44107-1505*

CAMPBELL, PAUL GARY, lawyer; b. Lancaster, Pa., Aug. 2, 1965; s. Guy Erb and Daisy Marie (Sellers) C.; m. Melinda Kay Breidenbaugh, May 28, 1988; children: Faith Ann, Gregory Paul, Joy Melinda. BA in Polit. Sci., Millersville U. Pa., 1986; JD, Widener U., 1989. Bar: Pa. 1989. Law clk. to Hon. Richard H. Horn, York County Ct. Common Pleas for 19th Jud. Dist., York, Pa., 1989-90; assoc. Law Offices D. Patrick Zimmerman, Lancaster, 1991-93, Law Offices Michael J. Rostolsky, Lancaster, 1993-96; pvt. practice, Holtwood, Pa., 1997—. Photographer, firefighter, fin. sec. Pequea (Pa.) Vol. Fire Co., 1991—; supr. Martic Twp., Pequea, 1992-98. Mem. Lions (pres. Tucquan, Pa. 1994-95). Republican. Avocations: hunting, sports, woodworking, reading. Home: 168 Pinnacle Rd W Holtwood PA 17532-9673 Office: PO Box 148 Holtwood PA 17532-0148

CAMPBELL, POLLYANN S., lawyer; b. Zanesville, Ohio, Oct. 26, 1949; d. Walter Frederick and Ann Marie Stuenkel; m. John William Campbell II, Apr. 3, 1970 (div. Oct. 1990); children: Georgia Ann, John William III. BA cum laude, Shorter Coll., 1970; JD magna cum laude, Woodrow Wilson Coll. of Law, 1981. Bar: Ga. 1981, U.S. Dist. Ct. (no. dist.) Ga. 1981. Assoc. Lipshutz, Frankel, Greenblatt, King and Cohen, Atlanta, 1982-85; dist. underwriter, counsel Stewart Title Guaranty Co., Atlanta, 1985-87; state counsel Transamerica Title Ins. Co., Atlanta, 1987-90; appointed div. counsel Commonwealth Land Title Ins. Co. and Transamerica Title Ins. Co., Atlanta, 1990-96; apptd. Ga. State Coun., 1996—, asst. v.p., 1997—; presenter Ga. Real Estate Closing Attys. Assn. seminar, 1991, Commonwealth Land Title Ins. Co. seminar, 1992, other seminars. Editor-in-chief Woodrow Wilson Jour. Law, 1979-81. Mem. coun. Luth. Ch. of Nativity, Austell, Ga., 1982, 89-91, pres., 1990-91; mem. Rudisill Meml. Handbell Choir, 1987-96. Mem. ABA, Ga. Bar Assn., Atlanta Bar Assn., Am. Land Title Assn. (former state ct. mem. of judiciary com.). Office: Commonwealth Land Title Ins Co Transnation Title Ins Co 990 Hammond Dr NE Ste 770 Atlanta GA 30328-6176

CAMPBELL, R. NELSON, financial executive; b. Smyrna, Tenn., Oct. 24, 1964; s. Ralph and Dorothy (Anderson) C. BSBA, U. Ark., 1986. Fin. analyst Merrill Lynch Capital Mkts., N.Y.C., 1986-88; assoc. Nomura Securities Internat., N.Y.C., 1988-90; asst. v.p. mergers and acquisitions Daiwa Am. Strategic Advisors Corp., N.Y.C., 1990-92; v.p. bus. devel., treas. OsteoArthritis Scis., Inc., Cambridge, Mass., 1992-96; CFO EntreMed, Inc., 1997—. Vol. Habitat for Humanity, N.Y.C., 1989, Boston, 1992. Mem. Fin. Analysts Fedn., Inst. for Chartered Fin. Analysts, Assn. for Investment Mgmt. and Rsch., Licensing Execs. Soc., Profl. Assn. Diving Instrs. (divemaster), Delta Upsilon, Beta Gamma Sigma, Beta Alpha Psi, Omicron Delta Kappa. Republican. Office: Entre Inc 9640 Medical Center Dr Rockville MD 20850

CAMPBELL, RENODA GISELE, human resources administrator; b. L.A., May 4, 1963; d. Rumby D. and Margarete (Alexander) C. BA, Loyola Marymount U., L.A., 1985. Mgmt. exec. Direct Mgmt. Group, L.A., 1989-90, assoc. pers. mgr., 1991-98; label mgr. E Pluribus Unum Recordings, L.A., 1994-98; office mgr. World Wide Web Assocs., San Luis Obispo, Calif., 1998-99, human resources mgr., 1999—. Office: World Wide Web Assocs 225 Prado Rd San Luis Obispo CA 93401-7363

CAMPBELL, RICHARD ALDEN, electronics company executive; b. Bend, Oreg., July 31, 1926; s. Corlis Eugene and Lydia Amney (Peck) C.; m. Edna Mary Seaman, June 12, 1948; children: Stephen Alden, Douglas Niall (dec.), Carolyn Joyce. B.S. in Elec. Engring., U. Ill., 1949, M.S. in Elec. Engring., 1950. With TRW Inc., Redondo Beach, Calif., 1954-87, exec. v.p., 1979-87; bus. cons., profl. co. dir. Rolling Hills Estates, Calif., 1987—; bd. dirs. Novadyne Computer Systems, Inc. Patentee in radio communications. Bd. dirs. U. Ill. Found., Hugh O'Brian Youth Found. With USN, 1944-46. Recipient Alumni Honor award U. Ill. Coll. Engring. Mem. IEEE (life), Am. Electronics Assn. (pres. 1969, dir. 1970), Phi Kappa Phi, Tau Beta Pi, Eta Kappa Nu, Sigma Tau, Pi Mu Epsilon, Phi Eta Sigma, Rolling Hills Country Club, Rancheros Visitadores Club, Los Caballeros Club. Republican.

CAMPBELL, RICHARD BRUCE, lawyer; b. Phila., Jan. 5, 1947; s. George B. and Edith (Neithammer) C.; m. Patricia Ann James, Mar. 7, 1981; children: Ron Martin, Rebecca Joi. BA, U. S.C., 1968, JD, 1974. Bar: U.S. Dist. Ct. S.C. 1975, U.S. Ct. Appeals (4th cir.) 1976, U.S. Ct. Appeals (5th cir.) 1983, Colo. 1985, U.S. Dist. Ct. Colo. 1986, U.S. Ct. Appeals (fed. cir.) 1989, Fla. 1989, U.S. Dist. Ct. (mid. dist.) Fla., U.S. Ct. Appeals (11th cir.) 1992. Law clk. to presiding justice U.S. Dist. Ct., Columbia, S.C., 1975; ptnr. Henderson & Salley, Aiken, S.C., 1975-80; atty. TVA, Knoxville, 1980-85; ptnr. Wells, Love & Scoby, Boulder, Colo., 1986-89; shareholder Carlton, Fields, Ward, Emmanuel, Smith & Cutler, P.A., Tampa, Fla., 1989—; lectr. in field. Contbr. articles to profl. jours. Served to capt. USAF, 1968-72. Mem. ABA, Am. Arbitration Assn. (panelist), Fla. Bar Assn., Colo. Bar Assn., Hillsborough County Bar Assn. Avocations: travel, skiing, photography. Office: Carlton Fields Ward Emmanuel Smith & Cutler PC PO Box 3239 Tampa FL 33601-3239

CAMPBELL, RICHARD RICE, retired newspaper editor; b. Athens County, Ohio, Mar. 25, 1923; s. Arthur Donald and Marguerite (Rice) C.; m. Margaret Jandes, Feb. 9, 1946; children: Christopher, Constant. A.B. summa cum laude, Ohio U., 1947; M.A., Kent State U., 1977. With Cleve. Press, 1947-77, asst. city editor, 1959-62, chief editorial writer, 1962-66, assoc. editor, 1966-68, mng. editor, 1968-77; on leave Scripps-Howard Newspapers rep. to Newspaper Systems Devel. Group, 1975; editor Columbus (Ohio) Citizen-Jour., 1977-86; editorial promotion adv. Scripps Howard Newspapers, 1986-87; columnist Suburban Newspapers, 1989-94. Trustee Ohio U., 1985-93, Libr. Bd., Columbus, 1986-91; mem. Ohio Supreme Ct. Bd. Commrs. on Discipline, 1989-94. With AUS, 1943-46. Recipient Alumni award outstanding achievement journalism Ohio U., 1962, Carr Van Anda award, 1983. Mem. Sawmill Athletic Club, Scioto Country Club, Kit Kat Club, Torch Club (pres. 1992-93), Phi Beta Kappa, Sigma Delta Chi, Sigma Pi. Methodist. Home: 1243 Kenbrook Hills Dr Columbus OH 43220-4900

CAMPBELL, ROBERT, architect, writer; b. Buffalo, Mar. 31, 1937; s. R. Douglas and Amy (Armitage) C.; m. Janice Jaye Gold, Feb. 2, 1969 (div. 1990); 1 child, Nicholas. AB magna cum laude with highest honors, Harvard U., 1958, MArch, 1967; MS in Journalism, Columbia U., 1960. Registered architect, Mass. Writer, editor Parade mag., 1960-63; designer Benjamin Thompson Assocs., 1968-69; assoc. Sert Jackson & Assocs., 1967-75; architecture critic Boston Globe, 1973—; pvt. practice architecture Cambridge, Mass., 1975—; cons. Am. Acad. Arts and Scis., Whitehead Inst., Boston Symphony Orch., Mayors Inst. for City Design, City of San Francisco; lectr. in field; mem. vis. faculty U. N.C. Sch. Architecture, Charlotte, 1979-94; Sam Gibbons Eminent scholar, U. South Fla.; vis. scholar MIT, 1991-94; artist-in-residence Am. Acad. Rome, 1997. Author: Cityscapes of Boston: An American City Through Time; contbg. editor Architectural Record mag., Preservation mag.; contbr. articles to profl. jours.; published poet, photographer. Mem. adv. bd. U. Va. Sch. Architecture; mem. Mid-Cambridge Neighborhood Assn.; propr. Boston Athenaeum. Recipient Francis Kelley prize, 1967; named Julia Amory Appleton traveling fellow, 1967, Nat. Endowment for Arts design fellow, 1975; grantee Graham Found., 1991; recipient Pulitzer Prize for criticism, 1996. Fellow AIA (nat. design com., medal for criticism 1980), Am. Acad. Arts and Scis.; mem. Boston Archtl. Ctr. (hon. life), Boston Soc. Architects, Am. Archtl. Found. (bd. regents), Cambridge Club, St. Botolph Club, Tavern Club, Examiner Club, Century Assn. (N.Y.C.), Saturday Club, Phi Beta Kappa. Democrat. Address: 54 Antrim St Cambridge MA 02139-1102

CAMPBELL, ROBERT AYERST, accounting company executive; b. Montreal, Que., Can., July 15, 1940; s. James Kenneth and Doris Victoria (Ayerst) C.; m. Cynthia Abbey, Aug. 17, 1963; children: Colin Ayerst, David Arthur, Sarah Reid. BBA, Clarkson U., 1961; MBA, U. Colo., 1966. CPA. Staff acct. Touche Ross, Montreal, 1961-63; mgr. Touche Ross, Rochester, N.Y., 1968-75; ptnr.-in-charge Touche Ross Internat., Tokyo, 1975-78; audit ptnr.-in-charge Touche Ross, Milw., 1978-82; mng. ptnr. Touche Ross, Dallas, 1982-90; exec. dir. internat. Deloitte & Touche LLP U.S., Wilton, Conn., 1990-95; Asia Pacific regional mng. ptnr. Deloitte Touche Tohmatsu Internat., 1995—, exec. com., 1995—; bd. dirs. Deloitte & Touche LLP U.S.A.; asst. dir. admissions Clarkson U., Potsdam, N.Y., 1963-65, instr. acctg., 1966-68. Treas., dir. Am. Sch. in Japan, Tokyo, 1976-78;. Mem. AICPA, Tex. Soc. CPAs, Beta Gamma Sigma, Beta Alpha Pi, Milw. Country Club, Dallas Club, Genessee Valley Club. Republican. Presbyterian. Home: 37 Granite Way Grantham NH 03753-0482 Office: Deloitte & Touches Ten Westport Rd Wilton CT 06897-0820

CAMPBELL, ROBERT CHARLES, minister, theology educator; b. Chandler, Ariz., Mar. 9, 1924; s. Alexander Joshua and Florence (Betzner) C.; m. Lotus Idamae Graham, July 12, 1945; children: Robin Carl, Cherry Colleen. AB, Westmont Coll., 1944; BD, Eastern Baptist Theol. Sem., 1947, ThM, 1949, ThD, 1951, DD (hon.), 1974; MA, U. So. Calif., 1959; postgrad., Dropsie U., 1949-51, U. Pa., 1951-52, NYU, 1960-62, U. Cambridge, Eng., 1969; DLitt (hon.), Am. Bapt. Sem. of West, 1972; HHD (hon.), Alderson-Broaddus Coll., 1979; LHD (hon.), Linfield Coll., 1982; LLD (hon.), Franklin Coll., 1986. Ordained to ministry Am. Bapt. Ch., 1947; pastor 34th St. Bapt. Ch., Phila., 1945-49; instr. Eastern Bapt. Theol. Sem., Phila., 1949-51; asst. prof. Eastern Coll., St. Davids, Pa., 1951-53; assoc. prof. N.T. Am. Bapt. Sem. of West, Covina, Cal., 1953-54, dean, prof., 1954-72; gen. sec. Am. Bapt. Chs. in U.S.A., Valley Forge, Pa., 1972-87; pres. Eastern Bapt. Theol. Sem., Phila., 1987-89, ret.; Vis. lectr. Sch. Theology at Claremont, Calif., 1961-63, U. Redlands, Calif., 1959-60, 66-67, Fuller Theology Seminary, Calif., 1992-97; Bd. mgrs. Am. Bapt. Bd. of Edn. and Publ., 1956-59, 65-69; v.p. So. Calif. Bapt. Conv., 1967-68; pres. Am. Bapt. Chs. of Pacific S.W., 1970-71; Pres. N.Am. Bapt. Fellowship, 1974-76; mem. exec. com. Bapt. World Alliance, 1972-90, v.p., 1975-80; mem. exec. com., gov. bd. Nat. Council Chs. of Christ in U.S.A., 1972-87; del. to World Council of Chs., 1975, 83, mem. central com., 1975-90. Author: Great Words of the Faith, 1965, The Gospel of Paul, 1973, Evangelistic Emphases in Ephesians, Jesus Still Has Something To Say, 1987. Home: 125 Via Alicia Santa Barbara CA 93108-1769

CAMPBELL, ROBERT DAVID, minerals and metals executive; b. Teaneck, N.J., May 5, 1947; s. Robert Wesley and Phyllis May Julich; m. Elizabeth I. Young, June 15, 1978; 1 child, Ariel. BS, Syracuse U., 1969. Trader C. Tennant Sons & Co., N.Y.C., 1969-73, Cargill, N.Y.C., 1974-75; mng. dir. Amalgamated Metal Corp., Zug, Switzerland, 1975-79; pres. Amalgamet Inc., N.Y.C., 1978-80; v.p. Samincorp Inc., N.Y.C., 1980-84; pres. RST Resources, Inc., N.Y.C., 1984-93; pres., CEO Global Minerals & Metals Corp., N.Y.C., 1993—. Mem. N.Y. Copper Club, Metropolitan Club, Cannon Point South (dir. 1983-95). Avocations: tennis, scuba, sailing, skiing. Home: 45 Sutton Pl S New York NY 10022-2444

CAMPBELL, ROBERT EMMETT, retired health care products company executive; b. Passaic, N.J., 1933. Grad., Fordham U., 1955, Rutgers U., 1962. Vice chmn., dir. Johnson & Johnson, New Brunswick, N.J.; ret., 1995. Chmn. bd. trustees Fordham U., 1992-98, Robert Wood Johnson Found., 1999—; chmn. bd. dirs. Cancer Inst. N.J., 1995—. Home: 40 Lake Dr New Brunswick NJ 08902-4830

CAMPBELL, ROBERT HEDGCOCK, investment banker, lawyer; b. Ann Arbor, Mich., Jan. 16, 1948; s. Robert Miller and Ruth Adele (Hedgcock) C.; m. Katherine Kettering, June 17, 1972; children: Mollie DuPlan, Katherine Elizabeth, Anne Kettering. BA, U. Wash., 1970, JD, 1973. Bar. Wash. 1973, Wash. State Supreme Ct. 1973, Fed. 1973, U.S. Dist. Ct. (we. dist.) Wash. 1973, Ct. Appeals (9th cir.) 1981. Assoc. Roberts & Shefelman, Seattle, 1973-78, ptnr., 1978-85; sr. v.p. Lehman Bros., Inc., Seattle, 1985-87, mng. dir., 1987—; bd. dirs. Pogo Producing Co.; dir., treas. Nat. Assn. Bd. Lawyers, Hinsdale, Ill., 1982-85; pres., trustee Wash. State Soc. Hosp. Attys., Seattle, 1982-85; mem. econs. dept. vis. com. U. Wash., 1995-97; mem. Law Sch. dean's adv. bd. U. Wash., 1999—. Contbr. articles to profl. jours. Trustee Bellevue (Wash.) Schs. Found., 1988-91, pres., 1989-90; nation chief Bellevue Eastside YMCA Indian Princess Program, 1983-88; trustee Wash. Phikeia Found., 1983-91, Sandy Hook Yacht Club Estates, Inc., 1993-98; mem. Wash. Gov.'s Food Processing Coun., 1990-91. Republican. Avocations: skiing, wind surfing, bike riding, physical fitness, golf. Home: 8604 NE 10th St Medina WA 98039-3915 Office: Lehman Bros Columbia Seafirst Ctr 701 5th Ave Ste 7101 Seattle WA 98104-7016

CAMPBELL, RONALD NEIL, magazine designer; b. Morristown, N.J., Mar. 7, 1926; s. Carroll Francis and Emily Ruth (Peters) C.; m. Jule Gallina, Sept. 22, 1956; 1 son, Bruce G. B.F.A., R.I. Sch. Design, 1951. With Fortune mag., N.Y.C., 1952-82; art dir. Fortune mag., 1974-82; freelance writer Sports Illustrated, CASE Currents, Graphis mag.; freelance graphic designer, lectr., 1951—; mem. adv. bd. Internat. Editorial Design Forum; design cons. Harvard Mag., 1985-95, Harvard Bus. Rev., 1987-90. Served with USNR, 1944-46. Recipient merit awards Art Dirs. Club N.Y., merit awards Communication Arts Mag., merit awards Art Direction Mag., Page One award Am. Newspaper Guild, 2 Silver awards Editorial Design Forum. Mem. Soc. Illustrators (Gold and Silver medals), Am. Inst. Graphic Arts (merit awards), Soc. Publ. Designers (hon. bd. dirs., merit awards), Univ. and Coll. Designers Assn., U.S.S. Bon Homme Richard Assn. Home: 37 Barton Rd Flemington NJ 08822-5929 Office: 136 Waverly Pl Apt 8A New York NY 10014-6822

CAMPBELL, SCOTT ROBERT, lawyer, former food company executive; b. Burbank, Calif., June 7, 1946; s. Robert Clyde and Jenevieve Anne (Olsen) C.; m. Teresa Melanie Mack, Oct. 23, 1965; 1 son, Donald Steven. BA, Claremont Men's Coll., 1970; JD, Cornell U., 1973. Bar: Ohio 1973, U.S. Dist. Ct. (so. dist.) Ohio 1974, Minn. 1976, Calif. 1989, U.S. Dist. Ct. (no. dist.) Calif. 1989, U.S. Ct. Appeals (9th cir.) 1989, U.S. Dist. Ct. (cen. and so. dists.) Calif. 1990, U.S. Ct. Appeals (5th cir.) 1991, U.S. Tax Ct. 1991. Assoc. Taft, Stettinius & Hollister, Cin., 1973-76; atty. Mpls. Star & Tribune, 1976-77; sr. v.p., gen. counsel, sec. Kellogg Co., Battle Creek, Mich., 1977-89; ptnr. Furth Fahrner Mason, San Francisco, 1989—; U.S. del. ILO Food and Beverage Conf., Geneva, 1984; participant, presenter first U.S.-USSR Legal Seminar, Moscow, 1988; speaker other legal seminars. Mem. ABA, Ohio Bar Assn., Minn. Bar Assn., Calif. Bar. Assn. Office: Furth Fahrner & Mason 1000 Furth Bldg 201 Sansome St San Francisco CA 94104-2303

CAMPBELL, SELAURA JOY, lawyer; b. Oklahoma City, Mar. 25, 1944; d. John Moore III and Gyda (Hallum) C. AA, Stephens Coll., 1963; BA, U. Okla., 1965; MEd, Chapel Hill U., 1974; JD, N.C. Cen. U., 1978; postgrad. atty. mediation courses, South Tex. Sch. of Law, Houston, 1991, Atty. Mediators Inst./Dallas, Dallas, 1992. Bar: Ariz 1983; lic. real estate broker, N.C.; cert. tchr. N.C. With flight svc. dept. Pan Am. World Airways, N.Y.C., 1966-91; lawyer Am. Women's Legal Clinic, Phoenix, 1987; charter mem. Sony Corp. Indsl. Mgmt. Seminar, 1981; guest del. Rep. Nat. Conv., Houston, 1992; judge all-law sch. mediation competition for Tex., South Tex. Sch. Law, Houston, 1994. Mem. N.C. Cen. U. Law Rev., 1977-78. People-to-People del. People's Republic of China, 1987; guest del. Rep. Nat. Conv., Houston, 1992. Mem. Ariz. Bar Assn., Humane Soc. U.S., Nat. Wildlife Fedn., People for the Ethical Treatment of Animals, Amnesty Internat., Phi Alpha Delta. Republican. Episcopalian. Avocations: climbed Mt. Kilimanjaro, 1983, also Machu Pichu, Peru, Mt Kenya, Africa, horseback riding, photography. Home: 206 Taft Ave Cleveland TX 77327-4539

CAMPBELL, STANLEY RICHARD, library services director; b. Oneida, Ky., Mar. 4, 1949; s. Pearl Campbell and Virginia Joe (Burks) Smith; m. Donna Carol Estridge, Mar. 15, 1975; children: Jennifer Andrea, Ian Mathew. BA, Berea Coll., 1972; MA, U. Ky., 1976, MSLS, 1977. Reference libr. Centre Coll., Danville, Ky., 1977-81, dir. libr. svcs., 1981—; mem. steering com. Coun. Ind. Ky. Colls. and Univs., Lexington, Ky., 1984-92; pres. Ky. Libr. Network, Frankfort, Ky., 1988-89. Mem. sch. coun. Jennie Rogers Sch., Danville, 1992—; bd. dirs. West T-Hill Cmty. Theatre, Danville, 1988—, pres. 1994—. Mem. ALA, Ky. Libr. Assn. (chmn. acad. divsn. 1986-87). Avocations: acting, directing. Home: 461 Fitzpatrick St Danville KY 40422-1635 Office: Centre Coll Grace Doherty Library 600 W Walnut St Danville KY 40422-1309*

CAMPBELL, STEWART CLAWSON, retired sales executive, artist; b. Salt Lake City, Aug. 18, 1903; s. Alexander Stewart and Alice Young (Clawson) C.; m. Mary M. McIntyre, June 27, 1942 (dec. July 1983); children: Stewart, Jeffrey, David (dec.), James, Scott, Judith. Student, U. Utah, 1928-31. Pres. Mormon Mission Conf., Dresden, Germany, 1924-28; surveyor Wasatch Gas Co., Salt Lake City, 1928-31, United Gas Sys., Houston, 1931-32; warehouse supr. Maceys Dept. Store, N.Y.C., 1932-35; overseer Alaska Rural Rehab. Corp., Palmer, 1935-39; regional adminstr. Nat. Youth Adminstrn., Cleve., 1939-41; spl. asst. Fed. Civil Def. Emergency Adminstrn., Washington, 1941-42; pres. Utah Wonderland Stages, Salt Lake City, 1946-51; regional adminstr. Fed. Civil Def. Adminstrn., 1952-56; gen. sales mgr. O.C. Tanner Co., Salt Lake City, 1956-75; ret., 1975. One-man shows include Wilma Wayne Gallery, London; maker Petrohlyphs replicas (ancient Indian images in stone), Galerie Royal, Paris, 1984; conceived (new art form) Tower-Mosaic for Human Rights Space Movement and Tower: Mosaic; proposed meml. to Am.'s ten pioneer astronaut heroes; originator of painting with fire art form. Lt. col. USAF, 1942-46. Named to Hon. Order of Ky. Colonels, 1953. Mem. LDS Ch. Avocations: reading, alpine skiing, ice skating, ballroom and contemporary dancing. Home: Apt 10 A 777 E South Temple Salt Lake City UT 84102-1274

CAMPBELL, STEWART FRED, foundation executive; b. St. Louis, June 29, 1931; s. Archibald Stewart and Charlotte (Ehrmann) C.; m. Ann Abbey Hudson, Dec. 18, 1954; children: Karen Ann, Deborah Ann. B.S., Lehigh U., Bethlehem, Pa., 1954; M.B.A., NYU, 1961. With Mfrs. Hanover Trust Co., N.Y.C., 1958-64; asst. sec. Mfrs. Hanover Trust Co., 1962-64; with Duke Endowment, N.Y.C., 1964-79, asst. treas., 1967-73, treas., 1973-79; sec.-treas. Alfred P. Sloan Found., N.Y.C., 1979-86, fin. v.p., sec., 1986—; treas. Doris Duke Trust, 1973-79, Angler B. Duke Meml., Inc., 1973-79, Nanaline H. Duke Fund, 1973-79; asst. treas. Duke Power Co., 1968-75; bd. dirs. Pocono Hotels Corp., 1992—, v.p., 1993-95, chmn. bd., 1995—. Treas. Essex unit N.J. Assn. Retarded Children, 1967-72, trustee, 1966-74; trustee Meml. Home of Upper Montclair, 1987-96, pres., 1990-95. Mem. Delta Phi. Clubs: Rockefeller Center (N.Y.C.); Montclair Golf; Skytop (Pa.). Home: 3 Wendover Rd Montclair NJ 07042-3031

CAMPBELL, SUSAN CARRIGG, secondary education educator; b. Copaigue, N.Y., Dec. 8, 1946; d. Richard Carrigg and Mildred Josephine (Schneider) C. BS cum laude, SUNY, Oswego, 1968; MA, Adelphi U., 1992. Cert. secondary tchr., N.Y. Tchr. Brentwood (N.Y.) Pub. Schs., 1968—; co-developer learning skills program Brentwood (N.Y.) Pub. Schs., 1985-89, co-chairperson sch. improvement team, 1990-92, 93-94, 95, mem. summer curriculum writing project, 1993, adv. program com., 1993-94, conflict resolution trainee, 1994; adv. Student Leaders Club, Brentwood, N.Y., 1991; coord. Art Enrichment Show, 1986-91. Named Tchr. of Yr. Brentwood East Mid. Sch. PTA, 1995-96. Mem. L.I. Coun. Social Studies, Brentwood Tchrs. Assn., Kappa Delta Pi, Pi Gamma Mu. Democrat. Lutheran. Avocations: reading, walking beaches, gardening.

CAMPBELL, TALMAGE ALEXANDER, newspaper editor; b. Big Spring, Tex., Dec. 1, 1939; s. Thomas L. and Wanda (Mayfield) C.; m. Karen Sue Morris, May 13, 1967; 1 child, Robert. BA, Pepperdine U., 1961. Reporter, news editor The News-Advertiser, L.A., 1958-65; reporter, photographer The Daily Breeze, Torrance, Calif., 1965-72, asst. city editor, city editor, 1972-81; mng. editor The Beacon-News, Aurora, Ill., 1981-90, exec. editor, 1990-91; mng. editor The News-Herald, Willoughby, Ohio, 1991-93, exec. editor, 1993—. Trustee Lincoln Christian Coll. Mem. Am. Soc. Newspaper Editors, Cleve. Press Club, Mentor Rotary Club. Mem. Ch. Christ. Avocation: biblical history. Office: The News-Herald 7085 Mentor Ave Willoughby OH 44094-7900

CAMPBELL, TENA, judge; b. Wendell, Idaho, Dec. 11, 1944. BA, U. Idaho, 1967; MA in French Lit. with honors, Ariz. State U., 1970, JD, 1977. Bar: Utah 1977, U.S. Dist. Ct. Utah 1977, U.S. Ct. Appeals (10th cir.) 1982. Tchr. French Twin Falls (Idaho) Sch. Dist., 1967-69, Tempe (Ariz.) H.S., Phoenix Jr. Coll., 1972-73; assoc. atty. Johnson Durham and Moxley, Salt Lake City, 1977-79, Fabian and Clendenin, Salt Lake City, 1979-81; dep. county atty. Salt Lake County, Salt Lake City, 1981; asst. U.S. atty. criminal divsn. Office of U.S. Atty. Dist. Utah, 1981-95; judge U.S. Dist. Ct. Utah, 1995—. Mem. Utah Bar Assn., Ft. Douglas HIdden Valley Country Club. Office: US Dist Ct Utah Rm 235 US Ct House 350 S Main St Salt Lake City UT 84101-2106*

CAMPBELL, THOMAS CORWITH, JR., economics educator; b. Enfield, Va., Mar. 19, 1920; s. Thomas Corwith and Pearl (Gravatt) C.; m. Burdine Gordon, Apr. 17, 1943; children—Thomas Corwith III, Maxwell Gordon. A.B., Lynchburg Coll., 1942; M.A., U. Pitts., 1947, Ph.D., 1948; student, U. Wis., summer 1947. Mem. faculty W.Va. U., 1948—, asst. to assoc. prof., 1948-58; asst. dean Coll. Commerce, 1955-64, prof., 1958-80, dean, 1964-68; vis. prof. Va. Commonwealth U., 1980-91. Contbr. articles to profl. jours. Adviser to Ministry of Econ. Planning and Devel. Govt. of Kenya, 1968-70; economist U.S. Bur. Mines, 1974-77, Dept. of Energy, 1977—; Chmn. Gov.'s Council Econ. Advisers, 1963-65; mem. Charleston Regional Export Expansion Council, 1964—. Served to lt. USNR, 1942-46; capt. Res. Mem. Am. Econ. Assn., AAUP, Soc. Cincinnati, Beta Gamma Sigma. Mem. Christian Ch. Home: 4014 Fauquier Ave Richmond VA 23227-4040

CAMPBELL, THOMAS DOUGLAS, lawyer, consultant; b. N.Y.C., Jan. 5, 1951; s. Edward Thomas and Dorothy Alice (Moore) C.; m. Mary Anne Makin, Dec. 22, 1978; 1 child, Kristen Anne. BA, U. Del., 1972; JD, U. Pa., 1976. Bar: Del. 1977. Law clk. Law Offices Bayard Brill & Handleman, Wilmington, Del., 1974-77; govt. affairs rep. Northeastern U.S. Std. Oil Co. Ind., 1977-78; Washington rep. Std. Oil Co., Ind., 1978-85; pres. Thomas D. Campbell and Assocs., Inc., Alexandria, Va., 1985—; govt. affairs rep. Northeastern U.S., Std. Oil Co. Ind., 1977-78. With U.S. Army, 1968-69, Del. Air N.G., 1969-77. Mem. ABA, Del. Bar Assn., Congl. Awards Found. (chmn. bd. dirs.), Phi Beta Kappa, Phi Kappa Phi, Omicron Delta Epsilon, Omicron Delta Kappa. Republican. Episcopalian. Home: 517 Queen St Alexandria VA 22314-2512 also: 300-30 Great Cruz Bay Rd Saint John VI Office: 517 Queen St Alexandria VA 22314-2512

CAMPBELL, THOMAS EMORY, author, researcher; b. Greensboro, Ga., June 9, 1935; s. Joseph Emory and Mary Lou (Brake) C. BA, Mercer U., 1957. Actor, dir. Henry St. Playhouse, N.Y.C., 1965-69, Flat Rock Playhouse, N.C., 1970-73; pres. JM Emory Pub., Greensboro, 1994-97; writer Franklin Chronicle, 1997—. Author: The Burning of Greensboro, 1994; appearances include Actors Equity, N.Y.C., 1967-72; dir. Hilton Head (S.C.) Playhouse, 1973-75. With USAF, 1959-63. Democrat. Baptist. Avocations: hiking, swimming, dancing, gardening. Home: PO Box 451 Carrabelle FL 32322-0451

CAMPBELL, THOMAS J., chiropractor, legislator; b. Bklyn., Oct. 27, 1954; s. Charles Marvin and Edna Mary (Sacer) C.; m. C. Lynn Hearn, July 2, 1983. AA in Social Scis., Fla. Tech. U., 1974; BA in Police Sci. and Adminstrn., Seattle U., 1977; DC, Life Chiropractic Coll., 1983; postgrad. in orthopedics, L.A. Chiropractic Coll., 1984-90. Diplomate Am. Acad. Pain Mgmt.; cert. chiropractic rehab. dr. Nat. Bd. Chiropractic Examiners-Physiotherapy; lic. chiropractor, Wash., Fla. Pvt. practice Chiropractic Spinal Care, Inc., 1984—. Mem. Wash. State Ho. of Reps., 1993-96, 99-2000. With inf. U.S. Army, 1977-79, capt. USAR/ARNG, 1979-85. Recipient Appreciation for Svc. award Chiropractic Disciplinary Bd., 1989-93, Gov. Appreciation Certificate Wash. State Disciplinary Bd. Fellow Internat. Coll. of Chiropractors; mem. Am. Chiropractic Assn. (alt. del. House of Dels. 1988-92), Wash. State Chiropractic Assn. (chmn. mem. com. 1984-85, dist. 4A 1985-86, dir. exec. bd. 1985-88, v. chmn. disciplinary bd. 1990-93, pres. award outstanding achievement in the mem. com. 1985, legislative affairs com. 1986, Dist. of the Yr. award 1985-86, named Chiropractor of the Yr. 1987, 89, 90, 91, Appreciation award for outstanding svc to the profession, 1994, Exceptional Svc. award 1994), Fla. Chiropractic Assn., Pierce County Chiropractic Assn., Chiropractic Rehabilitation Assn. (bd. dirs.), Elks (Tacoma Lodge # 174), Am. Legion. Republican. Avocations: scuba diving, boating, fishing. E-mail: Campbell @qa.net. Home: PO Box 443 Spanaway WA 98387-0443

CAMPBELL, THOMAS J., congressman; b. Chgo., Aug. 14, 1952; s. William J. and Marie Campbell; m. Susanne Martin. BA, MA in Econs. with highest honors, U. Chgo., 1973, PhD in Econs. with highest dept. fellowship, 1980; JD magna cum laude, Harvard U., 1976. Law clk. to presiding justice U.S. Ct. Appeals (D.C. cir.), 1976-77; law clk. to Justice Byron R. White U.S. Supreme Ct., Washington, 1977-78; assoc. Winston & Strawn, Chgo., 1978-80; White Ho. fellow Office Chief of Staff and White Ho. of Counsel, Washington, 1980-81; exec. asst. to dep. atty. gen. Dept. Justice, Washington, 1981; dir. Bur. Trade Competition FTC, Washington, 1981-83, head del. to OECD, Paris, com. experts on restictive bus. practices, 1982, 83; mem. 101st-105th Congresses from Calif. 12th Dist., 1989-92; mem. com. on sci., space and tech., com. on judiciary, banking, fin. and urban affairs 101st Congress from Calif. 12th Dist., 1989-92; mem. 104th - 105th Congress (now 106th Congress) from Calif. 15th Dist., 1995—; prof. Stanford Law Sch., 1983-89; mem. Congressional Com. on Banking and Fin. Svcs., 1997—, Internat. Rels., 1997—. Referee Jour. Polit. Economy, Internat. Rev. Law and Econs. Mem. San Francisco Com. on Fgn. Relations. Mem. ABA (antitrust sect., coun. 1985-88, program chmn. 1983-84). Office: US Ho of Reps 2442 Rayburn House Office Bldg Washington DC 20515-0515

CAMPBELL, TIMOTHY REID, financial services company executive; b. Sparta, Ill., Apr. 25, 1946; s. Floyd and Dorothy Mae (Patton) C.; m. Sara Lou Claussen, Apr. 18, 1970; children: Timothy Scott, Catherine Elizabeth. AB, MacMurray Coll, 1968; postgrad., U. Ill., 1968-69, U. Hartford, 1972; MA in Adminstrn., U. Ill. at Springfield, 1975; grad., Pub. Affairs Inst., 1995. Legis. staff intern Ill. State Senate, Springfield, 1968-69, appropriations staff, 1969-71; project dir. Eagleton Inst. Politics, Hartford, Conn., 1971-73, Rutgers U., New Brunswick, N.J., 1971-73; asst. to Senate pres. Ill. State Senate, Springfield, 1973-75, staff dir. Rep., 1975-78; asst. v.p. govt. rels. Aetna Life & Casualty, Hartford, 1979-87; v.p. govt. affairs Travelers Ins. Cos., Hartford, 1987-94; v.p. govt. rels. Travelers Group, N.Y., 1994-96, v.p. state govt. rels., 1996-98; sr. v.p., dir. state govt. rels. divsn. Citigroup, 1998—; bd. dirs. Ins. Fedn. Pa.; mem. exec. com. Nat. Conf. State Legislatures, Denver, 1976-78; chair governing bd. Manifesto Ins. Group, Tallahassee, Fla., 1992-98. Chmn. Farmington Valley YMCA, Simsbury, Conn., 1992-93, dir. 1987-93; chmn. Rep. Town Com., Canton, Conn., 1982-88; trustee MacMurray Coll., Jacksonville, Ill., 1976-83, 94-99; dir. Sci. Mus. Conn., West Hartford, 1994, 97—; apptd. by gov. to Conn. Adv.Commn. on Intergovtl. Rels., 1996—; trustee Conn. Policy and Econ. Coun., 1996—. Inducted into Samuel K. Gove Ill. Legis. Internship Hall of Fame, 1995. Mem. Am. Soc. Pub. Adminstrn., Ins. Assn. Conn. (mem. exec. com. 1987—, chmn. exec. com. 1993-94). Avocations: reading, travel. Home: 2 Orchard Hill Rd Canton CT 06019-2129 Office: 1 Tower Sq Hartford CT 06183-0001

CAMPBELL, WILBUR HAROLD, research plant biochemist, educator; b. Santa Ana, Calif., Apr. 23, 1945; s. Russell Carton and Vivian (Yates) C.; m. Ellen Roth, June 6, 1981. AA, Santa Ana Coll., 1965; BA, Pomona Coll., 1967; PhD, U. Wis., 1972. Postdoctoral U. Ga., Athens, 1972-73, Mayo Clinic, Rochester, Minn., 1973-74, Mich. State U., East Lansing, 1974-75; asst. prof. Coll. Environ. Sci. and Forestry. SUNY, Syracuse, 1975-80, assoc. prof., 1980-85; assoc. prof. Mich. Technol. U., Houghton, 1985-86, prof., 1986—, adj. prof. Dept. Chemistry and Chem. Engring, 1990—, coord. Pytotech. Rsch. Ctr., 1990—; pres. & CEO The Nitrate Elimination Co., Inc.; guest prof. Botanisches Inst., U. Bayreuth, Fed. Republic Germany, 1982; vis. scientist Molecular Biology Computer Rsch. Resource Harvard U., 1987; vis. prof. U. Stockholm, 1991-92; vis. scholar various Japanese Univs., 1995. Mem. editorial bd. Plant Physiology, 1982-92, editor: Plant Physiology, 1994—; contbr. numerous articles to profl. jours. Recipient Excellence in Rsch. award Mich. Tech. U., 1988, Disting. Faculty award Mich. U. Bd. Govs., 1989; Underwood fellow John Innes Centre Norwich, Eng., 1998. Fellow Japan Soc. for Promotion Sci; mem. AAAS, Am. Chem. Soc., Protein Soc., Am. Soc. of Plant Physiologists, Am. Soc. Agronomy/Crop Sci. Soc. Am., Japanese Soc. Plant Physiologists, Plant Growth Regulator Soc. Am., N.Y. Acad. Sci., Internat. Soc. for Plant Molecular Biology, Scandinavian Soc. Plant Physiology, France Soc. Plant Physiology, Sigma Xi. Home: 334 Hecla St Lake Linden MI 49945-1323

CAMPBELL, WILL DAVIS, writer; b. Miss., July 18, 1924; s. Lee Webb Campbell and Hancie Bea Parker; m. Brenda Rita Fisher, 1946; children: Penny Elizabeth, Bonnie Ruth, Lee Webb II. Student, La. Coll., Pineville, 1941-42; AB, Wake Forest U., 1948, HHD (hon.), 1984; student, Tulane U., 1948-49; BDiv, Yale U., 1952; LittD (hon.), U. of the South, Sewanee, Tenn., 1993; HHD (hon.), Mercer U., 1996. Author: Brother to a Dragonfly, 1977 (named 1 of 10 books of 1970's worthy of surviving, Time Mag., 1 of best books of 1977, N.Y. Times, finalist Nat. Book award, Christopher award, Lillian Smith prize), The Glad River, 1982 (1st prize for fiction Friends of Am. Writers), Providence, 1993, The Stem of Jesse, 1995, And Also With You, 1997. Recipient Lyndhurst prize, 1980, Alex Haley Meml. award, 1992, Tenn. Gov.'s award for the arts, 1994, Gov.'s Humanities award, 1995, Lifetime Achievement award Tenn. ACLU, 1997, The Richard Wright prize, 1998.

CAMPBELL, WILLIAM, research analyst, educator. Student, Bryn Mawr Conservatory Music, 1984-86. Print shop asst. Independence Hall Nat. Park, Phila., 1986; vis. instr. Gifted Opportunity Ctr., Lynchburg, Va., 1997; rsch. analyst The Beckley Found., 1998—; instr. Fellowship Christian Acad., Madison Heights, Va., 1997—, Gifted and Talented Devel. Ctr., Charlotte, N.C., summer 1998. Alt. del. Rep. Nat. Conv., San Diego, 1996; vice-chmn. Campbell County (Va.) Rep. Com., 1996, 98—, chmn., 1996-98; legis. dist. chmn. 22nd Dist. Rep. Com., 1997-98. Recipient Cert. of Recognition, Gov. Va., Richmond, 1997. Mem. Nat. Assn. for Gifted Children. Episcopalian. Avocations: scrabble, military history, polo.

CAMPBELL, WILLIAM AUBREY, law educator; b. Springfield, Mo., Mar. 30, 1940; s. Aubrey and Clastel (Richardson) C.; m. Lynnette Humphreys, June 29 1963; children: Alistair, Anne, Katherine. BA, Rhodes Coll., 1962; LLB, Vanderbilt U., 1965. Bar: N.C. 1976. Asst. prof. U. N.C., Chapel Hill, 1965-66, assoc. prof., 1969-74, prof. pub. law and govt., 1974-91, Gladys Hall Coates prof. pub. law govt., 1991—; mem. com. on contraceptive rsch. NAS, Washington, 1988-90. Author: Property Tax Collection, 1988, Guidebook for North Carolina Registers, 1994, (with others) Healthcare Facilities Law, 1991. Bd. dirs., pres. Conservation Trust for N.C., Raleigh, 1992—. Lt. USN, 1966-69. Mem. N.C. Bar Assn. (coun. real property sect. 1994-97). Democrat. Presbyterian. Office: U NC Chapel Hill Inst Govt CB 3330 Knapp Bldg Chapel Hill NC 27599-3330

CAMPBELL, WILLIAM BUFORD, JR., materials engineer, chemist, forensic consultant; b. Clarksdale, Miss., Nov. 23, 1935; s. William Buford and Bertha Lucille (Atkins) C.; m. Joan E. Stakem, June 29, 1963 (div. 1983); children: Lisa Anne, William Buford II, Heather Katherine, Matthew Rush (dec.). B in Ceramic Engring., Ga. Inst. Tech., 1958, MS in Engring., 1960; AM in Mineralogy, Inorganic Chemistry, Harvard U., 1962; PhD in Materials Engring., Ohio State U., 1967; postgrad., MIT, 1963-65, Ohio State U., 1969-72, NYU, 1980. Registered profl. engr., Ga., Ala. Asst. prof. dept. ceramic engring. Ohio State U., Columbus, 1967-69, assoc. prof., 1969-74; chief biomed. engring. dept. Doctor's Hosp., Morristown, Tenn., 1974-76; assoc. prof. engring. sci. and mechanics U. Tenn., Knoxville, 1974-77; sr. ptnr. Campbell, Churchill, Zimmerman & Assocs., Cons., Knoxville, 1977-84; cons., pvt. practice Biomed. Engring. and Forensic Sci., Knoxville, 1984—; adj. prof. Coll. Applied Sci., East Tenn. State U., 1998—; ptnr. Brae Arden Farms Ltd., Phila., Tenn., 1979-83, tech. dir., chief exec. officer Southeastern Mobility Co., Inc., Phila., Tenn., 1977-84; founder Biomed. Systems Inc., Knoxville, 1986; project engr. TVA, 1987-89; dir. EPRI Ctr. for Materials Fabrication, Battelle Meml. Inst., Columbus, Ohio, 1989-90, dir., program mgr. Innovation and Tech. Transfer, Battelle Meml. Inst., Columbus, 1990; mng. ptnr. Performance Cons., Knoxville, Tenn., 1991—. Patentee: Holds 3 U.S. Patents; contbr. articles to profl. jours. Mem. Adminstrv. Bd. Bearden United Meth. Ch., 1982-85; chmn. exec. com. The Ch. of the Redeemer, Concord, Tenn., 1985-87; mem. fin. com. Americans for Responsible Govt, 1984-85, fin. com. 50th Am. Presidential Inaugural, 1984-85, Nat. Adv. Bd. on Tech. and the Disabled; trustee Lakeshore Mental Health Insts., Dept. Mental Health, State of Tenn., 1986—; bd. dirs. Direct Braille Slate Fund, 1998—, Vols. of Am., Knoxville, 1987-90, Tenn. Tech. Devel. Corp., 1998—, Hist. Tenn. Theater Found., 1997—; mem. adv. bd. Knoxville Mus. Art, 1987-88; mem. Tenn. Sci. and Tech. Adv. Coun., State Tenn., 1993-98. Maj. Tenn. State Guard, 1995—. Recipient Cert. Recognition, NASA, 1973, Freeman award Am. Coun. for the Blind, 1976, Recognition award ASTM, 1997. Fellow Am. Inst. Chemists (cert. chemist), Am. Acad. Forensic Sci., Am. Ceramic Soc. (abstracter and reviewer 1962—, nat. programs and meetings com. 1968-72, div. chmn. 1969-70, other offices, life mem.); mem. ASTM (liaison mem. for ceramics and med., surg. materials and devices 1975—, Recognition award 1997—), Nat. Soc. Profl. Engrs., Am. Soc. for Engring. Edn., Am. Soc. for Nondestructive Testing, Nat. Inst. Ceramic Engrs. (life), Phi Lambda Upsilon, Tau Beta Pi (Eminent Engr. 1974), Sigma Xi (rsch. awards 1958, 60, 71), KERAMOS, others. Republican. Office: Performance Cons PO Box 51825 Knoxville TN 37950-1825

CAMPBELL, WILLIAM CECIL, biologist; b. Derry, No. Ireland, June 28, 1930; s. Robert John and Sarah Jane (Patterson) C.; m. Mary Mastin, Feb. 24, 1962; children: Jenifer, Peter, Betsy. B.A., Trinity College, Dublin, Ireland, 1952; MSc, U. Wis., 1954, PhD, 1957. With Merck Sharp & Dohme Rsch. Labs., Rahway, N.J., 1957-90, rsch. assoc., 1957-63, rsch. fellow, 1963-66, sr. rsch. fellow, 1966, dir. parasitology, 1966-72; dir. Merck Sharp & Dohme Vet. R & D Lab., Ingleburn, Australia, 1972-73; sr. investigator Merck Sharp & Dohme Rsch. Labs., Rahway, N.J., 1973-76, dir. basic parasitology, 1977-78, sr. dir., 1978-84, sr. scientist, 1984-90; Dana fellow Drew U., Madison, N.J., 1990—; adj. prof. N.Y. Med. Coll., Valhalla, 1985—, U. Pa., 1981—, Drew U., 1992—. Editor: Trichinella and Trichinosis, 1983, Chemotherapy of Parasitic Diseases, 1986, Ivermectin and Abamectin, 1989; mem. editorial bd. Exptl. Parasitology, others; contbr. articles to prof. jours. Recipient Dirs. Sci. award Merck & Co. Inc., 1987, Discoverers award Pharm. Mfg. Assn, 1989, Kitasato medal, 1990; Fulbright grantee, 1953; Kohler fellow U. Wis., 1955. Fellow Royal Soc. Tropical Medicine and Hygiene; mem. Am. Soc. Parasitology (pres. 1987), Internat. Commn. on Trichinellosis (pres. 1980-84), N.Y. Soc. Tropical Medicine (pres. 1970-71), N.J. Soc. Parasitology (pres. 1976-77), Summit Playhouse Assn. (pres. 1991-94), Med. History Soc. N.J. (pres. 1994-96). Avocations: community theater, poetry, painting. Office: Drew Univ Hall Of Scis Madison NJ 07940

CAMPBELL, WILLIAM EDWARD, mental hospital administrator; b. Kansas City, Kans., June 30, 1927; s. William Warren and Mary (Bickerman) C.; m. Joan Josselyn Larimer, July 26, 1952; children: William Gregory, Stephen James, Douglas Edward. Student, U. Nebr., 1944-45, M.S., 1975; student, U. Mich., 1945, Drake U., 1948; B.A., U. Iowa, 1949, M.A., 1950; Ph.D. in Psychology, U. Nebr., Lincoln, 1980. Psychologist Dept. Pub. Instrn., State of Iowa, 1951-52; hosp. adminstr. Mental Health Inst., Cherokee, Iowa, 1952-68; dir. planning and rsch. Dept. Social Svcs., State of Iowa, 1968-69; supt. Glenwood State Hosp. Sch., Iowa, 1969—, Clarinda Mental Health Inst., Iowa, 1979—; assoc. prof. mental health adminstrn. Northwestern U., Chgo., 1982—; pres., bd. dirs. River Bluffs Community Mental Health Ctr.; dir. Shared Mental Health Svcs., Clarinda/Glenwood; founder, chmn. Regional Drug Abuse Adv. Council; adj. prof. Sch. Pub. Health U. Minn., also preceptor grad. students in mental health adminstrn.; vis. faculty Avepane U., Caracas, Venezuela; adj. prof. Coll. Medicine and Health Adminstrn. Tulane U.; vis. staff mem. U. Nebr. Med. Ctr.-Creighton U. St. Joseph Med. Ctr. dept. psychiatry, 1969—. Author works in field. UN spl. cons. to Venzuela for UNESCO; bd. dirs. Polk County Mental Health; v.p., bd. dirs. Mercy Hosp., Coun. Bluffs, Iowa; state pres. United Cerebral Palsy; charter mem., bd. dirs. Pub. Broadcasting Sta. KIWR, Council Bluffs, Iowa, Glenwood-Mills County Econ. Devel. Found., Inc., 1985—; chartered mem., bd. dirs. Mills County Econ. Devel., 1987, Glenwood Resource Ctr., 1993—; apptd. State of Iowa Dept. Human Svcs. Exec. Mgmt. Team, 1997. Served with AUS, 1944-46; col. Res. Decorated Army Commendation medal; recipient Meritorious Service medal U.S. Army, 1982. Fellow Assn. Mental Health Adminstrs. (nat. com. chmn. 1970); mem. Assn. Med. Adminstrs., Am. Hosp. Assn. (nat. governing bd. psychiat. services sect., charter panelist nat. adv. panel on mental health services, mem. governing body psychiat. services sect.), Iowa Hosp. Assn., Health Planning Council of Midlands, Assn. Univ. Programs in Health Adminstrn. (mem. nat. task force on edn. of mental health adminstrs.), Am. Assn. on Mental Deficiency (chmn. adminstrn. sect. Region 8), Nat. Rehab. Assn., Assn. for Retarded Children, Mental Health Assn., Phi Beta Kappa. Office: Office of Supt Glenwood State Hosp Glenwood IA 51534

CAMPBELL, WILLIAM H., career officer; b. Kaukauna, Wis., Jan. 5, 1940. Commd. U.S. Army, advanced through grades to lt. gen., 1997; dir. info. info. sys. command, control, comm. and computers U.S. Army, Washington, 1997—. Office: Office Dir Info Sys for Command Control Comm and Computers 107 Army Pentagon Washington DC 20310-0107

CAMPBELL, WILLIAM LEROY, retired public utility executive, consultant; b. Tamaqua, Pa., Jan. 20, 1939; s. Alvin H. and Ruth E. (Cornelius) C.; m. Catherine A. Hurley, Mar. 28, 1964; children: William L. Jr., Craig S., Kyle J. BS in Bus., Drexel U., 1961. Programmer, analyst Pa. Power & Light Co., Allentown, 1961-62, sr. sys. analyst, 1964-66, sr. sys. analyst, 1967-73, mgr. bus. info. sys., 1973-84, mgr. computer svcs., 1984-93, mgr. info. solutions, 1993-94; pvt. practice cons. Allentown, 1995; cons., transition mgr. Computer Aid, Inc., Allentown, 1996—; CW4 U.S. Army (ret.). Mem., leader, asst. scoutmaster Boy Scouts Am. Troop #29, 1998-99. Mem. Hon. First Defenders (comdr. Allentown chpt. 1997-98), PPL Gold Credit Union (v.p. 1998-99), Rural Sportsmen's Assn. (fin. sec. 1998-99), Slatington Am. Legion. Republican. Presbyterian. Avocations: bicycling, golf. Home: 216 N 39th St Allentown PA 18104-5112 Office: Computer Aid Inc 1390 Ridgeview Dr Allentown PA 18104-9300

CAMPBELL, WILLIAM STEEN, publishing executive, writer, speaker; b. New Cumberland, W.Va., June 27, 1919; s. Robert N. and Ethel (Steen) C.; m. Rosemary J. Bingham, Apr. 21, 1945 (dec. Dec. 1992); children: Diana J., Sarah A., Paul C., John W. Grad., Steubenville (Ohio) Bus. Coll., 1938. Cost acct. Hancock Mfg. Co., New Cumberland, 1938-39; cashier, statistician Weirton Steel Co., W.Va., 1939-42; travel exec. Am. Express Co., N.Y.C., 1946-47; adminstr., account exec. Good Housekeeping mag., 1947-55; pub. Cosmopolitan mag., 1955-57; asst. dir. circulation Hearst Mags., N.Y.C., 1957-61; gen. mgr. Motor Boating mag., 1961-62; v.p., dir. circulation Hearst Mags., 1962-85; pres. Internat. Circulation Distbrs., 1978-81, Mags., Meetings, Messages, Ltd., 1986—; with Periodical Pubs. Svc. Bur. subs. Hearst Corp., Sandusky, Ohio, 1964-85, v.p., chief exec., 1964-69, pres., chief exec., 1970-85; dir. Audit Bur. Circulations, 1974-86, Periodical Pubs. Svc. Bur., 1964-85, Nat. Mag. Co., Ltd., London, Randolph Jamaica Ltd., Omega Pub. Corp. Fla., Hearst Can. Ltd., 1964-85; former chmn. Ctrl. Registry, Mag. Pubs. Assn.; chmn. bd trustees Hearst Employees Retirement Plan, 1971-85; mem. pres.'s coun. Brandeis U., 1974-94; chmn. nat. corp. and found. com. U. Miami, 1979-85; dir. Broadway Assn., 1985-90, v.p., 1988-90; keynote spkr. Fifth Ann. Hospitality Industry Luncheon, Santa Barbara, Calif., 1996. Bd. dirs. Santa Barbara Rep. Club, 1993-94, Lobero Theatre Found., 1994-96, v.p., 1995-96. Lt. col. USAF, 1942-46, ETO. Recipient Lee C. Williams award Mag. Fulfillment Mgrs. Assn.; Torch of Liberty award Anti-Defamation League, 1979. Mem. Campbell Clan Soc., Mil. Order of World Wars (chaplain), Masons, Cosmopolitan Club (chaplain). Home and Office: 1150 Coast Village Rd Santa Barbara CA 93108-2740

CAMPBELL, WILLIAM YATES, investment banker; b. Rochester, N.Y., Sept. 30, 1953; s. Frederick William and Marjorie (Smith) C.; children: Courtney, Elizabeth, Yates. BA, Albion (Mich.) Coll., 1976; MBA, Bowling Green (Ohio) State U., 1977. Registered investment advisor, SEC, registered securities prin. Credit analyst Mich. Nat. Bank of Detroit, Troy, 1978; loan rev. officer Mich. Nat. Bank of Detroit, Clawson, 1978-79; mgr. credit adminstrn. Mich. Nat. Bank of Detroit, Troy, 1979; v.p. comml. lending Mich. Nat. Bank of Detroit, 1979-82; group head spl. lending Mich. Nat. Bank of Detroit, Clawson, 1982-83; v.p., head comml. lending Standard Bank, Troy, 1983; v.p. investment banking First Mich Corp., Detroit, 1983-84, s.v.p., 1984-85; sr. v.p., co-mgr. investment banking First Mich. Corp., Detroit, 1985-88; chmn., mng. dir. W.Y. Campbell & Co. Investment Banking, Detroit, 1988—; chmn. Peninsula Capital Ptnrs., Detroit, 1995—; pres. Comerica Capital Markets Corp., Detroit, 1995—; mng. dir. Griffon Capital Ptnrs. LLC, Detroit, 1999—. Mem. Detroit Zool. Soc., Friends of Detroit Pub. Libr.; Founders Soc. of Detroit Inst. Arts; dir. Grosse Pointe Farms/City Little League. Mem. U. Liggett Sch. Alumnae Assn., Grosse Pointe Club, Country Club of Detroit, Les Cheneaux Club, Yondotega Club, St. Clair Flats Shooting Co. Avocations: fly fishing, hunting, golf, tennis, antique boats.

CAMPBELL-RAY, KECIA LYNN, elementary school teacher. BSeD, Memphis State U., 1988; MSeD, Trevecca Nazarene U., 1993; postgrad., Tenn. State U. Elem. sch. tchr. Cherokee County Schs., Canton, Ga., 1989-94; network sys. adminstr., instr. tech. Aquinas Coll., Nashville, 1994-95; elem. sch. tchr. Wilson County Schs., Lebenon, Tenn., 1996—; prof. tech. Lipscomb U., Nashville, 1995—. E-mail: keciar@bellsouth.net.

CAMPER, DENIECE ANN, special education educator; b. Kansas City, Mo., Sept. 20, 1954; d. Walter F. and Esther Lee (Culbertson) McIntyre; m. Timothy Harold Camper, June 20, 1981; s. Timothy Harold Jr., Shay Addison. BS in Edn., S.W. Bapt. U., 1976; MA in Spl. Edn., U. Mo., 1982. 1st grade tchr. Raytown (Mo.) C-2 Dist., 1976-77; 3rd and 4th grade tchr. Blue Springs (Mo.) R-IV, 1977-87, tchr. learning disabilities, 1987—. Mem. ASCD, Internat. Reading Assn., Coun. Exceptional Children, Learning Disabilities Assn. Mo., Mo. State Tchrs. Assn. Avocations: folk painting, piano playing. Home: 3211 S Owens School Rd Independence MO 64057-3215

CAMPER, JOHN JACOB, press secretary; b. Toledo, Sept. 8, 1943; m. Cleraine Ugucciono, Mar. 27, 1971 (div. May 1981); 1 child, Sarah; m. Mary C. Galligan, Jan. 9, 1988; 1 child, Joseph. BA, Kenyon Coll., 1964. Reporter Detroit News, 1965-68; reporter, critic Chgo. Daily News, 1968-78; editorial writer Chgo. Sun-Times, 1979-84; dept. head external relations Regional Transp. Authority, Chgo., 1984-85; media coord. Chgo. World's Fair Authority, 1985; reporter Chgo. Tribune, 1985-90; assoc. chancellor for pub. affairs U. Ill., Chgo., 1990-97; dep. press sec. Mayor of Chgo., 1997—; v.p. Chgo. Pub. Rels. Forum, 1995-97, pres., 1997-98. Bd. dirs. Family Svc. Mental Health Ctr. of Oak Park and River Forest, 1990-97. Recipient Peter Lisagor award Chgo. Headline Club, 1983, UPI award, Chgo., 1983, Stick-O-Type, Chgo. Newspaper Guild, 1983, Nat. Assn. Black Journalists award, 1987. Home: 1846 W Newport Ave Chicago IL 60657-1024 Office: 602 City Hall 121 N Lasalle St Chicago IL 60602-1202

CAMPER, JOHN SAXTON, public relations and marketing executive; b. Trenton, N.J., Apr. 24, 1929; s. Thomas Emory and Mildred Ruth (Burke) C.; m. Ferne Arlene Clanton; children: Susan Jennifer, John Saxton III. BS in History and Econs., U. Nebr., 1968. Enlisted U.S. Army, 1948, commd. to 1st lt., advanced through ranks to maj., 1972, ret., 1972; regional mktg. officer First Bank System, Mont., 1978-83; lectr., instr. mktg. and advt. pub. rels.; pres. Camper Comm., Helena, 1983—; dir. Profl. Devel. Ctr., Mont., 1984-91. Decorated Legion of Merit. Mem. Helena Advt. Fedn. (1st pres., founder), Rotary Internat. (dist. gov. 1998-99). Republican. Methodist.

CAMPER, MICHELLE GWEN, community health nurse; b. Flushing, N.Y., Feb. 21, 1965; d. William Henry and Mamie Alexandria (O'Quinn) C. AAS, Queensboro C.C., N.Y., 1988; student, Planned Parenthood Fedn. Am., 1999. Staff nurse Dorchester Gen. Hosp., Cambridge, Md., 1990-93; HIV coord., Tb coord. Caroline County Health Dept., Denton, Md., 1993—; cmty. health edn. aids prevention Caroline County Health Dept., Denton, Md., 1993—. Voting mem. State of Md. Comty. Planning Group for Prevention of HIV Transmission, regional work group co-chair; active Comty. Planning Group State of Md. AIDS, 1994-98. Named Outstanding Minority student Queensboro C.C., Bayside, N.Y., 1988. Mem. Nat. Black Nurses Assn., Nat. Assn. Sickle Cell Disease, Assn. Nurses in AIDS Care. Democrat. Baptist. Home: 503 Penn St Hurlock MD 21643-3548 Office: Caroline County Health Dept PO Box 10 Denton MD 21629-0010

CAMPHOR, JAMES WINKY, JR., educational administrator; b. Balt., Mar. 16, 1927; s. Emma Rosetta (Lewis) Butler; m. Lillie Mae Gilliard (div. Sept. 1976); children: Yvonne, Michael, Yolande; m. Florine Alston Camphor, Aug. 10, 1980. BS, Coppin Coll., 1951; MA, Coppin State Coll., 1971. Tchr. Dept. Edn., Balt., 1951-53; tchr. Dept. Juvenile Svcs., Cheltenham, Md., 1953-75, demonstration tchr., 1972-75; behavior specialist Dept. Health and Mental Hygiene, Montgomery County, Md., 1975-87, ednl. supr., 1987—; cons. Fantastic Buddies Travel, Balt., 1980-94. Co-author: (study) Social Studies in the Training School, 1963. Mem. adv. bd. Foster Grandparents Assn., Prince George County, Md., 1991-94, Nat. Assn. Sickle Cell Disease, Balt., 1984-94, chmn. Walk-A-Thon, Balt., 1991; supt. Sunday sch. Emmanuel Cmty. Ch., Balt., 1945; pres. Am. Fedn. State County Mcpl. Employees Assn., Assn. State County Employees Montgomery County, 1991. Recipient Comty. Svc. award Nat. Assn. Sickle Cell Disease, 1988, Presdl. citation Nat. Assn. in Higher Edn., 1992, Gov.'s Citation award William Donald Shafer, Annapolis, Md., 1994, Commitment to Edn. award City Coun. of Balt., 1994. Mem. Black Profl. Men Inc., Bus. and Profl. Coun. (pres. 1989-94), Comty. Men (comty. mem., bus. mgr. 1985-92), Lucky Ten Inc. (charter, pres. 1990-94), Elks, Phi Beta Sigma (pres. 1990-94). Democrat. Avocations: reading, tutoring, traveling, collecting pipes, singing. Home: 3308 Lauri Rd Baltimore MD 21244-1324 Office: Dept Health and Mental Hygiene 3100 Gracefield Rd Silver Spring MD 20904-1870

CAMPHOUSE, MARK DAVID, music educator, dean, composer, conductor; b. Oak Park, Ill., May 3, 1954; s. William Henry and Esther C.; m. Elizabeth Ann Curtis, June 20, 1982; children: Elizabeth Curtis Camphouse, Briton Curtis Camphouse. B in Music, Northwestern U., 1975, M in Music, 1976. Vis. instr. music U. Okla., Norman, 1976-77, St. Cloud (Minn.) State U., 1977-78; asst. prof. music Blackburn Coll., Carlinville, Ill., 1980-84; music dir. and conductor N.Mex. Music Festival, Taos, 1978-82; assoc. prof. music Radford (Va.) U., 1984—; assoc. dir. Va. Govs. Sch. Arts, Radford, 1986-89; acting dean music New World Sch. Arts, Miami, Fla., 1998—. Composer numerous symphonic poems. Midwest regional coord. Citizens for Haig, Jacksonville, Ill., 1978-79. mem: Nat. Band Assn. (1st Prize music composition 1991, bd. dirs. 1998—), Am. Bandmasters Assn., Music Edn. Nat. Conf., Am. Sympony Orch. League, Coll. Band Dir. Nat. Assn. Republican. Methodist. Avocations: racquetball, flag collecting. E-mail: mcamphou@runet.edu. Home: 106 Hidden Valley Dr Radford VA 24141 Office: Radford U Dept Music PO Box 6968 Radford VA 24142

CAMPI, JOHN G., newspaper publishing executive. V.p. promotion and cmty. affairs The Daily News, N.Y.C. Office: The Daily News 450 W 33rd St Fl 3 New York NY 10001-2681*

CAMPIGLIA, MICHAEL EDWARD, association executive; b. Bklyn., Mar. 11, 1947; s. Dominic Nicholas and Helen Elizabeth (Grzegorzewski) C.; m. Rose Romeo, Nov. 30, 1968; children: Michelle R., Maria R. BA in Sociology, U. Tampa, 1973; MA in Bus. Adminstrn., Webster U., 1984. Commd. 2d lt. U.S. Army, 1967, lt. col., 1967-90, ret., 1990; dep. exec. dir. Fed. Bar Assn., Washington, 1990-97, exec. dir., 1997—. Recipient Bronze Star with "V" device U.S. Army, 1968, Legion of Merit, 1990. Mem. The Ret. Officers Assn., Am. Soc. Assn. Execs., Greater Washington Soc. Assn. Execs., Lakepointe Townhome Homeowners Assn. (bd. dirs. 1994—, pres. 1995—). Republican. Roman Catholic. Avocations: golf, jogging, reading. Office: Fed Bar Assn 2215 M St NW Washington DC 20037

CAMPION, ALAN, chemistry educator; b. Tampa, Fla., May 12, 1951; s. Harold Henry and Alice (Arias) C.; m. Ellen Blair Smith, Oct. 20, 1990. BA, New Coll., 1972; C.Phil., UCLA, 1976, PhD, 1977. Postdoctoral fellow NSF, 1979; from asst. prof. chemistry to assoc. prof. chemistry U. Tex., Austin, 1980-87, prof. chemistry, 1988—, Dow prof. chemistry, 1993—, chmn. dept. chemistry and biochemistry, 1991-95; dir. Ctr. Condensed Matter Spectroscopy, U. Tex. Austin, 1989—. Recipient Camille and Henry Dreyfus Tch.-Scholar award The Dreyfus Found., 1982, Coblentz Meml. Prize in Molecular Spectroscopy The Coblentz Soc., 1987; IBM predoctoral fellow, 1975, 76, Alfred P Sloan Rsch. fellow Alfred P. Sloan Found., 1983. Mem. AAAS, Am. Chem. Soc., Am. Physical Soc., Am. Vacuum Soc., Sigma Xi. Office: U Tex Austin Dept Chemistry & Biochemistry Austin TX 78712

CAMPION, DANIEL RAY, editor; b. Oak Park, Ill., Aug. 23, 1949; s. Raymond Edward and Wilma Frances (Dougherty) C. AB, U. Chgo., 1970; MA, U. Ill., Chgo., 1975; PhD, U.Iowa, 1989. Indexer Libr. Resources, Inc., Chgo., 1971-72; prodn. editor Encyc. Britannica, Chgo., 1972-74; tchg. asst. U. Ill., Chgo., 1974-76; editl. asst. Follett Pub. Co., Chgo., 1977-78; tchg. and rsch. asst. U. Iowa, Iowa City, 1978-84; sr. test editor ACT, Inc., Iowa City, 1984—; vis. asst. prof. English U. Iowa, 1991-95. Author: (poems) Calypso, 1981, Peter De Vries and Surrealism, 1995; co-editor: Walt Whitman: The Measure of His Song, 1981, 2d edit. 1998. Mem. U. Ill. Pres. Coun., Urbana, 1992—, Mus. Contemporary Art, Chgo., 1996—; life mem. Art Inst. Chgo., 1973—. Recipient Festival of Arts Poetry award U. Chgo., 1967, All Nations Poetry award Triton Coll., River Grove, Ill., 1975, Ill Arts Coun. Literary award, Chgo., 1979, Sustainer Achievement award U. Ill., 1994-95. Mem. Nat. Coun. Tchrs. English, Midwest Modern Lang. Assn., MLA, Soc. Study Midwestern Lit., Authors Guild, Sierra Club, Cousteau Soc. Office: ACT 2201 N Dodge St Iowa City IA 52243

CAMPION, JANE, director, screenwriter; b. Wellington, New Zealand; d. Richard and Edith Campion. BA in Anthropology, Victoria U., Wellington; Diploma of Fine Arts, Chelsea Sch Arts, London; Diploma in Direction, Australian Film and T.V. Sch., 1984. Dir., screenwriter Peel: An Exercise in Discipline, 1982 (also editor, Palme d'Or short film category Cannes Internat. Film Festival 1986, Diploma of Merit melbourne Film Festival, 1983, finalist Greater Union awards, Australian Film Inst. awards), (video dir. and prodr.) Mishaps of Seduction and Conquest, 1983-84, A Girl's Own Story, 1983 (Rouben Mamoulian award 1984 Best overall short film Sydney Film Festival 1984, Unique Artist Merit Melbourne Film Festival 1984, Best Direction, BestScreenplay, Best Cinematography Australian Film Inst. 1984, First Prize Cinestud Amsterdam Film Festival, 1985, Best Film Cinestud 1985, First Prize Festival and Press prize), Passionless Moments, 1984 (also prodr. dir., writer, with Gerard Lee and dir. photography) Passionless moments, 1984,or, Unique Artist Merit Melbourne Film Festival 1984, Best Exptl. Film Australian Film inst. 1984, Most Popular Short Film Sydney Film Festival 1985), screened at Cannes, 1986, After Hours, 1984 (XL Elders award Best Short Fiction, Best Short Fiction Melbourne Internat. Film Festival 1985), Sweetie, 1988, (Georges Sadoul prize Best Fgn. Film, Best Dir., Best Actress, Best Film Australian Critics awards 1990, New Generation award L.A. Film Critics, 1990, Best Fgn. Film Spirit of Independence awards 1990), The Piano, 1993 (Palme d'Or Cannes Internat. Film Festival 1993, Academy Award Best Original Screenplay 1994, Best Picture, Best Dir., Best Cinematography, 66th Acad. Awards, Australian Film Inst. awards, Australian Film Critics, Southeastern Film Critics Assn., others, Best Fgn. Film Chgo. Film Critics, Caesar awards); dir. An Angel at my Table, 1990 (Byron Kennedy award, Spl. Jury prize, Annual Elvira Notari award Best Woman Dir., Agia Scuola Italian Min. Culture, Best Film Si presci award Panel Internat. Critics, Best Film O.C.I.C. award Christian journalists, Best Film for Young Audiences Cinema e Ragazzi Italian film critcs prize, Critics award Toronto Film FEstival, Most popular film in the Forum, Otto Debelius prize Berlin Film Festival, Best Fgn. Film Spirit of Independence Awards), (TV) Two Friends, 1986 (Golden Plaque T.V. category Chgo. Internat. Film Festival 1987, Best Dir., Best Telemovie, Best Screenplay AFI awards 1987; composer: Feel the Cold (from A Girl's Own Story), 1983, (play) The Portrait of A Lady, 1995. *

CAMPION, ROBERT THOMAS, manufacturing company executive; b. Mpls., June 23, 1921; s. Leo P. and Naomi (Revord) C.; m. Wilhelmina Knapp, June 8, 1946; 1 son, Michael. Student, Loyola U., Chgo., 1939-41, 46-48. C.P.A., Ill. With Alexander Grant & Co., Chgo., 1946-57; ptnr. Alexander Grant & Co., 1954-57; with Lear Siegler, Inc., Santa Monica, Calif., 1957—; pres. Lear Siegler, Inc., 1971-85, chief exec. officer, dir., 1971-86, chmn., 1974-86; pvt. investor, 1987—. Served with AUS, 1942-46. Mem. AICPA, Ill. Soc. CPAs, Bel Air Country Club, Jonathan Club, La Quinta Country Club. Republican. Office: Blair House # 406 10490 Wilshire Blvd Los Angeles CA 90024-4646

CAMPION, THOMAS FRANCIS, lawyer; b. Bklyn., Aug. 15, 1935; s. Thomas Francis and Genevieve Agnes (Schantz) C.; m. Virginia Grosscup, Aug. 21, 1965; children: Caroline, Michael. AB, Fordham U., 1957; LLB, Cornell U., 1961. Bar: N.J. 1961, U.S. Dist. Ct. N.J. 1961, U.S. Ct. Appeals (3d cir.) 1965, U.S. Supreme Ct. 1966, U.S. Dist. Ct. D.C. 1970, N.Y. 1988. Law clk. to judge Appellate Div.-Superior Ct. N.J., 1961-62; assoc. Shanley & Fisher, Newark and Morristown, N.J., 1962-67; ptnr. Shanley & Fisher, Morristown, 1968—; bd. on trial atty. cert. N.J. Supreme Ct., 1982-89, chmn., 1987-89, chmn. disciplinary oversight com., 1994—. Contbr. articles to profl. jours. Mem. N.J. Gov.'s Mgmt. Commn., 1970. 1st lt. USAR, 1957-61. Fellow Am. Bar Found., Am. Coll. Trial Lawyers; mem. ABA, N.J. Bar Assn. (past chmn. jud. and county prosecutor appointments com., civil cts. task force), Essex County Bar Assn., Morris County Bar Assn., Assn. Fed. Bar N.J. (pres. 1980-82), Univ. Club (N.Y.C.). Office: Shanley & Fisher 131 Madison Ave Morristown NJ 07960-6097

CAMPISI, DOMINIC JOHN, lawyer; b. San Jose, Calif., Apr. 30, 1944; s. Dominic Albert and Mary Elizabeth (Cukes) C.; m. Mary Beth Gillick, Jan. 5, 1969; children: Anne Elizabeth, Megan Moran, Catherine Marie. BA, U. Santa Clara, Calif., 1966; M in Pub. Affairs, Princeton U., 1968; JD, Yale U., 1974. Nat. field rep. Cmty. Rels. Svc., Washington, 1968, 71; clk. U.S. Ct. Appeals, Seattle, 1974-75; assoc. Morrison & Foerster, San Francisco, 1975-80; ptnr. Evans Latham Harris & Campisi, San Francisco, 1980—; dir. Cuvaison Winery, Calistoga, Calif., 1989—; chmn., vice chmn. trust and estate litigation com. sect. Real Property Probate and Trust, Chgo., 1984-96, chmn. malpractice com., 1996—. Author: Estate & Trust Litigation, 1981-96; contbr. chpt. to book, articles to Jour. Real Property Probate and Trust. With U.S. Army, 1969-71. Fellow Am. Coll. Trust & Estate Counsel; mem. Nat. Coll. Probate Judges, Internqt. Acad. Estate and Trust Law. Avocations: creative writing, photography, skiing. Office: Evans Latham Harris & Campisi 1 Post St Ste 600 San Francisco CA 94104-5210

CAMPMAN, CHRISTOPHER KULLER, consulting company executive; b. Bryn Mawr, Pa., May 25, 1949; s. Curtis Oscar Campman and Agnes R. (Kuller) Baberick; m. Sarah Ann Gladish, July 15, 1972; 1 child, Kurt Christopher. AS in Bus. Adminstrn., Montgomery County C.C., 1987. Asst. dir. solid waste Montgomery County, Norristown, Pa., 1970-84; owner, pres. C.K. Campman, Inc., Cons., Lansdale, Pa., 1984—. Chmn. bd. dirs.

park and recreation adv. bd. Upper Gwynedd Twp., Pa., 1986—. Mem. Am. Pub. Works Assn. (assoc.), Nat. Solid Waste Mgmt. Assn., Montgomery County Pub. Works Assn. (sec. 1978—), Solid Waste Assn. N.Am. (tech. dir. Swana). Republican. Lutheran. Avocations: golf, skiing, fresh-water fishing, hunting. Home: 934 Patriot Dr Lansdale PA 19446-5529 Office: CK Campman Inc 934 Patriot Dr Lansdale PA 19446-5529

CAMPO, TODD RUSSELL, principal, law enforcement educator; b. Dansville, N.Y., Oct. 25, 1953; s. Frank James and Shirley May (Mothorpe) C.; m. Jo Ann Marie Rocco; children: Christy Ellen, Todd Russell Jr., Joshua James. BS in Edn., SUNY, Oswego, 1976; MA in Religion magna cum laude, Liberty U., 1989; MA summa cum laude, Simon Greenleaf Sch. Law, 1991; PhD summa cum laude, Trinity Theol. Sem., 1997; grad. Internat. Inst. Human Rights, U. Strasbourg (France), 1990; honor grad., L.A. Police Acad., 1998. Prof. Chafer Theol. Sem., Huntington Beach, Calif., 1989—; prin. Hawthorne (Calif.) Christian Sch., 1990-96; apologist Reasons to Believe, Pasadena, Calif., 1989-91; minister of edn. Hawthorne Christian Sch., 1990-96; elder, min. Grace Ch., Fountain Valley, 1990—. Sponsor World Vision, 1988—, Wycliff Bible Translators, 1992—. Capt. USMC, 1976-83. Named A.A.U. Nat., North Am. and World Bench Press Champion, 1998. Mem. Assn. for Christian Schs. Internat., Christian Leadership Assn., Grace Evang. Soc., Am. Legion. Republican. Mem. Christian Ch. Avocations: family, reading, systematic theology, philosophy, pilot. Home: 14871 Mayten Ave Irvine CA 92606-2655 Office: LA Police Dept 1358 N Wilcox Ave Los Angeles CA 90038

CAMPOLETTANO, THOMAS ALFRED, contract manager; b. Long Island City, N.Y., Feb. 13, 1946; s. Barney and Mary (Felner) C.; m. Kathy Lee Clemons, Mar. 19, 1989; 1 stepchild, Christopher; children by previous marriage: Lisa, Jennifer, Tricia. AAS, Nassau Coll., 1971; BA, U. South Fla., 1977; postgrad., Am. Grad. U., 1980-85, Touro Coll., 1980-85. Cert. profl. contract mgr. Cost/price analyst Grumman Aero. Corp., Bethpage, N.Y., 1963-70; sr. cost/price analyst Potter Instrument Co., Plainview, N.Y., 1970-73; prin. fin. analyst, govt. liaison Space Systems div. Honeywell, Inc., Clearwater, Fla., 1973—; prof. Honeywell Fed. Contracting Tng. program (recipient 1992 Honeywell Fin. Achievement award). Author: Profit Proposal Initiatives, 1990; co-author: Weighted Guidelines Profit, 1984. With USN, 1963-66, Vietnam. Recipient Apollo Space Program commendation, NASA, 1969. Mem. Nat. Contract Mgmt. Assn., Fin. Exec. Inst. (mem. com. on govt. bus. 1985), Def. Industry Offset Assn., U.S. Track & Field, Road Runners Club Am. Republican. Roman Catholic. Avocation: long-distance and marathon running, golf. Home: 8412 Parkwood Blvd Seminole FL 33777-2710 Office: Honeywell Inc 13350 Us Highway 19 N Clearwater FL 33764-7290

CAMPOS, BRUNO, actor; b. Rio de Janeiro, Brazil, Dec. 3, 1974. T.V. and movie actor. T.V. series include The Last Don, 1997, Jesse, 1998—, also T.V. guest appearances. Office: c/o SDB Ptnrs Inc Ste 902 1800 Ave of the Stars Los Angeles CA 90067*

CAMPOS, JORGE, professional soccer player; b. Acapulco, Guerrero, Mexico, Oct. 15, 1966; s. Alvaro Campos Gonzalez and Lucina Navarrete de Campos. Goalkeeper Dolphins of Acapulco, Mex., 1984-85, Cruz Azul, Mex., Pumas, Mex., L.A. Galaxy, Atlante FC, Mex., Mexican Nat. Team, 1991; champion Concacaf, 1989; second pl. Am. Cup, 1993; champion Gold Cup, 1993, USA Cup, 1996. Recipient Mexican championship medal UNAM, 1991, league runners-up medal Am. MLS, L.A. Galaxy, 1996; named Best Goalkeeper, Mex. League, 1991, 92, 93, 94, 95. Avocations: surfing, basketball, volleyball, tennis, listening to music. Office: Club Deportino Socialy Cultural Cruz Azw AC, Antiguo Camino Xochimilco No 100, La Noria CP 16030, Mexico*

CAMPOS, ROBERT, construction company executive. Labor leadman Kiewit Constrn. Co., 1958; postal clk. U.S. Post Office, 1958-59; apprentice carpenter N.P. Dodge-Maple Village, 1959-61, Kiewit Constrn. Co., 1961-63; carpenter, foreman, supt. Sides Constrn. Co., 1963-77; pres. Campos Constrn. Co., Omaha, 1977—; bd. dirs. Bank of Bellevue, Douglas County Bank and Trust. Bd. dirs. United Way of Midlands, 1988-93, Safety and Health Coun. of Greater Omaha, 1996—, Omaha Cmty. Found., 1997—; chmn. parades and festivals Omaha Hispanic Coalition, 1984-90; mem. adv. bd. Score Bus. Info. Ctr., Small Bus. Assn., 1996—, Storz Cancer Inst., 1996-97; mem. Mayor of Omaha Police Adv. Com., 1987-88. Recipient Daniel J. Gross H.S. award, 1988, South H.S. award, 1988, Outstanding Contractor U.S. Army Corps Engrs., 1990, Human Rels. award Omaha Edn. Assn., 1991, Vol. of Yr. award Midwest N.E. Voter Registration Edn. Project, 1992, Champion Small Bus. of Yr. award Nebr. Bus. Devel. Ctr., 1993, Outstanding Builder award Star Bldg. Sys., 1994, Nebr. Hispanic Man of Yr., Nebr. Land Days North Platte, 1997, numerous others; Campos Scholarship award named in his honor Gross H.s., 1986. Mem. Associated Gen. Contractors, Greater Omaha C. of C. (mem. sports coun. 1993-96, youth leadership adv. bd. 1993-95, chmn. minority affairs 1997—), VFW, Am. Legion, Am. G.I. Forum, Rotary. Fax: (402) 733-8241. Office: Campos Constrn Co 3827 S 42d St Omaha NE 68107

CAMPOS, SANTIAGO E., federal judge; b. Santa Rosa, N.Mex., Dec. 25, 1926; s. Ramon and Miquela Campos; m. Patsy Campos, Jan. 27, 1947; children: Theresa, Rebecca, Christina, Miquela Feliz. J.D., U. N.Mex., 1953. Bar: N.Mex. 1953. Asst., 1st asst. atty gen. State of N.Mex., 1955-57; judge 1st Jud. Dist. N.Mex., 1971-78; judge U.S. Dist. Ct. N.Mex., Santa Fe, 1978—, sr. judge, 1992—. Served as seaman USN, 1944-46. Mem. State Bar of N.Mex., First Jud. Dist. Bar Assn. (hon.), Hon. Order of Coif. Office: US Dist Ct PO Box 2244 Santa Fe NM 87504-2244

CAMPOS-ORREGO, NORA PATRICIA, lawyer, consultant; b. Lima, Peru, Sept. 3, 1959; came to U.S., 1984; d. Victor M. and Ofelia A. Campos. BA, Cath. U. Peru, 1979, LLB, 1983, Lawyer, 1984; JD magna cum laude, InterAm. U. P.R., San Juan, 1989. Bar: P.R. 1989, Peru, 1984. Legal asst. women's affairs commn. P.R. Gov.'s Office, San Juan, 1988-89, lawyer women's affairs commn., 1989-93; lawyer women's affairs commn. P.R. Gov.'s Office/Immigration Law Practice, Miami, Fla., 1993-94; women's discrimination cons. San Juan, P.R., 1994-95; pvt. practice Miami Beach, 1995—. Co-author: How to Write Public Police and Internal Process to Sexual Harassment Claims, 1989; editor Law Sch. Mag., 1988-89. All Am. scholar U. P.R., 1988-89. Mem. ABA, InterAm. Bar Assn., P.R. Bar Assn., Peru Bar Assn. Roman Catholic. Avocations: sightseeing, reading, dancing, walking.

CAMPOS-PONS, MARIA MAGDALENA, artist; b. Matanzas, Cuba, 1959. Student, Nat. Sch. Art, Havana, Cuba, 1980, Higher Inst. Art, Havana, Cuba, 1985, Mass. Coll. Art, 1988. Prof. aesthetic and painting Higher Inst. Art, Havana, Cuba, 1986-89; asst. curator The Space Gallery, 1992; co-coord. aesthetic and fine art seminar Revolution and Culture Mag., Cuba, 1989-90; vis. prof. RISD, R.I., 1994, Mass. Coll. Art, Boston, 1995, 96, Sch. Mus. Fine Arts, Boston, 1997. One-woman shows include Gallery L, Havana, 1985, Kennedy Bldg. Gallery, Mass. Coll. Art, Boston, 1988, Castle of Royal Force, Havana, 1989, Embassy Cultural House, London, Ont., Can., 1990, Banff Ctr. Arts, Can., 1990, SOHO 20 Gallery, N.Y.C., 1991, Gallery Burning, Montreal, Can., 1991, Burnaby Art Gallery, B.C., Can., 1991, Gallery La Ctrl./Powerhouse, Montreal, 1992, Akin Gallery, Boston, 1993, Latin Am. Gallery, N.Y.C., 1993, Miami Dade C.C., Gallery North, Fla., 1994, Bunting Inst. Radcliffe Coll., Mass., 1994, Martha Schneider Gallery, Chgo., 1996, The Caribbean Cultural Ctr., N.Y.C., 1997, The Photographers Gallery, Saskatoon, Can., 1997, U. de Antioquia & Centro Colombo Americano, Colombia, 1997, Ambrosino Gallery, Coral Gables, Fla., 1997, Martha Schneider Gallery, Chgo., 1997, Mario Diacono Gallery, Boston, 1997, Hallwalls, Buffalo, 1998, MoMA, N.Y.C., 1998; group shows at Ctr. Fine Arts, Miami, 1996, DNA Gallery, Provincetown, Mass., 1996, Craiger/Dane Gallery, Boston, 1996, Wadsworth Atheneum, Hartford, 1997, Howard Yezerski Gallery, Boston, 1997, Addison Gallery Am. Art, Philips Acad., Andover, Mass., 1997, Smithsonian, Washington, 1997, 98, Nat. Gallery Can., Ottawa, 1998, numerous others; represented in permanent collections; performer The Seven Powers Come by the Sea, 1992, La Voz del Silencio/The Voice of Silence, 1993, Letter to my Mother, 1994, 95, 96, others; reviewer in field; contbr. articles to profl. jours.; juror numerous competitions; curatorial project Articule Gallery, Montreal, 1991, Inst. Contemporary Art, Boston, 1992. Office: care Schneider Gallery 230 West Superior Chicago IL 60610

CAMPS, JEFFREY LOWELL, financial services company general agent; b. Rye, N.Y., Mar. 1, 1954; s. Lowell C. and Helen (Place) C.; m. Judith B. Nelson, July 31, 1982; children: Ashley, Brooke. BS, Colo. State U., 1978. CLU; charter fin. cons. With mktg. mgmt. program John Hancock Fin. Svcs., Boston, 1979-81; sales mgr. Lowell Camps Gen. Agy., N.Y.C., 1981-87; gen. agt. John Hancock Fin. Svcs., N.Y.C., 1988—. Bd. dirs. N.Y. Ctr. for Fin. Studies, N.Y.C., 1989—, Estate Planning Coun., 1997—. Mem. Gen. Agt. and Mgrs. Assn. (bd. dirs. 1988-95, pres. 1992-93), John Hancock Gen. Agts. Assn. (bd. dirs. 1992-93), CLU and ChFC (officer N.Y.C. chpt. 1991-97, pres. 1995-96), N.Y.C. Estate Planning Coun. (bd. dirs. 1997—), Westchester Country Club. Avocations: tennis, golf. Office: John Hancock Fin Svcs 122 E 42nd St Rm 1903 New York NY 10168-1999

CAMRON, ROXANNE, editor; b. Los Angeles; d. Irving John and Roslyn (Weinberger) Spiro; m. Robert Camron; children: Ashley Jennifer, Erin Jessica. B.A. in Journalism, U. So. Calif. West Coast fashion and beauty editor, Teen mag., Los Angeles, 1969-70; sr. editor Teen mag., 1972-75, editor, 1976—; pub. relations rep. Max Factor Co., 1970; asst. to creative dir. Polly Bergen Co., 1970-71; lectr. teen groups; freelance writer. Active Homeowners Assn. Mem. Am. Soc. Exec. Women. Office: Teen Mag 6420 Wilshire Blvd Los Angeles CA 90048-5502

CAN, SUMER, research electrical engineer; b. Koyulhisar, Sivas, Turkey, Dec. 24, 1947; came to Can., 1974; came to U.S., 1980; s. Mahmut Celalettin and Bedriye (Erzurumlu) C.; m. Aysel Pala, Oct. 6, 1972; children: Argun Dennis, Tankut Uzay. BS, Tech. U. Istanbul, Turkey, 1972; MS in Applied Sci., U. Toronto, Ont., Can., 1977; postgrad., U. Santa Clara, 1981-83. Registered profl. engr., Can., Turkey. Lectr., researcher Tech. U. Istanbul, 1972-74; teaching and research asst. U. Toronto, 1974-78; electrical engr. Litton Systems Ltd., Ont., Can., 1978-80; sr. engr. Nat. Semiconductor, Santa Clara, Calif., 1980-81; prin. engr., scientist Sperry Univac and Control Data, Santa Clara, 1981-84; sr. design engr. Signetics Corp., Sunnyvale, Calif., 1984—. Contbr. articles to profl. jours.; patentee in field. Mem. IEEE, Circuits and Systems Soc. of IEEE, Electron Devices Soc. of IEEE, Assn. Profl. Engrs. of Turkey, Assn. Profl. Engrs. of Ont. Home: 7050 Rainbow Dr # 9 San Jose CA 95129-4524 Office: Signetics Corp 811 E Arques Ave Sunnyvale CA 94086-4523

CANADA, GEOFFREY, social welfare administrator. Grad., Bowdoin Coll., Harvard U. Supr. Camp Freedom, Center Ossipe, N.H.; dir. Robert White Sch., Boston; head children's program Rheedlen Ctrs. for Children and Families, N.Y.C., 1983—, pres., CEO, 1990—. Author 2 video essays. Bd. trustees the City Project, Geel Inc., The N.Y. Black Child Devel. Inst., The Door, The Neighborhood Family Svcs. Coalition. Recipient Gov. award for African Ams. of Distinction, Spirit of the City award Cathedral St. John the Devine, Common Good award Bowdoin Coll., Robin Hood Found. Heroes of Yr. award, Heinz award for human condition. Office: Rheedlen Ctrs for Children and Families 2770 Broadway New York NY 10025-2805*

CANADA, MARY WHITFIELD, librarian; b. Richmond, Va., June 13, 1919; d. Waverly Thomas and Ruth Bradshaw (Smith) C. B.A. magna cum laude, Emory and Henry Coll., 1940; M.A. in English, Duke U., 1942; B.S. in L.S., U. N.C., 1956. Asst. circulation dept. Duke U. Library, 1942-45, undergrad. librarian, 1945-55, reference librarian, 1956-85, asst. head reference dept., 1967-79, head dept., 1979-85. Contbr. articles to profl. jours. Mem. exec. com. Friends of Duke U. Library. Duke U. grantee Can., 1979, 81. Mem. ALA (life; initiated performance evaluation discussion group), Southeastern Library Assn. (sec. coll. and univ. sect., chmn. nominating com. reference services div., also chmn. div.), N.C. Library Assn. (chmn. nominating com., chmn. newspaper com., chmn. coll. and univ. sect.), Alumni Assn. Sch. Library Sci. U. N.C. (pres.), Va. Hist. Soc. (life), Va. Geneal. Soc., DAR (chpt. regent), Friends of Va. State Archives, Campus club (Duke U.), Planning Adv. Com. N. Cen. Durham, Va. Mus. Beta Phi Mu. Methodist. Home: 1312 Lancaster St Durham NC 27701-1132

CANADAY, RICHARD A., lawyer; b. Alton, Ill., Aug. 26, 1947. AB, Stanford U., 1969; JD, U. Calif., 1973. Bar: Oreg. 1973, Wash. 1987. Ptnr. Miller, Nash, Wiener, Hager & Carlsen, Portland, Oreg. Mem. ABA, Oreg. State Bar, Wash. State Bar Assn. Office: Miller Nash Wiener Hager & Carlsen 111 SW 5th Ave Ste 3500 Portland OR 97204-3699

CANADY, CHARLES TERRENCE, congressman, lawyer; b. Lakeland, Fla., June 22, 1954; m. Jennifer Houghton, Oct. 1996. BA, Haverford Coll., 1976; JD, Yale U., 1979. Mem. 44th dis. Fla. Ho. of Reps., 1984-90, mem. Marketable Record Title Act Study Commn., 1985-86, majority whip, 1986-88, mem. crime prevention and law enforcement study com., 1987-88; mem. 103rd-106th congresses from FL 12th dist., 1992—; mem. counsel Ctrl. Fla. Regional Coun., 1983-84. V.p. United Cerebral Palsy, Polk County, 1982-83; bd. dirs. Big Brothers & Big Sisters, 1984-85. Recipient Allen Morris award Fla. Ho. of Reps., 1986, Legislator of the Yr. Fla. Assn. Realtors, 1986, Spec Leadership award Save Our Home and Lands, 1986; named Most Valuable Legislator in Growth Mgmt. Fla. Regional Coun. Assn. Mem. ABA, Lakeland Bar Assn., Lakeland C. of C., Winter Haven C. of C. Republican. Presbyterian. Office: US Ho Reps 2432 Rayburn Bldg Washington DC 20515-0912*

CANALES, JAMES EARL, JR., foundation administrator; b. San Francisco, Nov. 6, 1966; s. James Earl Canales Sr. and Maritsa M. (Solorzano) Espinoza. BA, Stanford U., 1988, MA, 1989. English tchr., class dean San Francisco Univ. H.S., 1989-91, dir. admissions, 1991-93; program assoc. The James Irvine Found., San Francisco, 1993-95, program officer, spl. asst. to pres., 1995-97, chief adminstrv. officer, corp. sec., 1997—; sec., bd. dirs. Nat. Ctr. for Nonprofit Bds., Washington. Chair, bd. dirs. Larkin St. Youth Ctr., San Francisco, 1992—; bd. dirs., Nat. Assn. for Cmty. Leadership, Indpls., 1994-97; trustee San Francisco Day Sch., 1996—. Andrew W. Mellon Edn. Found. fellow, 1988-89. Mem. Stanford Alumni Assn. (bd. dirs. 1997—). Democrat. Roman Catholic. Home: 21 Carmel St San Francisco CA 94117 Office: The James Irvine Found Steuart 2500 One Market San Francisco CA 94105

CANAN, JANINE BURFORD, psychiatrist, poet; b. L.A., Nov. 2, 1942; d. Lewis Marion and Mary Alene Burford; m. Michael James Canan, Aug. 31, 1963 (div.). BA in French with distinction, Stanford U., 1963; postgrad., U. Calif., Berkeley, 1963-68; MD, NYU, 1976. Resident in psychiatry Herrick Hosp., Berkeley, 1976-78, courtesy staff psychiatrist, 1979-88; resident in psychiatry Mt. Zion Hosp., San Francisco, 1978-79; pvt. practice psychiatry Berkeley, 1979-92; courtesy staff psychiatrist Gladman Hosp., Oakland, Calif., 1980-92; staff psychiatrist Eden Children Ctr., Hayward, Calif., 1980-81; pvt. practice Port Townsend, Wash., 1994-98, Sonoma, Calif., 1998—; psychiatric cons. Berkeley Women's Ctr., 1979-88, Russell Ho. Low-Fee Clinic, Berkeley, 1980-88; faculty cons. U. Calif., Berkeley, 1980-81; provider psychiatrist HEALS, Berkeley, 1980-92, Kitsap Physicians Svcs., Port Townsend, 1994-98; founder, dir. Ctr. Integration, Port Townsend, 1994-98; evaluations psychiatrist Wash. State Dept. Social & Health Svcs., Port Townsend, Port Angeles, 1994. Author: (poems) Of Your Seed, 1977, The Hunger, 1979, Who Buried the Breast of Dreams, 1981, Daughter, 1981, Shapes of Self, 1982, Her Magnificent Body, New & Selected Poems, 1986, Goddess Poems, 1997, Love, Enter, 1998, Changing Woman, 1999; translator: Star in My Forehead: Poems by Else Lasker-Schueler, 1999; editor: She Rises like the Sun: Invocations of the Goddess by Contemporary American Women Poets, 1989 (Susan Koppelman award 1990), The Rhyme of the Aged mariness: Last Poems of Lynn Lonidier, 1999; contbr. poems to lit. jours. Mem. NOW, Poets & Writers. Democrat. Avocation: music. E-mail: jancanan@vom.com. Home and Office: 772 Ernest Dr Sonoma CA 95476

CANAN, MICHAEL JAMES, lawyer, author; b. Washington, Sept. 28, 1941; s. Robert Harvey and Molly Cornelia (Brown) C.; 1 child, Jennifer Michelle. BA, Stanford U., 1963; JD, U. Calif., Berkeley, 1966; LLM in Taxation, NYU, 1972. Bar: Calif. 1969, Fla. 1972. Assoc. Holland & Knight, Lakeland, Fla., 1972-74; ptnr. Canan & Harris, Lakeland, 1974-76, Canan, Murphy & Clark, Lakeland and Tampa, Fla., 1976-84, Dean Mead Edgeton Bloodworth, Orlando, Fla., 1984-86, Baker & Hostetler, Orlando, 1986, Steel Hector & Davis, Miami, Fla., 1986-93; pvt. practice Law Office Michael J. Canan, Orlando, Fla., 1993-98; atty. Gray, Harris and Robinson, P.A., 1998—. Author: Qualified Retirement plans, 1977, 14th edit., 1999, West's Federal Practice, 1979, part 20, 1992, West's Legal Forms, 1981, ed edit., vol. 8, 1991, 98; (computer software) West's Model Benefit Plans, 1990, Qualified Retirement Plans, 1991, Fringe and Welfare Plans, 1992, Volume Submitter Plans, 1992, IRS Retirement Plan Submittal Package, 1997, Tech Soft Pension Plans, 1998-99; co-author: Employee Fringe and Welfare Benefit Plans, 1990, 10th edit., 1999. Vol. Peace Corps, Venezuela, 1966-67. Capt. USAF, 1967-71. *

CANARY, NANCY HALLIDAY, lawyer; b. Cleve., Apr. 21, 1941; d. Robert Fraser and Nanna (Hall) Halliday; m. Sumner Canary, Dec. 1975 (dec. Jan. 1979). BA, Case Western Res. U., 1963; JD, Cleve. State U., 1968. Bar: Ohio 1968, Fla. 1972, U.S. Dist. Ct. (no. dist.) Ohio 1975, U.S. Supreme Ct. 1974. Law clk. to presiding judge Ohio Ct. Appeals, Cleve., 1968-69; ptnr. McDonald, Hopkins & Hardy, Cleve., 1969-83, Thompson, Hine and Flory, Cleve., 1984—. Trustee Beck Ctr. for Cultural Arts, Lakewood, Ohio, 1980-90, Ohio Motorists Assn., 1989-95, Ohio Chamber Orch.; trustee, mem. devel. adv. com. Fairview Gen. Hosp., Cleve., 1980-96; chairperson Sumner Canary Lectureship com. Case Western Res. U. Law Sch.; bd. dirs. Comerica Bank & Trust Co., F.S.B., 1993—. Mem. Ohio State Bar Assn., Cleve. Bar Assn., Palm Beach County Bar Assn., Estate Planning Coun. Cleve., Estate Planning Coun. Palm Beach County, Gulf Stream (Fla.) Golf Club, Westwood Country Club (Cleve.). Republican. Avocations: music, horseback riding. Home: 12500 Edgewater Dr Cleveland OH 44107-1677 also: 200 N Ocean Blvd Delray Beach FL 33483-7126 Address: Thompson Hine & Flory 127 Public Sq Ste 3900 Cleveland OH 44114-1291

CANAVAN, CHRISTINE ESTELLE, state legislator; b. Dorchester, Mass., Jan. 25, 1950; m. Paul Canavan; 2 children. Grad., Massasoit C.C., 1983; BS summa cum laude, U. Mass. RN, Mass. Rep. dist. 10 Mass. Ho. of Reps., Boston; vice chair on human svcs. and elderly affairs com.; mem. ins. com., husing and urban devel. com. Mass. Ho. of Reps., Boston; vice chair human svcs. and elderly affairs com. Mass. Ho. of Reps.; mem. Brockton (Mass.) Sch. Com., 1990—, vice chair, 1992—. Mem. Amvets, Mass. Nurses Assn., Polish White Eagles Inc. Democrat. Roman Catholic. Home: 29 Mystic St Brockton MA 02302-2825 Office: Mass Ho of Reps Mass State House Boston MA 02133

CANAVAN, CHRISTOPHE R., municipal manager; b. Flemington, N.J., Apr. 2, 1973; s. Robert James Canavan and Marilyn Lavish. BA in Polit. Sci., Am. U., 1995, MPA, 1996. Student activities advisor Am. U., Washington, 1995-96; asst. twp. mgr. Lower Gwynedd Twp., Spring House, Pa., 1996-97; acting twp. mgr. Lower Gwynedd Twp., Spring House, 1997, asst. twp. mgr., 1997—. Sec., bd. mem. North Pa. Vol. Fire Co., North Wales, 1997-99. Mem. ASPA, Internat. City/County Mgmt. Assn., Assn. Pa. Mcpl. Mgrs., Pi Sigma Alpha, Phi Sigma Sigma. Avocations: reading, golf, politics, physical fitness, travel. E-mail: ccanavan@voicenet.com. Office: Lower Gwynedd Twp 1130 N Bethlehem Pike Spring House PA 19477

CANAVAN, PATRICK JOSEPH, artist; b. Pitts., Dec. 21, 1927; s. Estus Gilmore; m. Christine Jane Withroe, Sept. 6, 1949; children: Philip Lynn, Kandie Jo. BSBA, Miami U., 1952; MFA in Painting, Md. Inst. Coll. Art, 1965. Assoc. prof. fine arts/painting U. Md., Catonsville, 1968-90. One-man shows include Balt. Mus. Art, 1962. With USN, 1945-47. Recipient award Pollack/Krasner Found., 1990, Visual Arts fellowship Pa. Counsel Arts, 1992.

CANBY, WILLIAM CAMERON, JR., federal judge; b. St. Paul, May 22, 1931; s. William Cameron and Margaret Leah (Lewis) C.; m. Jane Adams, June 18, 1954; children—William Nathan, John Adams, Margaret Lewis. A.B., Yale U., 1953; LL.B., U. Minn., 1956. Bar: Minn. 1956, Ariz. 1972. Law clk. U.S. Supreme Ct. Justice Charles E. Whittaker, 1958-59; asso. firm Oppenheimer, Hodgson, Brown, Baer & Wolff, St. Paul, 1959-62; asso., then dep. dir. Peace Corps, Ethiopia, 1962-64; dir. Peace Corps, Uganda, 1964-66; asst. to U.S. Senator Walter Mondale, 1966; asst. to pres. SUNY, 1967; prof. law Ariz. State U., 1967-80; judge U.S. Ct. Appeals (9th cir.), Phoenix, 1980-96, sr. judge, 1996—; chief justice High Ct. of the Trust Ter. of the Pacific Islands, 1993-94; bd. dirs. Ariz. Center Law in Public Interest, 1974-80, Maricopa County Legal Aid Soc., 1972-78, D.N.A.-People's Legal Services, 1978-80; Fulbright prof. Makerere U. Faculty Law, Kampala, Uganda, 1970-71. Author: American Indian Law, 1998; also articles; note editor: Minn. Law Rev, 1955-56. Precinct and state committeeman Democratic Party Ariz., 1972-80; bd. dirs. Central Ariz. Coalition for Right to Choose, 1976-80. Served with USAF, 1956-58. Mem. State Bar Ariz., Minn. Bar Assn., Maricopa County Bar Assn., Phi Beta Kappa, Order of Coif. Office: US Ct Appeals 9th Cir US Courthouse Rm 6445 230 N 1st Ave Phoenix AZ 85025-0230

CANCE, WILLIAM GEORGE, surgeon; b. Waterbury, Conn., June 14, 1957. MD, Duke U., 1982. Diplomate Am. Bd. Surgeons. Intern Barnes Hosp., Washington U., St. Louis, 1982-83, resident in gen. surgery, 1983-84, 86-88; fellow in surg. oncology Meml. Sloan Kettering Cancer Ctr., 1988-90; asst. prof. surgery U. N.C., Chapel Hill, 1990-95, chief sect. surg. oncology, 1993—, assoc. prof. surgery, 1995-99, prof. surgery, 1999—, James F. Newsome M.D. Endowed term prof. in surg. oncology, 1998-2003; mem. staff U. N.C. Hosps., 1990—. Fellow Am. Coll. Surgeons (George H.A. Clowes Jr. Meml. Rsch. Career Devel. award 1994); mem. Assn. Acad. Surgery, Soc. Surg. Oncology, Soc. Univ. Surgeons. Office: Univ NC Dept of Surgery 3010 Old Clinic Bld CB 7210 Chapel Hill NC 27599

CANCRO, ROBERT, psychiatrist, educator; b. N.Y.C., Feb. 23, 1932; s. Joseph and Marie E. (Cicchetti) C.; m. Gloria Costanzo, Dec. 8, 1956; children: Robert, Carol. Student, Fordham U., 1948-51; M.D., SUNY, 1955. Intern Kings County Hosp., Bklyn., 1955-56; resident in psychiatry Kings County Hosp., 1956-59; attending staff Gracie Sq. Hosp., N.Y.C., 1959-66; clin. instr. SUNY Downstate Med. Ctr., Bklyn., 1959-66; staff psychiatrist Menninger Found., Topeka, Kans., 1966-69; cons. Topeka State and VA Hosps., 1967-69; prof. dept. psychiatry U. Conn. Health Ctr., Farmington, 1970-76; prof., chmn. dept. psychiatry NYU Med. Ctr., 1976—; dir. N.S. Kline Inst. Psychiat. Research, 1982—; cons. psychiat. edn. br. NIMH; biol. scis. sect. NIMH. Editor 10 books.; Contbr. articles on schizophrenia to profl. jours. Recipient Freida Fromm-Reichmann award, 1975, Strecker award, 1978, Dean award, 1981, Lehmann award, 1992. Fellow A.C.P., Am. Coll. Psychiatrists, Am. Psychiat. Assn.; mem. Am. Psychol. Assn., Assn. Am. Med. Colls., Am. Assn. Social Psychiatry (pres.-elect 1982-84), N.Y. Acad. Scis., AAAS, AMA. Home: 118 Mclain Rd Mount Kisco NY 10549-4932 Office: NYU Med Ctr 550 1st Ave New York NY 10016-6481

CANDAGE, HOWARD EVERETT, insurance management consultant, agent, broker; b. Blue Hill, Maine, Sept. 23, 1952; s. Aubrey Llewellyn and Evelyn Edsley (Carter) C.; m. Jeri-Lynn Moore, Nov. 3, 1979; children, Chelsea Alyssa, Curran Aubrey. Cert., Am. Inst. Property and Liability Underwriters, 1984, Ins. Inst. Am., 1989, 90, 98. CPCU. Ind. comml. fisherman Blue Hill, Maine, 1970-79; ins. agt. J.T. Rosborough, Inc., Ellsworth, Maine, 1979-80, W.C. Ladd & Sons, Inc., Rockland, Maine, 1980-86; br. mgr. W.C. Ladd & Sons, Inc., Damariscotta, Maine, 1986-89; resident v.p. W.C. Ladd & Sons, Inc., Damariscotta, 1988-90; ptnr. Cole-Harrison Agy. of Maine, Inc./Atlantic Yacht Insurers, Ltd., Kennebunk, 1990-93; mktg. mgr. Hanover Ins. Co. Maine, Scarborough, 1993-96; owner Ins. Resources, Gorham, Maine, 1996-98; pres. H.E. Candage, Inc., Portland, Maine, 1998—; pres., Maine Marine Industry Assocs., Freeport, 1982-83; appointed adj. faculty mem. Ctrl. Maine Tech. Coll., 1998—. *Founded HE Candage, Inc. in response to a strong need for independent, objective advice to both insurance practitioners and insurance consumers. Twenty years experience in insurance practice brings clients a high level of value in risk management. agency operations, insurance litigation and industry mergers and acquisitions. Recent accomplishments include performance improvement for many insurance firms and the successful completion of several large mergers in the continuing consolidation of insurance and financial services.* Recipient Chmn's. award Am. Assn. Mng. Gen. Agts., 1992. Mem. Am. Soc. Appraisers, Am. Mgmt. Assn. (cert.), Soc. Chartered Property and Casualty Underwriters (treas. Maine chpt. 1990-92, v.p. 1992-93, pres.-elect

1993-94, pres. 1994-95), Nat. Soc. of Chartered Property and Casualty Underwriters (nat. chpt. affairs com.), Ind. Ins. Agts. Assn. Maine (chmn. com. 1983-84, 91-92, bd. dirs. 1990-93, Young Agt. of Yr. 1987), Soc. Ins. Rsch., Soc. Ins. Counselors (cert.), Am. Soc. Appraisers. Avocations: woodworking, travel, photography. Home: 6 Meadow Crossing Dr Gorham ME 04038-2058 Office: Marine Trade Ctr 2 Portland Fish Pier Ste 214 Portland ME 04101-4633

CANDELARIA, NASH, writer; b. L.A., May 7, 1928; s. Ignacio Nuanez and Flora Rivera Candelaria; m. Doranne Godwin, Nov. 27, 1955; children: David, Alex. BS, UCLA, 1948. Rsch. chemist Don Baxter, Inc., Glendale, Calif., 1948-52; tech. editor N.Am. Aviation, Inc., Downey, Calif., 1953-54; promotion supr. Beckman Instruments, Inc., Fullerton, Calif., 1954-59; promotion specialist Northrop Nortronics, Anaheim, Calif., 1959-65; account exec. Hixon Jorgensen Advt. Agy., L.A., 1965-67; advt. and sales promotion mgr. Varian Assocs., Palo Alto, Calif., 1967-82; pvt. practice fiction writer Palo Alto, 1982-85; mktg. writer Daisy Sys., Mountain View, Calif., 1985-87; mktg. comm. mgr. Hewlett-Packard Co., Palo Alto, 1987-92; ret., 1992; pvt. practice fiction writer Santa Fe, 1992—; lectr. Rutgers U., Newark, 1987. Author: Memories of the Alhambra, 1977, Not by the Sword, 1982 (Am. Book award 1983), Inheritance of Strangers, 1985, The Day the Cisco Kid Shot John Wayne, 1988, Leonor Park, 1991, Uncivil Rights and Other Stories, 1998; author of short stories, novels and articles. 1st lt. USAF, 1952-53. Mem. Nat. Assn. for Chicana and Chicano Studies (Cert. of award 1983), Western Writers Am., PEN Internat. Writers Assn., Sin Fronteras/ Writers Without Borders. Avocations: writing, reading, investments. Home: 111 E San Mateo Rd Santa Fe NM 87505

CANDELAS, TERESA BUSH, special education educator; b. Ft. Eustis, Va., Jan. 28, 1956; d. John Gilbert and Juanita Margaret (Ingram) Bush; m. Jose Antonio Candelas, May 21, 1979 (dec.); children: Deanna, Tony, John, Kristopher, Angelina. BA in Edn., U. Fla., 1993, MEd in Spl. Edn., 1998. Cert. tchr. spl. edn., learning disabilities, mental retardation. Tchr. self-contained mentally handicapped Sch. Bd. Alachua County, Archer, Fla., 1993—. Mem. sch. adv. bd. Archer Cmty. Sch., 1994—; host family Spanish Heritage, Gainesville, Fla., 1992-96. Mem. PTA, Coun. for Exceptional Children, U. Fla. Alumni Assn., Alachua County Edn. Assn. Roman Catholic. Avocations: woodworking, sewing, camping. Home: 4332 NW 26th Ter Gainesville FL 32605-1639

CANDER, LEON, physician, educator; b. Phila., Oct. 7, 1926; s. Joseph Harry and Anna (Glick) C.; m. Geraldine Piontkowski, Dec. 11, 1954; children—Alan Drew, Harris Scott. MD, Temple U., 1951. Rsch. fellow in physiology Grad. Sch. Medicine, U. Pa., 1952-56; resident in medicine Beth Israel Hosp., Boston, 1956-58; asst. in medicine Harvard U. Med. Sch., Boston, 1957-58; practice medicine specializing in pulmonary medicine Boston, Phila. and San Antonio, 1958—; sr. instr. medicine Tufts U. Med. Sch., Boston, 1958-60; asst. prof. medicine Hahnemann Med. Coll., Phila., 1960-63, assoc. prof., 1963-66, clin. prof. medicine, 1985-97; prof., chmn. dept. physiology and medicine U. Tex. Med. Sch., San Antonio, 1966-72; chmn. dept. medicine, dir. med. edn. Daroff div. Albert Einstein Med. Ctr., Phila., 1972-80, head sect. of chest diseases, dir. med. edn., 1980-88; head sect. of chest diseases Mt. Sinai Hosp., Phila., 1988-96; prof. medicine Jefferson Med. Coll., Phila., 1972-89; clin. prof. Hahnemann Med. Coll., Phila., 1985-97; mem. Nat. Adv. Coun. on Black Lung; nat. cons. U.S. Dept. Labor Black Lung Program, 1978—. Soc. Editor: (with J. H. Moyer) Aging of the Lung, 1963. Research fellow Nat. Acad. Scis., 1954-55. Fellow ACP; mem. Am. Thoracic Soc., Am. Physiol. Soc. Home: 317 Cherry Ln Wynnewood PA 19096-1710 Office: City Ave Med Ctr Bala Cynwyd PA 19004

CANDIB, MURRAY A., business executive, retail management consultant; b. Chelsea, Mass., Sept. 16, 1915; s. Jacob and Fannie (Einbinder) C.; m. Claudette Aggie, Oct. 8, 1972 (dec. Dec. 1991); children: Nancy, Rachel, David, Caroline; m. Maureen Davis, July 30, 1995. *Wife Maureen is an attorney counsel to the Children's Psychiatric Center of Miami. Daughter Nancy, who was living in Switzerland, has moved to New York and is with Brown Harris Realtors. She has two children, Cristina and Francesca. Daughter Rachel Tannenbaum lives on a ranch in Tucson, Arizona with husband Adam and their daughter Batie. She trains show horses. Son David since graduating Emory University, works as a market analyst at Solomon Smith Barney in Atlanta, Georgia. Daughter Caroline is married to Enrique Suarez, an engineer. They reside in Miami.* B.A., Boston U., 1950. Founder King's Dept. Store Inc., 1949; Pres. Canco Enterprises, Worcester, Mass. Credited with being the pioneer of self-service dept. stores; subject of articles in Fortune Mag., Harvard Bus. Rev. and profl. jours. Founder, life trustee, soc. mem. Mt. Sinai Hosp., Miami Beach, Fla.; benefactor Miami Heart Inst.; bd. dirs. Temple Emanu-El, Miami Beach; charter mem. Rep. Presdl. Task Force, 1981—, U.S. Senatorial Club, 1981—, Nat. Rep. Senatorial Com.; mem. Fla. Victory Com. Brandeis U. fellow, 1966; recipient Human Relations award Am. Jewish Com., Nat. Community Service award Jewish Theol. Sem. of Am., 1965, Man of Yr. award Mental Health Clinic, Mt. Sinai Hosp., N.Y.C., Man of Yr. award Boys Wear Industry of N.Y., Hall of Fame award U. Mass. Mem. Am. Heart Assn., Shriners, Masons, Westview Country Club Miami. Avocations: tennis, golf, painting, boating. Office: 306 Main St Worcester MA 01608-1550

CANDIDO, A. MICHAEL, contracting company executive, real estate manager; b. Falls Church, Va., June 23, 1953; s. Albert Babbitts and Rose Marie (Naturale) C.; m. Joyce Mary Baratta, Sept. 27, 1975; children: Rosalie, Elizabeth, Jacqueline, Allison. BA in Acctg., William Paterson U., 1975. Office mgr. J. Moore & Co., Livingston, N.J., 1973-79; v.p. J. Moore & Co., Livingston, 1979-95, pres., 1995—; pres. Essex Realty Co., Cedar Grove, N.J., 1991—; adj. prof. Kean U. N.J., Union, 1988-93. Mem. Essex Fells (N.J.) Zoning Bd., 1995—; trustee Steamfitters Local 475, Warren, N.J., 1995—; chmn. bldg. and grounds com. Notre Dame Ch., No. Caldwell, N.J., 1997—; active MCAA Industry Fund, Washington, 1999—. Mem. MCA-PAC (treas. 1998), Mech. Contractors Assn. (treas. 1998—), Essex Fells Country Club, Bay Head Hist. Soc. Roman Catholic. Avocations: golf, photography, books, music, fishing. Office: J Moore & Co 118 Naylon Ave Livingston NJ 07039

CANDIDO, ANTHONY NICHOLAS, artist, educator; b. N.Y.C., Sept. 5, 1924; s. John and Anna (Romano) C.; m. Bonnie Evans, Aug. 1959 (div. 1964); 1 child, Lesley; m. Nancy Catherine Meehan, Dec. 9, 1967. BArch, Ill. Inst. Tech., 1954. Archtl. designer I. M. Pei, N.Y.C., 1954-57; prof. art and arch. Cooper Union, N.Y.C., 1959-61, 1963-65; adj. prof., 1958—; adj. prof. CCNY, 1967-93; freelance artist, N.Y.C., 1957—; vis. prof. U. Calif., Berkeley, 1961-63, Cornell U., Ithaca, N.Y., 1966, U. Ill., Chgo., 1967; designer, constrn. supr. U.S. Pavilion Expo 70 Japan, Davis, Brody Architects, N.Y.C., 1969; spkr. in field. One-man shows include Area Gallery, N.Y.C., 1963, Attitudes Gallery, Colo., 1975, Wooster St. Gallery, 1985, Internat. Design Forum Asahikawa, Hokkgido, Japan, 1985, Cooper Unions Houghton Gallery, N.Y., 1993; exhibited in group shows at Exhbn. Momentum, Chgo., 1952-54, St. Mark's on the Bowery, 1964, Different Realities, Spectrum Gallery, 1967, Betty Parsons Gallery, 1973, Nippon Club, 1976, Betty Parsons, 1981, Inst. Contemporary Art, Boston, 1984, Prince Street Gallery, N.Y.C., 1986, Philippe Briet Gallery, N.Y.C., 1990, Can. Ctr. for Arch., Montreal, 1997-98. Finalist Toronto City Hall Competition, 1958. With archives of Am. art br. Smithsonian (I.M.PEI). 1st lt. USAAF, 1943-45, ETO. Democrat. Home and Studio: 463 West St Apt A-1111 New York NY 10014-2040 Office: Cooper Union Cooper Sq New York NY 10014

CANDIDO, ARTHUR ALDO, publishing and distribution company executive; b. Corona, Queens, N.Y., June 6, 1960. BA, CUNY, 1982. Ops. mgr. Scholium Internat. Inc., Port Washington, N.Y., 1982-91, pres., 1991—. Mem. Spl. Librs. Assn., Am. Booksellers Assn. Office: Scholium Internat Inc PO Box 1519 Port Washington NY 11050-0306

CANDLAND, DOUGLAS KEITH, educator; b. Long Beach, Calif., July 9, 1934; s. Horace George and Erma Louise (Downing) C.; m. Mary Homrighausen, June 18, 1959; children: Kevin, Christopher, Ian. A.B., Pomona Coll., 1956; Ph.D., Princeton U., 1959. Research fellow U. Va., 1959-60, Delta Primate Center, 1967-68, Pa. State U., 1968-69, U. Stirling, Scotland, 1972-73, Cambridge (Eng.) U., 1977-78, U. Mysore (India), 1983; asst. prof. psychology Bucknell U., 1960-64, assoc. prof., 1964-67, prof., 1967—, prof. animal behavior, 1985—, Presdl. prof., 1973-80, head program in animal behavior, 1968—, pres. div. teaching of psychology, 1976-77, head dept. psychology, 1970-75, Class of 1956 lectr., 1971; vis. scholar U. Calif., Berkeley, 1996-97. Author: Exploring Behavior, 1961, Psychology: The Experimental Approach, 1968, 2d edit., 1978, Emotion, Bodily Change, 1961, Emotion, 1979, Feral Children and Clever Animals, Reflections on Human Nature, 1993, Living Fossils of the Mind, 1997, Handbook of Comparative Psychology, 1998; contbr. chpts. to profl. books; editor The Primates, 1968-78, Animal Behavior, 1979-89; assoc. editor Animal Learning and Behavior, 1976-84, Teaching of Psychology, 1976-84, Am. Jour. Primatology, 1980-84; cons. editor Jour. Comparative Psychology, 1988-94. Bd. dirs. Wildlife Preservation Trust Internat. (chmn. conservation 1989-94), Pa. Cinema Register, 1976-79, 86-89. Recipient award Lindback Found., 1971; Harriman award Bucknell U., 1979. Fellow Am. Psychol. Assn. (award for disting. contbn. to edn. 1978); mem. Brit. Psychol. Assn., Psychonomic Soc., Internat. Soc. Primatologists, Animal Behavior Soc. (chmn. policy and planning). Home: 125 Stein Ln Lewisburg PA 17837-1742 Office: Psych Dept Bucknell U Lewisburg PA 17837

CANDLER, JAMES NALL, JR., lawyer; b. Detroit, Jan. 25, 1943; s. James Nall and Lorna Augusta (Blood) C.; m. Jean Ward McKinnon, Mar. 8, 1974; children: Christine, Elizabeth, Anne. AB, Princeton U., 1965; JD, U. Mich., 1970. Bar: Mich. 1970. Assoc. Dickinson Wright PLLC, Detroit, 1970-77, ptnr., 1977—; adj. prof. real estate planning U. Detroit Sch. of Law, 1975-80. Bd. dirs. Detroit Inst. Ophthalmology Grosse Pointe Park, Mich., 1983—, chmn., 1994—. Lt. USNR, 1965-67. Mem. State Bar Mich. (chmn. real property law sect. 1998-99), Am. Coll. of Real Estate Lawyers, Grosse Pointe Club (chmn. 1987-89), Country Club of Detroit. Republican. Avocations: sailing, golf, platform tennis. Home: 211 Country Club Dr Grosse Pointe MI 48236-2901 Office: 500 Woodward Ave Ste 4000 Detroit MI 48226-3423

CANDLER, JOHN SLAUGHTER, II, retired lawyer; b. Atlanta, Nov. 30, 1908; s. Asa Warren and Harriet Lee (West) C.; m. Dorothy Bruce Warthen, June 13, 1933; children: Dorothy Warthen (Mrs. Joseph W. Hamilton, Jr.), John Slaughter, Jr. A.B. magna cum laude, U. Ga., 1929; J.D., Emory U., 1931. Bar: Ga. bar 1931. Dep. asst. atty. gen. State of Ga., 1951-68; chmn. sect. fiduciary law State Bar Ga., 1964-65. Trustee Ga. Student Ednl. Fund, 1950—, Kappa Alpha Scholarship Fund, 1955-86, pres., 1970-72; trustee Lovett Sch., 1952-59; mem. USO Coun. of Ga., 1969—, pres., 1974-75; trustee St. Philip's Cathedral, 1957-67, sr. warden, 1955, lay reader, 1971-96. Col. USAR, 1941-46. Decorated Army Commendation Ribbon. Fellow Ga. Bar Found.; mem. ABA, Atlanta Bar Assn., Lawyers Club Atlanta, Atlanta Estate Planning Coun. (pres. 1963-64), Am. Legion (post cmdr. 1949-50), Ret. Officers Assn., Res. Officers Assn. U.S. (state pres. 1946), Mil. Order World Wars, English Spkg. Union, Kiwanis, Masons, Piedmont Driving Club, Capital City Club, Commerce Club, Ft. McPherson Officers Club, Oglethorpe Club (Savannah), Army-Navy Club (Washington), Phi Beta Kappa, Phi Kappa Phi, Phi Delta Phi, Kappa Alpha Order, Sigma Delta Chi. Home: 413 Manor Ridge Dr NW Atlanta GA 30305-3509*

CANDLISH, MALCOLM, manufacturing company executive; b. Liverpool, Eng., Aug. 23, 1935; came to U.S., 1963; s. Norman Dennis Candlish and Jane Jefferson (Grieves) Downey; m. Jasmine Rosemary Cresswell, Apr. 15, 1963; children: Fiona, Vanessa, Sarah, John. BSc, London Sch. Econs., 1956. Mgr. mktg., asst. mgr. prodn. Beecham Products, Brazil, Eng., 1958-63; product mgr. Colgate Palmolive, N.Y.C., 1963-65; prin. McKinsey and Co., N.Y.C., Cleve., Toronto, Melbourne and Sydney, Australia, 1965-77; pres., sr. v.p. mktg. Wilson Sporting Goods, Chgo., 1977-83; pres. Samsonite Corp., Denver, 1983-89; chmn., CEO Sealy, Inc. (formerly Ohio Mattress Co.), Cleve., 1989-92, First Alert, Inc., Aurora, IL, 1992-94; bd. dirs. Am. Mut. Life Assurance Co., Des Moines, Black & Decker Corp., Towson, Md. Bd. dirs. Mile High United Way, Denver, 1985-89. Lt. British Army, 1956-58. Mem. Luggage and Leather Goods Mfrs. Am. (bd. dirs. 1984-89), Econ. Club (founding mem.). Republican. Avocations: lit., philosophy, sports.

CANDREIA, PEGGY JO, financial analyst; b. Pawhuska, Okla., Aug. 23, 1944; d. Joseph Leonard and Wilma Jane (Brook) C. Student, U. Ozarks, 1965. Supr. credit and collections Credit Bur. Bartlesville, Okla., 1965-69; credit rep. Shell Oil Co., Tulsa, 1969-88; owner, mgr. Georgeous Car Care, Tulsa, 1988-90; fin. analyst H.A. Chpaman Inst., Children's Med. Ctr., Tulsa, 1990—, fin. coord. Children's Med. Network Telethon, 1994-99. Founder local chpt. Parents and Friends of Lesbians and Gays, Tulsa, 1988-90; v.p. Tulsa Oklahomans for Human Rights, 1988-89; bd. dirs. Follies Rev., Tulsa, 1993-97, Broken Arrow Cmty. Playhouse, 1998—; mem. steering com. and host com. Names Project, Tulsa, 1990—, co-chmn. ctrl. region logistics, Washington, 1996. Republican. Roman Catholic. Avocations: designing homes, travel, skiing, fundraising, drawing. Homee: 1525 N College Ave Tulsa OK 74110-2719

CANDRIS, LAURA A., lawyer; b. Frankfort, Ky., Apr. 5, 1955; d. Charles M. and Dorothy (King) Sutton; m. Aris S. Candris, Dec. 22, 1974. AB with distinction in polit. sci., Transylvania Coll., 1975; postgrad., U. Pitts., 1975-77, U. Fla., 1977-78; JD, U. Pitts., 1978. Bar: Fla. 1978, U.S. Dist. Ct. (mid. dist.) Fla. 1978, U.S. Ct. Appeals (4th cir.) 1980, Pa. 1981, U.S. Dist. Ct. (we. dist.) Pa. 1982, U.S. Ct. Appeals (3d cir.) 1983. Assoc. Coffman, Coleman, Andrews & Grogan, Jacksonville, Fla., 1978-80, Manion, Alder & Cohen, Pitts., 1981-85; assoc. Eckert, Seamans, Cherin & Mellott, Pitts., 1985-86, ptnr., 1987-96, vice chmn. labor and employment law dept, mem. practice mgmt. com., mem. strategic planning com.; ptnr. Meyer Unkovic & Scott, LLP, Pitts., 1996—, chair labor, employment law and employee benefits sect.; mem. litigation and transactions depts. Meyer Unkovic & Scott, LLP; counsel Nat. Assn. Women in Constrn. (chpt. 161), Pitts., 1985-86. Contbr. over 30 articles to profl. jours. including Forum Reporter, Pers. Law Update, Employment Law Inst. manuals, and Reference Manual for the 34th Annual Mid-West Labor Law Conf. Coun. mem. O'Hara Twp., 1986-96; mem. O'Hara Twp. Planning Commn., 1990; bd. dirs. Tri-State Employers Assn., 1991-93, Parent and Child Guidance Ctr., 1991—, v.p. exec. com., 1998-99, pres. 1999; treas., mem. exec. com. SMC Bus. Couns., 1993-94, bd. dirs., 1993-96; bd. dirs. Big Bros. & Big Sisters Greater Pitts., 1998—. Nat. Merit Found. scholar 1972-75; named Ky. Col., 1974. Mem. ABA (EEO com. labor sect., labor and employment law com. litigation sect.), Fla. Bar Assn., Pa. Bar Assn. (employment sect.), Allegheny County Bar Assn. (coun. on professionalism, employment and fed. cts. sect., hdqrs. com. and pers. subcom.), Soc. Hosp. Attys. Western Pa., Pitts. Human Resources Assn., Women's Bar Assn. Western Pa. Republican. Avocations: skiing, traveling, bicycling, reading. Office: Meyer Unkovic & Scott LLP 1300 Oliver Bldg Pittsburgh PA 15222

CANE, DAVID E., chemistry educator; b. N.Y.C., Sept. 22, 1944. BA, Harvard U., 1966, AM, 1967, PhD, 1971. NIH Postdoctoral fellow Eidgenossiche Technische Hochschule NIH, Zurich, Switzerland, 1971-73; asst. prof. Brown U., Providence, 1973-78, assoc. prof., 1978-80, prof., 1980—, chmn. dept. chemistry, 1983-89, Vernon K. Krieble prof. chemistry; vis. prof. U. Chgo., 1980; cons. Smith Kline and French Labs., Phila., 1984-85, Lederle Labs., Pearl River, N.Y., 1986-88; sci. adv. bd. KOSAN Biosci., San Francisco, 1996—; chmn. Gordon Conf. Natural Products, New Hampton, N.H., 1982; co-chmn. Gordon Conf. Enzymes, Coenzymes & Metabolic Pathways, Meriden, N.H., 1996. Mem. editl. bd. Bioorganic Chemistry, 1983—, Jour. Antibiotics, 1983—, Chem. Revs., 1987-89, Topics in Sterochemistry; assoc. editor Jour. Organic Chemistry, 1995—; contbr. articles to profl. jours. Recipient Research Career Devel. award NIH, 1978-83; fellow Japan Soc. Promotion Sci., 1983, Alfred P. Sloan Found., 1978; NIH Fogarty Sr. Internat. fellow, 1989; John Simon Guggenheim Meml. Found. fellow, 1990; Disting. Vis. fellow Christ's Coll., U. Cambridge, 1989-90; recipient Fulbright Grant-in-Aid, 1990. Mem. Am. Chem. Soc. (Ernest Guenther award 1985), Royal Soc. Chemistry (Simonsen lectr. 1990-91), Kitasato Inst. (Microbial Chemistry medal, 1995). *

CANE, MARK ALAN, oceanography and climate researcher; b. Bklyn., Oct. 20, 1944; s. Philip and Ida Deborah C.; m. Barbara Jane Haak, Oct. 28, 1968; children: Laura, Jacob. BA, Harvard U., 1965, MS, 1968; PhD, MIT, 1975. Earth scientist NASA, 1975-79; assoc. prof. oceanography MIT, Cambridge, 1979-84; Doherty sr. scientist Lamont Doherty Earth Obs. of Columbia, Palisades, N.Y., 1984-97; G. Unger Vetlesen prof. earth and climate scis. Columbia U., N.Y.C., 1998—. Contbr. articles to profl. jours. Organizer Student Non-Violent Coord. Conv., Ala., 1965. Fellow AAAS, Am. Meteorol. Soc. (Sverdup gold medal 1993), Am. Geophys. Union; mem. Oceanography Soc., N.Y. Acad. Scis. Democrat. Jewish. Achievements include prediction of climate variations known as El Nino and the Southern Oscillation. Office: Lamont Doherty Earth Obs Rte 9W Palisades NY 10964

CANEDY, NANCY GAY, comptroller, accountant, educator; b. North Adams, Mass., May 29, 1932; d. Donald Otis and Florence Gay (Hicks) C.; m. Leonard C. Goldman, July 19, 1963 (div.); 1 child, David Bennett. BS in Bus., Skidmore Coll., Saratoga Springs, N.Y., 1954; MS in Bus., SUNY, Albany, 1962; postgrad., Rensselaer Poly. Inst., 1971-72, Loyola U., Balt., 1973-74. Cert. tchr., N.Y. Instr. bus. Skidmore Coll., Saratoga Springs, 1955-61; asst. prof. bus. SUNY, Albany, 1961-69; assoc. prof. Towson (Md.) State U., 1972-76; asst. mgr. Whitcomb Summit Co., Inc., Florida, Mass., 1976-78; assoc. prof. Mass. Coll. Liberal Arts, North Adams, 1978-81; cost acctg. mgr. Tansitor Electronics, Bennington, Vt., 1981-85; vis. lectr. SUNY, Albany, 1985-86; pres. Bennett Bus. Communications, Ames, Iowa, 1986-88; comptr. Dodge Machine Co., Inc., Hoosick Falls, N.Y., 1990—. Bd. dirs. Shaftsbury (Vt.) Hist. Soc., 1982-96, pres., 1984-86; bd. dirs. Park McCollough House, North Bennington, Vt., 1984-86; pres. Shaftsbury Bicentennial Com., Shaftsbury, 1990-91. Episcopalian. Avocations: collecting antiques, geneology, travel, hiking, fishing. Office: Dodge Machine Co Inc PO Box 178 Hoosick Falls NY 12090-0178

CANEPA, CATHY, psychiatrist; b. N.Y.C., Jan. 8, 1951; d. Tito Enrique and Florence (Lessing) C.; m. Daniel Robert Neuspiel, Apr. 12, 1987; children: Juliana, Samuel. BA magna cum laude, Columbia U., 1979; MD, Yeshiva U., 1988. Diplomate Am. Bd. Med. Examiners, Am. Bd. Psychiatry & Neurology. Actress N.Y.C., 1973-80; psychiat. resident N.Y. Hosp.-Cornell Med. Ctr., White Plains, N.Y., 1988-94; instr. psychiatry Albert Einstein Coll. Medicine of Yeshiva U., Bronx, N.Y., 1994-97; dir. partial hosp. & women's program St. Vincent's Hosp. Westchester, White Plains, 1997—. Mem. Am. Psychiat. Assn., Phi Beta Kappa. Home: 8 Antony Rd White Plains NY 10605-2906 Office: 5 Old Mamaronectz Rd White Plains NY 10605

CANEPA, JOHN CHARLES, banking consultant; b. Newburyport, Mass., Aug. 26, 1930; s. John Jere and Agnes R. (Barbour) C.; m. Marie Olney, Sept. 13, 1953; children: Claudia, John J., Peter C., Milissa L. A.B., Harvard U., 1953; M.B.A., NYU, 1960. With Chase Manhattan Bank, N.Y.C., 1957-63; sr. v.p. Provident Bank, Cin., 1963-70; past pres., chmn. bd., CEO Old Kent Fin. Corp., Grand Rapids, Mich., 1970-95; past pres., past chief exec. officer Old Kent Bank & Trust Co., Grand Rapids, 1970-95; consulting prin. Crowe Chizek, Grand Rapids, Mich., 1995—. Served with USN, 1953-57. Office: Crowe Chizek 400 Riverfront Plaza Grand Rapids MI 49503

CANER, GEORGE COLKET, JR., lawyer; b. Boston, Oct. 12, 1925; s. George Colket and Mary (Paul) C.; m. Judith Brentlinger, Mar. 14, 1953; children: Grace G., Daniel F., Sarah H. A.B., Harvard U., 1946, LL.B., 1951. Bar: Mass. 1951, U.S. Ct. Appeals (1st Cir.) 1954, U.S. Supreme Ct. 1974. Assoc. Ropes & Gray, Boston, 1951-56, ptnr., 1965-96; asst. U.S. atty. Dept. Justice, Boston, 1957-60; trustee Brookline Savs. Bank, Mass., 1965—. Served to cpl. U.S. Army, 1943-45. Episcopalian. Home: 355 Hammond St Chestnut Hill MA 02467-1224 Office: Ropes & Gray 1 International Pl Boston MA 02110-2624

CANES, BRIAN DENNIS, professional services company official; b. London, July 14, 1945; came to U.S., 1982.; s. Jules Joel and Freda Rica (Gavronsky) C.; m. Melanie Maxine Segal, June 29, 1969; 1 child, David. B.Sc, U. Witwatersrand, Johannesburg, Republic of South Africa, 1967; student, Inst. Actuaries, London. Systems mgr. Shepley & Fitchett Consulting Actuaries, Johannesburg, 1968-75; asst. v.p. William M. Mercer Ltd., Toronto, Ont., Can., 1975-80; controller William M. Mercer Ltd., Toronto, 1980-82; prin. William M. Mercer-Meidinger-Hansen, N.Y.C., 1982-87; sr. systems cons. The Wyatt Co., N.Y.C., 1987-93; asst. dir. systems Ernst & Young ABC, N.Y.C., 1993-96; sr. mgr. Ernst & Young Mgmt. Cons., 1996—. Office: Ernst & Young 750 7th Ave Fl 17A New York NY 10019-6827*

CANES, MICHAEL EDWIN, trade association administrator, economist; b. Jerusalem, Israel, Dec. 24, 1941; came to U.S., 1943; m. Mary Patricia Ferron, July 11, 1970; children: Brandice, David, Aran. BS, U. Chgo., 1963, MBA, 1965; MSc, London Sch. Econs., 1966; PhD, UCLA, 1970. Economist The Ctr. for Naval Analyses, Arlington, Va., 1969-72; asst. prof. U. Rochester (N.Y.), 1972-74; sr. economist and dep. dir. Am. Petroleum Inst., Washington, 1974-78, dir., 1978-82, v.p., 1982—. Contbr. articles to profl. jours. Mem. Am. Economic Assn., Internat. Assn. of Energy Economists, Western Economic Assn. Office: Am Petroleum Inst 1220 L St NW Washington DC 20005-4018

CANESTRARI, RONALD, state legislator. Assemblyman dist. 106 N.Y. State Assembly, 1989—. Address: 731 Legislative Office Bui Albany NY 12248*

CANFIELD, EDWARD FRANCIS, lawyer, business executive; b. Phila., Apr. 7, 1922; s. Frank James and Eunice C. (Sullivan) C.; m. Janet Powell Trotter, 1952 (div. 1991); children: Andrew Trotter, Janet Powell; m. Margaret Harvey O'Brien, 1993. B.A., St. Joseph's U., 1943; J.D., U. Pa., 1949. Bar: Pa. 1949, D.C. 1972. Practice in Phila., 1949-51; with RCA, 1953-60; with Philco-Ford Corp., 1960-69, corp. dir. govt. planning and mktg., 1961-69; pres. Leisure Time Industries, Inc., 1969; mng. ptnr. Casey, Scott & Canfield, 1971-93; ptnr. Canfield & Smith, Washington, 1993—. Lt. comdr. USNR, ret. Mem. Fed. Bar Assn., D.C. Bar Assn., Phila. Bar Assn., Congl. Country Club (Bethesda, Md.), Overbrook Golf Club (Bryn Mawr, Pa., Atlantic City (N.J.) Country Club. Home: 1 Andover Rd Haverford PA 19041-1002 Office: Canfield & Smith Fed Bar Bldg 1815 H St NW Ste 1001 Washington DC 20006-3604 also: 1518 Walnut St Ste 1200 Philadelphia PA 19102-3419

CANFIELD, ELIZABETH FRANCES, lawyer; b. Fairport, Mo., Aug. 19, 1913; d. James Arthur and Bertha Mae (Ashley) Foard; m. Robert Roe Canfield, May 7, 1933 (dec. Sept. 1994); children: James Robert, Philip Roe. LLB, LaSalle Law Sch., 1949. Bar: Ill. 1950. Pvt. practice Rockford, Ill., 1950-97; spl. asst. atty. gen. State of Ill., 1974-84; ret. Rockford, Ill., 1997; asst. atty. gen. State Ill., 1974-84; lectr. in field. Women's divsn. chmn. United Fund Dr., Rockford, 1951; bd. trustees Ct. St. United Meth. Ch.; bd. dirs. Family Consultation Svc. Rockford; mem. blue ribbon adv. com. to Mayor of Rockford; elected mem. Dist. 58 Sch. Bd.; bd. dirs. Wesley Willows Retirement Home; bd. trustees North Rockford Convalescent home, Willows Health Ctr. Mem. AAUW, LWV (hon. life, Rockford pres. 1946-48), Winnebago County Bar Assn. (chmn. com. 1950—), Quota Internat. Exec. Women's Svc. (Rockford pres. 1980-82, mem. internat. by-laws and dist. gov.), Philanthropic-Ednl. Orgn. Republican. Methodist. Avocations: writing, reading, swimming, travelling, opera, theater. Office: Canfield Law Offices 202 W State St Ste 1100 Rockford IL 61101-1158

CANFIELD, GRANT WELLINGTON, JR., management consultant; b. L.A., Nov. 28, 1923; s. Grant Wellington and Phyllis Marie(Westland) C.; m. Virginia Louise Bellinger, June 17, 1945; 1 child, Julie Marie. BS, U. So. Calif., 1949, MBA, 1958. Personnel and indsl. relations exec. L.A., 1949-55; employee relations cons., regional mgr. Mchts. and Mfrs. Assn. L.A., 1955-60; v.p., orgnl. devel. cons. Hawaii Employers Council, Honolulu, 1960-75; pres., dir. Hawaiian Ednl. Council, 1969-92, chmn., CEO, 1989-92, chmn. emeritus, 1992; prin. cons. Grant W. Canfield CMC, 1993—; faculty assignments Calif. State U., L.A., 1957-59, U. So. Calif., 1958-59, U. Hawaii, 1963-72; exec. v.p. Hawaii Garment Mfrs. Assn., 1965-75, Assn. Hawaii Restaurant Employers, 1966-75; exec. dir. Hawaii League Savs. Assns., 1971-78; exec. dir. Pan-Pacific Surg. Assn., 1980-81, exec. v.p., 1982-83; exec. dir. Hawaii Bus. Roundtable, 1983-89; sec., treas. Econ. Devel. Corp. Honolulu, 1984-85; sec., treas. Hawaii Conv. Park Council, Inc., 1984-86, hon. dir., 1986-88. Co-author: Resource Manual for Public Collective Bargaining, 1973. Bd. dirs. Hawaii Restaurant Assn., 1974-76, bd. dirs. Hawaii chpt. Nat. Assn. Accts., 1963-67, nat. dir., 1965-66; bd. dirs. Vol. Service Bur. Honolulu, 1965-66, pres., 1966-68; bd. dirs. Vol. Info. and Referral Service

Honolulu, 1972-75, Goodwill Vocat. Tng. Ctrs. of Hawaii, 1973-81, Girl Scout council Pacific, 1961-65, 71-72; bd. dirs. Hawaii Com. Alcoholism, 1962-71, co-chmn., 1964-68; pres., dir. Friends of Punahou Sch., 1972-75; mem. community adv. bd. Jr. League Honolulu, 1968-70; exec. bd. Aloha council Boy Scouts Am., 1962-65; bd. regents Chaminade U., 1983-85. Served to 1st lt. inf. AUS, 1943-46. Decorated Bronze Star, Purple Heart, Combat Inf. badge. Mem. ASTD, Am. Soc. Assn. Execs. (cert. assn. exec.), Inst. Mgmt. Cons. (cert.), Soc. for Human Resource Mgmt., Healdsburg Mus. and Hist. Soc. (chmn. exec. com. 1993-95, dir. 1994—, pres. 1995-97), Santa Rosa Symphony Assn. (bd. dirs. 1993—, mem. exec. com. 1995-97), Rotary, Masons. Home: 1950 W Dry Creek Rd Healdsburg CA 95448-9747

CANFIELD, HOLLY BETH, legal nurse consultant; b. Buffalo, Nov. 21, 1970; d. Lowell Alonzo and Marilyn Marie (Hamann) Henry. BSN magna cum laude, U. Buffalo, 1995. RN, N.Y. Nurse Dept. VA Med. Ctr., Buffalo, 1995, Caro Med. Ctr., Buffalo, 1995-96, Geneva B. Scruggs Comty. Health Care Ctr., Buffalo, 1996-97; legal nurse cons. Magner & Love, P.C., Buffalo, 1997-98; nurse cons. Brown & Tarantino, LLP, Buffalo, 1998—. Lucie Stanton Nursing scholar U. Buffalo, 1992-95. Mem. Western N.Y. Paralegal Assn., Inc., U. Buffalo Alumni Assn., Sigma Theta Tau. Democrat. Lutheran. Avocations: inline skating, ice skating, stamp collecting, reading current research materials. Home: 10 Slate Creek Dr Apt 11 Cheektowaga NY 14227-2952 Office: Brown & Tarantino 1500 Rand Bldg 14 Lafayette Sq Buffalo NY 14203

CANFIELD, JAMES, art director. Art dir. Oreg. Ballet, Portland, 1988—. Office: Oregon Ballet 1120 SW 10th Ave Portland OR 97205-2400*

CANFIELD, JOHN DOUGLAS, English educator, writer, consultant; b. Washington, Feb. 4, 1941; s. Austin Francis and Gertrude Canfield; m. Pamela Eden Crotty, Sept. 7, 1963; children: Robert Alan, Bret Douglas, Colin Geoffrey. AB, U. Notre Dame, 1963; MA, Johns Hopkins U., 1966; PhD, U. Fla., 1969. Tchr. Radnor (Pa.) Sr. H.S., 1964-65; grad. asst. tchg. Johns Hopkins U., Balt., 1965-66; asst. prof. UCLA, 1969-74; assoc. prof. U. Ariz., Tucson, 1974-79, prof., 1979-94, Regents' prof., 1994—. Author: Nicholas Rowe and Christian Tragedy, 1977, Word as Bond in English Literature from the Middle Ages to the Restoration, 1989, Tricksters and Estates: On the Ideology of Restoration Comedy, 1997 (Outstanding Acad. Bk. award Choice Mag. 1997), Heroes and States: On the Ideology of Restoration Tragedy, 1999; mem. editl. bd. Restoration, 1983—; mem. adv. bd. Eighteenth-Century Studies, 1996-99. Coach, referee Am. Youth Soccer Orgn., 1983—. Recipient Tchg. Excellence award Burlington Resources Found., 1991, Sherill Creative Tchg. award U. Ariz. Found., 1993, Ariz. Prof. of Yr., Coun. for Advancement and Support of Edn., 1993. Mem. MLA (chair exec. com. divsn. on restoration and early 18th century Brit. lit.), Am. Soc. 18th Century Studies (chair Clifford Prize com. 1990-91), Western Soc. 18th Century Studies (exec. sec. 1972-74), Group for Early Modern Cultural Studies (co-founder). Democrat. Avocations: hunting, soccer. E-mail: dcanfield@dakotacom.net and jdcanfie@u.arizona.edu. FAX: 520-621-7397. Home: 1802 W Ahmed Ave Tucson AZ 85704 Office: Univ Ariz Dept English 445 Modern Lang Bldg # 67 Tucson AZ 85721

CANFIELD, JUDY OHLBAUM, psychologist; b. N.Y.C., May 15, 1947; d. Arthur and Ada (Wood) Ohlbaum; m. John T. Canfield (div.); children: Oran David, Kyle Danya. BA, Grinnell Coll., 1963; MA, New Sch. Social Rsch., 1967; PhD, U.S. Internat. U., 1970. Psychologist Mendocino State Hosp., Talmage, Calif., 1968-69, Douglas Coll., New Westminster, BC, Can., 1971-72, Family & Childrens Clinic, Burnaby, BC, Can., 1971-72; psychologist, trainer, cons. VA Hosp., Northampton, Mass., 1972-75; dir. New England Ctr., Amherst, Mass., 1972-76; dir., psychologist Gateways, Lansdale, Pa., 1977-78; asst. prof., psychologist Hahnemann Med. Ctr., Phila., 1978-84; pres., dir. Inst. Holistic Health, Phila., 1978-85; psychologist, cons. Berkeley, Calif., 1986—. Mem. task force, tng. com. Berkeley Dispute Resolution Svc., 1986-89; mem. measure H com. Berkeley United Sch. Dist., 1987-88. Mem. APA, Nat. Register Health Svc. Providers in Psychology, Nat. Assn. Advancement Gestalt Therapy (steering com. 1990), Calif. Psychol. Assn., Alameda County Psychol. Assn. (info.-referral svc. 1989—), Assn. Humanistic Psychology. Avocations: piano, horseback riding, ice skating. Office: 2031 Delaware St Berkeley CA 94709-2121

CANFIELD, ROBERT CLEO, lawyer; b. St. Joseph, Mo., Sept. 10, 1938; s. Robert Charles Canfield and Nadine (Ressler) Thomas; m. Patricia Joan Harms, June 8, 1958; children: Tamara, Robert, Michael. AB, DePauw U., 1960; LLB, U. Mich., 1963. Bar: Mo. 1963, U.S. Dist. Ct. (we. dist.) Mo. 1964. Assoc. Watson, Ess, Marshall & Enggas, Kansas City, Mo., 1963-72, ptnr., 1972-92; sr. v.p., gen. counsel, sec. DST Sys., inc., Kansas City, 1992—. Mem. exec. bd. Boy Scouts Am., Kansas City, 1982—. Mem. ABA, Mo. Bar Assn., Kansas City Club. Republican. Methodist. Home: 9722 Sagamore Rd Shawnee Mission KS 66206-2314 Office: DST Systems Inc 333 W 11th St Kansas City MO 64105-1634

CANFIELD, STELLA STOJANKA, artist, art gallery owner; b. Varna, Bulgaria, Jan. 17, 1950; emigrated to W. Germany, 1980, came to U.S., 1985; d. Stamat and Pepa-Despenna (Blisnacova) Bogdanov; m. Peter Petrov, Feb. 28, 1971 (div. Mar. 1988); children: Nicoletta, Peter; m. Michael Canfield, Mar. 27, 1988; adopted children: Jennifer, Paul. M, U. Phys. Edn. and Sports, Sofia, 1973. Lic. sport phys. therapy, Bulgaria. Phys. edn. and sports pedagogue H.S., Tolbuhin, Bulgaria, 1974-75, Med. U., Sofia, Bulgaria, 1975-76, middle and H.S., Sofia, 1976-80; owner Stella restaurant, Dusseldorf, Germany, 1982-83; with Oberheid Ceramic Studio, Dusseldorf, 1983-85; retail sales rep. The Ltd., Walnut Creek, Calif., 1989-90; savs. rep. Calif. Savs. & Loans, Montclair, 1990-92. Bd. dirs. Coupeville (Wash.) Arts Ctr., 1993—; treas., exhibitor Penn Cove Gallery, Coupeville, 1995—. Recipient 3 awards Tulip Festival, La Conner, Wash., 1994, 2 awards, 1995, 96, 2 awards, 1997, 1 award, 1998. Mem. Youth Coalition, Northwest Watercolor Soc. Avocations: languages, reading, travel, sports, gardening. Home: PO Box 1676 5 NW 8th St Coupeville WA 98239

CANGEMI, JOSEPH PETER, psychologist, consultant, educator; b. Syracuse, N.Y., June 26, 1936; m. Amelia Elena Santaló, Oct. 6, 1962; children: Michelle, Lisa Ann. BS, SUNY, Oswego, 1959; MS, Syracuse U., 1964; EdD, Ind. U., 1974; LittD (hon.), William Woods U., 1996. Diplomate Am. Bd. Vocat. Experts, Am. Bd. Forensic Examiners, Am. Coll. Counselors; diplomate in profl. counseling Am. Acad. Forensic Examiners, Internat. Acad. Behavioral Medicine, Counseling and Psychotherapy; cert. sch. psychologist, counselor, N.Y. Instr. Syracuse Pub. Schs., 1959-60, vocat. rehab. coord., rsch. assoc., 1961-65; instr. asst. dir. Carol Morgan Sch., Santo Domingo, Dominican Republic, 1960-61; asst. head basketball coach SUNY C.C., Syracuse, 1962-63, lectr., chmn. dept. psychology evening-extension divsn., 1962-65, vis. lectr., 1966; supr. edn. Orinoco Mining divsn. U.S. Steel Corp., Ciudad Piar, Venezuela, 1965-66; supr. tng. and devel. Orinoco Mining divsn. U.S. Steel Corp., Puerto Ordaz and Ciudad Piar, Venezuela, 1966-68; asst. prof. psychology Western Ky. U., Bowling Green, 1968-75, assoc. prof., 1975-79, prof., 1979—; project dir. U. Los Andes, Merida, Venezuela, Inter-Am. Devel. Bank, Washington, Western Ky. U., 1975-77; cons. R.R. Donnelley & Sons, Coca Cola, Gould Corp., Eaton Corp., Firestone Corp., Uniroyal/Goodrich Tire and Rubber Co., Gen. Tire and Rubber Co., Jefferson Smurfit, Std. Products, Tyson Foods, others; host Conversation program Western Ky. U. Divsn. Radio, TV Film, 1968-71. Author: Higher Education and the Development of Self-Actualizing Personalities, 1977, La Administracion Participativa, 1983, (with Casimir Kowalski) Perspectives in Higher Education, 1983, Higher Education in the United States and Latin America, 1983, (with George Guttschalk) Effective Management, 1980, (with Casimir Kowalski and Jeffrey Claypool) Participative Management: Employee Management Cooperation, 1985, Chinese edit., 1990, (with Mario Noronha) Marketing Y Venda, Portuguese edit., 1992, (with Casimir Kowalski) Andersonville Prison, Lessons in Organizational Failure, 1993, (with Carl Kreisler) Raymond C. Gibson-Distinguished Kentuckian, Renowned Educator and Statesman: An Anthology, 1996, (with Mario Noronha, Casimir Kowalski, George Guttschalk) Falhas Organizaciones, Portuguese edit., 1996, (with Tatyana Ushakova and Casimir Kowalski) Leadership for the 21st Century, Russian edit., 1997, Russian Academy of Sciences, Polish edit., 1997, (with Casimir Kowalski and Richard Zelichowski) Heroes of Solidarity, 1999, (Casimir Kowalski and K. Habib Khan) Leadership Behavior, 1998; editor: Educator's Svc. Bull., 1971-72, Psychology-A Quar. Jour. Human Behavior, 1977—, Jour. Human Behavior and Learning, 1983-90, Orgn. Devel. Jour., 1983-89; mem. editl. bd. Archivos Panamenos de Psicologia, 1968-88, Coll. Student Jour., 1973—, Faculty Rsch. Bull. of Western Ky. U., 1977-88, Jour. Instructional Psychology, 1977—, Counseling and Values, 1979-84, Technol. Horizons in Edn. Jour., 1979-92 Edn., 1976—, Jour. Fgn. Psychology, Russia, 1996—, Chinese Jour. Applied Psychology, 1999—, Forensic Examiner, 1998—; contbr. over 400 articles, chpts. to profl. publs. Trustee William Woods U., 1988—; bd. dirs. COCITE (Cooperativa de Ensino Superior de Technicas Avancadas de Gestao e Informatica) Technol. U., Lisbon; mem. Ho. of Goa, Lisbon, Portugal, 1996—. Recipient certs. and awards U.S. Army Armor Sch., 1974; Eaton Corp., 1974, 76, Brazilian Acad. Humanities, 1976, Nat. Autonomous U. Nicaragua, 1976, ICETEX, Colombia, 1977, Colombian Nat. Assn. Indsl. Engrs., 1977, Decreto award City of Bucaramanga, Colombia, 1976, 77, Quality Control Assn., 1979, Decreto award State of Santander, Colombia, 1977, Excellence in Productive Tchg. award Western Ky. U. Coll. Edn., 1979, 91, Firestone Tire and Rubber Co. award, 1978, 81, Profl.-Tech. Socs. award, 1983, Coll. Student Jour. and Models of Excellence award, 1983, Disting. Pub. Svc. award Western Ky. U., 1983, Excellence in Pub. Svc. award Coll. Edn., 1983, Disting. Alumnus award SUNY, Oswego, 1983; award from Uniroyal-Goodrich Tire and Rubber Co., 1986, Excellence in Rsch. and Creativity award Coll. Edn., Western Ky. U., 1987, United Rubber Workers/Internat. Brotherhood Elec. Workers and Firestone Tire & Rubber Co. award, 1991; featured personality Orgn. Devel. Jour., 1989, Jour. Edn. award, Project Innovation, 1992 (featured on cover and in summer issue); Bridgestone-Firestone award Valencia, Venezuela, 1994, Outstanding Contbn. award Southea. divsn. Redman Industries, 1996. Mem. ACA (regional chmn. com. internat. edn. 1976 life), Nat. Vocat. Guidance Assn. Profl., Internat. Coun. Psychologists (area chmn. Ky.), Assn. Specialists in Group Work (charter), Panamanian Psychol. Assn. (hon.), Southea. Psychol. Assn., Ky. Acad. Arts and Scis. (life), Internat. Assn. Edn. and Vocat. Guidance, Nat. Assn. Gifted (bd. dirs. 1973), Colombian Nat. Soc. Indsl. Engrs. (hon.), Romanian Acad. Scis. (hon.), Internat. Registry Orgn. Devel. Profls., RODC, InterAm. Soc. Psychology, Acad. Mgmt., Soc. Psychology in Mgmt., Capitol Arts Assn., Alumni Assn. SUNY-Oswego, Ind. U. Alumni Assn. (life), Gold Key, Pi Kappa Delta, Psi Chi, Sigma Delta Psi, Sigma Tau Delta, Phi Delta Kappa. Club: Bowling Green Country. Home: 1409 Mt Ayr Cir Bowling Green KY 42103-4708 Office: Western Ky U Dept Psychology Bowling Green KY 42101

CANHAM, PRUELLA CROMARTIE NIVER, retired educator; b. Statesboro, Ga., Dec. 4, 1924; d. Esten Graham and Mary Lee (Jones) Cromartie; m. Robert E. Niver June 4, 1946 (div. 1965) m. David L. Canham July 26, 1985; 1 child, Peddy Niver Hayhurst Moran; grandchild, Matthew William Hayhurst. BS in Bus. and Music, Ga. So. U., 1944; postgrad., various univs. tchr. voice, piano, chorus and bus. career maths. North Ft. Myers H.S., Fla.; former sec. Statesboro Air Base, Ga., Warner Robbins Air Base, Macon, Ga.; former tchr. Westside Sch., Bulloch County, Ga., Southside Sch., Opelika, Ala. *Pruella was an Honor Graduate at Statesboro, GA High School in 1941 and received a BS from Georgia Southern University in 1944. She has received numerous awards including Who's Who of American Colleges and Universities, 1944, Personalities of the South, 1980-82, Directory of Distinguished Americans, 1981, Community Leaders of America, 1981, The Biographical Roll of Honor for Distinguished Service to the Arts, Community, State and Nation, 1981, 2,000 Notable Americans, 1982, 2,000 Distinguished Southerners, 1982, Distinguished Americans First Edition for State and Connunity Service to the Arts, 1982, The World's Who's Who of Women, 1983; Community Leaders of America, 1987.* Mem. Singers Club of L.I.; guest spkr., panelist various cultural orgns. in Fla. and so. states; soloist various chs. and schs.; music cons. local theater groups; mem. Fla. State Secondary Music Instructional Materials Coun. Nominee Gannett Found. Heart of Gold Humanatarian award, 1981; named Vocal Solo. Lit. Music Specialist State of Florida, Lee County Florida Tchr. of the Year, 1987, nominee Nat. Tchr. Hall of Fame, 1998; recipient Nat. Libr. Poet's Editor's Choice award, 1994; cert. Appreciation Nat. Park Trust, 1995, Lee County Sch. Dist. Fla., 1991. Mem. AAAS, Am. Ch. Dirs. Assn., Fla. Music Educator Assns., Music Educator's Nat. Conf., Lee County Alliance of the Arts (charter), Fla. Vocal Assn. (past coord., state bd.), Nat. Assn. of Tchrs. of Singing in Am. and Cand., So. Fla. Symphony and Chorus Assn., Am. Guild of Organists, Fla. League of the Arts (past pres. and bd. dirs., hon. life, 1998—), Lee County Retired Tchrs. Assn., Fla. Vocal Assn., Am. Choral Assn., Internat. Soc. Poets (disting. mem. 1994, merit award, 1995), others. Home: 1271 Burtwood Dr Fort Myers FL 33901-8711

CANIPAROLI, VAL WILLIAM, choreographer, dancer; b. Renton, Wash., Sept. 12, 1951; s. Francisco and Leonora (Marconi) C. Student, Wash. State U., 1969-71, San Francisco Ballet Sch., 1971-72. Dancer San Francisco Opera, 1973; dancer San Francisco Ballet, 1974—, rehearsal asst., 1985—; co-dir. OMO, San Francisco, 1985; choreographer San Francisco Opera, 1987, 90; res. choreographer Ballet West, 1994—. Choreographer (ballets) Street Song, 1980, Pacific Northwest Ballet, Seattle, 1980, 91, The Bridge, 1998, Love-lies-Bleeding, 1982, San Francisco Ballet, 1982— including Aria, 1998, Slow, 1998, Ciao Marcello, 1997; Hamlet and Ophelia, 1985, In Perpetuum, 1990, Oakland (Calif.) Ballet, 1983-87, Aubade, 1985 (Isadora Duncan award), Narcisse, 1987, Israel Ballet, Tel Aviv, 1985, Ballet West, Salt Lake City, 1987—, Ririe Woodbury Dance Co., 1988, Ritual, 1990, A Door is Ajar, 1990, Honk Kong Ballet, 1990, Richmond Ballet, 1989, Pitts. Ballet, Theatre, 1990, 1990, Jacob's Pillow Dance festival, 1990, Pulcinella, 1991, Concerto Grosso, 1992, Seeing Stars, 1993, Lady of the Camellias, Ballet Fla., 1993, Ballet West, 1994, Lambarena, 1995, Capriccio, Chgo. Lyric Opera, 1994, Bow Out, Richmond Ballet, 1995, San Francisco Symphony Pops, 1995, 96, Prawn Watching, Ballet West, 1996, Djangology, Richmond Ballet, 1997, Open Veins, Atlanta Ballet, 1998, Book of Alleged Dances, Ballet West, 1998. Nat. Endowment Arts fellowship grantee, 1981—. Fellow Calif. Arts Coun. Coreographers. Avocations: music, theatre, dance. Home: 81 Lansing St Apt 405 San Francisco CA 94105-2638 Office: San Francisco Ballet 455 Franklin St San Francisco CA 94102-4471

CANIPE, STEPHEN LEE, educational administrator; b. Jan. 9, 1946; s. Clayton Lee and Edna Jeanette (Farmer) C.; m. Sharon Wilbourne, Apr. 1, 1972; children: Martha Murray, David Jacob. BS in Biology cum laude, Appalachian State U., 1968; MS in Biology, Mich. State U., 1973; EdD in Ednl. Adminstrn., Duke U., 1982. Lab. asst. USPHS, Savannah, Ga., 1968-69; tchr. h.s. biology Charlotte, N.C., 1969-76, asst. prin., 1976-77; N.C. sci. cons. Raleigh, 1977-78; supr. ednl. svcs. Duke Power Co., Charlotte, 1978-79, dir. employee comms., 1979-81, dir. adminstrn. and devel., 1981-83; prin. West Lincoln Sr. H.S., Lincolnton, N.C., 1983-86, Lincoln County Sch. of Tech., 1987-93; dir. media and tech. Mooresville (N.C.) Sch. Dist., 1993-94; prin. J.M. Alexander Mid. Sch., Charlotte-Mecklenburg Sch. Dist., 1994-96; project mgr. ABC Challenge Grant, Greensboro, N.C., 1997—; instr. Cen. Piedmont C.C., 1976-78; adj. prof. Gaston Coll., 1984-95; cons. Project ALIVE, 1979-81; instr., prin. exec. program U. N.C., Chapel Hill, 1991-95; apptd. gov.'s Adv. Coun. for Tech. and Vocat. Edn., 1991-96, Gov.'s permanent com. on Work Force Preparedness, 1992-96; state chmn. Telecomms. Users Networked for Edn., 1991; pres., founder Lakeshore Consulting, Inc., 1996—; mem. N.C. Adv. Task Force on Tech. Edn., 1996—; mem. tchr. adv. panel Davidson Coll., 1993—. Author: Valuing the Environment, 1975, High School Animal Behavior, 1977, School Retrofit Analysis System, 1983. Charter mem. Metrolina Environ. Concern Assn., 1970-77; mem. mayor's energy adv. com., 1979. Mem. NEA, ASCD, N.C. Alliance Sci. and Math. (tchr. edn. adv. com. 1992), Rotary, Civitan, Phi Delta Kappa, Kappa Delta Pi, Beta Beta Beta. Episcopalian. Home: 3035 Pisgah Pl Apt B Greensboro NC 27455-3275

CANITZ, HENRY CHARLES, food company executive; b. Milw., Feb. 12, 1962; s. Henry Carl and Arlene Norma Canitz; m. Cathryn Ann Simske, Aug. 27, 1983; children: Brian, Shannon. BS in Mech. Engring., U. Wis., 1985; MBA in Supply Chain Mgmt., Mich. State U., 1994. Cert. transp. and logistics mgr. Sr. engr. McDonnell Douglas, Long Beach, Calif., 1986-92; staff mgr. GTE Supply, Irving, Tex., 1994-96; dir. logistics planning CellStar Corp., Carrollton, Tex., 1996-97; dir. supply chain mgmt. ConAgra Refrigerated Prepared Foods, Downers Grove, Ill., 1997—. Contbr. articles to profl. jours. Tchr. Jr. Achievement, Chgo., 1999. Grad. scholar Mich. State Logistics Coun., 1993. Mem. Am. Soc. Transp. and Logistics, Coun. Logistics Mgmt. (Grad. scholar 1993, track chair 1994-99), Warehousing Edn. and Rsch. Coun., Beta Gamma Sigma. Avocations: model trains, small aircraft. Fax: 630-512-1768. E-mail: HCanitz@crfc.com. Office: ConAgra Refrigerated Prepared Foods 2001 Butterfield Rd Downers Grove IL 60515

CANIZARES, CLAUDE ROGER, astrophysicist, educator; b. Tucson, June 14, 1945; s. Orlando and Stephanie (Bolan) C.; children: Kristen, Alexander. BA, Harvard U., 1967, MA, 1968, PhD, 1972. Rsch. staff MIT, Cambridge, 1971-74, asst. prof. physics, 1974-78, assoc. prof., 1978-84, prof., 1984-97, Bruno Rossi prof. exptl. physics, 1997—, dep. dir. Ctr. for Space Rsch., 1989-90, dir. Ctr. for Space Rsch., 1990—; assoc. dir. NASA-Chandra X-ray Obs. Ctr.; chair Space Sci. Adv. Com., 1992-93; chair NRC Space Studies Bd., 1994—; chair space sci. adv. com. NASA, 1993-94, mem. Space Earth Sci. Adv. Com., Washington, 1986-88; mem. adv. coun. NASA, 1992—; mem. Astron. Astrophysics Survey Com. NRC, Washington, 1989-91; bd. trustees Associated Univs., Inc., 1997—. Contbr. over 100 articles to profl. jours. Royal Soc. vis. fellow, Cambridge, Eng., 1981-82, Alfred P. Sloan Found. fellow, 1980-84; NASA grantee, 1975—. Fellow Am. Phys. Soc.; mem. NAS, AAAS, Am. Astron. Soc., Internat. Astron. Union, Internat. Acad. Astronautics (corr.), Phi Beta Kappa, Sigma Xi. Achievements include first implementation of studies in x-ray spectroscopy and plasma diagnostics of supernova remnants, clusters of galaxies. Office: MIT 70 Vassar St 37-241 Cambridge MA 02139-4309

CANJAR, PATRICIA MCWADE, psychologist; b. Pitts., Mar. 14, 1932; d. Robert Malachai McWade and Lillian Kathryn (Seidenstricker) Robb; m. Lawrence N. Canjar, Aug. 4, 1951 (dec. Nov. 1972); 1 son, R. Michael; m. James M. McDonald, Sept. 24, 1977. A.A., Carlow Coll., 1951; B.A., U. Detroit, 1973; M.A., 1975. Lic. psychologist, Mich. Psychologist, Robinwood Clinic, Detroit, 1973-77, Psychol. Resources, Birmingham, Mich., 1977-80, Realistic Living Ctr., Warren, Mich., 1983-85, Behavior Ctr., Birmingham, 1980-84; with Eastwood Cmty. Clinic, Big Beaver, Mich., 1984-94; ret. 1994. Mem. Nat. YWCA Spl. Commn., Boston, N.Y.C. and Washington, 1967; bd. dirs. YWCA, Pitts., 1961-65, Detroit, 1965-67; asst. coordinator United We Sing, Pitts. Music Festival, 1955-65; pres. Carnegie Mellon Women's Club, Pitts., 1963-65, U. Detroit Faculty Wives' Club, 1968-70; mem. State of Mich. Fair Campaign Practices Commn., 1968-70; treas. Grandview Beach Assn., 1982-84, pres., 1984-87. Fellow Am. Psychol. Assn.; mem. Mich. Assn. Profl. Psychologist, Mich. Assn. Alcohol and Drug Abuse Counselors. Democrat. Roman Catholic.

CANN, NANCY TIMANUS, retail yacht sales executive; b. Balt.; d. E. Frank Timanus and Ruth F. (Herman) Schell; m. Craig Shimer; children: Justin Ronald, Heather Sharp, Heath Shimer. Grad., Balt. Bus. Coll., 1967. Pres. Crusader Yacht Sales, Inc., Annapolis, Md., 1982—; bd. dirs. Bayfarers. Mem. Yacht Architects and Brokers Assn. (v.p. 1989-91, 92-94, chmn. membership com. 1989-92, bd. dirs. 1992-99, pres. 1994-96, boat dealer adv. com. 1999—). Avocation: sailing. Home and Office: 7078 Bembe Beach Rd Annapolis MD 21403-3616

CANN, STEVEN J., political science educator; b. Oct. 30, 1944. BS, N.D. State U., 1970, MA, 1972; PhD, Purdue U., 1977. Assoc. prof. Idaho State U., Pocatello, 1977-85; prof. polit. sci. Washburn U., Topeka, 1985—. Author: Administrative Law (2nd edition); Contbr. to profl. jours. With USN, (E-4) 1966-68. Pres. Kansas Chpt. Amer. Soc. for Public Admin. Office: 1700 SW College Topeka KS 66621-0001

CANN, WILLIAM FRANCIS, judge; b. Somerville, Mass., Oct. 10, 1922; s. William Arthur and Frances (Hardy) C.; m. Cynthia Marden Batchelder, Dec. 10, 1994; children: Ellen Lockhart, Allan Craig Watts, Melinda Lea Cann. Student, Tufts U., 1940-42; LLB, Boston U., 1948; grad., Nat. Coll. State Judiciary, Reno, 1972. Bar: Mass. 1948, N.H. 1959, U.S. Supreme Ct. 1970. Sr. claim examiner Am. Mut. Liability Ins. Co., Wakefield, Mass., 1948-60; law asst. Office Atty. Gen., State N.H., Concord, 1960-61; asst. atty. gen. Office Atty. Gen., State N.H., 1961-67, dep. atty. gen., 1967-71; assoc. justice N.H. Superior Ct., 1971-87, sr. justice, 1988—, former chmn. sentence rev. div.; lectr. trial advocacy Franklin Pierce Law Ctr.; mem. N.H. Supreme Ct. Jud. Conduct Com., 1985-93; vice-chmn. Supreme Ct. study com. on jud. preformance evaluation; mem. Supreme Ct. long-range planning task force. Past mem. adv. bd. Cmty. Corrections Ctr., N.H. State Prison. With USAAF, 1942-45. Mem. N.H. Bar Assn. (former mem. com. on cooperation with the cts.), Merrimack County Bar Assn., N.H. Rose Soc. (pres. 1989-91). Office: 36 Roger Ave Concord NH 03301-4631

CANNADAY, PAUL BENJAMIN-DIELMAN, handicap resources educator, consultant; b. Gardnier, Maine, Nov. 25, 1959; s. Travis Gene Cannaday and Merilynn Ruth (Jordan) Dielman; m. Amy Joanne Miller, May 18, 1985 (div. Aug. 1990); m. Marjo Wimmer, May 14, 1994. BS in Theater Arts and Comm., Eastern Mich. U., 1985; cert. in computer ops., Washtenaw C.C., 1992. Crisis counselor Ozone House, Ann Arbor, 1977-78; housing helpline coord. SOS Cmty. Crisis Ctr., Ypsilanti, Mich., 1988-89; tech. dir., set designer, light and sound designer Barrier Free Theater, Ann Arbor, 1989; design analyst Ann Arbor Ctr. for Ind. Living, 1989-90; microcomputer specialist Washtenaw C.C., Ann Arbor, 1991-92; tech. dir., set designer, light designer Diversibility Theater, Ann Arbor, 1992-94; programmer Oakland/Macomb Ctr. for Ind. Living, Sterling Hghts., Mich., 1994; instr. handicap studies Washtenaw C.C., Ann Arbor, 1998—; founder Phys. Handicap Resources for Electronic Equipment, Handicaps United Means Accountability by All Nations, Barrier-free Records Hall of Fame, Handicap Solution Line, Handicap Greetings, Disabling Motion Picture Studio; founder Wag Your Tail Pet Sitting; cons. in field. Author: Princess' Wheels, 1995, Nine People, 1995, Prince Able, 1996, Dignity: A Historical And Candid Peek at the Handicap Culture, Handicap Childhood vs. Society, Common Sense Guide to Handicap and Able-Bodied Relationship, The Complete Handicap Book: The Past, Present and Future of the Handicap Culture, Barrier-Free Workbook, 1997, Fairy Tales for Children of All Abilities, 1995, Speaking of Handicap People, 1997, Why and a Collection of Other Poems, 1997, Handicap People Are Coming, 1996, 500 Questions and Answers for Elderly Handicapped People, 1997, Physicalism: A Pictorial Look at Handicap People, 1997, Marble Ramps, 1998, Animal Speaking, 1998, Two Legs to Dance, 1998, Two Alike, 1999, Guiding Angel, 1999, See No Disability, 1999, Zakie, 1999, Tests Disabilities, 1999, I'm Proud to Be a Circle, 1999, 5 Milleniums of Disabled Culture and History; author numerous poems; contbr. articles to profl. jours. Vol. Americore/Vista, 1991-92; active Paws with a Cause, 1995—; bd. dirs. Epilepsy Ministries, Brighton, Mich., 1982-84, Diversability Theater, 1992-93; mem. ADAPT, Ann Arbor, 1997—, ARRIVAL, Ypsilanti, 1987-88, Avenues, Sacto., Calif., 1995—; housing coord. for handicap persons Washtenaw Assn. for Cmty. Advocacy, Ann Arbor. Mem. Handicap Hist. Soc. (founder), Orgn. of Am. Historians, Internat. Pet Sitters' Assn. Democrat. Avocations: chess, music, theater, movies. E-mail: disablenet.aol.com. Home: 4971 Wixson Croswell MI 48422

CANNALIATO, VINCENT, JR., investment banker, mathematician; b. Bklyn., July 12, 1941; s. Vincent and Margaret (Mancuso) C.; m. June A. Marino, Apr. 8, 1967; children: Amy June, Kimberly Dawn, Douglas Vincent. BS in Math., Fordham U., 1963; MA in Math., Bklyn. Coll. CUNY, 1964; grad. cert. in system design, U. Pa., 1970. Systems analyst N.Y. Tel. Co., N.Y.C., 1969-70; account exec. CIT Leasing Corp., N.Y.C., 1970-72; v.p. Kidder Peabody & Co., Inc., N.Y.C., 1972-80, head leasing and project financing group corp. fin. dept., 1977-80; sr. v.p., mng. dir. and head leasing/project fin. grp. Smith Barney, Harris Upham & Co., Inc., N.Y.C., 1980-90; mng. dir., first v.p., head Merchant Banking Group Sanwa Bus. Credit Corp., N.Y.C., 1990-91; founder, pres. Commodore Capital Corp., N.Y.C., 1991—, Commodore Securities Capital, N.Y.C., 1996—, Argosy Ventures, 1997-98; bd. dirs. Nortankers, Inc., mem. audit com., 1989-90; vis. instr. Southwestern Grad. Sch. Banking, 1976-77; speaker law jour. seminars equip. leasing industry, 1986-87; adv. bd. U.S. Mcht. Marine Acad., 1974-90, chmn., 1977-90; instr. math. U. Md., 1966-69; mem. maritime adv. com. Dept. Transp., 1982-84, chmn. fin. subcom., 1983-84. Co-author: U.S. Taxation of International Operations, 1975, 77, 87; Oil and Gas Taxes/Natural Resources Service, 1979; World Leasing Yearbook, 1980, 81; Handbook of Modern Finance, 1999. Exec. bd., curriculum chmn. Gifted Child Soc., 1975-82; nation chief Rampo Indian Guides and Princesses, Western Hills YMCA, 1980-83; bd. dirs. Tomorrow Children's Fund, 1987-96, exec. bd. 1989-96; mem. parish coun. St. Elizabeth Roman Cath. Ch., 1986-88, pres., 1987-88. Capt. U.S. Army, 1963-69. Decorated Bronze Star. Mem. Equipment Leasing Assn. (bd. dirs. exec. com., nominating com. 1984-87, fed. legis. com. 1975-84, chmn. keyman com. 1978-83, chmn. membership com. 1982-83, chmn. academia awareness task force 1988-92, vice chmn. large ticket lessors com. 1994-97, chmn. 1995-97), Acad. Magical Arts, Inc.

(life), Met. Club (N.Y.C.). Office: Commodore Capital Corp 150 E 58th St Fl 15 New York NY 10155-0002

CANNELL, CHARLES FREDERICK, psychologist, educator; b. Antrim, N.H., Sept. 10, 1913; s. William J.B. and Hattie (Morse) C.; m. Martha Phyllis Osgood, Aug. 23, 1937; children—John Charles, Edward Lincoln. AB, U. N.H., 1936; MA, Ohio State U., 1940, PhD, 1952. Head field sect., div. program surveys Bur. Agrl. Econs., Dept. Agr., 1942-46; mem. staff Inst. Social Rsch., Survey Rsch. Ctr., 1946-84, program dir., 1963-84, rsch. scientist emeritus, 1984—; mem. faculty U. Mich., 1954-84, prof. psychology in communication, 1962-84, prof. emeritus, 1984—; cons. Nat. Center for Health Services Research, Nat. Center Health Stats. Author: (with R.L. Kahn) The Dynamics of Interviewing, 1957, Techniques for Evaluating Interviewer Performance, 1975, Experiments in Interviewing Techniques, 1979; contbr. (with R.L. Kahn) chpts. to Handbook of Social Psychology, 1968, (with P.V. Miller and L. Oksenberg) Sociological Methodology, 1981, chpts. to Survey Interviewing, 1985, (with L. Oskenberg) to Telephone Survey Methodology, 1988, articles to profl. jours. Fellow APA, Am. Statis. Assn.; mem. AAUP, Am. Assn. Pub. Opinion Rsch., Am. Psychol. Soc. Home: 13 Heatheridge St Ann Arbor MI 48104-2757

CANNELL, CYNDY MICHELLE, elementary school principal; b. Salt Lake City, Utah, July 27, 1948; d. Nick M. and Eugenie E. (Pfanmuller) Fasselin; m. Peter Anthony Cannell, Oct. 13, 1973; children: Peter John, David. BA, U. Utah, 1970, MA, 1973. Cert. adminstr., supr. severly handicapped, spl. edn., emotionally handicapped, gifted and talented. Tchr. Hab Ctr., 1973-74, Hill View Elem Sch., 1974-78; coord. spl. needs. Granite Sch. Dist., Salt Lake City, 1978-79, tchr. leader youth in custody, 1979-80, coord. spl. edn., 1980-84; asst. prin. Western Hills Elem. Sch., Salt Lake City, 1984-85; prin. Webster Elem. Sch., Salt Lake City, 1985-90, Plymouth Elem. Sch., Salt Lake City, 1990-95, Twin Peaks Elem. Sch., Salt Lake City, 1995—; mem. state strategic planning com. for edn., 1990-91, elem. prin. adv. com., 1990-96, spl. edn. strategic planning com., 1990-91, exec. class size steering com., 1990, ptnrs. in edn. com., 1985—, sch. lunch com., 1989-91, emer. preparedness com., 1989-90; mem. Women's State Legis. Coun., Utah, 1991-92; co-coord. Corp. Games, 1988—. Contbr. articles to profl. mags. Prin. rep. to state PTA Community Involvement Commn., 1989-90, Oquirrh South PTA Coun., 1989; mem. Utah Youth Village Scholarship Com., 1996—. Named Outstanding Educator of Yr. Nat. PTA Phoebe Apperson Hearst, 1990, Outstanding Adminstr. Utah Congress of Parents and Tchrs., 1989-90, Region V PTA, 1988-90. Mem. Granite Assn. Elem. Sch. Prins. (sec. 1998—, Innovator of Yr. 1997-98), Granite Assn. Sch. Adminstrs. (sec., treas. 1990-91) Utah Assn. Sch. Adminstrs., Nat Assn. Elem. Adminstrs., Granite Assn. Sch. Adminstrs. Avocations: skiing, reading, tennis, golf, travel. Home: 10331 S 2375 E Sandy UT 84092-4422 Office: Twin Peaks Elem 5325 S 1045 E Salt Lake City UT 84117-7229

CANNELL, JOHN REDFERNE, lawyer; b. Cambridge, Mass., Apr. 3, 1937; s. John and Thyra (Larson) C.; m. Elizabeth Ann May, May 28, 1960; children: John R. Jr. (dec.), James C., William H. AB, Princeton U., 1958; LLB, Columbia U., 1961. Bar: N.Y. 1961. Assoc. Simpson Thacher & Bartlett, N.Y.C., 1961-70, ptnr., 1970-95, of counsel, 1996—; gov. Am. Bus. Council, Singapore, 1982-85, vice chmn., 1984-85. Trustee Kessler Inst. for Rehab., West Orange, N.J., 1986-97, vice chmn., 1989-92, chmn., 1992-95; trustee Henry H. Kessler Found., 1992—, chmn., 1996-99; trustee Marcus Ward Home, Maplewood, N.J., 1996—; dir. Kessler Rehab. Corp., 1992—, Kessler Med. Rehab. Rsch. and Edn. Corp., 1997—; bd. dirs. New Alternatives for Children, Inc., 1996—. Mem. ABA, Assn. of Bar of City of N.Y., Montclair Golf Club, Montclair Racquet Club, Univ. Club, Singapore Cricket Club, Tanglin Club. Episcopalian. Avocations: squash, golf. Office: Simpson Thacher & Bartlett 425 Lexington Ave Fl 14 New York NY 10017-3903

CANNELL, ROBERT QUIRK, agricultural sciences educator; b. Isle of Man, Mar. 20, 1937; married; 2 children. BSc in Agrl. with 1st class honors, King's Coll., U. Durham, Newcastle-upon-Tyne, U.K., 1959; PhD, U. Newcastle-upon-Tyne, 1968. Agronomist fertilizer devel. sect. Shell Chem. Co. Ltd., London, 1959-61; lectr. crop physiology dept. agr. U. Newcastle-upon-Tyne, 1961-70; rsch. fellow. Fulbright scholar dept. agronomy/plant genetic U. Minn., St. Paul, 1968-69; prin. sci. officer, head field studies dept. Agrl. and Food Rsch. Coun., Letcombe Lab., Oxfordshire, 1970-84; dir. Welsh Plant Breeding Sta., prof. agrl. botany U. Coll. Wales, Aberystwyth, 1984-87; prof., head crop and soil environ. scis. Va. Poly. Inst. and State U., Blacksburg, 1987-94, dir. Va. Agrl. Expt. Sta., assoc. dean rsch., 1994—; internat. cons., lectr. in field; mem. FAO panel of experts on agrl. mechanization, Rome, 1981; assessor for U.K. Overseas Devel. adminstrn. on conservation tillage project, 1980, 82. Contbr. numerous articles and abstracts to profl. jours., chpts. to books; editl. bd. Agrl. Water Mgmt., Outlook on Agr., Soil and Tillage Rsch. Recipient Pres.'s award Va. Turfgrass Coun., 1992. Fellow Inst. Biology; mem. Am. Soc. Agronomy, Brit. Soc. Soil Sci., Inst. Biology London, Internat. Soc. Soil Sci., Internat. Soil Tillage Rsch. Orgn., Nat. Inst. Agrl. Botany, Royal Agrl. Soc. Eng., Soil Sci. Soc. Am. (mem. internat. soil sci. award com. 1992-94), Sigma Xi. Office: VA Polytechnic Inst & State Univ Sea Grant Blacksburg VA 24061-0402*

CANNELLA, DEBORAH FABBRI, elementary school educator; b. Statesville, N.C., Sept. 7, 1949; d. Raymond Joseph and Sylvia (Sides) Fabbri; m. S.J. Garciga, Apr. 16, 1970 (div. 1990); children: Jennifer, Melissa, Bryan; m. Frank Cannella, July 1, 1994. Student, U. So. Fla., 1970, 91—; Presch. Edn. degree, Montessori Inst. Am., 1984; BS in acctg., U. So. Fla., 1995; postgrad., U. South Fla., 1995-98. Cert. Montessori Presch. Edn., Kansas City, Mo. Tchr. presch. Montessori Acad. of Temple Terr., Fla., 1982-87; tchr. 1st grade St. John's Parish Day Sch., Tampa, Fla., 1987—. Facilitator Bay Area Assn. Ind. Schs. Profl. Day, 1990, mem. program com., 1990-92; bd. dirs. Tampa Prep. Parent's, grad. reception, 1987-88. Mem. Assn. for Childhood Edn., Tampa Mus. of Art, Tampa Bay Performing Arts Ctr., Mus. Sci. and Tech. Episcopalian. Avocations: walking, reading, baking. Office: St John's Parish Day Sch 906 S Orleans Ave Tampa FL 33606-2941

CANNING, JOHN RAFTON, urologist; b. Evanston, Ill., Dec. 5, 1927; s. Claude E. and Martha C. Canning; m. Elizabeth Learned, Sept. 11, 1948; 1 dau., Sarah Blee; m. Jacqueline Maartense, Apr. 3, 1970; children—John R., Richard, Roberta. B.A., Lake Forest (Ill.) Coll., 1951; M.D., Northwestern U., 1955, M.S., 1956. Diplomate: Am. Bd. Surgery, Am. Bd. Urology. Intern St. Luke's Hosp., Chgo., 1955; resident in gen. surgery VA Hosp., Hines, Ill., 1956-60; resident in urology VA Hosp., 1966-68; chest fellow Presbyn.-St. Luke's Hosp., Chgo., 1963; asst. chief vascular surg. sect. VA Hosp., Hines, 1960-66; asst. chief urology surg. sect. VA Hosp., 1968, chief urology, 1969—; asst. prof. urology Loyola U. Stritch Sch. Medicine, Maywood, Ill., 1969-82, prof. urology, 1982—; chmn. dept. Loyola U. Stritch Sch. Medicine, 1979-86. Fellow A.C.S.; mem. AMA, Ill. Urol. Soc. (exec. com.), Chgo. Urol. Soc. (pres. exec. com.), Chgo. Med. Soc., Soc. Univ. Urologists. Club: Chgo. Yacht. Office: Loyola U Stritch Sch Medicine Dept Urology Maywood IL 60153

CANNISTRARO, NICHOLAS, JR., newspaper executive; b. Waltham, Mass., Oct. 7, 1939; s. Nicholas and Audrey Phyllis (Hager) C.; m. Margaret Clement Clark, Sept. 30, 1961; children: Melissa Greer Salvesen, Margaret Clement Miller. B.A., Harvard U., 1961. Account exec. Young & Rubicam, N.Y.C., 1965-68; account supr. Erwin Wasey Co., N.Y.C., 1968-69; product mgr. Gillette Co., Boston, 1969-71; v.p. mktg. Bristol-Myers Corp., N.Y.C., 1971-82; v.p. advt. and mktg. Washington Post, 1982-92, sr. v.p., 1992-92; sr. v.p., chief mktg. officer Newspaper Assn. Am., Vienna, Va., 1993-96; pres., gen. mgr. The Newspaper Nat. Network, N.Y.C., 1997—. Bd. dirs. Md. Hall for Creative Arts Found., Advt. Coun. Lt. USN, 1961-65. Mem. Annapolis Yacht Club, Naval Acad. Sailing Squadron. Republican. Avocations: sailing; offshore racing. Home: 1865 Milvale Rd Annapolis MD 21401-5922 Office: Newspaper Nat Network 711 3rd Ave New York NY 10017-4014

CANNON, BENNIE MARVIN, physical education educator; b. Goshen Pike, Ala., Aug. 20, 1942; s. L.D. and Gussie Lee (Canty) C.; m. Vercilla Brown, Aug. 27, 1966; children: Steven Marvin, Jonathan Benjamin, Noah Christopher. AA, Chgo. City Coll., 1964; BS, Upper Iowa U., 1968; postgrad., U. Ill., 1971-76. Cert. phys. edn., safety and driver edn. tchr., Ill. Tchr. elem. phys. edn. Chgo. Pub. Schs., 1968-69, tchr. gen. sci., 1969-71, tchr. secondary phys. edn., driver's edn., 1971-78, 79—. Fitness specialist del. Dwight David Eisenhower Found., Spokane, Wash., 1992, Driver Edn. Profl. del. Dwight David Eisenhower Found., Spokane, 1996. Mem. AAPHERD, Ill. Assn. Health, Phys. Edn., Recreation and Dance (Quarter Century award Chgo. dist. 1993, Quarter Century Club award state dist. 1994), Nat. Sci. Tchrs. Assn., Ill. H.S. and Coll. Driver Edn. Assn., Nat. Fedn. News, Am. Fedn. Tchrs., Phi Zeta Tau. Democrat. African Methodist Episcopal. Avocations: baseball, basketball, skating, tennis, bicycling. Home: 8419 S Indiana Ave Chicago IL 60619-5606

CANNON, CARL N., publisher; b. Albany, Ga., Aug. 14, 1943. Pub. Fla. Times-Union, Jacksonville, 1990—; v.p. Morris Comm. Corp., Augusta, Ga., 1990—. Office: Fla Times-Union One Riverside Ave Jacksonville FL 32202-4904

CANNON, CHARLES C., JR., military career officer; b. Jasper, Ala., Feb. 19, 1943; m. Karen Cannon; children: Dianne, Curtis. Grad., U. Tex., Arlington; BA in History, Fla. Inst. Tech., MS in Logistics Mgmt.; grad., Army Command/Gen. Staff Coll. Commd. 2nd lt. U.S. Army, 1967, advanced through grades to maj. gen., 1995; various positions including exec. officer petroleum distbn. U.S. Army, Korea; logistics programmer Dept. of the Army, asst. exec. officer to dep. chief of staff for logistics, divsn. support command exec. officer 1st Cavalry Divsn., 1982; advance operational fellow Dept. of the Army, Ft. Leavenworth, Kans., 1985-87; dir. bulk fuels 200th Theater Army Material Mgmt. Ctr. Dept. of the Army, comdr. 8th Inf. Divsn. (Mechanized) Support Command, chief logistics planning divsn. on the joint staff, 1991-92; comdr. 3d Corps Support Command Dept. of the Army, Wiesbaden, Germany, 1992-94; vice dir. for logistics Joint Staff Dept. of the Army, 1994-96, asst. dep. chief of staff for logistics, 1996; comdr. for support, Implementation Force Dept. of the Army, Zagreb, Croatia, 1996; asst. dep. chief of staff for logistics Dept. of the Army, Washington, 1996—. Decorated Def. Disting. Svc. medal, Def. Superior Svc. medal, Legion of Merit with oak leaf cluster, Bronze Star medal with V device and three oak leaf clusters, Purple Heart, Def. Meritorious Svc. medal, Army Meritorious Svc. medal with three oak leaf clusters, Air medal, Army Commendation medal with V device and five oak leaf clusters, Army Achievement medal. Office: US Army 500 Army Pentagon Washington DC 20310-0500

CANNON, CHRISTOPHER B., congressman; b. Salt Lake City, Oct. 20, 1950; m. Claudia Fox, 1978; 7 children. BS, Brigham Young U., 1974, JD, 1980; postgrad., Harvard U., 1974-75. Bar: Utah 1980. Atty., 1979-83; dep. assoc. solicitor U.S. Dept. Interior, 1983, assoc. solicitor, 1984-86; owner Cannon Industries, 1987—; mem. 105th Congress (now 106th Congress) from 3d Utah dist., 1996—; mem. Resources, Judiciary, and Sci. coms. Republican. Office: US House of Reps 118 Cannon Bldg Washington DC 20515-4403

CANNON, DAVID JOSEPH, lawyer; b. Milw., Aug. 6, 1933; s. George W. and Florence (Dean) c.; m. Carol Nevins, Mar. 10, 1962; children: Charles, Courtney. BS, Marquette U., 1955, JD, 1960. Bar; Wis. 1960, U.S. Dist. Ct. (ea. dist.) Wis. 1960, U.S. Ct. Appeals (7th cir.) 1969, U.S. Ct. Appeals (8th cir.) 1976, U.S. Dist. Ct. (we. dist.) Wis. 1976, U.S. Ct. Appeals (5th cir.) 1978, U.S. Ct. Appeals (4th cir.) 1997. Atty. Cannon & Cannon, Milw., 1960-66; asst. dist. atty. Milw. County Dist. Atty., 1966-68, dist. atty., 1968; U.S. atty. Dept. Justice Ea. Dist. Wis., Milw., 1969-73; ptnr. Michael, Best & Friedrich, Milw., 1973—. Home: 1520 Sunset Dr Elm Grove WI 53122-1629 Office: Michael Best & Friedrich 100 E Wisconsin Ave Ste 3300 Milwaukee WI 53202-4108

CANNON, DYAN, actress; b. Tacoma, Jan. 4, 1937; m. Cary Grant (div.); 1 dau., Jennifer. Student, U. Wash.; studied with Sanford Meisner. Former model; TV appearances include Diane's Adventure, Harlequin's Diamond Girl, 1998; Broadway appearances include Ninety-Day Mistress; with road company How to Succeed in Business Without Really Trying; motion pictures include Bob and Carol and Ted and Alice, 1969 (Acad. award nomination), Doctors' Wives, 1970, Le Casse, 1970, The Anderson Tapes, 1971, The Love Machine, 1971, Such Good Friends, 1971, Doctors' Wives, 1971, The Last of Sheila, 1973, Shamus, 1973, Shamus, 1972, Child Under a Leaf, 1974, Revenge of the Pink Panther, 1978, Heaven Can Wait, 1978, Coast to Coast, 1980, Honeysuckle Rose, 1980, Author, Author, 1982, Deathtrap, 1982, Caddyshack II, 1988, The End of Innocence (also dir. and prod. screenwriter), 1990, The Pickle, 1993, One Point of View, That Darn Cat, 1997, Out to Sea, 1997, 8 Heads in a Duffel Bag, 1997, Drop Dead, 1998; appeared in TV movie Virginia Hill Story, 1974, Lady of the House, 1978, Having It All, 1983, Master of the Game, 1984, Arthur the King, 1985, Jenny's War, 1985, Rock and Roll Mom, 1988, Jailbirds, 1991, Christmas in Connecticut, 1992, Based on an Untrue Story, 1993, A Perry Mason Mystery: The Case of the Jealous Jokester, 1995, The Rockford Files: If the Frame Fits..., Beverly Hills Family Robinson, 1997, The Sender, 1997, Allie & Me, 1997, That Darn Cat, 1997, Out to Sea, 1997, Drop-Dead, 1998; dir., writer, producer short live action film Growing Pains: Number One, 1976 (Acad. award nomination); (TV series) Ally McBeal, 1997. Named Best Actress of Yr., Nat. Assn. Theater Owners. *

CANNON, ELIZABETH ANNE, special education educator; b. Chgo., May 22, 1946; d. Peter Francis and Mary Patricia (Tangney) Foley; m. Martin Francis Cannon, July 10, 1982. BSEd, Chgo. Tchrs. Coll., 1969; MS in Spl. Edn. Learning Disabilities, Chgo. State U., 1982, MA in Edn. Adminstrn. and Supervision, 1988; postgrad., Northeastern Ill. U., 1988, Colo. State U., 1992-94, U. Denver, 1992-94. Cert. elem. and secondary tchr., adminstr., spl. edn., EMH, TMH, ED, BD, LD, gifted, supervision and adminstrn. spl. edn., Ill., Colo. Sch. clk. Chgo. Pub. Schs., summer 1965-69, tchr. spl. edn. mentally handicapped, 1969-90, tchr. regular and spl. summer schs., 1970-76; tchr. adult edn. City Colls. Chgo., 1971-81; tchr. spl. edn. Lake Mid. Sch. Denver Pub. Schs., 1992—; cooperating tchr. trainer Chgo. State U., Roosevelt U., U. Ill., Denver Metro Coll., U. Colo.; mem. local sch. coun., 1974-90, prin.'s adv. coun., 1974-90, mem. PTA Chgo. Bd. Edn., 1969-90. Leader Girl Scouts Chgo. St. Barnabus Sch., 1968-72; mem. Archbishop's Guild (Denver) Mother of Perpetual Help Circle. Recipient Gov.'s Master Tchr. award State of Ill., Springfield, 1983, Tchr. of Merit award Chgo. Bd. Edn., Dists. 16, 19, 1974-88, PTA, Chgo., 1974-88. Mem. ASCD, AAUW, Coun. Exceptional Children (Ill. chpt.), Am. Fedn. Sch. Adminstrs., Colo. Assn. Sch. Execs., Coun. Learning Disabilites, Kappa Delta Pi, Delta Kappa Gamma Internat. (Denver chpt.). Democrat. Roman Catholic. Avocations: swimming, hiking mountain trails, camping, bike riding, arts and crafts. Home: 2041 S Wolff St Denver CO 80219-5044

CANNON, FRANCIS V., JR., academic administrator, electrical engineer, economist; b. Poughkeepsie, N.Y., Nov. 1, 1935; s. Francis Vincent and Marietta Elizabeth (Yerry) C.; m. Margaret Ann Klisart; children: JoAnn, John, Joseph. BSEE, Milw. Sch. Engring., 1963; MSEE, Marquette U., 1969; PhD, U. Wis.-Milw., 1987. Registered profl. engr., Wis. Technician Oster Mfg. Co., Milw., 1959-60, AC Sparkplug div. Gen. Motors Corp., Milw., 1960; instr. Milw. Sch. Engring., 1963-70, acad. dean, 1970-79, v.p. acads., 1979-85, exec. v.p., provost, 1985-89, chancellor, 1989-92; pres. De Vry Inst. Tech., Dallas, 1992—; cons. engr. Systems Design Co., Milw., 1964-75; adj. prof. U. Wis.-Milw., 1987. Contbr. articles to profl. jours. Officer East Side Community Coun., Milw., 1965-79; chmn. East Side Transit Study Com., Milw., 1975; mem. Gov.'s Coun. on Econ. Issues, 1990-92. Named Disting. Tchr. Milw. Sch. Engring., 1969, Outstanding Tchr. Salgo-Noren Found., N.Y.C., 1970. Mem. IEEE (sect. officer 1965-73, edn. award 1974), Am. Soc. Engring. Edn. (com. chmn. 1976-79), Engrs. and Scientists Milw. (pres. 1978-79), Wis. Econ. Edn. Coun. (bd. dirs.), Wis. Soc. Profl. Engrs. (chpt. pres. and officer 1976-82), Am. Legion (exec. com. 1987-90), Irving C. of C. (bd. dirs. 1993—, chmn. 1999-2000), Irving Symphony Orch. Assn. (bd. dirs., pres. 1996—), Rotary. Republican. Roman Catholic. Avocations: golf, cross-country skiing, fishing, camping. Home: 7706 Brookview Ct Irving TX 75063-3177 Office: De Vry Inst Tech 4800 Regent Blvd Irving TX 75063-2439

CANNON, GARLAND, English language educator; b. Fort Worth, Dec. 5, 1924; m. Patricia Richardson, 1947; children—Margaret, India, Jennifer, William. B.A. in English, U. Tex., 1947, Ph.D. in English Linguistics, 1954; M.A. in English, Stanford U., 1952. Instr. U. Hawaii, Honolulu, 1949-52; instr. U. Tex., Austin, 1952-54, U. Mich., Ann Arbor, 1954-55; asst. prof. speech U. Calif.-Berkeley, 1955-56; acad. dir. Am. U. Lang. Ctr., Bangkok, Thailand, 1956-57; asst. prof. English U. Fla., Gainesville, 1957-58; vis. prof. linguistics U. P.R., 1958-59; asst. prof. linguistics Columbia U., N.Y.C., 1959-62; dir. English lang. program for Afghanistan Columbia U., Kabul, 1960-62; assoc. prof. Northeastern Ill. U., Chgo., 1962-63, Queens Coll., CUNY, 1963-66; assoc. prof. English Tex. A&M U., College Station, 1966-68; prof. English Tex. A&M U., 1968—; vis. prof. humanities U. Mich., 1970-71; vis. prof. linguistics Kuwait U., 1979-81; vis. prof. linguistics Inst. Teknologi Mara, Kuala Lumpur, 1987; vis. summer prof. Cambridge U., 1980, Oxford U., 1974, MIT, 1969, U. Wash., 1967; lectr. throughout world. Author: Sir William Jones, Orientalist: A Bibliography, 1952, Biography, 1964, A History of the English Language, 1972, An Integrated Transformational Grammar of the English Language, 1978, Sir William Jones: A Bibliography of Primary and Secondary Sources, 1979, Historical Change and English Word-Formation, 1987, Oriental Jones: The Life and Mind of Sir William Jones, 1990, Arabic Loanwords in English, 1994, (with A. Pfeffer) German Loanwords in English, 1994, Japanese Loanwords in English, 1996; editor: The Letters of Sir William Jones, 1970 (Book of Yr. Sunday London Telegraph 1970), Objects of Enquiry: The Life and Influences of Sir William Jones, 1995; contbr. numerous articles to profl. jours. Recipient Disting. Achievement award Tex. A&M U., 1972; Indian Govt. grantee, 1984; Linguistic Soc. Am./Am. Council Learned Socs. grantee, 1984; Am. Philos. Soc. grantee, Eng., 1964, 66, 74. Mem. MLA (exec. com. gen. linguistics discussion group 1982-85, chmn. 1984, 85, exec. com. present-day-English 1986-89, 94-97, exec. com. lexicography 1986-89, chmn. 1989, rep. to del. assembly 1985-88), Am. Dialect Soc. (exec. coun. 1989-93), Dictionary Soc. N.Am., South Asian Lit. Assn. (pres. 1979-85). Office: Tex A&M U Dept English College Station TX 77843

CANNON, GRACE BERT, immunologist; b. Chambersburg, Pa., Jan. 29, 1937; d. Charles Wesley and Gladys (Raff) Bert; m. W. Dilworth Cannon, June 3, 1961 (div. 1972); children: Michael Quayle Cannon, Susan Radcliffe Cannon Antolin, Peter Bert Cannon. AB, Goucher Coll., 1958; PhD, Washington U., St. Louis, 1962. Fellow Columbia U., N.Y.C., 1962-64, Columbia U. Coll. Physicians and Surgeons, N.Y.C., 1964-65; staff fellow NIH Nat. Cancer Inst., Bethesda, Md., 1966-67; cell biologist Litton Bionetics, Inc., Kensington, Md., 1972-80, head immunology sect., 1980-85; dir. sci. ImmuQuest Labs., Inc., Rockville, Md., 1985-88; pres. Biomedical Analytics, Inc., Rockville, Md., 1988; mgr. ATLIS Fed. Svcs., Inc., Silver Spring, Md., 1991-95; dir. ATLIS Fed. Svcs., Inc., Rockville, Md., 1995-97; sr. assoc. United Info. Sys., Inc., Bethesda, Md., 1998—; Mem. contract rev. coms. Nat. Cancer Inst., 1983-87. Contbr. articles to profl. jours. Mem. Pub. Svc. Health Club, Bethesda, Md., 1984—, sec., 1990—; mem. bd. Cmty. Ministries Rockville. Grantee USPHS, 1959-65, NSF, 1959. Mem. AAAS, Am. Assn. for Cancer Rsch., N.Y. Acad. Sci., Sigma Xi. Home and Office: 4905 Ertter Dr Rockville MD 20852-2203

CANNON, HERBERT SETH, investment banker; b. Bklyn., Dec. 3, 1931; s. Joseph and Gertrude (Kimmel) C.; m. Edith Marks, June 20, 1954; children: Naomi Sue, Nina Louise. B.A., Washington and Jefferson Coll., 1953; student, Cornell U. Law Sch., 1953-54; LL.B., Fordham U., 1960. Salesman Manhattan Scalloping & Embroidery Co., N.Y.C., 1956-57; stock broker Hirsch & Co., N.Y.C., 1956-61, Wineman, Weiss & Co., N.Y.C., 1961-62; pres. Weis, Voisin, Cannon, Inc., N.Y.C., 1963-70; chmn. bd. Elgin Nat. Industries, Inc., N.Y.C., 1967-70; chmn. bd., pres. Cannon, Jerold & Co., Inc., 1970-73; chmn. bd. PUD Industries, Inc., 1971-83, CitiWide Capital Corp., 1984-88, CitiWide Securities Corp., 1984-88; pres. Cannon Enterprises Inc., real estate devel., investment bankers and fin. cons., Boca Raton, Fla., 1975-93; chmn. bd. Holistic Services Corp., 1979-83; pres. HSC Consulting, Inc., 1997—. Past trustee Washington and Jefferson Coll. Served with AUS, 1954-56. Mem. Young Pres. Orgn., World Bus. Council, Metro Pres. Orgn. Home and Office: 23402 Savona Ct Boca Raton FL 33433-6935 *Make it happen.*

CANNON, HUGH, lawyer; b. Albemarle, N.C., Oct. 11, 1931; s. Hubert Napoleon and Nettie (Harris) C.; m. Jo Anne Weisner, Mar. 21, 1998; AB, Davidson Coll., 1953; BA (Rhodes scholar) Oxford U., 1955, MA, 1960; LLB, Harvard U., 1958; children: John Stuart, Marshall, Martha Janet. Bar: N.C., 1958, D.C., 1978, S.C., 1979; mem. staff U. N.C. Inst. Govt., Chapel Hill, 1959; mem. firm Sanford, Phillips, McCoy & Weaver, Fayetteville, 1960; asst. to Gov. of N.C., Raleigh, 1961; dir. adminstrn. State of N.C., 1962-65, state budget officer, 1963; mem. and mng. ptnr. Sanford, Cannon, Adams & McCullough, Raleigh, 1965-79; pvt. practice, Charleston, S.C., 1979—; mem. Everett, Gaskins, Hancock and Stevens attys., Raleigh, 1990—; v.p. fin. Palmetto Ford, Inc., Charleston, 1979—. Parliamentarian NEA, 1965—; pres. Friends of Coll., Raleigh, 1963; alt. del. Democratic Nat. Conv., 1964; chief parliamentarian, 1976, 80, 84, 88, 92, 96; bd. govs. U. N.C., 1972-81; trustee Davidson Coll., 1966-74, N.C. Sch. Arts, 1963-72. Author: Cannon's Concise Guide to Rules of Order, 1992. Mem. Phi Beta Kappa, Omicron Delta Kappa, Phi Gamma Delta. Democrat. Episcopalian. Home: PO Box 31820 Charleston SC 29417-1820 Office: 1625 Savannah Hwy Charleston SC 29407-2236

CANNON, ISABELLA WALTON, mayor; b. Dunfermline, Scotland, May 12, 1904; came to U.S., 1916; d. James and Helen Bett (Seaman) Walton; m. Claude M. Cannon. BA, Elon Coll., 1924, LLD (hon.), 1978. Tchr. pub. schs.; head dept. stats. French Purchase Commn., Washington; fin. officer UN, Washington; with N.C. State U. Library; mayor of Raleigh, N.C., 1977-79. *Elected the first female mayor of any of the 50 state capitals, providing a leadership role-model for women in the political arena. The four-year Leadership Fellows program established in her honor at Elon College is significant in training the next generation of leaders in education, environment, and civic issues. Recently inducted into the National Women's Hall of Fame, a continuation of a high level of activity in community matters with widespread recognition as Isabella turns 95 years old. Received the Governor's Award of the Order of the Long Leaf Pine, the highest honor in North Carolina.* V.p. Women in Bus. Adv. Council, N.C. Conservation Council, Women's Polit. Caucus; charter mem. Wake County Dem. Women; organizer, pres. Univ. Park Assn., Raleigh; civic sponsor, mem. bldg. com. Raleigh Little Theatre; mem. Univ. Neighborhood Planning Council, N.C. Child Advocacy, N.C. Commn. Bicentennial of U.S.; bd. dirs. Mordecai Sq. Hist. Soc.; chmn. Wade CAC; mem. devel. bd. YWCA Acad. of Women; chairperson Keep Am. Clean Sweep; bd. dirs. Raleigh Symphony Orch.; mem. Women's Forum of N.C.; mem. Coll. Presdl. Electors, Centennial Com.; bd. dirs., historian St. Luke's Home, Raleigh liaison RSVP bd., Raleigh Bicentennial Task Force 1988-92, Martin Luther King Jr. Celebration Com., 1989-92; precinct chair numerous polit. orgns. Recipient Disting. Alumnus award Elon Coll., 1983, Medallion award, 1991, Isabella Cannon Rm. named in her honor Elon Coll., 1987, Isabella Cannon Leadership Fellows Program established in 1991, Lifetime Achievement award Theatre in the Park, Govt. award YWCA Acad. Women, 1988, Role Model Leader award N.C. State U., 1991, Mentor of Distinction award Women Bus. Adv. Coun., 1994; Isabella Cannon Arboretum Intership established in her honor N.C. State U., 1991; inductee Nat. Women's Hall of Fame, 1998. Mem. N.C. Sr. Citizens Assn. (pres.), Elon Coll. Alumni Assn., Delta Kappa Gamma. Mem. United Ch. of Christ. *The motivation which directs my life and activities is my profound belief in the democratic process and the response each citizen should make to its demands. This response includes taking an active part in political and governmental affairs, whether it be local community service or state or national matters. It is of basic importance for citizens to study the issues before their governmental bodies, communicate with their representatives and then vote faithfully. Only through wide-spread involvement in our communities can we meet the ideals of democratic society, no matter how small a part we play.*

CANNON, JAMES ANTHONY, advertising agency executive; b. N.Y.C., May 31, 1938; s. Anthony and Beatrice (McDonagh) C.; m. Anne E. Sheridan, Nov. 25, 1961; children—Lisa, Patrick, Anthony, Kathleen, Thomas, Maureen, Sheila. B.B.A., Pace U., 1968. Cost account mgr. Equitable Life Assurance Soc., N.Y.C., 1958-67; with Batten, Barton, Durstine and Osborne (now BBDO Internat.), N.Y.C., 1967-86; exec. v.p., chief fin. officer, BBDO Worldwide, 1989-90, vice chmn., chief fin. officer, 1990—; contr. Omnicom Group, 1986, dir. fin. ops., 1988—. With USMC, 1955-58. Roman Catholic. Home: 757 Charnwood Dr Wyckoff NJ 07481-1011 Office: BBDO Worldwide Inc 1285 Avenue Of The Americas New York NY 10019-6028*

CANNON, JOHN, actor, performing arts association executive; b. Chgo., Mar. 26, 1927; s. John Thomas and Margaret (Stewart) C.; m. Gertrude (Trudy) Weincek, June 11, 1951; children—Michael, Constance. Student, Western Res. U., 1940-41. Pres. Nat. Acad. TV Arts and Scis., N.Y.C., 1969—; nat. vice-chmn. from Nat. Acad. TV Arts and Scis., 1972, chmn., 1974-76; founder full opportunity com. TV Acad. Encouragement of Minorities Peoples in Television. Free-lance host, interviewer, moderator, narrator, newscaster, actor, writer, producer, numerous network shows, newsreels, comml., feature films, 1947—; appeared: Golden Age of TV, N.Y.C., 1950-60; premier interviewer: NBC's Monitor, 1961—. Served with AUS, 1943-46. Decorated Bronze Star. Mem. Institut Francais, Sommelier Soc. N.Y. Club: West Side Tennis. Office: Nat Acad TV Arts & Sci 111 W 57th St Ste 1020 New York NY 10019-2271*

CANNON, JOHN, investment consultant; b. Phila., Jan. 17, 1930; s. John F. and Anne (Carlin) C.; m. Edythe Marple Grebe, Aug. 16, 1952; children: John III, Lynne, Anne. BS, U. Pa., 1954; MBA, Drexel Inst. Tech., 1956. Fin. analyst Bishop & Hedberg, Inc., Phila., 1956-58; rep. Stone & Webster Securities Corp., Phila., 1958-62; nat. sales mgr. municipal bond dept. Hallowell & Sulzberger, Phila., 1962-64; pres., dir. AMA Investment Advisers, Inc., Blue Bell, Pa., 1964-91, AMA Family Funds, Inc., Blue Bell, 1967-71, AMA Money Fund, 1982-91, Med. Tech. Fund., Inc., 1979-88, Emerging Med. Tech. Fund, 1984-88; dir. AMA Svcs. Inc., 1986-91; bd. dirs. Oppenheimer/Rochester Funds, Limited Term New York Mcpl. Fund, Neuberger & Berman Fixed Income Funds, Oppenheimer Convertible Bond Fund, Oppenheimer/Rochester Fund Mcpls.; v.p. Janney, Montgomery, Scott, Inc., 1972-73; chmn., bd. dirs. CDC Capital Mgmt., Inc., Blue Bell, 1998-99. *John Cannon has over thirty years experience in the financial service industry including senior positions in brokerage, mutual fund management and investment consulting. He served as president, director and chief executive officer of several mutual funds and mutual fund management companies from 1967 to 1991. He has a strong background in portfolio management, marketing and mergers and acquisitions of mutual fund companies. He created the first medical sector mutual fund in 1979 and Emerging Medical Technology Fund in 1984. He is currently serving as an independent director of several Oppenheimer and Neuberger Berman mutual funds.* With USMCR, 1950-51. Mem. Fin. Analysts Am., Phila. Securities Assn., No-Load Mut. Fund Assn. (gov. 1979-89), Mfrs. Golf and Country Club (Oreland, Pa., pres. 1988-90), Masons. Home and Office: 531 Willow Ave Ambler PA 19002-6013

CANNON, JOHN, III, lawyer; b. Phila., Mar. 19, 1954; s. John and Edythe (Grebe) C. BA, Denison U., 1976; JD, Dickinson Sch. Law, 1983. Bar: Pa. 1983, Hawaii 1986, U.S. Dist. Ct. (ea. dist.) Pa. 1983, U.S. Ct. Appeals (3d cir.) 1985. Account exec. PRO Services, Inc., Flourtown, Pa., 1976-79; br. officer mgr. PRO Services, Inc., Pitts., 1979-80; law clk. Montgomery County Ct. of Common Pleas, Norristown, Pa., 1983-84; assoc. Rawle & Henderson, Phila., 1984-88; comml. litigation counsel CIGNA Corp., Phila., 1988-90; counsel CIGNA Internat. Fin. Svcs. Divsn., Phila., 1990-93; sr. counsel CIGNA Internat., Phila., 1993-95, v.p., sr. counsel, 1995-97, sr. v.p., chief counsel, 1997—; sr. v.p., chief counsel CIGNA Healthcare, Bloomfield, Conn., 1999—, Conn. Gen. Life Ins. Co., Bloomfield, Conn., 1999—; bd. dirs. CIGNA Stu Zychie, Warsaw, Poland, INA Himawari Life Ins. Co. Ltd., Tokyo; v.p. Life Ins. Co. N.Am., 1998—; trustee U.S.-China Legal Coop. Fund, Washington, 1998—. Comments editor Dickinson Internat. Law Ann., 1983. Mem. ABA, Pa. Bar Assn., Hawaii State Bar Assn., Kappa Sigma (pres. 1975-76), Gamma Xi (v.p., trustee 1982-86). Republican. Episcopalian. Office: Cigna Cos PO Box 7716 2 Liberty Pl Philadelphia PA 19192

CANNON, JOHN J(OSEPH), real estate sales and marketing executive; b. London, Jan. 29, 1954; came to U.S., 1963; s. Charles and Anne (Strogen) C.; m. Elena M. Manna; children: Ryan Scott, Taylor. Student, Pace U., 1972-74; BBA in Real Estate cum laude, Baruch Coll., 1976. Lic. real estate broker, N.Y. Corp. facilities rep. Volkswagen of Am., Englewood Cliffs, N.J., 1979-81; real estate negotiator The Chase Manhattan Bank, N.Y.C., 1981-82; regional mgr. real estate Pepsico, Pizza Hut, Inc., Wichita, Kans., 1983-85; regional dir. of real estate T.G.I. Fridays, Inc., Dallas, 1985; sales dir. The Beechwood Orgn., North Hills, N.Y., 1986, M.J. Raynes, Inc., N.Y.C., 1987-88; pres. Cannon Enterprises, N.Y., 1988-91; dir. sales The KLAR Orgn., East Meadow, N.Y., 1991-93; dir. real estate leasing ICON Internat., N.Y.C., 1993-96; mng. dir. RAK Group, N.Y.C., 1996—; cons. real estate Audio Exchange, Inc., Hicksville, N.Y., 1984—. Named one of Outstanding Young Men of Am., 1985. Mem. NACORE, L.I. Builders Inst. (treas. sales and mktg. coun. 1989, v.p. 1990-91), Nat. Assn. Home Builders, Inst. Residential Mktg. Assn. Home Builders, Inst. Residential Mktg., Beta Gamma Sigma. Republican. Roman Catholic. Avocations: modern art collector, tennis. Home: 15 Farmington Ln Melville NY 11747-4016 Office: RAK Group 680 5th Ave New York NY 10019-5429

CANNON, KIM DECKER, lawyer; b. Salt Lake City, Oct. 15, 1948; s. Morris Nibley Cannon and Bette Jeanne (Decker) Sage; m. Jane B. Howard, June 10, 1972 (div. Sept. 1985); children: Sage, Meredith; m. Susan Margaret Clinch, Sept. 6, 1986; 1 child, Grace. AB, Dartmouth Coll., 1970; JD, U. Colo., 1974. Bar: Wyo. 1974, U.S. Dist. Ct. Wyo. 1974, U.S. Ct. Appeals (10th cir.) 1974. Ptnr. Burgess & Davis, Sheridan, Wyo., 1974-90, Burgess, Davis, Carmichael & Cannon, Sheridan and Cheyenne, Wyo., 1990-94, Davis & Cannon, Sheridan and Cheyenne, 1994—. Pres. Sheridan County Fulmer Pub. Librs., 1980-85, Wyo. Theater, Inc., Sheridan, 1986-91, Wyo. Outdoor Coun., Lander, 1987-91; chmn. Wyo. Environ. Quality Coun., 1992-96; active Commn. on Jud. Conduct and Ethics, 1997—; mem. Rhodes Scholarship selection com., Wyo., 1998—. Mem. Sheridan Bar Assn. (pres. 1982). Avocations: polo, training horses, fly fishing, skiing. Home: PO Box 401 Big Horn WY 82833-0401 Office: Davis & Cannon 40 S Main St Sheridan WY 82801-4222

CANNON, LOUIS SIMEON, journalist, author; b. N.Y.C., June 3, 1933; s. Jack and Irene (Kohn) C.; m. Virginia Oprian, Feb. 2, 1953 (div. 1983); children: Carl, David, Judy, Jack; m. Mary L. Shinkwin, Sept. 7, 1985. Student, U. Nev., 1950-51, San Francisco State U., 1951-52. Reporter Lafayette Sun, Calif., 1957; editor Newark (Calif.) Sun, 1957-58, Merced Sun Star, Calif., 1958-60, Contra Costa Times, Calif., 1960-61, San Jose (Calif.) Mercury News, Calif., 1961-69; Sacramento corr. San Jose Mercury News, Calif., 1965-69; Washington corr. Ridder Pubs., Washington, 1969-72; reporter The Washington Post, L.A., 1972-96, spl. corr., 1997—. Author: Official Negligence: How Rodney King and the Riots Changed Los Angeles and the LAPD, 1998, President Reagan: the Role of a Lifetime, 1991, Reagan, 1982, Ronnie and Jesse, 1969, Reporting: An Inside View, 1977, The McCloskey Challenge, 1972. Recipient Gerald R. Ford prize Gerald Ford Libr., 1988, Merriman Smith award White House Corrs. Assn., 1986, Aldo Beckman award, 1984, Washington Journalism Rev. award, 1985, Disting. Reporting of Pub. Affairs award Am. Polit. Sci. Assn., 1968. Mem. Soc. of Profl. Journalists, Authors Guild. Home: PO Box 436 Summerland CA 93067-0436

CANNON, LYNNE MARPLE, investment management company executive; b. Phila., Oct. 14, 1955; d. John and Edythe (Grebe) C.; m. Richard W. Baksa, 1999. BA, Ohio Wesleyan U., 1977. Employee PRO Services Inc., Flourtown, Pa., 1979-82; asst. sec. PRO Services Inc., Blue Bell, Pa., 1982-86; v.p. AMA Investment Advisers Inc. (formerly PRO Svcs. Inc.), Blue Bell, 1986-92; v.p., sec. AMA Family of Funds, Inc., 1986-92; v.p. Independence Capital Mgmt., Inc., Horsham, Pa., 1992-95, Independence Capital Group of Funds, Inc., 1992-95; sr. v.p. relationship mgmt. FPS Svcs., Inc., King of Prussia, Pa., 1995-98; v.p. First Data Investor Svcs. Group, Inc., 1998—; dir. FPS Broker Svcs., Inc., 1996-98; dir. devel. Stratton Mgmt., Inc., 1995—; chmn. sml. funds com. Investment Co . Inst., 1994—; dir. The Stratton Funds, Inc., Plymouth Meeting, Pa., 1995—. Vol. Plant Ambler Inc., Pa., 1983—. Mem. Mut. Fund Edn. Alliance (bd. govs. 1990-91), Phila. Saddle Club (bd. dirs., v.p.), Wodehouse Soc. Republican. Episcopalian. Home: 219 Forest Ave Ambler PA 19002-5903 Office: First Data Investor Svcs Group 3200 Horizon Dr King Of Prussia PA 19406

CANNON, MAJOR TOM, special education educator; b. Anniston, Ala., Nov. 11, 1932; s. Thomas Albert and Sallie Mae (James) C. BA in Liberal Arts, Samford U., 1961; postgrad., So. Bapt. Theol. Sem., 1961-62, Tulane U., 1962-63, Auburn U., 1963-64; MEd in Counseling, U. Ga., 1968; postgrad., U. S.C., 1971, 81, 84, Francis Marion Coll., 1979-80, Western Md. Coll., 1980, S.C. State Coll., 1981-85, U. Charleston, 1993, The Citadel, Charleston, S.C., 1996-97. Cert. prin., guidance counselor, spl. edn. tchr., S.C. English tchr. North Whitfield H.S., Dalton, Ga., 1964-65, Savannah (Ga.) H.S., 1965-66; guidance counselor Savannah Pub. Schs., 1966-79; dir. spl. svcs. Marlboro County Sch. Dist., Bennettsville, S.C., 1979-80, coord. programs for handicapped, 1980-81; tchr. trainable mentally retarded Edisto Mid. Sch., Orangeburg, S.C., 1981-86; tchr. learning disabled Norman C. Toole Mid. Sch., Charleston, S.C., 1986-88; tchr. learning disabled Berkeley Mid. Sch., Moncks Corner, S.C., 1988-97, chmn. dept. spl. edn., 1991-94; specialist learning disabilities Berkeley County Sch. Dist., Moncks Corner, 1995-97; resource C.E. Murray H.s., Greeleyville, S.C., 1997—; labor resources technician City of Savannah, 1979; presenter in field; mem. Strategic Planning Com. for Berkeley County Sch. Dist., 1993-97, Sch. Improvement Coun., 1996-97. Contbr. poetry to Great Poems of the Western World, 1990, Our World's Favorite Gold and Silver Poems, 1991, Perceptions, 1994, Am. Poetry Annual, 1994; author resource manuals and videotaped lessons. Charter Rep. Nat. Com., 1992—, Rep. Presdl. Task Force, 1989—, Rep. Nat. Commn. on Am. Agenda, 1996, Nat. Rep. Senatorial Com., 1990—; at-large del. Rep. Party Platform Planning Com.; mem. Ga. Com. on Children and Youth, 1968. With USN, 1953-57. Recipient Nat. Def. Edn. award U.S. Office of Edn., 1966-67, GE Found. award, 1971, Rep. Presdl. Legion of Merit, 1992-98, Rep. Presdl. award, 1994, Rep. Presdl. Order of Merit, 1997. Mem. ASCD, ASPCA, Nat. Authors Registry, Coun. for Exceptional Children, Am. Pers. and Guidance Assn., Am. Sch. Counselors Assn. (Ga. coord.), Nat. Assn. Sch. Counselors., Am. Legion, VFW (life), Ga. Assn. Educators, Ga. Pers. and Guidance Assn., Palmetto Tchrs. Assn., Sierra Club, Nature Conservancy, Nat. Resources Def. Coun., World Wildlife Soc., Defenders of Wildlife, Am. Assn. Ret. Persons, Humane Soc. U.S., Phi Delta Kappa, Kappa Delta Pi. Republican. Baptist. Avocations: coin collecting, pets, scientific experiments, historical studies. Home: 324 Tulane Dr Ladson SC 29456-6235

CANNON, MARK WILCOX, government official, business executive; b. Salt Lake City, Aug. 29, 1928; s. Joseph Jenne and Ramona (Wilcox) C.; m. Ruth Marian Dixon, Dec. 28, 1956 (div. Jun. 1992); children: Lucile Cannon Tredway, Mark, Kristen Cannon Brown. m. Betty Ann Schomann, June 25, 1993. Student, Deep Springs Coll., 1944-46; BA, U. Utah, 1949; MA, Harvard U., 1954, MPA, 1955, PhD, 1961. Missionary Ch. Jesus Christ of Latter-Day Saints, Argentina, 1949-52; rsch. analyst Utah Found., 1953; sec. Utah Sch. Merit Study Com., 1954; instr. Brigham Young U., 1955, chmn. dept. polit. sci., 1961-64; mem. staff U.S. Senator W.F. Bennett, 1961, 62-63; adminstrv. asst. to U.S. congressman Henry A. Dixon, 1956-61; mem. staff Inst. Pub. Adminstrn., N.Y.C., 1964-72; dir. urban devel. program Inst. Pub. Adminstrn., Venezuela, 1964-65; dir. internat. programs Inst. Pub. Adminstrn., N.Y.C., 1965-68; dir. Inst. Pub. Adminstrn., 1968-72; adminstrv. asst. to chief justice of U.S., 1972-85; staff dir. Commn. on Bicentennial of U.S. Constn., 1985-88; vice chmn., bd. dirs. Geneva Steel; exec. v.p. Geneva Devel., 1988-89; vice chair Cannon Industries, 1989-96; venture capitalist, 1989—; guest scholar Woodrow Wilson Internat. Ctr. for Scholars, 1989. Author: (with R. Joseph Monsen) The Makers of Public Policy: American Power Groups and Their Ideologies, 1965; (with others) Partnership for Progress: Atlanta-Fulton County Consolidation, 1969, Urban Government for Valencia, 1973, Views From The Bench: The Judiciary and Constitutional Politics, 1985; contbg. author: Development Administration in Latin America, 1973; contbr. articles to profl. jours.; mem. editorial bd. Judicature, 1975-76. Trustee Inst. Pub. Adminstrn. Recipient ann. award Western Polit. Sci. Assn., 1963. Mem. Nat. Acad. Pub. Adminstrn., Internat. Studies Assn. (sec. 1962-63). Home: 8360 Greensboro Dr Apt 917 Mc Lean VA 22102-3543 *Much of my motivation, orientation, and values stem from a conviction of the masterful leadership of a perfect personal God who is exemplary in His knowledge and utilization of eternal laws to promote the eternal progress and happiness of each human being, partially by providing a complicated earthly learning environment and by permitting people to deal freely with individual and social problems, thereby providing laboratory opportunities for the flourishing of character, knowledge, and wisdom.*

CANNON, NANCY GLADSTEIN, insurance agent; b. San Francisco; d. Richard and Caroline Gladstein; m. Robert L. Cannon; 1 child, Richard Michael. BA, San Francisco State U.; JD, U. West Los Angeles, 1980. Agt. State Farm Ins. Co., Pacific Palisades, Calif., 1984-99, Thousand Oaks, Calif., 1999—. Mem. bd. govs. Pacific Palisades Civic League, 1987-91, Community Coun., 1988-89; bd. dirs. YMCA, Pacific Palisades, 1989-93, Sunset Mesa Property Owners Assn., 1991-93. Mem. Pacific Palisades C. of C., Santa Monica C. of C., Malibu C. of C., L.A. Athletic Club. Republican. Avocations: sailing, paddle tennis. Home: PO Box 1228 Agoura Hills CA 91376-1228

CANNON, PATRICK D., federal offical, broadcaster; married; five children. Comm. specialist Mich. Dept. Labor, Bur. Workers' Disability; staff rsch. specialist; dir. Senate Ctrl. Office, Audio Comm. Divsn.; exec. dir. Mich. Commn. Disability Concern, Lansing, 1988-97, Mich. Commn. Blind, Lansing, 1997—; bd. dirs. Capital Area Transp. Authority; mem. Pres.'s Com. Employment People with Disabilites; apptd. U.S. access Bd., 1995; presentor in field. Mem. Pres.'s com. Employment of People with Disabilities, Gov.'s com. People with Disabilities, Access Bd., 1995—, Advanced Am. with Disabilities Act Tng. Network, Capital Area Ctr. Indep. Living, All Peoples' Theater, Riverwalk Theater; bd. trustees BoarsHead Theater, Capitol Area Transp. Authority; co-chair Gov.'s State Am. with Disabilites Act Implementation Task Force; chair Mich. Am. with Disabilities Act Steering Com.; trainer Windmills; active People's Theatre, Easter Seal Soc., St. Vincent Home. Mem. Nat. Rehab. Assn.. Avocations: baseball, movies, theater, hotdogs, sunshine. Office: Mich Commn Blind PO Box 30652 Lansing MI 48909-8152 Office: Mich Commn on Disability Concerns PO Box 30015 Lansing MI 48909-7515

CANNON, PATRICK FRANCIS, public relations executive; b. Braddock, Pa., Mar. 2, 1938; s. Peter J. and Kathleen (Donnelly) C.; children by previous marriage: Patrick F. Jr., Elizabeth Kathleen; m. Jeanette Krema, Nov. 22, 1986. BA, Northwestern U., 1969. Ops. mgr. Compact Industries, Albert Lea, Minn., 1968-72; pub. info. dir. Dept. Pub. Works, Chgo., 1970-72; acct. exec. Humes & Assocs., Chgo., 1972-77; freelance journalist, cons. Oak Park, Ill., 1977-79; mgr. pub. rels. and prodn. Lions Clubs Internat., Oak Brook, Ill., 1979—. Editor: Water in Rural America, 1973, Wastewater in Rural America, 1974, We Serve: A History of the Lions Clubs, 1991; contbr. articles to profl. jours. and mags.; exec. producer, writer (pub. TV documentaries) With Very Little...Blindness Prevention in Developing Countries, 1991, The Search for Light, 1993, A Dangerous Time for Kids, 1997. Exec. dir. Civic Arts Coun. Oak Park, 1977-79; bd. dirs. interpreter coun. Oak Park Tour Ctr., 1978-82, mem. vol. svc. com. Frank Lloyd Wright Home and Studio Found., 1988-94, mem. pub. programs com., 1995-96, chmn. Wright Plus Housewalk, 1996; mem. bd. advisors U.S. Internat. Film and Video Festival. Named PR All Star 1996, Inside PR Mag. Mem. Lions (pres. 1983-84). Roman Catholic. Avocations: history, horse racing. Home: 243 Iowa St Oak Park IL 60302-2347 Office: Lions Clubs Internat 300 W 22d St Oak Brook IL 60523-8815

CANNON, ROBERT EUGENE, librarian, public administrator, fund raiser; b. Elkhorn, Wis., Dec. 20, 1945; s. Wendell Eugene and Louise Marie (Bredehoeft) C.; m. Miriam Ruth Hillson, May 25, 1974; 1 child, Allison. BA in Music, Calif. State U., L.A., 1967; postgrad. Ariz. State U., 1967-68; MLS, U. So. Calif., 1970; M in Pub. Adminstrn., San Diego State U., 1978. Adult svcs. libr. Tucson Pub. Libr., 1969-70, Altadena Libr. Dist., 1970-71; head tech. processing, regional coord. San Diego County Libr., 1971-76; asst. dir. Tulare County Libr., Visalia, Calif., 1976-78; dir. Kern County Libr., Bakersfield, Calif., 1978-86; exec. dir. Pub. Libr. of Charlotte and MacKlenburg County, N.C., 1986—; mem. bd. dirs. Mecklenburg County Law & Govt. Libr., Inc., 1992—; sec.-treas. Pub. Lib. Charlotte & Mecklenburg County, 1986—; sec. Mus. New South, 1991-93, bd. dirs., 1991-97; former mem. Leadership Charlotte; founder Novello Festival of Reading, 1991—, ProSearch Info. Svc., 1991-96; founder Internat. Bus. Libr., 1994—, Virtual Libr., 1995—, Digital Children's Libr. Project, 1998—, BizLinks, 1998—; co-founder Charlotte's Web, 1995—; bd. visitors Sch. Info. & Libr. Sci. U. N.C., Chapel Hill; steering com. Charlotte Alliance Info. Referral Svcs., 1995-97; mem. Internat. Network Pub. Librs. Bertelsman Found., Germany, 1996—. Named N.C. Libr. Dir. of Yr. N.C. Pub. Libr. Dirs. Assn., 1995; recipient Pegasus award Pub. Rels. Soc. Am., 1998. Mem. ALA, N.C. Libr. Assn., Charlotte/Mecklenburg Coalition for Literacy, 1988-89, Kern County Hist. Records Commn. (vice chmn. 1978-86), Southeastern Libr. Assn. (treas., chmn. conf. com. 1993-95), Mecklenburg Hist. Assn., Cultural Edn. Collaboration (bd. dirs.). Office: Pub Libr Charlotte & Mecklenburg County 310 N Tryon St Charlotte NC 28202-2176

CANNON, ROBERT HAMILTON, JR., aerospace engineering educator; b. Cleve., Oct. 6, 1923; s. Robert Hamilton and Catharine (Putnam) C.; m. Dorothea Alta Collins, Jan. 4, 1945 (dec. Apr. 1988); children: Philip Gregory, Douglas Charles, Beverly Jo, Frederick Scott. David John, Joseph Collins, James Robert; m. Vera Berlin Crie, May 27, 1989. B.S., U. Rochester, 1944; Sc.D. (du Pont fellow), MIT, 1950. Rsch. engr. Baker Mfg. Co., Evansville, Wis., 1946-50; instr. MIT, 1949-50; research engr. Bendix Aviation Research Labs., Detroit, 1950-51; with Autonetics div. N.Am. Aviation Inc., Downey, Calif., 1951-57; supr. automatic flight control systems, 1951-54, systems engr. inertial nav. instruments and systems, 1954-57; assoc. prof. mech. engring. MIT, 1957-59; mem. faculty Stanford U., 1959-74, prof. aeros. and astronautics, 1962-74, dir. Guidance and Control Lab., 1960-69; chief scientist USAF, 1966-68; asst. sec. U.S. Dept. Transp. Washington, 1970-74; chmn. div. engring. and applied sci. Calif. Inst. Tech., Pasadena, 1974-79; Charles Lee Powell prof. aeronautics and astronautics Stanford U., 1979—, chmn. dept., 1979-90, dir. aerospace robotics lab., 1980—; chmn. sci. adv. com. to dir. aerospace robotics emeritus Gen. Motors Corp., 1979-84; bd. dirs. Key Tronic Corp; mem. Draper Corp., 1975—; bd. dirs. Parkin Hannifin Corp.; vice chmn. sci. adv. bd. USAF, 1968-70; chmn. assembly of engring. NRC, 1974-75, chmn. energy engring. bd., 1975-81, mem. aeros. and space engring. bd., 1975-79, 85-92, ocean studies bd., 1991—, mem. governing bd., 1976-78; mem. Boeing Corp. Tech. Adv. Council, 1984—, R.R. Donnelley Tech. Adv. Coun., 1984-89, Comsat Tech. Adv. Com., 1985-87; chmn. Gen. Electric Space Sta. Adv. Bd., 1985-87; chmn. Pres.'s Com. on Nat. Medal of Sci., 1984-88; chmn. NASA Flight Telerobotic Servicer Commn., 1987-91; mem. tech. adv. coun. United Techs. Corp., 1989-92; commn. underwater vehicles Marine Bd. Author: Dynamics of Physical Systems, 1967; also articles. Served to lt. (j.g.) USNR, 1944-46. Fellow AIAA (dir. 1968-70), Am. Acad. Arts and Scis., Internat. Acad. Astronautics; mem. Nat. Acad. Engring. (councillor 1975-81), Sigma Xi, Theta Chi (chpt. pres. 1943-44), Tau Beta Pi. Presbyterian. Participated devel. hydrofoil boats, automatic flight control, inertial guidance instruments and systems, space vehicle control, drag free satellite, gyro test of gen. relativity, tech. assessment of climatic impact of stratospheric flight, wave-actuated upwelling pump, flexible robot and space robot control systems, underwater free-flying robots, autonomous task-commanded helicopter, nat. energy alternatives. Office: Stanford U Dept Aeronautics & Astronautics Durand Bldg Rm 357 Stanford CA 94305-8468*

CANNON, STEVE, non-profit organization administrator; b. New Orleans, Apr. 10, 1935; s. Eugene Charles and Lillie (St. Cyr) C. BA, U. Nebr., 1956; MA, London Sch. Econs., 1960. Prof. humanities Lincoln (Pa.) U., 1968-69, York Coll., Queens, N.Y., 1970-71, Hunter-CUNY, N.Y.C., 1971-72, Medgar Evers-CUNY, N.Y.C., 1971-72; dir. A Gathering of the Tribes, N.Y.C., 1990—. Author: Groove, Bang and Jive Around, 1969; author (plays) Trilogy, 1996, OOPS, 1997, Marvelous, 1997; editor-in-chief A Gathering of the Tribes Mag., 1990—. Home and Office: Bet C&D 2d Fl 285 E Third St New York NY 10009

CANNON, WILLIAM BERNARD, retired university educator; b. Cascade, Iowa, Nov. 10, 1920; s. Charles Bernard and Irma (White) C.; m. Jeanne Adair Ketchum, Aug. 16, 1944; children: Julia, Dominic, William, Robert. Ph.B., U. Chgo., 1947; M.A., 1949. Budget examiner Bur. Budget, 1951-54, 59-62; asst. v.p. U. Chgo., 1954-59, v.p. programs and projects, 1968-74; dean Lyndon B. Johnson Sch. Pub. Affairs, U. Tex. at Austin, 1974-75; v.p. bus. and fin. U. Chgo., 1976-83, prof., 1976-89, prof. emeritus, 1989—; asst. chief, office legis. reference for health, edn. and welfare programs Bur. Budget, 1962-65, chief edn., manpower and sci. div., 1965-67; dep. chmn. Nat. Endowment for the Arts, 1968. Mem. selection com. Rockefeller Pub. Service Awards, 1976-81; mem. Midwest selection com. H.S. Truman Scholarship Program, 1977-87. Served with AUS, 1943-46. Mem. Phi Beta Kappa. Home: 2102 Bowman Ave Austin TX 78703-2306

CANO, JUVENTINO, manufacturing company executive; b. Estapillo, Mex., 1956; cam to U.S., 1974; m. Hermila Cano; 3 children. Grad., Benito Juarez H.S., Tecoman, Mex. Pres., CEO Cano Container Corp., Aurora, Ill.; mem. adv. bd. Merchants Bank, Aurora, Joseph Corp., Aurora. Mem. Aurora Sch. Bus. Partnership; bd. dirs. Aurora Econ. Devel. Commn., Mercy Svc. Found., Waubonsee C.C. Found.; mem. exec. bd. Aurora Cmty. Mobilization Adv. Bd. Recipient Mfg. Firm of Yr. award, 1993, Hispanic 500 award Hispanic bus. Mag., 1994. Mem. USHCC (bd. dirs. Region IV 1997, Region IV Hispanic Businessman of Yr. 1995), Aurora Hispanic C. of C. (pres. bd. dirs.), Greater Aurora C. of C. (bd. dirs.), Urban League (bd. dirs.). Fax: (630) 585-7501. Office: Cano Container Corp 2300 Raddant Rd Ste A Aurora IL 60504

CANO, KRISTIN MARIA, lawyer; b. McKeesport, Pa., Oct. 27, 1951; d. John S. and Sally (Kavic) C. BS in Biochemistry, Pa State U., 1973; MS in Forensic Sci., George Washington U., 1975; JD, Southwestern U., 1978; LLM in Securities Regulation, Georgetown U., 1984. Bar: Calif. 1978, U.S. Dist. Ct. (cen., no. and so. dists.) Calif. 1984, U.S. Dist. Ct. Ariz., 1988, U.S. Supreme Ct. 1988, U.S. Ct. Appeals (9th cir.) 1992. Assoc. Yusim, Cassidy, Stein & Hanger, Beverly Hills, Calif., 1979-81, Walker and Hartley, Newport Beach, Calif., 1981-82, Milberg, Weiss, Bershad, Spethrie & Lerach, San Diego, 1984; pvt. practice Newport Beach, 1984—. Bd. dirs., v.p. Sandcastle Community Assn., Corona del Mar, Calif., 1987-97; active Leadership Tomorrow Class of 1994. Mem. Orange County Bar Assn., Balboa Bay Club. Democrat. Roman Catholic. Avocations: ballet, ice skating, bicycling, photography, golf. Office: 1 Corporate Plaza Dr Ste 110 Newport Beach CA 92660-7924

CANO, MARIO STEPHEN, lawyer; b. Miami, Fla., Sept. 2, 1953; s. Mario Arturo Cano and Irene H. Moreno; m. Johanna Marie Van Rossum, Oct. 13, 1979. AA, Miami Dade Jr. Coll., 1973; BA, Fla. Internat. U., 1975; JD, U. Santa Clara, 1978. Bar: Fla. 1979, U.S. Dist. Ct. (so. dist.) Fla. 1979, U.S. Ct. Claims 1979, U.S. Tax Ct. 1979, U.S. Ct. Mil. Appeals 1979, U.S. Ct. Appeals (9th cir.) 1979, U.S. Dist. Ct. (no. and mid. dists.) Fla. 1980, U.S. Dist. Ct. (no. dist.) Calif. 1980, U.S. Ct. Appeals (3d cir.) 1980, U.S. Ct. Internat. Trade 1981, U.S. Ct. Appeals (11th cir.) 1981, U.S. Ct. Appeals (6th and 10th cirs.) 1983, U.S. Supreme Ct. 1983, Nebr. 1984, U.S. Dist. Ct. Nebr. 1984, U.S. Dist. Ct. (no. dist.) Okla. 1984, U.S. Dist. Ct. Hawaii 1984, U.S. Ct. Appeals (2d, 4th, 5th, 7th 8th and D.C. cirs.) 1984, N.Y. 1985, U.S. Dist. Ct. (no., we., ea. and so. dists.) N.Y. 1985, U.S. Ct. Appeals (1st cir.) 1987, U.S. Dist. Ct. (no. and so. dists.) Tex. 1988, U.S. Dist. Ct. (ea. dist.) Wis. 1988, U.S. Dist. Ct. (we. dist.) Pa. 1988, U.S. Dist. Ct. (no. dist.) Ill. 1991, Mass., 1998, U.S. Dist. Ct. Mass. 1999. Assoc. Orta and Assocs., Miami, 1979-80, Law Office of J. Ramirez, Coral Gables, Fla., 1980, Law Office of I.G. Lichter, Miami, 1980-82, Gelb & Spatz, Miami, 1982; pvt. practice Coral Gables, 1982—. Mem. Cuban Am. Bar Assn., Nat. Assn. Criminal Def. Lawyers. Democrat. Fax: (305) 448-2121. Office: Ste 600 2121 Ponce De Leon Blvd Coral Gables FL 33134-5222

CANO-BALLESTA, JUAN, Spanish language educator; b. Murcia, Spain, Mar. 12, 1932; s. José Cano and Marcelina Ballesta; m. Mercedes Cano, Sept. 12, 1969. PhD, Ludwig Maximilian U., Munich, 1961. Lektor U. Göttingen, Germany, 1962-65; asst. prof. Spanish Yale U., New Haven, 1966-71; assoc. prof. Boston U., 1971-75; prof. U. Pitts., 1976-83; Commonwealth prof. U. Va., Charlottesville, 1983—, acting chmn. dept. Spanish and Italian, 1984-85. Author: La Poesia de Miguel Hernández, 1962, La poesia espaÑola entre purera y revolución, 1972, 2d edit. 1996, Literatura y tecnologia; las letras españolas ante la revolución industrial, 1981, Las estrategias de la imaginacion, 1994; editor: Poesia y prosa de guerra de Miguel Hernández, 1977, En torno a Miguel Hernández, 1978, Articulos sociales, politicos y de critica literaria de Mariano J. de Larra, 1982, El rayo que no cesa de Miguel Hernández, 1988, Viento del pueblo de Miguel Hernández, 1989, Nuevas amistades de J. Gracia Hortelano. Fellow Morse Research Soc. Yale U., 1968-69, Am. Council Learned Socs., Madrid, 1975-76, Ctr. for Advanced Studies U. Va., 1983-84. Mem. MLA, Internat. Assn.

Hispanists, Southeastern Medieval Assn., Am. Assn. Tchrs. Spanish and Portugese. Office: U Va Dept Spanish & Italian Charlottesville VA 22903

CANOFF, KAREN HUSTON, lawyer; b. Medford, Oreg., May 15, 1954; d. Loyd Stanley and Donna Lou (Wall) Huston; m. Lawrence Scott Canoff, May 30, 1981; children: Vincent Jared, Alyssa Rae. BS, U. Oreg., 1977; JD cum laude, Lewis & Clark Coll., 1981. Bar: Oreg. 1981, U.S. Dist. Ct. Oreg. 1982, U.S. Ct. Appeals (9th cir.) 1985, Calif. 1985, U.S. Dist. Ct. (so. dist.) Calif. 1985, U.S. Dist. Ct. (cen. dist.) Calif. 1986, U.S. Ct. Appeals (fed. cir.) 1991. Fin. cons. Stretch & Sew, Inc., Eugene, Oreg., 1975-78; assoc. Margaretta Eakin P.C., Portland, Oreg., 1981-82, 83, Gary M. Bullock, Portland, 1982-83, Markowitz & Herbold, Portland, 1983-86; ptnr. Dorazio, Barnhorst & Bonar, San Diego, 1986-89, shareholder, 1989; ptnr. Hyde & Canoff, San Diego, 1990-96; divsn. counsel Nielsen Dillingham Builders, Inc., San Diego, 1996—; instr. People's Law Sch., Eugene, Oreg., 1978. Author: (with others) Legal Resource Guide, 1983; contbr. articles to profl. jours. Mem. Multnomah County Vol. Lawyers, Portland, Oreg., 1982-83, San Diego Vol. Lawyers Program, 1985-96, Vols. in Parole, San Diego, 1986-87, Charlotte Baker Soc., 1992-93; judge pro tem San Diego County mcpl. Ct., 1988—, San Diego Superior Ct, 1991—, 4th Dist. Ct. Appeals, 1995—; mem. nat. panel comml. arbitrators Am. Arbitration Assn., 1991-96; active Girl Scouts Am. Finalist San Diego Women Who Mean Bus. awards, 1995, 96, 97; recipient Am. Jurisprudence award, 1979. Mem. Calif. State Bar Assn. (bus. law, labor and employment, pub. law and real property sects.), San Diego County Bar Assn., (appellate ct. com. 1987—, editor It's the Law 1987, alternative dispute resolution sec. 1990-95, arbitration com. 1990-96, client rels. com. 1990-96, bus law, comml. law, constrn. law, corp. counsel and labor and employment law sects., editor Bar Briefs 1992, mem. ethics com. 1996), Lawyers Club San Diego (bd. dirs. 1988-91, editor Lawyers Club News 1986-88), Assn. Bus Trial Lawyers, Am. Corp. Counsel Assn., Associated Gen. Contractors (legal issues com.), Constrn. Defect Def. Action Coalition, Nat. Assn. Women Bus. Owners (bd. dirs. 1993-96, sec. 1993-94, chair govt. affairs 1995-96), Mortgage BAnkers Assn. Am. (legal issues com. 1987-89), Phi Beta Kappa.

CANONI, JOHN DAVID, lawyer; b. Newton, Mass., May 11, 1939; s. John Joseph and Olga Elizabeth (Mangini) C.; m. Katherine Ariadna Bryant, Aug. 18, 1962; children: Lisa Ann, Peter Christopher, John Charles, Scott Francis. BA, Amherst Coll., 1960; LLB, Yale U., 1963. Bar: N.Y. 1964, U.S. Ct. Appeals (2d cir.) 1966, U.S. Ct. Appeals (3d cir.) 1967, U.S. Ct. Appeals (4th cir.) 1968, U.S. Ct. Appeals (1st cir.) 1969, U.S. Supreme Ct. 1971, U.S. Ct. Appeals (7th cir.) 1972. Assoc. Townley & Updike, N.Y.C., 1963-71, 1971-95; ptnr. Nixon, Hargrave, Devans & Doyle LLP, N.Y.C., 1995—; mem. Lt. Gov.'s Task Force on Plant Closings, N.Y., 1984-85. Mem. N.Y. State Bar Assn. (chmn. labor & employment law sect. 1983-84), Yale Club. Republican. Roman Catholic. Home: 20 High Meadows Mount Kisco NY 10549-3847 Office: Nixon Hargrave Devans & Doyle LLP 437 Madison Ave New York NY 10022-7001

CANOVA-DAVIS, ELEANOR, biochemist, researcher; b. San Francisco, Jan. 18, 1938; d. Gaudenzio Enzio and Catherine (Bordisso) Canova; m. Kenneth Roy Davis, Feb. 10, 1957; children: Kenneth Roy Jr., Jeffrey Stephen. BA, San Francisco State U., 1968, MS, 1971; PhD, U. Calif., San Francisco, 1977. Lab. asst. Frederick Burk Found. for Edn., San Francisco, 1969-71; rsch., tchg. asst. U. Calif., San Francisco, 1972-77, asst. rsch. biochemist, 1980-84; NIH postdoctoral fellow U. Calif., Berkeley, 1977-80; sr. scientist Liposome Tech., Menlo Park, Calif., 1984-85, Genentech, Inc., South San Francisco, 1985—. Contbr. articles to profl. jours. Recipient Nat. Rsch. Svc. award NIH, 1977-80, Honors Convocation award San Francisco State U., 1966; grantee Chancellor's Patent Fund, U. Calif., San Francisco, 1976, Earl C. Anthony Trust; grad. div. fellow U. Calif., San Francisco, 1972-73. Mem. Am. Chem. Soc., Calif. Scholarship Fedn., Sequoia Woods Country Club, Protein Soc., Am. Soc. Mass Spectrometry. Roman Catholic. Avocations: reading, sewing, bridge. Home: 1203 Edgewood Rd Redwood City CA 94062-2728 Office: Genentech Inc 1 DNA Way South San Francisco CA 94080-4990

CANSECO, JOSE, professional baseball player; b. Havana, Cuba, July 2, 1964; s. Jose and Barbara (dec.) C.; m. Esther Haddad, October 25, 1988. With Oakland (Calif.) Athletics, 1982-92, 97—, Tex. Rangers, 1992-94, Boston Red Sox, 1994-96; outfield/designated hitter Toronto Bluejays, 1997-98; with Tampa Bay Devil Rays, 1999—. Appeared in instructional video, Jose Canseco's Baseball Camp, 1989. Named Minor League Player of Yr. The Sporting News, 1985, MVP So. League, 1985, Am. League Rookie of Yr. The Sporting News, 1986, Baseball Writers' Assn. Am., 1986, Sporting News Am. League All-Star Team, 1986, 88-92, Sporting News Am. League Silver Slugger Team, 1988, 90-91, Am. League MVP Baseball Writers' Assn. Am., 1988, Sporting News Comeback Player of Yr., 1994, MVP Am. League, 1988; first player to have 40 home runs and 40 stolen bases in same season, 1988; mem. Championship Team, 1989. Mem. Am. League All-Star Team, 1986, 88, 89, 90, 92. Office: Tampa Bay Devil Rays, Toronto Blue Jays/Skydome, One Tropicana Dr, Saint Petersburg, FL Canada M5V1J1*

CANSLER, DENISE ANN, real estate executive; b. St. Louis, Apr. 19, 1959; d. Jerold Fredrick and Sandra Louise (Hartling) Wesling; m. Lowell Todd Cansler, June 28, 1996. Student, Mo. So. State Coll., 1977-78, Comml. Coll., 1980-86, Northlake Coll., 1986-87, Comml. Investment Real Estate Inst., Chgo., 1991-94. Lic. real estate broker, Okla., Tex., Ark.; lic. auctioneer, Tex.; cert. comml. investment member Comml. Investment Real Estate Inst. Comml. real estate agt. GLA & Assocs., Dallas, 1980-82; dir. mktg. Beltway Devel. Co., Dallas, 1982-86; v.p. Montfort Mgmt., Inc., Dallas, 1986-87; pres. Comml. Property Svcs., Dallas, 1987-90; dir. sales comml. real estate Tipton Group, Dallas, 1990-91; sr. v.p. sales mgmt., comml. real estate mktg. and investment banking Kennedy-Wilson, Internat., Dallas, 1991-94; v.p. client svcs. Prentiss Properties, Ltd., Inc., 1995-96; regional dir. comml. mortgage origination Wells Fargo Bank, 1996—; regional dir. Wells Fargo, 1996—; speaker Inst. Real Estate Mgmt., 1992, Nat. Assn. Indsl. Office Parks, Internat. Assn. Corp. Real Estate Execs., Comml. Investment Brokers Group; comml. real estate advisor, property and asset mgr. Vol. campaign Addison (Tex.) City Coun., 1982-86, Cumberland Children's Home, Denton, Tex., 1990-92; vol. road com. Argyle City Coun., 1990. Mem. Nat. Assn. Indsl. Office Parks, Real Estate Transfers-Dallas, Internat. Assn. Corp. Real Estate Execs., Asset Mgrs. Breakfast Group (sponsor Dallas chpt. 1991—, San Antonio chpt. 1991—), Cert. Comml. Investment (mem. North Tex. chpt. 1991—), Addison Bus. Assn., N. Tex. Comml. Assn. Realtors, Mortgage Bankers Assn., Urban Land Inst., The Real Estate Coun. Home: 2771 Harbinger Ln Dallas TX 75287-5904

CANSLER, LESLIE ERVIN, retired newspaper editor; b. Hickory, N.C., Sept. 16, 1920; s. Leslie Ervin and Mabel Pearl (Braswell) C.; m. Marie Muriel Olwell, Aug. 19, 1944 (div.); children: David, Robert, James.; m. Elizabeth Marie Walters; 1 dau., Leslie Anne. B.A., Wake Forest U., 1941. News editor Daily Advance, Elizabeth City, N.C., 1941; reporter Raleigh (N.C.) Times, 1941-42, 46, city editor, 1946-47; with News-Jour. Co., Wilmington, Del., 1947-88; day mng. editor News-Jour. Co., 1966-68, mng. editor, 1968-76, assoc. Sunday editor, 1976-79, Sunday editor, 1979-80, assoc. editor, 1980-89. Served with USNR, 1942-45. Mem. Sigma Phi Epsilon. Republican. Episcopalian. Home: 11 Bristol Way New Castle DE 19720-3906

CANTELLA, VINCENT MICHELE, stockbroker; b. Boston, Oct. 27, 1917; s. Michele and Josephine (Sapienza) C.; m. Josephine R. Castanien, Nov. 19, 1944; children: Betsy Ann, David V., Steven M. BS, Boston U., 1939. Mng. ptnr. Cantella & Co., Boston, 1952-74; ptnr. Josephthal & Co., Boston, 1974-78, 1974-78; pres. Cantella & Co. Inc., 1979, 1979-97; chmn. Cantella & Co. Inc., 1997—; mem. Boston Stock Exchange, 1953—, bd. govs., mem. exec. com., 1963-74, 79-91, chmn. exec. com., 1971-73, chmn. bd. govs., 1973-74; pres. Boston Stock Exchange Clearing Corp., 1964-68; mem. Midwest Stock Exchange, 1965-72, Pacific Coast Stock Exchange, 1965-78, N.Y. Stock Exchange, 1969-78, Detroit Stock Exchange, 1963-76, P.B.W. Stock Exchange, 1970-73, Am. Stock Exchange, 1972-75. Ret. Maj. USMC, World War II. Mem. Hyannis Yacht Club (assoc.), Carlouel Yacht Club, Boston Athletic Club. Home: 635 Lewis Wharf Boston MA 02110-3924 Office: One Court St Boston MA 02108

CANTELON, JOHN EDWARD, academic administrator; b. Warroad, Minn., June 20, 1924; s. Arthur Edward and Georgia (Turnbull) C.; m. Joy Elizabeth Norton, Aug. 16, 1953; children: Barbara Jean, Charles Norton. Student, U. Man., 1941-42; B.A., Reed Coll., 1948; Ph.D., Oxford U., 1951; D.H.L., Hebrew Union Coll.-Jewish Inst. Religion, 1972. Ordained to diocese of Oreg., 1952; pastor Fairmont Presbyn. Ch., Eugene, Oreg., 1952-53; mem. staff Christian Assn., U. Pa., 1953-57; asso. sec. div. higher edn. United Presbyn. Ch., Phila., 1957-60; univ. chaplain, asso. prof. U. So. Calif., 1960-67; prof. U. So. Calif. Sch. Relgion, 1967-70; vice provost, dean U. So. Calif. Coll. Letters, Arts and Scis., 1972-76; v.p. undergrad. studies U. So. Calif. (Coll. Letters, Arts and Scis.), 1972-76, Bicentennial prof., 1976; provost, v.p. for acad. affairs Central Mich. U., Mt. Pleasant, 1976-86; prof. Central Mich. U., 1976-89, provost emeritus, 1986; v.p. for acad. affairs Walden U., 1991-94, chancellor, 1995-99, chancellor emeritus, 1999—; pres. Middle Mich. Devel. Corp. Author: Higher Education and the Campus Revolution, 1969, Terrorism and the Moral Majority, 1984. Served with AUS, 1943-46. Recipient Gov. Gen.'s medal acad. excellence Neepawa Collegiate Inst., 1941. Mem. Newcomen Soc., Phi Beta Kappa, Phi Kappa Phi, Blue Key, Skull and Dagger, Sigma Iota Epsilon. Home: Portland Plz # 1201 1500 SW 5th Ave Portland OR 97201

CANTELON, PHILIP LOUIS, historian; b. Ft. Wayne, Ind., Nov. 7, 1940; s. Philip Eccles and Marie (Gehrke) C.; m. Eileen S. McGuckian, Feb. 14, 1989. AB, Dartmouth Coll., 1962; MA, U. Mich., 1963; PhD, Ind. U., 1971. Asst. prof. Williams Coll., Williamstown, Mass., 1968-77; Fulbright prof. Kyushu Nat. U./Seinan Gakuin U., Fukuoka, Japan, 1978-79; pres., CEO, History Assocs. Inc., Rockville, Md., 1980—; exec. sec. Nat. Coun. Pub. History, Washington, 1979-81, Soc. History in Fed. Govt., Washington, 1979-80, pres., 1995-96; chmn. Montgomery County Hist. Preservation Commn., 1985-91; pres. Montgomery County Hist. Soc., Rockville, 1991-95, Peerless Rockville Historic Preservation, Ltd., 1996—. Author: Crisis Contained, 1980, The History of MCI, 1993, The Roadway Story, 1996; editor: The American Atom, 1989, Corporate Archives and History, 1993. Mem. Orgn. Am. Historians (chair com. on rsch. and access to hist. documentations 1999), Oral History Assn., Cosmos Club (chair, mem. admissions com. 1993-94, bd. mgmt. 1995-99, v.p. 1999—). Home: 11807 Dinwiddie Dr Rockville MD 20852-4459 Office: History Assocs Inc 5 Choke Cherry Rd Ste 280 Rockville MD 20850-4004

CANTER, HOWARD RAPHAEL, nuclear engineer; b. Newark, June 21, 1932; s. Albert M. and Florence (Smith) C.; m. Phyllis Yoskalka, June 14, 1954; children: Judith Platkin, Mark, Janet Butler. BS, U.S. Naval Acad., 1954; BS in Marine Engring., Webb Inst., 1960, MS in Naval ARchitecture, 1960, postgrad., 1957-60. Registered profl. engr., N.J., Wash. Commd. ens. USN, 1954, advanced through grades to capt., 1974, chief engr. USS Dale, 1963-64, with Divsn. Naval Reactors, 1965-72, ship design mgr., project mgr., 1972-74, ret., 1974; asst. to pres. Burns and Roe, Inc., Oradell, N.J., 1974-76, divsn. dir., 1976-84, v.p., 1980-84; pres., CEO At-Sea Incineration, Parsippany, N.J., 1984-85; v.p., COO Magnetic Bearings Inc., Croton, Conn., 1988-90; dep. asst. sec. weapons complex reconfiguration U.S. Dept. Energy, Washington, 1991-94, tech. dir. fissile material disposition, 1994-96, acting dir. office fissile material disposition, 1997; cons. in field. Contbr. articles to profl. publs. Recipient award Am. Bur. Shipping, 1954. Mem. ASME, Soc. Naval Architects and Marine Engrs., Am. Nuclear Soc. Office: Dept Energy 1000 Independence Ave SW Washington DC 20585-0002

CANTER, JAMIE A., web designer, marketing consultant; b. Houston, Aug. 27, 1974; d. Roland Alexander and Charlotte Ruth Brinkley; m. Gregory Wayne Canter, June 21, 1997. BFA, Southwestern U., 1998. Mktg. mgr. Whorton Ins., Austin, Tex., 1996; network adminstr. Whorton Ins., Austin, 1996-98; web designer Alline Consulting, Austin, 1998—. Mem. Soc. Profl. Journalists. Avocation: reading. E-mail: allineco@aol.com. Office: Alline Consulting PO Box 270085 Austin TX 78727

CANTER, RALPH RAYMOND, psychology educator, research director; b. Indpls., Apr. 9, 1921; s. Ralph Raymond and Rose Etta (Durham) C.; m. Marjorie Louise Streed, May 3, 1923; children—James R., Philip C. A.B., DePauw U., 1943; M.A., Ohio State U., 1947, Ph.D., 1949; postgrad., UCLA, 1961. Asst. prof. psychology U. Calif., Berkeley, 1949-55; assoc. scientist Rand Corp., Santa Monica, Calif., 1956-58; asst. to pres. System Devel. Corp., 1958-60, dir. personnel, 1960-64, dir. Wash. corp. office, 1964-68; dir. manpower research Office Sec. of Def., Washington, 1968-74; chief manpower and personnel research Army Research Inst., Alexandria, Va., 1974-79; chief Army Research Inst. Sci. Office, Ft. Harrison, Ind., 1979-83; adj. prof. psychology Purdue U. Sch. Sci., Indpls., 1982-85; cons. indsl./organizational psychology, 1983—. Contbr. articles to profl. jours. Served to lt. USN, 1943-46. Fellow Am. Psychol. Assn., Soc. Indsl. Orgnl. Psychologists; mem. Human Factors Soc., Soc. Ret. Execs., AAAS. Congregationalist. Home: 14518 41st Avenue Ct NW Gig Harbor WA 98332-9003

CANTER, STANLEY D., retired marketing consulting company executive; b. N.Y.C., Dec. 10, 1923; s. Frank and Rose (Posner) K.; m. Florence Salom, Dec. 1987; children: Leonard A., Robert G. B.S., Coll. City N.Y., 1944; M.A., Columbia, 1947. Econ. analyst Econometric Inst., N.Y.C., 1944-45; dir. mktg. rsch. McCann-Erickson, 1947-57; sr. v.p., dir. Ogilvy & Mather, 1957-73; pres. Canter, Achenbaum, Assocs., N.Y.C., 1974-89. Served with USAAF, 1945-46. Mem. AAAS, Inst. Math. Statistics, Am. Statis. Assn., Am. Mktg. Assn., Market Rsch. Coun. Home: 201 E 79th St Apt 8E New York NY 10021-0833

CANTERBURY-COUNTS, W. DOUGLAS, psychologist; b. Lancaster, Pa.; s. William L. Jr. and Marion E. (Winters) Counts; m. Belinda Jaya Canterbury, Mar. 12, 1977; 1 child, William Andrew Hanuman. BA, So. Calif. Coll., 1979; MDiv, Ea. Bapt. Theol. Sem., 1983; PhD, Temple U., 1989. Pvt. practice roofing contractor Calif. & Pa., 1976-88; counselor Pathways Counseling Svc., Swarthmore, Pa., 1985-86; psychotherapist, clin. coord. dept. medicine Temple U., Phila., 1985-88; pvt. practice clin. psychologist Lake Worth and Sebastian, Fla., 1989—; lectr. Temple U., Coll. Edn., Phila., 1983-86; adj. prof. Fla. Atlantic U., Boca Raton, 1990—; cons. Goodwill Industries, Inc., West Palm Beach, Fla., 1995—, River Sch., Sebastian, 1995—; founder, pres. Ctr. for Sacred Psychology, 1992. County del. Delaware County Crisis Intervention and Suicide Prevention, Media, Pa., 1981-83; chairperson bereavement com. Fla. chpt. NAMES Project AIDS Meml. Quilt, Sebastian, 1997—; bd. dirs. River Fund, Sebastian, 1997—. Sgt. USMC, 1969-75. Mem. APA, Nat. Acad. Neuropsychology, Fla. Psychol. Assn., Ctr. for Jungian Studies SE Fla, Inc. (v.p. 1990-96). Democrat. Avocations: T'ai Chi Ch'uan, Tae Kwon Do, camping, white water rafting. E-mail: sacredpsyc@aol.com. Fax: 561-582-0520. Office: PO Box 1365 1627 US Hwy #1 Roseland FL 32957-1365

CANTILLI, EDMUND JOSEPH, safety engineering educator, writer; b. Yonkers, N.Y., Feb. 12, 1927; s. Ettore and Maria (deRubeis) C.; m. Nella Franco, May 15, 1948; children: Robert, John, Teresa. AB, Columbia U., 1954, BS, 1955; cert., Yale Bur. Hwy. Traffic, 1957; PhD in Transp. Planning, Poly. Inst. Bklyn., 1972; postgrad. in urban planning and pub. safety, NYU, 1968-71. Registered profl. engr., N.Y., N.J., Calif.; profl. planner, N.J.; cert. safety profl. (BCSP); cert. planner (AICP). Supervising engr. safety rsch. and studies Port Authority of N.Y. & N.J., 1955-69; prof. transp. and safety engring. Poly. U., N.Y.C., 1969-90; pres. Urbitran Assocs., 1973-81; exec. dir., chmn. bd. Internat. Inst. for Safety Trans., Inc., 1977—; pres. EJC Safety Assocs., Inc., 1989—; tchr. Italian, algebra, traffic engring., urban planning, transp. planning, urban and transp. geography, land use planning, aesthetics, environment, indsl., traffic and transp. safety engring., human factors engring., ethics for engrs.; cons. transp. and traffic safety engring., community planning, traffic engring., transp. planning, accident reconstrn., environ. impacts, 1969—; vis. prof. transp. safety engring. Inst. Superior Técnico, Lisbon, 1987—; advisor to doctorate students Poly. U., CUNY, 1969-94, Politecnico di Milano, U. Trieste, Italy, 1980—; consulting forensic engr., accident reconstructionist, expert witness transp. accident litigation including hwy. traffic, railroad, rail rapid transit, pedestrian accidents, 1969—. Author: Programming Environmental Improvements in Public Transportation, 1974, Transportation and the Disadvantaged, 1974, Transportation System Safety, 1979; editor: Transportation and Aging, 1971, Pedestrian Planning and Design, 1971; editor, contbr.: Traffic Engineering Theory and Control, 1973; editor and calligrapher There Is No Death That Is Not Ennobled by So Great A Cause, 1976; contbr. over 200 articles to profl. jours. and trade jours.; developer daylight running lights, methods of severity evaluation of accidents, identification, priority-setting and treatment of roadside hazards, transp. system safety methodology; expert systems for improving traffic safety; introduced diagrammatic traffic signs, collision energy-absorption devices. With U.S. Army, 1945-49, 50-51. Fellow ASCE, Inst. Transp. Engr., Nat. Acad. Forensic Engrs.; mem. NSPE, Am. Planning Assn. (charter), Am. Inst. Cert. Planners (cert.), Am. Soc. Safety Engrs., N.Y. Acad. Scis., Nat. Assn. Profl. Accident Reconstrn. Specialists, Internat. Assn. for Accidents and Traffic Medicine, Human Factors Soc., System Safety Soc., Sigma Xi. Home: 134 Euston Rd West Hempstead NY 11552-1024 Office: PO Box 63 New York NY 10029-0063

CANTILO, PATRICK HERRERA, lawyer; b. Santiago, Chile, Mar. 19, 1954; came to U.S., 1965; s. Luis M. and Yvonne (Cantilo) Herrera-Cantilo; m. Kathryn Gail Goltra, June 18, 1977; children: Michael, Daniel, Nicholas. BA, U. Tex., 1977, JD, 1980. Bar: Tex. 1980, U.S. Dist. Ct. (we. dist.) Tex. 1983, U.S. Dist. Ct. (no. dist.) Tex. 1988, U.S. Dist. Ct. (ea. and so. dists.) Tex. 1989, U.S. Ct. Appeals (5th cir.) 1989, U.S. Ct. Appeals (4th cir.) 1994, U.S. Supreme Ct. 1994. Counsel to receiver Tex. Bd. Ins., Austin, 1980-83; assoc. Davis & Davis P.C., Austin, 1983-85; ptnr. Davis, Cantilo, Welch & Ewbank, Austin, 1985-86; of counsel Freytag, Perry, LaForce, Rubinstein & Teofan, Austin, 1986-87; ptnr. Rubinstein & Perry, Austin, 1987-93, Cantilo, Maisel & Hubbard LLP, Austin, 1993-99, Cantilo & Bennett LLP, Austin, 1999—; chmn. fin. subcom. HMO adv. com. Tex. Bd. Ins., 1986. Contbr. articles to profl. jours. Mem. ABA, Tex. Bar Assn., Travis County Bar Assn., Austin Young Lawyers Assn., Nat. Assn. Ins. Commrs. (liquidators task force adv. com. 1986, chmn. fin. subcom., adv. com. HMO 1986, mem. receiver's handbook com. 1991), Soc. Ins. Receiver's Charter Prin., Nat. Assn. HMO Regulators-Nat. Assn. Ins. Commrs. (joint com., adv. com. 1986, continuation of benefits working group, contracts and svcs. 1989). Democrat. Roman Catholic. Home: 4508 Anikawi Dr Austin TX 78746-1628

CANTLIFFE, JERI MILLER, artist, art educator; b. Alliance, N.C., Nov. 25, 1927; d. Rufus Faye Miller and Viola Elizabeth (Ireland) Miller Smith; m. Lawrence R. Cantliffe Jr., Sept.1, 1949; children: Eileen M., David L., Geri Lyn, Lisa Ann, Jonathan M. BA, Meredith Coll., 1949; M in Art Teaching, Wesleyan U., 1967; postgrad., Paier Sch. Art, New Haven, 1974-76. Designer Stephenson Appliance Co., Raleigh, N.C., 1949-50; lab. asst. N.C. State Coll., Raleigh, 1950, Hoffman-LaRoche Pharms., Clifton, N.J., 1951-52; art tchr. Horace Wilcox Tech. Sch., Meriden, Conn., 1962-66; workshop tchr. Park & Recreation Dept., Haddam and Wallingford, Conn., 1970-84, YWCA, Meriden, 1970-85, Middletown (Conn.) Art Guild, 1970-90, instr. in arts and crafts, 1989; workshop tchr. Community Art Ctr., Kensington, Conn., 1977-79; freelance artist specializing in home portraits, 1980—; creative memories cons. One-woman shows include Cen. Bank, Meriden, 1977, 79, 82, Meriden Pub. Libr., 1981, 84 (commd. artists, Woman of Yr. in Arts award 1979), Cheshire (Conn.) Pub. Libr., 1982, Phoenix Mut. Life Inst. Co., Hartford, Conn., 1982, New Haven Pub. Libr., 1983, 86, Greene Art Gallery, Guilford, Conn., 1984, Meredith Coll., Raleigh, 1984, Lord Proprietor's Inn, Edenton, N.C.; juried mem. shows include Salamagundi, N.Y.C., New Haven Paint & Clay, Friends of New Britain (Conn.) Mus., Meriden Arts & Crafts (Frederick Flatow award 1979, Butler Paint award 1980, Alan Reid Meml. prize watercolor 1986), Middletown (Conn.) Art Guild (1st prize watercolor 1977, 78, 92, 93), Guilford Art League, 1994, Brush & Palette, New Haven, Milford (Conn.) Fine Arts, Mt. Carmel Art Assn., Hamden, Conn., Wis. Watercolor Show, Glastonbury (Conn.) Art Guild, The New Group, New Haven, Conn. Classic Arts, Conn. Acad. Fine Arts, Am. Penwomen, Fairfield, Conn.; invitational shows include Jewish Home for the Aged, New Haven, Art-on-the-Mountain, Wilmington, Vt., Wesleyan Showcase, Middletown Showcase (Most Popular award 1979), Glastonbury C. of C., AAUW Art Show, Soundview Ann. Art Show, Greeley Nat. Art Show, 1990, Brownstone Group, Meriden, 1990-94, Art Cache Gallery, Vt., 1990-94, Ariz. Arts & Crafts Market Gallery, 1990-92; illustrator Meriden Calendar, Meriden City Hall Christmas Card, Meriden Centennial Quilt. Co-chmn. Commn. on the Arts, Meriden, 1975-76. Recipient Redstone Mfg. award Mum Art Festival, Bristol, Conn., 1978, Best in Show award Middletown Annual Winter Show, 1978. Judges Tricolor award Cmty. Art League, Kensington, 1978, Most Popular Vote award Middletown Showcase, 1979, Middletown Art Guild, 1992, Rick Ciburi 1st prize award Cheshire Art League, 1981, Best in Show (watercolor) Bridgeport Art League, 1982, Women in Leadership award Middlesex County C. of C., 1992, Women in Leadership award YMCA, 1993, 1st pl. award/Best in Show award Bus. Bur. for the Arts, Denver, 1995, 96, Best in Show award Springfield Pub. TV Showcase, 1996, 97; named Woman Yr. in Arts Meriden-Record Jour., 1981, Meriden Girls Club, 1982, Meredith Coll., 1984, Meriden YWCA, 1992, 100 Exceptional Women 1893-1993, 1993, Susan Buckman Meml. award MCAA, 1998. Mem. Nat. League Am. PEN Women (nat. membership chair for the arts 1990-94, bd. dirs., sec. 1990-92, 92-94, nat. art show com. 1990-94, br. membership chair 1993-94, judge nat. art show Fayetteville, Ark. br. 1995, pres. Fairfield County br. 1988-92, corr. sec. 1992, v.p. 1986-88, 1st prize watercolor 1993, nat. art bd. 1990-94), PEN Women (state art co-chair 1988-89), Colo. Artists Assn., Rotary (youth exch. com., internat. com. chair youth exch. officer Meriden club, club svc. chair 1993, mem. scholarship com. 1993-94, dist. internat. com. 1993-94, Paul Harris fellow Meriden Rotary 1992). Congregationalist. Avocations: camping, embroidery, quilting.

CANTONI, GIULIO LEONARDO, biochemist, government official; b. Milan, Italy, Sept. 29, 1915; s. Umerto L. and Nella (Pesaro) C.; m. Gabriella S. Sobrero, May 29, 1965; children: Allegra, Serena. M.D., U. Milan, 1939. Research asst. dept. pharmacology Oxford U., Eng., 1940; instr. NYU, N.Y.C., 1943-45; asst. prof. L.I. Coll. Medicine, N.Y., 1945-48; sr. fellow Am. Cancer Soc., N.Y.C., 1948-50; assoc. prof. Western Res. U., Cleve., 1950-54; chief lab. cellular pharmacology NIMH, NIH, Bethesda, Md., 1954-56, chief lab. gen. and comparative biochemistry, 1956-96; prof. emeritus NIMH, NIH, Bethesda, 1996—. Patentee 3-Deazaaristeromycin and uses. Mem. Nat. Acad. Scis., Am. Acad. Arts and Scis., Biochem. Soc. Eng., Am. Soc. Biol. Chemists. Home: 6938 Blaisdell Rd Bethesda MD 20817-3039 Office: NIMH Bldg 36 Room 3D-06 9000 Rockville Pike Bethesda MD 20892-0001*

CANTONI, LOUIS JOSEPH, psychologist, poet, sculptor; b. Detroit, May 22, 1919; s. Pietro and Stella (Puricelli) C.; m. Lucile Eudora Moses, Aug. 7, 1948; children: Christopher Louis, Sylvia Therese. AB, U. Calif., Berkeley, 1946; MSW, U. Mich., 1949, Ph.D., 1953. Personnel mgr. Johns-Manville Corp., Pittsburg, Calif., 1944-46; social caseworker Detroit Dept. Pub. Welfare, 1946-49; counselor Mich. Div. Vocat. Rehab., Detroit, 1949-50; conf. leader, tchr. psychology, coordinator family and community relations program Gen. Motors Inst., Flint, Mich., 1951-56; from assoc. prof. to prof., dir. rehab. counseling Wayne State U., Detroit, 1956-89. Author books and monographs including: The 1939-1943 Flint Michigan Guidance Demonstration, 1953, Marriage and Community Relations, 1954; (with Mrs. Cantoni) Counseling Your Friends, 1961, Supervised Practice in Rehabilitation Counseling, 1978, Writings of Louis J. Cantoni, 1981, Essays, Theses and Projects in Rehabilitation Counseling, 1989; (with Mrs. Cantoni) Theoretical Underpinnings of Practice in Family Service Agencies, 1990; (poetry) With Joy I Called to You, 1969, Gradually The Dreams Change, 1979, A Festival of Lanternes, 1994; editor: Placement of the Handicapped in Competitive Employment, 1957; poetry editor Cathedral Digest, 1973-75; co-editor: Preparation of Vocational Rehabilitation Counselors Through Field Instruction, 1958; prin. editor: (poetry) Golden Song Anthology, 1985; editor jours. Mich. Rehab. Assn. Digest, 1961-63, Grad. Comment, 1963-64; bibliography, books and reprints placed in Reuther Libr. Archives Wayne State U., Detroit; contbr. articles, revs., poems and illustrations to jours. Judge Mich. regional and nat. essay and poetry contests, 1965-77; bd. dirs. Mich. Rehab. Assn., 1962-64, 78-79, Mich. Rehab. Conseling Assn., 1985-87. Served to 2d lt. AUS, 1942-44. Recipient award for leadership and service Mich. Rehab. Assn., 1964, Mich. Rehab. Counseling Assn., 1985, 87, 88, Outstanding Service award Mich. State Bd. Edn., 1989; South and West ann. poetry award, 1970; Award for Meritorious Service Wayne State U., 1971, 81, 86, 87, 89; Outstanding Service award Poetry Soc. Mich., 1984; Excelence in Poetry award Pig's Wing Press, 1997. Fellow AAAS; mem. AAUP, APA, Coun. of Rehab. Counselor Educators (sec. 1957-58, chmn. 1965-66), Nat. Rehab. Assn., Nat. Congress of Orgns. of the Physically Handicapped, Nat. Assn. of the Physically Handicapped, Nat. Alliance for the Mentally Ill,

Am. Inst. Econ. Rsch., Poetry Soc. Am., Mich. Rehab. Assn. (pres. 1963-64), Detroit Rehab. Assn. (pres. 1958), Mich. Counseling Assn., Mich. Career Devel. Assn., Mich. Assn. for Humanistic Edn. and Devel. (Outstanding Svc. award 1997), Mich. Employment Counselors Assn., Mich. Assn. for Marriage and Family Counseling, Internat. Inst. Met. Detroit, World Poetry Soc. (Edwin A. Falkowski Meml. award 1990), Acad. Am. Poets, Detroit Inst. Arts, Friends of Detroit Pub. Libr., Friends of Marshall M. Fredericks Sculpture Gallery, Soc. for Study of Midwestern Lit., U.S. Hist. Soc., Italic Studies Inst., USN Meml., Internat. Sculpture Ctr., Nat. Sculpture Soc., Sculptors Guild Mich., Lladro Collectors Soc., Birmingham-Bloomfield Art Assn., Psychology and the Arts, Poetry Soc. Mich., Detroit Film Soc., Detroit Zool. Soc., Poetry Resource Ctr. Mich., Univ. Club, Scarab Club (Detroit), Phi Kappa Phi, Phi Delta Kappa. Democrat. Episcopalian. Achievements include research in theory and practice of counseling and psychotherapy, psychosocial aspects of disabling conditions, therapeutic and vocational counseling with disabled persons, workplace accommodation for the disabled, vocational rehabilitation of the severely disabled. Home: 2591 Woodstock Dr Detroit MI 48203-1062 *His destination, when he set out, was pure poetry, although he did not recognize it. He came to cherish the gifts of sun, rain, a walk in the woods, a brightening smile. His wife radiates the clear beauty of mature women. His children, albeit circuitously, took on his values. He feels near to man and God and views death as another beginning. He has reached his destination many times and welcomes sunset as well as sunrise, conflict as well as calm. He knows now that much of his life has been pure poetry.*

CANTOR, ALAN BRUCE, management consultant, computer software engineer; b. Mt. Vernon, N.Y., Apr. 30, 1948; s. Hoaward and Muriel Anita C.; m. Judith Jolanda Szrka, Mar. 1, 1987; 1 child, Alec Brandon. BS in Social Scis., Cornell U., 1970; MBA, U. Pa., 1973. Mgmt. cons. M & M Risks Mgmt. Svcs., N.Y.C., 1974-78; nat. svcs. officer spl. projects divsn. Marsh & McLennan Risk Mgmt. Svcs., L.A., 1980-81; sr. v.p. sr. cons. prin. Warren, Mc Veigh & Griffin, Inc., 1981-82; founder, pres. Cantor & Co., 1982—; co-mgr. Air Travel Rsch. Group, N.Y.C., 1977-79; instr. risk mgmt. program Am. Mgmt. Assn.,; lectr. Risk and Inst. Mgmt. Soc. Conf., 1975-87; seminars How to Use Spreadsheets in Risk Mgmt., 1986-89, How to Use Computers in Risk Mgmt., 1989-93. Copyright airline industry model; contbr. articles to profl. jours.; creator, developer, copyright RISKMAP risk mgmt. software products, 1982-98, Exposure Base Mgmt. System (EBMS), 1985, 86, patient care monitoring system, 1985-92, Med. Quality Mgmt. Systems Plus, 1991-99, MQMS Plus Windows version, 1997-99, COLTS corp. overal legal tracking system, 1984, 86, 87, 89, 90, 91, 93, 94, RISKMAP ins. schedules system, 1989. Cons., vol. Urban Cons. Group, N.Y.C.; elder Beverly Hills Presbyn. Ch., 1991—; co-project dir. East European Orphans Toy Ministry, 1999—. Mem. Cornell Alumni Assn. N.Y.C. (bd. govs., program chmn.), Cornell Alumni Assn. So. Calif., Wharton Bus. Sch. Club (N.Y.C., chmn., mem. adv. com. L.A.), L.A. Athletic. Office: Cantor & Co 9100 Wilshire Blvd Beverly Hills CA 90212-3415

CANTOR, BERNARD JACK, patent lawyer; b. N.Y.C., Aug. 18, 1927; s. Alexander J. and Tillie (Henzeloff) C.; m. Judith L. Levin, Mar. 25, 1951; children—Glenn H., Cliff A., James E., Ellen B., Mark E. B. Mech. Engring., Cornell, 1949; J.D., George Washington U., Washington, 1952. Bar: D.C. 1952, U.S. Patent Office 1952, Mich. 1953; registered patent atty. U.S., Can. Examiner U.S. Patent Office, Washington, 1949-52; pvt. practice Detroit, 1952-88; ptnr. firm Harness, Dickey & Pierce, Troy, Mich., 1988—; lectr. in field. Contbr. articles on patent law to profl. jours. Mem. exec. council, legal officer Detroit Area Boy Scouts Am., 1972—. Served with U.S. Army, 1944-46. Recipient Ellsworth award patent law George Washington U., 1952, Shofar award Boy Scouts Am., 1975, Silver Beaver award, 1975, Disting. Eagle award, 1985. Fellow Mich. State Bar Found.; mem. ABA, Mich. Bar Assn. (dir. econs. sect., arbitrator State of Mich. grievance com.), Detroit Bar Assn., Oakland Bar Assn., Mich. Patent Law Assn., Am. Arbitration Assn. (arbitrator), Cornell Engring. Soc., Am. Technion Soc. (bd. dirs. Detroit 1970—), Pi Tau Sigma, Phi Delta Phi, Beta Sigma Rho. Home: 5685 Forman Dr Bloomfield Hills MI 48301-1154 Office: Harness Dickey & Pierce 5445 Corporate Dr Troy MI 48098-2617

CANTOR, CHARLES ROBERT, biochemistry educator; b. Blkyn., Aug. 26, 1942; s. Louis and Ida Dianne (Banks) C. AB summa cum laude, Columbia U., 1963; PhD, U. Calif., Berkeley, 1966. Asst. prof. chemistry Columbia U., N.Y.C., 1966-69, assoc. prof. chemistry and biol. scis., 1969-72, prof., 1972-81; prof., chmn. genetics and devel., dep. dir. Comprehensive Cancer Ctr. Coll. Phys. and Surgs. Columbia U., 1981-89; dir. Human Genome Ctr. Lawrence Berkeley Lab, 1988-90; prof. molecular biology U. Calif., Berkeley, 1989-92; prof. biomed. engring. Boston U., 1992—, chmn., 1992-98, dir. Ctr. for Advanced Biotech, 1995—; prof. pharmacology, 1995—; prin. scientist human genome project Dept. Energy, 1990-92; chief sci. officer Sequenom, Inc., 1998—; Sherman Fairchild vis. scholar Calif. Inst. Tech., 1975-76; mem. biophysics and biophys. chemistry study sect. NIH, 1971-75; mem. cell and molecular basis of disease rev. com. Nat. Inst. Gen. Med. Scis., 1977-81, coun. mem., 1986-89; mem. ozone update com. NRC, 1983, mem. rsch. opportunities in biology com., 1985-89, com. on the human genome, 1986-89, com. on bits of power, 1995-96; trustee Cold Spring Harbor Lab., 1977-83; mem. proposal rev. panel Stanford Sychrotron Radiation Lab., 1976-88; mem. U.S. Nat. Commn., Internat. Union Pure & Applied Biophysics, 1986-94, vice chmn., 1988-91, chmn., 1991-94; sci. adv. bd. Hereditary Disease Found., 1987-89; mem. coun. Human Genome Orgn., 1989-92, v.p. 1990-92, pres. America's, 1991—; chmn. DOE Department of energy Human Genome Coordinating com., 1989-92; adv. com. Searle Scholars program, 1987-93, chair, 1993-94, mem. adv. com. program in parasite biology MacArthur Found., 1990-93; mem. sci. adv. coun. Roswell Park Cancer Inst. 1992—; sci. adv. com. European Molecular Biology Lab., 1989-94; bd. sci. counselors Nat. Ctr. for Biotechnology Info., Nat. Libr. Medicine, 1990-95; cons. Incynte Pharm. Inc., 1992-98; mem. coun. Internat. Union Pure and Applied Biophysics, 1993—; vis. com. biology Brookhaven Nat. Lab., 1986-89; bd. dirs. and chair sci. adv. com. Avitech Diagnostics, Inc. (formerly ATGC Inc.), 1992-1997; mem. nomenclature com. IUBMB, 1989-97; chair adv. com. European Bioinformatics Inst., 1993-94; mem. USDA Genome Adv. Com., 1992—; co-chair biotech. adv. coun. Fisher Sci., 1994—; mem. biology adv. com. Lawrence Livermore Nat. Lab., 1995—; mem. sci. adv. com. Sequenom, Inc., Sequenom Instruments GmbH, 1995—, Soane Biosci. Inc., Caliper, Inc., 1996—; mem. FASEB concensus conf. on fed. funding, 1995—; quest scholar Quest Diagnostics, Inc., 1997-99; mem. biotech. coun. DOE, 1996—; mem. unconventional pathogen countermeasures adv. com. DARPA (Defense Advanced Projects Research Agency , 1996—. Author: (with Paul R. Schimmel) Biophysical Chemistry, I, II, III, (with Cassandra L. Smith) Genomics; assoc. editor Ann. Rev. Biophysics, 1983-93. Recipient Fresenius award Phi Lambda Upsilon, 1972; Eli Lilly award in biol. chemistry Am. Chem. Soc., 1978; Alfred P. Sloan fellow, 1969-71; Guggenheim fellow, 1973-74; Nat. Cancer Inst. outstanding investigator grantee, 1985, Analytica prize, 1988; ISCO prize, 1989, Sober prize ASBMB, 1990. Fellow AAAS; mem. Am. Acad. Arts and Scis., Nat. Acad. Sci., Am. Soc. Biol. Chemists, Am. Chem. Soc., Biophys. Soc. (mem. coun. 1977-81), Soc. Analytical Cytology, Harvey Soc., Am. Soc. Human Genetics, Biomed. Engring. Soc., Japanese Biochem. Soc. (hon.). Home: 526 Stratford Ct # E Del Mar CA 92014-2723 Office: Sequenom Inc 11555 Sorrento Valley Rd San Diego CA 92121

CANTOR, DONALD JEROME, lawyer; b. Stamford, Conn., May 11, 1931; s. Albert Adelbert and Lillian (Schoenfield) C.; m. Lois Levin (div.); children: Rachel, Elizabeth, Michael; m. Patricia Kirby, June 19, 1977; children: Jonathan, Stephanie. AB, Harvard Coll., 1953, LLB, 1959. Bar: Conn. 1959. Lawyer Gilman & Marks, Hartford, Conn., 1959-60, Levin & Hultgren, Hartford, 1960-64; ptnr. Levin, Hultgren & Cantor, Hartford, 1964-71, Hyman & Cantor, Hartford, 1971-76, Hyman, Cantor & Seichter, Hartford, 1976-85, Hyman, Cantor, Seichter & Klau, Hartford, 1985-92, Hyman, Cantor & Klau, Hartford, 1992—; corporator Mt. Sinai Hosp., Hartford; lectr. U. Conn. Law Sch., Hartford; founder, first pres. Conn. League Abortion Law Reform; co-founder, counsel Gender Identity Clin. Author: Escape From Marriage, 1971; co-author: Child Custody, 1989; contbr. articles to Am. Jurisprudence Trials, Atlantic Monthly, The Humanist. Founder, 1st pres. Conn. League for Abortion Law Reform; co-founder., counsel Gender Identity Clinic. Mem. Conn. Bar Assn., Hartford County Bar Assn. (chmn. family rels. sect. 1972-73), Tolland County Bar Assn. Jewish. Avocations: crossword puzzles, travel, reading, softball, children. Home: 49 High Farms Rd West Hartford CT 06107-1544 Office: Hyman Cantor & Klau 21 Oak St Hartford CT 06106-8003

CANTOR, GEORGE NATHAN, journalist; b. Detroit, June 14, 1941; s. Harold and Evelyn (Grossman) C.; m. Sheryl Joyce Bershad, Dec. 7, 1975; children: Jaime, Courtney. B.A., Wayne State U., 1962. Reporter, editor Detroit Free Press, 1963-77; columnist Detroit News, 1977—; commentator WWJ-Radio, Detroit, 1981-90, WXYZ-TV, Detroit, 1982-90; editl. page writer Detroit News. Author: The Great Lakes Guidebook, 3 vols., 1978-80. Bd. dirs. Greater Detroit Area Hosp. Council, 1983. Recipient Malcolm Bingay Wayne State U., 1962; recipient Paul Tobenaw Meml. Columbia U., 1980, Disting. Achievement UPI, 1982. Mem. Phi Beta Kappa. Jewish. Office: Detroit News 615 W Lafayette Blvd Detroit MI 48226-3197*

CANTOR, HERBERT I., lawyer; b. N.Y.C., Dec. 10, 1935; s. David and Ethel C.; m. Lynn Hardie, July 8, 1972; children: David, Susan. BA in Chemistry, NYU, 1965; JD, Cath. U. Am., 1970. Bar: Md. 1970, U.S. Dist. Ct. Md. 1970, D.C. 1971, U.S. Dist. Ct. D.C. 1971, U.S. Ct. Appeals (5th, D.C. and fed. cirs.) 1971, U.S. Supreme Ct. 1974, U.S. Ct. Appeals (4th cir.) 1981, U.S. Ct. Claims 1987. Patent examiner U.S. Patent Office, Washington, 1965-67; agt. Jacobi, Davidson & Jacobi, Washington, 1967-68; pvt. practice Washington, 1968-70; with Kraft, Cantor & Singer, Cantor & Lessler, Washington, 1971-85; ptnr. Cantor & Lessler, Washington, 1982-85, Wegner, Cantor, Mueller & Player, Washington, 1985-94; Evenson, McKeown, Edwards & Lenahan, Washington, 1994—; adj. prof. Law Ctr. Georgetown Univ., Washington, 1988-89. Assoc. editor Cath. U. Law Rev., 1969-70. Mem. ABA, Am. Chem. Soc., Fedn. Internat. des Conseils Propriete Industrielle, Am. Intellectual Property Assn. Office: Evenson McKeown Edwards & Lenahan 1200 G St NW Ste 700 Washington DC 20005-3839

CANTOR, JAMES ELLIOT, lawyer; b. Detroit, Mar. 14, 1958; s. Bernard J. and Judith (Levin) C.; m. Susan Elaine Finger, Dec. 26, 1983; children: Tilly Samantha, Brian Alexander. BS in Natural Resources, U. Mich., 1980; JD, Cornell U., 1986. Bar: Alaska 1986. Assoc. Perkins Coie, Anchorage, 1986-91; asst. atty. gen. environ. sect. Alaska, Atty. Gen.'s Office, Anchorage, 1991-98, supervising atty. transp. sect., 1998—. Mem. Eagle River (Alaska) Pk. and Recreation Bd. of Suprs., 1989-95, chmn., 1991-92; dir. Anchorage (Alaska) Trails and Greenways Coalition, 1994-97; commissioner Mcpl. of Anchorage; adv. commission Heritage Land Bank, 1999—. Mem. Anchorage Inn of Ct. Avocations: dog sled racing. Office: Atty Gen Office 1031 W 4th Ave Ste 200 Anchorage AK 99501-5903

CANTOR, MELVYN LEON, retired lawyer; b. Boston, Aug. 13, 1942; s. Manuel and Adeline (Raffel) C.; m. Susan Gershen, June 7, 1964 (div. Jan. 1981); children: Matthew, Douglas; m. Kathryn Gabler, Jan. 3, 1982; 1 child, Joanna. BA, U. Vt., 1964; LLB magna cum laude, U. Pa., 1967. Bar: N.Y. 1969, U.S. Dist. Ct. (so. and ea. dists.) N.Y. 1971, U.S. Ct. Appeals (2nd cir.) 1971, U.S. Ct. Appeals (3d cir.) 1974, U.S. Ct. Appeals (5th cir.) 1986, U.S. Supreme Ct. 1987. Law clk. to Hon. Stanley A. Weigel U.S. Dist. Ct., San Francisco, 1967-68; assoc. Simpson, Thacher & Bartlett, N.Y.C., 1968-74, ptnr., 1974-97; of counsel, 1998—; adj. prof. Yeshiva U. Benjamin Cardozo Sch. Law, N.Y.C., 1977-81. Contbr. numerous articles to profl. jours. Fellow Am. Coll. Trial Lawyers; mem. ABA, Am. Law Inst., Bar Assn. of City of N.Y., Fed. Bar Coun. Office: Simpson Thacher & Bartlett 425 Lexington Ave Fl 14 New York NY 10017-3954

CANTOR, MORTON B., psychiatrist; b. St. Louis, June 21, 1924; s. William and Sarah (Goldberg) C.; m. Cecilia Lola Gersch; children: Jonathan, David. BA in Chemistry, U. N.C., Chapel Hill, 1943; MD, St. Louis U., 1947. Diplomate Am. Bd. Psychiatry and Neurology, Nat. Bd. Med. Examiners. Intern Morrissania City Hosp., Bronx, N.Y., 1947-48, resident in neurology, 1948-49; resident psychiatrist Bklyn. State Hosp., 1949-52; lectr., supr. Karen Horney Inst. and Clinic, N.Y.C., 1955-59; faculty, asst. dean Postgrad. Ctr. Mental Health, N.Y.C., 1959-69; faculty supr. Westchester Ctr. For Study of Psychoanalysis and Psychotherapy, White Plains, N.Y., 1973—; faculty, clin. assoc. prof. N.Y. Med. Coll., Valhalla, N.Y., 1975—; assoc. attending psychiatrist Westchester County Med. Ctr., Valhalla, 1972—. Contbr. articles to profl. jours.; co-editor: Affect: Psychoanalytic Theory and Practice, 1983, Psychoanalysis and Severe Emotional Illness, 1990. Capt. U.S. Army, 1952-54. Fellow Am. Psychiat. Assn. (life), Am. Acad. Psychoanalysis (treas. 1967-72, jour. editor 1978-92); mem. Assn. Advancement Psychoanalysis (pres. 1965-67). Avocation: sculpting. Home and Office: 141 Stone Oaks Dr Hartsdale NY 10530-1151

CANTOR, NORMAN FRANK, history educator, writer; b. Winnipeg, Man., Can., Nov. 19, 1929; came to U.S., 1951, naturalized, 1968; s. Max W. and Elizabeth (Niznick) C.; m. Mindy Mozart, Aug. 25, 1957; children: Howard, Judith. B.A. with honors, U. Man., 1951; M.A., Princeton U., 1953, Ph.D. (Porter Ogden Jacobus fellow), 1957; postgrad. (Rhodes scholar), Oxford (Eng.) U., 1954-55; LL.D. (hon.), U. Winnipeg, 1973. Instr. Princeton U., 1955-59, asst. prof. history, 1959-60; asso. prof. Columbia U., 1960-65, prof., 1965-66; Leff prof. Brandeis U., 1966-70; disting. prof. SUNY, Binghamton, 1970-76; provost for grad. studies SUNY, 1974-75, v.p. acad. affairs, 1975-76; vice chancellor for acad. affairs U. Ill., Chgo., 1976-78; dean faculty Arts and Sci. NYU, 1978-81, prof. history, sociology and comparative lit., 1981—, dir. Inst. Cultural Analysis, 1981-87; Fulbright prof. Tel Aviv U., 1987-88; affiliated prof. NYU Sch. Law, 1982-88; vis. disting. prof. Adelphi U., 1988-89; lectr. Inst. for Secular Jewish Humanism, Farmington Hills, Mich., 1996—. Author: Church, Kingship and Lay Investiture, 1958, Medieval History, 1963, How to Study History, 1967, The English, 1968, Western Civilization, 1972, Twentieth Century Culture, 1988, Inventing the Middle Ages, 1991, The Civilization of Middle Ages, 1993, The Medieval Reader, 1994, Medieval Lives, 1994, The Sacred Chain, 1994, The Jewish Experience, 1997, The American Century, 1997. Imagining the Law, 1997, Encyclopedia of the Middle Ages, 1999. Am. Council Learned Socs.-Can. Council fellow, 1960. Fellow Royal Hist. Soc. Office: NYU History Dept 42 Bayview Ave Sag Harbor NY 11963-3040

CANTOR, RUSTY SUMNER, artist; b. N.Y.C., Aug. 6, 1927; s. Charles and Mollie (Kaufman) Sumner; m. Paul Arthur Cantor, Aug. 30, 1953 (dec. Sept. 1980); children: Lesley Cantor-Fallihee, Matt Geoffrey. presenter in field. Solo exhibits include Inst. of Am. Indian Art Mus., Santa Fe, 1984, Mill Valley (Calif.) City Hall, 1991, AIA, Oakland, Calif., 1994, Bade Mus., Berkeley, Calif., 1996, SoMar, San Francisco, 1997, The Atrium @ 600 Townsend, 1999, others; two-person show Gallery on the Rim, San Francisco, 1995; group exhibits include Lynnhouse Gallery, East Bay Bronze, Antioch, Calif., 1995, Fourth World Congress on Women, Beijing, 1995, Berkeley (Calif.) Art Ctr., 1995, Ritz Carlton Sculpture Gallery, San Francisco, 1995, NAWA Lever House, N.Y.C., 1995, ISE Art Found., N.Y.C., 1996, Bechtel Gallery Stanford U., 1996, NAWA Traveling exhibit, 1996—; Prieto Gallery, Mills Coll., Oakland, 1996, Design Ctr., San Francisco, 1996, N.Y.C., 1996, 99, Somar, San Francisco, 1999, numerous others; represented in collections Nat. Mus. Women in the Arts, Washington, Inst. Am. Indian Art Mus., Santa Fe, Am. Embassy, New Delhi, Art in Embassies Program, Washington, Many Horses Gallery, L.A., numerous pvt. collections. Group leader Noetic Soc.; advisor, pres. N.C. Womens Caucus for the Arts (nat. bd. mem.). Mem. Nat. Assn. Women Artists, Women's Caucus for Art (bd. dirs.), Pacific Rim Sculptor Group. Avocations: reading, traveling, theatre, cinema. E-mail: rustycan@lmi.net. Home and Studio: 2512 9th St Ste 14 Berkeley CA 94710-2542

CANTOR, SAMUEL C., lawyer, company executive; b. Phila., Mar. 11, 1919; s. Joseph and Miryl (Ginzberg) C.; m. Dorothy Van Brink, Apr. 9, 1943; children: Judith Ann Stone, Barbara Ann Palm. BSS, CCNY, 1940; JD, Columbia, 1943. Bar: N.Y. 1943, U.S. Dist. Ct. (so. and ea. dists.) N.Y. 1951, U.S. Supreme Ct 1969, D.C. 1971. Asst. dist. atty. N.Y.C., 1943-48; legislative counsel N.Y. State Senate; counsel N.Y.C. Affairs Com. N.Y. State Senate, 1949-59; mem. firm Newcomb, Woolsey & Cantor, Newcomb & Cantor, N.Y.C., 1951-59; 1st dep. supt. ins. State of N.Y., 1959-64, acting supt. ins., 1963-64; 2d v.p., gen. solicitor Mut. Life Ins. Co. N.Y., 1964-66, v.p., gen. counsel, 1967-72, sr. v.p., gen. counsel, 1973-74, sr. v.p. law and external affairs, 1974-75, sr. v.p. law and corp. affairs, 1975-78, exec. v.p. law and corp. affairs, 1978-84; counsel Rogers & Wells, 1984-89; bd. dir. Mut. Life Ins. Co N.Y., Mony Reins. Corp., Monyco, Inc., Key Resources, Inc., Mony Advisors, Inc.; chmn. exec. com. N.Y. Life Ins. Guaranty Corp., 1974-84; mem. spl. com. on ins. holding holding cos. N.Y. Supt. Ins., 1967, N.Y. State select com. pub. employee pensions, 1973. Contbr. articles to Golf and other mags., legal and ins. jours. Fellow Am. Bar Found.; mem. Ins. Fedn. N.Y. (pres. 1967-68), Am. Bar Assn., N.Y. State Bar Assn., Am. Life Conv. (v.p. N.Y. State 1965-70), Am. Coun. Life Ins. (chmn. legal sect. 1977, chmn. legis. com. 1977-78, N.Y. State v.p. 1977-84), Health Ins. Assn. Am. (chmn. govt. rels. com. 1975, chmn. health care com. N.Y. State 1974-80), Assn. Life Ins. Counsel (dir.), Am. Judicature Soc., Bar Assn. City N.Y., N.Y. Law Inst., Nat. Attys. Assn., N.Y. State Dist. Attys. Assn., Union Internationale des Avocats, Columbia U. Law Sch. Alumni Assn. (dir.). Clubs: Mason. (N.Y.C.), University (N.Y.C.); Met., Univ. (Washington); Fort Orange (Albany, N.Y.); Sawgrass Country, Marsh Landing, Ponte Vedra (Fla.); La Costa Country (Carlsbad, Calif.); Confrérie des Chevaliers du Tastevin; Fairview Country (Greenwich, Conn.); Royal Dornoch Golf (Scotland), Am. Seniors Golf Assn., U.S. Golf Assn. (committeeman). Home: 10 Audubon Ln Greenwich CT 06831-2501 also: 22 Little Bay Harbor Dr Ponte Vedra Beach FL 32082-3707

CANTORE GREEN, JEAN, secondary education educator; b. Alexandria, Va., Aug. 16, 1953; d. Thomas Anthony and Dorothy Joan (Mahony) Cantore; m. David Michael Green, Jan. 27, 1980; children: Thomas Scott, Jared Andrew. BA in English summa cum laude, SUNY, Albany, 1974, MA in English summa cum laude, 1976; student, Albany Law Sch., 1978-79. Cert. secondary sch. tchr. English and Spanish, N.Y., Mass. English tchr. Niskayuna Schs., Schenectady, N.Y., 1976-77, East Greenbush (N.Y.) Schs., 1977-78, Brighton Ctrl. Schs., Rochester, N.Y., 1979—; asst. prof. English, SUNY, Albany, 1979. Coach Little League Brighton Baseball, Rochester, 1991—. Recipient Tchr. of Yr. award Tufts U., 1986, Outstanding Educator award Cornell U., 1987, Outstanding Tchr. Tribute, Tufts U., 1995, Univ. Rochester Phi Beta Kappa Tchr.-Scholar Recognition award, 1982, 94. Mem. NEA, Nat. Coun. Tchrs. English, Autism Soc. Am., Parent-Tchr.-Student Assn., Parents Advocation Support Svcs., Phi Beta Kappa. Avocations: gardening, writing, art collecting, music, swimming. Office: Brighton High Sch 1150 Winton Rd S Rochester NY 14618-2299

CANTRELL, CAROL WHITAKER, educational administrator; b. Cin., July 25, 1951; d. James Ross and Edna M. Whitaker; m. David F. Justus, Jan. 23, 1970 (div. May 1981); 1 child, Holly; m. Pierce E. Cantrell Jr., May 24, 1986; 1 child, Janette. BS, West Tex. A&M U., 1973, postgrad., 1973; postgrad., Tex. A&M U., 1974, 88. Dir. adminstrn. and budgets Tex. Engr. Experiement Sta., College Station, 1984-87, asst. agt. dir., 1987-97, assoc. agy. dir., 1997—; asst. vice chancellor Tex. A&M U. Sys., College Station, 1987—. Regents life fellow Tex. A&M U. System, 1998—; grantee USIA, 1998. Mem. Soc. Rsch. Adminstrs., Nat. Coun. Univ. Bus. Officers, Tex. Assn. Sr. State U. Bus. Officers, Exec. Women in Govt., Nat. Coun. Univ. Rsch. Adminstrs., Mu Phi Epsilon. Avocations: music, piano. E-mail: c-cantrell@tamu.edu. Office: Tex A&M U Sys Room 301 WERC College Station TX 77845

CANTRELL, DONNA ALEXANDER, county commissioner finance; b. Middletown, Ohio, June 26, 1960. BS, U. Ky., 1982, MSc, 1987. Fin. analyst Office of Fin. Mgmt., Fin. Cabinet Commonwealth of Ky., 1988-90, economist, legis. rsch. commn., 1990-93; commr. fin. dept. Lexington-Fayette Urban County Govt., Lexington, Ky., 1993—. Office: Lexington-Fayette County Fin Dept 200 E Main St Lexington KY 40507-1310

CANTRELL, JOHN L., language educator; b. Aug. 24, 1945; s. Mance and Maglene (Conley) C. BA, Morehead State U., 1967; MA, la Universidad de Coahuila, Saltillo, Mex., 1971; postgrad., Miami U. Spanish tchr., dir., performing arts instr. Piqua (Ohio) City Schs., 1967-72, Hamilton (Ohio) City Schs., 1972-86, Springfield (Ohio) City Schs., 1987-98; ret., 1998; tchr. Spanish Wittenberg U., 1999—; Spanish instr. Clark State C.C., 1997-98. V.p. Civic Theatre, Springfield, 1987-89; bd. dirs. Ohio Lyric Theatre, Springfield, 1989-90. Recipient Ohio Gov.'s award for excellence in arts, 1992, Outstanding Citizen award Moose Lodge, 1970, Outstanding Educator award Jaycees, 1981. Mem. NEA, S.W. Ohio Edn. Assn. (chmn. fgn. langs. 1980-82), Ohio Edn. Assn., Ohio Tchrs. Assn. (bd. dirs., theatre dir. 1992), Ohio Theatre Alliance, Ednl. Theatre Assn., Phi Kappa Delta, Theta Kappa Epsilon (v.p. 1966-67). Home: 1853 Winding Trl Springfield OH 45503-2816

CANTRELL, LANA, actress, singer, lawyer; b. Sydney, Australia, Aug. 7, 1943; d. Hubert Clarence and Dorothy Jean (Thistlethwaite) C. JD, Fordham Law Sch., 1993. Bar: N.Y. 1994. Former of counsel Ballon Stoll Bader & Adler, N.Y.C.; assoc. Sendroff & Assocs. PC, N.Y.C., 1996—. Singer supper clubs, TV programs, Australia, 1958-62; U.S. debut: TV show The Tonight Show, NBC, 1962; rec. artist RCA and Polydor Records, 1967—(Grammy award as Most Promising New Female Artist, Nat. Assn. Rec. Arts and Scis. 1967); recs. include Lana!, Act III, And Then There Was Lana, The Now of Then!. Pres. Thrush, Inc.; U.S. rep. Internat. Song Festival, Poland, 1966, UN Internat. Women's Year Concert, Paris, France, 1975. Recipient 1st prize Internat. Song Festival Poland, 1966; 1st Internat. Woman of Yr. award Feminist Party, 1973. Office: 300 E 71st St New York NY 10021-5234

CANTRELL, ROBERT WENDELL, otolaryngologist, head and neck surgeon, educator; b. Neosho, Mo., Apr. 25, 1933; s. Lloyd L. and Ruby R. Moffett; m. Young Hi Lee, Feb. 6, 1964; children: Mark L., Elizabeth L., Victoria L., Robert Wendell Jr. Student, U.S. Naval Acad., 1952-55; AB, George Washington U., 1956, MD, 1960. Diplomate Am. Bd. Otolaryngology, 1969.. Intern N.Y. Hosp-Cornell U., 1960-61; resident in otolaryngology Nat. Naval Med. Center, Bethesda, Md., 1965-69; chmn. dept. otolaryngology Naval Regional Med. Center, San Diego, 1969-76; Fitz-Hugh prof. dept. otolaryngology-head and neck surgery U. Va., 1976—; acting v.p., provost U. Va. Health Scis. Ctr., Charlottesville, 1995-96, v.p., provost, 1996—; bd. dirs. Am. Bd. Otolaryngology, 1980-98, exec. v.p., 1990-98. Mem. editorial bd. Laryngoscope, 1976-88, Annals of Otology, Rhinology and Laryngology, 1977-88, Am. Jour. of Otolaryngology, 1978-82, Archives of Otolaryngology, 1979-88; contbr. numerous articles to profl. jours. Mayor, Oakmont, Md., 1968-69. Capt. USN, 1961-76, USNR, 1976-91. Am. Heart Assn. fellow, 1959; recipient Huron W. Lawson prize, 1960. Mem. AMA, Am. Acad. Otolaryngology-Head and Neck Surgery (pres. 1987), Am. Acad. Facial Plastic and Reconstructive Surgery (v.p. So. sect. 1980-83), Triological Soc. (v.p. So. sect. 1989-90, Mosher award 1974), Am. Soc. Head and Neck Surgery (pres. 1985-86), Soc. Univ. Otolaryngologists (pres. 1982), Am. Broncho-Esophagological Assn. (pres. 1988-89), Am. Larynbgol. Assn. (coun. 1988-90, treas. 1990-95, pres.-elect 1995, pres. 1996-97), Am. Otol. Soc., Alpha Omega Alpha. Home: 1925 Owensville Rd Charlottesville VA 22901-8824 Office: U Va Health Sci Ctr Office of VP and Provost PO Box 179 Charlottesville VA 22908-0179

CANTRELL, (THOMAS) SCOTT, newspaper music critic; b. Ft. Smith, Ark., Nov. 14, 1949; s. Bert Thomas and Elizabeth Winstel (Scott) C. BFA, So. Meth. U., 1971; MS, Rensselaer Poly. Inst., 1974. Prodr., announcer Sta. WMHT, Schenectady, N.Y., 1973-86; music critic Times Union, Albany, N.Y., 1981-87, Rochester, N.Y., 1987-90; classical music editor Kansas City (Mo.) Star, 1990—; freelance contbr. N.Y. Times, High Fidelity, Musical Am., Ovation, Classical and various other publs., 1973—; organist, choirmaster various chs., Albany, 1971-87. Recipient Deems Taylor award ASCAP, 1987, 89. Mem. Am. Guild of Organists, Music Critics Assn. N.Am. (exec. bd. 1989—, pres. 1993-97). Episcopalian. Avocations: travel, art, architecture, reading, cuisines. Office: The Kansas City Star 1729 Grand Blvd Kansas City MO 64108-1458

CANTRELL, SHARRON CAULK, secondary school educator; b. Columbia, Tenn., Oct. 2, 1947; d. Tom English and Beulah (Goodin) Caulk; m. William Terry Cantrell, Mar. 18, 1989; 1 child, Jordan; children from previous marriage: Christopher, George English, Steffenee Copley. BA George Peabody Coll. Tchrs., 1970; MS Vanderbilt U., 1980; EdS Mid. Tenn. State U., 1986. Tchr., Ft. Campbell Jr. High Sch., Ky., 1970-71, Whitthorne Jr. High Sch., Columbia, Tenn., 1977-86, Spring Hill (Tenn.) High Sch., 1986—; chmn. edn. Homecoming '86 Maury County Schs., Columbia, 1984-86. Mem. NEA, AAUW (pres. Tenn. div. 1983-85), Maury County Edn. Assn. (pres. 1983-84), Tenn. Edn. Assn., Assn. for Preservation Tenn. Antiquities, Maury County C. of C., Friends of Children's Hosp., Phi Delta Kappa. Mem. Ch. of Christ. Home: 5299 Main St Spring Hill TN 37174-2449 Office: Spring Hill High Sch 1 Raider Ln Columbia TN 38401-7346

CANTRELL, STEPHANIE ANN, nurse; b. Kansas City, Oct. 23, 1963; d. Charles L. and Allison Lee (Wolverton) O'Donnell; m. Michael Cantrell, June 27, 1998; children: Stephen K., Mathias J., Lindsey R. ADN, Southea. C.C., Keokuk, Iowa, 1985. Cert. ACLS, mobile intensive care nurse, trauma nurse specialist, psychiatric and mental health nurse. Staff nurse psychiat. svcs. St. Mary Hosp., 1985-90; emergency rm., trauman nurse, staff nurse Blessing Hosp., Quincy, Ill., 1990-93, employee health coord., 1992-95, patient care supr. child and adolescent and psychiat. svc., 1995—; attendee Soviet Am. Psychiat. Nursing Conf., Moscow, St. Petersburg, 1987. Mem. Assn. Hosp. Employee Health Profls.

CANTRELL, WILLIAM ALLEN, psychiatrist, educator; b. Everton, Ark., Nov. 6, 1920; s. William E. and Vida (Vinson) C.; m. Joyce Laree Hobbs, Jan. 17, 1945; children: Mary Elizabeth, William Robert. B.S., McMurry, 1940; M.D., U. Tex., 1943. Rotating intern U.S. Naval Hosp., Corona, Calif., 1943-44; resident neuropsychiatry U. Tex. Med. Br. Hosps., 1947-49; asst. prof. neuropsychiatry U. Tex. Med. Br., 1949-54; practice medicine specializing in psychiatry Houston, 1951-63; prof. psychiatry Baylor Coll. Medicine, Houston, 1963-90, prof. emeritus, 1990—; chief psychiatry service Meth. Hosp., Houston, 1966-73. Mem. med. adv. com. Tex. Bd. Mental Health and Mental Retardation, 1965-73, chmn., 1965-69, 72-73; bd. dirs. Tex. Assn. Mental Health, 1965-72. Served to lt. M.C. USNR, 1944-47. Fellow Am. Psychiat. Assn. (br. pres. 1958-59), Am. Coll. Psychiatrists; mem. Tex. Med. Assn., Tex. Neuropsychiat. Assn. (v.p. 1958-59), Central Neuropsychiat. Assn. (v.p. 1974-75), Central Neuropsychiat. Assn. (pres. 1976-77), Tex. Psychiat. Soc. (pres. 1980-81), Houston Psychiat. Soc. (pres. 1956). Home: 5018 Loch Lomond Dr Houston TX 77096-2724*

CANTRIL, ALBERT H(ADLEY), public opinion analyst; b. N.Y.C.; s. Hadley and Mavis Katherine Cantril; m. Susan Bradford Davis. AB, Dartmouth Coll., 1962; PhD, MIT, 1966. Asst. to Bill Moyers The White House, Washington, 1965-67; cons. to dir. Bur. of the Budget, Washington, 1967; spl. asst. to asst. sec. East Asian and Pacific affairs Dept. of State, Washington, 1967-69; exec. sec., com. on def. social sci. rsch. Nat. Acad. Scis., Washington, 1969-70; cons. Dem. Nat. Com. and candidates, Washington, 1971-74; dir. rsch. Commn. Op. of U.S. Senate, Washington, 1975-76; pres. Nat. Coun. on Pub. Polls, Washington, 1976-81, Bur. Social Sci. Rsch., Inc., Washington, 1981-86; fellow and rsch. fellow Inst. of Politics Harvard U., Cambridge, Mass., 1986-88; cons. ABA, 1989-96; cons. pub. opinion rsch. with Susan Davis Cantril ACLU Found., 1991-93, Woodrow Wilson Internat. Ctr. for Scholars, 1996—; mem. editl. adv. bd. Pub. Opinion Quar., 1985-89; trustee Nat. Coun. on Pub. Polls, 1982-94; adj. prof. internat. politics Fletcher Sch. Law and Diplomacy, Tufts U., Medford, Mass., 1991-94. Author: The Opinion Connection: Polling, Politics and the Press, 1991, Agenda for Access: The American People and Civil Justice, 1996; co-author: Hopes and Fears of the American People, 1971, Polls: Their Use and Misuse in Politics, 1972, 2d edit., 1980, Live and Let Live: American Public Opinion about Privacy at Home and at Work, 1994; editor: Polling on the Issues, 1980, Psychology, Humanism and Scientific Inquiry: The Selected Essays of Hadley Cantril, 1988. Recipient Mecklin award Dartmouth Coll., 1962. Mem. Am. Assn. Pub. Opinion Rsch. Avocations: jazz, tennis.

CANTU, CARLOS, holding company executive. With Cook Internat., Memphis, 1958-71; pres., CEO The Terminix Internat. Co., Memphis, 1971-92, Svc Master Co., Downers Grove, Ill., 1994—. Office: SVM Holdings Corp 2300 Warrenville Rd Downers Grove IL 60515-1765*

CANTÚ, NORMA V., federal official; b. Brownsville, Tex., Nov. 2, 1954. BS summa cum laude, Pan Am. U., 1973; JD, Harvard U., 1977. Bar: Tex. 1978, U.S. Dist. Ct. (so. dist.) Tex. 1979, U.S. Dist. Ct. (we. dist.) Tex. 1981, U.S. Ct. Appeals (5th and 11th cirs.) 1982, Calif. 1985, U.S. Ct. Appeals (10th cir.) 1986, U.S. Dist. Ct. (no. dist.) Tex. 1992. Tchr. English Brownsville, 1974, San Antonio, 1979; intern nursing home task force Office of Atty. Gen. Tex., 1977-78; staff atty. Chicana rights project Mex. Am. Legal Def. and Ednl. Fund, 1979-83, nat. dir., 1983-92, regional counsel, 1985-93; asst. sec. for civil rights Office for Civil Rights U.S. Dept. of Edn., Washington, 1993—; cons. NEA, Nat. Assn. Sch. Lawyers, Dept. of Edn., CRESST ctr. testing UCLA. Mem. exec. com. Avance Parent Child Tng. Program, 1990, 92, bd. dirs., 1990—; pro bono legal counsel YWCA San Antonio; mem. City San Antonio Health Facilities Commn., City of San Antonio Com. Drafting Regulations, Tex. Human Rights Commn., 1992, Ctr. Hispanic Health Policy Devel., 1992. Recipient Appreciation award Tex. Senate, 1993, Leadership award Hispanic Mag., 1993, Reynaldo G. Garza award Hispanic issues sect. State Bar Tex., 1993. Office: Dept of Education Office for Civil Rights 330 C St SW Ste 5000 Washington DC 20201-0001*

CANTUS, H. HOLLISTER, government relations consultant; b. N.Y.C., Nov. 16, 1937; s. Howard J. and Eleanor (Hollister) C.; m. Barbara Jane Park, Feb. 7, 1961; children: Charles Hollister, Jane Scott. BA, Williams Coll., 1959. Mem. prof. staff Com. on Armed Services U.S. Ho. Reps., Washington, 1970-74; dep. asst. sec. def. U.S. Dept. Def., Washington, 1974-75; dir. congl. relations U.S. Energy Research and Devel. Adminstrn., Washington, 1975-77; group v.p. bldg. systems United Technologies Corp., Washington, 1977-87; assoc. adminstr. NASA, 1987-88; group v.p. missiles and space Lockheed Corp., Washington, 1988-94; sr. v.p. ICF Kaiser Internat., Inc., Fairfax, Va., 1994-97; CEO The ILEX Group, McLean, Va., 1997—; bd. dirs. Aerospatiale, Inc. Capt. USNR, 1961-83. Fellow AIAA (assoc.); mem. Georgetown Club, Farmington (Va.) Country Club, Capitol Hill Club. Republican. Episcopalian. Office: The ILEX Group 8000 Towers Crescent Dr ste 1350 Vienna VA 22182-2700

CANTWELL, CHRISTOPHER WILLIAM, artist; b. Atwater, Calif., Dec. 24, 1960; s. Donald Byron and Ann Louise Cantwell; m. Susan Rebecca Moore, Sept. 19, 1982 (div. 1997); children: Claire Elyse Moore, Katie Lynn Moore. Owner, artist Christopher W. Cantwell Woodworks, Modesto, Calif., 1979-82, Oakhurst, Calif., 1982—; cons. Internat. Union for conservation of Natural Resources, Cambridge, Eng., 1991—. Contbr. art book Jewelry Boxes, 1996; exhibited at Del Mano Gallery, 1990, 98, Furniture Soc. Conf., San Francisco, 1998; represented in permanent collections Irving Lipton Collection, White House Ornament Collection. Youth advisor Oakhurst Luth. Ch., 1992-96. Mem. Am. Craft Coun., World Wildlife Fund, Program for Belize, Good Wood Alliance (CITES Liaison 1994—). Democrat. Avocations: rock climbing, skiing, fishing. Home and Office: PO Box 1736 Oakhurst CA 93644-1736

CANTWELL, DENNIS MICHAEL, finance company executive; b. Milw., Apr. 21, 1943; s. Paul and Maureen C.; m. Kathleen Gray, May 16, 1970; 1 child, Jennifer. BA, Marquette U., 1966; MBA, Northwestern U., 1968. Various acctg., systems and analysis positions Chrysler Corp., 1968-74; mgr. internat. systems Chrysler Fin. Corp., Troy, Mich. and Paris, 1975-77; dir. fin. Chrysler Fin. Corp. Subs., London, 1977-81; asst. treas. Chrysler Fin. Corp., Troy, 1982-86; v.p. strategic planning Chrysler Fin. Corp., Southfield, Mich., 1986-90, v.p. corp. fin. and devel., 1990-95, v.p., treas., gen. mgr. funding process, 1995—. Mem. Fin. Execs. Inst., Am. Fin. Svcs. Assn. (bd. dirs.). Office: Daimler Chrysler Corp 27777 Franklin Rd Southfield MI 48034-2337*

CANTWELL, JOHN DALZELL, JR., management consultant; b. Davenport, Iowa, July 17, 1909; s. John D. and Mary Edna (Taylor) C.; m. Margaret Jean Simpson, Apr. 30, 1938; children: C.J., John Dalzell III. BSME, U. Iowa, 1932; MBA, U. Pa., 1934. Registered profl. engr., Ill. Planner, Caterpillar Tractor Co., 1935; plants engr. Bettendorf Co. (Iowa), 1936-40; asst. to v.p. Thilmany Pulp & Paper Co., Kaukauna, Wis., 1941-42; div. engr. U.S. Gypsum Co., Chgo., 1943-48; mgr. home appliance div. Murray Corp. Am., 1949-53; v.p. mfg. Trane Co., 1954-61; v.p. Carrier Corp., 1961-74; exec. v.p. Carrier Air Conditioning Co., 1962-74; sr. assoc. McCormick & Co., Tarrytown, N.Y., 1974-82. Pres., Cantwell-Conteville Family Assn, 1978-89. Served to lt. (s.g.) USNR, World War II. Mem. Am. Legion, Masons, Phi Delta Theta. Republican. Presbyterian. Home: Sandpiper Village K4 1224 Village Creek Ln Mount Pleasant SC 29464-3186

CANTWELL, JOHN WALSH, advertising executive; b. Fall River, Mass., July 16, 1922; s. William J. and Esther (Walsh) C.; m. Evelyna Dyson; children from previous marriage: Sharon, Peter, Paul. BS in Econs., Holy Cross Coll., 1944; MA, Georgetown U., 1945; postgrad., Columbia U., 1949-50. Asst. sales mgr. Internat. Milling Co., 1947-48; v.p. mgmt. supr. Compton Advt., N.Y.C., 1948-60; sr. v.p. mgmt. supr. Sullivan, Stauffer Colwell & Bayles, N.Y.C., 1960-65; pres., CEO Pritchard, Wood (advt.), N.Y.C., 1965-68, Parkson Advt. Agy., Inc., 1968-69; sr. v.p. J.B. Williams Co., Inc., 1968-69; pres. Jack Cantwell, Inc., 1970—; chmn., CEO Dolphin Med. Acoustics, Ltd., 1997-99; CEO Essex Labs., Ltd., Ft. Lauderdale, 1999—. Office: Essex Towers 340 Sunset Dr Ste 1405 Fort Lauderdale FL 33301-2653

CANTWELL, ROBERT, lawyer; b. Buffalo, Sept. 12, 1931; s. Thomas and Helen (Robinson) C.; m. Barbara Hurlbert, Oct. 19, 1963; children: Robert, Helen Virginia, Sara Elizabeth. AB, Cornell U., 1953, JD, 1956; LLM, NYU, 1959. Bar: N.Y. State bar 1956. Assoc. firm Jaeckle, Fleischmann & Mugel (and predecessor firm), Buffalo, 1956-62; mem. legal dept. Colgate-Palmolive Co., N.Y.C., 1962-68, London dep. gen. counsel, 1972-73, v.p., gen. counsel, 1973-86, sec., 1974-86; v.p., sec., gen. counsel Roblin Industries, Inc., Buffalo, 1968-72; ptnr. Serchuk, Wolfe and Zelermyer, White Plains, N.Y., 1986-87, Cantwell and Chen, N.Y.C., 1988-89; pvt. practice Greenwich, Conn., 1989—. Mem. ABA, N.Y. State Bar Assn., Assn. of Bar of City of N.Y., Am. Soc. Corp. Secs., Saturn Club (Buffalo), Belle Haven, Greenwich Horseneck Club. Home and Office: 5 Meadow Dr Greenwich CT 06831-4504

CANTWELL, THOMAS, geophysicist, electrical engineer; b. Buffalo, June 25, 1927; s. Thomas and Helen (Robinson) C.; children: Elizabeth Raye, Thomas III, Douglas. BSChemE, MIT, 1948, MSChemE, 1949; MBA, Harvard, Boston, 1951; PhD in Earth Sci., MIT, 1960. Registered profl. engr., Tex.; lic. geologist, Calif. Project engr. nuclear engrng. dept. MIT, Cambridge, 1951-58, mem. faculty, 1958-65; pres. Mandrel Industries, Houston, 1966-70, Petroleum Holdings, Inc., Houston, 1970-78, Ind. Exploration, Inc., Houston, 1978-84, Tech. Computer Graphics, Inc., Houston, 1984—. With U.S. Army, 1946-47. Fellow Royal Geographic Soc.; mem. IEEE, Soc. Exploration Geophysicists, Am. Assn. Petroleum Geologists. Achievements include patent for Helium Leak Detector. Home: 3949 Ann Arbor Dr Houston TX 77063-6301 Office: Tech Computer Graphics Inc 3949 Ann Arbor Dr Houston TX 77063-6301

CANTWELL, WILLIAM PATTERSON, lawyer; b. Saranac Lake, N.Y., Dec. 2, 1921; s. Francis Barry and Genevieve (Godfrey) C.; m. Hendrika Antonia Bestebreurtje, June 19, 1947; children: Peter F., Rebecca D., Christopher A. BA with highest honors, Williams Coll., 1942; JD, Yale U., 1948. Bar: N.Y. 1948, Colo. 1953. Assoc. Moot, Sprague, Marcy & Gulick, Buffalo, 1948-52, Holland & Hart, 1953-64; ptnr. Sherman & Howard, 1964-87, of counsel, 1988-95; vis. lectr. law U. Denver, 1956-60, 64-65, U. Colo., 1962, 87, U. Miami, 1976; lectr. various continuing legal edn. insts. and legal meetings; reporter on Uniform Marital Property Act Nat. Conf. Commrs. on Uniform State Laws, 1980-83. Contbr. articles to profl. jours. Recipient Treat award Nat. Coll. Probate Judges for Probate Excellence, 1983. Mem. ABA (ho. of dels. 1964-66, 73-78, chmn. real property probate and trust law sect. 1971-72), Am. Coll. Trust and Estate Counsel (pres. 1975-76, Trachtman lectr. 1980), Colo. Bar Assn. (pres. 1970-71, gov. 1959-65, chmn. taxation law sect. 1959-60, probate and trust law sect. 1960-61), Denver Bar Assn. (pres. 1962-63, award of merit 1969), Order of Coif (hon.). Home: 700 West 140 North Driggs ID 83422

CANUP, SHERRIE MARGARET, foreign languages educator; b. Thomaston, Ga., Dec. 18, 1946; d. J.B. and Lucille Evelyn (Parham) C. BA, Ga. Coll., 1969, MEd, 1976; EdS, West Ga. Coll., 1990. Tchr. Griffin (Ga.)-Spalding County Sch. System, 1969-91; head. dept. fgn. lang. Griffin H.S., 1992—. Mem. NEA, Ga. Assn. Educators, Fgn. Lang. Assn. Ga., Profl. Assn. Ga. Educators, Griffin Spalding Assn. Educators. Republican. Home: 1110 W Poplar St Apt K4 Griffin GA 30224-2666 Office: Griffin HS 1617 W Poplar St Griffin GA 30224-2038

CANZONIER, WALTER JUDE, shellfish aquaculturist; b. New Brunswick, N.J., Feb. 6, 1936; s. Joseph V. and Mary M. (Patterson) C. BS, St. Peter's Coll., Jersey City, 1957; postgrad., Rutgers U., 1957-64. Teaching asst. dept. zoology Rutgers U., New Brunswick, N.J., 1958-59, rsch. asst. dept. oyster culture, 1960-67, rsch. assoc., 1968-71, 81-87; rsch. fellow Inst. Marine Biology, CNR, Venice, Italy, 1971-77; dir. Coastal Resources Applied Rsch. Lab., Venice, 1977-80; dir. R & D, Aquarius Assocs., Port Noris, N.J., 1987—; mem. tech. coms. Italian Ministry Sanita and Ministry Merchant Marine, 1974-80, Interstate Shellfish Sanitation Conf., 1980—; cons. on marine sci. UNESCO, France, 1978—. Contbr. over 45 articles to sci. jours. in N.Am., Europe and Asia. Organizer, treas. Point Pleasant Beach (N.J.) Taxpayers Assn., 1963-70; bd. dirs. N.E. Regional Aquaculture Ctr., 1992-98, N.J. Taskforce for Revitalization of Shellfish Industry, 1997. Recipient numerous grants from pub. agys. in N.Am. and Europe, 1971—. Mem. Nat. Shellfisheries Assn., Soc. Invertebrate Pathology, World Aquaculture Soc. N.J. Aquaculture Assn. (trustee 1989—, pres. 1991-99). Achievements include development of shellfish sanitation guidelines and regulations for state and national health agencies in North America and Europe; design of marine research and aquaculture facilities in Asia, Europe and North America. Home: 44 Cowart Ave Manasquan NJ 08736-3102 Office: Aquarius Assocs PO Box 662 Port Norris NJ 08349-0662

CAO, HEPING, biologist, researcher; b. Pingxiang, Jiangxi, China, Feb. 15, 1964; came to U.S., 1991; s. Shengwen Cao and Shuzhen Huang; m. Rin Lin, June 28, 1991; 1 child, Nancy L. BS in Agr., Jiangxi Agrl. U, Nanchang, China, 1984; MS in Agr., Southwestern Agrl. U., 1987; PhD, Pa. State U., 1994. Instr. physiology and biochemistry of plant steriod hormone Jiangxi Agrl. U., 1987-88; grad. asst. molecular biology plant devel. rsch. Chinese Acad. Scis., Beijing, 1988-91; grad. asst. physiology, genetics, biochemistry rsch. Pa. State U., Univ. Pk., 1991-94; vis. rsch. assoc biochemistry and molecular biology Mich. State U., East Lansing, 1994-95; postdoc. rsch. assoc. biochemistry and molecular biology Tex. Tech U., Lubbock, 1996-97, Iowa State U., Ames, 1997—. Contbr. articles to Jour. Protein Chemistry, Jour. Plant Physiology, Plant Physiology, Physiologia Plantarum, Nature Jour., Jour. Biol. Chemistry, Jour. Plant Growth Regulation, Plant Growth Regulation, Chinese Sci. Bull. Recipient Creative Student award Jiangxi Province, 1986, Hon. Mention award Pa. State U., 1993, 94, Wilton R. Earle award Soc. for In Vitro Biology,1994. Mem. AAAS, Am. Soc. Plant Physiologists. Achievements include discovery of a critical factor important in crop yield; designed cloning method for a gene critical to crop protein quality; rsch. in expressing a gene important for resisting insects by crops and a gene for crop yield and quality. Home: 135 Dotson Dr Apt B 21 Ames IA 50014-7685 Office: Iowa State U Dept Biochem Biocphysics 2154 Mol Biol Bldg Ames IA 50011

CAO, JIE-YUAN, electronics engineer, researcher; b. Shanghai, July 24, 1944; s. Zong-Quan and Pei-Li (Zheng) C.; m. Ai-Yu Lu, Dec. 8, 1973; 1 child, Wei-Wei. BS, Beijing Poly. Inst., 1966; MSc, Shanghai Jiao Tong U., 1981. Engr. Microwave Tech. Rsch. Inst., Du Yuan, 1966-78; lectr. Shanghai Jiao Tong U., 1981-87, rsch. fellow, 1990-95; vis. scientist Internat. Ctr. Theoretical Physics, Trieste, Italy, 1988-89; sr. scientist EXB Tech. Inc., Sunnyvale, Calif., 1995-97, Kaifa Tech, Inc., Sunnyvale, 1998-99, Oplink Comm. Inc., San Jose, 1999—. Co-author: Optical Fiber Transmission Technology, 1988; patentee in field. Mem. IEEE, Chinese Comm. Soc., Internat. Soc. Optical Engrng., Optical Soc. Am. Achievements include work on a novel manufacturing method for plastic optical fiber star couplers. Avocations: photography, stamp collecting. Home: 3076 San Juan Ave Santa Clara CA 95051-1640 Office: Oplink Comm Inc 3475 N First St San Jose CA 95131

CAO, THAI-HAI, industrial engineer; b. Saigon, Republic of Vietnam, July 8, 1954; came to U.S., 1975; s. Pho Thai and Anh Ngoc (Nguyen) C.; m. Hue Thi Tran, June 29, 1979; children: Quoc-Viet Thai, Quoc-Nam Thai, Huyen-Tran Thai, Uyen-Phuong Thai. BS in Indsl. Engring., U. Wash., 1980; grad., Gen. Electric Mfg. Mgmt. Prgm., 1982. Mfg. engr. GE, San Jose, Calif., 1980-82; mgr. mfg. engring. and quality assurance Broadcast Microwave div. Harris Corp., Mountain View, Calif., 1982-85; mgr. mfg. engring. John Fluke Mfg. Co., Everett, Wash., 1986-90; mgr. quality engring. Advanced Tech. Labs., Bothell, Wash., 1990—; sr. prin. electronic process engr. Primex Aerospace Co., 1990—; cons. total quality mgmt. Vinatek. Mem. Am. Soc. Quality Control (chmn. membership com. 1987-88), Soc. Vietnamese Profls. (pres. 1988), Soc. Mfg. Engrs., Inst. Indsl. Engrs., Am. Prodn. and Inventory Control. Avocations: reading, travel. Home: 23502 22nd Ave SE Bothell WA 98021-9553

CAO, WEIBIAO, physiologist, researcher; b. Tong Xiang, Zhejiang, China, Oct. 1, 1964; p. Songfa Cao and Baona Shen; m. Liping Zhang, Apr. 9, 1988; 1 child, Yi. MD, Zhejiang Med. U., 1986; MSc, Peking Union Med. Coll., Beijing, 1991. Resident Peking Union Med. Coll. Hosp., Beijing, 1986-88, resident, chief resident, 1991-93, attending physician, 1993-95; postdoctoral rsch. asst. dept. medicine U. Calgary, Can., 1995-96, R.I. Hosp., Brown U. Sch. Medicine, Providence, 1996—. Author: Respiratory Medicine, 1997. Recipient 1st prize for sci. advancement award Ministry Pub. Health China, 1997; sci. rsch. grantee Ministry Pub. Health China, Chinese Acad. Med. Scis., 1992, 93, 94. Mem. Am. Physiol. Soc., Am. Motility Soc. (Young Investigator award 1998), Am. Gastroenterol. Assn. E-mail: WeibiaoúCao@bBrown.edu. Fax: 401-444-5890. Office: RI Hosp Brown U Sch Medicine 593 Eddy St SWP-520 Providence RI 02903

CAOUETTE, JOHN BERNARD, insurance company executive; b. New Bedford, Mass., Oct. 5, 1944; s. Bernard Adrian and Constance Mary (Donahue) C.; m. Margaretta Johnson, Jan. 30, 1966; children: Tristen Michelle, Brian Willis. BA, Calif. State U., Long Beach, 1969; MBA, U. Calif., Berkeley, 1970. With Citibank, San Francisco, 1970-71; mgr. swaps and global securities, v.p. Citibank, Jakarta, Indonesia, 1971-72, Hong Kong, 1972-79, N.Y.C., 1979-82; mgr. fgn. exch. and money markets Continental Grain Co., N.Y.C., 1982-86; chmn., CEO Capital Markets Assurance Corp., N.Y.C., 1986-98; vice chmn. MBIA Ins. Corp., N.Y.C., 1998—; chmn. Assn. Fin. Guaranty Insurors, 1990-91. Author: Managing Credit Risk: The Next Great Financial Challenge, 1998; contbr. articles to various publs. With U.S. Army, 1965-67, Vietnam. Office: MBIA Ins Corp 885 3rd Ave New York NY 10022-4834

CAPALBO, CARMEN CHARLES, director, producer; b. Harrisburg, Pa., Nov. 1, 1925; s. Joseph and Concetta (Riggio) C.; m. Patricia McBride, July 9, 1950 (div. June 1961); children: Carla, Marco. Student, Yale Sch. Drama. prodns. include: dir., co-prodr. (plays) Juno and the Paycock, Shadow and Substance, Dear Brutus, Awake and Sing, The Threepenny Opera, The Potting Shed, A Moon for the Misbegotten, The Cave Dwellers, The Rise and Fall of the City of Mahagonny; dir. (opera) The Good Soldier Schweik, (plays) A Connecticut Yankee, Seidman and Son, The Strangers, The Sign in Sidney Brustein's Window, Enter Solly Gold, Slowly, By Thy Hand Unfurled, The Chosen; also TV prodn. The Power and the Glory; story cons.: Studio One, 1951-52; cons. The Bronx: After the Fires, Conversation with Eddie, 1983; prodn. mgr. Emlyn Williams as Charles Dickens, 1952-53, Jean-Louis Barrault-Madeleine Renaud Co., 1952; dir., prodr., writer 200 radio plays. Served with AUS, 1944-45. Decorated Bronze Star, Purple Heart. Recipient spl. Tony award 1956, Obie award 1956. Mem. League N.Y. Theatres, Dirs. Guild Am., Soc. Stage Dirs. and Choreographers, Dramatists Guild, League OffBroadway Theatres (co-founder 1958, exec. bd. 1958-60), Royal Philatelic Soc. (London). Address: 500 2nd Ave New York NY 10016-8606

CAPALDI, ELIZABETH ANN DEUTSCH, psychological sciences educator; b. N.Y.C., May 13, 1945; d. Frederick and Nettie (Tarasuck) Deutsch; m. Egidio J. Capaldi, Jan. 20, 1968 (div. May 1985). AB, U. Rochester, 1965; PhD, U. Tex., 1969. Asst. prof. dept. psychol. scis. Purdue U., West Lafayette, Ind., 1969-74, assoc. prof., 1974-78, prof., 1979-86, asst. dean Grad. Sch., 1982-86, head dept. psychol. scis., 1983-88, sec.-treas. council of grad. dept. psychology, 1986-88; prof. U. Fla., Gainesville, 1988—, provost, v.p. acad. affairs, 1996—; spl. asst. to pres., U. Fla., 1991-96. Author: Psychology, 1989, 4th edit., 1996; cons. editor Jour. Exptl. Psychology, 1991-96; assoc. editor Psychonomic Bull. Rev., 1993-98; contbr. articles to profl. jours. NIMH grantee, 1984-94, NSF grantee, 1995-98. Fellow AAAS, APA, Am. Psychol. Soc. (mem. governing bd. 1991-96, pres. 1999); mem. Psychonomic Soc. (mem. governing bd. 1992-97), Midwestern Psychol. Assn. (sec.-treas. 1988-90, pres. 1991), Sigma Xi. Home: 4140 NW 44th Ave Gainesville FL 32606-4518 Office: U Fla Office of Provost Tigert 235 Gainesville FL 32611

CAPALDINI, MARK LAURENCE, online information service executive; b. Bluefield, W.Va., Feb. 10, 1954; s. Louis Aloysius and Marie Pia (Frigo) C.; m. Laura Jane Hotchkiss, June 25, 1983. BS in Engring. Sci., Yale U., 1975; MBA, Harvard U., 1979. Sr. cons. Arthur Andersen & Co., N.Y.C., 1975-77; asst. to the pub. The Washington Post, 1979-80, asst. controller, 1980-82, asst. to the dir. circulation, 1982, zone mgr. home delivery, 1983, mgr. circulation ops., 1983-86; acct. exec. Claritas, Inc., Alexandria, Va., 1986-87, v.p. media, 1987-91, sr. v.p. mktg., 1991-92, exec. v.p., 1992-94; pres. LEGI-SLATE, Inc., Washington, 1994-97; pres., CEO Congressional Information Svc., Inc., Bethesda, Md., 1997—; discussion leader Am. Press Inst., Reston, Va., 1985-93; faculty mem. mgmt. ctr. Poynter Inst. for Media Studies, St. Petersburg, 1987-95. Bd. dirs. Yale Alumni Fund, New Haven, Conn., 1985-90, Information Industry Assn., Found. for Independent Higher Edn., 1998—, Washington. Mem. Young Presidents Orgn. Avocations: stewardship, choral music, photography, tennis. Office: Congressional Information Svc Inc 4520 East West Hwy Ste 800 Bethesda MD 20814-3389

CAPALDO, GUY, obstetrician, gynecologist; b. Bisaccia, Italy, Jan. 1, 1950; came to U.S., 1958; s. Arturo Nunziante and Maria Carmela (Ciani) C.; m. Kathy Nicita, Apr. 20, 1985. BSEE magna cum laude, U. Dayton, 1972; MS, Ohio State U., Columbus, 1973; MD, Med. Coll. Ohio, 1978. Diplomate Am. Bd. Ob-Gyn; cert. clin. densitometrist Internat. Soc. Clin. Densitometry. Research asst. Ohio State U., 1973-75; resident in ob-gyn Med. Coll. Ohio, Toledo, 1978-82; practice medicine specializing in ob-gyn Mansfield, Ohio, 1982—; chief ob-gyn. dept. Mansfield Gen. Hosp., 1985—; lab. dir. Mansfield (Ohio) Ob-Gyn Assocs. Contbr. articles to profl. jours. Clinic physician Plan Parenthood, Mansfield, 1982—. Pres. scholar U. Dayton, 1968-72, Univ. fellow Ohio State U., 1972-75. Fellow Am. Coll. Ob-Gyn; mem. AMA, Ohio State Med. Assn., Richland County Med. Soc. Avocations: reading, fishing, traveling, golfing. Office: Mansfield Ob-Gyn Assocs 500 S Trimble Rd Mansfield OH 44906-3483

CAPANNA, ALBERT HOWARD, neurosurgeon, neuroscientist; b. Utica, N.Y., May 12, 1947; m. Dawn McLouth; children: Christine, Alicia, Albert II, Danielle, Gabriella, Guy, Brianna, Gianna, Beau. BA, U. Tex., 1970; MD, Wayne State U., 1974. Med. intern St. John Hosp., Detroit, 1974, resident in gen. surgery, 1974-75; resident in neurosurgery Wayne State U., Detroit, 1975-79; fellow in microneurosurgery U. Zurich, 1979; stereotactic fellow U. Paris, 1980; fellow in pediatric neurosurgery Hosp. for Sick Children, Toronto, 1980; pvt. practice Las Vegas, Nev., 1983—; chief staff Sunrise Hosp., Las Vegas, 1993-94; chief neurosurgery Univ. Med. Ctr., Las Vegas; clin. prof. U. Nev. Sch. Medicine, 1991—. Mem. Rocky Mountain Neurosurgical Soc. (sec. 1998—). Office: Internat Neurosci Cons 820 Shadow Ln Ste 302 Las Vegas NV 89106-4105

CAPANO, EDWARD ANDREW, publishing company executive; b. Bklyn., Oct. 31, 1941; s. Louis Vincent and Mary Margaret (Kennedy) C.; m. Margaret Ann Gallagher, Apr. 18, 1964; children—Kathleen, Christopher, John Emmett, Elizabeth. B.A., St. John's U., 1964. Asst. to v.p. Publ. Corp, Greenwich, Conn., 1966-67; assoc. pub. National Rev., N.Y.C., 1968-91, pub., 1991—, also bd. dirs.; bd. dirs. Nat. Review Mag., Conservative TV Network, Am. Conservative Union, Townhall; mem. adv. bd. U.S. English Found., Conservative TV Network. Vice pres., treas. Human Life Found., N.Y.C., 1973—, Ad Hoc Com. in Def. of Life, N.Y.C., 1973—, Nat. Com. Cath. Laymen, N.Y.C., 1978—; fundraiser Buckley for Mayor, N.Y.C., 1965, Buckley for Senate, 1972. Roman Catholic. Avocations: tennis, bike riding, golf. Home: 5 Wychview Dr Westfield NJ 07090-1820 Office: Nat Review 215 Lexington Ave New York NY 10016-6023*

CAPASSO, FEDERICO, physicist, research administrator; b. Rome, June 24, 1949; came to U.S., 1976; D in Physics summa cum laude, U. of Rome, 1973. Researcher Fondazione Bordoni, Rome, Italy, 1974-76; vis. scientist Bell Labs., Holmdel, N.J., 1976-77, mem. tech. staff, 1977-78; mem. tech. staff Lucent Technologies (formerly AT&T), Murray Hill, N.J., 1978-87, head quantum phenomena and device rsch. dept., 1987-97, head semicondr. physics rsch. dept., 1997; co-chmn. Internat. Semiconductor Device Rsch. Symposium, Charlottesville, Va., 1995; chmn. Internat. Conf. on Advances in Semiconductors and Superconductors, Newport Beach, 1988, 90; program co-chmn. Picosecond Electronics and Optoelectronics Conf., Lake Tahoe, 1987; program com., mem. of 20 internat. confs.; invited lectr. at over 140 internat. confs. Editor 4 books; mem. editl. bd. Il Nuovo Cimento, Applied Physics Letters, Semiconductor Sci. and Tech.; holder 30 U.S. patents, more than 50 fgn. patents; contbr. over 200 articles to profl. jours. Recipient award N.Y. Acad. Scis., 1993, Gold medal Heinrich Welker Meml., 1994, Vinci Excellence award LMVH, 1995, medal Materials Rsch. Soc., 1995, Electronics Letters Premium award Inst. of Elec. Engrs. (London), 1995, Bell Labs. fellow award, 1997, John Price Wetherill medal Franklin Inst., 1997, Rank prize, 1998, Capitolium prize, 1998, Alessandro Volta Meml. medal, 1999; named hon. mem. Franklin Inst., 1997. Fellow AAAS (Newcomb Cleveland prize 1995), IEEE (David Sarnoff award 1991, Leos W. Steifer Sci. Achievement award 1998), Lasers and Electroptics Soc. (Sci. Achievement award 1998), NAS, Am. Phys. Soc., Optical Soc. Am., Internat. Soc. for Optical Engring., Nat. Acad. Engring., Am. Acad. Arts and Scis. Office: Lucent Technologies 700 Mountain Ave New Providence NJ 07974-1208

CAPASSO, FRANK LOUIS, secondary school educator; b. N.Y.C., Apr. 30, 1943; s. Louis and Marie Francis (Fiermonte) C.; m. Diane Patricia Webster, July 8, 1967; children: Ann Marie, Eleanor, Elizabeth. BA in History, Iona Coll., 1964; MS in Edn., Fordham U., 1976, MA in History, 1995. Tchr. Intermediate Sch. 148, N.Y.C., 1965-92, Truman H.S., N.Y.C., 1992—; mentor N.Y.C. Bd. Edn., 1993-97; acting chairperson Intermediate Sch. 148, 1985-91, cooperating tchr., 1997. Mem. Nat. Coun. Social Studies, Mid. State Coun. Social Studies, United Fedn. Tchrs. (chpt. leader 1986-91, Ely Tractenberg award 1975-76). Democrat. Roman Catholic. Home: 48 Pratt St New Rochelle NY 10801-4339

CAPDEVIELLE, XAVIER O., builder, constructor; b. Paris, Aug. 26, 1956; came to U.S., 1991; s. Marcel and Monique (Poulet) C.; m. Martine Valluy, June 7, 1983; 1 child, Victoria. MBA, Inst. Européen des Affairs, 1981. Lic. comml. pilot. Mgr. fin. Satam Brazil, Rio de Janeiro, 1981-84; gen. mgr. Satam Argentina, Buenos Aires, 1984-88; pres., CEO Cader S.A., Buenos Aires, 1988-93, So. Cross Group, Miami, Fla., 1991—; pres. Outinord Argentina & Hormigones Especiales, Buenos Aires, 1997—. 1st. lt. French Air Force, 1977-79. Mem. Aeroclub France (rep. Paris 1991), Grove Isle Yacht and Tennis (Miami), Buenos Aires Lawn Tennis. Home: 3 Grove Isle Dr Apt 1110 Miami FL 33133-4109 Office: Outinord Universal Svc 115 NW 167th St North Miami Beach FL 33169

CAPE, JAMES ODIES E., fashion designer; b. Detroit, Nov. 18, 1947; s. Odies E. and Juanita K. (Brandon) C. Student, Henry Ford C.C., 1973-75, Am. Acad. Dramatic Arts, N.Y.C., 1975-76, Pace U., 1977-78. Trapeze artist Mills Bros. Circus, 1962; skater Ice Capades, 1971-72; creator, dir., instr. skating program City of Southfield, Mich., 1972, 73; haute couture designer James E. Cape & Assocs., Dearborn, Mich., 1986—; mem. Marji Kunz scholarship award com. Wayne State U., Detroit. Film reviewer Times-Herald Newspapers, 1989-90; clothing designs pub. in various mags. and newspapers; creations for TV and stage including the Emmys, The Am. Music Awards, Dick Clark-ABC Prodns., Showtime Spl. "Aretha", Trump Castle, Atlantic City, The Chgo. Theater, Kennedy Ctr., Washington, Radio City Music Hall; co-prodr. Eartha Kitt, A Night in Paris; spl. commd. designs various celebrities; spl. publicity creations for Detroit Inst. Arts, Am. Lung Assn.; producer, host TV show "Town Talk." Recipient Pre-silver, bronze medals U.S. Figure Skating Assn., 1969, Citation award City of Dearborn, 1994, Wayne County (Mich.) Resolution award, 1993, Spl. Tribute award State of Mich. Ho. of Reps., 1994. Mem. AFTRA, Actors Equity, Soc. for Cinephiles. Home: James E. Cape and Associates 500 N Rosevere Dearborn MI 48128

CAPE, RONALD ELLIOT, retired biotechnology company executive; b. Montreal, Que., Can., Oct. 11, 1932; came to U.S., 1967, naturalized, 1972; s. Victor and Fan C.; m. Lillian Judith Pollock, Oct. 21, 1956; children: Jacqueline R., Julie A. AB in Chemistry, Princeton U., 1953; MBA, Harvard U., 1955; PhD in Biochemistry, McGill U., Montreal, 1967; post-grad., U. Calif., Berkeley, 1967-70. Customs, purchasing and advt. clk. Merck and Co., Ltd., Montreal, 1955-56; pres. Profl. Pharm. Corp., Montreal, 1960-67; chmn. bd. Profl. Pharm. Corp., 1967-73; pres. Cetus Corp., Emeryville, Calif., 1972-78; chmn. bd. Cetus Corp., 1978-91; founding chmn. Darwin Molecular Corp., 1992—; mem. adv. coun. dept. molecular biology Princeton U.; adj. prof. bus. adminstrn. U. Pitts.; vis. prof. biochemistry Queen Mary Coll., U. London; bd. dirs. Advanced Bioconcept Inc., Interactive Scis., Inc., Neutrogena Corp., The Found. Nat. Medals of Sci. & Tech., 1992—; founder, bd. dirs. Bay Area Biosci. Ctr., 1989—; mem. bus. adv. com. Neurobiol. Techs. Inc.; mem. sci. adv. bd. Can. Med. Discoveries Fund; mem. standing com. bus. devel. MEd. Rsch. Coun. (Can.); mem. bus. affairs com. Ann. Revs., Inc., 1975-80; mem. impacts of applied genetics adv. panel to Office Tech. Assessment; mem. adv. com. on life scis. Natural Scis. and Engring. Rsch. Coun. Can.; mem. bd. dirs. Whitehead Inst., Cambridge, Mass. Mem. Rockefeller U. Coun.; bd. dirs. U. Calif. Art Mus. Coun., Berkeley, 1974-76; trustee Head-Royce Schs., Oakland, Calif., 1975-80, Rockefeller U., 1986-90, San Francisco Conservatory Music, The Keystone Ctr., 1987-93; bd. dirs. San Francisco Opera Assn., mem. budget and fin. com., 1992—, U. Waterloo Inst. for Biotech. Rsch.; mem. bus. adv. com. U. Calif., Berkeley; mem. Berkeley Roundtable on Internat. Economy; mem. sci. adv. bd. Bio-Technology Mag., 1987—; trustee Princeton U., 1989-93; mem. bd. regents Nat. Libr. of Medicine, 1989-92; scientific adv. bd. Med. Rsch. Coun., Can., standing com. bus. devel. Fellow AAAS, Am. Acad. Arts and Scis., Am. Soc. Microbiology (Found. for Microbiology lectr. 1978-79); mem. Can. Biochem. Soc., Fedn. Am. Scientists, Royal Soc. Health, Soc. Indsl. Microbiology, Indsl. Biotech. Assn. (founding mem., pres. 1983-85, dir.), N.Y. Acad. Scis., Princeton Club of N.Y., Commonwealth Club of Calif., Sigma Xi. Jewish. Office: 220 Montgomery St Ste 1010 San Francisco CA 94104-3419

CAPECCHI, MARIO RENATO, genetecist, educator; b. Verona, Italy, Oct. 6, 1937; m. 1963. BS, Antioch Coll., 1961; PhD in Biophysics, Harvard U., 1967. Soc. fellows, jr. fellow biophysics Harvard U., 1966-68, from asst. prof. to assoc. prof. biochemistry med. sch., 1968-73; prof. Biology U. Utah, 1973-88; prof. human genetics U. Utah Sch. Medicine, Salt Lake City, 1973—; investigator Howard Hughes Inst./U. Utah, Salt Lake City, 1988—; disting. prof. human genetics Howard Hughes Inst./U.Utah, 1993—. Recipient Biochemistry award Am. Chem. Soc., 1969, Bristol-Myers Squibb award, 1992, Gairdner Found. Internat. award Gairdner Found. (Can.), 1993, Gen. Motors Corp. Alfred P. Sloan Jr. Prize, 1994, Molecular Bioanalytics Prize, 1996, Kyoto Prize in Basis Scis., 1996, Franklin medal Franklin Inst., 1997, Baxter award, AAMC, 1998. Mem. NAS, Am. Biochemical Soc., Am. Soc. Biol. Chemistry. Achievements include research in gaining an understanding of how the information encoded in the gene is translated by the cell, elucidating the mechanism of genetic recombination in mouse embryo-derived stem (ES) cells, developing gene targeting in the mouse, gaining an understanding of embryonic and neuronal mammalian development through the use of gene targeting. Office: Howard Hughes Med Inst Univ Utah 15 N 2030 E Rm 5100 Salt Lake City UT 84112-5331*

CAPECELATRO, MARK JOHN, lawyer; b. New Haven, June 2, 1948; s. Ralph Ettore and Mary Louise (Scialla) C.; m. Jane Beals, June 19, 1971; children: Christopher Beals, Kate Rowley, Jonathan Mark. BA, Colgate U., 1970; JD, U. Conn., 1973. Bar: Conn. 1973. Assoc. Ells, Quinlan, Eddy & Robinson, Canaan, Conn., 1973-77; ptnr. Ells, Quinlan & Robinson, Canaan, 1977-90, Capecelatro & Nelligan, Canaan, 1991—; bd. advisors Canaan Nat. Bank, 1982—; mortgage counsel People's Bank, Canaan and Hartford, Conn., 1983—; trustee Sharon (Conn.) Hosp., 1984-91, vice chmn., 1990-91, chmn. exec. com., 1990-91; trustee Salisbury Congl. Ch., 1990-98, vice chmn., 1990-93, chmn., 1993-98, fin. com., 1998—. Bd. dirs. Housatonic Homemaker Health Aide, West Cornwall, Conn., 1977-80, Housatonic Day Care Ctr., Inc., Lakeville, Conn., 1981-90, Salisbury Pub. Health Nursing, Lakeville, 1983-85, Salisbury Vol. Ambulance Svcs., Salisbury Winter Sports Assn., 1983-87, Salisbury (Conn.) Congl. Ch., Salisbury Vol. Ambulance Assn., Inc., 1997—; mem. adv. com. Parkside Med. Svcs. Corp., 1988-93. Mem. ABA, Conn. Bar Assn., Litchfield County Bar Assn., Assn. Trial Lawyers Am., Conn. Assn. Trial Lawyers, Nat. Assn. Criminal Def. Lawyers. Republican. Avocations: guitar, fishing, skiing, canoeing, kayaking. Home: 196 Belgo Rd Lakeville CT 06039-1003 Office: Capecelatro & Nelligan 117 Main St Canaan CT 06018-2463

CAPEHART, BARNEY LEE, industrial and systems engineer; b. Galena, Kans., Aug. 20, 1940; s. Samuel Alfred and Mary Jane (Bliss) C.; m. Lynne Carol Fowler, Sept. 2, 1961; children: Thomas David, Jeffrey Donald, Cynthia Diane. BSEE, U. Okla., Norman, 1961, MEE, 1962, PhD, 1967. Instr. elec. engring. U. Okla., 1965-67; mem. tech. staff Aerospace Corp., San Bernardino, Calif., 1967-68; asst. prof. indsl. and systems engring. U. Fla., Gainesville, 1968-72; assoc. prof. indsl. engring. U. Tenn., 1972-73; assoc. prof. indsl. and systems engring. U. Fla., 1973-79, prof., 1979—, asst. chmn., 1987-88; cons. Martin Marietta Corp., U.S. Naval Tng. Device Ctr., State of Fla., Hicks and Assocs., Casazza, Schultz & Assocs.; nat. lectr., Assn. Energy Engrs.; expert witness in energy and safety cases; chmn. Regional Energy Action Com., 1977-79; Region IV adv. group on appropriate tech. Dept. of Energy, 1978-80; mem. Local Energy Action Program, 1980-81; cons. U.S. Dept. Energy, Dep. Asst. Sec. for Bldg. Techs., Washington, 1989-90. Author books in field; editor Internat. Jour. Energy Systems, 1985-88; contbr. articles to profl. jours. Pres. Fla. League Conservation Voters, 1984-86; grad. Leadership Gainesville, 1984; dir. U. Fla., 1990-95; dir. U. Fla. Indsl. Assessment Ctr., 1995—. Decorated Air Force Commendation medal; Barney Capehart Day proclaimed by Alachua County, Fla., May 26, 1987, City of Gainesville, Dec. 21, 1987; recipient Palladium medal Am. Assn. Engring. Socs., 1988. Fellow AAAS, IEEE (energy com. 1988—), Inst. Indsl. Engrs. (dir. energy mgmt. divsn. 1986-87); mem. Audubon Soc. (Fla. chpt. Conservationist of Yr. 1987), Fla. Conservation Found., Assn. Energy Engrs., Fla. Blue Key, Sigma Xi, Sigma Tau, Alpha Pi Mu, Tau Beta Pi, Eta Kappa Nu. Home: 1601 NW 35th Way Gainesville FL 32605-4846 Office: U Fla Dept Indsl & Systems Engring 303 Weil Hall Gainesville FL 32611-2083

CAPEHART, CRAIG EARL, lawyer; b. Indpls., Oct. 13, 1951; s. H. Earl, Jr. and Harriet Jane (Holmes) C.; m. Lynn Dee Barker, Dec. 29, 1988 (div. Dec. 3, 1997); 1 child, Kelly Anne. BA, George Washington U., 1974, MA, 1976, MBA, Ind. U., 1978, JD, 1988. Bar: Ind. 1989, N.Y. 1989, U.S. Dist. Ct. (no. and so. dists.) Ind. 1989, D.C. 1991, Minn. 1991, U.S. Dist. Ct. Minn. 1992, U.S. Supreme Ct. 1992. Internat. analyst Abbott Lab., N. Chgo., 1978-80; mgr. consulting Arthur Andersen & Co., Chgo., 1980-81; v.p., gen. mgr. MPMS, Inc., Northfield, Ill., 1981-84; prin. MMC, Inc., Lake Bluff, Ill., 1984-87; atty. IBM, Armonk, N.Y., 1989-94, Capehart Law Office, Indpls., 1994—; dir. Capehart Farms, Inc., Washington, Ind., 1986—. Trustee Epsilon Edn. Found., Washington, 1980—; v.p. Chgo. Alumni Sigma Chi, Chgo., 1981-84. Mem. Am. Intellectual Property Law Assn., Computer Law Assn., Ind. Software Assn., Venture Club of Ind., Columbia Club (fin. com. 1996—). Republican. Avocation: pvt. pilot. Home: 11526 Creekside Ln Carmel IN 46033 Office: Capehart Law Office 136 E Market St Ste 860 Indianapolis IN 46204-3204

CAPEK, BRENDA JOYCE, social worker; b. St. Cloud, Minn., May 23, 1941; d. Harold I. and Sylvia E. (Nissen) Hendrickson; m. John E. Wanner, June 29, 1963 (div. Sept. 1974); children: Mark J. Wanner (dec.), Jason B. Wanner; m. Richard Capek, June 22, 1986. BA, Augsburg Coll., 1963; MA, U. Chgo., 1965. Lic. clin. social worker; cert. advanced image relationship therapist; cert. alcohol and drug counselor. Caseworker Chgo. Child Care Soc., 1965-67, United Cerebral Palsy, Chgo., 1972-74, Elk Grove Village (Ill.) Mental Health, 1972-76; social worker Luth. Home & Svc. for the Aged, Arlington Heights, Ill., 1976-78; dir. Luth. Social Svcs. of Ill., Villa Park, 1978-95; pvt. practice Downers Grove, Ill., 1995—. Alma Dickerson scholar Augsburg Coll., 1962, grad. sch. scholar Luth. Ch. Mo. Synod, 1963-65. Lutheran. Avocations: sewing, boating, swimming, scuba, traveling. Home and Office: 5516 Katrine Ave Downers Grove IL 60515-4217

CAPELLAN, ANGEL, small business executive; b. Zorraquin, Spain, Apr. 10, 1942; s. Sotero Capellan and Damasa Gnozalo; m. Sonia C. Guadalupe, Aug. 27, 1971; children: Carlos Manuel, Amaya Isabel. *Ángel Capellán is 1st generation immigrant to U.S. The Capellán family is traced directly to the end of 1590's and has remained for 400 years in Santurde, Spain. Spouse Sonia is high school administrator and teacher with licenses in Administration, Spanish, and ESL. For 28 years she has worked in NYC School System and recently in Nassau County School System. Son Carlos is graduate from Regis High School in Manhattan and now student at Johns Hopkins University, with double major in international relations and Spanish, and member of Beta Theta Pi since 1997. Daughter Amaya is entering the 2003 class at Princeton University in the fall of 1999.* Licentiate degree, U. Madrid, 1968; MA, NYU, 1969, NYU, 1970; PhD, NYU, 1977. Tchr. Colegio Santa Maria, Spain, 1962-66; instr. Spanish Hunter Coll., N.Y.C., 1969-78; dir. lang. arts South Bronx campus Sch. New Resources, Coll. New Rochelle, N.Y.C., 1978-83; assoc. dean Eugenio Maria de Hostos Community Coll., N.Y.C., 1983-84; pres. LEA, Book Distbrs. & Links-Lazos, Internat. Computer Systems, N.Y.C., 1984—; judge CEPI Literary Prizes, N.Y.C., 1972-89; founder, pub. Españoles en USA. Contbr. articles to profl. jours.; author of book revs., poems, and stories; author: Hemingway and the Hispanic World, 1985, Paisajes renacidos, 1982; contbg. author: Gran enciclopedia Rialp, Tomo 20, 1974, Tomo 23, 1974. Pres. Coun. Spanish Residents N.Y. Consular Area, 1997—; U.S. rep. Gen. Coun. for Emigration, Madrid, 1998—. Juan March fellow Juan March Found., Madrid, 1969-70, Fulbright scholar Fulbright Found., 1968-69; Elias Ahuja fellow Fulbright Found., Madrid, 1968-69. Mem. MLA, Am. Assn. Tchrs. Spanish and Portuguese, Am. Booksellers Assn., Assn. Empresarios Y Profesionales (U.S., Spain). Roman Catholic. Avocations: reading, stamp collecting, writing. Home and Office: 17023 83rd Ave Jamaica NY 11432-2101

CAPELLE, MADELENE CAROLE, opera singer, educator, music therapist; b. Las Vegas, Nev., July 29, 1950; d. Curtis and Madelene Glenna (Healy) C. BA, Mills Coll., 1971; MusM, U. Tex., 1976; postgrad., Ind. U., 1976-77; diploma cert., U. Vienna, Austria, 1978; postgrad. in creative arts, Union Coll. Cert. K-12 music specialist, Nev.; cert. hypnotherapist, hypnoanaesthesiologist. Prof. voice U. Nev., C.C. So. Nev., Nev. Sch. for the Arts, Las Vegas, 1986—; music therapist Charter Hosp., Las Vegas, 1987—; pvt. practice music therapy, Las Vegas, 1989—; music specialist Clark County Sch. Dist., Las Vegas, 1989—; contract music therapist Nev. Assn. for Handicapped, Las Vegas, 1990; guest voice coach U. Basel, Switzerland, 1992; presenter concerts in Kenya, self-esteem workshops for children and adult women; artist-in-residence, Nev., Wyo., S.D., Oreg., Idaho, N.D., Utah, 1988—; mem. cons. roster Wyo. Arts Cou., 1988—; cons. U.S. rep. Princess Margaret of Romania Found.; workshops in music therapy and humor therapy Germany, Austria, Switzerland; workshop day treatment program dir. Harmony Health Care; judge Leontyne Price Nat. Voice Competition; creative arts cons. Utah Festival Opera; artistic cons. Utah Fest Opera. Opera singer, Europe, Asia, S.Am., U.S., Can., Australia, 1978—; roles include Cio Cio San in Madama Butterly, Tosca, Turandot and Fidelio, Salome Electra; community concerts artist; featured PBS artist Guess Who's Playing the Classics; featured guest All Things Considered PBS radio, 1985; co-writer (one-woman show) The Fat Lady Sings, 1991 (Women's Awareness award), The Undone Divas: Hysterical/Historical Perspective (Nev. Humanities grant 1996) ; concerts Africa, Kenya, Somalia; concerts for Jugaslavian Relief throughout Europe; guest soloist national anthem San Francisco 49ers. Pres., founder, cons. Children's Opera Outreach, Las Vegas, 1985—; artist Musicians Emergency Found., N.Y.C., 1978-82; vol. Zoo Assn., Allied Arts, Ziegfeld Club (first Junior Ziegfeld Young Woman of Yr.), Las Vegas, 1979—; clown Very Spl. Arts, Nev., Oreg., S.D., 1989-90; goodwill and cultural amb. City of Las Vegas, 1983; panelist Kennedy Ctr., Washington, 1982; artist Benefit Concerts for Children with AIDS; mem. Nev. Arts Alliance, Make a Wish Found., Lyric Opera of Las Vegas; CEO Outreach for Creative Arts, Opera Piccolo; ednl. outreach cons. Utah Fest Opera. Named Musician of Yr. Swiss Music Alliance, 1993; recipient Congl. Cert. of Merit for work in the arts, 1993, 96; Nev. Humanities Torr grantee. Mem. Internat. Platform Assn., Nat. Assn. Tchrs. Singing (featured guest spkr.), Performing Arts Soc. Nev., Cultural Arts Soc. (co-founder 1995), Brown Bag Concert Assn. (bd. dirs.), Make a Wish Found., Las Vegas Lyric Opera (bd. dirs.). Democrat. Features on Women's Cable Network. Avocations: gardening, refinishing antique furniture, gourmet cooking, puppetry magic, pet therapy. Home: 3266 Brentwood St Las Vegas NV 89121-3316

CAPELLE, STEPHEN H., federal judge; b. 1947. JD, U. Tex., 1972. Apptd. magistrate judge we. dist. U.S. Dist. Ct. Tex., 1987. Fax: (512) 916-5668. Office: 200 W 8th St Austin TX 78701-2325

CAPELLE-FRANK, JACQUELINE AIMEE, writer; b. Fond du Lac, Wis., Dec. 23, 1935; d. Ira Richard and Aimee Cecilia (Dignin) Capelle; divorced; children: P. Malachi, Tamara, Daria Frank-Weber. AA, Edison C.C., Naples, Fla., 1986; cert., U. Cambridge, Eng., 1991, U. Oxford, Eng., 1992, Paris Am. Acad., 1992; BA, Fla. Internat. U., 1994. part-time instr. Internat. Coll., 1999. Author: (children's book) What's a Library, 1974, (anthologies) Poetic Voices of America, 1996, 97. Mem. Collier County Hist. Soc. (bd. dirs. 1994—, pres. 1997-99), Nat. Trust for Hist. Preservation, Mus. Trustee Assn., Cooperstown Art Assn. Republican. Presbyterian. Avocations: reading, travel, country walks, gardening, swimming. Home: 143 4th Ave N Naples FL 34102-8421

CAPELLI, JOHN PLACIDO, nephrologist; b. Hammonton, N.J., May 23, 1936; s. John L. and Marie C.; m. Patricia Ann Verna, Nov. 4, 1961; children: John L., Elizabeth Ann, David S. BS in Biology, Villanova U., 1958; MD, Jefferson Med. Coll., 1962. Diplomate: Am. Bd. Internal Medicine (Nephrology). Intern Michael Reese Hosp., Chgo., 1962-63; resident Thomas Jefferson U. Hosp., 1963-65, NIH fellow in nephrology, 1965-67, Martin E. Rehfuss chief resident internal medicine, 1967-68; practice medicine specializing in nephrology Haddonfield, N.J., 1968—; clin. prof. medicine U. Medicine and Dentistry N.J., 1995—; pres. Lourdes Med. Assn., P.A. and Health Mgmt. Svcs. Orgn., Inc., 1995—, Nephrology Network for N.J., P.C., 1995—; dir. div. clin. pharmacology Jefferson Med. Coll., Phila., 1968-69; dir. hemodialysis unit Our Lady of Lourdes Med. Ctr., Camden, N.J., 1969—, dir. div. nephrology and transplantation, 1974—, chief of staff, 1980-86, v.p. med. affairs, 1987—; clin. prof. medicine Thomas Jefferson U., Phila., 1974—; mem. chronic renal disease adv. com. N.J. Dept. Health, 1969-79, chmn., 1971-73, 74-75; pres. Health Mgmt. Svcs. Orgns., Inc., 1995—, N.J. Renal Mgmt., 1996—. Discovered extra-renal source of renin in uterus, 1968; contbr. articles to med. jours. Named to Order of Knights St. Gregory, 1995. Mem. Am. Soc. Nephrology, Internat. Soc. Nephrology, Renal Physicians Assn. (pres. 1977-79), AMA, Med. Soc. N.J., Am. Soc. Artificial Internal Organs, Southeastern Organ Procurement Found., Nat. Kidney Found. Roman Catholic. Office: Haddon Renal Med Specialists 35 Kings Hwy E Haddonfield NJ 08033-2009

CAPEN, CHARLES CHABERT, veterinary pathology educator, researcher; b. Tacoma, Sept. 3, 1936; s. Charles Kenneth and Ruth (Chabert) C.; m. Sharron Lee Martin, June 27, 1968. DVM, Wash. State U., 1960; MS, Ohio State U., 1961, PhD, 1965. Diplomate Am. Coll. Vet. Pathologists (pres. 1978-79, coun. 1975-81). Instr. dept. vet. pathology Ohio State U., Columbus, 1962-65, asst. prof. dept. vet. pathology, 1965-67, assoc. prof., 1967-70, prof., 1970—, prof. endocrinology Coll. Medicine, 1972—, chmn. dept. vet. pathobiology, 1981-94, chmn., 1982-94, interim chmn. dept. bioscis., 1994-97; chmn., 1997—; Israel Doniach Meml. lectr. Brit. Endocrine Soc. meeting, Manchester, 1989; plenary lectr. Italian Soc. Endocrinology Congress, Pisa, 1995. Editor: (series) Animal Models of Human Disease, 1979-96; mem. editorial bd. Lab. Investigation, 1988—, Vet. Pathology, 1986-87, Am. Jour. Pathology, 1984-88, Exptl. and Toxicologic Pathology, 1990—, Food and Chem. Toxicology, 1993—, Drug and Chem. Toxicology, 1994—, Toxicology and Ecotoxicology News, 1993—, Handbook on Rat Tumor Pathology WHO/IARC, 1991-96. Mem. Opera Columbus, 1982—, Columbus Symphony Assn., 1972—. Recipient Disting. scholar award Ohio State U., 1993, Dean's Tchg. Excellence award for grad. edn. Coll. Vet. Medicine, 1993, Disting. Vet. Alumnus award Wash. State U., 1997, Career Achievement award in canine rsch. Am. Vet. Med. Found., 1997. Mem. Inst. Medicine/NAS, AVMA (nat. Borden rsch. award 1975, small animal rsch. award 1984, Gaines rsch. award 1987, excellence in canine rsch. award 1995, George Scott Meml. award of Toxicology Forum 1997), U.S. Can. Acad. Pathology (coun. 1989-92), Soc. Toxicol. Pathologists (pres. 1997-98). Avocations: wildlife and nature photography, travel. Office: The Ohio State U Dept Vet Bioscis 1925 Coffey Rd Columbus OH 43210-1005

CAPENER, REGNER ALVIN, electronics engineer, minister, author, inventor; b. Astoria, Oreg., Apr. 18, 1942; s. Alvin Earnest and Lillian Lorraine (Lehtosaari) C.; divorced; children: Deborah, Christian, Melodie, Ariella; m. Della Denise Melson, May 17, 1983; children: Shelley, Danielle, Rebekah, Joshua. Student, U. Nebr., 1957-58, 59-60, Southwestern Coll., Waxahachie, Tex., 1958-59, Bethany Bible Coll., 1963-64. Ordained minister Full Gospel Assembly Ch., 1971. Rsch. engr. Lockheed Missiles & Space Corp., Palo Alto, Calif., 1962-64; engr., talk show host Sta. KHOF-FM, Glendale, Calif., 1966-67; youth min. Bethel Union Ch., Duarte, Calif., 1966-67; pres. Intermountain Electronics, Salt Lake City, 1967-72; assoc. pastor Full Gospel Assembly, Salt Lake City, 1968-72, Long Beach (Calif.) Christian Ctr., 1972-76; v.p. Refuge Ministries, Inc., Long Beach, 1972-76; pres. Christian Broadcasting Network-Alaska, Inc., Fairbanks, 1977-83; gen. mgr. Action Sch. of Broadcasting, Anchorage, 1983-85; pres., pastor House of Praise, Anchorage, 1984-93; chief engr. KTBY-TV, Inc., Anchorage, 1988-93; pres. R & DC Engring., Anchorage, 1993—; area dir. Christian Broadcasting Network, Virginia Beach, 1977-83; cons., dir. Union Bond and Trust Co., Anchorage, 1985-86; author, editor univ. courses, 1984-85; dep. gov. Am. Biog. Inst. Rsch. Assn., 1990—. Author: Spiritual Maturity, 1975, Spiritual Warfare, 1976, The Doctrine of Submission, 1988, A Vision for Praise, 1988, Ekklesia, 1993, For the Marriage of the Lamb Has Come, 1996, Open Letters to the Ekklesia, 1997; author, composer numerous gospel songs; creator numerous broadcasting and electronic instrument inventions. Sec., Christian Businessmen's Com., Salt Lake City, 1968-72; area advisor Women's Aglow Internat., Fairbanks, 1981-83; local co-chmn. campaign Boucher for Gov. Com., Fairbanks, 1982; campaigner for Boucher, Anchorage, 1984, Clark Gruening for Senate Com., Barrow, Alaska, 1980; TV producer Stevens for U.S. Senate, Barrow, 1978; fundraiser City of Refuge, Mex., 1973-75; statewide rep. Sudden Infant Death Syndrome, Barrow, 1978-82; founder Operation Blessing/Alaska, 1981; mem. resch. bd. advisors Am. Biog. Inst., 1990—; advisor Anchorage chpt. Women's Aglow Internat., 1990-91. Mem. Soc. Broadcast Engrs., Internat. Soc. Classical Guitarists (sec. 1967-69), Alaska Broadcaster's Assn., Nat. Assn. Broadcasters, Anchorage C. of C. Republican. Avocations: musician, ancient history, ancient langs. Office: R & DC Engring 709 S 7th St Sunnyside WA 98944-2218 *The word "impossible" need never be a part of the vocabulary of one whose life is intertwined with the Lord Jesus Christ. I have learned that there are no problems in life which do not have clear and definitive solutions when approached from the standpoint of a personal relationship with Jesus Christ.*

CAPERS, DOMINIC, professional football coach; b. Cambridge, Ohio, Aug. 5, 1950. BS in Psychology and Phys. Edn., Mount Union Coll.; MA in Adminstrn., Kent State U. Grad. asst. Kent State U., 1972-74, U. Wash.; defensive backs coach U. Hawaii, 1975, defensive coach, 1976; defensive asst. coach San Jose State, 1977, U. Calif., 1978-79; defensive backs coach U. Tenn., 1980-81, Ohio State, 1982-83, Phila. Stars (USFL), 1984, Balt. Stars (USFL), 1985, New Orleans Saints, 1986-91; defensive coord. Pitts. Steelers, 1992-94; head coach Carolina Panthers, 1995-98; defensive coord. Jacksonville Jaguars, 1999—. Office: Jacksonville Jaguars ALLTEL Stadium One ALLTEL Stadium Pl Jacksonville FL 32202*

CAPERTON, ALBERT FRANKLIN, newspaper editor; b. Hemphill, W.Va., Dec. 31, 1936; s. Albert Harrison and Viola (Hicks) C.; m. Elizabeth Moreland, Jan. 29, 1960; children—Catherine Elizabeth, Robert Harrell. B., Northwestern State U., 1962; M.Jour., Columbia U., 1965; cert. Advanced Mgmt. Program, Harvard U., 1982. Reporter Richmond News Leader, Va., 1962-64; reporter St Petersburg Times, Fla., 1965-67, Tampa Tribune, Fla., 1967-69; asst. city editor Miami Herald, Fla., 1969-72; Broward County editor Miami Herald, Fort Lauderdale, Fla., 1972-75; exec. editor Macon Telegraph & News, Ga., 1975-78, Virginian-Pilot & Ledger Star, Norfolk, 1978-84; mng. editor Indpls. News, 1984-90, Indpls. Star, 1990-95; exec. editor Indpls. (Ind.) Star and News, 1995—. Pres. Crossroads of Am. Coun. Boy Scouts of Am., Indpls., 1991-92; trustee Christian Theol. Sem. With USAF, 1954-57. Mem. Am. Soc. Newspaper Editors, Rotary. Mem. Diciples of Christ. Avocations: reading, tennis. Home: 6432 Landborough North Dr Indianapolis IN 46220-4351 Office: Indianapolis Star 307 N Pennsylvania St Indianapolis IN 46204-1811

CAPERTON, RICHARD WALTON, automobile repair company executive, educator, consultant; b. Waynesburg, Pa., Jan. 11, 1948; s. Walton Greene Caperton and Sareta (Campbell) Garetson ; children: Richard Walton Jr., Christa Elizabeth. Grad. high sch., Naples, Fla. Asst. mgr. W.T. Grant

Co., Naples, 1967-75; pres., chief exec. officer, gen. mgr. R&R Automotive Inc., Naples, 1975-95, CEO, 1996; pres., chief exec. officer AAMGO Auto Parts Inc., Naples, 1987-91; pres. Caperton Properties, 1977—, Nu U Mktg., 1991-95, Caperton Consulting, 1994—; instr. Walker Tech. Inst., 1996-97; advt. cons. Edwards Publs., 1998—. Bd. dirs. East Naples Civic Assn., 1979-80; v.p. Fla. Sports Park, Naples, 1997, pres., 1997-98, bd. dirs., 1987—; mem. adv. bd. J. L. Walker VoTech, 1991-95; apptd. to Fla. New Motor Vehicle Arbitration Bd., 1994-97. Fellow Automobile Svc. Assn., Rotary (bd. dirs. Naples East 1987-96, v.p. Naples East 1990-91, pres. 1996-97). Republican. Methodist. Avocations: golf, scuba diving, boating, shooting. Home: 233 Hughes St Seneca SC 29672-2373

CAPICE, PHILIP CHARLES, television production executive; b. Bernardsville, N.J., June 24, 1931; s. Philip Joseph and Angelina Mary (Togno) C.;. B.A., Dickinson Coll., 1952; M.F.A., Columbia U., 1954. Production supr., assoc. program dir. Benton & Bowles Inc., N.Y.C., 1954-64, Vice pres. in charge program devel., 1965-69; dir. spl. programs CBS-TV Network, N.Y.C., 1969-74; sr. v.p. creative affairs Lorimar Prodns., Burbank, Calif., 1974-78; pres. Lorimar TV, Burbank, Calif., 1978-79; ind. producer Lorimar Productions, Culver City, Calif., from 1979; pres., chief exec. officer Raven's Claw Productions, Los Angeles, Calif. Since 1974, exec. producer Dallas, Eight Is Enough, The Blue Knight, Two Marriages, Helter Skelter, Sybil (Emmy Award, 1977, Peabody Award, 1977), Green Eyes (Peabody Award, 1978, Humanitas Prize, 1978), Eric, Widow, Studs Lonigan, A Man Called Intrepid, The Runaways, The Prince of Central Park, A Question of Guilt, Some Kind of Miracle (Christopher Award, 1978), Returning Home, Conspiracy of Terror, Hunter, Married: The First Year, The Rivermen, Mary and Joseph: A Love Story, The Stranger Within, A Matter of Life and Death, Bunco, Some People Like Us, Private Sessions, others. Trustee Dickinson Coll. Recipient Emmy award, 1977, Peabody award, 1977, 78. Mem. Acad. TV Arts and Scis., The Caucus for Producers, Writers and Dirs.

CAPITAN, WILLIAM HARRY, university president emeritus; b. Owosso, Mich., Feb. 7, 1933; s. Harry and Anthe (Sarris) C.; m. Dolores Marie Randolph, Sept. 19, 1959; children: Rita, Edwin. B.A., U. Mich., 1954; postgrad., Queens U.; postgrad. (Ulster Am. fellow), 1954-55; M.A., U. Minn., 1958, Ph.D., 1960. Instr. philosophy U. Minn., 1959-60, U. Md., 1960-62; asst. prof., assoc. prof., chmn. dept. Oberlin (Ohio) Coll., 1962-70; dean fine arts, v.p. acad. affairs, acting pres. Saginaw Valley State U., U. Ctr., Mich., 1970-74; v.p. acad. affairs, dean faculty, acting pres. W.Va. Wesleyan Coll., Buckhannon, 1974-79; pres. Ga. Southwestern U/, Americus, 1979-95; pres. emeritus Ga. Southwestern Coll., Americus, 1996—; adj. prof. U. Ga., 1996; ednl. cons. Sangamon State U., Ill., Evergreen State Coll., Bd. Govs. State Colls. and Univs. Ill. Author: Introduction to the Philosophy of Religion, 1972, Speak For Yourself, 1987; editor: (with D.D. Merrill) Metaphysics and Explanation, Art, Religion, and Mind, 1967. Bd. dirs. Saginaw Symphony Orch., 1970-74, Project Save, Buckhannon C. of C., Sumter County United Way; trustee Charles L. Mix Meml. Fund., Inc., 1979-96; pres. Americus Sumter County C. of C., 1985; v.p. Hellenic-Am. C. of C., Atlanta. Am. Council Lerned Socs. fellow Paris, 1967-68. Mem. Am. Soc. Aesthetics, Am. Philos. Assn., Rotary (pres. 1990-91), Beta Theta Phi, Omicron Delta Kappa, Phi Kappa Phi, Phi Delta Kappa. Episcopalian. Office: GA Southwestern State U Americus GA 31709 *Clarity of objectives, persistence, and Christian respect for persons have guided me in whatever of value I have accomplished. My failures came when I wasn't very clear about what I was doing. America rewards, supports, and buoys up those with initiative. This is why my parents were able to go from "rags to riches" and I from illiterate to lettered. We Americans help one another, and we shape our institutions to help, too. May we ever remain so.*

CAPIZZI, MICHAEL ROBERT, prosecutor; b. Detroit, Oct. 19, 1939; s. I.A. and Adelaide E. (Jennelle) C.; m. Sandra Jo Jones, June 22, 1963; children: Cori Anne, Pamela Jo. BS in Bus. Adminstrn., Ea. Mich. U., 1961; JD, U. Mich., 1964. Bar: Calif. 1965, U.S. Dist. Ct. (so. dist.) Calif. 1965, U.S. Ct. Appeals (9th cir.) 1970, U.S. Supreme Ct. 1971. Dep. dist. atty. Orange County, Calif., 1965-68; head writs, appeals and spl. assignments sect., 1968-71, asst. dist. atty., dir. spl. ops., 1971-86; legal counsel, mem. exec. bd. Interstate Organized Crime Index, 1971-79; legal counsel, mem. exec. bd. Law Enforcement Intelligence Unit, 1971-95, chief asst. dist. atty., 1986-90, dist. atty., 1990-99; instr. criminal justice Santa Ana Coll., 1967-76, Calif. State U., 196-87. Commr. City Planning Commn., Fountain Valley, Calif., 1971-80, vice chmn. 1972-73, chmn. 1973-75, 79-80; candidate for Rep. nomination Calif. Atty. Gen., 1998. Fellow Am. Coll. Trial Lawyers; mem. Nat. Dist. Attys. Assn. (bd. dirs. 1995-96, v.p. 1996-99), Calif. Dist. Attys. Assn. (outstanding prosecutor award 1980, v.p. 1995, pres. 1996), Calif. Bar Assn., Orange County Bar Assn. (chmn. cts. com. 1977, chmn. coll. of trial advocacy com. 1978-81, bd. dirs. 1977-81, sec.-treas. 1982, pres. 1984). Office: PO Box 1938 Santa Ana CA 92702

CAPIZZI, ROBERT LAWRENCE, physician; b. Phila., Nov. 20, 1938; s. Nunzio B. and Nancy (Gatto) C.; m. Barbara Ann Kain, July 10, 1965; children: Robert, Marc, Tara Ann, Mary Catherine. B.S., Temple U., Phila, 1960; M.D., Hahnemann Med. Coll., Phila., 1964. Asst. prof. medicine and pharmacology Yale U., New Haven, 1972-75, assoc. prof. medicine and pharmacology, 1975-77, acting chief sect. med. oncology, 1976-77; chief div. med. oncology U. N.C., Chapel Hill, 1977-79, co-dir. div. hematology and oncology, 1980-82; dir. Comprehensive Cancer Ctr., sect. head hematology and oncology Bowman Gray Sch. Medicine, Wake Forest U., Winston-Salem, N.C., 1982-91; exec. v.p. worldwide R&D U.S. Bioscience, West Conshohocken, Pa., 1991-96; Magee prof., chmn. dept. medicine Jefferson Med. Coll., Phila., 1996—; Mem. study sect. Cancer Clin. Investigation Rev. Com., NIH, 1982-85. Served to maj. U.S. Army, 1969-72. Investigator, Howard Hughes Med. Inst., Yale U., 1976-77; recipient Faculty Devel. award Pharm. Mfrs. Assn., Yale U., 1974-76. Mem. Am. Soc. Clin. Oncology (program com. 1983, membership com. 1983), Am. Fedn. Clin. Research (program com. 1983), Piedmont Oncology Assn. (bd. dirs. 1982-91, chmn. 1985-91), Am. Soc. Clin. Investigation. Roman Catholic. Office: Dept Medicine Rm 821 Jefferson Med Coll Philadelphia PA 19107

CAPLAN, EDWIN HARVEY, university dean, accounting educator; b. Boston, Aug. 24, 1926; s. Henry and Dorothy (Nathanson) C.; m. Ramona Hootner, June 20, 1948; children—Gary, Dennis, Jeffrey, Nancy. BBA, U. Mich., 1950, MBA, 1952; PhD, U. Calif., 1965. CPA, Calif., Mich. Ptnr. J.J. Gotlieb & Co., CPAs, Detroit, 1953-56; prof. acctg. Humboldt State U., 1956-61, U. Oreg., 1964-67; prof. U. N.Mex., Albuquerque, 1967-91, assoc. dean Sch. Mgmt., 1982-83, dean Sch. Mgmt., 1989-90, prof. emeritus, 1991—; cons. in field. Contbr. articles to profl. jours. 1st lt. U.S. Army, 1944-46. Mem. AICPA, Am. Acctg. Assn., Inst. Mgmt. Accts. Home: 8201 Harwood Ave NE Albuquerque NM 87110-1517

CAPLAN, HELENE MOSES, psychologist; b. N.Y.C., Apr. 29, 1967; d. Bernard T. and Barbara S. (Haber) Moses; m. Morris Aaron Caplan, June 18, 1995. BA, U. Rochester, 1988; MA, Mich. State U., 1992, PhD, 1996. Lic. psychologist Commonwealth of Pa., 1998, Commonwealth of Va., 1999. Psychology intern Springfield Hosp. Ctr., Sykesville, Md., 1994-95; psychology assoc. Howard County Mental Health Ctr., Columbia, Md., 1995-96; staff psychologist Therapeutic Alts., Pemberton, N.J., 1996; staff psychologist Girard Med. Ctr., Phila., 1997—, mem. med. staff assn. and ethics com. Co-author: (book chpt.) Manual of Developmental Psychopathology, 1995. Mem. APA, Rsch. Soc. on Alcoholism, Mil. Spouses' Club (sec.). Avocations: fitness, travel, gardening. Office: Navy Family Svcs Ctr Naval Air Sta Oceana Virginia Beach VA 23456

CAPLAN, L(AZARUS) DAVID, manufacturing company executive; b. Montreal, Que., Can., May 24, 1940. B in Commerce, McGill U., 1961; sr. mgrs. program, Harvard U., 1979. Articled for Riddell, Stead & Co., Chartered Accts., 1961-64; with Pratt & Whitney Can., Montreal, 1964—, v.p. fin. and adminstrn., 1976-80, exec. v.p., 1980-84, pres., chief oper. officer, 1984-85, pres., chief exec. officer, 1985-94; chmn., CEO, 1994—; past chmn. Aerospace Industries Assn. Can.; past chmn. Indsl. and High Tech. Equipment Sectorial Adv. Group on Internat., co-pres. Greater Montreal 1995 Centraide Campaign. Mem. Can. Inst. Chartered Accts., Bus. Coun. on Nat. Issues, Gen. Aviation Mfrs. Assn. (chmn. 1999—). Avocations: bridge, golf. Office: Pratt & Whitney Can, 1000 Marie Victorin Blvd, Longueuil, PQ Canada J4G 1A1

CAPLAN, LOUIS ROBERT, neurology educator; b. Balt., Dec. 31, 1936; s. Carl Clarence and Bess Pauline (Cohen) C.; m. F. Brenda Fields, Nov. 28, 1963; children: Laura, Daniel, Jonathan, David, Jeremy, Benjamin. BA cum laude, Williams Coll., 1958; MD summa cum laude, U. Md., 1962. Diplomate Am. Bd. Internal Medicine, Am. Bd. Psychiatry and Neurology. Intern to jr. asst. resident Boston City Hosp., 1962-64; resident Harvard Neurol. Unit, Boston, 1966-69; cerebrovascular fellow Mass. Gen. Hosp., Boston, 1969-70; neurologist Beth Israel Hosp., Boston, 1970-78; asst. prof. Harvard Med. Sch., Boston, 1970-78, prof. neurology, 1999; chief neurologist Michael Reese Hosp., Chgo., 1978-84; prof. neurology U. Chgo., 1980-84; chief neurologist New England Med. Ctr., Boston, 1984-97; prof., chmn. dept. neurology Tufts U., Boston, 1984-97, prof. medicine, 1989-97; neurologist Beth Israel Deaconess Med. Ctr., Boston, 1998—. Author: Stroke: A Clinical Approach, 1986, 2d edit., 1993, Consultations in Neurology, 1987, The Effective Clinical Neurologist, 1990, Vertebrobasilar Arterial Disease, 1991, (with others) Cerebral Small Artery Disease, 1993, Management of Persons with Stroke, 1993, Brainstem Localization and Function, 1993, Intercerebral Hemmorhage, 1994, Family Guide to Stroke, 1994, Brain Ischemia—Basic Concepts and Clinical Relevance, 1995, Stroke Syndromes, 1995, Posterior Circulation Disease, 1996; Neurologic Disorders: Course and Treatment, 1996, Primer on Cerebrovascular Diseases, 1997, (with others) Clinical Neurocardiology, 1999; contbr. more than 350 articles to profl. jours. Bd. dirs. Solomon Schecter Day Sch., Boston, 1977-78, Chgo., 1983-85. Capt. U.S. Army, 1962-64. Recipient House Officer Teaching prize Michael Reese Hosp., 1980. Fellow Am. Acad. Neurology, Am. Neurol. Assn., Stroke Coun. Am. Heart Assn. (chmn. 1987-89, sci. adv. com. 1990—), Royal Soc. of Medicine; mem. Coun. Med. Specialties Socs. (rep. 1982-90), Chgo. Neurol. Soc. (chmn. 1984-85), Boston Soc. Neurology and Psychiatry (pres. 1988-89), Chgo. Heart Assn. (chmn. stroke com. 1979-84), Australian Neurol. Soc. (hon.), German Neurol. Assn. (hon.), Phi Beta Kappa, Alpha Omega Alpha. Democrat. Jewish. Office: Beth Israel Deaconess MC Dept Neurology 330 Brookline Ave Dept Boston MA 02215-5400

CAPLAN, RICHARD MELVIN, retired medical educator, musician, author; b. Des Moines, July 16, 1929; s. Carl and Iylene Edith (Lambe) C.; m. Fredda Ellen Sideman, June 15, 1952; children: David, Joel, Daniel, Aaron. BS, Iowa State U., 1949; MA, U. Iowa, 1951, MD, 1955. Diplomate Am. Bd. Dermatology. Resident dept. dermatology U. Mich. Med. Ctr., Ann Arbor, 1958-61; asst. prof. dermatology U. Iowa Coll. Medicine, Iowa City, 1961-65, assoc. prof., 1965-69, prof., 1969-97, dir. Office of Med. Edn., 1969-70, asst. dean for continuing med. edn., 1970-74, assoc. dean for continuing med. edn., 1974-91, acting head dept. dermatology, 1976-78, vice chmn. dept. dermatology, 1978-90, dir. program in med. humanities, 1981-91, prof. emeritus dermatology and program in biomed. ethics, 1997—. Author/editor 3 books; contbr. numerous chpts. to books, more than 120 articles to profl. jours. Bd. dirs., pres. Hillel Found., U. Iowa, Iowa City, 1965-83; bd. dirs. Preucel Sch. Music, Iowa City, 1995-97; founder, bd. dirs. The Younger Stamfords, Iowa City, 1988—. Capt. USAF, 1955-58. Recipient numerous awards. Fellow Am. Acad. Dermatology; mem. AMA, Am. Dermatol. Assn., Soc. for Med. Coll. Dirs. Continuing Med. Edn. (sec.-tres. 1978-80, pres. 1981-82, historian 1990-95), Am. Osler Soc. (bd. dirs. 1991-94), Soc. for Health and Human Values, Iowa Med. Soc., Johnson County Med. Soc., Iowa Dermatol. Soc. (pres. 1968-69), Phi Beta Pi, Alpha Epsilon Pi, others. Avocations: music (piano, composition), gardening, Sherlock Holmes. Office: U Iowa 1-104 MEB Iowa City IA 52242

CAPLES, ANNE L., healthcare consultant, former nursing educator; b. Norfolk, Va., Dec. 16, 1939; d. Martin H. and Alice (Leigh) C. Diploma in nursing, Orange (N.J.) Meml. Hosp., 1961; BSN, U. Va., 1964; MA, Ea. Mich. U., 1980; cert., Villanova U., 1984. RN, Mich., Pa., N.J., N.Y. Head nurse, ICU St. Luke's Med. Ctr., N.Y., 1965-69; staff nurse Rutland (Vt.) Hosp., 1969-70; coord. inservice edn. Beekman Downtown Hosp., N.Y., 1970-72; staff nurse St. Mary's Hosp., London, 1972-73; dir. staff devel. Helene Fuld Hosp., Trenton, N.J., 1973-74; asst. DON, staff devel. Hurley Med. Ctr., Flint, Mich., 1974-78; asst. prof. nursing U. Mich., Ann Arbor, 1978-81; dir. nursing St. Luke's Hosp., Bethlehem, Pa., 1981-86; dir. edn. Healthcare Info. Network, Princeton, N.J., 1986-88; dir. teleconf. networks Annenberg Ctr., Eisenhower Med. Ctr., Rancho Mirage, Calif., 1988-92; pres. Internat. Healthcare, Inc., Denver, 1992-96; healthcare cons., Grand Island, Fla., 1996—; mem. adv. bd. Telerounds, U. Ariz., 1991—; establisher stds. Satellite Continuing Edn. Credit for Healthcare Profls. Media rev. columnist Date Line; exec. producer Bright Horizons in Respiratory Care. Organizer Baker Neighborhood, Baker Guardian Angels; rep. to Denver Inter-Neighborhood Coop. Fellow Am. Soc. for Healthcare, Edn. and Tng. of Am. Hosp. Assn. (bd. dirs. 1990, past pres. 1982, Disting. Svc. award, Past Pres.'s award Mich. chpt., cert. of appreciation San Diego chpt., chair 1996 ann. conf. com.); mem. AAUW (charter mem.), Nat. Nursing Staff Devel. Orgn., Internat. Assn. for Continuing Edn. and Tng., Alliance for Continuing Edn., Sigma Theta Tau.

CAPLES, RICHARD JAMES, dance company executive, lawyer; b. Balt., June 7, 1949; s. Delphin Delmas and Louise Skinner (Leigh) C. BA, Yale U., 1971; MA, Johns Hopkins U., 1974; JD, Cornell U., 1977. Bar: N.Y. 1978, U.S. Dist. Ct. (so. and ea. dists.) N.Y. 1978. Assoc. Donovan Leisure Newton & Irvine, N.Y.C., 1977-81, Shearman & Sterling, N.Y.C., 1981-83; exec. dir. Santa Fe Festival Theater, 1983-84, Lar Lubovitch Dance Co., N.Y.C., 1984—; dir. Doug Varone and Dancers, N.Y.C., 1995—; dir. Dance/USA, Washington, 1995—, also sec. bd., 1998—; bd. dirs. Park 58 Corp., , N.Y.C., 1989—, pres. 1994—; dir. Dean Dance and Music Found., N.Y.C., 1981-84. Mem. Am. Soc. Internat. Law, N.Y. State Bar Assn., Am. Coun. on Germany, Johns Hopkins Alumni Assn. (bd. dirs. N.Y.C. chpt. 1988-92), Univ. Club, Yale Club, Johns Hopkins Club (Balt.). Episcopalian. Home: 470 Park Ave New York NY 10022-1903 Office: Lar Lubovitch Dance Co 625 Broadway Ste 11 H New York NY 10012-2611

CAPLIN, JERROLD LEON, health physicist; b. Phila., Jan. 25, 1930; s. Samuel Harry and Katherine (Socloff) C.; children: Sally C. Daniels, Patricia Graham Reed. AB, Temple U., 1951, postgrad., 1952-53, Vanderbilt U., 1951-52. Supervisory health physicist U.S. Army C.E., Ft. Belvoir, Va., 1959-61; health physicist AEC, U.S. Nuclear Regulatory Commn., Washington, 1961-81, ret., 1981; cons., 1981—; guest lectr. radiation sci. Georgetown U. Grad. Sch., 1987-97; sr. scientist Advanced Sys. Tech., Inc., 1993-97; photographer, newspaper editor, sci. writer, 1983—. Co-author, editor Manual Respiratory Protection Against Airborne Radioactive Materials, 1976. Active Nat. Mus. of Women in Arts, Friends of the Nat. Zoo, Friends of the Kennedy Ctr. Lt. USNR, 1953-58. AEC Radiol. Physics fellow Vanderbilt U., 1951-52. Mem. AAAS, ASTM, Am. Nat. Standards Inst., Am. Conf. Gov. Indsl. Hygienists (chm. com. 1977-83), Am. Assn. Physics Tchrs., Am. Film Inst., Internat. Radiation Protection Assn., U.S. Naval Inst., Nat. Wildlife Fedn., Nat. Geog. Soc., Nat. Trust for Hist. Preservation, Health Physics Soc., Smithsonian Instn. (resident assoc. 1970—), Wilderness Soc., Libr. of Congress Assocs., Com. Sci. Investigation of Claims of the Paranormal Assn. Home and Office: 9 Goodport Ln Gaithersburg MD 20878-1001

CAPLIN, MORTIMER MAXWELL, lawyer, educator; b. N.Y.C., July 11, 1916; s. Daniel and Lillian (Epstein) C.; m. Ruth Sacks, Oct. 18, 1942; children: Lee Evan, Michael Andrew, Jeremy Owen, Catherine Jean. BS, U. Va., 1937, LLB, 1940; JSD, NYU, 1953; LLD (hon.), St. Michael's Coll., 1964. Bar: Va. 1941, N.Y. 1942, D.C. 1964. Law clk. to Hon. Armistead M. Dobie U.S. Ct. Appeals (4th cir.), Richmond, 1940-41; assoc. Paul, Weiss, Rifkind, Wharton & Garrison, N.Y.C., 1941-42, 45-50; prof. law U. Va., Charlottesville, 1950-61, vis. prof. law, 1965-87; prof. emeritus, 1988—; ptnr. Perkins, Battle & Minor, Charlottesville, 1952-61; U.S. commr. IRS, Washington, 1961-64; sr. ptnr. Caplin & Drysdale, Washington, 1964—; mem. Pres.'s Task Force on Taxation, 1960; bd. dirs. Danaher Corp., Washington, Fairchild Corp., Chantilly, Va., Presdl. Realty Corp., White Plains, N.Y.; mem. pub. rev. bd. Arthur Andersen & Co., Chgo., 1980-88; reorgn. trustee Webb & Knapp, Inc., 1965-72. Author: Proxies, Annual Meetings and Corporate Democracy, 1953, Doing Business in Other States, 1959; editor-in-chief Va. Law Rev., 1939-40; contbr. numerous articles on tax and corp. matters to profl. jours. Past chmn. bd. dirs. Nat. Civic Svc. League, Am. Coun. on Internat. Sports; past chmn. nat citizens adv. com. Assn. Am. Med. Colls.; trustee U. Va. Law Sch. Found., Wolf Trap Found. Performing Arts, Shakespeare Theatre, Washington, Peace Through Law Found., Washington; bd. overseers U. V.I.; chmn. adv. bd. Hospitality and Info. Svc., Washington; chmn. Coun. for Arts, U. Va.; past pres. Atlantic Coast Conf.; emeritus trustee George Washington U.; mem. bd. visitors U. Va., 1992-97; pres., bd. dirs. Indigent Civil Litigation Fund. Cited as mem. of initial landing force Normandy Invasion, USN; recipient Va. State Bar and Va. Soc. CPAs award, 1960, Achievement award Tax Soc. of NYU, 1962, Judge Learned Hand Human Rels. award Am. Jewish Com., 1963, 93, Alexander Hamilton award U.S. Treasury Dept., 1964, Disting. Svc. award Tax Execs. Inst., 1964. Fellow Am. Bar Found., Am. Tax Policy Inst., Am. Coll. Tax Counsel; mem. ABA (ho. of dels. 1980-92, mem. fed. jud. com. 1993-96, ALI-ABA com. continuing profl. edn.), Am. Law Inst. (life), N.Y. State Bar Assn., Va. Bar Assn., D.C. Bar Assn., D.C. Bar Found. (adv. com.), Univ. Club (N.Y.C., Washington), Fed. City Club, Colonnade Club (Charlottesville), Order of Coif, Phi Beta Kappa, Phi Beta Kappa Assocs., Omicron Delta Kappa. Democrat. Jewish. Avocations: swimming, tennis, hiking. Home: 5610 Wisconsin Ave Apt 18E Chevy Chase MD 20815-4415 Office: One Thomas Circle NW Washington DC 20005-5802

CAPLINGER, PATRICIA E., family nurse practitioner; b. St. Louis, Oct. 6, 1956; d. Julius G. and Wanda L. (Guthrie) Kissel; child from previous marriage, Jeremy Michael Frederiksen; m. Ray E. Caplinger, Dec. 26, 1995. ADN, St. Louis C.C., 1977; BSN, U. State N.Y., 1982; FNP, U. Colo., Denver, 1985. RN, Colo.; CNOR, CNRN; cert. family nurse practitioner. Med. case mgmt. supr. Intracorp., Denver; clin. mgr. Rehab. Svcs. Corp., Eureka, Calif.; family nurse practitioner Burre Clinic, Eureka; pvt. practice Eureka; dir. PM&R Marian Health Ctr., Sioux City, Iowa; family nurse practitioner St. John's Physicians and Clinics, Lebanon, Mo. Mem. ANA (nursing scholar), ARN, AANP. Home: 23241 Red Oak Dr Lebanon MO 65536-5895

CAPLOW, THEODORE, sociologist; b. N.Y.C., May 1, 1920; s. Samuel Nathaniel and Florence (Israel) C.; m. Margaret Mary Pettit, 1981. AB, U. Chgo., 1939; PhD, U. Minn., 1946. Mem. faculty U. Minn., 1945-60; prof. sociology Columbia U., 1961-70; chmn. dept. sociology U. Va., Charlottesville, 1970-78, 84-86; Commonwealth prof. U. Va., 1973—; vis. prof. U. Bordeaux, France, 1950, U. Aix-Marseille, France, 1951, U. Utrecht, Netherlands, 1954-55, Stanford, 1957, P.R., 1959, U. Bogota, Colombia, 1962, Sorbonne, Paris, France, 1968-69, Institut d'Etudes Politiques, Paris, 1983, U. Rome, 1984, U. Oslo, 1986; pres. Mendota Research Group Inc., 1957-65. Author: Sociology of Work, 1954, Principles of Organization, 1964, Two Against One, 1968, L'Enquête Sociologique, 1970, Toward Social Hope, 1975, Peace Games, 1989, American Social Trends, 1991, Perverse Incentives, 1994; sr. author: The Academic Marketplace, 1957, The Urban Ambience, 1964, Middletown Families, 1982, All Faithful People, 1983, Recent Social Trends in the United States, 1960-90, 1991, Systems of War and Peace, 1995. Served with AUS, 1943-45, PTO. Decorated Purple Heart. Mem. Tocqueville Soc. (pres. 1979-83), Am. Sociol. Assn. (sec. 1983-86), Farmington Hunt Club (Charlottesville), Century Club (N.Y.C.), Tarratine Club (Dark Harbor, Maine). Home: Twin Springs 793 Reas Ford Rd Earlysville VA 22936-2306

CAPOBIANCO, ANNA THERESA, retired patient education specialist; b. Bklyn., Dec. 1, 1931; d. Carmen and Loretta (Botte) C. Diploma, St. Mary's Hosp. Sch. Nursing, 1952; BSN, St. John's U., 1957; MSN, Cath. U. Am., 1961; PhD, NYU, 1975. Cert. diabetes educator, N.Y. Staff nurse St. Mary's Hosp., Bklyn.; faculty St. Mary's Hosp. Sch. Nursing, Bklyn.; per diem nurse St. Giles Orthopedic Hosp., Bklyn., Meml. Hosp., N.Y.C.; instr. NYU, N.Y.C.; cons. dept. test devel. Nat. League Nursing, N.Y.C.; asst. coord. patient edn., diabetes case mgr. St. Mary's Hosp. of Bklyn.; ret., 1994. Mem. ANA, Sigma Theta Tau.

CAPOBIANCO, TITO, opera director; b. La Plata, Argentina, Aug. 28, 1931; m. Gigi Elena; 2 children. MA in Music, U. Buenos Aires, 1956; MusD (hon.), Duquesne U., 1988; LittD (hon.), Ind. U. Pa., 1988; LHD (hon.), LaRoche Coll., Pitts., 1989. Prof. U. Chile, Santiago, 1954-56; tech. dir. Teatro Colon, Argentina, 1958-62; gen. dir. Chile Opera Co., La Plata, 1959-61, 1967-70; artistic dir. Cin. Opera, 1961-65, Cin. Opera Festival, 1961-65; gen. dir. Canary Islands Opera Festival, 1973-75; artistic dir. San Diego Opera, 1975-77, gen. dir., 1977-83; gen. dir. Pitts. Opera, 1983-97, artistic dir., 1997—. Founder, San Diego Opera Ctr., 1977, Verdi Opera Festival, San Diego, 1978, Young Am. Opera Condrs. Program, 1980, dir., producer maj. opera cos. in Argentina, Australia, France, Fed. Republic of Germany, Holland, Italy, Mex., Spain and, U.S., including, N.Y.C., Phila., Houston, San Francisco, Washington, Met. Opera, prof. acting and interpretation, Acad. Vocal Arts, Phila., 1962-68, founder, gen. dir., Juilliard Sch. Music, N.Y.C., Am. Opera Ctr., 1968-71, dir. opera studies, Music Acad. West, 1983; prof. acting, staging, and interpretation Yale U. Sch. Music, 1983-90; prof. acting, staging and interpretation, Dunguesne U. Sch. Music, 1990, trustee Nat. Inst. Music Theater, 1981—; bd. dirs. Opera Am., 1985-87; founder Pitts. Opera Ctr., 1986; dir., Council of Arts, Argentina, 1959-61 (Named One of Ten Best Talents in Argentina 1968); Operatic debut in I Pagliacci, Teatro Argentino, La Plata, 1953; theatre debut, State Co., Buenos Aires, 1954. Named Hon. citizen Balt., New Orleans, and Miami; recipient Cavaliere award (Italy), 1979; decorated officer Order Arts and Letters (France), 1984, Gov. of Penn. Artist of the Year Award, 1997. Office: 801 Penn Ave Fl 3 Pittsburgh PA 15222-3609

CAPOLARELLO, JOE R., photojournalist; b. Bklyn., Sept. 6, 1961; s. Carmelo and Grace (Auditore) C. Cert. news prodn. and tech., Inst. New Cinema Artists, N.Y.C., 1981; cert. TV News Video Workshop, U. Okla., Norman, 1986; cert. TV News Feature Workshop, Internat. Film & TV Workshops, Rockport, Maine, 1987; cert. Leadership in Broadcast Photojournalism, The Poynter Inst. for Media Studies, St. Petersburg, Fla., 1992. Photojournalist, videotape editor, field producer W.Va. Jour. Sta. WSWP-TV, Beckley, W.Va., 1982-83; photojournalist Eyewitness News Sta. WABC-TV, N.Y.C., 1983; photojournalist Bus. Times, ESPN, N.Y.C., 1984, Broadcast News Svc., N.Y.C., 1984, Cable News Network, Inc., N.Y.C., 1984—, Entertainment Tonight, Paramount Pictures Corp., N.Y.C., 1988-91, Fox News at Seven, The Ten O'Clock News, Sta. WNYW-TV, N.Y.C., 1988-91, USA Today: The Television Show, Grant Tinker/Gannett East Prodns. Inc., N.Y.C., 1988-89, Preview: the best of the new, TV Program Enterprises, N.Y.C., 1990; photojournalist Personalities Twentieth Century Fox Film Corp., N.Y.C., 1991. Mem. Acad. TV Arts and Scis., Nat. Hon. Broadcasting Soc., TV and Radio Working Press Assn., Nat. Press Photographers Assn. Democrat. Avocation: traveling. Home: 1 Liberty St Little Ferry NJ 07643-2303 Office: Cable News Network 5 Penn Plz Fl 21 New York NY 10001-1810

CAPON, EDWIN GOULD, church organization administrator, clergyman; b. Boston, Apr. 1, 1924; s. Gould and Helen (Wood) C.; m. Norma Jean Wilcoxson (div. Jan. 1971); children: Peter Lawrence, Jonathan Edwin; m. Esther Constance Nicastro, Sept. 5, 1975. AB, Harvard U., 1947; STM, Andover-Newton Theol. Sem., 1949. Ordained to ministry Swedenborgian Ch., 1949. Min. Bridgewater (Mass.) New Ch., 1948-51, Elmwood (Mass.) New Ch., 1949-55, Detroit New Ch., Royal Oak, Mich., 1977-79; v.p. Swedenborg Sch. Religion, Cambridge, Mass., 1953-55; pres. Swedenborg Sch. Religion, Cambridge and Newton, Mass., 1955-77; pastor San Francisco Swedenborgian Ch., 1979-90; interim min. St. Paul Swedenborgian Ch., 1991-92, min., 1992-94; pres. The Swedenborgian Ch., Newton, 1992-98, chmn. coun. mins., 1956-67. Trustee Urbana (Ohio) U., 1966-80, 92—; v.p. Mass. Coun. Chs. Avocations: hiking, mountain climbing in New England.

CAPONE, ALPHONSE WILLIAM, retired industrial executive; b. Pitts., Oct. 22, 1919; s. Aniello and Mary (Manzione) C.; m. Eleanor M. Polis, Aug. 16, 1947 (dec. Nov. 1972); 1 child, Margaret Ellen; m. Alvira L. Petty, July 5, 1975. B.B.A., Duquesne U., 1942; postgrad., Harvard U., 1959, Am. U. Sch. Internat. Service, Washington, 1965, Brookings Instn., 1966. With Koppers Co., Inc., Pitts., 1946-84; mgr. fin. dept. internat. ops. Koppers Co., Inc., 1964-67, asst. treas., 1958-67, v.p., chief fin. officer, treas., 1967-77, sr. v.p., chief fin. officer, 1978-84; chmn. bd. Gordon Terminal Svc. Co., Aeolian Enterprises, Inc., Latrobe, Pa., 1993—. Bd. dirs. Duquesne U., chmn., 1979-87. Served to lt. USNR, 1943-46. Mem. AICPA, Pa. Inst. CPAs, Fin. Execs. Inst. (dir., pres. Pitts. chpt. 1974-75), Pitts. C. of C., World Affairs Council Pitts., Duquesne U. Alumni Assn. (past pres., gov.), Am. Mgmt. Assn. (v.p. charge fin. council 1977-79), Machinery and Allied Products Inst. (fin. council), Conf. Bd. (council fin. execs.), Harvard Advanced Mgmt. Assn.,

Harvard Bus. Sch. Assn. Pitts., Duquesne Club. Home and Office: PO Box 4540 Eighty Four PA 15330-0540

CAPONE, ANTONIO, psychiatrist; b. Afragola, Naples, Italy, Feb. 18, 1926; came to U.S., 1954; s. Giulio and Giovanna (Fico) C.; m. Maria Morello, Mar. 21, 1957; children: Antonio Jr., John, Walter. MD, U. Naples, 1953. Diplomate Am. Bd. Med. Psychotherapists, Am. Bd. Psychiatry and Neurology, Internat. Acad. Behavioral Medicine, Am. Bd. Forensic Examiners. Intern Ospedale Incurabili, Naples, 1953-54, St. Francis Hosp., Jersey City, 1954-55; resident physician St. Clare's Hosp., Denville, N.J., 1955-56; hon. staff Butler Hosp., Providence, 1995—; chief psychiatry John E. Fogarty Meml. Hosp., North Smithfield, R.I., 1969-79, Pawtucket (R.I.) Meml. Hosp., 1971-80, St. Joseph Hosp., Providence, 1971-94; clin. asst. prof. psychiatry and human behavior Brown U. Med. Sch., Providence, 1980-95; med. dir. St. Joseph Ctr. for Psychiat. Svcs., Providence, 1987-94; hon. staff St. Joseph Hosp., Providence, 1995—, Pawtucket Meml. Hosp., 1995—; cons. John E. Fogarty Meml. Hosp., North Smithfield, 1995—; chief psychiat. cons. R.I. Divsn. Vocat. Rehab., Providence, 1967-72; med. advisor Dept. HEW, 1967-95; clin. elective course leader Brown Med. Sch., Providence, 1980-95. Contbr. articles to profl. jours. Various presentations on mental health and alcoholism, Lions Club, Kiwanis, TV, and radio. Fellow Am. Psychiat. Assn. (pres. R.I. dist. br. 1968-70, mem. peer rev. com. 1982-95, mem. fellowship com. 1984-95, mem. ad hoc on referral svc. 1987-88); mem. AMA, R.I. Med. Soc., Providence Med. Assn., Psychiatry and Neurology, Pan Am. Med. Assn., Am. Soc. Vienna. Roman Catholic. Avocations: piano playing, gardening, jogging, walking, traveling. Address: PO Box 8988 Atlanta GA 31106-0988

CAPONE, LUCIEN, JR., management consultant, former naval officer; b. Bristol, R.I.; s. Lucien and Louise Dolores (Malafronte) C.; m. Charlotte Loretta Lammers, July 22, 1950; children: Lucien, Judith Ann. B.S., U.S. Naval Acad., 1949; grad., Naval Postgrad. Sch., 1955, Indsl. Coll. Armed Forces, 1967; M.S. in Bus. Adminstrn, George Washington U., 1967, postgrad., 1970-71. Commd. ensign USN, 1949, advanced through grades to rear adm., served on destroyers Atlantic Fleet, 1949-54, mem. staff Office Chief Naval Ops. Dept. of Navy, 1955-57, exec. officer U.S.S. Huse, 1957-59; staff, comdr. Middle East Force USN, Persian Gulf, 1959-61; head plans, programs, and requirements br. Naval Communications System Hdqrs. USN, Washington, 1961-63; comdg. officer U.S.S. Hammerberg, 1963-64; dep. chief of staff Def. Comm. Agy., Washington, 1964-66; comdg. officer U.S.S. Dahlgren, 1967-69; asst. comdr. plans, programs, requirements Naval Telecommunications Command USN, Washington, 1969-72; comdg. officer U.S.S. Richmond K. Turner, 1972-74; dep. dir. nat. mil. command system tech. support Def. Comm. Agy., Washington, 1974-76; dir. command and control tech. ctr. Def. Comm. Agy., 1976-78; dep. dir. command and control Def. Communications Agy. USN, 1976-78; dir. Inter-Am. Def. Coll., Washington, 1978-79; exec. Booz, Allen & Hamilton, Inc., McLean, Va., 1979-97, v.p., 1983-88, sr. v.p., 1988-97; bd. dirs., operating coun. Booz, Allen & Hamilton, Inc., McLean, 1988-97. Decorated Legion of Merit, Def. Superior Service medal with oak leaf cluster. Mem. IEEE, AIAA, Armed Forces Communications and Electronics Assn. (past pres. D.C. chpt.). Office: Booz Allen & Hamilton Inc 8283 Greensboro Dr Ste 700 Mc Lean VA 22102-3838

CAPONE, LUCIEN, III, lawyer; b. Balt., June 10, 1951; s. Lucien Jr. and Charlotte (Lammers) C.; m. Julia Smith, Oct. 17, 1950; children: William Justice, Margaret Grey. BA, N.C. State U., 1973; JD, Wake Forest U., 1977. Bar: N.C., D.C., U.S. Ct. Appeals (4th cir.), U.S. Ct. Mil. Appeals, U.S. Supreme Ct. Asst. atty. gen. N.C. Dept. Justice, Raleigh, 1977-86, spl. dep. atty. gen., 1986-91; univ. counsel U. N.C. Greensboro, 1991—; bd. dirs. CACREP, Alexandria, Va. Comdr. JAGC, USN, 1982—. Mem. Nat. Assn. Coll. and Univ. Attys., N.C. Bar Assn. Avocation: certified flight instructor. Office: U NC 1000 Spring Garden St Greensboro NC 27412-0001

CAPONE, ROBERT JOSEPH, physician, educator; b. East Orange, N.J., Sept. 10, 1938; s. Jules Gerald and Alice Annette (Franklin) C.; m. Emily Rose Erb, Oct. 9, 1965; children: Robert Joseph II, Jeffrey Jules. AB, Columbia U., 1960; MD, Cornell U., 1964. Diplomate Am. Bd. Internal Medicine, Am. Bd. Cardiovascular Medicine. Asst. prof. medicine Brown U., Providence, 1972-79, assoc. prof. medicine, 1979-86, prof. medicine, 1986-91; dir. coronary care R.I. Hosp., Providence, 1972-91; prof. medicine U. Rochester, N.Y., 1991-94, chief clin. cardiology, 1991-94; prof. medicine Albany (N.Y.) Med. Coll., 1994—; interim head cardiology Albany (N.Y.) Med. Ctr., 1996—. Fellow ACP, Am. Coll. Cardiology (gov. R.I. 1989-91), Am. Heart Assn. Coun. on Clin. Cardiology/. Home: 14 Wildwood Ct Clifton Park NY 12065-2736 Office: Albany Med Coll Divsn of Cardiology MC-44 47 New Scotland Ave Albany NY 12208-3412*

CAPONE, VINCE, health system administrator. MS in Health Care Sys., Cen. Mich. U., 1979. CEO Ctr. Ind. Health Sys., 1998—. Office: 2001 W 86th St Indianapolis IN 46260

CAPONEGRO, ERNEST MARK, stockbroker, financial planner; b. Hoboken, N.J., Feb. 8, 1957; s. Joseph Edmund and Anne (DiPietro) C.; m. Ida Teresa Russo, Aug. 23, 1987; children: Ernest Joseph, Mathew Vincenzo. BS in Econs., Fairleigh Dickinson U., 1985; cert. in fin. planning, Adelphi U., 1987. With corp. fin. E.F. Hutton, N.Y.C., 1979-81; investment broker Philiphs Appel and Waldin, N.Y.C., 1981; securities broker, C.F.P. Prudential-Bache Securities, N.Y.C., 1982-90; asst. mngr. Shearson Lehman Bros., N.Y.C., 1989-90, securities broker/CFP, 1990-91; v.p., dir. corp. fin. and mktg. Emanuel & Co./Investment Bankers, N.Y.C., Chgo., Boca Raton, Fla., 1991-94; v.p. Gilford Sec., N.Y.C., 1995—; pres./owner Integrity Planning & investments, LLC, 1998. Republican. Roman Catholic. Home: 168 Cliff Rd Brick NJ 08724-4708 Also: 168 Cliff Rd Brick NJ 08724-4708 Office: 2803 Bridge Ave Point Pleasant NJ 08742

CAPONETTI, JAMES DANTE, botany educator; b. Boston, Mar. 15, 1932; s. Michael Angelo and Maria Lucia (Cammarata) C.; m. Marilyn Joan Messieri, June 18, 1966; children: Ann Marie, James Michael. BS in Pharmacy, Mass. Coll. Pharmacy, 1954, MS in Pharmacy, 1956; AM in Biology, Harvard U., 1959, PhD in Biology, 1962. Registered pharmacist, Mass., Tenn. Grad. teaching asst. Mass. Coll. Pharmacy, Boston, 1954-56, Harvard U., Cambridge, Mass., 1956-61; asst. prof. U. Tenn., Knoxville, 1961-71, assoc. prof., 1971-84, prof. botany, 1984—, assoc. dept. head, 1986-92; exec. asst. to dept. head, 1992—. Grantee Knoxville Utilities Bd., 1988, Tenn. Wildlife Resources Agy., Nashville, 1990-91. Fellow AAAS, Tenn. Acad. Sci. (sec. 1966-77, pres. 1979, disting. svc. award 1989); mem. Am. Fern Soc. (treas. 1976—), KC. Roman Catholic. Office: U Tenn Dept Botany Knoxville TN 37996-1100

CAPONITI, JAMES, federal government official; m. Arlene Caponiti; 3 children. BS in Bus. Adminstrn., U. Md. With Cost of Living Coun., 1973; economist Office of Subsidy Adminstrn., Maritime Adminstrn./Dept. Transp., from 1974; dir. Office of Sealift Support Maritime Adminstrn./Dept. Transp., Washington, 1994-96, assoc. adminstr. for nat. security, 1996—; detailed to Mcht. Marine subcom. U.S. Ho. of Reps., 1993. Recipient Bronze Medal award Maritime Adminstrn., 1984, Silver Medal award Dept. Transp., 1996. Office: Maritime Adminstrn/Dept Transp National Security 400 7th St SW Rm 7300 Washington DC 20590-0001*

CAPORALE, D. NICK, lawyer; b. Omaha, Sept. 13, 1928; s. Michele and Lucia Caporale; m. Margaret Nilson, Aug. 5, 1950; children: Laura Diane Stevenson, Leland Alan. B.A., U. Nebr.-Omaha, 1949, M.Sc., 1954; J.D. with distinction, U. Nebr.-Lincoln, 1957. Bar: Nebr. 1957, U.S. Dist. Ct. Nebr. 1957, U.S. Ct. Appeals 8th cir. 1958, U.S. Supreme Ct. 1970. Judge Nebr. Dist. Ct., Omaha, 1979-81, Nebr. Supreme Ct., Lincoln, 1982-98; of counsel Baird Holm Law Firm, 1998—; lectr. U. Nebr., Lincoln, 1982-84. Pres. Omaha Community Playhouse, 1976. Served to 1st lt. U.S. Army, 1952-54, Korea. Decorated Bronze Star; recipient Alumni Achievement U. Nebr.-Omaha, 1972. Fellow Am. Coll. Trial Lawyers, Internat. Soc. Barristers; mem. Order of Coif. Office: Baird Holm Law Firm 1500 Woodmen Tower Omaha NE 68102

CAPORASO, PAT MARIE, art dealer; b. Englewood, N.J., Nov. 27, 1952; d. Pasquale and Florence (Lieberman) C. BFA, Pratt Inst., Bklyn., 1974. Asst. dir. to dir. Leo Castelli, N.Y.C., 1977-84, 84-91; pvt. art dealer, cons., 1991—; cons. La. Mus., Denmark, Yamanaka Fine Arts Ctr., Kyoto, Japan; expert J. Johns, R. Lichtenstein, R. Rauschenberg, E. Kelly, F. Stella, C. Twombly and numerous others; mus. clients include Albright-Knox Art Gallery, N.Y., Balt. Mus. of Art, Ctr. George Pompidou, Paris, Art Inst. of Chgo., Contemporary Arts Ctr., Ohio, Corcoran Gallery of Art, D.C., George Eastman House, Internat. Mus. of Photography, N.Y., Tel Aviv Art Mus., Israel, others; corp. clients include Am. Express, N.Y., Bank of Am. Corp. Art Collection, Chase Manhattan Bank, N.A., Coca-Cola, Ga., Estee Lauder, N.Y., Exxon, N.Y., Walt Disney, Calif., numerous others.

CAPOUANO, ALBERT D., lawyer; b. Montgomery, Ala., 1945. BS, U. Ala., 1967, JD, 1970; LLM in Taxation, NYU, 1971. Bar: Ala. 1970, Fla. 1973. Mem. Dean, Mead, Egerton, Bloodworth, Capouano & Bozarth P.A., Orlando, Fla. Mem. Fla. Bar (computer law sect. 1984-87), Ala. State Bar. Office: Dean Mead Egerton Bloodworth Capouano & Bozarth 800 N. Magnolia Ave # 1500 PO Box 2346 Orlando FL 32802-2346 also: 800 N Magnolia Ave Ste 1500 Orlando FL 32803-3269*

CAPOZZI, LOU, public relations executive. CEO Manning, Selvage & Lee, N.Y.C. Office: Manning Selvage & Lee 79 Madison Ave New York NY 10016-7880*

CAPP, MICHAEL PAUL, physician, educator; b. Yonkers, N.Y., July 1, 1930; s. Michael and Mary (Bybel) C.; children: Marianne, Michael, Steven, John; m. Constance Whitehead, Jan. 4, 1989. B.S., Roanoke Coll., Salem, Va., 1952; M.D., U. N.C., 1958. Diplomate: Am. Bd. Radiology (treas. 1982-85, v.p. 1985, pres. 1987-89, now exec. dir.). Lab. instr. physics Roanoke Coll., 1952; teaching asst. Grad. Sch. Physics, Duke, 1952-54; intern in pediatrics Duke Med. Center, 1958-59, resident in radiology, 1959-62, assoc. in radiology, 1962, asst. prof., 1963-66, assoc. prof., 1966-70, dir. diagnostic div., dept. radiology, 1967-70, asst. prof. pediatrics, 1968-70, radiologist in charge pediatric cardiology, 1962-70; dir. Duke Med. Center (Pediatric Radiology Program), 1965-70, Duke Med. Center (Med. Students Teaching Program Diagnostic Radiology), 1965-66; prof., chmn. dept. radiology U. Ariz. Coll. Medicine, Tucson, 1970-93; chief of staff Ariz. Med. Center, Univ. Hosp., 1971-73; exec. dir. Am. Bd. of Radiology, Tucson, 1993—; mem. NRC com. on Radiology, James Picker Found., 1972; exec. dir. Am. Bd. Radiology, 1993—. Contbr. articles to profl. jours. Mem. AMA, Am. Coll. Radiology, Am. Roentgen Ray Soc. (pres. 1990), Am. Assn. U. Radiologists (exec. com. 1970, Gold medal 1988), Am. Heart Assn. (pres. coun. on cardiovascular radiology 1976-78), Am. Bd. Radiology (exec. dir. 1993—), Radiol. Soc. N. Am. (chmn. sci. exhibits com. 1976-79), N.Am. Soc. Cardiac Radiologists (pres. 1975), Nat. Acad. Scis., N. Y. Acad. Scis., Pima County Med. Soc., Ea. Radiol. Soc. (sci. program chmn. 1967, v.p. 1973—), Soc. for Pediatric Radiology, Soc. for Chmn. Acad. Radiology Depts. (pres. 1977), Inst. Medicine, Sigma Pi Sigma. Home: 5200 N Valley View Rd Tucson AZ 85718-6123 Office: Ste 3200 5255 E Williams Cir Tucson AZ 85711-7401

CAPPE, MELVIN SAMUEL, economist; b. Toronto, Ont., Canada, Dec. 3, 1948; s. David and Patricia (Wise) C.; m. Marline Linda Pliskin, Nov. 5, 1971; children: Daniel, Emily. BA, U. Toronto, 1971; MA, U. Western Ont., 1972. Sr. analyst, chief Treasury Bd. Secretariat, Ottawa, Ont., 1975-78; chief Dept. Fin., Ottawa, 1978-82; asst. dept. minister Consumer & Corp. Affairs, Ottawa, 1982-90; dep. sec. Treasury Bd. Secretariat, Ottawa, 1990-94; dep. minister Environment Canada, Ottawa, 1994-96; dep. min. Human Resources Devel. Canada, 1996-99; clerk of the Privy Coun. Ottawa. Office: Langevin Block, Rue Wellington St, Ottawa, ON Canada K1A 0A3

CAPPELLO, EVE, international business consultant; b. Sydney, Australia; d. Nem and Ethel Shapira; children: Frances Soskins, Alan Kazdin. BA, Calif. State U., Dominguez Hills, 1974; MA, Pacific Western U., 1977. Singer, pianist, L.A., 1956-76; profl. devel. and mgmt. staff tng., 1977—; instr. Calif. State U.; counselor Assoc. Tech. Coll., L.A.; instr. St. Mary's Coll., U. Judaism, U. So. Calif., Loyola Marymount U.; founder, pres. A-C-T Internat.; founder WIN Internat.; invited speaker World Congress Behavior Therapy, Israel, Melbourne U., Australia; newspaper columnist, 1976-79. Author: Let's Get Growing, 1979, The New Professional Touch, 1988, Dr Eve's Garden, 1984, Act, Don't React, 3d edit. 1988, The Game of the Name, 1985, The Perfectionist Syndrome, 1990, Why Aren't More Women Running the Show?, 1994, Great Sex After 50; contbr. articles to profl. jours. Inducted into Bus. and Profl. Women Internat. Hall of Fame, 1994. Mem. Internat. Platform Assn. (bd. dirs., affirmative action com., bd. govs.), Book Publicists So. Calif., Pasadena C. of C., Toastmasters, Alpha Gamma. Home: 518 S El Molino Ave Apt 303 Pasadena CA 91101-3448

CAPPETTA, ANNA MARIA, art educator; b. New Haven, Feb. 14, 1949; d. Alfonso M. and Elvira (Bove) Cavaliere; m. Vincent John Cappetta, July 17, 1971. BS in Art Edn., So. Conn. State U., 1971, MS in Spl. Edn., 1973, MS in Supervision/Adminstrn., 1980, MS in Art Edn., 1981. Sub. tchr. West Haven (Conn.) Sch. System, 1971; art educator/coord. North Haven (Conn.) Sch. System, 1971—; adj. prof. art So. Conn. State U., New Haven, 1984-92; cons. Area Coop. Ednl. Svcs., Conn., 1987—. Co-author: (mag.) Art Education, 1990, School Arts, 1986—, Impace II Experienced Teachers Handbook, 1992; contbg. editor School Arts mag., 1991—. Recipient North Haven Tchr. of Yr. award, 1986, Conn. Celebration of Excellence award, 1987, 90, 92, Nat. Art Educator award, 1988, 89, Conn. Art Educator award, 1989, 95, North Haven Tchr. of Yr. award, 1989. Fellow Nat. Coun. Basic Edn.; mem. Nat. Art Edn. Assn. (nat. elem. dir. 1991-95, Nat. Art Educator award 1988, 89, advisory 1994, Briefing Paper Series 1993), Conn. Art Edn. Assn. (Conn. Art Educator award 1989, 95), Nat. Women's Art Caucus, Phi Delta Kappa (co-editor newsletter 1987-89), Delta Kappa Gamma. Home: PO Box 1399 19 Johnson Ln Madison CT 06443-2212

CAPPIELLO, ANGELA, church grants administrator; b. New Hyde Park, N.Y., July 6, 1954; d. Augustine and Angela (Tamburello) C. Cert. meeting and conv. mgmt., NYU, 1988, cert. assn. mgmt., 1989, cert. food and beverage mgmt., 1989, cert. travel mgmt., 1990, cert. hotel and motel mgmt., 1991, cert. in fin. controls, 1992, cert. mgmt. practices, 1998. Cert. meeting profl., assn. exec. Mgr. meetings and convs. N.Y. Libr. Assn., N.Y.C., 1987-89; conf. coord. ASCE, N.Y.C., 1989; mgr. meetings and confs. Coun. Cons. Orgns., N.Y.C., 1990-91; asst. to pres. Goodstein Devel. Corp., N.Y.C., 1991-93; asst. meetings mgr. Nat. Episcopal Ch., N.Y.C., 1993-96, dir. grants program, 1996—. Mem. NAFE, Am. Soc. Assn. Execs., Meeting Planners Internat. (bd. dirs. N.Y. chpt. 1991-93), N.Y. Soc. Assn. Execs., Profl. Conf. Mgrs. Assn., Religious Conf. Mgrs. Assn., Nat. Assn. for Advancement Fat Acceptance (bd. dirs. 1983-86). Home: 36 New Hyde Park Rd New Hyde Park NY 11040-4935 Office: Nat Episcopal Church 815 2d Ave New York NY 10017-4503

CAPPIELLO, FRANK ANTHONY, JR., investment advisor; b. Trenton, N.J., Jan. 5, 1926; s. Frank A. and Rose Marie (Clapis) C.; m. Marie Therese Rhodes, June, 1954; children: Frank Rhodes, Annmarie, Elaine. A.B., U. Notre Dame, 1949; postgrad., Cornell U. Law Sch., 1949-50; M.B.A., Harvard U., 1954. Supr. rate research Va. Electric and Power Co., Richmond, 1954-61; mgr. research dept. Alexander Brown & Sons, 1961-67; v.p. Securities Monumental Life Ins. Co., 1968-74; fin. v.p. Monumental Corp., 1970-80; pres. Monumental Capital Mgmt., Inc., Balt., 1974-80, Dowbeaters, Inc., Summit, N.J. and Balt., 1981-83, McCullough, Andrews and Cappiello, Inc., Balt. and San Francisco, 1983—; founder, dir. Bank of Md., 1985-90; chmn. Cappiello-Rushmore Mutual Funds, Bethesda, Md., 1993—; TV panelist Wall St. Week, 1970—; disting. visiting prof. fin. Loyola Coll., Balt., 1986—; mem. adv. investment com. Md. State Retirement Systems. Author: Finding the Next Super Stock, 1982, From Main Street to Wall Street, 1988. Trustee Balt. City Pension System; mem., commr. Md. State Econ. and Community Devel. Commn., 1977-80. Served with U.S. Marine Corps, 1950-52. Mem. Fin. Analysts Fedn. (chmn., dir.), Balt. Security Analysts Soc. Roman Catholic. Clubs: Univ., Harvard (N.Y.C.); Hamilton Street (Balt.). Home: 19 Buchanan Rd Baltimore MD 21212-3324 Office: 10751 Falls Rd Ste 250 Lutherville Timonium MD 21093-4552

CAPPITELLA, MAURO JOHN, architect; b. N.Y.C., N.Y., July 11, 1934; s. Gaetano and Maria (D'Errico) C.; m. Christine Wilhelmine Otte, Oct. 11, 1964; children: Mark, Christina, Nicole. BS in Architecture, CCNY, 1956; postgrad., Columbia U., 1960-62; M in Urban Planning, NYU, 1967. Registered architect, N.Y., N.J.; lic. Nat. Coun. Archtl. Registration Bds.; profl. planner, N.J. Designer Garfinkel & Marenberg, N.Y.C., 1956-57; architect Western Electric Co., Inc., N.Y.C., 1957-68; cons. architect Norwood, N.J., 1968-76, Upper Saddle River, N.J., 1976—. Served to 1st lt. U.S. Army, 1957-59. Recipient Anton Vegliante award 1993. Mem. AIA (N.J. liaison rep. to N.J. State Bd. Archs. 1997—), N.J. Soc. Architects (bd. dirs. 1983-84, 87-89, 93-96), Architects League No. N.J. (bd. dirs. 1980-83, 89-91, 94-96, sec. 1984-85, v.p. 1985, 1st v.p. 1986, pres.-elect 1987, pres. 1988, 93, Dir. of Yr. award 1980, 81, Vegliante award 1993), Soc. 3d U.S. Inf. Divsn. U.S. Army, Saddle River Tennis Club, Rotary. Republican. Roman Catholic. Office: 332 E Saddle River Rd Saddle River NJ 07458-2108

CAPPO, JOSEPH C., publisher; b. Chgo., Feb. 24, 1936; s. Joseph V. and Frances (Maggio) Cacioppo; m. Mary Anne Cappo, May 7, 1967; children: Elizabeth, John. BA, DePaul U., 1957. Reporter, Hollister Publs., Wilmette, Ill., 1961-62; reporter Chgo. Daily News, 1962-68, bus. columnist, 1968-78; columnist Crain's Chgo. Bus., 1978—, pub., 1979-89; v.p. Crain Communications, Inc., 1981-89, sr. v.p. group. pub., 1989-95, sr. v.p. internat., 1996—; pub. Advt. Age, 1989-92, publishing dir, 1992—; dir. Assn. Area Bus. Publs., 1982-88, pres., 1985-86. Bd. dirs. Off the Street Club, Chgo., 1981—, Chicago Advt. Fedn., 1987-93, Mus. of Broadcast Communications, 1984-1990, Ill. Coun. on Econ. Edn., 1990-95. With U.S. Army, 1959-61. Recipient award Ill. Press Assn., 1962, (with other Daily News staffers) Nat. Headliner award, 1966, Disting. Alumni award DePaul U., 1975, Page One award Chgo. Newspaper Guild, 1978, Peter Lisagor award Sigma Delta Chi, 1978, Outstanding Achievement award in Communication, Justinian Soc. Lawyers, 1979, Champion award YWCA of Met. Chgo., 1984, Media Svc. award Chgo. Lung Assn., 1990. Author: Future Scope: Success Strategies for the 1990's and Beyond, 1990. Mem. Internat. Advt. Assn. (world bd. 1994—, sr. v.p. 1996-98, world pres. 1998—), Econ. Club (Chgo.), Bus. and Econ. Writers (bd. govs. 1984-89), Ill. Small Business Advisory Commn., 1986-90, Delta Mu Delta (hon.). Roman Catholic. Office: Crain Communications Inc 740 N Rush St Chicago IL 60611-2546

CAPPON, ANDRE ALFRED, management consultant; b. Bucharest, Romania, Mar. 26, 1948; came to U.S., 1965; s. Otto and Frederica (Steuermann) C. BSc, MIT, 1970; MS, Columbia U., 1971. Analyst OECD, Paris, 1971-77; mgr. Arthur Andersen & Co., N.Y.C., 1977-80; v.p. Booz, Allen & Hamilton, Inc., N.Y.C., 1980-87; ptnr. Oliver, Wyman & Co., N.Y.C., 1987-91; pres. The CBM Group Inc., N.Y.C., 1992—; prof. Lycee Francais N.Y., N.Y.C., 1970-71; lectr. Am. Coll., Paris, 1974-76. Home: 531 Main St Apt 602 New York NY 10044-0109 Office: The CBM Group Inc 575 Madison Ave Ste 1006 New York NY 10022-2511

CAPPS, CINDY M., computer systems analyst; b. Stockton, Calif., Dec. 1, 1964; d. Nathan Cameron Doyel and Charlotte Blanche (Epler) Gezi. Student, Calif. State U., Sacramento, 1982-83; AA, MTI Bus. Coll., Sacramento, 1984. Supr. All Am. Mini Storage, Sacramento, 1988-89; mng. contr. The Royce Cos., Roseville, Calif., 1990-93; contr. Calif. Comml., Sacramento, 1993-95; gen. ptnr., operator Sierra Micro, Fair Oaks, Calif., 1995-98; help desk analyst Shared Med. Sys., Sacramento, Calif., 1998—. Mem. NOW, NAFE, Nat. Abortion and Reproductive Right Action League. Presbyterian. Avocations: writing, reading, waterpolo, swimming, softball. Office: Shared Med Sys 3321 Power Inn Rd Ste # 300 Sacramento CA 95826

CAPPS, DAVID EDWARD, JR., assistant dean; b. Atlanta, Nov. 1, 1946; s. David Edward Capps Sr. and Mary Elinor (Tyner) Roberts; m. Jamie Renee Gibson, Dec. 28, 1982. AA, Clarke Meml. Coll., 1967; BS, U. So. Miss., 1969, MS, 1977. Resident hall dir. Ga. So. U., Statesboro, 1977-80; asst. dir. student activities Embry-Riddle Aero. U., Daytona, Fla., 1980-83; summer youth counselor C.E.T.A., Crystal River, Fla., 1983; admissions specialist Pasco Hernando C.C., New Port Richey, Fla., 1984-85, continuing edn. specialist, 1985-86; asst. dean of students Pasco Hernando C.C., Brooksville, Fla., 1986—. With USN, 1969-73. Mem. Fla. Assn. C.C.'s, Rotary. Baptist. Avocations: jazz, movies, good restaurants, quality time with wife. Home: 905 Cedar Dr Brooksville FL 34601-2214 Office: Pasco Hernando CC Brooksville FL 34601

CAPPS, ETHAN LEROY, oil company executive; b. Sherman, Tex., Dec. 2, 1924; s. Ethen Daniel and Annie Mae (Anderson) C.; m. Emily Ann Tyson, Sept. 8, 1951; children—Richard LeRoy, Nancy Elizabeth. B.S., Tex. A&M U., 1948; grad., Advanced Mgmt. Program, Harvard U., 1965. C.P.A., Tex. With Tenn. Gas Transmission Co., Houston, 1948-59; asst. treas., budget dir. Tenn. Gas Transmission Co., 1960-61; chief acct. Midwestern Gas Transmission Co., Houston, 1959; v.p. Tenneco Corp., Houston, 1961-63; adminstrv. v.p., controller Tenneco Oil Co., Houston, 1963-73; v.p., treas. Tenneco Inc., 1974-84, v.p. fin. mgmt. devel. and ins. and loss control, 1984-86, ret., 1986. Elder First Presbyn. Ch., Houston. Clubs: Petroleum (Houston), Racquet (Houston). Home: 6206 Cedar Creek Dr Houston TX 77057-1804

CAPPS, JAMES LEIGH, II, lawyer, reserve military career officer; b. Brunswick, Ga., Dec. 17, 1956; s. Thomas Edwin Sr. and Betty Marie (Greenhill) C.; m. Nancy Ann Fisher, June 25, 1978; children: Bonnie Lynn, James Leigh III. AA, Seminole C.C., Sanford, Fla., 1976; BA in History, U. Cen. Fla., 1981; JD, U. Fla., 1987. Bar: Fla. 1987, U.S. Ct. Mil. Appeals 1988, Colo. 1990, U.S. Ct. Appeals (4th cir.) 1997. Enlisted USAF, 1976, advanced through grades to maj., 1995; med. svc. specialist USAF, MacDill AFB, Fla., 1977-79; air weapons dir. USAF, Germany, 1982-84; claims officer USAF, Homestead AFB, Fla., 1987-88, area def. counsel, 1988-90; dep. staff judge adv. USAF, Onizuka AFB, Calif., 1990-93; atty. office of state atty. 18th Jud. Ct., Sanford, Fla., 1994; assoc. Dominick Salfi Law Offices, Maitland, Fla., 1993-94, of counsel, 1994—; pvt. practice, 1996—; sr. res. judge adv. Moody AFB, Ga., 1996-99; civilian contract officer for Naval Air Warfare Ctr. USN, Orlando, Fla., 1999—; assigned to 16th Air Force Hdqs., Aviano AFB, Italy, Operation Joint Endeavor, 1996; atty. Vietnam Vets. Ctrl. Fla., 1998—; implementation force Dayton Peace Accords UN. Maj. USAFR, 1993—. Recipient McCarthy award for legal svc. Air Combat Command, 1995. Mem. DAV, VFW, Fla. Sheriff's Assn. (hon.). Democrat.

CAPPS, LOIS RAGNHILD GRIMSRUD, congresswoman, school nurse; b. Ladysmith, Wis., Jan. 10, 1938; d. Jurgen Milton and Solveig Magdalene (Gullixson) Grimsrud; m. Walter Holden Capps, Aug. 21, 1960 (dec.); children: Lisa Margaret, Todd Holden, Laura Karolina. BSN with honors, Pacific Luth. U., 1959; MA in Religion, Yale U., 1964; MA in Edn., U. Calif., Santa Barbara, 1990. RN, Calif.; cert. sch. nurse, Calif.; jr. coll. instr., Calif. Asst. instr. Emanuel Hosp. Sch. Nursing, Portland, Oreg., 1959-60; surgery flr. nurse Yale/New Haven Hosp., 1960-62, head nurse, out patient, 1962-63; staff nurse Vis. Nurse Assn., Hamden, Ct., 1963-64; sch. nurse Santa Barbara (Calif.) Sch. Dists., 1968-70, 77-98; dir. teenage pregnancy and parenting project Santa Barbara, 1985-86; mem. 105th Congress (now 106th Congress) from 22d Calif. dist., Washington, 1998—; mem. sci. com., internat. rels. com. U.S. Congress, campaign finance reform task force, budget task force, Calif. ISTEA task force, congrl. caucus women's issues, congrl. task force tobacco and health, diabetes caucus, congrl. caucus on the arts; instr. Santa Barbara City Coll., 1990—. Bd. dirs. Am. Heart Assn., Santa Barbara, 1989—, The Adoption Ctr., Santa Barbara, 1986-90, Family Svc. Agy., Santa Barbara, 1994—, Stop AIDS Now, Santa Barbara, 1994—, Santa Barbara Women's Polit. Com., 1991—; instr. CPR, first aid, ARC, Santa Barbara, 1985—; bd. dirs. Pacific Luth. Theol. Sem. Democrat. Lutheran. Fax: (202) 225-5632. E-mail: lois.capps@mail.house.gov. Home: 1724 Santa Barbara St Santa Barbara CA 93101-1025 Office: US House of Reps 1118 Longworth HOB Washington DC 20515-0522

CAPPS, RICHARD HENRY, minister; b. Columbia, S.C., June 22, 1944; s. Henry Eddie and Maude Cecile (Simpson) Crapps; m. Joyce Dianne Wood, Aug. 2, 1968; children: Richard Henry (Hank) Jr., Elizabeth Cecille. AA, North Greenville Coll., 1965; BA, Furman U., 1967; ThM with honors, New Orleans Bapt. Theol. Sem., 1970, DMin, 1978. Ordained minister So. Bapt., 1965. Pastor Fairfield Bapt. Ch., Winnsboro, S.C., 1964-68, Society Hill Bapt. Ch., Oakvale, Miss., 1969-71, First Bapt. Ch., Gaston, S.C., 1971-79; interim pastor First Bapt. Ch., Cheraw, S.C., 1968; sr. pastor Laurel Bapt. Ch., Greenville, S.C., 1979-82; dir. missions South Roanoke Bapt. Assn.,

Greenville, 1982-93, Liberty Bapt. Assn., Thomasville, N.C., 1993-98; area dir. Piedmont/Western NC Prison Fellowship, Winston-Salem, NC, 1998—; S.S. enlargement campaign cons. S.C. Bapt. State Conv., 1981-82; pack cons. N.Am. Mission Bd., Atlanta, 1988-95; state disaster relief coord. N.C. Bapt. Men., Cary, 1989-93; ch. growth cons. Bapt. State Conv. of N.C., Cary, 1996-98. Contbr. articles to profl. publs. Bd. dirs. Greenville Boys Choir, 1986-90, Transplant Recipient Suport Sys., Pitt County Meml. Hosp., Greenville, 1991-93; mem. Greenville Choral Soc., 1990-93; mem. religion in schs. task force Pitt County Schs., Greenville, 1993; vice chmn. chaplains bd. Davidson Correction Ctr., Lexington, N.C., 1996-98. Recipient Am. Legion award, 1965, Vol. of the Year, Davidson Correctional Ctr., 1997. Mem. Dir. of Missions Conf. (pres. 1986-87, treas. 1987-98), Thomasville C. of C., Lexington Ministerial Assn., Gaston Ruritan Club (chaplain 1973-77). Democrat. Avocations: roses, antiques/collectibles, walking, collecting stamps and coins. Home: 198 Creekside Dr High Point NC 27265-9209 Office: Western/Piedmont NC Prison Fellowship Office Winston Salem NC 27103

CAPPS, SUSAN MARIE, elementary school educator; b. Marianna, Fla., Feb. 28, 1964; d. Price Alton Kent and Anna (Reece) Robinson; m. Gregory Mark Capps, Oct. 26, 1985; children: Mark, Grant. BS in Edn., Ga. Southwestern State U., 1990. Cert. tchr., Ga. Elem. sch. tchr. Lee County Elem. Sch., Lee County Sch. Sys., Leesburg, Ga., 1991-94, West Gordon Elem. Sch., Valdosta (Ga.) City Schs., 1994—. Mem. Profl. Assn. Ga. Educators. Methodist. Avocations: reading, spending time with family, travel, computers. E-mail: susanúcapps@yahoo.com. Office: West Gordon Elem Sch 813 W Gordon St Valdosta GA 31601

CAPPS, THOMAS EDWARD, utilities company executive, lawyer; b. Wilmington, N.C., Oct. 31, 1935; s. Edward S. Jr. and Agnes (Rhodes) C.; m. Jane Paden, Sept. 13, 1963; children: Ashley R., Leigh C. AB, U. N.C., 1958, JD, 1965. Bar: Fla. 1975, N.C. 1966. Sr. counsel Carolina Power & Light Co., Raleigh, N.C., 1970-74; v.p., gen. counsel Boston Edison Co., 1974-75; sr. ptnr. Steel Hector & Davis, Miami, Fla., 1975-84; exec. v.p. Va. Power, Richmond, 1984-86; pres. Dominion Resources, Inc., Richmond, 1986—, chief exec. officer, 1990—, chmn. bd. dirs., 1992—; bd. dirs. Bassett (Va.) Furniture Industries, Inc., NationsBank Corp., Petersburg Long Distance, Inc. Bd. dirs. Va. Blood Svcs., 1986. Lt. USCG, 1959-62. Mem. ABA, Bd. of Bar Overseers, N.C. Bar Assn., Fla. Bar Assn., Mass. Bar Assn. Episcopalian. Office: Dominion Resources Inc PO Box 26532 Richmond VA 23261-6532*

CAPPS, THOS E., diversified financial services company executive; b. 1935. With Dominion Resources, Richmond, 1984—, pres., COO, 1986, pres., CEO, 1990, chmn., pres., CEO, 1992. Office: Dominion Resources Inc 120 Tredegar St Richmond VA 23219-4072*

CAPRA, LINDA ANN, elementary education educator; b. Bklyn., Mar. 23, 1948; d. John Khoury and Sadie (Nobile) Grayeb; m. Joseph Vincent Capra, June 25, 1971; children: Lauren, Alena. BA cum laude, CUNY, 1969, MS in Early Childhood Edn. cum laude, 1972. Cert. tchr. N-6 and Reading, N.Y. Grade 1 tchr. N.Y.C. Bd. Edn., Bklyn., 1979-74, Headstart tchr., 1972, Title I tchr. strengthening early edn., 1974-79, chpt. I math. specialist, 1979-84, chpt. I math./computer staff developer, 1984-94; grade 1 tchr. N.Y.C. Bd. Edn., Bayside, N.Y., 1994-97; computer software reviewer N.Y.C. Bd. Edn., Bklyn., 1984—; tchr. pre-K Bayside (N.Y.) Bd. Edn., 1998—; chpt. leader United Fedn. Tchrs., N.Y.C., 1988-94, 96—; various coms., N.Y.C. Bd. Edn. Recipient Newsday Good Health grant, L.I., N.Y., 1994. Mem. Nat. Coun. Tchrs. Math., Kappa Delta Pi. Avocations: walking, bicycling, painting. Office: PS 213 Queens 23102 67th Ave Flushing NY 11364-2706

CAPRARO, FRANZ, accountant; b. Uder-Eichsfeld, Thuringia, Germany, Nov. 19, 1941; came to U.S., 1959; s. Ernst Capraro and Lia (Loeschmann) Baeuscher; m. Daniela DiPauli, Dec. 26, 1964; 1 child, Monica L. BBA cum laude, U. Miami, 1964. CPA, Fla. Ptnr. Deloitte Haskins & Sells (name now Deloitte & Touche), Miami, 1966-84; exec. v.p. The Wolfson Initiative Corp., Miami, 1984-95; v.p. The Novecento Corp., Miami, 1984-95, Washington Storage Co., Miami, 1984-95, The Foundlings, Inc., Miami Beach, 1984-95, The Hampton Roads, Inc., Miami Beach, 1984-95; pvt. practice acctg. Davie, Fla., 1995-96; ptnr. Grau & Co., P.A., Miami, 1996—; treas. The Jour. of Decorative and Propaganda Arts, Miami, 1986-98; attended Nat. Security Forum, U.S. Air War Coll., Montgomery, Ala., 1993. Mem. exec. com. U. Miami Citizens Bd., Coral Gables, 1987—; treas. Mitchell Wolfson Family Found., Miami, 1985—; bd. dirs. Louis Wolfson II Media History Ctr., Miami, 1987-95; trustee Greater Miami Opera Fin. Com., 1991-96. 1st lt. U.S. Army Fin. Corps, France, 1965-66. Recipient Certificate of Appreciation City of Miami Beach, 1987; named Honorary Conch City of Key West, 1987. Mem. AICPA, Fla. Inst. CPAs, Schlaraffia Costa Aurea (treas. 1986-87), U.S. Air War Coll. Alumni Assn. (life). Roman Catholic. Avocations: reading, travel. Home: 2821 SW 116th Ave Fort Lauderdale FL 33330-1418 Office: Grau & Company PA 111 NE 1st St Fl 5 Miami FL 33132-2517

CAPRIATI, JENNIFER MARIA, professional tennis player; b. N.Y.C., Mar. 29, 1976; d. Stefano and Denise (Deamicis) Capriati. Profl. tennis player, 1990—. Winner: (jr. singles) French Open, 1989, U.S. Open, 1989, (jr. doubles, with McGrath) Italian Open, 1989, Wimbledon, 1989, (singles) P.R. tournament, 1990, San Diego, 1991, Can. Open, 1991, (doubles, with M. Seles) Italian Open, 1991; finalist (singles) Phila., 1990; semifinalist (jr. singles) French Open, 1988, (singles) Wimbledon, 1991, U.S. Open, 1991, Boca Raton, 1991, German Open, 1991; recipient Gold medal 1992 Olympics. Avocations: dancing, swimming, reading, music, golf. Office: Internat Mgmt Group care Barbara Perry 22 E 71st St New York NY 10021-4911*

CAPRIGLIONE, RALPH RAYMOND, geologist, educator; b. Chgo., Dec. 7, 1968; s. Peter C. and Helen T. (Benthey) C. BS in Earth Sci., Northeastern Ill. U., 1994. Geologist Indsl. Comml. Environ., Lansing, Ill., 1994-95; field technician Environ. Monitoring and Technologies, Morton Grove, Ill., 1995-96; geologist Integrated Environ. Solutions, Schererville, Ind., 1996-98, Bradburne Briller & Johnson, LLC, Chgo., 1998—; adj. prof. Moraine Alley C.C., Palos Hills, Ill., 1998—. Sec. Spl. Forces Assn., Chgo., 1995—; mem. Chgo. Coun. on Fgn. Rels. Mem. Chgo. Acad. Scis. Republican. Roman Catholic. Avocations: astronomy, scuba diving, off-road driving, exercise, rifle shooting. Home: 15513 Elm St South Holland IL 60473-1360

CAPRIO, ANTHONY S., university president; b. Providence, Apr. 12, 1945; s. Salvatore and Esther (Iafrati) C. BA, Wesleyan U., 1967; MA, Columbia U., 1969, PhD, 1973. Asst. prof. langs. and fgn. studies Lehman Coll., CUNY, Bronx, 1971-76; assoc. prof. Cedar Crest Coll., Allentown, Pa., 1976-80; prof., adminstr. Am. U., Washington, 1980-89; provost Oglethorpe U., Atlanta, 1989-96; pres. Western New Eng. Coll., Springfield, Mass., 1996—; mem. Nat. Humanities Faculty, 1977—; bd. dirs. Tuition Exch. Inc.; mem. College Bd. So. Regional Coun. Author: Reflets de la femme, 1973, En Français, 1976, 3d edit., 1985; also over 100 articles, book chpts. and revs. on pedagogy, lit. and transl. to profl. jours. including Columbia Dictionary of Modern European Lit., A Critical Bibliography of French Lit., others. Recipient Adminstr.-Faculty award for outstanding performance Am. U., 1984, Disting. Adminstr. and Educator award Greater Washington Assn. Fgn. Lang. Educators, 1986. Mem. Am. Translators Assn., Am. Assn. Higher Edn., Am. Assn. Univ. Adminstrs., Kiwanis, Phi Beta Kappa (assoc.), Omicron Delta Kappa, Phi Beta Delta, others. Office: Western New Eng Coll Office of President 1215 Wilbraham Rd Springfield MA 01119-2612

CAPRIOLE, SISTER CARMEN MARIA, geriatric nurse; b. Methuen, Mass.; d. Morris and Constance (Magri) C. Diploma, Burbank Hosp., 1978; AAS, Maria Coll., 1972; BSN, Worcester (Mass.) State Coll., 1982; MS, Springfield Coll., 1990. RN, Mass.; cert. gerontology nurse, nursing adminstrn ANCC; cert. in trauma nursing Emergency Nursing Assn. Asst. head nurse Meml. Hosp., Worcester, 1978-81; staff devel. coord. Bancroft House Health Care, Worcester, 1982-86; community health nurse Easter Seals Soc., Worcester, 1986-87; missionary nurse leper colony Peoples Republic of Benin, 1987-88; health care coord. for elderly Religious Venerini Sisters, Worcester, 1988—; staff devel. coord. Lincoln Nursing & Rehab. Ctr., Worcester, 1990-91; dir. nursing Lincoln Nursing and Rehab. Ctr., Worcester, Mass., 1991-92; dir. nursing edn. Keystone Nursing and Rehab. Ctr., Leominster, Mass., 1991-93; dir. health and edn. Jewish Healthcare Ctr., Worcester, Mass., 1994—. Capt. Army Nurse Corps, USAR, 1991—. Mem. ANA (cert. gerontology nurse, nursing adminstrn.), Sigma Theta Tau (Epsilon Beta chpt.). Home: 31 Indian Hill Rd Worcester MA 01606-2609 Office: Jewish Healthcare Ctr 629 Salisbury St Worcester MA 01609-1120

CAPRIOLI, JOSEPH, ophthalmologist; b. Deer Park, N.Y., May 15, 1954; m. Tracey Caprioli, June 1993; 1 child, Isabella; children from previous marriage: Peter, Joseph, Jessica, Marie. BS, SUNY, Stony Brook, 1975; MD, SUNY, Buffalo, 1979; MA Privatum, Yale U., 1993. Diplomate Nat. Bd. Med. Exmainers, Am. Bd. Ophthalmology; lic. physician, N.Y., Pa., Conn. Dir. Glaucoma Sect., 1984—; intern Yale U. Sch. Medicine, New Haven, 1979-80, resident ophthalmology, 1984-88, asst. prof. ophthalmology, dir. glaucoma svc., 1984-97, assoc. prof. ophthalmology, 1988-93, prof. ophthalmology, 1993-97; fellow glaucoma Wills Eye Hosp., Phila., 1983-84; acting chmn. Yale U. Sch. Medicine, New Haven, 1993-95; prof. ophthalmology, dir. glaucoma sect. UCLA/Jules Stein Eye Inst., L.A., 1997—; lectr. Ill. Soc. for Preservation of Blindness, 1992; mem. basic sci. and clin. glaucoma panels, planning subcom. Nat. Adv. Eye Coun., NIH, 1990, visual scis. A study sect. NIH/Nat. Eye Inst., 1992-94, chmn., 1994—; steering com. Advanced Glaucoma Intervention Study, NIH, 1988-91; lectr. in field. Book rev. editor Ophthalmic Surgery, 1984-89; mem. editl. bd. Ophthalmic Surgery, 1989—, Am. Jour Ophthalmology, 1991—, Investigative Ophthalmology and Visual Sci., 1992—, Jour. Glaucoma, 1991-94; editor: Ophthalmology Clinics of North America: Contemporary Issues in Glaucoma, 1991; contbr. articles to profl. jours., chpts. to books. Recipient Jules Francois prize, 1989, Alcon Rsch. Inst. award, 1992, Rudin prize for glaucoma rsch., 1996; grantee Hoechst-Roussel Pharms., Inc., 1985-86, NIH/Nat. Eye Inst., 1987-89, 93—, New Haven Found., 1988-89, Merck Sharp & Dohme, 1989-90, 92-93, Alcon Pharms., 1989-90, Robert Leet and Clara Guthrie Patterson Trust, 1989-92, Alcon Rsch. Inst., 1992, Lewis Rudin Glaucoma prize, 1997. Fellow ACS, Am. Acad. Ophthalmology (mem. quality of care com. glaucoma panel 1988—, chmn. 1991—); mem. Am. Ophthalmological Soc., Assn. for Rsch. in Vision and Ophthalmology, Internat. Soc. Eye Rsch., Am. Glaucoma Soc., Soc. Neurosci., Glaucoma Soc. of Internat. Gongress Ophahtlmology, New Eng. Ophthalmol. Soc. Avocations: piano, cabinetmaking, fitness. Office: Jules Stein Eye Inst Dept Opthalmology 100 Stein Plz # 2-118 Los Angeles CA 90095-7065

CAPRON, ALEXANDER MORGAN, lawyer, educator; b. Hartford, Conn., Aug. 16, 1944; s. William Mosher and Margaret (Morgan) C.; m. Barbara A. Brown, Nov. 9, 1969 (div. Dec. 1985); m. Kathleen West, Mar. 4, 1989; children: Jared Capron-Brown, Charles Spencer West Capron, Christopher Gordon West Capron, Andrew Morgan West Capron. BA, Swarthmore Coll., 1966; LLB, Yale U., 1969; MA (hon.), U. Pa., 1975. Bar: D.C. 1970, Pa. 1978. Law clk. to presiding judge U.S. Ct. Appeals, Washington, 1969-70; lectr., research assoc. Yale U., 1970-72; asst. prof. law U. Pa., 1972-75, vice dean, 1976, assoc. prof., 1975-78, prof. law and human genetics, 1978-82; exec. dir. Pres.'s Commn. for Study of Ethical Problems in Med. and Biomed. and Behavioral Rsch., Washington, 1980-83; prof. law, ethics and pub. policy Law Ctr. Georgetown U., Washington, 1983-84, inst. fellow Kennedy Inst. Ethics, 1983-84; Topping prof. law, medicine and pub. policy U. So. Calif., L.A., 1985-89, Univ. prof. law and medicine, 1989—, Henry W. Bruce prof. law, 1991—; co-dir. Pacific Ctr. for Health Policy and Ethics, L.A., 1990—; mem. bd. advisors Am. Bd. Internal Medicine, 1985-95, chmn., 1991-95; cons. NIH, mem. recombinant DNA com., 1990-95, mem. subcom. on human gene therapy, 1984-92; chmn. Congrl. Biomed. Ethics Adv. Commn., 1987-91; mem. Joint Commn. on Accreditation of Healthcare Orgns., 1994—, mem. ethics adv. com., 1984-85; mem. Nat. Bioethics Adv. Commn., 1996—. Author: (with Katz) Catastrophic Diseases: Who Decides What?, 1976, (with others) Genetic Counseling: Facts, Values and Norms, 1979, Law, Science and Medicine, 1984, supplements, 1987, 89, 2d edit., 1996, (with others) Treatise on Health Care Law, 1991; contbr. articles to profl. jours. Bd. mgrs. Swarthmore Coll., 1982-85; bd. trustees The Century Found. Fellow AAAS, Am. Coll. Legal Medicine (hon.), Hastings Ctr. (Inst. Society, Ethics and Life Scis., bd. dirs. 1975-98); mem. Inst. Medicine NAS (bd. dirs. 1985-90), AAUP (exec. com. Pa. chpt.), Am. Soc. Law, Medicine and Ethics (pres. 1988-89), Swarthmore Coll. Alumni Soc. (v.p. 1974-77). Office: U So Calif Law Sch University Park Los Angeles CA 90089-0071

CAPRON, JOHN M., lawyer; b. Mt. Vernon, Ohio, Apr. 14, 1942. AB, Kenyon Coll., 1964; LLB, U. Pa., 1967. Bar: Pa. 1968, Ga. 1971. Mem. Fisher & Phillips, Atlanta. Mem. Federalist Soc. (labor and employment sect.), Employers' Resource Group, Inc. (v.p.), State Bar Ga. Office: Fisher & Phillips 945 East Paces Ferry NE 1500 Resurgens Plz Atlanta GA 30326*

CAPSHAW, KATE (KATHY SUE NAIL), actress; b. Ft. Worth, 1953; m. John Capshaw (div.); 1 child: Jessica; m. Steven Spielberg, Oct. 12, 1991; 1 child: Sasha. Student, U. Mo. Actress: (feature films) A Little Sex, 1982, Indiana Jones and the Temple of Doom, 1984, Best Defense, 1984, Dreamscape, 1984, Windy City, 1984, Power, 1986, Spacecamp, 1986, Ti Presento un'Amica, 1988, Black Rain, 1989, Love at Large, 1990, My Heroes Have Always Been Cowboys, 1991, Love Affair, 1994, Just Cause, 1995, How to Make an American Quilt, 1995, Duke of Groove, 1995, The Locusts, 1997, Life During Wartime, 1997; (TV series) The Edge of Night, Black Tie Affair, 1993, (TV movies) Missing Children: A Mother's Story, 1982, The Quick and the Dead, 1987, Her Secret Life, 1987, Internal Affairs, 1988, Next Door, 1994; actress, prodr.: The Love Letter, 1999. Mem. Screen Actors Guild, AFTRA. Office: CAA care Kevin Huvane 9830 Wilshire Blvd Beverly Hills CA 90212-1804*

CAPSHAW, TOMMIE DEAN, judge; b. Oklahoma City, Sept. 20, 1936; m. Dian Shipp; 1 child, Charles W. BS in Bus., Oklahoma City U., 1958; postrad., U. Ark., 1958-59; JD, U. Okla., 1961. Bar: Okla. 1961, Wyo. 1971, Ind. 1975. Assoc. Looney, Watts, Looney, Nichols and Johnson, Oklahoma City, 1961-63, Pierce, Duncan, Couch and Hendrickson, Oklahoma City, 1963-70; trial atty., v.p. Capshaw Well Service Co., Liberty Pipe and Supply Co., Casper, Wyo.; sr. adminstrv. law judge Evansville, Ind., 1973-75, 96-99; hearing office chief adminstrv. law judge Chgo., 1977-78; sr. adminstrv. law judge, 1999—; acting appeals coun. mem., Arlington, Va., 1980, acting chief adminstrv. law judge, 1984; mem. faculty U. Evansville, 1977, Sch. Law Ill. U., 1988—, So. Ind. U., 1990; lectr. in field. Author: A Manual for Continuing Judicial Education, 1981, Practical Aspects of Handling Social Security Disability Claims, 1982, Judicial Practice Handbook, 1990, A Quest for Quality, Speedy Justice, 1991; contbr. numerous articles to profl. jours., chpt. to textbook. Mem. adv. coun. Boy Scouts Am., scoutmaster, den leader, 1969—, Nat. Jud. Coll. U. Nev.; bd. dirs. Casper Symphony, 1972-73, Casper United Fund, 1972-73, Midget Football Assn., Casper, 1972-73, German Twp. Water Dist., 1984-85; pres. Evansville Unitarian Universalist Ch., 1984-86; performer Evansville Philharmonic Orch., 1986-98. Recipient Kappa Alpha Order Ct. of HOnor award, 1962, Silver Beaver award Boy Scouts Am., 1980, presentation for vol. svc. contbg. betterment of cmty. Office Hearings and Appeals, 1992, presentation outstanding jud. mentor tng. Supreme Ct. Iowa, 1992, presentation disting. mentor tng. Fla. Jud. Coll., 1992. Mem. Okla. Bar Assn., Okla. County Bar Assn. (v.p. 1967), Wyo. Bar Assn., Evansville Bar Assn. (jud. rep. 1986-87, James Bethel Gresham Freedom award 1988), Young Lawyers Assn., Assn. Adminstrv. Law Judges HHS (bd. dirs. 1979-82, presentation dedicated svc. advancing jud. edn. 1992), Oklahoma City U. Alumni Assn. (bd. dirs. 1965). Home: 6105 School Rd # 6 Evansville IN 47720

CAPSOURAS, BARBARA ELLEN, college official; b. Niagara Falls, N.Y., Nov. 10, 1951; d. Joseph John and Wanda M. (Sczepanska) Horvath; m. John David Capsouras, Nov. 20, 1981; children: Cristina, Alexi. Student, Trenton State Coll., 1969-70; AA in Bus. Adminstrn. with high honors, County Coll. of Morris, 1982; postgrad., Fairleigh Dickinson U., 1983-84. Cert. family day care provider, N.J. Adminstrv. asst. tech. ops. Warner-Lambert Co., Morris Plains, N.J., 1970-79, adminstrv. asst. internat. mfg., 1979-80, adminstrv. asst. internat. mktg., 1980-83, pub. affairs coord., 1983-89; dir. alumni rels. County Coll. Morris, Randolph, N.J., 1990—, bd. dirs., mem. adv. bd. Child Care Ctr., 1990-93. Mem. AAUW, N.J. Consortium Alumni Profls., County Coll. of Morris Alumni Assn. (adv. bd. 1990—, mgr. campaign steering com. 1990-93, mgr. alumni annual fund 1990—), NOW, Nat. Parks and Conservation Assn., High Life Ski Club (officer 1972—, mem. race team, recipient various tennis and skiing awards). Avocations: tennis, jogging, swimming, bicycling, skiing. Office: County Coll Morris 214 Center Grove Rd Randolph NJ 07869-2007

CAPSTAFF, GENEVIEVE MACKEEBY, humanities educator; b. Paterson, N.J., Nov. 5, 1916; d. John Wesley and Josephine Claire (Pinckney) MacKeeby; m. Albert Lant Capstaff, Nov. 3, 1934 (div. Apr. 1945); 1 child, Judith Capstaff Heinrich. PhB, DePaul U., 1963, MA, 1968; CAS, No. Ill. U., 1973; PhD, Columbia Pacific U., 1975. Tchr. English, Reavis H.S., Burbank, Ill., 1966-68; prof. humanities Moraine Valley C.C., Palos Hills, Ill., 1968-86, prof. emeritus, 1986—, adj. prof., 1986-99; lectr., spkr. in field. Contbr. articles to German Shorthair Pointer News, Am. Kennel Club Gazette, 1964—. Mem. AAUW, German Wirehaired Pointer Club Am. (dir. 1960—), German Wirehaired Pointer Club Ill. (dir. 1963-90, treas. 1995-96, pres. 1997). Republican. Anglican. Avocation: breeding, showing and hunting German Wirehaired Pointers. Home: 13909 Will Cook Rd Orland Park IL 60467-1237

CAPUANO, MICHAEL EVERETT, congressman; b. Somerville, Mass., 1952; s. Andrew and Rita (Garvey) C.; m. Barbara Teebagy, 1974; children: Michael, Joseph. BA in Psychology, Dartmouth Coll., 1973; JD, Boston Coll., 1977; postgrad., Boston U. Bar: Mass. 1977. Alderman Ward 5 Somerville, 1977-79, alderman-at-large, 1985-89, mayor, 1990-99; congressman 8th Dist. Mass., 1999—; mem. Ho. Dem. Leadership team (regional whip), Ho. Com. on Banking and Fin. Svcs., subcoms. on Captial Mkts., Securities and Govt. Sponsored Enterprises, Com. on Sci., subcom. on Tech. Elected congressman Nov. 1998 with 82% of the vote. Office: 1232 Longworth HOB Washington DC 20515*

CAPUTI, MARIE ANTOINETTE, university official; b. Newport, R.I., Aug. 14, 1935; d. Saverio and Madeline (Esposito) C. AB, Barnard Coll., 1957; MS in Social Work, Columbia U., 1959; PhD, St. Louis U., 1978. Lic. social worker, Fla. Field instr. Columbia U., N.Y.C., 1962-64; social worker ob.-gyn. dept. Bronx (N.Y.) Mcpl. Hosp., 1964-65; generic supr. Maimonides Med. Ctr., Bklyn., 1965-75; asst. prof. Grad. Sch. of Social Work U. Wis., Madison, 1978-83; instr. dept. continuing edn. Edgewood Coll., Madison, Wis., 1982-85; asst. prof., dir. faculty svcs. region II Cardinal Stritch Coll., Milw., 1984-89; ptnr. Midwest Ctr. for Human Svcs., Madison, 1982-89; assoc. prof., dir. grad. and continuing edn. St. Thomas U., Miami, Fla., 1989-92, coord. Earth Literacy Programs, 1993-94; asst. to v.p. for acad. affairs Lynn U., Boca Raton, Fla., 1993, dir. Instnl. Rsch., Instnl. Effectiveness, 1994—; faculty mentor Walden U., 1993—; researcher, specialist U. Wis. Survery Rsch. Lab., Madison, 1982-84; rsch. cons. North Chicago VA Med. Ctr., 1984-89; cons. U. Wis. Hosp. & Clinics, Madison, 1987; adj. asst. prof. NYU Grad. Sch. Social Work, N.Y.C., 1967-69. Contbr. articles to profl. jours. Lavanburg Cornerhouse scholar, 1957-59; VA fellow, 1975-78. Mem. NASW, AAUW, Assn. of Institutional Rsch. Democrat. Avocations: opera, photography, classical music, theater, gardening. Home: 7120 SW 41st Pl Davie FL 33314-3182 Office: Lynn U 3601 N Military Trl Boca Raton FL 33431-5598

CAPUTO, A. RICHARD, judge. AB, Brown U., 1960; LLB, U. Pa., 1963. Judge U.S. Dist. Ct. (mid. dist.) Pa., 1997—. Office: 235 N Washington Ave Scranton PA 18501

CAPUTO, DAVID ARMAND, university president, political scientist educator; b. Brownsville, Pa., Aug. 30, 1943; s. Armand and Marie E. (Smalstig) C.; m. Alice M. Glotfelty, June 27, 1964; children—Christopher, Elizabeth, Jeffrey. BA, Miami U., Oxford, Ohio, 1965; MA, Yale U., 1967, MPhil, 1968, PhD, 1970. Mem. faculty Purdue U., 1969—, prof. polit. sci., 1977—, head dept., 1978-87, dean Sch. Liberal Arts, 1987-95; pres. Hunter Coll., CUNY, N.Y.C., 1995—. Author: Urban America: The Policy Alternatives, 1976; co-author: Urban Politics and Decentralization, 1974; editor: Politics of Policy-Making in America, 1977. Ruling elder Central Presbyn. Ch., Lafayette, Ind., 1981—. Woodrow Wilson nat. fellow, 1965-66; NSF faculty fellow, 1977; Fulbright fellow, Italy, 1985; Lilly fellow, 1985; Bologna chair Fulbright sr. fellow, Italy, 1993. Mem. Am. Polit. Sci. Assn., Am. Soc. Public Adminstrn., Midwest Polit. Sci. Assn., So. Polit. Sci. Assn., Phi Beta Kappa, Omicron Delta Kappa. Office: Hunter Coll CUNY 695 Park Ave New York NY 10021-5024

CAPUTO, GREGORY MICHAEL, physician, educator; b. May 18, 1954; s. Joseph Vincent and Mary (Pisapia) C.; m. Leesa, June 10, 1978; children: Jennifer, Michael. BA in Biol. Sci., U. Del., 1976; MD, U. Md., 1980. Diplomate Am. Bd. Internal Medicine, Am. Bd. Infectious Disease. Intern Thomas Jefferson U. Hosp., Phila., 1980-81; clin. asst. prof. dept. medicine, 1987-90; resident Milton S. Hershey Med. Ctr., Pa. State U. Coll. Medicine, Hershey, Pa., 1981-83; fellow divsn. infectious diseases Milton S. Hershey Med. Ctr., Pa. State U. Coll. Medicine, Hershey, 1983-84; from asst. prof. to prof. medicine Pa. State U., Hershey, 1990-98, prof., 1998—; chief, Divsn. Gen. Internal Medicine Milton S. Hershey Med. Ctr., Hershey, Pa.; staff Med. Ctr. Del., Wilmington, 1985-90, Union Hosp., Elkton, Md., 1985-90, St. Francis Hosp., Wilmington, 1985-90, Alfred I. duPont Inst., Wilmington, 1990-95, U. Hosp., Milton S. Hershey Med. Ctr., 1990—, med. dir. diabetes amputation prevention program, 1993—, dir. Cecil County Lyme Disease Clinic, Elkton, 1988-90; cons. Assn. Acad. Health Ctrs., Am. Lyme Disease Found., 1992—; lectr. in field. Author: (chpt.) Comprehensive Textbook of Pulmonary Medicine, 1991, The Foot in Diabetes, 2d edit., 1994; co-author: (chpt.) Comprehensive Textbook Pulmonary Medicine Update, 1995, (computer program) The Prevention Guides for Clinicians and Patients, 1996; co-editor: Medical Consultation, 1997; reviewer New Eng. Jour. Medicine, Chest, Clin. Infectious Diseases, Diabetes Care; contbr. articles to profl. jours. Recipient Fletcher Brown award, 1975, Disting. Physician award, 1995; Harvard Med. Sch. fellow, 1984-85, C. Everett Koop Inst. fellow Dartmouth Coll., 1996, 97; Ellis scholar, 1976. Fellow ACP; mem. Am. Soc. Microbiology, Soc. Gen. Internal Medicine, Am. Diabetes Assn., Phi Beta Kappa, Phi Kappa Phi, Beta Beta Beta, Alpha Omega Alpha. Avocations: music, tennis, hiking. Office: Divsn Gen Internal Medicine Milton S Hershey Med Ctr Hershey PA 17033

CAPUTO, JOHN DAVID, philosophy educator; b. Oct. 26, 1940; s. Peter Joseph and Florence Agnes (Binns) C.; m. Mary Kathryn Boyle, June 8, 1968; children: David, Paul, Kathryn Elizabeth. BA, LaSalle U., 1962; MA, Villanova U., 1964; PhD, Bryn Mawr Coll., 1968. Instr. philosophy St. Joseph's U., 1965-68; asst. prof. Villanova (Pa.) U., 1968-72, assoc. prof., 1972-76, prof. philosophy, 1976—, dept. chmn., 1972-80; adj. prof. Fordham U. Grad. Sch., 1985-87; vis. prof. Duquesne U., 1978, Fordham U., 1980. David R. Cook chair philosophy, 1993—. Author: The Mystical Element in Heidegger's Thought, 1978, Heidegger and Aquinas: An Essay on Overcoming Metaphysics, 1982, Radical Hermeneutics, 1987, Against Ethics, 1993, Demythologizing Heidegger, 1993, Deconstruction in a Nutshell, 1997, The Prayers and Tears of Jacques Derrida, 1997, Of God, the Gift and Postmodernism, 1999. Am. Coun. Learned Socs. grantee, 1972, 83-84; Nat. Endowment Humanities grantee, 1985, 91-92. Mem. Am. Cath. Philos. Assn. (v.p. 1986-87, pres. 1986-87), Am. Philos. Assn. (exec. com. 1986—, nat. bd. officers 1992-95), Hegel Soc. Am., Heidegger Conf. Am., Metaphys. Soc. Am., Soc. for Phenomenology and Existential Philosophy (exec. ci-dir. 1992-95). Democrat. Roman Catholic. Home: 14 Harrow Cir Wayne PA 19087-3852 Office: Villanova U Dept Philosophy Villanova PA 19085

CAPUTO, JOSEPH ANTHONY, university president; b. Jersey City, May 10, 1940; s. Anthony and Virginia (Bennett) C.; m. Linda Mary Ryan, Sept. 4, 1965; children: Christine D., David R. BS, Seton Hall U., 1962, MS, 1964; PhD, U. Houston, 1967. Research assoc. Duke U., Durham, N.C., 1967-68; prof. dept. chemistry SUNY Coll.-Buffalo, 1968-77, chmn. dept. chemistry, 1974-77; dean sch. sci. and math. S.W. Tex. State U., San Marcos, 1977-79, v.p. acad. affairs, 1979-81; pres. Millersville (Pa.) U., 1981—; mem. task force on transfer articulation Mid. States Commn. on Higher Edn., 1993-94, visitation team chair, 1987-92; mem. State Sys. Higher Edn. Commn. of Pres., 1981—, vice chair, 1982-84, chmn., 1984-86, mem.-at-large, 1995-96; bd. dirs. Acad. for Profession of Tchg., 1987-89; mem. Task Force on Acad. Quality and Enrollment Mgmt., chair, 1988-90; mem. tchr. edn. accreditation coun. Coun. of Ind. Colls., 1997. Contbr. numerous articles to profl. jours. Chmn. bd. Pa. State Athletic Conf., 1983, mem., 1981—; mem. Gov. Transition Team, 1982; mem. adv. bd. Commonwealth of Pa. Ben Franklin Partnership Program, 1983, N.E. Tier Ben Franklin

Tech. Ctr., 1988; bd. dirs. Lancaster Area Arts Coun., 1987-89, Lancaster Gen. Hosp. Found., 1989—, Harrisburg U. Ctr. Consortium, 1987-92, Lancaster Chamber Commerce and Industry, 1985-88, Urban League Lancaster County, 1988-93, St. Joseph Hosp. Neumann Svcs., Inc., 1983-85, Econ. Devel. Coun. Lancaster, 1997—, SICO Found., 1997—; mem. capital allocations com. Lancaster Gen. Health Alliance Fin., 1995, strategic planning and mktg. com., 1995-96; mem. Pa. Adv. Coun. for Migrant Edn., 1988-92; mem. 30th anniversary com. of 100, Lancaster County Human Rels. Commn., 1994; hon. chair Lancaster br. NAACP, 1990, Spanish Am. Civic Assn., mem. capital campaign com., 1988, 96-97. Recipient Elaine J. Washington award Urban League of Lancaster County, 1994; SUNY Rsch. Found. fellow and grantee, 1969-70, 73-74; NSF grantee, 1972-73, 75-77; Am. Chem. Soc. grantee, 1969-72; Sigma Xi grantee, 1976. Mem. AAAS, Am. Chem. Soc., Am. Assn. State Colls. and Univs. (com. on profl. devel. 1988-92, vice chair 1991, chair 1992, found. bd. dirs. 1984-87, policies and purposes com. 1982-85, 94-97, 98—), Am. Coun. on Edn. (Commn. on Leadership Devel. 1992-95, exec. com. 1996—), Pa. Assn. Colls. and Univs. (treas. 1991, v.p. 1992, chmn. 1993-94, bd. dirs. 1991-95, Commn. for Univs. 1981—, vice chair 1982-84, chmn. 1984-86), Renaissance Group (exec. com. 1994-96, chair 1994-95), Sigma Xi, Phi Sigma Pi, Phi Eta Sigma, Phi Kappa Phi. Home: 10 Hemlock Ln Millersville PA 17551-1701 Office: Millersville U of Pa Office of Pres PO Box 1002 Millersville PA 17551-0302

CAPUTO, KATHRYN MARY, paralegal; b. Bklyn., June 29, 1948; d. Fortunato and Agnes (Iovino) Villacci; m. Joseph John Caputo, Apr. 4, 1976. AS in Bus. Adminstrn., Nassau C.C., Garden City, N.Y., 1989. Legal asst. Jacob Jacobson, Oceanside, N.Y., 1973-77; legal asst., office mgr. Joseph Kaldor, P.C., Franklin Square, N.Y., 1978-82, William H. George, Valley Stream, N.Y., 1983-89; exec. legal asst., office adminstr. Katz & Bernstein, Westbury, N.Y., 1990-93; sr. paralegal and office adminstr. Blaustein & Weinick, Garden City, N.Y., 1993—; instr. adult continuing edn. legal sec. procedures Lawrence (N.Y.) H.S., 1992—. Spl. events coord. Bklyn.-Queens Marriage Encounter, 1981, 82, 83, 85, 86; mem. Lynbrook Civic Assn. Mem. L.I. Paralegal Assn. Avocations: traveling, reading, theatre, gardening. Office: Blaustein & Weinick 1205 Franklin Ave Garden City NY 11530-1629

CAPUTO, LUCIO, trade company executive; b. Monreale, Italy, May 22, 1935; s. Giuseppe and Gioacchina (Spinnato) C.; came to U.S., 1967. Law Degree, Palermo U., 1957, Journalism Degree, 1958, Degree in Polit. Sci., 1960, postgrad. Econs., 1961; m. Maria Luisa Mayr, Oct. 5, 1967; 1 child, Giorgio. Journalist, Italy, 1950-65. Bar: Italy, 1961. Assoc. Studio Legale Caputo-Orlando, Palermo, Sicily, 1960-62; ofcl. Italian Fgn. Trade Inst., 1962-82, market researcher, Libya, Cyprus, 1963, dep. trade commr., London, 1964-67, dir. study mission S.E. Asia, 1967, Italian trade commr., Phila., 1967-71, N.Y.C., 1972-82; founder Italian Wine Promotion Ctr., N.Y.C., 1975—, Italian Tile Ctr., 1979—, Italian Fashion Ctr., 1980—, Italian Shoe Ctr., 1981—, ITAL Trade Ctr., N.Y.C., 1981—; pres. Ital Trade USA Corp., 1982-86; pres. Italian Wine and Food Inst., 1984—; organizer ann. Italian Week on 5th Ave., N.Y.C.; exec. v.p., bd. dirs. Gruppo Esponenti Italiani, 1974—; adv. bd. Italy-Am. C. of C., 1972-82; U.S. rep. Verona Fair Org., 1980—; chmn. Internat. Trade Ctr., Inc., 1987—; exec. dir. Gruppo Ristoratori Italiani, 1988-90; vice chmn, bd. dirs. Nat. Wine Coalition, 1990—; chmn. bd. dirs. European Wine Coun., 1993—, chmn. bus. adv. coun. for gov., 1996—; bd. dirs. Am. Soc. Italian Legions of Merit. Signer agreement between Italy and People's Republic of China, 1967; editor trade mags.: Italy Presents, Quality (English, French, Spanish, German), 1962-64; contbr. articles to Italian mags. and newspapers. Lt. Italian Air Force, 1959-61. Named Cavaliere Ufficiale nell' Ordine al Merito della Republica Italiana, 1972, Commendatore, 1981, Grande Ufficiale, 1996. Mem. Sommelier Soc. Am., Italian Sommelier Soc., Italian Bar Assn., Italian Journalist Assn., Fgn. Consular Assn. Phila., Soc. Fgn. Consuls N.Y., Am. Soc. Italian Legions of Merit (bd. dirs.), World Trade Ctr. Club. Roman Catholic. Office: 1 World Trade Ctr Ste 7885 New York NY 10048-7885

CAPUTO, PHILIP JOSEPH, author, journalist, screenwriter; b. Chgo., June 10, 1941; s. Joseph and Marie Ylonda (Napolitan) C.; m. Jill Esther Ongemach, June 21, 1969 (div. 1982); children: Geoffrey Jacob, Marc Antony.; m. Marcelle Lynn Besse, Oct. 30, 1982 (div. 1985); m. Leslie Blanchard Ware, June 4, 1988. B.A. in English, Loyola U., Chgo., 1964. Mem. staff Chgo. Tribune, 1968-72; fgn. corr. Europe, Middle East, USSR, 1972-77; freelance writer, 1977—; screenwriter Mercury-Douglas Prodns., Paramount, 1987—. Author: A Rumor of War, 1977, Horn of Africa, 1980, Del Corso's Gallery, 1983, Indian Country, 1987, Means of Escape, 1991, Equation for Evil, 1996, Exiles, 1997; contbr. to N.Y. Times, L.A. Times, Boston Globe, Esquire, others. Served with USMCR, 1964-67, Vietnam. Recipient award Ill. AP, Ill. United Press award, Green Gavel award ABA, Overseas Press Club award, Pulitzer prize, Sidney Hillman award, others. Mem. Authors Guild, Nat. Writers Union. Democrat. Roman Catholic. Address: care Aaron Priest Lit Agy 708 3rd Ave New York NY 10017-4201*

CAPUTO, RICHARD KEVIN, social work educator, researcher; b. Bklyn., Sept. 11, 1948; s. Salvatore and Emily (Speciale) C. BA, Bklyn. Coll., 1970; MA, Iowa State U., 1972; MSW, Ariz. State U., 1978; PhD, U. Chgo., 1982. Lic. social worker, Pa. Mental health specialist I Ariz. State Hosp., Phoenix, 1973-75, mental health specialist II, 1975-76; dir. dept. rsch. United Charities of Chgo., 1982-87; asst. prof. U. Pa., Phila., 1987—. Author: Management and Information Systems in Human Services, 1988, Welfare and Freedom American Style, 1991; contbr. articles to profl. jours. Mem. NASW, Am. Acad. Polit. and Social Sci., Am. Evaluation Assn., Am. Sociol. Assn., Coun. Social Work Edn. (cert.). Office: U Pa Sch Social Work 3701 Locust Walk Philadelphia PA 19104-6214

CAPUTO, SALVATORE, critic; b. Plainfield, N.J., Dec. 18, 1952; s. Nicola and Antonietta (Rivezzi) C.; m. Joan Louise Kocurek, June 8, 1984; children: Christopher Michael, David Nicholas. BA, Rutgers U., 1975. News clerk Courier News, Bridgewater, N.J., 1975-77, reporter, asst. entertainment editor, 1977-81; copy editor Arizona Republic, Phoenix, Ariz., 1981-89, pop culture reporter, 1989-90, pop music critic, 1990-97; freelance writer, 1997—.

CAPUTO, WAYNE JAMES, surgeon, podiatrist; b. Newark, Feb. 18, 1956; s. James Vincent and Jennie (DeMaio) C.; m. Phyllis A. Grillo, Nov. 20, 1984; children: Karla, Stefanie. BS in Biology, Syracuse U., 1978; DPM, N.Y. Coll. Podiatric Medicine, 1982. Diplomate Am. Bd. Podiatric Surgery. Clin. asst. prof. N.Y. Coll. Podiatric Medicine, N.Y.C., 1984-89; chief dept. podiatric surgery Clara Maass Med. Ctr., Belleville, N.J., 1987—, Columbus Hosp., Newark, 1995—; dir. residency in podiatric surgery Union (N.J.) Hosp., 1990—. Contbr. articles to profl. jours. Fellow ACS, Am. Coll. Dermatologists. Office: Clara Maass Profl Med Ctr 5 Franklin Ave Belleville NJ 07109-3532

CARABELLO, BLASE ANTHONY, cardiology educator; b. Reading, Pa., Aug. 5, 1947; s. Charles Anthony and Fern June (Houck) C.; m. Susan Jane Beidman, Aug. 15, 1970 (div. June 1977); 1 child, Charles; m. Catherine Wheatley, Apr. 9, 1989; children: Nicholas, Blaise. BA, Gettsburg Coll., 1969; MD, Temple U., 1973. Diplomate Am. Bd. Internal Medicine, Am. Bd. Cardiology. Intern in Medicine Mass. Gen. Hosp., Boston, 1973-74, resident in Medicine Harvard Med. Sch., 1974-75, sr. resident in Medicine Harvard Med. Sch., 1975-76; fellow in Cardiology Peter Bent Brigham Hosp., Boston, 1976-78, cardiologist, 1978-79; asst. prof. Medicine U. Va. Hosp., Charlottesville, 1979-81; dir. Diagnostic Cardiology Temple U., Phila., 1981-85; prof. Medicine Med. U. S.C., Charleston, 1985-95, dir. clin. rsch., 1990-99; Charles Ezra Daniel prof. medicine U. S.C., Charleston, 1995-99; chief of med. svcs. Houston VA Med. Ctr., 1999—; vice chmn. medicine Baylor Sch. of Medicine, Houston, 1999—. Author: Cardiology Pearls, 1993; contbr. articles to profl. jours. Beta-Blockade grantee Pub. Health Svc., 1988-89, Dept. Va. Pub. Health grantee, 1989-94. Fellow Am. Coll. Cardiology, Am. Heart Assn. (coun. on circulation, chmn. com. on cardiac catheterization); mem. Am. Soc. Clin. Investigation, Alpha Omega Alpha. Avocation: fine dining. Home: 5303 Huisache St Bellaire TX 77401 Office: Dept Medicine VA Hosp Houston TX 77030

CARAHER, MICHAEL EDWARD, systems analyst; b. Indpls., Dec. 22, 1953; s. Gregory Thomas and Mary Margaret (Shevlin) C.; m. Jan. 6, 1979 (div. 1986); children: Joseph Michael, Erin Michelle. BA, Butler U., Indpls., 1976. Systems mgr. Alexander Typesetting, Indpls., 1984-88; systems specialist for Weimer Graphics divsn. Shepard Poorman Comm. Corp., Indpls., 1988-94; sys. mgr. Shepard Poorman Comm. Corp., 1994-96, Ind. State Budget Agy., Indpls., 1996—. Vice precinct committeeman Ind. Dem. Party, Indpls., 1972-78, precinct committeeman, 1994. Mem. Ancient Order of Hibernians. Democrat. Roman Catholic. Home: 5205 E Washington St Indianapolis IN 46219-6325

CARALEY, DEMETRIOS JAMES, political scientist, educator, author; b. N.Y.C., June 22, 1932; s. Christopher and Stella (Psaras) C.; m. Jeanne Benner (div.); children: James Christopher (dec.), David Andrew, Anne Leslie; m. Vilma Mairo Bornemann, 1988; 1 child, Lisa Anne. B.A. summa cum laude, Columbia U., 1954, Ph.D., 1962. Mem. faculty Barnard Coll. and Columbia U., N.Y.C., 1959—; prof. polit. sci. Barnard Coll. and Columbia U., 1968—, Janet H. Robb prof. social scis., 1980—; editor Polit. Sci. Quar., 1973—; dir. Grad. Program in Pub. Policy and Adminstrn. Columbia U., 1978-85, chmn. Barnard dept. polit. sci., 1965-95; pres. Acad. Polit. Sci., 1992—; vis. scholar Russell Sage Found., 1995-96. Author: Politics of Military Unification, 1966, New York City's Deputy Mayor—City Administrator, 1966, Party Politics and National Elections, 1966, (with R. H. Connery) Governing the City, 1969, City Governments and Urban Problems, 1977, American Political Institutions in the 1970's, 1976, (with M.A. Epstein) The Making of American Foreign and Domestic Policy, 1978, Doing More With Less, 1982, (with R. H. Connery) National Security and Nuclear Strategy, 1983, The President's War Powers, 1984, Volatilities in the New World Politics, 1993, Critical Issues for Clinton's Domestic Agenda, 1994, (with B.B. Hartman) American Leadership, Ethnic Conflict, and the New World Politics, 1997; contbr. American Politics and Public Policy, 1978, Urban Policymaking, 1979. Mem. North Tarrytown Zoning Bd. Appeals, 1970-71; mem. North Tarrytown Bd. Trustees, 1971-73, dep. mayor and acting mayor, 1972-73; chmn. North Tarrytown Planning Bd., 1977-79; mem. N.Y.C. Police Commr.'s Research Adv. Bd., 1979-85. Served with USNR, 1954-56. Mem. Am. Polit. Sci. Assn., Acad. Polit. Sci. (bd. dirs., pres. 1992—), Phi Beta Kappa. Club: University (N.Y.C.). Democrat. Office: Columbia Univ Barnard Coll Dept Polit Sci New York NY 10027 also: Acad Polit Sci/Polit Sci Quar 475 Riverside Dr Ste 1274 New York NY 10115-1299

CARAM, DOROTHY FARRINGTON, educational consultant; b. McAllen, Tex., Jan. 14, 1933; d. Curtis Leon and Elena (Santander) Farrington; m. Pedro C. Caram, June 7, 1958; children: Pedro M., Juan D., Hector L., Jose M. BA, Rice U., 1955, MA, 1974; EdD, U. Houston, 1982; postgrad., U. Madrid, 1957. Tchr. Houston Ind. Sch. Dist., 1955-56, 56-60, St. Mark's Episcopal Ch., Houston, 1964-65; substitute tchr. St. Vincent De Paul Cath. Sch., Houston, 1965-68; mgr. med. office Houston, 1983; dir. Fed. Home Loan Bank, Little Rock, 1976-82; pres. Inst. Hispanic Culture, Houston, 1983, 93; chmn. bd., pres. Inst. Hispanic Culture, 1984; with Houston Ednl. Excellence Program, 1980; mem. task force Tex. Edn. Agy., 1981-83; mem. adv. coun. Nat. Inst. Neurol. and Communicative Disorders and Stroke, 1972-76; pres. IDM Satellite Comm. of Tex. Divsn., Inc., 1990, chmn. bd., 1998—; asst. to pres. U. Houston, 1991-94, ret., 1994. Mem. coun. Miller Theater, Houston, 1976—; bd. dirs. Houston Pops, 1983-87, United Way Tex., 1991-94; mem. tadk force Quality Integrated Edn., Houston, 1972; bd. dirs. United Way Tex., Gulf Coast, 1989-95, mem. exec. bd., sec.; mem. Civil Commn. houston, 1983-85; bd. mgrs. Harris County Hosp. Dist., 1988-90; founder, bd. dirs. Houston Hispanic Forum, 1985, pres., 1989-90; chmn. bd. Teatro Bilingue de Houston, 1989-90; pres. Mexican Cultural Inst. Houston, Inc., 1997; bd. civic ctr. Southmain Ctr. Assn., 1998; bd. dirs. Harris County Hosp. Dist. Found., 1997—, Houston Ind. Sch. Dist., 1996—, chmn. peer com. magnet and vanguard schs., 1996—; mem. adv. bd. Theater Under Stars, End Hunger Network, Career and Recovery, Jobs for Progress of Tex. Gulf Coast, Inc., AAMA; bd. dirs. Majestic Seas Aquarium, 1998—. Recipient Willie Velasquez Outstanding Hispanic Citizenship award, 1994; named Col. of Yr., United Way Tex. Gulf Coast, 1992; decorated Lady in Court if Isabel La Catolica by King Carlos (Spain), 1984. Mem. Cedars Club (pres. 1978). Roman Catholic. Home: 2603 Glen Haven Blvd Houston TX 77025-2132

CARAM, EVE LA SALLE, English educator, writer; b. Hot Springs, Ark., May 11, 1934; d. Raymond Briggs and Lois Elizabeth (Merritt) La Salle; m. Richard George Caram, Apr. 19, 1965 (div. Apr. 1978); 1 child, Bethel Eve. BA, Bard Coll., 1956; MA, U. Mo., 1977. English instr. Stephens Coll., Columbia, Mo., 1974-79, 82; fiction writing grad. instr. Sch. Profl. Writing U. So. Calif., L.A., 1982-87; English lit. and writing instr. Calif. State U., Northridge, 1983—; sr. fiction writing instr. The Writers' Program UCLA, 1983—; fiction contest judge Calif. State U., Long Beach, 1992, 94, writer's conf. spkr., 1985-87, 94; spkr., mem. panel Tex. Am. Studies Assn., Wichita Falls, 1998. Author: (novel) Dear Corpus Christi, 1991, Wintershine, 1994; editor: Palm Readings, Stories from Southern California, 1998; fiction editor West/Word, 1991. Mem. AAUP, Assn. Calif. State Profs., Nat. Assn. Tchrs. English, Poets and Writers, PEN Ctr. U.S.A. West. Democrat. Avocations: swimming, beach walks, outdoors. Home: 3400 Ben Lomond Pl # 121 Los Angeles CA 90027 Office: UCLA Ext The Writers Program 10995 Le Conte Ave Los Angeles CA 90024 also: Calif State U English Dept 1811 Nordoff Northridge CA 91330

CARAMEROS, GEORGE DEMITRIUS, JR., natural gas company executive; b. El Paso, Tex., Mar. 1, 1924; s. George Demitrius and Esperanza (Purdy) C.; m. Verna Narcissus Easterling, May 26, 1944; children: Cecille (Mrs. George Shannon), Cynthia (Mrs. John Blevins), Cathy (Mrs. David Patton), George Demitrius III, Carl. B.A., U. Tex., El Paso, 1947. With El Paso Natural Gas Co., 1948-80; mgr. new projects devel. subs. El Paso Products Co., 1957-60; mng. dir. El Paso Europe-Afrique, Paris, France, 1960-65; adminstrv. asst. to chmn. bd. El Paso Natural Gas, N.Y.C., 1965-66; asst. v.p. El Paso Natural Gas Co., N.Y.C., 1966-70, v.p., 1970-73; exec. v.p. El Paso Europe-Afrique, N.Y.C., 1973-75; exec. v.p. The El Paso Co., 1975-78, vice chmn., 1978-80; pres. El Paso LNG Co., Houston, 1975-78, chmn., 1978-80, also bd. dirs.; chmn. Internat. Gas Devel. Corp., 1980-85; v.p. Groupe Internat. des Importateurs de Gaz Naurel Liquifie, 1988-92. Served with AUS, World War II. Decorated Bronze Star, Combat Inf. badge. Mem. Interstate Natural Gas Assn. Am. (dir.), Lakeside Country Club. Presbyterian. Home: 660 Shartle Cir Houston TX 77024-5503 Office: Ste 1760 1200 Smith St Houston TX 77002

CARAMIA, PHILIP DOMINICK, government official; b. Fairfield, Calif., May 7, 1955; s. Dominick Joseph and Genevieve Marie Caramia; m. Penney Marie Harwell, Sept. 30, 1989. BA in Polit. Sci., La. State U., 1984; MPA, North Tex. State U., 1987. Cert. govt. fin. mgr. Salesman Gibsons, Shreveport, La., 1973-74; shipping mgr. J.C. Penney, Shreveport, 1974-84; sr. evaluator GAO, Dallas, 1985—. Editor newsletter Countdown to Fountain Place, 1988. Del. Tex. Dem. Primary Conv., Dallas, 1988. Recipient leadership giving award Combined Fed. Campaign, 1998; Hatton Sumners fellow North Tex. State U., 1984. Mem. ASPA, Nature Conservancy, Am. Automobile Assn., World Ski Assn., CF/JM Homeowners Assn. Avocations: golf, travel writing, corporate correspondence, pruning. E-mail: c aramiap.dalro@gao.gov. Office: GAO 1999 Bryan Ste 2200 Dallas TX 75201

CARAS, JOSEPH SHELDON, life insurance company executive; b. Lawrence, Mass., Aug. 3, 1924; s. Joseph and Bessie Esther (Kasanoff) C.; m. Adele Salett, June 8, 1947; children: Richard, David, Susan. BA, Bowdoin Coll., 1948. CLU. With Met. Life Ins. Co., 1949-55; asst. mgr. Waltham, Mass., 1951-55; with New Eng. Mut. Life Ins. Co., 1955-88; 2d. v.p. mktg. Boston, 1967-71, sr. v.p. mktg. services, 1971-81, sr. v.p. mktg., 1982-88, ret., 1989; pres. New Eng. Nat., 1981-86; dir. New Eng. Nat. of N.Y., Covenant Life Ins. Co., InterNEL Corp.; exec. dir. Nat. Fin. Mktg. Group, 1988-93. Mem. Swampscott (Mass.) Town Meeting, 1972-78; past pres. Temple Emanu-El, Marblehead, Mass. Served with USAAF, 1943-45. Decorated Air medal. Mem. Life Ins. Mktg. Research Assn. (past chmn. sales com. and mktg. services com.), Agy. Mgmt. Tng. Council, Assn. Advanced Life Underwriters, Nat. Assn. Life Underwriters, Am. Soc. C.L.U.'s. Home: 11603 Losano Dr Boynton Beach FL 33437-1927

CARAS, ROGER ANDREW, author, motion picture company executive, television correspondent, radio commentator; b. Methuen, Mass., May 24, 1928; s. Joseph J. and Bessie (Kasanoff) C.; m. Jill Langdon Barclay, Sept. 5, 1954; children: Pamela Jill, Barclay Gordon. Student, Northeastern U., 1948-49, Western Res. U., 1949-50; BA in Cinema, U. So. Calif., 1952; LittD, Rio Grande Coll., 1979; LLD, U. Pa., 1984; DSc, SUNY, 1987. Asst. to v.p., also nat. dir. merchandising for U.S. and Can., Columbia Pictures Corp., 1955-65; v.p. Stanley Kubrick's Polaris Prodns., N.Y.C., 1965-68, Hawk Films Ltd., London, Eng., 1965-68; coll. lectr. on wildlife and conservation, 1955—; sci. editor Armed Forces Radio and TV Service, 1963-68; adj. prof. lit. Southampton Coll., 1975-78; lectr. U. Pa. Sch. Vet. Medicine, 1978-84, bd. overseers, 1981—; adj. prof. animal ecology U. Pa., 1984—. Columnist, Register & Tribune Syndicate, Ladies Home Jour., 1977-82, Newsday, 1980-87, star, CBS radio show, Pets and Wildlife; TV corr., ABC-TV, 20/20 TV News Feature (Emmy award 1990); Author: Antarctica: Land of Frozen Time, 1962, Dangerous to Man, 1964, Wings of Gold, 1965; pseudonym Roger Sarac: The Throwbacks, 1965, The Custer Wolf, 1966, Mammals of North America, 1966, Last Chance on Earth, 1966, Sarang, 1968, Monarch of Deadman Bay, 1969, Source of the Thunder, 1970, Panther, 1970, Death as a Way of Life, 1971, The Private Lives of Animals, 1974, Venomous Animals of the World, 1974, Sockeye, 1975, The Roger Caras Pet Book, 1976, A Zoo in Your Room, 1975, The Forest, 1979, Mysteries of Nature, 1979, Yankee, 1979, Amiable Little Beasts, 1980, The Roger Caras Dog Book, 1980, A Celebration of Dogs, 1982, A Roger Caras Treasury, 1984, Cats, 1985, Dogs, 1985, The Endless Migration, 1985, Mara Simba, 1985, A Celebration of Cats, 1986, Animals in Their Places, 1987, A Cat Is Watching, 1989, Roger Caras' Treasury of Great Horse Stories, 1990, A Dog is Listening, 1991, The Cats of Thistle Hill, 1994, A World Full of Animals, 1994, The Venemous Animals and Poisonous Plants of North America, 1994, A Most Dangerous Journey, 1995, The Roger Caras Dog Book, 3d edit., A Perfect Harmony, 1996, The Bond, People and Their Animals, 1997; contbg. editor: Geo Mag, 1979-84; book critic Boston Globe, 1994-95, Phila. Inquirer, 1994—, Miami Herald, 1994—. Assoc. curator rare books Cleve. Mus. Natural History; mem. adv. coun. Ariz.-Sonora Desert Mus.; mem. adv. bd. Zero Population Growth; v.p. zoo and wildlife com. Morris Animal Found.; v.p. Humane Soc. U.S.; pres., chief oper. officer ASPCA, 1991-99, pres. emeritus, 1999—; bd. visitors Duke Primate Ctr., 1992—; bd. dirs. World Soc. Protection of Animals, 1993—; mem. adv. coun. The Disney Co., 1994—. Recipient Joseph Wood Krutch medal, 1977, Scroll of Achievement Hai-Bar Soc., Israel, 1977, Arbor Day TV award, 1982, 1st recipient Oryx award Israel, 1983, 1st recipient Humanitarian award Am. Vet. Med. Assn., 1986, George T. Angell Humanitarian award Mass. Soc. Prevent Cruelty to Animals, 1987, James Herriot award Humane Soc. U.S., 1991, Ellis Island medal, 1996. Fellow Royal Soc. Arts, Rochester Museum and Sci. Center; mem. Authors League, Outdoor Writers Assn., Dog Writers Am., Westminster Kennel Club (mem. bd. govs., dog show com.), Mensa, Blue Key, Delta Kappa Alpha (past nat. pres.). *I don't know what happens next but at least I can say that so far I have lived for more than my own gratification. I have believed in what I have done. You have to be able to say that.*

CARASSO, ALFRED SAM, mathematician; b. Alexandria, Egypt, Apr. 9, 1939; came to U.S., 1962; s. Samuel and Renee (Ades) C.; m. Beatrice Kozak, June 12, 1964; children: Adam Leonard, Rachel Lisa. BSc in Physics, U. Adelaide, Australia, 1960; PhD in Math., U. Wis., 1968. Meteorologist Bur. Meteorology, Adelaide, 1960-62; rsch. asst. grad. sch. U. Wis., Madison, 1962-68; asst. prof. math. Mich. State U., East Lansing, 1968-69; asst. prof. math. U. N.Mex., Albuquerque, 1969-72, assoc. prof., 1972-76, prof., 1976-81; mathematician Nat. Inst. Standards and Tech., Gaithersburg, Md., 1982—; cons. Los Alamos (N.Mex.) Nat. Lab., 1972-81, Inst. Def. Analyses's Ctr. Computing Scis., Bowie, Md., 1996—. Contbr. articles to profl. jours. Mem. Am. Math. Soc., Soc. for Indsl. and Applied Math., Cosmos Club. Jewish. Achievements include rsch. in the math. and computational theory of ill-posed problems in partial differential equations, integral equations and deconvolution, holomorphic semigroup theory, time reversal in dissipative evolution equations, inverse heat conduction problems, image deblurring, blind image restoration, applications in system identification, ultrasonics, electromagnetics; invented "slow evolution" constraint in ill-posed continuation problems for partial differential equations; patents for new approach in image deblurring. Office: Nat Inst Stds and Tech Math & Computational Scis Gaithersburg MD 20899

CARAVATT, PAUL JOSEPH, JR., communications company executive; b. New Britain, Conn., Dec. 13, 1922; s. Paul Joseph and Bessie (Avery) C.; m. B. Laura Bennett, June 22, 1946; children—Cynthia Diane, Suzanne Laura. AB, Dartmouth, 1945, MBA, 1947. With Nat. Dairy Assn., 1947-49, Young & Rubicam, 1949-50; advt. mgr. Hunting and Fishing mag., 1950-52, Biow Co., 1952-56; v.p. Ogilvy, Benson & Mather, 1956-59; sr. v.p. Foote, Cone & Belding, 1960-64, LaRoche, McCaffrey & McCall (advt. agy.), N.Y.C., 1964-66; pres. Carl Ally, Ind. (advt. agy.), N.Y.C., 1966-67; chmn. bd., chief exec. officer Marschalk Co., Inc. (mem. Interpublic Group of Cos.), N.Y.C., 1967-69; sr. v.p., dir. Interpub. Group Cos., N.Y.C., 1970-72; pres., chief exec. officer, dir. Caravatt Communications, 1971-86, Newtel World Communications, N.Y.C., 1971-86; pres., chief exec. officer Caravatt Mktg., Norwalk, Conn., 1986—; exec. dir. Vision Fund divsn. The Lighthouse, 1994-97. Mem. SAR, Spl. Interest Video Assn. (pres., exec. dir. 1988-97), Newcomer Soc., Univ. Club (N.Y.C.), Ednl. Found. of Spl. Interest Marketers and Prodrs. (pres. 1997—), Zeta Psi. Congregationalist. Home: 274 Westport Rd Wilton CT 06897-4723

CARB, STEPHEN AMES, lawyer; b. Bklyn., Nov. 27, 1930; s. Alfred Benjamin and Betty (Pocost) C.; m. Sarah Rover, Dec. 24, 1971; 1 son, Daniel; children by previous marriage—Alison, Brian, Evan. AB, Colgate U., 1952; LLB, Columbia, 1955. Bar: N.Y. 1958. Since practiced in N.Y.C.; asso. firm Carb, Luria, Cook & Kufeld, N.Y.C., 1958-61; partner Carb, Luria, Cook & Kufeld, 1961—; bd. dirs. Reliastar Life Ins. Co. N.Y., Entran Devices, Inc. Served to lt. (j.g.) USNR, 1955-58. Mem. ABA, Assn. Bar City N.Y., Phi Kappa Tau, Phi Alpha Delta. Home: 254 E 68th St New York NY 10021-6012 Office: 521 5th Ave New York NY 10175-0003

CARBAJAL, MICHAEL, boxer; b. Phoenix, Sept. 17, 1967. named Jr. Flyweight Champion, Internat. Boxing Fedn., 1990, World Boxing Corp., 1993.

CARBALLO, FERNANDO ANTHONY, gastroenterologist, hepatologist; b. Chgo., Nov. 29, 1961; s. Fernando T. and Carmen L. (Lamas) C.; m. Noreen Patricia Henehan, June 4, 1988; children: Sarah, Andrew, Carmen. BS in Biology, Loyola U., Chgo., 1983; MD, Autonomous U., Guadalajara, Jalisco, Mexico. Diplomate Am. Bd. Internal Medicine and Gastrenterology. Fifth Pathway N.Y. Med. Coll., Valhalla, 1989-90; internal medicine intern West Suburban Hosp. Med. Ctr., Oak Park, Ill., 1990-91; internal medicine resident MacNeal-Rush Presbyn. St. Luke's Med. Ctr., Chgo., 1993-95; fellow in digestive disease Rush Presbyn. St. Luke's Med. Ctr., Chgo., 1993-95; gastroenterologist, hepatologist Sterling Rock Falls Clin., Sterling, Ill., 1995-97, Summit Digestive Disease and Liver Specialists, Oakbrook Terrace, 1998—; cons. Credentials Com., KSB Hosp., Dixon, Ill., 1996-97, Quality Assurance and Improvment Com., CGH Hosp., Sterling, 1996-97. Mem. AMA, Am. Gastroenterol. Assn., Am. Coll. Gastroenterology, Am. Soc. for Gastrointestinal Endoscopy. Republican. Roman Catholic. Avocations: computers, golf. Office: Milw Digestive Disease Cons 2901 W River Pky Ste 414 Milwaukee WI 53215

CARBAUGH, JOHN EDWARD, JR., lawyer; b. Greenville, S.C., Sept. 4, 1945; s. John Edward and Mary Lou (McCarley) C.; m. Mary Middleton Calhoun: children: John, Martha, Leacy, Miller. BA, U. of South, 1967; JD, U. S.C., 1973, postgrad., 1967-69; postgrad., Georgetown U., 1977-79. Bar: S.C. 1973, U.S. Ct. Appeals (4th cir.) 1982, U.S. Supreme Ct. 1982. With White House Staff, Washington, 1969-70; campaign dir. re-elect Thurmond campaign Washington, 1970-73; legis. asst. U.S. Senate, Washington, 1974-82; pvt. practice Washington, 1982—; bd. dirs. Westech. Internat., Inc., Washington Watch, Inc., Splty. Materials and Mfg., Inc., Tech. Holdings, Inc., The Stealth Corp., Inc.; mem. Pres. Commn. on Econ. Justice, Washington, 1985-87. Author: The Revisionists, 1991, We Need Each Other: U.S.-Japan Relations Approach the 21st Century, 1992; co-author: A Program for Military Independence, 1980; contbr. articles to profl. jours. Rep. Nat. Platform Staff, 1976, 80, 84, 88, 92, 96; Presdl. Transition Team, 1980-81. Sgt. USAR, 1969-77. Mem. Met. Club. Republican. Presbyterian. Avocations: tennis, travel, horticulture. Office: 1300 17th St N Ste 1100 Arlington VA 22209-3873

CARBERRY, MICHAEL GLEN, advertising executive; b. N.Y.C., Nov. 8, 1941; s. Glen Michael and Grace (Brennan) C.; m. Dianne Helen Riggs, Oct. 18, 1969; children: Glen, John, Catherine. BS, Manhattan Coll., 1963; MBA, Columbia U., 1968. Account exec. SSC&B, N.Y.C., 1968-69; account supr. Wells, Rich & Greene, N.Y.C., 1969-71; advt. mgr. U.S. Postal Svc., Washington, 1971-72; v.p., dir. Porter, Novelli & Assocs., Washington, 1972-79; chmn., CEO Henry J. Kaufman & Assocs., Washington, 1979-98; ptnr., gen. mgr. Earle Palmer Brown, Washington, 1998—; adj. prof. Georgetown U., Washington, 1984—. Pres. Am. Cancer Soc., D.C. divsn., 1995-96; bd. dirs. The Washington Ballet, 1994—. 1st. lt. USMC, 1963-66, Vietnam, col. USMCR, 1968-92. Mem. Marine Corps Res. Officers Assn. (nat. v.p. 1985-86), Marine Corps Assn. (bd. dirs. 1987-91), N.Y. Athletic Club, Kenwood Country Club (Washington). Roman Catholic. Avocations: running, scuba diving. Office: Earle Palmer Brown 6400 Goldsboro Rd Bethesda MD 20817

CARBINE, JAMES EDMOND, lawyer; b. Scotts Bluff, Nebr., June 3, 1945; s. Edmond Horace Carbine and Mabel (Porterfield) Hukle; m. Marianne Lemly, Aug. 5, 1972; 1 child, Matthew. BA, Mich. State U., 1967; JD, U. Md., 1972. Bar: Md. 1972. Assoc. Weinberg and Green, Balt., 1972-79, ptnr., 1980-96, chmn. litigation dept., 1985-95; pvt. practice Balt., 1996—; panel mem. Nat. Press Club Symposium, 1974. Reporter Govs. Landlord Tenant Commn., Md., 1973-76; mem. Mayor's Bus. Roundtable, Balt., 1983-85; bd. dirs. Greater Homewood Community Corp., Balt., 1980-82; trustee Roland Park Found., 1986-87; bd. dirs. Md. Vol. Lawyers Svc., 1991—. With U.S. Army, 1968-70. Named one of Outstanding Young Men Am., Jaycees, 1977. Mem. ABA (computer litigation com., corp. coun. com., co-chair trial practice com. 1994-97), Md. Bar Assn., Balt. City Bar Assn., Nat. Press Club (panelist 1974). Avocation: outdoor sports. Office: 111 S Calvert St Ste 2700 Baltimore MD 21202-6143

CARBINE, SHARON, lawyer, corporation executive; b. Bryn Mawr, Feb. 14, 1950; d. Thomas Joseph and Mary Teresa (Loftus) Carbine. BA, Temple U., 1972, JD, 1974, LLM in Taxation, 1977. Bar: Pa. 1974, Tex. 1981; CPA, Tex. Atty. Altemose Cos., Ctr. Square, Pa., 1974-75; law clk. to presiding justice Ct. Common Pleas, Phila., summer, 1975; tax atty. Provident Mut. Life Ins. Co., Phila., 1975-77, Emhart Corp., Farmington, Conn., 1977-78; tax sr. Peat Marwick Mitchell & Co., Phila., 1978-79; legal counsel to gov.'s chief energy advisor Tex. Energy and Natural Resources Adv. Coun., Austin, 1979-80; tax atty. Sun Co., Inc., Dallas, 1980-82; pvt. practice law Haverford, Pa., 1982-83; tax atty. Ebasco Svcs., Inc., N.Y.C., 1983-84; pvt. practice law King of Prussia, Pa., 1985-88; asst. treas., mgr. corp. taxation PQ Corp., Valley Forge, Pa., 1988-89; law clk. to presiding judge Superior Ct. Pa., Bala Cynwyd, 1989-90; tax atty. Fidelity Mut. Life Ins. Co., Radnor, Pa., 1991; ins. agent Sun Fin Group, Radnor, Pa., 1992-93; dir. regional mktg. Gen. Am. Life Ins. Co., Plymouth Meeting, Pa., 1993-94; v.p., gen. counsel Commonwealth Trust Co., Wilmington, Del., 1995—; software trainer Rsch. Inst. Am. Group, 1996-97; sr. info. tech. analyst VWR Corp., 1998; tech. svc. mgr. LegalEdge Software, 1999—. Vol. Rep. Party, 1964—; mem. Jaycees, Phila., 1978-79, Austin, Tex., 1979-80; bd. dirs. Rep. Women of the Main Line, Bryn Mawr, Pa., 1983, 93. Mem. Brehon Law Soc., Internet Bus. Alliance. Roman Catholic. Home: 150 E Wynnewood Rd # 4-C Wynnewood PA 19096-1532

CARBO, TONI (TONI CARBO BEARMAN), information scientist, university dean; b. Middletown, Conn., Nov. 14, 1942; d. Anthony Joseph and Theresa (Bauer) Carbo; m. David A. Bearman, Nov. 14, 1970 (div. Nov. 1995); 1 child, Amanda Carole. AB, Brown U., 1969; MS, Drexel U., 1973, PhD, 1977. Bibliog. asst. Am. Math. Soc., Math. Revs., 1962-63; supr. Brown U. Phys. Scis. Library, Providence, R.I., 1963-66, 67-71; subject specialist U. Wash. Engring. Library, Seattle, 1966-67; teaching and research asst. Drexel U., 1971-74; exec. dir. Nat. Fedn. Abstracting and Indexing Services, Phila., 1974-79; cons. for strategic planning and new product devel. Instn. Elec. Engrs., London, 1979-80; exec. dir. U.S. Nat. Commn. on Libraries and Info. Sci., Washington, 1980-86; dean U. Pitts. Sch. Info. Sci., 1986—; mem. adv. com. U.S. Dept. Commerce, Patent and Trademark Office, 1987-90; trustee Engring. Info., Inc., 1985-87; Lazerow lectr. U. Ind., 1984; Schwing lectr. La. State U., 1988; lectr. No. Ohio Am. Soc. Info. Sci./Spl. Librs. Assn., 1990, Beta Phi Mu, Phila., 1992; Sigma chpt. lectr. Drexel U.; mem. U.S. Adv. Coun. Nat. Info. Infrastructure, 1994-96; mem. U.S. del. G-7 Info. Soc. Conf.; bd. mem. Pa. Info. Hwy. Consortium, 1994—; Miles Conrad lectr. Nat. Fedn. Abstracting & Info. Svcs., 1997; Biennial Srygley lectr. Fla. State U., 1997, 8th Nasser Sharify lectr. Pratt U., 1997. Co-editor Internat. Info. and Libr. Rev., 1989-92, editor, 1993—; contbr. articles to profl. jours., mem. editorial bds. profl. jours. Bd. dirs. Greater Pitts. Literacy Coun.; mem. presdl. adv. com. Carnegie Libr. of Pitts. Recipient Disting. Alumni award Drexel U. Coll. Info. Studies, 1984, 100 Most Disting. Alumni award, 1992, 100th Anniversary medal Drexel U., 1992, silver anniversary award U.S. Nat. Commn. Librs. & Info. Sci., 1996. Fellow AAAS (chmn. sect. T 1992-93, coun. 1997—), Inst. Info. Scientists, Spl. Librs. Assn. (rsch. com. 1987-92, internat. rels. com. 1991); mem. ALA (coun. 1988-92, 50th Anniversary Honor Roll 1996), Am. Soc. for Info. Sci. (chmn. planning and nominations com. 1990-91, chmn. networking com., chmn. 50th ann. conf., pres. 1989-90, Watson Davis award 1983), Pa. Libr. Assn. (adv. bd. Pa. Gov.'s Conf. on libr. and info. svcs., Disting. Svc. award 1996), Nat. Info. Standards Orgn. (bd. dirs. 1987-90), Internat. Fedn. for Info. and Documentation (co-chair U.S. nat. com. 1990—, chair info. structures and policies com. 1997—, chair global info. infrastructure and superhwys. taskforce 1993-96, mem. coun. 1997—), Assn. for Libr. and Info. Sci. Edn. (bd. dirs. 1996—, pres. 1997-98), Laurel Initiative (bd. dirs. 1990-93), Ctr. for Democracy and Tech. (bd. dirs. 1996—, chair 1999—), Internat. Women's Forum of Western Pa., 3 Rivers Connect (bd. dirs. 1998—, exec. com. 1998—, planning com. 1998—). E-mail: carbo@sis.pitt.edu. Fax: 412-624-5231. Home: 263 Maple Ave Pittsburgh PA 15218-1523 Office: U Pitts Sch Info Sci 135 N Bellefield Ave Pittsburgh PA 15213-2609

CARBON, MAX WILLIAM, nuclear engineering educator; b. Monon, Ind., Jan. 19, 1922; s. Joseph William and Mary Olive (Goble) C.; m. Phyllis Camille Myers, Apr. 13, 1944; children: Ronald Allen, Jean Ann, Susan Jane, David William, Janet Elaine. BSME, Purdue U., 1943, MS, 1947, PhD, 1949. With Hanford Works divsn. GE, 1949-55, head heat transfer unit, 1951-55; with rsch. and advanced devel. divsn. Avco Mfg. Corp., 1955-58, chief thermodynamics sect., 1956-58; prof., chmn. nuclear engring. and engring. physics dept. U. Wis. Coll. Engring., Madison, 1958-92, emeritus prof., collateral faculty, 1992—, acting assoc. dean for rsch., 1995-96; group leader Ford Found. program Singapore, 1967-68; mem. adv. com. on reactor safeguards, 1975-87; chmn. spl. com. for integral fast reactor U. Chgo., 1984-94, chmn. spl. adv. com. for nuclear tech. program Argonne (Ill.) Nat. Lab., 1995—; mem. INPO Nat. Nuclear Accrediting Bd., 1990-94; mem. nuclear safety rev. and audit com. Kewaunee Nuclear Power Plant, 1993-96. Author: Nuclear Power: Villain or Victim, 1997. Capt. ordnance dept. AUS, 1943-46. Named Disting. Engring. Alumnus, Purdue U. Fellow Am. Nuclear Soc.; mem. AAAS, Sigma Xi, Tau Beta Pi. Office: U Wis Engring Rsch Bldg Madison WI 53706

CARBONE, DAVID A., academic administrator. BA, Rutgers U., 1979; MA, U. No. Iowa, 1981; EdD, U. Albany, 1992. Residence dir., fellow, adminstrv. asst., adminstrv. dir. U. Albany; analyst N.Y. State Senate; acctg. supr. LeBouef, Lamb, Am. List Counsel & Am. List Counsel; contract trainer Bergen County Coll.; dir. Hudson County C.C., Jersey City; dir., project mgr. N.J. State Dept. Edn., Trenton; presenter Hudson County Econ. Devel. Corp., Rotary Internat. Contbr. articles to profl. jours. Scholarship benefactor Hudson Cath. H.S., 1997-98;; mem. founder's club N.J. Performing Arts Ctr., 1997—, N.J. State Aquarium, 1992; petit juror Hudson County Supr. Ct., 1997; writer sch. facilities plan Sch. Dist. South Brunswick, 1992. Rsch. grantee Wartburg Coll., 1980, 81, NSF, 1973, Assn. for Study of Higher Edn., 1987. Mem. Assn. C.C. Continuing Edn. Adminstrs. (treas. 1997-98), Network of Tng. and Edn., N.J. Coll. Pers. Assn. (treas. 1994-97), Am. Coll. Pers. Assn., Rutgers Alumni Assn., Kiwanis. Office: NJ State Dept Edn Trenton NJ

CARBONE, PAUL PETER, oncologist, educator, administrator; b. White Plains, N.Y., May 2, 1931; s. Antonio and Grace (Cappelieri) C.; m. Mary Iamurri, Aug. 20, 1954; children—David, Kathryn, Karen, Kim, Paul J., Mary Beth, Matthew. Student, Union Coll., Schenectady, 1949-52; M.D., Albany (N.Y.) Med. Coll., 1956. Diplomate: Am. Bd. Internal Medicine; cert. medical oncology. Joined USPHS Hosp., 1956; intern USPHS Hosp., Balt., 1956-57; resident in internal medicine USPHS Hosp., San Francisco, 1958-60; resident NIH, Bethesda, Md., 1961-63; mem. staff Nat. Cancer Inst., NIH, Bethesda, Md., 1960-76; chief medicine br. Nat. Cancer Inst., NIH, 1968-72, asso. dir. for med. oncology, div. cancer treatment, 1972-76, dep. clin. dir., 1972-76; clin. prof. Georgetown U. Med. Sch., 1971-76; lectr. hematology Walter Reed Army Inst. Research, 1962-76; prof. medicine and human oncology U. Wis., Madison, 1976—, dir. div. clin. oncology, 1976-80, chmn. dept. human oncology, 1977-87; dir. Wis. Comprehensive Cancer Ctr., 1978-97; assoc. dean for program devel. U. Wis. Med. Sch., 1992—; assoc. dean program devel. U. Wis. Med. Sch. Contbr. profl. jours. Decorated USPHS Commendation medal; recipient Trimble Lecture award Md. Chirurgical Faculty, 1968; Lasker award clin. cancer chemotherapy, 1972; Rosenthal award for improvement in clin. cancer care, 1977, Medal of Honor Am. Cancer Soc., 1987, Jeffrey A. Gottlieb Meml. award M.D. Anderson Cancer Ctr., U. Tex., 1990; NIMMO vis. prof. Royal Adelaide Hosp., Adelaide, Australia, 1989. Master ACP (bd. govs. Wis. chpt. 1986-90); mem. AMA, Am. Soc. Clin. Oncology (pres. 1972-73, Outstanding Achievement award 1995), Am. Soc. Clin. Investigation, Assn. Am. Physicians, Am. Assn. Cancer Rsch. (pres. 1978-79), Am. Fedn. Clin. Rsch., Alpha Omega Alpha. Home: 1353 Boundary Rd Middleton WI 53562-3831 Office: U Wis Comprehensive Cancer Ctr 600 Highland Ave Rm K6546 Madison WI 53792-0002

CARBONI, LISA WILSON, education educator; b. Akron, Ohio, Dec. 1, 1964; d. Jack Lee and Gloria Kay (Revay) Wilson; m. Michael Paul Carboni, June 8, 1989; 1 child, Jessica Katherine. BS, Kent State U., 1986, MEd, 1990; MEd, U. N.C., Chapel Hill, 1996. Cert. tchr., Md., N.C. Tchr. Frederick (Md.) County Schs., 1986-88; dist. gifted coord. Minerva (Ohio) Local Schs., 1988-90; gifted/talented specialist Howard County Pub. Sch. Sys., Columbia, Md., 1990-92, team leader, educator, 1992-94; tchr. Chapel Hill-Carrboro Schs., 1994-95; clin. assoc. Duke U., Durham, N.C., 1998—; instr., supr. student tchrs. U. N.C., Chapel Hill, 1995—; instnl. design cons., Durham, N.C., 1995—; instr., course developer Towson (Md.) State U., 1992-94; curriculum and assessment writer Md. State Dept. Edn. and Howard County Schs., 1991-94. Mem. ASCD, Nat. Coun. Tchrs. Math., Am. Edn. Rsch. Assn., Phi Delta Kappa. Office: U NC Chapel Hill CB # 3500 212 Peabody Hall Chapel Hill NC 27514

CARCELLO, JOSEPH VINCENT, accounting educator; b. Queens, N.Y., Dec. 13, 1959; s. Vincent Neil and Judith (Bush) C.; m. Terri Lynn Osgood; children: Jane, Stephen, Karen, Sarah. BS, SUNY, Plattsburgh, 1982; MA, U. Ga., 1984; PhD, Ga. State U., 1990. CPA, Ga. Sr. acct. Ernst & Whinney, Atlanta, 1984-86; asst. mgr. fin. svcs. Confed. Life Ins. Co., Atlanta, 1986-87; asst. prof. U. North Fla., Jacksonville, 1991-93; assoc. prof. U. Tenn., Knoxville, 1993—. Contbr. articles to profl. jours. Recipient Acctg. Excellence award Pugh & Co. Acctg., 1997. Mem. AICPA, Am. Acctg. Assn. (treas. 1997—, ann. meeting planning com. 1997—), Inst. Internal Auditors (cert.), Inst. Mgmt. Accts. (cert., Robert Beyer gold medal 1984). Republican. Evang. Christian. Avocations: weight lifting, jogging, college football. Office: U Tenn 601 Stokely Mgmt Ctr Knoxville TN 37996-0560

CARD, JAMES CONRAD, coast guard officer; b. Melrose Park, Ill.; m. Jean Howell, June 14, 1964; children: Tim, Peter. BS, USCG Acad., 1964; MS in Naval Architecture, MSME, MIT, 1970; grad., Indsl. Coll. Armed Forces, 1986. Commd. ensign USCG, 1964, advanced through grades to vice adm., 1997; assigned to USCG cutters Winona, Dexter and Barataria; naval arch. USCG Hdqs., Washington; marine insp. Marine Safety Officer, Balt.; chief ship design br. marine tech.-hazardous materials div. USCG Hdqs.; comdg. officer Marine Safety Office, St. Louis; chief mcht. vessel inspection and documentation divsn. USCG Hdqs.; comdg. officer Marine Safety Office and Group, L.A., Long Beach, Calif.; chief ops. 11th Coast Guard dist.; chief staff 13th Coast Guard Dist., Seattle; comdr. 8th Coast Guard Dist., New Orleans; asst. commandant for marine safety and environ. protection Office Marine Safety, Security & Environ. Proction USCG Hdq., 1994-97; comdr., vice admiral USCG Pacific Area, 1997—; vice commandant USCG, Washington, 1999—. Decorated Legion of Merit with oak leaf clusters; apptd. vice commandant Pres. of U.S., 1998. Mem. Soc. Naval Archs. and Marine Engrs., Am. Soc. Naval Engrs., Royal Instn. Naval Archs. Office: Vice Admiral James C Card Vice Commandant USCG 2100 2nd St SW Washington DC 20593*

CARD, ORSON SCOTT (BYRON WALLEY), writer; b. Richland, Wash., Aug. 24, 1951; s. Willard Richards and Peggy Jane (Park) C.; m. Kristine Allen, May 17, 1977; children: Geoffrey, Emily, Charles, Zina. BA in Theater, Brigham Young U., 1975; MA in English, U. Utah, 1981. Editor Brigham Young U. Press, Provo, Utah, 1974-76; assoc. editor Ensign mag., Salt Lake City, 1976-78; sr. editor Compute! Publs., Greensboro, N.C., 1983; game design cons. Lucasfilm Games, 1989-92; instr. Brigham Young U., U. Utah, U. Notre Dame, Appalachian State U., Clarion West Writer's Workshop, Cape Code Writers Conf., Antioch Writers Workshop; columnist "You Got No Friends in This World", Science Fiction Review, 1979-86, "Book to Look For", Fantasy and Science Fiction, 1987—, "Gameplay", Compute!, 1988—. Author: (fiction) Capitol, 1978, Hot Sleep, 1978, A Planet Called Treason, 1979, Songmaster, 1980 (Hamilton/Brackett award 1981), Unaccompanied Sonata and Other Stories, 1981, Hart's Hope, 1982, The Worthing Chronicle, 1983, A Woman of Destiny, 1983, Ender's Game, 1985 (Nebula award 1985, Hugo award 1986, Hamilton/Brackett award 1986), Speaker For The Dead, 1986 (Nebula award 1986, Hugo award 1987, Locus award 1987), Hatrack River, 1986 (Hugo award nomination 1986, World Fantasy award 1987), Wyrms, 1987, Seventh Son, 1987 (Locus award best fantasy 1988, Hugo award nomination 1988, World Fantasy award nomination 1988), Cardography, 1987, Eye for Eye, 1987 (Hugo award 1988, Locus award nomination 1988), Treason, 1988, Red Prophet, 1988 (Locus award 1989), Prentice Alvin, 1989, Folk of the Fringe, 1989, The Abyss, 1989, Maps in a Mirror, 1990, The Worthing Saga, 1990, Xenocide, 1991, The Memory of Earth, 1992, Lost Boys, 1992, The Call of Earth, 1992, The Changed Man, 1992, Flux, 1992, Cruel Miracles, 1992, Monkey Sonatas, 1993, The Ships of Earth, 1993, A Storyteller in Zion, 1993, Earthfall, 1994, (with David Dollahite) Turning Hearts, 1994, (with Kathryn H. Kidd) Lovelock, 1994, Earthborn, 1995, Alvin Journeyman, 1995 (Locus award 1996), Pastwatch: The Redemption of Christopher Columbus, 1996, Children of the Mind, 1996, Treasure Box, 1996, Stone Tables, 1997, Homebody, 1998, Heartfire, 1998, Enchantment, 1999, Ender's Shadow, 1999; (nonfiction) Listen, Mom and Dad, 1978, Saintspeak, 1981, Ainge, 1982, Characters and Viewpoint, 1988, How to Write Science Fiction and Fantasy, 1990 (Hugo award for non-fiction 1991); (plays) The Apostate, 1970, In Flight, 1970, Across Five Summers, 1971, Of Gideon, 1971, Stone Tables, 1973, A Christmas Carol, 1974, Father, Mother, Mother, and Mom, 1974, Liberty Jail, 1975, Rag Mission, 1977, Fresh Courage Take, 1978, Elders and Sisters, 1979, Wings, 1982; editor: Dragons of Darkness, 1981, Dragons of Light, 1983; author numerous audio and videoplays; contbr. short stories and essays to Fantasy & Sci. Fiction, Windows Sources and other mags. Recipient John W. Campbell award World Sci. Fiction Conv., 1978, Hugo award nominations World Sci. Fiction Conv., 1978, 79, 80, Nebula award nominations Sci. Fiction Writers of America, 1979, 80, Utah State Inst. of Fine Arts prize, 1980. Mem. Sci. Fiction Writers Am., Authors Guild. Democrat. Mormon. Office: care Barbara Bova Lit Agy 3951 Gulf Shore Blvd N Ph 1B Naples FL 34103-3639*

CARDALENA, PETER PAUL, JR., lawyer, educator; b. Bklyn., Dec. 19, 1943; s. Peter Paul and Rose Rita (Femenella) C.; m. Rosalie Brunetti, Sept. 22, 1962; children: Peter Paul III (dec.), Lisa, Kim, Gina, Damian. AAS, St. John's U., Jamaica, N.Y., 1978, BS, 1980; JD, Touro Law Sch., 1984. Bar: N.Y. 1985. Supr. N.Y.C. Transit Authority, 1965—; sole practice law Floral Park, N.Y., 1984—; assoc. prof. law St. John's U., Jamaica, 1985—; lectr. Katharine Gibbs Sch., N.Y.C., 1986—; legal advisor Nassau Co. Shields, 1985—, Sch. Adminstrs. Assn., Albany, N.Y., 1986—. Editor periodical Call Box, 1985; contbr. articles to profl. jours. Named Mem. of the Yr. Nassau Co. Shields, 1986. Mem. ABA, Nassau County Bar Assn., Bklyn. Bar Assn., Columbian Lawyers Assn. (Serafin Calabrese award 1984), N.Y.C. Transit Police Dept., Lt.'s Benevolent Assn. (counsel 1987—, exec. sec. 1987—), Nassau County Shields (counsel 1985—, Mem. of Yr. 1986). Roman Catholic. Home and Office: 37 Fern St Floral Park NY 11001-3207

CARDAMONE, RICHARD J., federal judge; b. Utica, N.Y., Oct. 10, 1925; s. Joseph J. and Josephine (Scala) C.; m. Catherine Baker Clarke, Aug. 28, 1946; 10 children. BA, Harvard U., 1948; LLB, Syracuse U., 1952. Bar: N.Y. 1952. Pvt. practice law Utica, 1952-62; judge N.Y. State Supreme Ct., 1963-71, Appelate div. 4th Dept. N.Y. State Supreme Ct., 1971-81, U.S. Ct. Appeals (2d cir.), Utica, 1981—. Lt. (j.g.) USNR, 1943-46. Mem. Am. Law Inst., N.Y. State Bar Assn., Oneida County Bar Assn. Roman Catholic. Office: US Ct Appeals 10 Broad St Utica NY 13501-1233

CARDENAS, DIANA DELIA, physician, educator; b. San Antonio, Tex., Apr. 10, 1947; d. Ralph Roman and Rosa (Garza) C.; m. Thomas McKenzie Hooton, Aug. 20, 1971; children: Angela, Jessica. BA with highest honors, U. Tex., 1969; MD, U. Tex., Dallas, 1973; MS, U. Wash., 1976. Diplomate Nat. Bd. Med. Examiners, Am. Bd. Phys. Medicine & Rehab., Am. Bd. Electrodiagnostic Medicine. Asst. prof. dept. rehab. medicine Emory U., Atlanta, 1976-81; instr. dept. rehab. medicine U. Wash., Seattle, 1981-82, asst. prof. dept. rehab. medicine, 1982-86, assoc. prof. dept. rehab. medicine, 1986-92, prof. rehab. medicine, 1992—; med. dir. rehab. medicine clinic U. Wash. Med. Ctr., Seattle, 1982; project dir. N.W. Regional Spinal Cord Injury System, Seattle, 1990—; mem. Accreditation Coun. for Grad. Med. Edn. Residency Rev. Com., 1995-96. Editor: Rehabilitation & The Chronic Renal Disease Patient, 1985, Maximizing Rehabilitation in Chronic Renal Disease, 1989; acad. editor Archives of Phys. Medicine and Rehab., 1997—; contbr. articles to profl. jours. Co-chairperson Lakeside Sch. Auction Student Vols., Seattle, 1991; bd. dirs. CONSEJO Counseling & Referral Svc., 1994-96, co-chairperson internat. rels. com., 1995-98. Mem. Am. Spinal Injury Assn. (chairperson rsch. com. 1991, bd. dirs. 1994—), Am. Acad. Phys. Medicine and Rehab. (chairperson rsch. adv. and advocacy com. 1997—), Am. Congress of Rehab. Medicine (chairperson rehab. practice com. 1980-84, Ann. Essay Contest winner 1976), Am. Assn. Electrodiagnostic Medicine, Nat. Inst. Child Health and Human Devel. (rsch. subcom. 1996-99), Inst. of Medicine Nat. Acad. Sci. (com. on assessing rehab. sci. and engring, 1996-97, com. on injury prevention and control 1997-99). Avocations: art collecting, sewing, painting. Office: Univ Wash Dept Rehab Med Box 356490 1959 NE Pacific St Seattle WA 98195-0001

CARDENES, ANDRES JORGE, violinist, music educator; b. Havana, Cuba, May 2, 1957; came to U.S., 1958; s. Andres Manuel and Arlene (Cuevas) C. Student, Ind. U., 1975-80; diploma, Meisterkurse Zurich, Switzerland, 1977. Asst. prof. music Ind. U., Bloomington, 1980-82; prof. music Espoo Festival, Helsinki, Finland, 1982; prof. U. Utah, Salt Lake City, 1982-85; prof. music U. Mich., 1987-89; mem. artistic com. Utah Symphony, Salt Lake City, 1983-85; cons. in field; bd. dirs. Intermountain-West Music Festival, Salt Lake City, 1984-88; artistic dir. Strings in the Mountains Chamber Music Festival, Steamboat Springs, Colo.; prof. violin studies Carnegie Mellon U., 1989—. Concertmaster Utah Symphony, Salt Lake City, 1982-85, San Diego Symphony, 1985-86, Pitts. Symphony, 1987—; concert violin soloist, 1981—; 1985-86; editor: Concerto by Ramiro Cortes, 1983; performer worldwide Nuclear Arms Freeze, 1980—. Cultural amb. UNICEF, 1980—; chmn., co-founder Underprivileged Arts Student San Diego Soc.; cultural chmn. Make-a-Wish Found. of Pitts. Recipient Bronze medal Queen Elizabeth Internat. Violin Competition, Brussels, 1980, Bronze medal Sibelius Internat. Violin Competition, Helsinki, 1980, Bronze medal Tchaikovsky Internat. Violin Competition, Moscow, 1982, Bronze medal Internat. Violin Competition, Indpls., 1986, Pitts. Classical Artist of Yr., 1998, Starling Found. endowed chair Carnegie-Mellon U., 1998. Mem. Young San Diegans Soc. (bd. dirs.). Roman Catholic. Club: Machista (Bloomington) (pres. 1978—). Home: 4729 Bayard St Pittsburgh PA 15213 Office: Pittsburgh Symphony Orch Heinz Hall 600 Penn Ave Ste 1 Pittsburgh PA 15222-3259

CARDER, MARY ALICE, dietitian; b. St. Louis, Dec. 24, 1942; d. Clement Matthew and Helen Marguerite (Gaghen) Weber; m. Terry L. Carder, Apr. 15, 1972. BS in Foods and Nutrition, Incarnate Word Coll., 1967; MS in Dietetic Edn., Ind. U., 1971. Registered dietitian. Dir. nutrition and dietetics N.W. Manor Nursing Home, Indpls., 1970-80; asst. therapeutic dietitian Meth. Hosp. Ind., Indpls., 1970-71, head therapeutic dietitian, 1971-72, asst. dir. nutrition therapy, 1972-75, dir. dietetic internship, 1975-94; instr. Sch. of Nursing DePauw U., Greencastle, Ind., 1975-94; instr. Marian Coll., Indpls., 1992-94; dir. nutrition svcs. ARAMARK/The Uniontown (Pa.) Hosp., 1994—. Mem. The Am. Dietetic Assn., Pa. Dietetic Assn., Pitts. Dietetic Assn. Republican. Roman Catholic. E-mail: uniontlc@sgi.net. Office: The Uniontown Hosp 500 W Berkeley St Uniontown PA 15401-5596

CARDER, PAUL CHARLES, advertising executive; b. Oak Park, Ill., Jan. 27, 1941; arrived in Can., 1967; s. Lawrence E. and Irene (Zahler) C.; children from previous marriage: Greg Lawrence, Tracy Allison; children: Leigh Rebecca Kamping-Carder, Amanda Rachel Kamping-Carder. BA, U. Mich., 1962; MBA, Harvard U., 1964. Account exec. Ogilvy & Mather, N.Y.C., 1964-65; v.p. Ogilvy & Mather Can., Ltd., Toronto, Ont., Can., 1966-73; v.p., dir. client svcs. Doyle Dane Bernbach, Toronto, 1974-77; sr. v.p., mng. dir. Vicker & Benson, Ltd., Toronto, 1978-83; pres., chief exec. officer Carder Gray Advt., Inc., Toronto, 1983-90, DDB Needham Worldwide, Toronto, 1990-94; ret., 1994; dean, faculty Bus. and Creative Arts George Brown Coll.; adj. prof. Queen's U. Sch. Bus., 1995-96; prin. The Paladin Co., pvt. investment firm. Dir. Nat. Ballet Can., Toronto, 1984-90, Thousand Islands Playhouse, 1995—, Heart and Stroke Found. of Ont., 1997—. Mem. Inst. Can. Advt. (dir., treas. 1988-90), dir. Harvard Bus. Sch. Club of Toronto. Liberal party of Ontario. Avocations: tennis, skiing.

CARDER, THOMAS ALLEN, nuclear energy industry emergency planner, educator; b. Marion, Ind., June 6, 1949; s. Otto Leroy and Mary Madeline (Dobson) C.; m. Barbara Gail Rice, June 24, 1978; children: Damian Bruce, Eric Thomas, Kimberly Rose. Student, Ind. U., 1970-72, 76, Ky. Coll. Tech., 1967-68, So. Ill. U., 1986—. Registered emergency med. technician, Ind., Pa., Va., Ill. Cyclotron project technician Ind. U., Bloomington, 1971-73; radiation safety officer, instr., technician Ind. Emergency Mgmt. Agy., Indpls., 1973-81; coord. emergency planning North Anna Power Sta., Mineral, Va., 1981-82; nuclear specialist Energy Cons., Inc., Harrisburg, Pa., 1982-84; emergency planner Ill. Power Co., Clinton, 1984-88; sr. emergency planner Tex. Utilities, Comanche Peak Sta., 1988-95; pres., CEO Childcare Action Project Christian Analysis of Am. Culture, 1995—; radiation safety adv., mem. Mahomet (Ill.) Emergency Svcs. and Disaster Agy., 1985-88. Author: Handling of Radiation Accident Patients by Paramedical and Hospital Personnel, 1981, 2d edit., 1991, Strengths/Needs Analysis Project, 1994. Mem. Health Physics Soc. Baptist. Avocations: computers, electronics, woodworking. Home: PO Box 177 Granbury TX 76048-0177

CARDEW, WILLIAM JOSEPH, bank executive; b. Bklyn.; s. William and Lillian (Davis) C.; m. Janet Markel; children: Brian, Timothy, Nancy, Terence, Christopher. BBA, Pace U., 1958. Sr. v.p. Chem. Bank, N.Y.C., 1955-80; pres. Fidelity Comml. Fin. Co. subs. Fidelity Union Bank, Newark, 1980-85; vice chmn., COO Merchants Bank N.Y., N.Y.C., 1985—, also bd. dirs. Office: Mchts Bank of NY 275 Madison Ave New York NY 10016-6507*

CARDIFF, ROBERT DARRELL, pathology educator; b. San Francisco, Dec. 5, 1935; s. George Darrell and Helen (Kohfield) C.; m. Sally Joan Bounds, June 23, 1962; children: Darrell, Todd, Shelley. BS, U. Calif., Berkeley, 1958, PhD, 1968; MD, U. Calif., San Francisco, 1962. Intern King's County Hosp., Bklyn., 1962-63; resident in pathology U. Oreg., Portland, 1963-66; NIH fellow U. Calif., Berkeley, 1966-68; mem. faculty med. sch. U. Calif., Davis, 1971—, prof. pathology med. sch., 1977—, chair dept. pathology, 1990-96; dir. Ctr. for Med. Informatics U. Calif. Davis Healthcare System, Davis, 1996-98; mem. sci. adv. bd. Contra Costa Cancer Fund, Walnut Creek, Calif., 1985—; mem. Univ.-Wide AIDS Task Force, Berkeley, 1984-87; vis. prof. Sun-Yat Sen U. Med. Sci., Peoples Republic of China, 1985, 93. Mem. editorial bd. Human Pathology, 1992—, Tumor Markers, 1992—, Internat. Jour. Oncology, 1992—; contbr. articles to profl. jours. Lt. col. U.S. Army, 1968-71. Recipient Triton Rsch. award Triton Bioscis., Inc., 1985, Kaiser Found. Teaching award U. Calif. Med. Sch., Davis, 1985, Disting. Teaching award U. Calif., Davis, Sadusk award Peralta Cancer Inst., 1986, Faculty Rsch. award U. Calif. Med. Sch., 1988, Affirmative Action award U. Calif. Davis Med. Ctr., 1991, others. Mem. AAUP (exec. com. 1983-85), Pluto Soc., Internat. Acad. Pathology, Internat. Aassn. Breast Cancer (bd. dirs. 1984—), Sacramento Pathology Soc. (bd. dirs. 1985-96),

No. Calif. Pathology Soc. (pres. 1990-96), Coll. Am. Pathology, Sigma Xi. Avocations: basketball, skiing, jogging. Office: U Calif Med Sch Dept Pathology MS1ARm 3453 Davis CA 95616

CARDILLO, JOHN POLLARA, lawyer; b. Ft. Lee, N.J., July 1, 1942; s. John E. and Margaret (Pollara) C.; m. Linda Bentey, Sept. 25, 1976; children: John Thomas, Joseph Pollara, Margaret Celia, Mark Luigi. BA, Furman U., 1964; postgrad., W.Va. U., 1965; JD, U. S.C., 1968. Bar: S.C. 1968, N.Y. 1970, Fla. 1972, U.S. Ct. Appeals (2d cir., 4th cir. 5th cir. 11th cir.) 1972, U.S. Dist. Ct. (ea. and so. dists.) N.Y. 1972, U.S. Dist. Ct. S.C. 1968, U.S. Dist. Ct. (so. and mid. dists.) Fla. 1974, U.S. Tax Ct. 1972, U.S. Supreme Ct. 1984. Assoc. Cardillo & Corbett, N.Y.C., 1968-71, Mays & McLellan, Columbia, S.C., 1971-72, Sorokoty, Monaco & Cervelli, Naples, Fla., 1972-75; ptnr. Monaco, Cardillo & Keith, P.A., Naples, 1975-96, Cardillo, Keith & Bonaquist, P.A., 1997—. Mem. Furman U. Alumni Bd. Dirs., 1984-89; active Environ. Adv. Coun., Collier County, Fla., 1983-87, past chmn.; past pres. Pine Ridge Civic Assn.; bd. dirs. YMCA Collier County, past pres., 1978-80, United Arts Coun. of Collier County, pres., 1991-92, bd. dirs. Big Bros., 1974-76; past pres. Naples Leadership Sch., 1987-88; mem. Leadership Collier, 1992; mem. Gov.'s Task Force on Drug Abuse, 1985; bd. advisors Gene and Mary Sarazen FDN, 1997—; bd. trustees Edison C.C., 1998-99. Mem. ATLA, ABA, Am. Arbitration Assn. (arbitrator), Acad. Fla. Trial Lawyers, Fla. Bar (20th jud. cir., bd. govs. 1992—), Fla. Criminal Def. Attys., Collier County Bar Assn. (past pres.), S.C. Bar Assn., Assn. Bar City N.Y., Maritime Law Assn., Naples Area C. of C. (bd. dirs. 1990-95, pres. 1994-95). Home: 395 Ridge Dr Naples FL 34108-2933 Office: Cardillo Keith & Bonaquist PA 3550 Tamiami Trl E Naples FL 34112-4999

CARDIN, BENJAMIN LOUIS, congressman; b. Balt., Oct. 5, 1943; s. Meyer M. and Dora (Green) C.; m. Myrna Edelman, Nov. 24, 1964; children: Michael, Deborah. BA cum laude, U. Pitts., 1964; JD with honors, U. Md., 1967; LLD (hon.), U. Balt., 1990; LHD (hon.), U. Md., 1993, Balt. Hebrew U., 1994, Goucher Coll., 1996. Bar: Md. 1967. Pvt. practice law Balt., 1967-87; mem. Md. Ho. of Dels., 1967-86, chmn. ways and means com., 1974-79, speaker of house, 1979-86; mem. 100-106th Congresses from 3d Md. Dist., Washington, 1987—; asst. Dem. whip 100-105th Congresses from 3d Md. Dist., Washington; ways and means com., budget com., health subcom. 100-106th Congresses from 3d Md. Dist., Washington, steering com. Dem. caucus, 1991—, com. on stds. and ofcl. conduct, 1991—; chmn. Med. Legal Svcs. Corp., 1988-95; commr. Commn. on Security and Cooperation in Europe, 1993—. Contbr. articles to profl. jours. Bd. visitors U. Md. Sch. Law, 1993—; trustee St. Mary's Coll., 1988—. Recipient Small Bus. Coun. of Ams. Congrl. award, 1993, Nat. Multiple Sclerosis Soc. Rep. of the Yr. award, 1993, Israel Freedom award, 1992, U. Md. Law Sch. Alumni Assn. Cardin Pro Bono award, 1990, Ann. Hogan Meml. award Common Cause of Md., 1987, Friend of Psychiatry award Md. Psychiat. Soc., 1988, The Alliance to End Childhood Lead Poisoning: H. John Heinz III Leadership award, 1994, Hunting S. Williams award The Coalition for a Lead Safe Environment, 1995, Vernon Eney award Md. Bar Found., 1996, others. Mem. ABA (Pro Bono Public award 1989), Md. Bar Assn., Baltimore City Bar Assn. Democrat. Jewish. Office: US Ho Reps Rm 104 Cannon House Office Bldg Washington DC 20515*

CARDIN, SUZETTE, nursing educator; b. Attleboro, Mass., Feb. 4, 1950; d. Wilfred W. and Vera E. (Broadbent) C.; m. Edward R. Barden, May 10, 1986; children: Luke Edward, Helen Elizabeth. Diploma, Children's Hosp. Sch. Nursing, Boston, 1970; BSN, Southeastern Mass. U., 1974; MS, U. Md., 1978; DNSc, UCLA, 1995. RN, Calif. Nursing instr. Fall River (Mass.) Diploma Sch. Nursing, 1974-76; staff nurse SICU Johns Hopkins Hosp., Balt., 1977-78; dir. critical care nursing Med. Ctr. Hosp. Vt., Burlington, 1978-83; nurse mgr. UCLA Med. Ctr., 1984-98, performance improvement coord., 1998—; asst. adj. prof. UCLA Sch. Nursing, 1998—. Co-editor: Personnel Management in Critical Care Nursing, 1989, Critical Care Nursing, 1992, 96; mem. editl. bd. Dimensions of Critical Care Nursing, 1989—, Clin. Issues in Critical Care Nursing, 1989-92, AONE Leadership Perspectives, 1993-96. Recipient award Profl. Businesswomen, 1973, award Maxicare Ednl. & Rsch. Found., 1993, Nurse Mgr. Leadership Excellence award AONE, 1994. Fellow Am. Acad. Nursing; mem. AACN (chair various coms., co-editor CCRN newsletter 1985-86, mem. cert. com. 1984-85, liaison AANN cert. bd. 1986-88, pres. Vt. chpt. 1979-81, mem. program com. 1987-88, NTI com. 1987-88), Am. Heart Assn., Children's Hosp. Alumnae Assn., Sigma Theta Tau (co-editor newsletter Gamma Tau chpt. 1987-89). Home: 2102 Farrell Ave Redondo Beach CA 90278-1819

CARDINAL-COX, SHIRLEY MAE, education educator; b. Morann, Pa., May 6, 1944; d. Thomas Joseph and Mary Louise (Nemish) Giza; m. Leland Dean Cox, May 9, 1998; children: Julie Ann, Karen Lee. BS, Lock Haven U., 1966; MEd, Pa. State U., 1970. Tchr. Bald Eagle Nittany Corp., Mill Hall, Pa., 1966-68; tchr., supr. Pa. State U., University Park, 1968-76; tchr., chairperson State Coll. (Pa.) Area Schs., 1968-76; primetime educator Oregon-Davis Corp., Hamlet, Ind., 1984—; instr., cons. Dept. Edn., Indpls., 1979—, cons. energy edn., 1980-85, educator linker, 1981—, rep. prime time, 1987—; instr. Ancilla Coll., Donaldson, Inc., 1976—; chair for evaluation North Ctrl. Accreditation Assn., 1988-89, leadership team, 1996; mem. leadership team North Ctrl. Regional Lab., 1991-92, 93— (steering com. 1996-97), Fermi Nat. Accelerator Lab., 1994—; mem. leadership team, strategic teaching and reading field reference person North Ctrl. Regional Ednl. Lab., 1998. Author: Energy Activities with Learning Skills, 1980. Chmn. publicity com. Rep. Orgn. Plymouth, Ind., 1983—; mem. Teacher Talk, Ind. Gov's. Com., 1988-89. Recipient Mankind and Edn. award U.S. Jaycees and Ind. Jaycees, 1981. Mem. Ind. State Tchr. Assn., Marshall County Reading Assn., Pa. State U. Club, Proficiency Bd. Accreditation (chairperson 1996), Phi Delta Kappa (v.p. programs South Bend chpt. 1992-93, v.p. membership 1994-95), Pi Lambda Theta, Sigma Kappa (chmn. Parent Club), Tri Kappa. Roman Catholic. Avocations: reading, aerobics, jogging, biking, tennis. Home: 10101 Turf Ct Plymouth IN 46563-9494

CARDINALE, DREW ANTHONY, language educator; b. Bklyn., June 11, 1969; s. John Vincent and Marielena Lauretta (Perrone) C. Student, Pa. State U., 1988-91; BA in Spanish and Latin, Muhlenberg Coll., 1991; MA in Romance Philology, U. N.C., 1993. Tchg. asst. U. N.C., Chapel Hill, 1991-93; adj. instr. Raritan Valley C.C., Somerville, N.J., 1993-94; tchr. Spanish and Latin Delbarton Sch., Morristown, N.J., 1994-97, Bklyn. Friends Sch., 1997—. Democrat. Episcopalian. Avocations: music, tennis, theater, travel. Office: Bklyn Friends Sch 375 Pearl St Brooklyn NY 11201-3760

CARDINALI, ALBERT JOHN, lawyer; b. N.Y.C., Apr. 24, 1934; s. John and Ines (Clara) C.; m. June DuRose Seaman; children: Kathleen, John, Raymond, Kenneth, Scott, Jeffrey. B.A., CCNY, 1955; LL.B., Columbia U., 1958; LL.M., NYU, 1965. Bar: N.Y. 1961. Asso. Thacher, Proffitt & Wood, N.Y.C., 1960-68, partner, 1969—. Served with AUS, 1958-60. Mem. ABA, N.Y. State Bar Assn., Assn. Bar City N.Y. Clubs: Shenorock Shore (Rye, N.Y.); University (N.Y.C.). Home: 244 North St Rye NY 10580-1520 Office: Thacher Proffitt & Wood 2 World Trade Ctr New York NY 10048-0203

CARDINALLI, MARC PATRICK, lawyer; b. Ft. Lewis, Wash., Nov. 19, 1954; s. Guy Fredrick and Patricia Marie (DeWalt) C.; m. Deane Peacock, May 10, 1992. BA in Journalism, U. Nev., 1979; JD, U. of the Pacific, Sacramento, 1986. Bar: Nev. 1986, Calif. 1987. Student atty. Sacramento County Pub. Defender's Office, 1983-86; assoc. David Allen & Assocs., Sacramento and Reno, 1986-88; pvt. practice Reno, 1988; dep. atty. gen. State of Nev., Carson City, 1989-94; asst. gen. counsel U. and C.C. Sys. of Nev., Las Vegas, 1994-96; sr. asst. gen. counsel U. and C.C. Sys. of Nev., 1996-97; adminstrv. code officer U. Nev., Las Vegas, 1998—; mem. Nev. Atty. Gen.'s Com on Alt. Dispute Resolution, Com. on Continuing Legal Edn., 1990-94; instr. Nev. Atty. Gen.'s office continuing legal edn., 1994. Contbg. editor: Nevada Evidence Bench Book, 1985; contbg. author: So You Want to Go to Law School, 1989. Mem. Carson City Gang Task Force, 1989-91; mem., atty. gen.'s rep. Nev. Fed./State Jud. Com., 1990-94; rep. U.S. Justice Dept. Summit on Corrections, 1992; chair edn. com. Temple Emanuel, Reno, 1993-94; co-chair Nat. RFRA Lobbying Com., Carson City, 1993; pres. 5th Ave. Townhouse Owners Assn., Carson City, 1993-94; bd. dirs. Carson City United Way, 1993-94; instr. Congregation Ner Tamid post b'nai mitzvah class, Las Vegas, 1996—. Scholar Ahamson Found., Sacramento, 1985, Sacramento Bee, 1985. Mem. Nat. Assn. Coll. and University Attys. (com. on info. svcs. 1994-98, reporter com. on litig. and alt. dispute resolution 1995-98, CLE com. 1998—). Democrat. Jewish. Avocations: archaeology, gourmet cooking, travel, reading, educational pursuits. Office: UNLV Box 451077 4505 S Maryland Pkwy Las Vegas NV 89154-9900

CARDMAN, LAWRENCE SANTO, physics educator, research administrator; b. Mt. Vernon, N.Y., Oct. 7, 1944; s. Michael L. and Alice (Willis) C.; m. Helen-Andrea Fox; children: Andrew Lawrence, Michael Allan, Zena Maria. BA, Yale U., 1966, PhD in Physics, 1972. Instr. physics Yale U., New Haven, Conn., 1971-72, rsch. assoc., 1972; NAS/NRC postdoctoral fellow Nat. Bur. Stds., 1972-73; asst. prof. U. Ill., Urbana, 1973-78, assoc. prof., 1978-82, prof., 1982-95, adj. prof., 1995—; co-prin. investigator nuclear physics lab. U. Ill., Champaign, 1982-89, 92; dep. assoc. dir. physics Continuous Electron Beam Accelerator Facility, Newport News, Va., 1993-96; assoc. dir. for physics Thomas Jefferson Nat. Accelerator Facilities, Newport News, Va., 1996—; vis. scientist Centre D'Etudes Nucleaire Saclay, France, 1980-81, Continuous Electron Beam Accelerator Facility, Newport News, Va., 1989-90; adj. prof. Coll. William and Mary, Williamsburg, Va., 1995—. Contbr. over 50 articles to profl. jours. Nat. Acad. Scis.-NRC Postdoctoral Rsch. fellow, 1972-73. Fellow Am. Phys. Soc.; mem. Sigma Xi. Avocations: woodworking, electronics, computers, cooking.

CARDONA, MANUEL, physics educator; b. Barcelona, Catalonia, Spain, July 9, 1934; s. Juan and Angela (Castro) C.; m. Inge Hecht; children: Michael, Angela, Steven. Licenciado en Ciencias, U. Barcelona, 1955; DSc, U. Madrid, 1958; MSc, Harvard U., 1958, PhD, 1959; hon. degree, Brown U.; Dr. (hon.), U. Autónoma de, Madrid, 1985, U. Autónom de, Barcelona, 1985, U. Regensburg, Germany, 1994, Sherbrooke U., Can., 1994, U. La Sapienza, Roma, 1995, U. Toulouse, 1998. Mem. tech. staff RCA Labs, Zurich, Switzerland, 1959-61, Princeton, N.J., 1961-64; assoc. prof. physics Brown U., Providence, 1964-66, prof. physics, 1966-71; dir. Max Planck Inst. for Solid State Rsch., Stuttgart, Germany, 1971—; adj. prof. U. Stuttgart, 1973—, U. Konstanz, 1990—. Editor-in-chief Solid State Comm., Oxford, Eng., 1992—; mem. bd. editors Physica Status Solidi, Berlin, 1971—; assoc. editor Phys. Rev. Letter, Upton, N.Y., 1989-92; editor Solid State Sci. Series Springer, 1975—; author: Modulation Spectroscopy, 1969, Fundamentals of Semiconductors, 1995, 2d edit., 1999; others; contbr. numerous articles to profl. jours. Recipient Max Planck Rsch. prize, 1994, Principe de Asturias Found. award, 1988, Great Cross of Order of Alfonso X el Sabio, Spain, 1987, N. Monturiol medal Govt. of Catalonia, 1984, J.M. Marci von Kronland medal Czechoslovak Spectroscopy Soc., Prague, 1989, Sci. prize Catalonian Sci. Found., 1990, Medaglia Tersiana U. Pavia, Italy, 1992, Ernst Madi medal Czech Phys. Soc., 1999. Fellow Am. Phys. Soc. (Frank Isakson award 1984, John Wheatley award 1997); mem. NAS of U.S. (ordinary mem.), Acad. Scis. of Barcelona (corr. mem.), European Phys. Soc., Germany Phys. Soc., Academia Europaea, Royal Acad. Scis. of Spain (corr. mem.), Internat. Union Pure and Applied Physics (chmn. semicondrs. commn. 1996—). Lutheran. Office: Max Planck Inst, Heisenbergstr 1, 705969 Stuttgart Germany

CARDONA, RODOLFO, Spanish language and literature educator; b. San Jose, Costa Rica, Jan. 17, 1924; came to U.S., 1943, naturalized, 1950; s. Jose Ismael and Julia (Cooper) C.; m. Electra Ducas, Aug. 1, 1954; children: Eleni Maria, Alexander Xavier, Michael Anthony, Christopher Pericles. B.A., La. State U., 1946; Ph.D., U. Wash., Seattle, 1953. Consul of Costa Rica, San Diego, 1943-44; asst. instr. fine arts and Spanish La. State U., 1946-47; asst. prof. Am. Inst. Fgn. Trade, Phoenix, 1947-48; instr. U. Wash., 1948-53; hon. consul Costa Rica, Seattle, 1948-53; asst. prof. Western Res. U., also hon. consul Costa Rica, Cleve., 1953-56; asst. prof., then assoc. prof. Chatham Coll., Pitts., 1956-60; prof., then chmn. dept. Hispanic langs. U. Pitts., 1961-69; hon. consul Costa Rica, Pitts., 1956-69; prof. Spanish, chmn. dept. Spanish and Portuguese U. Tex., Austin, 1969-78; Univ. prof., dir. Univ. Profs. Program Boston U., 1978-88, prof. emeritus, 1991—. Author: Ramón: A Study of Gómez de la Serna and His Works, 1957; co-author: Visión del esperpento; editor: Novelistas españoles de hoy, 1959, La sombra de Benito Pérez Galdós, 1964, Doña Perfecta, 9th edit., 1984, Greguerias, 9th edit., 1997, La viuda blanca y negra by R. Gomez de la Serna, 1988, Galdós ante la literatura y la historia, 1998; Novelistas españoles de postguerra, 1977; co-editor: Teatro selecto de Galdós, 1973; founder, editor: Anales galdosianos; contbr. articles to profl. jours. Andrew Mellon postdoctoral fellow, 1960-61; grantee Am. Council Learned Socs., 1967-68; grantee Univ. Research Inst., 1973-74; fellow Nat. Endowment Humanities, 1973-74. Mem. Phi Beta Kappa, Phi Kappa Phi, Pi Mu Epsilon, Phi Sigma Iota. Mem. Easthern Orthodox Ch. Home: 17 Beethoven St Boston MA 02119-3108*

CARDONE, BONNIE JEAN, photojournalist; b. Chgo., Feb. 21, 1942; d. Frederick Paul and Beverly Jean (Johnson) Rittschof; m. David Frederick Cardone, June 9, 1963 (div. 1978); children: Pamela Susan, Michael David. BA, Mich. State U., 1963. Editorial asst. Mich. State Dental Assn. Jour., Lansing, 1963-64; asst. editor Nursing Home Adminstr. mag., Chgo., 1964-65; asst. editor Skin Diver Mag., L.A., 1976-77, sr. editor, 1977-81, photographer, 1981—, exec. editor, 1981-97, editor, 1997-99. Author: Fireside Diver, 1993; co-author: Shipwrecks of Southern California, 1989. Mem. Santa Monica Blue Fins Club (treas. 1975-76, pres. 1977-78, 91-92, sec. 1985-86, v.p. 1987-88), Calif. Wreck Divers Club, Hist. Diving Soc. (bd. dirs. 1997). Avocation: skiing.

CARDOZA, AVERY, writer, publisher; b. Bklyn., Feb. 11, 1957. Owner Cardoza Pub., Washington, 1981, Open Rd. Pub., Washington, 1993—; owner software pub. co. for multi-media windows games on CD-ROMS, Cardoza Entertainment. Author: Winning Casino Blackjack for the Non-Counter, 1981, How to Win at Gambling, 1991, Complete Guide to Successful Publishing, 1995, How to Play Winning Poker, 1987, Gambler's PlayBook, 1991, Casino Craps for the Winner, 1982, Beat the House Companion, 1992, Basics of Winning Baccarat, 1992, Basics of Sports Betting, 1991, Winning Casino Play, 1994; co-author: Las Vegas Guide, 1995; gaming expert casino simulation software Beat the House, 1992. Avocation: international travel. Office: Cardoza Pub 132 Hastings St Brooklyn NY 11235-3054

CARDOZIER, VIRGUS RAY, higher education educator; b. Montgomery, La., Apr. 2, 1923; s. James C. and Lelia M. C.; m. Nancy Pattison Fyfe, Dec. 29, 1955. B.S., La. State U., 1947, M.S., 1950; Ph.D., Ohio State U., 1952; postgrad., U. Mich., 1967. Adult edn. tchr. and supr. La. schs., 1947-50; edn. specialist in industry, 1952-57; assoc. prof. Coll. Edn., U. Tenn., Knoxville, 1957-60; prof., chmn. rural edn. U. Md., College Park, 1960-70; prof. higher edn. U. Md., 1968-70; v.p. for acad. affairs U. Tex. of Permian Basin, Odessa, 1970-74; prof. higher edn. and behavioral sci. U. Tex. of Permian Basin, 1970-82, pres., 1974-82; sr. acad. policy adviser U. Tex. System, 1982-83; prof. higher edn. U. Tex., Austin, 1983-97, prof. emeritus, 1997—; vis. prof. Pa. State U., 1968; vis. scholar UCLA, 1983; sec.-treas. Coun. Coll. and Univ. Presidents, Tex., 1979-82; bd. dirs. Am. Assn. State Colls. and Univs., 1981-82; cons. in field. Author: American Higher Education: An International Perspective, 1987, Colleges and Universities in World War II, 1993, The Mobilization of the United States in World War II, 1995; co-author, editor: Important Lessons from Innovative Colleges and Universities, 1993, University of Texas-Permian Basin: A History, 1998; contbr. articles to profl. jours. With U.S. Army, 1943-45, PTO. Named Outstanding Grad. Ohio State U. Centennial Celebration, 1969. Mem. Am. Sociol. Assn., Am. Assn. for Higher Edn., Acad. Polit. and Social Scis., Assn. for Study of Higher Edn., Nat. Assn. of Scholars, Phi Delta Kappa. Office: U Tex Coll Edn Austin TX 78712

CARDOZO, BENJAMIN MORDECAI, lawyer; b. N.Y.C., May 15, 1915; s. Sidney Benjamin and Eva Cecile (Mordecai) C.; m. Barbara Ruth Schaffer, Sept. 21, 1941; children: Enid Cardozo Lamcn, Ellen Cardozo Sonsino. BA, Dartmouth Coll., 1937; postgrad., Columbia U., 1938; JD, NYU, 1941. Bar: N.Y. State bar 1942, U.S. Supreme Ct. bar 1947, Conn. bar 1954. Mem. staff Moreland Commn. Workmen's Compensation Investigation, N.Y. State, 1941, Office Alien Property, U.S. Dept. Justice, Washington, 1946-49; assoc. Cardozo & Nathan, N.Y.C., 1949-51, Cardozo & Cardozo, P.C., N.Y.C., 1952—; pvt. practice, N.Y.C. Mem. ABA, New York County Lawyers Assn., Assn. Bar City N.Y., Yale Club, Met. Club. Home: 325 E 79th St New York NY 10021-0954 Office: 488 Madison Ave Rm 1100 New York NY 10022-5702

CARDOZO, OSCAR F., engineering executive; b. Mar. 11, 1941. BS in Automation and Control, Cvut-Praha, Prague, Czech Republic, 1966, MS in Automation and Control, 1971. Computer test engr. ZPA Čakovice, Prague, 1966-70; rsch. assoc., prof. physics U. Mayor de San Andres, La Paz, Bolivia, 1972-74; test and component engr. DSC Comm., Santa Clara, Calif., 1976-86; sr. component engring. mgr. Symmetricom, San Jose, Calif., 1986—. E-mail: ocardozo@MINDSPRING.COM. Home: 641 Tenth Ave Menlo Park CA 94025-1807

CARDOZO, RICHARD NUNEZ, marketing, entrepreneurship and business educator; b. Mpls., Feb. 13, 1936; s. William Nunez and Miriam (Honig) C.; m. Arlene Rossen, June 29, 1959; children: Miriam, Rachel (dec.), Rebecca. AB, Carleton Coll., 1956; MBA, Harvard U., 1959; PhD (Ford Found. fellow, Kaiser fellow), U. Minn., 1964. Asst. prof. bus. adminstrn. Harvard U., 1964-67; assoc. prof. mktg. U. Minn., 1967-71, prof., 1971—, Curtis L. Carlson chair in entrepreneurial studies, 1987—; dir. Center for Exptl. Studies in Bus., 1969-73, chmn. dept. mktg., 1975-78; dir. Case Devel. Ctr., 1980—, Entrepreneurial Studies Ctr., 1987—; dir. Nat. Presto Industries, Brownstone Distbg.; Fulbright lectr. Hebrew U., Jerusalem, 1980; vis. prof. bus. adminstrn. Harvard U., Grad. Sch. Bus., 1982-83; cons. in field. Author: (with others) Problems in Marketing, 4th edit, 1968; Product Policy: Cases and Concepts, 1979; contbr. articles to profl. jours. Served with USAR, 1961. Fulbright fellow London Sch. Econ., 1956-57. Mem. Am. Mktg. Assn., AAAS, Product Devel. and Mgmt. Assn., Acad. Mgmt. Home: 1007 Pine Tree Trail Stillwater MN 55082-5918 Office: U Minn 3-306 Carlson Sch Mgmt Minneapolis MN 55455

CARDUS, DAVID, physician; b. Barcelona, Spain, Aug. 6, 1922; came to U.S., 1957, naturalized, 1969; s. Jaume and Ferranda (Pascual) C.; m. Francesca Ribas, July 19, 1951; children: Hellena, Silvia, Bettina, David. BA, BS, U. Montpellier (France), 1942; MD magna cum laude, U. Barcelona, 1949, diploma in cardiology, 1956; D honoris causa, Autonomous U. Barcelona, 1993. French Govt. fellow dept. cardiology Hosp. Boucicaut and Hosp. de la Pitié, Paris, 1953-54; fellow U. Manchester, 1957; rsch. assoc. Lovelace Found., Albuquerque, 1957-60; NIH trainee Summer Inst. Math. for Life Scientists U. Mich., 1966; mem. active med. staff Inst. for Rehab. and Rsch. Baylor Coll. Medicine, Houston, 1960—, prof. dept. rehab., 1969—, prof. dept. physiology, 1973—, dir. Biomath. Program, 1966-69, dir. biomath. com. Sch. Grad. Studies, 1968-69, head exercise lab., 1960—, head cardiopulmonary lab., 1969—; adj. prof. math. scis. Rice U., 1970—, adj. prof. stats., 1989—. Chmn. bd. dirs. Inst. Hispanic Culture, Houston; vice chmn. Gordon Conf. on Biomaths., 1970; pres. Am. Inst. Catalan Studies, 1980—. Recipient 1st prize for exhibit Am. Urol. Assn., 1967, 1st prize for sci. exhibit 5th Internat. Am. Cong. of Rehab. Medicine, 1968, Gold medal for demonstration use of computers and telecomm. in rehab. 6th Internat. Congress Phys. Medicine and Rehab., 1972, August Pi Sunyer prize Inst d' Estudis Catalans, 1968, Elisabeth and Sidney Licht award for sci. writing Am. Congress Phys. Med. and Rehab., 1980, Narcis Monturiol medal Generalitat de Catalunya, Spain, 1985, Catalunya Enfora prize Inst. Catalan de Cooperación Iberoamericana Fundación Bertran, 1987, Commendation of Isabel la Católica (Spain), 1980, Creu de Sant Jordi Generalitat de Catalunya, 1992, Joan d'Alos award Centre Cardiovascular Sant Jordi, Barcelona, Spain, 1996. Mem. Am. Coll. Cardiology, Am. Coll. Chest Physicians, Am. Coll. Sports Medicine, Am. Congress Rehab. Medicine, Am. Physiol. Soc., Am. Statis. Assn., Internat. Soc. for Gravitational Physiology (pres. 1993), Fedn. Am. Socs. Exptl. Biology, Spanish Profls. in Am. (pres. 1984-85), N.Y. Acad. Scis., Societat Catalana Biologia, Sigma Xi. Home: 17207 Bonnard Cir Spring TX 77379-6275 Office: Baylor Coll Med 1333 Moursund St Houston TX 77030-3405

CARDWELL, HAROLD DOUGLAS, SR., rehabilitation specialist; b. Varnell, Ga., July 17, 1926; s. Arlie Amber and Hettie Ellen (Eledge) C.; m. Priscilla Dean Rumley, July 3, 1954; children: Harold Douglas, Jr., Ruth Ellen Cardwell-Landau. AA, Daytona Beach C.C., 1972; student, U. Fla., 1970; BA, Fla. Tech. U., 1974; postgrad., Clemson U., 1975. Registered landscape architect, Fla. Chem. operator Fercleve Chem. Corp., Oak Ridge, Tenn., 1945-46; draftsman C.M. Price Constrn. Co., Daytona Beach, Fla., 1947-48; bookkeeper, expediter W.A. Cardwell Constrn. Co., Gatlinburg, Tenn., 1948-49; office mgr., sales rep. J.H. Gordon Lumber Co., St. Augustine, Fla., 1949-51; asst. mgr. King Bros. Lumber Co., St. Augustine, 1951-56; pvt. practice landscape architect Port Orange, Fla., 1956-67; sr. rehab. specialist State of Fla. Divsn. of Blind Svcs., Daytona Beach, 1967—. Vice chmn. Daytona Beach Preservation Bd., 1987—; adv. mem. task force Daytona Beach City Govt., 1987; vice chmn. Volusia County Hist. Commn., Deland, Fla., 1989-92; mem. adv. bd. Volusia County Hist. Preservation Bd., Deland, 1992-94; adv. mem. Flagler Centennial Com., Tallahassee, Fla., 1986; pres. Fla. Anthropol. Soc., Gainesville, 1988-89. Recipient Historian of Yr. award Volusia County Hist. Commn., 1988, Lazarus award for Preservation, Fla. Anthropol. Soc., 1988. Mem. Am. Hort. Therapy Assn. (registered hort. therapist, nat. treas. 1978-80), Fla. Nurserymen and Growers Assn. (bd. dirs. 1963-64, 68-69), Halifax Hist. Soc. (bd. dirs. 1974—), Fla. Hist. Soc., Lions (Pres.' award in leadership Port Orange/South Halifax club 1988). Democrat. Methodist. Avocations: history, anthropology, historical tools, pre-historic tools, writing, research. Home: 1343 Woodbine St Daytona Beach FL 32114-5740 Office: State of Fla Divsn Blind Svcs 1111 Willis Ave Daytona Beach FL 32114-2808

CARDWELL, KENNETH HARVEY, architect, educator; b. Los Angeles, Feb. 15, 1920; s. Stephen William and Beatrice Viola (Duperrault) C.; m. Mary Elinor Sullivan, Dec. 30, 1946; children: Kenneth William, Mary Elizabeth, Ann Margaret, Catherine Buckley, Robert Stephen. A.A., Occidental Coll.; A.B., U. Calif.-Berkeley; postgrad., Stanford U. Lic. architect, Calif. Draftsman Thompsen & Wilson Architects, San Francisco, 1946-48, Michael Goodman, Architect, Berkeley, Calif., 1949; architect W.S. Wellington, Architect, Berkeley, 1950-59; prin. Kolbeck, Cardwell, Christopherson, Berkeley, 1960-66; prof. dept. arch. U. Calif.-Berkeley, 1950-82; prin. Kenneth H. Cardwell Architect, Berkeley, 1982—. Author: Bernard Maybeck, 1977. Pres. Civic Art Commn., Berkeley, 1963-65; mem. Bd. Adjustments, 1967-69, Alameda County Art Commn., 1969-72. Served to 1st lt. USAAF, 1941-45. Decorated D.F.C.; decorated Air medal with 3 oak leaf clusters; Rehman fellow, 1957; Graham fellow, 1961; recipient Berkeley citation U. Calif., 1982. Fellow AIA; mem. Alpha Rho Chi. Home and Office: 1210 Shattuck Ave Berkeley CA 94709-1413

CARDWELL, LARRY, executive director Toledo Youth Commission; b. Hamilton, Ohio, Jan. 18, 1951. BA, Bluffton Coll., 1973; MA, Bowling Green State U., 1976. Sr. parole officer Ohio State Parole Bd., Columbus, 1973-77; counselor, warden dept. corrections State of Ohio, Columbus, 1977-90, drug czar, 1990-92; exec. dir. youth commn. City of Toledo, 1992-95, with adminstrn. dept. neighborhoods, 1995—. Mem. Profl. Officials Northwestern Ohio, 50 Men and Women Orgn. Office: City of Toledo Adminstrn Dept Neighborhood 1 Government Ctr Ste 1800 Toledo OH 43604-2275*

CARDWELL, NANCY LEE, editor, writer; b. Norfolk, Va., Apr. 2, 1947; d. Joseph Thomas Cardwell and Martha (Bailey) Underwood. B.A. in Econs., Duke U., 1969; M.S. in Journalism, Columbia U., 1971. Copy editor Wall Street Jour., N.Y.C., 1971-73, reporter, 1973-76, editor fgn. dept. and Washington bur., 1977-80, night news editor, 1981-83, nat. news editor, 1983-87, asst. mng. editor, 1987-89; sr. editor Bus. Week mag., N.Y.C., 1989-91; editor Habitat World, Habitat for Humanity Internat., Americus, Ga., 1991-94; dir. comms. Craver, Matthews, Smith & Co., Falls Church, Va., 1994-95; freelance editor/writer, 1994—. Episcopalian.

CARDY, ANDREW GORDON, hotel executive; b. Brockville, Ont., Can.; s. Roland Hastings and Jean Davidson (Gordon) H.; m. Alice Elizabeth Cochrane, Sept. 18, 1948; 3 children. B. Commerce, U. Toronto (Ont.), 1941. Gen. mgr. Prince Edward Hotel, Windsor, Ont., 1951-52, Sheraton Connaught Hotel, Hamilton, Ont., 1952-54, Sheraton Brock Hotel, Niagara Falls, Ont., 1954-55, Sheraton Hotel, Rochester, N.Y., 1955-56, King Edward Sheraton Hotel, Toronto, 1956-68, Royal York Hotel, Toronto, 1968-78; v.p. central region Can. Pacific Hotels, 1971-78, pres., chief exec. officer, dir., 1978-86; chmn., CEO CP Hotels, 1980-86; pres. Gorbay Co. Ltd,

1986—; dir. Journeys End Corp., Can. Pacific Airlines Ltd.; bd. govs. Ryerson Poly. Inst., 1978-81; mem. Bd. Trade of Met. Toronto. Gov. Canadian Corps of Commissionaires, Toronto, 1990—; With Royal Canadian Arty., 1942-45. Decorated Mil. Cross (Can.), Knight Grace Mil. and Hospitaller Order St. Lazarus of Jerusalem.; mem. Most Noble Order of Crown of Thailand. Mem. Toronto Hotel Assn., Ont. Hotel and Motel Assn. (pres. 1973-74), Met. Toronto Conv. and Visitors Assn. (hon. dir.), Hotel Assn. Can. (pres. 1974-75), Royal Can. Mil. Inst. Mem. United Ch. of Can. Clubs: Lambton, Golf and Country, Toronto Bd. of Trade, Royal Can. Military Inst.

CARE, NORMAN SYDNEY, philosophy educator; b. Gary, Ind., Dec. 20, 1937; s. J. Norman and Anne (Baron) C.; m. Barbara Lou Bassett, Aug. 17, 1958; children: Steven Brooks, Jennifer Lorraine. BA, Ind. U., 1959; MA, U. Kans., 1961; postgrad., Oxford U., 1962-63; PhD, Yale U., 1964. Instr. Yale U., New Haven, 1964-65; asst. prof., assoc. prof., prof. philosophy Oberlin (Ohio) Coll., 1965—. Author: On Sharing Fate, 1987, Living with One's Past, 1996; editor: Readings in Theory of Action, 1968; author essays and revs., 1965—. Recipient Teaching Excellence award Sears-Roebuck Found., 1991. Mem. AAUP, Am. Philos. Assn. Office: Oberlin Coll King Bldg Oberlin OH 44074

CAREK, DONALD J(OHN), child psychiatry educator; b. Sheboygan, Wis., Aug. 10, 1931; s. Peter and Rose (Gergisch) C.; m. Frances M. Schaefer, Jan. 28, 1956; children—Carla, Thomas, Therese, Peter, Mary Beth, Christopher. MD, Marquette U., 1956. Diplomate Am. Bd. Psychiatry and Neurology (examiner in child psychiatry, psychiatry). Intern Walter Reed Army Hosp., 1956-57; resident U. Mich. Hosps., 1959-63; pediatrician Fort Meyer Dispensary, Arlington, Va., 1958-59; instr. psychiatry U. Mich., Ann Arbor, 1962-65, asst. prof., 1965-66; dir. day care Children's Psychiat. Hosp., Ann Arbor, 1965-66; assoc. prof. psychiatry and pediatrics Med. Coll. Wis., Milw., 1966-74, acting chmn. div. human behavior, 1970-73, prof. psychiatry, 1974-76; pres. med. staff Milw. Psychiat. Hosp., 1971-73; prof. psychiatry and pediatrics, chief youth divsn. Med. U. S.C., Charleston, 1976-96, emeritus prof. psychiatry, 1996—. Co-author: Guide to Psychotherapy, 1966; author: Principles of Child Psychotherapy, 1972; mem. editorial bd. Am. Jour. Child & Adolscent Psychiatry, 1988-93; contbr. articles to profl. jours. Bd. dirs. Cedarcrest Girls Residential Treatment Ctr., 1969-71. Capt. USAR, 1956-59. Fellow Am. Acad. Child Psychiatry (com. on adolescent psychiatry 1979-85, com. on psythotherapy 1986-90), Am. Psychiat. Assn., Am. Coll. Psychiatrists (membership com. 1991-94, 95-98); mem. AMA, Am. Orthopsychiatry Assn., AAAS, Am. Psychosomatic Soc., Soc. Profs. Child Psychiatry, S.C. Med. Assn. (mental health com. 1992-93), S.C. Dist. Cr. Am. Psychiat. Assn., Charleston County Med. Soc., S.C. State Bd. Med. Examiners (med. disciplinary commn. 1992-95), Alpha Omega Alpha, Alpha Sigma Nu, Best Doctors in America Southeast Region, 1995. Fellow Am. Acad. Child Psychiaty (com. on adolscent psychiatry 1979-85, com. on psychotherapy 1986-90), Am. Psychiat. Assn., Am. Coll. Psychiatrists (membership com. 1991-98); mem. AMA, AAAS, Am. Orthopsychiatry Assn., Am. Psychosomatic Soc., Soc. Profs. Child Psychiatry, S.C. Med. Assn. (mental health com. 1992-93), S.C. Dist. Cr. Am. Psychiat. Assn., Charleston County Med. Soc., S.C. State Bd. Med. Examiners (med. disciplinary commn. 1992-95), Alpha Omega Alpha, Alpha Sigma Nu. Roman Catholic. Home: Apt. 12 329 Harbor Pointe Dr. Mount Pleasant SC 29464 Office: Med Univ SC 171 Ashley Ave Charleston SC 29425-0001

CAREN, ROBERT POSTON, aerospace company executive; b. Columbus, Ohio, Dec. 25, 1932; s. Robert James and Charlene (Poston) C.; m. Linda Ann Davis, Mar. 27, 1963; children: Christopher Davis, Michael Poston. B.S., Ohio State U., 1953, M.S., 1954, Ph.D., 1961. Sr. physicist N.Am. Aviation, Columbus, 1959-60; assoc. research scientist research and devel. div. Lockheed Missiles and Space Co., Inc., Palo Alto, Calif., 1962-63, research scientist, 1963-66, sr. mem. research lab., 1966-69, mgr. def. systems space systems div., 1969-70, mgr. infared tech. R & D div., 1970-71, research dir., 1972-76, chief engr., 1976-86, v.p. gen. mgr. R & D div., 1986—, corp. v.p. sci. and engring., 1987-98; chmn. LITEX Inc., 1998—; bd. dirs. LITEX Corp., Superconducting Tech. Inc.; mem. U.S./Israel Sci. and Tech. Commn., 1997—. Contbr. articles to profl. jours. Mem. dean's adv. coun. Ohio State U., Calif. Poly. State U.-St. Louis Obispo, U. So. Calif., U. Calif., L.A., U. Calif., Davis. Fellow AIAA, AAAS, AAS; mem. NAE, IEEE (sr.), Am. Astron. Soc., Am. Def. Preparedness Assn. (past chmn. rsch. divsn.), Am. Phys. Soc., Aerospace Industries Assn. (past chmn. tech. and ops. coun.), Calif. Coun. on Sci. and Tech., Sigma Pi Sigma, Pi Mu Epsilon. Patentee in field. Home: 6039 Gleneagles Cir San Jose CA 95138-2372 Office: 340 N Westlake Blvd Ste 210 Westlake Village CA 91362

CARESS, STANLEY MALCOLM, political science educator; b. Alhambra, Calif., Jan. 30, 1951; s. Hyman and Diana (Margulies) C.; m. Lori Margolin, Sept. 5, 1992. BA, Calif. State U., San Jose, 1972, MA, 1974; PhD, U. Calif., Riverside, 1978. Lectr. Calif. State U., Long Beach, 1982-92; prof. State U. West Ga., Carrollton, 1992—; vis. prof. U. Nev., Las Vegas, 1996-97; assoc. dir. Ctr. for Future Democracy, Fountain Valley, Calif., 1990—. Contbr. articles to profl. jours. Dem. nominee Calif. State Assembly, 1984, 92. Mem. Am. Soc. for Pub. Adminstrn. (exec. coun. Ga. chpt.), Am. Polit. Sci. Assn., Western Polit. Sci. Assn., Ga. Polit. Sci. Assn. Jewish. Avocation: organic gardening. Home: 7738 Post Rd Winston GA 30183 Office: State U West Ga Carrollton GA 30187

CARET, ROBERT LAURENT, university president; b. Biddeford, Maine, Oct. 7, 1947; s. Laurent J. and Anne (Santorsola) C.; m. Elizabeth Zoltan; children: Colin Ready, Katherine Ready, Katalyn Ford, Kellen Ford. BA, Suffolk U., 1969; PhD, U. N.H., 1974; DSc (hon.), Suffolk U., 1996; DHL (hon.), Nat. Hispanic U., 1997. Dean Coll. Natural and Math. Scis. Towson (Md.) State U., 1981-87, prof. chemistry, 1994—, assoc. v.p., 1985-86, exec. asst. to pres., 1986-87, provost, exec. v.p., 1987-95; pres. San Jose (Calif.) State U., 1995—. Author: (with A.S. Wingrove) Quimca Organica, 1984, Study Guide and Answer Book to Organic Chemistry, 1981, Organic Chemistry, 1981, (with P. Plante) Myths and Realities in Higher Education Administration, 1990, (with K. Denniston and J.J. Topping) Principles and Applications of Organic and Biological Chemistry, 1995, 2d edit., 1997, Principles and Applications of Inorganic, Organic and Biological Chemistry, 1992, 2d edit., 1997, Foundations of Inorganic, Organic and Biological Chemistry, 1995; contbr. articles to profl. jours. Chmn. Baltimore County Higher Edn. Adv. Bd., Towson, 1989—; co-chmn. Balt. Sci. Fair/Kiwanis, Towson, 1983-88; bd. dirs. San Jose Repertory Theater, San Jose Opera, Calif. State U. Inst. Recipient Employee Incentive award State of Md., 1987, Outstanding Chemistry Tchr. award Md. Inst. Chemists, 1971, Award for Excellence Suffolk U. Gen. Alumni Assn., 1986; Lester A. Pratt fellow U. N.H., 1972, Albert W. Diniak fellow, U. N.H., 1972. Mem. AAUP (Towson State U. chpt., mem. exec. com. 1978-81, v.p. 1975-80, divsn. and dept. rep. 1975-80), Am. Assn. Higher Edn., Am. Assn. Univ. Adminstrs. (Md. membership rep. 1986—), Am. Coun. on Edn., EDUCOM (instl. rep. 1986-87), Am. Chem. Soc. (Chesapeake sect. alt. counselor 1979-87, mem. exec. com. 1978-87, mem.-at-large 1978-79, various coms. 1978-87), Am. Assn. State Colls. and Univs. (adv. bd. 1986—, Kellogg Leadership bd. 1989—, state rep. 1989—, joint venture Silicon Valley bd. dirs. 1997, co-chair econ. devel. team 1996—, co-chair econ. property coun. 1998—), Silicon Valley Mfg. Group (bd. dirs.), San Jose C. of C. (bd. dirs.), Sigma Xi (Towson State U. chpt. pres. 1975-76), Sigma Zeta, Phi Beta Chi, Omicron Delta Kappa. Avocations: jogging, tae kwon do, cross country skiing, golf. Office: San Jose State U One Washington Sq San Jose CA 95192-0002

CARETTO, ALBERT ALEXANDER, chemist, educator; b. Baldwin, N.Y., May 16, 1928; s. Albert A. and Mary (Magnasco) C.; m. Virginia L. Ahman, Apr. 30, 1960; children—Joseph A., Ann M. B.S., Rensselaer Poly. Inst., 1950; Ph.D., U. Rochester, 1954. Postdoctoral research Brookhaven Nat. Lab., Upton, N.Y., 1954-56, U. Calif. at Berkeley, 1956-57; asst. prof. Carnegie Inst. Tech., Pitts., 1957-58, 59-64; assoc. prof. Carnegie Inst. Tech., 1964-67; research chemist U. Calif. at Livermore, 1958-59; with CERN (European Lab. for Nuclear Research), Geneva, Switzerland, 1964-65; prof. Carnegie-Mellon U., Pitts., 1967-95; chmn. dept. chemistry Carnegie-Mellon U., 1970-74; with European Lab. Nuclear Research, CERN, Geneva, Switzerland, 1974-75. Contbr. articles to profl. jours. Sch. Bd. dir., 1979-85; dir. Pa. Gov.'s Sch. for the Scis., 1982-94. Mem. AAAS, Am. Chem. Soc. (chair Pitts. sect., 1996), Am. Phys. Soc., Sigma Xi, Phi Kappa Phi. Home: 43B Bethany Dr Pittsburgh PA 15215-1207 Office: Carnegie-Mellon U Dept Chemistry Pittsburgh PA 15213

CAREW, RODNEY CLINE, batting coach, former professional baseball player; b. Gatun, Panama, Oct. 1, 1945; m. Marilynn Levy, Oct. 1970; children: Charryse, Stephanie. Second baseman Minn. Twins, 1967-78; first baseman Calif. Angels, 1979-85; batting coach Anaheim Angels (formerly Calif. Angels). Named Am. League Rookie of Year, Sporting News, 1967, Am. League Rookie of Year, Baseball Writers' Assn. Am., 1967; winner Am. League Batting Title, 1969, 72-75, 77-78; named to Am. League All-Star Team, 1967-84, Sporting News All-Star Team, 1967-69, 72-75, 77-78; named Am. League Most Valuable Player, 1977; inductee Baseball Hall of Fame, 1991.

CAREY, ANTHONY MORRIS, lawyer; b. Balt., May 31, 1935; s. Anthony Morris and Louise (Waterman) C.; m. Eleanor MacKey, Oct. 7, 1967. AB, Princeton U., 1957; LLB, Harvard U., 1963; MLA, Johns Hopkins U., 1970. Bar: Md. 1963, U.S. Dist. Ct. (fed. dist.) Md. 1965, U.S. Supreme Ct. 1968. Assoc. Venable, Baetjer & Howard, Balt., 1963-67, ptnr., 1972-79, 87—; chmn. environ. dept., asst. atty. gen. State of Md., Balt., 1967-69; spl. asst. for energy affairs HUD, Washington, 1979-81; pres. Carey-Tidewater, Inc., Balt., 1981-86; regional dir., gen. counsel HEC Energy Corp., Balt., 1986-87; bd. dirs. Carey Machinery Supply Co., Inc., Balt.; former exec. sec. Md. Bd. Ethics. Former trustee Citizen's Planning and Housing Assn.; former dir. Nat. Civic League, Denver, 1979-90; chmn. bd. trustees Balt. Sch. for the Arts Found., current chmn. emeritus bd. overseers; vice chmn. Lillie Carroll Jackson Mus.; trustee Robert Garrett Fund for Surg. Treatment of Children. Capt USAF, 1957-60. Mem. ABA, Md. State Bar Assn., Ivy Club, Hamilton St. Club. Democrat. Episcopalian. Avocations: skiing, hiking, reading. Office: Venable Baetjer & Howard 1800 Merc Bank & Trust Bldg 2 Hopkins Plz Ste 2100 Baltimore MD 21201-2982

CAREY, ARTHUR BERNARD, JR., editor, writer, columnist; b. Phila., May 16, 1950; s. Arthur Bernard and Mary Louise (Lynch) C.; m. Katherine Ann White, Apr. 14, 1973 (div. Feb. 1980); m. Tanya Marie Walters, July 17, 1982; 1 child, Edward Lynch. A.B., Princeton U, 1972; M.S., Columbia U., 1975. Editor Fedn. Telephone Workers of Pa., Phila., 1972-74; reporter Bucks County Courier Times, Levittown, Pa., 1975-77, Phila. Inquirer, 1977—. Author: In Defense of Marriage, 1984, The United States of Incompetence, 1991; editor: That's Livin', 1984. Term trustee The Episcopal Acad., Merion, Pa., 1982-88, alumni trustee, 1990-93; mem. com. to nominate alumni trustees Princeton U., 1989-92. Recipient Edward J. Meeman Conservation award Scripps-Howard Found., 1977, Best Story of the Yr. award Nat. Conf. Sunday Mags., 1983, George Washington Honor medal Freedoms Found., 1984, Disting. Journalism award Epilepsy Found. Am., 1997, Robert Joplin Sci. Writers award Am. Orthopedic Foot and Ankle Soc., 1998; Robert E. Sherwood Traveling fellow Columbia U., 1975; best feature story Pa. Soc. Newspaper Editors, 1986, 91. Mem. Soc. Profl. Journalists (best newsfeature N.J. chpt. 1979). Democrat. Episcopalian. Avocations: running; weight lifting; carpentry; antique jeeps. Home: 928 Clover Hill Rd Wynnewood PA 19096-1631 Office: Phila Inquirer 400 N Broad St Philadelphia PA 19130-4099

CAREY, CHASE, broadcast executive. Chmn., CEO Fox TV, L.A. Office: Fox TV 10201 W Pico Blvd Los Angeles CA 90035-2606*

CAREY, DEAN LAVERE, fruit canning company executive; b. Biglerville, Pa., Nov. 29, 1925; s. Earl E. and Ann Olivia (Newman) C.; m. Doris M. Dugan, July 21, 1949; children—Philip D., Juanita Ann. B.S., U. Pitts., 1949. With Knouse Foods Corp., Inc., Peach Glen, Pa., 1949—; contr. Knouse Foods Corp., Inc., 1955-59, asst. gen. mgr., 1960-62, gen. mgr., 1963-65, pres., 1966—, also dir. Dir. Blue Cross, Harrisburg, Pa.; chmn. Capital Blue Cross, Harrisburg. Served with USNR, 1944-46. Mem. Pa. Chamber Bus. and Industry (bd. dirs.). Lutheran. Clubs: Am. Legion, Masons, Shriners. Office: Knouse Foods Coop Inc 800 Peach Glen Idarille Rd Peach Glen PA 17375-0001*

CAREY, DREW, actor; b. Cleve., May 23, 1958. Acting debut on The Tonight Show, 1991; actor (film): Coneheads, 1993, (tv movies) Freaky Friday, 1995, Sex, Drugs and Freedom of Choice, 1998, (tv series) The Drew Carey Show, 1995—, Whose Line Is It Anyway?, 1998; prodr.: Whose Line Is It Anyway?, 1998, The Drew Carey Show, 1995—; tv guest appearances include: The Torkelsons, 1991, Late Night with Rita Sever, 1998, Star Search, 1988, George Carlin Show, 1995, Lois & Clark: The New Adventures of Superman, 1993, Home Improvement, 1991, Ellen, 1994, Sabrina, the Teenage Witch, 1996, Weird Al Show, 1997, Dharma & Greg, 1997, Larry Sanders Show, 1992; star comedy spls. for Showtime: Full Frontal Comedy, Drew Carey, Human Cartoon; author: Dirty Jokes and Beer, 1997; host 25th Ann. Am. Music Awards, 1999. Winner TV Guide award Editor's Choice, 1999, People's Choice award for best actor in a new series, CableACE award. Office: Warner Bros Domestic Television Dist 4001 N Olive Ave Burbank CA 91522*

CAREY, E. FENTON, federal agency associate administrator. BS in Mech. and Aerospace Engring., U. Del., MS in Mech. and Aerospace Engring.; PhD in Aeronautical Engring., Naval Postgrad. Sch. Officer USN, 1970-90; various positions U.S. Dept. Def., Washington, 1980-90, U.S. Dept. of Energy, Washington, 1990-96; assoc. adminstr. for rsch., tech. and analysis, RSPA U.S. Dept. of Transp., Washington, 1996—; contbg. author Tech. for Nat. Security, 1988; major mgmt. assignments in Dept. of Def., Dept. of Energy. Contbr. articles on space and laser tech. and sci. and tech. policy to profl. jours. Mem. Am. Inst. Aeronautics and Astronautics, N.Y. Acad. Scis., Am. Astronautics Soc. (bd. dirs.), Sigma Xi, Tau Beta Pi. Office: Rsch/Spl Programs Adminstrn Dept Transp 400 7th St SW Washington DC 20590

CAREY, EDWARD JOHN, utility executive; b. N.Y.C., Jan. 16, 1944; s. Edward John and Mary Elizabeth (Hopkins) C.; m. Maureen A. McCullough, June 4, 1977. B.A., Fordham U., 1971. With N.Y. Central R.R., 1962-68; with Consol. Edison Co., N.Y.C., 1968—. Bd. dirs. Salvation Army, Greater N.Y. Adv. Bd. Home: 17 Richmond Hls Irvington NY 10533-2301 Office: 4 Irving Pl New York NY 10003-3502

CAREY, ELLEN, artist; b. N.Y.C., June 18, 1952. BFA, Kansas City Art Inst., 1976; MFA, SUNY, Buffalo, 1978. One woman shows include Concord Gallery, N.Y.C., 1985, Zone, Springfield, Mass., 1986, Real Art Ways, Hartford, Conn., 1986, Art City, N.Y.C., 1986, Simon Cerigo, N.Y.C., 1987, Internat. Ctr. of Photography, N.Y., 1987, John Good Gallery, N.Y.C., 1989, Schnider-Bluhm-Loeb Gallery, Chgo., 1990, Nat. Acad. of Scis., Washington, 1992, Jayne H. Baum Gallery, N.Y.C., 1992, 94, Gallery 954, Chgo., 1994, Nina Freudenheim Gallery, Buffalo, N.Y., 1995; exhibited in numerous group shows including Dayton (Ohio) Art Inst., 1993, The Dallas Mus. of Natural History, 1993, Rochester Mus. of Sci. Ctr., Rochester, 1993, L.A. Mus. of Natural History, Charles and Emma Frye Art Mus., Omniplex Sci. Ctr., Seattle, 1993, Fernback Mus. of Natural History, Atlanta, 1993, Calif. Acad. of Scis., 1993, Cleve. Mus. of Natural History, 1993, Tatischeff Gallery, N.Y.C., 1993, Mus. of Modern Art, 1994, U. N.C., Greensboro, 1993-94, Herter Gallery, U. Mass., Amherst, Mass., 1993-94, Palazoo de Exhbns., Rome, 1993-94, Art Inst. of Chgo., 1994, Caldwell (N.J.) Coll., Artspace, New Haven, Conn., 1994, Akron Art Mus., 1994, Ansel Adams Ctr. for Photography, San Francisco, 1994, Park Avenue Atrium, N.Y.C., 1994, Charter Oak Cultural Ctr., Hartford, 1995, Kingsborough Cmty. Coll. Art Gallery, Bklyn., 1995; represented in permanent collections Albright-Knox Art Gallery, Art Inst. of Chgo., Bell Atlantic, Bklyn. Mus. of Art, Chase Manhattan Bank, Coca Cola Corp., First Bank of Mpls., Fogg Mus., Harvard U., Internat. Ctr. of Photography, Mus. of Fine Arts, many others; contbr. articles to profl. jours. Home: 588 Broadway New York NY 10012-5404*

CAREY, ERNESTINE GILBRETH (MRS. CHARLES E. CAREY), writer, lecturer; b. N.Y.C., Apr. 5, 1908; d. Frank Bunker and Lillian (Moller) Gilbreth; m. Charles Everett Carey, Sept. 13, 1930; children: Lillian Carey Barley, Charles Everett. BA, Smith Coll., 1929. Buyer R. H. Macy & Co., N.Y.C., 1930-44, James McCreery, N.Y.C., 1947-49; Carey writer and lectr. Book reviewer, 1949—, syndicated newspaper articles, 1951, (with Lillian Moller Gilbreth) (McElligott medallion Assn. Marquette U. Women 1966); author: Jumping Jupiter, 1952, Rings Around Us, 1956, Giddy Moment, 1958, (with Frank B. Gilbreth, Jr.) Cheaper by the Dozen, 1949 (Prix Scarron French Internat. Humor award 1951, over 50 translations), Belles on Their Toes, 1951; contbg. author: Smith Voices—Selected Works by Smith College Women, 1990, 99; lifetime papers represented in collections at Smith Coll.; also mag. articles and book revs. Bd. dirs. Right to Read, Inc., 1968—, co-chmn., 1967; lay adv. com. Manhasset (N.Y.) Bd. Edn.; trustee Manhasset Pub. Libr., 1953-59, v.p., 1956-59; trustee Smith Coll., 1967-72; active in care-preservation and current student use of Frank B. and Lillian M. Gilbreth lifetime papers at Purdue U. Montgomery award Friends of Phoenix Pub. Libr., 1981, honored guest Ariz. Lib. Friends, 1994; recipient Internat. Mgmt. award: the Gilbreth Medal, Soc. for Advancement of Mgmt., 1996. Mem. Authors Guild Am. (life mem., mem. guild council 1955-60), PEN, North Shore Club, Smith Coll. Club (asst. chmn. scholarship com. L.I. chpt. 1950-59), Soc. Advancement Mgmt., Smith Coll. Club (vice chmn. scholarship com. Phoenix chpt.), 7 Coll. Conf. Coun. Club (Phoenix). Home: 701 W Herbert Ave Apt 64 Reedley CA 93654-3951

CAREY, FRANCIS JAMES, investment banker; b. Balt., Mar. 24, 1926; s. Francis James and Marjorie (Armstrong) C.; m. Emily Norris Large, June 8, 1956 (dec. Apr. 1997); children: Francis James III, Elizabeth P. Carey Boden, Henry Augustus, Emily Norris, Frances Carey MacMaster. Student, Princeton, 1943-44; A.B., U. Pa., 1945, J.D., 1949. Bar: Pa. 1950. Law sec. to justice Supreme Ct. Pa., 1950-51; with firm Reed Smith Shaw & McClay, Phila., 1951-87, counsel, 1987-92; mem. faculty U. Pa., 1946-47; bd. mgrs., mem. exec. com. Western Savs. Bank, 1970-82; chmn., CEO, bd. dirs. Carey Diversified LLC 1998—; pres., bd. dirs. W.P. Carey & Co.Inc., Carey Fiduciary Advisors Inc., Corporate Property Assn. 10 Inc. and affiliates, Corp. Property Assocs. 10 Inc., Carey Institutional Properties, Inc.; pres., trustee W.P. Carey Found., 1990—; mem. bus. adv. com. Bus. Coun. f or UN, 1994—; trustee Investment Program Assn., 1990—, chmn., 1998 —; mem. Senatorial Trust, 1992—. Mem. Com. of Seventy, Phila., 1957-58; mem. Lower Gwynedd Twp. (Pa.) Planning Commn., 1962-75, sec., 1962-65; trustee Germantown Acad., Fort Washington, Pa., 1961—, pres., 1966-72; overseer Sch. Arts and Scis., U. Pa., 1983-90; mgr. Law Alumni Soc., U. Pa., 1962-66. Served to lt. USNR, 1943-45, PTO. Mem. ABA, Pa. Bar Assn. (chmn. real property, probate and trust law sect. 1966-67, chmn. conf. group to cooperate with Pa. Land Title Assn. 1970-77), Phila. Bar Assn. (chmn. com. on civil legislation 1962), Soc. Mayflower Descendants in State of N.Y., Fourth Street Club, St. Anthony Club (Phila.), Sunnybrook Golf Club (Plymouth Meeting, Pa.), Racquet & Tennis Club, The Brook Club, St. Anthony Club (N.Y.), Abenakee Club (Biddeford Pool, Maine), Biddeford Pool Yacht Club. Republican. Episcopalian. Home: 485 Lewis Ln Ambler PA 19002-5116 Office: Carey Diversified LLC 50 Rockefeller Plz New York NY 10020-1605

CAREY, GERALD JOHN, JR., research institute director, former air force officer; b. Bklyn., Oct. 1, 1930; s. Gerald John and Madeline (McNamara) C.; m. Joan Bennett, Apr. 24, 1954; children: Gerald John, III, Cathleen, John Kevin, Daniel. B.S., U.S. Mil. Acad., 1952; M.S. in Aero. Engring, Tex. A&M U., 1961. Commd. 2d lt. USAF, 1952, advanced through grades to maj. gen., 1978; pilot trainee Victoria, Tex., 1953; flight instr. Laredo, Tex., 1954-56; asst. air attache Tokyo, 1958-61; aero. engr. Air Force Systems Command, Andrews AFB, Md., 1963-66; flight comdr. Seymour Johnson AFB, 1967; ops. officer Udorn, Thailand, 1969-70; wing comdr. 1st and 56th Tactical Fighter Wings, Tampa, Fla., 1973-75; asst. dep. chief of staff ops. Tactical Air Command Hdqrs., Langley AFB, Va., 1975-78; comdr. USAF Tactical Air Warfare Center, Eglin AFB, Fla., 1978-81; ret., 1981; assoc. dir. Rsch. Inst. Ga. Inst. Tech., Atlanta, 1981—. Mem. USAF Sci. Adv. Bd., 1995. Decorated Legion of Merit, D.S.M., D.F.C. with 2 oak leaf clusters. Mem. Air Forces Assn., Daedalians, Tau Beta Pi, Sigma Gamma Tau. Office: Ga Inst Tech Rsch Inst Atlanta GA 30332

CAREY, GRAHAM FRANCIS, engineering educator; b. Cairns, Queensland, Australia, Nov. 14, 1944; came to U.S., 1968; s. Lionel Dudley and Alma Lilian Carey; m. Kira Iljins, Jan. 13, 1968; children: Varis, Tija. BS, U. Queensland, 1965, BS with honors, 1966; MS, U. Wash., 1970, PhD, 1974. Registered profl. engr., Tex. Research engr. Boeing Co., Seattle, 1968-70; research prof. U. Wash., Seattle, 1974-76; prof. aerospace engring. U. Tex., Austin, 1977—, dir. Computational Fluid Dynamics Lab., 1986—; U.S. rep. Fenomech Conf., Germany, 1978, U.S.-Germany, Germany, 1981; lectr. Summer Rsch. Inst., Australia, 1984; Cray lectr., Adelaide, Australia, 1991; plenary lectr. Finite Element Meeting, Finland, 1993, summer grad. program, 1995, Finland Conf., 1996; keynote lectr. CTAC '97, Australia, 1996, Brazil Conf., 1997, EMAC '98, Australia, 1998; adj. fellow Minn. Supercomputer Inst., Mpls., 1986; Richard B. Curran Centennial chair in engring., 1998—; lectr. in field. Author: Introduction to Finite Element Methods, 1974, Finite Element Series, vols. I-VI, 1980-86, Circuit Device and Processes Simulation, 1996, Computational Grids: Generation, Adaptation and Solution Strategies, 1997; editor: Finite Elements in Fluids, 1984, Parallel Supercomputing: Methods, Algorithms and Applications, 1989, Finite Element Modeling of Environmental Problems, 1995; editor (internat. jour.) Comms. in Numerical Methods in Engring., 1984—; contbr. numerous articles to profl. jours. Recipient Ex-Student's Assn. Tchg. Excellence award, 1995. Mem. AIAA, Soc. for Indsl. and Applied Math., Am. Acad. Mechanics, Soc. for Engring. Sci., Soc. for Computer Simulation, U.S. Assn. for Computation of Mechanics, Internat. Assn. for Computational Mechanics (fellows award 1998). Office: U Tex Austin Dept Aerospace Engring WRW 111 Computational Fluid Dy Austin TX 78712

CAREY, HARRY, JR., actor; b. Saugus, Calif., May 16, 1921; s. Harry and Olive (Fuller) C.; m. Marilyn Frances Fix; children: Steven, Melinda, Thomas, Patricia. Served with U.S. Navy, 1942-45, PTO. Home: PO Box 3256 Durango CO 81302-3256

CAREY, J. EDWIN, lawyer; b. N.Y.C., Aug. 29, 1923; s. Edwin J. and Nora L. (Greene) C.; m. Marian G. Burke, May 23, 1954; children—Brianne, Christopher. Student, Manhattan Coll., 1941-43; LL.B., St. John's U., 1951. Bar: N.Y. bar 1951. Pvt. practice N.Y.C., 1951-89; with Hill, Rivkins, Carey, Loesberg, O'Brien, Mulroy and Hayden (and predecessors), 1990—; counsel Hill Rivkins et al; Lectr. admiralty law Practicing Law Inst., 1959—. Served with inf. AUS, 1943-46, ETO. Mem. ABA, N.Y. State Bar Assn., Maritime Law Assn. U.S. (chmn. membership com. 1958-60, membership sec. 1960-66, sec. 1966-69, 1st v.p. 1970-72, pres. 1972-74), U.S. del. internat. confs. UN, Comité Maritime International (titular mem.), Union Internationale des Avocats, Am. Judicature Soc., Assn. Average Adjusters, Ins. Soc. N.Y., St. Thomas More Soc. (pres. 1948-49), Phi Delta Phi. Clubs: Arcola Country (Paramus, N.J.). Home: 393 Carriage Ln Wyckoff NJ 07481-2306 Office: 90 West St New York NY 10006-1039*

CAREY, JAMES HENRY, banker; b. Elizabeth, N.J., May 22, 1932; s. Charles C. and Adelyne (Bilyeu) C.; m. Nancy Mershon Ferrenz, Aug. 14, 1954; children: Jane Meredith, Christopher James, George Mershon, David James. BA cum laude, Brown U., 1953; postgrad., Sch. Bus. Adminstrn., N.Y. U., 1956-59. With Chase Manhattan Bank, N.Y.C., 1955-86; asst. v.p. Chase Manhattan Bank, 1961-63, v.p., 1963-68, exec. v.p., 1976-86; exec. v.p. Hambro Am. Bank & Trust Co., N.Y.C., 1968-69; pres. Hambro Am. Bank & Trust Co., 1969-72, also bd. dirs.; pres., chmn. bd. First Empire Bank N.Y. (formerly Hambro Am. Bank & Trust Co.), N.Y.C., 1972-75; exec. v.p. Chase Manhattan Corp., N.Y.C., 1976-86; pres., CEO The Berkshire Bank N.Y., N.Y.C., 1989-92; mng. dir. Briarcliff Fin. Assocs., N.Y.C., 1992—; bd. dirs. Midland Co., Airborne Freight Corp., The S.G. Cowen Group of Mut. Funds (6). Bd. dirs. The Rayburn Found., Am. Mus. Flyfishing, U.S. Com. for UNICEF. Lt. (j.g.) USNR, 1953-55. Mem. The Dorset (Vt.) Field Club, Mid Ocean Club (Bermuda), The Sky Club, Phi Beta Kappa, Delta Tau Delta. Episcopalian. Home: PO Box 859 Manchester VT 05254-0859 Office: Briarcliff Fin Assocs PO Box 859 Manchester VT 05254

CAREY, JAMES WILLIAM, university dean, educator, researcher; b. Providence, Sept. 7, 1934; s. Cyril Joseph and Rita Miriam (Lyons) C.; m. Elizabeth Theresa Gilman, Sept. 7, 1957; children: William, Timothy, Daniel, Matthew. B.S., U. R.I., 1957; M.S., U. Ill., 1959, Ph.D., 1963. Prof. U. Ill., Urbana, 1963-67; dir. Inst. Communications Research, U. Ill., Urbana, 1969-76; dean Coll. Communications U. Ill., Urbana, 1979-92; prof. Pa. State U., State College, 1967-68, U. Iowa, Iowa City, 1976-79; CBS prof. Columbia

U., N.Y.C., 1993—; assoc. mem. Ctr. for Advanced Study, 1975; bd. dirs. PBS, Ill. Humanities Coun., Poynter Inst. for Media Studies, Peabody Awards in Broadcasting. Book review editor: Communication Research: An Internat. Quar., 1974-82; cons. and contbg. editor: Jour. Communication, 1981-83, Communication yearbook I, II, III, 1981-83; editor: Sage Ann. Revs. of Communication Research, 1982-87, Communication, 1985—; mem. editorial bd.: Journalism Quar., 1974—, Journalism Monographs, 1974—, Mass Communication Rev., 1974—, Studies in the Anthropology of Visual Communication, 1981—, Can. Communications Jour., 1980-83; contbr. articles to profl. jours. NEH fellow, 1975, Gannett Ctr. for Media Studies fellow Columbia U., 1985. Mem. Assn. Edn. in Journalism (pres. 1978-79), Assn. Schs. and Depts. Journalism (pres. 1982-83). Democrat. Roman Catholic. Home: 15 Claremont Ave # 33 New York NY 10027-6802 Office: Columbia U 512 Journalism Rm 201 New York NY 10027*

CAREY, JANA HOWARD, lawyer; b. Huntsville, Ala., Apr. 20, 1945; d. Ernest Randall and Mary Regna (Baites) Howard; m. James Johnston Hale Carey, Jan. 15, 1983. BS in Home Econs., Auburn U., 1967; MS in Audiovisual Communications, Towson State U., 1973; JD, U. Balt., 1976. Tchr. Hampton High Sch., Melbourne, Australia, 1967; home economist U. Ga., Athens, 1967-70, devel. specialist state youth program, 1970-72; devel. specialist state youth program U. Md., College Park, 1972-73; clk. appellate div. Pub. Defender's Office, Balt., 1974; assoc. Venable, Baetjer & Howard, Balt., 1975, 76-84, ptnr., 1984—, past chair labor and employment group, 1995-97. Author: The Developing Law on Equal Employment Opportunity for the Handicapped: An Overview and Analysis of the Major Issues, 1978, The Rehabilitation Act of 1973: Its Impact on Employee Selection Practices, 1978, Accommodations for the Handicapped: What Is the Employer's Duty?, 1979, Employee Handbooks: Practical Pointers for Avoiding a Handbook Horros Case, 1984, Recent Developments on the Rights of the Handicapped, Disabled or Injured Worker, 1985, The Developing Law on AIDS in the Workplace, 1987, AIDS: The Victim's Right in the Workplace, 1987, Employment Contracts in Maryland: New Lessons from Old Law, 1989, Checklist for Counseling the Corporate Defendant in an Employment Lawsuit, 1990, How the ADA & FMLA Interact With an Employer's Policies Concerning Absenteeism & Leave Due to Employee Medical Condition, 1993, Fear of AIDS & Hospital Liability, 1993, Fear of AIDS Cases, Court Offers New Guidance for Health Care Industry, 1994; co-author: Employers' Growing Problems-Sorting Out ADA, FMLA and Worker's Compensation Issues, 1995, Beware the Native Tongue: National Origin and English-Only Rules, 1995, Legal Aspects of the Employment Relationship: An Introduction for the General Practitioner, 1978; profl. articles editor U. Balt. Law Rev., 1974; contbr. articles to legal jours. Bd. dirs. Mcpl. Mus. Balt. City, 1984-86, Balt. New Directions for Women, 1979-84, also past pres.; women's mgmt. devel. program Goucher Coll., Balt., 1982-84; mem. affirmative action com. United Way Ctrl. Md., Balt., 1983-84; mem. joint Medicolegal Com. on AIDS of Med. and Chirurgical Faculty State of Md., 1987—; mem. vis. bd. U. Balt., 1986-88; mem. St. Mary's Coll. Pres.' Coun.; mem. United Way Task Force on AIDS, 1988—; mem. Gov.'s Exec. Coun. on Substance Abuse, 1989-90. Mem. ABA (coun., labor law sect., EEO com., former chair program divsn. of com. on EEI law, former co-chair insts. and mtgs. com., mem. EEOC liaison com.), Nat. Assn. Women Lawyers (gender bias com.), Fed. Bar Assn. (dep. chmn. labor rels. 1978), Md. Bar Assn., Bar Assn. Balt. City (CUE labor law adv. com.), Loophole Law Club, CWENS, Mortar Bd., Alpha Gamma Delta (past chpt. pres.), Alpha Lambda Delta, Omicron Delta Kappa, Omicron Nu. E-mail: jhcarey@venable.com. Office: Venable Baetjer & Howard 1800 Mercantile Bank & Trust Bldg Two Hopkins Plaza Baltimore MD 21201

CAREY, JOHN, lawyer, judge; b. Phila., June 11, 1924; s. Henry Reginald and Margaret Howell (Bacon) C.; m. Patricia F. Frank, Feb. 24, 1951; children: Henry Frank, John, Douglas, Jennifer Patricia. Grad., Milton Acad., 1942; B.A., Yale U., 1947; LL.B., Harvard U., 1949; LL.M. in Internat. Law, N.Y.U., 1965; LL.D., U. W.I., 1985. Bar: Pa. 1950, N.Y. 1957. Practiced in Phila., 1949-55, N.Y.C., 1956-87; asst. dist. atty. Phila., 1952-54; cons. spl. com. fed. loyalty-security program Assn. Bar City N.Y., 1955-56; ptnr. Coudert Bros., 1961-87; justice N.Y. Supreme Ct., 1987; judge Westchester County Ct., White Plains, N.Y., 1988-94; mem. faculty NYU Law Sch., 1966-73; jud. hearing officer N.Y. State, 1995—. Author: UN Protection of Civil and Political Rights, 1970; editor: United Nations Law Reports, 1966—. Mem. Rye (N.Y.) City Coun., 1964-68, 72-74, mayor, 1974-82; alt. mem. UN Subcommn. on Prevention Discrimination and Protection of Minorities, 1966-82, 84-91, mem. 1983; alt. U.S. rep. UN Human Rights Commn., 1968; trustee Little Harbor Chapel, Portsmouth, N.H. Mem. ABA, Internat. Bar Assn., N.Y. State Bar Assn., Assn. Bar City N.Y., Am. Soc. Internat. Law (v.p. 1987-88), Coun. on Fgn. Rels., Phi Beta Kappa. Home: 860 Forest Ave Rye NY 10580-3145 Office: County Ct House White Plains NY 10601

CAREY, JOHN, English language educator, literary critic; b. London, Apr. 5, 1934; s. Charles William and Winifred Ethel (Cook) C.; m. Gillian Mary Booth, Aug. 13, 1960; children—Leo, Thomas. BA, St. John's Coll., Oxford, Eng., 1957; PhD, Oxford U., 1960. Lectr. Christ Church Coll., Oxford, 1958-59; research fellow Balliol Coll., Oxford, 1959-60; tutorial fellow Keble Coll., Oxford, 1960-64, St. John's Coll., 1964-75; Merton prof. English lit. Oxford U., 1976—; prin. book reviewer Sunday Times, London, 1977—; hon. fellow St. John's Coll., Balliol Coll., Oxford, fellow British Acad., 1996. Author: Milton, 1969, The Violent Effigy, 1973, Thackeray: Prodigal Genius, 1977, John Donne: Life, Mind and Art, 1981, Original Copy: Selected Reviews and Journalism, 1987, The Faber Book of Reportage, 1987, The Intellectuals and the Masses, 1992, The Faber Book of Science, 1995, The Faber Book of Utopias, 1999. Served to lt. Brit. Army, 1953-54. Fellow Royal Soc. Lit. Avocations: bee-keeping; gardening; swimming. Home: 57 Stapleton Rd, Headington Oxford England Office: Merton Coll, Oxford England

CAREY, JOHN ANDREW, investment company executive; b. Glendale, Calif., May 27, 1949; s. John Nelson and Dorothea Ruth (Bordwell) C.; m. Harriet Ruth Stolmeier, June 19, 1982; children: Julia Scott, Elizabeth Bordwell. B.A., Columbia U., 1971; A.M., Harvard U., 1972, Ph.D., 1979. Chartered fin. analyst. Teaching fellow Harvard U., Cambridge, Mass., 1973-78; sr. council rep. Yankelovich, Skelly & White, Stamford, Conn., 1977-79; analyst Pioneer Investment Mgmt., Inc., Boston, 1979-81, sr. analyst, 1981-83, v.p., 1983-98, sr. v.p., 1998—; v.p. Pioneer Scout, Inc., Boston, 1984-89, v.p. Pioneer Fund, 1987—, Pioneer Equity-Income Fund, 1992—, Pioneer Income Fund, 1994-96, Pioneer Variable Contract Trust, 1995—. Author: Judicial Reform in France before the Revolution of 1789, 1981. Treas., Newton Hist. Soc., Mass., 1983-87. Mem. Assn. for Investment Rsch. and Mgmt., Boston Security Analysts Soc., Boston Athenaeum, Harvard Club of Boston. Republican. Episcopalian. Home: 16 Ridge Hill Farm Rd Wellesley MA 02482-7312 Office: Pioneer Group Inc 60 State St Ste 3 Boston MA 02109-1820

CAREY, JOHN CLAYTON, pediatrician; b. Balt., 1946. MD, Georgetown, 1972. Diplomate Am. Bd. Med. Genetics, Am. Bd. Pediatrics. Prof pediatrics U. Utah Med. Ctr., Salt Lake City. Author: Medical Genetics, 1999, Care of the Child with Trisomy 18/13, 1996; contbr. over 140 articles to profl. jours. Med. advisor Support Orgn. Trisomy 18/13, Utah Parent Ctr., Hope Network. Office: U Utah Med Ctr Pediatrics 413 Med Edn Bldg 50 N Medical Dr Salt Lake City UT 84132-0001

CAREY, JOHN EDWARD, information services executive; b. Albany, N.Y., Sept. 21, 1949; s. John Edward and Lillian Rose (Murdock) C.; m. Nicolette Anne Yianilos, Oct. 26, 1974; children: Theodore, Anna. BA, Tulane U., 1971. Pres. FOI Svcs., Inc., Rockville, Md., 1976-95, Gaithersburg, Md., 1995—. Office: FOI Svcs Inc 11 Firstfield Rd Gaithersburg MD 20878-1704

CAREY, JOHN JESSE, academic administrator, religion educator; b. Ft. Wayne, Ind., Oct. 13, 1931; s. Edmund Othmar and Frieda Louise (Jesse) C.; m. Sally Ann Stanback, Mar. 30, 1954 (div. Dec. 1967); children: Sarah, Mary Lynn, Beth; m. Mary Charlotte McCall, May 22, 1969; children: Joanna, Jessica. AB, Duke U., 1953, PhD, 1965; BD, Yale U., 1956, MST, 1957. Ordained to ministry Presby. Ch. Chaplain Catawba Coll., Salisbury, N.C., 1957-60; univ. chaplain Fla. State U., Tallahassee, 1960-62, assoc. dean students, 1962-63, asst. dean Grad. Sch., 1965-66, dean of students, 1966-67, v.p. student affairs, 1967-68, prof. religion, 1968-86; pres. Warren Wilson Coll., Swannanoa, N.C., 1986-88; Pendergrass prof. religion Fla. So. Coll., Lakeland, 1988-89; Wallace M. Alston prof. Bible and religion Agnes Scott Coll., Decatur, Ga., 1989-91, emeritus prof. religious studies, 1999—. Author: Carlyle Marney: A Pilgrim's Progress, 1980; editor: The Death of God Debate, 1967, Tillich Studies, 1975, Kairos and Logos, 1978, Theonomy and Autonomy, 1984, Doing and Being, 1988, The Sexuality Debate in North Am. Chs. 1988-95, 1995. Recipient Standard Oil Co. Excellence in Teaching award, Fla. State U., 1973, R.R. Oglesby Disting. Service award, Fla. State U., 1980. Mem. Soc. for Values in Higher Edn. Club: Yale (N.Y.C.).

CAREY, JOHN LEO, lawyer; b. Morris, Ill., Oct. 1, 1920; s. John Leo and Loretta (Conley) C.; m. Rhea M. White, July 15, 1950; children: John Leo III, Daniel Hobart, Deborah M. BS, St. Ambrose Coll., Davenport, Ia., 1941; JD, Georgetown U., 1947, LLM, 1949. Bar: Ind. 1954. Legislative asst. Sen. Scott W. Lucas, 1945-47; spl. atty. IRS, Washington, 1947-54; since practiced in South Bend; ptnr. Barnes & Thornburg, 1954—, now of counsel; law prof. taxation Notre Dame Law Sch., 1968-90. Trustee LaLumire Prep. Sch., Laporte, Ind. Served with USAAF, World War II; to lt. col. USAF, Korean War. Decorated D.F.C., Air medal. Mem. ABA (bd. govs. 1986-89, treas. 1990-93), Ind. Bar Assn. (pres. 1976-77), St. Joseph County Bar Assn., Signal Point Country Club. Home: H H 28 Ocean Reef Club Key Largo FL 33037 Office: 600 1st Source Bank Ctr 100 N Michigan St South Bend IN 46601-1610

CAREY, JOHN PATRICK, III, lawyer; b. N.Y.C., Oct. 31, 1955; s. John Patrick Jr. and Emily Smith (Warner) C.; m. Jane Alden Hopkins, June 21, 1980; children: William Nelson, Timothy Jarvis, John Patrick IV. AB, Georgetown U., 1978; JD, Geortetown U., 1983. Bar: N.Y. 1984, D.C. 1985. Asst. to pres. Georgetown U., Washington, 1978-80; law clk. to Hon. June L. Green U.S. Dist Ct. for D.C., Washington, 1983-85; assoc., of coun. Paul, Hastings, Janofsky & Walker, Washington, 1985-93; chief counsel Office of Presdl. Pers., The White House, Washington, 1993; gen. counsel Fed. Emergency Mgmt. Agy., Washington, 1993-97; sr. exec. v.p. MBNA Am. Bank, N.A., Wilmington, Del., 1997—; mem. adv. coun. IRS, Washington, 1998—; v.p., trustee South Kent (Conn.) Sch. Corp., 1991-98. Assoc. counsel pers. office Office of Presdl. Transition, Washington, 1992-93; bd. govs. Georgetown U., 1988-92; trustee Wilmington Music Sch., 1997-98; dir. Russian Ballet Theatre of Del., 1997-98. Georgetown U. Law Ctr. law fellow, 1982-83. Mem. ABA, D.C. Bar, Georgetown U. Alumni Assn. (senator 1992—). Democrat. Roman Catholic. Office: MBNA Am Bank NA 1100 N King St Wilmington DE 19884-0162

CAREY, KEITH GRANT, editor, publishing executive; b. Oakland, Calif., Jan. 13, 1958; s. Richard William and Juanita May (Yost) C.; m. Lois Lynn Schuricht, Oct. 15, 1994. BA in History with honors, San Jose State U., 1980. Tchr. Chaparral H.S., Las Vegas, 1981-82; pers. mgr. Grecian Health Spa, Palo Alto, Calif., 1982-83, Palos Verdes Health Spa, San Pedro, Calif., 1983-86; prodn. mgr., mng. editor U.S. Ctr. World Mission, Pasadena, Calif., 1986—. Mng. editor Global Prayer Digest, 1992—. Avocations: cooking, jogging. Office: USCWM Global Prayer Digest 1605 E Elizabeth St Pasadena CA 91104-2721

CAREY, PAUL RICHARD, biophysicist; b. Dartford, Kent, Eng., June 17, 1945; arrived in Can., 1969; s. Charles Richard and Winifred Margaret (Knight) C.; m. Julia Smith, Sept. 4, 1966 (div. May 1991); children: Emma, Sarah, Matthew; m. Marianne Pusztai, Mar. 7, 1992. BS in Chemistry with honors, U. Sussex, Eng., 1966, PhD, 1969. Postdoctoral fellow Nat. Rsch. Coun., Ottawa, Ont., Can., 1969-71, rsch. officer, 1971-94; mgr. Ctr. for Protein Structure Design, head protein lab. Inst. for Bio. Scis., Ottawa, Ont., Can., 1987-93; prof. dept. biochemistry Case Western Res. U., 1995—; mem. internat. adminstrv. com. Internat. Conf. on Lasers and Biol. Molecules, 1987—, adj. prof. Dept. Biochemistry, U. Ottawa, 1987-94, prof., 1994; prof. dept. biochemistry Case Western Reserve U. Author: Biochemical Applications of Raman and Resonance Raman Spectroscopies, 1982; contbr. over 170 articles to profl. jours.; patentee in field. Mem., past pres. Ottawa br. Amnesty Internat., 1980—. Fellow Chem. Inst. Can.; mem. Am. Chem. Soc., Can. Protein Engring. Network (Adminstrv. body 1990-93), Internat. Network Protein Engring. Ctrs. Achievements include first demonstration of resonance Raman spectroscopy providing vibrational spectrum of a substrate or drug in active site of an enzyme; generation of first quantitative relationship between active site bond lengths and reactivity by combining resonance Raman spectroscopy, enzyme kinetics and x-ray crystallography; elucidation of mechanism of sunlight degradation of biological insecticide from B. thuringiensis; research on use of lasers in fingerprint detection. Avocations: literature, music, birding. Office: Case Western Res U Dept Biochemistry Cleveland OH 44106-4935

CAREY, PETER KEVIN, reporter; b. San Francisco, Apr. 2, 1940; s. Paul Twohig and Stanleigh M. (White) C.; m. Joanne Dayl Barker, Jan. 7, 1978; children: Brendan Patrick, Nadia Marguerite. BS in Econs., U. Calif., Berkeley, 1964. Reporter San Francisco Examiner, 1964; reporter Livermore (Calif.) Ind., 1965-67, editor, 1967; aerospace writer, spl. projects and investigative reporter San Jose (Calif.) Mercury, 1967—. Recipient Pulitzer prize for internat. reporting Columbia U., 1986, George Polk award L.I. U., 1986, Investigative Reporters and Editors award, 1986, Jessie Meriton White Svc. award Friends World Coll., 1986, Mark Twain award Calif.-Nev. AP, 1983, staff team Pulitzer prize for gen. reporting, Columbia U., 1990, Thomas L. Stokes award Washington Journalism Ctr., 1991, Malcolm Forbes award Overseas Press Club of Am., 1993, Gerald Loeb award UCLA Grad. Sch. Mgmt., 1993, Best of the West, First Amendment Funding Inc., 1993, 95, Pub. Svc. award Calif. Newspapers Pub. Assn., 1996, Fairbanks award for pub. svc. AP, 1996; NEH profl. journalism fellow, Stanford U., 1983-84. Mem. Soc. Profl. Journalists, Investigative Reporters and Editors. Avocation: classical piano. Office: San Jose Mercury-News 750 Ridder Park Dr San Jose CA 95131-2432

CAREY, ROBERT MUNSON, university dean, physician; b. Lexington, Ky., Aug. 13, 1940; s. Henry Ames and Eleanor Day (Munson) C.; m. Theodora Vann Hereford, Aug. 24, 1963; children: Adonice Ames, Alicia Vann, Robert Josiah Hereford. BS, U. Ky., 1962; MD, Vanderbilt U., 1965; Doctor Honoris Causa, Fed. U. Ceara, Brazil, 1998. Diplomate Am. Bd. Internal Medicine, Am. Bd. Endocrinology and Metabolism, Nat. Bd. Med. Examiners. Intern in medicine U. Va. Hosp., Charlottesville, 1966; jr. asst. resident in medicine N.Y. Hosp.-Cornell Med. Ctr., N.Y.C., 1966-69, sr. asst. resident, 1969-70; instr. endocrinology, dept. medicine Vanderbilt U. Sch. Medicine, Nashville, 1970-72; postdoctoral fellow in medicine St. Mary's Hosp. Med. Sch., London, 1972-73; asst. prof. internal medicine, endocrinology and metabolism U. Va. Sch. Medicine, Charlottesville, 1973-76, assoc. prof., 1976-80, prof., 1980—, James Carroll Flippin prof. medical sci. and dean, 1986—, assoc. dir. Clin. Rsch. Ctr., 1975-86, head. div. endocrinology and metabolism, dept. internal medicine, 1978-86, chmn. gen. faculty, chmn. med. adv. com., chmn. exec. com., 1986—; attending staff U. Va. Hosp., Charlottesville, 1973—, pres. clin. staff, 1977-79, vice chmn. med. policy com., 1986—, adv. bd. 1986—; mem. study sect. on exptl. cardiovascular scis. NIH, 1982-85; mem. cardiovascular and renal adv. com. USDA, 1988—; vis. prof. div. nephrology, U. Miami Med. Sch., Fla., 1979, 83, 84, Hosp. das Clinicas da Univ., Fed. do Ceara, Forteleza, Brazil, 1981, hypertension div. Mt. Sinai Sch. Medicine, N.Y.C., 1981, div. pediatric endocrinology N.Y. Hosp.-Cornell Med. Ctr., 1981, dept. endocrinology St. Vincent's Hosp., Univ. Coll., Dublin, Ireland, 1982, depts. physiology and endocrinology Mayo Grad. Sch. Medicine, Rochester, Minn., 1984, div. rsch. Cleve. Clinic Found., 1984, Genentech, Inc., San Francisco, 1984, divs. endocrinology and metabolism U. Mass., U. Pa. Sch. Medicine, Boston U. Med. Sch., 1984, U. N.C. Sch. Medicine, 1985, Harvard Med. Sch., Boston, 1987, Jefferson Med. Coll., 1988; Bley Stein vis. prof. endocrinology U. So. Calif., 1987; Pfizer vis. prof. in pharmacology U. Chgo., 1988; co-organizer 3d Internat. Meeting on Peripheral Actions of Dopamine, Charlottesville, 1989; v.p. Va. Ambulatory Surgery, Inc., 1986—; speaker, presenter numerous nat. and internat. profl. meetings and congresses. Author: (with E.D. Vaughn) Adrenal Disorders, 1988; co-editor: Hypertension: An Endocrine Disease, 1985; mem. editorial bd. Jour. Clin. Endocronlogy and Metabolism, 1981-84, Hypertension jour., 1983-84, Am. Jour. Physiology: Heart and Circulatory Physiology, 1987-89, Am. Jour. Hypertension, 1987—; author over 150 articles, revs., papers for profl. jours., contbr. 19 chpts. to books. Mem. exec. com. and fin. com. U. Va. Health Services Found., 1986—; bd. dirs. Va. Kidney Stone Found., Inc., 1986—, The Harrison Found., Inc. U. Va., 1986—, Dyslexia Ctr., Charlottesville, 1986—. Surgeon (lt. comdr.) USPHS, 1966-68, res., 1968—. Recipient Attending Physician of Yr. awrd dept. internal medicine U. Va. Med. Ctr., 1983-84, Disting. Alumnus award and Founder's medal Vanderbilt U.; USPHS fellow Vanderbilt U., 1970-72; recipient numerous NIH grants as co-prin. and prin. investigator, 1972—. Fellow Am. Coll. Physicians (program com. regional meeting 1987), Coun. for High Blood Pressure Rsch. AMA (program com. 1984-86, exec. and long rang planning coms. 1992—); mem. Inst. Medicine of NAS, Am. Heart Assn. (established investigator 1975-80), Va. affiliate Am. Heart Assn. (bd. dirs. 1977-83, pres. 1979-80, Disting. Service award), The Endocrine Soc. (fin. com. 1988—, chair devel. com. 1991-92), Am. Fedn. Clin. Rsch. (so. sect. councilor 1978-81, nominating com. 1982), So. Soc. Clin. Investigation (nominating com. 1982, sec.-treas. 1985-86), Inter-Am. Soc. for Hypertension, Am. Soc. Clin. Investigation, Am. Clin. and Climatol. Assn., Am. Soc. Hypertension (intersocietal affairs com. 1986—), Internat. Soc. Hypertension, Assn. Am. Physicians, AMA, Albemarle County Med. Soc., Med. Soc. Va., Assn. Am. Med. Coll.s Coun. of Deans, Inst. of Medicine, Nat. Acad. of Scis., The Raven Soc., Alpha Omega Alpha (Disting. Med. Alumnus award Vanderbilt U. 1994). Home: Pavilion Vi East Lawn Charlottesville VA 22903 Office: U of Va Sch Medicine PO Box 395 Charlottesville VA 22902-0395

CAREY, RONALD, former labor union leader. Pres. local union Internat. Brotherhood of Teamsters, Long Island City, NY; pres. Internat. Brotherhood of Teamsters, Washington. *

CAREY, RUSSELL CHRISTOPHER, university administrator, lawyer; b. July 1, 1969. AB, Brown U., 1991; JD, Suffolk U., 1995. Bar: Mass. 1995. Asst. dean student life Brown U., Providence, 1994-95, 96-97; asst. dist. atty. Commonwealth of Mass., Northampton, 1995-96; asst. to provost Brown U., 1996-97, sec. univ., exec. asst. to pres., 1997—. E-mail: Russell_Carey@Brown.edu. Office: Brown Univ Univ Hall Brown U Providence RI 02912 Home: 63 Dexterdale Rd Providence RI 02906-2707

CAREY, SARAH COLLINS, lawyer; b. N.Y.C., Aug. 12, 1938; d. Jerome Joseph and Susan (Atlee) Collins; m. James J. Carey, Aug. 28, 1962 (div. 1977); 1 child, Sasha; m. 2d John D. Reilly, Jan. 27, 1979; children: Sarah, Katherine. BA, Radcliffe Coll., 1960; LLB, Georgetown U., 1965. Bar: D.C. 1966, U.S. Supreme Ct. 1977. Soviet specialist USIA/U.S. Dept. State, 1961-65; assoc. Arnold & Porter, Washington, 1965-68; asst. dir. Lawyers Com. for Civil Rights, Washington, 1968-73; ptnr. Heron, Burchette, Ruckert & Rothwell/predecessor firms, Washington, 1973-90; chair CIS Practice Steptoe and Johnson, 1990—; cons. Ford Found., 1975-83, Carnegie Corp., 1984-88. Contbr. articles to profl. jours. Bd. dirs. New Transcentury Found., Washington, 1982-90, Overseas Edn. Fund, 1982-92, Inst. for Soviet-Am. Rels., 1983-95, Russia-Am. Enterprise Fund, 1993-95, Defense Enterprise Fund, 1994—, Georgetown U. Sch. Law Inst. for Pub. Representation, 1971-85, Am. Arbitration Assn., 1975-82; bd. dirs. Eurasia Found., 1993—, chmn. bd. 1994—; bd. dirs. Women's Fgn. Policy Group. Mem. Coun. on Fgn. Rels., Atlantic Coun. Democrat. Office: 1330 Connecticut Ave NW Washington DC 20036-1704

CAREY, THOMAS DEVORE, baritone, educator; b. Bennettville, S.C., Dec. 29, 1931; s. Ernest Govan and Beatrice (Devore) C.; m. Carol Brice, Dec. 27, 1969. Student, CCNY, 1954-58, Stuttgart Musikhochschule, 1960-62, Muskhochschule of Munich, 1962-65. Mem. faculty U. Okla., Norman, 1969—, assoc. prof. voice, 1971-77, prof., 1977—, Regents prof. music, 1994—; bd. dirs. Am. Exchange Bank, Norman; mem. faculty Inst. Mus. Studies, Graz, Austria, summers 1980—. Concert debut Town Hall, N.Y.C., 1957; operatic debut as Giorgio Germont in La Traviata, Nederland Opera Co., 1962; appeared as Absolom in German premiere Lost in the Stars, Stuttgart Opera, 1963; created role of Mel in opera The Knot Garden, London Royal Opera, 1971; appeared as Joe in London prodn. Show Boat, 1971; Japan debut in Tokyo, 1991. Mem. Norman Human Relations Bd., 1973—; bd. dirs. Okla. Arts and Humanities Council; founder Okla. Cool Kids Opera Camp, 1996. Served with AUS, 1951-53. Recipient Concert Artist Guild award, 1957, Marian Anderson award Munich Internat. Competition, 1961, Okla. Artist award Gov. of Okla., 1976, Disting. Svc. award U. Okla., 1985; winner s'Hertogenbosch Internat. Competition, 1961, Brussels Internat. Competition, 1962; named Okla. Musician of Yr. (with wife), 1977; John Hay Whitney grantee, 1960-62, Walter M. Sullivan grantee 1959, Martha Baird Rockefeller grantee, 1962-64; inductee Okla. Higher Edn. Hall of Fame, 1997. Mem. Screen Actors Guild, Nat. Assn. Tchrs. Singing, AAUP, Okla. Music Tchrs. Assn., Am. Guild Musical Artists, Music Educators Nat. Conf., Pi Kappa Lambda. Lodge: Lions. Home: 801 Jona Kay Ter Norman OK 73069-4215 Office: U Okla Sch Music 560 Parrington Oval Rm 109A Norman OK 73019-3040

CAREY, V. GEORGE, farmer, state legislator; b. Milford, Del., May 2, 1928; s. Vinal H. and Hessie Mae (Phillips) C.; m. Jeanette Messick, Oct. 2, 1948; children: Dennis, Karen Sue, Dale. Grad., Milford High Sch. Farmer, pres. Carey Farms, Inc., Milford; mem. Del. Ho. of Reps., Dover, 1984—, chmn. natural resources and environ. control com., mem. agr. com.; mem. State Commn. for Preservation of Farm Land and the Environ. Legacy. Sunday sch. tchr. Slaughter Neck Meth. Ch., 20 yrs., also past chmn. fin. com.; former mem.Gov.'s Select Com. on Farm Adv. Com. Mem. Milford and Milton C. of C., Delmarva Poultry Improvement Assn., Milford Hist. Soc., Milton Hist. Soc., Friemds of Milford and Milton Librs., Del. State Farm Bur. Home: RR 1 Box 161 Milford DE 19963-9728 Office: Ho of Reps Legislative Hall Dover DE 19901

CAREY, W. DAVID P., hotel executive; m. Kathy Carey; 4 children. BSEE, Stanford U.; MBA with distinction, Santa Clara U., JD cum laude. Assoc. Carlsmith Tichman Case Mukai and Ichiki; exec. v.p., gen. counsel Outrigger Hotels, Inc., Honolulu, 1986-88, pres., 1988—, CEO, 1994—. Mem. Hawaii Tourism Authority. Mem. ABA, Hawaii Hotel Assn., Urban Land Inst., Hawaii State Bar Assn., Young Pres.' Orgn., Hawaii Bus. Roundtable, Beta Gamma Sigma. Avocations: soccer, golf. Office: Outrigger Hotels and Resorts 2375 Kuhio Ave Honolulu HI 96815-2939

CAREY, WILHELMINA COLE, management consultant; b. Jan. 29, 1928; d. John and Estell (Swinton) Cole; children: Gilbert Flemin and Tyrone Sr. AA, BS, MBA, PhD; student, St. Elizabeths Hosp., Washington, 1960. Cert. profl. housekeeper. Exec. housekeeper, 1951-58; LPN, LPN supr. St. Elizabeths Hosp., 1960-65; asst. hosp. houskeeping officer, 1965-78, hosp. housekeeping officer, 1978-89, fed. govt. employee, 1960-87, govt. employee, 1987-91, dep. chief logistics mgmt. br., 1984-91; cons., owner Carey and Hester, Inc., Washington, 1991—; spkr. in field. Founder, curator mgr. St. Elizabeths Hosp. Mus.; sr. citizens program coord. Upper Rm. Bapt. Ch., D.C. Office of Aging; mktg. edn. tchr. Arlington Pub. Schs. Avocations: reading, working with seniors, touring, sports. Home and Office: Carey & Hester Inc 33 54th St SE Washington DC 20019

CAREY, WILLIAM BACON, pediatrician, educator; b. Phila., Dec. 6, 1926; s. Henry Reginald and Margaret (Bacon) C.; m. Ann Lord McDougal, July 21, 1956; children: Katharine Blayney, Laura Bacon Carey-Anniballi, Elizabeth McDougal. BA, Yale U., 1950; MD, Harvard U., 1954. Diplomate Am. Bd. Pediatrics. Intern Phila. Gen. Hosp., 1954-55; resident in pediatrics Children's Hosp. of Phila., 1955-57, 59-60; practice medicine specializing in pediatrics Media, Pa., 1960-89; dir. sect. on behavioral pediatrics Children's Hosp. Phila., 1989—; instr. pediatrics U. Pa. Sch. Medicine and Children's Hosp. Phila., 1961-73, assoc. in pediatrics, 1973-79, clin. asst. prof., 1979-82, clin. assoc. prof., 1982-90, clin. prof., 1990—. Co-editor: Developmental-Behavioral Pediatrics, 1983, 3d edit., 1999, Clinical and Educational Applications of Temperament Research, 1989, Prevention and Early Intervention: Individual Differences as Risk Factors for the Mental Health of Children, 1994; co-author: (with S.C. McDevitt) Coping with Children's Temperament—A Guide for Professionals, 1995, (with M. Jablow) Understanding Your Child's Temperament, 1997; contbr. articles to profl. jours.; developer Infant Temperament Questionnaire, 1970; co-developer Toddler Temperament Scale, 1978, Behavioral Style Questionnaire, 1976, Middle Childhood Temperament Questionnaire, 1980, Early Infancy Temperament Questionnaire, 1990. Bd. dirs. Benchmark Sch., Media, Pa., 1989—; pres. Friends of Wyck (House), Germantown, Phila. Capt. M.C.,

U.S. Army. 1957-59. Fellow Am. Acad. Pediat. (rsch. grantee 1975, 80, 85, Aldrich award 1991, Practitioner Rsch. award 1992); mem. Inst. Medicine of NAS, Am. Pediatric Soc., Soc. Rsch. in Child Devel., Ambulatory Pediatric Assn., Soc. for Devel. and Behavioral Pediatrics (exec. coun. 1983-85, pres.-elect 1989-90,pres. 1990-91), Phila. Pediatric Soc. (bd. dirs. 1969-71), Franklin Inn Club, Phi Beta Kappa. Home: 511 Walnut Ln Swarthmore PA 19081-1140

CAREY, WILLIAM POLK, investment banker; b. Balt., May 11, 1930; s. Francis J. and Marjorie A. (Armstrong) C. Grad., Pomfret Sch., 1948; student, Princeton, 1948-50; BS in Econs., U. Pa., 1953; ScD. (Hon.), Ariz. State U., 1998. V.p., gen. mgr. A. J. Orbach Co., Plainfield, N.J., 1955-58; prin. W. P. Carey & Co., Bloomfield, N.J., 1958-63; pres., dir. Internat. Leasing Corp., N.Y.C., 1959-89; chmn. exec. com., dir. Hubbard, Westervelt & Mottelay, Inc. (now Merrill Lynch Hubbard, Inc.), N.Y.C., 1964-67; dept. head Loeb, Rhoades & Co. (now Lehman Bros.), N.Y.C., 1967-71; vice chmn. investment banking bd., dir. corporate finance duPont Glore Forgan Inc., 1971-73; pres., dir. W.P. Carey & Co., Inc. and affiliates, N.Y.C., 1973-83, chmn., 1983—; gen. ptnr. Corp. Property Assocs. (CPA), N.Y.C., 1978-97, chmn. CPA series of pub. ltd. partnerships and real estate investment trusts, 1979—; chmn. Carey Instnl. Properties, N.Y.C., 1991—, chmn. exec. com. Carey Diversified LLC, 1997—; adv. com. U.S. Treasury Dept., 1986-92. Trustee Johns Hopkins U.; adv. bd. Johns Hopkins Sch. Advanced Internat. Studies; life trustee Gilman Sch. Balt.; trustee, mem. exec. com. Rensselaerville (N.Y.) Inst., 1979—; chmn. bd. trustees Oxford Mgmt. Ctr. Assocs. Coun., 1984-94, hon. trustee 1994—; mem. coun. mgmt. Templeton Coll., Oxford U., 1970-95; chm. St. Elmo Found., W.P. Carey Found.; vis. com. econs. U. Pa.; dir. (hon.) Edmund Niles Huyck Preserve, Inc.; mem. leadership com. James A. Baker III Inst. for Pub. Policy Rice U.; gov. Nat. Assn. Real Estate Investment Trusts, 1993-97. 1st lt. USAF, 1953-55. Estab. William Polk Carey prize in econs., Carey term chairs in econs. and fin. U. Pa., Carey chair in math. Pomfret Sch., Carey prize in math. Calif. Inst. Tech., Armstrong law prize Ariz. State U. Mem. Soc. Mayflower Descs. (gov. emeritus), The Pilgrims, The Brook, Racquet and Tennis Club, Univ. Club, Penn Club (N.Y.), St. Elmo Club (Phila. and N.Y.C.), Maryland Club, Delta Phi. Episcopalian. Home: 525 Park Ave New York NY 10021-8141 also: Fullerlea Rensselaerville NY 12147 Office: 50 Rockefeller Plz New York NY 10020-1605

CARFORA, JOHN MICHAEL, economics and political science educator; b. New Haven, Conn., July 24, 1950; s. John Michael and Rose Mary (Mitro) C.; m. Linda Louise Palmer, July 22, 1972; 1 child, Rachel Ellen. BS, U. New Haven, 1973, MPA, 1975; MS in Econs. and Polit. Sci., London Sch. Econs., 1978; AM, Dartmouth Coll., 1985; EdM, Harvard U., 1993. Rsch. asst. London Sch. Econs. and Polit. Sci., 1980-81; lectr. polit. sci. Albertus Magnus Coll., New Haven, 1982-83; lectr. econs. and quantitative analysis U. New Haven, 1982-83; program cons. Dartmouth Coll., 1984-85, asst. prof. internat. econ. Sch. Internat. Tng., 1985-90; v.p. rsch. and acad. affairs, dir. Soviet-Am. projects Global-Genesis, Internat. Cons., 1989-91, dir. east and west projects, 1992-94; asst. dean for rsch. and sponsored programs Ind. State U., Terre Haute, 1994-95; dir. grants and sponsored programs Simmons Coll., Boston, 1995-97; asst. dir. grants and contracts Dartmouth Coll., Hanover, N.H., 1997—; ednl. cons. USSR Acad. Mgmt., Moscow, 1991-92; vis. asst. prof. def. Harvard U., 1979-80; vis. sr. lectr. Poly. of Ctrl. London, 1980; vis. asst. prof. internat. rels. So. Conn. State U., New Haven, 1982; cons. Commonwealth Acad. Mgmt., Moscow, 1992-94; lectr. in field. Contbr. articles to profl. jours. With USAR, 1970-76. Recipient Roy E. Jenkins award, 1972; fellow Radio Free Europe-Radio Liberty, 1979, Internat. Rsch. and Exchs. Bd., 1981-84. Mem. Am. Assn. Advancement Slavic Studies, Nat. Assn. Fgn. Student Advisors (internat. educators), Am. Acad. Polit. Sci., Am. Econ. Assn., Am. Polit. Sci. Assn., Nat. Coun. Univ. Rsch. Adminstrs., Acad. Polit. Sci., N.E. Slavic Assn., Soc. Rsch. Adminstrs., Royal Acad. Pub. Adminstrn. (Eng.), Atlantic Econ. Soc., Am. Friends of the London Sch. Econs. (Conn. program chmn. 1981-85, N.H.-Vt. program chmn. 1985-87, alumni bd. dirs. 1983-92). Office: Dartmouth Coll Office Grants and Contracts 11 Rope Ferry Rd Hanover NH 03755-1404

CARGERMAN, ALAN WILLIAM, lawyer; b. Chgo., Jan. 17, 1945; s. Harry and Bertha (Snider) C.; m. Linda Swanson Leifheit, July 28, 1990; children from previous marriage: Jack Marshall, Jill Faith. Student, U. Ill., 1961-64; LLB, DePaul U., 1970. Bar: Ill. 1970. Editorial writer Commerce Clearing House, Inc., Chgo., 1969-70; asst. state's atty. Ogle County, Oregon, Ill., 1970-72; assoc. judge 15th Jud. Cir. Ill., Oregon, 1972-90; with Fearer, Nye, Ahlberg & Chadwick, Oregon, 1991-96, of counsel, 1996—; lectr. Ill. Jud. Conf., 1981—, Nat. Jud. Coll., 1982; vice chmn. Northwest Ill. Criminal Justice Commn., 1971. Author Ill. Judges Assn. Manual History of the Illinois Judicial System, 1984. Mem. Ill. Commn. on Am. Constn. Bicentennial, 1985-87; chmn. Ogle County Commn. on Bicentennial, Oreg., 1987-91; mem. spl. com. on courtroom standards Ill. Supreme Ct., 1991-93. Fellow Ill. Bar Found.; mem. ABA, Ill. State Bar Assn. (sec. criminal law sect. 1971), Ogle County Bar Assn. (sec. 1971), Am. Judicature Soc., Ill. Judges Assn. (dir. Chgo. 1977-83, 86-89, jud. selection and retention com. 1981-84, spl. task force on dispute resolution 1985-87, publs. com. 1988-90, pub. affairs com. 1988-90), Ill. Jud. Conf. (chmn. study com.), Conf. Chief Cir. Judges (rules com. Chgo. 1981-87, chmn. 1988-90). Office: Fearer Nye Ahlberg & Chadwick 209 S 5th St Oregon IL 61061-1800

CARGILE, MICHAEL EDWARD, advertising agency executive; b. New Orleans, Jan. 8, 1942; s. Duncan Edward Cargile and Marguerite (Choppin) McCormick; m. Susan Elizabeth Walter, Nov. 26, 1966; children: Christopher, Heather. BA, U. Miss., 1963. Sales mgr. Cleve. Ad. Club, 1966-68; account exec. Watts, Lee and Kenyon, Cleve., 1968-71; account supr. Marschalk Interpublic, Cleve., 1971-75; pres. The Jayme Orgn., Cleve., 1982-89; gen. mgr. Fahlgren Martin, Interpub., Cleve., 1990-92; pres., owner Communiquik, Cleve., 1992-98; exec. v.p. Adcom Comm., Inc., Cleve., 1998—. Author: Spike's Grand Adventure, 1998. Trustee Cleve. Health Mus., 1976-80, Cuyahoga Valley Line Bath, Ohio, 1988—; pres. Hiram Ho. Bd. Trustees, Chagrin Falls, 1975—; trustee Hist. Warehouse Dist., 1990-98; mem. Mayor's Pub. Rels. Com., Cleve., 1991—; trustee Cleve. Zoological Soc., 1999—. Named Exec. of Yr. Exec. Women Internat., Cleve., 1987. Mem. Cleve. Art Assn. (trustee 1992), Hillbrook Country Club, The Country Club (Pepper Pike, Ohio). Avocations: golf, antique collection. Home: 20725 Shaker Blvd Cleveland OH 44122-2621 Office: Adcom Comm Inc 1330 Old River Rd Cleveland OH 44113-1222

CARGILL, ROBERT MASON, lawyer; b. Atlanta, Nov. 15, 1948; s. George Slade Jr., and Emma Elizabeth (Matthews) C.; m. Sharon McEver, June 12, 1971; children: Ansley Lauren, Kristin Lucille. BS summa cum laude, Ga. Inst. Tech., 1970; JD magna cum laude, Harvard U., 1973. Bar: Ga. 1973, D.C. 1975. Assoc. atty. Hansell & Post, Atlanta, 1976-81, ptnr., 1981-89; ptnr. Jones, Day, Reavis & Pogue, Atlanta, 1989—. Lt. USNR 1973-76. Mem. Swedish Am. C. of C. Atlanta (chmn. bd. dirs.), Japan Am. Soc. of Ga. (bd. dirs.), Swiss Am. C. of C. (Atlanta chpt. bd. dirs.), World Trade Ctr. Atlanta (bd. dirs.), Cherokee Town Country Club. Methodist. Avocations: tennis, travel. Home: 230 Colewood Way NW Atlanta GA 30328-2923 Office: Jones Day Reavis & Pogue 303 Peachtree St NE Ste 3500 Atlanta GA 30308-3242

CARGILL, URSULA BARDOT, university official; b. Buffalo, Aug. 2, 1963; d. Alton Elmore and Madge Evelyn (Bullard) C. BS, Morgan State U., Balt., 1981, MBA, 1983; PhD, SUNY, Buffalo, 1994. Zone mgr. Ford Motor Co., Dearborn, Mich., 1986-90; assoc. dean admission Colgate U., Hamilton, N.Y., 1994-98; coord. multicultural recruitment, coord. transfer admissions, 1994-98; dir. undergrad. acad. svcs. Stern Sch. Bus. NYU, 1998—. Contbg. author: High School to Employment Transition, 1994. Bd. trustees Liberation in Truth Unity Fellowship Ch., Newark, 1994—; bd. dirs. Foothills Coun. Girl Scouts U.S.A., 1997-98. Office: NYU Stern Sch Bus Undergrad Coll 40 W 4th St Ste 800 New York NY 10012 Address: 138 Brighton Ave Apt 29 Belleville NJ 07109-3548

CARGO, DAVID FRANCIS, lawyer; b. Dowagiac, Mich., Jan. 13, 1929; s. Francis Clair and Mary E. (Harton) C.; children: Veronica Ann, David Joseph, Patrick Michael, Maria Elena Christina, Eamon Francis. AB, U. Mich., 1951, M of Pub. Adminstrn., 1953, JD, 1957. Bar: Mich. 1957, N.Mex. 1957, Oreg. 1974. Practice in Albuquerque, 1957, asst. dist. atty., 1958-59; mem. N.Mex. Ho. of Reps., 1962; gov. N.Mex., 1967-71; practice law Santa Fe, 1970-73, Portland, Oreg., 1973-83. Chmn. Four Corners Regional Commn., 1967-71, Oil and Gas Conservation Commn.; chmn. N.Mex. Young Reps., 1959-61, Clackamas County Rep. Ctrl. Com.; mem. Israel Bond Com.; former mem. bd. govs. St. John Coll.; bd. dirs. Albuquerque Tech. Vocat. Sch.; chmn. governing bd. Albuquerque Tv.I. C.C.; mem. Albuquerque City Pers. Bd.; adv. bd. mem. N.Mex. State Fair; exec. bd. Found. for Open Govt. With AUS, 1953-55. Named Man of Yr. Albuquerque Jr. C. of C., 1964; recipient Outstanding Conservationist award N.Mex. Wildlife Assn., 1969, 70. Mem. Mich. Bar Assn., Oreg. Bar Assn., N.Mex. Bar Assn., Albuquerque Bar Assn., Isaac Walton League (past v.p. N.Mex.), World Affairs Coun. Oreg. (pres.), Interstate Oil and Gas Compact, Isaak Walton League Oreg., Hispano C. of C., Am. Leadership Conf. (bd. dirs.), Nat. Fedn. Blind. Home: 6422 Concordia Rd NE Albuquerque NM 87111-1228 Office: 400 Gold Ave SW Albuquerque NM 87102-3283

CARGO, WILLIAM IRA, ambassador, retired; b. Detroit, Feb. 27, 1917; s. Ira Wiles and Nina (Lathrop) C.; m. Margaret Grace Ludwig, June 21, 1938; children: David Paul, Ruth. AB, Albion Coll., 1937, LLD, 1963; AM, U. Mich., 1938, PhD, 1941; student Russian lang., Naval Tng. Sch., Boulder, Colo., 1944-45; LLD, Waynesburg Coll., 1970. Instr. polit. sci. U. Mich., 1941-42, Colo. Coll., 1942-43; staff Dept. State, 1943-78; staff Bur. UN Affairs, 1946-53, dep. dir. office dependent area affairs, 1952; assigned Nat. War Coll., 1953-54; adviser U.S. delegations Gen. Assembly, Trusteeship Council Sessions, 1946-53; alternate U.S. rep. UN Com. on Non-self-governing Terrs., 1952; U.S. rep. UN vis. mission Trust Terrs. Tanganyika, Italian Somaliland, Ruanda-Urundi, 1951; assigned to U.S. Mission to NATO and European regional orgns. in connection with spl. internat. trade problems, Paris, 1954-57; dep. dir. Office of UN Polit. and Security Affairs, Dept. State, 1957-58, dir., 1958-61; dep. U.S. rep. Internat. Atomic Energy Agy., Vienna, Austria, 1961-63; dep. chief of mission, minister-counselor Am. embassy, Karachi and Rawalpindi, Pakistan, 1963-67; dep. U.S. rep. to NATO minister, Brussels, 1967-69; career minister U.S. Fgn. Service, 1969; dir. policy planning staff Dept. State, Washington, 1969-73; U.S. ambassador to Nepal, 1973-76; sr. insp. Fgn. Service Inspection Corps., Washington, 1976-78; cons. Fgn. Service Inspection Corps., 1979-83; adviser U.S. delegation Gen. Assembly, 1957, Gen. Conf. of IAEA, Vienna, 1958; alt. U.S. rep. Gen. Conf. of IAEA, 1961, 62; adviser U.S. del. Conf. Discontinuance Nuclear Weapons Tests, Geneva, 1959; vice-chmn. U.S. del. Conf. to Amend Single Conv. Narcotic Drugs, Geneva, 1972. Co-author: (autobiography) Wherever the Road Leads, 1997. Served with USNR, 1944-46. Recipient Meritorious Service award Dept. State, 1958. Mem. AAAS, Phi Beta Kappa, Delta Sigma Rho, Phi Mu Alpha, Am. Fgn. Svc. Assn., DACOR. Methodist. Home: Vantage House # 313 5400 Vantage Point Rd Columbia MD 21044

CARHART, HOMER W(ALTER), research scientist; b. Orange, Calif., May 21, 1914; s. Walter D. and Ethel (Shepherd) C.; m. Julia M. Holzapfel, June 15, 1940; children: Martha Jean, David Henry. BS, Dakota Wesleyan U., 1934; MA, U. S.D., 1935; PhD in Organic Chemistry, U. Md., 1939. Asst. prof. Gallaudet Coll., Washington, 1939-42; rsch. chemist Naval Rsch. Lab., Washington, 1942-52, head fuels br., 1952-70, head chem. dynamics br., 1970-86, dir. Navy Tech. Ctr. for Safety and Survivability, 1986-94, sr. scientist emeritus, 1994—; mem. sec. of treas. Blue Ribbon Com. on Tanker Hazards, 1962-63; USN mem., del. Am., Brit., Can., and Australian Quadripartite Coms. on Fuels, 1964-94; mem. USN Working Group in Submarine Atmosphere Control, 1966-71; mem. Nat. Acad. Scis./NRC Com. on Hazardous Materials, 1966-75, chmn. Elec. Hazards Panel, 1966-75, chmn. Electrostatics Panel, 1969-75, chmn. indsl. hazards com., 1982-89; fire panel mem., spl. cons. NASA Apollo 204 (Fatal) Fire Rev. Bd., 1967; mem. exec. group, dir. Navy Labs. Planning Panel for Enhanced Aircraft Carrier Survivability, 1967-68; chmn. USN Panel on Hydrogen as a Potential Fuel, 1973, USN Inter-Labs. Com. on Pers. Adminstrn., 1973-75; chmn. dir. Navy Labs. Advanced Tech. Objectives Working Group for Fire Rsch., 1973-76; mem. Coordinating Rsch. Coun. Diesel Com., 1950-66; chmn. Ignition Quality Investigation Group, 1956-66, Compression Ignition Adv. Group, 1960-65; chmn. Aviation Fuel Safety Task Force (Adv. to FAA), 1974-76; chmn. NAS/NRC Com. on Indsl. Hazards, 1982-89; mem. Dept. of Labor Joint Soviet/Am. Task Force on Safety in the Chem. Industry, 1991. Contbr. articles to profl. publs.; patentee in field. Recipient USN Meritorious Civilian Svc. award, 1945, Dept. of Navy Recognition of Achievement award, 1975, USN Superior Civilian Svc. award, 1965, USN Disting. Civilian Svc. award, 1979, Winning Team, Federally Employed Women, Inc. award, 1989, Robert Dexter Conrad award for outstanding achievemnet in naval sci. and engring., 1991, Naval Rsch. Lab. Lifetime Achievement award, 1994, Harry C. Bigglestone award for excellence in written comm. of fire protection concepts, 1990, Jack Bono Engring. Comms. award, 1995, Ann. Homer W. Carhart award for excellence in damage control/fire protection established by Chief of Naval Ops; elevated to rank of Meritorious Sr. Exec. by Pres. Bush, 1989, Naval Rsch. Lab. Award for Innovation, 1998. Mem. Am. Chem. Soc. (alt. councilor 1954-56), Chem. Soc. Washington (mgr. 1953, mem. com. on rels. and status com. 1954, chmn. budget com. 1957, chmn. edn. com. 1965-66, chmn. long range planning com. 1967-70), Combustion Inst. (charter), U.S. Naval Inst., Naval Submarine League, Surface Navy Assn., Navy League U.S., Phi Kappa Phi, Sigma Xi. Avocations: musical composition, plant hybridization, photography. Office: Naval Rsch Lab Code 6108 Washington DC 20375

CARILLO, MARY, broadcaster, tennis analyst; b. Queens, N.Y., Mar. 15, 1957; m. Bill Bowden; 2 children. Profl. tennis player, 1977-80; winner French Open Mixed Doubles, 1977; tennis analyst CBS Sports, 1986—. Author: Tennis My Way with Martina Navratilova, Rick Elstein's Tennis Kinetics. Named Best Commentator Tennis Mag., 1988-91, World Tennis mag., 1986, Broadcaster of Yr. Womens Tennis Assn., 1981, 85. *

CARINO, AURORA LAO, psychiatrist, hospital administrator; b. Angeles, The Philippines, Jan. 11, 1940; came to U.S., 1967; d. Pedro Samson and Hilaria Sanchez (Paras) Lao; m. Rosalito Aldecoa Carino, Dec. 2, 1967; children: Robert, Edwin, Antoinette. AA, U. of the East, Manila, 1961; degree in medicine, U. of the East, Quezon City, The Philippines, 1966. Lic. psychiatrist N.Y., Conn., Fla.; cert. Am. Bd. Psychiatry and Neurology. Resident in pediatrics U. of the East-R.M. Meml. Hosp., Quezon City, 1966-67; rotating intern Stamford (Conn.) Hosp., 1967-68; resident in psychiatry Norwich (Conn.) Hosp., 1968-71, staff psychiatrist, 1971-75; staff psychiatrist, unit chief, acting clin. dir. Harlem Valley Psychiat. Ctr., Wingdale, N.Y., 1975-80; svc. chief Fla. State Hosp., Chattahoochee, 1982-83; unit chief Hudson River Psychiat. Ctr., Poughkeepsie, N.Y., 1983-89, dep. med. dir., acting clin. dir., 1989-90, asst. to clin. dir., 1990-93, dep. med. dir.-admissions, 1993-97; cons. Dept. Mental Hygiene, Dutchess County, Poughkeepsie, 1976—. Mem. Am. Psychiat. Assn. Republican. Roman Catholic. Avocations: gardening, country music, recording/listening to spiritual enhancement. Home: 10 Millbank Rd Poughkeepsie NY 12603-5112

CARINO, LINDA SUSAN, business consultant; b. San Diego, Nov. 4, 1954; d. DeVona (Clarke) Dungan. Student, San Diego Mesa Coll., 1972-74, 89-90. Various positions Calif. Can. Bank, San Diego, 1974-77, ops. supr., 1977-80, ops. mgr., 1980-82; asst. v.p. ops. mgr. First Comml. Bank (formerly Calif. Can. Bank), San Diego, 1982-84; v.p. data processing mgr. First Nat. Bank, San Diego, 1984-91; v.p. conversion adminstr. Item Processing Ctr. Svc. Corp., Denver, 1991-92; mgr. computer ops. FIserv, Inc., Van Nuys, Calif., 1992-93; v.p., data processing mgr. So. Calif. Bank, La Mirada, Calif., 1993-94, v.p. tech. support mgr., 1994-96; ind. cons. First Nat. Bank of Ctrl. Calif., Salinas, Calif., 1996-97; project mgr. EDS Corp., Burbank, Calif., 1997-98; customer group mgr. EDS Corp., Charlotte, N.C., 1998—. Democrat. Avocations: swimming, bicycling, camping, knitting, sewing. Home: 21308 Nautique Blvd Apt 102 Cornelius NC 28031-6413 Office: EDS Corp 9014 Research Dr Charlotte NC 28262-8507

CARIOLA, ROBERT JOSEPH, artist; b. Bklyn., Mar. 24, 1927. Grad., Pratt Inst. Art Sch., 1954; student, Pratt Graphic Ctr., 1958-59. Instr. art La Salle Acad., Oakdale, N.Y., 1963-65; instr. creative painting workshop Nat. Art League, Douglaston, Queens, N.Y.; condr. art workshops in mixed media painting Bd. Continuing Edn. One-man shows include Long Beach Mus., N.Y., 1985, East Meadow Libr. Gallery, 1990, Merrick Symphony Performance Lobby of Hall, 1990; exhibited in group shows including Boston Mus. Printmakers Exhbn., 1962, Corcoran Gallery Art, Washington, 1963, Pa. Acad. Fine Arts, Phila., 1963, Vatican Pavilion-N.Y. World's Fair, 1964, Nat. Acad. Design, N.Y.C., 1970, Signature Gallery, Va., 1986, Cath. Mus. Arts and Antiquities, Olympic Towers, N.Y.C., 1995-96; represented in permanent collections Landing Gallery, Woodbury, 1990—, Soundview Gallery, Pt. Jefferson, N.Y., 1990—; contbr.: Illustrator Writer's Ann., 1958, Sign Mag., 1971, art mags.; executed murals in Sr. Citizen Ctr., Wantagh, N.Y., 1989, comty. rm. St. Johns Luth. Ch., Merrick, N.Y., 1992, also schs.; created, installed 4-sided Indian Monument dedicated to Meroke Tribe Indians-1643, Merrick, N.Y., 1993; painted murals and mosaics in 4 chapels; created metal, wood, and concrete sculptures, faceted stained glass windows St. Johns Cemetery Mausoleum, Queens, N.Y. Recipient Ann. Painting prize Hofstra, 1957, Purchase award Hofstra, 1957, Operation Democracy prize Locust Vally, N.Y., 1958, 1st prize for painting John Kennedy Cultural Ctr. Bankers Trust, 1971, Grumbacher Cash award Silvermine Artists Guild, New Canaan, Conn., 1976, Best in Show award Bayshore C. of C. Art Festival, 1979, 1st prize Long Beach (N.Y.) Mus., 1984; grnatee Tiffany Grants, 1965, 66, N.Y. State Creative Arts Program, 1988, Nassau County, 1989, Wantagh Creative Arts Program, 1992; subject of feature article in Equine Images, fall, 1991. Address: 1844 Gormley Ave Merrick NY 11566-3009

CARIOTI, BRUNO M., civil engineer; b. St. Andrea, Catanzaro, Italy, Nov. 3, 1929; came to U.S., 1935; s. Vincenzo and Caterina (Stillo) C.; m. Ida Annamaria Schmutz, July 16, 1955; children: Daniela, Laura. BCE cum laude, CCNY, 1951; MS in Engring., Princeton U., 1961. Registered profl. engr., N.Y. Commd. ensign Civil Engrs. Corps USN, 1953, advanced through grades to comdr., 1965; project mgr. USN Contracts for Missile and Space Prog. USN, Cape Canaveral/Missile Range, 1961-63; cons. U.S. Naval Mission to Chile, Valparaiso, 1963-68; engring. dir. U.S. Naval Forces, Danang, South Vietnam, 1968-69, Naval Facilities Engring. Command, Washington, 1969-70; dep. pub. works dir. U.S. Naval Dist., Washington, 1970-74; constrn. dir., cons. Iranian Navy, 1974-79; retired USN, 1974; sr. cons. Royal Commn. for Jubail and Yanbu, Riyadh, Saudi Arabia, 1979-95, cons. indsl. and infrastructure devel., privatization, fin., 1995—; conf. participant Internat. Environ. Protection, Washington, 1990, World Conf. on Desalination and Water Reuse, Washington, 1991; speaker numerous other internat. engring. confs. and seminars. Contbr. tech. articles on earthquake engring. and ocean engring. to profl. jours.; author Master Plan for Devel. Chilean Navy Shipyards, 1967. Project mgr. Alliance for Progress Program, Chile and South America, 1963-68; head damage assessment and disaster relief Govts. of Chile and Iran for major earthquakes, 1965, 75; project mgr. for master plans of the Cities of Jubail and Yanbu, Saudi Arabia, tech. and econs. feasibility studies for indsl. projects, corrosion mitigation, privatization financing studies for conversion of the pub. works, budget revs., contracts award evaluations, devel. of design criteria and tech. stds., contract claims adjudications for Saudi indsl. and urban devel. programs. Decorated Bronze Star, Navy Commendation medal, Chilean Navy Diploma of Merit. Fellow ASCE; mem. Nat. Soc. Profl. Engrs., Soc. Am. Mil. Engrs., U.S. Naval Inst, Marine Tech. Soc., Jacque Cousteau Soc. Roman Catholic. Avocations: scuba diving, underwater photography, tennis, bridge. Home and Office: 4238 Embassy Park Dr NW Washington DC 20016-3619

CARIOU, LEN JOSEPH, actor, artist, director; b. Winnipeg, Can., Sept. 30, 1939. Student, St. Paul's Coll. Profl. tng., Guthrie Theatre, Mpls., Stratford Shakespeare Festival; profl. debut Damn Yankees, Winnipeg Rainbow Stage Theatre, 1959; joined Man. Theatre Center, 1961, appeared in The Threepenny Opera, Mr. Roberts; mem. Stratford (Ont.) Shakespeare Festival, 1961-65, appeared in Cyrano de Bergerac, Cariolanus, 1981, Taming of the Shrew, 1981, The Tempest, 1982, Julius Caesar, 1982, Arms and the Man, Timon of Athens, Chichester (Eng.) Festival, 1964; mem. Guthrie Theatre, Mpls., 1966, assoc. dir., 1972, appeared in The House of Atreus, King Lear, dir. The Crucible, Of Mice and Men; appeared in Othello, Goodman Theatre, Chgo., 1969, Much Ado about Nothing, The Three Sisters, Henry V Am. Shakespeare Festival, Stratford, Conn., 1969, Traveller in the Dark, Los Angeles, 1985, The Anastasia Game, Merrimack Repertory Theater, Lowell, Mass., 1990, Mountain, George Street Playhouse, Lucille Lortel Theater, 1990; Broadway plays include Applause, 1970, Nightwatch, 1972, A Little Night Music, 1973, Cold Storage, 1978, Sweeney Todd, 1979 (Tony award for best actor 1979), Dance a Little Closer, Up from Paradise, 1983, Teddy and Alice, 1987, Master Class '86, Roundabout Theater, N.Y.C., Day Six, Baldwin Youth Theater, N.Y.C., 1987, Measure for Measure, Lincoln Ctr., 1989, Speed of Darkness, 1990, Touch of the Poet, 1992, Papa: The Legendary Lives of Ernest Hemingway, 1994; film appearances include A Little Night Music, 1977, The Four Seasons (One Man 1976 winner Best Actor Can. Genie award), 1981, Lady in White, 1987, Getting Out, 1994, Executive Decision, 1996; TV appearances include Surviving, 1985, Stolen Dreams, 1986, There Were Times Dear, 1987, Killer in the Mirror, 1988, Miracle on I 88, 1993, The Seawolf, 1993, Witness to the Execution, 1994, The Man in the Attic, 1995, A Dream is a Wish Your Heart Makes, 1995, Derby, 1995, Never Talk to Strangers, 1995, The Outer Limits, 1995, The Annette Finicello Story, 1995, The Dan Jansen Story, 1996, The Summer of Ben Tyler, 1996; TV series Swift Justice; dir. plays The Petrified Forest, 1974, Death of a Salesman, Edmonton, 1984. Office: Paradigm c/o Joel Rudnick 10100 Santa Monica Blvd Fl 25 Los Angeles CA 90067-4003*

CARISTO-VERRILL, JANET ROSE, international management consultant; b. Quincy, Mass., Jan. 30, 1945; d. John J. and Adelaide Caristo; m. Richard M. Verrill, Mar. 31, 1984 (dec. Feb. 1995). BS, Boston U., 1968; diploma in social anthropology, Lady Margaret Hall, Oxford, Eng., 1974; M in Internat. Mgmt., Am. Grad. Sch. Internat. Mgmt., 1982. Social studies tchr. Boston, Pembroke & Cohasset Schs., Mass., 1969-81; summer planner, reunions MIT Alumni Office, Cambridge, 1973-76; pres. Macro Projects Internat., Wayland, Mass., 1984—; advisor Govt. Can., 1985, Nepal, 1986, Nizhny Novgorod, 1994, Algeria, 1994, Bosnia, 1996, 97, Habitat for Humanity, Belfast Unltd., 1994-96; guest spkr. energy conf. Govt. Turkey, Ankara, 1997; NGO del. UN Sci. & Tech. Commn., N.Y.C., 1993. Author: Civilian Military Cons. Corps, 1992,96;contbr. Macro Problems and World Projects, 1998. Filmmaker, vol. Mother Theresa's Hosps., Calcutta, India, summer 1980; vol. U.s. peace Corps, Nigeria, 1964-66, U.S./China People's Friendship, Cambridge, 1982-83; guest White House Conf. Trade & Devel. No. Ireland, 1995; participant Friends Raoul Wallenberg Conf., Stockholm, 1997; adv. com. MIT Dewey Libr., Cambridge, 1993—. Mem. Internat. Assn. Macro-Engring. Socs. (dir. 1996—), Macro Engring. (pres. Boston chpt. 1985—), United Oxford & Cambridge U. Club (London), English Spkg. Union, Boston Ctr. Internat. Visitors, Oxford & Cambridge Club New Eng., Brookline Bird Club. Roman Catholic. Avocations: poetry, birdwatching, gardener, music, art and literature. Office: Macro Projects Internat Inc 174 Pelham Island Rd Wayland MA 01778-2513

CARITHERS, HUGH ALFRED, physician, retired; b. Winder, Ga., July 21, 1913; s. Hugh A. and Starr (Blasingame) C.; m. Cornelia Davis Morse, July 27, 1942; children: Susan (Mrs. John F. Callender), Hugh Alfred, Starr (Mrs. Roy W. Waddell). A.B., Emory U., 1933, M.D., 1937. Diplomate: Am. Bd. Pediatrics. Intern Germantown Dispensary, Phila., 1937-39; resident St. Christophers Hosp. of Phila., 1939-40, Bellevue Hosp., N.Y.C., 1940-41; practice medicine specializing in pediatrics Jacksonville, Fla., 1945—; chief pediatrics Jacksonville Hosps. Edn. Program, 1958-69; chief dept. pediatrics St. Vincent's Hosp., 1952-64, staff pres., 1956-58; clin. prof. pediatrics U. Fla. Coll. Medicine, 1969-98. Mem. editorial bd. Am. Jour. Deseases of Children, 1970-79. Served with M.C. AUS, 1941-45. Recipient award for rsch. Am. Acad. Pediatrics, 1994. Fellow Am. Pub. Health Assn.; mem. Fla. Pediatric Soc. (pres. 1949-50), Duval Med. Soc. (pres. 1963-64, Fla. Yacht Club, The River Club (Jacksonville), Phi Delta Theta, Alpha Kappa Kappa, Alpha Omega Alpha. Clubs: Fla. Yacht, The River (Jacksonville). Home: 3010 Saint Johns Ave Jacksonville FL 32205-9103 Office: 2121 Paris St Jacksonville FL 32204

CARIUS, ROBERT WILHELM, mathematics and science educator, retired naval officer; b. Peoria, Ill., Jan. 4, 1929; s. Henry Clarence and Mary Magdalen (Wilhelm) C.; m. Geraldine Mary Sullivan, Mar. 16, 1957; children: Patricia, Mary, Linda, Robert, Daniel, Sara. B.S. in Naval Sci, U.S. Naval Acad., 1951; B.S. in Aero. Engring, U.S. Naval Postgrad. Sch., 1958; M.S. in Nuclear Engring, Iowa State Coll., 1959. Commd. ensign USN, 1951, advanced through grades to rear adm., 1977, served with Fighter Squadron 74, 1953-56, served with U.S.S. Bennington, 1959-61, project mgr. U.S. AEC, 1964-65, served with Air Anti-Submarine Squadron 33, 1962-63, command officer Air Anti-Submarine Squadron 29, 1966-68, exec. officer

U.S.S. Princeton, 1968-70, R & D br. head Dept. Navy, 1970-71; command officer U.S.S. New Orleans USN, San Diego, 1971-73; mem. staff Anti-Submarine Wing Pacific USN, 1973-77; comdr. Anti-Submarine Wings Atlantic, Naval Air Sta. USN, Jacksonville, Fla., 1977-79; with aviation programs Dept. Navy USN, from 1979; instr. physics Ark. Coll., Batesville, 1983-85, asst. prof. physics, 1986—; bd. govs. USO, Jacksonville. Mem. exec. bd. United Way of Jacksonville, N.E. Fla. coun. Boy Scouts Am.; pres. Independence County United Way. Decorated Legion of Merit, Air medal, Meritorious Service medal; recipient Spl. award United Way of Jacksonville, 1979. Mem. U.S. Naval Acad. Alumni Assn., Assn. Naval Aviation, Ret. Officers Assn., Ark. Hist. Soc., Batesville Symphony Assn., Naval Helicopter Assn., U.S. Naval Inst., Jacksonville C. of C. (gov.). Roman Catholic. Club: Rotary. Home: 2630 Antioch Rd Cave City AR 72521-9249 Office: Lyon Coll Batesville AR 72501 *Personal integrity and honesty to oneself have been key elements in my life's philosophy. Attempting to understand the people you work with and treating them as you prefer to be treated were other essential principles. Lastly, always do your very best in all endeavors, and you never have to look over your shoulder with regret.*

CARKIN, GARY BRYDEN, performing arts educator; b. York, Maine, Oct. 5, 1940; s. Laurence Earl and Beatrice Fillmore (Bryden) C.; m. Pachareeya Erawan, Jan. 1, 1961. BA, U. N.H., 1963; MA, U. N.Mex., 1977; PhD, Mich. State U., 1984. Actor Players' Theater of New Eng., Manchester, N.H., 1968-70; vis. prof. Thammasat U., Bangkok, Thailand, 1970-74; actor, tchr. U. N.Mex., Albuquerque, 1975-77, Mich. State U. Performing Arts Co., East Lansing, 1977-80; Fulbright scholar Thailand, 1980-81; assoc. prof. N.H. Coll., Manchester, 1982—; vis. prof. Ramkhamhaeng U., Bangkok, 1981; theater dir. Manchester Youth Theater, 1986-91; property mgr. Carkin Properties, Manchester, 1991—. Author: How to Succeed in the USA, 1997. Avocations: travel, architecture, music, films. Home: 40 Cascade Cir Manchester NH 03103-6905

CARL, ROBERT E., retired marketing company executive; b. Sept. 1, 1927; s. Elmer T. Carl and Marion R. (Pack) C.; m. Linda Arlene Sutton, Aug. 30, 1967; children: Melanie Ruth, Robert Brady, Camber Carleen. BS, U. Kans., 1950; cert. in real estate, So. Meth. U., 1965; cert. in investment analysis, N.Y. Inst. Fin., 1967. V.p. sales promotion Riverside Press, Inc., Dallas, 1951-54; pres., COO Jones-Carl, Inc., Dallas, 1954-62; v.p. mktg. comms. Modern Am. Corp., Dallas, 1962-70; v.p. sales Dunn Properties of Tex., Inc., Dallas, 1970-71; sr. v.p. mktg. svcs. Vantage Cos., Dallas, 1971-84; pres. Mktg. Mgmt. Sys., Dallas, 1984-90; v.p. The Premium Group, Inc., 1990-92; mem. Dallas Cable TV Bd., 1981-83; co-founder Liberty Christian High Sch. (Dallas), 1996. Recipient Chevalier and Legion of Honor Degrees Internat. Supreme Coun. of Order of De Molay, 1957, Silver Anvil award Pub. Rels. Soc. Am., 1958. Mem. Sales and Mktg. Execs. Dallas (pres. 1976-77, Disting. Salesman's award 1954), S.W. Found. Free Enterprise (pres.1 975-76), Tex. Indsl. Devel. Coun., Nat. Assn. Corp. Real Estate Execs., Sales and Mktg. Execs. Internat. (sr. v.p.), Nat. Assn. Indsl. and Office Parks, Big D Club, Toastmasters (pres. 1966), Press Club Dallas, Greater Dallas Pachyderm Club (bd. dirs.), Park City Club (bd. govs. 1989-92), Masons (32d degree), Shriners. Contbr. articles to profl. jours. Home: 4209 Gloster Rd Dallas TX 75220-3819

CARLE, HARRY LLOYD, social worker; b. Chgo., Oct. 26, 1927; s. Lloyd Benjamin and Clara Bell (Lee) C.; m. Elva Diana Ulrich, Dec. 29, 1951 (div. 1966); adopted children: Joseph Francis, Catherine Marie; m. Karlen Elizabeth Howe, Oct. 14, 1967 (dec. Feb. 1991); children: Kristen Elizabeth and Sylvia Ann (twins), Eric Lloyd; m. Diane Wyland Gambs, May 23, 1993. BSS, Seattle U., 1952; MSW, U. Wash., 1966. Pacific N.W. regional dir. Collegiate Coun. UN, 1952-53; rep. indsl. placement and employer rels. State of Wash., Seattle, 1955-57; parole and probation officer Seattle and Tacoma, 1957-61; parole employment splst., 1961-63, vocat. rehab. officer, 1963-64; clin. social worker We. State Hosp., Ft. Steilacoom, Wash., 1964-66, U.S. Penitentiary, McNeil Is., Wash., 1964-66; exec. dir. Shohomish County Cmty. Action Coun./Social Planning Coun., Everett, Wash., 1966-77; employment and edn. counselor Pierce County Jail Social Svcs., Tacoma, 1979-81; dir. employment devel. clinic coord. vocat. program North Rehab. Facility King County Divsn. Alcoholism and Substance Abuse, Seattle, 1981-90; counselor Northgate Outpatient Ctr. Lakeside Recovery, Inc., Seattle, 1991; staff deve. cons. Counseling for Ind. Living, Newport, R.I., 1992; ret., 1998; cmty. orgn. agy./problems mgmt. cons., 1968-92; cons. to pres. Geneal. Inst., Salt Lake City, 1974-78. Vol. Vis. Nurse Svc. Wash. Hospice and Home Care, Montlake Terrace, Wash., 1996-98; mem. social svc. project staff Pacific Luth. U., Tacoma, 1979-81. Served with USN, 1944-46. U.S. Office Vocat. Rehab scholar, 1965-66; named First Honoree Hall of Success Iowa Tng. Sch. for Boys, 1969. Mem. NASW, Seattle Geneal. Soc. (pres. 1974-76), Soc. advancement Mgmt. (chpt. exec. v.p. 1970-71), Acad. Cert. Social Workers, Henckel Family Nat. Assn., Seattle Japanese Garden Soc. (v.p. 1993-96), various hist. and geneal socs. in Pa. and Ill. Roman Catholic. Home: Poem Rising Garden 258 Two Crane Ln NW Poulsbo WA 98370-9700

CARLEN, SISTER CLAUDIA, librarian; b. Detroit, July 24, 1906; d. Albert B. and Theresa Mary (Ternes) C. AB in Library Sci., U. Mich., 1928, MA in Library Sci., 1938; LHD (hon.), Marygrove Coll., 1981, Loyola U., Chgo., 1983, Sacred Heart Major Sem., 1989; LittD (hon.), Cath. U. of Am., 1983. Asst. librarian St. Mary Acad., Monroe, Mich., 1928-29; asst. librarian Marygrove Coll., Detroit, 1929-44, librarian, 1944-69, library cons., 1970-71; on leave as index editor New Cath. Ency., 1963-67, Cath. Theol. Ency., 1968-70; library cons. grad. div. Casa Santa Maria, N.Am. Coll., Rome, 1971-72; libr. St. John's Provincial Sem., Plymouth, Mich., 1972-80, libr. emeritus, 1980-82, scholar-in-residence, 1982-85, archivist, 1985-88; rschr. Bentley Hist. Libr., U. Mich., Ann Arbor, 1989-97; supr. orgn. and servicing Community Ctr. Libraries staffed by vols.; bd. dirs. Corpus Instrumentorum, Inc., v.p., 1969-70; mem. instructional materials com. Mich. Curriculum Study; cons. McGraw Hill Ency. World Biography, 1968-72, World Book Ency., 1969-70; mem. working group on uniform headings for liturgical works Internat. Fedn. of Libr. Assns., 1972-75. Author: Guide to Encyclicals of the Roman Pontiffs, 1939, Guide to the Documents of Pius XII, 1951, Dictionary of Papal Pronouncements, 1958; editor: Papal Encyclicals, 1740-1981, 1981, Papal Pronouncements, 1991; editor: column At Your Service, Cath. Library World, 1950-52; Reference Book Rev. Sect., 1952-64, 66-72; Books for the Home column; monthly news release, Nat. Cath. Rural Life Conf., 1952-61; mem. editl. bd. Vatican Archives: An Inventory and Guide, 1997; mem. adv. bd.: The Pope Speaks, 1953-88, Pierian Press, 1972; contbr.: Catholic Bookman's Guide, 1961, Dictionary Western Chs, 1969, Ency. Dictionary of Religion, 1979, Translatio Studii, 1973. Trustee Marygrove Coll., Detroit, 1976-79, vice chmn. bd., 1977-79. Recipient Disting. Alumna award U. Mich. Sch. Libr. Sci., 1974, Domitilla award Marygrove Coll., 1991, Gabriel Richard award Mich. Cath. Libr. Assn., 1998. Mem. ALA (coun. 1958-61, 68-71), Cath. Libr. Assn. (chmn. com. membership 1946-49, chmn. Mich. unit 1952-54, chmn. coll. and univ. sect. 1954-56, chmn. publs. com. 1961-62, pres. 1965-67, Jerome award 1993), Mich. Libr. Assn. (chmn. coll. sect. 1956-57, chmn. recruiting com. 1959-60), Accademia Olubrense (Pietrabissara, Italy, charter), Am. Friends of Vatican Libr. (co-founder, v.p.), Phi Beta Kappa, Phi Kappa Phi, Beta Phi Mu. Home: 2301 Sandalwood Cir Apt 215A Ann Arbor MI 48105-1379 *To form the habit of reading good books so that reading becomes a necessity in one's life is a sure means of continual development and growth; a means of attaining that poise of spirit and richness of mind that should mark every professional person; a means by which the mind acquires new light, the will new incentives, the heart new desires, and life new ideals.*

CARLEN, PETER LOUIS, neuroscientist educator, science administrator; b. Edmonton, Alta., July 22, 1943; m. 1970; 2 children. MD, U. Toronto 1967. Intern Montreal (Que., Can.) Gen. Hosp., 1967-68, resident internal medicine, 1968-69; instr. neurophysiology, dept. zoology Hebrew U., Jerusalem, 1969-70; resident neurology U. Toronto, 1970-72; fellow neurophysiol. neurobiol. unit Hebrew U., Jerusalem, 1972-74; sr. physician, head neurol. program Addiction Rsch. Found. Clin. Inst., 1974-94; staff neurologist Toronto Western Hosp., U. Toronto, 1974; rsch. assoc. Playfair Neurosci. Unit U. Toronto, 1979-89, assoc. prof. dept. medicine and physiology, 1981-88, prof. dept. medicine & physiology, 1989—; dir. neurosci. unit Toronto Hosp., 1989—. Fellow Can. Neurol. Soc., Am. Acad. Neurology; mem. AAAS, Soc. Neurosci., Can. Physiol. Soc. Office: U Toronto-Playfair Neurosci Toronto Hosp-WD, 399 Bathurst St, Toronto, ON Canada M5T 2S8

CARLEONE, JOSEPH, aerospace executive; b. Phila., Jan. 30, 1946; s. Frank Anthony and Amelia (Ciaccia) C.; m. Shirley Elizabeth Atwell, June 29, 1968; children: Gia Maria, Joan Marie. BS, Drexel U., 1968, MS, 1970, PhD, 1972. Civilian engring. trainee, mech. engr. Phila. Naval Shipyard, 1963-68; grad. asst. in applied mechanics Drexel U., Phila., 1968-72, postdoctoral rsch. assoc., 1972-73, NDEA fellow, 1968-71, adj. prof. mechanics, 1974-75, 77-82; chief rsch. engr. Dyna East Corp., Phila., 1973-82; chief scientist warhead tech. Aerojet Ordnance Co., Tustin, Calif., 1982-88. v.p., gen. mgr. warhead systems div. GenCorp. Aerojet Precision Weapons, Tustin, 1988-89; v.p., dir. armament systems, Aerojet Electronics Systems Divsn., Azusa, Calif., 1989-94, v.p. tactial def. and armament products., Aerojet, Calif. 1994-97, v.p. ops., 1997—. Editor: Tactical Missile Warheads, 1993. Mem. ASME,, AIAA, NDIA. Sigma Xi, Tau Beta Pi, Pi Tau Sigma, Phi Kappa Phi. Contbr. articles to profl. jours.; rschr. explosive and metal interaction, ballistics, projectile penetration, impact of plates. Home: 2112 Campton Cir Gold River CA 95670-8302 Office: Aerojet PO Box 13222 Sacramento CA 95813-6000

CARLESIMO, P. J. (PETER J. CARLESIMO), professional basketball coach; b. Scranton, Pa., May 30, 1949. Grad., Fordham U., 1971. Asst. basketball coach Fordham U., Bronx, N.Y., N.H. Coll., Manchester; mem. staff Wagner Coll., Staten Island, N.Y.; head coach Seton Hall U., South Orange, N.J., 1982-94, Portland Trailblazers, 1994-97, Golden State Warriors, Oakland, Calif., 1997—. Office: Golden State Warriors 1011 Broadway Oakland CA 94607-4027*

CARLESON, ROBERT BAZIL, public policy consultant, corporation executive; b. Long Beach, Calif., Feb. 21, 1931; s. Bazil Upton and Grace Reynolds (Wilhite) C.; m. Betty Jane Nichols, Jan. 31, 1954 (div.); children: Eric Robert, Mark Andrew, Susan Lynn; m. Susan A. Dower, Feb. 11, 1984. Student, U. Utah, 1949-51; B.S., U. So. Calif., 1953, postgrad., 1956-58. Adminstrv. asst. City of Beverly Hills, Calif., 1956-57; asst. to city mgr. City of Claremont, Calif., 1957-58; sr. adminstrv. asst. to city mgr. City of Torrance, Calif., 1958-60; city mgr. City of San Dimas, Calif., 1960-64, Pico Rivera, Calif., 1964-68; chief dep. dir. Calif. Dept. Public Works, 1968-71; dir. Calif. Dept. Social Welfare, 1971-73; U.S. commr. welfare Washington, 1973-75; pres. Robert B. Carleson & Assocs., Sacramento, Calif. and Washington, 1975-81; chmn. Robert B. Carleson & Assocs., Washington, 1987-93, San Diego, 1993—; pres. Innovative Environ. Svcs. Ltd., Vancouver, B.C., Can., 1992; spl. asst. to U.S. pres. for policy devel. Washington, 1981-84; prin., dir. govt. rels. KMG Main Hurdman, Washington, 1984-87; dir. transition team Dept. HHS, Office of Pres.-Elect, 1980-81; spl. adviser Office of Policy Coordination; sr. policy advisor, chmn. welfare task force Reagan Campaign, 1980; bd. dirs. Fed. Home Loan Bank of Atlanta, 1987-90, I.E.S., Ltd., Can., Transenviro Co., USA, Churchill Co., USA; adv. com. Fed. Home Loan Mortgage Corp., 1985-87; mem. strengthening family policy coun. Nat. Policy Forum, Washington, 1994. *Robert Carleson is considered Ronald Reagan's voice in welfare policy matters. He achieved this right initially through service on Governor Reagan's welfare reform task force of 1970 and then as the chief architect and implementor of the successful welfare reform program of 1971-72. Later, as U.S. Commissioner of Welfare, his assignment was to carry Reagan style welfare reforms to the other States and to oppose efforts to enact a guaranteed income. He authored the successful 1981 Reagan national welfare reforms. As a private citizen he warned against the welfare reform of 1988 which added over 3 million persons to welfare, but this was rectified by the welfare reform of 1996 which contained his long held proposal to replace the 1935 family welfare program with finite appropriations to the States and requiring work for benefits.* Adv. coun. gen. govt. Rep. Nat. Com., Washington, 1980-81; sr. fellow Free Congress Found., 1994—; chmn. Am. Civil Rights Union, 1998—. Officer USN, 1953-56. Clubs: Masons, Rotary (pres. 1964), Army & Navy (Washington), Capitol Hill, Fairfax Hunt. Home and Office: 1911 Willow St San Diego CA 92106-1823

CARLETON, DON EDWARD, history center administrator, educator, writer; b. Dallas, Jan. 22, 1947; s. Edward Preston and Wilma Jo (Smith) C.; m. Suzanne Marie Young, Jan. 2, 1974; children: Ian Alexander, Aunna Fleur. BS, U. Houston, 1969, MA, 1974, PhD, 1978. Tchr. Friendswood Ind. Sch. Dist., Tex., 1969-71; teaching fellow U. Houston, 1971-75; research asst. Southwest Ctr. for Urban Research, Houston, 1974-75; dir. Houston Met. Research Ctr., 1975-79, Barker History Ctr., Austin, 1979-91, Ctr. for am. History, U. Tex., Austin, 1991—; urban adv. editor Handbook of Texas, Austin, 1983-95; sr. lectr. dept. history U. Tex., Austin, 1985—, Dept. Journalism, 1997—; cons. Amon Carter Mus., Ft. Worth, 1983, Birmingham Pub. Libr., Ala., 1978. Editorial bd. Southwestern Hist. Quar., 1980-90; author: Who Shot the Bear?, 1984, Red Scare!, 1985, (Coral Tullis best book award Tex. Hist. Assn. 1986), "A Breed So Rare": The Life of J.R. Parten, Liberal Texas Oilman, 1896-1992, 1998 (Tex. Inst. Letters Book award 1998); contbr. articles to profl. jours. Mem. Tex. Hist. Records adv. bd., Austin, 1984-87; advisor City of Austin Arts Commn., 1985; youth organizer McGovern-Shriver campaign, Houston, 1972. Recipient Presdl. Excellence award U. Tex., Austin, 1982; J.R. Parten fellow in Archives Am. History, 1989—; Parten Found. grantee, 1982; O'Connor Found. grantee, 1982; Tex. State Hist. Assn. grantee, 1983. Fellow Tex. State Hist. Assn., Tex. Inst. Letters; mem. Philosophical Soc. Tex., Orgn. Am. Historians, Western History Assn., U. Tex. Club, Headliners Club Austin, Tex. Democrat. Avocations: reading; travel. Office: U Tex Ctr Am History SRH 2.101 Austin TX 78713-7330

CARLETON, JOSEPH GEORGE, JR., lawyer, state legislator; b. Bklyn., July 21, 1945; s. Joseph G. and Ellen (Gabriel) C. AB, Dartmouth Coll., 1969; JD, Boston U., 1972. Atty. Calderwood & Ouellette, Dover, N.H., 1972-79; pvt. practice Wells, Maine, 1979-83, 88—; atty., ptnr. Patterson Carleton & Mongue, Wells, 1983-88; mem. Maine Ho. of Reps., Augusta, 1990-98, asst. Rep. leader, 1994-96. Chmn. Wells Site Rev. Bd., 1985-86; town meeting moderator Town of Wells, 1983—; mem. adv. bd. York County Tech. Coll., 1996—. Sgt. N.H. Air N.G., 1966-74. Mem. Wells C. of C. (pres. 1984), Elks, Masons. Republican. Avocations: golf, history, politics. Home and Office: PO Box 369 Wells ME 04090-0369

CARLETON, MARY RUTH, foundation administrator, consultant; b. Sacramento, Feb. 2, 1948; d. Warren Alfred and Mary Gertrude (Clark) Case; m. Bruce A. Hunt, Jan. 21, 1989. BA in Polit. Sci., U. Calif.-Berkeley, 1970, MJ, 1974; postgrad., San Diego State U. TV news anchorwoman, reporter Sta. KXAS-TV, Ft. Worth, 1974-78, Sta. KING-TV, Seattle, 1978-80, Sta. KOCO-TV, Oklahoma City, 1980-84; news anchor, reporter Sta. KTTV-TV, L.A., 1984-87; news anchor Sta. KLAS-TV, Las Vegas, Nev., 1987-91, KTNV-TV, 1991-93, Sta. UNLV-TV, 1993-94; broadcast instr. Okla. Christian Coll., 1981-84, UCLA, 1985-87, U. Nev.-Las Vegas, 1991-94; pub. speaking cons.; dir. UNLV Women's Ctr., 1991-94; news dir. univ. news Sta. UNLV-TV, 1992-94; asst. dean devel. San Diego State U., 1994-97; v.p./dir. devel. Scripps Found., 1997—. Bd. dirs. World Neighbors, Oklahoma City, 1984-89, Allied Arts Coun. So. Nev.-Las Vegas, 1988-94, Nev. Inst. for Contemporary Art, 1988-94; bd. dirs. United Way, Las Vegas, 1991-94, secret witness bd., 1991-94, Las Vegas Women's Coun., 1993-94, Friends of Channel 10, 1991-94. Named Best Environ. Reporter, Okla. Wildlife Fedn., 1983, Disting. Woman of So. Nev., Woman of Achievement Las Vegas Women's Coun., 1990; recipient Broadcasting award UPI, 1981, Nat. award for best documentary, 1990, Tri-State award for best newscast, 1990, Emmy award, L.A., 1986, L.A. Press Club award 1986, 90, Nat. award for documentaries UPI, 1990, Woman of Achievement Media award Las Vegas C. of C., 1990. Mem. AARP (mem. nat. econ. issues team 1992-94, state legis. com.)Women in Comm. (Clarion award 1981, Best Newscaster 1990), Soc. Prol. Journalists, Press Women, Investigative Reporters, Sigma Delta Chi. Democrat. Roman Catholic. Avocations: tennis, gourmet cooking. Office: San Diego State U Coll Health & Human Svcs 5500 Campanile Dr San Diego CA 92182-0002

CARLETON, RICHARD ALLYN, cardiologist; b. Providence, Mar. 15, 1931; s. Russell Francis and Margaret Rexford (Bristol) C.; m. April Michele Plumb, Jan. 29, 1975; children: Susan, Bradford, Margaret, Jennifer, Mary. A.B., Dartmouth Coll., 1952; M.D., Harvard U., 1955. Intern Harvard Service, Boston City Hosp., 1955-56, resident and fellow in cardiology, 1956-59; from asst. prof. to prof. medicine U. Ill., 1962-68; chief cardiology, prof. medicine Rush-Presbyn.-St. Luke's Med. Center, Chgo., 1968-72; chief med. service and cardiology San Diego VA Hosp., also prof. medicine U. Calif., San Diego, 1972-74; prof., chmn. dept. medicine Dartmouth Coll. Med. Sch., 1974-76; prof. med. sci., chief cardiology divsn. Meml. Hosp., Brown U. Med. Sch., Providence, 1976-97; physician-in-chief Meml. Hosp., 1982-95; prin. investigator NIH heart disease prevention program, 1982-96; chmn. R.I. Health Coord. Com., 1978-81; mem. Nat. Heart, Lung and Blood Adv. Coun., HHS, 1984-88. Contbr. articles to med. publs. Chmn. Population Panel, Nat. Cholesterol Edn. Program, 1988-90; chmn. R.I. Prevention Coalition, 1997—; bd. dirs. Hospice Care R.I., 1998—. Served to lt. comdr. M.C. USNR, 1960-62. Recipient Sci. award R.I. Gov., 1989. Mem. ACP, Am. Soc. Clin. Investigation, Assn. U. Cardiologists, Am. Coll. Cardiology, Am. Heart Assn. (recipient Gold Heart award 1993, coun. clin. cardiology and epidemiology), Soc. Behavioral Medicine, R.I. Audubon Soc. (bd. dirs. 1997—). Club: Barrington (R.I.) Yacht. Office: Memorial Hosp Pawtucket RI 02860

CARLEY, CHARLES TEAM, JR., mechanical engineer; b. Greenville, Miss., Dec. 27, 1932; s. Charles Team and Ruby (McClendon) C.; m. Shirley Holland, May 28, 1955; children: Karen, Mary McClendon, Charles Team III, Holland. BS, Miss. State U., 1955; MS, Va. Poly. Inst., 1960; PhD, N.C. State U., 1965. Engr. Gen. Elec. Co., 1955; instr. Va. Poly. Inst., 1958-60; asst. prof. Miss. State U., 1960-61; Ford Found. fellow N.C. State U., 1961-64; assoc. prof. Miss. State U., 1964-68, prof., 1968-93, head mech. engring. dept., 1969-80, head mech. and nuclear engring. dept., 1981-90, prof., dept. head emeritus, 1993—; head Petroleum Engring., 1990-93; prin. C.T. Carley & Assoc., 1993—; chmn. Miss. Tech. Adv. Bd. on Boiler and Pressure Vessel Safety, 1974-87; mem. ABET Engring. Accreditation Commn., 1981-86; mem. ABET Related Accreditation Commn., 1992-96, chmn., 1994-95; Fulbright sr. lectr. U. Buenos Aires, 1986, U. Catamarca, 1987. Chmn. Miss. Rep. Mcpl. Exec. Com., 1968-89. With USNR, 1955-58. Mem. ASME (v.p. region XI 1972-74, sr. v.p. edn. 1986-90, gov. 1990-92), Miss. Acad. Scis. (pres. 1976-77), Engrs. Coun. Miss. (pres. 1970-71), Sigma Xi, Omicron Delta Kappa, Phi Kappa Phi. Home: 213 Windsor Rd Starkville MS 39759-2137

CARLEY, GEORGE H., state supreme court justice; b. Jackson, Miss., Sept. 24, 1938; s. George L. Jr. and Dorothy (Holmes) C.; m. Sandra M. Lineberger, 1960; 1 child, George H. Jr. AB, U. Ga., 1960, LLB, 1962. Bar: Ga. 1961. Pvt. practice Atlanta and Decatur, Ga., 1961-71; ptnr. McCurdy & Candler, Decatur, Ga., 1971-79; also spl. asst. atty. gen. Office. Atty. Gen.; judge Ct. Appeals Ga., 1979-89, chief judge, 1989-91, presiding judge, 1991-93; justice Supreme Ct. Ga., Atlanta, 1993—; chmn. bd. visitors U. Ga. Law Sch., 1995-96. Bd. Visitors U. Ga. Law Sch.; past pres. U. Ga. Law Sch. Assn. Coun., 1989-90, active, 1986-91; trustee Ga. Legal History Found., Inc.; active Holy Trinity Episc. Ch., Decatur. Mem. ABA, State Bar Ga., Ga. Bar Found., Lawyers Club Atlanta, Old Warhorse Lawyers Club (pres. 1997-98), Joseph Henry Lumpkin Am. Inn of Ct. (pres. 1994-95), Pythagoras Lodge, Scottish Rite. Office: Supreme Court 504 State Judicial Bldg Atlanta GA 30334-9007*

CARLEY, JAMES FRENCH, chemical and plastics engineer; b. N.Y.C., July 16, 1923; s. Benjamin Lambert and Helen Jeanne (French) C.; m. E. Lucille Heitz, June 6, 1947 (div. Apr. 1955); children: James French, Ben Lewis; m. Marilyn Jo Mullens, July 29, 1955 (div. Apr. 1976); 1 dau., Katherine Jeanne; m. Nancy Kay Paquette, Nov. 7, 1981 (div. June 1987). B.S. in Chem. Engring., Cornell U., 1944, B.Ch.E. (now M.Ch.E.), 1947, Ph.D., 1951. Research chem. engr. DuPont Co., Wilmington, Del., 1950-55; engring. editor Modern Plastics, N.Y.C., 1955-59; asso. prof. chem. engring. U. Ariz., Tucson, 1959-62; tech. dir. Prodex Corp., Fords, N.J., 1962-64; devel. asso. Celanese Plastics Co., Clark, N.J., 1964; prof. chem. engring. and engring. design and econ. evaluation U. Colo. at Boulder, 1964-76; research engr. oil shale project Lawrence Livermore Nat. Lab. (Calif.), 1976-83, research engr. composites and polymers tech., 1983-86, quality assurance specialist, 1986-89, polymer engr., 1989-92; ret., 1992, cons. engr., 1980—; Instr. Cornell U., Ithaca, N.Y., 1949-50; lectr. U. Del. extension at Wilmington, 1952-54; vis. prof. mech. engr. U. Colo., Boulder, 1988-89. Contbr. articles to profl. jours., books; tech. editor Modern Plastics mag., 1982-88. Served to ensign USNR, 1943-46. Fellow Soc. Plastics Engrs. (pres. Rocky Mt. chpt. 1968-69); mem. Am. Inst. Chem. Engrs., Sigma Xi, Tau Beta Pi. Home: 579 Ruby Rd Livermore CA 94550-5158

CARLILE, CHRISTOPHER BLAKE, military officer, pilot; b. Paragould, Ark., July 22, 1962; s. Donald Gene and Jo Ann (Dinwiddie) C.; m. Sandra F. Pickett, Oct. 28, 1989; 1 child, Chelsea Brook. BS, Ark. State U., 1988; aviation officer course, Ft. Rucker, Ala., 1989, pilot, 1990; test pilot, Maintenance Coll., Ft. Eustis, Va., 1990; MBA, Embry-Riddle Coll., 1998. Commd. U.S. Army, 1988, advanced through grades to maj., 1988; exec. officer 1-145th Aviation Regiment Ft. Rucker, 1989; platoon leader 7-159th Aviation Regiment Stuttgart, Germany, 1990-92; prodn. control officer 7-159th Aviation Regiment Giebelstadt, Germany, 1992-93; co. comdr. A-5-158th Aviation Regiment Wiesbaden, Germany, 1993-95; exec. officer 1st Aviation Bn. Ft. Knox, Ky., 1995—. Mem. Army Aviation Assn. of Am. (treas. 1989-96). Republican. Avocations: golf, hunting, fishing. Office: 4th Cavalry Brigade Rm 330 Bldg 6581 Fort Knox KY 40121

CARLILE, HENRY DAVID, poet, writer, educator; b. San Francisco, May 6, 1934; s. Aurelio Antonio Prieto and Grace Edna Harris; m. Sandra Jean McPherson, July 22, 1966 (div. 1984); 1 child, Phoebe; m. Genevieve Jane Long, Aug. 20, 1995. AA, Grays Harbor Coll., Aberdeen, Wash., 1960; BA, U. Wash., 1962, MA, 1967. Instr. Portland (Oreg.) State U., 1967-69, asst. prof. English, 1969-72, assoc. prof., 1972-79, prof., 1980—; vis. lectr. U. Iowa, Iowa City, 1978-80. Author: The Rough-Hewn Table, 1971, Running Lights, 1981, Rain, 1994. Served with U.S. Army, 1953-56. Recipient Fiction Syndicated award PEN, 1986; Nat. Endowment for Arts Discovery grantee, 1971, Poetry fellow, 1976; Ingram Merrill Found. fellow, 1985. Office: Portland State U PO Box 751 Portland OR 97202

CARLILE, JANET LOUISE, artist, educator; b. Denver, Apr. 26, 1942; d. Jessie Crawford and Alice Essie (Locker) C.; m. David Hildebrand, Sept. 1, 1963 (div. 1968). BFA, Cooper Union, 1966; MFA, Pratt Inst., 1971. Prof. Bklyn. Coll., CUNY, 1971—; founder Incline Village (Nev.) Fine Arts Ctr., 1966-68; instr. Sch. Visual Arts, N.Y.C., 1968-70, Printmaking Workshop, N.Y.C., 1971, Scarsdale (N.Y.) Studio Workshop, 1971-73, SUNY-Stony Brook, L.I., 1976, Bard Winter Coll., Rhinebeck, N.Y., 1980; head printmaking, asst. dir. Bklyn. Mus. Art Sch., 1971-77; dir. Bklyn. Coll. Press, 1977—; cons. Woodstock (N.Y.) Sch. Art, 1980-84; judge Alpine Artists Show, Ouray, Colo., 1989, Landscape Ptg. Show, Woodstock Art Assn., 1995. One-woman shows include Blue Mt. Gallery, N.Y.C., 1980, Stetson U., DeLand, Fla., 1995, Fairleigh Dickinson Coll., Teaneck, N.J., 1995; exhibited in group shows at Associated Am. Artists Gallery, N.Y., 1971-81, Bklyn. Mus., 1976, Ulster County Artists Show, N.Y. State Coun. Show, 1984, Alpine Artists Show Ouray County, 1987; design for IRT Bklyn. Mus. Sta. Sec. San Juan Vista Landowners Assn., Ridgway, Colo., 1980-86. Recipient full scholarship Cooper Union, N.Y.C., 1962-66, Hirshorn Purchase prize, Soc. Am. Graphic Artists, 1969, Grad. fellowship Pratt Inst., Bklyn., 1971, Best of Show award, Alpine Artists Show Ouray County, 1987, NEA Workshop grant Colo. Coun. Arts, 1991, Creative Incentive award CUNY, 1992. Mem. Ouray (Colo.) County Arts Assn. (pres. 1991-93). Avocations: hiking, backpacking, skiing, yoga, rock climbing. Home: PO Box 1004 Ouray CO 81427-1004 Office: Brooklyn Coll Art Dept Bedford at Ave H Brooklyn NY 11210

CARLIN, BETTY, educator; b. N.Y.C.; d. Samuel and Rose Sara (Bernstein) Grossberg; m. Arthur S. Carlin, July 18, 1953 (dec.); children: Lisa Anne Skinner, James Howard. BA, UCLA, 1952; MA, U. Calif., Berkeley, 1955. Educator L.A. Sch. Dist., 1952-55; owner Carlin's Shoes, L.A., 1952-68; educator Berkeley (Calif.) Sch. Dist., 1957-58; master tchr. spl. programs Calif. State Coll., Hayward, 1967-84; educator U. Calif., Berkeley, 1984-86; tchr. demonstrator C.V.U. Sch. Dist.; student tchr. supr. Calif. State U., Hayward; co-owner Art-Car Corp., 1978-88. Creator ednl. videos for children Study in Characteristics of an Effective and Loving Mother, Children's Play as Related to Intelligence, An Eclectic Approach to Teaching Reading. Mem. Nat. Tchrs. Assn., Calif. Tchrs. Assn., Commonwealth Club, San Francisco Opera Guild. Avocations: swimming, opera, theater, gardening, vocal study.

CARLIN, CLAIR MYRON, lawyer; b. Sharon, Pa., Apr. 20, 1947; s. Charles William and Carolyn L. (Vukasich) C.; children: Eric Richard, Elizabeth Marie, Alexander Myron. BS in Econs., Ohio State U., 1969, JD, 1972. Bar: Ohio 1973, Pa. 1973, U.S. Dist. Ct. (so. dist.) Ohio 1973, U.S. Dist. Ct. (no. dist.) Ohio 1975, U.S. Supreme Ct. 1976, U.S. Ct. Claims, 1983, U.S. Tax Ct. 1985. Staff atty. Ohio Dept. Taxation, Columbus, 1972-73; asst. atty. City of Warren, Ohio, 1973-75; assoc. McLaughlin, DiBlasio & Harshman, Youngstown, Ohio, 1975-80; ptnr. McLaughlin, McNally & Carlin, Youngstown, 1980-98, Carlin & Vasvari, LLC, Poland, Ohio, 1998—. Mem. editl. bd. Ohio Trial mag. Mem. Trumbull County Bicentennial Commn., Ohio, 1976; v.p. Svcs. for the Aging, Trumbull County, 1976-77; mem. Pres.' Club Ohio State U. With Ohio NG, 1972-82. Mem. ATLA (bd. govs. 1996—, trustee PAC 1996-98), ABA, Ohio State Bar Assn. (negligence law com. 1991—), Ohio State Bar Coll., Mahoning County Bar Assn. (chmn. legal edn. com. 1985-86, counsel 1986-87), Ohio Acad. Trial Lawyers (trustee 1988-92, polit. action com. chmn. 1991, exec. com. 1991-97, treas. 1992-93, sec. 1993-94, pres.-elect 1994-95, pres. 1995-96), Mahoning-Trumbull Acad. Trial Lawyers (pres. 1991), Ohio State U. Alumni Assn. (pres. Trumbull County chpt. 1985—), Cath. War Vets. (Ohio state commdr., Vet. of Yr. 1988), Rotary. Democrat. Roman Catholic. Home: 3524 Hunters Hill Poland OH 44514 Office: Carlin & Vasvari LLC PO Box 5369 62 S Main St Poland OH 44514

CARLIN, DENNIS J., lawyer; b. Chgo., Aug. 23, 1941; s. Herbert E. and Lillian (Schnelder) C.; m. Fern Carlin, Nov. 25, 1964; children: Gregory A., H. David, Stuart B. BBA, U. Wis., 1963; JD, DePaul U., 1967; LLM in Taxation, Georgetown U., 1971. Bar: Ill. 1967; CPA. Auditor Checkers, Simon & Rosner, Chgo., 1963-67; assoc. tax ct. litigation divsn. IRS, Washington, 1967-71; ptnr. Frankel, McKay, Orlikoff, Denten & Kostner, Chgo., 1971-77, Horwood & Carlin, Chgo., 1977-82; ptnr. Gardner, Carton & Douglas, Chgo., 1982—, vice-chmn. Contbr. articles to profl. jours. Mem. atty. div. Jewish United Fund; bd. dirs. Coun. for Jewish Elderly. Mem. ABA, Am. Coll. Tax Counsel, Chgo. Bar Assn. (former chmn. fed. tax com.), Nat. Strategy Forum, Ill. State Bar, NYU Inst. Fed. Taxation, DePaul U. Alumni Coun., Am. Israeli C. of C., Twin Orchard Country Club. Avocations: golf, skiing, reading, music, theatre. Office: Gardner Carton & Douglas Quaker Tower Suite 3400 321 N Clark St Ste 3000 Chicago IL 60610-4762

CARLIN, DONALD WALTER, retired food products executive, consultant; b. Gary, Ind., Aug. 27, 1934; s. Walter Joseph and Mabel (Ebert) C.; m. Kathleen Susan McCone, Jan. 21, 1961; children: Michael Scott, Karen Mary, Mark Steven. BS in Engring, U. Notre Dame, 1956; LLB, U. Mich., 1959; grad., Advanced Mgmt. Program, Harvard U., 1978. Bar: Ind. 1959, Ill. 1960. Assoc. to ptnr. Soans, Anderson Luedeka & Fitch, Chgo., 1960-72; sr. atty. Kraft Inc., Glenview, Ill., 1972-73, v.p., asst. gen. counsel, 1974-79, sr. v.p., gen. counsel, 1979-81, sr. v.p., gen. counsel, sec., 1981-86, v.p., assoc. gen. counsel, 1986-89; v.p., dep. gen. counsel Kraft Gen. Foods, Northfield, Ill., 1989-92. Mem. bd. visitors Sch. Medicine, U. Calif.-Davis, 1990—. Mem. ABA (hon.) (com. corp. law depts. sect. bus. law), Assn. Gen. Counsel (emeritus), Westmoreland Country Club (bd. dirs. 1989-94, pres. 1993-94), Notre Dame Club (Chgo.), Iron Country Club. Home and Office: 333 Regent Wood Rd Northfield IL 60093-2762 also: 73-106 Galleria Ct Palm Desert CA 92260

CARLIN, GEORGE DENIS, comedian; b. N.Y.C., May 12, 1937; m. Brenda Hosbrook, 1961; 1 child, Kelly. Radio announcer Sta. KJOE, Shreveport, La., Sta. WEZE, Boston, Sta. KXOL, Ft. Worth, Sta. KDAY, L.A. Numerous TV appearances on Merv Griffin Show, Mike Douglas Show, Tonight Show (over 130), numerous other TV variety shows; regular on TV programs, Away We Go, 1967, John Davidson Show, 1966, Shining Time Station, 1992—, The George Carlin Show, sitcom on Fox TV, 1994-95; syndicated TV spl. The Real George Carlin, 1973; miniseries Streets of Laredo, 1995; movies include: With Six You Get Eggroll, 1968, Car Wash, 1976, Americathon, 1979, Outrageous Fortune, 1987, Justin Case, 1988, Bill & Ted's Excellent Adventure, 1989, Working Trash, 1990, Bill and Ted's Bogus Journey, 1990, Prince of Tides, 1991; albums include: At the Playboy Club Tonight, Burns and Carlin, 1960, Take-Offs & Put-Ons, 1967, FM/AM, 1972 (Grammy Award Best Comedy Record), Class Clown, 1972, Occupation: Foole, 1973; Toledo Window Box, 1974, An Evening with Wally Londo Featuring Bill Slaszo, 1975, The Original George Carlin, 1972, On The Road, 1977, Indecent Exposure, 1978, A Place for My Stuff, 1982, The Carlin Collection, 1984, Carlin On Campus, 1984, Playin' With Your Head, 1986, What Am I Doing In New Jersey, 1988, Parental Advisory—Explicit Lyrics, 1990, Jammin' in New York, 1992 (Grammy Award Best Spoken Comedy Album, 1994), Back in Town, 1996, You Are All Diseased, 1999; cable TV stand-up comedy specials include: On Location-USC Concert, 1977, On Location-Phoenix Concert, 1978, Carlin At Carnegie, 1982, Carlin On Campus, 1984, Playin' With Your Head, 1986, What Am I Doing In New Jersey, 1988, George Carlin—Doin' It Again, 1990 (Cable Ace award Best Stand Up Comedy Spl.), George Carlin: Jammin' in New York, 1992 (Cable Ace award Best Stand Up Comedy Spl.) Back In Town, 1996 (Cable Ace Awards: Best Stand-Up Comedy, Best Writing-Variety Spec.); 40 Years of Comedy, 1997, You Are All Diseased, 1999; author: Sometimes A Little Brain Damage Can Help, 1983, Brain Droppings, 1997. Office: Carlin Prodns 11911 San Vicente Blvd Los Angeles CA 90049-5086

CARLIN, HERBERT J., electrical engineering educator, researcher; b. N.Y.C., May 1, 1917; s. Louis Aaron and Shirley (Salzman) C.; children—Seth Andrew, Elliot Michael; m. Mariann J. Hartmann, June 29, 1975. B.E.E., Columbia Coll., 1938, M.E.E., 1950; Ph.D. in Elec. Engring., Poly. Inst. N.Y., 1947. Engr. Westinghouse Corp., Newark, 1940-45; from asst. to assoc. prof. Poly. Inst. Bklyn., 1945-60, prof., head electrophysics, 1960-66; J. Preston Levis prof. engring. Cornell U., Ithaca, N.Y., 1966—, dir. elec. engring., 1966-75; mem. adv. panel Nat. Bur. Standards, Boulder, Colo., 1967-70; mem. rev. com. Lehigh U., Bethlehem, Pa., 1966-74, U. Pa., Phila., 1979-82; vis. prof. Ecole Normale Superieure, Paris, 1964-67, MIT, Boston, 1973-74; vis. scientist Nat. Ctr. for Telecommunications, Issy Les Moulineaux, France, 1979-80; vis. lectr. U. Genoa, Italy, summer 1973, U. London, Dec. 1979, The Technion, Haifa, Israel, Mar. 1980, Tianjin U., China, summer 1982, Univ. Coll., Dublin, Ireland, summer 1983, Polytech. of Turin, Italy, summer 1985, 91, Fed. Polytech., Lausanne, Switzerland, summer 1992. Co-author: Wideband Circuit Design, 1997. Fellow NSF, 1964; recipient Outstanding Achievement award U.S. Air Force, 1965. Fellow IEEE (chmn. profl. group on circuit theory 1955-56, Centennial medal 1985). Home: 8 Highland Park Ln Ithaca NY 14850-1452 Office: Cornell U 201 Phillips Hall Ithaca NY 14853-5401

CARLIN, JOHN WILLIAM, archivist, former governor; b. Salina, Kans., Aug. 3, 1940; s. Jack W. and Hazel L. (Johnson) C.; m. Ramona Hawkinson, 1962 (div. 1980); children: John David, Lisa Marie; m. Lynn Lady, 1997. BS in Agr., Kans. State U., 1962, PhD (hon.), 1987. Farmer, dairyman Smolan, Kans., 1962-79; mem. Kans. Ho. of Reps., 1971-79, speaker of ho., 1977-79; gov. State of Kans., Topeka, 1979-87; pres. Econ. Devel. Assocs., Inc., 1987-92; partner Carlin & Associates, Topeka, KS, 1989-95; vice-chmn. Midwest Superconductivity, Inc., Lawrence, KS, 1990-94; partner Clark Publishing, Inc., Topeka, KS, 1991-95; archivist of the U.S. Nat. Archives & Records Admin., Washington, DC, 1995—; vis. prof. pub. adminstrn. and internat. trade Wichita State U., 1987-88; chmn. Nat. Govs. Assn., 1984-85, Midwestern Govs. Conf., 1982-83. Democrat. Lutheran. Home: 18201 Allwood Ter Olney MD 20832-1716 Office: Nat Archives & Records Admin 7th & Pennsylvania Ave Washington DC 20408 also: 8601 Adelphi Rd Rm 4200 College Park MD 20740-6002

CARLIN, SIDNEY ALAN, music publisher, arranger; b. Tulsa, Okla., Aug. 18, 1925; s. A. William and Lee Carlin; m. Janne Harriett Miller, Sept. 29, 1950 (div.); children: Kevin David, Christopher Paul (dec.); m. Mary Elizabeth Barlett, Dec. 1, 1972 (dec.). Student, U. So. Calif., 1943-47; studies with, Ernst Toch and George Antheil, 1948-50. Prin. Carlin Music Pub. Co., 1955—; conductor Sierra Pops Community Orchestra, Oakhurst, Calif., 1986—; guest conductor Ventura (Calif.) All-City Orchestra, 1975, Young Philharmonic Orchestra, Compton, Calif., 1977; conductor-clinician Campbell Union Sch. Dist., Los Gatos, Calif., 1980, many other appearances as guest conductor. Pub. The Orchestral Classics for the Young Series, since 1955, Classics for the Young String Orchestra Series, since 1955. Mem. Oakhurst C. of C. (pres.), Nat. Sch. Orch. Assn. Office: Carlin Music Pub Co PO Box 2289 Oakhurst CA 93644-2289

CARLIN, STEWART HENRY, accounting executive; b. Colo. Springs, Colo., Dec. 27, 1952; s. William Henry and Jean (Stewart) C.; m. Martha Self, June 10, 1978; children: Melissa, Kristyn. BS in Indsl. Mgmt., Ga. Tech, 1974; MS in Acctg., Stetson U., 1975. CPA, Fla. Mgr. G,P,H, & D, CPAs, Daytona Beach, Fla., 1975-78; treas. Carlin's TV & Appliance, Daytona Beach, Fla., 1978-83; controller Atlanta News Agy., Atlanta, 1983-85; controller, treas. Camelot Distbg. Co., Atlanta, 1985-89; controller CISU, Atlanta, 1989-90; pres. Acctg. Consultants of Cobb, Marietta, Ga., 1990—; chmn. Olympic CPA Vols., Atlanta, 1990-96; co-chmn. Course Ops., Marietta, 1991-97, Charity Ball/Silent Auction, Atlanta, 1991-96. Mem. Scottish Rite Festival, Atlanta, 1990-96, CPAs in Industry, Govt. & Edn., Atlanta, 1985-96, chmn. 1992-94; v.p. Hospice, 1992-94, pres. Marietta Rotary Club, 1995-96, mem. fin. com. Mt. Zion Meth. Ch., 1990-96, recreation com., 1990-94, adminstrn. coun., 1992-96. Mem. AICPA, Ga. Soc. CPAs, Marietta Metro Rotary Club. Republican. Avocations: golf, reading, cooking, writing. Office: Acctg Consultants of Cobb 1744 Roswell Rd Ste 200 Marietta GA 30062-3979

CARLINER, DAVID, lawyer; b. Washington, Aug. 13, 1918; s. Louis and Cassie (Brooks) C.; m. Miriam Kalter, Jan. 24, 1944 (dec. Aug. 9, 1994); children: Geoffrey Owen, Deborah Joan (Mrs. Robert Remes). *Miriam K. Carliner emigrated from Germany in 1936 at age 15. She graduated from George Washington University in 1942 and took graduate courses at Catholic University. Her professional career was highlighted by a study for a Congressional Task Force on Poverty dealing with the educational track system and its effect on African-American students, relied upon in Hobson v. Hansen in 1963, to restructure teaching methods in D.C. public schools. She coordinated training for 27,000 Head Start employees teaching in preschools for disadvantaged children, became Women's Action Program Director in the Department of Health and Human Services, and served on the D.C. Civilian Complaint Review Board, acting on police misconduct.* Student, Am. U., 1935-36, U. Va., 1936-38; student in law, U. Va., 1938-40; LLB, Nat. U., 1941. Bar: Va. 1940, D.C. 1946. Atty. JAG Office Army Dept., Washington, 1946; Washington rep. New Coun. Am. Bus., Washington, 1946-48; pvt. practice, 1948-50; ptnr. Wasserman and Carliner, 1950-67; of counsel Chapman Duff and Lenzini, 1968-74; ptnr. Carliner and Gordon, 1974-84, Carliner and Remes P.C., Washington, 1984-99, Carliner, Remes and Mirbagheri-Smith, 1999—; vis. lectr. Fgn. Svc. Inst., Dept. State, USIA, Harvard U., 1985. Author: Rights of Aliens, 1977; co-author The Rights of Aliens and Refugees, 1990. Nat. bd. dirs. ACLU, 1965-83, gen. counsel, 1976-79; chmn. Internat. Human Rights Law Group, 1978-86, Washington Home Rule Com., 1966-70; co-chmn. D.C. Com. for Re-Orgn. Plan, 1967-68; chmn. Washington chpt., mem. nat. exec. coun. Am. Jewish Com., 1969-71; mem. nat. adv. coun. Amnesty Internat., 1969—; Bd. dirs. Am. Coun. for Nationalities Svcs., 1977-89, Internat. League for Human Rights; trustee Washington Inst. Values in Pub. Policy, 1984-88. With AUS, 1941-45. Recipient Oliver Wendell Holmes award, 1966, Human Rights award Ctr. for Human Rights and Constl. Law, 1994, Isaiah award Am. Jewish Com., 1998. Mem. ABA (chmn. immigration and nationality com. adminstrv. law sect. 1979-83, mem. coun. adminstrv. law sect. 1983-87, Brookings Instn. coun., Washington 1995—), Fed. Bar Assn. (chmn. com. immigration and naturalization 1961-62), D.C. Bar (vice chmn. opinions com. ethics 1974-76, bd. dir. 1980-83), Va. State Bar, Am. Law Inst., Am. Immigration and Naturalization Lawyers Assn. (Jack Wasserman Meml. award 1994), Cosmos Club (Washington). Home: 2941 Chesapeake St NW Washington DC 20008-2114 Office: 903 Commerce Bldg 1700 K St NW Washington DC 20006-3817

CARLINER, GEOFFREY OWEN, economist, director; b. Washington, Sept. 21, 1944; s. David and Miriam (Kalter) C.; m. Astrid Synnove Skrikerud, July 31, 1971; children: Anders Benjamin, Hannah Emily Brooke. AB cum laude, Harvard U., 1966; MA, U. Calif., Berkeley, 1968, PhD, 1972. Rsch. assoc. U. Wis., Madison, 1971-73; asst. prof. U. Western Ont., London, Ont., Can., 1974-80; sr. staff economist Coun. of Econ. Advisors, Washington, 1980-83, staff dir., 1983-84; exec. dir. Nat. Bur. of Econ. Rsch., Cambridge, Mass., 1984-95; dep. dir. Inst. for Internat. Econs., Washington, 1995-97; prin. Charles River Assocs., Boston, 1997—; vis. asst. prof. U. Calif., Berkeley, 1976-77. Co-editor: Politics and Economics in the Eighties, 1991; contbr. articles to profl. jours. Recipient Joint Coun. of Econ. Edn. award, 1976. Mem. Am. Econ. Assn., Conf. for Rsch. on Income and Wealth (exec. com. 1985-95), Internat. Seminar on Internat. Trade (steering com. 1988-95). Office: Charles River Assocs 200 Clarendon St Ste T-33 Boston MA 02116-5021

CARLING, FRANCIS, lawyer; b. N.Y.C., Nov. 2, 1945; s. James Andrew and Mary Amelia (Lorenzo) C.; m. Elisabeth Morse Kelley, Aug. 30, 1969 (div. Apr. 1979); 1 child, Duncan Campbell; m. Christina Ellen Black, Sept. 28, 1991; children: Graham Black, Gillian Kirova. AB, Fordham U., 1967; JD, Yale U., 1970. Bar: Conn. 1970, U.S. Dist. Ct. Conn. 1971, N.Y. 1972, U.S. Dist. Ct. (so. and ea. dists.) N.Y. 1972, U.S. Ct. Appeals (2nd cir.) 1972, U.S. Supreme Ct. 1973, U.S. Dist. Ct. (no. dist.) Ohio 1978, U.S. Ct. Appeals (3d cir.) 1980, U.S. Dist. Ct. (we. dist.) N.Y. 1981, U.S. Ct. Appeals (6th cir.) 1986, U.S. Ct. Appeals (4th cir.) 1990. Staff atty. New Haven Legal Assistance Assn., 1970-72; assoc. Sullivan & Cromwell, N.Y.C., 1972-80; assoc. Winthrop, Stimson, Putnam & Roberts, N.Y.C., 1980-82, ptnr., 1982-97; ptnr. Collazo Carling & Mish LLP, N.Y.C., 1997—. Author: Move Over: Students, Politics, Religion, 1969. Bd. dirs. Big Bros., Inc., N.Y.C., 1974—, pres., 1993-95; v.p. Friends of Afghanistan, Inc., N.Y.C., 1985-90; bd. dirs. Vol. Cons. Group, Inc., N.Y.C., 1988-97. Mem. ABA, N.Y. State Bar Assn., Assn. Bar City N.Y., Union Club. Democrat. Episcopalian. Avocation: music. Home: 205 E 69th St New York NY 10021-5402 Office: Collazo Carling & Mish LLP 747 3rd Ave New York NY 10017-2803

CARLINI, JAMES, management consultant; b. Berwyn, Ill., Aug. 27, 1954; s. Harvey Reno and Helen Dorothy (Stan) C.; m. Holly R. Haupin, Sept. 29, 1979. MusB, Roosevelt U., 1976, BS in Computer Sci., 1978; MBA in Mgmt. Info. Systems and Mktg., DePaul U., 1982. Info. systems designer Western Electric div. Bell Labs., Naperville, Ill., 1977-79; software engr. Motorola, Schaumburg, Ill., 1979-81; mgr. Ill. Bell, Chgo., 1981-83; dir. telecommunications and computer hardware cons. Arthur Young & Co., Chgo., 1983-86; pres. Carlini & Assocs., Inc., Hinsdale, Ill., 1986—; adj. prof. Technol. Inst. Northwestern U., Evanston, Ill., 1986—, grad. sch. bus. DePaul U., Chgo., 1986-89; dir. Teledata Hong Kong; mem. adv. bd. COMDEX. Editorial adv. bd. mem. Cabling Bus. Mag.; contbr. articles to profl. jours. Pres. Mental Health Bd., Berwyn, 1983. Recipient Northwestern U. Alumni Prof.'s award, 1995, Disting. Tchg. award Northwestern U., 1996. Mem. Assn. Cabling Profls. (dir. End User Coun.), Internat. Trade Assn., Data Processing Mgmt. Assn. (bd. dirs. 1988-96, Chgo. chpt. pres. 1994-96, Spkrs. award, Outstand Instrs. award 1993), Intelligent Bldg. Inst. (chmn. definitions com.), DAV (citation 1979), Federal Comms. Bar Assn. Roman Catholic. Avocations: yachting, golf. Office: Carlini & Assocs Inc 120 E Ogden Ave Ste 206 Hinsdale IL 60521-3546

CARLINO, GUY THOMAS, construction executive; b. N.Y.C., Sept. 2, 1928; s. Peter T. and Beatrice (Logerfo) C.; m. Berniece Ruth Horth, Sept. 28, 1952; children: Margaret M., Peter T., Sharon S., James C. Student, U. Louisville, 1946-49. Pres. GTC Inc., 1993—; bd. dirs. Am. State Corp., Am. State Bank, Hub States LLC. Pres. Washington Twp. Sch. Found., Indpls., 1975, Indpls. Day Nursery Assn., 1982, Day Nursery Found. Sgt. U.S. Army, 1950-52. Mem. Indpls. Athletic Club, Gyro Club, Svc. Club. Office: GTC Inc 151 N Delaware St Indianapolis IN 46204-2526

CARLIP, HILLARY, author, screenwriter; b. L.A., Oct. 20, 1956; d. Allen Robert and Miriam Rhea (Lieverman) C. Student, U. Calif., Santa Cruz, 1975-76. Various positions as actress, juggler, fire-eater, comedienne, sketch writer, TV writer, screenwriter, artist; chair fundraising and publicity Aviva Ctr.-Sterlings, L.A., 1991—. Author: Girl Power, 1995, Zine Scene, 1998. Mem. SAG, AFTRA, Writers Guild Am., Actors Equity, Am. Soc. Composers and Pubs., BMI. Office: PO Box 2635 Los Angeles CA 90078-2635

CARLISLE, ERVIN FREDERICK, university provost, educator; b. Delaware, Ohio, Mar. 20, 1935; s. Ervin Frederick C. and Winnifred (Lucas) Pope; children: Lindy, Rebecca, Ginna, Jana; m. Barbara, Sept. 28, 1973. BA, Ohio Wesleyan U., 1956; MA, Ohio State U., 1957; PhD, Ind. U., 1963. Mem. faculty Ohio U., Athens, 1962-63, DePauw U., Greencastle, Ind., 1963-66; asst. prof. dept. English Mich. State U., East Lansing, 1966-68, assoc. prof., assoc. chmn. dept. English, 1968-72, prof., 1972-79, chmn. dept. English, 1979-81, asst. to pres., 1981-85; provost, exec. v.p. for acad. affairs Miami U., Oxford, Ohio, 1985-89; sr. v.p., provost Va. Poly. Inst. and State U., Blacksburg, 1989-94; William E. Lavery prof. Va. Poly. Inst. and State U., 1995—. Editor: American Poetry and Prose, 1970; author: The Uncertain Self, 1973, Loren Eiseley, 1983. Served to 1st lt. USAF, 1957-60. NEH fellow, 1972-73; NEH grantee, 1978, 80. Mem. MLA (chmn. lit. and sci. divsn. 1983). Home: Three Meadow Mountain 2406 Clover Hollow Rd Newport VA 24128-3529 Office: Dept English Va Poly Inst and State U Blacksburg VA 24061*

CARLISLE, HENRY C., author; b. Sept. 14, 1926. BA, Stanford U., 1950, MA, 1952. Tradebook editor Alfred A. Knopf, 1954-59, Rinehart & Co., 1959-61. Author: Voyage to the First of December, 1972, The Land Where the Sun Dies, 1975, The Jonah Man, 1984, repub., 1999, (with Olga Andreyev Carlisle) The Idealists, 1999. Home: 1100 Union St San Francisco CA 94109

CARLISLE, JAMES PATTON, clergyman; b. Miami Beach, Fla., May 7, 1946; s. William Olin and Evelyn Obie (Ogden) C.; m. Laima Kristina Launags; 1 child, Alexandra Ji-Anne. BA, Auburn U., 1969; MDiv, Emory U., 1976. Ordained to ministry Methodist Ch., 1975. Adminstrv. asst. Radney for Lt. Gov. Ala. campaign, 1969-70; asst. adminstr. Lee County Head Start, Auburn, Ala., 1970-72; assoc. pastor 10th St. United Meth. Ch., Atlanta, 1974-76; dir. continuing edn. N. Ga. Ann. Conf., United Meth. Ch., Atlanta, 1975-78; program dir. Ctr. for Profl. Devel. in Ministry, Lancaster, Pa., 1978-80; pres. Carlisle Leadership Group, 1984—, The Creative Leader Group; dir. Ctr. for Profl. Devel. in Ministry, Lancaster Theol. Sem., 1980-90; exec. dir. Ctr. for Creative Ch. Leadership, 1990-97; distbr. Edward de Bono Thinking Methods, Mexico; dir. programs and continuing edn. events; leader career planning events for clergy Uniting Ch. of Australia, Australia and N.Z., 1983; cons. mem. task force Pastoral Counseling Center, Lancaster, 1980-81; mem. nat. consultation on ch. ministry systems and racism, edn. and tng. for ethnic minorities Nat. Council Chs., 1983; elder N.Y. Ann. Conf. United Meth. Ch. Mem. Nat. Vocat. Guidance Assn., Assn. Clin. Pastoral Edn., Soc. Advancement Continuing Edn. for Ministry, Assn. for Creative Change (profl. mem.), Omicron Delta Kappa. Contbr. articles to profl. jours. Home and Office: 1722 Niblick Ave Lancaster PA 17602-4826 *As leaders we must engage ourselves and others in the mysterious adventure of life; whether through prayer and contemplation, social action or the adventure of living, engage life.*

CARLISLE, MARGO DUER BLACK, government official; b. Providence; d. Thomas F. Jr. and Margaret MacCormick Black; m. Miles Carlisle; children: Mary Hamilton, Tristram Coffin. BA, Manhattanville Coll. Legis. asst. Senator James A. McClure, Washington, 1973; staff mem. budget comm. task force U.S. Senate, Washington, 1974-75, exec. dir. steering com., 1975-80; staff dir. Senate Rep. Conf., Washington, 1981-84; exec. dir. Coun. for Nat. Policy, Washington, 1985-86; asst. sec. for legis. affairs Dept. Def., Washington, 1986-89; v.p. for govt. rels. The Heritage Found., Washington, 1989-90; chief staff Senator Thad Cochran, Washington, 1991-97; cons. Nat. Security, 1997-98; commr. Commn. to Assess the Orgn. of Fed. Govt.; staff dir. nat. security and fgn. policy subcoms. for Rep. platform, 1984, Washington. Contbr. articles on govt. policy to profl. jours. Trustee Phila. Soc., Washington, 1987-88, 93—, pres., 1995-96; bd. advisors, Marine Corps U., 1995—. Catholic. Avocations: sailing, scuba diving. Office: Office of Sen Thad Cochran 326 Russell Bldg Washington DC 20510-0008

CARLISLE, PATRICIA KINLEY, mortgage company executive, paralegal; b. Royston, Ga., Sept. 21, 1949; d. Luther Clark Kinley and Ann Busby Carey; children: Angela Renee, William Clark, Matthew Vincent. Grad., Suburban Inst. Real Estate, Tucker, Ga., 1978; grad. with honors, Lanier Tech. Sch., Oakwood, Ga., 1983; postgrad., Gainesville Coll., 1986, Maryville Coll., 1986. Lic. real estate salesperson, Ga. Fin. analyst, then pers. mgr. Citicorp Acceptance Co., Inc., St. Louis, 1983-89; exec. v.p., v.p. purchasing, regional sales mgr. George-Ingraham Corp., Stone Mountain, Ga., 1989-90; sr. loan officer Terrace Mortgage Co., Atlanta, 1990-92; dir. client svcs. Paynter & Everett, P.C., 1992-96; v.p., dir. client svcs. Feagin & Assocs., P.C., Atlanta, 1996-97; dir. client svcs. Chapin & Assocs., 1997—, 1997—; owner, mortgage broker Legacy Mortgage Co., Atlanta, 1998—; broker, owner Crowne Realty Group, Atlanta, 1999—; pres., owner Crowne Point Realty, 1999—. Mem. NAFE, Forsyth County Bd. Realtors, Aircraft Owners and Pilots Assn., Female Execs. North Atlanta, AAPMW, Ga. Mortgage Brokers Assn., MBAG. Avocations: computers cons. and tng., boating, travel, reading, walking, art collecting. Home: PO Box 467364 Atlanta GA 31146-7364

CARLISLE, RONALD DWIGHT, nursery owner; b. Bismarck, N.D., Oct. 28, 1940; m. Neva Carlisle, May 18, 1968. BS, Black Hills State Coll., 1966. Policy issue mgr. Provident Life Ins. Co., Bismarck, N.D., 1966-83; workers compensation commr. Bismarck, 1983-85; delivery driver Premium Beverage, Bismarck, 1985-86; owner trees N M Ore, Bismarck, 1986—; mem. N.D. Legislature. Chair Dist. 52-Dist. 30, Bismarck; del. Rep. State Conv., 1976, 78, 80, 82, 84, 86, 88, 90, 92, 94, 96, 98. With USN, 1958-62. Recipient Guardian of Small Bus. award NFIB, 1991. Mem. Am. Vets. (life), N.D. Nursery Assn., Elks, NRA. Address: PO Box 222 Bismarck ND 58502-0222

CARLL, ELIZABETH KASSAY, psychologist; b. May 4, 1950; d. Michael B. and Mary Kassay; m. Alan A. Carll, June 17, 1972. BA, Hofstra U., 1972, MA, 1976, PhD, 1978. Diplomate Am. Bd. Med. Psychotherapy. Pvt. practice clin. psychologist Huntington and Centerport, N.Y., 1979—; dist. psychologist Kings Pk. (N.Y.) Sch. Dist., 1981-86, chairperson psychol. svcs., 1986-89; adj. asst. prof. Hofstra U., Hempstead, N.Y., 1978-89; nat. presentations and publs. on family conflict, trauma intervention, aftermath of violence, eating disorders intervention, frequent media interviews. Contbr. numerous articles to profl. publs. Mem. APA Nat. Disaster Response Adv. Com., N.Y. State Psychol. Assn. (chair com. disaster/crisis response, chair task force on violence, chair pub. edn. com.), Suffolk County Psychol. Assn. (pres. 1991-93), Nat. Register Health Svc. Providers in Psychology, Internat. Soc. for Traumatic, Stress, Anxiety Disorders Assn. Am., World Fedn. for Mental Health, N.Y. State Psychol. Assn. (co-chmn. pub. edn. com.). Office: 4 Bittersweet Ct Centerport NY 11721-1703

CARLO-ALTIERI, GERARDO A., federal judge. Bankruptcy judge for P.R., U.S. Bankruptcy Ct, San Juan, 1994—. Office: US Bankruptcy Ct Federico Degetau Fed Bldg 150 Carlos Chardon Ave 490 San Juan PR 00918

CARLOCK, JANET LYNNE, middle school educator; b. Bowling Green, Ky., July 31, 1956; d. Dorris Dixon and Sarah Jane (Coates) C. BS in Elem. Edn., Western Ky. U., 1978, MA in Elem. Edn., 1980, cert. rank I in edn. adminstrn., 1995. Cert. tchr., Ky. Tchr. Owen County Elem. Sch., Owenton, Ky., 1979-86, Richardsville (Ky.) Elem. Sch., 1986-88, Henry Moss Mid. Sch., Bowling Green, Ky., 1988—; resource tchr. Ky. Internship Program, Frankfort, 1986—. Recipient Oustanding Young Educator, Jaycees, 1995. Mem. ASCD, Ky. ASCD, Ky. Mid. Sch. Assn., Nat. Mid. Sch. Assn., Ky. PTA, Nat. Coun. Social Studies, Internat. Reading Assn., Three Springs Reading Coun. (sec. 1992—), Parent/Tchr. Orgn. (bd. dirs. 1992—), Phi Eta Sigma. Office: Henry Moss Mid Sch 2565 Russellville Rd Bowling Green KY 42101-5200

CARLOCK, MAHLON WALDO, financial consultant, former high school administrator; b. Plymouth, Ind., Sept. 17, 1926; s. Thorstine Clifford and Katheryn G. (Gephart) C.; m. Betty L. Dobbs, Aug. 27, 1954; children: Mahlon W. II, Rhena M., Shawn R. BS, Ind. U., 1951, MS, 1956. Tchr. jr. high Martinsville Schs. Corp., Brooklyn, Ind., 1952-53; tchr. high sch. Indpls. Pub. Schs., 1953-63, asst. to dean of boys, 1963-73, asst. dean of boys, 1973-75, bus. mgr., 1976-87; fin. cons. Indpls., 1987-93; property builder, owner Ind.; lectr. on fin. and real estate; condr. seminars on estate planning and trust; income tax preparer. Sgt. U.S. Army, 1945-47. Mem. NEA (life), Indpls. Adminstrs., Ind. Bus. Edn. Assn., Indpls. Edn. Assn. (rep. 1958-63). Republican. Baptist. Lodge: Masons. Avocation: investing in real estate. Home and Office: 9705 E Michigan St Indianapolis IN 46229-2564 *Personal philosophy: You must always feel that Christ is beside you in everything you do.*

CARLOS, MICHAEL C., wine, spirits and linen service wholesale executive; b. 1927. Chmn. bd., dir., co-CEO Nat. Distbg. Co., Inc., Atlanta. Office: Nat Distbg Co Inc One National Dr SW Atlanta GA 30336*

CARLOTTI, RONALD JOHN, food scientist; b. Martins Ferry, Ohio, Sept. 20, 1942; s. John Peter and Mary Rose (Pilla) C.; m. Eileen Theresa Dorsey, May 17, 1969; children: Lori Ann, Christina Maria, Jennifer Ann, Theresa Maria. Student, Wheeling (W.Va.) Jesuit Coll., 1960-63; BS, Ohio State U., 1964; MS, W.Va. U., 1966, PhD, 1970; MM, Aquinas Coll., 1996. Postdoctoral fellow Dept. Biochemistry, U. Iowa, Iowa City, 1971-72; asst. rsch. scientist Pediatrics Dept., U. Iowa, Iowa City, 1973-74; corp. nutritionist Kellogg Co., Battle Creek, Mich., 1974-77; mgr. nutrition/basic rsch. Frito Lay div. Pepsico, Dallas, 1977-82, prin. scientist new products, 1982-85; sr. rsch. scientist Amway Corp., Ada, Mich., 1985-89; dir. food sci. and tech. Country Home Bakers, Grand Rapids, Mich., 1990-93; pres. Carlotti and Assocs., Grand Rapids, 1994; pres., CEO Natura Inc., Lansing, Mich., 1995—; tech. rep. Snack Food Assn., Crystal City, Va., 1978-82, Grocery Mfrs. of Am., Washington, 1975-77; nutritionist Am. Frozen Food Assn., Washington, 1990-93. Contbr. articles to profl. jours. Pres. Mary Immaculate Sch. Bd., Dallas, 1981-83. Recipient Lovable Spud award, Nat. Potato Promotion Bd., Denver, 1981. Mem. Am. Chem. Soc., Am. Assn. Cereal Chemists, Inst. Food Tech. Roman Catholic. Achievements include start-up of new biotechnology-based food and chemical ingredients company, development of first nutritionally improved (low fat/low calorie) prototype of Doritos light tortilla chips, of new high potency dry dog food for Amway Corp., of a series of nutritionally improved fruit pies for diabetics, of a specially formulated pumpkin pie which will not allow for the growth of pathogenic bacteria innoculated after baking in testing required to verify that the product can be stored at ambient temperature for up to five days; initiation of tech. and regulatory functions for corporate products. Home: 6921 Maplecrest Dr SE Grand Rapids MI 49546-9208 Office: Natura Inc 3900 Collins Rd Ste 1007 Lansing MI 48910-8543

CARLOTTI, STEPHEN JON, lawyer; b. Providence, Apr. 28, 1942; s. Albert Edward and Rose C.; m. Nancy Ann Arnold, Sept. 16, 1961; children: Stephen J., Cristina C. AB, Dartmouth Coll., 1963; LLB, Yale U., 1966. Bar: R.I. 1966, U.S. Ct. Mil. Appeals 1967, U.S. Ct. Appeals (9th cir.) 1969, U.S. Dist. Ct. R.I. 1970, U.S. Supreme Ct. 1972. Assoc. Hinckley, Allen, Salisbury & Parsons, Providence, 1966, 70-72; ptnr. Hinckley, Allen, & Snyder, Providence, 1972-89, 91, mng. ptnr., 1986-89, 92-96; with The Mut. Benefit Life Ins. Co., Newark, 1989-91; bd. dirs. Fleet Nat. Bank., Accessories Assoc., Inc., W.P.I. Group, Inc. Chmn. Town Com., 1975-76; trustee Roger Williams U., 1978-93, Health Provider Svcs., R.I. Pub. Expenditures Coun. Capt. JAGC, U.S. Army, 1967-70. Mem. ABA, R.I. Bar Assn., R.I. Country Club, Univ. Club. Republican. Roman Catholic. Avocations: golf, tennis, sailing. Office: Hinckley Allen & Snyder 1500 Fleet Ctr Providence RI 02903-2319

CARLOZZI, CATHERINE L., corporate communications consultant, writer; b. Berea, Ohio, July 25, 1953; d. Charles Henry and Carol Louise (Jones) Bader; m. Nicholas Carlozzi, Jan. 4, 1975. BA in English summa cum laude, Denison U., 1975; MA in English with distinction, U. Wis., 1976. Tchg. asst. U. Wis., Madison, 1976-77; editor Visual Edn. Cons., Madison, 1977-78; copywriter advt. Walnut Equipment Leasing, Ardmore, Pa., 1978-79; assoc. nat. dir. publs. Laventhol & Horwath, Phila., 1979-84; sr. assoc., mgr. spl. projects, v.p. Brown Boxenbaum, N.Y.C., 1984-91; prin. Carlozzi Comm. Cons., Cedar Grove, N.J., 1991—. Trustee Montclair, N.J. Art Mus., 1993—. Recipient Dir.'s award Montclair Art Mus., 1994. Mem. N.Y. Women in Comm. (Liz Hoover award 1999), Internat. Assn. Bus. Communicators, N.Y. Women's Agenda, Phi Beta Kappa. Avocation: sailing. Home and Office: 334 Crestmont Rd Cedar Grove NJ 07009-1908

CARLQUIST, SHERWIN, biology and botany educator; b. L.A., July 7, 1930; s. Robert William and Helen (Bauer) C. BA, U. Calif., Berkeley, 1952, PhD, 1956; postgrad, Harvard U., 1956. Assoc. prof. Claremont Grad. Sch., Calif., 1967-93, asst. prof. botany, 1956-61; prof. biology Pomona Coll., Claremont, 1976-93. Author: Japanese Festivals, 1965, Island Life, 1965 (Gleason award N.Y. Bot. Garden), Comparative Plant Anatomy, 1961, Hawaii: A Natural History, 1970, Island Biology, 1974, Ecological Strategies of Xylem Evolution, 1975, Comparative Wood Anatomy, 1988, Natural Man, 1991, Man Naturally, 1996, Outsiders, 1996, The Natural Male, 1999; contbr. articles to profl. jours. Recipient career award Bot. Soc. Am., 1977, Allerton award, 1992, Asa Gray award Am. Soc. Plant Taxonomists, 1993, Margaret Getman Svc. to Students award U. Calif., Santa Barbara, 1996, Fellows' medal Calif. Acad. Scis., 1996, Career award Santa Barbara Bot. Garden, 1996. *I would like to be remembered for initiating a fusion between plant ecology and wood anatomy; also for outlining how dispersal to islands occurs and what evolutionary trends occur on islands. In pursuing these interests, the pleasure of attempting creative and original work in scientific discovery and in written and graphic presentation of those discoveries is my chief motivation.*

CARLS, ALICE CATHERINE, history educator; b. Mulhouse, France, June 14, 1950; came to U.S., 1977; d. Victor Adrien Clement and Lise Simone (Ebersolt) Maire; m. Stephen Douglas, June 25, 1977; children: Philip, Elizabeth, Paul. BA, Sorbonne U., Paris, 1970, MA, 1972, PhD, 1976. Instr. Union U., Jackson, Tenn., 1983-85; grad. instr. U. Tenn., Martin, Tenn., 1984; asst. prof., polit. sci. Lambuth Coll., Jackson, 1985-88, asst. prof., history, polit. sci., 1988-92; asst. prof. history U. Tenn., Martin, 1992-96, assoc. prof. history, 1996—, dept. chair, 1997—; mem. editl. bd. Am. studies Polish-Am. Hist. Assn., N.Y.C., 1991-93; exec. com., 1989-91; Ea. European corr. Ctr. Pub. Justice, Washington, 1981-97, mem. editl. bd., 1998—; feature scholar U. Tenn., Martin, 1999. Author: La Ville Libre de Dantzig en crise ouverte, 1982; translator: La Vie qu'il faut choisir (Jan Kochanowski), 1992, Le Cavalier polonais (Wladyslaw Grzedzielski), 1991, Echapper à ma tombe (Jozef M. Rostocki), 1995, Une mouche dans ma soupe (Jozef M. Rostocki), 1998; contbr. articles to profl. jours. Mem. Bicentennial Com., Ad-hoc Bicentennial Com., Jackson, 1987; alt. dir. Ad-hoc Com. Memories Life Bemis Jackson, 1991-92; dir. Ad-hoc Com. Polish Week, Sterling, Kans., 1982. Grantee Herbert Hoover Instn. for War, Revolution and Peace, 1984, Herbert Hoover Pub. Libr. 1979, Deutscher Akademischer Austausch Dienst 1975, French Ministry Fgn. Affairs 1973-75; recipient Internat. Scholar award U. Tenn., Martin, 1999—. Mem. Am. Hist. Assn., UN Assn.-USA, Polish-Am. Hist. Assn., Am. Assn. for Advancement of Slavic Studies, Polish Studies Assn., Ctr. for Pub. Justice. Presbyterian.

CARLS, JUDITH MARIE, physical education educator, golf coach; b. Moline, Ill., Aug. 16, 1940; d. Orville Allen and Eleanor Lou (Shollenberger) Meyers; m. Larry Michael, Dec. 21, 1966 (div. June 1971). BA in Phys. Edn., U. No. Iowa, 1962; MA, Western Ill. U., 1982. Cert. educator/adminstr. K-14, Ill. Phys. edn. instr. John Deere Jr. H.S., Moline; dep. chmn. phys. edn. Moline H.S., 1965-93; dir. golf schs. Recreation Pk. Golf Course, Long Beach, Calif., 1993—; part-time instr., student tchr. supr. Calif. State U., Fullerton, 1994—; dir. jr. golf City of Long Beach, Calif., 1996—; cons. LPGA Jr. Golf Program, L.A., 1993-94; dir. Jr. Golf. in the City of Long Beach, 1997—. Campaign, fundraiser Tim Bell State Rep., Moline, 1980-84. Named to Ill. Coaches Hall of Fame, 1993. Mem. NEA, Ladies Profl. Golf Assn. (mid-west sect. 1982—), Ill. Phys. Edn. Assn. (govt. affairs office 1989-93), Phi Kappa Phi. Republican. Lutheran. Avocations: travel, hiking, biking. Home: 2814 32nd Avenue Dr Moline IL 61265-6956

CARLSEN, JAMES CALDWELL, musicologist, educator; b. Pasco, Wash., Feb. 11, 1927; s. Theodore N. and Eunice (Caldwell) C.; m. Mary Louisa Baird, May 1, 1949; children: Philip C., Douglas A., Susan A., Kristine L. B.A., Whitworth Coll., 1950; M.A., U. Wash., 1958; Ph.D., Northwestern U., 1962. Pub. sch. tchr. Almira, Wash., 1950-53; pub. sch. tchr. Portland, Oreg., 1953-54; mem. faculty Whitworth Coll., 1954-63, U. Conn., 1963-67; prof. music U. Wash., Seattle, 1967-92, head div. systematic musicology, 1968-92, ret., 1992, emeritus prof. music, 1992—; rsch. assoc. Stäatliches Institut für Musikforschung, West Berlin, Germany, 1973-74; adj. prof. psychology U. Wash., 1979-92; vis. lectr. Instituto Investigaciones Educativas, Buenos Aires, 1981, Ind. U., 1985, Centro de Investigacion en Educacion Musical del Collegium Musicum, Buenos Aires, 1994; vis. scholar U. Bergen, Norway, 1986; disting. vis. prof. music Aichi U. Edn., Japan, 1992; Housewright eminent scholar chair in music Fla. State U., 1998. Author: Melodic Perception, 1965; editor Jour. Research in Music Edn, 1978-81; assoc. editor Psychomusicology, 1980—; cons. editor Jour. Music Perception and Cognition, Japan, 1998—. Condr. Spokane Symphonic Band, Wash., 1957-60; music dir. Walla Walla Choral Soc., 1997. Served with AUS, 1945-47. Danforth Tchr. Study grantee, 1960-61; grad. fellow Presbyn. Ch., 1961-62; Fulbright-Hays grantee, 1973-74; recipient Soc. Rsch. in Music Edn. Sr. Researcher award, 1994. Mem. AAUP, Music Educators Nat. Conf., Music Edn. rsch. Coun. (past chmn.), Coll. Music Soc., Soc. for Music Perception and Cognition, Internat. Soc. Music Edn. (chmn. rsch. commn. 1976-80), Internat. Soc. Music Edn. Rsch. Commn. Seminars (hon. life), Internat. Soc. Music Edn. (hon. life), Walla Walla Symphony Soc. (bd. dirs. 1997—). Home: 845 Fern Ct Walla Walla WA 99362-8857

CARLSEN, JANET HAWS, retired insurance company owner, mayor; b. Bellingham, Wash., June 16, 1927; d. Lyle F. and Mary Elizabeth (Preble) Haws; m. Kenneth M. Carlsen, July 26, 1952; children: Stephanie L. Chambers, Scott Lyle, Sean Preble, Stacy K., Spencer J. Cert., Armstrong Bus. Sch., 1945; student, Golden Gate Coll., 1945-46. Office mgr. Cornwall Warehouse Co., Salt Lake City, 1950-55, Hansen's Ins., Newman, Calif., 1969-77; owner Carlsen Ins., Gustine, Calif., 1978-97. Mem. city coun. City of Newman, 1980-82, mayor, 1982-94; bd. dirs. ARC, Stanislaus, Calif., 1982-83, Tosca, 1993-98; bd. dirs. Stanislaus County Area Agy. on Aging, 1995—, chairperson, 1996-99; bd. dirs. Calif. state com. TACC Commn. on Aging, 1996-98; grand marshal Newman Fall Festival, 1989; v.p. ctrl. divsn. League of Calif. Cities, 1989-90, pres. 1990, 91; bd. dirs. Sr. Opportunity Svc. Ctr., 1993-96, 97-98, Sr. Opportunity Svc. Program of Stanislaus County, 1995-96; chairperson Ctrl. Valley Opportunity Ctr., 1996-98; mem. Stanislaus County Vision Com., 1997—; bd. dirs. Gt. Valley Ctr., 1997—. Named Soroptimist Woman of Achievement, 1987, Soroptimist Woman of Distinction, 1988, Outstanding Woman, Stanislaus County Commn. for Women, 1989, Newman Rotary Club Citizen of Yr., 1993-94, Woman of Yr. Calif. State Assembly Dist. 26, 1994, Ambassador, City of Newman, 1997—. Mem. Booster Club (Newman) Soroptimist Club. Mormon. Home: 1215 Amy Dr Newman CA 95360-1003

CARLSEN, JOHN RICHARD, engineer; b. Palo Alto, Calif., June 16, 1970. Attended, San Jose State U., 1988-91, De Anza Coll., 1992-93, 97—, Austin C.C., 1995. Engring. contractor Nolan K. Bushnell, Mountain View, Calif., 1988-89; engring. contractor Iguana Entertainment, Inc., Sunnyvale, 1991-93, sr. hardware engr., 1993-96; engring. contractor AAPPS Corp., Sunnyvale, Calif., 1989, Media Vision, Inc., Fremont, Calif., 1991-92; advanced layout engr. Altera Corp., San Jose, 1996-99; pres. Carlsen Electronic Rsch., Sunnyvale, 1988-93. Mem. IEEE, Soc. Tech. Comm. Achievements include design of interfaces and software tools for development of video games on Sony Playstation, Sega Saturn, Super Nintendo and Atari Jaguar; contributing designs for PC and Macintosh multimedia cards; creation of fully-custom CMOS integrated circuits, topological design rules, layout training program for college graduates. Home: 1592 Heatherdale Ave San Jose CA 95126-1308 Office: Carlsen Comm PO Box 1032 Santa Clara CA 95052-1032

CARLSEN, MARY BAIRD, clinical psychologist; b. Salt Lake City, Utah, Aug. 31, 1928; d. Jesse Hays and Susannah Amanda (Bragstad) Baird; m. James C. Carlsen, May 1, 1949; children: Philip, Douglas, Susan, Kristine. Student, St. Olaf Coll., 1946-47; BA, Whitworth Coll., 1950; MA, U. Conn., 1967; PhD, U. Wash., 1973. Profl. organist, piano tchr. Wash., Oreg., Ill., Conn., 1949-68; staff counselor Presbyn. Counseling Svc., Seattle, 1976-79; pvt. practice clin. psychologist, marriage therapist, cognitive, devel. psychology, career devel. Seattle, 1978-95; cons. creative aging Walla Walla, 1996—; chmn. sr. adult adv. coun. Seattle Parks Dept., 1975-76; adv. bd. Northwest Ctr. for Creative Aging, 1995-98; mem. steering com. Quest Learning Inst., Walla Walla, Wash., 1997—; mem. nat. adv. bd. Ctr. for Creative Retirement, Asheville, N.C., 1998—. Author: Meaning-Making: Therapeutic Processes in Adult Development, 1988, Creative Aging: A Meaning-Making Perspective, 1991, 2d edit., 1996, Transformational Meaning-Making and the Practices of Career Counseling, 1991; contbr. chpt. to book and articles to profl. jours. Grantee PEO Rsch., 1972, U. Wash. Women's Guidance Ctr., 1972. Mem. APA, Am. Soc. Aging.

CARLSEN, RUSSELL ARHTUR, city manager; b. Cleve., Sept. 25, 1945. AA in Law Enforcement, Monterey Peninsula Coll., 1995; BA in Sociology, U. Wash., 1977, BA in History, 1977. Property mgr. Calif., 1983-86; housing mgr. Cmty. Devel. Commn. L.A. County, 1986-88; dep. city mgr. City of Fontana, Calif., 1988-91; mgmt. cons. Calif., 1991-95; city mgr. City of Big Bear Lake, Calif., 1995—. Mgmt. cons. many orgns; divsn. del. League of Calif. Cities Pub. Safety Policy Com., Sacramento, 1998—. With U.S. Army, 1969-71. Named Hon. Citizen San Juan Batista, 1993; recipient Key to the City City of Soledad, 1994. Mem. Internat. City Mgrs. Assn., Rotary Internat., Phi Alpha Alpha. Fax: 909-866-6766. E-mail: citymanager@citybigbearlake.com. Office: City of Big Bear Lake PO Box 10000 39707 Big Bear Blvd Big Bear Lake CA 92315

CARLSMITH, JAMES MERRILL, psychologist, educator; b. New Orleans, Apr. 12, 1936; s. Leonard Eldon and Hope (Snedden) C.; m. Lyn Kuckenberg, July 27, 1963; children—Christopher, Kimberly, Kevin. A.B., Stanford U., 1958; Ph.D., Harvard U., 1963. Asst. prof. Yale U., 1962-64; from asst. prof. to prof. psychology Stanford U., 1964—, asso. dean grad. studies, 1972-75; fellow (Center for Advanced Study in Behavioral Scis.), 1975. Author: Social Psychology, 1970, Methods of Research In Social Psychology, 1976. Dir. Boys Town Center, 1980—. Office: Stanford U Dept Psychology Stanford CA 94305

CARLSMITH, ROGER SNEDDEN, chemistry and energy conservation researcher; b. N.Y.C., Oct. 2, 1925; s. Leonard Eldon and Hope (Snedden) C.; m. Thelma Kathleen Sutton, July 31, 1954; children: David, Nancy Lynn. AB in Chemistry cum laude, Harvard, 1948; MSCE, MIT, 1950. Rsch. engr. Oak Ridge (Tenn.) Nat. Lab., 1950-62, group leader, 1962-70, sect. mgr., 1970-78, prog. dir. conservation and renewable energy, 1978-94; ret., 1994; mem. Gov.'s Energy Task Force, Tenn., 1972-74, adv. com. Fed. Power Commn., Washington, 1973; bd. dirs. Am. Coun. Energy Efficient Economy, Washington, Tenn. Citizens Wilderness Planning. Author: (book with others) World Energy Conference Survey of Energy Resourses, 1974. Sgt. USAF, 1943-46. Recipient Sadi Carnot medal for achievements in energy conservation rsch. Dept. Energy, 1996. Mem. AAAS, Sierra Club, The Wilderness Soc. Achievements include research and development of advanced technology for improved energy efficiency, alternative energy sources, environmental impacts of energy, energy and the economy. Home: 1052 W Outer Dr Oak Ridge TN 37830-8641

CARLSON, ALLAN CONSTANTINE, historian; b. Des Moines, May 7, 1949; s. Harry Bernard and Constance Ann Carlson; m. Elizabeth Cecelia Belin, July 1, 1972; children: Anders, Sarah-Eva, Anna, Miriam. AB, Augustana Coll., 1971; PhD in European History, Ohio U., 1978. Asst. dir. office for govtl. affairs Luth. Coun. in the U.S.A., Washington, 1975-78; asst. to pres., history lectr. Gettysburg (Pa.) Coll., 1979-81; exec. v.p. The Rockford (Ill.) Inst., 1981-86, pres., 1986-97; pres. The Howard Ctr. for Family, Religion & Soc., 1997—; mem. Coun. on Families in Am., N.Y.C., 1991—; cons. Family Rsch. Inst., Moscow, 1995—, U.S. Dept. Justice, Washington, 1986-87, U.S. Dept. Edn., Washington, 1986-88; gen. sec. World Congress Families in Prague, The Czech Republic, 1997, Geneva, Switzerland, 1999. Author: The New Agrarian Mind, 1999, From Cottage to Work Station, 1993, The Swedish Experiment in Family Politics, 1990, Family Questions, 1988; co-author: The Family: Is it Just Another Lifestyle Choice?; contbr. articles to profl. jours. Commr. The Nat. Commn. on Children, Washington, 1988-93; adv. bd. project SHARE U.S. Dept. Health Human Svcs., Washington, 1983-85; leader Boy Scouts of Am., dist. chmn., 1995-96. NEH fellow Am. Enterprise Inst., 1979; recipient George Washington Honor medal Freedoms Found. Valley Forge, 1985, 87. Mem. Phila. Soc. (1st v.p. 1986-87), Rotary (pres. 1994-95), John Randolph Club (bd. dirs., sec. 1993-95), Lutherans for Life (bd. dirs. 1987-92), Phi Beta Kappa. Lutheran. Home: 1324 Camp Ave Rockford IL 61103-7104 Office: The Howard Center 934 N Main St Rockford IL 61103-7061

CARLSON, ARNE HELGE, former governor; b. N.Y.C., Sept. 24, 1934; s. Helge William and Kerstin (Magnusson) C.; children by previous marriage: Arne H. Jr., Anne Davis; m. Susan Shepard, July 12, 1985; 1 child, Jessica Shepard. BA, Williams Coll., 1957; postgrad., U. Minn., 1957-58. Mem. advt. staff Control Data, Bloomington, Minn., 1962-64; councilman Mpls. City Council, 1965-67; ind. businessman Mpls., 1968-69; legislator Minn. Ho. Reps., St. Paul, 1970-78; state auditor State of Minn., St. Paul, 1978-90, gov., 1991-98; chmn. bd. IDS Mut. Fund Group, Mpls., 1999—; bd. dirs. Minn. Land Exch. Bd., St. Paul; trustee Minn. State Bd. Investment, St. Paul, 1979—. Bd. dirs. Exec. Coun., St. Paul; sec. Minn. Housing Fin. Agy., St. Paul, 1979-91; past pres. Pub. Employees Retirement Assn., St. Paul, 1985-88; mem. Nat. Gov.'s Assn., Midwest Gov.'s Assn., Great Lakes Govs.; mem. Nat. Ednl. Goals Panel of Nat. Gov.'s Assn. Bush Found. Leadership fellow, 1971; recipient Children's Champion award Minn. Children's Def. Fund, Nat. Audubon Soc. award, Small Bus. Guardian award Nat. Fedn. Ind. Businesses, 1994, Great Blue Heron award N.Am. Waterfront Mgmt. Plan/U.S. Fish & Wildlife Svc., 1995; named Rep. of Yr. Nat. Ripon Soc., 1993. Bd. dirs. Exec. Coun. St. Paul, sec. Minn. Housing Fin. Agy., St. Paul, 1979-91; past pres. Pub. Employees Retirement Assn., St. Paul, 1985-88; mem. Nat. Gov.'s Assn. (chmn. com. on human resources, mem. Nat. Ednl. Goals Panel), Rep. Gov.'s Assn., Midwest Gov.'s Assn., Great Lakes Govs. Republican. Avocations: reading, squash, University of Minnesota basketball and football games. Home: 22005 Iden Ave N Forest Lake MN 55025-9329 Office: IDS Mut Fund Group Ste 2810 901 Marquette Ave Minneapolis MN 55402-3268

CARLSON, ARTHUR EUGENE, accounting educator; b. Whitewater, Wis., May 10, 1923; s. Paul Adolph and Dorothy Adeline (Cooper) C.; m. Lorraine June Bronson, Aug. 19, 1944; 1 child, George Arthur. EdB, U. Wis., Whitewater, 1943; MBA, Harvard U., 1947; PhD, Northwestern U., 1954. Instr., Ohio U., 1947-50; lectr. Northwestern U., 1950-52; from asst. prof. to prof. accgt. Washington U., St. Louis, 1952-88, prof. emeritus, 1988—; vis. prof. U. Hawaii, 1963-64. Author: College Accounting, 1967, 7th edit., 1993; Accounting Essentials, 1973, 5th edit., 1991. Chmn. Robert Meml. Endowment Fund., University City, Mo., 1972-98, trustee Police and Fire Pension Bd., 1979-88. Mem. Inst. Mgmt. Accts. (past pres.), Assn. Systems Mgmt. (past pres., Disting. Service award 1973), Soc. Profs. Emeriti Washington U. (pres. 1995, disting. bus. alumni awards com. 1998—). Republican. Episcopalian. Lodge: Kiwanis (pres. 1969). Avocation: bowling, gardening. Home: 801 S Skinker Blvd # 9A Saint Louis MO 63105-3228

CARLSON, ARTHUR W., lawyer; b. Chgo., Oct. 3, 1945; s. Arthur W. Sr. and Florence (Maul) C.; m. Jeri S. Waite, June 28, 1986; children: Mackenzie Waite Carlson, Sara Elizabeth Carlson. AB, Pomona Coll., 1967; JD, Duke U., 1971. Bar: Calif. 1972. Prin. Angle, Carlson & Goldrick, Santa Barbara, Calif., 1994—. Pres., bd. trustees Santa Barbara Mus. Natural History, 1990-93, 94-95. Office: Angle Carlson & Goldrick 200 E Carrillo St Ste 310 Santa Barbara CA 93101-7143

CARLSON, BRIAN JAY, health facility executive; b. Mpls., Mar. 21, 1956; s. John Russell and Shirley Mae Joan (Warholm) C.; m. Ann Margaret Grabau, May 26, 1979; children: Daniel Jordan, Katja Mari, Anja Matia, Peder Christian. BA in Bus. and Hosp. Adminstrn., Concordia Coll., 1978; MSA in Instl. Adminstrn., U. Notre Dame, 1986. From dir. ops. to v.p. ops. St. Joseph's Med. Ctr., Brainerd, Minn., 1978-95; pres., CEO Lake View Meml. Hosp. & Home, Two Harbors, Minn., 1995—; 2nd v.p., affiliated mem. St. Luke's Hosp. and Regional Trauma Ctr., Duluth, Minn., 1998—; engring. cons. St. Joseph's Med. Ctr., Brainerd, 1984-95. Fellow Am. Coll. Healthcare Execs.; mem. Am. Hosp. Assn., Brainerd C. of C. (mktg. expansion com. 1984-94). Democrat. Avocations: woodworking, tennis, racquetball, golf, softball. Office: Lake View Meml Hosp 325 11th Ave Two Harbors MN 55616-1300

CARLSON, BRUCE, career officer; b. Hibbing, Minn., Oct. 3, 1949; m. Vicki Martens; children: Jani, Bryan, Scott. BA, U. Minn., 1971; grad., USAF Fighter Weapons Sch., 1979; MA, Webster U., 1980; grad. (disting.), MA, Coll. Naval Warfare, 1989. Commd. 2d lt. USAF, 1971, advanced through grades to maj. gen., 1998; pilot USAF, Holloman AFB, N.Mex., 1973-74; air controller, instr. pilot USAF, Royal Thai AFB, Thailand, 1974-75; instr. pilot, flight examiner USAF, Bergstrom AFB, Tex., 1975-77; pilot, fighter weapons instr. pilot USAF, Myrtle Beach AFB, S.C., 1977-80; aide to comdr. Hdqs. Tactical Air Command, Langley AFB, Va., 1980-82; wing weapons officer, ops. officer Hdqs. Tactical Air Command, Shaw AFB, S.C., 1982-85; tactical sys. requirements officer Office of low Observables Tech., Sec. of Air Force, Washington, 1985-88; dir. advanced programs Hdqs. Tactical Air Command, Langley AFB, Va., 1989-91; vice comdr. 366th Wing USAF, Mountain Home AFB, Idaho, 1991-93; sr. mil. asst. to under sec. of def. acquisition Office of Sec. Def., Pentagon, Washington, 1993-95, also sr. mil. asst. to dep. sec. def., 1993-95; comdr. 49th Fighter Wing Holloman AFB, N.Mex.1996; dir. Global Power Programs, dir. ops. requirements, DCS ops. Office Asst. Sec. of Air Force for Acquisition, Washington, 1996-98, dir. ops. requirements, DCS, air and space ops., 1998—. Decorated def. disting. svc. medal, Legion of Merit, meritorious svc. medal with two oak leaf clusters, Air Force commendation medal with two oak leaf clusters. Office: USAF Dir Ops Requirements 1480 Air Force Pentagon Washington DC 20330-1480

CARLSON, BRUCE MARTIN, anatomist; b. Gary, Ind., July 11, 1938; s. Martin E. and Esther (Granquist) C.; m. Jean Ann Hyslop, Aug. 18, 1968; children: Martin, James. BA, Gustavus Adolphus Coll., 1959; MS, Cornell U., 1961; MD, PhD, U. Minn., 1986. Exchange scientist Inst. of Devel. Biology, Moscow, 1965-66; Fulbright fellow Hubrecht (Netherlands) Inst., 1973-74; Joshiah Macy scholar U. Helsinki, Finland, 1981-82; exchange scientist Inst. of Physiology, Prague, Czechoslovakia, 1971; asst. prof. of anatomy to prof. U. Mich., Ann Arbor, 1966—, prof. biology, 1979—, chmn. dept. anatomy and cell biology, 1988—, rsch. scientist Inst. Gerontology, 1989—; fellow Fetzer Inst., Kalamazoo, Mich., 1990-96, trustee, 1998—; mem. study sects. NIH, 1986-90, Nat. Bd. Med. Examiners, 1994-96. Author: The Regeneration of Minced Muscles, 1972, Patten's Foundations of Embryology, 1974, 4th edit. 1981, 5th edit. 1988, 6th edit. 1996, Regeneration (in Russian), 1986, Human Embryology and Developmental Biology, 1994, 99; editor: From Message to Mind, 1988, Regeneration and Transplantation, 1990, numerous others. Recipient Disting. Alumni award Gustavus Adolphus Coll., 1979, Newcomb-Cleveland prize AAAS, 1972, 650th Anniversary medal, Charles U., Prague. Fellow AAAS, Russian Acad. Natural Scis.; mem. Am. Assn. of Anatomists (nominating com. 1991, exec. com. 1994, pres. 1997-99), Am. Soc. Zoologists (divsn. chmn. 1987-89), Am. Soc. Ichthyologists and Herpetologists, Assn. of Anatomy, Cell Biology and Neurobiology Chairpersons (pres. 1995), Soc. of Devel. Biologists, Internat. Soc. of Devel. Biology. Lutheran. Achievements include invention of techniques of free muscle transplantation. Home: 3838 Curlew Ln Ann Arbor MI 48103-9404 Office: U Mich Dept Anatomy & Cell Biology Ann Arbor MI 48109

CARLSON, CAROLIN MCCORMICK FURST, civic worker; b. Williamsport, Pa., Apr. 20, 1934; d. S. Dale and Esther Caroline (McCormick) Furst O'Brien; m. Elton Frederic Carlson, Sept. 15, 1956 (dec. 1970); children: Eric Dale, Margaret Cora, Dwight Leonard. BA, Smith Coll., 1955. Dir. emerita First Nat. Bank of Port Allegany, Pa.; class fund sec. Abbot class Phillips Acad., Andover, Mass., 1951—; chmn. Abbot 40th Reunion, 1991. Contbr. articles to weekly paper Reporter-Argus, 1961-87. Jr. choir dir. Gethsemane Evang. Luth. Ch., Port Allegany, 1971-82, charter lay asst., 1972-74, 84-90, congl. sec., 1973-93, Theos chpt. exec. dir. and grief counselor, 1972-76, chmn. bicentennial celebration com., 1975-76, pres. Luth. Ch. Women, 1959-61, treas., 1962-65, 84-85, program chmn., 1976-80, sr. choir, 1983-86, Emporium Ministerium grief counselor, 1984-87; chmn. noon hour cultural series S.W. Smith Meml. Pub. Libr., 1972-74, 77-78, bd. dirs., 1977-78, v.p. spl. events, 1978-82, book selection, 1977-82, 94-95, pres., 1985-88, adv. bd. McKean Literacy Team, 1991-94; active children's story hour, hosp. bookcart Pike County Pub. Libr., 1997—, Port Area Cmty. TV, 1981-92; den mother Allegany Highland Coun. Boy Scouts Am., Port Allegany, 1967-70, 76-79, sec., 1976-79, merit badge counselor, 1984-92; asst. troop leader Keystone tall Tree coun. Girl Scouts U.S., 1969-74; charter driver Meals on Wheels, 1972-92; adv. bd. Charles Cole Meml. Hosp., 1988-95, long-range planning, 1990-91; adv. bd. dirs. McKean Count y Children & Youth Svcs., 1980-83; v.p. Port Allegany High Sch. Band Boosters, 1982-85; chmn.

United Way, 1984, 85; bd. dirs. Port Allegany Area Econ. Devel. Corp., 1984-95, solicitation chmn. capital funds drive, 1987-90; grants com. McKean County Coun. of Arts, 1990-93. Recipient award Luth. Ch. Am., 1975. Mem. Smith Coll. Alumnae Assn., Abbot Acad. Alumnae Assn., Port Allegany Woman's Club (treas. 1957-60, 66-67, 94-95, auditor 1965, 82, sec. 1963-65, 70-71, 2d v.p. 1967-68, 71-72, pres. 1977-79, choir 1961-95, Woman of Yr. 1995, hon. mem. 1996—), Pike County C. of C., McKean County Women's Club (sec. 1958-60, 66-68, treas. 1970-72, 1st v.p. 1972-76), Order Eastern Star, Bristol Village. Republican. Home: 334 Robin Rd Waverly OH 45690-1521

CARLSON, CHRISTOPHER TAPLEY, lawyer; b. N.Y.C., Mar. 7, 1949; s. David Bret and Jane (Tapley) C.; m. Jane Fisher, Aug. 22, 1970; children: Caroline, Jonathan. Bar: Mass. 1973, U.S. Supreme Ct. 1980. Assoc. Hale and Dorr, Boston, 1973-79, jr. ptnr., 1979-83, sr. ptnr., 1983-89; ptnr. Gilmore Rees and Carlson, Franklin, Mass., 1989—; mem. estate planning curr. com. Mass. Continuing Edn. New Eng. Law Inst., Inc., Boston, 1982-93; mem. exec. com. Boston Estate Planning Council, 1987-91; mem. Boston Estate Planning and Probate Forum, 1989—; lectr. Law Boston U. Sch. Law, 1982-84. Trustee William Lawrence Camp, Center Tuftonboro, N.H., 1975-90. Fellow Am. Coll. Trust and Estate Counsel; mem. Weston Golf Club. Office: Gilmore Rees & Carlson 20 Walnut St Wellesley MA 02481-2104

CARLSON, CURTIS LEROY, corporate executive; b. Mpls., July 9, 1914; s. Charles A. and Letha (Peterson) C.; m. Arleen Martin, June 30, 1938; children: Marilyn Carlson Nelson, Barbara Carlson Gage. BA in Econs., U. Minn., 1937. Salesman, Procter & Gamble Co., Mpls., 1937-39; founder, pres. Gold Bond Stamp Co., Mpls., 1938-73, pres., chmn. bd. dirs., CEO, 1973-98; chmn. bd. dirs. Carlson Cos., Inc., 1998—; pres. MIP Agy., Inc.; chmn. bd. Radisson Hotel Corp., Radisson Group Inc., Carlson Real Estate Co., Inc., Carlson Holdings, Inc., Carlson Leasing, Inc., TGI Friday's Inc., Dallas, Nordic-Am. Travel, Inc., K-Promotions, Inc., Carlson Mktg. Group, Carlson Travel Group; chmn. Carlson Hospitality Worldwide, Gold Points Corp. Sr. v.p., bd. trustees U. Minn. Found.; chmn. emeritus Swedish Coun. Am.; bd. dirs., founder Boys Club Mpls.; trustee emeritus Minn. Meetings; mem. emeritus adv. bd. U. Minn. Curtis L. Carlson Sch. of Mgmt., U. Minn.; mem. Royal Round Table, Swedish Coun. Am.; mem. Hennepin Ave. Meth. Ch. Mem. Trading Stamp Inst. Am. (dir., founder, pres. 1959-60), Sigma Phi Epsilon (mem. bd. govs.), Mpls. Club, Northland Country (Duluth), Minikahda Club, Ocean Reef Yacht (Key Largo), Palm Bay (Miami), Masons, Shriners, Jesters. Office: Carlson Cos Inc PO Box 59159 Carlson Pky Minneapolis MN 55459

CARLSON, CYNTHIA JOANNE, artist, educator; b. Chgo.; d. Ivan Morris and Ruth (Holmes) C. BFA, Sch. Art Inst., Chgo., 1965; MFA, Pratt Inst., Bklyn., 1967. Instr. Phila. Coll. Art., 1967-72, U. Colo., Boulder, 1972-73; asst. prof. painting Phila. Coll. Art., 1973; assoc. prof. Phila Coll. Art., 1979-82; prof. Phila. Coll. Art., 1982-87, Queens Coll., CUNY, 1987—. One-person shows include Allen Meml. Art Mus., Oberlin, Ohio, 1980, Hudson River Mus., Yonkers, N.Y., 1981, Milw. Art Mus., 1982, Pam Adler Gallery, N.Y.C., 1983, Albright-Knox Art Gallery, Buffalo, 1985, Queens Mus., Flushing, N.Y., 1990, Charles More Gallery, Phila., 1990-96, AIR Gallery, N.Y.C., 1992, Neuberger Mus., Purchase, N.Y., 1999; exhibited in group shows The Contemporary Art Ctr., Cin., 1980, Whitney Mus. Art, N.Y.C., 1980, Hayden Art Gallery, MIT, Cambridge, 1981, Jacksonville (Fla.) Art Mus., 1982; represented in permanent collections Guggenheim Mus., N.Y.C., Bklyn. Mus. Art, Phila. Mus. Art, Richmond (Va.) Mus. Fine Arts, Denver Art Mus., Allen Meml. Art Mus., Oberlin; commns. include L.A. Metro Rail Sys., 1992-93, Criminal Justice Ctr., Phila., Dept. Arts and Culture, 1995. Grantee NEA, 1975, 78, 81, 87, Creative Artists Pub. Service, 1978. Mem. NOW, Amnesty Internat., Coll. Art Assn. Home: 139 W 19th St New York NY 10011-4105 Office: CUNY Queens Coll Art Dept Klapper # 172 Flushing NY 11367-0904

CARLSON, DALE ARVID, university dean; b. Aberdeen, Wash., Jan. 10, 1925; s. Edwin C.G. and Anna A. (Anderson) C.; m. Jean M. Stanton, Nov. 11, 1948; children: Dale Ronald, Gail L. Carlson Manahan Joan M. Carlson Lee, Gwen D. Carlson Lundgren. AA, Grays Harbor Coll., 1947; BSCE, U. Wash., 1950, MS, 1951; PhD, U. Wis., 1960. Registered profl. engr., Wash. Water engr. City of Aberdeen, 1951-55; asst. prof., assoc. prof., prof., chmn. dept. civil engring. U. Wash., Seattle, 1955-76; dean (Coll Engring.) U. Wash., 1976-80, dean emeritus, 1980—, dir. Valle Scandinavian Exch ., 1980—; chmn. dept. civil engring. Seattle U., 1983-88, acting dean sci. and engring., 1990, dean sci. and engring., 1990-92; vis. prof. Tech. U. Denmark, Copenhagen, 1970, Royal Coll. Agr., Uppsala, Sweden, 1976, 78. Contbr. articles to profl. jours. Mem. exec. bd. Pacific N.W. Synod Luth. Ch. in Am., chmn. fin. com., 1980-84, treas., 1986-87, bd. edn., fin. com. Evang. Luth. Ch. in Am., 1987-91; v.p. Nat. Luth. Campus Ministry, 1988-91; treas. N.W. Washington synod Evang. Luth. Ch. in Am., 1996—; mem. exec. bd. Nordic Heritage Mus., 1981-86; bd. dirs. Hearthstone Retirement Ctrs., 1984-93, Evergreen Safety Coun., 1980-86. With AUS, 1943-45. Named Outstanding Grad. Weatherwax High Sch., Aberdeen, 1972, Outstanding Grad. Grays Harbor Coll., 1947; guest of honor Soppeldagene, Trondheim, 1978. Mem. ASCE, Am. Soc. Engring. Educators, Am. Acad. Environ. Engring., Water Pollution Control Fedn., Am. Water Works Assn., Am. Scandinavian Found., Swedish Water Hygiene Assn., Swedish Am. C. of C. (bd. dirs. 1994-99), Rainier Club, Chi Epsilon (hon.). Home: 9235 41st Ave NE Seattle WA 98115-3801 Office: U Wash 103 Wilson Box 352130 Seattle WA 98195-2130

CARLSON, DALE BICK, writer; b. N.Y.C., May 24, 1935; d. Edgar M. and Estelle (Cohen) Bick; children: Daniel, Hannah. BA, Wellesley Coll., 1957. Lic. wildlife rehabilitator, 1991. Pres. Bick Pub. House, 1993—; founder, pres. Bick Pub. House, 1993—. Author children's books, adult books 1961—, including: Perkins the Brain, 1964, The House of Perkins, 1965, Miss Maloo, 1966, The Brainstormers, 1966, Frankenstein, 1968, Counting Is Easy, 1969, Your Country, 1969, Arithmetic 1, 2, 3, 1969, The Electronic Teabowl, 1969, Warlord of the Genji, 1970, The Beggar King of China, 1971, The Mountain of Truth (Spring Festival Honor book, named Am. Library Assn. Notable Book), 1972, Good Morning Danny, 1972, Good Morning, Hannah, 1972, The Human Apes, 1973 (named Am. Library Assn. Notable Book), Girls Are Equal Too, 1973 (named Am. Library Assn. Notable Book), Baby Needs Shoes, 1974, Triple Boy, 1976, Where's Your Head?, 1971 (Christopher award), The Plant People, 1977, The Wild Heart, 1977, The Shining Pool, 1979, Lovingsex for Both Sexes, 1979, Boys Have Feelings Too, 1980, Call Me Amanda, 1981, Manners That Matter, 1982, The Frog People, 1982, Charlie the Hero, 1983, 1984-85: The Jenny Dean Science Fiction Mysteries, The Mystery of the Shining Children, The Mystery of the Hidden Trap, The Secret of the Third Eye, The James Budd Mysteries, The Mystery of Galaxy Games, The Mystery of Operation Brain, 1985, Miss Mary's Husbands, 1988, Basic Manuals in Wildlife Rehabilitation Series (6 vols.), 1993-94, Basic Manuals for Friends of the Disabled Series, 1995-96, Living With Disabilities, 1997, Wildlife Care for Birds and Mammals, 1997, Stop the Pain: Meditations for Teenagers, 1998, Confessions of a Brain-Impaired Writer: A Memoir, 1998. Mem. Authors League Am., Authors Guild. Address: 307 Neck Rd Madison CT 06443-2755

CARLSON, DAVID BRET, lawyer; b. Jamestown, N.Y., Aug. 16, 1918; s. David Albert and Gertrude (Johnson) C.; m. Jane Tapley, Apr. 12, 1947; children: Christopher Tapley, David Kurt, Nancy Berners-Lee. A.B., Brown U., 1940; LL.B., Harvard U., 1947. Bar: N.Y. 1947, U.S. Supreme Ct. 1972. Assoc. Debevoise & Plimpton, N.Y.C., 1947-53, ptnr., 1953-87. Contbr. articles to profl. pubs. Mem. ABA, N.Y. State Bar Assn., Bar Assn. City of N.Y. Home: PO Box 32 275 W Falmouth Hwy West Falmouth MA 02574

CARLSON, DAVID EMIL, physicist; b. Weymouth, Mass., Mar. 5, 1942; s. Emil Algot and Anne Alice (Salomaa) C.; m. Mary Ann Lewinski, June, 1966; children: Eric, Darcey. B.S. in Physics, Rensselaer Poly. Inst., 1963; Ph.D. in Physics, Rutgers U., 1968. Research scientist U.S. Army Nuclear Effects Lab., Edgewood Arsenal, Md., 1968-69; head photovoltaic device research RCA Labs., Princeton, N.J., 1970-83; dep. gen. mgr., dir. research Solarex Thin Film Div., Newtown, Pa., 1983-86, gen. mgr., 1986-88, v.p., 1988-98; chief scientist Solarex, 1999—. Contbr. articles to profl. jours. Served to capt. Signal Corps U.S. Army, 1968-70, Vietnam. Decorated Bronze Star medal; recipient Ross Coffin Purdy award Am. Ceramic Soc., 1976, Outstanding Achievement award RCA Labs., 1973, 76, Walton Clark medal Franklin Inst., 1986, Karl W. Boer Solar Energy medal of merit U. Del. and Internat. Solar Energy Soc., 1995. Fellow IEEE (co-recipient Morris N. Liebmann award 1984, William R. Cherry award 1988); mem. Am. Phys. Soc., Am. Vacuum Soc., Sigma Xi. Patentee in field; inventor amorphous silicon solar cell, 1974. Home: 1 Buckingham Dr Princeton NJ 08540-4313 Office: Solarex 3601 La Grange Pkwy Toano VA 23168 *My career in science has resulted from a curiosity about the workings of nature and a desire to use the phenomena and materials of nature to benefit society.*

CARLSON, DAVID NOEL, landscape architect, sculptor; b. Janesville, Wis., Feb. 5, 1938; s. Harold Raymond and Martha Ellen (Erickson) C.; m. Connie Kay Anderson, June 10, 1961; children: Scott, Bruce, Erik, Heather. Metall. Engr., U. Wis., 1959, BS in Landscape Architecture, 1964. Registered landscape architect, Ill. Landscape architect Milw. County Park Commn., 1965-68, William Nelson & Assocs., Milw., 1968-70; chief landscape architect City of Chgo., 1970-72; landscape architect Lipp/Wehler Ptnrs., Winfield, Ill., 1972-77; prin., owner D.N. Carlson & Assocs., Chgo., 1977-84; supt. planning Peoria (Ill.) Park Dist., 1984-89; gen. mgr. design group Green View Nursery, Dunlap, Ill., 1989-92; group leader landscape architecture State Farm Ins., Bloomington, Ill., 1992—; owner, landscape architect David N. Carlson & Assocs., Peoria, Ill., 1998—; design cons. Peoria City Beautiful, 1988-89, 95-96, J.S. James Co., Northbrook, Ill., 1977-84, Constitution Garden, Peoria, 1988-89. Author: (book of poetry) Reflected Visions, 1995. Mem. Peoria City Beautiful, 1986-88. Recipient Gold Key landscape architecture-recreation Chgo. Area Homebuilders Assn., 1974-79, Silver key landscape architecture-planning Chgo. Area Homebuilders Assn., 1977-78, gold award Wis. Landscape Fedn., Waukesha, 1993, merit award Ill. Landscape Contractors Assn., East Peoria, 1995. Mem. Am. Soc. Landscape Architect, Profl. Grounds Mgmt. Soc., Soc. Am. Registered Archs. Democrat. Avocations: tennis, writing, poetry. Home: 905 E Melbourne Ave Peoria IL 61603-2023 Office: State Farm Ins 1 State Farm Plz Bloomington IL 61710-0001

CARLSON, DESIREE ANICE, pathologist; b. Clinton, Iowa, June 10, 1950; d. Donald Richard and Bernice Elfriede (Jacobs) C.; m. Helmut Gunther Rennke; stepchildren: Stephanie Rennke, Christianne Rennke. MD, Duke U., 1975. Diplomate in anat. and clin. pathology, blood banking and cytopathology Am. Bd. Pathology. Resident in pathology U. Wash., Seattle, 1975-76, N.E. Deaconess Hosp., Boston, 1976-77, Peter Bent Brigham Hosp., Boston, 1977-79; pathologist W. Roxbury VA Med. Ctr., Boston, 1979-82; med. dir. blood bank Univ. Hosp., Boston, 1982-90; assoc. chief pathology N.E. Meml. Hosp., Stoneham, Mass., 1990-93; chief pathology Brockton (Mass.) Hosp., 1993—; asst. prof. pathology Boston U. Sch. Med., 1982—; cons. pathology Brigham and Women's Hosp., Boston, 1984-95; mem. adv. bd. ARC, Dedham, 1982-96. Contbr. articles to profl. jours., book chpts. Recipient Outstanding Contbd. Article award Med. Lab. Observer, 1988. Mem. Coll. Am. Pathologists (N.E. regional commr. 1991—), Am. Med. Women's Assn., Am. Assn. Blood Banks, Mass. Med. Soc. (coms.), Mass. Pathology Soc., N.E. Pathology Soc., N.E. Pathology Soc. (sec. 1996-98, treas. 1998—). Republican. Presbyterian. Avocations: aerobic exercise, bicycling, hiking. Office: Brockton Hosp 680 Centre St Brockton MA 02302-3395

CARLSON, DEVON MCELVIN, architect, educator; b. Topeka, Dec. 1, 1917; s. Gustave Elvin and Gertrude M. (Swanson) C.; m. Mary E. Ackley, June 14, 1949; children: Mitchell Lans, Martha Sue, Judith Ann, Peter DeVon. BS in Architecture, U. Kans., 1941; BS in Archtl. Engring. with honors, U. Colo., 1947; MS in Architecture, Columbia U., 1949. Mem. faculty U. Colo., 1943-81, prof., chmn. dept. architecture and archtl. engring., 1959-62, dean Sch. Architecture, 1962-70, dean Coll. Environ. Design, 1970-71, dean emeritus, 1981—, mem. steering com. Creative Arts Program, 1959-80; lectr. civic and profl. groups; past mem. Colo. Bd. Examiners Architects, pres., 1964-65. Co-author: An Approach to Architectural Design, 1950, Architecture/Colorado, 1966; contbr. articles to profl. jours. Past mem. Boulder Landmarks Bd.; advisor emeritus Nat. Trust for Hist. Preservation; mem. Colo. Hist. Preservation Rev. Bd., 1980-84, 85-93. Recipient Stearns award 1972, Disting. Alumnus award U. Kans., 1984; Columbia U. scholar, 1948. Fellow AIA (bd. dirs. Colo. chpt. 1966-67, pres. 1969, nat. scholarship com. chmn. 1977-78, mem. nat. com. on hist. resources 1978—, Silver medal Western Mountain region 1980, Carlson Lecture series established in his honor 1981); mem. Nat. Coun. Archtl. Registration Bds. (exam-devel. com. 1962-76, 87-93, chmn. 1975, editor Handbook 1976), Colo. Soc. Architects (pres. 1980), Assn. Coll. Schs. Architecture, Am. Soc. Engring. Edn. (past chmn. Colo. chpt.), Boulder C. of C., Rocky Mountain Liturg Art Assn., Hist. Boulder, Hist. Denver, Soc. Archtl. Historians, Scarab Club, Triangle Club, Rotary (bd. dirs.), Tau Beta Pi, Delta Phi Delta, Chi Epsilon. Address: 5472 White Pl Boulder CO 80303-1227

CARLSON, DONALD OTTO, magazine publisher, editor; b. Gary, Ind., Oct. 4, 1926. BA in Journalism, History, English, Ind. U., 1949. Spot news reporter Walla Walla (Wash.) Union Bulletin; mem. staff Inside Mich., Vance Pub. Corp., Chgo.; editor various, Chgo. and N.Y.C.; prin., owner CMN Assocs., Inc., Calif., 1964—. Editor, pub. Automated Builder, 1974—. Founder Automated Builders Consortium, 1993, ABC Saved shelter, 1999. Recipient five nat. journalism awards. Mem. Soc. Profl. Journalists, Wood Truss Council Am. (hall of fame 1988), Wood Found. Inst. (co-founder 1980).

CARLSON, E. DEAN, state official. Sec. Dept. Transp., Topeka. Office: Transp Dept Docking State Office Bldg Fl 7 Topeka KS 66612-1568*

CARLSON, EDWARD C., anatomy educator; b. Iron Mountain, Mich., Feb. 22, 1942; s. Clarence H. and Rachel O. (Olsen) C.; m. Pam R. Carlson, 1995; children: Scott Edward, Susan Rebecca. BA, Bethel Coll., 1964; PhD, U. N.D., 1970. Spl. instr. dept. biology Bethel Coll., St. Paul, 1964-66; instr. anatomy U. Ariz., Tucson, 1970-72, asst. prof., 1972-77; assoc. prof. human anatomy U. Calif., Davis, 1977-81, prof., 1981—; chmn. dept. anatomy and cell biology U. N.D., Grand Forks, 1981—; rsch. anatomist Calif. Primate Rsch. Ctr., Davis, 1982-85, rsch. affiliate, 1985—; co-dir. N.D. Diabetes Ocular Rsch. Ctr., Grand Forks, 1988—. Contbr. articles to profl. jours. Rsch. grantee Juvenile Diabetes Found., 1978-80, NIH, 1979-82, 81-85, Exptl. Program to Stimulate Competitive Rsch., NSF, 1987-91. Mem. Am. Assn. Anatomists, Am. Assn. Pathologists, Am. Soc. Cell Biology, Soc. Devel. Biology, Microcirculatory Soc. Avocations: running, fishing, skiing. Office: U ND Dept Anatomy & Cell Biol Grand Forks ND 58202

CARLSON, ELIZABETH ANNE, library director; b. Nov. 25, 1944. MLIS, Wayne State U., Detroit; B.A., N. Park Coll., Chicago. Libr. dir. White Lake Cmty. Libr., Whitehall, Mich., 1984—. E-mail: whieac@lakeland.lib.mi.us.

CARLSON, FREDA ELLEN, educator, consultant; b. Wilmington, Ohio, Jan. 4, 1914; d. Heber W. and Hazel (Reed) Custis; m. Raymond A. Carlson, June 15, 1940; children: Susan Ann Lapp, Philip Reed. MA in Adminstrn., Toledo U., 1967, MA in Teaching and Reading, EdS, 1972. Tchr. elem. Highland Sch., Sylvania, Ohio, 1963-68; from tchr. to supr. Lucas County Schs., Toledo, 1968-76; cons. to tchrs. Lucas County Schs., 1969-76, ret., 1976; tchr. adult continuing edn. Toledo U., 1961-76. Guardian ad litem Ohio Juvenile Ct., 1976-84: Sarasota County High Sch. Acad. Olympics, 1991—. Recipient Woman of Toledo award St. Vincent Hosp. Guild, 1984. Mem. Internat. Reading Assn. (pres. 1980-81), Nat. Middle Sch. Assn. (sec. 1978-79), AAUW (1st v.p. 1990—), Phi Delta Kappa, Pi Lambda Theta (pres. 1970-72), Delta Kappa Gamma (pres. 1974-76), Phi Kappa Phi. Republican. Lutheran.

CARLSON, GARY R., publishing executive; b. Ishpeming, Mich.; s. James H. and Vivian M. (Maki) C.; m. Mardee G. Parkinson, Aug. 21, 1963 (div.Apr. 21, 1991); children: Bruce S., Robyn L.; m. Maryanne Koschier, June 25, 1994. BA Far Eastern Langs. and Lit., U. Mich., 1969. Sales rep. John Wiley and Sons, Ann Arbor, Mich., 1970-72; editor John Wiley and Sons, N.Y.C., 1972-80, pub., 1980-84; pres. SoftPress, Inc., Monroe, N.Y., 1984-86; v.p., dir. acquisitions W.H. Freeman and Co./Scientific Am. Books, N.Y.C., 1986-92; v.p., editor-in-chief Macmillan Coll. Pub., Inc., N.Y.C., 1992-94; v.p., editorial dir., publisher Wadsworth Pub. Co., Belmont, Calif., 1994—. Editor: (textbooks and trade books) General Chemistry by James B. Brady, 1975, Organic Chemistry by T.W.G. Solomons, 1976, Fundamentals of General, Organic and Biological Chemistry by John R. Holom, 1978, Basic Inorganic Chemistry by A. Cotton and G. Wilkinson, 1977; contbg. author: The Videodisc Book, 1984. With USAF, 1963-69, Taiwan. Mem. Am. Assn. Pubs. Office: Wadsworth Pub Co 10 Davis Dr Belmont CA 94002-3002*

CARLSON, GEORGE ARTHUR, artist; b. Elmhurst, Ill., July 3, 1940; s. William Emanuel and Mathilda Katherine (Jorgensen) C.; m. Pamela Gustavson Hatzenbiler, May 9, 1981; children: Solon Emil, Andra Sean, Erin Hatzenbiler Vaughan, Eric Hatzenbiler. Student, Am. Acad. Art, Chgo., U. Ariz., Tucson. lectr. 1st U.S./Soviet Art Summit, Tretyakov Mus., Moscow, 1989. One man exhbns. include Indpls. Mus. Art, 1979, 85, Smithsonian Inst., Washington, 1982, Southwest Mus., L.A., 1988, Autry Western Heritage Mus., 1993, Gilcrease Mus., Tulsa, 1994, Ft. Worth Zoo Art Gallery, 1995-96; one man shows include Saks Gallery, Colorado Springs, Colo., 1972, Kennedy Galleries, N.Y.C., 1976, Bishop Galleries, Scottsdale, Ariz., 1977, Stremmel Galleries, Reno, 1978, 81, Grand Cen. Galleries, N.Y.C., 1980, O'Grady Galleries, Chgo., 1977, 83, Gerald Peters Gallery, Santa Fe, N.Mex., 1977, 85, 88, 92, Gerald Peters Gallery, Dallas, 1987, Farber Gallery Fine Arts, Indpls., 1989, Kneeland Gallery, Sun Valley, Idaho, 1990, 93, 94, Fenn Galleries, 1993; featured in group exhbns. including Phoenix Art Mus., Denver Art Mus., Denver Natural History Mus., Penrose Library at U. Denver, Gillette Pub. Library, Wyoming, Nat. Acad. Western Art, Oklahoma City, 1973-87, The Peking Exhibit, Beijing, Peoples Republic of China, 1981, Artists of Am. Show, Denver, 1981-87, Nat. Sculpture Soc., N.Y.C., 1982-83, 86, 90, Mus. Western Art, Denver, 1985, Gilcrease Mus., Tulsa, 1985, Ft. Smith (Okla.) Art Ctr., 1986, Kyoto (Japan) World Expn. Hist. Cities, 1987, Sonoma County Mus., Santa Rosa, Calif., 1987, Western & Wildlife Mus., Jackson Hole, Wyo., 1988, Amerika Haus, Berlin, 1990, Nat. Acad. Design, N.Y.C., 1990, Hubbard Mus., Riudoso, N.Mex., 1990, Hakone Open-Air Mus.,Tokyo, 1991, Denver 7 Show Nat. Cowboy Hall of Fame, 1992, 93, others; represented in pub. and corp. collections including Indpls. Mus., Genesee Mus., Rochester, N.Y., Denver Pub. Library, Denver Natural History Mus., Los Angeles Athletic Club, Cherokee Nat. Hist. Soc., Chakota, Okla., Corning (N.Y.) Mus., Anshutz Collection, Denver, Outdoor Mus. Art, Denver, Rockwell Mus., Pitts., Bank of Am., Las Vegas, Boatmans Bankshare, Inc., St. Louis, Brownsville (Tex.) Nat. Bank, Mountain States Bank, Denver, Rocky Mountain Bank, Denver, Sierra Nev. Arts Mus., Reno, Nat. Cowboy Hall of Fame, Oklahoma City, Mobile Oil Corp.; represented in various pvt. corp. and mus. collections, including U.S. Embassy, Copenhagen, Tucson Mus. Art, Manville Corp., Denver, L.A. Athletic Club, Rockwell Internat., others; sculptures include Bill Cosby, 1979, Bill Harrah, 1981, Early Day Miner, Washington Park, Denver, 1980, Of One Heart, Genesee Country Mus., 1982, Of One Heart, Mus. of Outdoor Arts, Englewood, Colo., 1985, I'm the Drum, Bank Am., Las Vegas, 1987, The Greeting, Genesee Mus., 1988, Eiteljorg Mus., 1989, Paul Robeson Cen. State U., Wilberforce, Ohio, 1990, Phylicia Rashad, 1991, I'm the Drum, Colo. Springs Fine Arts Ctr., 1994, Old Blue, Amon Carter Mus., Ft. Worth, 1995, Ennis Cosby, 1997, Mane of Wind-Neck of Thunder, Kirkland, Wash., 1999; featured in various bibliographies and films. Served with USAR, 1963-69. Recipient gold medal Nat. Acad. Western Art, 1974, 78, 80, 85, 89, Prix de West, 1975, Silver medal, 1976, 81, 88, Robert Lougheed award, 1989, Gold medal, 1989; Merit award Western Rendezvous Show, 1983. Mem. Nat. Sculpture Soc., Nat. Acad. Western Art (Gold medal 1974, 78, 80, 85, (2) 1989, Best of Show 1975, Silver medal 1976, 81, 88). Address: PO Box 28 Harrison ID 83833-0028 also: Erin Vaughan Pvt Dealer Franktown CO 80116

CARLSON, GUSTAV GUNNAR, anthropology educator; b. Gwinn, Mich., Nov. 21, 1909; s. Axel Victor and Brita Christina (Mattson) C.; m. Edith Elizabeth Erickson, Nov. 15, 1933; children: Karen Elizabeth Carlson Ogden, Eric Gustav. AB, No. Mich. U., 1932; MA, U. Mich., 1934, PhD, 1940. Instr. anthropology U. Cin., 1936-40, asst. prof. anthropology, 1940-43, assoc. prof. anthropology, 1946-52, prof. anthropology, 1952-80, head dept. sociology & anthropology, 1961-69, head dept. anthropology, 1969-77, prof. emeritus, 1980—; vis. prof. U. Yunnan, China, 1945; cons. in field. Rockefeller Found. fellow, 1933; recipient A.B. Cohen award Excellence in Univ. Tchg. U. Cin., 1961-62, Disting. Alumni award No. Mich. U., 1981. Mem. Phi Beta Kappa, Sigma Xi. Avocations: gardening, photography, bread baking.

CARLSON, JAMES ROY, animal science educator; b. Windsor, Colo., Mar. 9, 1939; married; two children. BS, Colo. State U., 1961; MS, U. Wis., 1964, PhD in Biochemistry, 1966. From asst. prof. animal sci. Wash. State U., 1966-70, assoc. prof. animal sci., 1971-75, chmn. grad. program nutrition, 1973-83, prof. animal sci., 1976-96, assoc. dean of rsch., 1996—; chmn. dept. animal sci. Wash. State U., 1982-93, assoc. dir. agr. rsch. ctr., 1993-94, assoc. dean agr. rsch. ctr., 1994—. Mem. Am. Inst. Nutrition, Am. Soc. Animal Sci., Soc. Exptl. Biol. Medicine. Office: Washington State Univ Coll Agr & Home Econom Rsch Ctr Agr Rsch Ctr Pullman WA 99164-6240

CARLSON, JANET FRANCES, psychologist, educator; b. Newport, R.I., Oct. 3, 1957; d. Robert Carl and Alice Marion (Orina) C.; m. Kurt Francis Geisinger, Sept. 22, 1984. BS summa cum laude, Union Coll., Schenectady, 1979; MA in Clin. Psychology, Fordham U., 1982, PhD in Clin. Psychology, 1987. Lic. psychologist, N.Y.; cert. sch. psychologist, N.Y., Conn. Clin. psychology intern Conn. Valley Hosp., Middletown, Conn., 1983-84; rsch. fellow Schering-Plough Found., Bronx, N.Y., 1984-85; psychologist I Creedmoor Psychiat. Ctr., Queens Village, N.Y., 1985-86; psychologist Hallen Sch., Mamaroneck, N.Y., 1986-88; asst. prof. psychology Fordham U., Bronx, N.Y., 1988-89; asst. prof. sch. and applied psychology Fairfield (Conn.) U., 1989-93, dir. sch. and applied psychology programs, 1989-90; asst. prof. counseling and psychol. svcs. SUNY, Oswego, 1993-95, assoc. prof., 1995-98, prof., 1998—, assoc. dean Sch. Edn., 1998—; cons. N.Y.C. Bd. Edn. Office Rsch., Evaluation and Assessment, 1988-92; vis. asst. prof. psychology LeMoyne Coll., Syracuse, N.Y., 1992-93. Recipient Sugarfree scholarship, 1984-85, Sigma Xi Grant-in-Aid of Research, 1984-85. Mem. APA, Am. Ednl. Rsch. Assn., NASP, Ea. Psychol. Assn., N.Y. State Psychol. Assn., Northeastern Ednl. Rsch. Assn. (editor newsletter 1988-91, bd. dirs. 1990-93, pres. 1995-96), N.Y. Assn. Sch. Psychologists, Sigma Xi, Psi Chi (charter), Phi Kappa Phi (charter, pres. 1995-96). Avocations: wildlife preservation, conservation issues.

CARLSON, JOHN DENNIS, JR., accountant; b. St. Petersburg, Fla., Oct. 7, 1969; s. John Dennis and Peggy Lynn (Neese) C.; m. Paula Jean Waterstradt, Aug. 13, 1994. BS, U. Mich., 1991, MS, 1992, MBA, 1995. CPA. Fin. planner Am. Express Fin. Svcs., Ann Arbor, Mich., 1992-94; assoc. PriceWaterhouseCoopers LLP, Chgo., 1995-96, sr. assoc., 1996-98; mgr. PriceWaterhouseCoopers LLP, Mich., 1998—. Mem. AICPA, Ill. CPA Soc., U. Mich. Bus. Ch. Club of Chgo. Home: 2848 Pittsfield Blvd Ann Arbor MI 48104 Office: PriceWaterhouseCoopers LLP 400 Renaissance Dr Detroit MI 48243-1507

CARLSON, JOHN EARL, lawyer; b. Seattle, May 18, 1952; s. William Richard and H. Joan (Fitzpatrick) C.; m. Audrey Fucilla, Aug. 31, 1984; children: William Grant, Andrew Ivan. AA, Wenatchee Valley Coll., 1972; BA, U. Wash., 1975; JD, U. Puget Sound, 1978. Bar: Wash. 1975, Ill. 1980, Calif. 1980. Asst. to pres. ABA, Chgo., 1978-80; assoc. Lawler, Felix & Hall, L.A., 1980-84; assoc. Brobeck, Phleger & Harrison, San Francisco, 1984-86, ptnr., 1986—. Bd. visitors Sch. Law, U. Puget Sound, Tacoma, 1982—. Mem. ABA (nat. v.p. law student divsn. 1977-78), Wash. State Bar Assn., Bar Assn. of San Francisco (chmn. bridge the gap com. 1985-87), State Bar of Calif., Ill. State Bar Assn. Roman Catholic. Avocations: basketball, skiing, running, art. Office: Brobeck Phleger & Harrison Spear St Tower 1 Market Plz San Francisco CA 94105

CARLSON, J(OHN) PHILIP, lawyer; b. Shickley, Nebr., Apr. 16, 1915; s. Christopher Theodore and Klara Louise (Blomquist) C.; m. Maryjo Suverkrup, Oct. 14, 1950. AB, Wayne State Coll., 1935; MA, Columbia U., 1967; JD, Georgetown U., 1951. Bar: D.C. 1952, U.S. Dist. Ct. D.C. 1952, U.S. Ct. Appeals D.C. cir. 1952, U.S. Supreme Ct. 1957, U.S. Ct. Mil. Appeals 1970, D.C. Ct. Appeals 1972. Tchr., athletic coach high schs. of Bristow, Nebr., 1935-37, Carroll, Nebr., 1937-38, Ashland, Nebr., 1938-42; vets. rels. advisor OPA, Washington, 1946-47; tng. specialist Dept. Navy, 1947-56; minority counsel House Com. on Govt. Ops., 1956-80; pvt. practice, Washington, 1980-93. Bd. dirs. Fellowship Sq. Found., Reston, Va., 1961-86,

Peter Muehlenberg Meml. Assn., 1972-86. Capt. USAAF, 1942-45; ETO. Congl. Staff fellow Am. Polit. Sci. Assn., 1964-65, 66-67; Decorated D.F.C., Air medal with oak leaf cluster; recipient Meritorious Svc. award Am. Nat. Standards Inst., 1984, Meritorious Svc. award Fellowship Square Found., 1986. Mem. ABA, Fed. Bar Assn., D.C. Bar Assn., Am. Judicature Soc., Am. Econ. Assn., Air Force Assn., Res. Officers Assn., Metropolitan Club, Capitol Hill Club, George Town Club, Nat. Econs. Club, Belle Haven Country Club. Republican. Lutheran. Home: 2206 Belle Haven Rd Alexandria VA 22307-1100

CARLSON, KATHLEEN BUSSART, law librarian; b. Charlotte, N.C., June 25, 1956; d. Dean Allyn and Joan (Parlette) Bussart; m. Gerald Mark Carlson, Aug. 15, 1987. BA in Polit. Sci., Ohio State U., 1977; JD, Capital U., 1980; MA in Libr. and Info. Sci., U. Iowa, 1986. Bar: Ohio 1980 (inactive). Editor Lawyers Coop. Pub. Co., Rochester, N.Y., 1980-83; asst. state law libr. State of Wyo., Cheyenne, 1987-88, state law libr., 1988—. 2d v.p., bd. dirs. Wyo. coun. Girl Scouts U.S., Casper, 1990-92, 1st v.p., bd. dirs., 1993-96. Mem. Am. Assn. Law Librs. (sec.-treas., state, ct. and county SIS 1992-95, SCCLL edn. com. 1991-92, chair grants com. 1997-98, nominating com. 1998-99, indexing legal periodical lit. adv. com. 1993-96, chair 1994-96, scholarship com. 1996-98, citation format com. 1998—), Western Pacific Assn. Law Librs. (pres. 1996-97), Wyo. Libr. Assn. (sec. acad. and spl. librs. sect. 1990-92, pres. 1994-95), Bibliog. Ctr. for Rsch. (trustee 1991-95), Kappa Delta, Beta Phi Mu, Zonta Internat. Avocations: arts and crafts, baking. Home: 911 E 18th St Cheyenne WY 82001-4722 Office: State Law Libr Supreme Ct Bldg 2301 Capitol Ave Cheyenne WY 82002

CARLSON, KENNETH GEORGE, data processing executive; b. Duluth, Minn., Dec. 14, 1949; s. George Bernard and Laura Anna (Larson) C.; m. Stephanie Venn Petersen, Sept. 20, 1969; children: Laura, Anna. BSEE, U. Minn., 1972. Cert. in data processing; cert. systems profl. Systems programmer U. Minn. Computer Ctr., Mpls., 1969-74; dept. mgr. United Computing System, Kansas City, Mo., 1974-80; computer scientist Computer Scis. Corp., Falls Church, Va., 1980-82; pres., chmn. bd. LSS Data Systems, Mpls., 1982-86, 87—; v.p. Minn. Supercomputer Ctr., Mpls., 1986-87, asst. to exec. v.p., 1987-90; data processing advisor Johnson Community Coll., Overland Park, Kans., 1975-78; bd. dirs., chief fin. officer Superior Resources, Duluth, 1985—. Mem. Minn. Regional Network (corp. sec. 1987-88). Republican. Mem. United Ch. of Christ. Avocations: cross country skiing, downhill skiing, travel. Office: LSS Data Systems 6423 City W Pkwy Eden Prairie MN 55344-3246

CARLSON, LARRY VERNON, insurance company executive; b. Geneseo, Ill., Apr. 15, 1943; s. Vernon L. and Marjorie I. (Daniels) C.; m. Janet E. Dingwell; children: Kathleen J. Carlson Smith, Laurel E. Carlson Lewis. BS, Iowa Wesleyan Coll., 1965. CLU. Salesman Northwestern Mut. Life, Mt. Pleasant, Iowa, 1965-68; tng. asst. Northwestern Mut. Life, Milw., 1968-71; dir. devel. Northwestern Mut. Life, South Bend, Ind., 1971-81; gen. agt. Northwestern Mut. Life, Columbus, Ohio, 1981—. Chmn. bd. dirs. Goodwill Rehab. Ctr., Columbus, 1991-93; pres. Worthington Hills Civic Assn., Columbus, 1983-84. Mem. CLU Assn. (pres. Columbus chpt. 1993-94), Northwestern Mut. Gen. Agts. Assn. (pres. 1993-94), Gen. Agts. and Mgrs. Assn. (pres. 1982-83, Nat. Mgmt. award 1991), Rotary (Group Study Exch. 1977). Republican. Methodist. Avocations: tennis, golf, travel. Home: 7626 Oakhurst Ln Columbus OH 43235-1642 Office: Northwestern Mut Life 580 S High St Columbus OH 43215-5644

CARLSON, LEROY THEODORE, JR., telecommunications industry executive; b. 1946. AB, Harvard U., 1968, MBA, 1971. Fin. analyst, mgr. fin. analysis and planning, mgr. acctg. Singer Corp., 1971-74; v.p. Telephone and Data Systems, Inc., 1974-78, exec. v.p., 1978-81, pres., 1981-86, pres., CEO, 1981—; chmn. bd. Am. Paging Sys., Inc., 1998; chmn. bd. Am. Paging, Inc., TDS Telecomm., U.S. Cellular Corp., Am. Portable Telecom. Mem. U.S. Telephone Assn. (bd. dirs.), Nat. Rural Telecom. Assn. (bd. dirs.). Office: Telephone & Data Sys Inc 30 N La Salle St Ste 4000 Chicago IL 60602-2507*

CARLSON, LOREN MERLE, political science educator; b. Mitchell, S.D., Nov. 2, 1923; s. Clarence A. and Edna M. (Rosenquist) C.; m. Verona Gladys Hole, Dec. 21, 1950; children: Catherine Ann, Bradley Reed, Nancy Jewel. BA, Yankton Coll., 1948; MA, U. Wis., 1952; JD, George Washington U., 1961. Bar: S.D. 1961, U.S. Supreme Ct. 1976. Asst. dir. Govt. Rsch. Bur., U. S.D., 1949-51; orgn. and methods examiner Dept. State, Washington, 1951-52; asst. dir. legis. rsch. State of S.D., 1953-55, dir., 1955-59, budget officer, 1963-68; rsch. asst. to U.S. Senator from S.D., 1959-60, adminstrv. asst., 1960-63; dir. statewide edn. svcs. U. S.D., Vermillion, 1968-74, dean continuing edn., 1974-87, assoc. prof. polit. sci., 1968-79, prof., 1979-89, emeritus prof. polit. sci., 1989—; hwy. laws study dir. U. S.D. Law Sch., Vermillion, 1963; mng. editor U. S.D. Press, 1985-89, sr. editor, 1989-93; chmn. Model Rural Devel. Commn., Dist. II, State of S.D., 1972-74; chmn. Region VII Planning Commn. on Criminal Justice, S.D., 1969-74; vice-chmn. South East Coun. of Govts., 1989-90, chmn., 1993-97. Author: (with W.O. Farber and T.C. Geary) Government of South Dakota, 1979; contbr. articles profl. publs. Mem. Vermillion City Coun., 1980-90, 91-92, pres. 1982-90; mem. S.D. Humanities Found., 1989-97; bd. dirs. Vermillion Devel. Co., pres., 1987; mem. Vermillion Golf Course/Rsch. Market Analysis Study Rev. Com., 1993-94; mem. Vermillion Facilities Task Force, 1996-97; Rep. candidate State Ho. of Reps., 1986; hon. life trustee U. S.D. Found., 1998. Named Outstanding Young Man Pierre Jaycees, 1959. Fellow Nat. Univ. Continuing Edn. Assn.; mem. ASPA, S.D. Adult Edn. Assn. (chmn. 1973-74), Karl Mundt Found., Spirit Mound Trust, Nat. Meml. Mt. Rushmore Soc., Farber Found. (exec. bd. dirs. 1993-98), Vermillion Quarterback Club, Pi Sigma Alpha, Pi Kappa Delta. Republican. Lutheran. Home: 229 Catalina Ave Vermillion SD 57069-3319 Office: U SD Dept Polit Sci Vermillion SD 57069

CARLSON, LYNDON RICHARD SELVIG, state legislator, educator; b. Mpls., Apr. 18, 1940; s. Lyndon C. and Shirley (Gittens) C.; m. Carole Moss, Dec. 7, 1968; children: Tonya, Lyndon Jr., Philip. BS, Mankato State U., 1964. Mem. Minn. Ho. of Reps., St. Paul, 1972—. Recipient Pub. Svc. award Met. State U., 1983, Carroll award Minn. Vocat. Assn., 1990, Disting. Svc. award U. Minn. Extension Svc., 1990. Mem. Nat. Conf. State Legislatures (edn. com. 1987) Washington, Minn. Fedn. Tchrs. Office: Minn Ho of Reps 279 State Office Bldg Saint Paul MN 55155-1288

CARLSON, MARGARET EILEEN (PEGGY CARLSON), counselor, hypnotherapist; b. Seattle, July 20, 1946; d. Patrick William and Dorothy Christina (DeMello) Hurley; m. Jerome Cathey, Sept. 6, 1968 (div. Feb. 1994); 1 child, Michael Patrick; m. Eric VictorCarlson, Jan. 20, 1996; children: Grace, Nick. BS, Bastyr U., 1995, MA, 1998. Retail store owner Seattle, 1973-94; counselor, hypnotherapist pvt. practice, Seattle, 1995—. Named for Outstanding Cmty. Svc. U. C. of C., Seattle, 1992. Home: 4808 NE 41st St Seattle WA 98105-5112 Office: 3216 NE 45th Pl #105 Seattle WA 98105

CARLSON, MARGUERITE T., science educator; b. Altus, Okla., May 7, 1957; d. Edward A. and Anne M. (McGuire) Carlson; divorced; children: Michael, James. BS, Manhattan Coll., 1979; MA, Montclair State U., 1982; postgrad., NYU. Tchr. sci. Chelsea H.S., N.Y.C. Bd. Edn. Recipient Ellen and Ralph Merz scholarship Acad. of the Holy Angels, Demarest, N.J., 1994. Mem. Bergen County Zool. Soc. (bd. dirs. 1992—).

CARLSON, MARIAN BILLE, geneticist, researcher, educator; b. Princeton, N.J., Oct. 19, 1952; d. B.C. and L.W. Carlson; m. Stephen P. Goff, Oct. 15, 1977; children: Sarah Carlson, Thomas Carlson. BA summa cum laude, Harvard U., 1973; PhD with distinction, Stanford U., 1978. Asst. prof. genetics Columbia U., N.Y.C., 1981-87, assoc. prof., 1987-88, prof., 1988—, prof. microbiology, 1991—; mem. genetic basis of disease rev. com. NIH, 1991-95; mem. sci. adv. com. Damon Runyan-Walter Winchell Cancer Rsch. Fund, 1992-96. Assoc. editor Genetics, 1988-95, 97—; mem. editl. bd. Molecular and Cellular Biology, 1987—, Current Opinion in Genetics and Devel., 1991—, Microbiol. and Molecular Biol. Rev.; contbr. chpts. to books, articles to profl. jours. Mem. basic sci. adv. com. March of Dimes, 1993-95, mem. sci. adv. coun., 1996—; coun. mem. Harvey Soc., 1998—. NSF fellow, 1973-76, Jane Coffin Childs fellow, 1976-81; recipient Irma T. Hirschl Career Sci. award, 1982-87, Lamport award for basic rsch. Columbia U., 1987, Faculty Rsch. award Am. Cancer Soc., 1988-92, NIH Merit award, 1996. Fellow AAAS, Am. Acad. Microbiology; mem. Genetics Soc. Am. (bd. dirs. 1994-96), Am. Soc. Microbiology (lectr. ASM Found. for Microbiology 1990-91), Phi Beta Kappa, Sigma Xi. Office: Columbia U 701 W 168th St New York NY 10032-2704

CARLSON, MARILYN C., travel service company executive; b. Mpls.; m. Glen Nelson; children: Diana, Wendy, Curtis C. Student, U. Sorbonne, Paris, Inst. Hautes Etudes Econ., Geneva; degree in internat. econs. with honors, Smith Coll., 1961; DBA (hon.), Johnson & Wales U.; DHL (hon.), Coll. St. Catherine, Gustavus Adolphus Coll. Securities analyst Paine Webber, Mpls.; co-owner Citizens State Bank, Waterville, Minn., 1971—; COO Carlson Cos., Inc., Mpls., 1997—, pres., CEO, 1998—, also bd. dirs.; vice chair Carlson Holdings, Inc., 1991—; co-chair Carlson Wagonlit Travel, 1994—; disting. vis. prof. Johnson & Wales U. Pres. United Way Mpls., campaign chair, 1984; bd. dirs. United Way Am.; chair Super Bown Task Force, Mpls.; bd. dirs. U.S. Nat. Tourism Orgn., 1996—, Ctr. for Internat. Leadership, 1990—; mem. Internat. Adv. Coun., 1996—; mem. disting. adv. coun. Coll. of St. Catherine, 1989—; mem. Bretton Woods Com., 1986—; hon. bd. dris. Svenska Inst., Stockholm, 1993—; mem. adv. bd. Hubert H. Humphrey Inst. Pub. Affairs, 1992-96; co-founder Minn. Women's Econ. Roundtable, 1974—; chair Minn. Super Bowl Task Force, 1992; chair, founder Midsummer Internat. Festival of Music; co-chair New Sweden '88; past bd. dirs. Guthrie Theatre, Greater Mpls. coun. Girl Scouts U.S., Jr. Achievement, Jr. League Mpls., KTCA Pub. TV, Minn. Congl. Award, Minn. Opera Co., Women's' Assn. Minn. Symphony Orch.; trustee Smith Coll., Northampton, Mass., 1980-85, Macalester Coll., St. Paul, 1974-80. Named Woman of Yr., Minn. Exec. Women in Tourism, Sales Exec. of Yr., Sales and Mktg. Exec. of Mpls., Person of Yr., Travel Agt. mag., 1997, Woman of Yr. Roundtable for Women in Foodsvc., 1995, Outstanding Individual in Tourism, Minn. Office of Tourism, 1992, Woman of Yr., Minn. Exec. Women in Tourism, 1991-92; recipient Minn. Congl. award for initiative and svc. to cmty., cert. of commendation State of Minn., Cmty. Svc. award YWCA, Independence award Vinland Nat. Ctr., Cmty. Svc. award Park-Nicollet Med. Ctr., Outstanding Mktg. Exec. of Yr. award, Minn. Distributive Edn. Club Am., Career Achievement award Sales and Mktg. Execs. Mpls., Outstanding Achievement award United Way Mpls., Extraordinary Leadership award Greater Mpls. C. of C., Disting. Svc. award United Way of Am., 1984-90, Nat. Caring award Caring Inst., 1995, Outstanding Bus. Leader award Northwood U., 1995. Mem. Hennepin County Med. Soc. Auxiliary, Jr. League Mpls., Minn. Meetings, Smith Coll. Alumni Assn., Smith Club Mpls., Woodhill Country Club, Mpls. Club, N.W. Tennis Club, Nat. Ctr. for Social Entrepreneurs, Com. of 200, Minn. Orchestral Assn., Orphei Dranger, Alpha Kappa Psi. Office: Carlson Cos Inc PO Box 59159 Minneapolis MN 55459-8200*

CARLSON, MARVIN ALBERT, theater educator; b. Wichita, Kans., Sept. 15, 1935; s. Roy Edward and Gladys (Nelson) C.; m. Patricia Alene McElroy, Aug. 20, 1960; children—Geoffrey, Richard. B.S., U. Kans., 1957, M.A., 1959; Ph.D., Cornell U., 1961. Instr. speech and drama Cornell U., Ithaca, N.Y., 1961-62, asst. prof., 1962-66, assoc. prof. theatre arts, 1966-73, prof., 1973-79, chmn. dept., 1966-68, 73-78; dir. Cornell U. (Univ. Theatre), 1963-64, 65-66; prof. theatre and drama Ind. U., Bloomington, 1979-86, prof. comparative lit., 1984-86, disting. prof., 1986—; exec. officer PhD program in theatre Grad. Ctr. CUNY, 1986-95; Sidney E. Cohn chair in theatre CUNY, 1988—; Walker-Ames lectr. U. Wash., 1994. Author: Andre Antoine's Memories of the Theatre-Libre, 1964, The Theatre of the French Revolution, 1966, The French Stage in the Nineteenth Century, 1972, The German Stage in the Nineteenth Century, 1972, Goethe and the Weimar Theatre, 1978, The Italian Stage from Goldoni to D'Annunzio, 1981, Theories of the Theatre, 1984, The Italian Shakespearians, 1985, Places of Performance, 1989, Theatre Semiotics, 1990, Deathtraps, 1993, Performance, 1996, Voltaire and the Theatre of the Eighteenth Century, 1998. Recipient George Jean Nathan award, 1994, ATHE Career Achievement award, 1995; Guggenheim fellow, 1968, Ind. U. Soc. for Humanities fellow, 1993. Fellow Am. Theatre Assn.; mem. Am. Soc. Theatre Rsch., Internat. Assn. Theatre Critics, Am. Theatre in Higher Edn., Internat. Fedn. Theatre Rsch. Home: 421 3rd St Brooklyn NY 11215-2854 Office: CUNY Grad Grad Ctr Program in Theatre 33 W 42nd St New York NY 10036-8099

CARLSON, MARY ISABEL (MARIBEL CARLSON), county treasurer; b. Kinsley, Kans., July 26, 1931; d. Paul Doak and Minnie (Huser) Owen; m. Merle Dean Carlson, Aug. 16, 1952 (dec. 1984); children: James Dean, Gary Lee, Tommy Owen. Grad., Am. Bus. Coll., 1950; postgrad., Hays State U., 1992. Pvt. sec. Equitable of Iowa, Wichita, Kans., 1950-51; exec. sec. Wichita Jr. C. of C., 1951-52; sec. Etling & Beezley, Attys. at Law, Kinsley, 1952-55; dep. Edwards County Register of Deeds, Kinsley, 1967; ins. clk. Taylor & Sons, Ins., Kinsley, 1969-84; treas. County of Edwards, Kinsley, 1984—. Clk. election bd. Logan Twp., Edwards County, 1960-70, judge, 1960-70. Mem. Kans. County Treas. Assn., South Cen. Dist. Kans. County Treas. Assn. (pres. 1990-91, v.p. 1989-90, sec.-treas. 1988-89, hostess spring mtg. 1990). Republican. Methodist. Avocations: reading newspapers, watching TV. Office: Edwards County Treas PO Box 246 Kinsley KS 67547-0246

CARLSON, MELINDA SUZANNE, librarian; b. LaPorte, Ind., Jan. 15, 1949; d. E. Stewart and Margaret S. Carlson. BA, Colo. Women's Coll., 1972; MAL, U. Denver, 1975. Media specialist Brown County Libr., Green Bay, Wis., 1975-78; audiovisual and interlibr. loan cons. Ea. Shore Regional Libr., Salisbury, Md., 1978-81; libr. cons. Washington, 1981-83; libr. ops. mgr. USA Today, Arlington, Va., 1983-90; rsch. analyst USA Today, Arlington, 1990-93; rsch. supr. ABC News, Washington, 1993—; cons. Newspaper Assn. of Am., Reston, Va., 1991-92. Mem. ALA, Spl. Librs. Assn., Investigative Reporters and Editors. E-mail: melinda.s.carlson@abc.com. Office: ABC News 1717 DeSales St NW Washington DC 20036

CARLSON, MITCHELL LANS, international technical advisor; b. Boulder, Colo., Nov. 24, 1951; s. DeVon M. and Mary (Ackley) C. BA in History and Internat. Affairs, Lewis and Clark Coll., 1974; MA in Environ. Planning, UCLA, 1978; postgrad., U. Calif., Berkeley, 1978-80. Rsch. asst. Sch. Architecture and Urban Planning UCLA, 1977-78; project planner Calif. Energy Resource Conservation and Devel. Commn., Riverside, Calif., 1977-78, Vastu-Shilpa Found., Ahmedabad, India, 1978-79; with UNHCR, WFP, UNDP UNOps., 1974-92; chief tech. adviser UN (UNDP), Bahambang, Cambodia, 1992-95, Kigali, Rwanda, 1996-97, Sarajevo, Bosnia, 1998—. Avocations: bicycling, photography, swimming, tennis. Home: 5472 White Pl Boulder CO 80303-1227 Office: UNDP Bosnia PO Box 1608 New York NY 10163-1608

CARLSON, NATALIE TRAYLOR, publisher; b. St. Paul, Feb. 15, 1938; d. Howard Ripley and Maxine (Johnson) Smith; m. James S. Carlson, Oct. 6, 1990; children: Drew Michael, Dacia Lyn, Dana Ann. BA, Jacksonville (Ala.) State U., 1975. Dir. Madison County Assn. of Mental Health, Huntsville, Ala., 1966-67; campaign mgr. U.S. Senatorial Race, No. Ala., 1968; pub. rels. Anniston Acad., 1970-76; journalist The Anniston Star, 1970-74, The Birmingham News, 1972-76; dir. Ala. affiliate, Am. Heart Assn., Birmingham, 1976-77; mgr. San Vincent New Home div., San Diego County Estates Realty, 1978-79; dir. sales Blake Pub. Co., San Diego, 1980-86; pres., owner Century Publ., San Diego, 1986—. Alternate del. at large Rep. Nat. Conv., San Francisco, 1964; fin. chmn. Madison County Rep. Exec. Com., Huntsville, Ala., 1966-69; pres. Madison County Rep. Women, Huntsville, 1967, 68; Diocesan Conv. del. Grace Episcopal Ch., Ala., 1975; active Nat. Rep. Party, 1962—; mem. St. James Episcopal Ch., Newport Beach, 1990—, mem. scholarship com., mem. welcomer's com.; mem. Nat. Rep. Pres.'s Club, 1996-97. Recipient 1st Pl. AP Newswriting award, 1971, 72, 73, 1st place So. Heart Assn. Profl. Staff award for profl. paper Am. Heart Assn., 1977; nominee Outstanding Woman of Yr., Huntsville Area Jaycees, 1967. Mem. Long Beach Area C. of C., Palm Springs C. of C., Greater Del Mar C. of C., Huntington Beach C. of C., Beverly Hills C. of C., Soroptimist Internat. (Huntington Beach), Kappa Kappa Gamma. Avocations: boating, reading, traveling.

CARLSON, NEIL RYAN, computer scientist; b. South Bend, Ind., Dec. 8, 1964; s. Marlyn Gilbert and Norma Fay Carlson. BA in Psychology, U. Mich., 1988; MS in Psychology, Purdue U., 1993. Sys. adminstrn. programmer Target Software, Inc., Cambridge, Mass., 1993-97; applications engr. Tropix, Inc., Bedford, Mass., 1997—; cons. Studio-E, Boston, 1993—; advisor Perkin Elmer Software Coun., 1998—. Mem. Soc. Biomolecular Screening. Avocations: chess, reading, running. E-mail: carlsonr@tropix.com. Home: 394 Riverway #3 Boston MA 02115

CARLSON, NORMAN A., government official; b. Sioux City, Iowa, Aug. 10, 1933; s. Albert N. and Esther (Hollander) C.; m. Patricia Helen Musser, Sept. 8, 1956 (dec. Feb. 1994); children: Lucinda M., Gary N.; m. Phyllis J. Rohan, May 23, 1997. B.A., Gustavus Adolphus Coll., 1955; M.A., State U. Iowa, 1957, Princeton U., 1966. Parole officer Dept. Justice, U.S. Penitentiary, Leavenworth, Kan., 1957-58; casework supr. Fed. Correctional Inst., Ashland, Ky., 1958-60; asst. supr. instl. programs Fed. Bur. Prisons, Dept. Justice, Washington, 1960-62; project officer Fed. Bur. Prisons, Dept. Justice, 1962-65, exec. asst. to dir., 1966-70; dir. Fed. Bur. Prisons, 1970-87; sr. fellow Hubert Humphrey Inst. Pub. Affairs, U. Minn., Mpls., 1987-88; prof. dept. sociology U. Minn., Mpls., 1988-98. Nat. Inst. Pub. Affairs fellow Princeton U., 1965-66; recipient Arthur S. Flemming award, 1972, Roger W. Jones award for exec. leadership, 1978, Atty. Gen.'s award for exceptional service, 1981. Mem. Am. Correctional Assn. (past pres., mem. exec. com., E.R. Cass award 1981). Home: 11410 115th St N Stillwater MN 55082-9231

CARLSON, P(ATRICIA) M(CELROY), writer; b. Guatemala City, Guatemala, Feb. 3, 1940; (parents Am. citizens); d. James Benjamin and Alene (Jones) McElroy; m. M.A. Carlson, Aug. 20, 1960; children: Geoffrey, Richard. BA, Cornell U., 1961; MA, Cornell, 1966, PhD, 1974. Instr., lectr. psychology and human development Cornell U., Ithaca, N.Y., 1973-78; mem. bd. dirs. Bloomington Restorations, Inc., 1982-84. Author: (with M. Potts, R. Cocking and C. Copple), Structure and Development in Child Language, 1979, Audition for Murder, 1985, Murder is Academic, 1985, Murder is Pathological, 1986, (with Richard Darlington) Behavioral Statistics, 1987, Murder Unrenovated, 1988, Rehearsal for Murder, 1988, Murder in the Dog Days, 1991, Murder Misread, 1991, Bad Blood, 1991, Gravestone, 1993, Bloodstream, 1995, Renowned Be Thy Grave, 1998, eleven short stories. Chair Ithaca Environ. Commn., 1975-78; bd. dirs. Historic Ithaca, 1976-77. Mem. Mystery Writers Am. (bd. dirs. 1990-92), Sisters in Crime (internat. sec. 1990-91, v.p. 1991-92, pres. 1992-93). Address: Vicky Bijur Literary Agy 333 W End Ave New York NY 10023-8128*

CARLSON, PAUL ROBINS, Presbyterian minister, author; b. Bklyn., Dec. 10, 1928; s. Rudolph Frederick and Betty (Robins) C.; m. Myrtle Elizabeth Warner, Aug. 5,1950; children: Paul Robins Jr., Timothy Eric. BA in History, Barrington Coll., 1954; MDiv, Pitts. Theol. Sem., 1960; MPA, SUNY, 1970; EdD, NYU, 1979. Sec. for publicity World Coun. of Chs., Geneva, 1960-62; assoc. dir. info. Presbyn. Ch. USA, N.Y.C, 1962-64; assoc. dir. comm. United Ch. of Christ, N.Y.C, 1967-70; assoc. for interpretation World Coun. Chs., N.Y.C, 1970-73; exec. dir. United Chs. Northeastern Pa., Scranton, 1980-83; adjunct instr. U. Scranton, 1980-86; served Presbyn. Chs. N.Y., PA, Ohio, 1964-91; min. Silver Lake Presbyn. Ch., Brackney, Pa., 1996—; Bd. dirs. Nat. Christian Leadership Conf. for Israel, N.Y.C., 1980-86, United Way, Scranton, 1982-84; pres. Interfaith Coun. S.W. Queens, N.Y., 1973-79; corr. Religious News Svc., N.Y.C., 1960-86. Author: God's Church--Not Ours, 1965, The 13th American, 1973, Our Presbyterian Heritage, 1973, O Christian! O Jew!, 1974, Before I Awake, 1975. Chmn. UN Day, Scranton, 1985. Recipient Brotherhood award Interfaith Coun. S.W. Queens, 1975, Edn. award Nat. Conf. Christians and Jews, Queens-Nassau Divsn., 1978. Avocations: writing, photography, travel. Home: PO Box 72 Montrose PA 18801-0072 Office: Silver Lake Prebtyn Ch Wilkes-Barre Tpke Brackney PA 18812

CARLSON, RALPH WILLIAM, JR., food products company executive; b. Oak Park, Ill., Dec. 28, 1936; s. Ralph W. and Evelyn Marie (Benson) C.; m. Donna Drevs, Feb. 9, 1963; children: Daniel, Karen Carlson Lombardi, Susan Carlson Franklin, Robert, Kathleen. B.A., Mich. State U., 1958; M.B.A., U. Chgo., 1965; J.D., De Paul U., 1976. Bar: Ill. Group product mgr. The Kendall Co., Chgo., 1966-70; dir. mktg. Ovaltine Products Co. div. Sandoz, Inc., Chgo., 1970-76; mgr. new products Arco Polymers, Inc. subs. Atlantic Richfield Co., Chgo., 1976-78; mgr. internat. fleet ops. Arco Transp. Co., Long Beach, Calif., 1978-81; dir. mktg. planning Arco Solar Industries, Woodland Hills, Calif., 1981-85; sr. mgr. trademark licensing Sunkist Growers, Inc., Ontario, Calif., 1986—. part-time instr. mktg. UCLA, 1989—; judge CORO So. Calif., 1995—. Mem. Oak Park (Ill.) Sch. Bd., 1976-78; bd. dirs. Phila. Maritime Exchange, 1978-79; trustee Cornelia Connelly Sch., 1990-94. Served to lt. USNR, 1958-63. Mem. ABA, Am. Mktg. Assn., Calif. Solar Energy Soc. (dir. 1983-85), U.S. Naval Inst., Delta Chi. Republican. Roman Catholic. Club: Economic (Chgo.); Newfoundland of So. Calif. (bd. dirs. 1985-93). Home: 9117 Wagner River Cir Fountain Vly CA 92708-6449 Office: Sunkist Growers Inc 720 E Sunkist St Ontario CA 91761-1861

CARLSON, RANDY EUGENE, insurance executive; b. Central City, Nebr., Jan. 5, 1948; s. Ned Conrad and Bonnie Lee (Norgard) C.; m. Lorraine Marie Cordsen, Sept. 16, 1967; children: Lance, Brent. BA in Edn., Wayne State Coll., 1970. Tchr., coach Elgin (Nebr.) Pub. Schs., 1970-72, Lewiston (Nebr.) Consol. Schs., 1972-74, North Platte (Nebr.) Pub. Schs., 1974-78; sales assoc. Franklin Life Ins. Co., North Platte, 1977-79; mng. gen. agt. Life Investors Ins. Co., North Platte, 1979—; trustee Fortunaires Found., Davenport, Iowa, 1980—; bd. dirs. Life Investors Ownership Trust, Cedar Rapids, Iowa, Life Investors Gen. Agt. Coun., 1993—; mem. Communicating for Agr. Scholarship and Edn. Found., 1985—. Contbr. articles to profl. jours. Mem. North Platte Booster Club, 1983—; designed plan for Nebr. High Sch. Football Playoff Sys., 1973; bd. dirs. Gt. Plains Regional Med. Ctr., 1997—; mem. bd. Physician-Hosp. Orgn., 1998—. Mem. Nat. Assn. Life Underwriters (local pres. 1985-86, state membership chmn. 1986-87, local chmn. life underwriter polit. action com. 1993-95, mem. state lupac bd. 1997—), Nebr. State Life Underwriters Assn. (regional v.p. 1988-89), Gen. Agts. and Mgrs. Assn., North Platte C. of C. (bd. dirs. 1986-91, vice chmn. 1988-89, chmn. 1989-90, chmn. bus. and edn. com. 1991-96), North Platte Am. Legion, North Platte Country Club. Republican. Lutheran. Avocations: golf, fishing, spectator sports. Home: 3301 W F St North Platte NE 69101-5866 Office: Carlson and Assocs Inc 717 S Willow St PO Box 969 North Platte NE 69103-0969 *Personal philosophy: The price you will pay for success is far less than the price you will pay for mediocrity.*

CARLSON, RICHARD GREGORY, accountant; b. Chgo., Aug. 24, 1949; s. Richard George and S. Diane (Russell) C.; m. Annette Claire Bonneville, Aug. 30, 1969 (div. May 1982); children: Scott Richard, Amy Kristin; m. Pamela Catherine Punzelt, Sept. 25, 1982. BBA, Western Mich. U., 1971. CPA, Ill. With Deloitte & Touche, Chgo., 1971—, ptnr., 1980—, dir. Chgo. real estate svc. ctr., 1980-91, mem. nat. real estate com., 1982-91, dirs. client svcs. and devel., 1985-88, mem. Chgo. exec. com., 1985-88, mng. ptnrs. adv. coun., 1986-88, mng. dir. nat. real estate svcs., 1991—, nat. dir. real estate cons. svcs., 1997—. Author: Real Estate Accounting and Reporting Handbook, 1995; editor Real Estate Accounting and Taxation Journal, 1991-93, Real Estate Strategies, 1991—; contbr. articles to profl. jours. Mem. MIT Real Estate Cir., 1995—; adv. bd. Ctr. Real Estate Studies Ind. U.; mem. bd. advisors Real Estate Fin. Jour., 1993—; bd. dirs. Western Mich. U. Found., 1986, mem. investment com., 1986-88, 91-97, mem. exec. com., 1988-97, vice-chmn., 1992-93, chmn. 1994-97; bd. dirs. Pin Oak Homeowners Assn., treas. 1982-86. With USAR, 1971-77. Recipient Disting. Acctg. Alumni award Western Mich. U., 1987, Disting. Alumni award 1993. Mem. AICPA, Am. Acctg. Assn. (Midwest regional steering com. 1983-87), Ill. Soc. CPAs, Internat. Coun. Shopping Ctrs., Western Mich. U. Alumni Assn. (bd. dirs. 1984-91, treas. 1984-86, pres. 1986-88), Nat. Assn. Real Estate Cos., Nat. Realty Com. (bd. dirs., exec. com. 1992—), Nat. Coun. Real Estate Investment Fiduciaries (acctg. com. 1985—, pres. elect 1997, membership com. 1992-98, bd. dirs. 1993-99, pres. 1998-99), Plaza Club (Chgo.), Westmoreland Country Club (Wilmette, Ill., bd. dirs. 1988-92, treas. 1988-92), Ironwood Country Club (Palm Desert, Calif.). Republican. Office: Deloitte & Touche 2 Prudential Plz Chicago IL 60601

CARLSON, RICHARD WARNER, journalist, diplomat, federal agency administrator, broadcast executive; b. Boston, Feb. 10, 1941; adopted s. W.E. and Ruth Miriam (Rafuse) C.; m. Patricia Caroline Swanson; children:

Tucker McNear, Buckley Peck. Student, U. Miss., 1961-62; LLD (hon.), Calif. Western U., 1988. Editl. asst. L.A. Times, 1962-63; writer, columnist UPI, San Francisco, Sacramento, 1963-66; investigative reporter, anchorman ABC-TV, San Francisco, 1966-71; anchorman, polit. editor ABC-TV, L.A., 1971-75; anchorman Sta. KFMB-TV (CBS), San Diego, 1975-77; prodr., writer, dir. documentary films NBC-TV, Burbank, Calif., 1974; anchorman, host Carlson & Co., CBS-TV, San Diego, 1975-76; sr. v.p. Gt. Am. First Bank, San Diego, 1977-84; dir. USIA/Voice of Am., Washington, 1985-91; U.S. amb. to Republic Seychelles, 1991-92; pres., CEO Corp. for Pub. Broadcasting, 1992-97; CEO Kingwood Pub. TV, Washington, 1997-99; bd. dirs. Exec. Info. Svc., Radio Voyager, Inc.; lectr., cons. in field. Chmn. San Diego Coalition, 1980-81; gov. Scripps Meml. Hosps., La Jolla, 1981-90, Banff (Can.) TV Festival, 1996—, Am. Ctr. Children's TV, 1996—; mem. Calif. State Rep. Ctrl. Com., 1982-85; appointed Pres.'s Coun. Peace Corps, 1982-84; mem. La Jolla Planned Dist. Bd., 1982-84; bd. dirs. Sharp Hosp. Found., 1983—, Scripps Inst. Medicine and Sci., 1995—; mem. La Jolla Town Coun., 1983-85; mem. San Diego Crime Commn., 1984-85; trustee Fund for Am. Studies, 1988-91; mem. Rosalind Russell Arthritis Found., 1985-91; dir. Georgetown Club, 1995—. Recipient investigative reporting awards AP, 1968, 76, 77, awards news analysis, 1968, 69, 75, Nat. Headliners award, 1968, Emmy award best investigative reporting, 1977, Golden Mike award best documentary, 1972, investigative reporting, 1975, best commentary, 1975, George Foster Peabody award, 1976, L.A. Press Club Grand award, 1976, San Diego Press Club award, 1976, 77, 79, Friend of Lithuania award Knights of Lithuania, 1988, Jose Marti award Cuban Am. Polit. Soc., Miami, Fla., 1988, Broadcast Pioneer award, 1997. Mem. Nat. Press Club, Thunderbird Country Club (Rancho Mirage, Calif.), Mid-Ocean Club (Tuckerstown, Bermuda), Georgetown Club, Met. Club, DACOR, The Pilgrims (N.Y.C.), Am. Ambs. Episcopalian. Home: Tulip Hill 7718 Georgetown Pike Mc Lean VA 22102-1431 Office: Gately-Carlson Ste 900 725 15th St NW Washington DC 20005

CARLSON, ROBERT CODNER, industrial engineering educator; b. Granite Falls, Minn., Jan. 17, 1939; s. Robert Ledin and Ada Louise (Codner) C.; children: Brian William, Andrew Robert, Christina Louise. BSME, Cornell U., 1962; MS, Johns Hopkins U., 1963, PhD, 1976. Mem. tech. staff Bell Tel. Labs., Holmdel, N.J., 1962-70; asst. prof. Stanford (Calif.) U., Stanford, 1970-77; assoc. prof. Stanford (Calif.) U., 1977-82, prof. indsl. engring., 1982—; program dir., lectr., cons. various spl. programs U.S., Japan, France, 1971—; cons. Japan Mgmt. Assn., Tokyo, 1990—, Raychem, Menlo Park, Calif., 1989—, GKN Automotive, London, 1989—, Rockwell Internat., L.A., 1988—; vis. prof. U. Calif., Berkeley, 1987-88, Dartmouth Coll., Hanover, N.J., 1978-79; vis. faculty Internat. Mgmt. Inst., Geneva, 1984, 88. Contbr. articles to profl. jours. Recipient Maxwell Upson award in Mech. Engring. Cornell U., 1962; Bell Labs. Systems Engring. fellow, 1962-63, Bell Labs. Doctoral Support fellow, 1966-67. Mem. Ops. Rsch. Soc. Am. (chmn. membership com. 1981-83), Inst. Mgmt. Scis., Inst. Indsl. Engrs., Am. Soc. Engring. Edn., Am. Prodn. and Inventory Control Soc. (bd. dirs. 1975-81), Internat. Material Mgmt. Soc., Tau Beta Pi, Phi Kappa Phi, Pi Tau Sigma, Soc. of Enophiles Club (Woodside, Calif.). Avocations: wine tasting, travelling. Office: Stanford Univ Dept Indsl Engring/Engring Mgmt Stanford CA 94305

CARLSON, ROBERT EDWIN, lawyer; b. Bklyn., Oct. 11, 1930; s. Harry Victor and Lenore Marie (Hanrahan) C.; m. Maureen Eleanor Donnelly, Aug. 24, 1963; children: John T., Katherine L., Elizabeth A., Robert E. Jr. BS, U. Oreg., 1953; JD, U. Calif., San Francisco, 1958; LLM, Harvard U., 1963. Bar: Calif. 1959, U.S. Dist. Ct. (ctrl. dist.) Calif. 1959, U.S. Ct. Appeals (9th cir.) 1959. Assoc. Kindel & Anderson, L.A., 1958-63, ptnr., 1963-67; ptnr. Agnew, Miller & Carlson, L.A., 1967-80, Hufstedler, Miller, Carlson & Beardsley, L.A., 1980-88, Paul, Hastings, Janofsky & Walker, L.A., 1988—; pres. Constl. Rights Found., L.A., 1978-80, L.A. County Bar Found., 1988-89; mem. exec. com. bus. sect. L.A. Bar Assn., 1982-89; bd. dirs. Legal Aid Found., L.A. Bd. dirs. Westridge Sch. for Girls, Pasadena, Calif., 1985-91, Trust for Pub. Land, San Francisco, 1987—; chair bd. Skid Row Housing Trust, L.A., 1989—; bd. visitors Santa Clara Law Sch., 1986-92. With U.S. Army, 1953-55. Recipient Griffin Bell award Dispute Resolution Svcs., Inc., 1992, Katherine Krause award Inner City Law Ctr., 1996. Mem. ABA (mem. securities com., co-chair com. devel. investment svcs., mem. task force to prepare guidebook for dirs. mut. funds 1995, chairperson youth edn. for citizenship, Chgo. 1982-85), Calif. State Bar (mem. corp. com. 1990—), Valley Hunt Club, Chancery Club, Calif. Club. Democrat. Avocations: hiking, tennis, reading, skiing. Office: Paul Hastings Janofsky & Walker 555 S Flower St Fl 23 Los Angeles CA 90071-2300*

CARLSON, ROBERT ERNEST, freelance writer, architect, lecturer; b. Denver, Dec. 6, 1924; s. Milton and Augustine Barbara (Walter) C.; m. Jane Frances Waters, June 14, 1952 (div. June 1971); children: Cristina, Bob, Douglas, Glenn, James. BS in Archtl. Engring., U. Colo., 1951. Registered architect, Colo. Architect H.D. Wagener & Assocs., Boulder, Colo., 1953-75; pvt. practice architect Denver, 1975-82; health and promotion cons. Alive & Well Cons., Denver, 1982-85; freelance writer Denver, 1985—; mem. Colo. Gov.'s Coun. for Fitness, Denver, 1975—; state race walking chmn. U.S. Track & Field, Denver, 1983—; bd. dirs. Colo. Found. for Phys. Fitness, Denver, 1987—; lectr. in field. Author: Health Walk, 1988, Walking for Health, Fitness and Sport, 1996. Vol. Colo. Heart Assn., 1985—, Better Air Campaign, 1986-87, Cystic Fibrosis, 1989-91, Multiple Sclerosis Soc., 1988-91, Qualife, 1989—, March of Dimes, 1989, United Negro Coll. Fund, 1989, bd. trustees, 1990. With U.S. Army, 1943-46, ETO. Decorated Bronze Star; named One of Ten Most Prominent Walking Leaders in U.S.A., Rockport Walking Inst., 1989. Mem. Colo. Author's League, Phidippides Track Club (walking chmn. 1981-85), Rocky Mountain Rd. Runners (v.p. 1983-84), Front Range Walkers Club (founder, pres. Denver chpt. 1985—), Lions (bd. dirs. 1965-72). Episcopalian. Avocations: racewalking, skiing, cross-country skiing, orienteering. Home and Office: 2261 Glencoe St Denver CO 80207-3834

CARLSON, ROBERT JAMES, bishop; b. Mpls., June 30, 1944; s. Robert James and Jeanne Catherine (Dorgan) C. B.A., St. Paul Sem., 1964, M.Div., 1976; J.C.L., Catholic U. Am., 1979. Ordained priest Roman Catholic Ch. 1970. Asst. St. Raphael Ch., Crystal, 1970-72; assoc. St. Margaret Mary Ch., Golden Valley, 1972-73, adminstr., 1973-76; vice chancellor, dir. Vocation Office, 1976-79, dir., 1977; pastor St. Leonard of Port Maurice, Mpls., 1982-84; aux. bishop St. Paul and Mpls., Mpls., 1983-94; vicar Eastern Vicariate Archdiocese of St. Paul and Mpls., Mpls., 1984-94; apptd. coadjutor Bishop of Sioux Falls, S.D., 1994-95; apptd. bishop Sioux Falls, 1995—; pres., bd. dirs. Nat. Evangelization Teams, 1991—; chmn. bishop com. on vocations Nat. conf. Cath. Bishops, 1992-95, chmn. subcom. on youth, 1993-96; mem. bishops com. on laity, 1993-96; pub. CD-Rom Treasure of the Cathedrals, 1996. Author: Going All Out: An Invitation to Belong, 1985. Pres. Nat. Found. Cath. Youth Ministry, Washington, 1989-97; bd. dirs. St. Paul Sem., 1993—; Episcopal moderator Nat. Cath. Com. on Scouting, 1993-97, USA/Can. coun. Serra Internat., 1996; bd. dirs. Mt. Angel Sem., Portland, Oreg., 1995—; bd. dirs. St. John V. Coll. Sem., U. St. Thomas, St. Paul, 1997—; bd. govs. N.Am. Coll. Rome, 1997—; bd. dirs. Hennich-Glennon Sem., St. Louis, 1998—. Recipient Friendship award Knights and Ladies of St. Peter Claver, 1990, St. De LaSalle Meml. award Cretin High Sch. Alumni Assn., 1990. Mem. Canon Law Soc. Am. Avocations: hunting, raising Golden Retrievers. Office: The Chancery 523 N Duluth Ave Sioux Falls SD 57104-2714

CARLSON, ROBERT LEE, engineering educator; b. Gary, Ind., May 22, 1924; s. Herman and Eva (Larson) C.; m. Betty Christine Nelson, Oct. 21, 1950; children—David Lee, Richard Ray, Karen Christine, Robert Lee, Carol Lynn. B.S., Purdue U., 1948, M.S., 1950; Ph.D., Ohio State U., 1962. Research engr. Battelle Inst., Columbus, Ohio, 1950-62; research engr. U.S. Steel Research Lab., Monroeville, Pa., 1962-63; research asso., lectr. Stanford, 1963-66; prof. Ga. Inst. Tech., Atlanta, 1966—; invited lectr. Internat. Union Theoretical and Applied Mechanics, 1960; cons. EIMAC div. Varian Assos., USAF Flight Dynamics Lab.; invited lectr. Internat. Conf. on Theoretical Concepts and Numerical Analysis of Fatigue, 1992. Contbr. to: Folke Odquist Vol. 1967; contbr. articles to profl. jours. Served with AUS, 1943-45. Recipient Charles Dudley medal ASTM, 1959. Mem. Am. Soc. for Exptl. Stress Analysis (chmn. S.E. chpt. 1968-69), Sigma Xi, Pi Tau Sigma, Tau Beta Pi. Home: 830 Morning Creek Ln Suwanee GA 30024-3790 Office: Ga Inst Tech Dept Aerospace Engring Atlanta GA 30332*

CARLSON, ROBERT MICHAEL, artist; b. Bklyn., Nov. 19, 1952; s. Sidney Carlson and Vickey (Mihaloff) Woodward; m. Linda Schneider; m. Mary Elizabeth Fontaine, Feb. 24, 1984; 1 child, Nora. Student, CCNY, 1970-73; studied with Flora Mace and Joey Kirkpatrick, Pilchuck Glass Sch., 1981, studied with Dan Dailey, 1982. Teaching asst. Pilchuck Sch., Stanwood, Wash., 1986, 88, mem. faculty, 1989-90, 92, 95; mem. faculty Pratt Fine Arts Ctr., Seattle, 1988-90, Penland (N.C.) Sch. Crafts, 1994, Bild-Werk Sch., Germany, 1996; mem. artists adv. com. Pilchuck Sch., 1989, 90; vis. artist Calif. Coll. Arts and Crafts, Oakland, 1989, Calif. State U., Fullerton, 1991, blossom summer program Kent State U., Ohio, 1991, U. Ill., Urbana-Champaign, 1993, Toledo Mus. of Art Sch., 1994; visual-artist-in-residence Centrum Found., Port Townsend, Wash., 1992. One-man shows include Foster White Gallery, Seattle, 1987, 90, 92, The Glass Gallery, Bethesda, Md., 1988, Heller Gallery, N.Y.C., 1989, 95, Betsy Rosenfield Gallery, Chgo., 1991, 92, MIA Gallery, Seattle, 1994, others; exhibited in group shows at Traver Gallery, Seattle, 1984, 89, Mindscape Gallery, Evanston, Ill., 1984, 86, Tucson Mus. Art., 1984 (Purchase award), 86 (Award of Merit), Hand and Spirit Gallery, Scottsdale, Ariz., 1985, 86, Craftsman Gallery, Scarsdale, N.Y., 1985, Robert Kidd Gallery, Birmingham, Mich., 1985, 88, Gazebo Gallery, Gatlinburg, Tenn., 1985, The Glass Gallery, Bethesda, Md., 1986 (Jurors award), 91, 92, 94, Artists Soc. Internat., San Francisco, 1987 (Critics Choice award), William Traver Gallery, Seattle, 1987, 90, 91, 92, Japan Glass Artcrafts Assn., Tokyo, 1987, Heller Gallery, 1988, 89, 90, 91, 93, 94, 95, 96, 97, Washington Sq. Ptnrs., 1988, Foster White Gallery, 1988, 90, Bellvue Art Mus., Wash., 1988, 91, 94, Am. Arts and Crafts Inc., San Francisco, 1989, Mus. Craft and Folk Art, San Francisco, 1989, Great Am. Gallery, Atlanta, 1989, Dorothy Weiss Gallery, San Francisco, 1989, Habitat Gallery, Farmington Hills, Mich., 1990, 93, Philabaum Gallery, Tucson, 1990, Greg Kucera Gallery, Seattle, 1990, Connell Gallery, Atlanta, 1990, Net Contents Gallery, Bainbridge Island, Wash., 1991, Seattle Tacoma Internat. Airport Installation, 1991, 95, Pratt Fine Arts Ctr., Seattle, 1991, Crystalex, Novy Bor, Czechoslovakia, 1991, Whatcom County Mus., Bellingham, Wash., 1992, Art Gallery West Australia, 1992, 1004 Gallery, Port Townsend, 1992, Bainbridge Island Arts Coun., 1992, MIA Gallery, 1993, Betsy Rosenfield Gallery, Chgo., 1993, Blue Spiral Gallery, Asheville, N.C., 1995, Huntington Mus., 1996, Salem Art Assn., 1996, Judy Yovens Gallery, Houston, 1997, Internat. Glass Art Exchange, Tucson, 1997, Habatat Gallery, Boca Raton, Fla., 1998, Habatat Gallery, Farmington Hills, Mich., 1998, Tampa (Fla.) Mus. Art, 1998; represented in permanent collections Corning (N.Y.) Mus. Glass, Tucson Mus. Art, Toledo Mus. Art, Glasmuseum Frauenau, Germany, Glasmuseum Ebeltoft, Denmark, Valley Nat. Bank, Phoenix, Fountain Assocs., Portland, Oreg., Iceland Air Co., Reykjavik, Iceland, Crocker Banks, L.A., Davis Wright Tremain, Seattle, Meiwa Trading Co., Tokyo, Safeco Ins. Corp., Seattle, Crystalex Corp., L.A. County Mus. Art. Fellow Tucson Pima Arts Coun., 1987, NEA, 1990. Mem. Glass Art Soc. (conf. lectr. 1991, bd. dirs. 1992-94, v.p. 1993-94, pres. 1995). Office: PO Box 11590 Bainbridge Is WA 98110-5590

CARLSON, ROBERT WELLS, physician, educator; b. Concord, Calif., Apr. 14, 1952; s. Robert L. Carlson and Mae E. Fox. BS in Biol. Sci., Stanford U., 1974, MD, 1978. Diplomate Am. Bd. Internal Medicine, Am. Bd. Med. Oncology. Intern Barnes Hosp., St. Louis, 1978-79, resident, 1979-80; resident Stanford (Calif.) Univ. Hosp., 1980-81; fellow Stanford U., 1981-83, clin. asst. prof., 1983-85, asst. prof., 1985-92, assoc. prof., 1992-97, prof., 1997—; assoc. chief for clin. affairs div. oncology, 1994-96; exec. officer No. Calif. Oncology Group, Palo Alto, Calif., 1984-87, group chmn., 1987-91. Bd. dirs. Theatreworks, Palo Alto, 1994—. Recipient Career Devel. award Am. Cancer Soc., 1987-90. Fellow ACP; mem. Am. Soc. Clin. Oncology, Am. Assn. Cancer Rsch. Office: Stanford U Oncology Day Care Clinic Stanford Med Ctr H0274 Stanford CA 94305

CARLSON, ROGER ALLAN, manufacturing company executive, accountant; b. Mpls., Dec. 12, 1932; s. Carl Albert and Borghild Amanda (Anderson) C.; m. Lois Roberta Lehman, Aug. 20, 1955; children: Gene, Bradley. *Wife Lois Lehman Carlson is researching her family history and genealogy. Three great grandfathers fought with the Union army in the American Civil War. She is a member of the Daughters of Union Veterans, Grand Army of the Republic. Son, Gene Allan Carlson is an automotive engineer with General Motors Corporation, Pontiac, Michigan. He has a BS in Industrial Technology from the University of Wisconsin, 1989 and an MS in Manufacturing Management from the GMI Institute, 1995. Son, Bradley Robert Carlson is a consultant in investment management and media, New York City. He has a BS in Journalism and Psychology from the University of Wisconsin, 1987, and an MS in Public Policy from the John F. Kennedy School of Government, Harvard University, 1992.* BBA, U. Minn., 1954. CPA, Minn. Investment mgr. Mayo Found., Rochester, Minn., 1963-83; controller Luth. Hosp. and Homes Soc., Fargo, N.D., 1983-84; v.p., treas. Crenlo Inc., Rochester, 1984-94, also bd. dirs., part owner; instr. seminars, 1971, 82. Pres. Ability Bldg. Ctr., Rochester, 1974-75, United Way, Olmsted County, Minn., 1980; trustee Minn. Charities Rev. Coun., Mpls., 1981-83; bd. dirs., dir. Samaritan Bethany, Inc., Rochester, Minn., 1991-95. Capt. U.S. Army, 1955-57. Mem. Am. Inst. CPA's, Minn. Soc. CPA's, Nat. Assn. Accts. (pres. So. Minn. chpt. 1969). Avocations: hunting, fishing, genealogy. Home: 4915 Sussex Pl Excelsior MN 55331-9217 Office: Crenlo Inc 1600 4th Ave NW Rochester MN 55901-2573

CARLSON, SCOTT BRANDON, state agency administrator; b. Salina, Kans., May 29, 1957; s. Dennis Eugene and Marilyn Yvonne (Swanson) C. BS in Agr., Ft. Hays State U., 1979; postgrad., U. Kans., 1997—. Farmer, rancher Falun, Kans., 1980-91; program coord. Kans. Conservation Commn., Topeka, 1994-98, non-point source pollution control program mgr., 1998—. Maj. Kans. Army Nat. Guard, 1996—. Mem. ASPA, NG Assn. U.S., Am. Legion. Republican. Lutheran. Avocations: fly fishing, sailing. E-mail: scarlson@scc.state.ks.us. Home: 4039 Parkway Ct Lawrence KS 66047 Office: Kans Conservation Commn 109 SW 9th Ste 500 Topeka KS 66612

CARLSON, SHARON LEE, archivist; b. Kalamazoo, Mich., Dec. 2, 1962; d. Andrew Raymond and Linda Inara (Volfarts) C.; m. Mark Anthony Dunham, Aug. 13, 1983 (div. Aug., 1989). BS, We. Mich. U., 1986, MPA, 1991. Cert. archivist Acad. Cert. Archivists. Cert. coord. Mich. Inst. Human Resource Devel., Kalamazoo, 1986-912; curator We. Mich. U., Kalamazoo, 1991-95, archivist, 1996—; dir. Mich. Alliance Conservation Cultural Resources, 1997—; mem. Mich. Commn. Preservation Archtl. Records, 1995—. Mem. ALA, Am. Hist. Assn., Mich. Archival Assn. (dir. 1996—), Stuart Area Restoration Assn. (chairperson 1986—), Soc. Am. Archivists, Phi Alpha Theta. Home: 430 Elm St Kalamazoo MI 49007-3232 Office: Archives and Regional History Collections Western Mich U Kalamazoo MI 49008-1272

CARLSON, STEPHEN CURTIS, lawyer; b. Mpls., Mar. 22, 1951; s. Curtis Harvey and Edna Mae (Pfunder) C.; m. Patricia Jane Brown, Aug. 21, 1976; children: Elizabeth Buckley, Susan Pfunder, Julie Desloge. AB magna cum laude, Princeton U., 1973; JD, Yale U., 1976. Bar: Minn. 1977, Ill. 1977, U.S. Dist. Ct. Minn. 1977, U.S. Dist. Ct. (no. dist.) Ill. 1977, U.S. Ct. Appeals (7th and 8th cirs.) 1977, U.S. Ct. Appeals (6th cir.) 1987, U.S. Ct. Appeals (9th cir.) 1989, U.S. Dist. Ct. (cen. dist.) Ill. 1991. Law clk. to presiding justice Minn. Supreme Ct., St. Paul, 1976-77; assoc. Sidley & Austin, Chgo., 1977-83, ptnr., 1983—. Rep. precinct capt. 1st Ward 11th Precinct, Chgo., 1985-91; pres. Dearborn Park Unit One Townhomes Condominium Assn., 1987-88; sec. Dearborn Park Prairie Single Family Homes Assn., 1997—. Mem. ABA, Ill. Bar Assn., Chgo. Bar Assn., Am. Inns of Ct., Legal Club (sec.-treas. 1997—), Nordic Law Club (v.p. 1987-90, pres. 1990-91), Princeton Club, Yale Club, Mid-Day Club, Civil War Roundtable, Phi Beta Kappa. Presbyterian. Avocations: theater, opera, symphony. Home: 1323 S Federal St Chicago IL 60605-2716 Office: Sidley & Austin 1 First Natl Plz Chicago IL 60603-2003

CARLSON, SUSAN SPEVACK, medical director, family physician; b. N.Y.C., July 20, 1945; d. Jerome S. and Ruth (Sporn) Spevack; m. Robert Howard Carlson, Dec. 27, 1970; 1 child, Christopher Randall. BA, Skidmore Coll., 1967; MD, Columbia U., 1973. Diplomate Am. Bd. Family Practice, Am. Bd. Quality Assurance and Utilization Rev. Physicians, Am. Bd. Med. Mgmt. Med. officer USPHS, Sitka, Alaska, 1973-86; med. dir. Mt. Edgecumbe Hosp., Sitka, 1986—. Contbr. articles to profl. jours. Pres. Alaska divsn. Am. Cancer Soc., 1984-86 (Vol. Leadership award 1988); bd. dirs. Sitka Summer Music Festival, 1985-94. Fellow Am. Acad. Family Physicians; mem. AAUW (treas. 1981-83), Commd. Officers Assn. Home: PO Box 1867 Sitka AK 99835-1867 Office: Mt Edgecumbe Hosp 222 Tongass Dr Sitka AK 99835-9416

CARLSON, SUZANNE OLIVE, architect; b. Worcester, Mass., Aug. 20, 1939; d. Sigfrid and Helga (Larson) C. BS, R.I. Sch. Design, 1963. Jr. ptnr. Dingnam-Fauteux & Partners, Worcester, 1969-70; ptnr. Richard Lamoureux Asso., Worcester, 1970-75, Herron & Carlson (AIA), Worcester, 1975-96; architect Edgecomb, Maine, 1997—; Guest lectr. Holy Cross Coll., 1969-70. Chmn. Worcester Hist. Commn., 1976-88; trustee Worcester Heritage Soc., 1982-88, Park Spirit of Worcester Inc., 1987—, Lincoln County Hist. Assn.; trustee Worcester Girls Inc. of Worcester, pres. 1989-92, sec. 1994—; trustee Performing Arts Sch. Worcester, 1977-86, v.p. 1980-85; trustee Cultural Assembly Greater Worcester, 1981-86, v.p., 1982-83; pres. Edgecomb Hist. Soc., 1997—. Recipient European Honors Program grant Rome, Italy, 1961-62; recipient AIA School medal for excellence, 1963. Mem. AIA (exec. bd. Ctrl. Mass. chpt. 1969-71, sec.-treas. 1970-71, v.p. 1971-72, pres. 1972-73), Mass. Soc. Architects (exec. bd. 1972-74, v.p. 1975, pres. 1976), New Eng. Regional Coun. Architects (pres. 1977), New Eng. Antiquities Rsch. Assn. (membership chair 1982-84, 90-94, resource devel. chair 1994—, graphics dir. jours. 1982—, publs. chair 1995—, trustee 1990—). Home and Office: Suzanne O Carlson Architect 94 Cross Point Rd Edgecomb ME 04556-3208

CARLSON, THEODORE JOSHUA, lawyer, retired utility company executive; b. Hartford, Conn., Jan. 4, 1919; s. John and Hulda (Larson) C.; m. Jacqueline L. Coburn, Apr. 25, 1953; children: Stephanie, Christopher J., Victoria, Antoinette. AB, Montclair State U., 1940; JD, Columbia U., 1948, AM, 1951; postgrad., U. Chgo., 1942. Bar: N.Y. 1948. Assoc. Gould & Wilkie, N.Y.C., 1948-54, ptnr., 1954-96, sr. ptnr., 1970-96, of counsel, 1997—; dir. Central Hudson Gas & Electric Corp., Poughkeepsie, N.Y., 1968-89, chmn., prin. officer, 1975-89; mem., chmn. fin. and audit com. N.Y. State Energy Rsch. Devel. Authority, 1980-88; dir. Empire State Electric Energy Rsch. Com., Edison Electric Inst., 1976-79; chmn. exec. com. Energy Assn. N.Y. State, 1976-77, 82-83, N.Y. Power Pool, 1977-78; dir., mem. exec. com. Mid-Hudson Pattern, Inc., Poughkeepsie, N.Y.; chmn. bd. dirs. Christian Herald Assn. and related cos., 1985-92. Author: A Design For Freedom. Pres. United Fund Rockville Centre, N.Y., 1966; chmn. adv. bd. Westchester County Salvation Army, 1977-80, State of N.Y., 1977-83; chmn. Greater N.Y. Adv. Bd., 1988-91; chmn. bd. trustees King's Coll., 1982-89. Capt. USAAF, 1942-46. Mem. ABA, N.Y. Bar Assn., Assn. of Bar of City of N.Y. (chmn. pub. utility sect. com. on post admissions-legal edn. 1970-73), Rotary (hon.). Office: Gould & Wilkie 1 Chase Manhattan Plz New York NY 10005-1401

CARLSON, THOMAS A., federal judge; b. 1942. BA, U. Notre Dame, 1964; JD, U. Mich., 1967. Asst. atty. gen. State of Mich. Atty. Gen.'s Office, 1969-79; magistrate judge U.S. Dist. Ct. (ea. dist.) Mich., Detroit, 1979—. With U.S. Army, 1967-69. Fax: (313) 234-5495. Office: US Dist Ct Ea Dist Mich 673 US Courthouse 231 W Lafayette Blvd Detroit MI 48226

CARLSON, THOMAS DAVID, lawyer; b. Mpls., Aug. 17, 1944; s. David W. and Grace M. (Laser) C.; m. Jane A. Gleeson; children: Amy A., Ryan T., Madeline Jane. BA, Colgate U., 1966; JD cum laude, U. Minn., 1969. Bar: Minn. 1969, U.S. Dist. Ct. Minn. 1969, U.S. Supreme Ct. 1973. Law clk. to Hon. Earl R. Larson U.S. Dist. Ct. (fed. dist.) Minn., Mpls., 1969-70; assoc. Best & Flanagan, Mpls., 1970-74, ptnr., 1974-91; ptnr. Lindquist & Vennum, Mpls., 1991—. Fellow Am. Coll. Trust & Estate Counsel; mem. ABA, Minn. State Bar Assn., Hennepin County Bar Assn., Mpls. Club, Minikahda Club, Colgate Silver Puck club (bd. trustees). Office: Lindquist & Vennum 4200 IDS Ctr Minneapolis MN 55402

CARLSON, THOMAS EDWARD, bankruptcy judge; b. 1947; m. Cynthia Hustad. BA, Beloit Coll., 1969; JD, Harvard U., 1975; LLM, NYU, 1985. Bar: Calif. 1976; U.S. Dist. Ct. (no. dist.) Calif. 1977, U.S. Dist. Ct. (cen. dist.) Calif. 1984, U.S. Ct. Appeals (9th cir.) 1978. Law clk. to Hon. Thomas Roberts U.S. Supreme Ct., R.I., 1976-77; law clk. to Hon. Donald Wright Supreme Ct. Calif., 1977-78; assoc. atty. Cooper, White & Cooper, San Francisco, 1978-84; dep. staff dir. Ninth Cir. Ct. Appeals, San Francisco, 1984; judge U.S. Bankruptcy Ct. No. Dist. Calif., San Francisco, 1985—. Mem. Nat. Conf. Bankruptcy Judges. Office: US Bankruptcy Ct Calif PO Box 7341 235 Pine St San Francisco CA 94120*

CARLSON, THOMAS JOSEPH, real estate developer, lawyer, former mayor; b. St. Paul, Jan. 12, 1953; s. Delbert George and Shirley Lorraine (Willardson) C.; m. Chandler Elizabeth Campbell, July 15, 1973; 1 child, Thomas Chandler. BA, George Washington U., 1975; JD, U. Mo., Kansas City, 1979. Reporter Springfield (Mo.) News-Leader, 1975-76; editor Buffalo (Mo.) Reflex, 1976-77; assoc. Woolsey Fisher, Springfield, 1980-83; pvt. practice law Springfield, 1983-86; ptnr. Carlson & Clark, 1986-93, Carmichael, Carlson, Gardner & Clark, Springfield, 1993-94; mayor City of Springfield, 1987-93; U.S. Bankruptcy trustee Springfield, 1982-98; pvt. practice, 1994-98; CEO, Resorts Mgmt., Inc., 1995—; lectr. in field. Contbr. articles to profl. jours. Mem. Springfield City Coun., 1983-87, 97—, Airport Bd. Springfield, 1994-97; chmn. Springfield-Branson Leadership Com., 1993—. Mem. Mo. Bar Assn. (Disting. Young Lawyer award 1989). Presbyterian. Office: 205 W Walnut Ste 200 Springfield MO 65806-2115

CARLSON, WALTER CARL, lawyer; b. Chgo., Sept. 14, 1953; s. LeRoy T. and Margaret (Deffenbaugh) C.; m. Debora M. DeHoyos, June 20, 1981; children: Amanda, Greta, Linnea. BA, Yale U., 1975; JD, Harvard U., 1978. Bar: Ill. 1978, U.S. Dist. Ct. (no. dist.) Ill. 1978, U.S. Supreme Ct. 1991. Law clk. to presiding justice U.S. Dist. Ct. No. Dist., Chgo., 1978-80; ptnr. Sidley & Austin, Chgo., 1980—; dir., mem. audit com. Telephone and Data Sys., Inc., Chgo., 1981—; bd. dirs., chmn. audit com. U.S. Cellular Corp., 1989—, Aerial Comm., Inc., 1996—. Pres. Dist. 65 Sch. Bd., Evanston, Ill. Mem. ABA, U.S. Supreme Ct. Hist. Soc., Am. Judicature Soc., Chgo. United. Office: Sidley & Austin 1 First Natl Plz Chicago IL 60603-2003

CARLSON, WILLIAM CLIFFORD, defense company executive; b. Detroit, Feb. 7, 1937; s. William and Marion Lucille Carlson; m. Jane Elder, Jan. 28, 1960 (div. Jne 1987); children: David, Scott, Jennifer Carlson-Burns; m. Linda Darlene Reid, June 6, 1991. BS in Edn., U. N.Mex., 1959; MS in Physics, U.S. Naval Postgrad. Sch., Monterey, Calif., 1965; MS equivalent, U.S. Naval War Coll., Newport, R.I., 1975. Commd. U.S. Navy, 1959, advanced through ranks to rear admiral, officer, 1959-92; mgr. ASW combat sys. Naval Sea Sys. Command U.S. Navy, Washington, 1982-88, asst. dep. cmdr. Naval Sea Sys. Command, 1988-91, cmdr. Naval Undersea Warfare Ctr., 1991-92; ret. U.S. Navy, 1992; dir. advanced programs Scientific Atlanta Instrumentation Group, 1993-94; v.p. mktg. & sales Scientific Atlanta SPS Group, 1994-95; dir. surface ship ASW combat system programs Lockheed Martin, Syracuse, N.Y., 1995—. Mem. Acoustical Soc. Am., U.S. Naval Inst., U.S. Navy League, Surface Warfare Assn. Avocations: trout fishing, fly tying, skiing. Home: 3996 Pompey Hollow Rd Cazenovia NY 13035-9523 Office: Lockheed Martin PO Box 4840 Syracuse NY 13221-4840*

CARLSON, WILLIAM DWIGHT, college president emeritus; b. Denver, Nov. 5, 1928; m. Beverley Ann Bradshaw, 1950; children: Susan Elaine, Earl Dwight. DVM, Colo. State U., 1952, MS, 1956; PhD in Radiology and Radiation Biology, U. Colo., 1958. Prof., chmn. dept. radiology and radiation biology, founder Colo. State U., 1964-68, pres. rsch. found., 1964-68, acting dir., 1966-68; prof. radiation biology, adminstr. Am. studies U. Wyo., Laramie, 1968-79, pres., 1968-79; pres. emeritus U. Wyo., 1989—; affiliate prof. radiology, radiation biology Colo. State U., Fort Collins, 1968-80; CEO St. John's Hosp., Jackson Hole, Wyo., 1980-84; prin. vet. Cooperative State Research Service USDA, Washington, 1984-88, assoc. adminstr. Office Grants and Program Systems, 1984-94, acting adminstr. Coop. State Rsch., Edn., and Extension Svc., 1994-95; mem. USDA Nat. Agr. Research Com., 1985-95; joint coun. Food and Agr. Scis., 1985-95; nat. cons. vet medicine to surgeon gen. USAF, 1970-75; trustee Wyo. Blue Shield/Blue Cross, 1976-85, chmn. bd. trustees, 1982-83; adv. dir. Wyo. Indsl. Devel. Corp., 1968-79; commr. Wyo. Western Interstate Commn. Higher Edn., 1968-79; mem. pres. coun. Land Grant Colls. and State Univs., 1968—; pres. coun. Western

Athletic Conf., 1968-79; exec. com. Assn. Western Univs., 1970-79; regional adv. com. Inst. Internat. Edn., 1969-79; mem. scholarship com. Marathon Oil Co., 1977-79. Author: Veterinary Radiology, 3d edit, 1978; editor procs. Internat. Symposium on the Effects of Ionizing Radiation of the Reproductive System, 1964; contbr. articles to profl. jours. Exec. com. Longs Peak council Boy Scouts Am., 1966-80, pres., 1974-76, v.p., North Central region, 1970-74; regional chmn. Nat. Eagle Scout Assn., 1975-80, Silver Beaver award, 1974; bd. dirs. U. Wyo. Found., 1968-79; bd. visitors Air U., Maxwell AFB, 1972-75; mem. Yellowstone Park Assn. Bd., 1974-86, mem. emeritus, 1986—, vice-chmn., 1976-83; mem. 4H Found. Bd., 1994-95; vol. interpretive divsn. Nat. Park Svc. Yellowstone Nat. Park, 1996-97; vol. ct.-apptd. spl. advocate for abused children, 1997—. Named Outstanding Young Man of Yr. Colo. Jr. C. of C., 1960, Top Prof. Colo. State U., 1961, U.S. Vet. of Yr. Am. Animal Hosp. Assn., 1967, hon. alumni Colo. State U., 1971; recipient William E. Morgan award Colo. State U., 1989, Supervisory award Women's Action Taskforce, USDA, 1995, Group Honor award USDA, 1992. Fellow AAAS; mem. AVMA (trustee ins. trust 1985-87), Nat. Acad. Practice (treas. 1988-96, coun. 1988-96, founding mem. vet. medicine acad. 1986—), Am. Coll. Vet. Radiology (founding, diplomate), Nuclear Medicine Soc. Am. (nat. trustee 1964-68), Wyo. Med. Soc., Am. Vet. Radiology Soc. (charter, pres. 1965), Laramie C. of C. (bd. dirs. 1968-79), Wyo. Hosp. Assn. (dir. 1982-84, sec.-treas. 1983), Nat. Cowboy Hall of Fame (hon. life mem.), Rotary (bd. dirs. 1965-84, 95—). Home: 900 Whitney Ct Denton TX 76205-8248

CARLSON-NELSON, MARILYN, advertising executive. Chmn., pres., CEO Carlson Cos., Inc., Mpls., 1998—; bd. dirs. Exxon Co., U.S. West. Office: Carlson Cos Inc Carlson Pkwy PO Box 59159 Minneapolis MN 55459*

CARLSON-PICKERING, JANE, gifted education educator; b. Providence, Sept. 17, 1954; d. Arthur Julius and Laura Helen (Extovicz) Carlson; m. Allan Thomas Pickering, Nov. 2, 1980; children: Lauren, Taylor. BS in Art Edn., R.I. Coll., 1976, MEd in Art and Indsl. Arts Edn., 1983. Cert. elem. tchr. (life), R.I., gifted edn. tchr. Profl. photographer Ted Pickering Studios, Warwick, R.I., 1973—; calligraphy tchr. Warwick Adult Edn., 1978; secondary tchr. graphics arts Warwick Sch. Dept., 1976-78, secondary tchr. gifted program, 1978-83; elem. gifted program coordinator and tchr. Chariho Sch. System, Wyoming, R.I., 1983-94, multiple intelligences program dir., tchr. M.I. Smart!, 1994—; computer coord. Charing Elem. Schs., 1998—; mem. Commr.'s Task Force on Vocat. and Indsl. Arts Edn., Providence, 1984-85, Commr.'s Task Force on Gifted and Talented Edn., 1991-92, Chariho K-12 Curriculum Coun., 1992—, tech. com., 1993—; aerial photographer for Aerovisions, 1988-92; adj. faculty mem. R.I. Coll., 1996—; cons. R.I. Dept. Edn., 1996—; tchr. R.I. Found. Tchrs. in Tech. Program, summer 1998. Recipient First Pl. award photography contest Warwick Arts Found., 1984, Tchr. award Invent Am., 1991, Lunar Disc Program Tchr. Tng. Cert. NASA, 1991; grantee R.I. Found. Tchrs. Tech. Pilot Program, 1997. Mem. NEA, ASCD, State Advs. Gifted Edn., Nat. Student Art Edn. Assn. Club (treas. 1971-72), Epsilon Pi Tau. Avocations: photography, golf, biking, travel. Home: 209 Blueberry Ln West Kingston RI 02892-1818 Office: Chariho Sch Dept Switch Rd Wood River Junction RI 02894

CARLSSON, BO AXEL VILHELM, economics educator; b. Ulricehamn, Sweden, July 22, 1942; s. Carl Axel Valentin and Dagmar Elisabet (Karlsson) C.; m. Glenda Joyce Bishop, Dec. 28, 1965; children: Eric, Mark, Amy. BA, Harvard U., 1968; MA, Stanford U., 1970, PhD, 1972; Docent, Uppsala U., Sweden, 1980. Sr. rsch. assoc. Indsl. Inst. Econ. & Social Rsch., Stockholm, Sweden, 1972-84, dep. dir., 1977-81; Umstattd prof. indsl. econs. Case Western Res. U., Cleve., 1984—, chmn. dept. econs., 1984-87; assoc. dean rsch. and grad. programs Weatherhead Sch. Mgmt., 1996—; vis. scholar MIT, 1982; cons. World Bank, Washington, 1983-87, Swedish Fedn. Industries, Stockholm, 1984-89; min. of fin. Stockholm, 1993-94, Econ. Commn. for L.Am., 1996; project dir. Sweden's Tech. Sys., Stockholm, 1987—; mem. Indsl. and Sci. Coun., Nat. Bd. Tech. Devel., 1987-98; chair sci. adv. bd. Danish Rsch. Unit for Indsl. Dynamics, 1996—. Author: Technology and Industrial Structure, 1979, Industrial Subsidies, 1980, Swedish Industry Facing the 80s, 1981; editor: Industrial Dynamics, 1989, Technological Systems and Economic Performance, 1995, Technological Systems and Industrial Dynamics, 1997. Mem. Swedish cultural orgns. Mem. Europe Assn. Rsch. Indsl. Econs. (pres. 1983-85, exec. com.), Am. Econ. Assn., Ea. Econ. Assn. (bd. dirs. 1989-92), Internat. J.A. Schumpeter Soc. (prize selection com. 1988-90, 94-96), Assn. Christian Economists. Methodist. Home: 2708 Rochester Rd Cleveland OH 44122-2167 Office: Case Western Res Univ Weatherhead Sch Mgmt Dept Econs Cleveland OH 44106-7206

CARLSSON, PER ARVID EMIL, pharmacologist, educator; b. Uppsala, Sweden, Jan. 25, 1923; s. Gottfrid and Lizzie (Steffenburg) C.; m. Ulla-Lisa Christoffersson, Dec. 29, 1945; children: Bo, Lena, Hans, Maria, Magnus. MD, PhD, U. Lund, Sweden, 1951. Assoc. prof. dept. pharmacology U. Lund, 1956-59; prof. pharmacology U. Göteborg, Sweden, 1959-89, prof. emeritus, 1989—; vis. scientist Lab. of Chem. Pharmacology, Nat. Heart Inst., Bethesda, Md., 1955-56. Recipient Anders Jahre's Med. prize U. Oslo, 1974, Wolf prize in medicine, Jerusalem, 1979, Gairdner Found. award, Toronto, Can., 1982, 2d Ann. Bristol-Myers award for disting. achievement in neurosci. rsch., 1989, Japan prize in psychology and psychiatry Sci. and Tech. Found. Japan, 1994, Lieber prize for rsch. in schizophrenia Sci. Coun. of Nat. Alliance for Rsch. in Schizophrenia and Depression, 1994, rsch. prize Lundbeck Found., Denmark, 1995, Golden Kraepelin medal Max Planck Inst. Psychiatry, Munich, 1997, numerous others. Fellow Med. Soc. Gothenburg (hon.), World Fedn. Socs. Biol. Psychiatry (hon.), Collegium Internat. Neuropsychopharmacologicum (hon.), Academia Medicinae and Psychiatriae (hon.); mem. NAS (fgn. assoc.), Royal Soc. Sci. and Arts (Gothenburg), Japanese Pharmacological Soc. (fgn.), Am. Coll. Neuropsycholpharmacology (fgn.), German Pharmacological Soc. (corr.), Royal Swedish Acad. Sci., Acad. Europaea. Home: Torild Wulffsgatan 50, S-41319 Göteborg Sweden Office: U Gothenburg, Dept Pharm, S-41390 Göteborg Medicinaregatan 7, Sweden

CARLSTON, JOHN A., allergist; b. N.Y.C., Nov. 9, 1932; s. Ramon R. and Genevieve P. (Poss) C.; m. Jean L. Lawson, June 21, 1958; children: Ann, Kimberly, Susan. BS in Biology and Philosophy, Coll. of Holy Cross, 1954; MD, Yale U., 1958. Diplomate Am. Bd. Allergy and Immunology. Intern Akron (Ohio) Gen. Hosp., 1958-59, resident in internal medicine, 1959-61; fellow in allergy U. Pitts., 1961-62; instr. medicine in allergy U. Ill., Chgo., 1962-64; assoc. in medicine Northwestern U., Chgo., 1964-69; active staff in medicine Virginia Beach (Va.) Gen. Hosp., 1969—; assoc. prof. in medicine Eastern Va. Med. Sch., Norfolk, Va., 1974—; Bd. cert. Allergy, 1974, 77, 80, 83, 87, 93. Contbr. articles to profl. jours. Lt. col. U.S. Army Med. Corps, 1967-69. Fellow Am. Coll. Allergy and Immunology, Am. Acad. Allergy and Immunology; mem. Va. Allergy Assn., S.E. Allergy Assn., Va. Beach Med. Soc. (pres. 1976), Allergy Rehab. Found. (cons.). Republican. Episcopal. Avocations: go, travel, skiing, golf, tennis. Office: Asthma and Allergy Specialists Ltd 1704 Sir William Osler Dr Virginia Beach VA 23454-3083

CARLTON, ALFRED PERSHING, JR., lawyer; b. Raleigh, N.C., Aug. 27, 1947; s. Alfred P. and Katherine (Singleton) C.; children: Mary Elizabeth, Troy Eugene. BSBA, U. N.C., 1969, JD, 1975; MPA, U. Dayton, 1973. Bar: N.C. 1975, U.S. Dist. Ct. (ea. dist.) N.C. 1975, U.S. Ct. Appeals (4th cir.) 1976, U.S. Supreme Ct. 1993. Pvt. practice Raleigh, 1975-77; counsel N.C. Bankers Assn., Raleigh, 1977-79; sec., gen. counsel Bancshares N.C., Inc., Raleigh, 1979-82; adj. prof. law Campbell U., Buies Creek, N.C., 1979-82; ptnr. Sanford, Adams, McCullough & Beard, Raleigh, 1983-89; shareholder McNair & Sanford, Raleigh, 1990-95; ptnr. The Sanford Holshouser Law Firm, Raleigh, 1995—. Mem. City of Raleigh Hist. Properties and Hist. Dists. Commn., 1978-82; mem. exec. bd. Occoneechee coun. Boy Scouts Am., 1983-94; trustee U. N.C. at Wilmington, 1997—. Served to 1st lt. Med. Svc. Corps, USAF, 1970-73. Fellow Am. Bar Found.; mem. ABA (ho. of dels. 1987—, chair of the house 1996-98, bd. govs. 1996-98), N.C. Bar Assn. (bd. govs. 1981-82, 92-95), Am. Law Inst., N.C. Legis. Rsch. Commn. (study com. on pub. financing 1985-88). Democrat. Episcopalian. Avocations: tennis, gardening. Office: The Sanford Holshouser Law Firm PO Box 2447 Raleigh NC 27602-2447

CARLTON, BRUCE J., transportation company executive; b. Detroit, Sept. 10, 1948. Assoc. adminstr. policy and internat. trade Dept. Transp., Washington, 1995—. Office: Dept Transp 400 7th St SW Washington DC 20590

CARLTON, CAROLE GASSETT, medical/surgical nurse; b. Thomaston, Ga., Sept. 8, 1941; d. Oliver M. and Nan (Slaughter) Gassett; m. Frederick Michael Carlton, Apr. 22, 1967; children: Michelle Leigh, Andrea Lynne. AS, Ga. Southwestern Coll. Nursing, Americus, 1964, student, 1960-64. Cert. kidney transplant nurse. Staff nurse Phoebe Putney Meml. Hosp., Albany, Ga., 1964-65; office nurse Albany, 1965-68; nurse, med.-surg unit St. Clare's Hosp., Schenectady, N.Y., 1982-83; nurse kidney transplant, open heart surgery SUNY Health Sci. Ctr., Syracuse, 1983-89; neurosurg. adolescent and pediatrics unit nurse Crouse Irving Meml. Hosp., Syracuse, 1989—. Avocations: horticulture, crafts and sewing, camping, reading. Home: 701 Hudson St Syracuse NY 13219-1007

CARLTON, CHARLES MERRITT, linguistics educator; b. Poultney, Vt., Dec. 12, 1928; s. Clarence Rann and Margaret Louise (Pennell) C.; m. Mary MacDonald, Aug. 31, 1957; children: David, John, Stephen. A.B., U. Vt., 1950; M.A., Middlebury Coll., 1951; Ph.D., U. Mich., 1963. Instr. Mich. State U., East Lansing, 1958-62; asst. prof. U. Mo., Columbia, 1962-66; prof. French and Romance linguistics U. Rochester, N.Y., 1966—; asst. dir. NDEA French Inst., U. Vt., Burlington, summer 1964; lectr. U.S. State Dept Seminars, Brasov, Romania, summer 1972, U. Ky., Cluj, Romania, summer 1977; reader NEH, 1974—, dept edn. title VI programs, 1993; Fulbright lectr., 1971-72, Romania, 1986, Brazil. Author: Studies in Romance Lexicology, 1965, A Linguistic Analysis of a Collection of Late Latin Documents Composed in Ravenna Between A.D. 445-700: A Quantitative Approach, 1973, Romanian Poetry in English Translation: An Annotated Bibliography and Census (1740-1996), 1997; bibliographer: Romanian Language and Linguistics, 1973, 75-91, Comparative Romance Linguistics Newsletter; co-translator: (G. Doca) Acquisition Grammar of Romanian, 1995, (A. Marino) The Biography of the Idea of Literature, 1996; editor: Comparative Romance Linguistics newsletter, 1970-71. Fulbright fellow, Paris, 1950-51; fellow NSF, summer 1965, Nat. Def. Fgn. Lang., summer 1970; Fulbright grantee, 1974, 78, 82, 88, Romania, IREX grantee, 1982, 91. Mem. Am. Assn. Advancement Slavic Studies, Am. Assn. Tchrs. Spanish and Portuguese, Am. Romanian Acad., N.Am. Catalan Soc., Romanian Studies Assn. Am., Soc. Romanian Studies, UN Assn. Rochester, Rennes-Rochester Sister City Assn. (steering com.), Sigma Delta Pi. Home: 3 Thornfield Way Fairport NY 14450-3023

CARLTON, DEAN, lawyer; b. Fort Worth, Nov. 4, 1928; s. Robert Ardine and Marjorie (Box) C.; m. Mary Ellen Williams, Sept. 9, 1949; children: Robert Mark, Scott Duane, Mary Ann. BS, Tex. A&M Coll., 1949; LLB, So. Methodist U., 1952. Bar: Tex. 1952, U.S. Supreme Ct 1968. Pvt. practice Dallas, 1952-78; propr. The Carlton Firm, P.C., Dallas, 1970-98, Fiedler, Akin, Frank & Carlton, P.A., Dallas, 1998—. Mem. City of Richardson Bd. Adjustment, 1966-67, Tex. Water Code Adv. Com., 1968-70; co-founder, chmn. Dallas Martini Found. and Trust, 1970-85. Mem. ABA, Tex. Bar Assn., Tex. Aggie Bar Assn. (pres. 1974-75), Dallas Bar Assn., Richardson Bar Assn. (pres. 1968), Tex. A&M 12th Man Found. (exec. com. 1980-86, pres. 1985). Home: 7038 Spring Valley Rd Dallas TX 75240-2719 Office: Fiedler Akin Frank & Carlton PA 450 N Central Plaza III 12801 N Central Expy Ste 450 Dallas TX 75243-1799

CARLTON, DENNIS WILLIAM, economics educator; b. Boston, Feb. 15, 1951; s. Jay and Mildred C.; m. Jane R. Berkowitz, 1971; children: Deborah, Rebecca, Daniel. BA summa cum laude, Harvard U., 1972; MS in Ops. Research, MIT, 1974, PhD in Econs., 1975. Instr. econs. MIT, Cambridge, Mass., 1975-76; asst. prof. econs. U. Chgo., 1976-79, assoc. prof., 1979-80; prof. U. Chgo. Law Sch., 1980-84, U. Chgo. Grad. Sch. Bus., 1984—; with Lexecon, Chgo., 1977—. Author: Market Behavior Under Uncertainty, 1984 (Outstanding Dissertation award 1984), (with J. Perloff) Modern Industrial Organization, 1994; co-editor Jour. Law and Econs., 1980—. Recipient P.W.S. Andrews prize Jour. Indsl. Econs., 1979. Mem. Am. Econ. Assn., Econometric Soc., Phi Beta Kappa. Jewish. Office: Univ Chgo Grad Sch Business 1101 E 58th St Chicago IL 60637-1511

CARLTON, DONALD MORRILL, research, development and engineering executive; b. Houston, July 20, 1937; s. Spencer William and Ruth (Morrill) C.; m. Elaine Yvonne Smith, Jan. 28, 1961; children: Donna Kay, Spencer Frank, Monica Elaine. BA, U. St. Thomas, Houston, 1958; PhD, U. Tex., Austin, 1962. Mem. staff, then group leader Sandia Corp., Albuquerque, 1962-65; with Tracor, Inc., Austin, 1965-69; asst. dir. research Tracor, Inc., 1968-69; pres., chmn. bd. Radian Corp., Austin, 1969-95; pres., CEO Radian Internat., LLC, Austin, 1996-98, ret., 1998; chmn. adv. coun. Inst. Nuclear Power Ops., 1998; bd. dirs. Ctrl. and S.W. Corp., Concert Investment Series U. St. Thomas, Houston, Nat. Instruments Corp. Past chmn. natural sci. adv. coun. U. Tex., Austin, mem. Engring. Found. adv. coun., mem. adv. coun. Electric Power Rsch. Inst.; chmn. Texans for Jud. Election Reform. Mem. Nat. Coal Coun. (exec. com.), Am. Chem. Soc., Tex. Taxpayers and Rsch. Assn. (past chmn.), Austin C. of C. (past dir.), Tex. C. of C. (past chmn.). Home: Apt 4 2305 Barton Creek Blvd Unit 4 Austin TX 78735-1648 Office: Radian Internat LLC PO Box 201088 8501 N Mo Pac Expy Austin TX 78720-1088

CARLTON, ERIC L., lawyer; b. Birmingham, Ala., May 4, 1948. BA magna cum laude, Vanderbilt U., 1970; JD cum laude, Harvard U., 1973. Bar: Ga. 1973, Ala. 1976, Fla. 1994. Mem. Burr & Forman, Birmingham, Ala. Fellow Am. Coll. Mortgage Attys.; mem. ABA, State Bar Ga., Birmingham Bar Assn., Ala. State Bar (mem. state bd. of bar examiners 1979-82), Phi Beta Kappa. Office: Burr & Forman LLP 3100 South Trust Tower 420 20th St N Box 830719 Birmingham AL 35283*

CARLTON, MICHAEL, magazine editor. Exec. editor Southern Living, Birmingham. Office: Southern Living 2100 Lakeshore Dr Birmingham AL 35209-6721*

CARLTON, PAUL KENDALL, JR., air force officer, physician; b. Roswell, N.Mex., May 13, 1947; s. Paul Kendall and Helen C. (Sweat) C.; m. Dorothea Janice Prichard, July 5, 1969; children: Paul Kendall III, Christianne Joy, Stephanie Jill, Luke Jeffrey. BS, U.S. Air Force Acad., 1969; MD, U. Colo., Denver, 1973. Diplomate Am. Bd. Surgery. Commd. 2d lt. U.S. Air Force, 1969, advanced through grades to maj. gen., 1995; resident in surgery Wilford Hall Med. Ctr., San Antonio, 1973-78; comdr. USAF Hosp. Torrejon, Madrid, 1985-88, Scott Med. Ctr., Scott AFB, Ill., 1988-91; command surgeon Air Edn. and Tng. Command, San Antonio, 1991-94; comdr. Wilford Hall Med. Ctr., San Antonio, 1994-99. Decorated Air medal, Legion of Merit (2). Fellow ACS (gov. 1992-96). Avocations: hunting, flying. Office: Air Force Med Ops Agy Bolling AFB 110 Julu Ave Rm 405 Washington DC 30332-7050

CARLTON, STEVEN NORMAN, retired professional baseball player; b. Miami, Fla., Dec. 22, 1944. Student, Miami Dade Jr. Coll. Pitcher St. Louis Cardinals, 1965-71, Phila. Phillies, 1972-86, San Francisco Giants, 1986, Chgo. White Sox, 1986, Cleve. Indians, 1987, Minn. Twins, 1987-88. Recipient Nat. League Cy Young Meml. award, 1972, 77, 80, 82; named lefthanded pitcher Nat. League All-Star Team, Sporting News, 1968, 69, 71, 72, 74, 77, 79, 80, 81, 82, Pitcher of Yr. Sporting News, 1972, 77, 80, 82; inducted into Baseball Hall of Fame, 1994. Address: care MLB Players Alumni Assn 1631 Mesa Ave Ste C Colorado Springs CO 80906-2917*

CARLTON, TERRY SCOTT, chemist, educator; b. Peoria, Ill., Jan. 29, 1939; s. Daniel Cushman and Mabel (Smith) C.; m. Claudine Fields, 1960; children: Brian, David. B.S., Duke U., 1960; Ph.D. (NSF grad. fellow 1960-63), U. Calif., Berkeley, 1963. Mem. faculty Oberlin (Ohio) Coll., 1963—, prof. chemistry, 1976—, chmn. dept., 1980-83; vis. prof. chemistry U. N.C., Chapel Hill, 1976. Co-author: Composition, Reaction and Equilibrium, 1970. Mem. Am. Chem. Soc. Home: 165 Fairway Dr Oberlin OH 44074-1420 Office: Oberlin Coll Dept Chemistry Oberlin OH 44074

CARLUCCI, GINO DOMINIC, JR., urban planner, policy analyst; b. Milford, Mass., July 2, 1952; s. Gino Dominic and Antonietta Italia C.; m. Pandora Patricia Grewe, Oct. 11, 1980; children: Michael Grewe, Nathan Anthony. AB in Govt., Georgetown U., 1974; M in Urban and Regional Planning, U. New Orleans, 1978. Cert. planner Am. Inst. Cert. Planners. Coastal resources analyst La. Dept. Transp. and Devel., Baton Rouge, 1977-78; dir. environ. affairs City of New Orleans Mayor's Office, 1978-81, dir. analysis, planning, 1981-85; sr. planner Morphy, Makofsky, Mumphrey, Masson, 1985-89; prin. PGC Assocs., Franklin, Mass., 1989—; spl. lectr. U. New Orleans, 1982; town planner Town of Sherborn, Mass., 1995—. Prodr.: (video) The Impacts of Growth in Franklin, 1994. Bd. dirs. Metocomet Land Trust, Franklin, Mass., 1988-93, Tri-Town Cmty. Devel. Corp., Bellington, Mass., 1994-95; alumni interviewer admissions office Georgetown U., Washington, 1994—; den leader, asst. scoutmaster Boy Scouts Am., Franklin, 1990—; mem. Franklin Indsl. Devel. Fin. Com., 1989—. Mem. Am. Inst. Cert. Planners (cert. planner), Am. Planning Assn. (La. chpt., Outstanding Planning award 1985), Mass. Assn. Cons. Planners. Avocations: gardening, sports.

CARLUCCI, JOSEPH P., lawyer; b. Port Chester, N.Y., Aug. 21, 1942; m. Elizabeth Smith; children: Susan Elizabeth, Kathleen Ann. B.A. in Econs., Georgetown U., 1964; J.D., Fordham U., 1967. Bar: N.Y. 1969. Ptnr. Pierro & Carlucci, Port Chester, N.Y., 1969-76; pvt. practice law, Rye, N.Y., 1977-78; mng. ptnr. Cuddy & Feder, White Plains, N.Y., 1979—; chief legis. counsel to N.Y. senator from Westchester County, 1971-73; chief counsel N.Y. State Select Com. on State's Economy, 1973-74. Trustee Village of Port Chester, 1974-77; chmn. Port Chester Indsl. Devel. Agy., 1974-76; mem. Westchester County Econ. Devel. Coun., 1976-80, Narcotics Guidance Council of Port Chester, 1970-74; chmn. Met. N.Y. YMCA Key Leaders Conf., 1984; mem. Parents Coun. Wheaton Coll., 1986-87; bd. dirs. Port Chester YMCA, 1970-79, sec., 1972-77, v.p., 1978; mem. Port Chester Govt. Study Commn., 1971-73; commr. of appraisal White Plains and Greenburgh Urban Renewal; counsel to Sound Shore Hotline, 1973-74; mem. Port Chester Pub. Employees Rels. Bd., 1973-77; mem. adv. bd. dirs. Salvation Army, 1973-77; adv. bd. Security Title and Guaranty Co., 1986-90; bd. dirs. Rye YMCA, 1979-87, pres., 1982-85, trustee, 1989—; trustee Rye Hist. Soc., 1979-83, 90-96 sec., 1980-81, v.p., 1982-83, 92-94, pres., 1994-96; interviewer Georgetown U. Alumni Admissions Program, 1988-96; bd. visitors Pace U. Sch. Law, 1990—; bd. dirs. Vol. Ctr. United Way Westchester County, 1991-97; mem. Westchester div. Cardinal's Com. for the Laity, 1991—, vice-chmn., 1992, chmn., 1993-95; mem. paralegal curriculum adv. com. SUNY/Westchester C.C., 1994; mem. bd. dirs. March of Dimes Birth Defects Found., 1994-96, Westchester Bus. Partnership, 1995-98. Recipient Golden R award Rennaissance Project, Inc., Gold Man award YMCA, 1985, Cmty. Svc. award Rotary Internat. Club, 1995. Mem. ABA (vice chmn. econs. of law practice com. on lawyering skills 1984-85), NY State Bar Assn., Westchester County Bar Assn. (real property com. 1978-82), Port Chester-Rye Bar Assn. (sec. 1970-75, pres. 1976, 77, bd. dirs Student Assistance Svcs. alcohol and drug abuse prevention program 1989-95, adv. bd. 1995—), Westchester C.C. Found. (bd. dirs. 1997—), Coveleigh Club (bd. govs. 1978-86, sec. 1979, v.p. 1980, pres. 1981-84) (Rye); Georgetown U. Met. Club (bd. dirs. 1980-82), Rye Town-Port Chester Rep. Club (co-founder, v.p. 1972), Hundred Club Westchester, Inc. (bd. dirs.).

CARLUCCI, MARIE ANN, nursing administrator, nurse; b. N.Y.C., Apr. 22, 1953; d. Clarence Hugh and Anna Rebecca (Mills) McNamee; m. Paul Pasquale Carlucci, Aug. 18, 1973; children: Christine, Patricia. Diploma in nursing, Mt. Vernon Hosp. Sch. Nursing, N.Y., 1974; BS in Behavioral Sci. summa cum laude, Mercy Coll., 1991; MPH, N.Y. Med. Coll., 1997. Cert. emergency nurse; cert. nurse adminstr. Staff nurse Mt. Vernon (N.Y.) Hosp., 1974-82, Lawrence Hosp., Bronxville, N.Y., 1982-84; staff nurse No. Westchester Hosp., Mt. Kisco, N.Y., 1984-91, asst. dir. nursing, mem. nurse mgmt. and ethics coms., 1991-94; asst. DON svcs. Ferncliff Manor, Yonkers, N.Y., 1994-95, dir. nursing svcs., 1995-98; dep. dir. nursing svcs. Taylor Care Ctr., Westchester, N.Y., 1998—. Religious edn. tchr. St. John and St. Mary's Ch., Chappagua, N.Y., 1984—; campaign mgr. Com. to Elect Paul P. Carlucci, Chappaqua, 1990; mem. Surrogate Decision Making Com., N.Y. Commn. Quality Care for Mentally Disabled; mem. bd. trustees Field Home-Holy Comforter, 1995—. Mem. N.Y. State MR/DD Nurses Assn., St. John and St. Mary's Women's Assn., Psi Chi, Phi Gamma Mu. Roman Catholic. Home: 23 Pineview Rd # 5 Mount Kisco NY 10549-3935 Office: Taylor Care Ctr Westchester 25 Bradhurst St Hawthorne NY 10595

CARLUCCI, PAUL V., publishing company executive. Various sales positions N.Y. Daily News, mgr. account sales Retail City; advt. mgr. N.Y. divsn. R.H. Macy, Inc., 1979-80, councilor, 1979-80, adminstr., advt. dir., 1981-83; sr. v.p. sales promotion Midwest divsn. R.H. Macy, Inc., Kansas City, Mo., 1983-85; sr. v.p. sales promotion Macy's N.J., 1985-89; sr. v.p., dir. mktg. Caldor, Inc., Norwalk, Conn., 1989-93; pres. News Am. FSI, Inc. subs. News Corp. Ltd., N.Y.C., 1993-95; CEO, News Am. Pub., Inc., N.Y.C., 1995-97; chmn., CEO News Am. Mktg., Norwalk, Conn., 1997—. Office: News Am Mktg 301 Merritt 7 PO Box 5102 Norwalk CT 06856*

CARLUCCIO, SHEILA COOK, psychologist; b. Carbondale, Pa., Nov. 10, 1954; d. Harry Thomas and Elizabeth Mary Cook; m. Robert Carluccio, Feb. 28, 1987; 1 stepchild, Robert Jr. BA, Marywood Coll., 1982, MA, 1987. Lic. psychologist. Sign lang. interpreter for hearing-impaired Scranton (Pa.) State Sch. for Deaf, 1984-86, psychology intern, 1986; staff clin. psychologist Devereux Found., Chester, N.J., 1987-88, Hope House, Dover, N.J., 1989-94, U. Scranton, Pa., 1994-95; pvt. practice Dickson City, Pa., 1993—. One woman art shows include Sterling Hotel, Wilkes-Barre, Pa., Sol Hemma, Uniondale, Pa., 1980; exhibited at Suraci Gallery, Scranton, Pa., 1979; contbr. poems to lit. jours. Human svc. team mem. Morris County Human Svc. Orgn., Dover, 1992. Mem. APA (assoc.), Am. Deafness and Rehab. Assn. (assoc.), Pa. Psychol. Assn. Psi Chi. Roman Catholic. Avocations: musician, vocalist, artist, writer. Office: 123 Huntington Dr Dickson City PA 18519-1150

CARLYON, DIANE CLAIRE, nurse; b. Butte, Mont., Nov. 5, 1950; d. Roy and Claire Jenny (Madison) C.; (div.); children: Michael Wade Jr., Tammy Michelle. BSN, U. Tenn., 1987. Cert. std. first aid/CPR instr., ARC; cert. CPR instr., Am. Heart Assn. Staff nurse Oakland Naval Hosp., Calif., Kimberly Nurses, Memphis; staff nurse, staff nurse Meth. Cen. Hosp., Memphis; utilization mgmt. Qual-Med Health Plan, Bellevue, Wash.; utilization mgmt./quality assurance coord. Gen. Hosp. of Everett; IV infusion specialist Homedco, Redmond, Wash.; clin. field coord. Vis. Nurse's of N.W. Everett, Everett, Wash., 1991-95; infusion therapy coord. Vis. Nurses Svcs. of N.W., Seattle, 1995—, staff devel. specialist, 1998—; mem. adv. coun. Wellspring Adult Care. Mem. Meth. Hosp. Staff Adv. Bd., Assistance Impaired Nursing Students Com., Egyptian God of Leadership Soc., Snohomish County AIDS Task Force Consortium, 1991—, Ryan White Care Funds Planning Coun., Snohomish County AIDS Walk Com., 1994-97; bd. mem. AIDS Project Snohomish County, 1996—; task force Home Care of Wash., VRE. Mem. ANA, Tenn. Nurses Assn. (task force HIV), Wash. Nurses Assn., Intravenous Nurse Soc., Continuing Nursing Edn. (com.). Home: 23000 Edmonds Way Apt 408 Edmonds WA 98020-8205 Office: Vis Nurses Svcs NW Seattle WA 98037

CARMACK, COMER ASTON, JR., steel company executive; b. Phenix City, Ala., June 26, 1932; s. Comer Aston and Mary Kate (Mills) C.; AS, Marion Mil. Inst., 1951; BS, Ala. Poly. Inst., 1954; m. Blanche Yarbrough, Nov. 30, 1957; children: Comer Aston, Mary Kate. Project mgr. Muscogee Iron Works, Columbus, Ga., 1956-58, v.p. engring., 1958-73, pres., 1973-91, chmn. bd. dirs. 1991—; pres. Universal Drives & Svcs., 1985-89; pres. M.K. Realty, Columbus, 1985-91, chmn. bd. dirs. 1991—. Past bd. dirs. Better Bus. Bur. With USAFR, 1954-56. Registered profl. engr., Calif. Mem. ASTM, Nat. Soc. Profl. Engrs., Ga. Soc. Profl. Engrs., Ga. Archtl. and Engring. Soc. (past pres., bd. dir. Columbus chpt.), Order of Engr., Chattahooche Valley Safety Soc., Columbus Country Club. Methodist. Office: Muscogee Iron Works 1324 11th Ave Columbus GA 31901-2202

CARMACK, MILDRED JEAN, retired lawyer; b. Folsom, Calif., Sept. 3, 1938; d. Kermit Leroy Brown and Elsie Imogene (Johnston) Walker; m. Allan W. Carmack, 1957 (div. 1979); 1 child, Kerry Jean Carmack Garrett. Student, Linfield Coll., 1955-58; BA, U. Oreg., 1967, JD, 1969. Bar: Oreg. 1969, U.S. Dist. Ct. Oreg. 1980, U.S. Ct. Appeals (9th and fed. cirs.) 1980, U. S. Claims Ct. 1987. Law clk. to Hon. William McAllister Oreg. Supreme Ct., Salem, 1969-73, asst. to ct., 1976-80; asst. prof. U. Oreg. Law Sch., Eugene, 1973-76; assoc. Schwabe, Williamson & Wyatt, Portland,

Oreg., 1980-83, ptnr., 1984-96, ret., 1996; writer, lectr., legal educator, Oreg., 1969—; mem. exec. bd. Appellate sect. Oreg. State Bar, 1993-95. Contbr. articles to Oreg. Law Rev., 1967-70. Mem. citizen adv. com. State Coastal Planning Commn., Oreg., 1974-76, State Senate Judiciary Com., Oreg., 1984; mem. bd. visitors Law Sch. U. Oreg., 1992-95. Mem. Oreg. State Bar Assn., Order of Coif.

CARMAN, ANNE, management consultant; b. Kansas City, Mo., Mar. 17, 1942; d. Martin Albert and Areleta Laynelle (Burditt) Utterback; m. Robert G. Stevens, Dec. 30, 1989; children: James Powell Carman Jr., Christopher Tully Carman. BS in Edn., U. Mo., 1965, MA, 1968, PhD, 1983. Coord. women's studies U. Mo., Columbia, 1977-81, mgr. ann. giving, 1981-83; dir. ann. giving Found., So. Ill. U. Found., Carbondale, 1983-85, dir. major gifts, 1985-86, pres., 1986-88; mem. bus. adv. com. So. Ill. U., Carbondale, 1987-88, 91-97; v.p. Coun. for Advancement and Support Edn., Washington, 1988-90, The Aspen Inst., Washington, 1990-92, The Points of Light Found., Washington, 1993-96; sr. ptnr. Fin. Mgmt. Ptnrs., Annapolis, Md., 1992—. Bd. dirs. Greater D.C. Cares, 1993-97, Support Ctr. of Washington, 1993—. Avocations: sailing, hiking, bicycling, reading. Home: 1690 Coventry Pl Annapolis MD 21401-6422 Office: Fin Mgmt Partners 1690 Coventry Pl Annapolis MD 21401-6422

CARMAN, GARY O., hospital administrator. BS, SUNY, Buffalo, 1962, MS in Spl. Edn., 1965; cert. advanced studies in spl. edn., Syracuse U., 1968, PhD in Spl. Edn., 1972. Dir. spl. edn. and spl. svcs. Yonkers (N.Y.) Pub. Sch. System, 1972-75; pres., CEO Julia Dyckman Andrus Meml., Yonkers, 1975—. Contbr. articles to profl. jours. Bd. dirs. Salvation Army, 1977-88, chair bd. dirs. 1986-87; mem. Mayor of Yonkers Blue Ribbon Task Force for selection of Bd. Edn., 1988-90; mem. Yonkers 2000 Com., 1989-91; bd. dirs. Alliance for Children and Families, 1998—; chair Westchester Behavioral Healthcare Network, 1996-98; governing bd. Internat. Coun. for Exceptional Children, 1980-83. Named Paul Harris fellow Yonkers Rotary Club, 1987. Mem. Nat. Assn. of Homes and Svcs. for Children (bd. dirs. 1984-87, pres. 1996-97, v.p. 1994-96, other coms.), Child Welfare League of Am. (com. on quality improvement, evaluation and rsch. 1995—), Institut Internat. d'Edn. Specialisee (bd. dirs. 1990—, chmn. internat. congress, chair Am. delegratio to Internat. Congress in Vienna 1992-96). Office: Julia Dyckman Andrus Meml Yonkers NY 10701

CARMAN, GEORGE HENRY, retired physician; b. Albany, N.Y., Sept. 23, 1928; s. Simon Peter and Mary (Whish) C. BA, Cornell U., 1948, MD, 1951. Diplomate: Am. Bd. Internal Medicine, Am. Bd. Cardiovascular Disease. Intern, then asst. resident in medicine Barnes Hosp., St. Louis, 1951-53; asst. resident in medicine Salt Lake County Gen. Hosp., 1955-56; chief resident VA Hosp., Salt Lake City, 1956-57; fellow cardiovascular diseases U. Utah Coll. Medicine, 1957-60; practice medicine specializing in cardiology and internal medicine Dallas, 1960-89; attending physician Baylor U. Med. Center, 1960-89; mem. clin. faculty U. Tex. Southwestern Med. Sch., Dallas, 1960-89; clin. prof. internal medicine U. Tex. Southwestern Med. Sch., 1972-89; ret., 1989. Served to 1st lt. M.C. AUS, 1953-55. Fellow ACP (emeritus), Am. Coll. Cardiology (emeritus); mem. AAAS, Am. Heart Assn. (emeritus fellow coun. clin. cardiology), Confrerie de Chaine des Rotisseurs (comdr.), Cornell Club (N.Y.), Phi Beta Kappa, Alpha Omega Alpha. Episcopalian. Home: # 19-D 3525 Turtle Creek Blvd Apt 19-d Dallas TX 75219-5514

CARMAN, GREGORY WRIGHT, federal judge; b. Farmingdale, N.Y., Jan. 31, 1937; s. Willis B. and Marjorie (Sosa) C. Exch. student, U. Paris, 1956-57; BA, St. Lawrence U., 1958; JD, St. John's U., 1961; Judge Adv. Gen. honors grad., U. Va. Law Sch., 1962. Bar: N.Y. 1961. Atty. Carman, Callahan & Sabino, Farmingdale, N.Y., 1964-83; councilman Town of Oyster Bay, N.Y., 1972-81; mem. 97th Congress from 3d Dist. N.Y., 1981-82; U.S. Congl. del. I.M.F. Cong., 1982; judge U.S. Ct. Internat. Trade, N.Y.C., 1983—, acting chief judge, 1991, now chief judge; statutory mem. Jud. Conf. U.S., 1991. Capt. AUS, 1962-64. Fellow Am. Bar Found.; mem. ABA, N.Y. State Bar Assn. (cts. and cmty. com.), N.Y. State Defs. Assn., Criminal Cts. Bar Assn., Nassau County Bar Assn., Nassau Lawyers Assn., St. John's Law Rev. Republican. Episcopalian. Office: US Ct Internat Trade 1 Federal Plz New York NY 10278-0001*

CARMAN, JOHN HERBERT, elementary education educator; b. New Brunswick, N.J., Feb. 5, 1937; s. John Herbert and Lillian Elizabeth (Twyman) C.; m. Linda Kyle, Aug. 26, 1979. BA in Bus. Adminstrn., Rutgers U., 1960, postgrad., 1977-85; elem. teaching cert., Trenton State Coll., 1965; postgrad., Kean Coll., 1979-81. Cert. K-8 tchr., N.J. Tchr. Jr. High Sch., New Brunswick, 1961-81, Lincoln Elem. Sch., New Brunswick, 1981-98; baseball coach St. Peter's Grammar Sch., 1971-1995; coord. summer playgrounds New Brunswick Recreation Dept., 1956-89. Trustee Rutgers U., New Brunswick, 1986-92, 1996—, mem. Kirkpatrick Chapel com., 1981-85, mem. St. Michaels Chapel com., 1981-83, treas., 1991-98; co-chair Friends of the Geology Mus., 1995—; active Procter Found., 1992—. With U.S. Army, 1962. Recipient Loyal Son of Rutgers award Rutgers U., 1978, Meritorious Svc. award, 1991, Gov.'s Tchr. Recognition award, 1998, Middlesex County Vocat. Schs. award, 1998; named New Brunswick Citizen of Week, 1980, Alec Baker award KC, 1984, Colgate-Palmolive award for edn. achievement, 1992; 1937 state scholar Rutgers U., 1956-60; named to St. Peter's Hall of Fame, 1996. Mem. N.J. Edn. Assn., Middlesex County Edn. Assn., New Brunswick Edn. Assn., St. Peter's Athletic Assn., Rutgers Coll. Alumni Assn. (corr. sec., v.p., pres.-elect 1982-85, pres. 1985-86, Phonothon All Star Team 1991-97, Hall of Fame 1997). Episcopalian. Avocations: sports, reading, theater, musical programs. Home: PO Box 602 Mount Desert ME 04660-0602 Office: Kyles Keep 110 Main St Bar Harbor ME 04660

CARMAN, ROBERT EUGENE, elementary school educator; b. Malden, Mo., July 21, 1940; s. Beauford Lav and Margaret Lav (Wiseman) C.; m. Betty Ann Robertson, July 1963 (div. 1968); m. Nada Joyce Shoemaker, Nov. 2, 1968; children: Jason Austin, Justin Aaron (dec.). BS in Edn., Southeast Mo. State Coll., 1962; MS in Combined Scis., U. Miss., 1966, cert., 1988. Cert. tchr., Mo. Tchr. math. Malden (Mo.) High Sch., 1962-67; tchr. math. Hazelwood Jr. High Sch., Florissant, Mo., 1967-72, supr. math., 1972-92, ret., 1992; early childhood and elem. edn. instr. U. Mo., St. Louis, 1993-95; mid. level specialist SMILE Inst., St. Louis, 1989; cons. pub. schs., St. Louis, 1989-91, 96-99, St. Genevieve, Mo., 1990, Riverview Gardens Sch. Dist., St. Louis County, Mo., 1990, Mehlville, Mo., 1990-95, St. Charles, Mo., 1991, Wentzville, Mo., 1994, others, including Glencoe Pub. and Mimosa Pub., Milliken Pub.; program cons. Math. and Sci. Edn. Ctr., 1986-91. Author: Using Cooperative Techniques and Manipulatives to Teach Core Competence and Key Skills, 1989, Supermarket Math, 1993; editor books, software, manipulatives, articles, Math. Tchr., 1984—. Named Hazelwood Jr. High Sch. Tchr. of Yr., 1992-93. Mem. ASCD, Educators Greater St. Louis (bd. dirs. 1984-86, pres. 1988-89, newsletter editor 1986-88, Educator of Yr. 1991-92, chmn. student support spring conf. 1995), Mo. Coun. Tchrs. Math. (pres. 1992-93, exec. bd. 1988-90, chmn. jr. h.s. math. contest 1988-90, chair contest test writing, gen. chmn. spring meeting 1991, Educator of Yr. 1991-92), Nat. Coun. Tchrs. Math. (chmn. student exhibit St. Louis Cen. Regional conf. 1988, chmn. mid grades conf. program 1991, chmn. workshop support Springfield Cen. Regional conf. 1995), Am. Philatelic Soc. Avocation: stamp collecting. Home: 3125 Matlock Dr Florissant MO 63031-1519

CARMAN, SUSAN HUFERT, nurse coordinator; b. Detroit, Oct. 2, 1940; d. Theodore Louis and Margaret L. (O'Connor) Hufert; children: Amy E., Holly C., John T. BSN, Johns Hopkins U., 1964; MEd, Northeastern U., 1975; MS in Health Care Adminstrn., Simmons Coll., 1988. Instr. psychiat. nursing Salem (Mass.) Hosp. Sch. Nursing, 1975-78, Curry Coll., Milton, Mass., 1978-80; editor Beacon Comm. Corp., Acton, Mass., 1980-84; writer health promotion Honeywell Inc., Waltham, Mass., 1984-85; mgr. mental health unit Heritage Hosp., Somerville, Mass., 1986-87; specialist adult psychiatry Mass. Dept. Mental Health, Boston, 1987-93; clinician intensive clin. svcs. MHMA, Boston, 1994-96; dir. Arbour Counseling Svcs. Boston, 1996—; with SHC Assocs., Boston, 1993—; bd. dirs. Com. to End. Elder Homelessness, Boston, Mass., 1993-99, Dept. Social Svcs., Lowell, sec., 1982-92. Chair health com. Jamaica Plain (Mass.) Tree of Life/Arbol da Vida, 1994—; docent Arnold Arboretum, Boston, 1989—. Mem. ANA, Mass. Nurses Assn. Avocations: travel, reading, walking, classical music.

CARMEAN, JERRY RICHARD, broadcast engineer; b. Greenfield, Ohio, Apr. 2, 1938; s. Cloyde B. and Mary F. (Hedges) C.; m. Patricia H. Carmean; 1 child, Steven. BS in Edn., Ohio U., 1965, BS in Elec. Engring., 1984. Registered profl. engr., Ohio; lic. FCC gen. class radiotelephone operator. Tchr. New Philadelphia (Ohio) High Sch., 1965-66; broadcast engr. Ohio U. Telecommunications Ctr., Athens, 1966-81, dir. engring., 1981-92; pvt. broadcast engring. cons., 1992—; cons. Sta. WLGN, Logan, Ohio, 1964—; tech. cons. Sta. 4VEH, Cap hatien, Haiti. Served with U.S. Army, 1961-64. Mem. NSPE, Ohio Soc. Profl. Engrs., Antique Wireless Assn., Soc. Broadcast Engrs., Men for Missions Internat., Athens County (Ohio) Amateur Repeater Assn., The Planetary Soc., Rotary. Avocations: astronomy, photography, amateur radio, antiques. Home: 16341 Calico Ridge Rd Logan OH 43138-9416 Office: Sta WLGN Logan Broadcasting Co 1 Radio Ln Logan OH 43138-8762

CARMEL, SIMON J(ACOB), anthropologist; b. Balt., Apr. 30, 1938; s. Joseph and Ann (Miller) C. BA in Physics, Gallaudet U., 1961; MA in Anthropology, Am. U., 1980, PhD in Anthropology, 1987. Physicist Nat. Bur. Standards, Gaithersburg, Md., 1961-81; lectr. Gallaudet U., Washington, 1982-87; assoc. prof. dept. liberal arts Nat. Tech. Inst. Deaf, Rochester (N.Y.) Inst. Tech., 1988—; condr. workshops on deaf folklore and culture, U.S., Can., Finland, Greece, Russian Fedn., Ukraine, 1978—; adj. prof. George Washington U., Washington, 1982-83; folklorist, rschr. Author: International Hand Alphabet Charts, 1975, 2d edit., 1982, International CISS SKI Technical Signs for Racers and Officials, 1990; columnist Skiingly Yours, 1967-76; editor U.S. Deaf Skiers Newsletter, 1968-76; actor plays at Frederick Hughes Meml. Theatre, Washington, 1964-69. Active publicity com. Frederick Hughes Meml. Theater, 1970-71; gen. chmn. Lake Placid Organizing Com. Sports for Deaf (CISS) World Winter Games for Deaf, 1971-75, alpine ski tech. del., 1971-91. Recipient Bronze medallion Internat. Com. Sports for Deaf, 1977, Dissertation fellowship award Am. U. Grad. Honor Awards Com., 1984, William C. Stokes award Nat. Assn. Deaf, 1985, Edward Miner Gallaudet award Gallaudet U. Alumni Assn., 1997; grantee Gallaudet U. Alumni Assn., 1981-84; Fulbright scholar/rschr. in Moscow, 1994; inducted into Am. Athletic Assn. Deaf Hall of Fame, 1982, Nat. congress Jewish Deaf Hall of Fame, 1987; one of three recipients Nat. Vol. awards program Nat. Ctr. for Voluntary Action, 1974. Mem. Am. Anthrop. Assn., Soc. for Anthropology in Cmty. Colls., Am. Folklore Soc., Nat. Assn. Deaf, Nat. Congress Jewish Deaf, Am. Athletic Assn. Deaf (chmn. internat. rels. com. 1991-95), U.S. Ea. Amateur Ski Assn. (chmn. ea. deaf skiers com. 1967-73, presenter workshops 1967-74, fund raiser 1970-73), U.S. Deaf Skiers Assn. (ea. v.p. 1968-72, pres. 1972-76, advisor 1976-92, various other positions), Soc. World Deaf Magicians (sec.-gen. 1990—, chair organizing com. 6th world festival, Rochester, Apr. 14-22, 1996), Empire State Assn. Deaf, Internat. Brotherhood Magicians, Soc. Am. Magicians, Rochester Magicians Club, Soc. of U.S.-Can. Deaf Magicians, Soc. of World Deaf Magicians, Moscow Magic Club (Russia), Phi Delta Kappa. Jewish. Avocations: reading books, miniature kite flying, magic, snow skiing, travel, museums. Home: 25 Branchbrook Dr Henrietta NY 14467-9717

CARMEN, IRA HARRIS, political scientist, educator; b. Boston, Dec. 3, 1934; s. Jacob and Lida (Rosenman) C.; m. Sandra Vineberg, Sept. 6, 1958; children: Gail Deborah, Amy Rebecca. BA, U. N.H., 1957; MA, U. Mich., 1959, PhD, 1964. Asst. prof. Ball State U., 1963-66; assoc. prof. Coe Coll., 1966-68; prof. polit. sci. U. Ill., 1968—; recombinant DNA adv. com. NIH, 1990-94; participant meetings on China-U.S. genetic engring. rsch. and policy rels., Beijing, 1991, European-U.S. human genetic experimentation and policy rels., London, Paris, Rome, 1995; program organizer Human Genome Orgn. internat. meeting, Heidelberg, 1996; vis. scholar Yale Law Sch., 1981; vis. lectr. Tamkang U., Taiwan, 1991. Author: Movies, Censorship, and the Law, 1966, Power and Balance, 1978, Cloning and the Constitution, 1985; co-prin. investigator Sociogenomics in Advanced Species, Consilience in Theory and Practice; contbr. articles to profl. jours. Sr. advisor Bush-Quayle Nat. Jewish Campaign Com., 1988; mem. Pres. George Bush's Inaugural Educators Adv. Com., 1989; guest del. Rep. Nat. Conv., 1992; mem. Rep. Nat. Com., Nat. Jewish Coalition, Empower Am. Recipient Clarence Berdahl award U. Ill., 1980, 87, 90, All-Campus award for excellence in undergrad. teaching, 1980, William F. Prokasy award, 1995, Harriet and Charles Luckman award, 1995; grantee U. Ill. Mem. AAAS, Am. Polit. Sci. Assn., Human Genome Orgn., Phi Beta Kappa. Office: U Ill Dept Polit Sci Urbana IL 61801

CARMEN, JULIE, actress; b. Millborn, N.J., Apr. 4, 1960. Appeared in films The Milagro Beanfield War, 1988, Neon Empire, 1989, Kiss Me a Killer, 1991, Cold Heaven, 1992, In the Mouth of Madness, 1995, The Omen, 1995, Africa, 1996, King of the Jungle, 1999, Everything's George, 1999; TV appearances include True Women, 1997, Gargantua, 1997. Office: Met Talent Agy 4526 Wilshire Blvd Los Angeles CA 90010-3801*

CARMENT, THOMAS MAXWELL, accounting educator, consultant, researcher; b. Cleve., Mar. 13, 1945; s. Charles Albert and Helen Marie C.; m. Deborah Lee Grant, Sept. 7, 1968; children: Rebecca L. Carment Schiehing, John M., David T. BA in Econs., Okla. State U., 1967, MBA, 1971, PhD in Bus. Adminstrn., 1991. CPA, Okla. Fin. analyst Ford Motor Co., Detroit, 1969-71; mktg. rep. Burroughs Corp., Detroit, 1971-72; asst. divsn. treasury mgr. Conoco, Inc., Houston, 1972-77; v.p. Power Pak Co., Inc., Conroe, Tex., 1977-78; prof. acctg. Northeastern State U., Tahlequah, Okla., 1979—; chmn. faculty adv. com. Okla. State Regents for Higher Edn., Oklahoma City, 1995-96; cons. Intelligent Media, Venice, Calif., 1995-99; cons. LSCI, Colorado Springs, Colo., 1992-99. Author various procs. Pres., mem. exec. com. Goodwill Industries, Muskogee, Okla., 1993-96; pres. faculty coun. Northeastern State U., 1993-95; scoutmaster Boy Scouts Am., 1987-99. Recipient Dist. award of merit and Scoutmaster Awd. of Merit, 1998, Boy Scouts Am., 1995; travel grantee, 1990, 96, 99, summer rsch. grantee, 1984. Mem. AAUP, Am. Acctg. Assn., Inst. Mgmt. Accts., Okla. Soc. CPAs, Acad. Internat. Bus., Optimist Club (exec. com. 1995-98, pres. 1999—). Democrat. Presbyterian. Avocations: bicycling, hiking, camping, travel. Office: Northeastern State U 600 N Grand Ave Tahlequah OK 74464-2301

CARMI, GIORA, illustrator; b. Kfar Malal, Israel, Sept. 17, 1944; s. Avraham and Miriam (Lozovick) C.; m. Avia Frenkel, May 19, 1965 (div. Jan. 1997); children: Ilil, Ore, Liane. Student, Bezalel Acad. Art and Design, Jerusalem, 1967-71. Freelance graphic designer and illustrator Israel, 1972-85; tchr. illustration Israel Inst. Tech., Tel Aviv, 1983-84, tchr. typography, 1983-84; freelance illustrator N.Y.C., 1985—; bd. dirs. Israeli Assn. Graphic Designer, Tel Aviv, 1983-85, judge nat. design competition, 1984. Designer, illustration many mags., newspapers and pvt. cos. in Israel, 1972-85; author, illustrator: And Shira Imagined, 1988, Night Farm, 1989; illustrator 15 books in Israel, 20 books in U.S., 1972—; illustration N.Y. Times, Wall St. Jour., others, 1985—; one person exhbn. of abstract drawings, Galerie Roswitha Tittel, Cologne, Germany, 1998. Lt. Israel mil., 1962-65. Recipient 1st pl. Simon Rockover award Am. Jewish Press Assn., 1988, 90, 1st pl. Sydney Taylor Book award Assn. Jewish Librs., 1991. Avocations: poetry, philosophy, music, literature. Home and Office: 82 Wayne St Apt 6 Jersey City NJ 07302-3543

CARMICHAEL, ALEXANDER DOUGLAS, engineering educator; b. Sliema, Malta, July 19, 1929; s. Adam and Jane (Hamilton) G.; m. Rose Margaret Whittaker, Sept. 1, 1951; children—Gillian Ruth, Alison Rose, Peter Stewart. B.Sc., Plymouth Tech. Coll., London U., 1949; Ph.D., Cambridge U., 1958. Chief engr. Dracone Developments Ltd., London, Eng., 1960-61; sr. project engr. No. Research and Engring. Corp., Cambridge, Mass, 1961-64; research fellow Imperial Coll. Sci. and Tech., London, 1964-68; tech. adv. English Electric Co. Ltd., Rugby, 1968-70; prof. power engring. MIT, 1970-96; prof. emeritus, 1996—. Fellow Soc. Naval Archs. and Marine Engrs. (v.p. N.E. region 1991-94), Whitworth Soc. (London). Home: 69 Otis St Newton MA 02460-1816 Office: MIT Dept Engring Cambridge MA 02139

CARMICHAEL, DAVID BURTON, physician; b. Santa Ana, Calif., Sept. 12, 1923; s. David Burton and Phyllis (Adams) C.; m. Ava Louise Smith, Dec. 26, 1944; children: Catherine Ann, Heather Sue, Linda L., Ava L. Student, Graceland Coll., 1940-42; B.A., M.D., U. Iowa, 1946; postgrad., Harvard U., 1949-50; LL.D. (hon.), Graceland Coll., Iowa, 1985. Diplomate: Am. Bd. Internal Medicine. Clin. and research fellow medicine Mass. Gen. Hosp., Boston, 1949-50; cons. cardiovascular diseases U.S. Naval Hosp., San Diego, Camp Pendleton, 1956-86; cons. cardiovascular diseases U.S. VA, 1960-82; chief dept. medicine Scripps Meml. Hosp., La Jolla, Calif., 1961-63, 65-67; chief staff Scripps Meml. Hosp., 1970-71; clin. prof. medicine U. Calif. at San Diego, 1968—; pres. De Anza Lab. Corp., 1962-72, Carmichael-Carson Med.-Clin. Lab. Corp., 1962-75; sr. ptnr. Med. Clinic; founding med. dir. Cardiovascular Inst. Scripps Meml. Hosps., 1985-96; pres. Orange County Pioneer Coun., 1993-94; trustee GDE Systems, Inc., 1992-94. Contbr. articles to profl. jours. Trustee Millicent Rogers Mus., Taos, N.Mex., 1986-90, Graceland Coll., Iowa, 1987—, Rancho de los Golondrinas Mus., Santa Fe, 1989—. Served to rear adm., med. insp. gen. USNR. Decorated Legion of Merit; recipient Alumni Disting. Service award Graceland Coll., 1967. Fellow ACP (gov. So. Calif. region III 1972-76, Laureate award 1991), Am. Coll. Cardiology (dir., sec. 1975, trustee 1979-85, Disting. Fellow award 1994), Am. Coll. Chest Physicians; mem. AMA (chmn. specialty soc. and service delegation 1985-87, 93-96, mem. grad. med. edn. adv. com. 1983—89, chmn., 1985-87, chmn. sect. council on clin. cardiology, Disting. Svc. award 1997), Am. Heart Assn., San Diego County Heart Assn. (pres. 1959-60), San Diego Biomed. Research Inst. (pres. 1958-59, 62-63, vice chmn. residency rev. com. internal medicine 1971-78), San Diego Soc. Internal Medicine (pres. 1959-61). Republican. Mem. Reorganized Ch. of Jesus Christ of Latter-day Saints (elder). Home: 8333 Calle Del Cielo La Jolla CA 92037-3033 *This country, with its Christian heritage, gives to the vast majority the opportunity to serve and often, the chance to excel. The guidance of parents and instructors should never be forgotten, nor should the sacrifices of those who have allowed us to preserve our freedom.*

CARMICHAEL, DONALD SCOTT, lawyer, business executive; b. Toledo, Feb. 19, 1912; s. Grey Thornton and Edna Earle (Jaite) C.; m. Mary Glenn Dickinson, May 28, 1940; children: Mary Brooke McMurray, Pamela Hastings Keenan. AB, Harvard U., 1935, student Sch. Law, 1935-37; LLB, U. Mich., 1942. Bar: Ohio 1942. Staff dept. law City of Cleve., 1938-40; chief renegotiation br. Cleve. Ordnance Dist., War Dept., 1942-46; practiced in Cleve., 1946; asst. sec. Diamond Alkali Co., 1946-48, sec., 1948-57, gen. counsel, 1957-58; v.p.-gen. counsel Stouffer Corp., 1959-60, exec. v.p., 1960-64; practiced in Cleve., 1964-71; pres. Schrafft's divsn. Pet, Inc., N.Y.C., 1971-75, Sportsvc. Corp., Buffalo, 1975-80; pres. Del. North Cos., Inc., Buffalo, 1980-89, vice chmn., 1989—; officer, dir. various corps. Editor: F.D.R.; Columnist, 1947; Contbr. to law revs. Mem. Cuyahoga County Charter Commn., 1959—; chmn.; mem. Cleve. Met. Services Commn., 1957-59, President's Task Force on War Against Poverty, 1964; Del. Democratic Nat. Conv., 1960, 64; mem. Cuyahoga County Dem. Exec. Com.; Chmn. bd. trustees Cuyahoga County Hosps., 1958-64, Urban League, Karamu House. Mem. ABA, Ohio Bar Assn., Cleve. Bar Assn., Union Club Cleve., Chagrin Valley Hunt Club, Harvard Club N.Y.C., River Club N.Y.C., Buffalo Club, Phi Gamma Delta. Home: Hardscrabble Rd Lyme NH 03768 Office: Del N Cos 438 Main St Ste 800 Buffalo NY 14202-3297

CARMICHAEL, IAN STUART EDWARD, geologist, educator; b. London, England, Mar. 29, 1930; came to U.S., 1964; s. Edward Arnold and Jeanette (Montgomerie) C.; m. Kathleen Elizabeth O'Brien; children by previous marriages: Deborah, Graham, Alistair, Anthea; stepchildren: Michael, Megan Handron. B.A., Cambridge U., Eng., 1954; Ph.D., Imperial Coll. Sci., London U., 1958. Lectr. geology Imperial Coll. Sci. and Tech., 1958-63; NSF sr. fgn. sci. fellow U. Chgo., 1964; mem. faculty U. Calif.-Berkeley, 1964—, prof. geology, 1967—, chmn. dept., 1972-76, 80-82, assoc. dean, 1976-78, 85—, assoc. provost, 1986—, dir. Lawrence Hall of Sci., 1996, acting dir. botanical garden, 1996—. Author: Igneous Petrology, 1974; editor-in-chief Contbns. to Mineralogy and Petrology, 1973-90; contbr. numerous papers to profl. jours. Guggenheim fellow, 1992; recipient Arthur L. Day medal Geol. Soc. Am., 1991. Fellow Royal Soc. London, Mineral Soc. Am. (Roebling medal 1997), Mineral Soc. Gt. Britain (Schlumberger medal 1992), Am. Geophys. Union (Bowen award 1986), Geol. Soc. of London (Murchison medal 1995). Office: U Calif Berkeley Dept Geology & Geophysics Berkeley CA 94720

CARMICHAEL, JAMES VINSON, JR., library and information science educator; b. Atlanta, Nov. 27, 1946; s. James Vinson and Frances Elizabeth (McDonald) C.; m. Karen Bryce Powers, June 18, 1969 (div. Sept. 1973). BA, Emory U., 1969, MLN, 1977; PhD, U. N.C., 1988. Inventory control clk. Lockheed Aircraft, Marietta, Ga., 1969; logistics asst. Lockheed Aircraft, Marietta, 1969-70; trust adminstrv. asst. Trust Co. Bank, Atlanta, 1970-76; ref., instrn. libr. Ga. Coll., Milledgeville, Ga., 1977-81; instr. U. N.C., Chapel Hill, 1988-89; instr. U. N.C., Greensboro, 1988-89, asst. prof. libr., info. scis., 1989-95, assoc. prof. libr., info. sci., 1995—. Editor: (monographic series) Beta Phi Mu, 1995—, Daring To Find Our Names: The Search for Lesbigay Library History, 1998; contbr. articles to profl. jours. Recipient Louis Round Wilson award Southeastern Libr. Assn., 1988, Franklin M. Garrett award Atlanta Hist. Soc., 1990. Mem. ALA (chair libr. history round table 1995-96, mem. com. status of women 1993-96), N.C. Libr. Assn. (Ray Moore award 1992, 94), Assn. Libr. and Info. Sci. Edn. Home: 2403 Cottage Pl Greensboro NC 27455-2912

CARMICHAEL, JOE, lawyer. BA, S.W. Mo. State U., 1969; JD, U. Ark., 1974. Atty. Carmichael, Gardner and Clark, Springfield, Mo., 1992. Chmn. Mo. State Dem. Party. Office: Ste 800 901 Saint Louis St Springfield MO 65806

CARMICHAEL, JUDY LEA, record industry executive, concert jazz pianist; b. Lynwood, Calif., Nov. 27, 1952; d. John Alvin and Jeanne Pauline (Boock) Hohenstein. Student, Calif. State U., Long Beach, 1970-73, Calif. State U., Fullerton. Owner C&D Prodns., N.Y.C., 1989—; chmn. jazz fellowships com. NEA, Washington, 1990-91; featured on Nat. Pub. Radio, Marian McPartland's Piano Jazz, 1990, Morning Edition Nat. Pub. Radio, also TV programs Entertainment Tonight, CBS, Sunday Morning with Charles Kuralt, 1993. Performed as pianist at Breda Jazz Festival, The Netherlands, 1986, Carnegie Hall, N.Y.C., 1988, 89, Rio de Janeiro, 1989, Peggy Guggenheim Mus., Venice, Italy, 1990, Am. Acad., Rome, 1990, 91, USIA Tour, Portugal, 1991, Spain, 1991, India, 1988, China, 1992, Singapore, 1994, S. Am., 1996, major U.S. tours 1993-95, also L.A., Zurich, Switzerland, Paris, Cannes, France; performer Stanford Symphony Pops with Skitch Henderson, 1997; author (music) Judy Carmichael's Complete Book of Stride Piano, 1987, You Can Play Stride Piano, 1996; producer, artist (LP's) Jazz Piano, 1983, Two Handed Stride, 1980, (CD's) Trio, 1989, Old Friends, 1991, Pearls, 1985, ...And Basie Called Her Stride, 1993, Judy, 1994, Chops, 1995, PianoDisc, 1995, QRS piano rolls, 1996, (CD and player piano formats) High on Fats and Other Stuff, 1997; featured on CBS Sunday Morning with Charles Osgood; jazz editor Sheet Music mag., 1989-90; contbr. numerous articles to profl. jours. NEA fellow, grantee; Grammy award nominee, 1980; chosen to be Steinway artist, 1986; nominated for Mac award Manhattan Assn. Cabarets and Clubs for Stage Show with Steve Ross, 1996. Avocations: golf, softball, tennis, skiing.

CARMICHAEL, LYNN PAUL, family practice physician; b. Louisville, Sept. 15, 1928; s. Donald Palmer and Vivian Iris (Linler) C.; m. Joan Pauline Steinlight, June 26, 1954; children: John Kevin, Cynthia Gail, Jon Christian. Student, Ind. U., 1945-48; MD, U. Louisville, 1952. Diplomate Am. Bd. Family Practice. From intern to battalion surgeon U.S. Army, San Antonio, Korea, 1952-54; pvt. practice Mooresville, Ind., 1954-55; pvt. gen. practice Miami, 1955—; fellow Harvard Med. Sch., Boston, 1953-54; faculty U. Miami, 1965—; test com. Nat. Bd. Med. Examiners, 1976-79; residency rev. com. Accreditation Coun. for Grad. Med. Edn., Chgo., 1972-75; cons. Pub. Health Svc., Washington, 1976-90. Med. support ARC, Cuba, 1962, Medishare, Haiti, 1995. Decorated bronze star U.S. Army, 1953, Primary Care Achievement for Edn. Pew Found., 1996. Mem. AMA, Soc. Tchrs. Family Medicine (founding pres. 1967-70, founding editor 1978-83), Am. Acad. Gen. Practice, Inst. of Medicine Nat. Acad. Sci. (sr. membership 1995). Avocations: cycling, swimming. Home: 3661 N Campbell Ave # 205 Tucson AZ 85719-1527 Office: U Miami Dept Family Med 600 Alton Rd # 501 Miami Beach FL 33139-5502

CARMICHAEL, MARY ALICE, artist, genealogist; b. Colon, Panama, Nov. 28, 1936; came to U.S., 1937; d. Donald Croom and Mary Alice (Gatling) Beatty; m. James Donald Carmichael, Oct. 28, 1961; children: James Donald Jr., Beatty Payseur, Daniel Troy. *Husband, James Donald, is vascular surgeon, graduated Medical Doctor, 1958 Johns Hopkins, fourth* *generation physician; fellow American College of Surgeons, Southern Surgical, Southern Vascular Associations; timber farmer. Son, Don Jr. is prsident/owner of Champion Golf, fundraising for non-profits; son, Beatty is president/owner of Success Products; son, Troy, computer programmer and president/owner DanCar, Inc. Both father, Donald Croom Beatty, and mother, Mary Alice Gatling Beatty, pioneer aviators, both installed Alabama Aviation Hall of Fame. Father organized and led Latin American Expedition 1931-1932, inducted 1935 as Fellow Royal Geographical Society of London, inducted 1934 as fellow of The Explorer's Club New York immediately after Admiral Richard Byrd.* BA, Howard Coll., 1960. Contbr. articles to profl. jours. Organizing mem. Ala. Men's Hall of Fame, 1988—; mem. Women's Com. of 100 of Birmingham, pres. 1989-91; steering com. Reynold's Hist. Soc., 1988—. Named one of Outstanding Young Women of Am., 1972-73. Mem. DAR (Outstanding Jr. Mem. award 1968, Most Outstanding Hist. Paper award 1988), Soc. Mayflower Descendants Ala. (gov. 1990-94, registrar 1985-94), Rotary. Presbyterian. Avocations: art, genealogy, photography, travel. Home: 2857 Canterbury Rd Birmingham AL 35223-1201

CARMICHAEL, RICHARD E., government official, financial manager, educator; b. Montclair, N.J., June 14, 1941; s. Charles Walter and Helen May (Buchanan) C.; m. Inez K Alexander, Oct. 6, 1984; children: Gregory, Andrew. BS in Econ., Monmouth U., 1970; MBA in Fin., Pace U., 1972; PhD, Calif. Coast U., 1997. Divsnl. controller Mfrs. Hanover Corp., N.Y.C., 1972-82; v.p. market planning and rsch. Bank Am. Corp., San Francisco, 1982-84, 1st Interstate Bank Calif., L.A., 1984-88; ptnr. Findata Corp., Balt., 1988-91; budget mgr. dist. Md. U.S. Bankruptcy Ct., Balt., 1991-97; br. chief credit programs SBA, Washington, 1997—; faculty assoc. Johns Hopkins U. Sch. Bus., Balt., 1991-99; asst. prof. Newberry (S.C.) Coll., 1999—. Author: Evolution Economics, 1995, Politics & Economics in America, 1997. Rep. Methodist. Avocations: tennis, swimming. Home: 9 Arlen Rd Apt K Baltimore MD 21236-5144

CARMICHAEL, VIRGIL WESLY, mining, civil and geological engineer, former coal company executive; b. Pickering, Mo., Apr. 26, 1919; s. Ava Abraham and Roseell (Murphy) C.; m. Emma Margaret Freeman, Apr. 1, 1939 (dec.); m. Colleen Fern Wadsworth, Oct. 29, 1951; children: Bonnie Rae, Peggy Ellen, Jacki Ann. BS, U. Idaho, 1951, MS, 1956; PhD, Columbia Pacific U., San Rafael, Calif., 1980. Registered profl. geol., mining and civil engr., geologist, land surveyor. Asst. geologist Day Mines, Wallace, Idaho, 1950; mining engr. De Anza Engring. Co., Troy, Idaho, Santa Fe, 1950-52; hwy. engring. asst. N.Mex. Hwy. Dept., Santa Fe, 1952-53; asst. engr. U. Idaho, 1953-56; minerals analyst Idaho Bur. Mines, 1953-56; mining engr. No. Pacific Ry. Co., St. Paul, 1956-67; geologist N.Am. Coal Corp., Cleve., 1967-69, asst. v.p. engring., 1969-74, v.p., head exploration dept., 1974-84; travel host Satrom Travel and Tour, Bismarck, N.D., 1988-92; advisor photogeology for People to People "Hard Rock" Minerals Del. to China, 1981; leader People to People Coal Mechanization Del. to China, 1982; advisor (photogeology) to Carbocol, Colombia, S.A., 1984-85; mem. Bismarck Scottish Rite Children's Hearing Impairment Bd., 1991-97. *Virgil Carmichael served with the U.S. Naval Reserve, Pacific Theater Operations, 1944-46. He is a past member of the American Institute Mining and Metallurgical Engineers, American Mining Congress Board of Governors (Western Division), Rocky Mountain Coal Mining Institute (vice-president), New York Academy of Science and International Platform Association. He has provided preliminary geological and engineering studies for major operating U.S. coal mines including Colstrip, Montana, Falkirk and Coteau, North Dakota, Quarto and Manor Lands, Ohio, Florence and Oneida, Pennsylvania and Sabine Mines in Texas.* Asst. chief distbr. Emergency Mgmt. Fuel Resources of N.D., 1968-92; bd. dirs., chmn. fund dr. Bismarck-Mandan Orch. Assn., 1979-83; 1st v.p., bd. dirs., chmn. fund dr. Bismarck Arts and Galleries Assn., 1982-86; mem. and spl. advisor (Minerals) Nat. Def. Exec. Res., 1983—; mem. Fed. Emergency Mgmt. Agy., 1983—; mem. adv. bd. Bismarck Salvation Army, 1988—, chmn., 1993-95; sci. rsch. bd. N.D. Acad. Sci. Found., 1986-91. Recipient A award for sci. writing Sigma Gamma Epsilon; J.C. Penney Golden Rule award finalist, 1996. Mem. Am. Inst. Profl. Geologists (past pres. local chpt.), Breezy Shores Resort and Beach Club (bd. dirs. 1986—), Kiwanis (past pres., dist. lt. gov., dist. chmn. internat. found. 1991—), Masons (past master, trustee 1987-92, N.D. Masonic Found. 1987-92, 94-99, chmn. 1990-92, 97-99, Mason of Yr. Bismarck lodge 1992, Gen. Grand Masters award Cryptic Mason Med. Rsch. Found., Scottish Rite (Knight Comdr. Cross of Honor, Royal Order of Scotland), York Rite (Knight Templar Cross of Honor, Knight of York Cross of Honor), Bismarck Lodge Found., Elks (life). Republican. Home: 1013 N Anderson St Bismarck ND 58501-3446

CARMICHAEL, WILLIAM DANIEL, consultant, educator; b. Denver, Sept. 5, 1929; s. Fitzhugh Lee and Anna Devona (Sullivan) C.; m. Faith Young, June 21, 1958; children: Amy, Philip Fitzhugh, Daniel Owen. AB, Yale, 1950; MA, MPA, Princeton, 1952, PhD, 1959; BLitt (Rhodes scholar), U. Oxford (Eng.), 1955; LLD (hon.), U. W.I., 1989. Legislative analyst U.S. Bur. Budget, 1955-56, budget analyst, 1956-57; lectr. econs. and pub. affairs Princeton, 1957-60, asst. prof., 1960-62; dir. undergrad. program Woodrow Wilson Sch. Pub. and Internat. Affairs, 1958-62; prof. econ. policy, dean Grad. Sch. Bus. and Pub. Adminstrn., Cornell U., 1962-68; rep. Ford Found., Brazil, 1968-71; head Ford Found., Latin Am. and Caribbean, 1971-77, Middle East and Africa, 1977-81; v.p. for developing country programs Ford Found., 1981-89; exec. dir. Ea. European programs Inst. Internat. Edn., N.Y.C., 1989-93; cons. on edn. and econ. devel., 1993—. Mem. exec. com. Human Rights Watch; bd. dirs. So. African Legal Svcs. and Edn. Program. Mem. Coun. on Fgn. Rels., Assn. Am. Rhodes Scholars, Phi Beta Kappa. Home and office: 603 W Lyon Farm Dr Greenwich CT 06831-4363

CARMICLE, LINDA HARPER, psychotherapist; b. Westmore, Tenn., Oct. 20, 1937; d. Noel Franklin and Mary Frank (Caldwell) Harper; m. Jerrel B. Carmicle, June 2, 1956; children: Roxanna Linn Carmicle Lynch, Jerry Noel. AA, St. Petersburg Jr. Coll., 1968; BSW with honors, Tex. Women's U., 1975, MA, 1977; PhD in Psychology, Fielding Inst., Santa Barbara, Calif., 1992. Lic. profl. counselor, marriage and family therapist; cert. eating disorder specialist; cert. group psychotherapist; supr. for LPCs. Dir. Galaxy Ctr., Garland, Tex., 1975-78; counselor Saudi Arabia Internat. Sch., Daharan, 1978, Dallas County Family Ct. Counselors, Dallas, 1979-83; pvt. practice psychotherapy Dallas and Plano, Tex., 1983—; mem. faculty S.W. Group Psychotherapy Inst., 1995; mem. adj. faculty Tex. Women's U., Denton, 1976-78, rep. Coun. on Social Work Edn., 1977; mem. adj. faculty Amber U., 1996—, LeTourneau U., 1999—. Contbr. articles to profl. jours., chpt. to book. Active Custer Rd. United Meth. Ch. Named Miss Sr. Plano, 1998. Mem. Am. Assn. Christian Counselors, Tex. Assn. Marriage and Family Therapy, Dallas Group Psychotherapy Soc., Internat. Assn. Eating Disorder Profls. Methodist. Avocations: grandchildren, aerobics, gourmet vegetarian cooking, piano, therapy dog. Home and Office: 3105 Santana Ln Plano TX 75023-3630

CARMIN, ROBERT LEIGHTON, retired geography educator; b. Muncie, Ind., Nov. 28, 1918; s. Zora and Florelda May (Harrison) C.; m. Marie Jane Carr, Nov. 2, 1940 (dec. 1981); children—Thomas Nelson, James Harrison. B.S. in Edn, Ohio U., 1940; M.A., U. Nebr., 1942; Ph.D. (Salisbury fellow geography), U. Chgo., 1953. Instr. geography Mich. State U., 1942-44, asst. prof., 1947-50; cartographer OSS, 1944-45; from asst. prof. to prof. geography U. Ill., 1951-62; dir. Center Latin Am. Studies, 1959-62; head Latin Am. studies unit U.S. Office Edn., 1962; dean Coll. Scis. and Humanities, 1962-80; prof. geography Ball State U., from 1962, now ret.; Cons. lang. devel. br. U.S. Office Edn., 1963-64; cons. NSF, 1964-76; internat. programs com. Am. Assn. State Colls. and Univs., 1966-76; com. geography Nat. Acad. Sci.-NRC, 1961-66; sec.-treas. Asso. Univs. for Internat. Edn., Inc., 1968-70, v.p., 1970-72; U.S. del. 6th Gen. Assembly Pan Am. Inst. Geography and History, Buenos Aires, Argentina, 1961. Author: Anápolis, Brazil: Regional Capital of an Agricultural Frontier, 1953; also articles.; coeditor: Geographic Research On Latin America-Benchmark 1970, 1971. Pan Am. World Airways travel fellow Brazil, 1948; adviser AID, Brazil, 1965; grantee U.S. Office Edn., Brazil, 1948-49; Office Q.M. Gen. Brazil, 1956; Fulbright scholar U. de Cuyo, Mendoza, Argentina, 1958; grantee U. Ill. Research Bd., Brazil, 1961; grantee Am. Assn. Colls. Tchr. Edn., Peru, 1963. Mem. Ill. Acad. Sci. (geography sect. 1955-56), Conf. Latin Americanist Geographers (co-founder, dir. 1971-72), Ind. Acad. of Social Scis. (dir. 1967-68), Assn. Am. Geographers (past pres. West Lakes div., ofcl. rep. to Internat. Council Edn. for Teaching, Brazil 1963), Assn. Latin Am. Studies (past pres.), Nat. Council Geog. Edn., Assn. dos Geografos Brasileiros, Latin Am. Studies Assn., Sigma Xi, Sigma Delta Pi. Home: 12401 N 22nd St Apt A-206 Tampa FL 33612-4670 Office: Ball State U Dept Geography Muncie IN 47306 *In a time of trial one of my professional mentors taught me the value of the aphorism: "Everything is important, but nothing is important." Give it your best, but don't fret when things aren't perfect—the world doesn't revolve around you alone.*

CARMODY, ARTHUR RODERICK, JR., lawyer; b. Shreveport, La., Feb. 19, 1928; s. Arthur R. and Caroline (Gaughan) C.; m. Renee Aubry, Jan. 26, 1952 (div. 1980); children: Helen Bragg, Renee, Arthur Roderick, Patrick, Timothy, Mary, Virginia, Joseph; m. Mary Wells, Sept. 1, 1990. Grad. with honors, N.Mex. Mil. Inst.; BS, Fordham U., 1949; LLB, La. State U., 1952. Bar: La. 1952, U.S. Supreme Ct. 1971. Mem. firm Wilkinson, Carmody & Gilliam and its predecessors, Shreveport, 1952—; bd. dirs. Kansas City So. Transport Co., Kansas City, Shreveport and Gulf Terminal Co., Shreveport Braves Baseball Club (Tex. League), Sta. KDAQ-FM Pub. Radio, pres., 1991, chmn., 1992, RED River Pub. Radio Newtwork; mem. Shreveport Steamer (World Football League) Partnership; pres. Touchdown Club of Shreveport, 1960. Author: Legal Problems in the Development and Mining of Lignite, 1976; legal history columnist Shreveport Bar Review, 1995—; La. adv. editor The Insurance Bar, 1961—. Chmn. Met. Shreveport Zoning Bd. Appeals, 1959-72; pres. bd. trustees Jesuit H.S., 1976-82; chmn. bd. govs. Loyola Found. Shreveport, 1991-94; trustee Schumpert Med. Ctr., 1965-85; bd. dirs. La. State U. Found., Baton Rouge, Agnew Day Sch., Shreveport, 1970-82, Ridgewood Montessori Sch.; nat. bd. dirs. N.Mex. Mil. Inst., Roswell, 1967-68 (named to Alumni Hall of Fame 1994); adv. coun. La. State U., Shreveport, 1982-86; govs. ad hoc com. for preparation rules and regulations for mining and reclamation of lignite in the State of La., Dept. Conservation, 1978-79; select com. mem. for rev. stds. jud. conducts Supreme Ct. of La., 1994-98. 1st lt. USAR, 1948-50. Recipient Alumni Achievement award Fordham U., 1995; named Hon. Alumnus, elected to Ring of Honor Loyola Coll. Prep., 1993. Master Am. Inns of Ct.; fellow Am. Coll. Trial Lawyers, La. Bar Assn. (mem. com. on lawyer and judicial conduct 1996-98); mem. ABA, Fed. Bar Assn., Shreveport Bar Assn., U.S. Supreme Ct. Hist. Soc., Fifth Fed. Cir. Bar Assn., Federalist Soc., North La. Hist. Soc., La. Hist. Assn., Confederate Meml. Lit. Soc., Nat. Soc. SAR (pres. Galvez chpt. 1997), Scribes Soc., Supreme Ct. of La. Hist. Soc., Univ. Assocs. of La. State U., Am. Judicature Soc., La. Law Inst., Trial Attys. Am., Nat. Assn. R.R. Trial Counsel, Internat. Assn. Def. Counsel, La. Assn. Def. Counsel, Nat. Acad. Law and Medicine, Am. Arbitration Assn. (panel arbitrators), Mid-Continent Oil and Gas Assn. (exec. com. 1984—), La. R.R. Assn. (exec. com. 1992—), Tarshar Soc., La. Assn. Bus. and Industry, Nat. Legal Ctr. for the Pub. Interest, Pub. Affairs Rsch. Coun., Shreveport C. of C. (dir. 1968-70), Kansas City So. Hist. Soc., Railway and Locomoitve Hist. Soc., Soc. Hosp. Counsel, La. Civil Svc. League, La. State U. Found., Res. Officers Assn., North La. Civil War Round Table, U.S. Horse Cavalry Assn., Soc. for Mil. History, Soc. for Civil War History, Federalist Soc., Sovereign Mil. Order of Malta, Phi Delta Phi, Kappa Alpha. Home: 255 Forest Ave Shreveport LA 71104-4506 Office: Wilkinson Carmody & Gilliam 1700 Beck Bldg 400 Travis St Shreveport LA 71101-3108

CARMODY, EDMOND, bishop; b. Moyvane, Kerry, Ireland, Jan. 12, 1934. Student, St. Brendan's Coll., Killarney, St. Patrick Seminary, Carlow, Ireland. Ordained priest San Antonio, 1957; missionary Peru, 1984-89; consecrated titular bishop Mortlach, 1988; consecrated aux. bishop San Antonio, 1988; consecrated bishop Tyler, Tex., 1992. Office: Diocese of Tyler Chancery 1015 ESE Loop 323 Tyler TX 75701-9663*

CARMODY, JAMES ALBERT, lawyer; b. St. Louis, Nov. 21, 1945; m. Helen Tippy Valin, mar. 22, 1969; children: Paul Valin, Leigh Christin. BA, Vanderbilt U., 1967; JD, U. Ark., 1973. Bar: Tex. 1974, U.S. Dist. Ct. (so. dist.) Tex. 1974, U.S. Ct. Appeals (5th, 9th and 10th cirs.) 1975, U.S. Supreme Ct., 1996. Assoc. Mabry & Gunn, Texas City, Tex., 1974-75; mcpl. ct. judge Texas City, Tex., 1975; assoc. Chamberlain & Hrdlicka, Houston, 1975-78, ptnr., 1978-89; ptnr. Keck Mahin & Cate, Houston, 1989-94, Carmody & Yokubaitis, L.L.P., Houston, 1995—. Assoc. editor U. Ark. Law Rev., 1973. Incorporator, Gulf Coast Big Bros. and Sisters, Inc., Galveston County, Tex., 1975; mem. St. Maximillian Cath. Community Bldg. Com., Houston, 1985-88. Served to lt. USN, 1967-71. Mem. Galveston County Jr. Bar Assn. (pres. 1975, Outstanding Young Lawyer award 1975), Harris County Bar Assn. (arbitrator fee dispute com. 1997—), Entrepreneurship Inst. Houston (chmn. 1991-94), Greater Houston Partnership (Mex. and Ams. com.), Delta Theta Phi (master insp. 1983-85, dean Houston alumni senate 1988, bd. dirs. Found.). Republican. Roman Catholic. Avocations: ham radio, international travel, satellite communications. E-mail: carmody@lawyer.com. Home: 15910 Congo Ln Houston TX 77040-2120

CARMODY, MARGARET JEAN, retired social worker; b. Wauwatosa, Wis., Aug. 5, 1924; d. Peter and Gertrude Francelia (Brown) Galijas; m. James Matthew Carmody, Apr. 3, 1971. BA, Marquette U., 1945; MA, U. Chgo., 1949. Social worker Denver Gen. Hosp., 1950-51; Fulbright fellow France, 1951-52; med. social work cons. U. Ill., Chgo., 1954-60; health scientist, adminstr. USPHS, Washington, 1960-96; ret., 1996. Mem. Acad. Cert. Social Workers. Democrat. Roman Catholic. Home: Garfield Apts 5410 Connecticut Ave # 705 Washington DC 20015

CARMONA, JOSÉ ANTONIO, Spanish language educator, English language educator; b. Remedios, Las Villas, Cuba, Mar. 9, 1960; came to U.S., 1971; s. Felix and Maria Gloria (Reyes) C. BA, Drew U., 1983; MA, Columbia U., 1984, EdM, 1986, postgrad in Hispanic culture & lit. U.S., 1986—. Cert. Spanish tchr. K-12, N.J., ESL. Spl. edn. tchr. grades 5, 6. P.S. 121 N.Y. Bd. Edn., N.Y.C., 1984; ESL instr. Hispanic Inst. Rsch. & Devel., Paramus, N.J., 1985-86; adj. prof. of Spanish Bergen C.C., Paramus, 1985-87; instr. Spanish Drew U., Madison, N.J., 1987-91; ESL instr. Emerson Adult Edn. Program, Union City, N.J., 1988-89; adj. assoc. prof. Spanish County Coll. of Morris, Randolph, N.J., 1988; adj. prof. Spanish Coll. St. Elizabeth, Convent Station, N.J., 1990; instr., coord. ESL and Spanish Hudson County C.C., West N.Y., N.J., 1990-94, asst. prof. ESL, modern lang. coord., 1994-96; supr. student tchrs. of Spanish William Paterson Coll., Wayne, N.J., 1996; assoc. prof. modern langs./ESL Daytona Beach (Fla.) C.C., 1996—; case worker Angel Guardian Home, Bklyn., 1983; coord. Hispanic Leadership Program, St. Elizabeth Coll., Convent Station, 1989-90, Gov.'s Sch. on the Environ. Stockton State Coll., Pomona, N.J., 1989-93, co-dir. 1993; faculty adviser Hispanic House students, Drew U., Madison, 1987-91, acad. adviser and counselor to 1st and 2nd yr. students, other adminstrv. duties; freelance translator, 1985—; lectr. and or presenter at many ednl. confs. in N.J. and out of state, 1988—. Author: Adolescent Blues (poetry) 1992, Distinct Voices: A Multicultural Anthology for ESL Writers, 1996; co-author: Mixed Media: Authentic Reading for the Beginning ESL Student (text), 1993, Topics and Trends: First Authentic Readings for ESL Writers, 1994 (text); contbr. over 40 poems to Spanish and English mags, 1988—. Mem. Hispanic Affairs Adv. Com. Dept. Community Affairs, Trenton, N.J., 1989-91,community, Affirmative Action Com., Drew U., Madison, 1989-91; adv. bd. mem. Drew U. EOF program, Madison, 1990-95, Selective Svc. Bd., West N.Y., 1992-96; bd. dirs. Jose Marti Scholarship Fund, Union City, 1979—, Hudson County 4-Coll. Consortium, 1992. Recipient Hon. Literary Essay award Cuban Lions Club in Exile, Union City,1976, Outstanding Alumnus award N.J. Ednl. Opportunity Fund Profl. Assn., Newark, 1989, Golden Poet award World of Poetry, Calif., 1989, Frances B. Sellers award, Drew U. E.O.F. Alumni Assn., Madison, 1990. Mem. NEA (rev. panel bd. dirs. higher edn. jour. Thought & Action 1996-99, plaque for svc. to the jour. 1999), MLA, Fgn. Lang. Educators N.J., N.Y. Met. Assn. for Devl. Edn., TESOL (N.J. higher edn. rep. 1992-96), Hispanic Assn. for Higher Edn., Circulo Cultural Pan Am., Acad. Am. Poets, Trio (N.J. bd. dirs. 1991-92), Fla. Assn. Cmty. Colls., United Faculty Fla., Halifax Club (Daytona Beach, Fla.), Sigma Delta Pi, Kappa Delta Pi., Epsilon Omega Psi. Roman Catholic. Avocations: writing, reading, dancing. Home: 7 Birchtree Way Palm Coast FL 32137-9326 Office: Daytona Beach CC 1200 Internat Speedway Blvd Daytona Beach FL 32120-2811

CARMONY, MARVIN DALE, linguist, educator; b. nr. Richmond, Ind., Feb. 27, 1923; s. Harry Edgar and Ellen (Brown) C.; m. Mary Joan Nicholson, May 31, 1947; children—Ronald Dee, Kathryn Lynn. Student, Valparaiso Tech. Inst., 1941-42, Olivet Nazarene U., 1947-49; A.B., Ind. State U., 1950, M.A., 1951; Ph.D., Ind. U., 1965. Radio operator Am. Airlines, Chgo., 1942-44; tchr. high schs. Pendleton and Shelbyville, Ind., 1953-59; from instr. English to assoc. prof. English and linguistics Ind. State U., Terre Haute, 1959-69, prof., 1969-88, assoc. dean Coll. Arts and Scis., 1970-86; co-founder Ind. Place-Names Survey (now Hoosier Folklore), 1968, dir., 1968-70; co-founder Ind. Names (now Hoosier Folklore), 1970, gen. editor, 1970-88. Author: (with D.F. Carmony) Indiana Dialects in Their Historical Setting, 1972, rev. edit., 1979, (with Ronald Baker) Indiana Place Names, 1975; also articles. Trustee Olivet Nazarene U., 1967-70, mem. alumni bd. dirs., 1995—. With U.S. Mcht. Marine, 1944-46; vet. USCG. Am. Council Learned Socs. fellow, 1964-65. Mem. Am. Dialect Soc. (adv. bd. publs. 1972-77, 82-86, pres. 1981-82), Soc. Wireless Pioneers, Am. Names Soc. (editorial bd. Names 1977-84), Linguistic Soc. Am., Nat. Soc. XVII Century Colonial Dames (Disting. Svc. award 1975), Phi Delta Lambda, Phi Delta Kappa, Sigma Tau Delta. Home: 227 Madison Blvd Terre Haute IN 47803-1911

CARNAHAN, BRICE, chemical engineer, educator; b. New Philadelphia, Ohio, Oct. 13, 1933; s. Paul Tracy and Amelia Christina (Gray) C. BS, Case Western Res. U., 1955, MS, 1957; PhD, U. Mich., 1965. Lectr. in engring. biostats. U. Mich., Ann Arbor, 1959-64; asst. prof. chem. engring. and biostatics U. Mich., 1965-68, assoc. prof., 1968-70, prof. chem. engring., 1970—; vis. lect. Imperial Coll., London, England, 1971-72; vis. prof. U. Pa., 1970, U. Calif.-San Diego, 1986-87; mem., chmn. Curriculum Aids for Chem. Engring. Edn. com. Nat. Acad. Engring., 1974-75. Author: (with H.A. Luther and J.O. Wilkes) Applied Numerical Methods, 1969, (with J.O. Wilkes) Digital Computing and Numerical Methods, 1973; Editorial bd.: Jour. Computers and Fluids, 1971—, Computers and Chemical Engineering, 1974—. Mem. communications com. Mich. Council for Arts, 1977—. Recipient Chem. Engr. of Yr. award Detroit Engring. Soc., 1987, 3M award Am. Soc. for Engring. Edn., 1990. Mem. AAAS, Am. Inst. Chem. Engrs. (Computers in Chem. Engring. award 1980, chmn. CAST div. 1981), Assn. for Computing Machinery, Soc. for Computer Simulation, Sigma Xi, Sigma Nu. Home: 1605 Kearney Rd Ann Arbor MI 48104-4065

CARNAHAN, JOHN ANDERSON, lawyer; b. Cleve., May 8, 1930; s. Samuel Edwin and Penelope (Moulton) C.; m. Katherine A. Halter, June 14, 1958; children: Peter M., Allison E., Kristin A. BA, Duke U., 1953, JD, 1955. Bar: Ohio 1955. Pvt. practice Columbus, Ohio, 1955-78; ptnr. Arter & Hadden, Columbus, 1978—; lectr. Ohio Legal Ctr. Inst., 1969, 73-74. Editor Duke Law Jour., 1954-55; chmn. bd. editors Ohio Lawyer, 1986-91; contbr. articles to profl. jours. Chmn. UN Day, Columbus, 1960; pres. Capital City Young Republican Club, 1960; bd. dirs. Columbus Cancer Clinic, pres., 1978-81; bd. dirs. Columbus chpt. ARC, 1979-87; mem. governing bd. Hannah Neil Mission, Inc., 1974-78; chmn. Duke Alumni Admissions Adv. Com., 1965-79. Named one of Outstanding Young Men of Columbus, 1965. Fellow Am. Bar Found. (life, chmn. Ohio fellows 1988-95), Am. Coll. Trust and Estate Counsel, Columbus Bar Found. (life); mem ABA (ho. of dels. 1984-95), Ohio State Bar Found. (trustee 1986-90), Nat. Conf. Bar Pres. (Ritter award for outstanding contbns. adminstrn. justice 1987), Ohio State Bar Assn. (coun. of dels. 1965-67, exec. com. 1977-81, 82-85, pres.-elect 1982-83, pres. 1983-84), Columbus Bar Assn. (bd. govs. 1970-72, sec.-treas. 1974-75, pres. 1976-77, Professionalism award 1996), Athletic Club of Columbus, Kit Kat Club (past pres.). Presbyterian. E-mail: jac5830@aol.com. Home: 767 S 5th St Columbus OH 43206 Office: Arter & Hadden 10 W Broad St Ste 21 Columbus OH 43215-3418

CARNAHAN, MEL, governor, lawyer; b. Birch Tree, Mo., Feb. 11, 1934; s. A.S.J. and Mary Kathel (Schupp) C.; m. Jean Anne Carpenter, June 12, 1954; children: Roger, John Russell, Robin, Thomas. BA, George Washington U., 1954; JD, U. Mo.-Columbia, 1959. Lt. gov. State of Mo., 1988-93, gov., 1993—; majority fl. leader Mo. Ho. of Reps., Jefferson City, 1965-66; state treas. State of Mo., 1980-84. 1st lt. USAF, 1954-56. Named Outstanding Democrat Mo. Ho. of Reps., 1965, St. Louis Globe, 1965. Mem. Mo. Bar Assn., Order of Coif, Kiwanis (pres. Rolla chpt.), Masons, Shriners. Baptist. Home: PO Box 698 Rolla MO 65402-0698 Office: Office of the Governor PO Box 720 Jefferson City MO 65102-0720

CARNAHAN, ORVILLE DARRELL, retired state legislator, retired college president; b. Elba, Idaho, Dec. 25, 1929; s. Marion Carlos and Leola Pearl (Putnam) C.; m. Colleen Arrott, Dec. 14, 1951; children: Karen, Jeanie, Orville Darrell, Carla. B.S., Utah State U., 1958; M.Ed., U. Idaho, 1962, Ed.D., 1964. Vocat. dir., v.p. Yakima Valley Coll., Yakima, Wash., 1964-69; chancellor Eastern Iowa Community Coll. Dist., Davenport, 1969-71; pres. Highline Coll., Midway Wash., 1971-76; assoc. Utah Commr. for Higher Edn., Salt Lake City, 1976-78; pres. So. Utah U., Cedar City, 1978-81, Salt Lake Community Coll., Salt Lake City, 1981-90; pres. emeritus Salt Lake Community Coll. (formerly Utah Tech. Coll.), Salt Lake City, 1990—; mem. Utah Ho. of Reps.; cons. to various orgns. Active Boy Scouts Am. Served with U.S. Army, 1952-54, Korea. Mem. Am. Vocat. Assn., NEA, Idaho Hist. Soc., Utah Hist. Soc., Alpha Tau Alpha, Phi Delta Kappa, Rotary Internat. Mem. Ch. of Jesus Christ of Latter-Day Saints. Home: 2112 Quailbrook Dr Salt Lake City UT 84118-1120 Office: Salt Lake Community Coll 4600 S Redwood Rd Salt Lake City UT 84123-3197

CARNAHAN, ROBERT NARVELL, lawyer; b. Littlefield, Tex., Nov. 22, 1928; s. C.D. and Wilma L. (Hartness) C.; children from previous marriage: Cynthia, Michael, Christopher; m. Natalie Kay Kowalik, May 8, 1993. BBA, Tex. Tech. Coll., 1950; JD with honors, U. Tex.-Austin, 1957. Bar. Tex. 1956. Asst. county atty. Potter County, Tex., Amarillo; ptnr. Stokes, Carnahan & Fields, Amarillo; sole practice, Corpus Christi, Tex. Contbr. articles to profl. jours. 1st lt. USAF, 1954. Named one of top ten young lawyers in Am., Nat. Jaycees, 1967. Mem. State Bar Tex., Nueces County Bar Assn., Tex. Trial Lawyers Assn., Tex. Assn. Criminal Def. Lawyers, Am. Judicature Assn. Office: 730 Wilson Plz Corpus Christi TX 78476

CARNAHAN, ROBERT PAUL, civil engineer, educator, researcher, consultant; b. Bradenton, Fla., July 22, 1936; s. Robert Dewey and Marion (Wilbur) C.; m. Geraldine Schott, July 30, 1938; children: Robert P. Jr., Christopher T., Sean P. BCE, U. Fla., 1959; MS in Sanitary Engring., U. N.C., 1964; PhD, Clemson U., 1973. Registered profl. engr., Fla., Va., Md. Commd. 2d lt. U.S. Army, 1959, advanced through grades to lt. col., 1975; co. comdr. 92d Engring. Battalion, Ft. Bragg, N.C., 1960-61; project officer U.S. Environ. Hygiene Agy., Edgewood Arsenal, Md., 1961-63; instr. Med. Field Service Sch., San Antonio, 1966-68; sr. environ. engr. 20th Pvt. Med. Unit, Socialist Republic of Vietnam, 1968-69; project officer U.S. Army Med. Research and Devel. Command, Washington, 1973-75; project devel. officer U.S. Army Material Devel. and Research Ctr., Ft. Belvior, Va., 1975-79; divsn. chief EPA br. U.S. Army Med. Bioengring. Rsch. and Devel. Lab, Frederick, Md., 1979-80; adj. research prof. dept. of chemistry Am. U., 1976-77; adj. prof. dept. civil, mech. and environ. engring. George Washington U., 1979-80; asst. prof. dept. civil engring. and mechs. U. South Fla., 1980-84; assoc. prof. dept. civil engring. and mechs. U. South Fla., 1984-89, prof. dept. civil engring. & mechs., 1989-93, assoc. dean rsch. Coll. of Engring., 1993—. Contbr. numerous articles to profl. jours. Decorated Legion of Merit, Bronze Star with oak leaf cluster, Meritorious Service Medal with oak leaf cluster, Army Commendation medal with oak leaf cluster; recipient Silver medal for research and devel. Am. Def. Preparedness Assn., Rsch. award U.S. Dept. of Army Rsch., Comdr.'s award for tech. Meradcom. Mem. ASCE, Nat. Soc. Profl. Engrs., Am. Inst. Chem. Engrs., Am. Chem. Soc., Water Pollution Control Fedn., Am. Water Works Assn., N.A. Membrane Soc., Internat. Desalination Assn., Am. Desalting Assn. (Hall of Fame 1998), Fla. Engring. Soc., Internat. Assn. Water Pollution Research, Am. Acad. Environ. Engrs. (cert.), Sigma Xi, Chi Epsilon, Tau Beta Pi. Democrat. Roman Catholic. Home: 506 Terrace Hill Dr Tampa FL 33617-3850 Office: U South Fla Coll Engring Rsch Office 4202 E Fowler Ave Tampa FL 33620-9951

CARNASE, THOMAS PAUL, graphic designer, typographic consultant; b. Bronx, N.Y., Sept. 15, 1939. Assoc. B.F.A., N.Y.C. Community Coll., 1959. Assoc. designer Sudler & Hennessey, Inc., N.Y.C., 1959-64; pres., designer Bonder & Carnase Studio, Inc., N.Y.C., 1964-68; v.p., ptnr. Lubalin, Smith, Carnase, Inc., N.Y.C., 1969-79; pres. Carnase, Inc., N.Y.C., 1979—, Carnase Computer Typography, N.Y.C., 1979—, World Typeface Ctr., Inc., N.Y.C., 1981—; mem. adv. com. N.Y.C. Community Coll., 1977—; guest lectr./juror art dirs. clubs, schs., univs. throughout world. Exhibited in group show

Whitney Mus. Am. Art, N.Y.C.; editor Ligature jour., 1981—; designer numerous typefaces; represented in permanent collection at Cooper Hewitt Nat. Design Mus. Recipient award of Excellence, Communication Arts mag.; cert. of Distinction Creativity mag. Mem. N.Y. Art Dirs. Club, N.Y. Type Dirs. Club, Soc. Publ. Designers, Am. Inst. Graphic Arts. Office: Carnase Inc 30 E 21st St New York NY 10010-7215

CARNEAL, DREW ST. JOHN, lawyer; b. N.Y.C., Nov. 12, 1938. BA, Princeton U., 1960; LLB, U. Va., 1963. Ptnr. Cabell, Moncure & Carneal, 1963-85; atty. City of Richmond, Va., 1985-88; sr. v.p., gen. counsel Ownes & Minor, Inc., 1989—. Author: (book) Richmond's Fan District, 1996. Trustee Richmond Hist. Found. Bd. Office: Owens & Minor 4800 Cox Rd Glen Allen VA 23060-6292*

CARNEAL, GEORGE UPSHUR, lawyer; b. N.Y.C., May 31, 1935. AB, Princeton U., 1957; LLB, U. Va., 1961. Bar: Va. bar 1961, D.C. bar 1962. Law clk. to judge U.S. Ct. Appeals, D.C. Circuit, 1961-62; asso. firm Hogan & Hartson, Washington, 1962-68; partner Hogan & Hartson, 1973—; spl. asst. to sec. Dept. Transp., Washington, 1969-70; gen. counsel FAA, Washington, 1970-73; lectr. Georgetown U. Law Ctr., 1965-68; chmn. bd. trustees D.C. Bar Clients Security Trust Fund, 1973-78; gen. counsel Nat. Aeronautic Assn., 1984—. Decisions editor: Va. Law Rev, 1960-61; contbr. articles to legal jours. Bd. govs. Flight Safety Found., 1982-95; mem. exec. com. Princeton U. Alumni Coun., 1984-87. Mem. ABA, Fed. Bar Assn., Bar Assn. D.C., Raven Soc., Order of Coif. Clubs: Princeton (pres. 1984-86), Aero (pres. 1982) (Washington), Metropolitan, Chevy Chase. Office: Hogan & Hartson 555 13th St NW Ste 800E Washington DC 20004-1161

CARNEAL, PAMELA LYNN, technical recruiter, technical, freelance writer; b. Barberton, Ohio, Sept. 27, 1956; d. Doyle Glenn and Annie Majorie (Tucker) Roach; m. Thomas Clarence Miracle, July 8, 1978 (div. Dec. 1982); 1 child, Thomas Clarence Jr.; m. Gregory Brooks Carneal, June 16, 1984. AA in Journalism and Comm., Allegheny County C.C., Pitts., 1988; BA in Journalism and Comm. cum laude, Point Park Coll., 1991. Engring. writer, editor Bettis Atomic Power Lab.-Westinghouse, West Mifflin, Pa., 1989-99; assoc. recuiter Tech. Job Finders, San Diego, 1999—; tech. writer, freelance writer and editor, West Mifflin, 1992—. Avocations: aviculture, health and fitness, meditation, computers ad Internet, sport trucks. Home and Office: just the write words 4225 Lebanon Church Rd West Mifflin PA 15122-2718

CARNECCHIA, BALDO M., JR., lawyer; b. Hackensack, N.J., Sept. 2, 1947; s. Baldo M. Carnecchia and Cleo (Gerhart) Harper; m. Barbara Wolf, Mar. 1, 1969; children: Brian B., Justin W., Laura A. BS, Pa. State U., 1969; JD, Villanova U., 1972; LLM, Harvard U., 1973. Bar: Pa. 1972, U.S. Dist. Ct. (ea. dist.) Pa., U.S. Ct. Appeals (3d cir.) 1973, U.S. Supreme Ct. 1994. Legal writing asst. Boston U., 1973; assoc. Montgomery, McCracken, Walker & Rhoads, Phila., 1973-79, ptnr., 1979—; adj. prof. law Villanova (Pa.) Law Sch.; mem. corp. exec. bd. Phila. Mus. of Art; mem. legal com. of Wharton/Spencer Stuart Directors Inst. Editor Villanova U. Law Rev., 1971-72. Mem. ABA, Pa. Bar Assn., Phila. Bar Assn. Clubs: Harvard, The Union League. Home: 220 N Ithan Ave Villanova PA 19085-1936 Office: Montgomery McCracken Walker & Rhoads 123 S Broad St Fl 24 Philadelphia PA 19109-1099

CARNEIRO, MERVYN JOSEPH, mechanical engineer; b. Jabalpur, India, May 4, 1966; s. Felix Philip and Verona (Fernandes) C.; m. Smita Anne Maria Carneiro, Sept. 9, 1995; children, Ana Denise, Nikhil Felix. BS in Mech. Engring., Jabalpur U., 1989; MS, U. Wis., Milw., 1992. Cer. Engr.-in-tng., certify Assoc. Safety Professional. Design engr. Larsen and Toubro Ltd., Bombay, 1989-90; project engr. Safety Cons. Engrs., Schaumburg, Ill., 1992-95; process safety specialist Chilworth Tech., Monmouth Junction, N.J., 1995—. Contbr. articles to profl. jours. Mem. Am. Soc. Safety Engrs., Phi Kappa Phi. Office: Chilworth Tech Inc 11 Deerpark Dr Ste 204 Monmouth Junction NJ 08852-1923

CARNEIRO, RONALDO DOS SANTOS, surgeon; b. Rio de Janeiro, Mar. 17, 1946; m. Mary Alice Schuch; 3 children. BS, Cath. U. Rio Grande do Sul, Porto Alegre, Brazil, 1964; MD, Fed. U. Rio Grande do Sul, Porto Alegre, 1970. Diplomate Am. Bd. Plastic Surgery, Am. Bd. Surgery of the Hand; lic. physician, Brazil; lic. physician, surgeon, Pa., Calif. Intern Emergency Hosp. of Porto Alegre, Fla., 1968-69; preceptor dept. thoracic surgery Cath. U., Rio de Janeiro, 1969; preceptor in hand surgery Santa Casa Hosp., Rio de Janeiro, 1969; intern, resident Union Meml. Hosp., Balt., 1971-75, preceptor in hand surgery, 1975; resident in plastic surgery Allentown (Pa.) and Sacred Heart Hosp. Ctr., 1975; fellow in hand surgery dept. orthop. Jackson Meml. Hosp. and U. Miami (Fla.) Affiliated Hosps., 1977; maytag fellow in plastic surgery, fellow in exptl. microsurg U. Miami Sch. Medicine, 1978, assoc. prof. dept. orthop. and rehab., 1987, assoc. prof. clin. surgery, 1989-92; instr. hand surgery dept. orthop. Med. Sch. of U. Rio Grande do Sul, 1979-85; chief of hand surgery Hosp. Independencia, Porto Alegre, 1979-85; pvt. practice Western Hand Ctr., Downey, Calif., 1985-87; chief sect. hand surgery dept. plastic surgery Cleveland Clinic Naples, Fla.; tchg. asst. lab. classes and rsch. Physiology Exptl. Inst., Med. Sch. Fed. U. of Rio Grande do Sul, 1967-68; with microsurgery lab. Union Meml. Hosp., Balt., 1974-75, U. Miami, 1978; instr. orthop. residents and med. students in hand surgery svc. dept. orthop. and rehab., U. Miami Sch. Medicine, 1987-91; vis. prof. Louisville Inst. Hand and Microsurgery, 1986; illustrious vis. prof. Sindicato Dos Medicos de Santa Maria, Brazil, 1989; internat. invited prof. IX Bolivian Nat. Meeting Orthop. and Traumatology, 1990, XVI Ecuadorian Nat. Meeting Orthop. and Traumatology, 1990, Venezuelan Nat. Meeting Hand Surgery, 1990, 1st Nat. Panamanian Congress, 1991, XVII Nat. Meeting Colombian Soc. Surgery of the Hand, 1990, XXV Regional Meeting So. Br. Brazilian Soc. Surgery of the Hand, 1st Ann. Internat. Meeting of Orthop. in Panama, 1992; cons. Children's Med. Svcs., Fla., 1987; presenter in field. Contbr. numerous articles to profl. jours. Named 1 of Best Drs. in Am., S.E. Region, 1996-97, 1998; rsch. grantee Biomatrix, Inc., U. Miami, 1987-88. Mem. Am. Soc. Surgery of the Hand, Am. Soc. Plastic and Reconstructive Surgeons, Brazilian Hand Soc. (pres. so. br. 1985), Brazilian Plastic Surgery Soc., Brazilian Soc. for Surgery of the Hand, Brazilian Med. Soc., Colombian Soc. Hand Surgery, Ecuadorian Soc. Orthop., Internat. Fedn. Socs. for Surgery of the Hand (com on infections of the hand), Venezuelan Soc. Hand Surgery, Fla. Hand Soc., Soc. Orthop. Surgeons De Santa Cruz De La Sierra Bolivia, S.Am. Hand Soc. (hon.). Office: Cleve Clinic Fla 6101 Pine Ridge Road Ext Naples FL 34119-3900

CARNELL, RICHARD SCOTT, law educator; b. Bronxville, N.Y., June 20, 1953; s. Corbin Scott and Carol Beth (Young) C. BA in History magna cum laude, Yale U., 1975; JD, Harvard U., 1982. Bar: Calif. 1982, U.S. Dist. Ct. (no. dist.) Calif. 1982, U.S. Ct. Appeals (9th cir.) 1984, U.S. Supreme Ct. 1987. Assoc. Broad, Schulz, Larson & Wineberg, San Francisco, 1982-84; atty. Bd. Govs., FRS, Washington, 1984-87; counsel to com. on banking, housing, and urban affairs U.S. Senate, Washington, 1987-88, sr. counsel to com. on banking, housing, and urban affairs, 1989-93; asst. sec. fin. instns. Dept. Treasury, Washington, 1993-99; assoc. prof. law Fordham U., N.Y.C., 1999—. Episcopalian. Office: Fordham U Sch Law 140 W 62nd St New York NY 10023-7485

CARNELLA, FRANK THOMAS, information executive; b. N.Y.C., Nov. 30, 1934; s. Frank Thomas and Mary Catherine (De Leonard) C.; m. Diane Christine Wissemann, Oct. 28, 1961; children: China Michele, John Alexander. BA, Fordham Coll., 1955; postgrad., Harvard U., 1956. Various staff and exec. mgmt. positions IBM Corp., N.Y.C., 1956-84, v.p. devel. svcs. and ops. internat. MarketNet, 1984-87; sr. v.p. devel. svcs. Chem. Bank, N.Y.C., 1987-88; exec. v.p. Tex. Commerce Bank, Houston, 1988-92; sr. v.p. tech. planning Chem. Bank, N.Y.C., 1992-96; sr. v.p. developing and distributed tech. svcs. Chase Manhattan Bank, N.Y.C., 1996—; bd. dirs. Electronic Check Clearing House Orgn., Fin. Svcs. Tech. Consortium, Open User Recommended Solutions. Trustee Houston Grand Opera, 1989-90; bd. dirs. Juv. Diabetes Found., Houston, 1991-92, pres. 1992-93; adv. dir. Lions Eye Bank Found., Houston, 1992-93. Avocations: lit., appreciation of music and visual arts, social tennis. Office: Chase Manhattan Bank 95 Wall St New York NY 10005-4201 Address: 7133 E Bronco Dr Paradise Vly AZ 85253-3185

CARNER, CHARLES ROBERT, JR., screenwriter, director; b. Chgo., Apr. 30, 1957; s. Charles Robert Carner Sr. and Barbara (Shields) Traeger. BA, Columbia Coll., 1978. Asst. to dir. TV show Dummy, Chgo., 1978; casting asst. film My Bodyguard, Chgo., 1979; story editor Tony Bill Prodns., Venice, Calif., 1979-81; screenwriter Fred Weintraub Prodns., Beverly Hills, Calif., 1981-82, Catalina Prodn. Group, Sherman Oaks, Calif., 1983-84, Trian Prodns./CBS-TV, Los Angeles, 1984-85; screenwriter, dir. Tristar Prodns., Los Angeles, 1985-89. Author: (screenplays) Seduced, 1985, Gymkata, 1985, Let's Get Harry, 1986, Blind Fury, 1988, Eyes of a Witness, 1991; writer, dir. TV series Midnight Caller, 1990, Reasonable Doubts, 1992, The Untouchables, 1993, TV movie A Killer Among Friends, 1992, One Woman's Courage, 1994, Vanishing Point, 1997, The Fixer, 1997. Active East African Wildlife Soc., Kenya, Los Angeles, 1984—. Recipient Best Student Film award Chgo. Internat. Film Festival, 1978. Mem. NRA (life), Writers Guild Am., Sierra Club (life). Roman Catholic.

CARNER, GEORGE, foreign service executive, economic strategist; b. N.Y.C., Sept. 2, 1945; s. Joseph Carner Ribalta and Esther Cadefau; m. Michele Colette Delamotte, Apr. 20, 1968; children: Shawn L., Deric A. BA in Internat. Affairs, U. N.C., 1965; postgrad., Inst. Polit. Sci. La Sorbonne, Paris, 1966; MA in Internat. Affairs, George Washington U., 1971; student, Fgn. Svc. Inst., 1975. Internat. trade specialist U.S. Dept. Commerce, Washington, 1967-71; asst. program officer Agy. for Internat. Devel., Rabat, Morocco, 1971-75; dep. program officer Agy. for Internat. Devel., Kabul, Afghanistan, 1976-79; program planning officer Agy. for Internat. Devel., Manila, 1979-82; officer-in-charge India Agy. for Internat. Devel., Washington, 1982-84, chief policy plan/eval. DP/AFR, 1984-86; dep. mission dir. Agy. for Internat. Devel., Dakar, Senegal, 1986-88; mission dir. Agy. for Internat. Devel., Tunis, Tunisia, 1988-91, Antan, Madagascar, 1991-94, Managua, Nicaragua, 1994-98, Guatemala City, Guatemala, 1998—; speaker, panelist Nat. Assn. of Schs. Pub. Affairs and Adminstrn., Honolulu and N.Y.C., 1981, 83, Harvard U., Boston, 1984. Contbr. articles to profl. jours. and procs. Recipient Superior Honor award Agency for Internat. Devel., Washington, 1978, Presdl. Meritorious Svc. award The White House, 1987. Mem. Am. Fgn. Svcs. Assn., East-West Ctr., Rotary. Avocations: listening to jazz, art, scuba diving, nature walks. Office: USAID Guatemala Unit 3323 APO AA 34024-3323

CARNES, EDWARD E., federal judge; b. 1950. BS, U. Ala., Tuscaloosa, 1972; JD, Harvard U., 1975. Asst. Ala. atty. gen. Office Atty. Gen., 1975-92; cir. judge U.S. Ct. Appeals (11th cir.), Montgomery, Ala., 1992—. Office: Frank M Johnson Jr Fed Bldg US Courthouse 15 Lee St Ste 410 Montgomery AL 36104-4055*

CARNES, JAMES EDWARD, electronics executive; b. Cumberland, Md., Sept. 27, 1939; s. Roy Clifton and Alta (Wigfield) C.; m. Nancy Louise Zolto, Nov. 27, 1977; 1 stepchild, Gillian. BS in Engring. Sci., Pa. State U., 1961; MA in Elec. Engring., Princeton U., 1967, PhD in Elec. Engring., 1970; PhD (hon.), Thomas Edison State Coll., 1994, Kean U., 1998. Mem. tech. staff RCA Labs., Princeton, N.J., 1969-77; mgr. tech. application RCA Consumer Electronics, Indpls., 1977-80, dir. new products lab, 1980-82, div. v.p. engring., 1982-87; v.p. consumer electronics and info. scis. David Sarnoff Rsch. Ctr. (subs. SRI Internat.), Princeton, N.J., 1987-90, pres., COO, 1990-93, pres., CEO, 1993—; sr. v.p. SRI Internat., 1990-95; chmn. bd. Sensar, Inc., Princeton, N.J., 1992—, Orchid Biocomputer Inc., 1995-97, Sarnoff Digital Comm., Inc., 1996-97; dir. Sarnoff Real Time Inc., Sarif, Inc., Delsys Pharm. Corp., Orchid Biocomputer, Inc., Sarnoff Digital Comms., Nova Corp., SRI Internat.; short course lectr. UCLA, 1978-81, Am. U. Washington, 1976, Ctrl. Poly. Inst., London, 1974. Contbr. articles to profl. jours.; inventor. Campaign chmn. Princeton Area United Way, 1992, bd. dirs., 1992-94, 1st v.p., 1993-94; chmn. bd. trustees United Way Greater Mercer County, 1994-96; chmn. sci. adv. bd. Rider Coll., 1990-92; trustee Rider U., 1993—, Ind. Coll. Fund. N.J., 1990-96, Thomas Edison State Coll. Found., 1992—, Am. Boychoir Sch., 1995—, MSM Regional Coun., 1997—; mem. bd . overseers N.J. Inst. Tech., 1993-98. Lt. USN, 1961-65. Recipient David Sarnoff Outstanding Achievement award RCA, 1981, Engr. of Yr. award Ctrl. N.J. Engring. Coun., 1991, Humanitarian award NCCJ, 1994, Citizen of Yr. award Mercer County C. of C., 1996, N J. Tech. Coun. High Tech. Hero award, 1999; named to Jr. Achievement Bus. Hall of Fame, 1998. Fellow IEEE (Centennial medal 1984, Region I award 1993); mem. Nat. Acad. Engring., Pa. State U. Alumni Assn. (coun., exec. com., Outanding Engr. Alumnus award 1992, Pres. and Exec. dir. award 1995, Disting. Alumnus award 1996, v.p. 1997—). Avocations: flying; sports. Home: 47 W Shore Dr Pennington NJ 08534-2122 Office: Sarnoff Corp 201 Washington Rd Princeton NJ 08540-6449

CARNES, JOSEPH SYDNEY, clergyman; b. Memphis, Dec. 2, 1929; s. Samuel Leslye and Marion Rachel (Weaver) C.; m. Annie Frank Rutledge, June 22, 1952; children: Jane Ann, Joseph Sydney Jr., James Rutledge, John David. BS, Memphis State U., 1956; MDiv, Tex. Christian U., 1962, D Ministry, 1979. Ordained to ministry Christian Ch. (Disciples of Christ), 1949; cert. pastoral counselor Parkland Hosp., Dallas. Min. of membership 1st Christian Ch, Eugene, Oreg., 1962-65; sr. min. 1st Christian Ch, Nampa, Idaho, 1965-72, Lakeview Christian Ch., Dallas, 1972-81, Oak Cliff Christian Ch., Dallas, 1981—; pres. Christian Chs. in Idaho, Boise, 1971. Co-author: Communion Meditations, 1966. Founding dir. Nampa Christian Housing, 1967; bd. dirs. Mercy Hosp., Nampa, 1968-72, Idaho Mental Health Dept., 1969-72. Col. Tex. State Guard, chief chaplains, 1972-94. Mem. Mil. Chaplains Assn. U.S.A. (local pres. 1972—), Masons (33d degree, chaplain 1988-95), Lions (local pres. 1981-82), Order Ea. Star. Republican. Avocations: fishing, hunting, world travel. Home: 3738 Cripple Creek Dr Dallas TX 75224-3701 Office: 1222 Kiest Blvd Dallas TX 75224

CARNES, JULIE ELIZABETH, federal judge; b. Atlanta, Oct. 31, 1950; m. Stephen S. Cowen. AB summa cum laude, U. Ga., 1972, JD magna cum laude, 1975. Bar: Ga. 1975. Law clk. to Hon. Lewis R. Morgan U.S. Ct. Appeals (5th cir.), 1975-77; spl. counsel U.S. Sentencing Commn., 1989, commr., 1990-96; asst. U.S. Atty. U.S. Dist. Ct. (no. dist.) Ga., Atlanta, 1978-90, judge, 1992—. Office: US Courthouse 75 Spring St SW Ste 2167 Atlanta GA 30303-3309

CARNESALE, ALBERT, university chancellor; b. Bronx, N.Y., July 2, 1936; two children: Keith, Kimberly. BME, Cooper Union, 1957; MS, Drexel U., 1961, LLD (hon.), 1993; PhD, N.C. State U., 1966, LLD (hon.), 1997; MA (hon.), Harvard U., 1979; DSc (hon.), N.J. Inst. Technology, 1984. Chief Def. Weapons System U.S. Arms Control and Disarmament Agy., Washington, 1969-72; prof. N.C. State U., Raleigh, 1972-74; prof. and acad. dean John F. Kennedy Sch. of Govt. Harvard U., Cambridge, Mass., 1981-91; dean John F. Kennedy Sch. of Govt., 1991-95; provost Harvard U., Cambridge, 1994-97; chancellor UCLA, 1997—. Author: (books) New Nuclear Nations: Consequences for US Policy, Fateful Visions: Avoiding Nuclear Catastrophy, Superpower Arms Control: Setting the Record Straight.. Gano Dunn award for Outstanding Achievement, Cooper Union, N.Y.C. Mem. Am. Nuclear Soc., Am. Soc. Engring. Edn., Assn. for Pub. Policy Analysis and Mgmt., Coun. on Fgn. Rels., Inst. for Strategic Studies. Office: U of California Office of the Chancellor 405 Hilgard Ave Los Angeles CA 90095-1405

CARNEY, ARTHUR WILLIAM MATTHEW, actor; b. Mt. Vernon, N.Y., Nov. 4, 1918; s. Edward M. and Helen (Farrell) C.; m. Jean Myers, Aug. 15, 1940, remarried Mar. 1977; children: Eileen, Brian, Paul; m. Barbara Isaac. Student pub. schs. Mem., Horace Heidt Orchestra, 1936-39, vaudeville and club entertainer, 1939-40; radio performer, 1942-44, 45-49; TV actor featured in comedy and dramatic roles with The Honeymooners, The Chevy Show, Morey Amsterdam, Henry Morgan, Jackie Gleason, Studio One, Kraft Theatre, 1949—, Omnibus, Climax, Playhouse 90, others; Rope Dancers, 1957-58, Harvey, 1958; actor in Broadway plays Take Her She's Mine, 1961-62, The Odd Couple, 1965, Lovers, 1968, Prisoner of Second Avenue, 1972-73; actor in motion pictures The Yellow Rolls Royce, 1964, Harry and Tonto, 1974, W.W. and the Dixie Dancekings, 1975, Won Ton Ton, 1976, The Late Show, 1977, Movie Movie, 1978, House Calls, 1978, Sunburn, 1979, Going in Style, 1979, Defiance, 1980, Roadie, 1980, Steel, 1980, Take This Job and Shove It, 1981, St. Helens, 1981, Better Late than Never, 1983, The Muppets Take Manhattan, 1984, Firestarter, 1984, The Naked Face, 1985, Where Pigeons Go To Die, 1990, The Last Action Hero, 1993; appeared in TV movies Death Scream, 1975, Katherine, 1975, Lanigan's Rabbi, 1976, Scott Joplin, King of Ragtime, 1978, The Naked Face, 1984, A Doctor's Story, 1984, Terrible Joe Moran, 1984, Bitter Harvest, 1981, Izzy and Moe, 1985. Served with U.S. Army, 1944-45. Recipient TV Acad. Emmy award for outstanding humor program, 1960, Emmy award for individual achievement, 1953, 54, 55, 68, Sylvania award, 1954, 59, Acad. award as best actor Harry and Tonto, 1974, Best Actor award Nat. Soc. Film Critics, 1977. Mem. Screen Actors Guild, AFTRA, Actors Equity. Club: Players. *

CARNEY, BRADFORD GEORGE YOST, lawyer, educator; b. Balt., Oct. 25, 1950; s. Blanchard Donald and Anne Carolyn (Yost) C.; m. Gail Elaine Hasson, Jan. 6, 1973; children: Jason Bradford, Brandon Burroughs. BA, Washington Coll., 1972; JD, U. Balt., 1976. Bar: Md. 1977, U.S. Dist. Ct. Md. 1978, U.S. Supreme Ct. 1982. Ptnr. Callahan, Calwell, Laudeman, Balt., 1982-87; ptnr. Weinberg and Green, Balt., 1987-96; of counsel Royston, Mueller, McLean & Reid, L.L.P., 1996—; asst. prof. law Villa Julie Coll., Stevenson, Md., 1983-97, assoc. prof., 1997—. Bd. trustees Boys' Latin Sch., Md., 1988-93. Mem. ABA, Nat. Assn. Criminal Def. Lawyers, Md. State Bar Assn., Balt. City Bar Assn., Balt. County Bar Assn., Md. Criminal Def. Attys. Assn., U. Balt. Alumni Assn. (bd. govs. 1984-87), Boys' Latin Sch. Alumni Assn. (bd. dirs. 1983-88, pres. 1986-88). Home: 474 Five Farms Ln Lutherville Timonium MD 21093-2954 Office: Royston Mueller McLean & Reid LLP 102 W Pennsylvania Ave Towson MD 21204-4526

CARNEY, DANIEL L., program and financial management consultant; b. Taunton, Mass., June 12, 1947; s. Lawrence Vincent and Jeannette B. (Piche) C.; m. Patricia Anne Morse, Feb. 14, 1970; children: Michael Sean, Jennifer Lynn. BS, USCG Acad., 1969; MBA in Fin. Mgmt., George Washington U., 1976; postgrad., Def. Sys. Mgmt. Coll., 1991. Cert. govt. fin. mgr., 1996. With USCG, 1969-92; exec. officer group Sandy Hook USCG, N.J., 1982-86; exec. officer supply ctr. USCG, Bklyn., N.Y., 1986-89; project officer, chief of logistics, fleet renovation & modernization USCG, Washington, 1991-92; asst. program mgr. sys. to automate and integrate logistics Dept. Transp., Booz Allen & Hamilton, Bethesda, Md., 1992-93; bus. mgr. Navy extremely high frequency satellite program Dept. Def., Booz Allen & Hamilton, Crystal City, Va., 1993; fin. mgr. composite healthcare sys. Dept. Def., Booz Allen & Hamilton, Falls Church, Va., 1993-97; mem. team to replace fin. mgmt. info. sys. for U.S. Senate Booz Allen & Hamilton, Falls Church, Va., 1997—; team leader for the decennial census Bur. Census; fin. advisor USCG Credit Union, Boston, 1977-79. Firefighter Arnold Vol. Fire Dept., Md., 1993—, treas., 1994—; basketball coach Our Lady of Perpetual Help, Highlands, N.J., 1983-88. Mem. Am. Soc. Mil. Comptrollers. Roman Catholic. Avocations: basketball, travel. Home: 578 Kevins Dr Arnold MD 21012-2066 Office: Booz Allen & Hamilton Inc 5109 Leesburg Pike Falls Church VA 22041-3208

CARNEY, DAVID JOHN, computer scientist, music theorist; b. Bklyn., Aug. 22, 1942; s. Francis John and Edith (Murphy) C. MusB, Cath. U. of Am., 1963; MusM, U. So. Calif., 1966; D of Musical Arts, Boston U., 1981, MS, 1985. Instr. Oberlin (Ohio) Conservatory, 1967-69; asst. prof. Boston U., 1972-79; software engr. Intermetrics, Inc., Cambridge, Mass., 1984-87; mem. rsch. staff Inst. for Def. Analysis, Alexandria, Va., 1987-92; sr. mem. tech. staff Software Engring. Inst., Pitts., 1992—. Author: Principles of CASE Tool Integration, 1994; contbr. articles to profl. jours.; composer choral and orchestral compositions, 1970-77; staff organist King's Chapel, Boston, 1969-74; asst. condr. Handel & Haydn Soc., Boston, 1973-76. Dir. Omnibus Concerts, Boston, 1974-77. Mem. Phi Beta Kappa. Office: Software Engring Inst 4500 5th Ave Pittsburgh PA 15213-2612

CARNEY, DEBORAH LEAH TURNER, lawyer; b. Great Bend, Kans., Aug. 19, 1952; d. Harold Lee and Elizabeth Lura (Dillon) Turner; m. Thomas J.T. Carney, Mar. 20, 1976; children: Amber Blythe, Sonia Briana, Ross Dillon. BA in Human Biology, Stanford U., 1974; JD, U. Denver, 1976. Bar: Kans. 1977, U.S. Dist. Ct. Kans. 1977, U.S. Ct. Appeals (10th cir.) 1982, Colo. 1984, U.S. Dist. Ct. Colo. 1984, U.S. Supreme Ct. 1989, U.S. Claims Ct. 1990. With Turner & Boisseau, Great Bend, 1976-84, of counsel, 1984-93; assoc. Lutz & Oliver, Arvada, Colo., 1984-85; prin. Deborah Turner Carney, P.C., Golden and Lakewood, Colo., 1985-92; shareholder Carney Law Office, Golden, Colo., 1992-95; owner Carney Law Office, 1995—. Author (newsletter) Profl. Solutions, 1984, (chpt.) Courtroom Handbook; editor Apple Law newsletter, 1984-86; contbr. articles to profl. jours. Pres. Canyon Area Residents for the Environment (C.A.R.E.), 1998. Mem. Colo. Trial Lawyers Assn., 1st Jud. Dist. Bar Assn. (Colo.), Genesee Daytime Bookclub (co-chair 1997-98), Kiwanis (bd. dirs. Denver club 1988-90, trustee 1990-92, sec. 1992-93). Republican. Avocations: horses, dancing, computers. E-mail: deb@carneylaw.net. Office: 21789 Cabrini Blvd Golden CO 80401-9488

CARNEY, DENNIS JOSEPH, former steel company executive, consulting company executive; b. Charleroi, Pa., Mar. 19, 1921; s. Walter Augustus and Ann (Nandor) C.; m. Virginia M. Horvath, June 12, 1943 (dec. Jan. 1984); children—Colleen A., Dennis Joseph, Glenn P., Lynn C., Dianne V. B.S. in Metallurgy, Pa. State U., 1942; Sc.D., Mass. Inst. Tech., 1949. With U.S. Steel Corp., Pitts., 1942-74; gen. supt. U.S. Steel Corp., 1963-65, v.p. long range planning, 1965-68, v.p. applied research, 1968-72, v.p. research, 1972-74; v.p. ops. Wheeling-Pitts. Steel Corp., 1974-75, exec. v.p., dir., 1975-76, pres., 1976-85, chief operating officer, 1976-77, chief exec. officer, 1977-85, chmn. bd., 1978-85; ret., 1985; pres. Intra-Continental Cons. Co, Fort Lauderdale, Fla., 1985—. Author: (with others) Gases in Metals, 1956. Bd. dirs. Wheeling (W.Va.) Coll. Served to lt. (j.g.) USNR, 1943-46. Fellow Am. Soc. Metals (Grossmann award Pitts. chpt. 1959, trustee 1972—); mem. Am., Brit., Internat. iron and steel insts., Am. Inst. Mining, Metall. and Petroleum Engrs. (McKune award 1951, Benjamin F. Fairless award 1978), Am. Iron and Steel Engrs., Sigma Xi, Tau Beta Pi, Sigma Nu. Clubs: South Hills Country (Pitts.), Duquesne (Pitts.) (dir.); Laurel Valley Country, Fox Chapel Country. Home and Office: 3900 N Ocean Dr Apt 3C Fort Lauderdale FL 33308-5936

CARNEY, JOHN MICHAEL, professional football player; b. Hartford, Conn., Apr. 20, 1964. Degree in mktg., U. Notre Dame, 1987. Place kicker Tampa Bay (Fla.) Buccaneers, 1988-89, San Diego Chargers, 1990—. Named to Sporting News NFL All-Pro Team, 1994, selected to Pro Bowl, 1994. Holds NFL record for most consecutive field goals (29), Nov. 1992-Sept. 1993; tied for NFL field goals (34), 1994. Office: Qualcomm Stadium Jack Murphy Field care San Diego Chargers PO Box 609609 San Diego CA 92160-9609*

CARNEY, JOSEPH BUCKINGHAM, lawyer; b. Greensburg, Ind., July 8, 1928; s. Edward O. and Grace Rebecca (Buckingham) C.; m. Constance J. Caylor, July 8, 1950; children: Elizabeth, Joseph Buckingham Jr., Julia, Sarah. AB, DePauw U., 1950; LLB, Harvard U., 1953. Bar: D.C. 1953, Ind. 1953, U.S. Dist. Ct. (so. dist.) Ind. 1953, U.S. Supreme Ct. 1957, U.S. Ct. Appeals (7th cir.) 1961; ind. cert. mediator. Assoc. Hogg, Peters & Leonard, Ft. Wayne, Ind., 1953-54; assoc. Baker & Daniels, Indpls., 1957-62, ptnr., 1962-95, mem. mgmt. com., 1993-94, sec., 1994, of counsel, 1996—; mem. lawyers com. Nat. Ctr. State Cts., Williamsburg, Va., 1985—; assoc. Environ. Law Inst., Washington. Chmn. bd. dirs. Parkinson Awareness Assn. Ctrl. Ind., Inc.; past pres. Interfaith Homes, Inc., Indpls.; past chmn., elder Northwood Christian Ch., Indpls. 1st lt. U.S. Army, 1954-57. Recipient Disting. Alumni award DePauw U., 1984. Mem. ABA, Ind. Bar Assn., Indpls. Bar Assn., Am. Judicature Soc., 7th Cir. Bar Assn. (pres. 1983-84), Univ. Club, Indpls. Athletic Club, Columbia Club, Contemporary, Lawyers Club Indpls. (past pres.), Phi Eta Sigma, Phi Gamma Delta (bd. dirs. 1974-78, sec. 1976-78, pres. 1980-82), Phi Gamma Delta Ednl. Found. (bd. dirs., pres. 1996-98). Avocations: scuba diving, travel, photography. Office: Baker & Daniels 300 N Meridian St Ste 2700 Indianapolis IN 46204-1782

CARNEY, KAREN ROSE, music educator, jazz, popular, classical pianist; b. Canton, Ohio, Dec. 9, 1940; d. Alex and Rose (Burky) Winkelman; 1 child, Miles. BMus, Baldwin-Wallace Coll., 1961; postgrad., Case Western Res. U., 1961; MA in Music, Ohio State U., 1980, PhD in Music, 1983. Cert. music tchr., N.C., Ohio. Accompanist, staff musician dance dept. Ohio State U., Columbus, 1983-85; asst. prof. N.C. Wesleyan Coll., Rocky Mount, 1985-87, U. S.D., Vermillion, 1987-88; pianist, spl. events The Ohio State U., Columbus, 1988-90; lectr., choir accompanist Fayetteville (N.C.) State U.,

1990-91; instr. performing arts Meth. Coll., Fayetteville, N.C., 1990-91; asst. prof. Lincoln U., Pa., 1991-93; assoc. prof. Paine Coll., Augusta, Ga., 1993-95, Winston-Salem (N.C.) State U., 1995—; PRAXIS item writer Ednl. Testing Svc., Princeton, N.J., 1997; com. music edn. UNC/NCCC Articulation Agreement, Chapel Hill, N.C., 1997; clinician Nat. Group Piano Symposium, U. Okla., Norman, 1985; judge music contests, Ohio, North Carolina, South Dakota. *Karen's classical music teachers include Guilford Plumley, Theodore Lettvin, and Richard Tetley-Kardos. Due to her love of the harmonies of jazz-popular music, she studied in this idiom with Dave Robertson in Los Angeles, and briefly with Jerry Coker at the University of Tennessee-Knoxville. Karen performs as a solo pianist, and collaborates with musicians for diverse events. She serves as an advisor to Chapter 7 of the Collegiate Music Educators National Conference at Winston-Salem State University. Her research interests are in perception and psychology. Karen's hobby is ballroom dancing.* Vol. tchr., performer Winston-Salem/Forsyth County Pub. Schs., 1997—; vol. pianist Baltic Country Manor, 1992—, nursing and retirement homes, Winston-Salem, 1995—; guest organist, pianist various chs., N.C. and Ohio. Recipient rsch. grant Lilly-Lincoln Univ., 1992, Cert. of Recognition Winston-Salem State U. Friends of O'Kelly Libr., 1997. Mem. Am. Fedn. Musicians, Coll. Music Soc., Intercollegiate Music Assn., Internat. Assn. Jazz Educators, Music Educators Nat. Conf.; Music Tchrs. Nat. Assn. (coll. faculty cert. in piano), Am. Mensa, Mu Phi Epsilon, Pi Kappa Lambda. Home: 4195 Spirea Drive Wilmington NC 28403 Office: Winston-Salem State U Martin Luther King Jr Dr Winston Salem NC 27110

CARNEY, MARTIN JOSEPH, JR., university administrator; b. Cleve., Jan. 17, 1954; s. Martin Joseph and Norma Mary (O'Brien) C.; m. Cynthia Lee Bardar, Oct. 11, 1980; children: Elizabeth Ann, Martin Joseph III, Mary Alana. BS in Bus. Adminstrn., John Carroll U., University Heights, Ohio, 1976; MS in Adminstrn., U. Notre Dame, 1980. Dir. fin. aid Ursuline Coll., Pepper Pike, Ohio, 1977-78, asst. dir. admissions, 1978-82; dir. fin. aid Borromeo Coll. Ohio, Wickliffe, 1978-82; assoc. dir. fin. aid U. Toledo, Ohio, 1982-87; assoc. dir. Office Fin. Assistance Svcs. U. Miami, Coral Gables, Fla., 1987-90, dir. Office Fin. Assistance Svcs., 1990—; mem. adv. bd. USA Group, Indpls., 1993-95, 97—, Nellie Mae, Boston, 1995—; mem. sch. adv. group for Edn. First, Tampa, 1997—; fin. aid adv. coun. Fla. Dept. Edn., Tallahassee, 1997—. Baseball coach Western Area Little League, Weston, Fla., 1990—, football and baseball coach YMCA, Weston, 1990—. Mem. Nat. Assn. Student Fin. Aid Adminstrs., So. Assn. Student Fin. Aid Adminstrs., Fla. Assn. Student Fin. Aid Adminstrs. (sec. 1995-97, outstanding svc. awards 1996, 97). Avocations: reading Western novels, gardening, softball, travel. Office: U Miami Rhodes House 37E 1204 Dickinson Dr Coral Gables FL 33146-2503

CARNEY, MICHAEL, orchestra leader; b. N.Y.C., Nov. 27, 1937; s. Edward M. and Jacqueline (Soutar) C.; m. Lisa Marshall, May 9, 1997. BA, Northwestern U., 1959. Securities analyst Butcher & Sherrerd Co., Phila., 1964-66; investment mgr. Barnes & Tucker Co., Haverford, Pa., 1966; orchestra leader Michael Carney Music, N.Y.C., 1970—; mem. vis. com. Northwestern U. Sch. Music., Evanston, Ill., 1983—. Trustee Boys Club N.Y., 1981—. Republican. Clubs: River, Meadow, Bohemian. Home: 200 E 71st St New York NY 10021-5137 Office: 305 Madison Ave New York NY 10017-6213

CARNEY, ROBERT ALFRED, health care administrator; b. Winnipeg, Man., Can., Feb. 24, 1916; s. Thomas Alfred and Opal Edna (Fogle) C. (parents Am. citizens); m. Jacqueline Briscoe, May 15, 1943; children: Thomas A., Roberta L., Richard D. BA, Denison U., 1938. Lic. hosp. and nursing home adminstr. Accountant Nat. Cash Register Co., 1938-41; accountant, auditor, controller Miami Valley Hosp., Dayton, O., 1941-47; asst. dir. Ochsner Found. Hosp., New Orleans, 1947-48; adminstrv. dir. Jewish Hosp., Cin., 1948-61; assoc. exec. dir. Jewish Hosp., 1961-68, exec. dir., 1968-78; cons. mgmt. and employee relations Children's Hosp. Med. Center, Cin., 1979; adminstr. Marjorie P. Lee Home for Aged, Cin., 1980-89; dir. spl. projects Twin Towers Retirement Community, Cin., 1989-92; interim adminstr. Auglaize Acres County Nursing Home, Wapakoneta, Ohio, 1990-91; adminstr. Lincoln Ave. and Crawford's Home for the Aged, 1993-96; cons. Drake Ctr., 1996-97; adj. assoc. prof. hosp. adminstrn. Coll. Pharmacy U. Cin., 1969-78; adj. faculty mem., grad. program hosp. adminstrn. Xavier U., Cin., 1970-78; trustee Health Careers Greater Cin., 1956-85, 1st v.p., 1970-85; mem. exec. com., trustee Health Careers of Ohio, 1973-81, treas., 1976-79; trustee Am. Nurses Assn. Nat. Retirement Plan, 1973-75; pres. Withrow H.S. PTA, 1969-71; mem. bd., pres. Bapt. Home Benevolent Soc., 1974-88; mem. bd. Jewish Fedn. Cin., 1969-70, 72-73; mem. racial isolation task force Cin. Pub. Schs., 1972-73, mem. adv. com. for sch. lic. practical nursing, 1973; mem. home health svcs. adv. com. Cin. Dept. Health, 1972—, chmn., 1974-76, 96—; mem. adv. com. Lic. Practical Nurse Assn. Ohio, 1979-85; mem. Ohio Commn. Nursing, 1973-75, Am. Bd. Med. Specialists, 1977-80; sec. Ohio Coun. on Nursing Needs and Resources, 1978-81; bd. dirs., sec., treas. Fedn. for accessible Nursing Edn. and Licensure, 1984—; chmn. Greater Cin. Nursing Home assn., 1985—. Trustee emeritus Assn. Ohio Philanthropic Homes, 1993—. Recipient Outstanding Preceptor award Xavier U., 1974. Mem. Am. Coll. Hosp. Adminstrs. (life), Am. Hosp. Assn. (life), Ohio Hosp. Assn. (life), Nat. League for Nursing (dir. 1977-81), Ohio League for Nursing (dir. 1968-76, v.p. 1973-76), Greater Cin. Hosp. Council, Am. Pub. Health Assn., Assembly of Hosp. Schs. Nursing (chmn. bd. 1977-78), Eagle Scout Assn. (life), Sigma Chi, Phi Mu Alpha. Baptist. Lodge: Masons. Home and Office: 2721 Grandin Rd Cincinnati OH 45208-3414

CARNEY, ROBERT ARTHUR, restaurant executive; b. Haddonfield, N.J., Aug. 20, 1937; s. George Albert and Margeret (Hollworth) C.; m. Janellen Sockol, may 31, 1996; 1 child, Lynn Ann. *Wife Janellen, BS 1982 University of New Haven, worked for fifteen years in various management positions for the Mariott Hotel Corporation. Daughter Lynn Guerrieri, BS Rutgers U., is employed in the operating room at The Thomas Jefferson Hospital, Philadelphia. She received a BSN from Thomas Jefferson University-College of Health and Sciences in 1993 where she graduated first in her class. Lynn and her husband, Mark, have one child, Emily, born in 1996.* BA, Ursinus Coll., 1963. Procurement agt. Campbell Soup Co., Paris, Tex., 1963-69; mgr. procurement Campbell Soup Co., Salisbury, Md., 1969-72; dir. procurement Campbell Soup Co., Camden, N.J., 1972-78; v.p. procurement Burger King Corp., Miami, 1978-82; v.p. purchasing Pizza Hut, Inc., Wichita, 1982-95; sr. v.p. procurement Long John Silver's, Inc., Lexington, Ky., 1995-99. Mem. editl. adv. bd. Supplier Selection and Mgmt. Report. Mem. dean's adv. bd. Ala. State U. Capt. U.S. Army, 1958-60. Mem. Nat. Restaurant Assn. Roman Catholic. Home: 3154 Maria Dr Lexington KY 40516-9616

CARNEY, ROBERT THOMAS, lawyer; b. Youngstown, Ohio, Mar. 28, 1947; s. Thomas P. and Mildred B. (Keeling) C.; m. Victoria L. Schrecengost, May 21, 1977; children: Brian, Michael. BS in Physics, Northwestern U., 1969; JD, Georgetown U., 1972. Bar: Ohio 1972, D.C. 1974, U.S. Ct. Appeals (fed. cir.), U.S. Ct. Fed. Claims, U.S. Tax Court, U.S. Patent and Trademark Office, U.S. Supreme Ct. Law clk. U.S. Dist. Ct., Cleve., 1972-73; trial atty. tax divsn U.S. Dept. Justice, Washington, 1973-79; ptnr. tax atty. Lee, Toomey & Kent, Washington, 1979-88, Dow, Lohnes & Albertson, Washington, 1988-90, Rogers & Wells, Washington, 1990-96; ptnr. Fulbright & Jaworski, Washington, 1996-98, Ernst & Young, Washington, 1998—; adj. prof. Georgetown U. Law Sch., Washington, 1987—. Mem. Murdoch Inn of Ct. (master, sec.-treas.). Office: Ernst & Young 1225 Connecticut Ave NW Ste 700 Washington DC 20036-2621

CARNEY, ROGER FRANCIS XAVIER, retired army officer; b. Bklyn., Oct. 20, 1933; s. Frank Clement and Clara Helen (Muller) C.; m. Linda Ann Bowlus, Aug. 11, 1963 (div. Mar. 1993); children—Kevin James, Stephen Jason, Brian Andrew. B.S., Purdue U., 1960, M.S. in Indsl. Adminstrn., 1963; grad. U.S. Army Command and Gen. Staff Coll., 1975, U.S. Army War Coll., 1979; MA, U. Conn., 1992. Commd. 2d lt. U.S. Army, 1960, advanced through grades to lt. col., 1976; comdr. 583d Ordnance Co., Muenster, W.Ger., 1969-72; research and devel. coordinator Army Materiel Command Field Office, Kirtland AFB, N.Mex., 1972-74; logistic staff officer CENTAG Signal Support GP (NATO), Seckenheim, W.Ger., 1975-78, chief nuclear weapons logistic element G4, 1978; comdr. 15th Ordnance Battalion, Darmstadt, W.Ger., 1978-80; prof. mil. sci. head dept. Worcester Poly. Inst. (Mass.), 1980-84; prof. mil. sci., head dept. Fitchburg State Coll. (Mass.), 1980-84; prof. mil. sci., head dept. Nichols Coll., Dudley, Mass., 1982-84, dean student affairs, 1985-98, dir. Robert C. Fischer Inst., Nichols Coll. Mem. Worcester Com. Fgn. Rels., Worcester Econ. Club (exec. com.), Mil. Adv. Coun. Ctr. for Def. Info. Mem. Bd. of dirs. Internat. Ctr. of Worcester; Decorated Legion of Merit, Bronze Star, 2 Meritorious Service medals, Army Commendation medal. Mem. Assn. U.S. Army, Assn. Former Intelligence Officers, Am. Legion, Ret. Officers Assn., U. Conn. Alumni Assn., Purdue Alumni Assn., Alpha Sigma Phi (pres. Purdue U. chpt. 1959-60), Pi Lambda Theta. Democrat. Christian. Home: PO Box 5000 Dudley MA 01571-5000

CARNEY, TIMOTHY MICHAEL, diplomat; b. St. Joseph, Mo., July 12, 1944; s. Clement Egan Carney and Jane (Byrne) Booth; m. Tep Demaz Baker, 1973 (div. 1983); 1 child, Anne; m. Victoria Anne Butler, May 28, 1983. BS, MIT, 1966; postgrad., Cornell U., 1975-76. Joined Fgn. Svc., 1966; 3d sec. and vice consul Am. Embassy, Saigon, Maseru, Phnom Penh, 1967-75; first sec. Am. Embassy, Bangkok, 1980-83; counsellor of embassy for polit. affairs Am. Embassy, Pretoria, South Africa, 1983-86; counsellor of embassy in polit. affairs Am. Embassy, Jakarta, Indonesia, 1987-90; prin. officer, consul U.S. Consulate, Udorn, Thailand, 1978-80; dir. Asian affairs Nat. Security Coun., Washington, 1991-92; dir. info./edn. divsn. UN Transitional Authority for Cambodia, Phnom Penh, Cambodia, 1992-93; cons. to UN UNOSOM, Somalia, 1993-94, UNOMSA, South Africa, 1993-94; dep. asst. sec. of state for south Asian affairs Dept. State, Washington, 1994-95; amb. to Sudan Dept. State, Khartoum, 1995—. Author: Kampuchea: Balance of Survival, 1981; and monograph; contbr. articles to profl. jours. Mem. ethnozoology working group of species survival commn. Internat. Union for Conservation of Nature, Switzerland, 1987-90; life mem. Mzuri Wildlife Found., Zambia, Zimbabwe E. and South Africa Wildlife Socs. Mem. Siam Soc. (life). Avocations: photography, hunting.

CARNEY, WILLIAM PATRICK, medical educator; b. Dillon, Mont., July 1, 1938; s. Thomas James and Helen Catherine (Ballard) C.; children: Christopher Patrick, Mark Daniel; m. Sharon Loreta Sonnek, Aug. 14, 1965. BA, St. Thomas U., Kenmore, Wash., 1960; BS, Western Mont. U., 1962; PhD, U. Mont., 1967; MPH, Johns Hopkins U., 1976. Cert. secondary tchr. in biol. scis. Rsch. assoc. Minot (N.D.) State U., 1967-69; commd. lt. USN, 1969, advanced through grades to capt., 1986; rsch. parasitologist Naval Med. Rsch. Inst., Bethesda, Md., 1969-70, 74-75; dir. parasitology dept. Naval Med. Rsch. Unit No. 2, Jakarta, Indonesia, 1970-74; dep. dir. Naval Med. Rsch. Unit No. 2, Taipei, Taiwan, 1976-79; lab. and scientific dir. Naval Med. Rsch. Unit No. 2, Jakarta, 1979-81; program mgr. Naval Med. Rsch. Devel. Command, Bethesda, 1981-84; lab. dir. Naval Bioscis. Lab., Oakland, Calif., 1984-87; prof., dir. grad. program Uniformed Svcs. U., Bethesda, 1987-91, ret., 1991; project mgr. schistosomasis rsch. project in Cairo Med. Svc. Corp. Internat., Arlington, Va., 1991-95; prof., dep. chair dept. preventive medicine Uniformed Svcs. U., Bethesda, Md., 1995—; exec. com. bd. dirs. Gorgas Meml. Inst., Bethesda; cons. Vector Biology and Control Project, Arlington, 1989-94, Am. Inst. Biol. Scis., Washington, 1987—. Contbr. articles to profl. jours. Adult leader Boy Scouts Am., Taipei, 1976-79. Decorated Legion of Merit. Mem. Am. Soc. Parasitologists, Am. Soc. Tropical Medicine and Hygiene, Helminthological Soc. Washington, Sigma Xi, Phi Sigma. Republican. Roman Catholic. Avocations: scuba diving, auto repair, carpentry, masonry, welding. Office: Uniformed Svcs U Dept Preventive Medicine 4301 Jones Bridge Rd Bethesda MD 20814-4712

CARNEY STALNAKER, LISA ANN, gerontological and home health nurse; b. Oak Hill, W.Va., Nov. 17, 1953; d. John Jr. and Ruth Marie (Love) Vegh; 1 child, Jonathan Michael; m. Calvin Gene Stalnaker. AD, Parkersburg Community Coll., 1974. RN, Ohio; cert. gerontol. nurse. Staff nurse Marietta (Ohio) Meml. Hosp., 1974; nursing supr. Fairview Manor, Beverly, Ohio, 1987-88; staff nurse Heartland of Marietta, 1988—; mem. nurse's aide tng. program Health Care and Retirement Corp., Toledo, 1989—; staff developer Heartland of Marietta, 1989, asst. dir. nurses, 1990-94; dir. nursing Harmar Place, Extended Care & Rehab. Ctr., Marietta, 1994-96, Interim Health Care, Marietta, 1997; mgr. clin. practice Olster Health Svcs., Parkersburg, W.Va., 1997—; lectr. continuing edn. for nurses Ohio Nurses Assn., 1993-94; instr. adult edn. nurse aide tng. program, Washington County Career Ctr., Marietta, 1997—. Home: RR 1 Box 322 Whipple OH 45788-9749

CARNICERO, JORGE EMILIO, aeronautical engineer, business executive; b. Buenos Aires, Argentina, July 17, 1921; came to U.S., 1942, naturalized, 1950; s. Alberto and Ana (Sulimeau) C.; m. Jacqueline Joanne Damman, Feb. 22, 1946; children—Jacqueline Denise, Jorge Jay. Student, U. LaPlata, Argentina, 1939-41, Aero. Engr., Rensselaer Poly. Inst., 1945. Chief engr. Dodero Airlines, Argentina, 1945, Flota Aerea Mercante, Argentina, 1945-46; v.p. Air Carrier Svc. Corp., Washington, 1946, exec. v.p., 1947-55, chmn. bd. dirs., dir., 1955-88; past chmn., bd. Dyncorp (formerly Calif. Ea. Aviation, then Dynalectron Corp.); pres., bd. dirs. Blue Cove, Inc., N.Y., Inter-Properties, Inc., Del., Trans-Am. Aero. Corp., Del., Round Hill Devel. Ltd., Jamaica. Bd. visitors Sch. Fgn. Service, Georgetown U., Washington; mem. council Rensselaer Poly. Inst., Troy, N.Y., adv. bd. mem. mech., aero. and mechanics dept.; bd. dirs. Internat. Eye Found., Washington. Fellow Royal Aero. Soc.; mem. Argentine-Am. C. of C. (bd. dirs.), Univ. Club, Met. Club, Congl. Country Club, Georgetown Club. Home: 3949 52nd St NW Washington DC 20016-1925 Office: 1313 Dolley Madison Blvd Mc Lean VA 22101-3926

CARNIOL, PAUL J., plastic and reconstructive surgeon, otolaryngologist; b. N.Y.C., Sept. 26, 1951; s. David A. and Diane (Hadler) C.; m. Renie Rich, Jan. 3, 1976; children: Michael P., Alan R., Eric T. BA, NYU, 1972; MD, U. Pa., 1976. Diplomate Am. Bd. Otolaryngology, Am. Bd. Cosmetic Surgery, Am. Bd. Med. Examiners, Am. Bd. Facial Plastic and Reconstructive Surgery. Surg. residency U. Pa., Phila., 1976-77, plastic and reconstructive surg. residency, 1981-83; surg. residency North Shore U. Hosp., Manhasset, N.Y., 1977-78; head and surg. residency, otolaryngology, clin. tchg. fellow Harvard Med. Sch., Boston, 1978-81; attending plastic surgeon, head and neck surgery Overlook Hosp., Summit, N.J., 1983—; clin. asst. prof. U. Medicine and Dentistry of N.J., Newark; cons. aesthetic, reconstructive and pediatric plastic surgery; mem. bd. examiners Am. Bd. Cosmetic Surgery; instr. courses on lasers in plastic surgery, also numerous lectrs., TV presentations in field; chief sect. otolaryngology Overlook Hosp., 1992-97, Summit, N.J., otolaryngology resident tng. rotation; clin. asst. prof. U. Medicine and Dentistry N.J.; police surgeon, New Providence, N.J. and Summit. Editor: Laser Skin Rejuvenation, 1998; spl. editor Am. Jour. Cosmetic Surgery; contbr. articles to profl. jours. Interviewer for admissions com. U. Pa., Phila., 1987—. Recipient Community Svc. award Ciba-Geigy, Summit, 1978, Found. award NYU, 1972, Alumni Gold Medal award NYU, 1972. Fellow ACS, Am. Acad. Otolaryngoloyy, Head and Neck Surgery, Am. Acad. Cosmetic Surgery, Am. Acad. Facial Plastic and Reconstructive Surgery (dir. courses lasers facial plastic surgery and cosmetic surgery cosmetic body conturing surgery, 1996-98, care com., chmn. new tech. and surg. devices com.), N.J. Acad. Medicine, Am. Rhinologic soc.; mem. AMA, Internat. Soc. Cosmetic Laser Surgery (bd. dirs.), N.J. Med. Soc. (coun. on comm.), N.J. Acad. Otolaryngology (pres. 1993-96, 97—), Union County Med. Soc. (planning com. 1986-89, chmn. program com., exec. com., bd. dirs., treas.), Phi Beta Kappa. Avocations: golf, fishing, horseback riding. Office: Summit Med Group 9 Deforest Ave Summit NJ 07901-2123

CARNOCHAN, JOHN LOW, JR., retired aluminum company executive, consultant; b. Hagerstown, Md., Oct. 19, 1918; s. John Low and Susan (Long) C.; m. Emily Kent Linton, July 3, 1943; children: John, David, Susan, Jean, Carol, Robert. AB, Western Md. Coll., 1940, MEd, 1947; EdD, Columbia, 1963. Tchr. pub. schs., Washington County, Md., 1941-53; vice-prin. schs., Hagerstown, Md., 1953-55; prin., Maugansville, Md., 1955-56, Williamsport, Md., 1956-61; ednl. TV project coordinator, Harrison, N.Y., 1961-62; asst. to state supt. schs. Md. Dept. Edn., Balt., 1962-63; asst. supt. county schs., Frederick Md., 1963-64, supt. county schs., 1964-76; mgr. community relations Eastalco Aluminum Co., Frederick, 1976-84; cons., 1984-87; prin. Carnochan, Felton & Gardiner Ednl. and Communications Cons., 1986—; treas., past chmn. bd. dirs. Home Care Research, Inc. Past chmn. Md. Adv. Council Vocat. Tech. Edn.; treas. Frederick Arts Ctr. Found., Inc. Served from pvt. to capt., AUS, 1941-46, lt. col. Res. (ret.). Danforth fellow, 1974. Mem. Am. Assn. Sch. Adminstrs., Md. Assn. Sch. Supts. (past pres. and legis. chmn.), Public Relations Soc. Am., Md. C. of C. (past v.p.), Frederick C. of C., Phi Delta Kappa, Delta Kappa Pi. Home: 4829 Round Hill Rd Frederick MD 21702-3535

CARNOCHAN, WALTER BLISS, retired humanities educator; b. N.Y.C., Dec. 20, 1930; s. Gouverneur Morris and Sibyll Baldwin (Bliss) C.; m. Nancy Powers Carter, June 25, 1955 (div. 1978); children—Lisa Powers, Sarah Bliss, Gouverneur Morris, Sibyll Carter; m. Brigitte Hoy Fields, Sept. 16, 1979. A.B., Harvard, 1953, A.M., 1957, Ph.D., 1960. Asst. dean freshmen Harvard U., 1954-56; successively instr., asst. prof., assoc. prof., prof. English, Stanford (Calif.) U., 1960-94, prof. emeritus, 1994—, chmn. dept. English, 1971-73, dean grad. studies, 1975-80, vice provost, 1976-80, dir. Stanford Humanities Ctr., 1985-91, Anthony P. Meier Family prof. humanities, 1988-91, Richard W. Lyman prof. humanities, 1993-94, Richard W. Lyman prof. emeritus, 1994—, acting dir. Stanford Humanities Ctr., 1999; mem. overseers com. to visit Harvard Coll, 1979-85. Author: Lemuel Gulliver's Mirror for Man, 1968, Confinement and Flight: An Essay on English Literature of the 18th Century, 1977, Gibbon's Solitude: The Inward World of the Historian, 1987, The Battleground of the Curriculum: Liberal Education and American Experience, 1993, Momentary Bliss: An American Memoir, 1999. Trustee Mills Coll., 1978-85, Athenian Sch., 1975-88, Univ. Art Mus., Berkeley, Calif., 1983-96, 98—. Home: 138 Cervantes Rd Portola Valley CA 94028-7725 Office: Stanford U Dept English Stanford CA 94305-2087

CARNS, MICHAEL PATRICK CHAMBERLAIN, air force officer; b. Junction City, Kans., June 23, 1937; s. Edwin Hugh John and Jeanette Anne (Chamberlain) C.; m. Victoria Greco, July 29, 1973; children: Michelle, Marc. BS, USAF Acad., Colorado Springs, Colo., 1959; MBA, Harvard U., 1967; postgrad., Royal Coll. Def. Studies, London, 1977. Commd. 2d. lt. USAF, 1959, advanced through grades to gen., 1991; dep. comdr. for ops. 81st Tactical Fighter Wing, RAF Bentwaters, Eng., 1978-79; comdr. 354th Tactical Fighter Wing, Myrtle Beach AFB, S.C., 1979-80, 57th Fighter Weapons Wing, Nellis AFB, Nev., 1980-82; dir. ops. Rapid Deployment Joint Task Force, U.S. Cen. Command, MacDill AFB, Fla., 1982-84; dep. chief of staff for ops. and intelligence, dep. chief of staff ofr plans Hdqrs. Pacific Air Forces, Hickam AFB, Hawaii, 1984-86; comdr. 13th Air Force, Clark Air Base, The Philippines, 1986-87; dep. comdr. in chief, chief of staff U.S. Pacific Command, Camp H.M. Smith, Hawaii, 1987-89; dir. Joint Chief of Staff, Washington, 1989-91; vice chief of staff Hqrs. USAF, Washington, 1991-94; pres., exec. dir. Ctr. for Internat. Polit. Economy, N.Y.C., CA, 1995; bd. dirs. Cordant Techs., M Internat, Mission Rsch. Corp., Burdeshaw Assocs., Global Health Alliance. Decorated D.S.M. with 2 oak leaf clusters, Def. D.S.M. with oak leaf cluster, Silver Star, Legion of Merit with 3 oak leaf clusters, DFC, Air medal with 10 oak leaf clusters; Gallantry Cross with palm (Vietnam), Most Noble Order of Crown 1st class (Thailand), Republic of Korea Order of Nat. Security Merit, Gudseon medal; recipient Outstanding Achievement medal Govt. of the Philippines. Home: 966 Coral Dr Pebble Beach CA 93953-2503

CARO, ANTHONY (ALFRED CARO), sculptor; b. New Malden, Surrey, Eng., Mar. 8, 1924; s. Alfred and Mary (Haldinstein) C.; m. Sheila May Girling, Dec. 17, 1949; children: Timothy Martin, Paul Gideon. M.A., Christ's Coll., Cambridge U., Eng., 1944; grad., Royal Acad. Schs., London, 1952; D.Litt. (hon.), East Anglia U., York U., Toronto, Ont., Can., Brandeis U. Asst. to Henry Moore, 1951-53; part-time tchr. sculpture St. Martin's Sch. Art, London, 1953-79; tchr. sculpture Bennington Coll., Vt., 1963, 65; founder Triangle Artists' Workshop, U.S.A.; guest lectr. Artists' Workshop, Maastricht, The Netherlands; vis. artist workshops Barcelona, Spain, Berlin, 1987, U. Alberta, Red Deer Coll., Alberta, Can., 1989; mem. coun. Slade Sch. Art, 1982—. Sculpture commd. by Nat. Gallery Art, Washington, 1977; one-man shows include, Galleria del Naviglio, Milan, Italy, 1956, Gimpel Fils Gallery, London, 1957, Whitechapel Art Gallery, London, 1963, Andre Emmerich Gallery, N.Y.C., 1964, 66, 68, 70, 72, 74, 77, 78, 79, 81, 82, 84, 86, Washington Gallery Modern Art, 1965, Kasmin Ltd., London, 1965, 67, 71, 72, David Mirvish Gallery, Toronto, Ont., Can., 1966, 71, 74, Galerie Bischofberger, Zurich, Switzerland, 1966, Kroller-Muller Mus., Netherlands, 1967, Hayward Gallery, London, 1969, Kenwood House, Hampstead, Eng., 1974, 81, Galleria dell'Ariete, Milan, 1974, Richard Gray Gallery, Chgo., 1975, 86, Watson/de Nagy Gallery, Houston, 1975, Mus. Modern Art, N.Y.C., 1975, Lefevre Gallery, London, 1976, Everson Mus., Syracuse, N.Y., 1976, Tel Aviv Mus., 1977, Piltzer-Rheims, Paris, 1977, Waddington & Tooth, London, 1977, Emmerich Gallery, Zurich, 1978, Harkus Krackow Gallery, Boston, 1978, 81, Knoedler, London, 1978, 82, 83, 84, 86, 89, 91, Wentzel, Hamburg, 1978, Ace, Venice, Calif., 1978, Kahsahara, Japan, 1979, 90, Glasgow, 1980, Acquavella Gelleries, N.Y., 1980, Galerie Andre, Berlin, 1980, Downstairs Gallery, Edmonton, Alta, Can., 1981, Galerie Wentzel, Cologne, Ger., 1982, 84, 85, 88, Gallery One, Toronto, 1982, 85, 87-88, 90, Knoedler & Waddington Galleries, London, 1983, Galerie de France, Paris, 1983, Acquavella Galleries, N.Y.C., 1984, 86, Brit. Council touring exhbn., Tel Aviv, N.Z., Australia, Germany, 1977-79, Madrid, Barcelona, Bilbao, Valencia, Spain, 1986, Mus. Fine Arts, Boston, 1980, Constantine Grimaldis Gallery, Balt., 1987, 89, Galerie Renée Ziegler, Zurick, 1988, Tate Gallery, 1991, numerous others; exhibited in group shows at 1st Paris Biennale, 1959 (sculpture prize), Battersea Park Open Air Exhbn., 1960, 63, 66, Gulbenkian Exhbn., London, 1964, Documenta III Kassel, 1965, Jewish Mus., N.Y.C., 1966 (David Bright prize), Venice Biennale, 1958, 66, Pitts. Internat., 1967, 68, Met. Mus. Art, 1968, Sao Paulo, 1969 (sculpture prize), U. Pa., 1969, Everson Mus., Mus. Modern Art, N.Y.C., 1975; represented in permanent collections Walker Art Gallery, Minn., Mus. Fine Arts, Houston, Boston, Dallas, Mus. Modern Art, N.Y.C., Phila. Mus. Art, Cleve. Mus. Art, Detroit Inst. Arts, Solomon R. Guggenheim Mus., N.Y.C., Yale U. Art Gallery, New Haven, numerous others. Trustee Tate Gallery, London, 1982, Fitzwilliam Mus., Cambridge, 1984. Served in Fleet Air Arm of Royal Navy. Decorated comdr. Order Brit. Empire; presented key to city N.Y.C., 1976; hon. fellow Christ's Coll., Cambridge, Royal Coll. Art, London, 1986, U. Surrey, England, 1987, Knighted, 1987. Mem. Am. Acad. and Inst. Arts and Letters (hon.).

CARO, EVELYN INGA ROUSE, writer; b. Monterey Park, Calif., June 2, 1956; d. Coburn Whitehead and Marcelaine (Ulvick) Rouse; m. Johnny Caro, Dec. 19, 1982; children: Jessica Lynn, Juan Abram, Matthew Jason, Ruben Emmanuel. Author: A Prelude to Summer, 1990, (novel) The Trial of Adam Smith, 1995 (play); contbr. poetry and articles to various publs. Elder 7th-day Adventist Ch., 1995—. Home: 9266 Valley View Ave Whittier CA 90603-1957

CARO, JESUS JAIME, medical researcher; b. Bogota, Colombia, May 11, 1959; came to U.S., 1992; s. Jose Jaime and Graciela (de la Torre) C.; m. Heidi Ann Hunting, June 11, 1983; children: Elena, Anthony, Alexandra. Cert. and diploma, Bishop's Coll. Sch., Lennoxville, Que., Can., 1976; diploma health scis., Champlain Regional Coll., Lennoxville, Que., Can., 1978; MD, CM, McGill U., Montreal, Que., Can., 1983. Asst. prof. McGill U., Montreal, 1987—; sci. dir. Caro Rsch., Concord, Mass., 1993—. Contbr. articles to profl. jours. Fellow ACP; mem. AMA, Mass. Med. Soc. Office: Caro Rsch 336 Baker Ave Concord MA 01742-2107

CARO, ROBERT ALLAN, author; b. N.Y.C.; s. Benjamin and Cele (Mendelow) C.; m. Ina Joan Sloshberg, June 9, 1957; 1 child, Chase Arthur. AB cum laude, Princeton U., 1957; DLitt (hon.), Merrimack Coll., 1983; LHD (hon.), New Sch. for Social Rsch., 1997. Reporter New Brunswick (N.J.) Home News, 1957-59, Newsday, Garden City, N.Y., 1960-66; Nieman fellow Harvard U., Cambridge, Mass., 1965-66; historian, biographer, 1967—. Author: The Power Broker: Robert Moses and the Fall of New York, 1974 (Pulitzer prize for biography 1975, Francis Parkman prize Soc. Am. Historians 1975, 1 of 100 Best Nonfiction Books Written in English during the 20th Century), The Years of Lyndon Johnson: The Path to Power, 1982 (Nat. Book Critics award for biography 1983, Tex. Inst. Arts and Letters award for non-fiction 1983), The Years of Lyndon Johnson: Means of Ascent, 1990 (Nat. Book Critics Cir. award for biography 1991). Bd. dirs. Fund for City N.Y., N.Y. Soc. Libr. Theatre for New Audience.que. Recipient Soc. of Silurians award, 1964, Deadline Club, 1964, 65, spl. citation N.Y. chpt. AIA, 1975, H.L. Mencken prize Free Press Assn., 1983, award in lit. Am. Acad. and Inst. Arts and Letters, 1986, Lifetime Achievement in Arts award Guild Hall Acad. Arts, 1992; co-recipient ann. polit. book award Washington Monthly, 1975, 83, 91. Fellow Soc. Am. Historians (Francis Parkman prize); mem. Authors Guild Am. (bd. dirs.

1976—, pres. 1980-82), PEN Am. Ctr. (mem. exec. bd. 1986-88, v.p. 1989-92), Century Club. Office: Robert A Caro Inc 250 W 57th St New York NY 10107

CARO, WILLIAM ALLAN, physician; b. Chgo., Aug. 16, 1934; s. Marcus Rayner and Adeline Beatrice (Cohen) C.; m. Ruth Fruchtlander, June 15, 1959 (dec.); children: Mark Stephen, David Edward; m. Joan Peters, Oct. 18, 1997. Student, U. Mich., 1952-55; BS in Medicine, U. Ill., 1957, MD, 1959. Diplomate Am. Bd. Dermatology (bd. dirs. 1981-91, v.p. 1989-90, pres. 1990-91). Intern Cook County Hosp., Chgo., 1959-60; resident in internal medicine U. Ill. Research and Ednl. Hosps., 1960-61; resident in dermatology Hosp. of U. Pa., 1961-62, 64-66; Earl D. Osborne fellow dermal pathology Armed Forces Inst. Pathology, Washington, 1966-67; asst. in medicine U. Ill. Coll. Medicine, 1960-61; asst. instr. U. Pa. Med. Sch., 1961-62, 64-66; asst. prof. dermatology Northwestern U. Med. Sch., 1967-73, assoc. prof. clin. dermatology, 1973-81; practice medicine specializing in dermatology Chgo., 1967—; chief dermatology sect. MacDonald Army Hosp., Fort Eustis, Va., 1962-64; attending physician Chgo. Wesley Meml. Hosp., 1969-72, Northwestern Meml. Hosp., 1972—, mem. med. exec. com., 1977-79; attending pathologist, cons. dermatologist VA Lakeside Hosp., Chgo.; cons. Children's Meml. Hosp., Rehab. Inst. Chgo.; Mcpl. Tb Sanitarium of Chgo., 1968-74; affiliate pathologist Evanston (Ill.) Hosp.; prof. clin. dermatology Northwestern U. Med. Sch., 1981—. Editor trans.: Chgo. Dermatol. Soc., 1971-73; editorial bd., Cutis, 1975—; asso. editor Year Book Pathology and Clin. Pathology, 1977-80. Mem. medicine adv. bd. U. Ill. Coll. Medicine, 1988—; trustee Northwestern Meml. Hosp., Chgo., 1986-87, bd. dirs., 1988-91; bd. dirs. Northwestern Meml. Corp., 1987—, exec. com., 1988-91. Served as capt. M.C. USAR, 1962-64. Mem. AMA, Am. Acad. Dermatology (Gold award sci. exhibit 1970), Chgo. Dermatol. Soc. (pres. 1983-84), Am. Dermatol. Assn. (bd. dirs. 1993-98), Am. Soc. Dermatopathology (bd. dirs. 1995—, pres.-elect 1995-96, pres. 1996-97), Internat. Soc. Dermatology, Pacific Dermatol. Assn., Dermatology Found., Soc. Investigative Dermatology, U. Ill. Med. Alumni Assn. (exec. bd. 1977-80), Alpha Omega Alpha, Phi Kappa Phi. Office: 676 N Saint Clair St Chicago IL 60611-2927

CAROFF, PHYLLIS M., social work educator; b. Bklyn., Feb. 22, 1924; d. Harry and Irene (Lesser) Friedman; m. Joseph Caroff, May 16, 1943; children—Michael, Peter. B.A., Douglass Coll., 1944; M.S.W., N.Y. Sch. Social Work, 1947; D.S.W., Columbia U., 1969. Caseworker ARC, 1944-45; caseworker, student supr. Community Service Soc., N.Y.C., 1956-61; from lectr. to assoc. prof. Hunter Coll. Sch. Social Work, N.Y.C., 1961-76, prof., 1976-87; dir. Postmasters Program in Advanced Clin. Social Work, 1977-87; pvt. practice psychotherapy N.Y.C., 1964—; cons. VA Hosp., N.Y.C., 1977-85, USPHS Hosp., S.I., 1974—; mem. adv. bd. Found. Thanatology, 1976—; mem. profl. adv. com. Grad. Program in Social Work, Inst. Health Professions, Mass. Gen. Hosp., 1980-86. Author: (with others) Before Addiction, 1973; editorial bd. Clin. Social Work Jour., 1972—, Jour. Gerontol. Social Work, 1978—; editor: (with others) Social Work in Health Services: An Academic Practice Partnership, 1980, A New Model in Academic/Practice Partnership, 1985, Psychosocial Advances in Clinical Social Work, 1985. Mem. exec. com. of bd. Planned Parenthood N.Y.C., 1974-79, chmn. rsch. and evaluation com., 1974-77, bd. dirs., 1971-86. Named Disting. Practitioner, Nat. Acad. Practice in Social Work, 1983; NIMH fellow, 1964-65; various grants. Fellow Am. Orthopsychiat. Assn., N.Y. Acad. Medicine; mem. AAUP, Nat. Assn. Social Workers (chmn. clin. council 1981-84, mem. peer rev. adv. com. 1982-84), N.Y. State Soc. Clin. Social Work Psychotherapists. Home: 15 W 81st St New York NY 10024-6022

CAROLAN, DOUGLAS, wholesale company executive. BS, Western Mich. U., 1964. Store mgr. to dir. mktg. div. Nat. Tea Co., 1962-83; sr. v.p. Associated Wholesale Grocers, Inc., Kansas City, Kans., 1983-86, chief ops. officer, exec. v.p., sec., 1986—; CEO, pres. Associated Wholesale Grocers, Inc., 1998—; bd. dirs. UMB Bank, Food Mktg. Inst. Bd. dirs. Kans. City area food bank Harvesters. Office: Assoc Wholesale Grocers Inc PO Box 2932 Kansas City KS 66110-2932

CAROLAND, WILLIAM BOURNE, structural engineer; b. Clarksville, Tenn., July 9, 1929; s. Enoch Arden and Jennie Wimberly (Bourne) C.; m. Eloise Joyce Crickard, June 3, 1957; children: Richard Bradley, Jennifer Dorothy. Student, U. Tenn., 1947-52. Registered profl. engr., Ky., Tenn., Ind., Mich. Fla., W.Va., land surveyor, Ky. Survey party chief King & Clark Engrs., Clarksville, 1955-56, Michael Baker Jr., Inc., Jackson, Miss., 1956-57; asst. designer Michael Baker Jr., Inc., Charleston, W.Va., 1957-62; project supr. Michael Baker Jr., Inc., Louisville, 1962-63; designer Michael Baker Jr., Inc., Charleston, 1963-64; bridge designer Vogt, Ivers & Assocs., Cin., 1964-65; sr. structural engr. Brighton Engring., Frankfort, Ky., 1965-73; chief bridge engr. Beam, Longest & Neff, Indpls., 1973-79; with Am. Cons. Engrs., Lexington, Ky., 1979—, chief bridge engr., 1988—. Contbr. papers to profl. publs. With U.S. Army, 1952-55. Recipient Welded Steel Design award Lincoln Arc Welding Found., 1974, Welded Steel Design hon. mention, Lincoln Arc Welding Found., 1975, Bridge Design award Prestressed Concrete Inst., 1977, 92. Mem. Am. Concrete Inst., Post-Tensioning Inst. Avocations: woodworking, photography. Home: 604 S Broadway St Georgetown KY 40324-1136 Office: Am Cons Engrs PLC Ste 301 400 E Vine St Lexington KY 40507-1518 *When I was growing up my father always told me there is no such word as can't. Over the years I have come to agree with this. If we believe and work hard it can be done.*

CAROLLO, JOE, mayor; b. Cuba, 1955; came to U.S., 1961; m. Mari Ledon; children: Joe Jr., Cristina, Caroline, Kelley. AA in Gen. Studies, Miami Dade C.C.; BA in Internat. Rels., Fla. Internat. U., BS in Crimnal Justice. Police officer City of Miami, 1975, commr., 1979-96, mayor, 1996—; past chmn. bd. dirs. Miami Sports and Exhbn. Authority; co-organizer Maritime Pk. and Port Expansion Project. Office: Mayor's Office 3500 Pan American Dr Miami FL 33133-5504*

CAROLLO, RUSSELL, journalist; b. New Orleans. BJ, La. State U.; M.History, Southeastern La. U. Spl. projects reporter Dayton Daily News. Winner 1998 Pulitzer prize for nat. reporting; U. Mich. Journalism fellow, Internat. Ctr. for Journalists fellow, Japan; recipient Investigative Reporters and Editors awards (3), Harvard U. Goldsmith award, White House Corr. Assn. Edgar A. Poe award, Soc. Profl. Journalists Nat. Award for Investigative Reporting, John Hancock award. Office: Dayton Daily News Cox Newspapers Inc 45 S Ludlow St Dayton OH 45402*

CAROME, PATRICK JOSEPH, lawyer; b. Cleve., Nov. 20, 1957; s. Edward Francis and Jeanne Marie (Carrabine) C.; m. Elsie Elizabeth Orr, Oct. 7, 1989. BA, Boston Coll., Chestnut Hill, Mass., 1980; JD, Harvard U., 1983. Bar: Mass. 1984, D.C. 1985, U.S. Dist. Ct. D.C. 1985, U.S. Ct. Appeals (D.C. cir.) 1987, U.S. Supreme Ct. 1988, U.S. Ct. Appeals (4th cir.) 1989, U.S. Ct. Appeals (9th cir.) 1993, U.S. Ct. Appeals (10th cir.) 1999. Law clk. to Judge Milton Pollack, U.S. Dist. Ct. for So. Dist. N.Y., N.Y.C., 1983-84; staff atty. Washington Post, 1984-86; staff counsel select com. to investigate covert arms trans. U.S. Ho. of Reps., Washington, 1987; assoc. Wilmer, Cutler & Pickering, Washington, 1986-87, 88-90, ptnr., 1991—. Mem. ABA (vice chmn. com. on govt. info. and right to privacy com. adminstrv. law sect. 1988-90, chmn. 1990-94). Office: Wilmer Cutler & Pickering 2445 M St NW Ste 500 Washington DC 20037-1487

CARON, ANITA JO, secondary education educator; b. Somerset, Ky., Feb. 16, 1962; d. Norman Eugene and Judy Kay (Godbey) Hurt; m. Steven Glenn Caron, Mar. 27, 1982; children: Stephanie Jo, Jonathan Derek. BA, Berea Coll., 1984; MA, Ea. Ky. U., 1991. Tchr. Pulaski County H.S., Somerset, 1986-87, No. Jr. H.S., Somerset, 1987-93, Southwestern H.S., Somerset, 1993—. Contbg. author: History of Casey County, 1992. Fellow Ky. Writing Project; mem. NEA, Nat. Coun. Tchrs. English, Ky. Edn. Assn., Pulaski County Edn. Assn., Columbia Scholastic Press Assn. Democrat. Methodist. Avocations: reading, traveling, photography. Home: 12653 N Highway 1247 Eubank KY 42567-9006 Office: Southwestern High Sch 1765 Wtlo Rd Somerset KY 42503-3721

CARON, ERNIE MATTHEW, airport executive; b. Morinville, Alta., Can., Sept. 15, 1938; m. Ellen Kinsella; 4 children. Grad., Banff Sch. Advanced Mgmt., 1977. V.p. eastern region Can. Airlines Internat., v.p. customer svc., v.p. properties and facilities, v.p. airports N.Am.; pres., CEO Calgary Airport Authority, 1992—; vice-chmn. Calgary Econ. Devel. Authority Adv. Coun., 1996—, Can. Airports Coun., pres. com. of mgmt. bd. dirs. Calgary Conv. and Visitors Bur., 1994—. Mem. Calgary Rotary Club. Avocations: racing horses, skiing, golfing. Office: Calgary Airport Authority, 2000 Airport Rd NE, Calgary, AB Canada T2E 6W5*

CARON, WILFRED RENE, lawyer; b. N.Y.C., July 23, 1931; s. Joseph Wilfred and Eva Caron; m. Anne Theresa Flanagan, AUg. 2, 1958. JD, St. John's U., 1956. Bar: N.Y. 1956, D.C. 1977, U.S. Dist. Ct. D.C. 1977, U.S. Dist. Ct. (no. dist.) N.Y. 1957, U.S. Dist. Ct. (so. and ea. dists.) N.Y. 1961, U.S. Ct. Appeals (2d cir.) 1965, U.S. Ct. Appeals (3d cir.) 1973, U.S. Ct. Appeals (5th cir.) 1977, U.S. Ct. Appeals (6th cir.) 1973, U.S. Ct. Appeals (8th cir.) 1975, U.S. Ct. Appeals (9th cir.) 1976, U.S. Ct. Appeals (D.C. cir.) 1975, U.S. Supreme Ct. 1961. Law clk. to chief judge N.Y. State Ct. Appeals, 1956-59; spl. asst. atty. gen. N.Y., 1959-60; assoc. Goldman & Drazen, 1960-64, Corner, Finn, Cuomo & Charles, N.Y.C., 1964-69; asst. gen. counsel Ronson Corp., Woodbridge, N.J., 1969-71; assoc. gen. counsel Securities Investor Protection Corp., Washington, 1972-80; gen. counsel U.S. Cath. Conf., Inc., Washington, 1980-87, Nat. Conf. Cath. Bishops, 1980-87, Cath. Telecom. Network Am., Inc., N.Y.C., 1981-88; ptnr. O'Connor & Hannan, Washington, 1987-88; sr. advisor Office of Policy Devel., U.S. Dept. of Justice, Washington, 1988-90; appellate counsel Travelers Ins. Co., 1990-92. Contbr. articles to profl. jours. ADv. bd. St. Thomas More Inst. Legal Rsch., St. John's U. Sch. Law, N.Y.C., 1981-92; exec. bd. Ctr. for Ch.-State Studies, DePaul U. Law Coll., Chgo., 1982—. Served to 1st lt. U.S. Army, 1952-54, Korea. Mem. ABA, D.C. Bar Assn., N.Y. Bar Assn., VFW, Am. Legion. Roman Catholic. Home: 44 Old Main Rd Little Compton RI 02837-1321

CARONIS, GEORGE JOHN, insurance executive; b. Columbus, Ohio, Dec. 8, 1933; s. John George and Effie (Zarafonetis) C.; m. Shirley Ann Milburn, June 7, 1958; 1 child, Kevin M. BA, Ohio State U., 1955, MA, 1960. CLU; ChFC; chartered property and casualty underwriter; CFP. Asst. dean of men Ohio State U., Columbus, 1957-60; assoc. gen. agt. Tice Ins. Co., Columbus, 1960-74; v.p. pensions and estate planning Midland Mut. Life Ins. Co., Columbus, 1974-77; v.p. bus. devel. Bank One Trust Co., Columbus, 1977-79; v.p. fin. svcs. Kientz and Co., Columbus, 1979-82; dir. mktg. Nationwide Ins. Cos., Columbus, 1982-87; mktg. mgr. Aetna Life and Casualty Co., Columbus, 1987-89; v.p. advanced underwriting Western Res. Life Assurance Co., Clearwater, Fla., 1989-91, v.p. mktg., 1991—; sr. v.p. Asset Accumulation Group, Aegon U.S.A., 1994-98; exec. v.p. Aegon Equity Group, 1998—; bd. dirs. Mass. Fidelity Trust Co. 1st lt. U.S. Army, 1955-57. Recipient Thomas Arkle Clark award Alpha Tau Omega, 1955, Ralph D. Mershon award Ohio State U., 1990. Fellow Life Mgmt. Inst.; mem. Ohio State Alumni Assn. (nat. pres. 1983-85), Ohio State U. Found. (nominating com.), Nat. Assn. Life Underwriters, Am. Soc. CLU and Chartered Fin. Consultants. Home: 1371 River Oaks Ct Oldsmar FL 34677-4829 Office: Western Res Life Assurance PO Box 5068 Clearwater FL 33758-5068

CAROOMPAS, CAROLE JEAN, artist, educator; b. Oregon City, Oreg., Nov. 14, 1946; d. John Thomas and Dorothy Lietta (Dirks) C. BA, Calif. State U., Fullerton, 1968; MFA in Painting, U. So. Calif., 1971. Instr. El Camino Coll., Torrance, Calif., 1971-72; vis. artist Calif. State U., Northridge, 1972-75; instr. Immaculate Heart Coll., L.A., 1973-76; vis. artist Calif. State U., Fullerton, 1976-78; instr. U. Calif., Irvine, 1976-80, Claremont (Calif.) Grad. Sch., 1976-79, Art Ctr. Coll. of Design, Pasadena, 1978-86, UCLA Extension, L.A., 1984-93; assoc. prof. fine arts Otis Coll. Art and Design, L.A., 1981—; vis. artist Anderson Ranch Art Ctr., Aspen, Colo., 1996, 98. One-woman shows include Jan Baum Art Gallery, L.A., 1978-82, Karl Bornstein Gallery, L.A., 1985, L.A. Contemporary Exhbns., 1989, U. Calif., Irvine, 1990, Sue Spaid Fine Art, L.A., 1992, 94, P.P.O.W., N.Y.C., 1994, Otis Coll. of Art and Design Art Gallery, 1997-98, Mark Moore Gallery, Santa Monica, 1997, 99; exhibited in group shows at Pasadena Mus. Art, 1972, Whitney Mus. of Art, 1978, Mus. Modern Art, N.Y.C., 1976, L.A. County Mus., 1982, Corcoran Gallery of Art, 43d Biennial Exhbn. of Contemporary Am. Painting, Washington, 1993, Under Contstrn. Armory Ctr. for Arts, Pasadena, 1995, Armand Hammer Mus. of Art, L.A., 1996, Art Gallery, L.A., 1997, L.A. County Mus. Art, 1996, Beaver Coll., 1996, L.A. Mcpl. Art Gallery, 1997; also a vocalist; recordings include 2 individual albums and inclusion in TheRecord: 13 Vocal Artists; contbr. articles to The Paris Rev., Dreamworks, Whitewalls. NEA grant, 1987, 93, Faculty Devel. grant New Sch. of Social Rsch., 1989, Support grant Esther and Adolph Gottlieb Found., 1993; John Simon Guggenheim Meml. fellow, 1995. Office: Otis Coll Art and Design 9045 Lincoln Blvd Los Angeles CA 90045-3505

CAROTHERS, A. J., scriptwriter; b. Houston, Oct. 22, 1931; s. A.J. and Vivian (Gibson) C.; m. Caryl Enid Volkman, Nov. 7, 1959; children: Cameron, Christopher, Andrew. BA, UCLA, 1954. Assoc. prodr. Playhouse 90 CBS TV, L.A., 1958-60; contract writer Walt Disney Prodns., Burbank, Calif., 1961-68; writer-prodr. Lorimar, Culver City, Calif., 1986-87; guest lectr. UCLA; writer, co-exec. prodr. Music Ctr. Spotlight Awards, 1989-99. Author: (screenplays) Miracle of the White Stallions, 1962, Emil and the Detectives, 1964, The Happiest Millionaire, 1967, Never a Dull Moment, 1968, Hero At Large, 1980, The Secret of My Success, 1987; (TV movies) The Making of a Male Model, 1984, Summer Girl, 1983, Forever, 1977, The Thief of Bagdad, 1978; creator, author, cons. (TV series) Nanny and the Professor, 1970-72; creator, writer (TV mini-series) Friends, 1979; creator, writer, exec. producer (TV series) Goodnight, Beantown, 1982-83, (mus. play) Busker Alley, 1994; writer (TV series) Studio One, 1958, My Three Sons, 1960-61, The Dupont Show, 1960-61, The Investigators, 1961, (TV spl.) Goldilocks, 1971. V.p. Fraternity of Friends, L.A., 1986—. With U.S. Army, 1954-56. Recipient Disting. Artists award, Club 100 of L.A. Music Ctr., 1990; Gold Lone Star award, Houston Film Festival, 1982; named Disting. Alumnus, KinKaid Sch., 1997. Mem. Motion Picture Acad., UCLA Theater Arts Alumni Assn. (bd. dirs. 1984-88). Home and Office: 2333 Canyonback Rd Los Angeles CA 90049-6812

CAROTHERS, CHARLES OMSTED, retired orthopedic surgeon; b. Medina, N.Y., Aug. 2, 1923; s. Thomas Abbott and Helen Flavia (Olmsted) C.; children from a previous marriage: Thomas Abbott, Stephen Cole, Lisa Booker; m. Lucille Klau, June 20, 1971. B.A., Williams Coll., 1944; M.D., Harvard U., 1946; M.S. in Orthopedic Surgery, U. Tenn., 1954. Diplomate Am. Bd. Orthopedic Surgery. Intern Cin. Gen. Hosp., 1946-47; head bone research project Naval Med. Research Inst., Bethesda, Md., 1949; resident in gen. surgery U. Cin., 1949-51; resident in orthopedic surgery U. Tenn., 1951-54; practice medicine specializing in orthopedic surgery Cin., 1954-98; ret.; chief orthopedic sect. Bethesda Hosps., ret. 1988; mem. staff Univ. Med. Sch., Univ. Hosp. Cin. Pres., chief exec. officer Cin. Playhouse in the Park, 1974-88. Served with USN, 1949-51. Recipient Post-Corbett award for Contbn. to the arts, 1986. Mem. AMA, ACS, Am. Acad. Orthopedic Surgery, Clin. Orthopedic Soc., Am. Assn. Surgery Trauma, Mid-Am. Orthopedic Assn., Soc. Colonial Wars Ohio (dep. gov. 1979-82, gov. 1975-76), Wequetonsing Assn., Ocean Reef Club, Literary Club, Univ. Club, Losantiville Country Club, Cin. Country Club. Episcopalian. Home: 1 Walsh Pl Cincinnati OH 45208-3424 Office: 250 William H Taft Rd Cincinnati OH 45219-2660

CAROTHERS, ROBERT LEE, academic administrator; b. Sewickley, Pa., Sept. 3, 1942; s. Robert Fleming and Mary (Skinner) C.; children: Robert Kennedy, Shelley Rye, Matthew K. Ruane. BS, Edinboro U., 1965; MA, Kent State U., 1966, PhD, 1969; JD, U. Akron, 1980. Bar: Pa. 1981. Prof. English, dean, v.p. Edinboro U., 1968-83; pres. S.W. State U., Marshall, Minn., 1983-86; chancellor Minn. State U. Sys., St. Paul, 1986-91; pres. U. R.I., Kingston, 1991—. Author: Freedom and Other Times, 1972; John Calvin's Favorite Son, 1980. Served with AUS, 1960-68. Avocation: fishing. Home: 56 Upper College Rd Kingston RI 02881-2022 Office: U RI Office of Pres 75 Lower College Rd Ste 7 Kingston RI 02881-1966

CAROVANO, JOHN MARTIN, not-for-profit adminstrator,conservationist; b. Tacoma, May 9, 1935; s. John and Elda C. (Martin) C.; m. Barbara Bevins, June 14, 1958; children: Kristen, Kathryn. B.A., Pomona Coll., 1957, LL.D., 1979; M.A., U. Calif. at Berkeley, 1961, Ph.D., 1965; LL.D., Hamilton Coll., 1974. Research asst., teaching fellow U. Calif. at Berkeley, 1959-63; instr. econs. Hamilton Coll., Clinton, N.Y., 1963-65; asst. prof. Hamilton Coll., 1965-68, asso. prof., 1969-74, acting provost, 1971-72, provost, 1972-74, pres. coll., 1974-88; dir. N.Y. office The Nature Conservancy, 1988-94, planned giving officer, 1994—; financial economist Office Tax Analysis, U.S. Dept. Treasury, Washington, 1968-69; chmn. N.Y. Com. of Selection, Rhodes Scholarship Trust, 1978-82; trustee Commn. on Ind. Colls. and Univs. N.Y., 1980-83. Mem. Democratic Com., Clinton, 1970-74. Served with AUS, 1957-58. Home: 26 St Agnes Ln Albany NY 12211-2058 Office: Nature Conservancy 415 River St Troy NY 12180-2834

CAROZZA, DAVY ANGELO, Italian language educator; b. Montenerodomo, Italy, Oct. 10, 1926; came to U.S., 1947, naturalized, 1952; s. Nicola and Maria A. (Mariotti) C.; m. Anna G. Carozza, Feb. 3, 1952; children—Daniel, Walter, Janet, Paolo. B.A. summa cum laude, Cath. U. Am., 1956, M.A. (Woodrow Wilson fellow), 1957, Ph.D. (Woodrow Wilson fellow), 1964. Tchr. Italian, 1943-47; lectr. summer sessions Cath. U. Am., 1957-65, lectr. in French, 1960-61; instr. Italian and French U. Md., College Park, 1961-64; asst. prof. Italian U. Md., 1964-65; lectr. Sch. Advanced Internat. Studies, Johns Hopkins U., 1964-65; asso. prof. comparative lit. U. Wis., Milw., 1965-68; prof. U. Wis., 1968-92, prof. emeritus, 1992—, chmn. dept., 1967-69, 73-76, coordinator M.A. program in Fgn. Lang. and Lit., 1976-86; prof. Scuola Italiana Middlebury Coll., Vt., 1990—; vis. asso. prof. comparative lit. Northwestern U., Evanston, Ill., 1966; mem. panel discussion on Dante Georgetown U. Forum radio program, 1965; adviser, coordinator Italian program for adults and children Cardinal Stritch Coll., 1971-73; mem. symposia on Baroque U. Ky., 1965, Cath. U. Am., 1975. Author: European Baroque, 1976, Petrarch's Secretum, 1989; contbr. book revs. and articles to lit. jours. Served with AUS, 1948-52. U. Wis. grantee, (8 awards) 1966-87. Mem. Midwest MLA (pres. 1969-70, exec. com. 1970-71), MLA (exec. council 1969-70), Internat., Am. Comparative lit. assns., Renaissance Soc. Am., Dante Soc. Am., Internat., Am. assns. tchrs. Italian, Am. Assn. Tchrs. French, Am. Assn. Tchrs. Spanish and Portuguese, Phi Beta Kappa, Delta Epsilon Sigma, Phi Kappa Phi. Home: 36 Turkey Hill Rd N Westport CT 06880-3943 Office: U Wis Dept English & Comparative Lit Milwaukee WI 53201

CARP, LARRY (LARRY CARP), lawyer; b. St. Louis, Jan. 26, 1926; s. Avery and Ruth C. Student, U. Mo., Columbia, 1944; cert., Sorbonne U., Paris, 1946; BA, Washington U., St. Louis, 1947; postgrad., Grad. Inst. Internat. Studies, Geneva, 1949; JD, Washington U., St. Louis, 1951. Bar: Mo. 1951, U.S. Dist. Ct. (ea. dist.) Mo. 1951. Mem. U.S. Dept. of State, Washington, 1951-53; mem. staff Senator Paul H. Douglas (Dem. Ill.), Washington, 1953-54; assoc. Fordyce, Mayne, Hartman, Renard, and Stribling, St. Louis, 1954-63; sole practice St. Louis, 1963-68; ptnr. Carp & Morris, St. Louis, 1968-90, Carp, Sexauer and Carr, St. Louis, 1990-94, Carp and Sexauer, St. Louis, 1994—; assoc. counsel, acting chief counsel U.S. Senate Subcom. on Constitutional Rights, Washington, 1956; mem. St. Louis Regional U.S. Export Expansion Coun., 1964-74; mem. Mo. Commn. on Human Rights, 1966-78, vice chmn., 1977-78; vice chmn., bd. dirs. Pastoral Counselling Inst. for Greater St. Louis, 1964-91; mem. bd. trustees The Acad. Sci., St. Louis, 1984—, asst. treas., 1992—; mem. adv. bd. George Engelmann Math. and Science Inst., 1992-96; bd. dirs. St. Louis Ctr. for Internat. Rels.; advisor Ethiopian Cmty. Assn. St. Louis, 1995—; legal advisor Image, Inc., St. Louis, 1998—. Co-author: (musicals) Pocahontas, The Pied Piper, Androcles; author: (musicals) For the Love of Adam, The Red Ribbon, Famous Last Words, God Knows!; contbr. articles to newspapers and mags. on subjects relating to immigration and nationality law. Mem. Common Cause, 1966-78, chmn. Mo. chpt., 1973-75; bd. dirs. Internat. Inst. of Metro St. Louis, 1980-86, English Speaking Union, St. Louis, 1985—; trustee St. Louis Ctr. for Internat. Rels., 1998—. With U.S. Army, 1944-46, ETO. Decorated (2) Battle Stars; Rotary Internat. fellow Grad. Inst. Internat. Studies, Geneva, 1948-49; award for Outstanding Service in Recognition of Spl. Needs of Hispanic Community IMAGE, St. Louis, 1984. Fellow Am. Acad. Matrimonial Lawyers; mem. ABA (immigration law coord. com., chmn. gen. practice sect. 1981-86), Mo. Bar Assn., Bar Assn. Met. St. Louis (chmn. internat. law and trade com. 1973-79, chmn. immigration law com. 1989-92), Am. Immigration Lawyers Assn., St. Louis Ctr. for Internat. Rels. (bd. dirs. 1998—), Phi Delta Phi. Fax: 314-727-0308. Office: Carp and Sexauer Ste 325 225 S Meramec Ave Saint Louis MO 63105-3511

CARP, STEVEN SCOTT, plastic surgery; b. Aug. 5, 1961. BS, Mich. State U., 1983; MD, Wayne State U., 1987. Pvt. practice plastic surgery Canton, Ohio. E-mail: gostate@sssact.com. Office: 4410 Executive Cir Canton OH 44718

CARPENTER, ALLAN, author, editor, publisher; b. Waterloo, Iowa, May 11, 1917; s. John Alex and Theodosia (Smith) C. BA, U. No. Iowa, 1938. Founder, editor, publisher Tchrs. Digest mag., 1940-48; dir. pub. relations Popular Mechanics mag., 1943-62; founder, 1962, since pres. Carpenter Pub. House, Inc., Chgo.; founder Infordata Internat. Inc., 1970-89, chmn. bd., dir., 1970-89; partner, editor Index to U.S. Govt. Periodicals, 1972-90, ret. Author over 230 nonfiction books including Between Two Rivers, Iowa Year By Year, 1940, 3d edit., 1997, 52 vol. Enchantment of America state series, 52 vol. New Enchantment of America, 52 vol. Enchantment of Africa, 38 vol. Enchantment of Latin America, 20 vol. Illinois, Land of Lincoln, 1968, All About the U.S.A., 1986, 7 vol. The Mighty Warriors, 1987, 4 vol. Encyclopedia of the Midwest, 1988, Encyclopedia of the Central West, 1990, Encyclopedia of the Far West, 1990, Facts About the Cities, 1992, 2d rev. edit., 1996, World Almanac of the U.S.A., 1993, 2d rev. edit., 1996, 3d edit., 1998, Between Two Rivers Iowa Year By Year, 1998; creator, editor 16 vol. Popular Mechanics Home Handyman Ency., 1962; founder, pub. Index to Readers Digest, 1980-90, Index to Alternative Health Periodicals, 1998—. Pres., chmn. Chgo. Businessmen's Symphony Orch., 1942-65; founder, 1954; since pres. Music Council Met. Chgo.; prin. bass violist non-profl. symphony orchs., 1935—; chief lay officer 2d Presbyn. Ch., Evanston, Ill., 1954-77. Mem. Soc. Wilson Descendants, Inc. (pres. 1955-93, chmn. 1994, founder James "Tama Jim" Wilson award), Arts Club Chgo., East Bank Club. Home and Office: 175 E Delaware Pl Suite 4602 Chicago IL 60611 *Plain stubbornness, at least rugged determination, has been a dominant element in whatever success I may have achieved. On the many occasions when I have failed or fallen short, I might have done better to have held on longer. When I have been confident of ultimate success and have held on to that confidence without fail, I have generally managed to make it.*

CARPENTER, AMY LYNN, elementary education educator; b. Limestone, Maine, July 2, 1972; d. Gregory Owen and Dorothy Diane (Rhodes) C. BS, Ohio U., 1994; MS, Ashland U., 1996; MSc, U. Dayton, 1998. Elem. tchr. Logan Elm Schs., Circleville, Ohio, 1994—. Mem. Nat. Coun. Tchrs. English. Methodist. Avocations: cinema, walking. Office: Logan Elm Schs 28158 Kingston Pike Circleville OH 43113-9741

CARPENTER, AMY TACY, architect; b. Abington, Pa., July 20, 1970; d. Frederick John and Marlen Julia Livezey; m. Stephen M. Carpenter, Jan. 4, 1992. BArch, Temple U., 1993. Registered arch., Pa. Intern arch. Stevens Luchanko Arch., Glenside, Pa., 1991-94; project mgr. Mike Rosen & Assocs., Phila., 1994-97; sr. project mgr. The Martin Archtl. Group, Phila., 1997—; promotional mgr. for music band Ruder Than You. Co-designer: Pavillion at Beaux Arts Ball, Phila., 1997 (1st pl. award Found. for Architecture/ELF-ATOCHEM). Mem. AIA, Nat. Assn. Archtl. Registration Bds. Avocations: softball, swimming, travel. Office: The Martin Archtl Group 240 N 22d St Philadelphia PA 19103

CARPENTER, ANNE BETTS, pathologist, physician, immunologist; b. Richmond, Va.; d. Earnest Betts and Anne Catherine (Gentry) C.; m. William Willett Reed, Feb. 14, 1992; 1 child: Timothy William Reed. BSN, Duke U., 1972, MSN, 1978; PhD, Medical Coll. Va., 1983; MD, Marshall U., 1993. Diplomate Am. Bd. Immunology, Am. Bd. Pathology. Fellow in cytopathology U. Ky., Lexington, 1997-98; resident in pathology Marshall U., Huntington, W.Va., 1994-97; asst. prof. microbiology, immunology Marshall U., Huntington, 1996-98; dir. immunology St. Margaret Meml. Hosp., Pitts., 1986-90; asst. prof. pathology U. Pitts., 1986-90; pathologist King's Daughter's Med. Ctr., Ashland, Ky., 1998-99; vice chmn., prof. pathology Marshall U., Huntington, W.Va., 1999—; voting mem. immunology svcs. panel FOA. Author: Manual for Clinical Immunology, 1994, Primer on Clinical Care, 1996, Quality Control in Clinical Immunology, 1997, Manual of Rheumatologic Rehabilitation, 1997. Recipient Quittner award Marshall U., Huntington, W.Va., 1997. Fellow Assn. of Med. Lab. Immunologists, Coll. Am. Pathologists (mem. immunology com., 1995-97, coun. mem. 1997), Assn. Clinical Pathologists, Alpha Omega Alpha. Avocations: gardening, cooking, traveling.

CARPENTER, ARTHUR LLOYD, education educator; b. Wayne, Mich., July 11, 1927; s. Arthur Betz and Mildred C. (Cunningham) C.; m. Madeline Mae Daue, Aug. 1, 1953; children: Thomas Wayne, James Paul, Lee Arthur. BS, Ea. Mich. U., 1951; MS, Mich. State U., 1956; postgrad. studies, Wayne State U., 1957, U. Mic., 1958-66. Cert. elem., secondary tchr. (permanent), Mich. Tchr. Jefferson Consol. Schs., Monroe, Mich., 1951-53, Plymouth (Mich.) Comty. Schs., 1953-55; asst. prof. edn. U. No. Iowa, Cedar Falls, 1956-64; coord. instrnl. materials Wayne-Westland Comty. Sch., Wayne, Mich., 1964; asst. prof. edn. Ea. Mich. U., Ypsilanti, Mich., 1964-90; cons. Iowa and Mich. schs., 1957-90, Fed. Correctional Prison, Milan, Mich., 1966; cons. with Nat. Coun. Accreditation of Tchr. Edn. Nebr. Wesleyan U., Lincoln, 1969. Film producer: 12 films for U. No. Iowa, 1957-64; Slide sets and F.S. 14 produced for U. No. Iowa, 1957-64; contbr. articles to 15 profl. publs.; photography reproduced in numerous mags.; book reviewer for several publishers. Recipient Red Balloon award Detroit Assn. Film Tchrs., 1970, 2d prize in Wayne Behling Meml. Photographic Contest, Ann Arbor, Mich., 1987. Mem. Wayne Hist. Soc. (bd. dirs., pres.), Mich. Bird Banders Assn. (pres.), Mich. Audubon Soc. (com. chmn.), Washtenaw Audubon Soc. (pres.), Mich. Natural Area Coun., Mich Photographic Hist. Soc. Home: 3646 S John Hix Rd Wayne MI 48184-1047

CARPENTER, BARRY KEITH, chemistry educator, researcher; b. Hastings, Sussex, U.K., Feb. 13, 1949; came to U.S., 1973; s. George Henry and Gladys Mable Carpenter. BSc with honors, Warwick U., Coventry, Eng., 1970; PhD, U. Coll., London, 1973. Postdoctoral fellow Yale U., New Haven, 1973-75; asst. prof. Cornell U., Ithaca, N.Y., 1975-81, assoc. prof., 1981-85, prof., 1985—; cons. Hoffman-La Roche, Inc., Nutley, N.J., 1985-97, Astra AB, Sodertalje, Sweden, 1989-95, Union Carbide, Linde divsn., Tarrytown, N.Y., 1991, Eastman Kodak Co., Rochester, N.Y., 1997—, Exxon Chem. Co., 1997, Bristol-Myers Squibb Co., 1998—; R.A. Welch Found. lectr. Yale U., New Haven, 1989, Bergman lectr., 1992; Louis Jacob Bircher lectr. Vanderbilt U., Nashville, 1993; vis. prof. U. New South Wales, Sydney, Australia, 1997. Author: Determination of Organic Reaction Mechanisms, 1984; sr. editor Jour. Organic Chemistry, 1992—. NATO fellow, 1973, A.P. Sloan Found. fellow, 1980, J.S. Guggenheim Found. fellow, 1986; Av. Humboldt Found. grantee, 1990. Fellow AAAS; mem. Am. Chem. Soc. (Cope Scholar award 1997, James Flack Norris award 1999), Royal Soc. Chemistry. Office: Cornell U Dept Chemistry 328 Baker Lab Ithaca NY 14853-1301

CARPENTER, BETTY O., writer; b. Montreal, June 1, 1926; d. Harry and Dorothy (Schacher) Shmerling; m. David G. Ostroff, Apr. 6, 1946 (div. 1972); children: Jack Ostroff, Lucy Ostroff Harrow; m. Russell William Carpenter, Jr., Oct. 2, 1976 (dec.); stepchildren: Annette Marie Carpenter Freedman, Cynthia Carpenter Jefferson, Lori Carpenter Bembry. BA in Edn., Bklyn. Coll., 1947, MA in Edn., 1953; PhD in Adminstrn., NYU, 1973. Cert. sch. supt., prin., N.J., guidance counselor, elem. tchr., N.Y. Tchr. elem. grades N.Y.C. Pub. Schs. 54 and 139, Bklyn., 1946-54, 62; asst. prin. Pub. Sch. 139, Bklyn., 1962-67; adminstrv. asst. pers. Ctrl. Office Bd. of Edn., N.Y.C., 1968-70; asst. supt. Plainfield (N.J.) Pub. Schs., 1970-74; supt. schs. Glen Rock (N.J.) Pub. Schs., 1974-84; ret. Author: Curriculum Guide to Public Schools of America, 1991, Tutoring for Pay, 1991, (book of poetry) Musings, The Brosh (Bionic Replacement of Species Humanoid), 1998, Lady of the Lake, 1999. Trustee Glen Rock Libr. Bd., 1974-80, United Fund Bd., Glen Rock, 1975-77; vice chmn. Iredell County Bd. of Adjustment N.C., 1990-95; fellow mem. Lake Owners Gathered in Concern, N.C., 1985-88. Recipient Founders Day award NYU, 1973, Adminstrv. Leadership award NACEL, 1984. Mem. Soc. Children's Book Writers and Illustrators, Romance Writers Am., Nat. Writers Assn., Bergen County Supts. Assn. (pres.-elect), Nat. Scrabble Assn., Am. Contract Bridge League. Avocations: sculpture, golf, water aerobics, computers, bridge. Home: 11730 N 91st Pl Scottsdale AZ 85260-6866

CARPENTER, CAROL SETTLE, communications executive; b. Schenectady, N.Y., Oct. 22, 1953; d. Carl Oscar and Ursula Elsen (McEldowney) Settle; m. R. Jay Carpenter, May 4, 1985; children: Reilly, Evie. BBA, Rochester Inst. Tech., 1975; postgrad., Inst. Children's Lit., 1988-91. Mgmt. trainee Lincoln First Bank, Rochester, N.Y., 1976-77; investment sec. Blyth Eastman Dillon, Scottsdale, Ariz., 1977-79; stockbroker E.F. Hutton, Scottsdale, 1979, Rauscher Pierce Refsnes, Scottsdale, 1979-81; exec. v.p. RL Kotrozo Inc., Scottsdale, 1981-85; asst. v.p. United Bank Ariz., Phoenix, 1985-88; asst. v.p. investments Citibank, Phoenix, 1988-91; freelance greeting card designer Phoenix, 1991; v.p. Warning Comm., Inc., Phoenix, 1992—. Staff vol. Crisis Nursery, Phoenix, 1987; co-pres. Khalsa Sch. Parent Coun., 1994-95; bd. dirs. Khalsa Montessori Elem. Schs., 1995—; mem. Contemporary Art Forum. Named Khalsa Sch. Parent of Yr., 1994-99. Mem. Phoenix Country Club, Phi Gamma Nu. Republican. Presbyterian. Avocations: music, art, writing for children. Home: 374 E Verde Ln Phoenix AZ 85012-3012

CARPENTER, CHARLES ALBERT, English language educator; b. Hazelton, Pa., June 8, 1929; s. Charles Albert and Frances Mary (Kenyon) C.; m. Randi Rothrock Carpenter, Nov. 4, 1950 (div. 1985); children: Carol, Linda, Janet, Diane; m. Martha Jean Clow Casella, Dec. 27, 1992. BA, Allegheny Coll., 1951; Ma in Libr. Sci., Kent State U., 1952; MA in English, Cornell U., 1960, PhD in English, 1963. Circulation libr. Dickinson Coll., Carlisle, Pa., 1952-54; head libr. Muskingum Coll., New Concord, Ohio, 1954-55; libr. Goldwin Smith Libr. Cornell U., Ithaca, N.Y., 1955-61; instr. in English U. Del., Newark, 1962-64, asst. prof. English, 1964-67; asst. prof. English SUNY, Binghamton, 1967-70, assoc. prof. English, 1970-81, prof., 1981-95; prof. emeritus Binghamton U., 1995—. Author: Bernard Shaw and the Art of Destroying Ideals: The Early Plays, 1969, Modern British Drama, 1979, Modern Drama Scholarship and Criticism 1966-80: An International Bibliography, 1986, Modern Drama Scholarship and Criticism 1981-1990: An International Bibliography, 1997, Dramatists and the Bomb: American and British Playwrights Confront the Nuclear Age, 1945-64, 1999; contbr. articles to profl. publs.; editl. bd. Modern Drama, 1974-92, Studies in America Drama, 1945-Present, 1986-92. Samuel S. Fels fellowship Cornell U., 1961-62, summer faculty fellowship Nat. Endowment for the Humanities, 1978, faculty rsch. fellowship U. Awards Com., 1979, grant in aid. Mem. Eugene O'Neill Soc., Harold Pinter Soc. Democrat. Avocations: duplicate bridge, senior softball. Home: 908 Lehigh Ave Vestal NY 13850-3808

CARPENTER, CHARLES COLCOCK JONES, physician, educator; b. Savannah, Ga., Jan. 5, 1931; s. Charles Colcock Jones and Alexandra (Morrison) C.; m. Sally R. Fisher, Nov. 29, 1958; children—Charles Morrison, Murray Douglas, Andrew Fisher. A.B., Princeton, 1952; M.D., Johns Hopkins, 1956. Diplomate: Am. Bd. Internal Medicine (mem. bd. 1976—, exec. com. 1980—, chmn. 1983-84). Intern Johns Hopkins Hosp., 1956-57, resident, 1957-59, 61-62; practice medicine, specializing in infectious disease Balt., 1962-73; asst. prof. medicine Johns Hopkins, 1962-67, assoc. prof., 1967-69, prof., 1969-73; physician-in-chief Balt. City Hosps., 1969-73; prof., chmn. dept. medicine Case Western Res. Sch. Medicine, 1973-86; physician-in-chief Case Western Res. Univ. Hosp., 1973-85; prof. medicine Brown U., 1986—, dir. Internat. Health Inst., 1993—; dir. Cholera Research Program, Johns Hopkins Center Med. Research and Tng., Calcutta, India, 1962-64; chmn. cholera panel U.S.-Japan Coop. Med. Sci. Program, 1965-72; mem. U.S.-Japan Coop. Med. Sci. Program (U.S. del.), 1973—, chmn., 1990—; mem. adv. bd. Sch. Medicine Johns Hopkins U., 1982-97; mem. Nat. Adv. Coun. Allergy and Infectious Diseases, 1985-89; chmn. extramural cons. AIDS exec. com. NIH, 1986-87, nat. adv. com. for AIDS, NIH, 1992-93; chmn. adv. coun. AIDS Rsch., NIH, 1995—. Trustee Internat. Ctr. for Infectious Disease Rsch., Bangladesh, 1979-83, Internat. Child Health Found., 1985-96, Miriam Hosp., 1992-97. Sr. asst. surgeon USPHS, 1959-61. Fellow ACP (master 1992), AAAS (chmn. med. scis. sect. 1994-96); mem. Inst. Medicine NAS, Am. Soc. Clin. Investigation, Assn. Am. Physicians (sec. 1975-81, councillor 1981-86, v.p. 1986-87, pres. 1987-88), Infectious Diseases Soc. Am. (Smadel medal 1991), Johns Hopkins Soc. Scholars, Johns Hopkins Med. and Surg. Assn. (pres. 1995-97), Order of the Sacred Treasure (Japan). Home: 12 Half Mile Rd Barrington RI 02806-4104

CARPENTER, CHARLES CONGDEN, zoologist, educator; b. Denison, Iowa, June 2, 1921; s. Harry Alonzo and Myrtle Ruth (Barber) C.; m. Mary F. Pitynski, Sept. 2, 1947; children—Janet Eleanor, Caryn Sue, Geoffrey Congden. B.A., No. Mich. Coll. Edn., Marquette, 1943; postgrad., Tarleton State Coll., Stephenville, Tex., 1943-44, Stanford U., 1944, Wayne U., 1945; M.S., U. Mich., 1947, Ph.D., 1951. Lab. asst. zoology No. Mich. Coll. Edn., 1941-43; teaching asst. zoology U. Mich., 1946; asst. herpetology and mammalogy Biol. Sta., summer 1948, teaching fellow zoology, 1947-51, instr. zoology, 1951-52; instr. U. Okla. Biol. Sta., Norman, summer 1952; instr. U. Okla., 1953, asst. prof. zoology, 1953-59; assoc. prof. zoology, curator reptiles U. Okla. and; assoc. prof. zoology, curator reptiles U. Okla. Biol. Sta., 1959-66, prof. zoology, curator reptiles, 1966-87, prof. emeritus zoology, curator emeritus reptiles and amphibians, 1988; rsch. assoc. in herpetology Dallas Zoo, 1980; expdns. and field studies U. Mich. Paleontol. Expdn., Kans. and, Colo., 1947, Jackson Hole Research sta., Grand Teton Nat. Park, 1951, field trips throughout, Mexico and; S.W., U.S., 1979—; Galapagos Islands Expdn., 1962; expdns. to islands of Gulf of Calif., 1964; invited scientist mem. Galapagos Internat. Sci. Project to Galapagos Islands, Ecuador and; Cocos Island, 1964—; sec. Animal Research Council, Oklahoma City Zoo, 1972-74, 78—, chmn., 1980. Contbr. articles to profl. jours. Served with AUS, 1943-46. Recipient Disting. Alumni award No. Mich. U., 1972; Regents award U. Okla., 1980; numerous grants NSF; numerous grants N.Y. Zool. Soc.; numerous grants U. Okla. Alumni Devel. Fund; numerous grants U. Okla. Research Inst., 1951—. Fellow Animal Behavior Soc. (sec. 1966-68), Okla. Acad. Sci. (pres. 1970, Outstanding Scientist award 1991), Herpetologist League (v.p. 1972-73, pres. 1974-75); mem. Am. Ornithologists Union, Am. Soc. Zoologists, Am. Inst. Biol. Sci., Ecol. Soc. Am., Am. Soc. Ichthyologists and Herpetologists, Wilson Ornithol. Soc., Southwestern Assn. Naturalists (bd. govs. 1965-68, pres. 1968-69, permanent sec. 1971-76, W. Frank Blair award 1987), Am. Soc. Mammalogists, Brit. Ecol. Soc., Soc. Study Amphibians and Reptiles, Explorers Club, Wilderness Soc., Nature Conservancy, Sigma Xi, Phi Kappa Phi, Phi Sigma. Home: 1218 Cruce St Norman OK 73069-4440 Office: U Okla Dept Zoology 730 Van Vleet Oval Norman OK 73019-6120

CARPENTER, CHARLES ELFORD, JR., lawyer; b. Greenville, S.C., Nov. 3, 1944; s. Charles Elford and Mary Charlotte (Campbell) C.; m. Nancy Townsend, June 8, 1968; children: Charlotte Elizabeth, John Morrison. BA, Furman U., 1966; JD, U. Va., 1969; MPA, U. S.C., 1976. Bar: Va. 1969, S.C. 1972, U.S. Dist. Ct. S.C. 1974, U.S. Ct. Appeals (4th cir.) 1978, U.S. Ct. Appeals (11th cir.) 1984, U.S. Supreme Ct. 1983. Assoc. Leatherwood, Walker, Todd & Mann, Greenville, 1969, Richardson, Plowden, Grier & Howser, Columbia, S.C., 1974-78; ptnr. Richardson, Plowden, Carpenter & Robinson, P.A., Columbia, S.C., 1978—; mem. com. on grievances and discipline S.C. Supreme Ct., 1986-89, 1996; spkr. Law Seminars, Inc., Columbia, 1987, Outline for Post-Trial Practice, 1988, 89, 90; mem. S.C. Supreme Ct. Bd. Law Examiners. Editor Appeal and Error, S.C. Jurisprudence; contbr. articles to legal jours. Mem. bd. visitors Presbyn. Coll., Clinton, S.C., 1983-87; trustee James H. Hammond Sch., Columbia, 1986-89, Trinity Presbytery; pres. A.C. Flora PTO; elder Eastminster Presbyn. Ch. Capt. U.S. Army, 1969-72. Fellow Am. Acad. Appellate Lawyers; mem. ABA (speaker appellate process program 1990, editor Appellate Practice Jour. 1989—, co-chair oral arguement subcom. litigation sect., mem. task force on unreported opinions 1996—), S.C. Bar Assn. (mem. Richland County fee dispute com. 1984-88, speaker 1987, appellate practice, panel mem. proposed rules of appellate practicefor S.C. Bar ann. meeting 1989, mem. practice and procedure com., health and hosp. law subcom., appellate rules subcom., chmn. merit selection of judges subcom., alternative dispute resolution com. 1993—), Richland County Bar Assn., S.C. Def. Trial Attys. (chmn. amicus curiae com. 1981-85), Forest Lake Club, St. Andrews Soc., Tarantella Club, Columbia Ball Club, Torch Club (pres.). Avocations: reading, hunting, tennis, fishing. Office: Richardson Plowden Carpenter & Robinson PA 1600 Marion St # 7788 Columbia SC 29201-2913

CARPENTER, CHARLES FRANCIS, lawyer; b. Raleigh, N.C., Apr. 3, 1957; s. William Lester and Mattie Frances (Wallace) C.; m. Heidi Ann Athanas, June 14, 1980. BA with honors, U. N.C., 1979, JD, 1982. Bar: N.C. 1982, U.S. Dist. Ct. (mid. dist.) N.C. 1982, U.S. Dist. Ct. (ea. dist.) N.C. 1986, U.S. Ct. Appeals (4th cir.) 1986, U.S. Dist. Ct. (we. dist.) N.C. 1988. Assoc. Newsom, Graham, Hedrick, Murray, Bryson & Kennon, Durham, N.C., 1982-87; ptnr. Newsom, Graham, Hedrick, Bryson & Kennon, Durham, 1988-93; pvt. practice, Charles F. Carpenter, P.A., Durham, 1993-98; ptnr. Pulley, Watson, King & Lischer, P.A., Durham, 1998—. Trustee N.C. Conf. United Meth. Ch., 1993—; mem. exec. bd. Occoneechee Coun. Boy Scouts Am., 1988—. Mem. ABA, N.C. State Bar, N.C. Bar Assn., Durham County Bar Assn. (medico-legal com. 1994—, bd. dirs.), Order of the Old Well, Honorable Order of Ky. Colonels, Phi Beta Kappa. Democrat. Avocations: karate, golf, softball, jogging, skiing, soccer. Home: 1325 Arnette Ave Durham NC 27707-1601 Office: 905 W Main St Ste 21 F Durham NC 27701-2076

CARPENTER, DANA LYNN, elementary educator; b. El Paso, Tex., Sept. 15, 1966; d. Joseph Alvie and Lena (Lupo) C. BS in Elem. Edn., U. Houston, 1990; MEd, Sam Houston State U., 1997. Cert. tchr., Tex. Pre-first grade tchr. Black Elem. Sch., Houston, 1990-91, spl. edn. pre-kindergarten-5 tchr., 1991-92, pre-1st grade tchr. ESL, 1992-94, 1st grade tchr., 1994-95, 2nd grade ESL tchr., 1995-97, Title I reading specialist/ESL, 1997—; tchr., reading specialist Sam Houston State U., Huntsville, 1995-97. Active PTA, Houston, 1990—; sponsor C.H.I.C.K.E.N. Club, Houston, 1990—; com. chair Make A Difference Day, Black Elem. Sch., 1995—. Sam Houston State ESL/Bilingual Dept. grantee, 1995-97. Mem. Nat. Coun. Tchrs. English, Internat. Reading Assn., Kindergarten Tchrs. Tex., Greater Houston Area Reading Coun. Republican. Roman Catholic. Avocations: book clubs, reading, in-line skating, travel, NASCAR racing. Office: Black Elem Sch 160 Mill Stream Ln Houston TX 77060-4114

CARPENTER, DAVID RONNIE, artist; b. Waterville, Maine, July 22, 1955. AS, Vernon Regional Jr. Coll., 1986; BS, Wayland Bapt. U., 1986. Works exhibited at State House Mus., Augusta, Maine, 1990, Sunflower-Cluster Dog Show, Wichita, Kans., 1993, Fryburg (Maine) Fair Art Exhibit, 1998, Windsor (Maine) Art Fair Exhibit, 1998 (first place excellence in visual art 1998), Augusta Civic Ctr., 1998; various portraits commd. by pvt. collectors; represented in permanent collections at Judy's Art Gallery, Fairfield; staff writer Art Calender Mag., 1995, Morning Sentinal, 1995. Recipient Nat. Crabbie award 2nd Annual Art Calender, 1995, 2nd place excellence in visual art award Maine Sportsman's Soc., 1998. Mem. Maine Art Commn., Ctrl. Maine Artists Assn. Home: 4 Burns St Fairfield ME 04937 Office: Cliff Duphiney 132 Main St Fairfield ME 04937

CARPENTER, DAVID WILLIAM, lawyer; b. Chgo., Aug. 26, 1950; s. William Warren and Dorothy Susan (Jacobs) C.; m. Jane Ellen French, Aug. 18, 1973; children: Johanna Lindsay, Julie Rachel. BA, Yale U., 1972; JD, Boston U., 1975. Bar: Mass. 1975, U.S. Ct. Appeals (1st cir.) 1977, D.C., Ill., U.S. Dist. Ct. (no. dist.) Ill. 1979, U.S. Ct. Appeals (D.C. cir.) 1980, U.S. Ct. Appeals (3d and 7th cirs.), U.S. Supreme Ct. 1981, U.S. Ct. Appeals (10th cir.) 1985, (8th cir.) 1986, (9th and 11th cirs.) 1987, (2d and 5th cirs.) 1990. Law clk. to presiding justice U.S. Ct. Appeals (1st cir.), Portland, Maine, 1975-77, U.S. Supreme Ct., Washington, 1977-78; assoc. Sidley & Austin, Chgo., 1978-82, ptnr., 1982—; lectr. Ill. Inst. Tech., Chgo., 1980-82. Bd. dirs., sec. Chgo. Coun. for Young Profls., 1985-90; bd. dirs., exec. com. Brennan Ctr. for Justice, N.Y.C., 1995—. Democrat. Mem. United Ch. Christ. Home: 1660 N Burling St Chicago IL 60614-5157 Office: Sidley & Austin 1 First Natl Plz Chicago IL 60603-2003

CARPENTER, DELBERT STANLEY, educational administration educator; b. Wichita Falls, Tex., May 18, 1950; s. Delbert Stanley Sr. and Ruby Elizabeth (Green) S.; m. Noralyn Gray, July 13, 1973 (div. Mar. 1986); m. Janet Ann Stewart, July 15, 1989 (div. June 1993); m. Linda Jan Meerdink Evans, June 15, 1994; 1 child, Susanne Gray Carpenter; stepchildren: Robert Scott Evans, Peter Clark Evans. BS, Tarleton State U., 1972; MS, East Tex. State U., 1975; PhD, U. Ga., 1979. Actuarial technician A.S. Hansen, Inc., Dallas, 1972-74; grad. asst. cen. housing office East Tex. State U., Commerce, 1974-75; men's resident dir. Oglethorpe U., Atlanta, 1975-77; grad. asst. rsch., tchg., counseling and human devel. dept. U. Ga., Athens, 1977-79; dean students U. Ark., Monticello, 1979-81; asst. dir. devel. Tex. A&M U., College Station, 1982-84, from asst. prof. ednl. adminstrn. to assoc. prof., 1985-95, prof., 1995—. Mem. editl. bds. various profl. jours.; contbr. articles to profl. jours. Named Outstanding Doctoral Alumnus, Students Affairs Administrn. U. Ga., 1995, Disting. Tchg. award Assn. Former Students Coll. of Edn., 1996. Mem. Assn. for the Study Higher Edn. (exec. dir. 1987—, Disting. Svc. award 1996), Am. Coll. Pers. Assocs. (Annuit Coeptis award 1995), Nat. Assn. Student Pers. Adminstrn., South Assn. for Coll. Student Affairs (Melvene Hardee award 1997), Alpha Phi Omega (pres., bd. dirs. 1986-90, Nat. Disting. Svc. award 1990, trustee endowment fund 1996—, chair 1997—), Alpha Chi. Avocations: golf, reading, travel. Home: 1111 12th Man Cir College Station TX 77845-8979 Office: Tex A&M U 517 Harrington College Station TX 77843

CARPENTER, DERR ALVIN, landscape architect; b. Sunbury, Pa., Jan. 18, 1931; s. Alvin Witmer and Katharine (Rockefeller) C.; m. Helen Longden Hedge, Apr. 10, 1954; children: Mary Katharine Carpenter Denault, Melissa Sue Carpenter Sciumbata. B.S., Pa. State U., 1953. Registered landscape architect. Chief landscape architect La. State Parks, Baton Rouge, 1955-58; asst. dir. City Parish Planning Com., Baton Rouge, 1958-62; chief planning and engrng. Pa. State Parks, Harrisburg, 1962-67; pres. Derr A. Carpenter & Assocs., Camp Hill, Pa., 1967-73; v.p. Smith, Miller & Assocs. Inc., Camp Hill and Kingston, Pa., 1973-86, Rettew Assocs. Inc., Mechanicsburg and Lancaster, Pa., 1987-90; self employed landscape architect Mechanicsburg, 1990—; lectr. Pa. State U., Harrisburg Area C.C., 1973-90, Susquehanna U.; mem. legis. com. pa. Recreation and Park Soc., University Park, 1982-90; bd. dirs. Pa. State Arts and Architecture Alumni Bd., University Park, 1985-95. Mem. Camp Hill Shade Tree Commn., 1968-87; councilman Tree of Life Luth. Ch., Linglestown, 1994-98; bd. dirs. Park Adv. Bd., Cumberland County, Pa., 1978-84; bd. dirs. YMCA, Harrisburg, 1974-80, Capital Region Econ. Devel. Corp., 1988-93; chair Zoning Commn., 1989, Dauphin County Open Space Commn., 1989-92. With U.S. Army, 1953-55. Pa. State U. Alumni fellow, 1984. Fellow Am. Soc. Landscape Architects (trustee 1977-80, pres. chpt. 1973-77, nat. ethics com. chmn. 1984-87, dir. legislation 1968-90, Disting. Svc. award 1981, cert. appreciation 1984); mem. Susquehanna River Tri-State Assn. (pres. 1980-82, Leadership award 1982, bd. dirs.), Pa. Nursery Mktg. Adv. Coun. (chmn. 1976-77, bd. dirs. Outstanding Achievement award 1972), Pa. State Alumni Assn. of Harrisburg (pres. 1983-85, bd. dirs., Leadership award 1985). Republican. Lutheran. Lodges: Torch (bd. dirs. 1976-81), Rotary (bd. dirs. 1968-82), Masons. Avocations: gardening, hiking, reading, printing, massage.

CARPENTER, DONALD BLODGETT, real estate appraiser; b. New Haven, Aug. 20, 1916; s. Fred Donald and Gwendolen (Blodgett) C.; m. Barbara Marvin Adams, June 28, 1941 (dec. Aug. 1978); m. 2d, Lee Burker McGough, Dec. 28, 1980 (div. Apr. 1987); children—Edward G., John D., William V., Andrew J., Dorothy J. and James J. McGough. PhB, U. Vt., 1938; postgrad., Sonoma State U., 1968-69, Mendocino C. Coll., 1977, Coll. of Redwoods, 1984-85. Reporter Burlington (Vt.) Daily News, 1938-39; guide chair operator Am. Express Co., N.Y. World's Fair, 1939; underwriter G.E.I. Corp., Newark, 1939-40; sales corr. J. Dixon Crucible Co., Jersey City, 1940-41, asst. office mgr., priorities specialist, 1941-42; sales rep. J. Dixon Crucible Co., San Francisco, 1946-52; field supr. Travelers Ins. Co., San Francisco, 1952-58; gen. agt. Gen. Am. Life Ins. Co., San Francisco, 1958-59; western supr. Provident Life & Accident Ins. Co., San Francisco, 1959-60; brokerage supr. Aetna Life Ins. Co., San Francisco, 1960-61; maintenance cons. J.I. Holcomb Mfg. Co., Mill Valley, Calif., 1961-68; ednl. svc. rep. Marquis Who's Who, Inc., Mill Valley, Calif., 1963-68; sales rep. Onox, Inc., Mendocino, Calif., 1965-68; tchr., coach Mendocino Jr.-Sr. High Sch., 1968; real property appraiser Mendocino County, 1968-81; instr. Coll. of Redwoods, 1985-87; real estate appraiser Carpenter Appraisal Svcs., 1982-88, ret., 1988. Active numerous civic orgns.; co-chmn. Citizens for Sewers, 1971-72; mem. Mendocino County Safety Coun., 1981; sponsor mem. Mendocino Art Ctr., 1965-96. With USNR, 1942-46; lt. comdr., comdg. officer res. unit, 1967-68, ret., 1968. Sec. of Navy Commendation with ribbon, 1946, other awards, certificates; companion Mil. Order World Wars (life); named Cmty. Sportsman of Yr., 1971. Mem. Res. Officers Assn. U.S. (life, chpt. pres. 1954-56, state v.p. 1958-61), Ret. Officers Assn. (life, chpt. survivors assistance area counselor 1979-96, chpt. scholarship com. 1986-91), Save-the-Redwoods League, Marines Meml. Assn., Mendocino County Employees Assn. (dir. 1981), Mendocino County Hist. Soc., Mendocino Hist. Rsch. Inc. (docent 1982-88), Nat. Assn. Uniformed Svcs. (life), Mendocino Coast Geneal. Soc. (pres. 1991-93), Nat. Ret. Tchrs. Assn., Calif. Ret. Tchrs. Assn., Naval Order U.S. (life), Naval Res. Assn. (life), Navy League U.S. (life), U.S. Naval Inst. (life), Am. Diabetes Assn., Alumni Assn. U. Vt. (founding pres. San Francisco Alumni Club 1964), Mendocino Coast Stamp Club (charter, dir. 1983-96, pres. 1994, v.p. 1995), Rotary Internat. (club pres. 1975-76, dist. gov. area rep. 1977-78, dist. ambassadorial scholarship com. 1978-81, 89-90, dist. group study exchange com. 1981-88, 90-93, club historian 1989-96, dist. foun. alumni com. 1991-92, Paul Harris fellow 1979—, Rotarian of Yrs. 1969-88, Dist. Gov. award 1974, 76, 96, Cert. Achievement for outstanding svc. 1993-94), Am. Legion (post comdr. 1972-73, State Citation for outstanding cmty. svc. 1972, past comdrs. Calif., life), VFW, Vt. Hist. Soc., Mendocino Coast Land Devel. Corp. (dir. 1991-97, exec. v.p. 1995-97), Mendocino Cardinal Booster Club (charter, life, pres. 1971), U. Vt. Catamount Club (charter), U. Vt. Chittenden County Alumni Assn., Old Mill Club, Kappa Sigma (Scholarship-Leadership award 1937-38). Republican. Congregationalist. Home: 100 Wake Robin Dr Shelburne VT 05482-7529

CARPENTER, EDMUND NELSON, II, retired lawyer; b. Phila., Jan. 27, 1921; s. Walter S. and Mary (Wootten) C.; m. Carroll Morgan, July 18, 1970; children: Mary W., Edmund Nelson III, Katherine R.R., Elizabeth Lea; stepchildren: John D. Gates, Ashley du Pont Gates. AB, Princeton U., 1943; LLB, Harvard U., 1948; LLD (hon.), Widener U., 1985, U. Del., 1999. Bar: Del. 1949, U.S. Supreme Ct. 1957. Assoc. Richards, Layton & Finger, Wilmington, Del., 1949-53, ptnr., 1953-78, dir., 1978-91, pres., 1982-85; retired, 1991; dep. atty. gen. State of Del., 1953-54, spl. dep. atty., 1960-62; chmn. Del. Superior Ct. Jury Study Com., 1963-66, Del. Supreme Ct. Cts. Consol. Com., 1985-87; mem. Del. Gov.'s Commn. Law Enforcement and Adminstrn. Justice, 1969; chmn. Del. Supreme Ct. Adv. Com. on Profl. Fin. Accountability, 1974-75, Del. Jud. Nominating Commn., 1977-83, Del. Superior Ct. Study Com., 1991-92; mem. Long Range Cts. Planning Com., 1976-89, Del. Ct. Common Pleas Study Com., 1992, Del. Supreme Ct. Com. on Judicial Code of Conduct, 1991-93; co-chmn. Del. Justice Ctr. Com., 1994-97; mem. lawyers adv. com. U.S. Ct. Appeals (3d cir.) 1975-80, chmn., 1975-77; chmn. local rules com. U.S. Dist. Ct. Del., 1978-83, Del. Ct. on the Judiciary Rules Com., 1996-98; bd. dirs. Bank of Del., Barclay's Bank. Trustee Wilmington Med. Ctr., 1965—, U. Del., 1971-77, Princeton U., 1974-85, 86-91, Winterthur Mus., 1991-99, World Affairs Coun. Wilmington, 1968-80, Woodrow Wilson Found., 1985—, Lawrenceville Sch., 1953-74, trustee emeritus, 1974—; trustee Nat. Humanities Ctr., 1995-98; bd. dirs. Good Samaritan Inc., 1973—, pres., 1998—; mem. Del. Health Care Injury Ins. Study Commn., 1976-80. With U.S. Army, 1942-46, 50-52. Decorated Bronze Star, Soldier's medal, Chinese Order of the Flying Cloud with four battle stars; recipient 1st State Disting. Svc. award, Del. State Bar Assn., 1984, Josiah Marvel Cup award Del. State C. of C., 1990, Benjamin Franklin Disting. Pub. Svc. award Am. Philos. Soc., 1996. Fellow Am. Coll. Trial Lawyers, Am. Bar Found.; mem. ABA (ho. of dels. 1979-86), Del. State Bar Assn. (pres. 1971-72, Presdl. citation 1987), ATLA, Am. Judicature Soc. (bd. dirs. 1974-83, exec. com. 1978-80, v.p. 1980-81, pres. 1981-83, Justice award 1991). Home and Office: 600 Center Mill Rd Wilmington DE 19807-1502

CARPENTER, EDWARD KEARNEY, writer, editor; b. Atlanta, Mar. 17, 1932; s. Otto William and Katherine (Kearney) C.; m. Ruth Corn, Aug. 31, 1958 (div. Dec. 1977); m. Joanna Clapp, Mar. 18, 1986. BA, Haverford (Pa.) Coll., 1954; MA, U. Pa., Phila., 1958. Assoc. editor Indsl. Design Mag., N.Y.C., 1960-64; sr. editor Progressive Archiecture, N.Y.C., 1964-69; contbg. editor Design & Environ., N.Y.C., 1970-72, Environ. Design, N.Y.C., 1972-78; corr. at large Archtl. Forum, N.Y.C., 1972-75; editor Oyster River Press, Durham, N.H., 1991—; cons. IBM, Poughkeepsie, N.Y., 1983. Author: The Best in Environmental Graphics, 1975, 37 Design and Environment Projects, 1976, Urban Design Case Studies, 1977, The Best in Exhibition Design, 1977, 78, 80, 82, 84, 86, 89, 91, 94, Design Case Studies, 1979, Design Review 25, 1979; writer, rschr.: Frommer's India on $5 and $10 a Day, 1976; contbr. articles to mags. and encys. Commr. Historic Dist. Commn., Durham, 1990-94. Sgt. U.S. Army, 1957-60, Korea. Mem. Nat. Audubon Soc. (life). Avocations: reading, sailing, skiing, hiking, canoeing.

CARPENTER, ELIZABETH JANE, communications executive; b. Cleve., Mar. 29, 1949; d. Robert E. and Joan Jaffe. BA, Western Coll., Oxford, Ohio, 1970. Pub. rels. asst. Lennen & Newell/Pacific, Honolulu, 1970-73; account exec. Marschalk Advt., Cleve., 1973-76; cons. Carpenter Advt. & Pub. Rels., Cleve., 1976-80; internat. pub. rels. mgr. Wang Labs., Inc., Boston, 1980-82, advt. mgr., 1982-87; mgr. worldwide comm. CSS Digital Equipment Corp., Merrimack, N.H., 1987-92, advt. mgr. U.S. Svcs. group, 1992—; assoc. producer Am. Treasure, TV spl., 1986, The Entrepreneurs, TV spl., 1986-87; owner Carpenter Antiques, Dennis, Mass. Mem. Cape Cod Antiques Dealers Assn., Boston Advt. Club, Boston Club. Office: Digital Equipment Corp 3 Results Way Marlborough MA 01752-3087

CARPENTER, ELIZABETH SUTHERLAND, journalist, author, equal rights leader, lecturer; b. Salado, Tex., Sept. 1, 1920; d. Thomas Shelton and Mary Elizabeth (Robertson) Sutherland; m. Leslie Carpenter, June 17, 1944; children: Scott Sutherland, Christy. BJ, U. Tex., 1942; PhD (hon.), Mt. Vernon Coll., Austin Coll. Reporter UP, Phila., 1944-45; propr. with husband of news bur. representing nat. newspapers Washington, 1945-61; exec. asst. to Vice Pres. Lyndon B. Johnson, 1961-63; pres. sec., staff dir. to Mrs. Johnson, 1963-69; v.p. Hill & Knowlton, Inc., Washington, 1972-76; cons. LBJ Library, Austin, Tex.; asst. sec. Dept. Edn., 1980-81; with White House Com. on Aging, 1998—; co-chmn. ERAmerica, 1976-81. Author: Ruffles and Flourishes, 1970, Getting Better All the Time, 1987, Unplanned Parenthood, 1994. Recipient Woman of Year award in field of politics and pub. affairs Ladies Home Jour., 1977, Disting. Alumnae award U. Tex., 1974-75; named to Tex. Women's Hall of Fame, 1985. Mem. Nat. Women's Polit. Caucus (founding mem. 1971), Women's Nat. Press (pres. 1954-55), Alpha Phi, Theta Sigma Phi (Nat. Headliners award 1962). Clubs: Press (Washington); Headliners (Headliner award), Univ. (Austin). Home and Office: 116 Skyline Dr Austin TX 78746-3643*

CARPENTER, FLORENCE ERIKA, retired human services adminstrator; b. Rochester, N.Y., July 28, 1913; d. William Rice and Alice Leah (Harman) Foster; m. Lawrence Edmund Carpenter, Oct. 30, 1937 (dec. June 1968); children: Luke, Susan, Michael, Patricia Carpenter-Light. BA, U. Rochester, 1935. Cert. nursing home adminstr., cert. case worker, N.Y. With rsch. dept. Eastman Kodak Co., Rochester, 1936-42; social worker Monroe County Dept. Social Svcs., Rochester, N.Y., 1960-62; med. social worker Strong Meml. Hosp., Rochester, 1966-71, Organized Home Care, 1962-64; exec. dir. Regional Coun. on Aging (now Life Span), Rochester, 1971-79; adminstv. svcs. Wayne, Ontario, Seneca and Yates counties Soc. for Prevention Cruelty to Children, Rochester, 1979-80; interim dir. Monroe County Mental Health Assn., Rochester, 1980; adminstr. Home and Family Svcs., Rochester, 1980-88, ret., 1988. Bd. dirs. Monroe County Dept. Health, 1988-94, Family Svcs., Rochester; pres., bd. dirs. Monroe County Mental Health Chpt., 1993-95, Rushville (N.Y.) Health Ctr., 1980-97; chmn. Liberal Party Monroe County, 1966; bd. dirs. Unitarian-Universalist Ch. Canandaigua, 1991-94. Recipient plaque Monroe County Mental Health Chpt., 1985, Monroe County Dept. Health, 1989. Mem. Am. Assn. Ret. Persons (N.Y.S. vote coord. 1988-92, mem. nat. legis. com. 1992-93), LWV (treas., bd. mem. 1948-97). Home: 5050 County Road 11 Rushville NY 14544-9704

CARPENTER, FRANK CHARLES, JR., retired electronics engineer; b. L.A., June 1, 1917; s. Frank Charles and Isobel (Crump) C.; A.A., Pasadena City Coll., 1961; B.S. in Elec. Engring. cum laude, Calif. State U.-Long Beach, 1975, M.S. in Elec. Engring., 1981; m. Beatrice Josephine Jolly, Nov. 3, 1951; children—Robert Douglas, Gail Susan, Carol Ann. Self-employed design and mfgr. aircraft test equipment, Los Angeles, 1946-51; engr. Hoffman Electronics Corp., Los Angeles, 1951-56, sr. engr., 1956-59, project mgr., 1959-63; engr.-scientist McDonnell-Douglas Astronautics Corp., Huntington Beach, Calif., 1963-69, spacecraft telemetry, 1963-67, biomed. electronics, 1967-69, flight test instrumentation, 1969-76; lab. test engr. Northrop Corp., Hawthorne, Calif., 1976-82, spl. engr., 1982-83; mgr. transducer calibration lab. Northrop Corp., Pico-Rivera, Calif., 1983-86. Served with USNR, 1941-47. Mem. IEEE (life), Amateur Radio Relay League. Contbr. articles to profl. jours. Patentee transistor squelch circuit; helicaland whip antenna. Home: 2037 Balearic Dr Costa Mesa CA 92626-3514

CARPENTER, GENE BLAKELY, crystallography and chemistry educator; b. Evansville, Ind., Dec. 15, 1922; s. Leland A. and Juanita (Blakely) C.; m. Elizabeth E. Corkum, Apr. 15, 1949; children—Jonathan R., Anne E. B.A., U. Louisville, 1944; M.A., Harvard U., 1945, Ph.D., 1947. NRC fellow Calif. Inst. Tech., 1947-48, research fellow, 1948-49; instr. Brown U., 1949-52, asst. prof., 1952-56, asso. prof., 1956-63, prof., 1963-88, prof. emeritus, 1988—; Guggenheim fellow U. Leeds, Eng., 1956-57; vis. prof. U. Groningen, The Netherlands, 1963-64; Fulbright-Hayes lectr. U. Zagreb, Yugoslavia, 1971-72; vis. scientist Oak Ridge Nat. Lab., 1980, U. Göttingen, Fed. Republic of Germany, 1987, U. Canterbury, Christchurch, New Zealand, 1989. Author: Principles of Crystal Structure Determination, 1969; Contbr. articles to sci. jours. Mem. Am. Crystallographic Assn., Am. Chem. Soc. Home: 8 Angell Ct Providence RI 02906-4118 Office: Brown U Dept Chemistry Providence RI 02912

CARPENTER, GORDON RUSSELL, lawyer, banker; b. Denton, Tex., Feb. 6, 1920; s. Solomon Lafayette and Grace L. (Fowler) C.; m. Muriel E. James, Sept. 18, 1943 (dec.); m. Mary Alice Borah, Aug. 4, 1962. BS, North Tex. State U., 1940; postgrad., Georgetown U., 1941-42; LL.B., So. Meth. U., 1948. Bar: Tex. 1947, U.S. Supreme Ct. 1960. Announcer KDNT, Denton, Tex., 1940-41; spl. agent FBI, 1941-46; exec. sec. Southwestern Legal Found., Dallas, 1947-56; exec. dir., 1956-58; adminstrv. asst. to dean Law Sch. So. Meth. U., 1951-58, asst. prof. law, 1956-68; trust officer 1st Nat. Bank, Dallas, 1958-60, v.p., 1960-79; v.p., sr. fin. planning officer InterFirst Bank, Dallas, 1979-84. Bd. regents Tex. Sch. Trust Banking, 1981-82; bd. trustees Hatton W. Sumners Found., 1959—, exec. dir., 1985-95; chmn. North Tex. State U. Ednl. Found.; chmn. Luth. Med. Sys. Tex. Found., 1980-83; vice chmn. Farmers Br. Hosp. Authority, 1976-77. Recipient Pres.'s award State Bar Tex., 1963, Bd. Dirs. award, 1971, Gene Cavin award for excellence in con. legal edn., 1998. Fellow Tex. Bar Found.; mem. ABA (chmn. publs. com. mineral andnatural resources law sect. 1958-64), State Bar Tex. (chmn. cont. legal edn. com. 1952-54, 58-66, chmn. real estate, probate and trust law sect. 1964-65), Dallas Bar Assn. (dir. 1960-61, 65-66, chmn. centennial com. 1972-73), Dallas Bar Found. (trustee, sec.-treas.), Tex. Bankers Assn. (chmn. trust divsn. 1980-81), Soc. Former Spl. Agts. FBI (pres. 1963), Brookhaven Country Club, Masons, Delta Theta Phi. Republican. Presbyterian. Office: 325 N Saint Paul St Ste 2800 Dallas TX 75201-3809

CARPENTER, HOYLE DAMERON, music educator emeritus; b. Stockton, Calif., Aug. 8, 1909; s. William Horace and Mabel (Hanna) C.; m. Rose Mick, Feb. 24, 1968. MusB, U. Pacific, 1930; MusM, U. Rochester, 1932; PhD, U. Chgo., 1951-57; postgrad., U. Calif., Berkeley, 1949-50. Instr. Ft. Hays (Kans.) State Coll., 1942-44; asst. prof. Grinnell (Iowa) Coll., 1944-57; asst. prof. music Rowan U., Glassboro, N.J., 1957-60, assoc. prof., 1960-61, prof., 1961-76, prof. emeritus, 1976—. Author: Teaching Elementary Music Without a Supervisor, 1959, also edits. Holyoke's Instrumental Assistant, 1959, Crequillon Pisne me peult venir, 1962; also several poster sets on music, 1970; also articles; writer program notes for Hollybush Festival, Lenape Chamber Players, Craftsbury Chamber Players, 1980—, Allegro Soc.; book reviewer various jours. Treas. Gloucester County Mental Health Assn., 1963-68; committeeman Glassboro Dem. Com., 1964; v.p. Glassboro Dem. Club, 1964-66. Mem. AAUP, Am. Musicological Soc., Music Tchrs. Nat. Assn. (sec. Ea. divsn. 1962-64), Music Educators Nat. Conf., Renaissance Soc. Am., Am. Guild Organists, Internat. Musicological Soc., N.J. Music Tchrs. Assn. (pres. 1961-63), Phi Kappa Lambda. Home: 512 S Woodbury Rd Pitman NJ 08071-1636

CARPENTER, J. SCOTT, vocational school educator. Supr. Penta County Vocat. Sch., Perrysburg, Ohio, supr. student svcs. & admissions. Named Nat. Vocat. Tchr. of Yr., 1993, Nat. Bus. Tchr. of Yr. Office: Penta County Voc Sch 30095 Oregon Rd Perrysburg OH 43551-4533

CARPENTER, JAMES FARLIN, consultant; b. Denver, Apr. 1, 1960; s. Charles H. and Lillian R. (Griffith) C.; m. Nancy Rhyme, Aug. 15, 1987; children: Emma, Nicholas. BA in Polit. Sci., U. Colo., 1985. Staff asst. U.S. Rep. Timothy E. Wirth, Washington, 1980-84; ops. dir. Wirth for U.S. Senate, Denver, 1985-86; assoc., cons. Nat. Strategies, Washington, 1987-88; dep. state dir. U.S. Senator Timothy Wirth, Denver, 1988-93; cons. Pub. Decisions, Denver, 1993-94; press sec. to gov. State of Colo., Denver, 1995-99; dir. Gonzales Consulting Svcs. Inc., 1999—. Active Dem. Party, Denver, 1978—; mem. 18th jud. dist. nominating com. Mem. Pub. Rels. Soc. Am., Denver Athletic Club. Avocations: hiking, teaching, home remodeling.

CARPENTER, JANET SHARKEY, nursing researcher; b. Detroit, Aug. 21, 1966; d. William Francis and Bibiana Eulalia (Leone) Sharkey; m. John Willard Carpenter III, June 30, 1990. BSN, Oakland U., 1988; MSN in Nursing, U. Ky., 1992, PhD in Nursing, 1996. Cert. Advanced Oncology Nurse, Oncology Nursing Soc. Staff nurse Harper Hosp., Detroit, 1988-90; clin. mgr., staff nurse St. Joseph Hosp., Lexington, Ky., 1990-94; rsch. and tchg. asst. U. Ky., Lexington, 1992-96, postdoctoral rsch. fellow, 1996-98; asst. prof. Vanderbilt U. Sch. Nursing, 1998—. Contbr. articles to profl. jours. Bd. dirs. Ky. divsn. Am. Cancer Soc., 1994-98. Recipient New Investigator award Oncology Nursing Soc., 1999. Mem. Oncology Nursing Soc. (Svc. award Bluegrass chpt. 1994, 95, 97), Soc. Behavioral Medicine, Florence Nightingale Soc., So. Nursing Rsch. Soc., Sigma Theta Tau. Office: Rm 508 Godchaux Hall 21st Ave South Nashville TN 37240

CARPENTER, JOHN HOWARD, director, screenwriter; b. Carthage, N.Y., Jan. 16, 1948; s. Howard Ralph and Milton Jean (Carter) C; m. Sandra Ann King, Dec. 1, 1990; 1 child, John Cody. Student, U. So. Calif., 1972. Co-writer, editor, composer: (short film) The Resurrection of Bronco Billy, 1970 (Academy award best live action short subject 1970); writer, prodr., dir., composer: (films) Dark Star, 1974; writer, dir., composer: (films) Assault on Precinct 13, 1976, Halloween, 1978, The Fog, 1980, Escape from New York, 1981, Prince of Darkness, 1987, They Live, 1988; writer, prodr., composer: (films) Halloween II, 1981; prodr., composer: (films) Halloween III: Season of the Witch, 1982; dir.: (films) The Thing, 1982, Starman, 1984, Memoirs of an Invisible Man, 1992, In the Mouth of Madness, 1994, Escape from L.A., 1996, Vampires, 1998; (TV movies) Elvis, 1979; dir., composer: (films) Christine, 1983, Big Trouble in Little China, 1986; exec. prodr.: (films) The Philadelphia Experiment, 1984, (TV movies) John Carpenter Presents Body Bags, 1993; writer: (films) The Eyes of Laura Mars, 1978, Black Moon Rising, 1986, (TV movies) Zuma Beach, 1978, Better Late Than Never, 1979, El Diablo, 1990, Blood River, 1991; writer, dir.: (TV movies) Someone's Watching Me!, 1978; composer: (films) Halloween V: The Revenge of Michael Myers, 1989. Mem. ASCAP, Dirs. Guild Am. West, Writers Guild Am. West. Avocations: music, helicopter piloting. Office: ICM 8942 Wilshire Blvd Beverly Hills CA 90211-1934*

CARPENTER, JOHN MARLAND, engineer, physicist; b. Williamsport, Pa., June 20, 1935; s. John Hiram and Ruth Edith (Johnson) C.; children: John Marland, Kathryn Ann, Susan Marie, Janet Elaine; m. Rhonda DeCardy, 1991. BS in Engring. Sci, Pa. State U., 1957; MS in Nuclear Engring, U. Mich., 1958, PhD, 1963. Fellow Oak Ridge Inst. Nuclear Studies, 1957-60; postdoctoral fellow Inst. Sci. and Tech., U. Mich., 1963-64, mem. faculty univ., 1964-75, prof. nuclear engring., 1973-75; vis. scientist nuclear tech. br. Phillips Petroleum Co., 1965; solid state sci. div. Argonne (Ill.) Nat. Lab., 1971-72, 73; physics div. Los Alamos Sci. Lab., 1973; sr. physicist solid state sci. div., mgr. intense pulsed neutron source project Argonne Nat. Lab., 1975-77, program dir., 1977-78, tech. dir., 1978—; vis. scientist Japanese Lab. for High Energy Physics, 1982, 93; mem. U.S. del. to USSR on fundamental properties of matter, 1977; mem. indsl. and profl. adv. coun. Coll. Engring. Pa. State U., 1984-87; mem. nat. steering com. for Advanced Neutron Source, 1986-95, mem. exec. com.; mem. grad. faculty Iowa State U., 1988-93; mem. internat. sci. coun. AUSTRON, Austria, 1993—; co-founder Internat. Collaboration on Advanced Neutron Sources, 1977; mem. external rev. com. Accelerator Prodn. Tritium Project Los Alamos Nat. Lab., 1995-98; mem. internat. adv. com. Scientific Coun. on Condensed Matter Investigations with Neutrons, Russian Ministry of Sci. and Tech., 1996—; mem. steering com. spallation neutron source Oak Ridge Nat. Lab., 1996-98, sci. adv. com. for spallation neutron source, 1998—; vis. scientist Rutherford Appleton Lab., 1997—; mem. exec. com., sr. sci. advisor SNS, 1998—. Author: (with Motoharu Kimura) Living with Nuclei, 1993, editor. Presdl. appointee vis. com. dept. nuclear engring. MIT, 1989-95. Recipient Disting. Service award U. Mich. Dept. Nuclear Engring., 1967, L.J. Hamilton Disting. Alumnus award, 1977, Disting. Performance award for work at Argonne Nat. Lab. U. Chgo., 1982, Ilja M. Frank prize Joint Inst. for Nuclear Physics, 1998. Fellow Condensed Matter Physics Divsn, Am. Phys. Soc.; mem. Am. Nuclear Soc. (sect. chmn. 1974-75), Neutron Scattering Soc. Am. (mem. subcom. on pulsed spallation sources 1993—, mem. pulsed source steering com.). Patentee nuclear instrumentation, neutron scattering, time dependent neutron thermalization, pulsed spallation neutron sources, neutron scattering instrumentation, structure and dynamcs of amorphous solids. Office: Argonne Nat Lab Intense Pulsed Neutron Source Argonne IL 60439

CARPENTER, JOT DAVID, landscape architect, educator; b. San Francisco, Mar. 19, 1938; s. Jot Thomas and Gretchen Marie (Johnston) C.; m. Claire Marie Dunn, Aug. 8, 1962; children: Jot David, Sean Michael, Kevin Patrick. B.L.A., U. Ga., 1960; M.L.A., Harvard U., 1962. Registered landscape architect, N.Y., Ohio. Landscape architect T.J. Wirth Assocs., Billings, Mont., 1965-68; asst. prof. dept. hort. Cornell U., Ithaca, N.Y., 1968-72; assoc. prof., chmn. dept. landscape architecture Ohio State U., Columbus, 1972-76, chmn. dept. landscape architecture, 1976-87, prof., 1987—; vis. scholar Kyoto U., Japan, 1985, Chongqing Inst. Architecture and Engring., People's Republic of China, 1984, 87; dir. Landscape Arch. Found., Washington, 1977-87, v.p., 1981, sec., 1982-83; mem. Ohio Bd. Landscape Arch. Examiners, 1973-76, CLARB Uniform Nat. Examination Com., Syracuse, N.Y., 1975-77. Author: Landscape Construction Workbook, 1975; editor: Handbook of Landscape Architectural Construction, 1976; editl. adv. bd. Landscape Planning, 1978-85; chmn. editl. adv. com. Landscape Architecture Mag., 1984-87, 93-96. Bd. dirs. Columbus Conv. & Visitors Bur., 1977-92; mem. Planning Comm., Upper Arlington, Ohio, 1978-82, Ohio Land Use Planning Task Force, 1974, Ohio Motorists Svcs. Signing Adv. Bd., 1989-93. 1st lt. USAF, 1962-65. Fellow Am. Soc. Landscape Architects (treas. 1973-74, v.p. 1976-78, pres. 1978-79, Pres.'s medal 1982, Ohio chpt. medal 1982); mem. Coun. of Educators in Landscape Architecture, Internat. Fedn. Landscape Architects, Phi Kappa Phi, Sigma Lambda Alpha. Roman Catholic. Home: 1801 Elmwood Ave Columbus OH 43212-1111 Office: Ohio State-Knowlton Sch. Architecture Dept Landscape Architecture 190 W 17th Ave Columbus OH 43210-1320

CARPENTER, KENNETH JOHN, nutrition educator; b. London, May 17, 1923; came to U.S., 1977; s. James Frederick and Dorothy (George) C.; m. Daphne Holmes, June 22, 1944 (dec. 1974); 1 child, Roger Hugh; m. Antonina Pecoraro, June 18, 1977. BA, U. Cambridge, Eng., 1944, PhD, 1948, ScD, 1974. Mem. sci. staff Rowett Inst., Aberdeen, Scotland, 1948-56; lectr., then reader in nutrition U. Cambridge, 1956-77; prof. nutrition U. Calif., Berkeley, 1977-91. Author: History of Scurvy and Vitamin C, 1986, Protein and Energy, 1994, Beriberi, WhiteRice and Vitamin B, 1999; editor: Pellagra, 1982. Kellogg fellow Harvard U., 1955-56, Commonwealth fellow Cen. Food Tech. Rsch. Inst., Mysore, India, 1961, fellow Sidney Sussex Coll., Cambridge, U.K., 1961-77. Fellow Am. Inst. Nutrition (Atwater medal 1993, Hatch medal 1993); mem. History of Sci. Soc. Avocations: art history, gardening. Home: 6201 Rockwell St Oakland CA 94618-1350 Office: U Calif Dept Nutritional Sci Berkeley CA 94720-3104

CARPENTER, KENNETH RUSSELL, international trading executive; b. Chgo., May 22, 1955; s. Kenneth and Margaret (Lucas) C.; 1 child, Matthew. AS in Aviation, Prairie State Coll., Chicago Heights, Ill., 1979. Respiratory therapist Harvey, Ill., 1980-83; dir., owner, ptnr. Pulmonary Therapy Inc., Harvey, 1983-91; v.p. Home Air Joliet Ltd., Harvey, 1984—; dir., owner Air Systems Internat. Export/Import Med. Equipment, Chicago Heights, 1981—, Air Systems, Ft. Lauderdale, 1991—, Home Ortho Ltd., Harvey, 1985—; pres., CEO Profl. Yacht Svcs., Inc., Chicago Heights, 1987-94; owner CLZ Exporting Inc., Chicago Heights, 1993-95; owner, CEO, Profl. Yacht Svcs., Chicago Heights, 1997—, Info. Plus Inc., Chicago Heights, 1997—; dir. pub. rels. Lansing (Ill.) Med. Group, 1990; dir. pulmonary rehab. Cardio-Pulmonary Assocs., Munster, Ind., 1990—, CLZ Exporting, 1992—; maj. importer/exporter of durable med. oxygen equipment worldwide, KRLC Mktg., 1996—. Pilot CAP, 1979-86. With USN, 1973-77. Mem. Am. Assn. Respiratory Therapy (cert.), Nat. Assn. Med. Equipment Suppliers, Ill. Assn. of Med. Equipment Suppliers, Am. Biog. Inst., Steger C. of C., Ill. C. of C. Avocations: flying, boating, computer programming. Home and Office: 23030 Miller Rd Steger IL 60475

CARPENTER, LUCAS ADAMS, III, English educator, writer; b. Elberton, Ga., Apr. 23, 1947; s. Lucas Adams Jr. and Maria (Wasilenkov) C.; m. Judith Leidner, Sept. 3, 1972; 1 child, Meredith. BS in English, Coll. of Charleston, 1968; MA in English, U. N.C., 1974; PhD in English, SUNY, Stony Brook, 1982. Math tchr. Charleston (S.C.) County Schs., 1972-74; tchg. asst. SUNY, Stony Brook, 1974-79; asst. prof. English Suffolk C.C., Riverhead, N.Y., 1979-83, assoc. prof. English, 1983-85, asst. to pres., 1984-85; assoc. prof. English Emory U., Oxford (Ga.) Coll., 1985-92, prof. English, 1992—. Author: John Gould Fletcher and Southern Modernism, 1990, A Year for the Spider, 1973; contbr. poems, stories, articles, and revs. to prof. jours. Sgt., U.S. Army, 1965-68, Vietnam. Recipient Fulbright fellowship, Belgium, 1999—. Avocation: golf. Office: Emory U Oxford Coll Hamill St Oxford GA 30267

CARPENTER, MARY CHAPIN, singer, songwriter; b. Princeton, N.J., 1958; d. Chapin and Mary Bowie. BA, Brown U., 1981, D (hon.), 1996. Owner GETAREALJOB Music and Why Walk Music. Albums: Hometown Girl, 1987, State of the Heart, 1989, Shooting Straight in the Dark, 1990, Come On Come On, 1992, Stones in the Road, 1994, A Place in the World, 1996, Party Doll and Other Favorites, 1999; recs. on CBS, 1987—. Grammy recipient for Best Female Country Vocal Performance for four consecutive years, 1992, 93, 94, 95, Country Album of the Yr., "Stones in the Road", 1995; named Top Female Vocalist by Country Music Assn., 1992, 93, Acad. of Country Music Awards Top New Female Vocalist, 1990, Top Female Vocalist, 1993. Mem. ASCAP. Office: Borman Entertainment 2d Fl 1303 16th Ave S Nashville TN 37212-2923*

CARPENTER, MARY LAURE, hospital administrator; b. South Bend, Ind., Oct. 17, 1953; d. Daniel Pierre and Elizabeth Ann (Arigan) Laure; m. Gregory John Ingrassia, Oct. 26, 1974 (div. 1981); m. David James Carpenter, Dec. 30, 1983 (div. 1995). Exch. student, France, 1970; student, U. Mo., St. Louis, 1972-74; BA, DePaul U., Chgo., 1988. With Christian Hosp. N.E., St. Louis, 1974-78; patient account mgr. Faith Hosp., Creve Coeur, Mo., 1978-81; telephone collector Tri-County Accounts Bur., Wheaton, Ill., 1981; Medicaid supr. Ingalls Meml. Hosp., Harvey, Ill., 1981-82; owner Medicare Claims Svc., Berkeley, Ill., 1982-84; ops. mgr. Superior Med. Supply, Elmhurst, Ill., 1984-85; bus. mgr. Forest Health Sys.-Forest Hosp., Des Plaines, Ill., 1985-86; asst. adminstr. Vencor/Sycamore (Ill.) Hosp., 1986-89; patient accounts mgr. Linden Oaks Hosp., Naperville, Ill., 1989-91; bus. office mgr. Vencor Hosp. Chgo., Northlake, Ill., 1991-95; pres. Vision Health, Inc., St. Charles, Ill., 1995-96, health care fin. cons., 1996—; lectr. in field. Mem. Am. Guild Patient Acctg. Mgrs. (v.p. 1979-80, Pres.'s award, 1980, Journalism award 1979), Health Care Fin. Mgmt. Assn., Midwest Hosp. Credit Mgr. Assn. (bd. dirs. 1976-79). Avocations: needlework, woodworking, furniture restoration, piano. Office: Vision Health Inc PO Box 828 Saint Charles IL 60174-0828

CARPENTER, MICHAEL ALAN, financial services executive; b. London, Mar. 24, 1947; came to U.S., 1971; s. Walter and Kathleen Mary C.; m. Mary Aughton, Mar. 1, 1975; children—Nicholas James, Abigail Lee. B.Sc. with joint honors, U. Nottingham, Eng., 1968; M.B.A., Harvard U., 1973. Bus. analyst Mond div. Imperial Chem. Industries, Runcorn, Eng., 1968-71; cons., mgr. Boston Cons. Group, 1973-78, v.p., 1978-83; v.p. Gen. Electric Co., Fairfield, Conn., 1983-86; exec. v.p. Gen. Electric Credit Corp., Stamford, Conn., from 1986; also exec. v.p. GE Financial Services Inc.; joined Kidder Peabody & Co. Inc., 1989, chmn., pres., CEO, 1990-94; head life and annuity bus. Travelers Ins. Co., Hartford, 1994—; also exec. v.p. Travelers Group, Hartford, 1994—, vice chmn., chmn., CEO, pres. life and annuity; formerly chmn. Gen. Electric Venture Capital Corp. Baker scholar Harvard Bus. Sch., 1973. Office: CitiGroup 388 Greenwich St New York NY 10013*

CARPENTER, MICHAEL H., lawyer; b. Huntington, W.Va., Mar. 3, 1953. BA, Ohio State U., 1974, JD, 1977. Bar: Ohio 1977. Former ptnr. Jones, Day, Reavis & Pogue, Columbus, Ohio; ptnr. Zeiger & Carpenter, Columbus, 1994—. Mem. Phi Beta Kappa, Order of Coif. Office: Zeiger & Carpenter 1600 Huntington Ctr 41 S High St Columbus OH 43215-6101*

CARPENTER, MYRON ARTHUR, manufacturing company executive; b. Jacksonville, Ill., Nov. 12, 1938; s. Paul Floyd and Margaret Esther (Lewis) C.; m. JoAnn Fisher, June 22, 1963. BA in Acctg, U. Ill., 1960. C.P.A., Mo. Staff acct. Arthur Young & Co., St. Louis, 1960-67; audit mgr. Arthur Young & Co., 1967-71; controller Bank Bldg. & Equipment Corp., St. Louis, 1972-78; v.p., treas. Bank Bldg. & Equipment Corp. Am., St. Louis, 1978-82, v.p. fin., treas., 1982-83; sr. v.p., chief fin. officer Bank Bldg. & Equipment Corp. Am., 1983-90; v.p. fin., adminstrn. Gemco, Inc., Collinsville, Ill., 1991—. Author: (with Neal W. Beckman) Purchasing for Profit, 1979. Served with U.S. Army, 1961. Mem. AICPA, Mo. Soc. CPAs, Delta Phi.

CARPENTER, NOBLE OLDS, banker; b. Cleve., May 8, 1929; s. John W. and Maribel (Olds) C.; m. Ann Lindemann, Oct. 13, 1956 (dec. Aug. 1987); children: John L., Noble Olds, Robert W.; m. Sharon D. D'Atri, Aug. 11, 1990. A.B. cum laude, Princeton, 1951. Cert. comml. lender. Comml. Lending div. Am. Bankers Assn. Vice pres. Central Nat. Bank, Cleve., 1951-65; chmn., pres., chief exec. officer, dir. Central Trust Co. of Northeastern Ohio, N.A., Canton, 1965-91; dir. Bank One, Akron, Ohio, 1991-97; mem. Internat. Exec. Svc. Corps.; dir. Mountain Lake Tree & Land Co., Ltd. Dep. sheriff Stark County; bd. dirs. Aultman Hosp. Devel. Found., Blue Coats, Inc., Greater Canton Partnership; trustee State Troopers of Ohio. Named outstanding Young Man of Year Jr. C. of C., 1965. Mem. Cleve. Pres. Orgn., Brookside Country Club. Home: 3423 Croydon Dr NW Canton OH 44718-3221 Office: 1 Central Plz S Canton OH 44702

CARPENTER, NORMAN ROBLEE, retired lawyer; b. Cambridge, Mass., Aug. 26, 1932; s. Norman Roblee and Mary P. (Hannigan) C.; children: Kevin D., Cynthia L., Kathryn Carpenter Nelson. BA, Dartmouth Coll., 1953; JD, U. Mich., 1960. Bar: Minn. 1960. Assoc. Faegre & Benson, Mpls., 1960-67, ptnr., 1969-98; dep. atty. gen. State of Minn., St. Paul, 1967-69; dir. Walter Judd Found., Mpls., 1963-70. Contbr. articles to profl. jours., short stories and poetry to lit. mags. Bd. regents Augsburg Coll., Mpls., 1970-82; chmn. bd. YMCA Camp Warren, Mpls., 1978-80, Charter Commn., City of St. Louis Park, Minn., 1965-67; trustee Plymouth Congl. Ch., Mpls., 1978-82; bd. dirs. Citizens League, Mpls., 1970-74, The Loft, 1994—; mem. Hennepin County Adv. Commn. on Chem. Dependency, 1977-79; vol. United Way, 1983-92. Capt. USMC, 1953-55. Mem. ABA, Minn. Bar Assn., Hennepin County Bar Assn., Dartmouth Coll. Alumni Coun., Minikahda Club. Republican. Home: 3430 List Pl Apt 906 Minneapolis MN 55416-4578 *All I ask in life is my share of the close ones.*

CARPENTER, PATRICIA, music educator; b. Del Rosa, Calif., Jan. 21, 1923; d. Daniel James and Dorothy Helen (Clock) C. BA cum laude, UCLA, 1944; PhD, Columbia U., 1971; student composition and theory with, Arnold Schoenberg, 1942-49; student piano with, Ethel Leginska, 1943-48; student conducting with, Leon Barzin, 1949-52. Instr. Barnard Coll., N.Y.C., 1964-70; asst. prof. Barnard Coll., 1970-78, assoc. prof., 1978-79, prof. music, 1979-89, prof. emerita, 1989—; chmn. undergrad. theory, 1968-69, chmn. grad. theory, 1969—, chmn. dept. music, 1974—. Condr. San Bernardino (Calif.) Cmty. Orch. and Chorus, 1947-48; author: The Janus-Aspect of Fugue: An Essay in the Phenomenology of Musical Form, 1971, Arnold Schoenberg: The Musical Idea, 1995, also articles. Alice M. Ditson fellow Columbia U., 1955-56; Ingram Merrill Found. fellow in musicology, 1967-68. Mem. Am. Musicol. Soc., Coll. Music Soc., Am. Soc. Aesthetics (sec. Eastern div. 1966-67), Soc. Music Theory (exec. bd. 1980—, v.p. 1991—). Home: 260 Colonel Green Rd Yorktown Hts NY 10598-6022 Office: Barnard Coll Music Dept New York NY 10027

CARPENTER, PATRICIA LYNN, author; b. Washington Court House, Ohio, Oct. 15, 1940; d. William Daniel Lower and Lorena Ellen (Butcher) Harding; m. Homer Pack, Dec. 24, 1959 (div. Oct. 1973); children: Lorena Ann Giuricich, Steven Riley, Gregory Allen; m. Jeffrey David Carpenter, May 10, 1980; stepchildren: Jeffrey David II, Jennifer Michelle, Janett

Marie. Student, Ohio State U., 1958-59. Sunday sch. tchr. various chs., Columbus, Ohio, 1968—; clk. typist various jobs, Columbus, 1968-77; clk. typist State of Ohio, Columbus, 1977-79, clerical specialist, 1979-85; treas. Westview Alliance Ch., Columbus, 1981-82; bible study tchr. Inner City Ministries, Columbus, 1990-92. Author: A Collection of Spiritual Poems and Thoughts, 1995, Poems and Thoughts for the Soul, 1997, Poems and Blessings to Enrich Your Life, 1998, Poems and Thoughts to Stay True to the Savior--No Matter What, 1998, 'Love' Poems and Thoughts from the Father's Heart, 1998, Poems and Thoughts On: Being Used by God!, 1999. Named Mother of the Yr. Hilltop Ch. of God, 1995. Republican.

CARPENTER, PAUL LYNN, cardiologist; b. Fairmont, Minn., Jan. 14, 1946; s. Orlo Earnest and Mae Elizabeth (Poulson) C.; m. Rhoda Ann Jordeth, Mar. 15, 1969); children: Amy Elizabeth, Emily Anne, Abigail Lynn. BSChE, U. Minn., 1968, MD, 1974. Diplomate Am. Bd. Internal Medicine. Chem. engr. 3M Co., St. Paul, 1968-69, USPHS, Cin., 1970-71; extern So. Bapt. Hosp., Ailoun, Jordan, 1975; resident in internal medicine Northwestern Hosp. U. Minn., Mpls., 1975-78, fellow in cardiology, 1978-80; invasive cardiologist Ctrl. Plains Clinic, Sioux Falls, S.D., 1980-81, North Ctrl. Heart, Ltd., Sioux Falls, 1981—; asst. clin. prof. dept. medicine U. S.D. Sch. Medicine, Sioux Falls, 1982-90, assoc. clin. prof. dept. medicine, 1990-98; clin. prof. medicine U. S.D. Sch. Medicine, 1998—; chmn. cardiac care com. Mckennan Hosp., Sioux Falls, 1984-98, co-dir. cardiac cath lab., 1988-99, dir. cardiac rehab., 1990-99; pres. North Ctrl. Heart, Ltd., 1984-85. Girls basketball coach YMCA, Sioux Falls, 1987-96; girls coach Sioux Falls Soccer Assn., 1991-94, 98—; Sunday sch. tchr. Ctrl. Bapt. Ch., Sioux Falls, 1987-94. Fellow Am. Coll. Cardiology (gov. S.D. 1987-90), Am. Coll. Chest Physicians; mem. ACP, AMA, S.D. State Med. Assn., Christian Med. Soc. (life), Alpha Omega Alpha, Tau Beta Pi. Avocations: Civil war and native American history, travel, sports, fishing. Office: No Ctrl Heart Ltd 911 E 20th St Sioux Falls SD 57105-1042

CARPENTER, PHYLLIS JEAN, medical/surgical nurse; b. Phila., Aug. 3, 1958; d. George Anthony Sr. and Phyllis Janet (Adamson) K. BA in Spanish, Portuguese, Temple U., 1980; BSN, Thomas Jefferson U., 1988. Staff nurse Thomas Jefferson U. Hosp., Phila., 1988-96, clin. staff nurse III, charge nurse, clin. coord. nurse, 1996—. Mem. Del. Valley Nursing Assn. for Healthcare Quality.

CARPENTER, RICHARD NORRIS, lawyer; b. Cortland, N.Y., Feb. 14, 1937; s. Robert P. and Sylvia (Norris) C.; m. Elizabeth Bigbee, Aug. 1961 (div. June 1975); 1 child, Andrew Norris; m. Leslie Nordby, July, 1991. BA magna cum laude, Syracuse U., 1958; LLB, Yale U., 1962. Bar: N.Y. 1962, N.Mex. 1963, U.S. Dist. Ct. (no. dist.) N.Y., U.S. Dist. Ct. N.Mex., U.S. Ct. Appeals (D.C. and 10th cirs.), U.S. Supreme Ct. Assoc. Breed, Abbott & Morgan, N.Y.C., 1962-63, Bigbee Law Firm, Santa Fe, 1963-78; ptnr. Carpenter Law Firm, Santa Fe, 1978-97, Carpenter & Nixon L.L.P., Santa Fe, 1997—; spl. asst. atty. gen., State of N.Mex., 1963-74, 90-96; sec. Bokum Corp., Miami, Fla., 1969-70. Mem. adv. bd. Interstate Mining Compact, N.Mex., 1981-88; elder 1st Presbyn. Ch., Santa Fe, 1978-80, 86-89, trustee, 1975-77, pres., 1977; bd. dirs. Santa Fe Community Coun., 1965-67, St. Vincent Hosp. Found., Santa Fe, 1980-84; trustee Santa Fe Prep. Sch., 1981-84, pres., 1982-84; trustee St. Vincent Hosp., 1980-86, 87—, chmn. 1985-86, 90-93, 98—; bd. dirs. Santa Fe YMCA, 1964-69, pres., 1969; trustee Santa Fe Prep. Permanent Endowment Fund., 1987-90. Rotary Found. fellow, Panjab U., Pakistan, 1959-60. Mem. ABA, N.Mex. Bar Assn., 1st Jud. Bar Assn., N.Y. State Bar Assn., The Best Lawyers of Am., Phi Beta Kappa, Pi Sigma Alpha, Phi Beta Phi. Home: 1048 Bishops Lodge Rd Santa Fe NM 87501-1009 Office: PO Box 1837 Santa Fe NM 87504-1837

CARPENTER, ROXANNE SUE, realtor; b. Lebanon, Pa., Mar. 16, 1952; d. John Harold and Viola Helen (Miller) Ristenbatt; m. Richard Lee Carpenter, Jan. 30, 1971 (div. May 1989); children: Keith Scott, Jeffrey Alan. Lic. real estate salesperson, Pa. Computer operator Good Samaritan Hosp., Lebanon, 1969-82; legal sec. Allen H. Krause, Esquire, Lebanon, 1982; personal sec. Judge John Walter, Lebanon County Courthouse, Lebanon, 1983-87; realtor Suburban Realty, Annville, Pa., 1986-95, Re/Max of Lebanon County, Cleona, Pa., 1995—. Deaconess, mem. consistory St. Mark's United Ch. of Christ, Lebanon, 1990-93; solicitor United Way Lebanon County, 1985-92; pres. Lebanon Women of Today, 1986-87, chmn. Today's Woman, 1985, 86; mem. Lebanon County Dem. Com., 1988—; mem. adv. bd. Big Bros. and Big Sisters, sec.-treas., 1984-86; project chmn. Muscular Dystrophy Lebanon County, 1982-86. Recipient various awards, including Outstanding Officer of Yr. award Lebanon Women of Today, 1987, Pa. Assn. Realtors Excellence Club award, 1988, 89, 90, Pa. Assn. Realtors Excellence Club "Gold" award, 1990. Mem. Nat. Assn. Realtors, Pa. Assn. Realtors (excellence club life mem. 1990, chmn. spl. events com. 1998), Lebanon County Bd. Realtors (chmn. spl. events com.), RE/MAX of Lebanon County Exec. Club, 1996, RE/MAX of Lebanon County 100% Club, 1997, 98, Lebanon County Assn. of Realtors (1997, 98 Winners Cir. award), Lebanon County Builders Assn., Lebanon Jaycee Women (chmn. Serena Lodge auction 1985), Pres. Club, Lebanon Jaycettes (v.p. 1982, pres. 1984, project chmn. 1985, 86, Jaycette of Yr. 1983, Pres. of Yr. 1984). Democrat. Avocations: horticulture, crocheting and stitchery. Home: 670 Prescott Dr Lebanon PA 17046-8710 Office: Re Max of Lebanon County 209 W Penn Ave Cleona PA 17042-3230

CARPENTER, SHARON QUIGLEY, municipal official. Tchr. history St. Louis Pub Schs.; elected recorder of deeds City of St. Louis, 1980—; mem. Mo. Reapportionment Commn. Dem. Committeewoman 23rd ward St. Louis, 1964—; chair Dem. Ctrl. Com. St. Louis; founding mem, 1st chair, bd. dirs. Maria Droste Residence, St. Louis; mem. Mo. Commn. on Intergovernmental Rels, 1996—, adv. bd. Cath. Youth Coun., St. Louis., 1997—. Mem. Recorders' Assn. Mo. (past pres.). Office: City of St Louis Office Recorder of Deeds Market & Tucker Aves Rm 126 Saint Louis MO 63103*

CARPENTER, SHEILA H., critical care and medical/surgical nurse; b. Lava Hot Springs, Idaho, July 14, 1937; d. William Boland and Esther Edsall (Hunt) Hunt; m. Bill L. Carpenter, Aug. 8, 1987: children: Beth Ann Huser Bender, Roger Dean Huser II, Amy Jo Huser Gaines, James Frank Huser, Ronald Edward Huser, William Thomas Huser. Student, Sul Ross Coll., Alpine, Tex., 1955-56; Assoc. degree, N.Mex. State U., Carlsbad, 1985, postgrad. RN, N.Mex., Colo. Office nurse Drs. McCollum and Smith, Carlsbad, 1985-86; asst. coord. med. floor Guadalupe Med. Ctr., Carlsbad, 1986—, staff nurse ICU, cardiac rehab. and pacemaker clinic, CCU; with hospice and home health, Carlsbad, 1996-97; coord. quality asurance and infection control Landrum Homes, Inc., Carlsbad, 1997-99; asst. to cardiologist with Thalium Scans. Active in ch. activities, Chpt. A of PEO. Mem. ACLS (cert.), Swan-Ganz (cert.). Home: 1409 N Country Club Cir Carlsbad NM 88220-4115

CARPENTER, SHEILA JANE, lawyer; b. Kyoto, Japan, Oct. 16, 1950; d. Chester Elwin and Betty (Boulger) C.; m. William Joseph McCarthy, May 26, 1973; 1 child, Diana Elizabeth. BA, Purdue U., 1972; JD, Yale U., 1975. Bar: Md. 1975, U.S. Dist. Ct. Md. 1976, D.C. 1977, U.S. Dist. Ct. D.C. 1978, U.S. Supreme Ct. 1980, U.S. Dist. Ct. (no. dist.) Ohio 1980, U.S. Claims Ct. 1982, U.S. Ct. Appeals (D.C. cir.) 1983, U.S. Ct. Appeals (4th and Fed. cirs.) 1984. Assoc. Weinberg & Green, Balt., 1975-77; assoc. Sutherland, Asbill & Brennan, Washington, 1977-82, ptnr., 1982-96; ptnr. Jorden Burt Boros Cicchetti Berenson & Johnson LLP, Washington, 1996—; pub. svc. com. Sutherland, Asbill & Brennan, 1990-94, chair, 1990-92, litigation group Washington office, 1991-93. Contbr. articles to profl. jours. Mem. ABA (vice chmn. excess surplus lines and reins. com. TIPS sect. 1992-94, chair elect 1994-95, chair 1995-96, vice chair pub. regulation ins. commn. TIPS sect. 1995—), Md. Bar Assn., Phi Beta Kappa. Office: Jorden Burt Boros Et Al Ste 400E 1025 Thomas Jefferson St NW Washington DC 20007-0805

CARPENTER, SHIRLEY M. (SAM), career officer. BA, U. Va., 1960; student, Squadron Officer Sch., 1967; disting. grad., Air Command and Staff Coll., 1976; MS, Troy State U., 1976; student, Nat. War Coll., 1982. Commd. 2d lt. USAF, 1960, advanced through grades to maj. gen., 1990; C-135B aircraft comdr., C-141A flight examiner 44th Air Transport Squadron, Travis AFB, Calif., 1962-68; pilot Trans World Airlines, 1968-69; wing standardization officer 514th Mil. Airlift Wing, McGuire AFB, N.J., 1969-75; ops. officer 702d Mil. Airlift Squadron, McGuire AFB, 1976-79, comdr., 1979-81; vice comdr. 514th Mil. Airlift Wing, McGuire AFB, 1981; res. adviser to comdr. in chief Mil. Airlift Command, Scott AFB, Ill., 1982-85; dep. chief USAF Res., Washington, 1985-89; mobilization asst. to comdr. Air Mobility Command, Scott AFB, 1989-95; mil. exec., mil. adviser to chmn. Res. Forces Policy Bd., Washington, 1995—. Contbr. articles to profl. jours. Decorated D.S.M., Legion of Merit, Air medal, Rep. Vietnam Gallantry Cross with Palm, Rep. Vietnam Campaign Medal. Recipient Award for excellence in rsch. and writing Air Force Assn., 1982. Office: Res Forces Policy Bd 7300 Defense Pentagon Washington DC 20301-7300

CARPENTER, STANLEY HAMMACK, retired military aviation organization executive; b. Hattiesburg, Miss., Jan. 21, 1926; s. Henry Herbert and Esther Mae (Cooper) C.; m. Catherine Jane Sadler, Nov. 29, 1946; children: Stanley Hammack, Louise N., Catherine D., Mary C. BS, Tulane U., 1946; U.S. Naval Postgrad. Sch., 1956; Aero. Engr., Calif. Inst. Tech., 1957; MS, U. So. Calif., 1982; cert. safety profl.; Enlisted U.S. Navy, 1944. Commd. 2d lt. U.S. Marine Corps, 1946, advanced through grades to col., 1968; comdg. officer Marine Detachment USS Breckinridge (AP-176), 1948-49; Korean combat tours in amphibian tractors, 1950-51, Skyraider and Bird Dog pilot, 1953-54; aircraft maintenance officer, Edenton, N.C., 1957-58; liaison officer Naval Weapons Center, China Lake, Calif., 1959-62; comdg. officer air base squadron Far East, 1962, A4E Squadron, 1963-65; aide to asst. sec. navy for research devel., 1965-68; Viet Nam combat tour officer in charge Chu-Lai Air Base, comdg. officer Marine Wing Support Group, 1968-69; staff officer, dir. def. research engring., 1969-71; asst. chief of staff and div. chief Marine Corps Devel. Center, Quantico, Va., 1971-74; ret., 1974; aero. engr., sr. program mgr. Unified Industries, Inc., Springfield, Va., 1975-86; exec. dir. Marine Corps Aviation Assn., 1988-93. Decorated Legion of Merit, Air medal. Mem. Marine Corps Aviation Assn., First Marine Div. Assn., Marine Corps Assn., Assn. Naval Aviation, Tailhook Assn., Marine Corps Res. Officers Assn., Ret. Officers Assn., Marine Corps League, Navy League, Marine Corps Heritage Found., Naval Aviation Mus. Found., Marine Corps Univ. Found., Marine Corps Scholarship Found., U.S. Naval Inst., Chosin Few, Aircraft Owners and Pilots Assn., Tulane U. Alumni Assn., Calif. Inst. Tech. Alumni Assn., U. So. Calif. Alumni Assn., Order of Daedalians, Phi Beta Kappa, Omicron Delta Kappa, Kappa Sigma, Kappa Delta Phi. Roman Catholic. Home: 8404 Bound Brook Ln Alexandria VA 22309-2136

CARPENTER, SUSAN ANN, financial planner; b. Huntington Park, Calif., Nov. 10, 1944; d. Clarence William and Lillian Mary (Reed) M.; m. Robert Ray Carpenter, Jan. 9, 1993; children: Lorrie King, Letitia Martin, Tania Radecki, Lance Brooks, Landry Carpenter, India Brooks, Shelli Carpenter. Degree, Coll. of Fin. Planning, 1991. CFP. Co-owner Jhirmack of Ctrl. L.A., 1974-82, Recur-L Systems Inc., L.A., 1979-90; fin. advisor IDS/Am. Express Fin. Advisors, Riverside, Calif., 1985—. Mem. Internat. Assn. of Fin. Planners, Soroptimist Internat. of Running Springs, Soroptimist Internat. of the Foothills, Inc (pres., v.p., rec. sec., treas., Soroptimist of Yr. 1990). Avocations: hiking, puzzels. Home: PO Box 2285 Running Springs CA 92382-2285 Office: Am Express Fin Advisors 5055 Canyon Crest Dr Riverside CA 92507-6015

CARPENTER, TED GALEN, political scientist; b. Ladysmith, Wis., Oct. 1, 1947; s. Jay Dee and Magdalene (Stuner) C.; m. Barbara Lynette Bethke, May 11, 1968; children: Lara, Amber, Brian. BA, U. Wis., Milw., 1970, MA in History, 1971; PhD in History, U. Tex., 1980. Rsch. assoc. ideas and action project U. Tex., Austin, 1980-83; fgn. policy analyst Cato Inst., Washington, 1985-87, dir. foreign policy studies, 1987-95, v.p. def. and fgn. policy studies, 1996—; cons. Profl. Mgmt. Resources, Austin, Tex., 1983-84. Author: A Search for Enemies: America's Alliances After the Cold War, 1992, Beyond NATO; Staying Out of Europe's Wars, 1994, The Captive Press; Foreign Policy Crises and the First Amendment, 1995; editor: Collective Defense or Strategic Independence: Alternative Strategies for the Future, 1989, NATO at 40: Confronting a Changing World, 1990, America Entangled: The Persian Gulf Crisis and Its Consequences, 1991, The Future of NATO, 1995, Delusions of Grandeur: The United Nations and Global Intervention, 1997; co-editor: The U.S.-South Korean Alliance; Time for a Change, 1992, NATO Enlargement: Illusions and Reality, 1998; mem. editl. bd. Jour. Strategic Studies; mem. editl. adv. bd. Mediterranean Quar.; contbr. articles to profl. jours. Mem. Soc. Historians Am. Fgn. Relations, Acad. Polit. Sci. Mem. Unitarian Ch. Office: Cato Institute 1000 Massachusetts Ave NW Washington DC 20001-5400

CARPENTER, WILL DOCKERY, chemical company executive; b. Moorhead, Miss., July 13, 1930; s. Horace Aubrey and Celeste (Brian) C.; m. Hellen E. Dodd, Mar. 26, 1960; children: Celeste, Bill. BS in Agronomy, Miss. State U., 1952; MS in Plant Physiology, Purdue U., 1956, PhD in Plant Physiology, 1958; grad. exec. program in bus. adminstrn., Columbia U., 1980. Research biochemist Monsanto Co., St. Louis, 1958-60, agrl. research chemist, 1960-61, staff agrl. devel., 1961-65; mgr. market devel. Monsanto Agrl. Div., St. Louis, 1965-71; dir. product devel. Monsanto Agrl. Products Co., St. Louis, 1971-77, dir. environ. ops., 1977-80, dir. environ. mgmt./environ. policy staff, 1980-84, gen. mgr. tech., 1984-86; v.p. technology Monsanto Agrl. Co., St. Louis, 1986-90, v.p., gen. mgr. new products, 1990-92; chmn., bd. dirs. Agridyne Techs. Inc. Served to capt. U.S. Army, 1952-54, Korea. Fellow Weed Sci. Soc. Am. (treas. 1975, pres. 1980); mem. Indsl. Biotech. Assn. (bd. dirs. 1986—), Chem. Mfrs. Assn. (chmn. environ. mgmt. com. 1982-84, chmn. chem. warfare disarmament com. Washington 1985—), North Cen. Weed Control Conf. (pres. 1977, hon. mem. 1982). Office: 456 Conway Meadows Dr Chesterfield MO 63017-9625

CARPENTER, WILLIAM MORTON, English educator, writer; b. Cambridge, Mass., Oct. 31, 1940; s. James M. and Dorothy N. (Sauer) C.; m. Joanne Laventis, 1962 (div. 1987); 1 child, Matthew; m. Donna Gold; 1 child, Daniel. BA, Dartmouth Coll., 1962; PhD, U. Minn., 1967. Instr. U. Minn., Mpls., 1963-67; asst. prof. U. Chgo., 1967-72; mem. faculty dept. lit. Coll. of Atlantic, Bar Harbor, Maine, 1972—, faculty dean, 1983-89; bd. dirs. Maine Acad. Coalition, Augusta. Author: The Hours of Morning, 1981, Rain, 1986, Speaking Fire at Stones, 1992, A Keeper of Sheep, 1994. Recipient Neruda prize U. Okla., 1979, Contemporary Poetry award Assoc. Writing Program, 1981, Black Warrior Rev. prize U. Ala., 1984, Morse prize Northeastern U., 1985; NEA fellow, Venice, Italy, 1985, Inst. for Human Ecology fellow 1989—, Yaddo Ctr., fellow 1984, MacDowell Colony fellow, 1985. Office: Coll of Atlantic 105 Eden St Bar Harbor ME 04609-1105

CARPENTER-MASON, BEVERLY NADINE, health care and quality assurance nurse consultant; b. Pitts., May 23, 1933; d. Frank Carpenter and Thelma Deresa (Williams) Carpenter Smith; m. Sherman Robert Robinson Jr., Dec. 26, 1953 (div. Jan. 1959); 1 child, Keith Michael; m. David Solomon Mason Jr., Sept. 10, 1960; 1 child, Tamara Nadina. Grad. in nursing, Shadyside Hosp. Sch. Nursing, Pitts.; BS, St. Joseph's Coll., North Windham, Maine, 1979; MS, So. Ill. U., 1981; PhD, Columbia Pacific U., 1995. RN, Pa., D.C., Fla.; cert. pediatric nurse practitioner. Staff nurse med. surgery, ob-gyn neonatology and pediatrics Pa., N.Y., Wyo., Colo. and Washington, 1954-68; mgr. clinician dermatol. svcs. Malcolm Grow Med. Ctr., Camp Spring, Md., 1968-71; pediatric nurse practitioner Dept. Human Resources, Washington, 1971-73; asst. dir. nursing Glenn Dale Hosp., Md., 1973-81; nursing coord. medicaid div. Forest Haven Ctr., Laurel, Md., 1981-83, spl. asst. to supr. for med. svcs., 1983-84; spl. asst. to supt. for quality assurance Burr. Habilitation Svcs., Laurel, 1984-89; exec. asst. quality assurance coord. Mental Retardation Devel. Disabilities Adminstrn., Washington, 1989-91; also bd. dirs., 1989—; asst. treas. Am. Bd. Quality Assurance Utilization Rev. Physicians, 1988-94, chair exam. com., 1990-93; ret. Mental Retardation Devel. Disabilities Adminstrn., Washington, 1991; bd. dirs. Quality Mgmt. Audits, Inc., 1991-94; coord. quality assurance health svcs. div. UPARC, Clearwater, Fla., 1993-94; owner, prin. BCM Assocs., 1992—; cons., lectr. in field; case study editor, mem. jour. editorial bd. Am. Coll. Med. Quality, 1985—, chmn. publs. com., 1987—, asst. treas., 1988-93; mem. Am. Bd. Quality Assurance and Utilization Rev. Physicians, 1984-95; chief proctor ABQAURP exam. com., 1995-97; mem. exec. com. Am. Found. for Edn. in Healthcare Quality, 1995—; bd. dirs. Dist. V, Fla. Dept. HHS, 1997—. Author: Quality Assurance: Toward a Paradigm of Universality, 1995; contbr. articles to profl. jours. Mem., star donor ARC Blood Drive, Washington, Md., 1975-91; chair nominations com. Prince Georges Nat. Coun. Negro Women, Md., 1984-85; mem. health and human svcs. bd. Fla. Dept. Children and Families, 1997—, cons. Dist. XI, 1998; bd. dirs. Pinnellas County (Fla.) County Coun., Pinnellas County WAGES Coalition, 1999. Recipient awards Dept. Air Force and D.C. Govt., 1966-92, Della Robbia Gold medallion Am. Acad. Pediatrics, 1972, John P. Lamb Jr. Meml. Lectureship award East Tenn. State Y., 1988, Woman of Yr., 1990, 91, 92, 93, 94, 95, 96. Fellow Am. Coll. Med. Quality; mem. NAFE, Am. Assn. Mental Retardation (conf. lectr. 1988), Am. Coll. Utilization Rev. Physicians, Assn. Retarded Citizens, Healthcare Quality Inst., Top Ladies of Distinction (1st v.p. 1986-91), Internat. Platform Assn., Order Ea. Star (Achievement award Deborah chpt. 1991), Am. Bd. Quality Assurance Utilization Rev. Physicians (Chmn. of Yr. award 1992, presdl. citation, Calvin R. Openshaw Svc. award 1993), Pipers Meadow Home Owners Assn. (sec. 1993—), Soroptomist Internat. (Achievement in Healthcare award 1997), Pinellas Soroptomist (sec. 1999). Democrat. Avocations: studying languages, traveling, reading, writing, collecting antiques.

CARPER, JAMES DAVID, magazine editor; b. Rochester, Minn., Apr. 18, 1956; s. John Mark and Jane E. (Reidenbaugh) C.; m. Penny C. Bardzinski, Aug. 25, 1984. BS in Journalism, Northwestern U., 1979. New products editor Profl. Builder Mag., Chgo., 1980-82; assoc. editor Profl. Builder Mag., Des Plaines, Ill., 1982-84, mng. editor, 1984-88, exec. editor, 1988-89, editor-in-chief, 1994-97; editor-in-chief Hotels Mag., Des Plaines, 1990-94; freelance writer, magazine cons., 1997—; editor Appliance mag., Oak Brook, Ill. Co-author: Using Building Systems, 1990; author foreword to Internat. Hotel and Resort Design 2, 1992; contbr. to Funk and Wagnalls yearbooks, 1983, 84, 85. Mem. Nat. Assn. Real Estate Editors (pres. 1989), Global Hoteliers Club (founder). Avocations: travel, foreign languages, gardening, running.

CARPER, THOMAS RICHARD, governor; b. Beckley, W.Va., Jan. 23, 1947; s. Wallace Richard and Mary Jean (Patton) C.; m. Martha Stacy, Jan. 1, 1986; children: Christopher Thomas, Benjamin Michael. B.A. in Econs., Ohio State U., 1968; M.B.A., U. Del., 1975. Indsl. devel. specialist Del. div. Econ. Devel., Dover, 1975-76; state treas. State of Del., Dover, 1976-83; mem. 98th-102nd Congresses from Del., Washington, 1983-93; governor of Del., 1993—. Fund-raising chmn. Big Bros.-Big Sisters of Del., 1985, 93; hon. chair Del. Spl. Olympics, 1987—; bd. vice chair Jobs for America's Grads., 1996—. Lt. USN, 1968-73, capt. Res., 1973-91. Mem. Nat. Govs. Assn. (vice chmn. 1997-98, chmn. 1998—). Democrat. Presbyterian. Office: Office of the Governor Tatnall Bldg William Penn St Dover DE 19901

CARPER, WILLIAM BARCLAY, management educator; b. Winchester, Va., Apr. 3, 1946; s. Roy Silas and Evadnyr Joyce (Arthur) C.; m. Brenda Carol Campbell, Aug. 20, 1966 (div. Sept. 1994); children: Melissa Paige, Jonathan Barclay; m. Andrea Lynn Sikes, Mar. 15, 1997; 1 stepson, Christopher Paul Sikes. BA, U. Va., 1968; MBA, Coll. William & Mary, 1976; PhD, Va. Poly. Inst. and State U., 1979. Instr. Va. Poly. Inst. and State U., Blacksburg, 1976-79; asst. prof. Auburn (Ala.) U., 1979-81, George Mason U., Fairfax, Va., 1981-87; assoc. prof. mgmt. Ga. So. U., Statesboro, 1987-92, prof., 1992-95, dept. head., 1987-90, assoc. dean., 1989-95; dir. ctr. for mgmt. devel., 1993-94; dean Coll. U. West Fla. Coll. Bus., Pensacola, 1995—; prof. mgmt. U. West Fla., Pensacola, 1995—; dir. small bus. programs George Mason Inst., 1983-85; pres. Strategic Mgmt. Systems, Inc., Statesboro and Pensacola, Fla., 1987—; cons. Nat. Health Advisors, Ltd., McLean, Va., 1983-95, Can. Mfrs. Inst., Washington, 1986-95. Jour. reviewer Acad. Mgmt. Rev., Jour. Mgmt., Rev. Bus. and Econ. Rsch., Mgmt. Sci.; mem. editl. bd. Jour. Global Info. Mgmt., Jour. of Mktg. and Theory Practice; contbr. articles to profl. jours. USAFR advisor Montgomery County Composite Squadron CAP, Blacksburg, 1977-79; coach Youth League Soccer and Football, Auburn, Ala. and Vienna, Va., 1980-86; mem. exec. com. cub scouts Boy Scouts Am., Vienna, 1982-83; pres. Statesboro High Sch. Quarterback Club, 1991-92; mem. Leadership Pensacola, 1998-99. Decorated DFC, Air medal with 3 oak leaf clusters; recipient Disting. Faculty Mem. award George Mason U., 1984; grantee SBA, 1983-84, Commonwealth of Va., 1984-86, State of Ga., 1994-95. Mem. Acad. Mgmt. (dissertation award com.), Ea. Acad. Mgmt., So. Mgmt. Assn. (program com. 1981-82, bd. dirs. 1989-92, mem. teaching excellence com. 1992-94), Decision Scis. Inst. (program com. 1991-92), S.E. Region Decision Scis. Inst. (program com. 1985-86, v.p. industry liaison 1986-87, v.p. planning and devel. 1987-88, sec. 1990-91, coun. mem. 1992—, coun. chair 1994-98, nominations com. 1996), Inst. Mgmt. Sci. (editor Southeastern chpt. Proceedings Jour. 1987, coun. 1986—, program chmn. 1986-87, sec.-treas. 1987-88, v.p. 1988-89, pres. 1989-90, Disting. Svc. award 1992), So. Bus. Adminstrn. (bd. dirs. 1998—), Soc. Advancement Mgmt. (Disting. Svc. award 1985), Aircraft Owners and Pilots Assn., Mid-Day Optimist Club (membership dir. 1989-91, bd. dirs. 1989-91), 5 Flags Rotary, Leadership Pensacola, U. Va. Alumni Assn. (Pensacola chpt. treas. 1997-98, bd. dirs. 1997—, pres. 1998—), Delta Sigma Phi, Beta Gamma Sigma, Phi Kappa Phi. Methodist. Avocations: boating, scuba diving, golf, private pilot. Office: Dean's Office Coll of Bus U West Fla Pensacola FL 32514-5752

CARR, ALBERT ANTHONY, retired organic chemist; b. Covington, Ky., Dec. 20, 1930; s. Albert Anthony and Virginia Charlotte (Wendel) C.; children: Virginia I., Michael P., Gregory J., Jerome R. BS, Xavier Univ., 1953, MS, 1955; PhD, Univ. Fla., 1958; LLD (hon.), Xavier U., 1994. Rsch. chemist Wm. S. Merrell Co., Cin., 1958-65; sect. head Merrell Nat. Labs., Cin., 1965-76; sr. sect. head Richardson-Merrell Inc., Cin., 1976-85; assoc. scientist Merrell Dow Rsch. Inst., Cin., 1985-88, sr. assoc. scientist, 1988-92; disting. scientist Marion Merrell Dow Rsch. Inst., Cin., 1992-95; disting. rsch. fellow Hoechst Marion Roussel, Cin., 1995-97; lectr. Xavier U., 1962-68; ind. cons. to pharm. industry, 1997—; cons. in field, 1997—. Contbr. articles to profl. jours.; patentee in field. Named Chemist of Yr., Cin. Am. Chem. Soc., 1987; recipient Disting. Scientist award Tech. Soc. Coun. Engrs., 1988, Am. Chem. Soc. award Creative Invention, 1993, Perkin medal, Am. Sect. Soc. Chem. Industry, 1999. Mem. AAAS, Am. Chem. Soc. (Creative Invention award 1993), N.Y. Acad. Scis. Achievements include selection of 14 of the many compounds he discovered for devel.; survival of 7 to be tested in humans.

CARR, ARTHUR CHARLES, psychologist, educator; b. Buffalo, Nov. 27, 1918; s. John E. and Katherine (Haas) C. B.S., Buffalo State Tchrs. Coll., 1941; M.A., Tchrs. Coll. Columbia U., 1946; Ph.D., U. Chgo., 1952; postgrad., William Alanson White Inst., 1953-54, Inst. Group Therapy, 1957-58, N.Y. Soc. Clin. Psychologists, 1954, 60. Diplomate: Am. Bd. Examiners in Profl. Psychology, N.Y. State Edn. Dept. Trainee clin. psychology VA, 1947-52; sr. clin. psychologist Creedmoor State Hosp., Queens Village, N.Y., 1952-56; prin. clin. psychologist N.Y. State Psychiat. Inst., N.Y.C., 1956—; ret.; asst. prof. psychology Adelphi Coll., Garden City, N.Y., 1952-56; asso. prof. med. psychology, dept. psychiatry Coll. Physicians and Surgeons, Columbia U., 1956-71, prof., 1971-78, prof. emeritus, 1978—; prof. psychology in psychiatry Cornell U. Med. Coll., 1978—. Author: (with Shervert Frazier) Introduction to Psychopathology, 1964, (with Herbert Hendin, William Gaylin) Psychoanalysis and Social Research, 1965; author, editor: (with others) Loss and Grief, 1970, Psychosocial Aspects of Terminal Care, 1972, The Terminal Patient, 1973, Anticipatory Grief, 1974, Bereavement: Its Psychosocial Aspects, 1975, Grief, Selected Readings, 1975, The Mouth in Critical and Terminal Illness, 1980, Education of the Medical Student in Thanatology, 1981, Adolescent Marijuana Abusers and their Families, 1981, Bernard Schoenberg: Contributions to Psychiatry, Education of the Health Professional, Thanatology and Ethical Values, 1984, Principles of Thanatology, 1987, Psychodynamic Psychotherapy of Borderline Patients, 1989; editor-in-chief: Man and Medicine, 75-80; cons. editor, 1980—; editorial bd., cons. editor: Jour. Projective Techniques, 1967-73; asso. editor: Jour. Abnormal Psychology, 1966 70, Jour. Thanatology, 1971—; contbr. articles to profl. jours. Served to maj. AUS, 1941-46. Fellow Am. Psychol. Assn., Soc. Projective Techniques (dir. 1961-64, pres. 1971-72); mem. Eastern, N.Y. State psychol. assns., N.Y. Soc. Clin. Psychologists. Home: 560 Riverside Dr New York NY 10027-3202

CARR, BESSIE, retired middle school educator; b. Nathalie, Va., Oct. 10, 1920; d. Henry C. and Sirlena (Ewell) C. BS, Elizabeth City Coll., N.C., 1942; MA, Columbia U. Tchrs. Coll., 1948, PhD, 1950, EdD, 1952. Cert. adminstr., supr., tchr. Prin. pub. sch., Halifax, Va., 1942-47, Nathalie-Halifax County, Va., 1947-51; prof. edn. So. U., Baton Rouge, 1952-53; supr. schs. Lackland Schs., Cin., 1953-54; prof. edn. Wilberforce U., Ohio, 1954-55; tchr. Leland Sch., Pittsfield, Mass., 1956-60; chair math. dept., tchr. Lakeland Mid. Sch., N.Y., 1961-83. Founder, organizer, sponsor 1st Math Bowl and Math Forum in area, 1970-76; founder Dr. Bessie Carr award Halifax County Sr. High Sch., 1962. Mem. Nat. Women's Hall of Fame. Mem. AAUW (auditor 1970-85), Delta Kappa Gamma (auditor internat. 1970-76), Assn. Suprs. of Math. (chair coordinating council 1976-80), Ret. Tchrs. Assn., Black Women Bus. and Profl. Assn. (charter mem. Senegal, Africa chpt.). Democrat. Avocations: travel, photography, souvenirs.

CARR, BOB, former congressman, lawyer; b. Janesville, Wis., Mar. 27, 1943; s. Milton Raymond and Edna (Blood) C.; m. Kathleen Smith; 1 child, Alexandra Anne; stepchildren: Jennifer McCloskey, Christopher McCloskey. BS, U. Wis., 1965, JD, 1968; postgrad., Mich. State U., 1968-69. Bar: Wis. 1968, Mich. 1969, U.S. Supreme Ct. 1973. Mem. staff of minority leader Mich. State Senate, 1968-69; adminstrv. asst. to atty. gen. State of Mich., Lansing, 1969-70, asst. atty. gen., 1970-72; counsel to spl. joint com. on legal edn. Mich. Legislature, Lansing, 1972; mem. 94th-96th, 98th-103rd Congresses from 6th (now 8th) Mich. Dist., Washington, 1975-80, 83; appropriations com., 1983-95, chmn. transp. subcom. appropriations, 1993-95; sr. v.p. The Jefferson Group, Inc., 1996-98; ptnr. Henry J. Kaufman & Assocs., Washington, 1997-99, Carr Minjack Co., Washington, 1999—; mgmt. cons., 1995—. Office: Ste 412 2233 Wisconsin Ave NW Washington DC 20007-4122

CARR, BOBBY G., legislative staff member. BA in History, Tex. Luth. U., 1983. Legis. aide Tex. Ho. Reps.; mem. congl. and media affairs U.S. Dept. Agriculture, Washington, 1989-90; lead press rep. U.S. Pres. George Bush, Washington, 1990-92; media and pub. rels. cons., tour coord. Clean Across Am. Tour, 1993; sr. account Stern, Nathan & Perryman, Dallas; press officer Southwestern Bell Tel., Topeka, Kans.; assoc. dir. Hill Rsch. Clients, 1995; mgr. pub. affairs practice Burson-Marsteller; chief staff Congresswoman Heather Wilson, Washington, 1998—; comm. dir. Am. Soc. Engring. Mgmt. Fax: 202-225-4975. Office: 2404 Rayburn Washington DC 20515 also: 625 Silver Ave SW Albuquerque NM 87102

CARR, CAROLYN KINDER, deputy director National Portrait Gallery; b. Providence, R.I., Feb. 23, 1939. BA in Art History, Smith Coll.; MA in Art History, Oberlin Coll.; PhD in Art History, Case Western Reserve U. Instr. art history Kent (Ohio) State Univ., 1963-65, 67-68; art critic Akron (Ohio) Beacon Jour., 1968-73; chief curator Akron Art Mus., 1978=83; asst. dir. for collections Nat. Portrait Gallery, Washington, 1984-90, dep. dir., 1991—; vis. lectr. Akron U., Spring 1975, '76; organizer numerous art exhbitions Akron Art Mus., 1978-83, Nat. Portrait Gallery, 1984—. Contbr. articles to art publs. including Nat. Portrait Gallery, The Dictionary of Art, Am. Art, The Am. Art Jour., Dialogue, Currier Gallery of Art Bull.; author: art catalogs for exhibitions at Akron Art Mus., Chrysler Mus. of Art, Nat. Portrait Gallery and Smithsonian Instn. Office: Nat Portrait Gallery 8th and F Sts Washington DC 20560

CARR, CASSANDRA COLVIN, communications company executive; b. Champaign, Ill., Nov. 14, 1944; d. A.B. and Irene Colvin; m. Edward M. Carr, Nov. 27, 1970. BA, Vanderbilt U., 1966; MA, U. Tex., 1973. Div. mgr. revenue requirements Southwestern Bell Telephone Co., Austin, Tex., 1985; div. mgr. congl. asst. program Southwestern Bell Telephone Co., Washington, 1986; dir. govt. rels. Southwestern Bell Corp., St. Louis, 1986-87, mng. dir. govt. rels., 1987-88, v.p. fin., treas., 1988, sr. v.p. fin., treas., 1988-90; v.p. revenues and pub. affairs Southwestern Bell Corp., Austin, Tex., 1990—; sr. v.p. human resources Southwestern Bell Corp., San Antonio, Tex. Commr. St. Louis Regional Conv. and Sports Complex Authority; bd. dirs. The Arch Funds, Inc., St. Louis, The Conf. Bd., N.Y.C., Found. Women's Resources, Austin. Recipient YWCA Leader award YWCA of St. Louis, 1988. Mem. Fin. Execs. Inst., Nat. Assn. Corp. Treasurers, St. Louis Club, Forest Hills Country Club. Office: SBC Communications Inc PO Box 2933 175 E Houston 6th fl San Antonio TX 78299-2933

CARR, CHARLES JELLEFF, pharmacologist, educator, toxicology consultant; b. Balt., Mar. 27, 1910; s. Joshua Barney and Pearl (Jelleff) C.; children: Daniel Jelleff, Noel Edward, Joseph Barney; m. Sallie D. Wenner, May 15, 1980. B.S. (Garvan scholar), U. Md., 1933, M.S., 1934, Ph.D. (Emerson fellow), 1937; D.Sc. (hon.), Purdue U., 1964. Teaching asst. pharmacology Sch. Medicine, U. Md., 1934-35, instr., 1935-37, asst. prof., 1937-39, assoc. prof., 1939-50, prof., 1950-55, adj. prof., 1957-91, prof. emeritus dept. pharmacology and exptl. therapeutics, 1991—; prof., chmn. dept. pharmacology Purdue U., 1955-57; chief pharmacology unit Psychopharmacology Service Center, NIMH, Bethesda, Md., 1957-63; chief sci. analysis br., life scis. div. Army Research Office, Office Chief Research and Devel. U.S. Army, Arlington, Va., 1963-67; dir. Life Scis. Research Office, Fedn. Am. Socs. for Exptl. Biology, Bethesda, 1967-77; exec. dir. Food Safety Council, Columbia, Md., 1977-80; sci. counsellor Food Safety Council, 1980-82; spl. lectr. Georgetown U. Sch. Medicine; instr. physicians course chem. warfare Emergency Med. Svc., Balt. Third Civilian Def. Region, 1943; cons. The Nutrition Found., 1982-84; exec. dir. Food Safety Coun., 1977-79, sci. counsellor, 1979-82; dir. life sci. rsch. Fedn. Am. Socs. for Exptl. Biology, 1967-77, dir. emeritus, 1977—; chief sci. analysis br. life scis. divsn. Army Rsch. Office, Office of Chief of Rsch. and Devel., Dept. Army, 1963-67; chief pharmacology unit Psychopharmacology Svc. Ctr., NIMH, 1957-63. Author: (with Krantz) Pharmacologic Principles of Medical Practice, 7th edit, 1969; also numerous sci. articles. Merit badge councilor for chemistry and pub. health Boy Scouts Am., 1957-67. Recipient U.S. Army Meritorious Civilian award, 1965, 68; U. Edinburgh fellow, 1986. Fellow N.Y. Acad. Scis., Am. Coll. Neuropsychopharmacology (life), Acad. Toxicological Scis.; mem. Am. Pharm. Assn. (life), Am. Chem. Soc. (life), Am. Assn. Pharm. Sci., Internat. Soc. Regulatory Toxicology and Pharmacology (sec., mng. editor Regulatory Toxicology and Pharmacology Jour., Internat. Achievement award 1993), Soc. Toxicology, Cosmos Club (Washington), Sigma Xi, Kappa Psi. Office: U Md Dept Pharmacology Expt Ther 6546 Bellview Dr Columbia MD 21046-1054*

CARR, CHARLES LOUIS, retired religious organization administrator; b. Rockport, Ind., Sept. 9, 1930; s. Louis E. and Loris B. (Lindsey) C.; m. Shirley R. Cron, Nov. 15, 1950; children: Kathleen Carr Wright, Charles Stephen, Jeffrey Louis, David Wayne. Student, Ind. State U., 1949-50, So. Bapt. Theol. Sem., 1965-67; BS, Oakland City U., 1978, DD, 1994. Ordained to ministry Gen. Assn. Gen. Bapts., 1957. Pastor East Oolitic Gen. Bapt. Ch., Bedford, Ind., 1959-63, Mt. Zion Gen. Bapt. Ch., Indpls., 1963-65, Hunsinger Lane Gen. Bapt. Ch., Louisville, 1965-67; missionary to Saipan Mariana Islands, 1967-73; exec. dir. Gen. Bapt. Fgn. Mission Soc., Poplar Bluff, Mo., 1973-96; ret., 1996; pastor Wyatt United Meth Ch., 1997—, Dogwood United Meth Ch., 1997—. Author: Seed, Soil and Seasons, 1988; contbr. articles to various publs. Home: 706 S 9th St Poplar Bluff MO 63901-5639

CARR, CYNDA ANNETTE, elementary education educator; b. Harper, Kans., June 6, 1948; d. Don Edward and Raquel Ann (Daniels) C. BA, Wichita (Kans.) State U., 1974, MEd, 1980. Tchr. Unified Sch. Dist. 361, Anthony, Kans., 1974—; steering com. Kans. Tchr. of Yr., 1995—; tchr. cons. Kans. Geographic Alliance, 1992—, Delta Kappa Gamma, 1981—, state editor, 1993—. Trainer Wheatbelt area coun. Girl Scouts U.S., Hutchinson, Kans., 1980-83, 85-92, bd. dirs., 1987-91, active various coms. and task forces; neighborhood chmn. Anthony coun. Girl Scouts U.S., 1985-91, troop leader, 1976-84, 88-89; bd. dirs. Harper County chpt. Am. Cancer Soc., Anthony, 1986—, Anthony United Way, 1987-89; mem. Leadership Harper County, 1994-95; activities counselor Camp Hope/Am. Cancer Soc., 1987; Sunday sch. tchr., mem. choir 1st Congl. Ch., 1990—; sponsor Kids for Saving Earth, 1991—; mem. Soil Conservation Earth Team, 1992—; Golden Gift Leadership/Mgmt. Seminar, 1995; Young Careerist Anthony Business and Profl. Women's Club, 1976. Named Tchr. of Yr. Harper County Conservation Dist., 1992; recipient Silver Pen award Kans. Edn. Assn., 1987, Thanks Badge award Girl Scouts U.S., 1988, Contbn. to Conservation award Anthony Republican, 1992, Nat. Educator award Milken Family Found., 1994, Diana award Epsilon Sigma Alpha, 1985. Avocations: calligraphy, collecting hippos. Home: 401 S Kansas Ave Anthony KS 67003-2624 Office: Anthony Elem Sch 215 S Springfield Ave Anthony KS 67003-2550

CARR, CYNTHIA, lawyer; b. San Antonio, Nov. 4, 1953; d. Robert Claude Carr and Alta Mae (Bletsch) Holmes; m. Marc Allan Wallman; children: Lydia Michael, Aidan Holmes. BA, Austin Coll., 1975; JD, Harvard U., 1984; LLM, NYU, 1990. Bar: N.Y. 1985, Conn. 1988. Coord. Cambodian sect. Internat. Rescue Com., Bangkok, Thailand, 1980-81; legal intern Mental Health Legal Advisers Com., Boston, 1982-83; assoc. White & Case, N.Y.C., 1984-87; assoc. gen. counsel, exec. dir. planned giving Yale U., New Haven, 1988—; vis. lectr. Yale U. Law Sch., New Haven, 1988-90. Vol. Peace Corps, West Africa, 1975-77, 79-80; bd. dirs. Yale Law Sch. Early Learning Ctr.; mem. charitable mini bd. Trusts & Estates mag., 1996—; trustee Yale U. Hong Kong Charitable Trust. Mem. ABA, Conn. Bar Assn. (mem. charitable giving exempt orgns. subcom.), Trusts and Estates Mag. (charitable giving mini bd. mem.). Home: 30 Hawley Rd Hamden CT 06517-2128 Office: Yale U PO Box 2038 265 Church St New Haven CT 06510-7013

CARR, DANIEL BARRY, anesthesiologist, endocrinologist, medical researcher; b. N.Y.C., Apr. 6, 1948; s. Andrew Joseph and Florence (Glassman) C.; m. Justine M. Meehan, Nov. 11, 1978; children: Nora, Rebecca, Andrew. BA, Columbia U., 1968, MA, 1970, MD, 1976. Diplomate Am. Bd. Internal Medicine (subsplty. bds. Endocrinology and Metabolism, Anesthesiology, Pain Mgmt.). Intern Columbia-Presbyn. Med. Ctr., N.Y.C., 1976-78; resident med. svc. Mass. Gen. Hosp., Boston, 1978-79, endocrine fellow, 1979-82, staff physician endocrine unit, 1982-94, clin. assoc. physician, clin. rsch. ctr., 1982-84, fellow in anesthesiology, 1984-86; dir. analgesic peptide research unit, 1986-94, staff physician anesthesia svc. and co-dir. anesthesia pain unit, 1986-91, dir. divsn. pain mgmt., 1991-94; anesthetist, 1992-94; instr. medicine Harvard U. Med. Sch., 1982-84, asst. prof., 1984-88; assoc. prof., 1988-94; rsch. staff Shriners Burns Inst., Boston, 1986-94; Saltonstall prof. Pain Rsch. in Anesthesia and Medicine Tufts-New England Med. Ctr., 1994—; co-chair acute and cancer pain mgmt. guideline panels, Agy. for Health Care Policy and Rsch., U.S. Dept. Health and Human Svcs., 1990-94; med. dir. Pain Mgmt. Program Tufts-New England Med. Ctr., 1995—; vice-chair rsch. Dept. Anesthsia, New England Med. Ctr., 1994—; pain trials registry coord. Cochrane Collaboration, 1998—; mem. Gov. Mass. spl. commn. pain mgmt., 1993-98. Editor-in-chief IASP Pain: Clinical Updates, 1993—; mem. editl. bd. Clin. Jour. Pain, 1988—, Jour. Clin. Anesthesia, 1995—, Anesthesia and Analgesia, 1996-99; contbr. articles, rsch. reports, essays, revs. to profl. lit. Daland fellow Am. Philos. Soc., 1980-83. Mem. Am. Pain Soc. (mem. bd. dirs. 1994—), Am. Acad. Pain Medicine (mem. bd. dirs. 1995-98), France-Am. Pain Soc. (pres. 1996-98), Am. Soc. Anesthesiologists, Internat. Assn for Study Pain (coun. 1996—), Endocrine Soc., Soc. for Neurosci., Internat. Anesthesia Rsch. Soc., Assn. Univ. Anesthetists, Alpha Omega Alpha. Research on pain, analgesic peptides and stress responses; relationship between analgesia and clinical outcome; systematic reviews and guidelines for improved pain treatment in hospital, hospice, and home care settings. Office: New Eng Med Ctr-Dept Anesthsia 750 Washington St Boston MA 02111-1526

CARR, DAVID MICHAEL, editor, writer; b. Mpls., Sept. 8, 1956; s. John Lawrence and Joan (O'Neill) C.; m. Jill Rooney, Sept. 17, 1994; children: Erin and Meagan (twins), Madeline. BFA, U. Minn., 1981. Writer Twin Cities Reader, Mpls., 1981-84; editor Corp. Report Minn., Mpls., 1986-87, Minn. Lawyer, Mpls., 1990-93, Twin Cities Reader, Mpls., 1993-95, Washington City Paper, 1995—; mem. alumni selectin com. journalism dept. U. Minn., Mpls., 1985; comm. cons., Mpls., 1990-93; com. mem. Assn. Alternative Newspapers, Washington, 1995; columnist Family Times Mag., Mpls., 1995; spkr. addiction and recovery various orgns., Mpls. and Washington, 1988-96. Recipient Page One award Soc. Profl. Journalists, Mpls., 1983-86, 93, 94, 95, Nat. Victory award, Washington, 1991, award Assn. Alternative Newspaper Columnist, Assn. Alternative Newspapers Media Column award, 1997; named Alumni of Distinction, U. Minn., Mpls., 1995. Home: 4838 Davenport St NW Washington DC 20016-4355 Office: Washington City Paper 2390 Champlain St NW Washington DC 20009-2620*

CARR, DAVID TURNER, physician; b. Richmond, Va., Mar. 12, 1914; s. John Ernest and Mary Lela (King) C.; m. Rosemary Rudow, June 18, 1948 (div. 1953); 1 child, Jennifer Anne Carr Oderkirk; m. Christine Nadeau, Dec. 27, 1979. Student, U. Richmond, 1931-33; M.D., Med. Coll. Va., 1937; M.S. in Medicine, Mayo Grad. Sch. Medicine, 1947. Intern, then asst. resident Grady Hosp., Atlanta, 1937-39; resident chest diseases Bellevue Hosp., N.Y.C., 1940-41; fellow medicine Mayo Clinic, 1943-47, cons. medicine, 1947-79, chmn. dept. oncology, 1975; dir. Mayo Comprehensive Cancer Center, 1975; assoc. dir. Center for Cancer Control, 1976-79; prof. medicine Mayo Med. Sch., 1964-79, M.D. Anderson Hosp. and Tumor Inst., Tex. Med. Center, Houston, 1979-92. Mem.-at-large bd. dirs. Am. Lung Assn., 1959-74, v.p., 1971-72; bd. dirs. Rochester Civic Theatre, 1951-70, pres., 1965-67; bd. dirs. at large Am. Cancer Soc., 1967-74, pres. Minn. div., 1974-75. Fellow ACP, AAAS; mem. Central Soc. Clin. Research, Internat. Assn. for Study Lung Cancer (v.p. 1974-76, pres. 1976, treas. 1976-82), Am. Thoracic Soc. (v.p. 1963-64), Rochester C. of C. (pres. 1959-60); hon. mem. Peruvian Anti-Tb Assn. Spl. research on pulmonary diseases. Home and Office: 103 Lockgreen Pl Richmond VA 23226-1744

CARR, DAVIS HADEN, lawyer; b. Richmond, Va., July 21, 1940; s. Frederick Clifton Jr. and Bernice (Haden) C.; m. Judith A. Guerry, Aug. 1959 (div. Apr. 1979); children: Wendy Carr Conners, Julia Carr Stewart; m. Martha Cash, Feb. 12, 1983. BEE, U. Va., 1961; JD, Vanderbilt U., 1970. Bar: Tenn. 1970, Ky. 1989. Assoc. Boult, Cummings, Conners & Berry PLC, Nashville, 1970-74; ptnr. Boult, Cummings, Conners & Berry PLC, 1974—; mng. ptnr. Boult, Cummings, Conners & Berry, 1984-94, chmn., 1995—. Active Leadership Nashville, 1977-78, chmn. alumni assn., 1978-79, bd. trustees 1997—; pres. Cumberland Museums, Nashville, 1978-80; bd. dirs. Greater Nashville Arts Found., 1991-97; bd. dirs. Jr. Achievement Mid. Tenn., 1991-, chmn., 1995-97; trustee Vol. State Horesemen's Found., 1988-; mem. bd. trustees, exec. com. Fisk U., 1996—; bd. dirs. Nashville Downtown Partnership, 1994—, chmn., 1994-95, exec. com., 1994—. Mem. ABA, Tenn. Bar Found., Tenn. Bar Assn., Nashville Bar Found., Nashville Bar Assn., Vanderbilt U. Law Alumni Assn. (bd. dirs.), Cumberland Club (pres. 1986-87), Nashville City Club, Belle Meade Country Club, Nashville Area C. of C. (gen. counsel, mem. exec. com. 1992-96, bd. govs.). Home: Martlesham Heath 1344 Carnton Ln Franklin TN 37064 Office: Boult Cummings Conners & Be PO Box 198062 Nashville TN 37219-8062

CARR, EDWARD A., lawyer; b. Borger, Tex., July 31, 1962. AB with distinction, Stanford U., 1984; JD, UCLA, 1987. Bar: Tex. 1988, D.C. 1989, U.S. Dist. Ct. (so. dist.) Tex. 1989, U.S. Ct. Appeals (5th cir.) 1989, U.S. Ct. Appeals (fed. cir.) 1989. Assoc. Vinson & Elkins, Houston, 1988-97, ptnr., 1997—; lectr. in field. Contbr. articles to profl. jours., contbg. author: (6-vol. book set) Business and Commercial Litigation in Federal Courts, 1998, mem. editl. bd. UCLA Law Review, 1986-87. Fellow Tex. Bar Found. (life); Mem. ABA (sects. antitrust law, litigation), Am. Judicature Soc. (life), Coll. State Bar Tex., D.C. Bar, Fed. Bar Assn. (sect. fed. litigation), State Bar Tex., Houston Bar Assn. Address: Vinson & Elkins LLP 2300 First City Tower 1001 Fannin St Houston TX 77002-6706

CARR, EDWARD ALBERT, JR., medical educator, physician; b. Cranston, R.I., Mar. 3, 1922; s. Edward Albert and Florence (Hodge) C.; m. Nancy Albosta, Dec. 27, 1952; children: Sharon L., Cynthia F. A.B. summa cum laude, Brown U., 1942; M.D. cum laude, Harvard, 1945. Rsch. fellow, instr. pharmacology Harvard Med. Sch., 1948-51; exch. fellow St. Bartholomew's Hosp., London, 1952-53; mem. faculty U. Mich. Med. Sch., Ann Arbor, 1953-74, prof. pharmacology, 1962-74, prof. internal medicine, 1967-74, dir. program investigative clin. pharmacology, 1962-74; mem. sr. staff Univ. Hosp., 1957-74; dir. Upjohn Center Clin. Pharmacology, 1966-74; prof. medicine, prof. and chmn. dept. pharmacology Med. Sch., U. Louisville, 1974-76; prof. medicine, pharmacology and therapeutics Med. and Dental Sch., SUNY, Buffalo, 1976-92, emeritus prof. medicine, pharmacology and therapeutics, 1992—, chmn. dept. pharmacology and therapeutics, 1976-88; mem. sr. staff, chmn. therapeutics com. Louisville Gen. Hosp., 1974-76; lectr. U. Helsinki, 1972, Autonomous U. Barcelona, 1974, Japan Med. Assn., 1977, Swedish Acad. Pharm. Scis., Stockholm, 1977, Esteve Found. Symposium, Mallorca, 1988; cons. Ann Arbor VA Hosp., 1954-74, Louisville VA Hosp., 1974-76, Buffalo VA Hosp., 1976—, Erie County Med. Ctr., 1978-92; hon. vis. prof. Prince Henry and Prince of Wales Hosp., Sydney, Australia, 1973. Co-author: Radioisotopes in Biology and Medicine, 1964; also articles. Mem. Nat. Joint Commn. on Prescription Drug Use, 1976-80; mem. coop. studies evaluation com. U.S. VA, 1980-83; chmn. pharmacology com. Am. Inst. Biol. Scis., Walter Reed Army Inst. Rsch., 1985-86; vol. Niagara Hospice, 1992—, bd. dirs., 1992-95, 96—. Fellow ACP (emeritus); mem. Am. Thyroid Assn. (emeritus), Am. Soc. Pharmacology and Exptl. Therapeutics (emeritus) (exec. com. clin. pharmacology div. 1984-86), Am. Soc. Clin. Pharmacology and Therapeutics (pres. 1974-75, Henry W. Elliott award 1981), Soc. Nuclear Medicine (emeritus), Ctrl. Soc. Clin. Rsch. (emeritus), Endocrine Soc. (emeritus), Phi Beta Kappa, Sigma Xi, Alpha Omega Alpha. Home: 2 Gothic Ledge Lockport NY 14094-9702

CARR, GARY THOMAS, lawyer; b. El Reno, Okla., July 25, 1946; s. Thomas Clay and Bobbye Jean (Page) C.; m. Ann Elizabeth Smith, Jan. 5, 1985. AB, Washington U., St. Louis, 1968, BSCE, 1972, JD, 1975. Bar: Mo. 1975, U.S. Dist. Ct. (ea. and we. dists.) Mo. 1975, U.S. Ct. Appeals (8th cir.) 1977, U.S. Ct. Appeals (fed. cir.) 1980, U.S. Ct. Appeals (5th cir.) 1991. Jr. ptnr. Bryan, Cave, McPheeters & McRoberts, St. Louis, 1975-83, ptnr., 1984—; lectr. law Washington U., 1978-82, adj. prof., 1982-85; sec., dir. Bruton-Stroube Studios, Inc., 1978—, bd. dirs. Trustee Parkview Subdiv. Assn., St. Louis, 1982-90. 1st lt. U.S. Army, 1968-71, Vietnam. Mem. ABA, Mo. Bar Assn., St. Louis Bar Assn., Order of Coif. Club: Mo. Athletic (St. Louis). Avocations: racquet sports, woodworking, hunting, fishing, scuba. Office: Bryan Cave 1 Metropolitan Sq 211 N Broadway Saint Louis MO 63102-2733

CARR, GEORGE FRANCIS, JR., lawyer; b. Bklyn., Feb. 11, 1939; s. George Francis and Edith Frances (Schaible) C.; m. Patricia Louise Shiels, Jan. 30, 1965; children: Frances Virginia, Anne McKenzie, Margaret Elizabeth. BA, Georgetown U., 1961; LLB, Harvard U., 1964. Bar: Ohio 1964, U.S. Dist. Ct. Ohio 1964. Assoc. Kyte, Conlan, Wulsin & Vogeler, Cin., 1964-70, ptnr., 1970-78; ptnr. Frost & Jacobs, Cin., 1978-82; sec., counsel Baldwin-United Corp., Cin., 1982-84, v.p., spl. counsel, 1984-85; sole practice Cin., 1985-86; ptnr. Douglas, Carr and Pettit, Milford, Ohio, 1987-88; staff v.p., assoc. gen. counsel Penn Cen. Corp., Cin., 1988-92, Gen. Cable Corp., Highland Heights, Ky., 1992-95; sales assoc. Comey & Shepherd Realtors, Inc., Cin., 1996-97; real estate sales devel. and investment Re/Max MKR Ptnrs., Cin., 1997—. Bd. dirs. Ctr. for Comprehensive Alcoholism Treatment, Cin., 1975-87, pres., 1980-83; bd. dirs. NCCJ, Cin., 1975-82. With U.S. Army, 1965-67. Roman Catholic. Avocations: physical fitness, hiking, farming. Home: 7150 Ragland Rd # 4 Cincinnati OH 45244-3148 Office: Re/Max MKR Ptnrs 7800 Laurel Ave Cincinnati OH 45243-2609*

CARR, GEORGE LEROY, physicist, educator; b. Upperco, Md., Dec. 11, 1927; s. William Grason and Florence May (Miller) C.; m. Phyllis Allegra Wenger, Mar. 9, 1952; children: Cynthia L., G. Lawrence, Melinda S. B.S., Western Md. Coll., 1948, M.Ed., 1959; Ph.D., Cornell U., 1969. Tchr. physics, chmn. sci. dept. Balt. County Schs., 1948-51, 53-61, 64-65; instr. physics Cornell U., Ithaca, N.Y., 1963-64; asst. prof. Western Md. Coll., Westminster, 1965-66; prof. physics U. Mass., Lowell, 1966-96, pres. univ. coun., 1981-83, coord. physics svc. lab., 1987-96, prof. emeritus, 1996—; cons. Phys. Sci. Study Com., 1957-61, Balt.-Washington area coordinator, 1958-61; instr. NSF Summer Inst., Fla. State U., 1959, Converse Coll., 1961; cons. Intermediate Sci. Curriculum Study, 1971—. Author: (with others) PSSC Physics, 1960, 65, 70, Secrets of the Nucleus, 1967, General Principles of Experimental Physics, 1982, 2d edit., 1986. Fundamentals of Experimental Physics, 1988. Served with U.S. Army, 1951-53. Mem. Am. Phys. Soc., Am. Assn. Physics Tchrs., Am. Geophys. Union, Nat. Sci. Tchrs. Assn., Phi Delta Kappa, Phi Kappa Phi, Sigma Xi. Methodist. Home: 2 Gifford Ln Chelmsford MA 01824-2023 Office: 1 University Ave Lowell MA 01854-2827

CARR, GERALD FRANCIS, German educator; b. Pitts., Dec. 29, 1930; s. James Patrick and Hannah (Sweeney) C.; m. Irmengard Rauch, June 12, 1965; children: Christopher, Gregory. BEd, Duquesne U., 1958; MA, U. Wis., 1960, PhD, 1968. Instr. in German Duquesne U., Pitts., 1960-62, asst. prof. German, 1964-68; tchg. asst. U. Wis., Madison, 1962-64; asst. prof. German Ea. Ill. U., Charleston, 1968-70, assoc. prof. German, 1970-75, prof. German, 1975-87; prof. German Calif. State U., Sacramento, 1987—. Co-editor: Linguistic Method: Essays in Honor of Herbert Penzl, 1979, The Signifying Animal: The Grammar of Language and Experience, 1980, Language Change, 1983, The Semiotic Bridge, 1989, On Germanic Linguistics, 1992, Insights in Germanic Linguistics I, 1995, II, 1996, Semiotics Around the World, 1996, Interdigitations: Essays for Irmengard Rauch, 1998; series editor: Studies in Old Germanic Languages and Literatures; assoc. editor Interdisciplinary Jour. for Germanic Linguistics and Semiotic Analysis. Cpl. USMC, 1951-54. Dist. tchg. fellow U. Wis., 1966. Mem. MLA, Internat. Assn. for Semiotic Studies (co-dir. 5th congress 1994), Am. Coun. Tchrs. Fgn. Lang., Semiotic Soc. Am., Am. Assn. Tchrs. of German, Soc. German Philology, Calif. Fgn. Lang. Tchr. Assn., Semiotic Circle Calif., Kappa Phi Kappa, Delta Phi Alpha. Avocations: books, antiques. Office: Calif State U 6000 J St Sacramento CA 95819-2605

CARR, GERALD PAUL, former astronaut, business executive, former marine officer; b. Denver, Aug. 22, 1932; s. Thomas Ernest and Freda (Wright) C.; divorced; children: Jennifer, Jamee, Jeffrey, John, Jessica, Joshua; m. Patricia Musick, Sept. 14, 1979. BS in Mech. Engring., U. So. Calif., 1954; BS in Aero. Engring., U.S. Naval Postgrad. Sch., 1961; MS in Aero. Engring., Princeton U., 1962; DSc (hon.), St. Louis U., 1976. Registered profl. engr., Tex. Commd. 2d lt. USMC, 1954, advanced through grades to col., 1974, ret., 1975; jet fighter pilot U.S., Mediterranean, Far East, 1956-65; astronaut NASA, Houston, 1966-77; comdr. 3d Skylab Manned Mission, 1973-74; sr. v.p. CAMUS, Inc., Huntsville, Ark.; adv. bd. Nat. Space Soc., Space Dermatology Found., Eldorado Bank. Bd. trustees U. of the Ozarks. Recipient Group Achievement award NASA, 1971, Distinguished Service medal, 1974; Gold medal City of Chgo., 1974; Gold medal City of N.Y., 1974; Alumni Merit award U. So. Calif., 1974; Distinguished Eagle Scout award Boy Scouts Am., 1974; Robert J. Collier Trophy, 1974; Robert H. Goddard Meml. trophy, 1975; FAI Gold Space medal; others; inductee Astronaut Hall of Fame, 1997. Fellow Am. Astronautical Soc. (Flight Achievement award 1975); mem. NSPE, Marine Corps Assn., Marine Corps Aviation Assn., Soc. Exptl. Test Pilots, U. So. Calif. Alumni Assn., Tau Kappa Epsilon. Presbyterian. Home and Office: PO Box 919 Huntsville AR 72740-0919

CARR, GILBERT RANDLE, retired railroad executive; b. Rockford, Ill., Jan. 4, 1928; s. Audra Clifford and Marjorie (Lantz) C.; m. Marion Minnie Heinemann, Mar. 28, 1953; children: John W., James M. B.S. in Accounting and Mgmt, U. Ill., 1950. With Arthur Andersen & Co. (C.P.A.s), Chgo., 1950-57; with C.& N. W. Transp. Co., 1957-88, comptroller, 1967-79, v.p., comptroller, 1979-88. Served with AUS, 1946-47. Lutheran. Home: 1425 Linden Ave Park Ridge IL 60068-5545

CARR, GLADYS JUSTIN, publishing company executive, editor, writer; b. N.Y.C.; d. Jack and Mollie (Marmor) C. B.A., Smith Coll., M.A.; postgrad., Cornell U. Sr. editor Prentice-Hall, Inc., Englewood Cliffs, N.J., 1969; exec. editor Cowles Communications, Inc., N.Y.C., 1969-71; editorial dir. Am. Heritage Press, N.Y.C., 1971-75; sr. editor McGraw-Hill, Inc., N.Y.C., 1975-81, editor in chief, editorial dir., chmn. editorial bd., 1981-89, v.p., pub., 1988-89; v.p., pub. HarperCollins Pubs., Inc., N.Y.C., 1989—. Pub. and editor books by James Baldwin, Anthony Burgess, Erica Jong, Erma Bombeck, Philip Caputo, Brenda Maddox, Stuart Woods, Leon Uris, others; contbr. articles, revs. and poetry to profl. jours. Marjorie Hope Nicholson trustee fellow Smith Coll.; vis. Ford Found. fellow, Walter Francis Wilcox fellow Cornell U. Mem. PEN Am. Ctr., Women's Media Group, Phi Beta Kappa. Club: Smith Coll. (N.Y.C.). Home: 920 Park Ave New York NY 10028-0208 also: 1 Boulder Ln East Hampton NY 11937-1047 Office: HarperCollins Pubs Inc 10 E 53rd St Fl Cellar1 New York NY 10022-5299

CARR, GLENNA DODSON, economics educator; b. Asheville, N.C., Jan. 7, 1927; d. Harry D. and Ruth (Gatling) Dodson; m. Thomas Deaderick Carr, May 20, 1961; 1 child, Susan Catherine. BS, James Madison U., Harrisonburg, Va., 1948; MS, Fla. State U., Tallahassee, 1951; EdD, U. Fla., 1959. Asst. prof. U. Fla., Gainesville, 1952—, prof., 1977—, prof., dir. Ctr. for Econ. Edn., 1977—; bd. dirs. AV-Med Santa Fe Inc.; chair bd. dirs. Santa Fe Health Care, Inc. Contbr. numerous articles to profl. jours. Democrat. Presbyterian. Avocation: tennis. Home: 1546 SW 35th Pl Gainesville FL 32608-3530 Office: U Fla Ctr for Econ Edn 186 Norman Hall Gainesville FL 32611-2053

CARR, HAROLD NOFLET, investment corporation executive; b. Kansas City, Kans., Mar. 14, 1921; s. Noflet B. and Mildred (Addison) C.; m. Mary Elizabeth Smith, Aug. 5, 1944; children: Steven Addison, Hal Douglas, James Taylor, Scott Noflet. B.S., Tex. A&M U., 1943; postgrad., Am. U., 1944-46. Asst. dir. route devel. Trans World Airlines, Inc., 1943-47; exec. v.p. Wis. Central Airlines, Inc., 1947-52; mem. firm McKinsey & Co., 1952-54; pres. North Central Airlines, Inc., Mpls., 1954-69; chmn. bd. North Central Airlines, Inc., 1965-79; chmn. Republic Airlines, Inc., 1979-84, chmn. exec. com., 1984-86; chmn. Carr and Assocs., 1986—; professorial lectr. mgmr. engring. Am. U., 1952-62; dir. Gov.'s Sound, Ltd., Cayman Water Co., Metro Airlines, Inc., First Nat. Bank Byran (Tex.) Cayman Mile, Ltd.; mem. bd. nominations Nat. Aviation Hall of Fame; mem. exec. adv. coun. Nat. Register Prominent Americans and Internat. Notables, Minn. Aviation Hall of Fame. Trustee Tex. A&M Rsch. Found., Internat. Inst. for Effective Communication; mem. Pres.'s Coun. of Advisors, Tex. A&M U. Chancellor's Century Coun. Mem. Nat. Aero. Assn., World Bus. Coun., Am. Mgmt. Assn., nat. Trust Historic Preservation, Pine Beach Peninsula Assn., Am. Econ. Assn., Tex. A&M Former Students Assn., Beta Gamma Sigma. Episcopalian. Clubs: Nat. Aviation, Aero (Washington), Minneapolis, Twelfth Man Found. (dir., Coll. Sta., Tex.), Tex. A&M Century, Racquet (Miami), Gull Lake Yacht (Brainerd, Minn.), Wings (N.Y.C.), Stearman Alumnus (Wichita, Kans.), Briarcrest Country.

CARR, IRIS CONSTANTINE, artist, writer; b. Smyrna, Turkey, Aug. 4, 1922; d. John and Julia Kyrides Constantine; m. Herman Edgar Carr Jr., 1947; 3 children. Diploma in dental nursing, Boston Sch. Dental Nursing, 1942; BA, Simmons Coll., 1970, postgrad., 1990-91; postgrad., DeCordova Mus. Sch., 1986—. Anesthetist for oral surgeon, Boston, 1942-43; exec. med. sec. Boston Evening Clinic, 1943-44; lab. sec., dir. Boston Dispensary, 1944-45, Children's Hosp., Boston, 1944-47; editl. asst. Internat. Rsch. and Publs., 1947—; developed improved interlibr. loan svc. Wellesley Coll. Libr., 1964; demonstrator watercolor technique Needham (Mass.) Arts Festival, 1996. *Iris Carr is the editorial assistant for Herman E. Carr, Jr., M.D. for two published articles, 1998, on the history of Boston University School of Medicine. She received the first prize of $100 from The Wellesley Society of Artists on April 19, 1998. She exhibited in a one-person show with eight paintings, all media at the Needham Travel Service Bureau. She had portraits exhibited at Massachusetts Medical Society, 1998, Needham Public Library, whose holdings display early N.C. Wyeth paintings, 3 paintings at Massachusetts Bay Community College. Her paintings are shown twice a year at Needham Art Association and Wellesley Society of Artists.* One woman show at Needham Village Gallery, 1991, Needham Travel Svc. Bur., 1998-99; group shows include Mass. Med. Soc., 1999, Needham and Wellesley Art Assn., 1999, Needham Libr., 1999; contbr. articles to profl. publs.; contbg. editor Mass. Med. Soc. Alliance. Recipient over 10 awards for pastel, watercolor and oil paintings. Mem. Mass. Med. Soc. Alliance (pub. rels. com. 1985-94, contbg. editor 1995—), Dedham Art Assn. (featured artist), Wellesley Soc. Artists (bd. dirs., registration com. 1994—), Needham Art Assn. (bd. dirs., publicity com., pres. 1989-90, co-inaugurated 1st art gallery 1990), Nat. Mus. Women in Arts. Democrat. Home: 14 Ingleside Rd Needham MA 02492-4239

CARR, JACQUELYN B., psychologist, educator; b. Oakland, Calif., Feb. 22, 1923; d. Frank G. and Betty (Kreiss) Corker; children: Terry, John, Richard, Linda, Michael, David. BA, U. Calif., Berkeley, 1958; MA, Stanford U., 1961; PhD, U. So. Calif., 1973. Lic. psychologist, Calif; lic. secondary tchr., Calif. Tchr. Hillsdale High Sch., San Mateo, Calif., 1958-69, Foothill Coll., Los Altos Hills, Calif., 1969—; cons. Silicon Valley Companies, U.S. Air Force, Interpersonal Support Network, Santa Clara County Child Abuse Council, San Mateo County Suicide Prevention Inc.,Parental Stress Hotline, Hotel/Motel Owners Assn.; co-dir. Individual Study Ctr.; supr. Tchr. Edn.; adminstr. Peer Counseling Ctr.; led numerous workshops and confs. in field. Author: Learning is Living, 1970, Equal Partners: The Art of Creative Marriage, 1986, The Crisis in Intimacy, 1988, Communicating and Relating, 1984, 3d edit., 1991, Communicating with Myself: A Journal, 1984, 3d edit., 1991; contbr. articles to profl. jours. Mem. Mensa. Club: Commonwealth. Home: # 5-2G 390 N Winchester Blvd Santa Clara CA 95050 Office: Foothill College 12345 El Monte Rd Los Altos CA 94022-4597

CARR, JAMES FRANCIS, lawyer; b. Buffalo, May 7, 1946; s. Maurice Kilner and Cecelia Francis (Harmon) C.; children: James Robert, Marguerite Louise. BS, USAF Acad., 1968; JD, George Washington U., 1971. Bar: D.C. 1972, Mich. 1972, Pa. 1972, U.S. Dist. Ct. D.C. 1972, U.S. Ct. Appeals (D.C. cir.) 1972, U.S. Supreme Ct. 1975, Colo. 1979, U.S. Dist. Ct. Colo. 1979, U.S. Ct. Appeals (10th cir.) 1979. Atty. Unity Ctr., Meadville, Pa., 1971-73; asst. pros. atty. Genesee County, Flint, Mich., 1973-79; sr. asst. atty. gen. State of Colo., Denver, 1979-82, 85—; assoc. Sumners, Miller & Clark, Denver, 1982-83, Miles & McManus, Denver, 1983-85; mem. Colo. Bd. Law Examiners, 1992—. Contbr. articles to profl. jours. Mem. Mich. Pub. Consultation Panel of Internat. Joint Commn., 1976-78; treas. Denver South High Sch. PTSA, 1988-91, pres., 1991-93; athletic dir. Most Precious Blood Sch., 1988-90; bd. dirs. Pioneer Jr. Hockey Assn., 1988-90. Mem. ABA (house of dels. 1997—, chair commn. on mental & physical disability law, 1998—, commn. on mental and phys. disability law 1995—, chmn. 1998—, tort and ins. practice sect., chmn. environ. law com. 1978-81, liaison jud. adminstrn. divsn. 1987-90, chmn. govt. liability com. 1988-89, 92-93, chmn. emerging issues com. 1996-97, sect. sec. 1997-99, mem. coun. govt. and pub. sector lawyers divsn. 1991-97, editor-in-chief The Brief 1981-87, spkr. ann. meeting 1991-94), ATLA, Denver Bar Assn. (chmn. pub. legal ednl. com. 1989-91, del. 1997—), Colo. Bar Assn. (spkr. ann. meetings 1991-95, chmn. health law sect. 1993-94, chmn. law edn. com. 1993-96, coun. licensure, enforcement and regulation, spkr. ann. meetings 1992-97, chmn. profl. discipline com. 1992-93, 98-99, program chmn. ann. meeting 1993-94, chair publs. com. 1995-97), Colo. Bd. Law Examiners. Democrat. Roman Catholic. Home: 1801 S Fillmore St Denver CO 80210-3507 Office: Atty Gen Office 1525 Sherman St Fl 5 Denver CO 80203-1760

CARR, JAMES GRAY, judge; b. Boston, Nov. 14, 1940; s. Edmund Albert and Anna Frances C.; m. Eileen Margaret Glynn, Dec. 17, 1966; children: Maureen M., Megan A., Darrah E., Caitlin E. AB, Kenyon Coll., 1962; LLB, Harvard U., 1966. Bar: Ill. 1966, Ohio 1972, U.S. Dist. Ct. (no. dist.) Ill. 1966, U.S. Dist. Ct. (no. dist.) Ohio 1970, U.S. Supreme Ct. 1980. Assoc. Gardner & Carton, et al., Chgo., 1966-68; staff atty. Cook County Legal Asst. Found., Evanston, Ill., 1968-70; prof. U. Toledo Law Sch., 1970-79; U.S. magistrate judge U.S. Dist. Ct., Toledo, 1979-94, U.S. dist. judge, 1994—; adj. prof. law Chgo. Kent Law Sch., 1969, Loyola U., Chgo., 1970; reporter, juvenile rules com. Ohio Supreme Ct., Columbus, 1971-72; reporter, mem. nat. wiretap com. U.S. Congress, Washington, 1976-77. Contbr. articles to profl. law jours. Founder, bd. dirs. Child Abuse Ctr., Toledo, 1970-84; active Lucas County Mental Health Bd., Toledo, 1984-89, Lucas County Children Svcs. Bd., Toledo, 1989-94. Fulbright fellow, 1977-78. Mem. ABA (reporter, elec. survey stds. 1979-80, mem. task force on tech. and law enforcement 1995—, mem. task force on jury initiatives 1995—), Toledo Bar Assn. (bd. dirs.), Phi Beta Kappa. Roman Catholic. Office: US Dist Ct 203 US Courthouse 1716 Spielbusch Ave Toledo OH 43624-1363

CARR, JAMES PATRICK, lawyer; b. Cheverly, Md., Apr. 13, 1950; s. Lawrence Edward Jr. and agnes (Dyer) C.; m. Mona L. Kyle, May 28, 1986; children: James P. Jr., Kristin, Kevin, Sean. BA, U. Notre Dame, 1972, JD, 1976. Bar: Md. 1976, Calif. 1977, U.S. Dist. Ct. (cen. dist.) Calif. 1977, U.S. Dist. Ct. (so. dist.) Calif. 1986. Assoc. Carr, Jordan et al, Washington, 1976-77; ptnr. Breidenbach, Swainston et al, L.A., 1977-84, Harney, Wolfe, Shaller & Carr, L.A., 1984-88, Carr & Shaller, L.A., 1988-89; pvt. practice law L.A., 1989—. Mem. Am. Bd. Trial Advs., Assn. Trial Lawyers Am., Consumer Attys. Calif., Consumer Attys. Assn. L.A. Democrat. Roman Catholic. Office: 11755 Wilshire Blvd Ste 1170 Los Angeles CA 90025-1539

CARR, JAMES REVELL, museum executive, curator; b. Bryn Mawr, Pa., Aug. 11, 1939; s. Clinton DeWitt and Asta Marie (Knudsen) C.; m. Mary Elizabeth Bump, June 25, 1963 (div. Oct. 1986); children: James Revell III, George McKelvy; m. Barbara Palmer, Apr. 15, 1989. BA, Rutgers U., 1962; MA, U. Pa., 1969. Teaching asst. U. Pa., Phila., 1968-69; archeologist N.J. State Mus., Trenton, 1968-69; rsch. assoc. Mystic Seaport Mus. Inc., Mystic, Conn., 1969-70, chief curator, 1970-78, dir., 1978—, pres., 1988—; pres. Internat. Congress Maritime Mus., Liverpool, Eng., 1984-87, Coun. Am. Maritime Mus., 1981-84; trustee Nat. Trust for Historic Preservation, Washington, 1983-92; accreditation commr. Am. Assn. Mus., Washington, 1988-94; chmn. Nat. Maritime Heritage Task Force, Washington, 1981-84. Author: Amerikanische Schiffsbuilder, 1976; contbr. chpts. to books, articles to profl. jours.; TV commentator Operation Sail, WBZ-TV, Boston, 1976, with Peter Jennings on ABC-TV, 1986, Columbus Celebration, Pub. Broadcast Sta., 1992. Corporator Lawrence and Meml. Hosp., New London, Conn., 1979-86; mem. vestry Calvary Ch., Stonington, Conn., 1978-81; mem., sec. Navy Adv. Com. Naval History. Lt. USNR, 1962-67. Mem. Am. Antiquarian Soc., Century Assn., Newcomen Soc., Off-Soundings Club. Avocations: running, skiing, sailing. Office: Mystic Seaport 75 Greenmanville Ave Mystic CT 06355-0990*

CARR, JAY PHILLIP, critic; b. N.Y.C., Aug. 19, 1936; s. Andrew Joseph and Florence (Glassman) C.; m. Nancy Lou Hutchison, Oct. 27, 1962 (div. Oct. 1978); children: Diane Elizabeth, Richard Joseph, Julia Veronica; m. Stacey Cooke Vaughan, May 3, 1996. B.S., City Coll. N.Y., 1958. Reporter Jersey City Jour., 1957; editorial asst., amusement dept. staff writer N.Y. Post, 1957-64; drama and music critic Detroit News, 1964-83; critic-at-large Boston Globe, 1983-88, film critic, 1988—. Served with AUS, 1960-62. Named Chevalier Ordre des Arts et Lettres (France), 1989; George Jean Nathan award for dramatic criticism, 1971-72. Office: Boston Globe 135 Morrissey Blvd PO Box 2378 Boston MA 02107-2378

CARR, JESSE METTEAU, III, lawyer, engineering executive; b. Roanoke, Va., Sept. 3, 1952; s. Jesse Metteau Jr. and Martha Ann (Niday) C.; m. Amelia Kathryn Tynes, May 6, 1983 (div. Oct. 1985). BSEE, La. State U., 1974, JD, 1977. Bar: La. 1978, Tex. 1979; registered profl. engr., Tex., Wash., Oreg., Pa., Ind., La., Miss., Ill. Elec. engr. Southeastern Chem., Reserve, La., 1974-77; control systems engr. J.E. Sirrine Co., Houston, 1977-83; pvt. practice cons. Houston, 1983-84; control systems engr. Jacobs Engring., Houston, 1985-86; mng. gen. ptnr. Carr/Sperry Design, Houston, 1985-87, Tech. Ventures Group, Houston, 1987-90; v.p. Intellex Corp., Houston, 1986-92, pres., 1992—, also bd. dirs.; mng. gen. ptnr. Tech. Ventures Group, Houston, 1987-90; v.p. East Tex. Co., Inc., 1994—; bd. dirs. Mimics Inc., Houston, East Tex. Co., Washington, Ga. Cub Scout leader Boy Scouts Am., Houston, 1987-90. Mem. IEEE, ABA, La. Bar Assn., Tex. Bar Assn., Am. Inst. Chem. Engrs., Internat. Soc. Pharm. Engrs., Am. Soc. Agrl. Engrs., S.W. Assn. Biotech. Cos., Instrument Soc. Am., Assn. Energy Engrs., Tau Beta Pi, Omicron Delta Kappa, Eta Kappa Nu. Republican. Methodist. Avocations: skiing, backpacking.

CARR, KENNETH MONROE, naval officer; b. Mayfield, Ky., Mar. 17, 1925; s. Samuel Norman and Nancy Elmore (Monroe) C.; m. Mary Elizabeth Pace, June 10, 1949. Student, U. Louisville, 1944-45; B.S., U.S. Naval Acad., 1949. Served as enlisted man U.S. Navy, 1943-45, commd. ensign, 1949; advanced through grades to vice adm., 1977; mem. commissioning crew U.S.S. Nautilus, 1954; comdg. officer U.S.S. Flasher, 1964-67, U.S.S. John Adams, 1967-68; mil. asst. to Dep. Sec. Def., 1973-77; comdr. submarine force Atlantic Fleet, Norfolk, Va., 1977-80; vice dir. Strategic Target Planning, Offutt AFB, Nebr., 1980-83; later dep. comdr. U.S. Atlantic Fleet, Norfolk, Va., 1983-85; chmn. US Nuclear Regulatory Commn., 1989-91; bd. dirs. MDM Svcs. Corp. Decorated D.S.M. (4), Legion of Merit (2). Baptist. Clubs: Army Navy Country, Army Navy Town, N.Y. Yacht, Thames. Home: 2322 Ft Scott Dr Arlington VA 22202-2207

CARR, LARRY DEAN, financial services executive; b. Mt. Vernon, Ill., Apr. 22, 1947; s. Jewell Dean and Mary Janet (Lawrence) C.; m. Jean Ann Swanson, May 12, 1973; 1 child, Lisa Diane. BS in Fin., U. Ill., 1969. CPCU. Analyst Allstate Ins. Co., Northbrook, Ill., 1970-75; controller Svc. Rev. Allstate Ins. Co., Arlington Heights, Ill., 1975-76; regional controller Allstate Ins. Co., Rochester, N.Y. and Murray Hill, N.J., 1976-80; exec. info. dir. Allstate Ins. Co., Northbrook, 1980-82, dir. mktg., 1982-83; v.p. Crum and Forster Personal Ins. Co./U.S. Fire Ins. Co., Basking Ridge, N.J., 1983-84, sr. v.p., 1984-85, exec. v.p., 1985-86, chmn. bd. dirs., chief exec. officer, 1986-90, also bd. dirs.; CEO Viking Inc. Co., 1986-90, Nat. Gen. Ins.Co., 1986-91; exec. v.p. Motors Ins. Corp., 1991; founding dir., chmn. bd. dirs. New Covenant Trust Co., N.A., 1997-99. Treas., bd. dirs. Somerset Hills YMCA, Basking Ridge, 1984-85; trustee Kent Place Sch., 1989-90; mem. adv. bd. Resource Ctr. for Women and Their Families, 1989-90; pres., CEO Presbyn. Ch. Found., 1993-99; dir. Jarvie Commonweal Svc., 1994-99, Ky. Shakespeare Festival, 1997. Served with USAR, 1969-74. Mem. Pres.' Assn., Am. Mgmt. Assn., Delta Sigma Pi. Republican. Presbyterian. Avocations: swimming, skiing. Office: 800 S 4th St Apt 1410 Louisville KY 40203-2146

CARR, LAWRENCE EDWARD, JR., lawyer; b. Colorado Springs, Colo., Aug. 10, 1923; s. Lawrence Edward and Lelah R. (Rubert) C.; m. Agnes Isabel Dyer, Dec. 26, 1946; children—Mary Lee, James Patrick, Lawrence Edward III, Eileen Louise, Thomas Vincent. B.S., U. Notre Dame, 1948, LL.B., 1949; LL.M., George Washington U., 1954. Bar: Colo. 1949, D.C. 1952, Md. 1961. With Travelers Ins. Co., 1949-51; practiced in Washington, 1952—; sr. ptnr. Carr Goodson Warner, P.C., Washington, 1984—. Mem. adv. coun. U. Notre Dame Coll. Law, 1985—. With USMCR, 1943-46, 51-52; col. Res.; ret. Fellow Am. Bar Found.; mem. ABA (ho. of dels. 1973-75), Bar Assn. D.C. (dir. 1969-71, pres. 1974-75), Internat. Assn. Ins. Counsel, D.C. Def. lawyers Assn. (pres. 1978-79), Bar Assn. D.C. Rsch. Found. (pres. 1985-86). E-mail: lec@cgu-law.com. Home: 111 Storm Haven Ct Stevensville MD 21666-3707 Office: Carr Goodson Warner PC 400 East Tower 1301 K St NW Ste 400E Washington DC 20005-3300

CARR, LES, psychologist, educator; b. Bklyn., Mar. 7, 1935; s. Samuel and Sarah (Berman) C.; children: Lincoln Damian, Sharon Rose, Lewis Wade, Faith Theresa. BA, NYU, 1957; MA, New Sch. for Social Rsch., N.Y.C., 1959; Ph.D., Vanderbilt U., 1963. Diplomate Am. Bd. Med. Psychotherapists (fellow); lic. psychologist, Calif.; cert. psychologist R.I. Rsch. and clin. intern Rockland State Hosp., N.Y.C. Dept. Mental Hygiene, 1958-59; cons. clin. psychologist to sr. clin. psychologist Ctrl. State Hosp., Nashville, 1962-64; sr. coord. psychol. svcs. U. R.I., Providence, 1963-68; prof., chmn. psychology dept., dean Summer Sch., Salve Regina Coll., Newport, R.I., 1966-70, v.p. acad. affairs, 1969-71; project dir. Newport Hosp., 1967-71; pres. Lewis U., Lockport, Ill., 1971-76; chmn. bd., dean faculty Columbia Pacific U., San Rafael, Calif., 1977—; pres., chmn. bd. dirs. Elder 100 Plus, Inc., Petaluma, Calif.; chmn. bd. dirs. Sr. Univ., B.C., Can., 1994—; staff psychologist San Quentin State Prison, 1989—; former ednl. cons. to sultan and min. of edn., Oman. Past chmn. R.I. Gov.'s Task Force on Mental Health Rehab.; chmn. bd. dirs. Sr. U., Richmond, Can.; mem. nat. adv. coun. Profl. Children's Sch., N.Y.C.; past chmn. adv. bd. dirs. Comprehensive Mental Health Ctr., Newport; past bd. dirs. Regional Ballet Soc., Joliet, Ill., R.I. Rehab. Assn.; past chmn. bd. trustees St. Mary's Acad., Nauvoo, Ill.; past mem. exec. com. R.I. Gov.'s Commn. on Vocat. Rehab. With U.S. Army, 1958. Mem. APA, Calif. Psychol. Assn., Marin Psychol. Assn. Home: 148 Wilson Hill Rd Petaluma CA 94952-9430

CARR, MARIE PINAK, book distribution company executive; b. Buffalo, June 17, 1954; d. Henry and Hildegard (Poech) Pinak; m. Richard Wallace Carr, Oct. 18, 1980; children: Katharine Marie, Ann Louise, Elizabeth Ashby. BS, Syracuse U., 1976. Cancer microbiologist Nat. Cancer Inst., Rockville, Md., 1976-78; mktg. specialist Precision Sci., Washington, 1978-80; art importer Dicmar Trading Co., Inc., Washington, 1981-83; book dist. Dicmar Trading Co., Silver Spring, Md., 1983—. Co-author: The Willard Hotel, 1986. Bd. dirs. Salvation Army Women's Aux., Washington, 1982—, pres., 1990-91; bd. dirs. Am. Cancer Soc., Washington, 1988-90; co-chmn. Nat. Cancer Ball, 1989, 90; active Jr. League Washington, 1987-90. Mem. Washington Club. Republican. Roman Catholic. Avocations: gardening, collecting textiles, tennis, travel. Office: Dicmar Trading Co Inc 4057 Highwood Ct NW Washington DC 20007-2131

CARR, MAURICE KIRK, JR., publishing executive; b. Dallas; s. Maurice Kirk and Effie Mae Carr; m. Jennifer Shinkle; children: Maurice Kirk III, Alexander Blakley. BBA, Tex. Tech U. Sales rep. Wall St. Jour., Dallas, 1968-70, Cin., 1970-73; sales rep. Wall St. Jour., Detroit, 1973-75, dist. mgr., 1975-78; advt. mgr. Wall St. Jour., N.Y.C., 1980-85, eastern regional mgr., 1985-94, advt. svc. dir., 1995—; adv. dir. Asian Wall St. Jour., Hong Kong, 1978-80. Named Outstanding Alumnus Tex. Tech. U. Mass Communications Dept., 1983, G.D. Crain Award, 1998. Mem. Bus. Mktg. Assn. (pres. N.Y. chpt. 1984, nat. treas. and chmn. 1987-88), Landmark Club, Halloween Yacht Club, Stamford Yacht Club. Avocations: tennis, sailing, skiing, exercise. Office: Wall St Jour 1155 S Ave of Americas New York NY 10170-0002

CARR, MICHAEL LEON, professional sports team executive, former professional basketball player; b. Wallace, N.C., Jan. 9, 1951; m. Sylvia Carr. Student, Guilford Coll., Greensboro, N.C. With Pat Pavers, Eastern Basketball Assn., Hamilton, Pa., 1973-74, Eastern Basketball Assn., Scranton, 1974-75; basketball player Israel Sabras, Israel, 1974-75, St. Louis Spirits, ABA, 1975-76; with Detroit Pistons, 1976-79; basketball player Boston Celtics, 1979-85, scout, 1985-91, dir., community relations, 1991-94, sr. exec. v.p., 1994-98, also dir. basketball ops., exec. v.p. corp. devel. Author: Don't Be Denied: My Story, 1987. NCAA Nat. Championship, 1973, first team All-American, NCAA, 1974; MVP, Israel Sabras; All-Rookie team, ABA; NBA All-Defensive Second Team, 1979, led NBA in steals, 1979, mem., NBA Championship Teams, 1981, 84. ABA All-Rookie Team, 1976. Mem., NAIA Championship Team, 1973. Office: Boston Celtics 151 Merrimac St Boston MA 02114-4720*

CARR, OSCAR CLARK, III, lawyer; b. Memphis, Apr. 9, 1951; s. Oscar Clark Carr Jr. and Billie (Fisher) Carr Houghton; m. Mary Leatherman, Aug. 4, 1973; children: Camilla Fisher, Oscar Clark V. BA in English with distinction, U. Va., 1973; JD with distinction, Emory U., 1976. Bar: Tenn. 1976, U.S. Dist. Ct. (we. dist.) Tenn. 1977, U.S. Dist. Ct. (no. dist.) Miss. 1977, U.S. Ct. Appeals (6th cir.) 1985, U.S. Ct. Appeals (5th cir.) 1995; cert. mediator, Tenn. Assoc. firm Glankler Brown, PLLC (formerly Glankler, Brown, Gilliland, Chase, Robinson & Raines), Memphis, 1976-82, chief mgr. Glankler Brown PLLC, 1998—, ptnr., 1982—, chief mgr., 1998—. Bd. dirs. Memphis Ballet Soc., 1980, Memphis-Shelby County Unit Am. Cancer Soc., 1985—, Memphis Oral Sch. for Deaf, 1988-91; treas., vestryman St. John's Episcopal Ch., Memphis, 1988-91, sr. warden, 1991; mem. Commn. on Ministry Diocese of West Tenn., 1987-90, King of Carnival Memphis, 1994; pres., dir. Juvenile Diabetes Found. Memphis chpt., 1998; bd. dirs. Carnival Memphis. Mem. ABA, Tenn. Bar Assn.(western dist. coun. environ. law 1992—), Memphis and Shelby County Bar Assn. (bd. dirs. 1985-87), bd. dirs. Carnival Memphis, 1997—, atty. Memphis Country Club, 1998—, U. Va. Alumni Assn. Office: Glankler Brown PLLC 1700 One Commerce Sq Memphis TN 38103

CARR, PATRICIA ANN, community health nurse; b. Teaneck, N.J., Dec. 6, 1949; d. John O. and Elizabeth (Nestor) Olsen. Diploma, Mt. Sinai Hosp. Sch. Nursing, N.Y.C., 1970. RN, Ga., Fla.; AIDS cert. RN. Asst. DON Taylor Meml. Hosp., Hawkinsville, Ga., 1979-81; staff nurse ICU Shands Teaching Hosp., Gainesville, Fla., 1981-82; staff nurse Venice Hosp., 1982-84; field nurse Fla. Home Health Svcs. Sarasota Inc., 1986-93; regulatory compliance coord. Fla. Home Health Svcs., Sarasota, 1993-96; program clin. coord. Cmty. AIDS Network, Inc., Sarasota, 1996-98; clin. studies coord. Infectious Diseases Assocs., Sarasota, 1998—. Contbr. articles to publs. Mem. APHA, Assn. Nurses in AIDS Care, Home Health Nurses Assn., Intravenous Nurses Soc., Assn. Practitioners in Infection Control, Assn. Clin. Rsch. Profls. Office: Infectious Diseases Assocs 1425 S Osprey Ave Ste 1 Sarasota FL 34239-2900

CARR, PATRICIA WARREN, adult education educator; b. Mobile, Ala., Mar. 24, 1947; d. Bedford Forrest and Mary Catherine (Warren) Slaughter; m. John Lyle Carr, Sept. 26, 1970; children: Caroline Elise, Joshua Bedford. BS in Edn., Auburn U., 1968, MEd, 1971. Tchr. DeKalb County Schs., Atlanta, 1969-70; counselor Dept. Defense Schs., Okinawa, Japan, 1972-75; tchr. Jefferson County Schs., Jefferson, Ga., 1975-76; counselor Clarke County Schs., Athens, Ga., 1976-78; tchr. Fairfax County Schs., Adult and Community Edn., Fairfax, Va., 1980—; instrnl. supr. Vol. Learning Program; coord. Enrichment for Srs. Program Fairfax Area Agy. on Aging and Adult and Cmty. Edn., 1985-89; cons. State Va. Dept. Edn., 1984—, Va. Assn. Adult and Cmty. Edn., 1987, Commn. on Adult Basic Edn., 1988; instr. George Mason U., Fairfax, 1985. Tchr. Met. Meml. United Meth. Ch., Washington, 1981—; co-leader McClean, Va. troop Girl Scouts U.S., 1985-88. Mem. Am. Assn. Adult and Community Edn., Smithsonian Nat. Assocs., No. Va. Assn. Vol. Adminstrs., Va. Assn. Adult and Community Edn., Greater Washington Reading Coun. Methodist. Avocations: tennis, horseback riding. Office: Fairfax County Adult & Community Edn Woodson Adult Ctr 9525 Main St Fairfax VA 22031-4006

CARR, PAUL HENRY, physicist; b. Boston, May 12, 1935. BS in Physics, MIT, 1957, MS in Physics, 1961; PhD in Physics, Brandeis U., 1966. Solid state research physicist Air Force Rsch. Lab. (formerly Rsch. Lab.), 1962-67; chief microwave acoustics br. Rome Air Devel. Ctr. (formerly Air Force Cambridge Research Labs.), 1967-77; chief components tech. br. Rome Air Devel. Ctr. (formerly Air Force Cambridge Research Labs.), Hanscom AFB, Mass., 1977-95, asst. chief antennas and components div. of electromagnetics directorate, 1977-95; tech. cons. Rome Lab., Bedford, Mass., 1995-97; ret., 1997; adv. group on electron devices, working group on microwave devices Office Under sec. Def. for Research and Engring. Contbr. articles to profl. jours.; patentee suface wave delay line with quater-wave taps, acoustic surface wave frequency synthesizer. 1st lt. Ordnance Corps U.S. Army, 1960-62. Recipient Marcus D. O'Day Meml. award for best paper, 1967, Guenter Loeser Meml. award for sci. achievement, 1973, Outstanding Tech. Achievement of Quarter award Air Force Systems Command, 1976. Fellow IEEE (chmn. Boston sect. on sonics and ultrasonics 1973-74, mem. tech. program coms. Ultrasonics Symposia 1971-89, chmn. tech. program coms. Ultrasonics Symposia 1976, com. microwave and microwave monolithic cirs. symposium 1986-89, chmn. Boston sect. microwave theory and techniques 1989-90, 94-95), Am. Phys. Soc. Office: Air Force Rsch Lab AFRL/SNHA 31 Grenier St Bedford MA 01731-3008 *Have the courage to create and the wisdom to choose love and truth.*

CARR, PAUL WALLACE, actor; b. New Orleans, Jan. 31, 1934; s. Edward Sidney and Elaine Grace Carr; children: Alexandra, Christina, Michael. Grad., Am. Theatre Wing, 1953. Actor, dir. L.A. Repertory Co., 1990—. Actor over 50 feature films, over 300 guest starring TV roles, over 100 stage prodns. Broadway, off-Broadway, L.A. and regional theatres. Recipient awards L.A. Weekly Newspaper, 1987, Dramalogue Mag., L.A., 1994. Democrat. Avocations: skiing, sailing, fishing.

CARR, RICHARD RAYMOND, editor, public relations administrator; b. Des Moines, Jan. 26, 1934; s. Raymond William and Myra Reuss (Stevens) C.; m. Kathryn S. Chapman, Jan. 9, 1954; children: Rochelle Carr Needham, Stephen Todd Carr. BJ, Kans. State U., 1956. News editor Headlight & Sun, Pittsburg, Kans., 1956-60; pub. rels. adminstr. Pittsburg State U., 1960-85; pub. rels. advisor Tri-Lakes Cmty. Theatre, Branson, Mo., 1985-87; mng. editor Alumni Today quar. jour. Ctrl. Mo. State U., Warrensburg, 1988-99, ret., 1999. Mem. Soc. Profl. Journalists, Kansas City Press Club, Alpha Tau Omega (trustee chpt.), Lions Club (past pres.), Kiwanis Club (past pres.). Methodist. Avocations: reading, collecting, history. E-mail: rcarr@iland.net. Home: 99 Hawthorne Hill Dr Warrensburg MO 64093-2904

CARR, ROBERT S., federal judge; b. 1946. BS, Furman U., 1967; JD, U. S.C., 1971. Bar: S.C. 1971. Legis. asst. to Senator Strom Thurmond, U.S. Senate, Washington, 1971; law clk. to Hon. Robert F. Chapman, U.S. Dist. Ct. for Dist. S.C., Columbia, 1971-72; pvt. practice, Columbia, 1972-75; magistrate judge for S.C., U.S. Magistrate Ct., Charleston, S, 1975—. With USAR, 1968. Office: Hollings Jud Ctr Broad and Meeting Sts Charleston SC 29401

CARR, ROBERT WILSON, JR., chemistry educator; b. Montpelier, Vt., Sept. 7, 1934; s. Robert Wilson and Marie (Soucy) C.; m. Betty Lee Elmer, June 21, 1958; children: Kevin, Terrell, Kathryn. B.S., Norwich U., 1956; M.S., U. Vt., 1958; Ph.D., U. Rochester, 1962. NIH fellow Harvard U., 1963-65; asst. prof. U. Minn., 1965-69, assoc. prof., 1969-75, prof. dept. chem. engring. and materials sci., 1975—; vis. prof. U. Cambridge, 1971-72, MIT, 1995; guest prof. U. Göttingen, Fed. Republic Germany, 1982. Asst. editor: Jour. Phys. Chemistry, 1970-80. Served to 1st lt. U.S. Army, 1963. NSF fellow, 1971-72; Fulbright fellow, 1982. Mem. Am. Chem. Soc., Am. Aviation Hist. Soc., Interam. Photochem. Soc., Am. Inst. Chem. Engrs., Sigma Xi. Mem. Congregational Ch. Home: 5722 Harriet Ave Minneapolis MN

55419-1807 Office: U Minn Dept Chem Engring & Material Scis Minneapolis MN 55455

CARR, RONALD EDWARD, ophthalmologist, educator; b. Newark, N.J., Sept. 17, 1932; s. Frank Edward and Mildred (Sasso) C.; m. Nancy May Gould, June 8, 1957; children: Peter Richardson, Jacqueline Marie, Timothy Edward. A.B., Princeton U., 1954; M.D., Johns Hopkins U., 1958; M.Sc., NYU, 1963. Intern Bellevue Hosp., N.Y.C., 1958-59; resident NYU Med. Ctr., N.Y.C., 1959-63; clin. assoc. NIH, Bethesda, Md., 1963-64, assoc. ophthalmologist, 1964-65; asst. prof. ophthalmology NYU Med. Ctr., 1965-67, assoc. prof., 1967-71, prof., 1971—. Author: Visual Electrodiagnosis, 1981, Electrodiagnostic Testing of the Visual System, 1990. Served to lt. comdr. USPHS, 1963. Recipient Knapp award AMA, 1966. Fellow Am. Acad. Ophthalmology, ACS; mem. Am Ophthal. Soc., N.Y. Ophthal Soc., Assn. Research in Ophthalmology. Republican. Episcopalian. Clubs: Princeton, Stone Horse Yacht. Home: 130 E End Ave New York NY 10028-7553 Office: NYU Med Ctr 530 1st Ave New York NY 10016-6481

CARR, ROXANNE MARIE, mortgage company executive; b. Mpls., Jan. 26, 1940; d. John A. and Lyla Jeannette (Coombs) Johnson; m. Rodney R. Levin, Sept. 7, 1993; children: Kurt Allen Carr, Karen Lee Carr Davis. Student, Calif. State U., Long Beach, 1968. Lic. real estate broker; cert. Dept. Real Estate approved instr., 1992. West coast regional v.p. ARCS Mortgage, Inc., San Luis Obispo, Calif., 1973-94; divsn. pres. and corp. sr. v.p. The Mortgage House, Inc., San Luis Obispo, 1995—; instr. real estate fin. Cuesta Coll.; bd. dirs. Cuesta Title Guaranty Co., San Luis Obispo, 1995—, Building Industry Assn., San Luis Obispo, 1996—, Econ. Forecast Project, U. Calif., Santa Barbara, 1996—, Mission Cmty. Bank, 1998—. Author: Financing Workbook for Real Estate Professionals, 1972, rev., 1994. Active various cmty. orgns.; bd. dirs. United Way of San Luis Obispo, 1994— ; vol. 1995 Kiss the Pig Fund Raiser; chair tech. bus. support campaign Cuesta C.C., San Luis Obispo, 1996-97; bd. dirs. Cure 2000 Leukemia Rsch.; task force Welfare to Work County of San Luis. Named Bus. Woman Yr. Telegram-Tribune, 1994. Mem. Rotary (various). Lutheran. Avocations: bicycling, travelling, reading, music. Office: The Mortgage House Inc 733 Marsh St San Luis Obispo CA 93401-3901

CARR, ROY ARTHUR, agricultural products applied research, development and commercialization processing organization executive; b. Toronto, Aug. 21, 1929; s. Arthur Edwin and Ruth Adelaide (Milligan) C.; m. Elizabeth Anne Gladman, Aug. 23, 1958; 1 son, Robert A. BASc in Chem. Engring. with first class honors, U. Toronto, 1952. Supr. quality control Procter and Gamble Co., 1952-55, supr. applied devel, 1955-58, quality control mgr., 1958-61, plant chem. engr., 1961-66; sect. head process engring. Anderson-Clayton Foods, Tex., 1966-68, div. head process engring., 1968-70, asst. tech. dir., 1970-71, plant mgr., 1971-72; mgr. engring. devel. Hunt-Wesson Foods, Calif., 1972-74, assoc. rsch. dir., 1974-75, dir. quality assurance, 1975-78, dir. consumer rels., 1976-78; dir. mfg. Canbra Foods, Alta., Can., 1978-80, v.p. ops., 1980-84; exec. dir. POS Pilot Plant Corp., Saskatoon, Sask., Can., 1984-85, pres., 1985—; pres. Internat. Oil Mill Supts., 1991-92; chmn. bd. dirs. AgWest Biotech., 1990-93; vice chmn. bd. dirs. Internat. Ctr. Agrl. Sci. and Tech., 1991; chmn., bd. dirs. Nuvotech Ventures Internat., 1993-95; bd. dirs. Canbra Foods. Contbr. papers to profl. confs., articles to jours. Served to lt. COTC RCEME Corp, 1948-51. Mem. Am. Oil Chemists Soc. (pres. 1989-90, pres. Can. sect. 1986-87), Can. Inst. Food Sci., Inst. Food Technologists, Canola Coun. Can. (tech. com.). Office: POS Pilot Plant Corp, 118 Veterinary Rd, Saskatoon, SK Canada S7N 2R4

CARR, STEPHEN HOWARD, materials engineer, educator; b. Dayton, Ohio, Sept. 29, 1942; s. William Howard and Mary Elizabeth (Clement) C.; m. Virginia W. McMillan, June 24, 1967; children: Rosamond Elizabeth, Louisa Ruth. BS, U. Cin., 1965; MS, Case Western Res. U., 1967, PhD, 1970. Coop. engr. Inland divsn. GM, Dayton, 1960-65; asst. prof. materials sci. and engring. and chem. engring. Northwestern U., Evanston, Ill., 1970-73, assoc. prof., 1973-78, prof., 1978—, dir. Materials Rsch. Ctr., 1984-90, asst. dean engring., 1991-93, assoc. dean engring., 1993—; cons. in field. Contbr. articles to profl. jours. Recipient Outstanding Alumni Achievement award U. Cin. Coll. Engring., 1993. Fellow Am. Soc. for Metals Internat., Am. Phys. Soc.; mem. AIChE, Soc. Automotive Engrs. (Ralph R. Teetor award 1980), Plastics Inst. Am. (Ednl. Svc. award 1975), Am. Chem. Soc., Soc. Plastics Engrs., Materials Rsch. Soc. Achievements include patents in plastics and textiles fields. Home: 2704 Harrison St Evanston IL 60201-1216 Office: Northwestern U 2145 Sheridan Rd Evanston IL 60208-0834

CARR, STEPHEN W., lawyer; b. Providence, Mar. 16, 1943. AB cum laude, Amherst Coll., 1965; JD cum laude, Harvard U., 1968. Bar: Mass. 1968. Law clk. to Hon. John Spaulding Mass. Supreme Judicial Ct., 1968-69; mem. Goodwin, Procter & Hoar, LLP, Boston. Mem. ABA (bus. law sect.), Mass. Bar Assn., Boston Bar Assn. Office: Goodwin Procter & Hoar LLP Exchange Pl Boston MA 02109-2803*

CARR, THOMAS DEADERICK, astronomer/physics educator, science administrator; b. Ft. Worth, Jan. 2, 1917; m. 1961; 1 child. BS, U. Fla., 1937, MS, 1939, PhD in Physics, 1958. Physicist, head blast measurement sect. Ballastic Rsch. Lab., Aberdeen Proving Ground, Md., 1940-45; civilian scientist U.S. Navy Bur. Ordanance, 1946; physicist, head antenna and propagation sect. Air Force Missile Test Ctr., Patrick AFB, Fla., 1950-56, staff mem. directorate range devel., 1950-56; asst. prof. to assoc. prof. U. Fla., Gainesville, 1958-66, assoc. chmn., 1976-78, chmn. astronomy, 1985-88, prof. astronomy and physics, 1979—, dir. Radio Obs., 1985-92. Mem. Am. Phys. Soc., Am. Astron. Soc., Am. Geophys. Union. Office: U Fla Radio Observatory 211 Space Scis Rsch Bldg Gainesville FL 32611-2055*

CARR, THOMAS ELDRIDGE, lawyer; b. Austin, Tex., Aug. 16, 1953; s. Peter Gordon and Margaret (Johnson) C.; children: Christopher Allen, Austin Thomas. BA, Tex. Tech U., 1975, JD, 1977. Bar: Tex. 1978, U.S. Dist. Ct. (no. and we. dist.) Tex. 1978, U.S. Ct. Appeals (5th cir.) 1981, U.S. Supreme Ct. 1982. Assoc. Morgan, Gambill & Owen, Ft. Worth, 1978-81; ptnr. Morgan, Owen, & Carr, Ft. Worth, 1981-85; ptnr. Quillin, Owen & Thompson, Ft. Worth, 1985-87; ptnr. Owen, Wilson & Carr, Ft. Worth, 1987-91; ptnr. Owen & Carr, Ft. Worth, 1991-94; ptnr. Lane, Ray, Wilson, Carr & Steves, Ft. Worth, 1994—. Co-author: Of Counsel to Classrooms: A Resource Guide to Assist Attorneys and Teachers in Law Focused Education. Active Benbrook City Council, Tex., 1984-86, Benbrook Park and Recreation Bd., 1981-84; mem. exec. bd. Longhorn coun. Boy Scouts Am., 1983-86; mem. Home Rule Charter Commn., Benbrook, 1983. Selected Outstanding Young Lawyer of Tarrant County, 1990. Mem. ABA (chmn. com), Ft. Worth Tarrant County Young Lawyers Assn. (pres. 1983), State Bar Tex. (chmn. sch. law sect. 1991, bd. dirs. 1998—, treas., sec. 1988), Tex. Young Lawyers Assn. (bd. dirs. 1984-86), Ridglea Country Club. Office: 6115 Camp Bowie Blvd Ste 200 Fort Worth TX 76116-5500

CARR, TIMOTHY BERNARD, librarian; b. Pitts., Nov. 22, 1955; s. Joseph Hurson and Margaret Elizabeth (O'Donnell) C.; children: Julia Elizabeth, Timothy Cahill. BA, U. Pitts., 1982, MLS, 1986. Libr. asst. Duke U., Durham, N.C., 1984-85; libr. U.S. News & World Report Mag., Washington, 1985-86; libr. Marymount U., Arlington, Va., 1986-89, head pub. svcs., 1989-90; br. libr. Anacostia Mus. Smithsonian Inst., Washington, 1991-93, br. libr. Nat. Postal Mus., 1993—. English adv. com. Arlington County Pub. Schs., 1987-88. Sgt. U.S. Army, 1975-79. Recipient commendation medal U.S. Army, 1978, sr. parachutists badge, 1978, pathfinder badge, 1978. Mem. ALA, Soc. History Fed. Govt. Office: Smithsonian Inst Librs Nat Postal Mus Br MRC 570 Washington DC 20560

CARR, WALTER JAMES, JR., research physicist, consultant; b. Knob Noster, Mo., May 6, 1918; s. Walter James and Alice Frances (Koch) C.; m. Winifred Walker Schultz, Mar. 21, 1953; children: James Lawrence, Robert David. BSEE, U. Mo., Rolla, 1940; MEE, Stanford U., 1942; DSc in Physics, Carnegie-Mellon U., 1951. Engr. Westinghouse Electric R&D, Pitts., 1942-51, section mgr., 1951-57, adv. physicist, 1957-65, mgr. solid state theory, 1965-70, cons., 1970-85; cons., 1985—; physicist Atomic Energy Establishment, Harwell, Eng., 1962. Author: AC Loss and Macroscopic Theory of Superconductors, 1983. Named to Acad. Elec. Engring., U. Mo., Rolla, 1981. Fellow Am. Phys. Soc., IEEE; mem. University Club. Avocations: tennis. Home: 1460 Jefferson Heights Rd Pittsburgh PA 15235-5220 Office: Westinghouse S&T Ctr 1310 Beulah Rd Pittsburgh PA 15235-5098

CARR, WILEY NELSON, hospital administrator; b. Dayton, Ohio, Dec. 29, 1940; s. Russell Earl and Anna Lee (Stroud) C.; m. Grace Elizabeth Brown, June 4, 1960 (div.); children: Wiley Nelson, Alison Mary Ann, G. Elizabeth, Joshua William, Joy Kathleen; m. Sharon L. Kersey, Aug. 22, 1997. Student, Miami U., Oxford, Ohio, 1959-62; BSJ, Ohio U., 1963, MS, 1964; MBA, Xavier U., Cin., 1974. Lic. nursing home adminstr., Ky. Dir. pub. rels. Western Coll. for Women, Oxford, 1964-67, dir. devel., 1967-70; dir. devel. and community rels. St. Elizabeth Med. Ctr., Covington, Ky., 1970-74, asst. adminstr., 1974-83; v.p., chief operating officer St. Elizabeth Med. Ctr., Edgewood, Ky., 1983-90; pres., CEO, Porter Meml. Hosp., Valparaiso, Ind., 1990—; bd. dirs. BetterCare, Inc., Cin.; sec. Tri-State Healthcare Laundry, Edgewood, 1989-90. Pres. Tri-State Community Cancer Orgn., Cin., 1988—; bd. dirs. United Way Porter County, Community Devel. Corp., Valparaiso, N.W. Ind. Forum, YMCA Valparaiso. Fellow Am. Coll. Healthcare Execs.; mem. Ind. Hosp. Assn. Republican. Methodist. Avocations: golf, hiking, swimming. Home: 1716 Beachview Ct Crown Point IN 46307-9315 Office: Porter Memorial Hospital 814 Laporte Ave Valparaiso IN 46383-5898

CARR, WILLARD ZELLER, JR., lawyer; b. Richmond, Ind., Dec. 18, 1927; s. Willard Zeller and Susan (Brownell) C.; m. Margaret Paterson, Feb. 15, 1952; children: Clayton Paterson, Jeffrey Westcott. BS, Purdue U., 1948; JD, Ind. U., 1951. Bar: Calif. 1951, U.S. Supreme Ct. 1963. Ptnr. Gibson, Dunn & Crutcher, Los Angeles, 1952—; mem. nat. panel arbitrators Am. Arbitration Assn.; former labor relations cons. State of Alaska; lectr. bd. visitors Southwestern U. Law Sch.; mem. adv. council Southwestern Legal Found., Internat. and Comparative Law Ctr. Trustee Calif. Adminstrv. Law Coll.; bd. dirs. Employers' Group, Calif. State Pks. Found., Los Angeles coun. Boy Scouts Am.; mem. Mayor's Econ. Devel. Policies Com.; past chmn. Pacific Legal Found.; past chmn. men's adv. com. Los Angeles County-USC Med. Ctr. Aux. for Recruitment, Edn. and Service; past chmn. bd. Wilshire Republican Club; past mem. Rep. State Central Com.; past mem. pres.'s coun. Calif. Mus. Sci. and Industry; mem. Nat. Def. Exec. Res., Los Angeles World Affairs Coun.; bd. dirs., sec. Los Angeles Police Meml. Found.; past chmn. Los Angeles sect. United Way; mem. adv. com. Los Angeles County Human Rels. Commn., commr., Calif. State World Trade Commn.; Los Angeles chpt. ARC. Fellow Am. Bar Found.; mem. ABA (past chmn. com. benefits to unemployed persons, econ. and resources controls com. of corp., banking and bus. law sect.; internat. labor rels. law com. of labor and employment law sect., also com. devel. of law under Nat. Labor Rels. Act), Internat. Bar. Assn. (past chmn. labor law com. of bus. law sect.), chmn. Labor Employment Com., The Federalist Soc., Calif. Bar Assn., L.A. County Bar Assn., L.A. C. of C. (past chmn. 1991), Calif. C. of C. Home: 2185 Century Hl Los Angeles CA 90067-3516 Office: Gibson Dunn & Crutcher 333 S Grand Ave Ste 4400 Los Angeles CA 90071-3197

CARR, WILLIAM H(ENRY) A., public relations executive, author; b. Albany, N.Y., Nov. 25, 1924; s. John Joseph and Ruby (Sokol) C.; m. Brooks Boeke, Nov. 18, 1984; stepchildren: Stephen (dec.), Christine, Jennifer, John, Brooks, Beth. Student, U. Chgo., 1944-46. Reporter City News Bur., Chgo., 1943-44, Chgo. Sun, 1944-45, Chgo. Times, 1945-46; news editor ABC, Chgo., 1946-47; pub. relations specialist John Price Jones Co., N.Y.C., 1949-52; assoc. dir. pub. rels. United Community Def. Svcs., N.Y.C., 1952-55; reporter, editor N.Y. Post, N.Y.C., 1955-64; cons. INA Corp., Phila., 1967-71; dir. pub. info. Commonwealth of Pa., Harrisburg, 1971; pres., CEO Jack Raymond & Assocs., Inc., N.Y.C. and Indpls., 1977—. Author: Beauty in the White House, 1961, Those Fabulous Kennedy Women, 1961, What Is Jack Paar Really Like?, 1962, The Basic Book of the Cat, 1962, Medical Examiner, 1963, J.F.K., A Complete Biography, 1963, Diplomatic Immunity (as Eleanor Sydell), 1966, The Age of the Wife Swappers (as John T. Warren), 1966, Savage Scalpel (as Alain Rothstein), 1968, Black Gold, 1969, Perils: Named and Unnamed, 1967, The Emergence of Red China, 1966, The DuPonts of Delaware, 1964 (Best Book of Yr., Friends of Am. Writers), From Three Cents a Week..., 1975, The New Basic Book of the Cat, 1978, Up Another Notch: Institution Building at Mead, 1989, Genentech: An Oral History, 1997. Mem. Md. Gov.'s Task Force on Crime Prevention and Cmty. Involvement, 19669; mem. exec. com. Pa. Pub. Com. for Humanities, 1971-76; bd. dirs. 500 Festival Assocs., 1988-93, Ind. Internat. Coun., 1988—, Phoenix Theatre, Indpls.; pres. Hemlock Soc. Ind., 1994—, Ind. Advocates for Arts, 1994-97; pres. Ind. Citizens for Arts, 1994-97. Recipient Albert Schweitzer medal for humanitarianism, Animal Welfare Inst., 1961. Mem. Authors Guild Am., Aircraft Owners and Pilots Assn., Pub. Rels. Soc. Am., Internat. Assn. Bus. Communicators, Confrerie Chevaliers du Tastevin de Bourgogne, Columbia Club Indpls., Overseas Press Club, Nat. Press Club, N.Y. Press Club, Indpls. Press Club. Office: Jack Raymond & Assocs Inc 5235 Roland Dr Indianapolis IN 46228-2242

CARRA, ANDREW JOSEPH, advertising executive; b. Bklyn., July 30, 1943; s. Andrew Sylvester and Grace (Santoro) C.; m. Eileen Lynn Campbell, Aug. 6, 1966; children: Christopher Andrew, Allison Lynn, Courtney Lauren. BA, St. Bonaventure U., 1966. Asso. editor Sport Mag., Macfadden-Bartell, N.Y.C., 1967-71; mng. editor publs. div. Spencer Mktg. Services, N.Y.C., 1971-73; assoc. pub. Camping Jour. mag. Davis Publs., N.Y.C., 1973-82; account supr. Robert Marston and Assocs., N.Y.C., 1982-83; v.p., dir. pub. relations Colarossi Griswold Inc., N.Y.C., 1983-84; pres. AC&R Pub. Relations, Inc., N.Y.C., 1984-86; dir. McCann-Erickson Inc., N.Y.C., 1987-96; creative dir. BBB Group Ltd., Hackensack, N.J., 1996—. Author: Complete Guide to Hiking and Backpacking, 1977, How to Go Camping, 1978; Contbr. chpts. to books, articles to periodicals. Mem. Outdoor Writers Assn., Am. Soc. Mag. Editors, Nat. Wildlife Fedn. Democrat. Roman Catholic. Home: 157 Fairfield Pl Fairfield CT 06430-5605 Office: BBB Group Ltd 364 Summit Ave Hackensack NJ 07601-1413

CARRADINE, KEITH IAN, actor, singer, composer; b. San Mateo, Calif., Aug. 8, 1949; s. John Richmond Reed and Sonia (Sorel) C.; m. Sandra Will, Feb. 6, 1982, 2 daughters: Martha Campbell Plimpton, Sorel; 1 son, Cade Richmond. Student in drama, Colo. State U., 1967. Appeared on Broadway in Hair, 1969-70, L.A. prodn., 1969, Foxfire, 1982-83 (Outer Critics Circle award 1983), L.A. prodn., 1985-86, The Will Rogers Follies, 1991-92 (Tony nomination best performance leading actor in a musical 1991); N.Y. Shakespeare Festival prodn. Wake Up, It's Time to go to Bed, 1979; film appearances include: A Gunfight, 1970, McCabe and Mrs. Miller, 1970, Idaho Transfer, 1971, Grasslands, 1971, Emperor of the North, 1972, Antoine and Sebastian, 1973, Joe and Margherito, 1973, Thieves Like Us, 1973, Nashville, 1975 (Acad. and Golden Globe awards, Best Original Song for "I'm Easy" 1975), Lumiere, 1975, (also contbr. music) Welcome to L.A., 1976, Old Boyfriends, 1976, The Duellists, 1977, Pretty Baby, 1978, An Almost Perfect Affair, 1979, The Long Riders, 1980, Southern Comfort, 1981, Choose Me, 1983, Maria's Lovers, 1984 (lyricist Maria's Story), Trouble in Mind, 1986, The Inquiry, 1986, Backfire, 1986, The Moderns, 1987, Street of No Return, 1988, Cold Feet, 1988, The Bachelor, 1989, Daddy's Dyin, Who's Got the Will?, 1990, Criss Cross, 1991, The Ballad of the Sad Cafe, 1991, Andre, 1994, Wild Bill, 1994, The Tie That Binds, 1994, 2 Days in the Valley, 1995, A Thousand Acres, 1996, Standoff, 1998, (cameo) Sgt. Pepper's Lonely Hearts Club Band, 1978; TV films include: Man on a String, 1972, The Godchild, 1974, Scorned and Swindled, 1984, Blackout, 1984, A Winner Never Quits, 1985, Half a Lifetime, 1985, Eye on the Sparrow, 1987, Stones for Ibarra, 1987, My Father, My Son, 1988, The Revenge of Al Capone, 1988, The Forgotten, 1989, Confessional, 1989, Judgment, 1990, Payoff, 1990, Is There Life Out There?, 1994, Journey to Mars, 1995, Trial by Fire, 1995, The Last Stand At Saber River, 1996, The Oath, 1996, Keeping The Promise, 1997, (mini-series) A Rumour of War, 1980, Chiefs, 1983 (Emmy award nominee 1983), Murder Ordained, 1986, Confessional, 1989, In the Best of Families: Bitter Blood, 1994, Dead Man's Walk, 1995, (pilot movie) Last Chance, 1995; narrations include: Hot on the Trail: The Untold West, 1993, Baseball Documentary Series, 1994, The West Documentary Series, 1995; albums include: I'm Easy, 1976, Lost and Found, 1978. Presented a star on Hollywood Walk of Fame, 1993. Mem. Acad. Motion Picture Arts and Scis., Greenpeace Found., Cousteau Soc., Sierra Club. Democrat. Episcopalian. *

CARRADINI, LAWRENCE, comparative biologist, science administrator; b. Astoria, N.Y., Apr. 18, 1953; s. George John and Florence (Camuti) C.; m. Susan Marie Peterson, Sept. 23, 1972 (divorced); 1 child, Daniel Lawrence. BS in Zoology, Columbia Pacific U., 1989, MS in Vertebrate Reproductive Physiology and Physiol. Ecology, 1992. From technician to lab. supr. Charles River Labs., Wilmington, Mass., 1978-91, rschr., 1991; sr. scientist, mgr. biol. labs. Mass. Health Rsch. Inst., Boston, 1992-96; chief labs. Mass. Biologic Labs., U. Mass. Med. Sch., Boston, 1996—; co-chmn. Instnl. Animal Care and Use Com., State Lab. Inst./Orphan Biologies Inst. Mass. Pub. Health and Mass. Biologics Lab.; apptd. to State DPGS task force on procurement practices; mem. Lake Survey, U. N.H., Salem, 1982-83; instr. Internat. Children's Vaccine Tng. Program. Mem. editl. bd. Internat. Jour. Advances in Contraceptive Delivery Systems; contbr. articles to Jour. Lab. Animal Sci., Jour. Am. Vet. Med. Assn. Officer, selectman apptd. mem. 208 Water Quality Study Com., Salem, N.H., 1981-82, chmn., selectman apptd. mem., 1982-83; mem. adv. bd. Internat. M.C. Chang Meml. Festschrift; bd. dirs. Lowell Celebrates Kerouac, Inc. N.Y. State Regents scholar, 1971. Mem. Soc. for Cryobiology, Nat. Am. Assn. Lab. Animal Sci., Am. Assn. Lab. Animal Sci. (New Eng. chpt., cert. nat. lab. animal technologist, item writer technician cert. examination program), Lab. Animal Mgmt. Assn., Internat. Platform Assn., N.Y. Acad. Scis. Democrat. Achievements include development of reliable method to cycle estrus in syrian hamsters; co-development of commercially available cryopreserved 1-cell mouse embryos for use in media assays; co-application of 1-cell technology toward development of commercially available cryopreserved, fertilized, pronuclear-staged mouse oocytes for DNA microinjection; development of central technical services group Massachusetts Public Health Biologics Laboratory of Orphan Biologics Inst. Home: PO Box 8797 Lowell MA 01853-8797 Office: 305 South St Boston MA 02130-3515

CARRAHER, JOHN BERNARD, lawyer; b. Denver, Feb. 13, 1934; s. Thomas Peter and Mary Agnes (Carroll) C.; m. Carol J. Steffens Carraher, June 28, 1958; children: Steven, Constance, Lee Anne, Patti. BS, Regis Coll., Denver, 1956; LLB, Denver U., 1958. Bar: Colo., U.S. Dist. Ct. 1959. Pvt. practice pvt. practice, Denver, 1958-80; lawyer, shareholder, dir. Feder, Morris, Tamblyn & Goldstein, Denver, 1980-96; of counsel Michael R. Dice & Co. LLC, Denver, 1996-97, Bryant and Van Nest LLC, Denver, 1997—; lectr. advanced estate planning symposium U. Denver, 1993, Guardianship Symposium, 1997. Contbr. articles to profl. jours. Coord. Risen Christ Parish Edn. Program, Denver, 1968-71; mem. jud. adv. coun. Colo. Supreme Ct., 1987-93; lectr. Nat. Bus. Inst., Eau Claire, Wis., 1992, 94. Named Presidency Colo. Mcpl. Judges Assn., 1984-85; mem. Nat. Hon. Soc., 1992. Fellow Am. Acad. Forensic Scis. (lectr. Cin. 1990, L.A. 1991, New Orleans 1992, Boston 1993, Seattle 1995, co-chair edn. jurisprudence sect. 1996, 97); mem. Denver Probate Ct. Vis. program, Greenwood Village Ct. Mediation Program, Greenwood Village Ct. Jud. Intern Program Colo. Bar Assn. (bd. govs. 1984-85), Colo. Trial Lawyers Assn. (lectr. 1989), Am. Colo. Denver Arapahoe Bar Assn., Elder Law Adv. Coun. U. Denver Inst. for Advanced Legal Studies (coun. co-chair 1995-97). Avocations: skiing, reading. Office: Bryant & Van Nest LLC 3300 E 1st Ave Denver CO 80206-5810

CARR-ALLEN, ELIZABETH, real estate and mortgage broker, metaphysician; b. Ithaca, N.Y., May 24, 1939; d. John Franklin II and Helen Louise (Ziegler) C.; m. Robert Kern Mansur, Sept. 7, 1980 (div. 1982). Student, U. Rochester, 1957-60; BA, U. Edinburgh, Scotland, 1962, MA in English Lit., 1962; PhD in Metaphysics, 1992, DDiv, 1993; grad., Realtors Inst. Lic. real estate broker, Fla.; cert. residential specialist. With various advt. pub. rels. firm N.Y.C., 1962-72; dir. comm. Unishield, Inc., N.Y.C., 1972-74; dir. pub. rels. Thermasol Ltd., N.Y.C., 1974-76; v.p., CFO Sports Mktg., Inc., N.Y.C., 1976-80; sales dir. Found. Investments, Highland Beach, Fla., 1980-85; dir. mktg. Concordia Properties, Highland Beach, 1985-86; pres. Sunstone Realty, Inc., Boca Raton, 1987-94, World Investors Realty, 1995-98, The Carr-Allen Group, 1998—. Mem. NRA, NAFE, AULV, Nat. Assn. Realtors, Fla. Assn. Realtors, Women's Coun. Realtors, South Palm Beach Assn. Realtors, Mensa, Intertel. Avocations: motorcycling, scuba diving, pistol/rifle shooting, crystals, healing. Home: 8705 Eagle Run Dr Boca Raton FL 33434-5433

CARRASQUILLO, RAMON LUIS, civil engineering educator, consultant; b. San Juan, P.R., July 28, 1953; s. Ramon L. and Abigail Carrasquillo; m. Gladys Mateu (div. 1983); children: Ramon L. Jr., Jessica Marie; m. Peggy Musser, 1985; children: Travis Andrew, Austin Mathew, Bryant Matthew. BSCE, U. P.R., 1975; MSCE, Cornell U., 1978, PhD, 1980. Registered profl. engr., Tex. Grad. rsch. asst. Cornell U., Ithaca, N.Y., 1976-79; asst. prof. civil engring. U. Tex., Austin, 1980-84, assoc. prof. civil engring., 1984-89, prof. civil engring., 1989—, researcher, 1980—; pres. CFX, Inc., Excellence in Engring., 1996—, Ceniza Internat., Inc., 1996—; ptnr. Carrasquillo Assocs., Austin, Tex., 1980—, assoc. dir. Internat. Ctr. for Aggregates Rsch., Austin, 1992-96; pres. Rainbow Materials, Inc., 1994—, bd. dirs. Children's Advocacy Found., 1999. Co-author: Production of High Strength Concrete, 1986, also papers in field. Bd. dirs. Children's Advocacy Found., 1999—. Recipient Lockheed Ft. Worth Tchg. Excellence award, 1995; Austin Industries fellow, 1991—; Dec. 14, 1995 named Ramon Carrasquillo Day, Austin. Fellow Am. Concrete Inst. (T.Y. Lin award 1990); mem. ASTM, ASCE, Tex. Aggregates and Concrete Assn. (Outstanding Speaker award 1980), Am. Concrete Inst. Office: U Tex 10100 Burnet Rd Bldg 18B Austin TX 78758-4445

CARRAWAY, MELVIN J., protective services official; m. Karen Carraway; children: Rachel, Maya. BMus, Heidelberg Coll., 1975; grad., FBI Nat. Acad., 1984. Comdr. enforcement divsn. Ind. State Police, supt., 1997—; exec. dir. Ind. State Emergency Mgmt. Agy./Dept. of Fire and Bldg. Svcs. With U.S. Army. Office: Ind State Police 100 N Senate Ave Indianapolis IN 46204

CARREAU, PIERRE, chemical engineering educator; b. Montreal, Que., Can., Nov. 14, 1939; m. 1963; 3 children. BSc, U. Montreal, 1963, MSc, 1965; PhD in Chem. Engring., U. Wis., 1968. Asst. chem. engr. Ecole Polytechnique, 1964-65; asst. prof. to assoc. prof. chem. engring. U. Montreal, 1968-80, chmn. dept., 1973-79, prof., 1980—. Mem. Chem. Inst. Can., Can. Soc. Chem. Engrs., Soc. Rheology, Am. Inst. Chem. Engrs., SPE. Office: Ecole Polytechnique, Box 6079 Suc Centre-Ville, Montreal, PQ Canada H3C 3A7

CARREKER, JOHN RUSSELL, retired agricultural engineer; b. Cook Springs, Ala., Aug. 15, 1908; s. John Robert and Cora Selina (Polk) C.; m. Helen Mackey Garrett, Feb. 10, 1934; children: Joan Louise, James Russell. BS, Ala. Poly. Inst. (now Auburn, U.), 1930, MS, 1933. Agrl. engr. Civilian Conservation Corps, Dadeville, Ala., 1933-34, USDA-SCS, Anniston, Ala., 1935-38; rsch. agrl. engr. USDA-SCS & Agrl. Rsch. Svc., Watkinsville, Ga., 1938-58; rsch. lia. rep. USDA-SCS & Agrl. Rsch. Svc., Athens, Ga., 1958-61; rsch. leader USDA-Agrl. Rsch. Svc., Athens, 1961-73; ret., 1973. Author over 80 tech. papers on erosion control, irrigation and water mgmt. on farm land. Chmn. PTA, Athens, 1950; pres. Civitan Club, Athens, 1948, Residents Assn., Atlanta, 1986. Recipient Outstanding Alumnus award Auburn U., 1991. Fellow Am. Soc. Agrl. Engrs. (emeritus) Soil and Water Engring. award 1970), Soil and Water Conservation Soc. (life fellow); mem. SAR.

CARREL, MARC LOUIS, lawyer, policy advisor; b. Buffalo, Aug. 31, 1967; s. Jerome D. and Judith E. (Fish) C. BA with distinction, U. Mich., 1988; JD, U. Pa., 1993. Bar: Calif., 1993, D.C., 1995. Staff asst. U.S. Senate Com. Agriculture, Nutrition, and Forestry, Washington, 1989, calender clk., 1989-90; assoc. cons. Office of Calif. State Assemblyman Richard Polanco, Sacramento, 1994; legis. cons. Office of Calif. State Senator Richard Polanco, Sacramento, 1994-96; counsel Calif. State Senate Dem. Caucus, Sacramento, 1995-96; legis. policy cons. to Calif. Assembly Spkr. Cruz M Bustamante, Sacramento, 1997, counsel, 1997-98; dep. issues dir. Jane Harman for Gov., 1998; sr. cons. Office of Assemblymem. Cruz M. Bustamante, 1998; policy dir. Cruz M. Bustamante for Lt. Gov., 1998; transition dir. Office of Lt. Gov.-Elect, 1998-99, sr. advisor to Lt. Gov., 1999—; mem. Legis. Task Force Land Use, Sacramento, 1995, L.A. Fiscal Crisis Working Group, Sacramento, 1995, Calif. Organized Investment Network Econ. Devel. Com., 1996; co-chair Ins. Reinvestment Task Force, Sacramento, 1995; staff Gov.-Elect's Agr. Water Transition Task Force, 1998; mem. rural devel. strategic plan steering com. USDA; coord. Gov.'s Emergency Freeze Assistance Task Force, 1999; mem. designee State Job Tng. Coord. Coun., 1999—. Sec. Pa. Law Equal Justice Found., Phila., 1990-92; comm. dir. Arlo Smith for Atty. Gen. '94, San Francisco, 1993; co-chair Young Leadership Divsn., Sacramento, 1996-97; trustee Jewish Fedn. Sacramento Region, 1996-97; bd. dirs. Jewish Cmty. Rels. Coun., Sacramento, 1997—, vice-chair, 1998—; cofounder, sec. Jewish Civic Action Network, 1997-99; mem. Sacramento Policy Adv. Com., 1998-99, chair, 1999—; commr. Human Rights/Fair Housing Commn., Sacramento, 1999—. Recipient U.S. Atty.'s Office Spl. Achievement award, Buffalo, 1991; William J. Branstrom Freshman prize, 1986. Mem. Am. Polit. Items Collectors, State Bar Calif., D.C. Bar, Sacramento Bar Assn., U. Mich. Alumni Assn., U. Pa. Law Alumni Soc. Avocation: collector of political paraphernalia. Office: Office of Spkr State Capitol Rm 219 Sacramento CA 95814-4906

CARRELL, DANIEL ALLAN, lawyer; b. Louisville, Jan. 2, 1941; s. Elmer N. and Mary F. (Pfingst) C.; m. Janis M. Wilhelm, July 3, 1976; children: Mary Monroe, Courtney Adele. AB, Davidson Coll., 1963; BA, Oxford U., 1965, MA, 1969; JD, Stanford U., 1968. Bar: Va. 1972, U.S. Dist. Ct. (ea. dist.) Va. 1972, U.S. Ct. Appeals (4th cir.) 1975, U.S. Dist. Ct. (we. dist.) Va. 1985. Asst. prof. U.S. Mil. Acad., West Point, N.Y., 1968-71; assoc. Hunton & Williams, Richmond, Va., 1971-79, ptnr., 1979-95; prin. Carrell & Rice, Richmond, Va., 1996—. Active Richmond Rep. Com., 1974—; co-counsel Dalton for Gov. campaign, Richmond, 1977; counsel Obenshain for Senate campaign, Richmond, 1978; treas. Va. Victory '92; state fin. chmn., mem. fin. com., state ctrl. com. and budget com. Rep. Party Va., 1993-96; bd. dirs. Southampton Citizens Assn., v.p., 1985-94; pres. Davidson Coll. Alumni Assn., 1987-88; trustee Davidson Coll., 1987-88; bd. dirs. Needles Eye Ministries, 1986-90, mem. adv. bd., 1990—; elder, trustee Stony Point Reformed Presbyn. Ch., 1993—; moderator James River Presbytery Presbyn. Ch. Am., 1998. Rhodes scholar, 1962; recipient Award of Merit Sports Illustrated Mag., 1963. Mem. ABA (chmn. exemption and Noerr Doctrine com. 1986-87, antitrust sect.), Va. Bar Assn. (chmn. young lawyers joint law-related edn. com. 1978-79, young lawyers fellow award 1980), Va. State Bar (chmn. com. on legal edn. and admission to bar 1984-91, bd. govs. sect. edn. lawyers 1992—), Richmond Bar Assn., Christian Legal Soc., Westwood Club. Avocations: tennis, basketball, theatre, concerts. Home: 3724 Custis Rd Richmond VA 23225-1102 Office: Carrell & Rice 7275 Glen Forest Dr Richmond VA 23226-3772

CARRELL, HAMMEL LEE, jewelry designer; b. Lovington, N.Mex., Dec. 3, 1941; s. Hammel and Sudie Lee (Foust) C.; m. Linda Lee Koch; 1 child, Sativa Sunny Day January. BA, Ea. N.Mex. U., 1965; BFA, N.Mex. State U., 1973, MA, 1974; MFA, U. Kans., 1977. Owner, mgr. Fuego Del Sol, Cloudcroft, N.Mex., 1971-74, Platoro Del Fuego, Las Cruces, N.Mex., 1972-74; instr. design U. Kans., Lawrence, 1974-77; co-owner, mgr. The Oxbow Gallery, Lawrence, 1976-77; asst. prof. art No. Ariz. U., Flagstaff, 1977-80; designer, planner Carrell Carpet and Interiors, Austin, 1980-82; owner Creative Solutions, Austin, 1982-84; dir., founder The Austin Sch. of Jewelry and Design, Austin, 1984-97; owner New Horizon Studio, Austin, 1988—, Reflections of the West Gallery, Spicewood, 1998—; juror N.Mex. Designer-Craftsmans show, 1978, Albuquerque Designer-Craftsman competition, 1981, N.Mex. State U. Art Undergrad. Shows, 1972-74, Grad. and Faculty Shows, 1973-74. One-man shows include Contemporary Jewelry show N.Mex. State Fair, 1972, Tex. Christian U., 1973, N.Mex. Gallery, 1973, Gallery Plus, Los Alamos, N.Mex., 1974, Nat. Metal Invitational Traveling Exhibit, U.S., Australia and New Zealand, 1975, Grad. Thesis Exhibit, Lawrence, Kans., 1977, S.W. Metalsmithing Exhbn., 1979, The Westside Gallery, Phoenix, 1980-82, Columbine Gallery, Breckenridge, Colo., 1984, Magic Mountain Gallery, Taos, N.Mex., 1985, Applied Arts Gallery, Austin, Tex., 1986, Littlefield Gallery, Austin, 1987, Red Poppy Gallery, Georgetown, Tex., 1988-90, El Taller Gallery, Austin, 1994-95, Spirit Echos Gallery, Austin, 1995—, Western Design Conf., 1998. Elected v.p. Art Students League N.Mex. State U., elected student rep. to faculty meetings. With USAF, 1966-70. Assistantship N.Mex. State U., U. Kans.; grantee Matthey-Johnson Inc. Mem. Delta Sigma Pi, Alpha Rho Gamma. Avocations: writing, painting, jewelry, sculpture, ceramics. Office: PO Box 196 Spicewood TX 78669-0196

CARRELL, TERRY EUGENE, manufacturing company executive; b. Monmouth, Ill., July 1, 1938; s. Roy Edwin and Caroline Hilma (Fillman) C.; m. Bonnie Lee Clements, July 11, 1964; children: Philip Edwin, Andrew David Sr. AB, Monmouth Coll., 1961; MBA, Calif. State U., L.A., 1967; D of Bus. Adminstrn., U. So. Calif., 1970; AAS, Ivy Tech. State Coll., 1991. Sr. engr. N.Am. Aviation, 1962, prin. engr. reconnaissance and comm., 1963-67; mgr. avionics analysis and techs. B-1 divsn. Rockwell Internat., 1967-73; dir. engring. Morse Controls divsn., 1973-74; gen. mgr. Morse Controls divsn. Incom Internat. Inc., 1974-78; pres. indsl. divsn. Morse Controls, 1978-80, pres., 1980-82; pres. Heim Bearings, 1982-85; gen. mgr. Stewart-Warner Corp., 1985-88; pres. Stewart Warner South Wind Corp., 1988-95, Stewart Warner Electronics Corp., 1991-95; pres., COO Nartron Corp., 1995-97; pres. Image Moulding and Frame, Inc., Image Arts, Inc., 1997—, TECorp, Inc., 1997—, Best Weld, Inc., 1998—; cons.; lectr. U. So. Calif., 1967-70. Contbr. articles to profl. jours; patentee in field. Mem. Hudson (Ohio) Econ. Devel. Com., 1979-82; bd. dirs., coun. commr. Boy Scouts Am., 1980-85, mem. nat. coun., 1980-85; mem. service rev. panel United Way of Summit County, 1980. NDEA fellow, 1961-63. Mem. Hudson C. of C. (trustee 1976-78), Boating Industry Assn. (chmn. steering task force 1974-85), Am. Boat and Yacht Coun. (dir. 1980-88). Office: 1315 W 18th St Anderson IN 46016-3800

CARREN, JEFFREY P., lawyer; b. Chgo., Oct. 8, 1946. AB with high honors, U. Ill., 1968; JD, Northwestern U., 1972. Bar: Ill. 1973, U.S. Dist. Ct. (no. dist.) Ill. 1973, U.S. Ct. Appeals (7th cir.) 1976, U.S. Supreme Ct. 1980. Formerly ptnr. Winston & Strawn, Chgo.; ptnr. Laner, Muchin, Dombrow, Becker, Levin & Tominberg Ltd., Chgo., 1994—. Editor notes and comments Northwestern U. Law Rev., 1971-72/. Edmund James scholar. Mem. ABA (tax sect.), Ill. State Bar Assn. (employee benefits sect. coun.), Chgo. Bar Assn. (employee benefits com), Am. Arbitration Assn. (panel arbitrators), Phi Eta Sigma. Office: Laner Muchin et al 515 N State St Chicago IL 60610-4325

CARRERA, RODOLFO, nuclear engineer, physicist; b. Barcelona, Spain, Dec. 18, 1953; came to U.S., 1978, naturalized, 1990; s. Rodolfo and Rosario (Zabaleta) C.; m. Elena Montalvo, Jan. 7, 1978. BS, Poly. U., Madrid, 1975; MS, U. Wis., 1979, PhD, 1983. Rsch. engr. Spanish Nuclear Agy., Madrid, 1975-77; rsch. asst. nuclear engring. dept. U. Wis., Madison, 1978-83; rsch. fellow physics dept. Inst. Fusion Studies U. Tex., Austin, 1983-86, project mgr. Ctr. Fusion, 1986-88, chief scientist Ctr. Fusion, 1988-91, lectr. mech. engring. and physics dept., 1984-90; tech. dir. Valley Rsch. Corp., Austin, 1991—; rsch. asst. Sci. Applications, Inc., Boulder, Colo., summer, 1982; lectr. in major plasma and and nuclear rsch. labs. and univs., U.S. and overseas; referee to major plasma and nuclear sci. and engring. tech. jours. Contbr. articles, reports to Plasma and Nuclear Sci. and Engring.. Mem. AAAS, IEEE, Am. Nuclear Soc., Am. Phys. Soc., Am. Chem. Soc., Materials Info. Soc. Achievements include development of a kinetic theory of thermal barrier in tandem mirrors, theory for non linear dynamics of magnetic islands in high-temperature tokamak plasmas; design and analysis of fusion ignition experiment; creation of a new sys. for distribution of R&D equipment for sci.

CARRERAS, FRANCISCO JOSÉ, retired university president, foundation executive; b. San Juan, P.R., May 13, 1932; s. Francisco and Antonia (Muriente) C.; m. Ana Elisa Carreras, Mar. 29, 1964; children: Inés María, María Soledad, Irene María, Marianne, Francisco José, María del Pilar. Student, Instituto Superior de Estudios Clásicos, Havana, Cuba, 1954-57; BA, Universidad Pontificia de Comillas, Santander, Spain, 1959; MA, Fordham U., 1960; PhD, Universidad Pontificia Gregoriana, Rome, 1966. Mem. faculty U. P.R., Rio Piedras Campus, 1962-69, acad. asst. to dir., 1967-69, dir. humanities dept., 1967-68; pres. Cath. U. P.R., Ponce, 1969-81; academician P.R. Acad. Arts and Scis., 1970; exec. dir. Angel Ramos Found., Inc., San Juan, P.R., 1984—; mem. P.R. State Commn. on Post-Secondary Edn., 1973; dir. Banco Popular de P.R. Author: Filosofía de la Coordinación de José Vasconcelos, 1971, Incógnita y Revelación, 1981; also articles. Adv. Sociedad Puertorriqueña UNESCO, 1973; pres. P.R. Endowment for Humanities, 1977; bd. dirs. Angel Ramos Found., 1977; bd. dirs. Damas Hosp., 1978, P.R. Acad. Arts and Scis., 1980; adv. bd. dirs. Orgns. Universidades Católicas de América Latina, 1976. Mem. Fundación Puertorriqueña Humanidades (pres. 1977), Ponce Sales and Mktg. Execs. Assn., Alpha Phi Omega, Phi Delta Kappa. Roman Catholic. Clubs: Rotary, Lions. Home: 1 St C-16 Villas Del Pilar Rio Piedras PR 00926-9078 Office: Angel Ramos Found Inc PO Box 362408 San Juan PR 00936-2408

CARRERE, CHARLES SCOTT, judge; b. Dublin, Ga., Sept. 26, 1937; 1 son, Daniel Austin. B.A., U. Ga., 1959; LL.B., Stetson U., 1961. Bar: Fla. 1961, Ga. 1960. Law clk. U.S. Dist. Judge, Orlando, Fla., 1962-63; asst. U.S. atty. Middle Dist. Fla., 1963-66, 68-69, chief trial atty., 1965-66, 68-69; ptnr. Harrison, Greene, Mann, Rowe & Stanton, 1970-80; judge Pinellas County, Fla., 1980-96; vis. prof. law Stetson Coll. Law, 1997-98, Cumberland Law Sch., 1998-99. Recipient Jud. Appreciation award St. Petersburg Bar Assn., 1996, Alumnus of Yr. award Stetson Student Bar Assn., 1998. Mem. State Bar Ga., Fla. Bar, Phi Beta Kappa. Presbyterian. Address: PO Box 22034 Gateway Mall Sta Saint Petersburg FL 33742

CARRERE, TIA (ALTHEA JANAIRO), actress; b. Honolulu, 1967; d. Alexander and Audrey Janairo. Profl. model. Film appearances include: Zombie Nightmare, 1987, Aloha Summer, 1988, Showdown in Little Tokyo, 1991, Harley Davidson and the Marlboro Man, 1991, Wayne's World, 1992, Rising Sun, Fatal Mission, 1990, Instant Karma, 1990, True Lies, My Generation, The Immortals, Learning Curves, Hollow Point, Bad with Numbers, Jury Duty, 1995, High School High, 1996, Top of the World, Kull the Conqueror, 1997, Scar City, 20 Dates, 1998; TV guest appearances include The A-Team, 1986, MacGyver, 1986, 88, Tour of Duty, 1987, Tales for the Crypt, 1992, The New Hollywood Squares, Murphy's Law, General Hospital, 1983-85, The Road Raiders, 1989, Fine Gold, 1990; TV movies include Natural Enemy, 1997, Dogboys, 1998; presenter The MTV Movie Awards, 1992, (spl.) Circus of the Stars. Recipient Female Star 1994 award NATO/Sho West. Office: United Talent Agy 9560 Wilshire Blvd Fl 5 Beverly Hills CA 90212-2400*

CARRETTA, ALBERT ALOYSIUS, lawyer, educator; b. N.Y.C., Dec. 23, 1907; s. Vincent and Concetta (De Florio) C.; m. Gertrude Elizabeth Lynch, Nov. 29, 1934; children: Albert Aloysius, John Vincent, William Joseph. B.S., CCNY, 1930; J.D., Georgetown U., 1940; postgrad., N.Y. U. Bar: D.C. 1940, Va 1941. Instr. econs., fin. Coll. City N.Y. Sch. Bus. and Civic Adminstrn., 1930-34; fin. analyst, atty. SEC, Washington, 1934-42; instr. finance Columbus U., Washington, 1935-36; bus. specialist OPA, Washington, 1942-44; lectr. corp. law, corp. finance, unfair trade practices, fed. antitrust legislation Catholic U. Am., Wash., 1942-54; instr. fin. U. Calif., 1945; vice chief, bd. mem. services and sales renegotiation sect. Navy Dept., Washington, 1946-47; lectr. accounting dept., sch. fgn. service Georgetown U., 1946-52; practice law Washington and Arlington, Va., 1947-52; mem. FTC, 1952-54; practice law Washington, 1954-82. Pres. Cath. Charities No. Va., 1955-57. Served with USN, 1944-45. Decorated Knight Order of the Star of Italian Solidarity; Albert A. Carretta Bldg., Alexandria, Va. named in his honor by century old trade assn. client, 1987. Mem. ABA, Va. Bar Assn., KC. Democrat. Roman Catholic. Home: 4076 Fountainside Ln Fairfax VA 22030-6089

CARREY, JIM, actor; b. Toronto, Ont., Can., Jan. 17, 1962; s. Percy and Kathleen Carrey; m. Melissa Womer, 1986 (div.); 1 child, Jane. Performances include (TV series) The Duck Factory, 1984, In Living Color, 1990-94; (TV films) Mike Hammer: Murder Takes All, 1989, Doing Time on Maple Drive, 1992; (films) Finders Keepers, 1984, Once Bitten, 1985, Peggy Sue Got Married, 1986, The Dead Pool, 1988, Earth Girls Are Easy, 1989, Pink Cadillac, 1989, High Strung, 1991, Ace Ventura: Pet Detective, 1993 (also screenwriter), The Mask, 1994, Dumb and Dumber, 1994 (MTV Movie awards), Batman Forever, 1995, Ace Ventura: When Nature Calls, 1995, The Mask's Revenge, 1996, Liar, Liar, 1996 (Blockbuster Entertainment award), The Cable Guy, 1996 (MTV Movie award), The Truman Show, 1997 (Golden Globe Best Performance award, MTV Movie award), Simon Birch, 1998, In My Life, 1998 (TV), Man on the Moon, 1999. Office: UTA 9560 Wilshire Blvd Fl 5 Beverly Hills CA 90212-2401*

CARREY, NEIL, lawyer, educator; b. Bronx, N.Y., Nov. 19, 1942; s. David L. and Betty (Kurtzburg) C.; m. Karen Krysher, Apr. 9, 1980; children: Jana, Christopher; children by previous marriage: Scott, Douglas, Dana. BS in Econs., U. Pa., 1964; JD, Stanford U., 1967. Bar: Calif. 1968. Mem. firm, v.p. corp. DeCastro, West, Chodorow, Inc., L.A., 1967-97; of counsel Jenkens & Gilchrist, L.A., 1997—; instr. program legal paraprofls., U. So. Calif., 1977-89; lectr. U. So. Calif. Dental Sch., 1987—, Employee Benefits Inst., Kansas City, Mo., 1996; legal cons. 33rd Dist. Calif. PTA, 1997—. Author: Nonqualified Defered Compensation Plans-The Wave of the Future, 1985. Officer Vista Del Mar Child Care Ctr., L.A., 1968-84; treas. Nat. Little League Santa Monica, Calif., 1984-85, pres., 1985-86, coach, 1990-95; coach Bobby Sox Softball Team, Santa Monica, 1986-88, bd. dirs., 1988, umpire in chief, 1988; referee, coach Am. Soccer Youth Orgn., 1989-95; curriculum com. Santa Monica-Malibu Sch. Dist., 1983-84 comm. health adv. com., 1988-95, chmn., 1989-95, sports and phys. edb adv. com., 1991—, chmn., 1991—, dist. com. for sch. based health ctr., 1991-94, title/gender equity com., chmn. 1992—, athletic study com., chmn., 1989-91, fin. adv. com., 1994, ad hoc com. dist. facilities chmn., 1998; dir. The Santa Monica Youth Athletic Found., 1995— (exec. comm. 1997-98, v.p. 1998—); dir. The Small Bus. Coun. of Am. 1995—, dir. Santa Monica H.S. Booster Club, 1995-97, dir. Santa Monica Bay Rep. Club, 1995-96, Santa Monica Police Activities League, 1995-97, v.p. fin., 1997-98, pres.-elect, 1998—; pres. Gail Dorin Music Found., 1994—; v.p. Sneaker Sisters, 1996—; pres. Santa Monical Jr. Rowing, 1997—; legal cons. 33d Dist. Calif. PTA, 1997—; recreation and parks commr. City of Santa Monica, 1999—; sec. Santa Monica Leaders Club, 1999—. Mem. LWV (dir. 1997—), U. Pa. Alumni Soc. (pres. 1971-79, dir. 1979-87), Mountaingate Tennis Club, Alpha Kappa Psi (life). Jewish. Home: 616 23rd St Santa Monica CA 90402-3130 Office: 12100 Wilshire Blvd Fl 15 Los Angeles CA 90025-7120

CARRICK, KATHLEEN MICHELE, law librarian; b. Cleve., June 11, 1950; d. Michael James and Genevieve (Wenger) C. BA, Duquesne U., Pitts., 1972; MLS, U. Pitts., 1973; JD, Cleve.-Marshall U., 1977. Bar: Ohio 1977, U.S. Ct. Internat. Trade 1983. Rsch. asst. The Plain Dealer, Cleve., 1973-75; head reference SUNY, Buffalo, 1977-78, assoc. dir., 1978-80, dir., asst. prof., 1980-83; dir., assoc. prof. law case Western Res. U., Cleve., 1983—; cons. Mead Data Central, Dayton, Ohio, 1987-91. Author: Lexis: A Research Manual, 1989; contbr. articles to profl. jours. Fellow Am. Bar Found.; mem. ABA, Am. Law Inst., Am. Assn. Law Librs., Assn. Am. Law Schs., Scribes. Home: 1317 Burlington Rd Cleveland OH 44118-1212 Office: Case Western Res U 11075 East Blvd Cleveland OH 44106-5409

CARRICO, DEBORAH JEAN, special education teacher; b. East St. Louis, Ill., Dec. 6, 1948; d. Leo Anthony and Edna Linda (Willett) C. BS, Murray State U., 1972; MA, Calif. State U., L.A., 1978. Cert. tchr., Calif. Tchr. Bonita Unified Sch. Dist., San Dimas, Calif., 1973-74, L.A. County Office Edn., Downey, 1974—; mentor L.A. County Office of Edn., 1989—. Bd. dirs. Hope House, Anaheim, Calif., 1988—. Mem. Coun. for Exceptional Children, Phi Kappa Phi. Democrat. Roman Catholic. Avocations: photography, videography, educational technology. Office: LA County Office Edn 9300 Imperial Hwy Downey CA 90242-2813

CARRICO, HARRY LEE, state supreme court chief justice; b. Washington, Sept. 4, 1916; s. William Temple and Nellie Nadalia (Willett) C.; m. Betty Lou Peck, May 18, 1940 (dec. 1987); 1 child, Lucretia Ann; m. Lynn Brackenridge, July 1, 1994. Jr. cert., George Washington U., 1938, JD, 1942, LLD, 1987; LLD, U. Richmond, 1973, Coll. William & Mary, 1993. Bar: Va. 1941. With Rust & Rust, Fairfax, Va., 1941-43; trial justice Fairfax, Va., 1943-51, pvt. practice, 1951-56; judge 16th Jud. Cir., Va., 1956-61; justice Va. Supreme Ct., Richmond, 1961-81, chief justice, 1981—; chmn. bd dirs Nat. Ctr. for State Cts., 1989-90. With USNR, 1945-46. Recipient Alumni Profl. Achievement award George Washington U., 1981. Mem. McNeill Law Soc., Conf. Chief Justices (bd. dirs. 1985-91, 1st v.p. 1987, pres.-elect 1988, pres. 1989-90, co-chmn. nat. jud. coun. 1991-97), Order of Coif, Phi Delta Phi, Omicron Delta Kappa. Episcopalian. Office: Va Supreme Ct 4th Fl 101 N 9th St Richmond VA 23219-2335*

CARRICO, VIRGIL NORMAN, physician; b. Cumberland, Md., Aug. 28, 1940; s. Virgil Norman and Lucille E. (Gnagy) C.; m. Nina Lois Lemper, Aug. 17, 1963; children: Pamela Beth Carrico-Miller, Sandra Kelly (dec.). BA, Wabash Coll., 1962; MD, Ind. U., 1966. Diplomate Am. Bd. Family Practice. Intern Marion County Gen. Hosp., Indpls., 1966-67; resident in family practice Akron (Ohio) City Hosp., 1970-72, chief resident in family practice, 1972, assoc. dir. family practice residency, 1972; chief family practice Bryan Cmty. Hosp., past chmn. bd. dirs. home health care; past mem. undergrad. med. edn. subcom. Med. Coll. Ohio, Toledo, past preceptor cmty. medicine, clin. asst. prof. family medicine, clin. prof. family medicine; past preceptor preventive medicine and family practice Ohio State U.; chief of staff Bryan Cmty. Hosp., 1977-78, preceptor Bryan Area Health Edn. Ctr., chmn. continuing med. edn. com.; med. dir. Bryan Area Health Edn. Ctr.; past pres., bd. dirs. Bryan Med. Group, Inc. Contbr. articles to profl. jours. Trustee YWCA, Bryan, Ohio, v.p., 1990-92; bd. dirs. United Fund, pres., 1990-92; bd. dirs. Jr. Achievement, 1981-83, Bryan Area Found. Capt. USAF, 1967-70. Fellow Am. Acad. Family Physicians (bylaw coms. 1989, 90, 91, 92, nat. chmn. 1993, chmn. patient care svcs. commn. 1988-89, chmn. mem. svcs. commn. 1989-90); mem. Soc. Tchrs. Family Medicine, Ohio Acad. Family Medicine, Am. Acad. Family Medicine, Williams County Med. Soc. (rpes. 1976-79, sec.-treas., v.p. 1980-83), Ohio Acad. Family Physicians (del. to ho. of dels. 1972-85; pres. Fulton County chpt. 1973-85, chmn. resident affairs subcom., nominating com., student awards, fin. com., ref. com. of the ho. of dels.; treas. 1985-87, v.p. 1987-89, bd. dirs. 1983-92, pres.-elect 1990-91), Rotary Internat. Avocations: golf, traveling, reading. Office: Bryan Med Group 442 W High St Bryan OH 43506-1681

CARRIER, GEORGE FRANCIS, applied mathematics educator; b. Millinocket, Maine, May 4, 1918; s. Charles Mosher and Mary (Marcaux) C.; m. Mary Casey, June 30, 1946; children: Kenneth, Robert, Mark. Degree in Mech. Engr., Cornell U., 1939, PhD, 1944. From asst. prof. to prof. Brown U., 1946-52; Gordon McKay prof. mech. engring. Harvard U., 1952-72, T. Jefferson Coolidge prof. applied math., 1972-88, emeritus, 1988—; mem. coun. emeritus Cornell U. Engring. Coll. Co-author: Functions of a Complex Variable, 1966, Ordinary Differential Equations, 1968, Partial Differential Equations, 1976; assoc. editor: Quar. Applied Math. Former trustee Rensselaer Poly. Inst., Troy, N.Y. Recipient Von Karman prize ASCE, 1977, Pres.'s Nat. medal sci. NSF, 1990. Fellow Am. Acad. Arts and Scis., Brit. Inst. Math. and Its Applications (hon.); mem. ASME (hon., Timoshenko medal 1978, Centennial medal 1980), NAS (Applied Math. and Numerical Analysis award 1980), AIAA (Dryden medal 1989), Soc. Indsl. and Applied Math. (Von Karman prize 1979), Nat. Acad. Engring., Am. Philos. Soc., Am. Phys. Soc. (Fluid Dynamics prize 1984), Internat. Soc. Interaction Mechs. and Math., Sigma Xi. Office: Harvard U Divsn of Engring and Applied Scis Pierce 317 Cambridge MA 02138

CARRIER, RONALD EDWIN, university administrator; b. Bluff City, Tenn., Aug. 18, 1932; s. James Murphy and Melissa (Miller) C.; m. Edith Marie Johnson, Sept. 7, 1955; children: Michael Lavon, Linda Lois Carrier Frazee, Jennine Marie Thomas. BS, Ea. Tenn. State U., 1955; MS in Econs., U. Ill., 1957, PhD in Econs., 1960. Assoc. prof. econs. U. Miss., Oxford, 1960-63; dir., prof. Bur. Bus. and Econ. Research, Memphis State U., 1963-66, provost, v.p. acad. affairs, 1966-71; pres., chancellor James Madison U., Harrisonburg, Va., 1971—; pres. Ctr. for Innovative Tech., Herndon, Va., 1986-87; bd. dirs. Clark/Bardes, Inc., Inst. for the Study of Terrorism, Sorensen Inst., Universal Systems, Inc., Universal Corp.; chmn. Coun. Pres.'s Va. Colls., 1975, Ctr. for Innovative Tech. Author: Plant Locations: A Theory and Explanations, 1968; contbr. articles and monographs to profl. publs. Mem. White House Conf. Balance Econ. Growth; mem. Va. Indsl. Facilities Study Commn., 1972-75; chmn. Va. Land Use Adv. Com., 1974-77, Va. Gov.'s Electricity Costs Commn., 1975—; mem. Va. Gov.'s Energy Resource Adv. Commn., 1975-76, Gov.'s Regulatory Reform Adv. Bd., 1983, Joint Subcom. to Study Coal Slurry Pipeline Feasibility, 1983; bd. dirs. WVPT Pub. TV. Earheart fellow 1958-60; recipient Ben Franklin award Memphis Printing Industry, 1966, faculty award East Tenn. State U., 1955, Disting. Svc. award Jr. C. of C., 1965, Virginian of Yr. award Va. Assn. Broadcasters, 1982; named Outstanding Virginian, FHA, 1990; cultural laureate Va.; named Outstanding Virginian FFA, 1991. Mem. Assn. Higher Edn. Execs., Omicron Delta Kappa, Omicron Delta Gamma, Sigma Phi Epsilon. Methodist. Home: PO Box 570 Basye VA 22810-0570 Office: James Madison U MSC 8803 250 E Market St Harrisonburg VA 22801-4131

CARRIER, WARREN PENDLETON, retired university chancellor, writer; b. Cheviot, Ohio, July 3, 1918; s. Burly Warren and Prudence (Alfrey) C.; m. Marjorie Jane Regan, Apr. 3, 1947 (dec.); 1 child, Gregory Paul; m. Judy Lynn Hall, June 14, 1973; 1 son, Ethan Alfrey. Student, Wabash Coll., 1938-40; AB, Miami U., Oxford, Ohio, 1942; MA, Harvard U., 1948; PhD, Occidental Coll., 1962. Asst. prof. English U. Iowa, 1949-52; assoc. prof. Bard Coll., 1953-57; lit. faculty Bennington, 1955-58; vis. prof. Sweet Briar (Va.) Coll., 1958-60; prof. Deep Springs (Calif.) Coll., 1960-62, Portland (Oreg.) State U., 1962-64; prof., chmn. English dept. U. Mont., Missoula, 1964-68; assoc. dean. prof. English and comparative lit., chmn. comparative lit. Livingston Coll., Rutgers U., 1968-69; dean Coll. Arts and Letters, San Diego State U., 1969-72; v.p. acad. affairs U. Bridgeport, Conn., 1972-75; chancellor U. Wis., Platteville, 1975-82. Author: The Hunt, 1952, Bay of the Damned, 1957, Toward Montebello, 1966, Leave Your Sugar for the Cold Morning, 1977, The Diver, 1986, Death of a Chancellor, 1986, An Honorable Spy, 1992, Murder at the Strawberry Festival, 1993, An Ordinary Man, 1997; founder Quar. Rev. of Lit.; editor: Guide to World Literature, 1980; co-editor: Reading Modern Poetry, 1955, 68, Literature from the World, 1981; assoc. editor: Western Rev., 1949-51; contbr. articles, poems, revs. to lit. mags. Mem. Jud. Commn. Wis. Vol., Am. Field Service attached to Brit. Army, India-Burma, 1944-45. Recipient award for poetry Nat. Endowment for Arts, 1972; Colladay prize for poetry, 1986. Mem. Nat. Coun. Tchrs. English, Royal Soc. Arts, Wis. Acad. Arts and Scis., Phi Beta Kappa. Home: 69 Colony Park Cir Galveston TX 77551-1737

CARRIGAN, DAVID OWEN, history educator; b. New Glasgow, N.S., Can., Nov. 30, 1933; s. Ronald and Marion Constance (Hoare) C.; m. Florence Catherine Nicholson, June 21, 1958; children: Nancy, Janet, David, Glen, Sharon, Douglas. B.A., St. Francis Xavier U., 1954; M.A., Boston U., 1955; Ph.D., U. Maine, 1966. Asst. prof. history St. Francis Xavier U., 1957-61, assoc. prof., 1961-67; assoc. prof. history Wilfred Laurier U., 1967-68; prin., dean arts Kings Coll., U. Western Ont., 1968-71; pres. St. Mary's U., Halifax, N.S., 1971-79; prof. St. Mary's U., 1979—. Outhor: Canadian Party Platforms, 1867-1968, 1968, Crime and Punishment in Canada: A History, 1991, Juvenile Delinquency in Canada a History, 1998; contbrs. articles to profl. jours. Former trustee Inst. Research on Public Policy; past mem. Can. Council; past bd. dirs. Can. Assn. for Treatment and Study of Families. Mem. Am. Hist. Assn., Phi Kappa Phi. Office: St Mary's Univ, Halifax, NS Canada B3H 3C3

CARRIGAN, JIM R., arbitrator, mediator, retired federal judge; b. Mobridge, S.D., Aug. 24, 1929; s. Leo Michael and Mildred Ione (Jaycox) C.; m. Beverly Jean Halpin, June 2, 1956. Ph.B., J.D., U. N.D., 1953; LL.M. in Taxation, NYU, 1956; LLD (hon.), U. Colo., 1989, Suffolk U., 1991, U. N.D., 1997. Bar: N.D. 1953, Colo. 1956. Asst. prof. law U. Denver, 1956-59; vis. assoc. prof. NYU Law Sch., 1958, U. Wash. Law Sch., 1959-60; Colo. jud. adminstr., 1960-61; prof. law U. Colo., 1961-67; partner firm Carrigan & Bragg (and predecessors), 1967-76; justice Colo. Supreme Ct., 1976-79; judge U.S. Dist. Ct. Colo., 1979-95; mem. Colo. Bd. Bar Examiners, 1969-71; lectr. Nat. Coll. State Judiciary, 1964-77, 95; bd. dirs. Nat. Inst. Trial Advocacy, 1971-73, 78—, chmn. bd. 1986-88, also mem. faculty, 1972—; adj. prof. law U. Colo, 1984, 1991—; bd. dirs. Denver Broncos Stadium Dist., 1996—. Editor-in-chief: N.D. Law Rev., 1952-53, Internat. Soc. Barristers Quar., 1972-79; editor: DICTA, 1957-59; contbr. articles to profl. jours. Bd. regents U. Colo., 1975-76; bd. visitors U. N.D. Coll. Law, 1983-85. Recipient Disting. Svc. award Nat. Coll. State Judiciary, 1969, Outstanding Alumnus award U. N.D., 1973, Regent Emeritus award U. Colo., 1977, B'nai Brith Civil Rights award, 1986, Thomas More Outstanding Lawyer award Cath. Lawyers Guild, 1988, Oliphant Disting. Svc. award Nat. Inst. Trial Advocacy, 1993, Constl. Rights award Nat. Assn. Blacks in Criminal Justice (Colo. chpt.), 1992, Disting. Svc. award Colo. Bar Assn., 1994, Amicus Curiae award ATLA, 1995. Fellow Colo. Bar Found., Boulder County Bar Found.; mem. ABA (action com. on tort system improvement 1985-87, TIPS sect. long range planning com., 1986-97; coun. 1987-91, task force on initiatives and referenda 1990-92, size of civil juries task force 1988-90, class actions task force 1995-97), Colo. Bar Assn., Boulder County Bar Assn., Denver Bar Assn., Cath. Lawyers Guild, Inns. of Ct., Internat. Soc. Barristers, Internat. Acad. Trial Lawyers (bd. dirs. 1995—), Fed. Judges Assn. (bd. dirs. 1985-89), Am. Judicature Soc. (bd. dirs. 1985-89), Tenth Circuit Dist. Judges Assn. (sec. 1991-92, v.p. 1992-

93, pres. 1994-95), Order of Coif, Phi Beta Kappa. Roman Catholic. Office: Judicial Arbiter Group 1601 Blake St Ste 400 Denver CO 80202-1328

CARRIGAN, MICHAEL ANDREW, journalism educator, journalist, writer; b. Oakland, Calif., Oct. 30, 1949; s. George Richard and Emelie Elizabeth (Glover) C.; m. Cora Suzanne Leigh, June 7, 1973; children: Ashley, Molly. BS in Naval Sci., U.S. Naval Acad., 1973; MA in Journalism, U. Nev., 1997. Cert. airline transport pilot FAA. Commd. ensign USN, 1969, advanced through grades to lt. comdr., naval officer, 1969-91; newspaper reporter Lahontan Valley News, Fallon, Nev., 1992-96; prof. Truckee Meadows C.C., Reno, 1996—, U. Nev., Reno, 1996—; advisor The Echo Newspaper, Reno. Author: (short story) The Chessmen, 1997 (Short Story of Yr., Anthology Mag. 1997), (novel) One Virginia Summer, 1999, Insiders' Guide to Reno/Tahoe, 1999; co-author (anthology) Nevada Sampler, 1997. Mem. Rep. Ctrl. Com., Reno, 1997—, Sparks (Nev.) Citizen Adv. Bom., 1998—. Recipient Journalist of Merit, Nev. Press Assn., 1994. Mem. Soc. Profl. Journalists, Ret. Officers' Assn. Republican. Roman Catholic. Avocations: flying, fishing, golf. E-mail: WWCarrigan@aol.com. Home: 3393 Alpland Ln Sparks NV 89434 Office: TMCC 7000 Dandini Blvd Reno NV 89434

CARRIGG, JAMES A., retired utility company executive; b. 1933. Student, Union Coll., 1951-53; AAS in Electrical Engring. Tech., Broome C.C. From safety cadet to gen. mgr. N.Y. State Electric & Gas Corp., Ithaca, 1958-82; v.p. N.Y. State Electric & Gas Corp., Binghamton, 1982-83, pres., dir., 1983-86, pres., COO, 1986-88, chmn., CEO, 1988-90, chmn., pres., CEO, 1991-96; ret., 1996; bd. dirs. Security Mut. Life Ins. Co., N.Y. Bd. dirs. Broome County Cmty. Charities, Inc., Dr. G. Clifford and Florence B. Decker Found.; trustee Pub. Policy Inst. of Bus. Coun. N.Y. State, Inc. Mem. Broome County C. of C. (former chmn.). Office: NY State Electric & Gas Corp PO Box 3607 4500 Vestal Pkwy E Binghamton NY 13902-3607

CARRIKER, ROBERT CHARLES, history educator; b. St. Louis, Aug. 18, 1940; s. Thomas B. and Vivian Ida (Spaunhorst) C.; m. Eleanor R. Gualdoni, Aug. 24, 1963; children: Thomas A., Robert M., Andrew J. BS, St. Louis U., 1962, AM, 1963; PhD, U. Okla., 1967. Asst. prof. Gonzaga U., Spokane, Wash., 1967-71, assoc. prof., 1972-76, prof. history, 1976—. Author: Fort Supply, Indian Territory, 1970, 90, The Kalispel People, 1973, Father Peter De Smet, 1995; editor: (with Eleanor R. Carriker) Army Wife on the Frontier, 1975, (with William L. Lang) Great River of the West, 1999; book rev. editor Columbia mag., 1987—. Mem. Wash. Lewis and Clark Trail Com., 1978—; commr. Wash. Maritime Bicentennial, Olympia, 1989-92; bd. dirs. Wash. Commn. for Humanities, Seattle, 1988-94. Burlington No. Found. scholar, 1985, 96; recipient Disting. Svc. award Lewis and Clark Trail Heritage Found., 1989. Mem. Wash. State Hist. Soc. (trustee 1981-90, v.p. 1993—), Western Hist. Assn., Phi Alpha Theta (councilor 1985-87). Roman Catholic. Avocations: travel, photography, cartography. Office: Gonzaga U 502 E Boone Ave Spokane WA 99258-0001

CARRINGTON, J(OSEPH) P(ETER) (JOSSIF PETER BARTOLOTTI), nutritionist, psychoanalyst, research scientist, educator; b. N.Y.C., Mar. 13, 1948; s. Nicholas S. and Yolanda Virginia (Luisi) B.; 1 child, Joseph Nicholas. Cert. advanced study, N.Y. Inst. Advanced Study, 1974; EdM, Harvard U., 1985; postgrad. in nuclear engring., MIT, 1985. Cert. psychol. assessment/analysis provider; lic. nutritionist. Med. nutritionist N.Y., 1970—, psychoanalyst, psychotherapist, 1985—; sr. fellow, prof. med. nutrition and theoretical physics N.Y. Inst. Advanced Study, N.Y.C., 1980—; founder Eugenics Corp., Del., 1994—; TV and radio guest ABC Nat. Network, 1992; host of Carrington Nutrition radio programs, WNN Radio, WSHE Radio, Fla., 1989. Electorate sr. governing bd. Harvard U. Fellow N.Y. Inst. Advanced Study (sr., pub. info. dir. on NASA 1983—, Albert Einstein Gold medal of Sci. 1985); mem. N.Y. Acad. Sci., Harvard Alumni Assn., Harvard Club, Phi Delta Kappa. Avocations: theoretical physics, Chinese medicine, natural scis., relativity, nutritional eugenics. Office: Eugenics Corp PO Box 770514 Coral Springs FL 33077-0514

CARRINGTON, MICHAEL DAVIS, criminal justice administrator, educator, consultant; b. South Bend, Ind., Mar. 9, 1938; s. Herman Lakin and Margaret (Davis) C.; m. Lynn Ogden, Feb. 8, 1958; children: Michael O. (dec.), Jill A., Elizabeth A., Gretchen L. BA, Ind. U., 1970; MALS, Valparaiso U., 1971. Parole officer State of Ind., South Bend, 1970-71; chief probation officer St. Joseph County, South Bend, 1971-74; dir. pub. safety City of South Bend, 1974-76, mayor's asst., 1976-80; adj. assoc. prof., dir. safety, security, police Ind. U., South Bend, 1979-94; presdl. appointment as U.S. Marshal Northern Dist. of Ind., South Bend, Ind., 1994—; cons. in pvt. security Pan Am. Games, Indpls., 1987; security advance agt. Olympic Torch Relay, Ind., 1984, Hands Across Am., Ind., 1986. Recipient Sagamore of Wabash award, 1984; named Ky. Col., 1984, Hon. Big. Brother of Yr., 1974, Outstanding Residential Faculty Mem. awrd Ind. U. South Bend Sch. Pub. and Environ. Affairs, 1992. Mem. Am. Soc. Indsl. Security, Assn. of Threat Assessment Profls. Methodist. Avocation: travel, reading, walking, working. Office: U.S. Marshal Robert A. Grant Fed Bldg 204 S Main St Rm 233 South Bend IN 46601-2115

CARRINGTON, PAUL DEWITT, lawyer, educator; b. Dallas, June 12, 1931; s. Paul and Frances Ellen (DeWitt) C.; m. Bessie Meek, Aug., 1952; children: Clark DeWitt, Mary Carrington Coults, William James, Emily Carrington Bell. BA, U. Tex., 1952; LLB, Harvard U., 1955. Bar: Tex. 1955, Ohio 1962, Mich. 1967. Practice Dallas, 1955; teaching fellow Harvard U., 1957-58; asst. prof. law U. Wyo., 1958-60, Ind. U., 1960-62; assoc. prof. Ohio State U., 1962-65; prof. U. Mich., 1965-78; dean Duke U. Sch. Law, Durham, N.C., 1978-88, prof., 1978—; reporter civil rules adv. com. Jud. Conf. of U.S., 1985-92. Author: (with Meador and Rosenberg) Justice on Appeal, 1977, (with Meador and Rosenberg) Appellate Courts, 1994, (with Babcock) Civil Procedure, 1977, 3d edit., 1983, Stewards of Democracy, 1999. Mem. Ann Arbor (Mich.) Bd. Edn., 1970-73; pres. Pvt. Adjudication Ctr., Inc., 1988-94, chmn., 1995—. With U.S. Army, 1955-57. Guggenheim fellow, 1988-89. Fellow Am. Bar Found.; mem. ABA, Am. Law Inst. Episcopalian. Office: Duke U Sch Law Durham NC 27708-0362

CARRINGTON, VIRGINIA GAIL (VEE CARRINGTON), professional society administrator, librarian; b. Dodge City, Kans., Apr. 20, 1949; d. Virgel Troy and Betty Lou (Rynerson) F.; Lynn Nugent Friesner, Aug. 4, 1971 (div. Feb. 1985); m. Paul Henry Carrington, Apr. 4, 1987. BA, Kans. Wesleyan, 1971; MS, U. Ill., 1972; MA, Kans. State U., 1978. Sci. cataloger Kans. State U. Libr., Manhattan, 1972-74, humanities bibliographer, 1974-78; dir. libr. devel. State Libr. Kans., Topeka, 1978-84; libr. network dir. Kans. Libr. Network, Topeka, 1982-84; edn. officer Pub. Libr. Assn. ALA, Chgo., 1984-86; pres. Carrington Cons., Waterbury, Conn., 1986-97; promotion coord. Assn. Coll. and Rsch. Librs. ALA, Middletown, Conn., 1997—; mgr. mem. svcs. Mattatuck Mus., Waterbury, 1992-97. Asst. editor: Guide to Reference Books, 11th ed., 1994; asst. to editor: Guide to Reference Books Supplement to 10th ed., 1990. Mem. ALA (Continuing Libr. Educator Network and Exch. Roundtable, Ind. Librs. Exch. Roundtable), Am. Soc. Assn. Execs., New England Libr. Assn. Democrat. Methodist. Avocations: travel, reading. E-mail: vcarrington@ala-choice.org. Home: 130 Melbourne Ter Waterbury CT 06704-1843 Office: CHOICE Assn Coll and Rsch Librs 100 Riverview Ctr Ste 290 Middletown CT 06457-3445

CARRINO, MICHAEL, writing educator; b. Bklyn., Jan. 3, 1949; s. Pasquale and Rita Carrino; m. Thelma Morgan; 1 child, Marc. BS, Plattsburgh State U., 1971, MS, 1975; MFA, Norwich U., 1984. Tchr. Elem./Jr. H.S., N.Y., Vt., 1971-79; gen. edn./writing cons. N.Y.C., Vt., 1975—; program coord. Washington West Tchr.'s Ctr., Waitsfield, Vt., 1979-83; writing instr. Plattsburgh-SUNY, 1988-98. Author: (poetry) Some Rescues, 1994, Under This Combustable Sky, 1998. Office: SUNY English Dept Plattsburgh NY 12901

CARRISON, DALE MITCHELL, emergency medicine physician; b. Macomb, Ill., Sept. 24, 1939; married. AA in Police Sci., Santa Ana Coll., 1966; BS in Criminology, Calif. State U., Long Beach, 1968; MS in Biology, Calif. State U., San Bernardino, 1983; DO, Coll. Osteo. Medicine Pacific, 1987. Diplomate Am. Bd. Emergency Medicine; cert. ACLS instr./profider, ATLS provider. Dep. sheriff Orange County (Calif.) Sheriff's Dept., 1964-71; spl. agt. FBI, L.A. and Portland, Oreg., 1971-76; pres., gen. mgr. Carrison Enterprises, Inc., So. Calif., 1976-83; rotating intern Flint (Mich.) Osteo. Hosp., 1987-88; resident in emergency medicine Cook County Hosp., Chgo., 1988-91; asst. dir., attending physician dept. emergency medicine Univ. Med. Ctr., Las Vegas, 1991-92, Emergency Physicians' Med. Group, Univ. Med. Ctr., Las Vegas, Nev., 1992-94; dir., attending physician dept. emergency medicine Emergency Physicians' Med. Group, Univ. Med. Ctr., Las Vegas, 1995—; asst. prof. emergency medicine dept. family medicine Coll. Osteo. Medicie of Pacific, 1993—; clin. prof. surgery U. Nev. Sch. Medicine, Las Vegas, 1994—; med. dir. Sexual Assault Nurse Examiner, Univ. Med. Ctr., 1994—, vice chmn., staff physician dept. trauma medicine, 1994-96; bd. dirs. Emergency Physicians' Med. Group, San Francisco, 1994—, Nev. regional dir., 1996—; regional clin. coord. Coll. Osteo. Medicine of Pacific, Pomona, Calif., 1994—; med. dir. emergency med. svcs., Lake Mead Recreational Area, Henderson, Nev., 1993—; med. dir., tactical physician Las Vegas Met. Police Dept. SWAT Team, 1995—; instr. Heckler & Koch Internat. Tng. Divsn. for Tactical Emergency Medicine, Sterling, Va., 1995—; med. dir. Las Vegas Motor Speedway, 1995—; med. dir. Nev. region Sports Car Club Am., Las Vegas, 1993-98; mem. coun., reviewer Health Insight, Las Vegas, 1995—; med. dir. emergency med. svcs. Nat. Park Svc., Death Valley, Calif., 1992—; staff physician emergency dept. Gottlieb Meml. Hosp., Melrose Park, Ill., 1990-91, Lakeland Med. Ctr., Elkhorn, Wis., 1989-91, Westlake Cmty. Hosp., Melrose Park, 1989-91; presenter, rschr. in field. Contbr. articles to profl. publs. With USN, USNR, 1956-61, maj. Med. Corps USAR, 1987-95. Fellow Am. Coll. Emergency Physicians; mem. Am. Osteo. Assn. (Nev. del., bur. student affairs), Nev. Osteo. Med. Assn. (v.p., pres.), Coll. Osteo. Medicine of Pacific Alumni Assn. (past pres.), Wilderness Med. Assn., Internat. Coun. Motorsports Scis.

CARRMUN, L. CONKLIN, police chief; b. Norfolk, Va., Aug. 6, 1941. AS cum laude, Tidewater C.C., Chesapeake, Va.; diploma, FBA Nat. Acad. Patrolman Chesapeake Police Dept., 1966, sgt., 1970, lt., 1973, capt., 1978, lt. col., dep. chief, 1990, col., chief, 1997. Named Hon. Citizen Elizabeth City, Exec. of the Yr. Tidewater chpt. Internat. Assn. Adminstrv. Profls., 1999; recipient City Star Performer award. Mem. FBI Nat. Acad. Assocs. (pres. Va. chpt. 1984), So. Police Inst. Alumni Assn., Va. State Crime Assn. (state pres. 1991-92), Mason. Office: 304 Albemarle Dr Chesapeake VA 23322

CARRO, CARL RAFAEL, executive search consultant; b. N.Y.C., Mar. 16, 1961; s. John and Victoria (Eugenia) C.; m. Inna Liban, Nov. 17, 1984. BA in Polit. Sci., Econs., Columbia U., 1983. With fin. svcs. Union Bank of Switzerland, 1983-87; cons. Korn Ferry Internat., N.Y.C., 1987-89; sr. exec. recruiter The Gap, Inc., N.Y.C., 1989-90; v.p. Exec. Placement Consultants subs. R.H. Macy & Co., N.Y.C., 1991-94; mng. dir. Exec. Search Cons. Internat., Inc., N.Y.C., 1994—. Republican. Roman Catholic. Avocations: karate, hiking, bicycling, old houses, chess. Office: Exec Search Cons Internat 350 5th Ave Ste 5501 New York NY 10118-5599

CARROL, EDWARD NICHOLAS, psychologist; b. Newark, June 22, 1943; s. Wilfred and Ruth (Gluck) C.; m. Anne Marie McDonald, May 27, 1973 (div. May 1989); 1 child, Abbe Galen; m. Virginia Paisley Herbruck, Oct. 6, 1996. BA, Columbia U., 1965; MA, NYU, 1970, U. Del., 1975; PhD, U. Del., 1979. Diplomate Am. Acad. Pain Mgmt. Dir. pain clinic VA Med. Ctr., Cleve., 1979—. *Dr. Carrol's professional focus has been in three main areas: the development of a four-drug regimen for the treatment of end-stage, metastatic cancer pain; the application of anti-convulsant medication of neuropathic, deafferentation, central pain syndromes; refinement of protocols for the electroanesthetic techniques of transcutaneous nerve stimulation and neuroprobe to the management of peripheral nerve injury, post-amputation stump pain, post-thoracotomy hyperesthesia, arthralgia and especially radicular pain.* Mem. Internat. Assn. Study of Pain, Midwest Pain Soc. Republican. Jewish. Avocations: dogs, classical and country music. Home: 21490 Claythorne Rd Shaker Hts OH 44122-1964 Office: VA Med Ctr Pain Clinic 10701 East Blvd Cleveland OH 44106-1702

CARROLL, ADORNA OCCHIALINI, real estate executive; b. New Britain, Conn., Aug. 24, 1952; d. Antonio and Mary Ida (Reney) Occhialini; m. Christoper P. Buchas, Sept. 7, 1974 (div. Nov. 1982); 1 child, Jenna Rebecca; m. John Francis Carroll, Oct. 15, 1983; children: Jordan Ashley, Sean William. BA in Philosophy, Cen. Conn. State U., 1975; grad., Realtors Inst., 1989. Lic. real estate broker; accredited buyer rep. Dir. therapeutic recreation program Ridgeview Rest Home, Cromwell, Conn., 1974, Meadows Convalescent Home, Manchester, Conn., 1975, Andrew House Health Care, New Britain, 1976; owner, mgr. Liquor Locker, Newington, Conn., 1977-87; owner, broker A.O. Carroll & Co., Newington, 1985-93, A. O. Carroll & Agostini Co., Kensington, Conn., 1994—; ptnr. Marco Realty & Devel. Co., Newington, 1978-97, Dynamic Directions, Inc., ednl. and sales tng. cons., 1997—. Mem. Nat. Assn. Realtors (dir. 1995, 96, 97, 98, 99, multiple listing policy forum 1993, legis./polit. forum 1993, mem. svcs. com. 1994, 96, 97, recruitment and retention forum 1994, state fiscal affairs com. 1995, personal asst. working group 1995, vice chair membership devel. and promotion forum 1996, 97, edn. forum 1995, cons. and meetings com. 1996-97, vice chmn. mktg. forum 1998, chmn. mktg. forum 1999, mem. lic. law com. 1999), Conn. Assn. Realtors (pres.-elect 1996, state pres. 1997, v.p.-at-large 1992-94, vice-chair legislation 1991, mem. legis. policy & RPAC coms. 1991, conv. com. 1990, polit. affairs com. 1988, 89, chair state MLS task force 1994, chair agy. task force 1994, 95, chair personal assts. 1995, chair comms./tech. com. 1995), Greater New Britain Assn. Realtors (local dir. 1991, 92, chair legislation & nominating coms. 1991-92, pres. 1990, 93, 96, chair bylaws com. & state conv. 1990, pres.-elect 1989, chair programs & polit. affairs & AM HM WK 1988, spkr. 1989—, Realtor of Yr. 1991, state dir. 1995), Nat. Package Store Assn., Conn. Package Store Assn. (legis. lobbyist 1984-88, pres. 1986-88, Disting. Svc. award 1985), Greater Hartford Package Store Assn. (pres. 1981-82), Marchegian Soc. New Britain (pres. 1992, corr. sec. & chair budget 1991), Newington C. of C. (bd. dirs. 1987-88, chmn. legis. 1988). Avocations: furniture refinishing, racquetball, softball, golf. Home: 23 Occhialini Ct Newington CT 06111-4754 Office: AO Carroll & Agostini Co 742 Worthington Rdg Berlin CT 06037-3233

CARROLL, AILEEN, retired librarian; b. Mason, Wis., Aug. 7, 1914; d. John P. and Mary (Noonan) C. BA, De Paul U., 1938; MA, Northwestern U., 1940; MLS, Rosary Coll., 1965. Tchr. Chgo. Pub. Schs., 1940-52; systems media dir., libr. organizer Cook County Pub. Schs., 1952—. Author and pub. of children's poetry. Vol. St. Vincent's Orphanage, Chgo., Sacred Heart Home for the Aged, Chgo. Recipient scholarship AAUW, 1991. Mem. AAUW (Western Springs, Ill.), LWV, Rep. Club of Oak Park, Art Group of Western Springs. Home: 712 Courtland Cir Western Springs IL 60558-1945

CARROLL, BARRY JOSEPH, manufacturing and real estate executive; b. Highland Park, Ill., Jan. 22, 1944; s. Wallace Edward and Lelia (Holden) C.; m. Barbara Ann Pehrson, July 16, 1965; children: Megan, Sean, Deirdre, Colleen, Oona. Student, Boston Coll., 1961-63; AB, Shimer Coll., 1966; MBA, Harvard U., 1969. Lic. real estate broker, Ill. Account rep. Amerad Advt. Service, Chgo., summers 1966, 67; staff analyst Jamesbury Valve Co., Worcester, Mass., 1968; asst. to pres. Am. Gage & Machine Co., Elgin, Ill., 1969; pres. J.C. Deagan Co., Chgo., 1969-77; v.p. Internat. Metals & Machines, Des Plaines, 1977-92, also bd. dirs.; v.p. Katy Industries, Elgin, 1984-94, also bd. dirs.; pres. Katy Comm., Inc. (WIVS-AM, WXRD-FM, WAIT AM/FM), 1986-92, Sta. W45AJ-TV, Rockford, Ill., 1989-92; v.p., bd. dirs. Pehrson-Long Assocs., Real Estate Mgmt., Am. Machine & Sci. Inc., CRL Inc., Carroll Internat. Corp. (chmn. 1992). Author: (monograph) Talking with Business, 1986; author of appendix/editor: What I Do Best: The Biography of Wallace Edward Carroll, 1992; editor/author: Private Means/Public Ends, 1987; author: Lake Forest, A Very Special Place, 1996; producer, dir. indsl. films, including In There Punching, 1965. Spl. asst. U.S. Sec. Edn., Washington, 1983-84; Presdl. Exch. exec., Washington, 1983-84; bd. govs. United Rep. Fund, Chgo., 1986-92; mem. Nat. Inst. Edn. Commn. Edn. and Tech., U.S. Dept. Edn., 1984-85; trustee Shimer Coll., 1970—, chmn. bd. trustees, 1975-78; trustee Barat Coll., Lake Forest, 1983—, life trustee, 1999—; trustee St. Xavier U., Chgo., 1988-94, Lake County Regional Sch. Bd., 1993—; bd. trustees Am. Ireland Fund, 1982—, sec., 1991—; bd. dirs. Lake Forest Symphony, 1970—, Pageant of Peace/Nat. Christmas Tree, 1987—, Lake Forest Music Inst., 1991—, Roosevelt U., Chgo., 1996—, U. Ill. Eye Rsch. Inst., 1996—; bd. dirs. Chgo. Crime Commn., 1993—, treas., 1994-98; mem., chmn. Lake Forest Cultural Arts Commn., 1997—; chair adv. bd. Inst. Metro. Affairs, 1998—. Shimer fellow Shimer Coll., Mt. Carroll, Ill., 1972, Shimer Hero award Shimer Coll., Waukegan, Ill., 1980, Dr. Letters, 1995. Mem. Woods Hole Oceanographic Inst. Assn., Ill. Mfrs. Assn. (bd. dirs. 1989—), Assn. for Mfg. Tech. (bd. dirs. chmn. pub. affairs com. 1988-93), Onwentsia Club (Lake Forest), Chgo. Club, Met. Club (Washington), East Chop Beach Tennis and Yacht Clubs (Martha's Vineyard Island), Edgartown Yacht Club, Bath and Tennis Club (Palm Beach, Fla.), Soc. Colonial Wars in the State of Ill. (treas. 1988-94, gov. 1998—). Avocations: flying, sailing, skiing, scuba diving, photography. Office: Carroll Internat Corp 2340 Des Plaines Ave Des Plaines IL 60018-3212

CARROLL, BRENDA SANDIDGE, retired civic worker; b. Leonardtown, Md., May 1, 1952; d. Ronald and Erma (McKay) Sandidge; m. Leo Elmer Carroll, Dec. 19, 1970; 1 child, Jennifer. BA, St. Mary's Coll. Md., 1989. Libr. acquisitions technician St. Mary's Coll., St. Mary's City, Md., 1989-95; ret., 1995. Vol. Mary's Song Ctr. Soup Kitchen, Lexington Park, Md., 1995—, St. Mary's County Literacy Coun., 1985—, St. Michael's Sch., 1977-83, St. Mary's County Hist. Preservation Com., 1986—; asst. food coord. Christmas in April, Hollywood, Md., 1991—; mem. play com., bd. govs. Ridge (Md.) Lions Club, 1997—; vol. Ridge VFW; meal deliverer Meals on Wheels, St. Mary's County, Md., 1997—.

CARROLL, CHARLES MICHAEL, music educator; b. Otterbein, Ind., Mar. 5, 1921; s. James William and Catherine Doretta (Bohan) C.; m. Mary Lipford Rosenbush, Sept. 4, 1951; children: Charles Michael, Mary Catherine, Theresa Jane, William Rosenbush. BM, Ind. U., Bloomington, 1949; MM, Fla. State U., Tallahassee, 1951, PhD, 1960. Asst. coordinator music services Ind. U., 1949-50; instr. music Fla. State U., 1950-53; concert mgr. symphony orchs. Toledo, Washington, Savannah, Ga., 1953-58; prof. music Pensacola (Fla.) Jr. Coll., 1960-64; prof. St. Petersburg (Fla.) Jr. Coll., 1964-89, chmn. communications dept.; music critic Tallahassee Democrat, 1950-53, St. Petersburg Evening Independent, 1976-86. Author: The Great Chess Automaton, 1975; contbr. articles to profl. jours., and encyclopaedias. Served to capt., AUS, 1942-46, ETO. Mem. Am. Symphony Orch. League (v.p. 1955-56), Am. Musicol. Soc. (nat. council 1974-77, chmn. chpt. 1974-76), Am. Soc. Eighteenth-Century Studies (exec. bd. region 1974-82, regional pres. 1979-80), Coll. Music Soc. (editor 1979-83, nat. council 1978-81, chmn. chpt. 1979-80), Société d'Etudes Philidoriennes (conseiller bibliographique 1988—). Home: 1701 80th St N Saint Petersburg FL 33710-3703

CARROLL, CORLIS FAITH, artist; b. Troy, N.Y., Oct. 11, 1950; d. Thomas Francis and Dorothy May (Sellingham) C.; children: Heather Elise Hewitt, Heidi Carroll Hewitt. BA summa cum laude, U. Albany, 1994. Artist, 1983—. Represented in private collections. Mediator Matrimonial and Cmty. Dispute Resolution. Mem. Phi Beta Kappa. Home: PO Box 309 Slingerlands NY 12159-0309

CARROLL, DAVID JOSEPH, actor; b. Stratford, N.J., July 9, 1979; s. David Ronald and Mary Jane (Popko) C. Student, Ctr. Talented Youth, 1991-92, ROGATE, 1991-92, Sch. Visual Arts, 1997—. Actor: (TV comls.) Rock & Roll Easter Eggs, 1989, British Knights, 1989, America's Funniest Home Videos, 1990, French Toast Clothes, 1990, Pizza Hut, 1990, Burger King, 1990, (films) Cadillac Man, 1989, Thank You and Goodnight, 1990. Mem. Screen Actors Guild. Avocations: biking, golf, computer animation, swimming, roller blading. Home: 385 Harlingen Rd Belle Mead NJ 08502-5313

CARROLL, DAVID LEE, museum administrator; b. Torrance, Calif., May 11, 1965; s. Ralph Marvin and Virginia Rose (McKey) C. BS in mgmt. info. systems, Colo. State U., 1988; MA in arts adminstrn., Ind. U., 1997. Tech. analyst United Airlines, Englewood, Colo., 1988-92; sr. tech. analyst Westin Hotels & Resorts, Seattle, 1992-94; cons. Galileo Internat., Englewood, 1994-95; assoc. dir. adminstrn. Ind. U. Art Mus., Bloomington, 1997, 1997—; docent Nat. Mus. of Women in the Arts, Washington, 1994; vol. sales asst. Fuel Gallery, Seattle, 1993-94. Sec. Denver Young Democrats, 1990-91; mem. Toastmasters Internat., 1992-93. Home: 817 W 11th St Bloomington IN 47404-3233 Office: Indiana University Art Museum Bloomington IN 47405

CARROLL, DIAHANN, actress, singer; b. N.Y.C., July 17, 1935; d. John and Mabel (Faulk) Johnson; m. Monte Kay (div.); m. Fredde Glusman (div.); m. Robert DeLean, 1975 (dec. 1977); m. Vic Damone, 1987. Student, N.Y. U. Began career as model; actress: motion pictures, including Claudine (Nominated for Acad. award as best actress by the Acad. Motion Picture Arts and Scis. 1974), Carmen Jones, Porgy and Bess, Hurry Sundown, Paris Blues, The Split. The Five Heartbeats, 1991, Eve's Bayou, 1997; on Broadway in No Strings, House of Flowers; appeared in: play Same Time, Next Year; TV series Julia, Dynasty, 1984-87, Lonesome Dove, 1994; TV movies Death Scream, 1975, I Know Why the Caged Bird Sings, 1979, Sister, Sister, 1982, Murder in Black and White, 1990, A Perry Mason Mystery: The Case of the Lethal Lifestyle, 1994, The Sweetest Gift, 1998, Motown 40: The Music is Forever, 1998, Having Our Say: The Delany Sisters' First 100 Years, 1999; TV miniseries Motown 40: The Music is Forever, 1998. Address: William Morris Agy Inc care Peter Levine 151 S El Camino Dr Beverly Hills CA 90212-2704*

CARROLL, EARL HAMBLIN, federal judge; b. Tucson, Mar. 26, 1925; s. John Vernon and Ruby (Wood) C.; m. Louise Rowlands, Nov. 1, 1952; children—Katherine Carroll Pearson, Margaret Anne. BSBA, U. Ariz., 1948, LLB, 1951. Bar: Ariz., U.S. Ct. Appeals (9th and 10th cirs.), U.S. Ct. of Claims, U.S. Supreme Ct. Law clk. Ariz. Supreme Ct., Phoenix, 1951-52; assoc. Evans, Kitchel & Jenckes, Phoenix, 1952-56, ptnr., 1956-80; judge U.S. Dist. Ct. Ariz., Phoenix, 1980—; spl. counsel City of Tombstone, Ariz., 1962-65, Maricopa County, Phoenix, 1968-75, City of Tucson, 1974, City of Phoenix, 1979; designated mem. U.S. Fgn. Intelligence Surveillance Court by Chief Justice U.S. Supreme Ct., 1993-99; chief judge Alien Terrorist Removal Ct., 1996-01. Mem. City of Phoenix Bd. of Adjustment, 1955-58; trustee Phoenix Elem. Sch. Bd., 1961-72; mem. Gov.'s Council on Intergovtl. Relations, Phoenix, 1970-73; mem. Ariz. Bd. Regents, 1978-80. Served with USNR, 1943-46; PTO. Recipient Nat. Service awards Campfire, 1973, 75, Alumni Service award U. Ariz., 1980, Disting. Citizen award No. Ariz. U., Flagstaff, 1983, Bicentenial award Georgetown U., 1988, Disting. Citizen award U. Ariz., 1990. Fellow Am. Coll. Trial Lawyers, Am. Bar Found.; mem. ABA, Ariz. Bar Assn., U. Ariz. Law Coll. Assn. (pres. 1975), Phoenix Country Club, Sigma Chi (Significant Sig award 1991), Phi Delta Phi. Democrat. Office: US Dist Ct US Courthouse & Fed Bldg 230 N 1st Ave Ste 6000 Phoenix AZ 85025-0005

CARROLL, ELIZABETH LEE, educator English; b. Charleston, S.C., Oct. 22, 1970; d. Ephraim Mikell and Elizabeth Cave C. BA in English, Appalachian State U., 1993; MA in English, U. Vt., 1997. Instr. English Wilkes C.C., Wilkesboro, N.C., 1997—. Grad. Teaching fellow U. Vt., Burlington, 1996-97. Mem. Nat. Coun. Tchrs. English, Modern Lang. Assn. Avocations: snowboarding, surfing, travel, backpacking, horseback riding. Home: 4663 Big Hill Rd Todd NC 28684 Office: Wilkes C C Collegiate Dr Wilkesboro NC 28697

CARROLL, FRANK JAMES, lawyer, educator; b. Albuquerque, Feb. 10, 1947; s. Francis J. and Dorothy (Bloom) C.; m. Marilyn Blume, Aug. 9, 1969; children: Christine, Kathleen, Emily. BS in Acctg., St. Louis U., 1969; JD, U. Ill., 1973. Bar: Iowa 1973, U.S. Dist. Ct. Iowa, U.S. Tax Ct., U.S. Ct. Appeals (8th cir.); CPA, Mo., Iowa. Acct. Arthur Young & Co., St. Louis, 1969-70; shareholder Davis, Brown, Koehn, Shors & Roberts, P.C., Des Moines, 1973—; lectr. law Drake U. Law Sch., Des Moines, 1976-86, lectr. Sch. of Bus., 1988-92; bd. dirs. Newton Mfg. Co., Pella Plastics, Inc. Mem. commr.'s adv. group IRS, Washington, 1989; mem. grad. tax adv. bd. U. Mo. Kansas City Sch. Law, 1995. Mem. ABA, Iowa Bar Assn. (chair bus. law sect. 1995-98), Polk County Bar Assn., Des Moines C. of C., Wakonda Club, Des Moines Variety Club (bd. dirs. 1998), Beta Gamma Sigma. Home: 5725 Harwood Dr Des Moines IA 50312-1203 Office: Davis Brown Koehn Shors Roberts PC 666 Walnut St Ste 2500 Des Moines IA 50309-3904

CARROLL, GEORGE JOSEPH, pathologist, educator; b. Gardner, Mass., Oct. 14, 1917; s. George Joseph and Kathryn (O'Hearn) C. BA, Clark U., Worcester, Mass., 1939; MD, George Washington U., 1944. Diplomate Am.

Bd. Pathology. Intern Worchester City Hosp., 1944-45; resident in medicine Doctors Hosp., Washington, 1945-46; resident in pathology Sibley Hosp., Washington, 1948-49, VA Hosp., Washington, 1949-50; asst. pathologist D.C. Gen. Hosp., 1950-51, assoc. pathologist, 1951-52; pathologist Louise Obici Meml. Hosp., Suffolk, Va., 1952—; sec. med. staff Louise Obici Meml. Hosp., 1956-59, chief of staff, 1959-60, 67-69; pathologist Chowan Hosp., Edenton, N.C., 1952-71, Southampton Meml. Hosp., Franklin, Va., 1952—, Greensville Meml. Hosp., Emporia, Va., 1961—; instr. pathology Georgetown U. Sch. Medicine, 1950-52; instr. bacteriology Am. U., Washington, 1950-51; assoc. clin. prof. pathology Med. Coll. Va., Richmond, 1968-70; clin. prof. pathology Va. Commonwealth U., 1970—; prof. dept. pathology Eastern Va. Med. Sch., Norfolk, 1974—; sec.-treas. Va. Bd. Medicine, 1967-86, treas., 1971-86. Contbr. articles to med. jours. Served with U.S. Army, 1946-48. Fellow ACP, Coll. Am. Pathologists, Am. Soc. Clin. Pathologists (bd. dirs. 1969—, pres. 1977—), Internat. Acad. Pathology; mem. AMA, So. Med. Assn. (Va. councilor 1965-70, pres. 1973-74), Med. Soc. Va., 4th dist. Med. Soc. (pres. 1968-70), Seaboard Med. Soc. (pres. 1957), George Washington Med. Soc., Tri-County Med. Soc. (pres. 1971-73), Am. Soc. Clin. Pharmacy Therapeutics, Va. Soc. Pathology (pres. 1973-74), Soc. Nuclear Medicine, Am. Assn. Blood Banks, Am. Cancer Soc. (bd. dirs. Va. div. 1955-62), Va. Med. Svc. Assn. (bd. dirs. 1960-71), Rotary. Home: 219 Northbrook Ave Suffolk VA 23434-6647 Office: Louise Obici Meml Hosp 1900 N Main St PO Box 1100 Suffolk VA 23434-4345

CARROLL, GLADYS HASTY, author; b. Rochester, N.H., June 26, 1904; d. Warren Verdi and Emma Frances (Dow) Hasty; m. Herbert A. Carroll, June 23, 1925; children: Warren Hasty Carroll, Sarah Carroll Watson. AB, Bates Coll., Lewiston, Maine, 1925, LittD, 1945; AM (hon.), U. N.H., 1934; LittD, U. Maine, 1939; LHD, Nasson Coll., 1975. Author: novels and nonfictions, including As the Earth Turns, 1933, current edit., 1995, A Few Foolish Ones, 1935, Neighbor to the Sky, 1937, Head of the Line, 1942, While the Angels Sing, 1947, West of the Hill, 1949, Christmas Without Johnny, 1950, Dannybrook, 1952, new edit., 1978 (tape of book sponsored by hist. socs. in South Berwick, Maine and the Dannybrook Hist. Found.), One White Star, 1954, Sing Out the Glory, 1957, Come With Me Home, 1960, Only Fifty Years Ago, 1962, To Remember Forever, 1963, The Road Grows Strange, 1965, The Light Here Kindled, 1967, Christmas Through the Years, 1968, Man on the Mountain, 1969, Years Away From Home, 1972, Next of Kin, 1974, Unless You Die Young, 1977, The Book That Came Alive, 1979, Winge over Berwick Academy, 1992; also short stories; contbr. to mags.; author stories appearing as screenplays on TV, in anthologies, large print edits. adj. prof. various doctoral coms.; founder Dunnybrook Hist. Found., 1985. Recipient Deborah Morton award Westbrook, Coll., 1987, Maryann Hartmann award U. Maine, Orono, 1995. Mem. Phi Beta Kappa. Home: 8 Earls Rd South Berwick ME 03908-2157

CARROLL, HOLBERT NICHOLSON, political science educator; b. Charleroi, Pa., June 30, 1921; s. James Russell and Mary Leola (McDonough) C. A.B., U. Pitts., 1943, M.A., 1947; postgrad., Yale U., 1943-44; Ph.D., Harvard U., 1953. Faculty U. Pitts., 1946-48, 50—, prof. polit. sci., 1960-90, prof. emeritus, 1990—, chmn. dept., 1960-68; teaching fellow Harvard U., 1949-50; Cons. Brookings Instn., 1959. Author: The House of Representatives and Foreign Affairs, 1958, rev. edit., 1966, A Study of the Goverance of the University of Pittsburgh, 1972; contbr. chpt. to: The Congress and America's Future, 1965, rev. edit., 1973; book rev. editor: Am. Polit. Sci. Rev., 1979-81. Served with AUS, 1943-46, CBI. Mem. Am. Polit. Sci. Assn., Phi Beta Kappa, Omicron Delta Kappa. Office: U Pitts Dept Polit Sci 4L0a Forbes Quad Pittsburgh PA 15260

CARROLL, HOWARD WILLIAM, state senator, lawyer; b. July 28, 1942; s. Barney M. and Lyla (Price) C.; m. Eda Stagman, Dec. 1, 1973; children: Jacqueline, Barbara. BBA, Roosevelt U., 1964; postgrad., Loyola U., 1964-65; JD, DePaul U., 1967. Bar: Ill. 1967. Staff atty. Chgo. Transit Authority, 1967-71; pvt. practice, 1971-74; ptnr. Carroll & Sain, Chgo., 1974—; mem. Ill. Senate, Springfield, 1973-99, asst. minority leader, 1993-99, chmn. appropriations com., 1977-93; mem. Legis. Info. System Commn., Ill. Comprehensive Health Ins. Bd.; vice chmn. State Employees Suggestion Award Bd.; mem. fed. budget and taxation com. State-Fed. Assembly; mem. Assembly Com. on State's Legis. Fiscal Affairs and Oversight; prof. complemental faculty Rush U. Coll. Health Scis., Chgo.; lectr. in field. Mem. Ill. Ho. of Reps., 1971-72; chmn. fin. com. Chgo. and Cook County Dem. Crtl. Com., 1982-84, treas., 1984—; committeeman 50th Ward Dem. Orgn., 1980—; mem. platform com. Ill. Dem. Com., 1974—; former mem. youth adv. bd. Dem. Nat. Com.; del. nat. and Ill. Dem. convs.; v.p. Young Dem. Clubs Am., 1971-73, also former gen. counsel; mem. exec. bd. Atlantic Alliance Young Polit. Leaders, 1970-73; active numerous civic orgns.; mem. exec. com. Jewish Nat. Fund, 1977—; founder Howard W. Carroll Found. Recipient numerous awards, 1971, including cert. of appreciation Decalogue Soc. Lawyers, 1972, Hemophilia Found. Ill., 1988, City Colls. Chgo., 1992, Disting. Svc. award State of Israel Bonds, 1974, Self-Help Assn., 1986, citation for meritorious svc. DAV, 1986, Legislator of Yr. award Child Care Assn. Ill., 1988, Ill. Coun. on Long Term Care, 1988, Outstanding Legislator award Am. Acad. Ophthollmology, 1989, Legis. Advocacy award Ill. Coun. for Gifted, 1991, Founders medal Montay Coll., 1992; named Ill. Health Care Outstanding Legislator of Yr., 1995. Mem. Chgo. Bar Assn. (Disting. Lawyer and Legislator award 1974), Zionist Orgn. Chgo., Masons (32d degree), B'nai B'rith (bd. dirs. West Rogers Park, chmn. Anti-Defamation League 1978-80, mem. exec. com. and chmn. spl. events Greater Chgo. coun., bd. dirs. Budlong Woods chpt.). Home: 2929 W Albion Ave Chicago IL 60645-4203 Office: Office of Senate Members State Capitol Springfield IL 62706 also: 47 W Polk St Ste 3 Chicago IL 60605-2000

CARROLL, IRWIN DIXON, engineer; b. Many, La., Nov. 6, 1934; s. Andrew Dixon and Elizabeth Margaret (Irwin) C.; m. Claudia Laverne Bratcher, June 27, 1958; children: Richard Irwin, Claudia Elizabeth. BS in Mech. Engring., So. Meth. U., 1957, MS in Elec. Engring., 1967. Registered profl. engr., Tex. Design engr. Tex. Instruments, Dallas, 1957-66, engring. supr., 1966-71, engring. mgr., 1971-75, ops. mgr., 1975-77, European div. mgr., 1977-79, mfg. ops. mgr., 1979-80, dept. mgr., 1980-85; dept. mgr. George A. Greene Co., Campbell, Calif., 1985-86; cons. engr. Irwin Carroll Assocs., Dallas, 1986-88; dir. joint devel. programs, site mgr. Applied Materials, Inc., Austin, Tex., 1988—; tech. program dir. Semiconductor Equip. and Materials Inst., Dallas, 1983-85, speaker Zurich, Switzerland, 1986; mem. info. sys. adv. com. U.S. Dept. Commerce, 1990-96. Chmn. Zion Luth. Sch. Bd., Dallas, 1985-89; bd. dirs. Jr. Achievement of Ctrl. Tex., 1991-93, Japan-Am. Soc. of Austin, 1990-95, Austin Symphony Orch., 1994-97; pres. Austin Children's Mus., 1991-97; active Austin Choral Union, 1994-96; pres. Austin Comty. Found., 1996—. Mem. ASME, Greater Austin C. of C. (bd. dirs. 1991-95), Rotary. Lutheran. Home: PO Box 923 Salado TX 76571-0923 Office: Design Tech Group Inc (Roti-Chef Grills) PO Box 1056 Salado TX 76571

CARROLL, J. SPEED, lawyer, financial executive; b. Sherman, Tex., Apr. 23, 1936; s. Horace Bailey and Mary Joe (Durning) C.; m. Martha Coleman Huff, Apr. 12, 1957; 1 child, Charles Durning. BA, U. Tex., 1957; LLB, Harvard U., 1962. Bar: N.Y. 1964, U.S. Supreme Ct. 1971, Japan (fgn. legal cons.) 1993-95. Assoc. Cleary, Gottlieb, Steen & Hamilton, N.Y.C. and Paris, 1963-70; ptnr. Cleary, Gottlieb, Steen & Hamilton, N.Y.C., London, Tokyo, 1971-97; counsel Cleary, Gottlieb, Steen & Hamilton, 1997—; mng. dir. Emerging Markets Partnership, Washington, 1997—; cons. fgn. law Nagashima & Ohno, Tokyo, 1964-65; instr. Internat. Law Inst., Washington, 1973-83; bd. dirs. Mitsubishi Trust and Banking Corp., U.S.A., N.Y.C., Am. Opera Projects, Inc., Performance Zone, Inc. Contbr. chapters to books and articles to profl. jours. Mem. Coun. on Fgn. Rels., N.Y.C., 1973—; trustee Parker Sch. Internat. and Comparative Law Columbia U., 1992—. Lt. USNR, 1957-59. Knox fellow Harvard U., 1962-63. Office: Emerging Markets Partnership 2001 Pennsylvania Ave NW Washington DC 20006-1850*

CARROLL, JAMES, author; b. Chgo., Jan. 22, 1943; s. Joseph F. and Mary A. (Morrissey) C.; m. Alexandra Marshall, May 21, 1977; children: Elizabeth, Patrick. B.A., St. Paul's Coll., Washington, 1966, M.A., 1968. Author: (novels) The Winter Name of God, 1974, Madonna Red, 1976, Mortal Friends, 1978, Fault Lines, 1980, Family Trade, 1982, Prince of Peace, 1984, Supply of Heroes, 1984, Firebird, 1989, Memorial Bridge, 1991, The City Below, 1994, (memoir) An American Requiem, 1996 (Nat. Book award in nonfiction). Mem. Authors League, PEN. Office: Houghton Miflin Co 222 Berkeley St Boston MA 02116-3748*

CARROLL, JAMES EDWARD, lawyer; b. Milford, Mass., July 9, 1952; s. James William and Anna (Bertoni) C.; m. Nancy Louise Baker, Oct. 12, 1974; children: Jonathan Patrick, Benjamin James, Jeremy David. BS, Fairfield U., 1974; MA, U. R.I., 1977; JD cum laude, Suffolk U., 1983. Bar: Mass. 1983, U.S. Dist. Ct. Mass. 1984, U.S. Ct. Appeals (1st cir.) 1984, U.S. Tax Ct. 1989, U.S. Supreme Ct. 1995. Tchr. Prout Meml. High Sch., Wakefield, R.I., 1974-76, Walpole (Mass.) High Sch., 1976-83; assoc. Gaston Snow & Ely Bartlett, Boston, 1983-86; trial atty. U.S. Dept. Justice, Washington, 1986-88; assoc. Hale & Dorr, Boston, 1988; ptnr. Peabody & Arnold, Boston, 1988-95; founding ptnr. Cetrulo & Capone, LLP, Boston, 1995—; mem. criminal justice panel, U.S. Dist. Ct. Mass., 1993—. Contbr. articles to law rev. Bd. dirs. Am. Cancer Soc. Mem. ABA, Mass. Bar Assn. (speaker 1991-92), Boston Bar Assn., Nat. Assn. Criminal Def. Attys., Supreme Jud. Ct. Hist. Soc., Phi Delta Phi. Roman Catholic. Avocations: running, baseball, football, children's soccer. Home: 139 Lawndale Rd Mansfield MA 02048-1621 Office: Cetrulo & Capone 53 State St Boston MA 02109-2804

CARROLL, JAMES J., lawyer; b. Chgo., Jan. 10, 1948. BS magna cum laude, DePaul U., 1969, JD summa cum laude, 1972. Bar: Ill. 1972, U.S. Tax Ct. 1980, U.S. Supreme Ct. 1981. Of counsel Sidley & Austin, Chgo., 1972—, ptnr., 1978-95; dir., pres. Wrigley Mgmt. Inc., Chgo., 1995—; lectr. Ill. Inst. for Continuing Legal Edn. Editor-in-chief DePaul Law Rev., 1971-72. Sec. Lakewood Estates Homeowners Assn.; bd. dirs. David and Ruth Barnow Found., 1979, Wrigley Family Found., 1993-99. With USAR, 1970-76. Mem. Ill. State Bar Assn. (chmn. children's rights subcom. 1972-73), Chgo. Bar Assn. (probate practice com. 1977-88, lectr.), Law Club Chgo., Legal Club Chgo., Phi Eta Sigma, Beta Alpha Psi. Office: Wrigley Mgmt Inc 400 N Michigan Ave Ste 1100 Chicago IL 60611-4163

CARROLL, JANE HAMMOND, artist, author, poet; b. Greenville, S.C., May 15, 1946; d. Charles Kirby and Margaret (Cooper) Hammond; m. Robert Lindsay Carroll Jr., Feb. 3, 1968; children: Jane-Gower, Robert Lindsay III. BA, U. S.C., 1968. Tchr. A.C. Flora High Sch., Columbia, S.C., 1968-70; exec. field dir. N.E. Ga. Girl Scout Coun., Athens, 1970-71; asst. dir. AID-Vol. Greenville, 1971-73; author, artist Winston Derek Pubs., Nashville, 1985—. Author, artist: Grace, 1987 (Gov.'s Collection 1988), Intimate Moments, 1987 (Gov.'s Collection), (art book) Dayspring, 1989; one-person shows include Williams Salon, Atlanta, 1989, 92, 93, 94, 95, 99, Galerie Timothy Tew, Jenny Pruitt Realty, 1989, Ariel Gallery, Atlanta, 1996; group shows include Fine Art Mus. of the South, Mobile, Beyond the Wall, 1990, Mus. Archives, Washington, 1992, Internat. Pastel Show, Ga., 1991, 95, Savannah Nat. (1st pl. award in drawing), Telfare Mus. Savannah, 1995, Telfare Art Fair, 1995, Ariel Gallery, 1995—, Calloway Garden, 1998; permanent collections represented Greenville Meml. Hosp., S.C., Embassy Suites, Ill., Macan Motor Cars, Ga., Jenny Pruitt Reality, Ga., and others; commns. include Landscape, Portraits, family, others; pub. and pvt. collections; included in art book Orchard. Bd. mgr. Greenville Jr. League, 1971-73; artist for fundraiser Rehab. Edn. for Handicapped Adults and Children, Atlanta, 1992-95; vol. artist Arts in the Atlanta Project, 1993. Mem. Nat. League Am. Pen Women (chair art's program 1984—, Achievement award 1987, 89, 93, 94, 95, 96, 97, 98), Atlanta Artist Club (v.p. 1984-85, Merit mem.). Presbyterian. Avocations: travel, reading, outdoor activities, yoga. Home and Office: 2979 Majestic Cir Avondale Estates GA 30002-1611

CARROLL, JEANNE, public relations executive; b. Oak Park, Ill., May 20, 1929; d. John P. and Mary (Noonan) Carroll; BA, U. London, 1950; MA, Northwestern U., 1951; m. Harold M. Kass, Apr. 1966. Bus. girls editor Charm Mag., N.Y.C., 1951-53; pub. relations dir. Rosary Coll., River Forest, Ill., 1953-66; chmn. publicity Am. Cancer Soc., bd. dirs. W. and S.W. Suburban Unit, 1967—; med. adminstr., asst. to Dr. Harold Kass, Oak Park, Ill., 1969—; pub. rels. cons., 1993—. Pub. relations counselor in Midwest for Brown U., 1962; dir. pub. relations Mundelein Coll., 1968; producer radio show for teen-agers, Chgo., 1954; lectr. sci. devels. Bell Labs. for AT&T, 1954; participant annual Sun-Times seminars for coll. journalists MacMurray Coll., Jacksonville Ill. Chmn. March of Dimes campaign for Chgo., ednl. TV Channel 11, River Forest, 1963; trustee DePaul U., Chgo., chmn. Soc. Fellows dinner; chmn. Oak Park Hosp. Ben Din Dan, 1971-80; mem. com. library Internat. Relations, 1975-82; mem. bd. Arden Shores, sch. for boys, 1984—; bd. dirs. Globe Theatre Ctr.; mem. adv. bd. USO, mem. com. USO Celebration D-Day Activities, Chgo., 1994. Recipient Excellence award for coll. brochures Am. Coll. Pubs. Com., 1957; medal of recognition for work in pub. relations Bishop Fulton Sheen, 1960; Humanitarian award Performing Arts Ctr. and Citizens Com., Chgo., 1976; award DuSable Mus., 1978. Mem. Ill. Assn. Coll. Admissions Counsellors (pres.), Assn. Coll. Pub. Relations Assn., Family Service Assn. Am. (past bd. dirs.), Acad. Hosp., Pub. Relations, Ill. (pres.), Chgo. (pub. relations dir., med. soc. auxs.), Oak Park Hosp. (pres. women's aux. 1986-89), West Suburban Hosp. Med. Ctr. Aux. (life). Home: 712 Courtland Cir Western Springs IL 60558-1945

CARROLL, JOANNE ZLATE, elementary education educator; b. Cleve., Jan. 24, 1950; d. Joseph Albin and Sophia Anne (Kastelic) Zlate; m. James William Carroll, Aug. 12, 1988. MusB, Otterbein Coll., 1972; MEd, Cleve. State U., 1988. Cert. music, computer science, Ohio. Tchr. gen. and instrumental music Berkshire Local Schs., Burton, Ohio, 1972-79; tchr. gen., instrumental music and computer sci. Wickliffe (Ohio) City Schs., 1982-96; tchr. computer sci. Wickliffe Elem. Sch., 1996—; bd. dirs. Wickliffe Sch. Employees Credit Union, 1995—. Mem. NEA, Ohio Edn. Assn., Wickliffe Educators Assn., Delta Omicron.

CARROLL, JOHN DOUGLAS, mathematical and statistical psychologist; b. Phila., Jan. 3, 1939; s. John Joseph and Nolie Fay (Godwin) C.; m. Sylvia Stevens Booma, Jan. 2, 1965; children: Gregory Alan, Steven Douglas. BS with honors, U. Fla., 1958; PhD, Princeton U., 1963. Research asst. dept. psychology Yale U., 1961-63; math.-statis. psychologist Bell Labs., Murray Hill, N.J., 1963-65, 66-89; bd. govs., prof. mgmt. and psychology Rutgers U., Newark, 1990—; asst. prof. indsl. engring. and ops. research NYU, 1965-66, adj. assoc. prof. stats., 1968-70; acting prof. psychology U. Calif.-San Diego, 1975-76; acting prof. social sci. U. Calif.-Irvine, 1975-76; adj. prof. stats. Baruch Coll., CUNY, 1971, adj. prof. mktg. U. Pa., 1978-79; Procter & Gamble adj. prof. of mktg. U. Pa., 1987-89; vis. rsch. prof. cognitive sci. U. Calif. Irvine, 1993. Contbr. numerous articles and chpts. to profl. pubs.; author computer programs for multidimensional analysis of behavioral sci. data; assoc. editor: Psychometrika, 1973—, Jour. Exptl. Psychology, 1978-88; mem. editl. bd. Jour. Classification, 1984—, Jour. Mktg. Rsch., 1994—; editor Methodika, 1987-93. Ednl. Testing Service psychometric fellow, 1958-61; NIMH fellow, 1959-61. Fellow AAAS, APA (active Div. 5, pres.-elect 1990-91, pres. 1991-92, APA Disting. Sci. Contbn. award 1989), Am. Psychol. Soc. (William James fellow 1989), Am. Statis. Assn. (program chair stats. in mktg. sect. 1992, chair stats. in mktg. sect. 1993-94, mem. exec. com. 1991-95); mem. Psychometric Soc. (trustee 1971-77, 81-83, 84-87, 93-96, pres. 1975-76, mem. editl. coun. 1975-81), Classification Soc. N.Am. (governing coun. 1974-77, pres. 1980-83, bd. dirs. 1984-96), Internat. Fedn. Classification Socs. (rep. to coun. 1984—, v.p./pres.-elect 1995, pres. 1996—), Soc. Multivariate Exptl. Psychology (editl. adv. bd. 1980-81, pres. 1982-83), Ea. Psychol. assn., Psychonomic Soc., Soc. Math. Psychology, Am. Mktg. Assn., Assn. for Consumer Rsch., Soc. for Consumer Psychology, Inst. for Ops. Rsch. and Mgmt. Scis., Phi Beta Kappa, Sigma Xi, Beta Gamma Sigma. Home: 14 Forest Dr Warren NJ 07059-5802 Office: Rutgers U Grad Sch Mgmt Fac of Mgmt/Mgmt Edn Ctr 111 Washington St Newark NJ 07102-1820

CARROLL, JOHN L., federal judge; b. 1943. BA, Tufts U., 1965; JD magna cum laude, Samford U., 1974; LLM, Harvard U., 1975. Law prof. Mercer U. Sch. Law, 1985-86, U. Ala., Ga. State U.; magistrate judge State of Ala., Montgomery, 1986—; mem. Jud. Conf. Adv. Com. on Civil Rules; mem. Fed. Jud. Ctr. Magistrate Judges Edn. Com. Contbr. articles to profl. jours. With USMC, Vietnam. Fax: 334-223-7114. Office: US Courthouse 15 Lee St Montgomery AL 36104

CARROLL, JOHN SAWYER, newspaper editor; b. N.Y.C., Jan. 23, 1942; s. John Wallace and Margaret (Sawyer) C.; m. Kathleen Kirk, May 1, 1971 (div. Sept. 1982) children—Kathleen Louise, Margaret Adriane; m. Lee Huston Powell, Nov. 1985. B.A., Haverford Coll., 1963. Reporter Providence Jour. - Bull., 1963-64; reporter Balt. Sun., 1966-72, Vietnam, 1967-69, Middle East, 1969, Washington Bur., 1969-72; city editor, met. editor Phila. Inquirer, 1973-79; exec. v.p., editor Lexington Herald-Leader, Ky., 1979-91; editor, sr. v.p. Balt. Sun, 1991—; v.p. Times Mirror Co., 1998—; bd. dirs. Am. Soc. Newspaper Editors, Pulitzer prize juror, 1987, 89, 94, Pulitzer prize bd., 1994—. Served with U.S. Army, 1964-66. Nieman fellow Harvard U., 1971-72; vis. journalist fellow Queen Elizbeth House, U. Oxford, 1988. Home: 1009 Poplar Hill Rd Baltimore MD 21210-1223 Office: Baltimore Sun Calvert & Centre Sts Baltimore MD 21278

CARROLL, JOSEPH J(OHN), lawyer; b. N.Y.C., Sept. 18, 1936; s. James J. and M. Catherine (Molloy) C.; m. Barbara Ann Lediger, May 16, 1959; 1 child, Barbara Ann (dec.). BS, Manhattan Coll., 1958; LLB, St. John's U., 1963; LLM, NYU, 1968. Bar: N.Y. 1964, U.S. Supreme Ct. 1967, D.C. 1978. Ins. underwriter Atlantic Mut. Ins. Co., N.Y.C., 1959-63; pub. adminstrn. intern N.Y. State Housing Fin. Agy., N.Y.C., 1963-64, adminstrv. asst., 1964-67; assoc. Mudge, Rose, Guthrie, Alexander & Ferdon, N.Y.C., 1967-77, ptnr., 1977-95; of counsel Sullivan & Donovan, LLP, N.Y.C., 1995—. Mem. ABA (health law and urban, state and local govt. sects.), N.Y. State Bar Assn. (mcpl. health law sects.), Am. Health Lawyers Assn., Am. Soc. Law, Medicine and Ethics.

CARROLL, JULIAN MORTON, lawyer, former governor; b. Paducah, Ky., Apr. 16, 1931; s. Elvie B. and Eva (Heady) C.; m. Charlann Harting, July 22, 1951; children: Kenneth Morton, Iva Patrice, Bradley Harting, Ellyn Kriston. AA, Paducah Jr. Coll., 1952; AB, U. Ky., 1954, LLB, 1956. Bar: Ky. 1956. Ptnr. Emery & Carroll, Paducah, 1960-68; mem. Ky. Ho. of Reps., 1962-71, speaker, 1968-71; lt. gov. State of Ky., 1971-74, gov., 1974-79; of counsel Reed, Scent & Walton, Paducah, 1968-71; ptnr. Carroll & Assocs., Frankfort, Ky., 1980—; chmn. Nat. Conf. Lt. Govs., 1974, Nat. Govs. Assn., 1978-79. Trustee Paducah Jr. Coll., Regency U. Lt. USAF, 1956-59. Recipient Minerva award U. Louisville, 1977, Man of Yr. award Advt. Club Louisville, 1978. Mem. ABA, Ky. Bar Assn., Franklin County Bar Assn., Optimist Club, Phi Delta. Democrat. Avocation: golf. Home: Deer Run Farm Frankfort KY 40601 Office: Carroll & Assocs 25 Fountain Pl Frankfort KY 40601-1942

CARROLL, KAREN, art educator. Dir. grad. programs in art edn. Md. Inst. Coll. Art, Balt. Named Nat. Higher Edn. Art Educator, Nat. Art Edn. Assn., 1992. Office: Maryland Inst Coll of Art 1300 W Mount Royal Ave Baltimore MD 21217-4134*

CARROLL, KENT, book publishing executive. Pub., exec. editor. Carroll and Graf Pub. Inc., N.Y.C., 1983—. Office: Carroll & Graf Pub Inc 19 W 21st St Ste 601 New York NY 10010-6805*

CARROLL, KENT JEAN, retired naval officer; b. Newton, Iowa, Aug. 22, 1926; s. Lee A. and Mabel E. (McCormick) C.; m. Betty M. Harrington, Mar. 29, 1947; children: Craig, Debra Carroll Rollins, Lance S., Maureen Burt. Student, U. Notre Dame, 1946; grad., U.S. Naval Postgrad. Sch., 1955, Naval War Coll., 1960, Army War Coll., 1965; B.A. in Internat. Affairs, George Washington U., 1965. Ensign U.S. Navy, 1946, advanced through grades to vice adm., 1979; service in Korea and Vietnam; comdr. U.S.S. Sablefish, 1959-60, Submarine Div. 81, Div. 82, 1968-69, 69, U.S.S. Blue Ridge, 1970-72, Amphibious Squadron 10, 1972-73, Task Force 65, 1974-75, Naval Inshore Warfare Command, Atlantic Fleet, 1974-75, U.S. Naval Forces Marianas, 1975-77; dir. J-4 OJCS, Washington, 1977-81; comdr. Mil. Sealift Command, Washington, 1981-83. Decorated Navy D.S.M. with cluster, Def. D.S.M., Legion of Merit with 2 clusters; recipient John Paul Jones award Navy League, 1977; Presdl. citation for humanitarian svc., 1976, Rev. William Corby C.S.C. award U. Notre Dame, 1995. Mem. Country Club N.C., Hospice (bd. dirs. 1994—). Home: Country Club NC 1600 Morganton Rd X 30 Pinehurst NC 28374-6862

CARROLL, LUCY ELLEN, choral director, music coordinator, educator; b. N.Y.C., Oct. 11; d. Edward Joseph and Lucy Sophie (Czapszys) C. B in Music Edn., Temple U., 1968; MA, Trenton State Coll., 1973; D in Musical Arts, Combs Coll. Music, Phila., 1982. Cert. tchr. music, N.J., Pa., Nat. Cert., 1991. Tchr. music Log Coll. Jr. High Sch., Pa., 1968-72, Ind. (Pa.) High Sch., 1972-73; tchr. music William Tennent High Sch., Warminster, Pa., 1973-98, dir. mus. theater, 1973-98; choir dir. St. John Bosco Parish Choir, 1999—; music coord. Centennial Schs., 1991-98; founder, dir. Madrigal Singers, Warminster, Pa., 1971-98; choral dir. Cabrini Coll., Radnor, Pa., 1974-77, First Day Singers, Phila., 1979-83, Combs Coll. of Music, Phila., 1981-84, 87-88; choral adjudicator various Music festivals, 1973—; organist, Carmel of Phila, 1997—; theatre dir., Villa Joseph Marie (Holland), 1998-99; guest lectr. mus. seminars, convs., and writers' confs.; del. Internat. Arts Conf., Cambridge, Eng., 1992; columnist Polyphony mag. Singer (operas Ambler Festival) Street Scene, 1970, Death of Bishop of Brindisi (premiere); (Robin Hood Dell) La Boheme; dir. (jazz theater piece N.Y.C.) Murder of Agamemnon, 1980, (musi. drama) Power of Love (1705), 1986, (outdoor music theater) Vorspiel (Pa. Historic Commn. 1989); contbr. articles to profl. jours., also sci. fiction to sci. fiction mags. and anthologies. Choir dir. St. John Basco, Hatboro, 1999—. Recipient awards Writers of Future, 1985, 87, Andrew Ferraro award Combs Coll. Music, 1989, plaque for svc. to music Bucks County Commr., 1991, Disting. Citizen prize Southampton Twp., 1994, Harmony award Country Gentlemen Nat. Soc. for Preservation and Encouragement Barbershop Quartet Singing in Am., 1994; Scholar-In-Residence, Pa. Hist. and Museum Commn.; named Humanities Spkr. for 2000, Pa. Humanities Coun. Mem. Am. Choral Dirs. Assn., Sci. Fiction Fantasy Writers of Am., Theatre Assn. Pa., Del. Valley Composers (choral cons. 1988-90), Hist. Soc. Pa., Smithsonian Assocs., Music Fund Soc. of Phila., The Sonneck Soc. for Am. Music, Pa. Music Educators Assn. (adv. bd. 1986-87), Ephrata Cloister Assocs., Sigma Alpha Iota. Republican. Roman Catholic. Avocations: travel, writing fiction. E-mail: LucyCarroll@worldnet.att.net. Home: 712 High Ave Hatboro PA 19040-2418

CARROLL, M(ARGARET) AILEEN, member of Canadian parliament; b. Halifax, N.S., Can., June 1, 1944; m. D. Kevin Carroll, Nov. 11, 1968; children: Joanna, Daniel. BA, St. Mary's U., Halifax, 1965; BEd, York U., Toronto, Ont., Can., 1989. Adminstr. Law Firm of Carroll, Heyd, 1990—; M.P. from Barrie-Simcoe-Bradford Ho. of Commons, Can.; mem. justice and environ. coms.; vice chair Ctrl. Ont. Caucus; v.p., major shareholder Canadiana Curtains, Barrie, Ont., Inc., 1976-88; chair bd. referees, Unemployment Ins. appeals process, 1994-95; mem. Ont. Film Rev. Bd., 1990-91; formerly with Can. Internat. Devel. Agy., Toronto, and Province of Ont. Fed.-Provincial Affairs Secretariat, Toronto. Elected alderman Ward 2, City of Barrie; past chair capital campaign New Barrie Pub. Libr.; past chair St. Joseph's H.S. Pvt. Bd.; past mem. bd. dirs. Barrie Food Found. Fax: 613-996-7923. Office: House of Commons, 125 Confederation Bldg, Ottawa, ON Canada K1A 0A6 and: Constituency Office, 7 Anne St S, Unit 4, Barrie Ont Canada L4N 2C4

CARROLL, MARIE-JEAN GREVE, educator, artist; b. Paterson, N.J., Dec. 19, 1930; d. William John and Charlotte Marie (Kranich) McGill; m. Theodore R. Greve, Nov. 4, 1950 (div. Oct. 1979); children: Richard W. Greve, Helen E. Greve Beard, Theodore A. Greve; m. William P. Carroll, 1981 (div. 1989). BA in Art Edn., William Paterson Coll., Wayne, N.J., 1971; MA in Visual Art, 1976. Cert. art tchr., N.J. Art tchr. Pequannock (N.J.) Elem. Sch., 1971-72, Passaic Valley High Sch., Little Falls, N.J., 1972-77, 85-86, Ramapo High Sch., Franklin Lakes, N.J., 1986—. Works exhibited at shows in Fla. galleries, 1983, Longboat Key Art Gallery, 1983, 84, Manatee Art Gallery, 1984, Pike County Art Show, Milford, Pa., 1994, 95, 96, N.J. Printmakers Coun., Sommerville, 1998, Paterson Pub. Libr., 1998. Recipient art awards. Mem. NEA, Bergen County Edn. Assn., N.J. Edn. Assn., Nat. Art Edn. Assn. Avocations: swimming laps, golf.

CARROLL, MARSHALL ELLIOTT, architect; b. Durham, N.C., May 14, 1923; s. Dudley Dewitt and Eleanore (Elliott) C.; m. Dorothy Jane Grune, Mar. 28, 1953; married; children: Jane Dudley, Marshall Elliott, Frederick Grune. AB, Harvard Coll., 1943; student, Grad. Sch. Design, 1947-51. Assoc. G. Milton Small & Assos. (architects and engrs.), Raleigh, N.C., 1957-60; various positions to dep. exec. v.p. AIA, Washington, 1960-71; ptnr. Vincent G. Kling & Ptnrs., Phila., 1971-73; exec. asst. architect U.S. Capitol, 1973-89; ind. archtl. cons., 1989—; mem. exec. com. U.S. com. Internat.

Coun. on Monuments and Sites, 1978-96, vice chmn., 1980-88, chmn., 1988-91, fellow, 1995, internat. v.p., mem. internat. exec. com., 1990-96; pres. Hist. Am. Bldgs. Survey and Hist. Am. Engring. Record Found., 1996—; mem. exec. com., chmn. com. on archtl. conservation Nat. Inst. for Conservation, 1975-85, vice chmn., 1983-85; lectr. Nantucket (Mass.) Preservation Inst., 1979-87; hist. preservation cons. for restoration of Arneri Palace, Korcula, Croatia, 1987—, for restoration of Tex. State Capitol, 1989-91. Project dir. master plan for U.S. Capitol, 1976-81, U.S. Senate Office Sys. Rsch. Project, 1976-81, Thurgood Marshall Judiciary Office Bldg., Washington, 1986-89, restoration studies Russell and Dirksen Senate Office Bldgs., 1979-82, Capitol Hill Graphics Sys., 1977-81, Archtl. Graphic Stds., 6th, 7th, 8th edits., 1964-88. Pres. N.C. Symphony Soc., 1955-60; mem. exec. com. U.S. com. Internat. Ctr. for Conservation in Rome, 1973-89; alt. bd. dirs. Pennsylvania Ave. Devel. Corp., 1973-89; mem. Nat. Capitol Meml. Commn., 1973-89; alt. mem. U.S. Adv. Coun. on Hist. Preservation, 1973-89; chmn. governing bd. Village of Drummond, Md., 1976-77, treas., 1974-76; mem. gen. com. in charge Westtown Sch., Pa., 1993—; mem. D.C. Zoning Commn., 1987-89, D.C. Bd. Zoning Adjustment, 1987-89; mem. U.S. Commn. Fine Arts, Old Georgetown Bd., 1989-98, alt., 1998—. Capt. USNR, 1944-46, 51-53. Fellow AIA (chmn. com. on archtl. graphic stds. 1976-80, 84-88, mem. com. on hist. resources 1981-89, Octagon restoration com. 1990—), Assn. Preservation Tech. (pres. 1980-83); mem. Lambda Alpha. Democrat.

CARROLL, MATTHEW SHAUN, reporter; b. Milton, Mass., Aug. 5, 1954; s. John Joseph and Marilyn Jane (McGrann) C.; m. Elaine Husk Cushman, June 25, 1983; children: Kasey, Alexander, Leigh, Kenneth. BA, Northeastern U., 1979. Owner, pub. Post, Boston, 1977-78; wire editor Middlesex News, Framingham, Mass., 1979-83; asst. city editor Boston Herald, 1983-87; reporter Boston Globe, 1987—. Tutor Boston Pub. Schs., 1992—. Office: Boston Globe 135 Morrissey Blvd Boston MA 02125-3338*

CARROLL, MICHAEL M., academic dean, mechanical engineering educator; b. Thurles, County Tipperary, Ireland, Dec. 8, 1936; came to U.S. 1960; s. Timothy and Catherine (Gleeson) C.; m. Carolyn F. Gahagan, Oct. 31, 1964; children—Patricia, Timothy J. B.A., Univ. Coll., Galway, Ireland, 1958, M.A., 1959; Ph.D., Brown U., 1965; DSc, Nat. U. Ireland, 1979, LLD (hon), 1992. Asst. prof. mech. engring. U. Calif., Berkeley, 1965-69, assoc. prof., 1969-73, prof., 1973-83; Shell disting. chair Shell Cos. Found., 1983-88; dean George R. Brown Sch. Engring., Burton J. and Ann McMurtry prof. engring. Rice U., Houston, 1988-98, prof. engring., 1998—; bd. dirs. Daniel Industries Inc.; cons. TerraTek Labs., Salt Lake City, 1976-84, Thoratec Lab., Berkeley, Calif., 1976-84, Sci. Applications Internat., La Jolla, Calif., 1984—, JAG Industries, Trinidad, Calif., 1984—, Sandia Labs., Albuquerque, 1991—, Brit. Petroleum, Houston, 1991—, Adams Golf, 1998—. Contbr. articles to profl. jours.; mem. editorial bds. of tech. jours. Fellow ASME, Am. Acad. Mechanics (pres. 1994-95), Am. Acad. Arts and Scis.; mem. NAE, Am. Soc. Engring. Edn. (gov. bd., deans coun. 1992—), Soc. Engring. Sci. (bd. dirs., v.p., pres.), Sigma Xi. Roman Catholic. Avocations: crossword puzzles, golf, play writing. Home: 48 T Huxley Ln Missouri City TX 77459-1901 Office: Rice U Sch Computational & Applied Math PO Box 1892 MS 134 Houston TX 77251-1892*

CARROLL, PETE, professional football coach; b. San Francisco, CA, Sept. 15, 1951. Head coach N.Y. Jets, 1994-95; defensive coordinator San Francisco 49ers, 1995-96; head coach New England Patriots, 1997—. Office: New England Patriots Foxboro Stadium Rt 1 Foxboro MA 02035*

CARROLL, PHILIP JOSEPH, engineering company executive; b. New Orleans, Sept. 24, 1937; s. Philip Joseph and Rosemary Agnes (McEntee) C.; m. Charlene Marie Phillips, Jan. 3, 1959; children: Philip III, Kenneth, Bruce. BS in Physics, Loyola U., New Orleans, 1958; MS in Physics, Tulane U., 1961. Petroleum engr. Shell Oil Co., New Orleans, L.A., N.Y.C. and Midland, Tex., 1961-73; dir. energy conservation div. U.S. Dept. Commerce, Washington, 1973-74; exec. dir. Nat. Ind. Energy Conservation Coun., Washington, 1974; regional engr., mgr. so. exploration and prodn. Shell Oil Co., New Orleans, 1974-75; div. mgr. prodn., western exploration and prodn. Shell Oil Co., Houston, 1975-78, gen. mgr. prodn., western ops., 1978-79, gen. mgr. plans and integration, 1979, v.p. pub. affairs, 1979-85; mng. dir. Shell Internat. Gas, Shell Internat. Petroleum Co., London, 1985-86; sr. v.p. adminstrn. Shell Oil Co., Houston, 1986-88, exec. v.p. adminstrn., 1988-93, pres., CEO, 1993-98, mem. bd. dirs., 1990; chmn., CEO Fluor Corp, Irvine, 1998—; bd. dirs. Boise Cascade Corp. Bd. dirs. Am. Petroleum Inst., Cen. Houston, Tex. Med. Ctr., Am. Air Mus.; trustee Com. for Econ. Devel., 1991—, Baylor Coll. Medicine, Boys & Girls Clubs of Am.; mem. Gov.'s Bus. Coun. (Tex.), Nat. Petroleum Coun., Conf. Bd., 1991—, Nat. Action Coun. for Minorities in Engring., 1993—, bd. dirs.; adv. bd. mem. Salvation Army; bd. adminstrs. adv. bd. mem. Ctr. Bioenviron. Rsch., Tulane U. Mem. 25 Yr. Club Petroleum Industry, Tchefuncta Country Club (Covington, La.), River Oaks Country Club, Champions Golf Club. Avocation: golf. *

CARROLL, RAY DEAN, SR., veterinarian; b. Barry, Tex., Oct. 19, 1927; s. James William and Blanche Estelle (Jordan) C.; m. Lula Pearl Mayfield, June 6, 1957; children: James William, Ray Dean Jr. Assoc., Hillsboro Jr. Coll., 1948; BS in Animal Sci., Tex. A&M U., 1950, DVM, 1957. Vet. Carroll & Harpe Animal Hosp., Corsicana, Tex., 1957—; instr. Navarro Coll., Corsicana, 1970-95. Author: Beef Cattle Science Handbook, vol. 16, 1979. Mem. found. bd. Navarro Coll., 1985—, vice-chmn., trustee, 1990. With USN, 1945-46, 51-52. Mem. AVMA, Tex. Polled Hereford Assn. (pres. 1992-96), Navarro County Ext. Beef Commn. (chmn. 1960—). Democrat. Methodist. Home: 2203 Highland Cir Corsicana TX 75110-1611 Office: Carroll & Harper Animal Hosp 2508 W 2nd Ave Corsicana TX 75110-2520

CARROLL, ROBERT LYNN, biology educator, vertebrate paleontologist, museum curator; b. Kalamazoo, May 5, 1938; s. John Henry and Arvella Mae (Wickerham) C.; m. Helen Louise Swaim, June 22, 1961 (dec. Jan. 1972); 1 child, David Lynferd; m. Anna Di Turi, Sept. 26, 1987. BS, Mich. State U., 1959; MA, Harvard U., 1961, PhD, 1963. NRC postdoctoral fellow McGill U., Montreal, Que., Can., 1962-63, asst. prof. zoology, 1964-69, assoc. prof. biology, 1969-74, prof. biology, 1974—, Strathcona prof. zoology, 1987—; curator vertebrate paleontology Redpath Mus., McGill U., 1965—, dir., 1985-90, 98-99, chmn. dept. biology, 1990-95; vis. prof. biology Sir George Williams U., Montreal, 1965-66. Author: Vertebrate Paleontology and Evolution, 1987, Patterns and Processes of Vertebrate Evolution, 1997; co-author: Paleontology—The History of Life, 1989; editor Lepospondyli, 1998; co-editor: Paleontology, The Evolutionary History of Amphibians, 1999; assoc. editor Can. Jour. Earth Scis., 1984-93, Jour. Vertebrate Paleontology, 1989-92; cons. editor Trans. Royal Soc. Edinburgh: Earth Scis., 1993—. Recipient Billings medal for contbns. to paleontology Geol. Assn. Can.; NSF postdoctoral fellow Brit Mus., London, 1963-64. Fellow Royal Soc. Can., Linnean Soc.; mem. Soc. Vertebrate Paleontology (pres. 1982-83), Soc. for Study Evolution, Paleontol. Soc. (Schuchert award 1978), Am. Soc. Zoologists, World Congress Herpetology (treas. 1989-94). Avocations: hiking, singing. E-mail: robertc@shared1.lan.mcgill.ca. Office: Redpath Mus/McGill Univ, 859 Sherbrooke St W, Montreal, PQ Canada H3A 2K6

CARROLL, ROBERT W., retired business executive; b. Ossining, N.Y., May 29, 1923; s. John Francis and Catherine Veronica (Coyne) C.; m. Mary Bernardine Dugan, June 1, 1946; children: Kevin, Dennis, Terrence, Maura, Monica. Student, Sch. Commerce, NYU, 1952-56, Mgmt. Inst., 1957. With N.Y. Cen. R.R., 1942-68, asst. to sec., 1953-54, asst. sec., 1954-59, sec., 1959-68; sr. asst. sec. Penn Cen. Transp. Co., 1968-70, sec., 1971-76, also former v.p., sec., dir. several railroad, real estate, trucking and fin.-oriented subsidiaries, 1971-76; exec. dir. adminstrn. Law Offices La Brum and Doak, Phila., 1976-88; prin. Robert W. Carroll & Assoc., Mgmt. Cons., Radnor, Pa., 1989-93; corp. sec. Pitts. and Lake Erie R.R. Co., 1959-79; v.p., sec., dir. Montour R.R. Co., Montour Land Co., Youngstown and So. Ry. Co., 1959-79; rep. Kissel Blake Orgn., Inc., 1983-89. Served with USCGR, 1942-46. Recipient Legion of Honor Chapel of the Four Chaplains, 1984. Mem. ABA (law office adminstrv. assoc. 1985-89), Internat. Assn. Legal Adminstrs. (bd. dirs. 1987-88, v.p. 1987—, pres.-elect Phila. chapter 1988), VFW, Soc. Friendly Sons St. Patrick, Pa. Soc. K.C. (4), World Affairs Coun. Phila., Am. Soc. of Corp. Secs., Inc., Overbrook Golf Club (Bryn Mawr, Pa.). Home: 9 Ridgewood Rd Wayne PA 19087-3713

CARROLL, ROBERT WAYNE, mathematics educator; b. Chgo., May 10, 1930; s. Walter Scott and Dorothy (Le Monnier) C.; m. Berenice Jacobs, Sept. 7, 1957 (div. June 1974); children: David Leon, Malcolm Scott; m. Alice von Neumann, Sept. 1974 (div. Mar. 1977); m. Joan Miller, Jan. 1979. B.S., U. Wis., 1952; Ph.D., U. Md., 1959. Aero. research scientist NASA, Cleve., 1952-54; NSF postdoctoral fellow, 1959-60; asst. prof. Rutgers U., 1960-63, assoc. prof., 1963-64; assoc. prof. math. U. Ill., Urbana, 1964-67, prof., 1967-97, prof. emeritus, 1997—. Author: Abstract Methods in Partial Differential Equations, 1969, Transmutation and Operator Differential Equations, 1979, Transmutation, Scattering Theory and Special Functions, 1982, Transmutation Theory and Applications, 1985, Mathematical Physics, 1988, Topics in Soliton Theory, 1991; co-author: Singular and Degenerate Cachy Problems, 1976; assoc. editor Jour. Applicable Analysis, 1970—; contbr. over 150 articles to math. and physics jours. Served with U.S. Army, 1954-57. Mem. Am. Math. Soc. Avocation: study of foreign languages. Home: 1314 Brighton Dr Urbana IL 61801-6417 Office: Univ Ill Math Dept Urbana IL 61801

CARROLL, ROGER CLINTON, medical biology educator; b. Mt. Clemens, Mich., Sept. 28, 1947; s. Lee Stanley and Evelyn Marie (Badgett) C.; m. Andrea Kristine Skrec, Sept. 13, 1969; children: Brian Roger, Alicia Helene. BS, Cornell U., 1969, PhD, 1977. Rsch. assoc. U. Calif. San Diego, LaJolla, 1976-78; rsch. assoc. U. Okla. Health Sci. Ctr., Oklahoma City, 1978-79, asst. prof. dept. pathology, 1979-80, adj. asst. prof. dept. biochemistry, dept. physiology, 1980-84; assoc. prof. dept. med. biology U. Tenn. Med. Ctr., Knoxville, 1984-90, prof. dept. med. biology, 1990—, prof. dept. surgery, 1993—; asst. mem. Okla. Med. Rsch. Found. (Merrick award 1984), Oklahoma City, 1982-84; cons. Nat. Heart Lung and Blood Inst., 1985— (grantee 1980-90). Co-editor: (jour.) Seminars in Thrombosis and Hemostasis, vol. 1, 1995; contbr. articles to profl. jours., chpts. to books. Mem. Am. Heart Assn. (thrombosis coun., rsch. com. chmn., peer rev. com. chmn., Tenn. affiliate, grantee 1981-84, 1987—), Sigma Xi. Democrat. Roman Catholic. Avocations: swimming, tennis, gourmet cooking. Home: 706 Ala Dr Knoxville TN 37920-6364 Office: U Tenn Med Ctr Grad Sch Medicine 1924 Alcoa Hwy Knoxville TN 37920-1511

CARROLL, ROSSYE O'NEAL, college administrator; b. Corsicana, Tex., Sept. 27, 1929; s. Thearon Andrew and Elnora (Cook) C.; m. Neverro Jean Randle, June 6, 1958 (div. June 1982); children: Arnett, Brenda, Marvin, Stephen, Rossye Jr., Sheila, Vicky, Karen, Edwin; m. Bertha Lee Johnson, Aug. 23, 1982. BA, U. Nev., Las Vegas, 1982; AAS, C.C. of So. Nev., North Las Vegas, 1989. Cert. secondary edn. tchr., Nev. Instr. 523 Field Tng. Squadron USAF, Las Vegas, 1969-75, propulsion supt. 247th Field Maintenance, 1975-76; propulsion supt. 2d Field Maintenance USAF, Shreveport, La., 1976-78; supr. maintenance Meadows Mall, Las Vegas, 1978-79; substitute tchr. Clark County Sch. Dist., Las Vegas, 1979-84; asst. to dean for Nellis Zone continuing edn. C.C. of So. Nev., North Las Vegas, 1984—. Mem. choir 2d Bapt. Ch., Las Vegas, 1990—. Sr. master sgt. USAF, 1950-78. Recipient Air Force Commendation medal, 1975, Meritorious Svc. medal, 1978. Mem. AAUP, NEA, Nat. Coun. Instructional Adminstrs., Nev. Faculty Alliance. Democrat. Baptist. Avocations: guitar, choir, basketball. Home: PO Box 9856 Las Vegas NV 89191-0856 Office: C C So Nev 4475 England Ave Ste 217 Las Vegas NV 89191-6506

CARROLL, ROY, academic administrator; b. England, Arkansas, Dec. 8, 1929; m. Eleanor Kate Moorefield, 1953; children: Jane, Linda. BA cum laude, Ouachita Baptist Univ., 1951; MA, Vanderbilt Univ., 1959, PhD, 1964. Math. tchr. Baker High Sch., Columbus, Ga., 1955; asst. prof. History and Political Sci. Mercer Univ., Macon, Ga., 1959-65; prof. History, chm. Dept. Hist. and Political Sci. Armstrong State Coll., Savannah, Ga., 1965-69; prof. History, chm. Dept. History Appalachian State Univ., Boone, N.C., 1969-79; v.p. planning gen. adminstrn. U. N.C. System, 1979-90, 91-96; sr. v.p., v.p. acad. affairs, 1996—; interim chancellor U. N.C., Asheville. 1990-91; mem. N.C. Justice Edn. and Tng. Standards Commn., 1979-90, chmn. Planning Com. of the Commn., 1981-88; mem. adv. bd. Inst. Transp. Rsch. and Edn., Rsch. Triangle Park, 1980—; mem. bd. dirs. Western N.C. Devel. Assn., 1990-91, N.C. State Employees Credit Union, 1990-91, Rsch. Triangle Inst., 1996—. Contbr. articles to profl. jours. infantry officer U.S. Army, 1951-53, Japan, Korea. Fulbright scholar, Eng., 1958-59. Home: 6811 Huntingridge Rd Chapel Hill NC 27514-8673 Office: U North Carolina Gen Adminstrn PO Box 2688 Chapel Hill NC 27515-2688

CARROLL, STEPHEN DOUGLAS, chemist, research specialist; b. Clarendon, Ark., Nov. 2, 1943; s. Albert Genson and Wilma Mae (Hill) C.; m. Nonnie Lee Dyer, June 8, 1991; children: Geoffrey Genson, Raymond Loyd. BA, Hendrix Coll., 1965; MS, U. Ark., 1970. Del. chemist Chicopee Mfg. Co., North Little Rock, Ark., 1969-73, Mgr. Quality Assurance, 1973-80; cons. self employed, Clarendon, Ark., 1980-82; rsch. asst. U. Ark., Marianna, 1982-87, rsch. specialist, 1987-98, rsch. assoc., 1998—. Mem. Am. Chem. Soc. Democrat. Methodist. Avocations: photography, writing, painting. Office: U Ark Highway 1 Byp Marianna AR 72360

CARROLL, THOMAS COLAS, lawyer, educator; b. Phila., Jan. 5, 1943; s. George Colas and Mary F. (Dempsey) C.; m. Peg Kelly, June 19, 1966; children: Kevin, Beth Ann. BS, St. Joseph's U., 1964; JD, Villanova U., 1967. Bar: Pa. 1967, U.S. Ct. Appeals (3d cir.) 1967, U.S. Ct. Appeals (D.C. cir.) 1988, U.S. Ct. Appeals (11th cir.) 1990, U.S. Supreme Ct. 1975. Assoc. Wolf, Block, Schorr & Solis-Cohen, Phila., 1967-69; staff atty., chief of family div., asst. chief fed. div. Defender Assn. of Phila., 1969-75; ptnr. Carroll Creamer Carroll & Duffy, Phila., 1975-80, Carroll & Carroll, Phila., 1980-89; sole practitioner Phila., 1989-93; ptnr. Carroll & Cedrone, Phila., 1993—; adj. prof. law Villanova (Pa.) U., 1972—; lectr. Pa. Trial Lawyers Assn., Pa. Criminal Def. Lawyers Assn.; chmn. criminal justice act selection com. for ea. dist. Pa., 1980-89. Assoc. editor Law Review. Mem. Am. Arbitration Assn. (arbitrator), U. Pa. Am. Inn of Ct., Order of the Coif. Avocation: sailing. Office: Pub Ledger Bldg Ste94 150 S Independence Mall W Philadelphia PA 19106-3413

CARROLL, THOMAS JOHN, retired advertising executive; b. St. Paul, Aug. 15, 1929; s. William H. and Neva (Saller) C.; m. Eleanor Rose Schmid, Aug. 27, 1955; children: David G., Thomas John, Ann Catherine, Robert G., Paul William. BA, St. Mary's Coll., Winona, Minn., 1952; cert., Grad. Sch. Mgmt., UCLA, 1977. Pharm. salesman A.H. Robins, Davenport, Iowa, 1955-70; advt. salesman Modern Medicine mag., Chgo., 1970-72; advt. exec. D'Arcy, McManus & Massius, St. Paul, 1972-73; dir. mktg. communications AMA, Chgo., 1973-92; cons. Carroll Media Svcs., LaGrange Park, Ill., 1992—. Editor Synergy mag., 1975-92, The Voice Quar., 1996—. Dir. pub. rels. St. Francis Xavier Sch. Bd., La Grange, Ill., 1977-79, Organist St. Francis Xavier Ch., La Grange, 1964-91; bd. trustee La Grange Park Libr. Dist., 1994—, v.p.; adminstrv. assoc. St. Francis Xavier Ch., La Grange, 1976-96. Mem. Phar. Advt. Coun., Midwest Healthcare Mktg. Assn. (bd. dirs.), Med. Mktg. Assn., Am. Guild Organists, Chgo. Area Theatre Orgn. Enthusiasts, La Grange Field Club, La Grange Tennis Assn. (past pres.), St. Francis Xavier Men's Club. Republican. Roman Catholic. Home and Office: 333 N Edgewood Ave La Grange Park IL 60526-5505

CARROLL, THOMAS LAWRENCE, JR., film and video producer; b. Kansas City, Mo., Apr. 3, 1931; s. Thomas Lawrence C. and Anna Alberta (Davis) Kelley; m. Carol Dieringer, May 4, 1997; children: Catherine Spencer, Cadence Beth, Thomas Leigh, Susan Davis. BA, U. N.C., 1953. Film prodn. assoc. Audio Prodns., Inc., N.Y.C., 1955-57; writer-dir. Paul Hance Prodns., Inc., N.Y.C., 1957-59; freelance writer, producer, dir. Norwalk, Conn., 1959-75; pres. In-sight Into Communication, Inc., Westport, Conn., 1975—; dir. rsch. and writing U.S. Internat. Transp. Exposition, 1982, Internat. Trade Fairs, 1959, 60, 62. Prin. works include (documentaries) The American Navy in Vietnam, 1967, The Small Boat Navy, 1967, Tool Steel Today, 1974, Last Days of the Warrior, 1975, The Trestle at Ju'aymah, 1980, Introducing the Breed Air Bag, 1984, Safe Handling of Sulfuric Acid, 1985, The Saint Thomas Choir School, 1988, Introducing the Wadsworth Athaneum, 1988, Warehouse Operating Procedures, 1992, Sleep Better...Live Better, 1993, USS Houston...The Galloping Ghost, 1996, sales, tng. and corp. presentations. First student mgr. Sta. WUNC-FM, U. N.C., 1953. Home and Office: 22 Great Hill Rd Newtown CT 06470-1951

CARROLL, WILLIAM, publisher. Mgr., dir. Auto Book Press Coda Publs., San Marcos, Calif. Office: Auto Book Press Coda Publs Bin 711 San Marcos CA 92079-0711

CARROLL, WILLIAM JEROME, civil engineer; b. Los Angeles, Nov. 23, 1923; s. William Jerome and Adeline Marie (Verden) C.; m. Louise May Judson, June 6, 1944; children—Charisse Jean, Charles Gary, Christine Louise, Pamela Ann. B.S., Calif. Inst. Tech., 1948, M.S., 1949. Indsl. waste engr. Los Angeles County Engr., 1949-51; engr. James M. Montgomery (Cons. Engr., Inc.), Pasadena, Calif., 1951-56; v.p. James M. Montgomery (Cons. Engr., Inc.), 1956-69, pres., 1969-85, chmn. bd., 1985-90; vice chmn. bd. Montgomery Watson, 1991-98. Served with USAAF, 1943-46. Named So. Calif. Engr. of Yr., 1983; recipient Disting. Alumni award Calif. Inst. Tech., 1996. Mem. NAE, ASCE (nat. bd. dirs. 1976—, nat. v.p. 1986-87, pres. elect 1988, pres. 1988-89, Pres.'s medal 1997), Acad. Engrs. Russian Fedn., World Fedn. Engring. Orgns. (pres. 1991-95), Am. Acad. Environ. Engrs. (diplomate, pres. 1980—, Hoover medal 1994, Gordon Maskew Fair award 1992), Am. Water Works Assn., Water Pollution Control Fedn., Cons. Engrs. Assn. Calif. (pres. 1972), Alumni Assn. Calif. Inst. Tech. (pres. 1976), Pasadena C. of C., Am. Assn. Engring. Socs. (Kenneth Roe award 1992). Republican. Clubs: Jonathan (Los Angeles); Univ. (Pasadena). Home: 342 Starlight Crest Dr La Canada Flintridge CA 91011-2839 Office: Montgomery Watson Inc 300 N Lake Ave # 1200 Pasadena CA 91101-4109

CARROLL, WILLIAM KENNETH, law educator, psychologist, theologian; b. Oak Park, Ill., May 8, 1927; s. Ralph Thomas and Edith (Fay) C.; m. Frances Louise Forgue; children: Michele, Brian. BS in Edn., Quincy Coll., Ill., 1950, BA in Philosophy, 1950; MA, Duquesne U., 1964; STL, Catholic U., 1965; PhD, U. Strasbourg, France, 1968; JD, Northwestern U., 1972. Bar: Ill. 1972, U.S. Dist. Ct. (no. dist.) Ill 1972, U.S. Ct. Appeals (7th cir.) 1973; lic. clin. psychologist, Ill. Asst. editor Franciscan Press, Chgo., 1955-60; asst. prof. psychology and religion Carlow Coll., Pitts., 1962-65, Loyola U., Chgo., 1968-70; staff atty. Fed. Defender Program, Chgo., 1972-75; prof. law John Marshall Law Sch., Chgo., 1975—; bd. dirs. Am. Inst. Adlerian Studies, 1982—; law reporter ABA Criminal Justice Mental Health Standards Project, 1981-83; cons. legal issues, Am. Psych. Assn.; standing com. on mental health law, Illinois. Author: (with Kosnik et al.) Human Sexuality, 1977; Eyewitness Testimony, Strategies and Tactics, 1984; contbg. author: By Reason of Insanity, 1983, Law for Illinois Psychologists, 1985. Bd. dirs. Chgo. Sch. Profl. Psychology, 1978-82; mem. bd. advisors Ill. Sch. Profl. Psychology, 1985. Recipient Am. Juris award, 1970; U. Chgo. scholar, 1968-69. Fellow Inst. Social and Behavioral Pathology (chmn. 1987—); mem. ABA, AAUP, APA (Outstanding Contbn. to Psychology award 1998, com. on legal issues 1995—), Ill. Psychol. Assn., Cath. Theol. Soc. Am. Avocation: pvt. pilot. Office: John Marshall Law Sch 315 S Plymouth Ct Chicago IL 60604-3968

CARROLL, WILLIAM MARION, financial services executive; b. Harrisburg, Oreg., May 7, 1932; s. Richard Eldon Carroll and Carolyn Flora (Williams) Bowles; m. Alma Louise Holmes; children: Kris, Karolyn, Mary. Student, Drake U., 1949-50; BCE, Oreg. State U., 1952; postgrad., US Corps Engrs, Anchorage, 1953, LaSalle U. Extension, Chgo., 1953-54. Civil engr., water resources U.S. Army CE, various locations, 1953-55; constrn. engr. U.S. Geol. Survey, Tacoma, 1956-58; owner, chief exec. officer Carroll Constrn. Co., Portland, Oreg., 1958-68; chmn., ptnr. Oakdell Cos., San Antonio, 1968-76; chmn., owner J C Corp., Bakersfield, Calif., 1972-75; owner, dir. Civic Savs. & Loan Assn., Irving, Tex., 1975-78; owner, CEO Metro Properties, Metro Fin., Dallas, 1977—; chmn., CEO The Seaford Group, Dallas, 1985—, Tri-Mark Constrn. Mgmt. Inc., Fla., Tex., Calif., 1984—; dir. Property Solutions USA, Inc.; chmn. Tri Source In. Mem. ASCE, Am. Soc. Mil. Engrs., Nat. Asbestos Coun., Am. Geophys. Union, Am. Vets, Am. Legion, Alpha Tau Omega, Masons, Shriners. Republican. Avocations: golf, tennis, fishing. Home and Office: 9396 Huebner Rd Bldg B San Antonio TX 78240-1505

CARROTHERS, ALFRED WILLIAM ROOKE, retired law educator; b. Saskatoon, Sask., Can., June 1, 1924; s. William Alexander and Agnes Elizabeth (Godber) C.; m. Margaret Jane Macintosh, July 1, 1961; children: Matthew, Jonathan, Alexandra. B.A., U. B.C., 1947, LL.B., 1948; LL.M., Harvard U., 1951, S.J.D., 1966. Lectr. Faculty Law, U. B.C., 1948-50, asst. prof., 1952-55, assoc. prof., 1955-60, prof., 1960-64; dir. U. B.C. Inst. Indsl. Relations, 1960-62; asst. prof. Faculty Law, Dalhousie U., Halifax, N.S., 1951-52; dean Faculty Law, U. Western Ont., London, 1964-68; pres., vice chancellor U. Calgary, Alta., 1969-74; pres. Inst. for Research on Pub. Policy, 1974-77; prof. common law Faculty of Law, U. Ottawa, Ont., Can., 1981-89, prof. emeritus, 1989—; founding chmn. Public Service Adjudication Bd., B.C., 1977-80; chmn. Commn. of Inquiry into Redundancies and Layoffs, Fed. Dept. Labour, 1978-79; Mem. Adv. Commn. to Minister No. Affairs and Nat. Resources on Devel. of Govt. N.W. Terrs., 1965-66; mem. Prime Minister's Task Force on Labour Relations, 1966-68; pres. Assn. Univs. and Colls. Can., 1972-73. Author: The Labour Injunction in British Columbia, 1956, Labour Arbitration in Canada, 1961, Collective Bargaining Law in Canada, 1965, 2 edit. (with E.E. Palmer and Wesley Rayner), 1986; contbr. articles to profl. jours. Mem. Law Soc. Upper Can., Canadian Bar Assn., Vancouver Club. Home: 7034 Tamarin Pl, Brentwood Bay, BC Canada V8M 1C6*

CARROTHERS, GERALD ARTHUR PATRICK, environmental and city planning educator; b. Saskatoon, Sask., Can., July 1, 1925. BArch, U. Man., Can., 1948, MArch, 1951; MCP, Harvard U., 1953; PhD, MIT, 1959. Lectr. architecture U. Man., Winnipeg, 1948-52; research asst. regional sci. Mass. Inst. Tech., Cambridge, 1953-56; asst. prof. town and regional planning U. Toronto, Ont., Can., 1956-60; assoc. prof. to prof. city planning U. Pa., Phila., 1960-67; chmn. dept. city planning U. Pa., 1961-65; founding dir. Inst. Environ. Studies, 1965-67; prof. York U., Downsview, Ont., 1968—; founding dean faculty environ. studies York U., 1968-76; chmn. U. Toronto-York U. Joint Program in Transp., 1971-78; adviser Central Mortgage and Housing Corp., Can., 1967-77; vis. prof. U. Nairobi, Kenya, 1978-80; registrar Ont. Profl. Planners' Inst., 1990-92. Fellow World Acad. Art and Sci., Royal Archtl. Inst. Can., Can. Inst. Planners (councillor 1968-70); mem. Am. Inst. Cert. Planners, Regional Sci. Assn. (pres. 1970-71). Home: 24 Bertmount Ave, Toronto, ON Canada M4M 2X9 Office: York U Faculty Environ Studies, 4700 Keele St, North York, ON Canada M3J 1P3

CARROW, LEON ALBERT, physician; b. Chgo., Jan. 18, 1924; s. Charles and Mollie (Sachs) C.; m. Joan Twaddell, June 21, 1974; children by previous marriage—Elizabeth, James. B.S., U. Chgo., 1945, M.D., 1947. Intern Cook County Hosp. and Chgo. Lying-in Hosp., 1947-48; resident Chgo. Wesley Meml. Hosp., Chgo. Maternity Center, 1949-51; sr. attending physician in obstetrics and gynecology Northwestern Meml. Hosp., 1954-91, sr. attending physician emeritus, 1991—, also past chief of staff; asso. prof. obstetrics and gynecology Northwestern U. Med. Sch., 1967-73, prof. clin. obstetrics and gynecology, 1973-91, prof. emeritus, 1991—. Contbr. articles to profl. jours. Served with AUS, 1944-46; to capt. USAF, 1952-53. Fellow A.C.S.; mem. Ill., Chgo. med. socs., AMA, Chgo. Gynecology Soc., Am. Soc. Cytology, Central Assn. Obstetrics and Gynecology. Home: 566 Cedar St Winnetka IL 60093-2338

CARROW, MILTON MICHAEL, lawyer, educator; b. N.Y.C., Sept. 13, 1912; s. Samuel and Ethel (Berlin) C.; m. Betsey Wood Hall, Nov. 2, 1940 (div. 1968); children: David M., Thomas E., Deborah, James H., Emily W.; m. Eve Wagner Cooper, Feb. 28, 1969 (div. 1986); m. Barbara M. Barski, Nov. 2, 1996. AB, Syracuse U., 1933, postgrad., 1933-34; JD, Harvard U., 1937. Bar: N.Y. 1938. Assoc. Legal Aid Soc., Rochester, N.Y., 1937-38, Lincoln Epworth & Nathan Sweedler, 1938-42, Emil Schlesinger, 1946-48; pvt. practice, 1948-53; ptnr. Lavine & Carrow, N.Y.C., 1953-59, Landis, Carrow, Benson & Tucker, N.Y.C., 1959-70, Carrow, Bernson, Hoeniger, Freitag & Abbey, 1970-73; dir. Ctr. for Adminstrv. Justice, ABA, 1973-77, Nat. Center for Adminstrv. Justice, Consortium of Univs. of Washington Met. Area, 1977-79; pres. Nat. Center for Adminstrv. Justice, 1979-82; adj. asst. prof. Law Sch. NYU, 1964-68; vis. prof. Nat. Law Ctr., George Washington U., 1973-80; adj. prof. Georgetown U. Law Ctr., 1980-81; rsch. prof. pub. policy George Washington U., 1983—; mem. faculty appellate judges seminar Inst. Jud. Adminstrn., 1969, 70; cons. Nat. Adv. Com. Civil Disorders, 1967; vice chmn. Weston (Conn.) Charter Commn., 1965-66; counsel UN We Believe, 1962-72; vis. intervenor XVIII Internat. Congress of

Adminstrv. Scis., Madrid, 1980; U.S. rep. to standing com. on law and sci. of pub. adminstrn. Internat. Inst. Adminstrv. Scis., 1982; cons. Block Island Charter Commn., 1988-89. Author: Background of Administrative Law, 1948, The Licensing Power in New York City, 1968, (with J.D. Nyhart) Law and Science in Collaboration, 1983: editor: (with Robert Paul Churchill and Joseph J. Cordes) Democracy, Social Values and Public Policy, 1998; also articles; editor Working Paper series, Grad. Program in Public Policy, 1985—. Dir. Washington Ctr., George Washington U., 1988—. With AUS, 1943-46. Mem. ABA (chmn. sect. adminstrv. law 1971-72), Assn. of Bar of City of N.Y. (chmn. com. adminstrv. law 1964-67). Home: 914 25th St NW Washington DC 20037-2101 Office: George Washington Univ Funger Hall Rm 507 2201 G St NW Washington DC 20052

CARRUS, GERALD, broadcast executive; b. 1926. V.p., contr. Metromedia, Inc., N.Y.C., 1964-72; sr. v.p. Metromedia Radio, N.Y.C., 1972-79; chmn. Infinity Broadcasting Corp., N.Y.C., 1988-96; with CBS Station Group, 1996—. Office: CBS Station Group 14th Fl 40 W 57th St New York NY 10019-4001*

CARRUTH, DAVID BARROW, landscape architect; b. Woodbury, Conn., June 28, 1926; s. Gorton Veeder and Margery Barrow (Dibb) C.; children: Kathryn Paige, Todd David, Peter Richmond. Grad., U.S. Mcht. Marine Acad., 1946; B.S. in Land Planning, Cornell U., 1951; M. in Landscape Architecture, 1952. Lic. landscape architect, N.Y.; nat. cert. landscape architect. Landscape architect, assoc. Clarke & Rapuano, Inc. (cons. engrs., landscape architects), N.Y.C., 1952-70; pres. Kane and Carruth, landscape architects, Pleasantville, N.Y., 1970-83; founder site design, environ. planning DE Assocs., 1983-89; ptnr. Wells & Carruth, Landscape Architects, P.C., Carmel, N.Y., 1989-92; mem. N.Y. State Bd. Landscape Architecture, 1970-80; pres. Coun. Landscape Archtl. Registration Bds., 1975, Interprofl. Coun. on Registration, 1975, Landscape Archtl. Registration Bds. Found., 1976; trustee Bayard Cutting Arboretum, 1969-92. Mem. Katonah-Lewisboro Sch. Bd., 1963-73; bd. dirs. Clark Garden, 1983-92. With USNR, 1944-46. Fellow Am. Soc. Landscape Architects. Home: 601 Stoneleigh Ave Unit 113 Carmel NY 10512-3936

CARRUTH, HAYDEN, poet; b. Waterbury, Conn., Aug. 3, 1921; s. Gorton Veeder and Margery Tracy Barrow (Dibb) C.; m. Sara Anderson, Mar. 14, 1943; 1 child, Martha Hamilton; m. Eleanore Ray, Nov. 29, 1952; m. Rose Marie Dorn, Oct. 28, 1961; 1 child, David Barrow II; m. Joe-Anne McLaughlin, Dec. 29, 1989. AB, U. N.C., 1943; MA, U. Chgo., 1948; LLD, New Eng. Coll., 1987, Syracuse U., 1993. Editor-in-chief Poetry mag., 1949-50; assoc. editor U. Chgo. Press, 1950-51; project adminstr. Intercultural Publs. Inc., N.Y.C., 1952-53; poetry editor Harper's mag., 1977—; poet-in-residence Johnson State Coll., 1972-74; adj. prof. U. Vt., 1975-78; prof. English Syracuse (N.Y.) U., 1979-91, prof. emeritus, 1991—. Author: The Crow and the Heart, 1959, Journey to a Known Place, 1961, Norfolk Poems, 1962, Appendix A, 1963, North Winter, 1964, Nothing for Tigers, 1965, Contra Mortem, 1967, After the Stranger, 1965, For You, 1970, The Clay Hill Anthology, 1970, The Voice That Is Great Within Us, 1970, The Bird-Poem Book, 1970, From Snow and Rock, from Chaos, 1973, Dark World, 1973, The Bloomingdale Papers, 1975, Loneliness, 1976, Aura, 1977, Brothers, I Loved You All, 1978, Almanach du Printemprs Vivarois, 1979, Working Papers, 1982, The Mythology of Dark and Light, 1982, The Sleeping Beauty, 1982, If You Call This Cry a Song, 1983, Effluences from the Sacred Caves, 1983, Asphalt Georgics, 1985, Lighter than Air Craft, 1985, The Oldest Killed Lake in North America, 1985, The Selected Poetry of Hayden Carruth, 1986, Mother, 1986, Sitting In: Selected Writings on Jazz, Blues & Related Topics, 1986, Sonnets, 1989, Tell Me Again How the White Heron Rises and Flies Across the Nacreous River at Twilight Toward the Distant Island, 1989, Collected Shorter Poems, 1946-91, 92, Suicides and Jazzers, 1992, Collected Longer Poems, 1994, Selected Essays and Reviews, 1995, Scrambled Eggs and Whiskey, 1996, Reluctantly, 1998, Beside the Shadblow Tree, 1999; mem. editl. bd. Hudson Rev., 1971—. Sr. fellow N.Y. Found. Arts, 1993. Recipient Vachel Lindsay prize, 1954, Bess Hokin prize, 1956, Levinson prize, 1958, Ann. Poetry award Brandeis U., 1959, Harriet Monroe Poetry prize U. Chgo., 1960, Helen Bullis prize U. Seattle, 1962, Carl Sandburg prize, 1963, Emily Clark Balch prize, 1964, Gov.'s medal State of Vt., 1974, Shelley award Poetry Soc. Am., 1978, Lenore Marshall prize, 1979, Morton Zabel prize, 1968, Whiting Writers award, 1986, Sarah Josepha Hale award, 1988, Ruth Lilly Poetry prize, 1990, Nat. Book Critics Circle award in poetry, 1993, Lannan award for poetry, 1995, Nat. Book award for Poetry, 1996; fellow Bollingen Found., 1962, John Simon Meml. Guggenheim Found., 1965, 79, sr. fellow Nat. Endowment for Arts, 1988; grantee Nat. Found. on Arts and Humanities, 1967, 74. Home: RR 1 Box 128 Munnsville NY 13409-9549

CARRUTH, PATTI JO, nursing director; b. San Diego, Sept. 1, 1958; d. Robert William and Constance (Cooper) Berg; m. Christopher James Peterson, June 6, 1981 (div. Apr. 1988); m. Denis Grady Carruth, Oct. 7, 1989; 1 child, Savannah Rose. BSN, San Jose State U., 1980. Cert. oncology nurse, Oncology Nursing Soc. Staff RN ortho/neuro Washington Hosp., Fremont, Calif., 1981-89, asst. mgr. ortho/neuro, 1989-92; dir. in-patient and out-patient oncology Touro Infirmary, New Orleans, 1992-96, oncology clin. specialist, 1996; clin. rsch. assoc. Alton Ochsner Med. Found. Hosp., New Orleans, 1996-97; clin. edn. specialist vascular access HOC Corp., Atlanta, 1997—. Mem. Nat. Assn. Vascular Access Networks, New Orleans Oncology Nurses (dir.-at-large 1993-94, mem. program planning 1994, Metro Atlanta Oncology Nursing chpt. 1998—). Republican. Baptist. Avocations: arts and crafts, gardening, horseback riding. Home: 661 Laurel Wood Dr SW Marietta GA 30064-3970 Office: HOC Corp 2109 O'Toole Ave San Jose CA 95131-3593

CARRUTHERS, CATHARINE, federal judge; b. 1954. BA, U. N.C., 1975; JD, Wake Forest U., 1980. Bar: N.C. 1980. Assoc. Billings Burns & Wells, Winston-Salem, 1982-84; ptnr. Allman Spry Leggett & Crumpler, Winston-Salem, 1985-95; law clk. to Hon. Rufus W. Reynolds, U.S. Bankruptcy Ct. for Mid. Dist. N.C., Winston-Salem, 1980-81, bankruptcy judge, 1995—. Office: US Bankruptcy Ct 226 S Liberty St Winston Salem NC 27101-5211

CARRUTHERS, CLAUDELLE ANN, occupational and physical therapist; b. Chgo., Nov. 23; d. Veronica Josephine Walker. AA, Golden Valley Luth. Coll., Minn., 1981; BS in Occupational Therapy, U. Minn., 1984; M in Phys. Therapy, U. Iowa, 1991; PhD, U. Minn., 1995. Lic. occupational therapist, Iowa, phys. therapist, Iowa, Minn.; cert. occupational therapist, Minn. Dir., supr., occupational therapist Rehab. Specialists, Inc., Minnetonka, Minn., 1984-86; supr., occupational therapist St. Therese Home, Inc., Mpls., 1986-88; dir., supr., occupational therapist Allied Health Alternatives, Inc., Mpls., 1988-89; occupational therapist St. Luke's Hosp., Cedar Rapids, Iowa, 1989-91; occupational therapist, phys. therapist Fairview Riverside Med. Ctr., Mpls., 1991—; instr., rschr. U. Minn., 1992-95; prof. occupational and phys. therapy Coll. of St. Catherine, 1995—; research in field of virtual reality, neurology/kinesiology; mem. adv. bd. occupational therapy program Anoka Tech. Coll., 1992—; mentor for occupational and phys. therapy students Coll. of St. Catherine's, St. Paul, 1992; mentor for occupational and phys. therapy and women athlete's of color U. Minn. Author publs. in field. Human rights commr. City of Plymouth, 1994—; mem. allocation panel United Way Mpls., 1992; mem. Minn. Zoo, 1986—. Recipienntt Vol. Basketball award Courage Ctr., Golden Valley, Minn., 1987, 89. Mem. Am. Phys. Therapy Assn. (student rep. 1981-83), Iowa Occupational Therapy Assn., Minn. Occupational Therapy Assn., Am. Occupational Therapy Assn., Occupational Therapy Minn.-Dak Assn. (panel presentor 1992), Glende Ski Club (2d v.p. 1987), Martin Luther King Tennis Club, Alpha Kappa Alpha. Avocations: doll collecting, stamp collecting, tennis, skiing, racquetball.

CARRUTHERS, JOHN ROBERT, scientist; b. Toronto, Ont., Can., Sept. 12, 1935; came to U.S., 1959, naturalized, 1976; s. William Elwood and Florence Isabelle (Dyment) C.; m. Nancy Louisa Millar, May 28, 1957; children: Wendy Ann, Michael John. B.Sc., U. Toronto, 1959, Ph.D., 1966; M.S., Lehigh U., Bethlehem, Pa., 1961. With Bell Labs., Allentown, Pa., 1959-63, Murray Hill, N.J., 1967-77; research asst. and asst. prof. U. Toronto, 1963-67; with NASA, Washington, from 1977; program dir. materials processing in space Office Space and Terrestrial Applications, 1977-81; dept. mgr. Materials Research Lab. Hewlett-Packard, Palo Alto, Calif., 1981-84; dir. components rsch. Intel Corp., Hillsboro, Oreg., 1984—; co-chmn. exec. tech. adv. bd. Semicondr. Rsch. Corp. Contbr. articles to profl. jours. Pres. Berkeley Heights PTA, N.J., 1971-72. Recipient Exceptional Service medal NASA, 1981; Ford Found. fellow, 1963-64; McAllister Found. fellow, 1964-65. Mem. IEEE. Patentee in field. Home: 20134 SW Tremont Way Beaverton OR 97007-8591 Office: Intel Corp Hillsboro OR 97124

CARRUTHERS, NORMAN HARRY, Canadian province supreme court justice; b. Augustine Cove, P.E.I., Can., Oct. 25, 1935; s. Lorne C.H. and Jean R. (Webster) C.; m. Diana C. Rodd, May 8, 1943; children: Susan, Karen, John. BSc, Mt. Allison U., 1956, BEd, 1961; LLB, Dalhousie U., 1967. Prodn. asst. C.I.L., Calgary, Alta., 1956-59; sch. tchr. Calgary Sch. Bd., Alta., 1961-64; lawyer Foster, MacDonald, Carruthers, P.E.I., Can., 1968-80; chief judge P.E.I., 1980-85, chief justice supreme ct., 1985—. Recipient Smith Shield Dalhousie Law Sch., 1967. Mem. Can. Jud. Council, Inst. for Adminstrn. Justice, Can. Judges Conf. Lodge: Rotary. Home: 16 Trafalgar St, Charlottetown, PE Canada C1A 3Z1 Office: Supreme Ct, 42 Water St PO Box 2000, Charlottetown, PE Canada C1A 8B9

CARRUTHERS, PHILIP CHARLES, public official, lawyer; b. London, Dec. 8, 1953; s. J. Alex and Marie Carruthers. BA, U. Minn., 1975, JD, 1979. Bar: Minn. 1979, U.S. Dist. Ct. Minn. 1979, U.S. Ct. Appeals (8th cir.) 1979. Assoc. Nichols & Kruger, and predecessor firm, 1979-81; ptnr. Nichols, Kruger, Starks and Carruthers, Mpls., 1982-84, Luther, Ballenthin & Carruthers, Mpls., 1985-93; pvt. practice Mpls., 1994—; pros. atty. City of Deephaven, Mich., 1979—, City of Woodland, Mich., 1980—; mem. Minn. Ho. of Reps., 1987—, majority leader, 1993-96, spkr. of the ho., 1997-98. Co-author: The Drinking Driver in Minnesota: Criminal and Civil Issues, 1982; note and comment editor Minn. Law Rev., 1978-79. Mem. Met. Coun. of Twin Cities Area, St. Paul, 1983-87. Mem. Minn. Trial Lawyers Assn. (bd. govs. 1982-86), Minn. State Bar Assn., Hennepin County Bar Assn. Democratic Farmer-Labor Party. Roman Catholic. Home: 6018 Halifax Pl Brooklyn Center MN 55429-2440 Office: 217 State Office Bldg Saint Paul MN 55155-1288

CARRUTHERS, S. GEORGE, medical educator, physician; b. Londonderry, No. Ireland, Sept. 18, 1945; came to Can., 1977; s. Moses and Alice McKeague (Nicholl) C.; m. Gillian Margaret Devon, Oct. 4, 1969; children: Alison, David, Bruce, Michael. MB, BCh, Queen's U., Belfast, No. Ireland, 1969, MD, 1975. Diplomate Am. Bd. Internal Medicine, Am. Bd. Clin. Pharmacology (sec.-treas. 1996-98, chair 1998—). Intern Royal Victoria Hosp., Belfast, 1969-70; tchr. Belfast City Hosp./Queen's U. Belfast, 1970-75; Fogarty Internat. fellow NIH Kans. U. Med. Ctr., Kansas City, 1975-77; asst. prof. U. Hosp./U. Western Ont., London, Can., 1977-82, assoc. prof., 1982-87, prof. dept. medicine, 1987-88, 95—, prof. dept. pharmacology and toxicology, 1987-88, 95—; Carnegie and Rockefeller prof., head dept. medicine Dalhousie U., Halifax, N.S., Can., 1988-95; physician-in-chief Victoria Gen. Hosp., Halifax, 1988-91, pres. med. staff, 1992-93; chief medicine London Health Scis. Ctr., St. Joseph's Hosp., 1995—; bd. commrs. Victoria Gen. Hosp., 1992-93; rep. Brit. Med. Assn., London, 1973-75; Richard Ivey prof., chmn. dept. medicine U. Western Ont., 1995—; pres. Foyle Coll. OBA, 1993-94; chmn. Cardio-Cerebrovascular Rsch. Adv. Coun.; bd. dirs. Heart and Stroke Found. Can., 1998—; Osler lectr. Royal Coll. Physicians and Surgeons Can. and Can. Soc. Internal Medicine, 1998. Co-author: Handbook of Clinical Pharmacology, 1978, 2d edit., 1983. Fellow ACP (gov. Ont. 1998—), Royal Coll. Physicians Can., Royal Coll. Physicians, Am. Coll. Clin. Pharmacology; mem. Am. Soc. Clin. Pharmacology and Therapeutics (nominating com. 1989, v.p. 1991-92, awards com. 1992-98, sci. program com. 1995—, bd. dirs. 1997—, vice chmn. sci. program com. 1998-99, chmn. 1999—), Can. Soc. for Clin. Pharmacology (pres. 1984-86, Piafsky Young Investigator award 1982, Disting. Achievement award 1992), Can. Hypertension Soc. (pres. 1990-91, bd. dirs. 1988-92, Disting. Svc. award 1995), Can. Assn. Profs. Medicine (pres. 1994-95), Can. Inst. Acad. Med., Brit. Pharm. Soc., West Haven G & C Club. Presbyterian. Avocations: travel, reading. Home: 2 Tobin Ct, London, ON Canada N6K 3Y3 also: LHSC Victoria-South St Camp, Rm N587 375 South St, London, ON Canada N6A 4G5 Office: N587 Victoria Campus, London Hlth Scis Ctr, London, ON Canada N6A 4G5

CARRUTHERS, THOMAS NEELY, JR., lawyer; b. Columbia, Tenn., Oct. 11, 1928; s. Thomas Neely and Ellen Douglas (Everett) C.; m. Dale Gilder Jones, Feb. 7, 1959; children: Thomas Neely III, Virginia Carruthers Smith, Catherine Everett. AB, Princeton U., 1950; LLB, Yale U., 1955. Assoc. Bradley, Arant, Rose & White, Birmingham, Ala., 1955-63, ptnr., 1963—, chair exec. com. and mng. ptnr., 1990-95. Mem. editorial bd. Yale Law Journal, 1953-55. Trustee Children's Hosp. Ala., pres. 1996-97, Ala. Shakespeare Festival, Leadership Ala., pres. 1995-96, chmn., 1996-97; trustee Birmingham Mus. Art., chmn., 1995—; chmn. Gov.'s Tax Reform Task Force, 1991-92, exec. sec. devel. com., 1992-93; bd. dirs., mem. dist. commn. Greater Birmingham Found., chmn., 1999—; bd. dirs. 2020 Birmingham Com.; bd. advisors Cumberland Law Sch., chmn., 1993-95; active Boy Scouts Am., Birmingham, exec. bd. Birmingham coun., silver beaver award, dist. Eagle Scout award. Recipient Thurmond Arnold Appellate Competition prize Yale U., 1954, Birmingham-So. Coll. medal Honor, 1992, award for pub. svc. Birmingham Bar, 1998, commendations: State Ala., Ala. Commn. Higher Edn., Jacksonville State U.; named to Ala. Acad. Honor, Humanitarian of Yr., 1997. Fellow Am. Bar Found.; mem. ABA, Internat. Bar Assn., So. Fed. Tax Inst. (trustee, past chmn., pres. 1993-94), Am. Coll. Tax Counsel, Am. Tax Policy Inst. (trustee), Am. Law Inst., Ala. Bar Assn., Birmingham Bar Assn., Mountain Brook Club, Birmingham Com. on Fgn. Rels., Rotary (pres. 1992-93). Episcopalian. Office: Bradley Arant Rose & White 1400 Park Place Tower 2001 Park Pl Ste 1400 Birmingham AL 35203-2736

CARSEY, MARCIA LEE PETERSON, television producer; b. South Weymouth, Mass., Nov. 21, 1944; d. John Edwin and Rebecca White (Simonds) Peterson; m. John Jay Carsey, Apr. 12, 1969; children: Rebecca Peterson, John Peterson. B.A. in English Lit., U. N.H., 1966. Exec. story editor Tomorrow Entertainment, L.A., 1971-74; sr. v.p. prime time series ABC-TV, L.A., 1978-81; founder Carsey Prodns., L.A., 1981; co-owner Carsey-Werner Co., 1982—; co-exec. producer TV series Oh Madeline, 1983; exec. producer The Cosby Show, 1984-92, A Different World, 1987-93, Roseanne, 1988-92, Chicken Soup, 1989-90, Grand, 1990, Davis Rules, 1991, You Bet Your Life, 1992-93, Frannie's Turn, 1992, Grace Under Fire, 1993, Cybill, 1995-97, 3rd Rock From The Sun, 1996—, Cosby, 1996—, Men Behaving Badly, 1996-97, Townies, 1996. Office: Carsey-Werner Prodns 4024 Radford Ave Bldg 3 Studio City CA 91604-2101*

CARSEY, TAMARA, paralegal; b. Athens, Ohio, Dec. 1, 1961; d. Kenneth B. McLain and Sandra K. (Grubb) Shrieves; m. Thomas Edward Carsey, Mar. 6, 1982; children: Kasandra Ann, Mindy Jo. Cert. paralegal, Tri-County Adult Edn. Ctr., Nelsonville, Ohio, 1995. Nurse's aide Hickory Creek Nursing Home, The Plains, Ohio, 1984; computer instr. Tri-County Adult Edn. Ctr., Nelsonville, 1985-96; sec. Gerald Hilferty & Assoc., Amesville, Ohio, 1986; secretarial cons. Rehab. Svcs. Commn., Athens, 1986-87; sec. AFSCME Ohio Coun. 8, Athens, 1987-96; staff rep. AFSCME Ohio Coun. 8, The Plains, 1996—; advisor computerized accounting adv. com. Tri-County Vocat. Sch., Nelsonville. Phone bank vol. S.E. Ohio Dems., Woker's Compensation issue 2, The Plains, 1997; mem. crowd control staff First Lady Visitation Ohio U., Athens, 1992. Democrat. Avocations: reading, crafts. Fax: 740-797-9712. Home: 10485 Porter Ln Athens OH 45701-9114 Office: AFSCME Ohio Coun 8 36 S Plains Rd The Plains OH 45780-1348

CARSON, ANDREW DOYLE, research psychologist; b. Dallas, Aug. 3, 1960; s. Doyle Irvin and Sarah Louise (Simmons) C.; m. Victoria Hutchinson McCain, Jan. 6, 1962; children: Emily, Nathaniel. AB cum laude, Harvard U., 1982; MS in Human Devel., U. Tex. at Dallas, Richardson, 1986; PhD in Edn!. Psychology, U. Tex., Austin, 1990. Tchr. spl. edn. Highland Acad., Dallas, 1983-85; adminstrv. dept. tutor U. Tex., Austin, 1985-88; cognitive rehab. therapist St. David's Hosp., Austin, 1988-89; psychol. intern Counseling Ctr., U. Md., College Park, 1989-90; asst. prof. counseling psychology Boston U., 1990-91, McGill U., Montreal, 1991-94; rsch. assoc. The Ball Found., Glen Ellyn, Ill., 1995-96, sr. rsch. assoc., 1996-97, dir. rsch., 1997-99, dir., 1999—. Contbr. articles to profl. jours. Chmn. grants com. New 200 Found., Wheaton, Ill., 1997-98; pres. Charter Sch. Assn., Wheaton, 1997. FCAR Que. New Rschr. grantee, 1992, Strong Rsch. Adv. Bd. grantee, 1989, 94, 95. Mem. APA (divsns. 1, 10, 15, 17), Soc. for Vocat. Psychology, Nat. Career Devel. Assn., Am. Ednl. Rsch. Assn. (career devel. spl. interest group program chair 1995-98, pres. 1998—), Am. Counseling Assn. Presbyterian. Avocations: drawing, writing, editorial and other cartoons. Office: The Ball Found 800 Roosevelt Rd Ste C120 Glen Ellyn IL 60137

CARSON, ARCH IRWIN, toxicology educator, preventive medicine physician; b. Cin., May 19, 1950; s. Arch Irwin and Inez Yvonne (McVay) C.; m. Sandra Gail Brock, Jan. 2, 1996; children: Alicia McDonald, Candace McDonald, Travis McDonald, Quint. BS, U. Cin., 1973, PhD, 1987; MD, Ohio State U., 1990. Diplomate Am. Bd. Preventive Medicine in Occupl. Medicine. Design engr. Millstone, Inc., Cin., 1969-73; rsch. technologist U. Cin., 1974-79, asst. prof., 1984-89; intern, clin. instr. NYU Med. Ctr., N.Y.C., 1990-91; asst. prof. toxicology U. Tex. Sch. Pub. Health, Houston, 1992—, dir. occupl. and environ. residency, 1998—, convenor occupl. and environ. health and aerospace medicine, 1998—; cons. in environ. toxicology, Houston, 1992—. Fellow in indsl. toxicology Nat. Inst. for Occupl. Safety and Health, 1979-81, fellow in combustion toxicology Owen Corning Fiberglas, 1982-83, fellow in toxicology Am. Lung Assn., 1984. Office: U Tex Sch Pub Health 1200 Herman Pressler 1030 Houston TX 77030

CARSON, BENJAMIN SOLOMON, neurosurgeon; b. Detroit, Sept. 18, 1951; s. Robert Solomon and Sonya (Copeland) C.; m. Lacena Rustin, July 6, 1975; children: Murray Nedlands, Benjamin Solomon Jr., Rhoeyce Harrington. BA, Yale U., 1973; MD, U. Mich., 1977; DSc (hon.), Gettysburg Coll., 1988, N.C. A&T, 1989, Andrews U., 1989, Sojourner-Douglas Coll., 1989, Shippenburg U., 1990, Jersey City State Coll., 1990, Southwestern Adventist Coll., 1992, U. Mass., Boston, 1992, Marygrove Coll., 1993, U. Detroit-Mercy, 1994, Spalding U., 1994, Western Md. Coll., 1994, Morgan State U., 1994, Long Island U., 1994, N.C. State U., 1994, Tuskegee U., 1995, Yale U., 1996, Del. State U., 1996, Med. U. South Africa, Medunsa, 1997, GMI Engring. and Mgmt. Inst., 1997, U. Del., 1997, Coll. William and Mary, 1998. Diplomate Am. Bd. Neurol. Surgery. Surg. intern Johns Hopkins Hosp., Balt., 1977-78, neurosurg. resident, 1978-82, chief resident, 1982-83; sr. registrar Sir Charles Gairdner Hosp., Perth, W. Australia, 1983-84; dir. pediatric neurosurgery Johns Hopkins Hosp., Balt., 1985—; bd. dirs. Kellogg Co. Author: Pediatric Neurooncology, 1987, Achondroplasia, 1988, Gifted Hands, 1989; contbr. jour. articles. Mem. med. adv. bd. Children's Cancer Found., Balt., 1987—; hon. med. chmn. Md. Red Cross, Balt., 1987—. Recipient Am. Black Achievement award Ebony mag., Hollywood, Calif., 1988, Cum Laude award Am. Radiol. Soc., Chgo., 1982, Candle award Morehouse U., Atlanta, 1989; Paul Harris fellow Rotary Internat., 1988. Mem. Am. Assn. Neurol. Surgeons, Congress Neurol. Surgeons, AAAS, Pediatric Oncology Group, Nat. Med. Assn. Seventh Day Adventist. Office: Johns Hopkins Hosp 600 N Wolfe St Baltimore MD 21287-0005*

CARSON, CHARLES HENRY, microwave engineer; b. Malden, Mass., July 18, 1930; s. Philip Stanley and Margaret (Mitchell) C.; m. Olivia Rose Marie Barto, Apr. 23, 1967; children: Cynthia, Craig. Student, Northeastern U., Boston, 1956, postgrad., 1966. Devel. engr. microwave Raytheon, Bedford, Mass., 1953-56; sr. engr., dept. mgr. Airtron Inc., Cambridge, Mass., 1956-58; co-founder, v.p., dir. ops. Ferrotec Inc., Newton, Mass., 1958-70; dir. corp. mkt. planning MA/COM, Burlington, Mass., 1970-75; chmn., founder, chief exec. officer Carson Assocs., Inc., Milford, Mass., 1975—; bd. dirs. Carson Assocs., Inc., Milford; co-founder, bd. dirs. Colonial Cablevision, Revere, Mass., 1976-86; co-founder, v.p. mktg., bd. dirs. Ferrotec Inc., Newton, 1958-70. Inventor in field; contbr. articles to profl. jours. Commr. Indsl. devel. Commn., Milford, 1968-70; minuteman Mass. Ind. Devel. Commn., 1969-73; bd. dirs. The Rosary Crusaders, 1993. With USN, 1948-53. Mem. U.S. Polo Assn. (del. 1986-96), R.I. Tuna Tournament (dep. dir. 1973-77), Galilee Tuna Club (pres. 1976-77), Newport Polo Club (del. 1989-90). Avocations: polo, giant tuna fishing, sailing, shooting. Office: Carson Assocs Inc 5 Kellett Dr Milford MA 01757-4013

CARSON, CHRISTOPHER LEONARD, lawyer; b. Washington, Dec. 28, 1940; s. Leonard O. and Evelyn (Watters) C.; m. Cynthia Caffey, Dec. 27, 1963; 1 dau., Melissa Ann. AB, Duke U., 1962; JD, U. Mich., 1965. Bar: N.Y. 1965, Fla. 1968, Ga. 1970. Assoc. Olwine, Chase, O'Donnell & Weyher, N.Y.C., 1965-66; ptnr. Hansell & Post, Atlanta, 1969-89, Jones, Day, Reavis & Pogue, Atlanta, 1989—. Contbg. author: Modern Real Estate Transactions; contbr. articles to legal publs. and mags. Bd. dirs., adv. coun. Atlanta Area Boy Scouts Am., 1974-80; bd. dirs. Young Life Urban Atlanta, 1983—. Lt. sr. grade USNR, 1960-69. Fellow Am. Coll. Coml. Fin. Lawyers; mem. ABA (Uniform Comml. Code Com., Subcoms. on Secured Transactions and Letter of Credit 1982—), Southeastern Bankruptcy Law Inst. (dir. 1973—, pres. 1980-81, chmn. 1981-82), Atlanta Bar Bankruptcy Sect. (chmn. 1981-82), Ga. Bar Uniform Code Com. (chmn. 1984-87), Cherokee Club. Republican. Baptist. Avocations: running, reading, traveling. E-mail: clcarson@jonesday.com. Office: Jones Day Reavis & Pogue 3500 SunTrust Plz 303 Peachtree St NE Ste 3500 Atlanta GA 30308-3242*

CARSON, CULLEY CLYDE, III, urologist; b. Westerly, R.I., Feb. 25, 1945; s. Culley Clyde Jr. and Dorothy (Scarborough) C.; m. Mary Jo McDonald, Aug. 10, 1970; children: Culley Clyde IV, Hilary. BS, Trinity Coll., 1967; MD, George Washington U., 1971. Diplomate Am. Bd. Urology. Intern Dartmouth Med. Ctr., 1971-72, resident surgery, 1971-73; fellow urology Mayo Clinic, 1975-78; instr. urology U. Minn. Mayo Med. Sch., 1978; asst. prof. urology Duke U. Med. Ctr., Durham, N.C., 1978-84; assoc. prof. Duke U. Med. Ctr., Durham, 1984-88, prof., 1988-93; prof., chmn. urology U. N.C., 1993—; chief urology Durham VA Hosp.; mem. new drug panel U.S. FDA; mem. exec. com. U.S. Pharmacopea. Author: Endourology, 1985, Atlas of Urologic Endoscopy, 1986, Impotence, 1992, 98, Complications of Invasive Procedures, 1995, Textbook of Erectile Dysfunction, 1999; editor-in-chief Mediguide to Urology, 1994—, Contemporary Urology, 1997—; contbr. chpts. to urol. texts. Maj. M.C., USAF, 1973-75. Recipient Calvin Klopp Rsch. award, 1971, Friedman rsch. prize, 1971, Cristol Mayo Alumni award, 1992; named Command Flight Surgeon of Yr., USAF, 1974; Rsch. fellow Am. Heart Assn., 1969, O'Dea travel fellow, 1978. Fellow ACS; mem. AMA, AAAS, Am. Urol. Assn., Internat. Soc. Urology, Am. Fertility Soc., Univ. Urol. Forum, N.Y. Acad. Scis., Mayo Alumni Assn., Gov.'s Club, Carolina Club, Trinity Club (Hartford), Sigma Xi, Psi Chi, Alpha Omega Alpha. Home: 2719 Spencer St Durham NC 27705-5720 Office: U NC Hosps Chapel Hill NC 27599-7235

CARSON, DAVID COSTLEY, psychologist, health care administrator; b. Oct. 18, 1921; s. William Henry and Eula Lee (Costley) C.; m. Barbara Dame, Aug. 22, 1946; children: Jonathan David, Laurel, Bruce Alan. BA, So. Meth. U., 1943; postgrad., U. Chgo., 1943-46; MA, U. Tex., 1950, postgrad., 1950-52. Psychologist Tex. State Youth Devel. Coun., Austin, 1952-53; counselor, planner Tex. Edn. Agy., Austin, 1953-67; project dir. Planning Commn. for Vocat. Rehab., Olympia, Wash., 1967-70; exec. dir. Group Health Coop. South Cen. Wis., Madison, 1972-76; pres. WindWatts, Inc., 1974—, Austin Health Maintenance Orgn., Inc., 1978-84; cons. health care adminstrn., 1969—. Author: Satellite HMO, 1972, Rehabilitation Advance, 1969; co-author: Rehabilitation in Washington State, 1968. Sec. Dane County Arts Commn., 1975-78; pres., bd. dirs. Austin Ballet Soc., 1955-67; pres. bd. trustees McDade Ind. Sch. Dist., 1986-89, pres., 1986-87. With M.C., U.S. Army, 1946-48. VA fellow, 1948-49. Mem. Nat. Audubon Soc. (bd. dirs. 1991-94), Audubon Coun. Tex. (pres. 1986-88), Bastrop County Audubon Soc. (pres. 1986-87), Phi Delta Kappa, Psi Chi. Home and Office: PO Box 369 Mc Dade TX 78650-0369

CARSON, EDWARD JOHN, book publisher; b. Winnipeg, Man., Can., Sept. 28, 1948; s. Roy Woodrow and Lillian Alice (Clemens) C.; m. Joyce Tooze, Oct. 31, 1952; children: Lindsay Alissa Hannah, Matthew Edward. BA with honors, U. Toronto, 1976; MA, York U., 1977; postgrad., U. Toronto, 1977-79. Lectr. U. Toronto, 1978-79; pub. Stoddart/Gen. Pub., 1980-85; v.p. pub. Random House of Can., 1986-91; exec. v.p. HarperCollins Can. Ltd., Scarborough, Ont., 1991-93, pres., CEO, 1993-97; pres., COO Distican, Richmond Hill, Ont., Can., 1997-98; lectr. Ryerson Poly. Inst., 1991-93, 96-97; program co-dir. Banff Pub. Workshop, 1989-90; profl. devel. coord. Book Pubs. Profl. Assn., 1988-90; bd. dirs. Trade Group, Can. Book Pubs. Coun., 1989-91, PEN Can., 1990-93; v.p. Can. Publs. Coun., 1997, pres., 1998—. Editor Rune; author: Scenes, 1977. Recipient E.J. Pratt award for poetry, 1973, 76, St. Michael's Coll. English award, 1976. Office: Distican, 35 Fulton Way, Richmond Hill, ON Canada L4B 2N4

CARSON, GORDON BLOOM, engineering executive; b. High Bridge, N.J., Aug. 1, 1911; s. Whitfield R. and Emily (Bloom) C.; m. Beth Lacy, June 19, 1937 (dec. Mar. 1998); children—Richard Whitfield, Emily Elizabeth (Mrs. Lee A. Duffus), Alice Lacy (Mrs. William P. Allman), Jeanne Helen (Mrs. Michael J. Gable). BSMechE, Case Inst. Tech., 1931, D Engring., 1957; MS, Yale U., 1932, ME, 1938; LLD, Rio Grande Coll., 1973. With Western Electric Co., 1930; instr. mech. engring. Case Inst. Tech., 1932-37, asst. prof., 1937-40, asso. prof. indsl. engring. charge indsl. div., 1940-44; with Am. Shipbldg. Co., 1936; patent litigation, 1937; research engr., dir. research Cleve. Automatic Machine Co., 1939-44; asst. to gen. mgr. Selby Shoe Co., 1944, mgr. engring., 1945-49, sec. of corp., 1949-53; sec., dir. Pyrrole Products Co., 1948-53; dean engring. Ohio State U., Columbus, 1953-58; v.p. bus. and finance, treas. Ohio State U., 1958-71; dir. Engring. Exptl. Sta., 1953-58, Accuray Corp., 1960-82, Cardinal Funds, Inc., 1962-98; exec. v.p. Albion (Mich.) Coll., 1971-76, exec. cons., 1976-77; asst. to chancellor, dir. fin. Northwood Inst., 1977-82; v.p. Mich. Molecular Inst., 1982-88; prin. Whitfield Robert Assocs., 1988—. Editor: The Production Handbook, 1958; cons. editor, 1972—; Author of tech. papers engring. subjects. Trustee White Cross Hosp. Assn., 1960-71; bd. dirs. Cardinal Funds, 1966-98; bd. d irs. Goodwill Industries, 1959-67, 1st v.p., 1963-64; bd. dirs. Orton Found., 1953-58; v.p. Ohio State U. Rsch. Found., 1958-71; v.p., chmn. adv. coun. Ctr. for Automation and Soc., U. Ga., 1969-71; Chmn. tool and die com. 5th Regional War Labor Bd., 1943-45; chmn. Ohio State adv. com. for sci., tech. and specialized personnel SSS, 1965-70; pres. Larkin Parking Condo Assn., Inc., 1992—. Fellow ASME, AAAS, Inst. Indsl. Engrs. (pres. 1957-58); mem. Columbus Soc. Fin. Analysts (pres. 1974-75), Fin. Analysts Fedn. (bd. dirs. 1964-65), C. of C. (bd. dirs., treas. 1952-53), Am. Soc. Engring. Edn., Assn. Univs. for Rsch. in Astronomy (bd. dirs. 1958-71), Midwestern Univs. Rsch. Assn. (bd. dirs. 1958-71), U.S. Naval Inst., Nat. Soc. Profl. Engrs. (life), Romophos, Sphinx, Sigma Xi (fin. com. 1975-89, nat. treas. 1979-89), Masons (32 deg.), Tau Beta Pi, Zeta Psi, Phi Eta Sigma, Alpha Pi Mu, Omicron Delta Epsilon. Home: 5413 Gardenbrook Dr Midland MI 48642-3402 Office: Whitfield Robert Assocs 5413 Gardenbrook Dr Midland MI 48642-3402 *Integrity is as essential as health or intelligence. And it cannot be put on and taken off as can a garment. You either have it or you don't. Integrity must be nurtured, bolstered, and reaffirmed, lest the naturally corrupting influences of life destroy it. Without integrity, democracy cannot survive. Without it, government becomes a mutual looting society, with the citizens paying the bills. No society can be free unless a heavy majority of its citizens has integrity, and demands it on the part of all associates.*

CARSON, HAMPTON LAWRENCE, geneticist, educator; b. Phila., Nov. 5, 1914; s. Joseph and Edith (Bruen) C.; m. Meredith Shelton, Aug. 14, 1937; children: Joseph II, Edward Bruen. AB, U. Pa., 1936, PhD, 1943. Instr. U. Pa., 1938-42; faculty Washington U., St. Louis, 1943-70; prof. biology Washington U., 1956-70; prof. genetics U. Hawaii, 1971-85, emeritus, 1985—; vis. prof. biology U. Sao Paulo, Brazil, 1951, 77. Author: Heredity and Human Life, 1963; Contbr. articles to profl. jours. Trustee B.P. Bishop Mus., Honolulu, 1982-88. Recipient medal for excellence in rsch. U. Hawaii, 1979, Leidy medal Acad. Natural Scis., Phila., 1985, Charles Reed Bishop medal Bishop Mus., Honolulu, 1992; Fulbright rsch. scholar zoology dept. U. Melbourne, Australia, 1961. Mem. Nat. Acad. Scis., Am. Acad. Arts and Scis., Genetics Soc. (pres. 1982), Soc. for Study Evolution (pres. 1971, George Gaylord Simpson award 1996), Am. Soc. Naturalists (pres. 1973), AAAS, Phi Beta Kappa, Sigma Xi. Address: Dept Genetics & Molecular Biology U Hawaii at Manoa Honolulu HI 96822 *As a life scientist, I study evolution with the tools of modern biology. Religious mysticism plays no role in either my scientific or philosophical thought. Each biological individual (man, mouse or fly) is unique in both genetic endowment and environmental experience. This fact is central to the ethics of a humanism that values each human life. The differences between us are mostly due to chance; some persons are more fortunate than others. Nevertheless, each has an equal right to be treated with dignity and forbearance.*

CARSON, JAY WILMER, pathologist, educator; b. Ki-Jang, Korea, Oct. 6, 1933; came to U.S., 1960; s. Han Kyu and Jin Chan (Son) Cha; m. Jennifer C. White, June 28, 1968 (dec. Aug. 1990); m. Teresa M. Alberda, July 14, 1995. MD, Seoul Nat. U., 1958. Diplomate Am. Bd. Pathology. Intern Bellevue Hosp. Ctr., N.Y.C., 1961-62; resident in pathology Albert Einstein Coll. Medicine, N.Y.C., 1963-66; fellow U. Montreal, Que., Can., 1967-68; chief anatomic pathology VA Hosp., Martinez, Calif., 1969-91; dir. cytopathology VA Med. Ctr., San Francisco, 1992-96; assoc. prof. U. Calif. Med. Sch., San Francisco, 1992—; aviation med. examiner FAA, Oklahoma City, 1987-96; assoc. clin. prof. U. Calif., Davis, 1985—; hosp. comdr. 6253d Army Hosp., Santa Rosa, Calif., 1994-96. Patentee needle aspiration device. Mem. chmn.'s adv. bd. Nat. Rep. Com., Washington, 1995-96. Col. USAR, 1971-96. Fellow Coll. Am. Pathologists; mem. Internat. Acad. Pathology, Assn. Mil. Surgeons U.S. (life), Res. Officers Assn. (life), U.S. Army War Coll. Alumni Assn. (life), Soc. U.S. Army Flight Surgeons (life). Avocations: skiing, sailing, music. Home: 1550 Sorrel Ct Walnut Creek CA 94598-4800 Office: VA Med Ctr 4150 Clement St San Francisco CA 94121-1598

CARSON, JOHN THOMPSON, JR., environmental consultant; b. Phila., Apr. 13, 1916; s. John Thompson and Agnes (Gillinder) C.; m. Margaret Evans, June 21, 1940; children: Frederick, Sylvia Hathaway. BS, Haverford Coll., 1938; MS, U. Pa., 1939. Tchr. Perkiomer Sch., Pennsburg, Pa., 1939-41; chmn. dept. biology George Sch., Newtown, Pa., 1941-64; exec. dir. Neshaminy Water Resources Authority, Doylestown, Pa., 1966-76; dir. Natural Resources Divsn., Bucks County, Doylestown, 1966-76; program dir. Del. River Basin Commn., West Trenton, N.J., 1976-78; pres. John Carson & Assocs., Inc., Doylestown, 1978—; adj. prof. environ. studies Del. Valley Coll., 1950-54; vis. prof. ecology Lehigh U., Bethlehem, Pa., 1968-69; lectr. environ. law U. Pa., 1978-79. Contbr. articles to profl. jours. Pres. Coun. Rock Little League, 1950-56; vice chmn. Bucks County Water & Sewer Authority, 1962-64, chmn., 1965; adv. com. Inst. Rsch. Land & Water Resources, Pa. State U., 1975-82; chmn. Doylestown Twp. Bd. Suprs., 1980-84, 94-99, vice chmn., 1985-93; chmn. Ctrl. Bucks Aquatic Performing Arts Ctr., 1998—. Recipient Samuel S. Baxter Meml. award Water Resources Assn., Del. River Basin, 1987, Haverford Coll. award, 1993, Pres. Achievement award Pa. Assn. Twp. Suprs., 1995, Am. Hometown Leader award Nat. Assn. Towns & Twps., 1996; named Watershed Man of Yr., Pa. Assn. Conservation Dists., 1974. Mem. Nat. Wildlife Fedn., Pa. Forestry Assn. (Conservation award 1971), Del. River Watershed Assn., Neshaminy Valley Watershed Assn. (pres. 1958-65). Republican. Mem. Soc. of Friends. Address: 412 Henley Ct Doylestown PA 18901-2508

CARSON, JULIA M., congresswoman; b. Louisville, July 8, 1938; 2 children. Ed. Ind. U., 1960-62, St. Mary of the Woods, 1976-78. Mem. In. Ho. of Reps., Indpls., 1972-76; mem. Ind. Senate, 1976-90; mem. 105th Congress from Indiana 10th Dist, 1997—. mem. Congressional Com. Banking and Fin. Svcs., 1997—, Vets. Affairs, 1997—. Vice pres. Greater Indpls. Prog. Com.; nat. Democratic committeewoman; trustee YMCA; bd. dirs. Pub. Service Acad. Recipient Woman of Yr. Ind. award, 1974; Outstanding Leadership award AKA; Humanitarian award Christian Theol. Sem. Mem. NAACP, Urban League, Nat. Council Negro Women. Baptist. Office: US Ho of Reps 1541 Longworth HOB Washington DC 20515-1410 Address: Ste 200 300 E Fall Creek Pkwy Indianapolis IN 46205-4261 also: 1541 Longworth HOB Washington DC 20515*

CARSON, LINDA FRANCES, gynecologic oncologist; b. Manchester, Conn., Feb. 8, 1952; d. Culley Clyde and Dorothy (Scarborough) C.; m. Bruce Allen MacFarlane, June 2, 1974 (div. 1988); children: Megan Carson, Ian Scarborough; m. Roderick Allen Barke, Jan. 13, 1989. BA, Conn. Coll., 1974; MD, George Washington U., 1978. Intern and resident Sinai Hosp. Balt., 1978-82; fellow in gynecologic oncology Barnes Hosp., St. Louis, 1982-83, U. Minn., 1983-86; dir. gynecologic oncology Hennepin County Med. Ctr., Mpls., 1986-89; dir. VA Gynecologic Svc., Mpls., 1989-90, dir. gynecol., 1990—, v.p. ob/gyn., 1994—; dir. div. gynecologic oncology U. Minn., Mpls., 1990—, assoc. prof. div. gynecologic oncology, 1991—; co-prin. investigator Gynecologic Oncology Group, 1990—; co-dir. Upper Midwest Trophoblastic Diseases Ctr. U. Minn., 1986—; dir. Women's Cancer Ctr., 1988—. Reviewer: Am. Jour. Obstetrics and Gynecology, 1989—, Gynecologic Oncology, Cancer, 1989—; contbr. articles to profl. jours. Fellow Am. Cancer Soc.; mem. AMA, Hennepin County Med. Soc., Internat. Soc. for Study Vulvar Disease, Mpls. Coun. Obstetrics and Gynecology, Minn. State Med. Soc., Minn. Women's Med. Soc., Soc. of Gynecologic Oncologists, Western Assn. Gynecologic Oncologists. Office: U Minn Dept Ob-Gyn Box 395 Mayo 420 Delaware St SE Minneapolis MN 55455-0374

CARSON, MARGARET MARIE, gas industry executive, marketing professional; b. Windber, Pa., Dec. 30, 1944; d. Peter and Margaret (Olenik) Buben; m. Brian Charles Scruby, June 6, 1975; stepchildren: Debbie, Victor, Chris, Kenneth. BA, U. Pitts., 1971; MS in Mgmt., Houston Bapt. U., 1985. Petroleum analyst Gulf Oil Co., Pitts., 1973-75, crude oil analyst, 1971-74, environ. coordinator, 1974-79, mgr. oil trading, Houston, 1980-84, mktg. dir., 1985; sales dir. Cabot Cons. Group, Houston, 1985-86; dir. competitor analysis and corporate strategy dept., Enron Corp., Houston, 1987—. Columnist: The Collegian, 1984-85. Bd. dirs. Indiana U., Pa., 1980-81. Mem. Am. Competitiveness Soc. (chmn. bd. dirs.), Internat. Energy Economists, Global Pacific Ptnrs. and Petroleum Economist Sessions, Univ. Club.

CARSON, MARY SILVANO, career counselor, educator; b. Mass., Aug. 11, 1925; d. Joseph and Alice V. Silvano; m. Paul E. Carson (dec.); children: Jan Ellen, Jeffrey Paul, Amy Jayne. BS, Simmons Coll.; MA, U. Chgo., 1970, postgrad., 1971, 72; postgrad., Ctr. Urban Studies, 1970, DePaul U., 1980. Cert. acad. counselor, Ill.; nat. cert. counselor. Mgr. S.W. Youth Opportunity Ctr., Dept. Labor, Chgo.; careers counselor Gordon Tech. H.S., Chgo., 1971-74; dir. Career and Assessment Ctr., YMCA Coll., Chgo., 1974-81; project coord. Career Ctr., Loop Coll., Chgo., 1981-85; mem. adv. bd. City-Wide Coll. Career Ctr.; bd. dirs. Loop YWCA, Chgo., coord. employment project, 1985-87; ESL tchr., Greece, 1990. Mem. ACA, TESOL, Am. Ednl. Rsch. Assn., Nat. Career Devel. Assn., Internat. Counseling Assn., Internat. Lyceum (London), Browning Soc., World Coun., English Speaking Union, Met. Club, Commonwealth Club, Pi Lambda Theta (chpt. pres. 1975).

CARSON, PAUL EUGENE, insurance examiner; b. Jan. 15, 1953. B in Bus. Adminstrn., Middle Tenn. State U., 1975; M in Accountancy, U. Mo., 1984. Legis. auditor Divsn. State Audit, Nashville, 1976-83; ins. examiner Tenn. Dept. Commerce and Ins., Nashville, 1987-94, Ariz. Dept. Ins., Phoenix, 1995—. E-mail: 104741.1305@compuserve.com. Home: 208 Chapel Ave Nashville TN 37206-2410

CARSON, SAMUEL GOODMAN, retired banker, company director; b. Glens Falls, N.Y., Oct. 6, 1913; s. Russell M.L. and Mary (Goodman) C.; m. Alice Williams, Oct. 14, 1939; children: Russell L., Frances Elizabeth (Mrs. Thomas E. Brady Jr.), Mary Goodman (Mrs. John A. Fedderke), Kathryn Williams (Mrs. Robert Richards), Samuel Goodman. B.A. magna cum laude, Dartmouth Coll., 1934. With Aetna Life Ins. Co., 1934-68; with Toledo Trust Co., 1967-84, exec. v.p., 1968, pres., 1969-84, chief exec. officer, 1970-84, chmn., 1976-84; chmn., dir. Toledo Trustcorp, Inc., 1976-84; dir. Bostwick-Braun Co., Kiemle-Hankins Co., Plastic Technologies, Inc., Carson Assocs., Inc. Mem. Ottawa Hills Bd. Edn., 1954-64; pres. United Appeal Greater Toledo Area, 1969, campaign chmn., 1964; Bd. dirs., trustee Toledo chpt. ARC, 1950—, chmn., 1959-61; trustee Toledo Hosp., 1960—, v.p., 1963-65, pres., 1966-69; bd. dirs. Community Chest Greater Toledo, 1962-65, pres., 1965; pres. Boys' Club Toledo, 1961-64, trustee, 1957—; trustee Toledo Mus. Art, 1967—, sec.-treas., 1969, v.p., 1973-78, pres., 1978-80. Recipient Service to Mankind award Sertoma Club Toledo, 1965, Man and Boy award Boys' Clubs Am., 1966, Pacemaker of Yr. award U. Toledo Coll. Bus. Adminstrn. Alumni Assn., 1969. Mem. Toledo Area C. of C. (trustee 1961-62, 73-76, pres. 1974-75), Phi Beta Kappa, Phi Gamma Delta. Republican. Conglist. Clubs: Rotarian, Toledo Country, Toledo. Lodge: Rotary. Office: 425 Madison Ave Toledo OH 43604-1229

CARSON, STEVEN LEE, newspaper publisher; b. N.Y.C., Mar. 23, 1943; s. Harold and Mathilde (Seidel) C.; m. Yvonne DeDrozizhki, Aug. 8, 1971 (dec. Feb. 1980). *Grandfather Samuel Seidel and his brother Max were models for I.J. Singer's 1930's novel The Brothers Ashkenazi. Uncle Henry Seidel was Undersecretary of Agriculture and Budget Director for Washington State and US Congressional Assistant, 1950's - 1960's. Cousin Max Steiner, Director of Music at Warner Brothers 1937-1967, won three Oscars. Cousin Dr. Dennis Carson discovered cure for a form of leukemia. Cousins Jan Peerce and Richard Tucker starred in the New York Metropolitan Opera. Cousin Robert Richter and wife Linda are judges on the District of Columbia Superior Court. Brother Michael Carson is producer of industrial shows in New York.* BA, NYU, 1964, MA, 1965. Archivist, conf. dir. Nat. Archives, Washington, 1967-73; chmn. White House Conf. Pres. & Children, Washington, 1974; editor, writer Manuscript Soc. News, Washington, 1987—; conf. dir. The Manuscript Soc., 1974-80; dir. history pavilion Hall of Fame Great Am., N.Y.C., 1964; editor Pres. Commn. Civil Disorders, Washington, 1968; TV commentator, lectr. in field. *Beyond his newspaper, historical and dramatic writings and lectures, Steven Lee Carson is a professional public speaker who has spoken in the Kremlin, the White House, the US Capitol, over the Voice of America and on national television. Honored as a speaker in the US Congressional Record, his fine arts investment topic is "Dealing with the Ayatollah, Einstein, Eleanor Roosevelt and Salvador Dali: The Fun, Challenge and Profit of Autograph and Manuscript Collecting." With humor and history, he also speaks on the human side of world leaders he has met such as the Dalai Lama and on Washington Folklore.* Author: Maximilien Robespierre, 1988, (plays) The Last Lincoln, Princess Alice; contbr. articles to profl. jours. Speechwriter The White House, U.S. Congress, Md. Ho. Dels., 1974—. Ford Found. fellow, 1964, Johns Hopkins U. Chas Carroll Fulton fellow, 1965; grantee Md. Commn. Humanities, 1986, 87, U.S. Dept. Interior, 1985; recipient NYU Heights Daily News Alumni award, 1964, Archival medal Republic of Korea, 1972, Internat. Psychohistory Assn. award, 1983, Lincoln Group of N.Y. award, 1988, 92, Surratt Soc. award, 1993; delivered ofcl. Lincoln Day Address, Ford's Theatre, Washington, 1996, Smithsonian lectr., 1999—. Fellow The Manuscript Soc.; mem. Nat. Press Club, Nat. Writers Union, Lincoln Group D.C. (pres. 1985-88), Wash. Ind. Writers, Lincoln Forum (trustee 1997—), Abraham Lincoln Inst. of the Mid. Atlantic (trustee 1997—), NYU Hon. Soc., NYU Soc. of the Torch. Avocation: collecting historic manuscripts & letters. Office: The Manuscript News 8811 Colesville Rd Ste 506 Silver Spring MD 20910-4332

CARSON, VIRGINIA HILL, oil and gas executive; b. L.A., Dec. 4, 1928; d. Percy Albert McCord and Flora May (Newking) Schultz; m. John Carson, Dec. 30, 1950 (dec.). BA in Internat. Relations, U. Calif., Berkeley, 1949; postgrad. Stanford U., 1948, UCLA, 1951. Gen. office worker UN, San Francisco, 1949; ind. oil and gas profl., U.S., Can., Cuba, 1953-73; supr., specialist Sun Exploration & Prodn. Co. (name changed to Oryx Energy Co.), Dallas, 1978-83, profl. analyst, 1983-92; lit. rschr. and freelance editor, 1992—. Mem. Dallas Coun. World Affairs, 1984—, Dallas Mus. Fine Arts, 1984—; vol. North Tex. Taping and Radio for the Blind, 1992—. Nominated to pres.'s coun. Am. Inst. Mgmt., N.Y.C., 1974. Address: PO Box 12530 Dallas TX 75225-0530

CARSON, WALLACE PRESTON, JR., state supreme court justice; b. Salem, Oreg., June 10, 1934; s. Wallace Preston and Edith (Bragg) C.; m. Gloria Stolk, June 24, 1956; children: Scott, Carol, Steven (dec. 1981). BA in Politics, Stanford U., 1956; JD, Willamette U., 1962. Bar: Oreg. 1962, U.S. Dist. Ct. Oreg. 1963, U.S. Ct. Appeals (9th cir.) 1968, U.S. Supreme Ct. 1971, U.S. Ct. Mil. Appeals 1977; lic. comml. pilot FAA. Pvt. practice law Salem, Oreg., 1962-77; judge Marion County Cir. Ct., Salem, 1977-82; assoc. justice Oreg. Supreme Ct., Salem, 1982-92, chief justice, 1992—. Mem. Oreg. Ho. of Reps., 1967-71, maj. leader, 1969-71; mem. Oreg. State Senate, 1971-77, minority floor leader, 1971-77; dir. Salem Area Community Council, 1967-70, pres., 1969-70; mem. Salem Planning Commn., 1966-72, pres., 1970-71; co-chmn. Marion County Mental Health Planning Com., 1965-69; mem. Salem Community Goals Com., 1965; Republican precinct commiteeman, 1963-66; mem. Marion County Rep. Central Exec. Com., 1963-66; com. predinct edn. Oreg. Rep. Central Com., 1965; vestryman, acolyte, Sunday Sch. tchr., youth coach St. Paul's Episcopal Ch., 1935—; task force on cts. Oreg. Council Crime and Delinquency, 1968-69; trustee Willamette U., 1970—; adv. bd. Cath. Ctr. Community Services, 1976-77; mem. comprehensive planning com. Mid-Willamette Valley Council of Govts., 1970-71; adv. com. Oreg. Coll. Edn. Tchr. Edn., 1971-75; pres. Willamette regional Oreg. Lung Assn., 1974-75, state dir., exec. com., 1975-77; pub. relations com. Williamette council Campfire Girls, 1976-77; criminal justice adv. bd. Chemeketa Community Coll., 1977-79; mem. Oreg. Mental Health Com., 1979-80; mem. subcom. Gov's Task Force Mental Health, 1980; you and govt. adv. com. Oreg. YMCA, 1981—. Served to col. USAFR, 1956-59. Recipient Salem Disting. Svc. award, 1968; recipient Good Fellow award Marion County Fire Svc., 1974, Minuteman award Oreg. N.G. Assn., 1980; fellow Eagleton Inst. Politics, Rutgers U., 1971. Mem. Marion County Bar Assn. (sec.-treas. 1965-67, dir. 1968-70), Oreg. Bar Assn., ABA, Willamette U. Coll. Law Alumni Assn. (v.p. 1968-70), Salem Art Assn., Oreg. Hist. Soc., Marion County Hist. Soc., Stanford U. Club (pres. Salem chpt. 1963-64), Delta Theta Phi. Office: Oregon Supreme Ct Supreme Ct Bldg 1163 State St Salem OR 97310-1331

CARSON, WILLIAM CHARLES, sales and marketing executive; b. Palmyra, N.J., Nov. 9, 1924; s. William and Carrie (Forderer) C.; m. Jean Gingerich, Apr. 1, 1950; children: William Scott, Colleen Jean, Caroline Grace. BA, Gettysburg Coll., 1949. Sales rep. Nat. Sugar Refinery Co., Phila., 1949-60; account exec. Metal Edge Industries, Barrington, N.J., 1960-70, sales mgr., 1970-80; gen. mgr. Metal Edge div. Lydall, Inc., Hartford, Conn., 1980-83; mktg. and sales mgr. Mefco, North Wales, Pa., 1983-90; ret. Campaign chmn. United Way, Berkeley Heights, N.J., 1966, bd. dirs. Burlington County, N.J., 1985—, sec., bd. dirs. Moorestown, N.J., 1984—. Served to cpl. U.S. Army, 1943-45, ETO. Decorated Bronze Star with oak leaf cluster, Purple Heart; recipient Presdl. citation, U.S. Army, Disting. Svc. medal N.J., Normandy medal (France). Mem. Am. Mgmt. Assn. (seminar chmn. 1972), Sales & Mktg. Execs. So. Jersey (v.p., bd. dirs. 1974-78), Am. Def. Preparedness Assn. (cons. 1984—, bd. dirs.), Def. Fire Protection Assn. (bd. advisors 1987—), Phi Kappa Psi (sec.). Republican. Avocation: golf. Home: 125 Somers Ct S Moorestown NJ 08057-3419

CARSON, WILLIAM MORRIS, manpower planning and development advisor; s. Edward Belmont and Frances Lucretia (Powell) C.; children: Lincoln Bruce Carson, Adrien Lee Allen, Anthony Lunt Carson, Karen Tracy Carson. BS, Columbia U.; MA, Johns Hopkins U.; postgrad., U. Chgo., London Sch. Econs. Cairo corr. MBS, 1951-53; asst. prof. Mid. East Studies, SAIS, 1955-56; tng. officer U.S. AID, 1958-64; indsl. rels. staff analyst ARAMCO, Dhahran, Saudi Arabia, 1964-70; mgr. mgmt. deve. and tng. Saudi Arabian Airlines, Jeddah, 1970-72; chief tng. sect. UN Devel. Programme, N.Y.C., 1973-75; mgr. mgmt. devel. and tng. Sulvania Tng. Ops., Waltham, Mass., 1975-76; dir. tng. Ingersoll-Rand Constrn. Svcs., Winston-Salem, N.C., 1977-79; sr. advisor manpower planning and devel. Internat. Human Resources Devel. Corp., Boston, 1979-83; gen. mgr. ITECO divsn. Saudi Tng. Svcs., Riyadh, Saudi Arabia, 1983-84; mng. dir. Arab Resources Devel. Corp., Mass., 1984-87; mgr. Turkish tech. projects GE Internat. Svc. Corp., 1987-92; prin. Carson & Assocs., Balt., 1992-96, Nat. Manpower Strategies, 1997—; cons. UN; Middle East Inst. fellow; Ford Found. area fellow. Co-author: International Manpower Planning: The Developing World, 1982; also articles. Recipient Outstanding Performance award AID. Fellow Royal Anthrop. Inst. Gt. Britain and No. Ireland, Inst. Comml. Mgmt.; mem. Assn. Internat Mgmt. Cons., Ineamus Meloria Honor Soc. Address: 1908 C St Forest Grove OR 97116-2308

CARSTEN, JACK CRAIG, venture capitalist; b. Cin., Aug. 24, 1941; s. John A. and Edith L. C.; m. Mary Ellis Jones, June 22, 1963; children: Scott, Elizabeth, Amy. BS in Physics, Duke U., 1963. Mktg. mgr. Tex. Instruments, Dallas, Houston, 1965-71; integrated circuits gen. mgr. Tex. Instruments, Houston, 1971-75; v.p. sales and mktg. Intel Corp., Santa Clara, Calif., 1975-79, v.p., microcomputer gen. mgr., 1979-82, sr. v.p., components gen. mgr., 1982-87; gen. ptnr. U.S. Venture Ptnrs., Menlo Park, Calif., 1988-90; venture capitalist Horizon Ventures LLC, Los Altos, Calif.; bd. dirs. Socket Comms., Inc., Comerica Bank-CA, and several privately held firms. Contbr. articles to profl.jours. Office: Tech Investments PO Box 704 Los Altos CA 94023-0704

CARSTENS, JANE ELLEN, retired library science educator; b. New Iberia, La., Apr. 19, 1922; d. Charles John and Marie Claudia (Blanchet) C. BA in Elem. Edn., U. Southwestern La., 1942; BS in LS, La. State U., 1945; MS in LS, Columbia U., 1955, DLS, 1975. Asst. libr. Hamilton Lab. sch. and instr. libr. sci. U. Southwestern La., Lafayette, 1942-54, asst. prof., 1954-65, assoc. prof., 1965-75; children's librarian/storyteller N.Y. Pub. Libr., N.Y.C., 1947, 48-49; vis. lectr. U. Minn., Mpls., 1955-56, summer 59, La. State U., Baton Rouge, summer 1958, State Coll. Iowa, Cedar Falls, summer 1963; prof. libr. sci. U. Southwestern La., Lafayette, 1975-94; vis. lectr. Syracuse U., summers 1962, 64, U. Tex., Austin, summers 1976-86, 89. Trustee Our Lady of Wisdom Cath. Ch. Named Tchr. of Yr., Amoco, 1982, Outstanding Alumna, U. Southwestern La., 1986; recipient Essae Culver Disting. Svc. award La. Libr. Assn., 1987, Alumni Faculty Excellence award Blue Key, 1990, Faculty Advisor of Yr. award U. Southwestern La. Student Govt. Assn., 1992, Point of Excellence award Kappa Delta Pi, 1992, Outstanding Tchr. award USL Found., 1994; Blue Key Faculty/Student Staff Directory dedicated to her, 1994-95. Mem. ALA, Assn. Libr. and Info. Sci. Edn., Assn. Libr. Svc. to Children (mem. Newbery award com. 1989-90), Am. Assn. Sch. Librs., La. Libr. Assn. (pres. 1959-60), Young Adult Libr. Svc. Assn., Lafayette Pub. Libr. Found., Univ. Women's Club, Phi Kappa Phi (pres. USL chpt. 1984-85), Delta Kappa Gamma (pres. Alpha chpt. 1988-90). Roman Catholic. Avocations: reading, walking. Home: 214 St Joseph St Lafayette LA 70506-4535 also: U Southwestern La PO Box 40298 Lafayette LA 70504-4535

CARSTENSEN, EDWIN LORENZ, biomedical engineer, biophysicist; b. Oakdale, Nebr., Dec. 8, 1919; s. August Hans and Opal Lois (Norwood) C.; m. Pam McDonald, Aug. 1, 1947; children: Richard Lorenz, Allen Brent, Laura Lee, Loretta Dee, Christina Marie. BS, Nebr. State Tchrs. Coll., 1941; MS, Case Inst. Tech., 1947; PhD, U. Pa., 1955. Mem. sci. staff div. war rsch. Columbia U., 1942-45; head lab. sect. U.S. Navy Underwater Sound Reference Lab., Orlando, Fla., 1945-48; rsch. assoc. Moore Sch. Elec. Engring., U. Pa., 1948-55, asst. prof. elec. engring., 1955-56; prin. investigator U.S. Army Biol. Lab., Fort Detrick, Frederick, Md., 1956-61; assoc. prof. elec. engring. U. Rochester, 1961-73, prof., 1973-88, Arthur Gould Yates prof. engring., 1988-90, Arthur Gould Yates prof. engring. emeritus, 1990—, dir. biomed. engring., 1971-83, prof. biophysics, 1981-90, univ. mentor, 1982—, sr. scientist in elec. engring., 1990—; dir. Rochester Ctr. for Biomed. Ultrasound, 1986-90. Author: Biological Effects of Transmission Line Fields, 1987; contbr. numerous articles to profl. publs. Fellow Acoustical Soc. Am., IEEE, Am. Inst. Ultrasound in Medicine; mem. Biophys. Soc., Biomed. Engring. Soc., Nat. Acad. Engring. Democrat. Home: 103 Eastland Ave Rochester NY 14618-1027 Office: U Rochester Dept Elec Engring Rochester NY 14627

CARSTENSEN, FRED V., economics educator; b. Seattle, Apr. 29, 1944; s. Vernon and Mary Buffum Carstensen; m. Mildred G. Eubanks, July 5, 1975; 1 child, Erin H. BA, Wis. U., 1966; MA, Yale U., 1969, PhD, 1976. Instr. The Coll., U. Chgo., 1970-71, 72-75; asst. prof. U. Va., Charlottesville, 1975-82; assoc. prof. U. Conn., Storrs, 1982-96, prof., 1996—, dir. Ctr. for Econ. Analysis, 1997—. Home: 3 Mallard Dr Bloomfield CT 06002-2227

CARSWELL, ALLAN IAN, physics educator; b. Toronto, Ont., Can., Oct. 4, 1933; s. Duncan and Margaret (McAskill) C.; m. Helen Alexandra Aird, June 2, 1956; children—Donald, Ruth, Diane. BS in Sci., U. Toronto, 1956, MA, 1957, PhD, 1960. NRC fellow U. Amsterdam, Holland, 1960-61; dir. optical physics lab. RCA Research Labs., Montreal, Que., Can., 1961-68; prof. physics York U., Toronto, 1968—; founder, pres. Optech Inc., Toronto, 1974—; chmn. physics com., Natural Scis. and Engring. Rsch. Coun., Ottawa, Ont., Can., 1977-81; mem. NASA Shuttle Lidar Group, Hampton, Va., 1977-79, Internat. Radiation Commn., 1984-96; prin. investigator and bd. dir. Inst. Space & Terrestrial Sci., 1988-95. Contbr. articles to profl. jours. Fellow Royal Soc. Can., Can. Aeros. and Space Inst.; mem. Can. Assn. Physicists (pres. 1985-86), Am. Meteorol. Soc. (chmn. com. on atmospheric laser studies 1984-87), Assn. Profl. Engrs. of Ont., Optical Soc. Am. Avocations: skiing, boating. Home: 17 Vallончliffe Rd, Thornhill, ON Canada L3T 2W6 Office: York U Dept Physics, Optech Inc, 100 Wildcat Rd, Toronto, ON Canada M3J 2Z9

CARSWELL, JANE TRIPLETT, family physician; b. Raeford, N.C., Feb. 26, 1932; d. Arthur Dula and Madeline Mapp (Warburton) C. Student, Flora Macdonald Coll., 1950-52; A.B. in Chemistry, U. N.C., 1954; M.D., Med. Coll. Va., 1958. Diplomate Am. Bd. Family Practice. Resident Med. Coll. Va., Richmond, 1958-61; practice medicine specializing in family medicine Harlan, Ky., 1961-62, Lenoir, N.C., 1962—. Chmn. Lenoir Human Relations Com., N.C., 1962-64; vice-chmn. Caldwell County Council Status of Women, Lenoir, 1976-78. Mem. Caldwell County Med. Soc. (pres. 1965), N.C. Acad. Family Physicians (N.C. Family Physician of Yr. award 1983), N.C. Med. Soc., Am. Acad. Family Practice (Nat. Family Dr. of Yr. award 1984). Presbyterian. Avocations: wildflowers; hiking; backpacking; skiing; photography. Office: 401 Mulberry St SW Lenoir NC 28645-5463

CARSWELL, LOIS MALAKOFF, botanical gardens executive, consultant; b. N.Y.C., Mar. 2, 1932; d. Arthur and Dora (Krechevsky) Malakoff; m. Donald Carswell, Oct. 12, 1957; children: Anne Carswell Tang, Alexander, Robert Ian. AB magna cum laude, Radcliffe Coll., 1953; cert. in bus. adminstrn., Harvard U. and Radcliffe Coll., 1954. Editor Dell Pub. Co., N.Y.C., 1954-56; publicist Ruth E. Pepper Co., N.Y.C., 1957-58; vol. Bklyn. Botanic Garden, 1964—, co-chmn. plant sales, 1967—, co-chmn. capital campaign, 1984-88, chmn. bd. dirs., 1989—; chmn. Coalition Living Mus. N.Y. State, N.Y.C., 1980—; cons. N.Y. State Natural Heritage Trust, 1982—; mem. bd. advisors Harvard Bus. Sch. of N.Y. Comty. Ptnrs., 1998—. Office: Bklyn Botanic Garden 1000 Washington Ave Brooklyn NY 11225-1008

CARSWELL, VIRGINIA COLBY, primary school educator, special education educator; b. Manchester, N.H., Aug. 10, 1923; d. Aretas Putnam and Lucille (Ford) Colby; m. Elwin Dow Carswell, Jan. 26, 1946 (dec. July 1997); children: Susan Lee Carswell-Hurdis, Debra Ann Carswell Roberts. Diploma, Elliot Hosp. Sch. Nursing, 1945; BS in Spl. Edn.-Elem. Edn., Brenau Coll., 1977, postgrad., 1978-80. Asst. dietitian Elliot Hosp., Manchester, N.H., 1946-58; tchr., head instr. Hi Hope Svc. Ctr., Lawrenceville, Ga., 1970-87; presch. tchr. Buford (Ga.) Meth. Presch., 1987—; child devel. internship Gainsville (Ga.) Coll., 1988-89. Recipient Outstanding Citizen award Woodman of the World Life Ins. Soc., 1981, Golden Rule award, J.C. Penney, 1984, Gene Willis award, Gwinnett County Assn. Retarded Citizens, 1987, Svcs. to Handicapped, Gwinnett Mental Health Assn., 1983, Leadership award Girl Scouts Am., 1970, Merit Mother award Am. Mothers Assn., 1980. Mem. Coun. Exceptional Children (Outstanding Profl. award 1987), Ga. Presch. Assn. (Disting. Cert. of Recognition 1998), So. Assn. Children under Six, Nat. Assn. Edn. Young Children (Disting. Cert. Recognition Profl. 1998), Am. Red Cross (instr. 1970—). United Methodist. Avocations: cooking, sewing, bowling, reading. Home: 80 Stonehedge Dr Buford GA 30518-2575

CARTA, FRANKLIN OLIVER, retired aeronautical engineer; b. Middletown, Conn., July 16, 1930; s. Salvatore and Anna (DeMauro) C.; m. Ann J. DiMauro, Sept. 25, 1954; children: Lisa Ann, Christopher Pace, Maura Ferragut. BS, MIT, 1952, MS, 1953. Rsch. asst. MIT Aeroelastics Lab., Cambridge, 1952-53; rsch engr. United Aircraft Rsch. Labs., East Hartford, Conn., 1953-60; aeroelastics engr. Cornell Aero. Lab., Buffalo, 1960; sr. engr./supr. aeromechanics United Tech. Rsch. Ctr., East Hartford, 1960-91; lectr. aero von Karman Inst., Rhode-St-Genese, Belgium, 1970, 77, Iowa State U., 1975, 77, 80—; panel mem. Adv. Group for Aerospace Rsch. and Devel. of NATO, 1979-84. Assoc. editor Jour. of Fluids and Structures, 1985-87; contbr. articles to profl. jours., chpts. to books. Assoc. fellow AIAA; fellow ASME (v.p. 1992-94, bd. dirs. Internat. Gas Turbine Inst. of ASME 1985-90, chmn. IGTI bd. dirs. 1988-89, Gas Turbine Power award 1967); mem. Sigma Xi, Tau Beta Pi, Gamma Alpha Rho. Achievements include patents in field; development of research on unsteady deep stall aerodynamics of wings and rotors, on turbomachinery coupled flutter.

CARTEN, FRANCIS NOEL, lawyer; b. Bryn Mawr, Pa., Dec. 25, 1935; s. Francis Patrick and Louise Cathleen (Leach) C. BS, U. Notre Dame, 1960; JD, Villanova U., 1964. Bar: Pa. 1967, N.Y. 1967, Conn. 1976. Assoc. Eyre, Mann & Lucas, N.Y.C., 1966-74; pvt. practice law, Danbury and Stamford, Conn., 1975-78; patent counsel TIE/communications, Inc., Shelton, Conn., 1978-79, Automation Industries, Inc., Greenwich, 1979-85; pvt. practice law, Stamford, 1985-88; pntr. Wyatt, Gerber, Meller & O'Rourke, L.L.P., 1988—. With U.S. Army, 1954-56. Mem. Am. Intellectual Property Law Assn., N.Y. State Bar Assn., N.Y. Intellectual Property Law Assn., Conn. Patent Law Assn., Seawanhaka Corinthian Yacht Club (Oyster Bay, N.Y.). Republican. Office: 1177 High Ridge Rd Stamford CT 06905-1211

CARTER, ALDEN RICHARDSON, writer; b. Eau Claire, Wis., Apr. 7, 1947; s. John Kelley and Hilda (Richardson) C.; m. Carol Ann Shadis Carter, Sept. 14, 1974; children: Brian Patrick, Siri Morgan. BA in English and Humanities, U. Kans., Lawrence, 1969; teaching cert. in English and History, Mont. State U., Bozeman, 1976. Officer USN, 1969-74; tchr. Marshfield (Wis.) H.S., 1976-80; writer pvt. practice, Marshfield, Wis., 1980—; spkr. on writing in 27 states. Author: Growing Season, 1984, Wart, Son of Toad, 1985, Sheila's Dying, 1987, Up Country, 1989, Robodad, 1990, Dogwolf, 1994, Between a Rock and a Hard Place, 1999, (with Wayne LeBlanc) Supercomputers, 1985, Modern China, 1986, Illinois, 1987, Colonies in Revolution, 1988, Darkest Hours, 1988, At the Forge of Liberty, 1988, Birth of the Republic, 1988, The Shoshoni, 1989, Last Stand at the Alamo, 1990, The Battle of Gettysburg, 1990, The Colonial Wars: Clashes in the Wilderness, 1992, The American Revolution: War for Independence, 1992, The War of 1812: Second Fight for Independence, 1992, The Mexican War: Manifest Destiny, 1992, The Civil War: American Tragedy, 1992, The Spanish-AMerican War: Imperial Ambitions, 1992, Battle of the Ironclads: The Monitor and the Merrimack, 1993, China Past-China Future, 1994, I'm Tougher Than Asthm!, 1996, Big Brothers Dustin, 1997, Seeing Things My Way, 1998, Dustin's Big School Day, 1999. Lt. USN, 1969-74. Recipient of several literary awards. Mem. Sierra Club, Soc. of Children's Book Writer and Illustrators, Coun. for Wis. Writers, Soc. of Midland Authors. Democrat. Avocations: canoeing, hiking. E-mail address: acartewriter@tznet.com. Home: 1113 W Onstad Dr Marshfield WI 54449-1732 Office: 210 W 29th Marshfield WI 54449

CARTER, ASHTON BALDWIN, physicist, educator, government agency executive; b. Phila., Sept. 24, 1954; s. William Stanley and Ann Baldwin C.; m. Ava Clayton Spencer, Aug. 6, 1983; children: William A., Ava Clayton. BA in Physics, Yale U., 1976, BA in Medieval History, 1976; PhD in Theoretical Physics, Oxford (Eng.) U., 1979. Analyst Office of Technology Assessment, Washington, 1980-81; rsch. analyst Office of Sec. Def., Washington, 1981-82; rsch. fellow MIT, Cambridge, 1982-84; asst. prof. Kennedy Sch. Govt., Harvard U., Cambridge, 1984-86, assoc. prof., 1986-88, Ford Found. prof. Sci. and Internat. Affairs, assoc. dir. Ctr. for Sci. and Internat. Affairs, 1988-90, dir. Ctr. for Sci. and Internat. Affairs, 1990-93; asst. sec. for internat. security policy U.S. Dept. Def., Washington, 1993-96; Ford Found. prof. Kennedy Sch. Govt., Harvard U., Cambridge, Mass., 1996—; Mem. Def. Sci. Bd., Washington, 1990-93, 97—; mem. Def. Polit. Bd., Washington, 1997—; advisor NAS, 1990—, AAAS, 1988—, White House Office of Sci. and Technology Policy, 1990-93, Joint Chiefs Staff; trustee MITRE Corp. Author: Directed Energy Missile Defense in Space, 1984; co-author: Ballistic Missile Defense, 1984, Managing Nuclear Operations, 1987, Beyond Spinoff: Military and Commercial Technologies in a Changing World, 1991, Soviet Nuclear Fission: Control of the Nuclear Arsenal in a Disintegrating Soviet Union, 1991, A New Concept of Cooperative Security, 1992, Cooperative Denuclearization: From Pledges to Deeds, 1993, Global Engagement: Cooperation and Security in the 21st Century, 1994, Preventive Defense: A New Security Strategy for America, 1999. Rhodes scholar, 1976; named Outstanding Young Man of Am., U.S. Jaycees, 1987. Mem. Am. Phys. Soc. (Forum award 1988), Coun. Fgn. Rels., Internat. Inst. Strategic Studies, Phi Beta Kappa. Office: Harvard U JFK Sch of Govt 79 JFK St Cambridge MA 02138-5801

CARTER, BARRY EDWARD, lawyer, educator, administrator; b. L.A., Oct. 14, 1942; s. Byron Edward and Ethel Catherine (Turner) C.; m. Kathleen Anne Ambrose, May 17, 1987; children: Gregory Ambrose, Meghan Elisabeth. A.B. with great distinction, Stanford U., 1964; M.P.A., Princeton U., 1966; J.D., Yale U., 1969. Bar: Calif. 1970, D.C. 1972. Program analyst Office of Sec. Def., Washington, 1969-70; mem. staff NSC, Washington, 1970-72; rsch. fellow Kennedy Sch., Harvard U., Cambridge, Mass., 1972; internat. affairs fellow Coun. on Fgn. Rels., 1972; assoc. Wilmer, Cutler & Pickering, Washington, 1973-75; sr. counsel Select Com. on Intelligence Activities, U.S. Senate, Washington, 1975; assoc. Morrison & Foerster, San Francisco, 1976-79; assoc. prof. law Georgetown U. Law Ctr., Washington, 1979-89, prof., 1989-93, 96—; exec. dir. Am. Soc. Internat. Law, Washington, 1992-93; acting undersec. for export adminstrn. U.S. Dept. Commerce, Washington, 1993-94, deputy undersec., 1994-96; vis. prof. law Stanford U. Law Sch., 1990; bd. dirs. Nukem, Inc., 1998—; chmn. adv. bd. Def. Budget Project, 1990-93; mem. UN Assn. Soviet-Am. Parallel Studies Project, 1976-87. Author: International Economic Sanctions: Improving the Haphazard U.S. Legal Regime, 1988 (Am. Soc. Internat. Law Cert. of Merit 1989); co-author: International Law, 3d edit., 1999; contbr. articles to profl. jours. With U.S. Army, 1969-71. Mem. ABA, Calif. Bar Assn., D.C. Bar Assn., Coun. on Fgn. Rels., Am. Soc. Internat. Law (hon. v.p. 1993-99, counselor, 1999—), Phi Beta Kappa. Democrat. Roman Catholic. Home: 2922 45th St NW Washington DC 20016-3559 Office: Georgetown U Law Ctr 600 New Jersey Ave NW Washington DC 20001-2075

CARTER, BUTCH, professional basketball coach, former sports team executive. Grad., Ind. U. Player L.A. Lakers, 1980, Ind. Pacers, N.Y. Knicks, Phila. 76ers; coach Middletown (Ohio) H.S., 1986; asst. coach Long Beach (Calif.) State U., U. Dayton, 1989-91, Milw. Bucks, 1991-96; asst. coach Toronto Raptors, 1997-98, head coach, 1998—. Named 1988 Ohio Coach of the Year, AP. Achievements include NBA record for most points scored in an overtime period, 1984. Office: Toronto Raptors, 20 Bay St Ste 1702, Toronto, ON Canada M5J 2N8*

CARTER, CAROL, artist, educator; b. Sumter, S.C., Sept. 22, 1955; d. Samuel and Jane (Downs) C.; m. Jeffrey B. Clark, Nov. 25, 1977; 1 child, Evan. BA, Principia Coll., 1977; MFA, Washington U., St. Louis, 1984. Gallery owner, oper. Rockport, Mass., 1976-79, St. Louis, 1976-79; tech. asst. photography Washington U., 1983, tchg. asst. three dimensional design, 1983-84; asst. B.Z. Wagman Gallery, St. Louis, 1985-86; watercolor instr. Fine Arts Inst. Washington U., 1985-92; vis. artist Metro Honors Art, St. Louis, 1988, 90, U. Denver, 1989; drawing instr. Sch. Architecture Washington U., 1989-90; watercolor instr. St. Louis C.C., 1995. One-woman shows include Keane-Mason Gallery, N.Y.C., 1981, B.Z. Wagman Gallery, 1986, 87, Diane Nelson Gallery, Laguna, Cal., 1990, Galleria Biagas, Detroit, 1993, Stein-Bartlow Gallery, Chgo., 1994, Duane Reed Gallery, St. Louis, 1995; exhibited at group shows at Bixby Gallery, St. Louis, 1988, Nan Miller Gallery, Rochester, N.Y., 1989, Wichita Art Mus., Kans., 1991, Springfield Art Mus., Mo., 1991, Strecker Gallery, Manhattan, Kans., 1993, R. Duane Reed Gallery, St. Louis, 1994. Recipient Internat. Exhbn. Watercolor award, 1981, Merit award William Woods Coll., 1983, Juror's award Bradley Nat., 1985, Grumbacher award Nat. Watercolor Show, 1988, Purchase award Springfield Art Mus., 1991, Fellowship award Mid Am Arts Alliance-Nat. Endowment for Art, 1995, Art award Nat. Assn. Women Bus. Owners, 1998. Mem. Art St. Louis. Christian Scientist. Avocation: running. Home: 4450 Laclede Ave Saint Louis MO 63108-2204*

CARTER, CHRIS, producer, director; b. Bellflower, Calif., Oct. 13, 1957; m. Dori Pierson, 1989—. Dir. The X-Files, 1993; writer The B.R.A.T. Patrol; composer (movie) In the Shadow of the Sun, 1980, (TV series) Rags to Riches, 1987; co-prodr. (TV series) Rags to Riches, 1989; exec. prodr., creator The X-Files, 1993, Millenium, 1996; prodr. (film): The X-Files, 1998; prodr. (TV series) Harsh Realm, 1999. Named one of Time Mags. Most Influential Ams., 1997. Office: Broder Kurland Webb Uffner c/o Elliott Webb 9242 Beverly Blvd Ste 200 Beverly Hills CA 90210-3731*

CARTER, CHRISTINE SUE, cardiac recovery nurse; b. Dover, Ohio, Feb. 22, 1958; d. Theodore Louis and Mary Louise (Rossi) Rondinella; m. Robert Keith Carter, Aug. 16, 1986; children: Amanda Marie, Timothy Robert. BSN, U. Akron, 1980. CCRN. Staff nurse gen. med. unit Riverside Meth. Hosp., Columbus, Ohio, 1980-82, staff nurse, charge nurse intermediate care unit, 1982-84, staff nurse, occassional charge nurse coronary care unit, 1984-87, asst. nurse mgr. invasive recovery unit, 1987—, mem. critical care edn. com., 1992—; speaker, lectr. in field; CPR instr. Mem., conf. speaker Am. Heart Assn., Columbus, 1985. Mem. AACN (cert.), Ohio Nurses' Assn., Sigma Theta Tau. Democrat. Roman Catholic. Avocation: child-rearing issues. Home: 2261 Lane Rd Columbus OH 43220-2962 Office: Riverside Meth Hosp 3535 Olentangy River Rd Columbus OH 43214-3998

CARTER, CLARENCE HOLBROOK, artist; b. Portsmouth, Ohio, Mar. 26, 1904; s. Clarence William and Hettie May (Holbrook) C.; m. Mary B. Griswold, May 4, 1929; children: John Holbrook, Peter Griswold, Clarence Blakesley. Student, Cleve. Sch. Art, 1923-27; studied abroad under, H. Hofman, Capri, Italy, summer 1927; PhD (hon.), Moravian Coll., 1994. Instr. Cleve. Mus. Art, 1930-37; asst. prof. painting and design Carnegie Inst. Tech., Pitts., 1938-44; guest instr. painting Cleve. Inst. Art, summer 1948, Mpls. Sch. Art., fall 1949, Lehigh U., 1954, Ohio U., 1955; Atlanta Art Inst., 1957; guest artist U. Iowa, Spring 1970; artist-in-residence Lafayette Coll., 1961-69, cons., 1970-71; guest artist Kent State U., 1975, Iowa State U., Ames, 1975; gen. supt. Fed. Art Project, Cleve. Dist., 1937-38. Represented in permanent collections: Met. Mus., Mus. Modern Art, Whitney Mus. Am. Art, Chase Manhattan Bank, Citibank, all N.Y.C., Bklyn. Mus., Phila. Mus. Art, Prudential Ins. Co. Am., Pfizer Co., N.Y.C., Mich. Bell, Detroit, Southwestern Bell, Allied Bank of Houston, Columbus Mus. Fine Arts, Cleve. Mus. Art, Schumacher Gallery Capital Univ., Columbus, Ohio, Toledo Mus. Art, San Francisco Mus. Modern Art, San Francisco, Stanford U. Mus. Art, Calif., Allentown Mus. Art, Pa., Los Angeles Athletic Club, Public Service Electric and Gas Co., Newark, Noyes Mus., Oceanville, N.J., Springfield (Mass.) Mus. Fine Arts, New Britain (Conn.) Mus. Am. Art, Newark Pub. Library, Arnot Art Mus., Elmira, N.Y., Meml. Art Gallery, Rochester, N.Y., Herbert F. Johnson Mus. Art, Cornell U., Ithaca, N.Y., Newark Mus., Montclair (N.J.) Art Mus., N.J. State Mus., Trenton, Fogg Art Mus. Harvard U., Mus. Fine Arts, Boston, Boston Pub. Library, Zimmerli Art Mus., Rutgers U., New Brunswick, N.J., Corcoran Gallery Art, Washington, Nat. Collection Art, Washington, Nat. Mus. Am. Art, Washington, Hirshorn Mus., Washington, U. Md. Art Gallery, College Pk., Ackland Art Mus. U. N.C., Chapel Hill, Davidson Coll. Art Gallery, N.C., Mead Art Mus. Amherst (Mass.) Coll., Colgate U., Hamilton, N.Y., Univ. Art Gallery, Va. Poly. Inst. and State U., Blacksburg, Strathmore Hall Arts Ctr., Butler Inst. Am. Art, Youngstown, Ohio, Allen Meml. Art. Mus., Oberlin Coll., Coll. of Wooster (Ohio) Art Center, Kent (Ohio) State U., Ohio U., Athens, Sheldon Swope Art Gallery, Terre Haute, Ind., Kalamazoo (Mich.) Inst. Arts, Atkins Mus., Nelson Gallery Art, Kansas City, Mo., Okla. Art Center, Oklahoma City, Mus. Art, U. Okla., Norman, U. Tex. Art Mus. at Austin, Philbrook Art Center, Tulsa, Norton Art Mus., West Palm Beach, Fla., Sheldon Meml. Art Gallery, U. Nebr., Lincoln, Pasadena (Calif.) Mus. Modern Art, Miami U., Fla., The Discovery Mus., Bridgeport, Conn., So. Ohio Mus. and Cultural Center, Portsmouth, Mus. Boymans-Van Beuningen, Rotterdam, Netherlands, Victoria and Albert Mus., London, Eng., Baukunst, Cologne, West Germany, Ursinus Coll. Gallery of Art, Collegeville, Pa., Mitchel Wolfson Jr. Collection, Macedonian Ctr. of Contemporary Art, Thessaloniki, Greece; executed murals for sect. of painting and sculpture, Treasury Dept., Portsmouth, Ohio and Ravenna, Ohio Post offices, murals for Cleve. Pub. Auditorium, David Sarnoff Research Ctr. Princeton U.; tapestry for Morris R. Williams Ctr. for Arts, Lafayette Coll, Easton, Pa.; represented by: Hirschl and Adler Galleries, N.Y.C., Fairweather Hardin Gallery, Chgo., Lewis A. Shepherd Works of Art, Worcester, Mass., F.B. Horowitz Fine Art, Hopkins, Minn., Harmon-Meek Gallery, Naples, Fla., David Lusenhop Fine Art, Cin.; retrospective one-man shows in largest cities; represented in exhibit 200 Years of Am. Painting, Tate Gallery, London, 1946; European tour of Modern Am. Art, 1955-56, Am. Trauma and Depression 1920/40; 10 paintings, Berlin, Hamburg, 1980-81, S.A.; gathering material for series of paintings for Alcoa S.S. Co., 1944. Recipient 1st prize oils, 1943, 1st prize water color, 1944, Popular prize, Painting in U.S., Carnegie Inst., 1943, First popularity prize, 1936, 1st prize for oils, 1940, 2d prize for oils, 1943, Youngstown, Ohio, Cleve, Butler medal for Life Achievement in Am. Art, Creative Arts award, 1972, Ohio Gov. award, 1984, N.J. Gov. award, 1976, 89, Walt Whitman Creative Arts award State of N.J., 1993; monograph with 100 full color reprodns. Clarence Holbrook Carter pub. by Rizzoli Internat. Publs., 1989. Mem. N.A.D. Conglist. Home: 251 Shire Rd Milford NJ 08848-1721 *My desire from early childhood was to be an artist. To this end I dedicated my life. I ordered my life to accomplish the ideals that I set for myself and would never let anything interfere with this end. I would only tolerate my best. I rigidly guarded my health to better perform my work. Part of my credo has always been not to allow myself to repeat any past successes. Rather, I prefer to stimulate myself constantly with new concepts. I never developed any theories, as I knew that they would fence me in. A free mobility is part of my everyday existence. For this reason the zest for creation never seems to flag.*

CARTER, CRIS, professional football player; b. Middletown, Ohio, Nov. 25, 1965. Student, Ohio State U. With Phila. Eagles, 1987-89; wide received Minn. Vikings, 1990—. Selected to Pro Bowl, 1993, 95; named to The Sporting News NFL All-Pro team, 1994. Holds NFL single-season record for most pass receptions, 122, 1994. Office: Minn Vikings 9520 Viking Dr Eden Prairie MN 55344-3898*

CARTER, DALE LAVELLE, professional football player; b. Covington, Ga., Nov. 28, 1969. Student, Ellsworth C.C., U. Tenn. Cornerback, punt returner Kansas City (Mo.) Chiefs, 1992-98, Denver Broncos, 1998—. Named to Coll. All-Am. 1st Team, Sporting News, 1990, 91; named to NFL Pro Bowl Team, 1994, 95, 96. Office: c/o Denver Broncos 13655 Broncos Pky Englewood CO 80112*

CARTER, DALE WILLIAM, psychologist; b. Woodbury, N.J., Jan. 27, 1949; s. Charles Elmer and Dorothy Adele (Seibold) C. BS, Wake Forest U., 1971; MS, Radford U., 1976; PhD, U. Ga., 1982. Tchr. Gaston Day Sch., Gastonia, N.C., 1971-73, Charlotte (N.C.) Country Day Sch., 1973-74; psychologist Roanoke County Schs., Salem, Va., 1976-83; psychologist Gwinnett County Schs., Lawrenceville, Ga., 1983-94, coord. psychol. svcs., 1994—; pvt. practice Lilburn, Ga., 1985-93, Norcross, Ga., 1994—; adj. prof. Mercer U., Atlanta, 1984-85; cons. N.E. Consulting Ctr., Lawrenceville, 1985-92; intern supervision Gwinnett County Schs., Lawrenceville, 1985—. Mem. APA (div. sch. psychology), Ga. Assn. Sch. Psychologists, Nat. Assn. Sch. Psychologists, Beta Beta Beta, Kappa Delta Pi, Phi Kappa Phi. Home: # 1907 6115 Abbott's Bridge Rd Duluth GA 30097 Office: Gwinnett County Schs 52 Gwinnett Dr Lawrenceville GA 30045-5624

CARTER, DANIEL PAUL, lawyer, educator; b. Massillon, Ohio, Mar. 22, 1948; s. Harry A. and Anna Jean (Steiner) C.; m. Regina Ranieri, July 9, 1983; children: Emily Hedges, Daniel Paul Jr., Anne Baldwin, Elizabeth Regina. BS, St. Joseph's Coll., Phila., 1971; JD, Villanova U., 1974. Bar: Pa. 1974, U.S. Dist. Ct. (ea. dist.) Pa. 1980, U.S. Ct. Appeals (3d cir.) 1981, U.S. Dist. Ct. (mid. dist.) Pa. 1985, U.S. Ct. Claims 1986, U.S. Dist Ct. (we. dist.) Pa. 1989, U.S. Supreme Ct. 1991, U.S. Ct. Appeals (1st cir.) 1995, U.S. Dist. Ct. (no. dist.) Ohio 1996. Asst. prof. of law, dir. admissions Widener U., Wilmington, Del., 1974-79; ptnr. LaBrum & Doak, Phila., 1979-86, Shaffer, Palma, Dougherty & Carter, West Chester, Pa., 1986-87, Murphy & O'Connor, Phila., 1988-90; founding ptnr. Timby Brown & Timby, Phila., 1990-96; ptnr., head environ. dept. Buckley King & Bluso, Cleve., 1996—; counsel jury study Delaware County, Media, Pa., 1976; adj. prof. law Widener U., 1984—. legal counsel Pa. Young Reps., 1977-78; regional legal counsel Young Rep. Nat. Fedn., 1978-79. Named One of Outstanding Young Men of Am., Jaycees, 1979. Mem. ABA, Del. County Bar Assn., Chester County Bar Assn., Phila. Bar Assn., Pa. Bar Assn. (vice chmn. law sch. liaison 1981-82). Republican. Presbyterian. Home: 30651 Brookwood Dr Pepper Pike OH 44124-5422 Office: Buckley King & Bluso 1400 Bank One Bldg Cleveland OH 44114-2652

CARTER, DANIEL ROLAND, lawyer; b. Shreveport, La., Aug. 6, 1956; s. Jerry Glen and Sandra Jane (Roland) Griffith; m. Lauri Ann Witek, Nov. 13, 1993. BA in Polit. Sci., La. Tech. U., 1979, BSChemE, 1983; JD, South Tex. Coll. Law, 1991. Bar: Tex. 1991, U.S. Dist. Ct. (so., no., ea. and we. dists.) Tex. Prodn. engr. Transco Exploration & Prodn. Co., Houston, 1982-83; transmission engr. Transcontinental Gas Pipe Line Corp., Houston, 1984-87, environ. engr., 1987-88, sr. environ. engr., 1988-91, atty., 1991-95; sr. assoc. Phillips & Akers, Houston, 1995-98; chief legal officer NATCO Group Inc., Houston, 1998—. Mem. Tex. Bar Assn., Houston Bar Assn., Tex. Soc. Profl. Engrs., La. Tech. Alumni Assn. (bd. dirs.), Phi Delta Phi, Tau Beta Pi, Phi Alpha Theta, Order of the Lytae. Republican. Baptist. Avocations: running, reading, wines, travel, cooking. Home: 1706 Lofty Maple Trl Kingwood TX 77345-1936 Office: NATCO Group Inc 2950 North Loop W Houston TX 77092-8839

CARTER, DAVID EDWARD, communications executive; b. Ashland, Ky., Nov. 24, 1942; s. Victor Byron and Lillie Elzena (Clarke) C.; m. Linda Louise Gibson, May 31, 1969; children: Christa Ann, Lauren Louise. AB, U. Ky., 1965; MS, Ohio U., 1967; MBA, Syracuse U., 1995; SMM, Harvard Bus. Sch., 1995, OPM, Harvard Bus Sch., 1998. Dir. advt. Wheeler & Williams Co., Ashland, 1965-66; instr. U. Ky., 1967-70; dir. communications Ky. Electric Steel Co., Ashland, 1970-77; pres. David E. Carter Inc., Ashland, 1977—; pres. Hollywood Ky. Corp. div. David E. Carter Inc., Ashland, Bangkok, Jakarta, Caracas, Hong Kong, 1986—; bd. dirs. Home Fed. Savs. & Loan Assn., Ashland, Decathlon Corp., Hanover Pub. Co.; exec. adv. bd. Ohio U. Sch. Bus.; alumni bd. dirs. U. Ky. Sch. Journalism; adj. prof. Thammasat U., Bangkok, 1992—. Scoutmaster, Tri-State Area Council Boy Scouts Am., 1970-77, dist. commr., 1977-78, recipient dist. award of merit, 1975, Recipient Clio award, N.Y.C., 1980, Disting. Alumnus award Ashland Community Coll., 1990. Mem. Nat. Acad. TV Arts and Scis. (3 Emmys for writing TV programs 1987), N.Y. Art Dirs. Club (2 Emmys for producing pub. TV program 1990, Am. Inst. Graphic Arts. Republican. Methodist. Author: It's Not the Money—It's The Principle, 1975, Book of American Trade Marks, 11 vols., 1972-89, Designing Corporate Symbols, 1975, Corporate Identity Manuals, 1976, Letterheads 7 vols., 1977-89, Ideas for Editors, 1977, Letterheads 5 vols. 1979-89, American Corporate Identity 5 vols. 1985-89, Designing Corporate Identity for Small Companies, 1985, How to Improve Your Corporate Identity, 1986, Logos of Major American Companies, 1989, International Corporate Design Symbols, 1990, Logos of Major World Corporations, 1990, World Corporate Identity, 1990; writer, producer: (TV series) Sassafrass, 1987-88; producer more than 12 sketches for The Johnny Carson Show, 1989-91 (2 Emmys, 1991). Avocations: sports collectibles, golf, photography. Home: 4727 Southern Hills Dr Ashland KY 41102-8213 also: 3225 W Gulf Dr Unit B-301 Sanibel FL 33957-5647 Office: PO Box 2500 Ashland KY 41105-2500

CARTER, DAVID GEORGE, SR., university administrator; b. Dayton, Ohio, Oct. 25, 1942; s. Richard Walter and Esther Mae (Dunn) C.; children: Ehrika Aileen, Jessica Faye, David George Jr. BS, Cen. State U., 1965; MEd, Miami U., 1968; PhD, Ohio State U., 1971. Cert. elem. tchr., Ohio. Prin. Dayton Pub. Schs., 1969-70, supr., 1970-71, unit facilitator, dist. supt., 1971-73; asst. and assoc. prof. Pa. State U., State College, 1972-77; assoc. dean and prof. edn. U. Conn., Storrs, 1977-82, assoc. v.p. acad. affairs, 1982-88; pres. East Conn. State U., Willimantic, 1988—. Contbr. articles to profl. jours. Bd. dirs. New England Regional Exch., Framingham, Mass., 1981-86, Haitian Health Found.; mem. Gov.'s Task Force on Jail and Prison Overcrowding. Named Young Man of Yr. Dayton C. of C., 1973, Disting. Alumnus Ctrl. State U., Wilberforce, Ohio, 1988; inducted into Donald K. Anthony Achievement Hall of Fame Ctrl. State U., 1993; recipient Roy Wilkins Civil Rights award NAACP, 1994; 39th Americanism award Conn. Am. Legion, 1994. Mem. Nat. Orgn. Legal Problems of Edn. (bd. dirs. 1980-83), NCAA (chair pres.' commn. divsn. III 1995—, pres.'s commn. 1991—), Am. Ednl. Rsch. Orgn., Phi Delta Kappa, Pi Lambda Theta, Phi Kappa Phi, Sigma Pi Phi. Home: 9 Charles Ln Storrs CT 06268-2308 Office: East Conn State U 83 Windham St Willimantic CT 06226-2211

CARTER, DAVID LAVERE, soil scientist, researcher, consultant; b. Tremonton, Utah, June 10, 1933; s. Gordon Ray and Mary Eldora (Hirschi) C.; m. Virginia Beutler, June 1, 1953; children: Allen David, Roger Gordon, Brent Ryan. BS, Utah State U., 1955, MS, 1957; PhD, Oreg. State U., 1961. Soil scientist USDA Agrl. Research Service, Corvallis, Oreg., 1956-60; research soil scientist, line project leader USDA Agrl. Research Service, Weslaco, Tex., 1960-65; rsch. soil scientist USDA Agrl. Rsch. Svc., Kimberly, Idaho, 1965-68, supervisory soil scientist, rsch. leader, 1968-86, supervisory soil scientist, rsch. leader, dir., 1986-96; pvt. cons. Kimberly, 1996—; cons., adviser to many projects and orgns. Contbr. articles to profl. jours.; author, co-author books. Recipient Emmett J. Culligan award World

Water Soc. Fellow Am. Soc. Agronomy (cert.), Soil Sci. Soc. Am. (cert.); mem. Soil Conservation Soc. Am. (Soil Conservation award 1985), AAAS, Internat. Soc. Soil Sci., Western Soc. Soil Sci., CAST, Internat. Soc. Soil Sci., OPEDA. Mormon.

CARTER, DAVID RAY, lawyer; b. Middletown, Ohio, Jan. 15, 1947; s. Vernon Robert and Lucy Lee (Harp) C.; m. Victoria Lee Hunt, Nov. 1, 1980; children: Mathew, Adam. BS, U. Fla., 1969; MS, Fla. State U., 1970; MD, U. Fla., 1974; JD, Stetson U., 1977. Bar: Fla. 1978. Assoc. Delzer, Coulter & Carter, Port Richey, Fla., 1978-87; pvt. practice, New Port Richey, 1987—; ptnr. Carter & Charnock, New Port Richey, 1990-92, Carter & Kelly, P.A., New Port Richey, 1996-97. Mem. Fla. Bar Assn. (exec. com. 1997-98, chmn. realtor-atty. joint com., Outstanding Svc. award 1997), Hernando County Bar Assn. (pres. 1982-84), Hernando County Assn. Realtors (atty.), Greater Clearwater Assn. Realtors. Republican. Avocations: tennis, scuba, bridge, boating, snow skiing. Home: 353 N Highland Ave Tarpon Springs FL 34689-8948 Office: 7419 Hwy 19 New Port Richey FL 34652

CARTER, DENNIS LEE, marketing professional; b. Louisville, Oct. 23, 1951; s. Bernard Lee and Opal Delores (Jaggers) C.; m. Janice Lea Herbert, Dec. 31, 1976; children: Serra Kimberly, Scott Winston. BSEE, BS in Physics, Rose Hulman Inst., Terre Haute, Ind., 1973; MSEE, Purdue U., 1974, DSc (hon.), 1996; MBA, Harvard U., 1981. Instr. elec. engring. tech. Purdue U., West Lafayette, Ind., 1975; collateral engr. Rockwell-Collins, Cedar Rapids, Iowa, 1975-76, design engr., 1976-79; product mktg. engr. Intel Corp., Santa Clara, Calif., 1981-83, software products mktg. mgr., 1983-85, tech. asst. to pres., 1985-89, end-user mktg. mgr., 1989-90, gen. mgr. end-user components divsn., 1990-91, dir. corp. mktg., 1991-92, v.p., dir. corp. mktg., 1992-98; v.p., dir. strategic mktg. Intel Corp., Santa Clara, 1998—. Inventor radio reception path monitor for a diversity sys., 1985. Episcopalian. Avocation: baseball fan. Office: Intel Corp RN5-20 2200 Mission College Blvd Santa Clara CA 95054-1549*

CARTER, DONALD J., wholesale distribution, manufacturing executive. CEO Home Interiors & Gifts, Dallas. Office: Home Interiors & Gifts 4550 Spring Valley Rd Dallas TX 75244-3705*

CARTER, DONALD K., architectural firm executive; b. Pitts., Apr. 27, 1942. BArch, Carnegie Mellon U., 1967; postgrad., U. Edinburgh, Scotland, 1969-70, Harvard U., 1974. Registered arch., Pa. Sr. planner Southwestern Pa. Regional Planning Commn., Pitts., 1970-73; arch., planner UDA Archs., Pitts., 1973-75, assoc., 1975-79, prin., 1979-87, mng. ptnr., 1987—, mng. prin. ptnr., 1987—; vis. critic in architecture Carnegie Mellon U.; vis. critic Grad. Sch. Internat. and Pub. Affairs U. Pitts. Prin. projects include East St. Valley Expressway, Pitts., The Oakland Plan, Pitts., Warren (Ohio) Downtown Plan and Streetscape Design, La Roche Coll., McCandless, Pa., Greater Pitts. Internat. Airport, Allegheny County, Pa., Walten Woods on the Lake, Erie, Pa., Thiel Coll., Greenville, Pa., Mpls.-St. Paul Airport, Hubbard Expressway Devel., Youngstown, Ohio, New Town of Chabarovice, Czech Republic, Steel Industry Heritage Project, Pitts., Novokuznetsk 2010 Plan, Siberia, Russia, many others; prin. architecture includes Gananda (N.Y.) Neighborhood Ctr., Scots Pavilion, Pitts., Warburton's Hot Bread Factory, Pitts., Froggy Roadhouse, Mt. Lebanon, Pa., Liberty Ctr., Pitts., Metropol Indsl. Ctr., Aliquippa, Pa., Clayton, Pitts., Hyatt Hotel at Chatham Ctr., Pitts., Carnegie Mellon Univ. Ctr., Pitts., Andy Warhol Mus., Pitts., Crawford Sq., Pitts., Pitts. Air and Space Mus., Clarksburg (W.Va.) Mcpl. Bldg., Thiel Coll. Howard Miller Ctr., others. Bd. dirs. Pitts. Downtown Partnership, 1994—, Found. for Abraxas, 1981-89, Pitts. Zool. Soc., 1989—, v.p., 1992—, Leadership Pitts. Alumni Assn., 1987-92, pres., 1990; mem. steering com. Leadership Pitts., 1988—, chair program com., 1991—; chair long range planning com. St. Andrew's Episc. Ch., Highland Park, Calif., 1989; mem. awards com. Greater Pitts. Commn. for Women, 1990-93; mem. awards jury Pitts. Best Deal, 1991—; mem. devel. panel chair Allegheny County 2001 Plan, 1991-92; chair La Roche Coll. Bd. Regents, 1993—; active Swissvale Borough Planning Commn., 1974-79, Swissvale Area Sch. Bd. Citizens Adv. Com., 1975, Regent Sq. Civic Assn. Bd., 1975-80, Wilkins Sch. Cmty. Ctr. Bd., 1979-83. 1st lt. U.S. Army Corps Engrs., 1967-69. Fellow AIA (chmn. design jury for Cin. chpt. Awards 1983, bd. dirs. Pitts. chpt. 1980-87, pres. 1983, bd. dirs. Charitable Assn. 1987-90); mem. Am. Inst. Cert. Planners, Am. Planning Assn., Pa. Soc. Archs. (bd. dirs. 1984-87), Urban Land Inst. (dist. coord. Pitts. area 1990—). Office: UDA Architects Gulf Tower 31st Fl 707 Grant St Pittsburgh PA 15219*

CARTER, DONALD PATTON, advertising executive; b. Richmond, Mo., July 30, 1927; s. R.D. and Lillian (Patton) C.; m. Susan Virginia Wurst, Apr. 22, 1950 (dec. Apr. 1980); children: Jeffrey, Stephen, Carol; m. Carol Holzrichter, Dec. 27, 1983. Student, U. Louisville, 1945-46; BS, U. Mo., 1948; MBA, U. Pa., 1950. With Continental Color Press, Inc., Kansas City, Mo., 1950-52; pres. Nasco, Inc., Kansas City, Kans., 1953-54; v.p., then pres. Biddle Co., Bloomington, Ill., 1955-68; pres. Post Keyes Gardner Inc., Chgo., 1968-78, also bd. dirs.; past chmn., pres. Cunningham & Walsh Inc., Chgo., N.Y., 1978-83; exec. v.p. Cunningham & Walsh Inc., N.Y., 1978-83, also bd. dirs.; chmn. bd. dirs. Modu-line Industries, 1982-97; tchr. econs. and bus. adminstrn. Kansas City (Mo.) Jr. Coll., 1950-52; trustee Thomson-McKinnon Mutual Funds, 1983-96, PIMCO Multi-Mgr. Mut. Funds, 1996—. *Donald P. Carter worked at the Continental Color Press Inc. in Kansas City, Missouri from 1950-52. In 1953 he formed Nasco in Kansas City, Kansas. He sold the company in 1955 and joined the first of several advertising agencies: the Biddle Company of Bloomington, Illinois, where he served as vice president, then president and with the board of directors from 1955-68. He was then president and with the board of directors of Post Keyes Gardner Inc. in Chicago, from 1968-78. He held the positions of president, chairman, executive vice president and with the board of directors of Cunningham & Walsh, in Chicago, from 1978-83 until his retirement.* With USNR, 1945-47. Named Young Man of Yr. Jr. C. of C., 1961. Mem. Knollwood Country Club, Bob O'Link Golf Club, Phi Kappa Psi. Home: 434 Stable Ln Lake Forest IL 60045-2799

CARTER, EDWARD CARLOS, II, librarian, historian; b. Rochester, N.Y., Jan. 10, 1928; s. Paul Epler and Elizabeth (Johnston) C.; m. Theresa Howard, Mar. 24, 1951 (div. 1976); 1 dau., Laura Coffin Carter (dec.); m. Louise Devine Bucknell, Oct. 11, 1976. AB, U. Pa., 1954, MA, 1956; PhD, Bryn Mawr Coll., 1962. Vis. lectr. history U. Pa., Phila., 1962-64; chmn. dept. history St. Stephen's Sch., Rome, 1965-69; prof. history Cath. U. Am., Washington, 1969-80; editor-in-chief Papers of Benjamin Henry Latrobe, Balt., 1970-95; adj. prof. history U. Pa., 1980—; librarian Am. Philos. Soc., Phila., 1980—; fellow Huntington Libr., Phila., 1989; mem. adv. coun. Phila. Ctr. Early Am. Studies, 1981—; mem. adv. bd. Hagley Found., 1984-86; mem. coun. Inst. Early Am. History and Culture, 1985-88; dir. Nat. Lewis and Clark Bicentennial Coun. Mem. editl. bd. Papers of Benjamin Franklin, 1985—, Papers of William Penn, 1978, Von Steuben Papers, 1976, Papers of Charles Willson Peale, 1980—; co-editor: Enterprise and Entrepreneurs in 19th and 20th Century France, 1976; editor: Microfich edit. Papers of Benjamin Henry Latrobe, 1976; Va. Jours. of Benjamin Henry Latrobe, 2 vols., 1977, Jours. of Benjamin Henry Latrobe: From Philadelphia to New Orleans, 1980, Latrobe's View of America, 1985, Beyond Confederation: Origins of the Constitution and American Identity, 1987, One Grand Pursuit: A Brief History of the American Philosophical Society, 1743-1993, 1993, Papers of Bejamin Henry Latrobe, 10 vol., 1995. Chmn. bd. trustees St. Stephen's Sch., Rome, 1982-85, 90-92. Served with U.S. Army, 1946-47. Fellow Huntington Libr., 1989. Mem. Ind. Rsch. Librs. Assn. (chmn. 1988-91), Am. Philos. Soc., Am. Antiquarian Soc. Clubs: Cosmos (Washington); Merion Golf (Ardmore, Pa.). Home: 15 S Valley Forge Rd Wayne PA 19087-4750

CARTER, EDWARD GRAYDON, editor; b. Canada, July 14, 1949; s. E.P. and Margaret Ellen C.; m. Cynthia Williamson, 1982; 4 children. Student, Carleton U., U. Ottawa. Editor The Can. Rev., 1973-77; writer Time, 1978-83, Life, N.Y.C., 1983-86; founder, editor Spy, 1986-91; editor N.Y. Observer, 1991-92; hon. editor Harvard Lampoon, 1989; editor in chief Vanity Fair, N.Y.C., 1992—. Mem. Washington (Conn.) Club. Avocation: fly fishing. Office: Vanity Fair 350 Madison Ave New York NY 10017-3704*

CARTER, ELEANOR ELIZABETH, business manager; b. Durham, N.C., July 16, 1954; d. Joseph William Jr. and Sheila Dale (Swartz) C. BS in Social Work, N.C. State U., 1977. Field worker family planning Wake County Health Dept., Raleigh, N.C., 1975-76; sales rep. Bristol-Myers Products, N.C., 1977-80; regional adminstn. asst. Bristol-Myers Products, Dallas, Tex., 1980; regional trainer Bristol-Myers Products, Washington, N.C., Va., 1980; sales adminstrn. mgr. corp. hdqrs. Bristol-Myers Products, N.Y.C., 1980-81; dist. supr. Bristol-Myers Products, Cin., 1981-82; account rep. Fuji Photo Film U.S.A., Inc., Cin., 1982-83; spl. account mgr. Fuji Photo Film U.S.A., Inc., Chgo., 1983-90; nat. account mgr. Fuji Photo Film U.S.A., Itasca, Ill., 1991-97, v.p. nat. accounts, 1997—. Mem. NAFE, Alpha Kappa Delta. Presbyterian. Avocations: jogging, horseback riding, travel, dancing. Office: Fuji Photo Film USA Inc 1285 Hamilton Pkwy Itasca IL 60143-1147

CARTER, ELLIOTT COOK, JR., composer; b. N.Y.C., Dec. 11, 1908; s. Elliott Cook and Florence (Chambers) C.; m. Helen Frost-Jones, July 6, 1939; 1 child, David. AB, Harvard U., 1930, AM, 1932, MusD (hon.), 1970; MusD (hon.), New Eng. Conservatory Music, 1961, Swarthmore Coll., 1956, Princeton U., 1967, Boston U., 1970, Yale, 1970, Oberlin Coll., 1970, Cambridge U., Eng., 1983. Music dir. George Balachine's Ballet Caravan, 1936-40; teacher St. John's Coll., Annapolis, Md., 1940-42; cons. O.W.I., 1943-44; tchr. Greek and math.; tchr. music theory and composition Peabody Conservatory, Balt., 1946-48; dir., pres. Amer. Section, International Soc. for Contemporary Music, 1946-52; assoc. prof. music Columbia U., N.Y.C., 1948-50; prof. of composition Queen's Coll., N.Y.C., 1955-56; tchr. in Am. studies Salzburg Seminars, Austria, 1958; lecturer, music seminar Princeton U., 1959-60; prof. of composition Yale U., New Haven, Conn., 1960-62; American delegate East-West Encounter, Tokyo, 1962; composer in residence Amer. Acad. in Rome, 1963, 1967, Amer. Sch., West Berlin, 1964; prof. of composition Julliard Sch. Music, New York, 1967-84; Andrew D. White Prof.-at-Large Cornell U., Ithaca, N.Y., 1967-68. Composer, symphonies/orchestral Symphony, Suite from Pocahontas (Juilliard publication awd., 1940), 1939, Symphony No. 1, 1942, Holiday Overture (1st prize, Independent Music Publishers Contest, 1945), 1944, Suite, From the Minotaur, 1947, Elegy, 1952, Variations for Orchestra, 1954-55, Double Concerto (Sibelius medal, 1961, Critics' Circle awd., 1961), Piano Concerto, 1964-65, Concerto for Orchestra, 1968-69, A Symphony of Three Orchestras, 1976, Penthode, 1984-85, A Celebration of Some 100 x 150 Notes, 1986, Oboe Concerto, 1988, Remembrance, 1988, Anniversary, 1989, Violin Concerto, 1990 (Grammy award "Best Contemporary Composition", 1994), Allegro Scorrevole, 1996 (Prince Rainier Found. Music award 1998), Clarinet Concerto, 1997; chamber/instrumental Canonic Suite (BMI publication prize, 1945), 1939, Pastoral, 1940, Elegy, 1941, Piano Sonata No.1, 1945-46, Woodwind Quintet, 1948, Cello Sonata, 1948, Eight Études and a Fantasy, 1949-50, Eight Pieces for Four Timpani/Recitative and Improvisation, 1950-66, String Quartet No.1, (1st prize International Quartet Competition, Liège, Belgium, 1953), 1950-51, Sonata, 1952, String Quartet No. 2 (Pulitzer prize for music, 1960, Critics' Circle awd., UNESCO awd., Naumburg awd., 1956), 1959, String Quartet No. 3, (Pulitzer prize for music, 1973), 1971, Canon for Three: In Memoriam Igor Stravinsky, 1971, Duo, 1973-74, Brass Quintet, 1974, A Fantasy About Purcell's Fantasia Upon One Note, 1974, Birthday Fanfare for Sir William Glock's 70th, 1978, Night Fantasies, 1980, Triple Duo, 1982-83, Changes, 1983, Canon for Four: Homage to William, 1984, Esprit rude/Esprit doux, 1984, Riconoscenza per Goffredo Petrassi, 1984, String Quartet No.4, 1986, Enchanted Preludes, 1988, 1994, Con Leggerezza Pensosa (Omaggio a Italo Calvino), 1990, Scrivo in Vento, 1991, Quintet for Piano and Winds, 1991, Trilogy for Harp and Oboe, 1992, Gra for clarinet alone, 1993, Figment for cello alone, 1994, Fragment for string quartet, 1994, esprit rude/esprit doux II, 1995, String Quartet No 5, 1995; 90 for piano, A Six-Letter Letter (for Paul Sacher's 90th Birthday) for English Horn alone, 1996, Luimen, 1997, Quintet for Piano and String Quartet, 1997, Tempo e tempi, 1998, Luimen, 1998; vocal,choral My Love is in a Light Attire, 1928, Tarantella, 1936, Harvest Home, To Music, Let's Be Gay, Heart Not So Heavy As Mine, Tell Me Where is Fancy Bred? 1938, The Defense of Corinth, 1941, Three Poems of Robert Frost, 1943, The Difference, The Harmony of Morning, 1944, Musicians Wrestle Everywhere, 1945, Emblems, 1947, A Mirror on whch to Dwell, 1975, Syringa, 1978, In Sleep, In Thunder, 1981, Of Challenge and Of Love, 1995; ballet Pochahontas, 1936, The Minotaur, 1947; opera What Next?, 1998; incidental music Philocetes, 1931, Mostellaria, 1936. Trustee Am. Acad. in Rome. Recipient Amer. Composers' Alliance prize, 1943; Acad.-Inst. awd. in Music, Amer. Acad. and Inst. of Arts and Letters, 1950; Guggenheim fellowships, 1945, 1950; Prix de Rome, 1953; Brandeis U. Creative Arts awd., 1965; Harvard Glee Club medal, 1967; Gold Medal, Amer. Acad. and Inst. of Arts and Letters, 1971; Handel medallion, 1978; Ernst von Siemens Musik-Preis, Munich, 1985; MacDowell medal, 1983, George Peabody medal, 1984; Nat. Medal of Arts, Nat. Endowment for the Arts, 1985; Commandeur dans l'Ordre des Arts et des Lettres, France, 1987; Commendatore in the Order of Merit of the Republic of Italy, 1991. Mem. League Composers (bd. dirs. 1939-52), Internat. Soc. Contemporary Music (bd. dirs. 1946-52, pres. U.S. sect. 1952), Nat. Inst. Arts and Letters, Am. Acad. Arts and Scis., Am. Composers Alliance (bd. dirs. 1939-52, treas. 1949-50), Acad. der Künste (Berlin), Acc. Santa Cecilia (Rome). Address: Boosey & Hawkes Inc 35 E 21st St New York NY 10010-6212

CARTER, EMILY ANN, physical chemist, researcher, educator; b. Los Gatos, Calif., Nov. 28, 1960; d. David and Rebecca (Blumberg) C.; m. Bruce E. Koel, 1994; 1 child, Adam. BS in Chemistry, U. Calif., Berkeley, 1982; PhD in Chemistry, Calif. Inst. Tech., 1987. Postdoctoral rsch. assoc. U. Colo., Boulder, 1987-88; asst. prof., physical chemistry UCLA, 1988-92, assoc. prof., 1992-94, prof., 1994—; mem. Defense Sci. Study Group, 1996-97. Mem. editl. bd. Jour. Phys. Chemistry and Surface Sci., 1994—, Encyclopedia Chemical Physics and Physical Chemistry 1996—, Chem. Phys. Letters, 1998—; contbr. numerous articles to tech. jours; given over 135 invited lectures. Recipient rsch. innovation recognition awards Union Carbide Co., 1990, 91, New Faculty award Camille and Henry Dreyfus Found., 1988; NSF Presdl. Young Investigator award, 1988, Dreyfus Tchr. Scholar award, 1992, Alfred P. Sloan fellow, 1993, Internat. Acad. of Quantum Molecular Sci. medal, 1993, Exxon faculty fellow, 1993, Peter Mark Meml. award Am Vacuum Soc., 1995, Dr. Lee vis. rsch. fellow Oxford U., 1996. Fellow Am. Vacuum Soc., Am. Phys. Soc.; mem. Am. Chem. Soc., Sigma Xi, Phi Beta Kappa. Democrat. Jewish. Avocations: theater, films, cooking, reading, tennis. Office: U California Dept Chem Box 951569 Los Angeles CA 90095-1569

CARTER, FRANCES MOORE, educator, writer; b. Washington; d. Joel Presley and Ora Emma Moore; m. Richard Dunn Carter, July 2, 1949 (dec. 1992); children: Karen Anne, Marcia Lee, Richard Dunn Jr. BA in English, Coll. of William and Mary, 1947; MA in Arts and Humanities, West Chester U., 1972; EdD in Edn. and Adminstrn., U. Pa., 1978. Cert. elem. and secondary tchr., secondary prin., curriculum and instrn. supr., supt., Pa. Elem. tchr. Chester-Upland Sch. Dist., Chester, Pa., 1968-69; tchr. in English and humanities Marple Newtown Sch. Dist., Newtown Square, Pa., 1969-78; adj. prof., English and edn. Villanova (Pa.) U., 1978-79; adj. prof. English and edn. St. Joseph's U., Phila., 1978-79; dir. career edn. Del. County Intermediate Unit, Media, Pa., 1979-83; dir. industry-edn. Del. County Partnership for Econ. Devel., Media, Pa., 1979-83; exec. dir. Chester (Pa.) Edn. Found., 1989-90; assoc. Career Solutions Planning Group, Paoli, Pa., 1990-93; pres. MicroGraph, Inc., Broomall, Pa., 1993-95; commr. Accrediting Commn. for Career Schs. and Colls. of Tech., Washington, 1990-94; bd. mem., exec. com., chair rev. com. Pa. State Bd. Pvt. Licensed Schs., Harrisburg, 1987-95; mem. Phila. Regional Labor Task Force, 1989-92. Author: (curriculum series) Employability and Life Skills Training, 1982, (book) Delaware County Job Planning Guide, 1982, Delaware County Training Resource Guide, 1983, Meeting the Challenge of Change, 1988; scriptwriter Cable TV series Solving the Job Puzzle, 1983. Chmn. bus./industry com. Partnership for Econ. Devel., Media, 1988-90; founder, dir. Clearinghouse for Edn./Industry, Delaware County, Pa., 1983-89; bd. mem., mem. exec. com., Resource Ctr. for Human Svcs., Phila., 1986-92, Leadership, Inc., Class of 1986-87; elder Presbyn. Ch. (U.S.A.), 1968—; bd. dirs. Girl Scouts of Del. County, Media, 1985-90, Girls Coalition S.E. Pa., sec., pres., 1983—; clk. of session Swarthmore (Pa.) Presbyn. Ch., 1993— elder, 1968—; mem. adv. bd. Pa. State U. (Lima campus), 1988—. Recipient Athena award Del. County C. of C., 1990, Educator of Yr. award, Nat. Assn. for Industry/Edn. Cooperation, 1989, Woman of Distinction award, Del. County Women's Commn., 1989, Disting. Svc. award, Del. County Coun., Media, 1988, Exemplary Achievement award Del. County Coun., 1984. Mem. Del. County Press Club (bd. dirs., chair comm. day 1987—), Phi Delta Kappa, Pi Lambda Theta, Mortarboard, Pi Beta Phi. Presbyterian. Avocations: reading, piano, theatre, sailing, travel. Home and Office: 77 S Rolling Rd Springfield PA 19064-2415

CARTER, FRANCES TUNNELL (FRAN CARTER), fraternal organization administrator; b. Springville, Miss.; d. David Atmond and Mary Annie (McCutcheon) Tunnell; m. John T. Carter; children: Wayne, Nell Branum. BS, U. So. Miss., 1946; MS, U. Tenn., 1948; EdD, U. Ill., 1954. Elem. sch. tchr. Thaxton, Miss., 1942-43, Cumberland, Miss., 1943-44; tchr. high sch. home econs. Randolph, Miss., 1944-45, Maben, Miss., 1946-47; instr. Wood Coll., Mathiston, Miss., 1948, East Central Jr. Coll., Decatur, Miss., 1948-49; prof. home econs. Clarke Coll., Newton, Miss., 1950-56; prof. Samford U., Birmingham, Ala., 1956-84; editor, children and youth products and resources Woman's Missionary Union, Birmingham, 1983-85; pres. CarterCraft, Inc., Birmingham, 1985-89; nat. exec. dir. Kappa Delta Epsilon, Birmingham, 1987—; vis. prof. Hong Kong Bapt. U., 1965-66, Anhui Normal U., People's Republic of China, 1987; tchr. workshops in China, 1988, 90, 92, 95; tchr. workshops in Indonesia, 1993; lectr. in symposium at invitation of Russian Edn. Ministry, Moscow, 1994, U. Nanjing, People's Republic of China, 1997; curriculum writer Bapt. Brotherhood Commn., 1986—; writer N.Am. Mission Bd., 1995—. Author: Sammy in the Country, 1960, Tween-Age Ambassador, 1970, Ching Fu and Jim, 1978; co-author: Sharing Times Seven, 1977, also short stories, articles; feature writer: Crusader Mag., 1986-95. Tchr. Sunday sch. Bapt. Ch., Birmingham, 1980—; mem., lt. col. CAP, 1968—, bd. dirs. Aerospace Edn. Ala. Wing, 1991-94, dir. pub. affairs regional S.E., 1994-95; v.p. Women's Civic Club of Birmingham, 1997—; placement officer ESL Sch., 1995—. Recipient Career Achievement award Profl. Fraternal Assn., 1988, Outstanding Alumnae award Wood Coll., 1992, Outstanding award Kappa Delta Pi, 1992, Brewer award for Aerospace Edn. Southeast region CAP, 1994; elected Birmingham's Woman of Yr., 1977, Birmingham's Vol. of Yr., 1980, Silver rep. Dist. 6 Ala. Nat. Silver Haired Congress, 1996—; named Ala. Silver Haired Legislator Dist. 55 Jefferson County, 1994-97, cert. Rosie the Riveter reunion, Little White House, Warm Springs, Ga., 1997. Mem. AARP (local pres. 1988-89, asst. state dir. 1989-93, Nat. Cmty. award 1992), Birmingham's Women C. of C. (pres. 1975-76), Nat. League of Am. Pen Women (3rd v.p. 1988-90, nat. pres. 1994-96), Ala. League of Pen Women (pres. 1970-72), Birmingham League of Am. Pen Women (pres. 1968-70, 76-78), Ala. Writers Conclave (pres. 1978-79), Ala. State Poetry Soc. (pres. 1979-82), Ala. Federated Women's Clubs (dist. dir. 1988-90, Outstanding Woman of Ala. Club award 1988), Freedoms Found. Valley Forge (pres. Birmingham Area chpt. 1990-91), Nat. Fellowship Bapt. Educators (sec. 1987-93), Birmingham Bus. and Profl. Club (pres. 1986-87), Am. Rosie the Riveter Assn. Inc. (founder, pres.), Kappa Delta Epsilon (nat. pres. 1980-85, co-dir. ESL Sch. 1994-98), Alpha Delta Kappa, Delta Kappa Gamma, Phi Delta Kappa. Home and Office: 2561 Rocky Ridge Rd Birmingham AL 35243-4442

CARTER, GALE BOATWRIGHT, hotel services executive; b. Toombs County, Ga., Dec. 20, 1949; d. Nathaniel O. Carter and Jeanne Cone Carter Evans; m. C.A. Goldenberg, Aug. 31, 1969 (div. May 1986); 1 child, Chadwick Ryan; m. Thomas Melvin Boatwright, July 13, 1991 (div. Sept. 1998). Student, U. Ga., 1967-69, Clayton Jr. Coll., 1971, Ga. State U., 1972. Br. ops. Nat. Bank Ga., Atlanta, 1972-74; sr. credit policy exec. Barnett Banks, Jacksonville, Fla., 1974-94, Enterprise Nat. Bank, Palm Beach, Fla., 1996; entrepreneur Courthouse Antiques, Walterboro, S.C., 1996-97; guest svc. rep. Hyatt Regency Westshore, Tampa, Fla., 1997—. Instr. Jr. Achievement, Orange Park, Fla., Am. Bankers Assn., New Port Rickey, Fla.; bd. dirs. Harbors Behavioral Health Inst., New Port Richey; participant Paint Your Heart Out, Red Cross Walkathon, St. John's Job Seekers Outreach, Charlotte, N.C.; loaned employee United Way; various other cmty. projects. Episcopalian. Avocations: grandmothering, reading, meditating, skiing, skating.

CARTER, GENE, federal judge; b. Milbridge, Maine, Nov. 1, 1935; s. K.W. and S. Loreta (Beal) C.; m. Judith Ann Kittredge, June 24, 1961; children: Matthew G., Mark G. BA, U. Maine, 1958, LLD (hon.), 1985; LLB, NYU, 1961. Bar: Maine 1962. Ptnr. Rudman, Winchell, Carter & Buckley (and predecessors), Bangor, Maine, 1965-80; assoc. justice Maine Supreme Jud. Ct., 1980-83; judge U.S. Dist. Ct. Maine, 1983-89, chief judge, 1989-96; chmn. adv. com. on rules of civil procedure Maine Supreme Jud. Ct., 1976-80. Chmn. Bangor Housing Authority, 1970-77; trustee Unity (Maine) Coll. Mem. Am. Trial Lawyers Assn., Internat. Soc. Barristers, Am. Coll. Trial Lawyers. Office: US Dist Ct 156 Federal St Portland ME 04101-4152

CARTER, GENE R., professional society administrator; b. Staunton, Va.. BA, Va. State U.; MA, Boston U.; EdD, Columbia U., 1973; LLD (hon.), Va. State U.; LittD, Old Dominion U. Various teaching and ednl. adminstrv. pos., 1960-92; exec. dir. ASCD, 1992—; cons. various colls. and univs.; adj. prof. Old Dominion U. Mem. vis. com. Lehigh U. Coll. Edn.; mem. bd. trustees So. Edn. Found.; mem. bd. dirs. Norfolk So. Corp.; mem. edn. commn. States Adv. Bd. Recipient Brotherhood citation Nat. Conf. of Christians and Jews, 1985, Presdl. citation Nat. Assn. Equal Oppty. in Higher Edn., 1985, Outstanding Sch. Supt. in Va. in 1985 award John F. Kennedy Ctr. for the Performing Arts, 1985, Nat. Supt. of the Yr. award Am. Assn. Sch. Adminstrs., 1988, Annual Leadership for Learning award Am. Assn. Sch. Adminstrs., 1990, Disting. Alumni award Teacher's Coll. Columbia U., 1991. Office: ASCD 1703 N Beauregard St Alexandria VA 22311-1714

CARTER, GEORGE EDWARD, education educator; b. Leominster, Mass., Sept. 16, 1934; s. Lester Earl and Anita (Bourque) C.; m. Carmen Ophelia Vazquez-Carter, Nov. 13, 1955 (wid. Sept. 1980); children: Lydia M. Carter-Zimmer, David Edward Carter, Russell George, Douglas Anthony; m. Betty K. Tonsing-Carter, Aug. 27, 1983; children: Eva Y Tonsing-Carter, Joseph Tonsing-Carter. BA, Calif. State U., Sacramento, 1961, MA, 1962; PhD, U. Oreg., 1970. Cert. tchr. Calif. Assoc. prof. U. Wis., LaCrosse, 1970-80; prof., scholar-in-residence UCLA, Calif. Polytech Pomona, U. Santa Clara, 1980-82; prof. Nat. U. of Lesotho, Roma, Lesotho, Africa, 1982-85; project coord. Acad. for Ednl. Devel., Maseru, Lesotho, 1985-88; prof., dir. acad. devel. Rhodes U., Grahamstown, S. Africa, 1988-93; adj. prof. Ind.-Purdue U., Ft. Wayne, 1993-94, 97—, U. S.C., Columbia, 1994-96, Wartburg Coll., Waverly, Iowa, 1997; cons. UN Devel. Program, Maseru, 1990-92, U.S. Agy. for Internat. Devel., 1988-90. Editor: Black Abolitionist Papers Project, 1982, Exploration in Ethnic Studies Jour., 1978-80. Fellow NEH, Yale U., 1973-74, Nat. Hist. Publs. Comm., Dartmouth Coll., 1968-69; Fulbright scholar Nat. U. Lesotho, 1982-85; rsch. grantee Rhodes U., Grahamstown, S. Africa, 1989-92. Mem. Am. Studies Assn., Anti-Slavery Internat., Assn. for Documentary Editing (nom. com. 1978), Nat. Assn. for Interdisciplinary Ethnic Studies (sec.-treas. 1975-81, pres. 1982), Fulbright Alumni Assn. Democrat. Quaker. Avocations: trout fishing, camping, biking, hiking, hunting. Home: 1809 Florida Dr Fort Wayne IN 46805-5036 Office: Ind-Purdue-Fort Wayne Fort Wayne IN 46805

CARTER, GEORGE KENT, oil company executive; b. Toledo, Nov. 5, 1935; s. Fred S. and Charlotte J. (Horen) C.; children from previous marriage: Caitlin, Seth; m. Kathleen Anne McKenna, July 22, 1990. AB, Stanford U., 1957, MBA, 1961. Various fin. positions Std. Oil of Calif., San Francisco, 1962-74, asst. treas., 1974, asst. comptr., 1974-81; comptr. Chevron U.S.A., Inc., San Francisco, 1981-83, v.p. fin., 1986-89; comptr. Chevron Corp. (formerly Std. Oil of Calif.), San Francisco, 1983-86, v.p. and treas., 1989—. Mem. Stanford Bus. Sch. Assn., Stanford U. Alumni Assn., Bankers Club. Office: Chevron Corp 575 Market St San Francisco CA 94105-2856 also: Chevron Corp PO Box 7643 San Francisco CA 94120-7643

CARTER, GEORGIAN L., minister; b. St. Mary's, Ga., July 3, 1939; d. Leroy Sr. and Abbie (Myers) Logan; m. Calvin L. Carter, Mar. 26, 1956; children: Janice Carter Slocumb, Arlette Carter Fletcher, Eric. AA, Prince Georges Community Coll., Largo, Md., 1973; cert., Dale Carnegie Sch., 1980. Ordained to ministry Deliverance Ch. of Christ, 1983. Clk., trustee Deliverance Ch. of Christ, Seat Pleasant, Md., 1968-87, Bible class tchr., 1983-89; sec., sick and shut-in ministry Full Gospel A.M.E. Zion Ch., Temple Hills, Md., 1989-92; mem. Live Oak Ch. of God, Hinesville, 1992, Sunday sch. tchr. of adult class, 1993—; with HUD, Washington, 1967-89;

tchr. noon-time Bible study U.S. State Dept. Fellowship, 1989-91; lay min. and leader Hines Estates Bible Study Group, 1993—. Asst. dir. Glenarden (Md.) Housing Authority, 1973-75. Democrat. Home: 909 Byrum Dr Hinesville GA 31313-5752 *Many of my desires for life conflicted with God's requirements. However, insight gained from the word of God has changed my way of thinking and has produced great rewards for my life.*

CARTER, GERALD EMMETT, retired archbishop; b. Montreal, Que., Can., Mar. 1, 1912; s. Thomas Joseph and Mary (Kelty) C. BTh, Grand Sem. Montreal, 1936; BA, U. Montreal, 1933, MA, 1940, PhD, 1947, LTh, 1950; DHL, Duquesne U., 1963; LLD (hon.), U. Western Ont., 1966, Concordia U., 1976, U. Windsor, 1977, McGill U., Montreal, 1980, Notre Dame (Ind.) U., 1981, St. Francis Xavier U., 1998; LittD, St. Mary's U., Halifax, 1980; lic. (hon.) Medieval Studies, LittD (hon.) Midieval Studies, Pontificial Inst. Medieval Studies, 1995; D of Sacred Letters (hon.), U. St. Michael's Coll., 1998; LLD (hon.), Assumption U., 1999. Ordained priest Roman Cath. Ch., 1937. Founder, prin., prof. St. Joseph Tchrs. Coll., Montreal, 1939-61; chaplain Newan Club McGill U., 1941-56; charter mem., 1st pres. Thomas More Inst. Adult Edn., Montreal, 1945-61; mem. Montreal Cath. Sch. Commn., 1948-61; hon. canon Cathedral Basilica Montreal, 1952-61; aux. bishop London and titular bishop Altiburo, 1961; bishop of London, Ont., 1964-78; archbishop of Toronto, 1978-90, ret., 1990; elevated to cardinal, 1979; Chmn. Episcopal Commn. Liturgy Can., 1966-73; mem. Consilium of Liturgy, Rome, 1965, Sacred Congregation for Divine Worship, 1970; chmn. Internat. Com. for English in the Liturgy, 1971; appointee Econ. Affairs Coun. of Holy See, 1981; vice pres. Can. Cath. Conf., 1973, Cath. Conf. of Ont., 1971-73; pres. Can. Conf. Cath. Bishops, 1975; mem. coun. Synod of Bishops, 1977. Author: The Catholic Public Schools of Quebec, 1957, Psychology and the Cross, 1959, The Modern Challenge to Religious Education, 1961, A Shepherd Speaks, 1981. Decorated companion Order of Can. Office: Chancery Office, 1155 Yonge St, Toronto, ON Canada M4T 1W2

CARTER, GLENN THOMAS, lawyer, clergyman; b. Beaumont, Tex., July 20, 1934; s. Glenmore Rust and Sarah Elizabeth (Woods) C.; m. Janette Lucile Mullikin, Aug. 1, 1954; children: Penny Lucile Loucks, Sylvia Lee De Vries. BA, Union Coll., 1956; JD, Emory U., 1967. Bar: Ga. 1968, Tex. 1969, D.C. 1976, Md. 1976, U.S. Dist. Ct. (no. dist.) Tex. 1981, Calif. 1984; ordained to ministry Seventh-day Adventist Chs., 1960. Pastor chs. in Tex., Wyo., Ga., 1956-65; spl. legal advisor Cumberland Conf. Seventh-day Adventists, Decatur, 1968-69; dir. trust svcs. and pub. affairs Texico and Tex. Conf. Seventh-day Adventists, Amarillo and Ft. Worth, Tex., 1969-76; assoc. dir. trust svcs. Gen. Conf. Seventh-day Adventists, Washington, 1976-80; dir. pub. affairs, assoc. dir. trust svcs. Southwestern Union Conf. Seventh-day Adventists, Burleson, Tex., 1980-82; bd. dir. trust svcs. Pacific Union Conf. Seventh-day Adventists, Westlake Village, Calif., 1982-85; dir. Trust Svcs. Gen. Conf. of Seventh-day Adventists, Washington, 1985—. Contbr. articles to ch. pubs. Recipient Am. Jurisprudence prize for litigation Lawyers Co-op, 1967. Mem. Rotary (Paul Harris fellow). Office: 12501 Old Columbia Pike Silver Spring MD 20904-6601

CARTER, GUY CHRISTOPHER, theologian; b. Feb. 21, 1951. BA, U. St. Thomas, 1973; MA, Marquette U., 1980, PhD, 1987; MDiv, Luth. Sch. Theology, Chgo., 1986. Parish pastor Evang. Luth. Ch. in Am., Sault St. Marie, Mich., 1986-89, Hameln, Germany, 1989-91, Bayonne, N.J., 1992-94, Fairview, N.J., 1994-98; adj. lectr. theology St. Peter's Coll., Jersey City, 1992-98, asst. prof. theology, 1998—. E-mail: gcemc@earthlink.net. Office: St Peters Coll Dept Theology 2641 Kennedy Blvd Jersey City NJ 07306-5943

CARTER, HAROLD O., agricultural economics educator; b. Eaton Rapids, Mich., Dec. 13, 1932; s. Ola Gay and Lillian Darlene (Fox) C.; m. Janet M. Edger, June 21, 1952; children: Teresa, Lisa, Brian, Michael, Alison. BS, Mich. State U., 1954, MS, 1955; PhD, Iowa State U., 1958. From asst. prof. to assoc. prof. agrl. econs. U. Calif., Davis, 1958-66; prof. to prof. emeritus U. Calif., 1966-93, 93—; chmn. dept. U. Calif., Davis, 1970-76, 87-89, dir. Agrl. Issues Ctr., 1985-96; vis. prof. Agrl. Coll. Sweden, Uppsala, 1967, Ctr. Agrl. Econs. U. Naples, Italy, 1972, dept. agrl. econs U. Sydney, Australia, 1984; economist Giannini Found. Agrl. Econs. Fellow Am. Agrl. Econs. Assn. (Outstanding Rsch. awards 1963, 67, 71, 75, 89, Best Jour. Article award 1968), Western Agrl. Econs. Assn. (Outstanding Extension award 1975, Outstanding Rsch. award 1962, 69, 71). Republican. Home: 550 Oak Ave Woodland CA 95695-3945 Office: U Calif Dept Agrl Econs Davis CA 95616

CARTER, HARRIET VANESSA, public relations specialist, congressional aide; b. N.Y.C.; d. Gerard Frederick and Eugenia Carter. BA in Spanish magna cum laude, Tulane U., 1969; MEd in Spanish, U. Ill., 1974; postgrad., U. D'Aix en Provence, France, 1972, U. Nice, France, 1974, U. Montreal, 1979, U. Vienna, 1980. Tchr. Spanish King Philip Jr. H.S., West Hartford, Conn., 1971-76, Irvington (N.J.) H.S., 1976-77, Closter (N.J.) Village Sch., 1977-78; tchr. Spanish, coord. acad. awards program Benjamin Sch., North Palm Beach, Fla., 1978-81; asst. to clin. dean., pub. rels. and med. residency coord. Am. U. of Caribbean Sch. Medicine, Miami, Fla., 1981-84; asst. dir. admissions Ross U. Sch. Medicine, N.Y.C., 1984; coord. ednl. tng., asst. to pres. United Schs. of Am., Miami, 1985-86; pub. rels. specialist edn., medicine, polit. govt., travel Miami, 1986—; coord. divsn. Latino studies Fla. Internat. U., Miami, 1987-88, promotions cons. in broadcasting, 1989-90, TV prodr., exec. asst. to program dir., 1990-91; TV prodr., co-host series Volunteer Miami Sta. WLRN-TV, 1991-92; congl. aide, 1993—; pub. rels. mgr. Voyager mag., Lake Park, Fla., 1981-82; instr. med. Spanish U. Conn. Med. Sch., Farmington, 1974, Mt. Sinai Hosp., Hartford, 1973; tchg. asst. in Spanish U. Ill., Urbana, 1970-71, fellow, 1970. Founder, editor (newsletter) Focus on Multi-Cultural Happenings, 1975-76; editor (newsletter) Am. Univ. of Caribean Sch. of Medicine, 1981-84; contbr. articles to profl. jours. Participant Hispanic leadership tng. program Cuban-Am. Nat. Coun., Miami, 1983; pub. rels. and comm. com. Leadership Miami, 1989—; vol. Miracle Telethon, Miami Children's Hosp., 1986, Rep. Nat. Conv., San Diego, 1996, Rep. Gov.'s. Assn. Ann. Conf., Miami, 1997; steering com. Jeb Bush for Gov., 1998; Jerry Lewis Labor Day Telethon, 1989, 93-95, auction Sta. WLRN-TV, Miami, 1990-94, vol.-a-thon for United Way Dade County, Sta. WPLG-TV, 1991; guide So. Govs.' Conf., Miami, 1985; active Greater Miami Ambs. Corps, 1985-92, Coun. Internat. Vis. Greater Miami. Semifinalist Miss Teenage Am. Contest; recipient Recognition award U.S. Ho. of Reps., 1991, cert. of merit for commitment to cmty. svc. Pres. of U.S., 1991; fellow U. Ill., 1969-70; scholar Govt. of Austria, 1980. Mem. NATAS, AAUW (co-chmn. com. on women 1980-81), Phi Beta Kappa, Phi Delta Kappa. Avocations: travelling, swimming, theater, tennis, reading. Office: 9357 Fontainebleau Blvd Ste 202 Miami FL 33172-4275

CARTER, HARRY ROBERT, fire chief; b. Neptune, N.J., July 29, 1947; s. Harry Barringer and Stella (Napiorkowski) C.; m. Jacalyn Roberta Miller, Apr. 29, 1972; children: Ellen, Kathleen, Todd. AA, Brookdale Coll., 1971; BA, Thomas Edison State Coll., 1975; BS magna cum laude, Jersey City State Coll., 1976; MA, Rutgers U., 1979; PhD, Western States U., 1984. Fire fighter Rahway (N.J.) Fire Dept., 1972-73; fire fighter Newark (N.J.) Fire Dept., 1972-77, fire capt., 1977-90, battalion fire chief, 1990-97, deputy fire chief, 1997—, dep. fire chief, 1997—; adj. prof. Ocean County Coll., Toms River, N.J., 1977-81; pres. Carter Fire Protection, Inc., Adelphia, N.J., 1980—; fire marshal N.J. Army Nat. Guard, 1981-91. Author: Management in the Fire Service, 1989, Managing Fire Service Finances, 1989, Understanding Fire Behavior, 1995, Strategic Planning and Fire Protection, 1996, Tactics in Fire Department Management, 1997, Firefighting Strategy and Tactics, 1998, Management in the Fire Service, 3d edit., 1998; contbr. articles to profl. jours. Vol. fire fighter, officer Howell Twp. Fire Co. # 1, Adelphia, N.J., 1971—, tng. officer, 1978-91, fire chief, 1991. Capt. USAR, 1966-96. Mem. ISFSI (bd. dirs. 1989—, 1st vice-chmn. bd. dirs. 1999), N.J. Soc. Fire Instrs. (bd. dirs. 1978-80, pres. 1980-82), Nat. Fire Protection Assn. (adv. coun. 1975-90), Internat. Assn. Fire Chiefs (scholarship 1975-76), Internat. Assn. Fire Fighters, Wall-Spring Lake Lodge F & AM, VFW, Am. Legion, Optimist Internat. Republican. Lutheran. Avocations: military music, playing the tuba, poetry, collecting military medals. Home: PO Box 100 Adelphia NJ 07710-0100 Office: Newark Fire Dept 34 Jersey St Newark NJ 07105-2209

CARTER, HELENA BONHAM, actress; b. Golders GreeN, London, England, May 26, 1966. Appeared in films, including Wings of the Dove, Hamlet, Mary Shelley's Frankenstein, A Room With A View, Howard's End, Mighty Aphrodite, Margaret's Museum (Best Actress award Can. Genie 1997), and others. Recipient Best Actress award L.A. Film Critics Assn., Boston Soc. Film Critics, Nat. Bd. of Rev., Soc. Tex. Film Critics; nominated Best Actress award Chgo. Film Critics Assn. Address: care UTA 9560 Wilshire Blvd Beverly Hills CA 90212-2427

CARTER, HENRY MOORE, JR., retired foundation executive; b. Portsmouth, Va., Mar. 10, 1932; s. Henry and Debbie (McCoy) C.; m. Martha Rhea Greene, Aug. 21, 1954; 1 dau., Ann Clair. BA, Randolph-Macon Coll., 1953; MA, Vanderbilt U., 1954. Tchr. English, Norfolk County Public Schs., Portsmouth, 1954-59; head dept. English Norfolk County Public Schs., 1957-59; headmaster Bollingbrook Sch., Petersburg, Va., 1959-66; dir. public relations Randolph-Macon Coll., Ashland, Va., 1966-68; dir. Randolph-Macon Fund, 1968-69, dir. devel., 1969-77; pres. Winston-Salem (N.C.) Found., 1977-97; pastmem. adv. com. Kate B. Reynolds Trust for Poor and Needy; chair bd. dirs. N.C. Ctr. for Nonprofits; former sec. Winston-Salem Campaign Coordinating Com. Past chmn., bd. dirs. coord. com. Winston-Salem Crime Stoppers; past chmn. Emergency Loan Fund; past mem. adv. bd. Mary Baldwin Coll.; trustee Southeastern Coun. Founds.; former chmn. N.C. Assn. Cmty. Founds; former sec.-treas. Twin City Devel. Corp; past chmn. bd. Forsyth Common Vision Coun.; bd. dirs. Old Salem Inc., Crosby Scholars Cmty. Partnership, Hospice Found., Forsyth Tech. Coll. Found. Carnegie fellow, 1953-54. Mem. Southeastern Coun. of Founds. (past chmn. bd. trustees), Forsyth Common Vision Coun. (past chmn. bd.). Republican. Methodist. Clubs: Litchfield Country, Torch, Piedmont. Lodge: Rotary. Office: 860 W 5th St Winston Salem NC 27101-2506

CARTER, HERBERT EDMUND, former university official; b. Mooresville, Ind., Sept. 25, 1910; s. George Benjamin and Edna (Pidgeon) C.; m. Elizabeth Winifred DeWees, Aug. 30, 1933; children—Anne Winsett, Jean Elizabeth. A.B., DePauw U., 1930, Sc.D., 1952; A.M., U. Ill., 1931, Ph.D., 1934, Sc.D., 1974; Sc.D., U. Ind., 1974, U. Ariz., 1984; L.H.D., Thomas Jefferson U., 1975. Instr. chemistry U. Ill., 1933-35, asso., 1935-37, asst. prof., 1937-43, asso. prof., 1943-45, prof., 1945-71, acting dean grad. coll., 1963-64, head dept. chemistry and chem. engring., 1954-67, vice chancellor for acad. affairs, 1967-71; coordinator interdisciplinary programs U. Ariz., Tucson, 1971-77; head dept. biochemistry U. Ariz., 1977-81; rsch. fellow Office Arid Lands Studies, 1981—, spl. asst. to v.p. rsch., 1984-90, coord. interdisciplinary programs, 1987-90; mem. Pres.'s Com. on Nat. Medal of Sci., 1963-66; mem. nat. sci. bd. NSF, 1963-76, chmn., 1970-74; mem. Citizens Commn. Sci., Law and Food Supply.; Mem. exec. com. div. chemistry and chem. tech. NRC, 1949-55, 57-68. Mem. editorial bd. Bio Chem. Preparations; editor-in-chief, Vol. I.; contbr. to tech. publs. Trustee Assn. Univs. for Argonne, 1980-83, Nutrition Found., 1972-85. Awarded Rector Scholarship, Rector Fellowship DePauw U.; Eli Lilly & Co., Annual award ($1,000 and bronze medal to biochemist under 35 years of age showing promise in research), 1943; Am. Oil Chemists Soc. award in lipid chemistry, 1966. Mem. Am. Chem. Soc. (dir., asso. editor Bio-Chemistry 1961-67, William H. Nichols medal N.Y. sect., also Spencer award Kansas City sect. 1969), Am. Inst. Nutrition (sec. 1945-47), Am. Soc. Biol. Chemists (editorial bd. 1951-60, editorial com. 1963-66, pres. 1956-57), Nat. Acad. Scis. (chmn. section biochemistry 1963-66, mem. council 1966-69), Blue Key, Phi Beta Kappa, Sigma Xi, Phi Eta Sigma, Lambda Chi Alpha, Gamma Alpha, Alpha Chi Sigma. Democrat. Presbyn.

CARTER, (WILLIAM) HODDING, III, foundation executive, former journalist, public official and educator; b. New Orleans, Apr. 7, 1935; s. William Hodding and Betty Brunhilde (Werlein) C.; m. Margaret A. Wolfe, June 21, 1957 (div. 1978); children: Catherine Ainsworth, Elizebeth Fearn, William Hodding IV, Margaret Lorraine; m. Patricia M. Derian, 1978. BA, Princeton U., 1957; LLD (hon.), Stetson Coll., 1980, Kenyon Coll., 1984; LittD (hon.), Tusculum Coll., 1983; LLD (hon.), George Washington U., 1986, N.Y. Inst. Tech., 1987; LHD (hon.), U. Maine, 1985, U. San Diego, 1991, Millsaps Coll., 1998. Reporter Delta Democrat-Times, Greenville, Miss., 1959-62, mng. editor, 1962-65, editor, assoc. pub., 1965-77; asst. sec. state for pub. affairs, dept. spokesman Dept. State, Washington, 1977-80; vis. prof. Am. U., 1980; anchorman and chief corr. Inside Story, PBS, 1981-84; chief corr., exec. editor Capitol Jour., PBS, 1985-86; pres. MainStreet TV Prodn. Co., 1985-95; Knight chair in pub. affairs journalism U. Md., 1995-98; pres. John S. and James L. Knight Found., 1998—; vis. prof. Duke U., 1990; op. ed. columnist Wall St. Jour., 1980-91. Author: The South Strikes Back, 1959, The Reagan Years, 1988; contbr. to books, newspapers and mags.; commentator on TV and radio; columnist Newspaper Enterprise Assn., 1992-95. Co-chmn. Young Dem. Clubs Miss., 1965-68; founding mem. Loyal Dems. of Miss., 1968; mem. Charter Commn. Dem. Party, 1973-74; del. Dem. Conv., 1968, 72, 76, Dem. Mini Conv., Kansas City, Mo., 1974; mem. campaign staff Johnson for Pres., 1964, Carter for Pres., 1976; mem. exec. com. So. Regional Coun., 1969-75, Miss. Dem. Party, 1976-79; trustee Princeton U., 1983-98; dir. Dreyfus Corp. Funds; bd. dirs. Twentieth Century Fund, Found. for the Mid South, Enterprise Corp. of the Delta; former chmn. adv. bd. Pew Ctr. for Civic Journalism; former chmn. Action Coun. for Peace in the Balkans. Nieman fellow Harvard U., 1965-66; recipient Editorial award Soc. of Profl. Journalists, 1961, Disting. Achievement award U. Calif. Sch. Journalism, 1972, 4 Emmy awards for pub. affairs TV, 1984-85, Edward R. Murrow award for best fgn. documentary, 1984. Mem. Coun. Fgn. Rels., Cosmos Club, Tarrantine Club. Episcopalian.

CARTER, IRENE LAVENIA, greeting card company owner, poet; b. Phila., Mar. 23, 1955; d. John and Gertrude M.; div.; children: Shawnette N., Tyesha C. Student, LaSalle Coll., 1979-82, Art Inst., Phila., 1997-99. Warehouser, team leader Proctor & Gamble, Hatboro, Pa., 1974—; vendor, crafter Family Affair, Abington, Pa., 1994-95, Hatboro, 1997—; supplier Expressions of You, Phila., 1996—. Author: (poetry books) Motherhood, 1994, Woman, 1995, Creator, 1996. Mem. Neighborhood Watch Against Drugs, Phila. Recipient Editor's Choice award, Internat. Soc. Poetry, 1994, award for edn., peace, equality, 1995. Democrat. Avocations: sports, songwriting, scrabble, poetry. Home and Office: 2188 Homer St Philadelphia PA 19138-1934

CARTER, JAINE M(ARIE), human resources development company executive; b. Chgo., Oct. 29, 1946; d. Bruno and Louise Kucinski; m. James Dudley Carter, Apr. 8, 1970; children: Paul, Todd. BS, Northwestern U., 1968; PhD, Walden U., 1988. Mgmt. cons. to bus., 1964-69; chmn. bd. Pers. Devel., Inc., Palatine, Ill., 1969—; dir. women's div. Lake Forest (Ill.) Coll. Advanced Mgmt. Inst., 1970—; writer, lectr., tchr., cons. mgmt. devel. programs; mem. faculty AMA; speaker weekly cable TV series Life Skills; chmn. bd. dirs. Carter & Carter Enterprises Inc., 1986—; pres., bd. dirs. Family Renewal Inst., 1991. Author: How to Train for Supervisors, 1969, Career Planning Workshop for Women, 1975, Training Techniques That Bring About Positive Behavioral Change, 1976, Assertive Management Role Plays, 1976, Understanding the Female Employee, 1976, Rx for Women in Business, 1976, New Directions Needed in Management Training Programs, 1980, The Burnout of Retirement, 1983, Successfully Working with People, 1984, Assertiveness Training for Supervisors, 1985, Successfully Managing People, 1986, The New Success, 1986, Employee Assistance Program Handbook, 1988, Stay Out of Your Own Way-And Get the Job You Want, 1989, He Works/She Works-Successful Strategies for Working Couples, 1996, syndicated columnist, script Howard, Balancing Work & Family. 1995; author, narrator TV series Executive Communications, 1988-89; moderator, content expert (TV spl.) Commitment to Quality, Nat. Tech. U., 1989; creator, prodr. Roboflex and Cammy animated video series, 1991; creator, prodr., host TV series Relationships, 1992, TV series Choices, 1992, 93, host radio talk show 1992—, TV interview show It's Your Business, 1993—; nat. newspaper columnist Scripps Howard News Svc., He Works/She Works, 1992—; co-host (radio talk show) Your Own Business!, 1993—. Mem. SAG, AFTRA, AGVA, Exec. Club Am., Am. Mgmt. Assn. *People can only be free when they are able to take personal responsibility for their actions, turn their back on the expectations of others, and confidently pursue their own unlimited realitites.*

CARTER, JAMES A., finance executive; b. Lakeland, Fla., July 25, 1926; s. William and LaTrelle (Morgan) C.; m. Mary Lois Barnes, Aug. 26, 1950; children: James A. Jr., Jeffrey M. BA in English Lit., The Citadel, 1950. Trainee to pres. various CIGNA corp. cos., Phila., 1954-80; pres. Lumbermens Mut. Ins. Co., Mansfield, Ohio, 1980-82; sr. Am. officer, exec. v.p. Tokio Marine and Fire Ins. Co., N.Y.C., 1982-84; pres. First Southern Ins. Co., Tampa, Fla., 1984-86; owner J.A. Carters Co., Inc., Tampa, 1986-90; owner, pres. Mgmt. Advisors Inc., Tampa, 1991-98; pres. JAC Realty Investments, Inc., Tampa, 1997—; co-owner Staffing Solutions, Tampa, 1999—. Contbg. author: Business Insurance Handbook, 1980. Lt. col. ret. U.S. Army infantry, 1945-46, WWII, 51-53, Korea. Decorated Combat Infantry badge and others. Democrat. Methodist. Avocations: fishing, gardening. Home and Office: 1215 S Roxmere Rd Tampa FL 33629-4225

CARTER, JAMES CLARENCE, university administrator; b. N.Y.C., Aug. 1, 1927; s. James Clarence and Elizabeth (Dillon) C. BS in Physics, Spring Hill Coll., 1952; MS in Physics, Fordham U., 1953; STL in Theology, Woodstock Coll., 1959; PhD in Physics, Cath. U. Am., 1956. Ordained priest Roman Cath. Ch., 1958. Instr., asst. prof. Physics Loyola U., New Orleans, 1960-67; assoc. prof. of Physics Loyola U., 1967—, v.p., 1970-74, pres., 1974-95, chancellor, 1995—; bd. dirs. Met. Area Com.; mem. higher edn. facilities com. State La., 1971-73, Am. Council's Commn. on Leadership in Higher Edn., 1975-78; bd. trustees Loyola U. Chgo., 1981-90; chmn. Mayor's Com. Ednl. Uses CATV, 1972. Contbr. articles to profl. jours. Mem. adv. com. New Orleans Pub. Library for the NEH Grant, 1975; bd. dirs. Greater New Orleans Area United Way, 1976-82, La. Ednl. TV Authority, 1977-83; bd. trustees Regis U., 1980-90, 94—, U. San Francisco, 1991—, St. Joseph's U., 1993—. Recipient Torch of Liberty award Anti-Defamation League of B'nai B'rith, 1983. Mem. Palmes Academiques, So. Assn. of Colls. and Schs. (exec. council of the commn. on colls.), Am. Phys. Soc., Am. Assn. Physics Tchrs., Assn. Jesuit Colls. and Univs. (chmn. acad. v.p. conf. 1971-74, chmn. 1991-94, exec. dir. 1996), Nat. Assn. Ind. Colls. and Univs. (bd. dirs. 1977-82), Am. Council Edn., Sigma Xi. Office: Loyola U Office of Chancellor 6363 Saint Charles Ave New Orleans LA 70118-6195

CARTER, JAMES FOLGER, obstetrician-gynecologist, consultant; b. Kingstree, S.C., Aug. 29, 1949; s. Almer Burnis and Mary Emma (Folger) C.; m. Deborah Josephine Cook, May 24, 1975; children: Jared Cook, Chad Michael Folger, Todd Joseph. BS, U. S.C., 1971, MD, 1975. Cert. in ob-gyn. Intern Richland Meml. Hosp., Columbia, 1975-76; resident in ob-gyn. Naval Regional Med. Ctr., San Diego, 1977-81; chief ob-gyn. Georgetown (S.C.) Meml. Hosp., 1990-92; with Charleston (S.C.) Meml. Hosp., VA Hosp., St. Francis Hosp.; asst. prof. ob-gyn. Med. U. S.C., Charleston, 1992—; tchr. advanced laparoscopic surgery, Charleston, 1992—. Author tchg. monograph; contbr. articles to med. jours. Bd. dirs. Tarahall Home for Boys, Georgetown County, 1995. Fellow ACOG, Assn. Advanced Laparoscopic Surgery, South Atlantic Assn. of Obstetricians and Gynecologists; mem. AMA, Am. Fertility Soc., S.C. Med. Assn. Office: Med U SC Dept Ob-gyn 171 Ashley Ave Dept Ob Charleston SC 29425-0001

CARTER, JAMES H., state supreme court justice; b. Waverly, Iowa, Jan. 18, 1935; s. Harvey J. and Althea (Dominick) C.; m. Jeanne E. Carter, Mar. 1959; children: Carol, James. B.A., U. Iowa, 1956, J.D., 1960. Law clk. to judge U.S. Dist. Ct, 1960-62; assoc. Shuttleworth & Ingersoll, Cedar Rapids, Iowa, 1962-73; judge 6th Jud. Dist., 1973-76, Iowa Ct. Appeals, 1976-82; justice Iowa Supreme Ct., Des Moines, 1982—. Office: Iowa Supreme Ct State House Des Moines IA 50319*

CARTER, JAMES HAL, JR., lawyer; b. Ames, Iowa, Sept. 25, 1943; s. James H. Sr. and Louise (Benge) C.; m. Sara N. Meeker, July 27, 1974; children: Janet, Faith, Katherine. BA, Yale U., 1965, LLB, 1969. Bar: N.Y. 1971, U.S. Dist. Ct. (so. dist.) N.Y. 1972, U.S. Dist. Ct. (ea. dist.) N.Y. 1975, U.S. Dist. Ct. (no. dist.) N.Y. 1992, U.S. Dist. Ct. (west. dist.) Mich. 1992, U.S. Dist. Ct. Conn. 1981, U.S. Ct. Internat. Trade 1980, U.S. Ct. Appeals (2nd cir.) 1971, U.S. Supreme Ct. 1976, U.S. Ct. Appeals (3rd and 5th cirs.) 1984, U.S. Ct. Appeals (fed. cir.) 1988, U.S. Ct. Appeals (3rd cir.) 1990. Fulbright scholar Cambridge U., Eng., 1965-66; law clk. U.S. Ct. Appeals (2d cir.), 1969-70; with Sullivan & Cromwell, N.Y.C., 1970, ptnr., 1977; lectr. internat. comml. arbitration Practicing Law Inst.; bd. dirs. Am. Arbitration Assn., Am. Assn. for Internat. Com. of Jurists, Am. Bar Found. Corr. editor: Internat. Legal Materials; contbr. articles to profl. jours. Mem. adv. bd. Southwestern Legal Found. Internat. and Comparative Law Ctr., Inst. for Transnational Arbitration. Mem. ABA (past chair internat. law and practice sect., former co-chmn. internat. comml. arbitration com.), U.S. Coun. Internat. Bus. (com. on arbitration), Am. Soc. Internat. Law (v.p.), Am. Law Inst., N.Y. State Bar Assn. (former chmn. internat. dispute resolution com.), Assn. of Bar of City of N.Y. (chmn. internat. affairs coun.), Coun. on Fgn. Rels. Office: Sullivan & Cromwell 125 Broad St Fl 28 New York NY 10004-2489

CARTER, JAMES HARVEY, psychiatrist, educator; b. Maysville, N.C., May 11, 1934; s. Thomas and Irene (Barber) C.; m. Jettie Lucille Strayhorn, Aug. 21, 1957 (dec. Sept. 1987); 1 child, James Harvey; m. Elsie Richardson, Aug. 26, 1988; 1 child, Saunia McDonald-Wilson. BS, N.C. Ctrl. U., Durham, 1956; MD, Howard U., 1966. Diplomate Am. Bd. Psychiatry and Neurology, Am. Bd. Forensic Examiners. Rotating intern Walter Reed Army Hosp., Washington, 1967; resident in gen. adult psychiatry Dorothea Dix/Duke Med. Ctr., Raleigh-Durham, N.C., 1969-70; assoc. dept. psycihatry Duke U., Durham, 1971-74, asst. prof., 1974-78, assoc. prof., 1978-83, prof., 1983—; sr. psychiatrist Dept. Correction, Raleigh, 1974—; lectr. N.C. Found. for Alcohol and Drug Studies, U. N.C., Wilmington, 1989-95. Editor Epikrisis. Bd. dirs. Gov.'s Inst. on Alcohol and Substance Abuse, 1992-94; co-founder Drug Action of Wake County, Raleigh. Served to Col. M.C., U.S. Army, 1958-94. Decorated Order of Mil. Merit; recipient Profl. Designation A, U.S. Army Surg. Gen., 1985; E.Y. Williams clin. scholar, 1994; Josiah Macy Faculty fellow, 1970-74; Falk fellow, 1971-72. Fellow Am. Psychiat. Assn. (vice chair com. on chronic mental illness), Orthopsychiat. Assn. Achievements include founding of various drug awareness programs. Avocations: gardening, horseback riding. Home: Duke U Med Ctr 3310 Pine Grove Rd Raleigh NC 27610 Office: Duke U Med Ctr PO Box 3106 Durham NC 27715-3106

CARTER, JAMES ROSE, JR., medical educator; b. Boston, Aug. 30, 1933; s. James Rose and Grace Marguerite (Dixon) C.; m. Betty Frances Chamberlain, 1955, (div. 1969); children: Christopher, Victoria; m. Susan Abbott Gear, Aug. 28, 1971. AB, Princeton U., 1955; MD, Columbia U., 1959. Diplomate Am. Bd. Internal medicine. Resident Mass. Gen. Hosp., Boston, 1959-61, 63-65; clin. fellow Nat. Heart Inst., NIH, Bethesda, Md., 1961-63; postdoctoral fellow dept. biochemistry Harvard U., Boston, 1965-67; asst. prof. medicine Harvard U. Sch. Medicine, 1967-71; assoc. prof. medicine U. Pa. Med. Sch., Phila., 1971-74; assoc. prof. to prof. medicine Case Western Res. U. Med. Sch., Cleve., 1974—; past chmn. Dept. of Medicine Metro Health Med. Ctr., Cleve., 1993; vice chmn. med. dept. Case Western Res. U. Med. Sch., Cleve., 1980-93, dir. dept. medicine Metro Health Med. Ctr., 1980-93; mem. metabolism study sect. NIH, 1975-78, rsch. study sect. Am. Heart Assn., Cleve. Contbr. articles to profl. jours. Sr. asst. surgeon USPHS, 1961-63. Fellow ACP; mem. AAAS, Am. Soc. Clin. Investigation (emeritus), Am. Fedn. Clin. Rsch., Innominatum Soc. (Cleve. sec.-treas. to pres. 1981-83), Pasteur Club (Cleve. pres. 1982). Democrat. Avocations: theater, classical music, skiing, travel. Office: Metro Health Med Ctr Dept Medicine 2500 Metrohealth Dr Cleveland OH 44109-1900

CARTER, JAMES SUMTER, oil company executive, tree farmer; b. Rock Hill, S.C., June 3, 1948; s. James Roy Jr. and Sumter Inez (McWatters) C.; m. Melinda Ruth Roberts, Mar. 25, 1972; children: James Sumter Jr., Stephanie Jane, Lauren Elizabeth. BSME, Clemson U., 1970; MBA, Tulane U., 1974. Mktg. staff Exxon Co. USA, Houston, 1974-79; dist. mgr. Exxon Co. USA, Linden, N.J., 1980-81; adv. Exxon Corp., N.Y.C., 1982-83; analysis mgr. Exxon Internat., Florham Pk, N.J., 1984-85; coord. mgr. Exxon Co. USA, Houston, 1986, exec. asst. to pres., 1987, distbn. mgr., 1988, downstream planning mgr., 1989, fuel products mgr., 1990-96, v.p. mktg., 1996—. Bd. dirs. Clemson U. Found., 1996—, Alley Theatre, Am. Hwy. Users Alliance, Channel 8 Assn. Cmty. TV, Tulane Parents Con., BBB, 1996—. Lt. U.S. Army, 1971-72. Mem. Am. Petroleum Inst., Petroleum Marketers Edn. Found. (bd. dirs. 1990-92), Forest Farmers Assn., Ben Tilman Soc., Lakeside Country Club, Petroleum Club Houston, Tau Beta Pi, Beta Gamma Sigma. Republican. Methodist. Avocation: restoration of S.C. plantation home. Office: Exxon USA 800 Bell St Houston TX 77002-7497

CARTER, JAMES THOMAS, contractor; b. N.Y.C., Dec. 27, 1952; s. Wendell Green and Carolyn Elizabeth (Smith) C.; m. Mary Jane Zellers, Oct. 8, 1985. Cert. airline transport pilot, flight instr., FAA, advanced open water diver, PADI. Charter pilot, flight instr. Pompano Air Ctr., Pompano Beach, Fla., 1976-78; profl. pilot Profl. Pilot Svcs., Ft. Lauderdale, Fla., 1978-79; aviation operative CIA, 1978-79; pres., pilot Carter Charter Co., Inc., Ft. Lauderdale, 1979-92; novelist Ft. Lauderdale, 1992-94; account exec. Power Line Components, Inc., Lighthouse Point, Fla., 1994-96; exec. dir. Advanced Tech., Inc., Ft. Lauderdale, 1996—; v.p. Advanced Mgmt. Svcs. Inc., Ft. Lauderdale, 1999—; mem. missile program Lockheed Missile and Space, Huntsville, Ala., 1995—, HRC program Smithsonian Astrophys. Obs., Cambridge, Mass., 1995-96, MIL-STAR program Electromagnetic Scis., Norcross, Ga., 1995—, J-STARS program, 1996—, Raytheon Missile Sys., Tucson, 1997—, GEC Marconi, Norcross, Ga., 1997. Author: Operation: Deepcover, 1994, A Twist of Fate, 1995, Stiletto, 1996, (poetry) Twilight, 1995, Christmas in the Snow, 1996. Recipient Editor's Choice award Nat. Libr. Poetry, 1996, 97. Mem. Aircraft Owners and Pilots Assn., Internat. Soc. Poets (disting.). Democrat. Presbyterian. Avocations: scuba diving, sailing, motorcycling, sea planes, snow skiing. Home: PO Box 30265 Fort Lauderdale FL 33303-0265 Office: Advanced Tech Components Inc 2717 E Oakland Park Blvd Fort Lauderdale FL 33306-1642 also: Advanced Mgmt Svcs Inc 2717 E Oakland Park Blvd Fort Lauderdale FL 33306-1642

CARTER, JAMES WALTON, fire chief; b. Jacksonville, N.C., July 3, 1945. Grad. h.S., Richlands, N.C.; Grad. Program Exec. Fire Officials, Nat. Fire Acad., Emmetsburg, Md., 1988. From fire fighter to battalion chief fire dept. City of Va. Beach, Va., 1970-76; battalion chief fire dept. City of Va. Beach, 1976-79, shift commdr. field ops., fire dept., 1979-83, tng. chief fire dept., 1983-84, fire marshal, 1984-85, dep. chief field ops. fire dept., 1988, dep. fire chief, 1997—. Office: City of Va Beach Mcpl Ctr Bldg 21 Virginia Beach VA 23456

CARTER, JANE FOSTER, agriculture industry executive; b. Stockton, Calif., Jan. 14, 1927; d. Chester William and Bertha Emily Foster; m. Robert Buffington Carter, Feb. 25, 1952 (dec. Dec. 1994); children: Ann Claire Carter Palmer, Benjamin Foster; m. Frank Anthony Bauman, Aug. 15, 1998. BA, Stanford U., 1948; MS, NYU, 1949. Pres. Colusa (Calif.) Properties, Inc., 1953—; owner Carter Land and Livestock, Colusa, 1965—; sec.-treas. Carter Farms, Inc., Colusa, 1975-94, pres., 1994—. Author: If the Walls Could Talk, Colusa's Architectural Heritage, 1988; author, editor: Colusa County Survey and Plan for the Arts, 1981, 82, 83, Implementing the Colusa County Arts Plan, 1984, 85, 86. Adv. mem. Calif. Gov.'s Commn. on Agr., Sacramento, 1979-82, Calif. Rep. Ctrl. Com., 1976-94; del. Rep. Nat. Conv., Kansas City, Mo., 1976, Detroit, 1980, Dallas, 1984; trustee Calif. Hist. Soc., 1979-89, regional v.p., 1984-89; mem. Calif. Reclamation Bd., 1982-96, sec., 1986-96; mem. Calif. Hist. Resources Commn., 1994—, vice chair, 1996-97, chair person, 1997-99; mem. Colusa Heritage Preservation Com., 1976—, chmn., 1977-83, vice chmn., 1983-91; bd. dirs. Colusa Cmty. Theatre Found., 1980—; bd. dirs. English-Speaking Union, San Francisco, 1992—, pres., 1993-95, v.p., 1995—; bd. dirs. The English-Speaking Union of the U.S., N.Y.C., 1995—, bd. dirs. Leland Stanford Mansion Found., Sacramento, 1992—; trustee Calif. Preservation Found., 1989-95. Recipient award of Merit for Historic Preservation Calif. Hist. Soc., 1989, Design award Calif. Preservation Found., 1990. Mem. Sacramento River Water Contractors Assn. (sec. 1992—, exec. com. 1974—), Francisca Club, Kappa Alpha Theta. Episcopalian. Avocations: travel, the arts, hist. preservation. Home and Office: 4746 River Rd Colusa CA 95932-4200

CARTER, JANICE JOENE, telecommunications executive; b. Portland, Oreg., Apr. 17, 1948; d. William George and Charline Betty (Gilbert) P. Student, U. Calif., Berkeley, 1964, U. Portland, 1966-67, U. Colo., Boulder, 1967-68; BA in Math, U. Guam, 1970; MBA, Golden Gate U., 1998. Computer programmer Ga.-Pacific Co., Portland, 1972-74; systems analyst ProData, Seattle, 1974-79; systems analyst, mgr. Pacific Northwest Bell, Seattle, 1979-80; data ctr. mgr. Austin Co., Renton, Wash., 1980-83; developer shared tenent svcs. Wright-Runstad, Seattle, 1983-84; system adminstr. Hewlett-Packard, Bellevue, Wash., 1984; global telecom. mgr. Nordstrom, Inc., Seattle, 1984-96; global telecomm. mgr. Hewlett-Packard Co., Palo Alto, Calif., 1996-98, 20th Century Fox, L.A., 1998—. Ski instr. Alpental, Snoqualmie Pass, Wash., 1984-87; bd. dirs. Educationally Gifted Children, Mercer Island, Wash., 1978-80; mem. curriculum com. Mercer Island Sch. Bd., 1992-95. Avocations: skiing, reading, German, French, traveling. Office: 20th Century Fox 2121 Ave of the Stars Los Angeles CA 90067

CARTER, JARED, poet; b. Elwood, Ind., Jan. 10, 1939; s. Robert Alton and Cleva Lois (Hackett) C.; m. Diane Haston, June 21, 1979; 1 child, Selene. BA, Goddard Coll., 1969. Writer-in-residence Knightstown (Ind.) H.S., 1977, Purdue U., West Lafayette, Ind., 1983, 86; vis. writer U. Hamburg, Germany, 1986; panelist for lit. Nat. Endowment for the Arts, Washington, 1985, 86. Author: Work, for the Night is Coming, 1981, After the Rain, 1993, Les Barricades Mystérieuses, 1999. Recipient Walt Whitman award Acad. Am. Poets, N.Y., 1980, New Writers award Great Lakes Colls. Assn., Phila., 1982, Gov.'s Arts award, Indpls., 1985, New Letters Literary award U. Mo., Kansas City, 1992, The Poets' prize Nicholas Roerich Mus., N.Y., 1995; Bridgman fellow Bread Loaf Writer's Conf., Middlebury, Vt., 1981, Literary fellow Nat. Endowment for the Arts, Washington, 1981, 91, John Simon Guggenheim Found. fellow, N.Y., 1983. Home: 1220 N State Ave Indianapolis IN 46201-1162

CARTER, JEAN ANNE, psychologist; b. Los Alamos, N.Mex., Dec. 19, 1951; d. Robert Emerson and Dorothy Jane (Williams) C.; m. Charles Joseph Gelso, Feb. 28, 1981; children: Philip, Charles, Brett, Catherine, Marie. BA in Psychology, Washington Coll., 1973; MA in Psychology, U. Md., 1976, PhD in Counseling Psychology, 1980. Staff assoc. Women's Med. Ctr. of D.C., Washington, 1978-81, dir. mental health clinic, 1981-83; pvt. practice Washington, 1981—; dir. Albemarle Psychol. Ctr., Washington, 1986—; adj. asst. prof. psychology U. Md., College Park, 1988—. Contbr. articles to profl. jours. Recipient Black award Outstanding Contbns. to Profl. Practice award Acad. of Counseling Psychology, 1997). Fellow APA (pres. divsn. counseling psychology); mem. Nat. Acads. of Practice (co-chair psychology, mem. NAP coun. 1996—, Disting. Practitioner), D.C. Psychol. Assn. Home: 16025 Jerald Rd Laurel MD 20707-2653 Office: #215 4501 Connecticut Ave NW Apt 215 Washington DC 20008-3702

CARTER, JEAN GORDON, lawyer; b. Fort Belvoir, Va., July 30, 1955; d. Thomas Laney and Cleone (Hunter) Gordon; m. Michael L. Carter, Sept. 17, 1977; children: Christina Jean, William Gordon. BS magna cum laude with honors in Accountancy, Wake Forest U., 1977; JD with high honors, Duke U., 1983. Bar: N.C. 1983; CPA; bd. cert. specialist in estates. Acct. Arthur Andersen & Co., Charlotte, N.C., 1977-80; atty. Moore & Van Allen, Raleigh, N.C., 1983-90; ptnr. Hunton & Williams, Raleigh, N.C., 1990—. Mem. Am. Coll. Trusts and Estates Coun., N.C. Bar Assn. (coun. estate sect. and healthcare sect. 1997—), Wake County Estate Coun. (pres. 1991-92), Order of Coif, Phi Beta Kappa. Democrat. Presbyterian. Avocation: reading. Home: 3913 Stratford Ct Raleigh NC 27609 Office: Hunton & Williams 1 Hannover Sq Raleigh NC 27601

CARTER, JEFFREY SCOTT, correctional officer; b. Sept. 23, 1967. BS corrections & juvenile svcs., Eastern Kentucky Univ., Richmond, KY, 1995, BS pol. sci., 1995. Platoon SST. USMC, Camp Pendleton, CA, 1986-90; chmn. Estill Co. Republican Party, Irvine, KY, 1996—; sch. tchr. Estill Co. Bd. Edn., Irvine, KY, 1992-98; correctional officer Fayette Co. Detention Ctr., Lexington, KY, 1999—. Home: 1085 Richmond Rd Irvine KY 40336

CARTER, JENNIFER LYN, English language educator; b. Lancaster, Pa., June 19, 1973; d. Clair Alan and Patricia Ann (Trimble) C. BA, Millersville U., 1995. Cert. tchr. English, Pa. Summer sch. tchr. Elizabethtown (Pa.) Area Mid. Sch., summer 1996, 97; long-term substitute tchr. English Elizabethtown Area H.S., 1996-97; tchr. English Kenwood H.S., Balt., 1997, Cocalico Sch. Dist., Denver, Pa., 1997—. Mem. NEA, Nat. Coun. Tchrs. English, Rho Kappa Chi. Republican. Avocations: walking, antiques, journal writing, traveling, restaurants. Home: 43 Crystal Dr Holtwood PA 17532-9739

CARTER, JIMMY (JAMES EARL CARTER, JR.), former President of United States; b. Plains, Ga., Oct. 1, 1924; s. James Earl and Lillian (Gordy) C.; m. Rosalynn Smith, July 7, 1946; children: John William, James Earl III, Donnel Jeffrey, Amy Lynn. Student, Ga. Southwestern Coll., 1941-42, Ga. Inst. Tech., 1942-43; BS, U.S. Naval Acad., 1946 (class of 1947); postgrad., Union Coll., 1952-53; LLD (hon.), Morris Brown Coll., 1972, Morehouse Coll., 1972, U. Notre Dame, 1977, Emory U., 1979, Kwansei Gakuin U., Japan, 1981, Ga. Southwestern Coll., 1981, N.Y. Law Sch., 1985, Bates Coll., 1985, Centre Coll., 1987, Creighton U., 1987; DEng (hon.), Ga. Inst. Tech., 1979; PhD (hon.), Weizmann Inst. Sci., 1980, Tel Aviv U., 1983, Haifa U., 1987; DHL (hon.), Cen. Conn. State U., 1985. Farmer, warehouseman Plains, Ga., 1953-77; mem. Ga. Senate, 1963-67; gov. State of Ga., Atlanta, 1971-75; President of United States, 1977-81; disting. prof. Emory U., Atlanta, 1982—; leader internat. observer teams Panama, 1989, Nicaragua, 1990, Dominican Republic, 1990, Haiti, 1990; host peace negotiations Ethiopia, 1989. Author: Why Not the Best?, 1975, A Government as Good as Its People, 1977, Keeping Faith/Memoirs of a President, 1982, Negotiation: The Alternative to Hostility, 1984, The Blood of Abraham, 1985, (with Rosalynn Carter) Everything to Gain: Making the Most of the Rest of Your Life, 1987, An Outdoor Journal, 1988, Turning Point: A Candidate, A State, and a Nation Come of Age, 1992, Talking Peace: A Vision for the Next Generation, 1993, Always a Reckoning, 1995. Mem. Sumter County (Ga.) Sch. Bd., 1955-62, chmn., 1960-62; mem. Americus and Sumter County Hosp. Authority, 1956-70; mem. Sumter County (Ga.) Library Bd., 1961; chmn. congl. campaign com. Dem. Nat. Com., 1974; founder Carter Ctr. Emory U., 1982; bd. dirs. Habitat for Humanity, 1984-87; chmn. bd. trustees Carter Ctr., Inc., 1986—, Carter-Menil Human Rights Found., 1986—, Global 2000 Inc., 1986—; chmn. Coun. of Freely-Elected Heads of Govt., 1986—; chmn. Coun. Internat. Negotiation Network, 1991—. Served to lt. USN, 1946-53. Recipient Gold medal Internat. Inst. Human Rights, 1979, Internat. Mediation medal Am. Arbitration Assn., 1979, Martin Luther King Jr. Nonviolent Peace prize, 1979, Internat. Human Rights award Synagogue Coun. Am., 1979, Conservationist of Yr. award, 1979, Harry S. Truman Pub. Svc. award, 1981, Ansel Adams Conservation award Wilderness Soc., 1982, Disting. Svc. award So. Bapt. Conv., 1982, Human Rights award Internat. League for Human Rights, 1983, World Meth. Peace award, 1985, Albert Schweitzer prize for Humanitarianism, 1987, Edwin C. Whitehead award Nat. Ctr. for Health Edn., 1989, Jefferson award Am. Inst. Pub. Svc., 1990, Phila. Liberty medal, 1990, Spirit of Am. award Nat. Coun. for Social Studies, 1990, Physicians for Social Responsibility award, 1991, Aristotle prize Alexander S. Onassis Found., 1991, Félix Houphouët-Boigny Peace prize UNESCO, 1995. Office: Carter Ctr 453 Freedom Pkwy 453 Freedom Pkwy Atlanta GA 30307-1400*

CARTER, JOAN PAULINE, investment company executive; b. Pitts., July 2, 1943; d. Paul Joseph and Hazel Elizabeth (Hykes) C.; m. John Aglialoro, 1979; children: Mark David Henderson, Liesl Ann Henderson. BA, Coll. of Wooster (Ohio), 1965. V.p. United Med. Corp., Haddonfield, N.J., 1973-85, pres., 1985—; bd. dirs. UM Holdings, Ltd., Haddonfield, N.J., Phila. Fed. Reserve Bd., Premier Rsch. Worldwide, Phila., Cybex Internat. Bd. trustees N.J. State Aquarium, Camden, 1995, Coll. Wooster, 1986—; mem. World Affairs Coun., Phila., 1982—. Mem. Drug Info. Assn., Union League (Phila.), N.Y. Women's Econ. Forum, CATO Inst. Republican. Office: UM Holdings Ltd 56 N Haddon Ave Haddonfield NJ 08033-2422*

CARTER, JOHN BOYD, JR., oil operator, bank executive; b. Ft. Worth, Oct. 19, 1924; s. John Boyd and Enlie (Corder) C.; m. Susie Ann Browne, Feb. 9, 1946 (div. Dec. 1968); children: Catherine Browne Malone, John Mason; m. Winifred Trimble Runnells, Feb. 23, 1970 (div. Jan. 1987); m. Elizabeth Langston Bayless, Apr. 29, 1987. Student, Kemper Mil. Sch., 1941-43, U. Tex., 1943-46, Babson Coll., 1946-47. Mortgage loan supr. Am. Gen. Investment Corp., 1947; ind. oil operator, 1948-49; sec., treas. Tex. Fund, Inc., 1949-52, mem. investment adv. bd., 1951-58; pres. Tex. Fund Rsch. and Mgmt. Assocs., 1950-52; ind. oil operator and fin. cons., 1952-58; Southwestern rep. Lehman Bros., 1959-65, gen. ptnr., 1965-77, mng. dir., 1970-77; sr. v.p., dir. Pogo Producing Co., 1977-86; former chair bd. dirs. Houston Nat. Bank; dir. Sterling Bank; chmn. bd. dirs. B.C.M. Tech., Inc.; pres., bd. dirs. High Prairie Ranch Co.; bd. dirs. Pogo Prodn. Co., Sterling Bancshares. Trustee Baylor Coll. Medicine, Howard Florey Inst., Melbourne, Australia. Bd. dirs. Robert Kleberg Found., Pvt. Enterprise Rsch. Corp. Tex. A&M U. Mem. Houston Soc. Fin. Analysts, Houston Com. on Fgn. Rels., Houston Country Club, U.S. Seniors Golf Assn., Bayou Club, Pilgrims Club (N.Y.C.), Brook Club (N.Y.C.), Sigma Alpha Epsilon. Home: 5422 John Dreaper Dr Houston TX 77056-4231 Office: 5757 Memorial Dr Houston TX 77007-8011*

CARTER, JOHN CHARLTON See HESTON, CHARLTON

CARTER, JOHN DALE, organizational development executive; b. Tuskegee, Ala., Apr. 9, 1944; s. Arthur L. and Ann (Bargyh) C.; m. Veronica Louise Helen Hopper, Oct., 12, 1986; children: Annelise Grace, Hopper Carter; AB, Ind. U., 1965, MS, 1967; PhD (NDEA fellow), Case Western Res. U., 1974. Dir. student affairs Dental Sch., Case Western Res. U., Cleve., 1974-75, asst. prof. applied behavioral sci., 1974-90, asst. dean orgn. devel. and student affairs, 1975-78; pres. John D. Carter and Assocs., Inc., Cleve., 1969—; ptnr. Portsmouth Cons. Group, 1984—; chmn. bd. Gestalt Inst. Cleve., 1974-80, chmn. orgn. and systems devel. program, 1980—, program dir., fin. dir. 1981-86, dir. corp. svcs., 1989-95, dean of faculty, 1992-96; pres. Orgn. and Systems Devel. Ctr., 1996—; mem. exec. bd. Nat. Tng. Labs., 1975-78; faculty Am. U., 1980-90, 94-96; mem. Nat. Tng. Labs., 1976—; bd. dirs. Behavioral Sci. Found., Cleve., Orgn. Devel. Network, 1999—; exec. bd. Fielding Inst., 1987-89; preceptor Shri Ram Chandra Yoga amd Meditation Mission, Sahag Marg, 1993—; Gestalt Inst. Cleve., 1996—; bd. mem. ODN Orgn. Devel. Network, 1999—. Mem. Internat. Assn. Applied Social Scientists, (cert. cons. Internat.), Kappa Alpha Psi (pres. Alpha chpt. 1964-65), Alpha Phi Omega. Author: Counselling the Helping Relationship, 1975, Managing the Merger Integration Process, 1986, Institutionalizing Change, 1995. Home and Office: 2232 Harcourt Dr Cleveland OH 44106-4622

CARTER, JOHN DOUGLAS, lawyer; b. Pendleton, Oreg., Feb. 6, 1946; s. Douglas Toner and Carmen Lucile (Cecil) C.; m. Diane Louise Werthen, Aug. 15, 1970 (div. 1977); m. Linda Louise Levy, Aug. 5, 1977; children: Courtney, Douglas, Christopher. AB, Stanford U.; LLB, JD, Harvard U. Bar: Calif. Law clk to Hon. J.F. Kilkenny U.S. Ct. Appeals (9th cir.), San Francisco, 1971-72; from assoc. to ptnr. Thelen, Marrin, Johnson & Bridges, San Francisco, 1972-82; chief litigation counsel Bechtel Power Corp., San Francisco, 1982-86; from asst. gen. counsel to sr. v.p. Bechtel Group, Inc., San Francisco, 1986-97, exec. v.p., 1997—; also bd. dirs. Bechtel Group, Inc., San Fransisco; pres. Bechtel Enterprises, San Fransisco, 1992-97; pres. Europe, Africa, Mid. East, S.W. Asia Bechtel Group, Inc., San Fransisco, 1997—; CFO, sr. officer pub. rels., internal audit Legis. Office, 1988-92; mem. chmn.'s leadership coun. Bechtel Group, Inc., 1996—. Editor: Construction Litigation: Representing the Contractor, 1986, 2d edit., 1992, Dow Jones Handbook of Joint Venturing, 1988, Construction Litigation Formbook, 1990. Mem. ABA, Calif. Bar Assn., San Francisco Bar Assn., Iternat. Bar Assn., San Francisco C. of C. (bd. dirs. 1988-92), Olympic Club, Bankers Club. Office: Bechtel Group Inc 50 Beale St San Francisco CA 94105-1813

CARTER, JOHN FRANCIS, II, lawyer; b. Washington, Dec. 21, 1939; s. John F. and Majorie (Thomas) C.; m. Marcia Wigby, June 26, 1966; children: J. F. III, Marion. AB, Princeton U., 1963; JD, U. Tex., 1970. Bar: Tex. 1970, U.S. Supreme Ct. 1977. Analyst Rotan Mosle, Houston, 1967-68; ptnr. Hutcheson & Grundy, Houston, 1970-90, mng. ptnr., 1990-94; sr. counsel Akin, Gump, Strauss, Hauer & Feld, Houston, 1996-98; atty. pvt. practice, Houston, 1998—; mem. State Bar Grievance Commn., Houston, 1976-79; internat. sr. advisor to dep. sec. U.S. Dept. Energy, 1994-96. Co-author: Incorporation in Texas, 1980. Chmn. Tex. Arts Alliance, 1981-82, Mcpl. Art Commn., Houston, 1988-90; pres. Arts Coun., Houston, 1983-84; chmn., sec. Harris County Dem. Party, Tex., 1988-90; mem. host com. Econ. Summit, Houston, 1989-90. Capt. U.S. Army, 1963-67, Vietnam. Mem. ABA (com. chair 1987-94), Houston Club, Tejas Breakfast Club, Univ. Cottage Club, Phi Delta Phi. Avocations: music, ballet, history. Office: The Carter Law Office 6631 Main St Ste 301 Houston TX 77030-2306

CARTER, JOHN LOYD, lawyer; b. Clayton, N.Mex., Oct. 2, 1948; s. John Allen and Ruth (Laughlin) C.; m. Dorel Susan Payne, Sept. 20, 1975; children: Matthew, Caroline, Susan. BA, So. Meth. U., 1970, JD cum laude, 1973. Bar: Tex. 1973, U.S. Ct. Appeals (5th and 11th cirs.) 1975, U.S. Supreme Ct. 1976, U.S. Dist. Ct. (so. dist.) Tex. 1974, U.S. Dist. Ct. (no. dist.) Tex. 1978, U.S. Dist. Ct. (ea. dist.) Tex. 1985. Assoc. Vinson & Elkins, Houston, 1973-80, ptnr., 1980—. Fellow Am. Coll. Trial Lawyers, Tex. Bar Found., Houston Bar Found. Office: Vinson & Elkins 2300 First City Tower Houston TX 77002-6760

CARTER, JOHN MACK, publishing company executive; b. Murray, Ky., Feb. 28, 1928; s. William Z. and Martha (Stevenson) C.; m. Sharlyn Emily Reaves, Aug. 30, 1948; children: Jonna Lyn, John Mack II. Student, Murray State Coll., 1944-46, LL.D., 1971; B.J., U. Mo., 1948, M.A., 1949; LL.D., St. John's U., 1983. Reporter Murray Ledger & Times, 1945; asst. editor Better Homes & Gardens mag., 1949-51; mng. editor Household mag., Topeka, 1953-57, editor, 1957-58; exec. editor Together mag., 1958-59; editor Am. Home mag., 1959-61; editor-in-chief McCall's mag., 1961-65; v.p. McCall Corp., N.Y.C., 1962-65; editor-in-chief Ladies Home Jour., 1965-74, pub., 1967-70; pres., chief operating officer Downe Communications Inc., 1972-73, chmn. bd., editor-in chief, 1973-77; pres. Am. Home Pub. Co., 1974-75; editor-in-chief Good Housekeeping mag., N.Y.C., 1975-95; dir. new mag. devel. Hearst Corp., N.Y.C., 1980—; pres. Hearst Mag. Enterprises. Bd. dirs. Future Homemakers Am., Am. Cancer Soc., Christian Ch. Found., Religion in Am. Life, Am. Bible Soc., Nat. Ctr. for Voluntary Action, Guideposts Mag. Served as lt. (j.g.) USNR, 1951-53. Recipient Walter Williams award for writing, 1949, Honor award for disting. service in journalism U. Mo., 1979, Faith and Freedom award Religious Heritage of Am., 1980, Quality of Life award for media Am. Lung Assn., 1986; named one of 10 Outstanding Men of Yr., U.S. Jr. C. of C., 1963, Pub. of Yr., Brandeis U., 1977, Headliner of Yr., Women in Communications, Inc., 1978, to Ky. Journalism Hall of Fame, 1983, Pub. of Yr., Mag. Pubs. Am., 1990. Mem. Kentuckians of N.Y. (pres.), Am. Soc. Mag. Editors (pres.), Sigma Delta Chi (pres. N.Y. chpt.). Office: Hearst Corp 959 8th Ave New York NY 10019-3795

CARTER, JOHN ROBERT, physician; b. Buffalo, Apr. 21, 1917; s. John Harvey and Gertrude Ann (Buckpitt) C.; m. Adelaide Briggs, May 8, 1943; children—Marilyn Anne, Jeanne Catherine. B.S., Hamilton Coll., 1939; M.D., U. Rochester, 1943. Diplomate: Nat. Bd. Med. Examiners. Intern State U. Iowa, 1943-44, resident, 1944-48, asst. dept. pathology, 1944, from instr. to asso. prof., 1944-55, prof., 1955-59; prof., chmn. dept. pathology and oncology U. Kans. Med. Center, 1960-66; prof. pathology dept. orthopedics Case Western Res. U., Cleve., 1981—, dir. Inst. Pathology, chmn. dept. pathology, 1966-81; prof. emeritus, 1987—, ret., 1995; cons. VA Hosp., U.S. Army Hosp., U.S. Penitentiary, Watkins Meml. Hosp.; Past chmn. pathology study sect. NIH; mem. pathology tng. grant com. Nat. Inst. Gen. Med. Scis.; mem. pathology adv. council Central VA Office; mem. sci. adv. bd. Armed Forces Inst. Pathology.; Bd. dirs. Univs. Asso. Research and Edn. Pathology; past pres. Mem. editorial bd.: Am. Jour. Pathology. Served to lt. USNR, 1946-48. Mem. AMA, AAAS, Cleve. Acad. Medicine, Path. Soc. Gt. Britain and Ireland, Am. Assn. Pathologists and Bacteriologists (past pres.), Internat. Acad. Pathology, Am. Soc. Clin. Pathology, Am. Soc. Exptl. Pathology, Am. Soc. Investigative Pathoogy, Coll. Am. Pathologists, Soc. Exptl. Biology, AAUP, Central Soc. Clin. Research, Phi Beta Kappa, Sigma Xi, Alpha Omega Alpha. Home: 36570 Ridge Rd Willoughby OH 44094-4106

CARTER, JOHN SWAIN, museum administrator, consultant; b. Exeter, N.H., May 11, 1950; s. John F. and Ethel Mae Carter; m. Karin Carter, Aug. 8, 1978; 1 child, Elsbeth. BS in Psychology, U. Mass., 1973; MA in History of Tech., U. Del., 1979. Editor The Am. Neptune, Salem, Mass., 1979-82; curator Peabody Mus. Salem, 1982-89; dir. Maine Maritime Mus., Bath, 1989-95; pres. Phila. Maritime Mus., 1995—, Independence Seaport Mus., 1990-96; vice chmn. Internat. Congress Maritime Mus., Oslo, 1987-93; dir. Phila. City Sail, Springside Sch. (v.p. 1996-98), Cushing Acad., 1999—, Herreshoff Marine Mus., 1991—, Merchant's Fund, 1995—, Pa. Fedn. Mus., 1997—. Author: Wood Book, 1980, (catalogs) Am. Traders, Maritime Arts, 1982. Mem. Am. Assn. Mus. (mem. coun. 1987-90), Coun. Am. Maritime Mus. (pres. 1986-90), Mus. Coun. Phila. (pres. 1991-93), Bostonian Soc., Union League, Corinthian Yacht Club, Phila. Cricket Club, Phila. Club, N.Y. Yacht Club, Crusing Club of Am., Edgartown Yacht Club, Royal Bermuda Yacht Club, Club Odd Volumes. Office: Independence Seaport 211 S Columbus Blvd Philadelphia PA 19106-3199

CARTER, JOHN THOMAS, retired educational administrator, writer; b. Mantee, Miss., Dec. 16, 1921; s. John Franklin and Mattie (George) C.; m. Frances Tunnell, Mar. 16, 1946; children: John W., Nell Carter Branum. Student Clarke Coll., 1940-42; student Miss. State U., 1942-43, BS, 1947; MS, U. Tenn., 1948; EdD, U. Ill., 1954. Cert. tchr. Tchr., prin. Maben Consol. Sch., Miss., 1946-47; faculty Wood Jr. Coll., Mathiston, Miss., 1947-48; faculty, farm supt. Clarke Coll., Newton, Miss., 1948-56; faculty, dean. Sch. Edn., Samford U., Birmingham, Ala., 1956-87; guest prof. Anhui Normal U., China, 1987, U. Ala. Birmingham, 1987-88; guest cons. to ednl. sys. in China, Indonesia, and Russia, 1988, 90, 91, 92, 93, 94, 95, 97. Author 6 books for children and youth, 1958-75, including: East is West, 1965; Witness in Israel, 1969; Sharing Times Seven, 1971. Regional dir. Aerospace Edn. CAP, 1970-84, 94. Served with U.S. Army, 1942-45, NATOUSA, ETO. Recipient Brewer award CAP, 1977, Crown Circle award Nat. Congress Aerospace Edn., 1983. Mem. Assn. Tchr. Educators (pres. 1970-71), Assn. Colls. for Tchr. Edn. (exec. bd. 1983-86), Assn. for Supervision and Curriculum Devel., Assn. Bapt. Educators (nat. coord. 1988—), Kiwanis, Kappa Delta Pi (treas. 1980-87), Phi Delta Kappa (v.p. 1982-83). Republican. Baptist. Avocations: flying; travel. Home: 2561 Rocky Ridge Rd Birmingham AL 35243-4442 Office: Samford U 800 Lakeshore Dr Birmingham AL 35229-0002

CARTER, JOSEPH CARLYLE, JR., lawyer; b. Mayfield, Ky., June 3, 1927; s. Joseph Carlyle and Cynthia Elizabeth (Stokes) C.; m. Dianne C. Dinwiddie, July 14, 1949; children: Joseph Carlyle, Hugh D., William H., Henry S., Dianne C. BA, U. Va., 1948, LLB, 1951. Bar: Va. 1951. Since practiced in Richmond; assoc. firm Hunton & Williams, Richmond, 1951-58, ptnr., 1958-93; mng. ptnr. Hunton & Williams, 1972-82; sr. counsel Hunton & Williams, Richmond, 1993—; dir. Albemarle Corp., 1994-96, Ethyl Corp., 1974-94. Trustee 2d Presbyn. Ch., Richmond, 1962—; chmn. Richmond Pub. Libr. Bd., 1967-77, mem., 1980-85; vice-chmn. Richard City Sch. Bd., 1990-94; trustee Colonial Williamsburg Found., 1977-93, Med. Coll. Va. Found., 1976—, pres., 1984-87; trustee U. Va. Law Sch. Found., 1985—, pres. 1988-98. Recipient Algernon Sidney Sullivan award, 1948. Mem. ABA, Va. Bar Assn., Richmond Bar Assn., Am. Law Inst., Am. Judicature Soc., Newcomen Soc. Presbyterian. Clubs: Commonwealth (Richmond), Country of Va. (Richmond). Home: 5102 Harlan Cir Richmond VA 23226-1637 Office: Hunton & Williams 951 E Byrd St Richmond VA 23219-4074

CARTER, JOSEPH EDWIN, former nickel company executive, writer; b. Jackson, Ga., Apr. 3, 1915; s. Charles Luther and Marilu (Holiman) C.; m. Virginia Meredith Crickmer, Apr. 8, 1939; children: Joseph Charles, Virginia Ann (Mrs. James Allan Colburn). B.S., Ga. Inst. Tech., 1937. Metallurgist Internat. Nickel Co., Huntington, W.Va., 1937-40; various positions Internat. Nickel Co., 1940-57, indsl. relations mgr., 1957-58, gen. supt., 1958-60; mfg. mgr. Huntington Alloy Products Div., 1960-62, v.p. mfg., 1962-67, exec. v.p., 1967-70, pres., 1971; v.p. Internat. Nickel Co. Can. Ltd., N.Y.C., 1971; exec. v.p. Internat. Nickel Co. Can. Ltd., 1972-73, pres., 1974-77; also dir.; chmn., chief exec. officer INCO Ltd., Toronto, Ont., Can., 1977-80; bd. dirs. Hamton Roads Pub. Co., Inc., Charlottesville, Va. Author: Living is Forever, 1990. Former mem. lay bd. St. Mary's Hosp.; past bd. dirs. Huntington Galleries, Huntington Pediatric Clinic. Served to maj. AUS, 1942-45. Decorated Bronze Star; Recipient Gold Knight of Industry award Nat. Mgmt. Assn., 1965. Mem. Am. Chem. Soc., W.Va. Mfrs. Assn. (pres. 1970-71), Phi Kappa Phi, Tau Beta Pi. Presbyterian (deacon). Clubs: Guyan Country, Lake Sunapee Country; University (N.Y.C.). Patentee in field. *

CARTER, KENNETH, state legislator, restauranteur; b. Scottsboro, Ala., Sept. 9, 1933; s. John and Bessie (Hennager) C.; m. Sylvia Ann Carter; children: Kenneth E., Michael S., Mitchell S., Matthew David. Restaurateur Carters 19th Hole, R.I., 1976—; mem. R.I. Ho. of Reps., Providence; mem.

fin. com., R.I. Ho. of Reps.; del. R.I. Constl. Conv., 1986. Mem. U.S. Selective Svc. Commn., State Crime Lab., Commn. on Criminal Justice, Town Dem. Com.; past pres. Pop Warner Football. Named Citizen of Yr., 1992, Quidnessett Grange. Mem. R.I. Police Chiefs Assn., Masons, Shriners, Elks. Office: 325 Railroad Ave Saunderstown RI 02874-1810*

CARTER, KENNETH CHARLES, geneticist; b. Flagstaff, Ariz., Nov. 28, 1959; s. James Frank and Norma (Barker) C. AA, AS, York Coll., 1980; BS in Biology, Abilene Christian U., 1983; PhD in Genetics, U. Tex. Med. Br., 1989. Grad. asst. U. Tex. Med. Br., Galveston, 1984-89; postdoctoral fellow U. Mass. Med. Sch., Worcester, 1989-93; scientist Human Genome Scis., Inc., Rockville, Md., 1993-98; pres. Internat. Genetics Assocs., Inc., Rockville, Md., 1998—. Contbr. articles to profl. jours. Recipient award for outstanding rsch. on aging Rose and Harry Walk Found., 1989, Muscular Dystrophy Assn., 1990, award for outstanding alumnus U. Tex. Med. Br., 1999; Kempner fellow J. B. Kempner Found., 1989, Human Genome fellow NIH, 1991. Mem. Am. Soc. for Cell Biology, AAAS, Microscopy Assn. Am., Thursday Group. Address: 11600 Brandy Hall Ln Gaithersburg MD 20878-2424

CARTER, LAURA LEE, academic librarian, psychotherapist; b. Iowa City, Apr. 9, 1955; d. Jack L. and Martha Ann (Shelton) C.; m. William Douglas Rolfe, Oct. 1, 1994. BA in East Asia Studies magna cum laude, U. Colo., 1977; M of Librarianship, U. Washington, 1979; grad. FALCON program, Cornell U., 1983; tng. in Chinese lang., Stanford Ctr., Taipei, Taiwan, 1983-84; MA in Third World History, U. Colo., 1988; MA in Transpersonal Counseling Psychol., Naropa Inst., Boulder, Colo., 1995. Internat. documents libr., asst. libr. Documents Divsn. Marriott Libr., U. Utah, Salt Lake City, 1979-82; original cataloger Norlin Libr., U. Colo., Boulder, 1986-89; internat. documents libr., asst. prof. Govt. Publs. Libr., U. Colo., Boulder, 1989-94; documents libr., asst. prof. Colo. State U., Ft. Collins, 1995-98; gen. ref. libr. Regis U., Denver, 1998—; part-time instr. Chinese and Japanese history dept history U. No. Colo., Greeley, 1987; invited participant/libr. collection devel. tour S.E. Asia, China and Japan, 1982; judge Most Notable Documents sect. Libr. Jour., 1994; organizer programs and confs.; lectr. and presenter in field. Contbr. book revs. to profl. publs., articles to periodicals. Participant Boulder County Big Sisters Program, 1992. Co-recipient READEX/GODORT/ALA Catherine Reynolds award, 1991, Univ. Colo. Program grant, 1990-91; Japan Found. Libr. Support grantee U. Utah, 1980-81; Nat. Resource fellow for Chinese lang. study Cornell U., 1982-83; tuition scholar Inter-Univ. Program for Advanced Chinese Lang. Studies, 1983-84. Mem. ALA (coord. internat. documents task force 1992-93, program chmn. internat. documents task force 1991). Avocations: gardening, hiking, biking, cooking. Home: 1508 Morning Dr Loveland CO 80538

CARTER, LOUVENIA MCGEE, nursing educator; b. Bradley, Oct. 12, 1934; d. Henry Battle and Emma (Cox) McGee; m. Harvey L. Carter Jr., Jan. 15, 1956; children: Harvey III, Christopher, Richard, Robert. Diploma, Northwestern State Coll., Natchitoches, La., 1955; BSN, Northwestern State Coll., 1961, MSN, 1979; PhD, Tex. Women's U., 1990. Svc. dir. Upjohn Health Care Svcs., Shreveport, La., 1979-81; staff nurse VA Med. Ctr., Shreveport, 1955-56, 60, 82; assoc. prof. Northwestern State U., Shreveport, 1982-97. Mem. ANA (cert. in nursing adminstrn.), Nat. Conf. Gerontol. Nurse Practitioners, Sigma Theta Tau. Home: 830 Erie St Shreveport LA 71106-1506

CARTER, MAE RIEDY, retired academic official, consultant; b. Berkeley, Calif., May 20, 1921; d. Carl Joseph and Avis Blanche (Rodehaver) Riedy; BS, U. Calif., Berkeley, 1943; m. Robert C. Carter, Aug. 19, 1944; children: Catherine, Christin Ann. Ednl. adv., then program specialist div. continuing edn. U. Del., Newark, 1968-78, asst. provost for women's affairs, exec. dir. commn. status women Office Women's Affairs, 1978-86; adv. bd. Rockefeller Family grant project, 1979-83. Regional v.p. Del. PTA, 1960-62; pres. Friends Newark Free Library, 1968-69; mem. fiscal planning com. Newark Spl. Sch. Dist., 1972. Recipient Outstanding Service award Women's Coordinating Council, 1977, 79; Spl. Recognition award, Nat. U. Extension Assn., 1977, award for credit programs, 1971, Creative Programming award, 1971, medal of distinction U. Del., 1998; AAUW grantee, 1968; Fulbright grantee, 1976; named to Delaware Women Hall of Fame, 1995. Mem. AAUW (past br. pres.), LWV, NOW, Women's Legal Def. Fund, Nat. Women's Polit. Caucus. Republican. Author: Research on Seeing and Evaluating People, 1982, (with Geis and Butler) Seeing and Evaluating People, 1982, revised, 1986, (with Haslett and Geis) The Organizational Woman: Power and Paradox, 1992; also papers, reports in field. Home: 604 Dallam Rd Newark DE 19711-3110

CARTER, MARSHALL NICHOLS, banker; b. Newport News, Va., Apr. 23, 1940; s. Marshall Sylvester and Préot (Nichols) C.; m. Mary Meehan, June 20, 1964; children: Christina Ann, Marshall William. BSCE, U.S. Mil. Acad., 1962; MS in Ops. Rsch., Systems Analysis, USN Postgrad. Sch., 1970; MA in Internat. Affairs, George Washington U., 1976. Commd. 2d lt. USMC, 1962, advanced through grades to maj., 1975; served in Vietnam, 1966-67, 70-71; resigned, 1976; White House fellow Dept. State, Washington, 1975-76; v.p. internat. dept. Chase Manhattan Bank, N.Y.C., 1976-78; dir. budgeting Chase Manhattan Corp., N.Y.C., 1978-81; product and prodn. risk mgmt. exec., div. exec. internat. trade procucts Chase Manhattan Bank, N.Y.C., 1981-84, sr. v.p. global securities svcs., 1988-91; exec. v.p. banking, sales and svcs. Chase Lincoln First Bank, Rochester, N.Y., 1985-88; pres., COO State St. Bank & Trust Co., Boston, 1991—; chmn. bd., pres., CEO, bd. dirs. State St. Boston Corp., 1992—; bd. dirs. CEDEL, Luxembourg; mem. exec. com. Livraison Valeurs Mobilieres, Luxembourg; mem. working group Group of Thirty, London, 1989—; mem. Sinai peacekeeping surveillance del. Dept. State, 1975, mem. internat. relief efforts, Guatemala, Italy, Mali., 1975. Sr. coord. Tri-State United Way, N.Y.C., 1989. Col. USMCR, 1985. Decorated Navy Cross, Bronze Star, Purple Heart. Mem. Internat. Soc. Securities Adminstrs. Republican. Roman Catholic. Avocations: flying, tennis, skiing. Office: State St Bank & Trust Co PO Box 351 225 Franklin St Boston MA 02110-2804*

CARTER, MELINDA, municipal official; b. Springfield, Ohio. BA in English lit., Ohio U.; JD, Capital U. Assoc. Beatty and Roseboro, Columbus, Ohio; spl. counsel to Ohio Atty. Gen. Columbus; exec. dir. New Salem Cmty. Reinvestment Corp., Columbus; exec. asst. to the dir. Equal Bus. Opportunity Commn., City of Columbus, exec. dir., 1996—. Mem. New Salem Missionary Bapt. Ch. Mem. Ohio U. Alumni Assn., Nat. Coalition of 100 Black Women, Network of Black Women for Justice, Alpha Kappa Alpha. Office: Equal Bus Opportunity Commn Mayor Office City of Columbus Columbus OH 43216

CARTER, MICHAEL ALLEN, college dean, nursing educator; b. Springfield, Mo., Feb. 13, 1947; s. William Franklin and Mary Alyne Kelly; m. Sarah Ann Jennings, July 4, 1969; 1 child, Elizabeth Ruth. BS in Nursing, U. Ark., 1969, MS in Nursing, 1973; D of Nursing Sci., Boston U., 1979. Cert. family nurse practitioner. Instr. U. Ark., Little Rock, 1972-73; nurse practitioner VA Hosp., Bedford, Mass., 1974-75; asst. prof. Boston U., 1975-76; asst. prof. U. Colo., Denver, 1976-79, assoc. prof., 1979-82; prof., coll. dean U. Tenn., Memphis, 1982—; chmn. Vis. Nurses Assn., Memphis. 1st lt. Nurse Corps, U.S. Army, 1969-71. Named Vol. of Yr. Salvation Army, Denver, 1978; recipient Better Life award Tenn. Health Care Assn., 1988. Fellow Am. Acad. Nursing; mem. Nat. Acads. Practice (Disting. practitioner). Home: 2933 Robin Rd Memphis TN 38111-2521 Office: U Tenn Coll Nursing 877 Madison Ave Memphis TN 38103-3408

CARTER, MICHAEL WAYNE, electrical engineer; b. Waverly, Tenn., Feb. 6, 1970; s. Jean (Warren) Hoffmann; m. Dana J. Carter, May 8, 1996. BS in Engring., Tex. Tech. U., 1996. Integration engr. Vertex Comm. Corp., Kilgore, Tex., 1996—. With U.S. Air Force, 1989-92. Mem. Am. Legion. Avocations: reading, exercizing. Office: Vertex Comm Corp 2600 N Longview St Kilgore TX 75662-6842

CARTER, NANETTE CAROLYN, artist; b. Columbus, Ohio, Jan. 30, 1954; d. Matthew Gameliel and Frances (Hill) C. BA, Oberlin Coll., 1976; MFA, Pratt Inst. of Art, 1978. Tchr. art Dwight Englewood Prep Sch., Englewood, N.J., 1978-87; profl. artist, 1987-92, CCNY, 1992-93; artist-in-residence Triangle Workshop, Pine Plains, N.Y.C., 1991. One-woman shows include Ericson Gallery, N.Y.C., 1983, N'Namdi Gallery, Detroit, 1984, 86, 92, Birmingham, Mich., 1989, 92, Cinque Gallery, N.Y.C., 1985, Montclair (N.J.) Art Mus., 1988, Jersey City (N.J.) Mus., 1990, June Kelly Gallery, SoHo, N.Y., 1990, Southampton (N.Y.) Coll., 1991, Franklin Marshall Coll., Lancaster, Pa., 1992, G.R. N'Namdi Gallery, Birmingham, Mich., 1992, 96, Kebede Fine Arts, L.A., 1992, Sande Webster Gallery, Phila., 1993, 95, June Kelly Gallery, N.Y.C., 1994, Alitash Kebete, L.A., 1995, Hodges-Taylor Gallery, Charlotte, N.C., 1997, June Kelly Gallery, N.Y.C., 1997, Sande Webster Gallery, Phila., 1997; exhibited in group shows including Bklyn. Mus., 1981, Newark Mus., 1985, Pa. Acad. Fine Arts, Phila., 1986, Clocktower Gallery, N.Y.C., 1986, Associated Am. Artists Gallery, N.Y.C., 1986, Wennigger Gallery Boston, 1987, Kenkelaba Gallery, N.Y.C., 1987, Fashion Moda Gallery, Bronx, N.Y., 1988, Studio Mus. in Harlem, N.Y., 1988, Louisa McIntosh Gallery, Atlanta, 1990, Sande Webster Gallery, Phila., 1990, East Hampton Ctr. for Contemporary Art, N.Y., 1990, Space Gallery, Cleve., 1991, Mary Ryan Gallery, N.Y.C., 1991, New Visions Gallery, Ithaca, N.Y., 1991, Bennington (Vt.) Coll., 1991, Bristol-Myers Squibb Co., Princeton, N.J., 1992; exhibited in group shows at The Rifle Gallery, Columbus, Ohio, 1991, The Nat. Mus. of Woman in the Arts, Washington, 1992, The Paine Webber Art Gallery, N.Y.C., 1993, Mus. Art, R.I. Sch. of Design, Providence, 1994, Pratt's Inst.'s Manhattan Ctr., N.Y.C., 1995, Skoto Gallery, N.Y.C., 1995, Phila. Mus. Art, 1996, Wayne State U., Detroit, 1996, Pitts. Ctr. for Arts, 1996, W.Va. Wesleyan Coll., Buckhannon, 1996, Yale U. Art Gallery, New Haven, 1996, Spelman Coll. Mus. Fine Art, Atlanta, 1996, and numerous others; represented in permanent collections Planned Parenthood, N.Y.C., Jane Zimmerli Art Mus., Rutgers U., New Brunswick, N.J., Jersey City Mus., Libr. of Congress, Washington, ARCO, Phila., Reader's Digest, Pleasantville, N.Y., Schomburg Libr., N.Y.C., Salomon Bros., N.Y.C., Newark Mus., Herbert Johnson Mu., Art, Cornell U., Ithaca, N.Y., Studio Mus. Harlem, N.Y., MCI Telecomm., Chgo., Times Mirror, N.Y.C., AT&T, N.J., IBM, Stamford, Conn., Lang Comm., Randolph, Vt., Merck Pharm. Co., Phila., Johnson & Johnson, Inc., New Brunswick, Pepsi-Cola, N.Y.C., Motown Corp., L.P., L.A., Am. Express, Mpls., Mus. Art R.I. Sch. Design, Providence, Yale Gallery of Art, New Haven, Conn., U.S.A. Assurance, San Antonio, Tex., Nextel Corp., L.A., GE, Fairfield, Conn., Cochran Found., La Grange, Ga., Rutgers Grad. Sch. Mgmt., Newark, ARCO, Phila., Magic Johnson Enterprises, L.A., Nissho Iwai Am. Corp., N.Y.C., and numerous others. Grantee Nat. Endowment for Arts, 1981, N.J. Coun. on Arts, 1985, N.Y. Found. for Arts, 1990, The Pollock-Krasner Found., 1994, Wheeler Found., N.Y.C., 1996.

CARTER, NELL, actress, singer; b. Birmingham, Ala., Sept. 13, 1948; d. Horace L. and Edna (M.) Hardy; m. Georg Krynicki, 1982 (div. 1992); m. Roger Larocque, May, 1992 (div.); children: Tracey, Joshua Bernard, Daniel. Student, Bill Russells Sch. Drama, 1970-73. Numerous radio and TV appearances in Ala.; numerous club appearances and concerts including Los Angeles Philharm; appeared in play and film: Hair; appeared in: films Modern Problems, 1981, Back Roads, 1981, The Grass Harp, 1995, The Crazysitter, 1995, The Proprietor, 1996, Fakin' Da Funk, 1997, Special Delivery, 1999; TV appearances include: Baryshnikov on Broadway, The Big Show, Christmas in Washington, Nell Carter, Never Too Old to Dream; star: TV series Gimme a Break, 1981-87, You Take the Kids, 1990-91, Hangin' with Mr. Cooper, 1993-94; TV movie Cindy, 1978, Final Shot: The Hank Gathers Story, 1992, Maid For Each Other, 1992; theatrical appearances include: Dude; Don't Bother Me, I Can't Cope; Jesus Christ Superstar; Bury the Dead; Rhapsody in Gershwin; Blues is a Woman; Black Broadway; Ain't Misbehavin', Fakin' Da Funk, 1997. Recipient Tony award; OBIE award; Drama Desk award; Soho News award for Ain't Misbehavin. Mem. AFTRA, SAG, Equity, NAACP (life). Democrat. Presbyterian. Office: care William Morris Agy c/o John Kimble 151 S El Camino Dr Beverly Hills CA 90212-2704*

CARTER, NEVILLE LOUIS, geophysicist, educator; b. Los Angeles, Aug. 21, 1934; s. Herman Louis and Maribelle (Sheller) C.; m. Susan Ruth Orton, Aug. 1, 1987; children from previous marriage: James Neville, Lindsay Louis, Jenifer June. A.B., Pomona Coll., 1956; M.A., UCLA, 1958, Ph.D., 1963; postgrad. (Fulbright fellow), U. Oslo, Norway, 1958-59. Research assoc. Inst. Geophysics, UCLA, 1963; research geologist Shell Devel. Co., Houston, 1963-66; assoc. prof. geology and geophysics Yale U., New Haven, 1966-71; prof. geophysics SUNY-Stony Brook, 1971-78; prof., head dept. geophysics, faculty assoc. Ctr. for Tectonophysics, Tex. A&M U., College Station, 1978-83; dir. Ctr. for Tectonophysics, Tex. A&M U., 1984-89; faculty assoc. Geodynamics Rsch. Inst., Tex. A&M U., 1984-96; prof. emeritus geology and geophysics Tex. A&M U., 1996—. Author, editor numerous publs. in field. Mem. Am. Geophys. Union (pres. tectonophysics sect. 1974-76), Sigma Xi. Home: PO Box 1442 Crescent City CA 95531-1442

CARTER, PAMELA LYNN, former state attorney general; b. South Haven, Mich., Aug. 20, 1949; d. Roscoe Hollis and Dorothy Elizabeth (Hadley) Fanning; m. Michael Anthony Carter, Aug. 26, 1971; children: Michael Anthony Jr., Marcya Alicia. BA cum laude, U. Detroit, 1971; MSW, U. Mich., 1973; JD, Ind. U., 1984. Bar: Ind. 1984, U.S. Dist. Ct. (no. dist.) Ind. 1984, U.S. Dist. Ct. (so. dist.) Ind. 1984. Rsch. analyst, treatment dir. U. Mich. Sch. Pub. Health and UAW, Detroit, 1973-75; exec. dir. Mental Health Ctr. for Women and Children, Detroit, 1975-77; consumer litigation atty. UAW-Gen. Motors Legal Svcs., Indpls., 1983-87; securities atty. Sec. of State, Indpls., 1987-89; Gov.'s exec. asst. for health and human svcs. Gov.'s Office, Indpls., 1989-91, dep. chief of staff to Gov., 1991-92; with firm Baker & Daniels, 1992-93; atty. gen. State of Ind., Indpls., 1993-96; partner Johnson & Smith, 1996-97; v.p., gen. counsel and sec. Cummins Engine Co., Inc., Columbus, Ind., 1998—. Author poems. mem. Cath. Social Svcs., Indpls., Jr. League, Indpls., Dem. Precinct, Indpls. Recipient Outstanding Svc. award Indiana Perinatal Assn., 1991, Community Svc. Coun. Ctrl. Ind., 1991, non-profl. healthcare award Family Health Conf. Bd. Dirs., 1991, award for excellence Women of the Rainbow, 1991; named Outstanding Young Woman of America, 1977, Breakthrough Woman of the Year, 1989. Mem. Nat. Bar Assn., Ind. Bar Assn., Coalition of 100 Black Women. Democrat. First African-American woman to hold title of Atty. Gen. in the nation, first woman atty. gen. in Ind. Avocations: gardening, hiking, traveling, reading. Office: Cummins Engine Co Inc Mail Code 60903 500 Jackson St Columbus IN 47201-6258*

CARTER, PAUL EDWARD, publishing company executive; b. Spokane, Wash., July 7, 1925; s. Richard Bert and Lula Selena (Jones) C.; m. Helen Barbara crosby, Nov. 2, 1950; children: Nancy, Thomas, Richard, Robert. BA in English and Journalism, Wash. State U., 1949. Advt. mgr. The Spokesman-Rev. and Spokane Daily Chronicle, 1949-87; advt. dir. Hobbs (N.Mex.) Daily News-Sun, 1987-91; western sales mgr. Slike Pub. Co., Harrisburg, Pa., 1983—; cons. various daily newspapers. Editor numerous ch., coll., club pubs., 1948—. Pres. Inland Empire coun. Boy Scouts Am., Spokane, 1971-73; divsn. chmn. United Way of Spokane County, 1955-68; pres. adv. bd. Spokane City U., 1977-83; bishopric LDS Ch., mem. high coun., young men's program leader, Sunday sch. supt., Elders Quorum pres., High Priest quorum leader, scoutmaster, explorer scout adviser. 1st lt. USAAF, WWII, 1943-46, USAF, Korea, 1950-52. Recipient Ramsey Oppenheim award Advt. Assn. of the West, 1962, Silver Beaver award Boy Scouts Am., 1973, Demolay Legion of Honor, 1955, Don Dirstine award Spokane Jr. C. of C., 1950, Disting. Svc. award Spokane Ctrl. Lions Club, 1958, 60 Yrs. Svc. Recognition award, 1997. Mem. Internat. Newspaper Advt. Execs. (dist. dir. 1989-92), Pacific N.W. Newspaper Advt. Execs. (pres. 1973-74), Soc. Profl. Journalists (pres. Coll. chpt.), Am. Press Inst. (del. 1958), SAR (pres. Salt Lake City chpt. 1997-98, pres. Utah Soc. 1999—), Spokane Advt. Club (pres. 1961-62, Advt. Man of the Yr. 1962, hon. life), Hobbs Rotary (pres. 1991-92, Rotarian of the Yr. 1989-90). Republican. LDS. Avocations: writing, computers, golf, rocks and minerals, church work. Home: 6280 Castleford Dr West Jordan UT 84084-6243

CARTER, PAUL MILTON, JR., federal agency administrator; b. Jan. 8, 1959. MA, Ind. U., 1984, PhD, 1997. Participant IREX Exchange Scholars with USSR, Moscow, 1985-86; vis. asst. prof. Cath. U. Am., Washington, 1988; pres., CEO Accuracy Hist. Prodns., Inc., Alexandria, Va., 1994-96; fgn. svcs. officer U.S. Dept. State, Washington, 1996—, Dept. State, Warsaw, Poland, 1996—.

CARTER, RICHARD, publisher, writer; b. N.Y.C., Jan. 24, 1918; s. Samuel J. and Alice (Kulka) C.; m. Gladys Chasins, Oct. 20, 1945; children—Nancy Jane, John Andrew. B.A., Coll. City N.Y., 1938. Music editor Billboard mag., 1940-46; staff organizer N.Y. Newspaper Guild, 1946-47; writer N.Y. Daily Mirror, 1947-49, N.Y. Daily Compass, 1949-52; pres. Millwood Publs., Inc., 1971-80; columnist The Racing Times, 1991-92, Daily Racing Form, 1992—. Author, contbr. mags., 1952—; Author: The Man Who Rocked the Boat, 1956, The Doctor Business, 1958, The Gentle Legions, 1961, Your Food and Your Health, 1964, Breakthrough: The Saga of Jonas Salk, 1966, Superswine, 1967, (with Curt Flood) The Way It Is, 1971, (under pseudonym Tom Ainslie) The Compleat Horseplayer, 1966, Ainslie's Jockey Book, 1967, Ainslie's Complete Guide to Thoroughbred Racing, 1968, The Handicapper's Handbook, 1969, Theory and Practice of Handicapping, 1969, Ainslie's Complete Guide to Harness Racing, 1970, Ainslie's Complete Hoyle, 1975, Ainslie's Encyclopedia of Thoroughbred Handicapping, 1978, How to Gamble in a Casino, 1979, (with Bonnie Ledbetter) The Body Language of Horses, 1980. Served with USAAF, 1942-45, PTO. Recipient George Polk Meml. award, 1952. Mem. Authors Guild, Nat. Assn. Sci. Writers, Nat. Turf Writers Assn. Address: 165 Pinesbridge Rd Ossining NY 10562-1317

CARTER, RICHARD BERT, retired church official, retired government official; b. Spokane, Wash., Dec. 2, 1916; s. Richard B. and Lula Selena (Jones) C.; BA in Polit. Sci., Wash. State U., 1939; postgrad. Georgetown U. Law Sch., 1941, Brown U., 1944, Brigham Young U. Extension, 1975-76; m. Mildred Brown, Sept. 6, 1952; children: Paul, Mark, Janis, David. *Immigrant surname ancestor: William Carter, blacksmith, glass blower, born February 12, 1821, Ledbury, Herefordshire, England; joined Church of Jesus Christ of Latter-day Saints, 1840; migrated to Nauvoo, Illinois 1841; married Ellen Benbow 1843 and posterity includes Church Apostle Jeffrey Roy Holland; served as scout in first Brigham Young pioneer company to Utah 1847; entered valley with advance party and plowed first half-acre ground July 23, 1847 before Brigham arrived; married second wife Harriet Temperance Utley, 1853, whose ancestor is Congregational Church minister Littlejohn Utley from whom also descends Apostle David Bruce Haight* Advt. credit mgr. Elec. Products Consol., Omaha, 1939-40; pub. affairs ofcl., investigator FBI, Washington, 1940-41, Huntington, W.Va., 1941, Houston, 1942, Boston, 1943, S. Am., 1943, Providence, 1944-45, N.Y.C., 1945, Salt Lake City, 1945, P.R., 1946-48, Phoenix, 1948-50, Washington, 1950-51, Cleve., 1952-55, Seattle, 1955-75, ret., 1975; assoc. dir. stake and mission pub. affairs dept. Ch. Hdqrs., Ch. of Jesus Christ of Latter-day Saints, Salt Lake City, 1975-77. Dist. chmn. Chief Seattle coun. Boy Scouts Am., 1967-68, coun. v.p., 1971-72, coun. commr., 1973-74, nat. coun. rep., 1962-64, 72-74; life mem., area II Nat. Eagle Scout Assn., 1984—. Mem. Freedoms Found. Valley Forge, Utah chpt., 1988—; bd. dirs. Salvation Army, 1963, United Way, 1962-63, mem. allocations com., 1962, 1987-88, JayCees, Omaha, Neb., 1939-40; organizer First Family History Lib., Seattle, 1971. Served to lst lt., Intelligence Corps, U.S. Army, 1954. Recipient Silver Beaver award Boy Scouts Am., 1964, Vigil Honor, 1971, Alumni Achievement award for Disting. Svc. Wash. State U., 1997; named Nat. Media Man-of-Month Morality in Media, Inc., N.Y.C., 1976. Mem. Profl. Photographers Am., Internat. Assn. Bus. Communicators, Am. Security Council (nat. adv. bd.), Internat. Platform Assn., Sons Utah Pioneers (pres. 1982, Disting. Svc. award 1985), SAR (pres. Salt Lake City chpt. 1987-88, Law Enforcement Commendation medal 1987, Meritorious Svc. medal 1989, Pres.-Gen.'s Program Excellence award, Oliver R. Smith medal 1990, Grahame T. Smallwood award 1990, Liberty medal 1991, Patriot medal 1992), Utah State Soc. (pres. 1989-90), Amicus Club of Deseret Found., chmn. membership com. 1988—, Gold Caduceus award, 1993, Wall of Honor), World Sr. Games (adv. com, 1987—), William Carter Family Orgn. (nat. pres.), Nat. Assn. Chiefs of Police (Am. Police Hall of Fame, John Edgar Hoover Distin. Pub. Svc. medal 1991, Nat. Patriotism medal, 1993), Scabbard and Blade, Crimson Circle, Am. Media Network (nat. adv. bd.), Utah Sheriffs' Assn. , Assn. Former Intelligence Officers, Soc. Profl. Journalists, Alpha Phi Omega, Pi Sigma Alpha, Phi Delta Theta. Mem. LDS Ch. (coord. pub. affars council Seattle area 1973-75, br. pres. 1944-45, seventies quorum pres. 1952, dist. pres. 1954-55, high priest 1958—, stake pres. counselor 1959-64, stake Sunday Sch. pres. 1980-81, temple staff 1987—). Clubs: Bonneville Knife and Fork (bd. dirs. 1982-85), Rotary (dir., editor The Rotary Bee, 1982-83, Paul Harris fellow 1982, Richard L. Evans fellow 1987, Best Club History in Utah award 1988, Best Dist. Newsletter award 1983, Rotarian of Month 1988, membership com. 1995—, club 24 found. bd. 1995—). Author: The Sunbeam Years-An Autobiography, 1986; assoc. editor FBI Investigator, 1965-75; contbg. author, editor: Biographies of Sons of Utah Pioneers, 1982; contbr. articles to mags. Home: 2180 Elaine Dr Bountiful UT 84010-3120 *Receiving good gifts brings happiness. Giving your time to serve others bring true joy.*

CARTER, RICHARD BONNER, systems specialist; b. Lancaster, S.C., Dec. 11, 1946; s. Samuel Hazel and Sue Simpson (McCain) C.; m. Patricia Joann Phillips, June 14, 1969; children: Jennifer Susan, Courtney Ann, Richard Bonner, II. BA in Math., Erskine, 1969. Programmer Springs Mills, Lancaster, 1969-77, systems analyst, 1977-83; systems specialist Springs Industries, Lancaster, 1983—. Youth leader Unity Assoc. Reformed Presbyn. Ch., Lancaster, 1973—, deacon, Lancaster, 1974-95, elder, 1996—; unit commr. Boy Scouts Am., Lancaster, 1990—; vice chmn. Buford Sch. Improvement Coun., Lancaster, 1998—. Avocations: woodworking, picture framing. Home: 3474 Unity Church Rd Lancaster SC 29720-8388 Office: Springs Industries PO Box 111 Lancaster SC 29721-0111

CARTER, RICHARD DUANE, business educator; s. Herbert Duane and Edith Irene (Richardson) C.; m. Nancy Jean Cannell, Sept. 3, 1955; 1 child, Erich Richardson. AB, Coll. William and Mary; MBA, Columbia U.; PhD, UCLA, 1968. Sr. advisor, dir. Taiwan Metal Industries Devel. Ctr. (under auspices of ILO), 1966-67; dir. UNDP, cons. svcs., Taiwan, 1966-67; chief exec. officer Human Resources Inst., Baton Rouge, La., 1968-70; liaison advisor Internat. Inst. Applied Systems Analysis, Vienna, Austria, 1975; U.S. rep., dir. indsl. mgmt. and cons. svcs. program UN Indsl. Devel. Orgn., Vienna, 1970-75; mem. East-West Trade and Mgmt. Commn., 1973-75; sr. advisor, dir. Korean Inst. Sci. and Tech. (under auspices of UN), Seoul, 1974-75; dean Sch. Bus. Quinnipiac Coll., Hamden, Conn., 1977-80; chmn. bd. TCG Industries, Inc., N.Y.C., 1980—; prof. mgmt., program coord. Fairfield (Conn.) U., 1980-84; founder, mng. dir. Internat. Mgmt. Consortium, Vienna, Westport and Millerton, N.Y., 1975—; assoc. mem. Seminar on Orgn. and Mgmt. Columbia U., 1975-89, vice-chmn. Seminar on Orgn. and Mgmt., 1976-89, chmn. rsch. and publ. com. Seminar on Orgn. and Mgmt., 1983-89; mng. dir. Wainwright & Ramsey Securities, Inc., N.Y.C., 1985—. Mem. editorial bd. Indian Adminstrv. and Mgmt. Rev., New Delhi, 1974-76; author: Management: In Perspective and Practice, 1970, The Future Challenges of Management Education, 1981; also numerous articles and revs. Trustee Dingletown Community Ch., Greenwich, Conn., 1978-87; mem. adv. coun. Calif. Coll. Tech., L.A., 1978—. Fellow Internat. Acad. Mgmt.; mem. Acad. Mgmt., Am. Mgmt. Assns. (pres.'s council, dir. 1976-77), N.Am. Soc. Corp. Planning, N.Am. Mgmt. Coun. (bd. dirs. 1983-87), Soc. Internat. Orgn. Devel., Mensa, Triple Nine Soc., Explorers Club, Sharon (Conn.) Country Club, Beta Gamma Sigma. *Success depends upon the art of optimizing the skills of confrontation, accommodation and cooperation.*

CARTER, RICHARD E(ITEL), legal association executive; b. Indpls., Oct. 30, 1935; m. Constance Crowder. BA, Butler U., 1958; LLB, Ind. U., 1961; postgrad., Common Market Sch., Luxembourg, summer 1963. Bar: Ind. 1961, D.C. 1966. Tchg. assoc., Krannert fellow Sch. Law Ind. U., Bloomington, 1961-63; litigation atty. Bur. Restraint of Trade, FTC, 1963-66; staff atty. Neighborhood Legal Svcs., Inc., 1966, mng. atty., 1967; project mgr. GWU-VISTA tng. project Neighborhood Legal Svcs. Program, Inc., 1967, acting exec. dir., dep. dir. law reform and edn., 1969-70; dir. Columbus Cmty. Legal Svcs. Program, Washington, 1970-71; asst. prof. Columbus Sch. Law, Cath. U. Am., Washington, dir. legal svcs. tng. program, 1971-76; dir. office of program support Legal Svcs. Corp., Washington, 1976-78; dir. Atty. Gen.'s Advocacy Inst. U.S. Dept. Justice, Washington, 1979-80, dir. Office Legal Edn., 1980-85; dir. divsn. for profl. edn. ABA, Chgo., 1985-93; exec. dir. com. on continuing profl. edn. Am. Law Inst.-ABA, Phila., 1993—; participant conf. on enhancing competence of lawyers Am. Law Inst.-ABA, 1981, Arden Ho. III nat. conf. on CLE of Bar, com. on continuing profl. edn., 1987, mem. adv. com. on study of CLE quality evaluation methods and stds. project, com. on continuing profl. edn., 1988-91; organizer course for clin. law tchrs., participant faculty Nat. Inst. for Trial Advocacy, summers 1974-75; organizer, instr. course in lawyering skills Asian Workshop for Legal Svcs. to Poor, Ford Found., summer 1974; mem. rev. com. for sr. v.p.

acad. affairs, on evaluation of CLE in Calif., U. Calif., fall 1986; mem. adv. com. on profl. edn. for dir. Inst. for Mgmt. of Lifelong Edn., Grad. Sch. Edn., Harvard U., 1991—. Inductee Acad. Law Alumni Fellows, Ind. U. Sch. Law, 1997. Fellow Am. Bar Found.; mem. FBA (mem. coun. on fed. litigation 1981-84), ABA (discussion leader workshop on in-ho. CLE 1983), Am. Law Inst. (elected), Assn. Continuing Legal Edn., D.C. Bar Assn. Office: Am Law Inst-ABA 4025 Chestnut St Philadelphia PA 19104-3054*

CARTER, RICHARD LELAND, neurosurgeon; b. Chgo., Oct. 17, 1958; s. John Malcom Sr. and Esther Elizabeth Carter; m. Bonnie Jean Carter, Oct. 27, 1990 (div. Feb. 1999); children: Kristen, Lindsay. BS, U. Mich., 1980, MD, 1984. Diplomate Am. Bd. Neurol. Surgery. Intern in gen. surgery U. Fla., Gainesville, 1984-85, resident in neurosurgery, 1985-90, chief resident in neurosurgery, 1990-91; neurosurgeon Bapt. Hosp., Miami, Fla., 1991-93, Meml. Healthcare Sys., Hollywood, Fla., 1993—; clin. asst. prof. neurosurgery U. Maimi, 1992-93. Contbr. chpts. to books, article to profl. jour. Fellow ACS; mem. Am. Assn. Neurol. Surgeons, Congress Neurol. Surgeons, Fla. Neurosurg. Soc. (bd. dirs. 1995-96, sec. 1997-98, pres-elect 1999). Avocations: rollerblading, skiing, scuba diving, art collecting. E-mail: mdrlc@aol.com. Office: Meml Healthcare Divsn Neurosurgery 1150 N 35th Ave # 300 Hollywood FL 33021

CARTER, ROBERTA ECCLESTON, therapist, counselor; b. Pitts.; d. Robert E. and Emily B. (Bucar) Carter; divorced; children: David Michael Kiewlich, Daniel Michael Kiewlich. Student Edinboro State U., 1962-63; BS, California State U. of Pa., 1966; MEd, U. Pitts., 1969; MA, Rosebridge Grad. Sch., Walnut Creek, Calif., 1987. Tchr., Bethel Park Sch. Dist., Pa., 1966-69; writer, media asst. Field Ednl. Pub., San Francisco, 1969-70; educator, counselor, specialist Alameda Unified Sch. Dist., Calif., 1970—; master trainer Calif. State Dept. Edn., Sacramento, 1984—; personal growth cons., Alameda, 1983—. Author: People, Places and Products, 1970, Teaching/Learning Units, 1969; co-author: Teacher's Manual Let's Read, 1968. Mem. AAUW, NEA, Calif. Fedn. Bus. and Profl. Women (legis. chair Alameda br. 1984-85, membership chair 1985), Calif. Edn. Assn., Alameda Edn. Assn., Charter Planetary Soc., Oakland Mus., Exploratorium, Big Bros. of East Bay, Alameda C. of C. (svc. award 1985). Avocations: aerobics, gardening, travel. Home: 1516 Eastshore Dr Alameda CA 94501-3118

CARTER, RODNEY, corporate finance executive; b. Roswell, N.Mex., Oct. 17, 1957; s. Powhatan Jr. and Beverly Jean (Tucker) C.; m. Dawn Denise Howes, Aug. 1, 1981; children: Meghan Alyssa, Brandon Matthew. BA, Tex. Tech U., 1980; MBA, So. Meth. U., 1983; M. in Internat. Mgmt., Am. Grad. Sch. Internat. Mgmt., Glendale, Ariz., 1983. Comml. banking officer Rep. Bank Dallas, N.A., 1983-86; asst. v.p. AmeriTrust Co., Dallas, 1986-87; financing project mgr. J.C. Penney Co., Inc., Dallas, 1988-90, corp. financing dir., 1990-92; mgr. fin. planning J.C. Penney Co., Inc., Plano, Tex., 1992-94; sr. v.p. fin. and planning, treas. J.C. Penney Life Ins. Co., Plano, 1994-97; fin. dir. EVA Team J.C. Penney Co., Inc., Plano, 1997-98, dir. portfolio mgmt., 1998—; fin. cons. North Am. Sound, Dallas, 1982, Jordan & Johnson, Inc., Dallas, 1986; bd. dirs. Fin. Exec. Inst. Advisor Jr. Achievement, Dallas, 1983-84; account vol. United Way, Dallas, 1983-86. Mem. Dallas C. of C. (internat. com. 1984-88, strategic planning forum), Am. Fin. Assn., Fin. Exec. Inst. Republican. Mem. Ch. of Christ. Avocations: golf, tennis, squash, sailing. Home: 5977 Willowross Way Plano TX 75093-5985 Office: JC Penney Co Inc 6501 Legacy Dr Plano TX 75024-3698

CARTER, RONALD MARTIN, SR., pharmaceutical company executive; b. Chgo., Nov. 18, 1925; s. Jack Edward and Anna (Press) C.; m. Joy Wolf, Nov. 14, 1946; children: Ronald M. Jr., Craig Alan. Student, U. Ill., 1942-43, 45-46. Sales mgr. Preston Labs., Inc., Chgo., 1948-52; v.p. Myers-Carter Labs., Inc., Phoenix, 1952-69, pres., 1969-75; pres. Carter-Glogau Labs., Inc., Glendale, Ariz., 1975-86, Steris Labs., Inc., Phoenix, 1987—, The Pharmikon Co., 1987—; cons. Internat. Exec. Service Corp., Stamford, Conn., 1985—. Served as cpl. U.S. Army, 1943-45. Mem. Drug, Chem. Allied Trades, Generic Pharm. Industry Assn., Nat. Assn. Pharm. Mfrs., Nat. Pharm. Alliance (pres. 1983-84). Democrat. Jewish. Clubs: Arizona, Plaza (Phoenix). Avocations: hunting, fishing. Home: 5707 N 40th St Phoenix AZ 85018-1108

CARTER, ROSALYNN SMITH, wife of former President of United States; b. Plains, Ga., Aug. 18, 1927; d. Edgar and Allie (Murray) Smith; m. James Earl Carter, Jr., July 7, 1946; children: John William, James Earl III, Donnel Jeffrey, Amy Lynn. Grad., Ga. Southwestern Coll.; DHL (hon.), Morehouse Coll., 1980; LLD (hon.), U. Notre Dame, 1987. Disting. fellow Inst. Women's Studies Emory U., Atlanta, 1990—; vice chair, bd. trustees The Carter Ctr., chair Mental Health Task Force Carter Ctr.; pres., bd. dirs. Rosalynn Carter Inst. of Ga. Southwestern State U.; co-founder Every Child by Two Campaign for Early Immunization. Author: First Lady from Plains, 1984, (with Jimmy Carter) Everything to Gain: Making the Most of the Rest of Your Life, 1987, Helping Yourself Help Others: A Book for Caregivers, 1994, Helping Someone With Mental Illness: A Compassionate Guide for Family, Friends and Caregivers, 1998. Bd. dirs. Friendship Force; bd. advisors Habitat for Humanity; mem. Ga. Gov.'s Commn. to Improve Svcs. for Mentally and Emotionally Handicapped, 1971; hon. chmn. Pres.'s Commn. on Mental Health, 1977-78. Recipient Presdl. Citation APA, 1982, Nathan S. Kline medal of merit Internat. Com. Against Mental Illness, 1984, Disting. Alumnus award Am. Assn. State Colls. and Univs., 1987, Dorothea Dix award Mental Illness Found., 1988, Dean's award Columbia U. Coll. Physicians and Surgeons, 1991, Notre Dame award for internat. humanitarian svc., 1992, Eleanor Roosevelt Living World award Peace Links, 1992, Nat. Caring award, The Caring Inst., 1995, Kiwanis World Svc. medal, Kiwanis Internat. Found., 1995, Jefferson award Am. Inst. for Pub. Svc., 1996, Into the Light award Nat. Mental Health Assn., 1997. Hon. fellow Am. Psychiat. Assn.

CARTER, ROY ERNEST, JR., journalist, educator; b. Ulysses, Kans., Apr. 7, 1922; s. Roy Ernest and Inez (Anderson) C.; m. Ruby Maxine Rice, Mar. 28, 1948; children: Phyllis Diane, Patricia Inez, Susan Dolores. BA, Ft. Hays State U., 1948; MA, U. Minn., 1951; PhD, Stanford U., 1954; Prof. h.c., U. Chile, 1982. Reporter, editor, editorial writer various newspapers, 1942-48, 51; high sch. tchr. Hutchinson, Kans., 1948-50; assoc. prof., chmn. dept. journalism Ohio Wesleyan U., 1951-52; acting assoc. prof. journalism Stanford U., 1952-54; research prof. journalism, mem. Inst. Research in Social Sci. of U. N.C., 1954-58; prof. journalism, sociology and internat. relations U. Minn., 1958-90, prof. emeritus, 1990—, prof. Ind. and Distance Learning Ctr.; lectr., Quito, Ecuador, 1961, Chile, Argentina, Uruguay, 1991; vis. prof. U. Chile, 1962-63, 82, U. Concepción, Chile, 1964, 66-68, 91, U. Costa Rica, 1971, 84, U. Pernambuco, Brazil, 1972, U. P.R., 1978-79, 86, Cath. U. Uruguay, 1987, U. del Salvador, Buenos Aires, 1989, Fla. Internat. U., 1992-96, U. Md., 1996—; cons. to mktg., pub. opinion rsch. firms, internat. orgns. Author: North Carolina Press-Medical Study, 1957, (with R.O. Nafziger, D.M. White et al.) Introduction to Mass Communication Research, 1963; Assoc. editor of: Journalism, Quarterly, 1958-63; Contbr. articles to sci. jours. Recipient Kellogg Found. grant Stanford, 1952-53, sr. Fulbright-Hays award Chile, 1962-63, sr. Fulbright-Hays award Costa Rica, 1971, sr. Fulbright award Argentina, 1989, Social Sci. Research Council grants, 1962, 68; Rotary fellow, Uruguay, 1987. Fellow Am. Sociol. Assn.; mem. Assn. Edn. Journalism, World Assn. Pub. Opinion Research, Sigma Delta Chi, Phi Kappa Phi. Episcopalian. Research in Costa Rica, 1975, 91, El Salvador and Chile, 1976, P.R., 1979, Uruguay, 1982-89, Colombia, 1993, Peru, 1994. Office: U of Minn Journalism Sch 206 Church St SE Minneapolis MN 55455-0488*

CARTER, RUTH B. (MRS. JOSEPH C. CARTER), foundation administrator; b. Charlotte, Vt.; d. Ira E. and Sadie M. (Congdon) Burroughs; m. Joseph C. Carter, June 28, 1935. PhB, U. Vt., 1931. Prin. Newton Acad., Shoreham, Vt., 1931-35; substitute tchr. Spaulding High Sch., Barre, Vt., 1931-35, Woodbury (Vt.) High Sch., 1935-36; tchr. Craftsbury Acad., Craftsbury Common, Vt., 1936-38; sales mgr., buyer Vt. Music Co., Barre, 1939-44; statistician Syracuse U., 1944-46; instr. English Temple U., Phila., 1946-47; records clk. sec. Phila., 1947-56; tchr. English Cen. High Sch., Phila., 1957, Springfield Twp. Sr. High Sch., Montgomery County, Pa., 1964-65; exec. dir. White-Williams Found., 1966-82, trustee, 1982-95. Author: (with Joseph C. Carter) Anchors Aweigh Around the World with Ernest Vail Burroughs, 1960, Pilgrimage to the Lovely Lands of our Ancestors, 1984. Recipient Humanitarian award Chapel of Four Chaplains, 1981, city coun. citation City of Phila., 1982, citation White-Williams Found., 1994. Mem. AAUW (admissions chmn. Phila. chpt. 1959-61, sec. 1961-64, treas. 1965-67), DAR (treas., historian, com. chmn., budget dir., regent Germantown chpt. 1983-86, 89-92, treas. 1992-95, registrar 1995— pub. rels. chmn. 1986—), Women for Greater Phila., New Eng. Hist. Geneal. Soc., Geneal. Soc. Vt., Soc. Mayflower Descs. (bd. dirs. 1983-84, sec. 1985-91), Temple U. Faculty Wives Club (rec. sec. 1983-86, sec. 1997—, pres. Old York group), Temple U. Women's Club, The English Speaking Union, Regent's Club (Phila. chaplain 1986-88). Republican. Methodist. Home: 40 Mount Carmel Ave Apt D2 Glenside PA 19038-3429

CARTER, S. DANIEL, corporate administrator, computer consultant, political consultant; b. Atlanta, Aug. 18, 1971; s. Lisa Ann Carter. BA, U. Tenn., 1994. State dir. Safe Campuses Now, Inc., Knoxville, Tenn., 1992-94; field rep. Security on Campus, Inc., Knoxville, Tenn., 1994-95, regional v.p., 1995-96; v.p. Security on Campus, Inc., King of Prussia, Pa., 1997—. Bd. dirs. Tenn. Victims' Coalition, Nashville, 1993, 96, East Tenn. Victims' Rights, Knoxville, 1994-95; corp. bd. dirs. Safe Campuses Now, Inc., Athens, Ga., 1992-97; mem. exec. com. Knox County Rep. Party, Knoxville, 1994—; vice chmn. Knox County Young Reps., Knoxville, 1997-98. Recipient Jeanne Clery Safe Campus award, 1994. Mem. Soc. Profl. Journalists (1st Amendment award 1998, assoc. mem.). Presbyterian. Avocations: photography, computers, politics. Home: 7505 Granda Dr Knoxville TN 37909-1730 Office: Security on Campus Inc Ste 205 601 South Henderson Rd King Of Prussia PA 19406

CARTER, SALLY PACKLETT, elementary education educator; b. Clovis, N.Mex., May 15, 1948; d. Charles Everett and Marion Jamie (Pippin) Gee; m. Leonard Gene Carter, Mar. 7, 1969; 1 child, Dale Lee. BS in Edn., Ctrl. Mo. State U., 1969, MS in Edn., 1981. Cert. vocat. home econs. grades 7-12, elem. edn. grades K-6, Mo., K-8 elem. edn., home econs. grades 7-12, Ariz. Home econ. tchr. Deepwater (Mo.) High Sch., 1969-71; tchr. grade 7 Deepwater (Mo.) Sch., 1971-73; tchr. grades 1 and 2 Davis R-12, Clinton, Mo., 1974-80; tchr. grade 5 Southeast Elem., Clinton, 1980-96; substitute tchr. Mesa, Ariz., 1996-97; tchr. grade 6 Fountain Hills (Ariz.) Middle Sch., 1997—. Mem. Nat. Coun. Tchrs. Math., Mo. State Tchrs. (pres. ctrl. dist. 1989-90), Clinton Tchrs. Assn. (pres. 1985, 90, 92), Ariz. Edn. Assn., VFW Ladies Aux. Post 1894, Delta Kappa Gamma (1st v.p. Mu. chpt. 1992-94, pres. Mu. chpt. 1994-96, Alpha Epsilon chpt. 1996—), Phi Kappa Phi. Avocations: reading, fishing, cooking, sewing. Home: 6316 E Quartz St Mesa AZ 85215-0943

CARTER, SANDRA JO, art therapist, costume designer, consultant; b. Canton, Ohio, Aug. 20, 1953; d. Albert John and Florence (Khoury) Mazzaferro; m. Alan James Carter, Aug. 5, 1972 (div. Nov. 1994); children: Lorien, Erin, Alan James Jr., McCall. BA, Mary Baldwin Coll., 1983. Tchr. art Trinity Christian Sch., Mt. Crawford, Va., 1983-85; resource specialist Grace Christian Sch., Staunton, Va., 1986-87; art therapist Augusta Hosp. Corp., Staunton, 1987—; with Assoc. MentL Health Profls., Staunton; costume designer Staunton Acad. Ballet, 1995—; art supr. Staunton Recreation Dept., 1997—. Republican. Mem. Christian and Missionary Alliance. Avocations: sewing, bicycling, piano playing. Office: Assoc Mental Health Profls 102 Mactanly Pl Ste E Staunton VA 24401-2316

CARTER, SHERRY, women's basketball coach; children: Kerri Michelle, Daniel Brooks III. AD, Anderson Jr. Coll., 1972; grad., U. S.C., 1974. Tchr. dept. phys. edn. Woodmont H.S., 1974-79, head women's basketball, track, volleyball, gymnastics coach, 1974-79; tchr., head dept. phys. edn. J.L. Mann Sch., 1980-82; head women's basketball coach Furman U., Greenville, S.C., 1982—, sr. woman adminstr., 1990-96; mem. cert. com. NCAA, 1994-95, chair So. conf. Golf. Com., 1993-94, chair So. Conf. Basketball Com., 1991—. Mem. Women's Basketball Coaches Assn. Office: Furman U Office of Sprots Info 3300 Poinsett Hwy Greenville SC 29613-1000

CARTER, SYLVIA, journalist; b. Keokuk, Iowa; d. Charles Sylvester and Frances Elizabeth (Smith) C. B of Journalism, U. Mo., 1968. Intern Quincy (Ill.) Herald-Whig, 1966, Detroit Free Press, 1967; reporter The N.Y. Daily News, 1968-70; successively gen. assignment reporter, edn. reporter, food writer, restaurant critic, food columnist Newsday, Melville, N.Y., 1970—; food writer, restaurant critic N.Y. Newsday, N.Y.C., 1985-95; founder, editor Kidsday Newsday, Melville. Author: Eats: The Best Little Restaurants in New York, 1988, Eats N.Y.C.: A Guide to the Best, Cheapest, Most Interesting Restaurants in Brooklyn, Queens and Manhattan, 1995; contbr. to Family Circle and other publs. Trustee Anne O'Hare McCormick Scholarship Fund, N.Y.C., 1988—. Mem. Newswomen's Club N.Y. (pres. 1990-92, bd. dirs., Front Page award 1982). Democrat. Presbyterian. Avocations: reading, collectibles, hiking, music, cooking. Home: 111 Waverly Pl New York NY 10011-9142 also: 46 Crescent Bow Ridge NY 11961-2915 Office: Newsday 235 Pinelawn Rd Melville NY 11747-4250

CARTER, TERRI GAY MANNS, Latin language educator; b. Centralia, Ill., Jan. 8, 1954; d. William Henry and Alfrieda (Kramer) Manns; m. Jerry William Carter, July 16, 1977; children: Emily Ann, Jerry William. BA, Tex. Tech U., 1975; MEd, U. North Tex., 1991, EdD, 1997. Secondary sch. Latin tchr. Big Spring (Tex.) Ind. Sch. Dist., 1975-78, Conroe (Tex.) Ind. Sch. Dist., 1978-89; secondary sch. Latin tchr. Grapevine (Tex.)-Colleyville Ind. Sch. Dist., 1989-98, curriculum writer, 1991—, insvc. preparer, 1992; chair dept. fgn. lang., 1994—. Lay minister Emmanuel Presbyn. Ch., Bedford, Tex., 1991-92. Mem. Classical Assn. So. U.S., Tex. Classical Assn., Am. Classical League, Tex. Fgn. Lang. Assn., Tex. Assn. for Gifted and Talented. Democrat. Avocation: reading. Home: 2600 Knoll Trl Euless TX 76039-2044 Office: Grapevine High Sch 3223 Mustang Dr Grapevine TX 76051-5998

CARTER, THOMAS ALLEN, retired engineering executive, consultant; b. Cin., July 12, 1935; s. Fernando Albert and Mary Gladys (Gover) C.; m. Janet Tucker, Oct. 14, 1956; children: Barry Everett, Duane Allen, Sarita Anne. AB, Jones Coll., 1980, BBA cum laude, 1982. Cert. constrn. insp. Enlisted USN, 1954, advanced through grades to master chief, ret., 1976; contract adminstr. Red Lobster Restaurants, Orlando, Fla., 1976-78; pvt. practice Orlando, 1978-80; sec. Blacando Devel. Corp., Orlando, 1980-84; chief engr. D.A.M.S., Inc., Orlando, 1984-91; constrn. cons., 1997—; estimator Ind. Mech. Design Co., Inc., 1996—. Mem. Fleet Res. Assn., Rafman Club Orlando, Am. Legion, Nat. Pinochle Assn. Democrat. Methodist. Avocations: bowling, tennis.

CARTER, THOMAS SMITH, JR., retired railroad executive; b. Dallas, June 6, 1921; s. Thomas S. and Mattie (Dowell) C.; m. Janet R. Hostetter, July 3, 1946 (dec. 1981); children: Diane Carter Petersen, Susan Carter Estes, Charles T., Carol Carter Koehler. BS in Civil Engring., So. Meth. U., 1944; MS in Engring. Mgmt., Kans. U., 1991. Registered profl. engr., Mo., Kans., Okla., Tex., La., Ark. Various positions Mo. Kans. Tex. R.R., 1941-44, 46-54, chief engr., 1954-61, v.p. ops., 1961-66; v.p. Kansas City So. Rlwy. Co., La. and Ark. Rlwy. Co., 1966-74; pres. Kansas City So. Rlwy. Co., 1973-86, also bd. dirs., chmn. bd., 1981-91; pres. La. and Ark. Rlwy. Co., 1974-86, also bd. dirs., chmn. bd., 1981-91, CEO, 1981-91; bd. dirs. Kansas City So. Industries, 1974-96, Georgetown Rail Equipment Co., 1995—, Assn. Am. R.R.'s, 1980-90, Snead Rsch. Inst., 1995—, Tex.-Mex. Rlwy. Co., Comml. Travel Inc., chmn. bd., 1996—; adj. prof. Rockhurst Coll., 1992-93; instr. Johnson County C.C., 1992-93. With C.E., AUS, 1944-46. Fellow ASCE; mem. Am. Rlwy. Engring. and Maintenance Assn. (life), NSPE, Hide-A-Way Lake Club. Home: 131 Clubview Dr Lindale TX 75771-5054

CARTER, VINCE, professional basketball player; b. Jan. 26, 1977. Grad., N.C. U., 1998. Forward Toronto (Can.) Raptors, 1998—; named NCAA Tournament All-East Regional Team, 1997, 98; mem. 1995 USA Basketball Jr. Team, World Championships. Established Embassy of Hope Found.; named Goodwill Amb., Big Bros./Big Sisters of Am. Recipient Schick Rookie of Yr. award 1998-99, selected Schick All-Rookie 1st Team. Office: c/o Toronto Raptors, 20 Bay St Ste 300, Toronto Ont CAN M5J 2N8*

CARTER, WILFRED WILSON, financial executive, controller; b. Providence, Feb. 22, 1923; s. Leo and Florence (Wilson) C.; m. Elsa Aulisio, June 17, 1950; children—Linda J., Donald J., Paul J., Gregory J. A.A., Roger Williams Coll., 1951; student, Bryant Coll., 1958-62. Sec., tax mgr. Nicholson File Co., East Providence, 1940-73; controller Columbia Chase Corp. (name changed to Chase Corp.), Braintree, Mass., 1973-84, v.p. fin., controller, 1984-88, CEO, pres., treas., CFO, 1988-91, chmn. bd. dirs., CEO, treas., 1991-93, chmn. bd. dirs., 1993-94; ret., 1994. Served with USAAF, 1942-46. Mem. Tax Exec. Inst. Episcopalian (vestryman 1968-76, 94, treas. 1968-76). Home: 40 Kennedy Blvd Lincoln RI 02865-3602

CARTER, WILLIAM GEORGE, III, career officer; b. Buffalo, June 18, 1944; s. William George Jr. and Elaine Ruth (Weber) C.; m. Linda Fay Yener, Oct. 2, 1965; children: Kris Ann, William George. BS, U. Tampa, 1972; MA, U. Shippensberg, 1982; MPE, U. Pitts., 1984. Commd. 2d. lt. U.S. Army, 1965, advanced through grades to lt. gen., 1995; various command and staff positions, 1964-77; exec. officer 3d Brigade, 1st Armored Div., Bamberg, Fed. Republic Germany, 1977-79; comdr. 1st Bn., 52d Inf., Bamberg, 1979-81, G3 1st Armored Div., VII U.S. Corps, Ansbach, Fed. Republic Germany, 1981-83; chief Plans and Integration Office, Hdqrs. U.S. Army, Washington, 1983-86; comdr. 1st Brigade, 4th Inf. Div., Ft. Carson, Colo., 1986-88; exec. asst. Office Chief of Staff Army, Washington, 1988-89; asst. div. comdr. 1st Inf. Div., Ft. Riley, Kans., 1989-91; comdr. Nat. Tng. Ctr., Ft. Irwin, Calif., 1991-93, 1st Armored Divsn., 1993-95; chief of staff Allied Forces So. Europe, 1995-97. Decorated DDSM with oak leaf cluster, DSM with oak leaf cluster, Legion of Merit with six oak leaf clusters, Bronze Star with V device and two oak leaf clusters, Purple Heart with oak leaf cluster. Mem. Soc. of the Big Red One, Alpha Chi. Avocations: golf, hunting.

CARTER, WILLIAM GERALD, non-profit corporation executive; b. Bethany, Mo., Jan. 12, 1929; s. William Young and Leah Genevieve (Cover) C.; m. Geralyn Gail Finlay, July 22, 1951; children: Kathryn Carter Gee, Karen Carter Winn, William Ralph. BSc, U. Mo., 1950. Assoc. editor Nat. Livestock Prodr., Chgo., 1950-51; comm. specialist Farmland Industries, Kansas City, Mo., 1953-54; advt. dir. MFA Oil Co., Columbia, Mo., 1954-58; ptnr. Neds & Wardlow Advt. Agy., Springfield, Mo., 1958-68; chmn., pres. Tri-State Pharm Co., Oklahoma City, 1968-81; real estate broker W.G. Carter Real Estate, Oklahoma City & Foster City, Calif., 1981-96; founder, chmn. Am. Acad. Vols. in Edn., Foster City, Calif., 1994—. Spl. agent intelligence U.S. Army, 1951-53. Named Young Man of Yr., C. of C., Springfield, 1964. Mem. Optimist Internat. (mem. various coms. 1981-89, v.p., bd. dirs. 1984, chair coms. 1985-87, v.p. Optimist Vols. for Youth, Inc. 1992-99). Republican. Methodist. Avocations: reading, writing. Home and Office: 247 Boothbay Ave Foster City CA 94404-3509

CARTER, WILLIAM HAROLD, SR., physicist, researcher, electrical engineer; b. Houston, Nov. 17, 1938; s. William Henry and Fannie (Augusta) C.; children: William Harold Jr., Elizabeth Lee. BSEE, U. Tex., 1962, MSEE, 1963, PhD, 1966. Rsch. asst. U. Tex., Austin, 1962-66; rsch. assoc. U. Rochester, N.Y., 1969-70; rsch. physicist Naval Rsch. Lab., Washington, 1971-93; prof. U. Nebr., Lincoln, 1981-82; instr. Johns Hopkin's U., Balt., 1989-93; program dir. NSF, Arlington, Va., 1993-95; vis. rsch. fellow U. Reading, Eng., 1976-77; vis. scientist applied physics lab. Johns Hopkin's U., Columbia, Md., 1991-92. Contbr. numerous articles to profl. jours. Cellist Alexandria (Va.) Symphony, 1979-88, Georgetown Symphony, 1981—. Capt. U.S. Army, 1967-69. Fellow Optical Soc. Am., Internat. Soc. for Optical Engring. (chmn. tech. coun. 1980-82, chmn. pub. com. 1981-83, chmn. fellows com. 1986); mem. IEEE (sr., conf. chmn. 1988), Am. Phys. Soc., Cosmos Club. Achievements include co-discovery of the quasi-homogeneous source model; research in optical coherence, in applications of speckle phenomena, and in processing images and data from optical sensors. Home: 8301 Cherry Valley Ln Alexandria VA 22309-2117 Office: NSF 4201 Wilson Blvd Arlington VA 22230-0001

CARTER, WILLIAM JOSEPH, lawyer; b. Balt., Sept. 1, 1949; s. Henry Merle and Florence (Rogan) C.; m. Monica Anne Urlock, July 17, 1976. BS in Psychology, Va. Poly. Inst., 1971; JD, Coll. William and Mary, 1974. Bar: Va. 1974, Pa. 1974, Md. 1980, U.S. Dist. Ct. D.C. 1981, U.S. Dist. Ct. Md. 1983, U.S. Dist. Ct. (ea. dist.) Va. 1985, U.S. Ct. Claims 1977, U.S. Tax Ct. 1977, U.S. Ct. Mil. Appeals 1975, U.S. Ct. Appeals (D.C. and 4th cirs.) 1979, U.S. Ct. Appeals (fed. cir.) 1982, D.C. 1980, U.S. Supreme Ct. 1977, U.S. Ct. Appeals (6th cir.) 1988, U.S. Ct. Appeals (3d and 5th cirs.) 1992. Commd. 2d lt. U.S. Army, 1971, advanced through grades to capt., 1974, served with JAGC, 1971-79, resigned, 1979; assoc. Carr, Jordan, Coyne & Savits, Washington, 1979-84; shareholder Carr, Goodson & Lee, P.C., 1984-95, Carr Goodson Lee & Warner Profl. Corp., Washington, 1996-98, Carr Goodson Warner Profl. Corp., Washington, 1999—; exec. com. deans adv. roundtable Coll. Arts and Scis., Va. Poly. Inst. Author: Appellate Practice Handbook for Maryland, Virginia and District of Columbia, 1996; editor: Appellate Practice Manual for the District of Columbia Court of Appeals, 1992. Mem. ABA, Md. Bar Assn., Bar Assn. D.C., Counsellors. Episcopalian. Avocations: ice hockey, tennis, music, scuba diving, skiing. Office: Carr Goodson Warner East Tower 1301 K St NW Ste 400 Washington DC 20005-3317

CARTER, WILLIAM RANDALL, educator, administrator; b. Rockford, Ill., Sept. 17, 1954; s. Harold B. and Alberta S. Carter; m. Billie Ann Crum, May 25, 1985; children: Christa, Brandon. BS, Tusculum Coll., 1977; MEd, East Tenn. State U., 1984. Mid. sch. sci. tchr. Greeneville (Tenn.) City Schs., 1977-92, head baseball coach, 1991-95, tchr. phys. edn., 1992-95, 96—, adminstr. summer enrichment program, 1997—, instrnl. coord., 1998—; career ladder tchr. evaluator Tenn. Dept. Edn., 1995-96; supervising tchr. for student tchrs. Tusculum Coll., Greeneville, 1996—. Mem. Greeneville Park and Recreation/Greeneville City Schs. Adv. Bd., 1998—. Named Coach of Yr., Region I, Tenn. Secondary Sch. Athletic Assn., 1995. Mem. NEA (del. 1998), Tenn. Edn. Assn. (del. 1999), Tenn. Assn. Health, Phys. Edn., Recreation, Greeneville Edn. Assn. (pres. 1998-99). Presbyterian. E-mail: carterr01@gcschools.net. Office: Greeneville City Schs 454 E Bernard Ave Greeneville TN 37745

CARTER, WILLIAM WALTON, physicist; b. Pensacola, Fla., Nov. 7, 1921; s. Eugene Hudson and Nannie (Ledyard) C.; m. Elizabeth Jean Dedick, June 11, 1945; children—Carolyn A., Susan J., Judith J., Paul W. B.S., Carnegie Inst. Tech., 1943; M.S., Calif. Inst. Tech., 1948, Ph.D., 1949. Atomic, thermonuclear Weapon research and devel., group leader weapons physics group, weapons div. Los Alamos Sci. Lab., 1949-59, project leader 1st thermonuclear weapon to enter regular nat. stockpile, also mem. joint working com.; chief scientist Army Missile Command, Redstone Arsenal, 1959-67; asst. dir. nuclear programs, def. research and engring. Office Sec. Def., Washington, 1967-71; assoc. dir. Harry Diamond Labs. U.S. Army, 1971-74, tech. dir., 1975-84, also chmn. staff devel. council; sr. scientist Pacific-Sierra Rsch., Arlington, Va, 1984-94; scientific cons. nuclear treaty monitoring, 1994—; designer, deployer instruments to verify nuclear treaties; chmn. steering com. Huntsville Rsch. Inst. Served to lt. USNR, 1944-46. Asso. fellow Am. Inst. Aeros. and Astronautics; mem. Am. Phys. Soc., AAAS, Am. Def. Preparedness Assn., Am. Inst. Physics, Assn. U.S. Army. Achievements include design of air samplers for worldwide network of sensors to monitor non-proliferation and nuclear test ban treaties.; installation first unit in Turkmenistan, 1994. Home: 1124 Ormond Ct Mc Lean VA 22101-2960

CARTER, YVONNE JOHNSON, writer, editor, English educator; b. Richmond, Va., July 31, 1949; d. John Miller and Lorraine (Brown) Johnson; m. Vernon L. Carter, Jr., Apr. 26, 1980. BA cum laude, St. Paul's Coll., 1971; MA, U. Md., 1979; PhD, Howard U., 1994. Contract specialist Dept. Def., Richmond, Va., 1972-75; edn. reporter Washington Afro-Am. Newspaper, 1980-82; writer-editor U.S. Dept. Army, Alexandria, Va., 1982-84; sr. editor Nat. Def. U., Washington, 1984-85; writer-editor USIA, Washington, 1985-91; lectr. Bowie (Md.) State U., 1994-96; writer-editor U.S. EEOC, Washington, 1995—; mem. Fed. Comm. Network, Washington, 1997—. Editor: The United States and the World Economy, 1984; editor (periodical) The Civil Rights Movement and the Legacy of Dr. King, 1989, (periodical) Two Cultures, Shared Values: Nigeria and the U.S., 1990; author (periodical) EEOC Mission, 1997. Mem. Habitat for Humanity, Atlanta, 1999, Corcoran Gallery Art, Washington, 1999, Nat. Hist. Preservation Soc., Washington, 1999, Smithsonian, Washington, 1999. Recipient Minority fellowship U. Md., 1978, Ivan Earle Taylor scholarship Howard U., 1992.

Mem. AAUP, AAUW, Alpha Kappa Alpha. Democrat. Baptist. Office: EEOC 1801 L St NW Washington DC 20036

CARTER, ZACHARY W., prosecutor. BA, Cornell U., 1972; JD, NYU, 1975. Bar: N.Y., U.S. Dist Ct. (ea. dist.) N.Y., U.S. Dist. Ct. (so. dist.) N.Y., U.S. Ct. Appeals (2d cir.), U.S. Supreme Ct. U.S. atty. Eastern Dist. N.Y., Bklyn., 1993—; magistrate judge U.S. Dept. Justice, Bklyn.; asst. U.S. atty. U.S. Dist. Ct. (ea. dist.) N.Y., 1975-80; mem. Patterson, Belknap, Webb & Tyler, 1980-81; exec. asst. dist. atty. King County Dist. Atty's. Office, Bklyn., 1982-87; exec. asst. to dep. chief adminstrv. judge N.Y. City Cts., 1987; judge criminal ct. City of N.Y., 1987-91; U.S. magistrate judge E.D.N.Y., 1991-93; U.S. atty. N.Y., 1993—. Mem. N.Y. Bar Assn. (mem. exec. com. criminal law sect.), Assn. Bar of the City of N.Y. (mem. com. to encourage judicial svc.). Office: US Attys Office US District Court 147 Pierrepont St Brooklyn NY 11201-1897*

CARTER-WOMMACK, BARBARA, retired educator; b. Decatur, Ga., Apr. 10, 1937; d. Robert Leonidas and Ruth Inez (Boyles) C.; m. Hines Lawrence Wommack, Mar. 21, 1974; 1 child, Beth. AB, LaGrange Coll., 1959; MEd, U. Ga., 1966, EdD, 1969. Ednl. asst. Brookhaven Meth. Ch., Atlanta, 1959-60; tchr. elem. DeKalb County Bd. Edn., Doraville, Ga., 1960-65; grad. tchg. asst. U. Ga., Athens, 1965-68; prof. reading Western Carolina U., Cullowhee, N.C., 1968-70, Ga. So. Coll., Statesboro, 1970-74; prof. Ga. Southwestern Coll., Americus, 1975-88; instrl. coord. Thomas Elem. Sch., Warner Robins, Ga., 1988-93; cons. So. Assn. Colls. and Schs., Atlanta, 1993-97; ret., 1997. Mem. Internat. Reading Assn. (Reading Tchr. Yr. S.W. Ga. Coun. 1976, Annette Hopson svc. award 1988, Ga. Hall of Fame 1994), Delta Kappa Gamma. Methodist. Avocations: gardening, travel, reading. Home: 424 Meadowlark Dr Albany GA 31707-3145

CARTHAY, R. JON, hand model, actor; b. Ellenville, N.Y., July 26, 1948; s. Alexander F. and Edith C.; m. Jane Brem, June 14, 1980. BA, Long Island U., 1971. Lic. pvt. pilot. Photographer's asst., 1977; profl. hand model Ford Models, Inc., N.Y.C., 1980—; actor Tranum Robertson Hughes, Inc, 1987-97, J. Michael Bloom, Inc., 1987-97. Author: New York Modelline, 1996; hands featured in ads for AmEx, Diners Club, Black Label, Absolut Vodka, Ernest and Julio Gallo, Remy Martin, Citibank, Freixenet, Tylenol, Carlsberg Beer, Pepsi, Schweppes, TDK, Ford, Bulova, Piaget, Dunkin Donuts, numerous others. Named Most Photographed Hands in the World Tranum Robertson Hughes, Inc., 1997. Mem. Am. Fedn. TV and Radio Artists, Screen Actors Guild. Avocation: flying, sailing. Office: N Y Modelline 339 E 58th St Ste 7E New York NY 10022-2250

CARTHEL, ANNE FAWVER, food products executive; b. Floydada, Tex., July 2, 1952; d. Ralph Carlton and Jonnie Louise (Ely) Fawver; m. Hulon Lon Carthel, Aug. 24, 1950; children: Casey Britten, Corey Brock, Cienna Beth. Student, S. Plains Jr. Coll., 1970-71, W. Tex. State U., 1971-75; BS, Wayland Bapt. U., 1979-80; cert. tchr., Tex. Tech. U., 1986-87. Cert. tchr., Tex. Tchr. English and reading Lockney (Tex.) Jr. H.S., 1980-81; tchr. English Floydada H.S., 1981, 86-87; tchr. phys. edn. A.B. Duncan Elem. Sch., Floydada, 1986-92; owner, mgr. Sagebrush Mills, Inc., Floydada, 1992—; com. mem. Dist. Goals Com., Floydada, 1986-87, Dist. Survey Com., Floydada, 1986-87, Dist. Survey Com., Floydada, 1987-88, Campus Long Range Plan Com., 1987-88. Sec. Floydada Execs. Homecoming, 1984-88; neighborhood chmn. Am. Cancer Soc., 1985-86; mem. Punkin' Days Festival Com., chmn., coord. Jump for Heart, Floydada, 1986-92; leader 4-H Club; vol. Floyd County Fair; mem. Floyd County-Floydada Econ. Devel. Bd., Floyd County Tourism Task Force; bd. dirs. South Plains Econ. Devel. Dist., 1994—; grant writer, adv. to bd. dirs. Floyd County Friends, 1995—; bd. dirs. Caprock coun. Girl Scouts U.S.A., 1998—. Named Women of Distinction, Caprock coun. Girl Scouts U.S.A., 1997; recipient Cmty. Builder award Tex. Masonic Lodge, 1998. Mem. Assn. Tex. Profl. Educators, Tex. Assn. Health, Phys. Edn., Recreation and Dance, Internat. Platform Assn., Am. Heart Assn. (v.p. programs 1992), Floydada C. of C. (pres. women's div. 1990-91, sec. 1991-92, Extra Mile award 1992). Baptist. Avocations: exercising, skiing, needlework. Home: 901 W Mississippi St Floydada TX 79235-2521

CARTIER, BRIAN EVANS, association executive; b. Providence, Apr. 12, 1950; s. Clarence Joseph and Mary Anna (Evans) C. BA, R.I. Coll., 1972; MEd, Springfield (Mass.) Coll., 1973. Exec. dir. Arthritis Found. Conn., Hartford, 1976-78, dep. exec. dir. N.Y. chpt., N.Y.C., 1979; exec. dir. Found. for Chiropractic Edn. and Research, Arlington, Va., 1979-90; exec. dir. Nat. Ct. Reporters Assn., 1990-98; chief of staff officer Natl. Assn. of Coll. Stores, Oberlin, 1998— Mem. Am. Mgmt. Assn.(cert. assn. exec.), Am. Soc. Assn. Execs, Greater Washington Soc. Assn. Execs., U.S. C. of C. Republican. Roman Catholic. Home: 3137 Northwood Ln Westlake OH 44145 Office: NACS 500 E Lorain St Oberlin OH 44074

CARTIER, CELINE PAULE, librarian, administrator, consultant; b. Lacolle, Que., Can., May 10, 1930; d. Henri Rodolphe and Irene (Boudreau) Robitaille; m. Georges Cartier, Nov. 29, 1952; children: Nathalie, Guillaume. Diplome superieur en pedagogie, U. Montreal, 1948, certificats en litterature et linguistique, 1952; diplome de bibliothecaire-documentaliste, Inst. Catholique, Paris, 1962; maîtrise en adminstrn. publique, Ecole Nationale d'Adminstrn. Publique, 1976; maîtrise en bibliothéconomie, U. Montreal, 1982. Dir. Bibliotheque Centrale, Commn. des ecoles catholiques, Montreal, 1964-73; dir. spl. collections U. Quebec, 1973-76, dir. sector librs., 1976-77; chief gen. libr. U. Laval, Que., 1977-78; gen. dir. libraries U. Laval, 1978-89; cons. Conseil CRC Cons., 1989—. Contbr. articles to profl. jours. Mem. Corp. des Bibliothecaires Profs. de Quebec. *The guiding principles of any profl. way of life are to some extent indentical to those which direct the personal life of individual: respect for a human being, dignity, and a sense of responsibility and fairness. Intellectual honesty in all its aspects together with a strong desire to achieve specific objectives or ideals constitute the best guarantee for satisfaction and success.*

CARTIER, CHARLES ERNEST, alcohol and drug abuse services professional; b. Chgo., Aug. 4, 1931; s. Charles E. and Kathryn (Hanlon) C.; m. JoAnne Murphy, July 12, 1958; children: Kevin, Julia, Theresa, Carol. BS in Commerce, DePaul U., 1953. Nat. cert. alcohol, drug and addictions counselor. Program asst. Alcoholism Svcs. of Cleve. (Ohio), Inc., 1983-84; community liaison coord. Merrick Hall Adolescent Chem. Dependency Program, Cleve., 1984-86; instr. D.W.I. Counter Attack Project Cleve. (Ohio) State Univ., 1984-92; clin. supr. Fresh Start, Inc., Cleve., 1986-91; rehab. therapist alcohol treatment program VA Med. Ctr., Brecksville, Ohio, 1991—; lectr. Cuya Hoga Community Coll., Sch. of Mental Health Tech., Cleve., 1987—; bd. mem., v.p. Exodus, Inc. Treatment Program, 1986-90. Sgt. U.S. Army, 1953-55. Mem. Nat. Assn. Alcoholism and Drug Abuse Counselors, Ohio Assn. Alcoholism and Drug Abuse Counselors (sec. 1986-91, Hinkle Meml. award for Outstanding Work in the Field of Alcoholism Counseling 1990, Superior Performance award 1997). Roman Catholic. Avocations: race walking, editorial writing. Home: 9049 Roosevelt Dr Northfield OH 44067-1222 Office: VA Med Ctr 10000 Brecksville Rd Cleveland OH 44141-3204

CARTIER, XAM CIARAN, writer; b. St. Louis, Oct. 7, 1955; d. Albert Wayne and Mary Carter Wilson; m. Darrell William Hayes; 1 child, Anáis Nicole. BS, U. Mo.; MS, St. Louis U.; postgrad., Golden Gate U. Writer, assoc. prodr. ABC-TV, Inc., San Francisco, 1979-88; novelist Random House, Inc., N.Y.C., 1988—; creative writing cons.-tchr. Calif. Poets-in-the-Schs., San Francisco, 1979-89, 91-94; assoc. prof. creative writing San Francisco State U., 1989-90, Oberlin (Ohio) Coll., 1991; assoc. prof. English and creative writing U. Wyo., Laramie, 1990-91; vis. prof. English Wayne State U., Detroit, 1990. Author: Be-Bop, Re-Bop, 1988, 91 (Most Notable Book of the Yr., N.Y. Times 1998), Muse-Echo Blues, 1991, 92 (Editors Choice 1991). Named Artist-in-Residence, Calif. Arts Coun., 1986-89, Mich. Arts Coun., 1990; Lit. fellow Calif. Arts Coun., 1989, Creative Writing fellow Nat. Endowment for the Arts, 1989, Honors-at-Entrance fellow Golden Gate U. Sch. Law, San Francisco, Grad. fellow St. Louis U. Avocations: painting, dancing, international traveling, foreign languages. Home: Apt 20 935 Solano Ave Albany CA 94706-1556

CARTLAND, BARBARA, author; b. Eng., July 9, 1901; d. Bertram and Polly (Scobell) C.; m. Alexander George McCorquodale, 1927 (div. 1933); m. Hugh McCorquodale, Dec. 28, 1936 (dec. 1963); children: Raine (Countess Spencer), Ian, Glen. Student pvt. girls' schs. in, Eng. Lectr., polit. speaker; TV personality (2 lecture tours), Can., 1940. Author hist. novels, biographies, material on health and phys. fitness; books include: (history) The Outrageous Queen: A Biography of Christina of Sweden, 1956, The Scandalous Life of King Carol, 1957, The Private Life of Charles II: The Woman He Loved, 1958, The Private Life of Elizabeth, Empress of Austria, 1959, Josephine, Empress of France, 1961, Diane de Poitiers, 1962, Metternich: The Passionate Diplomat, 1964; (biography) Ronald Cartland, 1942, Bewitching Women, 1955, Polly: The Story of My Wonderful Mother, 1956; (autobiography) The Isthmus Years: Reminiscences of the Years 1919-1939, 1943, The Years of Opportunity 1939-1945, 1948, I Search for Rainbows 1946-1966, 1967, We Danced All Night 1919-1929, 1970, I Seek the Miraculous, 1978; (non-fiction) Touch the Stars: A Clue to Happiness, 1935, You-in the Home, 1946, The Fascinating Forties: A Book for the Over-Forties, 1954, Marriage for the Moderns, 1955, Be Vivid, Be Vital, 1956, Love, Life and Sex, 1957, Look Lovely, Be Lovely, 1958, Vitamins For Vitality, 1959, Husbands and Wives, 1971, Etiquette Handbook, 1962, The Many Facets of Love, 1963, Sex and the Teenager, 1964, Living Together, 1965, The Pan Book of Charm, 1965, Woman, The Enigma, 1965, The Youth Secret, 1968, The Magic of Honey, 1970, Barbara Cartland's Book of Beauty and Health, 1972, Men Are Wonderful, 1973, Food For Love, 1975, Recipes for Lovers, 1977, Barbara Cartland's Book of Useless Information, 1977, Barbara Cartland's Book of Love and Lovers, 1978, Romantic Royal Marriages, 1981, Barbara Cartland's Etiquette for Love and Romance, 1984, Getting Older, Growing Younger, 1984, The Romance of Food, 1984, Barbara Cartland's Book of Health, 1985, A Year of Royal Days, 1988; (novels) Jigsaw, 1925, Sawdust, 1926, If The Tree Is Saved, 1929, For What?, 1930, Sweet Punishment, 1931, A Virgin in Mayfair, 1932, Just Off Piccadily, 1933, Not Love Alone, 1933, A Beggar Wished, 1934, Passionate Attainment, 1935, First Class, Lady?, 1935, Dangerous Experiment, 1936, Desperate Defiance, 1936, The Forgotten City, 1936, The Forgotten City, 1936, Saga at Forty, 1937, But Never Free, 1937, Broken Barriers, 1938, Bitter Winds, 1938, The Gods Forget, 1939, The Black Panther, 1939, Stolen Halo, 1940, Now Rough, Now Smooth, 1941, Open Wings, A Twenty-Third Novel, 1942, The Leaping Flame, 1942, The Dark Stream, 1944, After The Night, 1944, Yet She Follows, 1945, Escape From Passion, 1945, Armour Against Love, 1945, Out Of Reach, 1945, The Hidden Heart, 1946, Against The Stream, 1946, The Dream Within, 1947, If We Will, 1947, Against This Rapture, 1947, No Heart Is Free, 1948, No Heart Is Free, 1948, A Hazard of Hearts, 1949, The Enchanted Moment, 1949, A Duel of Hearts, 1949, The Knave of Hearts, 1950, The Little Pretender, 1950, Love Is An Eagle, 1951, A Ghost In Monte Carlo, 1951, Love Is The Enemy, 1952, Cupid Rides Pillion, 1952, Elizabethan Lover, 1953, Love Me For Ever, 1954, Desire of the Heart, 1954, The Enchanted Waltz, 1955, The Kiss of the Devil, 1955, The Captive Heart, 1956, The Coin of Love, 1956, Sweet Adventure, 1957, Stars In My Heart, 1957, The Golden Gondola, 1958, Love In Hiding, 1959, The Smuggled Heart, 1959, Love Under Fire, 1960, Messenger of Love, 1961, The Wings of Love, 1962, The Hidden Evil, 1963, The Fire of Love, 1964, The Unpredictable Bride, 1964, Love Holds the Cards, 1965, A Virgin in Paris, 1966, Love to the Rescue, 1967, Love is Contraband, 1968, The Enchanting Evil, 1968, The Unknown Heart, 1969, The Innocent Heiress, 1970, The Reluctant Bride, 1970, The Secret Fear, 1970, The Pretty Horse-Breakers, 1971, The Queen's Messenger, 1971, Stars in Her Eyes, 1971, Lost Enchantment, 1972, A Halo for the Devil, 1972, The Wicked Marquis, 1973, The Odious Duke, 1973, The Glittering Lights, 1974, A Sword to the Heart, 1974, Fire on the Snow, 1975, Bewitched, 1975, Call of the Heart, 1975, The Frightened Bride, 1975, The Impetuous Duchess, 1975, The Karma of Love, 1975, Love Is Innocent, 1975, The Husband Hunters, 1976, The Incredible Honeymoon, 1976, A Kiss for the King, 1976, Love in Hiding, 1976, Moon Over Eden, 1976, Never Laugh at Love, 1976, No Time for Love, 1976, Passions in the Sand, 1976, The Secret of the Glen, 1976, The Slaves of Love, 1976, The Wild Cry of Love, 1976, Conquered by Love, 1976, Love Locked In, 1977, The Mysterious Maid-Servant, 1977, The Wild Unwilling Wife, 1977, The Castle Made for Love, 1977, The Hell-cat and the King, 1977, Love and the Loathsome Leopard, 1977, The Love Pirate, 1977, The Marquis Who Hated Women, 1977, The Naked Battle, 1977, No Escape From Love, 1977, Punishment of a Vixen, 1977, The Saint and the Sinner, 1977, The Temptation of Torilla, 1977, A Touch of Love, 1977, A Duel with Destiny, 1977, The Magic of Love, 1977, A Rhapsody of Love, 1977, The Disgraceful Duke, 1977, Love at the Helm, 1977, The Chieftain without a Heart, 1978, A Fugitive from Love, 1978, The Ghost Who Fell in Love, 1978, Love Leaves at Midnight, 1978, Love, Lords and Lady-Birds, 1978, The Passion and the Flower, 1978, The Twists and Turns of Love, 1978, The Irresistible Force, 1978, The Judgement of Love, 1978, Lord Ravenscar's Revenge, 1978, Lovers in Paradise, 1978, A Princess in Distress, 1978, The Race for Love, 1978, A Runaway Star, 1978, Magic or Mirage?, 1978, Alone in Paris, 1978, Flowers for the God of Love, 1978, The Problems of Love, 1978, The Drums of Love, 1979, The Duke and the Preacher's Daughter, 1979, Imperial Spledor, 1979, Light of the Moon, 1979, Love in the Clouds, 1979, Love in the Dark, 1979, The Prince and the Pekinese, 1979, Love Climbs In, 1979, The Prisoner of Love, 1979, A Serpent of Satan, 1979, The Treasure of Love, 1979, The Dutchess Disappeared, 1979, A Nightingale Sang, 1979, The Dawn of Love, 1979, A Gentleman in Love, 1979, Only Love, 1979, Bride to the King, 1979. Women Have Hearts, 1979. Terror in the Sun, 1979, Who Can Deny Love?, 1979, Love Has His Way, 1979, The Explosion of Love, 1979, A Song of Love, 1980, Love for Sale, 1980, Lost Laughter, 1980, Free from Fear, 1980, The Goddess and the Gaiety Girl, 1980, Little White Doves of Love, 1980, Ola and the Sea Wolf, 1980, The Perfection of Love, 1980, The Prude and the Prodigal, 1980, Punished with Love, 1980, The Power and the Prince, 1980, Lucifer and the Angel, 1980, Signpost to Love, 1980, From Hell to Heaven, 1981, Pride and the Poor Princess, 1981, Count the Stars, 1981, Dollars for the Duke, 1981, Dreams Do Come True, 1981, The Heart of the Clan, 1981, In the Arms of Love, 1981, Touch a Star, 1981, Love in the Moon, 1981, A Night of Gaiety, 1981, The Waltz of Hearts, 1981, The Wings of Ecstasy, 1981, For All Eternity, 1981, For All Eternity, 1981, Afraid, 1981, Love in the Moon, 1981, Enchanted, 1981, Winged Magic, 1981, A Portrait of Love, 1981, The River of Love, 1981, Gift of the Gods, 1981, An Innocent in Russia, 1981, A Shaft of Sunlight, Pure and Untouched, 1981, Love Wins, 1982, Secret Harbor, 1982, Looking for Love, 1982, The Vibrations of Love, 1982, Lies for Love, 1982, Love Rules, 1982, Moments of Love, 1982, Riding to the Moon, 1982, Diona and a Dalmation, 1983, Wish for Love, 1983, A Very Unusual Wife, 1984, White Lilac, 1984, Temptation for a Teacher, 1985, A Witch's Spell, 1985, The Love Trap, 1986, Secret of the Mosque, 1986, Wanted: A Wedding Ring, 1987, A World of Love, 1987, Lovers in Lisbon, 1988, The Goddess of Love, 1988, Paradise in Penang, 1989, A Game of Love, 1989, Love is the Key, 1990, The Marquis Wins, 1990, Heaven in Hong Kong, 1990, Seek the Stars, 1991, Escape, 1991, Drena and the Duke, 1992, Love Strikes a Devil, 1992, The Windmill of Love, 1992, A Dynasty of Love, 1993, To Scotland and Love, 1993, Hidden by Love, 1992, The Queen of Hearts, 1993, The Cave of Love, 1993, Walking to Wonderland, 1993, A Duel of Jewels, 1993, and many, many others; series include "Camfield Romance" series, (editor only) "Barbara Cartland's Library of Love" series; novels also published under pseud. County councillor, Hertfordshire, chmn. St. John Coun., pres. Br. Royal Coll. Midwives, dep. pres. St. John Ambulance Brigade; chief lady welfare officer, Bedfordshire, 1941-45; founder Cartland Onslow Romany Trust. Decorated Dame Order of Brit. Empire, Dame of Grace St. John of Jerusalem; recipient Bishop Wright Air Industry award for contbn. to devel. aviation, 1984, Gold Medal of City of Paris for Achievement La Maire de la Ville, 1988; named Woman of Yr. by Nat. Home Furnishings Assn., 1981. Mem. Nat. Assn. Health (founder, pres. 1965), Oxfam (v.p.). Listed in Guiness Book of Records as having sold largest number of books in world, 750 million by 1999.

CARTLEDGE, RAYMOND EUGENE, retired paper company executive; b. Pensacola, Fla., June 12, 1929; s. Raymond H. and Meddie (Brookins) C.; m. Gale Perry, June 30, 1962; children: John R., Perri Ann, Susan R. BS, U. Ala., 1952; postgrad., Harvard Bus. Sch., 1970. With Procter & Gamble Co., 1955-56; with Union Camp Corp., Wayne, N.J., 1956-70, 80-94, pres., COO, 1983-86, chmn., pres., CEO, 1986-94; pres., CEO Clevepak Corp., White Plains, N.Y., 1971-79; chmn. Savannah Foods, 1996-97; past chmn. Am. Paper Inst., solid waste task force; trustee Am. Enterprise Inst.; trustee, life councillor The Conf. Bd.; bd. dirs. Union Camp Corp., Chase Brass Industries, Delta Airlines, The Sun Co., Blount, Inc., UCAR Internat.; past chmn. Inst. Paper Sci. and Tech., Nat. Coun. Paper Industry for Air and Stream Improvement, internat. bus. com. Am. Forest & Paper Assn.; past dir. The Pulp and Paper Fedn. Served with U.S. Army Airborne Infantry, 1952-55. Office: Ste 203 B 6 Skidaway Village Walk Savannah GA 31411-2913

CARTLIDGE, EDWARD SUTTERLEY, mechanical engineer; b. Trenton, N.J., Feb. 5, 1945; s. Leon James and Agnes Jean (Cinkay) C.; m. Marilyn Spinuzza, July 21, 1979. BS in Marine Engring, U.S. Mcht. Marine Acad., 1968; MS in M.E., N.J. Inst. Tech., 1971; MBA, Temple U., 1982. Registered profl. engr., Pa., Ill., Del., Md., N.J., Va., Wis., Calif. Marine engr. Seatrain Lines, 1968-69; performance engr. Foster Wheeler Corp., Livingston, N.J., 1969-71; cons. engr. Fluor, Sargent & Lundy, and Kuljian Corp., 1971-75; chief engr. Gimpel Corp., Langhorne, Pa., 1976-79; sr. research and devel. engr. Yarway Corp., Blue Bell, Pa., 1979-82; power utilities supr. Merck & Co., Inc., West Point, Pa., 1982-91; sr. project mgr. Conmec, Inc., Bethlehem, Pa., 1992-93, Edward S. Cartlidge, PE and Assocs., Blue Bell, 1993—; cons. Pharm. Utilities, Semiconductor, Steel Fab., Marine Indsl., Gideon; Christian fin. counselor, lectr., seminar leader. Served to comdr. USNR, 1968-91. Mem. Nat. Soc. Profl. Engrs. (chpt. pres.), Pa. Soc. Profl. Engrs. (Young Engr. of Yr. 1980), ASME, Instruments Soc. Am., Soc. Mfg. Engrs., Am. Soc. Metals, Soc. Naval Architects and Marine Engrs., Naval Reserve Assn., Nat. Fire Prevention Assn., Gideons Internat. Home: PO Box 62 Blue Bell PA 19422

CARTMELL, NATHANIEL MADISON, III, lawyer; b. N.Y.C., Oct. 22, 1951; s. Nathaniel Madison Jr. and Ruth Kincer (Davies) C.; m. Suzanne Cameron Pettus, Jan. 3, 1981; children: Nathaniel Madison IV, Edmund Winston, Samuel Chapman Davies. BA, Yale U., 1973; JD, Vanderbilt U., 1978. Bar: Calif. State 1983, D.C. 1980, Va. State 1978. Mem. faculty Williston Northampton Sch., Easthampton, Mass., 1973-75; assoc. Hunton & Williams, Richmond, Va., 1978-80, Washington, 1980-81; atty. U.S. Synthetic Fuels Corp., Washington, 1981; assoc. Pillsbury Madison & Sutro LLP, Washington, 1982-83, San Francisco, 1983-86; ptnr. Pillsbury Madison & Sutro, San Francisco, 1987—; mgr. Corp. and Securities Group, 1994-96. Alumni bd. dirs. Vanderbilt Law Sch., 1998—; alumni coun. Phillips Acad., 1997—. Mem. ABA (mem. fed. regulation of securities com., bus. law sect. 1990—), Calif. State Bar (mem. corps. com., bus. law sect. 1989-91). Episcopalian. Home: 24 Roble Ct Berkeley CA 94705-2836 Office: Pillsbury Madison & Sutro LLP 235 Montgomery St Fl 16 San Francisco CA 94104-3074

CARTMILL, GEORGE EDWIN, JR., retired hospital administrator; b. Plover, Wis., Dec. 26, 1918; s. George Edwin and Elsie Evelyn (Dobbie) C.; m. Helen Marie Heimburg, Feb. 20, 1948; children: George Thomas, William Charles, Sara Jane. BS, Cen. State Tchrs. Coll., Stevens Point, Wis., 1938; MS, Columbia U., 1947. High sch. tchr. Wis., 1938-41; asst. dir. Harper Hosp., Detroit, 1947-50; asso. dir., treas. Harper Hosp., 1950-52, dir., 1952—, pres., trustee, 1966-74; pres., chief exec. officer Harper-Grace Hosps., Detroit, 1974-83; trustee Harper-Grace Hosps., 1974-95; Mem. adv. com. hosps. div. W.K. Kellogg Found., 1956-61; pres. Greater Detroit Area Hosp. Council, 1952; trustee Blue Cross-Blue Shield of Mich., 1952-85, vice chmn. bd., 1962-85; v.p. Tri-State Hosp. Assembly, 1958-59; com. adminstrn. Wayne State U. Sch. Medicine, 1953-57, adj. asso. prof., 1972-86; trustee, v.p. Community Health, Inc., 1968; trustee Kresge Found., 1977-90; mem. Pres.'s Nat. Adv. Com. Health Facilities, 1968, Task Force on Medicaid and Related Programs, HEW, 1970. Hon. life mem. Detroit Med. Ctr. Served with AUS, 1941-45. Recipient Award of Merit Tri-State Hosp. Assembly, 1965; Meritorious Service award Mich. Hosp. Assn., 1966; Disting. Service award Wayne State U. Sch. Medicine, 1984. Fellow Am. Coll. Health Care Execs. (life fellow, regent 1970-72, Gold medal award 1974), Detroit Acad. Medicine (hon.); mem. Am. Dietetics Assn. (hon., adv. bd. 1963-69), Am. Hosp. Assn. (chmn. coun. adminstrv. practice 1959-62, trustee 1962-68, pres. 1966, Disting. Svc. award 1975), Mich. Hosp. Assn. (pres. 1958, trustee 1952-60), Assn. Am. Med. Colls. (exec. coun. 1970-72, chmn. coun. tchg. hosps. 1971-72), Country Club of Detroit, Dolphin Head Golf Club, Club Hilton Head S.C. Presbyterian. Home: 336 Kercheval Ave Grosse Pointe MI 48236-3063

CARTMILL, MATT, anthropologist, anatomy educator; b. Los Angeles, Jan. 4, 1943; m. Mary Kaye Brown, May 29, 1971; 1 child, Erica A. BA summa cum laude in Anthropology, Pomona Coll., 1964; MA, U. Chgo., 1966, PhD in Anthropology, 1970. Assoc. in anatomy Duke U., Durham, N.C., 1969-70, asst. prof. dept. anatomy, 1970-72, asst. prof. depts. anatomy and anthropology, 1972-74, assoc. prof., 1974-81, prof. dept. anatomy, 1981-88, assoc. prof. dept. anthropology, 1981-83, prof., 1983-88; prof. dept. biol. anthropology and anatomy, 1988—. Hon. Woodrow Wilson fellow, 1964, NSF fellow, 1964-69, Guggenheim fellow, 1985-86; NIH grantee, 1970, NSF grantee, 1982-85, 98; recipient Student AMA Med. Teaching award, 1971, 92, NIH Rsch. Career Devel. award, 1975-79, W.W. Howells award, 1994, G.P. Marsh award, 1994. Fellow AAAS; mem. Am. Assn. Phys. Anthropologists, Internat. Primatol. Soc., Sigma Xi (grantee 1968). Author: A View to a Death in the Morning, 1993; co-author: Human Structure, 1987; also numerous articles; mng. editor Internat. Jour. Primatology, 1980-88; editor Am. Jour. Phys. Anthropology, 1989-95; Mem. Am. Assn. Phys. Anthropologists (pres. 1997-99). Office: Duke U Med Ctr Dept Biol Anthrop and Anatomy Durham NC 27710

CARTON, CRISTINA SILVA-BENTO, elementary educator; b. Santiago, Beira Alta, Portugal, Jan. 23, 1928; came to U.S. Jan. 4, 1936; d. Mario Antunes and Alice (Silva) Bento; m. Jorge Luis Rodriguez, May 6, 1935; children: A. James DeCosta, Robert J. DeCosta, Wanda Rodriguez. BA, Queens Coll., 1968, MS, 1973; MA, SUNY, Stony Brook, 1983. Cert. elem. tchr. N.Y., Fla., ESOL tchr. Fla. Tchr. Our Lady of Loretto, Hempstead, N.Y., 1961-66, Hempstead Pub. Schs., Hempstead, 1968-70, Cen. Islip (N.Y.) Pub. Schs., 1970-87, Broward County Pub. Schs., Ft. Lauderdale, Fla., 1988—; DOP Coord., lead tchr. Pines Mid. Sch., 1990-96; DOP 6th grade tchr. Silver Trail Mid. Sch., 1996-98, 6th grade health and sci. tchr., 1998—; instr. philosophy Barry U., Miami, 1989-90. Mem. Nat. Cancer Assn., Stony Brook, N.Y., 1971-73; internat. chairperson AAUW, Stony Brook, 1970-73; fund raiser Dem. Party, Selden, N.Y., 1976. Recipient Fellowship for Study Abroad Gulbenkian Found., 1967. Mem. Nat. Edn. Assn., N.Y. State Tchrs. Assn., Cen. Islip Tchrs. Assn., Parent Tchrs. Assn. (membership chair 1970-75), Broward Tchrs. Union, Kappa Delta Pi, Phi Delta Kappa. Democrat. Avocations: travel, painting, reading, opera, ballet. Home: 410 NE 45th St Fort Lauderdale FL 33334-2314

CARTON, JAMES ALFRED, oceanographer, educator; b. Highland Park, Ill., July 10, 1954; s. Robert Wells and Jean (Keating) C.; m. Allison Joan Mankin, Aug. 15, 1983; children: Samuel, Molly. BSE, Princeton U., 1976, MA, 1980, PhD, 1983; MS, U. Wash., Seattle, 1979. Rsch. fellow theoretical physics Harvard U., Cambridge, Mass., 1983-85; asst. prof. U. Md., College Park, 1985-90, assoc. prof., 1990-97, prof., 1997—; co-chair adv. bd. Atlantic Climate Change Program, Silver Spring, Md., 1994—. Mem. adv. bd. Societ Jour. Phys. Oceanography, Moscow, 1990-94; contbr. articles to profl. jours. Mem. Am. Geophys. Union, Am. Meteorol. Soc., Sigma Xi (pres. College Park chpt. 1996—). Achievements include studying oceanic causes of low frequency climate variability. Office: Univ Maryland College Park MD 20742

CARTON, LONNIE CAMING, educational psychologist; b. Balt.; d. Daniel and Shirley (Cooper) Caming; m. Edwin B. Carton; children: Evan, Deborah, Paula. BS, Johns Hopkins U.; MS, U. Md.; PhD, Pa. State U. Tchr. Laurel (Md.) H.S.; instr. Pa. State U., State College, Temple U., Phila.; newspaper columnist Delaware County Times, Chester, Pa.; instr., then asst. prof. Tufts U., Medford, Mass., 1964-80; learning sys. cons. Tufts New Eng. Med. Ctr., Boston, 1968-73; broadcast journalist CBS Radio, N.Y.C., 1974—; family support sys. cons. Boston Ptnrs. in Edn., 1985—; ind. cons., lectr., workshop leader in field; guest appearances of various radio and TV shows. Author: Mommies, 1960, Daddies, 1963, Raise Your Kids Right, 1980, No is a Love Word, 1992; sr. editor Edn. Today, Boston, 1992-98; broadcast journalist Voice of Am., 1995-98; contbr. articles to profl. publs. Grantee Gannet Found., U.S. Dept. Edn., Mass. Dept. Edn., U.S. Dept. Hwy. Safety, Mass. Gov.'s Alliance Against Drugs; recipient Nat. Media award APA, 1978, 80, San Francisco State Broadcast Media award, 1983, Contbn. to Lives of Children award UNICEF, Margaret Sanger Soc. award Planned Parenthood, 1985, Don Bosco Friend of Youth award Salesian Soc., awards from Mass. Psychol. Assn., Nat. Commn. Against Drunk Driving, Gabriel Broadcaster's and Allied Communicators, Mass. Soc. Against Cruelty to Children, 1988;

named to One Hundred Most Remarkable Women in Mass., Boston Woman's Mag., 1989, Freedoms Found., George Washington medal for pub. comms., 1998. Avocations: tennis, spectator football, reading. Office: The Learning Ctr PO Box 204 Newton MA 02456

CARTON, ROBERT JOHN, environmental scientist; b. Ft. Monmouth, N.J., Nov. 23, 1943; s. John William and Ursula Juliet (Miller) C.; m. Christina Saunders, June 17, 1967; children: Sean Michael, Christina Noel. BA in Chemistry, LaSalle U., 1965; postgrad., Purdue U., 1965-66; MS in Environ. Sci., Drexel U., 1967; PhD in Environ. Sci., Rutgers U., 1974. Rsch. engr. E.I. DuPont, Wilmington, Del., 1967-69; chemist, environ. scientist U.S. EPA, Washington, 1972-92; environ. coord. U.S. Army Med. Rsch. and Materiel Command, Ft. DeTrick, Md., 1992—, Joint Vaccine Acquisition Program, Ft. Detrick, 1998—; pres. Truth About Fluoride, Inc., Buckeystown, Md., 1993-95. Editor: Fluoride Report, 1993-95. Pres. Nat. Fedn. Fed. Employees Local 2050/U.S. EPA, Washington, 1986-87, 89-90. Recipient Bronze medal U.S. EPA, 1973, 85. Mem. Internat. Acad. Oral Medicine & Toxicology, Internat. Soc. for Fluoride Rsch., Nat. Assn. Environ. Profls., Nat. Treasury Employees Union (chpt. 280). Methodist. Avocations: boating, gardening. Office: US Army Med Rsch and Materiel Command Ft Detrick MCMR-RCQ-E Frederick MD 21702-5012

CART-ROGERS, KATHERINE COOPER, emergency nurse; b. Jacksonville, Tex., Aug. 7, 1948; d. Raymond Jesse and June (Walker) Cooper; m. Frank E. Rogers, Sept. 25, 1981; 1 child, Natalie Christine Cart. Med. Technologist, St. Mary's, Galveston, Tex., 1967; BS in Nursing, Stephen F. Austin U., Nacogdoches, Tex., 1989; MA in Mgmt., Regent U., Virginia Beach, Va., 1995. Cert. emergency nurse, TNCC instr., and emergency nurse pediatric course instr. Pharmacology-toxicology researcher U. Tex. Med. Br., Galveston, 1967-68, Ohio State U., Columbus, 1968-72; physicians asst., lab. supr. Newborn Meml. Hosp., Jacksonville, 1975-78; lab. mgr. East Tex. Med. Ctr., Rusk, 1978-87; lab. supr. Nacogdoches Meml. Hosp., 1987-89, emergency rm. nurse, 1989-91; emergency rm. chrge nurse Kingwood (Tex.) Pla. Hosp., 1991-92; nursing cons. Thorstenson Eye Clinic, Nacogdoches, 1991-92; dir. surg. svcs. Thorstenson Ambulatory Surgery Ctr., Nacogdoches, 1992-93; dir. Emergency/Trauma Svcs., ETMC-Jacksonville, 1992—. Mem. AACN, Emergency Nurses Assn., Tex. Trauma Coords., Tex. Regional Adv. Coun. for Trauma Area G. Home: Rte 3 Box 2 Rusk TX 75785-9503

CARTWRIGHT, ALTON STUART, electrical manufacturing company executive; b. Casper, Wyo., Oct. 7, 1922; s. Alton Stuart and Blanche Susan (Harper) C.; m. Adelaide Frances Igoe, Dec. 22, 1951; children: Stuart Andrew, Matthew Alton, David Francis, Patrick Harper. B.S. in Elec. Engring, Oreg. State U., 1944; grad., Advanced Mgmt. Program, Harvard U., 1969. Registered profl. engr., Mass. With Gen. Electric Co., 1946-85; with Can. Gen. Electric Co. Ltd., 1970-85; exec. v.p. Can. Gen. Electric Co. Ltd., Toronto, Ont., 1972; pres. Can. Gen. Electric Co. Ltd., 1972-77, chmn. bd., chief exec. officer, 1977-85, also dir.; sr. mem. Conf. Bd. Served to 1st lt. AUS, 1942-46. Mem. No. Lake George Yacht Club, John's Island Club (Vero Beach, Fla.), Sigma Alpha Epsilon. Home: 676 Ocean Rd Vero Beach FL 32963-3516

CARTWRIGHT, BRIAN GRANT, lawyer; b. Seattle, May 29, 1947; s. John Brydonne and Helen Ruth (Engman) C.; m. Jean Claudia Libby, Jan. 5, 1975; children: Grant, Eliot, Bryce. BS, Yale U., 1967; PhD, U. Chgo., 1971; JD, Harvard U., 1980. Bar: D.C. 1981, U.S. Dist. Ct. D.C. 1981, U.S. Ct. Appeals (D.C. cir.) 1981, Calif. 1984. Law clk. U.S. Ct. Appeals (D.C. cir.), Washington, 1980-81, U.S. Supreme Ct., Washington, 1981-82; assoc. Latham & Watkins, L.A., 1982-88, ptnr., 1988—, mem. exec. com., 1994-98. Mem. L.A. County Bar Assn. (mem. exec. com., bus. & corps. law sect.). Office: Latham & Watkins 633 W 5th St Ste 3800 Los Angeles CA 90071-2007

CARTWRIGHT, CAROL ANN, university president; b. Sioux City, Iowa, June 19, 1941; d. Carl Anton and Kathryn Marie (Weishapple) Becker; m. G. Phillip Cartwright, June 11, 1966; children: Catherine E., Stephen R., Susan D. BS in Early Childhood Edn., U. Wis., Whitewater, 1962; MEd in Spl. Edn., U. Pitts., 1965, PhD in Spl. Edn., Ednl. Rsch., 1968. From instr. to assoc. prof. Coll. Edn. Pa. State U., University Park, 1968-72, from assoc. prof. to prof., 1972-79, dean acad. affairs, 1981-84, dean undergrad. program, vice provost, 1984-88; vice chancellor acad. affairs U. Calif., Davis, 1988-91, prof. human devel., 1988-91; pres. Kent (Ohio) State U., 1991—; founder, co-chair Alliance for Undergrad. Edn., 1986-88; trustee Akron Reg. Devel. Bd., 1991—, Akron Gen. Med. Ctr., 1991—; bd. dirs. KeyBank, N.A., Cleve., 1991—, Ohio Edison Co., Akron, 1992—, Republic Engineered Steels, Inc., Massillon, Ohio, 1992—, M.A. Hanna Co., Cleve., 1994—. Editorial bd. Topics in Early Childhood Special Education, 1982-88, Exceptional Education Quarterly, 1982-88. Pres., bd. dirs. Child Devel. Coun. of Center County, Title XX Day Care Contractor, 1977-80; bd. dirs. Center County United Way, State College, Pa., 1984-88, Urban League of Greater Cleve., 1997—; bd. mem. Davis (Calif.) Art Ctr., 1988-91, Davis Sci. Ctr., 1989-91; bd. dirs. Ohio divsn. Am. Cancer Soc., 1993—, nat. bd. dirs., 1993—. Mem. AAUW, Am. Coun. Edn., Am. Ednl. Rsch. Assn., Am. Assn. for Higher Edn., Nat. Assn. State Univs. and Land-Grant Colls., Coun. for Exceptional Children. Roman Catholic. Avocations: jogging, reading, traveling. Home: 1703 Woodway Rd Kent OH 44240-5917 Office: Kent State U Office of the President PO Box 5190 Kent OH 44242-0001*

CARTWRIGHT, KEROS, hydrogeologist, researcher; b. L.A., July 25, 1934; s. Eugene Ewing and Charlotte Lucy (Searle) C.; m. Sharon Miller, July 5, 1955 (dec.); children: Sylvia, Jennifer; m. Jennifer Elizabeth Moberley, Mar. 9, 1962 (div. Sept. 1988); children: David, Bridget; m. Madalene Rose Tierney, Feb. 16, 1990. AB in Geology, U. Calif., 1959; MS in Geology, U. Nev., 1961; PhD in Geology, U. Ill., 1973. Cert. profl. geologist, profl. hydrologist. Hydrogeologist Humboldt River Rsch. Project, Winnemucca, Nev., 1959-61; hydrogeologist Ill. State Geol. Survey, Champaign, 1961—, head hydrogeology and geophysics section, 1975-84, prin. scientist and head gen. and environ. geology group, 1984-88, prin. rsch. scientist, 1988-99, chief scientist emeritus, 1999—; adj. prof. geology No. Ill. U., DeKalb, 1979—, U. Ill., Urbana, 1985—; cons. pvt. practice in hydrogeology, N.Am. and Europe, 1968—, U.S. Environ. Protection Agy. Sci. Adv. Bd., Washington, 1983—, Savannah River Site Environ. Adv., Aiken, S.C., 1988—. Mem. editorial bd. Elsevier Sci. Publ. Jour. of Hydrology, 1982-85; contbr. articles to profl. jours. Named Disting. Lectr. Assn. Groundwater-Water Scientists and Engrs., 1987; recipient Cert. Appreciation U.S. Environ. Protection Agy., 1988. Fellow Geol. Soc. Am. (officer hydrogeology sect. 1975-78, chmn. 1978-79, editorial bd. Jour. Water Resources Rsch. 1975-81, Bull. 1981-83, Birdsall disting. lectr. 1987-88, governing coun. 1993—, chmn. publs. com., George B. Maxey Disting. Svc. award 1991), Explorers Club; mem. ASTM (vice chmn. subcom. D-14 1984-88), Am. Inst. Hydrology (editorial bd. Jour. Hydrological Sci. and Tech. 1985—), Am. Geophys. Union (assoc. editor 1975-81), Am. Water Resources Assn., Internat. Assn. Hydrogeologists (U.S. com. 1985-89). Avocations: farming. Office: Ill Geol Survey 615 E Peabody Dr Champaign IL 61820-6918

CARTY, ARTHUR JOHN, science policy advisor, research administrator; b. Hookergate, County Durham, Eng., Sept. 12, 1940; arrived in Can., 1965; naturalized, 1969; George M. and Evelyn Carty; m. Helene Cloutier, Sept. 3, 1967; children: Richard, Stephane, Roxanne. BSc, U. Nottingham, Eng., 1962, PhD, 1965; DSc (honoris causa), U. Rennes, France, 1986, Carleton U., Ottawa, Can., 1997, U. Waterloo, Can., 1997. Asst. prof. chemistry Meml. U. Nfld., St. John's, Can., 1965-67; asst. prof. chemistry U. Waterloo, Ont., Can., 1967-69, assoc. prof. chemistry, 1969-75, prof. chemistry, 1975-94, chmn. dept. chemistry, 1983-89, dean rsch., 1989-94; pres. Nat. Rsch. Coun. Can., Ottawa, Ont., 1994—; mem. Sch. Grad. Studies and Rsch. U. Ottawa, 1995—; dir. Guelph-Waterloo Ctr. for Grad. Work in Chemistry, 1975-79; chmn. chem. grants selection com. Nat. Scis. and Engring. Rsch. Coun. Can., 1980-81, mem. targeted rsch. com., 1992-95, chair internat. peer rev. com. Can. Microelectronics Corp., 1994; mem. rsch. grants reallocations com. Natural sci. and engring rsch coun. of Canada. 1997; mem. adv. bd. Steacie Inst. Molecular Scis., NRC, 1990-94; bd. dirs. Waterloo Ctr. for Groundwater Rsch., 1992-94, Ont. Ctr. for Materials Rsch., 1991-94, Can. Indsl. Innovation Ctr., 1990-94, Fields Inst. for Rsch. in Math. Scis., 1991-97; mem. mgmt. bd. Inst. for Chem. Scis. and Tech., 1989-94; mem. R&D adv. coun. Dept. Nat. Def., 1996—, Environment Can., 1996—; mem. internat. adv. bd. Asia Pacific Eco. Cooperation Ctr. for Tech. Foresight, Thailand, 1997—, numerous others. Mem. Waterloo Econ. Devel. Com., 1990-93; mem. internat. intellectual property com. Intelligent Mfg. Sys., 1992-94; mem. rsch. adv. com. Royal Victoria Hosp., London, 1993-94; bd. dirs. Can. Inst. Tech. for Environ., 1992-94, Ont. Ctr. for Environ. Techs. Applications, 1993-94; mem. selection com. phase II of program Network Ctrs. Excellence, 1994—; bd. dirs. Intelligent Mfg. Systems Corp., 1994—, Comm. Rsch. Ctr., 1995—; mem. exec. com. Soc. Chem. Industry, 1994—. Recipient Royal Soc. award Nuffield Found., 1974, Purvis award Soc. Chem. Industry, 1997; Officer of the Ordre Nat. du Mérite (France), 1998. Fellow Royal Soc. Can. (chmn. pub. awareness of sci. com. 1990-94); mem. Am. Chem. Soc., Can. Soc. for Chemistry (v.p. 1989-90, pres. 1990-91, Alcan award 1984, E.W.R. Steacie award 1995), Chem. Inst. Can. (Montreal medal 1996), Royal Soc. Sci. (policy com. 1998—). Office: Nat Rsch Coun Can, 1500 Montreal Rd Bldg M-58, Ottawa, ON Canada K1A 0R6

CARTY, DONALD J., airline company executive. Grad., Queen's U., Kingston, Ont., Harvard U. With Air Canada, Canadian Pacific Rwy.; gen. mgr. Montcel Distbrs. unit Celanese Can. Ltd., Montreal; sr. v.p. fin. Americana Hotels; v.p. profit improvement, v.p. ops. rsch. American Airlines, sr. v.p., controller, sr. v.p. airline planning, 1987-89; exec. v.p. fin. and planning AMR and Am. Airlines, DFW Airport, Tex., 1989-95; pres. AMR Airline group and Am. Airlines, Inc., DFW Airport, Tex., 1995-98; pres., CEO CP Air; chmn., CEO AMR Airline Group and Am. Airlines, Dallas-Ft. Worth Airport, 1998—; bd. dirs. Dell computer Corp., Can. Airlines Internat. Ltd.; adv. bd. Allendale Mut. Ins. Co. Bd. trustees Queen's U. Office: American Airlines Inc Dallas Fort Worth Airport PO Box 619616 Dallas TX 75261-9616*

CARTY, HEIDI MARLENE, educator, researcher; b. Salt Lake City, July 19, 1967; d. Richard Eathel Coon and Sharon (Pitcher) Smith; m. Shawn Patrick Carty. BS in Psychology with honors cum laude, Loyola U., 1992, MA in Rsch. Methodology and Stats., 1994, PhD in Rsch. Methodology and Stats., 1998. Rsch. asst. Loyola U. Med. Ctr., Maywood, Ill., 1993; rsch. asst. Loyola U., Chgo., 1993-94, grad. asst. statis. computing, 1992-94; statis. cons. Iota, Inc., Chgo., 1993-95; grad. asst. rsch. methodology Loyola U., Chgo., 1994-96; statis. cons., lectr. biology dept. AMA, Chgo., 1995-98; asst. prof. rsch. Hofstra U., Hempstead, N.Y., 1998—; part-time lectr. Loyola U., Chgo., 1992-96, U. San Diego, 1998—, statis. cons., 1996—. Contbr. articles to profl. jours. Recipient grad. assistantship Loyola U., 1992-94, 94-96; scholar Nat. AMBUCS, 1991. Fellow Am. Ednl. Rsch. Assn.; mem. APA, AERA, Psi Chi (pres.), Alpha Epsilon Delta. Avocations: sailing, reading, jogging, movies, theater. Office: Hofstra U 212 Mason Hall Hempstead NY 11561

CARTY, JOHN WESLEY, lawyer; b. Lansing, N.C., Oct. 29, 1923; s. John Arthur and Bertha (Eller) C.; m. Doris Frances Barnes, June 27, 1948; children: Dixie Lynne, John Jeffrey. BA, Buena Vista Coll., 1950; JD, Drake U., 1952. Bar: Iowa 1952, U.S. Dist. Ct. (so. dist.) Iowa 1952, U.S. Ct. Appeals (8th cir.) 1965. Assoc. Pryor, Hale, Plock, Riley & Jones, Burlington, Iowa, 1952-54; ptnr. Carty & Jones, Des Moines, 1960-75; pvt. practice Winfield, Iowa, 1955—; Bd. dirs. Farmers Nat. Bank, Winfield, Iowa, pres., chmn. 1985—; pres. Oxidex, Inc., Winfield, 1971—; broker, dir. Winfield Realty Co., 1956-98; pres., chmn. Winfield Health Care & Retirement Ctr., 1972-77; dir., sec., treas. Satellite Mill, Inc., 1961-63. Co-author: Business Law & The Cooperative, 1962; assoc. editor Drake U. Law Rev., 1951-52. City atty. City of Winfield, Iowa, 1954-89, City of Wayland, Iowa, 1962-70; mem. Henry County Conservation Bd., Mt. Pleasant, Iowa, 1972-74; chmn. Henry County Compensation Commn., 1987-92; sec. S.E. Iowa Planning Coun., 1973-74; dir. S.E. Iowa Health Care Coun., Ft. Madison, 1974-76; mem. Iowa Archaeol. Soc., 1991—; mem. commn. eminent domain Henry County, 1993-98. With combat infantry U.S. Army, 1944-46, ETO. Decorated Combat Infantryman's badge, Bronze star; recipient Spl. award Bur. Nat. Affairs, 1952, Annual award Greene County Conservation Bd., 1987. Mem. Henry County Bar Assn. (pres. 1961-62), S.E. Iowa Bar Assn. (pres. 1962), Iowa State Bar Assn., Iowa Archeol. Soc., Hawkeye Archeol. Soc., Am. Legion, VFW, Masons, Phi Alpha Delta. Presbyterian. Home: 1586 Oasis Ave Mount Union IA 52644-9506 Office: Carty Law Office Farmers Nat Bank Bldg Winfield IA 52659

CARTY, RAYMOND WESLEY, academic administrator; b. Carlinville, Ill., Jan. 26, 1956; m. Elaine Smith, Apr. 21, 1979; children: Brooke Angelyn, Devan Alicia. AA, Hannibal-LaGrange (Mo.) Coll., 1977; BS, S.W. Bapt. U., 1979; MA, Liberty U., 1990. Registered social worker, Ill. Youth therapist Macoupin County Mental Health Ctr., Ill., 1979-84; minister music and youth Charity Bapt. Ch., Carlinville, 1979-84; assoc. dir. admissions Hannibal-LaGrange Coll., 1984—, assoc. dean of admissions, 1987-95, dean of enrollment mgmt., 1995-98, v.p. for enrollment mgmt., 1998—. Named one of Outstanding Young Men of Am., 1988. Mem. Mo. Assn. Coll. Admissions Counselors, Ill. Assn. Coll. Admission Counselors. Baptist. Avocations: music, antique automobiles. Home: 15 Fairway Dr Hannibal MO 63401-3615 Office: Hannibal-LaGrange Coll 2300 Palmyra Rd Hannibal MO 63401-1919

CARUANA, JOAN, educator, psychotherapist, nurse; b. Bklyn., Dec. 11, 1941; d. Gaetano and Fanny Caruana. RN, St. Vincent Hosp. Sch. Nursing, 1961; BS, Boston Coll., 1964; MA, NYU, 1975; grad., Psychoanalytic Psychotherapy Study Ctr., 1992. Cert. clin. specialist in adult psychiat. mental health nursing; cert. psychiat. nurse practitioner. Instr. St. Vincent's Hosp. Sch. Nursing, N.Y.C., 1965-99; psychotherapist N.Y.C., 1987—. Mem. St. Vincent's Hosp. Sch. Nursing Alumnae Assn. (editor newsletter 1978—, pres. 1998—).

CARUS, ANDRE WOLFGANG, educational publishing firm executive; b. LaSalle, Ill., June 24, 1953; s. Milton Blouke and Marianne (Sondermann) C. MA, U. St. Andrews (Scotland), 1977; PhD, U. Cambridge (Eng.), 1981; MBA, U. Chgo., 1990. Editor Ernst Klett Verlag, Stuttgart, Fed. Republic Germany, 1979-81; instr., asst. to dir. curriculum lab. sch. U. Bielefeld (Fed. Republic Germany), 1981-82; project dir. reading Open Ct. Pub. Co., Peru, Ill., 1983-85, dir. reading, 1985-86, v.p., gen. mgr., 1986-88, pres., 1988-90; pres., chief operating officer Carus Pub. Co., Chgo., 1990—, bd. dirs. Mem. Am. Ednl. Rsch. Assn., Nat. Coun. for the Social Studies, Nat. Coun. Tchrs. of Math., Assn. for Supervision and Curriculum Devel., Am. Econ. Assn., Univ. Club Chgo., Quadrangle Club Chgo. Office: Open Court Pub Co 315 5th St Peru IL 61354-2859*

CARUS, MILTON BLOUKE, publisher children's periodicals; b. Chgo., June 15, 1927; s. Edward H. and Dorothy (Blouke) C.; m. Marianne Sondermann, Mar. 3, 1951; children: Andre, Christine, Inga. BS in Elec. Engring, Calif. Inst. Tech., 1949; postgrad., Mexico City Coll., summer 1949, U. Freiburg, Germany, 1949-51, Sorbonne U., Paris, 1951. Devel. engr. Carus Chem. Co., Inc., LaSalle, Ill., 1951-55; asst. gen. mgr. Carus Chem. Co., Inc., 1955-61, exec. v.p., 1961-64, pres., 1964—; pres., now advisor Carus Corp., Peru, 1967—; editor Open Ct. Pub. Co., 1962-67; pub., pres. Open Ct. Pub. Co., 1967-88, pub., 1988-89, chmn., 1989—; pub. Cricket mag., 1973-89; chmn. Ladybug mag., 1990—, chmn. Spider mag., 1994—; treas. Bookbird Internat. Bd. Books Young People, 1994—. Chmn. Ill. Valley Cmty. Coll. Com., 1965-67; pres. Internat. Baccalaureat N.Am. Inc., 1977, chmn., 1980-89; mem. IBO Coun., Geneva, 1977-94; co-trustee Hegeler Inst., 1968-89; mem. employment and tng. com. U.S. Chamber, 1981-85; mem. Nat. Coun. on Ednl. Rsch. Nat. Inst. Edn., Dept. Edn., 1982-85, vice chmn., 1983-85; trustee Parliament of World's Religious, 1988—; mem. Ill. Gov.'s Task Force on Sch.-to-Work, 1994—. Mem. Ill. Valley Indsl. Assn. (pres. 1970—), Chem. Mfrs. Assn. (dir. 1977-80), Ill. Mfrs. Assn. (dir. 1972-77, 1988—, chmn. edn. com. 1988—), LaSalle County Hist. Soc. (dir. 1979-85), Phila Soc., Ill. State C. of C. (edn. com. 1973—). Office: Carus Corp Hdqrs 315 5th St Peru IL 61354-2859*

CARUSO, AILEEN SMITH, managed care consultant; b. Albany, N.Y., July 25, 1949; d. Robert Vincent and Mary (Prince) Smith; 1 child, Patrick Michael. AAS in nursing, Russell Sage Jr. Coll., Albany, 1970; BSBA cum laude, Coll. St. Rose, 1994. RN, N.Y.; cert. case mgr. Staff nurse neuro and thoracic surgery units VA Hosp., 1970-71; staff nurse family practice Milton F. Gipstein, MD, Schenectady, N.Y., 1971-74; psychiat. nurse Peter F. Andrus, MD, Albany, 1977-81; coll. health nurse State U. N.Y., Albany, 1979-82; orthopedic staff nurse Rosa Road Orthopedics, Schenectady, 1980-82; coll. health nurse Union Coll., Schenectady, 1982-87; customer svc. rep. Empire Blue Cross, Albany, 1987-88; fin. planner N.Y. Life Ins., Albany, 1988-89; sr. mgr. Corp. Health Demensions, Troy, N.Y., 1989-94, dir. implementation and tng., 1994-96, dir. implementation and corp. case mgmt., 1996, v.p. implementation, 1997, v.p. ops., 1998—; advs. Gen. Elec. Corp. R&D Safety Com., Schenectady, 1992-94; chmn. profl. devel. Northeast N.Y. Health Promotion, Albany, 1994—; com. chair Schenectady Health Coalition, 1993-95; edn. and by laws com., com. chair govt. affairs Am. Occupational Health Nurses, Albany, 1994—, also mem. nominating com. Co-author: Occupational Health Services Administrative/Patient Management Manual. Pres. Ch. Women, St. George's Episcopal Ch., 1994-97, mem. exec. bd. dirs., 1989-97, sr. vestryman, mem. exec. search com., 1998-99, also lector; chmn. worksite program N.E. N.Y. Tobacco-Free Coalition, 1993-94; co-mgr. The Bookshop at St. Georges, 1993-95. Recipient Rector's Recognition award St. George's Ch., 1991. Mem. Am. Assn. Occupl. Health Nurses (chair govtl. affairs com.), Capital Dist. Occupl. Health Nurses (nominating com.), Schenectady County Health Promotion Consortium, Health Promotion Coun. of N.E. N.Y., Schenectady County Bus. and Profl. Women, Capital Dist. Case Mgmt. Assn., Alpha Sigma Lambda. Avocations; racquetball, boating, reading, golf. Home: 1156 Spearhead Dr Scotia NY 12302-3122 Office: Corp Health Dimensions 13 British American Blvd Latham NY 12110-1464

CARUSO, CHRISTOPHER L., state legislator; b. Bridgeport, Conn.. Grad., St. Vincent's Sch. Rad. Tech. Mem. Dist. 126 Conn. Ho. of Reps., 1991—; vice-chair commerce com., co-chair subcom. Tourism, mem. environ. com., mem. govt. adminstrn. and elections com., mem. labor and pub. employees com. Conn. Ho. of Reps. Mem. Bridgeport Dem. Town Com., 1981—, chmn., 1986-88; mem. Bd. Alderman, Bridgeport, 1983-91. Address: Legis Office Bldg Rm 5002 Hartford CT 06106*

CARUSO, DANIEL F., lawyer, judge, former state legislator; b. Greenwich, Conn., Dec. 12, 1957; s. Frederick A. Caruso and Ruth Collins. BA, U. Conn., 1980; JD, U. Vt., 1983. Bar: Conn. 1983, U.S. Dist. Ct. Conn. 1984. Atty. Paul M. Tymniak & Assocs., Fairfield, Conn., 1984-88; sole practice Fairfield, 1988-97; mem. Conn. Gen. Assembly, Hartford, 1989-94, asst. house minority leader, 1992-94, ranking mem. gen. law com., 1991; judge of probate Probate Dist. of Fairfield, 1995—; atty. Owens, Schine & Nicola, P.C., 1997—; co-chmn. House Rep. Policy Group on Drug Control Strategy; mem. gen. law com. Conn. Gen. Assembly, 1991-94, mem. judiciary com., 1989-94, mem. regulation rev. com., 1989-94. Mem., advisor Nat. Heritage Trust Adv. Bd., 1990-91; treas. Town of Fairfield, 1993-95, mem. bd. fin., 1985-89; del. Rep. Nat. conv., Houston, 1992. Mem. Kiwanis, Eagle Scouts Am., Pi Sigma Alpha, Phi Alpha Theta, Alpha Phi Omega. Roman Catholic. Home: 160 Fairfield Woods Rd Apt 61 Fairfield CT 06432-3348 Office: 53 Sherman St Fairfield CT 06430-5821

CARUSO, DAVID, actor; b. Queens, N.Y., Jan. 17, 1956; s. Charles and Joan C.; m. Sherry Maugans (div.); m. Rachel Ticotin (div.); 1 child, Greta. Appearances include (film) An Officer and a Gentleman, 1982, First Blood, 1982, Thief of Hearts, 1984, Blue City, 1986, China Girl, 1987, Twins, 1988, King of New York, 1990, Hudson Hawk, 1991, Mad Dog and Glory, 1993, Kiss of Death, 1994, Jade, 1995, The Split, 1997, Cold Around the Heart, 1997, The Split, 1998; (TV movies) Crazy Times, 1981, The First Olympics-Athens 1896, 1984, Into the Homeland, 1987, Rainbow Drive, 1990, Mission of the Shark, 1991, Judgement Day: The John List Story, 1993, Gold Coast, 1997; (TV series) N.Y.P.D. Blue, 1993-94 (Best Actor - Drama Golden Globe award 1994, Best Actor in Drama series Emmy award nominee 1994), Michael Hayes, 1997; (TV miniseries) Baseball, 1994, Gold Coast, 1997. Office: William Morris Agy c/o Scott Lambert 151 S El Camino Dr Beverly Hills CA 90212-2775*

CARUSO, KAY ANN PETE, elementary education educator; b. New Orleans, Sept. 23, 1944; d. John R. and Dorothy E. (LeBlanc) Pete; m. Frank J. Caruso III, Nov. 11, 1967; 1 child, Brian Joseph. BA, Southeastern La. U., 1966; MEd, U. New Orleans, 1981. Tchg. cert. La. Elem. tchr., libr., tchr. 5th grade reading Jefferson Parish Pub. Sch. Sys., Metairie, La., 1966—. Sec. Brother Martin H.S. Parent Club, New Orleans, 1992-94; tchr. rep. Alice Birney Sch. Parent/Tchr. Group, Metairie, 1979-83, 96-97; vol. Rep. Nat. Conv., New Orleans, 1990. Named tchr. of yr. Jefferson Parish C. of C. 1988, 95-96; recipient Barbara McNamara award for reading promotion Reading Is Fundamental program, 1989, Disting. Tchg. award Gifted and Talented Program Northwestern State U., 1995. Mem. AAUW (sec. 1996-98, v.p. 1998—), Jefferson Librs. Assn. (v.p., pres. 1984-88), Jefferson Fedn. Tchrs. (librs. chpt. rep. 1985-87), So. Assn. Colls. and Schs. (evaluator, com. chair 1980-98), AAUW (chpt. sec. 1996-98, v.p. 1998—, name grant honoree 1996), Delta Kappa Gamma (chpt. sec. 1984-86, v.p. 1988-90, pres. 1994-98, dir. South dist. 1997—, treas. 1998—). Avocations: reading, travel, genealogy. Office: Alice Birney Elem Sch 4829 Hastings St Metairie LA 70006-2676

CARUSO, MARK JOHN, lawyer; b. L.A., Apr. 27, 1957; s. John Mondella and Joyce Dorothy C.; m. Judy F. Velarde, Aug. 15, 1987. BS cum laude, Pepperdine U., 1979, JD, 1982. Bar: Calif. 1982, N.Mex. 1987, U.S. Dist. Ct. (ctrl. dist.) Calif. 1982, U.S. Dist. Ct. N.Mex. 1987, U.S. Dist. Ct. (no. and so. dists.) Calif. 1995, U.S. Ct. Appeals (9th cir.) 1983, U.S. Ct. Appeals (10th cir.) 1987. Pvt. practice, Burbank, Calif., 1982—, Albuquerque, 1987—; mem. House labor com., House consumer and pub. affairs com., House workers compensation oversight interim com., House ct. correction and justice interim com.; mem. N.Mex. Ho. of Reps., 1990-94, mem. jud. com., labor com., workers compensation oversight com., 1990-94; lobbyist Nat. Right to Work Com., 1984-86. Col., aide de camp to gov. State of N. Mex., 1987; chmn. N. Mex. Mcpl. Boundary Commn., 1988—; del. Rep. Nat. Conv., 1988, 92; lectr. breast implant litigation, Fen Phen diet drug litigation; Sandoval county chmn. George Bush for Pres., 1988. Recipient platinum award N.Mex. Free Enterprise Adv., 1986. Mem. ATLA, Breast Implant Litigation Group, Consumer Attys. of Calif., Albuquerque Hispano C. of C., Greater Albuquerque C. of C. Fax: 505-883-5012. Office: 4302 Carlisle Blvd NE Albuquerque NM 87107-4811

CARUSO, NICHOLAS DOMINIC, protective services official; b. Wilmington, Del., Feb. 2, 1957; s. Nicholas Anthony and Philomena Marie (Pelaia) C. BA in Polit. Sci., U. Del., 1985; MA in Liberal Arts, Widener U., 1991. Sr. analyst Bank of N.Y., Newark, 1985-89; police officer Wilmington Police Dept., 1989—. With U.S. Army, 1975-78, USN, 1979-83. Mem. Nat. Intelligence Study Ctr., Internat. Assn. of Stategic Studies, Acad. of Polit. Sci. Democrat. Roman Catholic. Avocations: book collecting, creative writing. Home: 909 W 21st St Wilmington DE 19802-3820 Office: Wilmington Police Dept 300 N Walnut St Fl 2 Wilmington DE 19801-3989

CARUSO, ROCCO ANDREW, television producer; b. Syracuse, N.Y., Jan. 6, 1964; s. Carmen Sam and Monica (Petta) C. BFA, SUNY, Purchase, 1987; postgrad, Yale U., 1987-90. Prodr. Caruso-Mendelsohn Prodns., N.Y.C., 1987—, HBO, N.Y.C., 1989-91, Warner Bros., 1992—. Assoc. prodr. TV show Shining Time Station, 1988, TNT Internat. Film Festival, 1990; segement prodr. TV show Salute to Superman's 50th Anniversary, 1987; prodr. music videos for HBO, 1990; prodr. films An Open Window, 1990, Judy Berlin, 1998. Recipient silver medal Photog. Soc. Am., 1988, best dramatic film award Melbourne (Australia) Film Festival, 1990, Un Certain Regard award Cannes Film Festival, 1992, Gold Hugo award Chgo. Internat. Film Festival, 1993. Mem. NATAS, Prodrs. Guild Am. Office: Caruso-Mendelsohn Prodns Tribeca Film Ctr 375 Greenwich St New York NY 10013-2376

CARUSONE, ALBERT ROBERT, writer; b. Ellwood City, Pa., Mar. 14, 1949; s. Albert D. and Dorothy (Lordo) C.; m. Gwendolyn Elaine Gettig, Oct. 12, 1974; children: Kristin Hilary, Kimberly Rebecca, Jamie Alyson. BS, U. Pitts., 1971, MA, 1972. Tchr. Penn Hills (Pa.) Sch. Dist., Bald Eagle Area H.S., Wingate, Pa.; reactor supr. Pa. State U., University Park; regional sales mgr. Accu Weather, State College, Pa., 1989-97; sales mgr. Keystone Scientific, Inc., Bellefonte, Pa., 1997-98. Author: Don't Open the Door After the Sun Goes Down, 1994, Sleepless Sleepover, 1995, Time's Up, 1996, Scout's Honor, 1996, Teacher's Pet, 1996, Cyber Sleuth, 1997, Soccer Rules, 1997, Hoop Magic, 1998, The Boy with Dinosaur Hands, 1998. Mem. Soc. Children's Book Writers and Illustrators, Authors Guild, Authors League of Am. Home: 1961 Old 220 Rd Howard PA 16841-4819

CARVAJAL, JORGE ARMANDO, endocrinologist, internist; b. Chiscas, Boyaca, Colombia, Dec. 20, 1935; came to U.S., 1963; s. Julio and Natividad (Caicedo) C.; m. Carlota Mellonunes Ribeiro, Sept. 5, 1965; children: Jorge Jr., Fernando, Eduardo. MD, U. Nacional Fac. Medicine, Bogota, Colombia, 1963. Diplomate Am. Bd. Internal Medicine, Am. Bd. Endocrinology. Resident Hosp. San Jose, Bogota, 1962-63; intern Meth. Hosp., Peoria, Ill., 1963-64; resident in medicine Meml. Hosp., Detroit, 1964-65, Mt. Sinai Hosp., Mpls., 1965-66, VA Med. Ctr., Long Beach, Calif., 1966-67; fellow in endocrinology VA Med. Ctr., L.A., 1967-69; asst. prof. U. Rosario, Bogota, 1969-72; fellow in metabolism U. Calif.-Davis, Sacramento, 1972-73; staff endocrinologist Kaiser-Permanente Hosp., Sacramento, 1973-75; staff physician VA Med. Ctr., Long Beach, Calif., 1975-76; pvt. practice Anaheim, Calif., 1976—; staff Anaheim Meml. Hosp., 1976—. Democrat. Roman Catholic. Avocations: jogging, reading. Home: 16562 Grimaud Ln Huntington Beach CA 92649-1828 Office: 1211 W La Palma Ave Ste 702 Anaheim CA 92801-2814

CARVALHO, JULIE ANN, psychologist; b. Washington, Apr. 11, 1940; d. Daniel H. and Elizabeth Cecilia (Gardiner) Schmidt; children: Alan R., Dennis M., Melanie D., Celeste A., Joshua E. BA with honors, U. Md., 1962, postgrad., 1973; MA, George Washington U., 1966; postgrad., Va. Poly. Inst., 1979-88. Social sci. rsch. analyst Mental Health Study Ctr., NIMH, 1963-67; edn. and tng. analyst Computer Applications, Inc., 1967-68; edn. program specialist Nat. Ctr. for Ednl. R&D, U.S. Office of Edn., Washington, 1969-70, program analyst, 1970-73; equal opportunity specialist Office of Sec., HEW, Washington, 1973-77; legis. program, civil rights analyst Office for Civil Rights Dept. Health and Human Svcs., Washington, 1977-85; ind. cons.; adj. lectr., No. Va. C.C., UMUC, George Mason U., Montgomery Coll., Strayer Coll., Shepherd Coll., Germanna Coll., U. Md. U. Coll., Prince William Hosp., Fairfax County Pub. Schs., Fairfax County Dept. Social Svcs., 1986—. Contbr. articles to profl. jours. Bd. dirs. Child Care Ctrs., 1970-76, HEW Employees Assn., 1973-78; mem. steering com. Alliance for Child Care, 1975-80. Mem. APA (panel condr. 1969—, editor Bull. of Peace Psychology 1991-98, divsn. 48), ASPA (condr. panels), Capitol Area Social Psychologists Assn. (conf. chmn. 1985, 93), Psychologists Soc. Responsibility, Federally Employed Women (nat. editor 1975-79), Fairfax County Assn. for the Gifted (pres. 1980), Psi Chi, Phi Alpha Theta, Alpha Sigma Lambda (hon.). Mailing Address: PO Box 11500 Alexandria VA 22312 Home and Office: 5927 Quantrell Ave Apt T3 Alexandria VA 22312-2762

CARVER, CALVIN REEVE, public utility company director; b. East Orange, N.J., Mar. 14, 1925; m. Emma G. Carver, Dec. 8, 1951 (dec. 1977); children: Marthanne G., Calvin Reeve Gilbert H.; m. June G. Carver, Jan. 10, 1982. B.S. in E.E., Cornell U., 1946. Vice pres. Syracuse Sub. Gas Co, East Syracuse, N.Y., 1952-68; v.p., then pres. City Gas Cos., Flemington, N.J., 1952-65, also bd. dirs.; v.p., then pres. Penn-Jersey Pipe Line, Short Hills, N.J., 1952-90, also bd. dirs.; v.p. Elizabethtown Gas, Elizabeth, 1965-75, also bd. dirs.; chmn. Lenape Resources, Bridgewater, 1981-86; pres. Pomfret Prodn. Co., Inc., Bridgewater, 1981-86, also dir.; exec. v.p. NUI Corp., Bedminster, N.J., 1969-86; bd. dirs. Elizabethtown Gas Co., Union, N.J., Penn-Jersey Pipe Line, Bradford, Vt., NUI Corp., Bedminster, N.J. Served with USN, 1943-47, lt., 1950-52. Republican. Congregationalist. Club: Short Hills.

CARVER, CRAIG R., lawyer; b. Aug. 5, 1948. AB with distinction, Stanford U., 1970; JD, U. Mich., U. Denver, 1974. Bar: Colo. 1974. Ptnr. Gibson, Dunn & Crutcher, Denver, 1982-96; mem., mgr. Alfers & Carver, L.L.C., Denver, 1996—. Bd. trustees Rocky Mountain Mineral Law Found., 1982-84, 92-94. Mem. ABA, Colo. Bar Assn., Denver Bar Assn. Office: Alfers & Carver LLC 730 17th St Ste 340 Denver CO 80202-3513

CARVER, DAVID HAROLD, physician, educator; b. Boston, Apr. 18, 1930; s. Elias and Lottie (Jaffe) C.; m. Patricia Jo Nair, Aug. 2, 1963; children: Randolph Nair, Rebecca Lynn, Leslie Allison. A.B. magna cum laude, Harvard U., 1951; M.D., Duke U., 1955. Intern Johns Hopkins Hosp., 1955-56; research fellow pediatrics Cleve. Met. Hosp., 1956-58; jr. asst. resident Children's Hosp. Med. Center, Boston, 1958-59; sr. asst. resident Children's Hosp. Med. Center, 1959-60, chief resident, 1960-61, USPHS spl. post doctoral research fellow Harvard Med. Sch., 1961-63; asst. prof. pediatrics Albert Einstein Coll. Medicine, 1963-66; assoc. prof., then prof. pediatrics Johns Hopkins U. Med. Sch., 1966-76; prof. pediatrics U. Toronto Med. Sch., 1976-88; physician-in-chief Hosp. Sick Children, Toronto, 1976-86; chmn. dept. pediatrics U. Toronto, 1976-86; prof., chmn. dept. pediatrics Robert Wood Johnson Med. Sch., 1988—; mem. study sect. USPHS Ctr. Disease Control, 1971-73; mem. provincial research grants rev. com. Ont. Ministry Health, 1977-83, chmn., 1981-83. Assoc. editor: Textbook of Pediatrics, 14th edit, 1968, 15th edit., 1972, 16th edit., 1977; editorial bd.: Pediatrics, 1973-79. Served with USPHS, 1956-58. Recipient Schaffer award clin. teaching Johns Hopkins U. Med. Sch., 1973, Bain award for clin. teaching Hosp. Sick Children, 1978, Kennedy sr. scholar, 1966-73. Mem. Am. Acad. Pediatrics (com. on infectious diseases 1973-79), Infectious Disease Soc. Am., Am. Soc. Virology, Internat. Soc. Interferon Research, Canadian Infectious Disease Soc., Am. Soc. Microbiology, Soc. Pediatric Research, Am. Pediatric Soc., Can. Pediatric Soc., Harvard Club Princeton. Home: 220 Sayre Dr Princeton NJ 08540-5852

CARVER, DOROTHY LEE ESKEW (MRS. JOHN JAMES CARVER), retired secondary education educator; b. Brady, Tex., July 10, 1926; d. Clyde Albert and A. Maurine (Meadows) Eskew; student So. Ore. Coll., 1942-43, Coll. Eastern Utah, 1965-67; BA, U. Utah, 1968; MA, Cal. State Coll. at Hayward, 1970; postgrad. Mills Coll., 1971; m. John James Carver, Feb. 26, 1944; children: John James, Sheila Carver Bentley, Chuck, David. Instr., Rutherford Bus. Coll., Dallas, 1944-45; sec. Adolph Coors Co., Golden, Colo., 1945-47; instr. English, Coll. Eastern Utah, Price, 1968-69; instr. speech Modesto (Calif.) Jr. Coll., 1970-71; instr. personal devel. men and women Heald Bus. Colls., Oakland, Calif., 1972-74, dean curricula, Walnut Creek, Calif., 1974-86; instr. Diablo Valley Coll., Pleasant Hill, Calif., 1986-87, Contra Costa Christian H.S.; ret., 1992; communications cons. Oakland Army Base, Crocker Bank, U.S. Steel, I. Magnin, Artec Internat.; presenter in field. Author: Developing Listening Skills. Mem. Gov's. Conf. on Higher Edn. in Utah, 1968; mem. finance com. Coll. Eastern Utah, 1967-69; active various cmty. drives. Bd. dirs. Opportunity Ctr., Symphony of the Mountain. Mem. AAUW, Bus. and Profl. Womens Club, Nat. Assn. Deans and Women Adminstrs., Delta Kappa Gamma. Episcopalian (supt. Sunday Sch. 1967-69). Clubs: Soroptimist Internat. (pres. Walnut Creek 1979-80 sec., founder region 1978-80); Order Eastern Star. Home: 20 Coronado Ct Walnut Creek CA 94596-5801

CARVER, GEORGE ALLEN, JR., lawyer; b. Washington, Nov. 8, 1940; s. George Allen and Barbara Ellen (Bristol) C.; m. Joan Page, Dec. 13, 1964; children: George Allen III, Robert William. BS, U.S. Mil. Acad., 1964; JD, U. Va., 1972. Bar: Va. 1972, D.C. 1978, U.S. Dist. Ct. (D.C. cir.) 1979, U.S. Ct. Appeals (9th cir.) 1986, U.S. Ct. Appeals (4th cir.) 1988. Trial atty. gen. crimes sect. Criminal divsn. U.S. Dept. Justice, Washington, 1972-76, trial atty. pub. integrity sect., 1976-81, dir. conflicts of interest crimes br., pub. integrity sect., 1981-88, dep. chief fraud sect., 1988-92, prin. dep. chief fraud sect., 1992-95, sr. counsel to chief asset forfeiture/money laundering sect., 1995-96, dep. chief, sr. counsel to the chief, 1996—. Capt. inf. U.S. Army, 1964-69. Decorated Silver Star, Bronze Star, Purple Heart. Avocations: photography, fishing, boating, walking, reading. Home: 6049 Makely Dr Fairfax Station VA 22039-1324 Office: US Dept Justice Criminal Div/Asset Forfeit/Money Launder 1400 New York Ave NE Washington DC 20002-1722

CARVER, JEFFREY A., writer; b. Cleve., Aug. 25, 1949; s. Robert D. and Mildred Sherrick Carver; m. Allysen Evans Palmer, Sept. 7, 1986; children: Alexandria, Julia. BA, Brown U., 1971; M of Marine Affairs, U. R.I., 1974. Scuba diving instr. Nat. Assn. of Underwater Instrs., Mass., R.I; Quahog diver Narragansett, R.I., 1974; word processing cons., Cambridge, 1984-85; webmaster The Star Rigger's Net, 1996—. Author: (novels) The Chaos Chronicles, vol. 1-3, Dragons in the Stars, 1992, Dragon Rigger 1993, From a Changeling Star, 1989, Down the Stream of Stars, 1990, The Infinity Link, 1984. Mem. Sci. Fiction and Fantasy Writers of Am., The Authors Guild. Avocations: reading, scuba diving, flying, camping with family. E-mail: jeff@starrigger.net. Office: Star Rigger Assocs 102 Melrose St Arlington MA 02474

CARVER, JOAN SACKNITZ, university dean; b. Spokane, Wash., Jan. 22, 1931; d. Weldon and Mabel (Swanson) S.; m. Jay Randall Carver, June 25, 1955; 1 child, James Randall (dec.). BA, Barnard Coll., 1953; MA, U. N.C., 1957; PhD, U. Fla., 1965. Exec. sec. Iranian del. to UN, N.Y.C., 1953-55; tchr. Lake Shore Jr. High Sch., Jacksonville, Fla., 1956-57; office mgr. Bartram Sch., Jacksonville, 1957-58; from asst. to assoc. prof. Jacksonville U., 1958-60, 63-75, prof., 1975—, chmn. div. social scis., 1982-83, dean Coll. Arts and Scis., 1983—, dir. Taft Seminars in Practical Politics, 1968-78; instr. employee seminars City of Jacksonville, 1969-82; evaluator ABT Assocs., Boston, 1975; mem. reaffirmation coms. So. Assn. Colls., Atlanta, 1983-97. Contbr. articles to profl. jours. Sec., bd. dirs. Jacksonville Cmty. Coun., Inc., 1976-80; commr. 1st Appellate dist. Jud. Nominating Commn., Tallahassee, 1983-87; commr. Jacksonville Mayor's Com. on Status of Women, 1984-88; bd. trustees St. John's Country Day Sch., Orange Park, Fla., 1984—, pres., 1993-95; chair career opportunities subcom. Def. Adv. Com. on Women in Svc., Washington, 1991-93; bd. dirs. Fla. Humanities Coun., 1993-97. Recipient Prof. of Yr. award Jacksonville, U., 1972, EVE award for achievement in edn. Fla. Times Union, Jacksonville, 1982; Seven Coll. Conf. nat. scholar Barnard Coll., 1949-53; grad. fellow U. Fla., 1960-63. Mem. Fla. Polit. Sci. Assn. (pres. 1975-76), Am. Soc. for Pub. Adminstrn. (pres. N.E. Fla. chpt. 1987-88), Women's Caucus for Polit. Sci.-South (pres. 1981-82), So. Polit. Sci. Assn. (membership chmn. 1983-91, rec. sec. 1993-94), Jacksonville Women's Network (pres. 1987-90), Phi Beta Kappa. Democrat. Episcopalian. Avocations: swimming, reading, gardening. Home: 46 15th St Jacksonville FL 32233-5722 Office: Jacksonville U 2800 University Blvd N Jacksonville FL 32211-3394

CARVER, JOAN WILLSON, publishing executive, artist; b. St. Paul; d. Stuart Van Vranken and Marie (Carlson) Willson; m. Norman F. Carver Jr., Aug. 15, 1953; children: Norman III, Cristina. BA, Smith Coll., 1950; postgrad., Yale U.sSch. Architectures, 1950-53. Architect Larson Playter Architects, Eau Claire, Wis., 1953, John W. King Assocs. Architects, Tokyo, 1954-55; designer Norman F. Carver Jr. Architect, Kalamazoo, 1958-78; v.p., treas. Documan Press Ltd., Kalamazoo, 1979—; editor World Architecture Calendars, 1982—; artist Joan Willson Carver Porcelains, Kalamazoo, 1981—; instr. ceramics Kalamazoo Arts Ctr., 1983—. Exhibited in group shows at Wichita (Kans.) Art Mus., Kalamazoo Art Ctr., Battle Creek (Mich.) Art Mus., Circle Gallery, Mich. Potters Assn., Six 17 Gallery, The Clay Studio, Lizards and Mice Gallery, Holland Area Arts Ctr., Dumont Gallery, 1997, Wearley Studio Gallery, 1997, 98; co-founder, editor Perspecta-Yale Achitecture Jour. Sustainer Kalamazoo Jr. League, 1971—; chmn. Kalamazoo Dental Clinic, 1972; bd. dirs. Kalamazoo Symphony Orch., 1975-78. Mem. Kalamazoo Inst. Arts (bd. dirs. 1966-73, 78-84, pres. bd. dirs. 1970-73, chmn. exhbns. 1967-73, 78-87, scholarship com. 1980—, edn. com. 1985—), Jr. League of Kalamazoo. Episcopalian. Clubs: Service of Kalamazoo (pres. 1969-70), Current Events (Kalamazoo) (pres. 1982-83, treas. 1986-87). Office: Documan Press Ltd 3201 Lorraine Ave Kalamazoo MI 49008-2003

CARVER, KENDALL LYNN, insurance company executive; b. Spencer, Iowa, Nov. 4, 1936; s. Marion and Letha G.; m. Carol Lee Spiers, July 1, 1961; children: Merrian, Kendra, Lee, Christine. BS, U. Iowa, 1958. Rep. field sales Washington Nat. Ins. Co., Evanston, Ill., 1958-73; regional dir. Washington Nat. Ins. Co., 1974-77; pres. Washington Nat. Ins. Co., N.Y.C., 1977—; CEO Washington Nat. Ins. Co., 1978-94; mng. dir. Kendall Carver and Assocs. LLC, 1996-98; chmn. fin. com. First Benefit Ins. Co. of Phoenix, 1996-98; also bd. dirs. First Benefit Inst. Co. of Phoenix, 1997; founder, pres., CEO Confirmation-Plus LLC, 1998—; bd. dirs. Life Ins. Coun. N.Y., chmn., 1991; chmn. bd. dirs. Security Adminstrs. Inc., Binghamton, N.Y.; cons. to ins. industry. Fellow Life Mgmt. Inst.; mem. Am. Coll. Life Underwriters, Life Ins. Council N.Y. (dir. 1979-82, 86-88). Republican.

CARVER, M. KYLE, secondary education educator. Tchr. sci. A.C. Reynolds Mid. Sch., Asheville, N.C.; mem. bd. trustees Mars Hill Coll., 1977—, N.C. Ednl. Coun. for Exceptional Children, 1986-94. First runner-up Outstanding Earth Sci. Tchr. N.C., 1992. Office: A C Reynolds Middle Sch 2 Rocket Dr Asheville NC 28803-9100*

CARVER, NORMAN FRANCIS, JR., architect, photographer; b. Jan. 27, 1928; m. Joan Willson, Aug. 15, 1953; children: Norman F. III, Cristina. Grad., Yale. Practice architecture Kalamazoo; prof. advanced photography Kalamazoo Inst. Arts, 1971-86; vis. lectr., critic Carnegie Inst. Tech., Mich. State U., Yale U., MIT, So. Ill. U.; guest lectr. King Faisal U., Saudi Arabia, 1981. Exhibited photography U.S. and abroad; photographs published in Aperture, House Beautiful, Horizon, others; author: Form and Space of Japanese Architecture, 1955, 2d edit., 1993, Silent Cities of Mexico and the Maya, 1966, rev. edit., 1986, Italian Hilltowns, 1979, rev. edit., 1995, Iberian Villages - Spain and Portugal, 1981, Japanese Folkhouses, 1984, North African Villages, 1989, Greek Island Villages, 1999. Recipient Fulbright awards to Japan, 1953-54, 64, silver medal Archtl. League, 1962, award Archtl. Record, 1960, 61, 62, Robert Hastings award Mich. Soc. Architects, 1987. Home: 3201 Lorraine Ave Kalamazoo MI 49008-2003

CARVEY, DANA, actor, stand up comedian; b. Missoula, Mont., Apr. 2, 1955; m. Paula Zwaggerman. Student communication arts, San Francisco U. Appeared in TV films Alone at Last, 1980, Whacked Out, 1981, Hot Shots, 1986; TV series One of the Boys, 1982, Blue Thunder, 1984, Saturday Night Live, 1986— (Emmy award Outstanding Individual Performance in Variety or Musical Program 1989, 90, 91, 93); appeared in films including Halloween II, 1981, Racing with the Moon, 1984, This is Spinal Tap, 1984, Tough Guys, 1986, Moving, 1988, Opportunity Knocks, 1990, Wayne's World, 1992, Wayne's World II, 1993, Clean Slate, 1994, The Road to Wellville, 1994, Trapped in Paradise, 1994, The Shot, 1996, (TV series) The Dana Carvey Show, 1996. Recipient Am. Comedy award, 1990. *

CARWILE, BILLIE NEWMAN, history educator; b. Campbell County, Va., Oct. 3, 1931; d. Warren Edgar and Ethel Martha (Moore) Newman; m. Revely Bomar Carwile, Sept. 10, 1949; children: Thomas Revely, Daniel Newman, David Neal, Revely B. Jr., Nancy Carwile Friend. BA, Lynchburg Coll., 1965; MEd, U. Va., 1969; advanced grad. studies, Va. Poly. Inst./U. Va./U. Pa., 1970-81. History instr. Lynchburg (Va.) Pub. Schs., 1965-86; adj. history prof. Cen. Va. C.C., Lynchburg, 1978—, Averette Coll., Danville, Va., 1988-92; reader Advanced Placement Exams Ednl. Testing Svc., Princeton, N.J., 1982-96; judge History Day, Soc. Va. History, Lynchburg, 1980—. Historian Old Dominion, Lynchburg, 1986—, U. D.C.; bd. dirs., sec. Campbell County Hist. Soc.; regent, vice regent Col. Charles Lynch Nat. Soc. DAR, Alta Vista, Va., 1995-99; state chmn. Monuments and Markers, U. D.C., 1991-95. Mellon Humanities grantee U. Va., 1966, Freedom Found. grantee FBI, 1980. Avocations: genealogy, archaeology. Home: 1520 Rivermont Ave Lynchburg VA 24503

CARWILE, NANCY RAMSEY, educational administrator; b. Pinehurst, N.C., Apr. 30, 1942; d. Ralston Rowan and Mary (Selden) Ramsey; m. C.L. Carwile Jr., June 29, 1963; children: Andrew Lewis, Lona Catherine. BA, Coll. William and Mary, 1963; MEd, U. Va., 1986, PhD, 1990. Tchr. Charlotte County Schs., Va., 1963-76, Appomattox (Va.) County Schs., Charlotte, 1976-87; faculty Southside Va. C.C., Keysville, 1988-90, adminstr., 1990-97; exec. dir. Govs. Sch. for Global Econs. and Tech., Keysville, 1997—; cons. Va. Dept. of Correctional Edn., 1987-88. Author: (with others) Sourcebook for USA Dependent Schools, 1993. Dir. Charlotte County United Way, 1965-67; mem. Va. Bd. for Correctional Edn., 1996—, Charlotte County Literacy Bd., 1988—; mem. edn. task force State Senator Dalton, Va., 1989; sec. Charlotte County Rep. Party, 1993, 95; lay leader Centenary United Meth. Ch., 1985-95; mem. Southside Va. Bus. and Edn. Commn., 1999—. Rsch. grant Appalachia Ednl. Labs., 1988; recipient Merit award for tchg. econs. day proclaimed Nancy Carwile day Va. Gov. Allen, 1997. Mem. Nat. PTA (life), Internat. Reading Assn., Nat. Coun. Tchrs. of Math. (dist. pres. 1990-92), Phi Beta Kappa, Phi Delta Kappa. Republican. Home: 235 Thomaswood Ln Cullen VA 23934-9714 Office: Gov Sch Global Econs and Tech 200 Daniel Dr Keysville VA 23947-9703

CARY, ANNE O., retired diplomat; b. Washington, Sept. 8, 1952; d. Charles O. and Jean (Cochran) C.; m. John F. McNamara, June 26, 1982; children: John McNamara, Elizabeth McNamara, James McNamara. Student, Trinity Coll., Dublin, Ireland, 1972-73; BA, U. Wis., 1973; MA, Stanford U., 1984. Internat. economist Civil Aeronautic Bd., Washington, 1974; fgn. svc. officer Dept. of State, Washington, 1974-76, U.S. Mission to European Community, Brussels, Belgium, 1976-78; fgn. svc. officer U.S. Emb., Port-au-Prince, Haiti, 1978-80, Paris, France, 1980-83, Addis Ababa, Ethiopia, 1985-87, New Delhi, India, 1987-89; fgn. svc. officer European Community Affairs, Dept. of State, Washington, 1989-91; consul gen. U.S. Consulate, Casablanca, Morocco, 1992-95; ret.; mem. Fgn. Svc. Res. Corps, 1995—. Dean Rusk fellow Georgetown U., Washington, 1991-92.

CARY, ARLENE D., retired hotel company sales executive; b. Chgo., Dec. 19, 1930; d. Seymour S. and Shirley L. (Land) C.; student U. Wis., 1949-52; BA, U. Miami, 1953; m. Elliot D. Hagle, Dec. 30, 1972 (div.). Pub. rels. acct. exec. Robert Howe & Co., 1953-55; sales mgr. Martin B. Iger & Co., 1955-57; sales mgr., gen. mgr. Sorrento Hotel, Miami Beach, Fla., 1957-59; gen. mgr. Mayflower Hotel, Manomet, Mass., 1959-60; with Aristocrat Inns of Am., 1960-72; v.p. mktg., McCormick Center Hotel, Chgo., 1972-93; ret. 1993. Active Nat. Women's Polit. Caucus, Internat. Orgn. Women Execs., membership promotion chmn., 1979-80, bd. dirs., 1980-81. Recipient Disting. Salesman award Sales and Mktg. Execs. Internat., 1977. Mem. Profl. Conv. Mgmt. Assn., Internat. Assn. Exposition Magmt., Hospitality Sales and Mktg. Assn. Internat., Meeting Planners Internat., Am. Soc. Assn. Execs., N.Y. Soc. Assn. Execs., Chgo. Soc. Assn. Execs., Ind. Hotel Alliance (sec. 1986—). Jewish. Home: 6007 N Sheridan Rd Apt 18H Chicago IL 60660-3063

CARY, CHARLES OSWALD, aviation executive; b. Boston, July 10, 1917; s. Charles P. and Adeline J. (Oswald) C.; m. Jean M. Cochran, May 8, 1948. Student, Northeastern U., 1937-39, MIT, 1941-42. With comml. airlines, 1936-44; supt. ops., gen. traffic mgr. Alaska Star Airlines, 1943-44; exec. asst. to chmn. CAB, 1944-46; spl. asst. to asst. sec. navy for air, 1946-48; mem. Civil Transp. Aircraft Evaluation and Devel. Bd., 1948-49; exec. sec. Air Coordinating Com., 1949-54; gen. sec. Air Transp. Moblzn. Survey, Nat. Security Resources Bd., 1950-51; dep. adminstr. Def. Air Transp. Adminstrn., 1951-54; dir. marketing & sales electronics div. Curtiss-Wright Corp., 1954-63; v.p. Hazeltine Corp., 1963-65; asst. adminstr. dept. transp. internat. aviation affairs FAA, 1965-78; spl. rep. of adminstr. FAA, Brussels, Belgium, 1978-79; ret. 1979; sr. lectr., dir. internat. studies Flight Transp. Lab., MIT, 1979-95; mem. U.S. del. 1st assembly Provisional Internat. Civil Aviation Orgn., 1945, U.S. dels. assemblies, 1947, 51, 53, 70, 74, 77; cons. to adminstr. FAA, 1963; bd. govs. Flight Safety Found., Washington, 1979-93; vice chmn. State of N.H. Aviation Users Adv. Bd., 1986-89, chmn., 1989-92. Fellow AIAA (assoc.); mem. Diplomatic and Consular Officers Club Ret. (Washington), Lake Sunapee Yacht Club. Home: 556 North Rd Sunapee NH 03782-2915

CARY, GREGORY J., dance center executive, dancer, choreographer, artist; b. N.Y.C., Mar. 29, 1951; s. Harold and Helen Marie (Kozal) C. BFA, The Julliard Sch., 1975. Dancer Danza de Mex., 1969-70, Kazuko Hirabayashi Dance Co., N.Y.C., 1971, Am. Ballet Theatre, N.Y.C., 1977-78, River Repertory, Poughkeepsie, N.Y., 1979-80; mem. faculty SUNY, New Paltz, 1980-85; ptnr. Cary-Roton Studio, Woodstock, N.Y., 1981-90; v.p., co-founder Kaatsbaan Internat. Dance Ctr., Tivoli, N.Y., 1991—; bd. dirs. Kaatsbaan Internat. Dance Ctr., 1991—. Set designer Paul Taylor Dance Co., 1975; commd. stained glass works include Celestial Pilgrimage, 1989, Epiphanies-Intuitive Perception of the Essential Meaning, 1990. Art in Pub. Pls. grantee Montgomery County, Md., 1990. Mem. N.Y. State Coun. on Arts (auditor). Avocations: skiing, antiques, art. Home: 840 Spencer Rd Woodstock NY 12498 Office: Kaatsbaan Internat Dance Ctr PO Box 482 Tivoli NY 12583-0482

CARY, NOEL DEMETRI, history educator; b. June 22, 1950. BS in Physics, U. Calif., Davis, 1971; MA in Astronomy, U. Va., 1973; PhD in History, U. Calif., Berkeley, 1988. Scientific programmer Computer Sci. Corp., Worcester, Mass., 1974-76, Informatics Inc., 1978-79; adj. asst. prof. Montana State Univ., 1986-87; instr. Swarthmore Coll., 1987-88; asst. prof. Coll. Holy Cross, 1989-93, assoc. prof., 1993—; vis. asst. prof. Oakland Univ., 1988-89. Author: The Path to Christian Democracy, 1996. Office: Coll Holy Cross Dept History Worcester MA 01610

CARY, SUZANNE, elementary education educator. Tchr. Mendenhall River Cmty. Sch., Juneau, Alaska; prin. Harborview Elem. Sch., Juneau, 1995—. Recipient State Elem. Tchr. of Yr. award State of Alaska, 1993. Office: Harborview Elem Sch 10014 Crazy Horse Dr Juneau AK 99801-8529

CARY, WALTER RAY, small business owner; b. Paris, Ill., Nov. 21, 1943; s. Walter and Mable (Vidito) C.; m. Judith Kay Shively, June 3, 1967; children: Thad, Alta. Store mgr. Irish Florist, Paris, 1958-67; cabinet maker Johnson's Planing Mill, Paris, 1967-86; owner, pres. Ray's Lock Shop, Paris, 1986—, RJC Enterprises, Terre Haute, Ind., 1992-98; pres., CEO JRC Inc., 1998—; owner, pres. Penske Truck Leasing, Terre Haute. Chmn. adminstrv. coun. 1st United Meth. Ch., Paris, 1991-94, 95—, chmn. bd. trustees, 1988-90; vol. instr. Sec. State Rules of Road. Office: RJC Enterprises 1296 Ft Harrison Rd Terre Haute IN 47804-1238

CARY, WILLIAM STERLING, retired church executive; b. Plainfield, N.J., Aug. 10, 1927; s. Andrew and Sadie C.; m. Marie B. Phillips; children: Yvonne, Denise, Sterling, Patricia. BA, Morehouse Coll., 1949, also D.D.; MDiv, Union Theol. Sem., 1952; LL.D., Bishop Coll.; D.D., Elmhurst Coll.; L.H.D., Allen U., Ill. Coll.; MDiv, Union Theol. Sem. Ordained to ministry Baptist Ch., 1948; pastor Butler Meml. Presbyn. Ch., Youngstown, Ohio, 1953-55, Interdenominational Ch. of Open Door, Bklyn., 1955-58, Grace Congl. Ch., N.Y.C., 1958-68; area minister Met. and Suffolk assns. N.Y. Conf. United Ch. Christ, 1968-75; pres. Nat. Council Chs., N.Y.C., 1972-75; conf. minister Ill. conf. United Ch. Christ, 1975—; chmn. United Ch. Christ Council Conf. Execs., Council Religious Leaders Met. Chgo., 1986-92; mem. governing bd. Nat. Council Chs.; mem. rep. consultation on ch. union United Ch. of Christ; mem. exec. council United Ch. of Christ; mem. Council on Ecumenism, Ch. World Service, Pres.'s Adv. Com. Vietnam Refugees; lectr. in field. Named One of 100 Most Influential Blacks in Am. for 1974-75 Ebony mag. Address: 206 Le Moyne Pky Oak Park IL 60302-1122

CARYL, WILLIAM R., JR., orthodontist; b. Syracuse, N.Y., Sept. 7, 1953; s. William R. and Joyce L. (Downs) C.; m. Deborah S. Auerbach, April 25, 1975; children: Mark R., David M. BA in Biology, SUNY, Buffalo, 1975, DDS, 1979; MS in Oral Biology, Loyola U. of Chgo., Maywood, Ill., 1981. Assoc. orthodontist William B. Drake, DDS, MS, Liverpool, N.Y., 1981-84; orthodontist pvt. practice, Camillus, N.Y., 1983—; mem. adv. bd. Fairmount Gardens, Syracuse, N.Y., 1994—; co-chair Ctrl. N.Y. Study Group for Dentofacial Abnormalities, 1993-95. Nat. ski patroler Nat. Ski Patrol System Camillus Ski Assn., 1969-71, 81-93. Mem. ADA, Am. Assn. Orthodontists, Am. Cleft Palate Craniofacial Assn., Syracuse Dental Seminar (program chair, sec. 1987-88, 88—, pres. 89, 89-90), Rotary Internat. (sec., pres. 1989-90). Avocations: sailing, skiing, bicycling, tennis, reading. Office: 5102 W Genesee St Camillus NY 13031-2327

CASA, DOUGLAS JAMES, sports medicine educator; b. Sept. 6, 1968. BS, Allegheny Coll., 1990; MS, U. Fla., 1993; PhD, U. Conn., 1997. Grad. asst. athletic trainer U. Fla., Gainesville, 1990-93; rsch. asst. U. Conn., Storrs, 1993-97; asst. prof. Berry Coll., Mount Berry, Ga., 1997-99, U. Conn., 1999—. E-mail: dcasa@berry.edu.

CASABIAN, EDWARD K., JR., secondary education educator; b. Boston, May 23, 1942; s. Edward K. and Mary (Kasabian) C.; m. Joan C. Ando, May 16, 1971; children: Mary C., Edward K. III. AB, Tufts U., 1964; MEd, Boston State Coll., 1965; CAGS, Boston U., 1971. Cert. tchr. English, social studies, cert. adminstr., Mass. Tchr. Bridgewater-Raynham Regional Sch. Dist., Bridgewater, Mass., 1965-82, tchr., chmn. dept. English, 1982—. Mem. NEA, Bridgewater-Raynham Edn. Assn. (2d v.p.), Nat. Coun. Tchrs. English, Mass. Coun. Tchrs. English. Avocations: athletics, reading, travel. Home: 193 South Dr Bridgewater MA 02324-2361 Office: Bridgewater-Raynham Regl HS 166 Mount Prospect St Bridgewater MA 02324-1352

CASABONNE, RICHARD J., publishing company executive; b. Apr. 27, 1945; m. Carol Casabonne; children: Meg, Peter. AB in Art, Brown U., 1967; MEd in Instrnl. Tech., Boston U., 1972. Various positions including dir. libr. svcs., 1972-76; dir. mktg. and sales UNICOM, microcomputer dealer, Providence, 1976-83; pres., COO, Computer Pub. Svcs., Inc., Lowell, Mass., 1983-86; pub. media, dir. mktg. Ramdom House Sch. Divsn., N.Y.C., 1986-88; v.p. sales and mktg. McGraw-Hill Ednl. Resouces, N.Y.C., 1988-89; pres. Franklin Watts, Inc. subs. Grolier, Inc., N.Y.C., 1989-90, pres. Grolier Pub. Co. divsn., 1990-91, pres. trade and internatl divsn. Grolier pub. group, 1991; pres. Casabonne Assocs Inc., mgmt. cons., Newton, Mass., 1980-86, 91-97, bd. dirs., 1980-97; pres., CEO, Steck-Vaughn Co. divsn. Harcourt Brace, Austin, Tex., 1997—; dir., cons. TALMIS, Inc., Chgo., 1979-86. Address: Steck-Vaughn Co 141 Dickerman Rd Newton MA 02461-1339 Office: PO Box 26015 Austin TX 78755-0015*

CASAD, ROBERT CLAIR, legal educator; b. Council Grove, Kans., Dec. 8, 1929; s. Clair L. and Eula Imogene (Compton) C.; m. Sally Ann McKeighan, Aug. 20, 1955; children: Benjamin Nathan, Joseph Story, Robert Clair, Madeleine. A.B., U. Kans., 1950, M.A., 1952; J.D. with honors, U. Mich., 1957; S.J.D., Harvard U., 1979. Bar: Kans. 1957, Minn. 1958, U.S. Dist. Ct. Kans. 1957; U.S. Ct. Appeals (10th cir.) 1985. Instr. law U. Mich., Ann Arbor, 1957-58; assoc. firm Streater & Murphy, Winona, Minn., 1958-59; asst. prof. law U. Kans., Lawrence, 1959-62, assoc. prof., 1962-64, prof., 1964-81, John H. and John M. Kane prof. law, 1981-97; John H. and John M. Kane prof. law emeritus, 1997; vis. prof. UCLA, 1969-70, U. Ill., 1973-74, U. Calif. Hastings Coll. Law, 1979-80, U. Colo., 1982, U. Vienna, 1986, U. Mich., 1986, U. Valladolid, 1988, Chuo U., 1992, U. Salamanca, 1995. Author: Jurisdiction and Forum Selection, 1988, Jurisdiction in Civil Actions, 1983, 2d edit., 1991, Expropriation Procedures in Central American and Panama, 1975, (with others) Kansas Appellate Practice, 1978, Civil Judgment Recognition and the Integration of Multiple State Associations, 1982, Res Judicata in a Nutshell, 1976; (with Fink and Simon) Civil Procedure: Cases and Materials, 2d edit., 1989, (with Gard) Kansas Code of Civil Procedure Annotated, 3rd edit., 1997; contbr. numerous articles to legal jours. Mem. civil code adv. com. Kans. Jud. Coun. 1st lt. USAF, 1952-53. Recipient Coblentz prize Sch. Law, U. Mich., 1957, Rice prize U. Kans. Law Sch., 1976, 83, 84, 88, 89, medal Dana Fund for Internat. and Comparative Legal Studies, 1981, Balfour Jeffrey Rsch. prize U. Kans., 1984; Ford fellow, 1965-66, fellow in law Harvard U., 1965-66, OAS fellow, 1976, NEH fellow, summer 1978; grantee Dana Fund for Internat. and Comparative Legal Studies. Mem. Am. Law Inst., ABA, Kans. Bar Assn., Order of Coif. Democrat. Home: 1130 Emery Rd Lawrence KS 66044-2515 Office: U Kans Sch Law Lawrence KS 66045*

CASADESUS, PENELOPE ANN, advertising executive, film producer; b. Calcutta, India, Sept. 20, 1940; came to U.S., 1980; d. Francis John and Betty (Walker) Copeland; m. Jean-Claude Casadesus, Jan. 20, 1960; children: Caroline, Sebastian. Gen. Cert. of Edn., Godolphin Sch., Eng. Head of prodn. S.S.C.B. Lintas, Paris, 1975-78, Grey-France, Paris, 1978-80; sr. v.p. Grey Advt., N.Y.C., 1980, exec. producer Internat. Health and Beauty div., 1991—; ind. film producer, 1984—. Author, producer (screenplays) Transvaal Episode, The Cuckoo. *

CASAGRANDA, ROBERT CHARLES, industrial engineer; b. Iron River, Mich., Oct. 8, 1939; s. Charles Casagranda and Lillian Otto Seppi; m. Sheila Adele Mikkola, Nov. 24, 1961; children: Gregory Charles, Wendy Jean, Jodi Marie, Renee Lynn. AA, Cerritos Coll., 1974. Sr. planner McDonnell Douglas, Long Beach, Calif., 1966-72; parts planner N. Am. Rockwell, El Segundo, Calif., 1972; quality analyst White Sunstrand, Belvidere, Ill., 1972-78; supr. Ares Inc., Port Clinton, Ohio, 1978-81; mgr. MFG. Systems-Ex-Cell-O, Rockford, Ill., 1981-84; mfg. con. Ingersoll Engrs., Rockford, 1984-88; project engr. Ingersoll Milling Machine Co., Rockford, 1988-90; sr. ptnr., owner, cons. The Mfg. Cons. Group, Inc., Rockford, 1990—. With U.S. Army, 1958-60. Mem. Soc. Mfg. Engrs., Soc. Mfg. Technologists. Home: 5450 Tam Oshanter Dr Rockford IL 61107-3764 Office: The Mfg Cons Group Inc 5450 Tam Oshanter Dr Rockford IL 61107-3764

CASALE, ALFRED STANLEY, thoracic and cardiovascular surgeon; b. Passaic, N.J., Nov. 28, 1955; s. Alfred Stanley and Regina Josephine (Cember) C.; m. Mary Louise Cavell, Aug. 1, 1976; 1 child, Katherine. BA, Johns Hopkins U., 1976, MD, 1980. Diplomate Am. Bd. Surgery, Am. Bd. Thoracic Surgery; cert. Surg. Critical Care. Intern Johns Hopkins U., Balt., 1980-81, resident in surgery, 1981-85, resident in thoracic surgery, 1985-88, asst. prof., 1988-90; surgeon Mid Atlantic Surg. Assocs., Morristown, N.J., 1990—, ptnr., 1993—. Contbr. articles to profl. jours. Dir. Madison YMCA, N.J., 1990-96, Am. Heart Assn., Morristown, 1990—, Kirby Child Care Ctr., Madison, 1992-96. Fellow Am. Coll. Surgeons, Am. Coll. Cardiology, Am. Coll. Chest Physicians; mem. Assn. Acad. Surgery (Resident Rsch. award 1984), Internat. Soc. Heart Transplantation, Soc. Thoracic Surgery. Avocations: skiing, tennis, fishing, shooting. Office: Mid Atlantic Surg Assoc 100 Madison Ave Morristown NJ 07960-6136

CASALE, PAUL JOSEPH, illustrator; b. Bklyn., Nov. 12, 1962; s. Louis and Lorraine Casale; m. Andrea Nora, Oct. 4, 1986; children: James Paul, Jessica Nora. BFA with honors, Pratt Inst., 1983. Freelance illustrator, 1983—. Illustrator book cover art: Thoroughbred Series, 1990-97, Saddle Club Series, 1995-98, for various book pubs., including Avon Books, Random House, Penquin Books, Houghton Mifflin, Scholastic Inc. Pratt scholar, 1979. Mem. Soc. Illustrators. Avocations: art instruction, photography, printmaking, bike riding, softball. Home: 609 Brookside Pl Cranford NJ 07016

CASALE, THOMAS BRUCE, medical educator; b. Chgo., Apr. 21, 1951; m. Jean M. Casale; 1 son, Jeffrey G. BS cum laude, U. Ill., 1973; MD, Chgo. Med. Sch., 1977. Diplomate Am. Bd. Internal Medicine, Am. Bd. Allergy and Immunology. Resident in internal medicine Baylor Coll. Medicine, Houston, 1977-80; med. staff fellow lab. clin. investigation NIAID, NIH, Bethesda, Md., 1980-84; from asst. prof. to prof. internal medicine U. Iowa, Iowa City, 1984-94, prof. internal medicine, 1994-96; dir. Nebr. Med. Rsch. Inst., 1996—; clin. prof. pediatrics Coll. Medicine U. Nebr., 1996—; clin. prof. medicine Creighton U., 1997—; chief med. staff fellow lab. clin. investigation, NIAID, NIH, Bethesda, 1982-83; attending physician VA Med. Ctr., Iowa City, 1984-96, staff physician, 1986-96, clin. investigator, 1991-96; asst. dir. tchg. allergy/immunology divsn. dept. internal medicine U. Iowa, Iowa City, 1989-92, acting dir., 1992, dir., 1993-96, faculty inerdisciplinary immunology grad. degree program U. Iowa, 1993-96; clin. prof. medicine Creighton U. Sch. Medicine, 1997—; reviewer over 15 profl. and scientific jours. Contbr. over 200 articles to profl. pubs.; mem. editl. bd. Jour. Allergy Clin. Immunology, 1988-93, clin. asthma revs., 1996—, Allergy & Clinical Immunology Internat., 1997—; editor Respiratory Digest, 1999—. Mem. asthma technical adv. group Am. Lung Assn., 1989-96. Lt. commdr. USPHS, 1980-83, USPHS Res., 1983—. Recipient Dr. John J. Sheinin Rsch. award Chgo. Med. Sch., 1977, Clin. Investigator VA, 1991-96, Am. Soc. Clin. Investigation, 1992; grantee Am. Acad. Allergy Immunology, 1981, Am. Coll. Allergy, 1984, Internat. Congress Allergology Clin. Immunology, 1985, 88, NIH, 1986-91, 87-90, 92-93, 93-94, VA Merit Rev., 1986-89, 89-92, 92-96, Environ. Health Sci. Core Ctr., 1990-96, CDC, 1994-95, Astra, U.S.A. Inc., 1996—, Zeneca Pharms., 1996-98, Novartis Pharms., 1997—, Sepracor, Inc., 1997, others. Fellow ACP, Am. Acad. Allergy Immunology (cutaneous allergy com. 1985-90, postgrad. edn. com. 1988-91, chmn. 1989-90, program com. dermatologic diseases sect. 1988-93, sec. 1989-90, vice chmn. 1990-91, chmn. 1991-92, prof. edn. coun. 1998—, chair 1998—, sec. 1993-95, vice chair 1995—, chmn. bronchoalveolar lavage com. 1991-95, 98—, others), Am. Coll. Allergy Immunology (profl. allergy/immunology edn. com. 1989-94); mem. Am. Fedn. Clin. Rsch., Am. Thoracic Soc. (sec. allergy immunology and inflammation scientific assembly 1990-91, chair-elect 1991-93, chair program com. 1992-93, chair 1993-95, long-range planning and policy com. sci. assembly on allergy immunology and inflammation 1991-96, sci. conf. com. 1991-93, bd. dirs. 1993-95, chair asthma adv. com. 1995—), Iowa Soc. Allergy Immunology (pres. 1987-89), Am. Assn. Immunologists, Midwest Sect. Am. Fedn. Clin. Rsch., Ctrl. Soc. Clin. Rsch., Am. Soc. Clin. Invest., Am. Lung Assn. (mem. rsch. coordinating com. 1996-99), European Respiratory Soc. Office: Nebr Med Rsch Inst 401 E Gold Coast Rd Ste 124 Papillion NE 68046-4194

CASALS, ROSEMARY, professional tennis player; b. San Francisco, Sept. 16, 1948. Profl. tennis player, 1968—; nat. championships and major tournaments include U.S. Open singles (finalist), 1970, 71, U.S. Open doubles, 1967, 71, 74, 82, U.S. Open mixed doubles, 1975, Wimbledon doubles, 1967, 68, 70, 71, 73; nat. championships and major tournaments include Wimbledon mixed doubles, 1971, 73, finalist with Dick Stockton, 1976; finalist with Dick Stockton Italian doubles, 1967, 70; finalist with Dick Stockton Family Circle Cup (winner), 1973, Wightman Cup, 1967, 76-81; Wightman Cup Bridgeston doubles championships (finalist), 1975, Spalding mixed doubles, 1976, 77, U.S. Tennis Assn. Atlanta doubles, 1976, Fedn. Cup, 1967, 76-81; winner 1st Virginia Slims tournament, 1970; 3d place Virginia Slims Championships, 1976, 4th place, 1977, 78; winner Murjani-WTA championship, 1980; Fla. Fed. Open doubles, 1980; pres. sports promotion co. Sportswoman, Inc., Sausalito, Calif., 1981—; Virginia Slims Legends Tour, 1995—; Mem. Los Angeles Strings team, World Team Tennis, 1975-77; founder Women's Sports Legends Inc. Virginia Slims Event tennis winner, 1986, doubles winner (with Martina Navratilova), 1988, 89; inducted in to Internat. Tennis Hall of Fame, Newport, R.I., 1996. Mem. Women's Internat. Tennis Assn. (bd. dirs.). Office: Sportswoman Inc PO Box 537 Sausalito CA 94966-0537

CASALS-ARIET, JORDI, physician; b. Viladrau, Girona, Spain, May 15, 1911; came to U.S., 1936, naturalized, 1946; s. Martin and Margarida (Ariet) Casals-A.; m. Ellen Evelyn Brock, Dec. 6, 1941; 1 dau., Christina. B.Ciencias, Instituto Nacional, Barcelona, Spain, 1928; Licenciado en Medicina y Cirurgia con Grado, U. Barcelona, 1934. Intern Med. Sch. Hosp., Barcelona, 1934-36; research asso. Cornell U. Med. Coll., N.Y.C., 1936-38; asso. Rockefeller Inst. Med. Research, N.Y.C., 1938-52; mem. staff Rockefeller Found., N.Y.C., 1952-74; prof. epidemiology Yale U., 1964-81, prof. emeritus, 1981—; vis. prof. dept. neurology Mt. Sinai Sch. Medicine, N.Y.C., 1981-84; professorial lectr. dept. neurology Mt. Sinai Sch. Medicine, 1984—. Contbr. articles to profl. jours. Served with Spanish Army, 1933. Recipient Kimble Methodology award Am. Pub. Health Assn., 1969. Fellow Am. Soc. Tropical Medicine and Hygiene (Taylor award 1968), Royal Soc. Tropical Medicine and Hygiene (hon.); mem. Soc. Exptl. Biology and Medicine, Harvey Soc., AAAS, N.Y. Acad. Medicine, N.Y. Acad. Scis., French Soc. Microbiology (hon.), Internat. Com. on Taxonomy of Viruses (life). Home: 25 Claremont Ave New York NY 10027-6802 Office: One Gustave L Levy Pl New York NY 10029

CASANOVA, ALDO JOHN, sculptor; b. San Francisco, Feb. 8, 1929; s. Felice and Teresa (Papini) C.; children: Aviva, Liana, Anabelle. BA, San Francisco State U., 1950, MA, 1951; PhD, Ohio State U., 1957. Asst. prof. art San Francisco State U., 1951-53; asst. prof. Antioch (Ohio) Coll., 1956-58; asst. prof. art Tyler Sch. Art, Temple U., Phila., 1961-64, Tyler Sch. Art, Temple U. (Italy campus), Rome, 1968-70; prof. art Scripps Coll., Claremont, Calif., 1966—; chmn. art dept. Scripps Coll., 1971-73; vis. prof. SUNY, 1981; faculty mem. Skowhegan Sch. Painting and Sculpture, Maine, summers 1973-74. One-man shows include Esther Robles Gallery, L.A., 1967, Santa Barbara (Calif.) Mus., 1967, Calif. Inst. Tech., 1972, Carl Schlosberg Fine Arts, L.A., 1977, SUNY, 1981; represented in permanent collections Whitney Mus., San Francisco Mus. Art, San Diego Mus. Sculpture Garden, Hirshhorn Collection, Cornell U., Columbus (Ohio) Mus., UCLA Sculpture Garden, Calif. Inst. Tech., Pasadena, Univ. Judaism, L.A., Air and Space Mus., Washington, Collection of Nat. Acad. of Design, N.Y.C., 1993, Robert Feldmuth Meml. Commn., W.M. Keck Sci. Ctr., Claremont, Calif., 1995, Newport Harbor Mus., Calif., 1996. Recipient Prix-de-Rome Am. Acad. in Rome, 1958-61; Louis Comfort Tiffany award, 1970. Fellow Am. Acad. in Rome; mem. NAD, NAS, Sculptors Guild, Nat. Sculpture Soc. Democrat. Roman Catholic. Office: Scripps Coll Art Dept Claremont CA 91711

CASARELLA, WILLIAM JOSEPH, physician; b. Dunmore, Pa., Nov. 17, 1937; s. Rocco F. and Madeline M. C.; m. Carolyn A. Hughes, June 18, 1966; children—Jennifer, Gregory. B.A., Yale U., 1959; M.D., Harvard U., 1963. Intern U. Pa. Hosp., 1963-64; resident in medicine Boston City Hosp., 1966-67; resident in radiology Columbia U.-Presbyn. Med. Center, 1967-70, attending radiologist, 1970-81; prof. radiology Columbia U. Coll. Physicians and Surgeons, N.Y.C., 1977-81; chmn. dept. radiology Emory U., Atlanta, 1981—; exec. assoc. dean Emory U. Sch. Medicine, Atlanta, 1986—; pres. Am. Bd. Radiology, 1998—. Contbr. articles to med. jours. Mem. nat. bd. dirs. Am. Cancer Soc. Served to capt. M.C. USAR, 1964-66. Fellow Am. coll. Radiology; mem. Soc. Cardiovascular Radiology (pres. 1979), Am. Heart Assn., Radiol. Soc. N. Am., N.Am. Soc. Cardiac Angiography, Assn. U. Radiologists, Eastern Radiol. Soc., N.Y. Roentgen Soc., Soc. Cardiac Angiography, Am. Roentgen Ray Soc. (exec. coun. 1988—), Soc. Chmn. Acad. Radiology Depts. (sec.-treas. 1989—, pres.-elect 1991). Home: 1109 Parker Pl NE Atlanta GA 30324-5402 Office: Emory Univ Hosp Dept Radiology 1364 Clifton Rd NE Atlanta GA 30322-1061*

CASARIEGO, JORGE ISAAC, psychiatrist, psychoanalyst, educator; b. Havana, Cuba, Apr. 25, 1945; came to U.S., 1960, naturalized, 1970; s. Isaac Alberto Casariego and Elena Mercedes Portela de Casariego. BS, U. New Orleans, 1967; MD, La. State U., 1969; postgrad., Balt.-Washington Psycho. Inst., 1983-90. Diplomate Am. Bd. Psychiatry and Neurology. Med. intern Jewish Hosp. Bklyn., N.Y.C., 1969-70; psychiat. resident N.Y. Med. Coll., N.Y.C., 1970-71, Walter Reed Army Hosp., Washington, 1971-73; chief psychiatry clinic U.S. Army Hosp., Heidelberg, Fed. Republic Germany, 1973-75; clin. instr. dept. psychiatry Sch. Medicine, U. Miami, Fla., 1976-78, asst. prof. psychiatry, 1978-82, clin. asst. prof., 1982-87, clin. assoc. prof., 1988—, chmn. continuing psychiat. edn. com., 1980-83; practice medicine specializing in psychiatry Miami, 1976—; mem. faculty Balt.-Washington Psychoanalytic Inst., 1991—, Fla. Psychoanalytic Inst., 1992—; med. dir. United Behavioral Health, Miami, 1996—; med. dirs. drug dependence outpatient unit VA Med. Ctr., Miami, 1976, dir. crisis intervention program, 1976-87, attending psychiatrist, 1976—, dir. divsn. psycho-therapy, 1987-89; attending psychiatrist Jackson Meml. Hosp., U. Miami Hosps., 1976—, Mercy Hosp.; sr. attending South Miami Hosp., Larkin Hosp., Doctor's Hosp., Highland Park Hosp., others; med. dir. United Behavioral Health; chmn. continuing psychiat. edn. com. U. Miami, 1980-83, others. Reviewer, contbr. articles Am. Jour. Psychiatry, other profl. pubs.; editor-in-chief The Tiger Rag (La. State U. Med Ctr.). Served with M.C., U.S. Army, 1971-75. NIH Tropical Medicine fellow, U. Recife, Brazil, 1968; recipient Physician's award AMA, 1977, 81, 87, 90. Fellow Am. Psychiat. Assn. (observer-cons. Coun. on Internal Orgn. 1979-81); mem. South Fla. Psychiat. Soc. (sec. 1988-89, chmn. membership com. 1978-80, chmn. Spanish speaking com. 1981-82, chmn. continuing med. edn. com. 1982-84, continuing edn. com. 1986-87, fellowship com. 1987, sec. 1988-89), Cuban Med. Assn. in Exile (mem. Fla. psychoanalytic tng. program faculty 1992—, Fla. Psychoanalytic Assn. (libr. com. 1991—, clin. svcs. com. 1991—, chmn. com. on continuing med. edn. 1992—, sec. 1992—), Am. Psychoanalytic Assn. (mem. continuing edn. com. 1992—) Aesculapians. Home and Office: 8600 SW 92nd St Ste 203 Miami FL 33156-7377

CASASENT, DAVID PAUL, electrical engineering educator, data processing executive; b. Washington, Dec. 8, 1942; s. Harold Kane and Delta (Fletchall) C.; m. Paula Timko; children: Candace, Erin, Maureen, Tod, Jon. BSEE, U. Ill., Urbana, 1964, MS, 1965, PhD, 1969. Prof. elec. engrng. Carnegie Mellon U., Pitts., 1969—; pres. Unicorn Systems, Inc., Pitts., 1983—; dir. Ctr. for Optical Data Processing, 1985. Editor: Optical Data Processing, 1978; contbr. more than 600 articles to tech. jours. Recipient Thomas K. Benedict award AIAA, 1979; named George Westinghouse prof. Carnegie-Mellon U., 1980. Fellow IEEE (local pres. 1971-72, Barry Carlton award 1976), Optical Soc. Am. (local pres. 1975-77), Soc. Photo-Optical Instrumentation Engrs. (gov. 1982-85, 87-90, pres. 1993, exec. bd.), Internat. Neural Network Soc. (gov. 1992-95, 1998-00, pres. 1999). Republican. Roman Catholic. Avocations: travel, basketball, volleyball. Home: 133 Woodland Farms Rd Pittsburgh PA 15238-2021 Office: Carnegie Mellon U Dept Elec & Computer Engrng Pittsburgh PA 15213-3890

CASAZZA, JOHN ANDREW, electrical engineer, business executive, educator; b. Bklyn., Jan. 3, 1924; s. John Andrew and Jane (Granata) C.; m. Madeline Russo, Apr. 24, 1949; children: John Anthony, Joan Bernadette Casazza Fram. Student, Cooper Union, 1941-43; BEE, Cornell U., 1945. Registered profl. engr., N.J. Successively system planning and devel. engr., gen. mgr. planning and rsch., v.p. planning and rsch. Pub. Svc. Electric & Gas Co., Newark, 1946-77; v.p. Stone & Webster Mgmt. Cons., N.Y.C., 1977-79; pres. Casazza, Schultz & Assocs., Inc., Arlington, Va., 1979-90; chmn. bd. CSA Energy Cons., 1991-97; pres. Am. Edn. Inst., 1994—; mem. energy engrng. bd. NRC, 1988-94; mem. rsch. adv. com. Elec. Power Rsch. Inst., Palo Alto, Calif., 1976-77; mem. U.S. Energy Assn. World Energy Conf., 1983-92; bd. dirs. Ga. Sys. Ops. Co., N.Y. State Reliability Coun. Contbr. numerous articles to profl. pubs. Pub. trustee N.J. Marine Scis. Consortium, 1973-79; treas. N.J. Energy Rsch. Inst., 1977; mem. N.J. Gov.'s Panel on Solar Energy, 1975-77. Ensign USN, 1943-45. Fellow IEEE (life, chmn. energy policy com. 1981-82, chmn. environ. quality com. 1984-85, U.S. activities bd. citation of honor 1985, Herman Halperin award 1990, U.S. activities bd. dirs. VII profl. leadership award 1992); mem. Internat. Conf. on Large High Voltage Electric Sys. (Exec. com. U.S. nat. com. 1974-93, Atwood assoc. 1986—, spl. citation 1982, Philip Sporn award 1994), Springfield Golf and Country Club. Roman Catholic. Avocations: golf, writing. Office: Am Edn Inst 8208 Donset Dr Springfield VA 22152-1810

CASCIANO, DANIEL ANTHONY, biologist; b. Buffalo, Mar. 1, 1941; s. Frederick James and Rose Ann C.; m. Gertrude Ann Tara, Aug. 22, 1964; children: Anne, Jonathan. B.S., Canisius Coll., 1962; Ph.D., Purdue U., 1971. Rsch. asst. Roswell Park Meml. Inst., Buffalo, 1963-64; rsch. asst. dept. biol. scis. Purdue U., Lafayette, Ind., 1965-66, tchg. asst., 1969, rsch. trainee, 1966-71; postdoctoral investigator U. Tenn., Oak Ridge Nat. Labs., 1971-73; rsch. biologist Nat. Ctr. Toxicol. Rsch., Jefferson, Ark., 1973—, program dir. divsn. mutagenesis rsch., 1976-78, dir. divsn. genetic toxicology, 1979-97; assoc. prof. dept. biochemistry and molecular biology U. Ark. for Med. Scis., Little Rock, 1974-90, prof. dept. biochemistry and molecular biology, 1990—; trainee NIH, 1966-71; dir. divsn. genetic and reproductive toxicology Nat. Ctr. Toxicol. Rsch., 1997—. Contbr. articles to profl. jours. Mem. Tissue Culture Assn., Environ. Mutagen Soc., AAAS, Beta Beta Beta. Home: 1921 Romine Rd Little Rock AR 72205-6723 Office: FDA Ctr Toxicological Rsch Jefferson AR 72079

CASCIANO, JOHN P., federal military program director; b. Phila.; m. Patricia M. Simmons; 1 child, John. BS in Langs. cum laude, Georgetown U., 1965, MA in Polit. Sci., 1972; grad. (disting.), Squadron Officer Sch., 1973, Air Command and Staff Coll., 1979; grad., NATO Def. Coll., Rome, 1983; grad. program in nat. security, Harvard U., 1991, grad. program nat./internat. security, 1994; CAPSTONE grad., Nat. Def. U., 1992; grad. jt. flag officer warfighting, Maxwell AFB, Ala., 1995. Commd. 2d lt. USAF, 1965, advanced through grades to maj. gen., 1995; chief intelligence divsn. Air Def. Command USAF, Hancock Field, N.Y.; intelligence watch officer, analyst, briefer, chief br. USAF, Nakhon Phanom Royal AFB, Thailand, 1969-70; intelligence plans and programs officer, tng./career devel. USAF, Washington, 1970-74; asst. prof. polit. sci., squadron faculty officer, dir. Air Force Acad. Assembly, USAF Acad., Colorado Springs, Colo., 1974-78; chief intelligence plans and policy divsn., dep. dir. plans Hdqrs. Strategic Air Command, Offutt AFB, Nebr., 1979-83; chief intelligence plans and programs br. Hdqrs. U.S. European Command, Stuttgart-Vaihingen, Germany, 1983-87; dir. warning and assessments Air Force Intelligence Agy., Washington, 1987-88; dir. policy, plans and programs, asst. chief of staff intelligence Hdqrs. USAF, Washington, 1988-91; dep. chief staff intelligence Hdqrs. Tactical Air Command, then Air Combat Command, Langley AFB, Va., 1991-93; dir. plans and requirements, asst. chief staff intelligence Hdqrs. USAF, Washington, 1993-94; cmdr. Air Intelligence Agy., dir Jt. Command Ctrl. Warfare Ctr., Kelly AFB, Tex., 1994-96; dir. intelligence, surveillance, reconnaisance Hdqrs. USAF, Washington, 1997—. Decorated Legion of Merit, meritorious svc. medal with two bronze oak leaf clusters, Republic of Vietnam Gallantry Cross with Palm, Air Force outstanding unit award with V device, Ordre nat. du Mérite with rank of officer, others. Office: Dept USAF/XOI 1480 Air Force Pentagon Washington DC 20330-1480

CASCIANO, PAUL, school system administrator. Prin. Moriches (N.Y.) Elem. Sch.; asst. supr. William Floyd Sch. Dist., Moriches, 1995—. Recipient Elem. Sch. Recognition award U.S. Dept. Edn, 1989-90. Office: William Floyd Sch Dist 240 Mastic Beach Rd Mastic Beach NY 11951-1028*

CASCINO, ANTHONY ELMO, JR., lawyer, insurance executive; b. South Bend, Ind., Aug. 21, 1948; s. Anthony E. and Lorayne (Allegretti) C.; m. Mary Anne Dory, July 28, 1973; children: Anthony Elmo, III, Christine Anne, Caroline Stephanie. B.A., Loyola U., Chgo., 1970; J.D., Ill. Inst. Tech., 1974; MMgt. Northwestern U., 1987. Bar: Ill. 1974, U.S. Dist. Ct. (no. dist.) Ill. 1974, U.S. Supreme Ct. 1986. Div. counsel CF Industries Inc., Long Grove, Ill., 1974-79; sec., gen. counsel Energy Coop., Inc., Rosemont, Ill., 1979-83; v.p., gen. counsel GHR Energy Corp., Good Hope, La., 1983; dep. gen. counsel AM Internat., Inc., Chgo., 1983-86; v.p. bus. devel. Multigraphics div. AM Internat., Mt. Prospect, Ill., 1986-88; exec. v.p., sec., gen. counsel, bd. dirs. United Fin. Group Inc. of Ill., Oak Brook, 1988-96; bd. dirs. Oak Brook Property and Casualty Ins. Co., First Oak Brook Corp. Syndicate, United Comml. Affiliated, Inc., Combined Adjustment Co., Inc., Central States Ins. Cons., Inc.; ptnr., exec. v.p. Tait Adv. Svcs., 1997; mem. inquiry bd. Atty. Registration and Disciplinary Commn., 1992-96; alt. trustee Ill. Ins. Exchange, 1988-97; arbitrator Cook County Mandatory Arbitration Program; lectr. Ill. Inst. Continuing Edn., 1986; mem. adv. com. on postgrad. programs, Ill. Inst. Tech., 1987-88. Hon. chmn. Tony C. and Carole Segal Patient Assistance Fund. Contbg. author: Commercial Damage, 1984. Mem. ABA, Fed. Energy Bar Assn., Ill. State Bar Assn., Chgo. Bar Assn., DuPage County Bar Assn., Art Inst. Chgo., Lyric Opera of Chgo. (Glencoe chpt.), Bar and Gavel Soc., DuPage Club, Union League Club (Chgo.), Club Internat. (Chgo.), Bob O' Link Golf Club. Democrat. Roman Catholic. Home: 385 Lincoln Ave Glencoe IL 60022-1521 Office: Tait Adv Svcs LLC 1 S Wacker Dr Ste 2700 Chicago IL 60606-4617

CASCINO, TERRENCE, neurologist; b. Chgo., Dec. 21, 1950; m. Ellen Riley, 1978; children: Jonathan, Jarett, Jeanine, Patrick. BA, Northwestern U., 1972; MD cum laude, Loyola U., 1975. Diplomate Am. Bd. Psychiatry & Neurology. Intern Presbyn.-St. Luke's Hosp., Chgo., 1976-77; resident Mayo Grad. Sch. Medicine, Rochester, Minn., 1977-80; fellow in neuro-oncology Meml. Sloan-Kettering Cancer Ctr., N.Y.C., 1980-82; cons. neurologist Mayo Clinic, Rochester, 1982—; from instr. to assoc. prof. Mayo Med. Sch., Rochester, 1982-84; vice chair dept. neurology Mayo Clinic, 1994—, prof. neurology, 1996—. Grantee North Ctrl. Cancer Treatment Group, Schering-Plough Pharms. Mem. AMA, Am. Acad. Neurology (spkr., co-chair ann. mtg. 1986, dir. courses), Minn. Med. Assn., Ctrl. Soc. Neurol. Rsch., Am. Soc. Clin. Oncology, N.Am. Soc. Neuro-Oncology, Am. Neurol. Assn. Office: Rochester Meth Hosp 201 W Center St Rochester MN 55902-3065*

CASCORBI, HELMUT FREIMUND, anesthesiologist, educator; b. Berlin, Germany, July 13, 1933; came to U.S., 1958; s. Gisbert and Isa (Ruckert) C.; m. Ann M. Morgan, Aug. 7, 1965; children: Alicia Maria, Kathryn Ann. M.D., U. Munich, W. Ger., 1957; Ph.D., U. Md., 1962. Prof., chmn. dept. anesthesiology Case Western Res. U., Cleve., 1980—. Mem. Am. Soc. Anesthesiologists, AMA, Assn. Univ. Anesthetists, Am. Soc. Pharmacology and Exptl. Therapeutics. Home: 2844 Fairmount Blvd Cleveland OH 44118-4059 Office: Univ Hosps of Cleve 11100 Euclid Ave Cleveland OH 44106-1736

CASE, CHARLES DIXON, lawyer; b. Manning, S.C., Mar. 23, 1952; s. James E. and Jennie (Stout) C.; m. Margie Toy, Aug. 28, 1982; children: J. Everett II, Elliot T. BS in Physics, N.C. State U., 1973; JD, Harvard U., 1977. Bar: N.C. 1977, U.S. Dist. Ct. (mid. and we. dists.) N.C., U.S. Supreme Ct. Environ. atty., ptnr. Moore & Van Allen, 1977-92; ptnr. Hunton & Williams, Raleigh, N.C., 1992—; adj. prof. law Campbell U., Buies Creek, N.C., 1981-84; hearing officer N.C. OSHA Safety and Health Rev. Bd., Raleigh, 1981-84; chmn. Wake County Bd. Adjustment, Raleigh, 1979-83; mem. N.C. Hazardous Waste Study Commn., 1982. Co-author: Toxic Tort and Hazardous Substance Litigation, 1995; contbr. articles to profl. jours. Pres. Coll. Phys. and Math. Scis. Found., N.C. State U. 1994-95, bd. dirs., 1991-98; bd. dirs. Jr. Achievement Ea. N.C., 1994-98, Camp Kanata; mem. bd. visitors N.C. State U., 1995—. Home: 1540 Carr St Raleigh NC 27608-2302 Office: Hunton & Williams PO Box 109 Raleigh NC 27602-0109

CASE, DAVID KNOWLTON, management consultant; b. Worcester, Mass., Mar. 26, 1938; s. Frederic Howard and Frances Mary (Knowlton) C.; m. Caroline Porter Richards, Feb. 2, 1974; children—Elizabeth, Sarah. BA, Yale U., 1961; grad. mktg. mgmt. program, Harvard U., 1973. Pub. relations rep. U.S. Steel Corp., Pitts., 1962-66; communications dir. John Hancock Ins. Co., Boston, 1966-70; asst. v.p. Shawmut Bank, Boston, 1970-76; devel. dir. Boston Ctr. for the Arts, 1977; dir. Plimoth Plantation, Plymouth, Mass., 1977-90, pres., CEO, 1990-96. Bd. assocs. ARTS/Boston, 1988—; pres. emeritus, hon. dir. English-Speaking Union, Boston; pres. emeritus, dir. Plymouth County Devel. Coun., 1988—; mem. adv. bd. S.E. Mass. Am. Automobile Assn., 1988—; mem. adv. bd. trustees Jordan Hosp., Plymouth; mem. external rels. com. Milton Acad. Recipient Golden Coin award Bank Mktg. Assn., 1973, Nat. award Bus. Com. Arts, N.Y., 1975, Leadership award Soc. Mayflower Descendants, 1994, Jackson Bowl award Milton Acad., 1995, Silver medal SAR, 1996, Lifetime Achievement award Mass. Office Travel and Tourism, 1997. Mem. Am. Assn. Mus., New Eng. Mus. Assn., Colonial Soc., Soc. Colonial Wars in Commonwealth of Mass., Yale Club (Boston and N.Y.), Harvard Club (Boston), Union Club (Boston), Duxbury Yacht Club (Mass.). Republican. Episcopalian. Home and Office: 378 River St Norwell MA 02061-2205 also: PO Box 361 205 Seapuit Rd Osterville MA 02655-0361

CASE, DAVID LEON, lawyer; b. Lansing, Mich., Sept. 22, 1948; s. Harlow Hoyt and Barbara Jean (Denman) C.; m. Cynthia Lou Rhinehart, Jan. 28, 1968; children: Beau, Ryan, Kimberly, Darren, Stephanie. BS with distinction, Ariz. State U., 1970, JD cum laude, 1973. Bar: Calif. 1973, U.S. Dist. Ct. (cen. dist.) Calif. 1973, U.S. Tax Ct. 1974, Ariz. 1976, U.S. Supreme Ct. 1997. Assoc. Willis, Butler & Scheifly, Los Angeles, 1973-75; from assoc. to mem. Ryley, Carlock & Applewhite, Phoenix, 1975—. Fellow Ariz. Bar Found.; mem. ABA (tax sect., corp. sect., probate and trust sect.), Ariz. Bar Assn., Ctrl. Ariz. Estate Planning Coun. (bd. dirs., pres. 1988-89), Beta Gamma Sigma. Republican. Presbyterian. Avocations: running, guitar, sports. Office: Ryley Carlock & Applewhite 101 N 1st Ave Ste 2700 Phoenix AZ 85003

CASE, DONNI MARIE, investment company executive; b. Chgo., Feb. 20, 1948; d. Donald Milton and Felecia Virginia (Krantz) Schuette; m. Lawrence Lee Hewitt, Apr. 20, 1996. BA in Econs., U. Ill., 1970. Vice chmn., nat. dir. mktg. intelligence Fin. Rels. Bd., Inc., Chgo., 1972—; bd. dirs. Inst. Bus. and Profl. Ethics Depaul U. Mem. Civil War Round Table Chgo. (trustee 1996—). Home: 2417 N Geneva Ter Chicago IL 60614-5914 Office: Fin Rels Bd Inc John Hancock Ctr 875 N Michigan Ave Chicago IL 60611-1803

CASE, DOUGLAS MANNING, lawyer; b. Cleve., Jan. 3, 1947; s. Manning Eugene and Ernestine (Bryan) C.; m. Marilyn Cooper, Aug. 23, 1969. BA, U. Pa., 1969; JD, MBA, Columbia U., 1973. Bar: N.Y. 1974, N.J. 1975, Calif. 1980, Ohio 1991. Assoc. Brown & Wood, N.Y.C., 1973-77; corp. counsel PepsiCo Inc., Purchase, N.Y. and Irvine, Calif., 1977-83, Nabisco Brands Inc., N.Y.C., East Hanover, N.J. and London, 1983-89; asst. gen. counsel Chiquita Brands Internat., Inc., Cin., 1989-92; prin. Douglas M. Case Law Offices Inc., Cin., 1993—; lectr. numerous seminars. Contbr. articles to profl. jours. Chmn. Olde Colonial Dist.; active Morris-Susssex Area Coun. Boy Scouts Am., 1986-88; sec., trustee Marble Scholarship Com., N.Y.C., 1983-88; bd. dirs. Cin. Opera Guild, 1994—, pres. 1997-98, chmn., 1998—. Mem. ABA, Internat. Bar Assn., Ohio State Bar Assn. (mem. internat. com. 1993—), Cin. Bar Assn. (chair solo and small firm practitioners com. 1995-97, continuing legal edn. chair internat. law com. 1994-96, sec. 1996-97, vice chair 1997-98, chair 1998—), Quality in Law (chmn. 1996-98), Grtr. Cin. Venture Assn., Munich Sister City Assn. of Greater Cin. (chmn. econ. devel. com. 1995-96), Greater Cin. Venture Assn., The Lawyers Club of Cin. (exec. com. 1995—, treas. 1996, sec. 1997, 2d v.p. 1998, 1st v.p. 1999), Morris County Golf Club, Columbia Bus. Sch. Club (N.Y.C., pres., bd. dirs. 1974-79), Kenwood Country Club, Cin. Opera Assn. (bd. dirs., exec. com. 1997-98). Avocation: golf. Office: 8700 Old Indian Hill Rd Cincinnati OH 45243-3724

CASE, EDWARD RALPH, manufacturing executive; b. Stamford, Conn.; m. Mary Ann B.; 4 children. BS, Georgetown U., 1969, MA, 1977; MBA, U. Va., 1984. Tchr. history Inst. Notre Dame, Balt., 1977-80; asst. dean Loyola Coll. Balt., 1980-82; dir. corp. fin. GM Corp., N.Y.C., 1984-89; treas. GM of Can. Ltd., Oshawa, Ont., 1989-91; dir. corp. devel. Campbell Soup Co., Camden, N.J., 1991-96; v.p., treas. Armstrong World Industries, Lancaster, Pa., 1996-98; v.p., controller Armstrong World Industries, Lancaster, 1998—; mem. corp. coun. Brookings Inst., Washington, 1997—. Vestryman St. Peter's Episcopal Ch., Phila., 1995-98. Georgetown U. fellow, 1972-74, Hyde fellow, U. Va., 1983-84. Mem. Nat. Assn. Corp. Treas., Fin. Execs. Inst. Avocations: parish, family, friends. Office: Armstrong World Industries Lancaster PA 17604

CASE, ELDON DARREL, materials science educator; b. Logan, Kans., Aug. 23, 1949; s. Eldon George and Ila Marie (Lewis) C.; m. Linda Lee Lubken, Aug. 29, 1975 (div. Mar. 1993); 1 child, Carl Allen; m. Rebecca J. Ervin, 1996. BA in Physics and Math., U. Colo., 1971; PhD in Materials Sci., Iowa State U., 1980. Rsch. asst. dept. materials sci. Iowa State U., Ames, 1976-80; NRC postdoctoral assoc. Nat. Bur. Standards, Gaithersburg, Md., 1980-82; rsch. engr. in materials sci. and mining engring. U. Calif., Berkeley, 1982-85; asst. prof. metallurgy, mechanics and materials sci. Mich. State U., East Lansing, 1985-88, assoc. prof., 1988—; cons. Indsl. Tech. Inst., Ann Arbor, Mich., 1990, Westinghouse, West Mifflin, Pa., 1991-92; judge Nat. Am. Indian Sci. and Engring. Fair, 1993-99. Contbr. more than 80 tech. articles to profl. jours. and conf. procs. including Jour. Materials Sci., Materials Sci. Engring., Applied Physics Letters. Speaker to sch. groups Okemos (Mich.) Pub. Schs., 1986-90; asst. with middle-sch. activities Episcopal Ch., East Lansing, 1988-92; judge Nat. Am. Indian Sci. and Engring. Fair, 1993-99. Recipient Tchr.-Scholar award Mich. State U., 1989, Withrow Excellence in Tchg. award Engring. Coll. Mich. State U., 1993, 95, 98; Regents scholar U. Colo., 1967-71; NRC postdoctoral assoc., 1980-82; grantee NASA, 1987, NSF, 1987-90, Mich. State U., 1989. Mem. AAUP, ASM, Nat. Inst. Ceramic Engrs., The Metall. Soc. (sec. structural materials div. 1988-91, chair non-metall. com. 1988-91), Am. Ceramic Soc. (pres. Mich. sect. 1998—), Sigma Xi. Democrat. Achievements include first neutron scattering study from microcracks in a polycrystalline ceramic; statistical analysis of water drop impact damage cracks in infrared windows; microwave sintering and joining of ceramics and ceramic composites; adhesion studies of diamond thin-films on brittle substrates; thermal-shock and thermal fatigue studies on ceramics and ceramic composites, microwave sintering and joining of ceramics. Home: 4469 Fairlane Dr Okemos MI 48864-2407 Office: Materials Sci and Mechanics Sci Dept East Lansing MI 48824

CASE, HADLEY, oil company executive; b. N.Y.C., Mar. 28, 1909; s. Walter Summerhayes and Mary Soule (Hadley) C.; m. Julie Marguerite Ill, June 8, 1935 (dec. Mar. 1975); children: Mary C. Durham, Julie Anne, Rosalie C. Clark, Deborah Joan; m. Elizabeth M. McCabe, Nov., 1975. Student, Kent (Conn.) Sch., 1924-29, Antioch Coll., 1929-33; DSc (hon.), Antioch U., 1991, DS (hon.), 1991. Geol. field work Australia, 1933-34, Tex., 1935-36; with geol. dept. Case, Pomeroy & Co., Inc., N.Y.C., 1936-39, v.p., 1939-41, pres., 1941-83, CEO, 1983-93, chmn. bd., 1983—, also bd. dirs.; pres., CEO Felmont Oil Corp., 1952-84; chmn. of bd., CEO Felmont Oil Corp. (merger Felmont and Homestake Mining Co.), 1972-84; dir. Homestake Mining Co., 1984-95, Brown Bros. Harriman Trust Co. Fla., 1986-93. Trustee Antioch U., 1987-93, Kent Sch., 1959-75, Brewster Acad., 1956-63, Boys' and Girls' Camps, Inc., Boston, 1971-76; trustee Hosp. St. Barnabas, Newark, 1942-59, pres. bd. trustees, 1949-52; bd. dirs. Greenwich Boys Club Assn., 1957-73, hon. mem., 1974—; trustee Naples (Fla.) Community Hosp., 1985-91; bd. dirs. Naples Philharm. Ctr. for Arts, 1988—; dir. The Conservancy, Naples, 1985-91; chancellor Kent Sch., 1985—, trustee, 1986—. Mem. Am. Inst. Mining and Metall. Engrs., Am. Petroleum Inst., Ind. Petroleum Assn. Am. (past v.p., dir.). Office: Case Pomeroy & Co Inc 529 5th Ave Fl 16 New York NY 10017-4684

CASE, HANK, wine importer, retired art educator, photographer; b. Danville, Ky., Jan. 12, 1938; s. Will Franklin and Margaret (Whitaker) C.; divorced; 1 child, J. Erin. BS, Ball State U., 1964, MA, 1966. Cert. master tchr., Ind. State Tchrs. Assn. Supr. of fine arts Anderson (Ind.) Cmty. Schs., 1964-96; instr. photography Anderson U., 1969-89; free-lance photographer Anderson, 1956—, cons. wine, 1981—; owner Hank Case Wine Imports, 1989—. Bd. dirs. Alliance of Indpls. Mus. of Art, 1992—. Mem. Art Educators Assn. Ind. (life), Commanderie du Bontemps de Medoc et des Graves (comdr. 1982—), Confrerie des Chevaliers du Tastevin (chevalier, redacteur 1984—), Confrerie de la Chaine des Rotisseurs (chevalier 1995—), L'Ordre Mondial des Gourmets Degustateurs, Internat. Wine and Food Soc., Indpls. Wine Soc. (pres. 1981-83), Theta Chi, Alpha Phi Gamma. Home: 823 W 7th St Anderson IN 46016-1056

CASE, JAMES HEBARD, lawyer; b. Lihue, Hawaii, Apr. 10, 1920; s. Adrial Hebard and Elizabeth (McConnell) C.; m. Suzanne Catherine Espenett, Sept. 18, 1948; children: Edward E., John H., Suzanne D., Russell L., Elisabeth D. Margueas, Bradford Case. AB, Williams Coll., 1941; JD, Harvard U., 1949. Bar: Hawaii 1949, U.S. Supreme Ct. 1985. Assoc. Pratt, Tavares & Cassidy, Honolulu, 1949-51, Carlsmith & Carlsmith, Hilo, Hawaii, 1951-59; ptnr. Carlsmith Ball, Honolulu, 1959—; bd. dirs. ML Resources, Honolulu. Trustee Hanahauoli Sch., Honolulu, 1970-82, Cen. Union Ch., Honolulu, 1984-88, Arcadia Retirement Residence, Honolulu, 1985-91. Lt. comdr. USNR, 1943-46, PTO. Mem. ABA, Hawaii Bar Assn., Hawaii Yacht Racing Assn. (bd. dirs. 1994—). Republican. Congregationalist. Clubs: Pacific (bd. dirs. 1978-82); Kaneohe Yacht (Honolulu). Avocations: sailing, tennis. Home: 3757 Round Top Dr Honolulu HI 96822-5043 Office: Carlsmith Ball PO Box 656 Honolulu HI 96809-0656

CASE, KAREN ANN, lawyer; b. Milw., Apr. 7, 1944; d. Alfred F. and Hilda M. (Tomich) Case. BS, Marquette U., 1963, JD 1966; LLM, NYU, 1973. Bar: Wis. 1966, U.S. Ct. Claims, 1973, U.S. Tax Ct. 1973. Ptnr. Meldman, Case & Weine, Milw., 1973-85, Meldman, Case & Weine div. Mulcahy & Wherry, S.C., 1985-87; Sec. of Revenue State of Wis., 1987-88; ptnr. Case & Drinka, S.C., Milw., 1989-91, Case, Drinka & Diel, S.C., Milw., 1991-97, CoVac, 1997—; lectr. U. Wis., Milw., 1974-78; guest lectr. Marquette U. Law Sch., 1975-78; dir. WBBC, 1998—. Mem. gov.'s Commn. on Taliesin, 1988, gov.'s Econ. Adv. Commn., 1989-91, pres.'s coun. Alverno Coll., 1988-94, nat. coun., 1998—; bd. dirs. WBCC, 1998—. Fellow Wis. Bar Found. (dir. 1977-90, treas. 1980-90); mem. ABA, Milw. Assn. Women Lawyers (founding mem., bd. dirs. 1975-78, 81-82), Milw. Bar Assn. (bd. dirs. 1985-87, law office mgmt. chair 1992-93), State Bar Wis. (bd. govs. 1981-85, 87-90, dir. taxation sect. 1981-87, vice chmn. 1986-87, 90-91, chmn. 1991-92), Am. Acad. Matrimonial Lawyers (bd. dirs. 1988-90), Nat. Assn. Women Lawyers (Wis. del. 1982-83), Milw. Rose Soc. (pres. 1981, dir. 1981-83), Friends of Boerner Bot. Gardens (founding mem., pres. 1984-90), Profl. Dimensions Club (dir. 1985-87), Tempo Club (sec. 1984-85). Contbr. articles to legal jours. Home: 2212 Harbour Ct Longboat Key FL 34228-4174 Office: CoVac 9803 W Meadow Park Dr Hales Corners WI 53130 *Delegate tasks for responsibility and accountability, then spend the resulting freed time nourishing your soul. Resign yourself to the fact that the tasks will not be completed as you would have, but they will be done, sometimes with more creativity. Give credit and praise away.*

CASE, KENNETH EUGENE, industrial engineering educator; b. Oak Ridge, Tenn., Aug. 12, 1944; s. Richard Thaddeus and Vera Lavone (Peyton) C.; m. Frances Lynn Curlee, Jan. 21, 1966; children: Kristin Lynn, David Rex. BSEE, Okla. State U., 1966, MS in Indsl. Engring., 1967, PhD in Indsl. Engring., 1969. Lic. profl. engr. Asst. prof. indsl. engring. Va. Poly. Inst., Blacksburg, 1969-73, assoc. prof. indsl. engring., 1973-74; mgmt. scientist GTE Data Services, Tampa, Fla., 1974-75; assoc. prof. indsl. engring. Okla. State U., Stillwater, 1975-78, prof., head indsl. engring., 1980-82, prof. inden. engring., 1978-87, regents prof. inden. engring., 1987—, dir. MS in Engring. and Tech. Mgmt. Program; quality control cons. Exxon, Honeywell, Ford, ATT, Abbott, 1973—; satellite sem./course instr. IBM, Motorola, Eastman Kodak, 3M, Honeywell, HP, DEC, 1985—; sr. examiner Malcolm Baldrige Nat. Quality Award Dept. Commerce, 1988, 89, 90, panel of judges, 1991, 92, 93. Co-author: Principles of Engineering Economic Analysis, 1977, 4th edit., 1998, Introduction to Industrial and Systems Engineering, 1977, 3d edit., 1993 (IIE Book of Yr. 1979), Profit Through Quality, 1978; contbr. numerous articles to profl. jours. Trustee Okla. State U. Amateur Radio Assn., Stillwater, 1977-96; com. chmn. troop 828 Boy Scouts Am., Stillwater, 1985-88; coun. chmn. Nat. Eagle Scout Assn., 1989-95. Named Outstanding Engring. Prof. Okla. State U., 1983, Disting. Eagle Scout Boy Scouts Am., 1986; recipient L.E. Tinker award Boy Scouts Am., Albert Holzman Disting. Edn. award, 1991, Regents Disting. Teaching award Okla. State U., 1992, Silver Beaver award Boy Scouts Am., 1994. Fellow Inst. Indsl. Engrs. (internat. pres. 1986-87, Award of Excellence 1980, Disting. Svc. award 1984), Am. Soc. Quality (past sect. chmn., editl. bd. Jour. Quality Tech. 1979-97, editl. bd. Quality Mgmt. Jour. 1993—, nat. dir. 1999—, Berg award 1978, cert. quality engr., cert. reliability engr., cert. quality auditor, cert. quality mgr.); mem. NAE (peer com. chair, com. membership sect. 8), NSPE, Okla. Soc. Profl. Engrs. (Okla. Outstanding Engr. 1987), Am. Soc. Engring. Edn. (George Westinghouse award 1989), Internat. Acad. Quality (academician 1990—, bd. dirs., editor IAQ Contact), Am. Prodn. and Inventory Control Soc. (cert. prodn. and inventory mgmt. 1990), Order of Arrow, Am. Radio Relay League (Conn.), Sigma Chi. Home: 2416 Tanglewood Cir Stillwater OK 74074-1717 Office: Okla State U Sch Indsl Engring and Mgmt Stillwater OK 74078-5018

CASE, KENNETH MYRON, physics educator; b. N.Y.C., Sept. 23, 1923. SB, Harvard U., 1945, MS, 1946, PhD, 1948. Rsch. assoc. Lawrence Radiation Lab., 1949-50, U. Rochester, 1950-51; prof. U. Mich., 1951-69, 1969-88; emeritus prof. physics Rockefeller U., 1988—; adj. prof. Inst. Nonlinear Studies, U. Calif., San Diego, 1988—, vis. prof., 1981-82, Lawrence Radiation Lab., 1956, 61, MIT, 1963-64; scientist Los Alamos Sci. Lab., 1944-45; mem. Inst. Adv. Study, Princeton, 1948-50, 56-57; cons. Rand Corp., Ramo-Woolridge Corp., La Jolla Inst. & Phys. Dynamics. Recipient Guggenheim fellow, 1963. Fellow Am. Phys. Soc. Home: 1429 Calle Altura La Jolla CA 92037-7802

CASE, LARRY D., agricultural education specialist; b. Norborne, Mo., Aug. 8, 1943; s. Burr Jr. and Eva Marie (Harper); m. Joy Leona Vandivort, June 18, 1966; children: Jeffrey Dale, Rebecca Joy, Matthew Edward. BS in Agriculture, U. Mo., 1966, MEd, 1972, EdD, 1983; LHD (hon.), SUNY, Cobleskill, 1990. Life cert. agriculture tchr. Tchr. Northwestern High Sch., Mendon, Mo., 1966, Orrick (Mo.) Sch. Dist., 1966-69; tchr. Lexington (Mo.) R-V Sch. Dist., 1969-73, vocat. dir., 1973-74; dir. vocat. edn. Lexington La-Ray Area Vocat. Sch., 1974-77; supr. agrl. edn. Mo. Dept. Elem. & Sec. Edn., Jefferson City, 1977-78, state dir. agrl. edn., 1978-84; ednl. program specialist-agriculture U.S. Dept. Edn., Washington, 1984—; chmn. bd. Future Farmers Am., Alexandria, 1984, Nat. Coun. for Vocat. Tech. Edn. in Agr., Alexandria, 1984-93, Nat. Postgrad. Agrl. Students Orgn., Alexandria, 1984; pres. Future Famrers Am. Found., Alexandria, 1984; adj. prof. Pa. State U., University Park. Contbr. articles on agrl. edn. and internat. travel related to agrl. edn. Active deacon Fredericksburg (Va.) Bapt. Ch., 1984—, Sunday sch. tchr., 1984—; pres. Motts Row Property Owners Assn., 1988-89. Recipient Hon. Am. Farmer degree Future Farmers Am., 1984, Citation of Merit, U. Mo. Coll. of Agr., 1990. Mem. Future Farmers Am. Alumni Assn. (life), Am. Vocat. Assn., Nat. Assn. State Suprs. Agrl. Edn. (sec. 1980-84), Nat. Vocat. Agr. Tchrs. Assn. (life), Nat. Planning Assn. (food and agr. com.), Phi Delta Kappa, Alpha Gamma Rho (nat. hon. mem.). Office: US Dept Edn 350 C St SW Washington DC 20202

CASE, MANNING EUGENE, JR., food products executive; b. Sioux City, Iowa, Mar. 19, 1916; s. Manning Eugene and Loretta (Seims) C.; m. Ernestine Bryan, July 26, 1941; children: Douglas Manning, Randall Bryan. A.B., Western Res. U., 1938, J.D., 1941. Bar: Ohio 1941. Asst. counsel B.F. Goodrich Co., Akron, 1941-52; sec., treas., gen counsel, dir. Perfection Industries, 1952-55; sec. Hupp Corp., 1955-57; v.p. service and fin. M&M Candies div. Mars Inc., 1957-60; asst. treas. Standard Brands Inc., N.Y.C., 1961-62, treas., 1962-68, v.p., treas., 1968-77, v.p., chief fin. officer, 1977-78, sr. v.p., chief fin. officer, 1978-80, sr. v.p. human resources, 1980-81; sr. v.p. human resources Nabisco Brands, Inc., Parsippany, N.J., 1981-82, sr. v.p., 1983-84. Served to col., JAGC U.S. Army, 1942-46. Mem. ABA, Phi Beta Kappa, Delta Sigma Rho, Omicron Delta Kappa, Beta Theta Pi, Phi Delta Phi. Clubs: Met., Morris County Golf, N.Y. Athletic, Royal Palm Yacht and Country. Home: 1717 Homewood Blvd Delray Beach FL 33445

CASE, MARGARET A., state legislator; b. Albany, N.Y., Feb. 15, 1938; d. Kosta Stefan and Mary Collins K.; m. Frank G. Case; children: Martin, Matthew. Student, Boston U.; BS, U. N.H., 1976. N.H. state rep. Dist. 6, Rockingham County, 1982-86, Dist. Rockingham 2, 1994—; mem. health, human svc., and elderly affairs coms. N.H. Ho. of Reps.; devel. tester. Mem. N.H. Assn. Realtors, Rockingham Woman's Coun. Realtors (v.p. 1993, pres. 1994), N.H. Womens' Coun. Realtors (sec. 1993-94, pres.-elect 1994-95). Address: 44 Beach Head Rd 22 Lakeshore Dr Nottingham NH 03290*

CASE, RICHARD PAUL, electronics executive; b. Akron, Ohio, May 13, 1935; s. Charles Robert and Barbara (Ebinger) C.; m. Virginia Carolyn Quallich, Sept 1, 1956; children: Duane, Ralph, Glenn, Ellen, Sarah, Eileen, Katherine, Melinda. BSEE, Case Inst. Tech., Cleve., 1956; MSEE, Syracuse U., 1985. Registered profl. engr., Conn. Tech. engr., then sr. programmer IBM, 1956-65; mgr. programming ctr. IBM, Kingston, N.Y., 1965-66, dir. systems architecture, 1966-71, dir. advanced systems, 1971-75; cons. to dir. rsch. Thomas J. Watson Rsch. Ctr. IBM, Yorktown Heights, N.Y., 1975-77, dir. advanced systems devel. Data Processing Product Group, 1977-78, dir. tech. ops. for System Products Div., 1979-81; v.p. devel. ops. Gen. Tech. Div. IBM, White Plains, N.Y., 1981-82; dir. product lab. IBM, Endicott, N.Y., 1983, v.p. for devel. Systems Tech. Div., 1983-84, dir. tech. pers. devel., 1984-86, dir. univ. rels. and tech. programs, 1986-87, dir. systems analysis, 1987-91; dir. tech. strategy devel. IBM, Armonk, N.Y., 1991-97; commr. Pres.'s Commn. on Critical Infrastructure Protection, Washington, 1997-98; ind. computer cons., 1998—; panelist Nat. Computer Conf., Anaheim, Calif., 1975, Comp-Con, Washington, 1975, 4th IEEE Careers Conf., 1985, NRC Panel on Reliability, Integrity and Privacy in Telecommunications, 1985-86, TECHWORLD Symposium, Washington, 1987, Ann. Jud. Conf. 2d Jud. Cir. U.S., Bolton Landing, N.Y., 1989, 2d Nat. Conf. on Ct. Mgmt., Phoenix, 1990; participant in Air Force Studies Bd. Workshop on Software Devel. and Procurement, Woods Hole, Mass., 1976; mem. sponsors adv. com. Ctr. for Integrated Systems, Stanford U., 1980-84; mem. adv. com. Office of Tech. Assessment, Congress of U.S., 1983; keynote speaker Conf. on Automation and Robotics, Pa. State U., 1983, Symposium on Bus. and the Creative Process, AIESEC, R.I., 1985, Computer Integrated Mfg. and Communications, Anaheim, Calif., 1985; speaker numerous symposiums and confs.; ind. computer cons., 1998—. Chmn. editorial bd. Systems Programming Series, 1975—; contbr. articles to profl. jours. Chmn. evaluation PFG Com., Met. N.Y. Synod, Luth. Ch. in Am., 1973-77; bd. dirs., treas. Mid-Hudson Philharm. Orch., 1974-77; bd. dirs. Binghamton Symphony Orch., 1983-84, Greenwich Symphony Orch., 1989—; trustee Wagner Coll., S.I., N.Y., 1982-88, Nat. Tech. U., 1984-88; trustee, chmn. exec. com. Computer Mus., Boston, 1989—; bd. dirs. nat. judge Nat. Math. Counts Found., 1992—. Recipient Outstanding Invention award IBM, 1965, award for excellence in principles of mgmt. and quantative methods Inst. Certification of Computer Profls., 1976. Fellow IEEE (various offices); mem. Assn. for Computing Machinery, Sigma Xi (assoc.), Tau Kappa Alpha, Tau Beta Pi, Eta Kappa Nu. Office: 40 Bush Ave Greenwich CT 06830-7067

CASE, RICHARD W., sports association executive; m. Barbara Case; two children. Sec. gen. USA Baseball (formerly U.S. Baseball Fedn.), 1980—; Bd. dirs. U.S. Olympic Com.; cons., advisor and dir. in field; producer instrnl. videotapes, books and brochures with a concentration in the areas of player and coach tng., vol. enlistment, accident prevention, juv. delinquency, and youth tournament operation in all sports. Recipient USA Baseball Pres.'s award, Am. Baseball Coaches Assn. award of honor, Centenary medal Juan Antonio Samaranch, Internat. Olympic Com. Pres., others; inducted into Nat. Jr. Coll. Athletic Assn. Hall of Fame, Nat. Assn. Intercollegiate Athletics Hall of Fame, Nat. Police Assn. Hall of Honor; recipient numerous hon. citizenship and commendation awards. Mem. Internat. Baseball Assn. (sec. gen.). Office: USA Baseball 3400 E Camino Campestre Tucson AZ 85716-5800*

CASE, ROBBIE, education educator, author; b. Barrie, Ont., Can., Aug. 2, 1944; came to U.S., 1989; s. Francis Elliot and Jesse Olga (Dunbar) C.; m. Donna Lee Crossan, Nov. 15, 1969 (div. 1976); 1 child, Rebecca Elswyth; m. Nancy Frances Link, July 23, 1980; children: Jonathan Elliot, Sarah Diane. BSc, McGill U., 1965; MA, U. Toronto, 1968, PhD, 1971. From asst. prof. to assoc. prof. edn. U. Calif., Berkeley, 1971-76; prof. edn. Ont. Inst. for Studies in Edn., Toronto, 1976-89, Stanford U., Palo Alto, Calif., 1989—; prof., dir. Laidlaw Centre Inst. Child Study, U. Toronto, 1993—; cons. Open Ct. Pub. Co., Chgo., 1994—. Author: Intellectual Development: Birth to Adulthood, 1985, The Mind's Staircase, 1992, The Role of Central Conceptual Structures in the Development of Children's Thought, 1996. Van Leer fellow, The Hague, 1976, Guggenheim fellow, 1978, Ctr. for Advanced Study in Behavioral Scis. fellow, 1987-88, Can. Inst. for Advanced Rsch. fellow, 1993—; recipient Disting. Contbn. to Knowledge award APA, 1996. Mem. Nat. Acad. Edn. Achievements include co-creation of RightStart: an early math program designed to teach number sense to children at risk for school failure. Office: Stanford U Ctr for Ednl Rsch Palo Alto CA 94305

CASE, ROSEMARY PODREBARAC, lawyer; b. Kansas City, Mo., Sept. 15, 1961; d. Eugene George and Mary Josephine (Musick) Podrebarac; m. Kevin Dudley Case, Apr. 30, 1994. BA in Math. and French, U. Kans., 1983; JD, Washington U., St. Louis, 1986. Bar: Kans. 1986, U.S. Dist. Ct. Kans. 1986, Mo. 1987, U.S. Dist. Ct. (we. dist.) Mo. 1987. Assoc. McAnany, Van Cleave & Phillips, P.A., Kansas City, Kans., 1986-90, shareholder, 1991—. Contbr. chpts. to legal handbooks. Bd. dirs. Caritas Clinics, Inc., Kansas City, 1995—. Mem. Mo. Bar, Kans. Bar Assn., Wyandotte County Bar Assn. (treas. 1990-92), Wyandotte County Bar Found. (bd. dirs., treas. 1993—). Office: McAnany Van Cleave & Phillips PA 707 Minnesota Ave 4th Fl PO Box 171300 Kansas City KS 66117-0300

CASE, STEPHEN H., lawyer; b. Trenton, N.J., Mar. 1, 1942. AB, Columbia U., 1964, LLB, 1968. Bar: N.Y. 1969, D.C. 1985. Assoc. Davis Polk & Wardwell, N.Y.C., 1968-75, ptnr., 1975—; adj. prof. law Georgetown U. Law Ctr., 1990-91, 95—; sr. advisor Nat. Bankruptcy Rev. Commn., 1996-97; trustee Columbia U., 1997—. Contbr. articles to profl. jours. Fellow Am. Coll. Bankruptcy; mem. ABA (chair ad hoc com. on uncertificated debt securities, 1985-92), Am. Law Inst., Assn. of Bar of City of N.Y., Nat. Bankruptcy Conf. (vice chair legis. com. 1992-96). Democrat. Avocations: opera, tennis, reading. Home: 7200 Glenbrook Rd Bethesda MD 20814-1243 Office: Davis Polk & Wardwell 450 Lexington Ave New York NY 10017-3911

CASE, STEPHEN M., business executive; b. Honolulu, Aug. 21, 1958; m. Joanne Case (div.); 3 children. BA in Polit. Sci., Williams Coll., 1980. With mktg. dept. Procter & Gamble, 1980-82; mng. new pizza devel. Pizza Hut divsn. PepsiCo, 1982-83; with Control Video, 1983-85, Quantum Computer Svcs., 1985-92; CEO America Online, 1992—, chmn., sr. exec. officer, 1995—. Named Entrepreneur of Yr. Inc. Mag., 1994. Avocation: reading political science and social history. Office: America Online 22000 AOL Way Dulles VA 20166-9302*

CASE, SYLVESTER QUEZADA, minister; b. La Vega, Dominican Republic, June 25, 1941; s. Sylvester and Digna Quezada; m. Juanita Rodriguez, Aug. 29, 1961; children: Larry, Alvin, Edward. BA in Theology, Andrews U., Berrien Springs, Mich., 1982, MDiv, 1985; MA in New Testament, Denver Bapt. Seminary, 1987. Ordained to ministry Seventh-day Adventists, 1987. Min. Mid. Am. Union Seventh Day Adventists, Lincoln, Nebr., 1984—; assoc. prof. biblical langs. & theology Union Coll., Lincoln; del. Mid Am. Union Seventh Day Adventists, Lincoln, 1984—. Named Outstanding Student of Yr. Am. Bible Soc. Mem. Soc. Bibl. Lit., Phi Kappa Phi, Alpha Mu Gamma. Republican. Home: 5910 English Park Ct Lincoln NE 68516-3220 *There is no crime in being inquisitive. On the contrary, one of the great joys of life radicates in finding things out for ourselves.*

CASE, THOMAS LOUIS, lawyer; b. Dallas, June 14, 1947; s. Donald L. and Ellen (Hanson) C.; m. Bonnie Nally, July 8, 1972. BA, Vanderbilt U., 1969, JD, 1972; cert. civil trial law, Tex. Bd. Legal Specialization. Bar: Tex. 1972, U.S. Dist. Ct. (no. dist.) Tex. 1973, U.S. Dist. Ct. (we. and ea. dists.) Tex. 1978, U.S. Dist. Ct. (so. dist.) Tex. 1979, U.S. Dist. Ct. (ea. dist.) Ark. 1981, U.S. Ct. Appeals (5th cir.) 1977, U.S. Supreme Ct. 1978, U.S. Ct. Appeals (8th cir.) 1984, U.S. Ct. Appeals (11th cir.) 1981. Assoc. Johnson, Bromberg, Leeds & Riggs, Dallas, 1972-77; ptnr. Bickel & Case, Dallas, 1977-84, St. Claire & Case, Dallas, 1984-93, Thomas L. Case & Assocs., P.C., Dallas, 1993—. Mem. ABA, Tex. Bar Assn., Tex. Assn. Def. Coun.,

Dallas Assn. of Def. Counsel, Dallas Bar Assn. Office: Thomas L Case & Assocs PC 5910 N Central Expy Ste 1450 Dallas TX 75206-5146

CASEBEER, LINDA LOUISE, medical educator; b. Boone, Iowa, Apr. 8, 1947; d. Paul Fredrick and Hazel Arlene (Wickstrom) Gallmeier; m. Norman Leslie Shillman, Dec. 22, 1968 (div. Oct. 1983); children: Holly, Lisa, Wendy, Rachael; m. Edwin Frank Casebeer Jr., July 23, 1988; 1 stepchild, John. BA in Polit. Sci., N.C. State U., 1969; MEd, The Citadel, Charleston, S.C., 1983; PhD in Instrnl. Systems Tech., Ind. U., 1991. Elem. tchr. Colleton County Sch., Roundo, S.C., 1970-73; tchr. Christ Luth. Presch., Hilton Head Island, S.C., 1979-82; instrnl. designer Meth. Hosp., Indpls., 1985-90, dir. acad. affairs dept., 1990-95; assoc. dir., asst. prof. U. Ala. Sch. Medicine, Birmingham, 1995—; mem. accreditation rev. com. Accreditation Coun. for Continuing Med. Edn., Chgo., 1993—. Contbr. poetry to profl. jours. Mem. Alliance Continuing Med. Edn. (rsch. award 1995, provider/industry award 1997), Am. Med. Informatics Assn. Democrat. Lutheran. Home: 1500 21st Way S Birmingham AL 35205-5002 Office: U Ala Sch Medicine 1521 11th Ave S Birmingham AL 35205-3503

CASEBERE, JAMES EDWARD, artist; b. Lansing, Mich., Sept. 17, 1953; s. James Louis Casebere and Katherine Ann (Young) Kudreiko. Student, Mich. State U., 1971-73; BFA, Mpls. Coll. Art and Design, 1976; postgrad., Whitney Mus. Study Program, N.Y.C., 1977; MFA, Calif. Inst. Arts, Valencia, 1979. prof. art Rockland C.C., Suffern, N.Y., 1985-88; vis. artist Boston Mus. Sch., 1989, Calif. Inst. Arts, Valencia, 1984, RISD, 1991, Cooper Union, N.Y.C., 1994, Sch. Visual Arts, N.Y.C., 1994-95, Parsons New Sch., 1995, Harvard U., 1996, Yale U., 1997-99. One-man shows include Neuberger Mus., SUNY Purchase, 1989, Art Mus., U.S. Fla., Tampa, 1989, Kuhlenschmidt/Simon Gallery, L.A., 1985, 88, Michael Klein, Inc., N.Y.C., 1987, 91, 93, 95, Mpls. Coll. Art and Design, 1985, Diane Brown Gallery, N.Y.C., 1984, Sonnabend Gallery, N.Y.C., 1982, 84, St. George Ferry Terminal Installation, Staten Island, N.Y., 1983-84, Cepa Gallery, Buffalo, N.Y., 1982, Franklin Furnace, N.Y.C., 1981, Vreg Baghoomian Gallery, 1990, Urbi et Orbi, Paris, 1990, Fac-Simile Gallery, Milan, 1990, Mus. Photographic Arts, San Diego, 1990, U. Iowa Mus. Art, 1991, Photographic Resource Ctr., Boston, 1991, Bruges (Belgium) La Morte Gallery, 1991, James Hockey Gallery, WSCAD Farnham, Eng., 1991, Birmingham (Ala.) Mus. Art, 1991, Galliani Gallery, Genoa, Italy, 1994, 96, Richard Levy Gallery, Albuquerque, 1994, Lisson Gallery, London, 1996, Ansel Adams Ctr., San Francisco, 1996-97, Williams Coll. Mus. Art, Williamstown, Mass., 1997, Windows, Brussels, 1997, Jean Bernier Gallery, Athens, Greece, 1997, Angela Ho Gallery, N.Y.C., 1997, Site Gallery, Sheffield, Eng., 1997, Sean Kelly Gallery, N.Y.C., 1998-99, Gallery Tanit, Munich, Germany, 1998, Oxford Mus. Modern Art, Eng., 1998-99, Centro Galego de Art Contemporanea, Santiago, Spain, 1999; exhibited in group shows at Walker Art Ctr., Mpls., 1987, Mus. Contemporary Art, Chgo., 1988, Mus. Fine Arts, Boston, 1993, Whitney Mus. Biennial, 1985, Nat. Mus. Am. Art, Washington, 1989, Mus. Modern Art, N.Y.C., 1991-92, 97, L.A. County Mus. Art, 1997, Whitney Mus., 1998, Carnegie Mus. Art, Pitts., 1998, Guggenheim Mus., 1999. Fellow N.Y. Found. for Arts, 1985, 89, 94, Nat. Endowment for Arts, 1982, 86, 90, John Simon Guggenheim Found., 1995. Studio: 303 E 8th St Apt 2F New York NY 10009-5211

CASEI, NEDDA, mezzo-soprano; b. Balt.; d. Howard Thomas and Lyda Marie (Graupman) Casey; m. John A. Wiles, Jr., 1971 (div. 1979); m. Samuel Strasbourger, 1983 (dec. 1987). Student, Mozarteum, Salzburg, Austria, 1959; B in Performing Arts Adminstrn. magna cum laude, Fordham U., 1982; studied voice with, William P. Herman, N.Y.C., Vittorio Piccinini, Milan, Italy, Loretta Corelli, N.Y.C.; also student piano, langs., modern dance, ballet. Tchr. master classes, lectr. univs. and festivals; judge vocal competitions for Met. Opera, Fulbright Scholarship, Rosa Ponselle Internat. Competition, Savannah Festival, George London Found. Competition, First Internat. Vocal Competition, Baku, Azerbaijan, and others; vis. prof. Aichi Prefectural U. Fine Arts and Music, Nagoya, Japan; guest prof. Flaine Festival/Paris Conservatory, Haut Savoie, France, Mannes Coll. Music, New Sch. Social Rsch., N.Y.C.; pvt. tchr. Operatic debut Theatre Royal de la Monnaie, Brussels, 1960, with La Scala, Milan, Met. Opera, N.Y.C., 1964; operatic performances at Met. Opera, 1964-86, Basel Stadttheater, Gran Liceo, Barcelona, Teatro Carlo Fenice, Genova, San Remo Festival, Trieste Opera, Opera du Rhin, Strasbourg, Salzburg Festspielhaus, Teatro San Carlo, Naples, Chgo. Lyric Opera, Bogota Opera, Caracas Opera, Pitts. Opera, Vancouver Opera, Cape Town Opera, Brno Opera, Bratislava Opera, Kosice Opera, Prague Opera, Miami Opera, Houston Opera, San Diego Opera, Hartford Opera, Phila. Opera, Toledo Opera, Dayton Opera, Memphis Opera, Mobile Opera, Los Angeles Opera, Boston Opera, N.J. Opera, Taipei Opera, Opera of Mexico City; performances in numerous mus. festivals, concert tours, also symphonic concerts, oratorios, recitals and operatic guest appearances in Europe, South Africa, Cen. Am., S.Am., Can., U.S., Far East, Middle East and Australia; performed on radio and TV in Holland, Belgium, Leipzig, Japan, U.S., German Dem. Republic, Fed. Republic of Germany, Hong Kong, Singapore; performed at White House, Washington; made various recs. Supraphon, Everest, Nonesuch, Concert Hall, Vanguard, CETRA, others; contbr. articles to profl. jours.; guest editor Opera Quar. Coord. mus. events and benefits for Internat. Ctr. for Disabled, Morningside Home, Aging in Am. Gerontol. Acad.; mem. adv. bd. Fordham U., 1984-99, Lincoln Ctr.; bd. dirs. Theatre for a New Audience, Am. Coun. for Arts, Nat. Cultural Alliance. Recipient Martha Baird Rockefeller Found. award, 1962, 64, Community Leaders and Noteworthy Americans, 1975-76, Woman of Achievement award, 1969, Outstanding Young Singers award, 1959. Mem. AFTRA, Actors Equity, Am. Guild Mus. Artists (nat. pres. 1983-93, chmn. emergency relief fund 1983-94), Nat. Assn. Tchrs. Singing (bd. govs.), The Players.

CASELLA, MARGARET MARY, artist, photographer; b. Bklyn., May 12, 1940; d. John August and Ann Elizabeth (Krajci) Butkovsky; m. Anthony Joseph Casella, Nov. 23, 1961; children: Paul Joseph, David John, Gregory Anthony. Cert. in Merchandising, Tobe-Coburn Sch., N.Y.C., 1961; BFA, L.I. U., 1982, MFA, 1984. lectr. in field. Photographer: (book) Garbage or Art?, 1990 (Gold award Photo Design Mag. 1990); exhibited in solo exhbns. Media Port Gallery, Port Washington Libr., 1989, Midtown Y Photography Gallery, N.Y.C., 1991, Grand Ctrl. Terminal, N.Y.C., 1991, others; group shows include U. Tex. at Arlington, Deutser Art Gallery, Houston, Heckscher Mus., Huntington, N.Y., Konica Plz., Tokyo, Elaine Benson Gallery, Bridgehampton, N.Y., Firehouse Gallery, Garden City, N.Y., The Visual Club, N.Y.C., Hillwood Art Mus., Greenvale, N.Y.; works in permanent collections of Mus. for Photography, Branschweig, Germany, Yergeau Musee Internat. d'Art, Montreal, Fine Art Mus. of L.I., Hempstead, N.Y., Houston fotofest Permanent Archives, Houston. Founder, dir. Art Upstairs Gallery, East Williston, 1983-91; co-chmn. Diet of the Arts, C.W. Post campus of L.I. U., 1992—. Mem. Advt. Photographers of N.Y., Profl. Women Photographers. Avocations: gardening, physical fitness, writing. Studio: Casella Photography 889 Broadway New York NY 10003-1212

CASELLA, PETER F(IORE), patent and licensing executive; b. June 5, 1922; s. Fiore Peter and Lucy (Grimaldi) C.; m. Marjorie Eloise Enos, March 9, 1946 (dec. Aug. 1989); children: William Peter, Susan Elaine, Richard Mark. BChE, Poly. Inst., Bklyn., 1943; student in chemistry, St. John's U., N.Y.C., 1940. Registered to practice by the U.S. Patent and Trademark Office, Can. Patent and Trademark Offices. Head patent sect. Hooker Electrochem. Co., Niagra Falls, N.Y., 1943-54; mgr. patent dept. Occidental Chem. Corp. (formerly Hooker Chem. Corp.), Niagra Falls, N.Y., 1954-64, dir. patents and licensing, 1964-81, asst. sec., 1966-81, ret., 1981; pres. TFA Products, Inc., Houston, Intra Gene Internat., Inc., Lewiston, N.Y., 1981-92; chmn. bd. In Vitro Internat., Inc., Linthicum, Md., 1983-86; cons. patents and licensing, Lewiston, N.Y., 1981—; Dept. Commerce del. on patents and licensing exchange, USSR, 1973, 90, Poland and German Dem. Rep., 1976. Editor: Drafting the Patent Application, 1957. Mem. Lewiston Bd. Edn., 1968-70. With AUS, 1944-46. Recipient Centennial citation Poly. Inst. Bklyn., 1955, Golden Jubilee Soc., 1993. Mem. ACS, AIChE, Assn. Corp. Patent Counsel (emeritus, exec. com. 1974-77, charter mem.), N.Y. Intellectual Property Law Assn. (Niagra Frontier chpt. pres. 1973-74, founder award 1974), Licensing Execs. Soc. (v.p. 1976-77, Trustees award 1977), Chartered Inst. Patent Agts. Gt. Britain (emeritus), Patent and Trademark Inst. Can., Internat. Patent and Trademark Assn. (emeritus), U.S. Trademark Assn., Nat. Assn. Mfrs. (patent com.), Mfg. Chemists Assn., Pacific Indsl. Property Assn., U.S. Patent Office Soc. (assoc.), U.S. Trademark Office Soc. (assoc.), Chemists Club (N.Y.C. chpt.), Niagra Club (Niagra Falls chpt. pres. 1973-74).

CASELLAS, GILBERT F., lawyer, business executive; b. Tampa, Fla., Aug. 2, 1952; s. John G. and Yolanda (Panier) C.; m. Ada Garcia-Casellas, Aug. 1, 1981; 1 child, Marisa Astrid. BA, Yale U., 1974; JD, U. Pa., 1977. Bar: Pa. 1977, U.S. Dist. Ct. (ea. dist.) Pa. 1979, U.S. Ct. Appeals (3rd cir.) 1980, U.S. Supreme Ct. 1988, U.S. Dist. Ct. (mid. dist.) Pa. 1989. Assoc. Montgomery, McCracken, Walker & Rhoads, Phila., 1977-78, 80-85, ptnr., 1985-93; law clk. to Hon. Leon Higginbotham U.S. Ct Appeals (3rd cir.), Phila., 1978-80; gen. counsel Dept. of Air Force, Washington, 1993-94; chmn. U.S. EEOC, Washington, 1994-98; ptnr. McConnell Valdés LLP, Washington, 1998-99; pres., COO The Swarthmore Group, Inc., West Chester, Pa., 1999—; lectr. U. Pa. Law Sch., Phila., 1985-89, 92-93; spl. counsel Phila. Human Rels. Commn., Phila., 1990-91; judge pro tem Phila. Ct. Common Pleas, 1992; chmn. bd. overseers Sch. Social Work, U. Pa., 1996—; bd. dirs. Prudential Ins. Co. Am. Trustee U. Pa., 1996—; sec., trustee Free Libr. Phila., 1990-93; bd. dirs. P.R. Legal Def. and Edn. Fund, 1998—. Recipient Citation award City Phila., 1986, Clarence Farmer Svc. award Phila. Commn. on Human Rels., 1995. Mem. ABA (mem. ho. dels. 1986-91, Spirit of Excellence award 1999), Am. Law Inst., Am. Arbitration Assn. (bd. dirs. 1998—), Hispanic Nat. Bar Assn. (nat. pres. 1984-85, Citation award 1985), Pa. Bar Assn. (mem. ho. dels. 1987-83), Phila. Bar Assn. (chmn. bd. govs. 1990), Phila. Bar Found. (trustee 1991). Office: The Swarthmore Group Inc 1646 W Chester Pike Ste 3 West Chester PA 19382-7979

CASELLAS, JOACHIM, art gallery executive; b. Gerona, Spain, Aug. 1, 1927; came to U.S., 1954; s. Juan and Dolores Farre (Carrera) C.; m. Elizabeth Reed Brannon, Mar. 17, 1952 (dec. Dec. 1984); m. Janice Mary Bezverkov, May 29, 1990. BA, Gerona Coll., 1948; MA, Sacred Heart Coll., 1953. Curator Mus. Provincial, Gerona, Spain, 1952; art appraiser Feist Co., N.Y.C., 1952-68, Mahan Co., New Orleans, 1968-72; pres. Casell Gallery, New Orleans, 1972—. One-man shows include Ft. Walton (Fla.) Beach Mus. Art, 1987. Mem. Ocean Springs Yacht Club. Republican. Episcopalian. Avocations: photography, plants. travel, antiques, boating. Home: 107 Shearwater Dr Ocean Springs MS 39564-4828 Office: Casell Gallery 818 Royal St New Orleans LA 70116-3115

CASELLAS, SALVADOR E., judge; b. 1935. BS in Fgn. Svc. cum laude, Georgetown U., 1957; LLB magna cum laude, U. P.R., 1960; LLM, Harvard U., 1961. Ptnr. Fiddler, Gonzalez & Rodriguez, 1962-72, 77-94; judge U.S. Dist. Ct. P.R., San Juan, 1994—; mem. P.R. Acad. Jurisprudence, P.R. Commn. on Bicentennial of U.S. Constn., 1987-89; aide to Sec. of U.S. Army, 1985-89, emeritus, 1990—. Dir. Alliance for Drug Free P.R., 1993-94. 1st lt. U.S. Army, 1961-62, Res., JAGC, 1963-67. Recipient Comdrs. medal Second U.S. Army, 1990, P.R. Nat. Guard medal, 1990. Mem. ABA, Am. Bar Found., P.R. Bar Assn., P.R. Bar Assn. Found., Caparra Country Club, Banker's Club. Office: US Dist Ct PR US Courthouse 150 Ave Carlos Chardon # 111 San Juan PR 00918-1703

CASELLI, VIRGIL P., real estate executive; b. San Francisco, May 29, 1940; s. Americo P. and Cressida N. C.; m. Mary T. McKeon, July 18, 1970; children—Monica, Megan, Virgil Paul. B.S., U. Calif., Berkeley, 1963; M.B.A., U. San Francisco, 1973. Security analyst Wells Fargo Bank, San Francisco, 1963-65; purchasing agt. Raychem Corp., Menlo Park, Calif., 1965-70; founding dir., v.p. 1st Montgomery Corp., San Francisco, 1970-72; div. mgr. Kaiser-Aetna Co., Oakland, Calif., 1972-75; chief exec. officer, exec. v.p., gen. mgr. Ghiradelli Sq., San Francisco, 1975-82; pres. Comml. Property Ventures, Inc., San Francisco, 1982—; CEO C.P. Ventures (named changed Comml. Property Ventures, Inc.), San Francisco, 1990—; bd. dirs. San Francisco Conv. and Visitors Bur., 1975-83, Cable Car Friends, San Francisco, 1975—, The Guardsmen, Francisco, 1977-79; pres. Fisherman's Wharf Mchts. Assos., 1976-77, San Francisco Parking and Garage Owners Assocs., 1977. Founder, pres., C.O.B., Com. to Save Cable Cars, 1979-87; trustee U. Calif.-Berkeley Found., 1981-89; bd. dirs. Golden Gate Nat. Parks Assocs., 1983—, chmn., 1983-87; mem. adv. com. U. San Francisco; mem. adv. coun. Bologna Ctr., Johns Hopkins U. Sch. Advanced Internat. Studies, 1985-92. Mem. Soc. Real Property Adminstrs., Bldg. Owners and Mgrs. Inst. Internat. Republican. Roman Catholic. Office: CP Ventures PO Box 1116 Belvedere Tiburon CA 94920-7032

CASEM, CONRADO SIBAYAN, civil, structural engineer; b. Luna, La Union, Philippines, Feb. 19, 1945; came to U.S., 1984; s. Pedro Nuesca and Francisca (Sibayan) C.; m. Corazon Nieveras Noble, May 7, 1972; children: Christopher, Conrado Jr. BSc in Civil Engring. cum laude, Feati U., Manila, 1967; M Engring. in Structural Engring., Asian Inst. Tech., Bangkok, 1970. Lic. profl. engr., N.Y., N.J., Ohio, Ill., Pa., Calif., Mass., Minn., Ont. Civil engr. Philippine Engring. & Constrn. Corp., Rizal, Philippines, 1970-73; structural engr. Morrison Knudsen Internat. Co., Singapore, 1973-75; design engr. Monenco (Asia) Ltd., Singapore, 1975-78; sr. engr. Montreal (Ont.) Engring. Co., 1978-83; sr. engr. Flour City Archtl. Metals, Glen Cove, N.Y., 1984-87, chief engr., 1987—. Recipient Scholarship Grant Asian Inst. Tech., Bangkok, 1968-70. Mem. ASCE, Assn. Profl. Engrs. Ont. Democrat. Roman Catholic. Achievements include structural engring. svcs. to exterior wall systems of bldgs. such as United Airlines Terminal at O'Hare Airport, Soc. Bank Tower, others; rsch. in the elastic flexural-torsional buckling of beam-columns by discrete elements tech. Office: Flour City Archtl Metals 125 Jericho Tpke Ste 100 Jericho NY 11753-1016

CASEY, BARBARA A. PEREA, state representative, school superintendent; b. Las Vegas, N.Mex., Dec. 21, 1951; d. Joe D. and Julia A. (Armijo) Perea; m. Frank J. Casey, Aug. 5, 1978. BA, N.Mex. U., 1972; MA, Highland U., Las Vegas, N.Mex., 1973. Instr. N.Mex. Highlands U., Las Vegas, 1972-74; tchr. Roswell Ind. Schs., Roswell, N.Mex., 1974-96; supt. Hondo Valley Pub. Schs., N.Mex.; mem. N.Mex. Ho. of Reps., 1984—; supt. Hondo (N.Mex.) Valley Pub. Schs., 1996—; instr. N.Mex. Mil. Inst., Roswell, 1977-82, Roswell Police Acad., 1984. N.Mex. advisor Nat. Trust for Hist. Preservation. Mem. NEA (Adv. of of Yr.), AAUW, Am. Bus. Women's Assn., N.Mex. Endowment for Humanities. Democrat. Roman Catholic. Avocations: hunting, reading, writing, poetry. Home: 1214 E 1st St Roswell NM 88201-7960*

CASEY, BARBARA JEANNE, magazine marketing official; b. Glen Cove, N.Y., Mar. 6, 1970; d. William Royal DeMeo and Barbara Louise (Anderson) Terry; m. John Edward Casey, Sept. 12, 1998. BA, U. So. Calif., 1992; MBA, Columbia U., 1998. Client svcs. rep. Christie's Inc., N.Y.C., 1992-93, adminstr., 1993-94, overseas liaison, 1994-96; assoc. mktg. mgr. Time Inc., N.Y.C., 1998—. Mem. jr. com. Search and Care, Inc., 1993—. Mem. Am. Mktg. Assn., Columbia Media Mgmt. Assn., Columbia Internet Bus. Group, Columbia Wine Soc., Columbia Women in Bus., Choate N.Y.C. Alumni Club (v.p. 1996-98, co-pres. 1998—), Doubles Club (assocs. com. 1993—), Delta Gamma (v.p. programming alumni club 1994-95). Avocations: dogs, tennis, golf, skiing, arts and entertainment. Home: 945 Fifth Ave Apt 5E New York NY 10021-2655 Office: Time & Life Bldg 12th Fl 1271 Avenue of the Americas New York NY 10020

CASEY, BERNARD J., lawyer; b. Pawtucket, R.I., June 4, 1942; s. Andrew J. and Theresa (Lennon) C.; m. Kathleen A. Wall; children: Brendan, B. John. A.B., Providence Coll., 1964; J.D., Catholic U., 1967. Bar: R.I. Supreme Ct. 1967, D.C. 1971, U.S. Supreme Ct. 1972, U.S. Cir. Ct. (D.C. cir., 4th cir., 6th cir.). Assoc., Gall, Lane & Powell, Washington, 1971-76, ptnr., 1976; ptnr. Reed Smith Shaw & McClay, Washington, 1976—, mem. exec. com. 1982-87, litigation group chief D.C., 1987-98. Bd. dirs. Cath. Charities, 1994—, chmn., 1997-98. Served to capt. AUS, 1967-71. Decorated Bronze Star medal. Mem. ABA (mem. litigation com.), D.C. Bar Assn., Barristers, Lawyers Club, Univ. Club (bd. govs. 1989-97, pres. 1990-92), Chevy Chase Country Club. Roman Catholic. Home: 3257 Worthington St NW Washington DC 20015-2354 Office: Reed Smith Shaw & McClay East Tower 1301 K St NW Ste 1100 Washington DC 20005-3317

CASEY, BEVERLY ANN, postmaster; b. Decaturville, Tenn., Aug. 6, 1949; d. Willie Hugh and Lillian Blanche (Ivy) Tillman; m. John Robert Casey, Jan. 19, 1969 (div. 1982); children: John Gary, Kimberly Jean. Student Jackson State C.C., 1982-84. Sec. State of Tenn., We. Inst., 1969-76; post office clk. U.S. Postal Service, Western Institute, 1977-82, postmaster, 1982-84; postmaster U.S. Postal Service, Pickwick Dam, Tenn., 1984—; officer-in-charge U.S. Postal Service, Michie, Tenn., 1984. Bd. dirs. Pickwick Med. Clinic, 1986; vol. Hardeman chpt. Saint Jude, Bolivar, Tenn., 1983, Hospice, 1996; mem. parents advancement com. Wesleyan Coll., 1991-94; town chmn. Reelfoot coun. Girl Scouts U.S., 1980-84, activities chmn., 1980-84, recipient Appreciation award, 1983. Named Outstanding 3d Class Postmaster 380 area U.S. Postal Service, 1984; recipient Vol. Service award Cystic Fibrosis Found., Tenn. Chpt., 1982, Vol. Appreciation Cert. Western Mental Health, 1984, cert. of appreciation Tenn. Partnership Missions, 1997. Mem. Nat. League of Postmasters (v.p. Tenn. br. 1984-86), 380 Postmasters Assn. (pres. 1983-84), U.S. Postal Service (dir.-at-large women's adv. coun. 1983-88). Baptist. Avocations: walking, gardening. Home: PO Box 363 Pickwick Dam TN 38365-0363 Office: US Postal Service Pickwick Dam TN 38365

CASEY, DANIEL L., school counselor; b. Litchfield, Minn., Sept. 19, 1942; s. Thomas Austin and Beatrice Lucille (Christie) C.; m. Janet E. Puffe, July 7, 1988; children: Jeffrey, Jennifer, Michele, Jason, Danielle. BS, Bemidji State U., 1988, MA, 1991; PhD, U. Minn., 1999. Cert. traumatologist; bd. cert. expert sch. crisis response. Firefighter, forester DNR/U.S. Forest Svc., 1968-93; prof. psychology Bemidji (Minn.) State U., 1993-94; counselor St. John's U., Collegeville, Minn., 1994-98; crisis mgmt. counseling and consultation Clear Lake, Minn.; adv. com. Internat. Crit. Incident Stress Found., Balt., 1987—. Author: (book) Rural Emergency Response, 1996; contbr. articles to profl. jours. Sgt. USAF, 1960-63, Hawaii. Gov.'s Coun., St. Paul, 1991. Mem. Am. Legion. Avocations: raising Paso Fino horses, hunting, fishing. Home: 11959 77th St Clear Lake MN 55319-9420

CASEY, DON, professional basketball coach; Married Dwynne Casey; 3 children: Leann, Michael, Sean. Formerly head coach Temple U., Phila.; asst. coach Chgo. Bulls (NBA), 1982-83, Los Angeles Clippers (NBA), 1983-84; head coach in Italian profl. basketball league, 1984-85; asst. coach Los Angeles Clippers, 1985-89, head coach, 1989-90; asst. coach Miami Heat, 1992-95, N.J. Nets, 1996—. Office: c/o NJ Nets 405 Murray Hill Pkwy East Rutherford NJ 07073-2136*

CASEY, EDWARD DENNIS, newspaper editor; b. Binghamton, N.Y., Apr. 16, 1931; s. Edwin John and Agnes Mary (Casey) C.; m. E. Jacqueline Wilson, July 13, 1957; children—Daniel, Jeanne, Edward, John. B.A., St. Bonaventure U., 1952; postgrad., Armed Forces Pub. Information Sch., 1953, Syracuse U. Grad. Sch. Journalism, 1954. News editor Sun-Bull., Binghamton, 1960-65; editor Daily Advance, Dover, N.J., 1965-71; exec. editor Capital-Gazette Newspapers, Annapolis, Md., 1971—. Vice pres. Community Chest of Anne Arundel County.; bd. dirs. Annapolis Symphony Orch.; pres. Annapolis/Bywater Boys and Girls Club. With U.S. Army, 1952-54. Recipient Pub. Service award A.P., 1964, Nat. Headliners award, 1965. Mem. AP Mng. Editors Assn., Am. Soc. Newspaper Editors, KC, Sigma Delta Chi. Roman Catholic. Home: 1517 Riverdale Dr Annapolis MD 21401-5839 Office: The Capital 2000 Capital Dr Annapolis MD 21401-3157

CASEY, EDWARD PAUL, manufacturing company executive; b. Boston, Feb. 23, 1930; s. Edward J. and Virginia (Paul) C.; m. Patricia Pinkham, June 23, 1950 (dec. Nov. 1996); children: Patricia Estes Casey Shepherd, Tyler Casey White, Jennifer Paul Casey Schwab, Sheila Pinkham Casey McManus, Virginia Louise Casey Pettengill; m. Mary Ann Patton, Mar. 28, 1998. AB, Yale U., 1952; MBA, Harvard Coll., 1955. With Davidson Rubber Co., Dover, N.H., 1950-65; COO McCord Corp., Detroit, 1965-78, pres., 1965-78; COO Ex-Cell-O Corp., Troy, Mich., 1978-81, CEO, pres., 1981-86, chmn., 1983-86; vice chmn. Textron Inc., 1986-87; pres. E. Paul Casey Assocs., 1987-89; mng. gen. ptnr. Metapoint Ptnrs., Peabody, Mass., 1989-97, chmn., 1997—; bd. dirs. Comerica Inc., Detroit, Wyman Gordon Co., Worcester, Mass. Trustee Henry Ford Health Care Sys., Detroit; pres. Hobe Sound Cmty. Chest, Fla. Mem. Engring. Soc. Detroit, Soc. Automotive Engrs., Chief Execs. Orgn., Harvard Bus. Sch. Club So. Fla., N.Y. Yacht Club (N.Y.C.), Yondotega Club (Detroit), Ea. Yacht Club (Marblehead, Mass.), Wig and Pen Club (London), Island Club, Hobe Sound Yacht Club (Jupiter Island, Fla.). Home: 330 S Beach Rd Hobe Sound FL 33455-2606

CASEY, GEORGE EDWARD, JR., construction executive; b. Cohasset, Mass., July 15, 1946; s. George Edward and Dorothea Evelyn (Oliver) C.; m. Linda Lauraine Bail, Aug. 24, 1974; children: Peter, Matthew. BS in Environ. Engring., Rensselaer Poly. Inst., 1968; MBA, U. Pa., 1974. V.p. Charter Adv. Co., Jacksonville, Fla., 1974-76; owner, mgr. Casey & Co., Brunswick, Maine, 1976-79; project mgr. Toll Bros., Inc., Huntingdon Valley, Pa., 1979-81, v.p., 1981-84, sr. v.p., 1984-89; v.p. Realen Homes, Berwyn, Pa., 1989-91; sr. v.p., chief fin. officer Realen Homes, Berwyn, 1992-95; pres., CEO Zaring Homes, Inc., Cin., 1995-98, also bd. dirs.; pres. Fla. Ops. Arvida, Weston, 1998—; bd. dirs. Robertson Bros. Builders, Inc. Trustee Am. Boychoir Sch., Princeton, N.J., 1986-88. Lt. USN, 1968-72, Vietnam. Decorated Bronze Star. Mem. Urban Land Inst., Wharton Real Estate Ctr., Patroons Rensselaer, Weston Hills Country Club, Lauderdale Yacht Club, Beta Gamma Sigma. Republican. Avocations: ocean sailboat racing, skiing, golfing, traveling. Home: 2617 Delmar Pl Fort Lauderdale FL 33301-1577 Office: Arvida 1205 Arvida Pkwy Weston FL 33327-1700

CASEY, GEORGE W., military career officer; b. Japan, July 22, 1948. BS in Internat. Rels., Georgetown U.; MA in Internat. Rels., U. Denver. Commd. 2nd lt. U.S. Army, 1970, advanced through grades to brig. gen., 1996, various positions, 1970-82; exec. officer 1st Battalion, 10th Infantry, 4th Divsn. U.S. Army, Ft. Carson, Colo., 1982-84; sec. gen. staff 4th Infantry Divsn. U.S. Army, Ft. Carson, 1984-85, comdr. 1st Battalion, 10th Infantry, 4th Divsn., 1985-87; congl. program coord. Office of the Chief of Legis. Liaison, Washington, 1988-89; spl. ast. to Chief of Staff U.S. Army, Washington, 1989-91; chief of staff 1st Cavalry Divsn. U.S. Army, Ft. Hood, Tex., 1991-93; comdr. 3rd Brigade, 1st Cavalry Divsn. U.S. Army, Ft. Hood, 1993-95; asst. chief of staff G-3 (ops.), V Corps. U.S. Army Europe, 1995; chief of staff V Corps. U.S. Army Europe and Seventh Army, Germany, 1995-96; asst. divsn. comdr. 1st Armored Divsn. U.S. Army Europe and Seventh Army, 1996-97; asst. dep. dir. politico-mil. affairs J-5 The Joint Staff, Washington, 1997—. Decorated Legion of Merit with 2 oak leaf clusters, Def. Meritorious Svc. medal, Meritorious Svc. medal, Army Commendation medal with oak leaf cluster, Army Achievement medal with oak leaf cluster. Office: The Joint Staff 5104 Joint Staff Pentagon Washington DC 20318-5104

CASEY, GERARD WILLIAM, food products company executive, lawyer; b. N.Y.C., Nov. 12, 1942; s. William Gerard and Bridget (Carmody) C.; m. Mary Howard, May 1, 1971; children: Jennifer, William, Thomas, Andrew, Patrick. BS in History, Fordham Coll., 1963; MA in History, NYU, 1966; JD, Fordham U., 1967. Bar: N.Y. 1969. Criminal investigator U.S. Army, U.S., Korea, 1967-69; v.p., gen. counsel Pepsi Cola Co., PepsiCo, Inc., Puchase, N.Y., 1969—; dir. Westchester County Legal Aid Soc., White Plains, N.Y., 1980—. Mem. Friendly Sons of St. Patrick, White Plains, 1987—; dir. Lincoln Hall Sch., Lincolndale, N.Y., 1988-91. Mem. ABA, N.Y. State Bar Assn. Roman Catholic. Office: PepsiCo Inc 700 Anderson Hill Rd Purchase NY 10577

CASEY, H(ORACE) CRAIG, JR., electrical engineering educator; b. Houston, Dec. 4, 1934; s. H.c. and Mae (Walls) C.; m. Jean Anne Merritt, June 14, 1960 (div. 1983); children: Anne, Michael; m. Jacqueline Lucas, Jan. 22, 1983. BSEE, Okla. State U., 1957; MSEE, Stanford U., 1959, PhD, 1964. Devel. engr. Hewlett-Packard, Palo Alto, Calif., 1957-62; mem. tech. staff Bell Labs., Murray Hill, N.J., 1964-79; chmn. dept. elec. engring. Duke U., Durham, N.C., 1979-94, prof. elec. engring., 1979—; mem. Dept. of Def. Adv. Group Electron Devices, Washington, 1975-79; bd. dirs. Acme Elec., 1984-91. Author: Heterostructure Lasers, 1978, Devices for Integrated Circuits: Silicon and III-V Compounds, 1999. Fellow IEEE (pres. Electron Devices Soc. 1988-89, editor centennial issue Trans. on Electron Devices 1984); mem. Am. Phys. Soc. Office: Duke U Dept Elec Engring Durham NC 27706

CASEY, JAMES B., librarian; b. Syracuse, N.Y., June 29, 1950; s. John Joseph and Louise (Countryman) C.; m. Diane Dates, Nov. 16, 1984; children: Nathan, Jeremy. MLS, SUNY, Geneseo, 1973; MA, Cleve. State U., 1979; PhD, Case Western Res. U., 1985. Head librarian Ohio Hist. Soc.,

Columbus, 1983-84; dir. Pickaway County Pub. Libr., Circleville, Ohio, 1984-92, Oak Lawn (Ill.) Libr., 1992—. Editor: Libby Prison Autograph Book, 1984. Recipient Health Literacy award Am. Numismatic Assn., 1980. Mem. ALA (mem. coun. 1996—). Avocation: numismatics. E-mail: jim-casey@lib.oak-lawn.il.us. Home: 9717 S Parkside Ave Oak Lawn IL 60453 Office: Oak Lawn Libr 9427 S Raymond Oak Lawn IL 60453

CASEY, JAMES FRANCIS, management consultant; b. Boston, May 22, 1935; s. James Francis and Elizabeth Mary (MacNeil) C.; m. Margaret Ann Flaherty, Jan. 22, 1977. BA in Philosophy cum laude, Weston Coll., 1957, BS/MS in Physics cum laude, 1962. Sales mgr. Xerox Corp., Stamford, Conn., 1963-79; dir. mktg. Computervision Corp., Bedford, Mass., 1979-82; v.p. CTX Corp., Sunnyvale, Calif., 1982-83; mktg. mgr. Hewlett-Packard Corp., Palo Alto, Calif., 1983-86; group mgr. Digital Equipment Corp., Maynard, Mass., 1986-92; mng. ptnr. Synergy Cons., Austin, Tex., 1992—; ptnr. Agincourt Capital Plc, Dublin, Ireland, 1997—; pres., CEO Mcpl. Utility Dist., State of Tex., 1998—; cons. numerous clients, including Hewlett-Packard Co., Ceridian, Lexis-Nexis, Raster Graphics, Inc., Reed Elsevier Plc. Group, others. Patron San Francisco Opera Co., 1982-99, San Francisco Orch., 1982-91; Friend Boston Symphony Orch., 1976-81; contbr. Austin Symphony Orch. Mem. Xerox-X, Am. Mgmt. Assn. (bd. dirs. 1962-65), Am. Electronic Assn. (mktg. com. chmn. 1989-91), Del. Valley Reprographic Soc. (v.p.1965-69), Jr. C. of C. (pres. Phila. chpt. 1965-69). Fax: (512)-436-6024. E-mail: casey78730@aol.com. Home and Office: 10123 Treasure Island Dr Austin TX 78730-3559

CASEY, JAMES LEROY, curriculum director; b. Bigham, Ill., July 6, 1942; s. Truman Alva and Juanita Clara (Boaz) C.; m. Kazuko Casey, Dec. 26, 1963. BA, Sophia U., Tokyo, 1974; MS in Edn., U. Soc. Calif., 1976, EdD, 1992. Enlisted USAF, 1959, rose through ranks to Master Sgt., retired, 1983; tchr. English as a fgn. lang. Wakanai H.S., Japan, 1964, Chitose (Japan) Am. Lang. Inst., 1970-72, Tomakami (Japan) Jr. Coll., 1972, Sophia U., Tokyo, 1973-75; pers. mgr. and tchr. English as fgn. lang. Berkeley House Lang., Tokyo, 1982-88; curriculum dir. Mid Pacific Coll., Honolulu, Hawaii, 1992—. Mem. VFW, Tokyo, (cmmdr. post 9450 Tokyo 1984-85, cmmdr. Japan dist. 1985-86, chaplin dept. Pacific area 1987-88), Elks (scholarship chmn. 1995—, dist. scholarship chmn. 1996—). Lutheran. Avocations: golf, computers, reading. Home: 94 619 Palai St Waipahu HI 96797

CASEY, JOHN ALEXANDER, lawyer; b. Wisconsin Rapids, Wis., Apr. 7, 1945; s. Samuel Alexander and Ardean A. AB, Stanford U., 1967; JD, U. Mich., 1970. Ptnr. Quarles & Brady, Milw., 1970—. Office: Quarles & Brady 411 E Wisconsin Ave Ste 2550 Milwaukee WI 53202-4497

CASEY, JOHN DUDLEY, writer, English language educator; b. Worcester, Mass., Jan. 18, 1939; s. Joseph Edward and Constance (Dudley) C.; m. Jane Barnes, June 10, 1967 (div. 1980); children: Maud, Nell; m. Rosamond Pinchot Pittman, June 27, 1982; children: Clare, Julia. BA, Harvard U., 1962, LLB, 1965; MFA, U. Iowa, 1968. Prof. English U. Va., Charlottesville, 1972-92, U. Iowa, 1998, U. Va., 1999—; lit. executor Estate of Breece D'J Pancake, 1979—; resident scholar Am. Acad. in Rome, 1990-91. Author: An American Romance, 1977 (runner up Ernest Hemingway award 1977), Testimony and Demeanor, 1979 (Friends Am. Lit. award 1980), Spartina, 1989 (Nat. Book award 1989), Supper at the Black Pearl, 1995, The Half-life of Happiness, 1998; contbr. stories (O. Henry award 1989), essays maj. nat. mags. including New Yorker, Esquire. With USAR, 1959-60. Guggenheim fellow, 1979-80, Nat. Endowment for Arts fellow, 1983, resident Am. Acad. in Rome, 1990-91; grantee Strauss living AAAL, 1992-97. Mem. PEN. Avocation: rowing. Office: U Va Dept English Bryan Hall Charlottesville VA 22903-3289 also: Michael Carlisle Carlisle & Co 24 E 64 St New York NY 10021

CASEY, JOHN PATRICK (JACK CASEY), public relations executive, political analyst; b. Syracuse, N.Y., July 19, 1928; s. Patrick Joseph and Ellen (Loftus) C.; m. Ursula Casey, Feb. 3, 1951 (div. 1975); children: Michael, Gretchen, John, Patrick; m. Mary Lou Butcher, May 2, 1982. BA, U. Toledo, 1958. Reporter Toledo Times, 1951-56; staff writer Detroit Free Press, 1956-61; spl. asst. to mayor City of Detroit, 1962-66; v.p. MG and Casey Communications Inc., Detroit, 1966-82; pres., chief exec. officer Casey Communications Mgmt. Inc., Southfield, Mich., 1982-90; chmn. Casey Butcher Ventures, Bloomfield Hills, Mich., 1990—; polit. analyst Sta. WJR-Radio, Detroit, 1966—, Sta. WDIV-TV, Detroit, 1978-87, WKBD-TV, Detroit, 1989—; speaker in field. Contbr. articles to various publs. Campaign mgr. Re-elect Mayor Cavanagh, Detroit, 1966; chmn. Commn. on Community Rels., City of Detroit, 1968-70. With U.S. Army, 1946-48. Recipient Page One awards Newspaper Guild, Detroit, 1957, 58; other awards for news coverage, pub. rels. Mem. Pub. Rels. Soc. Am. (pres. Detroit chpt. 1981-82, counselors acad., pub. affairs sect., inducted in Detroit chpt. Hall of Fame 1994), Plum Hollow Country Club, Mission Hills Country Club. Democrat. Avocations: classical music, reading, golf. Home: 3864 Vista Ln Orchard Lake MI 48323-1678 also: 12504 Prestwick Ct Rancho Mirage CA 92270-1481

CASEY, KAREN ANNE, banker; b. Bklyn., Oct. 5, 1955; d. Stanley Joseph and Helen Katherine (Kosowski) Mozeleski; m. Dennis Joseph Casey, May 14, 1977; children: Christopher Sean, Erin Michelle. BBA, Baruch Coll., CUNY, 1977. CPA, N.Y., CFP. Jr. acct. Coopers & Lybrand, N.Y.C., 1977-78, sr. acct., 1978-79, supr., 1979-81; asst. fin. contr. Gulf Internat. Bank, N.Y.C., 1981-82, fin. contr., 1982; v.p., fin. contr. Allied Irish Banks plc, N.Y.C., 1982-87, sr. v.p., fin. contr., 1988-89, sr. v.p. mgmt. support svcs., 1989-92, sr. v.p., CFO, Allied Irish Bank, 1992-94, sr. v.p., head pvt. fin. svcs., 1994—; bank rep. to Inst. Fgn. Bankers, 1984—, Inst. Cert. Fin. Planners, 1991—. Mem. Am. Inst. CPAs. Roman Catholic. Avocations: gardening, golf, tennis, reading. Office: Allied Irish Banks Plc 405 Park Ave New York NY 10022-4405

CASEY, KATHLEEN MARGARET, secondary education educator; b. Albany, N.Y., May 3, 1971; d. Albert S. and Ellen M. Casey. BA, SUNY, Albany, 1992, MA, 1994. Provisional tchg. cert., N.Y., Mich. Summer sch. tchr. East Greenbush (N.Y.) Ctrl. Schs., 1993—; social studies tchr. Laurens (N.Y.) Ctrl. Sch. Dist., 1995-96; social studies and math. tchr. Manchester (Vt.) Elem.-Middle Sch., spring 1997; social studies and sci. tchr. Maimonides Hebrew Day Sch., Albany, N.Y., fall 1997; social studies tchr. grade 9 Bethlehem Ctrl. H.S., Delmar, N.Y., spring 1998; social studies tchr. grades 9 and 10 Gloversville (N.Y.) H.S., 1998—. Mem. ASCD, N.Y. State Coun. for the Social Studies, Capital Dist. Coun. for the Social Studies, U. Albany Alumni Assn., Rep. Nat. Com. Avocations: running, cross stitching. E-mail: ktkc9294@aol.com. Home: 1 Cobblers Ln Rensselaer NY 12144 Office: Gloversville High Sch 199 Lincoln St Gloversville NY 12078

CASEY, KENNETH G., neurosurgeon, educator; b. N.Y.C., Oct. 6, 1950; s. Russell Kathleen Casey. BS, Georgetown U., Washington, 1972; MD, U. Medicine & Dentistry N.J., Newark, 1977. Asst. prof. neurosurgery U. Colo., Denver, 1986-89, U. Conn., Farmington, 1989-91, U. Pa., Phila., 1991-95, Hahnemann/Med. Coll. Pa., Phila., 1995—. Office: Cpup-U Pa 1 Graduate Plz Philadelphia PA 19146-1407

CASEY, KENNETH LYMAN, neurologist; b. Ogden, Utah, Apr. 16, 1935; s. Kenneth Lafayette and Lyzena (Payne) C.; m. Jean Louise Madsen, June 21, 1958; children—Tena Jeanette, Kenneth Lyman, Teresa Louise. B.A., Whitman Coll., Walla Walla, Wash., 1957; M.D. with honors, U. Wash., Seattle, 1961. Diplomate: Am. Bd. Neurology and Psychiatry. Intern in medicine Cornell U. Med. Center-N.Y. Hosp., 1961-62; USPHS officer lab. neurophysiology NIMH, 1962-64; fellow in psychology McGill U., Montreal, Que., Can., 1964-66; mem. faculty U. Mich. Med. Sch., Ann Arbor, 1966—; prof. neurology and physiology U. Mich. Med. Sch., 1978—; resident in neurology U. Mich Hosp., 1971-74; chief neurology svc. VA Med. Center, Ann Arbor, 1979—; sci. bd. dirs. Nat. Inst. Dental Rsch., 1984-88; sci. adv. com. Santa Fe Neurol. Inst., 1984—. Assoc. editor Clin. Jour. Pain, 1984—; editor-in-chief Am. Pain Soc. Jour. Pain Forum, 1991—; contbr. articles to profl. jours., chpts. to books. NIH Spl. fellow, 1964-66, grantee, 1966—; Bristol-Myers rsch. grantee, 1988-93. Fellow Am. Acad. Neurology; mem. Am. Physiol. Soc., Am. Acad. Neurology, Soc. Neurosci., Am. Pain Soc. (pres. 1984-85, F.W.L. Kerr Basic Sci. Rsch. award and lecture 1998), Internat. Assn. Study Pain, Phi Beta Kappa, Sigma Xi, Alpha Omega Alpha (J. J. Bonica disting. lectr. and awardee 1991). Unitarian. Home: 2775 Heatherway St Ann Arbor MI 48104-2852 Office: VA Med Ctr Neurology Svc 2215 Fuller Rd Ann Arbor MI 48105-2300

CASEY, KIMBERLYN LORETTRE, artist, painter, educator; b. Dexster, Maine, Apr. 10, 1964; d. Terry F. and Jeanette (Turcotte) Casey; m. Mar. 18, 1958. Student, Chautauqua Sch. Art; BS in Art Edn., U. N.H., Plymouth, 1982; postgrad., U. N.H., Durham, 1983-84, Mass. Coll. Art, Boston, 1985-86; MFA in Painting and Printmaking, CUNY, N.Y.C., 1997. Cert. tchr. K-12, N.H., Mass. Owner Creative Corner Studio Sch., Dover, N.H., 1991-95; tchr. workshops U. N.H., Durham, 1992-94; prof. art Plymouth (N.H.) State Coll., 1998—; mem. pilot program drawing early age Ipswich (Mass.) Pub. Schs., 1997. Contbr. articles to profl. jours. Recipient Vt. Studio Ctr. Alumni award, 1994, award Charles Edison Fund, 1995; Ruth Farkau scholar Chautauqua Instn. N.Y., 1996; N.H. Coun. on the Arts painting grantee and fellow, 1999. Fellow Coll. Art Assn.; mem. CHADD, ADD, ADHD Children, Kappa Delta Phi. Avocations: swimming masters, skiing, hiking, camping. Home: 244 Locust St Dover NH 03820-4034

CASEY, MARSHA, hospital executive. MS, U. Tex., Tyler, 1986; postgrad., U. Tex. Health Sci. Ctr., Houston. CEO Vanderbilt U. Hosp. and Clinic, 1998—. Office: 1161 21st Ave S Nashville TX 37232

CASEY, MICHAEL KIRKLAND, business executive, lawyer; b. Wheeling, W.Va., Jan. 24, 1940; s. Clyde Thomas and Joan Ferrell (McLure) C.; m. Mary Ann McCarten, Jan. 31, 1969 (div. 1999); children: Michael Kirkland II, Mary Larkin, Colin McCarten (dec.). Student, U. Notre Dame, 1957-58; BS, W.V. U., 1964; JD, George Washington U., 1967. Bar: D.C. 1974, U.S. Dist. Ct. D.C., U.S. Ct. Appeals (D.C. cir.), D.C. Ct. Appeals; lic. securities NASD series 7; cert. life, accident, health and variable contract ins. Hartford Life and Annuity Co., Nationwide Ins. Cos. Cons. to White House Washington, 1977-81; handled overseas Presdl. missions India, Western Europe, Brazil and Middle East, 1977-81; dir. White House Conf. on Small Bus., Washington, 1979-80; assoc. adminstr. for investment SBA, Washington, 1980-81; chmn. bd. MCW Internat. Ltd., Alexandria, Va., 1981-89; Washington rep. Nationwide Ins. Cos., 1990—; chmn. Entre Ireland Ltd., San Francisco, 1996—, Washington, 1996—, Dublin, 1996—; nat. adminstr. fringe benefits program U.S. Conf. Mayors, 1984-89; founding mem. Nat. Conf. Dem. Mayors; dir. Emerald Films Ltd., Dublin, 1999—. Advance man Kennedy for Pres. Com., 1968; asst. campaign mgr. Jackson for Pres. Com., 1968; spl. asst. to U.S. Senator Edmund S. Muskie, 1969-72; campaign mgr. Carter-Mondale Reelection Com. in Mo. and Ill., 1980; mem. Dem. Senatorial Campaign Com.; sponsor Habitat for Humanity Bicycle Challenge, 1999. With USMC, 1958-64. Recipient Presdl. Cert. Pres. of U.S., 1977, 78, 79, Disting. Svc. Plaque White House Commn. on Small Bus., 1980, Disting. Svc. award SBA, 1980. Mem. Irish Am. Partnership (Boston/Dublin), Marine Corps Heritage Found., U.S. Power Squadrons, Naval Order of U.S. (first enlisted marine to be inducted by vote), Carter Legacy Cir. (founder), Carter Ctr. (founder), Marines Meml. Assn. and Club (San Francisco), Old Dominion Boat Club, Belle Haven Country Club, Nat. Dem. Club. Roman Catholic. Home and Office: 400 Madison St Apt 2206 Alexandria VA 22314-1736

CASEY, MURRAY JOSEPH, physician, educator; b. Armour, S.D., May 1, 1936; s. Meryl Joseph and Gladice (Murray) C.; m. Virginia Anne Fletcher; children: Murray Joseph Jr., Theresa Marie, Anne Franklin, Francis Xavier, Peter Colum, Matthew Padraic. Student, Chanute Jr. Coll., 1954-55, Rockhurst Coll., 1955-56; AB, U. Kans., 1958; MD, Georgetown U., 1962; postgrad., Suffolk U. Law Sch., 1963-64, Howard U., 1965, U. Conn., 1977; MS in Mgmt., Cardinal Stritch Coll., 1984; MBA, Marquette U., 1988. Diplomate Nat. Bd. Med. Examiners, Am. Bd. Ob-Gyn. Intern USPHS Hosp.-Univ. Hosp., Balt., 1962-63; staff physician USPHS Hosp., Boston, 1963-64; rsch. staff Lab Infectious Diseases, Nat. Inst. Allergy and Infectious Diseases, NIH, Bethesda, Md., 1964-66; virologist, resident physician Columbia-Presbyn. Med. Ctr. also Francis Delafield Hosp., N.Y.C., 1966-69, USPHS sr. clin. trainee, 1969-70; fellow gynecol. oncology, resident dept. surgery Meml. Hosp. Cancer and Allied Diseases, Meml. Sloan-Kettering Cancer Ctr., N.Y.C., 1969-71; Am. Cancer Soc. fellow, 1969-71; ofcl. observer in radiotherapy U. Tex. M.D. Anderson Hosp. and Tumor Inst., Houston, 1971; vis. scientist Radiumhemmet Karolinska Sjukhuset and Inst., Stockholm, 1971; asst. prof. ob-gyn U. Conn. Sch. Medicine, 1971-75, asso. prof., 1975-80, dir. gynecologic oncology, 1971-80, also mem. med. bd.; prof., assoc. chmn. dept. ob-gyn U. Wis. Med. Sch., 1980-89; prof., chmn. dept. ob-gyn. Creighton U., Omaha, 1989-94; chief ob-gyn. and dir. gynecologic oncology St. Joseph Hosp., Creighton U. Med. Ctr., Omaha, 1989-94; dir. gynecologic oncology Creighton Cancer Ctr, 1996—; faculty coun. Creighton U., 1995—, acad. coun., 1992-93, 95—, instrnl. rev. bd. dirs., 1994—, rank and tenure com., cancer ctr. adv. bd., 1994—, sr. appts. and tenure com., 1998—; chief ob-gyn Mt. Sinai Med. Ctr., Milw., 1980-82, dir. gynecologic oncology, 1980-89, also mem. med. exec. com.; chmn. research adv. com., mem. council Conn. Cancer Epidemiology Unit. Editor, contbr. articles in sports medicine to profl. jours., chpts. to books; rsch. in oncogenesis and tumor immunology. Bd. dirs., mem. exec. com., chmn. profl. edn. com. Hartford unit Am. Cancer Soc., dir. Milw. divsn., exec. com. 1985-87, v.p., 1985-86, pres.-elect, 1986-87, 1st v.p. exec. com. Wis. divsn. 1987-89, bd. dirs., chmn. profl. edn. com., 1987-89, bd. dirs., 1989-96, exec. com. Nebr. divsn., 1989-93, pub. edn. and communications com., profl. edn. com. vice chair, 2nd v.p., 1990-91, 1st v.p., pres.-elect, 1991-92, pres., 1992-93, bd. dirs. Douglas County unit, 1993—; mem. mayor's adv. com. Cancer Survivors Park, City of Omaha, 1991-92; mem. Parks and Recreation Bd., City of Omaha, 1993-94; mem. med. svcs. 1980 Winter Olympic Games, Lake Placid, N.Y.; mem. med. supervisory team U.S. Nordic Ski Team. Lt. (j.g.) USPHS, 1962-64, lt. comdr., 1964-66; col. USAR, 1988-93. Fellow ACS, Am. Coll. Ob-Gyn; mem. AAAS, Soc. of Gynecol. Surgeons, Cen. Assn. Ob-Gyns., Am. Coll. Sports Medicine, N.Y. Acad. Scis., Am. Soc. Colposcopy, Am. Assn. Gynecologic Laparoscopists, Am. Fertility Soc., Soc. Gynecol. Oncologists, European Soc. Gynecol. Oncologists, New Eng. Assn. Gynecol. Oncologists (pres. 1980-81), Internat. Gynecol. Cancer Soc., Am. Radium Soc., Am. Soc. Clin. Oncology, Internat. Menopause Soc., N.Am. Menopause Soc., Internat. Assn. for Advancement of Humanistic Studies in Medicine, Soc. Meml. Gynecol. Oncologists (exec. bd. 1979-84; pres. 1982-83), Lake Placid Sports Medicine Soc. (v.p. 1981-84, pres. 1984-86), Am. Urogynecol. Soc., Assn. Mil. Surgeon, Cedarburg C. of C. (Ambassadors com. 1983—, dir. 1983-85, chmn. bus. indsl. program com. 1985, 87-88), St. George Soc., Milwaukee Gynecologic Soc., Omaha Ob-Gyn. Soc., Beta Gamma Sigma. Office: Creighton U Sch Medicine Dept Ob-Gyn 601 N 30th St # 4810 Omaha NE 68131-2137

CASEY, PAUL ARNOLD, writer, composer, photographer; b. Inglewood, Calif., Dec. 10, 1934; s. Paul Franklyn and Orilee Corinne (Gray) C. AA, UCLA, BA. Pres., genetics cons. CSCA Internat., Sun Valley, Calif.; pres., tech. advisor Solenz Corp., Wilmington, Del.; dramaturg L.A. Playwrights Group, 1996. Author poetry: Songs of Youth, 1951; writer TV show Lassie, 1969; photographer wildlife: Girl Scouts Calendar, 1995; developer breed of cat: Calif. Spangled, 1971-86; inventor power lens, 1967. With USN, 1953-54. Recipient Nat. Humane Soc. award, 1965; U.S. Govt. scholar, 1954. Mem. L.A. Playwrights Group (gen. sec. 1995-96, bd. dirs. 1998-99). Avocations: wildlife photography, astronomy, archaeology, natural power systems technology. Office: CSCA International PO Box 368 Sun Valley CA 91353-0368

CASEY, PAULA F., writer, speaker; b. Jacksonville, N.C., Dec. 10, 1953; d. Paul J. and Frances (Flora) C.; m. Richard L. Worden, Dec. 11, 1982 (dec. July 1988). BS in Comm., U. Tenn., 1975. Pres. Music City Foods Inc., Nashville, 1983—, Vote 70 Inc., Memphis, 1989—. Prodr. (videotape) Generations-American Women Win the Vote, 1989 (2nd place award Nat. Fedn. Press Women 1989); editl. coord.: The Perfect 36: Tennessee Delivers Woman Suffrage, 1998. Co-founder Memphis Women's Polit. Caucus, 1983; bd. dirs. YWCA of Greater Memphis, 1984-91; v.p. bd. trustees Nat. Ornamental Metal Museum, 1995—; active design rev. bd. Ctr. City Commn., Memphis, 1997—. Named for Leadership, YWCA of Greater Memphis, 1992, one of Memphis Pioneers and Role Models, Girls Inc., Memphis, 1996, one of Women Who Make A Difference, Women's News of the Mid-South, Memphis, 1997; recipient Vision award Women of Achievement of Memphis/Shelby County, 1994. Mem. Nat. Fedn. Press Women (exec. com., sec. 1997—). Methodist. Home and Office: Vote 70 Inc 109 N Main St Apt 812 Memphis TN 38103-5019

CASEY, PAULA JEAN, prosecutor; b. Charleston, Ark., Feb. 16, 1951; d. Arthur Clinton and Mildred Aleene (Underwood) C.; m. Gilbert Louis Glover II, Mar. 13, 1981. BA, Ea. Cen. (Okla.) U., 1973; JD, U. Ark., 1977. Staff atty. Ctrl. Ark. Legal Services, Hot Springs, Ark., 1977-79; dep. pub. defender 6th Jud. Dist. Pub. Defender, Little Rock, 1979; clinic supr. U. Ark. at Little Rock Law Sch., 1979-81, asst. prof., 1981-84, assoc. prof., 1984-92, prof., 1992-93, assoc. dean, 1986-90; legis. dir., chief counsel U.S. Senator Dale Bumpers, 1990-92; lobbyist Ark. Bar Assn., 1993; U.S. atty. Ea. Dist. Ark., 1993—; cons. for juvenile affairs 6th Jud. Dist. Judges, Ark., 1987. Author, editor: Poverty Law Practice Manual, 1985. Sec. Pulaski County Dem. Com., Little Rock, 1984-89; mem. Ark. Dem. Com., 1984-89; mem. Juvenile Adv. Group, Little Rock, 1985-89; mem. Gov.'s Task Force on Juvenile Cts., Ark., 1987; chmn. Ark. Dem. Jud. Com., 1987; bd. dirs. Ctrl. Ark. Legal Svcs., Little Rock, 1986-89. Named One of Top 100 Women in Ark., Ark. Bus. Pubs., 1996, 98, 99; recipient Gale Pettus Pontz award U. Ark.-Fayetteville Law Sch. Women Students Assn., 1994, award of merit Organized Crime Drug Enforcement Task Force, 1997. Fellow Ark. Bar Found. (bd. dirs.); mem. Ark. Bar Assn. (del. 1986-90), Am. Inns Ct., Overton Am. Inns of Ct. Democrat. Office: US Attys Office PO Box 1229 # P Little Rock AR 72203-1229

CASEY, RICHARD CONWAY, judge. BA, Holy Cross, 1955; JD, Georgetown U., 1958. Judge U.S. Dist. Ct. (so. dist.) N.Y., 1997—. Office: 500 Pearl St New York NY 10007

CASEY, RICHARD L., pharmaceutical executive. Pres., CEO, chmn. bd. Scios, Inc., Mountain View, Calif. Office: Scios Inc 2450 Bayshore Pkwy Mountain View CA 94043-1173

CASEY, RITA JO ANN, nursing administrator; b. Paulsboro, N.J., Nov. 19, 1942; d. George John and Louise Elizabeth (De Santis) Centofanti; m. Robert Joseph Casey, June 5, 1965; children: Joseph, Thomas. Diploma, Woman's Med. Coll. Hosp., 1963; BSN, Holy Family Coll., 1985. RN Pa. Staff nurse Woman's Med. Coll. Hosp., Phila., 1963-68; sch. nurse Bensalem (Pa.) Sch. Dist., 1979-83; coord. health svcs. Holy Family Coll., Phila., 1983—; sec. HFC Student Svcs. Mid. States Evaluation Com., Phila., 1991-92; mem. HFC Cmty. Svc. Adv. Bd., 1991—; mem. HFC Strategic Planning Com., Phila., 1993; ARC CPR instr., 1991—. Chartered orgn. rep. Boy Scouts Am., 1976—; pres. Bensalem H.S. Football Booster Club, 1988-89; sec. Bensalem Meml. Day Parade Com., 1989-94, Phila. Archdiocesan Cath. Com. Scouting, 1992—; co-founder Bensalem Tricentennial Commemorative Hist. Trail, 1993. Mem. Am. Coll. Health Assocs., Nat. Assn. Sch. Nurses, Nat. Athletic Trainers Assn., Southeast Coll. Health Nurses Assn., Med. Coll. Pa. Sch. Nursing Alumni Assn. (banquet chair 1963-94). Roman Catholic. Avocations: reading, boating, fishing, crocheting, needlepoint. Home: 2370 Ogden Ave Bensalem PA 19020-5211 Office: Holy Family Coll Grant & Frankford Aves Philadelphia PA 19114

CASEY, ROBERT J., international trade association executive; b. Youngstown, Ohio, July 18, 1923; s. Michael Francis and Anna Barbara (Siefert) C.; m. Phyllis Lou Lewis, May 20, 1950; children: Kathleen Ann, Robert J. II, Susan Elizabeth. BA, Kent State U., 1948; LLB, Youngstown U., 1954; JD, Ohio State U., 1956. Asst. dir. Ohio Bar Assn., Columbus, 1949-56; account exec. Ketchum, Inc., Pitts., 1956-60; v.p. Western Pa. Nat. Bank (Nat. City Bank), Pitts., 1960-65; dir. spl. svcs. PPG Industries, Pitts., 1965-69; dir. pub. info. Westinghouse Air Brake Co., Pitts., 1969-74, Amtrak, Washington, 1975-78; exec. dir. Ohio Rail Transp. Authority, Columbus, 1978-83; founder, exec. dir., chmn. High Speed Rail/Maglev Assn., Pitts., 1983. Contbr. articles on bank mktg. and transp. to profl. jours. Rep. candidate for Ho. of Reps., Pitts., 1976; del. Rep. Nat. Conv., Miami, Fla., 1972. 1st Lt. USAAC, 1945. Recipient Chmn.'s award High Speed Rail Assn., 1991. Mem. Am. Legion, Delta Upsilon. Avocations: skiing, collecting rare books, tennis, painting.

CASEY, ROBERT REISCH, lawyer; b. New Orleans, May 19, 1946; s. Robert Taylor Casey and Merlyn Lucille (Reisch) Weilbaecher. BBA in Acctg. magna cum laude, U. Notre Dame, 1968; JD, Tulane U., 1971; LLM in Taxation, NYU, 1973. Bar: La. 1971. Ptnr. Jones, Walker, Waechter, Poitevent, Carrere and Denegre, Baton Rouge, 1971—. Mem. bd. editors Tulane Law Rev., 1970-71. Mem. ABA (chmn. partnership com. tax sect. 1982-84, mem. coun. 1985-88, sec. 1988-90, vice chmn. 1989-91), Order of Coif, Beta Gamma Sigma, Beta Alpha Psi. Avocations: golf, French horn.

CASEY, RONALD BRUCE, journalist; b. Birmingham, AL, Aug. 21, 1951; s. J. B. and Ruby Lois (Sizemore) C.; m. Margaret Griffin Brooke, Feb. 3, 1979; children: Jefferson Brooke, Anna Heviges. BA, U. Ala., Tuscaloosa, 1973. Reporter Birmingham News, 1973-77, asst. city editor, 1977-79, editorial writer, 1979-90, editor editorial page, 1990—; adj. prof. journalism U. Ala. Bd. dirs. Family and Child Svcs., Birmingham, 1991—; mem. Leadership Birmingham. Recipient Nat. Headliners award Atlantic City Soc. Profl. Journalists, 1991, Pulitzer prize for editl. writing, 1991, Journalist of Yr. award Troy (Ala.) State U., 1993, award for editl. writing Nat. Edn. Writers Assn., 1995. Mem. Nat. Conf. Editorial Writers. Office: Birmingham News PO Box 2553 Birmingham AL 35202-2553

CASEY, THOMAS J., lawyer; b. Frankfurt, Germany, Feb. 24, 1952. BA magna cum laude, Boston Coll., 1973; JD with honors, George Washington U., 1977. Bar: Va. 1977, D.C. 1979, Mass. 1984, U.S. Supreme Ct. 1985. With ITT, Washington, 1973-75, antitrust div. U.S. Dept. Justice, 1975-78, Fed. Communications Commn., 1978-81, assoc. and ptnr. Mintz, Levin, Cohn, Ferris, Glovsky & Popeo, P.C., 1981-89, ptnr., 1983-89; ptnr., co-head of telecoms. and media group Skadden, Arps, Slate, Meagher & Flom, 1990-95, Merrill Lynch mng. dir., co-head of global comms. investment banking group, 1995-98; pres., dir. Pacific Capital Group, Inc., 1998—; vice chmn. bd., mng. dir. Global Crossing Ltd., 1998—. Co-author: Cable Television Law, 1983. Home: 150 S El Camino Dr Ste 240 Beverly Hills CA 90212-2733 also: 1-3 Prince's Gate, SW7 1QJ London England

CASEY, THOMAS JEFFERSON, investment banker, venture capitalist. Student, U.S. Naval Acad., 1964-65; MBA, Harvard U., 1970; PhD, U. London/Am. U., 1997—. Pres./COO New Eng. Furniture Group, Boston, 1968-71; chmn./CEO Commonwealth Industries, Inc., N.Y.C., 1971-75; pres./gen. mgr. Damson Oil Corp. AMEX, N.Y.C. and Houston, 1975-80; founder/chmn./CEO The Sovereign Group, Ltd., N.Y.C., 1980-90; chmn., CEO ENTECH, Inc., N.Y.C., 1991—; guest lectr. Wharton Grad. Sch. Bus. Adminstrn.; former mem. faculty internat. mgmt. Northeastern U. Sch. Mgmt. and Adminstrn., Boston; sr. fin./investment advisor to several Fortune 500 cos., sovereign fgn. govts. and internat. fin. instns. Avocations: golf, tennis, skiing, sailing, flying. Office: Advanced Environ Technols Inc 730 5th Ave Ste 900 New York NY 10019-4105

CASEY, THOMAS WARREN, graphic design company executive, architect; b. Columbus, Ohio, Dec. 9, 1942; s. Warren Vale and Martha Elizabeth (Greene) C.; m. Susan Henrietta Davis, Oct. 1, 1966. BArch, Ohio State U., 1966. Registered architect, N.Y. Draftsman Skidmore Owings & Merrill, Chgo., 1964-66; architect U.S. Peace Corps, Tanzania, 1966-69; designer Brooks Barr Graeber & White, Austin, Tex., 1969-71, Hardy Holzman Pfeiffer, N.Y.C., 1971-73; design dir. Paul Arthur & Assoc., N.Y.C., 1973-74; designer Page, Artibrio & Resen, N.Y.C., 1974-79; ptnr. Greenboam & Casey Assocs., Inc., N.Y.C., 1979-94, The Casey Group, New Canaan, Conn., 1994—; con. Conn. Trust for Hist. Preservation, 1995, U.S. Gen. Svc. Adminstrn., 1996, juror Print Casebook Awards, N.Y.C., 1988, Hotel Sales & Mktg. Assoc., N.Y.C., 1987-90, Soc. Environ. Graphic Design 1997 Design Awards; adj. prof. N.J. Sch. of Architecture, Newark, 1980-82; guest lectr. Harvard U., Boston, 1982, U. Cin., 1990. Pres. Friends of New Canaan Libr., 1998—. Recipient Print Casebook 7 award, 1987. Mem. AIA (hist. resources com. Acad. of Architecture for Health), Soc. Environ. Graphic Design (bd. dirs. 1985-90, 96—, pres. 1988-89), S.W. Pks. and Monuments Assn. (life), Conn. Trust for Hist. Preservation, Dutch Treat Club, Xi Grad. chpt. Phi Gamma Delta (Centennial Celebration com.), Gridiron Club of New Canaan. Democrat. Fax: (203) 966-0250.

CASEY-BEICH, MICHEAL LOUANNA, artist; b. Bloomington, Ill., Oct. 9, 1950; d. David George and Anne Lee (Williamson) Casey; m. Otto Gerkin Beich II, Dec. 24, 1977 (div. Mar. 10, 1991); children: Otto Gerkin III,

Rossie Anne, Oscar Casey. Grad. H.S., Bloomington, 1969. Avocations: cello, gardening, harp. Home Studio: 1107 E Jefferson St Bloomington IL 61701-4144 Office: Authentic ROPpp Art Galleries PO Box 3053 Bloomington IL 61702-3053 *Psalm 144: "Blessed be the Lord my strength which teacheth my hands to war, and my fingers to fight".*

CASH, ALAN SHERWIN, electronics assembly specialist; b. Chgo., Oct. 28, 1938; s. Edward A. and Mildred M. (Miller) C.; m. Carole M. Hoffman, July 31, 1966; children: Susan, Jody. BS in Indsl. Engring., U. Ill., 1961; MBA, Northwestern U., 1969. Registered profl. engr., Calif.; cert. electrostatic discharge engr. and technician. Sr. process engr. Cook Electric Co., Morton Grove, Ill., 1973-75; sr. indsl. engr. Motorola, Carol Stream, Ill., 1975-77; supr. indsl. engring. def. sys. divsn. Northrop Grumman, Rolling Meadows, Ill., 1977-80, mgr. tech. svcs. def. sys. divsn., 1980-84, mgr. advance mfg. tech. def. sys. divsn., 1984-86, mgr. tng. ctr. def. sys. divsn., 1986-95; tech. advisor/tng. specialist, 1995—; category C instr., examiner, ISO 9000 lead assessor Dept. Def., electrostatic discharge site coord., 1995—; engr. Nat. Soldering Std. Working Coms., 1990-93, mem. IPC J-stds. coms.-001, 002, 003, 004, 005, 006, 1990—, mem. IPC Term and Definitions Com. Mem. Nat. Assn. Radio and Telecomm. Engrs. (cert. engr., technician), Inst. Indsl. Engring. (pres. North Suburban Ill. chpt. 1982-83, program chmn. Dist. 8, 1984—, spouses program chmn. 1992 internat. conv., Midwest chpt. ESD assoc. libr. chmn., pres. 1998), Inst. Indsl. Engrs., Assn. Old Crows, U. Ill. Alumni Assn., Northwestern U. Alumni Assn., Northwestern Club Chgo., ESD Assn. (Midwest chpt.). Office: Northrop Grumman ESSS-DSD 600 Hicks Rd Rolling Meadows IL 60008-1098

CASH, DEAN W., military career officer; b. N.J., Dec. 28, 1946; m. Dee Cash; children: Mindy, Caitlin. Grad., Kearney State Coll., 1971; Masters Degree, Va. Poly. Inst., 1979; grad., Command and Gen. Staff Coll., 1986, Indsl. Coll. Armed Forces, 1992. Commd. officer U.S. Army Infantry, 1971, advanced through grades to maj. gen.; airborne inf. platoon leader 1st Bn., 60th Inf. U.S. Army Infantry, Ft. Richardson, Alaska; weapons platoon leader, co. exec. officer Bn. S-1/Bn. S-2 U.S. Army Infantry, Ft. Richardson; co. comdr., S-3 tng. officer 3d Inf. Regiment U.S. Army Infantry, Ft. Myer, Va.; with Spl. Warfare Ctr. U.S. Army Infantry, Ft. Bragg, N.C.; with 82d Airborne Divsn. U.S. Army Infantry, divsn. G-3 plans officer, dep. G-3, exec. officer 1/505th; with U.S. Army Europe (USAREUR) Staff, 1986-89; comdr. 4th Bn., 8th Inf. U.S. Army, Sandhofen, Germany, 1989; infantry sys. team chief Dept. of the Army; comdr. 2d Brigate, 1st Armored Divsn. U.S. Army, Baumholder, Germany, 1993; comdr. ops. group Combat Maneuver Tng. Ctr. U.S. Army, Hohenfels, Germany; asst. divsn. comdr. for maneuver of the 4th Inf. Divsn. U.S. Army, Ft. Hood, Tex., 1996; comdg. gen. Nat. Tng. Ctr. and Ft. Irwin U.S. Army, Calif.; comdr. U.S. Army Alaska U.S. Army, Fort Richardson, Alaska. Decorated Legion of Merit, Bronze Star, Meritorious Svc. medal, Army Commendation medal, S.W. Asia Svc. medal, Armed Forces Expeditionary medal. Office: US Army Alaska 600 Richardson Dr #5000 Fort Richardson AK 99505

CASH, DEANNA GAIL, nursing educator, retired; b. Coatesville, Pa., Nov. 28, 1940. Diploma, Jackson Meml. Hosp., 1961; BS, Fla. State U., 1964; MN, UCLA, 1968; EdD, Nova U., Ft. Lauderdale, Fla., 1983. Staff and relief charge nurse Naples (Fla.) Community Hosp., 1961-62; staff nurse Glendale (Calif.) Community Hosp., 1964-65; instr. Knapp Coll. Nursing, Santa Barbara, Calif., 1965-66; staff nurse, team leader Kaiser Found. Hosp., Bellflower, Calif., 1968-69; prof. nursing El Camino Coll., Torrance, Calif., 1969-96, ret., 1996; coord., instr. Internat. RN Rev. course, L.A., 1974-76; mentor statewide nursing program, Long Beach, Calif., 1981-88; clin. performance in nursing exam. evaluator Western Performance Assessment Ctr., Long Beach, 1981-96. Mem. ANA.

CASH, FRANCIS WINFORD, hotel industry executive; b. Buena Vista, Va., Mar. 16, 1942; s. Winsford McKinley and Elsie E. (Yates) C.; m. Judith R. Robey, Dec. 27, 1962; children: Jeri Cash Colton, Lori Cash Richards, Robin Cash Clark, David, Kristine. B.S. in Acctg, Brigham Young U., Provo, Utah, 1965. C.P.A., D.C. With Arthur Andersen & Co. (C.P.A.s), Washington, 1965-74; v.p., corp. contr. Marriott Corp., Washington, 1974-79; sr. v.p. corp. svcs. Marriott Corp., 1980-84; pres. Marriott Svc. Group, 1985-92; pres., dir. Nova Care, Inc., King of Prussia, Pa., 1992-95; chmn., pres., CEO, dir. Red Roof Inns, Hilliard, Ohio, 1995—; bd. dirs. Schneider Nat. Chmn. Washington area Boy Scouts Am. show, 1978; mem. bd. advisors Sch. Mgmt., Brigham Young U., 1987; mem. Presdl. Commn. on White House fellowships, 1985-89; bd. dirs. Washington Police Boys and Girls Clubs. Recipient Service award Boy Scouts Am., 1978, Beta Alpha Psi Outstanding Alumnus award Brigham Young U., 1984. Mem. LDS Ch. Office: Red Roof Inns Inc 4355 Davidson Rd Hilliard OH 43026-2491*

CASH, JOHNNY, entertainer; b. Kingsland, Ark., Feb. 26, 1932; s. Ray and Carrie (Rivers) C.; m. June Carter, Mar. 1, 1968; 1 child, John Carter; children by previous marriage: Rosanne, Kathleen, Cindy, Tara. H.H.D., Gardner-Webb Coll., 1971, Nat. U., San Diego, 1975; L.H.D. (hon.), Nat. U., San Diego, 1976. Pres. House of Cash, Inc., Song of Cash, Inc.; v.p. Family of Man Music, Inc.; Mem. adv. com. Peace Corps, Country Music Assn., John Edwards Meml. Found. Profl. composer, also, rec. artist; TV performer: the Johnny Cash Show, 1969-71; Author: (autobiography) Man in Black, 1975, (novel) Man in White, 1986; composer documentary rec. The True West; composer movie sound tracks Little Fauss and Big Halsy; recs. The Essential Johnny Cash, 1993; Johnny Cash: American Recordings, 1994; subject of documentary films Johnny Cash, the Man, His World, His Music; actor in movies A Gunfight, North and South, 1985, Stagecoach, 1986, Highwayman, 1990; albums: Water From the Wells of Home, 1988, The Sun Years, 1990, Boom Chicka Boom, 1990, Mystery of Life, 1991, Unchained (Grammy award 1998); TV documentary film Johnny Cash at San Quentin; promotional film United Way of America, 1972; co-writer, producer narrator: film The Gospel Road, 1972, Tennessee Nights, 1989, Return to the Promised Land, 1993, Radio Star - die AFN - Story, 1994. Hon. com. mem. Israel's 25th Anniversary. Served with USAF. Recipient No. 1 Hit Song award for Tennessee Flat Top Box, Country Music Assn., 1988, Golden Boot award, 1990, Grammy Living Legend award, 1993, Contempory Folk Album Grammy American Recordings, 1995; named to Country Music Hall of Fame, 1980, to Songwriter's Hall of Fame, 1984, to Rock-n-Roll Hall of Fame, 1992. Over 53 million albums sold. *

CASH, JUNE CARTER, singer; b. Maces Springs, Va., June 23, 1929; d. Ezra and Maybelle (Addington) Carter; m. John R. Cash; children: Rebecca Carlene, Rozanna Lea, John Carter. Student, Neighborhood Playhouse Sch. Dramatics, 1955-56; HHD (hon.), Nat. U., San Diego, 1977. Propr. June Carter Cash Antiques and Gift Shop, Hendersonville, Tenn. Singer with, Carter Family, 1939-43, with Carter Sisters (and mother), after 1943; performed on, Sta. XERF, Del Rio Tex., Sta. KWTO, Springfield, Mo.; mem. Grand Ole Opry, Sta. WSM, Nashville; TV appearances include John Davidson Show, Tennessee Ernie Show, Johnny Cash Show, others; films include: Thaddeus, Rose and Eddie, Country Music Holiday; TV movies: Stage Coach, Murder Coweta Country, The Baron, The Last Days of Frank and Jessie James, Keep on The Sunny Side, Appalachian Pride, Gospel Road, Country Music Caravan, Road to Nashville, Tennessee Jamboree, Gospel Road; TV spl. The Best of The Carter Family; songs recorded include: Baby It's Cold Outside, Music Music Music, Love Oh Crazy Love, Let Me Go Lover, Leftover Loving; contbr. to album Johnny Cash is Coming to Town, 1987; author: Among My Klediments, 1979, From the Heart, 1986, Mother Maybelle's Cookbook, 1989; co-author: Ring of Fire; appeared in film The Apostle, 1997. Address: House of Cash Inc 700 Johnny Cash Blvd Hendersonville TN 37075-2609*

CASH, (CYNTHIA) LAVERNE, physicist; b. Statesville, N.C., Oct. 7, 1956; d. William J. and Martha Lee (Stroud) C. BS, Appalachian State U., 1979; MS, Clemson U., 1982; AA, Mitchell C.C., 1976; PhD, Johns Hopkins U., 1999. Physicist U.S. Army Material Systems Analysis Activity, Aberdeen Proving Ground, Md., 1984-88; rsch. physicist U.S. Army Edgewood Rsch., Devel. and Engring. Ctr., Aberdeen Proving Ground, 1988—. Contbr. articles to profl. publs. Mem. Oak Grove Bapt. Ch, Bel Air, Md., singer in choir, sound engr., numerous others. Mem. Am. Phys. Soc., Sigma Phi Sigma, Pi Mu Epsilon, Phi Theta Kappa, Gamma Beta Phi. Baptist. Home: 100 Drexel Dr Bel Air MD 21014-2002

CASH, RALPH EUGENE, psychologist; b. Knoxville, June 1, 1947; s. Ralph Leon and Alice Kathryn (Barnewell) C.; m. Dana V. Wallace, June 10, 1972; 1 child, Christopher David. BS, U. Tenn., 1968; MA, NYU, 1974, PhD, 1979. Lic. psychologist, Fla. Psychologist in tng. Bellevue Psychiat. Hosp., N.Y.C., 1972-73; psychology intern Flatlands Community Mental Health Ctr., Bklyn., 1973-74, psychotherapist, 1974-75; cons., sch. psychologist Broward County (Fla.) Pub. Schs., 1976-79, program coord., 1979-80; pvt. practice psychologist Hollywood, Fla., 1980—; adj. prof. Nova U., Ft. Lauderdale, Fla., 1980; bd. dirs. Assn. Drug Abuse Prevention and Treatment, Tamarac, Fla., 1980—. With U.S. Army, 1969-71. Mem. Am. Psychol. Assn., Fla. Assn. Sch. Psychologists (exec. bd. 1980-95, pres.-elect 1995-96, pres. 1996-97), Broward Assn. Sch. Psychologists (founding mem., past pres., v.p.), Nat. Assn. Sch. Psychologists, Phi Beta Kappa, Phi Delta Kappa, Phi Eta Sigma, Phi Mu Alpha. Avocations: singing, guitar, jogging, scuba diving, travel. Office: 2699 Stirling Rd Ste 305B Fort Lauderdale FL 33312-6546

CASH, R(OY) DON, gas and petroleum company executive; b. Shamrock, Tex., June 27, 1942; s. Bill R. and Billie Mae (Lisle) C.; m. Sondra Kay Burleson, Feb. 20, 1966; 1 child, Clay Collin. BS in Indsl. Engring., Tex. Tech U., 1966. Former engr. Amoco Prodn. Co.; v.p. Mountain Fuel Supply, Salt Lake City, 1976-79; pres. Wexpro Co., Salt Lake City, 1979-80; pres., CEO Mountain Fuel Supply Co., Salt Lake City, 1980-84; pres., CEO Questar Corp., Salt Lake City, 1984-85, pres., chmn., CEO, 1985—, also bd. dirs.; bd. dirs. Zions Bancorp., Zions First Nat. Bank, Salt Lake City br. Fed. Res. Bank, Aegis Ins. Svcs., Inc., Energen Corp., Interstate Natural Gas Assn. of Am.; trustee Inst. Gas Technology, Chgo., 1986—; chmn. 1992-94. Trustee Holy Cross Hosp., 1987-90, Salt Lake Organizing Com. of 2002 Olympic Winter Games, 1991—, So. Utah U., 1992-97; bd. dirs. Utah Symphony Orch., Salt Lake City, 1983-86, 93—; Gas Rsch. Inst., 1991-93. Mem. Soc. Petroleum Engrs., Rocky Mountain Oil and Gas Assn. (bd. dirs., pres. 1982-84), Utah Mfrs. Assn. (bd. dirs. 1983-89, chmn. 1986), Pacific Coast Gas Assn. (bd. dirs. 1981-85, 87-97, chmn. 1993-94), Am. Gas Assn. (bd. dirs. 1989-95), Am. Petroleum Inst. (bd. dirs. 1986-91), Nat. Petroleum Coun., Ind. Petroleum Assn. of Am., Salt Lake Area C. of C. (bd. dirs. 1981-84, 89-92, chmn. 1991-92), Alta Club, The Country Club. Avocations: boating, skiing, tennis, fishing, hunting. Office: Questar Corp PO Box 45433 Salt Lake City UT 84145-0433*

CASHATT, CHARLES ALVIN, retired hydro-electric power generation company executive; b. Jamestown, N.C., Nov. 14, 1929; s. Charles Austin and Ethel Buren (Brady) C.; m. Wilma Jean O'Hagan, July 10, 1954; children: Jerry Dale, Nancy Jean. Grad. high sch., Jamestown. Bldg. contractor, Jamestown, 1949-50; 1954-58; powerhouse foreman Tri-Dam Project, Strawberry, Calif., 1958-66; power project mgr. Merced Irrigation Dist., Calif., 1966-92; ret. 1992; mem. U.S. com. large dams, 1988-92. Contbr. articles to ASCE pub. and books. Pres. Merced County Credit Union, 1981-82. Served with USAF, 1950-54. Mem. Am. Legion. Republican. Lodge: Elks, Odd Fellows.

CASHDOLLAR, DICK, protective services official; b. Butler, Pa., May 21, 1946. BS, USCG Acad., 1968; MBA, U. Miami, 1987. Commd. ensign USCG, 1968, advanced through grades to capt., 1990, ret., 1994; exec. dir. Pub. Safety Divsn., City of Mobile, Ala., 1994—. Mem. Internat. Assn. Police Chiefs, Internat. Assn. Fire Chiefs, Rotary. Office: Public Safety Divsn City of Mobile PO Box 1827 City Hall 205 Government St Mobile AL 36602-2613

CASHEN, HENRY CHRISTOPHER, II, lawyer, former government official; b. June 25, 1939; s. Raymond and Catherine C.; m. Leslie Renchard, June 28, 1967 (div. 1982); children: Raymond II, Hayley Holloway, Henry Christopher III; m. Diana Knowles Pryor, June 4, 1988. A.B., Brown U., 1961; grad., U. Mich. Law Sch., 1963. Bar: Mich. 1964, U.S. Supreme Ct. 1969. Mem. firm Dickinson, Wright, McKean & Cudlip, Detroit, 1964-69; dep. counsel to Pres. U.S., Washington, 1969-70, dep. asst. to, 1970-73; mem. firm Dickstein, Shapiro & Morin (and predecessor), Washington, 1973—. Mem. Barristers Soc., D.C. Mich. bar assns., Fed. Nat. Mortgage Assn. (bd. dirs. 1985-91), Country Club of Detroit, The Brook, Met. Club, Chevy Chase Club, Psi Upsilon Phi Delta Phi. Republican. Roman Catholic. Office: 2101 L St NW Washington DC 20037-1526

CASHIN, PATRICIA JEANNE (PAT CASHIN), artist, educator; b. Huntington, N.Y., May 16, 1931; d. Thomas Vincent and Alice Isabel (Feudtner) Gillman; children: Rachel Leigh Gish, Sean Tyler, Zachary Paul. BA in Art, Hofstra U., 1954; MA in Art, Wayne State U., 1965; postgrad., Miami U., Oxford,Ohio, 1969-71. Dept. head, instr. Mich. Luth. Coll., Detroit, 1965-66; interior designer Homestead House, Denver, 1972-77, Howard Lorton Galleries, Denver, 1977-84; art. tchr. St. Martha's Sch., Sarasota, Fla., 1990-99; artist in residence The Common Ground of the Arts, Detroit, 1965-67, Western Coll. for Women, Oxford, Ohio, 1970-72. One woman shows includes Johnson/Peterson Archs., Sarasota, 1995, The Seaside (Fla.) Inst., 1995, Fla. Collectors Gallery, Ft. Lauderdale, 1999; exhbns. include Detroit Artists Market, 1965, Rochester (Mich.) Biennial, 1965, The Common Ground of the Arts, Detroit, 1965, U. Mich., 1967, Cin. Art Mus., 1970, Brena Gallery, Denver, 1972, Spectrum Gallery, San Diego, 1986, San Diego Art Inst., 1986, L.D.L. Gallery, Atlanta, 1987, Wexford Gallery, Hilton Head, S.C., 1988, New Vision Gallery, Atlanta, 1989, Brenau U., Gainesville, Ga., 1989, Artforms Gallery, Sarasota, 1991, Joan Hodgel Gallery, Sarasota, 1991, 92, Veridian Gallery, N.Y.C., 1991, Raleigh Gallery, Dania, Fla., 1992, Clayton Gallery, Tampa, 1993, U.S. Garage, Sarasota, 1993, Ringling Mus. Art, Sarasota, Fla., 1994, 98, Park Ave. Armory, N.Y.C., 1995, The Open Studio Press, Wellesley, Mass., 1998, Sarasota County Arts Coun; represented in permanent collections U. Colo., Boulder, Brenau U., Lankford & Assocs., La Jolla, Calif., Office Environments, Inc., Hilton Head, S.C., Rene Brown & Assocs., Hilton Head, Diatech Diamond Corp., Charleston, S.C., Teco Electric Co., Tampa. Fellow Vt. Studio Colony, Johnson, 1988, The Seaside Inst., 1995; recipient Esther Longyear Murphy award Rochester Biennial, 1967. Avocations: travel, interior design, theater, music. Home: 1146 Patterson Dr Sarasota FL 34234-5854

CASHION, JOE MASON, home health care administrator; b. Lynchburg, Tenn., Jan. 24, 1938; s. Rufus and Mary (Mason) C.; m. Mary Soroka, July 31, 1973; children: Michael David, Steven Andrew. BS, U. Tenn., 1961; MBA, George Washington U., 1963; postgrad., Syracuse U., 1963, Cornell U., 1969. Adminstr. resident East Tenn. Baptist Hosp., Knoxville, 1962-63, asst. adminstr., 1965-66; Peace Corps hosp. adminstr. Dyer Maternity Ctr., Monrovia, Liberia, 1963-65; hosp. adminstr. Arabian Am. Oil Co., Dhahran, Saudi Arabia, 1966-73, Franklin County Hosp. & Nursing Home, Winchester, Tenn., 1973-75; pres. Mid. Tenn. Home Health Svc., Winchester, 1975—; owner Am. Homecare Alliance and United Home Care Network; health care cons. Trans World Airlines, Dubai, Hosp. Corp. Am., Saudi Arabia, Saudi Arabian Ministry of Health, Nat. Pub. Health Service, Liberia; mem. home health care profl. exchange to Republic of China with People-to-People program Spokane, Wash., 1987. Fellow Royal Soc. Health (London); mem. Nat. Assn. Home Care, Am. Coll. Healthcare Execs. (cert. healthcare exec.). Mem. Ch. of Christ. Lodge: Rotary (pres. Winchester 1979-80). Avocations: riding Tenn. walking horses, working on farm. Home and Office: Mid Tenn Home Health Svc PO Box 399 Winchester TN 37398-0399

CASHMAN, EDMUND JOSEPH, JR., investment banker; b. Rockville Center, N.Y., Aug. 31, 1936; s. Edmund Joseph and Mary (Hoare) C.; m. Susan Taylor, Nov. 28, 1964; children: Jeffrey, Robert, Mary Elizabeth. BA, St. Michael's Coll., 1958. Securities analyst Hayden, Stone Inc., N.Y.C., 1961-66; dir. rsch. Mason & Co., Newport News, Va., 1966-70; sr. exec. v.p., dir. Legg Mason Inc., Balt., 1970—; pres., dir. Legg Mason Income Trust and Tax-Exempt Trust, 1988—; bd. dirs. EA Engring. Sci. & Tech., Inc., Hire Quality, Inc. Trustee Boys Latin Sch., 1982-90, St. Michael's Coll., 1983—, Shephard and Enoch Pratt Hosp., 1985-92; bd. dirs. Worldwide Value Fund, Inc., 1986-97, dir. Bartlett Income Trust, 1997—, Tissue Bank Internat., 1992—, Cath. Charities, 1997—. Capt. USMCR, 1958-61. Mem. Nat. Assn. Security Dealers (bd. govs. 1982-84), St. Michael's Coll. Alumni Assn. (pres. 1983)., Center Club, Elhridge Club, Caves Valley Golf Club, Mill Reef Club. Republican. Roman Catholic. Home: 1717A Circle Rd Baltimore MD 21204-6443 Office: Legg Mason Wood Walker Inc 100 Light St Ste B2 Baltimore MD 21202-1099

CASHMAN, MICHAEL RICHARD, small business owner; b. Owatonna, Minn., Sept. 26, 1926; s. Michael Richard and Mary (Quinn) C.; m. Antje Katrin Paulus, Jan. 22, 1972 (div. 1983); children: Janice Katrin, Joshua Paulus, Nina Carolin. BS, U.S. Mcht. Marine Acad., 1947; BA, U. Minn., 1951; MBA, Harvard U., 1953. Regional mgr. Air Products & Chems., Inc., Allentown, Pa., 1959-64; then pres. so. div. Air Products & Chems., Inc., Washington, 1964-68; mng. dir. Air Products & Chems., Inc. Europe, Brussels, 1968-72; internat. v.p. Airco Indsl. Gasses, Brussels, 1972-79; pres. Continental Elevator Co., Denver, 1979-81; assoc. Moore & Co., Denver, 1981-84; prin. Cashman & Co., Denver, 1984—. Committeeman Denver Rep. Com., 1986—, congl. candidate, 1988; chmn. "Two Forks or Dust" Ad Hoc Citizens Com.. Lt. (j.g.) USN, 1953-55. Mem. Bldg. Owners and Mgrs. Assn., Colo. Harvard Bus. Sch. Club, Am. Rights Union, Royal Golf de Belgique, Belgian Shooting Club, Rotary, Soc. St. George, Phi Beta Kappa. Avocations: skiing, golf, sailing, guitar, opera. Home: 2512 S University Blvd Apt 802 Denver CO 80210-6152

CASHMAN, SUZANNE BOYER, health services administrator, educator; b. Phila., Apr. 14, 1947; d. Vincent Saul and Ethel (Wolf) Boyer; m. Daniel Cashman, Jan. 16, 1971; children: Adam, Rebecca, David. BA, Tufts U., 1969; MS, Cornell U., 1973; ScD, Harvard U., 1980. Sr. analyst Urban Sys. Rsch., Cambridge, Mass., 1979-82; cons. Mass. Dept. Pub. Health, Boston, 1982-83; spl. asst. to v.p. Brigham and Women's Hosp., Boston, 1983-85; assoc. dir. rsch. Boston U. Office Spl. Projects, 1985-89; asst. prof. Boston U. Sch. Pub. Health, 1985-96; evaluator Cmty. Oriented Primary Care, Boston, 1989-91; assoc. dir. Ctr. for Cmty. Responsive Care, Boston, 1991-97; pub. health cons. U. Mass. Med. Ctr., Worcester, 1998; assoc. prof. dept. family medicine, cmty. health Med. Sch. U. Mass., Worcester, 1999—; cons. Acad. Health Ctrs., Derby, Conn., Columbia, S.C., Atlanta and Balt., 1995-97. Co-editor: Community Oriented Primary Care, 1998; contbr. articles to profl. jours. Mem. leadership tng. program, chair alumni orgn. com. NCCJ, Boston, 1995—; co-chair H.S. METCO Program, Newton, Mass., 1995—. Mem. APHA, Assn. Tchrs. Preventive Medicine (conf. planner). Avocations: ballet dancing, sewing, cooking, jogging, gardening. Home: 17 Calvin Rd Newtonville MA 02460-2104 Office: U Mass Med Ctr Dept Family Medicine 55 Lake Ave N Worcester MA 01655-0008

CASIANO VARGAS, ULISES AURELIO, bishop; b. Lajas, P.R., Sept. 25, 1933. Ordained priest Roman Cath. Ch., 1967. Elected to bishop, 1976 bishop of Mayaguez, P.R., 1976—. Address: Diocese of Mayaguez PO Box 2272 Mayaguez PR 00681*

CASIDA, JOHN EDWARD, entomology educator; b. Phoenix, Dec. 22, 1929; s. Lester Earl and Ruth (Barnes) C.; m. Katherine Faustine Monson, June 16, 1956; children: Mark Earl, Eric Gerhard. B.S., U. Wis., 1951, M.S., 1952, Ph.D., 1954; D (hon.), U. Buenos Aires, 1997. Research asst. U. Wis., 1951-53, mem. faculty, 1954-63, prof. entomology, 1959-63; prof. entomology U. Calif.-Berkeley, 1964—; scholar-in-residence Bellagio Study and Conf. Center, Rockefeller Found., Lake Como, Italy, 1978; Messenger lectr. Cornell U., 1985; Sterling B. Hendricks lectr. USDA and Am. Chem. Soc., 1992—; dir. Environ. Chemistry and Toxicology Lab., 1964—; William Muriece Hoskins chair in chem. and molecular entomology U. Calif., Berkeley, 1996—; faculty rsch. lectr. U. Calif., Berkeley, 1998; lectr. in sci. Third World Acad. Scis., U. Buenos Aires, 1997. Author research publs. Served with USAF, 1953. Recipient medal 7th Internat. Congress Plant Protection, Paris, 1970, Disting. Svc. award USDA, 1988, Wolf prize in agr., 1993; Haight traveling fellow, 1958-59, Guggenheim fellow, 1970-71, Founder's award Soc. Environ. Toxicology and Chemistry, 1994, Kôrô-sho prize Pesticide Sci. Soc. Japan, 1995; Jeffery lectr. U. NSW, Australia, 1983. Mem. NAS, Royal Soc. U.K. (fgn.), Am. Chem. Soc. (Internat. award rsch. pesticide chemistry 1970, Spencer award in agrl. and food chemistry 1978), Entomol. Soc. Am. (Bussart Meml. award 1989, fellow 1989), Soc. Environ. Toxicology and Chemistry (Founder's award 1994), Soc. Toxicology (hon.). Home: 1570 La Vereda Rd Berkeley CA 94708-2036

CASIMIR, KENNETH CHARLES, adolescent forensic psychiatrist, educator; b. Irvington, N.J., July 5, 1961; s. Casey and Sophie (Piorkowski) Mroczkowski; m. Leeann Tate, Feb. 7, 1998. BS in Biology, BA in Psychology, Georgetown U., 1983; MD, Tex. Tech. U., 1989. Diplomate Am. Bd. Psychiatry. Intern N.Y. Med. Coll., Valhalla, 1989-90; resident in psychiat. St. Vincent's Hosp., N.Y.C., 1990-93; fellow in child and adolescent psychiatry Brown U., Providence, 1993-95; chief psychiatry adolescent forensic program Vernon (Tex.) State Hosp., 1995—; clin. asst. prof. psychiatry Health Scis. Ctr. Sch. Medicine, Tex. Tech U., Lubbock, 1996—; cons. to med. adv. com. Times Record News, Wichita Falls, Tex., 1997—. Mem. Am. Psychiat. Assn., Am. Acad. Child and Adolescent Psychiatry, Am. Acad. Psychiatry and Law, Tex. Soc. Psychiat. Physicians, Christian Med. Dental Soc. (psychiatry sect.), Rotary, Vernon, Tex., Psi Chi. Avocations: keyboards, basketball, travel, cinema. Fax: 940-553-2509. E-mail: kenneth.casimir@mhmr.state.tx.us. Office: Vernon State Hosp Adolescent Forensic Program PO Box 2231 Vernon TX 76385-2231

CASKEY, CHARLES THOMAS, biology and genetics educator; b. Lancaster, S.C., Sept. 22, 1938; m. Peggy Ann Pearce, 1960; children: Clifton, Caroline. Student, U. S.C., 1956-58; MD, Duke U., 1963; DSc (hon.), U. S.C., 1993. Diplomate Am. Bd. Internal Medicine. Intern, resident dept. medicine Duke Med. Sch., 1963-65; rsch. assoc. Nat. Heart & Lung Inst., Bethesda, Md., 1965-67, head sect. med. genetics, 1970-71; sr. investigator Lab. Biomed. Genetics NIH, Bethesda, 1967-70; chief sect. med. genetics, prof. medicine, prof. biochemistry Baylor Coll. Medicine, Houston, 1971—, investigator Howard Hughes Med. Inst., 1976—, dir. Robert J. Kleberg, Jr. Ctr. for Human Genetics, 1980-94, dir. med. scientist tng. program, 1982-93, prof. cell biology, 1982-94, dir. and prof. molecular genetics Inst. Molecular Genetics, 1985-92, prof. molecular genetics Inst. Molecular Genetics, 1985-94, Henry and Emma Meyer chmn. molecular genetics, 1987-94, dir. Human Genome Ctr., 1991-94, chmn. dept. molecular and human genetics, 1994-95; sr. v.p. rsch. Merck Rsch. Labs., 1995—; adj. prof. Baylor Coll. Medicine, Houston, 1995—; Josiah Macy, Jr. faculty scholar Med. Rsch. Coun. Cambridge (Eng.) U., 1979-80; dir. NATO ASI on Somatic Cell Genetics, 1980-81, NATO/EMBO/FEBS Spetsai European Molecular Biology Course, 1983, 87; Bernard Sachs lectr. Child Neurology Soc., 1993; Roy E. Moon disting. lectr. sci. Angelo State U., 1994; Samuel Rudin disting. vis. prof. Columbia U., N.Y.C., 1994; mem. biochem. test com. Nat. Bd. Med. Examiners, 1977-81, chmn. biochem. test com., 1981-84, mem. coord. com. for FLEX, 1984-86, mem.-at-large, 1984-88; chmn. sci. adv. bd. Xytronyx Inc., 1984-90; acad. assoc. Nichols Inst., 1987-92; liason mem. program adv. com. on human genome NIH, 1989-92; chair adv. panel forensic uses DNA tests U.S. Congress Office Tech. Assessment, 1989-90; mem. mapping the human genome adv. com. U.S. Dept. Energy, 1986-89; mem. adv. panel mapping the human genome U.S. Congress Office Tech. Assessment, 1987-88; mem. human genome coord. com. Dept. Energy, 1989-94; trustee, pres. Merck Genome Rsch. Inst., Inc., 1996—. Author: Somatic Cell Genetics, 1982; author: (with others) Prebiotic and Biochemical Evolution, 1971, Frontiers of Biology: The Mechanism of Protein Synthesis and Its Regulation, 1972, The Enzymes, 1974, The Kidney in Systemic Disease, 1976, Protein Synthesis, 1976, Molecular Mechanisms of Protein Biosynthesis, 1977, Tay-Sachs Disease Screening and Prevention, 1977, Nonsense Mutations and tRNA Suppressors, 1979, Strauss and Welt Diseases of the Kidney, 3d edit., 1979, Gene Amplification, 1982, Internal Medicine, 1983, Advances in Gene Technology: Human Genetic Disorders, 1984, After Barney Clark: Reflections on the Utah Artificial Heart Program, 1984, Pediatric Neurology, 1986, Clinical Endocrinology, 1986, Gene Transfer, 1986, Molecular Biology of Homo Sapiens, 1986, Medical and Experimental Mammalian Genetics: A Perspective, 1987, Human Genetics, 1987, Molecular Neurobiology in Neurology and Psychiatry, 1987, Current Neurology, vol. 9, 1988, Textbook of Internal Medicine, 1988, Nucleic Acid Probes in Diagnosis of Human Genetic Diseases, 1988, Molecular Genetics of Brain, Nerve, and Muscle, 1989, Molecular Genetics of Diseases of Brain, Nerve, and Muscle, 1989, The Metabolic Basis of Inherited Disease, 6th edit., 1989, PCR Technology: Principles and Applications of DNA Amplification, 1989, The Polymerase Chain Reaction, 1989, PCR Protocols: A Guide to Methods and Applications, 1989, Genetic Engineering, Principles and Methods, vol. 11, 1989, The Science and Practice of Pediatric Cardiology, vol. 1, 1990, Ribosomes and Protein Synthesis: A Practical Approach, 1990, Etiology of Human Disease at the DNA Level, 1991, PCR: A Practical Approach, 1991, Neurodegenerative Disorders: Mechanisms and Prospects for Therapy, 1991, Reproductive Risks and Prenatal Diagnosis, 1991, Antisense RNA and DNA, 1991, Biomonitoring and Carcinogen Risk Assessment, 1991, Legal and Ethical Issues Raised by the Human Genome Project, 1991, Advances in Forensic Haemogenetics, 1992, Gene Mapping - Using Law and Ethics as Guides, 1992, The Code of Codes, 1992, Antisense Strategies, 1992, Molecular Basis of Neurology, 1993, Genetic Engineering, Principles and Methods, 1993, Genetics and Society, 1993, numerous other chpts. to books; mem. editorial bd. Archives Biochemistry and Biophysics, 1975-78, Jour. Biol. Chemistry, 1978-83, Annals Intenal Medicine, 1980-83, Molecular Biology and Medicine, 1982-90, Somatic Cell and Molecular Genetics, 1983-94, Trends in Genetics, 1985-90, Genomics, 1987-90, Molecular and Cell Biology, 1988-90, Human Gene Therapy, 1990—, Jour. AMA, 1991-94, Genetic Epidemiology, 1992-94, Human Mutation, 1992—, Circulation, 1993—; mem. bd. reviewing editors Sci., 1991—. Mem. Human Genome Orgn., 1988—, pres., 1993—; mem. task force on genetics Muscular Dystrophy Assn., 1989-94. With USPHS, 1965-67. Recipient Borden Rsch. award, Disting. Alumnus award Duke U. Med. Sch., 1991, Wadsworth award N.Y. State Dept. Health, 1992, Svc. Merchandise Leadership award Muscular Dystrophy Assn., 1992, Basic Biomed. Rsch. prize Giovanni Lorenzini Med. Found., 1993, Lucy Wortham James Basic Rsch. award Soc. Surg. Oncology, 1994, Norberto Montalbetti Milan award, 1994, The Coriell medal Coriell Inst., 1995, 5th Milano award in memory of Norberto Montalbetti, 1995. Fellow AMA (founding), AAAS (sci. innovation program com. 1991-93), Am. Coll. Physicians, Am. Acad. Microbiology, Royal Soc. Medicine Found.; mem. Nat. Acad. Scis., Am. Fedn. Clin. Rsch., Am. Soc. Biochemistry and Molecular Biology, Am. Soc. Clin. Investigation, Am. Soc. Human Genetics, Am. Soc. Cell Biology, Am. Coll. Med. Genetics, Assn. Am. Physicians, Fedn. Am. Socs. for Exptl. Biology, N.Y. Acad. Scis., So. Soc. Clin. Investigation, Soc. Inherited Metabolic Disorders, Inst. Medicine Nat. Acad. Scis., Royal Soc. Medicine, Baylor Med. Alumni Assn. (disting. faculty mem. 1993), Alpha Omega Alpha. Home: 6402 Belmont St Houston TX 77005-3802 Office: Merck Rsch Labs Sumneytown Pike PO Box WP26-207 West Point PA 19486*

CASKEY, JUDITH ANN, educational director; b. San Antonio, Dec. 3, 1947; m. Robert D. Caskey, Jan. 1, 1977; 1 child, Kyle. BA, Baylor U., 1969, MS, 1970; postgrad., Tex. A&M U., 1971-76. Cert. supr., counselor, secondary edn., secondary English, history and Latin, Tex. Tchr. North Jr. H.S. Waco (Tex.) Ind. Sch. Dist., 1968-71; tchg. asst. Tex. A&M U., College Station, 1971-72; tchr. A&M Consol. Jr. H.S. A&M Consol. (Tex.) Ind. Sch. Dist., College Station, 1972-75; secondary curriculum coord. College Sta. Ind. Sch. Dist. 2, 1975-79; tchr. A&M Consol. (Tex.) Ind. Sch. Dist., College Station, 1979-81; tchr. Bellville Jr. H.S. Bellville (Tex.) Ind. Sch. Dist., 1981-82; tchr. Johnson City H.S. Johnson City (Tex.) Ind. Sch. Dist., 1982-90; tchr. Daingerfield H.S. Daingerfield (Tex.) Ind. Sch. Dist., 1990-94; field svc. region VIII Edn. Svc. Ctr., Mt. Pleasant, Tex., 1994-96, dir. instrn. region VIII, 1996—; ednl. cons., trainer Region XII Edn. Svc. Ctr., Waco, 1969-73, Region VI Edn. Svc. Ctr., Huntsville, Tex., 1974-79; nat. trainer Talents Unltd., Mobile, Ala., 1976-81. Facilitator Literacy Coun., Daingerfield and Mt. Pleasant, 1994-97; advisor Girl Scouts USA, College Station, 1973-80; crafts facilitator Blanco County Fair Assn., Johnson City, Tex., 1982-88. Mem. ASCD, Tex. Assn. Supervision and Curriculum Devel., Nat. Coun. Tchrs. English, Tex. Coun. Tchrs. English, Delta Kappa Gamma (pres. Nu chpt. 1985-88, Achievement award 1988; pres. Alpha Upsilon chpt. 1992-94). Avocations: reading, cooking, walking, researching, traveling, shopping. Office: Region VIII Edn Svc Ctr PO Box 1894 Mount Pleasant TX 75456-1894

CASLER, JANICE LOREEN, marketing professional, public relations executive; b. Charlottetown, Can., Nov. 28, 1958; d. Ivan Jack and Mildred June (Sherren) Newrick; m. Frederick C. Casler Sr., Nov. 26, 1983; 1 child, Frederick Jr. BA, Rollins Coll., 1989; postgrad., Holland Coll., Can., 1976-78. Dir. Osceola County Retired & Sr. Vol. Program, Kissimmee, Fla., 1985-87, 97-98; coord. vols. Orange County Retired & Sr. Vols. Program, Orlando, Fla., 1991-97; dir. mktg., pub. rels. Osceola County Coun. Aging, Kissimmee, 1998—. Recipient Disting. Svc. award Fla. Dept. Cmty. Affairs, 1998. Mem. Rotary, Greater Osceola/St. Cloud C. of C., Kissimmee/Greater Osceola County C. of C. Mem. LDS Ch. Avocations: reading, art, painting, crafts, Cub Scouts, biking. Home: 1899 Mathis Rd PO Box 701727 Saint Cloud FL 34770-1727 Office: Osceola County Coun Aging 1099 Shady Ln Kissimmee FL 34744-4973

CASNER, TRUMAN SNELL, lawyer; b. Balt., Oct. 9, 1933; s. A. James and Margaret (Snell) C.; m. Elizabeth Lyons, June 12, 1954 (dec. Aug. 1997); children—Richard Dana, Elizabeth Anne, Abigail Lee. BA cum laude, Princeton U., 1955; LLB cum laude, Harvard U., 1958. Bar: Mass. 1958. Law clk. to Chief Justice Raymond Wilkins, Mass. Supreme Judicial Ct., 1958-59; assoc. firm Ropes & Gray, Boston, 1959-68; partner Ropes & Gray, 1968—, mng. ptnr., 1994—; bd. dirs. State St. Corp., State St. Bank and Trust Co., Mass. Bus. Roundtable. Mem. Belmont Town Meeting, 1971-95; trustee, mem. exec. com. Belmont Hill Sch., 1966-94, pres. 1985-89, chmn. 1989—; sec., trustee, mem. exec. com. Pine Manor Coll., 1973-79; trustee Boston Mus. Sci., 1981-93, 94—, overseer, 1981—; mem. corp. Woods Hole Oceanographic Instn. Mem. ABA, Am. Law Inst., New Bedford Yacht Club, Comml. Club of Boston, Kittansett Club, Cruising Club of Am. Episcopalian. Home: 20 Rowes Wharf Apt 510 Boston MA 02110-3378 Office: Ropes & Gray One International Pl Boston MA 02110

CASO, ADOLPH, publishing company executive; b. Mirabella, Avellino, Italy, Jan. 7, 1934; came to U.S., 1947; s. Raffaele and Prisca (DeLuca) C.; divorced; children: Richard Anthony, Robert Ralph, Liana Cristina. BA, Northeastern U., 1957; AM, Harvard U., 1965. Dir. bilingual edn. Waltham (Mass.) Pub. Schs., 1964-83; pres., editor Branden Pub. Co. Inc., Boston, 1983—; teaching fellow Harvard U., Cambridge, Mass., 1964. Author: The Straw Obelisk, 1973, Lives of Italian Americans, 1976, Water and Life, 1979, America's Italian Founding Fathers, 1984, Bilingual Two Language Battery of Tests, 1985, Mass Media vs. The Italian Americans, 1986, Issues in Foreign Language and Bilingual Education, 1987, Pages and Windows, 1991, (with Joseph Kinney) Young Rocky--The Life of Rocky Castellani, 1983; co-author: Tuskegee Airmen; contbg. editor: Dante in the 20th Century, 1985; editor: On Crimes and Punishments (Cesare Beccaria), 1985, Romeo and Juliet—Original Text, 1992, Straw Obelisk, 2d edit., 1995, We, The People, 1995, others. Pres. PTA, Newton, Mass., 1965, Waltham Overseas Studies, 1966-69; founder, pres. Dante U. Found., Boston, 1976—. With Signal Corps, U.S. Army, 1957-62; col. U.S. Army Res., 1963-87. Decorated cavaliere Republic of Italy; Fulbright scholar, 1966. Mem. Sons of Italy (commr.). Roman Catholic. Avocations: music, art, swimming, walking, Italian cuisine. Office: Branden Pub Co Inc 17 Station St # 843 Brookline MA 02445-7371

CASO, PHILIP MICHAEL, financial services company executive, educator; b. N.Y.C., June 19, 1958; m. Suzanne Marie Marcil, Nov. 30, 1987. BS, NYU, 1981. Lic. Nat. Assn. Securities Dealers (series 7, 63, 4, 24, 8); lic. Dept. Ins., Life, Health and Annuity, Fla. Gen. mgr. Hallmark & Holland, Inc., N.Y.C., 1980-81; officer ops. mgr. Citicorp Capital Markets Group, N.Y.C., 1981-83; v.p. investments, registered rep. various fin. firms, 1983-86; v.p., br. mgr. Rosenkrantz, Lyon & Ross, Inc. and predecessor cos., Chgo., 1986-89; resident mgr., fin. cons. Pierce, Fenner & Smith, Inc., Pompano Beach, Miami Beach, Fla., 1989-91; resident mgr. Merrill Lynch, Miami Beach, 1991-96; v.p. Merrill Lynch Pvt. Client Group, Miami Beach, 1997—; instr. Broward Community Coll., CUNY, others, 1981-89; fin. expert, lectr. Celebrity Cruises, Miami, Fla., 1990—. Bd. curriculum advisors Broward C.C., Coconut Creek, Fla., 1990-91; founding mem. Fla. Grand Opera Leadership Coun., 1993—, Miami Beach Com. of One Hundred; appointee City of Hollywood (Fla.) Sister Cities Adv. Bd.; vice-chmn. budget adv. bd. City of Hollywood, Fla., 1998. Mem. Sales and Mktg. Execs. Internat. (past pres., So. Fla. chpt.), Fla. Bar Com., Miami Beach C. of C., Sommellier Guild, Beacon Coun.

CASON, JUNE MACNABB, musician, educator, arts administrator; b. Phila., June 21, 1930; d. Vernon C. and Eleanor (Scarlet) Macnabb; m. Roger Lee Cason, June 12, 1952; children: David Alan, Diane Louise, Nancy Lynn. Student, Eastman Sch. Music, Rochester, N.Y., 1948-52; grad., U. Houston, 1965-69; postgrad. in bus., U. Pa., 1984. Dir. youth chorus St. John's Episcopal Ch., Charleston, W.Va., 1956-63; soloist ch. and music groups, Charleston, 1957-63; founder, dir. music summer camp Episcopal Diocese W.Va., 1961-62; soloist Christ Ch. Cathedral, Houston, 1963-71, Gilbert and Sullivan Soc., Houston, 1970; pvt. tchr. voice, Houston, 1965-71, Wilmington, Del., 1971-92; tchr. voice San Jacinto Coll., Pasadena, Tex., 1969-71; founder, gen. mgr., soloist Minikin Opera Co., Wilmington, 1972-87; mem. faculty Wilmington Music Sch., 1973-77; mem. Del. Pro Musica, Wilmington, 1973-77, chmn., 1975-77; dir. music Immanuel Episcopal Ch., Wilmington, 1973-75; instr. music Albert Einstein Acad., Wilmington, 1975-76; v.p. Resource Ctr. for Performing Arts, 1982-86; chmn. Music Consortium New Castle County, 1982-84; devel. dir. Opera Delaware, 1988-92; trainer, cons. Nonprofit Mgmt. Devel. Ctr., La Salle U., 1989—; dir. devel. arts and humanities U. Del., 1992-99, MacIntyre Assocs., 1998—. Contbr. articles to profl. jours. Recipient Theta Eta award U. Rochester, 1952. Mem. Nat. Soc. Fundraising Execs., Coun. Advancement and Support of Edn., Met. Opera Guild, Sigma Alpha Iota (Sword of Honor 1971). Republican. Home: 1125 Grinnell Rd Wilmington DE 19803-5125 Office: Univ Del Devel Office Academy Bldg Newark DE 19716

CASON, MARILYNN JEAN, technological institute official, lawyer; b. Denver, May 18, 1943; d. Eugene Martin and Evelyn Lucille (Clark) C.; married. BA in Polit. Sci., Stanford U., 1965; JD, U. Mich., 1969; MBA, Roosevelt U., 1977. Bar: Colo. 1969, Ill. 1973. Assoc. Dawson, Nagel, Sherman & Howard, Denver, 1969-73; atty. Kraft, Inc., Glenview, Ill., 1973-75; corp. counsel Johnson Products Co., Inc., Chgo., 1975-86, v.p., 1977-86; mng. dir. Johnson Products Co., Inc., Lagos, Nigeria, 1980-83; v.p. internat. Johnson Products Co., Inc., Chgo., 1986-88; v.p., gen. counsel DeVry, Inc., Chgo., 1989-96; sr. v.p. adminstrn. gen. counsel, 1996—. Bd. dirs. Ill. chpt. Arthritis Found., Chgo., 1979—, chmn., 1991-93, trustee, Atlanta, 1993-96; bd. dirs. Internat. House, Chgo., 1986-92; bd. dirs. Ill. Humanities Coun., Chgo., 1987-96, chmn., 1993-96. Mem. ABA, Nat. Bar Assn., Cook County Bar Assn. (pres. community law project 1986-88). Club: Stanford (Chgo.) (pres. 1985-87). Home: 3108 Colfax St Evanston IL 60201-1842 Office: DeVry Inc 1 Tower Ln Ste 1000 Oakbrook Terrace IL 60181

CASON, NICA VIRGINIA, nursing educator; b. Edna, Tex.; 1 child, Cynthia Diane. Diploma, Lillie Jolly Sch. Nursing, 1965; BSN, U. Tex. Med. Br., Galveston, 1967; MSN, U. So. Miss., 1981. RN, Miss. Pub. health nurse Miss. State Dept. Health, Pascagoula, 1978; nursing instr. Miss. Gulf Coast Community Coll.-Jackson County Campus, Gautier, 1981-84, chair ADN program, 1984—. Col. USAFR, ret. Mem. NOADN, Nat. League Nursing, Sigma Theta Tau, Phi Kappa Phi.

CASON, ROGER LEE, retired chemical company executive, educator, consultant; b. Madison, Wis., Aug. 13, 1930; s. Hulsey and Eloise (Boeker) C.; m. June Ely Macnabb, June 12, 1952; children: David Allan, Diane Louise, Nancy Lynn. BS in Mech. Engring. with high distinction, U. Rochester, 1951, MS, 1952; MBA, U. Del., 1977. MA in Liberal Studies, U. Del., 1998. Registered profl. engr., Del. With E.I. DuPont de Nemours & Co., various locations, 1955-92, sr. mech. engr., prodn. supr., mech. supr., Houston, 1963-70, staff bus. analyst, Wilmington, Del., 1971-75, bus. analysis mgr., 1975-83, prin. cons., 1983-92; cons. to for profit, non-profit orgns., 1993—. Contbr. articles to profl. publs. Served with C.E.C., USN, 1952-55. Mem. Fla. Mgmt. Assn. (instl. dir. 1987-89), Wilmington Power Squadron (instr. courses 1977-80, 83-89, sec. 1985-86, exec. officer 1987-88, comdr. 1988-89, 95-96), Nat. Model R.R. Assn., Beta Gamma Sigma, Phi Beta Kappa, Sigma Xi (asso. mem.), Tau Beta Pi. Republican. Episcopalian. Home and Office: 1125 Grinnell Rd Wilmington DE 19803-5125

CASONI, RICHARD ALBERT, marine technologist, educator; b. Brockton, Mass., Nov. 1, 1940; Recipient Outstanding Avisor award Vocat. Indsl. Clubs of Am.; s. Aleramo and Jennie (Baldini) C.; m. Lourdeen Sheridan, Oct. 6, 1979; children: Richard, Elizabeth, Mario, Mauricio, Alexander. Student, Calvin Coolidge Coll., Boston, 1962, U. Mass., Boston, 1982, U. South Fla., 1992—, Manatee C.C., Bradenton, Fla., 1997—. Sr. tech. New Eng. Med. Ctr., Boston, 1963-67; field engr. Atlantic Rsch. Corp., Halifax, Mass., 1967-74; first officer U.S. Merchant Marine, Galveston, Tex., 1974-79; quality control insp. Cape Dory Yachts, East Taunton, Mass., 1979-82; gen. mgr. Parker Dawson Corp., Hingham, Mass., 1982-83; dept. head, instr. marine tech. South Shore Vocat. Tech. H.S., Hanover, Mass., 1983-89; instr. marine tech. Manatee Tech. Inst., Bradenton, Fla., 1989—; master instr. USCG Aux. Advisor Vocat. Indsl. Clubs of Am.; mem. Manatee County Job Shadow Program; asst. scoutmaster Troop 102, Boy Scouts Am.; resident mus. overseer/curator 1726 hist. farm Soc. for Preservation of New Eng. Antiquities; marine expert tech. edn. curriculum com. State of Fla., 1994-95. With U.S. Army, 1958-61. Mem. Am. Boat and Yacht Coun., Am. Soc. Naval Engrs., Soc. of Naval Architects and Marine Engrs. Avocations: reading, travel, boating, antiques.

CASPAR, DONALD LOUIS DVORAK, biophysics and structural biology educator; b. Ithaca, N.Y., Jan. 8, 1927; s. Caspar V. and Blanche (Dvorak) C.; m. Gwladys Williams, Dec. 20, 1962; children: Emma, David. BA in Physics, Cornell U., 1950; PhD in Biophysics, Yale U., 1955. Postdoctoral fellow Calif. Inst. Tech., 1954-55, MRC Lab. Molecular Biology, Cambridge, Eng., 1955-56; instr. biophysics Yale U., New Haven, 1956-58, asst. prof., 1958-59; rsch. assoc. Harvard U., Cambridge, Mass., 1962-63; lectr. Harvard Med. Sch., Boston, 1963-73; rsch. assoc. in pathology Children's Hosp. Med. Ctr., Boston, 1959-73; prof. of physics, rsch. prof. of structural biology Rosenstiel Basic Med. Scis. Rsch. Ctr., Brandeis U., Waltham, Mass., 1972-94, acting dir., 1987-88; prof. biol. scis. Inst. Molecular Biophysics Fla. State U., 1994—; mem. biophysics and biophys. chem. study sect. NIH, 1969-73; guest rsch. assoc. in biology Brookhaven Nat. Lab., 1973—, chmn. biology dept. vis. com., 1974-77, mem., 1996—; mem. nat. laser users facility steering com. Lab. for Laser Energetics, U. Rochester, N.Y., 1981-84; mem. sci. adv. com. European Molecular Biology Lab., Heidelberg, Germany, 1976-81; mem. neutron users adv. com., biology dept. Brookhaven Nat. Lab., 1980-81, 91—, mem. adv. com. scanning transmission electron microscope facility, 1985-86, mem. program adv. com. high flux beam reactor, physics dept., 1992—, Haworth disting. scientist, 1994-96; mem. sci. adv. com., structural biology ctr. Argonne Nat. Lab., 1989-94; adv. bd. Nat. Ctr. for Macromolecular Imaging, Baylor Coll. Medicine, 1995—; mem. editl. com. Ann. Revs. Biohysics and Bioengring., 1970-73; vis. prof. Inst. Molecular Biophysics, Fla. State U., 1994; rsch. fellow Japan Soc. for Promotion of Sci., Inst. Molecular Biology, Nagoya U., 1984. Contbr. articles, rsch. papers to profl. pubs. Grantee NIH, 1969-88, NSF, 1983-86, Guggenheim fellowship, 1994; recipient Outstanding Investigator award Nat. Cancer Inst., 1988—. Fellow Am. Acad. Arts and Scis.; mem. NAS, Biophys. Soc. (pres. 1991-92, nat. lectr. 1985), Am. Crystallographic Assn. (Fankuchen award 1992). Achievements include research in structural biology of viruses, membranes and protein interactions. Home: 911 Gardenia Dr Tallahassee FL 32312-3001 Office: Fla State U Inst Molecular Biophysics Tallahassee FL 32306-4380*

CASPARIS, ALEXANDER LAMAR, accountant; b. Odessa, Tex., May 21, 1956; s. Alexander Lamar and Marjorie Nell (Cain) C.; m. Tami Jo. Whitmire, Apr. 4, 1989 (div. Oct. 1993); children: Casi, Sandra; m. Cynthia Ann Parris, Sept. 15, 1994; children: Casi, Paul, Sandra, Adam, Caleb. BBA in Econs., Baylor U., 1978; MBA in Mgmt., U. Tex., 1995; postgrad., Nova Southeastern U., 1998—. CPA, Tex.; diplomate Am. Bd. Forensic Acctg. Asst. controller Abbott Bldg. Co., Odessa, Tex., 1979-82, Gibson's Distbg., Odessa, Tex., 1982-83; developer Paul Rochester Investments, Odessa, Tex., 1983-84; asst. controller Ingersol-Rand, Midland, Tex., 1984-86; acct. pvt. practice, Odessa, 1984-98; controller, MIS dir. Bus. Investment & Devel. Corp., Odessa, 1988-98; acct. Elms, Fairs & Co., Odessa, 1998—. Fundraiser YMCA, Odessa, 1978; city councilman City of Odessa, 1993-95; chmn. Leadership Odessa, 1991-92, Jr. Leadership Odessa, 1990-91; instr. Jr. Achievement, Odessa, 1994-95. Mem. Omnicron Delta Epsilon. Office: Elms Faris & Co 700 N Grant Ave Ste 800 Odessa TX 79761-4556

CASPER, BARRY MICHAEL, physics educator; b. Knoxville, Tenn., Jan. 21, 1939; s. Barry and Florence (Becker) C.; m. Nancy Carolyn Peterson, Aug. 25, 1979; children: Daniel Casper, Benjamin Casper, Michael Casper, Aaron Syverson, Jay Syverson, Kaarin Madigan. B.A., Swarthmore Coll., 1960; Ph.D. in Physics, Cornell U., 1966. From asst. prof. to prof. physics Carleton Coll., Northfield, Minn., 1966—, dir. tech. policy project, 1981—; rsch. fellow Stanford U., Calif., 1973-74, Harvard U., Cambridge, Mass., 1975-76, U. Minn., Mpls., 1976-77, MIT, 1980-81, U. Calif., San Diego, 1992-93; policy advisor to U.S. Sen. Paul Wellstone, 1991. Co-author: Revolutions in Physics, 1972, Powerline: First Battle of America's Energy War, 1981. Dir. Nuclear War Graphics Project, Northfield, 1981-89, Minn. Nuclear Weapons Freeze Campaign, 1983-84. Recipient Pub. Citizen award Minn. Pub. Interest Research Group, 1984. Mem. Am. Phys. Soc. (nat. council 1980-83; Forum on Physics and Soc. prize 1984), Fedn. Am. Scientists (nat. council 1970-74, 80-84, 91-95). Home: 100 Nevada St Northfield MN 55057-2341 Office: Carleton College Dept Physics Northfield MN 55057

CASPER, BERNADETTE MARIE, critical care nurse; b. Buffalo, Jan. 13, 1961; d. Frank David and Mary Ann (Zmozynski) C. BSN, D'Youville Coll., 1983, MS. Cert. BLS and ACLS instr./provider, critical care instr., N.Y. Staff/charge nurse, preceptor, clin. instr. faculty Millard Fillmore Hosp., Buffalo, 1983—. Bd. dirs. Villa Maria Acad., Buffalo. Mem. AACCN, AACN (legis. com. dist. 1), N.Y. Nurses Assn., Profl. Nurses Assn. (we. N.Y. dist. 1), Sigma Theta Tau (sec. Zeta Nu chpt.). Avocations: crafts, dancing, reading, travel, sports. Home: 5121 William St Lancaster NY 14086-9659 Office: Millard Fillmore Hosp 3 Gates Cir Buffalo NY 14209-1194

CASPER, CHARLES B., lawyer; b. Boise, Idaho, June 9, 1952; s. John Blaine and Joyce Lucile (Mercer) C.; m. Brenda Cheryl Bowers, Aug. 28, 1976; children: Timothy L., Jonathan B. BA, Yale U., 1974; JD, U. Va., 1977; MDiv, Princeton Theol. Sem., 1985. Bar: Utah 1977, U.S. Dist. Ct. Utah 1977, U.S. Ct. Appeals (10th cir.) 1978, U.S. Supreme Ct. 1982, Pa. 1985, U.S. Dist. Ct. (ea. dist.) Pa. 1989, U.S. Ct. Appeals (3d cir.) 1989, U.S. Dist. Ct. N.J. 1990, N.J. 1990. Assoc. Fabian & Clendenin, Salt Lake City, 1977-82, shareholder, 1982; assoc. pastor Arch St. United Meth. Ch., Phila., 1985-89; assoc. Montgomery, McCracken, Walker & Rhoads, LLP, Phila., 1989-92, ptnr., 1992—, vice chmn. litigation dept., 1996-98. Bd. dirs. Evangelical Svcs. for the Aging Found., 1996—, United Meth. Neighborhood Svcs., Phila., 1987-93, Parent-Infant Ctr., Phila., 1990-93; com. chair Utah Heritage Found., Salt Lake City, 1979-82; active Vol. Coun. Emergency Assistance, Phila., 1988-98, chair, 1998—. Recipient Svc. award Utah Heritage Found., 1982. Mem. ABA, Utah State Bar Assn., N.J. Bar Assn., Pa. Bar Assn., Phila. Bar Assn. Republican. Office: Montgomery McCracken Walker and Rhoads LLP 123 S Broad St Fl 24 Philadelphia PA 19109-1023

CASPER, EPHRAIM SAUL, medical oncologist; b. Chgo., Dec. 27, 1950; s. Irwin S. and Adele (Ohrenstein) C.; m. Chava Reyna Pollack, Mar. 15, 1982; children: Binyamin, David, Noam, Ilan, Sarah. BS, U. Ill., 1971; MD, Rush Med. Coll., 1974. Diplomate Am. Bd. Internal Medicine, Am. Bd. Med. Oncology. Intern Rush Presbyn.-St. Luke's Med. Ctr., Chgo., 1974-75, resdient in medicine, 1975-77; fellow in med. oncology Meml. Sloan-Kettering Cancer Ctr., 1977-79; asst. in medicine Rush Med. Coll., Chgo., 1974-77; clin. asst. physician Meml. Hosp., N.Y.C., 1979, asst. attending physician, 1980-87, assoc. attending physician, 1987-93, assoc. chmn. for clin. trials, dept. medicine, 1988-95, attending physician, 1993—; asst. prof. medicine Cornell U. Med. Coll., N.Y.C., 1979-87, assoc. prof. clin. medicine, 1987-94, prof. medicine, 1994—; chief med. oncology Meml. Sloan-Kettering Cancer Ctr. at St. Clare's, Denville, N.J., 1996—; dir. dept. of medicine Clin. Trials Office, 1988-95; mem. Institutional Rev. Bd., 1984-96, assoc. chmn. 1988-96; sarcoma com. ACS, 1995—. Jr. Faculty Clin. fellow Am. Cancer Soc., 1980-83; James scholar U. Ill. Fellow ACP; mem. Am. Assn. for Cancer Rsch., Am. Soc. of Clin. Oncology (program com. 1996—), AAAS, Cancer and Leukemia Group B. Office: Meml Sloan Kettering Cancer Ctr 23 Pocono Rd Denville NJ 07834-2954

CASPER, GERHARD, academic administrator, law educator; b. Hamburg, Germany, Dec. 25, 1937; s. Heinrich and Hertha C.; m. Regina Koschel, Dec. 26, 1964; 1 child, Hanna. Legal state exam., U. Freiburg, U. Hamburg, 1961; LL.M., Yale U., 1962; Dr.iur., U. Freiburg, Germany, 1964. Asst. prof. polit. sci. U. Calif., Berkeley, 1964-66; assoc. prof. law and polit. sci. U. Chgo., 1966-69, prof., 1969-76, Max Pam prof. law, 1976-80, William B. Graham prof. law, 1980-87, William B. Graham Disting. Svc. prof. law, 1987-92, dean law sch., 1979-87, provost, 1989-92; prof. law Stanford (Calif.) U., 1992—, pres., 1992—; vis. prof. law Cath. U., Louvain, Belgium, 1970, U. Munich, 1988, 91; bd. dirs. Ency. Britannica. Author: Realism and Political Theory in American Legal Thought, 1967, (with Richard A. Posner) The Workload of the Supreme Court, 1976; co-editor: The Supreme Ct. Rev., 1977-91, Separating Power, 1997. Fellow Am. Acad. Arts and Scis.; mem. Internat. Acad. Comparative Law, Am. Bar Found. (bd. dirs. 1979-87), Coun. Fgn. Rels., Am. Law Inst. (coun. 1980—), Oliver Wendell Holmes Devise (permanent com. 1985—), Am. Philos. Soc.

CASPER, LEONARD RALPH, American literature educator; b. Fond du Lac, Wis., July 6, 1923; s. Louis and Caroline (Eder) C.; m. Linda Velasquez-Ty, June 2, 1956; children: Gretchen Gabrielle, Kristina Elise. BA, U. Wis., 1948, MA, 1949, PhD, 1953. Grad. asst. U. Wis., 1949-51; instr. Cornell U., 1952-53; asst. prof. U. Philippines, 1953-56, Fulbright lectr., 1962-63, summer 1973; mem. faculty Boston Coll., 1956—, prof. contemporary Am. lit., 1963-93, prof. emeritus, 1993—; dir. creative writing U. R.I., summer 1958. Author: Robert Penn Warren: The Dark and Bloody Ground, 1960, The Wayward Horizon: Essays on Modern Philippine Literature, 1961, The Wounded Diamond: Studies in Modern Philippine Literature, 1964, New Writing from The Philippines: A Critique and Anthology, 1966, A Lion Unannounced: 12 Stories and a Fable, 1971, Firewalkers: Concelebrations 1964-1984, 1987, In Burning Ambush: Essays, 1985-90, 1991, The Opposing Thumb: Decoding Literature of the Marcos Regime, 1995, Sunsurfers Seen From Afar: Critical Essays, 1991-96, 1996, The Blood Marriage of Earth and Sky: The Later Novels of Robert Penn Warren, 1997, The Circular Firing Squad, 1999; contbg. author prefaces: 13 Kalisud, 1955, Brother, My Brother, 1960, The Selected Stories of Francisco Arcellana, 1963, A Stun of Jewels, 1963, Godkissing Carrion, 1964, Selected Stories of N. V.M. Gonzalez, 1964, After This Exile, 1965, Black or Otherwise, 1969, Scent of Apples, 1979, Distances: in Time, 1983, Salimbibig: Philippine Vernacular Literature, 1984, Ethnic Houses and Philippine Artistic Expression, 1988, Morning Song, 1990, Literature and Politics, 1993, Gentle Woman: Mary to the Filipinos, 1997; editor Six Filipino Poets, 1955, Modern Philippine Short Stories, 1962; co-editor: (with T.A. Gullason) The World of Short Fiction: An International Collection, 1962; contbg. editor Panorama, Manila, 1965-61, Drama Critique, 1956-62, Solidarity, Manila, 1966-78, Literature East and West, 1969-81, Aquila, 1975-79, Pilipinas, 1987—. Served with F.A., AUS, 1943-46. Recipient Ford Found. Pub. award, Nat. Coun. on Arts award, 1970, Rockefeller Found. Residency award, Bellagio, Italy, 1994; Stanford Creative Writing fellow, 1951-52; Bread Loaf Creative Writing scholar, 1961; rsch. grantee Am. Coun. Learned Socs.-Social Sci. Rsch. Coun., 1965, Asia Soc., 1965; Creative Writing grant Boston Coll.; rsch. travel grantee Am. Philos. Soc., 1968-69. Home: 54 Simpson Dr Framingham MA 01701-4076 Office: Dept English Boston Coll Chestnut Hill MA 02167

CASPER, MARIE LENORE, middle school educator; b. Honesdale, Pa., Mar. 26, 1954; d. Frank J. and Ellenore L. (Austin) Shedlock; m. Gerald Joseph Casper, Oct. 9, 1976 (dec. Oct. 1998); children: Julia Anne, Jennifer Marie. BA, Marywood Coll., 1976; masters equivalency cert., State of Pa., 1982. Cert. elem. and secondary social studies tchr., Pa. Substitute tchr. Western Wayne Sch. Dist., South Canaan, Pa., 1976-81, secondary and elem. tchr., 1981-86, chpt. 1 math. specialist, 1986-90, middle sch. social studies tchr., 1990—; social studies tchr. Wallenpaupack Area Sch. Dist., Hawley, Pa., 1980-81; corp. sec. Simply Elegant Homes & Constrn., Inc., Kresgeville and South Canaan, Pa.; coord. Western Wayne Middle Sch. (WW II commemorative com.). Contbr. articles to profl. publs. Mem. PTA R.D. Wilson Sch., Western Wayne Mid. Sch. Mem. NEA, Pa. State Edn. Assn., Pa. Mid. Sch. Assn., Waymart Hist. Soc., Western Wayne Edn. Assn., Wayne County Hist. Soc., Smithsonian Instn., Audubon Soc., Nat. Geog. Soc., Platform Assn., Am. Legion Aux. (life). Republican. Roman Catholic. Avocations: piano and vocal music, needlecraft, reading, antiques, genealogy. Home: PO Box 31 Lake Quinn Rd South Canaan PA 18459-0031 Office: Western Wayne Mid Sch RR 2 Box 376B Lake Ariel PA 18436-9802 also: Simply Elegant Homes & Cnst PO Box 937 Kresgeville PA 18333-0937

CASPER, RICHARD HENRY, lawyer; b. Chgo., Nov. 4, 1950; s. Edson Lee and Dorothy Ellen (Klemp) C.; m. Betty Gene Ward, Aug. 26, 1972; children: Terrance, Laura, Russell, Jeremy. AB, Bowdoin Coll., 1972; JD, Northwestern U., 1975. Bar: Wis. 1975, U.S. Dist. Ct. (ea. dist.) Wis. 1975. Assoc. Foley & Lardner, Milw., 1975-82, ptnr., 1982—. James Bowdoin scholar Bowdoin Coll, 1972. Mem. Wis. Bar Assn., Milw. Bar Assn., Order of the Coif. Office: Foley & Lardner Firstar 777 E Wisconsin Ave Milwaukee WI 53202-5367

CASPER, STEWART MICHAEL, lawyer; b. Fitchburg, Mass., Jan. 12, 1953; s. Irwin Stanley and Dorothy (Cohen) C.; children: Stacey Lynn, Allison Rose. BA, U. Mass., 1975; JD, Hofstra U., 1978. Bar: Conn. 1978, U.S. Dist. Ct. Conn. 1978, N.Y. 1985, U.S. Dist. Ct. (so. dist.) N.Y. 1987, U.S. Ct. Appeals (2d cir.) 1987, U.S. Supreme Ct. 1987. Assoc. McAnerney & Millar, Darien, Conn., 1978-80, Glazer Seelig & Glazer, Stamford, Conn., 1980-82, Arnold H. Rutkin PC, Westport, Conn., 1982-86; ptnr. Wynn Casper & de Toledo, Stamford, 1986-88, Casper & de Toledo LLC, Stamford, 1988—. Trustee Temple Beth El, Stamford, 1987-92. Mem. ATLA (state del. 1999—), Conn. Trial Lawyers Assn. (bd. govs. 1984-85, 87—, exec. com. 1990—, legis. com. 1990—, parliamentarian 1991-92, sec. 1992-93, treas. 1993-94, v.p. 1994-95, pres.-elect 1995-96, pres. 1996-97, immediate past pres. 1997-98), Conn. Bar Assn., Regional Bar Assn. Democrat. Jewish. Avocations: golf, photography. Office: Casper & de Toledo LLC 1111 Summer St Stamford CT 06905-5511

CASPER, WAYNE ARTHUR, state government official, educator; b. Detroit, June 10, 1949; s. Arthur Eugene and Arlene (Burke) C.; m. Catherine Adelle Lyons, Jan. 22, 1972; children: Catherine, Jeff. BS, U. Ariz., 1971, MS, 1979. Buyer City of Tucson, 1971-74, adminstrv. asst., 1974-75, asst. purchasing agt., 1975-81; procurement dir. State of Ariz., Phoenix, 1981-90; dir. procurement City of Tucson, 1990—; advisor, City of Mesa Risk Mgmt. Adv. Coun., 1983-88. Mem. Nat. Assn. State Purchasing Inst. (pres. 1991), Nat. Inst. Govtl. Purchasing (Ariz. chpt. treas. 1983, sec. 1984, v.p. 1985, pres. 1986). Roman Catholic. Office: City of Tucson PO Box 27210 Tucson AZ 85726-7210*

CASPERSEN, FINN MICHAEL WESTBY, diversified financial services company executive; b. N.Y.C., Oct. 27, 1941; s. Olaus Westby and Freda Caspersen; m. Barbara Caspersen, June 17, 1967. BA With honors in Econs., Brown U., 1963; LLB cum laude, Harvard U., 1966; DHL (hon.), Johns Hopkins U., 1999; various hon. degrees. Assoc. Dewey, Ballantine, Bushby, Palmer & Wood, N.Y.C., 1969-72; chmn. bd., chief exec. officer, mem. exec. com. Beneficial Corp., Wilmington, Del., 1976-98; chmn. bd. dirs., CEO Knickerbocker LLC; past bd. dirs., mem. exec. com. Beneficial Nat. Bank; chmn. bd. dirs. Beneficial Bank, Plc; bd. advisors Inst. Law and Econs., U. Pa.; chmn. Coalition for Better Transp.; co-chair Prosperity N.J.; chmn. U.S. Equestrian Team. Emeritus trustee Brown U.; moderator, bd. dirs. Shelter Harbor Fire Dist.; pres. O.W. Caspersen Found.; trustee BGCN Life Camp Inc.; chmn. bd. trustees Peddie Sch., Hightstown, N.J.; chmn. bd. trust Gladstone Equestrian Assn. Inc.; bd. dirs. Drumthwacket Found.; charter mem. Partnership for N.J., New Brunswick; bd. dirs. Coalition of Svc. Industries, Inc., Washington, 1982-95, vice chair, 1995—; chmn. World Pair Championship, 1993; mem. corp. Cardigan Mountain Sch., 1981-96; mem. exec. com. Harvard Resources Com.; trustee BGCN Life Camp Inc., John Carter Libr.; chmn. dean's adv. com. Harvard Law Sch.; dir. Clay Math. Inst. Lt. USCG, 1966-69. Recipient Pres.'s medal Johns Hopkins U., Ethics in Bus. award BBB, 1992, Gov.'s award Alexander Hamilton Econ. Devel., 1997, President's medal Brown U., 1997, Brightest Star award Boys and Girls Clubs Newark, Inc., 1997; nameCivic Leader of Yr., YMCA, 1982, Citizen of Yr., Morristown Meml. Hosp., 1993. Mem. Am. Fin. Svcs. Assn. (bd. dirs., chmn. govt. affairs com., chmn. membership com., adminstrn. com., past chmn.), Fla. Bar Assn., N.Y. Bar Assn., Harvard Club, Knickerbocker Club, Univ. Club, Wilmington Club. Office: Knickerbocker LLC 268 Main St Gladstone NJ 07934*

CASS, BARBARA FAY, elementary school educator; b. Vernon, Tex., Jan. 24, 1949; d. Jester Earl and Sylvia Louise (Bowden) Hunt; m. Millard Don Cass, Jan. 21, 1966; 1 child, Paula Sue Cass Threatt. BS, Tex. Tech U., 1985. Sec. Dr. Johnson, Plainview, Tex., 1973; receptionist Dr. T.M. Trimble, Wylie, Tex., 1973-75, Dr. Thomas Neal, Lubbock, Tex., 1987-88; bookkeeper Aledo (Tex.) Counter Top, 1976-77; receptionist med. records and ins. clk. care unit Trinity Oaks Hosp., Ft. Worth, 1977-78; substitute tchr. Lubbock Ind. Sch. Dist., 1986-87, DeSoto (Tex.) Ind. Sch. Dist., 1988-89; kindergarten tchr. home econs. Tyler St. Christian Acad., Dallas, 1989-94; tchr. 1st grade Robinwood Christian Acad., Seagoville, Tex., 1994-97; tchr. kindergarten, 1st grade Hope Christian Sch., Tijeras, N.Mex., 1998—. Baptist. Home: 9032 Walter Bambrook Pl NE Albuquerque NM 87122-2711

CASS, DAVID, economist, educator; b. Honolulu, Jan. 19, 1937; s. Phil and Muriel (Dranga) C.; m. Janice Vernon, Sept. 14, 1959 (div. July 1983); children—Stephen, Lisa. B.A., U. Oreg., 1958; Ph.D. in Econs. and Stats., Stanford U., 1965; D (hon.), U. Geneva, 1994. From asst. to assoc. prof. Yale U., New Haven, 1964-70; prof. econs. Carnegie-Mellon U., Pitts., 1970-74; prof. econs. U. Pa., Phila., 1974-88, Paul F. and E. Warren Shafer Miller prof. econs., 1988—; prof. econs. European Univ. Inst., Italy, 1996-97. Contbr. articles to profl. jours.; co-editor: Selected Readings in Macroeconomics from Econometrica, 1974; The Hamiltonian Approach to Economics, 1976. 1st lt. USAR, 1959-65. Guggenheim fellow, 1970-71; recipient Morgan prize U. Chgo., 1976; Sherman Fairchild Disting. Scholar Calif. Inst. Tech., 1978-79; NSF grantee, 1971-91. Fellow Am. Econ. Assn. (disting.), Econometric Soc.; mem. Phi Beta Kappa. Office: U Pa Dept Econs Philadelphia PA 19104

CASS, EDWARD ROBERTS (PETER), hotel and travel marketing professional; b. La Porte, Ind., Nov. 21, 1941; s. Edward Smith and Shirley (Mazur) C.; m. Marilyn Brooks, Apr. 1, 1967; children: Edward Brooks Cass, Alexander Brooks Cass. AB in History, Hamilton Coll., 1964; MBA in Mktg./Fin., Syracuse U., 1970. Dir. mktg., gen. sales mgr. Mohawk Airlines Inc., N.Y.C., 1964-72; sr. v.p., gen. mgr. The Travel Industry Assn. Am., Washington, 1972-78; gen. mgr., COO Tri-Met, Oreg. and Wash., 1978-81; v.p. unregulated activities Pacific Telecom, subsidiary of Pacificorp, Vancouver, Wash., 1982-83; pres., founder Transax Data Corp., Falls Church, Va., 1983-85; pres., CEO Transax Data divsn. of Jour. of Commerce Knight-Ridder Inc., Bridgewater, N.J., 1985-94, Preferred Hotels & Resorts Worldwide, Chgo., 1994—. Home: 101 Woodland Dr Oak Brook IL 60523-1416 Office: Preferred Hotels Resorts Worldwide 311 S Wacker Dr Ste 1900 Chicago IL 60606-6620

CASS, GLEN ROWAN, environmental engineer; b. Pasadena, Calif., Apr. 18, 1947; s. Robert Mervin and Marie (Segner) C.; m. Jean Elizabeth Annis, Dec. 18, 1976; 1 child, Robert Cass. BSME, U. So. Calif., 1969; MSME, Stanford U., 1970; PhD, Calif. Inst. Tech., 1978. Officer USPHS, Atlanta, 1970-73; from instr. to prof. engring. Calif. Inst. Tech., Pasadena, 1978—; clean air scientific adv. com. U.S. EPA, Washington, 1991-92; com. on haze in nat. parks and wilderness areas Nat. Rsch. Coun., Washington, 1990-93; rsch. adv. com. Health Effects Inst., Cambridge, Mass., 1993—; adv. com. ozone, fine particles, and regional haze EPA, 1996-98; cons. in field. Assoc. editor Aerosol Sci. and Tech., 1994-98; mem. editl. bd. Environ. Sci. Tech., 1998—. Environ. goals com. L.A. 2000, 1987-88; clean air com., Pasadena Lung Assn., 1977-85. Mem. Am. Chem. Soc., Am. Assn. Aerosol Rsch. (bd. dirs. 1996—). Office: Environ Engring Sci Dept Calif Inst Tech Pasadena CA 91125

CASS, RICHARD EUGENE, English language educator; b. Milw., Dec. 22, 1943; s. Eugene Franklin and Edna Mary (Welke) C.; m. Bonnie Jean Bauer Cass, Aug. 2, 1969; children: Richard Welke, Adrienne Jean, Valerie Ann. BA in English, Principia Coll., 1966; MS in Edn. Psychology, U. Wis., Milw., 1969, PhD in English Curriculum, 1973. Secondary educator Brown Deer (Wis.) Schs., 1966-68; instr. U. Wis., Milw., 1968-73, 83-94; chair English dept. Cedarburg (Wis.) Schs., 1974—; pres. Precision Writing Seminars, Whitefish Bay, Wis., 1988—; adjunct instr. Principia Col., Elsah, Ill., 1988—. Editor: (book) Voices From the Honorable Right Side, 1995. Sunday Sch. Supt. First Ch. Christ, Scientist, Whitefish Bay, Wis., 1992-94, 98-99; trustee First Ch. Christ, Scientist, Whitefish Bay, 1989-91; centennial historian Cedarburg (Wis.) Schs., 1995—. Named Herb Kohl fellow by Sen. Herb Kohl, 1996, Ozaukee County Educator of Yr., 1998. Mem. Indian Princes (chief, 1991-93). Christian Scientist. Avocations: skiing, tennis, sailing, chess. Office: Cedarburg HS Cedarburg WI 53012

CASS, ROBERT MICHAEL, lawyer, consultant; b. Carlisle, Pa., July 5, 1945; s. Robert Lau and Norma Jean (McCaleb) C.; m. Patricia Ann Garber, Aug. 12, 1967 (dec. Jan. 1999); children: Charles McCaleb, David Lau. BA, Pa. State U., 1967; JD, Temple U., 1971. Bar: N.Y. 1974; cert. arbitrator Aida Reins. and Ins. Arbitration Soc. Benefit examiner Social Security Adminstrn., Phila., 1967-68; mktg. rep. Employers Comml. Union Ins. Co., Phila., 1968-70; asst. sec. Nat. Reins. Corp., N.Y.C., 1970-77; asst. v.p. Skandia Am. Reins. Corp., N.Y.C., 1977-80; mgr. Allstate Reins. div., South Barrington, Ill., 1980-86, R.K. Carvill, Inc., Chgo., 1986-87; pres. R. M. Cass Assocs., Barrington, 1987—; v.p. Assurance Alliance, Inc., Crystal Lake, Ill., 1989; lectr. Ins. Sch. Chgo., Coll. of Ins. N.Y., U. Wis., Am. Inst. for Chartered Property Casualty Underwriters; bd. dirs. Legion Indemnity Co., Phila. Author: (with others) Reinsurance Contract Wording, Reinsurance Practices, 2d edit.; editor, reviewer: (with others) The Legal Environment of Insurance, 4th edit. Mem. ABA (tort and ins. practice sect., past chair com. on excess, surplus lines and reins. law, standing com. on professionalism, chmn. com. internat. tort and ins. law, liaison to ABA Ctrl. & East European Law Initiative, dispute resolution sect., past chair com. large complex case arbitration), Soc. CPCUs (past chair risk mgmt. sect. com., mem. excess, surplus and splty. lines sect. com., v.p., bd. dirs. Chgo. N.W. suburban chpt.), Am. Arbitration Assn. (panel arbitrators), Assn. Ind. Reins. Cons. (pres.), Internat. Assn. Ins. Receivers (publs. com., past chair membership com.), N.Y. State Bar Assn., Assn. Internat. de Droit des Assurances, Ill. Captive and Alternative Risk Funding Ins. Assn. (pres. bd. dirs.), Coalition Alternative Risk Funding Mechanisms (bd. dirs.), Assn. Internat. de Droit des Assurances. Home: 325 Old Mill Rd Barrington IL 60010-4734 Office: PO Box 1362 Barrington IL 60011-1362

CASS, RONALD ANDREW, dean; b. Washington, Aug. 12, 1949; s. Millard and Ruth Claire (Marx) C.; m. Valerie Christina Swanson, Aug. 24, 1969; children: Laura Rebecca, Alexander Stephan. BA with high distinction, U. Va., 1970; JD with honors, U. Chgo., 1973. Bar: Md. 1973, D.C. 1974, U.S. Dist. Ct. D.C. 1974, U.S. Ct. Appeals (D.C. cir.) 1974, U.S. Supreme Ct. 1977, Va. 1979. Law clk. to chief judge U.S. Ct. Appeals (3d cir.), Wilmington, Del., 1973-74; assoc. Arent, Fox, Kintner, Plotkin & Kahn, Washington, 1974-76; asst. prof. law U. Va. Sch. Law, Charlottesville, 1976-81; assoc. prof. law Boston U., 1981-83, prof., 1983-95; dean Boston U. Law Sch., 1990—; Melville Madison Bigelow prof. Boston U., 1995—; legal advisor Office Plans and Policy, FCC, Washington, 1987-88; mem. U.S. Internat. Trade Commn., Washington, 1988-90, vice chmn., 1989-90; cons. comm. program Aspen (Colo.) Inst., 1977-78, Adminstrv. Conf. U.S., Washington, 1980-87, Helsell, Fetterman, Martin, Todd & Hokanson, Seattle, 1984-85, Assn. Trial Lawyers Am., Phila., 1985-87, UN Conf. Trade and Devel., Geneva, 1991, U.S. Dept. Justice, 1998, Microsoft Corp., 1998-99; spl. cons. Nat. Econ. Rsch. Assn., Cambridge, Mass., 1990-94; adj. scholar Am. Enterprise Inst., Washington, 1993—; sr. fellow Internat. Ctr. Econ. Rsch., Turin, 1996-97, 1999—; sesquicentennial assoc. Ctr. Advanced Studies U. Va. Law Sch., 1980-81; mem. nat. adv. bd. Case Western Res. U. Sch. of Law, 1996-97; disting. lectr. U. Francisco Marroquin, Guatemala City, 1996. Author: Revolution in the Wasteland: Value and Diversity in Television, 1981, (with Colin S. Diver) Administrative Law: Cases and Materials, 1987, (with Colin S. Diver and Jack M. Beermann) Administrative Law: Cases and Materials, 2nd edit., 1994, 3rd edit., 1998, (with John R. Haring) International Trade in Telecommunications, 1998; contbr. articles and essays to profl. jours., also chpts. to books. Bd. dirs. Northwestern Va. Health Systems Agy., Culpeper, 1980, New Eng. Coun., 1995—; bd. govs. Sightsavers Internat., Washington, 1989-91; bd. dirs. Telecomm. Policy Rsch. Conf., Washington, 1989-92, sec.-treas. 1989-90, vice chmn., 1991-92; bd. dirs. New Eng. Legal Found., 1994—, New Eng. Coun., 1995—; bd. overseers Boston Bar Found., 1992-94, Supreme Jud. Ct. Hist. Soc., 1997—; sr. Europe Discussion Group, Ctr. for Strategic and Internat. Studies, 1989-96; bd. advisors George Mason U. Law Sch. Law & Econs. Ctr., 1996—, Inst. Dem. Comm., Boston, 1991-92, Fundación de la Commn. Social, Madrid, 1995—. Sr. fellow Internat. Ctr. Econ. Rsch., Turin, 1996-97. Fellow Am. Bar Found.; mem. ABA (adminstrv. law and regulatory practice sect., coun. 1993-95, chair 1998-99, legal edn. and admission bar sect., review commn. 1994-95), Am. Law Inst., Am. Law Deans Assn. (bd. dirs. 1995—, pres. 1995-97), Mont Pelerin Soc., Boston Bar Assn. (coun. 1992-95), Adminstrv. Conf. U.S. (pub. mem. 1990-95, govt. mem. 1988-90), Transatlantic Policy Network (U.S. Working Group), Spring Valley C. C., Order of Coif, Phi Beta Kappa, Bay Club. Republican. Jewish. Home: 36 Forest St Wellesley Hls MA 02481-6818 Office: Boston U Sch Law 765 Commonwealth Ave Boston MA 02215-1401

CASSADY, WILLIAM E., federal judge; b. 1950. Magistrate judge U.S. Dist. Ct. (so. dist.) Ala., 1985—. Fax: 334-694-4198. Office: 306 US Courthouse 113 St Joseph St Mobile AL 36602

CASSAGNERES, EVERETT, engineer, consultant, pilot; b. New Haven, Conn., Feb. 7, 1928; s. Eugene Francis and Alta Mun (Bryan) C.; children: Kirsten Joy, Bryan Ev. Grad. H.S., New Haven, Conn. Pres. Aero-Draft, Cheshire, Conn., 1977—; expert on Charles Lindbergh's Spirit of St. Louis airplane, 1965—, aircraft built by Ryan Aeron. Co., San Diego, 1956—. Author: Spirit of Ryan, 1984, The New Ryan, 1995. Mem. cycling com. Spl. Olympics, Nwe Haven, 1995. With U.S. Army, 1950-52. Mem. Am. Aviation Hist. Assn., Explt. Aircraft Assn. (Young Eagles Pilot 1995—), Charles A. and Anne Morrow Lindbergh Found., London Soc. Air Britain, Conn. Aero. Hist. Assn. (founding mem. 1961). Avocations: flying, skiing, hiking, canoeing, cycling. Home: PO Box 145 Cheshire CT 06410

CASSANDRAS, CHRISTOS GEORGE, engineering educator, consultant; b. Athens, Greece, Sept. 19, 1955; came to U.S., 1974; s. George and Venetsiana (Zervopoulou) C.; m. Carol Ellen Kamm, May 30, 1991; 1 child, Monica Georgia. BS, Yale U., 1977; MSEE, Stanford U., 1978; SM, Harvard U., 1979, PhD, 1982. Sr. systems engr. ITP Boston, Inc., Cambridge, Mass., 1982-84; asst. prof. U. Mass., Amherst, 1984-89, assoc. prof., 1989-93, prof. elec. and computer engring., 1993-97; prof. mfg. engring. Boston U., 1997—; cons., faculty affiliate Network Dynamics, Inc., Burlington, Mass., 1988—; vis. scholar Harvard U., Cambridge, Mass., 1990; vis. prof. U. Cath. de Louvain, Belgium, 1993. Author: Discrete Event Systems: Modelling and Performance Analysis, 1993; contbr. articles to profl. jours.; editor spl. issues various jours., 1990—. Fellow Lilly Found., 1991; rsch. grantee various fed. agys. and indsl. orgns., 1985—. Fellow IEEE (editor IEEE Transactions on Automatic Control 1994-98, editor-in-chief 1998—); mem. Inst. for Ops. Rsch. and Mgmt. Sci. (sr.), Control Systems Soc. (bd. govs.). Achievements include pioneering contributions to field of discrete event system theory and its applications to manufacturing, computer networks and transportation. Avocation: travel. Office: Dept Mfg Engring Boston U 15 Saint Marys St Boston MA 02215

CASSANO, VALERIE, women's health nurse; b. Bklyn., Oct. 12, 1955; d. Walter and Margaret (Cutrone) Turchak; m. Steve Cassano, Sept. 7, 1980; children: Jennifer, Stephanie. AAS, Kingsborough Community Coll., 1977. Charge nurse, labor/delivery State U. Hosp., Bklyn., 1977-87; staff nurse South Nassau Community Hosp., Oceanside, N.Y., 1989-91; dermatology office nurse Lawrence, N.Y., 1994—.

CASSARA, CATHERINE, journalism educator; b. Lowell, Mass., Mar. 19, 1954; d. Ernest and Beverly Benner Cassara. BA, U. Va., 1976; MA, Mich. State U., 1987, PhD, 1992. Asst. composing supr. Fairfax (Va.) Globe, 1977-79; asst. editor The Times, Springfield, Va., 1979; staff reporter The Pictorial, Old Saybrook, Conn., 1979-81, The Jour.-Tribune, Biddeford, Maine, 1981-84, The Lewiston (Maine) Sun, 1984-85; asst. prof. Bowling Green (Ohio) State U., 1992-98, assoc. prof., 1998—; writing coach, cons. various newspapers, 1996—. Author: (with others) News and Foreign Policy, 1999. Vol. Bridge Hospice, Bowling Green, 1995—. Knight fellowship Am. Soc. Newspaper Editors, 1996; recipient 1st Pl. spot news Maine Press Assn., 1985. Mem. Assn. for Edn. in Journalism and Mass Comm. (head interna. comm. divsn. 1996-97, vice head/program chair 1995-96), Am. Journalism Historians Assn. Unitarian Universalist. Avocation: hiking. E-mail: ccassar@bgnet.bgsu.edu. Office: Dept of Journalism Bowling Green State U Bowling Green OH 43403

CASSARA, FRANK, artist, printmaker; b. Partinico, Italy, Mar. 13, 1913; came to U.S., 1913, naturalized, 1936; s. Gaspare and Rosalia (Savarino) C.; m. Gretchen Jean Grathwohl, Dec. 28, 1946; children: Christina, Francesca. Student, U. Iowa, summer 1956, Atelier 17, Paris, summer 1958; M.S. in Design, U. Mich., 1954. Supr. easel painting sect. WPA, 1937; instr. Detroit Sch. Art, 1935-36, Soc. Arts and Crafts, Detroit, 1946-47; prof. U. Mich., Ann Arbor, after 1947, now prof. emeritus; instr. Nat. Music Camp, Interlochen, Mich., summers 1948-49. Illustrated manuscript published in Artists Proof, A Collectors Edition, 1963; one-man shows include: U. Man., Can., Winnipeg, Flint (Mich.) Inst. Arts, Toledo Mus., 1983, Kalamazoo Art Ctr., U. Maine, Orono, U. Ill., Urbana, U. Oreg., Corvallis, U. Nebr., Lincoln; group shows include: 7th Internat. Prints, Chgo. Art Inst., Mus. Palace Legion of Honor, San Francisco, Gallerie Nees Morphes, Athens, Greece, Bklyn. Mus., Achenbach Found. Graphic Arts, San Francisco, Okla. Art Ctr., Oklahoma City, Internat. Conf. Hand Papermakers, Boston, 1980, Internat. Papermakers, Birmingham Art Assn., Ella Sharp Mus. and Slusser Gallery; represented in permanent collections at Bibliotecque Nationale, Paris, Stadelijk Mus., The Netherlands, Libr. of Congress, USIA Agy., Nat. Mus. Am. Art, Smithsonian Instn., Washington; mural executed East Detroit Post Office, 1939, Sandusky (Mich.) Post Office, 1941, Lansing (Mich.) Water Conditioning Plant, 1941, renovated, 1989, Palio, Ann Arbor, 1996. Served with U.S. Army, 1942-46. Decorated 2 Bronze Stars.; Grantee Rackham Research Found., U. Mich., 1957-61, 68; Recipient over 50 awards in National and regional exhibitions. Mem. Ann Arbor Art Assn. (past pres., dir. 1954-62), Nat. Acad. Design. Innovator two white grounds for etching. Address: 1122 Pomona Rd Ann Arbor MI 48103-3045

CASSAVETES, NICK, film director, actor; b. N.Y.C., May 21, 1959. Dir., writer: Unhook the Stars/Décroche les étoiles, 1996 (Dirs.' Week award Fantasporto, Best Film, 1997); dir.: She's So Lovely/Call It Love, 1997; actor: A Woman Under the Influence, 1974, (TV) Reunion, 1980, Mask, 1985, The Wraith, 1986, Quiet Cool, 1986, Black Moon Rising, 1986, Assault of the Killer Bimbos, 1987, (TV) Shooter, 1988, Under the Gun, 1989, Blind Fury, 1989, Backstreet Dreams/Backstreet Strays, 1990, Delta Force 3: The Killing Game/Young Commandos, 1991, Sins of the Night, 1993, Sins of Desire, 1993, Body of Influence, 193, Twogether, 1994, Class of 1999 II: The Substitute, 1994, Mrs. Parker and the Vicious Circle/Mrs. Parker and the Round Table, 1994, Just Like Dad, 1995, Black Rose of Harlem/Machine Gun Blues/Pistol Blues, 1996, Me and the Gods, 1997, Face/Off, 1997, Conversations in Limbo, 1998, Panic, 1999, Life, 1999, The Astronaut's Wife, 1999; notable TV guest appearances include Matlock, 1986, The Convict, 1987. Office: c/o DGA 7920 Sunset Blvd Los Angeles CA 90046*

CASSCELLS, SAMUEL WARD, III, cardiologist, educator; b. Wilmington, Del., Mar. 18, 1952; s. Samuel Ward and Oleda (Dyson) C.; m. Roxanne Bell, Feb. 10, 1990; children: Sam, Henry, Lillian. BS cum laude, Yale U., 1974; MD magna cum laude, Harvard U., 1979. Intern then resident Beth Israel Hosp., Boston, 1979-82; cardiology fellow Mass. Gen. Hosp., Boston, 1982-85; Kaiser fellow clin. epidemiology Brigham and Women's Hosp. and Harvard Sch. Pub. Health, 1984-85; rsch. fellow Nat. Heart, Lung, and Blood Inst., Bethesda, Md., 1985-91; vis. scientist Scripps Inst. Medicine and Sci., LaJolla, Calif., 1991-92; chief cardiology, T.R. and M. O'Driscoll Levy prof. medicine U. Tex. Med. Sch., Houston, 1994—; chief cardiology Hermann Hosp., Houston, 1994—; assoc. dir. cardiol. rsch. Tex. Heart Inst. and St. Luke's Episc. Hosp., Houston, 1992—; med. dir. U. Tex. Telemedicine; founder Prizm Pharms., La Jolla, 1992—; cons. FDA, Advanced Rsch. Project Agy., NASA, NIH, VA. Mem. editl. bd. Circulation, 1992—, Am. Jour. Cardiology, 1992—, Tex. Heart Inst. Jour., 1992—, Vascular Medicine, 1995—, U.T. Lifetime Newsletter, 1996—; contbr. numerous articles to profl. jours. Mem. Am. Heart Assn. (Houston bd. dirs. 1992-96), Am. Fedn. Clin. Rsch., Am. Soc. Cell Biology, Soc. Vascular Biol. Medicine (bd. dirs.), Houston Cardiology Soc. (pres. 1995-96), Am. Coll. Cardiology, Assn. Univ. Cardiologists, Assn. Profs. of Cardiology, Chevy Chase (Md.) Club, Union Boat Club (Boston), Vicmead Hunt Club (Wilmington, Del.), Farmington Country Club (Charlottesville, Va.), City Tavern Club (Washington). Office: U Tex Med Sch 6431 Fannin St Houston TX 77030-1501

CASSEL, CHRISTINE KAREN, physician; b. Mpls., Sept. 14, 1945; d. Charles Moore and Virginia Julia (Anderson) C.; AB U. Chgo., 1967; MD U. Mass., 1976. Intern, resident in internal medicine Children's Hosp., San Francisco, 1976-78; fellow in bioethics, Inst. Health Policy Studies, U. Calif., San Francisco, 1978-79; fellow geriatrics Portland (Oreg.) VA Hosp., 1979-81; asst. prof. medicine and public health U. Oreg. Health Scis. U., 1981-83; asst. prof. geriatrics and medicine Mt. Sinai Med. Ctr., N.Y.C., 1983-85; prof. medicine, prof. pub. policy, chief gen. internal medicine, U. Chgo., 1985-95; prof. Geriatrics and medicine, Mt. Sinai, 1995—, chmn., Geriatrics and Adult Devel. Dept., 1995—. Bd. dirs. Lutheran Gen. Health Care Systems, Greenwall Found. Woodrow Wilson fellow, 1967; Henry J. Kaiser Family Found. faculty scholar, 1982-85; Hastings Ctr. fellow; Ctr. Advanced Study in Behavioral Sci. fellow, 1991-92; diplomate Am. Bd. Internal Medicine; Ch. Fellow Am. Geriatrics Soc., ACP (vice chair bd. regents 1991); mem. ACP (regent 1989—), NAS, Physicians for Social Responsibility (dir. 1983—, pres. 1988—), Soc. Health and Human Values (pres. 1986), Inst. of Medicine, Am. Bd. Internal Medicine (Chmn. 1998—), Am. Soc. Law & Medicine (bd. dirs.), Inst. of Medicine. Author: Ethical Dimensions in the Health Professions, 1981; Geriatric Medicine: Principles and Practice, 1984, 2d edit., 1990; Nuclear Weapons and Nuclear War: A Sourcebook for Health Professionals, 1984. Office: The Mount Sinai Medical Center 1 Gustave L Levy Pl New York NY 10029-6500*

CASSEL, DOUGLASS WATTS, JR., lawyer, educator, journalist; b. Balt., Aug. 29, 1948; s. Douglass Watts and Vivian Elizabeth (Keller) C.; m. Joan Ellen Steinman, June 1, 1974 (div. 1986); children: Jennifer Lynn, Amanda Hilary; m. Beatriz Cervantes, Sept. 10, 1988; 1 child, Magdalena Maria. BA, Yale Coll., 1969; JD, Harvard Law Sch., 1972. Bar: Md. 1972, D.C. 1973, Ill. 1976. Writer, rschr. Ralph Nader's Congress Project, Washington, 1972; lawyer USNR, Great Lakes Naval Base, Ill., 1973-76; from atty. to gen. counsel BPI, Chgo., 1976-91; journalist Chgo. Reader, 1989; exec. dir. DePaul U. Coll. Law Internat. Human Rights Law Inst., Chgo., 1990-98; dir. Northwestern U. Sch. Law Ctr. for Internat. Human Rights, Chgo., 1998—; legal advisor UN Truth Commn. for El Salvador, N.Y.C., 1992-93; human rights cons. U.S. Dept. State, Washington, 1997—; commentator WBEZ, Chgo., 1994—. Mem. ABA, Am. Soc. Internat. Law. Democrat. Roman Catholic. Avocation: swimming. Office: Northwestern U Sch Law 357 E Chicago Ave Chicago IL 60611-3069

CASSEL, JOHN ELDEN, accountant; b. Verden, Okla., Apr. 24, 1934; s. Elbert Emry and Erma Ruth (McDowell) C.; m. Mary Lou Malcom, June 3, 1953; children—John Elden, James Edward, Jerald Eugene. Plant mgr., also asst. gen. mgr. Baker and Taylor Co., Oklahoma City, 1966-71; paymaster, office mgr. Robberson Steel Co., Oklahoma City, 1971-76; pvt. investor, 1976—. Democrat. Methodist. Home: 2332 NW 118th St Oklahoma City OK 73120-7404

CASSEL, JOHN MICHAEL, plastic surgeon; b. Miami, Mar. 25, 1948; m. Robyn Cassel, July 12, 1987; children: (twins) Adrienne and Brandon. BS, U. Miami, 1972, MD, 1978. Diplomate Am. Bd. Plastic Surgery. Gen. surg. intern U. Va., Charlottesville, 1978-79, gen. surg. resident, 1979-80; gen. surg. resident Cedars-Sinai Med. Ctr., L.A., 1980-81; jr. resident in plastic surgery U. Miami Sch. Medicine, 1981-82, sr. resident in plastic surgery, 1982-83; microsurgery and hand surgery fellow Ralph K. Davies Med. Ctr., San Francisco, 1984; pvt. practice plastic surgery Miami, 1985—; clin. assoc. prof. plastic surgery U. Miami Sch. Medicine, 1984—. Fellow Am. Coll. Surgeons; mem. Am. Soc. Plastic & Reconstructive Surgeons, Am. Soc. Aesthetic Plastic Surgeons. Avocations: sculpture, stained glass, gem cutting, jewely design & fabrication. Office: 8950 N Kendall Dr Ste 100 Miami FL 33176-2144

CASSEL, NEIL JONATHON, business owner; b. Phila., Apr. 16, 1961; s. Arno and Sydney Marilyn (Applebaum) C. BBA, Temple U., 1983; MBA, St. Joseph's U., 1988. Interviewer The Data Group, Inc., Plymouth Meeting, Pa., 1982-83; salary analyst The Equitable, N.Y.C., 1983-84; compensation analyst L.S.I. Avionic Systems, Florham Park, N.J., 1984-85; pers. coord. Spain's Merit Store Div., Phila., 1987-90; regional recruiter PharMor, 1990; ptnr. Total Suburban Svcs., Ft. Washington, Pa., 1982-90; cons. Assoc. Orgnl. Cons., Ft. Washington, 1983-90; pres. TSS Ent., Ft. Washington, 1990—. Author, editor: Tidbits on Nothing, 1983; editor: The Czechmate, 1998-99; contbr. articles to profl. jours. Campaign coord. Dave Brown for Congress, Springfield Twp., 1978; com. person Montgomery County Pa.

Dems., Upper Dublin, 1982-83, 88-89; precinct capt. Hoeffel for Congress, Upper Dublin, 1986. Recipient Mitchell Cole award Upper Dublin S.D., 1979, Cert. of Recognition Montgomery County Planning Commn., 1975. Mem. Nat. Assn. Profl. Pet Sitters, Gen. Alumni Assn. Temple U., Pannonia Beneficial Assn., St. Joseph's U. Alumni Assn., Phi Gamma Nu (v.p. 1982), Cesky Terrier Club of Am. (v.p. 1997-99). Democrat. Jewish. Avocations: tennis, photography, theatre. Home: 1983 Audubon Dr Fort Washington PA 19025-1901

CASSEL, SEYMOUR, actor; b. Detroit, Jan. 22, 1937; s. Seymour Joseph and Pancretia Ann (Kearney) C.; m. Betty Lou Deering, Mar. 14, 1964; children: Lisa, Matthew, Dilyn. Grad., Northwestern High Sch., Detroit. Appeared in films including Shadows, 1960 (Critics award Venice Festival), Too Late Blues, 1962, The Killers, 1964, The Sweet Ride, 1968, Coogan's Bluff, 1968, Faces, 1968 (Best Supporting Actor award N.Y. Critics, Academy award nomination), The Revolutionary, 1970, Minnie and Moskowitz, 1971 (Best Actor award N.Y. Film Critics), The Last Tycoon, 1975, The Killing of a Chinese Bookie, 1976, Scott Joplin, 1977, Black Oak Conspiracy, 1977, Death Game, 1977, Valentino, 1977, Convoy, 1978, California Dreaming, 1979, Love Streams, 1984, Tin Men, 1986, Track 29, 1988, Dick Tracy, 1990, White Fang, 1990, Honeymoon in Vegas, 1992, In the Soup, 1992, Indecent Proposal, 1993, There Goes My Baby, 1993, Boiling Point, 1993, Imaginary Crimes, 1994, Handgun, 1994, Dark Side of Genius, 1994, Chasers, 1994, Anything for John, 1995, It Could Happen To You, 1994, Things To Do In Denver When You're Dead, 1995, Trees Lounge, 1996, This World, Then the Fireworks, 1996, Dream for an Insomniac, 1996, Cannes Man, 1996, Cameleone, 1996, Cosas que nunca te dije, 1996, Motel Blue, 1997, Obsession, 1997, The Treat, 1998, Ballad of the Nightingale, 1998, Relax. . .It's Just Sex, 1998, Emma's Wish, 1998, Irresistible, 1999, Cure for Boredom, 1999, others; dir. play Jesse and the Bandit Queens, 1978 (Best Dir. award); (TV series) Under Suspicion, 1994, Good Company, 1996; (TV mini-series) The Last Don, 1997. *

CASSELL, DEAN GEORGE, retired aerospace executive, management consultant; b. Bklyn., Sept. 25, 1928; s. George James and Blanche Mary (Duffy) C.; m. Roberta Francis Reid, June 5, 1954; children: Gerald, Leslie Ann, Geoffrey. BS, Georgetown U., 1951; postgrad., MIT, 1977. Support mgr. early warning program Grumman Aerospace, Bethpage, N.Y., 1963-69, program mgr., 1969-75, asst. to sr. v.p. aircraft and space, 1975-77, v.p. ops., 1977-81, dir. comml. devel. ctr., 1981-85, v.p. product integrity and environ. affairs, 1986-93; ret., 1993, pvt. practice mgmt. cons., 1994—; bd. dirs. Grumman Ohio Corp. Member execs. recycling rev. com. Suffolk County, Hauppauge, N.Y., 1990. With USN, 1953-60. Mem. L.I. Assn. (environ. com. 1986-93), U.S. C. of C., Rotary. Republican. Roman Catholic. Avocations: golf, gardening. Home: 764 Pat Dr West Islip NY 11795-3538

CASSELL, ERIC JONATHAN, physician; b. N.Y.C., Aug. 29, 1928; s. Hyman William and Anne (Lake) Goldstein; m. Joan M. Fishman; Oct. 17, 1957 (div. 1987); children: Justine, Stephen; m. Patricia M. Owens, May 26, 1990. BA, Queens Coll., 1950; MA, Columbia U., 1950; MD, NYU, 1954; DHL (hon.), Med. Coll. Pa., 1985. Intern 3d med. div. Bellevue Hosp., N.Y.C., 1954-55, asst. resident 3d med. div., 1955-56, 58-59, physician 3d, 4th med. div., 1965-66; USPHS trainee in infectious diseases Cornell U., N.Y.C., 1959-61, clin. prof. pub. health, 1971—; attending physician French Hosp., N.Y.C., 1961-74; assoc. attending physician Mt. Sinai (N.Y.) Hosp., 1966-71; assoc. dir. ambulatory care Community Med., Mt. Sinai, 1966-68; attending physician N.Y. Hosp., 1984—; clin. assoc. prof. medicine, NYU, 1965-66, Mt. Sinai Hosp., 1966-71; bd. dirs. Hasting's Ctr., Garrison, N.Y., 1975—; commr. Nat. Bioethics Adv. Commn., 1997—. Author: Healer's Art, 1976, Place of Humanities in Medicine, 1984, Talking With Patients (2 vols.), 1985, The Nature of Suffering, 1991, Doctoring: The Nature of Primary Care Medicine, 1997; editor: Changing Values in Medicine, 1979. Served to capt. M.C., U.S. Army, 1956-58. Master ACP; fellow N.Y. Acad. Medicine; mem. Inst. Medicine of NAS. Democrat. Jewish. Avocations: woodworking, metalworker. Office: 1550 York Ave New York NY 10028-5970

CASSELL, FRANK ALAN, university president, history educator; b. Hammond, Ind., Feb. 23, 1941; s. Frank Hyde and Marguerite Ellen Cassell; m. Elizabeth Ann Weber, Apr. 1, 1961; children: David Daniel Grande-Cassell, Jonathan Frank. BA, Wabash Coll., 1963; MA, Northwestern U., 1966, PhD, 1968. Prof. history U. Wis., Milw., 1967—, asst. chancellor, 1975-80, chair dept. history, 1980-89, interim dean social welfare, 1989-91; vice provost, dean Roosevelt U., Schaumburg, Ill., 1991-97; pres. U. Pitts., Greensburg, 1997—. Author: Merchant Congressman in the Young Republic: Samuel Smith of Maryland, 1752-1839, 1971; co-author: The University of Wisconsin-Milwaukee, 1992; editor: Seeds of Crisis, 1993 (Gambruinus prize 1994); contbr. numerous articles, book revs. to profl. publs. Planning commr. Arlington Heights (Ill.) Planning commn., 1995-97; dir. Northwest 2001, 1991-97; bd. dirs. Wis. State Hist. Preservation Rev. Bd., 1976-86. Woodrow Wilson scholar, 1963, 66; recipient Author's award Mo. Hist. Soc., 1986, others. Mem. HIst. Assn., Orgn. Am. Historians, Am. Coun. Edn., Rotary, Univ. Club of Pitts. Home: 430 Glenmeade Rd Greensburg PA 15601-1138 Office: U Pitts at Greensburg 1150 Mount Pleasant Rd Greensburg PA 15601-5860

CASSELL, FRANK HYDE, business educator; b. Chgo., Oct. 12, 1916; s. Frank V. Seymour and Mary Alicia (Robinson) C.; m. Marguerite Ellen Fletcher, Mar. 24, 1940; children: Frank Allan, Thomas W. (dec.), Christopher B. AB, Wabash Coll., 1939; postgrad., U. Chgo., 1946-47. Exec. Inland Steel Co., Chgo., 1948-68; U.S. rep. OECD, Amsterdam, 1966, Paris, 1967; on leave as dir. U.S. Employment Svc., Washington, 1966-68; prof. indsl. rels. Kellogg Grad. Sch. Mgmt., Northwestern U., 1968-85, prof. emeritus orgn. behavior and indsl. rels., 1985—; chmn. bd. employment rsch. and devel. inst. Northwestern U., 1987—; vis. prof. Inst. Am. Studies, Salzburg, Austria, 1957, Inst. Mgmt., Northwestern U., Burgenstock (Luzerne), Switzerland, 1975—; v.p. bd. dirs. Rehab. Inst. Chgo., 1960-66; cons. to govt. and industry in fields manpower, econ. and technol. devel., indsl. rels. and mgmt. Author: The Employment Service: An Organization in Change, 1968, (with Weber and Ginsberg) National Manpower Policies, 1969, (with Jean Baron) Collective Bargaining in the Public Sector, 1976; contbr.: Handbook of Business Strategy, Strategic Human Resources Planning, 1985, Handbook of Airline Economics, Emergence of Policy Bargaining, 1996; contbr. articles to profl. jours. Trustee Wabash Coll., 1967-71; chmn. Gov. Ill. Com. Unemployment, 1961-63; chmn. Winnetka (Ill.) Planning Commn., 1973-75; bd. dirs. Chgo. Urban League, 1953-92; bd. dirs., mem. exec. com. Means Services, Inc., 1974-82; co-chmn. Chgo. Mayoral Transition Com., 1983, Chgo. Mayor's Task Force on Steel and S.E. Chgo., 1984-86; adv. Northwestern U.-Am. Iron and Steel Inst. Steel Research Project, 1987-90; advisor set-aside contracts legis. for women and minorities Mayor's Blue Ribbon Panel, Chgo., 1990; hon. mem. White Mountain Apache Tribe, White River, Ariz., 1967; pres. Op. Able, Chgo., 1991-92; chmn. Employment Rsch. and Devel. Inst., 1990—. Recipient Disting. Svc. awards U.S. Dept. Labor, 1968, 73. Mem. Indsl. Rels. Assn. Chgo. (pres. 1957-58), Indsl. Rels. Rsch. Assn. (bd. dirs. 1966-69), Am. Econ. Assn., Nat. Planning Assn., Beta Gamma Sigma. Home: 9200 E Prairie Rd # 210 Evanston IL 60203-1640 Office: Northwestern U McCormick Sch Engring 2145 Sheridan Rd Evanston IL 60201-2926 Office: Employment R&D Inst 809 Ridge Rd Wilmette IL 60091-2489

CASSELL, KAY ANN, librarian; b. Van Wert, Ohio, Sept. 24, 1941; d. Kenneth Miller and Pauline (Zimmerman) C. B.A., Carnegie-Mellon U., 1963; M.L.S., Rutgers U., 1965; M.A., Bklyn. Coll., 1969. Reference librarian Bklyn. Coll. Library, 1965-68; adult svcs. cons. N.J. State Libr., Trenton, 1968-71; libr. cons.-vol. Peace Corps, Rabat, Morocco, 1971-73; adult svcs. cons. Westchester Libr. System, White Plains, N.Y., 1973-75; dir. Bethlehem Pub. Libr., Delmar, N.Y., 1975-81, Huntington (N.Y.) Pub. Libr., 1982-85; exec. dir. Coordinating Coun. Lit. Mags., N.Y.C., 1985-87; univ. libr. New Sch. for Social Rsch., 1987-88; assoc. dir. programs and svcs. br. librs. N.Y. Pub. Libr., 1989—; adj. faculty Grad. Sch. Libr. Sci., SUNY, Albany, 1976-78, Palmer Sch. Libr. and Info. Scis., L.I. U., 1986-90, Grad. Sch. Info. and Libr. Sci., Pratt Inst., 1994—; chmn. cmty. adv. com. Capital Dist. Humanities Program, Albany, 1980-81; bd. dirs. Literacy Vols. of Suffolk, Bellport, N.Y., 1981-85; chmn. N.Y.C. Sch. Libr. Sys. Coun., 1991-94; treas. Libr. Pub. Rels. Coun., 1993-98, v.p., pres.-elect, 1998—. Mem. ALA (pres. reference and adult svcs. divsn. 1983-84, chair membership com. 1991-95, coun. 1992—), N.Y. Libr. Assn. (pres. reference and adult svcs. sect. 1975-76), Feminist Press (bd. dirs.), Beta Phi Mu. Office: NY Pub Libr Office Programs & Svcs 455 5th Ave New York NY 10016-0118*

CASSELL, LUCILLE RICHARDSON, small business owner; b. Sikeston, Mo., Feb. 23, 1958; d. Glen and Cenia (McCaster) Richardson; m. Arthur Earl Cassell, Apr. 12, 1986; children: Christopher Glen, Bryan Mitchell, David Arthur, Aaron Lamar. A in Bus. Admintrn., S.E. Mo. State U., 1980; deaconess lic., Green Meml. Bible Inst.-Coll., Sikeston, 1982; B in Bus. Mgmt., Frederick Taylor U., 1997. Shoe packer Wohl Shoe Co., Sikeston, 1980-84; sales clk. J.C. Penney, Sikeston, 1984-85; bookeeper, teller Bank of Sikeston, 1985-86; computer operator Sta. KBSI-TV, Cape Girardeau, Mo., 1986-89; data clk. Falcon Cable TV, Sikeston, 1989-90; owner, mgr. Wee=Care Daycare Ctr., Charleston, 1990-99; pres. CBD Enterprises, Inc., Charleston, 1999—; owner Cassell Cmty. Devel. Corp., 1995—, Wee-Care Christian Acad. Pre-School, 1998. Author: The Best That I Can Be, 1995; patented disposable diapers, adult diapers; inventor in field. Vol. Mo. Delta Med. Ctr., Sikeston, 1990; participant walk-a-thons Cystic Fibrosis Found., Charleston, 1992; Sunday sch. tchr. Green Meml. Ch., Sikeston, 1985-86, Opportunity Ch., Charleston; leader Kid's Beat Program, Opportunity COGIC Drill Team, Fancy Bottoms Diapers (displayed in Black Inventors Mus., St. Louis), leader youth drill team. Mem. Ch. of God in Christ. Avocations: reading, volleyball, music, bowling. Fax: (573) 683-6670. E-mail: cbdenterprises@ldd.net. Home: PO Box 284 1210 Warren St Charleston MO 63834-1842

CASSELL, WILLIAM COMYN, retired college president; b. Vallejo, Calif., Oct. 8, 1934; s. Comyn R. and Emily E. (Duckwith) C.; m. Jeanne Taylor, Dec. 27, 1955; children: Paul, Susan, David. BA, Pomona Coll., 1956; MA, Claremont Grad. Sch., 1969; LHD (hon.), Lakeland Coll., 1977; LLD, William Penn Coll.; D in Bus. Adminstn., Won Kwang U.; MBA, Heidelberg Coll., DLitt. Broker Hornblower and Weeks, Inc., Orange, Calif., 1958-64; asst. to treas. Claremont (Calif.) Coll., 1964-65; dir. income trusts and bequests Calif. Inst. Tech., Pasadena, 1965-69; dir. devel. and pub. relations Menninger Found., Topeka, 1969-70; dir. devel. U. Denver, 1970-74; pres. Coll. of Idaho, Caldwell, 1974-80; pres. Heidelberg Coll., Tiffin, Ohio, 1980-96, pres. emeritus, 1996—; cons. Ford Found., Phelps-Stokes Fund, Congress of No. Marianas Islands, numerous colls. and govt. agys., 1966—; hon. royal consul gen. Nepal; bd. dirs. Fifth-Third Bank No. Ohio. Author: The Case for Deferred Giving, 1966, Deferred Giving Programs: Administration and Promotion, 1972; editorial adv. bd.: Ednl. Record. Mem. Parks and Recreation Commn., Claremont, 1967-69, City Council, Bow Mar, Colo., 1967-69; mem. adv. bd. Salvation Army, Caldwell, , Western Electric Fund; trustee Caldwell Meml. Hosp., chmn., 1976; mem. Idaho newspaper carrier scholarship selection com.; mem. Missions on Am. Mgmt. and Ednl. Techniques to Indonesia and Jamaica; mission leader Thailand on Edn. and Mgmt.; mem. White House Adv. Com. on Libr. and Tech., White House Conf.; mem. Ohio Higher Edn. Facilities Commn.; adv. com. chmn. bd. Western Ind. Coll. Funds; bd. dirs. Tiffin YMCA; bd. dirs. Ketchum/Sun Valley Transit Authority; jr. warden St. Thomas Episcopal Ch., Sun Valley. 1st lt. AUS, 1957-58. Recipient Brakeley award for Outstanding Coll. Devel. Am. Alumni Coun., 1968, Nat. Fund Raising Coun. award, 1969; named an Idaho Disting. Citizen, 1977, hon. VIP Sta. KIDO, Boise, Citizen of Yr. City of Tiffin, 1991. Mem. Coun. for Advancement of Support of Edn., Caldwell C. of C. (exec. bd. dir.), Tiffin C. of c. (bd. dirs.), Internat. Assn. Univ. Pres. (exec. com.), World Bus. Coun., North Cen. Accreditation Assn. (commr.), Am. Coun. on Edn. (commn. internat. edn.), Rotary (fellows selection com. dist., Citizen of Yr., Tiffin, Ohio 1991), Ketchum Sun Valley Rotary Club (bd. dirs.). *

CASSELL, WILLIAM WALTER, retired accounting operations consultant; b. Chgo., Apr. 10, 1917; s. Charles F. and E. Margaret (Jackson) C.; m. Rosamond Mary Fisher, May 13, 1944; children: Anne, Gerald, Douglas, Mary. Student, U. Wash., 1936-38, Syracuse U., 1943-44; grad., Am. Inst. Banking, 1957, Grad. Sch. Savs. Banking, 1965, Savs. Banks Mgmt. Devel. Program, U. Mass., 1970. Officer's asst. Syracuse (N.Y.) Savs. Bank, 1959-66, treas., 1966-71, v.p., 1971-75, sr. v.p., controller, 1975-77, exec. v.p., 1977-83, cons., 1983, also dir.; dir. State Bank of Chittenango, 1963-73, 1983—, Credit Bur. Syracuse, 1976-83, Consumer Credit Counseling Service, 1979-83; chmn. bd. dirs. State Bank of Chittenango, 1993—, SBC Fin. Corp., 1993—. Bd. dirs. Syracuse Symphony Orch., 1979-81, Opera Theater of Syracuse, 1982-84; pres. Madison County Hist. Soc., 1982-84. Served with U.S. Army, 1941-45, ETO. Decorated Bronze Star. Mem. Am. Inst. Banking, Fin. Execs. Inst. (pres. Syracuse chpt. 1971-72). Republican. Methodist. Clubs: Men's Garden of Am, Monarch of Syracuse. Home: 131 W Genesee St Chittenango NY 13037-1501 *To find happiness in little things each day; to be all I am capable of being, judged within the framework of my own real values and to make others glad I came this way—this is the measure of a life worthwhile: contentment, not complacency.*

CASSELLA, DENNIS GENE, county official; b. Pratt, Kans., Oct. 24, 1946; s. Barney Joseph and Norma Jeanne Cassella. AA, Sacramento C.C., 1970; BA in History/Polit. Sci., U. Calif., Davis, 1971; MPA, East Tex. State U., 1975. City pers. dir. City of Texarkana, Ark., 1971-75; dir. adminstrv. svcs. Ark. Dept. Local Svcs., Little Rock, 1975-76; dir. gen. svcs. County of Nevada, Calif., 1977—; dir. emergency svcs. County of Nevada, 1988—; sr. adj. prof. Golden Gate U., Sacramento, 1979—. Mem. Nevada City Police Cmty. Rels. Commn., Nevada City, 1991-93, Nevada City Bicentennial of the Constitution Commn., 1986—. Staff sgt. USAF, 1966-69. Mem. Nevada County Libr. Found. (pres. 1998-99), Gold Country Lions (pres. 1987), Am. Soc. for Pub. Adminstrn. E-mail: henryv@nccn.net. Office: County of Nev Gen Svcs 950 Maidu Ave Nevada City CA 95959

CASSELLA, WILLIAM NATHAN, JR., organization executive; b. Alton, Ill., July 14, 1920; s. William Nathan and Martha (Stanly) C.; m. Margaret Powers Crowley, June 22, 1946 (dec. Nov. 1987); children: John Woodson, Stephen Rowan, Mark Crowley, William Kent. A.B., U. Ill., 1942; M.S., Syracuse U., 1943; A.M., Harvard, 1951, Ph.D., 1953. Research asst. Pub. Adminstrn. Clearing House, Washington, 1946; instr., then asst. prof. polit. sci. U. Mo., 1948-54; with Nat. Mcpl. League, 1953-90, exec. dir., 1969-85, project coord., 1985-90; sr. assoc. Inst. Pub. Adminstrn., 1988—; rsch. assoc. Govt. Affairs Found., 1954-57; vis. assoc. prof. pub. adminstrn. Columbia, 1957; sr. rsch. assoc. Columbia (Met. Region Program), 1957-61; mem. adv. com. state and local govt. stats. Bur. Census, 1962-65, chmn., 1963-65; mem. area devel. adv. bd. Com. Econ. Devel., 1964-66; cons. Adv. Commn. Intergovtl. Rels., 1967-89. Author: Constitutional Aspects of Metropolitan Government, 1961, also articles; contbg. editor Nat. Civic Rev., 1954-85, chmn. editorial bd., 1969-85. Mem. Greenburgh (N.Y.) Bd. Edn., 1961-64; mem. Westchester County Planning Bd., 1962-97, vice chmn., 1967-72, chmn., 1973-97, Hudson River Valley Greenway Compact Commn., 1997—, Conservation Adv. Com., Dobbs Ferry, N.Y., 1997—; bd. dirs. Westchester County Indsl. Devel. Agy., 1976-83; trustee Pub. Adminstrn. Service, 1969-76; governing bd. Governmental Affairs Inst., 1969-76. Served to lt. USNR, 1943-46. Mem. Am. Polit. Sci. Assn., Am. Soc. Pub. Adminstrn., Govtl. Rsch. Assn., Internat. City/County Mgmt. Assn., Nat. Acad. Pub. Adminstrn., Regional Plan Assn. N.Y., Phi Beta Kappa, Alpha Kappa Lambda, Delta Sigma Pi, Omicron Delta Kappa, Pi Alpha Alpha. Episcopalian. Home: 100 Buena Vista Dr Dobbs Ferry NY 10522-3521 Office: Inst Pub Adminstrn 411 Lafayette St New York NY 10003

CASSELMAN, FREDERICK LEE, computer artist; b. Columbus, Ohio, Jan. 5, 1940; s. Carroll Dean Casselman and Marjory Evelyn Howard; m. Carol Esther Puffer, Nov. 23, 1968; children: Amy, Aaron. BEE, Ohio State U., 1963, MSEE, 1965. Sr. engr. GTE Corp., Needham, Mass., 1966-94. *Computer artist and creator of the online artist's project, Earth Echo, www.eartecho.com. Frederick Casselman's purpose is to create art with a sense of harmony and peace with the earth, the Cosmos, and within ourselves. The work is characterized by vibrant colors and organic patterns, reflecting that which we see in nature and sense in our souls. One online visitor responded with "O! Such Grace and Spirit." Another commented "Earth and the whole of the Cosmos lives within these images."* Exhibited in one-man shows at Boston Cyberarts Festival, 1999; author website The Earth Echo Project, 1996—; artist on-line-exhbn. Digital Americana, Orlando Mus. Art, 1998. Publicity dir. Framingham (Mass.) Cultural Coun., 1996—. E-mail: fred@earthecho.com. Home: 48 Florissant Ave Framingham MA 01701

CASSELMAN, WILLIAM E., II, lawyer; b. Washington, Pa., July 8, 1941; s. William E. and Lucy (Bobbs) C.; m. Mia Kang, June 15, 1993; children: Katharine Carr, Lee Wilson. BA, Claremont-McKenna Coll., 1963; postgrad., U. Madrid, 1963-64; JD, George Washington U., 1968. Bar: Va. 1968, D.C. 1972, U.S. Supreme Ct. 1975. Legis. asst. to Robert McClory U.S. Ho. of Reps., 1965-68; staff asst. Office of Pres., 1969, dep. spl. asst. to Pres., 1969-71, counsel to Pres., 1974-75; gen. counsel Gen. Svcs. Adminstrn., 1971-73; legal counsel to Vice Pres. U.S., 1973-74; ptnr. Ambrose & Casselman, P.C., 1975-79; pvt. practice Washington, 1979-82; ptnr. Dorsey & Whitney, 1982-84, Popham, Haik, Schnobrich & Kaufman, Ltd., Washington, 1985-93; of counsel Stairs Dillenback Finley & Merle, N.Y.C., 1993—; pvt. practice Washington, 1993—; mem. adminstrv. conf. U.S., 1971-73; adv. mem. Nat. Conf. Commrs. on Uniform State Laws, 1975; mem. Gerald R. Ford Commemorative Com., 1977-82; bd. dirs. gen. counsel, mem. fin. com., fellow Georgetown U. Ctr. for Internat. Bus. and Trade (formerly Nat. Ctr. Export-Import Studies), 1983-93. Recipient Disting. Alumni Achievement award George Washington U., 1975. Mem. ABA, Fed. Bar Assn. (chmn. gen. counsels com. 1973-74, nat. coun. 1974-79, Disting. Svc. commendation 1974), George Washington Law Assn. (bd. dirs. 1976-81), Nat. Trust for Hist. Preservation (mem. com. on legal svcs. 1978-80), Franklin Square Club, Nat. Lawyers Club, Delta Theta Phi, Theta Chi. Republican.

CASSELS, MARTHA BEASLEY, realtor, developer; b. Greenwood, S.C., Oct. 22, 1932; d. Hugh Alton and Ora Faith (Mitchell) Beasley; m. Marion Carlyle Crenshaw, Jr., June 25, 1953 (div. 1979); children: Marion Carlyle III, William Frank, Hugh Charles, Faith Byrd; m. Samuel Jones Cassels, III, Oct. 6, 1979. BA, Converse Coll., 1953. Cert. residential specialist Realtors Nat. Mktg. Inst., 1979. Tchr. Carr Jr. H.S., Durham, N.C., 1953-55, 1st Congl. Pre Sch., Branford, Conn., 1964-66; dir., tchr. Barfield Kindergarten, Durham, 1966-68; dir. Duke Meml. Pre Sch., Durham, 1968-74; sec. corp. Bob Gunter Realty, Inc., Durham, 1972-77; owner Crenshaw Co., Inc., Durham, 1977-79, Cassels Real Estate, Montgomery, Ala., 1980—; pres. Hampton Killingsworth, Inc. 1990—, Montgomery Area Bd. Realtors, Ala. Bd. Realtors, 1979—, Nat. Bd. Realtors, Chgo., 1974—. Elected mem. County Bd. Edn., Durham, 1972-79; bd. dirs. Scott & Zelda Fitzgerald Mus., Montgomery, 1986—; patron theatre dept. Ala. State U., Montgomery, 1994—; active Montgomery Zoo. Named Top Prodr., Montgomery Area Bd. Realtors, 1981; recipient Top Residential award Montgomery Area Bd. Realtors, 1982, 10 Consecutive Yrs. of Multi Millions award Montgomery Area Bd. Realtors, 1990. Mem. AAUW, YMCA, Greater Montgomery Home Builder Assn., Jr. Twentieth Century, Montgomery Area C. of C., C.E.O. Roundtable, Prattville C. of C. Episcopalian. Avocations: reading, grandchildren activities, swimming. Office: Cassels Real Estate 623 S Perry St Montgomery AL 36104-5890

CASSENS, NICHOLAS, JR., ceramics engineer; b. Sigourney, Iowa, Sept. 8, 1948; s. Nicholas and Wanda Fern (Lancaster) C.; B.S. in Ceramic Engring., Iowa State U., 1971, B.S. in Chem. Engring., 1971; M.S. in Material Sci. and Engring., U. Calif., Berkeley, 1979; m. Linda Joyce Morrow, Aug. 30, 1969; 1 son, Randall Scott, Jr. research engr. Nat. Refractories and Minerals Corp., Livermore, Calif., 1971-72, research engr., 1972-74, sr. research engr., 1974-77, staff research engr., 1977-84, sr. staff research engr., 1984—. Mem. Am. Ceramic Soc. Democrat. Patentee in field, U.S., Australia, S.Am., Japan, Europe. Home: 4082 Suffolk Way Pleasanton CA 94588-4117 Office: 1852 Rutan Dr Livermore CA 94550-7635

CASSERLY, CHARLEY, professional football team executive; b. Feb. 27, 1949; m. Bev Casserly; 1 daughter, Shannon. BS in Edn., Springfield Coll., M. in Guidance. Asst. coach Cathedral H.S., Springfield, Mass., 1969-72; athletic dir. Cathedral H.S., 1974-75; asst. Springfield Coll., 1973-74; tchr., football coach Minnechaugh H.S., Mass., 1975-76; joined Washington Redskins, NFL, 1977, went from intern in scouting dept., to full-time scout, to asst. gen. mgr., 1977-89, gen. mgr., 1989—. Office: Washington Redskins Dulles Internat Airport PO Box 17247 Washington DC 20041-7247*

CASSERLY, JAMES LUND, lawyer; b. Norfolk, Va., Dec. 26, 1951; s. James Robert and Patricia (Lund) C.; m. Kathleen Ann Flynn, Apr. 25, 1981; 1 child Laura Flynn. AB magna cum laude, Tufts Coll., 1973; JD, Columbia U., 1976. Bar: D.C. 1976, U.S. Dist. Ct. D.C. 1980, U.S. Ct. Appeals (D.C. cir.) 1981. Law clk. to trial judges U.S. Ct. Fed. Claims, Washington, 1976-77; law clk. to judge Marion Bennett U.S. Ct. Appeals Fed. Cir., Washington, 1977-78; assoc. Wilkinson, Cragun & Barker, Washington, 1978-82; assoc. Squire Sanders & Dempsey, Washington, 1982-85, ptnr., 1985-94; sr. legal advisor to Commr. Susan Ness FCC, Washington, 1994—. Home: 5345 Broad Branch Rd NW Washington DC 20015-1352 Office: FCC 445 12th St SW Washington DC 20554*

CASSETTA, SEBASTIAN ERNEST, industry executive; b. July 30, 1948; m. Linn Miller; children: Christopher, Sebastian III, Kathryn. BSBA, U. Denver, 1971; postgrad., Wharton Sch., U. Pa. Spl. asst. to gov./v.p. Nelson A. Rockefeller Albany, N.Y. and Washington, 1971-75; pres. Transec Inc., Dallas, 1975-80; v.p. internat. devel. Brinks, Inc., Darien, Conn., 1980-85; pres., chief exec. officer, mem. bd. dirs. Burns and Roe Securacom, Inc., Oradell, N.J., 1985-92; chmn., CEO Smart Phone Comms., Inc., Stamford, Conn., 1992—; bd. dirs. Brinks Europe, Paris; mem. U.S. Dept. of Commerce and Industry Sector Adv. Coun., 1983, U.S. Export Coun., 1984, V.P.'s Task Force on Terrorism, Washington, 1986, Nat. Def. Exec. Res., U.S. Dept. Commerce. Author: Winning America's Biggest Security Contract. Trustee Worcester (Mass.) Acad., 1983-90; dir. Christian edn. St. Michael's Episc. Ch., Dallas, 1976-80. Mem. Interactive Svcs. Assn., Nat. Info. Infrastructure Testbed, Am. Soc. Indsl. Security, Am. Nuclear Soc., Am. Def. Preparedness Assn., Nat. Security Indsl. Assn. (bd. dirs.), Young Pres. Orgn. (bd. dirs.), U.S. Rowing Assn. Office: SmartServ Online Inc One Station Place Stamford CT 06902

CASSIDY, BARRY ALLEN, physician assistant, clinical medical ethicist; b. Chgo., Aug. 28, 1947; s. Frank Thomas and Ann Marie (Panek) C.; m. JoAnn DeRue (div.); m. Robyn G. Lacher (div.); children: Colleen Osmond, Jason Lacher, Nathaniel Austin; m. Barbie A. Cassidy. Cert. physician assoc., Duke U., 1971; BS, Univ. State N.Y., Albany, 1992; PhD, Union Inst., 1995. Cert. physician asst. Physician assoc. Med. Offices of T.C. Rozema, MD, Waukegan, Ill., 1971-73; instr. in healthcare sci. Sch. Medicine George Washington U., Washington, 1973-75; med. cons. Medicolegal Rsch., Washington, 1975-79; CEO, dir. health svcs. Occucare, Inc., Research Triangle Park, N.C., 1979-81; v.p. Coastal Group, Inc., Durham, N.C., 1981-82; exec. v.p. So. Emergency Med. Assocs., Research Triangle Park, 1982-83; physician asst. Ariz. Heart Inst., Phoenix, 1983-86; pres. West Health Corp., Phoenix, 1986-87; thoracic and cardiovascular surgery asst. Mayo Clinic, Scottsdale, Ariz., 1987-96; assoc. prof., assoc. dir. physician asst. program Coll. Allied Health Scis. Midwestern U., Glendale, Ariz., 1996—; dir. physician asst. program Midwestern U., Glendale, 1998; adj. faculty S.W. Ctr. for Osteo. Med. Edn. and Health Scis., 1995-96; mem. Joint Bd. Regulation Physician Assts., 1998. Mem. editl. bd. Physician Assts. in Primary Care, 1985-88; inventor break-away catheter sys. Advisor on allied health Ill. Med. Soc., Chgo., 1972; advisor Gov.'s Health Licensure Commn., State of Ill., Chgo., 1972. Sgt. USAF, 1965-69. Mem. Ariz. Med. Assn., Ariz. Acad. Physician Assts., Hastings Ctr. for Med. Ethics (assoc.), Am. Soc. Law, Medicine and Ethics, Am. Acad. Physician Assts. (chmn. jud. affairs com., v.p. 1974). Jewish. Home: 6630 E Lafayette Blvd Scottsdale AZ 85251-3134 Office: Midwestern U Coll Coll Health Scis 19555 N 59th Ave Glendale AZ 85308-6813

CASSIDY, DAVID C., science educator; b. Richmond, Va., Aug. 10, 1945. BA, Rutgers U., New Brunswick, N.J., 1967, MS, 1970; PhD, Purdue U., West Lafayette, Ind., 1976, DSc (hon.), 1997. Rsch. fellow U. Calif., Berkeley, 1976-77; A.V. Humboldt fellow U. Stuttgart, Germany, 1977-80; asst. prof. U. Regensburg, Germany, 1980-83; assoc. editor Einstein Papers Princeton (N.J.) U. Press, Princeton and Boston, 1983-90; assoc. prof. Hofstra U., Hempstead, N.Y., 1990-96; prof. Hofstra U., Hempstead, 1996—. Author: Uncertainty: Life and Science of W. Heisenberg, 1992, Einstein and Our World, 1995; editor Papers of A. Einstein, 1983-90; mem. editl. bd. Physics in Perspective, 1997—, Isis, 1998—; contbr. articles to profl. jours. Recipient sci. writing award Am. Inst. Physics, 1993. Fellow Am. Phys. Soc. (sec.-treas. forum hist. physics 1994-98); mem. History of Sci. Soc. (chair Pfizer prize com. 1994-97, Pfizer award 1995, runner-up Watson-Davis prize

1996), N.Y. Acad. Scis. (chair sect. hist. philos. sci. 1994-97). Office: Hofstra U Natural Sci Program Hempstead NY 11549

CASSIDY, DAVID MICHAEL, lawyer; b. Amityville, N.Y., May 31, 1954; s. Paul Francis and Theresa Alice (Britts) C.; m. Janet Patricia Johnson, Aug. 26, 1978; children: Daniel B., Caitlin E. BA, SUNY, Stony Brook, 1981; JD, St. John's U., Jamaica, N.Y., 1985. Bar: N.Y. 1986. Assoc. Rivkin, Radler & Kremer, Uniondale, N.Y., 1985-92, ptnr., 1992—. Mem. Suffolk County Bar Assn., L.I. Assn. Office: Rivkin Radler & Kremer EAB Plz Uniondale NY 11556

CASSIDY, ESTHER CHRISTMAS, retired government official; b. Upper Marlboro, Md., Aug. 5, 1933; d. Donelson and Esther Christmas; divorced; children: William Keeling, Carroll Cassidy Drewyer, Daniel Clark. BA, Manhattanville Coll., 1955. Phys. scientist, R&D Nat. Bur. Standards, Gaithersburg, Md., 1955-73; sci. advisor U.S. Congressman Teno Roncalio, Washington, 1973-74; asst. dir. congl. affairs Energy R&D Adminstrn. Dept. Energy, Washington, 1974-78; dir. congl. and legis. affairs Nat. Inst. Stds. and Tech., Gaithersburg, 1978-98; ret., 1998. Contbr. articles to profl. jours. Mem. IEEE (sr.). Avocations: horse racing, golf.

CASSIDY, GEORGE THOMAS, international business development consultant; b. Jamaica, N.Y., Apr. 13, 1939; s. George Leo and Vivia P.M. (Sharpe) C.; m. Eileen Mary O'Shea, Nov. 25, 1967; children: George, Eileen, Patrick, Martin. BA, St. John's U., 1960. Officer Detroit Police Dept., 1964-66; fin. analyst Esso Internat., Inc., N.Y.C., 1966-69; asst. treas. Am. Standard, Inc., N.Y.C., 1969-74; dir. bus. devel. St. Regis Paper Co., Inc., N.Y.C., 1974-85; pres. SC Mgmt. Svcs. Corp., Wilton, Conn., 1985—; chmn. SC Mgmt. Svcs. Corp., Wilton, 1989—. Author: International Financial Management, 1987, Handbook of Budgeting, 1989, 93. Lt. USCG, 1960-64. Mem. L.I. Assn. (internat. trade advisor 1991—). Republican. Roman Catholic. Avocations: boating, antique automobiles. Home: 60 Evergreen Rd New Canaan CT 06840-2927 Office: SC Mgmt Svcs Corp PO Box 7458 Wilton CT 06897-7458

CASSIDY, JAMES MARK, construction company executive; b. Evanston, Ill., June 22, 1942; s. James Michael and Mary Ellen (Munroe) C.; B.A., St. Mary's Coll., 1963; m. Bonnie Marie Bercker, Aug. 1, 1964 (d. Dec. 1981); children: Micaela Marie, Elizabeth Ann, Daniel James; m. Patricia Margaret Mary Murphy, Sept. 15, 1984. Estimator, Cassidy Bros., Inc., Rosemont, Ill., 1963-65, project mgr., 1965-67, v.p., 1967-71, exec. v.p., 1971-77, pres., 1978—; trustee Plasterer's Health & Welfare Trust, 1971-92. Area fund leader constrn. industry salute to Boy Scouts Am., 1975; mem. pres.'s council St. Mary's Coll.; chmn. labor liaison com. Laborers Internat. Union N.Am. and Assn. Wall and Ceiling Industries, 1982-85, chmn. labor-mgmt. group, 1985-88; chmn. Chicagoland Assn. Wall and Ceiling Contractors' Carpenters Union Negotiating Team, 1983—. Served with U.S. Army, 1963-64, N.G., 1964-69. Mem. Chgo. Plastering Inst., Builder Uppers Club (pres. 1973-74), Chicagoland Assn. Wall and Ceiling Contractors (pres. 1976-79), Great Lakes Council, Internat. Assn. Wall and Ceiling Contractors (chmn. 1977), Constrn. Employers Assn. Chgo. (dir. 1976—, pres.-elect 1989-90, pres. 1991-93), chmn. com. labor-mgmt. relations 1983-93), Chicagoland Safety Council (dir. 1988-92), Joint Conf. Bd. Cook County (chmn. 1996-97, 98-99), Assn. Wall and Ceiling Industries Internat. (dir. 1978-81, 88-89, fin. v.p. 1990, 2d vp. 1991, pres.-elect 1992, pres. 1993), Park Ridge (Ill.) Country Club (dir. 1994-97), Eagle Creek Country Club (Naples, Fla.).

CASSIDY, JOHN FRANCIS, JR., industrial technology executive; b. Troy, N.Y., Nov. 26, 1943; s. John F. Sr. and Beverly A. (Blowers) C.; m. Paulina C. DiBacco, July 24, 1965; children: Rachel, Sean. BEE, Rensselaer Poly. Inst., 1965, MEE, 1967, PhD, 1969. Various R & D mgmt. positions GM, 1969-81; with control systems R & D GE Corp. R & D Labs., 1981-89; corp. dir. tech. mgmt. United Techs. Corp., 1989-92; dir. United Techs. Rsch. Ctr., 1992-93, v.p., 1993-98; sr. v.p. sci. and tech. United Techs. Rsch. Ctr., East Hartford, 1998—; vice chair bd. dirs. Rensselaer at Hartford. Bd. dirs. Convergence Electronics Transp. Assn., Convergence Ednl. Found., Detroit. Mem. IEEE (sr.), Soc. Automotive Engrs. (sr.), Conn. Acad. Sci. and Engring. Office: United Techs Rsch Ctr MS 129-04 411 Silver Ln East Hartford CT 06118-1127*

CASSIDY, JOHN HAROLD, lawyer; b. St. Louis, June 18, 1925; s. John Harold and Jennie (Phillips) C.; m. Marjorie Blair, Nov. 26, 1947; children: Patricia, John, Brian. AB, Washington U., 1949, JD, 1951. Bar: Mo. 1951, U.S. Dist. Ct. (ea. dist.) Mo. 1951, U.S. Ct. Appeals (8th crct.) 1951, U.S. Supreme Ct. 1955. Atty. U.S. Govt., St. Louis, 1951-56; pvt. practice St. Louis, 1956-59; atty. Crown Zellerbach Corp., San Francisco, 1959-61; atty. Ralston Purina Co., St. Louis, 1961-89, v.p., 1975-85, v.p., sec., sr. counsel, 1985-89. Served with U.S. Mcht. Marine, 1943-45. Mem. ABA, Mo. Bar Assn., St. Louis Bar Assn., Am. Soc. Corp. Secs. Republican.

CASSIDY, JOHN JOSEPH, hydraulic and hydrologic engineer; b. Gebo, Wyo., June 21, 1930; s. Valentine Patrick and Johannah Elizabeth (Johnson) C.; m. Alice Willman, Mar. 15, 1953; children: Val Patrick, Jon Allan, Debra Kay. BSCE, Mont. State U., Bozeman, 1952, MSCE, 1960; PhD, U. Iowa, 1964. Registered profl. engr., Mont., Calif., Wash., Idaho, Wyo., Nebr. Hwy. engr. U.S. Bur. Pub. Rds., Missoula, Mont., 1951-52; design engr. Mont. State Water Bd., Helena, 1954-58; instr. civil engring. Mont. State U., Bozeman, 1958-60; rsch. asst. in hydraulics U. Iowa, Iowa City, 1960-63; prof., chmn. civil engring. U. Mo., columbia, 1963-74; dir. Wash. Water Resources Ctr. Wash. State U., Pullman, 1979-81; chief hydrologic engr. Bechtel Corp., San Francisco, 1974-79, 81-85, mgr. hydraulics and hydrology, 1985-94, mgr. hydraulics and geotechnical svcs., 1994-95; ret., 1995; cons. dam safety Hydro Que., Montreal, 1993-94; cons. water resources Wyo. State Engrs. Office, Cheyenne, 1990-99; cons. dam design MK Corp., Boise, Idaho, 1980-81; cons. hydrology Gomez and Cajon, Bogota, Colombia, 1980-81; commn. Binacional de Yacryeta, Buenos Aires, Argentina, 1994-96, Hidroestudios, Bogota, Columbia, 1995-97, Consutoria Colombiana, 1998. Co-author: Hydrology for Engineers and Planners, 1974, Small and Mini Hydropower Systems, 1984, Engineering Hydraulics, 1988, 98, Design of Hydropower Systems, 1989. Chmn. fin. com. Walnut Creek (Calif.) United Meth. Ch., 1990-92. Served to cpl. U.S. Army, 1952-54. Bechtel fellow, 1987. Fellow ASCE (hon., Hunter Rouse Hydraulic Engring. award 1988, Hydraulic Structures medal 1996); mem. NAE, Internat. Assn. Hydraulic Rsch., U.S. Com. on Large Dams (dir. 1987-95), Internat. Commn. on Large Dams (com. chmn. 1987-96). Republican. Methodist. Avocations: woodworking, fly fishing. Home: 4400 Capitol Ct Concord CA 94518-1933

CASSIDY, KEVIN ANDREW, retired engineering company executive; b. N.Y.C., May 20, 1931; s. Joseph Aloyisius and Norine Beatrice (Mangan) C.; m. Mary Elizabeth Hennessey, Jan. 16, 1954; children: Kevin Andrew Jr., Mark Robert, Karen Marie, Richard Joseph. BCE, Manhattan Coll., 1953. Registered profl. engr., N.J. Engr. Standard Oil (Ind.), Whiting, Ind., 1953-59; project engr. Foster Wheeler, N.Y.C., 1959-69; project mgr. Foster Wheeler Energy Corp., Livingston, N.J., 1969-78, div. v.p., 1978-82; dir. Foster Wheeler Energy Ltd., Reading, Eng., 1982-96, Hytech, Moscow, 1989-94; v.p. Foster Wheeler Internat. Corp., Perryville, N.J., 1985-96; dir. Foster Wheeler Eastern Private Ltd., Singapore. Served with U.S. Army, 1954-56. Republican. Roman Catholic. Avocations: golf, skiing.

CASSIDY, RICHARD ARTHUR, environmental engineer, governmental water resources specialist; b. Manchester, N.H., Nov. 15, 1944; s. Arthur Joseph and Alice Ethuliette (Gregoire) C.; m. Judith Diane Maine, Aug. 14, 1971; children: Matthew, Amanda, Michael. BA, St. Anselm Coll., 1966; MS, U. N.H., 1969, Tufts U., 1972. Field biologist Pub. Service Co. of N.H., Manchester, 1968; jr. san. engr. Mass. Div. Water Pollution Control, Boston, 1968-69; aquatic biologist Normandeau Assocs., Bedford, N.H., 1969-70; hydraulic engr. New Eng. div. U.S. Army C.E., Waltham, Mass., 1972-77, environ. engr., Portland Dist., Oreg., 1977-81, supr., environ. engr., 1981—. Contbr. articles to books and profl. jours. Den leader Pack 164 and 598 Columbia Pacific council Cub Scouts Am., Beaverton, Oreg., 1982-83, Webelos leader, 1984-85, 90-91, troop 764 committeeman, 1985-87, asst. scoutmaster, 1992, scoutmaster, 1993-94 troop 598 scoutmaster, 1995—, Cascade Pacific council troop 598 Boy Scouts Am., 1985-87; mem. Planning Commn. Hudson, N.H., 1976-77. Recipient commendation for exemplary performance Mo.-Miss. flood, 1973, commendation for litigation defense, 1986, commendation for mgmt. activities, 1987, 91, Comdr.'s award for civilian svc., 1997. Mem. Am. Inst. Hydrology (cert., profl. ethics com. 1986, v.p. Oreg. sect. 1987-89, pres. Oreg. sect. 1990-92, nat. treas. 1995—), Internat. Tng in Communication (pres. West Way Club 1989-90), N.Am. Lake Mgmt. Soc. Democrat. Roman Catholic. Home: 7655 SW Belmont Dr Beaverton OR 97008-6335 Office: Portland Dist CE Chief Reservoir Reg & Water Quality PO Box 2946 Portland OR 97208-2946

CASSIDY, RICHARD THOMAS, hotel executive, defense industry consultant, retired army officer; b. Camp Keathley, Philippines, Aug. 16, 1916; s. William Henry and Lillie Christiana (Bergstresser) C.; m. Annette Nine, June 12, 1940; 1 child, Camille Gay Loo. BS, U.S. Mil. Acad., 1940; grad., Command and Gen. Staff Coll., 1945, U.S. Army War Coll., 1958; grad. in French, Army Lang. Sch., 1959. Commd. 2d. lt. U.S. Army, 1940, advanced through grades to lt. gen., 1971; dep. chief staff (Army Air Def. Command), 1956-57; Army attache to Iraq, 1959-61; comdg. gen. (4th Region, Air Def. Command), 1963, Arty. Brigade, U.S. Army, Europe, 1963-66; dir. Air Def., Pentagon, 1966-68; comdg. gen. Air Def. Center, comdt. Air Def. Sch., Ft. Bliss, Tex., 1968-71, Army Air Def. Command, Colorado Springs, Colo., 1971-73; ret., 1973; v.p. pub. relations and advt. El Paso Nat. Bank, 1973; pres. Paso del Norte Hotel Corp., El Paso, 1975-84; v.p., dir. Resort Am. Corp., 1973-84, 91—; v.p. Camelot, Inc., 1976-84; dir. Tex. Ind. Coll. Fund, 1981-82; cons. to Northrop Corp., Martin Marietta Corp., Norden Div. United Aircraft Corp., EG&G Corp., 1973-80. Chmn. Intergovt. Rels. Adv. Bd., El Paso, 1975-79; dir. Intercity Group Juarez, Mex./El Paso, 1977-81. Decorated D.S.M., Legion of Merit, Bronze Star, Army Commendation medal with 2 oak leaf clusters; recipient Conquistador award, Centennial Leadership award (Mentors of Today), City of El Paso, 1989. Mem. El Paso C. of C. (bd. dirs.). Home: 6006 Balcones Ct Villa 25 El Paso TX 79912 Office: Resort Am Corp Coronado Tower 6006 N Mesa St Ste 105 El Paso TX 79912-4611

CASSIDY, ROBERT CHARLES, JR., lawyer; b. Beaumont, Tex., May 16, 1946; s. Robert Charles and Peggy (Timken) C.; m. Leslie Fleming Iben, Sept. 2, 1949; children: Robert Charles III, Thomas Reinhard, Leslie Anne Vallandingham. B.A., Johns Hopkins U., 1968; J.D., U. Pa., 1973; LL.M., Georgetown U., 1977. Bar: Pa. 1973, U.S. Dist. Ct. D.C. 1975, U.S. Ct. Appeals (D.C. cir.) 1975, U.S. Ct. Internat. Trade 1982, U.S. Ct. Appeals (Fed. cir.) 1982. Asst. counsel Office of Legis. Counsel, U.S. Senate, 1973-75, internat. trade counsel Com. on Fin., 1975-79; gen. counsel Office of U.S. Trade Rep., Exec. Office of Pres., Washington, 1979-81; ptnr. Kaye, Scholer, Fierman, Hays & Handler, Washington, 1982-83, Wilmer, Cutler & Pickering, Washington, 1983—, internat. practice group leader, 1995—. With U.S. Army, 1968-70. Mem. ABA (chmn. internat. trade law com. 1986-90, counsellor internat. law sect. 1996-98), D.C. Bar Assn., Am. Soc. Internat. Law. Office: Wilmer Cutler & Pickering 2445 M St NW Ste 500 Washington DC 20037-1487

CASSIDY, SAMUEL H., lawyer, lieutenant governor, state legislator; m. Jillian Jacobellis; children: Rachael, Sarah, Alexandra, Samuel H. IV. BA, U. Okla., 1972; JD, U. Tulsa, 1975; postgrad., Harvard U., 1991. Bar: Okla., 1975, U.S. Supreme Ct. 1977, U.S. Ct. Appeals (10th cir.), 1977, Colo. 1982. Pvt. practice law, 1975—; mem. Colo. State Senate, 1991-94; lt. gov. State of Colo., 1994-95; pres. Jefferson Econ. Coun., 1995-97; pres., CEO Colo. Assn. Commerce and Industry, 1997—; bd. dirs. Capital Reporter; instr. U. Tulsa, 1978-81, Tulsa Jr. Coll., 1979; owner High Country Title Co.; developer of residential and commercial real estate, pres. Sam Cassidy, Inc. oil and gas exploration and production co., mem. agriculture and natural resources com., 1991-92, state, mil. and vet. affairs com., 1991-92, local govt. com. 1991, legal svcs. com. 1991-92, hwy. legis. review com. 1991-93, nat. hazards mitigation coun., 1992-93, appropriations com., 1993, judiciary com., 1993; pres. Econ. Devel. Coun. of Colo., 1997-98; exec. com. legis coun., 1993-94, senate svcs. com. 1993; elected Senate Minority Leader, 1993-94, exec. com. Colo. Gen. Assembly; sr. fellow U. Denver, 1997—. Bd. dirs. Colo. DLC, 1993-95, Leadership Jefferson County, Rocky Flats Local Impacts Initiative, dir.; chmn. bd. Arts Comm., Inc. Named Outstanding Legislator for 1991 Colo. Bankers Assn., ACLU Outstanding Legis. 1994; recipient Outsatnding Legis. Efforts award Colo. Counties, Guardian of Small Bus. award, NFIB, 1992, 94; fellow Gates Found., 1991, U. Denver sr. fellow. Mem. Colo. Bar Assn. (bd. gov. 1993-94), S.W. Colo. Bar Assn., Nat. Conf. State Legis. (Colo. rep., task force on state-tribe rels.), Rotary (hon. mem., sustaining Paul Harris fellow), Club 20 (bd. dirs.), San Juan Forum (chmn., bd. dirs.). Avocations: fine art photography, skiing, fishing. Home: 1390 Ash St Denver CO 80220-2409 Office: 1776 Lincoln St Ste 1200 Denver CO 80203-1029 *Leaders must nurture the positive. They must identify and promote issues which concern the whole community and the future of their grandchildren. They cannot indulge themselves in the profits of the politics of division. This is a vision which is hard to sell next November but which clearly distinguishes leaders from politicians.*

CASSIDY, TERRENCE PATRICK, JR., engineering consultant; b. Honolulu, May 21, 1964; s. Terrence Patrick Sr. and Lorraine C. BS Marine Engring., U.S. Merchant Marine Acad., 1987. 3d asst. engr. Crowley Maritime, Ft. Lauderdale, Fla., 1987-89; 2d asst. engr. D2-Meba-Amo, Dania, Fla., 1989-91, 1st asst. engr., 1991-92; project engr. Spectec Gen., Irvine, Calif., 1991; sr. project engr., corp. sec. Impact Engring., Inc., Ft. Lauderdale, 1992-97; v.p. Impact Engring. Inc., Ft. Lauderdale, 1995-97, also bd. dirs.; corp. sec. Impact Engring. Equipment, Inc., Ft. Lauderdale, 1993-97, v.p., 1995-97; CFO, Qualtair, Inc., Seattle, 1994-95, bd. dirs., 1994—; owner TC Internat., Ft. Lauderdale, Fla., 1997—; also bd. dirs. TC Internat., Ft. Lauderdale; sr. analyst Reliability Maintenance Sys., Inc., Ft. Lauderdale, 1998—. Lt. USNR. Mem. Soc. Naval Architects and Marine Engrs. Republican. Roman Catholic. Avocations: photography, skiing, boating, roller blading. Fax-954-771-5041. Office: PMB 200 1511 E Commercial Blvd Fort Lauderdale FL 33334-5717

CASSIDY, WILLIAM ARTHUR, geology and planetary science educator; b. N.Y.C., Jan. 3, 1928; s. John and Nellie (Briel) C.; m. Beverly J. Griffith, Aug. 29, 1959; children: Shauna Lynne, Laura Dawn, Brian John. B.S. in Geology, U. N. Mex., 1952; Ph.D. in Geochemistry, Pa. State U., 1961. Seismic computer Superior Oil Co. of Calif., Midland, Tex., 1952-53; research scientist Lamont Geol. Obs., Palisades, N.Y., 1961-67; assoc. to prof. geology and planetary sci. U. Pitts., 1968-80, prof., 1981-98, prof. emeritus, 1998—, trustee, 1998—; trustee Univ. Space Research Assn., Columbia, Md., 1975-82, chmn., 1978-79; chmn. meteorite working group Lunar and Planetary Sci. Inst., Houston, 1977-83. Contbr. articles to profl. jours. Served with USNR, 1945-46. Recipient Antarctic Svc. medal NSF, 1978; Fulbright student, 1953-54; grantee NSF, NASA. Mem. Am. Geophys. Union, Meteoritical Soc. (Barringer award 1995), Antarctican Soc. (Washington). Office: U Pitts 321 Old Engineering Hall Pittsburgh PA 15260-3303

CASSIERS, JUAN, diplomat; b. Middlekerke, Belgium, May 11, 1931; m. Daisy Lannoy, 1956; 4 children. Grad., St. Jean Berchmans Coll., Brussels, Belgium, Cath. U. Louvain, Belgium. Sec. Embassy of Belgium, Washington, 1962-67; dep. permanent rep. of Belgium to OECD Paris, 1970-73, permanent rep., 1987-91; min.-counsellor Beijing, 1974-76, Bonn, Fed. Republic Germany, 1976-79; head polit. and mil. affairs Ministry Fgn. Affairs, Brussels, 1979-81, prin. pvt. sec. to min. fgn. affairs, 1981, permanent rep. of Belgium to NATO, 1983-87; Belgian amb. to U.S. Washington, 1991-94; Belgian amb. to Holy See Rome, 1994-98. Decorated comdr. Ordre de Léopold, grand officier Ordre de Léopold II, grant officier Ordre de la Couronne; Harvard U. fellow, 1973-74. Avocations: reading, writing. Home: 48 rue Emile Bouilliot, 1060 Brussels Belgium Office: Embassy of Belgium, Via Giuseppe de Notaris 6A, 00197 Rome Italy

CASSILETH, PETER ANTHONY, internist; b. Bklyn., Aug. 16, 1937. MD, Columbia U., 1962. Diplomate Am. Bd. Internal Medicine, Am. Bd. Hematology, Am. Bd. Oncology. Intern Columbia Presbyn. Med. Ctr., N.Y.C., 1962-63, resident, 1963-65, fellow hematology-oncology, 1965-66, 68-69; prof. medicine U. Miami (Fla.) Sch. Medicine, 1975—. Mem. ACP, Am. Soc. Hematology, Am. Fedn. Cancer Rsch., ASCO. Office: U Miami Sch Med PO Box 016960 #D8-4 Miami FL 33101-6960 Office: U Miami Sch Medicine Hematology/Oncology Divsn 1475 NW 12th Ave Ste 3300 Miami FL 33136-1002

CASSILL, HERBERT CARROLL, artist; b. Percival, Iowa, Dec. 24, 1928; s. Howard Earl and Mary Elizabeth (Glosser) C.; m. Jean Kuniko Kubota, Aug. 23, 1951; children: Sarah Eden, J. Aaron. Student, Purdue U., 1944-45; B.F.A., State U. Iowa, 1948, M.F.A., 1950. Instr. printmaking State U. Iowa, Iowa City, 1953-57; prof., head dept. printmaking Cleve. Inst. Art, 1957-91, prof. emeritus, 1991—. One man shows include Oakland (Calif.) Art Mus., Ohio State U., Columbus, Cleve. Inst. Art, U. Wis., William Busta Gallery, 1990, 93, 96; group shows include Library of Congress, Washington, Bklyn. Art Mus., Bradford Internat. Invitational, 1984; represented in permanent collections, Mus. Modern Art, N.Y.C., Cleve. Mus. Art, Oakland Art Mus., San Francisco Art Mus., and others. Tiffany fellow printmaking, 1953. Mem. Coll. Art Assn. Home: 3084 Coleridge Rd Cleveland OH 44118-3556 Office: 11141 East Blvd Cleveland OH 44106-1710

CASSILL, RONALD VERLIN, author; b. Cedar Falls, Iowa, May 17, 1919; s. Howard E. and Mary (Glosser) C.; m. Karilyn Kay Adams, Nov. 23, 1956; children—Orin, Erica, Jesse. B.A., U. Iowa, 1939, M.A., 1947. Tchr. Writers Workshop, U. Iowa, 1948-52, 60-66; prof. Brown U., 1966—; reviewer for N.Y. Times, Book Week, Chgo. Sun Times. Author: Eagle on the Coin, 1950, Clem Anderson, 1961, 2d edit., 1990, Pretty Leslie, 1963, Writing Fiction, 1963, The President, 1964, The Father, 1965, The Happy Marriage, 1966, La Vie Passionnee of Rodney Buckthorne, 1968, In An Iron Time, 1969, Doctor Cobb's Game, 1970, The Goss Women, 1974, Hoyt's Child, 1976, Labors of Love, 1980, Flame, 1980, After Goliath, 1985, The Unknown Soldier, 1991; also short stories; editor Norton Anthology of Short Fiction, 1977, 2d edit., 1981, 3d edit., 1986, 4th edit., 1990, 5th edit., 1995, 6th edit., 1999, Anthology of Contemporary Fiction, 1987, 2d edit., 1997, 15x3, 1958, Patrimonies, 1988, Collected Stories of R.V. Cassill, 1989, The Man Who Bought Magnitogorsk, 1994, Late Stories, 1995; editor Norton Anthology Contemporary Fiction, 1997. Served to 1st lt. AUS, 1942-46. Mem. Phi Beta Kappa. Methodist. Home: 22 Boylston Ave Providence RI 02906-2413 *More important than talents or intelligence, luck or strength, is the knack for using these things and using weaknesses as well. This knack is a very mysterious thing. Perhaps it is no more than a determination or a strong desire to make use of the good as well as the bad. The creative process, by its nature, can't have any predetermined goals, but a faith in the infinite possibilities for shaping life tends to define and clarify the value of achievement as one goes along.*

CASSIMATIS, EMANUEL ANDREW, judge; b. Pottsville, Pa., Dec. 2, 1926; s. Andrew Emanuel and Mary H. (Calopedis) C.; m. Thecla Karambelas, June 2, 1952; children: Mary Ann Maza, John E., Gregory E. BA, Dickinson Coll., 1949, LLB, 1951, LLD (hon.) York Coll., 1991. Bar: Pa. 1951. Sole practice law, York, Pa., 1951-53, 55-57; assoc. Kain, Kain & Kain, York, Pa., 1953-55; ptnr. Stock & Leader, York, 1957-78; judge Ct. Common Pleas, York, Pa., 1978-96, sr. judge, 1996—; solicitor Springettesbury Twp., York, Pa., 1960-66, Sewer Authority, 1965-66; solicitor Wrightsville Borough, Pa., 1966-71, Mcpl. Authority, 1968-78, York Suburban Sch. Dist., 1970-77; faculty Pa. Coll. Judiciary, 1981, 82, 83; pres. Pa. Conf. State Trial Judges, 1989-90, chmn. spl. projects com., 1980-82, ann. meeting com., 1984-85, pres. Juvenile Ct. sect., 1988-89; mem. juvenile adv. com. Pa. Commn. Crime and Deliquency, 1996—; mem. Juvenile Ct. Judges' Commn. 1989-98, chmn., 1990-94; mem. Pa. three-judge breast implant coord. panel, 1993—. Pres. United Way of York County, 1964-65; co-chmn. steering com. York Community Audit for Human Rights, 1959; pres. Children's Growth and Devel. Clinic, 1974; trustee Meml. Osteopathic Hosp., 1963-80; bd. dirs. Capital Blue Cross, Harrisburg, Pa., 1970-79, Historic York, 1977-82. Served with U.S. Army, 1945-46. Named Young Man of Yr., York Jr. C. of C., 1960; Vol. of Yr., Pilot Club, 1965; Mem. Hall of Fame, William Penn Sr. High Sch., York, 1981; Nat. Juvenile Ct. Judge of Yr., CASA, 1995. Greek Orthodox. Lodges: Masons (hon. mem. supreme council). Home: 176 Rathton Rd York PA 17403-3720

CASSIMATIS, PETER JOHN, economics educator; b. Greece, Jan. 30, 1928; came to U.S., 1946, naturalized, 1946; s. John G. and Coula N. (Lourantos) C.; m. Margaret Ann Nell, Nov. 30, 1958; 1 son, Gregory. BCE, CUNY, 1953, MBA, 1961; PhD, New Sch. Social Research, 1967. Registered profl. engr., N.Y.; cert. cost analyst. Project mgr. several mgmt. and engring. cons. firms, 1953-64; prof. econs. and finance Fairleigh Dickinson U., Teaneck, N.J., 1964—; vis. prof. Center for Planning and Econ. Research, Athens, Greece, 1972-73. Author: Economics of the Construction Industry, 1970, Construction and Economic Development, 1975, The Construciton Industry in Greece, 1976, Engineering Economics, 1988, Managerial Economics, 1996; contbr. articles to profl. jours. Served with AUS, 1946-47. Research fellow Found. Econ. Edn., 1970. Mem. Am. Econ. Assn., Eastern Econ. Assn., Nat. Assn. Bus. Economists, Acad. Internat. Bus., World Future Soc., Fin. Mgmt. Assn. Home: 19 Lorraine Dr Eastchester NY 10707-2008 Office: Fairleigh Dickinson U Economics Dept Teaneck NJ 07666

CASSIN, JAMES RICHARD, broadcast educator; b. Port Huron, Mich., Oct. 7, 1933; s. Lloyd Gerald Cassin and Gladys Caroline (Smith) McCarron; m. Winnie Christine Carr, May 2, 1952; children: James R. II, Carolyn Marie Cassin Krecklow. BS in Journalism, Ball State U., 1982; MS in Radio-TV, Butler U., 1984. Enlisted USAF, 1951; served as pub. info. specialist USAF, Japan, Korea, Nev., Tex., Colo., Wis., 1951-71; ret. USAF, 1971; editor internal publs. Am. Fletcher Corp., Indpls., 1972-74; publicity dir. Amateur Athletic Union of U.S., Indpls., 1974-76; prof. broadcasting Def. Info. Sch., Ft. Benjamin Harrison, Ind., 1976-95; broadcast instr. Walker Career Ctr., Indpls., 1996-97; adj. prof. Marian Coll., Indpls., 1988-91, Butler U., Indpls., 1998—. Editor industry newspaper Dimensions (Best newspaper award Ind. Bus. Communicators, 1972); editor newletter Kaleidoscope (Award of Merit, Ind. Bus. Communicators, June 1972, Mar. 1973); editor Am. Fletcherline (Best newspaper award Ind. Bus. Communicators, 1974); editor AAU News Mag. (award of month Ind. Bus. Communicators, Feb., Apr., Dec. 1975, Mar. 1976). Mem. AFTRA, Air Force Pub. Affairs Assn., Armed Forces Broadcasters Assn., Am. Legion, USAF Thunderbird Alumni Assn., Def. Info. Sch. Alumni Assn., Track and Field Writers Assn. Lutheran. Avocations: creative writing, jogging, live theatre and music, amateur sports.

CASSINELLI, JOSEPH PATRICK, astronomy educator; b. Cin., Aug. 23, 1940; s. Herbert John and Louise (Schlottman) C.; m. Mary LeFever; children: Joseph Michael, Carolyn Marie, Mary Kathleen. BS in Physics, Xavier U., 1962; MS in Physics, U. Ariz., 1965; PhD in Astronomy, U. Wash., 1970. Research asst. Kitt Peak Nat. Obs., Tucson, 1963-65; research engr. Boeing Co., Seattle, 1965-66; postdoctoral research assoc. Joint Inst. for Lab. Astrophysics, Boulder, Colo., 1970-72; postdoctoral fellow U. Wis., Madison, 1972-73, asst. prof., 1973-77, assoc. prof., 1977-81, prof., 1981—, chmn. astronomy dept., 1986-89; vis. scientist Space Astronomy Lab., Utrecht, the Netherlands, 1975-76, Space Telescope Sci. Inst., 1991, High Altitude Obs., 1998; Donders chair U. Utrecht, 1985; sr. vis. fellow dept. physics and astronomy U. Glasgow, Scotland, 1998. Co-author: Introduction to Stellar Winds, 1999. Langley Abbot research fellow Harvard Smithsonian Ctr. for Astrophysics, 1981; Fulbright research fellow Sonnenborgh Obs., 1986. Mem. Am. Astron. Soc., Internat. Astron. Union. Roman Catholic. Home: 1520 Chandler St Madison WI 53711-2210 Office: U Wis Astronomy Dept 475 N Charter St Madison WI 53706-1507

CASSMAN, MARVIN, biochemist; b. Chgo., Apr. 4, 1936; s. Harry and Anna (Singer) C.; m. Alice M. Baker, June 24, 1972. BA, U. Chgo., 1954, BS, 1957, MS, 1959; PhD, Albert Einstein Coll. Medicine, 1965. Postdoctoral fellow U. Calif., Berkeley, 1965-67; asst. prof. U. Calif., Santa Barbara, 1967-75; adminstr. Nat. Inst. Gen. Med. Sci. NIH, Bethesda, Md., 1975-78, sect. chief, 1978-84, program dir., 1984-89, dep. dir., 1989-93, acting dir., 1993-96, dir., 1996—; mem. staff subcom. in sci., rsch. and tech. U.S Ho. of Reps., Washington, 1982-83; sr. policy analyst Office Sci. and Tech. Policy The White House, Washington, 1985-86. Recipient Sr. Exec. Svc. award USPHS, 1987, Pres. Meritorious award, 1991. Jewish. Avocations: music, racquetball. Home: 5608 Beam Ct Bethesda MD 20817-6303 Office: NIH Nat Inst Gen Med Sci 45 Center Dr MSC 6200 Bethesda MD 20892-6200*

CASSON, ALAN GRAHAM, thoracic surgeon, researcher; b. Birmingham, Eng., Apr. 22, 1958; arrived in Can., 1981; m. Sharon Margaret Coffey; 1 child, Angela. MB ChB, Manchester U., Eng., 1981; MSc, Meml. U., St.

John's, Nfld., Can., 1986. Asst. prof. surgery and oncology U. Western Ont., Can., 1991-93; asst. prof. surgery, program dir. thoracic surgery U. Toronto, Can., 1994-97; prof. thoracic surgery U. of Warwick, Eng., 1997-98; cons. thoracic surgery Hartland Hosp., Birmingham, Eng., 1997-98; prof. surgery, head divsn. thoracic surgery, dir. surg. oncology Dalhousie U., Halifax, N.S., Can., 1998—. Author: Oncogene Activation in Esophageal Cancer, 1992, Key Topics in Thoracic Surgery, 1999; contbr. chpts. to surg. textbooks and articles to profl. jours. Fellow Royal Coll. Surgeons Can., Am. Coll. Chest Physicians (young investigator award 1993), Am. Coll. Surgeons; mem. Am. Assn. Cancer Rsch., Soc. Cardiothoracic Surgeons of Great-Bratain and Ireland. Avocations: fly fishing, squash. Office: Divsn Thoracic Surg, 1278 Twr Rd Victoria Bldg 7-007, Halifax, NS Canada B3H 2Y9

CASSON, RICHARD FREDERICK, lawyer, travel bureau executive; b. Boston, Apr. 11, 1939; s. Louis H. and Beatrix S. C. AB, Colby Coll., 1960; JD, U. Chgo., 1963. Bar: Ill. 1963, Mass. 1964. Ptnr. Casson & Casson, Boston, 1967-68; assoc. counsel, corporate sec. Bankers Leasing Corp., 1968-75; asst. gen. counsel, corp. sec. Commonwealth Planning Corp., 1975-76; assoc. gen. counsel, asst. sec. Prudential Capital Corp., 1976-92; pres. Autumn Crest Corp., 1991-98; v.p. Casseden Corp.; career advisor Vt. Assocs. Capt. JAGC U.S. Army, 1964-67. Decorated Bronze Star. Jewish. Home and Office: PO Box 233 Randolph Center VT 05061

CASSON, RICK, member of Canadian parliament; b. Calgary, Alta., Can., Dec. 30, 1948. Mem. House of Commons Canadian Parliament, Ottawa, 1997—. Office: House of Commons, 251 Wellington Bldg, Ottawa, ON Canada K1A 0A6

CASSTEVENS, KAY L., federal official; b. Ft. Worth, July 4, 1949; d. Floyd C. and Shirley D. (Jackson) C. BJ cum laude, U. Tex., 1971; JD, George Washington U., 1979. Bar: D.C. 1980. Legis. aide Senator George McGovern, S.D., 1973-77; legis. dir. Rep. John F. Seiberling, Ohio, 1977-85; legis. dir. Sen. Tom Harkin, Iowa, 1986-91, chief of staff, 1991-92; asst. sec. legis. and congrl. affairs Dept. of Edn., Washington, 1993-97; dir. legis. affairs Office of V.P. of U.S., Washington, 1997—; dep. issues dir. to Geraldine Ferraro, Mondale-Ferraro Campaign, fall 1984; mem. rsch. staff Dukakis for Pres. Campaign, fall 1988; dep. campaign mgr. Ams. for Harkin Presdl. Campaign, 1991-92. Office: Office of the VP The White House Washington DC 20501

CAST, ANITA HURSH, small business owner; b. Columbus, Ohio, July 11, 1939; d. Charles Walter and Hulda Marie (Ramsey) Hursh; m. William R. Cast, Apr. 1, 1961; children: Jennifer, Carter, Meghan. BA, DePauw U., 1961. Ptnr. Cast Hursh and Assocs., Ft. Wayne, Ind., 1982—; pianist Words and Music, Ft. Wayne, 1983—; owner Anita Cast's Wearable Art, Ft. Wayne, 1986—; bd. dirs. Fort Wayne Philharmonic; exec. com. Arts United; past pres. Exec. Com. Ind. U. Friends of Music; bd. dirs. Ind. Endowment for the Arts; mem. Book of Soc. of 600 Internat. Violin Competition. Bd. dirs., pres. Am. Symphony Orch. League, vol., v.p., 1985-86; bd. dirs. WBNI Nat. Pub. Radio, Ft. Wayne; commr. Ind. Gov.'s Mansion Commn., 1987, Ind. Arts Commn., 1979-87; chmn., bd. dirs. Fine Arts Found., Ft. Wayne, 1988; pres. Ft. Wayne Philharmonic, 1977-79; pres., bd. dirs. Friends of Music, Ind. U., 1995-97; v.p. Leadership Ft. Wayne Adv. Bd., Ind. Endowment of the Arts; chmn. bd. Arts United of Greater Ft. Wayne, 1988-90; pres. Met. YMCA, Ft. Wayne, 1986—; mem. Mayor's Bicentennial Exec. Bd., 1989-94; mem. Ind. Cultural Congress Hon. Com.; cmty. adv. coun. Purdue U., Ft. Wayne; bd. dirs. Soc. of 600 Internat. Violin Competition; bd. dirs. Wawasee Area Conservancy Found. Lily Endowment Leadership fellow. Republican. Episcopalian. Avocations: music, cooking, tennis, reading, water sports. Home and Office: Anita Cast Wearable Art 4401 Taylor St Fort Wayne IN 46804-1913

CASTAGNA, WILLIAM JOHN, federal judge. Student, U. Pa., 1941-43; LLB, JD, U. Fla., 1949. Bar: Fla. 1949. Ptnr. MacKenzie, Castagna, Bennison & Gardner, 1970-79; judge U.S. Dist. Judge (mid. dist.) Fla., 1979—, now sr. judge. Democrat. *

CASTAGNETTO, PERRY MICHAEL, retail sales executive; b. San Francisco, Jan. 22, 1959; s. William Joseph and Patricia Mary (Williams) C. BA, San Jose State U., 1985. Asst. mgr. Emerald Hills Golfland, San Jose, 1978-85; dept. mgr. Orchard Supply Hardware, San Jose, 1987—; owner, pres. Castagnetto Enterprises, San Jose, 1991—; landscane and garden cons.; locksmith. Mem. Kappa Sigma (Outstanding alumni 1985, 87). Avocations: gourmet cooking, sculpting, fishing, camping. Home: 450 Avenida Arboles San Jose CA 95123-1428

CASTALDI, DAVID LAWRENCE, health care company executive; b. Logansport, Ind., Jan. 27, 1940; s. Lawrence J. and Ruth (Speitel) C.; m. Judith A. Pille, June 18, 1966; children: Valerie A., Maria C. BBA maxima cum laude, U. Notre Dame, 1962; MBA with distinction, Harvard U., 1966. Sec., dir. Mid-West Spring Mfg. Co., Inc., Chgo., 1961-71; with Baxter-Travenol Labs., Inc., 1971-87; exec. v.p. Artificial Organs divsn. Baxter-Travenol Labs., Inc., Deerfield, Ill., 1976-77; pres. hyland therapeutics divsn. Baxter-Travenol Labs., Inc., Glendale, Calif., 1977-87; founder, pres., CEO, bd. dirs. BioSurface Tech., Inc., Cambridge, Mass., 1987-94; bd. dirs. NABI (N.Am. Biologicals, Inc.), Bocan Raton, Fla., Ergo Sci. Corp., Charlestown, Mass., Biolink Corp., Middleboro, Mass., chmn. bd. dirs., 1995-98, CEO, 1996-98; chmn., bd. dirs. Cadent Med. Corp., Bedford, Mass., 1996—, CEO, 1998—. Mem. bd. of transplantation svcs. ARC, 1988-90, nat. skin adv. coun., 1990-92; mem. gov.'s biotech. subcom., 1991. With U.S. Army, 1962-64. Republican. Roman Catholic. Office: 19 Crosby Dr Ste 22D Bedford MA 01730-1401

CASTALDI, FRANK JAMES, environmental engineer, consultant; b. Elizabeth, N.J., May 24, 1947; s. Frank James and Anita (Arditi) C.; m. Keerocha Srithavatch, July 2, 1981; 1 child, Ann Elizabeth. BS in Civil Engring., N.J. Inst. Tech., 1969; ME in Environ. Engring., Manhattan Coll., Bronx, N.Y., 1971; PhD in Civil (Environ.) Engring., U. Tex., 1976. Registered profl. engr., Tex. Engr. Alexander Potter Assocs., N.Y.C., 1969; rsch. assoc. Manhattan Coll., 1969-71; design engr. Buck, Seifert and Jost Engrs., Englewood Cliffs, N.J., 1971-72; rsch. asst. U. Tex., Austin, 1972-76; project mgr., engr. Engring. Sci., Inc., Austin, 1976-84; sr. engr. Radian Internat. LLC a Dames & Moore Group Co., Austin, 1984-86; sr. staff engr., group leader Radian Internat. LLC, Austin, 1986-90, prin. engr., 1990—; chmn. Synfuels Wastewater Biotreatment Workshop Morgantown (W.Va.) Energy Tech. Ctr., 1983. Contbg. author: Applied Biotechnology for Site Remediation, 1994, Microbial Processes for Bioremediation, 1995, Standard Handbook of Hazardous Waste Treatment and Disposal, 1997; patentee in field. Mem. ASCE, Water Environ. Fedn., Internat. Assn. Water Quality. Roman Catholic. Avocation: numismatics. Office: Radian Internat LLC Ste 1 8501 N Missouri Pacific Exp Austin TX 78759-8399

CASTAÑEDA, JAMES AGUSTÍN, Spanish language educator, university golf coach; b. Bklyn., Apr. 2, 1933; s. Ciro Castañeda and Edna May Sincock; m. Terrill Lynn McCauley, Sept. 14, 1957; 1 child, Christopher James; m. Clara Luz, Dec. 9, 1991. BA summa cum laude, Drew U., 1954; MA, Yale U., 1955, PhD, 1958; Certificat d'Aptitude à l'Enseignement du Français à l'Etranger, Université Paris, 1957; student, Universidad de Madrid, 1957—; student summer inst. tchrs. fgn. langs., Purdue U., 1959. Asst. to assoc. prof. Spanish and French Hanover (Ind.) Coll., 1958-61; asst. prof. Spanish Rice U., Houston, 1961-63, assoc. prof. Spanish, 1963-67, prof. Spanish, 1967—; vis. prof. Spanish U. So. Calif., 1959, U. N.C., 1962, 68, Western N.Mex. U., 1970; Florence Purington vis. prof. Mt. Holyoke Coll., 1976-77; prof. summer program Hispanic studies in Spain Rice U., 1979, 82, 83-90, head freshman baseball coach, 1962-67, asst. varsity coach, 1962-83, chmn. dept. Classics, Italian, Portuguese, Russian and Spanish, 1964-72, moderator television series, 1964-67, 68-69, head golf coach, 1983-98; lectr., dir., adviser and sponsor numerous acad. and other coms. in field. Author: A Critical Edition of Lope de Vega's "Las paces de los reyes, y Judía de Toledo", 1962, introducción, edición, 1971, Agustín Moreto, 1974, Mira de Amescua, 1977, El esclavo del demonio, 1980; contbr. numerous articles to profl. jours. Chmn. interview team in Europe Kent Fellowship Program, 1968; active Internat. Good Neighbor Coun. Rose Meml. scholar Drew U., 1950-54, Varsity Club scholar, Alumni Assn. Meml. scholar, Fulbright scholar Université de Paris, 1956-57, scholar Instituto de Cultura Hispánica, 1971; Danforth fellow Yale U., 1954-58, teaching fellow 1958—; named Miembro Titular, Instituto de Cultura Hispánica de Madrid, 1972, Hon. Master Will Rice Coll., 1976, Spanish Tchr. of Yr. and Fgn. Lang. Tchr. of Yr., Tex. Fgn. Lang. Tchrs.' Assn., 1982; recipient Drew U. Alumni Achievement award in Humanities, 1973, Will Rice Coll. James St. Fulton Svc. award 1973, Bklyn. Cadets Alumni Assn. Achievement award, 1976, Spanish Heritage award 1982. Mem. Am. Assn. Spanish and Portugese (numerous coms. and offices), Am. Assn. Tchrs. French, Am. Coun. Tchrs. Fgn. Langs. (del. affiliate assembly, 1970-75), S. Ctrl. Modern Lang. Assn. (various coms. and offices), Houston Area Tchrs. Fgn. Langs. (various coms. and offices), Modern Lang. Assn. (various coms. and offices), Inst. Hispanic Culture Houston (founding mem. 1966, numerous other coms. and offices), Sigma Delta Pi (hon. pres. 1998). Office: Rice Univ # MS34 6100 Main St Houston TX 77005-1892

CASTANO, ELVIRA PALMERIO, art gallery director, art historian; b. Cin., July 23, 1929; d. John and Josephine C.; m. Carlo Palmerio, June 1, 1958 (dec.); 1 child, Marina. B Lit. Interpretation, Emerson Coll., 1950; postgrad., Pius XII Inst., Florence, Italy, 1954-55; student opera with Cesare Sturani. Curator Castano Art Gallery, Boston, 1965-78; dir. Castano Art Gallery, Needham, Mass., 1978—; rschr.mem Smithsonian Instn., Boston, 1988-89; performed voice Oub. Broadcasting Sys. Series, Nova, Italy, 1997; gov. adv. com., 1997; Vatican translator; interpreter Italian art specializing in Macchiaioli art; Italian interpreter Ritz Carlton Internat. Festival, (Italian) Mayor's Office Sister Cities Internat. Conv.; appointed sec. World Affairs Coun., Boston. Mem. Rep. Presdl. Task Force, Nat. Rep. Senatorial Com., Presdl. Inner Circle; active Boston chpt. UN; bd. dirs. Needham Hist. Soc.; vol. Sail Boston, 1992; del. Presdl. Trust, 1992; aapptd. Gov.'s Com. on Women's Issues; vol. Italian Interpreter for Mayor's Office Sister Cities Internat. Conv. Cardinal Spellman scholar; recipient Piramdello Lyceum award, I Migliori, 1997. Mem. UN, Boston U. Women's Coun., Boston Mus. Fine Arts, Boston Browning Soc., Fogg Art Mus. of Harvard U., Friends of Needham Libr., Archives Am. Art Boston, Alliance Francaise Boston, World Affairs Coun. Boston (sec.), Nat. Mus. Women in Arts, Needham Hist. Soc. (bd. dirs.), Nat. Italian Am. Found. Avocations: current events, internat. affairs, writing, travel, language study. Address: 50 Grove St Wellesley MA 02482

CASTANO, GREGORY JOSEPH, lawyer; b. Kearny, N.J., Feb. 17, 1929; s. Nicholas and Marianna (Prestinaci) C.; m. June Dwyer, Oct. 15, 1966; children: Gregory, Christopher, John, Timothy. BS, Seton Hall U., 1950; JD, Fordham U., 1953; LLM, NYU, 1956. Bar: N.J. 1956, U.S. Ct. Appeals (3d cir.) 1957, U.S. Supreme Ct. 1959, U.S. Tax Ct. 1974, N.Y. 1985. Sports writer Newark Star-Ledger, 1946-53; pvt. practice Harrison, N.J., 1959-78; atty. Bd. Adjustment, Harrison, 1978; judge Superior Ct. N.J., Jersey City, 1978-85; ptnr. Tompkins, McGuire & Wachenfeld, Newark, 1985-88, Waters, McPherson & McNeill, Secaucus, N.J., 1988—; asst. atty. Town of Harrison, 1959-64; asst. prosecutor County of Hudson, N.J., 1963-71; atty. Town of West New York, N.J., 1977-78, Town of Kearny, N.J., 1999; adj. prof. Seton Hall U. Sch. Law, Newark, 1988—; master com. to computerize criminal cts. Essex County; mediator U.S. Dist. Ct., Superior Ct. Mem. editorial bd., The Cath. Adv., 1976-78. Tax assessor Town of Harrison, 1964-78; del. N.J. Constl. Conv., 1964; mem. juvenile conf. com. Twp. West Caldwell, N.J., 1977-78; trustee Caldwell (N.J.) Coll., 1985-91, chmn. acad. affairs com. bd. trustees, 1987-91; chmn. County Govt. Transition Com., Hudson County, 1987-88; mem. Hudson County Community Coll. Blue Ribbon Task Force, 1992-93. With U.S. Army, 1953-55. Named Man of Yr., Kearny Jaycees, 1963, Alumnus of Yr., Dorf Feature Service, 1987. Fellow Am. Bar Found.; mem. ABA, N.J. Bar Assn., Hudson County Bar Assn. (Justice medallion 1985), Essex County Bar Assn., West Hudson Bar Assn. (pres. 1977-78), Assn. Fed. Bar N.J., Essex Fells Country Club. Home: 19 Sunset Rd West Caldwell NJ 07006-6540 Office: Waters McPherson & McNeill 300 Lighting Way PO Box 1560 Secaucus NJ 07096-1560

CASTBERG, EILEEN SUE, construction company owner; b. Santa Monica, Calif., Mar. 12, 1946; d. George Leonard and Irma (Loretta) Conroy; m. David Christopher Castberg, Oct. 27, 1967; children: Eric, Christopher. Grad. high sch., U. High Sch., L.A., 1964; certificate, Anthony Schs., 1990. Lic. real estate agt., Calif. Exec., co-founder Advanced Connector Telesis, Inc., Santa Ana, Calif., 1986-87; exec. Western Energy Engrs., Inc., Costa Mesa, Calif., 1987-89; owner Dave Castberg and Assoc., Inc., Ramona, Calif., 1989—; sales assoc. Ramona and Country Estates Realty, Keller Williams Realty, 1999—; cons. Watt Asset Mgmt., Santa Monica, 1990-91. Mem. choir Ramona Luth. Ch.; 3d v.p. Holy Cross Luth. Ch. Women's League, Cypress, Calif., 1983; bd. dirs., sec. San Diego Country Estates Timeshare, pres. Internmountain Republican Women's Fed. Mem. San Diego Bd. Realtors, Ramona Real Estate Assn. (bd. dirs.), Intermountain Rep. Women's Fedn. (past pres.), Ramona Christian Women's Club, San Vicente Valley Club. Republican. Avocations: statuary painting, singing, gardening, decorating, reading.

CASTEEL, DIANN BROWN, principal; b. Greeneville, Tenn., Dec. 16, 1953; d. Harold James Brown and Clara Ruth (Phillips) Johnston; m. Everette Kenneth Casteel, Oct. 7, 1972; children: Trisha DiAnn, Mary Camille, Cheyenne James. BS, East Tenn. State U., 1973, MA, 1976, EdD, 1994. Cert. tchr., Tenn. Tchr. Greene County Bd. Edn., Greeneville, 1973-90; dir. Project Choice, Greeneville-Greene County Ctr. for Tech., 1990-91; tchr. Doak Sch., Tusculum Sta., Tenn., 1992—; asst. prin. Chuckey Elem. Sch., Greene County Bd. Edn.; founder Iowa-Tenn. Student Exch. Program, Dayton and Greeneville, 1986-87; secondary educator, evening instr. Tusculum Coll., Greenville, Tenn., Guidance and Assessment for Single Parent/Displaced Homemaker Program, 1989-90. Founder, conor Hay Relief Program, Tenn., 1986-87; leader 4-H Club, Baileyton Elem. Sch., 1985-88; mem. Ottway United Meth. Ch., Greenville, 1985-92; v.p. Ottway United Meth. Women, Greeneville, pres., 1976; mem. women's group study exch. to India, Rotary Internat., 1989; mem. 1st Christian Ch., Greenville, Tenn., 1992—. Recipient Horse of Yr. award Appalachian Horse Show Assn., 1967, Outstanding Citizen award Ruritan Nat., 1986, 4-H Emerald Club Leader award, 1987, DIANA award Epsilon Sigma Alpha, 1990, Book of Golden Deeds award Greeneville (Tenn.) Exchange Club, 1992. Mem. NEA, Greene County Edn. Assn., East Tenn. Edn. Assn., Tenn. Edn. Assn., Internat. Platform Assn., U.S.S. Greenville, Inc., Kappa Delta Pi, Phi Delta Kappa. Democrat. Avocations: horses, creative cooking, reading, swimming. Home: 2545 Flatwoods Rd Greeneville TN 37745-8582 Office: Chuckey Elem Sch 1605 Chuckey Hwy Chuckey TN 37641-5447

CASTEEN, JOHN THOMAS, III, university president; b. Portsmouth, Va., Dec. 11, 1943; s. John Thomas and Naomi Irene (Anderson) C.; children: John Thomas IV, Elizabeth, Lars. BA with high honors, U. Va., 1965, MA, 1966, PhD, 1970; LLD, Shenandoah Coll. and Conservatory Music, 1984; DHL, Bentley Coll., 1992; hon. degree, Piedmont (Va.) C.C., 1992; DPA, Bridgewater Coll., 1993; D honoris causa, U. Athens, Greece, 1996. Asst. prof. English U. Calif., Berkeley, 1970-75; assoc. prof., dean admissions U. Va., Charlottesville, 1975-82; adj. prof. Va. Commonwealth U., Richmond, 1982-85; prof. English, pres. U. Conn., Storrs, 1985-90; pres. U. Va., 1990—, George M. Kaufman presdl. prof. of English, 1990—; bd. dirs. NCAA, Coun. for Higher Edn. Accreditation, Wachovia, Inc., Nellie Mae, Inc.; mem. Assn. Acad. Health Ctrs.' Coun. Health Scis. and Univ.; mem. com. Nat. Inst. on Alcohol Abuse and Alcoholism and Misuse on Coll. Campuses. Author: 16 Stories, 1981; contbr. articles to various publs.; mem. editl. adv. bd. The Presidency. Sec. edn. Commonwealth of Va., Richmond, 1982-85; trustee Mariner's Mus., 1990—, Coll. Entrance Exam Bd., N.Y.C., 1980-90, chmn. 1986-88; mem. So. Regional Edn. Bd., 1982-85. New Eng. Bd. of Higher Edn., 1986-90; mem. nat. adv. com. Nat. Domestic Violence Media Campaign, 1992—; dir. Am. Coun. on Edn., 1993-96. Recipient Outstanding Virginian award, 1993. Mem. Assn. Am. Univs. (exec. com.), So. Assn. Colls. and Schs. (chair commn. on colls. 1995-97, pres.-elect 1997, pres. 1998), Assn. Governing Bds. Colls. and Schs. (coun. of pres. 1992—), Keswick Club, Farmington County Club, Commonwealth Club (Richmond), Phi Beta Kappa. Episcopalian. Office: U Va Office of Pres Madison Hall PO Box 9011 Charlottesville VA 22906-9011

CASTEL, JEAN GABRIEL, lawyer; b. Nice, France, Sept. 17, 1928; s. Charles A. and Simone (Ricour de Quinsac) C. Lic., U. Paris, 1948; JD, U. Mich., 1953; SJD, Harvard U., 1957; LLD (hon.), Aix-Marseille, France, 1988. Created queen's counsel. From asst. prof. to assoc. prof. law McGill U., 1954-57; now prof. emeritus law Osgoode Hall Law Sch., York U., Toronto, Ont., Can. Author: International Law as Interpreted and Applied in Canada, 1978, Canadian Criminal Law: International and Transnational Aspects, 1981, Extraterritoriality in International Trade, 1988, The Canadian Law and Practice of International Trade, 1991, 2d edit., 1997, Canadian Conflict of Laws, 4d edit., 1997; editor: Can. Bar Rev., 1957-83. Mem. spl. group for settlement of disputes under Can.-U.S. Free Trade Agreement, 1989-93. Served with French Resistance, 1943-45. Decorated officer Order of Can., Chevalier Ordre Nat. du Merite, Chevalier Légion d'Honneur, Order of Ontario. Fellow Acad. Arts and Scis., Royal Soc. Can.; mem. Can. Bar Assn. (hon.), Internat. Acad. Comparative Law (assoc.).

CASTEL, NICO, tenor, educator; b. Lisbon, Portugal, Aug. 1, 1935; s. Felix and Margalitt (Castel) Kalinhoff; 1 child, Alexandra. B.A., Temple U., 1952. Artist in residence Mannes Coll. of Music, N.Y.C., 1980—; instr. diction and langs. Mannes Coll. Music, Manhattan Sch. Music, Juilliard Sch. Music, Israel Vocal Arts Inst., Tel Aviv, Finnish Nat. Opera, Helsinki, Aspen Festival, Colo.; diction coach Met. Opera; stage dir. opera; adj. faculty Boston U. Author: The Nico Castel Book of Ladino Songs, A Singers' Manual of Spanish Lyric Diction, The Complete Puccini, Verdi, Mozart Libretti with phonetics and translation; Debuts include, N.Y. City Opera, 1965, Metropolitan Opera, 1970; permanent artist, Metropolitan Opera; extensive concert tours, U.S., S.Am., Europe; tchr. master classes in multilingual diction and style. With U.S. Army, 1952-54. Mem. Am. Guild Mus. Artists. Democrat. Jewish. Home: 214 W 92nd St New York NY 10025-7440 Office: c/o Met Opera Lincoln Ctr New York NY 10023 Address: Mannes Col of Music 150 W 85th St New York NY 10024-4402*

CASTEL, P. KEVIN, lawyer; b. N.Y.C., Aug. 5, 1950; s. Peter A. and Mildred (Cronin) C.; m. Patricia A. McLernon; children: Jeanne Margaret, Allison Maureen. BS, St. John's U., Jamaica, N.Y., 1972, JD, 1975. Bar: N.Y. 1976, U.S. Dist. Ct. (so. and ea. dists.) N.Y. 1976, U.S. Ct. Appeals (2nd cir.) 1979, U.S. Supreme Ct. 1983, U.S. Ct. Appeals (fed. cir.), 1986, U.S. Ct. Appeals (10th cir.), 1988, U.S. Ct. Appeals (3rd cir.) 1989, U.S. Ct. Appeals (4th cir.) 1991, U.S. Ct. Appeals (7th cir.) 1995, U.S. Ct. Appeals (11th cir.) 1997. Law clk. to judge U.S. Dist. Ct. (so. dist.) N.Y., 1975-77; assoc. Cahill Gordon & Reindel, N.Y.C., 1977-83, ptnr., 1983—; mem. departmental disciplinary com. appellate divsn. 1st Dept., 1987-93, hearing panel chair, 1991-93, mem. policy com., 1997—. Articles editor St. John's Law Rev., 1974-75. Mem. mayor's panel Martin Luther King Jr. Inst. for Law and Social Justice, 1987-89; nat. chmn. ann. giving campaign St. John's U., 1994-95. Fellow Am. Bar Found., N.Y. Bar Found.; mem. N.Y. State Bar Assn. (mem. com. on cts. of appelate jurisdiction 1979-86, mem. com. fed. cts. of appelate jurisdiction 1979-86, mem. com. fed. cts. 1986-89, chmn. com. fed. practice 1989-91, exec. vice chmn. comml. and fed. litigation sect. 1991-92, chmn. 1993-94, mem. ho. of dels. 1994-95), Assn. of Bar of City of N.Y. (mem. com. profl. and jud. ethics 1994-97, mem. coun. on jud. adminstrn. 1997—), Fed. Bar Coun. (pres. elect 1998—, sec. 1983-85, trustee 1985-93, 97—, chmn. publs. com. 1984-95, chmn. program com. 1995-98, v.p. 1988-90), N.Y. County Lawyers Assn., Supreme Ct. Hist. Soc., St. John's U. Law Sch. Alumni Assn. (bd. dirs. 1991—, v.p. 1998—). Office: Cahill Gordon & Reindel 80 Pine St Fl 17 New York NY 10005-1790

CASTELE, THEODORE JOHN, radiologist; b. New Castle, Pa., Feb. 1, 1928; s. Theodore Robert and Anne Mercedes (McNavish) C.; m. Jean Marie Willse, Oct. 20, 1951; children: Robert, Ann Marie, Richard, Mary Kathryn, Thomas, Daniel, John. BS, Case Western Res. U., 1951, MD, 1957. Diplomate Am. Bd. Radiology, 1962. Intern then resident U. Hosps. Cleve., 1957-61, fellow, 1961-62; dir. of radiology Luth. Med. Ctr., Cleve., 1968-75, 77-89; chief of staff Luth. Med. Ctr., 1975-81; pres. Med. Ctr. Radiologists, Inc., Cleve., 1978-95; v.p. med. and copr. devel. Health Cleve. Inc., 1989-91; chmn. Lakeshore Radiology Inc., Cleve., 1991-96, emeritus chmn., 1996—; med. editor sta. WEWS-TV-ABC, Cleve., 1975—; chmn. bd. Med. Cons. Imaging Co., Cleve., 1981-97; asst. clin. prof. radiology Case Western Res. U. Chmn. Southwestern dist. Greater Cleve. coun. Boy Scouts Am., 1969, 73; mem. bd. med. cons. Cleve. Police Dept., pres., 1988-90; trustee Comty. Dialysis Ctr., chmn. 1997—; active Luth. Med. Ctr. Found., chmn. bd. trustees, 1969-75, pres., 1988-90; trustee Case Western Res. U., Blue Cross/Blue Shield Ohio, Greater Cleve. Hosp. Assn., Fairview Health, Luth. Med. Ctr., 1975-80, Fairview Hosp. Found., No. Ohio Lung Assn.; chmn. Health Mus. Cleve., 1996—, Humility of Mary Healthcare Sys., 1995-98; dir. Coun. Pub. Reps. for NIH, 1999—. With USN, 1946-47. Recipient Order of Merit award Boy Scouts Am., 1971, Silver Beaver award, 1972, Nat. Disting. Eagle Scout award, 1984, Frances Payne Bolton Sch. of Nursing Disting. Svc. award, 1990, Outstanding Philanthropist award Nat. Soc. of Fundraising Execs., 1991, Alumnus of the Yr. award Dept. Radiology of Case Western Res. U., 1996, LMC Found. Women's Bd. award, 1996, Luth. Hosp. award Fairview Health Sys. Bd., 1996, Midwest Nursing Rsch. Soc. Media award, 1998; named Knight of the Equestrian, Order of the Holy Sepulchre of Jerusalem, 1993—; recipient Magis award St. Ignatius H.S. Fellow Am. Coll. Radiology; mem. AMA (Physician Spkr. Gold award 1978, 80, Silver 1979, Bronze 1978, Benjamin Rush award 1989, Golden Achievement award Golden Age Ctrs., 1996, chmn. Ohio del. 1987-96), Ohio State Med. Assn. (5th dist. councilor 1977-79, Spl. award 1979, Disting. Svc. award 1997), Cleve. Radiol. Soc. (pres. 1969-70), Cleve. Med. Libr. Assn. (pres. 1996, 97-98), Case Western Res. U. Med. Alumni Assn. (pres. 1971-72, 91-92, Disting. Svc. award 1987, Spl. Trustees award 1997, Univ. medal 1998), Cleve. Acad. Medicine (pres. 1974-75, Disting. Mem. award 1990, Disting. Svc. award 1984, Spl. Honor award and portrait 1998), Ohio State Radiol. Soc. (Silver award 1990). Home: 18869 Canyon Rd Cleveland OH 44126-1703 Office: Case Western Reserve University School of Medicine Cleveland OH 44106

CASTELLANO, CHRISTINE MARIE, lawyer; b. Jacksonville, Fla., Jan. 10, 1966; d. James Todd and Constance Marie (Wallis) Drylie; m. Ralph Castellano, Sept. 15, 1997. BA summa cum laude, U. Colo., 1987; JD cum laude, U. Mich., 1990. Bar: Colo. 1990, Ill. 1991, U.S. Dist. Ct. Colo. 1991, U.S. Dist. Ct. (no. dist.) Ill. 1991, U.S. Dist. Ct. (ctrl. dist.) Ill. 1994, U.S. Ct. Appeals (10th cir.) 1991, U.S. Ct. Appeals (7th cir.) 1993, U.S. Supreme Ct. 1995. Clk. to chief judge Sherman G. Finesilver U.S. Dist. Ct. Colo., Denver, 1990-91; income ptnr. McDermott, Will & Emery, Chgo., 1991-96; ops. atty. Corn Products divsn. of CPC Internat. Inc., Summit-Argo, Ill., 1996-97; atty. Corn Products Internat., Inc., 1998—; adminstr. Family Law Project, Ann Arbor, Mich., 1988-91; judge Julius H. Miner Moot Ct., Northwestern U. Sch. Law, 1993-95, Northwestern U. Sch. Law Negotiation Competition, 1992-94. Writer newspaper The Res Gestae, 1987-90; editor yearbook The Quadrangle, 1988-90; contbg. editor Jour. of Law Reform, 1988-90. Vol. Lincoln Park Homeless Shelter, Chgo., 1991-92, Chgo. Cares, 1993-96; co. coord. Youth Motivation Program, 1991-96. Recipient Negligence Sect. award Mich. Bar Assn., 1990; Carl B. Gussin Meml. prize U. Mich., 1991; scholar Elk's, 1983-84, faculty U. Colo., 1983-84; U. Colo. grantee, 1987. Mem. ABA, Colo. Bar Assn., Ill. Bar Assn., Denver Bar Assn. (vol. teen ct. 1991), Chgo. Bar Assn., Chgo. Coun. Laywers, Women Law Students Assn., U. Colo. Alumni Assn., U. Mich. Alumni Assn., Moot Ct., Mortar Bd., Phi Beta Kappa, Pi Sigma Alpha. Democrat. Avocations: photography, ice skating, camping, hiking. Office: Corn Products Internat PO Box 345 Argo IL 60501-0345

CASTELLANO, JOSEPH ANTHONY, chemist, management consulting firm executive; b. N.Y.C., Oct. 28, 1937; s. Joseph John and Marie Antoinette (Gallo) C.; m. Rosalie Ann Fantaci, Aug. 28, 1960; children: Joseph, Thomas, Laura. BS in Chemistry, CCNY, 1959; MS in Chemistry, Poly. Inst. N.Y., 1964, PhD in Chemistry, 1969. Cert. profl. chemist; cert. community coll. instr. Research chemist Witco Chem. Co., Paterson, N.J., 1959-62; sr. research chemist Thiokol Chem. Corp., Denville, N.J., 1962-65; mem. tech. staff, project mgr. RCA Labs., Princeton, N.J., 1965-73; chmn., CEO Princeton Materials Sci., 1973-75; ops. mgr. Fairchild Camera and Inst. Corp., Palo Alto, Calif., 1975-77; mgr. ops. Kylex, Mt. View, Calif., 1977-78; pres. Stanford Resources, San Jose, Calif., 1978—; cons. scientist Princeton U., 1970-72; lectr. Rutgers U., Kent State U., SUNY-Binghamton, NASA Research Ctr., USAF Materials Lab., Office Naval Research, IBM Research Ctrs., RCA Labs., Motorola and various profl. and trade assns. Author: Handbook of Display Technology, 1992; publisher: Electronic Display World, The Electronic Display Industry Svc.; contbr. articles to profl. jours.; patents in field. Recipient RCA Doctoral Study award, RCA Labs. Outstanding Achievement award Indsl. Rsch. mag.'s IR-100 award, David Sarnoff Team award in Sci. Fellow Am. Inst. Chemists; mem. AAAS, Am.

Chem. Soc., Am. Assn. Advancement Sci., N.Y. Acad. Sci., Royal Chem. Soc., Soc. Info. Display, Profl. and Tech. Cons. Assn., Soc. Tech. Comm., N.Y. Acad. Sci., Sigma Xi. Roman Catholic. Home: 7017 Elmsdale Dr San Jose CA 95120-3225 Office: Stanford Resources Inc PO Box 20324 San Jose CA 95160-0324

CASTELLANO, VALEN EDWARD, biologist; b. Seattle, July 4, 1954; s. Edward Joseph and Florence Marie(Beaudette) C.; m. Mary Joan Coakley, Mar. 5, 1989. BS, Humboldt State U., 1980; MPA, Calif. State U., Turlock, 1995. Fisheries Aide Calif. Dept. Fish & Game, Eureka, 1980-81; rsch. asst. Oreg. Coop. Wildlife Rsch. Unit, Corvallis, 1981-84; fisheries tech. Coastal Fisheries Divsn. Tex. Parks & Wildlife Dept., Seabrook, 1984-86; fgn. fisheries observer Oreg. State U. Nat. Marine Fisheries Svc., Seattle, 1986-87; wildlife control agt. Wash. Dept. Wildlife, Olympia, 1988-89; agrl. biologist Merced Co. Dept. Agrl., Los Banos, Calif., 1989—. Mem. Am. Soc. Pub. Adminstrn., The Wildlife Soc. Avocations: hiking, golf, fishing. Office: Merced County Dept Agrl 342 D St Los Banos CA 93635-3601

CASTELLANOS, DIEGO ANTONIO, television personality, writer, educator; b. Guayama, P.R., Oct. 19, 1933; s. Felix Castellano and Mercedes Serrano; m. Pamela Joan Leggio, Oct. 3, 1981; children: Olivia, Felicia, Carlos. Grad., N.J. Mil. Acad., Sea Girt, 1960; MA, Montclair State U., 1973; EdD, Fairleigh Dickinson U., 1979; Journalism Cert., Marquette U., 1989. Lic. pilot. Announcer, prodr. Sta. WCAM, Camden, N.J., 1954-63; Sta. WSSJ, Camden, 1989-90; columnist, Spanish editor Cath. Star Herald, Camden, 1963-67; feature writer, corr. El Diario-La Prensa, N.Y.C., 1967; columnist, reporter Courier-Post, Camden, 1967-68; producer, dir., host N.J. Network, Trenton, 1971-72; radio talk show host, prodr. WTTM, Trenton, 1990; TV talk show host Sta. WPVI-TV 6/ABC, Phila., 1970—; dir. bilingual edn. N.J. State Dept. Edn., Trenton, 1970-75, dir. office of equal ednl. opportunity, 1979-84; co-anchor ann. Phila. Puerto Rican Parade broadcast, Sta. WPVI-TV 6/ABC; mem. nat. adv. bd. Children's TV Workshop, N.Y.C., 1971-82, chmn., 1977-79. Author: The Best of Two Worlds, 1983; co-author: Puerto Ricans on the US Mainland, 1972. Bd. dirs. Aspira of N.J., Newark, 1969-72; bd. dirs. N.J. Puerto Rican Congress, Trenton, 1970-78, v.p., 1975-76; mem. Pa. Gov.'s Commn. on Latino Affairs, 1996—. Commd. officer N.J. N.G., 1960. Recipient Presdl. Commendation for Outstanding Cmty. Svc., 1981; named Outstanding Young Man of Yr., Greater Camden Jaycees, 1967. Mem. Broadcast Pioneers, N.J. TESOL (bd. dirs. 1984-85). Avocations: flying, playing guitar. Home: 1495 Merrick Rd Yardley PA 19067-2760 Office: County Supt of Schs Hunterdon County Admin Bldg Flemington NJ 08822

CASTELLANOS, JESUS ANTONIO, federal judge; b. 1942. BA, Inter-Am. U., San German, P.R., 1963; LLB, Inter-Am. U., Hato Rey, P.R., 1968. Bar: P.R. 1970, U.S. Dist. Ct. P.R. 1976, U.S. Ct. Appeals P.R. 1982, U.S. Ct. Internat. Trade 1983. Atty., mgmt. asst. legal dept. Office Gen. Counsel, P.R. Water Resources Authority, Santurce, 1963-71; in-house counsel Commonwealth Resources Mgmt. Corp., Hato Rey, 1973-74; assoc. Francis, Doval, Colorado & Carlo, Hato Rey, 1974-76; legis. asst. to Hon. Jorge Luis Cordova, U.S. Ho. of Reps., 1976; asst. U.S. atty. U.S. Dept. Justice, Old San Juan, 1976; legis. asst. to Hon. Baltasar Corrado del Rio, U.S. Ho. of Reps., 1977-80; magistrate judge for P.R., U.S. Magistrate Ct., San Juan, 1980—; lectr. Legal Aid Clinic, U. P.R. Law Sch., 1974-76. Mem. ABA, FBA, Am. Judicature Soc., Inst. Jud. Adminstrn., P.R. Bar Assn. Office: Ruiz-Nazario Fed Bldg 150 Carlos Chardon Ave 181 San Juan PR 00918

CASTELLANOS, JULIO J(ESUS), banker; b. Havana, Cuba, Mar. 7, 1910; came to U.S., 1960, naturalized, 1967; s. Manuel de Jesus and Virginia (Justiniani) C.; B of Arts and Letters, De La Salle Coll., Havana, 1927; JD, Tulane U., 1933; DCL, U. Havana, 1934; student Fed. Res. System Examiner's Sch., 1964-65; m. Irene Machado, Dec. 27, 1976; children: Julio J., Maria, Ana Maria, Carlos. Bar: Cuba 1934. Tax commr. City of Havana, from 1934; sr. ptnr. Lopez Munoz & Castellanos, Havana; sec. gen. Banco de la Construccion, Havana, 1959-60; analyst Morgan Guaranty Trust Co. N.Y., N.Y.C., 1960-63; examiner Fed. Res. Bank N.Y., N.Y.C., 1963-66; v.p. Marine Midland Bank, N.Y.C., 1966-71; founder, organizer, sr. v.p., mgr. First Wis. Internat. Bank, N.Y.C., 1971-76; pres. Pan Am. Nat. Bank, Union City, N.J., from 1976; exec. rep. Banco de Intercambio Regional, N.Y.C., 1976-80; pres. Banco del Estado Holding Co. Inc., Atlanta, 1982-84; adviser Banco de Reservas de la Republica Dominicana, N.Y.C., 1982-84; N.Y.C. rep. Banco del Estado, Bogota, Colombia, 1978-84; N.Y. rep. Banco Hipotecario Dominicano, 1983-85; banking cons. law firm Reid & Priest, 1983-86; v.p. BHD Corp., real estate investments, 1984-86; pres., chief cons. Castellanos Cons. Group Inc., 1984—; v.p. IDOSA N.Y. Inc., 1984-85. Bd. dirs. Colombian-Am. Assn. Pan Am. Soc. of U.S., 1984-85. Recipient retirement recognition diploma First Wis. Internat. Bank, 1976, pub. recognition diploma Dr. Guillermo Belt, former Mayor Havana, 1979. Mem. Havana Bar Assn. (del. in exile 1994). Republican. Address: 510 E 85th St New York NY 10028-7430

CASTELLI, ALEXANDER GERARD, accountant; b. N.Y.C., May 3, 1929; s. Gerard and Carmela (Canzoneri) C.; m. Michelina Castelli, Jan. 8, 1961; children—Gerard, Alexander, JoAnn. B.S., N.Y. U., 1958. C.P.A., N.Y., Md., 1970. Chief accountant Daitch Crystal Dairies, Inc., Bronx, N.Y., 1965-68; asst. controller Alexander's, Inc., N.Y.C., 1968-70; v.p., treas. Bond Stores, Inc., N.Y.C., 1970-73; v.p. fin. McBrides, Inc., Washington, 1973-77; mng. ptnr. Castelli & Catudal, P.A., 1977—; bd. advisers Nat. Bank of Washington. Served with CIC AUS, 1951-53. Recipient Founder's Day award NYU, 1958. Mem. Am. Inst. CPA's, N.Y. State Soc. CPA's, Beta Gamma Sigma. Roman Catholic. Home: 10009 Gainsborough Rd Rockville MD 20854-4276 Office: 7925 Glenbrook Rd Bethesda MD 20814-2441

CASTELLINI, CLATEO, medical technology company executive; b. 1935. BA in Econs., Bocconi U., Milan, Italy, 1958; postgrad., Harvard U., 1973. With Lepetit, S.A. (became subs. Dow Chem. 1965), 1959-77; various mgmt. positions Becton Dickinson & Co., Franklin Lakes, N.J., 1978-89, pres. med. sector, 1989-94, chmn. bd. dirs., pres., CEO, 1994—. Office: Becton Dickinson & Co 1 Becton Dr Franklin Lakes NJ 07417-1880*

CASTELLINO, FRANCIS JOSEPH, university dean; b. Pittston, Pa., Mar. 7, 1943; s. Joseph Samuel and Evelyn Bonita C.; m. Mary Margaret Fabiny, June 5, 1965; children—Kimberly Ann, Michael Joseph, Anthony Francis. BS, U. Scranton, 1964; MS, U. Iowa, 1966, PhD in Biochemistry, 1968; LLD, U. Scranton, 1983; DSc (hon.), U. Waterloo, Ont., Can., 1994. Postdoctoral fellow Duke U., Durham, N.C., 1968-70; mem. faculty dept. chemistry & biochemistry U. Notre Dame, Ind., 1970—; prof. U. Notre Dame, 1977—; dean U. Notre Dame (Coll. Sci.), 1979—. Contbr. articles to profl. jours. NIH fellow, 395201968-70. Fellow N.Y. Acad. Scis., AAAS; mem. Am. Heart Assn., Am. Chem. Soc., Am. Soc. Biol. Chemistry. Roman Catholic. Office: Univ Notre Dame Col Sci 229 Nieuwland Sci Hall Notre Dame IN 46556-5670

CASTELLINO, RONALD AUGUSTUS DIETRICH, radiologist; b. N.Y.C., Feb. 18, 1938; s. Leonard Vincent and Henrietta Wilhelmina (Geffken) C.; m. Joyce Cuneo, Jan. 26, 1963; children: Jeffrey Charles, Robin Leonard, Anthony James. Student, Creighton U., Omaha, 1955-58, M.D., 1962. Diplomate: Am. Bd. Radiology. Rotating intern Highland Alameda County Hosp., Oakland, Calif., 1962-63; USPHS/Peace Corps physician Brazil, 1963-65; resident in diagnostic radiology Stanford U. Hosp., 1965-68, chief resident, 1967-68; asst. prof. radiology Stanford U. Med. Sch., 1968-74, assoc. prof., 1974-81, prof., 1981-93, chief diagnostic oncologic radiology, 1970-89, chief CT body scanning, 1979-89, dir. div. diagnostic radiology and assoc. chmn. dept. radiology, 1981-86, acting chmn. dept. diagnostic radiology and nuclear medicine, 1986-89; prof. emeritus Stanford U. Med. Sch., N.Y.C., 1993—; chair dept. radiology, Carroll and Milton Petrie chair Meml. Sloan Kettering Cancer Ctr., N.Y.C., 1990-98; prof. radiology Cornell Med. Sch., 1994-98; mem. U.S. Cancer del., People's Republic China, 1977. Co-editor: Pediatric Oncologic Radiology, 1977; assoc. editor; Lymphology, 1973-97, Investigative Radiology, 1985-94, Academic Radiology, 1994-97, Radiology, 1986-94, Postgrad. Radiology, 1986—; contbr. numerous rsch. papers to profl. jours., chpts. to books. Recipient T.F. Eckstrom Fund award, 1978; Guggenheim fellow, 1974-75. Mem. Internat. Soc. Lymphology (exec. com. 1975-85), Am. Coll. Radiology, Assn. Univ. Radiologists (exec. com. 1981-85), Radiol. Soc. N.Am., Soc. Cardiovascular and Interventional Radiology (charter), Am. Roentgen Ray Soc., Western Angiography Soc. (charter), Calif. Med. Assn. (adv. panel sect. radiology 1972-89), Calif. Radiol. Soc., Soc. Thoracic Radiology (charter), Soc. Cancer Imaging (charter), N.Am. Soc. Lymphology (charter, exec. com. 1982-86), Calif. Acad. Medicine, N.Y. Roentgen Soc., N.Y. Acad. Medicine, Am. Soc. Therapeutic Radiation Oncologists (hon.), Alpha Omega Alpha. Office: R-2 Tech Dept Radiology 325 Distel Cir Los Altos CA 94022

CASTELLON, CHRISTINE NEW, information systems specialist, real estate agent; b. Pittsfield, Mass., June 22, 1957; d. Edward Francis Jr. and Helen Patricia (Cordes) New; m. John Arthur Castellon, Oct. 1, 1988. BS in Elec. and Computer Engring., U. Mass., 1979; MBA, Northeastern U., 1986. Engr. microwave radio system design New Eng. Telephone Co., Framingham, Mass., 1979-82; mgr. minicomputer support group New Eng. Telephone Co., Dorchester, Mass., 1982-85; mgr. current systems planning/network svcs. NYNEX Svc. Co., Boston, 1985-87; mem. tech. staff computing environments Bellcore, Piscataway, N.J., 1987-90; assoc. dir. info. systems provisioning NYNEX Telesector Resources Group, N.Y.C., 1990-93; sales assoc. Weidel Realtors, Flemington, N.J., 1994—; speaker New Eng. Telephone Careers-In-Engring. Program, 1980-82. Leader 2d violin sect. Cen. Jersey Symphony Orch., Raritan Valley Community Coll., N.J., 1988—; prin. 1st violinist New Eng. Conservatory Extension Div., Boston, 1979-87; violinist Civic Symphony Orch., Boston, 1982-87; active UMASS Coll./Industry Adv. Com. Named Monument Mountain High Sch. valedictorian, 1975; recipient Arion Music award, 1975, cert. Applied Music and Theory Pittsfield Community Music Sch., 1975, Exceptional Merit award NYNEX, 1987. Mem. U. Mass. Alumni Assn. (coll./industry adv. com. for women), Northeastern U. MBA Alumni Assn. Roman Catholic. Home: 622 Old York Rd Neshanic Station NJ 08853-3600

CASTELLONE, NATALIE LYNNÉ, accountant; b. Mar. 1, 1968; d. Frank B. and Shirley M. Lusignau. B in Acctg., U. R.I., 1991; postgrad., Bryant Coll. CPA, R.I. Practice acctg., Johnston, R.I., 1991—. Fin. dir. Town of Johnston, 1997—. Mem. AICPA, R.I. Soc. CPAs. Home: 1603 Plainfield Pike G-9 Johnston RI 02919 Office: Johnston Town Hall 1385 Hartford Ave Johnston RI 02919

CASTEN, RICHARD FRANCIS, physicist; b. N.Y.C., Nov. 1, 1941; s. Daniel F. and Constance Mary (Bell) C.; m. Jo Ann Daly, June 6, 1964. BS magna cum laude, Coll. of the Holy Cross, 1963; PhD, Yale U., 1967. Postdoctoral fellow Niels Bohr Inst., Copenhagen, 1967-69, Los Alamos (N.Mex.) Sci. Lab., 1969-71; asst. scientist Brookhaven Nat. Lab., Upton, N.Y., 1971-73, assoc. scientist, 1973-76, scientist, 1977-81, sr. scientist, 1981—, group leader nuclear structure group, 1981-96; prof. physics, dir. A.W. Wright Nuclear Structure Lab. Yale U., New Haven, Conn., 1995—; chmn. N.Am. com. for Isospin Lab. Radioactive Beam Facility, 1989—; guest prof. U. Cologne, Germany, 1985—; mem. panel on basic nuclear data NAS, 1990-92; mem. long-range plan working group Nuclear Sci. Adv. Com., 1989, 95; mem. subcom. on implementation of long-range plan, 1991; mem. spl. emphasis panel NSF, 1993; U.S. rep. Megasci. Forum for Nuclear Physics, Subpanel on Intense Beams and Target Sys., 1997, 98; chair writing panel for White Paper on sci. opportunities with an advanced ISOL facility, 1997; chair ISAC/TRIUMF rev. com., 1997; mem. Nuc. Sci. Adv. Com., 1998, 99 and numerous other nat. and internat. coms.; invited spkr. over 100 internat. confs. Author: Nuclear Structure from a Simple Perspective, 1990, revised edit., 1999; co-author, editor: Algebraic Approaches to Nuclear Structure, 1993; mem. editl. bd. Nuclear Physics News Internat., Internat. Jour. Modern Physics, Jour. Physics G; editor 2 internat. conf. procs.; contbr. over 250 articles to profl. jours. Pres. Jo Ann and Richard Casten, Ltd., 1973—. Danforth fellow, 1963-67; recipient Sr. Alexander von Humboldt prize, 1983. Fellow AAAS, Am. Phys. Soc. (exec. com. divsn. nuclear physics 1991-93, chmn. task force to rev. jour. Phys. Rev. C 1995), Sigma Xi. Achievements include discovery of O(6) symmetry of IBA model and other experimental verifications of the IBA including extensive study of 168-Erc; co-inventor of consistent Q formalism; study of the evolution of nuclear structure with nucleon number; study of the valence p-n interaction; proposal of the NpNn scheme and P-factor; developed new signatures of nuclear structure; discovery of new global correlations of nuclear observables; discovery of new evidence for multi-phonon states in nuclei; co-discovery of anharmonic vibrator and tripartite correlations of nuclear observables; development of ARC method of complete spectroscopy; first uses of the GRID technique for nuclear structure studies; invention of the symmetry triangle of the IBA (the "Casten" triangle); study of phase/shape transitions in nuclei; first tests of coriolis mixing in nuclei; first evidence for large hexadecapole deformations in odd-A nuclei; study of Q-invariants; research with radioactive nuclear beams. E-mail: rick@riviera.physics.yale.edu. Office: Yale Univ Wright Nuc Structure Physics Dept 272 Whitney Av New Haven CT 06520

CASTENSCHIOLD, RENÉ, engineering company executive, author, consultant; b. Mt. Kisco, N.Y., Feb. 7, 1923; s. Tage and Juno (Hagemeister) C.; m. Martha Naomi Stinson, Dec. 14, 1947; children: Gail F., Frederick T., Lynn Castenschiold Jones. BEE, Pratt Inst., 1944. Registered profl. engr., N.Y., N.J., Pa.; registered profl. planner, N.J. Test engr. (Manhattan Project) GE, Pittsfield, Mass., 1944-45; design engr. GE, Schenectady, 1946-47; sr. product engr. Am. Transformer Co., Newark, 1947-50; design engr. Automatic Switch Co., Florham Park, N.J., 1951-57; chief customer engr. Automatic Switch Co., Florham Park, 1957-74, exec. engring. mgr., 1974-85; pres. LCR Cons. Engrs. P.A., Green Village, N.J., 1986—; lectr. N.J. Inst. Tech., Newark, 1967-79; adviser Underwriters Labs., Inc., Melville, N.Y., 1973-85; chmn. U.S. Tech. Adv. Group and U.S. del. Internat. Electotech. Commn., Geneva, 1981-90. *A leading authority on emergency and standby power systems for essential electrical loads. Since joining the Automatic Switch Company in 1951, he has pioneered in the research, design and standardization of automatic transfer switches and emergency generator controls. His accomplishments have increased reliability of alternate power for critical electrical loads, such as in hospitals, airports and communication facilities. Recipient of 14 patents and author of 40 published papers and articles, he successfully advanced closed-transition switching for computer and other essential loads, which are vulnerable to momentary losses of power. In recognition of his research and standardization of standby and emergency power systems, the National Electrical Manufacturers Association presented him with the prestigious James H. McGraw Award in 1986, and the Institute of Electrical & Electronic Engineers presented him with the 1990 Richard Harold Kaufmann Award.* Contbr. numerous articles and papers to profl. jours., chpts. to books, promulgation of numerous nat. and internat. elec. standards; patentee in fields transformer design, relays, automatic transfer switches and engine generator controls. Chmn. Bd. of Adjustment, Harding Twp., 1975-77, chmn. Planning Bd., 1982-85; dir. Civil Def., 1966-70; trustee Wash. Assn. N.J., Morristown, 1984-93, sec., 1985-88, v.p., 1989-92, pres., 1992-93; trustee Morristown Meml. Health Found., Inc., 1995—; co-chmn. Jefferson Soc., Morristown Meml. Hosp., 1995-98; vestryman Episcopal Ch., 1991-94. Named to Disting. Alumni Bd. Visitors, Pratt Inst., 1979; recipient Disting. Svc. award Morristown Nat. Hist. Park, 1993, achievement award Washington Assn. N.J., 1995. Listed in Danmarks Adel Aarbog, 1923—. Fellow IEEE (stds. bd. 1983-85, Achievement award 1988, Richard Harold Kaufmann award 1990), NSPE, Instrument Soc. Am., Nat. Elec. Mfrs. Assn. (chmn. automatic transfer switch com. 1982-88, James H. McGraw award 1986), Internat. Assn. Elec. Insps., Nat. Acad. Forensic Engrs., Coun. Engring. Splty. Bds. (cert. diplomate), Am. Cons. Engrs. Coun., Nat. Fire Protection Assn., Internat. Platform Assn., N.J. Christmas Tree Growers' Assn., Can. Stds. Assn., Nat. Elec. Safety Found., Nat. Forensic Ctr., Danish Am. Soc., Skytop Club (Pa.), The Morristown (N.J.) Club. Republican. Avocations: swimming, tree farming, photography, hiking. Home: PO Box 154 Lees Hill Rd New Vernon NJ 07976 Office: LCR Cons Engrs PA PO Box 2 Green Village NJ 07935-0002

CASTILE, RAND (JESSE RANDOLPH, III), retired museum director; b. N.C., July 15, 1938; s. Jesse Randolph II and Pauline Virginia (Simmons) C.; m. Sondra Meadow Myers, 1960; children: Leath Willow, Heather Rain. BA, Drew U., Madison, N.J., 1960; diploma, Urasenke Tea Ceremony, Kyoto, Japan, 1967; LHD (hon.), Drew U., 1992. With ARTnews, N.Y.C., 1963-65; dir. edn. Japan Soc., N.Y.C., 1967-71, dir. performing arts, 1981-86, dir. Japan House Gallery, 1971-86; dir. Asian Art Mus., San Francisco, 1986-94; ret.; vis. com. Met. Mus. Art, 1974—; sec., mem. U.S.-Japan Cultural and Ednl. Conf., 1972-86; mem. Maine Art Commn., 1997—. Author: The Way of Tea, 1971, 79; (exhbn. catalogue) Japanese Art Now: Tadaaki Kuwayama & Rikuro Okamoto, 1980, other catalogues; editor: Japanese Art Exhibitions with Catalogue in U.S., 1980; contbr. articles to profl. jours. Panelist Calif. Arts Coun., 1986-91; bd. dirs. West-East Coun. Cathedral Ch. of St. John the Devine, 1977-86, AAM/ICOM, 1982-85, Japan Soc. No. Calif., 1986-95, San Francisco Bay Area Dance Coalition, 1986-88, Rock and Roll Mus., San Francisco, 1988-89, U. San Francisco Ctr. for Pacific Rim, 1989-95, Seoul-San Francisco Sister City Com., 1987-93, Nat. Maritime Mus., San Francisco, 1989-93; mem. internat. adv. com. Ctr. for Internat. Contemporary Arts, 1989-95; chair co-chair gov. State Calif. awards for Art and Philanthropy, 1990-94, others. Fulbright-Hayes fellow, 1966-67; recipient Mayor's award of Honor for Arts and Culture, N.Y.C., 1982, Alumni Achievement award Drew U., Madison, N.J., 1987, Plowshares Humanitarian award, 1990. Mem. Assn. Art Mus. Dirs. (1974-95), Am. Assn. Mus. (bd. dirs. Internat. coun. 1982-86), Maine Arts Commn., Mus. Trustee Assn. (adv. coun. of dirs. 1989-95), Am. Fedn. Arts (nat. exhbn. com. 1980-95), Acad. Lacquer Rsch. Tokyo (Am. sec. 1977-86), Japan Soc. No. Calif. (bd. dirs. 1986-95), Century Assn., St. Croix Country Club, Herring Cove Golf Club.

CASTILLA, VINIVIO SORIA, professional baseball player; b. Oaxaca, Mexico, July 4, 1967. Grad. high sch., Mexico. With Atlanta Braves, 1991-92; shortstop Colo. Rockies, 1993—. Named Nat. League All-Star Team, 1995. Office: Colo Rockies 2001 Blake St Denver CO 80205-2000*

CASTILLO, DIANA MAY, religious organization administrator; b. Pontiac, Mich., July 22, 1945; d. John Robert and Ellen May (Steele) Burkhart. AA in Humanities magna cum laude, U. Cin., 1992, BA in English magna cum laude, 1994; postgrad. in Rescue Ministry, Rescue Coll., 1998—. Lic. real estate sales agt., W. Va.; notary pub., Ariz. Delayed birth cert. clk. State of W. Va. Dept. Health, Charleston, 1979-86; proofreader Anderson Publ. Co., Cin., 1987-88, Press Cmty. Papers, Cin., 1987-88; word processing specialist U. Cin., 1990-94; supr. Hope Cottages Women's Gospel Mission, Flagstaff, Ariz., 1996-98; intern Tucson Rescue Mission, 1996, Denver Rescue Mission, 1998—; writer, editor St. John Social Svc. Ctr., Cin., 1989; proofreader, desktop publisher Dept. English, U. Cin., 1994, Florence (Ky.) Bapt. Temple, 1994-95, editor, desktop publ., Beechgrove (Ky.) Boosters, 1995; juror Goodwin, Raup PC, Phoenix, 1998; spkr. in field of homelessness. Mem. editl. bd. Daily Sun, 1997; newsletter reporter Mountain Friends, 1998. Poll vol. Coconino County Bd. Elections, Flagstaff, Ariz., 1996-98; CPR instr. Am. Heart Assn., Charleston, W. Va., 1983, vol. respite care provider, United Home Care, Cin., 1987; vol. worship leader Women's Gospel Mission, Flagstaff, 1995-96; crisis response team Nat. Orgn. for Victim Assistance, Flagstaff, 1997-98; Bible study facilitator Coconino County Jail, Flagstaff, 1997-98; libr. asst. Flagstaff Christian Fellowship, 1997-98; pastoral counselor, Overcomers facilitator; victim witness vol., 1998; instr. English as 2d Lang., Sunnyside Bapt. Ch., Flagstaff, 1997; participant Quick Ct. Tng., Coconino County Law Libr., Flagstaff, 1997; facilitator Prison Fellowship, Flagstaff, 1998; grad. Citizen's Police Acad., Flagstaff, 1998. Presidential scholarship W. Va. State Coll., Institute, W. Va., 1985. Mem. Internat. Platform Assn., Internat. Union Gospel Missions, Women in Comm., Inc., Freelance Edtl. Assn., Golden Key, Alpha Sigma Kappa, Phi Kappa Epsilon. Republican. Baptist. Avocations: travel, singing, reading, photography, fine arts. Home: 4 S San Francisco St # 330 Flagstaff AZ 86001-5737

CASTILLO, JOHN E., councilman. City councilman Dist. 1 Houston, 1996—. Office: PO Box 1562 Houston TX 77251-1562*

CASTILLO, LEANNE MARLOW, artist, nurse; b. Lone Rock, Iowa, July 24, 1933; d. Lemuel Jess Marlow and Ida Mary Kollasch; m. Jozef Bednarz, July 6, 1953 (div. Jan. 1977); children: Barbara Goecke, Katherine Rike, Jan Christensen, John Bednarz, Angie Curell, Theresa Gerdis, Mary Palmer, Margaret Shellenberg, Rob Michael, Sandra Lamoreux, Sharon Bednarz; m. Cruz Castillo, July 14, 1983 (dec. Sept. 1987). Cert. in comml. design, Art Instrn. Inc., 1953; degree in nursing, Iowa Lakes C.C., 1980. LPN, Iowa. Staff nurse Algona (Iowa) Good Samaritan Home, 1980-83; charge nurse Westview Care Ctr., Britt, Iowa, 1983-86, 87—; staff nurse Pinal County Nursing Ctr., Florence, Ariz., 1986-87. Artist over 45 oil paintings Britt Hobo Kings and Queens, 1988—. Chair Britt Hobo Days Art Show, 1988-97. Mem. Iowa Artists, North Iowa Artist's League. Democrat. Roman Catholic. Home and Studio: Castillo Art Studio 54 S 1st St SE Britt IA 50423

CASTILLO, MARIO ENRIQUE, artist, educator; b. Rio Bravo, Mexico, Sept. 19, 1945; came to U.S., 1955, naturalized, 1965; s. Manuel Castillo and Maria Enriquez de Allen. *Mario's mother, Maria Enriquez De Allen, is a Nationally known folk artist. She has been recognized with an award and show in New York by the Women's National Caucus. His step-father, Mr. Allen was the Chair of the Photography Department at the Art Institute of Chicago. He is internationally known for his Egyptomania Architectural Photographs. Manuel Castillo, Mario's brother, lives in Uvalde, Texas and is well-known for his recyclable material art projects made for specific holidays* Cert. Ill. Inst. Design, 1964; BFA, Sch. of Art Inst. Chgo., 1969; MFA, Calif. Inst. of Arts, 1972; postgrad. U. So. Calif., 1969-70, Pasadena City Coll., 1977, Calif. State U. at L.A., 1980-81, Calif. State U., Dominguez Hills, 1986-88, East L.A. City Coll., 1982, Nat. U., Inglewood, Calif., 1989. Designer J.M. Pateros Studios, Inc., Chgo., 1965, Lukas & Assocs., Chgo., 1966; instr. Pilsen Settlement House, Chgo., 1967; comml. artist Chgo. Bd. Edn., 1968; instr. United Christian Cmty. Svc., Chgo., 1968-69; mural dir. Halsted Urban Progress Ctr., 1968, Dept. Human Resources, Chgo., 1969, McHenry Coll., Crystal Lake, Ill., 1992, No. Ill. U., DeKalb, 1993, Joliet Jr. Coll., Ill., 1994, Coll. of Lake County, Grayslake, Ill., 1994, U. Guadalajara, Ocotlan, Mex., 1995, SAIC & Lincoln Park Cultural Ctr., Chgo., 1996, Bemis Found., Omaha, 1996, Triton Coll., River Grove, Ill., 1997; tchg. asst. Calif. Inst. Arts, Valencia, 1970-72, instr., 1972-73; instr. Santa Monica (Calif.) City Coll., 1973; mem. faculty dept. art U. Ill., Champaign, 1973-76; comml. artist, L.A., 1977; instr. art Immaculate Heart Coll., Hollywood, Calif., 1979-80, Pacific Asian Consortium in Edn., 1980-81, E.C.F. Art Ctr., L.A., 1986-90, L.A. Unified Sch. Dist., 1986-90, Instituto Comercial Artistico, Maywood, Calif., 1987, Lexicon Sch. Languages, 1987-88, Plaza de la Raza, 1989-90; mem. faculty art dept. Columbia Coll., Chgo., 1990—; panelist at Northeastern Ill. U., Chgo., 1974, Coll. Art Assn., Chgo., 1975, Columbia Coll., Chgo., 1992, 94, 96, Chgo. Artist Coalition, 1993, Nat. Assn. Chicano Studies, Chgo., 1994, 96, Suburban Fine Arts Ctr., Highland Park, Ill., 1995, U. Guadalajara, Jalisco, 1995; presenter workshop Human Rights Portfolio, Chgo., 1994, Internat. Prints, Chgo., 1994, Humboldt Park, Chgo., 1995; guest lectr. Galeria J.M. Velazco, Mexico City, 1975, Centro de la Causa, Chgo., 1975, Latino Cultural House, Champaign, 1975, U. Ill., Champaign, 1975, 76, Corpus Christi (Tex.) State U., 1978; McHenry County Coll., 1991, 92, Northwestern U., 1991, Columbia Coll., Montebello Sch. Dist., 1990, No. Ill. U. DeKalb, 1993, Triton Coll., River Grove, Ill., 1993, 94, Prospectus Gallery, Chgo., 1993, Joliet (Ill.) Jr. Coll., 1994, St. Cloud (Minn.) State U., 1994, Mac Murry Coll., Jacksonville, Ill., 1994, Coll. of Lake County, 1994, Nat.- Louis U., Chgo., 1995, Melrose Park (Ill.) Pub. Libr., 1995, Mobil Art Gallery, Jacksonville, Ill., 1994, Northeastern U., Chgo., 1995, Harold Washington Libr., Chgo., 1995, Munster Ind. Cultural Ctr., 1995, U. Guadalajara, Ocotlan, Jalisco, 1995, 96, CCC Art Gallery, Chgo., 1995, Winnetka (Ill.) Cultural House, 1995, No. Ill. U., De Kalb, 1995, U. Guadalajara, La Barranca Campus, 1996, Lincoln Park Cultural Ctr., Chgo., 1996, Triton Coll., River Grove, 1996, 97; art juror Weisman Scholarship CCC, Chgo., 1993, Old Town Art Fair, Chgo., 1993, Hokin Gallery CCC, Chgo., 1995, Weisman Best of Show, Chgo., 1996; curator of art exhibitions U. Ill., Champaign, 1975, Columbia Coll., Chgo., 1994, 95, Triton Coll., 1995, No. Ind. Arts Assn., Munster, 1995, 11th Street Art Gallery CCC, 1995, Hokin Ctr. Gallery, Columbia Coll., 1996; interior designer El Mercado Co., L.A., 1981-83; regular performer musical program Noches Rancheras, East L.A., Calif., 1981-83; cons. in field. One-man shows include Scholarship and Guidance Assn., Chgo., 1968, Calif. Inst. of the Arts, Burbank, 1971, Valencia, Calif., 1972, Latino Cultural House, U. Ill., Champaign, 1976, Inst. For Hispanic Cultural Studies, Santa Monica, Calif., 1989, Orlando Gallery, Sherman Oaks, Calif., 1989, Sangre De Cristo Arts and Conf. Ctr., Pueblo, Colo., 1991, Prospectus Gallery, Chgo., 1991, 93, McHenry County Art Gallery, 1991, No. Ill. U. Art Gallery, DeKalb, 1993, Atwood Art Ctr., St. Cloud U., 1994, Mac Murry Coll., Jacksonville, Ill., 1994; numerous group shows including: Fresno Art Mus., Calif., 1991, San Francisco Art Mus., 1991, San Francisco Mus. of Modern Art, 1991, Albuquerque Mus., 1991, Denver Art Mus., 1991, 93, Expo, 1993, San

Antonio Mus. of Art, 1993, Nat. Mus. of Am. Art, 1993, . Chgo., 1993, 94, Chgo. Latino Film Festival, 1994, Las Artes Galeria, Omaha, 1994, Open Windows Gallery, Chgo., 1994, S. Suburban Coll., South Holland, Ill., 1994, Columbia Coll., Chgo., 1994, 95, J.R. Shapiro Gallery, Oak Park, 1994, Cath. Theological Union, Chgo., 1995, John Linsey Gallery, Oak Park, 1995, Hokin Gallery CCC, Chgo., 1995, Oak Park Art League, 1995, Pilsen Artist to Artist, Chgo., 1996, CCC Faculty Exhbn., Chgo., 1996, Richard Love Gallery, Chgo., 1996, La Llorona Gallery, Chgo., 1997, Prospectus Art Gallery, Ghgo., 1997, Mexican Fine Arts Ctr. Mus., 1997, Chgo. Hist. Soc., 1996, 97, Mus. Contemporary Art, Chgo., 1996, 97, numerous others; also film screenings U.S., Europe and Mexico; commd. muralist in public locations and pvt. residences; represented in permanent collections: Sara Lee Corp., Chgo., Mexican Mus. of Fine Arts, Chgo., San Francisco Mus. of Art, San Francisco Mus. of Contemporary Art, Tucson Mus. of Art, San Diego Mus. of Contemporary Art, Latino Inst., Chgo., Columbia Coll., Chgo., Bell Telephone Co., Chgo., Lake Meadows Assn., Chgo., Scholarship and Guidance Assn., Chgo., City of Chgo., San Antonio Art Mus., Guadalupe Cultural Arts Ctr., Denver, Evergreen State Coll., Olympia, Wash., Chicano Humanities and Art Coun., Denver, Ariztlan Inc., Phoenix, Mira, Chgo., Centro Cultural de La Raza, San Diego, San Diego Mus. Art, Albuquerque Mus., San Francisco Mus. Art, San Diego Mus. Contemporary Art, Denver Art Mus., Mex. Mus., San Francisco, Portland Art Mus., Nat. Mus. Am. Art, Washington, also numerous pvt. collections. Recipient numerous awards including: nat. gold medal, gold keys and certs. Scholastic Mag., 1963-65, cert. of merit N.Y. Times, 1965, 1st Prize award, Chgo. Police Dept., 1964, 1st Prize award Chgo. Assn. Commerce & Indus., 1965, 1st pl. U. Ill. Chicago LASP design competition, 1st prize Maldef Art Competition, 1989, 1st pl. ESDC's Archtl. Relief Design Competition for New Homes in Chgo., 1992; artist to represent midwest in nat. workshop, UCLA, 1988, artist to represent Latino culture in Spanish TV comml., 1989, 1st prize Homewood (Ill.) C. of C., 1967, 1st prize Fiesta del Quinto Sol, Chgo., 1974, 1st prize Mus. Sci. and Industry, Chgo., 1975, 1st prize for 18th St. banner design, Chgo., 1994; Am. Film Inst. grantee, 1972; Oakley fellow U. So. Calif., 1969-70; Scholarship and Guidance Assn. grantee, 1965-68, Ford Found. grantee, 1975; named Artst of Yr., Latino Inst., 1991. Composer numerous songs. Home and Studio: 10101 S Avenue M Chicago IL 60617-5925 Office: Columbia Coll Art Dept 600 S Michigan Ave Chicago IL 60605-1900

CASTILLO, RUBEN, judge; b. 1954. BA, Loyola U., 1976; JD, Northwestern U., 1979. Pvt. practice Chgo., 1979-84, Kirkland & Ellis, Chgo., 1991-93; dist. judge U.S. Dist. Ct. (no. dist.) Ill., 1994—; adj. prof. Northwestern U., 1988—. Mem. ABA, Latin Am. Bar Assn., Chgo. Bar Found., Chgo. Coun. of Lawyers (v.p. 1991-93). Office: U S Courthouse 2378 Dirksen Bldg 219 S Dearborn St Chicago IL 60604-1702*

CASTLE, EMERY NEAL, agricultural and resource economist, educator; b. Eureka, Kans., Apr. 13, 1923; s. Sidney James and Josie May (Tucker) C.; m. Merab Eunice Weber, Jan. 20, 1946; 1 child, Cheryl Diana Delozier. BS, Kans. State U., 1948, MS, 1950; PhD, Iowa State U., 1952, LHD (hon.), 1997. Agrl. economist Fed. Res. Bank of Kansas City, 1952-54; from asst. prof. to prof. dept. agrl. econs. Oreg. State U., Corvallis, 1954-65; dean faculty Oreg. State U., 1965-66, prof., head dept. agrl. econs., 1966-72, dean Grad. Sch., 1972-76, Alumni disting. prof., 1970, prof. univ. grad. faculty econs., 1986—; v.p., sr. fellow Resources for the Future, Washington, 1976-79; pres. Resources for the Future, 1979-86; vice-chmn. Environ. Quality Commn. Oreg., 1988-95. Editor: The Changing American Countryside: Rural People and Places, 1995; mem. editl. bd. Land Econs., 1969—. Recipient Alumni Disting. Service award Kans. State U., 1976; Disting. Service award Oreg. State U., 1984. Fellow AAAS, Am. Assn. Agrl. Economists (pres. 1972-73), Am. Acad. Arts and Scis. Home: 1112 NW Solar Pl Corvallis OR 97330-3640 Office: Oreg State U 227 Ballard Extension Hall Corvallis OR 97331-8538

CASTLE, ERIC F., administrator historic site. BA in Art History, So. Ill. U., 1967, MFA in Art History, 1971. Chmn., instr. art dept. Bay de Noc C.C., Escanaba, Mich., 1972-82; curator, dir. U.S. Army Med. Mus., Ft. Sam Houston, Tex., 1984-87; curatorial dir. Nat. Mus. of Transport, St. Louis, 1987-90; adminstr. Drake Well Mus., Titusville, Pa., 1990-93; hist. site adminstr. Washington Crossing (Pa.) Hist. Park, 1993—. V.p., pres. Upper Peninsula Crafts Coun., 1972-82; treas. Mich. C.C. Arts and Humanities Assn., 1972-82; devel. exhibit area and coord. exhibits for new Cmty. Performing Arts Ctr., 1972-82; chmn. steering com. Oil Region Heritage Park, 1990—; bd. dirs. Oil Creek and Titusville Railroad, 1990—; adv. com. Oil Prodn. Curriculum , 1990—; adv. bd. Venango County Area Vocat. Tech. Sch., 1990—; mem. Titusville Transp. Commn., 1990—. Sgt. U.S. Army, 1967-69. Office: Washington Crossing Hist Pk PO Box 103 Washington Crossing PA 18977-0103

CASTLE, GRACE ELEANOR, legal investigator; b. Waldport, Oreg., Feb. 13, 1943; d. James Everett and Ethel Grace (Smith) Elting; m. Terry Lynn Castle, Feb. 3, 1962; children: Nancy Kae Castle Cary, Tari Ann Castle Utterback. Cert. Legal Investigator. Investigator, paralegal William A. Barton, PC, Newport, Oreg., 1987-89; owner, operator Castle Investigations, Newport, 1989-96; mgr. investigations Paul J. Ciolino and Assocs., Inc., Chgo., 1996—. Co-author, editor: Advanced Forensic Civil Investigations, 1997; contbr. articles to profl. jours. Mem. Nat. Assn. Legal Investigators (editor 1993-98, regional dir. 1993, Pres.'s award 1997, 98), Nat. Assn. Profl. Process Servers (editor 1994-99), Nat. Assn. Criminal Def. Lawyers (assoc.), Oreg. Assn. Legal Investigators (pres. 1991-92), Huguenot Hist. Soc. New Paltz, N.Y. Avocations: historical research and writing, photography. Office: Paul J Ciolino and Assocs Inc Ste 1080 800 E Northwest Hwy Palatine IL 60067

CASTLE, HOWARD BLAINE, religious organization administrator; b. Toledo, July 15, 1935; s. Russell Wesley and Letha Belle (Hobbs) C.; m. Patricia Ann Haverty, Aug. 12, 1957; 1 child Kevin Blaine. AB, Marion Coll., 1958; postgrad., Valparaiso U., 1960. Pastor The Wesleyan Ch., Valparaiso, Ind., 1958-60, Toronto, Ohio, 1963-69; assoc. pastor Northridge Wesleyan Ch., Dayton, Ohio, 1960-63; exec. dir. gen. dept. youth Wesleyan Ch. Hdqrs., Marion, Ind., 1968-72, dir. field ministries gen. dept. Sunday schs., 1972-74, exec. dir. curriculum, 1980-81; mng. editor WIN Mag., Marion, Ind., 1969-72; asst. gen. sec. Gen. Dept. of Local Ch. Edn., Marion, Ind., 1974-80; gen. dir. estate planning Wesleyan Ch. Internat Ctr., Indpls., 1982—; Editor Ohio dist. The Wesleyan Ch., Columbus, 1961-69; gen. conf. del. The Wesleyan Ch., Anderson, Ind., 1968. Writer: Curriculum-Religious Adult Student/Teacher, 1982—, Light from the Word, 1982—. Mem. Christian Holiness Partnership, Christian Stewardship Assn., Christian Mgmt. Assn. Avocations: music, reading. Office: The Wesleyan Ch Internat PO Box 50434 Indianapolis IN 46250-0434 *Life's choices impact more than any other factor the measure of our successes and achievements. Circumstances cannot defeat one who chooses to rise above them by acting in accord with his choice.*

CASTLE, JAMES CAMERON, information systems executive; b. Peoria, Ill., Nov. 4, 1936; s. Charles Cameron and Betty Evelyn (Shaw) C.; m. Dorothy Patricia Gorbandt, June 7, 1958; children: James Charles, Patricia Elizabeth. BS, U.S. Mil. Acad., 1958; MSEE, U. Pa., Phila., 1963, PhD, 1966. Pres., chief exec. officer Honeywell Bull Network Info. Svcs., S.A., Paris, 1975-78; gen. mgr. GE, Daytona Beach, Fla., 1978-80; v.p. ops. Honeywell, Inc., Billerica, Mass., 1980-82; exec. v.p. Memorex Corp., Santa Clara, Calif., 1982-84; pres. TGB Info. Systems, Inc., N.Y.C., 1984-87; chmn., pres., chief exec. officer Infotron Systems Corp., Cherry Hill, N.J., 1987-91; CEO Teradata Corp., El Segundo, Calif., 1991-92; chmn., chief exec. officer U.S. Computer Svcs., Sacramento, 1992—; bd. dirs. Par Tech. Corp., New Hartford, N.Y., Leasing Solutions, Inc., San Jose, Calif., ADC Telecomms., Mpls., PMI Group, Inc., San Francisco, DST Systems, Kansas City, Chief Exec. Orgn., Bethesda, Md.; trustee West Point (N.Y.) Assn. Grads. 1st lt. U.S. Army, 1958-61. Mem. World Presidents Orgn.

CASTLE, JOHN KROB, merchant banker; b. Cedar Rapids, Iowa, Dec. 22, 1940; s. Clyo F. and Emma (Krob) C.; m. Marianne Sherman, Sept. 20, 1969; children: William Sherman, John Sherman, James Sherman, David Alexander. SB, MIT, 1963; MBA with high distinction, Harvard U., 1965; LHD (hon.), N.Y. Med. Coll., 1988. Assoc. Donaldson, Lufkin & Jenrette, Inc., N.Y.C., 1965-68, v.p., 1968-71, exec. v.p., 1971-73, mng. dir., 1973-80, chief operating officer, 1979-84, pres., 1980-86, chief exec. officer, 1985-86; pres., chief exec. officer Branford Castle, Inc., N.Y.C., 1986—; also founder, chmn., CEO Castle Harlan, Inc., N.Y.C., 1987—, also founder, chmn., chief exec. officer, 1987; gen. ptnr. Legend Capital Group L.P., N.Y.C.; chmn., gen. ptnr. Castle Harlan Ptnrs. III; bd. dirs. Sealed Air Corp., Morton's Restaurant Group, Inc., Dearborn Risk Mgmt., Inc., USSynthetic Corp., Statia Terminals Internat., N.V., Commemorative Brands, Inc., Universal Compression, Inc. Author: Financial Executives Handbook: Dividend Policy and Equity Financing, 1970, The Strategy of Corporate Financing: Packaging a Merger or Acquisition, 1971, Acquisition and Merger Negotiating Strategy, 1971; co-pub. Castle Connolly Guide, 1994, 95, 97, 98, Parent's Helper, 1996. Trustee N.Y. Med. Coll., chmn. bd., 1979-90; mem. corp. MIT, 1987-99; mem. vis. com. dept. econs; trustee The Whitehead Inst. for Biomed. Rsch., N.Y. Presbyn. Hosp., N.Y. Acad. Medicine, Internat. Ctr. for Disabled; chmn. Rhodes Scholar Selection Com., N.Y. State, 1986-90; endowed Castle Krob Fellowship for grad. study in econs. MIT, Castle Krob Fund for rsch. support at N.Y. Med. Coll., Castle Krob Devel. Chair in econs. MIT, John K. Castle Publs. Fund on Ethics, Politics and Econs., Yale U. Mem. Links Club, Met. Club, Harvard Club, N.Y. Yacht Club, Palm Beach Polo Club, Doubles Ltd., Club Collette. Home: 1095 N Ocean Blvd Palm Beach FL 33480-3230 Office: Castle Harlan Inc 150 E 58th St New York NY 10155-0002

CASTLE, JOSEPH LANKTREE, II, energy company executive, consultant; b. Germantown, Pa., July 25, 1932; s. George Scott and Frances (Murphy) C.; m. Sally Buckman Watson, May 4, 1957; children: Sallie Buckman Harder, Joseph Lanktree III, Kathryn Lanktree Van Blarcom. AB in English, Princeton U., 1954. V.p. Phila. Nat. Bank, 1954-66; ptnr. Butcher & Sherrerd, Phila., 1966-72; cons. Joseph L. Castle Assocs., Gladwyne, Pa., 1972-74; trustee The Reading Co., Blue Bell, Pa., 1974-80; CEO, Castle Energy Corp., Radnor, Pa., 1981—; bd. dirs. Mark Ctrs. Trust, Kingston, Pa., Charming Shoppes, Bensalem, Pa. Capt. U.S. Army, 1955-59. Republican. Presbyterian. Avocations: golf, fly fishing. Home: 1790 Aloha Ln Gladwyne PA 19035-1031 Office: Castle Energy Corp 100 Matsonford Rd Radnor PA 19087

CASTLE, MICHAEL N., congressman, former governor, lawyer; b. Wilmington, Del., July 2, 1939; s. J. Manderson and Louisa B. Castle. BA, Hamilton Coll., 1961; JD, Georgetown U., 1964. Bar: Del. 1964, D.C. 1964. Assoc. firm Connolly Bove and Lodge, Wilmington, 1964-73; ptnr. firm Connolly Bove and Lodge, 1973-75; dept. atty. gen. State of Del., 1965-66; ptnr. firm Schnee and Castle (P.A.), 1975-80; lt. gov. State of Del., Wilmington, 1981-85; prin. Michael N. Castle (P.A.), 1981—; gov. State of Del., 1985-93; mem. Congress from Del. (at large), 1993—; chmn. banking & fin. svcs. subcom. on Domestic & Internat. Monetary Policy, mem. edn. and workforce com., intelligence com.; mem. Del. Ho. of Reps., 1966-67, Del. State Senate, 1968-76, minority leader, 1976. Bd. dirs. Boys Club of Wilmington. Mem. Del. State Bar Assn., ABA, Council State Govts., Nat. Gov.'s Assn., Rep. Gov.'s Assn., Southern Gov.'s Assn. Republican. Roman Catholic. Office: US Ho of Reps 1227 Longworth Bldg Washington DC 20515-0801*

CASTLE, SANDIE, writer, playwright, artist; b. Balt., Jan. 1, 1954; d. John Thornton and Eileen (Burns) Berger; m. Francis Joseph Hartlove, June 19, 1976 (dec. Jan. 1982); m. Meyer David Baron, Dec. 31, 1984 (div. Dec. 1989); 1 child, Shawn Castle Hartlove Baron. Cert., Profl. Sch. Comml. Art, Balt., 1977; B in Liberal Arts, Notre Dame U. Md., Balt., 1997. Freelance writer, artist, lectr. Author: The Catholics Are Coming, 1986, Turning 30, 1989, A Child of God, 1995, plays include: Rhythm of Torn Stars, What the Shadow Knows; author: (anthologies) Exquisite Corpse, Push Cart Prize (Best of Small Press award for short story), Up Late; contbr. articles to mags.; guest TV and radio programs. Participant AIDS benefit Md. Food Com.; pub. rels. vol. Union Meml. Hosp. Md. State Poetry fellow; named Best New Poet/Performer, Md. Writers Coun. Mem. Sigma Tau Delta, Delta Epsilon Sigma, Alpha Sigma Lambda (Delta Chi chpt.). Avocations: collecting religious icons, gardening, flea market shopping.

CASTLE, WILLIAM EUGENE, retired academic administrator; b. Thomas, S.D., Sept. 5, 1929; s. Eugene Albert and Kathryn (Barkley) C.; m. Diane Lee Sklar, Aug. 8, 1963. B.S., No. State Tchrs. Coll., 1951; M.A., U. Iowa, 1958; Ph.D., Stanford U., 1963. Tchr. Faulkton (S.D) High Sch., 1951; instr. St. Cloud (Minn.) Tchrs. Coll., 1958-60, Central Wash. Tchrs. Coll., Ellensburg, 1961; asst. prof. U. Va., 1963-65; asso. sec. for research and sci. affairs Am. Speech, Lang. and Hearing Assn., Washington, 1965-68; dean Nat. Tech. Inst. for Deaf, Rochester Inst. Tech., N.Y., 1968-79; v.p. Nat. Tech. Inst. for Deaf, Rochester Inst. Tech., 1979-95, dir., 1977-95. Author: The Effect of Narrow Band Filtering on the Perception of Certain English Vowels, 1964. Served with USAF, 1952-56. Named Outstanding Alumnus, No. State Coll., 1984. Mem. Am. Speech Lang. and Hearing Assn., Alexander Graham Bell Assn. for Deaf (pres. 1982-84, 90-92). Home: Cypress Landing 104 Roanoke Ln Chocowinity NC 27817-8809 *Though it took more than one-fourth of the years I have thus far spent, a great sense of relief from skepticism and cynicism occurred for me when I reasoned within myself that life is the only absolute and that the greatest component of feeling and the finest advocacy are that of love, not just for fellow human beings but for all parts of life that reflect beauty. Without these two prime thoughts and without lifegiven talents, integrity, and flexibility for living cooperatively with others, I would have no sense of success.*

CASTLEBERRY, ARLINE ALRICK, architect; b. Mpls., Sept. 19, 1919; d. Bannona Gerhardt and Meta Emily (Veit) Alrick; m. Donald Montgomery Castleberry, Dec. 25, 1941; children: Karen, Marvin. B in Interior Architecture, U. Minn., 1941; postgrad., U. Tex., 1947-48. Designer, draftsman Elizabeth & Winston Close, Architects, Mpls., 1940-41, Northwest Airlines, Mpls., 1942-43, Cerny & Assocs., Mpls., 1944-46; archtl. draftsman Dominick and Van Benscotten, Washington, 1946-47; ptnr. Castleberry & Davis Bldg. Designers, Burlingame, Calif., 1960-65; prin. Burlingame, 1965-90. Recipient Smith Coll. scholarship. Mem. AIA, Am. Inst. Bldg. Designers (chpt. pres. 1971-72), Commaisini, Alpha Alpha Gamma, Chi Omega. Democrat. Lutheran. Home and Office: 1311 Parrott Dr San Mateo CA 94402-3630

CASTLEBERRY, CAROLYN P., mental health therapist and counselor; b. Oct. 13, 1952. MS in Counseling, So. Christian U., Montgomery, Ala., 1997. Mental health therapist South Ctrl. Mental Health, Andalusia, Ala., 1997; supr., counselor United Meth. Children's Home, Andalusia, 1997—. Email: juliacarolyn@yahoo.com. Home: HCR 36 Box 274 Evergreen AL 36401

CASTLEBERRY, JAMES NEWTON, JR., retired law educator, dean; b. Chatom, Ala., Dec. 28, 1921; s. James Newton and Nellie (Robbins) C.; m. Mary Ann Blocker, Feb. 12, 1944 (dec.); children: Jean, Nancy, James III (dec.), Elizabeth, Cynthia, Robert, Mary Ann. JD magna cum laude, St. Mary's U., 1952; diploma, Nat. U. Mex., 1960; diploma in teaching of comparative law, Strasburg, 1963. Bar: Tex. 1952. Asst. atty. gen. State of Tex., 1953-55; prof. law St. Mary's U., San Antonio, 1955-92, dean, 1978-89, dean emeritus, 1989—, ret., 1992; dir. St. Mary's U. Summer Program in Internat. and Comparative Law, Innsbruck, Austria, 1986-89; exec. dir. Tex. Ctr. for Legal Ethics and Professionalism, 1990-92; lectr. comparative law fgn. legal study tours Corp. for Profl. Confs., 1990—. Co-author: Water & Water Rights, 1970; contbr. articles to law jours. Bd. dirs. Preservation Tex.; trustee Tex. Supreme Ct. Hist. Soc. Mem. ABA, Am. Bar Found., San Antonio Bar Assn., Tex. Bar Found., San Antonio Bar Found., Tex. State Bar, Phi Delta Phi (internat. pres. 1977-79). Home: 7727 Woodridge Dr San Antonio TX 78209-2223*

CASTLEBERRY, MAY LEWIS, librarian, curator, editor; b. Midland, Tex., Sept. 26, 1954; d. Frank Petit and Katharine Elizabeth (Egan) Castleberry; m. Michael C. FitzGerald, June 11, 1976. Student, U. Tex.-Austin, 1972-74; BFA, BA, So. Meth. U., Dallas, 1974-76; MS, Columbia U., 1977-78; MA, NYU, 1987. Libr. Whitney Mus., N.Y.C., 1978—. Pub. artists and writers series, Whitney Mus. Am. Arts; dir.: Dal Vero, 1983, Could I Ask You Something?, 1984, The View, 1985, Annie, Gwen, Lilly, Pam and Tulip, 1986, Hiddenness, 1987, My Pretty Pony, 1988, Heat, 1989, Swimming, 1991, Ghost of Chance, 1991, The First Picture Book, 1991. Mem. Art Librs. Soc. N.Am. (George Wittenborn award 1979). Home: 41 5th Ave New York NY 10003-4319 Office: Whitney Mus of Am Art 945 Madison Ave New York NY 10021-2701

CASTLE-HASAN, ELIZABETH E., religious organization administrator; b. Balt., Nov. 1, 1950; d. John Thomas and Elizabeth Eliza (Wilson) Castle; m. Osborne Samuel James, Jr., Dec. 20, 1980 (div. Nov. 1993); children: Claudia C. Boulware, Richsharia D. Boulware, Kurtson E. Boulware, Curtis R. Boulware II; m. Edward N. Hasan, Dec. 12, 1994. AA in Criminal Justice, Valencia C.C., 1982; D of Systematic Theology (hon.), Interdenominational Theol. Sem. and Coll. of Theism, 1990; student, Love of God Theol. Sem., 1996—. Account exec. Sta. WEBB, Balt., 1975-77; liaison coord. Balt. City Jail, 1977-79; case mgr. Health and Rehabilitative Svcs., Cocoa, Fla., 1980-88; CEO Yissakar Ministries, Gainesville, Fla., 1989-94, Jabbok Ministries, Gainesville, 1991-94, Resurrected Life Ministries, Inc., Sarasota, Fla., 1994—; pres. The House of Bavaka (formerly, The House of La E'Shika), Sarasota, 1992—; CEO Resurrected Life Ministries Inc., 1994—, HEAT Ministries, 1996; bd. dirs. Jay Ministries, West Palm Beach, Fla., 1993. Author: The Prophet's Fast, 1996; co-author: Reflections in Lace, 1992; author: (poetry) Power, 1990 (honorary mention 1990); columnist, religious editor Mahogany Revue, Ocala, Fla., 1992-93; author short story, 1987 (honorary mention 1987); contbr. articles to newspaper. Chairperson com. for Aged and Disabled Persons, Gainesville, 1993, Sarasota Employment and Econ. Devel., 1996; chmn. grant com. Student Adv. Com. of Howard Bishop Mid. Sch., Gainesville, 1993; candidate City Commr. Dist. I, Gainesville, 1993, 95; mem. leadership bd. Sarasota County Coalition for the Homeless, 1994—, mem. exec. bd., 1995; mem. exec. com. Democratic Club, Sarasota, 1994; pres., bd. dirs. Family Self-Sufficiency Project, Sarasota, 1994—; cmty. liasion for Newtown Task Force; bd. dirs. Common Ground Cmty. Assn.; mem. Nat. Coalition Neighborhood Women. Recipient 1st Willie Bruton award U. Ctrl. Fla., 1982, Dr. Martin L. King scholarship, 1982. Mem. NAFE, Nat. Coalition of Neighborhood Women, God's Women of Power (pres. 1993), Gainesville Women's Network, Royal Venice Assn., Phi Beta Kappa, Chi Epislon. Democrat. Avocations: writing music, poetry, researching Old Testament studies. Office: Venice Housing Authority PO Box 49796 Sarasota FL 34230-6796

CASTLEMAN, ALBERT WELFORD, JR., physical chemist, educator; b. Richmond, Va., Jan. 7, 1936; s. Albert W. and Mildred L. Castleman; m. Heide Gisela Engel, Mar. 10, 1976; children: Sharon Beth, Robert Gill, Clifton Carl. BChemE, Rensselaer Poly. Inst., 1957; MS, Poly. Inst. Bklyn., 1963, PhD, 1969; PhD (hon.), U. Innsbruck, Austria, 1987. Leader chemistry rsch. group Brookhaven Nat. Lab., 1958-75; adj. prof. atmospheric chemistry depts. earth and space sci. and mechanics SUNY, Stony Brook, 1973-75; prof. chemistry, CIRES fellow U. Colo., Boulder, 1975-82; prof. chemistry Pa. State U., University Park, 1982—, prof. physics, Evan Pugh prof. chemistry, 1986—, adv. bd. Particulate Materials Ctr., 1987-94, mem. Ctr. for Materials Physics, 1993—, Eberly disting. chair in sci., 1999—; adv. bd. Ctr. for Nanoscale Sys. Materials Va. Commonwealth U., 1992—; vis. prof. Physics Inst., Leopold-Franzens U., Innsbruck, Austria, 1981, 84; mem. rev. com. chem. physics programs, Oak Ridge Nat. Lab., 1979, adv. com. to lab. dir. chem. physics programs, Health and Safety Div., 1987-90, chmn., 1990, mem. Dept. Energy rev. com. for chem. physics and radiol. physics program, 1985, Fulbright guest prof., 1990; adv. to Dept. Energy on chem. physics pertaining to energy related environmental programs, 1980; mem. ad hoc. panel on atmospheric chemistry Com. on Atmospheric Scis., NRC, NAD, 1980; mem. rev. com. for radiol. and environ. rsch. div. Argonne Univs. Assn. Argonne Nat. Lab., 1977-81, chemistry div., Argonne, 1988; mem. various rev. and adv. coms. Nat. Ctr. for Atmospheric Rsch., U.S. Dept. Energy U.S. Nuclear Regulatory Commn.; cons. Mfg. Chemists Assn., 1975-80, nuclear div. Oak Ridge Nat. Lab., 1976-86, E.I. Dupont de Nemours, 1989—; chmn. subcom. on ions, aerosols and radioactivity Internat. Commn. Atmospheric Electricity, 1976-80; sr. scientist von Humboldt awardee Tech. Hochschule Darmstadt, 1987, Philipps U., Marburg, Germany, 1988, U. Wuerzburg, 1998. Mem. editl. bd. Jour. Phys. Chemistry, 1985-88, sr. editor, 1988—; mem. edit. bd. Chem. Phys. Lett., 1995—, Jour. Cluster Sci., Internat. Jour. Mass Spectrometry and Ion Proc., 1987-90, Jour. Chem. Physics, 1985-87, Jour. Atmospheric Chemistry, 1982-94, Aerosol Sci. and Tech., 1982-86, Advances in Chem. Physics, 1995—; co-editor, mem. editl. bd. Zeitschrift fer Physick D., 1987-90; mem. chem. physics editl. adv. bd. Rsch. Trends; contr. articles to profl. jours. Recipient Sr. Scientist Alexander von Humboldt award, 1986, Sr. Scientist Fulbright award, 1990; Sherman Fairchild Disting. scholar, Calif. Inst. Tech., 1977; NSF Creativity Award grantee, 1985-87; Japanese Soc. for Promotion Sci. fellow, 1983, 97. Fellow AAAS, Am. Acad. Arts and Scis., , Am. Phys. Soc., N.Y. Acad. Scis.; mem. Nat. Acad. Scis., Am. Chem. Soc. (Creative Advances in Environ. Sci. and Tech. award 1988), Am. Geophys. Union, Am. Assn. Aerosol Rsch., Deutsche Bunsen-Gesellschaft Soc., N.Y. Acad. Scis., Materials Rsch. Soc., Sigma Xi, Phi Lambda Upsilon. Home: 425 Hillcrest Ave State College PA 16803-3419 Office: Pa State U Dept Chemistry 152 Davey Lab University Park PA 16802-6300

CASTLEMAN, BREAUX BALLARD, health management company executive; b. Louisville, Aug. 19, 1940; s. John Pryor and Mary Jane (Ballard) C.; m. Sue Ann Foreman (div. 1995); children: Matthew B., Shea B. BA in Econs., Yale U., 1962; postgrad., NYU, 1963. Mgmt. trainee Bankers Trust Co., N.Y.C., 1963-65; mng. dir. Castleman and Co., Houston, 1965-71; dir. program planning, econ. U.S. Dept. HUD, Ft. Worth, Dallas, 1971-73; v.p., office mgr. Booz Allen and Hamilton, Dallas, Houston, 1973-85; mng. dir. Castleman Group, Houston, 1985-87; CEO Kelsey-Seybold Clinic, P.A., Houston, 1987-95; pres. physician resources divsn. Caremark Internat., Inc., 1994-96; pres. Scripps Clinic, La Jolla, Calif., 1996-99. Contbr. articles to profl. jours. Candidate state legislature, Houston, 1968. Mem. Am. Med. Group Assn. (bd. dirs. 1996—), Planning Forum (chmn. 1985-86), Univ. Club San Diego. Office: Scripps Clinic 10666 N Torrey Pines Rd La Jolla CA 92037-1092

CASTLEMAN, LOUIS SAMUEL, metallurgist, educator; b. St. Johnsbury, Vt., Nov. 24, 1918; s. Max and Fannie (Svetkey) C.; m. Mildred Blanche Rubin, Jan. 25, 1948; children—Michael Z., David A., Steven J., Daniel J. B.S., Mass. Inst. Tech., 1939, D.Sc., 1950. Plant metallurgist Sunbeam Electric Mfg. Co., Evansville, Ind., 1939-41; sr. scientist, supr., acting sect. mgr. Westinghouse Atomic Power Div., Pitts., 1950-54; metall. specialist Gen. Telephone & Electronics Labs., Inc., Bayside, N.Y., 1954-64; prof. phys. metallurgy Poly. U., N.Y., 1964-89, prof. emeritus, 1989—; Cons. phys. metallurgy. With AUS, 1941-46; lt. col. Ret. Recipient Distinguished Tchr. award Poly. Inst. N.Y., 1975. Fellow AAAS; mem. Am. Soc. Metals (chpt. chmn. 1963-64), Am. Inst. Mining, Metall. and Petroleum Engrs., Am. Phys. Soc., Metal Sci. Club N.Y. (pres. 1973-74), Sigma Xi. Democrat. Jewish religion. Home: 120 Morris Ave C5 Rockville Centre NY 11570-4240 Office: 6 Metrotech Ctr Brooklyn NY 11201-3840

CASTLEN, PEGGY LOU, insurance company executive; b. Parkersburg, W.Va., Sept. 7, 1939; d. Ted and Nina Leone (Wehler) Swartz; m. Tom Mefford Castlen, June 16, 1962 (div. Oct. 30, 1987); children: Michael Alan, Thomas Matthew, Cynthia Anne. BS in Edn., Miami U., 1961; M of Human Resource Devel., Univ. Assocs., San Diego, 1983. Lic. personal lines ins. agt.; CPCU. Elem. tchr. various sch. systems, Dearborn, Mich., 1961-62, Chgo., 1962-64, Oxford, Bluffton, Ohio, 1964-65, 65-66; dir. Bluffton (Ohio) Community Nursery Sch., 1969-71; coord. Assn. for Effectiveness Trainers, Columbus, Ohio, 1974-77; ind. tng. cons. Columbus and Portland, Oreg., 1971-80; office svcs. mgr. NERCO, Inc., Portland, Oreg., 1980-85; personnel div. mgr. Nationwide Mut. Ins. Co., Portland, Oreg., 1985-89, field sales mgr., 1989-90; life co. human resources officer Nationwide Ins., Columbus, 1990-95, EEO/human resources officer, 1995-97, nat. enterprise EEO/employee rels. compliance officer, 1997—; cons., com. bd. mem. Jr. Achievement, Portland, 1981-85; assessor-cons., bd. dirs. Employment Connection, Beaverton, Oreg., 1980-85. Chmn. United Way Campaign Nationwide Regional Office, Portland, 1989; chmn. adv. com. Lake Oswego (Oreg.) Sch. Dist., 1985-88; elder, trustee United Presbyn. Ch., Beaverton, 1978-91, Columbus, 1975-77; mem. adv. bd. Downtown Cmty. Based Program, 1993—; com. chair, bd. dirs., asst. treas., YWCA, 1995—; com. mem. ARC, 1987-90; mem. human rels. bd. Franklin U., 1999—. Recipient Vol. of Yr. award Nationwide Civic Action Program, 1989; named to Drummer's Soc., 1990. Mem. Soc. for Human Resource Mgmt., Am. Mgmt. Assn., Profl. Ins. Pers. Adminstrs., CPCU Soc. (bd. dirs., editor newsletter), Nationwide Ins. Enterprise Human Resources Coun., Nat. Fed.

Credit Union (mem. com.). Presbyterian. Office: Nationwide Ins Co 1-26-14 One Nationwide Plz Columbus OH 43215

CASTNER, LINDA JANE, instructional technologist, nurse educator; b. Abilene, Tex., Feb. 16, 1943; d. Joseph Arthur and Jane Theora (Stickdorn) Kidwell; m. Harvey Robert Castner, June 12, 1965; children: Raymond Scott, David Alan, Susan Marie. BSN summa cum laude, Ohio State U., 1965, PhD in Edn., 1992; MSN, Marquette U., Milw., 1984. RN, Ohio. Pub. health nurse I Columbus Pub. Health Nurses, 1965-66; med./surg. instr. St. Joseph Hosp. Sch. Nursing, Joliet, Ill., 1967-68; part-time instr. Waukesha County Tech. Inst., Pewaukee, Wis., 1974-83; staff nurse med./surg. West Allis (Wis.) Meml. Hosp., 1981-82; asst. dir. TLC/instr. U. Rochester, N.Y., 1984-86; instructional designer Fuld Inst., Athens, Ohio, 1992-97, ednl. cons. in nursing, 1992-97; cons. in instrnl. technology Castner Cons., Worthington, Ohio, 1998—. Author/designer interactive videos: Physical Examination, 7 programs, 1994-95, Mosby Basic Skills Series, 4 programs, 1996-97, Pediatric Assessment, 1994. Mem. ANA, AAUW, Assn. Ednl. Comm. and Tech., Health Scis. Comm. Assn., Sigma Theta Tau. Avocations: reading, computers, boating. Home: 433 Olenwood Ave Worthington OH 43085-2245 Office: Castner Cons Instrnl Tech 433 Olenwood Ave Worthington OH 43085-2245

CASTON, J(ESSE) DOUGLAS, medical educator; b. Ellenboro, N.C., June 16, 1932; s. Lemuel Joseph and Myrtice Elizabeth (Vassey) C.; m. Marry Ann Keeter, June 1, 1958; children: John Andrew, Elizabeth Anne, Mary Susan. A.B., Lenoir Rhyne Coll., 1954; M.A., U. N.C., 1958; Ph.D., Brown U., 1961. Fellow Carnegie Instn., Washington, Balt., 1961-62; asst. prof. anatomy Case Western Res. U., Cleve., 1962-71, assoc. prof., 1971-76, prof., 1976-98, co-dir. Devel. Biology Ctr., 1971-77, prof. emeritus, 1999—; cons. Diamond Shamrock Corp., Cleve., 1975-77; coordinator Core Acad. Program, Sch. Medicine, 1985-94. Patentee folate assay, methotrexate assay; contbr. numerous articles to sci. jours., 1962—. Served with AUS, 1954-56. Fellow H.W. Wilson, 1956; grantee USPHS, 1963—, Cancer Soc., 1963—. Mem. Am. Chem. Soc., AAAS, Am. Soc. Zoologists and Developmental Biologists, Biophys. Soc., Soc. Cell Biology, Am. Assn. Anatomists. Episcopalian.

CASTOR, BETTY, academic administrator. Pres. Univ. South Fla., Tampa. *

CASTOR, CAROL JEAN, artist, teacher; b. Bend, Oreg., Feb. 3, 1944; d. Keith and Lena (Morara) Morrison; 1 child, William Franklin. BFA, U. Okla., 1967; postgrad., U. Tulsa, summer 1976, Art Student's League of N.Y., N.Y.C., summer 1984. Benedictine Oblate with Osage Monastery, Sand Spring, Okla. Dir. art dept. Jefferson Jr. High Sch., Oklahoma City, 1967-68; art instr. Vinita (Okla.) High Sch., 1976-80; profl. artist specializing in commd. portraiture Carol Castor Art Studio, Vinita, 1980—, profl. artist commd. for portraits of Native Ams. & Cowboys, 1980—; maintains Window Gallery on Mainstreet Vinita; bd. dirs. Craig Gen. Hosp., 1995—; artist-in-residence mural project Vinita Pub. Sch. Alternative Sch., 1998; artist-in-residence Vinita Pub. Schs., 1998-99. Represented in permanent collections at Vinita Pub. Libr., Craig Gen. Hosp., Vinita, 1st Nat. Bank & Trust, Vinita, Cowgirl Hall of Fame and Western Heritage Ctr., Ft. Worth, Okla. Hall of Fame, Oklahoma City, Okla. U. Med. Sch., Oklahoma City, Oklahoma U. Law Sch., Norman, Okla. U. Pharmacy Sch., Oklahoma City, Columbia Presbyterian Med. Ctr., N.Y.; featured in 2nd edit. of American Artists: An Illustrated Survey of Leading Contemporaries; portraits represented by Grand Ctrl. Galleries, N.Y.; artist cover illustration Oklahoma's Guide to Grand Lake; contbr. illustration to Labor of Love: The Life and Times of Vinnie Ream. Mem. Mayor's Adv. Com., Vinita, 1972-74; mem. bldg. com. Vinita Pub. Libr., 1974-75; charter mem. Vinita chpt. Okla. Alliance for Mentally Ill, 1986—; organizer, mem. com. Young Life, Vinita, 1987—; mem. com. for chronically and mentally ill Vinita Day Ctr. Inc., 1987—; organizer Ea. Trails Art Assn., 1972—, chmn. Art Invitational '98, Vinita; bd. dirs. Craig Gen. Hosp., 1995—; chmn. Med. Svcs. Corp., 1998—. Recipient Cmty. Svc. award Vinita C. of C., 1984, named to Hall of Fame, 1993. Mem. AAUW (pres. Vinita chpt. 1972-74, Best banner award nat. conv. 1979, Women of Achievement award 1985), P.E.O., Am. Soc. Portrait Artists. Democrat. Roman Catholic. Avocations: song writing, reading, piano, writing, poetry. Home and Studio: 121 Jennie Ln Vinita OK 74301

CASTOR, CHRISTINA PELAYO, critical care nurse; b. St. Louis, June 3; d. Jacobo E. and Abundia L. (Pelayo) C. AS in nursing, Ind. U., Gary, 1980; BSN, Purdue U., Hammond, Ind., 1983, MS in nursing, 1984; MD, U. Santo Tomas, Manila, The Philippines, 1989. RN, Calif., Ill., Ind., Mich.; CEN; cert. ACLS, PALS, mobile intensive care; cert. trauma nurse. Staff nurse/charge nurse Our Lady of Mercy Hosp., Dyer, Ind., 1980-85, 86, 87; office nurse Conrado P. Castor MD, Munster, Ind., 1984-90; staff nurse Humana Hosp., Hoffman Estates, Ill., 1990; staff nurse/charge nurse emergency rm. St. Margaret Hosp., Hammond, Ind., 1990—. Mem. Emergency Nurse's Assn.

CASTOR, JON STUART, electronics company executive; b. Lynchburg, Va., Dec. 15, 1951; s. William Stuart and Marilyn (Hughes) C.; m. Stephanie Lum, Jan. 7, 1989; 1 child, David Jon. BA, Northwestern U., 1973; MBA, Stanford U., 1975. Mgmt. cons. Menlo Park, Calif., 1981-96; pres. TeraLogic, Inc., 1996—. Dir. Midwest Consumer Adv. Bd. to FTC, 1971-73; v.p., bd. dirs. San Mateo coun. Boy Scouts Am., 1991-93; bd. dirs. Pacific Skyline Coun. Boy Scouts Am., 1994—; trustee Coyote Point Mus. Environ. Edn., San Mateo, 1992-95. Office: TeraLogic Inc 1240 Villa St Mountain View CA 94041-1124

CASTORA, JOSEPH CHARLES, history educator; b. N.Y.C., Nov. 20, 1946; s. Charles Carlo and Clara Mary (Toto) C. BA with hons., Manhattan Coll., 1968; MA, NYU, 1973, MPhil, 1979, PhD, 1990. Shipping coord. Amax, Inc., N.Y.C., 1969-83; adj. asst. prof. Manhattan Coll., N.Y.C., 1991—, Yeshiva U., N.Y.C., 1992. Recipient scholarship NYU, 1973-74, Lane Cooper fellowship, 1983-84. Mem. Am. Hist. Assn., Medieval Acad. Am., Am. Cath. Hist. Assn., Am. Classical League, Phi Alpha Theta. Roman Catholic. Avocations: classical music, opera. Home: 96-01 24th Ave East Elmhurst NY 11369 Office: Manhattan Coll Manhattan Coll Pkwy Bronx NY 10471

CASTORINO, SUE, communications executive; b. Columbus, Ohio, May 5, 1953; m. Randy Minkoff, Oct. 29, 1983. BS in Speech, Northwestern U., Evanston, Ill., 1975. Grad. fellow Ohio Gov.'s Sch., Columbus, 1975; producer, community affairs WBBM-TV (CBS all-news)), Chgo., 1975; news anchor, reporter Sta. WBBM, Chgo., 1981-86; news reporter WHTH-AM/FM, Newark, Ohio, 1975; news anchor, reporter WERE-AM (NBC all-news), Cleve., 1975-78, WWWE-AM (ABC), Cleve., 1978-81; founder, pres. Sue Castorino: The Speaking Specialist, Chgo., 1986—; guest lectr. various groups in bus., medicine, govt., law, sports, fin., worldwide, 1986—; leader media and presentation skills seminars; pvt. voice coach, 1986—; internat. exec. comm. tng. in media, crisis and issue mgmt. Author: North Shore Mag., 1987—; voice-over and on-camera talent, 1986—. Recipient Golden Gavel award Chgo. Soc. Assn. Execs., 1991, various news reporting awards AP, UPI, Chgo., 1981-86. Mem. Sigma Delta Chi. Avocations: sports, film, accomplished pianist. Office: The Speaking Specialist 435 N Michigan Ave Ste 2700 Chicago IL 60611-4008

CASTORO, ROSEMARIE, sculptor; b. Bklyn., Mar. 1, 1939; d. Michael Peter and Camille (Gallo) C. Student in painting, Mus. Modern Art, N.Y.C., 1955-56; BFA cum laude, Pratt Inst., Bklyn., 1963. Tchr. Sch. Visual Arts, N.Y.C., 1971, Hunter Coll., N.Y.C., 1972, Calif. State U., Fresno, 1973, Syracuse (N.Y.) U., 1975, U. Colo., Boulder, 1977, Stockton State U., N.J., 1983, Boston Mus. Sch., 1983; lectr. art Boston Mus. Sch. Art, 1971, 80, New Sch. Social Rsch., N.Y.C., 1972, 73, Phila. Coll. Art, 1974, Atlanta Coll. Art, 1974, Rome Art Assn., N.Y. State, 1975, Syracuse (N.Y.) U., 1975, U. Calif., Berkeley, 1976, Suzuki-Walker, Sausalito, Calif., 1976, Art Inst. Sch., Chgo., 1980, Pratt Inst., N.Y.C., 1982, 95, C.W. Post, L.I., N.Y., 1984, San Jose (Calif.) U., 1984, 85, N.J. Ctr. for Visual Arts, Summit, N.J., 1989, Ecole Nat. Superieure des Beaux-Arts, Paris, 1995. Solo shows include Tibor de Nagy Gallery, N.Y.C., 1971, 72, 73, 75, 76, 78, 81, 83, 85, 89, Hal Bromm Gallery, N.Y.C., 1976, 78, 79, 80, 83, 87, 91-92, Julian Pretto, N.Y.C., 1978, 79, Marion Deson, Chgo., 1981, Am. Ctr., Paris, 1983, Eaton/Shoen Gallery, San Francisco, 1984, 86, Newark Mus., 1991, Arnaud Lefebvre Gallery, Paris, 1993, 95, 97, 98, 99, Stella R Graphics, Paris, 1993; group shows include Bklyn. Mus., 1963, Tibor de Nagy Gallery, 1966, Stable Gallery, 1966, Dwan Gallery, N.Y.C., 1968, 69, Richard Feigen Gallery, N.Y.C., 1968, Paula Cooper Gallery, N.Y.C., 1969, 71, Vancouver (B.C., Can.) Art Gallery, 1970, Stadtische Kunsthalle, Dusseldorf, Germany, 1970, Allen Art Mus., Oberlin, Ohio, 1970, Hundred Acres Gallery, N.Y.C., 1970, 112 Greene St Gallery, N.Y.C., 1971, 72, Richard Gray Gallery, Chgo., 1972, Storm King Art Gallery, Mountainville, N.Y., 1972, 74, 75, Grapestake Gallery, San Francisco, 1975, 76, Moore Coll. Art, Phila., 1977, John Weber Gallery, N.Y.C., 1977, Hal Bromm Gallery, 1977, 81, 82, 85, 86, 87, Indpls. Mus. Art, 1978, Whitney Mus. Am. Art, N.Y.C., 1978, Nancy Lurie Gallery, Chgo., 1978, Smithsonian Instn., Washington, 1980, Hunter Mus. Art, Chatanooga, Tenn., 1980, Banco Gallery, Brescia, Italy, 1980, Hirshhorn Mus. and Sculpture Garden, Washington, 1981, Pratt Inst. Art Gallery, Bklyn., 1981, Eaton/Shoen Gallery, 1982, Maier Mus. Art, Lynchburg, Va., 1983, 90, Laguna Gloria Art Mus., Austin, Tex., 1985, Mus. Modern Art, N.Y.C., 1985, Newark Mus., 1987, Marvin Seline Gallery, Houston, 1990, Jan Baum Gallery, L.A., 1990, Stellar Graphics, Paris, 1992, Galerie Arnaud Lefebvre, Paris, 1993, 95-96, Henry St. Settlement, N.Y.C., 1993, Athenaeum Music & Arts Libr., La Jolla, Calif., 1995, 24 Hours for Life Gallery, N.Y.C., 1995, Beaumanoir, Le Leslay, France, 1995, and many, many others; commns. include Battery Park City, N.Y.C., 1978, GSA, Topeka, Kans., 1979, Am. Ctr., Paris, 1983, Athena Found., L.I., N.Y., 1986, Woodstock '94, Saugerties, N.Y., 1994, and others; permanent collections include Allen Art Mus., Oberlin, Ohio, Boca Raton (Fla.) Mus., Bank of Am., Calif., Chase Manhattan Bank, N.A., GSA, Washington, Mus. Modern Art, N.Y.C., Newark Mus., Univ. Art Mus., U. Calif., Berkeley, U. Mass., Woodward Found., Washington, and others. Treas. HIV-Arts, N.Y.C., 1994-97. Guggenheim fellow, 1971; grantee Woodward Found., 1970, CAPS, 1972, 74, NEA, 1974-75, 84-85, Tiffany Found., 1977, Pollock-Krasner Found., 1989-90, 97-98. Home and Studio: 151 Spring St New York NY 10012-3850

CASTRO, AMUERFINA TANTIONGCO, geriatrics nurse; b. Morong, Rizal, Philippines, July 30, 1942; d. Eusebio and Juana (Victorio) Tantiongco; m. El B. Castro, Apr. 6, 1966; children: Cesar, El Jr., Christopher. BSN, U. East, Quezon City, Philippines, 1963; MA in Nursing, NYU, 1975. Cert. in oncology and gerontology nursing. Mem. staff U. East Ramon Magsaysay Meml. Med. Ctr., Quezon City, 1963-64; mem. faculty St. Catherine Sch. Nursing, Quezon City, 1964-65; operating room nurse Fordham Hosp. and Union Hosp., Bronx, N.Y., 1966-69; staff nurse in chemotherapy rsch. Meml. Hosp.-Sloan Kettering, N.Y.C., 1969-74; charge nurse Greenbrook (N.J.) Manor Nursing Home, 1989—. Vice-chmn., trustee Found. Philippine-Am. Med. Soc. N.J., 1990—. Mem. ANA, N.J. Nurses Assn., Philippine Nurses Assn. Am. (bd. dirs., Nat. Svc. award 1988-90), Philippine Nurses Assn. N.J. (pres., adv. bd., Outstanding Mem. award 1986—), U. East Ramon Magsaysay Meml. Med. Ctr. Nursing Alumni Assn. U.S.A. (pres. 1988-92, mem. adv. bd., Outstanding Alumni in Cmty. Svc. award 1993, Spl. Recognition award 1998), Philippine Am. Med. Soc. N.J. Aux. (pres.), Sigma Theta Tau.

CASTRO, JAN GARDEN, author, arts consultant, educator; b. St. Louis, June 8, 1945; d. Harold and Estelle (Fischer) Garden; 1 child, Jomo Jemal. Student, Cornell U., 1963-65; BA, U. Wis., 1967; pub. cert., Radcliffe Coll., 1967; MA in Tchg., Washington U., St. Louis, 1974, MA, 1994. Life cert. tchr. secondary English, speech, drama and social studies, Mo. Tchr., writer St. Louis, 1970—; dir. Big River Assn., St. Louis, 1975-85; adj. prof. humanities Lindenwood Coll., 1980—; co-founder, dir. Duff's Poetry Series, St. Louis, 1975-81; founder, dir. River Styx P.M. Series, St. Louis, 1981-83; arts cons. Harris-Stowe State Coll., 1986-87. Contbg. author: San Francisco Rev. Books, 1982-85, Am. Book Rev., 1990-93, Mo. Rev., 1991, News Letters, 1993, 96, Tampa Rev., 1994—, The Nation, Am. Poetry Rev., Sculpture mag., 1997—; author books including Mandala of the Five Senses, 1975, The Art and Life of Georgia O'Keeffe, 1985, paperback edit., 1995; editor: River Styx mag., 1975-86; co-editor: Margaret Atwood: Vision and Forms, 1988; TV host and co-prodr. The Writers Cir., Double Helix, St. Louis, 1987-89. Mem. University City Arts and Letters Commn., Mo., 1983-84. NEH fellow UCLA, 1988, Johns Hopkins U., 1990, Camargo fellow, Cassis, France, 1996; recipient Arts and Letters award St. Louis Mag., 1985, Editor's award and editor during G.E. Younger Writers award to River Styx Mag., Coordinating Coun. for Lit. Mags., 1986, Arts award Mandrake Soc. Charity Ball, 1988, Leadership award YWCA St. Louis, 1988. Mem. MLA, CAA, Margaret Atwood Soc. (founder). Home: 7420 Cornell Ave Saint Louis MO 63130-2914 Office: Lindenwood College Saint Charles MO 63301

CASTRO, JOSEPH ARMAND, music director, pianist, composer, orchestrator; b. Miami, Ariz., Aug. 15, 1927; s. John Loya and Lucy (Sanchez) C.; m. Loretta Faith Haddad, Oct. 21, 1966; children: John Joseph, James Ernest. Student, San Jose State Coll., 1944-47. Mus. dir. Herb Jeffries, Hollywood, Calif., 1952, June Christy, Hollywood, 1959-63, Anita O'Day, Hollywood, 1963-65, Tony Martin, Hollywood, 1962-64, Tropicana Hotel, Las Vegas, Nev., 1980—, Desert Inn, Las Vegas, 1992-93; orch. leader Mocambo Night Club, Hollywood, 1952-54; soloist Joe Castro Trio, L.A., N.Y.C., Honolulu, 1952-65, Sands Hotel, Desert Inn, Las Vegas, 1975-80; mus. dir. Folies Bergere, 1980-89; with Joe Castro Trio with Loretta Castro, 1995—. Recs. include Cool School with June Christy, 1960, Anita O'Day Sings Rodgers and Hart, 1961, Lush Life, 1966, Groove-Funk-Soul, Mood Jazz, Atlantic Records, also albums with Teddy Edwards, Stan Kenton, Jimmy Borges with Joe Castro Trio, 1990, Loretta Castro with Joe Castro Trio, 1990, Honolulu Symphony concerts; command performance, Queen Elizabeth II, London Palladium, 1989, Concerts with Jimmy Borges and Honolulu Symphony Pops Concerts, 1991; jazz concert (with Nigel Kennedy) Honolulu Symphony, 1990; jazz-fest, Kailua-Kona, Hawaii, 1990; leader orch. Tropicana Hotel, 1989-94. With U.S. Army, 1946-47. Roman Catholic. Home: 2812 Colanthe Ave Las Vegas NV 89102-2026

CASTRO, JOSEPH RONALD, physician, oncology researcher, educator; b. Chgo., Apr. 9, 1934; m. Barbara Ann Kauth, Oct. 12, 1957. B.S. in Natural Sci., Loyola U., Chgo., 1956, M.D., 1958. Diplomate: Am. Bd. Radiology, 1964. Intern Rockford (Ill.) Meml. Hosp.; resident U.S. Naval Hosp., San Diego; assoc. radiotherapist and assoc. prof. U. Tex.-M.D. Anderson Hosp. and Tumor Inst., 1967-71; prof. radiology/radiation oncology U. Calif. Sch. Medicine, San Francisco, 1971-94, prof. emeritus radiation oncology, 1994—; vice-chmn. dept. radiation oncology U. Calif. Sch. Medicine, 1980-94; dir. particle radiotherapy Lawrence Berkeley Lab., 1975-99, faculty sr. scientist, 1991-94; mem. program project rev. com. NIH/Nat. Cancer Inst. Cancer Program, 1982-85. Author sci. articles. Past pres., chmn. bd. trustees No. Calif. Cancer Program, 1980-83. Served to lt. comdr., M.C. USN, 1956-66. Recipient Teaching award Mt. Zion Hosp. and Med. Center, San Francisco, 1972. Fellow Am. Coll. Radiology; mem. European Soc. Therapeutic Radiology and Oncology (hon.), Am. Soc. Therapeutic Radiology, Rocky Mountain Radiol. Soc. (hon.), Gilbert H. Fletcher Oncologic Soc. (past pres. 1988). Office: U Calif Radiology Oncology Dept L-75 San Francisco CA 94143

CASTRO, LAURA ELLEN, accountant; b. Columbus, Ohio, June 5, 1969; d. David Lee and Carolyn Ann Hamilton; m. Oscar James Castro, Sept. 6, 1997. BSBA, Ohio State U., 1991; MPA, George Washington U., Washington, 1996. CPA, Md. Auditor U.S. Gen. Acctg. Office, Washington, 1991-93, evaluator, 1993—. Recipient fellowship Wolcott Found., 1993. Mem. AICPA (Sells cert. with high distinction), LWV (chair voter svc. com. Alexandria, Va. 1997—), Am. Soc. for Pub. Adminstrn., Assn. Govt. Accts. (cert. govt. fin. mgr.), Am. Assn. for Budget and Program Analysis. Office: US Gen Acctg Office 441 G St NW Washington DC 20548

CASTRO, LEONARD EDWARD, lawyer; b. L.A., Mar. 18, 1934; s. Emil Galvez and Lily (Meyers) C.; 1 son, Stephen Paul. A.B., UCLA, 1959, J.D., 1962. Bar: Calif. 1963, U.S. Supreme Ct. 1970. Assoc. Musick, Peeler & Garrett, Los Angeles, 1962-68, ptnr., 1968—. Mem. ABA, Internat. Bar Assn., Los Angeles County Bar Assn. Office: Musick Peeler & Garrett 1 Wilshire Blvd Ste 2000 Los Angeles CA 90017-3876

CASTRO, RAUL HECTOR, lawyer, former ambassador, former governor; b. Cananea, Mexico, June 12, 1916; came to U.S., 1926, naturalized, 1939; s. Francisco D. and Rosario (Acosta) C.; m. Patricia M. Norris, Nov. 13, 1954; children—Mary Pat, Beth. B.A., Ariz. State Coll., 1939; J.D., U. Ariz., 1949; LL.D. (hon.), No. Ariz. U., 1966, Ariz. State U., 1972, U. Autonoma de Guadalajara, Mex. Bar: Ariz. bar 1949. Fgn. service clk. Dept. State, Agua Prieta, Mexico, 1941-46; instr. Spanish U. Ariz., 1946-49; practiced in Tucson, 1949-51; dep. county atty. Pima County, Ariz., 1951-54; county atty., 1954-58; judge Superior Ct., Tucson, 1958-64, Juvenile Ct., Tucson, 1961-64; U.S. ambassador to El Salvador, San Salvador, 1964-68, to Bolivia, La Paz, 1968-69; practice internat. law Tucson, 1969-74, Phoenix, 1980—; gov. Ariz., 1975-77; U.S. ambassador to Argentina, 1977-80; operator Castro Pony Farm, 1954-64. Pres. Pima County Tb and Health Assn., Tucson Youth Bd., Ariz. Horseman's Assn.; Bd. dirs. Tucson chpt. A.R.C., Tucson council Boy Scouts Am., Tucson YMCA, Nat. Council Christians and Jews, YWCA Camp; Bd. Mem. Ariz. N.G., 1935-39. Recipient Outstanding Naturalized Citizen award Pima County Bar Assn., 1964, Outstanding Am. Citizen award D.A.R., 1964; Pub. Service award U. Ariz., 1966; John F. Kennedy medal Kennedy U., Buenos Aires. Mem. Am. Fgn. Service Assn., Am. Judicature Soc., Inter-Am. Bar Assn., Ariz. Bar Assn., Pima County Bar Assn., Nat. Council Crime and Deliquency (bd. dirs.), Assn. Trial Lawyers Am., Council Am. Ambassadors, Nat. Assn. Trial Judges, Nat. Council Juvenile Ct. Judges, Fed. Bar Assn., Nat. Lawyers Club, Phi Alpha Delta. Democrat. Roman Catholic. Club: Rotarian. Office: 404 W Crawford St Nogales AZ 85621-2508

CASTRO, ROBERT R., retired surgeon; b. Lima, Peru, Sept. 16, 1929; came to U.S., 1961; s. Hector and Eloise (Serrano) C.; m. Nicole Godin, Oct. 10, 1959; children: Isabelle, Michael. MD, U. Paris, 1957. Diplomate Am. Bd. Surgery. Intern Augustana Hosp., Chgo., 1957-58; resident in surgery McGill U. Hosp., Montreal, Que., Can., 1958-61, U. Wis. Hosp., Madison, 1961-66; surgeon Norwest Hosp., Chgo., 1966-67, Ottawa (Ill.) Cmty. Hosp., 1967-81, Friesbie Meml. Hosp., Rochester, N.H., 1985—; pvt. practice, Barrington, N.H., 1985—. Lt. col. USAF, 1981-85. Fellow ACS, Am. Coll. Chest Physicians, Internat. Coll. Surgeons. Republican. Roman Catholic. Avocation: skiing. Home: 70-31 B Park Dr E Flushing NY 11367-1951

CASTRODAD, FELIX A., university administrator. Chancellor, prof. microbiology U. of P.R., Humacao, 1995, prof. microbiology, 1995—. Office: U PR Humacao U Coll Cuh Sta Humacao PR 00791*

CASTRO-KLAREN, SARA, Latin American literature educator; b. Arequipa, Sabandia, Peru, June 9, 1942; d. José Andrés and Zoila Rosa (Rivas) Castro-Valdivia; m. Peter F. Klaren, Sept. 3, 1962; 1 child, Alexandra. BA, UCLA, 1962, MA, 1965, PhD, 1968. Asst. prof. Dartmouth Coll., No. Hampshire, N.H., 1970-84; chief Hispanic div. Lib. of Congress Fed. Govt., Washington, 1984-86; prof. Latin Am. lit. Johns Hopkins U., Balt., 1986—. Author: El Mundo Magico de J.M. Arquedas, Lima, 1973, Mario Vargas Llosa, Analisis Introductorio, Lima, 1988, Escritura Sujeto y Transgresión, Mexico, 1989, Understanding Mario Vargas Llosa, U. S.C., 1990, Women's Writing in Latin America, Westview Press, 1991. Fellow Woodrow Wilson Ctr. for Scholars, Washington, 1977-78. Mem. MLA, AAUP, Latin Am. Studies Assn., Ibero-americana, Soc. Hispanists, Am. Assn. Colls. and Univs., Brazilian Studies Assn. Avocation: gardening. Office: Johns Hopkins U Hispanic and Italian Study 34 Charles St Baltimore MD 21201*

CASTRO-POZO, TALÍA, dancer, educator; b. Lima, Peru, Oct. 2, 1975; came to U.S., 1995; d. Jose and Renée Castro. Profl. degree in Ballet and Modern Dance, Nat. Ballet Sch., Lima, Peru, 1992; studied with Sergei Radchenko, Mabel Silvera Studio, Buenos Aires, 1992; student, Sch. Am. Ballet, 1995-96. Soloist Nat. Ballet, 1992-95; dancer/tchr. Arthur Murray Dance Studio, N.Y.C., 1996—; rep. Internat. Ballet Competition, U.S.A., 1994, World Ballet Competition, Osaka, Japan, 1995, 30th Course of Ballet and Modern, Varna, Bulgaria. Dancer in classical, contemporary, modern pieces including Don Quixote, Spring Waters, Spartacus, A Solas; featured dancer in film Summer of Sam. Dancer/choreographer Korean Army Festivities, Lima, 1992; dancer First Festival for Children's Rights, Lima, 1995. Recipient 1st Place award Latin Am. competition, 1989; Best Dancer of Yr. award Peruvian Press, 1991. Mem. Nat. Assn. Writers and Artists. Address: Jr Junin 246, Lima 17, Peru

CASTRUITA, RUDY, school system administrator. BA in Social Sci., Utah State U., 1966, MS in Sch. Adminstrn., 1967; EdD, U. So. Calif., 1983. Cert. adminstrv. svcs., std. secondary, pupil svcs. Dir. econ. opportunity program City of El Monte, Calif., 1966-67; secondary tchr., counselor, program coord. El Monte Union High Sch. Dist., 1967-75, asst. prin. Mountain View High Sch., 1975-80; prin. Los Alamitos (Calif.) High Sch. Los Alamitos Unified Sch. Dist., 1980-85; asst. supt. secondary divsn. Santa Ana (Calif.) Unified Sch. Dist., 1985-87, assoc. supt. secondary divsn., 1987-88, supt., 1988-94; supt. schs. San Diego County, 1994—; adj. prof. Calif. State U., Long Beach, 1981-88, mem. adv. com. dept. ednl. adminstrn., 1983-86; adj. prof. U. San Francisco, 1984-88; mem. State Tchr. of Yr. Selection Com., 1988, Student Tchr. Edn. Project Coun., SB 620 Healthy Start Com., SB 1274 Restructuring Com., Joint Task Force Articulation, State High Sch. Task Force; mem. Latino eligibility study U. Calif., mem. ednl. leadership inst.; mem. state adv. coun. Supt. Pub. Instrn.; Delta Epsilon lectr. U. So. Calif.; rep. Edn. Summit; mem. selection com. Calif. Ednl. Initiatives Fund; co-chair subcom. at risk youth Calif. Edn. Com., 1989; mentor supt. Harvard Urban Supt.'s Program, 1993—. Chair Orange County Hist. Adv. Coun., South El Monte Coordinating Coun.; mem. exec. coun. Santa Ana 2000; mem. articulation coun. Rancho Santiago C.C. Dist.; active Hacienda Heights Recreation and Pks. Commn., Santa Ana City Coun. Stadium Blue Ribbon Com.; exec. dir. Orange County coun. Boy Scouts Am.; mem. adv. com. Bowers Mus.; mem. exec. bd. El Monte Boys Club; hon. lifetime mem. Calif. PTA; bd. dirs. Santa Ana Boys and Girls Club, Orange County Philharm. Soc., Santa Ana Pvt. Industry Coun., El Monte-South El Monte Consortium, Drug Use is Life Abuse, EDUCARE sch. edn. U. So. Calif. Named Supt. of Yr. League United Latin Am. Citizens, 1989; state finalist Nat. Supt. Yr. award, 1992. Mem. ASCD, Assn. Calif. Sch. Adminstrs. (rep. region XVII secondary prins. com. 1981-85, presenter region XVII 1984, Calif. Supt. of Year award 1991, Marcus Foster award 1991), Calif. Sch. Bds. Assn. (mem. policy and analysis com.), Assn. Calif. Urban Sch. Dists. (pres. 1992—), Orange County Supts. (pres.), Santa Ana C. of C. (bd. dirs.), Delta Epsilon (pres. 1990-91), Phi Delta Kappa. Office: San Diego County Supt Office 6401 Linda Vista Rd San Diego CA 92111

CASTURO, DON JAMES, venture capitalist; b. McKeesport, Pa., Nov. 9, 1942; s. Charles and Elizabeth B. (Barno) C.; m. Judith K. Erkman, Aug. 22, 1964; children: Don J.E., Christian D.E. BA, Mich. State U., 1964; MBA, U. So. Calif., 1966. Participant mgmt. devel. program Mellon Bank, Pitts., 1966-67, investment rschr., 1967-69, asst. invesment officer, 1969-71, investment officer, 1971-73, asst. v.p., 1973-82; v.p. mgr. Venture Capital Investments, 1982-88; gen. ptnr. Point Venture Ptnrs., Pitts.; bd. dirs. GALT Technologies, Inc., Tri Foods, Inc., Lloyd's Food Products, Inc., Network Data Corp., Creativators, Inc., Meretek Diagnostics, Southdown Trading, Inc., The Steak-umm Co. Co-chmn. enrichment program Mich. State U.; bd. dirs. Upper St. Clair Athletic Assn. Mem. Pitts. Soc. Fin. Analysts (past pres., chmn. exec. com., dir.), Assn. for Investment Mgmt. and Rsch. (chartered fin. analyst), Nat. Venture Capital Assn., Pitts. Venture Capital Assn. (founding mem., past pres., bd. dirs.), Sigma Nu. Republican. Orthodox Catholic. Home: 2339 Morton Rd Pittsburgh PA 15241-3301 Office: Point Venture Ptnrs 3260 Usx Towers Pittsburgh PA 15219

CASWELL, FRANCES PRATT, retired English language educator; b. Brunswick, Maine, June 25, 1929; d. Harold Edward and Marian Elizabeth (Nicoll) Pratt; m. Forrest Wilbur Caswell, June 30, 1956; children: Lucy Caswell Hilburn, Helen Caswell Watts, Harold F. BA, U. Maine, 1951; MA, U. Mich., 1955. Tchr. English, Bridgton (Maine) High Sch., 1951-54, Grosse Point (Mich.) High Sch., 1955-56; instr. South Maine Tech. Coll., South Portland, 1968-84, chmn. dept., 1984-93; bd. dirs. Maine Vocat. Region 10. Athor: Growing Through Faith, A History of the Brunswick United Methodist Church, 1821-1996, 1996; contbg. author: Brunswick, Maine, 250 Years A Town, 1989. Pres. United Pejepscot Housing Inc., Brunswick, 1987-93. Mem. AAUW, Nat. Coun. Tchrs. English, Casco Bay Art League. Republican. Methodist. Avocations: painting, gardening.

CASWELL, HERBERT HALL, JR., retired biology educator; b. Marblehead, Mass., May 21, 1923; s. Herbert Hall and Grace (Parker) C.; m. Ethel Claire Preble, Mar. 28, 1948; children: Hal, Martha, William, Edward,

Thomas, Michael. B.S., Harvard U., 1948; M.S., UCLA, 1950; Ph.D, Cornell U., 1956. Prof. biology Eastern Mich. U., Ypsilanti, 1955-88, prof. emeritus, 1988, head dept. biology, 1974-88. Served to 1st lt. U.S. Army, 1942-46. Mem. Ecol. Soc. Am., Assn. Field Ornithol., Am. Inst. Biol. Scis., Sigma Xi. Home: 952 Sheridan St Ypsilanti MI 48197-2713

CASWELL, LINDA KAY, insurance agency executive; b. Canton, Ohio, Sept. 29, 1952; d. Lloyd Norman and Eva Mae (Clark) C. Grad. high sch., Canton, Ohio. Office mgr., sec. Harold Dickinson Architect, Canton, 1970-73; dist. mgr., sec., clk. Met. Life Ins., Canton, 1973-80, office mgr., 1980-86; brokerage assoc. Met. Brokerage, Canton, 1986-89; owner, pres. Golden Horizons Ins. Agy., Canton, 1987—. Avocations: cards, fishing, Golden Retreivers. Office: Golden Horizons Ins Agy 5874 Fulton Dr NW Canton OH 44718-1735

CASWELL, RANDALL SMITH, physicist; b. Eugene, Oreg., Feb. 7, 1924; s. Albert Edward and M. Constance (Edwards) C.; m. Jean M. Miller, June 14, 1945; children: William Edward, Virginia Lee, Anne Marden, Ellen Sue, Wendy Jean (dec.), Julia Constance. SB, MIT, 1947, PhD in Physics, 1951. Assoc. prof. physics U. Ky., 1950-52; rschr. particle solid state physics Oak Ridge Nat. Lab., 1952; physicist neutron physics Nat. Bur. Standards, 1952-69; dep. dir. Ctr. Radiation Rsch., 1969-78, chief nuclear radiation divsn., 1978-85; chief ionizing radiation divsn. Nat. Inst. Standards & Tech., Gaithersburg, Md., 1985-94, ret., 1994; adj. prof. physics Am. U. 1957-71; mem. Nat. Coun. Radiation Protection & Measurements, 1967-91; chmn. neutron measurements sect. Adv. Com. Standards Ionizing Radiation Measurement, Bur. Internat. des Poids et Mesures, 1969-89; mem. Internat. Commn. Radiation Units & Measurement, 1975—, sec., 1979—; chmn. sci. panel Com. Interagy. Radiation Rsch. and Policy Coord. Office Sci. and Tech. Policy, 1984-94. Assoc. editor Radiation Rsch., 1977-80. Fellow Am. Physics Soc.; mem. Radiation Rsch. Soc. Office: Nat Inst of Stds Tech Physics Rm C229 Radiation Physics Bldg 245 Gaithersburg MD 20899

CASWELL, REX ACE, sales executive; b. Havre de Grace, Md., Aug. 4, 1948; s. Lawrence Ace Caswell and Doris Virginia (Tollenger) Sellers; m. Nancy Catherine Thornburgh, Dec. 17, 1987; children: Shawna, Jonathan, Alexander. AA, Pensacola (Fla.) C.C., 1975; BA, U. North Fla., 1977; MA, U. Cin., 1978. Human resource mgmt. cons. U.S. Navy, Jacksonville, Fla., 1973-77; account dir. Performax Sys. Internat., Dayton, Ohio, 1979-85; account mgr. Maritz Motivation Co., Cin., 1985-88; sr. region dir. Lexis-Nexis, Dayton, 1988-97; dir. U.S. sales OneSource Info. Svcs., Cambridge, Mass., 1998—; cons. Paul Reed and Assocs., Dayton. Petty officer second class USN, 1970-77. Univ. grad. scholar U. Cin. Dept. Sociology, 1977; fellow InterUniversity Seminar of Soc. and the Armed Forces, U. Chgo., 1978. Episcopalian. E-mail: rexcaswell@onesource.com. Office: OneSource Info Svcs 150 Cambridge Park Dr Cambridge MA 02140-2322

CASWELL, ROBERT STEARNS, public relations director; b. Damariscotta, Maine, July 24, 1952; s. Stearns Dana and Gloria (Naylor) C.; m. Diane Lapointe, Aug. 23, 1975; children: Aimee Elizabeth, Jenna Leigh. BA, U. So. Maine, Gorham, 1974. Reporter The Courier Gazette, Rockland, Maine, 1975-80; pub. relations staff mem. Univ. So. Maine, Portland, 1980-83; exec. dir. media and community rels. Univ. So. Maine, 1983—; pres. Maine Pub. Rels. Coun., Portland, 1988-89; dir. Maine Press Assn., Orono, 1984-95. Producer Maine Pub. Broadcasting Network, Portland, 1982—; mem. campaign cabinet United Way, Portland, 1991-92, mem. comms. com., 1995—. Recipient Edward Bernays award for pub. rels. Maine Pub. Rels. Coun., 1990. Mem. Gorham C. of C. (pres. 1990-92), C. of C. Greater Portland Region (bd. dirs. 1993-94, comms. com. 1993—), Am. Assn. State Schs. and Univs. (pub. rels. adv. coun.). Avocations: jazz/blues collector, reading, sports. Office: U So Maine PO Box 9300 Portland ME 04104*

CASWELL, SALLY ELLEN, artist, art educator; b. Brockton, Mass., Nov. 1, 1941; d. Sherman Clarke Sr. and Eleanor Catherine Caswell; m. Carl Lewis Hayter, 1962 (div. June 1973); children: Dana Ward Hayter, Royce Evan Hayter; m. Leonard Linhares, Aug. 1976 (div. Aug. 1987). BFA, Mass. Coll. Art, Boston, 1965; MAT equivalency, R.I. Coll., 1978; MFA disting. thesis, U. Mass., 1990. Cert. lifetime tchr., R.I. Tchr. art-ceramics Johnston (R.I.) H.S., 1972-80, 83-84; tchr. painting, watercolor Attleboro (Mass.) Mus., 1980-83; tchr. advanced watercolor, drawing, design R.I. Sch. Design, Providence, 1986-94; adj. asst. prof. art C.C. R.I., Warwick, 1987—, dir. Knight Campus Art Gallery, 1995—; tchr. watercolor, spl. studies The Chautauqua (N.Y.) Instn., 1996—; fine artist, illustrator Swansea, Mass., 1965—; mem. arts festival com. Wickford (R.I.) Art Assn., 1982-83; mem. exec. bd. Pawtucket (R.I.) Arts Coun., 1986-88; mem. exec. bd. Nat. Mus. Women in Arts., R.I. chpt., 1997-99; art lectr. Fall River (Mass.) Art Assn., 1996—; contbg. artist fundraising raffle R.I. Watercolor Soc., Pawtucket, 1997. One-person shows include Bierstadt Gallery, New Bedford, Mass., 1990, Gallery 401, Providence, 1991, Windsor Gallery, Providence, 1991, South County Art Ctr., Wakefield, R.I., 1993, Wickford Art Assn. Gallery, 1993, South County Art Assn., Kingston, R.I., 1993, C.C. R.I., LIncoln, 1993, Nicole Saul-Kogut Gallery, Providence, 1994, 95, Pawtucket, 1995, Winds of March Gallery, Chautauqua, 1996, Providence Art Club, 1997, Spencer Gallery, Wickford, R.I., 1998, others; exhibited in group shows at U. Mass., Dartmouth, 1990, South Wharf Gallery, Nantucket, Mass., 1980-90, Hera Gallery, Wakefield, 1992, Cornwall Gallery, Jamaica Plain, Mass., 1992, South County Ctr. for Arts, Kingston, 1993, Woods-Gerry Gallery, R.I. Sch. Design, Providence, 1987-93, Copley Soc. Boston, 1993, 97, Mass. Coll. Art Tower Bldg. Alumni Gallery, Boston, 1993, Copley Soc. Boston, 1994, 95, 98, C.C. R.I. Galleries, 1987-96, Nicole Saul-Kogut Gallery, Pawtucket, 1989-96, Providence Art Club, 1996, Fall River Art Assn., 1996, Cape Cod Art Assn., 1997, R.I. Watercolor Soc., 1997, Providence Art Club, 1997, Wickford Art Assn., 1997, others; represented in permanent collections at U.S. Naval War Coll. Mus., Newport; also corp. collections; illustrator: An Anniversary Collection, 1984-1988: Winning Poems From the Pawtucket Arts Council Annual Poetry Competition, 1988, The Watchman: A Novel by G.R. Conrad, 1972, Objective Drawing Techniques-New Approaches to Perspective in Interior Space (Calvin Burnett), 1966. Supt. Sunday Sch. Ch. of the Mediator, Unitarian-Universalist, Providence, 1967; tchr. ESL Adult Sch., Warren, R.I., 1968-69; mem. exec. bd. Nat. Mus. Women in Arts, R.I. chpt. Recipient awards Providence Watercolor Club, 1981, 82, Fall River Art Assn., 1983, Bristol Art Mus., 1983, New Haven Paint and Clay Club, All Eng. and N.Y. Show, 1983, Providence Art Club Open Painting Exhbn., 1985, Japan/Am. Exch. Exhbn., R.I. Watercolor Soc., Pawtucket, Tokyo, Sako City, Japan, 1986, Bristol (R.I.) Art Mus. Invitational, 1986, Art of N.E. U.S.A. Exhbn., Silvermine Gallerie, New Canaan, Conn., 1988, R.I. Watercolor Soc., 1989, Duxbury Art Complex Mus. All New Eng. Exhbn., 1989, Am. Artist Mag., 1990, Wickford Art Assn., 1994, Providence Art Club Abstract/Representational Exhbn., 1996, Greater Fall River Art Assn. Ann. Regional Show, 1996. Mem. Wickford Art Assn. (program chair, juror), R.I. Watercolor Soc., Providence Art Club, Copley Soc. (Copley Artist), 19 on Paper. Avocations: cross-country skiing, sailing, art history, writing. Home and Studio: 611 Warren Ave Swansea MA 02777-3332

CASWELL, STEVEN JAMES, health care administrator; b. Pontiac, Mich., Feb. 9, 1957; s. Otis Warden and Bernice Chavis (Fernandez) C.; m. Janice Fern Tarica, June 24, 1984; children: Allison Brooke, Ashley Michelle. BA, Mich. State U., 1979, U. Md., 1987. Provider rels. Dental Benefit Providers, Bethesda, Md., 1989-92; sr. supr. Mid-Atlantic Med. Svcs., Rockville, Md., 1992—; bd. mem. Great Lakes Invitational Conf. Assn., Grand Rapids, Mich., 1975-79. Author: The Parenting Contract, 1992. Recipient Evans scholarship Western Golf Assn., Golf, Ill., 1975-79. Mem. Dobro Slovo. Jewish. Avocations: religious study, golf. Home: 12204 Milestone Manor Ln Germantown MD 20876-5912 Office: 4 Taft Ct Rockville MD 20850-5310

CASWELL, WILLIAM STEPHEN, JR., civil engineer; b. South Kingston, R.I., Feb. 2, 1962; s. William Stephen Caswell and Shirley Frances (Mason) Farrell; m. Joy Lynne Russo, Aug. 4, 1984; children: William Stephen III, Benjamin Perry. Registered profl. engr., N.H. Civil engr. N.H. Dept. Transp., Concord, 1984-89, CAD/D applications engr., 1989—. Planning bd. Boscawen (N.H.) Planning Bd., 1996—. Mem. R.I. Geneal. Soc., N.H. Hist. Soc. Baptist. Avocations: genealogy, hiking. Home: 3 Buxton Pl Boscawen NH 03303-1219 Office: NH Dept Transp PO Box 483 Concord NH 03302-0483

CATACOSINOS, WILLIAM JAMES, retired utility company executive; b. N.Y.C., Apr. 12, 1930; s. James and Penelope (Paleologos) C.; m. Florence Maken, Oct. 16, 1955; children: William, James. BS, NYU, 1951, MBA, 1952, PhD, 1962. Asst. editor 20th Century-Fox, N.Y.C., 1951-52; asst. dir. bus. mgmt. and adminstrn. Brookhaven Nat. Lab., Upton, N.Y., 1956-69; pres. Applied Digital Data Sys., Inc., Hauppauge, N.Y., 1969-77, chmn., CEO, 1977-82; chmn., CEO Market Span Corp. formerly L.I. Lighting Co., Hicksville, N.Y., 1984-98, also bd. dirs.; adj. asst. prof. NYU, 1962-64; chmn. bd. Corometrics Med., 1968-74; bd. dirs. Atlantic Bank N.Y.; adv. com., policy com. on strategic planning, bd. dirs. Edison Electric Inst., 1990-95. Bd. dirs. L.I. Assn., New N.Y. Alliance, Brookhaven Town Indsl. Commn., 1956-77, Am. Cancer Soc. Suffolk County chpt., 1969-77, Stony Brook Found., 1978-85; trustee Poly. Inst. N.Y., 1981-85; nat. chmn. Am. Soc. Prevention Cruelty to Children, 1981-83. With USN, 1952-56.

CATALANO, GERALD, accountant, oil company executive; b. Chgo., Jan. 17, 1949; s. Frank and Virginia (Kreiman) C.; m. Mary L. Billings, July 4, 1970; children: James, Maria, Gina. BSBA, Roosevelt U., 1971. CPA, Ill. Jr. acct. Drebin, Lindquist and Gervasio, Chgo., 1971; jr. acct. Leaf, Dahl and Co., Ltd., 1971-77, prin., 1978-80, ptnr. 1980-82; prin. Gerald Catalano, CPA, Chgo., 1982-83; ptnr. Barbakoff, Catalano & Assocs., 1983-87; pres. Barbakoff, Catalano & Caboor, Ltd., 1988-93, pres., Catalano, Caboor & Co., Ltd., 1993—; v.p. Tri-City Oil, Inc., Addison, Ill., 1983—; treas. Uncle Andy's, Inc., 1991-94; corp. officer Bionic Auto Parts, Inc.; bd. dirs. EDT, Inc., treas., 1993—; ptnr.PetCatMusic Publ., 1996—;owner IEP Record Group, 1996—. Pres. Young Dems., Roosevelt U., 1967-71; trustee U. Ill. Russo Scholarship Fund, 1989—; dir. Elmhurst Jaycees, 1976. Mem. AICPA, ASCAP (assoc.), NARAS (assoc.), Ill. CPA Soc., Theosophical Soc. Roman Catholic. Office: 1 S 376 Summit Ave Oakbrook Terrace IL 60181

CATALANO, JAMES ANTHONY, social worker; b. Lackawanna, N.Y., Nov. 5, 1954; s. George and Frances (McGowan) C. BA, Canisius Coll., 1977, Canisius Coll., 1992; MS, Columbia U., 1985, MA in Ednl. Psychology, 1999; MDiv, Weston Jesuit Sch. Theology, Cambridge, Mass., 1994, ThM, 1995. Cert. social worker, N.Y.; diploma clin. social work NASW, 1991. Caseworker Neighborhood Info. Ctr., Buffalo, N.Y., 1975-79; dir. Youth Svcs. Program Lincoln Community Ctr., Buffalo, N.Y., 1979-80; psychiatric social worker, discharge planner Bry-Lin Hosp., Buffalo, N.Y., 1981; social worker Cath. Charities of Western N.Y., Buffalo, N.Y., 1987-89; asst. to the dir. Inst. of Faith and Justice Canisius Coll., Buffalo, N.Y., 1989-90; pvt. practice Buffalo, N.Y., 1989—; relief worker Jesuit Refugee Svcs., San Salvador, El Salvador, 1985; chmn. Site Selection Com. for Residential Care Facilities, Buffalo, 1979-81; adv. to chmn. Pub. Svc. Commn. of N.Y., 1979-81; speaker on San Salvador Diocese of Buffalo, 1990-91; workshop leader Buffalo Taditional High Sch., Buffalo City High Sch. East Campus, 1988-89; com. mem. Dem. Orgn. Erie County, Buffalo, 1978-81. Recipient Vol. Svc. award VA, Syracuse, N.Y., 1982. Mem. NASW. Home and Office: 50 Glenwood Ave Jersey City NJ 07306-4606

CATALANO, JANE DONNA, lawyer; b. Schenectady, N.Y., Feb. 21, 1957; d. Alfred and Joan (Futscher) Martini; m. Peter Catalano, June 18, 1988. BA, SUNY, Plattsburgh, 1979; JD, Albany Law Sch., 1982. Bar: N.Y. 1983, U.S. Dist. Ct. 1983. Atty. Pentak, Brown & Tobin, Albany, N.Y., 1982-87, Niagara Mohawk Power Corp., Albany, 1987—. Mem. N.Y. State Bar Assn., Albany County Bar Assn. Home: 7 Blackburn Way Latham NY 12110-1943 Office: Niagara Mohawk Power Corp 111 Washington Ave Ste 305 Albany NY 12210

CATALANO, ROBERT ANTHONY, ophthalmologist, physician, hospital administrator, writer; b. Albany, N.Y., Nov. 24, 1956; s. Anthony Joseph and Ida Santa (Muscolino) C.; m. Madeline Faye Kalmer, Aug. 6, 1978; children: Christopher, Ruth, Thomas, Matthew. BS, Union Coll., Schenectady, 1978; MD, U. Va., 1982; MBA, Rensselaer Poly. Inst., 1992. Resident in ophthalmology Albany Med. Coll., 1983-86, vice-chmn. dept. ophthalmology, 1989-90, acting chmn., 1990-91; fellow in pediatric ophthalmology Wills Eye Hosp., Phila., 1986-87; v.p. med. affairs Olean (N.Y.) Gen. Hosp., 1991-93, COO, 1994-95, pres., CEO, 1995—; bd. dirs. Westlink Corp. Author: Atlas of Ocular Motility, 1989, Ocular Emergencies, 1992, Pediatric Ophthalmology: A Text/Atlas, 1994, When Autism Strikes, 1998; contbr. articles to profl. jours. Recipient Nat. Found. award March of Dimes Found., 1978, Robert D. Reinecke award Albany Med. Coll., 1985, Shannon award U. Va., 1982; Heed Found. fellow, 1986, Forty Under Forty award, 1993. Fellow Am. Acad. Ophthalmology; mem. Am. Coll. Physician Execs., Am. Coll. Healthcare Execs., Western N.Y. Hosp. Assn. (bd. dirs. 1992-95), So. Tier Healthcare Network (bd. dirs. 1994—), Alpha Omega Alpha. Roman Catholic. Office: Olean Gen Hosp 515 Main St Olean NY 14760-1598

CATALDI, PHYLLIS JEAN, writer, publisher of genealogies; b. Burlington, Wis., Apr. 4, 1927; d. Oliver L. and Thelma D. (Wallace) Kortendick; m. Horace A. Cataldi, Dec. 29, 1951; children: Marifrances, Vincent, Margaret, James, Lisa. BA, Mount Mary Coll., 1949; M in Creative Writing, U. Wis.-Milw., 1977; AD, Milw. Area Tech. Coll., 1969. Registered genealogist. Writer, broadcaster WDUZ, Green Bay, Wis., 1950-51; publicity writer WJJD, Chgo., 1951-52; univ. editor U. Wis.-Milw., 1964-67; publs dir. Alverno Coll., Milw., 1964-67; pub., rschr. Cataldi & Assocs., Inc., Shorewood, Wis., 1985—; cons. genealogist for various heirfinder orgns. Writer, pub.: (book) Family of William Kortendick, 1989, Millen Family, 1991; editor, pub. (book) Hardy Hill of Ky., 1993. Roman Catholic. Home and Office: 2516 E Menlo Blvd Shorewood WI 53211-2612

CATALDO, C. A., hotel executive; b. Chgo., Oct. 23, 1933. Student, Loyola U.; grad. bus. mgmt. program, Harvard U., 1973. Founder Hostmark Mgmt. Group, 1974—; past chmn., bd. dirs. Chgo. Convention and Tourism Bur. Active City of Hope Med. Ctr., Maryville Acad., Boy Scouts Am. Recipient Awards Nat. Restuarant Assn., award Holiday Inn's Top 10 Restaurant Mgrs., 1968, Innkeeper of Yr. award Holiday Inn, Spirit of Life award, Lifetime Achievement award Roosevelt U. Manfred Seinfeld Sch. in Hospitality Mgmt., 1998; med. rsch. fellowship established in his name City of Hope, 1982. Mem. Greater Chgo. Hotel/Motel Assn., Am. Hotel/Motel Assn. (bd. dirs.), Ill. Hotel and Motel Assn. (bd. dirs.). Office: Hostmark Mgmt Group 1600 Golf Rd #800 Rolling Meadows IL 60008

CATALDO, PATRICK A., JR., corporate training executive; b. New Rochelle, N.Y., Oct. 17, 1943; s. Patrick Anthony Sr. and Adele Linda (Pisani) C.; m. Kathleen Mary Mikoloski, July 12, 1969; children: Patrick Edward, Peter Anthony, Catherine Adele. BA, St. Francis Coll., 1966; MBA, Boston Coll., 1968; PhD, Grand Valley State Coll., 1987. Dir. Chamberlayne Jr. Coll., Boston, 1968-69; mgr. Honeywell, Waltham, Mass., 1969-74; v.p. Digital Equipment Corp., Maynard, Mass., 1974-94; chief exec. Digital Equipment Ireland, Dublin, Ireland, 1992-94; v.p. Bellcore, Red Bank, N.J., 1995-97, group v.p., 1999—; v.p. Home Depot, Atlanta, 1997-98; CLO SAIC, San Diego, 1999—. Office: Bellcore NVC 2Z-359B 331 Newman Springs Rd Red Bank NJ 07701-5699

CATALDO, ROBERT J., hotel executive; b. Chgo., Sept. 1, 1941. Pres., COO Hostmark Mgmt. Group, 1996—. Office: Hostmark Mgmt Group 1600 Golf Rd #800 Rolling Meadows IL 60008

CATALFO, ALFRED, JR. (ALFIO CATALFO), lawyer; b. Lawrence, Mass., Jan. 31, 1920; s. Alfio and Vincenza (Amato) C.; m. Caroline Joanne Mosca (dec. Apr. 1968); children: Alfred Thomas, Carol Joanne, Gina Marie; m. Gail Varney, 1988. BA, U. N.H., 1945, MA in History, 1952; LLB, Boston U., 1947, JD (hon.), 1969; postgrad., Suffolk U. Sch. Law, 1955-56, Am. Law Inst., N.Y.C., 1959. Bar: N.H. 1947, U.S. Dist. Ct. 1948, U.S. Ct. Appeals 1978, U.S. Supreme Ct. 1979. Pvt. practice Dover, N.H., 1948—; ptnr. Catalfo Law Firm, Dover, 1980—; county atty. Strafford County, Dover, N.H., 1949-50, 55-56; bd. immigration appeals U.S. Dept. Justice, 1953—; football coach Berwick Acad., South Berwick, Maine, 1944, Mission Catholic H.S., Roxbury, Mass., 1945-46. Author: Laws of Divorces, Marriages, and Separations in New Hampshire, 1962, History of the Town of Rollinsford, 1623-1973, 1973. Pres. Young Dems. of Dover, 1953-55; 1st vice-chmn. Young Dems., N.H., 1954-56; mem. Strafford County Dem. Com., 1948-75; vice-chmn. N.H. Dem. Com., 1954-56, 1st chmn., 1956-58, chmn. spl. activities, 1958-60; del. Dem. Nat. Conv., 1956-60, 76; chmn. N.H. Dem. Conv., 1958, conv. dir., 1960; mem. Dem. state exec. com., 1960-70; Dem. nominee for U.S. Senate, 1962; vice-chmn. Dover Cath. Sch. Com., 1969-71; mem. Dover Bd. Adjustment, 1960-65; apptd. lt. commdr. N.H. Govs. Mil. Staff. Pilot U.S. Naval Air Corp., lt. commdr. USNR, 1942-44. Recipient keys to cities of Dover, Somersworth, Concord, Berlin, Manchester and Rochester N.H., 6 nat. plaques DAV, 3 disting. svc. awards Am. Legion, Am. Legion Life Membership award, spl. recognition award Berwick Acad., 1985. Mem. ABA, N.H. Bar Assn., Strafford County Bar Assn. (v.p. 1966-67, pres. 1968-69), Assn. Trial Lawyers Am., N.Y. State Trial Lawyers Assn., Mass. Trial Lawyers Assn., N.H. Trial Lawyers Assn., Tex. Trial Lawyers Assn., Nat. Assn. Criminal Def. Lawyers, N.H. Assn. Criminal Def. Lawyers, Am. Judicature Soc., Phi Delta Phi, DAV (judge adv. N.H. dept. 1950-68, 72—; comdr. chpt. 1953-54, comdr. N.H. 1956-57), Am. Legion (life, chmn. state conv. 1967, 77, 84), Navy League, N.H. Hist. Soc., Dover Hist. Soc., Rollinsford Hist. Soc., Eagles Club, Sons of Italy, Lions, Elks, K.C. (grand knight 1975-77), Moose, Lebanese Club. Clubs: Eagles (Somersworth, N.H.), Sons of Italy (Portsmouth, N.H.). Lodges: Lions, Elks, K.C. (grand knight 1975-77), Moose, Lebanese (Dover). Home: 20 Arch St Dover NH 03820-3602 Office: 450 Central Ave Dover NH 03820-3451

CATALFO, BETTY MARIE, health service executive, nutritionist; b. N.Y.C., Nov. 2, 1942; d. Lawrence Santo and Gemma (Patrone) Lorefice; children—Anthony, Lawrence, Donna Marie. Grad. Newtown High Sch., Elmhurst, N.Y., 1958. Sec., clk. ABC-TV, N.Y.C., 1957-60; founder, lectr., nutritionist Weight Watchers, Manhasset, N.Y., 1964-75; founder, pres. Every-Bodys Diet, Inc. dba Stay Slim, Queens, N.Y., 1976—; dir. in-home program N.Y. State Dept. Health, N.Y.C., 1985—; founder, pres. Delitegul Diet Foods, Inc., 1988—; lectr. in field. Author: 101 Stay-Slim Recipes, 1983, Get Slim and Stay Slim Diet Cook Book, rev. ed., 1987, Diet Revolution, 1990, Holiday Cookbook, 1992, Fat Counts in Fast Food Spots, 1992, Choose to Loose!, 1993, You Are Not Alone, 1993, Eating Out, 1994, Change or Select, 1994, Calories Do Count!, 1994, Fat Free Receipes, 1994; author, dir., producer: (video) Dancersize for Overweight, 1986, Get Slim and Stay Slim Diet Cook Book, Eating Right for Your Life, Hello It's Me and I'm Slim, (videos) Stay Slim Line Dancing, 1989, Stay Slim Food Facts, 1989, Help Me Before I Give In, 1990, A New Year A New You!, 1991, Relax and Meditate, 1991, Come Shop with Me, 1991, Change or Accept, 1993, The Bag Lady, 1993, Sneak Eater, 1993, Sins That Every Dieter Makes, 1994, Stay Slim from Start to Finish, 1994, Here's Some Helpful Diet Tips, 1994, What Every Smart Dieter Knows, 1994, Mirror Mirror on the Wall, 1994, Weight Management Techniques, 1995; author, editor: (video) Eating Right For Life, 1985, Isometric Techniques for Weight Reduction, Dance Your Calories A-Weigh; author, producer: (video) Eating Habits, 1986—; (video) Isometric Techniques for Weight Reduction, 1986, Patience Is a Virtue When Weight Loss is the Goal, 1986, Slow Down you Eat to Fast, 1994, Always Giving Never Receiving, 1994, Relax and Don't You Worry, 1994; producer, dir.: (video) Positive and Negative Diet Forces, 1987, (video) Hello It's Me and I'm Thin, 1987, (video) Dance Your Calories A-Weigh, 1987, (video) Positive and Negative Diet Forces, 1987. Sponsor, lectr. St. Pauls Ctr., Bklyn., 1981—, Throgs Neck Assn. Retarded Children, Bronx, 1985—; active ARC, LWV, Am. Italian Assn., United Way Greenwich, Council Chs. and Synagogues, Heart Assn., N.Y. Meals on Wheels, 1985—, Health Assn. Fairfield County, Food Svcs. for Homeless People, 1993, 94, 95; chairperson, sponsor Battered Women, 1994—. Named Woman of Yr., Bayside Womens Club, N.Y., 1983, O, PK Woman of Yr., 1986—, Woman of Yr. Richmond Boys Club, 1987, Woman of Yr. Bronx Press Club Assn., 1987; recipient Merit award for Svc. Cath. Archdiocese of Bklyn., 1985, Merit award Svcs. Cath. Archdioces of Bklyn. and Queens, 1992, 93, 94, Community Service award Sr. Citizens Sacred Heart League Bklyn./Queens Archdiocese. N.Y. State Nutritional Guidance for Children Nat. Assn. Scis. Mem. Nat. C. of C. for Women (Woman of Yr. 1987, 90), Pres.'s Coun. on Nutrition, Roundtable for Women in Food Service, Bus. and Profl. Women's Club, Pres. Council for Phys. Fitness, Nat. Assn. Female Execs., Assn. for Fitness in Bus. Inc., Nat. Assn. Female Bus. Owners. Democrat. Roman Catholic. Club: Mothers Sacred Heart Sch. (chairperson 1979-82). Avocations: reading; travel, golf, family. Home: 21422 27th Ave Flushing NY 11360-2608 also: 58 Riverview Ct Greenwich CT 06831-4127 Office: 10005 101st Ave Ozone Park NY 11416-2601

CATALFOMO, PHILIP, retired university dean; b. Providence, Dec. 27, 1931; s. Antonio and Frances (Di Giuseppe) C.; m. Magdalena Wettstein, Jan. 8, 1962; children—Kristina, Anthony Werner. B.S., Providence Coll., 1953, U. Conn., 1958; M.S., U. Wash., Seattle, 1960, Ph.D., 1962. Mem. faculty Oreg. State U., 1963-75, prof. pharmacognosy, 1966-75, head dept., 1966-75; prof. pharmacognosy, dean Sch. Pharmacy, U. Mont., Missoula, 1975-86; dean coll. health scis. U. Wyo., Laramie, 1986-91; ret., 1991. Author research articles fungal metabolism. Served with AUS, 1953-55. Gustavus A. Pfeiffer Meml. research fellow, 1969-70. Home: 81800 Old Hwy # 93 Dayton MT 59914

CATANELLO, IGNATIUS ANTHONY, bishop; b. Bklyn., July 23, 1938. Student, Cathedral Prep. Sem.; BA, St. Francis Coll., Bklyn.; STB, Cath. U. Washington; MA, MS, St. John's U.; PhD, LLD, NYU; LLD (hon.), St. John's U., 1989. Ordained priest Roman Cath. Ch., 1966. With St. Rita's, L.I., 1966-76, St. Helen's, Howard Beach, N.Y., 1976-81, St. Ann's, Flushing, N.Y., 1981-86, O.L.O. Angles, Bay Ridge, N.Y., 1987-88; titular bishop Diocese of Deulto, 1994—; auxiliary bishop Diocese Bklyn., 1994—; adj. prof. St. John's U.; Episcopal liaison Nat. Holy Name Soc.; bd. govs. Maj. Sem., Huntington, N.Y.; co-chair Roman Cath.-Islamic Dialogue; vicar for evangelization Roman Cath. Diocese of Bklyn.; regional bishop Queens South; chair convocation on crime Religious Leaders of N.Y.C.; established bilateral com. Cath. and Ea. Orthodox. Revised, edited Cath.-Jewish Guidelines for Diocese of Bklyn. Recipient Builder of Brotherhood award Nat. Conf. on Christians and Jews, Disting. Svc. award State of N.Y. Mem. AAUW, Cath. Biblical Assn., Religious Edn. Assn. Office: St Johns U SJH-103 800 Utopia Pky Jamaica NY 11439*

CATANESE, ANTHONY JAMES, academic administrator; b. New Brunswick, N.J., Oct. 18, 1942; s. Anthony James and Josephine Marlene (Barone) C.; m. Sara Jean Phillips, Oct. 23, 1968; children: Mark Anthony, Michael Scott, Mark Alexander. BA, Rutgers U., 1963; M in Urban Planning, NYU, 1965; PhD, U. Wis., 1968. Asst. prof. city planning Ga. Inst. Tech., Atlanta, 1967-78, assoc. prof., 1968-73, chmn. doctoral studies com., 1970-73; James A. Ryder prof. transp. and planning, dir. Ryder program in transp. U. Miami, Coral Gables, Fla., 1973-75; dean Sch. Architecture and Urban Planning U. Wis., Milw., 1975-82; prof. architecture and urban planning, provost Pratt Inst., N.Y.C., 1982-84; dean Coll. Architecture, U. Fla., Gainesville, 1984-89; pres. Fla. Atlantic U., Boca Raton, 1989—, pres., prof., 1990—; sr. Fulbright prof., Colombia, 1971-72; sr. cons. State of Wis., 1965-67, sr. planner State of N.J., 1963-67; pres. A. J. Catanese & Assocs., Inc., 1967—; mem. pres. commn. NCAA, 1991-93. Author: Scientific Methods of Urban Analysis, 1972, New Perspectives on Urban Transportatio Research, 1972, Systematic Planning-Theory and Applications, 1970, Planners and Local Politics: Impossible Dreams, 1973, Urban Transportation in South Florida, 1974, Personality, Politics and Planning, 1978, Introduction to Urban Planning, 1979, Introduction to Architecture, 1979, The Politics of Planning and Development, 1984, Uban Planning, 1988; contbr. articles to profl. jours. Chmn. Mid. DeKalb County Dem. Party, 1969-71, mem. 5th Congl. Dist. Dem. caucus, 1971; aide-de-camp Gov.'s Office, State of Ga., 1971-72; mem. Ga. Dunes Studies Commn., 1972-73; bd. dirs. Archtl. Rsch. Ctrs. Consortium, 1976—; mem. Urban Policy Task Force, Carter presdl. campaign, 1976, 80; pres. Park West Redevel. Corp., 1976-78; chmn. Milw. City Plan Commn., 1978-82; bd. dirs. Goals for Milw. 2000, 1978-82, Environ. Edn. Found. Fla.; chmn. Gainesville (Fla.) Planning Bd., 1986-89. With USAR, 1961-63. Recipient fellowships State of N.J. Act of 1927, 1962-63, Werner Heisemann Found., 1963-65, Wis. Alumni Rsch. Found., 1965-68, Richard King Mellon Trust, 1966-67, Ford Found., 1967, Nat. Endowment Arts, 1980. Mem. Am. Inst. Planners (bd. govs., v.p. 1971-74), Am. Inst. Cert. Planners (mem. exec. com. 1971-74), Am. Planning Assn., Transp. Rsch. Bd., Regional Sci. Assn., Am. Acad. Polit. and Social Scis., Assn. Coll. Schs. Planning, Heritage Club, Wycliff Club, Tower Club. Office: Fla Atlantic U 777 Glades Rd PO Box 3091 Boca Raton FL 33431-0991

CATANIA, A(NTHONY) CHARLES, psychology educator; b. N.Y.C., June 22, 1936; s. Charles John and Elizabeth (Lattarulo) C.; m. Constance J. Britt, Feb. 10, 1962; children: William John, Kenneth Charles. BA in Psychology with highest honors, Columbia U., 1957, MA, 1958; PhD (NSF fellow), Harvard U., 1961. Postdoctoral research fellow Harvard U., 1961-

62; sr. pharmacologist Smith, Kline & French Labs., Phila., 1962-64; asst. prof. NYU, 1964-66, asso. prof., 1966-69, prof., chmn. dept. psychology, 1969-73; prof. dept. psychology U. Md. Baltimore County, Catonsville, 1973—; mem. psychobiology com. NSF, 1982-85; vis. prof. Keio U., Tokyo, 1992. Author: Learning, 1979, 4th edit., 1998; co-author: (with E. Shimoff and B.A. Matthews) Behavior on a Disk, 1989; editor: Contemporary Research in Operant Behavior, 1968; co-editor: (with T.A. Brigham) Handbook of Applied Behavior Analysis, 1978, (with S. Harnad) The Selection of Behavior: The Operant Behaviorism of B.F. Skinner, 1988, (with P.N. Hineline) Variations and Selections, 1996; editor: Jour. Exptl. Analysis Behavior, 1966-69, rev. editor, 1969-76, 83-91; assoc. editor: Behavioral and Brain Scis., 1980—; mem. bd. editors various jours.; contbr. articles to profl. jours.; contbr. chpts. to textbooks. Recipient James McKeen Cattell Sabbatical award, 1986-87, Outstanding Sci. Contbns. to Psychology award Md. Psychol. Assn., 1993, Outstanding Contbr. Behavior Analysis award No. Calif. Assn. Behavior Analysis, 1990; grantee NSF, 1965-67, 74-79, 82-88, USPHS grantee, 1967-73, 79-83; Fulbright sr. rsch. fellow, Wales, Bangor, 1986-87. Fellow Am. Psychol. Assn. (pres. of divsn. 25 1976-79, 96-98, Don Hake award divsn. 25); mem. Assn. Behavior Analysis (pres. 1982-83, chair publ. bd. 1992-95), Ea. Psychol. Assn. (dir. 1979-82), Soc. Exptl. Analysis of Behavior (pres. 1966-67, 81-83), Lang. Origins Soc. (program chair 1996). Home: 10545 Rivulet Row Columbia MD 21044-2420 Office: U Md Baltimore County Dept Psychology Baltimore MD 21250

CATANZARO, DANIEL FRANK, molecular biologist, educator; b. Sydney, Apr. 4, 1957; came to U.S., 1990; m. Cathy L. Budman; two children. BA in Biol. Scis. with honors, Macquarie U., 1978; PhD in Physiology and Molecular Biology, U. Sydney, 1986. Vis. rsch. biochemist U. Calif., San Francisco, 1985; lectr. in eukaryotic molecular genetics U. Sydney, 1986-90; asst. prof. physiology in medicine Cornell U. Med. Coll., 1990-95; assoc. prof. physiology in medicine Weill Med. Coll. Cornell U., N.Y.C., 1995—. Dep. editor basic sci. Am. Jour. Hypertension, 1999—; contbr. articles and revs. to profl. jours. Postgrad. scholar U. Sydney Faculty of Medicine, 1979-81; recipient investigatorship award Am. Heart Assn., 1995. Fellow AHA High Blood Pressure Rsch. Coun.; mem. Endocrine Soc., Am. Soc. Hypertension (Young Scholars award 1993). Office: Weill Med Coll Cornell U Cardiovascular Ctr A 863 1300 York Ave New York NY 10021-4805

CATANZARO, TONY, dancer; b. Bklyn.; s. Archie Achilles and Elvira (Alessandra) C.; children: Maya Vanesa, Antonio; m. Mara Beatiz Betancour, 1998. Student, Performing Arts, N.Y.C., 1961-64. Artistic dir. Bay Ballet Theatre, Tampa, Fla., 1994-95, City of Coral Gables, Fla., 1997—; dance panel Mass. Coun. for Arts and Humanities, 1978-80; mem. Com. for Pub. Action for Arts; mem. blue ribbon com. for Mass. arts lottery bill Spl. Commn. on Performing Arts; mem. hon. com. Dance/New Eng.; coach Internat. Ballet Competition, Moscow, 1981; staged first Nutcracker in Medellin, Colombia, 1995 (first nutcracker ever in S.A.); artistic dir. dance dept. Youth Ctr., Coral Gables, 1997—. Appeared with modern dance cos. Paul Sanansardo Co., 1963-64, Pearl Lang Co., 1966-70, Norman Walker, 1963-70, Harkness Ballet Co. II, 1967, N.J. Ballet Co., 1968-69, Ala. Ballet Co., 1969, Boston Ballet Co., 1969-70, 73-76, Joffrey Ballet, 1970-73, Dennis Waynes Dancers, Boston, 1977-78, artistic dir., choreographer, Boston Ballet Ensemble, 1980-81; prin. dancer, Boston Ballet Co., 1980-82; artistic dir. Ballet Acad. of Miami, 1984—, Ballet Theatre of Miami, 1985-96, Ballet Theatre of Miami Ensemble, 1989-95; leading dance roles in (Broadway) Annie Get Your Gun, 1966, Golden Boy; London Palaedium, 1968. Team coach for Am. team Internat. Ballet Competition, Varna, Bulgaria, 1994. With USNG, 1967-70. Office: 1809 Ponce De Leon Blvd Miami FL 33134-4418

CATASUS, JOSE MAGIN PEREZ, school psychologist; b. Santiago, Oriente, Cuba, Jan. 18, 1942; came to U.S., 1960; s. Magin Perez and Teresa (Losada) C.; m. Carol Lee Getty, Sept. 15, 1962 (div. Nov. 30, 1967); 1 child, Magin Scott; m. Lina Teresa Jubran, Nov. 13, 1982; children: Cristina Teresa, Adam Benjamin. AA, Miami-Dade Jr. Coll., 1971; BS, Fla. Internat. U., 1974, MS, 1976; PhD, Fla. State U., 1981. Cert. sch. psychologist, Fla. Med. technologist Quillian & Assocs., Coral Gables, Fla., 1965-74; screening specialist Dade County Schs., Miami, 1974-76; psychometrist Med. Psychiatric Ctr., Miami, 1974-77; specialist sch. psychology Palm Beach County Schs., W. Palm Beach, Fla., 1977-78; clin. instr. Fla. Internat. U., Miami, 1980-81, visiting instr., 1981-82; vis. instr. U. Fla., Gainesville, 1982-83; lead sch. psychologist Alachua County Schs., Gainesville, 1983—; cons. in field; adv. com. mem. Vocat. Edn. Fla. Internat. U., Miami, 1981-82. Founder Psychol. Svcs. Grad. Student Assn., Miami, 1975; coord. guest speakers XVI InterAm. Congress of Psychology, Miami, 1976; bd. dirs. Hispanic Human Resource Coun., West Palm Beach, 1977-78. Recipient Doctoral Fellowship Fla. State U., 1978. Mem. Nat. Assn. Sch. Psychologists, Fla. Assn. Sch. Psychologists, Fla. Soc. for Med. Technology. Democrat. Roman Catholic. Home: 6800 NW 26th Pl Gainesville FL 32606-6339 Office: Alachua County Schs Psychoednl Svcs 620 E University Ave Gainesville FL 32601-5448

CATCHPOLE, JUDY, state agency administrator; m. Glenn Catchpole; children: Glenda, Fred, Katie. BA in Edn., U. Wyo. CEO, state supt. pub. instrn. State Dept. Edn., Cheyenne, Wyo. Exec. dir. Wyoming Rep. Party. Mem. Wyo. Sch. Bds. Assn. (vice chmn.), Wyo. Early Childhood Assn. (pres.), Natrona County Bd. Trustees (chmn., treas.), Bd. Coop. Edn. Svcs. (treas.), Natrona County C. of C. Office: Wyo Dept Edn Hathaway Bldg 2nd Fl 2300 Capitol Ave Cheyenne WY 82002-0050*

CATE, DONALD JAMES, mechanical engineer, consultant; b. Concord, N.H., Apr. 5, 1933; s. Hiram W. and Jessie M. (Cochran) C.; m. Sara Jane Reiter, Apr. 19, 1958; 1 child, Elisabeth Rowena. BSME, U. N.H., 1955. Registered profl. engr., Pa. Various positions Bell of Pa., Harrisburg, 1955-67, mgr. interoffice facilities, 1967-85; mgr. interoffice facilities Bell Atlantic, Harrisburg, 1985-91; account rep. NEC Am., Harrisburg, 1992; engring. cons. Harrisburg, 1993—. Pres. Devon Manor Civic Club, Harrisburg, 1964, Tel. Pioneers Capital Coun., Harrisburg, 1983-84; treas. Market Sq. Presbyn. Ch., 1977-98, Family & Children's Svcs. of the Capitol Region, 1998, bd. dirs., 1996; treas. Family & Children's Svcs.; mem. Pa. Citizens for Better Libra., 1985—, White House Conf. on Libr. and Info. Svcs. Task Force, 1993—. Mem. Lower Paxton Twp. Lions Club (pres. 1978-79, 94-95, Lion of Yr. 1985, 86). Presbyterian. Avocations: biking, painting. Home and Office: 4502 Coventry Rd Harrisburg PA 17109-1638

CATE, PHILLIP DENNIS, art museum director; b. Washington, Oct. 19, 1944; s. Phillip Harding and Catherine (Watson) C.; m. Lynn Gumpert; children from previous marriage: Phillip Isaac, Anthony David. BA, Rutgers U., 1967; MA, Ariz. State U., 1970. Asst. to dir. Pa. Acad. Fine Arts, Phila., 1967-68; instr. Phila. Coll. Art, Phila., 1969-70; dir. University Art Gallery Rutgers U., New Brunswick, N.J., 1970-82, dir. Zimmerli Art Mus. (formerly University Art Gallery), 1983—. Author: (exhbn. catalogues) The Color Revolution: Color Lithography in France, 1978, The Circle of Toulouse-Lautrec, 1985, The Eiffel Tower a Tour de Force, 1989, From PIssarro to Picasso: Color Etching in France, 1992, The Spitir of Montmartre: Cabarets, Humor and the Avant-garde, 1875-1905, 1996. Mem. Assn. Art Mus. Dirs., Print Coun. Am., le Comité nat. de la gravure française. Home: 151 W 28th St New York NY 10001-6110 Office: Rutgers U Jane Voorhees Zimmerli Mus George & Hamilton Sts New Brunswick NJ 10001

CATE, RODNEY MICHAEL, academic administrator; b. Sudan, Tex., May 9, 1942; s. Tommy A. and Elsie P. (Cherry) C.; m. Patricia Cate, June 11, 1941; children: Brandi, Shani. BS in Pharmacy, U. Tex., 1965; MS in Family Studies, Tex. Tech. U., 1975; PhD in Human Devel. and Family Studies, Pa. State U., 1979. Asst. prof. Tex. Tech. U., Lubbock, 1978-79; asst. prof. Oreg. State U., Corvallis, 1979-83, assoc. prof., 1983-85; prof., dept. chmn. Washington State U., Pullman, 1985-90; assoc. dean Iowa State U., Ames, 1990-94; dir Sch. Family and Consumer Resources U. Ariz., Tucson, 1994—. Co-author: Courtship, 1992; editor: Family and Cons. Rsch. Jour., 1992; contbr. articles to profl. jours. Lt. USN, 1966-69. Mem. Am. Assn. Family and Cons. Scis. Assn. (James D. Moran Meml. Rsch. award 1991), Am. Psychol. Assn., Nat. Coun. on Family Rels., Internat. Soc. for the Study Personal Relationships. Democrat. Office: U Ariz Sch Family and Consumer Resources Bldg 33 Tucson AZ 85721-0033

CATELL, ROBERT BARRY, gas utility executive; b. Bklyn., Feb. 1, 1937; s. Joseph Daniel and Belle (Mishkind) Cicatelli; m. Joan Kathryn Weigand, June 25, 1971; children: Laura Anne, Erica Anne; children by previous marriage: Robert Edward, Carla Ann, Donna Theresa. BME, CCNY, 1958, MME, 1964. Registered profl. engr. Asst. v.p. Bklyn. Union Gas Co., 1974-78, v.p., 1978-82, sr. v.p., 1982-84, exec. v.p., 1984-86, exec. v.p., COO, 1986-90, pres., COO, 1990-91, pres., CEO, 1991-96; chmn., CEO Key Span Energy Corp. (formerly Bklyn. Union Gas Co.), 1996—; trustee Independence Savs. Bank, Bklyn., 1984—, Gas Rsch. Inst., 1992; chmn. adv. com. CCNY, 1986—; regional adv. com. Chase Bank. Bd. dirs. BKlyn. Bur. Comml. Svc., 1988, Bklyn. Botanic Garden, 1989; mem. N.Y. Serda Bd., N.Y.C. Partnership, N.Y. State Bus. Coun., N.Y. Gas Group. Mem. Am. Gas Assn., Soc. Gas Lighting. Avocations: swimming; golf; tennis. Office: Key Span Energy Corp One Metrotech Ctr Brooklyn NY 11201*

CATER, JUDY JERSTAD, librarian; b. San Francisco, Jan. 20, 1951; d. Theodore S. and Estelle E. (Christian) Jerstad; m. Jack E. Cater, Nov. 24, 1973; children: Joanne Jerstad, Jennifer Jerstad. AB, Mount Holyoke Coll., 1973; MS, Simmons Coll., 1974; MA, U. San Diego, 1984. Cert. libr., libr. tech., supr. chief adminstrv. officer. Cataloging libr. Palomar Coll., San Marcos, Calif., 1975-76, fine arts, evening reference libr., 1976-77, acquisitions libr., 1977-86, media svcs., acquisitions libr., 1988-90, chair, v.p. instrn. search, 1987-88, dir. libr. media ctr., 1986-88, 90-92, media svcs. libr., 1993-97, acquisitions libr., 1997—; cons., manuscript asst. Presidio Army Mus., Calif. Hist. Soc., San Francisco, 1974-75; rschr. Charles H. Brown Archaeol. Site, San Diego, 1977; adj. faculty mem. history dept., 1990—. Pres. Mount Holyoke Club of San Diego, 1982-86. Recipient stipend Simmons Coll. Sch. Libr. Sci., 1979, Girl Scouts of San Diego and Imperial Counties Disting. Leader award, 1990, Faculty Svc. award Palomar Coll., 1990, NISOD Excellence award, 1991. Mem. ALA, Calif. Libr. Assn. (sec. treas. 1986, membership chair 1987, minority scholarship com. 1991-93, awards and scholarships com. 1993—), Calif. Tchrs. Assn. (pres. Palomar Coll. chpt. 1979-80), Faculty Assn. Calif. Cmty. Colls., Am. Assn. Women in Cmty. and Jr. Colls. Episcopalian. Avocations: mystery fiction, needlepoint. Office: Palomar Coll Libr 1140 W Mission Rd San Marcos CA 92069-1415

CATES, CORAL J. HANSEN, nurse practitioner, respiratory therapist; b. Seattle, June 5, 1950; d. Raymond Leland and Rosalie (Van Deman) H. Cert. in respiratory therapy, Seattle Cen. Coll., 1975; BS in Nursing summa cum laude, Seattle U., 1987; M in Psychosocial Nursing magna cum laude, U. Wash., 1990. Registered respiratory therapist, Wash.; RN, Wash.; advanced RN practitioner with prescriptive authority; cert. clin. specialist in adult mental health/psychiat. nursing. Respiratory therapist Cura-Care Inc., Modesto, Calif., 1975-84, Northwest Hosp., Seattle, 1984-88; critical care and rehab. nurse University Hosp., Seattle, 1986-87; psychiat. nurse jail psychiat. health Seattle Dept. Pub. Health, 1991; psychiat. nurse Minerth-Meier Psychiat. Unit, Seattle, 1991—; pvt. practice psychotherapy/counseling adult mental health Seattle, 1991-97; nursinghome surveyor, bdg. home licensor, instl. nurse cons. Dept. Aging and Adult Svcs., Washington, 1997—. Contbr. letters to profl. jours. Profl. Nurse Traineeship grantee NIH, 1988-89. Mem. ANA, Assn. Advanced Practice Psychiat. Nurses, DAR, Sigma Theta Tau. Avocations: writing short stories, travel, running, collage. Office: PO Box 75193 Seattle WA 98125-0193

CATES, DENNIS LYNN, education educator; b. Dallas, Nov. 25, 1946; s. Robert N. and Wanda June (Boyd) C.; m. Sue Anne Sadler, Aug. 9, 1975. BA, Tex. Tech U., 1968, MEd, 1976, EdD, 1986; MA, Sul Ross State U., 1981. Cert. secondary edn. tchr., deficient vision, learning disabilities, mental retardation, supervision, mid-mgmt., orientation and mobility instr. Tchr. Eagle Pass (Tex.) Ind. Sch. Dist., Beeville (Tex.) Ind. Sch. Dist., Levelland (Tex.) Ind. Sch. Dist.; tchg. asst. Tex. Tech. U., Lubbock; asst. prof. West Tex. State U., Canyon, 1986-89; asst. prof. U. S.C., Columbia, 1989-95, dir. Ctr. for Excellence in Spl. Edn. Tech., 1992-93; assoc. prof. Cameron U., Lawton, Okla., 1995—; presenter numerous profl. confs.; field reviewer edn. jours. and pubs. Contbr. articles to profl. jours. Sgt. USAF, 1969-73. Consultation Tchrs. grantee, 1981-82. Mem. ASCD, AAUP, Nat. Coun. for Social Studies, Nat. Coun. Geographic Edn., Am. Assn. Mental Retardation, Internat. Assn. Spl. Edn., Am. Ednl. Rsch. Assn., Coun. for Exceptional Children (constn. and elections com. of tchr. edn. divsn., advisor student chpt.), Am. Coun. for Rural Spl. Edn. (bd. dirs.), Assn. Edn. and Rehab. for Blind and Visually Impaired (chairperson 1998—, newsletter editor Divsn. 3), Phi Delta Kappa. E-mail: dennisc@cameron.edu. Office: Cameron U Dept Edn Lawton OK 73505

CATES, GILBERT, film, theater, television producer and director; b. N.Y.C., June 6, 1934; s. Nathan and Nina (Peltzman) Katz; m. Jane Betty Dubin, Feb. 9, 1957 (div.); children: Melissa Beth, Jonathan Michael, David Sawyer, Gilbert Lewis; m. Judith Reichman, Jan. 25, 1987; stepchildren: Ronit Reichman, Anat Reichman. BS, Syracuse U., 1955, MA, 1965. Dean, prof. theatre, film and TV UCLA, 1990—; with Cates-Doty Prodns., Inc.; artistic dir. Gefen Playhouse, L.A., 1995—; com. mem. 1 drama dept. Syracuse U., 1969-73. TV prodr., dir. Haggis Baggis, 1959, Camouflage, 1961-62, Internat. Showtime, 1962-64, Hootenanny, 1962, To All My Friends on Shore, 1972, The Affair, 1974, After the Fall, 1974, Johnny, We Hardly Knew Ye, 1977, The Kid From Nowhere, 1982, Country Gold, 1982, Faerie Tale Theatre, 1982, Hobson's Choice, 1983, Consenting Adult, 1984, Child's Cry?, 1986, Fatal Judgement, 1988, One More Time, 1988, Muffin Man, 1989, Call Me Anna, 1990, Absolute Strangers, 1991, Overruled, 1992, Confessions-Two Faces of Evil, 1994, Innocent Victims, 1995; film prodr., dir.: The Painting, 1962, Rings Aroung the World, 1967, I Never Sang for My Father, 1970, Summer Wishes, Winter Dreams, 1973, Dragonfly, 1976, The Promise, 1978, The Last Married Couple in America, 1979, O God, Book II, 1980, Backfire, 1986; theatrical prodr.: You Know I Can't Hear You When the Water's Running, 1967, I Never Sang for My Father, 1968, The Chinese and Doctor Fish, 1970, Solitaire-Double Solitaire, 1971; dir.: Voices, 1972, Tricks of the Trade, 1980; prodr.: Ann. Acad. Awards, 1990-1995, 1997-99, To Life, America Celebrates Israel's 50th (CBS-TV), 1998, America Celebrates Ford's Theater (ABC-TV), 1999. Bd. dirs. Israeli Cancer Rsch. Fund, 1992-94. Recipient Best Short Film award Internat. Film Importers and Distbrs., 1962, Chancellor'smedal Syracuse U., 1974, Emmy award, 1991, Star on Hollywood Walk of Fame, 1994, Jimmy Doolittle award L.A. Theater, 1998, Lifetime Dirs. Achievement award Caucus of Prodrs., Writers and Dirs., 1998. Mem. Dirs. Guild Am. (hon. life award 1990, v.p. Ea. region 1965, Western region 1980—, pres. 1983-87, Robert B. Aldrich award 1989, nat. sec.-tras. 1997—), Acad. Motion Picture Arts and Scis. (bd. govs., chmn. bd. dirs. 1985-94), Women in Film (bd. dirs. 1993-94), League N.Y. Theatres, Friars Club (gov. 1980—). Office: 10920 Wilshire Blvd Ste 820 Los Angeles CA 90024-6510 *Craft is freedom.*

CATES, JO ANN, library administrator, writer; b. Ft. Worth, June 25, 1958; d. Charles Kimbrough and Lydia Joe (Sachse) C.; m. Joseph Daniel Frank, Oct. 28, 1989 (div.); children: Jacob Abraham Frank, Dec. 9, 1993, Mabel Rose Frank, Sept. 2, 1996. BS in Journalism, Boston U., 1980; MLS, Simmons Coll., 1984. Advt. asst. Boston Phoenix, 1978-79; med. serials asst. Mass. Gen. Hosp., Boston, 1979-80; editorial asst. Exceptional Parent Mag., Boston, 1980-81; libr. reference asst. Lesley Coll., Cambridge, Mass., 1981-84; head reference libr. Lamont Libr., Harvard U., Cambridge, Mass., 1984-85; chief libr. Poynter Inst. for Media Studies, St. Petersburg, Fla., 1985-91; head transp. libr. Northwestern U., Evanston, Ill., 1991-94; regional rsch. mgr. Ctr. for Bus. Knowledge Ernst & Young, 1997—; tchr. News Libr. and Newsroom Seminars Poynter Inst., 1990-91; mem. Harvard Com. on Instrn. Libr. Use, 1984, mem. adv. com. on book and serial budgets, 1991-94; cons. journalism orgns. Calif., Fla., Mass., 1984—; book reviewer Libr. Jour., Choice, 1985—, Am. Reference Book Annual, 1993—; knowledge mgmt. column editor B&F Divsn. Bull., 1999—. Author: Journalism: A Guide to the Reference Literature, 1990, 2d edit., 1997; editor Transp. Divsn. Bull., 1992-94; mem. editorial bd. Footnotes, 1991-94; contbr. articles to profl. jours. Mem. Transp. Rsch. Bd. Info. Svcs. Com., 1991-94; media intern Dem. Nat. Com., Boston, 1979-80. Scholar Women in Comm., 1976-78; Trustee scholar Boston U., 1978-80; Simmons Coll. grantee, 1982-84. Mem. Spl. Librs. Assn., Assn. for Edn. in Journalism and Mass Comm., Suncoast Info. Specialists (pres. 1990-91). Avocations: gourmet cooking, collecting books. Home: 1514 Central St Evanston IL 60201-1631

CATES, NELIA BARLETTA DE, diplomat of Dominican Republic; b. Santo Domingo, Dominican Republic, Dec. 21, 1932; d. Amadeo and Nelia (Ricart) Barletta; m. Miguel Morales Abreu, Oct. 29, 1953 (div. 1961); m. John Martin Cates, Nov. 19, 1976. Ed. in Argentina, Cuba and U.S.A.; diploma Duchesne Coll., 1950. Cultural attache Embassy of Dominican Republic, London, 1975-85, amb., permanent rep. to Internat. Maritime Orgn., 1985-94; pres. Compaña Editorial El Mundo S.A., La Habana, Cuba, 1994—. Mem. Maritime Orgn., 1985-86. Address: Erik Leonard Ekman 67, Arroyo Hondo Zona 5, Santo Domingo Dominican Republic also: EPS # P 7397 PO Box 02-5261 Miami FL 33102-5261

CATES, PHOEBE, actress; b. 1964; m. Kevin Kline, Mar. 5, 1989; 2 children: Owen, Greta. Actress: (feature films) Paradise, 1982, Fast Times at Ridgemont High, 1982, Private School, 1983, Gremlins, 1984, Date With An Angel, 1987, Shag: The Movie, 1988, Bright Lights, Big City, 1988, Heart Of Dixie, 1989, Gremlins II: The New Batch, 1990, I Love You to Death, 1990, Drop Dead Fred, 1991, My Life's in Turnaround, 1993, Bodies, Rest & Motion, 1993, Princess Caraboo, 1994, (TV mini-series) Lace, 1984, Lace 2, 1985, (TV movies) Baby Sister, 1983, (stage prodn.) The Nest of the Wood Grouse, N.Y. Shakespeare Festival, 1984. Sch. Am. Ballet scholar.

CATES, SUE SADLER, educational diagnostician; b. Ft. Worth, Aug. 7, 1947; d. Mary Jo (Merkt) Sadler; m. Dennis Lynn Cates, Aug. 9, 1975. BA, Baylor U., 1970; MEd, Sul Ross State U., 1977. Cert. tchr., counselor, ednl. diagnostician, Tex. Tchr. spl. edn. Eagle Pass (Tex.) Ind. Sch. Dist., 1974-76, Beeville (Tex.) Ind. Sch. Dist., 1976-80; supr., ednl. diagnostician Sinton (Tex.) Ind. Sch. Dist., 1980-81; counselor, diagnostician Snyder (Tex.) Ind. Sch. Dist., 1981-86; ednl. diagnostician Pampa (Tex.) Ind. Sch. Dist., 1987-89; elem. counselor Richland County Sch. Dist., Columbia, S.C., 1989-95; ednl. diagnostician Wichita Falls (Tex.) Ind. Sch. Dist., 1995-97, Graham (Tex.) Ind. Sch. Dist., 1997-98, Carrollton-Farmers Branch (Tex.) Ind. Sch. Dist., 1998—. Bd. dirs. Scurry County Sheltered Workshop, 1981-85, Tex. Assn. Children with Learning Disabilities, 1976-77, 81-83; coach Tex. Spl. Olympics, Beeville, and Sinton, 1978-81; mem. sanctuary choir Floral Heights United Meth. Ch., Wichita Falls, 1995—, Stephen min., 1992—; tchr. Sunday sch., youth coordinator, various other positions. Mem. Tex. Ednl. Diagnosticians' Assn., Council Exceptional Children, Council Ednl. Diagnosticians, Assn. Supervision and Devel., Nat. Assn. Workshop Dirs., NEA, Tex. State Tchrs. Assn., Tex. Classroom Tchrs. Assn., Am. Assn. Counseling and Devel., Tex. Assn. Counseling and Devel., Tex. Ednl. Diagnosticians Assn., AAUW, Phi Delta Kappa, Zeta Phi Eta. Democrat. Avocations: swimming, coin collecting, travel, singing, jewelry. Home: 4402 York St Wichita Falls TX 76309-4014

CATHCART, DAVID ARTHUR, lawyer; b. Pasadena, Calif., June 1, 1940; s. Arthur James and Martelle (Leeper) C.; m. Janet Eileen Farley, June 19, 1973; children: Sarah Emily, Rebecca Eileen. BA with gt. distinction, Stanford U., 1961; MA, Harvard U., 1966, LLB cum laude, 1967. Bar: Calif. 1968, U.S. Dist. Ct. (cen. dist.) Calif. 1969, U.S. Dist. Ct. (so., no. dists.) 1975, U.S. Dist. Ct. (ea. dist.) 1979, U.S. Ct. Appeals (9th cir.) 1975, U.S. Supreme Ct. 1979. Assoc. Gibson, Dunn & Crutcher, L.A., 1968-70, 72-75, ptnr., 1975—; legis. asst. U.S. Senate, Washington, 1971-72; mem. NLRB Adv. Com., 1994—. Editor-in-chief: Employment Discrimination Law Five-Year Cumulative Supplement, 1989, Employment-At-Will: A 1989 State-By-State Survey, 1990; contbr. chpts. to legal texts, articles to profl. jours. Bd. dirs. Western Ctr. on Law and Poverty, L.A., 1985-88, U.S.-S. Africa Leadership Devel. Program, 1992—, Ninth Judicial Circuit Hist. Soc., 1992—, mem. Andover Devel. Bd., 1995—. Woodrow Wilson fellow, 1961-62, Danforth fellow, 1961-64. Fellow Coll. of Labor and Employment Lawyers; mem. ABA (mem. coun. 1997—, mgmt. co-chair equal employment opportunity law com., 1994-96, sect. of labor and employment law, co-chair employment and labor rels. law com., 1985-88, litigation sect.), L.A. County Bar Assn. (chair labor & employment law sect. 1991-92), Am. Employment Law Coun. (chair 1993—), Internat. Bar Assn. (vice-chmn. labor com., bus. law sect. 1987-90, U.S. country rep. 1989-93), Chancery Club, City Club on Bunker Hill, Harvard Club N.Y.C., Phi Beta Kappa. Office: Gibson Dunn & Crutcher 333 S Grand Ave Los Angeles CA 90071-3197

CATHCART, HAROLD ROBERT, hospital administrator; b. Odebolt, Iowa, Mar. 9, 1924; s. Catham S. and Martha M. (Wells) C.; m. Tressa Bolt, July 20, 1951; 1 child, Tressa Ann. Student, Drake U., 1941-43; B.A., State U. Iowa, 1947; D.H.A., U. Toronto, Can., 1948. Fellow W.K. Kellogg Found., 1948-49; mem. staff Pa. Hosp., Phila., 1949-91; v.p. Pa. Hosp., 1960-70, pres., 1970-91; cons. Lomax Health Sys., Chalfort, Pa.; bd. dirs Haelan Health Corp., Houston; bd. trustees Waverly Heights Ltd., Gladwyne, Pa.; adj. prof. health care sys. Associated Faculty of U. Pa.; Hunter Group, Health Learning Sys., Witikar Saudi Arabia Ltd.; mem. U. Pa. Leonard Davis Inst. Adv. Coun.; mem. adv. com. Nat. Health Care Mgmt. Ctr., U. Pa. Bd. dirs. Am. Medico-Legal Found. Served with U.S. Army, 1943-46. Recipient Health Care award B'nai B'rith, 1988. Mem. Am. Hosp. Assn. (chmn. council of nursing 1967-68, council on manpower and edn. 1969-71, trustee 1972-74, chmn. bd. trustees 1976, speaker ho. dels. 1977, Disting. Service award medal 1983), Am. Coll. Health care Execs. (Gold medal 1986), Hosp. Assn. Pa. (pres. 1967-68, Disting. Service award 1977), Delaware Valley Hosp. Council, Greater Phila. Partnership. Fax: 215-893-4714. Home: 1400 Waverly Rd Villa 62 Gladwyne PA 19035-1296

CATHCART, LINDA, art historian. BA in Fine Arts, Calif. State U., Fullerton, 1969; MA in Art History, Hunter Coll., CUNY, 1972. Fulbright fellow Courtauld Art Inst., 1973-74; curator Albright-Knox Art Gallery, Buffalo, 1975-79; dir. Contemporary Arts Mus., Houston, 1979-87; prin. Linda Cathcart Gallery; organizer exhbns. in field, 1989-95; prof. art history UCLA, 1996, U. Tex., Austin, 1997. Office: 829 Hot Springs Rd Santa Barbara CA 93108-1108

CATHCART, ROBERT STEPHEN, mass media consultant; b. Los Angeles, Jan. 30, 1923; s. Stephen Joseph and Martha (Morley) C.; m. Dolores June Hawley, July 1, 1944; children: Linda L., Stephen P. A.B., U. Redlands, 1944, M.A., 1947; Ph.D., Northwestern U., 1953. Teaching fellow U. Redlands, 1946-47; instr. Purdue U., 1947-49; teaching fellow Northwestern U., 1949-51; instr. U. Md., 1953-55; prof. rhetorical theory Calif. State U. at Los Angeles, 1955-68; chmn. dept. communication Queens Coll., 1968-72; prof. communication theory, 1972-88; prof. emeritus Queens Coll., 1988—; cons. USN Officer Tng. Corps, U.S. Army Ordnance Ctr., Carnation Co.; mem. Pres.'s Adv. Commn. of Scholars, 1967; sr. visitor in philosophy Oxford (Eng.) U., 1966; vis. prof. Sophia U., Tokyo, 1974, U. Oreg., 1986, 89. Author: (with M. Laser and F. Marcus) Ideas and Issues, 1963, (with J. Dahl and Laser) Student, School and Society, 1964, Post Communication, 1966, rev. edit., 1983, (with L. Samovar) Small Group Communication, 1970, rev. edit., 1995, (with G. Gumpert) Inter/Media-Interpersonal Communication in a Media World, 1979, rev. edit., 1988, Television Stereotypes of Three Nations: France, U.S. and Japan, 1988, (with Susan Drucker) American Heroes in a Media Age, 1994. Lt. USNR, 1943-46, 51-53. Fax: 805-565-0357. Home: 829 Hot Springs Rd Montecito CA 93108-1108 Office: Queens Coll Flushing NY 11367

CATHER, PHYLLIS BAKER, pediatrics nurse; b. Bubbling Springs, W.Va., Aug. 7, 1936; d. Burzie Carmelias Sr. and Daisy Violet (Rowland) Baker; m. George William Cather Sr., Apr. 23, 1960; children: George William Cather, Jr., Natalie Jo Cather Miller, Marietta Dale Cather Walls, Edwin Baker Cather, Brian Lee Cather. Nursing diploma, Winchester (Va.) Meml. Hosp., 1957; BSN, Richmond (Va.) Profl. Inst., 1960. RN, Va.; cert. pediatric nurse, PALS. RN Stuart Circle Hosp., Richmond, 1957-58; pediatric RN Med. Coll. Va., Richmond, 1958-60; pediatric and nursery RN Winchester Meml. Hosp., 1960-79, 84-89; vol. sch. RN Winchester Meml. Hosp., Frederick County, 1973-84; pediatric RN Winchester Med. Ctr., 1990-98. Mem. Soc. Pediatric Nurses.

CATHEY, WADE THOMAS, electrical engineering educator; b. Greer, S.C., Nov. 26, 1937; s. Wade Thomas Sr. and Ruby Evelyn (Waters) C.; children: Susan Elaine, Cheryl Ann. BS, U. S.C., 1959, MS, 1961; PhD, Yale U., 1963. Group scientist Rockwell Internat., Anaheim, Calif., 1962-68; from assoc. prof. to prof. elec. engring. U. Colo., Denver, 1968-85, chmn. dept. elec. engring. and computer sci., 1984-85, chmn. faculty senate, 1982-83; prof. U. Colo., Boulder, 1985-97, rsch. prof., 1997—; pres. CDM Optics, 1996—; dir. NSF Ctr. Optoelectronic Computing Sys., Boulder, 1987-93; cons. in field, 1968—. Author: Optical Information Processing and Holography, 1978; contbr. articles to profl. jours.; inventor in field. Fellow

Croft, U. Colo., 1982, Faculty, U. Colo., 1972-73. Fellow IEEE, Optical Soc. Am. (topical editor 1977-79, 87-90), Soc. Photo-Optic Instrumentation Engrs. Achievements include extend focal depth and passive ranging in imaging systems, rsch. on matching image acquisiton and signal processing systems. Home: 228 Alpine Way Boulder CO 80304-0406 Office: U Colo Dept Elec Engring Boulder CO 80309

CATHOU, RENATA EGONE, chemist, consultant; b. Milan, Italy, June 21, 1935; d. Egon and Stella Mary Egone; m. Pierre-Yves Cathou, June 21, 1959. BS, MIT, 1957, PhD, 1963. Fellow, rsch. assoc. in chemistry MIT, Cambridge, 1962-65; rsch. assoc. Harvard U. Med. Sch., Cambridge, 1965-69, instr., 1969-70; rsch. assoc. Mass. Gen. Hosp., 1965-69, instr., 1969-70; asst. prof. dept. biochemistry Sch. Medicine, Tufts U., 1970-73, assoc. prof., 1973-78, prof., 1978-81; pres. Tech. Evaluations, Lexington, Mass., 1983—; sr. cons. SRC Assocs., Park Ridge, N.J., 1984-93; sr. investigator Arthritis Found., 1970-75; vis. prof. dept. chemistry UCLA, 1976-77; mem. adv. panel NSF, 1974-75; mem. bd. sci. counselors Nat. Cancer Inst., 1979-83; ind. cons. and writer. Mem. editl. bd. Immunochemistry, 1972-75; contbr. chpts. to books and articles to profl. jours. MIT Company Founders citation, 1989; NIH predoctoral fellow, 1958-62; grantee Am. Heart Assn., 1969-81, USPHS, 1970-81. Mem. AAAS, Am. Soc. for Biochemistry and Molecular Biology, Am. Assn. Immunologists, U.S. Power Squadron (past dist. lt. comdr.), Charles River Squadron (past comdr.). Avocations: photography, opera, fine arts. Office: Tech Evaluations PO Box 23 Lexington MA 02420-0001

CATINELLA, FRANK PETER, cardiovascular and thoracic surgeon; b. Nov. 25, 1952. MD, NYU, 1978. Staff surgeon dept. cardiovasc. surgery North Ridge Med. Ctr., Ft. Lauderdale, Fla., 1988—, dir. cardiovasc. surgery, 1994—. Office: 5609 N Dixie Hwy Ste 209 Fort Lauderdale FL 33334-4145

CATLETT, D. MARK, federal official; b. Martinsburg, W.Va., Apr. 22, 1952; s. Lyle S. and Marilyn D. (Sensel) C.; m. Sally A. Snapp, Aug. 3, 1974; children: A. Marisa, M. Ryan. BS in Polit. Sci. magna cum laude, W.Va. U., 1974, MPA, 1976. Budget analyst Dept. Vets. Affairs, Washington, 1976-81, divsn. chief, 1981-84, sect. chief, 1984-86, dep. dir. budget svc., 1986-88, acting dir., 1988-89, dep. asst. sec. budget, 1989-93, asst. sec. fin. and info. resources mgmt., 1993-95, asst. sec. mgmt., 1995-98, dep. asst. sec. budget, 1998—. Mem. Phi Beta Kappa. Presbyterian. Avocations: tennis, civil war history. Office: Department of Veterans Affairs Office of Mgmt 810 Vermont Ave NW Washington DC 20420-5289*

CATLETT, GEORGE ROUDEBUSH, accountant; b. Fairmount, Ill., Aug. 14, 1917; s. Shirley Tilton and Effie (Wehrman) C.; m. Martha Jane Beamsley, May 27, 1944; children—Stanley, Steven, Lawrence, David. B.S., U. Ill., 1939, M.S., 1940. C.P.A., Ill., other states. With Arthur Andersen & Co., Chgo., 1940-80; ptnr. Arthur Andersen & Co., 1952-75, sr. ptnr.er, 1975-80; cons. to govt. Contbr. articles to profl. jours. Pres. bd. dirs. U. Ill. Athletic Assn., 1964-65. Served to maj. AUS, 1942-46. Mem. Am. Inst. C.P.A.'s (council 1964-70, 76-79, v.p., dir. 1976-77), Ill. Soc. C.P.A.'s (pres. 1966-67), Am. Accounting Assn., Nat. Assn. Accountants, U. Ill. Alumni Assn. (dir. 1959-65), Univ. Club (Chgo.), Westmoreland Country Club (Wilmette, Ill.), Beta Theta Pi, Beta Gamma Sigma. Methodist. Home: One Arbor Ln # 104 Evanston IL 60201-1918

CATLETT, RICHARD H., JR., retired lawyer; b. Boston, May 1, 1921; s. Richard Henry and Martha Barton (Taylor) C.; m. Marion Frances Buckey, Apr. 3, 1948 (dec. Sept. 1967); children—Ross C. Rose, Richard H. III, Thomas Y., Maria C. Eldredge; m. 2d, Barbara Ann L'Orange, May 1, 1969. B.S. in Elec. Engring., Va. Mil. Inst., 1943; LL.B., U. Richmond, 1952. Engr. C&P Telephone Co., Richmond, Va., 1946-47, Catlett-Johnson Corp., Richmond, Va., 1947-50; assoc., ptnr. Christian & Barton, Richmond, Va., 1952-76; ptnr. McGuire, Woods, Battle, & Boothe, Richmond, Va., 1976-91, ret., 1991; bd. dirs. James River Corp. (now Ft. James Corp), Richmond, gen. counsel and sec., 1969-90; gen. counsel Signet Banking Corp., Richmond, 1985-89; adj. asst. prof. law U. Richmond, 1990-93. Chmn. City of Richmond Personnel Bd., 1971-80; mem. vestry St. James Episc. Ch., Richmond, 1954-75; dir. Westminster-Canterbury House, Richmond, 1985-89, chmn., 1987-89. 1st lt. U.S. Army, 1943-46, ETO. Mem. ABA, Va. State Bar (chmn. bus. law sect. 1971-72), Va. State Bar Assn. (chmn. bus. law sect. 1972-73). Clubs: Country of Va. (dir. 1966-69, 71-74), Commonwealth (Richmond). Home: 11 Robin Rd Richmond VA 23226-3205*

CATLEY-CARLSON, MARGARET, professional organization administrator; b. Nelson, B.C., Oct. 6, 1942; d. George Lorne and Helen Margaret (Hughes) Catley; m. Stanley F. Carlson, Oct. 30, 1970. BA with honors, U. B.C., 1966; postgrad., Inst. Internat. Relations, U. W.I., St. Augustine, Trinidad and Tobago, 1970; LLD (hon.), U. Regina, 1985; LittD (hon.), St. Mary's U., 1985; Fellow, Ryerson Poly. Inst. Concordia U., 1986, Mt. St. Vincent U., 1990. Joined Dept. External Affairs, Can., 1966; second sec. Can. High Commn., Colombo, Sri Lanka, 1968; with aid and devel. div. Dept. External Affairs, 1970-74; econ. counsellor Can. High Commn., London, 1975-77; v.p. Can. Internat. Devel. Agy., 1978, sr. v.p., acting pres., 1979-80; asst. under-sec. Dept. External Affairs, 1981-82; asst. sec. gen. UN; dep. exec. dir. ops. UNICEF, 1981-83; pres. Can. Internat. Devel. Agy., 1983-89; dep. minister Health and Welfare Country of Canada, 1989-92; pres. The Population Coun., N.Y.C., 1993—. Office: 1790 Broadway Suite 800 HRA New York NY 10019

CATLIN, AVERY, engineering and computer science educator, writer; b. N.Y.C., Jan. 29, 1924; s. Randolph and Hannah (White) C.; m. Edith J. Reed, Sept. 7, 1946; children: Avery W., Edith R., Beverly L., Frederic F. B.E.E., U. Va., 1947, M.A., 1949, Ph.D., 1960. Assoc. prof. elec. engring. and materials sci. U. Va., 1960-67, prof., 1967-82, univ. prof. computer sci., 1982-94, assoc. dean engring., 1967-74, exec. v.p., 1974-82, prof. emeritus, 1994—. Office: U Va Thornton Hall Charlottesville VA 22903-2442

CATLIN, FRANCIS IRVING, physician; b. Hartford, Conn., Dec. 6, 1925; s. Robert Irving and Frances Rose (Maleski) C.; m. Rebecca Vaughan Graham, June 11, 1948; children: Robert, Andrew, Martha. AA, Princeton U., 1949; MD, Johns Hopkins U., 1948, DSc, 1959. Diplomate: Am. Bd. Otolaryngology. Intern Union Meml. Hosp., Balt., 1948-49; resident in otolaryngology Johns Hopkins Hosp., Balt., 1950, 52-54; from instr. to assoc. prof. Johns Hopkins U. Med. Sch., Balt., 1956-72; prof. otorhinolaryngology and communicative scis. Baylor U. Med. Sch., Houston, 1972-91, prof. emeritus, 1991—; chief otolaryngology svc. Tex. Children's Hosp., 1972-91, emeritus staff, 1991—, mem. credentials com., 1989—. Contbr. articles to med. jours. Capt. M.C. USAF, 1950-52. Fellow Am. Otol. Soc.; mem. AMA, ASTM (F29 com. on anesthesia and respiratory equipment 1989—)Tex. Med. Soc., Am. Acad. Otolaryngology, Am. Coun. Otolaryngology, Am. Laryngological, Rhinological and Otol. Soc., Am. Speech and Hearing Assn. (life). Republican. Episcopalian. Home: 13307 Queensbury Ln Houston TX 77079-6013

CATOE, BETTE LORRINA, physician, health educator; b. Apr. 7, 1926; d. John Booker and Laura Beola (Adams) C.; m. Warren J. Strudwick, Sept. 17, 1949; children: Laura Christina, Warren J., William J. BS cum laude, Howard U., 1948, MD, 1951. Intern Freedmen's Hosp., Washington, 1951-52; pediat. resident Howard U./Freedman's Hosp., 1952-55; practice medicine specializing in pediatrics Howard U./Freedman's Hosp., Washington, 1956—; instr. bacteriology Howard U., 1955-57; mem. staff Providence Hosp., Columbia Hosp., Howard U. Hosp., Wash., Hosp. Ctr.; sch. health officer Dept. Health, Washington, 1960-64; clin. instr. Howard U., 1956-58; mem. D.C. Health Planning Adv. Coun., 1967-77, chmn. 1973-77; chmn. D.C. Devel. Disabilities Adv. Coun., 1970-74; mem. D.C. Mayor's Commn. on Food and Nutrition, 1971-72, Mayor's Commn. on Maternal and Child Health, 1978-84, appt. vice chmn. Pub. Benefit Corp., 1997; mem. D.C. Commn. Jud. Tenure and Disabilities, 1977—, chmn. Bd. Public Benefit Corp. of D.C., 1998—; bd. govs. St. Alban's Sch., 1978-84; bd. dirs. D.C. Health and Welfare Coun., 1968-73, pres., 1973-74; del. Democratic Nat. Conv., 1976; bd. dirs. Met. Washington Health and Welfare Coun., 1970-72, Parent Coun. of Washington, 1974-75, Met. Med. Founds., Inc., Silver Spring YMCA, 1977-80, Kingsburg Ctr., 1997—; mem. Mayor's Health Policy Coun.; chair emergency medicine com. Mem. AMA, D.C. Chirurg. Soc., D.C. Med. Soc. (bd. trustees 1996—), Nat. Med. Assn. (chmn. pediat. sect. 1981-83), Am. Med. Women's Assn., NAACP, Urban League, Assn. Comprehensive Health Planners (dir. 1975-77), Women's Aux. Medico-Chirurg. Soc., Jack and Jill Am., Century Club of Nat. Assn. negro Bus. and Profl. Women's Clubs (pres. 1985-89), Alpha Kappa Alpha, Links Club, Carrousels Club (nat. v.p. 1986-88, nat. pres. 1988-90), Women's Nat. Dem. Home: 1748 Sycamore St NW Washington DC 20012-1031 Office: 5505 5th St NW Washington DC 20011-6513

CATOE, PAUL, cultural organization administrator; b. Columbia, S.C.. Meteorologist WFLA-TV, Tampa, Fla., sta. mgr., gen. mgr., 1999; pres. Tampa Hillsborough Conv. & Vis. Assn., 1999—. Office: Tampa Hillsborough Conv & Vis Assn 400 N Tampa St Ste 1010 Tampa FL 33602*

CATOE, WILLIAM M., JR., federal judge; b. 1944. BS, The Citadel, 1966; JD, U. S.C., 1969. Bar: S.C. Law clk. to Hon. J. Robert Martin, Jr., U.S. Dist. Ct. for Dist. S.C., 1971-73; magistrate judge for S.C., U.S. Magistrate Ct., Greenville, 1978—; county atty. Lancaster County, S.C.; asst. solicitor 5th Jud. Circuit, S.C. Capt. U.S. Army. Office: 300 E Washington St Greenville SC 29601-2800

CATOLINE-ACKERMAN, PAULINE DESSIE, small business owner; b. Ft. Worth, Dec. 17, 1937; d. Byron Hillis and Dessie Elizabeth (Plumlee) Doggett; children: Sherry Lou, Brenda Lynn; m. Donald Ralph Ackerman, Feb. 19, 1993. BA in Bus. Mgmt. (labor rels. specialty), Hiram Coll., 1989. Notary public, Ohio. Sec. Gen. Am. Life Ins. Co., Ft. Worth, 1956-57, Kelly Girl Svcs., Youngstown, Ohio, 1965-69; legal sec. Burgstaller, Schwartz & Moore, Youngstown, 1962-65, Green, Schiavoni, Murphy & Haines, Youngstown, 1969-71, Flask & Policy, Youngstown, 1971-83; sec. Western Res. Care System, Youngstown, 1983-87, exec. sec., 1987-90; owner, mgr. Pauline's Place, Youngstown, 1993—; legal sec. Henderson, Covington, Stein, Donchess & Messenger Law Firm, 1993-94; exec. adminstrv. asst. to pres. CEO, sr. v.p. Internat. Renaissance Developers, Youngstown, 1994-96; owner Pauline's Place, 1996—; adminstrv. asst. to v.p. and client svc. mgr. Bank One Investment Mgmt. & Trust Group, Youngstown, 1996—. Pres. PTA, Cottage Hills, Ill., 1968-69, brownie and scout leader, 1968-69. Mem. Mahoning County Legal Secs. Assn. (v.p. 1973-74, editor monthly booklet 1974-75), Exec. Link, Missionary Group Club. Democrat. Methodist. Avocations: oil painting, reading poetry, tennis, swimming, horseback riding. Home: 3961 Cannon Rd Youngstown OH 44515-4604 also: Bank One Invst Mgmt Group 6 Federal Plz W Youngstown OH 44503-1410

CATON, TIMOTHY CHARLES, marketing professional; b. Lawrence, Mass., Sept. 30, 1976; s. Frederick Charles and Pamela Marie (Smith) C. BA in Polit. Sci. and Lit., Am. U., Washington, 1997. Staff writer Washington (D.C.) Inquirer, 1994-95, comm. dir., 1997; systems mgr. Office U.S. Rep. Tom Latham, Washington, 1995-97; project devel. coord. Integrated Food Tech.s Corp., Emmaus, Pa., 1998—. Mem. Congl. Staff Club, U.S. House Legis. Assts. Assn., Pi Sigma Alpha. Roman Catholic. Avocations: reading, traveling, the Internet, environmental issues. E-mail: tcaton@usa.net. Home: 4982 Wendi Dr W Zionsville PA 18092-2056 Office: Integrated Food Techs Corp PO Box 363 Emmaus PA 18049-0363

CATON-JONES, MICHAEL, film director; b. Broxburn, Scotland. Dir. (films) Scandal, 1989, Memphis Belle, 1990, Doc Hollywood, 1991, This Boy's Life, 1993, Rob Roy. Office: Creative Artists Agency 9830 Wilshire Blvd Beverly Hills CA 90212-1825*

CATRAMBONE, EUGENE DOMINIC, magazine editor; b. Chgo., June 5, 1926; s. Nicola and Maria Theresa (Catrambone) C.; m. Mary Gloria Gaimari, Mar. 26, 1951; children: Mary, Eugene Jr., Jane, David, Jill. BA, St. Benedict Coll., 1950; postgrad., Kans. State U., 1952-54; MA, DePaul U., 1960; postgrad., UCLA, 1962-63. Cert. secondary tchr., coll. instr., Calif. Tchr. high schs. Chgo., 1950-62, L.A., 1963-88; mng. editor Internat. Film Festival Mag.; tech. writer U. Chgo., 1956-59, Douglas Missile div. USN, L.A. and Ventura, Calif., 1962-75; reporter, editor Las Virgenes Enterprise, Calabasas, Calif., 1968-75; evening instr. L.A. City Coll., 1965-68. Author: Requiem for a Nobody, 1993, The Golden Touch: Frankie Carle, 1981; poems "Exit dust", 1982, "Tender Moments", 1996, "The Portrait", 1997; contbr. articles on edn. to profl. publs., 1959-60, feature stories to local newspapers, 1968-75. Sgt. U.S. Army, 1944-46. Recipient Fostering Excellence award L.A. Unified Sch. Dist., 1986-87, nominee Apple award, 1986. Mem. NEA (life), VFW, Ret. Tchrs. L.A., United Tchrs. L.A., Am. Legion, Westlake Village Men's Golf Club (pub. rels. editor 1986—, bd. dirs., pres. 1989—). Democrat. Roman Catholic. Avocations: coins, World War II history, golf, poetry. Home: 31802 Tynebourne Ct Westlake Village CA 91361 Office: Golden Touch Assocs 31802 Tynebourne Ct Westlake Village CA 91361

CATRAMBONE, KATHY, journalist; b. Chgo., Mar. 21, 1951; d. Joseph Benedict and Marian (Danza) C. BS in Journalism, No. Ill. U., 1973. Reporter Chronicle Pub., St. Charles, Ill., 1973-75; reporter, editor Pioneer Press, Oak Park, Ill., 1975-86, editor, exec. editor, 1988-91; freelancer, 1986-88, 94-95; editor-in-chief Press Publ., Elmhurst, Ill., 1991-94; editor Crain Comm., Chgo., 1995-98; editor/bureau chief Pioneer Press, 1998—; adj. prof. Medill Sch. Journalism Northwestern U., 1994-95, Columbia Coll., 1995. Founding editor Pioneer Press publ. Forest Park News; founding editor LaGrange Press, Bartlett Press, Countryside Press. Bd. dirs. Hubbard St. Dance Chgo., 1982—; organizer, fundraiser Catrambone Family Meml. Park, Chgo., 1997. Recipient Journalist of Yr. award Suburban Press Club, 1985, Best Interpretative or Investigative Series award Suburban Newspapers Am., 1985, various writing and editing awards Ill. Press Assn., 1977-95; named Disting. Almuna Mother Guerin H.S., 1987. Mem. Assn. Women Journalist (bd. dirs. 1994), Soc. Profl. Journalists, Chgo. Headline Club (bd. dirs. 1992-98), Tri-Taylor Hist. Dist. Assn. (vice-chmn. 1997). Avocations: dancing, traveling, Italian cooking, bicycle riding. Office: Pioneer Press 291 N Dunton Arlington Heights IL 60004

CATSIMATIDIS, JOHN ANDREAS, retail chain executive, airline executive; b. Nissiros, Greece, Sept. 7, 1948; came to U.S., 1949, naturalized, 1950; s. Andreas John and Despina (Emmanulides) C. BS in Engring., NYU, 1970. Chmn., chief exec. officer Red Apple Cos. (Gristedes, Red Apple stores), N.Y.C. and Ft. Lauderdale, Fla., 1970—, United Refining Inc., Warren, Pa., 1986-94; chmn., CEO Sloan's Supermarket, N.Y.C. Recipient Humanitarian award NCCJ, 1978, Am. Jewish Com., 1982, Nat. Kidney Assn., 1986; Entrepreneurship award NYU Bus. Sch., 1987. Mem. Westside C. of C. (vice chmn. 1975—). Clubs: New York Univ., Wings, Young Men Philanthrapic League, N.Y. Athletic. Office: Red Apple Group 823 11th Ave New York NY 10019-3557

CATTANEO, JACQUELYN ANNETTE KAMMERER, artist, educator; b. Gallup, N.Mex., June 1, 1944; d. Ralph John and Gladys Agnes (O'Sullivan) Kammer; m. John Leo Cattaneo, Apr. 25, 1964; children: John Auro, Paul Anthony. Student Tex. Woman's U., 1962-64. Portrait artist, tchr. Gallup, N. Mex., 1972; coord. Works Progress Adminstrn. art project renovation McKinley County, Gallup, Octavia Fellin Performing Arts wing dedication, Gallup Pub. Library; formation com. mem. Multi-modal/Multi-Cultural Ctr. for Gallup, N.Mex.; exch. with Soviet Women's Com., USSR Women Artists del., Moscow, Kiev, Leningrad, 1990; Women Artists del. and exch. Jerusalem, Tel Aviv, Cairo, Israel; mem. Artists Del. to Prague, Vienna and Budapest.; mem. Women Artists Del. to Egypt, Israel and Italy, 1992, Artist Del. Brazil, 1994, Greece, Crete and Turkey, 1996, Spain, 1996. One-woman shows include Gallup Pub. Libr., 1963, 66, 77, 78, 81, 87, Gallup Lovelace Med. Clinic, Santa Fe Station Open House, 1981, Gallery 20, Farmington, N.Mex., 1985—, Red Mesa Art Gallery, 1989, Soviet Restrospect Carol's Art & Antiques Gallery, Liverpool, N.Y., 1992, 97, N.Mex. State Capitol Bldg., Santa Fe, 1992, Lt. Govt. Casey Luna-Office Complex, Women Artists N.Mex. Mus. Fine Arts, Carlsbad, 1992, Rio Rancho Country Club, N.Mex., 1995, Carol's Art & Antiques, Liverpool NY, 1997; group shows include: Navajo Nation Library Invitational, 1978, Santa Fe Festival of the Arts Invitational, 1979, N.Mex. State Fair, 1978, 79, 80, Catharine Lorillard Wolfe, N.Y.C., 1980, 81, 84, 85, 86, 87, 88, 89, 91, 92, 4th ann. exhbn. Salmagundi Club, 1984, 90, 98, 3d ann. Palm Beach Internat., New Orleans, 1984, Fine Arts Ctr. Taos, 1984, The Best and the Brightest O'Brien's Art Emporium, Scottsdale, Ariz., 1986, Gov.'s Gallery, 1989, N.Mex. State Capitol, Santa Fe, 1987, Pastel Soc. West Coast Ann. Exhbn. Sacramento Ctr. for Arts, Calif., 1986-90, gov.'s invitational Magnifico Fest. of the Arts, Albuquerque, 1991, Assn. Pour La Promotion Du Patrimone Artistique Français, Paris, Nat. Mus. of the Arts for Women, Washington, 1991, Artists of N.Mex., Internat. Nexus '92 Fine Art Exhbn., Trammell Corw Pavilion, Dallas, Carlsbad (N.Mex.) Mus. Fine Art; represented in permanent collections: Zuni Arts and Crafts Ednl. Bldg., U. N.Mex., C.J. Wiemar Collection, McKinley Manor, Gov.'s Office, State Capitol Bldg., Santa Fe, Historic El Rancho Hotel, Gallup, N.Mex., Sunwest Bank. Fine Arts Ctr., En Taos, N.Mex., Armand Hammer Pvt. Collection, Wilcox Canyon Collections, Sadona, Ariz., Galaria Impi, Netherlands, Woods Art and Antiques, Liverpool, N.Y., Stewarts Fine Art, Taos, N.Mex., Rohoboth McKinley Christian Hosp. & Sacred Heart Cathedral, Gallup, NM. Mem. Dora Cox del. to Soviet Union-U.S. Exchange, 1990. Recipient Cert. of Recognition for Contbn. and Participation Assn. Pour La Patrinome Du Artistique Français, 1991, N.Mex. State Senate 14th Legislature Session Meml. # 101 for Artistic Achievements award, 1992, Award of Merit, Pastel Soc. West Coast Ann. Membership Exhbn., 1998, Holbein Award Excellence in painting, Pastel Soc. West Coast Internat. Juried Exhibition. Mem. Internat. Fine Arts Guild, Am. Portrait Soc. (cert.), Oil Painters of Am., Pastel Soc. of W. Coast (cert., Hobein award), Mus. N.Mex. Found., N.Mex. Archtl. Found., Mus. Women in the Arts, Fechin Inst., Artists' Co-op. (co-chair), Gallup C. of C., Gallup Area Arts and Crafts Council (nat. and internat. artist of distinction award 1997), Am. Portrait Soc. Am., Pastel Soc. N.Mex., Catharine Lorillard Wolfe Art Club of N.Y.C. (oil and pastel juried membership), Chautaugua Art Club, Oil Painters of Am., Soroptimists (internat. woman of distinction 1990), Salmagundi Art Club. Address: 210 E Green St Gallup NM 87301-6130

CATTANEO, MICHAEL S., heating and cooling company executive; b. Detroit, May 30, 1948; s. Alex and Bernadine (Krause) C.; m. Nancy Lucille Horsch, Sept. 6, 1969; children: Michael Alex, Jason Ryan. Cert., Lawrence Inst. Tech., 1970, Macomb Coll., 1977. Service tech. Reliable Heating and Cooling, Detroit, 1965-69; service supr. Artic Air Inc., Detroit, 1969-77; supt. Kropf Service Inc., Detroit, 1977-78; owner Greater Detroit Heating and Cooling, Inc., 1978—, J.B. Air Conditioning Inc., 1978—; mech., tech. educator, Career Prep. Ctr., Warren, Mich., 1982-83; tech advisor Macomb Prosecutor's Office div. consumer fraud, Mt. Clemens, Mich., 1985—. Mem. Italian Cultural Ctr. (Warren), Ams. Italian Origin. Republican. Roman Catholic. Avocations: fishing, hunting, competitive shooting and boating, bicycling, tennis, golf. Office: Greater Detroit Heating and Cooling Inc 18334 E 9 Mile Rd East Detroit MI 48021

CATTANI, DANTE THOMAS, artist, art teacher, writer; b. Perth Amboy, N.J., Nov. 14, 1922; s. Louis and Catherine (Paone) C.; m. Alice Barone, Jan. 11, 1947 (div. Dec. 1951); 1 child, Dorian Mark (dec. 1980); m. Elizabeth Ann Peirce, Sept. 2, 1957. Diploma in advt. design, Phila. Coll. Art, 1945; BFA, Temple U., 1970. Ptnr. Cattani-Strome Studio, Phila., 1944-53; artist Hoedt Studios, Phila., 1953-56; freelance artist Phila., 1956—; lectr. U. Pa., Phila., 1969, Beaver Coll., 1975; prof. drawing and anatomy Phila. Coll. Art, 1945-85, head anatomy dept., 1954-85; ret., 1985—. Author: The Human Form, 1960; asst. with mural (Allen Saalberg) Bloomingdale, N.Y.C., (Jean Francksen) Parkway House, Phila., Helen Caro Store, Phila.; exhibited in shows at Dubin, Owen Joseph, Phila., Butcher and More, Phila., Civic Ctr., Phila., Allentown Mus., Phila., Ocean County Artists Guild, N.J., Oceanside Belmar, N.J., and numerous others. Mem. Center City Residents, Phila., 1975-83. Recipient best of show award, Ocean County Cultural & Hist. Soc., Toms River, N.J., 1988, Grumbacher Medal, Ocean County Art Guild, Toms River, 1991. Mem. Ocean County Art Guild. Avocations: reading, crosswords, guitar, piano. Home: 52 Williamsburg Dr Toms River NJ 08755-6306

CATTANI, LUIS CARLOS, manufacturing engineer; b. Rosario, Santa Fe, Argentina, Oct. 14, 1962; came to U.S., 1987; s. Carlos Candido and Margarita Dora (Rebola) C.; m. Maria Andrea Marañon, Jan. 7, 1989. BSME, Cath. U. of Cordoba, Argentina, 1987; MSME, U. Detroit, 1989, DEng, 1993. Project engr. Modern Automation Specialties, Detroit, 1988-90; computer integrated mfg. mgr. Uni Boring Co. Inc., Howell, Mich., 1990-95, program mgr., 1996—; adj. prof. U. Detroit Mercy-Ford Motor Co., Dearborn, Mich., 1991—. Co-author (book) Advances in Control and Dynamic Systems, 1991; contbr. articles to profl. pubs. Mem. IEEE, ASME (assoc.), Robotics Internat., Computer and Automated Systems Assn., Soc. Mfg. Engrs. (chmn. Detroit chpt. 1991). Roman Catholic. Avocations: golf, soccer. Office: Uni Boring Co Inc 2280 W Grand River Ave Howell MI 48843-8515

CATTANI, MARYELLEN B., lawyer; b. Bakersfield, Calif., Dec. 1, 1943; d. Arnold Theodore and Corinne Marilyn (Kovacevich) C.; m. Frank C. Herringer; children: Sarah, Julia. AB, Vassar Coll., Poughkeepsie, N.Y., 1965; JD, U. Calif. (Boalt Hall), 1968. Assoc. Davis Polk & Wardwell, N.Y.C., 1968-69; assoc. Orrick, Herrington & Sutcliffe, San Francisco, 1970-74, ptnr., 1975-81; v.p., gen. counsel Transamerica Corp., San Francisco, 1981-83, sr. v.p., gen. counsel, 1983-89; ptnr. Morrison & Foerster, San Francisco, 1989-91; sr. v.p. gen. counsel APL Ltd., Oakland, Calif., 1991-95, exec. v.p., gen. counsel, 1995-97; bd. dirs. Golden West Fin. Corp., World Savs. & Loan Assn., ABM Industries Inc. Author: Calif. Corp. Practice Guide, 1977, Corp. Counselors, 1982. Regent St. Mary's Coll., Morega, Calif., 1986—, pres., 1990-92, trustee, 1990—, chmn., 1993-95; trustee Vassar Coll., 1985-93, The Head-Royce Sch., 1993—, Alameda County Med. Ctr. Hosp. Authority, 1998—; bd. dirs. The Exploratorium, 1988-93. Mem. ABA, State Bar Calif. (chmn. bus. law sect. 1980-81), Bar Assn. San Francisco (co-chair com. on women 1989-91), Calif. Women Lawyers, San Francisco C. of C. (bd. dirs. 1987-91, gen. counsel 1990-91), Am. Corp. Counsel Assn. (bd. dirs. 1982-87), Women's Forum West (bd. dirs. 1984-87). Democrat. Roman Catholic. Club: Women's Forum West.

CATTELL, HEATHER BIRKETT, psychologist; b. Carlisle, eng., Dec. 16, 1936; came to U.S., 1958; d. Wilfred B. and Anne Birkett; m. Russel B. Shields, June 10, 1958 (div. 1968); children: Vaughn, Gary, Heather Luanne; m. Raymond B. Cattell, May 9, 1981. BA, U. Hawaii, 1974, MA, 1977, PhD, 1979. Lic. clin. psychologist, Hawaii. Dir. rsch. Salvation Army, Honolulu, 1979-81; pvt. practice Honolulu, 1981—; lectr., workshop leader, U.S., Australia, Can., and United Kingdom, 1989—. Author: The 16PF: Personality in Depth, 1989, The Cattell Comprehensive Personality Inventory, 1998. Mem. Phi Beta Kappa. Office: 1188 Bishop St Ste 1702 Honolulu HI 96813-3307

CATTERALL, MARLENE, Canadian legislator; b. Ottawa, Ont., Can., Mar. 1, 1939; d. Paul and Isobel Petzold; m. Ron Catterall, July 14, 1962; children: Karen, Chris, Cheryl. Ed., Carleton U. Alderman City of Ottawa, 1976-85; coun. mem. Regional Municipality Ottawa-Carleton, 1976-85; mem. from Ottawa West Ho. of Commons, 1988-97, apptd. parliamentary sec. to pres. of treasury bd., mem. from Ottawa W., Nepeau, 1997—; apptd. dep. govt. whip, 1994; vice chair Procedure and House Affairs Com. Mem. Ottawa Women's Network, Bus. and Profl. Women's Club. Liberal. Roman Catholic. Office: House of Commons, Rm 451-S Centre Block, Ottawa, ON Canada K1A 0A6

CATTERALL, WILLIAM A., pharmacology, neurobiology educator; b. Providence, Oct. 12, 1946; s. William V. and Alice (Aldred) C.; m. Nancy Sharples; children: W. Douglas, Elizabeth R. BA in Chemistry, Brown U., 1968; PhD in Physiol. Chemistry, Johns Hopkins U., 1972. Postdoctoral research fellow Lab. of Biochem. Genetics NIH, Bethesda, Md., 1972-76, staff scientist, 1976-77; assoc. prof. dept. pharmacology U. Wash., Seattle, 1977-82, prof., 1982—, chmn. dept. pharmacology, 1984—, chmn. interdisciplinaty com. on neurobiology, 1986—. Editor Molecular Pharmacology, 1986-90; contbr. numerous articles to profl. jours. and textbooks. Recipient Young Scientist award Passano Found., 1981, Jacob Javits Neurosci award, NIH, 1984, 91, Basic Sci. Prize award Am. Heart Assn., 1992; numerous grants. Mem. Nat. Acad. Sci., Am. Soc. Pharmacology and Exptl. Therapeutics, Soc. for Neurosci., Am. Soc. Biol. Chemists, Neurosci. Research Program. Avocations: sailing, skiing. Office: Univ Wash Dept Pharmacology PO Box 357280 Seattle WA 98195-7280

CATTERTON, MARIANNE ROSE, occupational therapist; b. St. Paul, Feb. 3, 1922; d. Melvin Joseph and Katherine Marion (Bole) Maas; m. Elmer

John Wood, Jan. 16, 1943 (dec.); m. Robert Lee Catterton, Nov. 20, 1951 (div. 1981); children: Jenifer Ann Dawson, Cynthia Lea Uthus. Student, Carleton Coll., 1939-41, U. Md., 1941-42; BA in English, U. Wis., 1944; MA in Counseling Psychology, Bowie State Coll., 1980; postgrad., No. Ariz. U., 1987-91. Registered occupational therapist, Occupational Therapy Cert. Bd. Occupational therapist VA, N.Y.C., 1946-50; cons. occupational therapist Fondo del Seguro del Estado, Puerto Rico, 1950-51; dir. rehab. therapies Spring Grove State Hosp., Catonsville, Md., 1953-56; occupational therapist Anne Arundel County Health Dept., Annapolis, Md., 1967-78; dir. occupational therapy Eastern Shore Hosp. Ctr., Cambridge, Md., 1979-85; cons. occupational therapist Kachina Point Health Ctr., Sedona, Ariz., 1986; regional chmn. Conf. on revising Psychiat. Occupational Therapy Edn., 1958-59; instr. report writing Anne Arundel Community Coll., Annapolis, 1974-78. Editor Am. Jour. Occupational Therapy, 1962-67. Active Md. Heart Assn., 1959-60; mem. task force on occupational therapy edn. Md. Dept. of Health, 1971-72; chmn. Anne Arundel Gov. Com. on Employment of Handicapped, 1959-63; gov.'s com. to study vocat. rehab., Md., 1960; com. mem. Annapolis Youth Ctr., 1976-78; ministerial search com. Unitarian Ch. Anne Arundel County, 1962; curator Dorchester County Heritage Mus., Cambridge, 1982-83; v.p., officer Unitarian-Universalist Fellowship Flagstaff, 1988-93, v.p., 1993-97; co-moderator, founder Unitarian-Universalist Fellowship Sedona, 1994—, pres., 1997-98; citizen interviewer Sedona Acad. Forum, 1993, 94; vol. Respite Care, 1994—, VerdeValley Caregivers, 1996—. Mem. P.R. Occupl. Therapy Assn. (co-founder 1950), Am. Occupl. Therapy Assn. (chmn. history com. 1958-61), Md. Occupl. Therapy Assn. (del. 1953-59), Ariz. Occupl. Therapy Assn., Pathfinder Internat., Dorchester County Mental Health Assn. (pres. 1981-84), Internat. Platform Assn., Ret. Officers Assn., Air Force Assn. (Barry Goldwater chpt., sec. 1991-92, 94-98), Severn Town Club (treas. 1965, sec. 1971-72, 94-95), Internat. Club (Annapolis, publicity chmn. 1966), Toastmasters, Newcomers (Sedona, pres. 1986), Pathfinder, Zero Population Growth, Nature Conservancy, Delta Delta Delta. Republican. Home: 415 Windsong Dr Sedona AZ 86336-3745

CATTO, HENRY EDWARD, former government official, former ambassador; b. Dallas, Dec. 6, 1930; s. Henry Edward and Maurine (Halsell) C.; m. Jessica Oveta Hobby, Feb. 15, 1958; children: Heather, John, William, Elizabeth. BA, Williams Coll., 1952; JD (hon.), U. Aberdeen, 1990. Ptnr. Catto & Catto, San Antonio, 1955—; dep. rep. Orgn. Am. States, Washington, 1969-71; ambassador to El Salvador, 1971-73; U.S. chief protocol White House, Washington, 1974-76; ambassador to UN, Geneva, 1976-77; asst. sec. def. Pentagon, Washington, 1981-83; vice chmn. H & C Communications, 1983-89; amb. to U.K., 1989-91; dir. U.S. Info. Agy., Washington, 1991-93; adj. prof. U. Tex., San Antonio, 1993—; mem. Coun. on Fgn. Rels., N.Y.C., 1973; bd. dirs. Cullen-Frost Bankers; bd. dirs. Nat. Pub. Radio; vice chmn. The Aspen Inst., 1993—; chmn. Atlantic Coun. U.S., 1999—. Mem. Metro Club (Washington). Republican. Presbyterian. Office: 110 E Crockett St San Antonio TX 78205-2612

CATTO OF CAIRNCATTO, BARON STEPHEN GORDON, banker; b. Stanmore, Eng., Jan. 14, 1923; s. Thomas Sivewright and Gladys Forbes (Gordon) C. of C.; m. Josephine Innes Packer, July 28, 1948 (div. 1965); children: Innes G., Alexander G., Christian V.G. Menzies-Wilson, Ariane M.G.; m. Margaret Forrest, Jan. 27, 1966 (dec. June 1998); children: James S.G., Georgina L.G. Newman. Ed., Eton Coll., 1936-41, Trinity Coll., Cambridge, Eng., 1941-43. With Morgan Grenfell & Co. Ltd., London, 1948-79, dir., 1957-73, chmn., 1973-79; chmn. Morgan Grenfell Group plc, London, 1980-87; chmn. Yule Catto & Co. plc, London; bd. dirs., Times Newspapers Holdings Ltd., London. Chmn. exec. com. Westminster Abbey Trust, U.K., 1973-97; chmn. Royal Air Force Benevolent Fund, Eng., 1978-91. Flight lt. RAFVR, 1943-47. Fellow Chartered Inst. Bankers, Royal Coll. Pathologists (hon.). Clubs: Oriental (London); Melbourne (Australia). Avocations: music; gardening. Home: 41 William Mews, London SW1X 9HQ, England Office: 1st Fl, 12 Berkeley St, London W1X 5AD, England

CATUZZI, J(EROME) P(RIMO), JR., lawyer; b. N.Y.C., Aug. 23, 1938; s. J.P. Sr. and Ida (Ghezzi) C.; m. Chantal Mauricette Marais, Nov. 10, 1979; children: Daniella Firenze, Vanessa Carmen, Vanessita Lee. BA, Columbia U., 1958; JD, Georgetown U., 1961; LLM in Internat. Law, NYU, 1963; PhD in Internat. Bus., La Salle U., 1998. Bar: N.Y., D.C., Assesor Legal, Spain 1973. Assoc. Baker & McKenzie, N.Y.C. and Chgo., 1963-65; gen. counsel, exec. v.p. Royal Bus. Fund Corp. (Amex), N.Y.C., 1965-72; exec. v.p., gen. counsel Holmes Protection, Inc. (Amex); internat. counsel, mng. dir. Occidental S.A., Madrid and Geneva, 1972-84; counsel U.S. Consulate, Costa del Sol, Spain, Sotogrande, S.A.; U.S. gen. counsel Soparind S.A., N.Y.C. and Paris, 1984-86; resident U.S. ptnr. Belricz, Ferry, David, Lutz & Rochefort, N.Y.C., 1986-88; resident prin. J.P. Catuzzi, Jr. & Assocs., N.Y.C., 1989—; internat. counsel Colina la Ropa, S.A.; Mexico, 1987; adj. prof. law and fin. C.W. Post campus Long Island U., N.Y.C., 1985—; nat. lectr. Internat. Bus. Network, N.Y.C. and Santa Monica, Calif., 1980-84; internat. cons. Eums Pharma, S.A., Geneva, Switzerland, Prime Capital, Nassau, The Bahamas, Magellan, GmbH, MNG Industries, GmbH, Fed. Republic Germany, Mir Capital Corp., L.A. and Moscow, 1991-92, GEFI Holdings, Ltd., Gibraltar, ChartHouse Holdings, Ltd., Ireland, Galia, Ltd., Lausanne, Switzerland,, Centro Geotecnico, S.R.L., Rome, Geosaf, Inc., Montreal, Can., Hanover Trust House, Ltd., Ireland; internat. coun. Chropi, S.A., Greece, Igos Comm., S.A., Paris, Ireland, Pirme Capital Corp, Nassau, Bahamas, Lenzburg Capital Corp, Calgary, Alta., Can.; gen. internat. counsel Centrum European Securities, Ltd., Geneva, Switzerland; int. counsel golden Hat Resources, Inc., Vancouver, B.C., Canada; gen. counsel Orbis Capital Investment, Ltd., Dublin, Ireland. Legis. cons. to Gov. Rockefeller div. human rights State of N.Y., Albany, 1968-70; mem. legal com. N.Y. County Rep. Party, 1967-72. Mem. Confrerie des Chevalier du Tastevin (N.Y.C.) (chevalier 1985—), Knights of Malta. Roman Catholic.

CATZ, BORIS, endocrinologist, educator; b. Troyanov, Russia, Feb. 15, 1923; s. Jacobo and Esther (Galbmilion) C.; came to U.S., 1950, naturalized, 1955; m. Rebecca Schechter; children: Judith, Dinah, Sarah Lea, Robert. BS, Nat. U. Mexico, 1941, MD, 1947; MS in Medicine, U. So. Calif., 1951. Intern, Gen. Hosp., Mexico City, 1945-46; prof. adj., sch. medicine U. Mexico, 1947-48; research fellow medicine U. So. Calif., 1949-51, instr. medicine, 1952-54, asst. clin. prof., 1954-59, assoc. clin. prof., 1959-83, clin. prof., 1983—; pvt. practice, Los Angeles, 1951-55, Beverly Hills, Calif., 1957—; chief Thyroid Clinic Los Angeles County Gen. Hosp., 1955-70; sr. cons. thyroid clin. U. So. Calif.-Los Angeles Med. Center, 1970—; clin. chief endocrinology Cedars-Sinai Med. Ctr., 1983-87. Served to capt. U.S. Army, 1955-57. Boris Catz lectureship named in his honor Thyroid Research Endowment Fund, Cedars Sinai Med. Ctr., 1985. Fellow ACP, Am. Coll. Nuclear Medicine (pres. elect 1982), Royal Soc. Medicine; mem. AMA, AAAS, Cedars Sinai Med. Ctr. Soc. for History of Medicine (chmn.), L.A. County Med. Assn., Calif. Med. Assn., Endocrine Soc., Am. Thyroid Assn., Soc. Exptl. Biology and Medicine, Western Soc. Clin. Research, Am. Fedn. Clin. Research, Soc. Nuclear Medicine, So. Calif. Soc. Nuclear Medicine, N.Y. Acad. Scis., L.A. Soc. Internal Medicine, Collegium Salerni, Cedar Sinai Soc. of History of Medicine, Beverly Hills C. of C., Phi Lambda Kappa. Jewish. Mem. B'nai B'rith. Club: The Profl. Man's (past pres.). Author: Thyroid Case Studies, 1975, 2d edit., 1981. Contbr. numerous articles on thyroidology to med. jours. Home: 300 S El Camino Dr Beverly Hills CA 90212-4212 Office: 435 N Roxbury Dr Beverly Hills CA 90210-5027

CAUCHON, MARTIN, Canadian government official. Lic. in Civil Law, U. Ottawa, 1984; ML in Internat. Law, U. Exeter, 1990. Practiced civil and comml. law, 1985-93; mem. Parliament. Govt. of Can., Ottawa, Ont., 1993-95; pres. Liberal Party Can. Govt. of Can., Que., 1993-95; vice. chmn. standing com. pub. accts. Govt. of Can., 1994, chmn. Can.-France Inter-Parliamentary Assn., 1994-95, mem. standing com. human rights devel., 1994-96; sec. state responsible for Can. econ. devel. Govt. of Can., Montreal, Que., 1996—; re-elected to Parliament, Govt. of Can., Ottawa, 1997—; also mgr. Can.-Quebec infrastructure works agreement, cmty. futures program Govt. of Can. Office: Can Econ Devel, 264 W Block House Commons, Ottawa, ON Canada K1A OA6

CAUDILL, SAMUEL JEFFERSON, architect; b. Tulsa, June 5, 1922; s. Samuel Jefferson and Maymie Starling (Boulware) C.; m. Joy Maxwell, May 31, 1952; children: Jody Caudill Cardamone, Julie Hertzberg, Samuel Boone, Robert Maxwell, Anne Goertzen,. BArch, Cornell U., Ithaca, N.Y., 1946. Registered architect Colo., Calif., Idaho, Ariz. Prin. architect Samuel J. Caudill, Jr., Aspen, Colo., 1954-59, Caudill Assocs. Architects, Aspen, 1959-80; pres. Caudill Gustafson & Assocs. Architects, PC, Aspen, 1980-87, Caudill Gustafson Ross & Assocs., Architects, P.C., Aspen, 1987-92; pres., CEO Caudill Gustafson & Assocs., Architects, P.C., Aspen, 1992—; mem. Pitkin County Planning and Zoning Commn., Colo., 1955-58; mem. outdoor edn. com. Colo. Dept. Edn., 1966-68; chmn. Pitkin County Bd. Appeals, 1970; mem. Colo. Water Quality Control Commn., 1977-80. Wildlife rep. adv. bd. Bur. Land Mgmt. Dept. Interior, Grand Junction, Colo., 1969-75, 80-85; chmn. citizens adv. com. Colo. Hwy. Dept. for I-70 through Glenwood Canyon, 1975-92; chmn. Colo. Wildlife Commn., 1978-79. Recipient Outstanding Pub. Service Bur. Land Mgmt., 1975; named to Aspen (Colo.) Hall of Fame, 1998. Fellow AIA (Community Svc. award 1976, Architect of Yr. award 1992); mem. Colo. Soc. Architects (pres. 1983), Colo. Coun. on Arts and Humanities, Aspen C. of C. (pres. 1956-57), Masons, Shriners (Denver). Home: 1055 Stage Rd Aspen CO 81611-1096 Office: Caudill Gustafson & Assocs Architects PC 234 E Hopkins Ave Aspen CO 81611-1938

CAUDILL, TOM HOLDEN, governmental policy and analysis executive; b. St. Augustine, Fla., June 21, 1945; s. Julian Terrill and Alta Jane (Holden) C.; m. Virginia Mary Kauss, June 26, 1971; 1 child, Mara Julia. BA in History, East Tenn. State U., 1967, MA in Internat. Rels., 1977; MA in Mgmt. Sci., Webster U., 1980. Instr. English as second lang., polit. sci., mgmt. sci. U.S. Peace Corps, Loei, Thailand, 1970-73; instr. English as second lang., polit. sci., mgmt. sci. Steed Coll., Johnson City, Tenn., 1973-76; instr. Internat. Ctr. U. Tex., Austin, 1976-77; tng. specialist Air Tng. Command USAF, Lackland AFB, Tex., 1977-80; tng. specialist Logistics Command USAF, Wright-Patterson AFB, Ohio, 1980-81, logistics mgmt. specialist, 1981-85, chief, policy and procedures Internat. Logistics Ctr., 1985-88, chief policy and analysis, 1986—, chief plans and devel., 1988; dir. Arabian programs Internat. Logistics Ctr., 1991-95; exec. fellow Woodrow Wilson Sch. Govt. Princeton U., 1995-96; dep. dir. internat. programs Air Force Security Assistance Ctr., 1996; chief prodn. policy Hdqtrs. Air Force Material Command, Wright Patterson AFB, Ohio, 1997-99; dir. ops. mgmt. Air Force Security Assistance Ctr., Wright Patterson AFB, Ohio, 1999—; vis. instr. English as a second lang., polit. sci., mgmt. sci. Antioch Coll., Yellow Springs, Ohio, 1986—; asst. dep. plans policy mgmt. systems, 1988, dir. plans and policy, 1988, tech. lead integrated logistics support, acquisition logistics div., 1988—, instr. mgmt. sci. Author: Textbook in Logistics 1988, Policy Regulations/Procedural Instructions 1986—; contbr. articles to profl. jours., 1987—. Adminstr. Refugee Assistance Program, Greene County, Ohio, 1981-84, AFS chpt. v.p.; Scoutmaster Buckeye Trails coun. Girl Scout U.S., Yellow Springs, 1982-86; active Dayton (Ohio) Coun. on World Affairs, 1984—; pres. local chpt. Am. Field Svc., Greene County, 1988—. Mem LWV (fin. chm. Greene county chpt. 1987—). Democratic. Methodist. Avocations: traveling, scouting, reading, profl. rsch. writing. Home: 445 W South College St Yellow Springs OH 45387-1422 Office: Hdqs Air Force Material Cmd Air Force Security Asst Ctr AFSAC/OM Wright Patterson AFB OH 45433

CAUDLE, BEN HALL, petroleum engineering educator; b. Midlothian, Tex., Apr. 27, 1923. BS, U. Tex., 1943, PhD in Petroleum Engring., 1963. Prof. petroleum enging. U. Tex., 1963—. Mem. Nat. Acad. Engring., Soc. Petroleum Engrs. (hon., DeGolyer Disting. Svc. medal 1994). Office: Univ of Texas Dept of Petroleum Engring CDE2-502 MC C0300 Austin TX 78712*

CAUDRON, JOHN ARMAND, accident reconstructionist, forensic investigator; b. Compton, Calif., Sept. 26, 1944; s. Armand Robert and Evelyn Emma (Hoyt) C.; m. Marily Edith Fairfield, Mar. 16, 1968; children: Melita, Rochelle. AA, Ventura Coll., 1965; BA, Calif. State U., Fullerton, 1967; postgrad., U. Nev., 1975-78; MS, U. So. Calif., 1980. Dist. rep. GM, Reno, 1969-75; mgr. Snyder Rsch. Lab., Reno, 1976-78; v.p. Snyder Rsch. Lab., El Monte, Calif., 1978-82, pres., 1982—; prin. Fire and Accident Reconstruction, Walnut, Calif., 1985—. Pub. accident reconstrn. newsletter. With U.S. Army, 1967-69. Fellow Am. Bd. Forensic Examiners (bd. cert.); mem. ASCE, NSPE, Am. Soc. Safety Engrs., Nat. Fire Protection Assn., Geol. Soc. Am., Firearms Rsch. and Identification Assn. (pres. 1978—), Am. Soc. Metals, Nat. Safety Coun., Nat. Assn. Profl. Accident Reconstruction Specialists. Republican. Baptist. Avocations: hiking, traveling, photography. Office: Fire & Accident Reconstruction 21465 E Fort Bowie Dr Walnut CA 91789-5106

CAUDURO, RAFAEL, painter, muralist; b. Mexico City, Apr. 18, 1950. Study in indsl. design, U. Ilberoamericana, Mex., 1969-74. Prin. works include Mus. Modern aRt, Cuevas Mus., Alfa Cultural Ctr., Mex.; commnd. Postage stamp, Dept. Communs, Mexico City, 1985; murals includ Dept. Comms., Mexican, Vancouver, B.C., Can., 1986, London Underground, Paris Metro, City Coun., Mexico City, 1989; one-mans shows include Palace Fine Arts, Mexico City, 1984, Chrysler Mus., Norfolk, Va., 1986, Alfa Cultural Ctr., Monterrey, Mex., 1987, Mus. Modern Art, Mexico City, 1991, Casa de la Cultura Mex.-Japan, Mexico City, 1991, Children;s Mus. Manhattan, 1990, others; author: (bibliographies) Jorge A. Manrique, 1991, Albert Hijar, 1991, Taquel Tibol, 1991; co-author: Rafael Cuaduro, 1991, Elena Poniatowska, 1992, Donald Kuspit, 1994. Office: C/O Saturno 12, Cuernevaca, 62360 Morelos Mexico*

CAUFIELD, MARIE CELINE, religious organization administrator; b. Chgo., Aug. 11, 1929; d. John Patrick and Anna Marie (Clear) C. MA in Religious Edn., Fordham U., 1975; DMin in Creative Ministry, Grad. Theol. Found., Bristol, Ind., 1989. Elem. prin. St. Martin's Sch., Kankakee, Ill., 1952-64; missionary Congregation de Notre Dame, Guatemala, Ctrl. Am., 1964-71; dir. religious edn. St. Colomba, N.Y.C., 1971-75, St. Bernard, Pirtleville, Ariz., 1975-76; dir. Hispanic ministry Diocese of Providence (R.I.), Central Falls, 1976-81; dir. of the Office of Hispanic ministry Roman Cath. Diocese of Boise, 1981-96; nat. exec. dir. The Cath. Migrant Farmworker Network, 1996—. Author numerous poems; contbr. articles to profl. jours. Bd. dirs. Cath. Migrant Farmworkers' Network, Toledo, 1992—; founder Idaho's Cath. Golden Age Chpt., Boise, 1983-87. Grantee Am. Bd. Cath. Missions, 1991. Mem. Nat. Writers Assn., Fedn. of Returned Overseas Missioners (N.W. contact person 1990-94). Roman Catholic. Avocations: networking, writing, photography, walking, music. Home: 1111 N 17th St Boise ID 83702-3306 Office: Catholic Migrant Farmworker Network 1915 University Dr Boise ID 83706-3022

CAUGHLIN, STEPHENIE JANE, organic farmer; b. McAllen, Tex., July 23, 1948; d. James Daniel and Betty Jane (Warnock) C. BA in Family Econs., San Diego State U., 1972, MEd, 1973; M. in Psychology, U.S. Internat. U., San Diego, 1979. Cert. secondary life tchr., Calif. Owner, mgr. Minute Maid Svc., San Diego, 1970-75; prin. Rainbow Fin. Svcs., San Diego, 1975-78; tchr. San Diego Unified Sch. Dist., 1973-80; mortgage broker Santa Fe Mortgage Co., San Diego, 1980-81; commodity broker Premex Commodities, San Diego, 1981-84; pres., owner Nationwide Futures Corp., San Diego, 1984-88; owner, sec. Nationwide Metals Corp.; owner, gen. mgr. Seabreeze Organic Farm, 1984—. Sec. Arroyo Sorrento Assn., Del Mar, Calif., 1978—. Mem. Greenpeace Nature Conservancy, DAR, Sierra Club, Jobs Daus. Republican. Avocations: horseback riding, swimming, skiing, gardening. Home and Office: 3909 Arroyo Sorrento Rd San Diego CA 92130-2610

CAULDER, JERRY DALE, weed scientist; b. Gideon, Mo., Nov. 7, 1942. BA & BS, Southeast Mo. State U., 1964; MS, U. Mo., 1966, PhD in Agronomy/Plant Physiology, 1969. Rsch. asst. weed sci. U. Mo., 1966-70; mktg. devel. specialist Monsanto Co., 1969-71; mgr. Monsanto Co., Columbia, 1971-73; devel. assoc. Monsanto Co., 1973, tech. mgr. herbicides, 1973-74, mew product mgr., 1974-84; chmn., CEO Mycogen Corp., San Diego, 1984-97, chmn. emeritus, 1997—. Patentee in field. Achievements include research in coordination of the discovery, development and manufacture of herbicides and plant growth regulators. *

CAULEY, ALVIN PAUL, state government administrator; b. Washington, Sept. 25, 1936; s. L.C. and Helen Virginia (Campbell) C. BA, Temple U., 1978; MA, U. Va., 1983. EDP programmer, analyst GSA, Washington, 1958-64; EDP sys. analyst Washington, 1964-68; divsn. chief USDA Adminstrv. Svcs., Washington, 1968-74, asst. dir., 1974-79, exec. asst., 1979-83; bur. dir. City of Harrisburg, Pa., 1985-89; exec. asst. to majority leader Pa. Ho. of Reps., Harrisburg, 1990-91, spl. asst. to spkr., 1992-95, dir. house ops., 1995—; mem. exec. com. Nat. Conf. State Legislatures, Denver, 1994—, staff chair assembly on state issues, 1995—; bd. dirs. YMCA, Harrisburg, 1992-93; vice chair Black United Fund, Harrisburg chpt., 1987-89; mem. Pa. Dem. State Affirmative Action Com., Harrisburg, 1987. Judge election 3rd Ward, Harrisburg, 1987, committeeman, 1986; mem. Nat. Forum Black Pub. Adminstrn., Washington, 1987-89. Mem. NAACP (life), Nat. Assn. Ret. Fed. Employees (life), Internat. City Mgrs. Assn., U. Va. Alumni Assn. (life), Am. Legion. Avocation: reading. Home: 1355 Wandering Way Harrisburg PA 17110-2965

CAULFIELD, HENRY JOHN, physics educator. BA in Physics, Rice U., 1958; PhD in Physics, Iowa State U., 1962. Staff scientist Cen. Rsch. Labs. Tex. Instrument Inc., Dallas, 1962-67; tech. dirs. night vision dept. Raytheon Co., Melville, N.Y., 1968; prin. scientist Sperry Rand Rsch. Ctr., 1968-72; mgr. laser tech. dept. Block Engring. Inc., 1972-77; pres. Diversified Rsch. Corp., 1981-85; dir Ctr. for Applied Optics U. Ala., Huntsville, 1985-91; University Eminent Scholar, prof. physics Ala. Agrl. and Mech. U., Normal, 1991-97; disting. prof. physics Fisk U., 1997—; adj. prof. U. Louis Pasteur, France, Degli Studi di Cagliari, Italy, U. Ala., Huntsville, Vanderbilt; bd. dirs. Diversified Rsch. Corp., Phys. Optics Corp., Karmanos Cancer Inst., ImEdge Tech., N.E. Photosciences, AIA Optical Info. Processing team; mem. patent bd. Applied Optics, evaluation bd. NAS, NBS, adv. com. Mus. Holography, N.Y.C., hon. exec. bd. Nat. Inst. for Enging. Tech., Frederick, Md.; chmn. bd. Loki; curator Holography Works, N.Y. Mus. Holography, 1984; tchr. course Optical Info. Processing, Munich, Paris, London, Tel Aviv, 1986; tchr. course Strategic Infrared Systems, U. Ala., Huntsville, 1986. Author: (with Sun Lu) The Applications of Holography, 1972, (with Gregory Gheen) Optical Computing, 1990; editor: (with Jean Robillard) Industrial Applications of Holography, (with Christopher Tocci) Optical Interconnection Foundations and Applications, 1994, (with Mustafa A.G. Abushagur) Fourier Optics, 1995; editor: editor: Optical Memory and Neural Networks; former editor: Optical Engring.; former mem. editl. bd. Fiber and Integrated Optics, Applied Optics (info. processing editl. adv. bd., Laser Focus, Holography News, Microwave and Optical Tech. Letters, Jour. Neural Network, Computing Internat., Jour. Optical Computing, Optical Computing and Processing Jour., Math. Imaging; series editor: PWS Kent Pub. Co., 1988; publ. bd. Acad. Press; contbr. articles to profl. jours., chpts. to books, presentations to confs. and seminars; patentee in field. Fellow Optical Soc. Am. (Eastman lectr. 1982, 92), Soc. Photooptical-Instrumentational Engrs. (Svc. award, Gov.'s award, pres.'s award, Gabor award); mem. IEEE (sr.). Address: 4626 Delina Rd Cornersville TN 37047-5231

CAULFIELD, JAMES BENJAMIN, pathologist, educator; b. Mpls., Jan. 1, 1927; s. Linus Joseph and Olive Bell (Curtis) C.; m. Virginia Walsh, Jan. 28, 1950; children: Ann, John, Clare. BA, Miami U., Oxford, Ohio, 1947; BS, U. Ill., 1948, MD, 1950. Intern Henrotin Hosp., Chgo., 1950-51; resident U. N.C., Chapel Hill, 1951-52, U. Kans. Med. Ctr., Kansas City, 1954-55; vis. investigator Rockefeller Inst., N.Y.C., 1955-56; instr. pathology Harvard U., 1959-64, asst. prof., 1964-70, assoc. prof., 1970-75; asst. pathologist Mass. Gen. Hosp., Boston, 1960-64; assoc. pathologist Mass. Gen. Hosp., 1964-75; prof., chmn. dept. pathology U. S.C., 1975-85; prof. pathology U. Ala., Birmingham, 1985—; adj. prof. Med. U. S.C., Charleston, 1981-85; rsch. on collagen network of heart and changes associated with alterations in the network. Contbr. articles to profl. jours. Served with USN, 1944-46, 52-54. Mem. Am. Soc. Cell Biology, Am. Soc. Pathology, Internat. Acad. Pathology, Fedn. Exptl. Pathology, Electron Microscopy Soc., Internat. Study Group for Heart Research (treas. Am. sect. 1972-85), N.Y. Acad. Scis., Harvard Club, Boston Athenaeum Club, Sigma Xi, Phi Eta Sigma. Office: U Ala Dept Pathology 506 Kracke Bldg 619 19th St S Birmingham AL 35233-0001

CAULFIELD, W. HARRY, health care industry executive, physician; b. Waverly, N.Y., Aug. 22, 1936; m. Mary Sisk; children: Mary, Harry, James, Michael. AB, Harvard U., 1957, postgrad., 1976; MD, U. Pa., 1961. Diplomate Am. Bd. Internal. Medicine, Am. Bd. Cardiology. Rotating intern Hosp. U. Pa., 1961-62; resident Pa. Hosp., 1962-64; fellow in cardiology Georgetown U. Hosp., 1964-66; dir. ICU Kaiser Found. Hosp., San Francisco, 1969-75, asst. chief of staff, 1971-75, chief of staff, 1975-80; physician-in-chief, mem. exec. com. Permanente Med. Group, San Francisco, 1975-80, mem. internal medicine staff cardiology, 1968—, from exec. dir.-elect to exec. dir., 1990—; assoc. clin. prof. medicine U. Calif., San Francisco, 1971-96. Capt. U.S. Army Med. Corps, 1966-68. Fellow Am. Coll. Cardiology, Am. Heart Assn.; mem. AMA (adv. com. on group practice physicians 1994—, fedn. study consortium 1994—), San Francisco Med. Soc. (alt. del. to Calif. Med. Assn. 1992, del. 1993-94, managed care task force, leadership devel. com.), Calif. Med. Assn., Calif. Hosp. Assn. (membership com. 1987), Am. Hosp. Assn., Calif. Acad. Medicine, Am. Med. Group Assn. (trustee 1994—, vice chmn. bylaws com. 994, fin. com. 1996—), Soc. Med. Adminstrs., Am. Assn. Health Plans (bd. dirs. 1994—). Office: Permanente Med Group Inc 1950 Franklin St Oakland CA 94612-5103

CAULKINS, CHARLES S., lawyer; b. Great Bend, Kans., Sept. 22, 1949; s. Daniel P. Caulkins and Martha Taylor; m. Kelley D. Harris, Nov. 27, 1973; children: Kipp, Sloane, Sydney. BA, Monmouth Coll., 1971; JD, Creighton U., 1976; LLM in Labor Law, NYU, 1977. Bar: Kans. 1977, S.C. 1978, U.S. Dist. Ct. S.C. 1978, U.S. Ct. Appeals (4th and 10th cirs.) 1979, Fla. 1985, U.S. Dist. Ct. (so. dist.) Fla. 1985, U.S. Ct. Appeals (11th cir.) 1985, U.S. Supreme Ct. 1985. Ptnr. Thompson, Mann & Hutson, Greenville, S.C., 1977-84; mng. ptnr. Fisher & Phillips, Ft. Lauderdale, Fla., 1984—. Author: Florida Bar Journal, 1991. Office: Fisher & Phillips 1 Financial Plz Ste 2300 Fort Lauderdale FL 33394-0001

CAUSEY, ROBERT LOUIS, philosopher, educator, consultant; b. Los Angeles, Apr. 13, 1941; s. Robert Vester and Gertrude (Bloom) C.; m. Sandra Lee Shliff, Jan. 25, 1964; children—Britt Ann, Diane Sue. B.S., Calif. Inst. Tech., 1963; Ph.D., U. Calif., Berkeley, 1967. Asst. prof. dept. philosophy U. Tex., Austin, 1967-73, asso. prof., 1973-79, prof., 1979—, chmn. dept. philosophy, 1980-88; co-founder, assoc. dir. U. Tex. Artificial Intelligence Lab., 1984-97; cons. NSF, 1979-81; spkr. numerous cofs., univs., broadcasts; cons. to U.S. Army and various pvt. corps. and univs. Author: Logic, Sets, and Recursion, 1994, Unity of Science, 1977; co-author: Introduction to Artificial Intelligence and Expert Systems, Video-Course, 1988; contbr. articles and revs. to philos. and sci. jours.; author various edl. and exptl. computer programs. NSF fellow, NSF grantee, 1973-74, 79-81; U. Tex. Rsch. Inst. grantee, 1979; rsch. scientist, U.S. Army Rsch. Office grantee, 1984-89; U. Tex. Dean's fellow, 1997. Mem. AAAS, Am. Philos. Assn. (com. on computer use in philosophy 1994-97, rev. editor World Wide Web pages for Newsletter on Philosophy and Computers), Philosophy of Sci. Assn. (governing bd. 1980-81), Am. Assn. Artificial Intelligence, Southwestern Philos. Soc., Assn. for Computing Machinery, Soc. for Machines and Mentality. Achievements include development of new system for automated defeasible reasoning. Office: Univ Tex Dept of Philosophy Waggener Hall # 316 Austin TX 78712

CAUSEY-JEFFERY, TRACY ANN, art dealer, art historian; b. Salisbury, Md., Mar. 23, 1964; d. John Wesley and Charlotte Ann (Truitt) Causey; m. Mark Quinton Jeffery, Nov. 17, 1990. BA in Oriental Studies, U. Pa., Phila., 1986, BA in Internat. Rels., 1986; Degree in Asian Arts, U. London, 1989; cert. in Chinese lang., Donghai U., Taizhong, Taiwan, 1985; cert. in Small Bus. Adminstrn., Wor Wic C.C., 1991. Intern Chinese Works of Art Sotheby's N.Y., N.Y.C., 1986; asst. mgr., loan officer Mfrs. Hanover/Am. Gen., Upper Darby & Springfield, Pa., 1986-88; fair asst. Bluett & Sons Ltd., London, 1989; gallery asst. A&J Spoolman, London, 1989; asst. mgr. Platypus, Phila., 1991-92; owner, dir. Finer Side Galleries, Salisbury, Md., 1992—; sales cons. Martin Lawrence Galleries, N.Y.C., 1999—; bd. dirs. Salisburg (Md.) Wicomico Arts Coun., 1993; spl. events chair, v.p., pres. Art Inst. and Gallery, Salisbury, 1990-96; mem. adv. panel Spl. Project-Mrs. Glendering, Annapolis and Salisbury, 1996-97; prof. art listory U. Md. Eastern Shore, Princess Anne, 1996-97; lectr. Salisbury State U., 1995, 96; lectr. art Women's Bus. Network, Salisbury, 1996. Author: (poems) National Library of Poetry Anthology, 1993, 94, 95, Road Publishers Poetry Anthology, 1994. Bd. dirs. Downtown Salisbury Assn., 1995-97; v.p., pres. Art Inst. & Gallery Salisbury, 1990-97. Named Best Place to Buy Art on

Delmarva, Salisbury Pub. and Met. Mag., 1995. Mem. Nat. Orgn. Female Execs., Nat. Mus. Women in Arts, Salisbury Wicomico Arts Coun., Fells Point Creative Alliance. Avocations: dancing (ballet, jazz), writing poetry, goumet and ethnic cooking, teaching children, stargazing.

CAUTHEN, CHARLES EDWARD, JR., retail executive, business consultant; b. Columbia, S.C., Oct. 26, 1931; s. Charles Edward and Rachel (Macaulay) C.; m. Hazel Electa Peery, June 13, 1959; children: Portia Cauthen White, Rachel Cauthen Rohrer, Sara Cauthen Landfear, Sidney Cauthen Bullard. BA, Wofford Coll., 1952; cert. Charlotte Meml. Hosp. Sch. Hosp. Adminstrn., 1956; MS in Bus. Adminstrn. and Labor Mgmt., Kennedy-Western U., 1986, PhD in Bus. Adminstrn., 1986; LLD, Montreat-Anderson Coll., 1991. Asst. adminstr. Union Meml. Hosp., Monroe, N.C., 1956-58; adminstr. Lowrance Hosp., Inc., Mooresville, N.C., 1958-61; v.p., mgr. Va. Acme Market, Bluefield, W.Va., 1961-68; v.p. Acme Markets and A-Mart Stores (now Acme Markets of Tazewell, Va., Inc.), North Tazewell, Va., 1965-87, exec. v.p., 1968-71, pres., 1971-87; provost King Coll., Bristol, Tenn., 1987-89, pres., 1989-92; pres. Doran Devel. Corp., 1971-87, Big A Market, Inc., 1981-87; cons. in field. Author: Evaluation of the Small Company For Strategic Planning, Merger or Acquisition, 1987. Deacon, elder, trustee Westminster Presbyn. Ch., Bluefield, W.Va.; mem. Internat. Adv. Coun. Han Nam U., Korea, 1991; mem. exec. bd. Sequoyah Coun. Boy Scouts Am.; bd. dirs. Internat. Inst. Christian Studies, 1993-97, Family Inst., 1994—. Served to 1st lt. AUS, 1952-54. Mem. W.Va. Assn. Retail Grocers (v.p., dir. 1968-82), Va. Food Dealers Assn. (dir. 1978), Bluefield Sales Exec. Club (dir. 1965-67), Rotary (bd. dirs. 1966). Republican. Home and Office: 1626 King College Rd Bristol TN 37620-2735

CAUTHORNE-BURNETTE, TAMERA DIANNE, family nurse practitioner, healthcare consultant; b. Richmond, Va., Apr. 13, 1961; d. Robert Francis Cauthorne and Lois Avery (Lloyd) Cumashot; m. William Nichols Burnette, Dec. 3, 1983. BSN, U. Va., 1983; postgrad., Med. U. S.C., 1988; MSN, Old Dominion U., 1993, grad. cert. in women's studies, 1994; postgrad., Med. Coll. Va., 1994—. RN, Va.; family nurse practitioner. Staff nurse, charge nurse gynecology-oncology unit U. Va. Med. Ctr., Charlottesville, 1983, staff nurse, charge nurse high-risk labor and delivery, ICU, 1984-85; staff nurse, charge nurse, preceptor med. ICU Med. U. S.C., 1985-87, staff nurse ICU, 1988; staff nurse, charge nurse med.-surg. ICU, progressive care Stuart Cir. Hosp., Richmond, Va., 1988-90; staff nurse pediat. and neonatal ICU Childrens' Hosp. of the King's Dau., Norfolk, Va., 1990, staff nurse, team leader neonatal ICU, 1990-91; pvt. health care cons., 1993—; with Delmar Pub., 1994—; pres. The Foxmont Co., LLC, 1995—; with Sussex Ctrl. Health Ctr., 1995; men's responsibility clinic coord. Planned Parenthood, 1996; primary practitioner med. svcs. Va. League Planned Parenthood, 1997—; cons. Old Dominion U. Coll. Health Sci., Sch. Nursing, 1993—, undergrad. clin. facility, 1994—; condr. analysis of Russian and Ukrainian health care system; breast self-exam instr. Am. Cancer Soc., 1982—; presenter at profl. confs.; mng. mem. The Foxmont Co., L.L.C.; mem. adj. faculty Sch. Nursing U. Va., 1996; primary med. provider Va. League Planned Parenthood, 1997; mem. clin. faculty sch. of nursing Va. Commonwealth U., 1999. Contbg. author A Quick Reference for Health Assessment, 1997, Clin. Companion to Health Assessment and Physical Examination, 1998; contbr. articles to profl. jours. Vol. Ronald McDonald House, 1980-83; docent Spoleto Festival USA, 1984-92, MacArthur Meml. Mus., 1991; vol. receptionist info. ctr. Gibbes Art Gallery, 1987-89; vol. ARC Blood Donation Ctr., 1986-92; mem. U. Va. Coll. of Health Scis. Coun. Named Vol. of Yr., U. Va. Sch. Nursing. Fellow Internat. Pedagogical Acad./Moswoc. Order of Omega Nat. Honor Soc., Raven Honor Soc. U. Va., Sorenson Inst. Polit. Leadership U. Va.; mem. AACN, DAR, AAUW, Va. Coalition for Nurse Practitioners, U. Va. Sch. Nursing Alumnae Assn. (pres., CEO 1994—), Jr. League Va. (chair state pub. affairs com.), Virginians Patient Choice Coalition, Jr. League Norfolk and Virginia Beach (state pub. affairs vice chmn./lobbyist 1995), Daus. of Confederacy, Carolina Art Assn., S.C. Hist. Soc., Confederate Meml. Lit. Soc., U. Va. Coll. Health Scis. Coun., Alpha Delta Pi (chmn. nat. panhellenic rels. com., nat. by-laws and resolutions com.), Sigma Theta Tau. Avocations: riding, raising and showing thoroughbred racing horses, collecting sporting art, foxhunting.

CAUTHRON, ROBIN J., federal judge; b. Edmond, Okla., July 14, 1950; d. Austin W. and Mary Louise (Adamson) Johnson. BA, U. Okla., 1970, JD, 1977; MEd, Cen. State U., Edmond, Okla., 1974. Bar: Okla. 1977. Law clk to Hon. Ralph G. Thompson U.S. Dist. Ct. (we. dist.) Okla., 1977-81; staff atty. Legal Svcs. Ea. Okla., 1981-82; pvt. practice law, 1982-83; spl. judge 17th Jud. Dist. State Okla., 1983-86; magistrate U.S. Dist. Ct. (we. dist.) Okla., Oklahoma City, 1986-91, judge, 1991—. Editor Okla. Law Rev. Bd. dirs. Juvenile Diabetes Found. Internat., 1989—; mem. nominating com. Frontier Coun. Boy Scouts Am., 1987, Edmond Ednl. Endowment; trustee, sec. First United Meth. Ch., 1988-90. Mem. ABA, Okla. Bar Assn. (vice chmn. 1990), Okla. County Bar Assn. (bd. dirs. 1990— bench and bar com.), McCurtain County Bar Assn. (pres. 1986), Am. Judicature Soc., Nat. Assn. Women Judges, Fed. Bar Assn., Okla Assn. Women Lawyers, Nat. Coun. Women Magistrates (bd. dirs. 1990-91), Okla. Jud. Conf. (v.p. 1985), Am. Inns of Ct. (pres. elect 1990-91), Order of Coif, Phi Delta Phi. Office: US Courthouse 200 NW 4th St Ste 3108 Oklahoma City OK 73102-3029*

CAVA, MICHAEL PATRICK, chemist, educator; b. Bklyn., Feb. 13, 1926; s. Michael R. and Catherine (Lombardo) C.; m. Esther Laden, June 11, 1951; 1 son, John M. B.S., Harvard U., 1946; M.S., U. Mich., 1948, Ph.D., 1951. Postdoctoral fellow Harvard, 1951-53; from asst. prof. to prof. Ohio State U., 1953-65; prof. Wayne State U., Detroit, 1965-69; prof. chemistry U. Pa., Phila., 1969-85; prof. U. Ala., Tuscaloosa, 1985—; mem. study sect. NIH, 1987-91. Author: (with M.J. Mitchell) Cyclobutadiene and Related Compounds, 1967; also numerous articles. Alfred P. Sloan Found. fellow. Mem. Am. Chem. Soc. Research on organic sulphur, selenium and tellurium compounds; organic condrs., benzocyclobutenes, natural products chemistry. Home: 15 Northshore Dr Tuscaloosa AL 35406-2012 Office: U Ala Dept Chemistry Box 870336 Tuscaloosa AL 35487

CAVAGLIERI, GIORGIO, architect; b. Venice, Italy, Aug. 1, 1911; came to U.S., 1939, naturalized, 1943; s. Gino and Margherita (Maroni) C.; m. Norma Sanford, Jan. 31, 1942. D. Archtl. Engring, Sup. Sch. Engring., Milan, Italy, 1932; student spl. city planning, Sup. Sch. Architecture, Rome, 1934. Apprenticeship N.Y. office R. Candela, Balt. offices J.O. Chertkof, also; Benjamin Franklin, architect, prior to World War II; propr. own firm N.Y.C., 1946—; adj. prof. Sch. Architecture, Pratt Inst., 1956-69; trustee Nat. Inst. Archtl. Edn., chmn. trustees, 1957-60; academician NAD. *Drafted in 1935 during the Ethiopian war, was sent as a lieutenant of Air Force Engineers, to supervise construction of the Airport of El-Adem 16Km. South of Tobruk, Lybia. Dismissed in 1938 from the position of Instructor and lecturer at the Architectural and Engineering faculties of the Superior School of Engineering (Politecnico) of Milan, when anti-sematic laws were established in Italy, decided to emigrate to the U.S. Drafted in the U.S. Army Corps of Engineers in 1943. Landing in Normandy in the European campaign was decorated with five Battle Stars and a Bronze Star.* Prin. works in Milan, prior to World War II; prin. works include, Fenton Hall reconstrn. Fredonia (N.Y.) Coll., Astor Library restoration and conversion to N.Y. Pub. Theatre, N.Y. Shakespeare Festival, Jefferson Market Courthouse restoration and conversion to N.Y. Pub. Library, Branch Library, Riverdale, N.Y., N.Y. Pub. Library main bldg. Periodical Dept., Pub. Sch. 32, S.I., Kip's Bay br. library; assoc. architect Pension Bldg./Nat. Mus. Bldg. Arts, Washington; architect-in-charge Rosary Hall, U.S. Mil. Acad. Mus.; Eldridge St. Synagogue restoration, N.Y.C.; Chapel of the Good Shepherd reconstrn., Roosevelt Island, N.Y. Served with C.E. AUS, 1943-45. Decorated Bronze Star; recipient Honor award A.I.A., 1968, House Improvement award, 1961; Bard award, spl. citation City Club N.Y., 1968; Illuminated scroll Municipal Art Soc. N.Y., 1966; Clients award N.Y. State Assn. Architects, 1964; Gold medal honor architecture Archtl. League N.Y., 1956; winner 1st prize nat. competition auditorium Rome, 1935, 3d prize competition city hosp. Cuneo, Italy., 1938, hon. mention Armed Forces bldgs. Rome World's Fair, 1938, 3d prize N.Y.C. Bd. Edn. archtl. competition for modernization Bronx Jr. High Sch., 1967; certificate of merit for excellence in design N.Y. State Assn. Architects, 1976; 1st honor award ALA/AIA, 1976; Sidney L. Strauss Meml. N.Y. Soc. Architects, 1977; recipient award Excellence in Design N.Y.C. Art Commn., 1992, Design award for Preservation Gen. Svcs. Adminstrn., 1992; Outstanding Cert. for Competition N.Y.C. Bd. Edn., 1997. Fellow AIA (pres. N.Y. chpt. 1970-71, Disting. Architecture award 1985, Honor award 1986, Presdl. citation 1990, Medal of Honor N.Y. chpt. 1990); mem. Mcpl. Art Soc. N.Y. (pres. 1963-65, 4th Annual Preservation award 1992), Archtl. League N.Y. (v.p. 1961-63), Am. Soc. Interior Designers (v.p. 1984-85, 87-88, medal 1985), Fine Arts Fedn. N.Y. (pres. 1970-72, 74-76, Centennial Yr. honoree 1995), N.Y. Coun. Arts and Govt., N.Y.C. Victorian Soc. (Outstanding in Preservation award 1986). Democrat. Home: 75 Central Park W New York NY 10023-6011 Office: 250 W 57th St Ste 2016 New York NY 10107-2016

CAVALCANTE-FLEMING, MARIA A., preschool educator, language educator, translator; b. Sao Paulo, Brazil; came to U.S., 1981; d. Alfredo Bispo and Maria do Carmo Cavalcante; divorced; children: David Alfredo Fleming, Amanda Marie Fleming. BA in Edn., Oswaldo Cruz U., Brazil. Presch. tchr. St. Ann's Sch., Kaneohe, Hawaii, 1989-92, kindergarten aide, 1992-94; 3d grade tchr. St. Anthony Sch., Kalihi, Hawaii, 1994-96; presch. tchr. Aiea (Hawaii) Honwanji Presch., 1996—; tchr. ESL and Portuguese Windward Sch. for Adults, Kailua, Hawaii, 1996—; child care provider PATCH, Kaneohe, Hawaii, 1987-89. Painter in tempera and acrylics. Mem. Hawaii Assn. for Edn. of Young Children, Oahu Ednl. Employees fed. Credit Union, Tchrs. Club, Tchrs. Curriculum Assn. Roman Catholic. Avocations: reading, swimming, quilting, sewing, travel.

CAVALLARO, JOSEPH JOHN, microbiologist; b. Lawrence, Mass., Mar. 18, 1932; s. John and Salvatrice (Zappala) C.; m. Kathleen Frances Kraus, Dec. 2, 1972; children: Theresa Margaret, Sandra Marie, Elizabeth Camille, Danielle Kay, Gina Kathleen. BS, Tufts U., 1952; MS, U. Mass., 1954; PhD, U. Mich., 1966. Pub. health sanitarian Hartford (Conn.) Health Dept., 1954-55, 57-61; teaching assoc. dept. microbiology U. Mass., Amherst, 1961-62; rsch. virologist Med. Rsch. Labs., Charles Pfizer & Co., Groton, Conn., 1966-67; rsch. assoc. dept. epidemiology Sch. Pub. Health, U. Mich., Ann Arbor, 1967-70; microbiologist, diagnostic immunology tng. br. Ctrs. for Disease Control, Atlanta, 1971-86, research microbiologist anaerobic bacteria br., Ctrs. for Disease Control, 1986—; lectr. resident pathologists Grady Meml. Hosp., Atlanta, 1975; asst. prof. pathology Morehouse Sch. Medicine, 1982-85, clin. assoc. prof., 1986-97; adj. asst. prof. pathology and lab. medicine Emory U. Sch. of Medicine, 1985—; cons. Pan Am. Health Orgn., Colombia and Brazil, 1976, 77. Served with M.C., AUS, 1955-57. Registered specialist microbiologist Nat. Registry Microbiologist, Am. Acad. Microbiology. Fellow Am. Acad. Microbiology; mem. Am. Soc. Microbiology, Am. Assn. Immunologists, N.Y. Acad. Sci., KC, Sigma Xi. Democrat. Roman Catholic. Prin. author/co-author over 11 lab. manuals; contbr. articles to profl. jours., chpts. to books. Home: 1325 Balsam Dr Decatur GA 30033-2905 Office: 1600 Clifton Rd Atlanta GA 30333

CAVALLO, JO ANN, Italian language educator; b. Summit, N.J., May 21, 1959; d. Joseph Anthony and Jacqueline Amelia (Toth) C.; children: Maria Cristina, Alberto Joseph. Student, U. Florence, Italy, 1979-80, U. Valencia, Spain, 1980; BA, Rutgers U., 1981; student, Inst. French Studies, Avignon, 1982; MA, Yale U., 1984, PhD, 1987. Instr. dept. Italian Yale U., New Haven, 1983-86, instr. dept. Spanish, 1986-87, instr. Sch. Music, 1986-87; asst. prof. U. Wash., Seattle, 1987-88; assoc. prof. of Italian Columbia U., N.Y.C., 1988—; mem. sci. com. Boiardo Quincentennial Celebration, Italy, 1993-94; founder and program dir. Columbia U. Summer Program in Scandiano, Italy, 1995—. Author: (book) Boiardo's Orlando Innamorato: An Ethics of Desire, 1993. Recipient scholarship Nat. Italian Am. Found., Washington, 1986, fellowship grant Columbia U. Coun. for Rsch. in the Humanities, 1989, 90. Mem. MLA, Am. Assn. for Tchrs. of Italian, Am. Assn. of Italian Studies, Renaissance Soc. Am., Phi Beta Kappa. Roman Catholic. Home: 733 Buchanan St Toms River NJ 08753-7207 Office: Columbia Univ Italian Dept 514 Hamilton Hall New York NY 10027

CAVANAGH, CARROLL JOHN, business advisor, lawyer, principal art services company; b. N.Y.C., Nov. 11, 1943; s. Carroll and Mona (Schmid) C.; m. Valerie Ives Mixter (div.); children: Dorothy, Carroll III; m. Candida N. Smith, June 22, 1991; children: Hudson Nicholas, Gabriel Herald. BA, Yale U., 1964; JD cum laude, U. Pa., 1970; cert., Hague (The Netherlands) Acad. Internat. Law, 1969. Bar: D.C. 1979, Conn. 1970, N.Y. 1970. Assoc. Sullivan & Cromwell, N.Y.C., 1970-79; sec., gen. counsel Nat. Gallery of Art, Washington, 1979-85, trustee's coun., 1984-95; prin. asst. Paul Mellon, Upperville, Va., 1985-96; pres. Belvedere Found., 1993—. Lt. USNR, 1964-69. Clubs: Metropolitan (Washington), Union (N.Y.C.). Home: 43 W 13th St Apt 5F New York NY 10011-7908 Office: Art Assets LLC 1776 Broadway New York NY 10019-2002

CAVANAGH, DENIS, physician, educator. MB, ChB, U. Glasgow, Scotland, 1952. Diplomate: Am. Bd. Obstetrics and Gynecology. Former prof. gynecology and obstetrics, chmn. dept. St. Louis U. Sch. Medicine, 1966-77; prof. obstetrics, gynecology, dir. gynecologic oncology U. South Fla. Coll. Medicine, 1977—. Fellow ACS, ACOG, Am. Gyn-Ob Soc., Royal Coll. Obstetricians and Gynecologists; mem. South Atlantic Assn. Obstetricians and Gynecologists, Soc. Gynecol. Oncologists, Soc. Pelvic Surgeons. Office: 4 Columbia Dr Ste 529 Tampa FL 33606-3568

CAVANAGH, GERALD FRANCIS, business educator; b. Cleve., Sept. 13, 1931; s. Gerald Francis and Margaret Mildred (Gilmore) C. BS in Engring., Case Western Res. U., 1953; MBA, St. Louis U., 1958, Licentiate in Philosophy, 1959, MEd, 1960; Licentiate in Theology, Loyola U., Chgo., 1965; D in Bus. Adminstrn., Mich. State U., 1970; PhD, Loyola U., Balt., 1989, LHD (hon.), 1989. Ordained Jesuit Cath. priest, 1964. Assoc. prof. Wayne State U., Detroit, 1970-79; chair bus. ethics Santa Clara (Calif.) U., 1979-80; prof. U. Detroit, 1980-86; Gasson chair Boston Coll., 1986-87; acad. v.p. U. Detroit Mercy, 1989-92, provost, chancellor, 1992-95, chair bus. ethics, 1995—; trustee Fordham U., N.Y.C., 1974-80, Xavier U., Cin., 1981-84, Santa Clara U., 1991—; bd. chair U. Detroit, 1975-77; presenter in field. Author: Blacks in the Industrial World: Issues for the Manager, 1972, The Businessperson in Search of Values, 1976, American Business Values in Transition, 1976, Ethical Dilemmas in the Modern Corporation, 1988, American Business Values with International Perspectives, 4th rev. edit., 1998; contbr. articles to profl. jours. Mem. bd. ethics City of Detroit, 1994—. Mem. Internat. Assn. for Bus. and Soc., Acad. Mgmt. (Sumner Marcus award 1990), Soc. for Bus. Ethics, Theta Tau, Blue Key, Alpha Phi Omega (advisor), Beta Gamma Sigma, Tau Kappa Alpha, Alpha Sigma Nu. Office: Univ Detroit Mercy Lansing-Reilly Hall PO Box 19900 Detroit MI 48219-0900

CAVANAGH, HARRISON DWIGHT, ophthalmic surgeon, medical educator; b. Atlanta, July 22, 1940; s. William Edwards and Marie Corrine (Logue) C.; m. Lynn Ayres Gantt, Dec. 27, 1964; 1 dau., Catherine DuVal. *Confirmation Patent of Arms granted May 27, 1994 (liber X, folio 57) by Donald Begley, Chief Herald of Ireland, Dublin Castle: arms: Gules, a chevron between in chief two stag's heads caboshed and in the base a maltese cross all argent; crest: upon broad sword erect argent a stag's head caboshed gules within a chaplet of laurelvert fructured of the first; motto: Faoi Reir an tsolais. Grandfather William Edwards, born in 1869, Kinsale, Cork, emigrated to U.S. in 1896 and died in Leominster MA, 1943; second son of John Cavanagh (1836-1907) was born in Tralee, Co. Kerry. He was the commissioner of the Royal Irish Constabularyand died in Cork City.* A.B., Johns Hopkins U., 1962, M.D. (Joseph Collins scholar 1963-65), 1965; Ph.D. in Biology, Harvard U., 1972. Life diplomate Am. Bd. Ophthalmology. Intern Johns Hopkins Hosp., 1965-66, resident in ophthalmology, 1969-73; fellow corneal surgery Mass. Eye and Ear Infirmary, Boston, 1973-75; instr. ophthalmology Johns Hopkins Med. Sch., 1969-73; asst. prof. Harvard U. Med. Sch., 1975-76; mem. faculty Emory U., 1976-87, F. Phinizy Calhoun prof. ophthalmology, chmn. dept., 1978-87; prof. Georgetown U., Washington, 1987-91; Disting. Univ. prof., vice chmn. dept. ophthalmology U. Tex. Southwestern Med. Ctr., Dallas, 1991-95, W. Maxwell Thomas chair prof., 1995—; med. dir., assoc. dean clin. svcs. Zale Lipsky U. Hosp./U. Tex. Southwestern Med. Ctr.; vis. prof. Georgetown U., 1986-87; cons., chmn. visual scis. study sect A NIH, 1980-84; Heed Found. scholar, 1973-74; sci. adv. panel Nat. Soc. Prevention Blindness, Knights Templar Found.; civilian cons. USAF, 1983-86, USN, Bethesda Naval Hosp., 1989-91; mem. neuroscis. behavior study sect. NIH, 1989-93; organizing com. 3rd-4th Internat. Conf. on Confocal Microscopy and 4th-5th Internat. Conf. on 3D Image Processing in Microscopy, 1991—. Editor-in-chief Jour. Cornea, 1989-96; mem. editorial bd. Jour. Scanning, Bioimaging Jour.; contbr. articles to profl. jours. Recipient Heed medal lectr. U. Toronto, 1983, 2d Joseph Koplowitz lectr. Georgetown U., 1983, 14th Waldert lectr. U. Rochester, 1987, 5th Morton B. Sarver lectr. U. Calif., Berkeley, 1991, George Nissel lectr. Brit. Contact Lens Assn., 1997; 21st James McDonald lectr., Loyola U. Chicago, 1998, recipient Sr. Scientific Investigators award Rsch. to Prevent Blindness, Inc., 1996. Fellow ACS, Internat. Coll. Surgeons, Am. Acad. Ophthalmology (assoc. sect. govt. rels. and rsch. 1979-83, Honor Recognition award 1982, Whitney Sampson lectr. 1997), Royal Microscopy Soc., Royal Soc. Medicine; mem. Contact Lens Assn. Ophthalmologists Am. (pres. 1987, 20th Conrad Behrens medal lectr. 1989, Honor Recognition award 1988), Castroviejo Soc. Corneal Surgeons (pres. 1988-90, Honor Recognition awards 1987, 96), Keratorefractive Soc. (bd. dirs.), Internat. Eye Found. Eye Surgeons, New Eng. Ophthal. Soc., Assn. Rsch. in Vision and Ophthalmology (exec. sec.-treas. 1981-86, Honor Recognition award 1987), South-Ctrl. Eyebank Assn. (pres. 1997), Eye Bank Assn. Am. (bd. dirs. 1997-99), Johns Hopkins Club, Park Cities Club, Harvard Club (Dallas), Phi Beta Kappa. Republican. Episcopalian. Home: 27 Lakeside Park Dallas TX 75225-8110 Office: U Tex Southwestern Med Ctr Dept Ophthalmology 5323 Harry Hines Blvd Dallas TX 75235-7208

CAVANAGH, JOHN CHARLES, advertising agency executive; b. San Francisco, Dec. 19, 1932; s. John Timothy and Alicia Louise (McDowell) C.; m. Mary Ann Anding, Apr. 10, 1959; children: Karen, Brad. Student, U. Hawaii, 1950; BS, U. San Francisco, 1954. Pub. rels. rep. Kaiser Industries Corp., Oakland, Calif., 1956-58; pub. rels. mgr. Kaiser Cement & Gypsum Corp., Oakland, 1958-63; pub. relations dir. Fawcett-McDermott Assos. Inc., Honolulu, Hawaii, 1964-66; ops. v.p. Fawcett-McDermott Assos. Inc., 1966-69, exec. v.p., 1969-73, pres., dir., 1973-75; pres., dir. Fawcett McDermott Cavanagh Inc., Honolulu, 1975-87, Fawcett McDermott Cavanagh Calif., Inc., San Francisco, 1975-87; pres. The Cavanagh Group/Advt. Inc., San Francisco, Calif., 1987—. Served to 1st. lt. 740th Guided Missile Bn. AUS, 1954-56. Named Advt. Man of Yr. Honolulu Advt. Fedn., 1985. Mem. Pub. Rels. Soc. Am. (accredited, v.p. 1970, pres. Hawaii chpt. 1971), Advt. Agy. Assn. Hawaii (pres. 1973), Am. Assn. Advt. Agys. (chmn. Hawaii coun. 1980-81), Affiliated Advt. Agys. Internat. (chmn. 1984-85), Fountaingrove Country Club, Outrigger Canoe Club, Commonwealth Club of Calif. Home: 3750 Saint Andrews Dr Santa Rosa CA 95403-0945 Office: The Cavanagh Group 505 Sansome St Fl 10 San Francisco CA 94111-3106

CAVANAGH, JOHN HENRY, political economist; b. Boston, Aug. 20, 1955; s. James Ellsworth and Elizabeth (Brady) C.; m. Robin Broad, Apr. 26, 1982. BA, Dartmouth Coll., 1977; MPA, Princeton U., 1980. Asst officer econ. affairs UN Conf. on Trade and Devel., Geneva, 1977-78, 80-81; tech. officer World Health Orgn., Geneva, 1981-82; fellow Inst. for Policy Studies, Washington, 1983-95; co-dir. Inst. Policy Studies, Washington, 1996-97, dir., 1998—. Co-author: The World in Their Web, 1983, Alcoholic Beverages, 1985, From Debt to Development, 1986, Trade's Hidden Costs, 1988, Merchants of Drink, 1988, Trading Freedom, 1992, Plundering Paradise, 1993, Global Dreams: Imperial Corporations and the New World Order, 1994, Beyond Bretton Woods, 1994. Co-coord. Debt Crisis Network, Washington, 1984-89; advisor World Coun. Chs., Geneva, 1984-85; bd. dirs. Internat. Labor Rights Fund, Washington, 1987—, Philippine Devel. Forum, 1989-95, Inter-Hemispheric Resource Ctr., 1993—. Harbison fellow Princeton U., 1979. Democrat. Home: 214 Tulip Ave Silver Spring MD 20912-4202 Office: Inst for Policy Studies 1601 Connecticut Ave NW Washington DC 20009-1035

CAVANAGH, MICHAEL FRANCIS, state supreme court justice; b. Detroit, Oct. 21, 1940; s. Sylvester J. and Mary Irene (Timmins) C.; m. Patricia E. Ferriss, Apr. 30, 1966; children: Jane Elizabeth, Michael F., Megan Kathleen. BA, U. Detroit, 1962, JD, 1966. Bar: Mich. 1966. Law clk. to judge Ct. Appeals, Detroit, 1966-67; atty. City of Lansing, Mich., 1967-69; ptnr. Farhat, Story, et al., Lansing, Mich., 1969-73; judge 54-A Dist. Ct., Lansing, 1973-75, Mich. Ct. Appeals, Lansing, 1975-82; justice Supreme Ct., Lansing, 1983—, chief justice, 1991-94; Supreme Ct. liaison Mich. Indian Tribal Cts./Mich. State Cts.; supervising justice Sentencing Guidelines Com., Lansing, 1983-94, Mich. Jud. Inst., Lansing, 1986-94; bd. dirs. Thomas M. Cooley Law Sch., 1979-88; chair Mich. Justice Project, 1994-95, Nat. Interbranch Conf., Mpls., 1994-95. Bd. dirs. Am. Heart Assn. Mich., 1982—, chmn. bd. Am. Heart Assn. Mich., Lathrup Village, 1984-85; bd. dirs. YMCA, Lansing, 1978. Mem. ABA, Fed. Bar Assn., Ingham County Bar Assn., Inst. Jud. Adminstrn. (hon.), Inc. Soc. of Irish/Am. Lawyers (pres. 1987-88). Democrat. Roman Catholic. Avocations: jogging, racquetball, fishing. Office: Mich Supreme Ct 525 W Ottawa St Lansing MI 48933-1067

CAVANAGH, PETER ROBERT, science educator, researcher; b. Wolverhampton, Staffordshire, Eng., July 31, 1947; came to U.S., 1972; s. John Joseph and Dorothy Ann (Stokes) C.; m. Magda Margalova, Dec. 21, 1968 (div. 1979); 1 child, Sasha; m. Ann Elizabeth Vandervelde, Apr. 18, 1981; children: Drew, Chris, Jennifer. BEd, U. Nottingham, Loughborough Coll., 1968; PhD, U. London, Royal Free Med. Sch., 1972. Rsch. asst. Royal Free Med. Sch., London, 1968-72; asst. prof. Pa. State U., University Park, 1972-75, assoc. prof., 1975-81, prof., 1981-94, distng. prof. locomotion studies, kinesiology, biobehavioral health, medicine, orthpaedics, 1994—, dir. Ctr. for Locomotion Studies, 1986—; cons. U.S. Olympic Com., Colorado Springs, Colo., 1984-90, NASA, Houston, 1986—, various athletic shoe cos., U.S., Japan, Germany, 1978—; expert witness; sec. Am. Gait Lab. Accreditation Bd., 1995—. Author: The Running Shoe Book, 1980; co-author: Biomechanics and Physiology of Cycling, 1978, The Biomechanics of Distance Running, 1990, The Foot in Diabetes: A Bibliography, 1992, The Foot in Diabetes, 1994, Prevention, Protection and Recurrence Reduction of Diabetic Neuropathic Foot Ulcers, 1994; co-author: Prevention of Lower Extremity Amputation in Patients with Diabetes, 1996; mem. editl. bd. Posture and Gait, Foot and Ankle Internat., 1994—. Fellow Am. Coll. Sports Medicine (trustee 1987, Wolffe lectr. 1987); mem. Internat. Soc. Biomechanics (pres. 1995-97), Am. Soc. Biomechanics (pres. 1986-87, Borelli award 1994), Am. Diabetes Assn. (chmn. rsch. com. of foot coun. 1992-94), Internat. Soc. Electrophysiol. Assn. for Study Diabetes, Aerospace Med. Soc., Am. Soc. Gravitational and Space Biology, Am. Acad. Podiatric Sports Medicine (hon.), Orthopedic Rsch. Soc., Internat. Space Sta. Human Rsch. Facility Sci. Working Group NASA (chmn. musculoskeletal group 1995—), European Assn. Study Diabetes. Avocations: running, music, collecting British classic cars, flying. Office: Pa State U Ctr for Locomotion Studies 29 Recreation Bldg University Park PA 16802-5702

CAVANAGH, RICHARD EDWARD, business policy organization executive; b. Buffalo, June 15, 1946; s. Joseph John and Mary Celeste (Stack) C.; m. Patricia Sypher, 1995; 1 child, Katherine Ann. BA, Wesleyan U., Middletown, Conn., 1968; MBA, Harvard U., 1970. Assoc. McKinsey & Co. Inc., Washington, 1970-77, sr. cons., 1979, ptnr., 1980-88; exec. dir. fed. cash mgmt. U.S. Office Mgmt. and Budget, Washington, 1977-79; exec. dean Kennedy Sch. Govt. Harvard U., Cambridge, Mass., 1988-95; pres., CEO The Conference Board, Inc., N.Y.C., 1995—; mem. staff Carter-Mondale Policy Planning, 1976; cons. Carter-Mondale Presdl. Transition, 1976-77; domestic coord. Pres.' Reorgn. Project, The White House, Washington, 1978-79; mem. exec. com. Pres.' Pvt. Sector Survey on Cost Control, Grace Commn., 1982-83; mem. bus. adv. com. advanced study program Brookings Instn., 1983-86. Co-author: (with Donald K. Clifford Jr.) The Winning Performance: How America's High-Growth Midsize Companies Succeed, 1985, 2d edit., 1988 (pub. in 11 fgn. langs.). Mem. bd. judges Dively Award, Harvard U., 1984-94; mem. bd. visitors Georgetown U. Sch. Bus., 1985-92; trustee Ctr. for Excellence in Govt., 1985, 96—, Drucker Found., 1998—, Ednl. Testing Svc., 1997; trustee Wesleyan U., 1988—, vice chair, 1997—; trustee, dir. Black Rock Mut. Funds, 1994—; dir. Fremont Group, The Guardian Ins., Arch Chems.; trustee Airplanes Group, 1999—. With U.S. Army, 1968. Recipient Presdl. commendation, 1979, 80, 83; John Reilly Knox fellow, 1969, Clark fellow, 1969. Mem. Am. Soc. Pub. Adminstrn., Acad. Polit. Sci., Coun. on Fgn. Rels., Raimond Duy Baird Assn., Wesleyan U. Alumni Assn. (chmn. 1985-87), Met Club (D.C.), Harvard Club (N.Y.C.), Beta Theta Pi. Democrat. Roman Catholic. Home: 995 Memorial Dr Cambridge MA 02138-4842 Office: The Conference Board Inc 845 3rd Ave New York NY 10022-6601

CAVANAGH-MCKEE, KATHRYN, nurse; b. N.Y.C., July 11, 1938; d. Arthur James and Ethel (Adrian) Cavanagh; div.; children: Victoria, Carolyn. BA magna cum laude, Hunter Coll., CUNY, 1985; BSN, Hunter-Bellevue Sch. Nursing, 1988. RN, N.Y. Med.-surg. nurse N.Y. Hosp.,

N.Y.C., 1989-90; emergency room intern St. Luke's Hosp., N.Y.C., 1990-91; RN emergency dept. A.O. Fox Meml. Hosp., Oneonta, N.Y., 1991-93; emergency dept. asst. nurse care coord. St. Francis Hosp., Jersey City, 1994-95; staff nurse student health svcs. NYU, N.Y.C., 1995-98; Sr. staff nurse, IV team NYU Med. Ctr., N.Y.C., 1998—. Mem. Sigma Theta Tau. Home: 530 E 23rd St New York NY 10010-5022

CAVANAUGH, DENNIS M., federal judge. Bar: N.J. Magistrate judge for N.J., U.S. Magistrate Ct., Newark, 1993—. Office: US PO and Courthouse Bldg Rm 2060 Newark NJ 07102

CAVANAUGH, JAMES HENRY, medical corporate executive, former government official; b. Orange, N.J., Mar. 3, 1937; s. James H. and Madeline Rachel (McFerren) C.; m. Esther Sally Musselman, Jan. 20, 1962; children: Elizabeth Anne, Michael Patrick. BS, Fairleigh Dickinson U., 1959; MA, U. Iowa, 1961, PhD, 1964. Asst. adminstr. Princeton (N.J.) Hosp., 1961-62; asst. prof. hosp. and health care adminstrn. U. Iowa, 1964-66; spl. asst. to surgeon gen. USPHS, 1966-67, dir. office comprehensive health planning, 1967-68; dep. asst. sec. health and sci. affairs HEW, 1969-71; staff asst. for health affairs Pres. Nixon, The White House, 1971-73, asst. dir. domestic council, 1973-74, dep. dir., 1974-75; dep. chief White House staff for Pres. Ford, 1975-76; v.p. corp. devel. Allergan Pharms., Irvine, Calif., 1977-78, sr. v.p. sci. and planning, 1978-81; spl. cons. to Pres. Reagan, 1981; pres. Allergan Internat., 1981-82, SmithKline BioSci. Labs., 1983-85, Smith Kline & French Labs. US, Phila., 1985-88, HealthCare Investment Corp.; founding bd. dirs. Marine Nat. Bank, Santa Ana Calif.; bd. dirs. Nat. Ctr. for Genome Resources, MedImmune, Inc., Shire Pharms. Group, PLC, Leukosite, Inc. Mem. Pres.'s Export Council, 1981-85; bd. dirs. Proprietary Assn., 1980-82; trustee Nat. Com. for Quality Health Care, nat. chmn. 1988; trustee emeritus Calif. Coll. Medicine; mem. nat. adv. com. Am. Refugee Com. Recipient Disting. Alumnus award U. Iowa Coll. Medicine. Mem. Am. Hosp. Assn. (hon.), Pharm. Mfrs. Assn. (bd. dirs. 1986-88), Union League Club (Phila.). Episcopalian (vestryman). Home: 554 Dorset Rd Devon PA 19333-1845 Office: HealthCare Ventures LLC 44 Nassau St Princeton NJ 08542-4506

CAVANAUGH, JOSEPH THOMAS, museum director; b. Washington, Feb. 28, 1947; s. Joseph Thomas and Hester Ann (Burns) C.; m. Stephanie Louise Jacobson, Nov. 28, 1969; 1 child, Michael. BA, U. Ark., 1978. Historian Prairie Grove Battlefield State Park, Ark., 1978-81; exhibits tech. Goliad (Tex.) State Park, 1981-83; mus. curator Refugio (Tex.) County Mus., 1983-89; exec. dir. Dr. Pepper Mus. & Free Enterprise Inst., Waco, Tex., 1989—. Mem. Mus. Assn. South Tex. (pres. 1987), Mus. Assn. Waco (pres. 1992-93), Tex. Assn. Mus. (councilor-at-large 1994-98), Rotary. Roman Catholic. Avocations: photography, computers. Office: Dr Pepper Mus & Free Enterprise Inst 300 S 5th St Waco TX 76701-2115*

CAVANAUGH, KENNETH CLINTON, retired housing consultant; b. Fremont, Mich., Apr. 30, 1916; s. Frank Michael and Buryll Marie (Preston) C.; m. Barbara Blythe Boling, Feb. 24, 1979; children from previous marriage: Patricia Ann, James Lee, John Thomas. BS in Forestry, Mich. State U., 1939. County supr. Farm Security Adminstrn., USDA, Kalamazoo, 1939-43; community mgr. PHA, Willow Run, Mich., 1946-49; dir. fiscal mgmt. PHA, Washington, 1949-55, dir. elderly housing Housing & Home Fin. Agy., 1955-57; reg. dir. PHA, San Juan, P.R., 1957-58; dir. housing programs HUD, Washington, 1958-73; controller/dep. dir. San Francisco Housing Authority, 1973-78; pres. Ken C. Cavanaugh & Assocs., pvt. internat. housing and community devel. cons., Vista, Calif., 1978—; fin. finder Merrill Lynch-Huntoon Paige Co., San Francisco, 1979-81, Western Pacific Fin. Co., Newport Beach, Calif., 1981-83; gen. ptnr. The Knolls, Rogers, Ark., 1980-89. Exec. dir. Arlington (Va.) Youth Found., 1950-58; advisor Salvation Army adv. bd., Honolulu, 1985-88. Served to capt. USN, 1943-46, USNR, 1946-73. Recipient Superior Svc. award, Pub. Housing Adminstrn., 1956. Mem. Nat. Assn. Housing & Redevel. Ofcls., Ret. Officers Assn., Res. Officers Assn., Naval Res. Assn., Shadowridge Golf Club (Vista), Elks, Masons. Avocations: golf, travel. Home and Office: PO Box 749 Vista CA 92085-0749

CAVANAUGH, MARGARET ANNE, chemist; b. Dayton, Ohio, July 17, 1947; m. Joseph C. Cavanaugh. BS in Chemistry, U. Pitts., 1968; PhD in Phys. Inorganic Chemistry, Cath. U. Am., 1973. Asst. prof. chemistry and physics St. Mary's Coll., Notre Dame, Ind., 1975-79, assoc. prof., 1979-86, prof., chair, 1981-82, 85-89, acting dept. chair, 1981-82, 85-86; program officer chemistry divsn. NSF, Arlington, Va., 1989-91, program dir. chemistry divsn., 1991—; vis. asst. prof., postdoctoral rsch. assoc. chemistry U. New Orleans, 1973-75; vis. scientist UOP, Inc., 1983; mem. test devel. com. for advanced placement exam. in chemistry The Coll. Bd., 1988-91; lectr. Am. U., 1991, George Wash. U., 1990-92. Trustee U. Dayton, 1990—. Fellow Am. Inst. Chemists; mem. Am. Chem. Soc. (councilor 1984-90, women chemists com. 1982-88, chair 1988, meetings and expositions com. 1985-87, nominations and elections com. 1988-90, soc. com. on edn. assn. 1991-95, coun. com. pub. rels. chair 1994-96, com. on sci. 1997—, award for encouraging women into careers in chem. scis. 1995), Internat. Union Pure and Applied Chemistry, Sigma Xi, Iota Sigma Pi (editor 1981-87, v.p. 1987-90, pres. 1990-93, immediate past pres. 1993-96). Achievements include research in synthesis and reactions of transition metal compounds, particularly those containing metal clusters, unusual oxidation states, or proton interactions. Office: NSF Chemistry Divsn Rm 1055 Arlington VA 22230

CAVANAUGH, MARIANNE, secondary educator. BA, St. Joseph Coll., 1974; MA, Ctrl. Conn. State U., 1980; postgrad., U. Hartford, 1997—. Lectr. U. Conn., 1998—; head tchr., math K-12, 1992—, secondary math tchr., 1975—; presenter in field. Named Conn. Tchr. of Yr., 998, Middle Sch. Tchr. of Yr. Conn. Assn. of Schs., 1997. Mem. Nat. Coun. for Suprs. of Math., Assn. for Tchrs. of Math. in Conn., Nat. Coun. for Tchrs. of Math., Conn. Coun. for Leaders in Math., Nat. State Tchrs. of Yr. E-mail: awecav@aol.com. Office: Glastonbury High Sch Hubbard St Glastonbury CT 06033

CAVANAUGH, MICHAEL EVERETT, lawyer, arbitrator, mediator; b. Seattle, Dec. 23, 1946; s. Wilbur R. Cavanaugh and Gladys E. (Herring) Barber; m. Susan P. Heckman, Sept. 7, 1968. AB, U. Calif., Berkeley, 1973; JD, U. Wash., 1976. Bar: Wash. 1976, U.S. Dist. Ct. (we. dist.) Wash. 1977, U.S. Ct. Appeals (9th cir.) 1977, U.S. Dist. Ct. (ea. dist.) Wash. 1978. Staff atty. U.S. Ct. of Appeals (9th cct.) Calif., San Francisco, 1976-77; from assoc. to ptnr. Preston & Thorgrimson, Seattle, 1981-85; ptnr. Bogle & Gates, Seattle, 1985-97, assoc., 1977-81, ptnr., 1985-97; propr. Michael E. Cavanaugh, J.D., Arbitration and Mediation, Seattle, 1997—. Contbg. author: Employment Discrimination Law, 3d edit., 1995. Avocations: sailing, creative writing, music. Office: 1420 5th Ave Ste 2200 Seattle WA 98101-2333

CAVANAUGH, TOM RICHARD, artist, antiques dealer, retired art educator; b. Danville, Ill., July 19, 1923; s. Harry William and Hazel (Brown) C. B.F.A., U. Ill., 1947, M.F.A. (McLellan fellow), 1950. Art and ednl. dir. Springfield (Ill.) Art Assn., 1947-49; mem. faculty Kansas City Art Inst., 1952-55, Washington U. Sch. Art, St. Louis, 1955-56; emeritus prof. painting and drawing La. State U., Baton Rouge, 1957-83, ret., 1983; owner, dir. The Bay Street Studio, Boothbay Harbor, Maine, 1950—. One man shows, Chapellier Gallery, N.Y.C., 1963, La. State U., 1963, 78, Griffith-Menard Gallery, Baton Rouge, 1986; group shows include, Met. Mus. Art, 1950, Whitney Mus., 1951-58, Corcoran biennials, 1959, 61, Nelson Gallery Art, 1952, Joslyn Mus. Art, 1954, Mulvane Art Mus., 1955, Kans. State Coll., 1956, New Orleans Mus., 1959, Ark. Arts Center, 1961; represented in permanent collections, Mead Corp., N.Y.C., Joslyn Mus. Art, New Orleans Mus., others; executed mural Govt. Bldg., Baton Rouge; publication: Outstanding Educators of America, 1975. Served with U.S. Army, 1943-45. Fulbright fellow Italy, 1956-57; McDowell Colony fellow, 1973. Office: 2 Bay St Boothbay Harbor ME 04538-2142 Home: 8155 Gulf Blvd Navarre Beach FL 32566-7115

CAVANEAU, JERRY W., federal judge. Magistrate judge U.S. Dist. Ct. (ea. dist.) Ark., Little Rock. Office: 600 W Capitol Ave Ste 502 Little Rock AR 72201-3327

CAVANNA, DINO FRANCESCO, chemicals executive; b. Arona, Novara, Italy, Oct. 5, 1939; came to U.S., 1967; s. Carlo and Carla (Gelada) C.; m. Barbara Dziewulska, Nov. 30, 1946; children: Robert, Danielle. Degree in polit. and social scis., U. Milan, 1964; degree in internat. policy and indsl. diplomacy, Inst. Study Internat. Policy, Milan, 1965; degree in law, economy of European cmtys, Internat. Ctr. Studies and Documentation European Cmtys., Milan, 1966; postgrad., NYU, 1974. Exec. v.p. Indesit, Inc., N.Y.C., 1967-69, pres., 1969-82; pres. Indesit Mfg., Harrison, N.Y., 1982-89, Domestic Appliances Trading of Am., Inc., N.Y.C., 1989-91; exec. v.p. The Tartaric Chems. Co., N.Y.C., 1991—. Mem. Italy-Am. C. of C. (N.Y.C. chpt., bd. dirs. 1996—, mem. adv. com. 1997—), Larchmont (N.Y.) Shore Club (bd. dirs. 1994—), Famija Piemonteisa Cultural Found. (bd. dirs. 1991, mem. exec. com. 1996—), European-am. C. of C. U.S., Inc. (N.Y.C. chpt. bd. dirs. 1998—). Avocations: tennis, historical social studies. Home: 38 Howell Ave Larchmont NY 10538-3249 Office: The Tartaric Chems Corp 515 Madison Ave Rm 1902 New York NY 10022-5403

CAVARNOS, CONSTANTINE PETER, writer, philosopher; b. Boston, Oct. 19, 1918; s. Peter (Panagiotes) John and Irene (Maistrou) C. AB magna cum laude, Harvard U., 1942, AM, 1947, PhD, 1948. Tchg. asst. in philosophy Harvard U., Radcliffe Coll., 1945-46; teaching fellow in philosophy Harvard U., Cambridge, Mass., 1946-47; teaching asst. in philosophy Tufts U., Wellesley (Mass.) Coll., 1948-49; asst. prof. philosophy U. N.C., Chapel Hill, 1949-54; assoc. prof., prof. philosophy and Byzantine art Greek Orthodox Sch. Theology, Brookline, Mass., 1954-56; vis. assoc. prof. philosophy Wheaton Coll., Norton, Mass., 1965-67, Clark U., Worcester, Mass., 1967-68; pres. Inst. for Byzantine and Modern Greek Studies, Belmont, Mass., 1969—; adj. prof. philosophy and Byzantine art Hellenic Coll., Brookline, 1978-82. Author: A Dialogue between Bergson, Aristotle and Philologos, 1949, Byzantine Sacred Art, 1957, Anchored in God, 1959, Man and the Universe in American Philosophy, 1959, Symbols and Proofs of Immortality, 1964, Modern Greek Philosophers on the Human Soul, 1967, Byzantine Thought and Art, 1968, Modern Greek Thought, 1969, The Holy Mountain, 1973, Plato's Theory of Fine Art, 1973, 2d edit., 1998, The Classical Theory of Relations, 1975, Plato's View of Man, 1975, Orthodox Iconography, 1977, A Dialogue on G.E. Moore's Ethical Philosophy, 1979, Paths and Means to Holiness, 1980, Modern Orthodox Saints, Vols. I-XIII, 1971-99, St. Nectarios of Aegina, 1981, 2d edit., 1988, 95, The Future Life According to Orthodox Teaching, 1984, The Educational Theory of Benjamin Lesvos, 1984, Meetings with Kontoglou, 1985, Bysanttilainen Taide, 1987, The Goodness of God and the Self-Willed Wickedness of Man, 1987, St. Methodia of Kimolos, 1987, Smoking and the Orthodox Christian, 1988, Fasting and Science, 1988, The Hellenic-Christian Philosophical Tradition, 1989, New Library, Vol. 1, 1989, Vol. 2, 1992, Vol. 3, 1995, Immortality of the Soul, 1993, Guide to Byzantine Iconography, Vol. I, 1993, Vol. II, 1999, Pythagoras on the Fine Arts as Therapy, 1994, Biological Evolutionism, 1994, 2nd ed. 1997, Orthodox Christian Terminology, 1994, Cultural and Educational Continuity of Greece, 1995; editor: Greek Language and Culture: Their Vitality and Importance Today, 1995, Byzantine Churches of Thessaloniki, 1995, He Hiera Byzantine Techne, 1995, Spiritual Beauty, 1996, The Concept of Christian Love, 1996, The Seven Sages of Ancient Greece, 1996, Ecumenism Examined, 1996, Victories of Orthodoxy, 1997, St. Nectarios' Study on Holy Icons, 1997, Byzantine Chant, 1998, Fine Arts as Therapy, 1998, St. Photios The Great: Philosopher and Theologian, 1998, Dostoievsky's Philosophy of Man, 1998. Sheldon Travel fellow in philosophy, Harvard/Athens-Paris-Cambridge (Eng.)-Oxford, 1947-48, Fulbright Rsch. scholar U. Athens, 1957-59; recipient Archon of the Oecumenical Patriarchate, Constantinople, 1979, Ann. Faculty award Hellenic Coll., 1986, The Florovsky Theol. prize Ctr. for Traditionalist Orthodox Studies, 1992. Mem. Am. Philos. Assn., The Metaphysical Soc. of Am. (past treas. 1949), Internat. Inst. Arts & Letters, Revista de la Soc. Argentina of Philosophy, Plomaritan Soc. of Boston (past pres.), Ctr. de Estudios Bizantinos y Neohelénicos Fotios Malleros U. Chile (hon.). Greek Orthodox. Avocations: music, restoration of icons, walking. Home: 115 Gilbert Rd Belmont MA 02478-2200 Office: Inst Byzantine & Greek Studies 115 Gilbert Rd Belmont MA 02478-2200

CAVAT, IRMA, artist, educator; b. Bklyn.; children: Karina Cavat-Gore, Nika Cavat-Hoffman. Student, NYU, 1956, Alexander Archipenko Sch., Woodstock, N.Y., New Sch. for Social Rsch., N.Y.C., 1960-62. Prof. art U. Calif., Santa Barbara, 1964-91. One-woman shows include Gallery Sistina, Rome, 1961, 63, Santa Barbara Mus. Art, 1966, Phoenix Art Mus., 1967, Kennedy Gallery, N.Y.C., 1972, 74, 78, Arwin Galleries, Detroit, 1982, 84, 87, Feingarten Gallery, L.A., 1991, Cline Gallery, Santa Fe, 1995, Fielding Inst., Santa Barbara, Calif., 1996, others. Fulbright fellow, Rome, 1957-59. Avocations: poetry, travel. Office: Univ of California Dept Art Santa Barbara CA 93106

CAVE, ALFRED ALEXANDER, history educator, writer; b. Albuquerque, Feb. 8, 1935; s. Jerome Waite and Jane Harscher; m. Harriett Bennett, June 15, 1961 (div. July 1977); children: Ruth Anne, Laurence Andrew, Elizabeth Jane, Rachel Grace; m. Mary Sue Deisher, May 25, 1978. BA, Linfield Coll., McMinnville, Oreg., 11957; MA, U. Fla., 1959, PhD, 1961; DLitt (hon.), Salford (Eng.) U., 1990. Instr. U. Fla., Gainesville, 1960-61, CCNY, 1961-62; from asst. prof. to prof. U. Utah, Salt Lake City, 1962-73, dean humanities, 1967-73; prof. history U. Toledo, 1973—, dean arts and scis., 1973-90. Author: Jacksonian Democracy and the Historians, 1964, The Pequot War, 1996. Mem. AAUP (v.p. U. Toledo chpt. 1994—). Democrat. Roman Catholic. Home: 2434 Goddard Rd Toledo OH 43606-3207 Office: U Toledo Dept History Toledo OH 43606-3207

CAVE, KENT R., national park ranger; b. Elkin, N.C., Oct. 6, 1952; s. John Marvin and Bessie Irene (Dezern) C.; m. Annette Gail Pruitt, May 28, 1983; children: John Carlton, Jacob Reuben, Benjamin Pruitt. BA, Appalachian State U., 1974, student, 1974-76; student, U. Tenn., 1976-80. Editorial asst. Papers of Andrew Johnson, Knoxville, 1976-80; park ranger Blue Ridge Pkwy, Asheville, N.C., 1975-77, Great Smoky Mountains Nat. Park, Gatlinburg, Tenn., 1980-83; park ranger Andrew Johnson Nat. Hist. Site, Greeneville, Tenn., 1984-87, chief park ranger, 1987-88; chief park ranger Ft. Pulaski Nat. Monument, Savannah, Ga., 1988-97; info. officer NPS SE Region Incident Mgmt. Team, 1994—; staff park ranger, interpretation Gt. Smoky Mountains Nat. Park, Gatlinburg, Tenn., 1997—. Active Bull St. Bapt. Ch., Savannah, Ga., 1992-97, dir. Royal Ambassador youth group, 1993-97; active 1st Bapt. Ch., Gatlinburg, Tenn., 1997—, mem. missions com., 1998—. Hilton Smith fellow U. Tenn., 1980. Mem. Nat. Park Svc. Employees and Alumni Assn. (life), Savannah Fed. Exec. Assn. (pres. 1991), So. Hist. Assn., Appalachian Studies Assn. Avocations: woodworking, hiking, Am. history, early 20th century naval history. Office: Gt Smoky Mountains Nat Park Interpretation & Vis Svcs 107 Park Headquarters Rd Gatlinburg TN 37738-4102

CAVE, MAC DONALD, anatomy educator; b. Phila., May 14, 1939; s. Edward Joseph and Adeline Roberta (MacDonald) C.; m. Donna Kay Brainard, Jan. 1, 1989; children from previous marriage: Eric MacDonald, Heidi Lee. B.A., Susquehanna U., 1961; M.S., U. Ill., 1963, Ph.D., 1965. Instr. dept. anatomy U. Ill. Coll. Medicine, Chgo., 1964-65; asst. prof. U. Pitts. Sch. Medicine, 1967-72; assoc. prof. anatomy U. Ark. Med. Ctr., Little Rock, 1972-79, prof. anatomy, 1979—. Contbr. numerous articles to profl. jours. Am. Cancer Soc.-Swedish Am. exchange fellow, 1966; USPHS postdoctoral fellow Max Planck Inst., Tubingen, W. Ger., 1966-67. Mem. AAAS, Am. Assn. Anatomists, Am. Soc. Cell Biology, Am. Soc. for Microbiology, Sigma Xi, Pi Gamma Mu. Home: 5220 Crestwood Dr Little Rock AR 72207-5404 Office: U Ark Med Scis Dept Anatomy 4301 W Markham St Little Rock AR 72205-7101

CAVE, SKIP, company executive. Dir. R&D Intervoice, Inc. Address: Intervoice Inc 17811 Waterview Pkwy Dallas TX 75252-8016*

CAVELL, CHARLES G., printing company executive. BS in Econs., Mount Allison U., New Brunswick; postgrad., U. Western Ont., Sir George Williams U. With Bell Canada, Yellow Pages; with Tele-Direct Inc., v.p. mfg.; asst. to pres. Ronalds Pringtin, pres., CEO; pres., CEO BCE PubliTech Inc.; pres., COO Quebecor Printing Inc. a subsidiary Quebecor Inc., CEO, 1997—, also bd. dirs.; bd. dirs. Hydro-Quebec, Guillevin Internat. Inc., Royal Bank Equity Ptnrs. Ltd. subsidiary of Royal Bank. Office: Quebecor Printing Inc, 612 Saint-Jacques St, Montreal, PQ Canada H3C 4M8

CAVENDER, CATHERINE C., magazine editor; b. Anniston, Ala., Oct. 31, 1957; d. Henry J. and Annette (Hilley) C.; m. Michael D. Heneberry, Oct. 1, 1988. BA, Douglas Coll., New Brunswick, N.J., 1979. Editl. asst., asst. editor Redbook Mag., N.Y.C., 1979-83; promotion assoc. Parade Mag., N.Y., 1985; assoc. articles editor Mademoiselle Mag., N.Y.C., 1987-90; mng. editor YM Mag., N.Y.C., 1990-93; exec. editor Seventeen Mag., N.Y.C., 1993-94, McCall's Mag., N.Y.C., 1995—. Mem. Am. Soc. Mag. Editors. Address: Family Circle 375 Lexington Ave 9th Fl New York NY 10017-5514*

CAVENDER, MICHAEL CHARLES, broadcast news executive; b. Aurora, Ill., Mar. 15, 1954; s. Norbert Leon Cavender and Marilyn (Augustine) Clabaugh; m. Kathryn Harle, Aug. 14, 1976. BS in Journalism, No. Ill. U., 1976; MS in Journalism, Northwestern U., 1977. Exec. producer Sta. KMOL-TV, San Antonio, 1979-84; producer Sta. WMAQ-TV, Chgo., 1984-85; exec. producer Sta. WKRN-TV, Nashville, 1985-88; news dir. Sta. WTVF-TV, Nashville, 1988-92; v.p. news divsn. Sta. WTSP-TV, Tampa, Fla., 1992-97, Sta. WUSA-TV, Washington, 1997-99; news dir. CBS/ Atlanta, Atlanta, 1999—. Recipient Emmy award NATAS, 1987, 88, 92, 94, 97. Mem. Radio-TV News Dirs. Assn. (nat. bd. dirs. 1990-98, chmn. bd. dirs. 1996-97, trustee 1996—), Nashville chpt. Soc. Profl. Journalists (pres. 1989-90), Tampa Bay Soc., Ctr. Club, Montgomery Country Club. Avocations: golf, music, travel.

CAVENDER, PATRICIA PATTEN, director program; b. Louisa, Ky., Oct. 29, 1950; d. William Patten. B, Ohio U., 1972, M, 1974. Asst. dir. fundraising Ohio U., Athens, 1974-76, adj. prof. German, 1979-80, internat. advisor, 1981-84, asst. dir. admissions, 1984-87, asst. dir. alumni rels., 1989-93; dir. admissions U. W. Fla., Pensacola, 1987-89; dir. admissions Old Dominion U., Norfolk, Va., 1993-97, asst. v.p. enrollment svcs., 1995-97; dir. admissions Christopher Newport U., Newport News, Va., 1997—. Mem. NACAC, AACRAO. E-mail: pcavende@cnu.edu.

CAVENEE, WEBSTER K., director. Dir., prof. Ludwig Inst. for Cancer Rsch. U. Calif., LaJolla, 1991—. Office: Ludwig Inst 9500 Gilman Dr La Jolla CA 92093-0660

CAVENEY, WILLIAM JOHN, pharmaceutical company executive, lawyer; b. Wheeling, W.Va., Aug. 5, 1944; s. James Joseph and Esther Virginia (Ackermann) C.; AB cum laude, W.Va. U., 1966; JD, Vanderbilt U., 1969; LLM in Taxation, NYU, 1977, Advanced Profl. Cert. in Fin., Grad. Sch. Bus. Adminstrn., 1979; m. Margaret Carol Serota, Sept. 18, 1971; children: Ryan Benjamin, Christine Joanna. Bar: N.Y. 1972, U.S. Supreme Ct. 1976. Tax mgr. Arthur Andersen & Co., N.Y.C., 1969-73; tax atty. Texaco, Inc., N.Y.C., 1973-76; mgr. tax planning Norton Simon, Inc., N.Y.C., 1976-78; dir. tax planning Warner-Lambert Co., Morris Plains, N.J., 1978-79, corporate tax counsel, mem. tax planning com., 1979—; mem. Township Com., mayor, Millburn-Short Hills, N.J.; lectr. Taxation and internat. fin. CPA, N.Y. Council mem., auditor The Short Hills Assn.; trustee Rep. Club of Millburn, Short Hills; trustee Free Pub. Libr., Millburn, N.J., Cora Hartshorn Arboretum, Short Hills, N.J.; chmn. Hist. Preservation Commn., Millburn; mem. Zoning Bd. Adjustment, Millburn. Mem. AICPA, ABA (com. fgn. activities of U.S. taxpayers), N.Y. State Bar Assn. (mem. exec. com. tax sect.), N.Y. State Soc. CPAs, Tax Execs. Inst., (chmn. internat. tax steering com.), World Trade Inst. Contbr. articles to profl. jours. Home: 88 Stewart Rd Short Hills NJ 07078-1924 Office: 201 Tabor Rd Morris Plains NJ 07950-2614

CAVENY, LEONARD HUGH, mechanical engineer, aerospace scientist, consultant; b. Atlanta, Oct. 30, 1934; s. Elmer Leonard and Dorothy (Franklin) C.; m. Joyce Rodal, Apr. 10, 1957; children: Polly J., Rebecca R., Teresa L., Leslie Y., Susan C. BME, Ga. Inst. Tech., 1956, MSME, 1960; PhD in Mech. Engring., U. Ala., 1969. Registered profl. engr. Ala., 1965. Supr. aerothermodynamics Thiokol Chem. Corp., Huntsville, Ala., 1960-67; sr. tech. staff Princeton (N.J.) U., 1969-80; program mgr. Air Force Office Sci. Rsch., Washington, 1980-85; dep. dir. sci. and tech. Strategic Defense Initiative Orgn., Washington, 1985-93; dir. sci. & tech. Ballistic Missile Defense Orgn., Washington, 1993-97; cons. in field. Editor: Orbit-Raising and Maneuvering Propulsion, 1984; inventor in field. Lt. (j.g.) USN, 1956-59. Recipient Yuri Gagarin medal, Moscow, 1993. Fellow AIAA (chair elec. propulsion tech. com. 1984-86, chair Princeton sect. 1974-75, tech. chair internat. elec. propulsion conf. 1985, editorial adv. bd. 1988—, Wyld Propulsion medal 1997); mem. The Combustion Inst. Avocations: photography, construction, tennis. Home: 13715 Piscataway Dr Fort Washington MD 20744-6635

CAVERS-HUFF, DASIEA YVONNE, philosopher; b. Cleve., Oct. 24, 1961; d. Lawrence Benjamin and Yvonne (Warner) Cavers; m. Brian Jay Huff, July 26, 1986. BA, Cleve. State U., 1984, MA, 1990; postgrad., U. Md., 1986-90; PhD, U. Calif., Riverside, 1997; postgrad., Calif. So. Sch. Law, 1997—. Teaching asst. Cleve. State U., 1983-86; instr. Upward Bound program Case Western Res. U., Cleve., 1986; instr. U. Md., Coll. Park, Md., 1987-89; mem. faculty Charles County Community Coll., 1989-90; assoc. prof. Riverside Community Col., 1990—. U. Md. grad. fellow, 1986-87; Ford Found. predoctoral fellow, 1987-89. Mem. Am. Philos. Assn., Minority Grad. Student Assn. (co-chmn. U. Md. 1987-88). Democrat. Avocations: swimming, biking, gourmet cooking, jogging. Home: 25969 Andre Ct Moreno Valley CA 92553-6824 Office: Riverside City CollDivsn Humanities & Social Sci Riverside CA 92506

CAVERT, HENRY MEAD, physician, retired educator; b. Mpls., Mar. 30, 1922; s. William Lane and Mary (Mead) C.; m. June Lorraine Sederstrom, Jan. 27, 1946; children: John Mead (dec.), Harlan McCrea, Winston Peter. B.S. in Agrl. Biochemistry, U. Minn., 1942, M.D., 1951, Ph.D. in Physiology, 1952. Postdoctoral research fellow Am. Heart Assn., 1951-54; faculty U. Minn. Med. Sch., 1953-92, assoc. dean, 1964-92, prof. physiology, 1967-92, prin. investigator Gen. Clin. Rsch. Ctr., 1978-92, prof. emeritus, 1992—; Nat. Heart Inst. spl. rsch. fellow, vis. prof. biochemistry U. Edinburgh, Scotland, 1961-62; established investigator Am. Heart Assn., 1954-57; mem. program project com. B, Nat. Heart Inst., 1966-69; cons. Nat. Heart and Lung Inst., 1969-92. Author: (with A.J. Carlson and V. Johnson) Machinery of the Body, 5th edit., 1961; also numerous articles. Mem. met. bd. dirs. YMCA, Mpls., 1968-70, mem. endowment com., 1988—; mem. bd. mgmt. U. Minn. YMCA, 1955-57, 77-83, 84-90, chmn., 1968-70, chmn. capital campaign endowment, 1992-95, chmn. capital bldg. campaign, 1998-99; mem. bd. parish edn. Am. Luth. Ch., 1958-72, Luth. Health Care Bangladesh, 1994—; trustee Minn. Med. Found., 1958-92, chmn. scholarship and loan com., 1960-68, chmn. honors and awards com., 1970-76, mem. spl. grants com., 1981—, chmn. student fin. aid com., 1984-92, active 1992—, mem. planned giving com., 1991—. Mem. AMA, Assn. Am. Med. Colls. (chmn. com. student aspects internat. med. edn. 1966-68, steering com. group on student affairs 1967-68, com. internat. rels. med. edn. 1968-75), Am. Physiol. Soc., Minn. Acad. Medicine (pres.-elect 1989-90, pres. 1990-91), Minn. Med. Alumni Soc. (bd. dirs. 1992-98), Minn. Med. Assn. (pres.' award 1988, mem. various coms.), Sigma Xi, Phi Lambda Upsilon, Alpha Omega Alpha, Gamma Sigma Delta, Alpha Zeta. Home: 3328 48th Ave S Minneapolis MN 55406-2347

CAVES, PEGGY, medical/surgical nurse; b. Lodi, Calif., July 19, 1945; d. Burnerd Clette and Thelma Jean (Humphrey) Hamilton; m. Virgil Wayne Caves, Feb. 14, 1978 (div. June 28, 1995); children: Rhonda Pilcher Miller, Kelly Pilcher Rainwater, Shelly Pilcher Dennis; stepchildren: Shelly Deanne White, Leo Wayne, Karrie Ausbrooks, Billy. LPN, Kiamichi Vo-Tech, Hugo, Okla., 1982; Assoc. degree Sch. Nursing, Ea. Okla. State Coll., 1996. RN, Okla. Staff nurse Pushmataha Hosp., Antlers, Okla., Texoma Med. Ctr., Denison; dr. nursing Antlers (Okla.) Nursing Home; staff nurse Presby. Hosp., Oklahoma City; dir. nursing Choctaw Nursing Home, Antlers, Okla., 1992-93; staff nurse Med. Ctr. of Southeastern Okla., Durant, Okla., 1992; staff nurse outpatient dept., emergency room Choctaw Nation Hosp., Talihina, Okla., 1993-94; pvt. duty field nurse Superior Home Health, Talihina, 1994-95; dir. nurses Choctaw Nation Nursing Home, 1994—; field nurse Happy Hearts Home Health, Antlers; dir. nursing Choctaw Nation Nursing Home; field nurse Happy Hearts Home Health, Antlers, Okla., 1995—, staff nurse Pushmataha Hosp. Home: HC 70 Box 43 Antlers OK 74523-9402 Office: Happy Hearts Home Health Antlers OK 74523

CAVETT, DORCAS C., elementary educator; b. Alliance, Nebr., July 1, 1916; d. Theodore Ray and Bertha Esther Crawford; m. Alva Bayard Cavett, Dec. 27, 1947 (dec. Jan. 1994); 1 child, Dick. BSc, U. Nebr., Lincoln, 1937; MA, U. Nebr., 1949. Elem. tchr. pub. schs., Snyder, Nebr., 1937-38, Mitchell, Nebr., 1938-39, Des Moines, 1939-43, Lincoln, Nebr., 1949—; TV tchr. pub. schs. and U. Nebr., Lincoln, 1953; assoc. prof. U. Nebr., 1953-84. Mem. com. Cooper Found., Woods Bros. Found.; mem. Bereuter Mil. Selections, Lincoln. Capt. USMC, 1943-46. Recipient Amoco award for disting. tchg. U. Nebr., 1976. Mem. PEO, Am. Legion, Lincoln Univ. Club, Faculty Women's Club (treas.), TTT Soc. (pres.), Delta Kappa Gamma (sec.). Congregationalist. Home: 1835 High St Lincoln NE 68502-4824

CAVETT, VAN ANDREW, retired journalist; b. Memphis, Aug. 5, 1932; s. Van A. and Anne (Broyles) C.; m. Virginia Caroline Bradley, Sept. 26, 1959; children: Anne C., V. Andrew III. BA, Millsaps Coll., 1953; MS in Journalism, Northwestern U., 1957. Reporter The World News, Roanoke, Va., 1957; copy editor The Chattanooga Times, 1957-64; copy editor, reporter The Louisville Times, 1964-69, editorial writer, 1970-74, editorial page editor, 1974-86; editorial page editor The Courier Jour. & Louisville Times, 1986-88; comment pages editor The Morning Call, Allentown, Pa., 1989-97. With U.S. Army, 1953-55. Mem. Nat. Conf. Editl. Writers (pres. 1985). Episcopalian. Home: 309 W Brow Rd Lookout Mountain TN 37350-1111

CAVIGLI, HENRY JAMES, petroleum engineer; b. Colfax, Calif., Mar. 14, 1914; s. Giovanni and Angelina (Giachi) C.; m. Ruth Loree Denton, June 11, 1942; children: Henry James Jr., Robert D., Paul R., Loree Ann McIntire. BS in Petroleum Engring., U. Calif., Berkeley, 1937, MS in Mech. Engring., 1947. Sr. engr. Chevron Corp., Rio Vista, Calif., 1954-57, supt. No. Calif., 1958-69; mgr. non operated joint ventures Chevron Corp., LaHabra, Calif., 1970-76; cons. Cavigli & Mee, petroleum cons., Sacramento, Calif., 1976—. Author: Escapades in the Blue, 1996. Mem. sch. bd. Rio Vista High Sch., 1962-67. Maj. USAF, 1942-47. Decorated Bronze Star with 4 oak leaf clusters. Mem. Soc. Petroleum Engrs., Petroleum Prodn. Pioneers, Calif. Conservation Commn. Oil Producers (chmn. 1971-72), Sutter Club, C. of C., Lion, Sigma Xi, Theta Tau Epsilon. Republican. Roman Catholic. Achievements include research in mech. sampling-field oil tanks, determination of minimum chem., productivity index of pumping wells, rotating piston pressure recorder. Home: 6271 Eichler St Sacramento CA 95831-1864 Office: Cavigli & Mee PO Box 22815 Sacramento CA 95822-0815

CAVILL, KAREN A., writer, editor; b. Islip, N.Y., June 22, 1957; d. Henry and Joan (Brown) Wettingfeld. BA, Queens Coll., 1979. Co-founder, editor Sound Resources Ltd., Manhasset, N.Y., 1979-95, pub., editor-in-chief, 1995-97; freelance writer and editor, 1998—. Mem. NAFE.

CAVIN, KRISTINE SMITH, lawyer; b. Decatur, Ga., Mar. 26, 1969; d. Richard Theodore and Sherri (Nash) Smith; m. James Michael Cavin, May 13, 1995. BA, Furman U., 1991; JD, Calif. Western Sch. Law, 1995. Bar: Ga. 1995. Legal asst. Smith & Jenkins, P.C., Atlanta, 1991-92; intern child abuse and domestic violence unit San Diego City Atty.'s Office, 1995; assoc. Smith, Ronick & Corbin, L.L.C., Atlanta, 1995—. Recipient, NAtl. Assn. of Women Lawyers Outstanding Stud., 1995. Mem. ABA, Nat. Assn. Women Lawyers, Assn. Profl. Mortgage Women, Mortgage Bankers Assn. (assoc.), Ga. Bar Assn., Ga. Assn. for Women Lawyers, Ga. Real Estate Closing Attys. Assn. (sec. 1997—), Atlanta Bar Assn. Avocations: gourmet cooking, wine, gardening. Office: Smith Ronick & Corbin LLC 750 Hammond Dr NE Bldg 11 Atlanta GA 30328-5532

CAVIN, SUSAN ELIZABETH, sociologist, writer; b. Trion, Ga., Mar. 18, 1948; d. John Charles and Mary (Risk) C.; 1 child, Julian Samuel Cavin-Zeidenstein. BA, Vanderbilt U., 1970; MA, Rutgers U., 1973, PhD, 1978. Teaching asst., sociology Rutgers U., Newark, N.J., 1970-75; typesetter SoHo News, N.Y.C., 1976; asst. prof. sociology Green Mountain Coll., Poultney, Vt., 1979-83; lectr. women's studies Rutger's U., New Brunswick, N.J., 1984-91, asst. dir. women's studies, 1988-91; project dir. women in engring. sci. tech. program, 1991-97; assoc. prof. sociology Sch. Continuing Edn. NYU, 1998-99; rsch. scientist N.Y.C. Dept. Health, 1999—; cons. Gov.'s Study Commn. on Discrimination, Trenton, N.J., 1992; adj. asst. prof. sociology NYU, 1990-97, assoc. prof., 1998—. Author: Lesbian Origins, 1985, poetry book, 1973, (cd-rom) Alice in Techiland, 1997; founding editor: (newspapers) Radical Chick, 1992-95, Big Apple Dyke News (B.A.D. News), 1981-88, Green Mountain Dyke News, 1980, (jour.) Tribad, 1977-79. Named Outstanding Tchr. of Yr., Green Mountain Coll., Poultney, 1982-83, winner Declamation awards, Ga. High Sch. Assn., 1965, 66. Mem. Nat. Writers Union, Am. Sociol. Assn., Nat. Women's Studies Assn., N.Y. Acad. Scis. Democrat. Avocation: writing, poetry.

CAVINS, WILLIAM ROBERT, deacon, educator; b. Homestead, Pa., May 15, 1953; s. Samuel James and Joan ELizabeth (Witkowski) C.; m. Karen René Steele, Oct. 19, 1985; children: Zachary A., Suzannah E. AA, BA, U. Cen. Fla., Orlando, 1974; student, St. Meinrad Sem., Ind., 1975-76; MS, Nova U., Ft. Lauderdale, Fla., 1980. Cert. tchr., Fla.; ordained deacon Cath. Ch. Diocese of Orlando, 1996; commd. pastoral min. Roman Cath. Ch., 1993. Tchr. Sch. Bd. of Seminole County, Sanford, Fla., 1982-94, Lake Mary Elem. Sch., DeBary, Fla., 1994—; deacon St. Ann's Cath. Ch., De Bary, Fla., 1996—. Precinct leader Dem. Exec. Com., Lake County, Fla., 1981-82 (chmn. 1982); pres. Groveland/Mascotte C. of C., Fla., 1981-82. Recipient Tchr. Merit award Walt Disney World Co., Lake Buena Vista, Fla., 1990, 91, 94, Louie Camp award for creative teaching Fla. Coun. Elem. Edn., 1990. Mem. Seminole County Coun. Tchrs. Math., Seminole Edn. Coun., Seminole Edn. Assn., K.C. (founding grand knight Assisi coun.), Phi Delta Kappa (found. rep. 1989-90). Democrat. Roman Catholic.

CAVIOR, WARREN JOSEPH, communications executive; b. Boston, Sept. 18, 1929; s. Joel H. and Shirley (Miller) C.; m. Mariko Sanjo, Oct. 12, 1969; children—Mayu, Samuel. A.B. cum laude, Harvard, 1951; M.A., Columbia, 1952; postgrad., Oxford U., 1952-53. Asso. editor Forbes Mag., 1956-59; pres. Wall Street Consultants, Inc., N.Y.C., 1959-62, Warren J. Cavior & Co., N.Y.C., 1962-67; chmn. bd. Universal Communications Inc., N.Y.C., 1967-74; exec. v.p. Rogers, Cowan & Taplinger, Inc., N.Y.C., 1974-76; sr. v.p. Rogers & Cowan, Inc., N.Y.C., 1976-81; pres. Cavior Orgn., Inc., 1981—; chmn. The Am. Depositary Receipt Assn., 1993—; treas., dir. Wako Internat. Corp., 1962-67. Adv. bd.: Present Tense Mag. Chmn. Cavior Found., 1968—. Mem. Am. C. of C. in Japan. Home: 2 Fifth Ave New York NY 10011 Office: 60 E 42nd St New York NY 10165-0006

CAVITT, LORRAINE DIMINO, reading specialist, elementary educator; b. Norristown, Pa., Oct. 25, 1951; d. Augustus Richard and Frances Mary (Calabrese) DiMino; children: Rebecca Cavitt, Amanda Cavitt. BA, Villanova U., 1973; M in Reading, West Chester (Pa.) U., 1978; postgrad., Pa. State U., Great Valley, 1993. Cert. tchr., reading specialist, prin., Pa. Tchr. Methacton Sch. Dist., Norristown, 1976-78; reading specialist Upper Merion Area Sch. Dist., King of Prussia, Pa., 1978—. Developer edn. programs. Recipient tchg. grants. Mem. Delta Kappa Gamma. Avocations: running, reading, traveling. Home: 1852 Morgan Ln Collegeville PA 19426-2853 Office: Roberts Sch 889 Croton Rd Wayne PA 19087-2201

CAW, THOMAS WILLIAM, retired publisher and editor; b. Zanesville, Ohio, Nov. 21, 1929; s. William Hooper and Hazel Lavern Caw; m. Margaret Jane Derry, Dec. 26, 1951; children: Melanie Jane Caw Woods, Thomas Shepherd. Grad., Mergenthaler Linotype Sch., N.Y.C., 1950. Linotype operator The Pataskala (Ohio) Standard, 1950-76, editor, pub., co-owner, 1955-65, editor, pub., owner, 1965-96. Advisor, mem. com. Bicentennial book People Make the Difference, 1976; creator, bd. dirs. Pataskala Lost Arts Festival, 1972-75. Mem. Pataskala Planning Commn., 1965; mem. Pataskala Zoning Bd., 1967; bd. dirs. Licking County Red Cross, Newark, Ohio, 1977; mem. commn. Licking Meml. Hosp., Newark, 1977—; mem. exec. com. Boy scouts Am., Licking County, 1978-79; poll worker, pres. judge Licking County Bd. Elections, 1997—; mem. Comprehensive Planning com., Pataskala, 1998—; mem. adv. bd. YMCA, 1999. Cpl. USMC, 1951-53. Recipient Order of Merit award Licking County Boy scouts, 1980, Licking County Citizen of Yr. award, 1995, Cmty. Svc. award Masons, 1995, Paul S. Noblitt Sch. Bell award, 1982, Rotary Four Way Test award, 1998, numerous others. Mem. Ohio Newspaper Assn., Nat. Newspaper Assn., Soc. Profl. Journalists, Lions Club (bd. dirs., treas., sec., pres.), Pataskala C. of C. (charter mem., bd. dirs., Outstanding Citizen 1976). Seventh-day Adventist. Avocations: golf, reading, walking. Home: 289 Poplar St PO Box 1394 Pataskala OH 43062

CAWLEY, CHARLES M., banker. Grad., Georgetown U. Chmn., chief exec. officer MBNA Am. Bank N.A., Newark, Del.; pres., dir. MBNA Corp.; bd. dirs. MasterCard Internat. Mem. exec. com. bd. dirs. Am. Quality Found.; bd. regents Georgetown U. Office: MBNA America Bank N A 400 Christiana Road Newark DE 19713*

CAWNS, ALBERT EDWARD, computer systems consultant; b. Houston, Apr. 3, 1937; s. Harry William and Blanche Ophelia (Bays) C.; m. Sheila Mathie Climie, June 24, 1961; children: Elizabeth Carrick, Jennifer Kathryn. AB in Math., Drury Coll., Springfield, Mo., 1958; BS in Mech. Engring., U. Mo., Rolla, 1959, MS in Computer Sci., 1984; M Engring. Adminstrn., Washington U., St. Louis, 1965. Engr. White Rodgers Co., St. Louis, 1959-62, McDonnell Aircraft Co., St. Louis, 1962-64; v.p. Thomas Inc., St. Louis, 1964-82; pres. Talos Co., St. Louis, 1982—; adj. faculty Webster U., St. Louis, 1986-91, asst. prof. math. and computer sci., dir., M.S. in Comp. Sci. Prog., 1991—, assoc. prof. math. and computer sci., 1995—. Moderator Southeast Mo. Presbytery, 1971; mem. Gen. Assembly Mission Bd., Presbyn. Ch. U.S.A., 1973; trustee Westminster Presbyn. Ch., St. Louis, 1976; pres. alumni adv. coun. Sch. Engring., Washington U., St. Louis, 1990-92. Cpl. USMCR, 1954-62. Home: 7391 Stratford Ave Saint Louis MO 63130-4138 Office: Talos Co PO Box 3069 Saint Louis MO 63130-0469

CAWOOD, ALBERT MCLAURIN (HAP CAWOOD), newspaper editor; b. Harlan, Ky., Nov. 10, 1939; s. Frank Finley and C. Eugene (Barwick) C.; m. Sonia Barreiro, July 3, 1965; children: Romy Lanier, Shuly Xochitl. BA in English, Union Coll., 1962; MA in Journalism, Ohio State U., 1966. Asst. city editor Dayton (Ohio) Daily News, 1966, editorial writer, 1966-82, editorial page editor, 1982—. Vol. Peace Corps., Sierra Leone, 1962-64; chmn. Ohio Com. on Crime and Delinquency, 1969-70. Recipient Disting. Svc. award for Editorial Writing, Nat. Soc. Profl. Journalists, 1968, Walker Stone award for Editorial Writing, Scripps-Howard Found., 1984. Mem. Am. Soc. Newspaper Editors, Nat. Conf. Editorial Writers, Union Coll. Alumni Assn. (pres. 1985-87). Democrat. Home: 211 S Winter St Yellow Springs OH 45387-1730 Office: Dayton Daily News PO Box 1287 Dayton OH 45401-1287

CAWOOD, CHARLES DAVID, urologist; b. Lexington, Ky., May 22, 1937; s. Charles David and Helen Elizabeth (Rinke) C.; m. Susan Ruth O'Dell, June 10, 1962 (dec. July 1986); children: Todd Christopher, Amy Elizabeth; m. Charlotte Dee Barton, June 18, 1988; children: Elizabeth Ann Maddeaux, Scott Edward Maddeaux. BS cum laude, U. Ky., 1957; MD, U. Louisville, 1961. Diplomate Am. Bd. Urology. Intern St. Joseph's Infirmary, Louisville, 1961-62; urology resident Baylor Coll. of Medicine, 1964-68, instr. divsn. of urology, 1968-71, asst. clin. prof., 1971-83; assoc. chief of urology Ben Taub Gen. Hosp., 1968-72; ret., 1997; chief or urology St. Luke's Episcopal Hosp., Tex. Med. Ctr., 1991-94; clin. prof., dept. urology Baylor Coll. of Medicine; active staff St. Luke's Episcopal Hosp., The Meth. Hosp.; cons. staff Tex. Children's Hosp., Ben Taub Gen. Hosp., VA Hosp.; presenter in field; cons. Am. Cystoscope Makers Inc./Baxter, 1981-84, Advanced Clin. Products, 1988-90, N.Am. Med., 1994-98. Contbr. articles to profl. jours.; patentee in field. Mem. Harris County Med. Soc., Houston Urologic Soc., Am. Urol. Assn. (south ctrl. sect.), Tex. Assn. of Genitourinary Surgeons, Phi Beta Kappa.

CAWOOD, HOBART GUY, historic site administrator; b. Jonesville, Va., June 15, 1935; s. George Pope and Eula (Graham) C.; m. Shirley Ann Flanary, Dec. 22, 1956 (div. Oct. 1976); 1 child, Stephen Andrew; m. Adelaide Louise Wahlert, Sept. 10, 1977. BA, Emory and Henry Coll., Emory, Va., 1957, LLD (hon.), 1988; LHD (hon.), Pa. Coll. Podiatric Medicine, 1980; LLD (hon.), Thomas Jefferson U., 1987, Drexel U., 1987, Phila. Coll. Textiles and Sci., 1991. With Nat. Park Svc., 1958-91; pres. Old Salem Inc., Winston-Salem, N.C., 1991—; historian Cumberland Gap Nat. Hist. Park, 1958-60, Ft. Frederica Nat. Monument, 1960-61; supervisory historian Ft. Sumter Nat. Monument, 1961-62, Castillo de San Marcos Nat. Monument, 1962-63, Chickamuga and Chattanooga Nat. Mil. Park, 1963-67; park planner Washington Svc. Ctr., 1967-69; supt. Richmond Nat. Battlefield, Va., 1969-71, Independence Nat. Hist. Park, Phila., 1971-91. Bd. dirs. Phila. Conv. and Visitor Bur., 1977-83. With USAR, 1958-64. Recipient award for excellence of service, 1971, Disting. Svc. award, 1992, Dept. Interior; recipient 250th Anniversary medal Carpenters' Co., 1976, KC Cardinal Dougherty, 1976, Man of Yr. Chestnut St. Assn., 1976, Legion of Honor Chapel of Four Chaplains, 1976; citation for assistance with visit by Pres. France Pa. Legislature, 1976; recipient Hist. St. George's Gold medal St. George's United Meth. Ch., 1976, Bicentennial PA Soc. DAR, 1976, Unit Dept. Interior, 1977, Phila. Bowl Colonial Phila. Hist. Soc., 1977, Greater Am. Achievements Bicentennial Countil of Original 13 States, 1977, Honor award for Meritorious Service Dept. Interior, 1977, Disting. Service Phila. Flag Day Assn., 1978, Gold medal King of Sweden, 1980, Disting. Service Am. Legion, 1980, Achievement Communications Charles Morris Price Sch. Journalism, 1983; named Alumnus of Yr. Emory and Henry Coll., 1977; Gold medal award Phila. Pub. Relations Assn., 1986, Gold Medal award Phila. Pub. Relations Assn., 1986, Good Scout award Boy Scouts Am., 1986, Disting. Civilian Service award Sec. Army, 1987, award Baronial Order Magna Carta, 1988, medal of Achievement Friends of Wistar Inst., 1991, Ft. Mifflin Gallant Defender award, 1991. Republican. Methodist. Office: Old Salem Inc Box F Salem Sta Winston Salem NC 27108

CAWS, MARY ANN, French language and comparative literature educator, critic; b. Wilmington, N.C., Sept. 10, 1933; d. Harmon Chadbourn and Margaret Devereux (Lippitt) Rorison; m. Peter Caws, June 2, 1956 (div. 1987); children: Matthew, Hilary. BA, Bryn Mawr Coll., 1954; MA, Yale U., 1956; PhD, U. Kans., 1962; D.Humane Letters, Union Coll., 1983. Asst. instr. Romance Langs. U. Kans., Lawrence, 1957-62, asst. editor univ. press, 1957-58, vis. asst. prof., spring 1963; lectr. Barnard Coll. Columbia U., N.Y.C., 1962-63; mem. faculty Sarah Lawrence Coll., Bronxville, N.Y., 1963-64, Hunter Coll. CCNY, N.Y.C., 1966-88; prof. Grad. Sch. CCNY, N.Y.C., 1969-88, exec. officer comparative lit. program Grad. Sch., 1977-79, exec. officer French program Grad. Sch., 1979-86, Disting. prof. French and comparative lit. Grad. Sch., 1983—; prof. English CUNY, 1985—; Disting. prof. French, comparative lit., English Grad. Sch. CUNY, N.Y.C., 1987—; Phi Beta Kappa vis. scholar, 1982-83; dir. NIH summer seminars for coll. tchrs., 1978, 85; mem. faculty Sch. of Criticism and Theory, Dartmouth U., 1988, Sch. Visual Arts, 1993; professeur associé Université de Paris VII, 1993-94; co-chair Henri Peyre Inst. for the Humanities, 1980—, French Inst., 1997—; lectr. N.Y. Coun. for Humanities, 1992-96. Author: Surrealism and the Literary Imagination, 1966, The Poetry of Dada and Surrealism, 1970, The Inner Theatre of Recent French Poetry, 1972, The Presence of René Char, 1976, René Char, 1977, The Surrealist Voice of Robert Desnos, 1977, La Main de Pierre Reverdy, 1979, The Eye in the Text, Essays on Perception, Mannerist to Modern, 1981, André Breton, 1982, 96, The Metapoetics of the Passage, Architextures in Surrealism and After, 1982, Yves Bonnefoy, 1984, Reading Frames in Modern Fiction, 1988, Edmond Jabès, 1988, The Art of Interference: Stressed Readings in Visual and Verbal Texts, 1989, Women of Bloomsbury, 1991, Robert Motherwell: What Art Holds, 1996, Carrington and Lytton: Alone Together, 1996, The Surrealist Look: An Erotics of Encounter, 1997; co-author: Bloomsburg and France: Art and Friends, 1999; contbr. articles to profl. jours.; editor: Dada-Surrealism, 1972, co-editor, 1980—, Le Siècle éclaté, 1974-78, About French Poetry from Dada to Tel Quel, 1974, Selected Poetry Prose of Stéphane Mallarmé, 1982, Selected Poems of St.-John Perse, 1983, Writing in a Modern Temper, 1984, Textual Analysis, 1986, Perspectives on Perception: Philosophy, Art, and Literature, 1989, City Images, 1992, Joseph Cornell's Theater of the Mind: Selected Diaries, Letters and Files, 1994; co-editor: Selected Poems of René Char, 1992, Contre-Courants: Les femmes s'écrivent à travers les siècles, 1994, Écritures de femmes: Nouvelles Cartographies, 1996; translator: Poems of René Char, 1976, Approximate Man and other Writings of Tristan Tzara, 1975, Mad Love, 1987, The Secret Art of Antonin Artaud, 1998; co-translator: Poems of André Breton, 1984, Communicating Vessels, 1990, Daybreak, 1999; chief editor Harper Collins World Reader, 1994. Decorated officier Palmes Académiques, France; fellow Guggenheim Found., 1972-73 NEH, 1979-80, Fulbright traveling fellow, 1972-73, Rockefeller Found. fellow, 1994; Getty scholar, 1990. Mem. MLA (exec. coun. 1973-77, v.p. 1982-83, pres. 1983-84), Am. Assn. Tchrs. French, Assn. for Study Dada and Surrealism (pres. 1982-86), Internat. Assn. Philosophy and Lit. (exec. bd. 1982—, chmn. 1984), Acad. Lit. Studies (pres. 1985), Am. Comparative Lit. Assn. (exec. com. 1981, v.p. 1986—, pres. 1989-91). Home: 140 E 81st St New York NY 10028-1805 Office: CUNY Grad Ctr 33 W 42d St New York NY 10036-8003

CAWS, PETER JAMES, philosopher, educator; b. Southall, Eng., May 25, 1931; came to U.S., 1953; naturalized, 1995; s. Geoffrey Tulloh and Olive (Budden) C.; m. Mary Ann Rorison (div.); children: Hilary, Matthew; m. Nancy Breslin, Nov. 28, 1987; 1 child, Elisabeth. BS, U. London, 1952; MA, Yale U., 1954, PhD, 1956. Instr. natural sci. Mich. State U., 1956-57; asst. prof. philosophy U. Kans., 1957-60, assoc. prof., 1960-62, chmn. dept., 1961-62, Rose Morgan vis. prof., 1963; vis. prof. U. Costa Rica, 1961; exec. assoc. Carnegie Corp. N.Y., 1962-65, cons., 1965-67; prof. philosophy Hunter Coll., N.Y.C., 1965-82; chmn. dept. Hunter Coll., 1965-67; exec. officer Ph.D. program in philosophy CUNY, 1967-70, 81-82; Univ. prof. philosophy George Washington U., 1982—, dir. PhD Program in Human Scis., 1991-93; vis. prof. NYU, spring 1982, U.Md., spring 1985; tchr. New Sch. Social Research, 1965-67; mem. adv. bd. Learning Corp. of Am., 1968-74; vis. scholar U. Kent, Canterbury, Eng., 1993-94; lectr. Smithsonian Resident Assocs. Program, 1988-95; mem. Coun. Philos. Studies, 1965-71; bd. dirs. Coordinating Coun. Lit. Mags., 1969-70; mem. Scientists Inst. for Pub. Info., 1967—, treas., 1969-72, fellow, 1972—, dir., 1975-80, vice chmn., 1975-79; mem. editl. bd. Environment, 1972-78; mem. bd. advisers, history of physics program Am. Inst. Physics, 1966-75; mem. NRC, 1967-70, Assembly Behavioral and Social Scis., 1973-77; nat. lectr. Sigma Xi, 1975-77; dir. Bicentennial Symposium of Philosophy; cons. in humanities LWV, 1978; vis. scholar Phi Beta Kappa, 1983-84; 1st Philip Morris Disting. lectr. in bus. and soc. Baruch Coll., N.Y.C., 1986. Author: The Philosophy of Science, Systematic Account, 1965, Science and the Theory of Value, 1967, Sartre, 1979, Structuralism, The Art of the Intelligible, 1988, Structuralism: A Philosophy for the Human Sciences, 1997, Yorick's World: Science and the Knowing Subject, 1993, The Capital Connection, 1993, Ethics from Experience, 1996; editor: Two Centuries of Philosophy in America, 1980, The Causes of Quarrel: Essays on Peace, War, and Thomas Hobbes, 1989; mem. editl. bd. Jour. Enterprise Mgmt., 1976—, Philosophy Documentation Ctr.; mem. adv. bd. The News Jour., Wilmington, Del., 1998-99. Recipient Pres.'s medal Grad. Sch., CUNY, 1978; Am. Council Learned Socs. fellow, Paris, 1972-73; Rockefeller Found. humanities fellow, 1979-80. Fellow AAAS (v.p. 1967); mem. Am. Philos. Assn. (dir., chmn. com. on internat. coop. 1974-84), Fedn. Internat. des Socs. de Philosophie (commn. on policy 1979-88, comité dir. 1978-88), Philosophy of Sci. Assn. (del.), Soc. Gen. Systems Rsch. (pres. 1966-67), Soc. Am. de Philosophie de Langue Française (v.p. 1989-92, pres. 1992-94), Elizabethan Club, Washington Philosophy Club (pres. 1988-89), Phi Beta Kappa (hon. Alpha chpt. D.C.). Home: 237 Cheltenham Rd Newark DE 19711-3617 Office: George Washington U Dept Philosophy Washington DC 20052

CAWTHON, FRANK H., retired construction company executive; b. Kissimmee, Fla., Apr. 3, 1930; s. Benjamin Hill and Eva Elizabeth (Mullins) C.; m. Mary Elizabeth Dickert, July 10, 1959; 1 child, Frank H. Grad. high sch. Asst. sec.-treas. Orange Belt Truck & Tractor, Orlando, Fla., 1948-52, Murdock Constrn. Co., Inc., Orlando, 1954-59; sec.-treas. Amick Constrn. Co., Inc., Orlando, 1959-90; ret., 1990; bd. dirs. Amick Constrn. Co., Inc. Bd. dirs. Conway Little League, Orlando, 1977. With U.S. Army, 1952-54. Mem. Cen. Fla. Rd. Bldrs. Assn. Democrat. Lutheran. Avocations: oil painting, gardening, fishing. Home: 391 Brushwood Ln Casselberry FL 32708-4955 Office: Amick Constrn Co 401 Ferguson Dr Orlando FL 32805-1009

CAWTHON, WILLIAM CONNELL, operations management consultant; b. Roxton, Tex., Sept. 1, 1922; s. William Arthur and Lura (Denton) C.; m. Flora Keith Campbell, May 31, 1947; children: William Connell, Clark Campbell, Flora Keith. B.M.E., Cornell U., 1944; M.S.M.E., U. Tex., 1947; M. Automotive Engring., Chrysler Inst., Detroit, 1949. Mfg. exec. Chrysler Corp., Detroit, 1955-59; dir. purchasing Chrysler Corp., 1959-62; v.p. mfg. Am. Standard Corp., N.Y.C., 1962-66; v.p., dir. indsl. engring. and mfg. worldwide ITT, N.Y.C., 1966-68; exec. v.p. Weatherhead Co., Cleve., 1968-70; prin. William C. Cawthon (cons.), Hudson, Ohio, 1970-72; v.p., gen. mgr. parts div., textile machinery div. Rockwell Internat., Hopedale, Mass., 1972-73; v.p. mfg. No Telecom Ltd. (former No. Electric Co., Ltd.), Montreal, Que., Can., 1973-77; v.p. mfg. No. Telecom Inc., Nashville, 1973-80, v.p. ops., 1980-85, v.p. corp. devel., 1985-87; prin. William C. Cawthon Cons., Nashville, 1987—; mem. chancellor's council U. Tex. Served to lt. comdr. USNR, 1945-46, 51-53, PTO, Korea. Named Distinguished Grad. U. Tex., 1961. Fellow Boston U. Mfg. Roundtable; mem. Newcomen Soc. Republican. Mem. Ch. of Christ. Home and Office: 1024 Lynwood Blvd Nashville TN 37215-4512 *If I have made the places I have worked better places to work, and the places I have lived better places to live, I would suppose that would be success.*

CAWTHORN, ROBERT ELSTON, health care executive; b. Masham, Eng., Sept. 28, 1935; came to U.S., 1982; s. Gerald P. and Gertrude E. (Longster) C.; m. H. Susan Marshall, Jan. 15, 1960; children: Amanda, Liza. BA in Agriculture, Cambridge U., 1959. Various exec. positions Pfizer, Inc., Can., Africa, Mid. East and Europe, 1961-79; pres. Biogen S.A., Geneva, 1979-82, Rorer Internat., Fort Washington, Pa., 1982-83; exec. v.p. Rorer Group, Inc., 1982-84, pres., 1985-85, pres., chief exec. officer, 1985-86, chmn., chief exec. officer, from 1986; CEO Rhône-Poulenc Rorer, Inc. (formerly Rorer Group, Inc.), Collegeville, Pa., 1988-95; chmn. Rhone-Poulenc Rorer, Inc. (formerly Rorer Group, Inc.), Collegeville, Pa., 1988-96, chmn. bd. dirs., 1996—, chmn. emeritus, 1996—; chmn. Fisons plc, 1995-96; mng. dir. Global Health Care Ptnrs., DLJ Merchant Banking Ptnrs., 1996—; bd. dirs. Sun Co. Inc., CBS Corp. Bd. dirs. United Way Southeastern Pa., trustee, 1985-96; bd. dirs. Greater Phila. 1st. corp., 1986-95, World Affairs Coun. Pa., 1986-90, Internat. Bus. Forum, chmn., 1987-89; trustee The Baldwin Sch., 1984-86, U. Pa., 1992—, U. Pa. Med. Ctr., 1992—. Mem. Pharm. Mfrs. Assn. (bd. dirs. 1985-94), Greater Phila. C. of C. (bd. dirs. 1987—). Home: 50 Crosby Brown Rd Gladwyne PA 19035-1513 Office: DLJ Merchant Banking Ptnrs 401 E City Line Ave Ste 110 Bala Cynwyd PA 19004-1116*

CAWTHORNE, ALFRED BENJAMIN, education educator; b. Collingdale, Pa., Aug. 19, 1942; s. Alfred B. Sr. and Dorothy M. (Childs) C.; m. Beverly A. Parry, June 26, 1965; children: Alfred B. III, David H. BA, Eastern Nazarene Coll., Quincy, Mass., 1964; MEd, Northeastern U., 1972; EdD, Nova Southeastern U., 1997. Cert. secondary gen. sci., secondary biology, instrnl. tech. specialist, dir.-supr., all levels, Mass. Sci. tchr. Quincy Pub. Schs., 1964-97; adj. prof. biology Quincy Coll., 1966-78; adj. prof. biology and edn. Eastern Nazarene Coll., 1972-84; instr. biology, NSF programs U. Mass., Boston, 1984-98; adj. prof. instrnl. tech. Nova Southeastern U., Ft. Lauderdale, Fla., 1993-98; assoc. prof. tchr. edn. Eastern Nazarene Coll., 1997—; mem. exec. bd. Mass. Marine Educators, Boston, 1982-82; tech. cons. Quincy Pub. Schs., 1984-97, mem. supt.'s tech. task team, 1990—; coord. ednl. tech., distance edn. Eastern Nazarene Coll., 1998—, mem. distance edn. com., 1998. Designer sci. tchr. computer network, Quincy Pub. Schs. Trustee South Weymouth (Mass.) Ch. of the Nazarene, 1996-97, mem. choir, 1994—; Sunday sch. tchr. Wollaston Ch. of the Nazarene, Quincy, 1984-92, mem. ch. bd., 1984-92. Recipient Pathfinder award Mass. Computer Using Educators, Boston, 1995, Tandy Scholar award Tandy Corp., Tex., 1992. Mem. ASCD, NEA, Mass. Tchrs. Assn., Quincy Edn. Assn., Assn. Ednl. Computing Technologists. Mem. Church of the Nazarene. Avocations: computers, scuba diving, boating, sports. Home: 78 Willow Ave Quincy MA 02170-3726 Office: Eastern Nazarene Coll 23 E Elm Ave Quincy MA 02170-2905

CAWTHORNE, KENNETH CLIFFORD, retired financial planner; b. Manistee, Mich., Feb. 13, 1936; s. Clifford Haney and Marie Dorothy (Schimke) C.; m. Martha S. Zielinski, Aug. 23, 1958; children: Steven, Daniel, Cynthia, Thomas. BS cum laude, Central Mich. U., 1958. CPA, Mich.; lic. real estate broker, Ill.; cert. fin. planner; cert. life, health and accident ins. producer, Ill.; registered rep. Nat. Assn. Security Dealers. Sr. acct. Ernst & Ernst, CPAs, Grand Rapids, Mich., 1958-62; contr. Grand Rapids Sash and Door Co., 1962-67, Melling Forging Co., Lansing, Mich.,

1968-72; contr., treas., v.p. fin. Jovan, Inc. (name changed to Beecham Cosmetics, Inc.), Chgo., 1973-84; corp. v.p. mfg. ops. Quintessence Inc. (formerly Beecham Cosmetics, Inc.), 1984-89; fin. planner Tucker Assocs., Des Plaines, Ill., 1990-95; ret., 1996. Mem. AICPA, Inst. Cert. Fin. Planners, Nat. Assn. Life Underwriters. Home: 9297 Elmwood Ct Stanwood MI 49346-9305

CAWVEY, CLARENCE EUGENE, physician; b. Du Quoin, Ill., May 16, 1929; s. Clarence Eli and Lois Jane (Matheny) C.; m. Paulina Isabel Hincke, Sept. 12, 1953 (dec. Apr. 1973); children: Janet Edna, William Clarence, Paulina Ann, Jean Hincke; 1 stepchild, Douglas Lance Hester; m. Linda Mae Rice, Jan. 26, 1974. BA, Yale U., 1951; MD, U. Chgo., 1955. Diplomate Am. Bd. Family Practice. Intern Cook County Hosp., 1955-56; resident in psychiatry Brook Army Hosp., 1956-57; ptnr. Pickneyville (Ill.) Med. Group, 1958-98; ret., 1998; clin. asst. prof. Med. Sch. So. Ill. U., Springfield, 1976—, mem. adv. com. continuing med. edn., 1977—; dir., mem. exec. com. Ctrl. Ill. Profl. Rev. Orgn., Champaign, 1988—; bd. dirs., chmn. First Nat. Bank, Pinckneyville. Founding mem., pres. Perry County Health Dept., Pinckneyville, 1970. Capt. U.S. Army, 1956-58. Fellow Am. Acad. Family Physicians; mem. AMA, Ill. State Med. Soc. (del. 1960-70), Perry County Med. Soc. Republican. Methodist. Avocations: skiing, photography, travel, gardening. Home: 204 W Laurel St Pinckneyville IL 62274-1019

CAYEA, DONALD JOSEPH, lawyer; b. Bklyn., Mar. 3, 1948; s. Glendon Vernon and Marie Nicola (Gesualdo) C.; m. Elizabeth Mary Peck, Jan. 27, 1973 (div. Sept. 1975); m. Yvonne Karen Kemeny, Sept. 11, 1983 (div. Sept. 1989). BA, L.I. U., 1969; JD, Western New Eng. Coll., 1975. Bar: N.Y. 1976, U.S. Dist. Ct. (so. and ea. dists.) N.Y. 1978, D.C. 1979, U.S. Supreme Ct. 1979. Prin. Donald J. Cayea & Assoc., N.Y.C., 1976—; ptnr. Kroll & Tract, N.Y.C., 1988-90, Levitan, Frieland & Cayea, N.Y.C., 1990-94, Klepner & Cayea, N.Y.C., 1994-98, Brand, Cayea & Brand, LLC, N.Y.C., 1998—, Brand, Cayea & Brand LLC, 1998—; gen. counsel Entertainment USA, 1990—; lectr. Paralegal Inst., NYU, 1984—, adult edn. program Nassau County Bar Assn., Mineola, N.Y., 1978-79; panelist trial advocacy program Cardozo Law Sch., Yeshiva U., N.Y.C., 1984—; spkr. Ft. Lauderdale (Fla.) Film Festival, 1989, 90, Coun. on Mgmt. Worker's Compensation Update, N.Y.C., 1995, 96; guest panelist Property Loss Rsch. Bur., Washington, 1989, Chgo., 1991; spkr. coun. edn. mgmt., N.Y.C., 1995. Prodr.: (video) Dahmer, the Secret Life, 1993, (off Broadway) West Side Stories, Theatre Airelle, N.Y.C., 1993, Conversations with My Daughter; exec. prodr. (film) The Hunt for CM24; assoc. prodr. (film) Prague Duet; prodr. (theatre) The Remarkable Thing About Star Dust. Pres. Seascape Condominium, Westhampton Beach, N.Y., 1986-92; sponsor Richmond Roller Hocker Assn., Staten Island, N.Y., 1984-89; mem. Pres.'s Coun., L.I. Univ. Served in U.S. Army, 1970-71. Mem. ABA (editor TIPS publ. editorial bd. 1990-93), Assn. Trial Lawyers Am., N.Y. State Bar Assn., Internat. Bar Assn., Assn. of Bar of City of N.Y., New York County Lawyers Assn., Phi Epsilon Pi. Office: 720 5th Ave Fl 14 New York NY 10019-4107

CAYEN, MITCHELL NESS, biochemist; b. Montreal, Quebec, Can., Nov. 6, 1938; came to U.S., 1984; s. Benjamin and Herzelle (Ness) Cayen; m. Liliane Hoffman, Mar. 14, 1967 (div.); children: Ilene, Barry; m. Judy Rajczyk, Jan. 17, 1987; 1 child, Reuben. PhD, McGill U., 1965. Assoc. dir. drug metabolism Wyeth-Ayest Rsch., Princeton, N.J., 1984-89; sr. dir. drug metabolism and pharmacokinetics Schering-Plough Rsch. Inst., Kenilworth, N.J., 1989—; chmn. Gordon Rsch. Conf. on Drug Metabolism, 1985. Mem. editl. bd. Xenobiotica, 1985—, Chirality, 1993—, Drug Metabolism Revs., 1995—; contbr. over 100 articles to profl. jours. Fellow AAAS, Am. Assn. Pharm. Scientists, Coun. Arteriosclerosis, Am. Heart Assn.; mem. Internat. Soc. Study Xenobiotics (pres. 1992-93), Pharm. Mfrs. Assn. (exec. com. 1987-91, steering com. 1995-98). Home: 98 Autumn Ridge Rd Bedminster NJ 07921-1849 Office: 2015 Galloping Hill Rd Kenilworth NJ 07033-1310

CAYETANO, BENJAMIN JEROME, governor, former state senator and representative; b. Honolulu, Nov. 14, 1939; s. Bonifacio Marcos and Eleanor (Infante) C.; m. Vicky Tiu, 1997; children: Brandon, Janeen, Samantha. BA, UCLA, 1968; JD, Loyola U., 1971; D in Pub. Svc. (hon.), Loyola Marymount U., 1998. Bar: Hawaii 1971. Practiced in Honolulu, 1971-86; mem. Hawaii Ho. of Reps., 1975-78, Hawaii Senate, 1979-86; lt. gov. State of Hawaii, 1986-95, gov., 1994—; bar examiner Hawaii Supreme Ct., 1976-78, disciplinary bd., 1982-86; arbitration panel 1st Cir. Ct. State of Hawaii, 1986; adv. U. Hawaii Law Rev., 1982-84. Mem. bd. regents Chaminade U., 1980-83; mem. adv. council U. Hawaii Coll. Bus. Adminstrn., 1982-83; chmn. Western Gov.'s Assn., 1999. Recipient Excellence in Leadership Medallion Asia-Pacific Acad. Consortium for Pub. Health, 1991, UCLA Alumni award for excellence in pub. svc., 1993, Leadership award Harvard Found., 1996, Edward A. Dickson Alumnus of Yr. award UCLA, 1998. Democrat. Office: Office of Gov State Capitol 415 S Beretenia St 5th Fl Honolulu HI 96813

CAYNE, BERNARD STANLEY, editor; b. N.Y.C., Nov. 8, 1924; m. Helen M. Burgard, Apr. 11, 1953; children—Claudia Elizabeth, Douglas Andrew. Student, Cornell U., 1940-42; B.S., Moravian Coll., 1945; postgrad., U. Pa., 1945-46; research fellow, Harvard U., 1953-55; M.A., Columbia U., 1947. Head sci. dept. Adelphi Acad., 1946-47; instr. Bklyn. Coll., 1947-49; tchr. N.Y.C. Pub. Schs., 1948-49; head sci. sect., test devel. dept. Ednl. Testing Service, Princeton, N.J., 1949-53; dir. research Boston U. Coll. Basic Studies, 1953-54; sr. sci. editor Ginn & Co., Boston, 1955-61; v.p. Crowell-Collier Ednl. Corp., N.Y.C., 1961-68; exec. editor Collier's Ency., 1963-68, Collier's Ency. Yearbook, 1963-68; editor-in-chief Merit Students Ency., 1961-69, asst. editorial dir. corp., 1963-68; mng. editor, sch. div. Macmillan Co., 1968-69; editor-in-chief Ency. Americana, Danbury, Conn., 1969-90; v.p., editorial dir. Grolier, Inc., Danbury, 1980-90; creative dir. The Readfern Group, Newtown, Conn., 1990—. Chmn. bd. editors: Harvard Edn. Rev, 1954. Fellow AAAS, Am. Psychol. Soc.; mem. N.Y. Acad. Scis., Am. Ednl. Rsch. Assn., Phi Delta Kappa. Home: 8 Old Green Rd Sandy Hook CT 06482-1043 Office: The Readfern Group 100 Acre Wood PO Box 3431 Newtown CT 06470-3431

CAYNE, JAMES E., investment banker; b. 1934. With Bonn Bush Mach, 1954-66, Lebenthal and Co., 1966-69; pres., past sr. mng. dir. Bear Stearns and Co. Inc., also bd. dirs., CEO, pres., 1993—. Office: Bear Stearns & Co Inc 245 Park Ave Fl 9A New York NY 10167-0002*

CAYTON, MARY EVELYN, minister; b. Morgantown, W. Va., July 7, 1926; d. Adam Johnson and Dorothy Ena (Bigler) Cayton. Student, Internat. Bible Coll., San Antonio, Tex., 1955. Ordained minister Full Gospel Denomination, 1958. Clk. First Nat. Bank, Morgantown, 1945-51; founder, pastor Morgantown Revival Ctr., 1956-92; staff, controller's office W.Va. U., Morgantown, 1951-55, '58-84; chmn. Morgantown Revival Ctr. Assn., 1956—. Home and office: 1702 Tyrone Rd Morgantown WV 26508-5902 *I have found through life that "With Man some things are possible", but "With God nothing is impossible".*

CAZALAS, MARY REBECCA WILLIAMS, lawyer, nurse; b. Atlanta, Nov. 11, 1927; d. George Edgar and Mary Annie (Slappey) Williams; m. Albert Joseph Cazalas (dec.). *Her great-great-grandfather, General John Coffee, fought in the Battle of New Orleans. His wife, Mary Donelson, was niece of Mrs. Andrew Jackson. Their son, Major John A. Coffee, served in the Civil War. His daughter, Mary Stevens Coffee, married Dr. John George Slappey, prominent physician at Jeffersonville, Georgia. His grandfather was Hans (John) George Slappey, who fought in the Revolution, and his father was Robert Rutherford Slappey. His daughter, Mary Annie Slappey, married George Edgar Wiliams. His mother was Sarah Cobb of Kosiesco, Mississippi. He graduated from Mercer University and was Chief Dispatcher of Central of Georgia Railroad.* BS in Pre-medicine, Oglethorpe U., Atlanta, 1954; MS in Anatomy, Emory U., 1960; JD, Loyola U., 1967, Loyola U., New Orleans, 1967. RN, Ga. Gen. duty nurse, 1948-68; instr. maternity nursing St. Josephs Infirmary Sch. Nursing, Atlanta, 1954-59; med. rschr. in urology Tulane U. Sch. Medicine, New Orleans, 1961-65; legal rschr. for presiding judge La. Ct. Appeals (4th cir.), New Orleans, 1965-71; pvt. practice New Orleans, 1967-71, asst. U.S. atty., 1971-79; sr. trial atty. EEOC, New Orleans, 1979-84; owner Cazalas Apts., New Orleans, 1962—; lectr. in field. Contbr. articles to profl. jours. Bd. advisors Loyola U. Sch. Law, New Orleans, 1974, v.p. adv. bd., 1975; active New Orleans Drug Abuse Adv. Com., 1976-80; task force Area Agy. on Aging, 1976-80, pres. coun. Loyola U., 1978—; adv. bd. Odyssey House, Inc., New Orleans, 1973; chmn. womens com. Fed. Exec. Bd., 1974; bd. dirs. Bethlehem House of Bread, 1975-79. Named Hon. La. State Senator, 1974; recipient Superior Performance award U.S. Dept. Justice, 1974, Cert. Appreciation Fed. Exec. Bd., 1975-78, Rev. E.A. Doyle award, 1976, Commendation for tchg. Guam Legislature, 1977, Career Achievement award Mt. de Sales Acad., 1995. Mem. Am. Judicature Soc., La. Sate Bar Assn., Fed. Bus. Assn. (v.p. 1976—, pres. 1976-78, bd. dirs. 1972-75), Fed. Bar Assn. (1st v.p. 1973, pres. New Orleans chpt. 1974-75, nat. coun. 1974-79), Assn. Women Lawyers, Nat. Health Lawyers Assn., DAR, Bus. and Profl. Womens Club, Am. Heart Assn., Emory Alumni Assn., Oglethorpe U. Alumni Assn., Loyola U. Alumni Assn. (bd. dirs. 1974-75, 77, v.p. 1976), Jefferson Parish Hist. Soc., Sierra Club, Zonta, Leconte Hon. Sci. Soc., Phi Delta Delta (merged with Phi Alpha Delta pres. 1970-72, bd. dirs., vice justice 1974-75), Alpha Epsilon Delta, Phi Sigma. Democrat.

CAZAN, MATTHEW JOHN, political science educator; b. Beclean, Romania, Mar. 10, 1912; s. John and Marie (Sipos) C.; student U. Bucharest Law Sch., Youngstown Coll., Georgetown U. Sch. Fgn. Service; m. Sylvia Marie Buday, July 14, 1935; 1 son, Matthew John George. Lectr. Georgetown U., 1942-44; spl. lectr. Indsl. Coll. of the Armed Forces, 1947; asso. in Romanian Georgetown U. Inst. Langs. and Linguistics, 1949—, lectr. polit. sci. and econs. Sch. Fgn. Service, 1943-57; lectr. The Inst. Fgn. Service Officer Preparation, 1953—; lectr. polit. sci. George Washington U., 1963—; spl. employee U.S. Dept. of Justice, 1947-60, 63—; internat. claims analyst fgn. claims settlement commn., 1960-63. Chmn. Lobarca youth guidance com. Va. Gov.'s Conf. Youth. Mem. AAUP, Am. Polit. Sci. Assn., Am. Soc. Internat. Law, Conf. Democratic Theory, Pi Gamma Mu. Home: 6369 Lakeview Dr Lake Barcroft Estates Falls Church VA 22041 Office: Dept Justice Washington DC 20530

CAZEAUX, ISABELLE ANNE MARIE, retired musicology educator; b. N.Y.C., Feb. 24, 1926; d. François and Marie Anne (Fort) C. BA magna cum laude, Hunter Coll., 1945; MA in Musicology, Smith Coll., 1946; MS in Libr. Sci., Columbia U., 1961. Licence d'Enseignement, Ecole Normale de Musique, Paris, 1950; Première Médaille, Conservatoire Nat. de Musique, Paris, 1950. Sr. music cataloguer, head sect. music and phonorecords cataloguing N.Y. Pub. Libr., N.Y.C., 1957-63; mem. faculty Manhattan Sch. Music, N.Y.C., 1969-82; Alice Carter Dickerman prof. emeritus of music Bryn Mawr Coll., Pa., 1963-92, chmn. dept., 1978-92; vis. prof. Douglass Coll. Rutgers U., New Brunswick, N.J., 1978. Author: French Music in the 15th and 16th Centuries, 1975; editor: The Chansons of Claudin de Sermisy, 1974; translator: The Memoirs of Philippe de Commynes, 1969, 2d vol., 1973; contbr. articles to profl. jours. Recipient Libby van Arsdale prize Hunter Coll., 1945; Smith Coll. fellow Inst. Internat. Edn.; Martha Baird Rockefeller Fund grantee, 1971-72, Herman Goldman Found. grantee, 1971-72. Mem. Am. Musicol. Soc. (coun. 1968-70, com. on status of women 1974-76), Music Libr. Assn., Soc. Française de Musicologie, Internat. Musicol. Soc. Roman Catholic. Avocations: opera, concerts. Home: 415 E 72nd St New York NY 10021-4412

CEASAR, MITCHELL, lawyer; b. Bklyn., Jan. 10, 1954; s. Alfred and Eleanor (Weinreb) C.; m. Jenny Kleinman, Aug. 5, 1979. BA, Fla. Atlantic U., 1975; JD, Nova U., 1978. Bar: U.S. Dist. Ct. (so. dist.) Fla., U.S. Ct. Appeals (5th cir.), U.S. Ct. Appeals (11th cir.), U.S. Supreme Ct. Sr. ptnr. Mitchell Ceasar, P.A., Plantation, Fla., 1980—; adv. bd. Broward Fed. Savs. and Loan, Sunrise, Fla., 1980-88. Editor univ. newspaper Scepter, 1973, Atlantic Sun, 1975. Vice-chmn. Dem. Exec. Com. Broward, Ft. Lauderdale, Fla., 1975-76; mem. Broward County Com. Mass Transit, 1979; bd. dirs. Broward County Urban League, 1980; chmn. Broward County Exp. Auth. Recipient Appreciation award United Way, 1977. Mem. Fla. Bar Assn., West Broward Bar Assn. Democrat. Avocations: tennis, softball, politics, movies. Office: 8181 W Broward Blvd Ste 300 Fort Lauderdale FL 33324-2049

CEASOR, AUGUSTA CASEY, medical technologist, microbiologist; b. Birmingham, Ala., Feb. 22, 1943; d. Augustus and Willie Mae (Stubbs) C. *Parents Augustus and Willie Mae Ceasor, Cosmetologists, Founders/Owners of Ceasor's University of Cosmetology, Miami, Florida, 1958. Father invented the Weaver Webb automatic hair weaving machine in 1969. Mother, a Master Cosmetologist with teacher's certification taught in the public school system. Now retired, she enjoys her membership in Alpha Pi Chi Sorority. Sister Gwendolyn Lee Goolsby, Cosmetologist, Child Development Associate (CDA), Miami-Dade Community College, 1988, is now Owner/Director, Gwens Day Care Center. Sister Lucille E. Hilton, Jamaica New York, retired RN, now travels, enjoys her grandchildren and is a fashion designer. Sister Delores Edwards, Cosmetologist, has been a foster care parent for several years.* AS, SUNY, 1981; BS, So. Ill. U., 1981. Cert. clin. lab. scientist Nat. Cert. Agy. Lab. asst. Mt. Sinai Hosp., Miami Beach, Fla., 1967-68; lab. technician Coordinated Lab. Svcs., Jamaica, N.Y., 1969-71; med. technician Andrew Radar U.S. Army Health Clinic, Ft. Myer, Va., 1972-76; med. technologist Armed Forces Inst. Pathology, Washington, 1976-91, Dept. Army, Mil. Dist. Wash., Ft. Myer, Va., 1991-97; ret. Dept. of Army, 1997; cons. clin. lab. sci., 1997—; dept. asst. Webster U., Ocala, Fla., 1999; sci. fair judge Am. Soc. Microbiology, Washington, 1988-97; high sch. sci. mentor Minority Women in Sci., 1989—; speaker to profl. groups. Mem. editorial bd. Metroscope Newsletter, 1985-98, editor, 1989-98; tech. asst. Mycobacteriology Rsch., 1985-90. Active minority alumni scholarship com. So. Ill. U., Carbondale, 1981—; mem. Montgomery Knolls Cmty. Assn., Silver Spring, Md., 1983-96, v.p., chmn. safety and environ. com., 1984-85. Recipient Cert. of Meritorious Svc., 1991, Performance award, 1987, 89, 93, 95-97. Fellow Alpha Mu Tau (scholarship com. 1995-97); mem. Am. Soc. Clin. Lab. Sci. (minority forum sec. 1994-96, forum scholarship com. 1996—, chair forum scholarship com. 1997—), Am. Soc. Med. Tech. (mem. Region II Coun. 1986-93, 96-97, Region II microbiology chair 1988-89, Region II mem. chair 1990-93, Cert. of Recognition 1990), Internat. Soc. Clin. Lab. Tech. (cert. gen. supr.), Am. Bd. Bioanalysis, D.C. Soc. Med. Tech. (profl. and pub. rels. chair 1985-86, 92-93, program com. chair 1986-87, pres. 1987-88, microbiology chair 1988-89, awards chair 1988-98, Svc. award 1989, Mem. of Yr. 1989-90, Past Pres. award 1988, Disting. Svc. award 1991, Profl. Achievement award in Microbiology 1994), Capital Area Soc. for Clin. Lab. Sci. (pres.-elect 1995-96, pres. 1996-97, past pres. 1997-98). Roman Catholic. Achievements include research in unique toxin of mycobacterium ulcerans.

CEBALLOS, RUBEN ALBERTO, nursing researcher; b. Maracay, Aragua, Venezuela, Oct. 26, 1964; s. Antonio Alejandro Ceballos and Teresita Del Nino Jesus Barreto. ASN, Bunker Hill C.C., 1993; BS in Computer/Biology, Southwestern Adventist Coll., 1987. Jr. programmer Brandon Mfg., Keene, Tex., 1987-88; computer coord./inventory control mgr. New England Meml. Hosp., Stoneham, Mass., 1988-94; telemetry staff nurse New England Meml. Hosp., Stoneham, 1994-95; nurse case mgr. Fenway Cmty. Health Ctr., Boston, 1995-97, clin. nurse mgr., 1997-99; regional sr. clin. rsch. assoc. Pharma Rsch. Corp., Hamilton, Mass., 1999—. Bd. dirs. HIV/AIDS Nursing Cert. Bd., Reston, Va., 1998—; mem. Boston AIDS Consortium, 1997—. Avocations: music, movies. E-mail: ceballor@pharmaresearch.com. Home: 171 Essex St Hamilton MA 01982 Office: Pharma Rsch Corp 171 Essex St Hamilton MA 01982

CEBE, JUANITA, academic administrator; b. Erie, Pa., Dec. 24, 1952; d. Walter and Frances (Kosin) C. BSEd., Edinboro U. of Pa., 1974; MEd, Pa. State U., 1982; PhD, Gallaudet U., 1996. Cert. spl. edn. supr., elem. prin., secondary prin., speech correction, hearing impaired, Pa. Speech/lang. pathologist Ross County Bd. Edn., Chillicothe, Ohio, 1974-76, N.W. Tri-County I.U. #5, Edinboro, Pa., 1978-91; project devel. specialist Coll. for Continuing Edn., Gallaudet U., Washington, 1991-98; coordinator, mktg. and communication Coll. for Continuing Edn., Gallaudet Univ., Wash., D.C., 1998—. Editor: (books) Educational Interpreting: Into the 1990s, 1991, Bilingual Considerations in the Education of Deaf Students, 1992, Deaf Studies for Educators, 1992, Deaf Studies: What's Up?, 1992, Deaf Studies III: Bridging Cultures in the 21 Century, 1993. Pres.'s scholar Gallaudet U., Washington, 1988-89, 89-90, edn. fellow, 1988-90; edn. fellow Pa. State U., 1976-77. Mem. Kappa Delta Pi, Phi Delta Kappa. Avocations: swimming, sailing, sewing, jogging, ushering in theaters. Office: Gallaudet U/Conf Ctr 3115 800 Florida Ave NE Washington DC 20002-3660

CECCHETTI, GIOVANNI, poet, educator, literary critic; b. Pescia, Italy, July 12, 1922; came to U.S., 1948, naturalized, 1954; s. Agostino and Adorna (Fattorini) C.; m. Ruth Elizabeth Schwabacher, Dec. 27, 1953; children: Stephen G., Margaret F. Liceo Machiavelli, Lucca, 1939-40; Liceo Dante, Florence, Italy, 1940-41, Maturità classica, 1941; Lit.D., U. Florence, 1947. Lectr. to asst. prof. U. Calif. at Berkeley, 1948-57; assoc. prof., prof. Tulane U., 1957-65; prof. Stanford U., 1965-69, charge Italian program, 1965-69; prof. UCLA, 1969-91, Disting. prof., 1985-91, Disting. prof. emeritus, 1991—, chmn. dept. Italian, 1969-77; cons. U. Colo., U. Iowa, 1957; disting. vis. prof. Wake Forest U., U. Mich., U. Wis., 1994, U. Conn., 1997; disting. vis. internat. lectr. Author: La poesia del Pascoli, 1954, G. Verga, The She-Wolf and other stories, 1958, rev., 1973, Leopardi e Verga, 1962, Diario nomade, 1967, Il Verga maggiore, 1968, 70, 75, Impossible scendere, 1978, Giovanni Verga, a critical monograph, 1978, Le Operette morali, Tre studi con un poscritto sui Canti, 1979, G. Verga, Mastro-don Gesualdo, 1979, Il villaggio degli inutili, 1980, Nel cammino dei monti, 1980, G. Leopardi, Operette morali/Essays and Dialogues, 1982, Spuntature e intermezzi, 1983, Danza nel deserto, 1985, Favole spente, 1988, Proc. 1988 UCLA Leopardi Congress, 1990, Contrappunti/Counterpoints, an Anthology of Prose Writings, 1997, Voci di poesia, 1997; assoc. editor Forum Italicum; mem. bd. editors PMLA, Italica; contbr. essays and poems to European and Am. jours. Mem. sci. com. Schlesinger Found. With Italian Liberation Army, 1943-45. Decorated Star of Solidarity Italian Govt., knight and cavaliere ufficiale, Presdl. gold medal for spl. cultural and artistic merits Republic of Italy, Targa d'Oro Regione Puglia; Golden Spur (Belgium), 1982; honored with a Festschrift, 1988; grantee NEH, 1981; recipient Internat. prize for poetry and criticism, Italy, 1991; named Hon. Citizen City of Salerno, Italy, 1989. Mem. MLA, Am. Assn. Tchrs. Italian (Disting. Svc. award 1988), Am. Assn. Italian Studies (hon. pres. 1993), Dante Soc. Am., Leonardo Da Vinci Soc., Patrons of Italian Culture. Home: 1191 Lachman Ln Pacific Palisades CA 90272-2227 Office: U Calif Dept Italian Los Angeles CA 90095*

CECCOLA, RUSS, electrical engineer, writer; b. Phila., Aug. 29, 1966; s. Philip John and Irma Theresa (Bogash) C. BEE, Villanova U., 1988. Engr. PECO Energy Co., Phila., 1988-98. Author: Phantasmagoria Official Player's Guide, 1995, William Shatner's Tek War-The Official Strategy Guide, 1995, WarGames-Exclusive Strategy Guide, 1998. Republican. Roman Catholic. Avocations: computer/video games, comic books, movies, horror, Star Trek. Home: 121 Merion Ave West Conshohocken PA 19428

CECH, JOSEPH HAROLD, chemical engineer; b. Flint, Mich., Oct. 8, 1951; s. Hoseph, Jr. and Margaret Luella (Taphouse) C. BS in Chem. Engring., Mich. Tech. U., 1978. Trainee Menasha Corp., North Bend, Oreg., 1978-79; project engr. molded products div. Menasha Corp., Watertown, Wis., 1979-84; plastic devel. engr. Menasha Corp., Watertown, 1984-86, composite engr., coordinator, 1986-90, sr. process engr., 1990-92, process material supr., 1992-97, material/process mgr., 1996-97; tech./environ. mgr. Applied Molded Products Corp., Watertown, 1997—. With USN, 1971-75. Mem. Mensa, Soc. Plastic Engrs., Am. Inst. Chem. Engrs., Nat. Geog. Soc., Watertown Conservation Club. Methodist. Office: 426 S Montgomery St Watertown WI 53094-6132

CECH, THOMAS ROBERT, chemistry and biochemistry educator; b. Chgo., Dec. 8, 1947; m. Carol Lynn Martinson; children: Allison E., Jennifer N. BA in Chemistry, Grinnell Coll., 1970, DSc (hon.), 1987; PhD in Chem., U. Calif., Berkeley, 1975; DSc (hon.), U. Chgo., 1991; Drury Coll., 1994. Postdoctoral fellow dept. biology MIT, Cambridge, Mass., 1975-77; from asst. prof. to assoc. prof. chemistry U. Colo., Boulder, 1978-83, prof. chemistry and biochemistry also molecular cellular and devel. biology, 1983—, disting. prof., 1990—; rsch. prof. Am. Cancer Soc., 1987—; investigator Howard Hughes Med. Inst., 1988—; co-chmn. Nucleic Acids Gordon Conf., 1984; Phillips disting. visitor Haverford Coll., 1984; Vivian Ernst meml. lectr. Brandeis U., 1984, Cynthia Chan meml. lectr. U. Calif., Berkeley; mem. Welch Found. Symposium, 1985; Danforth lectr. Grinnell Coll. 1986; Pfizer lectr. Harvard U., 1986, Hastings lectr., 1992; Verna and Marrs McLean lectr. Baylor Coll. Medicine, 1987; Harvey lectr., 1987; Mayer lectr. MIT, 1987, HHMI lectr., 1989, T.Y. Shen lectr., 1994; Martin D. Kamen disting. lectureship, U. Calif., San Diego, 1988; Alfred Burger lectr. U. Va., 1988; Berzelius lectr. Karolinska Inst., 1988; Osamu Hayaishi lectr. Internat. Union Biochemistry, Prague, 1988; Beckman lectr. U. Utah, 1989; Max Tishler lectr. Merck, 1989; Abbott vis. scholar U. Chgo., 1989; Herriott lectr. Johns Hopkins U., 1990; J.T. Baker lectr., 1990; G.N. Lewis lectr. U. Calif., Berkeley, 1990; Sonneborn lectr. Ind. U., 1991; Sternbach lectr. Yale U., 1991; W. Pauli lectr., Zürich, 1992; Carter-Wallace lectr. Princeton U., 1992; Stetten lectr. NIH, 1992; Dauben lectr. U. Wash., 1992; Marker lectr. U. Md., 1993; Hirschmann lectr. Oberlin Coll., 1993; Beach lectr. Purdue U., 1993; Abe White lectr. Syntex, 1993; Robbins lectr. Pomona Coll., 1994; Bren lectr. U. Calif., Irvine, 1994; Wawzonek lectr. U. Iowa, 1994; Sumner lectr. Cornell U., 1994; Steenbock lectr. U. Wis., 1995; Murachi lectr. FAOB Congress, Sydney, 1995; Streck award lectr. U. Nebr., 1996; Gardner-Davern lectr. U. Utah, 1996, Priestley lectr. Pa. State U., 1996, Beckman lectr. Calif. Inst. Tech., 1996, Lemieux lectr. U. Alta., Can., 1997, Hogg Award lectr. MD Anderson Cancer Ctr., 1997, DeCoursey Nobel Lectr. Trinity U., 1998, Tschirgi lectr. U. Calif. San Diego, 1998. Assoc. editor Cell, 1986-87, RNA Jour.; mem. editl. bd. Genes and Development; dep. editor Sci. mag. Non-resident fellow Salk Inst.; trustee Grinnell Coll. NSF fellow, 1970-75, Pub. Health Svc. rsch. fellow Nat. Cancer Inst. 1975-77, Guggenheim fellow, 1985-86; recipient medal Am. Inst. Chemists, 1970, Rsch. Career Devel. award Nat. Cancer Inst., 1980-85, Young Sci. award Passano Found., 1984, Harrison Howe award, 1984, Pfizer award, 1985, U.S. Steel award, 1987, V.D. Mattia award, 1987, Louisa Gross Horowitz prize, 1988, Newcombe-Cleveland award AAAS, 1988, Heineken prize Royal Netherlands Acad. Arts and Scis., 1988, Gairdner Found. Internat. award, 1988, Lasker Basic Med. Rsch. award, 1988, Rosenstiel award, 1989, Warren Triennial prize, 1989, Nobel prize in Chemistry, 1989, Hopkins medal Brit. Biochem. Soc., 1992, Feodor Lynen medal, 1995, Nat. Sci. medal, 1995, Mike Hogg award, 1997, Wright prize, 1998; named to Esquire Mag. Register, 1985, Westerner of Yr. Denver Post, 1986. Mem. AAAS, Am. Soc. Biochem. Molecular Biology, NAS, Am. Acad. Arts and Scis., European Molecular Biology Orgn., RNA Soc. (v.p. 1993-96). Office: U Colo Dept Chem & Biochemistry PO Box 215 Boulder CO 80309-0215

CECI, JESSE ARTHUR, violinist; b. Phila., Feb. 2, 1924; s. Luigi Concezio and Catherine Marie (Marotta) C.; m. Catherine Annette Stevens, Aug. 5, 1979. BS, Juilliard Sch. Music, 1951; license de concert, L'Ecole Normale de Musique, Paris, 1954; MusM, Manhattan Sch. Music, 1971. Assoc. concertmaster New Orleans Philharm. Orch., 1953-54; violinist Boston Symphony Orch., 1954-59, N.Y. Philharm. Orch., N.Y., 1959-62, Esterhazy Orch., N.Y.C., 1962-68; concertmaster Denver Symphony Orch., 1974-89, Colo. Symphony Orch., 1989-95; over 50 performances of 22 major works; mem. Zimbler Sinfonietta, Boston, 1957-59; participant Marlboro Festival Chamber Orch. Vt., summmers 1960-62, 65, Marlboro Festival Chamber Orch. European-Israeli tour, 1965, Grand Teton Festival, Wyo., 1972, with Denver Duo, 1975—, N.Mex. Festival, Taos, 1980, Carmel (Calif.) Bach Festival, 1987—, Whistler (B.C., Can.) Mozart Festival, 1989-90, Bear Valley (Calif.) Festival, 1995—, Mendocino (Calif.) Festival, 1996—; mem. faculty Congress of Strings, Dallas, 1985, N.Y. Coll. Music, 1961-71, NYU, 1971-74, U. Colo., 1975-79; guest mem. faculty Univ. Denver, 1986; mem., assoc. concertmaster Casals Festival Orch., San Juan, P.R., 1963-77; violinist Cleve. Orch. fgn. tours, 1967, 73, 78, Cin. Symphony Orch. world tour, 1966; 1st violinist N.Y. String Quartet in-residence at U. Maine, Orono, summer 1969; guest violinist Fla. West Coast Symphony, Sarasota, 1993-98; concertmaster Minn. Orch., summers 1970-71, Denver Chamber Orch., 1985-90; guest concertmaster Pitts. Symphony Orch., Pitts., L.A., 1988, mem. N.Y. Philharmonia Chamber Ensemble in-residence at Hopkins Ctr., Dartmouth U., summer 1973; recitalist, Paris, 1963, Amsterdam, 1963, recitalist Carnegie Recital Hall, N.Y.C., 1963, Town Hall, N.Y.C., 1968, 70, Alice Tully Hall, N.Y.C., 1972; fgn. tour Pitts. Symphony Orch., 1989; soloist Royal Chamber Orch. Japan, 1997-98. Cpl. U.S. Army, 1943-46, PTO. Fulbright fellow Paris, 1951-52. Democrat. Roman Catholic. Office: Colo Symphony Orch 1031 13th St Denver CO 80204-2156

CECI, LOUIS J., former state supreme court justice; b. N.Y.C., Sept. 10, 1927; s. Louis and Filomena C.; m. Shirley; children—Joseph, Geraldine, David; children by previous marriage: Kristin, Remy, Louis. Ph.B., Marquette U., 1951, J.D., 1954. Bar: Wis. 1954, U.S. Dist. Ct. (ea. dist.) Wis.

1954, U.S. Dist. Ct. (we. dist.) Wis. 1987; cert. mediator-arbitrator. Sole practice Milw., 1954-58, 63-68; asst. city atty. City of Milw., 1958-63; mem. Wis. Assembly, Madison, 1965-66; judge Milw. County Ct., 1968-73, Milw. Circuit Ct., 1973-82; justice Wis. Supreme Ct., Madison, 1982-93, retired, 1993; res. judge State of Wis., 1993—; lectr. Wis. Jud. Confs., 1970-79. Lectr. Badger Boys State, Ripon, Wis., 1961, 1982-84; asst. dist. commr. Boy Scouts Am., 1962. Recipient Wis. Civic Recognition PLAV, Milw., 1970; recipient Community Improvement Pompeii Men's Club, Milw., 1971, Good Govt. Milw Jaycees, 1973, Community-Judiciary Pompeii Men's Club, 1982. Mem. ABA, Wis. Bar Assn., Dane County Bar Assn., Milw. County Bar Assn., Waukesha County Bar Assn., Am. Legion (comdr. 1962-63).

CECIL, BONNIE SUSAN, elementary education educator; b. Louisville, Sept. 29, 1951; d. Robert Lawrence and Mary Hedwig (Kluesner) C. BA in Edn., U. Ky., 1973; MS in Edn., Ind. U., 1978; postgrad., U. Louisville, 1988—. Tchr. grades 1-4 Roosevelt Cmty. Sch., Jefferson County, Ky., 1972-80; tchr. ages 6 and 7 Wandle Primary Sch., London, 1980-81; tchr. 1st grade Foster Elem. Sch., Jefferson County, 1981-82; tchr. ages 5-8 Brown Sch. Primary, Jefferson County, 1982—; co-dir., instr. writing process for tchrs. Ky. Writing Insts. I and II, Boone County, 1986-88; instr. writing process insvc. Jefferson County Pub. Schs., 1988-89, workshop presenter on environ. edn., 1990, 92, supr. student tchrs., 1989-90, 92, 94, 95, 97; instr. lang. arts U. Louisville, 1990-91; participant Fulbright Tchr. Exch. Program, London, 1980-81, Brown Sch. Dream Team, 1992; presenter ann. conf. Ky. Assn. Edn. Young Children-Louisville Assn. for Children Under Seven, 1990; presenter Cmty. Learning Resource Conf., 1992; participant Louisville Writing Project, 1984-85, premier class Leadership Edn., 1986-87. Tchr. rep. J. Graham Brown Sch. PTSA, 1983-90, 92-97; tchr. rep. site-based decision making coun., 1996—; bd. dirs. Roosevelt Cmty. Sch., Inc., 1973-76; creator, dir. summer reading and writing program Portland Mus., Louisville, 1985; treas. Louisville Homefront Performances, Inc., 1986-87, sec., 1988-90, bd. dirs. 1984-96. Recipient Golden Apple Achievement award Ashland Oil Co., 1989, Individual Tchr. Achievement award, 1992, Nat. Educator award Milken Family Found., 1994, ExCel award WHAS-TV and PNC Bank, 1995; named Jefferson County Elem. Tchr. of Yr., 1992, Ky. Elem. Tchr. of Yr., 1993, Ky. Tchr. of Yr., 1993, Milken Family Nat. Educator Project Mentor, 1998; grantee Ky. Arts Coun., 1986-87, Jefferson County Pub. Schs.-U. Louisville, 1989-91, U. Louisville, 1991, Rosenbaum Found., 1998; named Milken Virtual Workspace Mentor, 1998; inducted into The Commonwealth for Tchrs., 1998. Mem. ASCD, NEA, Assn. Childhood Edn. Internat., Nat. Coun. Tchrs. English (conf. presenter 1988, chmn., presenter nat. conf. 1992), Ky. Edn. Assn., Jefferson County Tchrs. Assn., Leadership Edn. Alumni Assn. Avocations: music, gardening, pets. Office: J Graham Brown Sch 546 S 1st St Louisville KY 40202-1816

CECIL, CHARLES HARKLESS, artist, educator; b. Kansas City, Mo., May 12, 1945; s. Charles F. and Alice (Harkless) C.; m. Isabelle Claude Jeanne Touren, Dec. 30, 1982; 1 dau., Charlotte Alice Marcelle. B.A., Haverford Coll., 1967; postgrad., Yale U., 1967-69. Co-dir. Studio Cecil-Graves, Florence, Italy, 1983-91; dir. Charles H. Cecil Studios, Florence, 1991—; instr. Villa Schifanoia, Grad. Studio Fine Arts, Florence, 1983-87. Exhibited in group shows at N.A.D., N.Y.C., 1979, 80, Dallas, 1983; represented in permanent collections at: Portrait Gallery, Haverford Coll., Pa., West Bend Gallery Fine Arts, Wis; executed: portrait Dr. Jonathon Rhodes for Am. Philos. Soc. NDEA grantee, 1967-69; Elizabeth Greenshields Found. grantee, 1970-73; John F. Stacey Found. grantee, 1980; recipient Julius T. Hallgarten First prize for oil painting, 1979, Benjamin Altman Second prize for landscape 155 Ann. Exhbn. Nat. Acad. Design, 1980. Home: Via Pandolfini 21, 50122 Florence Italy Office: Charles H Cecil Studios, Borgo San Frediano 68, 50124 Florence Italy

CECIL, DAVID ROLF, mathematician, educator; b. Tulsa, July 12, 1935; s. Neil McKinley and Ola Ethel (Turner) C.; m. Betty Lou Poe, June 14, 1958; 1 child, Eric Alan. Student (Pitts. Plate Glass Co. scholar), Carnegie Inst. Tech., 1954-55; B.A., U. Tulsa, 1958; postgrad (fellow), Tulane U., 1958-59; M.S., Okla. State U., 1960, Ph.D., 1962. Grad. teaching asst. Okla. State U., 1959-62; sr. research mathematician Atlantic Refining Co., 1962; asst. prof., then assoc. prof. math. North Tex. State U., Denton, 1962-69; prof. math. Butler U., Indpls., 1969-70, Tex. A&I U., Kingsville, 1970—; chmn. dept. Tex. A&I U., 1980-85; cons. Edn. Service Ctr. Region II, 1979-80, Air Force Office Sci. Rsch., Wilford Hall Med. Ctr., Tex., 1988-90; organizer Kingsville Computer Club, 1980; mem. credit com. Kingsville Area Educators Fed. Credit Union, 1979—. Contbr. articles to math. jours. Faculty fellow North Tex. State U., 1968-69; Faculty fellow Tex. A&I U., 1971-73. Fellow Tex. Acad. Scis.; mem. Assn. for Computing Machinery, Am. Statistical Assn., Sigma Xi. Methodist. Club: Kingsville Radio (pres. 1974). Office: Tex A&M U Kingsville Dept Math Kingsville TX 78363

CECIL, DONALD, investment company executive; b. N.Y.C., Jan. 3, 1927; s. Leopold and Viola C.; m. Jane Grossman, Mar. 5, 1953; children: Alec, Leslie (twins). BS in Applied Econs., Yale U., 1947. Sr. instl. rsch. analyst Eastman Dillon Union Securities, N.Y.C., 1961-63; from dir. instl. rsch. to sr. v.p. Shearson Hamill, Inc., N.Y.C., 1963-70; pres. Shearson Hamill Mgmt. Co., 1966-70; founding ptnr. Cumberland Assocs., N.Y.C., 1970-82; bd. dirs., trustee 45 Merrill Lynch domestic, global and offshore mutual funds and trusts; bd. dirs. Rycote Adv. Panel, Geneva, Switzerland, 1984—; chmn. valuation bd. Biotech. Investments, Ltd., London, 1986—; dep. chmn. Internat. Biotech. Trust Ltd., London, 1994—; chmn. dirs. svc. com., Investment Com. Inst., Washington, 1995-98. Chmn. Bd. Transp., Westchester County, White Plains, N.Y., 1978—; vice chmn. bd. trustees SUNY Purchase Coll. Found., 1987—; sponsor I Have a Dream Found., Mt. Vernon, N.Y., 1987—; chmn. bd. Friends of Neuberger Mus., Purchase, 1989-91. Mem. Chartered Fin. Analysts (cert.), N.Y. Econ. Club, N.Y. Soc. Security Analysts. Avocations: theater, travel, tennis. Office: Cumberland Assocs Rm 3803 1114 Avenue Of The Americas New York NY 10036-7775

CECIL, DORCAS ANN, property management executive; b. Greensboro, N.C., Mar. 31, 1945; d. George Joseph and Marianne Elizabeth (Zimmerman) Ernst; m. Richard Lee Cecil, June 8, 1968; children: Sarah, Matthew. BA, U. Ark., 1967. Pres. B & C Enterprises Property Mgmt., Ltd., O'Fallon, Ill., 1977-93, Cecil Mgmt. Group, Inc., O'Fallon and St. Louis, 1993—. Bd. dirs. O'Fallon Pub. Libr., 1983—, v.p., 1986-87, pres., 1987—; sec. St. Vincent de Paul Soc., 1987—; bd. dirs. Leadership Coun. Southwestern Ill., 1994—. Named Realtor of Yr., Belleville Area Assn. Realtors, 1994. Mem. Inst. Real Estate Mgmt. (cert., v.p. 1987, pres. St. Louis chpt. 1990, vice chmn. Nat. IREM std. coms. 1991—, regional v.p. 1992-93, governing councillor 1994—, nat. ethics and discipline hearing bd. 1994—), St. Louis Multi-Housing Coun., Profl. Housing Mgmt. Assn., Cmty. Assns. Inst., Nat. Assn. Realtors, Ill. Assn. Realtors (housing com. 1994—), Belleville Assn. Realtors (bd. dirs. 1991-94, Realtor of Yr. 1994), Mo. Assn. Realtors, Belleville Bd. Realtors C. of C. (bd. dirs. 1987-96, v.p. 1988—, pres. 1992-93), O'Fallon C. of C. Office: Cecil Mgmt Group Inc PO Box 459 O'Fallon IL 62269-0459

CECIL, LINDA MARIE, obstetrician/gynecologist; b. Huntsville, Tex., Apr. 10, 1944. MD, U. Tex., 1971. Diplomate Am. Bd. Ob-Gyn. Intern U. Tex., 1971-72, resident in ob-gyn, 1972-75; fellow in fetal maternal medicine Baylor U., 1979-80; staff Med. Ctr. Hosp., Conroe, Tex.; courtesy staff Meml. Hosp., Woodlands, Tex.; asst. clin. prof. Baylor Coll. Med. Mem. ACOG, AMA, Tex. Med. Assn., Tex. Assn. Ob-Gyn., So. Med. Assn. Fax: (409) 539-3349. Office: 500 Med Ctr Blvd # 240 Conroe TX 77304

CECIL, LOUIS ANTON, mathematics educator; b. Oak Pk., Ill., Dec. 19, 1940; m. Joan Rose Johnson, Dec. 15, 1962; children: Sutton Roberta, Cecil, Smith. BS, U. Minn., 1969. Cert. life tchr. secondary math., Wis. Insp. Honeywell, Mpls., 1959-65; math. educator Sheboygan (Wis.) Area Sch. Dist., 1969-99; track coach North H.S., Sheboygan, 1981-99. Named Melvin Jones fellow Lions Club Internat., 1992. Mem. Sheboygan Evening Lions (pres. 1978-79, zone chmn. Lions. Multiple Dist. 27B-1 1981-82, region chmn. 1984-87, Leo chmn. 1993-97, state Leo chmn. 1995-97, dist. sec.-treas. 1998-99), Elks Lodge #299. Democrat. Methodist. Avocations: participation in arts, golf, camping. Home: 1922 N 2nd St Sheboygan WI 53081-2916 Office: North H S 1042 School Ave Sheboygan WI 53083-4053

CECIL, MAXINE, critical care nurse; b. Healdton, Okla., Sept. 25, 1921; d. James Albert and Clara (Phelps) Metz; children: Harold E. Seals, James Michael Seals, David Ray Smith. LPN, Seventh Day Adventist Hosp., Ardmore, Okla., 1954; ADN cum laude, No. Okla. Coll., Tonkawa, Okla., 1979. RN, Okla. LPN Seventh Day Adventist Hosp., Ardmore, 1953-66; LPN, charge nurse at nursing homes Ardmore, 1966-74; LPN and RN Johnston Meml. Hosp., Tishomingo, Okla., 1974-80; RN Meml. Hosp. So. Okla., Ardmore, Okla., 1980-84; charge nurse Love County Med. Ctr., Marietta, Okla., 1988-90; charge nurse, RN Lakeland Manor, Inc., Ardmore, 1982—; nurse Meml. Convalescent Home, Ardmore, 1990—; pres. LPN Assn for Carter, Love, Johnston and Marshall Counties, 1963-70; mem. state bd. LPNs, 1968. Instr. first aid ARC, Ardmore, 1960-62; pathfinder dir. Seventh Day Adventist Ch., Ardmore.

CECIL, ROBERT SALISBURY, telecommunications company executive; b. Manila, Philippines, May 28, 1935; came to U.S., 1941; s. Robert Edgar and Susan Elizabeth (Jurika) C.; m. Louise Nuttal Millholland, Nov. 30, 1963; children: Scott Douglass, James Hilliard. BSEE, U.S. Naval Acad., 1956; MBA, Harvard U., 1962. Commd. 2d lt. USAF, 1956, advanced through grades to 1st lt., 1958, ret., 1960; dir. govt. programs IBM, Washington, 1976-77; corp. v.p. mktg. Motorola Inc., Schaumburg, Ill., 1977-84; pres. Cellular Group Lin Broadcasting, N.Y.C., 1984-91; chmn. Plantronics, Inc., Santa Cruz, Calif., 1992—; bd. dirs. GT Group Telecom., Xantrex, CW Saskfund III, Ltd. Mem. Lyford Cay Club, Vancouver Lawn Tennis and Badminton Club, Rotary Internat. Republican. Episcopalian. Office: Plantronics Inc, Plantronics Inc, 1703-560 Cardero St, Vancouver, BC Canada V6G 3E9

CECIL, WILLIAM A.V., landmark director; married; 2 children. Grad., Harvard U. bd. dirs. Pub. Svc. Natural Gas Co., Carolina Motor Club, N.C. Citizens for Bus. and Industry. Staff Chase Manhattan Bank N.Y., Washington; officer Chase Manhattan Bank N.Y., N.Y.C.; pres. The Biltmore Co., Asheville, N.C., 1979—. Pres. Southern Highlands Attractions Assn., N.C. Travel Council (recipient Charles J. Parker Travel award 1974), Asheville Area C. of C.; founder Ashevill/Buncombe County Tourism Dev. Authority. With British Navy, World War II. Mem. Historic House Assn. Am. (chmn., founder), Nat. Trust Historic Preservation. Fax: (704) 255-1139. Office: Biltmore Estate One North Pack Square Asheville NC 28801-3400*

CEDAR, PAUL ARNOLD, church executive, minister; b. Mpls., Nov. 4, 1938; s. Carl Benjamin and Bernice M. (Peterson) C.; m. Jean Helen Lier, Aug. 25, 1959; children: Daniel Paul, Mark John, Deborah Jean. BS, No. State Coll., Aberdeen, S.D., 1960; MDiv, No. Bap. Theol. Sem., 1968; Calif. State U., Fullerton, 1971; DMin, Am. Baptist Sem. of the West, 1973. Ordained to ministry Evang. Free Ch. of Am., 1966. Youth for Christ, crusade dir. Billy Graham Evang. Assn., Leighton Ford Team, 1960-65; pastor Evang. Free Ch., Naperville, Ill., 1965-67, Yorba Linda, Calif., 1969-73; exec. pastor 1st Presbyn. Ch. Hollywood, Calif., 1975-81; sr. pastor Lake Ave. Congl. Ch., Pasadena, Calif., 1981-90; pres. Evang. Free Ch. Am., Mpls., 1990-96; chmn., CEO Mission Am., 1995—; guest dean Billy Graham Sch. Evangelism, Mpls., 1983—; vis. prof. Fuller Theol. Sem., Pasadena, Talbot Theol. Sem., La Habra, Calif., Trinity Div. Sch., Deerfield, Ill. Author: How to Make Love Your Motive, 1977, Becoming a Lover, 1978, Seven Keys to Maximum Communication, 1980, Sharing the Good Life, 1980, Communicators Commentary, 1983, Strength in Servant Leadership, 1987, Mastering the Pastoral Role, 1991, Where Is Hope?, 1992, A Life of Prayer, 1998. Chmn. Internat. Lausanne Com., 1998; chmn. U.S. Lausanne Com. for World Evangelization, 1992—, Internat. Coalition, AD 2000 and Beyond Movement; mem. adv. bd. African Enterprise. Mem. Christian TV and Film Commn. (adv. bd.), Internat. Students, Ron Hutchcraf Ministries, Worldwide Leadership Coun., Caleb Ministries, Leadership Renewal Ctr., John M. Perkins Found., Nat. Prayer Com., Revival Prayer Fellowship, Barnabas Internat., Pioneer Clubs. Avocations: athletics, music, writing, carpentry. Office: Mission Am 5666 Lincoln Dr Ste 100 Edina MN 55436 *I am convinced that when all of life is over, only one thing will matter ultimately-fufilling the will of God.*

CEDARBAUM, MIRIAM GOLDMAN, federal judge; b. N.Y.C., Sept. 16, 1929; d. Louis Albert and Sarah (Shapiro) Goldman; m. Bernard Cedarbaum, Aug. 25, 1957; children: Daniel Goldman C., Jonathan Goldman C. BA, Barnard Coll., 1950; LLB, Columbia U., 1953. Bar: N.Y. 1954, U.S. Dist. Ct. (so. dist.) N.Y. 1956 U.S. Ct. Appeals (2d cir.) 1956, U.S. Ct. Claims 1958, U.S. Supreme Ct. 1958, U.S. Dist. Ct. (ea. dist.) N.Y. 1980, U.S. Ct. Appeals (5th and 11th cirs.) 1981. Law clk. to judge Edward Jordan Dimock U.S. Dist. Ct. (so. dist.) N.Y., 1953-54, asst. U.S. atty., 1954-57; atty. Dept. Justice, Washington, 1958-59; part-time cons. to law firms in litigation matters, 1959-62; 1st asst. counsel N.Y. State Moreland Act Commn., 1963-64; assoc. counsel Mus. Modern Art, N.Y.C., 1965-79; assoc. litigation dept. Davis, Polk & Wardwell, N.Y.C., 1979-83, sr. atty., 1983-86; acting justice Village of Scarsdale, N.Y., 1978-82, justice, 1982-86; judge U.S. Dist. Ct. (so. dist.) N.Y., 1986-98, sr. judge, 1998—; mem. com. defender svcs. Jud. Conf. U.S., 1993—; bd. vis. Columbia Law Sch.; trustee Barnard Coll.; co-counsel Scarsdale Open Soc. Assn., 1968-86. Mem. adv. com. on labor rels. Scarsdale Bd. Edn., 1976-77; mem. Scarsdale Bd. Archtl. Rev., 1977-78. Recipient Medal of Distinction Barnard Coll., 1991. Mem. Am. Law Inst., ABA (chmn. com. on pictorial graphic sculptural and choreographic works 1979-81, copyright com. fed. practice and procedure, 1983-84), N.Y. State Bar Assn. (chmn. com. on fed. legislation 1978-80, com. on dist., city, village and town cts., 1983-84), Assn. of Bar of City of N.Y. (com. on copyright and literary property, 1982-84, com. on the Bicentennial 1988-92), Fed. Bar Coun., Copyright Soc. U.S.A. (trustee, mem. exec. com. 1979-82), Supreme Ct. Hist. Soc. Jewish. Office: US Dist Ct US Courthouse 500 Pearl St Rm 1330 New York NY 10007-1312

CEDARS, MICHAEL G., plastic surgeon. BSEE, MIT, 1973; MD, U. Calif., San Francisco, 1977. Resident in plastic surgery UCLA, 1984; pvt. practice Berkeley Children's Hosp., Oakland, Calif.; med. staff Altabates Hosp. E-mail: cedarsm@sutterhealth.org. Office: Berkeley Ste 200 3000 Colby St Berkeley CA 94705-2058

CEDDIA, ANTHONY FRANCIS, university administrator; b. Boston, Mar. 4, 1944; s. Antonio John and Marie (Loungo) C.; m. Valerie Ann Mulkern, Apr. 15, 1966; children: Ann-Marie, Michael. BS in Edn., Northeastern U., 1965, MEd, 1968; EdD, U. Mass., 1980; postgrad. John F. Kennedy Sch. Govt., Harvard U., 1990; LLD (hon.), North Adams State Coll., 1990; cert. sr. exec. program in local govt., Harvard U., 1990; LLD (hon.), North Adams State Coll., 1990. Cert. counselor, secondary sch. tchr., Mass. Tchr. social studies, counselor Melrose High Sch., Mass., 1965-70; fin. aid and admissions ofcl. North Adams State Coll., Mass., 1970-73, dean of adminstrn, 1973-78, exec. v.p., 1978-81; acting pres. North Adams State Coll., Mass., 1979; pres. Shippenburg U. Pa., 1981—; chmn. bd. Univ. Ctr., State System Higher Edn., Harrisburg, 1987-90; chmn. Commn. Univs. of Pa., 1986-88; mem. Sico Found., Sico Oil Corp., 1983—; mem. adv. bd. Orrstown Bank, Shippenburg, 1984-87. Mem. Cumberland County Transp. Bd., 1990; trustee Chambersburg Hosp. Bd., 1989—; mem. exec. com. South Ctrl. Pa. coun. Boy Scouts Am., 1982—, adv. panel Nat. Army ROTC, 1984—, chair, 1990-92; bd. dirs. Ams. for the Competitive System, 1981-87; chair divsn. II steering com. NCAA, 1990-92. Recipient Disting. Alumni Northeastern U., 1979. Mem. Am. Assn. State Colls. and Univs. (editor 1982-86, chmn. com. rsch. and liaison, com. on policy and purpose 1987-90), Am. Assn. Higher Edn., Mid. States Assn. Colls. and Schs. (commn. on higher edn. 1986-92), Nat. Intercollegiate Athletic Assn. (coun.). Home: PO Box 606 Shippensburg PA 17257-0606 Office: Shippensburg U Office of Pres 1871 Old Main Dr Shippensburg PA 17257-2299*

CEDEL, MELINDA IRENE, music educator, violinist; b. Ft. Worth, July 31, 1957; d. Albert and Emilia Florence (Sylvester) C. Student, N.C. Sch. Arts, 1974-77; MusB Edn., U. S.C., 1979. Cert. tchr., S.C. Tchr. music Charleston (S.C.) County Pub. Schs., 1979-92; pvt. tchr. music, 1983—; concertmaster Brunswick (Ga.) Civic Orch., 1993-97, pers. mgr., 1995-96. Performed with Florence Symphony, Columbia Philharm., S.C. Chamber Orch., Augusta Symphony, Jacksonville Symphony Orch., Savannah (Ga.) Symphony, Hilton Head (S.C.) Symphony, Jacksonville Summer Symphonetta, Valdosta (Ga.) Symphony Orch.; musician Charleston Symphony, 1979-92, Charleston Symphony Chamber Orch., Long Bay (S.C.) Symphony; musician, mgr. Charlestowne String Quartet, 1983-92; condr. Charleston County Prep. Orch., 1983-84; performer Piccolo Spoleto, 1980-91; co-dir. Charleston County Strolling Strings. Mem. Am. Fedn. Musicians, Am. String Tchrs. Assn., Mensa, Kappa Phi Kappa. Avocations: sailing, water sports, reading, travel. Home: 220 Five Pounds Rd Saint Simons GA 31522

CEDERBERG, JAMES, physics educator; b. Oberlin, Kans., Mar. 16, 1939; s. J. Walter and Edith E. (Glad) C.; m. Judith Ness, June 10, 1967; children: Anna Sook, Rachel Eun. BA, U. Kans., 1959; MA, Harvard U., 1960, PhD, 1963. Lectr., rsch. assoc. Harvard U., Cambridge, Mass., 1963-64; asst. prof. St. Olaf Coll., Northfield, Minn., 1964-68, assoc. prof., 1968-80, prof., 1980—, Grace A. Whittier prof. sci., 1992—; councilor Coun. on Undergrad. Rsch., 1985-91, 92-95, pres. physics coun., 1985-88. Recipient Distinguished Service Citation awd., Am. Assn. of Physics Teachers, 1993. Mem. Am. Phys. Soc., Am. Assn. Physics Tchrs. Lutheran. Fax: 507-646-3968. E-mail: ceder@stolaf.edu. Office: St Olaf Coll 1520 Saint Olaf Ave Northfield MN 55057-1574 also: U Canterbury, Dept Physics & Astronomy, Christchurch New Zealand*

CEDERSTROM, GARY LYNN, professional baseball umpire; b. Bismarck, N.D., Oct. 4, 1955; s. George Herman and Gladys Edria (Collins) C.; m. Theresa Pope, 1994; children: Erin, Caitlin, Keaton. BS in Edn., Minot (N.D.) State Coll., 1979. Profl. umpire Midwest League Profl. Baseball Clubs, Burlington, Iowa, 1979-82, Eastern League Profl. Baseball Clubs, Plainville, Conn., 1982-83, Am. Assn. Profl. Baseball Clubs, Grove City, Ohio, 1983-96, Columbian Winter League, Barranquilla, 1984-85, P.R. Winter League, San Juan, 1985-86, Caribbean World Series, Mariciba, Venezuela, 1986, Dominican Republic Winter League, Santo Domingo, 1989—, Am. League Profl. Baseball Clubs, N.Y.C., 1997—. Named Alumni of Yr., Gamma Delta chpt., Sigma Tau Gamma, Minot State Coll., 1980-81. Mem. Elks. Avocations: reading, playing scrabble, crossword puzzles. Home: 2910 2nd Ave SW Minot ND 58701-3342

CEDOLINI, ANTHONY JOHN, psychologist; b. Rochester, N.Y., Sept. 19, 1942; s. Peter Ross and Mary J. (Anthony) C.; m. Clare Marie De Rose, Aug. 16, 1964; children: Maria A., Antonia C., Peter E. Student, U. San Francisco, 1960-62; BA, San Jose State U., 1965, MS, 1968; PhD in Ednl. Pscyhology, Columbia Pacific U., 1983. Lic. ednl. psychologist, sch. adminstr., marriage, family, child counselor, sch psychologist, sch. counselor, social worker, Calif.; Lic. real estate broker, Calif. Mng. ptnr. Cienega Valley Vineyards and Winery (formerly Almaden Vineyards) and Comml. Shopping Ctrs., 1968—; coord. psychol. svcs. Oak Grove Sch. Dist., San Jose, Calif., 1968-81, asst. dir. pupil svcs., 1977-81; dir. pupil svcs. Oak Grove Sch. Dist., San Jose, 1981-83; pvt. practice, ednl. psychologist Ednl. Assocs., San Jose, 1983—; co-dir. Biofeedback Inst. of Santa Clara County, San Jose, 1976-83; ptnr. in Cypress Ctr.-Ednl. Psychologists and Consultancy, 1978-84; cons., program auditor for Calif. State Dept. Edn.; instr. U. Calif., Santa Cruz and LaVerne Coll. Ext. courses; guest spkr. San Jose State U.; lectr., workshop presenter in field. Author: Occupational Stress and Job Burnout, 1982, A Parents Guide to School Readiness, 1971, The Effect of Affect, 1975; contbr. articles to profl. jours. and newspapers. Founder, bd. dirs. Lyceum of Santa Clara County, 1971—. Mem. NEA, Calif. Tchrs. Assn., Calif. Assn. Sch. Psychologists, Nat. Assn. Sch. Psychologists, Coun. for Exceptional Children, Calif. Assn. for Gifted, Assn. Calif. Sch. Adminstrs., Calif. Personnel & Guidance Assn., Biofeedback Soc. Am., Nat. Assn., Tau Delta Phi. Avocations: collecting antique furniture and coins, stained glass, wine making, classic cars. Home and Office: 1183 Nikulina Ct San Jose CA 95120-5441

CEDRASCHI, TULLIO, investment management company executive; b. Zurich, Switzerland, Oct. 4, 1938; s. Guido and Ida (Colombara) C. Degree in Civil Engring., Coll. Tech., Zurich, 1960; MBA, McGill U., 1968. Civil engr., project mgr. Conrad Zschokke, Zurich, 1960-61, Bur. D'Etudes Quoniam, Paris, 1961-63, BBR Switzerland and Can., 1963-65, R. R. Nicolet and Assocs., Montreal, 1965-66; with CN Investments, Montreal, 1968—, gen. mgr., 1973-77, pres., CEO, 1977—; bd. dirs. Cambridge Shopping Centres Ltd., Helix Investments, Freehold Resources Ltd. Mem. Montreal Soc. Fin. Analysts, Swiss-Can. C. of C., Hillside Tennis Club. Avocations: tennis, skiing. Home: # 605 2600 ave Pierre-Dupuy, Habitat 67 Cite du Havre, Montreal, PQ Canada H3C 3R6 Office: CN Investment Divsn Ste 1515, PO Box 11002 5 Pl Ville Marie, Montreal, PQ Canada H3C 4T2 also: Canadian National Railways, 935 de la Gauchetiere St, Montreal, PQ Canada H3C 3N4

CEDRIC, LYLE RUSSELL See HENDERSON, SKITCH

CEDRONE, LOUIS ROBERT, JR., critic; b. Balt., June 25, 1923; s. Louis and Lucia (Mazzola) C.; m. Nancy Nelson, Sept. 11, 1954; children—Linda, David. B.S., U. Md., 1951. With Balt. Evening Sun, 1951-92, drama-film critic, 1963-92, ret., 1992; corr. Variety, 1957-77, 82-85; TV show cablevision Critics Corner, 1982-85. Swimming instr. ARC, 1961-68. Served with inf. AUS, 1943-45. Decorated Purple Heart with oak leaf cluster, Bronze Star. Mem. Sigma Nu, Omicron Delta Kappa, Pi Delta Epsilon. Home: 9 Muirfield Ct Lutherville Timonium MD 21093-3905

CEFALO, ROBERT CHARLES, obstetrician, gynecologist; b. Boston, 1933. MD, Tufts U., 1959. Diplomate Am. Bd. Ob.-Gyn. Intern Chelsea Naval Hosp., Boston, 1959-60; resident in ob.-gyn. U.S. Naval Hosp., Oakland, Calif., 1961-64; prof. dept. ob-gyn. Med. Sch. U. N.C., Chapel Hill. Mem. ACOG, AMA, SGI. Office: U NC Med Sch 214 MacNider Chapel Hill NC 27599*

CELANT, GERMANO, curator. PhD in History of Modern Art, Genoa (Italy) U., 1975. Sr. curator contemporary art Solomon R. Guggenheim Mus., N.Y.C., 1989—. Collections arranged: Maplethorpe vs Rodin, Kunsthalle Dusseldorf, Germany, 1992, Robert Maplethorpe, Louisianne Mus., Denmark, 1992, Louise Nevelson, Palazzo Esposizioni, Rome, 1993, Keith Haring, Rivoli, Turin, Italy, 1994 and traveling to Malmö (Sweden) Konsthall, Seichtorhalley, Hamburg, Germany, Tel Aviv Mus. Art, 19994-95, Fundacion la Caixa, Madrid, 1995, Kunsthaus, Vienna, 1995-96, Mus. Contemporary Art, Sidney, 1996-97, The Italian Metamorphosis, 1943-1968, Solomon R. Guggenheim Mus., N.Y.C., 1994 and traveling to Milan and Wolfsburg, Claes Oldenburg, Nat. Gallery Art, Washington, 1995 and traveling to L.A., N.Y.C., Bonn, Germany, and London, (with Nancy Spector) Rebecca Horn, Solomon R. Guggenheim Mus., N.Y.C., 1993, Osmosis: Haim Steinbach & Ettorre Spalletti, Solomon R. Guggenheim Mus., N.Y.C., 1993, Joel-Peter Witkin Castello di Rivoli, Turin and The Solomon R. Guggenheim Mus., 1995-96, Piero Manzoni Sculpture Gallery, London, 1998; artistic dir. 1st Biennale di Firenze, 1997; curator 47th Biennale of Venice, 1998; contbg. editor Artforum & Interview; contbr. articles to popular mags. Office: Solomon R Guggenheim Mus 575 Broadway New York NY 10012-3230

CELELLA, JAN GERDING, retired legislative staff member; b. Cin., Dec. 10, 1935; d. Carlyn Henry and Kathryn Josephine (Simon) Wodraska; m. Philip Gary Celella, Apr. 8, 1989; children: Thomas Allen, Timothy James, Peggy Ann, Pamela Rose. Student, Thomas More Coll., 1972-75. Field rep. Congressman John B. Breckinridge, 6th Dist., Ky., 1973-79; dist. rep. Senator Wendell H. Ford of Ky., Covington, 1979-98; ret., 1998; Co-founder The Resource Bank. Contbr. articles to profl. jours. Bd. mem. No. Ky. U. ReEntry Ctr.; dir. Covington-Cin. Suspension Bridge Com.; bd. overseers Redwood Sch.; bd. mem. Louise Southgate Women's Ctr.; mem. Summit on Ky. Women, Women's Health Seminar Com.; mem. Elder Abuse Prevention Task Force, United Way; bd. dirs. March of Dimes Birth Defect Found.; mem. No. Ky. Chamber Quest com., new resident com. Named Outstanding Woman Ky. Post/No. Ky. U., 1988; recipient Walter L. Pieschel award C. of C., 1989, No. Ky. Area Devel. Dist. Cmty. Leadership award, 1992. Mem. Am. Bus. Women's Assn., No. Ky. C. of C. (transp. com.). Democrat. Roman Catholic. Avocations: travel, community service, grandchildren, photography, reading. Home: 944 Ravine Dr Villa Hills KY 41017-3679

CELENTANO, FRANCIS MICHAEL, artist, art educator; b. N.Y.C., May 25, 1928; s. Michael Anthony and Rafaela (Valentino) C. B.A., NYU, 1951, M.A. in Art History, 1957. Lectr. C.W. Post Coll., L.I., N.Y., 1961-63, N.Y. Inst. Tech., Old Westbury, N.Y., 1965-66; from assoc. prof. to prof. Sch. Art, U. Wash., Seattle, 1966-93. One-man shows include Howard Wise Gallery, N.Y.C., 1963, Foster/White Gallery, Seattle, 1971, 73, 75, 78, Diane

Gilson Gallery, Seattle, 1981, 82, Fountain Gallery, Portland, Oreg., 1983, Greg Kucera Gallery, Seattle, 1986, 89, 91, Safeco Plaza, Seattle, 1990, 95, Laura Russo Gallery, Portland, 1990, Woodside/Braseth Gallery, 1993, 95, 97; retrospective exhbn. Portland Ctr. for the Visual Arts, 1986, Whatcom County Mus., Bellingham, Washington, 1992; represented in permanent collections at Mus. of Modern Art, N.Y.C., Albright-Knox Mus., Buffalo, Seattle Art mus., Fed. Res. Bank of San Francisco, Wash. State Arts Commn., King County Arts Commn., Univ. Hosp., Seattle. Fulbright scholar Rome, 1958; fed. regional fellow in painting Western States Arts Fedn. Nat. Endowment for the Arts, 1990.

CELENTANO, LINDA NANCY, industrial designer; b. N.J., May 11, 1958; d. Edward and Ruth Celentano. Student design, U. Copenhagen, 1978; B Indsl. Design, Pratt Inst., 1980. Indsl. designer Lebowitz/Gould Design, N.Y.C., 1979-81, Smart Design, N.Y.C., 1981-85; product design dir. Medin Corp., Wallington, N.J., 1985-95; indsl. designer Pfizer Howmedica, 1995-97; prof. indsl. design Pratt Inst., N.Y.C., 1998—; lectr. Pratt Inst. Alumni Series, Bklyn., 1986-87. Published in Indsl. Design Mag., 1986, 90, Product Design II, 1987, Product Design VI, 1994, Internat. Design Yearbook, 1988, 89, N.Y. Times, 1990, ID Mag., 1990, New and Notable Product Design, 1991, Crain's N.Y. Bus., 1998, Design Exch., Toronto, 1998, also salad servers; represented in permanent collections Cooper-Hewitt Collection, N.Y.C., Nambe Picture Frames and Desk Top Accessories Chgo. Athenaeum Design Mus. Vol. Libr. for Recording for Blind, N.Y.C., 1990; co-founder Rowena Reed Kostellow Fund, 1990—, active exec. com.. Recipient Design Excellence award Indsl. Design Mag., 1986. Mem. Indusl. Designer Soc. Am. Lutheran. Avocations: cooking, travel, photography. Home: 325 Haywood Dr Paramus NJ 07652-3329 Office: 263 Franklin Ave Apt 33 Ridgewood NJ 07450-3251

CELENTINO, VICTOR GERARD, special education educator; b. Apr. 7, 1965. AA, Lansing (Mich.) C.C., 1987; BA, Olivet (Mich.) Coll., 1991; MA, Western Mich. U., 1998. Asst. voter registration clk. Lansing Twp. County Clk.'s Office, 1989-91; tchr. spl. edn. Dwight Rich Middle Sch., Lansing, 1992—. Trustee Lansing Twp., 1992—.

CELESIA, GASTONE GUGLIELMO, neurologist, neurophysiologist, researcher; b. Genoa, Italy, Nov. 22, 1933; came to U.S., 1959, naturalized, 1970; s. Raffaele Amadeo and Ottavia (Tortrino) C.; m. Linda Irene Pike, Aug. 1, 1964; children—Gloria, Laura. M.D., U. Genoa, 1959; M.S., McGill U., Montreal, 1965. Diplomate Am. Bd. Psychiatry and Neurology in Neurology, Am. Bd. Psychiatry and Neurology in Clin. Neurophysiology. Intern Madison Gen. Hosp., Wis., 1960; fellow neurophysiology U. Wis., Madison, 1960-62, asst. prof. neurology, 1966-69, assoc. prof., 1970-73, prof., 1974-79, 1979-83; resident in neurology Montreal Neurol. Inst./McGill U., Montreal, Que., Can., 1962-66; chief neurology service VA Hosp., Madison, 1979-83; chmn. dept. neurology Loyola U., Chgo., 1983—. Editor in chief: Electroenceph. Clin. Neurophysiol.; contbr. articles to profl. jours. Fellow Am. Acad. Neurology; mem. AMA, Am. EEG Soc., Am. Acad. Clin. Neurophychol. (pres. 1993-95), Am. Neurol. Assn., Ctrl. Assn. EEG, Wis. Neurol. Soc. Wis. Med. Alumni Assn., Wis. Neurol. Soc., Soc. Neurosci., Am. Epilepsy Soc., N.Y. Acad. Scis. AAAS, Sigma Xi. Office: Loyola Univ-Chgo Dept Neurology 2160 S 1st Ave Maywood IL 60153-3304

CELESTE, RICHARD F., ambassador, former governor; b. Cleve., Nov. 11, 1937; s. Frank C.; m. Dagmar Braun, 1962; children: Eric, Christopher, Gabriella, Noelle, Natalie, Stephen. B.A. in History magna cum laude, Yale U., 1959; Ph.B. in Politics, Oxford U., 1962. Staff liaison officer Peace Corps, 1963; dir. Peace Corps, Washington, 1979-81; spl. asst. to U.S. amb. to India, 1963-67; mem. Ohio Ho. of Reps., Columbus, 1970-74, majority whip, 1972-74; lt. gov. State of Ohio, Columbus, 1974-79, gov., 1983-91; mng. ptnr. Celeste & Sabety, Ltd., Columbus, Ohio; amb. to India New Delhi, 1997—. Mem. Ohio Dem. Exec. Com. Rhodes scholar Oxford U., Eng. Mem. Am. Soc. Pub. Adminstrn., Italian Sons and Daus. Am. Methodist. Office: Am Embassy New Delhi India Dept State Washington DC 20521-9000*

CELL, GILLIAN TOWNSEND, historian, educator; b. Birkenhead, Cheshire, Eng., June 5, 1937; came to U.S., 1962; d. Thomas Edmund and Doris Abigail (Clark) Townsend; m. John Whitson Cell, Oct. 19, 1962; children: Thomas K., Katherine A., John D. BA, U. Liverpool, Eng., 1959, PhD, 1964. Instr. U. N.C., Chapel Hill, 1965-66; asst. prof. U. N.C., 1966-70, assoc. prof., 1970-78, prof., 1978-91, affirmative action officer, 1981-83, chmn. dept. history, 1983-85, dean Coll. Arts and Scis., 1985-91; provost Lafayette Coll., 1991-93, Coll. of William and Mary, 1993—. Author: English Enterprise in Newfoundland; 1577-1660, 1969; editor: Newfoundland Discovered, 1982. Office: Coll William and Mary Office of Provost PO Box 8795 Williamsburg VA 23187-8795

CELLA, JOHN J., freight company executive; b. 1940; married. BBA, Temple U., 1965. Regional mgr. Japan ops. Airborne Freight Corp., Seattle, 1965-71, v.p. Far Ea. ops., 1971-72, sr. v.p. internat. div., from 1982, now exec. v.p. internat. div. Office: Airborne Freight Corp 3101 Western Ave Seattle WA 98121-1043

CELLAN-JONES, JAMES GWYNNE, television producer, director; b. Swansea, Wales, July 13, 1931; s. Cecil John and Lavinia Sophia (Dailey) C.-J.; m. Margaret Eavis, Apr. 2, 1959; children: Rory, Simon, Deiniol, Lavinia. BA, Cambridge U., 1952, MA, 1977. From callboy to prodn. mgr. BBC-TV, 1955-60, dir., 1960—, head of plays, 1976-79; mng. dir. Lawnsdale Prodns.; coun. mem. Dirs. and Prodrs. Rights Soc.; W.D. Thomas meml. lectr. Univ. Coll., Swansea, 1991; vis. artist-in-residence Verde Valley Sch., Sedona, Ariz., 1997, 99. Dir.: films The Forsyte Saga, 1966, Portrait of a Lady, 1968, The Way We Live Now, 1968, The Creative Impulse, 1970, The Roads to Freedom, 1970, Midsummer Nights Dream, 1971, The Nelson Affair, 1972, Caesar and Cleopatra, 1974, Jennie, 1974, Adams Chronicles, 1975, You Never Can Tell, 1976, School Play, 1977, Unity Mitford, 1980, The Day Christ Died, 1980, A Fine Romance, 1981, Mrs. Silly, 1982, The Comedy of Errors, Redundant or the Wife's Revenge, 1983; producer, dir. Oxbridge Blues, series, 1984 (3 U.S. Cable award 1987), Slip-Up, 1985, The Fortunes of War, 1986-87 (3 Brit. Academy awards, Brit. Critics award), Arms and the Man, 1988, A Perfect Hero, 1989-90, The Gravy Train Goes East, 1991, Maigret, 1992—, Harnessing Peacocks, 1993 (Golden Nymph award Monte Carlo TV Festival 1994), A Class Act, 1994, The Vacillations of Poppy Carew, 1994, Chouchou la Vie de Claude Debussy, 1995-96, May and June, 1996, McLibel-The McDonald's Libel Trial, 1997, Married 2 Malcolm, 1998. 2d lt. Royal Engrs., 1953-54, The Mcdonald Libel Trial, 1997. Fellow Royal Soc. Arts; mem. Dirs. Guild Am. (Series award 1976), Brit. Acad. Film and TV Arts (hon. life mem., vice chmn. 1979-83, chmn. 1983-85), Dirs. Guild Gt. Britain (coun. 1985—, chmn. 1992-94, vice-chmn. 1995—). Mem. Liberal Dem. Party. Home: 19 Cumberland Rd, Kew Surrey England Office: care London Mgmt Ltd, 2-4 Noel St, London W1, England

CELLI, JOSEPH, municipal government official; b. Yonkers, N.Y., Sept. 27, 1963. Grad. high sch., Yonkers, 1982. Owner Roof Care, Yonkers, 1986-92, Akron Bldg. Svcs., Yonkers, 1992-95, Metro Tech Ctr., Bklyn., 1995; dir. gen. svcs. City of Yonkers, 1996—. Office: City Hall 40 S Broadway 5th Fl Yonkers NY 10701-3715*

CELLUCCI, ARGEO PAUL, state official; b. Marlboro, Mass., Apr. 24, 1948; s. Argeo R. and Prisicilla Rose C.; m. Janet Garnett, 1971; children: Kate, Anne. BS, Boston Coll., 1970, JD, 1973. Atty. Kittredge, Cellucci and Moreira, Hudson, Mass., 1973-90; mem. charter commn. Hudson, 1970-71; selectman, 1971-77; state rep. Third Middlesex Dist., Mass., 1977-84; state senator Middlesex and Worcester Dists., Mass., 1985-90; gov. State of Mass., Mass., 1991—. Capt. USAR. Recipient Haskins and Fells Found. award, 1969. Mem. ABA, Mass. Bar Assn., Elks, Sons of Italy. Republican. Roman Catholic. Office: State House State House Rm 360 Boston MA 02133*

CELLUCCI, PETER T., principal. Prin. Wyomissing (Pa.) Area Jr./Sr. H.S., 1982—. Recipient Blue Ribbon Sch. award U.S. Dept. Edn., 1990-91. Office: Wyomissing Area Jr-Sr High Sch 630 Evans Ave Wyomissing PA 19610-2636

CELMINS, VIJA, artist, photographer; b. Riga, Latvia, 1939; came to U.S.; Student, Yale U.; MFA, UCLA, 1965. One-woman shows include Whitney Mus. Am. Art, N.Y.C., 1993; represented in permanent collections Sheldon Meml. Art Gallery and Sculpture Garden, U. Nebr., Lincoln, F.M. Hall Collection. Office: 745 5th Ave 4th Fl New York NY 10151

CELOTTA, ROBERT JAMES, physicist; b. N.Y.C., Nov. 18, 1943; s. Bart and Agnes Margaret (Comerford) C.; m. Beverly Kay Lauter, Nov. 20, 1966; children: Jennifer Ann, Daniel Wayne. BS in Physics, CCNY, 1964; PhD in Physics, NYU, 1969. Rsch. asst. IBM Watson Lab., N.Y.C., 1963-64; rsch. asst. dept. physics NYU, N.Y.C., 1964-69, instr., 1966-69; postdoctoral rsch. assoc. Joint Inst. Lab. Astrophysics, Boulder, Colo., 1969-71; physicist Nat. Inst. Standards and Tech., Gaithersburg, Md., 1971-86, fellow, 1987—; gen. com. Internat. Conf. on Physics of Electron and Atom Collisions, 1985-89; participant NSF-Nat. Coun. for Sci. and Tech. U.S.-Latin-Am. Coop. Sci. Program, 1984-86, U.S.-Spain Sci. Program, 1985-88, U.S.-Yugoslav Coop. Rsch. Program, 1978-87; vice-chair Gordon Conf. on Magnetic Nanostructures, 1997—. Series editor Methods of Exptl. Physics, 1981-95, Exptl. Methods in Phys. Scis., 1995—; mem. editl. bd. Rev. Sci. Instruments, 1982-85, vice chair Davisson-Germer Prize Com., 1990-91, chair, 1992-93, adv. com. on Magnetics and Magnetic Materials, 1996-97; contbr. articles to Phys. Rev. Letters, Phys. Rev., Jour. Vaccum Sci. Tech., Jour. Applied Physics, Applied Physics Letters, Revs. Sci. Instruments, Sci., Jour. Physics, Jour. Magnetism and Magnetic Materials, Jour. Chem. Physics, numerous others; contbr. to conf. procs. Recipient Disting. Young Scientist award Md. Acad. Scis., 1978, Edward V. Condon award U.S. Dept. Commerce, 1980, IR-100 award R & D Mag., 1980, 85, Fed. Lab. Consortium award Excellence in Tech. Transfer, 1988, William P. Slichter award Nat. Inst. Stds. and Tech., 1992. Fellow AAAS, Am. Phys. Soc., Am. Vacuum Soc. (Gaede-Langmuir prize 1994); mem. Washington Acad. Sci. (Outstanding and Disting. Career in Sci. award 1994). Achievements include patents for Absorbed Current Electron Polarization Detectors; Apparatus and Methods for Electron Spin Polarization Detection; Laser Controlled Nanolithography; developed photodetachment spectroscopy method for electron affinity measurement; pioneering measurements in polarized electron scattering from atoms and surfaces, scanning tunneling microscopy, surface magnetism and laser controlled atom deposition; developed the GaAs polarized electron source, the diffuse low energy polarization detector, and the technique of scanning electron microscopy with polarization analysis (SEMPA). Office: NIST B206 Metrology Bldg Gaithersburg MD 20899-8412

CENARRUSA, PETE T., secretary of state; b. Carey, Idaho, Dec. 16, 1917; s. Joseph and Ramona (Gardoqui) C.; m. Freda B. Coates, Oct. 25, 1947; 1 son, Joe Earl (dec.). B.S. in Agr., U. Idaho, 1940. Tchr. high sch. Cambridge, Idaho, 1940-41, Carey and Glenns Ferry, Idaho, 1946; tchr. vocat. agr. VA, Blaine County, Idaho, 1946-51; farmer, woolgrower, nr. Carey, 1946-95; mem. Idaho Ho. of Reps., 1951-67, speaker, 1963-67; sec. state Idaho, 1967-90, 91—; mem. Idaho Bd. Land Commrs., Idaho Bd. Examiners; pres. Idaho Flying Legislators, 1953-63; chmn. Idaho Legis. Council, 1964—, Idaho Govt. Reorgn. Com.; Idaho del. Council State Govts., 1963—. Elected ofcl., mem. BLM Adv. Coun., Boise Dist.; Rep. adminstr. Hall of Fame, 1978; sr. mem. State Bd. Land Commrs., 1967-96; dean Nations Secs. of State, 1967—. Maj. USMCR, 1942-46, 52-58. Named Hon. Farmer Future Farmers Am., 1955; inductee Agrl. Hall of Fame, 1973, Idaho Athletic Hall of Fame, 1976, Basque Hall of Fame, 1983, Idaho Hall of Fame, 1998. Mem. Blaine County Livestock Mktg. Assn., Idaho Wool Growers Assn. (chmn. 1954), Carey C. of C. (pres. 1952), U. Idaho Alumni Assn., Gamma Sigma Delta, Tau Kappa Epsilon. Republican. Office: Office of Sec State PO Box 83720 Boise ID 83720-3720

CENKNER, WILLIAM, religion educator, academic administrator; b. Cleve., Oct. 25, 1930; s. Joseph Paul and Sophia (Gladis) C. BA, Providence Coll., 1954; STB, Dominican Faculty, Washington, 1956, STL, 1959; PhD, Fordham U., 1969. Ordained priest Roman Cath. Ch., 1958. Lectr. Aquinas Coll. High Sch., Columbus, Ohio, 1959-64, St. Charles Coll., Columbus, 1962-64; asst. prof. religion Marist Coll., Poughkeepsie, N.Y., 1964-65; asst. prof. religion Cath. U. Am., Washington, 1969-73, assoc. prof., 1973-83, prof., 1983—, dean Sch. Religious Studies, 1985-93, Katharine M. Drexel prof. religious studies, 1998—; mem. exec. com. Am. Conf. on Religious Movements, Washington, 1988—. Author: The Hindu Personality in Education, 1976, A Tradition of Teachers: Sankara and Jagadgurus Today, 1983; editor: The Religious Quest, 1983, The Multicultural Church, 1995, Evil and the Response of World Religions, 1996. Chmn. Faiths in the World Com., Washington, 1985-93. Rsch. grantee Chauncy Stillman Found., India, 1969, C. VanderLinde Found., India, 1979, Nanzan Inst. Religion and Culture, Japan, 1983. Mem. Am. Acad. Religion, Cath. Acad. Scis. in U.S., Assn. Asian Studies, Am. Oriental Soc., Coll. Theology Soc. (pres. 1978-80), Internat. Assn. History of Religions. Roman Catholic. Office: Cath Univ of Am Sch of Religious Studies Washington DC 20064

CENSER, JACK RICHARD, history educator; b. Memphis, Dec. 8, 1946; s. Joseph B. and Dorothy Theresa (Jiedel) C.; m. Emily Jane Turner, May 23, 1976; children: Marjorie, Joel. BA, Duke U., 1968; MA, Johns Hopkins U., 1971, PhD, 1973. Asst. prof. history Coll. of Charleston, S.C., 1974-77; from asst. prof. to full prof. George Mason U., Fairfax, Va., 1977—, chmn. dept. history, 1995—; asst. dir. Urban Studies Program, Coll. Charleston, 1974-77. Author: Prelude to Power, 1976, the Press in the Age of Enlightenment, 1994; editor: Press in Pre-Revolution France, 1986. Fellow Ctr. for Met. Planning Johns Hopkins U., Balt., 1973-74, Am. Coun. Learned Socs., N.Y., 1989-90, Max Planck Inst., 1986, 89; Mellon fellow U. Pitts., 1978-89; grantee NEH, 1977, 98. Mem. Am. Hist. Assn. (Gershoy prize com.), Soc. for French Hist. Studies (mem. program com., 1978, 1979, 1980, 1989, 1999, prize com. 1978, 80, 89, v.p. 1989). Democrat. Jewish. Home: 4122 Lenox Dr Fairfax VA 22032-1111 Office: George Mason U Dept History Fairfax VA 22030

CENSITS, RICHARD JOHN, business consultant; b. Allentown, Pa., May 20, 1937; s. Stephen A. and Theresa M. Censits; m. Linda A. Malin, June 21, 1958; children: Debra, Mark, David. BS in Econs., U. Pa., 1958; MBA, Lehigh U., 1964. Sr. auditor Arthur Andersen & Co., 1958-62; mgr. acctg. Air Products & Chems., 1962-64; contr. Hamilton Watch Co., Lancaster, Pa., 1964-69; v.p., contr. IU Internat., Phila., 1969-75; v.p., CFO Campbell Soup Co., Camden, N.J., 1975-86; CEO, chmn. MedQuist Inc., Marlton, N.J., 1986-95; bd. dirs. Checkpoint Sys., Inc., MedQuist Inc., First Fla. Bank. Trustee U. Pa., 1989—. Mem. The Club of Pelican Bay and Quail Creek C. of C. Home and Office: 688 Annemore Ln Naples FL 34108-7520

CENTAFONT, LUCY ANN ALEXANDER, occupational therapy consultant; b. Anchorage, Alaska, Apr. 6, 1953; d. Robert C. and Lucy Ann (Morgan) Alexander; m. Richard A. Centafont, May 13, 1978; children: Ryan Alan, Jeffrey Richard, Lauren Ann. BS in Occupational Therapy, Temple U., 1977, MS, 1987; BS in Health Edn., Slippery Rock U., 1975. Occupational therapy cons. Bucks County Assn. for Retarded Citizens, Doylestown, Pa.; dir. occupational therapy Community Found. for Human Devel., Sellersville, Pa.; chief occupational therapy Rolling Hill Hosp., Elkins Park, Pa.; pvt. practice occupational therapy cons. Southampton, Pa. Mem. Am. Occupational Therapy Assn., Pa. Occupational Therapy Assn. (developmental disabilities spl. interest group, adminstrv. spl. interest group).

CENTGRAF, DAMIAN LOUIS, broadcast engineer; b. Bad Hamburg, Fed. Republic of Germany, Dec. 1, 1957; came to U.S., 1958; s. Damian and Sarah Barbara (Schmit) C.; m. Marie Cowart, 1998. AS in Broadcasting, Iowa Cen. Community Coll., Ft. Dodge, 1979; postgrad., Hastings Community Coll., 1983, Kearney State Coll., 1987-89, Armstrong State Coll., 1992-93, Tech. Coll. Low Country, 1995-97. Studio tech. Sta. KICB AM FM, Fort Dodge, Iowa, 1977-78, asst. chief engr., 1978-79; broadcast engr. Nebr. Rural Radio Assn., Stas. KRVN AM FM, KNEB AM FM, Lexington and Scottsbluff, Nebr., 1979-85; ops. engr. Nebr. Rural Radio Assn. Stas. KRVN-AM-FM, KNEB-AM-FM, Lexington and Scotts Bluff, Nebr., 1985-89; broadcast engr. Sta. WSHB Internat. Shortwave C.S. Monitor World Svcs., Cypress Creek, S.C., 1989-93, systems & network adminstr., 1993-97, chief engr., 1997—. Del. Iowa State Dem. Party, Des Moines, 1978. Mem. IEEE (newsletter editor 1999—), Soc. Broadcast Engrs. (vice chmn. 1983-84, frequency coord. 1983-85, chmn. 1985-86), Sons of Am. LEgion, Elks. Republican. Club: Nat. Street Rod Assn. (Memphis). Avocations: golfing, reading, building street rods and custom cars. Office: Sta WSHB 1030 Shortwave Ln Pineland SC 29934

CENTINI, BARRY J., airport administrator. Dir. Wilkes-Barre/Scranton Internat. Airport, 1989—. Office: Wilkes-Barre/Scranton Internat Airport 100 Terminal Rd Avoca PA 18641-2224*

CENTNER, CHRISTOPHER MARTIN, intelligence analyst, writer; b. San Diego, Calif., May 16, 1957; s. Richard L. and Margeret J. C. BFA, Md. Inst. Coll. of Art, Balt., 1980; M in Strategic Intelligence, Joint Mil. Intelligence Coll., Washington, 1990; M in Polit. Sci., Auburn U., Montgomery, Ala., 1995. Graphic designer various cos., Met. Washington, 1980-82; intelligence analyst Air Force Intelligence, Washington, 1986-90, chief combined arms br., 1990-91; graphic designer Defense Intelligence Agy., Washington, 1982-86, advisor chem. disarmament, 1991-97, sr. intelligence analyst, 1997—. Contbr. articles to mil. jours. Founder James B. Davis award for Auburn U. students, Montgomery, 1997—. Mem. U.S. Strategic Inst. Avocations: history, information warfare, foreign policy.

CENTO, WILLIAM FRANCIS, retired newspaper editor; b. St. Louis, Mar. 20, 1932; s. Frank and Augusta (Albietz) C.; m. Vera Ann Shaide, May 16, 1964. BS, St. Louis U., 1954. Gen. assignment reporter East St. Louis (Ill.) Jour., 1954-56; suburban editor Globe-Democrat, St. Louis, 1956-61; copy-editor Post-Dispatch, St. Louis, 1961-62; make-up editor Pioneer Press, St. Paul, 1962-65, wire editor, 1965-67, Sunday editor, 1967-73; graphics editor Pioneer Press & Dispatch, St. Paul, 1974-77; mng. editor St. Paul Dispatch, 1977-84; assoc. editor Pioneer Press, St. Paul, 1984-90; owner Give Me Rewrite, West St. Paul, 1990—; editor, pub. Letter from Minn., West St. Paul, 1995—. Editor: Fifty and Feisty APME: 1933 to 1983, 1983. Recipient numerous awards including Twin Cities Newspaper Guild Page 1 award Makeup 1st pl. award, 1969, 71, 74, 2d pl., 1971, 72, Award of Appreciation, AP Mng. Editors Assn., 1983. Mem. Soc. Profl. Journalists, AP Mng. Editors Assn. (bd. dirs. 1982-88). Roman Catholic. Avocations: painting, graphic design. Home: 111 Imperial Dr W Apt 103 West Saint Paul MN 55118-2226

CENTOFANTI, JOSEPH, accountant; b. Watervliet, N.Y., Oct. 2, 1965; s. Anthony Joseph and Mary Ann (Sutton) C. AS in Mgmt., Bentley Coll., 1987, BS in Acctg., 1987. CPA, Conn.; cert. Govt. Fin. Mgr.; cert. Fraud Examiner. Staff acct. Pannell Kerr Forster, Hartford, Conn., 1987-88, sr. acct., 1988-91; sr. acct. Kostin, Ruffkess and Co., West Hartford, Conn., 1991-92, supr., 1992-95, mgr., 1995—. Author: Audit Manual; contbr. articles to profl. jours. Treas. New Britain (Conn.) Jaycees, 1991-97, pres., 1993-95, v.p. membership, 1995-97. Mem. AICPA, Govt. Fin. Officers Assn. (spl. rev. com.), Assn. Cert. Fraud Examiners, Assn Govt. Accts., Conn. Soc. CPAs. Home: 205 Merigold Dr New Britain CT 06053-1445 Office: Kostin Ruffkess & Co LLC 345 N Main St Hartford CT 06117-2524

CENTOFANTI, JOYCE MICHELINA, artist, educator; b. Dec. 3, 1957. BFA, Mt. St. Mary's Coll., 1980; MFA, U. Mont., 1984; postgrad., N.Mex. Highlands U., 1998—. Artist/educator N.Mex. Arts, Santa Fe, 1984—; art tchr. Crownpoint (N.Mex.) Jr./Sr. High, 1990-95. E-mail: Flamingofarms@etsc.net.

CENTORINO, JAMES ROCCO, science educator, composer; b. Salem, Mass., Aug. 16, 1949; s. James Joseph and Nicoletta Nancy (DiFine); m. Susan Virginia Hasson, Aug. 26, 1989. BS, Boston Coll., 1971, MS, 1975; MusB, Boston Conservatory Music, 1981, MusM, 1994. Calif. state tchg. credential, secondary sch. phys. sci. Asst. mgr., clk. Danvers (Mass.) News Agy., 1963-75; music arranger, instr. mus. marching groups, Northeastern U.S.A., 1964-84; tchg. fellow Boston Coll., 1972-74; substitute sci. and music tchr. Boston area schs., 1974-80; sci. tchr. Winchester (Mass.) Pub. Schs., 1980-81, Needham (Mass.) Pub. Schs., 1982; physics and music tchr. Weston (Mass.) Pub. Schs., 1982-84; physics tchr. Natick (Mass.) H.S., 1984-85, El Camino Real H.S., Woodland Hills, Calif., 1985—; pres. Centorino Prods.; music and sci. coach Acad. Decathlon Team, Woodland Hills, 1991—; music composing cons. bands, drum and bugle corps, mus. groups, 1965—. Composer: Notes on a Triangle, 1983 (ASCAP award 1993), Christmas Love, 1984 (ASCAP award 1985), others, 1975—; composer, performer, prodr.: (mus. album) Footsteps in the Sand, 1991 (Album of Yr. 1991), Ivory, 1993 (Genesis award recognition 1994), It's Christmas Everywhere, 1997, Three Dreams For Solo Cello and Piano. Mem. ASCAP, Nat. Assn. Rec. Arts and Scis., Nat. Sci. Tchrs. Assn., Calif. Tchrs. Assn., United Tchrs. L.A., Sigma Xi, Pi Kappa Lambda, Phi Mu Alpha Sinfonia. Roman Catholic. Avocations: scriptwriting, furniture refinishing. E-mail: centorino@earthlink.net. Home: 23278 Aetna St Woodland Hills CA 91367-3101 Office: Centorino Prodns PO Box 4478 West Hills CA 91308-4478

CENTUORI, JEANINE GAIL, architecture educator; b. Newark, Apr. 13, 1959; d. Edmond and Janet (Galati) C.; m. Russell Rock, Sept. 15, 1992. BArch, The Cooper Union, 1983; MArch, Cranbrook Acad. Art, 1991. Registered architect, N.Y. Asst. prof. Kent (Ohio) State U., 1992—; faculty adv. com., undergrad. com. Sch. Arch. and Environmental Design/Kent State U., 1995—, gallery dir., 1992-94; adj. prof. dept. arch. U. Mich., Ann Arbor, 1990; guest critic U. Ark., 1993-94, Iowa State U., 1994, Parsons Sch. Design, 1993, U. Mich., 1993, U. Cin., 1990, film coord. Cranbrook Acad. Art, 1989-90; presenter and lectr. in field. One-woman shows include The Sculpture Ctr., Cleve., 1994; exhibited in group shows at The Sheet Project, Ames, Iowa, 1995, New Visions Gallery, 1994, Mcpl. Art Soc. Urban Ctr., N.Y.C., 1994 (1st Pl. Design award 1994), Oakland (Calif.) Mus., 1993, Kent (Ohio) State U. Faculty Show, 1993 (2d Pl. award 1994), The Sculpture Ctr., Cleve., 1993, The Trumbull Art Gallery, Warren, Ohio, 1993, The Artist Market, Detoirt, 1992, Cranbrook Art Mus., 1991, The Storefront for Art and Arch., N.Y.C., 1991, Cranbrook Acad. Art, 1990; editor: Architronic: The Electronic Jour. Arch., 1992—; contbr. articles to profl. jours. Rsch. grant Kent State U., 1995; Poplak Merit scholar, Cranbrook Acad. Art, 1990, Bd. Govs. Merit scholar, 1988; recipient AIA Cert. Achievement award The Cooper Union, 1983. Office: Kent State University School Arch Environ Design PO Box 5190 Kent OH 44242-0001*

CEPEDA, ORLANDO, retired professional baseball player; b. Ponce, P.R., Sept. 17, 1937; m. Miriam Cepeda; children: Orlando Jr., Hector, Malcolm, Ali Manuel. 1st baseman San Francisco Giants, 1958-66, St. Louis Cardinals, 1966-69, Atlanta Braves, 1969-72, Oakland (Calif.) Athletics, 1972, Boston Red Sox, 1973, Kansas City Royals, 1974; cmty. rep. San Francisco Giants, 1990—; lifetime .297 hitter with 379 home runs, 1,364 RBIs; appeared in 3 World Series; 11-time All-Star; hit over .300 9 times in career. Named Rookie of Yr. San Francisco Giants 1958, Comeback Player of Yr. St. Louis Cardinals 1966, Nat. League Most Valuable Player award 1967, Designated Hitter of Yr. award 1973; inductee P.R. Sports Hall of Fame, 1993, Baseball Hall of Fame, 1999. Office: c/o San Francisco Giants 3 Com Park San Francisco CA 94124*

CEPIELIK, ELIZABETH LINDBERG, educator; b. Syracuse, N.Y., Sept. 18, 1941; d. Herman Elroy and Kathryn Emily (Karl) Lindberg; m. Michael A. Zemel, Apr. 22, 1967 (div. Jan. 1973); 1 child, Molly; m. Martin Joseph Cepielik, Mar. 10, 1973; children: Jeffrey, Kristina, Julie. AA, Stephens Coll., Columbia, Mo., 1961; BA, San Jose State Coll., 1963; postgrad., Calif. State U., L.A., 1963-67. Tchr. Humphreys Ave. Sch., L.A., 1963-71; math. specialist Non-Pub. Schs. Program, L.A., 1971-84; tchr. Sheridan Street Sch., L.A., 1984—; receptionist Weight Watchers, Arcadia, Calif., 1987—. Editor News of Polonia. Vol. Sta. KPCC, Pasadena, Calif., 1988-94. Mem. DAR, Polish Nat. alliance (sec. lodge 1980—, sec. coun. 1983-93, treas. Woman's divsn. 1992-93), Swedish Am. Ctrl. Assn. (auditor 1987-90, sec. 1989—), Swedish Am. Women's Club, Polish Am. Congress (sec. 1990-93), Stephens Coll. Alumnae Club (pres. Pasadena chpt. 1967-68), Skandia (auditor, asst. sec. Pasadena lodge 1983—). Republican. Presbyterian. Mailing: 260 S Lake Ave # 243 Pasadena CA 91101-3002 Home: 260 S Lake Ave # 243 Pasadena CA 91101-3002

CEPPOS, JEROME MERLE, newspaper editor; b. Washington, Oct. 14, 1946; s. Harry and Florence (Epstein) C.; m. Karen E. Feingold, Mar. 7, 1982; children: Matthew, Robin. B.S. in Journalism, U. Md., 1969; postgrad., Knight-Ridder Exec. Leadership Program, 1989-90. Reporter, asst. city editor, night city editor Rochester (N.Y.) Democrat & Chronicle, 1969-

72; from asst. city editor, to nat. editor, to asst. mng. editor The Miami (Fla.) Herald, 1972-81; assoc. editor San Jose (Calif.) Mercury News, 1981, mng. editor, 1983-94, exec. editor, sr. v.p., 1995—; mem. nat. adv. bd. Knight Ctr. Specialized Reporting, U. Md.; mem. Accrediting Coun. on Edn. in Journalism and Mass Comm. Mem. AP Mng. Editors (bd. dirs.), Am. Soc. Newspaper Editors, Calif. Soc. Newspaper Editors (former mem. bd. dirs., past pres.), Soc. Profl. Journalists, Assn. for Edn. in Journalism and Mass Comm., Silicon Valley Capital Club. Home: 14550 Pike Rd Saratoga CA 95070-5359 Office: San Jose Mercury News 750 Ridder Park Dr San Jose CA 95131-2432

CERA, LEE MARIE, veterinarian; b. Chgo., June 24, 1950; d. Ernest Joseph and Gloria (Bonet) Cera. BS, St. Xavier Coll., 1971; BA, U. Ill., 1973, DVM, 1975; PhD in Pathology, U. Chgo., 1992. Clin. veterinarian U. Chgo., 1975-78; chief lab. services Office Animal Care, U. Chgo., 1978-80, dir., 1980-91; dir. lab. animal medicine Pathology Assocs. Inc., Chgo., 1991-93; asst. dean comparative medicine, dir. lab. animal medicine Loyola U. Chgo., 1993—; dir. program Davis Vet. Pathology Found., Sayre, Pa., 1977—; adv. Lincoln Park Zoo, Chgo., 1978—; cons. Orland Park Small Animal Hosp., 1980—. Contbr. articles to profl. jours. Recipient Pfizer award Pfizer Drug Co., 1974, Humane Soc. award, Lake County, 1974, Vet. Pathology award C.L. Davis, 1986, Honored Alumni award St. Xavier award, 1995; Cancer Soc. fellow, 1991-92. Mem. AVMA, Midwest Vet. Pathology Assn., C.L. Davis Found. for Vet. Pathology (Service award 1981), Am. Soc. Lab. Animal Practitioners, Assn. Wildlife Veterinarians. Roman Catholic. Avocations: dressage, Siberian huskies, wildlife pathology, wilderness camping, pet therapy, sailing. Office: Loyola U Stritch Sch of Medicine 2160 S 1st Ave Maywood IL 60153-5590

CERADSKY, SHIRLEY ANN, psychiatric nursing; b. Gravette, Ark., Feb. 8, 1944; d. Albert Raymond and Pansy Blanch (McGhee) Kelley; m. Kenneth Meade Ceradsky, June 15, 1968; children: Shane Thomas, Cameron Lee, Eric Tanner. Diploma, Wesley Sch. Nursing, 1966; student, Wichita State U., 1967-78, Carl Menninger Sch. Psychiatry, 1992-96. Cert. psychiat. nursing ANCC. Staff nurse Wesley Med. Ctr., Wichita, Kans., 1966, Siloam Meml. Hosp, Siloam Springs, Ark., 1966-67, Swedish Convenant Hosp., Chgo., 1967-68, U. Iowa Hosp., Iowa City, 1968-71, Charter Hosp., Wichita, 1988-89; charge nurse, staff nurse St. Joseph Med. Ctr., Wichita, 1971—, mem. quality assurance program, 1992-93, staff nurse adv. coun., 1994—; presenter nursing at night clin. ann. sessions Menninger Clinic, 1994. Contbr. article to profl. jours. Mem. Am. Psychiatric Nurses Assn. Democrat. Avocations: sewing, quilting. Home: 7121 E 40th Street Cir N Wichita KS 67226-2414 Office: St Joseph Medical Ctr 3600 E Harry St Wichita KS 67218-3713

CERAMI, ANTHONY, biochemistry educator; b. Newark, Oct. 3, 1940; s. Anthony and Hazel (Kirk) C.; m. Helen Vlassara, May 1, 1981; children: Carla, Ethan. B.S., Rutgers U., 1962; Ph.D., Rockefeller U., 1967. Asst. prof. biochemistry Rockefeller U., N.Y.C., 1969-72, assoc. prof., 1972-78, prof., 1978-91, head lab. med. biochemistry, 1972-91, dean grad. and post-grad. studies, 1986-91; pres. Picower Inst. for Med. Rsch., 1991-96; founder, bd. dirs. Alteon Inc., 1993-99. Editor Jour. Exptl. Medicine, 1981-93. Recipient Abbott Laboratories award Am. Society for Microbiology, 1994. Mem. NAS, AAAS, Am. Soc. Pharmacology and Exptl. Therapeutics, Am. Soc. Biochemistry and Molecular Biology, Am. Diabetes Assn., Internat. Diabetes Fedn., N.Y. Acad. Sci., Clin. Immunology Soc., Am. Assn. for Cancer Rsch., N.Y. Biotech. Assn., Protein Soc., Juvenile Diabetes Found. Internat., Am. Aging Assn., Am. Assn. Immunologists, Am. Chem. Soc., Am. Fedn. for Aging Rsch., Internat. Cytokine Soc., Internat. Endotoxin Soc. Home: Ram Island Dr Shelter Island NY 11964*

CERASO, CHRIS, dramatist, actor; b. Leechburg, Pa., Sept. 23, 1952; s. Anthony M. and Albena M. (Ferrando) C.; m. Carla Meadows, July 9, 1977. Ba in Theatre, Notre Dame U., 1974; MFA in Playwriting, Fla. State U., 1977. Actor, writer, tchr. Ensemble Studio Theatre; tchr. Manhattan Theatre Club; writer, tchr. Lincoln Ctr. Inst.; actor, writer Hartford Stage, Capital Repertory Co.; writer Plays for Living, Children's TV Workshop; writer, actor The 52nd Street Project; bd. dirs. Ensemble Studio Theatre, N.Y.C. Actor over 100 plays; actor (TV show) Law and Order; writer Another World; co-screenwriter (film based on original play Home Fires Burning) The Turning; author numerous plays and screenplays, including Sittin', The Red Forest and others. Recipient Gold Plaque writing for TV Chgo. Film Festival, (Passing Over,, co-written with brother, Michael), 1996, Bronze World medal radio writing Internat. Radio awards, 1996; play devel. grant Nat. Endowment, 1985.

CERCELLE, AUDREY LYNN, school psychologist; b. Shelby, Ohio, Apr. 23, 1966; d. Charles and Margaret (Nowakowski) Stuart; m. Timothy F. Cercelle; 1 child. BS, John Carroll U., 1988; MEd, Kent State U., 1989, EdD, 1991. Cert. sch. psychologist; lic. sch. psychologist. Sch. psychologist South Euclid Schs., Cleve., 1990-91, Brooklyn (Ohio) City Schs., 1991-93, Orange City Schs., Pepper Pike, Ohio, 1993—; pvt. practice Solutions Psychol. Cons., Westlake, Ohio, 1994—. Mem. Nat. Assn. Sch. Psychologists, Ohio Sch. Psychologists Assn., Cleve. Assn. Sch. Psychologists.

CERE, RONALD CARL, languages educator, consultant, researcher; b. N.Y.C., Oct. 22, 1947; s. Mindie Anthony and Edvige Clelia (Ruggero) C. BA, CUNY, 1968; MA, Queens Coll., 1969; PhD, NYU, 1974. Asst. prof. SUNY, Old Westbury, 1974-77, U. Ill., Urbana, 1977-80, U. Nebr., Lincoln, 1980-83, Gettysburg (Pa.) Coll., 1983-85; prof. Ea. Mich. U., Ypsilanti, 1985-90, 1990—; cons. Trinity Dynamics, N.J., Harcourt Brace Jovanovich, Harper & Collins, D.C. Heath, Prentice-Hall, Random House, Scott Foresman Pub. Cos., 1985—; speaker, presenter in field. Author: Los Fabulistas, 1969, Exito Comercial, 1990; contbr. articles to profl. jours. Recipient James C. Healy award NYU, 1974. Mem. MLA, ASTD, Am. Assn. Tchrs. Spanish and Portuguese (dir. career svcs.), Am.Coun. Teaching Fgn. Langs., Soc. for Intercultural Edn., Tng. and Rsch., Southern Conf. Lang. Teaching (bd. advisors). Home: 2245 Glencoe Hills Dr Apt 7 Ann Arbor MI 48108-3017 Office: Ea Mich U Dept Fgn Langs 219 Alexander Hall Ypsilanti MI 48197-2255

CEREGHINO, JAMES JOSEPH, health facility administrator, neurologist; b. Portland, Oreg., Oct. 27, 1937; s. Joseph Thomas and Amelia E. (Arata) C. BS, Portland State Coll., 1959; MD, U. Oreg., 1964; MS in Neurophysiology, Linfield U., 1971. Intern Good Samaritan Hosp., Portland, 1964-65; resident Good Samaritan Hosp. and Med. Ctr., Portland, 1965-68; rotating resident in neuropathology Sch. of Medicine U. Wash., 1967; rotating resident in child neurology U. Calif. Med. Ctr., San Francisco, 1968; rotating resident in psychiatry Med. Sch. U. Oreg., 1968; nerol. cons. pub. health svc.-health svcs. and mental health adminstrn.-neurol. and sensory disease control program HEW, Rockville, Md., 1968-70; staff neuroglogist epilepsy br. NIH HEW, Bethesda, Md., 1970-85; chief epilepsy br. convulsive, devel. and neuromuscular disorders program Nat. Inst. Neurol. Disorders and Stroke, Bethesda, Md., 1985-93; dir. rsch. Epilepsy Ctr. Oreg. Health Scis. U., Portland, 1993—; prof. dept. neurology Oreg. Health Scis. U., 1993—; attending neurologist VA Med. Ctr., Portland, 1993—; speaker in field. Editor-in-chief Epilepsia, 1986-94, emeritus, 1994-97, supplements editor, 1994-97; contbr. numerous articles to profl. jours. Capt. USPHS, ret. Fellow Am. Electroencephalographi Soc. (pub. rels. com. 1980-81); mem. Am. Acad. Neurology, Am. Epilepsy Soc. (constn. com. 1970-74, chmn. 1975, membership com. 1975, chmn. 1976, 77 chmn. edn. com. 1978, 79, 80, dir. continuing med. edn. 1981-83, 1st v.p. 1982-83, pres. 1983-84, v.p. to ILAE 1985-86, coun. 1985-94), Am. Neurologic Assn., Epilepsy Found. of Am. (profl. adv. bd. Washington chpt. 1969-93, v.p. 1973-75, speaker's bur. 1972-93, region IX rep. to EFA profl. adv. bd. 1996—, Epilepsy Internat. (libr. devel. com. 1981, chmn. 1981-85), U. Oreg. Med. Sch. Alumni Assn., Internat. League Against Epilepsy (edn. com. 1985-94, coun. 1985-94), Med. Soc. D.C. (sect. neurology and neurol. surgery 1971-94), Uniformed Svcs. Orgn. Neurologists (chmn. awards com. 1984-85), Epilepsy Assn. Oreg. (sec. 1993-97, pres. 1997—, region 9 rep. to Epilepsy Found. Am. 1996—), World Fedn. Neurology (epidemiology rsch group 1978—), Alzheimer's Rsch. Alliance Oreg. (exec. coun. 1994—, chmn. res. awards com. 1995—). Home: 525 SE 65th Ave Portland OR 97215-2038 Office: Oreg Health Scis Univ Epilepsy Ctr CDW-3 3181 SW Sam Jackson Park Rd Portland OR 97201-3011

CEREZO, ABRAHAM JOHNSON, social worker; b. San Francisco, Dec. 1, 1966; s. Abelardo Sumijit and Mapuana Jane (Kanoho) C.; m. Carrie Ann Warner; children: Brandon Keli'i, Cameron Kekoa. BA in Psychology, Sacramento State U., 1992, MS in Counseling, 1995. Youth care worker St. Patrick's Home for Children, Sacramento, 1990-92; field rsch. worker Inst. for Social Rsch., Sacramento, 1991-92; anger mgmt. spkr. South Sacramento Counseling Ctr., 1995—, intern in marriage, family and child counseling, 1995—; owner Cerezo's Martial Arts, Sacramento, 1995—; sch. age coord., trainer and curriculum specialist McClelland AFB, Calif., 1996—; social worker Family Alliance Foster Family Agy., 1998—; conflict mgmt. coord., spkr. Mark Hopkins Elem. Sch., Sacramento, 1994-95, conflict mgmt. coord., 1994-95; cmty. liaison South Sacramento Counseling Ctr., 1995—; founder Power Kicks; founder, chief instr. Cerezo's Martial Arts. Bd. dirs. South Sacramento Interfaith Partnership, 1995-96; mem. strategic planning com. Childrens Health, Sacramento, 1995—. Mem. ACA, Assn. for Multicultural Counseling and Devel., Calif. Assn. Marriage and Family Therapists. Avocations: Karate, camping, skating. Office: Cerezos Martial Arts 7213B Florin Mall Dr Sacramento CA 95823-2701

CEREZO, CARMEN CONSUELO, federal judge; b. 1940. BA, U. P.R., 1963, LLB, 1966. Pvt. practice, 1966-67; law clk. U.S. Dist. Ct., San Juan, 1967-72; judge Superior Ct., P.R., 1972-76, Ct. Intermediate Appeals, 1976-80; judge U.S. Dist. Ct., P.R., 1980-93, chief judge, 1993—. Office: Federico Degetau Fed Bldg Rm CH-131 150 Carlos Chardon Ave Hato Rey PR 00918-1761*

CERF, VINTON GRAY, telecommunications company executive; b. New Haven, June 23, 1943; s. Vinton Thruston and Muriel (Gray) C.; m. Sigrid L. Thorstenberg, Sept. 10, 1966; children: David, Bennett. BS, Stanford U., 1965; MS in Computer Sci., UCLA, 1970, PhD in Computer Sci., 1972; PhD (hon.), Capitol Coll., Gettysburg Coll., U. Balearic Islands, U. Lulea, Swiss Fed. Inst. Tech. Sys. engr. IBM Corp., 1965-67; prin. programmer UCLA, 1967-72; asst. prof. elec. engring. and computer sci. Stanford (Calif.) U., 1972-76; sr. programmer Jacobi Sys. Corp., Santa Monica, Calif., 1968-70; program mgr. info. processing techniques office Def. Advanced Rsch. Projects Agy., U.S. Dept. Def., Arlington, Va., 1976-81, prin. scientist, 1981-82; dir. sys. devel. MCI Comm. Corp., 1982-83; v.p. engring. MCI Digital Info. Svcs. Co., Washington, 1983-86; v.p. Corp. for Nat. Rsch. Initiatives, Reston, Va., 1986-94; sr. v.p. Internet arch. MCI Comm. Corp., Reston, 1994—. Author: A Practical View of Communication Protocols, 1979. Named to Datamation Hall of Fame, 1989; recipient Kilby award, 1995, Silver medal Internat. Telecomms. Union, 1995, Industry Legend award Computer and Comms. Industries Assn., 1996, NEC Computer and Comm. prize, 1996, Computer Networks and Smithsonian Leadership award, 1996, Nat. Medal of Tech., 1997; Marconi fellow, 1998. Fellow IEEE (Kobayashi award 1992, Alexander Graham Bell award 1997), AAAS, Assn. Computing Machinery (chmn. SIG Comm. 1987-91, coun. 1990-92, Software award), Internat. Fedn. Info. Processing, Internet Activities Bd. (chmn. 1979-82, 89-91), Internet Soc. (pioneer mem., trustee 1992—, pres. 1992-95, v.p. chpts. 1996-97, chmn. 1998-99); mem. Nat. Acad. Engrs., Sigma Xi. Office: MCI Data Svcs Divsn 2100 Reston Pkwy Rm 6002 Reston VA 20191-1218 *My entire working career has been focused on science and technology, in many forms—teaching, research, engineering management. The trait I have come to admire most among technical colleagues is absolute honesty in reporting or assessing results—blemishes and failures as well as successes.*

CERINO, ANGELA MARIE, lawyer, educator; b. Phila., Mar. 17, 1950; d. Salvatore and Mary Rose (Falivene) C. BA in Polit. Sci., Temple U., 1972, JD, 1976. Bar: Pa. 1976, U.S. Dist. Ct. (ea. dist.) Pa. 1982, Internat. Ct. Trade, 1988, U.S. Ct. Appeals, 1988. Assoc. Stein & Silverman, Phila., 1975-77; staff atty. Camden (N.J.) Regional Legal Services, 1977-78; sole practice Phila., 1978-83; asst. prof. Villanova (Pa.) U., 1980—; arbitrator Phila. Ct. of Common Pleas, 1978-84. Contbr. articles to profl. jours. Mem. Variety Charity for Handicapped Children, Phila., 1985-93. Mem. ABA (internat. law and labor coms.), Mid-Atlantic Regional Bus. Law Assn. (exec. dir. 1986-89, sec.-treas. 1989-90, 2d v.p. 1990-91, 1st v.p. 1991-93, pres. 1993-94), Am. Bus. Law Assn. Roman Catholic. Office: Villanova U Bartley Hall Villanova PA 19085

CERKLEWSKI, FLORIAN LEE, human nutrition educator, nutritional biochemistry researcher; b. Danville, Pa., May 28, 1949; s. Florian and Ruth C.; m. Irene Joan Farkas, June 9, 1973, children—Christopher Louis, James Andrew. B.S. in Nutritional Sci., Pa. State U., 1971; Ph.D., U. Ill., 1976. Postdoctoral fellow U. Cin., 1975-76; asst. prof. Marquette U., Milw., 1976-79; asst. prof. Oreg. State U., Corvallis, 1979-84, assoc. prof., 1984—. Contbr. articles to profl. jours. Recipient Nat. Inst. Dental Research New Investigator award, 1980-83, research investigator award, 1983-91; Oreg. Agrl. Experiment Sta. Research Investigator award, 1980—. Mem. Am. Soc. Nutrition Sci. Office: Coll Home Econs and Edn Oreg State U Corvallis OR 97331

CERMAK, JACK EDWARD, engineer, educator; b. Hastings, Colo., Sept. 8, 1922; s. Joseph and Helen (Herman) C.; m. Helen Jane Carlson, Dec. 17, 1949; children: Douglas Karl, Jonathan Joel. B.S., Colo. State U., 1947, M.S., 1948; Ph.D., Cornell U., 1959; NATO postdoctoral fellow, Cambridge U., Eng., 1961-62. Mem. faculty Colo. State U., Ft. Collins, 1947—; prof. charge fluid mechanics and wind engring. program, also dir. Fluid Dynamics and Diffusion Lab. Colo. State U., 1960-85; univ. disting. prof., 1986—, chmn. engring. sci. maj. program, 1963-72; pres., dir. Colo. State U. (Research Found.), 1965-72; pres. Cermak Peterka Petersen Inc., 1982—; cons. in field; mem. bd. mems. Univ. Corp. Atmospheric Research, 1966-67; pres., chmn. 10th Midwestern Mechanics Conf., 1966-67; dir. summer inst. fluid mechanics NSF, 1963, 65, 68, 72; chmn. 2d U.S. Nat. Conf. Wind Engring. Research, 1975, 5th Internat. Conf. Wind Engring., 1979; founding mem., pres. Wind Engring. Research Council, Inc., 1979-85; co-chmn. U.S.-Japan Seminar Lab. Simulation of Stratified Shear Flows; co-dir. NATO Advanced Study Inst., 1993; mem. Colo. Gov.'s Sci. and Tech. Adv. Council, Com. on Army Basic Research, NRC, 1979-83. Mem. editl. adv. bd. Indsl. Aerodynamics Abstracts, Mechanics Rsch. Communications; regional editor for U.S., Internat. Jour. Wind Engring.; mem. inernat. editl. bd. Wind and Structures; contbr. articles to profl. jours. Fellow AAAS, AIAA (assoc.), ASCE (chmn. engring. mechanics divsn. 1965, chmn. wind effects com. structural divsn. 1991, elected to hon. membership 1990), Am. Acad. Mechanics; mem. ASME (Freeman scholar 1974, disting. lectr. 1987-89), ASHRAE (mem. com. flow around bldgs.), NSPE (Outstanding Profl. Achievement award), Air and Waste Mgmt. Assn., Am. Soc. Engring. Edn. (chmn. mechanics divsn., Sr. Rsch. award 1987), Nat. Acad. Engring. (chmn. com. natural disasters, chmn. panel on wind engring. rsch.), Internat. Assn. Wind Engring. (chmn. bd. 1975-79, regional sec. N.Am. and S.Am. 1983—), Am. Meteorol. soc., Am. Geophys. Union, Instn. Civil engrs. (Scruton lectr. 1995), N.Y. Acad. Scis., Rotary, Sigma Xi (nat. lectr. 1976-77), Chi Epsilon (nat. honor). Home: 407 E Prospect Rd Fort Collins CO 80525-1058 *My thoughts and actions have been influenced always by a belief and an awareness that man, the near environment, and the far reaches of the universe are influenced by common natural laws. I believe that the order found in natural events, as revealed by scientific investigation, can someday become manifest in the behavior of man. Ultimately, through persistent and directed effort, I am confident that man will integrate religion, science, and technology to achieve harmony of man with man, and man with the environment. For the most part, my achievements and contributions to society can be attributed to the motivation and direction stemming from these convictions.*

CERNE, GERALD JOHN, biology educator; b. Amsterdam, N.Y., Jan. 30, 1941; s. John William and Virginia Rose (Saldas) C.; m. Elaine Julia Urban, June 17, 1961; children: Michael, Diana, Maryanne. BS, SUNY, Albany, 1962, MS, 1966. Cert. tchr., secondary prin., sci. supr., N.Y. Tchr. sci. South Colonie Schs., Albany, N.Y., 1962-95; cons. biology regents tests for Biol. Sci. Edn. N.Y. State Edn. Dept., Albany, 1968-79, cons., writer Bur. Continuing Edn.-Curriculum Devel., 1970-78; editor Solar Energy Project U.S. Dept. Energy, Albany, 1978; adj. prof. biology Schenectady (N.Y.) County C.C., 1969—; coord. sci. tchr. team South Colonie H.S., Albany, 1964-68, adminstrv. aide, 1974-75, cooperating tchr. student tchrs., 1965-95; mem. pres. adv. bd. Schenectady County C.C., 1979-81. Cons., writer curriculum, curriculum aids Bur. Sci. Edn., Bur. Continuing Edn., N.Y. State Edn. Dept., 1970-78; editor Solar Energy Project, U.S. Dept. Energy, 1978. Mem. N.Y. State United Tchrs., Sci. Tchrs. Assn. N.Y. State, N.Y. State Sci. Congress (dir. 1978-79), South Colonie Tchrs. Assn., Elks. Avocations: camping, fishing, gardening, reading, spoiling grandchildren. Home: 3305 Marie St Schenectady NY 12304-2228

CERNERA, ANTHONY JOSEPH, academic administrator; b. Bronx, N.Y., Mar. 21, 1950; children: Anthony, Philip, Thomas, Anne Marie. BA in History and Theol., Fordham U., 1972, MA in Religious Edn., 1974, PhD in Theology, 1987. Tchr./chmn. Aquinas High Sch., Bronx, N.Y., 1972-77; asst. exec. dir. Bread for the World Ednl. Fund, 1977-80; exec. dir. Bread for the World Ednl. Fund, N.Y.C., 1980-81; exec. asst. to pres. Marist Coll., Poughkeepsie, N.Y., 1981-84, asst. v.p. acad. affairs, dean acad. programs & svcs., 1984-85, v.p. coll. advancement, 1985-88; pres. Sacred Heart U., Fairfield, Conn., 1988—. Bd. dirs. Mt. St. Michael Acad., Fairfield County Cmty. Found.; also bus. adv. com., Commn. on Children Bus. Adv. Com. State of Conn., NCCJ Regional Chpt., Conn. Hospice, Inc.; v.p. exec. com. Conn. Conf. Ind. Colls. Office: Sacred Heart U Office of Pres 5151 Park Ave Fairfield CT 06432-1000*

CERNUDA, PALOMA, artist; b. N.Y.C., Feb. 18, 1948; s. Julio and Aida (Cusnier) C. BFA, Calif. State U., Long Beach, 1983; MFA, Hunter Coll., 1985. One-man shows include AFR Fine Art, Washington, 1987, 88; group shows include The Drawing Ctr., N.Y.C., 1985, Mus. Contemporary Hispanic Art, N.Y.C., 1986, Berkshire Mus., Pittsfield, Mass., 1986, AFR Fine Art, 1987, Lehman Coll. Art Gallery, Bronx, 1988, Anton Gallery, Washington, 1989, others. Resident grantee Yaddo, Saratoga Springs, N.Y., 1988; N.Y. State Found. for Arts fellow, 1987, NEA fellow, 1989, Brandywine Workshop vis. artist fellow, 1990. Home: 223 1st Ave Apt 3 New York NY 10003-2993*

CERNUGEL, WILLIAM JOHN, consumer products and special retail executive; b. Joliet, Ill., Nov. 19, 1942; m. Laurie M. Kusnik, Apr. 22, 1967; children: Debra, James, David. BS, No. Ill. U., 1964. CPA, Ill. Sr. supr. KPMG Peat Marwick, Chgo., 1964-70; asst. corp. contr. Alberto-Culver Co., Melrose Park, Ill., 1970-71, corp. contr., 1972—, v.p., 1974-82, v.p. fin., 1982-93, sr. v.p. fin., 1993—. Mem. bd. govs., treas. Gottlieb Meml. Hosp., Melrose Park; assoc. mem. bd. advisors Coll. Bus., No. Ill. U. Mem. AICPA, Am. Mgmt. Assn. (fin. coun.), Inst. Mgmt. Accts., Ill. Soc. CPAs, Fin. Exec. Inst., Lions. Home: 8111 Lake Ridge Dr Burr Ridge IL 60521-5977 Office: Alberto-Culver Co 2525 Armitage Ave Melrose Park IL 60160-1163

CERNY, CHARLENE ANN, museum director; b. Jamaica, N.Y., Jan. 12, 1947; d. Albert Joseph and Charlotte Ann (Novy) Cerny; children: Elizabeth Brett Cerny-Chipman, Kathryn Rose Cerny-Chipman. BA, SUNY, Binghamton, 1969. Curator Latin-Am. folk art Mus. Internat. Folk Art, Santa Fe, 1972-84, mus. dir., 1984—; adv. bd. C.G. Jung Inst., Santa Fe, 1990—. Mem. Mayor's Commn. on Children and Youth, Santa Fe, 1990-93, adv. bd. Recipient Exemplary Performance award State of N.Mex., 1982, Internat. Ptnr. Among Mus. award; Smithsonian Instn. travel grantee, 1976; Florence Dibell Bartlett Meml. scholar, 1979, 91; Kellogg fellow, 1983. Mem. Am. Assn. Mus. Internat. Coun. Mus. (bd. dirs. 1991—, exec. bd. 1991-95), Am. Folklore Soc., Mountain-Plains Mus. Assn., N.Mex. Assn. Mus. (chair membership com. 1975-77). Office: Mus Internat Folk Art PO Box 2087 Santa Fe NM 87504-2087*

CERNY, JOSEPH, III, chemistry educator, scientific laboratory administrator, university dean and official; b. Montgomery, Ala., Apr. 24, 1936; s. Joseph and Olaette Genette (Jury) C.; m. Barbara Ann Nedelka, June 13, 1959 (div. Nov. 1982); children: Keith Joseph, Mark Evan; m. 2d Susan Dinkelspiel Stern, Nov. 12, 1983. BS in Chem. Engring., U. Miss.-Oxford, 1957; postgrad. Fulbright scholar, U. Manchester, Eng., 1957-58; PhD in Nuclear Chemistry, U. Calif.-Berkeley, 1961; PhD in Physics (hon.), U. Jyväskylä, Finland, 1990. Asst. prof. chemistry U. Calif., Berkeley, 1961-67, assoc. prof., 1967-71, prof., 1971—, chmn. dept. chemistry, 1975-79, head nuclear sci. div., 1979-84, assoc. dir. Lawrence Berkeley Lab., 1979-84, dean grad. div., 1985—, provost for research, 1986-94, vice chancellor for rsch., 1994—; mem. Nat. Acad. Scis. Physics Commn., chair nuclear physics panel, 1983-86; mem. NASA Adv. Coun., Univ. Rels. Task Force, 1991-93, NRC Study of Rsch. Doctorates, 1992-95. Editor: Nuclear Reactions and Spectroscopy, 4 vols., 1974; contbr. numerous articles to field to profl. jours. Served with U.S. Army, 1962-63. Recipient E.O. Lawrence award AEC, 1974, A. von Humboldt sr. scientist award, 1985; named to U. Miss. Alumni Hall of Fame, 1988. Fellow AAAS, Am. Phys. Soc.; mem. Am. Chem. Soc. (Nuclear Chemistry award 1984), Assn. Grad. Schs. (v.p., pres. 1992-94). Democrat. Home: 860 Keeler Ave Berkeley CA 94708-1324 Office: U Calif 309 Sproul Hall Berkeley CA 94720-5900

CERNY, JOSEPH CHARLES, urologist, educator; b. Apr. 20, 1930; s. Joseph James and Mary (Turek) C.; m. Patti Bobette Pickens, Nov. 10, 1962; children: Joseph Charles, Rebecca Anne. BA, Knox Coll., 1952; MD, Yale U., 1956. Diplomate Am. Bd. Urology. Intern U. Mich. Hosp., Ann Arbor, 1956-57, resident, 1957-62; practice medicine specializing in urology Ann Arbor and Detroit, 1962—; instr. surgery (urology) U. Mich., Ann Arbor, 1962-64, asst. prof., 1964-66, assoc. prof., 1961-77, clin. prof., 1971—; chmn. dept. urology Henry Ford Hosp., Detroit, 1971—, chmn. emeritus urology Henry Ford Hosp., 1998; pres. Resistors, Inc., Chgo., 1960—; cons. St. Joseph Hosp., Ann Arbor, 1973—. Mem. editl. bd. Am. Jour. Kidney Diseases, 1988—; contbr. articles to profl. jours., chpts. to books. Bd. dirs., trustee Nat. Kidney Found. Mich., Ann Arbor, 1988—, chmn. urology coun., 1987—, exec. com., 1987—, pres., 1988—, emeritus trustee, 1997; bd. dirs. Ann Arbor Amateur Hockey Assn., 1980-83; pres. PTO, Ann Arbor Pub. Schs., 1980. Lt. USNR, 1956-76. Recipient Disting. Svc. award Transplantation Soc. Mich., 1982, Disting. Svc. award Nat. Kidney Found. Mich., 1993, Champion of Hope award Nat. Kidney Found., 1997. Fellow ACS (pres.-elect Mich. br. 1984-85, pres. 1985—); mem. Am. Acad. Med. Dirs., Am. Coll. Physician Execs., Internat. Soc. Urology, Am. Urol. Assn. (pres. Mich. br. 1980-81, pres. North Cen. sect. 1985-86, manpower com. 1987-88, 90-92, jud. rev. com. 1987-91, tech. exhibits 1987-88, fiscal affairs rev. commn. 1985-89, audit commn. 1992-96, chmn. 1995, exec. commn. 1993—, bd. dirs. 1994—, work force com., publs. com. 1995—, chmn. publs. com. 1999, Best Sci. Exhibit award 1978, Best Sci. Films award 1980, 82, audio-visual com. 1994—, program rev. com. 1994—, urology work force com. 1995—, jud. and ethics com. 1997—), Transplantation Soc. Mich. (pres. Mich. 1983-85), Am. Assn. Transplant Surgeons, Endocrine Surgeons, Soc. Univ. Urologists, Am. Assn. Urologic Oncology, Am. Fertility Soc., Am. Coll. Physician Execs., Am. Acad. Med. Dirs., S.W. Oncology Group, Barton Hills Country Club, Ann Arbor Racquet Club. Avocations: tennis, fishing, Civil War. Home: 2800 Fairlane St Ann Arbor MI 48104-4110 Office: Henry Ford Hosp Dept Urology 2799 W Grand Blvd Detroit MI 48202-2689

CERNY, LOUIS THOMAS, civil engineer, association executive; b. Berwyn, Ill., Mar. 7, 1942; s. Thomas Alois and Rosalia Patricia (Havranek) C.; m. Lana Sally Taylor, June 6, 1964; children—Leonard, David. BSCE, U. Ill., 1964, MS, 1965. Registered profl. engr., Ill., Miss. Rsch. asst. U. Ill., Urbana, 1964-65; various engring. positions Elgin, Joliet & Eastern Ry., Joliet, Ill., 1965-75; v.p., chief engr. Columbus & Greenville Ry., Miss., 1975-78; v.p. ops. Erie Western Ry., Huntington, Ind., 1978-79; exec. dir. Am. Ry Engring. Assn., Washington, 1979-94; exec. dir. engring. divsn. Assn. Am. Railroads, 1979-97, cons., 1997—; leader engring. dels. to China, 1983, 84. Contbr. articles to profl. jours.; patentee in field. Mem. Am. Railway Engring. and Maint.-of-Way Assn., Nat. Conf. Weights and Measures (assoc.). Unitarian. Avocations: travel; photography; hiking; astronomy.

CERNY, ROSANNE, librarian; b. N.Y.C., Apr. 8, 1947; d. George F. and Rose (Panzarella) C. AB, Hunter Coll., 1967; MLS, Rutgers U., 1969. Cert. pub. libr., N.Y. Children's libr. Ridgefield (N.J.) Free Pub. Libr., 1968-69; various positions N.Y. Pub. Libr., N.Y.C., 1970-89; asst. coord. childrens Queens Borough Pub. Libr., Jamaica, N.Y., 1989-90, coord. children's svcs., 1990—. Contbr.: Key to the Future, 1994. Mem. ALA (com. mem., Assn. for Libr. Svcs. to Children 1989—), Pub. Libr. Assn., N.Y. Libr. Assn. (Pied Piper award 1993, Randolph Caldecott Award Com. 1998-99). Avocations: storytelling, needlework, reading. E-mail: rcerny@queenslibrary.orgn. Office: Queens Borough Pub Libr 89-11 Merrick Blvd Jamaica NY 11432

CEROKE, CLARENCE JOHN, engineer, consultant; b. Chgo., Dec. 1, 1921; s. Paul Anthony and Anne (Krieger) C.; m. Violet Marie Lobonc, Sept. 21, 1947; children: Paul, Donald, Robert, Marie, Louise, Karen. BS in mech. Engring., Ill. Inst. Tech., 1943. Reg. profl. engr., Ill. Supr. product devel. U.S.I. Clearing, Chgo., 1969-74; engr. Panduit Corp., Tinley Park, Ill., 1974-75; design engr. Interlake Steel, Chgo., 1975-76; mgr. engring. AFL Industries, West Chicago, 1976-77; design engr. Castle Engring., Chgo., 1977-80; supr. Dreis and Krump, Chgo., 1980-81; project engr. Epstein Process Engring., Chgo., 1981-83; cons. engr. Beacon Engring., Homewood, Ill., 1983-84; engr. Espo Engring., Canton, Ohio, 1984—; owner Beacon Engring., Homewood, 1978—. Patentee in field; author books. Pres. St. Kilians Holy Name Soc., Chgo., 1960; coach Little League Baseball, Chgo., 1959. With USN, 1943-44. Mem. Mt. Carmel Alumni Assn., Pi Tau Sigma, Hall-Fame Racquet Club. Roman Catholic. Avocations: tennis, contract bridge, in plant safety and environmental research. Home: 4716 Magnolia Dr NE Canton OH 44705-2949 Office: Beacon 4716 Magnolia Rd NE Canton OH 44705-2949

CERONE, DAVID, academic administrator. Pres. Cleve. Inst. Music, 1985—. Office: Cleve Inst Music 11021 East Blvd Cleveland OH 44106-1705*

CERRA, FRANK BERNARD, dean; b. Oneonta, N.Y., Feb. 13, 1943; m. Kathie Krieger; children: Josh, Christa, Nicole. BA in Biology, SUNY, Binghamton, 1965; MD, Northwestern U., 1969. Diplomate Nat. Bd. Med. Examiners, Am. Bd. Surgery. Intern, resident in surgery Buffalo Gen. Hosp., 1969-74; staff surgeon U. Minn. Hosp. Clinic, Mpls.; prof. U. Minn. Med. Sch., 1981—; dean, prof. surgery U. Minn. Med. Sch., Mpls., 1995-96, sr. v.p. health scis., 1996—; clin. asst. instr. surgery SUNY, Buffalo, 1969-75, asst. prof. 1975-80, assoc. prof. surgery and biophysics, 1980; interim head surgery U. Minn., 1994-95, dean med. sch., 1995-96, provost acad. health ctr., 1996—; rsch. asst. pharmacology Upstate Med. Ctr., 1963-64; rsch. asst. transplantation Northwestern U., 1967-69; rsch. assoc. immunology and cardiovascular rsch. labs. Buffalo Gen. Hosp., 1972-73, SUNY, Buffalo, 1974-75; dir. surg. critical care, dir. nutrition support svcs. U. Minn. Hosp. and Clinic; vis. lectr. in exptl. surgery Harvard U., 1991; vis. prof. Rush Presbyn.-St. Lukes Med. Ctr., 1991. Editor Perspective in Critical Care, 1988-91, Critical Care Outlook, 1988-90, Critical Care Medicine, 1990—; mem. editl. bd. Drug Intelligence & Clin. Pharmacy Panel onCritical Care, 1982-87, Nutrition, 1982—, Critical Care Medicine, 1983—, Circulatory Shock, 1987-93, Shock, 1993—, Jour. Parenteral and Enternal Nutrition, 1987-93, Am. Jour. Surgery, 1987—, Current Opinion in Gen. Surgery, 1992—, Jour. Critical Care Nutrition; contbr. articles to profl. jours.; patentee preparation for the prevention of catabolism, preparation for nutrition support of immune function. Acute care com. Found. for Health Care Evaluation, 1983-86; adv. group Minn. Emerging Infections Program, 1995—. Clark Found. fellow, 1965-69, Kellogg Nutrition fellow, 1987-89, Surgical Infection Soc. Rsch. fellow, 1988-90, Soc. Critical Care Medicine Lilly Rsch. fellow, 1990-93, Svc. award fellow NIH, 1994-96; United Health Found. Rsch. Tng. grantee, 1972-73; recipient Owen Wangensteen award, 1987, Therapeutic Frontiers Rsch. award Am. Coll. Clin. Pharmacy, 1990, Disting. Investigator award Am. Coll. Critical Care Medicine, 1993. Fellow ACS (chmn. pre-postoperative care com. 1985-87), Am. Coll. Nutrition, Coll. Critical Care Medicine; mem. AMA, AAAS, Soc. Parenteral Alimentation, Soc. for Surgery the Alimentary Tract, Am. Soc. Parenteral and Enteral Nutrition (bd. govs. 1987-88), Soc. Critical Care Medicine (treas. 1990, pres. 1991-92), Assn. for Acad. Surgery, Assn. Internat. Anesthesistes-Reanimateurs D'Expression, Soc. Univ. Surgeons (exec. coun. 1984-85), Ctrl. Surg. Assn., Am. Assn. for the Surgery Trauma, Assn. for Surg. Edn., St. Paul Surg. Soc., Surg. Biology Club, Shock Soc., Soc. Internat. Surgery, Internat. Assn. for the the Surgery Trauma and Surg. Intensive Care, Am. Soc. for Artificial Internal Organs (membership com. 1994-95), Am. Soc. Home Care Physicisn, Hennepin County Med. Soc. Office: U Minn Hosps & Clinic Haward St at E River Rd Minneapolis MN 55455 Office: U Minn Health & Scis Ctr PO Box 501 420 Delaware St SE Minneapolis MN 55455-0374*

CERRELL, JOSEPH R., political scientist, consultant; b. N.Y.C., June 19, 1935. BA, U. of So. Calif., 1957. Exec. dir. Dem. Party of Calif., 1959-66; disting. vis. prof. Pepperdine U., Malibu, Calif., 1994—; exec. v.p. Palumbo & Cerrell, L.A., 1989-94; adj. prof. U. So. Calif., 1978-94. Pres. Calif. Mus. Found.; bd. dirs. Long Beach (Calif.) Aquarium. Mem. PRSA, Am. Assn. of Polit. Cons., Internat. Assn. of Polit. Cons., L.A. Pub. Affairs Officer Assn., Nat. Italian Am. Fedn. (bd. dirs.). Office: Cerrell Assocs Inc 2d Fl 320 N Larchmont Blvd Los Angeles CA 90004-3039*

CERRI, ROBERT NOEL, photographer; b. Boston, Dec. 25, 1947; s. Lawrence Alfred and Angelina (Arena) C.; m. Armande Dagenais. BA, Georgetown Coll., 1972. Dir., head counselor The Open Door, Boca Raton, Fla., 1972-77; actor, model Miami, 1977-79; photojournalist Newsweek/Nat. Geographic, Miami, 1979-85; comml. advt. photographer Miami, 1985-98; pres. Robert Cerri Photography (now RC Photo & Design), Miami, NY, LA, Orlando, The Caribbean, 1985—; ptnr. ADC Entertainment Inc., 1994—; pres. RC Photo & Design, 1999—. Mem. USGA, Acad. Model Aeronautics, Tasters Guild, U.S. Golf Assn., Meeting Profl. Internat., Nat. Trust for Historic Preservation, Williamsburg Preservation Soc., PGA Ptnrs. Club. Republican. Avocations: golf, inline skating, horseback riding, travel, model planes & rockets. Fax: 305-682-1577. E-mail: rcp-d@worldnet.att.net. Office: RC Photo & Design PO Box 801536 Aventura FL 33280-1536 also: PO Box 618121 Orlando FL 32861-8121

CERRITOS, RONALD, professional soccer player; b. San Salvador, El Salvador, Jan. 3, 1975. Forward San Jose Clash, 1997—; mem. All-Star West team, 1997. Named Honda's MVP, 1998. Office: c/o San Jose Clash Ste 100 3550 Stevens Creek Blvd San Jose CA 95117*

CERULLO, RUDY MICHAEL, II, psychology, theology educator, minister; b. Phila., Feb. 25, 1952; s. Rudy and Edith Elizabeth (Cullen) C.; m. Kathleen Marie Evans, June 10, 1993. BA, Oral Roberts U., Tulsa, 1973; MDiv, Fuller Theol. Sem., Pasadena, Calif., 1976, ThM, 1984; DMin, ThD, So. Calif. Theol. Sem., 1990; PhD, Vision Internat. U., Ramona, Calif., 1996; DDiv, Kingsway Theol. Sem., Des Moines, 1989. Ordained to ministry Assemblies of God, 1977; cert. pastoral counselor. Assoc. pastor Orange (Calif.) Covenant Ch., First Presbyn. Ch., Alhambra, Calif., Tri-City Assembly Ch., Covina, Calif., Woodland Hills (Calif.) Neighborhood Ch., Palm View Assembly of God Ch., Whittier, Calif., En Agape Christian Fellowship Ch., Alta Loma, Calif.; psychiat. hosp. program dir., clinician in pvt. practice Brea (Calif.) Hosp. Neuropsychiat. Ctr., Terrace Plaza Med. Ctr., Baldwin Park, Calif., Manor West Hosp., L.A., Buena Park (Calif.) Med. Ctr., Agape Counseling and Therapy Svcs., Anaheim; prof. theology So. Calif. Coll., Costa Mesa, Calif., 1979-83; prof. psychology/theology, acad. dean So. Calif. Theol. Sem., Stanton, 1989-92, Trinity Coll. of Grad. Studies, Orange, 1989-92; assoc. pastor Harmony Christian Fellowship Ch., Anza, Calif., 1994-96; pastor Discipleship Regency Christian Ctr., Downey, Calif., 1996—; prof. psychology/theology, psychology dept. dir. Vision Internat. U., Pomona, 1991—, Calif. Union U., Fullerton, 1991—, Calif. Grad. Sch. Theology, Rosemead, 1991—, New Hope U., Stanton, 1991—, Ctrl. U., Palos Verdes, Calif., 1991—; missionary to Republic of Korea, 1996-98; mem. faculty Benjamin U., Buena Park, Calif., 1998—; ch. Mason Bible Coll., Pomona, 1998—. Assoc. pastor New Gethsemane Ch. of God in Christ, Pomona, Claif., 1998—. Named Disting. counselor in field of Psychiat. Hosp. Devel., U.S. Pubs., Inc., 1990. Fellow ACA (student cert. sponsor 1988—). Republican. Avocations: Renaissance Faire actor, antique collecting. Home and Office: 207 Rosalynn Dr Glendora CA 91740-5173

CERVANTES, LUIS AUGUSTO, neurosurgeon; b. Torreon, Mex., Mar. 5, 1953; came to U.S., 1976; s. Luis Augusto and Gloria (Galindo) C.; m. Joann Frances Emanuele, Feb. 10, 1979; children: Luis III, Sara, Francis, Nicolas, Juan Carlos, Mary Teresa. MD, Nat. U. Mex., 1976. Intern Suburban Hosp., Bethesda, Md., 1977-78; resident in surgery Washington Hosp. Ctr., 1978-79; resident in neurology George Washington U., Washington, 1979-80, resident in neurosurgery, 1980-84; chief neurosurgery sect. dept. surgery Meml. Hosp. Burlington County, Mount Holly, N.J., 1992—. Fellow ACS, Internat. Coll. Surgeons; mem. Am. Assn. Neurol. Surgeons, Congress Neurol. Surgeons. Roman Catholic. Avocation: golf. Office: 110 Marter Ave Ste 309 Moorestown NJ 08057-3124

CERVANTES AGUIRRE, ENRIQUE, Mexican government official; b. Puebla, Mex., Jan. 20, 1935; married; 4 children. Student, Heroico Mil. Coll., Mex. Enlisted Mex. Mil., 1952, advanced through grades to brigidere gen., 1980, divsn. gen., 1982; dep. chief of staff 27/a Mil. Zone, Alcapulco; dep. chief of staff 35/a Mil. Zone, Chilpancingo; comdr. Mil. Zones; dir. gen. def. prodn., sec. nat. def. Govt. of Mex., Mexico City, 1995—. Office: Blvd Manuel Avila Camacho y, Avada Industri Militar, Col Lomas de Sotelo Mexico City 11640, Mexico*

CERVANTEZ, GIL LAWRENCE, venture capital company executive; b. Concord, Calif., July 14, 1944; s. Val J. and Laura E. (Verdugua) C.; m. Pamela A. Richmond, Feb. 14, 1965; children: Jeffrey, Thomas. BS, U. Oreg., 1965; MBA, U. Calif., Berkeley, 1972. V.p. Gt. Western Nat. Bank, Portland, Oreg., 1971-74, Heller Internat., San Francisco, 1975-76; dir. Control Data, San Francisco, 1976-79; sr. v.p. Century Bank, San Francisco, 1979-85; dir. syndications Pacificorp Ventures, Portland, 1988-90; pres. Latipac Fin., San Francisco, 1985-90; pres. A, G & T Investments, Inc., Walnut Creek, Calif., 1990—, also bd. dirs.; bd. dirs. CEO Terameth Industries, Inc., Walnut Creek, 1990—, also bd. dirs.; bd. dirs. Tyratech Industries. Lt. comdr. USN, 1965-71, Vietnam. Mem. Robert G. Sproul Assocs., U. Calif. Alumni Assn., Libr. Assocs., Smithsonian Assocs., Bear Backers, Commonwealth Club Calif. Republican. Roman Catholic. Avocations: skiing, fly fishing, flying. Home: 177 Ardith Ct Orinda CA 94563-4344 Office: A G & T Investments Inc PO Box 4689 Walnut Creek CA 94596-0689

CERVENY, KATHRYN M., educational administrator; b. Chgo., May 26, 1939; d. Roland John and Florence Anna (Cooke) Heidenfelder; children: Erick Joseph, Charles George. Student, Milw. Downer Coll., Lawrence U. Distbr., county mgr. Vanda Beauty Counselors, Orlando, Fla., 1965-80; sales assoc., adminstrv. asst. Resource Data Systems, Northbrook, Ill., 1981-87; dept. asst. Northwestern U., Evanston, Ill., 1987—; internat. conf. editl. asst. IEEE, 1994-97; pvt. piano tchr. Leadership trainer, dist. commr. Boy Scouts Am.; mem. exec. coun. bd. N.W. Suburban Coun., Mt. Prospect, Ill., 1993—. Recipient Silver Beaver award Boy Scouts Am. Mem. NAFE.

CERVONE, ANTHONY LOUIS, lawyer; b. Providence, Nov. 19, 1962; s. Anthony and Mary Gloria (Borrelli) C.; m. Joy D'Amico, Dec. 31, 1995. BA, R.I. Coll., 1984; JD, U. Bridgeport, 1988; Cert. Program Instrn. Lawyers, Harvard U., 1996. Bar: R.I. 1989, U.S. Dist. Ct. R. I. 1990, U.S. Ct. Appeals (1st cir.) 1991, U.S. Supreme Ct. 1996. Founder, prin. Cervone Law Firm, Cranston, R.I., 1989—; spl. coun. to The City of Providence, 1991-92; mem. bench-bar com. R.I. Superior Ct., R.I. Family Ct., R.I. Dist. Ct.; affiliate atty. Am. Ctr. for Law and Justice, The Rutherford Inst. Mem. ABA, ATLA, R.I. Bar Assn., R.I. Trial Lawyers Assn., Supreme Ct. Hist. Soc., Smithsonian Instn., Library of Congress. Avocations: snowboarding, rollerhockey, golf, surfing, cycling, triathlons. Home: 68 White Birch Ln Hope RI 02831-1106 Office: Renaissance Park 37 Sockanosset Crossroad Cranston RI 02920

CERVONI, ROBERT ANGELO, financial executive, consultant; b. N.Y.C., Feb. 2, 1953; s. Paul and Maria (Capogna) C.; m. Diane Eileen Peters, May 29, 1976 (div.); m. Michelle Lapenna Molinari, Aug. 9, 1998; children: Dana, Robert Ryan. BS in Acctg., L.I. U., 1975. CPA, N.Y. Audit mgr. Oppenheim Appel Dixon & Co., N.Y.C., 1975-82; contr. Trading Co. of the West, L.A., 1982-84; chief fin. officer Spear Securities, Inc., L.A., 1984-88, JMC Group, Inc., La Jolla, Calif., 1984-97; CFO, mng. dir. Weeden & Co., L.P., 1986—; cons. Forstmann Leff Assocs., N.Y.C., 1982-84, Instinet Corp., N.Y.C., 1983-84; bd. dirs. Weeden Securities Corp.; pres. Sci. Search Assoc., Inc., 1991-98; mng. dir. Fusion Fans LLC, 1998—, Web Investors LLC. Mem. AICPA, N.Y. Soc. CPAs, Nat. Soc. Compliance Profls., N.Y. Stock Exch. (allied mem.), Securities Industry Assoc. (legal and compliance divsn.). Office: Weeden & Co LP 145 Mason St Greenwich CT 06830-6605

CESARANI, SAL, fashion designer; b. N.Y.C., Sept. 25, 1941. Student, High Sch. of Fashion Industries, Fashion Inst. Tech., N.Y.C. Sportswear designer Bobbie Brooks, 1963-64; fashion coord. men's wear Paul Stuart, 1964-69; merchandising dir. men's and women's apparel Ralph Lauren/Polo, 1969-73, Country Britches, 1973-75, collection S. Blacker, 1976(Cesarani est. 1977), collection Jaymar Ruby, 1979, collection Pulliman/Spencer, 1984-86, collection Hartmarx (SJC Concepts est. 1979-93), 1986-87; commd. by U.S. Olympic Com. to design ceremonial uniforms of the Winter Olympics, 1980, lic. to W. Seitchek and Sons, Phila., 1995-97, lic. to Salvatore J. Cesarani, Italy, 1997—; lic. in Japan for Men's Apparel Collection, 1979—, lic. to Men's Furnishing & Acess in Japan, 1979, lic. Childrenswear, 1992, lic. in Japan Eyewear, 1992, lic. in Japan Leather Bay, 1992. Vol. NYU Med. Ctrs. Vol. Corp. Recipient Coty award, 1974, 75, 82. Mem. Coun. Fashion Designers Am. Office: care SJC Concepts 201 E 79th St New York NY 10021-0830

CESARIO, ROBERT CHARLES, franchise executive, consultant; b. Chgo., Apr. 6, 1941; s. Valentino A. and Mary Ethel (Kenny) C.; m. Susan Kay DePoutee; children: Jeffrey, Bradley. B.S. in Gen. Edn., Northwestern U., 1975; postgrad. in bus. adminstrn. DePaul U., 1975. Mgr. fin. ops. Midas Internat. Corp., Chgo., 1968-73; dir. staff ops. Am. Hosp. Supply Corp., McGaw Park, Ill., 1973-76; v.p. Car X Svc. Systems Inc., Chgo., 1976-78, v.p. oil svcs., 1983-84; v.p. Chicken Unltd. Enterprises Inc., Chgo., 1978-83; pres. Growth Strategies, Inc., 1984-87; pres. CEO Lube Pro's Internat., Inc., 1987—. Served with USMC, 1960-62. Office: Lube Pros Internat Inc 1630 W Colonial Pky Palatine IL 60067-4725

CESARIO, ROBERT JAMES, music educator, performer; b. Wauwatosa, Wis., June 23, 1951; s. James and Virginia (Morrone) C.; m. Sandra Kay Block, May 29, 1976; children: Anthony Robert, Anastasia Louise. BFA, U. Wis., Milw., 1974, MusM, 1978; MA, NE Mo. State U., 1977; ArtsD, U. No. Colo., 1990. Temp. asst. instr. NE Mo. State U., Kirksville, 1975-77; dir. instrumental music Mayville (N.D.) State Coll., 1978-79; dir. bands N.Mex. Highlands U., Las Vegas, 1979-82; dir. univ. bands Panhandle State U., Goodwell, Okla., 1982-83; mem. faculty, dir. instrumental music Rogers State Coll., Claremore, Okla., 1983-90; adminstr., curriculum coord. for music Tulsa Pub. Schs., 1990-98; dir. of bands Rice U., Houston, 1998—; conducting asst. U. No. Colo., Greeley, 1981-82; performer Tulsa Philharmonic, Okla. Sinfonia, Starlight Concert Band; soloist with various high sch. bands, coll. orchs. Composer: (music for band) Penache, 1987. Bd. dirs. Claremore Community Concerts Assn., 1983—, pres., 1985-88. Mem. Internat. Assn. Jazz Educators, Music Educators Nat. Conf., Coll. Music Soc., Coll. Band Dirs. Nat. Assn. (condr. nat. conducting symposium 1983, 84, nat. conv. 1985), Okla. Music Educators Assn. (condr. honor jazz ensemble 1985, 88, honor concert band 1989), Nat. Band Assn., World Assn. of Symphonic Bands and Ensembles, Tex. Bandmasters Assn., Tex. Music Educators Assn., Western Athletic Conf. Band Dirs. Assn., Phi Beta Mu. Democrat. Roman Catholic. Avocations: racquetball, microcomputers. Home: 5440 Braesvalley #181 Houston TX 77096 Office: Rice University MS 314 6100 Main St Houston TX 77005-1892

CESARIO, SANDRA KAY, women's health nurse, educator; b. Racine, Wis., May 3, 1955; d. Harold J. and Bernice (Ittner) Block; m. Robert J. Cesario, May 29, 1976; children: Tony, Anna. RN, St. Luke's Hosp., Racine, Wis., 1976; BSN, Ft. Hayes State U., Hays, Kans., 1985; MS, U. Okla., 1989; postgrad., Tex. Womans U., 1995—. Nursery charge nurse Kirksville (Mo.) Osteopathic Hosp., 1976-77; staff nurse NICU St. Joseph's Hosp., Milw., 1977-78; ob staff nurse N. Colo. Med. Ctr., Greeley, 1981-82; ob nursing instr. Luna Vo-Tech., Las Vegas, N.Mex., 1980-81; ob insvc. coord. Guymon (Okla.) Meml. Hosp., 1983; coord. ob nurse residency prog. Indian Health Svc., Oklahoma City, 1989-92; asst. prof. U. Okla., 1992—; mem. adj. clin. faculty Langston U., 1994. Mem. editl. rev. bd. Jour. Nursing Theory Constrn. and Testing. Mem. Assn. Womens Health Obstetrics and Neonatal Nursing, Okla. Nurses Assn., Okla. Nurses Found. (bd. dirs.), Am. Nurses Assn., Midwest Nursing Rsch. Soc., So. Nursing Rsch. Soc., Sigma Theta Tau. Home: 23135 S Cedar St Claremore OK 74017-0366

CESNIK, JAMES MICHAEL, union official, newspaperman, printer, consultant; b. Marshfield, Wis., Oct. 6, 1935; s. Ignatius Anthony and Mary Catherine (Bayuk) C.; m. Elizabeth Louise Havlik, Aug. 1, 1959 (div. 1987); children: Margaret Mary, Sarah Elizabeth, Michael Ignatius; m. Barbara E. Nelson, Jan. 1, 1990. B.A., St. John's U., Collegeville, Minn., 1958. Reporter, Rice Lake (Wis.) Chronotype, 1958; reporter, makeup, layout editor Mpls. Star & Tribune, 1958-64; internat. rep., asso. dir. research and info., dir. research and info. Newspaper Guild, AFL-CIO/CLC, Washington, 1965-75; editor Guild Reporter, 1973-93; v.p. Internat. Labor Press Assn., Washington, 1973-79; pres. Internat. Labor Press Assn., 1980-82, sec.-treas., 1984-87; editor Internat. Labor Comm. Assn. Reporter, 1983-84; sec.-treas. JBTM Enterprises Inc., 1989-91, pres., 1991—; pres. Signet Screen Printing and Embroidery, 1993—; Elijah P. Lovejoy lectr. So. Ill. U., 1970; cons., 1993—; publs. cons., 1993—. Mem. Falls Church (Va.) Democratic Com., 1970-84; founding mem. Falls Church Com. on Status of Women, 1975-76; pres. Montessori Sch. No. Va., 1970. Mem. Slovenian Heritage Com. Washington, Slovenian Choral Soc. Washington, Am. Slovenian Cath. Union, Soc. for Slovene Studies. Roman Catholic.

CETRON, MARVIN JEROME, management executive; b. Bklyn., July 5, 1930; s. Jack Student and Gertrude Leah C.; m. Gloria Rita Wasserman, June 29, 1955; children: Edward Jack, Adam Bruce. B.S. in Indsl. Engring and Indsl. Psychology, Pa. State U., 1952; MBA, Columbia U., 1959; PhD in Rsch. and Devel. Mgmt, Am. U., 1970. Civilian with U.S. Navy, 1951-71, chief rsch. and devel. planning Naval Material command, 1963-71; founder, pres. Forecasting Internat. Ltd., Arlington, Va., 1971—; adj. prof. Am. U., M.I.T., Ga. Inst. Tech.; Mem. research and devel. adv. com. USCG, 1974—. Author: Technological Forecasting: A Practical Approach, 1969, Technical Resource Management: Quantitative Methods, 1970, The Science of Managing Organized Technology, 4 vols, 1971, Industrial Applications of Technological Forecasting: Its Use in Research and Development Management, 1971, The Navy Technological Forcast, 3d edit, 1970, Technology Assessment in a Dynamic Environment, 1972, The Methodology of Technology Assessment, 1972, Quantitative Decision-aiding Techniques for Research and Development Management, 1972, Proc. NATO Advanced Study Institute on Technology Transfer, 1974, Industrial Technology Transfer, 1977, Encounters with the Future, A Forecast of Life into the 21st Century, 1982, Jobs with a Future, 1984, Schools of the Future, 1985, The Future of American Business, 1985; Great Job Shakeout: How to Find a New Career after the Crash, 1988, America at the Turn of the Century, 1989, American Renaissance: Our Lives at the Turn of the 21st Century, 1989, Educational Renaissance: How to Improve Our School by Turn of the 21st Century, 1990, Crystal Globe: The Have and the Have-Not of the New World Order, 1991, Probable Tomorrows: How Science and Technology Will Transform Our Lives in the Next Twenty Years, 1997, Cheating Death: The Promise and the Future Impact of Trying to Live Forever, 1998; editor in chief Tech. Assessment Jour., 1971-78. Served with USCG, 1954-56. Mem. Ops. Rsch. Soc. Am., IEEE, Tech. and Indsl. Mgmt. Soc., World Future Soc. Office: 3612 Boat Dock Dr Falls Church VA 22041-1413

CETRULO, JERRY, sculptor; b. Jersey City, N.J., Sept. 10, 1941; s. Gerardo Cetrulo and Eva Augustine; m. Renate Cetrulo, 1961 (div.); children: Michael, Mark, Heidi; m. Barbara Cetrulo, Aug. 2, 1998. Customer engr. IBM, Cranford, N.J., 1967—; instr. Am. Woodcarving Sch., Wayne, N.J., 1992—. With U.S. Army, 1959-62. Avocations: woodcarving, painting. Home: 18 Cayuga Ave Rockaway NJ 07866 Office: Am Woodcarving Sch 21 Pompton Plains Crossroad Wayne NJ 07470

CEURVELS, WARREN STEVEN, school system administrator; b. Bklyn., Mar. 30, 1944; s. Frank Augustus and Evelyn Lilian (Nerzig) C.; m. Denise Ann Saladini, Nov. 7, 1981; children: Matthew James, Frank Christopher. BA, Newark State Coll., 1967; MA, Montclair State Coll., 1969; EdD, Rutgers U., 1983. Cert. sch. bus. adminstr., supt., indsl. arts tchr., N.J. Indsl. arts tchr. Rahway (N.J.) Bd. Edn., 1965-66, Union County Regional Bd. Edn., Springfield, N.J., 1966-68; tng. supr. Ohaus Sch. Corp., Union, N.J., 1968-69; personnel analyst Montgomery County Pub. Schs., Rockville, Md., 1969-70; dir. continuing edn. Montclair (N.J.) State Coll., 1970-83, Ridgefield (N.J.) Bd. Edn., 1983-84; sch. bus. adminstr. Franklin (N.J.) Bd. Edn., 1987-88, Wanaque (N.J.) Bd. Edn., 1988—. Contbr. articles to profl. jours. Pres. Lake Community Property Owners Assn., Barry Lakes, N.J., 1984-85, treas., 1982-84. Mem. Nat. Ski Patrol, Passaic County Assn. Sch. Bus. Officials, N.J. Assn. Sch. Bus. Officials, Internat. Assn. Sch. Bus. Officials. Republican. Roman Catholic. Avocations: skiing, hunting, golf. Home: 12 Higgins Rd Vernon NJ 07462-3025 Office: Parsippany-Troy Hills Bd Edn 577 Vail Rd Parsippany NJ 07054

CEVETILLO, GERRI MARIE, manufacturing company executive; b. Bronx, N.Y., May 27, 1946; d. Gennaro Dominick and Jean Marie (Cucchiello) Luizzi; m. Louis Anthony Cevetillo, Aug. 6, 1967 (div. May 1978); children: Christopher Dante, Michael Gennaro. Mgr. mktg. J.F. Jeleko & Co., Armonk, N.Y., 1978-85; mgr. sales and mktg. Coltene Whaledent Dental Lab. Tech., Mahwah, N.J., 1985-90; gen. mgr. ULTRONICS, Mahwah, 1990—; cons. infection control Assn. Barber Bds. Am., 1996—; spkr. in field. Cons. Milady Publs., 1998-99, Hair Internat., 1998-99, Pivot Pt. Internat., 1999; contbr. articles to profl. jours. Mem. Am. Beauty Assn. (chair mktg./pub. rels. com. 1997—), Nat. Interstate Coun. State Cosmetology Bds. (mem. infection control com. 1994—), Nail Mfrs. Coun. (v.p. 1996—). Avocations: travel, sailing, public speaking. Home: 291 Sylvan Knoll Rd Stamford CT 06902-5344 Office: ULTRONICS 750 Corporate Dr Mahwah NJ 07430-2009

CEYER, SYLVIA T., chemistry educator. Grad. summa cum laude, Hope Coll., Holland, Mich.; PhD, U. Calif., Berkeley. Postdoctoral fellow Nat. Bur. Standards; faculty mem. dept. chemistry MIT, Cambridge, Mass., 1981—, asst. prof., J.C. Sheehan prof. chemistry. Recipient Recognition award for young scholars AAUW Ednl. Found., 1988, Nobel Laureate Signature awd. for Graduate Education in Chemistry, Am. Chemical Soc., 1993. Fellow NAS, Am. Phys. Soc., Am. Acad. Arts and Scis. Office: MIT 6-215 Dept Chemistry 77 Mass Ave Dept Cambridge MA 02139-4307

CHA, SE DO, internist; b. Seoul, Korea, Dec. 17, 1942; came to U.S., 1966, naturalized, 1977; s. Young Sun and Hee Joo (Chang) C.; m. Elsa Jane Greene, Dec. 21, 1974; 1 child, Elizabeth. M.D., Yon Sei U., 1966. Diplomate Am. Bd. Internal Medicine. Intern Presbyn.-U. Pa. Med. Ctr., Phila., 1966-67; resident in medicine Harrisburg (Pa.) Hosp., 1967-70; chief resident in medicine Roger Williams Gen. Hosp., Providence, 1970-71, cardiologist, 1973-75; fellow in cardiology Deborah Heart and Lung Center, Browns Mills, N.J., 1971-73, cardiologist, 1975—, asst. dir. adult cardiac catheterization lab., 1975-86, dir., 1987—; clin. asst. prof. U. Medicine and Dentistry N.J., 1987; instr. Brown U., Providence, 1973-75. Contbr. articles to profl. jours. Fellow ACP, Soc. for Cardiac Angiography; mem. AMA, Fedn. Clin. Rsch., Am. Heart Assn. Office: Deborah Heart and Lung Ctr Trenton Rd Browns Mills NJ 08015

CHA, SOYOUNG STEPHEN, mechanical engineer, educator; b. Inchon, Korea, June 25, 1944; came to U.S., 1974; s. Sang O. and Sook S. (Lee) C.; m. Young W. Park, Sept. 4, 1974. BS, Seoul (Korea) Nat. U., 1969; MS, Mich. State U., 1976; PhD, U. Mich., 1980. Project rsch. engr. Northrop corp., Rsch. Triangle Park, N.C., 1979-84; prof., dir. opto-mech. lab. U. Ill., Chgo., 1984—; spkr. in field. Guest editor Optics Lasers Engring., 4 vol. edit., 1992; contbr. over 90 articles to profl. and tech. jours. Dept. of Energy fellow, 1987, NASA fellow, 1994, USAF fellow, 1996. Mem. ASME (tech. com. 1983-87), Internat. Soc. Optical Engring. (conf. chair, cochair 1991—), Am. Soc. Aeronautics Astronautics (tech. com. 1994-97, 1998—), Visualization Soc. Japan (conf. co-chair 1998). Methodist. Achievements include patent for holographic velocimetry. Office: U Ill Chgo 2039 ERF 842 W Taylor St Chicago IL 60607

CHA, VICTOR D., government educator, consultant; b. N.Y.C., Oct. 27, 1961; s. Moon Young and Soon (Ock) C.; m. Hyun Jung; 1 child, Patrick Ellis. BA, Columbia U., 1983; MA, Oxford (Eng.) U., 1986; PhD, Columbia U., 1994. Rsch. assoc. East Asian Inst., Columbia U., N.Y.C., 1989-94; Fulbright scholar Inst. for Internat. Edn., N.Y.C., 1991-92; Nat. Security fellow John M. Olin Inst. for Strategic Studies, Harvard U., Cambridge, Mass., 1992-94; cons. Sci. Applications Internat. Corp., McLean, Va., 1998—; postdoctoral fellow Ctr. Internat. Security and Arms Control Stanford (Calif.) U., 1994-95, Nat. fellow Hoover Instn. on War,, 1998-99; prof. dept. govt. and Sch. Fgn. Svc., Georgetown U., Washington, 1995—; cons. The Pentagon, Washington; analyst CNN, AP and others. Author: Alignment Despite Antagonism: The United States-Korea-Japan Security Triangle, 1998; contbr. articles to profl. jours. Mem. Fulbright Assn., Am.

Polit. Sci. Assn., Oxford Soc., Assn. Asian Studies. FAX: 202-687-5858. Office: Dept of Govt 681 ICC Washington DC 20057

CHABEK, DANIEL JAMES, journalist, writer, public relations professional; b. Cleve., Apr. 8, 1915; s. Daniel James Sr. and Hattie (McLkovsky) C.; m. Margaret Pangrace, Oct. 28, 1939; children: Cynthia, Christopher. BS in Journalism, Ohio State U., 1936. Reporter Cleve. Press., 1936-52; pub. rels. rep. Ford Motor Co., Dearborn, Mich., 1952-58, Cleve., 1958-80; newspaper columnist North Ridgeville (Ohio) Light, 1980-88, Lakewood Sun Post, North Olmsted, Ohio, 1988—; adv. bd. Lakewood Sun Post, 1989—. Author: (stories) Lakewood Lore, 1998; contbr. articles to newspapers. Bd. trustees Lakewood Hist. Soc., 1989—; jury voter, mem. selection commn. City of Lakewood, 1993. Lt. (j.g.) USN, 1944-46, PTO. Mem. Soc. Profl. Journalists, Cleve. Press Club, Kiwanis (editor Kiwanigram 1982-89, Best Newsletter 14th divsn. award 1984). Avocations: running, calisthenics. Home and Office: 1592 Arthur Ave Lakewood OH 44107-3804

CHABOT, ELLIOT CHARLES, lawyer; b. Anniston, Ala., Mar. 29, 1955; s. Herbert L. and Aleen (Kerwin) C.; m. Christine H. Swan, July 3, 1998. BA with honors, U. Md., 1977; JD, George Washington U., 1980. Bar: D.C. 1980, U.S. Dist. Ct. D.C. 1981, U.S. Ct. Fed. Claims 1981, U.S. Ct. Internat. Trade 1981, U.S. Tax Ct. 1981, U.S. Ct. Appeals Armed Forces 1981, U.S. Temporary Emergency Ct. Appeals 1981, U.S. Ct. Appeals (D.C. cir.) 1981, U.S. Ct. Appeals (4th, 5th, 8th, 9th, 10th, 11th, fed. cirs.) 1982, U.S. Ct. Appeals (7th cir.) 1983. Applications analyst, atty., House Info. Systems U.S. Congress, Washington, 1980-81; project leader integrated law revision and retrieval project U.S. Congress, Washington, 1981-89; legal support project leader House Info. Systems U.S. Congress, Washington, 1989-95; webmaster internet law libr. U.S. Congress, Washington, 1994-99, legal sys. team leader House Info. Resources, 1995—; bd. dirs. Am. Revenue Assn., Rockford, Iowa, 1983-87, Threshold Services, Inc., Silver Spring, Md., 1984-89; v.p. Banor Housing Inc., Kensington, Md., 1987-88, 90—, dir. 1987—. Columnist Aspen Hill Gazette, 1987-96. Pres. Aspen Hill (Md.) Civic Assn., 1985-95, dir. 1995—; pres. Parkland Community Sch. Coun., Aspen Hill, 1983-87, 94-96, v.p., 1971-73, mem. coun. 1970-74, 82-96; chmn. community svcs. com. Greater Wheaton (Md.) Citizens Adv. Bd., 1986-92; chmn. Ga. Ave. Men's Shelter Adv. Bd., Aspen Hill, 1989-96, Community Edn. Devel. subcom. of Citizens Adv. com. to the Interagency Coordinating Bd. for Community Use of Ednl. Facilities and Svcs. , 1985-88; dist. 3 v.p. Montgomery County Civic Fedn., 1990-91; exec. com. Robert E. Peary High Sch. PTA, Aspen Hill, 1972-73; Montgomery County Coun. com. on re-use of Peary High Sch., 1986, task force to examine the regional dist. act, 1991; corr. sec. Area 2 adv. coun. Montgomery County Pub. Schs, 1972-74, adv. com. spl. edn. programs, 1974; commr. Gov.'s Commn. on Student Affairs, Md., 1976-77; adv. com. Aspen Hill Libr., 1972, 1986—; sec. Friends Aspen Hill Libr., 1994-96, dir., 1996—; rec. sec. Dist. 19 Dem. Club, Montgomery County, 1983-86, 2d v.p., 1986-89, 1st v.p., 1989-92; legal and acctg. div. steering com. Washington Israel Bonds, 1984-86; mem. exec. com. Allied Civic Group, Silver Spring, 1987-89, corr. sec., 1992-94; chmn. Kensington/Wheaton Human Svcs. Area Plan Adv. Group, 1988; mem. Sta. 21 com. Kensington Vol. Fire Dept., 1989; mem. Greater Layhill Community Night Com., 1989, Aspen Hill Master Plan Citizens Adv. com., 1990-94; sec. Montgomery County Dem. Party, 1994—, chmn. rules com., 1994—, chmn. Internet Svcs. com., 1995-99, mem. ballot questions adv. com., 1988, 90, 98, vice chmn. precint orgn. com. of the party opers. task force, 1991-92; area coord. Dist. 19, 1992-94, chmn. Precinct 13-43, 1987-92, treas. Precinct 13-45, 1978-85; mem. Wheaton Action Group, 1990-95; campaign chmn. Dist. 19 Democratic Team, 1989-90; chmn. Wheaton Woods Recreation Ctr. Adv. Com., 1990; dir. dist. 3 Montgomery Citizens Polit. Action Com., 1991-92; mem. Bauer Drive Community Ctr. Adv. Com., 1992—; vice chmn. homeless com. Temple Shalom, Chevy Chase, Md., 1992-93; sec. Montgomery County United Democrats, 1997—; mem. Md. State Dem. Ctrl. Com., 1994—. Recipient George Washington award, George Washington U., 1980, Donald R. Spivak award Montgomery County Interagency Coordinating Bd. Community Use of Edn. Facilities and Services, 1987, Total Quality Team award Chief Adminstrv. Office of U.S. Ho. of Reps., 1996; named One of Outstanding Young Men, U.S. C. of C., 1982, Ky. Col. Hon. Order Ky. Cols., 1967, Citizen of Yr. Greater Wheaton Citizen's Adv. Bd., 1990, One of the Federal 100 Federal Computer Week, 1994. Mem. ABA, Fed. Bar Assn., D.C. Bar Assn., George Washington U. Law Alumni Assn. (pres. Capitol Hill chpt. 1987-89, sec. 1985-87), Phi Alpha Delta (clk. Jay chpt. 1979-80), Omicron Delta Kappa. Home: 12929 Magellan Ave Rockville MD 20853-3037 Office: US Congress House Info Resources H2-641 Ford Ho Office Bldg Washington DC 20515-6165

CHABOT, HERBERT L., judge; b. N.Y.C., July 17, 1931; s. Meyer and Esther (Mogilansky) C.; m. Aleen Carol Kerwin, Jun. 16, 1951; children: Elliot C., Donald J., Lewis A., Nancy Jo. BA, CCNY, 1952; LLB, Columbia U., 1957; LLM, Georgetown U., 1964. Bar: N.Y. 1958. Staff counsel Am. Jewish Congress, 1957-60; law clk. U.S. Tax Ct., Washington, 1961-65, judge, 1978—; atty. Joint Congl. Com. Taxation, 1965-78. Del. Md. Constl. Conv., 1967-68. With U.S. Army, 1953-55. Mem. ABA, Fed. Bar Assn. Office: US Tax Ct 400 2nd St NW Washington DC 20217

CHABOT, STEVEN J., congressman; b. Cin., Jan. 22, 1953; s. Gerard Joseph and Doris Leona (Tilly) C.; m. Donna Daly, June 22; children: Erica, Randy. BA, Coll. William & Mary, 1975; JD, Salmon P. Chase Coll. of Law, 1978. Bar: Ohio; cert. tchr., Ohio. Tchr. St. Joseph Sch., Cin., 1975-76; atty. Cin., 1978-95; mem. city coun. City of Cin., 1985-90; commr. Hamilton County, Ohio, 1990-94; mem. U.S. House of Reps., Washington, 1995—; internat. rels., judiciary, sm. bus. coms. 105th Congress; mem. internat. rels. with Africa, internat. econ. policy & trade, comml. & adminstrv. law, crime, procurement, exports & bus. opportunities coms. Republican. Roman Catholic. Avocations: reading, spending time with family. Office: US House Reps 129 Cannon Bldg Washington DC 20515-3501*

CHABRAJA, NICHOLAS D., lawyer; b. Gary, Ind., Nov. 6, 1942. BA, Northwestern U., 1964, JD, 1967. Bar: Ind. 1967, Ill. 1968. Ptnr. Jenner & Block, Chgo., 1968-97; sr. v.p., gen. counsel Gen. Dynamics Corp., 1993-94, exec. v.p., bd. dirs., 1994-97, chmn. bd., CEO, 1997—; spl. counsel to Ho. of Reps. re-Impeachment Trial of Judge Harry E. Claiborne before U.S. Senate, 1986. Fellow Am. Coll. Trial Lawyers; mem. ABA, Ill. Bar Assn., Chgo. Bar Assn. Office: General Dynamics Corp 3190 Fairview Park Dr Falls Church VA 22042*

CHACE, WILLIAM M., university executive. PhD, Berkeley U., 1968. Pres. Emory U., Atlanta, 1994—. Recipient Richard W. Lyman award Stanford U., 1986, Woodrow Wilson Nat. Fellowship award. Office: Emory U 1380 S Oxford Rd Atlanta GA 30322

CHACE, WILLIAM MURDOUGH, university administrator; b. Newport News, Va., Sept. 3, 1938; s. William Emerson and Grace Elizabeth (Murdough) C.; m. JoAn Elizabeth Johnstone, Sept. 5, 1964; children: William Johnstone, Katherine Elizabeth. BA in English, Haverford Coll., 1961; MA in English, U. Calif., Berkeley, 1963; PhD in English, U. Calif., 1968; LLD (hon.), Amherst Coll., 1990, William Coll., 1992. Instr. Stillman Coll., Tuscaloosa, Ala., 1963-64; teaching asst. U. Calif., Berkeley, 1964-66, acting instr., 1967-68; asst. prof. English Stanford (Calif.) U., 1968-74, assoc. prof., 1974-80, prof., 1980, assoc. dean Sch. Humanities and Scis., 1981-85, vice provost for acad. planning and devel., 1985-88; pres. Wesleyan U., Middletown, Conn., 1988-94, Emory U., Atlanta, 1994—; dir. Sun Trust Banks; cons. to Hewlett-Packard, Hallmark Cards Inc., Hawaiian Ednl. Fund, Midwestern Mgmt. Assn.; vis. prof. The Coll. Aboard the Delta Queen, 1979, 80, 82, The Coll. in We. Europe and Brit. Isles, 1985; lectr. to Libr. Assocs. of Stanford U., 1976, 6th Internat. James Joyce Symposium, Dublin, 1977, MLA Ann. Conv., 1977, 78, Tufts U. Symposium, 1978, English Conf. of U. Calif., Berkeley, 1979, Eighth Internat. James Joyce Symposium, Dublin, 1982, IBM Internat. Bus. and Acad. Conf., Monte Carlo, 1984, Ezra Pound Centennial Colloquium, San Jose State U., 1985, Ann. Meeting of the Assn. of Grad. Liberal Studies Programs, St. Louis, 1986, Chico State U., La. State U., 1987, U. Utah Sch. of Medicine Pub. Lecture series, 1987, Northern Calif. Sci. Meeting of Am. Coll. Physicians, Monterey, Calif., 1987, 13th Internat. James Joyce Symposium, 1992; presenter Joyce and History conf. Yale U., 1990. Author: James Joyce: A Collection of Critical Essays, 1973, The Political Identities of Ezra Pound and T.S. Eliot, 1973, Lionel Trilling: Criticism and Politics, 1980, (with others) Graham Greene: A Revaluation, 1990; editor: (with Peter Collier) Justice Denied: The Black Man in White America, 1970, An Introduction to Literature, 1985, (with JoAn E. Chace) Making It New, 1972; contbr. numerous scholarly articles, revs. to profl. jours. Avocations: cycling, T'ai Chi, Jack Russell terriers. Office: Emory U Office of Pres Atlanta GA 30322

CHACHQUES, JUAN CARLOS, cardiac surgeon, researcher; b. Godoy, Santa Fe, Argentina, Jan. 8, 1944; arrived in France, 1980; s. Manuel Ernesto and Sara (Vaintrub) C.; m. Paula Dardan, Oct. 15, 1983; children: Emmanuel, Valerie, Maria-Paula. MD, U. Med. Sch., Rosario, Argentina, 1970; MS, U. Paris, 1989, PhD, 1993. Diplomate Argentinian Bd. Surgery, French Bd. Cardiovasc. Surgery. Resident in gen. surgery U. Hosp., Buenos Aires, 1970-74, chief of residents, 1974-75; resident in cardiovasc. surgery Broussais Hosp., Paris, 1981-86, asst. prof. cardiac surgery, 1988-94, staff surgeon cardiovasc. surgery, 1988—, assoc. prof., 1994—; dir. for surg. and clinical rsch. Nat. Inst. Health, Paris, 1990—; sr. rsch. Lab. for the Study of Cardiac Grafts and Prostheses, U. Paris, 1983—. Editor, author: Cardiomyoplasty, 1991, Heart Failure, 1994, Pathophysiology of Heart Failure, 1996, Cardiac-BioAssist, 1997; inventor method and apparatus for cardiac assistance (Cardiomyoplasty and Aortomyoplasty), surgical device for muscular expansion and electrostimulation, and cell therapy for heart failure (cellular cardiomyoplasty). Recipient prize French Acad. Surgery, 1985, French Acad. Scis. 1986, cardiology prize Acad. of Medicine of Argentina, 1988. Fellow Internat. Coll. Surgeons; mem. N.Y. Acad. Scis. (life), European Cir. of Cardiac Surgeons (founder 1991), French Assn. for Devel. of Rsch. in Cardiac Surgery (hon. pres.). Avocations: rowing, lawn tennis, country life, riding. Home: 116 rue de la Tour, 75116 Paris France Office: Broussais Hosp Dept Cardiovascular Surgery, 96 rue Didot, 75014 Paris France

CHACKO, GEORGE KUTTICKAL, systems science educator, consultant; b. Trivandrum, India, July 1, 1930; came to U.S., 1953.; s. Geevarghese Kuttickal and Thankamma (Mathew) C.; m. Yo Yee, Aug. 10, 1957; children: Rajah Yee, Ashia Yo Chacko Lance. MA in Econs. and Polit. Philosophy, Madras U., India, 1950; postgrad., St. Xavier's Coll., Calcutta, India, 1950-52; B in Commerce, Calcutta U., 1952; cert. postgrad. tng., Indian Stat. Inst., Calcutta, 1951; postgrad., Princeton U., 1953-54; PhD in Econometrics, New Sch. for Social Rsch., N.Y.C., 1959; postdoctoral, UCLA, 1961. Asst. editor Indian Fin., Calcutta, 1951-53; comml. corr. Times of India, 1953; dir. mktg. and mgmt. rsch. Royal Metal Mfg. Co., N.Y.C., 1958-60; mgr. dept. ops. rsch. Hughes Semicondr. div., Newport Beach, Calif., 1960-61; cons., 1961-62; ops. research staff cons. Union Carbide Corp., N.Y.C., 1962-63; mem. tech. staff Research Analysis Corp., McLean, Va., 1963-65, MITRE Corp., Arlington, Va., 1965-67; sr. staff scientist TRW Systems Group, Washington, 1967-70; cons. def. systems, computer, space, tech. systems and internat. devel. systems, assoc. in math. test devel. Ednl. Testing Service, Princeton, N.J., 1955-57; asst. prof. bus. adminstrn. UCLA, 1961-62; lectr. Dept. Agr. Grad. Sch., 1965-67; asst. professorial lectr. George Washington U., 1965-68; professorial lectr. Am. U., 1967-70, adj. prof., 1970; vis. prof. def. systems Mgmt. Coll., Ft. Belvoir, Va., 1972-73; vis. prof. U. So. Calif., 1970-71, prof. systems mgmt., 1971-83, prof. systems sci., 1983-94, prof. emeritus, 1994; prof. mgmt. U. Pertanian, Malaysia, 1996—, prin. investigator IRPA project, 1996-97; prof. U. Putra, Malaysia, 1997—; prof. tech. mgmt. Malaysian Grad. Sch. Mgmt., 1997—; chmn. MIT-UPM Grad. Program Tech. Mgmt., 1997—; sr. Fulbright prof. Nat. Chengchi U., Taipei, 1983-84, sr. Fulbright rsch. prof., 1984-85; prin. investigator and program dir. Tech. Transfer Project, Taiwan Nat. Sci. Coun., 1984-85; disting. fgn. expert lectr. Taiwan Ministry Econ. Affairs, 1986; sr. vis. rsch. prof. Taiwan Nat. Sci. Coun. Nat. Chengchi U., Taipei, 1988-89; sr. vis. rsch. prof. Dah-Yeh Inst. Tech., Dah-Tsuen, Chang-Hwa, Taiwan, 1993-94; vis. prof. Nat. Chengchi U., Taipei, 1993-94; v.p. program devel. Systems and Telecom. Corp., Potomac, Md., 1987-90; chief sci. cons. RJO Enterprises, Lanham, Md., 1988-89; cons. Med. Svcs. Corp. Internat., vector biology and control project U.S. Agy. for Internat. Devel., 1991; guest lectr. Tech. Univs. Tokyo, Taipei, Singapore, Dubai, Cairo, Warsaw, Budapest, Prague, Bergen, Stockholm, Helsinki, Berlin, Madras, Bombay, London, 1992, Yokohoma, Taipei, Hong Kong, Kuala Lampur, Madras, Bombay, Alexandria, Jerusalem, Cairo, Paris, London, 1993-94, Madrid, Bologna, Milan, Monte Carlo, Amsterdam, Vienna, Austria, Kuala Lampur, Bangkok, 1994; Bogta, Quito, Lima, Santiago, Buenos Aires, Rio De Janeiro, Johannesburg, Kuala Lumpur, 1996; USIA sponsored U.S. sci. emissary to Egypt, Burma, India, Singapore, 1987; USIA sponsored U.S. expert on tech. transferand military conversion 1st Internat. Conf. on Reconstrn. of Soviet Republics, Hannover, Germany, 1992; keynote speaker 2d annual conf. on mgmt. edn. in China, Taipei, Taiwan, 1989, world conf. on transition to advanced market economies, Warsaw, Poland, 1992, annual conv. Indian Inst. Indsl. Engring., Hyderabad, India, 1993, First Sino-South Africa Bilateral Symposium on Tech. Devel., Taipei, 1994, First Asia-Pacific Convention on Bus. mgmt. Edn., Kuala Lompen, 1996, Annual Conf. of Malasian Soc. of Ops. Rsch. and Mgmt. Scis, 1997; mem. internat. adv. com. on restructuring strategies for electronics info. industry Asian Inst. Tech. Workshop, 1994; mem. First Convention on Bus. and Mgmt. Edn., Kuala Lumpur, 1996, mem. Asian-Pacific Conf. on Mgmt. Sci., Malaysia, 1997. Author: Applied Statistics in Decision Making, 1971, Computer Aided Decision Making, 1972, Systems Approach to Public and Private Sector Problems, 1976, Operations Research Approach to Problem Formation and Solution, 1976, Management Information systems, 1979, Trade Drain Interperative of Technology Transfer: U.S. Taiwan Concomitant Coalistions, 1985, Robotics/Artificial Intelligence/Productivity U.S.-Japan Concomitant Coalitions, 1986, Technology Management: Applications to Corporate Markets and Military Missions, 1988, The Systems Approach to Problem-Solving: From Corporate Markets to National Missions, 1989, Toward Expanding Exports Through Technology Transfer: IBM Taiwan Concomitant Coalitions, 1989, Dynamic Program Management: From Defense Experience to Commercial Application, 1989, Decision-Making Under Uncertainty: An Applied Statistics Approach, 1991, Operations Research/Management Science: Case Studies in Decision Making Under Structured Uncertainty, 1993, Invoking Intercessory Prayer Power: Meditating Modern-day Miracles, 1997, Targeting Strategies for Continuous Competitiveness: 32 Corporate, Country, and Cross-national Information Technology (IT) Applications, 1988, Half-Indian, Half-Chinese, and All American, 1998; columnist: The Sunday Star, 1998—, Bus. Times, 1998—. Active Nat. Presbyn. Ch., Washington, 1967-84, mem. ch. coun., 1969-71, mem. chancel choir, 1967-84, co-dean ch. family camp, 1977, coord. life abundant discovery groups, 1979; chmn. worship com. Taipei Internat. Ch., 1984, founder, dir. Intercessory Prayer Power, 1984, mem. adult choir, 1983-85, 88-89, 93-96, chmn. membership com., 1985, chmn. stewardship and fin. com., 1985, chmn. com. Christian edn., 1988, Sunday Sch. supt., 1989, adult Sunday sch. leader, 1993; adult Sunday Sch. leader 4th Presbyn. Ch., Bethesda, Md., 1986-87, mem. sanctuary choir, 1985—; participant 9th Internat. Ch. Mus. Festival, Coventry Cathedral, 1992; mem. Men's Ensemble, 1986-93; mem. Ministry Com. Men of 4th Rep. to Session, 1990—; founder, dir. Prayer Power Partnership, 1990—; adult Sunday sch. leader Kuala Lumpur Internat. Ch., 1996—; mem. internat. adv. bd. Technol. Forecasting and Social Change, 1996—. Recipient Gold medal Inter-Collegiate Extempore Debate in Malayalam U. Travancore, Trivandrum, India, 1945, 1st pl. Yogic Exercises Competition U. Travancore, 1946, Jr. Lectureship prize Physics Soc. U. Coll., 1946, 1st prize Inter-Varsity Debating Team Madras, 1949, NSF internat. sci. lectures award, 1982, USIA citation for invaluable contbr. to America's pub. diplomacy, 1992, Commendation for 2 books on U.S. - Taiwan Technology Transfer by Presidential Palace, Taipei, 1993; Coll. scholar St. Xavier's Coll., 1950-52; Inst. fellow Indian Stat. Inst., 1951, S.E. Asia Club fellow Princeton U., 1953-54, Univ. fellow UCLA, 1961. Fellow AAAS (nat. coun. 1968-73, chmn. or co-chmn. symposia 1971, 72, 74, 76, 77, 78), Am. Astronautical Soc. (v.p. publs. 1969-71, editor Tech. Newsletter 1968-72, mng. editor Jour. Astronautical Scis. 1969-75); mem. Ops. Rsch. Soc. Am. (vice chmn. com. of representation on AAAS 1972-78, nat. coun. tech. sect. on health 1966-68, editor Tech. Newsletter on Health 1966-73), Washington Ops. Rsch. Coun. (trustee 1967-69, chmn. tech. colloquia 1967-68, editor Tech. Newsletter 1967-68, Banquet chmn. 1992-93), Inst. Mgmt. Scis. (rep. to Internat. Inst. for Applied Systems Analysis in Vienna, Austria 1976-77, session chmn. Athens, Greece 1977, Atlanta 1977), World Future Soc. (editl. bd. publs. 1970-71), N.Y. Acad. Scis., Soc. Scientific Mgmt. and Ops. Rsch. (Egypt, 1st hon. fgn. mem.), Inst. for Ops. Rsch. and the Mgmt. Scis. (founding, INFORMS 1994); Kiwanis (charter 1st v.p., Life-time Hickson fellow 1995), Costa Mesa North Club (charter pres.), Friendship Heights Club (charter dir., Outstanding Svc. award 1972-73, Life award), Bethesda Club (disting. divsn. one svc. award, 1968, 70, capital dist. chmn. 1967, 69-70, 71-72, inter divsn. chmn. Green Candle of Hope Dinner, 1965-82), Capital dist. Found. 1982, Taipei-Keystone Club (disting. dir., spl. rep. of internat. pres. and counselor to dist. of Republic of China 1983-86, Pioneer Premier Project award Asia-Pacific conf. 1986, Legion of Honor 1985), Bethesda Club (dir. 1967-69, 95, chmn. internat. rels. 1991—, chmn. hon. com. 1992—, numerous coms. 1966—). Democrat. Office: U So Calif Inst Safety and Sys Mgmt Los Angeles CA 90089-0021 *As one who was privileged to be born into a Christian family tracing itself to the founding in the year 52 of the Mar Thoma Syrian Church in Southwest India by Thomas the Doubting Disciple of Jesus Christ, I look upon the exciting encounters I have had with new ideas (such as Theory of Games) and new professions (such as Operations Research) as precious talents over which I exercise stewardship by enjoying excellence of effort and exposition toward a better tomorrow at home and abroad, as an Indian-American blest with a most supportive family.**

CHACÓN, HIPÓLITO RAFAEL, art historian, educator, art critic; b. Havana, Cuba, Oct. 20, 1963; came to U.S., 1970; s. Hipólito Feleciano and Manuela Marian Chacón. AB, Wabash Coll., 1985; MA, U. Chgo., 1986, PhD, 1995. Intern dept. cmty. edn. Met. Mus. Art, N.Y.C., 1984; slide collection cataloguer art dept. U. Chgo., 1985; grad. intern, asst. to curator David and Alfred Smart Mus., U. Chgo., 1986-88; asst. to curator dept. Africa, Oceania and the Ams. Art Inst. of Chgo., 1988-90, Hispanic studies coord., 1990-92; Owen Duston instr. art Wabash Coll., Crawfordsville, Ind., 1992-94; asst. prof. art history and criticism U. Mont., Missoula, 1994-98, assoc. prof. art history and criticism, 1998—; lectr. office continuing edn. U. Chgo., 1991-92; lectr., presenter in field. Contbr. articles to profl. jours.; author art catalogues. Mem. Mansfield Libr. and Archives Com., U. Mont., 1994; bd. dirs. Mont.-No. Wyo. Conf. United Ch. of Christ, 1997; mem. aesthetics com. and arts task force Univ. Congl. Ch., 1996; mem. program com. bolle Ctr. for People and Forests, 1997; mem. spkr.'s bur. Mont. Com. for Humanities, 1998; mem. City of Missoula Hist. Preservation Adv. Commn., 1997. George Lewes Mackintosh grad. fellow, 1985, rsch. fellow Spanish Ministry Fgn. Rels., 1990, Mont. Com. for Humanities, 1997; U. Chgo. scholar, 1985-94; grantee Wabash Coll., 1992. Mem. Renaissance Soc. Am., Soc. for Archtl. Historians, Coll. Art Assn., Assn. Latin Am. Art, Am. Soc. for Hispanic Art Hist. Studies, Phi Beta Kappa, Phi Kappa Phi. Office: U Mont Fine Arts 404B Missoula MT 59812

CHACON, MICHAEL ERNEST, computer networking specialist; b. L.A., Feb. 14, 1954; s. Ernest Richard and Teresa Marie (Venegas) C.; m. Virginia Marie; children: Mylan Graham, Aubrie Sarah, Christina Nabseth, Caitlyn Nabseth, Julia Anna. Student, Pierce Coll., 1972-74, Boise State U., 1980-82; BSBA, U. Phoenix, 1997. Sys. cons. MEC & Assocs., Riverside, Calif., 1986-91; regional mgr. Inacom Corp., Garden Grove, Calif., 1991-97; chief tech. officer Ascolta Tng. Co., Irvine, Calif., 1997—; cons. in field; lectr. Microsoft Corp., Bellvue, Wash., 1990-92; chief tng. officer Ascolta Tng. Co., Irvine, Calif.; bd. dirs. Info. Tech. Tng. Assn. Author: Understanding Networks, 1991; columnist Microsoft Cert. Profl. Mag.; contbr. articles to profl. jours. Named to Dean's List, Pierce Coll., 1973, 74. Mem. Lake Elsinore Sportsman Assn., L.A. World Affairs Coun., 3Com Adv. Coun. (pres. tech. adv. bd. 1986-92). Avocations: songwriting/composing, rocketry, shooting, photography. Office: Ascota Tng Co 2351 Mcgaw Ave Irvine CA 92614-5831

CHADBOURNE, JOHN FREDERICK, JR., engineering executive; b. Detroit, Oct. 10, 1948; s. John Frederick and Wilhelmina (Williams) C.; m. Deborah Ann Bennett, Aug. 13, 1968. BSChemE, U. Fla., 1970, MS in Engring., 1971, PhD in Environ. Engring., 1977. Staff cons. environ. sci. and engring. U. Fla., Gainesville, 1971-74; proprietor Environ. Cons. Svcs., Orlando, Fla., 1974-77; corp. environ. mgr. Lafarge Corp., Dallas, 1977-87, dir. environment and indsl. hygiene, 1992-94; v.p. tech. and regulatory affairs Systech Environ. Corp., Dallas, 1987-92; pres. Chadbourne Environment and Safety Programs Inc., Dallas, 1994—; vis. prof. environ. engring. so. Meth. U., 1997—. Author (book chpt.) Burning Hazardous Waste in Cement Kilns, 1989, 97. Mem. AAAS, AIChE, Air and Waste Mgmt. Assn. (com. chair 1977-97), N.Y. Acad. Scis. Achievements include having secured permits to replace fosssil fuel with hazardous waste on many cement kilns. Avocations: scuba diving, trekking, Wu Chi Chuan. Home: 13106 Roaring Springs Ln Dallas TX 75240-5643 Office: CESP Inc 13106 Roaring Springs Ln Dallas TX 75240-5643

CHADICK, SUSAN LINDA, executive search consulting executive; b. N.Y.C., 1952. BS, Hunter Col., 1973; MS, New Sch. for Soc. Rsch., N.Y.C., 1982. Cons. Boyle Kirkman Assoc., N.Y.C., 1976-78; human resources Am. Express, N.Y.C., 1978-86; cons. Gould and McCoy, N.Y.C., 1989-89; prin. Gould and McCoy, 1989-92, managing dir., 1992-94; partner Gould, McCoy and Chadick, 1994—. Active Brooklyn Hts. Synogogue, Bklyn. Mem. Fin. Woman's Assn., Internat. Assn. Corp. & Profl. Resources (v.p. annual meeting, 1986-94, co-chairperson N.Y. chpt., 1992-94). Office: Gould McCoy & Chadick 300 Park Ave New York NY 10022-7402

CHADWELL, JAMES RUSSELL, JR., controller; b. Shelbyville, Ky., Dec. 29, 1948; s. James Russell and Martha (Cinnamond) C.; m. Cecilia Pearce, Dec. 4, 1993; children: Cameron, Ellen, Jackson, Aaron. BS in Math., Ea. Ky. U., 1970; BBA in Acctg., U. Cen. Fla., 1975; MBA, U. Louisville, 1981. CPA, Ky. Auditor Ky. State Auditor's Office, Frankfort, 1975-80, audit mgr., 1981-84; comptr. Ky. Tchr.'s Retirement System, Frankfort, 1984—. Bd. dirs. Commonwealth Credit Union, 1988—, sec.-treas., 1992—. With U.S. Army, 1970-72. Mem. AICPA, Ky. Soc. CPAs, Assn. Govt. Accts. (pres. 1981-82, treas. 1983-84), Govt. Fin. Officers Assn. (spl. rev. com. 1991), Frankfort Earthday Alliance (treas.), U. Louisville Capital Region Alumni Club (pres. 1993-94, treas. 1994-97, Bicentennial com.), Sigma Chi. Democrat. Episcopalian. Avocations: running, hiking, tennis, racquetball, gardening. Office: Ky Tchrs Retirement System 479 Versailles Rd Frankfort KY 40601-3868

CHADWICK, CYDNEY MARIE, writer, art projects executive; b. Oakland, Calif.. MA, Kootenay Sch. of Writing, Vancouver, B.C., Can., 1996. Exec. dir. Syntax Projects for Arts, Penngrove, Calif., 1990—; writer Penngrove, Calif., 1993—. Author: Enemy Clothing, 1993 The Gift Horse's Mouth, 1994, Oeuvres, 1995, Persistent Disturbances, 1995, Interims, 1997. Office: AVEC PO Box 1059 Penngrove CA 94951-1059

CHADWICK, JOHN EDWIN, financial counselor and planner; b. Mpls., Feb. 6, 1957; s. Edwin Bazley and Roberta Mae (Brown) C.; m. Patti E. Andersen, June 20, 1997; 2 children. BA, Gustavus Adolphus Coll., St. Peter, Minn., 1979; cert., Am. Coll., Bryn Mawr, Pa., 1989. CFP. Feed ingredient merchandiser Pillsbury Co., Mpls., 1979-81; pres. Chadwick Co., Bloomington, Minn., 1982-84; v.p. sales Red Wing (Minn.) Bus. Systems, 1984-85; fin. counselor CIGNA, Mpls., 1985-88; prin. The Chadwick Group, Inc., Bloomington, Minn., 1989—. Founding chmn. Oak Grove Endowment Com., Bloomington, 1987—. Lutheran. Avocations: hunting, waterskiing. Office: The Chadwick Group Inc 1550 E 79th St Bloomington MN 55425-1139

CHADWICK, ROBERT, lawyer, judge; b. Jackson, Miss., Apr. 5, 1924; s. Hudson and Annie (Eley) C.; m. Helen Faye Josey, Apr. 5, 1953; children: Robert Hudson, Celia, Dan, Lea Ann, Robin. BA, Auburn U., 1950; JD, Miss. Coll., 1957; postgrad., U. So. Calif., 1973, 75-76. Bar: Miss. 1963, U.S. Supreme Ct. 1970, U.S. Ct. Mil. Appeals 1975, Ky. 1980, U.S. Dist Ct. (ea. dist.) Ky. 1987. Chief regulation staff div. pesticide regulation USDA, Washington, 1965-70; atty., ecologist div. enforcement EPA, Washington, 1970-75, chmn. com. pesticide misuse rev., 1975-79; asst. gen. counsel Presdl. Clemency Bd. White House Dept. Justice, Washington, 1975; pvt. practice law Frankfort, Ky., 1980-82, 83—; law judge parole bd. Corrections Cabinet, Frankfort, 1982-83; asst. dir. div. hazardous materials Ky. Dept. Natural Resources and Environ. Protection, Frankfort, 1983—; chmn. bd. Exis, Inc.; staff atty., gen. counsel Ky. Cabinet for Human Resources, 1989-90. Pres. PTA Oxon Hill (Md.) Jr. High Sch., 1974, Frankfort Audubon Soc., 1981-83. Cpl. U.S. Army, 1943-45. Mem. ABA, Nat. Assn. Adminstrv. Law Judges, Miss. State Bar Assn., Ky. State Bar Assn., Franklin County Bar Assn., VFW, Masons. Home and Office: 16 Ryswick Ln Frankfort KY 40601-3848

CHADWICK, WHITNEY, writer, art historian, educator; b. Niagara Falls, N.Y., July 28, 1943; d. Cecil George and Helen Louise (Reichert) C.; m. Robert Alan Bechtle, Nov. 5, 1983. BA, Middlebury Coll., 1965; MA, Pa. State U., 1968, PhD, 1975. From asst to assoc. prof. MIT, Cambridge, Mass., 1972-78; prof. of art San Francisco State U., 1978—; vis. asst. prof. U. Calif., Berkeley, 1977; vis prof. Stanford (Calif.) U., 1990. Author: Myth in Surrealist Painting, 1980, Women Artists and the Surrealist Movement, 1985, Women, Art and Society, 1990; co-editor: Significant Others, 1995; (monograph) Leonora Carrington, 1995, Mirror Images: Women, Surrealism and Self-Representation, 1998, Framed, 1998. Named NEH fellow, 1981, ACLS fellow, 1987, Mary Ingraham Bunting Inst. fellow, Cambridge, Mass., 1992-93. Mem. Coll. Art Assn. (bd. dirs. 1987-93). Office: San Francisco State U 1600 Holloway Ave San Francisco CA 94132-1722

CHAFE, WALLACE LESEUR, linguist, educator; b. Cambridge, Mass., Sept. 3, 1927; s. Albert J. and Nathalie (Amback) C.; m. Mary Elizabeth Butterworth, June 23, 1951 (div. 1980); children—Christopher, Douglas, Stephen; m. Marianne Mithun, Jan. 25, 1985. B.A., Yale U., 1950, M.A., 1956, Ph.D., 1958. Asst. prof. U. Buffalo, 1958-59; linguist Bur. Am. Ethnology, Smithsonian Instn., 1959-62; mem. faculty U. Calif.-Berkeley, 1962-86, prof. linguistics, 1967-86; prof. linguistics U. Calif., Santa Barbara, 1986-91, prof. emeritus, 1991—. Author: Seneca Thanksgiving Rituals, 1961, Seneca Morphology and Dictionary, 1967, Meaning and the Structure of Language, 1970, The Pear Stories, 1980, Evidentiality, 1986, Discourse, Consciousness, and Time, 1994. Served with USNR, 1945-46. Mem. Linguistic Soc. Am., Am. Psychol. Assn., Am. Anthrop. Assn. Office: Univ Calif Dept Linguistics Santa Barbara CA 93106*

CHAFE, WILLIAM HENRY, history educator; b. Boston, Jan. 28, 1942; s. William Robinson and Elsie (Crabtree) C.; m. Lorna Jane Waterhouse, July 12, 1964; children: Christopher Robert, Jennifer Elizabeth. AB, Harvard U., 1962; AM, Columbia U., 1966, PhD, 1971. Instr. Columbia Grammar Sch., N.Y.C., 1963-65, Vassar Coll., Poughkeepsie, N.Y., 1970-71; asst. prof. Duke U., Durham, N.C., 1971-74, assoc. prof., 1974-79, prof., 1979—, Alice Mary Baldwin prof. history, 1988—, acad. dir. Ctr. for Rsch. on Women, 1987-89, co-dir. Duke Oral History Program, 1974-82, sr. rsch. assoc. Duke Ctr. for Documentary Studies, chair, history dept., 1990-95; dean Faculty Arts and Scis. Duke U., Durham, 1995—. Author: The American Woman, 1972, Women and Equality, 1977, Civilities and Civil Rights, 1980 (R.F. Kennedy book award 1981), The Unfinished Journey, 1986, A History of Our Time, 1986, The Paradox of Change, 1991, Never Stop Running, 1993 (Sidney Hillman Found. book award 1994), The Road to Equality, 1994. NEH fellow, 1974-75, 84-85, Rockefeller Found. fellow, 1978, Guggenheim fellow, 1989-90; grantee Nat. Humanities Ctr., Rsch. Triangle Pk., N.C., 1981-82, Ctr. for Advanced Study, Palo Alto, Calif., 1989-90. Fellow Soc. Am. Historians; mem. Am. Hist. Assn. (chmn. nominating com., 1987-88), Orgn. Am. Historians (co-chmn. program com. 1981-82, chair nominating com. 1991, exec. bd. 1993-96, pres. 1998-98), Am. Studies Assn., So. Hist. Assn. Avocations: sailing, tennis. Office: Duke U PO Box 90046 Durham NC 27708-0046*

CHAFEE, JOHN HUBBARD, senator; b. Providence, Oct. 22, 1922; s. John S. and Janet (Hunter) C.; m. Virginia Coates, Nov. 4, 1950; children: Zachariah, Lincoln, John, Georgia, Quentin. BA, Yale U., 1947; LLB, Harvard U., 1950; LLD (hon.), Brown U., 1964, Providence Coll., 1965, U. R.I., 1965, Jacksonville U., 1970, Bryant Coll., 1979. Bar: R.I. 1950. 2d lt. USMC, Guadalcanal, Okinawa, 1942-45; capt., rifle co. commander USMC, 1951-53; practice law Providence, 1952-62, 73-76; mem. R.I. Ho. of Reps. 3d Dist. Warwick, 1957-62, minority leader, 1959-62; gov. State R.I., 1963-69; sec. Navy, 1969-72; mem. U.S. Senate from R.I., 1977—; chmn. environ. & pub. works com. 104th Congress; Chmn. Com. on Environ. and Pub. Works; me. Com. Fin., Joint Com. on Taxation, Select Com. on Intelligence. Chmn. Rep. Gov.'s Assn., 1967; Mem. corp. Yale, 1972-78; trustee Deerfield Acad., 1970-79. Recipient Disting. Health Svc. award Nat. Assn. Cmty. Health Ctrs., 1994, Nat. Environ. Quality award Natural Resources Coun. Am., 1995; inducted into Nat. Wrestling Hall of Fame, 1993; named legislator of yr. Nat. League Women Voters, 1992. Mem. R.I. Bar, Fed. Bar Assn. Episcopalian. Office: US Senate 505 Dirksen Senate Office Bldg Washington DC 20510-3902*

CHAFETZ, MARC EDWARD, lawyer; b. Boston, Apr. 21, 1953; s. Morris Edward and Marion (Donovan) C.; m. Andrea Laurie Barkan, Aug. 20, 1977; children: Drew Edward, Maria Caitlin. BA, Oberlin Coll., 1975; JD, U. Va., 1979. Bar: D.C. Ct. Appeals 1980, U.S. Dist. Ct. D.C. 1980, U.S. Ct. Appeals (D.C. cir.) 1982. Law clk. to presiding justice U.S. Dist. Ct., Bryan, Va., 1979-80; assoc. Fulbright & Jaworski, Washington, 1980-82; sr. counsel SEC, Washington, 1982-84; gen. counsel Health Communications Inc., Washington, 1984—, also bd. dirs.; assoc. Ballard, Spahr, Andrews & Ingersoll, Washington, 1984-87; pres. Health Comms., Inc., Washington, 1987-94; COO The Tech. Group, Balt., 1996-97; of counsel Tighe, Patton, Tabackman & Babbin, Washington, 1996; CEO Train, Inc., Washington, 1995—; mng. dir. Bozman Ptnrs., LLC, Washington, 1997—; sr. v.p., gen. counsel In Touch Techs. Ltd., Washington, 1998—. Contbr. articles to profl. jours. Trustee Health Edn. Found., 1979—, Nat. Child Rsch. Ctr., 1989-91; bd. dirs. Foodfit.com., Washington, 1998—. Mem. ABA, Fed. Bar Assn., D.C. Bar Assn. Home and Office: 5105 Chevy Chase Pky NW Washington DC 20008-2920

CHAFFEE, JAMES ALBERT, protective services official; b. Balt., Aug. 14, 1952; s. John Dempster and Elizabeth May (Holden) C.; m. Virginia Rose Braun, Oct. 4, 1980; children: Andrew James, Thomas John, Elizabeth Mary. AA, Alan Hancock Coll., 1973; BA, Chapman Coll., 1980; MBA, St. Thomas Coll., 1986. Lic. EMT, L.A. County; lic. police officer, Minn. Police officer Minnetonka (Minn.) Police Dept., 1976-87, police supr., 1982-87; pub. safety dir. City of Chanhassen, Minn., 1987-90; dir. security Walt Disney Co., Burbank, Calif., 1990—; dir. S.W. Metro Drug Task Force, Chanhassen, 1988-90; adv. com. 1991 U.S. Open, Chaska, Minn., 1989-90. Founding mem. Chanhassen Rotary Club, 1987, v.p., 1990; pres. Emblem Sch. Site Coun., Saugus, Calif., 1992. With USAF, 1972-76. Mem. Chief Spl. Agts. Assn. (dir. 1991—), Am. Soc. for Indsl. Security, Community Police and Security Team. Republican. Roman Catholic. Avocations: golf, softball, skiing, fishing. Office: Walt Disney Co 500 S Buena Vista St Burbank CA 91521-0004

CHAFFEE, PAUL CHARLES, newspaper editor; b. Racine, Wis., Aug. 10, 1947; s. Raymond Russell and Ellen Mary (Tiles) C.; m. Bonnie Louise Burmeister, Aug. 9, 1969. BA in Journalism, U. Minn., 1969. Reporter Grand Rapids (Mich.) Press, 1969-79, asst. met. editor, 1979-81; met. editor Saginaw (Mich.) News, 1981-88, editor, 1988—; founding mem. adv. bd. dept. journalism Ctrl. Mich. U., Mt. Pleasant, 1987—; past pres. bd. dirs. Mich. Assoc. Press Editl. Assn.; bd. dirs. Mid Am. Press Inst. Bd. dirs. Salvation Army, Saginaw, 1986—, St. Charles (Mich.) Cmty. Schs. Found., 1994—, Westlund Child Guidance Clinic, 1995—, Saginaw Bay Orch., 1996—; mem. Leadership Saginaw Steering Bd.; mem. steering com. Bridge Ctr. Racial Harmony. Mem. Am. Soc. Newspaper Editors, Mich. State U. Journalism Dept. Hispanic Adv. Assn., Saginaw Country Club. Avocations: gardening, horses. Office: Saginaw News 203 S Washington Ave Saginaw MI 48607-1283

CHAFFEE, PAUL DAVID, city official; b. Kansas City, Mo., Mar. 8, 1953; m. Marsha R. Isaacson; children: Ashley, Jennifer. BS in Econs., Kans. State U., 1975, M Regional and Cmty. Planning, 1982. Planning intern Wichita (Kans.) Urban Renewal Agy., 1976; coord. human resources City of Dodge City, Kans., 1977-78, asst. planner, 1978-86, dir. planning, 1986-88; city planner City of Shawnee, Kans., 1988-94, dir. planning, 1994—; mem. hist. adv. bd. Johnson County Mus., Shawnee, 1993—; mem. growth tech. forecast com. Mid-Am. Regional Coun., Kansas City, Mo., 1994—; mem. peripheral transp. com. Johnson County, Olathe, 1997—. Bd. dirs. Dodge City Area Arts Coun., 1978-81; bd. edn. United Sch. Dist. 443, Dodge City, 1985-88. Mem. Am. Inst. Cert. Planners, Am. Planning Assn. Lutheran. Home: 14409 W 72nd St Shawnee KS 66216-5519 Office: City of Shawnee 11110 Johnson Dr Shawnee KS 66203-2799

CHAFFEE, STEVEN HENRY, communication educator; b. South Gate, Calif., Aug. 21, 1935; s. Edwin Wilbur and Nancy Marion (Kinghorn) C.; m. Sheila M. McGoldrick, Sept. 20, 1958 (div. Apr. 1987); children: Laura, Adam, Amy; m. Debra Lieberman, Mar. 25, 1989; 1 child, Eliot. BA, U. Redlands, 1957; MS, U. Calif., 1962; PhD, Stanford U., 1965. News editor Angeles Mesa News Advertiser, L.A., 1957; reporter Santa Monica (Calif.) Evening Outlook, 1962; rsch. assoc. Stanford (Calif) U., 1963-65, prof. communication, 1981—, Janet M. Peck prof., 1986—; asst. prof. to assoc. prof. U. Wisconsin, Madison, 1965-72, prof., 1972-82, 85-86, Vilas rsch. prof., 1974-81; mem. com. on mass communication and polit. behavior Soc. Sci. Rsch. Coun., N.Y.C., 1973-77; sci. adv. com. on TV and behavior NIMH, Washington, 1979-82. Author: Communication Concepts I: Explication, 1991; co-author: Television and Human Behavior, 1978, To See Ourselves, 1994; author, editor: Political Communication, 1972; co-author, co-editor: Handbook of Communication Science, 1986; co-editor: The Beginnings of Communication Study in the United States, 1996; contbr. numerous articles to profl. jours. Campaign pollster Dem. Party, Dane Co., Wis., 1966-84. Lt (j.g.) USNR, 1958-61. Fellow Internat. Comm. Assn. (pres. 1982-83); mem. Am. Polit. Sci. Assn., Assn. for Edn. in Journalism and Mass Comm. (mem. exec. com. 1971-72, 86-87), Am. Assn. Pub. Opinion Rsch. Democrat. Avocations: swimming, biking. Office: Stanford U Dept Communication Bldg 120 Stanford CA 94305-2050

CHAFFIN, CEAN, producer. Film prodr.: (with Steve Golia) The Game, 1997, Fight Club, 1999. Recipient Best Music Video-Short Form Grammy award, 1995, 96. Office: Propaganda Films 940 N Mansfield Ave Los Angeles CA 90038-2300*

CHAFFIN, DON BRIAN, industrial engineering educator, research director; b. Sandusky, Ohio, Apr. 17, 1939; m. 1966; 3 children. B of Indsl. Engring., Gen. Motors Inst., 1962; MS in Indsl. Engring., U. Toledo, 1964; PhD in Engring., U. Mich., 1967. Registered profl. engr., Ohio; cert. prof. ergonomist. Quality ctrl. engr. New Departure Divsn. GM Corp., Ohio, 1960-62, inspection foreman, 1962-63; project engr. Micrometrical Divsn. Bendix Corp., Mich., 1963-64; asst. prof. phys. medicine U. Kans., 1967-68, asst. prof. indsl. engring., 1968-70, assoc. prof. indsl. engring., 1970-77; prof. indsl. and ops. engring. U. Mich., Ann Arbor, 1977-93, dir. Ctr. for Ergonomics, 1980-97, Johnson prof. indsl. engring. and biomedical engring., 1993—. Fellow Human Factors Soc. (Paul Fitts award 1992), Am. Indsl. Hygiene Assn. (Edward Baier award 1994), Ergonomics Soc., Am. Inst. Med. and Biol. Engring.; mem. NSPE, NAE, Am. Inst. Indsl. Engrs. (Baker Disting. Rschr. award 1991), Sigma Xi. Achievements include research on effects and applications of electromyography for measuring human performance, concepts of biomechanics for injury prevention in skeletal-muscle system; expanding the teaching of physiological, neurological and anatomical concepts related to the simulation of human motions and exertions in the design of operated systems in manufacturing and service organizations, and in vehicle operation and maintenance. Office: U Mich Ctr Ergonomics 1656 IOE Bldg Ann Arbor MI 48109-2117*

CHAFFIN, GARY ROGER, business executive; b. Satanta, Kans., June 6, 1937; s. Owen Charles and Leona Irene (Dale) C.; m. Charlotte Daisy Hawley, Aug. 17, 1958; children: Darcy Lea, Charla Cai, Darren Roger, Charles Dale. BA, U. Kans., 1960. Loan officer Limerick Fin., Lawrence, Kans., 1959-60; asst. mgr. Chaffin Grocery, Moscow, Kans., 1960-62; store mgr. Chaffin Inc. Gibson Discount Ctrs., 1962-68; gen. mgr. Chaffin Inc., Dodge City, Kans., 1968-85; pres. Chaffin, Inc., Dodge City, Kans., 1985—, Great S.W. BanCorp, 1978-97. Bd. dirs., sec. Dodge City C.C. Found., 1996-98; bd. dirs., v.p. Dodge City Area Cmty. Found. Republican. Methodist. Avocations: golf, travel. Home: 510 Clover St Dodge City KS 67801-2816 Office: Chaffin Inc PO Box 177 Dodge City KS 67801-0177

CHAFKIN, RITA M., physician, dermatologist; b. N.Y.C., Apr. 11, 1929; d. Joseph and Dora (Winslow) Melnick; m. Samuel Chafkin, June 29, 1952; children: Elise Ceil Perkins, Marc David Chafkin (dec.). BA, NYU, 1949; MD, NYU Med. Sch., 1953; cert. in dermatology, NYU Postgrad. Med. Sch., 1957. Diplomate Am. Acad. Dermatology, 1959. Intern in internal medicine Kings County Hosp., Bklyn., 1953-54; dermatology resident Bellevue Hosp., N.Y.C., 1954-55; postgrad. trainee NYU Postgrad. Med. Sch., 1955-56, fellow in dermatology, 1956-57; precepteeship with Dr. Marion Sulzberger; pvt. practice dermatology Modesto, Calif., 1958-94; assoc. clin. prof. dermatology U. Calif., Davis, 1975-97; clinic dir. dermatology Stanislavs County Med. Ctr., Modesto, 1958-97. Artist in mixed media. Bd. dirs. Stanislaus County Med. Ctr. Found., 1982-97, pres. 1984-85. Recipient Tchr. of the Yr. award Stanislaus County Med. Ctr., Modesto, 1988, Founder's Dinner honoree, 1992. Fellow Am. Acad. Dermatology; mem. AMA, Calif. Med. Soc., San Francisco Dermatology Soc., Stanislaus County Med. Soc. (pres. 1983-84), Pacific Dermatology Assn. (fin. com. 1959—). Hebrew.

CHAGALL, DAVID, journalist, author; b. Phila., Nov. 22, 1930; s. Harry and Ida (Coopersmith) C.; m. Juneau Joan Alsin, Nov. 15, 1957. Student, Swarthmore Center Coll., 1948-49; B.A., Pa. State U., 1952; postgrad., Sorbonne, U. Paris, 1953-54. Social caseworker State of Pa., Phila., 1955-57; sci. editor Jour. I.E.E., 1959-61; pub. relations staff A.E.I.-Hotpoint Ltd., London, 1961-62; mktg. research assoc. Chilton Co., Phila., 1962-63; mktg. research project dir. Haug Assos., Inc. (Roper Orgn.), Los Angeles, 1964-74; research cons. Haug Assos., 1976-79; investigative reporter for nat. mags., 1975—; host TV series The Last Hour, 1994—. Author: Diary of a Deaf Mute, 1960, The Century God Slept, 1963, The Spieler for the Holy Spirit, 1972, The New Kingmakers, 1981, The Sunshine Road, 1988, Surviving the Media Jungle, 1996; contbr.: Television Today, 1981, The Media and Morality, 1999; pub.: Inside Campaigning, 1983; contbr. Television Today, 1981, The Media and Morality, 1999, syndicated column, articles, revs., stories and poetry to mags., jours., newspapers; contbg. editor: TV Guide, L.A. Mag. Apptd. to Selective Svc. Bd., 1991; bd. dirs. Chosen Prophetic Ministries, 1991. Recipient U. Wis. Poetry prize, 1971; nominee Nat. Book award in fiction, 1972, Pulitzer prize in letters, 1973, Disting. Health Journalism award, 1978; Presdl. Achievement award, 1982; Carnegie Trust grantee, 1964. Home: PO Box 85 Agoura Hills CA 91376-0085

CHAGANTI, RAJU S., geneticist, educator, researcher; b. Samalkot, Andhra, India, Mar. 12, 1933; came to U.S., 1960; s. Sanyasi Raju and Seetasiromani (Vallury) C.; m. Seeta Ramam Kurada, Aug. 20, 1966; children: Seeta, Sara. BS with honors, Andhra U., 1954, MS, 1955; PhD, Harvard U., 1964. Diplomate Am. Bd. Med. Genetics. Mem. Med. Rsch. Coun. Radiobiology Unit, Harwell, Berks, U.K., 1967-71; rsch. assoc. N.Y. Blood Ctr., N.Y.C., 1971-73; assoc. investigator N.Y. Blood Ctr., 1973-76; asst. prof. Meml. Sloan-Kettering Cancer Ctr., N.Y.C., 1976-83; assoc. prof. Meml. Sloan-Kettering Cancer Ctr., 1983-87, prof., 1987—; William E. Snee chair Meml. Sloan-Kettering Cancer Ctr., N.Y.C., 1995—; profl. assoc. N.Y. Hosp., N.Y.C., 1979—. Editor: Genetics in Clinical Oncology, 1985; contbr. articles to profl. jours. Recipient research awards NIH, Nat. Cancer Inst., 1979—. Fellow AAAS, Am. Coll. Med. Genetics; mem. Am. Soc. Human Genetics, Harvey Soc. Achievements include research in the genetic basis of cancer development. Home: 325 E 79th St Apt 15C New York NY 10021-0900 Office: Meml Sloan-Kettering Cancer Ctr 1275 York Ave New York NY 10021-6007

CHAGNON, LUCILLE TESSIER, literacy and developmental learning specialist; b. Gardner, Mass., June 1, 1936; d. Fred G. Tessier and Alfreda C. (Ross) Noel; m. Richard J. Chagnon, Sept. 16, 1978; children: Daniel, David. BMus, Rivier Coll., Nashau, N.H.; adv. cert. in Human Resource Mgmt. and Cmty. Devel., Inst. Cultural Affairs, Chgo., 1969; MEd, Boston Coll., 1972. Educator N.H., 1960-73; internat. cons. Inst. Cultural Affairs, Chgo., 1973-79; staff tng. dir. CO-MHAR, Inc., Phila., 1979-81; pres., owner Chagnon Assocs., Collingswood, N.J., 1981-86; prin. Sacred Heart Sch., Camden, N.J., 1986-87; founder, dir. Lifeline Literacy Project, 1988-94; literacy and developmental learning specialist Rutgers U., Camden, 1989—; adj. grad. faculty dept. counseling psychology Temple U. Sch. Edn., Phila., 1985-90; sr. project staff Right Assocs., Phila., 1983-93. Author: (with Richard J. Chagnon) The Best is Yet to Be: A Pre-Retirement Program, 1985, Easy Reader, Learner, Writer, 1994, Voice Hidden, Voice Heard: A Reading and Writing Anthology, 1998. Bd. dirs. Camden County Literacy Vols. of Am., 1987-91, Handicapped Advocates for Ind. Living, 1988—; mem. Collingswood Bd. Edn., 1985-89. Mem. Nat. Learning Found. (adv. bd. 1997—), Brain-Based Edn. Network, Inst. Cultural Affairs, Internat. Reading Assn. Home and Office: 1 Courtland Ln Willingboro NJ 08046-3405

CHAHINE, MOUSTAFA TOUFIC, atmospheric scientist; b. Beirut, Lebanon, Jan. 1, 1935; s. Toufic M. and Hind S. (Tabbara) C.; m. Marina Bandak, Dec. 9, 1960; children: Tony T., Steve S. B.S., U. Wash., 1956, M.S., 1957; Ph.D., U. Calif., Berkeley, 1960. With Jet Propulsion Lab., Calif. Inst. Tech., Pasadena, 1960—; mgr. planetary atmospheres sect. Jet Propulsion Lab., Calif. Inst. Tech., 1975-78, sr. research scientist, mgr. earth and space scis. div., 1978-84, chief scientist, 1984—; vis. scientist MIT, 1969-70; vis. prof. Am. U., Beirut, 1971-72; regent's lectr. UCLA, 1989-90; mem. NASA Space and Earth Sci. Adv. Com., 1982-85; mem. climate rsch. com. Nat. Acad. Scis., 1985-88, bd. dirs. atmospheric scis. and climate, 1988—; chmn. sci. steering group Global Energy and Water Cycle Experiment World Meteorol. Orgn., 1988—; cons. U.S. Navy, 1972-76. Contbr. articles on atmospheric scis. to profl. jours. Recipient medal for exceptional sci. achievements NASA, 1969, NASA Outstanding Leadership medal, 1984, William T. Pecora award, 1989, Jule G. Charney award, 1991, Losey Atmospheric Scis. award AIAA, 1993. Fellow AAAS, Am. Geophys. Union, Am. Phys. Soc., Royal Soc., Am. Meteorol. Soc.; mem. Internat. Acad. Astronautics, Sigma Xi. Office: 4800 Oak Grove Dr Pasadena CA 91109-8001

CHAI, WINBERG, political science educator; b. Shanghai, China, Oct. 16, 1932; came to U.S., 1951, naturalized, 1973; s. Ch'u and Mei-en (Tsao) C.; m. Carolyn Everett, Mar. 17, 1966 (dec. 1996); children: Maria May-lee, Jeffrey Tien-yu. Student, Hartwick Coll., 1951-53; BA, Wittenberg U., 1955, DHL, 1997; MA, New Sch. Social Rsch., 1958; PhD, NYU, 1968; DHL, Wittenberg U., 1987. Lectr. New Sch. Social Rsch., 1957-61; vis. asst. prof. Drew U., 1961-62; asst. prof. Fairleigh Dickinson U., 1962-65; asst. prof. U. Redlands, 1965-68, assoc. prof., 1969-73, chmn. dept., 1970-73; prof., chmn. Asian studies CCNY, 1973-79; disting. prof. polit. sci., v.p. acad. affairs, spl. asst. to pres. U. S.D., Vermillion, 1979-82; prof. polit. sci., dir. internat. programs U. Wyo., Laramie, 1988—; chmn. Third World Conf. Found., Inc., Chgo., 1982—; pres. Wang Yu-fa Found., Taiwan, 1989—. Author: (with Ch'u Chai) The Story of Chinese Philosophy, 1961, The Changing Society of China, 1962, rev. edit., 1969, The New Politics of Communist China, 1972, The Search for a New China, 1975; editor: Essential Works of Chinese Communism, 1969, (with James C. Hsiung) Asia in the U.S. Foreign Policy, 1981, (with James C. Hsiung) U.S. Asian Relations: The National Security Paradox, 1983, (with Carolyn Chai) Beyond China's Crisis, 1989, In Search of Peace in the Middle East, 1991, (with Cal Clark) Political Stability and Economic Growth, 1994, China Mainland and Taiwan, 1994, revised edit. 1996, Hong Kong Under China, 1998; co-translator: (with Ch'u Chai) A Treasury of Chinese Literature, 1965. Haynes Found. fellow, 1967, 68; Ford Found. humanities grantee, 1968, 69, Pacific Cultural Found. grantee, 1978, 86, NSF grantee, 1970, Hubert Eaton Meml. Fund grantee, 1972-73, Field Found. grantee, 1973, 75, Henry Luce Found. grantee, 1978, 80, S.D. Humanities Com. grantee, 1980, Pacific Culture Fund grantee, 1987, 90-91. Mem. Am. Assn. Chinese Studies (pres. 1978-80), AAAS, AAUP, Am. Polit. Sci. Assn., N.Y. Acad. Scis., Internat. Studies Assn., NAACP. Democrat. Home: 1071 Granito Dr Laramie WY 82072-5045 Office: PO Box 4098 Laramie WY 82071-4098 *Born in China and educated in the United States, I feel privileged to have experienced two rich cultures. My goals include promoting better understanding of all cultures and peoples.*

CHAIFETZ, DAVID HARVEY, lawyer; b. Worcester, Mass., Nov. 6, 1942; s. Harry and Gertrude (Katz) C.; m. Edith Jakubs; children: Rosalyn, Pamela, Matthew. BS in Bus. Adminstrn., Clark U., 1965; JD, Boston Coll., 1968. Bar: Mich. 1968, U.S. Dist. Ct. (ea. dist.) Mich. 1968, U.S. Supreme Ct., 1995. Staff atty. Chrysler Corp., Highland Park, Mich., 1968-75; div. atty. Union Carbide Corp., N.Y.C., 1975-77, sr. div. atty., 1978-81; group counsel Union Carbide Corp., Danbury, Conn., 1981-85, asst. gen. counsel, 1985-92; gen. counsel Union Carbide Indsl. Gases Inc., Danbury, 1988-92; v.p., gen. counsel, sec. Praxair, Inc., Danbury, 1992—; bd. dirs. Conn. Legal Svcs., Middlebury, 1991-92, 97—, Conn. Yankee Coun., Boy Scouts of Am., 1994—. Mem. ABA (co-chair corp. counsel com. of internat. law sect. 1989-91), Conn. Bar Assn. (exec. com. corp. counsel sect. 1989—, com. to provide opportunities for minorities 1989—), Corporate Bar Assn. (chmn. pro bono com. 1990-93), Westchester-Fairfield Corp. Counsel Assn. (pres. 1988-89, bd. dirs. 1984-90), C. of C. (antitrust adv. coun. 1985—). Avocations: golf, travel. Office: Praxair Inc # MI-535 39 Old Ridgebury Rd Danbury CT 06810-5108

CHAIKEN, BERNARD HENRY, internist, gastroenterologist; b. Bklyn., Oct. 14, 1927; s. Max and Esther (Golland) C.; m. Mildred Gilbert, Dec. 5, 1950; children: Barry Glenn, Caryl Joy Gordon. Student, NYU, 1944-45; MD, U. Tex., Dallas, 1949. Diplomate Am. Bd. Internal Medicine, subspecialty Bd. Gastroenterology. Intern Boston City Hosp., 1949-50; resident physician Cushing VA Hosp., Framingham, Mass., 1950-51, Phila. VA Hosp., 1953-54; staff physician VA Hosp. Dallas, 1954-55, VA Hosp., East Orange, N.J., 1955-56; attending physician Overlook Hosp., Summit, N.J., 1956—, St. Barnabas Med. Ctr., Livingston, N.J., 1956—; vis. fellow Hosp. of U. Pa., Phila., 1954; clin. instr. Southwestern Med. Sch., U. Tex., Dallas, 1954-55; clin. asst. prof. medicine Seton Hall Coll. Medicine, Jersey City, 1956-58. Contbr. articles to med. jours. Capt. U.S. Army M.C., 1951-53. Fellow ACP, Am. Coll. Gastroenterology (Best Clin. Vignette Paper and Poster Presentation 1995); mem. Am. Soc. Internal Medicine, Am. Gastroenterol. Assn., Med. Soc. N.J., N.J. Gastroenterol. Soc. (pres. 1964-65). Avocation: collecting early American folk art. Home: 12 Taylor Rd Short Hills NJ 07078-2226 Office: 58 Chatham Rd Short Hills NJ 07078-2321

CHAIKIN, A. SCOTT, public relations executive. BA, Oberlin Coll. Group pres. Dix & Eaton, Cleveland, 1986; also bd. dirs.; pres., CEO Dix & Eaton, Cleve., 1994—. Mem. Pub. Rels. Soc. Am., Nat. Investor Rels. Inst., Cleveland Works, Great Lks. Theater Festival. *

CHAIKIN, ALYCE, artist; b. N.Y.C., Apr. 14, 1923; d. Morris and Sara (Kunin) C.; m. Harold Louis Kleinman, Sept. 10, 1944 (dec. Dec. 1986); children: George Michael, Thomas John. Cert., Parsons Sch. Design, N.Y.C., 1943; student, Bennington Coll., 1941, Fairfield U., 1962. Cartoonist Famous Studios subs. Paramount, N.Y.C., 1943-44; freelance illustrator various dept. stores, Bridgeport, Conn., 1948-52; freelance artist, 1952—; represented by Capricorn Galleries, Bethesda, Md., 1979—, Silvermine Galleries, New Canaan, Conn., 1979—; cons. interior decorator Fairfield (Conn.) U., 1963-64. Group shows include Invitational Conn. Gallery, Marlborough, 1990, Invitational Munson Gallery, New Haven, 1989, Hon. Artist Conn. Commn. on Arts, Hartford, 1988, Invitational Drawing Show, Huntsville (Ala.) Mus., 1987, Philip Desind Collection of Contemporary Realism, Butler Inst. of Am. Art, Youngstown, Ohio, 1987; represented in permanent collections Town of Fairfield, New Haven Paint and Clay, U. Conn. Health Ctr., Meml. Sloan-Kettering Cancer Ctr.; executed murals Park Ave., Temple, Bridgeport, 1958-59. 1st pres. Park City Hosp. Aux., Bridgeport, 1952-53. Recipient numerous awards for drawings including three best-in-show awards. Mem. Silvermine Guild Artists, New Haven Paint and Clay Club, Inc. Avocations: piano, knitting. Home and Studio: 8417 Olde Troon Dr Charlotte NC 28277-6521

CHAIKOF, ELLIOT LORNE, vascular surgeon; b. Toronto, Ont., Can., Apr. 9, 1957; s. Leo and Bayla (Appel) C.; m. Melissa Kershman, Aug. 7, 1983; children: Rachel, Adam. BA, Johns Hopkins U., 1979, MD, 1982; PhD, MIT, 1989. Diplomate Am. Bd. Surgery. Intern Mass. Gen. Hosp./Harvard Med. Sch., Boston, 1982-83, resident in gen. surgery, 1983-85, 89-91; asst. prof. Emory U. Sch. Medicine, Atlanta, 1992-98, fellow in vascular surgery, 1991-92, assoc. prof. surgery, 1998—; adj. prof. chem. engring. Ga. Inst. Tech. Contbr. to profl. publs. Mem. Am. Inst. Chem. Engrs., Am. Chem. Soc., Materials Rsch. Soc., Soc. Biomaterials, Phi Beta Kappa, Sigma Xi, Alpha Omega Alpha. Achievements include patent on antithrombogenic devices containing polysiloxanes. *

CHAIM, ROBERT ALEX, dean, educator; b. Stockton, Calif., Oct. 25, 1947; s. Alex Jr. and Carmen Lorraine (Rodriques-Lopez) C.; m. Diane Leonora Gregonis, May 30, 1971 (dec. 1973); m. Linda Jean Riley, Dec. 22, 1976. AA, San Joaquin Delta Coll., 1967; BA, Sacramento State Coll., 1970; cert. in secondary teaching, U. Pacific, 1972, ArtsD, 1980. Instr. English lang. U. Pacific, Stockton, 1973-77; lectr. lang. of law U. Pacific, Sacramento, 1977-95; asst. to dean McGeorge Sch. Law, Sacramento, 1977-81, asst. dean students, 1981-95; dean students Roger Williams U. Sch. Law, Bristol, R.I., 1995-98; cons. grammar, usage and linguistics numerous law orgns. and pvt. law firms, Calif. and R.I., 1978—; mem. curriculum com. law sch. U. San Fernando, Calif., 1979; mem. ABA/Assn. Am. Law Schs./Law Sch. Admission Coun. Joint Task Force on Fin. Aid, 1991-93. Editor-in-chief Stauffer Legal Rsch. Series, 1978-95; contbr. articles to scholarly books and profl. jours. Mem. Elk Grove (Calif.) Community Planning Adv. Couns., 1986-88, vice-chmn., 1987; mem. scholarship com. Centro Legal de Calif., Sacramento, 1987-90, curriculum adv. com. Elk Grove Unified Sch. Dist., 1988, scholarship com. Sacramento Country Day Sch., 1988; lectr., campus coord. Oak Park Sports and Edn. Found., Inc., 1989-95; bd. advisors St. Hope Acad. Youth Orgn., 1991-98. Recipient Meritorious Svc. award Asian-Am. Law Students Assn., Sacramento, 1986, 87, Outstanding Svc. award La Raza Law Students Assn., 1988. Mem. ABA (assoc., legal edn. and bar admissions sect.), Nat. Assn. Fgn. Student Affairs, Assn. Am. Law Schs. (mem. legal rsch. and writing sect., student svcs. sect., student svc. com. 1990-91, law admission coun. joint task force on fin. aid 1991-94), Lions Club (judge 53rd ann. multiple dist. four, final spkr. contest, 1990). Avocations: golf, cabinetry, gardening.

CHAIN, BOBBY LEE, electrical contractor, former mayor; b. Hattiesburg, Miss., Sept. 19, 1929; s. Zollie Lee and Grace (Sellers) C.; ; m. Betty Sue Green, June 30, 1967; children: Robin Ann, Laura Grace, Bobby Lee, John Webster. BS, U. So. Miss., Hattiesburg, 1974; DBA (hon.), William Carey Coll., Hattiesburg, 1983. Chief electrician Miss. Power & Light Co., Natchez, 1950-53; asst. to gen. supt. atomic energy plant Allegany Electric Co., Oak Ridge, 1954-55; owner, chmn. bd. Chain Electric Co., Hattiesburg, 1955, Chain Lighting & Appliance Co., Hattiesburg, 1960; owner, pres. Chainco, Inc., oil properties, Hattiesburg, 1974—; bd. dirs. Deposit Guaranty Nat. Bank, Jackson; adv. dir. Deposit Guaranty Nat. Bank, Hattiesburg; mem. Interstate Oil Compact Commn., 1972—; mem. nat. adv. coun. SBA, 1966-67; bd. dirs. Miss. Econ. Coun., 1991-93; mayor city of Hattiesburg, 1980-85. Past mem., past pres. Miss. Trustees Instns. Higher Learning; past mem. So. Regional Edn. Bd., Mississippians for Quality Edn.; past chmn. Commn. on Efficiency in Govt., Miss. Econ. Coun.; mem. Miss. State Workforce Devel. Coun.; chmn. Pearl River County Dist. Workforce Coun.; past bd. dirs. Pub. Edn. Forum of Miss.; mem. commissioning com. USS John C. Stennis CVN-74 Aircraft Carrier, 1995. With U.S. Army, 1950-51, Korea. Recipient Disting. Svc. award U. So. Miss., 1976, Hub award, 1979, Continuous Outstanding Svc. award, 1980, Liberty Bell award Forrest County Bar Assn., 1980, Svc. to Edn. award Phi Delta Kappa, 1980, Disting. Citizen award Pine Burr Area Coun. Boy Scouts Am., 1995; named to Hall U. So. Miss., Miss. Bus. Hall of Fame, 1994; Bobby L. Chain Tech. Ctr. named in his honor; Bobby L. Chain Hattiesburg Mcpl. Airport named in his honor; Paul Harris fellow Rotary Internat., 1990. Mem. Newcomen Soc. N.Am., U. So. Miss. Alumni Assn. (Outstanding Svc. award 1972, Sales and Mktg. Man of Yr. award 1981), Hattiesburg C. of C. (past dir.), Miss. Bus. Roundtable, Kiwanis, Hattiesburg Country Club (past pres.), U. So. Miss. Century Club, Shriners, Univ. Club, Plimsoll Club (New Orleans), Omicron Delta Kappa, Beta Gamma Sigma. Baptist. Home: 312 6th Ave Hattiesburg MS 39401-4294 Office: PO Box 2058 Hattiesburg MS 39403-2058

CHAIT, ANDREA MELINDA, special education educator; b. Buffalo, May 7, 1970; d. Marvin and Rochelle (Benatovich) C. BS in Health Edn., Ithaca (N.Y.) Coll., 1992; MEd in Spl. Edn., U. Fla., 1995, postgrad. in psychology, 1997—. Cert. tchr. health edn., N.Y.; cert. N.Y. State Mandatory Child Abuse and Neglect Tng. Program K-12; cert. tchr. spl. edn., Ga. Substitute tchr. Cortland (N.Y.) H.S., 1992; tchrs. aid, substitute Stanley G. Falk, Cheektowaga, N.Y., 1993; pvt. spl. edn. tutor Buffalo and Gainesville, 1992—; behavioral disorders tchr. Paul D. West Middle Sch., East Point, Ga., 1995-96; chair discipline com. spl. edn. dept. Paul P. West Middle Sch., East Point, Ga., 1995—. Vol. Task Force for Battered Women, Ithaca, 1991, nursing homes, Ithaca, 1991-92, Human Rights Orgn., Gainesville, 1993-94. Mem. ASCD, Coun. for Exceptional Children, Coun. for Children with Behavioral Disorders, Pi Lambda Theta, Kappa Delta Pi, Phi Kappa Phi. Jewish. Avocations: poetry, reading, drawing, painting, soccer. Home: 823 SW 56th Ter Gainesville FL 32607-3850

CHAIT, ARNOLD, radiologist; b. N.Y.C., Jan. 20, 1930; s. Irving and Tillie (Newman) C.; m. Joan Lois Oppenheim, Mar. 14, 1965; children: Andrea, Elizabeth, Caroline. BA, NYU, 1951; MD, U. Utrecht, Netherlands, 1957; MA (hon.), U. Pa., 1971. Diplomate: Am. Bd. Radiology. Intern Kings County Hosp., Bklyn., 1958; resident in pathology Manhattan Vets. Hosp., N.Y.C., 1959; radiology Kings County Hosp., 1959-62; instr. radiology SUNY, Bklyn., 1962-64, asst. prof. radiology, 1964-67, assoc. prof., 1967; asst. prof. radiology U. Pa., Phila., 1967-70, assoc. prof., 1970-74, prof., 1974-76; clin. prof. U. Pa., 1976—; chief vascular radiology Hosp. U. Pa., 1969-76, dir. dept. radiology Grad. Hosp., 1976—, pres. med. staff, 1981-83; prof. radiology Allegheny U. of the Health Scis., 1997—; cons. radiology Bklyn. VA Hosp., 1962-67, Phila. VA Hosp., 1969-76, Phila. Naval Hosp., 1975-76. Contbr. articles to profl. jours. Fellow Coll. Physicians Phila., Am. Coll. Radiology; mem. Pa., Phila County med. socs., Am., Roentgen Ray Soc., Phila. Roentgen Ray Soc. (pres. 1983-84), Radiol. Soc. N. Am., N.Y. Roentgen Soc., AAAS, Assn. U. Radiologists, Soc. Cardiovascular Radiology Am. Heart Assn. (council on cardiovascular radiology), Soc. Uroradiology, Soc. Cardiovascular and Interventional Radiology. Home: 835 Chauncey Rd Narberth PA 19072-1303 Office: Grad Hosp Radiology Dept One Graduate Plz Philadelphia PA 19146

CHAIT, JON FREDERICK, corporate executive, lawyer; b. Bakersfield, Calif., Aug. 9, 1950; s. Michael and Irene (Goddard) C.; m. Mary Lardner, Feb. 13, 1988; children: Jamie E., Meredith L. BA magna cum laude, UCLA, 1972, JD, 1975. Bar: Wis. 1975. Assoc. Foley & Lardner, Milw., 1975-79; assoc. Godfrey & Kahn, S.C., Milw., 1979-82, ptnr., 1982-89; exec. v.p., CFO Manpower Inc., Milw., 1989-98, also bd. dirs.; bd. dirs. Marshall & Ilsley Corp., Milw., M&I Data Svcs., Milw., Krueger Internat., Inc., Green Bay, Wis. Mem. ABA, Am. Soc. Corp. Secs., Univ. Club, Milw. Country Club, Milw. City Club, Phi Beta Kappa. Office: 5464 N Port Washington Rd Glendale WI 53217

CHAIT, MAXWELL MANI, physician; b. Linz, Austria, Nov. 7, 1947; came to the U.S., 1953; s. Morris and Eva (Lederman) C.; m. Lynne Robin Milstein C.; children: Alanna Rose, Daniel Lawrence, Michael Paul. BA magna cum laude, U. Utah, Salt Lake City, 1969; BS cum laude, U. Calif., San Francisco, 1969, MD, 1972. Diplomate Am. Bd. Internal Medicine, 1975, Am. Bd. Gastroenterology, 1977; lic. N.Y., Utah. Intern st. medicine U. So. Calif. Med. Ctr., L.A. County, 1972-73; resident in medicine Cornell Coop. Hosps., North Shore U. Hosp., Manhasset, N.Y., 1973-75; fellow GI Cornell Coop. Hosps., Meml. Sloan-Kettering Cancer Ctr., N.Y.C., 1975-77; attending physician White Plains (N.Y.) Hosp., 1977—; asst. attending physician St. Agnes Hosp., White Plains, 1977—, Columbia Presbyn. Med. Ctr., N.Y., 1993—; asst. clin. prof. medicine Coll. Physicians & Surgeons of Columbia U., 1993—; bd. dirs. Bd. Jewish Edn. Greater N.Y.; lectr. in field. Pres. Westchester Assn. of Hebrew Schs., 1992-94; former mem. bd. trustees Temple Israel of White Plains; coach baseball, softball, basketball Scarsdale Recreation Dept. Fellow Am. Coll. Gastroenterology, Am. Coll. Physicians; mem. Am. Gastroenterological Assn., Am. Soc. Gastrointestinal Study, N.Y. Acad. Gastroenterology, N.Y. Soc. Gastrointestinal Endoscopy, Westchester Acad. Medicine, Crohn and Colitis Found. of Am. (CMAC com.). Office: Hartsdale Med Group 180 E Hartsdale Ave Hartsdale NY 10530-3544

CHAIT, WILLIAM, librarian, consultant; b. N.Y.C., Dec. 5, 1915; s. Max and Mollie (Miller) C.; m. Beatrice L. Faigelman, June 13, 1937; 1 son, Edward Martin. B.A., Bklyn. Coll., 1934; B.L.S., Pratt Inst., 1935; M.S. in L.S, Columbia U., 1938. Library asst., br. librarian Bklyn. Pub. Library, 1935-45; service command librarian 2d Service Command AUS, 1945-46; chief in- service tng., personnel control Milw. Pub. Library, 1946-48; dir. Kalamazoo Pub. Library, 1948-56; dir. Dayton and Montgomery County Pub. Library, 1956-78, dir. emeritus, 1979—; mem. Library Cons., Inc. Pres. Kalamazoo Council Social Agys., 1954-55, Dayton City Beautiful Com., 1968-69; treas. Montgomery County Hist. Soc., 1968-69; trustee On-Line Computer Library Center, 1974-85, treas., 1976-79. Fulbright lectr. library sci. U. Tehran, 1969-70. Mem. Pub. Library Assn. (pres. 1964-65), ALA (treas. 1976-80, council 1981-85, chmn. personnel adminstrn. sect. 1958-60), Mich. Library Assn. (pres. 1955-56), Ohio Library Assn. (pres. 1964-65), S.C. Library Assn. Home: 38 Deer Run Ln Hilton Head Island SC 29928-4136 Office: 215 E 3rd St Dayton OH 45402-2103

CHAITMAN, HELEN DAVIS, lawyer; b. N.Y.C., July 5, 1941; d. Philip and Miriam (Pfeffer) D.; m. Edmund Chaitman, Feb. 29, 1964 (div. 1978); children: Jennifer, Alison; m. George B. Gelman, Oct. 21, 1979. AB cum laude, Bryn Mawr Coll., 1963; JD, Rutgers U., 1976. Bar: N.Y. 1976, N.J., U.S. Dist. Ct. N.Y., U.S. Dist. Ct. N.J., U.S. Ct. Appeals (3d cir.), U.S. Supreme Ct. Assoc. Paul, Weiss, Rifkind, Wharton & Garrison, N.Y.C., 1977-82; ptnr. Wilentz, Goldman & Spitzer, Woodbridge, N.J., 1983-87, Ross & Hardies, Somerset, N.J., 1987-99, Wolf Haldenstein Adler Freeman & Herz LLP, N.Y.C., 1999—. Author: The Law of Lender Liability, 1990; contbg. author: Commercial Damages, 1985; editor Emerging Theories of Lender Liability, 1985-87. Mem. ABA (chmn. comml. fin. svcs. com. 1994-97, sect. bus. law), Am. Law Inst. (sustaining mem. 1992-99), Pub. Law Inst. Home: The Farm 115 Fairview Rd Frenchtown NJ 08825-3013 Office: Wolf Haldenstein Adler Freeman & Herz LLP 270 Madison Ave New York NY 10016 also: Wolf Haldenstein Adler Freeman & Herz LLP 580 Howard Ave Somerset NJ 08873-1136

CHAITOVITZ, SAMUEL, judge. BA, Amherst Coll., 1956; JD, Harvard U., 1959. Chief adminstrv. law judge Fed. Labor Rels. Authority, Washington, 1994—. Office: Fed Labor Rels Authority Ste 440 607 14th St NW Washington DC 20424-0001

CHAJET, CLIVE, communications consultant; b. London, Feb. 27, 1937; came to U.S., 1950, naturalized, 1964; s. Henry W. and Anne (Kravis) C.; m. Bonnie Sue Loeb, Mar. 20, 1966; children: Lisa Ellen, Lori Menschell. BA, Columbia U., 1959. Acct. exec. Fuller, Smith & Ross, N.Y.C., 1960-63; designer Milprint, N.Y.C., 1963-65; exec. Gould Assocs., N.Y.C., 1965-72; founder Chajet Design Group, N.Y.C., 1972-83; chmn. Lippincott & Margulies, Inc., N.Y.C., 1983-96; chmn. Chajet Consultancy, 1997—; bd. dirs. Triarc Corp., 1994. Trustee Town Sch., N.Y.C., 1980-83; bd. dirs. 92nd St. YMHA, 1997—, Am. Jewish Congress. Mem. Package Designers Coun. (pres. 1980-82), University Club. Jewish. Author: Image by Design, 1991: From Corporate Vision to Corporate Reality, 1991, 2nd edit., 1997. Home: 1035 Fifth Ave New York NY 10028-0135 Office: Chajet Consultancy LLC 575 Madison Ave Fl 10 New York NY 10022-2511

CHAKRABARTI, SUBRATA KUMAR, marine research engineer; b. Calcutta, India, Feb. 3, 1941; came to U.S., 1964, naturalized, 1981; s. Asutosh and Shefali C.; m. Prakriti Bhaduri, July 23, 1967; children: Sumita, Prabal. BSME, Jadavpur U., Calcutta, India, 1963; MSME, U. Colo., 1965, PhDME, 1968. Registered profl. engr., Ill. Asst. engr. Kuljian Corp., Calcutta, 1963-64, Simon Carves Ltd., Calcutta, 1964; instr. engring. U. Colo., Boulder, 1965-66; hydrodynamicist CB&I Tech. Svcs. Co. (formerly Chgo. Bridge and Iron Co.), Plainfield, Ill., 1968-70, head analytical group, 1970-79, dir. marine rsch., 1979-95, dir. structural devel., 1995-96; pres. Offshore Structure Analysis, Inc., Plainfield, 1996—; vis. prof. U.S. Naval Acad., Annapolis, Md., 1986, 88, Indian Inst. Tech., Madras, 1996; presenter seminars in field. Author: Hydrodynamics of Offshore Structures, 1987, Nonlinear Methods in Offshore Engineering, 1990, Offshore Structure Modeling, 1994; editor: Fluid Structure Interaction in Offshore Engineering, 1994; tech. editor Applied Ocean Rsch., 1998—; mem. editl. bd. Applied Ocean Rsch., Marine Structures, Topics in Engring., Advances in Fluid Mechanics series; assoc. editor Energy Resources Tech.; contbr. numerous articles to profl. publs. and chpts. to books; patentee in field. Recipient Jadavpur U. Gold medal, 1963; U. Colo. fellow, 1968; named Outstanding New Citizen, 1981-82. Fellow ASCE (publ. com. waterway divsn., James R. Cross Gold medal 1974, Freeman scholar 1979), ASME (exec. com., editor jour. offshore mechanics and arctic engring. divsn. 1986-96, chmn. divsn., 1987-88; mem. awards com. 1983-96, tech. session devloper, chmn. 1983—, chmn. tech. program com. 1988-89, Ralph James award 1984, co-editor proc. internat. symposium, Offshore Mechanics and Arctic Engring. achievement award 1990, Ten Paper award 1991), AAAS; mem. NAS (design group, marine structures group 1989-91, chmn. 1992-95), Sigma Xi. Home: 191 N Weller Dr Plainfield IL 60544-8981 Office: Offshore Structure Analysis Inc 191 Weller Dr Plainfield IL 60544-8981

CHAKRABARTY, ANANDA MOHAN, microbiologist; b. Sainthia, India, Apr. 4, 1938; s. Satya Dos and Sasthi Bala (Mukherjee) C.; m. Krishna Chakraverty, May 26, 1965; children: Kaberi, Asit. BSc, St. Xavier's Coll., 1958; MSc, U. Calcutta, 1960, PhD, 1965. Sr. research officer U. Calcutta, 1964-65; research asso. in biochemistry U. Ill., Urbana, 1965-71; mem. staff Gen. Electric Research and Devel. Center, Schenectady, 1971-79; prof. dept. microbiology U. Ill. Med. Center, 1979-89; disting. prof., 1989—. Editor: Genetic Engineering, 1977, Biodegradation and Detoxification of Environmental Pollutants, 1982. Named Scientist of Yr. Indsl. Rsch. Mag., 1975, Univ. scholar U. Ill., 1989; recipient Inventor of Yr. award Patent Lawyers' Assn., 1982, Pub. Affairs award Am. Chem. Soc., 1984, Disting. Scientist award EPA, 1985, Merit award NIH, 1986, Pasteur award, 1991, Disting. Svc. award U.S. Army, 1993, Proctor & Gamble award, 1995. Mem. Am. Soc. Microbiology, Soc. Indsl. Microbiology, Am. Soc. Biol. Chemists. Home: 206 E Julia Dr Villa Park IL 60181-3340 Office: U Ill Med Ctr Dept Microbiology M/C 790 835 S Wolcott Ave Chicago IL 60612-7340

CHAKRAVARTHY, BALAJI SRINIVASAN, strategic management educator, consultant; b. Madras, Tamil-Nadu, India, July 16, 1947; came to U.S., 1974; s. V.S. and Sushila (Gopalachari) Vijayaraghavan; m. Kiran Karandikar, Sept. 3, 1976. B in Tech., Indian Inst. Tech., Madras, 1968; MBA, Indian Inst. Mgmt., Ahmedabad, India, 1970; D in Bus. Adminstrn., Harvard U., 1978. Asst. mgr. MIS Binny Ltd., Madras, 1970-71; exec. asst. to mng. dir. Telco, Poona, India, 1971-73, asst. mgr. cen. planning, 1973-75; asst. prof. Tulane U., New Orleans, 1978-81; assoc. prof. Wharton Sch. U. Pa., Phila., 1981-86; assoc. prof. Carlson Sch. U. Minn., Mpls., 1986-92, 94—, prof., 1991—, Spencer Chair prof., 1994—; dir. Strategic Mgmt. Rsch. Ctr., 95—; prof. Insead, Fountainebleau, 1992-94; cons. in field, Mpls. Author: Decision Making for Managers, 1974, Managing Coal, 1982, Managing the Strategy Process, 1991; assoc. editor Mgmt. Sci., 1990-92; mem. edit. bd. Strategic Mgmt. Jour., 1990—. Recipient Best Paper award The Planning Forum, 1984. Mem. Strategic Mgmt. Soc. (founder), Acad. Mgmt., Inst. for Mgmt. Sci. Avocations: jogging, squash, tennis, golfing. Office: U Minn 3-426 Carlson Sch Mgmt Minneapolis MN 55455

CHAKRAVORTY, RANES CHANDRA, surgeon, educator; b. Calcutta, India, Jan. 9, 1929; came to U.S., 1952; s. Pares Chandra and Sivani (Mazumdar) C.; m. Chitra Adhikari, Nov. 10, 1955; children: Aryaa, Agnis. MB, BS, U. Calcutta, 1949; MEd, Va. Poly. Inst. & State U., 1992. Cert. Royal Coll. Surgeons. Internship and residency U. Calcutta, 1949-52; resident Mt. Sinai Hosp., Chgo., 1952-53; from asst. resident to chief resident and fellow Meml. Sloan Kettering Cancer Ctr., N.Y.C., 1953-59; registrar Hammersmith Hosp., U. London, 1955; stagiaire Jules Bordet Cancer Ctr, Brussels, 1959, Gustave Roussy Cancer Ctr., Seine, France; asst. prof. surgery Inst. Postgrad. Med. Edn. and Rsch., Calcutta, 1960-62, prof., 1970-71; surgeon Chittaranjan Cancer Hosp., Calcutta, 1962-70; head dept. oncology RKM Sevapratishthan, Calcutta, 1961-70; asst. prof. Med. Coll. Va., Richmond, 1971-74; assoc. prof. U Va. Med. Sch., Charlottesville, 1974-80, prof., 1980—; chief surgery VA Med. Ctr., Salem, Va., 1974-94; dir. Health Care Ctr., Trinity Luth. Ch., Roanoke, Va., 1982-84; Squibb-Olin observer Meml. Sloan-Kettering Cancer Ctr., N.Y.C., 1966. Author, editor: Core Concepts in Cancer, 1983; editor Scalpel and Tongs, Am. Journal of Medical Philately, 1973—; mem. editl. bd. Vets. Health Systems Jour., 1997—, Jour. Indian Med. Assn., 1997—; also chpts. to books. Recipient Vth Subbarow Oration award Andhra State Med. Assn., 1968, Subodh Mitra medal 1st All India Chemotherapy Congress, 1980, GIECO Pub. Svc. cert., 1991, Calvert medal, 1995, A.K. Sen medal, 1995, J.B. Chatterjea medal, 1995. Fellow ACS (liaison fellow commn. on cancer 1974-94), Royal Coll. Surgeons (Eng.); mem. Soc. Surg. Oncology Soc. Head and Neck Surgeon, Am. Assn. for Cancer Edn., Brit. Assn. Surg. Oncology, Am. Assn. History of Medicine, Internat. Soc. History of Medicine, French Soc. for History of Medicine (fgn.), Va. Philatelic Fedn. (sec. 1981-82, pres. 1984-85, 92-93), Am. Topical Assn. (disting. topical philatelist 1992), AAPI (trustee 1990—), Univ. Calcutta Med. Alumni Assn. (pres. 1990-91), Am. Assn. Physician India, Rotary (chmn. internat. svcs. 1984-86). Democrat. Vedantist. Avocations: medical philately, astronomy, photography, computers, travel. Home: 5049 Cherokee Hills Dr Salem VA 24153-5848 Office: VA Med Ctr Salem VA 24153

CHALEFF, CARL THOMAS, brokerage house executive; b. Inpls., Nov. 21, 1945; s. Boris Carl and Betty J. (Miller) C.; m. Carolyn F. Heath, Apr. 26, 1970 (div. Apr. 1985); children: Fritz. Eric; m. Darlene Finkel, Dec. 13, 1987. BS in Econs., Purdue U., 1969; MBA in Fin., Xavier U., 1976. Asst. v.p. Am. Can Corp., N.Y.C., 1969-70; sales mgr. Am. Can Corp., Cin., 1970-73; account exec. Merrill Lynch, Cin., 1973-76; v.p. Oppenheimer, Chgo., 1976-81; assoc. dir. Bear Stearns & Co., Chgo., 1981-88; ptnr., mng. dir. CIBC Oppenheimer, 1988—. Pres. bd. dirs. Nat. Kidney Found.; exec. coun. U. Chgo. Childrens Hosp., Boy Scouts Am., 1992-94; bd. dirs. AIDS Care, Adler Planetarium & Mus., Chgo. Mem. Chgo. Bond Club, Am. Arbitration Assn., Nat. Bd. Arbitrators, East Bank Club, Rainbows (bd. dirs. 1984-96), Met. Club, Chgo. Mercantile Exch. Club, Chgo. Yacht Club, Ctr. for Excellence in Edn. (bd. dirs. 1990-92), Chgo. Filmmakers (bd. dirs. 1986-98). Avocations: sailing, skiing, tennis. Home: 55 W Goethe St Chicago IL 60610-7406

CHALK, EARL MILTON, retired art director; b. Deerlodge, Mont., Sept. 14, 1927; s. Forrest A. and Jeanette Curtis (Robinson) C.; m. Carole Estelle, Feb. 9, 1963 (div. 1974); children: Teri, Kevin, Quinn. BFA, U. Wash., 1953. Artist Facilities Boeing, Seattle, 1954-57; writer, artist Facilities Boeing, Renton, Wash., 1957-60; supr. mfg. Facilities Boeing, Seattle, 1960-65; sr. supr. planning Facilities Boeing, Auburn, Wash., 1965-71, art dir. mfg. engring., 1971-87; painter in oils, 1987—; co-mgr., owner Art Galary, 1967-74. Artist Puget Sound Group of North West Painters, Seattle, 1968-78, artist Puyallup, Wash., 1987—. 1st class petty officer USN, 1945-49. Recipient Rotary scholarship U. Wash., 1953. Mem. Grapha Techna. Avocations: bicycling, hiking, fishing, gardening, computers. Home and Office: 1803 7th Ave SE Puyallup WA 98372-4010

CHALK, JOHN ALLEN, SR., lawyer; b. Lexington, Tenn., Jan. 16, 1937. A.A., Freed-Hardeman Coll., 1956; B.S., Tenn. Tech. U., 1962, M.A., 1967; J.D., U. Tex., 1973. Bar: Tex. 1973, D.C. 1977; ordained to ministry Ch. of Christ, 1956. Pastor chs. Dayton, Ohio, 1956-60, Cookeville, Tenn., 1960-66, Abilene, Tex., 1966-71; assoc. Rhodes and Seamster, Abilene, 1973-74, Rhodes and Doscher, Abilene, 1974; ptnr. Rhodes, Doscher, Chalk and Heatherly,, Abilene, 1975-78; gen. counsel La Jet, Inc., Abilene, 1978-84, also v.p., sec; exec. v.p. Dabney Corp., 1984-86; pres. Dabney Capital, 1984-86; assoc. Gandy, Michener, Swindle, Whitaker & Pratt, Ft. Worth, 1986, ptnr., 1987-93; ptnr. Michener Larimore Swindle Whitaker Flowers Sawyer Reynolds & Chalk, Ft. Worth, 1993—; pres. Equity, Inc., 1982-90; bd. dirs. Osteo. Health Sys. Tex., Inc.; mem. strategic alliances com. for edn. Nat. Ct. Reporters Assn., 1994-95; cert. advanced mediator Dispute Resolution Svcs. Tarrant County, Tex.; Tex. court-approved mediator; mem. Panel of Neutrals, Am. Arbitration Assn.; contract mediator EEOC, Dallas, 1999—. Author: The Praying Christ, 1964, Three American Revolutions, 1970, Jesus' Church, 1970, The Christian Family, 1973, Great Biblical Doctrines, 1973, The Devil, You Say!, 1974; author numerous articles on U.S. Dept. Edn. postsecondary regulations, also articles on religion; presenter in field. Trustee Abilene Regional Mental Health Retardation Ctr., 1978-80, Christian Scholarship Found., Inc., Atlanta, 1980—, chmn. bd., 1992-93; chmn. Ailene Bicentennial Com., 1975-76; mem. nat. adv. coun. Am. United for Separation of Ch. and State, 1979-82, pres. bd. trustees, 1981-82; mem. nat. devel. coun. Abilene Christian U.; featured spkr. radio and TV programs Herald of Truth, 1966-69; trustee Osteo. Health Care Found., Inc., Ft. Worth, 1987-96, sec.-treas., 1990-91, sr. v.p., pres.-elect, 1991-92, pres., 1992-93; mem. Strategy for 2000, City of Ft. Worth, 1995—. Fellow Coll. of State Bar Tex., Tex. Bar Found. (life); mem. ABA (acting assoc. editor, mem. editl. bd. Family Adv. 1977-78), FBA, Am. Health Lawyers Assn., Am. Arbitration Assn. (panel arbitrators and mediators), Internat. Ctrs. for Arbitration (panel arbitrators and mediators), Tarrant County Assn. Mediators, Tex. Ct.-Approved Mediators, State Bar Tex., Ft. Worth Bar Assn. Home: 3601 Verde Vista Ct W Aledo TX 76008-3679 Office: Michener Larimore Swindle Whitaker 3500 City Ctr II Fort Worth TX 76102-4140

CHALKLEY, JACQUELINE ANN, retail company executive; b. Benson, Minn., Jan. 3, 1946; d. Vincent Otto and Dorothy Mildred (Alsaker) Kaehler; m. C. Wayne Callaway. BA in Art History cum laude, Brown U., 1967; MA, Columbia U., 1968; postgrad. in Contemporary Art, New Sch. for Social Rsch., N.Y.C., 1968-70; postgrad. in Ceramics, U. Md., 1970-72. Art tchr. Summit (N.J.) High Sch., 1968-70, Rockville (Md.) High Sch., 1970-74; adj. prof. ceramics Montgomery Coll., Rockville, 1974-78; owner Jackie Chalkley at Foxhall Square, Washington, 1978-99, Jackie Chalkley at Willard Collection, Washington, 1986-99, Jackie Chalkley at Chevy Chase Plz., Washington, 1989-99; juror Rhinebeck Craft Fair, 1981, New Eng. Buyers Market, Boston, 1982, Craft Art '82, Richmond, Va. Craft Show, 1983, Smithsonian Crafts Exhbn. '83, Smithsonian Instn. Women's Com. Craft Show, 1984, Annie Albers fashion show at Renwick Gallery, 1984, Morristown Craft Fair, 1984, Washington Craft Show, 1986, Potomac Craftsmen's Guild Show, 1987, Harrisburg Arts Festival, 1987, Ceramic Guild Washington, 1987, Washington Guild Goldsmiths, 1987, 18th Bienniel Exhbn. Creative Crafts Coun., 1988, others; appointee screening com. Piedmont Craftsman's Guild, Winston-Salem, N.C., 1983-86, D.C. Commn. Arts, 1983-85; mem. hon. com. Brandeis Art Exhbn., 1984; mem. hon. com. various exhbns. and fundraisers Textile Mus., 1984-86. Featured in Ceramics Monthly, 1994, Women's Wear Daily, 1995. Mem. hon. com. 2d Ann. 34th St. Art Fair, John Eaton Sch., 1985; mem. benefit com. Washington Charitable Fund, 1989; hon. bd. trustees D.C. chpt. Design Industries Found. for AIDS, 1989, 90; mem. auction ann. benefit com. Washington Project for Arts, 1989, 90, benefit com. Source Theater, 1993, benefit com. Corcoran Mus. Jazz Evening, 1993, honorary com. Lab Sch. Wash., 1992, honorary benefit com. Arena Stage Living Theater, 1997, 98; sponsor Wearable Art Fashion Show, Renwick Mus., 1993; juried Smithsonian Craft Show, 1994. Appeared on cover of Forecast Mag., 1978; recipient Best Taste in Washington award Washingtonian Mag., 1982, 1st Ann. Outstanding Accessories Merchandising award Accessories Mag., 1985; named one of 23 People to Watch in 1983, Washingtonian Mag., 1982; her apt. chosen as Residential Interior of Yr., Am. Soc. Interior Designers, 1985, 92; her store named 1986 Comml. Interior of Yr., Am. Soc. Interior Designers; nat. award for logo design Am. Corp. Identity, 1988, 91. Mem. Am. Craft Coun., Washington Fashion Group, James Renwick Craft Leaders Caucus, Friends of the Corcoran Gallery of Art, Friends of the Phillips Collection, Friends of the Textile Mus. Avocations: travel, food, modern dance, visual arts, swimming. Office: Jackie Chalkley 2130 Cathedral Ave NW Washington DC 20008

CHALL, JEANNE STERNLICHT, psychologist, educator; b. Shendishov, Poland, Jan. 1, 1921; came to U.S., 1927; d. Hyman and Eva (Kreinik) Sternlicht; m. Leo P. Chall, June 8, 1946 (div. 1964). BBA cum laude, CCNY, 1941; MA, Ohio State U., 1947, PhD, 1952; MA (hon.), Harvard, 1965; HLD, Lesley Coll., 1972. Rsch. asst. Ohio State U., Columbus, 1945-47, rsch. assoc., instr., 1947-49; instr. CCNY, 1950-52, asst. prof., 1952-62, assoc. prof., 1962-65, prof., 1965; vis. assoc. prof. Harvard U. Grad. Sch. Edn., Cambridge, Mass., 1963, prof., 1965-91, prof. emeritus, 1991; readability cons., 1950—; faculty summer sessions Tchrs. Coll., Columbia U., N.Y.C., 1958, 60-61; mem. Nat. Com. on Dyslexia and Related Reading Disorders, 1968-69, steering com. Project Literacy, U.S. Office Edn.; sec.-treas. Nat. Conf. on Rsch. in English, 1962, v.p. 1964-65, pres. 1965. Author: Readability: Research and Application, 1958, Learning to Read: The Great Debate, 1967, updated edit., 1983, 3d edit., 1996; co-author: (with Dale) A Formula for Predicting Readability, 1948, Readability Revisited: The New Dale-Challl Formula, 1995; (with Roswell) Diagnostic Test of Word Analysis Skills, 1956, 59, 78, 96, Diagnostic Assessments of Reading with Trial Teaching Strategies, 1992, Stages of Reading Development, 1983, 2d edit., 1996, Creating Successful Readers: A Practical Guide to Testing and Teaching at All Levels, 1994, Reading Difficulties: Effective Mehods for Successful Teaching, 1999; (with Jacobs and Baldwin) The Reading Crisis: Why Poor Children Fall Behind, 1990; (with Conard) Should Textbooks Challenge Students? The Case for Easier or Harder Books, 1991; (with Roswell, Fletcher, Richmond) Teaching Children to Read: A Step by Step Guide for Volunteer Tutors, 1998; (with Bissex, Conard, Harris-Sharples) Qualitative Assessment of Text Difficulty, 1996; (with Popp) Teaching and Assessing Phonics, 1996; contbr. articles to profl. jours. Recipient Andre Favat award Mass. Coun. Tchrs. Eng., 1979, Am. Edl. Rsch. Assn. award, 1982, 86, Edward L. Thorndike award APA, 1982, Disting. Rsch. award Nat. Conf. on Rsch. in English, 1993, Samuel T. Orton award Internat. Dyslexia Assn., 1996, Internat. Acad. Edn. award, 1997; named to the Reading Hall of Fame, 1979, Nat. Acad. Edn., 1979. Fellow APA; mem.

Nat. Assn. Remedial Teaching (chmn. program com. 1955), Nat. Reading Coun., Internat. Reading Assn. (dir. 1961-65, chmn. pre-conf. inst. 1959-61, membership com. 1958-60, Citation of Merit 1979), Am. Ednl. Rsch. Assn., Nat. Soc. for Study of Edn. (dir. 1972-78), Phi Delta Kappa. Home: 1558 Massachusetts Ave Cambridge MA 02138-2905 Office: Harvard U Grad Sch Edn Larsen Hall Appian Way Cambridge MA 02138

CHALLA, CHANDRASHEKAR DUTT, business educator; b. Nandyal, India, Feb. 7, 1959; came to U.S., 1988; s. Soma Sundaram and Bhramaramba Challa; m. Mahalakshmi Gollakota, Aug. 22, 1984; children: Chandni, Chirag. BTech in Mech. Engring., Kakatiya U., Warangal, India, 1981; MBA in Mktg., U. Delhi, India, 1983; PhD in Bus., Va. Commonwealth U., 1992. Asst. mgr. Garware Paints Ltd., Hyderabad, India, 1983-85; sales officer India Foils Ltd., Bombay, 1985-88; grad. tchg. asst. Va. Commonwealth U., Richmond, 1989-92; assoc. prof. Va. State U., Petersburg, 1992—. Mem. Hindu Ctr. Va., Richmond, 1988—, asst. editor, 1996—; mem. Indian Assn. Va., Richmond, 1988—, cricket capt., 1992-93. Microsoft instrnl. grantee, 1996-98, summer rsch. grantee Sch. Bus., Va. State U., 1998-99. Mem. S.E. Decision Scis. Inst. (v.p. planning and devel. 1998, track chair 1998), S.E. Inst. for Ops. Rsch. and Mgmt. Sci. (track chair 1995—), Decision Scis. Inst. Hindu. Avocations: traveling, reading fiction, playing tennis and cricket, listening to music, home improvement. E-mail: cchalla@vsu.edu. Office: Va State U Sch of Bus Box 9038 Petersburg VA 23806

CHALLELA, MARY SCAHILL, maternal, child health nurse; b. Hopedale, Mass., Nov. 30, 1927; d. James and Sarah Mary (Norton) Scahill; m. Charles V. Challela, May 29, 1976. BS, Boston U., 1954, MS, 1967, D in Nursing Sci., 1979. Staff nurse Mass. Gen. Hosp., Boston, 1949-51, U.S. Indian Svc., Ariz., 1951-52; sr. instr. Cleve. Met. Gen. Hosp. Sch. Nursing, 1954-66; asst. prof. Northeastern U., Boston, 1967-70; cons. Shriver Ctr., Waltham, Mass., 1970-72, dir. nursing univ. affiliated program, 1972-93; ret., 1993; mem. staff continuing edn. New Eng. Regional Genetics Group, 1990-92. Contbr. articles to profl. jours. Pres. Sacred heart Guild, Hopedale, 1972-74; chair Commn. on Disabilities, Hopedale, 1987-95; mem. strategic planning steering com. Hopedale Pub. Schs., 1999; with RCIA program Sacred Heart Ch., Hopedale, 1996—. Recipient Citizen Achievement award Mass. Assn. for Retarded Citizens, 1987, Excellence in Nursing award Sigma Theta Tau, 1987; Am. Assn. Mental Retardation fellow, 1988. Mem. ANA, Mass. Nurses Assn., Internat. Assn. Nurses in Genetics. Avocations: poetry, photography, aerobics, swimming.

CHALLONER, DAVID REYNOLDS, university official, physician; b. Appleton, Wis., Jan. 31, 1935; s. Reynolds Ray and Marion (Below) C.; m. Jacklyn Davnes Anderson, Aug. 30, 1958; children: David Harvey, Laura Reynolds, Britt-Davnes. B.S. cum laude, Lawrence Coll., Appleton, 1956; postgrad., Cambridge (Eng.) U., 1958; M.D. cum laude, Harvard, 1961. Resident in internal medicine Columbia Presbyn. Hosp., N.Y.C., 1961-63; research assoc. Nat. Heart Inst., Bethesda, Md., 1963-65; chief med. resident and endocrinology research fellow U. Wash., Seattle, 1965-67; prof. medicine, asst. chmn. dept. Ind. U. Sch. Medicine, Indpls., 1967-75; vis. scholar Inst. Medicine, Nat. Acad. Sci., 1974; dean St. Louis U. Sch. Medicine, 1975-82; v.p. health affairs U. Fla., Gainesville, 1982-98; dir. Inst. for Sci. & Health Policy U. Fla., Gainesville, Fla., 1998—; chmn. pres.'s com. on nat. med. sci. NIH, 1988-91, mem. dirs. adv. com., 1990-96; mem. com. sci., engring. pub. policy NAS, 1993-97; cons. Eli Lilly & co., NIH; mem. NAS Nat. Rsch. Coun. governing bd., 1997—; foreign sec. NAS, Inst. Med., 1998—. Served to lt. comdr. USPHS, 1963-65. Recipient Harvard Med. Alumni award, 1961, Dr. William Beaumont award AMA, 1982, Disting. Alumnus award Lawrence U., 1987. Fellow AAAS; mem. Inst. of Medicine (fgn. sec. 1998—), Am. Fedn. Clin. Rsch.pres. 1975), Inst. Medicine, Nat. Acad. Sci., Am. Soc. Clin. Investigation, Endocrine Soc., Am. Diabetes Assn., Assn. Am. Physicians, Boylston Soc., Am. Clin. and Climatol. Assn., Phi Beta Kappa, Alpha Omega Alpha, Beta Theta Pi. Clubs: Racquet (St. Louis); Cosmos (Washington). Home: 2715 NW 22nd Dr Gainesville FL 32605-2975 Office: U Fla PO Box 103204 Gainesville FL 32610-3204

CHALMERS, DAVID B., petroleum executive; b. Denver, Nov. 17, 1924; s. David Twiggs and Dorrit (Bay) C.; 1 child, David B. B.A., Dartmouth Coll., 1947; A.M.P., Harvard U., 1966. Various positions Bay Petroleum Co., Denver, 1951-55; various positions Tenneco Oil Co., Houston, 1955-67; v.p. Occidental Petroleum Corp., Houston, 1967-68; pres. Can. Occidental Petroleum Ltd., 1968-73; pres., chief exec. officer Petrogas Processing Ltd., 1968-73; officer Cansulex Ltd., 1968-73; chmn., chief exec. officer, dir. Coral Petroleum, Inc. and subs., Houston, 1973—. Served to lt. USMC, 1943-45, 49-50, Korea. Mem. Am. Petroleum Inst., Petroleum Club of Houston, Lochinvar Golf Club, Houston Racquet Club, Denver Country Club, Houston Club. Republican. Episcopalian. Home: 5600 San Felipe St # 4 Houston TX 77056-2613 Office: Coral Oil and Gas Inc 909 Texas Ste 202 Houston TX 77002-3007

CHALMERS, DAVID J., philosophy educator; b. Sydney, NSW, Australia, Apr. 20, 1966; s. John Phillip Chalmers and Julie Ann Kierath. BSc in Math. with honors, U. Adelaide, Australia, 1986; PhD, Ind. U., 1993. McDonnell fellow Washington U., St. Louis, 1993-95; asst. prof. U. Calif., Santa Cruz, 1995-97, assoc. prof., 1997-98, prof., 1998; prof. U. Ariz., Tucson, 1999—. Author: The Conscious Mind, 1996; mem. editl. bd. Jour. Consciousness Studies, Consciousness and Cognition, Psyche Am. Philos., Quarterly, Philos. Psychology, Trends in Cognitive Sci., Stanford Ency. Philosophy; contbr. articles to profl. jours. Rhodes scholar Rhodes Trust, Oxford, Eng., 1987. Mem. Assn. for Sci. Study Consciousness (chair bd. dirs.), Soc. for Philosophy and Psychology (mem. exec. com.). Office: Dept Philosophy Univ Ariz Tucson AZ 85721

CHALMERS, DIANA JEAN, office administrator; b. Harvey, Ill., Aug. 25, 1955; d. Melvin Earl and Rita Caroline (Zulfer) Besse; Michael Jon Chalmers, Mar. 18, 1972 (div.); children: Mikki Lynn, Robert Michael. Mgr. Pizza Hut, Richton Park, Ill., 1975-77; owner, operator D-Dusters, Hazel Crest, Ill., 1985-91; trustee Village of Hazel Crest, 1987-94; adminstrv. dir. Hazel Crest Area C. of C., 1990-95; office mgr. AAA Galvanizing, Joliet, Ill., 1995—. Author of poems. Founder Neighbors United Party, Hazel Crest, 1989; chmn. Hazel Crest Hazelnut Festival, 1986-90; coord. Hazel Crest Blood Donor Program, 1990-93; pres. Hazel Crest Girl's Softball. Home: 1013 Sterling #1 Joliet IL 60432 Office: AAA Galvanizing 625 Mills Rd Joliet IL 60433-2842

CHALMERS, JANE, broadcast executive. News reporter, documentary prodr. ITV, Edmonton, Alta., Can., 1981; co-host current affairs program CBC, Calgary; sr. prodr. 24 Hours CBC, Manitoba, exec., area prodr. 24 Hours News and Current Affairs, 1989-93, dir. radio, 1994-96; dir. radio/regional dir. Man. CBC/SRC, Winnipeg, 1996-99; regional dir. CBC/SRC, Manitoba, 1999—. Recipient Gold medals Internat. Film and TV Festivals of N.Y. and Columbus, Ohio, Human Right awards B'nai B'rith, Prix Anik, Michener award for journalism. Office: CBC-SRC, 541 Portage Ave, Winnipeg, MB Canada R3B 2G1*

CHALONER, ALICE BRAINERD, mathematics educator; b. Cleve., July 22, 1928; d. Arthur and Winifred (Kent) C.; m. James Byron Skellenger, July 30, 1947 (div. 1977); four children; m. Robert Canterbury, Aug. 31, 1978 (div. 1981). BA, Kent State U., 1967. From sys. analyst to mgr. human resourses Goodyear Tire & Rubber, Akron, Ohio, 1969-91; lectr. programming Kent (Ohio) State U., 1986-87; tutor maths. Learning Ctr. Akron, 1994-97; cons. human resources sys. Gdye Tire & Rubber. Mem. Akron Libr. Book Club, Portage Lakes Garden Club. Democrat. Avocations: reading, walking, dancing, gardening.

CHALSTY, JOHN STEELE, investment banker; b. Port Elizabeth, Republic of South Africa, Nov. 7, 1933; came to U.S., 1955, naturalized, 1964; s. Frederick H. and Sarah S. (Lamprecht) C.; m. Jennifer Blomefield, Feb. 16, 1957; children: Susan Chalsty Neely, Deborah Ann. B.Sc. in Chemistry and Physics, U. Witwatersrand, 1952, B.Sc. with honors in Chemistry, 1953, M.Sc., 1954; M.B.A. (Baker scholar), Harvard U., 1957. With Exxon Corp., N.Y.C., 1957-69; dir. Donaldson, Lufkin & Jenrette, Inc., N.Y.C., 1969—, chmn., 1986—; bd. dirs. IBP Inc., Occidental Petroleum Corp.; chmn. N.Y. Econ. Devel. Corp. Bd. dirs. Teagle Found. Inc., 1974—, chmn., 1997—; trustee Columbia U., St. Barnabas Med. Ctr.; chmn. Lincoln Ctr. Theater; bd. dirs. Am. Ballet Theater, N.Y. Philharm. Mem. Short Hills (N.J.) Club, Harvard Club, Univ. Club (N.Y.C.), Links Club. Office: Donaldson Lufkin & Jenrette Inc 277 Park Ave New York NY 10017-2016*

CHALUPA, VLASTISLAV JOHN, retired bank executive; b. Opava, Czechoslovakia, Nov. 4, 1919; came to U.S., 1952; s. Rudolf and Jana Chalupa; m. Marie Krckova, Apr. 21, 1947; children: Vlastislav John, Rudolf Pavel, Karel Václav. Grad., Bus. Acad., Brno, Czechoslovakia, 1941; LLD, Masaryk U., Brno, 1946, JD (hon.), 1990. lectr. internat. banking Am. Inst. Banking, Chgo., 1977-80; chmn. Mid-Am. Com. on Internat. Banking, Chgo., 1977-78, Nat. Assn. of Coms. on Internat. Banking, N.Y.C., 1978-79; mem. internat. banking Internat. C. of C., Paris, 1980-82. Acct. Cen. Bank of Savs. Assn., Brno, 1941-45; rsch. asst. theory of law Sch. Masaryk U., 1946; asst. legal dept. Slovenska Bank, Bratislava, Czechoslovakia, 1946-47; chmn. pres.' braintrust Nat. Socialist Party, Prague, Czechoslovakia, 1947-48; transl., clk. Carnegie Endowment for Internat. Peace, Paris, 1949-52; clk. internat. banking City Nat. Bank, 1952-55; asst. v.p. Continental Ill. Nat. Bank, Chgo., 1955-74, v.p., 1981-84; asst. v.p. Am. Nat. Bank, Chgo., 1975-81; ret. Author: (books) Rise and Development of a Totalitarian State, 1959, Catholic Politics? An Examination, 1986, An A-B-C-D of Politics, 1997, An Alphabet of Postmodern Politics, 1998, (textbooks) Principles of Science of Politics, 1990, II, 1991, Comments of Political Science, 1992; editor: (books) Three Years I-III, 1991, Sources to the History of the 3rd Resistance I-III, 1995, (periodicals) Směr, 1946, The Am. Bull., 1989-94, Survey of Political Science, 1991-92; co-editor: (periodicals) Plamen, 1948-49, The Cold War, 1952-59; mem. editl. bd.: Building a State, 1990-92, Studies, 1948-49; contbr. to profl. jours. Spkr. election campaign Czechoslovak Nat. Socialist Party, Moravia, 1946, organizer, leader sect. for sci. politics, Brno/Prague, 1946-49; coord. Czechoslovak Fgn. Inst. in Exile, Paris, 1949-62; v.p. Czechoslovak Nat. Coun. Am., Chgo., 1953-92; co-founder, dir. Internat. Inst. for Study of Politics Law Sch., Masaryk U., Brno, 1990-92; co-founder Ctr. for Czechoslovak Exile Studies of Palacky U., Olomouc, Czech Republic, 1992. Recipient Diploma of Appreciation, Nat. Coun. of City of Brno, 1945, award in appreciation of past contbns. Mid-Am. Com. on Internat. Banking, 1978, award of appreciation Nat. Assn. of Coms. on Internat. Banking, 1979, Commemorative medal Mil. Acad. Brno, 1992. Mem. Masaryk Sociol. Assn. Avocations: remodeling old farm, renovating and rebuiling old buildings, farming, writing. Home: 55 S Linden Ave Palatine IL 60067

CHAMBERLAIN, ADRIAN RAMOND, transportation engineer; b. Detroit, Nov. 11, 1929; s. Adrian and Leila (Swisher) C.; m. Melanie F. Stevens, May 19, 1979; children: Curtis (dec.), Tracy, Thomas (dec.). BS, Mich. State U., 1951, D Engring., 1971; MS, Wash. State U., 1952; PhD, Colo. State U., 1955; LittD, Denver U., 1974. Registered profl. engr., Colo. lic. real estate broker, Colo., 1981-91. Rsch. engr. Phillips Petroleum Co., 1955; rsch. coord., civil engr. Colo. State U., 1956-57, chief civil engr. sect., 1957-61, acting dean engring., 1959-61, v.p., 1960-66, exec. v.p., treas., governing bd., 1966-69, pres., 1969-80; chmn. bd. dirs. Univ. Nat. Bank, 1964-69, dir., 1964-74; pres., dir. Mitchell & Co., Inc., 1981-85; exec. v.p. Simons, Li & Assocs., Inc., 1985-87; pres., CEO, Chemagnetics, Inc., Ft. Collins, Colo., 1987-89; exec. dir. Colo. Dept. Hwys., Denver, 1987-91, Colo. Dept. Transp., 1991-94; with Parsons Brinckerhoff, Denver; chmn. NSF Commn. Weather Modification, 1964-66; mem. Nat. Air Quality Criteria Adv. Com., 1967-70; vice chmn. rsch. and tech. coord. com. Fed. Hwy Admiinstrn. of Transp. Rsch. Bd., NRC, 1991-94. Colo. commr. Western Interstate Commn. on Higher Edn., 1974-78; pres. State Bd. Agr. Sys., 1978-80; trustee Cystic Fibrosis Found., 1971-84, Univ. Corp. for Atmospheric Rsch., 1967-72, 74-81, chmn. bd. trustees, 1977-79; pres. Black Mountain Ranch, Inc., 1969-85; bd. dirs. Nat. Ctr. for Higher Edn. Mgmt. Sys., 1975-80, chmn. bd. dirs., 1977-78; bd. visitors Air U., USAF, 1973-76, chmn., 1975-76; exec. com. Nat. Assn. State Univs. and Land Grant Colls., 1976-80, pres.-elect, 1978-79, chmn., 1979-80; mem. adv. coun. to dir. NSF, 1978-81; chmn. Ft. Collins-Loveland Airport Authority, 1983-86; bd. dirs. Synergetics Internat. Inc., 1987-90; mem. exec. com. strategic hwy. rsch. commn. Transp. Rsch. Bd. NRC, 1989-93, chmn. strategic transp. rsch. study hwy. safety, 1989-90, exec. com., 1991-96, vice-chmn., 1992, chmn., 1993; mem. Gov.'s Cabinet, State of Colo., 1987-94; mem. Info. Mgmt. Commn., 1988-93. Fulbright student U. Grenoble, 1955-56. Mem. ASCE, Am. Assn. State Hwy. and Transp. Ofcls. (policy com. 1987-92, v.p. 1990-91, pres. 1991-92, bd. dirs. 1992-94, chmn. standing com. on adminstrn. 1993-94), Am. Trucking Assn. (v.p. for freight policy 1994-98, mng. dir. found. 1998), Order of Aztec Eagle, Mex., Sigma Xi, Tau Beta Pi, Phi Kappa Phi, Chi Epsilon. Home: 124 Idlewild Ln Winter Park CO 80482 Office: Parsons Brinckerhoff 1660 Lincoln St Ste 2000 Denver CO 80264-2001

CHAMBERLAIN, BRENDA KAY, member of Canadian parliament; b. Toronto, Can., Apr. 9, 1952; b. Brenda K. Borst; married; three children. Home day care owner, mgr. Guelph, Ontario, Can., 1979-83; adminstrv. asst. Guelph, 1984-87; trustee Wellington County Bd. Edn., Guelph, 1985-93, chair, 1987-90; mem. parliament Canadian Ho. of Commons, Ottawa, Ontario, 1993—; mem. standing com. on govt. ops., 1994-96, standing com. on fin., 1996-97, standing com. on human resources devel. and the status of persons with disabilities, 1998—; chair Nat. Liberal Caucus Com. on Econ. Devel., 1994-97, vice chair Can.-Mex. Friendship Group, 1995-97, parliamentary sec. Minister of Labour, 1997—. Mem. Liberal Party of Can. Office: House of Commons, 152 Confederation Bldg, Ottawa, ON Canada K1A 0A6

CHAMBERLAIN, CHARLES JAMES, railroad labor union executive; b. Ashton, Ill., Aug. 7, 1921; s. Charles Hubert and Katherine (Reitz) C.; m. Joyce Lois Swanson, June 27, 1942; children—Richard B., Charles M. Student pub. schs. With signal dept. C. & N.-W. Ry., 1938-57; grand lodge rep. Brotherhood of R.R. Signalmen, 1957-61, sec.-treas., 1961-67, pres., 1967—; Appointed Labor mem. by Pres. Carter to U.S. R.R. Retirement Bd., Chgo., 1977, reappointed, 1979-84, reappointed by Pres. Reagan, 1986-89, reappointed by Pres. Bush, 1989-92, ret. 1992; arbitrator Nat. Mediation Bd., 1996. Alderman DeKalb (Ill.) City Coun., 1949-57; pres. 4 Colonies Condo Assn., Crystal Lake, Ill., 1987—; chmn. St. John's Luth. Ch., Algonquin, Ill., 1990-91, 94—. Mem. Ry. Labor Execs. Assn. (chmn. 1970—). Home: 740 St Andrews Ln Apt 33 Crystal Lake IL 60014-7043

CHAMBERLAIN, DANIEL ROBERT, college president; b. Mexico, Mo., Aug. 22, 1932; s. Ray Willis and Marianne Elizabeth (Horine) C.; m. Joyce F. Books, June 22, 1952; children: Rodney, Mark, Anthony, Priscilla, Aletha, Cynthia, Marianne. BA, Upland Coll., 1953; M.A., Calif. State U., Los Angeles, 1957; postgrad., UCLA, 1958-59; D.Ed., U. So. Calif., 1967; PhD (hon.), Huntington Coll. Tchr., adminstr. Western Pilgrim Schs., El Monte, Calif., 1953-59; tchr. English and history Pasadena (Calif.) City Schs., 1959-63; chmn. div. profl. studies, acting pres. Upland Coll., 1963-65; asst. univ. dean for univ. wide activities SUNY, Albany, 1965-68; dean of coll. Messiah Coll., Grantham, Pa., 1968-76; pres. Houghton (N.Y.) Coll., 1976—; lectr. on higher edn. and social scis. in People's Republic of China, 1984, 87, 88, 89. Pres. Calif. youth Wesleyan Ch., 1954-64; chmn. bd. dirs. Mile High Camp, Barton Flats, Calif., 1959-65; pres. men's commn. Christian Holiness Assn., 1975-80; bd. dirs. Commn. Ind. Colls. and Univs.; chmn. Ind. Coll. Fund, N.Y., Western N.Y. Consortium Higher Edn., 1976—; mem. gen. bd. adminstrn. Wesleyan Ch., 1988-92; chmn. Western N.Y. Consortium Higher Edn., 1991-93; bd. dirs. N.Y. State Commn. on Ind. Colls. and Univs., 1994-97. Named One of 50 Most Outstanding Alumni, Calif. State U., L.A., 1997. Mem. Christian Coll. Consortium (chmn.), Council of Mennonite Coll. Deans (chmn.), Am. Assn. Higher Edn., Middle States Assn. Schs. and Colls. (evaluator, team chmn.), Wesleyan Edn. Council (chmn.), Lions, Phi Delta Kappa. Republican. Office: Houghton Coll Office of Pres Houghton NY 14744

CHAMBERLAIN, GEORGE ARTHUR, III, manufacturing company executive, venture capitalist; b. Boston, Sept. 14, 1935; s. George Arthur, Jr. and Mabel G. (Greene) C.; m. Judith Fehr, June 20, 1959; children—G. Randall, Cynthia L. A.B., Wheaton (Ill.) Coll., 1957; M.B.A., Harvard U., 1961. Loan officer Worcester County Nat. Bank, Mass., 1961-65; v.p. fin., treas. Anderson Corp., Worcester, 1966-69; with Digital Equipment Corp., Maynard, Mass., 1969-92, treas., 1976-83, v.p. mfg., engring., mktg. fin., 1983-92; exec. v.p. Capitol Techs. Inc., 1993-94; CFO Marcam Corp., Boston, 1994-97, Radnet, Inc., Cambridge, 1997—; trustee Consumers Savs. Bank, Worcester, 1970-85; adv. dir. ABN-AMRO Bank, Boston. Trustee Lawrence Acad., Groton, Mass.; past trustee Met. Ctr., Boston; bd. dirs. ARC Mass. Bay, 1986-94; overseer Sta. WGBH, Boston, 1988-94, Mus. Fine Arts, Boston, gov. sch., 1992—. With AUS, 1957-59. Mem. Fin. Execs. Inst.

CHAMBERLAIN, JEAN NASH, county government department director; b. Chgo., Oct. 14, 1934; d. William Edmund and Virginia Jean (La Fon) Nash; m. James Staffeld Chamberlain, Dec. 29, 1953; children: James W., William S., Caren T., Martha J. Student, U. S.C., 1951-53. Polit. dir. Tribune/United Cablevision, Huntington Woods, Mich., 1982; orgn. dir. polit. campaign, Oakland, Mich., 1983-84; dir. fin. Dan Murphy for Gov., Mich., 1985-86; exec. mgr. Greater Royal Oak (Mich.)/Oak Park C. of C., 1986-93. Vice chair Rep. com., Oakland County, Mich., 1971-73; chair Rep. 18th congl. dist., 1973-77; del. Rep. Nat. Conv., Kansas City, Mo., 1976; bd. dirs. Oakland County Mental Health Bd., 1976-93, chair 1984-86. Named among top thirty Outstanding Women State Mich., Mich's. Womens Commn., 1998. Mem. U.S. C. of C., Mich. State C. of C., South Oakland Boys and Girls Club (bd. dirs.), South Oakland Salvation Army (bd. dirs.), Harnack Firefighters Scholarship Fund (bd. dirs.), Woodward Dream Cruise (bd. chair). Roman Catholic. Avocations: tennis, bridge, sports, cooking. Office: Oakland County Exec Office Bldg 1200 N Telegraph Rd Pontiac MI 48341-1032

CHAMBERLAIN, JEFFREY SCOTT, history educator; b. Hartford, Conn., Sept. 4, 1958; s. John and Ruth Warren (Howe) C. BA in History, Bryan Coll., 1980; MDiv, Trinity Evang. Div. Sch., Deerfield, Ill., 1985, MA in Ch. History, 1986; PhD in Brit. History, U. Chgo., 1992. Vis. instr. ch. history Trinity Evang. Div. Sch., Deerfield, 1988-89; assoc. prof. history U. St. Francis, Joliet, Ill., 1992—; chair dept. history and polit. sci. U. St. Francis, Joliet, 1993—; chair acad. assembly U. of St. Francis, Joliet, 1996-97, chair undergrad. planning task force, 1997; instr. European cultural history tours Ea. Mich. U., Ypsilanti, 1997. Author: Accomodating High Churchmen: The Clergy of Sussex, 1700-1745, 1997; contbr. articles to profl. jours. Vol. Big Bros./Big Sisters, Joliet, 1995—; facilitator Choices for the 21st Century, Joliet, 1996, 1999. Mem. N.Am. Conf. Brit. Studies, Am. Soc. Ch. History, Am. Hist. Soc. Avocations: cycling, hiking, running, travel. Home: 906 Campbell St Joliet IL 60435-6934 Office: U of St Francis 500 Wilcox St Joliet IL 60435-6169

CHAMBERLAIN, JILL FRANCES, financial services executive; b. Chgo., Mar. 25, 1954; d. Chester Emery and Mary Edythe (Hurd) C. B.A. in Math. with honors, Ill. State U., 1975; M.B.A., U. Chgo., 1981. Programmer Arthur Andersen, Chgo., 1975-76; cons. Laventhol & Horwath, Chgo., 1976-77; fin. systems analyst U. Chgo. Hosp., 1978-80; v.p. CHI/COR Info. Mgmt., Inc., Chgo., 1980-87; systems designer GECC, Stamford, 1987-88; mgr. systems devel., GE Capital Corp., 1988-96; v.p. systems devel. RFS Retailer Fin. Svcs. 1996-97, v.p. ops. and customer svc., 1998—; cons. RMS Bus. Systems, Chgo., 1976-77. Mem. NAFE. Libertarian. Methodist. Avocations: reading, traveling, needlework. Office: GE Capital 1600 Summer St Stamford CT 06905-5125

CHAMBERLAIN, JOSEPH MILES, retired astronomer, educator; b. Peoria, Ill., July 26, 1923; s. Maurice Silloway and Roberta (Miles) C.; m. Paula Bruninga, Dec. 12, 1945; children: Janet Ann, Susan Louise, Barbara Jean. BS, U.S. Mcht. Marine Acad., 1944; BA, Bradley U., 1947; AM, Tchrs. Coll. Columbia, 1950, EdD, 1962. Instr. Columbia Jr. High Sch., Peoria, 1943; instr. nav. War Shipping Adminstrn., 1944-45; boys sec. YMCA, Peoria, 1946-47; instr. U.S. Mcht. Marine Acad., Kings Point, N.Y., 1947-50; asst. prof. U.S. Mcht. Marine Acad., 1950-52; asst. curator Am. Museum-Hayden Planetarium, N.Y.C., 1952-53; gen. mgr., chief astronomer Am. Museum-Hayden Planetarium, 1953-56, chmn., 1956-64; asst. dir. Am. Mus. Natural History, 1964-68; dir. Adler Planetarium, Chgo., 1968-91, pres., 1977-91, ret., 1991; prof. astronomy Northwestern U., 1968-78; professorial lectr. U. Chgo., 1968-71; led eclipse expdns. to Atlantic Ocean, 1972, 73, 94, Mexico, 1970, Can., 1954, 79, Ceylon, 1955, Pacific Ocean, 1977, 91, astro-geodetic expdns. to Can., 1956, 57, Greenland, 1958; dean coun. of sci. staff Am. Mus. Nat. History, 1960-62. Co-author: Planets, Stars and Space, 1957; author: Time and the Stars, 1964; also articles on popular astronomy. Active Boy Scouts Am., Met. Chgo. YMCA; trustee Lakeview Mus. Arts & Scis., Peoria, 1993—; bd. dirs. Heartland Water Resources Coun., 1995-98. Lt. USNR, 1945-46; staff Naval Res. Officers Sch. 1953-54, N.Y.C. Mem. Am. Astron. Soc., Internat. Astron. Union, Internat. Planetarium Dirs. Conf. (vice chmn. 1968-77, chmn. 1977-87), Am. Polar Soc., Am. Assn. Museums (mem. council 1965-77, v.p. 1971-74, pres. 1974-75), Mus. Trustee Assn. (bd. dirs. 1996—), Peoria Hist. Soc. (trustee 1993-96), Univ. Club (Chgo.), Ill. Valley Yacht Club, University Club (Chgo.), Phi Delta Kappa, Phi Kappa Phi, Kappa Delta Pi. Republican. Presbyn. (elder). Home: 510 W Thousand Oaks Dr Peoria IL 61615-1395

CHAMBERLAIN, KATHLEEN REUTER, English educator, dean; b. Cleve., Sept. 2, 1955; d. Robert Donald and Alice (McHugh) Reuter; m. Robert Allen Chamberlain, Jr., Nov. 25, 1989. BA summa cum laude, Cleve. State U., 1977; MA, U. N.C., 1981, PhD, 1986. Lectr. U. N.C., Chapel Hill, 1985-86; vis. asst. prof. Wake Forest U., Winston-Salem, N.C., 1986-89; asst. prof. Emory (Va.) & Henry Coll., 1989-92, assoc. prof., 1992—, assoc. dean, 1998—. Contbr. articles to profl. jours. Named Va. Prof. of the Yr. Carnegie Found./CASE, 1994. Mem. Am. Culture Assn. (mem.-at-large governing bd. 1995-99). Avocations: radio theater, community theater. Office: Emory & Henry Coll PO Box 947 Dept English Emory VA 24327

CHAMBERLAIN, KATHRYN BURNS BROWNING, retired naval officer; b. Rapid City, S.D., Jan. 17, 1951; d. George Alfred III and Mildred Doty Browning; m. Thomas Richard Masker, Apr. 19, 1975 (widowed Sept. 1978); m. Guy Caldwell Chamberlain III, Mar. 25, 1980 (div. Oct. 1988); children: Burns Doty, Anne Caldwell. BA, La. Tech. U., 1973; postgrad., Naval Postgrad. Sch., Monteray, Calif., 1978-79; MA, Auburn U., 1984; postgrad., U. Ill., 1994-96, Govs. State U., 1995-96. Ensign USN, 1974, ltjg., 1976, lt., 1978, advanced through grades to comdr., 1983, surface warfare designation, 1980, joint staff officer, 1986; comdg. officer Mil. Sealift Command Office USN, Alaska, 1986-88; comdr., exec. officer USNAVFAC, Newfoundland, Nfld., Can., 1991-94; cmty. planner City of Montgomery, 1998—. Mem. AAUW, Am. Planning Assn. Home and Office: 364 Felder Ave Montgomery AL 36104-5616

CHAMBERLAIN, OWEN, nuclear physicist; b. San Francisco, July 10, 1920; divorced 1978; 4 children; m. June Steingart, 1980 (dec.); m. Senta Pugh, 1998. AB (Cramer fellow), Dartmouth Coll., 1941; PhD, U. Chgo., 1949. Instr. physics U. Calif., Berkeley, 1948-50, asst. prof., 1950-54, assoc. prof., 1954-58, prof., 1958-89, prof. emeritus, 1989—; civilian physicist Manhattan Dist., Berkeley, Los Alamos, 1942-46. Recipient Nobel prize (with Emilio Segré) for physics, for discovery anti-proton, 1959, The Berkeley citation U. Calif., 1989; Guggenheim fellow, 1957-58; Loeb lectr. at Harvard U., 1959. Fellow Am. Phys. Soc., Am. Acad. Arts and Scis.; mem. Nat. Acad. Scis., Berkeley Fellows. Office: U Calif Physics Dept 367 Le Conte Hall Berkeley CA 94720

CHAMBERLAIN, ROBERT GLENN, retired tool manfacturing executive; b. Cedar Rapids, Iowa, Feb. 17, 1926; s. Glenn Arlie and Ora Margarite (Castle) C.; m. Jane Helen Newlin, June 13, 1946; children: Carole, James, Sue, Patricia, Tracey. B.S.M.E., Iowa State U., 1949; postgrad., U. Wis.Milw. With Link-Belt Speeder, Cedar Rapids, 1949-54; with Giddings & Lewis, Fond du Lac, Wis., 1954-83, group v.p. indsl. products, 1980-82, exec. v.p. machine tools, 1982-83, ret., 1983; pioneer numerical control programmer, 1954-59. Mem. PTO; v.p. Bay Lakes coun. Boy Scouts Am., Menasha, Wis., 1982-89, exploring chmn. in sch., Dallas, 1981, exploring chmn. Area 1 NC region, Oak Brook, Ill., 1977; bd. dirs. Evergreen Retirement Cmty., 1989-94. With USNR, 1944-46. Recipient Silver Beaver award Boy Scouts Am., 1974, Silver Antelope award, 1983. Mem. Masons. Home: W2728 Oakwood Beach Rd Markesan WI 53946-8904

CHAMBERLAIN, WILLARD THOMAS, retired metals company executive; b. New Haven, Nov. 22, 1928; s. Thomas Huntington and Alice Irene (Daley) C.; m. Harriet Halbert Keck, Nov. 20, 1965; children: Huntington Wilson, Amy Thatcher. B.E., Yale U., 1950; postgrad., Ill. Inst. Tech., 1951-53. With Armour Research Found., Chgo., 1951-53; asst. to tech. mgr.

Anaconda Brass div. Anaconda Corp., Waterbury, Conn., 1953-56, tech. supr., 1956-60; metall. mgr. Anaconda Brass div. Anaconda Corp., Torrington, Conn., 1960-61; mgr. devel. Anaconda Brass div. Anaconda Corp., Waterbury, 1961-62, lab. mgr., 1962-64, mgr. research-tech. ctr., 1964-67; mgr. Anaconda Brass div. Anaconda Corp., Valley Mills, 1967; mgr. Anaconda Brass div. Anaconda Corp., Ansonia, 1967-70, mgr. prodn. planning, 1970-71, v.p. mfg., 1971-72, exec. v.p. Brass div., 1972-74, pres., 1974-80; pres. Anaconda Industries, 1980; sr. v.p. Atlantic Richfield Co., 1980-82; pres. Arco Metals Co., 1982-85; sr. v.p. corp. affairs Atlantic Richfield Co., 1985-87; sr. v.p. govt. and pub. affairs ARCO, 1987-89; mem. So. Calif. bus. com. Econ. Literacy Council Adv. of Calif. Mem. exec. bd. Waterbury Republican Town Com., 1964-70; commr. Waterbury Bd. Fin., 1966-67, chmn. charter revision com., 1966-67; mem. exec. bd. Mattatuck council Boy Scouts Am., 1965-72, Waterbury Assn. for Retarded Children, 1965-66; co-chmn. Clergy-Industry Conf., 1965-66; campaign chmn. Valley United Fund, 1970-71; bd. dirs. United Way, Central Naugatuck Valley, 1974, The Banking Ctr., 1974-81, Western Conn. Indsl. Council, 1974-81, Calif. State U. Found., Found. for Am. Communications, Los Angeles Arts Council; trustee Calif. Mus. Found., Harvey Mudd Coll.; bd. trustees Greater Los Angeles Partnership for the Homeless; bd. dirs. L.A. Habitat for Humanity. Recipient Outstanding Civic Leader award, 1967. Mem. Copper Devel. Assn., Aluminum Assn. (dir.), Am. Soc. Metals, Yale Engring. Assn., Greater Waterbury C. of C. (bd. dirs. 1974), Alliance Aging Rsch. (bd. dirs.), Am. Petroleum Inst. (emerging issues task force), Brookings Instn. (coun. mem.), Calif. State U. Found. (bd. dirs., compensation planning com., chmn. investment com.), Calif. State U. Bus. Assocs., Constl. Rights Found. (bus. adv. coun.), Econ. Literacy Coun. Adv. Calif. (so. Calif. bus. com.), Found. Am. Communications (dir.), Hugh O'Brian Youth Found., Math. Engring. and Sci. Achievement (industry adv. bd.), Nat. Action Coun. for Minorities in Engring., Nat. Minority Supplier Devel. Coun. (bd. dirs.), Nat. Wetlands Policy Forum, Nat. Wildlife Fedn. (vice chmn. corp. conservation coun.), Vols. of Am., L.A., Town Hall, U.S. C. of C., World Affairs Coun., Univ. Club L.A., Yale Club, So. Calif. Presbyterian. Home: 721 Madre St Pasadena CA 91107-5662

CHAMBERLAIN, WILLIAM EDWIN, JR., management consultant; b. St. Louis, June 8, 1951; s. William Edwin Sr. and Grace (Salisbury) C. AA in Bus. Mgmt., Mesa (Ariz.) Community Coll., 1983; BBA, U. Phoenix, 1988. Tng. and human resources devel. specialist Motorola, Inc., Phoenix, 1979-87; pres., seminar speaker Chamberlain Cons. Svcs., Chino Valley, Ariz., 1987—. Curator, dir. ops. U.S. Wolf Refuge and Adoption Ctr. Mem. ASTD, Network for Profl. Devel. Avocations: wildlife preservation and management, hiking, backpacking, tennis, basketball, racquetball. *Personal philosophy: Better people make better workers and better workers make better people. A company's workforce is often its biggest investment, therefore efforts to develop its workers will often bring the biggest returns.*

CHAMBERLAIN, WILLIAM RHODE, county official; b. Clarendon, Tex., Feb. 1, 1944; s. William Park and Norma Evelyn (Rhode) C.; m. Brenda Kay Lane, Nov. 28, 1963; children: Shalane Chamberlain Wesley, Sheri Chamberlain Cooper. Student, Tex. A&M U., 1988-94, Amarillo (Tex.) Jr. Coll., 1993, Midwestern State U., 1993. County commr. Donley County, Clarendon, 1979-98; dir. Shamrock Savs. and Loans, Amarillo, 1985-88; v.p. Panhandle Grant Com., Amarillo, 1987; pres. Panhandle Judges and Commrs., Amarillo, 1990; conf. com. mem. West Tex. Judges and Commrs., 1990-92, chmn. nominations com., 1994. State Judges and Commns. Assn. Nomination Com., 1997-98. Recipient outstanding county official in West Tex. award, 1998. Mem. Free Mason (past master 1978, 32 Lubbock dist. dep. 1982). Democrat. Methodist. Home: HC 5 Box 40 Clarendon TX 79226-9322

CHAMBERLAIN, WILTON NORMAN, retired professional basketball player; b. Phila., Aug. 21, 1936. Student, U. Kans., 1954-58. Player Harlem Globetrotters, 1958-59, Phila. (later San Francisco) Warriors, 1959-65, Phila. 76ers, 1965-68, Los Angeles Lakers, 1968-73; coach San Diego Conquistadors, Am. Basketball Assn., 1973-74; co-founder, race dir. Suzuki Rock N Roll Marathon; owner Hundred Point Films. Actor, Conan The Destroyer, 1982; author: A View from Above, 1991. Player, Nat. Basketball Assn. All-Star Game, 1960-69, 71-73; rookie of yr. Nat. Basketball Assn., 1960; Most Valuable Player, Nat. Basketball Assn., 1960, 66-68, Nat. Basketball Assn. Playoffs, 1972; inducted Naismith Meml. Basketball Hall of Fame, 1978; named to Nat. Basketball Assn. 35th Anniversary All-Time Team, 1980; mem. Nat. Basketball Assn. Championship Team, 1967, 72; holder Nat. Basketball Assn. record for most points scored in one game with 100; selected to NBA Anniversary All-Time, 1996-97. Office: care NCH Entertainment, 14 Prince Arthur Ave # 205, Toronto, ON Canada M5R 1A9*

CHAMBERLAND, ANNA MARGARET PICKETT, communications professional, small business owner; b. Anchorage, Apr. 27, 1962; d. Peter and Beatrice Carol (Havercamp) P.; m. Carl D. Willis, Apr. 16, 1983 (div. 1986); m. William Chamberland Jr., July 11, 1998. Grad., Dimond H.S., Anchorage, 1980. Advt. salesperson, office mgr., prod./circulation mgr. Tundra Times, Anchorage, 1979-84; exec. editor Tundra Times, 1992-96; adminstrv. asst. Klukwan Forest Products, Anchorage, 1986-89; occupancy specialist Aleutian Housing Auth., Anchorage, 1989-90; editor Tanana Chiefs Conf., The Council, 1996-99; spl. asst. comm. Alaska Fedn. Natives, 1999—; owner AMPle Prodns., 1996—. Mem. Native Alaskan Profl. and Bus. Soc., Advt. Fedn., Alaska Bikers Advocating Tng. and Edn. (ABATE), ABATE of Tanana Valley, ABATE of Valdez. Home: PO Box 56920 North Pole AK 99705

CHAMBERLIN, DONALD DEAN, computer engineer; b. San Jose, Calif., Dec. 21, 1944. BS, Harvey Mudd Coll., 1966; PhD in Elec. Engring., Stanford U., 1971. Rsch. staff mem. IBM, San Jose, Calif., 1971—; adj. prof. Santa Clara U., 1992-95. Author: Using the New DB2: IBM's Object-Relational Database System, 1996, A Complete Guide to DB2 Universal Database, 1998; contbr. articles to profl. jours. Fellow Assn. Computing Machinery; mem. Nat. Acad. Engring., Inst. Elec. & Electronics Engrs. E-mail: chamberlin@almaden.ibm.com. Fax: 408-927-3215. Office: Almaden Research Ctr IBM 650 Harry Rd San Jose CA 95120-6001

CHAMBERLIN, ED, curator; b. Rochester, Mich., Nov. 11, 1958. BA, No. Mich. U., 1982. Mus. curator Grand Canyon Nat. Park, Ariz., 1981-89, Hubbell Trading Post Nat. Hist. Site, Ganado, Ariz., 1989-92, 97—; pk. curator Carlsbad (N.Mex.) Caverns Nat. Pk., 1992-93; regional curator Bur. Reclamation, Boulder City, Nev., 1993-97. Office: Hubbell Trading Post National Historic Site PO Box 150 Ganado AZ 86505-0150*

CHAMBERLIN, EDWARD ROBERT, career officer, educator; b. Boston, May 16, 1944; s. Joseph King and Ruth Louise (Cooper) C.; m. Sandra Jean Stratton, June 10, 1972; children: Jill, Courtney, Katherine, Rebecca. BBA, U. Wis., 1966; MBA, Harvard U., 1973. Commd. ensign USN, 1966, advanced through grades to rear adm., 1993; head data processing dept. Naval Air Sta., Jacksonville, Fla., 1973-75; supply officer USS Little Rock, Gaeta, Italy, 1976; instr. Navy Supply Corps Sch., Athens, Ga., 1976-79; weapons policy officer Aviation Supply Office, USN, Phila., 1980-82; supply officer USS Nimitz, Norfolk, Va., 1983-84; with Stock Point ADP Replacement project office Naval Supply Systems Command, Washington, 1985-88; asst. chief of staff logistics Naval Air Force Pacific, Coronado, Calif., 1989-90; exec. asst., asst. sec. of def. Office of Sec. of Def., Washington, 1991-92; exec. dir. Def. Logistics Agy., Alexandria, Va., 1993—. Pres. Parent Tchrs. Student Orgn., Churchville, Pa., 1982, 83; elder 1st United Presbyn. Ch., Dale City, Va., 1993, 94; mem. Pres.'s Com. Purchase From Blind and Disabled, Washington, 1998—; vol. Naval Credit Union, Vienna, Va., 1997—. Decorated Def. Superior Svc. (2), Legion of Merit (2). Avocations: swimming, jogging, biking. Office: Defense Logistics 8725 John J Kingman Rd Ste 2533 Fort Belvoir VA 22060-6221

CHAMBERLIN, EUGENE KEITH, historian, educator; b. Gustine, Calif., Feb. 15, 1916; s. Charles Eugene and Anina Marguerite (Williams) C.; m. Margaret Rae Jackson, Sept. 1, 1940; children: Linda, Thomas, Rebecca, Adrienne (dec.), Eric. *Father lost an infant daughter and wife by deaths and almost lost Eugene, 1921-22. In poor health, he struggled to keep Eugene, Agnes and Everett together until 1926, through an unsuccessful second marriage. Two of mother's sisters raised Agnes and Everett, but Eugene and father were together through many job and school changes, preparing him for life and work before Charles died from stroke, 1944. Aunt Mary Wilhelmine Williams (Stanford, Goucher College) urged him through two university degrees before her 1944 death. From their first 1938 meeting, wife Margaret helped him with career adjustments while raising a delightful family.* BA in History, U. Calif., Berkeley, 1939, MA, 1940, PhD, 1949. Tchr. Spanish, Lilian Lassen Union H.S. and Jr. Coll., Susanville, Calif., 1941-43; tchr. history Elk Grove (Calif.) Joint Union H.S., 1943-45; tchg. asst. history U. Calif., Berkeley, 1946-48; instr. history Mont. State U., Missoula, 1948-51, asst. prof., 1951-54; asst. prof. to prof. San Diego City Coll., 1954-78; prof. history San Diego Miramar Coll., 1978-83, San Diego Mesa Coll., 1983-86; ret.; part time cab driver San Diego Yellow Cab Co., 1955-74, 79, 86; vis. prof. history Mont. State Coll., Bozeman, summer 1953, U. Calif. Ext., 1964-68, San Diego State Coll., 1965-68, others; instr., coord. history lectr. San Diego C.C.-TV, 1969-77; prof. history MiraCosta Coll., 1998; mem. adv. com. Quechan Crossing Master Plan Project, 1989-90; historian San Diego First Ch. of the Brethren, 1954-98. Author numerous booklets on S.W. Am. history; numerous articles on Mexican N.W. to profl. jours. Recipient Merit award Congress of History San Diego County, 1978, award for dedicated svc. to local history San Diego Hist. Soc., 1991, Ben Dixon award Congress History, San Diego and Imperial Counties, 1997; Huntington Libr.-Rockefeller Found. grantee, 1952, Fulbright-Hays grantee, Peru, 1982. Mem. AAUP (various coms., nat. coun. 1967-70, pres. Calif. chpt. 1968-70, acting exec. sec. 1970-72, 50 Yr. Mem. 1999), San Diego County Congress of History (pres. 1976-77, newsletter editor 1977-78), Am. Hist. Assn. (life, Beveridge-Dunning com. 1982-84, chmn. 1984), Pacific Coast Coun. on Latin Am. Studies, Cultural Assn. of the Californias, The Westerners (Calafia, S.D. chpt.), E Clampus Vitus Squibob Chpt. (historian 1970-96, emeritus historian and archivist 1996—, chpt. pres. 1972-73, dir. proctor 1983-89, grand coun. mem. 1972-93, dir. T.R.A.S.H. 1979-93, pres. 1983-84), San Diego Hist. Soc. (hon. life), Phi Alpha Theta (sec. U. Calif. Berkeley chpt. 1947-48, organizer and faculty adv. Mont. State U. chpt. 1948-54). Democrat. Mem. Church of the Brethren. Home: 3033 Dale St San Diego CA 92104-4929

CHAMBERLIN, JOAN MARY, assistant principal, academic services director; b. Cleve., May 30, 1955; d. John A. and Patricia Irene (Mirous) Chesney; m. Alexis Lee Chamberlin, Apr. 24, 1976; children: Matthew James, Sarah Marie, Michael Alexis. BS in Edn., Kent State U., 1976, MED, 1992, EdS, 1996. Cert. asst. supt., prin., tchr., Ohio. Elem. tchr. Cleve. Diocese, 1976-78; mid. sch. tchr. Garfield Heights (Ohio) City Schs., 1978-79, elem. tchr., 1989-93, computer tchr., 1994-95, adult edn. dir., 1994-98, unit prin., 1998, EMIS dir., 1994—, asst. prin., 1993—, pupil svcs. dir., 1998—. Adminstrv. leader Garfield Heights Youth, Family and Teen Svcs., 1997-98; mem., officer St. Nick and St. Vincent De Paul, Garfield Heights, 1994—. Kurdziel grantee Henry and Kathryn Kurdziel Found., 1993-94; Ohio Classrm. Mgmt. grantee, 1997-98. Mem. ASCD, East Side Adult Edn. Roundtable. Roman Catholic. Avocations: piano playing, choir, swimming, camping, crafts. Home: 6404 Hathaway Rd Garfield Hts OH 44125-4926 Office: Garfield Heights City Schs 5640 Briarcliff Dr Garfield Hts OH 44125-4158

CHAMBERLIN, JOHN CHARLTON, federal agency administrator. B Indsl. Engring., Va. Poly. Inst., 1965; MBA, U. Pitts., 1968; grad. Program for Sr. Mgrs. in Govt., Harvard U., 1987. With U.S. EPA, Washington, 1974—, chief spl. analysis and regional ops. br., 1975-79, dep. dir. budget divsn., 1980-81, dep. comptr., 1981-84, dir. adminstrn., 1984—. Recipient Meritorious Exec. Presdl. Rank award, 1989. Office: US EPA Adminstrn Office 401 MST SW Washington DC 20460

CHAMBERLIN, JOHN STEPHEN, investor, former cosmetics company executive; b. Boston, July 29, 1928; s. Stephen Henry and Olive Helen (McGrath) C.; m. Mary Katherine Leahy, Oct. 9, 1954; children—Mary Katherine, Patricia Ann, Carol Lynn, John Stephen, Liane Helen, Mark Joseph. A.B. cum laude, Harvard U., 1950, M.B.A., 1953. Lamp salesman Gen. Electric Co., N.Y.C., 1954-57, mgmt. cons., 1957-60; mgr. product planning TV receiver dept. Gen. Electric Co., Syracuse, N.Y., 1960-63; mgr. mktg., gen. mgr. radio receiver dept. Gen. Electric Co., Utica, N.Y., 1963-70; exec. v.p., dir. Lenox Inc., Trenton, N.J., 1970-71; v.p., gen. mgr. housewares div. Gen. Electric Co., Bridgeport, Conn., 1971-74, v.p., gen. mgr. housewares and audio div., 1974-76; pres., chief exec. officer, dir. Lenox Inc., Lawrenceville, N.J., 1976-81, chmn., chief exec. officer, 1981-85; pres., chief operating officer Avon Products, Inc., N.Y.C., 1985-88; pvt. investor Princeton, N.J., 1988—; bd. dirs. Seasons, Inc., The Robbins Co., Health South Corp., Imagyn Techs. Inc., Papel Giftware, Inc.; chmn. bd. dirs. WNS, Inc., 1993—; sr. advisor Mancuso & Co., 1992-98. Trustee Med. Ctr. at Princeton, vice chmn. 1995, Woodrow Wilson Nat. Fellowship Found. Mem. Bedens Brook Club, Harvard Club N.Y.C., Nassau. Home: 182 Fairway Dr Princeton NJ 08540-2410

CHAMBERLIN, MICHAEL JOHN, biochemistry educator; b. Chgo., June 7, 1937; s. John Windsor and Marian (McMichael) C.; m. Caroline Marie Kane, Jan. 31, 1981. AB, Harvard U., 1959; PhD, Stanford U., 1963. Asst. prof. virology U. Calif., Berkeley, 1963-67, assoc. prof. molecular biology, 1967-71, assoc. prof. biochemistry, 1971-73, prof., 1973—, vice chmn. dept. biochemistry, 1983-88, prof. biochemistry and molecular biology, 1989—; mem. physiol. chemistry study sect. NIH, 1970-74, molecular biology study sect., 1980-84; mem. study sect. Am. Heart Assn., 1983-86. Mem. editorial bd. Jour. Biol. Chemistry, 1975-78, Biochemistry, 1993—; contbr. articles to profl. jours. Recipient Charles Pfizer award Am. Chem. Soc., 1974. Mem. NAS, AAAS, Am. Acad. Arts and Scis., Am. Soc. Biochemistry and Molecular Biology, Am. Soc. Microbiology, Am. Acad. Microbiology, Phi Beta Kappa, Sigma Xi. Office: U Calif Dept Molecular/Cell Biology 401 Barker Hall Berkeley CA 94720-3203

CHAMBERLIN, MICHAEL MEADE, lawyer; b. Omaha; s. Cecil Meade and Helen Gail (Russell) C. AB in Econs., Princeton U., 1972; JD, George Washington U., 1975. Bar: N.Y. 1976. Assoc. Shearman & Sterling, N.Y.C., 1975-83, ptnr., 1984-93; CEO, exec. dir. Emerging Markets Traders Assn., 1994—; v.p. Ascension Music, Inc.; chair the Dennis Keene Choral Festival, Inc. Mem. nat. coun. World Wildlife Fund. Avocations: conservation, running, choral music, skiing, flying.

CHAMBERLIN, ROBERT WEST, medical educator; b. Cleve., Feb. 15, 1929. BS, Princeton (N.J.) U., 1951; MD, Harvard Med. Sch., 1956; MPH, Johns Hopkins U., 1982. Diplomate Am. Bd. Pediatrics, Am. Bd. Med. Examiners. Intern The Mary Hitchcock Hosp., Hanover, N.H., 1956-57; resident Mass. Gen. Hosp., Boston, 1957-59; postdoctoral fellow Johns Hopkins Hosp., 1961-62, resident in preventive medicine, 1981-82; postdoctoral fellow U. Mich. Inst. for Social Rsch., Ann Arbor, 1966-67; dir. pediatric ambulatory svcs., asst. prof. pediatrics U. Ky. Med. Ctr., 1962-66; asst. and assoc. prof. of pediatrics and nursing U. Rochester Med. Ctr., 1967-82; med. dir. child devel. program Bur. of Spl. Med. Svcs., N.H. Divsn. of Pub. Health, 1984-89; assoc. prof. maternal and child health Dartmouth Hitchcock Med. Ctr., Hanover, 1984-89; adj. prof. sch. of health and human svcs. U. N.H., 1992—; adj. prof. pediatrics Dartmouth Med. Sch., 1992—. Contbr. articles to profl. jours. Capt. U.S. Army, 1959-61, med. officer, 1989-92; sr. surgeon USPHS, 1982-84. Fellow Am. Coll. of Preventive Medicine, Am. Acad. Pediatrics; mem. APHA (governing coun. rep. for sect. on maternal and child health 1984-85), Ambulatory Pediatric Soc. (bd. dirs. 1981-84), European Soc. of Social Pediatrics. Home: PO Box 12 Canterbury NH 03224-0012

CHAMBERLIN, WARD BRYAN, JR., public broadcasting executive; b. N.Y.C., Aug. 4, 1921; s. Ward Bryan and Elizabeth Frances (Nichols) C.; m. Lydia Gifford, Oct. 6, 1951; children: Carolyn, Margot. B.A. summa cum laude, Princeton U., 1946; LL.B., Columbia U., 1948. Bar: N.Y.State bar 1949. Practiced in N.Y.C., 1949-51; asst. counsel Mutual Security Agency, Washington, 1951-53; asso. counsel Def. Materials Procurement Agency, Paris, London, 1953-54, Gen. Dynamics Corp., N.Y.C., 1954-65; v.p., gen. counsel Internat. Exec. Service Corps, N.Y.C., 1965-68; v.p. Corp. for Pub. Broadcasting, N.Y.C., 1968-70; exec. v.p. Sta. WNET-TV, N.Y.C., 1970-72; pres. PACT, Inc., N.Y.C., 1972-73; sr. v.p. Pub. Broadcasting Service, N.Y.C., 1973-75; pres., gen. mgr. Sta. WETA-TV and WETA-FM, Greater Washington Ednl. Telecommunication Assn., Washington, 1975-90; chmn., CEO Am. Playhouse, N.Y.C., 1993—, Am. Documentaries, Inc., N.Y.C., 1993—; v.p., mng. dir. Sta. WNET-TV ednl. broadcasting, N.Y.C., 1994—. Trustee Princeton U., 1975-79; ambulance driver Am. Field Svc., Africa, Italy, India, 1942-45, bd. dirs. 1946—, chmn. bd. 1967-72, chmn. bd. trustees, 1972-74, bd. dirs. Outward Bound, 1980-84; trustee Earthwatch, Inc., 1981-89, Nat. Pub. Radio, 1983-89. Recipient John Phillips award Phillips Exeter Acad., 1978, Ralph Lowell award Corp. for Pub. Broadcasting, 1990, Pub. Svc. award Cath. U. Am., 1982. Mem. Century and Univ. Clubs (N.Y.C.), Army-Navy Country, Met. and Alibi Clubs (Washington), Ralph Lowell award Corp. for Pub. Broadcasting, 1990. Democrat. Office: Thirteen WNET 450 W 33rd St New York NY 10001

CHAMBERS, ANNE COX, newspaper executive, former diplomat; b. Dayton, Ohio. Student, Finch Coll., N.Y.C.; D in Pub. Svc. (hon.), Wesleyan Coll., 1982; DHL (hon.), Spelman Coll., 1983; LLD (hon.), Oglethorpe U., 1983; DHL (hon.), Brenau Coll., 1989; LLD (hon.), Clark Atlanta U., 1989. Chmn. bd. Atlanta Jour.-Constn.; Am. amb. to Belgium, 1977-81; bd. dirs. Cox Enterprises, Inc. Bd. dirs. Atlanta Arts Alliance, High Mus. Art, Cmtys. in Schs., MacDowell Colony, Forward Arts Found., Emory Mus. Art and Archaeology, N.Y. Bot. Garden, Coun. Am. Ambs., Chmn.'s Coun., Met. Mus. Art, Fr.-Am. Found., The Lacoste Sch. Arts; trustee Mus. Modern Art, Carter Ctr.; mem. internat. coun. Mus. Modern Art; mem. nat. com. Whitney Mus. Am. Art. Decorated Legion of Hon. (France). Mem. Coun. Fgn. Rels. Office: Atlanta Newspapers 1400 Lake Hearn Dr NE Atlanta GA 30319-1464

CHAMBERS, ANTHONY HOOK, Literature educator; b. Pasadena, Calif., July 1, 1943; s. J. Curtis and Pauline Klene Chambers. BA, Ponoma Coll., 1965; MA, Stanford U., 1968; PhD, U. Mich., 1974; MA (hon.), Wesleyan U., 1987. Asst. prof. Ariz. State U., Tempe, 1971-75, prof., 1998—; asst. to assoc. to prof. Wesleyan U., Middletown, Conn., 1975-98; resident dir. Associated Kyoto (Japan) Program, 1989-90; cons. NEA, Washington, 1987, 88, 93, 94, 97. Translator: A Tanizaki Feast: The International Symposium in Venice, 1998, The Secret Window: Ideal Worlds in Tanizaki's Fiction, 1995, The Reed Cutter and Captain Shigemoto's Mother: Two Novellas, 1993, New Leaves: Studies and Translations of Japanese Literature in Honor of Edward Seidensticker, 1993, Naomi, The Secret History of the Lord of Musashi and Arrowroot, 1983; translator numerous jours. and contbr. articles to profl. publs. Bd. dirs. Asian Arts Coun., Phoenix Art Mus., 1998—. Grantee Nat. Endowment for the Arts, 1992, Am. Philos. Soc., 1979; fellow Nat. Def. Edn. Act, 1968-70, Nat. Def. Fgn. Lang. fellowship, 1966-68, Japan Found. fellowship, 1977. Mem. Ariz. Assn. of Tchrs. of Japanese (pres. 1999—), Ariz. Lang. Assn., Assn. of Tchrs. of Japanese, Assn. for Asian Studies, Internat. House of Japan, Phi Kappa Phi. Avocations: reading, travel, music. Office: Dept Langs and Lits Airz State U PO Box 870202 Tempe AZ 85287-0202

CHAMBERS, CAROL TOBEY, elementary school educator; b. L.A., July 17, 1947; d. Joseph Richard and Jean Doris (Neal) Tobey; m. Joseph Price Chambers, June 8, 1973; 1 child, Ryan Leigh. Student, Ohio State U., 1965-67; BS in Edn., George Peabody Coll. Tchrs., 1969; postgrad., U. Tenn., 1971, Belmont U., 1971, 88, 96, Tenn. State U., 1980-83, Vanderbilt U., 1986, 92, Trevecca Coll., 1978, 89, 90, Tenn. Arts Acad., 1989, 94-96; arts seminar, workshop, Coll. of Santa Fe, 1997. Cert. tchr. elem. edn., K-12 art, Tenn. Tchr. 4th grade Metro-Nashville Pub. Sch., Nashville, 1969-70, tchr. art, music, 1970-71; tchr. 5th grade Harding Acad., Nashville, 1971-75, tchr. art K-8, 1977—; presenter workshops Mid-So. Assn. Ind. Schs., Nashville, 1986; vis. com. Oak Hill Sch., So. Assn. Colls. and Schs., Nashville, 1990, St. Berbard Acad., 1991; chair planning com. Harding Acad., Nashville, 1992-94, mem. 25th anniversary com.; fine arts chair St. Cecilia Acad. Parents Club, Nashville, 1991-93, mem. Parents Club; co-founder Art Tchrs. Guild, Nashville; organizer Youth Art Month Exhibit, Nashville, 1992—. V.p. in charge of art Children's Internat. Edn. Ctr., Nashville, 1985-90; mem. edn. coun. Frist Fine Arts Ctr.; mem. Cheekwood Fine Arts Ctr. and Bot. Gardens Edn. Dept., Nashville, 1987—; prodr. parent's seminar 1st Bapt. Ch., 1986; mem. edn. coun. Frist Ctr. Visual Arts, Nashville. Outstanding Tchr. of Humanities grantee Tenn. Humanities Couns., 1988. Mem. Nat. Art Edn. Assn., Tenn. Art Edn. Assn., Nat. Mus. Women in the Arts (charter). Baptist. Avocations: watercolor and calligraphy, traveling, singing, piano. Home: 722 Starlit Rd Nashville TN 37205-1210 Office: 170 Windsor Dr Nashville TN 37205-3719

CHAMBERS, CAROLYN SILVA, communications company executive; b. Portland, Oreg., Sept. 15, 1931; d. Julio and Elizabeth (McDonnell) Silva; widowed; children: William, Scott, Elizabeth, Silva, Clark. BBA, U. Oreg. V.p., treas. Liberty Comm., Inc., Eugene, Oreg., 1960-83; pres. Chambers Comm. Corp., Eugene, 1983-95, chmn., 1996—; chmn., CEO, bd. dirs. Chambers Constrn. Co., 1986—; bd. dirs., dep. chair bd. Fed. Res. Bank, San Francisco, 1982-92; bd. dirs. Portland Gen. Corp.; bd. dirs. U.S. Bancorp. Mem. Sacred Heart Med. Found., 1980—, Sacred Heart Gov. Bd., 1987-92, Sacred Heart Health Svcs. Bd., 1993-95, PeaceHealth Bd., 1995—; mem. U. Oreg. Found., 1980—, pres., 1992-93; chair U. Oreg. Found., The Campaign for Oreg., 1988-89; pres., bd. dirs. Eugene Arts Found.; bd. dirs., treas., dir. search com. Eugene Symphony; mem. adv. bd. Eugene Hearing and Speech Ctr., Alton Baker Park Commn., Pleasant Hill Sch. Bd.; chmn., pres., treas. Civic Theatre, Very Little Theatre; negotiator, treas., bd. dirs., mem. thrift shop Jr. League of Oreg. Recipient Webfoot award U. Oreg., 1986, U. Oreg. Pres.'s medal, 1991, Disting. Svc. award, 1992, Pioneer award, 1983, Woman Who Made a Difference award Internat. Women's Forum, 1989, U. Oreg. Found. Disting. Alumni award, 1995, Tom McCall awrd Oreg. Assn. Broadcasters, 1995, Disting. Alumni award U. Oreg., 1995, Outstanding Philanthropist award Oreg. chpt. Nat. Soc. Fund Raising Execs., 1994. Mem. Nat. Cable TV Assn. (mem. fin. com., chmn. election and by-laws com., chmn. awards com., bd. dirs. 1987-89, Vanguard award for Leadership 1982), Pacific Northwest Cable Comm. Assn. (conv. chmn., pres.), Oreg. Cable TV Assn. (v.p., pres., chmn. edn. com., conv. chmn., Pres.'s award 1986), Calif. Cable TV Assn. (bd. dirs., conv. chmn., conv. panelist), Women in Cable (charter mem., treas., v.p., pres., recipient star of cable recognition), Wash. State Cable Comm. Assn., Idaho Cable TV Assn., Community Antenna TV Assn., Cable TV Pioneers, Eugene C. of C. (first citizen award, 1985). Home: PO Box 640 Pleasant Hill OR 97455-0640 Office: Chambers Comm Corp PO Box 7009 Eugene OR 97401-0009

CHAMBERS, CHARLES MACKAY, university president; b. Hampton, Va., June 22, 1941; s. Charles McKay and Ruth Ellanora (Wallach) C.; m. Barbara Mae Fromm, June 9, 1962; children: Charles M., Catherine M., Christina M., Carleton M. BS, U. Ala., 1962, MS, 1963, PhD, 1964; JD, George Washington U., 1976. Bar: Va. 1977, D.C. 1978, U.S. Patent and Trademark Office, 1978, U.S. Supreme Ct. 1980, U.S. Dist. Ct. D.C. 1985, U.S. Ct. Appeals (D.C. cir.) 1987, U.S. Dist. Ct. (ea. dist.) Va. 1988, U.S. Ct. Appeals D.C., 1987, U.S. Ct. Appeals (4th cir.) 1990, Mich. 1994. Aerospace engr. NASA, Huntsville, Ala., 1962-63; rsch., teaching asst. U. Ala. Rsch. Inst., Huntsville, Ala., 1963-64; research fellow NASA, Cambridge, Mass., 1964-65; assoc. prof. U. Ala., Tuscaloosa, 1965-69; mng. dir. Univ. Assocs., Washington, 1969-72; prof., assoc. dean George Washington U., Washington, 1972-77; v.p., gen. counsel Council on Postsecondary Accreditation, Washington, 1977-83; exec. dir. Am. Inst. Biol. Sci., Washington, 1983-87; pres. Am. Found. Biol. Scis., Washington, 1987-93, Lawrence Tech. U., Southfield, Mich., 1993—; cons., evaluator commn. on instns. of higher edn. North Ctrl. Assn. Colls. and Schs., Chgo. Author: (with others) Understanding Accreditation, 1983; pub. BioScience; contbr. chpts. to books. Mem. Diocesan Adv. Coun., Arlington, Va., 1978-84, Fairfax County (Va.) Dem. Com., 1979-95; judge No. Va. Sci. Fair, 1976—; trustee, sec. Southeastern U., Washington, 1983-87; trustee BIOSIS, Inc., Phila. and London, 1991-93; mem. Oakland County (Mich.) Workforce Devel. Bd., 1996—. Recipient Olive Branch award Editors and Writers Com., N.Y.C., 1986, Citizenship award Am. Legion, 1959; postdoctoral fellow Nat. Sci. Found., 1964. Fellow AAAS; mem. ABA, AAUP, Am. Assn. Univ. Adminstrs. (pres. 1984-85), Engring. and Sci. Devel. Found. (bd. dirs., pres. 1996—, fellow Engring. Soc. 1997), Am. Coun. Edn. (bus. and higher edn. forum), Soc. Automotive Engrs., Nat. Soc. Black Engrs. (hon.), ESD-The Engring. Soc. (bd. dirs. 1999—), Circumnavigators Club, Econ. Club of Detroit (bd. dirs.), Cosmos Club, Phi Beta Kappa, Sigma Xi, Tau Beta Pi. Roman Catholic. Avocation: flying. Office: Lawrence Tech U 21000 W 10 Mile Rd Ste M351 Southfield MI 48075-1058

CHAMBERS, CHRISTOPHER HART, artist; b. N.Y.C., May 15, 1960; s. Joseph Charles and Patricia May (Hart) C.; m. Anita Ka-Wai Yeung, Nov. 25, 1989; children: Kaela Mei-Chee, Toran Jun-Yang. Student, Art Student's League, N.Y.C., 1976-78, SUNY, Purchase, 1978-79. Curator over 30 contemporary art exhbns. One-man shows Kleeblatt Gallery, 1984, Jim Diaz Gallery, 1985, Huntington (N.Y.) Arts Coun., 1987, A.S.A.G.E. Gallery, 1988, Sarah Rentschler Gallery, 1990, Andrew Zarre Gallery, 1994, V.I.A. Art, Inc., 1995, Grant Gallery, 1998-99; exhibited in numerous group shows, 1983—, including Stewart Neil Gallery, 1983, Gabrielle Bryers Gallery, 1983, GuGu Ernesto Gallery, Cologne, Germany, 1983, Milan Poly. Faculty Architecture, 1983, Cattedra Evan Pugh, Italy, 1983, Galleria Lo Zibbetto, Milan, 1983, John Gerstaadt Gallery, 1985, Sarah Rentschler Gallery, 1987, Louise Hallet Gallery, London, 1988, Bettal Gallery, 1991, Am. Icon, 1992, Cavaliero Gallery, 1993, Galerie Pelin Helsinki, 1994, Bronx River Art Ctr. and Gallery, 1995, Robert Wood Gallery, Syracuse, N.Y., 1995, Phyllis Weil and Co., 1995, 96, 97, 450 Broadway Gallery, 1996, 97, Livestock Gallery, 1996, 97, 98, Gen Art, 1996, 98, Santa Monica (Calif.) Mus., 1996, Stux/Cooper Gallery, 1997, Index Gallery, Osaka, Japan, 1997, FIA, Inc., Kyoto, Japan, 1997, Sala Franco, Trieste, 1997, Abraham Lubelski Gallery, 1998, Golstrom Gallery, 1998, Hartnett-Murray, 1999; contbr. art criticism to mags., including Flash Art, N.Y. Arts, Zing, dART. Studio: 187 Lafayette St 4th Fl New York NY 10013

CHAMBERS, CLARICE LORRAINE, clergy, educational consultant; b. Ossining, N.Y., Oct. 7, 1938; d. Willie and Louise (McDonald) Cross (dec.); m. Albert W. Chambers, June 9, 1962; children: Albert W., Cheryl L. Fultz. Diploma, Manna Bible Inst., Phila.; BS in Bibl. Studies, Trinity Coll. of Bible, Newburgh, Ind., 1983; MA in Bibl. Theology, Internat. Bible Inst. and Sem., Orlando, Fla., 1986. Ordained to ministry Pentecostal Ch., 1977. Master data specialist Naval Supply Dept., Phila., 1957-65; dir. tng., tchr. Opportunities Indsl. Ctr., Harrisburg, Pa., 1969-72; pub. info. asst. Pa. Dept. Revenue, Harrisburg, 1972-79; pastor Antioch Tabernacle United Holy Ch. of Am., Harrisburg, 1979—; Fin. sec. United Holy Ch. of Am., Greensboro, N.C., 1978-92, treas. no. dist., Linden, N.J., 1992-96; mem. screening team La. Dept. Edn., Baton Rouge, 1995. Mem. Harrisburg Sch. Bd., 1975—; pres. Pa. Sch. Bds. Assn., New Cumberland, 1992; bd. dirs. Nat. Sch. Bds. Assn., Alexandria, Va., 1993—, pres.-elect, 1999; trustee Shippensburg (Pa.) U., 1989-96. Recipient Cmty. Sv. award Ctrl. Pa. chpt. Nat. Assn. Black Accts., 1984, Harrisburg chpt. Black United Fund. Pa., 1989, Outstanding Leadership award Greater Harrisburg NAACP, 1987, award of svc. Coun. of Pub. Edn., 1995. Democrat. Avocations: singing, reading. Home: 147 Sylvan Ter Harrisburg PA 17104-1039 Office: Antioch Tabernacle UHC of Am 1920 North St Harrisburg PA 17103-1631

CHAMBERS, CLYTIA MONTLLOR, public relations consultant; b. Rochester, N.Y., Oct. 23, 1922; d. Anthony and Marie (Bambace) Capraro; m. Joseph John Montllor, July 2, 1941 (div. 1958); children: Michele, Thomas, Clytia; m. Robert Chambers, May 28, 1965. BA, Barnard Coll., N.Y.C., 1942; Licence en droit, Faculte de Droit, U. Lyon, France, 1948; MA, Howard U., Washington, 1958. Assoc. dir. dept. rsch. Coun. for Fin. Aid to Edn., N.Y.C., 1958-60; asst. to v.p. indsl. rels. Sinclair Oil Corp., N.Y.C., 1961-65; writer pub. rels. dept. Am. Oil Co., Chgo., 1965-67; dir. editorial svcs., v.p. Hill & Knowlton Inc., N.Y.C., 1967-77; sr. v.p., dir. spl. svcs. Hill & Knowlton Inc., L.A., 1977-90, sr. cons., 1990—; cons. and trustee Childen's Inst. Internat., L.A., 1988-93. Co-author: The News Twisters, 1971; editor: Critical Issues in Public Relations, 1975. Mem. Calif. Rare Fruit Growers (editor Fruit Gardener 1979—). E-mail: clytia@112358.com. Home: 11439 Laurelcrest Dr Studio City CA 91604-3872

CHAMBERS, CURTIS ALLEN, clergyman, church communications executive; b. Damascus, Ohio, Sept. 24, 1924; s. Binford Vincent and Margaret Esther (Patterson) C.; m. Anna June Winn, Aug. 26, 1946; children: David Lloyd, Curtis Allen II, Deborah Ann, Charles Cloyde. Th.B., Malone Coll., 1946; A.B., Ind. Wesleyan U., 1947; B.D., Asbury Theol. Sem., 1950; postgrad., Oberlin Grad. Sch. Theology, 1951-53; S.T.M., Temple U., 1955, S.T.D., 1960; D.D. (hon.), Lebanon Valley Coll., 1967. Ordained to ministry Evang. United Brethren Ch., 1954. Pastor 1st Ch., Cleve., 1951-53, Rockville Ch., Harrisburg, Pa., 1953-59; editor adult publs. Evang. United Brethren Ch., 1959-65; assoc. editor Ch. and Home mag., Dayton, Ohio, 1963-66; editor Ch. and Home mag., 1967-69; asst. editorial dir. Together and Christian Advocate, Meth. Pub. House, Park Ridge, Ill., 1969; editor Together mag., 1969-73; acting editorial dir. gen. periodicals United Meth. Ch., 1971-72, editorial dir., 1972-73; gen. sec. United Meth. Communications, 1973-84; gen. mgr. Alternate View Network, 1984-85; minister edn. and communication First United Meth. Ch., Shreveport, La., 1985-87, minister pastoral care and communication, 1987-88; minister program and communication St. Paul's United Meth. Ch., Monroe, La., 1988-90; religious communication cons. Nashville, 1990—; assoc. pastor Andrew Price United Meth. Ch., Nashville, 1991-94; book editor Evang. United Brethren Ch., 1965-68; co-editor Plan of Union, United Meth. Ch., 1965-68, Plan of Union, United Meth. Ch. (Book of Discipline), 1968, chmn. staff com. long range planning, 1969-72, mem. commn. on ch. union, 1965-68; dir. radio-TV relations gen. confs. Evang. United Brethren Ch., 1958, 62, 66, United Meth. Ch., 1966, 68; Chmn. commn. on ednl. media Nat. Council Chs., 1965-66, chmn. com. on audio visual and broadcast edn., 1962-65, exec. com. broadcasting and film commn., chmn. communications commn., 1975-78, v.p., 1975-78; chmn. Religious Communications Congress, 1980; named 1 of 12 editors sent to Middle East on fact-finding trip, 1969. Contbr. articles to religious lit. Served as capt. (chaplain) CAP, 1960-65. Recipient Distinguished Alumni award Malone Coll., 1967, Alumni of Year, 1978, Distinguished Alumni award Goshen High Sch. Alumni Assn., 1992; named to Communicators Hall of Fame United Met. Assn. Communicators, 1992. Mem. Aircraft Owners and Pilots Assn., United Meth. Assn. Communicators (v.p. 1968-72, Communicators' Hall of Fame 1992), World Assn. Christian Communications (central com., chmn. Jour. editorial bd. 1975-82, chmn. periodical devel. com., exec. com., sec. 1978-82), Asso. Ch. Press (hon. life), Religious Pub. Relations Council. Clubs: Chgo. Press (Dayton), Torch (Dayton). Home: 120 Saddle Tree Ct Hermitage TN 37076-1372 *When I was young I thought that anything was possible for me and that I had a long, long time to achieve it. With maturity I have come to a recognition of mortality, finitude, a limitation of time and opportunity. Thus my life has taught me three things: 1) Choose the best. Life is too precious to squander it on the second rate. 2) Live for others. The quality of one's life is enhanced rather than diminished as one shares himself/herself with others. 3) Fulfill your dreams. Tomorrow may never come; act now so that life's opportunities may not be lost forever.*

CHAMBERS, DONALD ARTHUR, biochemistry and molecular medicine educator; b. N.Y.C., Sept. 24, 1936. AB, Columbia U., 1959, PhD, 1972. Rsch. biochemist dept. surgery Harvard Med. Sch./Mass. Gen. Hosp., Boston, 1961-66; rsch. fellow in hematology dept. surgery Harvard Med. Sch./Beth Israel Hosp., Boston, 1967-68; faculty fellow in chem. biology Columbia U., N.Y.C., 1969-71; asst. rsch. biochemist Ctr. for Med. Genetics dept. medicine U. Calif. Med. Ctr., San Francisco, 1972-74, lectr. in biochemistry and biophysics, 1972-74, asst. prof. molecular biology and biochemistry, 1974-75; asst. prof. biol. chemistry and dermatology U. Mich., Ann Arbor, 1975-79, assoc. prof. biol. chemistry, 1979; prof. molecular biology U. Ill., Chgo., 1979—, prof. biol. chemistry, 1980—, rsch. prof. dermatology, 1981—, prof. biol. psychiatry, 1996; assoc. mem. Dental Rsch. Inst. U. Mich., 1978-79, adj. rsch. investigator Dept. Biol. Chemistry, 1979—; dir. Ctr. for Molecular Biology of Oral Disease, U. Ill., Chgo., 1979—, interim head dept. biochemistry, 1985, head dept. biochemistry, 1986—; vis. scholar Green Coll., Oxford U., 1989-93, hon. vis. fellow, 1993—; fellow Honors Coll., 1985—, Phi Kappa Phi lectr., 1991; nat. action com. Am. Assn. Dental Rsch., 1981—; study sect. rev. NIH, 1983-86, 92, 98—. Mem. editl. bd. Perspectives in Biology and Medicine. Recipient James Howard McGregor prize Columbia U., 1971; named Inventor of Yr., U. Ill., 1990; fellow in hematology NIH, 1967-68, fellow in chem. biology 1969-71; Rsch. grantee NIH, Am. Cancer Soc., Office of Naval Rsch., 1986—, Helene Curtis, Inc., 1988—, Tng. grantee NIH-NIGMS, 1975-79, NIH-NIAMDD, 1976-79, 77-80, NIH-NIDR-NIAMDD, 1980—, NIH-NCI, 1982-88. Mem. AAAS, Am. Assn. Med. Colls., Am. Chem. Soc., Am. Fedn. Clin. Rsch., Am. Soc. Biol. Chemistry, Am. Soc. Cell Biology, Am. Soc. Microbiology, Internat. Assn. Dental Rsch. (com. on rsch. progress 1982-85, chmn. 1984-85, chmn. grad. tng. forum com. exptl. pathology sect. 1983), Assn. Dept. Chmn. Biol. Chemistry, Chgo. Assn. Immunologists, Chgo. Cancer Assn., N.Y. Acad. Scis. (organizer meeting The Double Helix, 40 Yrs. 1993), Royal Soc. Medicine, Soc. Investigative Dermatology, Phi Kappa Phi, Sigma Xi. Achievements include patents (U.S., Can.) for method of determining periodontal disease, (with other) method of quantifying aspartate amino transferase in periodontal disease; research in role of cyclic nucleotides, prostaglandins, hormones and other regulatory factors in the regulation of cell function, proliferation and differentiation, in molecular medicine in neural-immune interactions, the regulatory mechanisms of host-microbial interactions, in the history and devel. of concepts in the bio-med. scis. Office: U Ill Coll Med Dept Biochemistry 1819 W Polk St # C 536 Chicago IL 60612-7331 Office: Ctr Molecular Biol Oral Diseases 801 S Paulina St # C 860 Chicago IL 60612-7210

CHAMBERS, HEIDI KNISKERN, English educator; b. Champaign, Ill., Feb. 9, 1967; d. Peter Jon Kniskern and Heather MacFarlane Odegaard Mapp; m. Anthony Kirk Chambers, June 20, 1992; 1 child, John Ramsay. BA in English, U. Ga., 1989, MEd in English, 1991; MEd in Adminstrn., Albany (Ga.) State U., 1997. Tchr. spl. edn. Early County H.S., Blakely, Ga., 1992-93; English tchr. Bainbridge (Ga.) H.S., 1993—. Pres. Bainbridge Svc. Club, 1996-97. Mem. ASCD, AAUW (pub. policy chair 1993-96), Nat. Coun. Tchrs. English, Alpha Delta Kappa. Avocations: travel, reading. Office: Bainbridge HS 1301 E College St Bainbridge GA 31717-4878

CHAMBERS, HELEN MCGRAW, pianist; b. Takoma Park, Md., Dec. 23, 1905; d. Fred and Mary (Graves) McGraw; m. Robert Chambers, Apr. 14, 1928. Artists diploma, Peabody Conservatory, 1930; student under Alfred Cortot, Ecole Normale de Musique, Paris, 1932. Developed reputation for playing good but unfamiliar pieces; played opening concerts 1st 2 Am. Music Festivals, Washington. Recipient first prize Walter W. Naumburg Found. competition, N.Y.C., 1930. Mem. Nat. Mus. Women in the Arts, Friday Morning Music Club. Home: 16401 Black Rock Rd Germantown MD 20874-3211

CHAMBERS, HENRY CARROLL, realty broker; b. Beaufort, S.C., July 23, 1928; m. Elizabeth Lee Brewer. BSCE, Clemson U., 1949. From ptnr. to v.p. Burton Block Co., 1952-65; pres., gen. mgr. Burton Block & Concrete Co., Inc., 1965-81; pres. Deerfield Sand & Mining Co., Inc., 1958-74, Branchville, S.C., 1963-73; pres. Chambers-Cleckley, Inc., 1967-74, Hilton Head Concrete, Inc., 1970-74, South Atlantic Leasing Corp., 1961-74; v.p. MSC, Inc., 1981-84; broker Beaufort Realty Co., 1982—; sec.-treas. Brays Island Plantation Co., 1987-91. Mayor City of Beaufort, 1969-91; chmn. Beaufort County Devel. Bd., 1958-63; pres., campaign chmn. Beaufort County United Fund, 1960-63, bd. dirs., 1963; ruling elder First Presbyterian Ch. Beaufort; nat. alumni coun. rep., bd. visitors, pres. statewide adv. com. Clemson U.; mem. Historic Beaufort Found., 1969-82, Gov.'s Beautification and Community Improvement Bd., 1971-74; chmn. Beaufort dist. Boy Scouts Am., 1959-60, pres. Coastal Carolina coun., 1968-69; pres., chmn. bd. Beaufort Acad., 1967-75. Named Beaufort Young Man of Yr., Beaufort Jaycees, 1961, Boss of Yr., 1969; recipient Rotary Bowl for civic svc. Rotary Club, Beaufort, 1970, Pub. Svc. award Nat. Trust for Hist. Preservation, 1978; Silver Beaver award Boy Scouts Am., Silver Antelope award; Disting. Svc. Key, Boys Clubs Am. Mem. AIA (hon. nat. and S.C. chpt.), Am. Soc. Landscape Architects (honor award 1987), Concrete Masonry Assn., Soc. Am. Mil. Engrs., Am. Concrete Inst., S.C. Asphalt Pavement Assn. (past bd. dirs.), S.C. Concrete Masonry Assn. (past pres. and bd. dirs.), S.C. Hist. Soc. (bd. curators, 1st v.p.), Beaufort County C. of C. (past bd. dirs.), Nat. Sorjourners, Beaufort Coun. Navy League, Sertoma Club (bd. dirs. Beaufort 1956-58, charter pres.), Masons, Scottish Rite, York Rite. Office: 210 Carteret St Beaufort SC 29902-5524

CHAMBERS, HENRY GEORGE, orthopedic surgeon; b. Portsmouth, Va., June 22, 1956; s. Walter Charles and Teresa Frances (Fernandez) C.; m. Jill Annette Swanson, June 10, 1978; children: Sean Michael, Reid Christopher. BA summa cum laude in Biochemistry, U. Colo., 1978; MD, Tulane U. Sch. Medicine, 1982. Diplomate Am. Bd. Orthopaedic Surgery. Commd. 2d lt. U.S. Army, 1978, advanced through grades to maj., 1988; intern Fitzsimmons Army Med. Ctr., Aurora, Colo., 1982-83; orthopaedic surgery resident Brooke Army Med. Ctr., Ft. Sam Houston, Tex., 1983-87, chief resident, 1986-87, staff orthopaedic surgeon to asst. residency program dir., 1987-89, asst. chief surgeon orthopaedic surgery svc., 1990-92; staff orthopaedic surgeon DeWitt Army Hosp., Ft. Belvoir, Va., 1987; pediatric orthopaedic fellow San Diego Children's Hosp., 1989-90; asst. prof. surgery Uniformed Svcs. U. Health Scis., Bethesda, Md., 1987—; asst. program dir. Brooke Army Med. Ctr. Orthopaedic Surgery, 1987-92; assoc. prof. U. Calif.-San Diego Med. Ctr., 1989—; pvt. practice San Diego, 1992—; chmn. dept. orthopedic surgery San Diego Children's Hosp., 1997—; med. dir. Motion Analysis Lab.; adj. prof. natural scis. Incarnate Word Coll., San Antonio, 1986—. Co-author: Long Distance Runner's Guide to Training, 1983; contbr. various articles to profl. jours. Physician St. Vincent de Paul Clinic for Homeless, San Diego, 1989—; v.p. United Cerebral Palsy. Recipient Comdrs. award for oustanding rsch. Brooke Army Med. Ctr., 1987. Fellow Acad. Cerebral Palsy Devel. Medicine (bd. dirs.), Pediatric Orthopedic Soc. N.Am., Am. Acad. Pediatrics, Acad. Orthopedic Soc., Orthopedic Rsch. Soc., Am. Acad. Orthopedic Surgeons, Physicians for Social Responsibility, Physicians Coun. for Responsible Medicine, We. Orthopedic Soc., World Wildlife Fedn., Wilderness Soc., Union Concerned Scientists, Friends of Earth, Handgun Control, Phi Beta Kappa. Democrat. Unitarian. Avocations: bicycling, weight lifting, golf, tennis. Home: 5458 Sandburg Ave San Diego CA 92122-4128

CHAMBERS, JACK A., educator; b. Hamilton, Ohio; s. Glen S. and H. Edna C.; m. Ruth Chambers; children: Melissa Ann, Wendy Colleen. AB, U. Miami; MA, U. Cin.; PhD, Mich. State U. Dir. computer ctr. Mansfield (Pa.) U., 1972-74; dir. computing and comms. Calif. State U., Fresno, 1974-86, Duquesne U., Pitts., 1986-89; exec. dir. computing and comms. Loyola Coll., Balt., 1989-90; planning and info. rsch. ctr. mgr. Fla. C.C., Jacksonville, 1990—. Co-author: (with others) (book) Computer Assisted Instruction: Its Use in the Classroom, 1983; (chpt.) Motivating Students for Lifetime Learning in New Directions in Education and Training Technology, 1985; author: chpt. in Facilitating Academic Software Development, 1988; editor: (books) Selected Papers Fifth InternatConference on College Teaching and Learning, 1994, Sixth Conference, 1995, Seventh Conference, 1996, Eighth Conference, 1997, Ninth Conference, 1998, Tenth Conference, 1999. Grantee: James McKeen Cattell Fund, Calif. State Dept. Edn., Calif. State Univ. System, NSF. Office: Fla CC at Jacksonville 501 W State St Jacksonville FL 32202

CHAMBERS, JERRY RAY, school system administrator; b. St. Joseph, Mo., Oct. 1, 1947; s. Ray Linden and Betty Allene (Roach) C.; m. Jacqueline Kaye Thomas, Feb. 11, 1967; children: Sandra Kaye, Jennifer Lynn. AS, Mo. Western State Coll., 1967; BA, U. Mo., Kansas City, 1969, MA in Edn. Adminstrn. and History, 1971; postgrad., U. Madras, India, 1974; PhD in Edn. Adminstrn., U. Mo., Kansas City, 1986. Tchr. Lillis High Sch., Kansas City, Mo., 1969; high sch. tchr. Sch. Dist. St. Joseph, Mo., 1969-80, dir. media svcs., 1980-90; supt. schs. Sch. Dist. Washington, Mo., 1990—; coun. pres. ITV Kansas City Pub. TV, 1981-90; assessor Mo. Prin. Assess Ctr., DESE, Jefferson City, Mo., 1987-90; bd. dirs. 353 Econ. Devel. Corp. Washington, 1991—, Network Ednl. Devel., St. Louis, 1993-96; exec. com. Coop. Sch. Dists. St. Louis. Author: Missouri Students Tune IN, 1987, History of Missouri Instructional Television, 1986, Beyond the Bullet Hole, 1988. Bd. dirs. Regional Bluffs Libr., St. Joseph, 1989, United Fund, Washington, 1992-95; campaign co-chmn. Earnings Tax Com., St. Joseph, 1988; chmn. edn. divsn. United Way, St. Joseph, 1986-89, bd. dirs. 1992; bd. dirs. Tri-County Fine Arts Ctr., 1992-97. Fulbright scholar U.S. Dept. Edn., 1974; recipient Alumni Achievement award U. Mo., Kansas City, 1988, Disting. Alumni award Mo. Western State Coll., 1990, Disting. Leadership award Nat. Assn. Com. Leadership, 1988, Key to City award City of St. Joseph Mayor, 1990, Pearce award as Mo. Supt. of Yr., 1999. Mem. Am. Assn. Sch. Adminstrs., Lions Club (Washington chpt., 1990-98, St. Joseph Host Club pres. 1989-90, exec. com. Cooperating Sch. Dists. Greater St Louis, 1996-98, pres. CSD 1999—). Avocations: basketball, tennis, reading, model railroading, nostalgia, baseball. Home: 2 Winchester Ct Washington MO 63090-5314 Office: School Dist Washington PO Box 357 220 Locust St Washington MO 63090-2829

CHAMBERS, JIM ARTHUR, educator; b. Mar. 30, 1940. PhD, Portland (Oreg.) State U., 1984. Prof. Washington State U., Pullman, 1988-89, Mesa State Coll., Grand Junction, Colo., 1989-92, Ind. State U., Terre Haute, 1992-96, Fla. Gulf Coast U., Fort Myers, Fla., 1997—. Home: 9163 N Cypress Dr Fort Myers FL 33912-5290 Office: Fla Gulf Coast U 10501 Blvd S Fort Myers FL 33965-6565

CHAMBERS, JOAN LOUISE, retired librarian, retired university educator and dean; b. Denver, Mar. 22, 1937; d. Joseph Harvey and Clara Elizabeth (Carleton) Baker; m. Donald Ray Chambers, Aug. 17, 1958. B.A. in English Lit., U. No. Colo., Greeley, 1958; M.S. in L.S., U. Calif.-Berkeley, 1970; M.S. in Systems Mgmt., U. So. Calif., 1985; cert., Coll. for Fin. Planning, 1989. Libr. U. Nev., Reno, 1970-79; asst. univ. libr. U. Calif., San Diego, 1979-81; univ. libr. U. Calif., Riverside, 1981-85; dean librs., prof. Colo. State U., Ft. Collins, 1985-97, emeritus dean and prof., 1997—; mgmt. intern. Duke U. Libr., Durham, N.C., 1978-79; sr. fellow UCLA Summer, 1982; cons. tng. program Assn. of Rsch. Libraries, Washington, 1981; libr. cons. Calif. State U., Sacramento, 1982-83, U. Wyo., 1985-86, 94, 95, U. Nebr., 1991-92, Calif. State U. System, 1993-94, Univ. No. Ariz., 1994, 95. Contbr. articles to profl. jours., chpts. to books. Bd. dirs. Consumers Union, 1996—. U. Calif. instl. improvement grantee, 1980-81; State of Nev. grantee, 1976, ARL grantee, 1983-84. Mem. Sierra Club, Beta Phi Mu, Phi Lambda Theta, Kappa Delta Phi, Phi Kappa Phi. Avocations: hiking, golfing, downhill and cross-country skiing, cycling, tennis. Home and Office: PO Box 1477 Edwards CO 81632-1477

CHAMBERS, JOE CARROLL, physician, consultant, educator; b. Bristol, Va., Aug. 12, 1932; s. Joseph Lemuel and Anna Chambers; m. Ruth Gwen Renfro Aycock, Dec. 20, 1956 (div. Apr. 1971); m. Bettye Anne Terry, Dec. 9, 1972; 1 child, Cynthia Anne. Student, East Tenn. State U., 1952; MD, U. Tenn., Memphis, 1956; MPH, U. N.C., 1962. Diplomate Am. Bd. Preventive Medicine. Intern Mid-States Bapt. Hosp., Nashville, 1957; health officer Tenn. Dept. Pub. Health, Johnson City, 1957-58; gen. asst. surgeon USPHS, Montgomery, Ala., 1958-60; dep. health officer, then health officer Jefferson County Health Dept., Birmingham, Ala., 1960-68; coord. regional med. program Med. U. S.C., Charleston, 1968; dir. Appalachian Regional Ctr. for Healing Arts, Johnson City, 1969-71; health dir. S.C. Dept. Health, Myrtle Beach, 1971-73, Aiken, S.C., 1974, Charleston, 1975-96; cons. Carealliance Health Svcs., Charleston, 1996—; clin. assoc. prof. preventive medicine and epidemiology Med. U. S.C., 1973—; adj. prof. Sch. Pub. Health U. S.C., 1977—. Pres. S.C. chpt. Am. Lung Assn., Columbia, 1989-91; mem. Preservation Soc. Charleston, 1972—; mem. Mayor's Task Force on Homeless, Charleston, 1985—; mem. stroke task force Am. Heart Assn., Columbia, S.C., 1998—. Mem. APHA, S.C. Pub. Health Assn. (pres. 1987-88, Hayne medal), So. Health Assn. (pres. 1985-86), Carolina Yacht Club, Delta Omega. Presbyterian. Avocations: culinary arts, music, sketching. E-mail: joe.chambers@carealliance.com. Home: 35 State St Charleston SC 29401 Office: Carealliance Health Svc 316 Calhoun St Charleston SC 29401

CHAMBERS, JOHN T., computer company executive; m. Elaine Chambers; 2 children. BS, BA, W.Va. U., JD; MBA, Ind. U. Sr. v.p. worldwide ops. Cisco Sys., Inc., San Jose, Calif., 1991-94, exec. v.p., 1994-95, pres., CEO, 1995—; bd. dirs. Clarify, Inc., San Jose, Arbor Software, Sunnyvale, Calif. Office: Cisco Sys Inc 170 W Tasman Dr San Jose CA 95134

CHAMBERS, JOHN WHITECLAY, II, history educator; b. West Chester, Pa., Aug. 6, 1936; s. John McCausland and Le-Arie P. C.; BS, Temple U., 1958; MA, San Francisco State Coll., 1965; PhD, Columbia U., 1973; m. Dorothy Roman, 1958; children: John Bret, Jeffrey Mark, Michael Adam; m. 2d, Amy Russo Piro, 1982; 1 child, Tacy Elizabeth. *Ancestor, John Chambers, yeoman Quaker farmer and his family, emigrated from Yorkshire, England to Pennsylvania in 1713, and purchased land in Chester County from William Penn's agent. By the mid-nineteenth century, the Chambers family farm, with manor house, "Hilltop," included more than 500 acres in London Britain Township, southeastern Chester County, Pa. Although the Quaker side of the family remained pacifists, Methodist Clark side fought in the Civil War in 97th Pennsylvania Volunteer Infantry Regiment (Chester County), with a brother, William Clark who was killed at Petersburg. Another brother, Jeptha Clark, cited for gallantry in storming of Fort Fisher, Wilmington, North Carolina* Reporter, Pasadena (Calif.) Ind. Star-News, 1958-60, San Rafael (Calif.) Ind.-Jour., 1960-61; news and documentary writer/producer KRON-TV, San Francisco, 1961-65; asst. prof. history Barnard Coll., Columbia U., N.Y.C., 1972-82, Rutgers U., New Brunswick, N.J., 1982-87, assoc. prof., 1987-93, prof. 1993—; dept. chair, 1997-98; Fulbright lectr. U. Rome, Spring 1982; project dir. Rutgers Ctr. Hist. Analysis, 1993-95. Nat. Endowment for Humanities grantee, 1974; humanities fellow Rockefeller Found., 1981-82, Vis. fellow Inst. Advanced Study, Princeton, 1995-96. Mem. Conf. on Peace Rsch. In History (pres. 1975-77), Am. Hist. Assn., Orgn. Am. Historians, Soc. Historians of Am. Fgn. Relations, Soc. Mil. History. Author: Three Generals on War, 1973; Draftees or Volunteers, 1975; The Eagle and the Dove: The Peace Movement and U.S. Foreign Policy, 1900-1922, 1976, 2d edit., 1991; The Tyranny of Change: America in the Progressive Era, 1890-1920, 1980, 2d edit., 1992; (with Warren Susman) American History Reading Lists, 3 vols., 1983; To Raise an Army: The Draft Comes to Modern America, 1987 (Best Book award, Soc. Mil. History, 1988, Best Book on Mil. History, 1987); (with Charles C. Moskos) The New Conscientious Objection: From Sacred to Secular Resistance, 1993; (with David Culbert) World War II Film and History, 1996; (with G. Kurt Piehler) Major Problems in American Military History, 1998. Ed-in-chief, Oxford Co. to Amer. Military History, 1999. Home: 10 Bunker Hill Dr Cranbury NJ 08512-3226 Office: Rutgers U 16 Seminary Pl New Brunswick NJ 08901-1108

CHAMBERS, JOHNNIE LOIS (TUCKER), retired elementary school educator, rancher; b. Crocket County, Tex., Sept. 28, 1929; d. Robert Leo and Lois K. (Slaughter) Tucker; m. R. Boyd Chambers; children: Theresa A., Glyn Robert, Boyd James, John Trox. BEd, Sul Ross State U., Alpine, Tex., 1971. Tchr. 1st and 2d grades Candelaria (Tex.) Elem. Sch., 1971-73; head tchr. K-8 Ruidosa (Tex.) Elem. Sch., 1973-77; head tchr. K-8 Presidio Ind. Sch. Dist. at Candelaria Elem. Sch., 1977-91, tchr. 2d and 3d grades, 1991-93, tchr. pre-kindergarten, kindergarten and 1st grade, 1993-98; acting prin. Candelaria Elem. and Jr. High, 1995-98, head tchr. pre-K to 8th grades, 1996-98, tchr. pre-K, kindergarten, 1st and 2d grades, 1996-98; mem. sight-base decision making, Presidio, 1991-94; mem. Chihuahuan Desert Rsch. Inst., Alpine, 1982-94. Leader Boy Scouts Am., Ruidosa and Candelaria, 1973-91, Cub Scout leader, 1973-91; chpt. mem. Sheriffs Assn. Tex., Austin, 1980. Recipient awards Boy Scouts Am., 1969, 83, winner Litter Gitter award, 1994-95. Mem. Tex. State Tchrs. Assn., Phi Alpha Theta. Avocations: hiking, camping, anthropologic digs, cave exploring, cooking. Home and Office: 99 Retirement Cir Candelaria TX 79843

CHAMBERS, JUDITH TARNPOLL, speech pathologist, audiologist; b. Newark, Mar. 17, 1940; d. Morris and grace Annette (Lambeck) Tarnpoll; m. John Darby Chambers, May 29, 1977; 1 child, Joshua. BA, Rutgers U., 1964; MA, Columbia U., 1966. Cert. audiologist, N.Y., Conn. Speech and lang. therapist League Sch., Bklyn.; lang. therapist BOCES, Elmsford, N.Y.; chief audiologist Royal Victoria Hosp., Montreal, Que., Can.; ind. dispensing audiologist Bridgeport, Conn.; speech and lang. pathologist Symphony Rehab. Svcs. Inc. Mem. Am. Speech-Lang.-Hearing Assn., Acad. Dispensing Audiologists, Am. Acad. Audiology (charter mem.).

CHAMBERS, JULIUS LEVONNE, academic administrator, lawyer; b. Montgomery County, N.C., Oct. 6, 1936. BA, N.C. Central U., 1958; MA, U. Mich., 1959; LLB, U. N.C., 1962; LLM, Columbia U., 1963. Bar: N.C. 1962, N.Y. 1986. Ptnr. Chambers, Ferguson, Watt, Wallas, Adkins, & Fuller, Charlotte, N.C., 1964-84; dir., counsel NAACP Legal Def. and Ednl. Fund, N.Y.C, 1984-92; chancellor N.C. Ctrl. U., Durham, N.C., 1993—; bd. dirs. RJR Nabisco Holdings. Trustee N.J. State Bd. of Higher Edn.; bd. visitors Harvard U., Columbia Law Sch.; trustee U. Pa., mem. bd. overseers Law Sch.; bd. dirs. Children's Def. Fund, Legal Aid Soc. N.Y. Mem. ABA (bd. editors ABA jour.), N.C. Bar Assn., Mecklenburg County Bar Assn., N.Y. State Bar Assn., Assn. of Bar of City of N.Y., Nat. Bar Assn., Assn. Black Lawyers N.C., Order of Coif, Order of Golden Fleece, Phi Alpha Theta. Office: NC Ctrl U 1801 Fayetteville St Durham NC 27707-3129

CHAMBERS, KENNETH CARTER, astronomer; b. Los Alamos, N.Mex., Sept. 27, 1956; s. William Hyland and Marjorie (Bell) C.; m. Jeanne Marie Hamilton, June 28, 1986; children: Signe Hamilton, William Hamilton. BA in Physics, U. Colo., 1979, MS in Physics, 1982; MA in Physics and Astronomy, Johns Hopkins U., 1985, PhD in Physics and Astronomy, 1990. Rsch. asst. dept. physics U. Colo., Boulder, 1982-83; rsch. asst. dept. physics and astronomy Johns Hopkins U., Balt., 1983-86; mem. instrument team Hopkins Ultraviolet Telescope, Balt., 1983-86; rsch. asst. Space Telescope Sci. Inst., Balt., 1986-90; postdoctoral fellow Leiden (The Netherlands) Obs. Leiden U., 1990-91; asst. prof. Inst. Astronomy U. Hawaii, Honolulu, 1991-98, assoc. prof., 1998—; Contbr. articles to Astrophys. Jour., Nature mag., Phys. Rev.; contbr. conf. procs. in field. Mem. Am. Astron. Soc. (Chretein award 1989), Am. Phys. Soc. Achievements include discovery of most distant known galaxy (4C41.17), of alignment effect in high redshift radio galaxies; research on observational cosmology, galaxy formation and evolution, active galaxies, observing techniques, spacecraft observations. Office: U Hawaii Inst Astronomy 2680 Woodlawn Dr Honolulu HI 96822-1839

CHAMBERS, KENTON LEE, botany educator; b. Los Angeles, Sept. 27, 1929; s. Maynard Macy and Edna Georgia (Miller) C.; m. Henrietta Laing, June 21, 1958; children: Elaine Patricia, David Macy. A.B. with highest honors, Whittier Coll., 1950; Ph.D. (NSF fellow), Stanford U., 1955. Instr. biol. scis. Stanford U., 1954-55; instr. botany, Yale U. 1956-58, asst. prof., 1958-60; assoc. prof. botany Oreg. State U., Corvallis, 1960-65, prof., 1965-90, prof. emeritus, 1991—, curator Herbarium, 1960-90; program dir. systematic biology NSF, Washington, 1967-68. NSF fellow, 1955-56. Mem. Bot. Soc. Am. (BSA Merit award 1990), Am. Soc. Plant Taxonomists, AAAS, Am. Inst. Biol. Scis., Calif. Bot. Soc. Democrat. Presbyterian. Clubs: Triad, Oreg. State U. Contbr. articles in field to profl. jours. Home: 4761 SW Hollyhock Cir Corvallis OR 97333 Office: Oreg State U Herbarium Botany Dept Corvallis OR 97331-2902

CHAMBERS, LETITIA PEARL CAROLINE, public policy consulting firm executive; b. Alva, Okla., Feb. 1, 1943; d. E. Wade and Anita (Sims) Chambers; m. Stephen Morelock, Mar. 1964 (div. 1970); 1 child, Melissa. BA, U. Okla., 1965; MS, Okla. State U., 1971, EdD, 1973. Tchr. Oklahoma City Pub. Schs., 1965-70, adminstr., 1973-74; dir. fed. programs N.Mex. State Edn. Agy., Santa Fe, 1974-75; sr. analyst US Senate Budget Com., Washington, 1976-77; staff dir. US Senate Spl. Com. on Aging, Washington, 1978, US Senate Com. on Labor & Human Resources, Washington, 1979-81; pres. Chambers Assocs., Inc., Washington, 1982—; U.S. rep. to the UN gen. assembly 51st Session, N.Y.C., 1996; pres. Coalition of Publicly Traded Partnerships, Washington, 1987—; dir. Adams Nat. Bank, Washington, 1989-94; treas. Nat. Infrastruction Bond Coalition; dir. Am. Assn. Budget Program Analysis, Stratego Investments, Prague, Cech Republic, 1997—; chief budget adv. Clinton/Gore Presdl. Transition, 1992-93; trustee Inst. Am. Indian Arts and Culture, Santa Fe, 1997—; bd. visitors U. Okla., 1995—. Author various senate reports, policy studies. Edler Chevy Chase (Md.) Presbyn. Ch., 1986-89; mem. Dem. Leadership Coun.; trustee Fed. City Coun. Recipient Disting. Alumni award U. Okla., 1998. Mem. Coun. for Excellence in Govt. (bd. dirs.), Ctr. Nat. Policy (trustee), Cosmos Club. Avocation: landscape gardening. Office: Chambers Assocs Inc 805 15th St NW Ste 500 Washington DC 20005

CHAMBERS, LISA M., psychiatric and mental health nurse; b. Pitts., Nov. 9, 1965; d. Paul and Rita M. (Beil) Koropal. BSN, U. Pitts., 1987. RN, Pa., N.Y. Staff nurse Western Psychiat. Inst. and Clinic, Pitts., 1987-89; staff nurse South Beach Psychiat. Ctr., S.I., N.Y., 1989-90, nursing supr. inpatient adolescent psychiat. unit; nurse clinician Western Psychiat. Inst. & Clinic, 1990-95; staff nurse Mercy Psychiat. Inst., Pitts., 1991—; nurse clinician Allegheny East Mental Health and Mental Retardation, 1992-93; mental health specialist Allegheny County Mental Health Dept., 1995—; nursing supr. Mercy Behavioral Health, Journey Home LTSR, 1996—. Mem. Pa. Nurses Assn. Home: 311 5th Ave Carnegie PA 15106-2324

CHAMBERS, LOIS IRENE, insurance automation consultant; b. Omaha, Nov. 24, 1935; d. Edward J. and Evelyn B. (Davidson) Morrison; m. Peter A. Mscichowski, Aug. 16, 1952 (div. 1980); 1 child, Peter Edward; m. Frederick G. Chambers, Apr. 17, 1981. Clk. Gross-Wilson Ins. Agy., Portland, Oreg., 1955-57; sec., bookkeeper Reed-Paulsen Ins. Agy., Portland, 1957-58; office mgr., asst. sec., agt. Don Biggs & Assocs., Vancouver, Wash., 1958-88, v.p. ops., 1988-89, automation mgr., 1989-91, mktg. mgr., 1991-94; automation cons. Chambers & Assocs., Tualatin, Oreg., 1985—; system mgr. Contractors Ins. Svcs., Inc., 1997—; chmn. adv. com. Clark Community Coll., Vancouver, 1985-93, adv. com., 1993-94. Mem. citizens com. task force City of Vancouver, 1976-78, mem. Block Grant rev. task force, 1978—. Mem. Ins. Women of S.W. Wash. (pres. 1978, Ins. Woman of Yr. 1979), Nat. Assn. Ins. Women, Nat. Users Agena Systems (charter; pres. 1987-89), Soroptimist Internat. (Vancouver)(pres. 1978-79, Soroptimist of the Year 1979-80). Democrat. Roman Catholic. Office: Chambers & Assocs 8770 SW Umatilla St Tualatin OR 97062-6340

CHAMBERS, MICHELE DENISE, technical writer; b. Atlantic City, N.J., Nov. 4, 1964; d. Frederick Lavan and Shirley Elizabeth (Boone) C. BA in Journalism, Rutgers U., 1987. Comm. asst. United Way Ctrl. N.J., Milltown, 1986; pub. affairs asst. Fed. Aviation Adminstn.-Atlantic City Internat. Airport, 1987-88; literacy coord., library asst. Atlantic City Library, 1988-91; tech. writer Hilton Sys. Inc., Cherry Hill, N.J., 1991-95, Universal Tech. Resource Svcs. Inc., Cherry Hill, N.J., 1995—. Contbr. articles to profl. jours. Home: 401 N Main St Apt 153B Williamstown NJ 08094-1461 Office: Universal Tech Resource Svc 950 N KingsHwy Ste 208 Cherry Hill NJ 08034

CHAMBERS, MILTON WARREN, architect; b. L.A., Aug. 5, 1928; s. Joe S. and Barbara N. (Harris) C.; m. Elizabeth M. Smith, Nov. 27, 1949; children: Mark, Michael, Daniel, Matthew. Student, Coll. of Sequoias, 1948-49, Harvard U., 1990. Lic. architect, Calif., Nev., Colo., Hawaii, Mont.; cert. Nat. Coun. Archtl. Registration Bds. Apprentice architect Kastner & Kastner Architects, Visalia, Calif., 1950-57; project architect Wurster, Bernardi & Emmons, Architects, San Francisco, 1958-63, Claude Oakland, Architect, San Francisco, 1964-65; chief architect Bank of Am., San Francisco, 1965-68; pres., owner Milton W. Chambers, Architect, San Rafael, Calif., 1969-82, The Chambers Group, Architects, Rancho Mirage, Calif., 1983—. Architect, designer St. Margaret's Episcopal Church, 1988. Foreman Marin County Grand Jury, San Rafael, 1976; mem. Archtl. Design Rev. Bd., Rancho Mirage, 1986—; trustee Marywood Sch., Rancho Mirage, 1990—. Cpl. U.S. Army, 1946-48, PTO, 50-51. Mem. AIA (pres. Calif. Desert chpt. 1986-87, 96&, dir. Calif. coun. 1989-90, 96—), Rotary Internat., Terra Linda Rotary Club (pres. 1975-76, dist. gov. 1993-94), Rancho Mirage Rotary Club (pres. 1986-87). Republican. Episcopalian. Avocations: playing the banjo and guitar. Office: The Chambers Group 44267 Monterey Ave Ste B Palm Desert CA 92260-2710

CHAMBERS, RAY WAYNE, security and loss control consultant; b. Cascade, W.Va., June 22, 1931; s. Robert and Mildred Ethel (Starrett) C.; m. Joan Roberta Tilley, Apr. 7, 1952; children: Rebecca H. Frase, Bonita I. Knight, Diana L. Sobalvarro. Cert. protection profl., mgmt. cons. Enlisted U.S. Army, 1949, advanced through grades to lt. col., 1971; sgt.-maj. tank battalion U.S. Army, Republic of Korea, 1952-53; U.S. Army, Europe, 1956-60, 62-65, 67-70; intelligence battalion ops. officer U.S. Army, Socialist Republic of Vietnam, 1966-67; dep. chief staff ops., intelligence command U.S. Army, ret., 1973; v.p. loss prevention Little Gen. Store div. Gen. Host Corp., Tampa, Fla., 1973-84; pres. Assets Protection Systems Assocs., Inc., Largo, Fla., 1985—; loss control cons. JRB Investigations Inc., Largo, 1986-87. Contbr. articles to profl. jours.. Bd. dirs. Del Prado Imperial Assn., Largo, chmn. neighborhood watch com., 1983-88. Decorated Bronze Star, Legion of Merit. Mem. Am. Soc. Indsl. Security (chmn. 1975-76, cert. 1976), Internat. Assn. Profl. Security Cons. (exec. dir. 1990-93), Retail Grocers Assn. Fla. (chmn. crime prevention 1983-85), Pinellas Assn. Pvt. Investigators (pres. 1986), Fla. Crime Prevention Officers Assn., Nat. Assn. Convenience Stores, Internat. Found. for Protection Officers, Assn. Counter Intelligence Corps Vets, Inst. Mgmt. Cons. Republican. Avocations: swimming, historial studies. Home and Office: Assets Protection Sys Assoc Inc 11113 Bella Loma Dr Largo FL 33774-4622

CHAMBERS, RICHARD LEON, retired Turkish language and civilization educator; b. Brundidge, Ala., Sept. 27, 1929; s. Cody Leon and Eunice Gertrude (Logan) C. BS in History, U. Ala., Tuscaloosa, 1950, MA in History, 1955; BS in Fgn. Svc., Georgetown U., 1951; MA in History and Oriental Studies, Princeton U., 1958, PhD in Near Ea. Studies, 1968. Lectr. history Am. U. in Cairo, 1958-59; asst. in instrn. Princeton (N.J.) U., 1960; instr. history St. Lawrence U., Canton, N.Y., 1960-62; instr. Turkish lang. and civilization U. Chgo., 1962-65, asst. prof., 1965-71, assoc. prof., 1971-95, dir. Ctr. for Mid. Ea. Studies, 1979-85, assoc. prof. emeritus, dir. devel. Ctr. for Mid. Ea. Studies, 1995—; co-founder, dir. Am. Rsch. Inst. in Turkey-Bosphorus U. summer Turkish lang. program, Istanbul, 1982-88; pres. Am. Rsch. Inst. in Turkey, Chgo. and Phila., 1985-88. Co-editor: Beginnings of Modernization in the Middle East: The 19th Century, 1968, Contemporary Turkish Short Stories, 1977; contbr. articles to profl. jours. and Ency. Brit. Recipient edn. award Am.-Turkish Coun., Washington, 1997; fellow German Acad. Exch. Svc., Munich, 1951-52, Ford Found., Princeton, 1955-57, rsch. fellow Am. Rsch. Inst. in Turkey, Istanbul, 1965. Mem. Mid. East Studies Assn. N.Am. (Svc. award 1998), Am. Assn. Tchrs. Turkic Langs., Turkish Studies Assn. (sec./treas. 1997—), Am. Hist. Soc., Am. Oriental Soc., Internat. Assn. Mid. Ea. Studies. Avocations: travel, reading, gardening, antiques. E-mail: r-chambers@uchicago.edu. Home: 5555 N Sheridan Rd Apt 807 Chicago IL 60640-1621 Office: U Chgo Ctr for Mid Eastern Studies 5828 S University Ave Chicago IL 60637-1515

CHAMBERS, ROBERT ARTHUR, entertainment director; b. Phila., Aug. 19, 1946; s. James Robert and Marjorie Evelyn (Weiss) C.; m. Alice Irene Bielak, July 25, 1968; children: Kathryn Evelyn, James Robert. BFA, U. Conn., 1975. Prodn. mgr. Bushnell Meml. Hall, Hartford, Conn., 1975-76; gen. mgr. Coconut Grove Playhouse, Miami, Fla., 1976-78; dir. show ops. Resorts Internat. Casino, Atlantic City, 1978-90; dir. lounge and theater Merv Griffin's Resorts Casino, Atlantic City, 1990-96; dir. entertainment Resorts Casino, Atlantic City, 1996-98, Sands Casino Hotel, Atlantic City, 1998—. With USN, 1967-73. Office: Sands Casino Hotel Indiana Ave and Brighton Pk Atlantic City NJ 08401

CHAMBERS, ROBERT HUNTER, III, college president, American studies educator; b. Winston-Salem, N.C., Oct. 24, 1939; s. Robert Hunter and Hildred (MacDonald) C.; m. Alice Louise Grant, Aug. 18, 1962 (div. 1995); children: Lisa, Grant. A.B., Duke U., 1962; B.D., Yale U., 1965; Ph.D., Brown U., 1969. Asst. prof., dean Davenport Coll. Yale U., New Haven, Conn., 1969-74; vis. fellow Clare Coll., Cambridge U., Eng., 1972-73; prof., dean Coll. Arts and Scis. Bucknell U., Lewisburg, Pa., 1975-84; vis. scholar Doshisha U., Kyoto, Japan, 1982; pres., prof. English Western Md. Coll., Westminster, 1984—; founding dir. Wellway Ctrs., Inc., Fort Worth, 1984-88, WMC Devel. Corp., 1985-88; presdl. chmn. Centennial Conf., Md. and Pa., 1986, 98-99; mem. segmental adv. com. State Bd. Higher Edn., Annapolis, Md., 1985-88; mem. internat. adv. coun. U. Buckingham, Eng.; mem. cmty. bd. Carroll Co. Health Svcs., Inc., 1988—; assoc. fellow Davenport Coll., Yale U. Author, editor: Twentieth Century Interpretations of All the King's Men, 1977. Contbr. articles to profl. jours. Bd. dirs. Ind. Coll. Fund of Md., Balt.,1984—; mem. coun. on grad. edn. Brown U., 1989; mem. City of Westminster Mayoral Task Force, 1990; co-chair spl. gifts Am. Heart Assn.; mem. task force on assessment Nat. Assn. Ind. Colls. and Univs., 1991-92, mem. commn. on state rels., 1992-95; mem. Gov.'s Edn. Policy Transition Team, 1994—; mem. Md. Citizens for Arts; bd. trustees Coun. of Ind. Colls. Rockefeller Brothers fellow, 1962-63; Nat. Endowment for the Humanities grantee, 1978, U.S.-Japan Friendship Commn. grantee, 1982; recipient Balt. Regional Coun. Govts. award, 1989. Mem. MLA, The Japan Soc., Higher Edn. Commn., Mid. States Assn. Colls. and Schs. (commr. 1985—, exec. com. 1986-91, vice chair 1987-89, chair 1990), Md. Ind. Coll. and Univ. Assn. (bd. dirs. 1984—, exec. com. 1985-88, 91—, budget com. 1985-89, 91, chair 1994-98), Am. Studies Assn., Coun. on Econ. Edn. in Md. (trustee 1), Internat. Assn. Univ. Presidents, Rotary (hon. 1990), Yale Club, Center Club, Phi Beta Kappa, Phi Kappa Assocs. Avocations: running, travel. Home: 1 College Hl Westminster MD 21157-4303 Office: Western Md Coll Office of the Pres 2 College Hl Westminster MD 21157-4303

CHAMBERS, ROBERT WILLIAM, financial company executive; b. Atlanta, Apr. 4, 1943; s. Robert William Chambers and Mary Emily (Martin) Nalley; m. Wendy Ann Treneer, Dec. 28, 1967 (div. 1979); 1 child, Robert William III. AB, Princeton U., 1965; MA, Indiana U., 1970, PhD, 1974. Assoc. instr. Ind. U., Bloomington, 1970-73; instr. Kans. State U., Manhattan, 1973-74; gen. mgr. Standard Cellulose Products Inc., Atlanta, 1974-75; mgr. sales, ops. Disposable Plastic Systems Inc., Marietta, Ga., 1975-77; asst. v.p., account exec. instl. sales Robinson-Humphrey Co. Inc., Atlanta, 1977-80; columnist, fin. reporter Atlanta Journal, 1980-81; account exec. Hill and Knowlton (J. Walter Thompson Group), Atlanta, 1981-83; sr. v.p., sales mgr. eastern div. Colonial Investment Svcs. Inc., Atlanta, 1983-90; sr. fin. cons. The Gwent Group, Atlanta, 1990-92; v.p., treas. Rabun Gap Film Corp., Atlanta, 1993—; dir. Bus. Svcs. Div. Porraro and Assocs., Atlanta, 1993-95; mgr. accts. divsn. Atlanta Rsch. and Trading, 1994-95; regional mktg. dir. Stephens, Inc., Atlanta, 1996-97; fin. reporter Atlanta Jour.-Constn., 1997-99; mktg. dir. Macey-Holland & Co., Atlanta, 1999—; Ga. correspondent The Economist, London, 1978-83, 99—; Am. Bankers Assn. fellowship, 1998. Mem. bd. Oglethorpe U. Art Mus., 1998—. Episcopal. Clubs: Piedmont Driving, Nine O'Clocks (Atlanta). Home: 335 Franklin Rd NE Atlanta GA 30342-2711 Office: RWC Ltd PO Box 421612 Atlanta GA 30342

CHAMBERS, RONALD D., book publishing executive; b. N.Y.C., Oct. 7, 1943; s. Burl W. and Blanche E. C.; m. Louise Callahan, June 10, 1966; children: Lalie Elizabeth, Richard Callahan. BA History, Coll. William and Mary, 1966; MA cum laude Latin Am. History, Univ. de las Ams., Mex., 1972. Sales rep. Coll. divsn. Prentice Hall, 1973-75, acquisitions editor edn. Coll. divsn., 1975-77; sr. acquisitions editor the Free Press Macmillan, 1977-80; editor in chief Praeger Publ., 1980-86, editor in chief, gen. mgr., 1986-93; v.p., edit. dir. Greenwood Pub. Group, 1993; dir. Naval Inst. Press, 1994. With USMC, 1967-70, Vietnam. Decorated Bronze Star. Office: Naval Inst Press 118 Maryland Ave Ste 2 Annapolis MD 21402-5034

CHAMBERS, THOMAS EDWARD, college president, psychologist; b. Cleve., Aug. 1, 1934; s. James Clyde and Mary Celestine (Malone) C. BA, U. Notre Dame, 1956, MA, 1962, PhD, 1976; MA, Holy Cross Coll., 1961. Lic. counselor, Ohio, La. Dir. student residences U. Notre Dame, Ind., 1969-73, dir. student activities, 1973-74, asst. v.p. student affairs, 1974-76; v.p. acad. affiars Ursuline Coll., Cleve., 1976-87; pres. Our Lady of Holy Cross Coll., New Orleans, 1987—; founder Internat. Student Leadership Inst., 1968; mem. exec. com. Sta. WLAE-TV, New Orleans, 1987—. Editor: For Leaders Only, 1975. Mem. exec. com. Met. Area Com., New Orleans, 1987—; bd. dirs. King's Coll., Wilkes-Barre, Pa., 1989—, St. Joseph Sem. Coll.; trustee Gilmour Acad., Cleve., 1978—, United Way. Recipient Nat. League Nursing award of Ohio Nat. League Nursing, 1986, Trustee award Cathedral High Sch., 1987. Mem. Am. Psychol. Assn., Am. Cath. Colls. and Univs., Plimsoll Club, Internat. House Club. Roman Catholic. Office: Our Lady of Holy Cross Coll 4123 Woodland Dr New Orleans LA 70131-7337

CHAMBERS-MANGUM, FRANSENNA ETHEL, special education educator; b. Meridian, Miss., June 27, 1957; d. Forrest S. and Betty (Wade) Chambers; 1 child, Richard Jomar Sullivan. BS, Jackson State U., 1979, MA, 1980, EdS, 1986. Cert. tchr., Miss., secondary adminstr., Miss. Chpt. tchr. Meridian Pub. Schs., 1979; tchr. spl. edn. Magee (Miss.) Pub. Sch., 1980-84; speech pathologist Heritage Sch. Learning Disability, Jackson, Miss., 1984-85; speech pathologist Canton (Miss.) Pub. Schs., 1985-86, spl. edn. tchr., 1986-88, pre-sch. coord., 1988-89; tchr. spl. edn. lang. delayed Jackson (Miss.) Pub. Schs., 1989-90, tchr. spl. edn., 1990—, mid. sch. reading tchr., 1993—; Miss. Writing Project cons. tchr., 1989—, Adult Edn. tchr. (ages 16-65). Writer and editor poems. Mem. Miss. Registrar Voters Com., Jackson, 1975—, Vista/Peace Corps, Jackson, 1980, NAACP, Jackson, 1982-85; bd. dirs., sec. and coord. Roshea Recovery Ctr., 1993—; tchr. Sunday sch., Jackson, 1992. Named Miss Miss. Elks, 1972-74, Miss Miss. Congeniality, Jaycees, 1972; Black Women's Assn. partial scholar, 1975. Mem. Miss. Writers of Am., Miss. Assn. Colls. and Evaluator Univs., Miss. Assn. Tchrs. (evaluator 1986—, Educator of Yr.), Learning Disabled Assn. Miss. Assn. Edn., Eastern Star, Daus. of Isis. Democrat. Avocations: writing poetry, public relations. Home: 1772 Casteel Dr Jackson MS 39204-3508 Office: Jackson Pub Schs 419 S President St Jackson MS 39201-5008

CHAMBLESS, ANNE DEVON, wig and make-up artist; b. Jacksonville, N.C., June 30, 1963; d. B.D. and Helen (Kolb) C.; m. Donald Edward Christopher, Nov. 15, 1986. BA summa cum laude, U. Richmond, 1985. Cutter, asst. to costume designer, wigs and make-up Univ. Players, U. Richmond, Va., 1983-87; stitcher, cutter, wardrobe, and wigs TheatreVirginia, Richmond, 1985-87; stitcher, wigs and make-up Juilliard Sch., N.Y.C., 1987-88, wig and make-up supr., 1988—; wig stylist Bershire Opera Co., Great Barrington, Mass., 1995-99; cutter N.Y. Shakespeare Festival, N.Y.C., 1988; make-up artist Life Mag., N.Y.C., 1997; wig and make-up artist PBS TV, 1996, 97. Nominee Daytime Emmy award NATAS, 1996-97. Baptist. Home: 3039 Ocean Pkwy Apt D2 Brooklyn NY 11235-8362 Office: Juilliard Sch 60 Lincoln Center Plz New York NY 10023-6588

CHAMBLISS, SAXBY, congressman; b. Warrenton, N.C., Nov. 10, 1943; m. Julianne Chambliss; 2 children. BA in Bus. Adminstrn., U. Ga., 1967; JD, U. Tenn., 1968. Atty., 1968—; mem. 104th Congress from 8th Ga. dist., 1995—; mem. agriculture, nat. security coms. 105th Congress from 8th Ga. dist., 1996—; mem. forestry, resource conservation & rsch., gen. farm commodities, risk mgmt. & specialty crops, mil. readiness, mil. rsch. & devel. coms. Republican. Office: US House of Reps 1019 Longworth Bldg Washington DC 20515-1008*

CHAMEIDES, STEVEN B., lawyer; b. N.Y.C., Sept. 6, 1946; s. Robert and Belle (Karpen) C.; m. Sandra R. Fetterman. BSE in Math. and Naval Architecture, U. Mich., 1967, JD, 1970. Bar: N.Y. 1971, U.S. Supreme Ct. 1975, D.C. 1976. Assoc. Haight, Gardner, Poor & Havens, N.Y.C., 1970-76, Arent, Fox, Kinter, Plotkin & Kahn, Washington, 1976-79; ptnr. Becker & Chameides, Washington, 1979-84, Chameides & Goldstein, Washington, 1985-89, Foley & Lardner, Washington, 1989—; dir. Transglobe Container Svc., Inc., Washington. Mem. Mid-Atlantic Cancer Rsch. Found., Washington, Internat. Found. Thrombosis Rsch., United Jewish Appeal Fedn., Washington. Lt. JAGC, USN, 1971-74. Mem. ABA, Maritime Law Assn., Soc. of Naval Archs. Avocations: sailing, flying. Office: Foley & Lardner Washington Harbour 3000 K St NW Fl 5 Washington DC 20007-5143

CHAMINGS, PATRICIA ANN, nurse, educator; b. Lakeland, Fla., June 21, 1940; d. Roy John and Esther Delilah (O'Steen) C. Diploma, Orange Meml. Hosp., 1961; BSN, U. Fla., 1964, M of Nursing, 1965; PhD, George Peabody Coll., 1978. Cert. nurse adminstr. advanced. Dir., assoc. prof. grad. program Vanderbilt U., Nashville, 1976-84; asst. dean Emory U., Atlanta, 1984-85; prof. U. N.C., Greensboro, 1985—, dean, 1985-90, dir. anesthesia edn. project, 1989-92; bd. trustees Wesley Long Cmty. Hosp., 1989-97; bd. dirs. N.C. Ctr. for Nursing, Health Svc. Ministry, N.C. Commn. on Mental Health, Devel. Disabilities and Substance Abuse Svcs., Wesley Long Cmty. Health Found. Named N.C. Nurse Educator of Yr., 1988; advanced nurse tng. grantee USPHS, 1989-92. Fellow Am. acad. Nursing; mem. Sigma Theta Tau Internat.

CHAMIS, CHRISTOS CONSTANTINOS, aerospace scientist, educator; b. Sotira, Greece, May 16, 1930; came to U.S., 1948; s. Constantinos and Anastasia (Kyriakos) C.; m. Alice Yanosko, Aug. 20, 1966; children: Chrysanthie, Anna-Lisa, Constantinos. BS in Civil Engring., Cleve. State U. 1960; MS, Case Western Res. U., 1962, PhD, 1967. Draftsman, designer Cons. Engring., Cleve., 1955-60; research asst. Case Western Res. U., Cleve., 1960-62, rsch. assoc., 1964-68; rsch. mathematician B. F. Goodrich, Brecksville, Ohio, 1962-64; aerospace engr. Lewis Rsch. Ctr., NASA, Cleve., 1968-78, sr. rsch. engr., 1978-86, sr. aerospace scientist, 1986—; cons. Lawrence Livermore Labs., Calif., 1974-79; adj. prof. Cleve. State U., 1968—, Akron U., 1980—, Case Western Reserve U., 1984—. Editor: Composites Analysis/Design, 1975, Test Methods and Design Allowables for Composites, 1979, 89; mem. editl. bd. Jour. Composites Rsch. and Tech., Reinforced Plastics and Composites, Internat. Jour. Damage Mechanics. Thoretical and Applied Fracture Mechanics. Contbr. numerous articles to sci. jours. Patentee in field for Intraply Hybrid Composites; researcher in hygrothermal composite micromechanics, computational composite mechanics-computer codes, high-temperature composite structures, structural tailoring of engine structures, computational simulation of progressive fracture, engine structures computational simulations, computational simulation/tailoring of coupled multi-discipline problems, and probabilistic structural analysis. Served with USMC, 1952-53. Fellow ASME, AIAA (assoc. editor 1986-88), ASCE, ASTM, Soc. Advancement Materials and Process Engring.; mem. Soc. Exptl. Mechanics, Soc. Automotive Engrs., Am. Soc. Metals, Am. Soc. Composites, Soc. Engring. Sci., Am. Ceramic Soc., Sigma Xi. Clubs: Dodoni, Hellenic U. Home: 24534 Framingham Dr Cleveland OH 44145-4902

CHAMLEE, ANN COMBEST, music educator; b. Waco, Tex., Jan. 5, 1934; d. Otis Carter Ray and Hazel Meharg; children: Ann Alisabeth Chamlee, Margaret Carter Chamlee Zabcik. BM, Baylor U., 1969, MM, 1987; postgrad., Sam Houston State U., 1978-82. Exec. sec. Rocketdyne, McGregory, Tex., 1953-56; legal sec. Brown Assocs., Temple, Tex., 1977-80; fashion salesperson The Rosebud, Temple, Tex., 1980-85; choir master, organist Concover Luth. Ch., Temple, Tex., 1984-89; piano tchr. Temple, Tex., 1964-87; music educator Temple Coll., 1988—; artist in schs. Cultural Activities Ctr., Temple, 1980—. Author: Music Fundamentals Workbook, 1989, Two Halves Make a Whole, 1985. Performer with Linda Kowalski Cmty. Concert Tour, Ind., 1978; music dir. Gatesville/Milam County Tex.; bd. dirs. City Fedn. Womens Club, Temple, Temple Civic Theatre, 1998—. Recipient Outstanding Cmty. Vol. award City Fedn. of Womens Club, 1991, U2 award Child Help, Inc., 1991, Musician of Yr. award Wildflower Guild, 1994. Mem. Nat. Music Tchrs. Assn., Tex. Coalition for Quality in Arts Edn. (bd. dirs. 1995—), Music Club of Temple (past pres. 1968-89), Ctrl. Tex. Music Tchrs. Assn. (past pres. 1970-72, 94-96), Tex. Music Tchrs. Assn. (conv. presenter 1993, 97), Nat. Piano Guild (judge 1980-97), Lions (bd. dirs. 1993-95, Hon. Lion or Yr. 1970, Lion of Yr. 1993). Office: Temple Coll 2600 S 1st St Temple TX 76504-7435

CHAMORRO, JUAN PABLO, financial analyst, marketing professional; b. Zaragoza, Aragon, Spain, Feb. 14, 1967; s. Angel and Fiorella Angela (Porta) C.; m. Kristin L. Andersen, Apr. 19, 1997. BBA, U. Mass., 1989; MBA, Columbia U., 1993. Fin. assoc. United Technologies, Pratt & Whitney, East Hartford, Conn., 1989-91; equity rsch. assoc. J.P. Morgan Investment Mgmt., N.Y.C., 1992; sr. fin. analyst AlliedSignal Inc., Morristown, N.J., 1993-94; regional mgr. AlliedSignal Flurochems. Europe B.V., Amersfoort, The Netherlands, 1994-95; product mgr. AlliedSignal Europe, Heverlee, Belgium, 1995-96; industry mktg. mgr. AlliedSignal, Inc., Morristown, N.J., 1996-98; mgr. global bus. analysis Pharmacia & Upjohn, Bridgewater, N.J., 1999—. Mem. Fin. Mgmt. Assn. Roman Catholic. Avocations: travel, tennis, history, reading. Home: 16 Collinwood Rd Maplewood NJ 07040 Office: Pharmacia & Upjohn 95 Corporate Dr Bridgewater NJ 08807

CHAMP, STANLEY GORDON, scientific company executive; b. Hoquiam, Wash., Feb. 15, 1919; s. Clifford Harvey and Edna Winnifred (Johnson) C.; m. Anita Knapp Wegener, Sept. 6, 1941; children: Suzanne Winnifred Whalen, Colleen Louise Szurszewski. BS, U. Puget Sound, 1941; MS, U. Wash., 1950; postgrad., MIT, 1955, 57, UCLA, 1959. Cert. tchr., adminstr., Wash. Tchr. Lake Washington Sch. Dist., Kirkland, Wash., 1942-48; prof. math. U. Puget Sound, Tacoma, 1948-51; supr. mathematician Puget Sound Naval Shipyard, Bremerton, Wash., 1951-55; rsch. specialist Boeing Co., Seattle, 1955-68; v.p. R.M. Towne & Assocs., Seattle, 1968-75; founder, pres. Dynac Scis., Tacoma, 1975—; cons. R.M. Towne Assocs., Seattle, Yantis Assocs., Bellevue, Wash. Contbr. articles to profl. jours.; patent method and apparatus determination soil dynamics insitu. Mem. N.Y. Acad. Sci., Phi Delta Kappa. Presbyterian. Avocation: model building. Home: 2709 84th Avenue Ct W Apt 12 Tacoma WA 98466-2770

CHAMPA, JOHN JOSEPH, telecommunications engineer, consultant; b. Columbus, Ohio, Oct. 16, 1944; s. Antonio John and Helen Catherine (Izzie) C.; m. Lendel Pauline Sloan, Aug. 7, 1965; children: Lea Christine Kuhn, Susan Catherine Muscat, Rebecca Lynn McLaughlin, Patrick John. BA, Ohio State U., Columbus, 1974; MA, Cen. Mich U., Mt. Pleasant, 1975; MS, Columbia Pacific U., San Rafael, Calif., 1985, PhD, 1986. Cert. telecom.

engr. Mem. U.S. police Fed. Protective Svc., Nashville & Columbus, 1972-74; safety engr. Borden Corp., Columbus, 1974-76; plant safety engr. Buckeye Steel Castings, Columbus, 1976-80; divsn. safety engr. Cooper Energy Svcs., Mount Vernon, Ohio, 1980-82; sr. safety engr. Goodyear Atomic Corp., Piketon, Ohio, 1982-83; corp. safety engr. Unisys Corp., Detroit, 1984-88; mgr., chief engr. Unisys Worldwide Videoconferencing, Detroit, 1988-94; dir. Multimedia Comms. Svcs., Plymouth, Mich., 1994—; exec. v.p. Radio Amateur Satellite Corp., Washington, 1988-91; adj. prof. Franklin U., Columbus, 1979-81. Inventor: Digital Video Switch for Videoconferencing, 1992; author: CD-ROM Unisys Multimedia and Videoconferencing Solutions; co-author: Am. Nat. Stds. Inst. (ANSI) Z241 Std.; contbr. articles to profl. jours. Capt. U.S. Army, 1967-71. Mem. Internat. Teleconferencing Assoc. (bd. dirs. 1993—, exec. com. 1996-97), Nat. Assn. Radio and Telecom. Engrs., Nat. Rifle Assn., Nat. Arbor Day Found., Nature Conservancy Mich. Chpt.-Great Lakes Soc., Nat. Geog. Soc., Mich. Bear Hunters Assn., Upper Peninsula Bear Houndsman Assn., Mich. United Conservation Clubs, Desktop Users Group, PictureTel Users Group, VFW (past post comdr. and trustee), Safari Club Internat., Am. Radio Relay League. Avocations: hunting, cartography, reading, amateur radio. Office: Unisys Corp 41100 Plymouth Rd Ste 350 Plymouth MI 48170-1892

CHAMPAGNE, DUANE WILLARD, sociology educator; b. Belcourt, N.D., May 18, 1951; children: Talya, Gabe, Demelza. BA in Math., N.D. State U., 1973, MA in Sociology, 1975; PhD in Sociology, Harvard U., 1982. Teaching fellow Harvard U., Cambridge, Mass., 1981-82, rsch. fellow, 1982-83; asst. prof. U. Wis., Milw., 1983-84; asst. prof. UCLA, 1984-91, assoc. prof., 1991-97, prof., 1997—; publs. dir. Am. Indian Studies Ctr., UCLA, 1986-87, assoc. dir., 1990, acting dir., 1991, dir., 1991—; adminstrv. co-head interdepartmental program for Am. Indian studies UCLA, 1992-93; mem. grad. rsch. fellowship panel NSF, 1990-92, minority fellowship com. ASA; cons. Energy Resources Co., 1982, No. Cheyenne Tribe, 1983, Realis Pictures, Inc., 1989-90, Sta. KCET-TV, L.A., 1990, 92, Salem Press, 1992, Book Prodns. Systems, 1993, Readers Digest, 1993, Rattlesnake Prodns., 1993. Author: American Indian Societies, 1989, Social Order and Political Change, 1992; editor: Native North American Almanac, 1994, Chronology of Native North American, 1994, Native American of the peoples Portrait, 1994; co-author: A Second Century of Dishonor: Federal Inequities and California Tribes, 1996, Service Delivery for Native American Children in Los Angeles County, 1996; editor: Native Am. Studies Assn. Newsletter, 1991-92; co-editor: Native American Activism: Alcatraz to the Longest Walk, 1997, Contemporary Native American Cultural Issues, 1999; book rev. editor Am. Indian Culture and Rsch. Jour., 1984-86, editor, 1986—; contbr. numerous articles to profl. jours. Mem. city of L.A. Cmty. Action Bd., 1993, L.A. County/City Am. Indian Commn., 1992—, chair, 1993, 95-97, v. chair, 1997—; mem. subcom. for cultural and econ. devel. L.A. City/County Native Am. Commn., 1992-93; bd. dirs. Ctr. for Improvement of Child Caring, 1993—, Greater L.A. Am. Indian Culture Ctr., Inc., 1993, Incorporator, 1993; bd. trustees Southwest Mus., 1994-97, Nat. Mus. Am. Indian, 1998—; Master of Coll. of Humanities and Social Sci., N.D. State U., 1996. Recipient L.A. Sr. Health Peer Counseling Cmty. Vol. Cert. of Recognition, 1996; grantee Rockefeller Found., 1982-83, U. Wis. Grad Sch. Rsch. Com., 1984-85, Wis. Dept. Edn., 1984-85, 87-88, 88-89, NSF, 1985-88, 88-89), Nat. Endowment for Arts, 1987-88, 91-92, NRC, 1988-89, Nat. Sci. Coun., 1989-90, John D. and Catherine T. MacArthur Found., 1990-91, Hayes Found., 1990-91, 92-93, Calif. Coun. for Humanities, 1991-92, Ford Found., 1990-92, Gale Rsch. Inc., 1991-93, 93-95, Rockwell Corp., 1991-93, GTE, 1992-93, Kellog Found., 1997—, Pequot Mus. and Rsch. Ctr., 1997-98, So. Calif. Indian Ctr., 1998; Fund for the Improvement of Post Secondary Edn., 1998—; Am. Indian scholar, 1973-75, 80-82, Minority fellow Am. Sociol. Assn., 1975-78, RIAS Seminar fellow, 1976-77; Rockefeller Postdoctoral fellow, 1982-83, NSF fellow, 1985-88, Postdoctoral fellow Ford Found., 1988-89. Avocations: chess, basketball. Home: 28012 Ridgecove Ct N Rancho Palos CA 90275-3377 Office: UCLA Am Indian Studies Ctr PO Box 951548 Los Angeles CA 90095-1548

CHAMPAGNE, RONALD OSCAR, academic administrator, mathematics educator; b. Woonsocket, R.I., Jan. 2, 1942; s. George Albert and Simone (Brodeur) C.; m. Ruth Inez DesRuisseux, Nov. 25, 1970. BA, Duquesne U., 1964; MA, Cath. U. Am., 1966, Fordham U., 1970; PhD, Fordham U., 1973. Instr. math. Sacred Heart U., Bridgeport, Conn., 1966-69; asst. prof. math. Manhattanville Coll., Purchase, N.Y., 1969-75, dir. advanced studies program, 1973-75; prof. math., v.p., dean of faculty Salem Coll., W.Va., 1975-82; prof. math., pres., trustee St. Xavier U., Chgo., 1982-94, pres. emeritus, 1994—; prof. philosophy, v.p. for devel. Roosevelt U., Chgo., 1996—; bd. dirs. Maria High Sch., Chgo., Tchrs. Acad. for Math. and Sci.; chmn. Chgo. adv. coun. St. Paul Fed. Bank; chmn. edn. sector Lincoln Found. for Bus. Excellence. Author: LP Spaces of Complex Valued Functions, 1966; A Formalization of the Dialectical Development of Intelligence, 1974. Mem. Mat. Assn. Am., Philosophy of Sci. Assn., Carlton Club, Econs. Club Chgo. Roman Catholic. Office: Roosevelt Univ 430 S Michigan Ave Chicago IL 60605-1301

CHAMPE, PAMELA CHAMBERS, biochemistry educator, writer; b. Oakland, Calif., Aug. 29, 1945; d. Robert Leroy and Leah June (Musser) Chambers; m. Sewell Preston Champe, June 28, 1969; stepchildren: Mark Adrian, Sewell Peter. BA, Stanford U., 1967; MS, Purdue U., 1969; PhD, Rutgers U., 1974. Instr. Rutgers Med. Sch., Piscataway, N.J., 1974-76; asst. prof. Robert Wood Johnson Med. Sch. (formerly Rutgers Med. Sch.) U. Medicine and Dentistry N.J., Piscataway, 1977-84, assoc. prof. Robert Wood Johnson Med. Sch., 1984-96; prof. Robert Wood Johnson Med. Sch., 1996—; lectr. several med. schs. and tng. programs. Co-editor: Gene Families of Collagen and Other Proteins, 1980; co-author: Biochemistry (Lippincott's Illus. Revs.), 1987, 2nd edit., 1994; co-author, co-editor: Pharmacology (Lippincott's Illus. Revs.), 1992, 2nd edit. 1997, Microbiology (Lippincott's Illus. Revs.), 1999. Health and Human Svcs. grantee, 1988-94; recipient Nat. award Basic Sci. Educator of the Yr., 1995. Mem. AAAS, Assn. Am. Med. Colls., N.Y. Acad. Scis., Alpha Omega Alpha. Avocation: malacology. Office: U Medicine and Dentistry NJ Robert Wood Johnson Med Sch 675 Hoes Ln Piscataway NJ 08854-5627

CHAMPION, CHARLES HOWELL, JR., retired army officer; b. Canton, Ga., Feb. 17, 1944; s. Charles Howell and Ethel Marie (Cooper) C.; m. Patricia Ann Little, Nov. 24, 1965; children: Charles Howell III, Danielle, Christopher, Jonathan, Alicia. BS in Biology, North Ga. Coll., 1967; MA in Health Facilities Mgmt., Webster U., 1977. Commd. 2d lt. U.S. Army, 1966, advanced through grades to col., 1989; asst. chief schedules acad. ops. Med. Field Svc. Sch., Ft. Sam Houston, Tex., 1967-68; commanding officer 3/45 Med. Air Ambulance, Long Binh, Vietnam, 1969-70, 15th Med. Air Ambulance, Grafenwoehr, Germany, 1971-74; force devel. test officer Acad. Health Scis., Ft. Sam Houston, Tex., 1975-80; med. tng. liason officer Tng. and Doctrine Command, Ft. Monroe, Va., 1980-84; chief force modernization Office Surgeon Gen., Washington, 1984-88, chief doctrine, policy and orgn., 1988-90; dep. command surgeon U.S. Army Forces Command, Ft. McPherson, Ga., 1990-96; ret., 1996; v.p. ops. Eagle Group Internat., Inc., Atlanta, 1996—; sr. faculty mem. Col. John R. Sperandeo Plans, Ops. Profl. Postgrad. Short Course, Denver, 1991, 93, 95; bd. dirs. Med. Svc. Corps U.S.A., Washington, 1992-94. Inducted into Order of Mil. Med. Merit, 1988; designated a disting. mem. Army Med. Dept. Regiment, 1996. Mem. Assn. Mil. Surgeons, Assn. U.S. Army, Army Aviation Assn. Am., Dustoff Assn., Retired Officers Assn., Army War Coll. Alumni Assn. Roman Catholic. Avocations: sailing, shooting, gardening. Home: 2800 Chelsea Pl NW Marietta GA 30064-1288 Office: Ste 100 3475 N Desert Dr Bldg 1 Atlanta GA 30344-5723

CHAMPION, (CHARLES) HALE, political science educator, former public official; b. Coldwater, Mich., Aug. 27, 1922; s. Paul Upham and Ruth Emma (Hungerford) C.; m. Marie Ozine Tifft, Aug. 21, 1952; children: Thomas Paul, Katherine Marie. B.A., Stanford U., 1952. Journalist UPI, Milw. Jour., Sacramento Bee, San Francisco Chronicle, Reporter mag., 1946-49, 52-58; legis. asst. to Congressman Andrew J. Biemiller of Wis., 1950; press and exec. sec. to Gov. Edmund G. Brown of Calif., 1958-60; dir. fin. State of Calif., 1961-66; dir. Boston Redevel. Authority, 1968-69; v.p. fin., planning and ops. U. Minn., Mpls., 1969-71; v.p. fin. Harvard U., Cambridge, Mass., 1971-76, exec. dean John F. Kennedy Sch. Govt., 1980-87; undersec. HEW, Washington, 1977-79; chief of staff to Gov. Michael S. Dukakis of Mass., Boston, 1987-88; lectr. John F. Kennedy Sch. Govt. Harvard U., 1989-91; mem. Presdl. Task Force Reorgn. Fed. Govt., 1966-67, Presdl. Task Force Role of Univ. in Urban Affairs, 1967-68; chmn. Mass. Joint Legis.-Exec. Com. Fed. Base Conversion, 1973-74; chmn. Presdl. Commn. on Nat. Health Ins., 1977-78. Bd. dirs. Kaiser Family Found., 1984-92, chmn., 1989-92; bd. dirs. Ctr. for Study of Social Policy, 1986—, chmn., 1998—. Served with AUS, 1942-46. Nieman fellow Harvard U., 1956-57; fellow John F. Kennedy Inst. Politics, 1967. Mem. Nat. Acad. Pub. Adminstrn. (trustee 1980-86). Democrat. Office: Harvard Univ John F Kennedy Sch Govt 79 Jfk St Cambridge MA 02138-5801

CHAMPION, KENNETH STANLEY WARNER, physicist; b. Sydney, NSW, Australia, Dec. 7, 1923; s. Cecil Alexander Buckingham and Ellen Catherine (Moxham) C.; m. Mavis Audrey Hinckley, Nov. 27, 1948; children: Annette, Gwendalyn, Geoffrey, Sandra. BS, U. Sydney, 1945; PhD, U. Birmingham, Eng., 1951. Asst. lectr. physics U. Queensland, Australia, 1946-49; rsch. fellow Australian Nat. U., 1949-52; rsch. assoc. MIT, Cambridge, Mass., 1952-54; asst. prof. physics Tufts U., Medford, Mass., 1954-59; rsch. scientist, sr. scientist Atmospheric Physics/Br. Chief, 1959-64; sr. exec. AF Cambridge Rsch. Labs./Phillips Lab., 1964-94; Brit. Coun. Rsch. scholar, 1947-49; vis. prof. U. Adelaide, Australia, 1964; presenter in field in 21 countries. Contbr. articles to 6 internat. profl. jours. Co-pres. PTA, Lexington, Mass., 1965-75. Fellow Phys. Soc. of London; mem. AIAA (assoc. fellow), N.Y. Acad. Scis., Am. Phys. Soc., Am. Geophys. Union, Am. Meteorol. Soc., Sigma Xi. Episcopalian. Achievements include being a pioneer in early plasma fusion oriented rsch.; pioneer in space rsch. with rocket and satellite measurements and development of internationally accepted atmospheric models. Home: 6 Rolfe Rd Lexington MA 02420-2308

CHAMPION, MARGE (MARJORIE CELESTE CHAMPION), actress, dancer, choreographer; b. L.A., Sept. 2, 1923; d. Ernest and Gladys (Basquette) Belcher; m. Art Babbitt (div.); m. Gower Champion, Oct. 5, 1947 (div. 1973); children: Blake (dec.), Gregg; m. Boris Sagal, Jan. 1, 1977 (dec. 1981). Student pub. schs., Los Angeles. stage debut L.A. Civic Opera, 1936; movie debut (under name Marjorie Bell) in The Castles, 1938; live action model for cartoon heroines in: Walt Disney prodns. Blue Fairy in Pinocchio, 1938, Snow White, 1937, Hippo and Storks in Fantasia; appeared on Broadway musicals Dark of the Moon, 1945, Beggar's Holiday, 1946; first profl. appearance with Gower Champion as Gower and Bell Normandie Roof, Montreal, Que., Can., 1947; N.Y. debut as Marge and Gower Champion at Hotel Plaza, 1947; weekly show Admiral Broadway Review, Dumont and NBC TV Network, 1949, Marge and Gower Champion Show, 1957; with husband staged dances for revues: Lend an Ear, 1949, Make A Wish, Small Wonder; movies include: Showboat, 1951, Lovely to Look At, 1952, Everything I Have is Yours, 1952, Give A Girl a Break, 1953, Three for the Show, 1955, Jupiter's Darling, 1955, The Swimmer, 1968, The Party, 1968, The Cockeyed Cowboy of Calico County, 1970, That's Entertainment, Part 2, 1976; various TV appearances, including TV show Toast of the Town, 1953; Three for Tonight, 1955, Shower of Stars, 1956, GE Theatre, 1957, Dinah Shore Show, 1958, Telephone Hour, 1960; acting debut Hemingway and All Those People, Indpls., 1958; title role: Sabrina Fair, 1960; choreographer: Queen of the Stardust Ballroom, 1975 (Emmy award), 1992, Day of the Locust, 1975; author: (with Marilee Zdenek) Catch the New Wind, 1972, God is a Verb, 1974; dialogue coach and choreographer: The Awakening Land, NBC-TV, 1978, Masada, ABC-TV, 1979, Diary of Ann Frank, NBC-TV, 1980, When the Circus Comes to Town, CBS-TV, 1980; appeared: TV series Fame, 1982; dir., choreography: TV prodn. I Do, I Do, 1983, Stepping Out, Berkshire Theatre Festival, 1988, 89, Lute Song, 1989, She Loves Me, 1990; dancer: 5-6-7-8, Dance!, Radio City Music Hall, 1983, No No Nanette, St. Louis Muny Opera, 1990. Recipient Legend of Dance award, 1991. Office: Fifi Oscard Agency, Inc. 24 W 40th St 17th Fl New York NY 10018-3904*

CHAMPION, MICHAEL EDWARD, physician assistant, clinical perfusionist; b. Oroville, Calif., Jan. 30, 1954; s. Robert Joseph and Shirley Anne (Rowland) C.; m. Marie S. Sittner, Oct. 8. 1990. AS, Cuyahoga C.C., 1980; BS, USNY, Albany, 1983; MEd, Boston U., 1986; M of Med. Sci., St. Francis Coll., 1996. Cert. physician asst., NCCPA, clin. perfusionist ABCVP. Enlisted U.S. Army, 1972, advanced through grades to maj., 1994; ret., 1994, aviation medicine physician asst., 1980-87; chief physician asst./perfusionist Letterman Army Med. Ctr., 1989-91; founding physician asst./perfusionist Madigan Army Med. Ctr., 1991-94; cardiac surgery mgr., chief physician asst/perfusionist Mercy Med. Ctr., Janesville, Wis., 1994-96; dir. cardiac svcs. Hutchinson (Kans.) Hosp., 1996-98; v.p. projects Champion Constrn., Inc., Wichita, Kans., 1997—; sr. PA/perfusionist Hays (Kans.) Med. Ctr., 1998—; clin. instr. U.S. Army Physician Asst. Program, 1981-84, U.S. Army Adult Nurse Practitioner Program, 1982; EMS instr. Fayetteville Tech. Inst., 1983; instr. MEDEX program U. Washington, 1992-95, MMS programs St. Francis Coll., Loretto, Pa., 1996—; CEO Champion and Assocs., LLC; organizer Surg. Physician Asst. course, Jamaica, 1995. Contbr. articles to profl. jours. Treas. Rock County Rep. Party, Janesville, 1994; mem. Red Cross, Am. Cancer Soc., EAA Young Eagles Program. Mem. Am. Acad. Physician Assts. (rsch. rev. com. 1984, profl. and continuing edn. com. 1988, vets. caucus bd. dirs. 1989-91, vets. caucus pres. 1991-92, chmn. pilots assn. 1995, chmn. vets. caucus awards 1992-95, jud. affairs com. 1994, vice chmn. surg. congress 1994-96, chmn. 1996-97, Outstanding Svc. award 1989), Wis. Acad. Physician Assts. (chair legis. com., sec. 1995, pres.-elect 1996), Soc. Army Physician Assts. (life, chief del. 1983-84, v.p. 1984-85, pres. 1985-86, 98-99), Assn. Physician Assts. in Cardiovascular Surgery, Assn. Mil. Surgeons of U.S. (life, Physician Asst. of Yr. 1992), Am. Soc. Extracorporeal Tech., Am. Heart Assn., Am. Acad. Med. Adminstrs., Am. Coll. Cardiovascular Adminstrs. Republican. Roman Catholic. Avocation: private pilot. Home: PO Box 66 Hays KS 67601

CHAMPION, MICHAEL RAY, health facility administrator; b. Plymouth, Ind., Aug. 15, 1954; s. James Osborne and Gloria Jean Champion. Diploma, Brackenridge Hosp. Sch. Nsg., 1978. RN, Tex. Staff nurse Brackenridge Hosp., Austin, Tex., 1973-80; DON DFW Preventative Medicine Ctr., Dallas, 1982; asst. dir. nurses Northaven Nursing Ctr., Dallas, 1983; dir. staff devel., asst. dir. nurses Meadowgreen, Dallas, 1986-90; asst. dir. nurses Treemont, Dallas, 1990, clin. svcs. coord. subacute, DON, 1991-92; DON svcs. Manor Care Health Svcs., Dallas, 1992-98; dir. of Nurses Four Seasons, Dallas, leader seminars, workshops in field. Top Ten Safety scholar Nat. Safety Coun. Mem. Assn. for Nurses in AIDS Care, Assn. Profl. Nurses, Nat. Fedn. LPNs, Tex. Nurses Assn. Home: 10823 Wallbrook Dr Dallas TX 75238-2942

CHAMPION, NORMA JEAN, communications educator, state legislator; b. Oklahoma City, Jan. 21, 1933; d. Aubra Dell and Beuleah Beatrice (Flanagan) Black; m. Richard Gordon Champion, Oct. 3, 1953 (dec.); children: Jeffrey Bruce, Ashley Brooke. BA in Religious Edn., Cen. Bible Coll., Springfield, Mo., 1971; MA in Comm., S.W. Mo. State U., 1978; PhD in Tech., U. Okla., 1986. Producer, hostess The Children's Hour, Sta. KYTV-TV, NBC, Springfield, 1957-86; asst. prof. Cen. Bible Coll., 1968-84; prof. broadcasting Evangel U., Springfield, 1978—; mem. Springfield City Coun., 1987-92, Mo. Ho. of Reps., Jefferson City, 1992—; adj. faculty Assemblies of God Theol. Sem., Springfield, 1987—, pres. coun.; chmn. bd. Berean U.; mem. Commn. on Higher Edn., Assemblies of God, 1998; frequent lectr. to svc. clubs, edn!. seminars; seminar spkr. Internat. Pentecostal Press Assn. World Conf., Singapore, 1989; announcer various TV commls. Contbr. numerous articles to religious publs. Mem. bd Mo. Access to Higher Edn. Trust, 1990—, Boys & Girls Town of Mo.; regional rep. Muscular Dystrophy Assn.; mem. adv. bd. Chameleon Puppet Theater, 1987; mem. exec. bd. Univ. Child Care Ctr., 1987; hon. chmn. fund raising Salvation Army, 1986; also numerous other bds., hon. chairmanships.; judge Springfield City Schs. Recipient commendation resolution Mo. Ho. of Reps., 1988; numerous award for The Children's Hour; Aunt Norma Day named in her honor City of Springfield, 1976. Mem. Nat. Broadcast Edn. Assn., Mo. Broadcast Edn. Assn., Nat. League Cities, Mo. Mcpl. League (human resource com. 1989, intergovtl. rels. com. 1990), Nat. Assn. Telecom. Officers and Advisors, PTA (life). Republican. Mem. Assemblies of God Ch. Avocations: gardening, reading, interior decoration. Home: 3609 S Broadway Ave Springfield MO 65807-4505 Office: Evangel Univ 1111 N Glenstone Ave Springfield MO 65802-2125

CHAMPLIN, CHARLES DAVENPORT, television host, book critic, writer; b. Hammondsport, N.Y., Mar. 23, 1926; s. Francis Malburn and Katherine Marietta (Masson) C.; m. Margaret Frances Derby, Sept. 11, 1948; children: Charles Jr., Katherine, John, Judith, Susan, Nancy. AB cum laude, Harvard U., 1947. Reporter Life mag., N.Y.C., 1948-49; corr. Life mag., Chgo., 1949-52, asst. editor, 1954-59; corr. Denver, 1952-54, Time mag., L.A., 1959-62, London, 1962-65; arts editor, columnist L.A. Times, 1965-91, prin. film critic, 1967-80, book critic, 1981—; host-commentator Ste. KCET-TV, L.A., ETV Network, Z Channel Cable TV, Bravo Channel, 1969-96; adj. prof. Loyola-Marymount U., L.A., 1969-86; adj. prof. U. So. Calif., 1986-96. Author: (with C. Sava) How to Swim Well, 1960, The Flicks, 1977, The Movies Grow Up, 1981, Back There Where the Past Was, 1989, George Lucas: The Creative Impulse, 1992, enlarged, 1997, John Frankenheimer: A Conversation, 1995, Woody Allen at Work, 1995, Hollywood's Revolutionary Decade, 1998; contbr. numerous articles to mags. and publs. Bd. dirs. Am. Cinemateque; trustee L.A. Film Tchrs. Assn. With U.S. Army, 1944-46, ETO. Decorated Purple Heart; recipient Order Arts and Letters, France, 1977. Mem. PEN, Nat. Book Critics Cir., L.A. Film Critics Assn., Authors Guild, Overseas Press Club. Democrat. Home: 2169 Linda Flora Dr Los Angeles CA 90077-1408

CHAMPLIN, EDWARD JAMES, classics educator; b. N.Y.C., June 3, 1948; s. Frank James and Marion Joan (Bazett) C.; m. Caroline Beatrice Llewellyn-Thomas, Dec. 29, 1972; children: James Christopher, Alexander Edward. BA, U. Toronto, Can., 1970, MA, 1972; DPhil, Oxford (Eng.) U., 1976. From instr. to assoc. prof. classics Princeton (N.J.) U., 1975-86, prof., 1986—, Cotsen prof. humanities, 1987—, master Butler Coll., 1995—; vis. fellow Alexander von Humboldt Found., Heidelberg, Germany, 1984-85, Christ Ch., Oxford, 1989-90. Author: Fronto and Antonine Rome, 1980, Final Judgments, 1991. Lt. Can. Army, 1967-70. Mem. German Archeol. Inst. (corr.). Episcopalian. Office: Princeton U Dept Classics 104 East Pine Bldg Princeton NJ 08544-1099

CHAMPLIN, RICHARD H., lawyer, insurance company executive; b. Enid, Okla., May 12, 1935; s. Paul B. and Ida Adelene (Johnson) C.; m. Katherine Gore, Apr. 4, 1961; children: Kimberly Kay, Margaret Ann, Christian Paul. BBA, U. Okla., 1957, JD, 1961. Bar: Okla. 1961. Asst. gen. counsel Lee Way Motor Freight Co., Oklahoma City, 1961-63, asst. sec., 1963-66, gen. counsel, 1966-69, v.p., gen. coun., 1969-81, sec., 1977-81; v.p., gen. counsel Mistletoe Express Svc., 1982-85, The Benham Cos., 1985-86; sr. v.p. C.L. Frates & Co., Oklahoma City, 1987—; v.p. BancInsure, Inc., 1987—. V.p. Oklahoma City All Sports Assn. With Signal Corps, AUS, 1957-58. Mem. Okla. Bar Assn., Transp. Lawyers Assn. (pres. 1987-88, Disting. Svc. award 1994, Lifetime Achievement award 1996), Oklahoma City Golf and Country Club, Econ. Club of Okla. Presbyterian. Home: 2300 NW 56th St Oklahoma City OK 73112-7704 Office: CL Frates & Co Box 26967 5005 N Lincoln Blvd Oklahoma City OK 73105-3336

CHAMPLIN, STEVEN KIRK, lawyer; b. Omaha, July 6, 1944; m. Marjorie Eckenberg, Mar. 15, 1969; children: Anne, Paul, Jane. BA, Vanderbilt U., 1966; JD, U. Minn., 1969. Bar: Minn. 1969, U.S. Dist. Ct. Minn., U.S. Ct. Appeals (8th cir.). Assoc. Dorsey & Whitney, Mpls., 1969-70, 71-72, 73-75, ptnr., 1976—; pub. defender Hennepin County, Mpls., 1972-73. Capt. U.S. Army, 1970-71. Mem. USTA. Home: 50 Myrtlewood Rd Wayzata MN 55391-9679 Office: Dorsey & Whitney 220 S 6th St Ste 2200 Minneapolis MN 55402-1498

CHAMPLIN, WILLIAM GLEN, clinical microbiologist-immunologist; b. Rogers, Ark., Sept. 10, 1923; s. Glen and Anna Champlin; m. Helen Elizabeth Garner, Feb. 2, 1951; 1 child, Steven. BS, N.E. Okla. State U., 1948; MS, U. Ark., 1965, PhD, 1971. Lab. dir. VA Med. Ctr., Fayetteville, Ark., 1955-65, clin. microbiologist, lab. dir., 1965-80; cons. ANL Med. Lab. Wash. Regional Med. Ctr. VA Med. Ctr., 1965-90; edn. coord. Antaeus Inst. Sch. Med. Tech., 1980-90; vis. prof. microbiology U. Ark., 1978-85. With U.S. Army, 1943-45. Mem. Am. Acad. Microbiology (specialist), Am. Soc. Clin. Pathologists (specialist), Sigma Xi.

CHAMPNEY, RAYMOND JOSEPH, advertising and marketing executive, consultant; b. N.Y.C., Aug. 6, 1940; s. Raymond Joseph and Florence (McConnell) C.; m. Anne Kelly, Jan. 10, 1976. Student, CCNY, 1961-63, NYU, 1965. With BBDO Advt., N.Y.C., 1964-66, McCann Erickson Advt., 1966-68, Clinton E. Frank Advt., 1968-71, Norman Craig & Kummel Advt., 1971-73, Doyle Dane Bernbach Advt., 1973-74, Guest Pub. Co., 1974-77, Bozell & Jacobs Advt., 1977-79; sr. v.p. Weekley & Assocs., 1980-84; pres. Weekley & Champney Advt. Weekley & Assocs., Dallas, 1984-86; pres., chief exec. officer Champney and Assoc. Advt., Dallas, 1986-92; pres. Champney Publicidad S.A. de C.V., Mexico City, 1987-92, Champney Fulfillment, 1987-92, RJC Internat., Bedford, Tex., 1992—; dir. gen. Osama Al Madany/RJC Internat., Saudi Arabia, 1994-97. Served with U.S. Army, 1959-61. Mem. Sales Mktg. Execs., Dallas Ad League, Am. Mgmt. Assn., Presidents Assn.,. Am. Soc. Travel Agts., Hotel Sales and Mktg. Assn., Better Bus. Bur., Dallas C. of C., HEB C. of C. Home: 2300 Marshfield Dr Bedford TX 76021-7300 Office: PO Box 1072 Bedford TX 76095-1072

CHAMPY, WILLIAM, JR., mathematician, educator, researcher, scientist; b. Orangeburg, S.C., July 23, 1949; s. Buster and Mamie (Brown) C.. BS in Profl. Chemistry, S.C. State Coll., 1977, MEd, 1985, postgrad.; cert. prodn. operator, Orangeburg-Calhoun Tech. Coll., Orangeburg, S.C., 1990; cert. computer operator, Orangeburg-Calhoun Tech. Coll., 1997. Cert. critical needs tchr. in sci.; lic. bus driver, S.C., armed security guard, small bus. owner, operator. Mgr., owner Champy's Night Club, Orangeburg, S.C., 1968-84; tchr. chemistry, physics, sci. Quinas H.S., Augusta, Ga., 1980; instr. math. Orangeburg-Calhoun Tech. Coll., Orangeburg, S.C., 1985-87; tchr. math Branchville (S.C.) H.S., 1987; coord. devel. lab., math instr. Denmark (S.C.) Tech. Coll., 1989-90; lab. mgr., adminstr. Voorhees Coll., Denmark, S.C., 1991-92; math instr. Midlands Tech. Coll., Columbia, S.C., 1994; security officer Security Force, Inc., 1992-94, Spartan Security, 1995-96, Pinkerton, Inc., 1988—, Sizemore Security, Columbia, 1996—; rsch. asst. dept. energy, divsn. ecology S.C. State U., Orangeburg; truck driver, laborer City of Columbia, 1980; edgefiler, tool sharpener Utica Tool Co., Inc., Orangeburg, 1982; security officer Wells Fargo, Orangeburg, 1990-92, Security Force, Inc., 1992-94, others; substitute tchr., bus driver Orangeburg Sch. Dist. # 5, 1988—; freelance personal income tax preparer, 1998—; coord. Swapop Tutoring Program S.C. State U./NASA, Orangeburg, 1998—; press operator, blademaker Frigidaire Corp., Orangeburg, 1998—; saw operator, laborer, inspector N.Am. Container, Orangeburg, 1996. Census enumerator, summer 1990; custodian, maint., set-up helper Episcopal Ch. of the Redeemer, 1997; field rep. U.S. Census Bur., 1997; security officer Am. Security, Inc. Mem. AAAS, ACS, NAACP, Nat. Inst. Sci., Am. Mgmt. Assn., S.C. State U. Nat. Alumni Assn., S.C. Tech. Edn. Assn., Nat. Inst. Sci., Nat. Soc. Black Engrs., Nat. Assn. Black Engrs., Ernest E. Just Sci. Club, Masons (sec.), Phi Delta Kappa, Omega Psi Phi. Avocations: pocket billiards, reading, fishing, hunting, checkers. E-mail: wchampy@scsu.edu. Home: 327 Champy Rd Orangeburg SC 29115 Office: SC State U Dept Energy Divsn Phytoplan Orangeburg SC 29117

CHAN, CARLYLE HUNG-LUN, psychiatrist, educator; b. Clarksdale, Miss., July 4, 1949; s. Henry Howe and Jennie (Wong) C.; m. Patricia Meyer, June 18, 1977; children: Christopher, Diana. BS, U. Wis., 1971; MD, Med. Coll. Wis., 1975. Diplomate Am. Bd. Psychiatry and Neurology. Resident in psychiatry U. Chgo., 1975-78; postdoctoral fellow R.W. Johnson clin. scholar Yale U. Sch. Medicine, 1978-80; asst. prof. Med. Coll. Wis., Milw., 1980-86, assoc. prof., 1986-98; prof. Med. Coll. of Wis., Milw., 1998—; dir. residency edn. Med. Coll. Wis., Milw., 1987—, prof., 1998—, vice chair edn. and informatics, 1997—, dir. continuing med. edn., 1990—; dir. catchment area Milw. County Mental Health Complex, 1981-82; chief psychiatrist Psychiatrist Ctr., Columbia Hosp., Milw., 1982-87; dir. continuing med. edn. Soc. Tchg. Scholars, 1994; dir. course annual psychiat. conf., 1982—; dir. Door County (Wis.) Summer Inst., 1987—. Asst. editor Asian-Am. Psychiatry Newsletter, Washington, 1983-84; assoc. editor Acad. Psychiatry Newsletter, 1991-94; contbr. articles to profl. jours. Bd. dirs. Planning Council for Mental Health and Social Service, 1983—. Jr. Faculty Devel. award NIMH, 1983-85; Community Devel. award Apple Computer Co., Milw., 1984. Fellow Am. Psychiat. Assn.; mem. Wis. Psychiat. Assn. (pres. Milw. chpt. 1990-91, chair edn. com. 1995—), Assn. Acad. Psychiatry (regional coord. 1987—, regional coord. dir. 1993-96, treas. 1996—), Am. Assn. Dirs. Psychiat. Residency Tng. (sec. 1994-95, pres.-elect 1995, pres. 1996, treas. 1990-92, program com. chair 1993-94), Wis. State Med. Soc., Milw. County Med. Soc. Med. Coll. of Wis., Soc. Teaching Scholars. Avocations: tennis, golf, running. Office: Med Coll Wis Dept Psychiatry 8701 W Watertown Plank Rd Milwaukee WI 53226-3548

CHAN, DAISY S. W., manufacturing engineer; b. Hong Kong, Sept. 25, 1961; came to U.S., 1995; d. Sze Kin Chan and Hau Ching Law; m. Kenneth Earl Olson, June 27, 1987; 1 child, Derick Olson. Diploma, Kwun Tong Tec Inst, Hong Kong, 1983, Hong Kong Polytechnics, 1986. Cert. indsl. engr. Asst. merchandiser Waterace Co., Hong Kong, 1982-84; sales rep. Tin Lung Co., Hong Kong, 1984-86; mktg. rep. R. H. Macy Corp., Hong Kong, Singapore, 1987-90; sr. merchandiser Esprit Corp., Singapore, 1990-92; prodn. engring. mgr. Circa Corp., San Francisco, 1995—. vol. Garment 2000/City Coll., San Francisco, 1995—. Mem. Rhinoceros Bus. Club (sec. 1998-99, v.p. edn. 1999—, medal 1998, Achievement and Contbn. award 1999). Avocations: jogging, diving, biking. E-mail: daisyc@joymail.com. Home: 164 Monterey St Brisbane CA 94005 Office: Circa Corp 1330 Fitzgerald Ave San Francisco CA 94124

CHAN, DANIEL CHUNG-YIN, lawyer; b. Kowloon, Hong Kong, June 5, 1948; came to U.S., 1969; s. David Chi-Kwong and Betty Wai-Lan (Kwok) C.; m. Mary Ching-Fay Wong, June 11, 1977; children: Pamila Wai-Sum (dec.), Derrick Ming-Deh. BA cum laude, Azusa Pacific U., 1972; postgrad., Calif. State U., L.A., 1973-75; JD, U. West L.A., 1983. Bar: Calif. 1984, U.S. Dist. Ct. (cen. dist.) Calif. 1984, U.S. Ct. Appeals (9th cir.) 1984, U.S. Dist. Ct. (so. dist.) Calif. 1985, U.S. Dist. Ct. (no. dist.) Calif. 1986. Mgr. Elegant Sewing Co., L.A., 1977; legal asst. Otto Frank Swanson Law Office, Marina Del Ray, Calif., 1978-84, assoc., 1984-87; pvt. practice, Pasadena, Calif., 1987—; legal counsel Chinese Grace Missions Internat., Inc., Duarte, Calif., 1984—, Diao Jiou Chinese Christian Ch. L.A., Highland Park, Calif., 1988—, Ruth Hitchcock Found. Mem. ABA, Assn. Trial Lawyers Am., So. Calif. Chinese Lawyers Assn., Am. Immigration Lawyers Assn., Delta Epsilon Chi, Alpha Chi. Office: 283 S Lake Ave Ste 219 Pasadena CA 91101-4818

CHAN, DANIEL SIU-KWONG, psychologist; b. Swatow, China, June 6, 1952; came to U.S., 1973; s. Hon-Kwong and Suet-Hing (Wong) C.; m. Rosario Arroyo, Dec. 14, 1985; children: Nathaniel Arroyo, Jennifer Arroyo. BA, Buena Vista Coll., 1977; MS, U. La Verne, 1980; PhD, U.S. Internat. U., 1984. Diplomate psychopharmacology; lic. psychologist, Calif. Dir. outreach program Chinese Cmty. Ch., San Diego, 1980-81; exec. dir. Chinese Social Svc. Ctr., San Diego, 1981-82; rehab. counselor Asian Rehab. Svcs., Inc., L.A., 1982-84; program dir. Hawthorne (Calif.) Cmty. Group Home, 1984-86; psychologist Pacific Clinics, Pasadena, Calif., 1986-89, Fairview Devel. Ctr., Costa Mesa, Calif., 1989—; pvt. practice, Monterey Park, Calif., 1989—; cons. psychologist Ingleside Hosp., Rosemead, Calif., 1991-95, Garfield Med. Ctr., Monterey Park, 1993—, Asian Youth Ctr., Rosemead, 1993-96, Allied Physicians of Calif., San Gabriel, 1993—, Project SHINE, Inc., Downey, Calif., 1982-88. Mem. APA, Prescribing Psychologists Register, Internat. Coll. Prescribing Psychologists, Calif. Psychol. Assn., Fairview Psychol. Assn. Republican. Presbyn. Avocations: classical music, reading, traveling. Fax: (626) 284-3926. Home: 11107 Mcvine Ave Sunland CA 91040-2121 Office: Atlantic Med Ctr 943 S Atlantic Blvd Ste 221 Monterey Park CA 91754-1066

CHAN, DAVID RONALD, tax specialist, lawyer; b. L.A., Aug. 3, 1948; s. David Yew and Anna May (Wong) C.; m. Mary Anne Chan, July 21, 1980; children: Eric, Christina. AB in Econs., UCLA, 1969, MS in Bus. Adminstrn., 1970, JD, 1973. Bar: Calif. 1973, U.S. Tax Ct. 1974, U.S. Ct. Appeals (9th cir.) 1974, U.S. Dist. Ct. (ctrl. dist.) Calif. 1980. Acct. Oxnard Celery Distbrs., L.A., 1968-73, Touche Ross & Co., L.A., 1970; tax prin. Kenneth Leventhal & Co. (name now E&Y Kenneth Leventhal Real Estate Group), L.A., 1973—. Contbr. chpts. to books and articles to profl. jours. Founder, dir. Chinese Hist. Soc. So. Calif., L.A., 1975—; mem. spkrs. bur. L.A. 200 Bicentennial, L.A., 1981; spkr. Project Follow Through, L.A., 1981, EY Tax Forum, UCLA Real Estate Forecast, Merril Lynch Symposium, Calif. CPA Soc. Recipient Forbes Gold medal Calif. Soc. CPAs, L.A., 1970, Elijah Watt Sells cert. AICPA, L.A., 1970, cert. recognition Chinese Hist. Soc. So. Calif., L.A., 1985. Mem. So. Calif. Chinese Lawyers Assn., L.A. County Bar Assn., Chinese Am. CPAs So. Calif., Asian Bus. League, Chinese For Affirmative Action. Republican. Avocations: Chinese cuisine, sports memorabilia, philately. Office: E&Y Kenneth Leventhal Real Estate Group 2049 Century Park E Ste 1700 Los Angeles CA 90067-3119

CHAN, HENRY ALBERT, minister; b. Grove, East Bank, Guyana, Jan. 7, 1946; came to U.S., 1967, naturalized, 1977; s. Clarence Kenneth and Ruby Verna (Milner) C.; m. Jean Flora Langdon, Apr. 26, 1969; children: H. Anthony, Andre Dwayne, Natasha Laura. BS, SUNY, Saratoga Springs, 1978; MBA, Dowling Coll., Oakdale, N.Y., 1980; D.Pub. Adminstrn., Nova Southeastern U., Ft. Lauderdale, Fla., 1981; DMin, U. of the South, Sewanee, Tenn., 1987; M.Sacred Theology, Gen. Theol. Sem., N.Y.C., 1990; PhD in Pastoral Psychology, Grad. Theol. Found., Donaldson, Ind., 1994; Cert. of Grad., Mercer Sch. Theology, Garden City, N.Y., 1982. Ordained to ministry, Episcopal Ch., 1983. Long-range planning analyst Blue Cross/Blue Shield, N.Y.C., 1980-83; curate and rector Ch. of the Transfiguration, Freeport, N.Y., 1983-87; interim priest Christ Ch., Brentwood, N.Y., 1987; rector St. Peter's Episc. Ch., Rosedale, N.Y., 1988—. Bd. dirs. Liberty Park Non-Profit Housing Corp., Freeport, 1984-87; mem. Freeport Village Human rights Commn., 1986-87; mem. Peale Ctr. for Christian Living, 1996—. Mem. Christian Clergy, Queens Fedn. Chs., C.G. Jung Found. for Analytic Psychology, Inc. Avocations: fishing, reading, travel within Caribbean region. Office: St Peters Episcopal Church 137-28 244th St Rosedale NY 11422-1828

CHAN, JACKIE, actor, director, writer; b. Hong Kong, Apr. 7, 1955; s. Charles and Lee-Lee C.; m. Lin Feng Chow; 1 child: J.C. Trained, Peking Opera Sch. Films include: Little Tiger of Guangdong, Little Tiger from Canton, Hand of Death, 1975, New Fist of Fury, Shaolin Wooden Men, 1976, To Kill with Intrigue, 1977, Snake in the Eagle's Shadow, Snake and Crane Arts of Shaolin, Magnificent Bodyguards, 1978, Drunken Master (Drunk Monkey on the Tiger's Eyes), Spiritual Kung Fu, The Fearless Hyena, Dragon Fist, 1979, The Young Master, Half a Loaf of King Fu, The Big Brawl, 1980, The Cannonball Run, 1981, Dragon Lord, Marvelous Fists, 1982, Winners and Sinners, The Fearless Hyena Part 2, Cannonball Run 2, Project A, 1983, Wheels on Meals, 1984, My Lucky Stars, 1985, Heart of the Dragon (First Mission), Police Story, Armour of God, 1986, Project A Part 2, Dragons Forever, 1987, Police Story II, 1988, Mr. Canton and Lady Rose, 1989, Armour of God II: Operation Condor, Island of Fire, 1990, Twin Dragons, Police Story III: Super Cop, City Hunter, 1992, Crime Story, Project S, 1993, Drunken Master II, Cinema of Vengeance, 1994, Dead Heat, 1995, (also stunt dir.) Rumble in the Bronx, 1996, First Strike, 1996, Burn Hollywood Burn, 1997, Rush Hour, Mr. Nice Guy, 1998, (TV) Who Am I?, 1998, Gorgeous, 1999, many others. Recipient Lifetime Achievement award MTV, 1995, Best Picture award Hong Kong Film, 1989, Best Action Choreography Hong Kong Film, 1996, 99, Maverick Tribute award Cinequest San Jose Film Festival, 1998. Office: c/o New Line Cinema Corp 116 N Robertson Blvd Fl 2 Los Angeles CA 90048-3103 also: Blue Train Entertainment 9333 Wilshire Blvd Beverly Hills CA 90210*

CHAN, JACK-KANG, undersea warfare engineer, mathematician; b. Toyshan, KwangTung, China, Oct. 20, 1950; came to U.S., 1975; s. David En-Shek and Yip-Ching (Yuen) C.; m. Suet-Fong Ng, June 3, 1982; children: Me-Fun, Kang-Ray. PhD in Elec. Engring., Poly. U., 1982, PhD in Math., 1990. Microwave engr. Sedco Systems div. Raytheon, Melville, N.Y., 1979-80; sr. mem. tech. staff Northrop Grumman Norden Sys., Melville, 1980—. Author papers in field. Mem. IEEE (reviewer signal processing 1989-90, vice chmn. L.I. signal processing chpt.), Am. Math. Soc., Math. Assn. Am., Soc. Indsl. and Applied Math. E-mail: jackúchan@ny.essd.northgrum.com. Fax: 516-719-4640. Home: 15316 58th Ave Flushing NY 11355-5523 Office: Northrop Grumman Norden Sys 65 Marcus Dr Melville NY 11747-4232

CHAN, LO-YI CHEUNG YUEN, architect; b. Canton, China, Dec. 1, 1932; came to U.S., 1942, naturalized, 1954; s. Wing tsit and Wai hing (Lei) C.; m. Mildred Wu, Sept. 1, 1957; children: Christopher, Leighton, Leicia. BA, Dartmouth Coll., 1954; MArch, Harvard U., 1959, postgrad. (Appleton fellow), 1959-60. Asso. firm I. M. Pei & Partners, N.Y.C., 1960-65; practice architecture N.Y.C., 1965—; Adj. asst. prof. architecture Columbia, 1963-67; vis. critic Coll. Architecture, Cornell U., 1965-68, Harvard U., 1976, 78, 80, Mass. Inst. Tech., 1977; panelist Am. Arbitration Assn., 1972-80. Bd. dirs. Parks Council, N.Y.C., 1971-85, pres., 1974; trustee Cmty. Svc. Soc., N.Y.C., 1977-86, Henry St. Settlement, 1980—, Lingnan Found., 1986—, chmn., 1990—, mem. N.Y.C. Art Commn., 1992-97, Berkshire Sch., 1992—; active N.Y. State Coun. Arts, 1993-96. With AUS, 1955-57. Nat. Endowment for Arts Design fellow, 1975-76. Fellow AIA (corp.); mem. Phi Beta Kappa. Home: 270 Riverside Dr New York NY 10025-5209 Office: Lo-Yi Chan FAIA Ste 8B 270 Riverside Dr Apt 8B New York NY 10025-5211

CHAN, MICHAEL CHIU-HON, chiropractor; b. Hong Kong, Aug. 31, 1961; came to U.S., 1979; s. Fuk Yum and Chun Wai (Ma) C. D of Chiropractic, Western States Chiropractic Coll., 1985; fellow, Internat. Acad. Clin. Acupuncture, 1986. Assoc. doctor Widoff Chiropractic Clinic, Phoenix, 1986, Horizon Chiropractic Clinic, Glendale, Ariz., 1986-88; dir. North Ranch Chiropractic Assoc., Scottsdale, Ariz., 1988-91; pvt. practice Phoenix, 1991—; founder Horizon Info. Group, 1996; dir. Neighborhood Chiropractic, Phoenix, 1988-89. Contbr. articles to profl. jours. Mem. Am. Chiropractic Assoc., Internat. Platform Assn., Coun. on Diagnostic Imaging, Paradise Valley Toastmaster Club. Avocations: golf, reading, traveling, computer. Office: 3302 W Thomas Rd # 3 Phoenix AZ 85017-5601

CHAN, PETER WING KWONG, pharmacist; b. L.A., Feb. 3, 1949; s. Sherwin T.S. and Shirley W. (Lee) C.; children: Kristina Dionne, Kelly Alison, David Shoichi. BS, U. So. Calif., 1970, D in Pharmacy, 1974. Lic. pharmacist, Calif. Clin. instr. U. So. Calif., 1974-76; staff clin. pharmacist Cedars-Sinai Med. Ctr., L.A., 1974-76; 1st clin. pharmacist in ophthalmology Alcon Labs., Inc., Ft. Worth, 1977—, formerly in Phila. monitoring patient drug therapy, teaching residents, nurses, pharmacy students, then assigned to Tumu Tumu Hosp., Karatina, Kenya, also lectr. clin. ocular pharmacology tng. course, Nairobi, Cairo, Athens, formerly dist. sales mgr. Alcon/BP, ophthal. products div. Alcon Labs., Inc., Denver; v.p., gen. mgr. Optikem Internat., Sereine Products Div., Optacryl, Inc., Denver, 1980-91; product mgr. hosp. pharmacy products Am. McGaw div. Am. Hosp. Supply Corp., 1981-83; internat. market mgr. IOLAB subs. Johnson & Johnson, 1983-86, dir. new bus. devel. Iolab Pharms., 1986-87, dir. Internat. Mktg., 1987-89, dir. new products mktg., 1989; bus. and mktg. strategies cons. to pharm. and med. device cos. Chan & Assocs., Northridge, Calif., 1989-98; regional mng. dir. Pacific Rim, Leiner Health Products, Inc., Carson, Calif., 1998—; ptnr., chmn., CEO PreFree Techs., Inc., 1992-96; med. dir., Clin Profl. Affairs, Nexstar Pharms., Inc., Boulder, 1996-97; ptnr. Vitamin Specialties Corp., 1993-95, JSP Ptnrs., Ltd., 1992—; med. dir., clin. and profl. affairs, Nexstar Pharm. Inc., Boulder, Colo.; regional Managing Dir. Pacific Aim Leiner Health Products, 1998—; bd, dirs. SUDCO Internat., L.A. Del. Am. Pharm. Assn. House of Dels., 1976-78, Calif. Youth Theatre at Paramount Studios, Hollywood 1986-87, 91—; bd. councillors U. So. Calif. Sch. Pharmacy, 1995—. Recipient Hollywood-Wilshire Pharm. Assn. spl. award for outstanding svc., 1974. Mem. Chinese Am. Pharm. Assn., Am. Pharm. Assn., Calif. Pharm. Assn., Hollywood-Wilshire Pharm. Assn. (bd. dirs. 1972-76), Am. Soc. Hosp. Pharmacists, Am. Pharm. Assn. Acad. of Pharmacy Practice, U. So. Calif. Assocs. (life), U. So. Calif. Gen. Alumni Assn., U. So. Calif. (steering com. lifescis. info. networking coun.), Granada Hills H.S. Highlanders Booster Club (bd. dirs. 1991, 92, 93, chmn.-Project 2000), QSAD Centurions, U. So. Calif. Lifetime Assocs., Gamma Epsilon Omega Alumni Assn. (bd. dirs.), Phi Delta Chi, NRA (life), Golden Eagle, Calif. Rifle and Pistol Assn. (life mem.). Republican. Home: 49 Bridgeport St Dana Point CA 92629-3242 Office: Leiner Health Products Inc 901 E 233rd St Carson CA 90745-6204

CHAN, PHILIP, dermatologist, army officer; b. Oceanside, N.Y., Oct. 14, 1946; s. Walter O. and Ann (Yee) C. BA, Harvard U., 1968; MD, Columbia U., 1972. Diplomate Am. Bd. Dermatology. Commd. capt. U.S. Army, 1973, advanced through grades to col., 1987; dermatologist Martin Army Cmty. Hosp., Ft. Benning, Ga., 1995-98; retired U.S. Army, 1998; adj. asst. prof. Uniformed Svcs. U. Health Scis., 1995-97. Editor (govt. pub.) Procs. of Vesicant Workshop, 1987; contbr. articles to profl. jours. Fellow Am. Acad. Dermatology; mem. AMA, Mensa, Assn. of Mil. Dermatologists. Avocations: teaching Reiki master with research interests, blues harmonica, ballroom dancing, writing. Home: 1285 Whisperwood Dr Columbus GA 31907-5883

CHAN, PHILIP J., medical educator; b. Malaysia, May 11, 1956; m. Hilda, 1981; 3 children. BA cum laude in biology, Kalamazoo Coll., 1979; MS in Physiology, Mich. State U., 1981, PhD in Physiology, 1983. Diplomate Am. Bd. Bioanalysis. Dir. sperm processing & IVF and embryo transfer lab. Kennedy Meml. Hosps./U. Med. Ctr., Cherry Hill, N.J., 1983-87; dir. labs. Hillcrest Fertility Ctr., Tulsa, 1987-89; dir. andrology/male reproduction and molecular biology labs. Loma Linda (Calif.) U. Obstetrics Med. Group, 1989—; mgr. info. sys. lab. computers and network Loma Linda U. Ob-Gyn. Med. Group, Inc., 1991—; from instr. to asst. prof. U. Medicine and Dentistry of N.J. Sch. Osteopathic Medicine, 1983-87; assoc. prof. Oral Roberts U. Sch. Medicine, 1987-89; from assoc. prof. to prof. Loma Linda U. Sch. Medicine, 1989—; mem. comparative medicine study sect. NIH, 1994—; insp. Coll. Am. Pathologists, 1993—. Contbr. articles to profl. jours. Recipient Walter-MacPherson First Pl. Rsch. award The Walter E. Macpherson Soc., 1997. Mem. AAAS, Am. Soc. Reproductive Medicine, Internat. Soc. Andrology, Am. Soc. Primatologists, Am. Assn. Bioanalysts, European Soc. Human Reproduction and Embryology, Soc. for Study of Reproduction. Office: Loma Linda U Fac Med Office Dept Ob-Gyn Ste 3950 11370 Anderson St Loma Linda CA 92354-3450

CHAN, RAYMOND, Canadian government minister; b. Hong Kong, Oct. 25, 1951; m. Maureen Chan, 1975; 2 children. B Applied Sci. in Engring. Physics, U. B.C., Vancouver, Can., 1977. Owner, operator restaurant, 1974-89; engr. TRIUMF Rsch. Ctr., U. B.C., 1977-93; mem. Parliament of Can., Ottawa, Ont., 1993—; Sec. of State (Asia-Pacific), 1993—. Office: Can Fed Cabinet Min, Can Fed Ministry, 307 Confederation Bldg, Ottawa, ON Canada K1A 0G2 also: # 221-4940 No 3 Rd, Richmond, BC Canada V6X 3A5

CHAN, SHIH HUNG, mechanical engineering educator, consultant; b. Chang Hwa, Taiwan, Nov. 8, 1943; came to U.S., 1964; s. Ping and Fu Zon (Liao) C.; m. Shirley Shih-Lin Wang, June 14, 1969; children: Bryan, Erick. Diploma Taipei Inst. Tech., Taiwan, 1963; MS, U. N.H., 1966; PhD, U. Calif.-Berkeley, 1969. Registered profl. engr., Wis. Asst. to assoc. prof. NYU, N.Y.C., 1969-73; assoc. prof. Poly. Inst. N.Y., N.Y.C., 1973-74; research staff mem. Argonne Nat. Lab., Ill., 1974-75; assoc. prof. U. Wis., Milw., 1975-78, prof. mech. engring., 1978-88, chmn. dept., 1979-89, Wis. Disting. prof. mech. engring., 1989—, dir. thermal engring. rsch. lab., 1997—, dean Coll. Engring. & Applied Sci., 1991—, honor chair prof. Yuan-Tze Inst. Tech., 1993—; cons. Argonne Nat. Lab., Ill., 1975—, Allen-Bradley Co., Milw., 1984, Gen. Electric Co., Schenectady, 1980, Teltech Resource Network, 1986—, Eclipse, Inc., 1988. Contbr. articles to profl. jours. Bd. dirs. Orgn. Chinese Americans, State of Wis., 1983—; v.p. Civic Club, Milw., 1984—, pres., 1985—. Served to 2d lt. Taiwan M.C., 1963-64. Recipient Outstanding Research award U. Wis.-Milw. Research Found., 1983, Research citation Assembly State of Wis., Madison, 1984, 1st Coll. Research award, 1987, Coll. Outstanding Rsch. award, 1987, Disting. Alumni award, 1991 ; grantee NSF, Dept. Energy, Argonne Nat. Lab., Office of Naval Research NASA Gas Rsch. Inst., 1969—. Fellow ASME; mem. Am. Nuclear Soc. (pres. Wis. 1982-83), Profl. Ergrs. State of Wis. Avocations: fishing, Tae-Kwon-do. Home: 3416 W Meadowview Ct Thiensville WI 53092-5110 Office: U Wis-Milw Dept of Mech Engring PO Box 784 Milwaukee WI 53201-0784

CHAN, SHU-PARK, electrical engineering educator; b. Canton, China, Oct. 10, 1929; came to U.S., 1951, naturalized, 1965; s. Chi-Tong and Shui-Ying (Mok) C.; m. Stella Yok-Sing Lam, Dec. 28, 1956; children: Charlene Li-Hsiang, Yau-Gene. BEE, Va. Mil. Inst., 1955; MEE, U. Ill., 1957, PhD, 1963. Instr. elec. engring. and math. Va. Mil. Inst., 1957-59; instr. elec. engring. U. Ill., 1960-61, rsch. assoc., 1961-62, asst. prof. math., 1962-63; assoc. prof. elec. engring. U. Santa Clara, 1963-68, prof., 1968-92, chmn. elec. engring. and computer sci. dept., 1969-84; Nicholson Family Chair prof. Santa Clara U., 1987-92, prof. emeritus, 1992—, acting dean Sch. Engring., 1987-88; founder, pres. Internat. Technol. U., Santa Clara, 1994—; pres. Chu Hai Coll., Hong Kong, 1995-96; prin. investigator NSF, NASA; Univ. fellow U. Ill., 1959-60; vis. spl. chair prof. elec. engring. dept. Nat. Taiwan U., 1973-74; spl. lectr. Acad. Sci., Peking, China, summer 1980; hon. prof. elec. engring. dept. U. Hong Kong, 1980-81; hon. prof. Anhuei U., China, 1982; spl. chair Tamkang U., Taipei, Taiwan, 1981; apptd. mem. J. William Fulbright Fgn. Scholarship Bd., 1991-93; founder, pres. Internat. Tech. U. Found., 1994—. Author: introductory Topological Analysis of Electrical Networks, 1969, (with others) Analysis of Linear Networks and Systems—A Matrix-Oriented Approach with Computer Applications, 1972, (with E. Moustakas) Introduction to the Applications of the Operational Amplifier, 1974; editor: Network Topology and Its Engineering Applications, 1975, Graph Theory and Applications, 1982. Chmn. bd., pres. Acad. Cultural Co., Santa Clara; founder, pres. China Exptl. U. Found., 1985—; chmn. Santa Clara County Bicentennial Chinese Festival Com.; pres. Chinese Arts and Culture Inst., 1976—; trustee Inst. Sino-Am. Studies, San Jose, Calif., 1971-76, West Valley-Mission C.C. Dist., Calif., 1988. Recipient Disting. Elec. Engring. Alumnus award U. Ill., 1983, 1991 Rschr. of Yr. award Sch. Engring., Santa Clara U., 1992, Courvoisier Leadership award in Edn., 1994; named Engr. of Yr. in Engring. Edn. San Francisco session AIAA, 1994, Chinese Am. Pioneer award Orgn. Chinese Ams., San Francisco, 1996; Hon. Prof. award S. China Normal U., Guangzhou, China, 1997—. Fellow IEEE (past chmn. circuit theory group San Francisco sect., chmn. asilomar conf. circuits and sys. 1970); mem. Am. Soc. Engring. Edn., Chineses Alumni Assn. U. Santa Clara (pres.), U. Santa Clara Faculty Club (pres. 1971-72), Sigma Xi, Tau Beta Pi, Eta Kappa Nu, Pi Mu Epsilon, Phi Kappa Phi. Home: 2085 Denise Dr Santa Clara CA 95050-4557 *I would like to attribute my personal success to the teaching of my father, the late General of the Army Chi-Tong Chan, who taught me the Four Principles of Goodness: Set a good goal in mind; acquire a good wealth of knowledge; exercise good self-discipline; and perform only good deeds.*

CHAN, SUNNEY IGNATIUS, chemist; b. San Francisco, Oct. 5, 1936; s. Sun and Hip-For (Lai) C.; m. Irene Yuk-Hing Tam, July 11, 1964; 1 son, Michael Kenneth. B.S. in Chem. Engring, U. Calif. at Berkeley, 1957, Ph.D. in Chemistry, 1960. Asst. prof. chemistry U. Calif. at Riverside, 1961-63; mem. faculty Calif. Inst. Tech., 1963—, prof. chem. physics, 1968-92, prof. biophys. chemistry, 1976-92, George Grant Hoag prof. biophys. chemistry, 1992—, exec. officer for chemistry, 1977-80, 89-94, master student houses, 1980-83, chmn. faculty, 1987-89; dir. Inst. of Chemistry, Academia Sinica, Taipei, Taiwan, 1997-99; v.p. Academia Sinica, Taipei, Taiwan, 1999—; R.T. Major lectr. U. Conn., 1998; Wilson T.S. Wang Disting. Internat. prof. Chinese U. Hong Kong, 1993; cons. in field. Author numerous articles in field. Guggenheim fellow, 1968-69; Sloan fellow, 1965-67; NSF Postdoctoral fellow, 1960-61; Reilly lectr. U. Notre Dame, 1973-74; Chan Meml. lectr. U. Calif., Berkeley, 1984; Fogarty fellow NIH, 1986. Mem. AAAS, Academia Sinica, Am. Chem. Soc., Chinese Am. Chem. Soc. (chmn. bd. 1988-97), Am. Phys. Soc., Am. Soc. Biochemistry and Molecular Biology, Biophys. Soc., So. Calif. Chinese Engrs. and Scientists Assn. (Progress award 1971), Chinese Collegiate Colleagues So. Calif. (v.p. 1970-71, pres. 1971-72), Chinese Am. Faculty Assn. (pres. 1988, Achievement award 1991), Phi Beta Kappa, Sigma Xi, Tau Beta Pi, Alpha Chi Sigma, Phi Tau Phi (pres. 1981-83). Home: 327 Camino Del Sol South Pasadena CA 91030-4107 Office: Calif Inst Tech Chem Dept Pasadena CA 91125

CHAN, TAK HANG, chemist, educator; b. Hong Kong, June 28, 1941; s. Ka King and Ling Yee (Yick) C.; m. Christina W.Y. Hui, Sept. 6, 1969; children—Juanita Y., Cynthia S. B.A., U. Toronto, 1962; M.A., Princeton U., 1963, Ph.D., 1965. Rsch. assoc. Harvard U., 1965-66; asst. prof. McGill U., Montreal, Que., Can., 1966-71, assoc. prof., 1971-77, prof. chemistry, 1977—, chmn. dept., 1985-91, dean sci., 1991-94; v.p., 1994-99. Contbr. articles to profl. jours. Killam fellow, 1983-85; recipient R.U. Lemieux award Can. Soc. Chem., 1993, Merck, Sharp and Dohme award, 1982. Fellow Royal Soc. Can.; mem. Chem. Inst. Can., Am. Chem. Soc., Royal Soc. Chemistry. Office: 801 Sherbrooke St, Montreal West, Montreal, PQ Canada H3A 2K6

CHAN, W. Y., pharmacologist, educator; b. Shanghai, China, Dec. 1, 1932; came to U.S., 1952, naturalized, 1968; m. Beatrice Ho Chan, June 11, 1961; children: Mina, Jennifer. BA, U. Wis., 1956; PhD in Pharmacology, Columbia U., 1961. Rsch. assoc. then asst. prof. biochemistry Weill Med. Coll. at Cornell U., N.Y.C., 1960-67, asst. prof. then assoc. prof. pharmacology, 1966-76, prof., 1976—, acting chmn., 1983-91; mem. basic pharmacology adv. com. Pharm. Mfrs. Assn. Found., 1973-80; mem. study sect. NIH, 1977, cons., 1981. Contbr. articles to profl. jours. Recipient NIH rsch. career devel. award, 1968-73, Irma T. Hirschl Career Scientist award, 1973-77; NIH grantee, 1965—. Mem. Am. Soc. Pharmacology and Exptl. Therapeutics, Soc. for Study of Reprodn., Soc. Exptl. Biology and Medicine, Harvey Soc., N.Y. Acad. Scis., AAAS. Research on pharmacology of neurohypophys hormones and polypeptides, uterine and cardiovascular-renal actins of oxytocin and vasopressin pathphysiology and pharmacology of dysmenorrhea. Office: Weill Med Coll of Cornell U 1300 York Ave LC-407 New York NY 10021-4805

CHAN, WAI-YEE, molecular geneticist; b. Canton, China, Apr. 28, 1950; came to U.S., 1974; s. Kui and Fung-Hing (Wong) C.; m. May-Fong Sheung, Sept. 3, 1976; children: Connie Hai-Yee, Joanne Hai-Wei, Victor Hai-Yue, Amanda Hai-Pui, Bessie Hai-Lui. BSc with first class honors, Chinese U. of Hong Kong, 1974; PhD, U. Fla., 1977. Tchg. asst. dept. biochemistry and molecular biology U. Fla., Gainesville, 1974-77; rsch. assoc. U. Okla., Oklahoma City, 1978-79, asst. prof. dept. pediats., 1979-82, assoc. prof., 1982-89, asst. prof. dept. biochemistry and molecular biology, 1979-82, assoc. prof., 1982-89; staff affiliate Pediat. Endocrine Metabolism & Genetic Svc., Okla. Children's Meml. Hosp., Oklahoma City, 1979-89, dir. Clin. Trace Metal Diagnostic Lab., 1979-85, asst. sci. dir. Biochem. Genetics and Metabolic Screening Lab., 1980-87; cons. VA Med. Ctr., Oklahoma City, 1981-87; co-sci. dir. State of Okla. Tchg. Hosp., 1982-87; prof. dept. pediats., biochemistry and molecular biology and cell biology, chief divsn. genetics and metabolic diseases, mem. Vincent T. Lombardi Cancer Rsch. Ctr., sci. dir., Molecular Genetics Diagnostic Lab., Georgetown U., Washington, 1989—. Editor 2 books and monograph; editor Jour. Endocrine Genetics, Jour. Am. Coll. Nutrition; contbr. articles to profl. jours. Assoc. mem. Okla. Med. Rsch. Found., Oklahoma City, 1987-89. Scholar Chinese U. Hong Kong, 1972-74, 73-74; NATO fellow, 1979; recipient Okla. Med. Rsch. Found. Merrick awrd, 1988. Mem. Am. Inst. Nutrition, Am. Soc. Biochem. Molecular Biology, Am. Soc. Human Genetics, Internat. Assn. Bio-Inorganic Scientists, N.Y. Acad. Sci., Am. Soc. Cell Biology, Soc. Pediat. Rsch., Am. Assn. Immunology, Endocrinology Soc., Am. Coll. Nutrition. Achievements include patent on application of pregnancy-specific glycoproteins and development of in-vitro diagnostic method for Wilson's Disease. Home: 10708 Butterfly Ct North Potomac MD 20878-4209 Office: Georgetown U Childrens Med Ctr Dept Pediatrics 3800 Reservoir Rd NW Washington DC 20007-2113

CHAN, WING-CHI, cultural organization administrator, musicologist; b. Hong Kong, Aug. 10, 1952; came to U.S., 1979; s. Hing and Mui-Fung (Leung) C.; m. Mina Chan, Jan. 1, 1979; children: Tidings, Leona, Dexter. BA, Chinese U., Hong Kong, 1978; MMus, No. Ill. U., 1981; postgrad., U. Amsterdam, 1991. Pres. Chinese U. Student Union, Hong Kong, 1977; rsch. asst. U. S.W. La., Lafayette, 1979; mgr. Charm's Trading Co., Houston, 1982; asst. to dir. coll. honors program U. Md., Catonsville, 1984-85; dir. devel. Washington Youth Orch., 1985-96; broadcaster Voice of Am. Radio, Washington, 1989-90; exec. dir. Nat. Chamber Orch., 1992; D.C. commr. Nat. & Cmty. Svcs., 1994-97; pres. Washington Cultural Internat. Inc.; v.p. Washington Symphony Orch., 1997—; lectr., spkr. U. Md., College Park, 1983, 84, Tenri (Japan) U., 1986, Kingston Poly., London, 1988, Hong Kong U., 1990; tour coord. Washington Youth Orch. to China, Honk Kong, Taiwan, Korea, Spain, France, Netherlands, and Russia, 1986-94; cons. NEA, Washington, 1989—, N.J. State Arts Coun., 1995, 97, S.C. Arts Commn., 1993; vis. assoc. prof. ShenYang Conservatory, China, 1992—; organizer conf. Asia 4th Pacific Life Underwriters Assns. Conf., Hong Kong, 1997; organizer seminar Aetna Sales Congr., Hong Kong, 1998. Recipient Supr. Svc. award Mayor of Washington, 1987. Mem. Assn. for Asian Studies, Am. Symphony Orch. League, Cultural Alliance Greater Washington. Office: Washington Cultural Internat Inc Nat Capital Station PO Box 77661 Washington DC 20013-8661

CHANCE, BRITTON, biophysics and physical chemistry educator emeritus; b. Wilkes Barre, Pa., July 24, 1913; s. Edwin M. and Eleanor (Kent) C.; m. Jane Earle, Mar. 4, 1938 (div.); children: Eleanor, Britton, Jan, Peter; m. Lilian Streeter Lucas, Nov. 1956 (div.); children: Margaret, Lilian, Benjamin, Samuel; stepchildren—Ann Lucas, Gerald B. Lucas, A. Brooke Lucas, William C. Lucas. B.S. and M.S., U. Pa., 1936, Ph.D. (E.R. Johnson Found. fellow), 1940; Ph.D., U. Cambridge, 1942, D.Sc., 1952; M.D. (hon.), Karolinska Inst., Stockholm, 1962; U. Buenos Aires; D.Sc. (hon.), Med. Coll. Ohio, 1974, Semmelweis U., Budapest, 1976; M.D. (hon.), Hahnemann Coll. and Hosp., 1977; D.Sc. (hon.), U. Pa., 1985, U. Helsinki, 1990; M.D. (hon.), U. Dusseldorf, Fed. Republic Germany. Acting dir. E.R. Johnson Found. U. Pa., Phila., 1940-41, dir., 1949-83, asst. prof. biophysics and phys. biochemistry, 1941-49, prof. biophysics and phys. biochemistry, grad. group of biophysics, 1947-49, chmn. dept. biophysics and phys. biochemistry, 1949-75, Eldridge Reeves Johnson prof. biophysics, dept. biophysics, 1964-75, prof. biochemistry and biophysics, 1975-83, Eldridge Reeves Johnson univ. prof. emeritus of biochemistry, biophysics and phys. biochemistry, 1983-92; Eldridge Reeves Johnson univ. prof. emeritus of biochemistry and biophysics and phys. biochemistry, and radiol. physics Sch. Medicine, U. Pa., 1992—; cons. NSF, 1952-55; mem. Pres.'s Sci. Adv. Com., 1959-60; mem. adv. council Nat. Inst. Alcohol Abuse and Alcoholism, 1971-75; mem. molecular control working group Nat. Cancer Inst., 1973—; dir. Inst. Structural and Functional Studies, Univ. City Sci. Ctr., Phila., 1982-90, dir. Inst. Biophys. and Biomed. Rsch., 1990—. Author: (with F.C. Williams, V. Hughes, E.F. McNichol, David Sayre) Waveforms, 1949, (with R.I. Hulsizer, E.F. McNichol, F.C. Williams) Electronic Time Measurements, 1949, Energy-linked Functions of Mitochondria, 1964, (with Q.H. Gibson, R. Eisenhardt, K.K. Lonberg-Holm) Rapid Mixing and Sampling Techniques in Biochemistry, 1964, (with R.W. Estabrook, J.R. Williamson) Control of Energy Metabolism, 1965, (with R.W. Estabrook, T. Yonetani) Hemes and Hemoproteins, 1966, (with others) Probes of Structure and Function of Macromolecules and Enzymes, 1971, Alcohol and Aldehyde, Vol. I, 1974, II, III, 1977, Tunneling in Biological System, 1979; rev. articles Advances in Enzymology, Vo. 12, 1951, Vol. 17, 1956, Ann. Rev. of Biochemistry, 1952, 70, 76, The Enzymes, Vol. II. Part 1, 1952, Vol. XIII, 1976, Ann. Rev. Plant Physiology, 1958, 68; Bd. editors: Physiol. Revs, 1951-54, FEBS Letters, 1973-75, BBA Reviews, 1972—, Photobiochemistry and Photobiophysics, 1979—; Contbr.: articles to Am., Brit., Swedish, German and Japanese Jours. Presdl. lectr. U. Pa., 1975; Julius L. Jackson Meml. lectr. Wayne State U., 1976; Da Costa oration Phila. County Med. Coll., 1976; Recipient Paul Lewis award for enzyme chemistry, 1950; Pres.'s Certificate of Merit for services, 1941-45, as staff mem. Radiation Lab. of M.I.T., 1950; Guggenheim fellow Stockholm, 1946-48; Harvey lectr., 1954; Phillips lectr., 1955, 65; Pepper lectr., 1957; Exchange scholar to USSR, 1963; Genootschapps medal Dutch Acad. Scis., 1965; Heineken medal, 1970; Keilin medal Brit. Biochem. Soc., 1966; Harrison Howe award, 1966; Franklin medal, 1966; Overseas fellow Churchill Coll., 1966; Herter lectr. NYU, 1968; Pa. award for excellence in life scis., 1968; Nichols award N.Y. sect. Am. Chem. Soc., 1970; Phila. sect. award, 1969; Redfearn lectr., 1970; Gairdner award, 1972; Post-Congress Festschrift Stockholm, 1974; Semmelweis medal, 1974; Nat. medal Sci., 1974, Benjamin Franklin medal Am. Philos. Soc., 1990; Troy C. Daniels lectr. U. Calif.-San Francisco, 1984; Pendergrass lectr. U. Pa., 1991, Christopher Columbus Discovery award in biomedical rsch. NIH, 1992. Fellow Am. Phys. Soc., IEEE (Morlock award 1961, Phila. sect. award 1984), AAAS, Am. Inst. Chemists; mem. NAS, Internat. Union Pure and Applied Biophysics (pres. 1972-75), Chem. Soc., Royal Soc. Arts, Biochem. Soc. Eng., Am. Soc. Biol. Chemists (Sober lectr. 1984), Am. Philos. Soc. (v.p. 1984-90), Am. Acad. Arts and Sci., Am. Physiol. Soc., Am. Acad. Orthopaedic Surgeons (Elizabeth Winston Lanier award 1981, Kappa Delta award 1986), Soc. Magnetic Resonance in Medicine (Gold medal 1988), Soc. Gen. Physiologists (council 1957-60), Am. Inst. Physics, Soc. for Neurosci., Biophys. Soc. (council 1959-62), Swedish Biochem. Soc., Royal Swedish Acad. Scis., Royal Acad. Arts and Scis., Sweden, Bavarian Acad. Scis., Acad. Leopoldina DDR, Max-Planck Gesellschaft für Forerung der Wissenschaften (fgn.), Argentine Nat. Acad. Sci., Royal Soc. London (fgn.), Harvey Soc., Sigma Xi, Tau Beta Pi. Clubs: Corinthian Yacht (Phila.); St. Anthony. Patentee in field of automatic steering devices, fast spectrophotometers, radar range and bombing devices, nuclear magnetic resonance photonmigration in tissues, optical imaging. Gold medal winner (yachting) 1952 Olympics. Office: Johnson Rsch Found Dept Biochemistry/Biophys D501 Richards Bldg U Pa Philadelphia PA 19104*

CHANCE, HENRY MARTYN, II, engineering executive; b. Pottsville, Pa., Jan. 16, 1912; s. Edwin M. and Eleanor (Kent) C.; m. Suzanne Sharpless, June 12, 1934; children: Edwin M. Suzanne, Barbara; m. Elizabeth Reese, Aug. 19, 1944; children: Steven K., James M., Henry Martyn III, Mark Raymond. Grad., Haverford Sch., 1930; B.S. in Civil Engring., U. Pa., 1934, LL.D. (hon.), 1983. Registered profl. engr., 7 states. Chemist, assayer Am. Smelting & Refining Co., 1934-36; with United Engrs. & Constructors, Inc., Phila., 1936—, pres., 1954-71, chmn., 1972-77, dir., cons., 1977—. Life trustee, mem. exec. bd. U. Pa., until 1982, emeritus trustee, 1982—; pres. Haverford Sch., 1962-70, mem. bd., 1962-72, life dir., 1974—; bd. mgrs. emeritus Franklin Inst.; mem. bd. overseers U. Pa. Mus. Named Engr. of Year Del. Valley, 1964. Home: 30 Lonsdale Ln Kennett Square PA 19348-2045 Office: 30 S 17th St Philadelphia PA 19103-4001

CHANCE, JANE, English literature educator; b. Neosho, Mo., Oct. 26, 1945; d. Donald William and Julia (Mile) C.; m. Dennis Carl Nitzsche, June, 1966 (div. Mar. 1969); 1 child, Therese; m. Paolo Passaro, Apr. 30, 1981; children: Antony Damian, Joseph Sebastian. BA in English with honors and highest distinction, Purdue U., 1967; AM in English, U. Ill., 1968, PhD in English, 1971. Lectr. U. Saskatchewan, Can., 1971-72, asst. prof., 1972-73; asst. prof. English, Rice U., Houston, 1973-77, assoc. prof., 1977-80, prof., 1980—; hon. rsch. fellow U. Coll. U. London, 1977-78; sec., Scientia, 1982-83, acting dir., 1983-84; dir. NEH Summer Seminar for Coll. Tchrs., 1985, NEH Inst. for Coll. Tchrs. on Medieval Women, summer 1997; pres. TEAMS, 1986-89; dir. med. studies program Rice U., 1986-92; resident Rockefeller Found., Bellagio, Italy, 1988; mem. Sch. Hist. Studies Inst. for Advanced Study, Princeton U., 1988-89; vis. rsch. fellow Inst. for Advanced Studies in Humanities, U. Edinburgh, summer, 1994; Eccles fellow Humanities Ctr., U. Utah, 1994-95; plenary spkr. Rocky Mountain Med. and Renaissance Assn., 1995; 2d annual lectr. on Italian archaeology Friends of Archaeology U. St. Thomas/Fedn. Italian Assns., Houston, 1997; semi-plenary spkr. 4th annual meeting Internat. Soc. for the Classical Tradition, 1998. Author: The Genius Figure in Antiquity and the Middle Ages, 1975, Tolkien's Art: A Mythology for England, 1979, Woman as Hero in Old English Literature, 1986, The Lord of the Rings: The Mythology of Power, 1992, Medieval Mythography: From Roman North Africa to the School of Chartres, Vol. 1, 1994 (South Ctrl. MLA book prize 1994), The Mythographic Chaucer: The Fabulation of Sexual Politics, 1995; translator: Christine de Pizan's Letter of Othea to Hector, 1990; editor: The Mythographic Art: Classical Fable and the Rise of the Vernacular in Early France and England, 1990, Medievalism in the Twentieth Century, Studies in Medievalism, vol. 2:2, 1983, The Inklings and Others, vol. 3:3, 1990; editor: Gender and Text in the Later Middle Ages, 1996; co-editor: Mapping the Cosmos, 1985, Approaches to Teaching Sir Gawain, 1986; gen. editor Focus Libr. Medieval Women, 1988—, Boydell & Brewer Libr. of Medieval Women, 1997—. NEH fellow, 1977-78, Guggenheim fellow, 1980-81, ACLS Travel grantee, 1982, Mellon leave Rice U., 1988, Disting. Faculty Tchg. fellow, 1995, Ctr. for Study Cultures fellow, 1998, Women's Ctr. IMPACT award Rice U., 1998. Mem. AAUP (Rice U. chpt. sec., treas. 1975-76), MLA, NCS, South Ctrl. Modern Lang. Assn., Scientia (acting dir. 1983-84, sec. 1982-83), Tex. Faculty Assn. (exec. com. 1995—, chpt. pres. 1998—, v.p. 1998—, Faculty Rights award 1998). Avocations: horseback riding, photography, cinema, travel. Office: Rice U Dept English MS 30 PO Box 1892 Houston TX 77251-1892

CHANCE, KENNETH DONALD, engineer; b. Denver, July 27, 1948; s. John Jefferson and Evelyn Pauline (Jacobs) C. AA, Red Rocks Coll., Golden, Colo., 1982. Stationery operating engr. EG&G Rocky Flats, Golden, 1980—.

CHANCE, PATTI LYNN, adult education educator; b. Oklahoma City, July 13, 1955; d. Claude R. and Margaret M. (Altman) Bruza; m. Edward W. Chance, Mar. 20, 1976. BA with highest honors, U. Okla., 1977; MEd, S.D. State U., 1987; PhD, Univ. Okla., 1992. Cert. elem. tchr., adminstr., secondary social studies tchr. Counselor Youth Svcs., Chickasha, Okla., 1977-80; elem. tchr. Lindsay (Okla.) Pub. Schs., 1980-81; jr. high tchr. Bethel (Okla.) Pub. Schs., 1981-84; coord. gifted and talented program Henryetta (Okla.) Pub. Schs., 1984-85, Grove Sch., Shawnee, Okla., 1985-86; instr. S.D. State U., Brookings, 1987-88; acad. counselor U. Okla., Norman, 1988-89; middle sch. tchr. Norman (Okla.) Pub. Schs., 1989-90; elem. asst. prin. Deer Creek Pub. Schs., Edmond, Okla., 1990-92; elem. prin. Deer Creek Pub. Schs., 1992-95; gifted edn. program specialist Clark County Sch. Dist., Las Vegas, 1995-98; asst. prof. Dept. Ednl. Leadership U. Nev., Las Vegas, 1998—; presenter, cons. in field. Contbr. articles to profl. publs. Mem. Coun. of Profs. of Instrl. Supervision, Nat. Assn. for Gifted Children, Nat. Assn. Elem. Sch. Prins., Nat. Middle Sch. Assn., Phi Beta Kappa. Home: 2012 Lady Lake St Las Vegas NV 89128-6721 Office: U Nev Dept Ednl Leadership 4505 Maryland Pkwy Box 453002 Las Vegas NV 89154-3002

CHANCELLOR, VAN, professional basketball coach; b. Louisville, Miss.; m. Betty Chancellor; children: John, renee. Student, East Ctrl. Jr. Coll., Decatur, Miss.; B.Math. and Phys. Edn., Miss. State U., 1965, MEd, 1974. Head coach boys' basketball Noxapater (Miss.) H.S.; head coach women's basketball U. Miss., Oxford; head coach, gen. mgr. Houston Comets, 1997—. Office: Houston Comets Two Greenway Plz #400 Houston TX 77046-3865*

CHANCELLOR, WILLIAM JOSEPH, agricultural engineering educator; b. Alexandria, Va., Aug. 25, 1931; s. John Miller and Caroline (Sedlacek) C.; m. Nongkarn Bodhiprasart, Dec. 13, 1960; 1 child, Marisa Kuakul. BS in Agr., BSME, U. Wis., 1954; MS in Agrl. Engring., Cornell U., 1956, PhD, 1957. Registered profl. agrl. engr., Calif. Prof. agrl. engring. U. California.-Davis, 1957-94; prof. emeritus; vis. prof. agrl. engring. U. Malaya, Kuala Lumpur, Malaysia, 1962-63; UNESCO cons. Punjab Agrl. U., 1976. Contbr. articles to profl. jours.; patentee transmission, planters, dryer, 1961-73. East/West Ctr. sr. Fellow, Honolulu, 1976. Fellow Am. Soc. Agrl. Engrs. (Kishida Internat. award 1984); mem. Soc. Automotive Engrs., Sigma Xi. Office: Univ of California Dept Biol & Agrl Engineering Davis CA 95616

CHANCE-REAY, MICHAELINE K., educator, psychotherapist; b. Gary, Ind.; m. Neville William Reay III. BS in English and Social Studies, Ball State U., 1966, MA in English and Social Studies, 1967; PhD in Humanities Edn., Ohio State U., 1984, MSW in Mental Health and Women's Studies, 1994. Tchr. Bolsa Grande H.S., Garden Grove, Calif., 1967-70; rsch. asst. U. Kans., 1970-73; tutor, substitute tchr. L.A. City Schs., 1973-74; tchr., co-chairperson dept. reading and language arts Morgan Mid. Sch., Yellow Springs, Ohio, 1975-78; tchg. assoc., acad. counselor, supr. humanities edn. Ohio State U., 1978-85; asst. prof. edn., asst. dir. reading and study ctr. Otterbein Coll., Ohio, 1987-90; adj. faculty elem. and secondary edn. Kansas State U., Manhattan, 1995—; adj. faculty Columbus State C.C., Ohio, 1986-94. Contbr. articles to profl. jours.; presentor in field. Dissertation Rsch. grantee Ohio State U., 1981, Spl. Rsch. grantee U. Rsch. Assn. Mem. NASW, Am. Culture Assn., Assn. Psychol. Type, Nat. Coun. Tchrs. English (mem. assembly Am. lit., mem. assembly lit. adolescents, mem. contemporary issues com., mem. assembly expanded perspectives learning), Western Am. Lit. Assn., Sierra Club, Phi Delta Kappa. Office: Kans State U. 248 Bluemont Hall Manhattan KS 66506-5300

CHANDLER, ALBERT BENJAMIN III, attorney general; m. Jennifer Chandler; children: Lucie Brasher, Albert Benjamin IV, Russell Branham. BA in History with distinction, U. Ky., JD, 1986. Bar: Ky. 1986. Assoc. Brown, Todd & Heyburn, Lexington, Ky., Reeves & Graddy, Versailles, Ky.; state auditor, atty. gen. Office of Atty. Gen., Ky. Recipient Achievement of the Yr. award Assn. Govt. Accts., 1993-94. Mem. ABA, Ky. Bar Assn. (named Outstanding Young Lawyer 1993), Woodford County Bar Assn. Office: Office of Atty Gen Ste 118 Capitol Bldg Frankfort KY 40601-2831

CHANDLER, ALFRED DUPONT, JR., historian, educator; b. Guyencourt, Del., Sept. 15, 1918; s. Alfred Dupont and Carol (Ramsay) C.; m. Fay Martin, Jan. 8, 1944; children: Alpine Douglass Chandler Bird, Mary Morris Chandler Watt, Alfred Dupont III, Howard Martin. AB, Harvard U., 1940, AM, 1947, PhD, 1952, LLD (hon.), 1995; PhD (hon.), U. Leuven, Belgium, 1976, U. Antwerp, Belgium, 1979; LHD (hon.), Babson Coll., 1982, Ohio State U., 1987; LLD (hon.), York U., Can., 1988, New England Coll., 1992. Research assoc. MIT, 1950-51, from instr. to prof., 1951-63; prof. history Johns Hopkins U., 1963-71, chmn. dept., 1966-70, dir. Center for Study Recent Am. History, 1964-71; Straus prof. bus. history Harvard U. Bus. Sch., 1971-89, prof. emeritus, 1989—; vis. fellow All Souls Coll., Oxford U., 1975; vis. prof. European Inst. Advanced Studies in Mgmt., Brussels, 1979; Walker-Ames vis. prof. U. Wash., 1981; cons. U.S. Naval War Coll., 1954; mem. Nat. Adv. Council on Edn. Professions Devel., 1970-71; chmn. adv. hist. com. U.S. AEC (renamed ERDA 1974), 1969-77. Author: Henry Varnum Poor, 1956, Strategy and Structure, 1962 (Newcomen award 1964), Giant Enterprise, 1964, The Railroads, 1965, (with Stephen Salsbury) Pierre S. duPont, 1971, The Visible Hand (Pulitzer and Bancroft prizes for 1978), (with Herman Daems) Managerial Hierarchies, 1980; (with Richard Tedlow) The Coming of Managerial Capitalism, 1985, Scale and Scope, 1990; editor Papers of Dwight D. Eisenhower, 5 vols, 1970; asst. editor: The Letters of Theodore Roosevelt, 4 vols, 1954; subject of The Essential Alfred Chandler, 1988. Trustee Park Sch., Brookline, Mass., 1957-63, chmn. bd., 1961-63; trustee Brookline Pub. Libr., 1959-63, Roland Park Sch., Balt., 1964-70, Johns Hopkins U., 1971-81, Eleutherian Mills-Hagley Found., 1981-95, hon. trustee, 1995—. Lt. comdr. USNR, 1940-45. Recipient Pulitzer prize for history, 1978, award Assn. Am. Pubs., 1991, Melamed prize, 1992; rsch. fellow Harvard U., 1955, Guggenheim fellow, 1958-59. Mem. Am. Acad. Arts and Scis., Econ. History Assn. (trustee 1966-70, pres. 1971-72), Orgn. Am. Historians (exec. bd. 1969-72), Soc. for History Tech. (exec. coun. 1972-75), Am. Hist. Assn. (Scholarly Distinction award 1997), Soc. Am. Historians, Mass. Hist. Soc. (coun. 1977-83), Bus. History Conf. (pres. 1977-78), Am. Antiquarian Soc., Am. Philos. Soc., Brit. Acad., Japan Acad., Acad. Mgmt. (Scholarly Contbn. to Mgmt. award 1985), St. Botolph Club (Boston), Nantucket Yacht Club (Mass.). Episcopalian.

CHANDLER, ALICE, higher education consultant, university president; b. Bklyn., May 29, 1931; d. Samuel and Jenny (Meller) Kogan; m. Horace Chandler, June 10, 1954; children: Seth, Donald. A.B., Columbia U., 1951, M.A., 1953, Ph.D., 1960. Instr. Skidmore Coll., 1953-54; lectr. Columbia U. Barnard Coll., 1954-55, Hunter Coll., CUNY, 1956-57; from instr. to prof. CCNY, 1961-76, v.p. instl. advancement, 1974-76, v.p. acad. affairs, 1974-76, provost, 1976-79, acting pres., 1979-80; pres. SUNY Coll., New Paltz, 1980-96; cons. in higher edn., 1996—; bd. dirs. Mohonk Mountain House. Author: The Prose Spectrum: A Rhetoric and Reader, 1968, The Theme of War, 1969, A Dream of Order, 1970, The Rationale of Rhetoric, 1970, The Rationale of the Essay, 1971, From Smollett to James, 1980, Foreign Student Policy: England, France, and West Germany, 1985, Obligation or Opportunity: Foreign Student Policy in Six Major Receiving Countries, 1989, Access, Inclusion and Equity: Imperatives for America's Campuses, 1997, Public Higher Education and the Public Good: Public Policy at the Crossroads, 1998, Paying the Bill for International Education: Programs, Purposes, and Possibilities at the Millenium, 1999. Lizette Fisher fellow. Mem. Lotos, Phi Beta Kappa.

CHANDLER, ARTHUR BLEAKLEY, pathologist, educator; b. Augusta, Ga., Sept. 11, 1926; s. Clemmons Quillian and Mary Isabella (Bleakley) C.; m. Jane Stoughton Downing, Sept. 2, 1953; children—Arthur Bleakley, John Downing. Student, U. Ga., 1943-44; M.D., Med. Coll. Ga., Augusta, 1948. Diplomate: Am. Bd. Pathology. Intern Baylor U. Hosp., Dallas, 1948-49; resident in pathology, NIH trainee in cancer dept. pathology Med. Coll. Ga., 1950-51, asst. in pathology, 1949-50, mem. faculty, 1949—, prof. pathology, 1962—, chmn. dept., 1975—; mem. coms. Nat. Heart, Lung and Blood Inst., 1969-93. Author papers in field, chpts. in books; mem. editorial bd.: Haemostasis, 1975-83, Pathology Research and Practice, 1987—. Trustee Young Mens Library Assn. Fund, 1962-72, Historic Augusta, Inc., 1966-69; Trustee Augusta-Richmond County Mus., 1965-87, Dan Printup Meml. Trust, 1985—, trustee Acad. Richmond County, 1984—. Served as officer M.C. AUS, 1951-53. Commonwealth Fund fellow Norway, 1963-64. Mem. AMA, Internat. Acad. Pathology, Internat. Soc. Thrombosis and Haemostasis,;Am. Assn. History Medicine, Coll. Am. Pathologists, Am. Assn. Pathologists, Am. Soc. Hematology, Am. Heart Assn. (fellow coun. arteriosclerosis, chmn. coun. on thrombosis 1979-80, chmn. com. on coronary lesions and myocardial infarctions 1980-82), Ga. Assn. Pathologists (pres. 1984-85), Ga. Heart Assn., Med. Assn. Ga., Richmond County Med. Soc. (trustee 1984—, sec. 1987, v.p. 1988), Sch. Medicine Alumni Assn. Med. Coll. Ga. (pres. 1996-97), Alpha Omega Alpha. Episcopalian. Home: 803 Milledge Rd Augusta GA 30904-4351 Office: Med Coll Ga Dept Pathology Augusta GA 30912

CHANDLER, BRUCE FREDERICK, internist; b. Bohemia, Pa., Mar. 26, 1926; s. Frederick Arthur and Minnie Flora (Burkhardt) C.; m. Janice Evelyn Piper, Aug. 14, 1954; children: Barbara, Betty, Karen, Paul, June. Student, Pa. State U., 1942-44; MD, Temple U., 1948. Diplomate Am. Bd. Internal Medicine, cert. specialty pulmonary disease. Commd. med. officer U.S. Army, 1948, advanced through grades to col., 1967; intern Temple U. Hosp., Phila., 1948-49; chief psychiatry 7th Field Hosp., Trieste, Italy, 1950; resident Walter Reed Gen. Hosp., Washington, 1949-53; battalion surgeon 2d Div. Artillery, Korea, 1953-54; chief renal dialysis unit 45th Evacuation Hosp. and Tokyo Army Hosp., Korea, Japan, 1954-55; various assignments Walter Reed Gen. Hosp., Fitzsimons Gen. Hosp., Letterman Gen. Hosp., 1955-70; comdg. officer 45th Field Hosp., Vicenza, Italy, 1958-62; pvt. practice internist Ridgecrest (Calif.) Med. Clinic, 1970-76; chief med. svc. and out-patients VA Hosps., Walla Walla, Spokane, Wash., 1976-82; med. cons. Social Security Adminstrn., Spokane, Wash., 1983-87; ret., 1987; lectr. in field of pulmonary disease. Panel mem. TV shows, 1964-70; contbr. articles to profl. jours. Decorated Legion of Merit. Fellow ACP, Am. Coll. Chest Physicians; mem. AMA, Am. Thoracic Soc., N.Y. Acad. Scis., So. European Task Force U.S. Army Med. Dental Soc. (pres., founder 1958-62). Republican. Methodist. Avocations: photography, travel, fishing, collecting books (especially by Jules Verne and Agatha Christie). Home: 6496 N Callisch Ave Fresno CA 93710-3902

CHANDLER, CHRISTOPHER MARK (CHRIS), professional football player; b. Everett, Wash., Oct. 12, 1965. Degree in econ., Wash. State U., 1988. Quarterback Indpls. Colts, 1988-89, Tampa Bay Buccaneers, 1990-91, Phoenix Cardinals, 1991-93, L.A. Rams, 1994, Houston Oilers, 1995-96, Atlanta Falcons, 1997—; mem. Pro Bowl team, 1997, NFC conf. champions, 1998-99, lost Superbowl 33 to Denver Broncos, 1999. Office: c/o Atlanta Falcons 1 Falcon Pl Suwanee GA 30024*

CHANDLER, DAVID, scientist, educator; b. Bklyn., Oct. 15, 1944. SB, MIT, 1966; PhD, Harvard U., 1969. Research assoc. U. Calif., San Diego, 1969-70; from asst. prof. to prof. U. Ill., Urbana, 1970-83; prof. U.Pa., Phila., 1983-85, U. Calif., Berkeley, 1986—; vis. prof. Columbia U., N.Y.C., 1977-78; vis. scientist IBM Corp., Yorktown Heights, N.Y., 1978, Oak Ridge Nat. Lab., 1979; cons. Los Alamos Nat. Labs., 1987-90; Miller rsch. prof., 1991; dir. de recherche Ecole Normale Superieure de Lyon, France, fall 1992; Christensen vis. fellow Oxford U., winter 1993, Hinshelwood lectr., 1993; Kolthoff lectr. U. Minn, 1994; faculty chemist Lawrence Berkeley Nat. Lab., 1996—, Miller rsch. prof., 1999—. Editor Chem. Physics, 1985—; mem. editl. bd. Jour. Statis. Physics, 1976-78, 94-96, Jour. Chem. Physics, 1978-80, Chem. Physics Letters, 1980-82, 91—, Molecular Physics, 1980-87, Theoretica Chimica Acta, 1988-89, Jour. Phys. Chemistry, 1987-92, Phys. Rev. E, 1995—, Adv. Chem. Phys., 1995—; mem. editl. adv. bd. PhysChemComm, 1999—; author books in field; contbr. articles to profl. jours. Recipient Bourke medal Faraday divsn. Royal Chem. Soc., Eng., 1985, Hirschfelder Theoretical Chemistry prize U. Wis., 1998, Humboldt Rsch. award, 1999; fellow Alfred P. Sloan Found., 1972-74, Guggenheim Found., 1981-82; Flygare Meml. lectr., 1989. Fellow AAAS, Am. Phys. Soc.; mem. NAS, Am. Acad. Arts and Scis., Am. Chem. Soc. (chmn. divsn. theoretical chemistry 1984, chmn. divsn. phys. chemistry 1990, Joel Henry Hildebrand award 1989, Theoretical Chemistry award 1996). Avocations: tennis; piano playing. Office: U Calif Dept Chemistry Berkeley CA 94720

CHANDLER, E(DWIN) RUSSELL, clergyman, author; b. L.A., Sept. 9, 1932; s. Edwin Russell Sr. and Mary Elizabeth (Smith) C.; m. Sandra Lynn Swisher, Aug. 24, 1957 (div. 1977); children—Heather, Holly, Timothy John; m. Marjorie Lee Moore, Dec. 21, 1978; 3 stepchildren. Student, Stanford U., 1950-52; B.S. in Bus. Adminstrn., UCLA, 1952-55; postgrad., U. So. Calif. Grad. Sch. Religion, 1955, New Coll., Edinburgh, Scotland, 1955-56; M.Div., Princeton Theol. Sem., 1958; grad., Washington Journalism Ctr., 1967. Ordained to ministry Presbyterian Ch., 1958. Asst. pastor 1st Presbyn. Ch., Concord, Calif., 1958-61; pastor Escalon Presbyn. Ch., Calif., 1961-66; reporter Modesto Bee, Calif., 1966-67; religion editor Washington Star, 1968-69; news editor Christianity Today, Washington, 1969-72; reporter Sonora Daily Union Dem., Calif., 1972-73; religion writer L.A. Times, 1974-92; interim pastor 1st Presbyn. Ch., Columbia, Calif., 1995-96. Author: The Kennedy Explosion, 1972, Budgets, Bedrooms and Boredom, 1976; co-author: Your Family—Frenzy or Fun?, 1977, The Overcomers, 1978, Understanding the New Age, 1988 (Silver Angel award 1989, Wilbur award 1989), Racing Toward 2001, 1992, Doomsday, 1993, Feeding the Flock, 1998; contbr. articles to profl. jours. Recipient Arthur West award United Methodist Communications Council, 1978, Faith and Freedom award Religious Heritage of Am., 1993; co-recipient Silver Angel award, Religion in Media, 1985. Mem. Religion Newswriters Assn. (pres. 1982-84, James O. Supple Meml. award, 1976, 1984, 86, John M. Templeton Reporter of Yr. award 1984, 87, 89), Phi Delta Theta. Republican. Avocations: travel; beekeeping; birdwatching. Home and Office: 698 Hillside Dr Solvang CA 93463-2156 also: 14304 Lake Vista Dr Sonora CA 95370-9692

CHANDLER, ELISABETH GORDON (MRS. LACI DE GERENDAY), sculptor, harpist; b. St. Louis, June 10, 1913; d. Henry Brace and Sara Ellen (Sallee) Gordon; m. Robert Kirkland Chandler, May 27, 1946 (dec.); m. Laci de Gerenday, May 12, 1979. Grad., Lenox Sch., 1931; pvt. study sculpture and harp. Mem. Mildred Dilling Harp Ensemble, 1934-45; prof. sculpture Lyme Acad. Fine Arts, 1976—, chair sculpture dept. Exhibited sculpture NAD, Nat. Sculpture Soc., Allied Artists Am., Nat. Arts Club, Pen and Brush, Lyme Art Assn., Mattatuck Mus., Catherine Lorillard Wolfe Art Club, Am. Artists Profl. League, Hudson Valley Art Assn., USIA, 1976-78, Lyme Art Ctr., 1979, retrospective exhbn. Lyme Acad. Fine Arts, 1987, Madison Gallery, 1987, Old State House, Hartford, Conn., 1989, Mellon Art Ctr., Wallingford, Conn., 1989, Fairfield U. Walsh Gallery, 1991, Brit. Mus., London, Am. Medallic Sculptors Assn. Traveling Exhbn., 1994, Slater Mus. Cropsey Found., 1995, Nat. Sculpture Exhbn. Lyme Acad. Fine Arts, 1995-96, Lever House, N.Y.C., 1996, America's Tower, 1996-98, Hillsdale (Mich.) Coll., 1997, Nat. Acad. Mus., N.Y.C., 1998; represented in permanent collections Aircraft Carrier USS Forrestal, Gov. Dummer Acad., James Forrestal Research Ctr. of Princeton U., Lenox Sch., James L. Collins Parochial Sch., Tex., Storm King Art Ctr., Columbia U., Pace U., White Plains, N.Y., St. Patrick's Cathedral, N.Y.C., McAuley Ctr., St. Joseph's Coll., West Hartford, Conn., Nat. Acad. Mus.; designed and executed Brookgreen Gardens medal, Forrestal Meml. Medal, Timoschenko Medal for Applied Mechanics, Benjamin Franklin Medal, Albert A. Michelson Medal, Jonathan Edwards Medal, Shafto Broadcasting Award Medal, Enrichment of Life medal Soc. Medallists, Adlai Stevenson bronze bust for Woodrow Wilson Sch. of Princeton U., 250 Ann. George Washington medal,Owen R. Cheatham bronze bust for Ga. Pacific Bldg., Atlanta, Messiah Coll., Grantham, Pa., Adlai E. Stevenson High Sch., Ill., Queen Anne's County Courthouse Square, Md., Our Lady Mercy Hosp., N.Y.C., pvt. collections. With mus. therapy div. Am. Theatre Wing, 1942-45; trustee The Lenox Sch., 1953-55; chmn. Associated Taxpayers Old Lyme, 1969-72; mem., trustee Brookgreen Gardens, S.C., 1989-97; life trustee Lyme Acad. Fine Arts, 1979—. Recipient 1st prize Bklyn. War Meml. competition, 1945, 1st prize sculpture Catherine Lorillard Wolfe Art Club, 1951, 58, 63, Gold medal, 1969, Founders prize Pen & Brush, 1954, 76, 78, Gold medal, 1957, 61, 63, 69, 74, 76, Am. Heritage award, 1968, Solo Show award, 1961, 69, 75, Thomas R. Proctor prize NAD, 1956, Dessie Greer prize, 1960, 79, 85, Sculpture prize Nat. Arts Club, 1959, 60, 62, Gold medal, 1971, Gold medal Am. Artists Profl. LEague, 1960, 69, 73, 75, prize, 1981, Anna Hyatt Huntington prize, 1970, 76, Harriet Mayer Meml. prize, 1961, Gold medal Hudson Valley Art Assn., 1956, 69, 74, Mrs. John Newington award, 1976, 78, Lindsey Morris Meml. prize Allied Artists Am., 1973, Gold medal, 1982, Sculpture prize Acad. Artists, 1974, Sydney Taylor Meml. prize Knickerbocker Artists, 1975, New Netherlands DAR Bicentennial medal, 1976, Pietro Montana Meml. prize Hudson Valley Art Assn., 1995, Citation, State of Conn., 1995; named Citizen of Yr., Town of Old Lyme, Conn., 1985. Fellow NAD (academician), Nat. Sculpture Soc. (coun. 1976-85, Tallix Foundry award 1979, John Spring Founder's award 1986, John Cavanaugh

Meml. prize 1991, Silver medal, citation 1992, Herbert Adams Meml. medal for svc. to Am. Sculpture), Am. Artists Profl. League, Internat. Inst. Arts and Letters; mem. Federation International de la Medaille, Nat. Arts Club, Allied Artists Am., Am. Medallic Art Soc., Pen and Brush, Catherine Lorillard Wolf Art Club, Lyme Art Assn. (pres. 1973-75), Coun. Am. Artists Socs. (dir. 1970-73), Am. Artists Profl. League (dir. 1970-73). Home and Studio: 2 Mill Pond Ln Old Lyme CT 06371-1118

CHANDLER, FAY MARTIN, artist; b. Norfolk, Va., Sept. 15, 1922; d. Howard Gresham and Alpine Douglas (Gatling) Martin; m. Alfred Dupont Chandler Jr., Jan. 8, 1944; children: Alpine C. Bird, Mary C. Watt, Alfred D. III, Howard Martin. BA, Sweetbriar Coll., 1943; MFA, Md. Inst. Coll. Art, Balt., 1967. Coord., dir. Fell's Point Gallery Md. Inst. Coll. Art, 1968-73; fellow Va. Ctr. Creative Arts, Sweetbriar, 1993; bd. dirs. Friends of Art-Sweetbriar Coll., Md. Inst. Alumni Coun., Boston Ctr. Arts, Nantucket Island (Mass.) Sch. Design & Arts; hon. bd. dirs. Mass. Vol. Lawyers for the Arts; chmn. bd. dirs. The Art Connection, Boston, 1995-99; mem. Arts in Edn. Adv. Coun. of Harvard Grad. Sch. Edn. One-woman shows include Kenneth Taylor Little Gallery, Nantucket, 1973, 76, Fells Point Gallery, Balt., 1974, 76, Mills Gallery, Boston, 1974-88, Main St. Gallery, Nantucket, 1977, Ensign-Sibley Gallery, Nantucket, 1978, Sibley Gallery, Nantucket, 1980-85, Billiard Room Gallery, Mass., 1980, Helen Shlien Gallery, Boston, 1980, Bodley Gallery, N.Y.C., 1980, St. Botolph Club, Boston, 1982, Stebbins Gallery, Mass., 1987, Bentley Coll., Waltham, Mass., 1987, Columbia (Md.) Ctr. for the Arts, 1987, Babcock Gallery Sweet Briar Coll., Va., 1993, Wenham (Mass.) Mus., 1993, Nantucket Island Sch. Design Gallery, 1994, Boston Ctr. For the Arts, 1995, Children's Mus., Boston, 1996, Decker Gallery/Md. Inst. Art, 1997, Stenbaum Krauss Gallery, N.Y.C., 1997-98. Papers and slides chosen to be preserved Schlesinger Libr., Radcliffe Coll., Cambridge, Mass. Mem. Cambridge Art Assn. Avocations: train trips, mystery books, philosophy. Home: 1010 Memorial Dr Apt 17E Cambridge MA 02138-4857 Studio: Engine House Studios 444 Western Ave Boston MA 02135-1016

CHANDLER, GEORGE FRANCIS, III, lawyer, naval architect; b. Winthrop, Mass., Dec. 15, 1940; s. George Francis Jr. and Phyllis (McKay) C.; children: Heather Suzanne, George Francis IV. BSME, Va. Poly. Inst., 1963; JD, Suffolk U., 1972. Bar: Mass. 1972, N.Y. 1973, N.J. 1978, U.S. Dist. Ct. Mass. 1972, U.S. Dist. Ct. (so. dist.) N.Y. 1973, U.S. Dist. Ct. (ea. dist.) N.Y. 1977, U.S. Dist. Ct. (so. dist.) Tex. 1990), U.S. Dist. Ct. N.J. 1977, U.S. Ct. Appeals (2d cir.) 1973, U.S. Supreme Ct. 1977, U.S. Ct. Appeals (4th cir.) 1978, U.S. Ct. Appeals (11th cir.) 1983, U.S. Ct. Appeals (1st cir.) 1984, U.S. Ct. Appeals (5th cir.) 1992 ; profl. engr., Mass. Naval architect Dept. BuShips USN, Boston, 1958-63, 67-72; assoc. Bigham, Englar, Jones & Houston, N.Y.C., 1972-78; ptnr. Hill, Rivkins & Hayden LLP (and predecessor firm), N.Y.C., 1978—; U.S. rep. to UNCITRAL for Electronic Commerce, 1991-96; mem. joint work group UNCITRAL/CMI, 1995-96; del. Comitè Maritime Internat., 1990, 98, CMI subcom. on H/V Rules, 1995-99, CMI steering commn. on transport law, 1997—; titulary mem. CMI Subcom. on Electronic B/L. Contbr. articles to profl. jours. Pres., founder Spl. Edn. PTA, Maplewood, N.J., 1984-87. Lt. USNR, 1963-67. Mem. ABA, Soc. Naval Archs. (chmn. N.Y. sect. 1986-87), Maritime Law Assn. (proctor, bd. dirs. 1993-96, chmn. com. on carriage of goods 1991-95, chmn. subcom. on electronic contracts of carriage 1990-91, chmn. electronic comm. com. 1995-99), Houston Maritime Arbitrators Assn. (founder, pres., bd. dirs. 1998—). Office: Hill Rivkins & Hayden LLP Ste 1515 712 Main St Houston TX 77002-3209

CHANDLER, HARRIETTE LEVY, management consultant, educator, legislator; b. Balt., Dec. 20, 1937; d. S. Lester and Reba K. Levy; m. Burton Chandler, July 12, 1959; children: Frank Levy, Victoria Jane, Edward Lee. BA, Wellesley Coll., 1959; MA, Clark U., 1963, PhD, 1973; MBA, Simmons Coll., 1983; PhD in Pub. Adminstrn. (hon.), Worcester State Coll., 1998. High sch. history tchr. Worcester (Mass.) Pub. Schs., 1959-61; polit. sci. prof. Clark U., Worcester, 1973-77; prof. polit. sci. Tufts U., Medford, Mass., 1977-78; exec. dir. nat women's com. Brandeis U., Waltham, Mass., 1978-81; cons. Prime Computer, Natick, Mass., 1983-84; mgr. documentation tng. Adelie Corp., Cambridge, Mass., 1984-85; mgr. mktg. svcs. Adelie Corp., Cambridge, 1985-87, prin., 1987-89; dir. communication Open Software Found., Cambridge, 1989; mgmt. cons. Chandler Assocs., 1990—. Author: U.S. Soviet Relations During World War II, 1982. Mem. Worcester Sch. Com., 1992-94, vice chmn., 1994, Mass Comm. on Common Core of Learning, 1994; state rep. 13th Worcester Dist., Mass. Legislature, 1995—, chair joint com. on health care, mem. steering and policy com.; chmn. com. on shareholder responsibility Clark U., 1982-86; chmn. bd. trustees Worcester Meml. Auditorium, 1987-89; founding mem. Worcester Women's Polit. Caucus, 1985, Worcester Com. Fgn. Rels.; mem. Worcester Econs. Club; corporator Dynam'y, Age Ctr. Worcester; incorporator Worcester Cmty. Found.; past pres. Jewish Healthcare Ctr.; vice chair health care Assembly on Fed. Issues, Nat. Coun. State Legislatures; mem. exec. com. Reforming States Group. Jewish. Avocations: walking, swimming, knitting, reading. Home: 7 Brook Hill Dr Worcester MA 01609-1314 Office: Ho of Reps Rm 130 State House Boston MA 02133

CHANDLER, HUBERT THOMAS, former army officer; b. Charleston, W.Va., Dec. 8, 1933; s. Hubert Paris and Eleanor Lee (Gay) C.; m. Mary Frances Ritter, June 4, 1955; 1 son, Thomas Ritter. Student, Morris Harvey Coll., Charleston, 1951-52, U. Louisville, 1952-53; D.D.S., Balt. Coll. Dental Surgery, 1957; grad., Army War Coll., 1974. Diplomate: Am. Bd. Prosthodontics. Commd. Dental Corps U.S. Army, 1957, advanced through grades to maj. gen., dep. to chief Dental Corps, 1975-78, dep. comdr. Med. Command; dental surgeon U.S. Army, Europe, 1979-82; asst. surgeon gen., chief Dental Corps U.S. Army, 1982-86, dir. personnel Med. Dept., 1983-85; assoc. dean for profl. devel. Dental Sch., U. Md., Balt., 1988-92. Exec. com. Transatlantic council Boy Scouts Am., 1980-82; chmn. trust fund Girl Scouts Europe, 1981-82; pres. European Assn. Rod and Gun Clubs, 1981-82, Am. German Friendship Club, Heidelberg, W. Ger., 1981-82. Decorated D.S.M., Bronze Star, Meritorious Service medal, Army Commendation medal. Fellow Am. Coll. Prosthodontists; mem. ADA. Office: 1714 Besley Rd Vienna VA 22182-2004

CHANDLER, J. HAROLD, insurance company executive; b. 1949. MBA, U. S.C. With Citizens & So. Nat. Bank S.C., Columbia, 1972-88, Citizens & So. Nat. Bank, Atlanta, 1988-91, NationsBank Corp., Atlanta, 1992-93; pres., CEO, chmn. Provident Companies, Inc., Chattanooga, Tenn., 1993—; bd. dirs. AmSouth Bancorporation, Herman Miller, Inc., Healthsource, Inc. Office: Provident Companies Inc 1 Fountain Sq Chattanooga TN 37402-1307*

CHANDLER, JAMES JOHN, surgeon; b. Dayton, Ohio, Nov. 13, 1932; s. James Kapp and Margaret Bertha (Paulson) C.; m. Fleur Elizabeth Varney, July 23, 1955; 1 child, Jennifer Hauge. A.B., Dartmouth Coll., 1954, diploma in medicine, 1955; M.D. cum laude, U. Mich., 1957. Diplomate in surg., critical care Am. Bd. Surgery. Intern Harvard Surg. Service, Boston City Hosp., 1957-58, jr. asst. resident, 1958; resident, chief resident in surgery, clin. fellow Am. Cancer Soc. U. Oreg. Hosps., Portland, 1961-64; instr. surgery U. Oreg. Hosps., 1964; sr. attending staff, chmn. surgery Med. Ctr. at Princeton, N.J., 1972-92; pres. med. and dental staff Med. Ctr. at Princeton, 1993-94; clin. prof. surgery Coll. Medicine and Dentistry N.J.-Robert Wood Johnson Med. Sch., Piscataway, 1976—; cons. in surgery Princeton U., Robert Wood Johnson U. Hosp.; bd. trustees Med. Ctr. of Princeton, 1993-94. Contbr. chpt. to book, articles to profl. jours. Bd. dirs. Trinity Counseling Svc., 1968—, chmn., 1968-72, 79-81; pres. Princeton Day Sch. PTA, 1976-78, trustee, 1976-81; active All Saints Episcopal Ch., Princeton, 1965—; mem. alumni coun. Dartmouth Med. Sch., 1981-86, Dartmouth Coll., 1983-86. Lt. USN, 1958-60; to lt. comdr. USNR, 1960-61. Fellow ACS (pres. N.J. chpt. 1976-77, gov. 1981-87), Am. Coll. Chest Physicians, Soc. Surg. Oncology; mem. Am. Soc. Clin. Oncology, Soc. Surgeons N.J., Med. Soc. N.J. (sec., chmn. surgery sect. 1967-69), Mercer County Med. Soc., Collegium Internationale Chirurgiae Digestivae, Soc. Surg. Alimentary Tract, Soc. Internat. Surgery, Alpha Omega Alpha. Home: 95 Russell Rd Princeton NJ 08540-6729 Office: 281 Witherspoon St Princeton NJ 08540-3210

CHANDLER, JAMES WILLIAMS, retired securities company executive; b. Adairville, Ky., Feb. 4, 1904; s. James Avery and Mary Nell (Williams) C.; m. Lelia Elizabeth Roemele, June 29, 1932. A.B., Centre Coll., Danville, Ky., 1925. With Stein Bros. & Boyce, Louisville, 1926-48, N.Y.C., 1948-49; ptnr. W.L. Lyons & Co., 1950-65; partner J.J.B. Hilliard, W.L. Lyons & Co., Inc., Louisville, 1965-81; sr. v.p. J.J.B. Hilliard, W.L. Lyons & Co., Inc., 1965-85. Trustee emeritus, past alumni dir. Centre Coll., Danville, Ky.; past jr. warden, sr. warden and treas. Calvary Episcopal Ch., Louisville; past trustee Bishop Dudley Meml. Fund; past conv. cel. Episcopal Diocese. Recipient Disting. Alumni award Centre Coll., 1983. Mem. Soc. Colonial Wars (past trustee), River Valley Club, Pendennis Club, Delta Kappa Epsilon. Republican. Home: 6209 Wolf Pen Branch Rd Harrods Creek KY 40027

CHANDLER, JOHN WESLEY, educational consultant; b. Mars Hill, N.C., Sept. 5, 1923; s. Baxter Harrison and Mamie (McIntosh) C.; m. Florence Gordon, Aug. 25, 1948; children: Alison, John, Jennifer, Patricia. Student, Mars Hill Coll., 1941-43; A.B., Wake Forest Coll., 1945, L.H.D. (hon.); B.D., Duke U., 1952, Ph.D., 1954; LL.D., Hamilton Coll., 1968, Colgate U., 1968, Williams Coll., 1973, Amherst Coll., 1974, Wesleyan U., 1978, North Adams State Coll., 1983; L.H.D., Wake Forest U., 1968, Trinity Coll., 1982, Middlebury Coll., 1983, Bates Coll., 1983, Beaver Coll. Instr. philosophy Wake Forest Coll., 1948-51, asst. prof., 1954-55; asst. prof. religion Williams Coll., 1955-60, assoc. prof., chmn. dept., 1960-65, Cluett prof. religion, 1965-68, acting provost, 1965-66, dean faculty, 1966-68; pres. Hamilton Coll., Clinton, N.Y., 1968-73, Williams Coll., Williamstown, Mass., 1973-85, Assn. Am. Colls., Washington, 1985-90; ednl. cons. Korn/Ferry Internat., Washington, 1990-91, Acad. Search Cons. Svc., 1992—. Contbg. author: Miscellany of American Religion, 1963, Masterpieces of Religious Literature, 1963, also jour. articles and revs. Trustee Williams Coll., 1969-73; bd. visitors Wake Forest Coll., 1971-77, 79-91; bd. dirs. Williamstown Theatre Festival, 1973-85, Sterling and Francine Clark Art Inst., 1973-85; pres. New Eng. Assn. Schs. and Colls., 1977-78, Assn. Ind. Colls. and Univs. Mass., 1977—; chmn. New Eng. Colls. Fund, 1978; trustee Duke U., 1985-94, chmn., 1993-94; trustee Randolph-Macon Woman's Coll., 1985-88, Phillips Collection, 1997—. Fulbright fellow India, 1963; Kent fellow. Mem. Phi Beta Kappa. Mem. United Ch. of Christ. Clubs: Williams; Cosmos (Washington). Office: 1818 R St NW Washington DC 20009-1604

CHANDLER, KENNETH A., newspaper editor; b. Westcliff-on-Sea, Essex, Eng., Aug. 2, 1947; came to U.S., 1974; s. Leonard Gordon and Beatrix Marie (McKenzie) C.; m. Linda Kathleen, Mar. 22, 1975; children—Bethany, Benjamin, Kathryn. Mng. editor N.Y. Post, N.Y.C., 1978-86; exec. editor Boston Herald, 1986-93; exec. prodr. Fox-TV's "A Current Affair", N.Y.C., 1993; editor The New York Post, N.Y.C., 1993—. Office: NY Post Ste 1910 1211 Avenue Of The Americas Fl 10 New York NY 10036-8790*

CHANDLER, KENT, JR., lawyer; b. Chgo., Jan. 10, 1920; s. Kent and Grace Emeret (Tuttle) C.; m. Frances Robertson, June 19, 1948; children: Gail, Robertson Kent. BA, Yale U., 1942; JD, U. Mich., 1949. Bar: Ill. 1949, U.S. Dist. Ct. (no. dist.) Ill. 1949, U.S. Ct. Claims 1958, U.S. Ct. Appeals (7th cir.) 1955. Assoc. Wilson & McIlvaine, Chgo., 1949-56, ptnr., 1957-94, spl. counsel to firm, 1994-98; of counsel Bell, Jones, Quinlisk & Palmer, Chgo., 1998—; bd. dirs. No. Trust Bank Lake Forest, 1969-90, A.B. Dick Co., 1971-79; dir. Internat. Crane Found., 1988—. Mem. zoning bd. appeals City Lake Forest (Ill.), 1953-63, chmn., 1963-67, mem. plan commn., 1955-69, chmn., 1969-70, pres. bd. local improvements, 1970-73, mem., 1973-78, mayor, 1970-73, mem. bd. fire and police commn., 1975-82, chmn., 1982-84. Served to maj. USMCR, 1941-46. Mem. ABA, Chgo. Bar Assn., Ill. State Bar Assn., Lake County Bar Assn., Legal Club Chgo., Law Club (pres. 1985-86), Univ. Chgo., Onwentsia Club (Lake Forest), Old Elm Club (Highland Park, Ill.). Republican. Presbyterian. Office: 200 W Adams St Ste 2620 Chicago IL 60606-5233

CHANDLER, KIMBERLEY LYNN, gifted education resource specialist; b. Waynesboro, Va., Sept. 28, 1961; d. Alden Hugh and Cecille Frances (Brooks) C. BA in Elem. Edn., Coll. William and Mary, 1984, MA in Edn./Gifted Edn., 1992, postgrad. Lic. educator, Va. Tchr. Fredericksburg (Va.) Pub. Schs., 1984-87, Henrico County Pub. Schs., Richmond, Va., 1987-98; gifted edn. resource specialist Hanover County Pub. Schs., Richmond, Va., 1998—; summer sch. coord. Henrico County Pub. Schs., 1996, 97, staff devel. presenter, 1996, 97; curriculum cons. Coll. of William and Mary, Williamsburg, Va., 1996; presenter in field.; mem. gifted edn. staff devel. talent bank, mem. tchr. stds. com. Va. Dept. Edn.; sch. renewal planning team facilitator Hanover County Pub. Schs. Author: (curriculum unit) Literary Reflections, 1992. Vol. Hanover Humane Soc., 1994—, Big Bros. and Big Sisters of Richmond, Barnett Mission Group. Grantee Henrico Edn. Found., 1997, Henrico Gifted Adv. Coun., 1997, Pntrs. in Arts grantee Richmond Arts Coun., 1996. Mem. Nat. Assn. for Gifted Children (Harry Passow Classroom Tchr. scholarship 1997, sec./treas. technol. divsn. 1997-99, sec./treas. profl. devel. divsn. 1997-99), Richmond Area Reading Coun., Va. Soc. for Tech. in Edn., Kappa Delta Pi (chpt. sec.). Home: 11444 New Farrington Ct Glen Allen VA 23059-1629 Office: Hanover County Pub Sch 200 Berkley St Ashland VA 23005-1302

CHANDLER, KRIS, computer consultant, educator; b. Cleveland Heights, Ohio, June 26, 1948; d. Gerhard A. and Hanna R. (Rittmeyer) Hoffmann; children: Karen, Heidi. BSBA with honors and spl. distinction, U. So. Colo., 1984, postgrad., 1984-85; MBA, U. Ark., 1987; PhD in C.C. Adminstrn., Colo. State U., 1993. Owner, mgr. V&W Fgn. Car Svc., Canon City, Colo., 1970-80; prin. The Chandlers, Computer Cons., Pueblo, Colo., 1982-88; ptnr. Jak Rabbit Software, 1989—; mem. faculty Pikes Peak C.C., chair computer info. systems dept., U. So. Colo., also mgr. Sch. Bus. microcomputer lab. Bd. dirs. Canon City Community Svc. Ctr., 1978-80, Canon City chpt. ARC, 1978-81. Mem. Assn. for Computing Machinery, Data Processing Mgmt. Assn. (advisor student chpt. Pikes Peak C.C. 1989—), Assn. for Info. Tech. Profls. (v.p. So. Colo. chpt.), U. So. Colo. Honors Soc. (pres.), U. So. Colo. Grad. Assn. (founder), Alpha Chi, Sigma Iota Epsilon. Home and Office: 401 S Neilson Ave Pueblo CO 81001-4238

CHANDLER, LAWRENCE BRADFORD, JR., lawyer; b. New Bedford, Mass., June 20, 1942; s. Lawrence Bradford and Anne (Crane) C.; m. Madeleine Bibeau, Sept. 7, 1963 (div. June 1984); children: Dawn, Colleen, Brad. BS in Bus. Adminstrn., Boston Coll., 1963; LLB, U. Va., 1966, JD, 1970. Bar: Mass. 1966, U.S. Supreme Ct. 1967, Va. 1970, W.Va. 1993; diplomate Nat. Bd. Trial Advocacy; advocate Am. Bd. Trial Advocates. Ptnr. Chandler, Franklin & O'Bryan, Charlottesville, Va., 1971—. Pres. Western Va. Chpt., 1992-93. Capt. U.S. Army, 1967-71. Mem. ABA, ATLA (chair state dels. 1993-94, exec. com. 1993-94, bd. govs. 1995—), Va. Trial Lawyers Assn. (pres. 1985-86), Am. Bd. Trial Advs. (pres. Va. chpt.), Nat. Bd. of Trial Advocacy (bd. examiners), Charlottesville Bar Assn., Assn. U.S. Army (pres. 1971-73), Am. Coll. Legal Medicine, Am. Soc. on Law, Medicine and Ethics, Am. Assn. Profl. Liability Attys. Roman Catholic. Home: 1445 Old Ballard Rd Charlottesville VA 22901-9469 Office: Chandler Franklin & O'Bryan PO Box 6747 Charlottesville VA 22906-6747

CHANDLER, MICHAEL D., city official. Alderman Chgo., 1995—. Office: 4325 W Roosevelt Rd Chicago IL 60624-3838*

CHANDLER, ROBERT CHARLES, healthcare consultant; b. Birmingham, Ala., Apr. 15, 1945; s. Coleman Duke and Myrtle (Cleveland) C.; m. Linda Watson, May 17, 1997; children—Jason Charles, Jonathan Robert. B.S. in Pharmacy, Samford U., 1968; M.S. in Hosp. and Health Adminstrn., U. Ala.-Birmingham, 1972. Registered pharmacist. Pharmacy intern Carraway Methodist Hosp., Birmingham, 1968-69; chief pharmacist Holy Family Hosp., Birmingham, 1969-70; v.p. Ft. Sanders Med. Ctr., Knoxville, Tenn., 1971-78; sr. v.p. Bapt. Med. Ctrs., Birmingham, 1978-79, exec. v.p. Princeton, 1979-85; pres. E. Tenn. Bapt. Hosp., Knoxville, 1985-90, The Bapt. Health System East Tenn., Knoxville, 1986-90, ptnr. Ward Howell Internat., 1991-98, LAI Worldwide, 1998—; bd. dirs. Am. Healthcare Sys. San Diego, 1988-90; chmn. bd. dirs. SunHealth Care Plans Tenn., 1986-88; bd. dirs. Ala. Quality Assurance Found., Birmingham, 1984-85, Ala. Med. Rev., Birmingham, 1980-84; adv. bd. Blue Cross/Blue Shield, Birmingham, 1983-85; liaison com. Jefferson County Med. Soc., Birmingham, 1984-85; various faculty appts. U. Ala., Birmingham, Emory U. Sch. Medicine, Atlanta. Div. chmn. United Way, Birmingham, 1984; bd. dirs. United Way Greater Knoxville, 1987-88, Knoxville Opera Co., 1988; Sunday Sch. tchr. Dawson Bapt. Ch., Birmingham; deacon chmn. 1st Bapt. Ch., Knoxville, 1988-90. Recipient Cert. Appreciation, Tenn. Gov. Ray Blanton, 1978, Disting. Service award Tenn. Com. on Employment of Handicapped, 1978, Award of Excellence Ala. Pub. Relations Council, 1979. Fellow Am. Coll. Hosp. Adminstrs.; mem. Birmingham Regional Hosp. Council (pres. elect 1985), Hosp. Alliance Tenn. (pres. 1987-88), Ala. Hosp. Assn. (trustee 1984-85), Birmingham C. of C. (chmn. health services com. 1980). Republican. Club: The Club (Birmingham). Lodge: Rotary (mem. group study exchange, 1977). Office: LAI Worldwide 191 Peachtree St NE Ste 800 Atlanta GA 30303-1747

CHANDLER, ROBERT LESLIE, public relations executive; b. Phila., Mar. 3, 1948; s. Joel leslie and Evelyn Laney (DeLaney) C.; m. Maureen O'Keefe, Mar. 21, 1970. AS, Atlantic C.C., 1969; BS, Bowling Green State U., 1971; MS, Ohio U., 1972; MBA in Hosp. Adminstrn., Wagner Coll., 1980. Dir. pub. rels. Athens Mental Health Ctr., Ohio, 1972; internal comms. editor, pub. affairs dept. Owens-Corning Fiberglas Corp., Toledo, 1972-74; dir. cmty. rels. Wyandotte Gen. Hosp., Mich., 1974-76; v.p. asst. adminstr. mktg./pub. affairs Meth. Hosp., Bklyn., 1976-82; exec. v.p. Burson-Marsteller Pub. Rels., N.Y.C., 1982-95; pres. Chandler-Chicco Agy., 1995. Mem. budget com. United Way Mich., 1975-76; bd. dirs. N.Y. chpt. Am. Heart Assn. Am. Heart Assn. N.J./N.Y. State scholar, 1969. Mem. Pub. Rels. soc. Am., Am. soc. Health Care Mktg. and Planning, Am. Coll. Healthcare Execs. (assoc. mem.), Sigma Delta Chi, Kappa Tau Alpha. Home: 525 W 22nd St Apt 6D New York NY 10011-1100 Office: Chandler Chicco Agy 450 W 15th St New York NY 10011-7097

CHANDLER, WILLIAM FREDERICK, physician, neurosurgeon; b. Chgo., July 25, 1945; s. George Marshall and Maxine Searle Chandler; m. Susan Elizabeth Chandler, Jan. 3, 1970; children: Scott, Justin. BA, Northwestern U., 1967; MD, U. Mich., 1971. Fellow in neurosurg. rsch. Karolinska Inst., Stockholm, Sweden, 1977; asst. prof. neurosurgery La. State U., New Orleans, 1977-79; prof. neurosurgery U. Mich., Ann Arbor, 1979—. Author: Carotid Artery Injuries, 1982, Ultrasound in Neurosurgery, 1989. 1st lt. USAR, 1972-77. Recipient Nat. Pres.'s award Mich. State Med. Soc., 1982, Disting. Svc. award Neurosurgery Sect. on Tumors, 1997. Mem. Congress Neurol. Surgeons (pres. 1992), Am. Assn. Neurol. Surgeons (bd. dirs. 1998—, Van Wagenen fellowship 1977), Soc. Neurol. Surgeons, Am. Acad. Neurol. Surgery, Mich. Assn. Neurol. Surgeons (pres. 1986-88). Presbyterian. Avocations: tennis, skiing. E-mail: wchndlr@umich.edu. Office: Univ Mich Med Ctr 1500 E Medical Center Dr Ann Arbor MI 48109

CHANDLER, WILLIAM KNOX, physiologist; b. Chgo., Oct. 13, 1933; s. William Knox and Margaret Belle (Colston) C.; m. Caroline Hardee Teague, June 6, 1957; children—William Knox, Janet Colston, Caroline Louise, Margaret Teague. A.B., U. Louisville, 1955, M.D., 1959. Postdoctoral fellow Physiol. Lab., Cambridge, Eng., 1962-65; staff asso. Lab. Biophysics, Nat. Inst. Neurol. Diseases and Blindness, Bethesda, Md., 1965-66; asso. prof. physiology Yale U. Sch. Medicine, 1966-72, prof., 1973—. Editor Physiol. Revs, 1968-74, Jour. Physiology, 1974-81, Jour. Gen. Physiology, 1990—. Served with USPHS, 1959-61, 65-66. Mem. NAS, Biophys. Soc., Physiol. Soc., Soc. Gen. Physiologists. Democrat. Home: 594 County Rd Guilford CT 06437-1035 Office: 333 Cedar St New Haven CT 06510-3206

CHANDLER-WALTON, MARCIA SHAW BARNARD, farmer; b. Arlington, Mass., Aug. 22, 1934; d. John Alden and Grace Winifred (Copeland) Barnard; m. Samuel Butler Chandler, Aug. 31, 1952 (dec. 1986); children: Shawn Chandler Seddinger, Mark Thurmond, Matthew Butler; m. Lewis S. Walton, June, 1998. BA, Francis Marion Coll., Florence, S.C., 1976; MEd, U. S.C., 1985. Resource person United Cerebral Palsy of S.C., Dillon, 1976-79; instr. English Horry-Georgetown Tech. Coll., Conway, S.C., 1980-81; farm owner, mgr. Dillon; drama critic Dillon (S.C.) Herald, 1986—. Author: (with others) Best of Old Farmer's Almanac, First 200 Years, 1991; cover artist So. Bell Telephone Directory, 1988, 90; artist Dillon County Lib., 1998. Bd. dirs., publicist, artist Dillon County Theatre, Inc., 1985—; publicist, bd. dirs., artist MacArthur Ave. Players, Dillon, 1990—; bd. dirs. Friends of Francis Marion U., 1985-95; pres. Dillon Area Arts Coun., 1980-85, Jr. Charity League of Dillon, 1960-75; nat. poetry judge DAR, 1982; Dunbar libr. com., Dillon County, 1999. Recipient Honorable Commendation for civic involvement S.C. Ho. Reps., Mar. 22, 1990. Mem. Cousteau Soc., Ctr. Environ. Edn., Internat. Fund Animal Welfare, World Wildlife Fund, Nature Conservancy, Sea Shepherd Conservation Soc., Humane Soc. U.S. Avocations: swimming, animal welfare activities, local theater, travel. Home: 309 E Reaves Ave Dillon SC 29536-1919

CHANDOR, STEBBINS BRYANT, pathologist; b. Boston, Dec. 18, 1933; s. Kendall Stebbins Bryant and Dorothy (Burrage) C.; m. Mary Carolyn White, May 30, 1959; children: Stebbins Bryant Jr., Charlotte White. B.A., Princeton U., 1955; M.D., Cornell U., 1960. Diplomate Am. Bd. Pathology. Intern Bellevue Hosp., N.Y.C., 1960-61, resident, 1965-66; resident Stanford U. Med. Ctr., Palo Alto, Calif., 1962-65; instr. Cornell U., Ithaca, N.Y., 1966; asst. prof. U. So. Calif. Med. Ctr., Los Angeles, 1969-73, assoc. prof., 1974-76; assoc. prof. SUNY, Stony Brook, 1976-80; prof., chmn. dept. pathology Marshall U. Sch. Medicine, Huntington, W.Va., 1981-91; assoc. dean for clin. affairs Marshall U. Sch. Medicine, 1990-91; prof., vice chmn. Sch. Medicine U. So. Calif., L.A., 1991—; pathologist Tripler Army Med Ctr, Honolulu, 1966-69; dir. immunopathology U. So. Calif., Los Angeles County Med. Ctr., 1969-76; dir. clin. lab. Univ. Hosp., Stony Brook, N.Y., 1978-80; dir. JMMS Labs., Huntington, W.Va., 1981-91; dir.labs. U. So. Calif. U. Hosp., L.A., 1991—. Contbr. articles to profl. jours. Pres. San Marino Tennis Found., 1975. Served to maj. USAR, 1966-69. Decorated Army Commendation medal; recipient Physicians Recognition award AMA, 1983, 86, 89, 93. Fellow Am. Assn. Med. Coll. (exec. coun. 1998—), Am. Soc. Clin. Pathologists (deputy commn. 1993-98, continuing edn., bd. dirs. 1990-96, chair by-law com., 1993-96, chmn. pathology group, 1993-98, v.p. 1997-98, pres.-elect 1998-99), Coll. Am. Pathologists (state commr. I&A program 1987-91, dist. commr. 1991—); mem. Calif. Soc. Pathologists (sec.-treas. 1974-75, pres. elect. 1975-76), Assn. Am. Pathologists, W.Va. Assn. Pathologists (pres. 1985-86), Assoc. Pathol. Chmn. Acad. Clin. Lab. Physicians and Scientists (rep. CAS 1991—, adminstrv. bd. 1997—), exec. coun. Am. Assn. Med. Colls. 1998—, L.A. Acad. Medicine, Princeton Club, Valley Club (v.p. 1975, bd. dirs. 1993), City Club (v.p. 1988-89, pres. 1989-90), San Gabriel Country Club, Valley Hunt Club. Republican. Episcopalian. Home: 855 S Oak Knoll Ave Pasadena CA 91106-4419 Office: U So Calif Sch Medicine 2011 Zonal Ave Los Angeles CA 90033-1034 *Have fun and make life enjoyable for those around you.*

CHANDRA, ABHIJIT, engineering educator; b. Calcutta, India, Jan. 4, 1957; came to U.S., 1980; s. Ramesh Kumar and Sandhya (Dey) C.; m. Dolly Day, June 4, 1984; children: Koushik, Shoma. B of Tech. with honors, Indian Inst. Tech., Kharagpur, India, 1978; MS, U. N.B., Fredericton, Can., 1980; PhD, Cornell U., 1983. Sr. rsch. engr. GM Rsch. Labs., Warren, Mich., 1983-85; asst. prof. U. Ariz., Tucson, 1985-89, assoc. prof. engring., 1989-95; prof. Mich. Tech. U., Houghton, 1995—; cons. Goodyear Tire and Rubber Co., Akron, Ohio, 1988-89, Advanced Ceramic Rsch., Tucson, 1990-95, ALCOA, Pitts., 1990-95. Author: Boundary Element Methods in Manufacturing, 1997; guest editor Internat. Jour. Solid Structures, 1994; contbr. over 70 articles to profl. jours. Alexander von Humboldt fellow, 1991; recipient Presdl. Young Investigator award NSF, 1987, Arc Welding Achievement award J. F. Lincoln Arc Welding Found., 1989. Fellow ASME (sec. So. Ariz. sect. 1988-89); mem. SME, Sigma Xi. Avocations: swimming, skiing, tennis, gardening, fiction writing.

CHANDRA, PRAMOD, art history educator; b. Varanasi, India, Nov. 2, 1930; came to U.S., 1964; s. Moti and Shanti (Devi) C.; m. Mary Carmen Lynn, 1981; children: Abhijit, Sasanka. B.S., Georgetown U., 1951; Ph.D., U. Bombay, 1964. Asst. curator Prince of Wales Mus. of Western India, Bombay, 1954-60; curator art and archaeol. sects. Prince of Wales Mus. of Western India, 1960-64; assoc. prof. U. Chgo., 1964-71, prof., 1971-80; George P. Bickford prof. Indian and South Asian art Harvard U., Cambridge, Mass., 1980—; founder, dir. Ctr. for Art and Archaeology, Am. Inst. Indian Studies, 1965-71; founder, pres. Am. Com. South Asian Art, 1963-71; hon. advisor on archaeology and mus. Govt. of Madhya Pradesh, India; guest curator Sculpture of India exhbn. Nat. Gallery Art, Washington, 1985. Author: Bundi Painting, 1959, Stone Sculpture in the Allahabad Museum, 1971, Studies in Indian Temple Architecture, 1974, The Cleveland Tuti-nama and the Origins of Mughal Painting, 1976, On the Study of Indian Art, 1983, Sculpture of India 3000 BC-1300 AD, 1985. Recipient Bharat Kala Bhavan award Banaras Hindu U., India; grantee NEH, 1976-80.

CHANDRA, ROB S., venture capitalist; b. Boulder, Colo., Apr. 15, 1966; s. S. and M. Chandra; m. Shikha Chandra, May 28, 1995. BA in Econs. cum laude, U. Calif., Berkeley, 1988; MBA, Harvard U., 1993. Analyst strategic planning dept. Lucky Stores, Oakland, Calif., 1985-86; gen. mgr. Calif. Bus. Weekly, Berkeley, 1986-87; sales asst. IBM, Oakland, 1987-88; assoc. Andersen Cons., Strategic Svcs., San Francisco, N.Y.C., London, 1988-91; mgr. McKinsey & Co., San Francisco, L.A., 1993-95; gen. ptnr. Commonwealth Capital Ventures, Wellesley, Mass., 1996—. Contbr. articles to profl. publs. Alumni class sec. class of 1993, Harvard Bus. Sch., Boston, 1993—. Mem. Nat. Venture Capital Assn., New Eng. Venture Capital Assn., MIT Enterprise Assn., Bus. Assocs. Club (Boston). Avocations: golf, tennis, basketball. Office: Commonwealth Capital Ventures 20 William St Ste 225 Wellesley MA 02481-4102

CHANDRAMOULI, RAMAMURTI, electrical engineer; b. Sholinghur, Madras, India, Oct. 2, 1947; s. Ramamurti and Rajalakshmi (Ramamurti) Krishnamurti; m. Ranjani, Dec. 4, 1980; children: Suhasini, Akila. BSc, Mysore U., 1965, BE, 1970, MEE, Pratt Inst., 1972; PhD, Oreg. State U., 1978. Instr., Oreg. State U., Corvallis, 1978; sr. engr. R & D group, tech. staff spacecraft datasystems sect. Jet Propulsion Lab., Pasadena, Calif., 1978-81; staff engr., design automation group Am. Microsystems Inc., Santa Clara, Calif., 1982-83; staff software engr. corp. computer-aided design Intel, Santa Clara, 1983-86; project leader computer-aided design Sun Microsystems, Mountain View, Calif., 1986-93; tech. mktg. engr. Mentor Graphics, San Jose, Calif., 1993-95; dir. Bist Products Logicvision, San Jose, 1995-98; product line mgr. test products Synopsys, Mountain View, Calif., 1998—; adj. lectr. Calif. State U., Fullerton, 1987—. Sec., South India Cultural Assn., L.A., 1980-81; bd. dirs. Am. Assn. East Indians. Mem. IEEE, IEEE Computer Soc., Sigma Xi, Eta Kappa Nu. Home: 678 Tiffany Ct Sunnyvale CA 94087-2439 Office: LV Software Inc 1735 N 1st St San Jose CA 95112-4529

CHANDRASEKARAN, BALAKRISHNAN, computer and information science educator; b. Lalgudi, Tamil Nadu, India, June 20, 1942; came to U.S., 1963; s. Srinivasan and Nagamani Balakrishnan; m. Sandra Mamrak, Oct. 21, 1978; 1 child, Mallika. B in Engring., Madras U., Karaikudi, India, 1963; PhD, U. Pa., 1967. Devel. engr. Smith Kline Instruments, Phila., 1964-65; rsch. specialist Philco-Ford Corp., Blue Bell, Pa., 1967-69; asst. prof. computer and info. sci. Ohio State U., Columbus, 1969-71, assoc. prof., 1971-77, prof., 1977-95; sr. rsch. scientist, 1995—; dir. Lab. for Artificial Intelligence Rsch., Columbus, 1983—; co-chmn. Symposium on Potentials and Limitations of Mech. Intelligence, Anaheim, Calif., 1971; chmn. Norbert Wiener Symposium, Boston, 1974; sci. dir. Summer Sch. on Computer Program Testing, SOGESTA, Urbino, Italy, 1981; vis. scientist Lawrence Livermore Nat. Lab., Livermore, Calif., summer 1981, cons. fall 1981; vis. scientist MIT Computer Sci. Lab., 1983; dir. NIH Artificial Intelligence in Medicine Workshop, 1984; organizer panel discussion on artificial intelligence and engring. ASME, 1985; vis. scholar Stanford U., 1990-91; keynote spkr. World Congress on Expert Sys., Mexico City, 1998. Editor: Diagrammatic Reasoning, 1995; co-editor Computer Program Testing, 1981; editor ACM Sigart Spl. Issue on Structure, Function, and Behavior, 1985; assoc. editor Artificial Intelligence in Engring., 1986—; mem. bd. editors Internat. Jour. Pattern Recognition & Artificial Intelligence, Med. Expert Systems, Artificial Intelligence in Engring.; assoc. editor Internat. Jour. Human-Computer Interactions, 1996—. Recipient Outstanding Paper award Pattern Recognition Soc., 1976; Moore fellow U. Pa., 1964-67. Fellow IEEE (editor-in-chief Expert Jour. 1990-94), Am. Assn. for Artificial Intelligence (chmn. workshops on diagrammatic reasoning 1992), Assn. for Computing Machinery; mem. Sys. Man and Cybernetics Soc. IEEE (v.p. 1974-75, pattern recognition com. 1969-72, assoc. editor Trans. 1973—, guest editor spl. issue on distributed program solving 1981). Democrat. Avocation: travel. Home: 2053 Iuka Ave Columbus OH 43201-1415 Office: Ohio State U Dept Computer and Info Sci 2015 Neil Ave Columbus OH 43210-1210

CHANDRASEKHAR, B(ELLUR) S(IVARAMIAH), physics educator; b. Bangalore, India, May 24, 1928; came to U.S., 1952; B.Sc. with honours, U. Mysore, (India), 1947; M.Sc., U. Delhi, 1949; D. Phil., Oxford U., (Eng.), 1952. Research assoc. physics U. Ill., Urbana, 1952-54, vis. prof., 1977-78; vis. scientist Oxford U., (Eng.), 1954-55; research physicist Westinghouse Research Labs., Pitts., 1955-59, fellow physicist, 1959-61, mgr. cryophysics sect., 1961-63, cons., 1963-64; prof. Western Res. U., Cleve., 1963-67; Perkins prof. physics Case Western Res. U., Cleve., 1967-88, prof. emeritus, 1988—, dir. labs., dept. physics, 1964-65, chmn. dept. physics, 1965-67, co-dir. Condensed State Ctr., 1965-67, co-chmn. dept. physics, 1967, dir. labs., 1967-69, dean sci., 1969-70, chmn. dept. biology, 1969-70, chmn. Univ. faculty senate, 1970-71, dean Western Res. Coll., 1972-76; guest prof. Meissner Inst., Garching, Germany, 1988-98; mem. NSF vis. com. (Nat. Magnet Lab), 1973-76; vis. prof. U. Ill., Urbana, 1978, Tata Inst. Fundamental Research, Bombay, 1980, Eidgenoessische Technische Hochschule, Zurich, 1980-81; cons. in physics. Author: Why Things Are the Way They Are, 1998. Rhodes scholar Oxford U., (Eng.), 1949-52; sr. vis. research fellow Imperial Coll. Sci. and Tech., London, 1961; DAAD fellow Meissner Inst., 1986; Fulbright research prof. Imperial Coll., London, U. Cambridge, 1978; Fulbright research prof. Meissner Inst., Garching. Fed. Republic Germany, 1984-85. Fellow Am. Phys. Soc. (mem. numerous coms., chmn. condensed matter physics div. 1975, councillor-at-large 1984-87, exec. com. 1987); mem. Cleve. Physics Soc. (pres. 1965-66), sigma Xi (chpt. v.p. 1965-66), Sigma Xi (chpt. pres. 1966-67). Address: Hollerweg 13, 82194 Groebenzell Germany

CHANDY, K. MANI, computer science educator. B Tech. in Elec. Engring., Indian Inst. Technology, Madras, 1965; MSEE, Polytechnic Inst. of Bklyn., 1966; PhD in Elec. Engring., MIT, 1969. Engr. Honeywell Electronic Data processing, Waltham, Mass., 1966-67; staff IBM Cambridge Scientific Ctr., 1969-70; asst. prof. computer scis. U. Tex., Austin, 1970-73, assoc. prof., 1973-78, prof., 1978-89; prof. computer scis. Calif. Inst. Technology, Pasadena, 1989—; Simon Ramo prof., exec. officer dept. computer scis Calif. Inst. Tech.; acting site dir. Ctr. for Rsch. in Parallel Computing, Caltech Site, 1994; acting chmn. dep. computer scis., 1978-79, chmn. 1983-85, Regent's chair, 1988-89; scientific adv. panel Advanced Systems Inst., B.C., Can., 1986-89; mem. NSF panels; lectr. in field. Assoc. editor: Jour. of Capacity Mgmt., 1983-88, Info. Executive, 1983-88, Jour. of Info. Econs., 1983-88. Recipient John Sherman Fairchild scholarship John Sherman Fairchild Found., 1987-88, A.A. Michelson award, Computer Measurement Group, Dallas, 1985. Fellow IEEE (Koji Kobayashi Computers and Comms. award 1995, assoc. editor: IEEE Transactions on Software Engring. 1985-87); mem. Assn. Computing Machinery, Soc. for Computer Simulation;. Office: Calif Inst Technology Computer Sci 256-80 Pasadena CA 91125*

CHANES, JEROME ALAN, non-profit organization administrator, public affairs analyst; b. N.Y.C., Mar. 29, 1943; s. Manuel S. and Berta (Gottlieb) C.; m. Eva Fogelman, June 19, 1988. BA, Yeshiva U., 1964, MSW, 1974; postgrad., Columbia U., 1966-68, Brandeis U., 1974-76. Nat. affairs dir. Nat. Jewish Community Rels. Adv. Coun., N.Y.C., 1983-96; assoc. dir. Nat. Found. Jewish Culture, N.Y.C., 1996—; adj. prof. Jewish communal issues Wurzweiler Sch. Social Work, Yeshiva U., N.Y.C., 1990—; rsch. fellow Ctr. for Jewish Studies, CUNY Grad. Ctr.; founding chmn. Project Ezra. Author: Antisemitism in America Today, 1995, A Profile of the American Jewish Community, 1998; contbr. articles to profl. jours., chpts. to books. Benjamin Hornstein fellow, 1974. Mem. Labor Zionist Alliance (nat. sec. 1988-90), Am. Zionist Movement (treas. 1988-90). Home: 60 Riverside Dr Apt 11G New York NY 10024-6170 Office: Nat Found Jewish Culture 330 7th Ave New York NY 10001-5010

CHANEY, GENE PAUL RUSS, trade association administrator; m. Jutta Suzanne Kobia, Dec. 9, 1995. AA in Acctg., Brookdale Coll., Lincroft, N.J., 1981; BS in Pers. Mgmt., Glassborough (N.J.) State U., 1979. Master plumber, N.J., Tex.; plumbing inspector, N.J. Master plumber Garnet Plumbing, Jackson, N.J., 1981-91; dir. tech. svcs. Nat. Assn. Plumbing, Heating & Cooling Contractors, Falls Church, Va., 1991-95; exec. dir. Internat. Assn. Plumbing & Mech. Ofcls., Walnut, Calif., 1995—; cons. plumbing industry; developer plumbing and mech. codes. Mem. Am. Soc. San. Engrs. Roman Catholic. Avocation: golf. Office: Internat Assn Plumbing & Mech Ofcls 20001 E Walnut Dr S Walnut CA 91789-2825

CHANEY, ROBERT GALEN, religious organization executive; b. LaPorte, Ind., Oct. 27, 1913; s. Clyde Galen and Maree (Francis) C.; m. Earlyne Cantrell, Oct. 4, 1947; 1 child, Sita. Student, Miami U., Ohio, 1931-33; DD, Coll. Universal Truth, 1954. Ordained to non-denominational ministry, 1939. Pastor various parishes, Eaton Rapids and Lansing, Mich., 1938-50; founder, pres. Astara, L.A., 1956-76, Upland, Calif., 1976—. Author: The Inner Way, 1962, Adventures in ESP, 1975, Mysticism: The Journey Within, 1979, The Power of Your Own Medicine, 1995, Visits to the Manger, 1996. Mem. Masons, Kiwanis. Republican. Office: Astara 792 W Arrow Hwy W Upland CA 91786

CHANEY, SARA JO, college official, clergywoman; b. July 10, 1954. BA, Ctrl. Meth. Coll., Fayette, Mo., 1976; MDiv, Garrett-Evang. Theol. Sem., Evanston, Ill., 1978; MA in English, U. Mo., 1989. Ordained to ministry United Meth. Ch., 1978. Clergywoman Wis. Conf., United Meth. Ch., 1978-87; exec. dir. Passages, Program for Survivors Domestic Violence and SexualAssault, Inc., 1990-97; dir. ch. rels. Ctrl. Meth. Coll., 1997—. E-mail: schaney@cmc.edu. Home: 2508 Park de Ville Pl Columbia MO 65203 Office: Ctrl Meth Coll 411 Central Methodist Sq Fayette MO 65248-1129

CHANEY, SHARON HENDERSON, secondary education educator, consultant; b. Fayetteville, Tenn., July 16, 1948; d. Eugene Wilson and Avis Marie (Tomerlin) Henderson; m. Carl William Chaney, Dec. 26, 1970; children: Daniel Eugene, Carl David. BA, Belmont U., Nashville, 1970; MA in Edn., Austin Peay State U., Clarksville, Tenn., 1975; EdD, Vanderbilt U., 1991. Cert. tchr. English and Latin, secondary prin., Tenn. Tchr. English and French, Springfield (Tenn.) H.S., 1971-76; tchr. English, Latin and French, Goodlettsville (Tenn.) H.S., 1983-86; tchr. advanced placement English and writing Hunters Lane Comprehensive H.S., Nashville, 1986—; adj. faculty Peabody/Vanderbilt U., Nashville, 1990-95, Belmont U., 1987-96; mem. writing assessment scoring com. State of Tenn., Nashville, 1994—; mem. adv. coun. on tchr. edn./cert. State Bd. Edn., Nashville, 1995—; cons., reader, presenter Coll. Bd. So. Regional Office, Atlanta, 1995—; facilitator trainee Nat. Bd. for Profl. Tchg. Standards, 1997; manuscript reviewer English Jour., 1993—. Contbr. articles to profl. jours. Pianist, Inglewood Bapt. Ch., Nashville, 1990-95; mem. choir First Bapt. Ch., Downtown, Nashville, 1995-98. Named Tchr. of Yr., Springfield H.S., 1976, Goodlettsville H.S., 1986, Hunters Lane H.S., 1990-91, Metro Secondary Tchr. of Yr., Met. Pub. Schs., Nashville, 1991, Career Ladder III, State of Tenn., 1986—. Mem. Nat. Coun. Tchrs. English (local arrangements conv. chmn. 1997-98), Tenn. Coun. Tchrs. English (bd. dirs., pres. 1997-98, Award for Excellence in Tchg. English 1994), Nashville Coun. Tchrs. English (pres., newsletter editor), Delta Kappa Gamma (chpt. pres., Golden Gift Leadership Mgmt. Sem. 1997), Alpha Delta Kappa (chpt. pres., state membership com.). Avocations: swimming, piano, travel, reading, writing. Home: 4315 Grandville Blvd Nashville TN 37207-1021

CHANEY, VERNE EDWARD, JR., surgeon, foundation executive, educator; b. Kansas City, Mo., July 16, 1923; s. Verne Edward and Adelaide (Hafner) C.; divorced; children: Christopher Edward, Steven Wood. B.S., Va. Mil. Inst., 1951; M.D., Johns Hopkins U., 1948, M.P.H., 1972. Diplomate: Am. Bd. Surgery, Am. Bd. Thoracic and Cardiac Surgery. Intern surgery Johns Hopkins U. Hosp., 1948-49, asst. resident, 1949-50, instr. anatomy, 1950-53; surg. resident N.C. Meml. Hosp., Chapel Hill, 1953-56; chief of surgery Albert Schweitzer Hosp., Deschappelles, Haiti, 1956-58; practice medicine specializing in thoracic surgery Monterey, Calif., 1958-61; pres. and founder Thomas A. Dooley Found.-INTERMED, Inc., N.Y.C., 1961—; clin. prof. surgery U. Miami, 1976—, clin. prof. epidemiology and pub. health, 1977—; founder, pres. INTERMED, Geneva, 1976—. Patentee in field. Served from pvt. to capt. M.C. U.S. Army, 1944, 51-53. Decorated Silver Star medal; decorated Bronze Star medal with V, Purple Heart U.S., Croix de Guerre France, Order of Million Elephants Laos; recipient Disting. Svc. award Sch. Medicine U. North Carolina, 1991. Fellow ACS, Am. Coll. Chest Physicians; mem. N.Y. State Med. Soc., N.Y. Acad. Medicine, Am. Pub. Health Assn., Internat. Health Soc. (pres. 1987-88), Nathan A. Womack Surg. Soc., Internat. Soc. Surgeons, Nat. Soc. Fund Raising Execs., Explorers Club. Republican. Episcopalian. Clubs: N.Y. Athletic, Sky, West Side Tennis. Home: 530 E 72nd St Apt 16E New York NY 10021-4863 Office: Dooley Found Intermed 420 Lexington Ave Rm 2428 New York NY 10170-2599

CHANEY, WILLIAM ALBERT, historian, educator; b. Arcadia, Calif., Dec. 23, 1922; s. Horace Pierce and Esther (Bowen) C. AB, U. Calif., Berkeley, 1943, PhD, 1961. Mem. faculty Lawrence U., Appleton, Wis., 1952—, George McKendree Steele prof. Western culture, 1966—, chmn. dept. history, 1968-71, 95-96; vis. prof. Mich. State U., summer 1958. Author: The Cult of Kingship in Anglo-Saxon England: The Transition from Paganism to Christianity, 1970; Contbr. profl. jours., encys. Jr. fellow Harvard Soc. Fellows, 1949-52; grantee Am. Council Learned Socs., 1966-67. Fellow Royal Soc. Arts; mem. MLA, AAUP, Am. Hist. Assn., Mediaeval Acad. Am., Am. Soc. Ch. History, Conf. Brit. Studies, Archeol. Inst. Am. Episcopalian. Home: 215 E Kimball St Appleton WI 54911-5720

CHANG, CHENG-SHIEN, reliability engineering executive, consultant; b. Silver Spring, Md., July 8, 1972; s. Shaw-Tai and Chuu-Joan (Soong) C. BS, U. Md., 1993, MS, 1994; PhD, East China Normal U., Shanghai, 1997. Cert. reliability engr. Am. Soc. Quality Control. Spl. rep. of pres. U. Md., College Park, 1995-96; v.p. Hope Chinese Sch., College Park, 1995-96; pres. Instant Computing Corp., Silver Spring, 1992-96; owner United Cons. Internat., College Park, 1995-96; pres. World Reliability/Quality Orgn.; sr. quality assurance analyst U. Md., College Park, 1993-95, info. tech. devel. specialist, 1995-96; exec. v.p. Taiwan Commn. for Pub. Safety; sr. lectr. China Productivity Ctr.; sr. adviser Jiang Su Info. Networks Ctr., China. Author: (software) Caprina, 1992; editor: China 5000, 1995. Mem. AAAS, N.Y. Acad. Sci., Ill. Acad. Sci., Miss. Acad. Sci., Rochester Acad. Sci., Libr. of Congress (nat. mem.). Achievements include copyrights for international reliability index, 15 software developments. Avocations: singing, acting. Home and Office: 15305 Watergate Rd Silver Spring MD 20905-5779

CHANG, CHING MING (CARL CHANG), business executive, mechanical engineer, educator; b. Nanking, China; came to U.S., 1967; m. Birdie S.C. Chang, Dec. 18, 1964; children: Andrew L.P., Nelson L.A. Dipl. Ing., Technol. U. Aachen, Germany, 1962; PhD, Technol. U. Aachen, 1967; MBA, SUNY, Buffalo, 1985. Registered profl. engr., N.Y., Va. Asst. prof. N.C. State U., Raleigh, 1968-73; sr. engr. to sr. devel. assoc. Praxair, Inc. (formerly Union Carbide Indsl. Gases), Tonawanda, N.Y., 1973-95, bus. devel. mgr., 1995-98; pres. CarlChang LLC Bus. Cons., Amherst, N.Y., 1998—; adj. prof. engring. SUNY, Buffalo, 1979—. Inventor, holder of five U.S. patents; contbr. articles to profl. jours. Named Person of Yr. Tech. Soc. Coun., Buffalo, 1986. Mem. NSPE (pres. Erie-Niagara chpt. 1980-81, Disting. Svc. award 1981, Basinsky award 1984, Engring. Educator of Yr. award 1990, Praxair Special Recognition award for Technol. Leadership, 1992, Basinski-Wohler award 1994), Niagra Internat. Trade Coun. Avocations: tennis, travel, computer games, mahjong. E-mail: cchangllc@aol.com. Office: CarlChang LLC PO Box 2451 Amherst NY 14231-2451

CHANG, CHING-I EUGENE, insurance executive; b. Taichung, Republic of China, June 16, 1938; came to U.S., 1965; s. Chang T. and Tsai (Chen) C.; m. Lucia S. Chen, Sept. 9, 1967; 1 child, Michael K. BBA, Chang Kung U., 1962; MS in Stats., Mich. State U., 1967. Chief actuary Chrysler Ins. Group, Troy, Mich., 1970-80; v.p. ITT Lyndon Ins. Group, St. Louis, 1980; asst. v.p. actuary Citizens Ins. Co. Am., Howell, Mich., 1980-85; pres., COO Lake States Ins. Co., Traverse City, Mich., 1985—; mem. Mich. Bilateral Trade Team to Taiwan, 1993—. Trustee Lake Superior State U., 1996—; mem. adv. bd. Boys and Girls Club of Grand Traverse, Mich., 1991—. Mem. Am. Acad. Actuaries, Soc. Actuaries (assoc.), Mich. Actuarial Soc. (pres. 1981-82), Internat. Actuarial Assn., Econ. Club Traverse City (pres. 1993-94). Avocation: tennis. Home: 6176 Singletree Williamsburg MI 49690-9570 Office: Lake States Ins Co 12935 W Bay Shore Dr PO Box 352 Traverse City MI 49685-0352

CHANG, CHONG EUN, chemical engineer; b. Seoul, Korea, Dec. 4, 1938; came to U.S., 1968; BS in Chem. Engring., Seoul Nat. U., 1964; PhD in Chem. Engring., U. So. Calif., 1973, MS in Mech. Engring., 1977. Asst. chief of lab. Hyundai Co., Seoul, 1964-68; postdoctoral rsch. assoc. U. So. Calif., L.A., 1973-75; sr. process engr. Allis-Chalmers Corp., Stansteel Products, L.A., 1976-78; mgr. process devel. Alpha Therapeutics Corp., L.A., 1979-81, sr. prin. scientist, 1981-92; v.p. RAAS, Inc., Agoura Hills, Calif., 1992-94; exec. advisor Korea Green Cross Corp., Seoul, Korea, 1996—. Contbr. articles to Jour. Crystal Growth, Internat. Jour. Heat and Mass Trans. With Korean Army, 1959-60. Archimedes Cir. scholar. 1971. Mem. AIChE. Achievements include patents for fractionation of blood plasma, albumin purification. Home: 5833 Briartree Dr La Canada Flintridge CA 91011-1826 Office: Korea Green Cross Corp 227 Kugal-ri Agoura Hills CA 91301-2082

CHANG, CHRIS C.N., physician, pediatric surgeon; b. Taiwan, China, June 20, 1943; s. Shu-Ming and Yu-Bow (Chow) C.; m. Rose Lee Chang, Mar. 4, 1972; children: Lynda, Steven. MD, Nat. Taiwan U., 1969. Intern Nat. Taiwan Univ. Hosp., 1968-69, resident in surgery, 1970-72; resident in surgery Albert Einstein Med. Ctr., Phila., 1972-76; resident in pediat. surgery St. Christopher's Hosp. for Children, Phila., 1976-78; dir. pediat. surgery Lehigh Valley Hosp., Allentown, Pa., 1993—. Fellow ACS, Internat. Coll. Surgeons, Am. Acad. Pediats.; mem. Am. Pediat. Surg. Assn. Fax: (610) 402-7901. Office: Lehigh Valley Hosp 401 N 17th St Ste 302 Allentown PA 18104-5051

CHANG, CLARENCE DAYTON, chemist; b. Tianjin, China, Mar. 8, 1933; came to U.S., 1939; s. Hsueh Tseng and Lucy Chang; m. Cheryl Schucker, June 28, 1958 (div. 1987); 1 child, Christopher E.; m. Elizabeth C. O'Donoghue, June 28, 1987; 1 child, Stephen D. AB, Harvard U., 1954. Project chemist Weyerhaeuser Co., Longview, Wash., 1954-55, Sugar Rsch. Found., N.Y.C., 1955-61; supr. M.W. Kellogg Co., Piscataway, N.J., 1961-70; sr. rsch. chemist Mobil R & D Corp., Princeton, N.J., 1970-74, rsch. assoc., 1974-81, rsch. scientist, 1981-84, sr. scientist, 1984—; sr. scientist Mobile Tech. Co., Paulsboro, N.J. Author: Hydrocarbons from Methanol, 1983; editor: Methane Conversion, 1988; also articles; over 190 U.S. patents in field. Mem. Catalysis Soc. (excellence in catalysis award 1984), Am. Chem. Soc. (E.V. Murfree award 1992), Chinese-Am. Chem. Soc. (bd. dirs. 1993), N.Am. Catalysis Soc. (E.J. Houdry award 1999). Office: Mobil Tech Co PO Box 480 Paulsboro NJ 08066

CHANG, DAVID PING-CHUNG, business consultant, architect; b. Shanghai, China, Dec. 10, 1929; came to U.S., 1941, naturalized, 1956; s. Hsin-Hai and Siang-Mei (Han) C.; m. Lorna Mickle, Jan. 22, 1955; children: Pamela R., Christopher R., David R., Jennifer R. Grad., Hotchkiss Sch., 1947; A.B., Princeton U., 1951; M.F.A., Princeton, 1953. Pvt. practice architecture N.Y.C., 1956-59, San Juan, P.R., 1959-68; v.p. ITT-Levitt & Sons, Inc., N.Y.C., 1969-71; pres. ESI Assos., Inc., N.Y.C., 1971; pvt. practice David Chang Assocs., 1972-81, pres., 1986—; v.p. Nike Inc., 1981-86; guest lectr. seminar indsl. housing MIT, 1971; dir. Huntington Comprehensive Service Center; fellow Amos Tuck Sch. Dartmouth Coll. Ctr. for Asia and Emerging Economies, 1997—. Contbg. editor: Jour. Indsl. Designers Soc. Am, 1969-70; Prin. works include: Academia San Jose, P.R., WAPA-TV Studios and Offices, P.R., City of Glen Cove (N.Y.) downtown renewal. Overseer World Affairs Coun. Oreg.; mem. CONSULTEC, Beijing; trustee Hotchkiss Sch., Internat. Trade Inst., Portland State U.; bd. dirs. Pacific Intercultural Inst., Pacific U. Recipient 1st prize U. P.R. indsl. design seminar, 1961, 1st prize for best comml. bldg. Urbe award P.R., 1966, 1st prize best edn1. bldg. Urbe award P.R., 1971; Archi award N.Y., 1972, 79. Mem. Colegio de Ingenieros de P.R., World Trade Ctr. (bd. govs.), Century Assn., Anglers Club (N.Y.C.), Univ. Club (Portland), Broad Brook Fishing, Chowder and Marching Soc. (East Barnard, Vt.). Democrat. Home: RR 2 Box 192 South Royalton VT 05068-9111 also: David Chang & Assocs PO Box 65 South Royalton VT 05068-0065

CHANG, DAVID WOOSUK, medical educator; b. Apr. 26, 1961. BS, U. Wis., 1983, MD, 1987. Asst. prof. M.D. Anderson Cancer Ctr., Houston, 1998—. E-mail: dchang@notes.mdacc.tmc.edu.

CHANG, DEBBIE I-JU, health services director. BS in Chem. Engring., MIT, 1984; MPH, U. Mich., 1987. Presdl. mgmt. intern Health Care Fin. Adminstrn. Office Legislation and Policy, 1987-89; sr. health policy advisor Senator Donald W. Riegle Jr., 1989-94; dir. office legis. and intergovt. affairs Health Care Fin. Adminstrn., Washington, 1994-98, co-chair steering com. Dept. Health and Human Svcs., 1997—, dir. divsn. coverage benefits and payments, 1998; dep. sec. for health care financing Medicaid, Balt., 1998—. Contbr. articles to profl. jours. Office: Medicaid of MD Dept Healthcare Financing 201 W Preston St Baltimore MD 21201*

CHANG, H. K., biomedical engineer, educator; b. Shenyang, Liaoning, China, July 9, 1940; came to U.S., 1963; s. En Shu and Li (Kwan) C.; m. Min-min Chou, Sept. 5, 1965; children: Y. Katharine, W. Michael. BCE, Nat. Taiwan U., Taipei, 1962; MCE, Stanford U., 1964; PhD in Biomed. Engring., Northwestern U., 1969. Asst. prof. SUNY, Buffalo, 1969-75, assoc. prof., 1975-76; assoc. prof. McGill U., Montreal, Que., Can., 1976-80, prof. biomed. engring., physiology and medicine, 1980-84; prof. biomed. engring. and physiology U. So. Calif., L.A., 1984-90, chmn. dept. biomed. engring., 1985-90; founding dean sch. engring., prof. chem. engring. Hong Kong U. Sci. and Tech., 1990-94; dean sch. engring., prof. chem. engring., prof. medicine U. Pitts., 1994-96; pres., Univ. prof. City U. Hong Kong, 1996—; mem. study sect. NIH, Bethesda, Md., 1987-90; hon. prof. Chinese Acad. Med. Scis., Beijing, 1987—, Peking Union Med. Coll., 1987—. Author: Respiratory Physiology: An Analytical Approach, 1989, Fluid and Solute Transport in the Airspaces of the Lungs, 1993; mem. editorial bd. Jour. Applied Physiology, 1979-85; contbr. over 100 articles to profl. jours.; patentee in field. Grantee Nat. Heart Lung Blood Inst., 1974-89. Fellow Hong Kong Instn. Engrs., Hong Kong Acad. Engring. Scis.; mem. ASCE (sr.) AIChE, Am. Inst. Med. and Biol. Engring. (founding fellow), Am. Physiol. Soc., Biomed. Engring. Soc. (sr.; bd. dirs. 1985—, pres. 1989-90), Am. Thoracic Soc. Office: City U Hong Kong, City U Hong Kong, Office of Pres Tat Chee Ave, Kowloon Hong Kong China

CHANG, HELEN CHUNG-HUNG, piano pedagogy specialist; b. Shanghai, July 20, 1937; d. Shou-Tsu Edward and Chen-Tze Kiang Hsiang; m. Nai Lin Chang; children: Tai Deborah, Huan Justina, Lan Samantha, Ling Patricia. *Husband Nai-Lin is a professor emeritus. Daughter Tai Deborah, BA Yale; JD University Pennsylvania; She is an Associate Editor for the University Pennsylvania Law Review; Assistant General Counsel, Time Warner; Treasurer, Board Managers, University Pennsylvania Law Alumni. Daughter Huan Justina, BA Dartmouth; M.D. Dartmouth Medical School. Her specialties include Rheumatology (Northwestern), Epidemiology (Center for Disease Control and Prevention). Robert Wood Johnson Clinical Scholar, University Chicago. Daughter Lan Samantha, BA Yale; MPA Harvard; MFA University Iowa; Stegner Fellow, Stanford; NEA Literature Grant. Daughter Ling Patricia, BA, MSEd Psychological Services, University of Pennsylvania; expected BAPT, MPT 2001 Thomas Jefferson University, First Degree Black Belt Taikwando.* BA cum laude, Mt. Mercy Coll., Cedar Rapids, Iowa, 1960; BMus cum laude, Lawrence U., 1980; postgrad. in pedagogical study, Am. Suzuki Inst., Stevens Point, Wis., 1972, 83, 88-89. Cert. tchr. Music Tchrs. Nat. Assn., Wis. Music Tchr. Assn., Suzuki Assn. of the Ams. Co-chair Fox Valley Keyboard Tchrs., Appleton, Wis., 1981-82, chair, 1982-83, treas., 1996-97; recital chair Suzuki Edn. Assn. of the Fox Valley, Appleton, 1984-96; judge regional competitions Wis. Music Tchrs. Assn., 1988-97, state competition, 1994, 95, others, coach numerous students. Mem. Northeast Wis. Chinese Assn. (Chinese lang. instr. 1972-76), Wis. Music Tchrs. Assn. (award of excellence 1981, 94), Music Tchr. Nat. Assn., Suzuki Assn. of the Ams., Suzuki Assn. of Wis.

CHANG, HENRY CHUNG-LIEN, library administrator; b. Canton, China, Sept. 15, 1941; came to U.S., 1964, naturalized, 1973; s. Ih-ming and Lily (Lin) C.; m. Marjorie Li, Oct. 29, 1966; 1 dau., Michelle. LL.B., Nat. Chengchi U., 1962; M.A., U. Mo., 1966; M.A. in L.S, U. Minn., 1968; Ph.D., 1974. Reader advisor Braille Inst. Am., Los Angeles, 1965-67; reference librarian U. Minn., Mpls., 1968-70, instr., librarian, 1970-72, asst. head govt. document div., 1972-74; library dir., lectr. in social scis. U. of the V.I., St. Croix, 1974-75; dir. div. libraries, museums and archeol. services, 1975-

88; dir. V.I. Library Tng. Inst., 1975-76; coordinator, chmn. V.I. State Hist. Records Adv. Bd., 1976-88; pres., libr. cons., 1988-89; dir. libr. svcs. Braille Inst. Am., L.A., 1990—; chmn. microfilm com. ACURIL, 1977-88; coordinator V.I. Gov.'s Library Adv. Council, 1975-87; mem. V.I. Bicentennial Commn., 1975-77, Ft. Frederik Commn., 1975-76; mem. adv. com. on research tng. Caribbean Research Inst., 1974-75; coordinator Library Conf., 1977-87; project dir. cultural heritage project Nat. Endowment for Humanities, 1979-83. Author: A Bibliography of Presidential Commissions, Committees, Councils, Panels and Task Forces, 1961-72, 1973, Taiwan Democracy, 1964-71: A Selected Annotated Bibliography of Government Documents, 1973, A Selected Annotated Bibliography of Caribbean Bibliographies in English, 1975, A Survey of the Use of Microfilms in the Caribbean, 1978, Long-Range Program for Library Development, 1978, Institute for Training in Library Management and Communications Skill, 1979; contbr. numerous articles and book revs. on libr. sci. to profl. jours. Chmn. bd. Eden Found. for the People with Disabilities, 1995—; chairperson nat. collection devel. com. NLS, Libr. of Congress, 1998. Served to 2d lt. Taiwan Army, 1962-63. Recipient Libr. Adminstrs. Devel. Program fellowship award, 1972, Cert. of Appreciation, Govt. V.I., 1985, L.A. Internat. Lions Club award, 1992, 95, Driver Safety award, 1993; named Mem. Staff of Yr., Coll. V.I., 1974-75; Nat. Commn. on Librs. and Info. Sci. grantee. Mem. ALA (counselor 1980-84), AAUP, Asian Pacific Am. Libr. Assn. (chmn. fin. com. 1993-96), Eden Found. for the People with Disabilities (chmn. bd. dirs. 1995—), Population Assn. Am., Am. Sociol. Assn., Chinese Am. Profl. Soc. Home: 7839 Svl Box Victorville CA 92392-5161 Office: Braille Inst Am 741 N Vermont Ave Los Angeles CA 90029-3594

CHANG, HOWARD FENGHAU, law educator, economist; b. Lafayette, Ind., June 30, 1960; s. Joseph Juifu and Mary Hsueh-mei C. AB in Govt. cum laude, Harvard Coll., 1982; M in Pub. Affairs, Princeton (N.J.) U., 1985; JD magna cum laude, Harvard U., 1987; SM in Econs., MIT, 1988, PhD in Econs., 1992. Bar: N.Y. 1989, D.C. 1989. Law clk. to hon. Ruth Bader Ginsburg U.S. Ct. of Appeals, Washington, 1988-89; asst. prof. law U. So. Calif. Law Sch., L.A., 1992-94, assoc. prof. law, 1994-97, prof. law, 1997-99; vis. assoc. prof. law Georgetown U. Law Ctr., Washington, 1996-97; vis. prof. law Stanford Law Sch., 1998; vis. prof. law U. Pa. Law Sch., Phila., 1999—. Supervising editor Harvard Law Rev., Cambridge, 1986-87. John M. Olin fellowship Dept. Econs. MIT, 1987, 90, 91; nat. merit scholar IBM, 1978. Mem. Am. Econ. Assn., Am. Law and Econs. Assn. Office: U Pa Law Sch Law Sch 3400 Chestnut St Philadelphia PA 19104-6204

CHANG, JACK CHE-MAN, imaging materials and media administrator; b. Shanghai, China, Nov. 19, 1941; came to U.S., 1958; s. Tse-Liang and Ho-Chen (Tyen) C.; m. Elizabeth P. Ng; children: Clara, Anthony. BA, Asbury Coll., 1961; MS, U. Ill., 1963, PhD, 1966. Rsch. chemist Eastman Kodak, Rochester, N.Y., 1967-73, lab. head, 1973-78, asst. dir. analytical scis. div., 1978-81, asst. dir. electrophotography divsn., 1981-84, mgr. advanced tech. devel. copy products, 1984-85, dir. chemistry Kodak rsch. labs. div., 1985-86, dir. corp. rsch. labs. divns., 1986-93; dir. photosci. rsch. divsn. Eastman Kodak, Rochester, 1993-96, v.p., dir. R&D, imaging materials and media, 1996—. Patentee in field. Mem. Am. Chem. Soc., Electrochem. Soc., Chinese Am. Chem. Soc. (bd. dirs. 1989-92). Home: 1198 Fox Holw Webster NY 14580-9150 Office: Eastman Kodak Co Imaging Materials and Media Rochester NY 14650-2210

CHANG, JAE CHAN, hematologist, oncologist, educator; b. Aug. 29, 1941; came to U.S., 1965; s. Tae Whan and Kap Hee (Lee) C.; m. Sue Young Chung, Dec. 4, 1965; children: Sung-Jin, Sung-Ju, Sung-Hoon. MD, Seoul (Korea) Nat. U., 1965. Diplomate Am. Bd. Internal Medicine, Hematology, Med. Oncology, Am. Bd. Pathology. Intern Ellis Hosp., Schenectady, N.Y., 1965-66; resident Harrisburg (Pa.) Hosp., 1966-69, fellow in nuclear medicine, 1969-70; fellow in hematology and ocology, instr. U. Rochester, N.Y., 1970-72; chief hematology sect. VA Hosp., Dayton, Ohio, 1972-75; from hematopathologist to co-dir. hematology Good Samaritan Hosp., Dayton, Ohio, 1975-88, co-dir. hematology, 1988—; asst. clin. prof. Ohio State U., Columbus, 1972-75; assoc. clin. prof. Wright State U., Dayton, 1975-80, clin. prof., 1980-99, prof., 1999—; co-dir. hematology and med. oncology fellowship program Wright State U., Dayton, 1993-98; cons. in field; adv. com. Greater Dayton Area chpt. Leukemia Soc. Am., 1977; trustee Montgomery County Soc. Cancer Control, Dayton, 1976-85, Dayton Area Cancer Assn., 1985-88, Cmty. Blood Ctr., 1982-86, Hipple Cancer Ctr., 1999—. Contbr. articles to profl. med. jours., essays to newspaper columns, and mags. Recipient Med. Econ. Essay Competition award 1990; fellow Nat. Cancer Inst., 1970-72. Fellow ACP, Am. Soc. Clin. Pathologists; mem. AAAS, Am. Soc. Hematology, Am. Fedn. Clin. Rsch., Am. Soc. Clin. Oncologists, Am. Assn. Cancer Rsch., Dayton Oncology Club, Dayton Soc. Internal Medicine (pres. 1989), Montgomery County Med. Soc. (dir. 1990-93). Home: 1905 Kresswood Cir Kettering OH 45429-1152 Office: Good Samaritan Hosp 2222 Philadelphia Dr Dayton OH 45406-1813 also: 2661 Salem Ave Ste 232 Dayton OH 45406-2933

CHANG, JANICE MAY, lawyer, administrator, notary public; b. Loma Linda, Calif., May 24, 1970; d. Belden Shiu-Wah (dec.) and Sylvia (Tan) C. BA, Calif. State U., San Bernardino, 1990, cert. paralegal studies, 1990, cert. creative writing, 1991; JD, LaSalle U., 1993; D in Naturopathy, Clayton Sch. Natural Healing, 1993; MS in Psychology, Calif. Coast U., 1997; PhD in Bus. Adminstrn., Columbia State U., 1997; postgrad., Calif. Coast U., 1999. Notary pub., Calif. Victim/witness contact clk.-paralegal Dist. Atty.'s Office Victim/Witness Assistance Program, San Bernardino, Calif., 1990; gen. counsel JMC Enterprises, Inc., Loma Linda, Calif., 1993-98; law prof. LaSalle U., Mandeville, La., 1994-97; corp. counsel, CFO JDS Assocs., Inc., Loma Linda, 1998-99, DJS, L.P., Loma Linda, 1998-99; with trust mgmt.-legal dept./trust svcs. Southeastern Calif. Assn. Seventh-Day Adventists, Riverside, 1998—; spkr. Internat. U. Graduation Ceremony/Conv., Las Vegas, 1998; sponsor La Sierra U. Student Employment Recognition Banquet, Riverside, Calif., 1999, La Sierra U. Path of the Just Tree Project, 1998, vol. La Sierra U., Riverside, Ca. Health Fair Expo, 1988, 89, Am. Red Cross First Aid & CPR classes, 1994—. Contbr. poetry to anthologies, including Am. Poetry Anthology, 1987-90, The Pacific Rev., 1991, The Piquant, 1991, River of Dreams, 1994, Reflections of Light, 1994, Musings, 1994 (Honorable Mention award 1994), Best Poems of 1995 (Celebrating Excellence award 1995, Inspirations award 1995), Am. Poetry Annual, 1996, Best New Poems of 1996, Interludes, 1996, Meditations, 1996, Perspectives, 1996 (Honorable Mention award 1996), Keepsakes, 1997 (Honorable Mention award 1997), Best Poems of 1997, Poetic Voices of America, 1997, The Isle of View, 1997, The Other Side of Midnight, 1997, Treasures, 1998, Best Poems of 1998, Writingscapes: Insights & Approaches to Creative Writing, 1998. Vol. ARC first aid and CPR La Sierra U., 1998, 99; donor Loma Linda Indonesian SDA Ch. Belden S. Chang Meml. Fund-Bldg. Annex, Loma Linda, Calif., 1998, 99. Recipient Poet of Merit award Am. Poetry Assn., San Francisco, 1989, Golden Poet award World of Poetry, Washington, 1989, Publisher's Choice award Watermark Press, 1990, Editor's Choice award The Nat. Libr. of Poetry, 1990-97, Pres.'s award for lit. excellence Iliad Press, 1995-97. Mem. APA, Nat. Notary Assn. Republican. Seventh-Day Adventist. Avocations: poetry writing, music, drama, lit., numismatics. Home: 11466 Richmont Rd Loma Linda CA 92354-3523 Office: Southeastern Calif Assn 7th-Day Adventists PO Box 8050 11330 Pierce St Riverside CA 92515-8050

CHANG, JEANNETTE, publishing executive. BS, CCNY. Advt. sales rep. Cosmopolitan mag. Hearst Mags., N.Y.C., 1973-77, fashion advt. mgr., 1977-79; dir. fashion mktg. Bazaar mag. Hearst Mags., N.Y.C., 1979-84; assoc. pub. Harper's Bazaar mag. Hearst Mags., N.Y.C., 1984-94, v.p., 1992-94, v.p., pub., 1994—; spkr. in field. Active City Meals on Wheels, Meml. Sloan Kettering Found., Susan G. Komen Breast Cancer Found. Named to YWCA Acad. of Women Achievers, 1992. Mem. Fashion Group Internat. (bd. dirs., chair cosmetic exec. women's com.). Office: Harper's Bazaar 1700 Broadway Fl 36 New York NY 10019-5905*

CHANG, JEFFREY CHAI, dentist, educator, researcher; b. Canton, China, Dec. 19, 1946; came to U.S., 1967; s. Po Wing and Wai Ming (Chan) C.; m. Frances Fuhnan Liang; children: Sheila Sai, Kenneth Kiu. BA with honors, Northeastern U., 1971; DDS, Georgetown U., 1976; MS in Dentistry, U. Tex. Dental Br., Houston, 1996. Commd. 2d lt. U.S. Army, 1976, advanced through grades to maj.; gen. dental officer Dental Corps U.S. Army, Ft. Bliss, Tex., 1976-79; officer-in-charge Dental Clinic U.S. Army, Pusan, Korea, 1979-80; asst. chief clinician dental activity U.S. Army, Ft. Momouth, N.J., 1980-83; chief dental emergency svc. dental activity U.S. Army, Ft. Hood, Tex., 1984-85; resigned U.S. Army, 1985; clin. asst. prof. Dental Sch. U. Calif., San Francisco, 1985-88; clin. asst. prof. NYU Coll. Dentistry, N.Y.C., 1988-90; asst. prof. U. Tex. Dental Br., 1990-92, assoc. prof., 1992—; cons. VA Med. Ctr., San Francisco, 1987-88, St. Barnabas Hosp., Bronx, N.Y., 1988-90, VA Med. Ctr., Houston, 1993—, ADA Coun. on Sci. Affairs, 1996—; scientist U. Tex. Houston Biomaterials Rsch. Ctr., 1996—. Contbr. articles, abstracts to profl. jours. Col. USAR, 1998—. Master Acad. Gen. Dentistry; fellow Am. Coll. Dentists, Delta Sigma Delta; mem. ADA, Am. Coll. Prosthodontists, Am. Assn. Dental Rsch., Internat. Assn. Dental Rsch., Chinese Am. Drs. Assn. (bd. dirs. 1994—), Am. Legion, Omicron Kappa Upsilon. Avocations: soccer, stamps, contemporary music, photography, hi-fi systems. Home: 4123 Custer Creek Dr Missouri City TX 77459-1545

CHANG, JENGHWA, biomedical and electrical engineer, medical physicist; b. Taipei, June 18, 1962; came to U.S., 1989; s. Tsen-Ming Chang and Yu-Jeng Huang; m. Shiaoching Gong. BS in Control Engring., Nat. Chiao-Tung U., Hsinchu, Taiwan, 1984, MS in Comm. Engring., 1986; MS in Elec. Engring., Poly. U. N.Y., 1991, PhD in Elec. Engring., 1995. Cert. med. dosimetrist, med. physicist. Rsch. and tchg. asst. Nat. Chiao-Tung U., Hsinchu, Taiwan, 1984-86; rsch. asst. Academia Sinica, Taipei, 1988-89, N.Y. Hosp.-Cornell Med. Ctr., N.Y.C., 1991-93; rsch. asst. prof. SUNY Health Sci. Ctr., Bklyn., 1993-98; clin. med. physicist Rahway (N.J.) Hosp., 1994-97, Peninsula Hosp. Ctr., Far Rockaway, N.Y., 1996-97; asst. attending physicist and asst. lab. mem. Meml. Sloan-Kettering Cancer Ctr., N.Y.C., 1997—. Contbr. chpt. to book, over 20 articles to profl. jours. Scholar for Spl. Tech. Chinese Min. Edn. Affairs, 1985, 86; named Excellent Officer award Chinese Marine Corps, 1988. Mem. IEEE, Am. Assn. Physicists in Medicine, AAAS, Radiol. and Med. Physics Soc. N.Y., Am. Soc. for Therapeutic Radiology Oncology. Achievements include pioneering in reconstructing tomographic images of biological tissues from scattered light source and verificatiion of intensity modulated beam for radiation treatment of cancers using electronic portal imaging devices. Avocations: music, philosophy, art, exercise. Office: Meml Sloan-Kettering Cancer Ctr Dept Med Physics 1275 York Ave New York NY 10021-6007

CHANG, JONATHAN LEE, orthopedist, educator; b. Lebanon, Pa., Feb. 22, 1959; s. Timothy Scott and Annabelle (Yee) C. Ed., U. Mich., 1980; MD, Duke U., 1984. Intern in surgery U. Va., Charlottesville, 1984-85, resident in surgery, 1985-86, resident in orthopedics, 1986-90; fellow in sports medicine Ky. Sports Medicine, Lexington, 1991; pvt. practice Orthop. Surgery and Sports Med. Group, Monterey Park, Calif., 1991—; clin. asst. prof. U. So. Calif., L.A., 1992—; bd. dirs. Anderson Unicom Group, Inc., Pasadena, 1996—; team physician El Monte (Calif.) H.S., 1991—; physician U.S. Olympic Com., 1999. Editl. bd. Jour. Musculoskeletal Medicine, 1993—; manuscript reviewer Medicine and Sci. in Sports and Exercise, 1996—; contbr. articles to profl. jours. Mem. Am. Orthopedic Soc. for Sports Medicine, James Smithson Soc., Calif. Med. Assn., Am. Acad. Orthop. Surgeons, Am. Coll. Sports Medicine, Los Angeles County Med. Assn., Nat. Athletic Trainers Assn., McCue Soc. Avocations: distance running, weight lifting, skiing, scuba diving, numismatics. Office: Orthopedic Surgery and Sports Medical Group 500 N Garfield Ave Ste 204 Monterey Park CA 91754-1242

CHANG, LEE-LEE, lawyer; b. Taipei, Taiwan, May 26, 1954; came to U.S., 1986; parents: T.S. and B.H. (Ong) C. LLB, Nat. Chung Hsing U., Taipei, 1976; JD, CUNY, 1990. Bar: N.Y. 1990. Chinese law specialist Stephen S. Lee & Assocs., Taipei, 1981-86; tchg. asst. CUNY Law Sch., Flushing, 1989-90; assoc. Wise, Lerman & Katz, P.C., N.Y.C., 1990-93; pvt. practice Flushing, 1994—; cons. Dorcas & Kalam Co., Hicksville, N.Y., 1994—; adv. bd. mem. Chgo. Title Ins. Co., Garden City, N.Y., 1996—. Co-author: A Practical Usage Guide to Commercial Papers in R.O.C., 1983, Chinese Businessman's Guide to American Law-Business Practice-Taxation, 1993. Mem. Christian Legal Soc. Avocations: tennis, golf, traveling, swimming, reading. Office: 13621 Roosevelt Ave 3d Fl Flushing NY 11354-5507

CHANG, LEROY L., physicist; b. Kaifung, China, Jan. 20, 1936; came to U.S., 1959; s. Hsin-Fu and Hsien-Hen (Lee) C.; m. Helen H. Chang, 1962; children: Justin, Leslie. BS, Taiwan U., 1957; MS, U. S.C., 1961; PhD, Stanford U., 1963. Mem. rsch. staff IBM T.J. Watson Rsch. Ctr., Yorktown Heights, N.Y., 1963-68, 69-75, mgr. molecular beam epitaxy, 1975-84, tech. planning staff, 1984-85, mgr. quantum structures, 1985-92; dean of sci. Hong Kong U. of Sci. Tech., 1993-98, v.p. acad. affairs, 1998—. Fellow IEEE (David Sarnoff award 1990), Am. Phys. Soc. (Internat. prize New Materials 1985); mem. NAS, NAE, Chinese Acad. Scis., Franklin Inst. (Stuart Ballantine award 1993), Academia Sinica. Office: Sch of Sci, Office of VP Acad Affairs, Hong Kong U of Sci & Tech, Kowloon Hong Kong

CHANG, LING WEI, sales executive; b. Taiwan, China, July 27, 1960; came to U.S., 1976; d. Thomas T.P. and Hou Hsin (Wang) C. BE, Cooper Union, 1982; MS, Syracuse U., 1989. Engr. Data Systems div. IBM Corp., Poughkeepsie, N.Y., 1982-85; sys. engr. U.S. mktg. and svcs. IBM Corp., N.Y.C., 1985-90; adv. mktg. rep. N.Y. gov. br. IBM U.S., N.Y.C., 1991-92; acct. mgr. N.Y. Pub. Svcs. IBM N.Am., N.Y.C., 1993-94; br. mgr. LEXIS-NEXIS, N.Y.C., 1994-95; nat. account mgr. Computer Assocs. Internat. Inc., N.Y.C., 1996-99; acct. exec. Compaq Svcs., N.Y.C., 1999—. Vol. City Hosp. Ctr. at Elmhurst, N.Y., 1978; jr. judge Nat. Energy Found., 1979-82; bd. mgrs. Queens Ctr. Pla. Condominium, 1990-92. Mem. Exec. Women's Golf Assn., Tau Beta Pi, Eta Kappa Nu. Avocations: piano, golf, skiing, tennis, investment stock. Home: 87-08 Justice Ave Apt 10D Elmhurst NY 11373-4580 Office: Compaq Computer Corp 2 Penn Plz Fl 8 New York NY 10121

CHANG, LYDIA LIANG-HWA, school social worker, educator; b. Wuhan, Hubei, China, Sept. 25, 1929; came to U.S., 1960; d. Shu-Tze Yu-Rou and Jian-Bung (Young) C.; m. Norman Stock, Aug. 20, 1998; children: Elizabeth Shu-Mei L. Ip, George Shu-Ang Lee. Diploma in Spanish and Lit., U. Sorbonne, Paris, 1959; MSW, NYU, 1963; cert. in advanced social work, Columbia U., N.Y.C., 1977, PhD in Social Work, 1980. Cert. social worker, cert. sch. bilingual social worker, N.Y. Supr. Cath. Charities, N.Y.C., 1969-71; dir. mental health cons. ctr. Univ. Settlement, N.Y.C., 1971-73; psychotherapist Luth. Med. Ctr., Bklyn., 1974-78; assoc. prof. U. Cin., 1978-80; asst. prof. Borough of Manhattan C.C., N.Y.C., 1983-86; bilingual sch. social worker N.Y.C. Bd. Edn., 1987-98, instr. for staff devel. program, 1991-98; psychotherapist Western Queens (N.Y.) Consultation Ctr., 1998—; cons. Cath. Social Svc. Bur., Cin., 1978-80; faculty advisor Borough of Manhattan C.C., 1983-86. Contbr. articles and poetry to various publs. Mem. adv. bd. Pub. Sys. of Schs., Cin., 1978-80, Orange County Asian Am. orgn., Goshen, N.Y., 1980-82; treas. U.S.-China Ednl. Fund, Hastins-on-Hudson, N.Y., 1994—; mem. Asian-Am. Dem. Assn., Queens, 1993—, Am. Voters Assn., Queens, 1986—; founder of the Shu-Tze Chang and Jian-Bung Young Chang Ednl. scholarship fund, China, 1996. Mem. NASW, Nat. Assn. Sch. Social Workers, Columbia Alumni Assn., Nankai Alumni Assn. (v.p. 1991-94). Episcopalian. Avocations: playing clarinet, singing, tai-chi-chuang, swimming, reading. Home: 77-11 35th Ave Apt 2P Jackson Heights NY 11372

CHANG, MARIAN S., filmmaker, composer; b. Atlanta, Aug. 19, 1958; d. C.H. Joseph and C.S. (Chun) C. BA in Music, Harvard U., 1981; MFA in Filmmaking, Columbia U., 1994. Composer, dir., choreographer Exptl. Theatre, Dance, Boston, 1981-88; composer for modern dance co. Performing Arts Ensemble, Boston, 1986-88; co-dir., choreographer, performer Theatre S., Boston, 1987-88; prodr., dir., writer, sound designer, composer N.Y.C., 1991—; founder, prodr. Shy Artists Prodns., Boston, N.Y.C., 1988-94. Recipient Mass. Artists Fellowship Program award in choreography, 1987, in music composition, 1988; recipient First Prize Kans. City Music Scholarship Competition, 1976, Nino Cerruti Film award, 1995; grantee N.Y. Coun. for the Humanities, 1998. Home: 220 E 27th St Apt 7 New York NY 10016-9234

CHANG, MICHAEL, tennis player; b. Hoboken, N.J., Feb. 22, 1972; s. Joe and Betty Chang. Round of 16 U.S. Open, N.Y.C., 1988, 89, 91, 94; round of 16 Wimbledon, London, 1989, 90, quarterfinalist, 1994; champion French Open, Paris, 1989, quarterfinalist, 1990, 91, finalist, 1995; semifinalist Australian Open, Melbourne, 1995, finalist, 1996; finalist U.S. Open, N.Y.C., 1996; champion Infiniti Open, L.A., 1996, Legg Mason Tennis Classic, Washington, 1996, Newsweek Champions Cup, Indian Wells, Calif., 1996; other tournaments include: semifinalist WCT Scottsdale (Ariz.) Open, 1987; champion Transamerica Open, San Francisco, 1988; semifinalist Volvo Tennis Indoor, Memphis, 1989, semifinalist, 1991; finalist Volvo Tennis L.A., 1989, 90, 93; champion Silk Cuts Championships, Wembley, Eng., 1989; semifinalist Sovran Bank Classic, Washington, 1990; champion Player's Ltd. Internat. Can. Open, Toronto, 1990; semifinalist Suntory Japan Open, Tokyo, 1991, 92; semifinalist Open de la Ville de Paris, 1991, 94; finalist Compaq Grand Slam Cup, Munich, 1991, 92; champion Diet Pepsi Indoor Challenge, Birmingham, Eng., 1991; semifinalist Thriftway ATP Championships, Cin., 1992, champion, 1993, 94, finalist, 1995; semifinalist Waldbaum's Hamlet Cup, L.I., N.Y., 1992; semifinalist Seiko Super Tennis, Tokyo, 1992, finalist, 1994, champion, 1995; semifinalist European Cmty. Championships, Antwerp, Belgium, 1992; finalist Salem Open, Hong Kong, 1992, champion, 1994, 95, champion, Osaka, 1993, champion, Kuala Lumpur, 1993, champion, Beijing, 1993, 94, 95; champion Volvo Tennis/San Francisco, 1992; champion Newsweek Champions Cup, Indian Wells, Calif., 1992, semifinalist, 1993; champion Lipton Internat. Players Championships, Key Biscayne, Fla., 1992; semifinalist Kroger St. Jude Internat., Memphis, 1993, finalist, 1998; Ford Australian Open, Melbourne, 1997, U.S. Open, N.Y.C., 1997; champion Indonesian Open, Jakarta, 1993; finalist Japan Open, Tokyo, 1994, semifinalist, 1995; champion Indonesian Men's Open, Jakarta, 1994; champion Comcast U.S. Indoor, Phila., 1994, finalist, 1995; champion AT&T Challenge, Atlanta, 1994, 95, Infiniti Open, L.A., 1996, U.S. Men's Clay Ct. Championships, 1997, Salem Open, Hong Kong, 1997, Legg Mason Tennis Classic, Washington, 1996, 97, Kroger St. Jude, 1997, Newsweek Champions Cup, Indian Wells, Calif., 1996, 97; finalist Sybase Open, San Jose, Calif., 1995, semifinalist, 1996, 1998; finalist ATP World Tour Championships, Frankfurt, Germany, 1995; mem. U.S. Davis Cup Squad, 1989-91; semifinalist du Maurier Open, Montreal, Canada, 1997; semifinalist Great Amer. Insurance ATP Championship, Cincinnati, Oh., 1997; semifinalist Heineken Open, Rosmalen, The Netherlands, 1997. Youngest player to win USTA Boys' Nat. Championships, 1987; youngest male to advance to semifinals of Super Series tournament, 1987; youngest male to win match at U.S. Open, 1987; youngest male to win match at Wimbledon, 1988; youngest player to win Super Series tournament, 1988; youngest player to be named to U.S. Davis Cup Squad, 1989; youngest male Grand Slam Champion in Open Era, 1989; youngest ever French Open Champion, 1989; first Am. since Tony Trabert to win French Open, 1989. Address: Advantage Internat 1751 Pinnacle Dr Ste 1500 Mc Lean VA 22102-3833*

CHANG, PARRIS HSU-CHENG, law-maker, political science educator, writer; b. Chikou, Chiayi, Taiwan, Dec. 30, 1936; came to U.S., 1961; s. Chao and Liu (Chen) C.; m. Shirley Hsiu-chu Lin, Aug. 3, 1963; children: Yvette, Elaine, Bohdan. BA, Nat. Taiwan U., 1959; MA, U. Wash., 1963; postgrad., Pa. State U., 1963-64; PhD, Columbia U., 1969, cert. Asian studies, 1966. Research polit. scientist U. Mich., Ann Arbor, 1969-70; asst. prof. polit. sci. Pa. State U., University Park, 1970-72; vis. fellow Australian Nat. U., Canberra, 1978; vis. scholar Inst. Sino-Soviet Studies, George Washington U., Washington, 1979; assoc. prof. polit. sci. Pa. State U., University Park, 1972-76, prof., 1976-97, dir. Ctr. for East Asian Studies, 1989-93; mem. Legis. Yuan Parliament, Taiwan, Republic of China, 1993—; prof. emeritus polit. sci., 1997—; cons. The Rand Corp., Santa Monica, Calif., 1975-82, BDM, Vienna, Va., 1975—, Voice of Am., Washington, 1982—, Dept. State, 1983-84, Titan Sys., Vienna, 1985—; assoc. China coun. Asia Soc., N.Y.C., 1976—; vis. prof. Columbia U., summer 1985, Sch. Internat. Studies, JFK Spl. Warfare Ctr., Ft. Bragg, N.C., 1985-86, Tokyo U. Fgn. Studies, 1986-87; pres. steering com. unrepresented Nations and Peoples Orgn., The Hague, 1993—, Taiwan Inst. for Polit. Econ. and Strategic Studies, 1994—. Author: Radicals and Radical Ideology in China's Cultural Revolution, 1973, Power and Policy in China, 1975, 3d edit. 1990, Elite Conflict in the Post-Mao China, 1981, 2d edit. 1983; co-author, co-editor: If China Crosses the Taiwan Strait, 1993, Chinese View of Future Warfare: Taiwan's Response, 1998; columnist Newsweek, 1985-87. Fellow Fulbright Council Internat. Exchange of Scholars, 1977; research grantee Social Sci. Research Council, 1972; travel grantee Internat. Research Exchange Council, 1982, 85. Fellow Japan Soc. for Promotion of Sci.; mem. Assn. Asian Studies (pres. Mid-Atlantic region 1976-77), Inter-Univ. Seminar on Armed Forces and Soc., Am. Polit. Sci. Assn. Fax: 886 2 2391 3760. Office: 3-2 Chingtao E Rd, Taipei Taiwan

CHANG, RODNEY EIU JOON, artist, dentist; b. Honolulu, Nov. 26, 1945; s. Alfred Koon Bo and Mary Yet Moi (Char) C.; m. Erlinda C. Feliciano, Dec. 4, 1987; children: Bronson York, Houston Travis, Rochelle Jessica. BA in Zoology, U. Hawaii, 1968; AA in Art, Triton Coll., 1972; DDS, Loyola U., 1972; MS in Edn., U. So. Calif., 1974; MA in Painting and Drawing, U. No. Ill., 1975; MA in Community Leadership, Cen. Mich. U., 1976; BA in Psychology, Hawaii Pacific U., 1977; MA in Psychology of Counseling, U. No. Colo., 1980; PhD in Art Psychology, The Union Inst., 1980; MA in Computer Art, Columbia Pacific U., 1989. Pvt. practice dentist Honolulu, 1975—; dir. SOHO too Gallery and Loft, Honolulu, 1985-89; freelance artist Honolulu, 1982—; curator Webfelt Mus. of Early Cyberart, Honolulu, 1996—; founder Pygoya Internat. Art Group, 1990—; founder Art Cap Group, Slap Caps Co., Honolulu, 1993; columnist Milk Cap News; dir. ann. Honolulu City Hall Hawaiian Computer Art Exhbn., 1990-92; speaker on art psychology and computer art, also numerous TV and radio interviews. Author: Mental Evolution and Art, 1980, Rodney Chang: Computer Artist, 1988, Commentaries on the Psychology of Art, 1980; host (radio show) Disco Doc Hour, Sta. KISA; one-man shows include Honolulu Acad. Arts, 1986, Shanghai State Art Mus., People's Republic of China, 1988, Retrospective Exhbn. 1967-87, Ramsay Gallery, Honolulu, 1987, Visual Encounters Gallery, Denver, 1987, The Bronx Mus. of the Arts, N.Y.C., 1987, Nishi Noho Gallery, N.Y.C., 1987, Eastern Wash. U. Gallery of Art, 1988, Salon de la Jeune Peinture, Paris, 1989, Holter Art Mus., Mont., 1989, Las Vegas Art Mus., 1990, Forum Art Sch. Gütershoh, Fed. Republic of Germany, 1990, Siggraph-Dallas, 1990, Tartu State Art Mus., Estonia/USSR, 1990, U. Oregon Continuation Ctr., Portland, 1991—, Kauai Art Mus., Hawaii, 1993, RC Gallery of Computer Art, Honolulu, 1994, Archtl. Design of the Pygoya Home Mus., 1994; conceived, produced 1st milk cap art exhbn., Arts of Paradise Gallery, Waikiki Beach, 1993. Judge Jr. Miss Contest, Honolulu, 1981. Served to capt., U.S. Army, 1973-74. Mem. ADA, Hawaii Dental Assn., Assn. of Honolulu Artists (pres. 1989), Nat. Computer Graphics, Acad. Gen. Dentistry, Hawaii Space Soc., Bernice Bishop Mus. Honolulu. Roman Catholic. Achievements include publication and issue of world's first pre-paid long distance telephone cards as signed and numbered, limited edition fine art prints, Pygoya Webmuseum of Cyberart on Internet, 1997; dir. Internet Programs, Las Vegas Art Mus. Office: 2119 N King St Ste 206 Honolulu HI 96819-4550

CHANG, SHIRLEY LIN (HSIU-CHU CHANG), librarian; b. Chia-yi, Taiwan, June 22, 1937; came to U.S., 1962, naturalized, 1977; d. Tzu-kun and Ying (Chang) Lin; m. Parris H. Chang, Aug. 3, 1963; children: Yvette Y., Elaine Y., Bohdan P. BA, Nat. Taiwan U., Taipei, 1960; postgrad. U. Wash., 1962-63; MLS, Columbia U., 1967; MA, Pa. State U., 1988. Libr. asst. Yale U., New Haven, 1964, Columbia U., N.Y.C., 1964-67; asst. ref. libr. Pa. State U., University Park, 1971-75; cataloguer Australian Nat. U., Canberra, 1978; catalog/ref. libr. Lock Haven U., 1979—, asst. prof., 1982-88, assoc. prof., 1988—. Author: Taiwan's Brain Drain and Its Reversal, 1999. Mem. ALA, Chinese-Am. Librs. Assn. (chmn. awards com. 1982-83), Asian/Pacific Am. Librs. Assn., Assn. for Asian Studies, Pa. Libr. Assn., Phi Beta Delta Honor Soc. Home: 1221 Edwards St State College PA 16801-6930 Office: Lock Haven U Stevenson Libr Lock Haven PA 17745

CHANG, SHU TING, fungal geneticist, mushroom biologist; b. Yuanping, Shanxi, China, Sept. 30, 1930; arrived in Australia, 1972; s. Huang-Kuan and Tsan-Li (Kuo) C.; m. Judy Li-Ju Lee; children: David Ming-Tsan, Barbara Ming-Wai, Judy Ming-Sze, Ernest Ming-Cheng, Jennifer Ming-Jing. BSc, Nat. Taiwan U., 1953; MSc, U. Wis., 1958, PhD, 1960; Diploma, Nat. Tsing Hua U., Taiwan, 1963; postgrad., Harvard U., 1966-67. Asst. lectr. in biology Chinese U. Hong Kong, 1960-61, lectr. in biology, 1961-70, sr. lectr. in biology, 1970-74, reader in biology, 1974-78, prof. biology, 1978-95, emeritus prof. biology, 1995—; dir. Hong Kong Microbial Resources Centres, 1990—; dir. Center for Internat. Svcs. to Mushroom Biotech., 1993-96; dir. Inst. Sci. and Tech., Chinese U. Hong Kong, 1985-92, dean Faculty of Sci., 1975-77, chmn. dept of biology, 1983-94, dir. of the office of student affairs,

1979-81. Author: The Chinese Mushroom, 1972, Edible Mushrooms and Their Cultivation, 1989Technical Guidelines for Mushroom Growing in Tropics, 1990, Hong Kong Mushrooms, 1995, Mushroom Biology: Concise Basics and Current Developments, 1997; editor: The Cultivation of Edible Mushrooms, 1978, Tropical Mushrooms, Biological Nature and Cultivation Methods, 1982, Genetics and Breeding of Edible Mushrooms, 1993, Mushroom Biology and Mushroom Products, 1993. Decorated officer Order Brit. Empire, 1994. Fellow World Acad. Art and Sci. (Stockholm), Internat. Inst. Biotech. (London), World Acad. Productivity Sci. (Stockholm); mem. Internat. Mushroom Soc. for the Tropics (pres.), Brit. Mycological Soc. (hon., life), Internat. Soc. for Mushroom Sci. (hon., life, Internat. Cooperation award for light industry 1990). Christian. Avocations: travel, reading, swimming. Home: 3 Britton Pl, McKellar, Canberra ACT 2617, Australia Office: Chinese U Hong Kong, Univ Sci Ctr Dept Biology, Shatin Hong Kong

CHANG, SUNG-JIN JAMES, management consultant; b. Harrisburg, Pa., Aug. 20, 1966; s. Jae C. and Sue Y. C. BA, Cornell U., 1988; MM, Northwestern U., 1992. Rsch. analyst Glassman Oliver Econ. Cons., Washington, 1988-90; analyst N.W. Airlines, Inc., Eagan, Minn., 1992-93; sen. staff planner United Airlines, Inc., Elk Grove Village, Ill., 1993-95; sr. mgr. Andersen Consulting-Strategic Svcs., Chgo., 1995—. Office: Andersen Consulting 161 N Clark St Chicago IL 60601-5300

CHANG, T. SUSAN, book editor; b. N.Y.C., Aug. 26, 1969; d. Nai Yong and Wei-Wen (Pu) Chang; m. Randall D. te Velde, 1998. BA magna cum laude, Harvard U., 1990. Asst. editor Oxford U. Press, N.Y.C., 1991-93; assoc. editor Cambridge U. Press, N.Y.C., 1993-95; editor Oxford U. Press, 1995—; book editor for Wole Soyinka, Henry Louis Gates Jr., Frank Lentricchia, Harold Bloom, Chinua Achebe, Stanley Fish, Cornel West, others. Mem. MLA, Am. Philol. Assn., Am. Studies Assn. Democrat. Avocations: ballroom dance, alto saxophone, cuisine, scuba diving.

CHANG, TAIPING, marketing executive, magazine publisher; b. Tainan, Taiwan, Apr. 20, 1949; came to U.S., 1975; d. Lanfeng Chang and Shuchun Liu; m. David R. Knechtges, June 7, 1976; 1 child, Jeanne Y. BA, Tunghai U., 1971, MA, 1974; PhD, U. Wash., 1981. Lectr. Tunghai U., Taichung, Taiwan, 1974-75; asst. prof. Pacific Luth. U., Tacoma, 1986-88; pub. Asia Pacific Bus. Jour., Seattle, 1988-94; pres. Asia Media Group, Inc., Seattle, 1989-94; asst. prof. Asian studies program U. Puget Sound, Tacoma, Wash., 1994-95; asst. prof. Asian langs. and lit. dept. U. Wash., Seattle, 1996—; bd. dirs. Chong-Wa Benevolent Assn., Seattle, No. Seattle (Wash.) C.C.; chmn. World Trade Club-Taiwan Forum, Seattle, 1991—. Editor: Editor-in-Chief, 1988. Named Woman of Yr., Asia Am. Soc., Seattle, 1990. Mem. Rotary Club. Office: Univ Wash Asian Lang Lit Dept Seattle WA 98195

CHANG, THOMAS MING SWI, medical scientist, biotechnologist; b. Swatow, Kwantang, China, Apr. 8, 1933; arrived in Can., 1952; m. Lancy Yuk Lan, June 21, 1958; children: Harvey, Victor, Christine, Sandra. BSc, McGill U., Montreal, Que., Can., 1957, MD, CM, 1961, PhD, 1965. Intern Montreal Gen. Hosp., 1961-62; rsch. fellow depts. physiology and chemistry McGill U., 1962-65, asst. prof. physiology, 1966-69, assoc. prof., 1969-72, prof. physiology, 1972—, dir. artificial organs rsch. unit, 1975-79, prof. medicine, 1975—, dir. artificial cells and organs rsch. ctr., 1979—, assoc. dept. chem. engring., 1985—, assoc. dept. chemistry, 1986—, prof. biomed. engring., 1990—; lab. and clin. rschr. med. scis., biotech., biomed. engring. Montreal, 1962—; mem. staff Royal Victoria Hosp.; hon. mem. staff Montreal Chinese Hosp., 1970—; cons. Montreal Children's Hosp., 1979—, Med. Rsch. Coun. fellow, 1962-65, scholar, 1965-68, career investigator, 1968-69; hon. prof. Nankai U., 1983—. Inventor artificial cells and blood substitutes; author: Artificial Cells, 1972, Biomedical Application of Immobilized Enzymes and Proteins, Vols. I and II, 1977, Artificial Kidney, Artificial Liver and Artificial Cells, 1978, Hemoperfusion-Kidney and Liver Supports and Detoxification, 1980, Hemoperfusion, 1981, Past, Present and Future of Artificial Organs, 1983, Microencapsulation and Artificial Cells, 1984, Hemoperfusion and Artificial Organs, 1985, Blood Substitutes, 1988, Blood Substitutes and Oxygen Carriers, 1993, Blood Substitutes: Principles, Methods, Products & Clinical Trials, Vol. I, 1997, II, 1998; editor-in-chief Artificial Cells, Blood Substitutes and Immobilization Biotechs.; sect. editor Internat. Jour. Artificial Organs, 1977—, Trans. Am. Soc. Artificial Organs, 1977—, BioTech Ann. Rev., 1995—; mem. editl. bd. Jour. Biomaterial Med. Devel. and Orgn., 1972-87, Jour. Membrane Sci., 1975-92, Jour. Bioengring., 1975-79, Jour. Enzyme and Microbial Tech., 1978-86. Decorated officer Order of Can., 1992—. Fellow Royal Coll. Physicians Can.; mem. Internat. Soc. Artificial Organs (trustee 1982-87, 89-92, congress pres. 1991, pres. 1994-96, immediate past pres. 1996-98), Can. Soc. Artificial Organs (pres. 1980-82), Internat. Soc. Artificial Cells, Blood Substitutes and Immobilization Biotech. (hon. pres. 1990—, hon. congress pres. 1994, 97), Internat. Soc. Microencapsulations (hon.). Office: Artificial Cells & Organs Rsch Ctr, 3655 Drummond St Rm 1005, Montreal, PQ Canada H3G 1Y6

CHANG, WEILIN PARRISH, construction and engineering educator, administrator, researcher; b. Mukden, Manchuria, China, May 26, 1947; came to U.S., 1985; arrived in Australia, 1997; s. Cheng-Chung and Chien-Min (Chen) C.; m. Lily Yuan, Oct. 20, 1973; children: Howard, Cynthia. BS, Nat. Taiwan U., 1969; MS, SUNY, Buffalo, 1973, PhD, 1975. Instr. SUNY, Buffalo, 1973; assoc. prof. Chung-Yuan Christian Coll., Chung-Li, Taiwan, 1975-77, Nat. Taiwan U., Taipei, 1977-78; asst. prof. King Abdul Aziz U., Jeddah, Saudi Arabia, 1978-80; gen. mgr. United Taiwan Constrn. Co., Jeddah, 1978-81; from assoc. to full prof. Chung-Yuan Christian U., Chung-Li, 1981-85; assoc. prof. Mesa State Coll., Grand Junction, Colo., 1986-87; assoc. prof. U. Fla., Gainesville, 1987-89, prof., dir. Sch. Bldg. Constrn., 1989-95, prof. Sch. Bldg. Constrn., 1995-96; prof., dean faculty built environ. and engring. Queensland U. Tech., Brisbane, Australia, 1997—; patent examiner Chinese Ministry Econs., Taipei, 1975-85; cons. Taiwan Gen. Contractors Assn., Taipei, 1983-85; trustee Am. Coun. for Constrn. Edn.; bd. dirs. Am. Inst. Constructors, CIB-Internat. Coun. for Bldg. Rsch. and Documentation; edn. advisor China Ministry of Constrn., 1993—; adv. prof. Tongji (China) U., 1998. Contbr. numerous articles to profl. jours. 2d lt. Chinese Marines, 1969-70. Recipient Klinger Constrn. Edn. award Am. Inst. Constructors, 1994, numerous rsch. grants, 1983—. Fellow Instn. Engrs. Australia, Australian Inst. Bldg.; mem. ASCE, Am. Inst. Constructors (bd. dirs.), Am. Assn. Cost Engrs., Am. Coun. Constrn. Edn., Sigma Lamda Chi, Phi Tau Phi. Avocations: philaticity, swimming. Office: Queensland U Tech, Garden Point, Brisbane Queensland 4001, Australia

CHANG, WILLIAM SHEN CHIE, electrical engineering educator; b. Nantung, Kiangsu, China, Apr. 4, 1931; s. Tung Wu and Phoebe Y.S. (Chow) C.; m. Margaret Huachen Kwei, Nov. 26, 1955; children: Helen Naiyee, Hugh Nai-hun, Hedy Nai-lin. BSE, U. Mich., 1952, MSE, 1953; PhD, Brown U., 1957. Lectr., rsch. assoc. in elec. engring. Stanford (Calif.) U., 1957-59; asst. prof. elec. engring. Ohio State U., 1959-62, asso. prof., 1962-65; prof. dept. elec. engring. Washington U., St. Louis, 1965-76, chmn. dept., 1965-71, dir. Applied Electronic Scis. Lab., 1971-79, Samuel Sachs prof. elec. engring., 1976-79; prof. dept. elec. and computer engring. U. Calif., San Diego, 1979—, chmn. dept., 1993-96. Author: Principles of Quantum Electronics, 1969; Contbr. articles to profl. jours. Fellow Am. Optical Soc., IEEE; mem. Am. Phys. Soc. Research on quantum electronics and guided wave optics. Home: 9654 Claiborne Sq La Jolla CA 92037-1172 Office: U Calif San Diego MS-0407 Dept Elec/Computer Engring La Jolla CA 92093-0407

CHANG, WUNG, researcher, lecturer, business advisor; b. Kangke Pyongbuk, Republic of Korea, Apr. 24, 1942; came to U.S., 1973; s. Jae Sun and Key Bok (Yoo) C.; m. Han Jin Yang, Nov. 14, 1970; children: Min, Won. *Wife, Han Jin Chang, is an RN and supervisor at Temple Community Hospital, Los Angeles. Son, Min Chang, is an attorney at law, with an LLM and JD from Duke Law School. Son, Won Chang, is also an attorney at law, with a JD from Cornell Law School. Won's wife, Jenny (Ko) Chang, is an attorney at law, with a JD from University of California Berkeley Law School.* MPA, Yon-Sei U., 1971; PhD in Bus. Mgmt., Union U., 1983. Editor-in-chief Korea Photo Times, Seoul, 1970-73; sec.-gen. Wum Found., L.A., 1986-87; sr. analyst Pacific Rsch. Inst., L.A., 1988-92; advisor Korea Travel News, Seoul, 1988-93; controller U.S. Top Capital Corp., L.A., 1991—; vice chmn. Mid-Wilshire Vocat. Tng. Ctr. divsn. Adult and Career Edn., L.A. Unified Sch. Dist. Adv. Coun., 1994-96; vol. lectr. The Korean Sr. Citizens Assn. of San Fernando Valley Coll, 1995-96; co-chmn. Internat. Rsch. Inst. Govt. and Pub. Adminstrn., L.A., 1995—; commentator Radio Korea, USA, 1997-98. Mem. Rep. Presdl. Adv. Commn., Washington, 1991; active Rep. Senatorial Com., Washington, 1991; nat. campaign advisor Rep. Senatorial Inner Circle, Washington, 1995—. Capt. Korean Army, 1966-70. Recipient Presdl. Order of Merit, 1991, Rep. Presdl. Task Force Wall of Honor, 1992. Avocations: fishing, swimming, music, baseball. Home: 7625 Radford Ave North Hollywood CA 91605-2858

CHANG, Y. AUSTIN, materials engineer, educator; m. P. Jean Ho, Sept. 15, 1956; children: Vincent D., Lawrence D., Theodore D. B.S. in Chem. Engring, U. Calif., Berkeley, 1954; Ph.D. in Metallurgy, U. Calif., 1963; M.S. in Chem. Engring, U. Wash., 1955. Chem. engr. Stauffer Chem. Co., Richmond, Calif., 1956-59; postdoctoral fellow U. Calif.-Berkeley, 1963; metall. engr. Aerojet-Gen. Corp., Sacramento, 1963-67; assoc. prof. U. Wis.-Milw., 1967-70, prof., 1970-80, chmn. materials dept., 1971-78, assoc. dean research Grad. Sch., 1978-80; prof. dept. materials sci. and engring. U. Wis., Madison, 1980—, chmn. dept., 1982-91, Wis. Disting. prof., 1988—; mem. summer faculty Sandia Labs., Livermore, Calif., 1971; vis. prof. Tohuku U., Sendai, Japan, fall 1987, MIT, Cambridge, fall 1991; NRC Disting. lectr. in material sci. Nat. Cheng Kung U., Tainan, Taiwan, 1987-88; adj. prof. U. Sci. Tech., Beijing, 1987—, hon. prof., 1995-96, adv. bd., 1996—; hon. prof. Ctrl. South U. Technology, Changsha, Hunan, 1996—. Co-author four books on phase equilibria and thermodynamic properties; co-editor four books; contbr. 300 scholarly articles in metall. and materials field to profl. jours. Mem. bd. Goodwill Residential Cmty., Inc., Milw., 1978-80; mem. Wis. Gov.'s Asian Am. Adv. Coun., 1980-82, Nat. Acad. Engring., 1996. Recipient Outstanding Instr. award U. Wis., Milw., 1972, Byron Bird award U. Wis., Madison, 1984. Fellow Am. Soc. Metals Internat. (Fellow award 1978, trustee 1981-84, Hall of Fame award Milw. chpt. 1986, Albert Easton White Disting. Tchr. award 1994, Albert Sauveun Achievement award 1996), Minerals, Metals and Materials Soc. (William Hume-Rothery award 1989, Educator award 1990, Fellow award 1991, Extraction and Processing lectr. award 1993, Mathewson award 1996); mem. NSPE, NAE, Orgn. Chinese Ams. (chpt. pres. 1979-81), Nat. Assn. Corrosion Engrs., Electrochem. Soc., Materials Rsch. Soc., Am. Phys. Soc., Sigma Xi, Tau Beta Pi, Phi Tau Phi, Alpha Sigma Mu (pres. 1984-85, hon. life). Office: U Wis 1509 University Ave Madison WI 53706-1538

CHANG, YI-CHENG, insurance agent; b. Guang Dong, China, June 24, 1943; came to U.S., 1974; s. Jin-Xin and Man-Hua (Ling) C.; m. Rufina Hoi Tong Chung, Sept. 6, 1975; 1 child, Wen Zhong. BS, Hong Kong Bapt. Coll., 1968; MS, Mich. State U., 1976. Owner Self-Strength Air Conditioning, Hong Kong, 1962-68; asst. lab. mgr. Micro Electronics, Hong Kong, 1968-70; purchasing mgr. Gen. Electronics, Hong Kong, 1970-73; material controller Coltronics Ltd., Hong Kong, 1973-74; purchasing agt. Reese Finer Foods, Elk Grove Village, Ill., 1976-79; import clk. Charlotte Charles, Inc., Chgo., 1979-80; purchasing agt. Commodity Communication Corp., Lombard, Ill., 1980-82; agt. N.Y. Life, Chgo., Ill., 1982—; spkr. at minority workshop and Chinese market conf. N.Y. Life, 1988-89; commentator Chinese radio and TV, Chgo.; speaker nat. Chinese Market conf., 1993-98, 2d Worldwide Chinese Life Ins. Congress, Malaysia, 1998, Internat. Ins. Conf., Guangzhou, China, 1996, Inst. Internat. Rsch., Washington, 1996, others. Author: Easy & Practical Ways of Learning Swimming, 1971; columnist Chinese newspapers; contbr. articles to profl. jours. Mem. Orgn. of Chinese-Ams., Chgo., 1983—; founder, bd. dirs. Chgo. Chinese TV, 1990—; bd. dir. Light-a-Lamp Edn. Found., 1988, 89. Mem. Nat. Assn. Life Underwriters (strategic planning com. 1995-96), Life Underwriters Assn., Chgo. Life Underwriters Assn. (bd. dirs. 1992-94), Chinese Alliance No. Ill., Chgo.-Chinese C. of C. (bd. dirs. 1998-99), Chinese Am. C. of C. and Professions, Million Dollar Roundtable. Avocations: cooking, gardening, writing. Office: 211 W 22nd Pl # 3 F Chicago IL 60616-1901

CHANG, YOON IL, nuclear engineer; b. Seoul, Korea, Apr. 12, 1942; came to U.S., 1965; s. Paul Kun and In Sil (Hahn) C.; m. Ok Ja Kim, Dec. 19, 1966; children: Alice, Dennis, Eugene. BS in Nuclear Engring., Seoul Nat. U., 1964; ME, Tex. A & M U., 1967; PhD, U. Mich., 1971; MBA, U. Chgo., 1983. Mgr. spl. projects Nuclear Assurance Corp., Atlanta, 1971-74; asst. nuclear engr. Argonne (Ill.) Nat. Lab., 1974-76, group leader, 1976-77, sect. head, 1977-78, assoc. div. dir., 1978-84, gen. mgr. IFR program, 1984-94, dep. assoc. lab. dir. for engring. rsch., 1994-96, assoc. lab. dir. for engring. rsch., 1997—. Recipient E. O. Lawrence award U.S. Dept. Energy, 1994. Fellow Am. Nuclear Soc. (Walker Cisler award 1997—). Home: 2020 Palmer Dr Naperville IL 60564-5664 Office: Argonne Nat Lab 9700 Cass Ave Argonne IL 60439-4803

CHANG-HASNAIN, CONSTANCE JUI-HUA, educator; b. Taipei, Taiwan, Oct. 1, 1960; came to U.S., 1978; d. Ping-Jen and Chia-Fu (Wan) Chang; m. Ghulam Hasnain, June 22, 1984; 1 child, Katherine Mei. BS, U. Calif., Davis, 1982; MS, U. Calif., Berkeley, 1984, PhD, 1987. Mem. tech. staff Bellcore, Red Bank, N.J., 1987-92; asst. prof. dept. elec. engring. Stanford (Calif.) U., 1992-95, assoc. prof., 1995; prof. elec. engring. and computer sci. U. Calif., Berkeley, 1996—. Contbr. articles to IEEE Jour. Quantum Electronics, Applied Phys. Letters, Photonics Tech. Letters, Jour. Lightwave Tech. Quantum fellow Am. Electronics Assn., 1984-87, David Sakrison prize, 1989; best paper Soviet-Am. Interacad. Workshop on Semiconductor Laser Physics, 1991; named Outstanding Young Elec. Engr. Eta Kappa Nu, 1991, Nat. Young Investigator NSF, 1992; Packard fellow David and Lucille Packard Found., 1992, Reid and Polly Anderson faculty scholar, 1992, Presdl. Faculty fellow. Fellow, IEEE (sr., assoc. editor Circuits and Devices mag. 1991—, chairperson semiconductor laser workshop 1991), Conf. Lasers and Electro-Optics (subcom. chair 1993), fellow Optical Soc. Am., Am. Phys. Soc. Achievements include patents for cross-coupled quantum well stripe laser array, for multiple wavelength laser array and method of making. Home: 4387 Ramora Dr Union City CA 94587 Office: U Calif Berkeley EECS Dept 571 Cory Hall Berkeley CA 94720

CHANG-MOTA, ROBERTO, electrical engineer; b. Caracas, Venezuela, Dec. 28, 1935; s. Roberto W. and Mary C. (Mota) Chang; m. Alicia Santamaria-Gonzales, May 4, 1968; children: Roberto Ignacio, Roxana Ivette, Ricardo Ignacio. DEE, U. Cen. Venezuela, 1960; MS, U. Ill., 1962; AR, Harvard U., 1970; PhD, U. Calif., 1983. Dir. sch. engring., prof. Ctrl. U., 1964-69; pro., dean Simon Bolivar U., 1971-77; pres. Colegio de Ingenieros de Venezuela, 1974-79; dir. Venezuelan Power Co., 1974-79; pres. Latin Am. Orgn. Engring., 1977-79, Corporoil, 1981-85, Audio Interface Corp., 1983-96; v.p. ESCA Corp., 1991-95; pres. 3R Corp., 1995—; spl. cons. Venezuelan Navy and Army, 1971-75, Venezuelan Congress, 1989-96; mem. tech. com. Venezuelan Supreme Election Coun., 1971-81, exec. dir., 1981-82, gen. dir., 1982-97; gen. dir. Consejo Nacional Electoral, 1991-98; cons. Ministry of Interior, 1990; v.p. Electronic Cir. Corp., 1991—; trustee Simon Bolivar U., 1985-98;. Gen. dir. Nat. Election Coun., 1985-99. Mem. IEEE, Am. Soc. Engring. Edn., Venezuelan Soc. Elec. and Mech. Engring. (pres. 1972-73), Instn. Elec. Engrs., Puerto Azul Club, Playa Pintada Club, Caracas Racquet Club. Roman Cath. Home: 7861 SW 180th St Miami FL 33157-6216 also: Prados del Este, Calle Colon Quinta Cumana, Caracas 1080, Venezuela

CHAN HON GOH, ballerina; b. Beijing, Feb. 1, 1969; arrived in Can., 1977; d. Choo Chiat and Lin Yee (Zhang) G. Dancer Goh Ballet Tng. Co., Vancouver, B.C., Can., 1986-87; corp de ballet dancer Nat. Ballet of Can., Toronto, 1988-90, second soloist, 1990-92, first soloist, 1992-93, prin. dancer, 1993—; advisor in dance Met. Toronto Arts Coun., 1992-94; guest artist The Royal Danish Ballet, Hong Kong Ballet, Singapore Dance Theatre, Washington Ballet,. Prin. full length ballet roles in The Sleeping Beauty, La Fille Mal Gardée, Don Quixote, Romeo & Juliet, Coppelia, The Merry Widow, The Nutcracker, Taming of the Shrew, Onegin, Swan Lake, Giselle, Cinderella, La Boutique Fantasque, Tales of Arabian Night, La Sylphide, Swan Lake; other dances include Sylvia Pas de deux, Paquita, Dream Dances, Divertimento No. 15, Les Sylphides, Theme and Variations, Désir, The Four Temperaments, La Ronde, Dahnis and Chloe, Mozartiana, Song of the Earth, LaBayadere Act II, Etudes, Napolie Act 3, Désir; ; Can. premieres include Concerto for Flute and Harp (John Cranko), 1990, The Leaves Are Fading (Antony Tudor), 1990, Pastorale (James Kudelka), 1990, Musings (Kudelka), 1991, The Actress (Kudelka), 1993, Now and Then (John Neumeier), 1993, The Four Seasons (Kudelka), 1997, Terra Firma, Forgotten Land (Kylian). Can. Coun. grantee, 1987; recipient Solo Seal award Royal Acad. Dancing, 1988, Prix de Lausanne, 1986, Silver medal Adelene Genee Comp., London. Avocations: reading, music, theatre. Office: Nat Ballet of Canada, 470 Queens Quay W, Toronto, ON Canada M5E 3K4

CHANIN, MICHAEL HENRY, lawyer; b. Atlanta, Nov. 11, 1943; s. Henry and Herma Irene (Blumenthal) C.; m. Margaret L. Jennings, June 15, 1968; children: Herma Louise, Richard Henry, Patrick Jennings. A.B., U. N.C., 1965; J.D., Emory U., 1968. Bar: Ga. 1968, D.C. 1981. Dir. So. Ctr. for Studies in Pub. Policy, Atlanta, 1968-69; asst. and acting legal officer 1st Coast Guard Dist., Boston, 1969-72; atty. Powell, Goldstein Frazer & Murphy, Atlanta, 1972-77; spl. asst. to sec. U.S. Dept. Commerce, Washington, 1977-78; dep. asst. to pres. The White House, Washington, 1978-81; ptnr. Powell, Goldstein, Frazer & Murphy, Washington, 1981—. Served to lt. USCGR, 1969-72. Mem. ABA, D.C. Bar Assn., State Bar Ga. Democrat. Office: Powell Goldstein Frazer & Murphy 1001 Pennsylvania Ave NW Fl 6 Washington DC 20004-2505*

CHANIN, ROBERT HOWARD, lawyer; b. Bklyn., Dec. 24, 1934; s. Frank and Irene (Goldfein) C.; m. Rhoda Paley, June 9, 1957; children: Jeffrey, Stacy, Lisa. BA, Bklyn. Coll., 1956; LLB, Yale U., 1959; MA, Columbia U., 1961. Bar: N.Y. 1959, D.C. 1969. Instr. in psychology New Haven Coll., 1956-59; staff atty. Law Sch. Columbia U., N.Y.C., 1959-62; assoc. Kaye, Scholer, Fierman, Hays & Handler, N.Y.C., 1962-68; gen. counsel NEA, Washington, 1968—, gen. counsel, dep. exec. dir., 1973-80; profl. lectr. George Washington U. Law Sch., Washington, 1973-80; ptnr. Bredhoff & Kaiser, P.L.L.C., Washington, 1980—; trustee NEA Ins. Trust, Washington, 1975—. Author: The Law and Practice of Teacher Negotiations, 1970, The Law and Practice of Teacher Negotiations, 1974; contbr. articles to profl. jours. Mem. Nat. Orgn. Lawyers for Edn. Assn. (pres. 1969—), Nat. Resource Ctr. for Consumers for Legal Svcs. (exec. com., bd. dirs. Washington chpt. 1975—). Office: Bredhoff & Kaiser 1000 Connecticut Ave NW Washington DC 20036-5398

CHANLATTE, LISANDRO JOSE, consultant; b. Danville, Va., Sept. 25, 1976; s. Jose D. and Elena (Garcia) C. BBA, Loyola U., 1997. Tytor French & Spanish Loyola U., New Orleans, 1995-97; internal cons. analyst JP Morgan, N.Y.C., 1998—. Alumni Assn. Loyola U. scholar, 1996. Mem. Internat. Student Assn. (pres., v.p. 1994-96), Loyola U. Martial Arts Club (pres., founder 1995-97). Delta Sigma Pi, Phi Eta Sigma. Roman Catholic. Avocations: Jujutsu, travel, music. Home: 207 E 37th St Apt 5J New York NY 10016 Office: JP Morgan 23 Wall St New York NY 10060

CHANNER, HAROLD HUDSON, television producer, interviewer; b. Detroit, Mar. 14, 1935; s. Harold Hudson and Grace (Sprunk) C.; m. Eileen McLanhagan, June 11, 1960 (div. 1974); children—Lisa Eileen, David Donald. BA, Wayne State U., 1959, MA, 1961; PhD, Ind. U., 1963. Instr. So. Ill. U., Edwardsville, Ill., 1963-64, Wayne State U., Detroit, 1965-66; asst. prof. Utah State U., Logan, 1966-67, Calif. State U., Long Beach, 1967-68, N.Y. State U., N.Y.C., 1968-71; pres., CEO Conversations, Inc., N.Y.C., 1973—, prodr., host TV interview series; prodr. over 1500 interviews. Comm. coord. Com. for UN. Served with U.S. Army, 1954-56. Mem. Acad. TV Arts and Scis. Avocations: reading; swimming; dancing. Home and Office: Conversations with Channer 241 W 36th St Apt 13F New York NY 10018-7511

CHANNING, CAROL, actress; b. Seattle, Jan. 31, 1923; d. George and Adelaide (Glaser) C.; m. Charles F. Lowe, Sept. 5, 1956; 1 son, Channing George. Student, Bennington Coll. Actress: (Broadway prodns.) No for an Answer, 1941, Let's Face It, 1941, Proof Through the Night, 1942, So Proudly We Hail, Lend an Ear, 1948 (Theatre World award, Critic's Circle award), Gentlemen Prefer Blondes, 1949, 51-53, Wonderful Town, 1953, Pygmalian, 1953, The Vamp, 1955, Show Business, 1959, Show Girl, 1961, George Burns-Carol Channing Musical Revue, 1962, The Millionairess, 1963, Hello Dolly, 1964-67, also revivial (Tony award for Best Actress, N.Y. Drama Critics Cir. award for Best Actress), Carol Channing with Her Stout-Hearted Men, 1970 (London Critics award), Four on a Garden, 1971, Cabaret, 1972, Festival at Ford's, 1972, Carol Channing and Her Gentlemen Who Prefer Blondes Revue, 1972, Jerry's Girls, 1984-85, Legends, 1986, (theatre tours) Lorelei, 1973-75, Carol's Broadway Revue; (films) First Travelling Saleslady, 1956, Thoroughly Modern Millie, 1967 (Golden Globe award as Best Supporting Actress 1967), Skidoo, 1968, Shinbone Alley (voice), 1971, Sgt. Peppers Lonely Hearts Club Band, 1978, Happily Ever After (voice), 1990, Hans Christian Andersen's Thumbelina (voice), 1994, The Line King: Al Hirschfield, 1996, others; (TV prodns.) Svengali and the Blonde, Three Men on a Horse, Crescendo; (TV appearences) The Love Boat, 1977, Alice in Wonderland, 1985, Where's Waldo? (voice), 1991, Addams Family (voice), 1992, The Magic School Bus (voice), 1994, The Line King: Al Hirschfeld, 1996, Homo Heights, 1998. Recipient Best Night Club Act award, 1957, 64, Spl. Tony award, 1968, Theatre World award for Bronze medallion City of N.Y., 1978, Lifetime Achievement Tony award, 1995. Christian Scientist. Office: William Morris Agy 151 S El Camino Dr Beverly Hills CA 90212-2775*

CHANNING, STOCKARD (SUSAN STOCKARD), actress; b. N.Y.C., Feb. 13, 1944. BA cum laude, Harvard U. Actress movies include The Fortune, 1975, The Big Bus, 1976, Sweet Revenge, 1977, The Cheap Detective, 1978, Grease, 1978, The Fish That Saved Pittsburgh, 1979, Safari 3000, 1982, Without a Trace, 1983, The Men's Club, 1986, Heartburn, 1986, A Time of Destiny, 1988, Staying Together, 1989, Meet the Applegates, 1990, Lunes de Fiel, 1992, Six Degrees of Separation, 1993, Married to It, 1993, To Wong Foo, Thanks for Everything, Julie Newmar, 1995, Smoke, 1995, Edie and Pen, 1996, The First Wives Club, 1996, Up Close and Personal, 1996, Moll Flanders, 1996, Twilight, 1998, Lulu on the Bridge (voice), 1998, Practical magic, 1998, The Red Door, 1999, Other Voices, 1999, Isn't She Great, 1999; tv movies include Girl Most Likely to..., 1973, Lucan, 1977, Silent Victory: The Kitty O'Neill Story, 1979, Not My Kid, 1985, The Room Upstairs, 1987, Echoes in the Darkness, 1987, Tidy Endings, 1988, Perfect Witness, 1989, Lincoln, 1992, David's Mother, 1994, Mr. Willowby's Christmas Tree, 1995, An Unexpected Family, 1996, Lily Dale, 1996, The Prosecutors, 1996, An Unexpected Life, 1998, The Baby Dance, 1998, tv series include Road to Avonlea, King of the Hill (voice), Batman Beyond, 1999. Office: ICM c/o Andrea Eastman 40 W 57th St New York NY 10019-4001*

CHANOCK, ROBERT MERRITT, pediatrician; b. Chgo., July 8, 1924; married; two children. BS, U. Chgo., 1945, MD, 1947, DSc (hon.), 1977. NRC fellow Children's Hosp., Cin., 1950-52; asst. prof. rsch. pediat. Coll. Medicine, U. Cin., 1954-56; asst. prof. epidemiology Sch. Hygiene and Pub. Health, Johns Hopkins U., 1956-57; surgeon USPHS, 1957-59, head respiratory viruses sect., 1959-61; chief lab. infectious diseases Nat. Inst. Allergy and Infectious Diseases, NIH, Bethesda, Md., 1968—; Nat. Found. Infantile Paralysis fellow, 1951-52; sr. rsch. fellow USPHS, 1956-57; virologist Children's Hosp. D.C., 1957—; mem. Internat. Nomenclature Com. Myxoviruses, 7th and 8th Internat. Microbiol. Congress; mem. Armed Forces Epidemiology Bd., Com. Acute Respiratory Disease, 1960-62; assoc. mem. Com. Influenza, 1963-74; dir. Internat. Ref. Ctr. Lab. Mycoplasms, WHO, 1962; mem. Internat. Com. Nomenclature Bacteria, 1966; clin. prof. Georgetown U., 1970-71; mem. nominating com. NAS, 1979-80; mem. sci. rev. com. Scripps Clin. and Rsch. Found., 1986-89. Recipient E. Mead Johnson award pediat. rsch., 1964, Squibb Gorgas medal Assn. Mil. Surgeons, 1972, Robert Koch medal Fed. Republic Germany, 1981, Virol prize ICT Internat., 1990, Bristol-Myers Squibb award, Albert B. Sabin Gold medal. Mem. NAS, Soc. Pediat. Rsch., Am. Soc. Microbiology, Am. Epidemiol. Soc., Am. Epidemiology, Am. Pediat. Soc., Am. Soc. Clin. Investigation, Soc. Exptl. Biology and Medicine, Assn. Am. Physicians, Royal Danish Acad. Scis. (fgn. mem.). Office: NIH 7 Center Dr Room 100 Bethesda MD 20892-0001

CHANTHANOM-GOOD, SUVAJEE, science educator; b. Bangkok, Aug. 15, 1964; d. Jetana Chanthanom and Amporn Pintong. BA in Sociology and Anthropology, Thammasat U., Bangkok, 1985; MSW, Delhi (India) U., 1988; MA, U. Pitts., 1992, PhD in Sociology, 1998'. Rschr. Child Workers in Asia, UNICEF, Bangkok, 1988-91, Asian Inst. Tech., Bangkok, 1989, UNHCR, UN, Bangkok, 1990; tchg. fellow U. Pitts., 1992-97, instr., 1998; asst. prof. Mahidol U., Bangkok, 1998—; asst. botanist Carnegie Mus., Pitts., 1997-98; ethnobiologist Phipps Conservatory, Pitts., 1996-97; interpreter UN, Bangkok, 1988-90. Mem. steering com. South Asian Caucus, 1994; vol. for edn. Carnegie Mus., Pa., 1997-98, Phipps Conservatory, Pa., 1997-98. Recipient Anandhamahidol Found. award King of Thailand, 1991-98, Bhumipol award, 1984, 85, 86. Mem. Internat. Sociology Assn. (presenter World Congress of Sociology 1994, 98), Am. Sociol. Assn., Western Pa. Conservancy. Avocation: collecting plants for conservatism and scientific purposes. Home: 66/119 Bangyai City, Bangyai Nondhapuri 11140, Thailand Office: Mahidol U, Faculty Social Sci Salaya, Nakorn Pathom Thailand

CHAO, BEI TSE, mechanical engineering educator; b. Soochow, China, Dec. 18, 1918; came to U.S., 1948, naturalized, 1962; s. Tse Yu and Yin T. (Yao) C.; m. May Kiang, Feb. 7, 1948; children: Clara, Fred Roberto. B.S. in Elec. Engring. with highest honor, Nat. Chiao-Tung U., China, 1939; Ph.D. (Boxer Indemnity scholar), Victoria U., Manchester, Eng., 1947. Asst. engr. tool and gage div. Central Machine Works, Kunming, China, 1939-41; asso. engr. Central Machine Works, 1941-43, mgr. tool and gage div., 1943-45; research asst. U. Ill., Urbana, 1948-50; asst. prof. dept. mech. engring. U. Ill., 1951-53, assoc. prof., 1953-55, prof., 1955-87, prof. emeritus, 1987—, head thermal sci. div., 1971-75, head dept. mech. and indsl. engring., 1975-87; assoc. mem. U. Ill. (Center for Advanced Study), 1963-64; cons. to industry and govtl. agys., 1950-94; vis. Russell S. Springer prof. mech. engring. U. Calif., Berkeley, 1973; mem. reviewing staff Zentralblatt für Mathematik, Berlin, 1970-82; mem. U.S. Engring. Edn. Del. to Visit People's Republic of China, 1978; mem. adv. screening com. in engring. Fulbright-Hays Awards Program, 1979-81, chmn., 1980, 81; mem. com. U.S. Army basic sci. rsch. NRC, 1980-83; Prince disting. lectr. Ariz. State U., 1984; bd. dirs. Aircraft Gear Corp., 1989-94. Author: Advanced Heat Transfer, 1969; tech. editor Jour. Heat Transfer, 1975-81; mem. adv. editl. bd. Numerical Heat Transfer, 1977-95; mem. hon. edit. bd. Internat. Jour. Heat and Mass Transfer, 1987-97, Internat. Comm. in Heat and Mass Transfer, 1987-97; contbr. numerous articles on mech. engring. to profl. jours. Recipient Outstanding Tchr. award Ill. Mech. Engring. Alumni, 1978, Max Jakob Meml. award ASME/Am. Inst. Chem. Engring., 1983; Tau Beta Pi Daniel C. Drucker eminent faculty award, 1985; Univ. scholar, 1985. Fellow AAAS, ASME (Blackall award 1957, Heat Transfer award 1971, William T. Ennor Mfg. Tech. award 1992), Am. Soc. Engring. Edn. (Outstanding Tchr. award 1975, Western Electric Fund award 1973, Ralph Coats Roe award 1975, Benjamin Garver Lamme award 1984, Centennial Medallion 1993); mem. Nat. Acad. Engring., Academia Sinica, Chiao-Tung U. Alumni Assn. (pres. Midwest sect. 1975-76), Tau Beta Pi, Pi Tau Sigma (hon.). Home: 101 W Windsor Rd Apt 6103 Urbana IL 61802-6697 Office: Univ Ill 264 Mech Engring Bldg 1206 W Green St Urbana IL 61801-2906

CHAO, CEDRIC C., lawyer; b. Cambridge, Mass., Apr. 9, 1950. BA, Stanford U., 1972; JD, Harvard U., 1977. Bar: Calif. 1977, U.S. Dist. Ct. (no. dist.) Calif. 1977, U.S. Ct. Appeals (9th cir.) 1979, U.S. Supreme Ct. 1988. Law clk.to Hon. William H. Orrick U.S. Dist. Ct. (no. dist.) Calif., San Francisco, 1977-78; asst. U.S. atty. U.S. Atty.'s Office, San Francisco, 1978-81; assoc. Morrison & Foerster, San Francisco, 1981-83, ptnr., 1983—; lawyer del. 9th cir. judicial conf., 1990-92; chair magistrate judge selection com. No. Dist. Calif., 1996. Author: Creating Your Discovery Plan, 1997. Named One of Calif.'s Top 25 Lawyers Under Age 45, Calif. Law Bus., 1994. Fellow Am. Bar Found.; mem. ABA (standing com. fed. judiciary, 1991-94), State Bar Calif. (com. profl. responsibility and conduct 1980-84, exec. com. litigation sect. 1986-91, vice chair 1989-90, chair 1990-91), San Francisco Bar Assn. (bd. dirs. 1988-90), Am. Law Inst., Asian Am. Bar Assn. Greater Bay Area (bd. dirs. 1977-82, pres. 1982), San Francisco C. of C. (bd. dirs. 1996—), World Affairs Coun. No. Calif. (trustee 1994—), Commonwealth Club Calif. (quar. chair 1989). Office: Morrison & Foerster 425 Market St Ste 3100 San Francisco CA 94105-2482*

CHAO, JAMES LEE, chemist; b. Lafayette, Ind., Sept. 4, 1954; s. Tai Siang and Hsiang Lin (Lee) C.; m. Juliana Meimei Ma, Apr. 4, 1992. BS in Chemistry, U. Ill., 1975, MS in Chemistry, 1976; PhD in Chemistry, U. Calif., Berkeley, 1980. Applications scientist IBM Instruments, Inc., Danbury, Conn., 1980-87; vis. assoc. prof. dept. chemistry Duke U., Durham, N.C., 1986-87, adj. asst. prof. dept. chemistry, 1987-91, adj. assoc. prof., 1992—; adv. scientist Materials Engring. Lab., IBM, Research Triangle Park, N.C., 1987—; cons. Lab. for Laser Energetics, U. Rochester, N.Y., 1979-80; postdoctoral fellow Lab. for Chem. Biodynamics, Lawrence Berkeley Lab., 1980; referee Applied Spectroscopy, 1982—, Applied Physics Letters, Jour. Applied Physics, 1989—; grant referee N.C. Biotech. Ctr., 1991—. Contbr. articles to profl. jours. Edmund James scholar, 1972-75, Dow Chem. scholar, 1977. Fellow N.Y. Acad. Scis., Am. Inst. Chemists; mem. Am. Chem. Soc. (chmn. N.C. sect. 1991, councillor 1993—, Marcus E. Hobbs svc. award 1995), Soc. for Applied Spectroscopy, Coblentz Soc., Triangle Coun. Engring. and Sci. Socs. (treas. 1992-94), Sigma Xi. Achievements include development of step-scan implementation for FT-IR spectrometers to study photothermal and time-resolved spectroscopies; first reported 2-D FT-IR correlation spectroscopy using step-scan; project leader for IBM environmental gaseous corrosion testing. Home: 7424 Ridgefield Dr Durham NC 27713-9503 Office: IBM Corp Dept CMZA 061 PO Box 12195 Research Triangle Park NC 27709

CHAO, JAMES MIN-TZU, architect; b. Dairen, China, Feb. 27, 1940; came to U.S., 1949; naturalized, 1962; m. Kirsti Helena Lehtonen, May 15, 1968. BArch, U. Calif., Berkeley, 1965. Registered arch., Calif., Ariz., Colo., Ill., N.Mex.; cert. instr. real estate, Calif. Intermediate draftsman Spencer, Lee & Busse, Archs., San Francisco, 1966-67; asst. to pres. Import Plus Inc., Santa Clara, Calif., 1967-69; job capt. Hammaberg and Herman, Archs., Oakland, Calif., 1969-71; project mgr. B A Premises Corp., San Francisco, 1971-79; constrn. mgr. The Straw Hat Restaurant Corp., San Francisco, 1979-81, mem. sr. mgmt., dir. real estate and constrn., 1981-87; mem. mktg. com. Straw Hat Coop. Corp., San Francisco, 1988-91; pvt. practice Berkeley, 1987—; dir. real estate Papillon Devel. Inc., 1998—; pres. Food Svc. Cons. Inc., 1987-89; pres., CEO Stratsac, Inc., 1987-92; prin. arch. Alpha Cons. Group Inc., 1991-98; v.p. Intersyn Industries Calif., 1993—; nat. tng. dir. Excel Telecom., Inc., 1995—; CEO Nuts and Bolts Books, 1997—; lectr. comml. real estate site analysis and selection for profl. real estate seminars; coord. minority vending program, solar application program Bank of Am.; guest faculty mem. N.W. Ctr. for Profl. Edn. Author: The Street-Smart Restaurant Development Handbook, 1996; patentee tidal electric generating system; author 1st comprehensive consumer orientated performance specification for remote banking transaction. Mem. AIA, Encinal Yacht Club (bd. dirs. 1977-78). Republican.

CHAO, JAMES S. C., maritime executive; b. Shanghai, China, Dec. 29, 1927; came to the U.S., 1959; s. Yi Jen and Yu Chin (Hsu) C.; m. Ruth Mu-Lan Chu, Nov. 12, 1951. BS, Nat. Maritime Coll., China, 1949; MBA, St. John's U., N.Y., 1964, DCS, 1979; LLD, Niagara U., N.Y., 1992. Cert. marine master certificate license. Marine officer, master port capt. Chinese Maritime Trust, Taiwan, 1949-59; asst. to dir. China Merchant Nav. Corp, N.Y.C., 1960-64; gen. mgr. exec. v.p. Foremost Maritime Corp., N.Y.C., 1964-69, pres., dir., 1969—; chmn. Foremost Group, N.Y.C., 1986—; adj. prof. St. John's U., N.Y.C., 1977-83, trustee; hon. prof. Dalian Maritime U., Dalian, China, 1987—; hon. prof., pres. Shanghai Maritime Coll., China. Author: (monograph) International Shipping: Prospects and Opportunities, 1982; co-author: (monograph) Rise and Decline of the U.S. Shipping and Shipbuilding Industries, 1993. Bd. advisors St. John's U. Coll. of Bus. Adminstrn., N.Y., 1971—; hon. trustee Shanghai Jiao Tong U., China.; trustee St. John's U., 1995—. Named Bus. Community Leader Fed. Reserve Bank of N.Y., 1976, 1981. Mem. Chinese Maritime Assn. (pres. 1964—), Soc. Maritime Arbitrators, Chinese Opera (hon. mem., bd. dir. 1969—), Chiao Tung U. Alumni Assn. in Am. (chmn. 1989—), Beta Gamma Sigma, Omicron Delta Epsilon (hon. mem.). Office: Foremost Maritime Group 420 Lexington Ave # 453-455 New York NY 10170-0002

CHAO, KWANG-CHU, chemical engineer, educator; b. Chongqing, China, June 7, 1925; came to U.S., 1954, naturalized, 1969; s. Chung-Pu and Jui-Pu (Chou) C.; m. Jiun-Ying Su, May 2, 1953; children: Howard Honshuen, Albert Honchi, Bernard Honwei. B.S., Nat. Chekiang U., 1948; M.S., U. Wis., 1952, Ph.D., 1956. Chem. engr. Taiwan Alkali Co., 1948-51, 52-54; research engr. Chevron Research Co., Richmond, Calif., 1957-63; asso. prof. Ill. Inst. Tech., Chgo., 1963-64, Okla. State U., 1964-68; prof. Purdue U., West Lafayette, Ind., 1968-93, Harry C. Peffer Disting. prof. chem. engring., 1989-93, Harry C. Peffer disting. prof. emeritus chem. engring., 1994—; cons. to industry, 1964—; lectr., internat. scientist Nat. Sci. Coun., Taiwan, 1989; hon. prof. Beijing U. Chem. Tech., 1984—, Zhejiang U., 1988—. Author: (with R.A. Greenkorn) Thermodynamics of Fluids, 1975; Editor: Applied Thermodynamics, 1968, Equations of State in Engineering and Research, 1979; Equations of State-Theories and Applications, 1986. Recipient Donald Katz award Gas Processors Assn., 1994. Fellow Am. Inst. Chem. Engrs. (editorial bd. jour., also Ind. Engring. Chem. Ann. Revs.); mem. Am. Chem. Soc., AAUP, Sigma Xi, Omega Chi Epsilon. Home: 2909 Henderson Ave West Lafayette IN 47906-1542

CHAO, MARSHALL, chemist; b. Changsha, Hunan, China, Nov. 20, 1924; came to U.S., 1955; s. Heng-ti and Hwei-yng C.; m. Patricia Hu, July 20, 1968; 1 dau., Anita J. B.S., Nat. Central U., Nanking, China, 1947; M.S., U. Ill., 1958, Ph.D., 1961. Tech. asst. Taiwan Fertilizer Co., Taipei, 1949-55; research chemist Dow Chem. Co., Midland, Mich., 1960-72, research specialist, 1973-80; research leader Dow chem. Co., Midland, Mich., 1980-86; sr. assoc. Omni Tech Internat., Ltd., Midland, 1986—. Author: Taiwan Fertilizers, 1951; editor newsletter Midland Chinese Christian Fellowship, 1987-94; contbr. articles to profl. jours.; patentee in field. Mem. Ch. Council Grace Bapt. Ch., Taipei, 1951-55; deacon 1st Baptist Ch., Midland, 1974-76. Univ. fellow U. Ill., 1957-60. Fellow Am. Inst. Chemists; mem. Am. Chem. Soc., Electrochem. Soc. (sect. chmn. 1973-74, 83-84, councilor 1974-76, 85—, vice chmn. 1964-65), Soc. Electroanalytical chemistry (charter), N.Y. Acad. Scis., Mensa, Sigma Xi, Phi Lambda Upsilon. Clubs: Midland Chinese (chmn. 1975-76), Tittabawassee Toastmasters (sec.-treas. 1976-77). Home: 1206 Evamar Dr Midland MI 48640-7213 Office: Omni Tech Internat Ltd 2715 Ashman St Midland MI 48640-4449 *A man's intrinsic worth is measured by the good he has done his fellow men. As for outward signs of success, such as recognition or rewards, he should much rather have people wondering why he didn't get them than have people wondering why he got them at all.*

CHAPANIS, ALPHONSE, human factors engineer, ergonomist; b. Meriden, Conn., Mar. 17, 1917; s. Anicatas and Mary (Barkevich) C.; m. Marion Amelia Rowe, Aug. 23, 1941 (div. 1960); children: Roger, Linda Chapanis Fox; m. Natalia Potanin, Mar. 25, 1960 (div. 1987). BA, U. Conn., 1937; MA, Yale U., 1942, PhD, 1943; DSc, U. Conn., 1998. Cert. Human Factors Profl. Prof. psychology The Johns Hopkins U., Balt., 1946-82; pres. Alphonse Chapanis, PhD, P.A., Balt., 1974-99; mem. tech. staff Bell Labs., Murray Hill, N.J., 1953-54; mem. adv. panel USAF Office Sci. Rsch., Washington, 1956-59; mem. com. on human factors NRC, Washington, 1980-85; liaison scientist Office Naval Rsch., Am. Embassy, London, 1960-61; cons. IBM, Yorktown Heights, N.Y. and Bethesda, Md., 1960-95, Loral Fed. Sys., Bethesda, 1995-96. Author: Research Techniques in Human Engineering, 1959, Man-Machine Engineering, 1965, Human Factors in Systems Engineering, 1996, The Chapanis Chronicles; 50 Years of Human Factors Research, Education, and Design, 1999; co-author: Applied Experimental Psychology, 1949; editor: Ethnic Variables in Human Factors Engineering, 1975; co-editor: Human Engineering Guide to Equipment Design, 1963; contbr. over 175 articles to profl. jours. Capt. USAAF, 1943-46. Recipient Disting. Contbn. for Applications in Psychology award APA, 1978, Outstanding Sci. Contbn. to Psychology, Md. Psychol. Assn., 1981, Outstanding Achievement in Behavioral and Social Sci. award Wash. Acad. Sci., 1997. Fellow AAAS, Soc. Engring. Psychologists (Franklin V. Taylor award 1963), Human Factors and Ergonomics Soc. (Paul W. Fitts award 1973, Pres.' Disting. Svc. award 1987), Ergonomics Soc. (hon.); mem. Internat. Ergonomics Assn. (Outstanding Contbn. award 1982). Achievements include patent (with others) on Correlation of Seismic Signals.

CHAPDELAINE, LORRAINE ELDER, gerontology nurse; b. Yonkers, N.Y., Sept. 29, 1939; d. Alexander Lindsay Elder and Evelyn Emma Flower Bellini; m. Bernard Grant Dostal, May 15, 1960 (div. Nov. 1972); children: Dana Arthur Dostal, Jeffrey Alexander Dostal. Diploma, Mass. Genl. Hosp. Sch. Nursing, Boston, 1961; BS cum laude, Elms Coll., Chicopee, Mass., 1990; MS, U. Mass., 1992. RN, Mass.; cert. gerontol. clin. specialist. Staff nurse Cooley Dickinson Hosp., Northampton, Mass., 1961-67, Holyoke (Mass.) Hosp., 1967-74; health svc. supr. Mountain View Nursing Home, Montgomery, Mass., 1979-85; staff nurse, supr. Port Charlotte (Fla.) Care Ctr., 1985-87; staff nurse Holyoke Geriatric Authority, 1987-89; temporary staff O'Connell Profl. Svc., Holyoke, 1987-90; asst. prof. clin. nursing U. Mass. Sch. Nursing, Amherst, 1992-93; clin. specialist/wound cons. Hampshire County Vis. Nurse Assn., Northampton, 1992-96; clin. specialist, vis. staff Vis. Nurse Svcs Western Mass., Holyoke, Mass., 1989—; grant writer, adminstr. Innovative Nurse-Managed Well Elderly Foot Clinics, 1993—; pvt. practice in nursing foot care, 1997—; lectr. in field; initiator, adminstr. grant-funded nurse-managed foot clinics for elderly poor.; prin. The Foot Care Nurse, Holyoke, 1997—. Mem. Nat. Gerontol. Nurses Assn., Advanced Practice Gerontol. Nurses Interest Group, Order Eastern Star (Worthy Matron 1981, 84), Sigma Theta Tau. Episcopalian. Avocations: music, gardening. Home and Office: Vis Nurse Svcs Western Mass 3 Vassar Cir Holyoke MA 01040-2627

CHAPDELAINE, PERRY ANTHONY, JR., public health physician, educator; b. Mason City, Iowa, Feb. 23, 1950; s. Perry Anthony Sr. and Ruby Elizabeth (McCurley) C.; m. Catherine Joan Tidwell, May 22, 1981; 1 child, Rachel Maria. BA in Sociology, St. Ambrose U., 1972; MD, Meharry Med. Coll., 1989, MSPH, 1992. Diplomate Am. Bd. Preventive Medicine. CEO, pres. AC Projects Inc., Franklin, Tenn., 1974-86; epidemiologist Meharry Med. Coll., Nashville, 1992-95, asst. prof., 1993-95, dir. preventive medicine residency program, 1995; chief med. physician City of Nashville, Metro Health Dept., 1995—; cons. St. Thomas Hosp. Clin. Ethics Ctr., Nashville, 1993-98, Nashville Prevention Mktg. Initiative, 1994-96; med. dir. Samaritan Recovery Cmty., Nashville, 1993-95; mem. Access Med Plus Peer Rev. Com., Nashville, 1996—. Co-editor: The John W. Campbell Letters, 1985 (Hugo award nominee 1986). Mem. Am. Assn. Pub. Health Physicians, Tenn. Pub. Health Assn., Alpha Chi, Alpha Omega Alpha. Avocations: writing, photography, dulcimer, hiking. E-mail: tonyúchapdelaine@mhd.nashville.org. Home: 7378 Walker Rd Fairview TN 37062 Office: City of Nashville, Davidson County Health Dept 311 23d Ave N Nashville TN 37203

CHAPEL, ROBERT CLYDE, stage director, theater educator; b. June 25, 1945; married. BA in TV, U. Mich., 1967, MA in Theatre, 1968, PhD in Theatre, 1974. Asst. prof. dept. theatre U. Ala., 1974-75; profl. actor L.A., 1975-77; dir. devel. Force Ten Prodns., L.A., 1977-78; v.p. prodn. Trans-Atlantic Enterprises, L.A., 1978-81; actor, dir. L.A., then N.Y.C., 1981-83; dir. BFA mus. theatre program U. Mich., 1983-84; coordinating dir. mus. theatre program Tisch Sch. of Arts NYU, N.Y.C., 1984-86; co-prodr. Shubert Archives Series Lyceum Theatre, N.Y.C., 1984-86; artistic dir. Music Theatre North, Potsdam, N.Y., 1986; freelance dir. N.Y.C., 1986-88; dir. mus. theatre program San Diego State U., 1988-90; prof., chair dept. drama U. Va., 1990—; mng. dir. Heritage Repertory Theatre, Charlottesville, Va., 1990-94, prodr., artistic dir., 1995—; chair Va. Film Festival, 1996—; chmn. pres. commn. on fine arts and performing arts U. Va., 1998—. Mem. SAG, AFTRA, Assn. for Theatre in Higher Edn., Nat. Assn. Schs. of Theatre, Actors Equity Assn., Soc. Stage Dirs. and Choreographers. Home: 1029 Hazel St Charlottesville VA 22902-4904

CHAPEL, THERON THEODORE, quality assurance engineer; b. Jackson County, Mich., Jan. 31, 1918; s. Theron Eugene and Monica Iris (Paton) C.; m. Lucy Eldredge, 1946 (dec. 1973); m. Sue Smith, 1990 (div. Aug. 1995); children: Robert, James. *Mr. Chapel's Great great great great great great great great great grandfather was William Brewster, the religious leader of the Plymouth Colony. His son, Jonathan Brewster, was deputy to the General Court of the Plymouth and Connecticut Colonies. Mr. Chapel's brother, Byron James was a farmer and plant manager for Jafra Cosmetics in Santa Monica, California. His father, Theron Eugene, taught school in several towns in Michigan. His wife, Lucy Eldredge, was a real estate salesperson in Michigan, and Mississippi. His sons are Robert, a former archivist at the University of Michigan, and James, a former auditor and finance officer for the State of Mississippi.* BA, Albion Coll., Mich., 1938; BSE, U. Mich., 1940. Analytical chemist Minn. Mining & Mfg. Co., Detroit, 1940-41; rubber compounder, 1941-43; R&D chemist The Simoniz Co., Chgo., 1946-51; quality control supr. The Simoniz Co., Chgo. and Kankakee, Ill., 1951-53; process devel. engr. Armour Pharm. Labs., Bradley, Ill., 1953-56; product control supr. Acheson Colloids Co., Port Huron, Mich., 1956-61; material treatment and processes quality control rep. Inspector of Naval Material, Chgo., 1962-63; shipbuilding quality control rep., supr. shipbuilding USN, Bay City, Mich., 1963-70; quality assurance specialist supr. Shipbuilding, Conversion & Repair USN, Pascagoula, Miss., 1970-72, quality assurance engr. supr. Shipbuilding, Conversion & Repair, 1973-93; ret. supr. Shipbuilding, Conversion & Repair, USN, Pascagoula, Miss., 1993. With U.S. Army, 1943-46. Mem. ASTM, Am. Soc. Nondestructive Testing, Am. Chem. Soc., Am. Soc. for Quality (sr.). Mem. LDS Ch. Avocations: philosophy, genealogy. Home: 114 Ethel Circle Apt. 3 Ocean Springs MS 39564-3742

CHAPELLE, SUZANNE ELLERY GREENE, history educator; b. Phila., Sept. 21, 1942; d. John Channing and Jessie Horn (Myers) Ellery; m. Michael Thomas Greene, Sept. 15, 1972 (dec. 1973); 1 child, Jennifer; m. Francis Oberlin Chapelle, Apr. 14, 1984. BA, Harvard U., 1964; MA, Johns Hopkins U., 1966, PhD, 1970. Asst. prof. Fed. City Coll., Washington, 1968-69; asst. prof. Am. history Towson State U., Balt., 1969-71; assoc. prof. Am. history Morgan State U., Balt., 1971-75, prof., 1975—. Author: Books for Pleasure, 1976; Baltimore: An Illustrated History, 1980; sr. author: Maryland: A History of its People, 1986; revisions author: A Child's History of the World, 1994. Bd. dirs. Md. Interfaith Coalition for the Environment, 1997—. Mem. Am. Hist. Assn., Am. Studies Assn. (mem. exec. bd. Chesapeake chpt. 1988-90), Popular Culture Assn. (bd. dirs. 1980-82), Orgn. Am. Historians, Md. Hist. Soc. (publs. com. 1998—), Mid-Atlantic Popular Culture Assn. (pres. 1977-80), Balt. County League Environ. Voters (exec. bd. 1992-96), Episcopal Diocese of Md. Com. on the Environ. (sec. 1994—), Ruxton-Riderwood Assn. (bd. govs. 1987-91), The Johns Hopkins Club, The Harvard-Radcliffe Club Md. Episcopalian. Home: 6021 Lakeview Rd Baltimore MD 21210-1033 Office: Morgan State U Hist Dept Baltimore MD 21251

CHAPIN, DEBORAH, artist; b. Ft. Collins, Colo., Jan. 15, 1954; d. Wallace Everett and Nancy Arlene (Jones) Chapin; m. Calvin Lee Keeler, May 25, 1979 (div. Sept. 1987). BS in Biology, Mary Washington Coll./U. Va., 1976; postgrad., USDA Grad. Studies, Washington, 1990-92. One-woman shows include Greenwich (Conn.) Workshop Galleries, 1987, Audubon Naturalist Soc., 1992, 94, 95, Gregg Gallery, N.Y., 1998; group shows include Balt. Museum of Art, 1980, Greenwich Workshop Galleries, 1983, 84, 85, Mystic (Conn.) Seaport Museum, 1984, 85, 86, 87, Md. Hist. Museum, Balt., 1989, Catharine Lorillard Exhbn., 1982, 83, 94, Salmagundi Open, N.Y.C., 1996, others; participant Arts-in-Embassies program, exhibited in Am. Embassies in Abu Dhabi, Quito, Ecuador, Sanaa, Yemen, Bogota, Colombia, Baku, Azerbaydzhanskaya. Mem. Artists Fellowship, Calif. Art Club, Artists of Am., Soc. Nat. des Beaux Arts, Am. Artists Profl. League, Nat. Arts Club. Avocations: hiking, swimming, still and video photography.

CHAPIN, DWIGHT ALLAN, columnist, writer; b. Lewiston, Idaho, June 16, 1938; s. Don Merle and Lucille Verna (Walker) C.; m. Susan Enid Fisk, Feb. 14, 1963 (div. 1973); children—Carla, Adam; m. Ellen Gonzalez, Aug. 10, 1983. B.A., U. Idaho, 1960; M.S. in Journalism, Columbia U., 1961. Reporter Lewiston Morning Tribune, Idaho, 1956-62; reporter, editor Vancouver Columbian, Wash., 1962-65; sportswriter Seattle Post-Intelligencer, 1965-67, Los Angeles Times, 1967-77; columnist San Francisco Examiner, 1977—. Co-author: Wizard of Westwood, 1973; contbr. numerous articles to popular mags. Served with USNG, 1962-68. Recipient Sports Writing award AP, Calif./Nev., 1968-69; Baseball Writing award Am. Assn. Coll. Baseball Coaches. Mem. Sigma Delta Chi (sports writing award Wash. state 1964, 65, 66). Democrat. Avocation: trading card and sports memorabilia collecting. Office: San Francisco Examiner 110 5th St San Francisco CA 94103-2918

CHAPIN, ELLIOTT LOWELL, retired bank executive; b. N.Y.C., Mar. 5, 1917; s. Gilbert Elliott and Elizabeth Lowell (Black) C.; m. Sarah Louise Root, Feb. 12, 1942; children: Bruce Elliott, Gilbert Russell. Student, NYU, 1935-36. Clk. S.I. Savs. Bank, N.Y., 1937-41, officer to pres., 1942-82, trustee, 1974-92, trustee emeritus, 1992-98, dir. emeritus, 1998—; dir. Instns. Group Info. Corp., N.Y.C., 1979-82. Bd. dirs. United Way of S.I., 1979-84; mem. S.I. distbn. com. Greater N.Y. Fund/United Way, 1984-86. Served to capt. U.S. Army, 1941-46; to lt. col. USAFR. Clubs: Richmond County Country, Richmond County Yacht, Staten Island. Lodge: Rotary. Home: 55 Westminster Ct Staten Island NY 10304-1313 Office: SI Savs Bank 15 Beach St Staten Island NY 10304-2713

CHAPIN, FRED, airport executive. Dir. ops. Charleston (S.C.) Internat. Airport. Office: Charleston Internat Airport Charleston Cty Aviation Authorty 5500 International Blvd Charleston SC 29418-6900

CHAPIN, MARY Q., arbitrator, mediator, writer, perfoming artist; b. Shepherdstown, W.VA., May 5, 1933; d. Guy Estil and Anne Mildred (Jones) Quisenberry; m. Edward John Chapin Jr.; children: John Edward, Susan Q. (dec.). SUNY Regent's Degree, 1985; AAS, SUNY, Binghamton, BS, 1991. Pers. adminstr. Mohawk Valley Psychiatric Ctr., Utica, N.Y., 1976-89; arbitrator Am. Arbitration Assn., N.Y.C., 1989-99; pres. Dispute Resolution Internat., New Hartford, N.Y., 1993—; neutral chair NYSDOL Office of Labor Mgmt., Albany, N.Y., 1993—; mem. adv. coun. on safety and security in N.Y. State schs. N.Y. State Dept. Edn., Albany, 1995-97; founder, mem., bd. dirs. Forum on Conflict and Concensus, 1993-94l chair Mohawk Valley Women's History Project, 1998—. Author: Woman's Suffrage: A Dream of Full Citizenship; author, performer An Afternoon with Susan B. Anthony; contbr. articles to profl. jours. Pres. Utica/Rome Metro League of Women Voters, 1992-97; coord. Com. on Met. Orgn., 1995-97; coord. of multicultural commn. League of Women Voters Edn. Fund, 1997; trustee Mohawk Valley Cmty. Coll., 1996—; mem. edn. com. Assn. Bd. of Trustees of C.C., 1997—; Utica C. of C., 1995-98. Recipient Found. award The Found. of SUNY at Binghamton, 1992, Recognition award NYS League of Women Voters, 1995, 97, Recognition award U.S. LWV Edn. Fund, 1998, Labor Mgmt. award Office of Mental Health, 1988. Mem. AAUW (v.p.), Central N.Y. Futurist, Bd. Neighborhood Ctr. Avocations: medical herbalist, human rights and women's rights. Home and Office: 56 Woodbrooke Rd New Hartford NY 13413

CHAPIN, MARYAN FOX, civic worker; b. Easton, Pa., Apr. 26, 1933; d. Louis Rodman and Mary Catherine (Cannon) Fox; m. Richard Chapin, Nov. 3, 1956; children: Aldus Higgins II, Margery Rodman, Marya Marsh, Richard Dickinson. AB, Vassar Coll., 1954. Sec. editorial office New Yorker Mag., Inc., 1954-55; mem. staff admissions office Harvard Coll., Cambridge, Mass., 1956; fin. cons. The Cheswick Ctr., 1982-86; contr. Chapin's Market, Cambridge, 1986-88; co-dir. Cambridge United Fund Campaign, 1959; bd. dirs. Vis. Nurse Assn., Cambridge, 1960-62; trustee Longy Sch. Music, 1974-75; pres. founding bd. trustees New Sch. Music, 1976-77; bd. dirs. Young Audiences of Mass., 1976-83, chairman, 1980-82; adv. bd. Wheelock Coll. Family Theatre, 1985-92; treas. Richards Libr., Georgetown, Maine; chmn., bd. trustees Bowdoin Summer Music Festival, 1997—. Mem. New Eng. Conservatory (bd. overseers 1987-92), Vincent Club. (bd. mgrs. 1961-67). Home: Knubble Rd Georgetown ME 04548

CHAPIN, MELVILLE, lawyer; b. Boston, Dec. 14, 1918; s. Edward Barton and Jeannette (Thomas) C.; m. Elizabeth Ann Parker, Sept. 6, 1940; children: Allan M., Elizabeth M. B.A., Yale U., 1940; J.D., Harvard U., 1943. Bar: Mass. 1943. Of counsel Warner & Stackpole LLP, Boston, 1954—; chmn. bd. dirs. H.B. Smith Co., Inc.; pres., trustee emeritus Phillips Acad.; chmn. emeritus, trustee Mass. Eye and Ear Infirmary and Found. Bd. dirs. Chewonki Found. Inc.; chmn. Yale U. Planned Giving, Coun. Mass. Hist. Soc.; trustee Sturbridge Village; mem. adv. com. Salvation Army; bd. dirs. dir. Bostonian Soc.; mem. leadership coun. New Bedford Whaling Mus.; mem. state adv. com. Salvation Army; v.p. Polly Hill Found. Fellow Am. Bar Found., Mass. Bar Found.; mem. ABA, Boston Bar Assn., Mass. Bar Assn., Internat. Bar Assn., Edgartown Yacht Club (trustee). Home: 15 Traill St Cambridge MA 02138-4738 Office: 75 State St Fl 6 Boston MA 02109-1807

CHAPIN, RICHARD, arbitrator, consultant; b. Boston, Dec. 25, 1923; s. Vinton and Elizabeth (Higgins) C.; m. Maryan Gainor Fox, Nov. 3, 1956; children: Aldus Higgins II, Margery Rodman, Marya Marsh, Richard Dickinson. Grad., Milton Acad., 1942; SB, Harvard U., 1944, MBA, 1949; LLD (hon.), Emerson Coll., 1972. Asst. to treas. Anderson, Davis & Platt, Inc., 1946; journeyman machinist Yale & Towne Co., 1947; various adminstrn. and instnl. positions Harvard Grad. Sch. Bus. Adminstrn., 1949-67; pres. Emerson Coll., Boston, 1967-75; cons.; dir. Norton Co., 1974-90; exec. dir. Cheswick Ctr., 1976-84, dir., 1984-95; bd.d irs. Advanced Mech. Tech., Inc., Alden Yachts, Inc., Nickerson Lumber Co., Splty, Aluminum Co.; bd. advisors Venture Capital Fund Am.; arbitrator N.Y. Stock Exch., Am. Stock Exch., Nat. Assn. Security Dealers. Trustee Higgins Found., Bigelow Lab. Ocean Sci. Served with USNR, 1942-46. Clubs: N.Y. Yacht, Harvard, Tavern, St. Botolph. Home: Knubble Rd HC 33 Box 1440 Georgetown ME 04548-9410 Office: 48 Brattle St Cambridge MA 02138-3705

CHAPIN, RICHARD EARL, librarian; b. Danville, Ill., Apr. 29, 1925; s. Harry W. and Lula May (Briggs) C.; m. Eleanor Jane Lang, Aug. 15, 1949; children: Robert Lang, David Brian, Rebecca Anne. AB, Wabash Coll., 1948; MS, U. Ill., 1949, PhD, 1954; LHD (hon.), Wabash Coll., 1991. Reference asst. Fla. State U., 1949-50; libr. asst. U. Ill., 1950-53, vis. prof., 1957; asst. dir., asst. prof. Sch. Libr. Sci., U. Okla., 1953-55; assoc. libr., assoc. prof. Mich. State U., East Lansing, 1955-59, dir. librs., prof. journalism, 1959-89, dir. librs. emeritus, prof. emeritus, 1989—; libr. advisor United Arab Emirates U., 1989-92; dir. Mich. State U. Press, 1986-90; cons. to govts., founds., colls., and univs.; bd. dirs. Ctr. for Rsch. Librs., 1978-83; bd. dirs. OCLC Users' Coun., 1980-83, pres., 1983. Contbr. articles to libr. periodicals and encys. Mem. East Lansing Human Relations Commn., 1966-69, chmn., 1969; mem. East Lansing Bd. Edn., 1970-74, 75, pres., 1973-74; bd. dirs. W.B. and Candace Thoman Found., 1991—. Served to lt. (j.g.) USNR, 1943-46. Mem. ALA, Mich. Library Assn. (pres. 1967), Assn. Research Libraries (bd. dirs. 1984-87), Blue Key, Sigma Chi, Phi Kappa Phi. Home: 2539 Koala Dr East Lansing MI 48823-7211

CHAPIN, ROY DIKEMAN, JR., automobile company executive; b. Detroit, Sept. 21, 1915; s. Roy Dikeman and Inez (Tiedeman) C.; m. Ruth Mary Ruxton, Oct. 29, 1937 (div.); children: Roy D., Christopher K., William R., Cicely P.; m. Loise Baldwin Wickser, July 17, 1965; children: Alexandra, Robert L., Loise B. A.B., Yale U., 1937. With Hudson Motor Car Co., Detroit, 1938-54; dir. Hudson Motor Car Co., 1946-54; asst. sales mgr. Hudson div. Am. Motors Corp., 1954-55; asst. treas., dir. Am. Motors Corp., 1954-55, v.p., treas., 1955, exec. v.p., 1956-66, exec. v.p., gen. mgr., 1966-67, chmn., chief exec. officer, 1967-78; bd. dirs. Coastal Corp. Mem. Elihu Soc., Country Club of Detroit, Detroit Club, Sankaty Head Club. Office: 333 W Fort St Ste 1960 Detroit MI 48226-3134

CHAPIN, SCHUYLER GARRISON, cultural affairs executive, university dean; b. N.Y.C., Feb. 13, 1923; s. L.H. Paul and Leila H. (Burden) C.; m. Elizabeth Steinway, Mar. 15, 1947 (dec. 1993); children: Henry Burden, Theodore Steinway, Samuel Garrison, Miles Whitworth; m. Catia Zoullas Mortimer, Sept. 15, 1995. Student, Longy Sch. Music, 1940-41; LHD (hon.), NYU, 1974, Hobart/William Smith Coll., 1974; DLitt (hon.), Emerson Coll., 1976; MusD (hon.), Mannes Coll., New Sch., 1990. Spot salesman NBC-TV, N.Y.C., 1947-51; gen. mgr. Tex and Jinx McCary Enterprises, N.Y.C., 1951-53; booking dir. Judson, O'Neill & Judd divsn. Columbia Artists Mgmt., 1953-59; dir. masterworks Columbia Records divsn. CBS, 1959-62, v.p. creative svcs., 1962-63; v.p. programming Lincoln Center for the Performing Arts, 1964-69; exec. producer Amberson Enterprises, N.Y.C., 1969-71; acting gen. mgr. Met. Opera, N.Y.C., 1972-73; gen. mgr. Met. Opera, 1973-75; dean faculty arts Columbia U., 1976-87; v.p. worldwide concert and artist activities Steinway & Sons, N.Y.C., 1990-92; commr. of cultural affairs City of N.Y., 1994—; cons. Carnegie Hall Corp., 1979-87. Author: (autobiography) Musical Chairs, 1977, Leonard Bernstein: Notes from a Friend, 1992, Sopranos, Mezzos, Tenors, Bassos and Other Friends, 1995. Past chmn. Bagby Music Lovers Found.; former chmn., trustee Am. Symphony Orch. League, 1985-92; trustee Naumburg Found., 1949, Richard Tucker Found., 1975-92, Am. Inst. for Verdi Studies, 1975, Bklyn. Philharm., 1978-92, Lenox Music Theatre Group, 1984, Lincoln Ctr. Theatre, 1985-94, Carnegie Hall Soc., 1987, Curtis Inst. Music, 1986, Pres.'s Com. on Arts and Humanities, 1982-90, Redwood Libr. and Athenaeum, 1990-96; chmn., exec. com. Franklin and Eleanor Roosevelt Inst., 1982—. Recipient N.Y. State Conspicuous service cross, 1951, Christopher award, 1971, Emmy awards 1972, 76, 80, Gold Medal Nat. Arts Club, 1983. Club: Century Assn. (N.Y.C.). Home: 655 Park Ave New York NY 10021-5937 *Throughout my career, and indeed my life, I have been fortunate to make my avocation my vocation. I've worked in, around, about and for the arts in a variety of ways. That, I hope, has brought as much happiness to others as it has to me. I have been privileged to be part of what a poet once called the Arts: the Signature of Man.*

CHAPLIN, DAVID DUNBAR, medical research specialist, medical educator; b. London, Aug. 28, 1952; came to U.S., 1952; s. Hugh Jr. and Alice Elizabeth (Dougherty) C.; m. Jane Ellen Bryant; children: Vernon H., Rosalind K., Daniel B. AB, Harvard U., 1973; MD, PhD, Washington U., St. Louis, 1980. Intern, then resident Parkland Meml. Hosp., Dallas, 1980-82; post-doctoral fellow dept. genetics Harvard U. Med. Sch., Boston, 1982-84; asst. prof. medicine Washington U. Sch. Medicine, St. Louis, 1984-91, prof. medicine, 1995—; assoc. investigator Howard Hughes Med. Inst., St. Louis, 1984—. Assoc. editor: The New Biologist, 1990-92, Diabetes, 1992-96; contbr. articles to profl. jours. Mem. grants com. Arthritis Found., Atlanta, 1989-92. Scholar Harvard U., 1972, 73; Jane Coffin Childs Fund for Med. Rsch. fellow, 1982-84. Mem. Am. Soc. Clin. Investigation, Am. Fedn. Clin. Rsch., Am. Assn. Immunologists, Am. Soc. Human Genetics, Alpha Omega Alpha. Democrat. Roman Catholic. Office: Howard Hughes Med Inst 4566 Scott Ave PO Box 8022 Saint Louis MO 63156-8022

CHAPLIN, GEORGE, newspaper editor; b. Columbia, S.C., Apr. 28, 1914; s. Morris and Netty (Brown) C.; m. Esta Lillian Solomon, Jan. 26, 1937; children: Stephen Michael, Jerry Gay. BS, Clemson Coll., 1935; Nieman fellow, Harvard U., 1940-41; HHD (hon.), Clemson U., 1989; LHD (hon.), Hawaii Loa Coll., 1990. Reporter, later city editor Greenville (S.C.) Piedmont, 1935-42; mng. editor Camden (N.J.) Courier-Post, 1946-47, San Diego Jour., 1948-49; mng. editor, then editor New Orleans Item, 1949-58; asso. editor Honolulu Advertiser, 1958-59, editor in chief, 1959-86, editor at large, 1986—; mem. selection com. Jefferson fellowships East-West Ctr.; chmn. Gov.'s Conf. on Year 2000, 1970; chmn. Hawaii Commn. on Year 2000, 1971-74; co-chmn. Conf. on Alt. Econ. Futures for Hawaii, 1973-75; charter mem. Goals for Hawaii, 1979-81; alt. U.S. rep. South Pacific Commn., 1978-81; chmn. search com. for pres. U. Hawaii, 1983; chmn. Hawaii Gov.'s Adv. Coun. on Fgn. Lang. and Internat. Studies, 1983-94; rep. of World Press Freedom Com. on missions to Sri Lanka, Hong Kong, Singapore, 1987. Editor, officer-in-charge: Mid-Pacific edit. Stars and Stripes World War II; editor: (with Glenn Paige) Hawaii 2000, 1973, Presstime in Paradise: The Life and Times of the Honolulu Advertiser 1856-1995, 1998. Bd. dirs. U. Hawaii Rsch. Corp., 1970-72, Inst. for Religion and Social Change, Hawaii Jewish Welfare Fund, Charleston Christian-Jewish Coun.; mem. bd. govs. East-West Ctr., Honolulu, 1980-89, chmn., 1983-89; mem. bd. govs. Pacific Health Rsch. Inst., 1984-90, 93-97, pres., 1995-96; bd. govs. Straub Med. Found., 1989-98, Hawaii Pub. Schs. Found., 1986-87; trustee Clarence T. C. Ching Found., 1986-95; mem. Temple K.K. Beth Elohim; Am. media chmn. U.S.-Japan Conf. on Cultural and Ednl. Interchange, 1978-86; co-founder, v.p. Coalition for Drug-Free Hawaii, 1987-90; panelist ABA Conf., 1989; mem. Civilian Adv. Group, U.S. Army, Hawaii, 1985-95; co-chair Hawaii State Commn. on Judicial Salaries, 1995-98. Capt. AUS, 1942-46. Decorated Star Solidarity (Italy), Order Rising Sun (Japan), Prime Minister's medal (Israel); recipient citations Overseas Press Club, 1961, 72, Headliners award, 1962, John Hancock award, 1972, 74, Distinguished Alumni award Clemson U., 1974, E.W. Scripps award Scripps-Howard Found., 1976, Champion Media award for Econ. Understanding, 1981, Judah Magnes Gold medal Hebrew U. Jerusalem, 1987, Herbert Harley award Am. Judicature Soc., 1991, Regents medal of distinction U. Hawaii, 1998; inductee Honolulu Press Club Hall of Fame, 1987. Mem. Honolulu Symphony Soc., Pacific and Asian Affairs Council (dir.), Internat. Press Inst., Am. Soc. Newspaper Editors (dir., treas. 1973, sec. 1974, v.p. 1975, pres. 1976), Friends of East-West Ctr., Country Club of Charleston, Harbour Club. Home: Ashley House 7AB 14 Lockwood Dr Charleston SC 29401-1126

CHAPLIN, GERALDINE, actress; b. Santa Monica, Calif., July 3, 1944; d. Charles and Oona (O'Neill) C.; 1 child, Shane. Ed. pvt. schs., Royal Ballet Sch., London. Motion pictures include Doctor Zhivago, 1965, Stranger in the House, 1967, I Killed Rasputin, 1968, The Hawaiians, 1970, La casa sin fronteras, 1971, Sur un arbre perche, 1971, Innocent Bystanders, 1972, Z.P.G., 1972, Le Marriage a la Mode, 1973, Ana y los lobos, 1973, The Three Musketeers, 1974, Verflucht dies Amerika!, 1974, La Banda de Jaider, 1974, The Four Musketeers, 1975, Nashville, 1975, Noroit, 1976, Buffalo Bill and the Indians, 1976, Welcome to L.A, 1977, Cria Cuervos, 1977, Elisa, Vida Mia, 1977, Roseland, 1977, In Memorium, 1977, Une Page d'Amour, 1977, Remember My Name, 1978, A Wedding, 1978, Los Ojos Vendados, 1978, L'Adoption, 1978, Mais ou et donc ornicar, 1979, Mama Cumple 100 Anos, 1979, La Viuda de Montiel, 1979, The Mirror Crack'd, 1980, Voyage en Douce, 1981, Les Uns et les Autres, 1981, Bolero, 1982, La Vie est un roman, 1983, Buried Alive, 1984, L'Amour par terre, 1984, Gentile Alouette, 1985, White Mischief, 1988, The Moderns, 1988, I Want to Go Back Home, 1989, The Return of the Musketeers, 1989, The Children, 1990, Buster's Bedroom, 1991, Chaplin, 1992, Hors Saison, 1992, The Age of Innocence, 1993, Words Upon the Window Pane, 1994, Century of Cinema, 1994, Para recibir el canto de los pajaros, 1995, Home for the Holidays, 1995, Olhos da Asia, 1996, Jane Eyre, 1996, Mother Theresa: In the Name of God's Poor, 1997, Cousin Bette, 1998; TV appearances include: (miniseries) The Word, 1978, The Odyssey, 1995 (specials) My Cousin Rachel, 1985, (movies) The Corsican Brothers, 1985, Duel of Hearts, 1992, A Foreign Field, 1994. Office: William Morris Agy c/o Ames Cushing 151 S El Camino Dr Beverly Hills CA 90212-2775*

CHAPLIN, HARVEY, wine and liquor wholesale executive; b. 1929. Chmn., CEO So. Wine Spirits of Am., Miami. Office: Southern Wine & Spirits 1600 NW 163rd St Miami FL 33169-5672*

CHAPLIN, HUGH, JR., physician, educator; b. N.Y.C., Feb. 4, 1923; m. Alice Dougherty, June 16, 1945; 4 children; m. Lee Nelken Robins, Aug. 5, 1998. A.B., Princeton U., 1943; M.D., Columbia U., 1947. Diplomate Am. Bd. Internal Medicine, Nat. Bd. Med. Examiners. Intern Mass. Gen. Hosp., Boston, 1947-48, resident, 1948-50; fellow in hematology Brit. Postgrad. Med. Sch., London, 1951-53; physician in charge Clin. Center Blood Bank, NIH, Bethesda, Md., 1953-55; Commonwealth Fund fellow Wright Fleming Inst. Microbiology, London, 1962-63; Josiah Macy Faculty scholar Wright Fleming Inst. Microbiology, 1975-76; instr. in medicine Washington U. Sch. Medicine, St. Louis, 1955-56, asst. prof. medicine and preventive medicine, 1956-62, asso. dean, chmn. admissions com., 1957-62, asso. prof., 1963-65, prof., 1965, William B. Kountz prof. preventive medicine, 1965-83; dir. IWJ Inst. of Rehab., St. Louis, 1964-72; prof. pathology, dir. Barnes Hosp. Blood Bank, St. Louis, 1983-91; emeritus prof. pathology and medicine, 1991—; mem. Am. Standards Com. for Blood Transfusion Equipment; mem. subcom. on transfusion problems NRC, 1959-62, mem. com. on blood and transfusion problems, 1963-67; chmn. ad hoc blood program research com. ARC, 1967-73, bd. govs., 1978-84. Assoc. editor Transfusion, 1960-98; contbg. editor Vox Sanguinis, 1960-79. Served with USNR, 1942-45. Mem. Am. Fedn. Clin. Research, Central Soc. Clin. Research, Am. Soc. Clin. Investigation, Assn. Am. Physicians, Am., Internat. socs. hematology, Brit. Med. Research Soc., Brit. Royal Soc. Medicine, Am. Assn. Blood Banks (sci. program com. 1959-60, Emily Cooley award 1968, Morton Grove-Rasmussen award 1985), Phi Beta Kappa, Alpha Omega Alpha, Sigma Xi. Office: Washington U Sch Medicine Box 8118 4949 Barnes Hospital Plz Saint Louis MO 63110-1003

CHAPLIN, JAMES CROSSAN, IV, securities firm executive; b. Sewickley, Pa., Mar. 20, 1933; s. James Crossan III and Gretchen (Brown) C.; m. Martha A. Tinker, May 19, 1956 (div. Jan. 1980); 1 son, W. Craig II; m. Carol C. Mullaugh, Apr. 12, 1980. Grad., Phillips Acad., 1951; A.B., Princeton U., 1955. With firm Chaplin McGuiness & Co. Inc. (now part of Parker/Hunter, Inc.), Pitts., 1959-74; v.p. retail ops. Chaplin McGuiness & Co. Inc. (now part of Parker/Hunter, Inc.), 1971-73, sr. v.p. mktg., 1973-82, sec.-treas., also dir., mem. exec. com., 1973-82; v.p. Parker/Hunter, Inc., 1974-82; chmn., treas. dir. Chaplin-Mullaugh, Inc., 1982—; bd. dirs. Rymac Mortgage Investment Corp. Pres. Sewickley Cemetery; treas. Old Sewickley Post Office Corp., 1986—, Leet Twp. Mcpl. Authority, 1975—; chmn. Sewickley Parking Authority, 1986—. 1st lt. USAF, 1956-59. Mem. Bond Club Pitts. (pres. 1971-72). Clubs: Duquesne (Pitts.), Allegheny Country (Sewickley), Princeton Club (N.Y.C.), Princeton Univ. Cottage Club (Princeton, N.J.). Home: 24 Myrtle Hill Rd Sewickley PA 15143-8700 Office: PO Box 567 435 Beaver St Sewickley PA 15143-1543*

CHAPLIN, PEGGY FANNON, lawyer; b. Guantanamo Bay Naval Base, Cuba, Nov. 22, 1940; d. Raymond Gerard Fannon and Joan Marie (Carguil) Boyce. BS, Johns Hopkins U., 1971; JD, U. Md., 1973; LLM in Internat. Comml. Law, Georgetown U., 1983. Bar: Md. 1973, U.S. Dist. Ct. Md. 1973, U.S. Ct. Internat. Trade 1975, U.S. Ct. Appeals (fed. cir.) 1986, (D.C. cir.) 1988. V.p. Vanguard Shipping & Import, Balt., 1972-77, F.W. Myers & Co., Inc., Balt., 1977-84; assoc. Ober, Kaler, Grimes & Shriver, Balt., 1984-91, ptnr., 1992-97; ptnr. Sandler, Travis & Rosenberg, P.A., Balt., 1997—; chair Johns Hopkins U. Inst. of Policy Studies com. Logistics and the Economy, 1996—. Contbr. articles to bar jours. Mem. Gov.'s Commn. World Trade Efforts, 1984, Balt. City Wage Commn., 1986-90, Md. Trade Policy Com., 1986; chair 2d Ann. Md. Internat. Trade Conf.; chair air cargo devel. com. BWI Econ. Devel. Coun., 1993-96. Mem. NAFTA (chpt. 19 roster), Md. State Bar Assn. (chair internat. comml. law sect. 1991-92), Women's Bar Assn. Md. (pres. 1977-78), Md. Internat. Trade Assn. (pres. 1984-86), Md. C. of C. (chmn. internat. trade com. 1984-97), Am. Arbitration Assn. (panelist), Am. Assn. Exporters and Importers (chmn. logistics com.). Office: Sandler Travis & Rosenberg PA 111 S Calvert St Ste 2700 Baltimore MD 21202-6143

CHAPMAN, ALGER BALDWIN, finance executive, lawyer; b. Portland, Maine, Sept. 28, 1931; s. Alger Baldwin Sr. and Elizabeth (Ives) C.; m. Beatrice Bishop, Oct. 30, 1983; children: Alger III, Samuel P., Andrew I., Henry H. BA, Williams Coll., 1953; JD, Columbia U., 1956. Bar: N.Y. 1957. Pres. Shearson, Hammill & Co., 1970-74; co-chmn. Shearson & Co., 1974-81; vice chmn. Am. Express Bank, 1982-85; chmn., chief exec. officer Chgo. Bd. Options Exchange, 1986-97; vice chmn. ABN Amro, Inc., 1996—; vice chmn. ABN AMRO Inc., 1997—; bd. dirs. ISO New Eng., HDO, Current Assets LLC. Clubs: Chgo., Racquet Club Chgo.; Metropolitan (N.Y.C.), Chgo. Club. Avocations: golf, skiing, reading. Home: 1500 N Lake Shore Dr Chicago IL 60610-6657 Office: ABN AMRO Inc 208 S Lasalle St Ste 300 Chicago IL 60604-1099*

CHAPMAN, ALLEN FLOYD, management educator, college dean; b. Dawson, N.Mex., Apr. 14, 1930; s. Thomas and Velma (Sylva) C.; m. Ann Bunker; children: Margaret Ann, Nancy Elizabeth. BS, U. Colo., 1951; D Bus. Adminstrn., Harvard U., 1965; MBS, Hartford Grad. Ctr., 1982. Commd. ensign USN, 1951, advanced through grades to lt., resigned, 1960; rsch. assoc. Harvard U., Boston, 1961-63; dean grad. sch. bus. C.W. Post Ctr., L.I. U., Greenvale, N.Y., 1963-77; prof. mgmt. Hartford (Conn.) Grad. Ctr., 1977-96, dean Sch. of Mgmt., 1977-79, 81-84, 87-89; prof. mgmt. Sch. Mgmt. Rensselaer at Hartford, 1996—; pres., founder various pvt. corps., N.Y., Conn., 1965—; cons. to various corps. and depts. and agys. of U.S. Govt. Patentee in field. Recipient Cert. for Patriotic Civilian Svc. U.S. Army, 1973. Home: 64 Great Hl Pond Rd Portland CT 06480-1315

CHAPMAN, ALVAH HERMAN, JR., newspaper executive; b. Columbus, Ga., Mar. 21, 1921; s. Alvah Herman and Wyline (Page) C.; m. Betty Bateman, Mar. 22, 1943; children: Dale Page Chapman Webb, Chris Ann Chapman Hilton. BS, The Citadel, 1942, hon. degree, 1971; hon. degree, Barry U., 1985, Fla. Internat. U., 1988, U. Miami, Coral Gables, Fla., 1989, U. Notre Dame, 1991. Bus. mgr. Columbus Ledger, 1945-53; exec. v.p., gen. mgr. St. Petersburg (Fla.) Times, 1953-57; pres., pub. Morning News and Evening Press, Savannah, Ga., 1957-60; exec. Knight-Ridder Newspapers, Inc., Miami, Fla., 1960-89; exec. com. Knight-Ridder Newspapers, Inc., 1960—, exec. v.p., 1967-73, pres., 1973-82, chief exec. officer, 1976-88, chmn., 1982-89, dir., chmn. exec. com., 1984-95; v.p., gen. mgr. Miami Herald, 1962-70, pres., 1970-82; lectr. Am. Press Insts., Columbia. Bd. dirs. Miami Coalition for a Drug-Free Community; mem. Pres.'s Drug Adv. Coun., 1989-92; chmn. emeritus Fla. Internat. U. Found.; founding chmn. Community Anti-Drug Coalitions Am.; chmn. We Will Rebuild, 1992-93, Gov.'s Commn. on Homeless, 1992-94, Community Partnership for Homeless, Inc., 1993—. Maj. USAAF, WWII. Decorated D.F.C. with 2 oak leaf clusters, Air medal with 5 clusters U.S., Croix de Guerre; named one of 5 Outstanding Young Men in Ga., 1951, Outstanding Young Man, Columbus Jr. C. of C., 1952, Dade County's Outstanding Citizen of 1968-69, Brigham Young U. Internat. Businessman of Yr., 1984; recipient Citadel Palmetto award, 1985, Isaiah Thomas award Rochester Inst. Tech., 1986, Joseph Wharton Statesman award, 1988, United Negro Coll. Fund's Disting. Svc. award, 1988, The Miami Herald Spirit of Excellence Lifetime Achievement award, 1989, Anne Ackerman Disting. Floridian award, 1991, LeRoy Collins Lifetime Achievement award Leadership Fla., 1992, United Way Dorothy Shula award for Volunteerism, 1994, Salvation Army Red Shield award, 1994, ARC Humanitarian of Yr. award, 1994, Health Found. of South Fla. Concern awardm 1995, Drum Maj. of Justice award Miami-Dade Cmty. Coll., 1996, Spirit of Martin Luther King Jr. Parade & Festivities Dinner Com. award, 1996, Citizen of Yr. award Gray Panthers North Dade, 1996, Resolution State Fla., 1996, Named Hon. Dir. Fla. C. of C., 1997. Mem. Newspaper Assn. Am., Am. Newspaper Pub. Assn. (chmn., pres. 1986-87), So. Newspapers Pubs. Assn. (pres. 1976). Methodist. Home: Grove Harbour 1690 S Bayshore Ln # 10ab Miami FL 33133-4073 Office: Knight Ridder Inc One Herald Plz Miami FL 33132-1693

CHAPMAN, ANTHONY BRADLEY, psychiatrist; b. Salem, Mass., June 22, 1938; s. Anthony Bredick and Gladys Gwendolyn (Poole) C.; m. Ella Mueller, Aug. 30, 1963; children: Bradley, Jeffrey. BS with honors, Northeastern U., 1961; MD, Stanford U., 1966. Diplomate Am. Bd. Psychiatry and Neurology. Rsch. asst. Harvard Med. Sch., Boston, 1957-61; intern Case-Western Res. U., Cleve., 1966-67; resident Johns Hopkins Hosp., Balt., 1967-69, fellow in behavioral medicine, 1967-69; fellow in child psychiatry U. Pa., Phila., 1969-71; pvt. practice Alexandria, Va., 1973—; dir. Attention Disorder Ctr. No. Va., Alexandria, 1991—; guest lectr. Children and Adults with Attention Deficit Disorder, Arlington, Va., 1990-96. Editor Hyperactive Child Newsletter, 1974-78. Maj. U.S. Army, 1971-73. Recipient Outstanding Tchr. award Am. Acad. Family Practice, 1976-81. Mem. Am. Med. Soc., Am. Psychiat. Electrophysiology Assn., Va. Med. Soc., Alexandria Med. Soc., Attention Deficit Disorders Profls. No. Va. (pres. 1990-92). Avocations: jazz, Brazilian music, tennis, skiing. Office: 2059 Huntington Ave Ste 108 Alexandria VA 22303-1602

CHAPMAN, CONRAD DANIEL, lawyer; b. Detroit, July 31, 1933; s. Conrad F. and Alexandrine C. (Baranski) C.; m. Carol Lynn DeBash, Sept. 1, 1956; children: Stephen Daniel, Richard Thomas, Suzanne Marie. BA, U. Detroit, 1954, JD summa cum laude, 1957; LLM in Taxation, Wayne State U., 1964. Bar: Mich. 1957, U.S. Dist. Ct. (so. dist.) Mich. 1957. Pres., chmn. bd. dirs. Powers, Chapman, DeAgostino, Meyers & Milia and predecessor firms, Troy, Mich., 1964—. Mem. ABA, Detroit Bar Assn., Oakland Bar Assn., Am. Arbitration Assn., Detroit Estate Planning Coun., Oakland Estate Planning Coun., Nat. Assn. Estate Planning Counc., Detroit Athletic Club, Detroit Golf Club, Elks. Office: Powers Chapman DeAgostino 3001 W Big Beaver Rd Ste 704 Troy MI 48084-3193

CHAPMAN, DELORES, elementary education educator; b. Chgo., June 22, 1945; d. John Calvin and Julia (Frazier) C. AA, Kennedy-King Coll., 1966; BA, Northeastern Ill. U., 1968, MA, 1979. Tchr. Chgo. Bd. Edn., 1968—; v.p. Chapman's Security Systems, Inc., Country Club Hills, Ill., 1990—; chpt. I reading tchr. Fed. Govt./Chgo. Bd. Edn., Chgo. Archdiocese, 1982-85; mem. profl. poers. adv. com. Carver Primary Sch., Chgo., 1990—, chmn. sci. fair, 1987-91; chmn. Emmanuel Christian Sch. Bd., Chgo., 1996. Vice chmn. Emmanuel Christian Sch. Bd., Chgo., 1992; dir. Emmanual Bapt. Ch. Children's Choir, 1973—. Chgo. Found. for Edn. grantee, 1992. Mem. NAACP, ASCD, Nat. Sci. Tchrs. Assn., Ill. Sci. Tchrs. Assn., Northeastern Ill. U. Alumni Assn., Ill. Coun. Tchrs. Math. Avocations: playing the piano, reading. Home: 18600 Village West Dr Hazel Crest IL 60429-2462

CHAPMAN, DONALD D., retired naval officer, lawyer; b. Thalia, Tex., Dec. 9, 1917; s. William Gardner and Bertha (Brown) C.; m. Norene Vernetta Elam, Dec. 30, 1942; children—Ronald Warren, Randall Douglas. B.A., Tex. Tech. Coll., 1939; LL.B., U. Tex., 1942; grad., Army Judge Adv. Sch., 1959. Bar: Tex., Va. bars. Commd. ensign U.S. Navy, 1942, advanced through grades to rear adm., 1968; gen. line duty, 1942-46; comdg. officer U.S.S. PC 792, 1945-46; asst. dist. legal officer Hdqrs. 8th Naval Dist., New Orleans, 1946-49; staff legal officer to comdr. Amphibious Force, U.S. Pacific Fleet, 1949-51; atty. Mil. Justice div. Office Judge Adv. Gen., 1951-55; staff legal officer to comdr. in chief U.S. Atlantic Fleet, 1955-58; dir. adminstrv. law div. Office Judge Adv. Gen., 1959-63; dist. legal officer Hdqrs. 14th Naval Dist., Pearl Harbor, Hawaii, 1963-66; chmn. bd. rev. Office Judge Adv. Gen., 1966-67, dir. adminstrv. law div., 1967-68, dep. judge adv. gen., 1968-71. Decorated Legion of Merit and; numerous service and area ribbons; recipient Distinguished Alumnus award Tex. Tech. Coll., 1968. Mem. Va., Tex. state bars, Judge Advocates Assn. (pres. 1975-76), Am., Fed., Inter-Am. bar assns. Home: 3400 N Piedmont St Arlington VA 22207-5362

CHAPMAN, GARY H., artist, educator. BS in Indsl. Arts, Berea Coll., 1984, BA in Art, 1984; MFA in Painting and Drawing, Cranbrook Acad. Art, 1986. lectr. Birmingham Mus. Art, Montgomery Mus. Fine Arts, Vanderbilt U., Nashville, Fla. State U., Tallahassee, U. Ga., Athens; vis. artist lectr. Wimbledon Sch. Art, London, Kent Inst. Art and Design, Canterbury, Eng., Carmarthenshire (Wales) Coll. Tech. and Art, U. Ulster, Belfast, No. Ireland. One-man shows include Blue Spiral 1 Gallery, Asheville, N.C., U. Miami The New Gallery, Coral Gables, Fla., U. Ga., The Main Gallery, Sch. Art, Athens, U. Cin., The Aranoff Ctr. DAAP Gallery, U. Art Mus., U. Southwestern La., Lafayette, Montgomery (Ala.) Mus. Fine Arts; group exhbns. include Birmingham (Ala.) Mus. Art, Southeastern Ctr. for Contemporary Art, Winston-Salem, N.C., Cummer Mus. Art, Jacksonville, Fla., Huntsville (Ala.) Mus. Art, Hunter Mus. Am. Art, Chattanooga, Columbus (Ga.) Mus. Art, Alexandria (La.) Mus. Art; represented in permanent collections Huntsville Mus. Art, Birmingham Mus. Art, Montgomery Mus. Fine Arts, Mobile (Ala.) Mus. Art, Fla. State U. Mus. Art, Tallahassee, and pvt. collections. Visual Arts fellow Nat. Endowment for the Arts, So. Arts Fedn., 1996; faculty rsch. grantee U. Ala., Birmingham, 1991, 93, 97, 98, fellow grantee Ala. State Coun. on the Arts, 1994-95. Office: c/o Blue Spiral One 38 Biltmore Ave Asheville NC 28801*

CHAPMAN, GERALD WESTER, educator; b. Rusk, Tex., July 20, 1927; s. Gerald Benson and Eunice (Wester) C.; m. Ruth Rimmer, Dec. 31, 1950 (div. 1967); children: Robin Chapman Stacey, Gerald Wester Jr.; m. Karen Carbone, Dec., 1968 (div. 1972). BA, So. Meth. U., Dallas, 1949, MA, 1951; PhD, Harvard U., 1957. Instr. Northwestern U., Evanston, Ill., 1954-57; instr. Harvard U., Cambridge, Mass., 1957-60, lectr., 1960-61, vis. prof., summer 1968, 70; asst. prof. U. Tex., Austin, 1961-62; assoc. prof. English, U. Denver, 1962-65, prof., 1965—, Phipps prof., 1967-76; mem. vis. com. dept. English, Harvard Bd. Overseers, Cambridge, 1967-73. Author: Edmund Burke: The Practical Imagination, 1967, Literary Criticism in England 1660-1800, 1966; editor: Essays on Shakespeare, 1965; co-founder, assoc. editor Denver Quar., 1966-76. John Simon Guggenheim fellow, 1977-78. Home: 2512 S University #709 Denver CO 80210-6162 Office: U Denver Denver CO 80208

CHAPMAN, GILBERT BRYANT, physicist; b. Uniontown, Ala., July 8, 1935; s. Gilbert Bryant and Annie Lillie (Stallworth) C.; m. Loretta Woodward, June 5, 1960 (dec. Sept. 1994); children: Annie L., Bernice M., Cedric N., David O., Ernest P., Frances Q.H., Gilbert Bryant III. BS in Math. and Chemistry, Baldwin Wallace Coll., Berea, Ohio, 1968; MS in Physics, Cleve. State U., 1973; MBA, Mich. State U., 1990; postgrad, Kent State U., Ohio, 1974-76. Phys. sci. technician NASA-Lewis Rsch. Ctr., Cleve., 1953-68, emission spectroscopist, 1968-75, materials engr., 1975-77; sr. rsch. engr. Ford Motor Co., Redford Twp., Mich., 1977-83, project engr., 1983-86; adv. materials testing specialist Chrysler Corp., Highland Park, Mich., 1986-89; adv. materials specialist Chrysler Corp., Madison Heights, Mich., 1989-91, advanced materials and product exec., 1991-95, advanced materials cons., 1995-98; sr. mgr. advanced materials and product devel. DaimlerChrysler Corp., Madison Heights, Mich., 1998—; chmn. auto. com. '87 Soc. Mfg. Engrs. Composites Group, Dearborn, 1987, chair bd., 1996; chmn. ind. adv. bd. NDE/Ctr., Iowa State U., Ames, 1989, 90; mem. indsl. adv. bd. Inst. for Mfg. Rsch., Wayne State U., Ctrl. State U., U. Tex.-Pan Am., U. Mich.-Dearborn; chair Internat. Symposium on Automotive Tech. and Automation Materials Conf., 1996, 98, Automotive Composites Consortium, 1996.

Contbr. articles to profl. jours., chpts. to books. Lay leader, elder SDA Ch. of Southfield, Mich., 1983-95; bd. trustees Mt. Vernon Acad., Ohio, 1972-76; lay adv. coun. Ohio Conf. SDA, 1974-77. With USAF, 1959-61. Recipient Group Achievement award, NASA Lewis Rsch. Ctr., 1970, Apollo Achievement award, 1968, Mayor Archer's Proclamation, Motor City Youth Fedn., 1994, Spirit of Detroit award Detroit City Coun., 1994; named one of Best and Brightest Profls., Dollars and Sense Mag., 1993, Black Engr. of Yr. and Career Achievement award Black Engrng. Mag., 1999. Fellow Am. Soc. Nondestructive Testing (cert. level III 6 NDT methods); mem. AAAS, ASM (polymer composites program com. paper 1986), ASTM, IEEE, SAE (award for excellence in oral presentation), Am. Chem. Soc., Am. Phys. Soc., Am. Soc. for Composites, Engrng. Soc. Detroit (sci. com., ASM/ESD Best Paper award 1993), Fedn. of Analytical Chemists, Nat. Tech. Assn. (Cleve. program com.), Soc. for Applied Spectroscopy (Cleve. vice chair, sec.), Soc. Mfg. Engrs. (chaired CMA adv. bd.), Soc. Physics Students (pres.), Internat. Symposium on Automative Tech. and Automation (chair materials conf. 1996). Achievements include patent for infrared inspection method for friction welds in thermoplastics and advanced vehicle concepts; development of low-frequency ultrasonic inspection methods for polymer composites and adhesive bond joints; co-development of D.C. arc method of determining work functions of refractory alloys, spectrochemical analysis of microgram-size samples. Home: 17860 Bonstelle Ave Southfield MI 48075-3452 Office: Chrysler Corp 30900 Stephenson Hwy Madison Heights MI 48071-1617 *The persistant pursuit of moral and ethical values, faith and the concomitant virtues while seeking to serve more effectively, can lead to a successful and satisfying life.*

CHAPMAN, GILBERT WHIPPLE, JR., publishing company executive; b. N.Y.C., July 1, 1933; s. Gilbert W. and Katherin (Bright) C.; m. Judith Coste, June 14, 1956; 1 child, Gilbert W. III. B.A., Yale U., 1956. Pub. McGraw-Hill, Inc., N.Y.C., 1958-72; exec. v.p., dir. Morgan Grampain, Inc., N.Y.C., 1971-75; pres. Pub. Group Esquire Inc., N.Y.C., 1975-78; pres., dir. Diversion Communications, Inc., N.Y.C., 1978-85, Kalo Communications, Inc., N.Y.C., 1985-91; pub. U.S. Banker Mag., 1985-91; chmn., CEO Cemark, Inc., 1991—. Trustee Village of Mill Neck, 1993—, Choate Sch., Walingford, Conn., 1978, L.I. Nature Conservancy, 1985-90, Pomfret (Conn.) Sch., 1986-91; bd. dirs. Planned Parenthood of Nassau County, 1985—, Cmty. Hosp., Glen Cove, 1986-90, North Shore U. Hosp., 1990-94. Mem. Racquet and Tennis Club, Piping Rock Club. Republican. Episcopalian. Home: Factory Pond Rd Locust Valley NY 11560-1405 Office: 13531 E Boundary Rd Midlothian VA 23112-3953

CHAPMAN, HUGH MCMASTER, banker; b. Spartanburg, S.C., Sept. 11, 1932; s. James Alfred and Martha (Marshall) C.; m. Anne Allston Morrison, Dec. 27, 1958 (dec. Mar. 1993); children: Anne Allston, Rachel Buchanan, Mary Morrison. BSBA, U. N.C., 1955. With Citizens & So. Nat. Bank S.C., 1958—, pres., 1971-74, chmn. bd., 1974-91; pres. Citizens & So. Corp., Atlanta, 1986-91; vice chmn. C&S/Sovran Corp., 1990-91; chmn. Nations Bank S., 1992-97; ret., 1997; bd. dirs. SCANA Corp., Inman Mills., PrintPack, Inc., West Point Stevens. Trustee East Lake Cmty. Fedn., Duke Endowment. 1st lt. USAF, 1955-57. Office: NationsBank Plz 54th Fl 600 Peachtree St Fl 54 Atlanta GA 30308

CHAPMAN, JAMES ALBION, novelist, publisher; b. Oakland, Calif., Nov. 10, 1955; s. David Duane and Esther June (Stormont) C. BA in English, U. Calif., Berkeley, 1978. Pub. Fugue State Press, N.Y.C., 1992—. Author: Our Plague: A Film from New York, 1993, The Walls Collide as You Expand, 1993, Glass: Pray the Electrons Back to Sand, 1995, In Candyland it's Cool to Feed on Your Friends, 1997. Office: Fugue State Press PO Box 80 New York NY 10276-0080

CHAPMAN, JAMES L. (JIM CHAPMAN), former congressman; b. Washington, Mar. 8, 1945. BBA, U. Tex.; JD, So. Meth. U. Dist. atty. Tex., 1977-85; mem. 99th-104th Congresses from 1st Tex. dist., Washington, 1985-96; mem. appropriations com.; ptnr. Arter & Hadden, Washington, 1996—. Home: 2691 Marcey Rd Arlington VA 22207-5231 Office: Arter & Hadden 1801 K St NW Ste 400K Washington DC 20006-1301*

CHAPMAN, JAMES PAUL, university official; b. Cleve., Nov. 11, 1943; s. Paul Edward and Alice (McDevitt) C.; m. Patricia Ann Daniel, Dec. 30, 1967; children: J. Daniel, Andrew A. BA, St. Meinrad Coll., 1965; MS in Edn., Ind. U., 1967, MA, 1967, PhD, 1972. Asst. dir. acad. affairs U. Ky., Madisonville Community Coll., 1972-74; asst. univ. budget dir. U. Ky., Lexington, 1974-76, spl. asst. to v.p. acad. affairs, 1975-80, asst. v.p. acad. affairs, 1981-82, asst. vice chancellor adminstrn., 1982-89, asst. chancellor, 1990-96, adj. prof. honors, 1994-98, faculty classics, 1976-98, vice chancellor pub. svc. and outreach, 1996-98; pres. Shawnee State U., 1998—; acad. cons. Indonesia, 1988, Croatia, 1994; coord. Coll. Bus. Mgmt. Inst., Lexington, 1987-91. Forum moderator Sta. WKYT-TV, Lexington, 1980-94. Co-chair Task Force Equality Pub. Schs., Fayette County, Ky., 1988-89; bd. dirs. Bluegrass chpt. NCCJ, Lexington, 1988-90; mem. Lexington Commn. Race Rels., 1988-98; trustee, overseer St. Meinrad Coll., 1991-97. Capt. U.S. Army, 1968-71, Vietnam. Decorated Bronze Star. Mem. So. Assn. Coll. and Univ. Bus. Officers, Assn. Gen. and Liberal Studies (exec. bd. 1984-86). Avocations: running, tennis. Home: 1840 Traveller Rd Lexington KY 40504-2006 Office: Shawnee State U 940 2d St Portsmouth OH 45662-4344

CHAPMAN, JEFFERSON, museum director; b. Kinston, N.C., Mar. 13, 1943; married; 2 children. BA in Anthropology, Yale U., 1965; MAT in History and Edn., Brown U., 1968; MA in Anthropology, U. N.C., 1973, PhD in Anthropology, 1975. Tchr. Webb Sch., Knoxville, Tenn., 1965-67, tchr., chmn. social studies dept., 1968-71, tchr. summer enrichment program, 1969, dir. Field Sch. in Archaeology, 1970-71; rsch. asst. prof. dept. anthropology U. Tenn., Knoxville, 1975—, rsch. assoc. prof., 1984—, curator archaeology Frank H. McClung Mus., 1981-90, dir., 1990—; part time tchr. Webb Sch. Knoxville, 1981—; peer reviewer Delores Archaeol. Project, Southwestern Colo., U.S. Dept. Interior, Water and Power Resources Sv. Project; periodic peer reviewer proposals submitted to Nat. Geog. Sof., NSF, NEH; chmn. Tenn. Archaeol. Adv. Coun., 1988—. Contbr. articles to profl. jours. Bd. advocates Planned Parenthood Assn. Knox County, 1985—; trustee Webb Sch. Knoxville, 1975-81, chmn., 1986—; bd. dirs. Knoxville Symphony Soc., 1977—; bd. dirs. Lamar House-Bijou, 1982-90, exec. officer, 1983-90; bd. dirs. Tenn. Children's Dance Ensemble, 1984-88, Thompson Ctr., 1984—; mem. Knoxville Bicentennial Hist. Com., 1990-91; mem. dir. search com. Knoxville Mus. Art, 1989, 91; mem. Arts Coun. Adv. Panel, 1984-86. Recipient Outstanding Young Educator award Farragut Jaycees, 1971, Disting. Alumnus award Webb Sch. Knoxville, 1991; named hon. fellow Lower Miss. Survey, Peabody Mus., Harvard U., 1987. Fellow Am. Anthropol. Assn.; mem. Am. Assn. Museums, Am. Soc. Conservation Archaeology (exec. bd. 1981-83), Archaeol. Soc. Am. (pres. East Tenn. chpt. 1982-83), Archaeol. Soc. N.C., Assn. Field Archaeology, Coun. Mus. Anthropology, Ala. Archaeol. Soc., Museums of Knoxville (treas. 1990—), Soc. Am. Archaeology (nominating com. 1983-90), Soc. Historic Archaeology, Soc. Profl. Archeologists (dir. at large 1981-83), Southeastern Archaeol. Conf., Southeastern Mus. Conf., Tenn. Anthropol. Assn. Home: 2229 Duncan Rd Knoxville TN 37919-9112 Office: Frank H McClung Mus U Tenn 1327 Circle Park Dr Knoxville TN 37996-3200*

CHAPMAN, JOHN ANDREW, association executive; b. Evanston, Ill., Oct. 12, 1928; s. Roger Edington and Margaret Holloway (Morgan) C.; m. Betsy Miller, June 23, 1951; children: Andrew K., Jean M., Margaret M., Peter S. BS, Northwestern U., 1950. Cert. Nat. Inst. for Orgn. Mgmt. Asst. dir. pub. rels. Northwestern U., Evanston, 1950-54; asst. mgr. Joliet Assn. Commerce, Ill., 1954-57; mgr. Twin Cities Area C. of C., Benton Harbor and St. Joseph, Mich., 1957-67; pres. Muskegon Area Devel. Council and C. of C., Mich., 1967-74, Charleston C. of C., W.Va., 1974-94; mng. dir. Kanawha Pastoral Counseling Ctr., 1994-98. Former mem. bd. dirs. Charleston Symphony; former chmn. Berrien County Planning Commn.; past treas. Tri-Cap, Inc. (tri-county anti-poverty program); past v.p. Southwestern br. Mich. Children's Aid Soc.; past sec. Bishop Whittemore Found.; past vestryman St. John's, St. Edward's and St. Gregory's Episcopal Chs.; past Warden St. Augustine's Episcopal Ch.; mem. emeritus Salvation Army, Charleston; active Charleston Job Corps; past treas. W.Va. Taxpayers Assn.; pres. Charleston Leadership Coun. Pub. Safety; bd. dirs. W.Va. Cmty. Police Inst., Eisenhower Math-Sci. Consortium; bd. dirs. Charleston Renaissance Corp. Served with USAF, 1951-52. Mem. W.Va. C. of C. Execs. (past pres.), Mich. C. of C. Execs. (past pres.), Am. C. of C. Execs. (bd. dirs.), So. Assn. C. of C. Execs. (past pres.), Anvil Club, Rotary (program chmn. Charleston 1981-82). Republican. Home: 209 Ashby Ave Charleston WV 25314-1009

CHAPMAN, JOHN EDMON, university dean, pharmacologist, physician; b. Springfield, Mo., July 5, 1931; s. Loran Edmon and Bertha Gay (Duncan) C.; m. Judy Jean Cox, Mar. 9, 1968. BEd, BS in Biology and Chemistry, Southwest Mo. State Coll., 1954; MD, U. Kans., Kansas City, Kans., 1958; MD (hon.), Karolinska Med. Inst., Stockholm, 1987. Diplomate Nat. Bd. Med. Examiners (mem.-at-large, 1980—, fin. com. 1989—, bylaws com. exec. bd.). Intern Kans. Med. Ctr., 1958-59; asst. chief med. staff U. Ariz., Tucson, 1959-60; resident and fellow in internal medicine and clin. pharmacology U. Kans. Med. Ctr., 1960-63; instr. medicine and pharmacology Sch. Medicine U. Kans., 1961-62, asst. to assoc. prof. pharmacology, 1962-67, asst. dean to assoc. dean student affairs, 1963-67, coordinator med. edn. for nat. def., 1963-67; assoc. dean for edn. Sch. Medicine Vanderbilt U., Nashville, 1967-75, dean Sch. Medicine, 1975—; co-chmn. Liaison Com. on Med. Edn., 1988; fgn. adj. prof. Karolinska Inst., Stockholm; mem., chair composite com. U.S. Med. Licensing Examiners, chmn., 1997—. Mem. steering com. Health Policy Agenda for Am. People, 1982-87; mem. exec. bd. Mid. Tenn. couns. Boy Scouts Am., Nashville, 1984—; active Leadership Nashville, 1985—; bd. dirs. Health Edn. Media Assn., Washington, 1973-84. Recipient Medal of Achievement, 1979, Crystal Gavel award in Internat. Medicine, 1986 Karolinska Med. Inst., Medal of Merit Rene Descartes Sch. of Medicine, Paris; named Winthrop Sterlin Disting. Lectr. U. Kans. Med. Ctr., 1982, William Root Prof. Med. Edn. U. Kans. Med. Ctr., 1982, William Root Prof. Med. Edn. U. Kans. Med. Ctr., 1985, Disting. Alumnus of Yr. U. Kansas Med. Ctr. Sch. of Medicine, 1988. Fellow ACP; mem. AMA (chmn. sect. on med. schs. 1981-83, founding mem. sect. on med. schs., del. ho. of dels., coun. on med. edn. 1989—, accreditation coun. for grad. med. edn.), Am. Coll. Clin. Pharmacology (life, regent 1972-82, 89—), Am. Soc. Clin. Pharmacology and Therpaeutics, Am. Acad. Mgmt., Am. Acad. Med. Adminstrn., Assn. Am. Med. Colls. (coun. deans, adminstrv. bd. coun. deans 1977-84, exec. coun. 1977-84), Soc. Med. Cons. to Armed Forces, Alpha Omega Alpha. Office: Vanderbilt U Sch Medicine D-3300 Med Ctr North 21st Ave S at Garland Ave Nashville TN 37232-2104

CHAPMAN, JOHN WILLIAM, JR., marketing executive; b. Greensboro, N.C., Mar. 4, 1955; s. John William and Mary Elizabeth (Arndt) C.; m. Judith Arlene Vos, Mar. 28, 1992. BS in Computer Info. Systems, Ohio State U., 1978. Project engr. AccuRay Corp., Columbus, Ohio, 1978-82, mktg. mgr., 1982-84; mgr. demonstrations and exhbns. Combustion Engrng., Columbus, 1984-90; project mgr. ABB Indsl. Sys. (formerly ABB Process Automation, Columbus, 1990-92; mgr. solutions ctrs. ABB Automation, Columbus, 1992—. Comm. chmn. disaster svcs. ARC, Columbus, 1988—; mem. Columbus Zoo Docent Assn., 1982—; pres. Cen. Ohio Amateur Radio Emergency Svc., 1988—. Mem. Tech. Assn. Pulp and Paper Industry. Avocations: amateur radio, scuba, skiing. Home: 743 Fleetrun Ave Gahanna OH 43230-3267 Office: ABB Indsl Sys 650 Ackerman Rd Columbus OH 43202-4500

CHAPMAN, LOREN J., psychology educator; b. Muncie, Ind., Jan. 5, 1927; s. Herbert L. and Lurana Gertrude (Treff) C.; m. Jean Marilyn Paulsen, June 6, 1953; children: Nancy, Laurence. AB cum laude, Harvard U., 1948; MS, Northwestern U., 1952, PhD, 1954. USPHS postdoctorate research fellow U. Chgo., 1954-56, instr., asst. prof., 1956-59; assoc. prof. U. Ky., Lexington, 1959-62; from assoc. prof. to prof. Southern Ill. U., Carbondale, 1962-67; prof. U. Wis., Madison, 1966-93, NIMH rsch. scientist, 1988-93; prof. emeritus, 1994—. Author: Disordered Thought in Schizophrenia, 1973; contbr. over 100 articles to profl. jours. Recipient Disting. Scientist award Soc. for Sci. Clin. Psychology, 1992; NIMH research grantee, 1952-97. Fellow AAAS, APA (Disting. Sci. award 1999); mem. Am. Psychopathol. Assn., Soc. Rsch. Psychopathology (pres. 1989, Joseph Zubin award 1992), Am. Psychol. Soc. (William James fellow 1995, Disting. Sci. award 1999). Home: 129 Richland Ln Madison WI 53705-4834 Office: Univ Wis Dept Psychology 1202 W Johnson St Madison WI 53706-1611

CHAPMAN, LORING, psychology, physiology educator, neuroscientist; b. L.A., Oct. 4, 1929; s. Lee E. and Elinore E. (Gundry) Scott; m. Toy Farrar, June 14, 1954 (dec.); children: Robert, Antony, Pandora (dec.). BS, U. Nev., 1950; PhD, U. Chgo., 1955. Lic. psychologist, Oreg., N.Y., Calif. Rsch. fellow U. Chgo., 1952-54; rsch. assoc., asst. prof. Cornell U. Med. Coll., N.Y.C., 1957-61; rsch. dir. Music Rsch. Found., N.Y.C., 1958-61; assoc. prof. in residence Neuropsychiat. Inst., UCLA, 1961-65; rsch. prof. U. Oreg., Portland, 1965; br. chief NIH, Bethesda, Md., 1966-67; prof., chmn. dept. behavioral biology, joint prof. human physiology Sch. Medicine U. Calif., Davis, 1967-81, prof. psychiatry and head Divsn. of Clin. Psychology, 1981-91; prof. emeritus Sch. Medicine U. Calif., 1991—, prof. neurology, 1977-81, prof. human physiology, 1977-81; asst. dean, rsch. affairs Sch. Medicine U. Calif., Davis, 1972-74; vice chmn. div. of sci. basic to medicine, 1976-79; Lic. psychologist, Calif. Author: Pain and Suffering, 3 vols, 1967, Head and Brain 3 vols, 1971, (with E.A. Dunlap) The Eye, 1981; assoc. editor courtroom medicine series updates, 1965-91; contbr. sci. articles to publs. Fogarty Sr. Internat. fellow, 1980; grantee NASA, 1969-80; grantee NIH, 1956-91; grantee Nat. Inst. Drug Abuse, 1971-80; recipient Thorton Wilson prize, 1958, Career award USPHS, 1964, Commonwealth Fund award, 1970. Mem. Am. Acad. Neurology, Am. Physiol. Soc., Am. Psychol. Assn., Royal Soc. Medicine (London), Am. Neurol. Assn., Am. Assn. Mental Deficiency, Aerospace Med. Assn., Soc. for Neurosci. Home: 205 Country Pl Sacramento CA 95831 Office: U Calif Med Ctr Dept Psychiatry 2315 Stockton Blvd Sacramento CA 95817-2201 *The first taste of the forbidden fruit in the distant gardens of genesis evoked a most deeply human question, beautifully phrased in antiquity, "And we, who are we, anyway?" I have been privileged to spend my working life sharing in the search for this understanding. The pace of progress has seemed rapid, but evil has come along with good, and now the terrible fragility of ourselves and our planet lies bare before us. We feel the need for immediate, practical, and wise answers ever more urgently, for our utmost yearning is to see the full flowering of who we, we human beings, are and can become.**

CHAPMAN, MAX C., investment company executive. Co-chmn. of bd., CEO Nomura Securities Internat., N.Y.C.; chmn. bd. Nomura Holding Am. Inc., 1996—. Office: Nomura Securities Internat 2 World Financial Ctr Bldg B New York NY 10281-1077*

CHAPMAN, MICHAEL WILLIAM, orthopedist, educator; b. Newberry, Mich., Nov. 29, 1937; m. Elizabeth Casady; adopted sons: Mark, Craig. AA, Am. River Coll., Sacramento, Calif., 1957; postgrad., U. Calif., Davis, 1957-58; BS, U. Calif., San Francisco, 1959, MD, 1962. Diplomate Am. Bd. Orthopaedic Surgery (ad hoc appeal com. 1986, site visitor 1986, certification renewal com. 1985-88, certification renewal com. chmn. 1986-88). Intern San Francisco Gen. Hosp., 1962-63, asst. chief orthopaedic surgery svc., 1971-79, acting chief orthopaedic surgery svc., 1972-73; resident in orthopaedic surgery U. Calif., San Francisco, 1963-67, asst. prof. dept. orthopaedic surgery, Sch. Medicine, 1971-76, assoc. prof. dept. orthopaedic surgery, Sch. Medicine, 1976-79; resident in orthopaedic surgery U. Calif. Hosps., San Francisco, 1963-64, Samuel Merritt Hosp., Oakland, Calif., 1964, Highland-Alameda County Hosp., Oakland, 1965, Children's Hosp. of the East Bay, Oakland, 1966, Shriners Hosp., Honolulu, 1966-67; fellow Nat. Orthopaedic Hosp., London, 1967-68; chmn. dept. orthopaedic surgery U. Calif., Davis, Sacramento, 1979—, prof. dept. orthopaedic surgery, 1981—; panelist Calif. Crippled Children Svcs. Panel in Orthopaedic Surgery; cons. VA Hospital, Martinez, Calif.; cons. staff Sutter Gen. Hosp., Sacramento, California; co-chmn. Zimmer Trauma Panel, 1983-84; vis. prof. Fresno Valley Med. Ctr., 1975, Dept. Orthopaedics, U. Calif., Davis, 1976, U. Hawaii, Honolulu, 1977; vis. prof., cons. to Surgeon Gen. U.S. Army, Europe, 1978; vis. prof. U. Basel, Switzerland, 1979, Phoenix Orthopaedic Residency Program, 1979, Stanford U., 1981, U. Hawaii, 1982, U. So. Calif., L.A., 1984, SUNY, Buffalo, 1985, U. Utah, 1985, U. Iowa Coll. Medicine, 1987, Duke U. Sch. Medicine, 1988, U. Calif. Irvine, Div. Orthopaedics, 1990, U. S.C., 1990, Mass. Gen. Hosp., Harvard U., 1990, Boston U., 1994, Stanford U., 1995, Med. Coll. Pa., 1996, numerous others; also guest lectr. numerous instns.; insp. for residency rev. com. ad hoc appeal com. Accreditation coun. for Grad. Med. Specialist Site, 1983-86. Editor: (with M. Madison) Operative Orthopaedics, 1988 (Best New Book in Clin. Medicine Assn. Am. Pubs.); contbr. more than 120 articles and numerous abstracts to profl. jours.; presenter exhibits, audiovisual programs, some 500 other presentations; cons. editor Skiing Mag., 1973-77; mem. bd. assoc. editors Clin. Orthopaedics and Related Rsch., 1982-85, Internat. Med. Soc. Paraplegia, 1972-80; reviewer Jour. Bone and Joint Surgery, 1980-85, trustee, 1995—; past reviewer New Eng. Jour. Medicine; patentee in field. With U.S. Army, 1968-70. Decorated Army Commendation medal; recipient Outstanding Tchg. award U. Calif., San Francisco, 1972, Outstanding Tchr. award U. Calif., Davis, 1984, 93; named One of Best 100 Doctors Am., Good Housekeeping Mag.; Fogarty Sr. Internat. fellow NIH, 1978-79, 80-81; grantee Johnson & Johnson, 1983-84, Zimmer Inc., 1983-85, 85-86, 87-90, Interpore Internat., 1985-86, 89-90, Collagen Inc., 1985-86, 88-89, Upjohn Inc., 1985-86, Orthopaedic Rsch. and Edn. Found., 1988-89. Mem. AMA (Physicians Recognition award 1989-96), ACS, Am. Acad. Orthopaedic Surgeons (bd. dirs. 1982-83, numerous coms.), Am. Orthopaedic Assn. (bd. dirs. 1985-86, pres. 1990-91, various coms.), Internat. Orthopaedic Assn., Assn. for Study of Internal Fixation (N.Am. chpt.), Internat. Soc. Orthopaedic Surgery and Traumatology, Internat. Soc. for Fracture Repair, Brit. Orthopaedic Assn., South African Orthopaedic Assn. (hon.), Am. Acad. Orthopaedic Surgeons, Am. Assn. for Surgery of Trauma, Am. Bd. Med. Spltys., Assn. Am. Med. Colls., Leroy C. Abbott Orthopaedic Soc., Austrian Trauma Assn., Paul R. Lipscomb Soc., Northwestern Med. Assn., Orthopaedic Rsch. Soc., Orthopaedic Trauma Assn., Sierra Club, U. Calif. San Francisco Alumni Assn., Western Orthopaedic Assn., Houston Orthopaedic Assn. (hon.), Calif. Med. Assn., Calif. Orthopaedic Assn., Sacramento-El Dorado Med. Soc., Wilson Interurban Orthopaedic Soc., Alpha Omega Alpha. Avocations: skiing, mountaineering, backpacking, tennis, bicycling. Office: U Calif-Davis Sch Med Dept Orthopedics 4860 V St Ste 3800 Sacramento CA 95817

CHAPMAN, MORRIS HINES, denominational executive; b. Kosciusko, Miss.; m. Jodi Francis; 2 children. Grad., Miss. Coll.; MDiv, D of Ministry, Southwestern Bapt. Theol. Sem.; hon. doctorates, S.W. Bapt. U., Miss. Coll. Pastor 1st Bapt. Ch., Albuquerque, 1974-79, Wichita Falls, Tex., 1979-92; pres. So. Bapt. Conv., 1990-92, pres., CEO, exec. com., 1992—; pres., CEO, exec. com., 1992—; pres. pastor's conf. So. Bapt. Conv., 1986, preacher Conv. Sermon, Las Vegas, 1989. Author: Faith: Taking God at His Word, The Wedding Collection. Office: Executive Committee Southern Baptist Convention 901 Commerce St Nashville TN 37203-3620*

CHAPMAN, ORVILLE LAMAR, chemist, educator; b. New London, Conn., June 26, 1932; s. Orville Carmen and Mabel Elnora (Tyree) C.; m. Faye Newton Morrow, Aug. 20, 1955 (div. 1980); children: Kenneth, Kevin; m. Susan Elizabeth Parker, June 15, 1981. BS, Va. Poly. Inst., 1954; PhD, Cornell U., 1957. Instr. chemistry Iowa State U., 1957-59, asst. prof., 1959-62, assoc. prof., 1962-65, Prof. chemistry, 1965-74; prof. chemistry UCLA, 1974—; cons. Mobil Chem. Co. Recipient NAS award, 1974, Founders prize Tex. Instruments, George and Freda Halpern award in photochemistry N.Y. Acad. Scis., 1978, Outstanding Patent of Yr. award Mobil Corp., 1992, Best Use of Info. Tech. in Edn. and Academia award Computer World/Smithsonian Instn., 1995, Computer World-Smithsonian Instn. award in Edn., 1995. Mem. Am. Chem. Soc. (award in pure chemistry 1968, Arthur C. Cope award 1978, Midwest award 1978, Havinga medal 1982, McCoy award UCLA, 1985). Home: 1213 Roscomare Rd Los Angeles CA 90077-2202 Office: UCLA Dept Chemistry 405 Hilgard Ave Los Angeles CA 90095-9000

CHAPMAN, PAUL H., author; b. Greenville, S.C., Apr. 8, 1921; s. Judson W. and Zena H. C. Student, Furman U. Founder, CEO Chapman Comp., Inc., 1954-83. Author: The Man Who Led Columbus to America, 1973, The Norse Discovery of America, 1981, Discovering Columbus, 1992, Columbus the Man, 1992, Spirit Pond Runestones, A Study in Linguistics, 1994; contbr. articles to profl. jours.; speaker in field. Founder of the Fdn. for Improvement of Justice, 1985— (chmn.). With U.S. Army Air Corps. Fellow in Epigraphic Soc.; recipient RootCutters award Inst. for the Study of Am. Cultures. Address: 2319 Waterton Ct Atlanta GA 30338-4516

CHAPMAN, PAULA ANNE, cultural organization administrator; b. Tiffin, Ohio, Sept. 15, 1960; d. Paul Everett and Mary Virginia (Brosious) Young; m. James Nelson Cook, Sept. 16, 1977 (div. Dec. 1981); children: Nichole Adele, Jessica Theresa, Samantha Rebekah; m. Harry N. Chapman, Dec. 10, 1988 (div.). BS in Psychology, Heidelberg Coll., 1982; MA in Polit. Sci., Bowling Green (Ohio) State U., 1987; MA in Adult Edn., Ball State U., 1996; postgrad., Nova Southeastern U., Ft. Lauderdale, Fla., 1997—; cert. in fundraising mgmt., Ind. U., 1997. Cert. fundraising exec. Child therapist Sandusky (Ohio) Youth Referral Svc., 1982-83; parole officer State of Ohio, Columbus, 1983-86; dep. dir. Seneca, Sandusky and Wyandot Commn. Mental Health Bd., Tiffin, 1987-88; program dir. WSOS Cmty. Action Commn., Fremont, Ohio, 1988-90; exec. dir. Tiffin Area C. of C./Seneca Indsl. & Econ. Devel. Corp., Tiffin, 1988-90; pres. Chapman Cmty. Devel. Cons., Tiffin, 1990-93; dir. devel. St. Francis Health Care Ctr., Green Springs, Ohio, 1993-94, St. Francis Coll., Fort Wayne, Ind., 1994-95; dir. of fund devel. Girl Scout Coun., Inc., Fort Wayne, 1995-97; exec. dir. McMillen Ctr. for Health Edn., Fort Wayne, 1997—; adj. prof. econs. Tiffin U., 1987-94; mem. ednl. adv. bd. Vanguard/Sentinel Vocat. Sch., Fremont, 1989-90; chmn. Tiffin Fair Housing Bd., 1985-90; bd. dirs. Ohio Indsl. Tng. Program, Sandusky, 1988-90, Pvt. Industry Coun., Fremont, Seneca County Revolving Loan Fund, Tiffin; chairperson adv. bd. WSOS. Candidate Seneca County Commr., 1992; mem. Grad. Ft. Wayne Leadership Works, 1994. Mem. NAFE, Nat. Soc. Fundraising Execs. (mem. N.W. Ind. cluster steering com.), Bus. and Profl. Women's Assn. (Young Career Woman of Yr. 1987, 89), Ft. Wayne C. of C. (mem. VIP com. Ambs. Club), Rotary (Ft. Wayne). Avocations: philanthropic studies. Home: 6808 Covington Creek Trl Fort Wayne IN 46804-2872

CHAPMAN, PETER HERBERT, investment company executive; b. Stockton, Calif., Mar. 6, 1953; s. Duff Gordon and Emalee (Sala) C.; m. Diane Chapman Clark; children: Charlotte Moseley, Alexander Clark. AB, Columbia U., 1977. V.p. Salomon Bros., Inc., N.Y.C., 1977-86, The First Boston Corp., N.Y.C., 1986-88; dir. Girozentrale Vienna, N.Y.C., 1989-91; sr. vp. Bessemer Group, Inc., N.Y.C., 1991-92; pres. Alpha Investment Mgmt., Inc., N.Y.C., 1992-94; exec. dir. CIBC Oppenheimer Corp., N.Y.C., 1993—; bd. dirs. C.D. Stimson Co., Seattle, 1988-92. Bd. dirs. Am. Internat. Sch., Florence, Italy, 1982-94. Mem. The Links Club, Racquet and Tennis Club, Piping Rock Club. Republican. Home: 923 Fifth Ave New York NY 10021-2649

CHAPMAN, RANDELL BARKLEY, family and emergency physician, medical educator; b. Altus, Okla., July 20, 1955; s. Dale Barkley and Doris Quay (Saunders) C.; m. Sydney Lee Ellison, Mar. 11, 1978 (div. Jan. 1999); children: Chase Creighton, Cory Lee, Sherry Jordan Barkley. BS in Microbiology, U. Okla., Norman, 1978; MD, U. Okla., Oklahoma City, 1983. Diplomate Am. Bd. Family Practice; lic. in healing arts, Kans. Intern in family medicine Okla. Meml. Hosp., Norman, 1983-84, resident in family medicine, 1984-86; emergency physician Norman Regional Hosp., 1986-87; pvt. practice, Bapt. Care Ctr., Yukon, Okla., 1987-89, Altus, Okla., 1989-91; clin. lab. dir. Family Health Ctr., Derby, 1991-95; prin. physician Rose Hill (Kans.) Med. Ctr., 1995—; mem. med. staff Via Christi Med. Ctr., St. Joseph Campus, Wichita, Kans., 1991—, St. Francis Campus, 1995—, Wesley Med. Ctr., Wichita, 1991—; clin. instr. Butler County C.C., 1991-95. Fellow Am. Acad. Family Practice, Assn. Emergency Physicians; mem. AMA (Physician's Recognition award with spl. commendation for self-directed learning 1995), Am. Coll. Sports Medicine, Assn. Emergency Physicians (charter), Kans. Acad. Family Practice, Sedgewick County Med. Soc. (alternate del. Kans. Med. Polit. Action Com. 1992-94), Sigma Phi Epsilon. Democrat. Methodist. Avocation: music, acting. Office: Box 247 1305 N Rose Hill Rd Rose Hill KS 67133-9466

CHAPMAN, RICHARD LEROY, public policy researcher; b. Yankton, S.D., Feb. 4, 1932; s. Raymond Young and Vera Everette (Trimble) C.; m. Marilyn Jean Nicholson, Aug. 14, 1955; children: Catherine Ruth Hoff, Robert Matthew, Michael David, Stephen Raymond, Amy Jean. BS, S.D. State U., 1954; postgrad., Cambridge (Eng.) U., 1954-55; MPA, Syracuse U., 1958, PhD, 1967. With Office of Sec. of Def., 1958-59, 61-63; dep. dir. rsch. S.D. Legis. Rsch. Coun., 1959-60; mem. staff Bur. of the Budget, Exec. Office of Pres., Washington, 1960-61; profl. staff mem. com. govt. ops. U.S.

Ho. of Reps., Washington, 1966; program dir. NIH, Bethesda, Md., 1967-68; sr. rsch. assoc. Nat. Acad. Pub. Adminstrn., Washington, 1968-72, dep. exec. dir., 1973-76, v.p., dir. rsch., 1976-82; sr. rsch. scientist Denver Rsch. Inst., 1982-86; mem. adv. com. Denver Rsch. Inst. U. Denver, 1984-86; ptnr. Milliken Chapman Rsch. Group Inc., Denver, 1986-88; v.p. Chapman Rsch. Group, Inc., Littleton, 1988-98; cons. U.S. Office Pers. Mgmt., Washington, 1977-81, Denver, 1986-98; cons. CIA, Washington, 1979, 80, 81, Arthur S. Fleming Awards, Washington, 1977-81; exec. staff dir., cons. U.S. Congressman Frank Denholm; lectr. on sci., tech., govt. and pub. mgmt. Author: (with Fred Grissom) Mining the Nation's Braintrust, 1992; contbr. over 70 articles and revs. to profl. jours. and congl. staff reports. Mem. aerospace com. Colo. Commn. Higher Edn., Denver, 1982-83; chmn. rules com. U. Denver Senate, 1984-85; bd. dirs. S.E. Englewood Water Dist., Littleton, 1984-88, pres. 1986-88; mem. strategic planning com. Mission Hills Bapt. Ch., 1986; bd. dirs. Lay Action Ministry Program, 1988-96, chmn. 1992-96; established Vera and Raymond Chapman Scholarship Fund, S.D. State U.; mem. Fairfax County Rep. Ctrl. Com., Va., 1969-71, Fairfax County Com. of 100, 1979-82. With U.S. Army, 1955-57, Korea, capt. Res. Syracuse U. Maxwell Sch. fellow, 1957-58, 63-64, Brookings Inst. fellow, 1964-65. Mem. Tech. Transfer Soc. (bd. dirs. 1987-95, Pres.'s award 1991, founder Colo. chpt., Thomas Jefferson award 1996), Fed. Lab. Consortium (nat. adv. com. 1989-98), S.D. State U. Found. (bd. dirs. 1992-98, vice chmn. 1994-96, chmn. bd. 1996-98), Southglen Country Club, Masons, KT, Order of DeMolay (Cross of Honor 1982), Rotary (fellow Internat. Found. 1954-55, Paul Harris fellow 1989). Republican. Avocations: hunting, fishing, golf, reading, gardening. *Treat all of life as an opportunity to learn and to contribute. As one enriches the lives of others, you receive great satisfaction and returns that cannot be imagined.*

CHAPMAN, ROBERT FOSTER, federal judge; b. Inman, S.C., Apr. 24, 1926; s. James Alfred and Martha (Marshall) C.; m. Mary Winston Gwathmey, Dec. 21, 1951; children: Edward, Foster, Winston. BS, U. S.C., 1945, LLB, 1949, LLD (hon.), 1986. Bar: S.C. 1949. Asso. firm Butler & Moore, Spartanburg, 1949-51; partner firm Butler, Chapman & Morgan, Spartanburg, 1953-71; U.S. dist. judge for S.C., 1971-81, U.S. cir. judge, 1981—. Chmn. S.C. Republican Party, 1961-63. Served to lt. USNR, 1943-46, 51-53. Recipient Nat. Patriot's award Congl. Medal of Honor Soc., 1985. Fellow Am. Coll. Trial Lawyers. Presbyn. (ruling elder). Home: Box 1043 Camden SC 29020 Office: US Ct Appeals 4th Ct PO Box 7097 Columbia SC 29202-7097

CHAPMAN, ROBERT JAMES, clinical psychiatrist, educator; b. Delaware, Ohio, July 10, 1936; s. Edward Samuel and Frances Mae (Stephenson) C.; m. Janice Holmes, June 18, 1960; children: Steven Holmes, Scott Edward, Erik Wellington. AB, Oberlin Coll., 1958; MD, Ohio State U., 1963. Diplomate Am. Bd. Psychiatry and Neurology. Instr., fellow, USPHS U. Rochester (N.Y.) Sch. Med., 1968-69; asst. prof. clin. psychiatry Dartmouth Med. Sch., Hanover, N.H., 1969-79, asst. prof. cmty. and family med., 1976-79, assoc. prof. clin. psychiatry, 1980-94, adj. assoc. prof. psychiatry, 1994—; dir. Robert Wood Johnson Primary Care/Physician Mgr. residency program Dartmouth Med. Sch., Hanover, N.H., 1977-79, dir. Fellowship Program in Rural Cmty. Psychiatry, 1979-81, dir. Comprehensive Alcoholism Svcs. program, 1973-75; dir. Mt. Ascutney Psychiat. Assocs., Windsor, Vt., 1984-94; dir. Choate Psychiat. Assocs., New London, N.H., 1995—. Contbr. chpts. to books, articles to profl. jours. Mem. steering com. Upper Valley Health Care Coalition, White River Junction, Vt./Lebanon, N.H., 1984-86; mem. Area Health Planning Coun., N.H., 1977-80; bd. dirs. Planned Parenthood Assn. Upper Valley, Lebanon, 1970-78; chmn. profl. adv. com. Hanover Vis. Nurse Svc., 1979-80. Sr. asst. surgeon with USPHS, 1964-66, with Peace Corps., Nigeria. Fellow Am. Psychiat. Assn.; mem. AMA, AAAS, N.H. Psychiat. Soc. (pres. 1983-84, chmn. ethics com. 1985-86), Am. Geriatrics Soc., Am. Assn. for Geriatric Psychiatry, Ad Hoc Com. for Def. of Health Care, Physicians for Social Responsibility. Avocations: camping, canoeing, photography, wilderness travel. Home: 33 Rip Rd Hanover NH 03755-1616 Office: Choate Psychiatric Assocs Aldrich House PO Box 1390 16 Beaver Meadow Rd Norwich VT 05055-9305

CHAPMAN, RONALD THOMAS, musician, educator; b. Bklyn., Dec. 16, 1933; s. William Leon and Rosamond (Walker) C.; m. Joyce Elaine Chase, Dec. 1966 (dec. May 1973); adopted child, Debra Anne (dec. July 1992); m. Virginia Marie Knochenhauer, Feb. 14, 1975 (dec. July 1989); stepchildren: Suzanne, Michael. BS cum laude, CUNY, 1982; MA in Teaching, Lehman Coll., 1983; PhD in Music in Higher Edn., NYU, 1989. Cert. tchr. music, N.Y., tchr. Spanish, N.Y. Toured with Leonard dePaur Infantry Chorus, 1953-55; mem. trio The Versatones, U.S. and Can., 1955-59; vocalist, 1978—; asst. dir. men's choir Kingsborough Community Coll., 1980-82; asst. to dir. mixed chorus Lehman Coll., CUNY, 1982-83; instr. voice NYU, N.Y.C., 1986—; instr. computer music for music teachers N.Y. Inst. Tech., N.Y.C., 1987; pvt. instr. voice, piano, guitar, computerized music, music theory, sight singing and music lit., 1980—; substitute tchr. Hempstead (N.Y.) Sch. Dist., 1983-85, mem. faculty, 1988-89, tchr. adult edn., ESL, 1993—, tchr. group piano, group voice in continuing adult edn. program, 1993—; instr. voice NYU, 1986—; bd. dirs. Cultural Environ, Queens, N.Y.; adjudicator N.Y. Singing Tchrs. Assn., 1995. Performed in Spain, Japan, Thailand, The Philippines, Eng., Jamaica, Can., Vietnam, P.R., Fed. Republic of Germany, Laos, Portugal and U.S. including N.Y.C., Atlanta and Miami; TV appearances on Johnny Carson Show, Arthur Godfrey Talent Scouts, Gary Moore Show, Tex and Jinx Falkenburg Show, many others; rec. artist for Columbia Records, RCA Records, Island in the Sun soundtrack; appeared in Broadway play Kwamina; appearing nightly Fox Hollow, 1978-93, Caterer/Restaurant, Woodbury, N.Y., 1978—; starred in Playboy Club and Hotel Chain, 1960-67, (movies) Rueda de Sospechosos, 1963, (revue) The Ronnie Chapman Show, 1968-69; debuted by singing and accompanying himself on piano a medley of Broadway Show Tunes and Internat. Art Songs in various langs. Carnegie Hall, 1991, 92, 93, 94, 95, 96; Cafe Trilussa, 1996-97, J. DeCarlos Restaurant, Huntington, N.Y., 1998—. Bd. dirs. Cultural Environment, Queens, N.Y., 1978—; apptd. dep. gov. Am. Biog. Inst. Rsch. Assn., 1992. Mem. Internat. Assn. for Rsch. in Singing (rsch. assoc. Found. for Rsch. Singing), Nat. Assn. Tchrs. of Singing, N.Y. Singing Tchrs. Assn., N.Y. State Sch. Music Assn. (cert. to adjucate "Voice"), Internat. Assn. Jazz Educators, Chopin Found. N.Y., Am. Assn. Choral Dirs., Music Educators Nat. Conf., Music Tchrs. Nat. Assn., Assoc. Music Tchrs. League N.Y., Internat. Platform Assn., Am. Choral Dirs. Assn., Phi Delta Kappa (v.p. programs NYU chpt. 1988-89), Pi Kappa Lambda, Kappa Delta Pi (chpt. 3d v.p. 1994—). Achievements include being awarded a design patent for invention of a portable back rest/supporter, 1993. Avocations: writing plays, composing music, painting, teaching voice and piano in home studio. E-mail: ronchainc@aol.com. Home and Office: 108 Glenmore Ave Hempstead NY 11550-6630

CHAPMAN, ROSALYN M., federal judge; b. 1943. BA cum laude, U. Mich., 1964; JD, Boalt Hall, 1967. Adminstrv. law judge Office of Adminstrv. Hearings State of Calif., 1977-95; apptd. magistrate judge cen. dist. U.S. Dist. Ct. Calif., 1995; arbitrator Fed. Mediation and Conciliation Svc. and Am. Arbitration Assn.; assoc. dir. Western Ctr. on Law and Poverty; lectr. UCLA Sch. Law. Fax: (213) 894-4949. Office: US Courthouse 312 N Spring St Los Angeles CA 90012-4701

CHAPMAN, SAMUEL GREELEY, political science educator, criminologist; b. Atlanta, Sept. 29, 1929; s. Calvin C. and Jane (Greeley) C.; m. Patricia Hepfer, June 19, 1949 (dec. Dec. 1978); children: Lynn Randall, Deborah Jane; m. Carolyn Hughes, June 1, 1991. A.B., U. Calif.-Berkeley, 1951, M.A., 1959. Officer Police Dept., Berkeley, 1951-56; police cons. Pub. Adminstrn. Service, Chgo., 1956-59; asst. prof. Sch. Police Adminstrn., Mich. State U., East Lansing, 1959-63; police chief Multnomah County, Portland, Oreg., 1963-66; asst. dir. Pres.'s Commn. on Law Enforcement and Adminstrn. of Justice, Nat. Crime Commn., Washington, 1966-67; prof. dept. polit. sci. U. Okla., Norman, 1967-91; prof. emeritus, 1991—; chmn. athletic council U. Okla., 1971-72, 79-80; adj. prof. criminal justice U. Nev., Reno, 1995—; assoc.'s disting. lectr., 1985-86. Author: Dogs in Police Work, 1960, The Police Heritage in England and America, 1962, Police Patrol Readings, 1964, rev. edit., 1970, Perspectives on Police Assaults in the South Central United States, 1974, Short of Merger, 1976, Police Murders and Effective Countermeasures, 1976, Police Dogs in North America, 1979, 2d. edit., 1990, Cops, Killers and Staying Alive: The Murder of Police Officers in America, 1986; Murdered On Duty: The Killing of Police Officers in America, 1998; contbr. chpts. to books, articles to profl. jours. Mem. Norman City Council, 1972-83, mayor pro-tem, 1975-76, 79-80, 81-83. Recipient Amoco Found. award, 1986. Mem. Alpha Delta Phi. Republican. Home and Office: 680 Kane Ct Reno NV 89512-1354

CHAPMAN, SUE TURNER, artist; b. Albany, Sept. 25, 1927; d. Charles and Isabel (Fite) T.; m. Robert Joseph Chapman, Oct. 4, 1954 (div. 1968); 1 child, Paul. Scorer auto races, 1947-68; staff artist Indpls. Blueprint, 1960-61; prodn. artist Pinarie Lithographing, Louisville, 1968-70; art dir. Humana, Louisville, 1970-77; dir. Floyd County Mus., New Albany, Ind., 1980-82; working backside thoroughbred race horses, 1979-86; freelance comml. artist, 1983—; presenter in field. One-woman shows, Ind., Ky., S.C., 1977—. Recipient 1st place watercolor Womans Club Louisville, 1981, Merit award, Best of Show award Ind. Heritage Arts, Brown County Art Gallery, Nashville, 1991, Merit award Southside Art League, Indpls., 1996. Democrat. Avocations: camping, photography, gardening. Home: 1244 S Whiskey Run Ranch Rd Milltown IN 47145-7302

CHAPMAN, WILLIAM, baritone; b. Los Angeles; s. William Cloud and Augusta Jane (Kiel) C.; m. Irene Veronica Meyer, Sept. 15, 1957; children—Alexa Maria, Teren Cloud. B.A. in Drama, U. So. Calif. Propr. vocal studio Los Angeles, 1967—; mem. faculty U.S. Internat. U. Performing Arts Sch., San Diego, 1971-86; mem. extension faculty UCLA. Leading baritone N.Y.C. Opera, 1956—, also other opera houses, U.S. and Europe; opened Spoleto Festival as Macbeth in Macbeth, 1957; leading performer: Menotti's Maria Golovin as produced by David Merrick, Broadway, Frank Loesser's Greenwillow, Alvin Theater, (original prodn.) Candide, Martin Beck Theater; Broadway appearances as Charlie in Shenandoan, 1978-79, also in N.Y.C. Center revival of South Pacific; appeared as Frank Maurrant for N.Y.C. Opera, also PBS-TV; TV appearances on Wonderful World of Disney; Columnist: Notes for the Singing Actor, Voice Mag.; appearing as Cecil B. DeMille in 1996-97 Nat. Touring Co. of Sunset Blvd. Rockefeller grantee; recipient DramaLogue award for performance, 1992, various certs. of appreciation. Mem. Screen Actors Guild, Actors Equity, Am. Guild Variety Artists, AFTRA.

CHAPMAN, WILLIAM ERVIN, elementary education educator; b. Spencer, WVa., Oct. 5, 1967; s. William Ervin and Allene (Hill) C. BA in Elem. Edn., Bethany Coll., 1990; MA in Elem. Edn./Sci., Marshall U. Grad. Coll., Huntington, 1997. Tchr. grades 5-8 Reedy (WVa.) Elem. Sch., 1990-91; tchr. grades 4-5 Walton (WVa.) Elem. Sch., 1991-92, tchr. grade 6, 1992-93; tchr. grades 6-8 Walton Middle Sch., 1993-94; tchr. grade 6 Spencer Middle Sch., 1994—; trainer Appalachian Edn. Lab., Charleston, 1994—; mentor Project CATS-Coord. Sci., 1995—. Co-author: (book) Forces in Nature: A Coordinated and Thematic Science Module, 1995-97. adult tchr. Penial United Methodist Ch., Spencer, 1995—, trustee, 1997—. Recipient Golden Apple Achiever award Ashland Oil Co., 1996-97. Mem. NEA, W.Va. Sci. Tchrs. Assn., W.Va. Edn. Assn., W.Va. Edn. Assn., Roane County Edn. Assn.. (pres. 1996—), Masons. Democrat. Methodist. Avocations: hunting, fishing, farming, rock hunting, painting. Home: RR 1 Box 60 Reedy WV 25270-9709 Office: Spencer Middle Sch. 102 Chapman Ave Spencer WV 25276-1310

CHAPMAN, WILLIAM S., state agency administrator; b. Lithonia, Ga., July 1937; married; four children. BS, North Ga. Coll., 1959; MBA, Furman U., 1973. With U.S. Army, 1959-79; v.p. Info. Sys. Am., Atlanta, 1980-93; asst. sec. state Atlanta, Ga., 1993-95; staff mem. Ga. Mil. Affairs Coordinating Com., Atlanta, 1996; state dir. Senator Max Cleland, Atlanta, 1997—. Office: Ste 1700 75 Spring St SW Atlanta GA 30303-3309

CHAPNICK, DAVID B., lawyer; b. N.Y.C., Apr. 24, 1939; s. H.M. and G. (Kraft) C.; m. Elaine Schlozman, Dec. 25, 1966; children: Adam Lawrence, Melissa Rachel. AB with honors, Union Coll., 1959; LLB, NYU, 1962. Bar: N.Y. 1963. Law clk. to Hon. Warren E. Burger U.S. Ct. Appeals (D.C. cir.), Washington, 1962-63; pvt. practice N.Y.C., 1963-67; assoc. Simpson Thacher & Bartlett, N.Y.C., 1967-69, ptnr., 1970—. Trustee Union Coll., Schenectady, N.Y., 1991—, vice chmn., 1995-96, chmn., 1998—. Mem. N.Y. State Bar Assn., Assn. Bar City N.Y. Office: Simpson Thacher & Bartlett 425 Lexington Ave Fl 15 New York NY 10017-3954*

CHAPOTON, JOHN EDGAR, lawyer, government official; b. Galveston, Tex., May 18, 1936; s. Otis Byron and Grace Donaldson (Wayman) C.; m. Sarah Eastham, Jan. 5, 1963; children: John Edgar, Clare Eastham. Student, Washington and Lee U., 1954-55; BBA with honors, U. Tex., 1958, LLB with honors, 1960. Bar: Tex. 1960, D.C. 1985. Assoc. Andrews, Kurth, Campbell & Jones, Houston, 1961-69; with Dept. Treasury, Washington, 1969-72, 81-84; tax legis. counsel Dept. Treasury, 1970-72, asst. sec. for tax policy, 1981-84; ptnr. Vinson & Elkins, Houston, 1972-81; mng. ptnr. Vinson & Elkins, Washington, 1984—. Chmn. law firms div. United Way Capital Area, Washington, 1988-90; bd. dirs. Boys and Girls Clubs Greater Washington, 1990—. Recipient Achievement award Tax Soc. NYU, 1984. Fellow Am. Coll. Tax Counsel (vice-chmn.); mem. ABA (sect. taxation), Tex. State Bar Assn., D.C. Bar Assn., Am. Law Inst. Republican. Episcopalian. Avocations: golf. Office: Vinson & Elkins LLP 1455 Pennsylvania Ave NW Washington DC 20004-1008*

CHAPPARS, TIMOTHY STEPHEN, lawyer; b. Cin., July 23, 1952; s. Gregory S. and Helen (Maragos) C.; m. Laurie A. Kress, Dec. 24, 1986 (div. Sept. 1987); m. Laurie A. Kress, Apr. 18, 1990; children: Alexander T., Jake A. BS, Duke U., 1974; JD, U. Cin., 1978. Assoc. Cox & Chappars, Xenia, Ohio, 1978-94, Bryant Law Office, Wilmington, Ohio, 1981—; trial atty. Pub. Defender's Office, Clinton County, Wilmington, 1978-88; lectr. So. State Jr. Coll., Wilmington, 1982. Mem. Ohio Bar Assn., Am. Trial Lawyers Acad., Ohio Acad. Trial Lawyers. Methodist. Avocations: tennis, piano, hiking, cycling, skiing. Home: 2025 Winding Brook Way Xenia OH 45385-9382 Office: PO Box 280 Xenia OH 45385-0280

CHAPPELL, ANNETTE M., university dean; b. Washington, Oct. 31, 1939; d. Joseph John and Annette B. (Harley) C.; m. Brian Thomas Flower, Sept. 3, 1960 (div. Mar. 1983); m. Frank Joseph Sanders, Apr. 8, 1985 (dec. 1995). BA in English, U. Md., 1962, MA, 1964, PhD, 1970. Lectr. European div. U. Md., Eng., 1965-66; instr. English U. Md., College Park, 1966-69; asst. prof. English Towson (Md.) U., 1969-72, assoc. prof., 1972-79, prof., 1979—, spl. asst. to pres., affirmative action officer, 1974-77; dean humanistic, social and managerial studies Towson (Md.) State U., 1977-82, dean Coll. Liberal Arts, 1982-95, assoc. v.p. acad. affairs, 1995-99. Contbr. articles to profl. jours. and book revs. to Ms Mag., Balt. Sun. Lay reader, chalicist All Saints Episcopal Ch., Reisterstown, Md., 1973—; pres. Baltimore County Commn. for Women, 1977-79; bd. dirs. Baltimore County Sexual Assault and Domestic Violence Center, 1978-83, pres., 1980-82. Mem. AAUP, MLA, Am. Assn. Higher Edn., Council Colls. Arts and Scis. (bd. dirs. 1984-86), Exec. Women's Council Md. (1st v.p. 1980, pres. 1981). Home: 105 Kenilworth Park Dr Baltimore MD 21204-2269 Office: Towson U Towson MD 21252

CHAPPELL, CHARLES FRANKLIN, meteorologist, consultant; b. St. Louis, Dec. 7, 1927; s. Hubert Guy and Wilma Halle (Lindsey) C.; m. Doris Mae Kennedy, Aug. 4, 1951; children—Christa Ann, Susan Lynne, Deborah Louise. B.S., Washington U., St. Louis, 1949; postgrad., St. Louis U., 1952-54; M.S., Colo. State U., 1967, Ph.D., 1971. Flight data engr. McDonnell Aircraft Co., St. Louis, 1950-55; weather forecaster U.S. Weather Bur., Kansas City, Mo., 1956-67; research assoc. Colo. State U., Ft. Collins, 1967-70; assoc. prof. Utah State U., Logan, 1970-72; research meteorologist NOAA, Boulder, Colo., 1972-79, research dir., 1979-87; head applied sci. group Nat. Ctr. for Atmospheric Research, Boulder, 1988-89, sr. scientist coop. program for operational meteorology edn. and tng., 1989-94; meteorologist cons., Boulder, 1995—; cons. meteorologist Midwest Weather Service, Kansas City, Mo., 1958-60. Assoc. editor Jour. Atmospheric Sci., 1984-87; contbr. articles to prof. jours. (Best Sci. Paper award in NOAA-Environ. Research Labs. 1981). Served as seaman 1st class USN, 1945-46. Recipient silver medal Dept. Commerce, 1957. Fellow Am. Meteorol. Soc.; mem. Nat. Weather Assn., Weather Modification Assn., Am. Geophys. Union. Avocations: hiking, painting, gardening, piano. Home and Office: 3110 Heidelberg Dr Boulder CO 80303-7010 *You can always accomplish more than you think, so do it.*

CHAPPELL, CHARLES RICHARD, space scientist; b. Greenville, S.C., June 2, 1943; s. Gordon Thomas and Mabel Winn (Ownbey) Chappell; m. Brenda Kay Taylor; 1 child, Christopher Richard. BA magna cum laude, Vanderbilt U., 1965; PhD in Space Sci., Rice U., 1968. Assoc. research scientist Lockheed Palo Alto (Calif.) Research Lab., 1968-70, research scientist, 1970-72, staff scientist, 1972-74; chief magnetospheric physics br. NASA-Marshall Space Flight Ctr., Huntsville, Ala., 1974-80, chief solar terrestrial physics div., 1980-87, assoc. dir. for sci., 1987-97; adj. prof. physics, dir. sci. and rsch. comm. Vanderbilt U., Nashville, 1997—; selected as Alternate Payload Specialist for the ATLAS-1 mission of the Space Shuttle, 1985; spl. asst. for environ. outreach to NASA adminstr., 1994-95; dep. dir. Global Learning and Observations to Benefit the Environment (GLOBE), a v.p. initiative, 1994-95; vis. profl. scholar Freedom Forum First Amendment Ctr., Vanderbilt U., 1996-97. Author: (ency.) Plasmasphere, 1970, Spacelab Mission, 1985; contbr. numerous articles to profl. jours. Recipient medal for Exceptional Sci. Achievement NASA, 1981, 84, Exceptional Svc. medal, 1998; NASA trainee, 1966-68. Mem. Am. Geophys. Union, Congress of Space Research, Phi Beta Kappa, Phi Eta Sigma. Methodist. Avocations: distance running, sailing. Home: 569 Midway Cir Brentwood TN 37027-5178 Office: Vanderbilt U 708 Baker Bldg Office Sci and Rsch Comm Nashville TN 37203

CHAPPELL, FRED DAVIS, English language educator, poet; b. Canton, N.C., May 28, 1936; s. James Taylor and Anne Mae (Davis) C.; m. Susan Nicholls, Aug. 2, 1959; 1 son, Christopher Heath. BA, Duke U., 1961, MA, 1964; LittD, U. N.C., 1989, Spring Hill Coll., 1991. Prof. English U. N.C., Greensboro, 1964—; adv. editor Skyhook, 1958-59, Red Clay Reader, 1964-65, Greensboro Rev., 1964—, Appalachian Heritage, 1977—, Denver Quar., 1984-90, Shenandoah, 1988—, Ga. Rev., 1990—. Author: It Is Time, Lord, 1963, The Inkling, 1965, Dagon, 1968, The World Between the Eyes, 1971, The Gaudy Place, 1972, Midquest, 1981, Moments of Light, 1982, Castle Tzingal, 1984, I Am One of You Forever, 1985, Source, 1985, The Fred Chappell Reader, 1988, First and Last Words, 1989, Brighten the Corner Where You Are, 1989, More Shapes Than One, 1992, C, 1993, Plow Naked, 1993, Spring Garden: New and Selected Poems, 1995, Farewell, I'm Bound To Leave You, 1996, A Way of Happening, 1998. Recipient Roanoke-Chowan Poetry prize N.C. Lit. Assn., 1979, Prix de Meilleur des Lettres Etrangers, 1973, N.C. award in lit. State of N.C., 1987, Bollingen prize for poetry, 1985, World Fantasy award World Fantasy Assn., 1992, 94, T.S. Eliot prize Ingersoll Found., 1993, Aiken Taylor Poetry award, 1996, Irene Lenore Heasley prize, 1999; named N.C. Poet Laureate, 1997; NDEA fellow, 1961-63; Rockefeller grantee, 1967-68, grantee Nat. Acad. Arts and Letters, 1968. Democrat. Avocations: books, wine, mischief. Office: U NC English Dept Greensboro NC 27412

CHAPPELL, JOHN CHARLES, lawyer; b. Minden, Nebr., Jan. 28, 1935; s. Charles Arthur and Eletta Hope (Pattison) C.; m. Joyce Joan Dawson, Sept. 1, 1957; children: Laura, Pamela, James, Allegra. B.S. in Edn., U. Nebr., 1956; JD, NYU, 1960. Bar: N.Y. 1960. Summer assoc. firm Dewey Ballantine, N.Y.C., 1959, assoc., 1960-68; ptnr. Dewey Ballantine LLP, N.Y.C., 1968—. Served to 1st lt. U.S. Army, 1957. Root-Tilden scholar NYU, 1956. Mem. ABA, N.Y. State Bar Assn., Assn. of Bar of City of N.Y., Univ. Club. Home: 2 Galloping Hill Cir Holmdel NJ 07733-1848 Office: Dewey Ballantine LLP 1301 Ave Of The Americas New York NY 10019-6022

CHAPPELL, MILES LINWOOD, JR., art history educator; b. Norfolk, Va., June 6, 1939; s. Miles Linwood Sr. and Melrose Clarice (Debnam) C.; m. Marcial Cassada, July 23, 1966; children: Ashley, Oliver, Picot. BS in Chemistry, Coll. William and Mary, 1960; PhD in Art History, U. N.C., 1971. Prof. art history dept. art and art history Coll. William and Mary, Williamsburg, Va., 1971—; chair dept.; Chancellor prof. art history Coll. William and Mary, 1987; artistic adv. bd. Interlochen Ctr. for Arts. Author: Cristofano Allori, 1984, Lodovico Cigoli, Disegni, 1992, The Fine Art of Drawing, 1993; co-author: Disegni dei Toscani, 1979, Lodovico Cigoli, tra manierismo e barocco, 1992, Renascence of the Florentine Baroque in "Dialoghi di storia dell'arte", 1998; formulator and co-author: Form, Function and Finesse: Drawings from the Herman Found., 1983; asst. editor: Studies in Iconography, 1978-80; adv. editor: Eighteenth-Century Life, 1980-84, 85—; contbr. articles on Renaissance, Baroque and Am. art to profl. jours. Mem. internat. survey of Jewish monuments, U. Ill., 1978. Harvard U. Ctr. for Italian Renaissance Studies fellow, Florence, 1980; Cité Internat. des Arts, 1995; recipient numerous rsch. grants. Mem. Kunsthistorisches Institut Florence, Phi Beta Kappa (Alpha chpt. award for scholarship 1987, v.p. 1992-93). Avocations: drawing, painting, music. Home: 139 Ridings Cv Williamsburg VA 23185-3903 Office: Coll William & Mary Dept Art History Williamsburg VA 23187

CHAPPELL, VERE CLAIBORNE, philosophy educator; b. Rochester, N.Y., Mar. 22, 1930; s. Vere Chambers and Edyth (Brown) C.; m. Sally Anderson, June 7, 1951 (div. June, 1963); children: Jennifer Helen, Jonathan Claiborne, David Lincoln; m. Sheryl Berglund, July 31, 1963; children: Vere Chambers II, Melissa, Addison Ward; step-children: Clayton Scott Templin, Jaime Templin Carlsen. B.A., Yale U., 1951, M.A., 1953, Ph.D., 1958; student, U. Heidelberg, Germany, 1953-54. Instr. Yale, 1954-57; instr. U. Chgo., 1957-61, asst. prof., 1961-63, assoc. prof., 1963-68, prof. philosophy, 1968-70, acting chmn. philosophy dept., 1964-65; prof., head philosophy U. Mass., 1970-74; acting assoc. provost, dean U. Mass. (Grad. Sch.), 1974-76, assoc. provost, 1977-78, prof. philosophy, 1978—; vis. prof. Ind. U., 1967, U. Ill., Chgo., 1967, U. Ill., Urbana, 1968, Notre Dame U., 1969, U. So. Calif., 1969-70, Smith Coll., 1973, 74, Mt. Holyoke Coll., 1982, 83, 85, 90, 91, 92; mem. Coun. for Philos. Studies, 1973-78. Co-author: Twenty-five Years of Descartes Scholarship, 1987; co-author: The Cambridge History of Seventeenth-Century Philosophy, 1998; editor: The Philosophy of Mind, 1962, The Philosophy of David Hume, 1963, Ordinary Language, 1964, Hume, 1966, Essays on Early Modern Philosophers, 1992, The Cambridge Companion to Locke, 1994, Descartes's Meditations, 1997, Locke: Oxford Readings in Philosophy, 1998, Hobbes and Bramhall on Liberty and Necessity, 1999; mng. editor: Rev. Metaphysics, 1954-56; asst. editor: Ethics, 1958-61; asst.-treas. Philos. Quar., 1959-69; cons. editor Random House Knopf, 1963-74; editl. cons.: Thoemmes Dictionary of Seventeenth-Century British Philosophers, 1995—. Fulbright fellow, 1953-54; Nat. Endowment for Humanities fellow, 1970. Mem. Am. Philos. Assn., Aristotelian Soc., Royal Inst. Philosophy. Home: 17 Harkness Rd Amherst MA 01002-9704 Office: U Mass Philosophy Dept Bartlett Amherst MA 01003

CHAPPELL, WILLARD RAY, physics educator, environmental scientist; b. Boulder, Colo., Feb. 27, 1938; s. Willard Bruce and Mildred Mary (Weaver) C.; m. Juanita June Benetin, Mar. 5, 1981; children: Ginger Ferguson, Robert Ferguson. B.A. in Math., U. Colo., 1962, Ph.D. in Physics, 1965; A.M. in Physics, Harvard U., 1963. Postdoctoral research assoc. Smithsonian Astrophys. Obs., Cambridge, Mass., 1965-66; postdoctoral research assoc. Lawrence Livermore Lab., Calif., 1966-67; asst. prof. physics U. Colo., Boulder, 1967-70, assoc. prof., 1970-73, prof., 1973-76; prof. physics, dir. Ctr. for Environ. Scis. U. Colo., Denver, 1976—; chmn. Dept. Energy Oil Shale Task Force, 1978-83; mem. adv. com. to dir. on health scis. Los Alamos Nat. Lab.; mem. Colo. Gov.'s Sci. Adv. Com., 1974-76, chmn., 1975-76. Author: Transport and Biological Effects of Molybdenum in the Environment, 1975. Served with U.S. Army, 1956-58. NSF fellow, 1962-65; grantee Fleishman Found., 1969-71, NSF, 1971-76, EPA, 1975-79, Dept. Energy, 1976-83, U.S. Bur. Mines, 1979-81. Mem. Am. Phys. Soc., AAAS, Soc. Environ. Geochemistry and Health (exec. com. 1981-83, 86-88, sec./treas. 1988—), Phi Beta Kappa. Democrat. Office: U Colo Environ Scis PO Box 173364 Denver CO 80217-3364

CHAPPELLE, LOU JO, physical therapist assistant; b. Watertown, N.Y., Mar. 7, 1952; d. Harold Joseph and Alice Jean (Marcellus) Getman; m. Richard George Tobey, Aug. 14, 1982 (div.); m. Gerald E. Chappelle, Sept. 14, 1996; stepson, Scott C. AA, Hudson Valley Community Coll., 1972; BSE, State U. Coll., Cortland, N.Y., 1974; AAS, St. Philips Coll., 1981. Cert. elem. and secondary tchr., N.Y. Educator phys. edn., coach Gilbertsville (N.Y.) Central Sch., 1974-79, 1000 Islands Jr.-Sr. High Sch., Sand Bay-Clayton, N.Y., 1980-82; phys. therapist asst. II N.Y. State Veteran's Home, Oxford, 1982-91; phys. therapy asst. F.F. Thompson Health Sys., Inc., Canandaigua, N.Y., 1992-98, SunDance Rehab Corp, Ontario County Health Facility, 1998, Finger Lakes Vis. Nurse Svc., 1999—. EMT Gilbertsville

(N.Y.) Emergency Squad, 1983-89. Capt. USAR, 1977-96. Decorated Army Achievement medal. Home: 4313 Deep Run Cove Canandaigua NY 14424

CHAPPEN, EDWARD PETER, physician; b. Carbondale, Pa., July 8, 1925; s. Peter E. and Amelia E. (Kouloumpy) C. BS, Pa. State U., 1946; MD, Jefferson Med. Coll., 1952. Diplomate Am. Bd. Psychiatry and Neurology. Intern Jefferson Med. Coll. Hosp., Phila., 1953; fellow Menninger Sch. Psychiatry; practice gen. psychiatry, Trenton, N.J., 1955—; resident in psychiatry Menninger Sch. Psychiatry, Topeka, Kans., 1967-70; staff psychiatrist Cen. Santa Clara County Mental Health Ctr., San Jose, Calif., 1970-71; mem., then chmn. staff St. Francis Hosp.; cons. in psychiatry Hamilton Hosp., Union Indsl. Home, Trenton. Mem. Trenton Mayor's Com. for Selection of Trenton Sister City, 1961, Trenton Landmarks Commn. for Hist. Preservation, Trenton Civic Improvements Com.; mem. spl. groups div. Del. Valley United Fund, 1958; treas. local chpt. Am. Assn. UN, 1960-61; mem. exec. bd. Greater Trenton chpt. People to People; exec. council, chmn. pub. relations com. Parnassos Greek Cultural Soc. of N.Y. Inc., 1963; mem. adv. com. for study sociology, death and dying Mercer County; mem. fine arts com. Anglican Cathedral of the Trinity, Trenton; bd. govs. Greater Trenton Symphony Assn., 1966-67; trustee Friends of Trenton Free Pub. Library, Vis. Nurse Assn. Trenton; bd. mgrs. Donnelly Meml. Hosp.; trustee Greek Orthodox Ch. St. George, Hamilton Twsp., N.J., 1962-64. Served to lt. (j.g.) USMC, 1954. Menninger Sch. Psychiatry fellow, 1970. Mem. N.Y. Acad. Scis., AMA, Am. Psychiat. Assn., Santa Clara-Monterey Counties Psychiat. Soc., Mercer County Med. Soc. (chmn. physician placement service com.), Navy League U.S., Internat. Platform Assn., Byzantine Fellowship, Pa. Soc., Assn. Mil. Surgeons U.S., UN Assn. U.S.A. (chpt. pres. 1966), Alumni Assn. Menninger Sch. Psychiatry, Princeton Soc. Archeol. Inst. Am., Trenton Mus. Soc., State House Dist. Assn., Douglass House Commn., Archeol. Inst. Am., Nat. Hist. Soc., Trenton Hist. Soc., Hist. Soc. Hamilton Twp., Nat. Trust Hist. Preservation, Trent House Assn., Symposium Soc. Trenton, Met. Mus. Art, Friends of Art Mus. Princeton U., Phi Alpha Sigma. Clubs: Architectoniki (Athens, Greece); Commd. Officers U.S. Naval Base (Phila.). Lodges: Rotary, Soc. of Mary, Masons (32 deg.), Shriners. Office: 476 Hamilton Ave Trenton NJ 08609-2711

CHAPPLE, ABBY, consumer communications consultant; b. N.Y.C., Aug. 17, 1939; d. Adolph Emil and Thelma (Pierce) Klueppelberg; m. Ross Victor Chapple (div.); m. Robert Alan Mewhinney (div.); m. David Marshall Walker. BA, Am. U., 1961, postgrad., 1961-65. Reporter Washington Star, 1966-81; pres. Chapple/Mewhinney Assocs., Annapolis, Md., 1981-82; spl. asst. to chmn. Consumer Product Safety Commn., Washington, 1982—; pres. Consumer Comm., Great Cacapon, W.Va., 1985; dir. retail program Upholstered Furniture Action Coun., 1986—. Founding editor Washington County Pickett, 1996. Pres. Friend of the Cacapon River, 1998—; bd. dirs. W.Va. Rivers Coalition, 1999—. Recipient Media award Dallas Mkt. Ctr., 1978, Home Furnishngs Hall Fame, 1979, Am. Soc. Interior Designers, 1985, Chmn.'s award Consumer Product Safety Commn., 1984. Mem. Internat. Furnishings and Design Assn. (Presdl. commendation 1991), Nat. Assn. Bus. Women, Women in Comm. (pres. Md. chpt. 1994), Rotary (program chair Berkeley Springs chpt.). Republican. Jewish. Home: Brandon Rd Largent WV 25422-0370 Office: Consumer Comms PO Box 370 Great Cacapon WV 25422-0370

CHAPPLE, JOHN H., professional sports team executive; b. Syracuse, N.Y., Apr. 8, 1953. Grad., Syracuse U.; postgrad., Harvard u. Former exec. v.p. ops. McCaw Cellular Comms., Inc.; former exec. v.p. AT&T Wireless Svcs.; pres., COO Orca Bay Sports and Entertainment parent co. of Vancouver Grizzlies (NBA), Vancouver Canucks (NHL), 1995—. Office: Orca Bay Sports & Entertainment, 800 Griffths Way, Vancouver, BC Canada V6B 661*

CHAPPLE, THOMAS LESLIE, lawyer; b. Canandaigua, N.Y., Nov. 28, 1947; s. Howard Leslie and Elizabeth Chapple; m. Shelly Smith, July 17, 1982; children: Adam Roger, Hannah Elizabeth. BA, Cornell U., 1970; JD, Albany Law Sch., 1973. Bar: N.Y. 1974, U.S. Supreme Ct. 1981, Va. 1992. Atty. assoc. Nixon, Hargrave, Devans & Doyle, Rochester, N.Y., 1973-76; sec., asst. gen. counsel Gannett Co., Inc., Arlington, Va., 1977-79; assoc. gen. counsel., sec. Gannett Co., Inc., Rochester, N.Y., 1979-81, v.p., assoc. gen. counsel, sec., 1981-91, gen. counsel, sec., 1991-95, sr. v.p., gen. counsel, sec., 1995—; sec. The Gannett Found., 1983-89. Mem. ABA, Assn. Corp. Counsel, N.Y. State Bar Assn., Sigma Pi. Republican. Methodist. Office: Gannett Co Inc 1100 Wilson Blvd Ste 2100 Arlington VA 22209-2299*

CHAPUT, CHARLES J., archbishop; b. Concordia, Kans., Sept. 26, 1944. Student, St. Fidelis Coll., Capuchin Coll., Cath. U., U. San Francisco. Ordained priest Roman Cath. Ch., 1970; consecrated bishop Diocese Rapid City, S.D., 1988. Bishop Rapid City, S.D., 1988-97; archbishop Denver, Colo., 1997—. Office: Catholic Pastoral Ctr 1300 S Steele St Denver CO 80210-4710*

CHAR, PATRICIA HELEN, lawyer; b. Honolulu, Mar. 23, 1952; d. Lincoln S. and Daisy Char; m. Thomas W. Bingham, Mar. 20, 1982; children: Matthew Thomas Bingham, James Nathan Bingham. BA, Northwestern U., 1974; JD, Georgetown U., 1977. Bar: Wash. 1977, U.S. Dist. Ct. (we. dist.) Wash. 1977, U.S. Dist. Ct. (ea. dist.) Wash. 1982, U.S. Ct. Appeals (9th cir.) 1981, U.S. Supreme Ct. 1984. Assoc. Bogle & Gates, Seattle, 1977-84; ptnr., mem. Bogle & Gates P.L.L.C., Seattle, 1984-99; of counsel Garvey, Schubert & Barer, Seattle, 1999—. Author: Ownership By a Fiduciary, 1997. Trustee Epiphany Sch., Seattle, YWCA, Seattle-King County-Snohomish County; vol. King County Big Sisters, United Way of King County, Seattle, 1987-90, Guardian Ad Litem Program, Seattle, 1987-93. Mem. ABA, Wash. State Bar Assn. (co-author chpts. 3 and 4 Wash. Civil Procedure Deskbook 1992). Office: Garvey Schubert & Barer 1191 2nd Ave # 1800 Seattle WA 98101-2939

CHAR, VERNON FOOK LEONG, lawyer; b. Honolulu, Dec. 15, 1934; s. Charles A. and Annie (Ching) C.; m. Evelyn Lau, June 14, 1958; children: Richard, Daniel, Douglas, Charles, Elizabeth. BA, U. Hawaii, 1956; LLB, Harvard U., 1959. Bar: Hawaii 1959. Dep. atty. gen. Office of Atty. Gen., Honolulu, 1959-60, 62-65; ptnr. Damon Key Char & Bocken, Honolulu, 1965-89, Char, Sakamoto, Ishii, Lum & Ching, Honolulu, 1989—. Chmn. Hawaii Ethics Commn., Honolulu, 1968-75, Hawaii Bicentennial Com., 1986-91, 1st Hawaii Jud. Conf., 1985. Mem. ABA (bd. govs. 1991-94), Hawaii Bar Assn. (pres. 1985), U. Hawaii Alumni Assn. (pres. 1989-90). Home: 351 Anonia St Honolulu HI 96821-2052 Office: Char Sakamoto Ishii Lum & Ching Davies Pacific Ctr 841 Bishop St Ste 850 Honolulu HI 96813-3957

CHARANIA, BARKAT, real estate consultant; b. Ahmedabad, Gujrat, India, June 27, 1941; came to U.S., 1961; s. Ismail and Zenabai Charania; m. Jerilyn Lee Scott, Apr. 10, 1962 (div. May 1970); children: Sultana, Ramzan, Kalvin, Kevin, Stephen; m. Maher Kurani, Oct. 11, 1970; children: Munira, Rahim, Munira Moon. Student, Alpena (Mich.) Community Coll., 1961-62, U. Calif., L.A., 1962-63, U. Pa., 1965-68, Lincoln Tech. Sch., 1983. Cert. comml. investment mem.; cert. hotel adminstr. Pres. Eurindus, Inc., Cherry Hill, N.J., 1965-83, Airline Inn, Inc., Atlanta, 1980-83; owner B.C. Investments & Realty Co., Atlanta, Ga., 1985—; pres. Southern Inn, Inc., Chattanooga, 1987—; owner B.C. Hospitality Mgmt. Co., Atlanta, 1987—; pres. Trident Devel. Corp., Charleston, S.C., 1989—, BJM Hospitality, Inc., 1993—, ICI Long Distance Inc., 1995—, Universal Connect Corp., 1995—; sr. assocs. Marcus & Millichap, Atlanta, 1996-97; cons. Pattni Holdings, Atlanta, 1984—, Esmail Internat., Inc., Atlanta, 1986—, Harbour Enterprise, Chattanooga, 1987—, Shin Inc., Chattanooga, 1987—, ABC Inc., Chattanooga, 1988—. Ga. coord. Agakhan Found. U.S.A., Atlanta, 1988; chmn. Southeastern Enterprising People's Assn., 1990, 91. Mem. Atlanta Bd. Realtors, Nat. Assn. Realtors, Realtor Nat. Mktg. Inst., Comml. Investment Real Estate Coun., Edn. Inst., Internat. Real Estate Inst., Ismaili Commerce Club (v.p. Atlanta chpt. 1982), S.E. Region (chmn. Agakhan econ. planning bd. for U.S.A.), Internat. Real Estate Fedn. Republican. Avocations: reading, traveling, swimming, tennis. Fax: 404-767-0714. Home: 4850 Woodvale Dr NW Atlanta GA 30327-4556 Office: 4505 Best Rd College Park GA 30337-5107 *People don't care how much you know until they know how much you care...about them. How far you go in life depends on your being tender with the young, compassionate with the aged, sympathetic with the striving, and tolerant of the weak and the strong. Because someday in life you will have all of these.*

CHARAP, STANLEY HARVEY, electrical engineering educator; b. N.Y.C., Apr. 21, 1932; s. William and Esther Charap; m. Marilyn Novick, Aug. 7, 1955; children: Joshua David, Lawrence Gordon. BS in Physics, Bklyn. Coll., 1953; PhD in Physics, Rutgers U., 1959. Mem. rsch. staff IBM T.J. Watson Rsch. Ctr., Yorktown Heights, N.Y., 1958-64; rsch. scientist Rsch. div. Am.-Standard Inc., Piscataway, N.J., 1964, supr. solid state physics, 1965-66, mgr. physics and electronics, 1966-68; assoc. prof. elec. and computer engring. Carnegie Mellon U., Pitts., 1968-71, prof., 1971—; prof. emeritus, 1997—; assoc. head dept. Carnegie Mellon U., Pitts., 1980-85, acting head dept., 1981-82, vice chmn. faculty senate, 1972-73, chmn. faculty senate, 1986-87, assoc. dir. Data Storage Systems Ctr., 1990-96; cons. Westinghouse Rsch. Ctr., Pitts., 1969-84; mem. tech. staff Bell Labs., Whippany, N.J., summer 1973; sr. vis. fellow U. Wales, Cardiff, spring 1976; vis. scientist Control Data Corp., Mpls., summer 1987. Editor: Physics of Magnetism, 1964; contbr. to Magnetism & Metallurgy, 1969; contbr. over 60 tech. articles to profl. jours. V.p. Sch. Advanced Jewish Studies, Pitts., 1989-91. Recipient Tech. Achievement award Nat. Storage Industry Consortium, 1998. Fellow IEEE; mem. IEEE Magnetics Soc. (sec.-treas. 1987-88, v.p. 1989-90, pres. 1991-92, past pres. 1993-94, editor-in-chief IEEE Trans. on Magnetics 1982-86, editl. bd. IEEE Press 1989-91, IEEE Tech. activities bd., liaison coun. 1993, gen. chmn. Joint INTERMAG-MMM conf. 1994, Disting. Lectr. 1996, Achievement award 1998), Am. Inst. Physics, Conf. on Magnetism and Magnetic Materials (treas. 1981-83, gen. chmn. 1986). Office: Carnegie Mellon U Dept Elec & Computer Engring 5000 Forbes Ave Pittsburgh PA 15213-3890

CHARBONNEAU, YVON, member of parliament; b. Mont-Saint-Michel, July 11, 1940; m. Raja Mammound; 4 children. BA in Classical Studies, Sem. de Mont-Laurier, 1959; degree in edn., U. Montreal, 1961, M degree in French Lit., 1968; M in Polit. Sci., U. Laval, 1980; D in Polit. Sci. and Internat. Rels., U. Que., Montreal, 1981. Prof. French and humanities Jean-Jacques-Olier Classical Day Sch., Verdun, 1961-69, Polyvalente de Mont-Laurier, Verdun, 1961-69; coop. worker Can. Internat. Devel. Agy., Sfax, Tunisia, 1965-67; pres. Que. Tchrs. Union, 1970-78, 82-88, spl. advisor, dir. comms. and internat. affairs, 1979-82, chair comm. on inquiry on hazardous wasts, 1989-90; v.p. pub. rels. environ. divsn. Groupe SNC-Lanvalin, 1990-92; pres., cons. for pub. affairs Premier and Consult Enjeu, 1992; v.p. planning and devel. Que. Labour Force Devel. Corp., 1993-94; mem. Nat. Assembly for the Bourassa, 1994-97; M.P. for Anjou-Rivere Des Prairies House of Commons, 1997—, mem. standing com. on the environ., mem. standing com. on procedure and house affairs, former mem. subcom. on pvt. mem.'s bus.; participant in internat. projects on edn., human rights, and the environment; mem. numerous Que. orgns. working in the fiels of the environment, edn., human rights, employment, and econ. and social devel. Mem. Liberal Party. Office: House of Commons, Rm 343 Confederation Bldg, Ottawa, ON Canada K1A 0A6*

CHARENDOFF, MARK STUART, educator; b. Toronto, Aug. 21, 1963; s. Nathan and Lillian (Zaid) C.; m. Susan Frances Cohen, Sept. 7, 1992. B Hebrew Letters, Darche Noam Coll., Jerusalem, 1985. Ordained rabbi, 1986. Asst. regional dir. B'nai B'rith Youth Orgn., Toronto, 1986-88; cons. B'nai B'rith Youth Orgn., 1994-95; dir. Judaic Cultural Devel. Jewish Cmty. Ctr. Toronto, 1988-94; program cons. Charles R. Bronfman Found., Montreal, Que., Can., 1992-95; dir. Jewish Ednl. Svcs. Jewish Cmty. Ctrs. Assn. N.Am., N.Y.C., 1994-98; v.p. Andrea and Charles Bronfman Philanthropies, N.Y.C., 1998—; mem. adv. bd. Washington Inst. for Jewish Leadership and Values, 1996—, Edah, 1997—, Nat. Ctr. for the Hebrew Lang., 1997—; chair Forum Jewish Educators, N.Y.C., 1990-93; mem. adv. coun. Joint Authority for Jewish Edn., N.Y.C., 1994—. Editor: Jewish Education and the Jewish Community Center, 1974. Bd. dirs. Coalition for Advancement Jewish Education, 1997—. Jewish. Avocations: sailing, biking, travel. Office: Andrea and Charles Bronfman Philanthropies 375 Park Ave 6th Fl New York NY 10152

CHARETTE, SHARON JULIETTE, library administrator; b. Woonsocket, R.I., Apr. 24, 1956; d. Roland Alfred Lionel and Juliette Cecile (Lavoie) C. BA in French and English, R.I. Coll., 1978; MLS, U. R.I., 1981; cert. in computer info. systems, Bryant Coll., 1989; student, RISD, 1989-91. Asst. serials Wheaton Coll., Norton, Mass., 1978-79, catalog asst., 1979-82, libr. acquisitions, 1982-86; dir. Learning Resources Ctr. New Eng. Inst. Tech., Warwick, R.I., 1986—; seamstress, designer, craftsman, 1976—. Chair Franco Am. com. R.I. Heritage Commn., Providence, 1987-90, treas., 1982-87, mem., 1978—. Mem. ALA, New England Libr. Assn., R.I. Libr. Assn., Mensa, TechACCESS of R.I. (bd. dirs., corr. sec. 1992-98, chair 1998—). Avocations: jewelry design, hist. costume reproduction, computers, music, theatre. Home: 147 Greenville Rd North Smithfield RI 02896-7422 Office: New Eng Inst Tech 2500 Post Rd Warwick RI 02886-2244

CHAREWICZ, DAVID MICHAEL, photographer; b. Chgo., Feb. 17, 1932; s. Michael and Stella (Pietrzak) C.; student DePaul U., 1957, Northwestern U., 1952; MA in Photography, Profl. Photographers Am. Inc., 1986; m. Catherine Uccello, Nov. 8, 1952; children: Michael, Karen, Daniel. Trainee, Merill Chase, Chgo., 1950-51; dark room technician Maurice Seymour, Chgo., 1951-52; photographer Oscar & Assos., Chgo., 1955-63; owner Dave Chare Photography, Park Ridge, Ill., 1963—; pres., owner C&C Duplicating, Inc., 1978-93. Pres. Oakton Parent Tchr. Club, 1968-69, del. dist. 64 caucus, 1970, 73; mem. centennial photo com., Park Ridge, Ill., 1973; mem. sponsoring com. Park Ridge Men's Prayer Breakfast 1982—. Served with AUS, 1952-54. Mem. Am. Soc. Photographers, Profl. Photographers Assn., Midstate Indsl. Photographers Assn. (treas. 1981, pres. 1984-85). Home: 739 N Northwest Hwy Park Ridge IL 60068-2541 Office: 1045 N Northwest Hwy Park Ridge IL 60068-1805

CHARFOOS, LAWRENCE SELIG, lawyer; b. Detroit, Dec. 7, 1935; s. Samuel and Charlotte (Salkin) C.; m. Jane Emerson. Student, U. Mich., 1953-56; LLB, Wayne State U., 1959. Bar: Mich. 1959, Ill. 1965. Pvt. practice Detroit, 1960-63; pres., partner Charfoos & Christensen, (P.C.), Detroit, 1967—; theatrical producer, legitimate theater mgr. Chgo., 1963-67; cons. med.-legal problems Mich. Med. Soc., Mich. Hosp. Coun., State Bar Mich., ATLA; mem. Com. U.S. Cts., 1995. Author: The Medical Malpractice Case: A Complete Handbook, 1974, Daughters at Risk, 1981, Personal Injury Practice, Technique and Technology, 1986; contbr. articles to profl. jours. Trustee Lawrence S. Charfoos Found. Elected to Inner Circle of Advocates, 1973. Mem. ABA, Mich. Bar Assn., Detroit Bar Assn. (past dir.), Am. Bd. Profl. Liability Attys. (founder, past pres.), Internat. Acad. Trial Lawyers, Plaintiff's Steering Com./Breast Implant Cases, Com. on U.S. Cts., State Bar Mich., 1995—. Office: 5510 Woodward Ave Detroit MI 48202-3804

CHARGAFF, ERWIN, biochemistry educator emeritus, writer; b. Austria, Aug. 11, 1905; came to U.S., 1928, naturalized, 1940; s. Hermann and Rosa C.; m. Vera Broido; 1 son, Thomas. Dr. phil., U. Vienna, 1928; Dr. phil. h.c, U. Basel, 1976; Sc.D. (hon.), Columbia U., 1976. Research fellow Yale U., 1928-30; asst. U. Berlin, Germany, 1930-33; research assoc. Inst. Pasteur, Paris, France, 1933-34; faculty Columbia U., 1935—, prof. biochemistry, 1952-74, prof. emeritus, 1974—, chmn. dept. biochemistry, 1970-74; vis. prof., Sweden, 1949, Japan, 1958, Brazil, 1959; vis. prof. Coll. de France, 1965, Naples, Palermo, Cornell, 1966, Stazione Zoologica, Naples, 1969. Author: Essays on Nucleic Acids, 1963, Voices in the Labyrinth, 1977, Heraclitean Fire, 1978, Das Feuer des Heraklit, 1979, Unbegreifliches Geheimnis, 1980, Bemerkungen, 1981, Warnungstafeln, 1982, Kritik der Zukunft, 1983, Zeugenschaft, 1985, Serious Questions, 1986, Abscheu vor der Weltgeschichte, 1988, Alphabetische Anschlaege, 1989, Vorlaeufiges Ende, 1990, Vermächtnis, 1992, Ueber das Lebendige, 1993, Armes Amerika: Arme Welt, 1994, Ein zweites Leben, 1995, Die Ausgicht vom 13 Stock, 1998, other lit. work in English and German; contbr. numerous articles to profl. jours.; editor: the Nucleic Acids, 3 vols., 1955, 60. Guggenheim fellow, 1949, 58; recipient Pasteur medal, 1949, Soc. Biol. Chemistry, Paris, 1961, Neuberg medal Am. Soc. European Chemists, 1958, Bertner Found. award Houston, 1965, C.L. Mayer prize French Acad. Scis., 1963, Dr. H.P. Heineken prize Netherlands Acad. Scis. Gregor-Mendel medal Leopoldina, 1973, Nat. Medal of Sci., 1975, medal N.Y. Acad. Medicine, 1980, Disting. Svc. award Columbia U., 1982, Johan-Heinrich Merck prize German Acad. Land. and Lit., 1984, Lit. prize City of Vienna, 1994. Fellow Am. Acad. Arts and Scis.; mem. Nat. Acad. Scis., Am. Philos. Soc.; fgn. mem. Royal Swedish Physiographic Soc., German Acad. Scis. Leopoldina. Home: 350 Central Park W Apt 13G New York NY 10025-6503

CHARITY, NADINE AMENT, educator, poet; b. Detroit, Nov. 23, 1949; d. Robert Malcolm and Clarice Ann (Stolker) Ament; m. Robert S. Bryson, Aug. 15, 1970 (div. 1979); children: Christine R. Tharpe, Robert T. Bryson; m. John Charles Charity, Nov. 26, 1987; 1 child, Edward M.C. Charity. BSEd, Centenary Coll., Shreveport, La., 1973, MEd, 1980; MLA, La. State U., Shreveport, 1993. Tchr. Southfield Schs., Shreveport, 1979-85, Bossier Parish Schs., Haughton, La., 1986—; tchr.-cons. Nat. Writing Project, Shreveport, 1990—. Author: (poetry) Sunday at Four, 1990—, Louisiana Literature, 1993, Cafe Review, 1994, Spectra, 1991-94. Cofounder River Cities Writers, Shreveport, 1992-94; poetry coord. Red River Revel, Shreveport, 1993—; mem. artist roster La. Divsn. of the Arts, Baton Rouge, 1994—' artist, judge Shreveport Regional Arts Coun. Art Break, 1994—. Mem. NEA, La. Edn. Assn. Avocation: reading. Home: 1908 Venus Dr Bossier City LA 71112 Office: Bossier Parish Sch Bd Benton LA

CHARKIEWICZ, MITCHELL MICHAEL, JR., economics and finance educator; b. Springfield, Mass., Sept. 29, 1946; s. Mitchell Michael Sr. and Helen (Nycz) C.; m. Sandra Isabel Miranda Amaral, June 30, 1970. BSBA, Am. Internat. Coll., 1969, MBA, 1984; postgrad., U. Conn., 1986-95. Prof. econs. Am. Internat. Coll., Springfield, 1985—, acting chmn. fin. dept., chmn. econs. dept., 1988-91; prof. econs. Ctrl. Conn. State U., New Britain, 1989—, Tunxis C.C., Farmington, Conn., 1986-91, Bay Path Coll., Longmeadow, Mass., 1995—, Springfield Tech. C.C., Springfield, Mass., 1999—; bus. tchr. Mt. Greylock Regional High Sch., Williamstown, Mass., 1969-71, Montachusett Regional Tech. High Sch., Fitchburg, Mass., 1971-74; unit mgr. Sports Prodns., Cleve., 1974; with sales and promotions San Antonio Spurs NBA, 1974-76; mgr. Bristol (Conn.) Racquet Club, 1976-80; sports dir. Sta. WBIS Radio, Bristol, 1980-85; regional tng. dir. Center Point Technologies, Chgo., 1997—; cons. Tecnomed, J. Trapp, CA, Caracas, Venezuela, 1989, De-Yang Devel. Corp. of Sci. and Tech., China, 1990; Yale Internat. studies faculty com. U. Kuwait; faculty info. tech. Springfield Tech. C.C., 1999. Author test bank for Principles of Economics (by Colander), 1993, Economics rev., 1994; author: (instrs. resource manual for) Money and Banking, 1995; editor AIC Sch. of Bus. Jour., 1988-91; referee jour. Iranian Econ. Rev., 1990; contbr. articles to profl. jours. Chmn. softball marathon Easter Seals, New Britain, 1985; celebrity chmn. Conn. Pub. TV, Hartford, 1980-84; mem. World Affairs Coun., Springfield, 1985-91; judge Internat. Chili Soc., L.A., 1980—. Recipient Appreciation award Optimist Club, Woodland Hills, Tex., 1976, San Antonio, 1976, Conn. Pub. TV, Hartford, 1982-84, Easter Seals, Conn., 1985, U. Kuwait, 1988. Mem. AAUP, Am. Econ. Assn., Ea. Econ. Assn., N.E. Bus. and Econs. Assn. (bd. dirs. 1992-98, treas. 1995-98), Western Mass. Econ. Devel. Assn., Conn. Internat. Trade Assn. (chmn. scholarship com.), New Eng. Coun. L.Am. Studies, Omicron Delta Epsilon (bd. dirs. 1988-91). Republican. Roman Catholic. Avocations: judging food contests, world travel. Address: 100 Ellison St Suffield CT 06078-2260

CHARLA, LEONARD FRANCIS, lawyer; b. New Rochelle, N.Y., May 4, 1940; s. Leonard A. and Mary L. Charla; m. Kathleen Gerace, Feb. 3, 1968 (div. Dec. 1988); children: Larisa, Christopher; m. Elizabeth A. Du Mouchelle, Aug. 27, 1993. BA, Iona Coll., 1962; JD, Cath. U., 1965; LLM, George Washington U., 1971. Bar: D.C. 1967, N.J. 1970, Mich. 1971. Tech. writer IRS, Washington, 1966-67; atty. adv. ICC, Washington, 1967, atty., 1968-69; mgmt. intern HEW, Washington, 1967-68; atty. Bowes & Millner, Transp. Cons., Newark, 1969-71; atty. legal staff GM, Detroit, 1971-85, sr. counsel, 1985-87, asst. gen. counsel, 1987-89; sr. v.p. Clean Sites Inc., Alexandria, Va., 1989-90; shareholder Butzel Long, Detroit and Birmingham, Mich., 1990—; mem. faculty Ctr. for Creative Studies, Coll. Art and Design, Detroit, 1978-89, adj. asst. prof., 1982-89; faculty art U. Mich., 1980, 84-89, adj. asst. prof. 1988-89. Author: Never Cooked Before/Gotta Cook Now!, 1999. Bd. dirs. Gt. Lakes Performing Artists Assocs., 1983-85; bd. dirs. Mich. Assn. Cmty. Arts Agys., 1983-89, 92-93, vice-chair, 1986-88, chair, 1988-89; bd. govs. Cath. U. Am. Alumni, 1982, v.p., 1993—; active Info. Network Superfund Settlements, 1988—; bd. regents Cath. U. Am., 1992—, Birmingham Bloomfield Art Assn., 1987-88, 94-95; bd. dirs. Friends of Modern Art, Detroit Inst. Arts, 1996—, v.p., 1998—. Fellow N.Y. State Regents, 1962; scholar Cath. U. Law Sch., 1962-65. Mem. ABA, Mich. State Bar Assn. (chmn. arts sect. 1980-81, arts comm. entertainment and sports sect. coun. 1979-88, 92—). Office: Butzel Long 1500 W Jefferson Ave Ste 900 Detroit MI 48216

CHARLES, ALLAN G., physician, educator; b. N.Y.C., Nov. 15, 1928; s. Harry G. and Alice (Grotzky) C.; m. Phyllis V. J. Vail, June 28, 1957; children: Della Marie, Aaron Joseph, David Jonathan. AB cum laude, NYU, 1948, MD, 1952. Diplomate: Am. Bd. Obstetrics and Gynecology. Intern Phila. Gen. Hosp., 1952-53; resident in obstetrics and gynecology Mt. Sinai Hosp., N.Y.C., 1955-57, Michael Reese Hosp., Chgo., 1957-60; clin. asst. Michael Reese Hosp., 1960-61, assoc. attending physician, 1961-69, attending physician, 1969—; co-dir. Michael Reese Hosp. (Rh-Investigative Clinic), 1963—, vice-chmn. dept. obstetrics and gynecology, 1971, pres. staff, 1978, bd. dirs., 1981-84; chief obstetrics and gynecology Michael Reese Hosp., 1990-99; chmn. rsch. and edn. found. Michael Reese Hosp. med. staff, 1996—; pvt. practice specializing in obstetrics and gynecology Chgo., 1960—; courtesy staff Chgo. Lying-In-Hosp.; clin. asst. prof. ob-gyn. U. Ill. Coll. Medicine, Chgo., 1960-64, Chgo. Med. Sch., 1964-72; clin. prof. Pritzker Sch. Medicine, U. Chgo., 1972-84; attending physician Northwestern Meml. Hosp., 1984-90; prof. clin. ob-gyn. Northwestern U., 1983; clin. prof. ob-gyn. U. Ill. Coll. Medicine, 1991. Author: Rh Iso Immunization and Erythroblastosis Fetalis, 1969; Contbr. articles to profl. jours. Fellow Am. Coll. Obstetricians and Gynecologists, Internat. Coll. Surgeons (chmn. Am. sect. obs. and gynec. 1979-83, sec., asst. treas. Am. sect.), Central Assn. Obstetricians and Gynecologists; mem. AMA, Ill., Chgo. med. socs., Chgo. Gynecol. Soc. (v.p. 1980—, sec. 1988-90, pres.-elect, 1992, pres. 1993-94). Developer substitute for uterine tube, Rh-sensitization. Home: 6854 S Bennett Ave Chicago IL 60649-1502 Office: Michael Reese Hosp Med Ctr Dept Ob/Gyn 29th and Ellis Ave Chicago IL 60616

CHARLES, BERTRAM, radio broadcasting executive; b. Boston, Jan. 26, 1918; s. Jacob H. and Annie L. (Kanter) Fein; m. Alberta Marie Carpenter, Sept. 4, 1948; children—Meredith Ann Trapp, Blair Carpenter Adams. Student, NYU, 1935-38. Reporter Bklyn. Daily Eagle, 1938-39, N.Y. Post, 1939-40; news and sports announcer Sta. WAOV, Vincennes, Ind., 1945; sportscaster Sta. WIRE, Indpls., 1945; dir. sports and pub. service Sta. WAKR, Akron, Ohio, 1946-48; program and sports dir. Sta. WVKO-AM-FM, Columbus, Ohio, 1948-49; sta. mgr. Sta. WVKO-AM-FM, 1949-53, v.p., 1953-71, pres., gen. mgr., 1971-82, ret. Trustee Columbus Zoo, Opera/Columbus, Upper Arlington Rotary Club; patron Columbus Art Gallery; past pres., chmn. bd. Charity Newsies; chmn. artistic com. Columbus Opera. Served with USAF, 1942-45; vice chmn. Upper Arlington Cultural Arts Commn. Named Columbus Father of Year, 1961; Paul Harris fellow Rotary Internat. Mem. Columbus Better Bus. Bur. (past dir.), Ohio Radio and TV Execs. (pres. 1957), Columbus Radio Broadcasters, Ohio Assn. Broadcasters (past dir.), Soc. Profl. Journalists (dir.), Ohio Sportscasters Assn. (past dir.), Nat. Football Found. Hall of Fame, Columbus Advt. Fedn. Clubs: York Temple Country, Maennerchor, Rotary (bd. dirs.), Agonis, Probus (pres.), Torch (pres.), Capital. Home: 2548 W Lane Ave Columbus OH 43221-3657 *Although I've prayed to God as if everything depended upon Him, I've worked all my life as if everything depended upon me.*

CHARLES, CAROL MORGAN, education educator; b. Loraine, Tex., Jan. 11, 1931; s. Joe M. and Lois F. C.; m. Ruth M. Kimbell, June 3, 1951; children: Gail, Timothy. B.A., Eastern N.Mex. U., 1953, M.A., 1957; Ph.D., U. N.Mex., 1961. Tchr., Estancia (N.Mex.) Schs., 1953-59; research asst., vis. prof. U. N.Mex., 1959-61; prof. edn. San Diego State U., 1961-66, 68—; prof. Tchrs. Coll., Columbia U., 1967-68; cons. govts. Brazil and Peru. Author: Educational Psychology, 1972, 2d rev. edit., 1976, Individualizing Instruction, 1976, 2d rev. edit., 1980, Schooling, Teaching Learning: American Education, 1978, The Special Student, 1980, Building Classroom Discipline, 1981, 4th rev. edit., 1992, 5th rev. edit., 1995, 6th rev. edit., 1998, Elementary Classroom Management, 1983, 2d rev. edit., 1994, Introduction to Educational Research, 1988, 2d rev. edit., 1994, 3rd rev. edit., 1998; contbr. articles to profl. jours. Recipient Disting. Teaching award, Outstanding Prof. award, Meritorious Performance award. Mem. ASCD, Assn. Tchr. Educators, AAUP, Phi Beta Kappa, Phi Delta Kappa. Home: 7239 Birchcreek Rd San Diego CA 92119-1627

CHARLES, CHERYL, non-profit and business executive; b. Seattle, Nov. 4, 1947; d. Tom E. Charles and Irene D. (Brown) Shelver; m. Robert E. Samples, Sept. 15, 1973; 1 child, Stician M. BA, U. Ariz., 1969; MA, Ariz. State U., 1971; PhD, U. Wash., 1982. Lic. secondary edn. Tchr. Phoenix Union H.S., 1969-71; staff assoc. Social Sci. Edn. Consortium, Boulder, Colo., 1971-72; social studies dept. chmn. Trevor Browne H.S., Phoenix, 1972-73; asst. dir. Essentia: Environ. Studies for Urban Youth, Olympia, Wash., 1973-75; nat. dir. Project Learning Tree, Tiburon, Calif. & Boulder, Colo., 1976-84; exec. dir. Project Wild, Boulder, 1981-93; pres. Sol y Sombra Found., Santa Fe, N.Mex., 1991—; exec. dir. Ctr. for Study of Cmty., Santa Fe, 1993—; COO The Santa Fe Group; owner Hawksong Assocs.; prin. investigator MacArthur Found., Chgo., 1993-94, Bradley Found., Milw., 1995—, Ednl. Found. Am., Westport, Conn., 1995—; project dir. McCune Found., Santa Fe, N.Mex., 1995-97; sr. dir. Banking Industry Tech. Secretariat, 1997—. Co-author: The Whole School Book, 1977; editor: Project Wild Elementary and Secondary Guide, 1983-92, Project Wild Aquatic Guide, 1987-92; co-editor, designer Windstar Jour., 1987-90. Mem. nat. adv. com. U. Mich. Coll. Engring., East Lansing, Mich., 1990-93; nat. judge Seiko Youth Challenge, 1994; bd. advisors Aspen (Colo.) Global Change Inst., 1990—; bd. trustees Hispanic Culture Found., Albuquerque, 1995-98; pres. bd. trustees Windstar Land Conservancy, 1996—; chair bd. trustees Windstar Found., 1995—. Recipient Leadership award U.S. Forest Svc., internat. region, 1985, L.B. Sharp award excellence in outdoor/environ. edn., 1993, Gold medal Pres. Environ. and Conservation Challenge award, Washington, 1991; named Profl. of Yr. Western Assn. Fish/Wildlife Agys., 1991. Mem. N.Am. Assn. Environ. Edn., Nat. Coun. Social Studies, N.Mex. First Town Hall, No. N.Mex. Grant Makers. Avocations: writing, horseback riding, dancing, cooking, reading. Office: The Santa Fe Group 3 N Chamisa Dr Ste 2 Santa Fe NM 87505-9463

CHARLES, ISABEL, university administrator; b. Bklyn., Mar. 10, 1926; d. James Patrick and Isabel (Roney) C. B.A., Manhattan Coll., 1954; M.A., U. Notre Dame, 1960, Ph.D., 1965; postgrad., U. Mich., 1968-69. Chmn. dept. English Bishop Watterson High Sch., Columbus, Ohio, 1954-59, St. Mary of the Springs Acad., Columbus, 1959-62; asst. prof. English Ohio Dominican Coll., Columbus, 1965-68; acad. dean, exec. v.p. Ohio Dominican Coll., 1969-73; asst. dean Coll. Arts and Letters, U. Notre Dame, 1973-75, acting dean, 1975, dean, 1976-82, asst. provost, 1982-87, assoc. provost, 1987-95; assoc. provost emerita U. Notre Dame, 1995—. Contbr. articles to profl. jours. Mem. MLA, Assn. Am. Colls. Home: 1802 Stonehedge Ln South Bend IN 46614-6341

CHARLES, LESLIE BERMANN, government official; b. Brunswick, Maine, Feb. 11, 1966; d. Max Meir and Catherine Marie (Grelck) B. BS, Georgetown U., 1988; MA, Johns Hopkins U., 1990; cert., Leningrad State U., Russia, 1989, Internat. Space U., 1997. Rsch. asst. Soviet Prog. of the Ctr. for Strategic & Internat. Studies, Washington, 1987-88; presdl. mgmt. intern NASA, 1990-92; budget analyst Goddard Space Flight Ctr. NASA, Greenbelt, 1990-91; policy analyst NASA, Washington, 1991-93, program analyst, 1993-94, internat. rels. specialist, 1994—; Russian lang. tutor Washington, 1987-88. Merrill fellow in security studies, 1989-90. Mem. Phi Beta Kappa. Avocations: dancing, weightlifting, aerobics, downhill skiing, white water rafting. Home: 1530 Key Blvd Apt 509 Arlington VA 22209-1537 Office: NASA Hdqrs Office of External Rels Washington DC 20546

CHARLES, RAY (RAY CHARLES ROBINSON), musician, singer, composer; b. Albany, Ga., Sept. 23, 1930; s. Bailey and Areatha Robinson; divorced; 9 children. Student music at sch. for blind, St. Augustine, Fla. TV appearances, Ray Charles' 50 Years in Music, Uh-Huh!, 1991, TV advertising, 1992—. Played with bands in South; organized trio; played on TV in Seattle; formed own band, 1954; rec. artist, Atlantic Records, 1952-59, ABC-Paramount, 1959-65, Tangerine Records, 1965-73, Crossover Records Co., 1973—; numerous TV, concert appearances.; albums include Message from the People, Volcanic Action of My Soul, Renaissance, Porgy and Bess, Brother Ray is At It Again, Rockin' With Ray, Friendship, Do I Ever Cross Your Mind, The Genius After Hours, From the Pages of My Mind, 1986, Just Between Us, 1988, Greatest Country and Western Hits, 1988, Genius Soul = Jazz, 1991, (with Willie Nelson) Seven Spanish Angels and Other Hits, Goin' Down Slow, The Real Ray Charles, 1986, Wish You Were Here Tonight, Would You Believe, 1990, (with Milt Jackson) Soul Brothers Soul Meeting, 1989, Birth of a Legend, 1992, The Session Vol. 2, 1992, My World, 1993, Blue and Jazz, 1994, and others; sang in We Are the World, 1985. Established (Ray Charles) Robinson Foundation. Recipient New Star award down beat Critics poll, 1958, 61-64, Image award NAACP; named number 1 male singer 16th Internat. Jazz Critics Poll, 1968; 10 Grammy awards; Grammy Lifetime Achievement award, 1987; best soul/R & B artist Down Beat critics poll, 1984; named to Playboy Jazz and Pop Hall of Fame, Songwriters Hall of Fame; hon. life chmn. Rhythm and Blues Hall of Fame; gold records include Ray Charles' Greatest Hits, 1962, Modern Sounds in Country and Western Music, Vol. 1 1962, Vol. 2, 1963, Ray Charles: A Man and His Soul, 1967; inducted into the Rock and Roll Hall of Fame, 1986; Leadership awd., NAFEO, 1991; Lifetime Achievement award Ebony Mag., 1993; Grammy award, Best R&B Song 1994 for "A Song for You." Address: care Ray Charles Entertainment 2107 W Washington Blvd Los Angeles CA 90018-1536*

CHARLES, ROBERT BRUCE, lawyer; b. Portsmouth, Va., Aug. 23, 1960; s. Roland Wilbur Charles Jr. and Doris Anne (Hassell) Barbineau; m. Marina Timasheff, Oct. 16, 1988; 1 child, Nicholas Westcote. AB, Dartmouth Coll., 1982; MA, Oxford U., 1984; JD, Columbia U., 1987. Bar: N.Y. 1989, Conn. 1989, Maine 1990. Law clk. to judge U.S. Ct. Appeals (9th cir.), Seattle, 1987-88; assoc. Kramer, Levin, Nessen, Kamin & Frankel, N.Y.C., 1988-91; assoc. Weil, Gotshal & Manges, N.Y.C., 1991-92, Washington, 1993-95; dep. assoc. dir. office of policy devel The White House, Washington, 1992-93; chief staff, chief counsel nat. security, internat. affairs and criminal justice subcommittee U.S. Ho. of Reps., Washington, 1995—; prof. govt. and cyberlaw Harvard U. Extension Sch., 1998-99; summer assoc. The White House, Washington, 1982-84, Supreme Ct. India, 1985. Contbr. articles to profl. jours., chpts. to books. Active Coun. on Fgn. Rels. Theodore Roosevelt Assn. Officer USNR, 1998—. Keasbey Scholar, Phila. 1982, Tony Patino Fellow Columbia, 1984. Republican. Avocations: distance running, cycling, hiking, writing. Office: US Ho Com on Govt Reform US Congress Rayburn HOB Rm B-373 Washington DC 20515

CHARLES, WALTER, actor; b. East Stroudsburg, Pa., Apr. 4, 1945; s. Theodore Edmund and Catherine Alexandra (Carstensen) Jacobsen. MusB, Boston U., 1968. Appeared in Broadway shows La Cage Aux Folles, Aspects of Love, Me & My Girl, Cats, Sweeney Todd, Grease, Knickerbocker Holiday, Call Me Madam, A Christmas Carol, Sunset Blvd., others; off Broadway, Wit; films: A Fine Mess, Weeds, Fletch Lives, Prancer, TV programs Cagney & Lacey, Kate & Allie, Law & Order, 1981 Tony Awards, PBS Great Performances, 1983 Grammy awards, All My Children, others, also various nat. tours, regional and stock theatrical prodns., commls. and voice-overs. Recipient Best Actor in Musical award Bay Area Drama Critics, 1984.

CHARLESWORTH, ARTHUR THOMAS, mathematics and computer science educator; b. Gainesville, Fla., Nov. 8, 1944; s. Arthur Riggs and Martha Jean (Hamilton) C.; m. Josephine Ann Owenby, Sept. 10, 1966; 1 child, Jonathan David. BS in Math., Stetson U., 1966; AM in Math., Duke U., 1968, PhD in Math., 1974; MS in Computer Sci., U. Va., 1983. Trajectory analysis engr. Apollo support dept. GE, Daytona Bch., Fla., 1966-67; instr. Jacksonville (Fla.) U., 1968-69, Randolph-Macon Coll., Ashland, Va., 1969-71; asst. prof. Queens Coll., Charlotte, N.C., 1974-76; asst. prof. U. Richmond, Va., 1976-82, assoc. prof., 1982-89, prof., 1989—; sec. astronomy, math., physics sect. Va. Acad. Sci., 1977-78, chmn., 1978-79; treas. Md., D.C., Va. sect. Math. Assn. Am., 1980-82. Contbr. articles to profl. jours. Chmn. Trinity Meth. Comsn. on Missions, Richmond, 1981. Research grantee NASA Langley Rsch. Ctr., Hampton, Va., 1987, 88, 89, 90, 91, 92. Mem. IEEE, Assn. Computing Machinery, Omicron Delta Kappa, Sigma Xi. Avocations: hiking, rock collecting. Office: U Richmond Dept Math/Computer Sci Richmond VA 23173

CHARLEY, NANCY JEAN, communications professional; b. LaCrosse, Wis., Jan. 6, 1956. A in Bus. Adminstrn., Midway Coll., 1992, A in Computer Info. Systems, 1993, BBA, 1994, postgrad. Office mgr. for neurologist, Lexington, Ky., 1985-88; health unit coord. acute care hosp., Lexington, 1979-91, health unit coord. trainer, 1992-93, coord. order comms., order mgmt. trainer mgmt. info. system, 1988-95; system support analyst Mgmt. Info. Systems, 1994-96, sys. support analyst, patient auditor trainer, 1996-97; clin. informatics analyst Ctrl. Bapt. Hosp., Lexington, 1997-98; application analyst Appalachian Regional Healthcare, Lexington, 1998—; freelance cons. Contbg. author: Health Unit Coordinating Expanding the Scope of Practice, 1999. Mem. Nat. Assn. Health Unit Coords. (support cons. 1990, edn. bd. 1990-95, chmn. continuing edn. com. 1991-93, mem. several ad hoc coms.), Midway Coll. Alumnae Assn. Avocations: Tai Chi, Swedish massage, ice skating, dance, water activities. Office: Appalachian Regional Healthcare Corp Ctr 1220 Harrodsburg Rd Lexington KY 40533

CHARLIER, ROGER HENRI, oceanography, geography, and geology educator; b. Antwerp, Belgium, Nov. 10, 1921; came to U.S., 1946, naturalized, 1948.; s. Armand Adolphe Joseph and Pauline Bernardine (Uyterhoeven) C.; m. Marie Helen Glennon (dec. 1956); m. Patricia Mary Simonet, June 17, 1958; children: Constance C.P., Jean Armand-Leonard. Lic. in Pol. Adminstrn. Sci., Free U. Brussels, 1941, lic. in sci., 1945; PhD magna cum laude, Friedrich-Alexander U., Erlangen, Germany, 1947; diploma, Indsl. Coll. Armed Forces, Washington, 1952; Postdoctorate diploma, McGill U., Can., 1953; LittD magna cum laude, U. Paris, 1957, DSc summa cum laude, 1958. Chmn. dept. geography Polycultural U., Washington, 1951-52; chmn. dept. phys. scis. Finch Coll., N.Y., 1952-55; chmn. dept. geology and geography Hofstra U., N.Y., 1955-58; prof. earth scis. Parsons Coll., Fairfield, Iowa, 1960-61; adj. prof. Union Grad. Sch., 1980-95; extraordinary prof. Vrije U. Brussels, 1971-87; prof. geology, geography and oceanography Northeastern Ill. U., Chgo., 1961-87; prof. U. de Bordeaux I, France, 1970-74, 76-78; prof. emeritus Northeastern Ill. U., 1986—, Vrije U. Brussels, 1988—; bd. dirs., v.p. European ops. Environ. Planning Group Inc., Houston, Moscow and Chicago, 1993-97; hon. prof. U. Bordeaux, 1986—; vis. prof. Polycultural U., summer 1953, 54, 55, U. Minn., 1959-60, DePaul U., Chgo., 1965-67, U. Autonoma de Baja, Calif., 1966-67, U. Md., 1974-76, 79-80, 83, U. Bordeaux, 1970-74, 83-84; guest lectr. NYU, 1953-57; vis. lectr. CUNY, 1957-58, U. Aix-Marseille, France, 1958-60; prof. suppléant U. Paris, 1958-59; dep. dir. UN Relief and Rehab. Adminstrn., 1945-46; dir. USNDEA Title III, 1967, 69; spl. cons. Ill. Supt. Pub. Instrn., 1967, 68, 70, 71; exec. dir. Inst. Devel. of Riverine and Estuarine Studies, 1974-76, exec. pres., 1980—; exec. advisor Internat. Divsn. Dolmen Engring., Belgium, 1982-84; sci. advisor SOPEX N.V., Antwerp, 1988-89, HAECON N.V., Ghent, Belgium, 1985-89, 90-99. Author: The World Around Us, 1978, Economic Oceanography, 1980, Marine Science and Technology, 1982, Tidal Energy, 1982, Ocean Energies, 1993, Coastal Protection Management, 1998; co-author: Seaweeds of Europe, 1994, Benthos and Eutrophication, 1996; assoc. editor U. So. Fla. Lang. Quar., 1956-77, Hexagon, 1961-63; cons. editor Oceanic Abstracts, 1965-89; mem. editl. bd. Newsletter Internat. Geog. Union, 1954-56, Lang. Quar., 1956-78, Hexagon Bull. R&D, 1961-63, Oceanic Abstracts, 1965-85. Maj. Belgian Mil. Intelligence, 1940-45, WWII. Decorated Cross of Resistance, Cross Polit. Prisoners, Order of Leopold (Belgium), knight Order Academy Palms (France), medal WWII with crossed swords and thunderbolts (Belgium), Campaign medal, War Vol. medal WWII, medal Campaign (Belgium), medal Mérite Touristique (Belgium); recipient award Carnegie Found., 1953, Prix at Médaille d'Excellence, Belgium, 1939, Presdl. Merit award, 1980, Book awards Belgian Univ. Found., 1988, 96, Médaille d'Or Lettres, Arts et Scis., France, 1979, Grande Médaille Univ. Bordeaux, 1974, gold medal Encouragement du Progrès, France, 1974, Paul-Henri Spaak Meml. prize, 1992; Kellogg Found fellow, 1983-84; Fulbright scholar, 1975-76; Oceanographic Found. Monaco grantee, 1968, Belgian Nat. Found. Sci. Rsch. grantee, 1977-79, 83-87, 89-91, grantee IREX, 1969, NATO, 1979-80, 90-91, NAS, 1979. Fellow Geol. Soc. Am., N.J. Acad. Sci. (pres. 1954-57, past pres. 1957-58); mem.NAS, AAUP, Internat. Assn. for History of Oceanography, Belgian Acad. Scis. (mem. environ. commn.), Royal Belgian Soc. Geog. Studies, Royal Flemish Assn. Engrs., European Fedn. Consulting Engrs. Assns., Order Consulting Engrs. (Belgium), Letters and Fine Arts (France), Marine Tech. Soc. (edn. com.). Office: Haecon Inc, 110 Deinsesteenweg, B-9031 Drongen Belgium

CHARLIP, RALPH BLAIR, career officer; b. Detroit, July 16, 1952; s. Jack Edward and Dorothea (Steinman) C.; m. Cynthia Lanell Sallas, May 23, 1987. BA, U. Ariz., 1976, MPA, 1977. Commd. 2nd lt. USAF, 1978, advanced through grades to lt. col., 1994; squadron comdr. USAF Regional Hosp., Langley AFB, Va., 1978-79, dir. patient adminstrn., 1979-80, plant mgr., 1980-81; dir. med. resource mgmt. USAF Clinic Andersen, Andersen AFB, Guam, 1981-82; dir. patient adminstrn. Malcolm Grow USAF Med. Ctr., Andrews AFB, Md., 1983-84; intern Data Systems Design Ctr., Gunter AFB, Ala., 1984-85; health policy devel. officer USAF Hdqs., Bolling AFB, Washington, 1985-89; dir. patient adminstrn. USAF Med. Ctr., Wright-Patterson AFB, Ohio, 1989-92; assoc. dir. med. svcs. Air Nat. Guard Hqrs., Andrews AFB, 1992-94; dir. plans integration and mktg. Dept. Def. Health Svcs. Region VII, Ft. Bliss, Tex., 1994-96; comdr. 423 Clinic, Upwood, U.K., 1996-97; adminstr. aerospace med. Armstrong Lab., Brooks AFB, Tex., 1997; dep. comdr. 59 Med. Support Group, Lackland AFB, Tex., 1997-99; assoc. adminstr. strategic mgmt. 59 Med. Wing, Lackalnd AFB, 1999—. Author (book) Your Health Benefits, 1989. Fellow Am. Coll. Healthcare Execs., Am. Acad. Med. Adminstrs. Office: 59 MDW/ADM Lackland AFB TX 78236

CHARLSON, ROBERT JAY, atmospheric sciences educator, scientist; b. San Jose, Calif., Sept. 30, 1936; s. Rolland Walter and Harriet Adele (Stucky) C.; m. Patricia Elaine Allison, Mar. 16, 1964; children: Daniel Owen, Amanda Marcella. B.S. in Chemistry, Stanford U., 1958, M.S. in Chemistry, 1959; Ph.D. in Atmospheric Scis., U. Wash., 1964; postgrad. (Fulbright scholar), London U., 1964-65; PhD (hon.), Stockholm U., 1993. Rsch. engr. Boeing Co., Seattle, 1959-62; rsch. asst. prof. dept. civil engring. U. Wash., Seattle, 1965-69, assoc. prof. atmospheric chemistry, 1969-71, assoc. prof. civil engring. and geophysics, 1971-74, prof. atmospheric chemistry in civil engring. geophysics and environ. studies, 1974-94, prof. atmospheric scis., 1985-98, adj. prof. chemistry, 1985-96, prof., 1996-98, prof. emeritus, 1998—. Author: (with S.S. Butcher) An Introduction to Air Chemistry, 1972; assoc. editor: Jour. Applied Meteorology, 1971-73; coeditor: Global Biogeochemical Cycles; mem. editorial bd. Jour. Boundary Layer Meteorology, 1971-86, Water, Air and Soil Pollution, 1971-85; contbr. articles on atmosphere chemistry to profl. jours.; patentee in field. Corecipient Gerbier/Mumm award World Meteorol. Orgn., 1988; grantee USPHS, EPA, NSF, NASA, NOAA. Fellow Am. Meteorol. Soc., Am. Geophys. Union; mem. AAAS, Am. Chem. Soc., Sigma Xi, Phi Lambda Upson (hon.). Office: U Wash Dept Atmospheric Scis Box 351640 Seattle WA 98195-1640

CHARLTON, BETTY JO, retired state legislator; b. Reno County, Kans., June 15, 1923; d. Joseph and Elma (Johnson) Canning; BA, U. Kans., 1970, MA, 1976; m. Robert Sansom Charlton, Feb. 24, 1946 (dec. 1984); children: John Robert, Richard Bruce. Asst. instr. polit. sci. and western civilization U. Kans., Lawrence, 1970-73; legis. adminstrv. svcs. employee State of Kans., Topeka, 1977-78, legis. aide gov's. office, 1979; mem. Kans. Ho. of Reps., 1980-95, ret., 1995.

CHARLTON, GORDON RANDOLPH, physicist; b. Newport News, Va., Aug. 30, 1937; s. George Randolph and Sarah Louise (Harper) C.; children: George Thomas, Anne Louise. BSc, Ohio State U., 1957; MSc in Physics, W.Va. U., 1960; PhD in Physics, U. Md., 1966, M of Gen. Adminstrn. in Applied Mgmt., 1996. Charge de recherches Ecole Poly. Lab., Paris, 1966-69; asst. physicist high energy physics div. Argonne (Ill.) Nat. Lab., 1969-72; rsch. assoc. Stanford (Calif.) Linear Accelerator Ctr., 1972-73; rsch. fellow physics dept. U. Toronto (Ont., Can.), 1973-75; sr. physicist divsn. high energy physics Office of Sci., U.S. Dept. Energy, Washington, 1975—. Contbr. articles to Phys. Rev., Phys. Rev. Letters, Physics Letters. Mem. Am. Phys. Soc., U.S. Croquet Assn. E-mail: gordon.charlton@pobox.com. Office: US Dept Energy SC-221 Office Sci 1000 Independence Ave SW Washington DC 20585-0001

CHARLTON, GORDON TALIAFERRO, JR., retired bishop; b. San Antonio, Sept. 29, 1923; s. Gordon Taliaferro and Enid Lynn (Jones) C.; m. Landon Cutler Crump, Dec. 23, 1948; children—Virginia, David, Duncan. B.A., U. Tex-Austin, 1944; M.Div., Va. Sem., 1949, D.D. (hon.), 1974. Ordained priest Episcopal Ch. Asst. rector St. James Ch., Houston, 1949-51; rector St. Mathews Ch., Fairbanks, Alaska, 1951-54; personnel sec. Overseas dept. Nat. Council Episcopal Ch., N.Y.C., 1954-58; rector Christ Ch., Mexico City, 1958-63, St. Andrews Ch., Wilmington, Del., 1963-67; asst. dean Va. Sem., Alexandria, 1967-73; dean Sem. of Southwest, Austin, Tex., 1973-82; Suffragan bishop Episcopal Diocese of Tex., Houston, 1982-89, ret., 1989. Served to lt. (j.g.) USNR, 1943-46; PTO. Episcopalian.

CHARLTON, JESSE MELVIN, JR., management educator, lawyer; b. Livonia, La., May 12, 1916; s. Jesse Melvin and Anna Lela (Medlin) C.; m. Mary Camp, Oct. 4, 1941; children: Jesse Melvin, Frances Anne. B.S., La. State U., 1937, M.B.A., 1938; J.D., Harvard U., 1951. Bar: U.S. Ct. Mil. Appeals 1952, U.S. Supreme Ct 1963, D.C. 1951. Instr. U. Ala., 1938-40; commd. 2d lt., inf. U.S. Army, 1940; advanced through grades to col. U.S. Army (Judge Adv. Gen.'s Corps), 1962; dep. comdr. Judge Adv. Gen. Sch., Charlottesville, Va., 1962-64; ret., 1964; mem. faculty U. New Orleans Coll. Bus., 1964-81, prof. mgmt., 1971-81, prof. emeritus, 1981—; asst. dean coll. bus. U. New Orleans, 1967-71, dean grad. sch., 1978-80. Author handbook; co-editor: Statistical Abstract of Louisiana, 5th edit, 1974. Decorated Bronze Star. Mem. D.C. Bar Assn. Republican.

CHARLTON, JOHN KIPP, pediatrician; b. Omaha, Jan. 26, 1937; s. George Paul and Mildred (Kipp) C.; m. Susan S. Young, Aug. 15, 1959; children: Paul, Cynthia, Daphne, Gregory. AB, Amherst Coll., 1958; MD, Cornell U., 1962. Intern Ohio State U. Hosp., Columbus, 1962-63; resident in pediatrics Children's Hosp., Dallas, 1966-68, chief resident in pediatrics, 1968-69; fellow in nephrology U. Tex. Southwestern Med. Sch., Dallas, 1969-70; pvt. practice medicine specializing in pediatrics, Phoenix, from 1970; chmn. dept. pediatrics Maricopa Me.d Ctr., Phoenix, 1971-78, 84-93, pres. med. staff, 1991; med. dir., bd. dirs. Crisis Nursery, Inc., 1977—; dir. Phoenix Pediatric Residency, 1983-85, Phoenix Hosps. affiliated pediatric program, 1985-88; clin. assoc. prof. pediatrics U. Ariz. Coll Medicine. Author articles and book revs. in field. Pres. Maricopa County Child Abuse Coun., 1977-81; bd. dirs. Florence Crittenton Svcs., 1980-83, Ariz. Children's Found., 1987-91; mem. Gov.'s Coun. on Children, Youth and Families, 1984-86. Officer M.C., USAF, 1963-65. Recipient Hon. Kachinaaward for volunteerism, 1980, Jefferson award for volunteerism, 1980, Horace Steel Child Advocacy award, 1993; named Clin. Sci. Educator of Yr., U. Ariz., 1997, 99. Mem. Am. Acad. Pediatrics, Ariz. Pediatric Soc., Maricopa County Pediatric Soc. (past pres.). Home: 6230 E Exeter Blvd Scottsdale AZ 85251-3060 Office: Maricopa Med Ctr 2601 E Roosevelt St Phoenix AZ 85008-4973

CHARLTON, SHIRLEY MARIE, educational consultant; b. Nashville, Nov. 20, 1934; d. Ottis Ruby and Irene Lenoir (Cabler) C.; children: David Matthew Christian Sironen, Charlton Gwynn Cabler Sironen. BS, George Peabody Coll. Tchrs., 1954; MA in Ednl. Adminstrn. and Supervision, U. Tenn., Chattanooga, 1970. Cert. supr., Tenn. Classroom tchr. Albany (Ga.) Pub. Schs., 1954-55, 56-57, Orlando (Fla.) Pub. Schs., 1960-61, Grand Forks (N.D.) Pub. Schs., 1962-65; TV and resource tchr. Chattanooga Publ Schs., 1965-67, supr., 1967-97; cons., 1997-99. Mem. NEA, Tenn. Edn. Assn., Chattanooga Edn. Assn. (charter mem. negotiating team 1979-81), Alpha Delta Kappa (v.p. 1981-83). Episcopalian. Avocations: history, genealogy, acting, art, music.

CHARM, JOEL BARRY, manufacturing company executive. BA in Chemistry, U. Mass., 1965; MS in Radiation Biology and Environ. Health, U. Mich., 1967; cert. advanced mgmt. program Columbia U., 1977. With Dow Chem. Co., Midland, Mich., 1968-73, radiation safety officer, 1968-73, chief indsl. hygienist dept. chem. prodn., 1970-72, research specialist in indsl. hygiene, 1972-73; corp. mgr. indsl. hygiene Miles Labs., Elkhart, Ind., 1973-75; mgr. occupational health and toxicology Allied Corp., Morristown, N.J., 1975-77, dir. corp. product safety and integrity, 1977-96, dir. occupational health and product safety, 1996-97; leader Product Stewardship Ctr. of Excellence, 1996-97; pres. Charm HS&E Internat. Inc., Randolph, N.J., 1998—; spkr., lectr. on ISO-14000 toxic substances control, indsl. hygiene, OSHA, radiation, pollution control at univs., profl. meetings; chmn. U.S. Technical Adv. Group on ISO-14000. Author profl. reports and papers. NIH fellow, 1967. Mem. Am. Acad. Indsl. Hygiene (diplomate), Am. Indsl. Hygiene Assn. (chmn. com. product safety and health), Ind. Indsl. Hygiene Soc. (bd. dirs.), Mich. Indsl. Hygiene Soc. (bd. dirs. 1969-70), Health Physics Soc., ASTM (rec. sec. air sampling methodology and occupational safety and health criteria), Am. Soc. Safety Engrs. (profl.), N.J. Indsl. Hygiene Soc. Office: Charm HS&E Internat 15 Springhill Rd Randolph NJ 07869-4324

CHARNAS, FRAN ELKA, theatre director, educator, author; b. Cleve.; d. Morris and Zelda (Wymor) C. BFA in Theatre, Ohio U., 1968; MA in Theatre, Emerson Coll., 1981. Producer, dir. East Cleveland (Ohio) Music Theatre, 1972-74; mem. faculty Boston Conservatory, 1980—; adminstrv. dir. Summer Inst. in Mus. Theatre, Boston, 1984; presenter and cons. in field. Dir., choreographer (mus.) The All Night Strut, 1975—, (TV spl.), 1988; dir. (mus.) Party of One, 1989, (opera) Look What A Wonder Jesus Has Done, 1990; co-author, dir. (mus.) Sheboppin, 1987; dir. various plays and mus.; author, dir. In the Groove, 1998. Mem. New Eng. Theatre Conf. Avocations: antiques, travel. Office: The Boston Conservatory 8 Fenway Boston MA 02215-4099

CHARNAS, MICHAEL (MANNIE CHARNAS), investment company executive; b. Cleve., Sept. 24, 1947; s. Max and Eleanor (Gross) C.; m. Mimi F. Stein, June 10, 1990; 1 child from previous marriage, Matthew; 1 child, Max. BBA, Ohio State U., 1969, MBA, 1971. Page Ohio Ho. of Reps., 1969; mem. Ohio Staters, Inc., 1969; fin. analyst Addressograph-Multigraph, Inc., Cleve., 1971-73; asst. to pres., dir. planning and budget 1st Nat. Supermarkets, Inc. (Pick-N-Pay), Cleve., 1975-78, asst. to pres., v.p. planning and budgets, 1978-79, sr. v.p. fin., adminstr., 1979-81; sr. v.p., CFO, adminstrv. officer 1st Nat. Supermarkets, Inc. (Pick-N-Pay), Hartford, Conn., 1981-86; founder Charnas Mktg. and Investment Co., 1986—; pres., owner Indsl. Pallet and Packaging Co., Beachwood, Ohio, 1986-94; regional v.p. Pallet Pallet, Inc. (formerly Indsl. Pallet and Packaging Co.), Toronto, 1995-97; bd. dirs. Gorman-Lavelle Corp. Jewish. Avocations: tennis, reading, collecting modern classic cars. Office: Charnas Mktg and Investment Co 23811 Chagrin Blvd Ste 160 Beachwood OH 44122-5525

CHARNEY, CRAIG RUSSELL, pollster, political scientist; b. N.Y.C., Oct. 27, 1956; s. Roy L. and Lena (London) C. BA, Brandeis U., Waltham, Mass., 1977; MPhil, Oxford U., 1979; DEA, Sorbonne U., Paris, 1986. Polit. reporter The Star, Johannesburg, South Africa, 1980-81; assoc. editor Mgmt. Mag., Johannesburg, 1982-83; instr. polit. sci. Yale U., New Haven, 1989-90; rsch. fellow Wits U., Johannesburg, 1991-92; ptnr. Rsch. Initiatives, Johannesburg, 1992-93; pollster South African Broadcasting Corp., 1994-95; sr. analsyt Penn & Schoen Assocs., N.Y.C., 1996-97; pres. Charney Rsch., N.Y.C., 1997—. Contbr. articles to profl. jours. Mem. Am. Polit. Sci. Assn., Nat. Writers Union. Office: Charney Rsch 2nd Fl 5 W 102nd St New York NY 10025

CHARNEY, EVAN, pediatrician, educator; b. N.Y.C., Feb. 24, 1933. BA, Cornell U., 1954; MD, Albert Einstein Coll. Medicine, 1960. Intern, resident Strong Meml. Hosp, N.Y.S., 1960-63; from asst. to assoc. prof. pediatrics Strong Meml Hosp., U. Rochester, N.Y., 1963-75; prof. pediatrics, chief pediatrics dept. Sinai Hosp. Balt., Johns Hopkins U., 1975-87; prof., chmn. dept. pediatrics U. Mass. Med. Ctr., Worcester, 1987-98. 1st lt. Ordnance Corps, U.S. Army, 1954-56. Recipient Armstrong award Ambulatory Pediatric Assn., 1982; Markle scholar Acad. Medicine, 1968-73. Fellow Inst. Medicine NAS; mem. Am. Acad. Pediatrics. Home: 146 Stiles Rd Boylston MA 01505-1504 Office: U Mass Med Ctr Worcester Found Campus 222 Maple Ave Shrewsbury MA 01545-2732

CHARNEY, MELVIN, artist, architect, educator; b. Montreal, Que., Can., Aug. 28, 1935; s. H. and F. (Cassack) C.; m. Ann Korsower, May 29, 1960; 1 child, Dara Alexandra. B.Arch., McGill U., Montreal, 1958; M.Arch., Yale U., 1959. Registered architect, Que. Prin. Melvin Charney, Architect, Montreal, 1964—; prof. U. Montreal, 1964—; mem. architects com. Am. Acad.

Arts and Scis., Boston, 1968-69; co-dir. task force on housing Govt. of Can., Ottawa, Ont., 1970-71; mem. adv. com. Can. Centre for Architecture, Montreal, 1983-89; bd. dirs. Conseil des Arts et des Lettres, Quebec, 1994—; invited prof. to numerous univs. One-man shows include Harvard U., 1977, Art Gallery of Ont., Toronto, 1978, Musee d'Art Contemporain, Montreal, 1979, Inst. for Art and Urban Resources, N.Y.C., 1979, Can. Cultural Ctrs., Paris and Brussels, 1980, Mus. Contemporary Art, Chgo., 1982, Richard Gray Gallery, Chgo., 1982, 49th Parallel, Centre for Can. Contemporary Art, N.Y.C., 1982, 87, Agnes Etherington Art Centre, Kingston, Ont., 1983, represented Can. at the 42nd Venice Biennale, 1986, René Blouin Gallery, Montreal, 1987, 88, Ctr. for Canadian Art, N.Y., 1987, Sable-Castelli Gallery, Toronto, 1988, 91, 92, 93, maj. retrospective, Can. Centre for Architecture, Montreal, 1991-92, de Beyrie Gallery, Paris, 1994, Israel Mus., Jerusalem, 1995, Power Plant Gallery Contemporary Art, Toronto, 1995; exhibited in group shows at Montreal Mus. Fine Arts, 1972, 83, Musee d'Art Moderne de la Ville de Paris, 1973, Institut d'Art Contemporain, Montreal, 1975, 76, XXI Olympic Games, Montreal, 1976, John Weber Gallery, N.Y., 1979, Max Protetch Gallery, N.Y.C., 1979, Los Angeles Inst. Contemporary Art, 1980, Vancouver Art Gallery, 1980, Centre George Pompidou, 1980, Musee du Que., 1981, 83, 85, Akademie der Kunst, Berlin, 1983, Kunstverein, Stuttgart, 1983, Mus. Contemporary Art, Chgo., 1984, Internationalen Bauausstellung, Berlin, 1984, 17th Trianale di Milano, 1985, Le Musee du Que., 1985, Centre internat. d'art contemporain, Montreal, 1985, Musee d'art Comtemporaine du Montreal, 1987, 91, Power Plant, Contemporary Art at Harbourfront, Toronto, 1988, The Canadian Ctr. for Architecture, Montreal, 1989, Musee du Quebec, 1989, 91, Nat. Mus. of Contemporary Art, Seoul, S. Korea, 1990, Mus. des Jacobins, Morlaix, France, 1991, Canadian Pavilion, V Biennale di Architettura, Venice, 1991, Passages, Centre d'art contemporain, Troyes, France, 1992, Musée national d'art moderne, Paris, 1994, Centre Cultura Contemporania, Barcelona, 1994, Royal Festival Hall Galleries, London, 1995, Manchester City Art Gallery, 1995, others; sculpture comms. The Can. Tribute to Human Rights, Ottawa, 1986, Urban Sculpture Garden for Can. Ctr. for Architecture, montreal, 1987, Place Berri, Montreal, 1991; represented in permanent collections Nat. Gallery Can., Ottawa, Can. Council Art Bank. Ottawa, Art Gallery Ont., Toronto, Musee d'art contemporain, Montreal, Can. Ctr. for Architecture, Montreal, Mus. Contemporary Art, Chgo., IBM Collection, Chgo., Fonds Nat. d'Art Contemporain, Paris, Musee du Quebec, Montreal Mus. Fine Arts, Frac Basse Normandie, France, Art Gallery Hamilton. Contbr. articles to profl. publs. Recipient Arts award Minister des Affaires Culturelles, 1967, research award Humanities and Social Scis. Council, 1971, Berlin Arts award Deutcher Akademischer Austanschdienst, 1982, Sr. Arts award Can. Council, 1983, 87. Mem. Royal Can. Acad., Can. Artists Reps., Ordre des Architectes du Que. Home: 3620 Marlowe Ave, Montreal, PQ Canada H4A 3L7*

CHARNIAK, EUGENE, computer scientist, educator; b. Chgo., June 2, 1946; s. Samuel and Dora (Nussman) C.; m. Lynette Mills, Feb. 19, 1972. AB with honors, U. Chgo., 1967; MS, MIT, 1968, PhD, 1972. Researcher artifical intelligence lab. MIT, Cambridge, 1972-73, Inst. for Semantic Studies, Geneva, 1972-73; vis. prof. Yale U., New Haven, 1977-78; asst. prof. Brown U., Providence, 1978-81, assoc. prof., 1981-84, prof., 1984—, chair dept. computer sci., 1991-97. Author: Artificial Intelligence Programming, 1980, 2d edit., 1987, Introduction to Artificial Intelligence, 1985, Statistical Language Learning, 1993; editor: Cognitive Sci., 1977-84; contbr. articles to profl. jours. Fellow Am. Assn. for Artifical Intelligence (councilor 1983-86); Sr. mem. IEEE, Cognitive Sci. Soc. (bd. dirs. 1977-79, editorial bd. 1984—), Assn. for Computational Linguistics (editorial bd. 1988-91). Office: Brown U Dept Computer Sci Box 1910 115 Waterman St Providence RI 02912-9016*

CHARNIN, JADE HOBSON, magazine executive; b. N.Y.C., Mar. 12, 1945; d. John Louis Campo and Elizabeth (Anne) Stanton; m. David Alan Hobson, Dec. 30 (div. 1972); m. Martin Charnin, Dec. 18, 1984. BA, NYU, 1967. Asst. editor Glamour mag., N.Y.C., 1970; accessory editor Vogue mag., N.Y.C., 1970-78, fashion editor, 1978-81, fashion dir., 1981-86, creative dir. fashion, 1987-88; v.p., dir. creative svcs. for fashion and design group Revlon, Inc., 1988; exec. creative dir. Mirabella Mag., 1988-94; fashion dir.. N.Y. Mag., 1994-98; freelance journalist, 1999—; cons. editor Self mag., N.Y.C., 1979-81; freelance contbr. to House & Garden. Costumer coord. for off broadway shows Upstairs at Oneals, 1981, Laughing Matters, 1989, Martin Charnin, the Hits and the M.S.'s, 1990. Mem. ASPCA, Am. Hort. Soc., Nat. Mus. Women in the Arts, Hort. Soc. N.Y. (bd. dirs.), Humane Soc. N.Y. (bd. dirs.), Animal Protection Inst. Democrat. Avocations: gardening, opera, ballet, theater, skiing.

CHARNIN, MARTIN, theatrical director, lyricist, producer; b. N.Y.C., Nov. 24, 1934; s. William and Birdie (Blakeman) C.; m. Lynn Ross, Mar. 2, 1958 (div.); 1 son, Randy; m. Genii Prior, Jan. 8, 1962 (div.); 1 dau., Sasha; m. Jade Hobson, Dec. 1985. BA, Cooper Union, 1955. Acting stage debut West Side Story, 1957; also appeared in The Girls Against the Boys, 1959; writer: lyrics and sketches Fallout Revue, 1959; lyricist: revue Pieces of Eight, 1959, Little Revue, 1960, Hot Spot (Broadway), 1963, Zenda, 1963, Mata Hari, 1967; lyricist, dir. Ballad for a Firing Squad, 1968; lyricist: Two by Two, 1970; conceived and directed: revue Nash at Nine (Broadway), 1973; dir.: revue Music! Music!, 1974; lyricist, dir., creator: Annie (Tony award for lyrics), 1977 (2 Drama Desk awards for lyrics and direction); dir. 4 nat. cos., 1978, also London prodn., 1978; dir. Bar Mitzvah Boy, London, 1978; lyricist: I Remember Mama, 1979; lyricist, dir., co-book writer The First (2 Tony nominations), 1981; lyricist: TV spl. Feathertop, 1961, Jackie Gleason Show, 1961; conceived and produced: TV spl. the Women in the Life of a Man, 1970 (2 Emmy awards); conceived, produced, directed and wrote TV spls. George M, 1970, Jack Lemmon in 'S Wonderful, 'S Marvelous, 'S Gershwin (2 Emmy awards), 1972 (Peabody award for Broadcasting), Jack Lemmon in Get Happy—The Music of Harold Arlen, 1973, Dames at Sea, 1972, Cole Porter in Paris, 1973, Annie and the Hoods, 1974, The Annie Xmas Show, 1977, C'mon Saturday, 1977; author: TV spls. The Giraffe Who Sounded Like Ol' Blue Eyes, 1976, Annie: A Theatre Memoir, 1977; dir. On the Swing Shift, A Backer's Audition, 1983; creator, writer, dir. Upstairs at the O'Neals, 1983; dir. Jokers at Goodspeed, 1986, An Evening of Neil Simon at the Public Theater, 1986; creator, writer, dir. The No-Frills Revue, 1987; dir. Cafe Crown at the Public Theater, 1988, Cafe Crown on Broadway, 1989, Laughing Matters, Off Broadway Sid Caeser and Co., Annie 2, 1990, N.Y. premiere Jules Feiffers Carnal Knowledge, 1991; lyrics and dir. Annie Warbucks at Goodspeed, Mata Hari, N.Y., 1996; producer N.Y. Shakespeare Festival Evenings for Joseph Papp, 1990, 91; one show Rainbow and Stars, N.Y.C.; lyrics, co-writer, dir. Winchell, 1991; lyrics, dir. Galileo, 1992, Annie Warbucks, 1993; dir. Loose Lips Revue, 1995, Can Can, rev. 1995; dir. Jeanne, Montreal, 1996. Office: care Richard Ticktin 1345 Avenue Of The Americas New York NY 10105-0302

CHAROCHAK, DALE MICHAEL, county official; b. Pitts., Apr. 18, 1955; s. Michael and Alice (Nazak) C.; m. Kathleen Gallagher. BS in Biochemistry, U. Pitts., 1977. Contr. County Controller's Office, Pitts., 1977-80; contract supr. Dept. Aviation, Pitts., 1980-84, chief property adminstr., 1984-91; chief contract adminstr. Pitts. Internat. Airport, 1991—. Dem. committeeman Moon, Pa., 1982-98, sch. bd. dir., legis. rep., 1983-85; bd. trustees Montour (Pa.) Football Orgn., 1979-81; Pa. state commr. Am. Wallyball Assn.; asst. scoutmaster Boy Scouts Am., Montour. Mem. Am. Assn. Airport Execs. (bd. dirs. acad. com.), Pitts. Aero Club. Byzantine Catholic. Avocations: basketball, softball, parasailing, wallyball, photography. Home: 131 Greenlea Dr Coraopolis PA 15108-2609 Office: Pitts Internat Airport PO Box 12370 Ste 4000 Pittsburgh PA 15231-0370

CHAROS, EVANGELOS NIKOLAOU, economics educator; b. Larnaca, Cyprus, Sept. 13, 1953; s. Nicos Demetriou Charos and Alexandra Charou; m. Maryann Andrews, Oct. 2, 1976; children: Nikolas, Alexandra, Melanie. Bs in Math., U. N.H., 1975, MA in Econs., 1978, PhD in Econs., 1984. Instr. Nasson Coll., Springvale, Maine, 1980-83; asst. prof. Merrimack Coll., North Andover, Mass., 1983-88; assoc. prof. econs. Merrimack Coll., 1988-94; prof. econs., 1994—; asst. dir. computer svcs. U. N.H., Durham, 1976-80. Asst. editor, data base mgr. Internat. Bus. Conditions Digest, 1980-83. Mem. Am. Econ. Assn., Northeast Bus. & Econs. Assn., Internat. Assn. Bus. Forecasters, Omicron Delta Epsilon. Greek Orthodox. Home: 1 Center Dr Dover NH 03820-4646

CHARPAK, GEORGES, physicist, nuclear scientist; b. Dabrovica, Poland, Aug. 1, 1924; naturalized in France, 1946; s. Maurice and Anna (Szapiro) C.; m. Dominique Vidal, 1953; children: Yves, Nathalie, Serge. Student, Ecole des Mines de Paris, 1945-47, BSc in Engring., 1948; D of Physics, Coll. of France, 1954; PhD in Physics, Collège de France, 1954; hon. doctorate, U. Geneva, 1977, U. Thessalonica, Greece, 1993, Vrije Univ. Brussels, 1994, U. Coimbra, Portugal, 1994, U. Ottawa, Canada, 1995. Lic. civil mining engr. Prof. Centre Nation de la Recherche Scientifique, 1948-59, Centre Européen pour la Recherche Nucléaire, Geneva, 1959—; rschr. Cern Lab. for Particle Physics, Geneva; Joliot-Curie prof. Ecole Supérieure de Physique et Chimie de la Ville de Paris, 1984—. Contbr. articles to profl. jours. With French Army, prisoner of war, Dachau. Decorated chevalier Legion of Honor, Mil. Cross 39-45, Croix de Guerre (France); recipient Ricard prize European Physics Soc., 1980, High Energy and Particle Physics prize, 1989, Nobel prize for physics, 1992. Mem. NAS (fgn. assoc.), French Acad. Scis. (Commissariat prize of Atomic Energy 1984), Austrian Acad. Scis. (hon.), Russian Acad. Scis. (fgn.), Lisboa Acad. Scis. (corr.). Achievements include invention of multiwire proportional chambers, drift chambers, diverse types of flash chambers without photography; development of particle detectors in high energy physics, installations for biological research using Beta-ray imagery; research in nuclear structure by reactions. Home: 2 rue de Poissy, 75005 Paris France Office: CERN Lab for Particle Physics, CH 1211 Geneva 23, Switzerland

CHARPENTIER, GAIL WIGUTOW, private school executive director; b. N.Y.C., Mar. 10, 1946; d. Jacob M. and Ethel (Israel) Wigutow; m. Peter Jon Charpentier; children: Elisabeth Marie, Matthew Kyle. BA, CUNY, 1967; MA, New Sch. Social Research, N.Y.C., 1976; postgrad., LaSalle U. Lic. social worker; cert. adminstr. of spl. edn. Tchr. Spl. Service Pub. Sch., Bronx, N.Y., 1967-73; adminstr. Boston City Hosp., 1973-76; dir. Monson Devel. Ctr., Palmer, Mass., 1976; residential dir. Kolburne Sch., New Marlboro, Mass., 1976-79; exec. dir. Berkshire Meadows, Housatonic, Mass., 1979—; researcher Nat. Opinion Research Ctr., N.Y.C. and Boston, 1973-76; trainer residential child care, Mass., 1978—; mem. human rights bd. Oakdale Found., Great Barrington, 1980—. Recipient Community Criminal Justice award Justice Resource Inst., 1984. Mem. NAFE, Am. Assn. Mental Retardation, Mass. Assn. Approved Pvt. Schs. (bd. dirs. 1982-84, ins. trustee 1984-87, svc. award 1982), New Eng. Assn. for Child Care, Internat. Assn. for Retts Syndrome, Berkshire Profl. Women, Hop Brook Club (pres.). Avocations: skiing, tennis, sailing, bass fishing, golf. Home: Orchard House PO Box 406 Tyringham MA 01264-0406 Office: Berkshire Meadows 249 N Plain Rd Housatonic MA 01236-9736

CHARPENTIER, KEITH LIONEL, school system administrator; b. Attleboro, Mass., Mar. 6, 1959; s. David L. and Matilda (Marchand) C.; m. Catherine Joan Fleming, July 29, 1989. AS, Mitchell Coll., 1980; BS, Plymouth State Coll., 1982, MEd in Guidance and Counseling, 1992. Cert. phys. edn. and health sci. tchr., N.H.; cert. reality therapist; cert. guidance dir., N.H. Health sci. tchr. SAU #23 Sch. System, Woodsville, N.H., 1982-84; counselor F.L. Chamberlain Sch., Lyman, N.H., 1984-86; spl. edn. tchr. Blue Mt. Union Sch., Wells River, Vt., 1985-86; dean of students, counselor Pike (N.H.) Sch. Inc., 1986-93; guidence counselor New Found Mid. Sch., Bristol, N.H., 1993-98, dean students, vice prin., 1998—; instr. assoc. level Crisis Prevention Inst., Brookfield, Wis., 1989—, Drug/Alcohol Edn., Meredith, N.H., 1988—, Life Skills Edn., Granville, Ohio, 1987—; pvt. provider outpatient counseling Divsn. Children, Youth and Families, Dept. Health and Human Svcs., State of N.H., 1992—. Vol. firefighter, capt. Haverhill Corner Fire Dept. Recipient Mitchell Coll. Athletic Trainers award, 1980. Mem. ASCD, ACA, Nat. Athletic Trainers Assn., Nat. Mid. Sch. Assn. Avocations: sports, coaching, skiing, fishing, hunting, photography, gardening. Home: RR 151 Rockcreek Acr North Haverhill NH 03779

CHARPIE, ROBERT ALAN, physicist; b. Cleve., Sept. 9, 1925; s. Leonard Asbury and Dorothy (McLean) C.; m. Elizabeth Downs, July 12, 1947; children: Richard Alan, Carol Elizabeth, David Wayne, John Robert. B.S. with honors, Carnegie Inst. Tech., 1948, M.S., 1949, D.Sc. in Theoretical Physics, 1950; D.H.L., Denison U., 1965; D.Sc., Alderson-Broaddus Coll., 1967; LL.D., Marietta Coll., 1975; D.Sc., Boston Coll., 1982. With Westinghouse Electric Corp., 1947-50; with Oak Ridge Nat. Lab., 1950-51, tech. asst. to research dir., 1952-54, asst. research dir., 1954-58, dir. reactor divsn., 1958-61; mgr. adv. devel. Union Carbide Corp., 1961-63, gen. mgr. devel. dept., 1963-64, dir. tech., 1964-66, pres. electronics divsn., 1966-68; pres. Bell & Howell Co., Chgo., 1968-69; pres. Cabot Corp., Boston, 1969-86, also. bd. dirs.; chmn. Cabot Corp., Waltham, Mass., 1986-88, Ampersand Ventures, Wellesley, Mass., 1988—; trustee Mitre Corp., Boston, 1966-82, chmn., 1972-82; dir. Champion Internat. Corp.; sec. gen. adv. com. AEC, 1959-63; mem. Nat. Sci. Bd., 1969-76; sci. sec., editor-in-chief proc., also asst. U.S. mem. 7 nation adv. com. 1st Internat. Conf. Peaceful Uses Atomic Energy, 1955; coordinator U.S. fusion research exhibit, 2d Conf., 1958; chmn. invention and innovation panel U.S. Dept. Commerce, 1965-67. Gen. editor: Internat. Monograph Series on Nuclear Energy, 1955-60; editor: Progress Series in Nuclear Energy, 1955-60, Jour. Nuclear Energy, 1955-60. Mem. Oak Ridge Bd. Edn., 1957-61; pres. Byram Hills Central Sch. Dist., 1966-68; trustee Carnegie Inst. Tech., 1962—. Recipient Alumni Merit award Carnegie Inst. Tech., 1957. Fellow Am. Phys. Soc., Am. Nuclear Soc. (dir.); mem. N.Y. Acad. Sci., Nat. Acad. Engring., Sigma Xi, Tau Beta Pi, Phi Mu Epsilon. Office: Ampersand Ventures 55 William St Ste 240 Wellesley MA 02481-4003

CHARRON, HELENE KAY SHETLER, retired nursing educator; b. West Bloomfield, N.Y., Nov. 17, 1937; d. Ellis John and Helene Esther (Moore) Shetler; m. Ronald W. Charron, July 1964; children: Michele Gefell, Andrea Hagen. Diploma, Rochester State Hosp. Sch., N.Y., 1958; BS in Nursing, U. Rochester, 1964, MS in Nursing Edn., 1965. Staff nurse Strong Meml. Hosp., Rochester, 1958-60; head nurse Monroe Community Hosp., Rochester, 1961-63; coord. psychiat. nursing Monroe Community Coll., 1965-87; mental hygiene staff devel. specialist Rochester Psychiat. Ctr., 1982-83; chairperson dept. nursing Monroe Community Coll., Rochester, 1987-95; ptnr. Initiatives in Nursing Edn., West Bloomfield, N.Y., 1995—; cons., lectr. on integration of Computer Assisted Instruction and Interactive Video Disk in nursing curricula and hosp. staff devel. Writer numerous instructional computer programs, videotapes and games in field. Office: 9148 Dugway Rd West Bloomfield NY 14585-0196

CHARRON, JOSEPH L., bishop; b. Redfield, SD, Dec. 30, 1939. ordained priest June 3, 1967. Asst. Theology prof. St. John's U., Collegeville, MN, 1970-76; asst. gen. sec. U.S. Catholic Conf., 1976-79; assoc. gen. sec. Nat. Conf. of Catholic Bishops, 1976-79; Kansas City Provincial dir. CPPS, 1979-87; aux. bishop Diocese of St. Paul/Minneapolis, 1990-93; bishop Diocese of Des Moines, 1994—; mem. Soc. of Precious Blood, Kansas City Province, 1961—; mem. Catholic Theological Soc. of Amer.; mem. Nat. Conf. of Catholic Bishops/U.S. Catholic Conference admin. comm. Office: Chancery PO Box 1816 Des Moines IA 50306-1816*

CHARRON, PAUL RICHARD, apparel company executive; b. Schenectady, N.Y., Aug. 24, 1942; s. Richard Armand and Helen Marie (Barringer) C.; m. Kathy Lyn Herdt, June 29, 1974; children: Bradley, Ashley. BA, U. Notre Dame, 1964; MBA, Harvard U., 1971. Brand mgr. Procter & Gamble Corp., Cin., 1971-78; category mgr. Gen. Foods Corp., White Plains, N.Y., 1978-81; sr. v.p. sales, mktg. Cannon Mills Co., N.Y. and N.C., 1981-83; pres., chief operating officer Atwater Group, Inc., St. Paul, 1983-87; pres., chief oper. officer Brown & Bigelow, St. Paul, 1983-87; exec. v.p. VF Corp., Wyomissing, Pa., 1988-94; chmn., CEO Liz Claiborne Inc., N.Y.C., 1994—. Lt. USN, 1964-69, Vietnam. Decorated Meritorious Service medal. Office: Liz Claiborne Inc 1441 Broadway Fl 22 New York NY 10018-2088

CHARRON, SUSAN E., mental health nurse; b. Attleboro, Mass., Aug. 16, 1959; d. Allan Richard and Shirley Ann (Pitts) England; m. Mark Edward Charron, 1986; children: Mark Edward II, Matthew A., Bethany Marie. BA in Psychology, Southeastern Mass. U., North Dartmouth, 1981; ADN, R.I. Community Coll., Lincoln, 1984. Cert. tchr., Mass. Nurse Wrentham (Mass.) State Sch. Mem. ANA, Mass. Nursing Assn.

CHARRY, MICHAEL R(ONALD), musician, conductor; b. N.Y.C., Aug. 28, 1933; s. Harold Paul and Sylvia C.; m. Jane Thoms, Mar. 31, 1956; children: Stephen Walter, Barbara. Student, Oberlin Conservatory Music, 1950-52; BS, Juilliard Sch. Music, 1955, MS in Orch. Conducting, 1956; studies with, Jean Morel, Pierre Monteux, Hans Schmidt-Isserstedt, George Szell. Mem. faculty Mannes Coll. Music, 1988-99, head, orch. conducting, 1989-99, music dir. Mannes Coll. Music Orch., 1989-99; chmn. Music Consortium of Nashville, 1977-79, Nashville Inst. Arts, 1979-80. Condr., pianist, José Limón Modern Dance Co. tours, Europe, 1957, South and Central Am., 1960, Far East, 1963, asst. condr., prin. oboist, R.I. Philharmonic, 1960-61, music dir., condr., Canton Symphony Orch., 1961-74, apprentice condr., Cleve. Orch., 1961-65, asst. condr., Cleve. Orch., 1965-72, music dir., condr., Nashville Symphony Orch., 1976-82, Peninsula Music Festival, 1978-82; guest condr. concerts, operas, U.S. and Europe; assoc. prof. orchestral conducting, dir. orchestral activities, Syracuse U. (N.Y.), 1983-85, prof., mus. dir. orchestral and opera programs Boston U. Sch. Music, 1984-87. With U.S. Army, 1958-60. Fulbright scholar, 1956-57; Martha Baird Rockefeller grantee, 1975, Elizabeth Ring Mather and William Gwinn Mather Fund grantee, 1991, 94; recipient Alice M. Ditson award Columbia U., 1981, Spl. Merit award Tenn. Arts Commn., 1982. Mem. Am. Symphony Orch. League, Condrs. Guild (bd. dirs. 1983-95, 1st v.p. 1989-91, pres. 1991-93).

CHARTERS, ALEXANDER NATHANIEL, retired adult education educator; b. Verdant Valley, Alta., Can., Aug. 22, 1916; came to U.S., 1948, naturalized, 1957.; s. Alexander Allen and Louisa Magdalena (Kern) C.; m. Margaret Anne MacNaughton, Mar. 29, 1952; children: A. William, David W., John C., Louisa A. Vike. *Dr. Margaret Anne Charters is a consumer educator, born in Prince Albert, Saskatchewan, Canada, September 25, 1925 and naturalized a U.S. citizen. BHSC, Saskatchewan, 1946, SM, Chicago, 1947, PhD, Syracuse, 1971. She and her husband are professional colleagues in the field of Adult Education. She has had an international and national career in consumer studies. She served as an Associate Professor at Syracuse University, from 1971-95. She also served as director of consumer studies and of an MA program in the College of Human Development, and an S.U. board member of the American Council of Consumer Interests.* BA, U. B.C., 1938; PhD, U. Chgo., 1948. Tchr. pub. schs., Fernie, B.C., 1939-41, Vancouver, 1941-42; asst. to dean Univ. Coll., Syracuse U., 1948-50, asst. dean, 1950-52, dean, 1952-64, asst. prof. Sch. Edn., 1950-54, assoc. prof., 1954-59, prof., 1959-83, prof. emeritus, 1983—, area chmn. for adult edn., 1950-73, univ. v.p. for continuing edn., 1964-73; vis. mem. faculty U. Chgo., 1958; delegate Conf. on Adult Edn., UNESCO, 1972; observer, del., Tokyo, 1972, Paris, 1985; coord. US participation pvt. sector CONFINTEA V, Hamburg, 1997, mem. U.S. del. team, 1997; cons. UNESCO Inst. for Edn., 1998; mem. standing com. 5th World Conf. on History of Adult Edn., 1991; mem. steering com. Internat. Assocs., 1991—; chmn. program com. Internat. Conf. Rethinking Adult Edn. for Devel., Ljubljana, Slovenia, 1993; adv. S. Rodriguez U., Caracas, Venezuela, 1994; external examiner adult edn. U. Madras, 1996; presenter edn. conf., Jena, Germany, 1996; cons. in adult edn. Inst. Pedagogida Rural, Venezuela, 1998; founding cons. Academic Inst. Educators of Adults, 1998; cons. to numerous acad. instns. Author numerous books and publs. multi-media formats. Mem. bd. Ctr. Study Liberal Edn. Adults, 1957-67, chmn., 1964-65; mem. Internat. Coun. for Adult Edn. (hon. 1998); founding mem., treas. Internat. Congress U. Adult Edn., 1962-67; mem. N.Y. State Adv. Bd. on Continuing Higher Edn.; chmn. Galaxy Conf. Adult Edn. Orgns., 1969; chmn. priorities com. Cmty. Chest and Coun.; trustee, dir. Chautauqua Inst., Laubach Literacy Internat., Ctrl. N.Y. UN Assn., Syracuse World Affairs Edn. Orgns.; mem. U.S. Nat. Com. UNESCO, presenter 5th world assembly, Cairo, 1994; bd. visitors U. Pitts., Washington U., St. Louis; founding mem., bd. dirs. Coalition Adult Edn. Orgn., 1964-82; exec. bd. dirs. Westminster Manor Ctr.; bd. dirs., treas. Vandercamp Conf. and Recreation Ctr., 1991-95, Ctrl. N.Y. Presbytery Conf. Ctr., 1991; mem. Park Ctrl. Presbyn. Ch. With Royal Can. Naval Vol. Res., 1942-45. Recipient William Pearson Tolley medal for disting. leadership in adult edn. Syracuse U., 1986, Lifetime Achievement award Ctrl. N.Y. Coalition on Adult and Cont. Edn. Mem. Assn. Continuing Higher Edn. (pres. 1947-48, Leadership citation 1973), Am. Assn. Adult Continuing Edn. (Pioneer award 1980), Nat. U. Continuing Edn. Assn. (pres. 1965-66, Bitner award 1973), Internat. Coun. Adult Edn. (founder 1972, chair documentation 1974, coord. confs., mem. Internat. Adult and Continuing Edn. Hall of Fame 1996), Internat. Soc. Comparative Adult Edn. (founding pres. 1992), Acad. Inst. Educators of Adults (founding cons. 1998), Ctrl. N.Y. Coalition on Adult and Continuing Edn. (lifetime achievement award 1998), Rotary (Internat. Paul Harris fellow 1992), Beta Theta Pi. Presbyterian (clk. of session, elder). Home: 216 Lockwood Rd Syracuse NY 13214-2035

CHARTERS, ANN, biographer, editor, educator; b. Bridgeport, Conn., Nov. 10, 1936; d. Nathan and Kate Danberg; m. Samuel B. Charters, Mar. 14, 1959; children: Mallay, Nora Lili. AB, U. Calif.-Berkeley, 1957; MA, Columbia U., 1960, PhD, 1965. Mem. faculty Colby Jr. Coll., New London, N.H., 1962-64; lectr. Columbia U., 1964-65; asst. prof. Am. lit. N.Y.C. Community Coll., 1967-70; assoc. dean of the coll. Brown U., 1989-90; prof. Am. lit. U. Conn., Storrs, 1974—. Author: Nobody—Life and Times of Bert Williams, 1967, Kerouac, 1973, 2d edit., 1986, I Love—Story of Vladimir Mayakovsky and Lili Brik, 1979, The Story and Its Writer, 5th edit., 1998, The Beats: Literary Bohemians in Post-War America, 1983, Beats and Company: A Portrait of a Literary Generation, 1986, The Viking Portable Beat Reader, 1992, Major Writers of Short Fiction, 1993, The Viking Portable Jack Kerouac Reader, 1995, Selected Letters of Jack Kerouac, 1995, (with Samuel Charters) Literature and Its Writers, 1997; author intro. Penguin Classic edit. Three Lives and Q.E.D. (Gertrude Stein), On the Road (Jack Kerouac). Office: U Conn Dept English Box U-25 Storrs Mansfield CT 06269

CHARTIER, VERNON LEE, electrical engineer; b. Feb. 14, 1939; s. Raymond Earl and Margaret Clara (Winegar) C.; m. Lois Marie Schwartz, May 20, 1967; 1 child, Neal Raymond. BSEE, BS in Bus., U. Colo., 1963. Registered profl. engr., Pa.; cert. electromagnetic compatibility engr. Rsch. engr., cons. Westinghouse Electric Co., East Pitts., Pa., 1963-75; prin. engr. high voltage phenomena Bonneville Power Adminstrn., Vancouver, Wash., 1975-95; power sys. EMC cons. Portland, 1995—. Contbr. articles to profl. jours. Fellow IEEE (past fellow com. 1993-96, Herman Halperin Transmission and Distbn. award 1995); mem. IEEE Power Engring. Soc. (chmn. transmission and distbn. com. 1987-88, chmn. fellows com. 1990-92), Internat. Conf. Large High Voltage Electric Sys. (W.G. 36.01 EMC Aspects of Corona and Magnetic Fields, Attwood Assoc. award 1999), Bioelectromagnetics Soc., Internat. Electrotech. Commn. (U.S. rep. to subcom. on High Voltage Lines & Traction Sys.), Chartier Family Assn. Baptist. Home and Office: 13095 SW Glenn Ct Beaverton OR 97008-5664

CHARTOFF, ROBERT IRWIN, film producer; b. N.Y.C.; s. William and Bessie Chartoff; children: Jenifer, William, Julie, Charley, Miranda. AB, Union Coll., 1955; LLB, Columbia U., 1958. Producer: numerous films including Double Trouble, 1967, Point Blank, 1967, The Split, 1968, Leo the Last, 1969, They Shoot Horses Don't They, 1969, The Strawberry Statement, 1970, The Gang That Couldn't Shoot Straight, 1971, The New Centurions, 1972, The Mechanic, 1972, Up the Sandbox, 1972, Busting, 1974, Peeper, 1975, The Gambler, 1975, Rocky, 1976 (Acad. award for best picture), Nickelodeon, 1976, New York, New York, 1977, Valentino, 1977, Comes A Horseman, 1978, Uncle Joe Shannon, 1978, Rocky II, 1979, Raging Bull, 1980, True Confessions, 1981, Rocky III, 1982, The Right Stuff, 1983, Rocky IV, 1985, Beer, 1986, Rocky V, 1990, Straight Talk, 1992. Office: Chartoff Prodns Inc 1250 6th St Ste 101 Santa Monica CA 90401-1612

CHARTON, MARVIN, chemist, educator; b. Bklyn., May 1, 1931; s. William and Elsie (Halpern) C.; m. Barbara Israel, Aug. 28, 1955; children—Michael, Sarah, Deborah. B.S., Coll. City N.Y., 1953; M.A., Bklyn. Coll., 1956; Ph.D., Stevens Inst. Tech., 1962. Instr. chemistry Pratt Inst., Bklyn., 1956-61; asst. prof. Pratt Inst., 1961-64, asso. prof., 1964-67, prof., 1967—, chmn. dept., 1969—; vis. prof. Polymer Rsch. Inst., Poly. U., Bklyn., 1985—. Editor: Advances in Quantitative Structure Property Relationships, 1996; co-editor: Topics in Current Chemistry, vol. 114, 1983; contbr. articles to profl. jours. Fellow AAAS, Intrasci. Rsch. Found.; mem. Am. Chem. Soc., Internat. Group for Correlation Analysis in Chemistry, Internat. QSAR Soc., Royal Chem. Soc. London, N.Y. Acad. Scis., Sigma Xi. Home: 1 Grace Ct Brooklyn NY 11201-4195

CHARTRAND, APRIL MARTIN, designer; b. Ft. Worth, July 19, 1957; d. Joseph E. and Daisy E. (Pitts) Martin. AA, Fashion Inst. Design, L.A., 1978, Santa Barbara (Calif.) City Coll., 1982; BA, San Francisco State U., 1982. Jr. asst. buyer Macys Calif., San Francisco; owner April, San Francisco. Numerous solo and group exhibitions shows including pvt. collections. Organizer Bay Area Women Artist Network. Home: 150 Page St Apt 43 San Francisco CA 94102-5837

CHARTRAND, ROBERT LEE, information scientist; b. Kansas City, Mo., Mar. 6, 1928; s. Joseph Sterling, Jr. and Isabel Christine (Doherty) C.; m. Eleanor Salmon, Oct. 9, 1967; children: Leslie, Kevin; stepchildren: James, Jennifer. B.A., U. Mo., Kansas City, 1948, M.A., 1949; postgrad., La. State U., 1949-50, U. Mo., 1956. Staff Whatsoever Circle Community House, 1950; supr. phys. recreation welfare dept. City of Kansas City, Mo., 1951; Mem. tech. staff Thompson-Ramo-Wooldridge (TRW), Denver and Canoga Park, Calif., 1959-61; with fed. system div. IBM Corp., Bethesda, Md., 1961-64; mgr. advanced systems mktg. IBM Corp., 1964; mgr. applications devel. Planning Research Corp., Washington, 1964-66; specialist in info. sci. Congressional Research Service, Library of Congress, Washington, 1966-77; sr. specialist in info. policy and tech. Congressional Research Service, Library of Congress, 1977-88, sr. fellow in info. policy and tech., 1988-90; Fulbright-Hays lectr., 1968, UN lectr., 1979; cons. Pres.'s Commn. on Population Growth and Am. Future, 1970-71, U.S. Commn. Civil Rights, 1972-78, George Washington U., 1975-77, UNESCO, 1977, Exec. Office of Pres., 1977-82, Office of Tech. Assessment, 1979-89, NAS, 1981-83, Nat. Acad. Pub. Adminstrn. Sr. Res. Assoc., 1995—, sr. cons. Global Disaster Info. Network, 1997—, IRS, 1985-86, Dept. Energy, 1986, Fed. Election Com., 1976-77, U.S. Dept. Commerce, 1985-88, GSA, 1983, 86, 92—, OMB, 1995-97, Fed. Emergency Mgmt. Agy., 1986-88, NASA, 1993, Carnegie Commn. on Sci., Tech. and Govt., 1993-94, NLM, 1994-95, Turner Edn. Svcs., 1994-96, World Future Soc., 1997—; adj. fellow Ctr. for Strategic and Internat. Studies, 1990-95; mem. STI bd. NAS/NRC, 1990-91, mapping sci. com., 1990-93; mem. adv. coun. Nat. Inst. Urban Search and Rescue, 1991—; adj. prof. Am. U., 1974-78; lectr. U.S. Info. Agy., 1977; sr. lectr. UN Devel. Program, 1979; vis. prof. UCLA, 1982, U. Pitts., 1989, 1991—; spl. advisor Open Systems Conf. Bd., 1990-94, Internat. Green Cross, 1993-94; mem. program adv. bd. Govt. Tech. Leadership Inst., 1998—; mem. adv. com. U.S. CSC, 1973-80, White House Conf. on Libr. and Info. Svcs., 1979-80; adv. NSF, 1977-79; mem. planning panel for toxicology and environment NLM, 1991-92; mem. adv. panel Dept. State, 1978-84; NLM, 1985-86, 91-92; mem. adv. bd. Chem. Abstracts Svc., 1979-84, Info. Inst., 1983-86, Econ. Devel. Found., 1985-90, Ency. Libr. and Info. Sci., 1986—, Internat. Design for Extreme Environments Assembly, 1991-95, Internat. Energy Mgmt. & Engr. Soc., 1993, 94—, S.W. Fla. Emergency Adv. Bd., 1993—, Collier County Disaster Recovery Coalition Com., 1995—; mem. bd. visitors Emergency Mgmt. Recovery Inst., 1987-89; proj. devel. cons. U. Mo., Kansas City, 1985-89, White House Conf. Libr. and Info. Svc., 1990-91; spl. cons. U. Mo. Sys., 1991, 93; nat. bd. dirs. Alliance of Info. and Referral Sys, 1994—; bd. govs. Naples Inst., 1994-97, Internat. Coun. for Computer Commns., 1994—, sr. adv. Stennis Ctr. Pub. Svc., 1998—. Author: Systems Technology Applied to Social and Community Problems, 1971, Computers and Political Campaigning, 1972, (with others) State Legislature Use of Information Technology, 1978, Opportunities for the Use of Information Resources and Advanced Technologies in Congress, 1993; also congl. studies; editor, contbg. author: Information Support, Program Budgeting and the Congress, 1968; editor, contbg. author: Computers in the Service of Society, 1972, Critical Issues in the Information Age, 1991; editor: Hope for the Cities: A Systems Approach to Human needs, 1971; co-editr, contbg. author: Information Technology Serving Society, 1979, Strategies and Systems for Disaster Survival, 1989; editorial bd.: Law and Computer Tech, 1968-82, The Information Society, 1979—, Hazard, 1979-95, Futures Res. Quar., 1987—, Am. Fedn. Info. Processing Socs. Washington Report, 1989-90; editorial adviser: Rutgers Jour. Computers and the Law, 1970-72, ASK, 1982-86, ASIS Bull., 1979-91; cons. editor: Info. Storage and Retrieval, 1969-74, SIAM News, 1976-79; contbr. articles to profl. jours. Trustee Windham Coll., 1974-76, Engring. Info., 1980-83, Capital Children's Mus., 1982-86; vice chmn. Friends of Montgomery County Libr., 1984-87; cons. advisor Smithsonian Inst., 1986-90; bd. dirs. Friends of Libr. Collier County, Fla., 1991—, v.p., 1993-95, pres.-elect, 1994, pres., 1995-96; mem. Leadership Collier Masters, 1996-97, class chmn., 1997-98, mem. adv. com., 1997-99; mem. MPA adv. com. Fla. Gulf Coast U., 1997—. Decorated Cavaliere Ufficiale Italy; recipient Interagy. Com. on ADP award, 1976, Test of Time award, 1979, Alumni Achievement award U. Mo., Kansas City, 1984, Internat. Emergency Mgmt. and Engring. Soc. Life Achievement award, 1993, Outstanding Svc. award, 1994; named to Govt. Computer News Hall of Fame, 1988. Fellow AAAS (sect. chmn. 1983-84); mem. Am. Soc. Info. Sci. (cons. editor bull. 1974-90, cert. appreciation 1976, award of merit 1985, Pioneer award 1988), Naval Intelligence Profls., Cosmos Club, Forum Club, Kenwood Golf and Country Club, Kensington Golf and Country Club, Naples Bath and Tennis Club. Unitarian. Home: 1558 B Oyster Catcher Pte Naples FL 34105-2434 *If there is to be a future, every effort must be expended by technologists and humanitarians alike to meld their philosophies and pragmatic undertakings. The global dimensions and impacts of mankind's major initiatives are inextricably related, and the ancients were prescient in their avowal that "where there is no vision, the people perish."*

CHARWAT, ANDREW FRANCISZEK, engineering educator; b. Poland, Feb. 10, 1925; came to U.S., 1945; s. Franciszek and Wanda (Niec) C.; m. Halina M. Stieglitz, Aug. 18, 1948; 1 child, Danuta K. Charwat McCall. M Engring., Stevens Inst. Tech., 1948; PhD, U. Calif., Berkeley, 1952. Aerodynamicist Propulsion Research Corp., Los Angeles, 1952-53; designer Northrup Aircraft Corp., Los Angeles, 1953-55; prof., dept. mech. and aerospace engring. UCLA, 1955-92, prof. emeritus, 1992—; cons. to numerous industry and govt. agys., 1955—; expert witness various legal cases; dir. Univ. Study Ctr., Lyon and Grenoble, France, 1986-88. Contbr. over 80 articles and research papers. Guggenheim fellow, 1962. Office: UCLA Dept Mech Aerospace & Nuc Engring PO Box 951597 Los Angeles CA 90095-1597

CHASANOW, DEBORAH K., federal judge; b. 1948. BA, RUtgers U., 1970; JD, Stanford U., 1973. Pvt. practice atty. COle & Groner, Washington, 1975; asst. atty. gen. State of Md., 1975-79; chief criminal appeals divsn. Md. Atty. Gen.'s Office, 1979-87; U.S. magistrate judge U.S. Dist. Ct. Md., 1987-93, dist. judge, 1993—; instr. law schs. U. Balt., U. Md., 1978-84. Mem. Fed. Magistrate Judges Assn., Md. Bar Assn., Prince George's County Bar Assn., Montgomery County Bar Assn., Women's Bar Assn., Marlborough Am. Inn. Ct. (pres. 1988-90), Wrangler's Law Club, Phi Beta Kappa. Office: US Courthouse 6500 Cherrywood Ln Rm 465A Greenbelt MD 20770-1249*

CHASANOW, HOWARD STUART, judge, lecturer; b. Washington, Apr. 3, 1937; 1 child from previous marriage, Andrea; m. Deborah Hovis Koss, May 15, 1983. BA, U. Md., 1959, JD, 1961; LLM, Harvard U., 1962. Bar: Md. 1961, U.S. Supreme Ct. 1965. Asst. states atty. Prince George County, Upper Marlboro, Md., 1963-64, dep. states atty., 1964-68; judge Dist. Ct., Upper Marlboro, 1971-77, 7th Jud. Cir., 1977-90; judge Ct. Appeals of Md., 1990—; lectr. Sch. Law U. Md., Balt., 1973—, Nat. Jud. Coll., Reno, 1980—, Am. Acad. Jud. Edn., 1984—; founder Prince George's County Drinking Driving Sch.; chmn. adv. bd. Sentencing Guidelines, Md., 1982-90, chmn. jud. adminstrn. sect., 1982-84; mem. Md. Commn. on Criminal Sentencing Policy, 1996—; mem. standing com. on rules of practice and procedure Ct. Appeals, 1985-90; mem. govs. task force to Revise Criminal Code, 1992—. Contbr. law rev. articles. Served with USAF, 1968-69. Office: Ct Appeals Md Prince George County Courthouse PO Box 399 Upper Marlboro MD 20773-0399

CHASE, ALISON M., adult nurse practitioner; b. Cin., Jan. 27, 1940; d. William Rowell and Katharine Chase; m. Joseph C. Hill, Apr. 15, 1983. BA, Ripon Coll., 1963; BS in Nursing, Columbia Prsbyn. Sch. Nursing, 1966; MS in Nursing, Simmons Coll., 1997. Cert. adult nurse practitioner. Adult nurse practitioner Harvard Cmty. Health Plan, Boston, M$Ds., 1972-96; ind. practitioner, 1996—. Mem. ANA, North Shore Nurse Practitioners Assn., Sigma Theta Tau.

CHASE, ALYSSA ANN, editor; b. New Orleans, Dec. 23, 1965; d. John Churchill and Alexandra Andra (de Monsabert) C.; m. Robert Brian Rebein, July 1, 1995; 1 child, Alexandra Maria Rebein. BA in Lit. in English, U. Kans., 1988; BA in Studio Art magna cum laude, SUNY, Buffalo, 1994. Asst. editor Dial Books for Young Readers, N.Y.C., 1989-90; assoc. editor Holiday House, Inc., N.Y.C., 1990-92, Buffalo (N.Y.) Spree Mag., Buffalo, N.Y., 1992-95; copy editor, writer The Riverfront Times and St. Louis Mag., St. Louis, Mo., 1995-97; mng. editor St. Louis Mag., 1997-98; editor RCI Premier Mag., Indpls., 1998—; freelance copy writer, proofreader, copy editor and/or rschr. Harper Collins Children's Books, N.Y.C., 1990-92, Morrow Jr. Books, N.Y.C., 1990-92, Tambourine Books, N.Y.C., 1990-92, Lothrop, Lee & Shepherd Books, N.Y.C., 1990-92, Dorling Kindersley, Inc., N.Y.C., 1990-92, The Humanist: Prometheus Books, 1993, Printing Prep, Buffalo, 1994, Georgette Hasiotis, Buffalo, 1994, August Tavern Creek Developers, St. Louis, 1996; tchg. artist, docent coord., tour guide The Arts in Edn. Inst. of Western N.Y., Cheektowaga, N.Y., 1995. Mem. Phi Beta Kappa. Avocations: painting, writing childrens books, travel, gardening, running. Home: 306 N Ridgeview Dr Indianapolis IN 46219-6127*

CHASE, CHEVY (CORNELIUS CRANE CHASE), comedian, actor, author; b. Woodstock, N.Y., Oct. 8, 1943; s. Edward Tinsley and Cathalene Crane (Widdoes) C.; m. Jayni Chase, 1982; children: Cydney Cathalene, Caley Leigh, Emily Evelyn. B.A. in English, Bard Coll., 1967; CCS, Inst. Audio Rsch., 1970. Artist MGM Records, 1968; writer for Mad mag., 1969; actor Groove Tube, Pasta Prodns., 1967-71; writer, actor Gt. Am. Dream Machine, 1971; dir., writer, actor, Nat. Lampoon Theatre Co., 1972-74; writer, actor Sat. Night Live TV show, 1975-76 (Emmy award 1975-76); appeared on TV in Paul Simon Spl., host of The Chevy Chase Show, 1993; appeared in films Foul Play, 1978, Oh Heavenly Dog, 1980, Caddyshack, 1980, Seems Like Old Times, 1981, Under the Rainbow, 1981, Modern Problems, 1981, Vacation, 1983, Deal of the Century, 1983, Fletch, 1984, European Vacation, 1985, Spies Like Us, 1985, Follow That Bird, 1985, The Three Amigos, 1986, Caddyshack II, 1988, Funny Farm, 1988, The Couch Trip, 1988, Christmas Vacation, 1989, Fletch Lives, 1989, Nothing But Trouble, 1991, L.A. Story, 1991, Memoirs of an Invisible Man, 1992, Hero, 1992, Last Action Hero, 1993, Cops and Robbersons, 1994, Man of the House, 1995, National Lampoon's Vegas Vacation, 1997, Snow Day, 1999. Recipient award for best script in comedy variety spl. Writers Guild, award best supporting actor in comedy variety series Nat. Acad. TV Arts and Scis. Mem. Am. Fedn. Musicians, Stage Actors Guild, Actors Equity, AFTRA. Democrat. Office: Cornelius Prods PO Box 257 Bedford NY 10506-0257

CHASE, CLINTON IRVIN, psychologist, educator, business executive; b. Aug. 14, 1927; m. Patricia Cronenberger; 1 child. B.S. in Psychology with honors, U. Idaho, 1950, M.S. in Adminstrn., 1951; Ph.D. in Ednl. Psychology, U. Calif.-Berkeley, 1958. Asst. to dean students Wash. State U., 1951-52; sch. psychologist Piedmont Pub. Schs., Calif., 1957-58; asst. prof. ednl. psychology Idaho State U., 1958-61, Miami U., Oxford, 1961-62; asst. prof. ednl. psychology Ind. U., Bloomington, 1962-64, assoc. prof., 1964-68, prof., 1968-95; prof. emeritus Indiana U., Bloomington, 1995—; assoc. dir. Bur. Evaluative Studies and Testing Ind. U., Bloomington, 1962-70, dir., 1970-89, chmn. dept. ednl. psychology, 1970-74; dir. Ind. Testing and Evaluation Svc., Bloomington, 1976-87, Ind. Ctr. for Evaluation, 1988-94; owner, mgr. Ind. Testing and Evaluation Svc., 1990—. Author: (with H. Glenn Ludlow) Readings in Educational and Psychological Measurement, 1966, Elementary Statistical Procedures, 1967, 3d edit., 1984, Measurement for Educational Evaluation, 1974, 2d edit., 1978, (with L.C. Jacobs) Developing and Using Tests Effectively, 1992, Contemporary Assessment for Educators, 1999. Served with USN, 1945-46; to capt. USAF, 1952-55. Named Ky. Col., 1998. Fellow Am. Psychol. Assn., Am. Ednl. Research Assn., Nat. Council on Measurement in Edn., Phi Beta Kappa, Kappa Delta Pi. *The careful establishment of objectives, and the persistant pursuit of objectives, are the primary ingredients of achievement.*

CHASE, COCHRANE, advertising agency executive; b. Berwyn, Ill., Feb. 6, 1932; s. Henry Cochrane and Roselyn (Scott) C.; m. Janis Valeria Kueber, June 19, 1954; children—Katherine Ann, Anthony Scott, Lisa Marie. B.A., Wesleyan U., 1954. With steel warehousing div. Jessop Steel Co., Broadview, Ill., 1956-62; mgr. sales Jessop Steel Co., 1961-62; with Jessop Steel Calif., Santa Fe Springs, 1963-64; asst. mgr. market research Ducommun Metals & Supply Co., Los Angeles, 1964-65; v.p. Newport Advt. Inc., Newport Beach, Calif., 1965; pres. Cochrane Chase, Livingston & Co., Inc., Irvine, Calif., 1966, chmn. bd., chief exec. officer, 1966-88; chmn. emeritus AC&R/CCL, Irvine, Calif., 1988-89. Co-author: Marketing Problem Solver, 1973, Newport Financial Planner, 1985. Served with USNR, 1954-56. Home: 2162 Papaya Dr La Habra CA 90631-7917

CHASE, DONALD JACOB, film journalist, film producer; b. New Britain, Conn., Aug. 25, 1944; s. Anthony Daniel and Helen Rochelle (Chudzik) Cieszynski. BA magna cum laude, Boston U., 1965; postgrad., Columbia U., 1965-66. Freelance journalist various met. newspapers, 1977—. Author: Filmmaking: The Collaborative Art, 1975; contbg. editor: Pictures Will Talk (K.L. Geist), 1977, Something Wonderful Right Away (Jeffrey Sweet), 1978; editor numerous books on film, TV, theatre; critic Film Comment mag., 1991—. Avocations: swimming, gymnastics, french language and culture. Office: Even Keel Prodns 325 E 80th St New York NY 10021-0665

CHASE, DORIS TOTTEN, sculptor, video artist, filmmaker; b. Seattle, 1923; d. William Phelps and Helen (Feeney) Totten; m. Elmo Chase, Oct. 20, 1943 (div. 1972); children: Gregary Totten, Randall Jarvis Totten. Student, U. Wash., 1941-43. lectr. tours for USIA in S.Am., 1975, Europe, 1978, India, 1972, Australia, 1986, Eastern Europe, 1987; vis. lectr., presenter U. Colo., Boulder, Mary Mount Coll., N.Y., the Kitchen Ctr. for Film & Video, Nat. Film Bd. of Can., Toronto, N.Y. Grad. Sch. One-woman shows include Ruth White Gallery, N.Y.C., 1967, 69, 70, Fountain Gallery, Portland, Oreg., 1970, U. Wash. Henry Gallery, 1971, 77, 98, Wadsworth Athenum, Hartford, Conn., 1973, Hirshhorn Mus., Washington, 1974, 77, Anthology Film Archives, N.Y.C., 1975, 80, 83, Donnell Libr., N.Y.C., 1976, 79, 83, 92, Performing Arts Mus. at Lincoln Ctr., 1976, Mus. Modern Art, N.Y.C., 1978, 80, 87, 93, 98, High Mus., Atlanta, 1978, Herbert Johnson Mus., 1982, A.I.R. Gallery, N.Y.C., 1983-85, Art in Embassies, USIS, 1984-88, Inst. Contemporary Art, London, 1989, Woodside/Braseth Gallery, 1990, 92, John F. Kennedy Ctr., 1990, Seattle Arts Mus., 1990, 92, 95, Mus. N.W. Art La Conner Wash., 1995; circulating exhibit Western Mus. Assn., 1970-71, Am. Inst. Archs., Seattle, 1994, Friesen Gallery, Seattle, 1997, 98; represented in permanent collections Finch Coll. Mus., N.Y.C., Mus. Modern Art, N.Y.C., Seattle Art Mus., Ashai Shimbum, Tokyo, Georges Pompidou Ctr., Paris, Battelle Inst., Mus. Fine Arts Boston, Milw. Art Inst., Art Inst. Chgo., Mus. Fine Arts Houston, Frye Art Mus., Seattle, Nat. Collection Fine Arts, Smithsonian Instn., Washington, Wadsworth Athenum, N.C. Mus. Art, Raleigh, Mus. Modern Art, Kobe, Japan, Pa. Acad. Art, Phila., Portland Art Mus., Vancouver (B.C.) Art Gallery, Montgomery (Ala.) Mus. Fine Art, Hudson River Mus., N.Y.C., Tacoma Art Mus.; works represented in archival collections Ctr. for Film and Theatre Rsch., U. Wis., Madison, U. Wash., Seattle; executed monumental kinetic sculpture Kerry Park, Seattle, Lake Park, Anderson, Ind., Expo '70, Osaka, Japan, Sculpture Park, Atlanta, Met. Mus. Art, N.Y.C., Montgomery Mus. Fine Arts, Seattle Ctr., 1999; multi-media sculpture for 4 ballets, Opera Assn. Seattle; included in Sculpture in Park program N.Y.C., Playground of Tomorrow ABC-TV, L.A.; prodr. Doris Chase Dance Series, 1971-81, Concept Series, 1980-84; prodr. By Herself Series: Table for One (with Geraldine Page), 1985, (with Anne Jackson) Dear Papa, 1986, (with Luise Rainer) A Dancer, 1987, (with Priscilla Pointer) Still Frame, 1988, (with Joan Plowright) Sophie, 1989, The Chelsea, 1994. Recipient honors and awards at numerous festivals in U.S. and fgn. countries; grantee Nat. Endowment for Arts, Am. Film Inst., 1988, N.Y. State Coun. for Arts, Mich. Arts Coun., Seattle Art Commn., 1992, Jerusalem Film Festival, 1987, Berlin Film Festival, 1985, 87, Athens Film Festival, 1995, London Film Festival, 1986, Am. Film Inst. Festival, 1987, 94, Retirement Rsch. Found., 1994, Lockwood Found., Herzman Family Found., Seattle Center Found., NEA, NYSCA; subject of documentary Doris Chase: Portrait of the Artist, PBS, 1985; subject of book and video: Artist in Motion, 1993; recipient Wash. Gov.'s Art award, 1992. Mem. Actors Studio (writer, dirs. wing 1986). All work in film and video in collection and archives of Mus. Modern Art, N.Y.C. Address: Chelsea Hotel 222 W 23rd St New York NY 10011-2301

CHASE, EDITH NEWLIN, preschool educator, poet; b. Plainfield, Ind., June 6, 1905; d. Eli J. and Mary Etta (Pickett) Newlin; m. Heman Lincoln Chase III, Jan. 21,1933; children: Margaret C. Perry, Ellen Chase. Student, Olney Friends Sch., Barnesville, Ohio, 1920-23, Indpls. Pub. Libr., 1924, Bank St. Coll., N.Y.C., 1929, 31, Bank St. Coll., 1932. Birthright mem. Religious Soc. Friends. Tchr. Hessian Hills Sch., Croton on Hudson, N.Y., 1929, Spring Hill Sch., Litchfield, Conn., 1931-34; tchr. Manhasset Bay Sch., Port Washington, N.Y., 1934-37, resident dir., 1934-35, co-dir., 1935-37; owner, dir. Chase Preschool, Alstead, N.H., 1940-45, 50-63; summer counselor Mill Hollow Children's Camp, East Alstead, N.H., 1928-31. Author: Small Window Panes, 1978, Twigs From My Tree, 1984, The New Baby Calf, 1984, Waters, 1993, Secret Dawn, 1996; co-author Another Here & Now Story Book Bank Street, 1937. Mem. Ladies Cir. of Alstead 2nd Ch., N.H., 1940-84. Mem. AARP, Poetry Soc. N.H. Congregationalist. Avocations: building our home, gardening, English folk dance, reading, surveyor's helper.

CHASE, EDWARD THORNTON, lawyer; b. Palo Alto, Calif., June 25, 1942; s. Edward Tinsley Chase and Cathalene (Crane) Widdoes; m. Joan Gregory Chase, Dec. 4, 1982; children: Lila Gregory, Edward Browning. BA, Harvard U., 1964; LLB, U. Pa., 1967. Bar: N.Y. 1969, U.S. Dist. Ct. (so. and ea. dists.) N.Y. 1970, U.S. Supreme Ct. 1981. Assoc. Botein, Hays, Sklar & Herzberg, N.Y.C., 1968-70, Legal Aid Soc., N.Y.C., 1970-78; pvt. practice N.Y.C., 1978—; ptnr. Chase & Greenberg, N.Y.C., 1980-82; trial techniques instr. Nat. Inst. for Trial Advocacy, N.Y.C., 1978-81; arbitrator Civil Ct., City of N.Y., 1981; mem. Mayor's Adv. Coun. on Juvenile Facilities and Programs, N.Y.C., 1973-74. Mem. ATLA, Assn. of the Bar of the City of N.Y., N.Y. State Trial Lawyers Assn. Office: Ste 4500 60 E 42nd St New York NY 10165

CHASE, ERIC LEWIS, lawyer; b. Princeton, N.J., Sept. 21, 1946; s. Harold William and Bernice Mae (Fadden) C.; m. Jamie Campbell, Dec. 29, 1979; children: Eric Campbell, Kathryn Dianne, John Harold. BA, Princeton U., 1968; JD cum laude, U. Minn., 1974. Bar: N.J. 1974, D.C. 1975, U.S. Ct. Appeals (3d cir.) 1979, U.S. Supreme Ct. 1981, U.S. Claims Ct. 1982, U.S. Tax Ct. 1982, N.Y. 1983. Trial atty. FCC, 1974-78; asst. U.S. atty. Dist. N.J., Newark, 1978-80; ptnr. Margolis Chase, Verona, N.J., 1980-90, Hannoch Weisman, Roseland, N.J., 1990-93, Bressler, Amery & Ross, Florham Park, N.J., 1993—; prof. law of war Marine Corps Command and Staff Coll., Quantico, Va., 1990—. Author: Automobile Dealers and the Law, 1994, 6th edit., 1999; contbr. articles on law and mil. to profl. publs., including N.Y. Times, Washington Post, Newsweek mag. With USMC, 1968-71; col. Res., ret. Mem. ABA (mem. task force on internat. criminal ct.), N.J. State Bar Assn. (franchise com. 1997—). Office: Bressler Amery & Ross 325 Columbia Tpke Ste 8 Florham Park NJ 07932-1212

CHASE, J. VINCENT, shopping center executive, justice of the peace; b. N.Y.C., Nov. 5, 1949; m. Addie Lee Pickus, Sept. 3, 1983. BS, U. Bridgeport, 1972. Pers. adminstr. Ins. Svcs. Office, N.Y.C., 1972-77; gen. mgr. pers. John Wiley & Sons, N.Y.C., 1977-79; pers. dir. CitiCorp, N.Y.C., 1979-83; pres., owner Colonial Square Shopping Ctr., Stratford, Conn., 1983—; mem. Conn. Ho. of Reps., Hartford, 1980-96, dep. minority leader, 1990-96; asst. treas. Conn. Office of the State Treasurer, Hartford, 1997-98; chief investigator U.S. Ho. of Reps., Washington, 1998—. Founding bd. dirs. Shang Wheeler Meml. Mus.; bd. dirs. ARC, Kennedy Ctr., Union Cemetery Assn., Stratford Vis. Nurse Assn.; trustee Conn. Am. Parkinson Disease Assn.; Stratford Rep. Town Com.; candidate for U.S. Ho. of Reps. from 3d Dist. Conn., 1990. Recipient Outstanding Svc. award Stratford Tenants' Coun., 1982, Man of Yr. award Stratford Civitan Club, 1983, Alumnus of Yr. award U. Bridgeport, 1990, Legislator of Yr. award Conn. Profl. Ins. Agts. Assn., 1991, Legislator of Yr. award Conn. Assn. Optometrists, 1993, Legislator of Yr. award Conn. Chiropractic Assn., 1994, Legislator of Yr. award Conn. Adoption Coun., 1996, Legislator of Yr. award U.S. Humane Soc., 1997. Mem. U. Bridgeport Alumni Assn. (bd. dirs.), Washington D.C.-Conn. Soc., Masons, Scottish Rite. Congregationalist. Office: Colonial Square Shop Ctr PO Box 44 2420 Main St Stratford CT 06615-5951

CHASE, JAMES KELLER, retired artist, museum director, educator; b. Logansport, Ind., May 18, 1927; s. James Howard and Agnes (Keller) C.; m. Marcelle Pierard, Dec. 29, 1969; 1 son, Henrik Clovis. B.S., Ball State U., Muncie, Ind., 1952, doctoral fellow, 1972-74; M.A., Mich. State U., 1963. Art supr. Chili (Ind.) schs., 1952-53, Sturgis (Mich.) schs., 1953-57; asst. prof. Western Mich. U., 1957-60; tchr. edn. TV on camera Central Mich. U., 1960-65; prof., chmn. fine arts dept. Northwood U., Midland, Mich., 1964-74; dir. Saginaw (Mich.) Mus., 1975-77, Ariz. Capitol Mus., Phoenix, 1978-81, McPherson Coll., 1982-87; art instr. Maricopa County, 1982-89; ret., 1989; vis. prof. Western Mich. U., Saginaw Valley U., Delta Coll., Saginaw, Johns Hopkins U. at Ariz. State U.; mem. Mich. Higher Edn. Commn., 1967, Mich. Creativity Com., 1966; bd. dirs. Midland Ctr. Arts, 1967-71, Thompson Draw, Tonto Nat. Forest. Author: Nine Fine, 1977; contbr. articles to edn. jours., newspapers, mags.; exhibiting artist state, regional and nat. shows. Pres. Sands East II Homeowners Assn., 1987-89, sec., 1989-96; vol. ct. vis. guardianship rev. project Ariz. Superior Ct., 1994—. Mem. Am. Assn. Museums, Ariz. Adminstrs. Assn., Central Ariz. Museums Assn., Ariz. Hist. Assn. Home: 3075 N 83rd Pl Scottsdale AZ 85251-7316 *Creating, sharing and understanding art and beauty adds truth and vibrance to life.*

CHASE, JAMES RICHARD, retired college president; b. Oxnard, Calif., Oct. 7, 1930; s. James Warren and Nina Marie (Fiscus) C.; m. Mary Corinne Sutherland, Dec. 16, 1950; children: Kenneth Richard, Jennifer Corinne. B. Theology, Biola Coll., 1951; B.A., Pepperdine U., 1953, M.A., 1954; Ph.D., Cornell U., 1961. Instr. Biola Coll., La Mirada, Calif., 1953-57; prof., chmn. dept. humanities Biola Coll., 1959-65, v.p. acad. affairs, 1965-70, pres., 1970-82; pres. Wheaton (Ill.) Coll., 1982-93, pres. emeritus, 1993—; teaching asst. Cornell Univ., Ithaca, N.Y., 1957-59; bd. dirs. World Christian Tng. Ctr., 1970-82; bd. dirs. Christian Coll. Coalition, 1977-79, chmn. bd., 1977-79; bd. dirs. Mission Aviation Fellowship, 1975-81, chmn. bd., 1978-81; bd. dirs. Western Coll. Assn., 1980-82. Mem. Nat. Assn. Ind. Colls. and Univs. (dir. 1980), Assn. Ind. Calif. Colls. and Univs. (mem. exec. com. 1978-82), Am. Assn. Bible Colls. (dir. 1974-80), Nat. Assn. Intercollegiate Athletics (pres. adv. com. 1976-82), Nat. Assn. Evangelicals (exec. com. 1984-92), We. Assn. Schs. and Colls. (sr. commn. 1981-82), Am. Assn. Pres. Ind. Colls. and Univs. (dir. 1980-85, v.p. 1982-85), Speech Communication Assn., Christian Coll. Consortium (chmn. 1976), Coalition (chmn. 1976), Fedn. Ind. Ill. Colls. and Univs. (exec. com., chmn. bd. 1989-91). Baptist.

CHASE, JOHN DAVID, university dean, physician; b. Detroit, Sept. 24, 1920; s. Clyde Harrison and Bonnie Lucille (Fogas) C.; m. Edwarda I. Walther (Layne), June 18, 1985; 1 child from previous marriage, Robert Winslow. AB, Wabash (Ind.) Coll., 1942; MD, Western Res. U., 1945. Diplomate: Am. Bd. Internal Medicine. Intern Detroit Receiving Hosp., 1945-46; resident in internal medicine Wayne State U. Hosp., 1948-52; teaching fellow Nat. Heart Inst., 1952; with VA, 1952-78; dep. assoc. chief med. dir. academic affairs VA, Washington, 1970-73; chief med. service VA Hosp., Tacoma, 1973-74; chief med. dir. VA Central Office, Washington, 1974-78; assoc. dean clin. affairs U. Wash. Sch. Med., Seattle, 1978-81, dean Sch. Medicine, 1981-82, dean emeritus, 1983—; mem. nat. adv. council Heart and Lung Inst., 1968-70, Regional Med. Programs, 1970-73, Nat. Library Medicine, 1971-73; mem. Nat. Adv. Council VA Edn., 1973, Nat. Adv. Council Health Services Planning and Resources, 1976, Fed. Coordinating Council Sci., Engring. and Tech., 1976-78, Nat. Adv. Council Health Planning and Devel., 1976—; bd. govs. Armed Forces Inst. Pathology, 1976-78. Mem. Inst. Medicine, 1982—. Served with M.C. USNR, 1946-48. Recipient Distinguished Service award Wayne State U. Med. Sch., 1976. Fellow ACP, Am. Coll. Chest Physicians; mem. Assn. Mil. Surgeons U.S., AMA (ho. dels.), Am. Hosp. Assn. (trustee 1976-78). Home: 1356 E 8th St Port Angeles WA 98362

CHASE, LUCIUS PETER, lawyer, retired corporate executive; b. Rochester, N.Y., Jan. 1, 1902; s. Lucius A. and Beatrice (Tucker) C.; m. Virdelle Simpson, June 13, 1925. AB, U. Wis., 1923, JD, 1925; LLD, Lakeland Coll., 1972. Former spl. asst. to atty. gen. U.S.; former gen. counsel, sr. v.p. Kohler Co., Wis., 1925-71; bd. dirs., 1936-84, mem. exec. com., 1936-84; dir. emeritus Kohler Co., Wis., 1984-96, Citizens Bank of Sheboygan.;

Trustee, chmn. emeritus Lakeland Coll., Sheboygan. Contbr. articles profl. jours. Served as col. AUS, World War II. Decorated Silver Star, Legion of Merit with oak leaf cluster, Purple Heart; Croix de Guerre with palm France; officer Order of Leopold (Belgium). Mem. VFW, Wis. Bar Assn., Am. Legion, Mil. Order Purple Heart, Order of Coif, Scabbard and Blade, Rotary, Alpha Sigma Phi, Gamma Eta Gamma. Methodist. Home: 650 N Lake Howard Dr Apt 7H Winter Haven FL 33881-3134

CHASE, MARIA ELAINE GAROUFALIS, publishing company executive; b. Chgo., Jan. 9, 1957; d. Byron L. and Irene (Mathews) Garoufalis. BS, Manchester Coll., 1979. CPA, Ill. Sr. mgr. Ernst & Young, Chgo., 1979-92; contr., v.p. fin. Fox Valley Press, Inc., Plainfield, Ill., 1994—. Bd. trustees rep., Alumni Assn. bd. dirs. Manchester Coll.; bd. dirs. St. Nectarios Greek Orthodox Ch. Ladies' Soc., Palatine, Ill., 1985-92, pres., 1989-90. Mem. AICPA, AMA, NAFE, Internat. Newspaper Fin. Execs., Ill. CPA Soc., Manchester Coll. Acctg. Alumni Assn., Greek Women's Univ. Club. Avocations: personal fitness, tennis, cooking. Office: Fox Valley Press Inc 3101 N Us Highway 30 Plainfield IL 60544-9604

CHASE, MARILYN, journalist; b. L.A.. AB in English, Stanford U., 1971; MS in Journalism, U. Calif., Berkeley, 1973. News reporter Arlington (Va.) News, 1974-75; reporter Arlington Jour., 1975-76; stringer N.Y. Times, 1976-78; reporter Wall St. Jour., San Francisco, 1978-94; health columnist Wall St. Jour., 1994—. Office: Wall St Jour 201 California St San Francisco CA 94111-5002

CHASE, MERRILL WALLACE, immunologist, educator; b. Providence, Sept. 17, 1905; s. John Whitman and Bertha H. (Wallace) C.; m. Edith Steele Bowen, Sept. 5, 1931 (dec. 1961); children: Nancy Steele (Mrs. William W. Cowles), John Wallace, Susan Elizabeth (dec. 1985); m. Cynthia Hambury Pierce, July 8, 1961. AB, Brown U., 1927, ScM, 1929, PhD, 1931, ScD honoris causa, 1977; ScD honoris causa, Rockefeller U., 1988; MD honoris causa, U. Münster, Fed. Republic Germany, 1974. Instr. biology Brown U., 1931-32; staff mem. Rockefeller Inst. Med. Research, 1932-79; prof. immunology and microbiology, head lab. immunology and hypersensitivity Rockefeller U., 1956-79; med. adv. council Profl. Ednl. and Research Task Force, Asthma and Allergy Found. Am., 1955-83. Editor: (with C.A. Williams) Methods in Immunology and Immunochemistry, Vol. 1, 1967, Vol. 11, 1968, Vol. III, 1970, vols. IV, 1977, and V, 1976. Fellow Am. Acad. Allergy (hon., Disting. Svc. award 1969), Am. Coll. Allergists (hon.), Am. Acad. Arts and Scis.; mem. AAAS, Am. Assn. Immunologists (pres. 1956-57), Am. Soc. Microbiology (program chmn. 1959-61), Harvey Soc., N.Y. Acad. Scis., N.Y. Allergy Soc. (hon.), Nat. Acad. Sci. Republican. Universalist-Unitarian. Spl. research hypersensitivity to simple chem. allergens, studies Kveim antigen in sarcoidosis, studies tuberculins and mycobacterial antigens. Office: Rockefeller U 1230 York Ave # 73 New York NY 10021-6399

CHASE, NICHOLAS JOSEPH, lawyer, educator; b. Windsor, Conn., Jan. 9, 1913; s. Michael and Lucy A. (Sinisgalli) C.; m. F. Louise Dooley, Dec. 27, 1936; children: Stephen Edward, Mary Ann, Michael Dooley, Clare Lucia, Martha Louise. AB in Philosophy, Cath. U. Am., 1933, AM in Politics, 1934; Columbian fellow, Brookings Instn., 1934-35; JD magna cum laude, Georgetown U. Law Sch., 1940. Bar: D.C. 1939, U.S. Ct. Appeals 1940, U.S. Ct. Claims 1940, U.S. Supreme Ct. 1943, Md. 1950, U.S. Mil. Ct. Appeals, 1949-65, U.S. Emergency Ct Appeals, 1952-62. Pvt. practice Washington, 1939—; adminstrv. asst. Pub. Works Admin., 1935-40; atty. Leahy & Hughes, Washington, 1940-47; prof. law Cath. U. Am., 1943-45; gen. coun. Chevy Chase Village, Md., 1943-48; prof. law Georgetown U., Washington, 1946-66; prin. Chase & Williams, Washington, 1948-52, Chase & McChesney, Washington, 1952-62, Chase & Colton, Washington, 1963-66; mem. adv. com. Fed. Rules of Criminal Prodedure for U.S. Cts., 1940-49; mem. com. on Rules for Mcpl. and Superior Cts., 1943-63; mem. D.C. Coun. Law Enforcement, 1950-59; judge moot ct. Georgetown U., 1959-66, Prettyman Criminal Law Clinic, 1956-66; arbitrator Am. Arbitration Assn., 1970—, trial specialist, 1940-65; mem. Jud. Conf. D.C. Cir., 1952-62; def. counsel U.S. Dist. Ct. for D.C., 1941-66. Author: Federal and Washington, D.C. Relations, 1801-1933, publs. on Adams Meml., Miscellaneous Essays: 1994, Essays of Prof. Anon, 1997-98, Washington Adams Memorial and Centennial of Cath. U. Am., Moments: 1913-98; assoc. editor Washington D.C. Bar Jour., 1951-59. Past chm. bd. trustees Hawthorne Sch., Washington, 1969-74; adminstr. 1st dist. Columbia Bar Assn. CLE Inst., 1960-61; bd. dirs. Rehoboth Art League, 1949-58. Mem. ABA, Bar Assn. D.C. (1st v.p., bd. dirs. 1958-63), Georgetown Alumni Assn. (mem. bd. govs. 1958-62), Cath. U. Am. Alumni (pres. 1952-54), Columbia Hist. Soc. (chmn. memls. and plaques com.), Congrl. Country Club, Nat. Press Club, Counsellors Club (founder), St. Thomas More Legal Soc. (pres. Washington chpt. 1968-70), Touchdown Club (Washington, founder), John Carroll Soc. (founder), Kenwood Country Club, Rehoboth Country Club, Pi Epsilon (Nat. Journalism), Blue Key (nat. extra curricula), Phi Delta Phi (nat. legal). Home: West Hills 5205 Oakland Rd Chevy Chase MD 20815

CHASE, NORMAN ELI, radiologist, educator; b. Cin., June 29, 1926; s. Oscar and Irene (Gindy) C.; m. Joan Salkover, Oct. 1, 1954; children: Stephen Owen, Diana Stephanie. Student, Ohio U., 1946; B.S., U. Cin., 1950, M.D., 1953. Intern Kings County Hosp., Bklyn., 1953-54; resident radiology Columbia Presbyn. Med. Center, 1956-58, instr., asso., 1959-61; asst. prof. N.Y. U. Med. Center, 1961-64, asso. prof., 1964-67, prof. radiology, 1967—, chmn. dept. radiology, 1969—; dir. radiology Bellevue Hosp., 1965-73, asso. dir. radiology, 1973—; sr. cons. radiology Manhattan VA Hosp., 1969—; cons. N.Y. Infirmary, 1971—. Served with USAAF, 1944-45. Fellow N.Y. Acad. Medicine, Council Cerebrovascular Disease; mem. Harvey Soc., Assn. Univ. Radiologists, Am. Coll. Radiology (pres. N.Y. state chpt. 1983), Am. Soc. Neuroradiology (pres. 1971), Am. Heart Assn., Am. Assn. Neurol. Surgeons, N.Y. Roentgen Soc. (pres. 1978-79), Radiol. Soc. N.Am. (2d v.p. 1980-81). Research and publs. on cerebrovascular disease and new imaging techs. Office: 550 1st Ave New York NY 10016-6481

CHASE, PEARLINE, adult education educator; b. Lake Providence, La., Jan. 25, 1949; d. Willie and Rebecca (Thompson) C. BS in Liberal Studies and Math., So. U., 1970; MS in Math. Edn., La. Tech. U., 1977; EdM in Adminstrn. Planning Social Policy, Harvard U., 1984, EdD, 1987. Tchr. Caddo Parish Schs., Shreveport, La., 1970-78, East Carroll Parish Schs., Lake Providence, La., 1980-81; program coord., staff asst. Harvard U., Cambridge, Mass.; exec. asst. to pres. Ky. State U., 1985-86, assoc. v.p. acad. affairs, 1986-87, v.p. student affairs, 1987-88; dir. bd. programs and policy analysis City Colls. Chgo., 1988-89; v.p. acad. affairs Paul Quinn Coll., Dallas, 1990-92; cons. Wilmington Inst., Dallas, 1992-96; assoc. prof. math. DeVry inst. Tech., Irving, Tex., 1996—. Teaching fellow U. Okla., Norman, 1981-83; fellow Congl. Black Caucus, Washington, 98th Congress, U.S. Ho. of Reps., Woodrow Wilson fellow; T.H. Harris scholar. Mem. Nat. Coun. Tchrs. Math., Nat. Assn. Devel. Educators, Alpha Kappa Alpha, Phi Delta Kappa. Office: DeVry Inst 4800 Regent Blvd Irving TX 75063-2440

CHASE, RANDAL STUART, communication educator, consultant; b. Payson, Utah, Aug. 3, 1949; s. Irel Lynn and Louise (Barton); m. Deborah Johnsen, Feb. 1, 1971; children: Michelle, Randal Field, April, William Irel, Michael Darwin, Adam Paul. BS in Mass Comm. magna cum laude, U. Utah, 1987, MS in Comm., 1991, PhD in Comm., 1997. Program dir. Sta. KSL-FM, Salt Lake City, 1972-73; pres., CEO, Chase Media, Inc., Salt Lake City, 1973-83, Chase Cons. Inc., Salt Lake City, 1986—; instr. Sandy (Utah) Inst. LDS Ch. Ednl. System, 1994—; adj. prof. Westminster Coll., Salt Lake City, 1994—; assoc. prof. Salt Lake C.C., Salt Lake City, 1993—, comm. dept. head, 1996—; cons. media, bus. comm. and tech. to 30 firms, Salt Lake City, 1984—. Creator Internet Interactive Labs. on TV ratings, Telecomm., 1993; producer radio talk show KCPX Youth Talk, 1986-87. Bishop LDS Ch., Sandy, Utah, 1977-83, mem. high coun. LDS Granite Stake, 1994—. Recipient Farr scholarship U. Utah, Salt Lake City, 1988-89. Mem. Internat. Comm. Assn., Speech Comm. Assn., Assn. Educators in Journalism and Mass Comm., Western Speech Comm. Assn., Media History Soc., Utah Info. Tech. Assn., Kappa Tau Alpha, Phi Kappa Phi. Avocations: history, genealogy, sports. Home: 9231 Solena Way Sandy UT 84093-2628 Office: Salt Lake CC 4600 S Redwood Rd Salt Lake City UT 84123-3145

CHASE, ROBERT ARTHUR, surgeon, educator; b. Keene, N.H., Jan. 6, 1923; s. Albert Henry and Georgia Beulah (Bump) C.; m. Ann Crosby Parker, Feb. 3, 1946; children: Deborah Lee, Nancy Jo, Robert N. B.S. cum laude, U. N.H., 1945, DSC (hon.), 1993; M.D., Yale, 1947. Diplomate: Am. Bd. Surgery, Am. Bd. Plastic Surgery. Intern New Haven Hosp., 1947-48, asst. resident, 1949-50, sr. resident surgery, 1952-53, chief resident surgeon, 1953-54; mem. faculty Yale Sch. Medicine, 1948-54, 59-62, asst. prof. surgery, 1959-62; mem. faculty U. Pitts., 1957-59, resident plastic surgeon, also teaching fellow, 1957-59; attending surgeon VA Hosp., W. Haven, Conn., 1959-62, Grace New Haven Community Hosp., 1959-63; prof., chmn. dept. surgery Stanford Sch. Medicine, 1963-74, Emile Holman prof. surgery, 1972—; prof. surgery U. Pa., 1974-77; attending surgeon Pa. Hosp., Hosp. U. Pa., Grad. Hosp., Phila., 1974-77; pres., dir. Nat. Bd. Med. Examiners, Phila., 1974-77; prof. anatomy Stanford (Calif.) U., 1977—; Cons. plastic surgery Christian Med. Coll. and Hosp., Vellore, S. India, 1962; cons. to surgeon gen. USAF, 1970—; Benjamin K. Rank prof. Australasian Coll. Surgeons, 1974. Author: Atlas of Hand Surgery; Editor: Videosurgery, 1974—; editorial bd.: Med. Alert Communication; Contbr. articles to profl. jours. Served to maj. M.C. AUS, 1949-57. Recipient Francis Gilman Blake award Yale Sch. Medicine, 1962, Henry J. Kaiser award Stanford U. Sch. Medicine, 1978, 79, 84, 86, 90, 93, Calif. Golden Apple award 1991, Albion William Hewlett award, 1992, Pettee award U. N.H., 1998. Fellow ACS, Australasian Coll. Surgeons (hon.); mem. NAS, Am. Assn. Plastic Surgeons (hon.), Calif. Acad. Medicine (pres.), San Francisco Surg. Soc., Am. Surg. Assn., Santa Clara County Med. Soc., Conn. Med. Soc., Am. Soc. Surgery Hand (pres.), Am. Assn. Clin. Anatomists (hon., pres.), Am. Soc. Cleft Palate Rehab., Am. Assn. Surgery Trauma, Plastic Surgery Rsch. Coun., AMA, Soc. Clin. Surgery, Western Surg. Assn., Pacific Coast Surg. Soc., Am. Assn. Plastic Surgery (hon.), James IV Assn. Surgeons, Am. Cancer Soc. (clin. fellowship com.), Found. Am. Soc. Plastic and Reconstructive Surgery (dir.), Soc. Univ. Surgeons, Inst. Medicine (exec. com. 1976, coun. 1986—), Am. Soc. Most Venerable Order Hosp., St. John of Jerusalem, Halsted Soc., South African Soc. Surgery Hand (hon.), South African Soc. Plastic and Reconstructive Surgery (hon.), Am. Soc. Clin. Anatomists (hon., pres.)Phi Beta Kappa, Sigma Xi. Home: 797 N Tolman Ln Stanford CA 94305-1045 Office: Stanford U Div Anatomy 1215 Welch Rd Palo Alto CA 94305-5102

CHASE, SANDRA LEE, clinical pharmacist, consultant; b. Oak Park, Ill., July 31, 1959; d. William Warren and Charlene Lois (Johnson) C.; m. Christopher Paul Bloch, Sept. 8, 1984; children: Kyle Thaddeus, Matthew William. Student, Mich. State U., 1977-80; BS in Pharmacy, U. Mich., 1983, PharmD, 1984. Lic. pharmacist, Del., Mich., Pa. Rsch. asst. U. Mich., Ann Arbor, 1980-81; pharmacy intern Three Rivers (Mich.) Hosp., 1981, Cmty. Pharmacy, Ann Arbor, 1980-83; pharmacy intern, grad. intern St. Francis Hosp., Wilmington, Del., 1982-83; resident in hosp. pharmacy Thomas Jefferson U. Hosp., Phila., 1984-85, clin. pharmacist in cardiopulmonary medicine, 1985-89; sr. med. info. coord. ICI Pharms. Group, Wilmington, Del., 1989-92; clin. pharmacist Thomas Jefferson U. Hosp., Phila., 1989-93, clin. pharmacist drug use policy and clin. svcs., 1993-98; clin. specialist Spectrum Health, Grand Rapids, Mich., 1999—; adj. asst. pharmacy Temple U. Coll. Pharmacy, 1997-98; clin. instr. in pharmacy practice Phila. Coll. Pharmacy and Sci., Phila., 1985-87, clin. asst. prof., 1987-88, clin. assoc. prof., 1988-98; instr. critical care cardiopulmonary medicine in nursing Episcopal Hosp., Phila., 1986-88, Thomas Jefferson U. Hosp., Phila., 1985-91, Our Lady of Lourdes Med. Ctr., Camden, N.J., 1988-91; coord., prof. pharmacology and drug therapeutic for advanced nursing practice course Sch. Nursing, Ctr. for Profl. Devel., U. Pa., Phila., 1994—; adj. prof. pharmacy Coll. Pharmacy Ferris State U., 1999—; mem. Pa. Osteoporosis Soc. Bd., 1996-98; presenter in field. Mem. editl. bd. RN, Med. Econs.; referee AHFS Drug Info., Am. Druggist, Am. Jour. Hosp. Pharmacy, Nursing 96 Drug Handbook, Nursing 97 Drug Handbook, Pharmacotherapy, RN Mag., Annals of Pharmacotherapy, U. Hosp. Consortium Monographs; contbg. editor RN Mag., mem. editl. bd.; contbr. numerous articles to profl. jours. Mem. adv. bd. Nursing Mothers Network; bd. dirs. Coll. Pharmacy Alumni Soc., 1991-97, 99-00. Mem. Am. Coll. Clin. Pharmacy, Mid-Atlantic Coll. Clin. Pharmacy, Am. Soc. Health Sys. Pharmacists, Am. Pharm. Assn., Del. Pharm. Soc. (conv. com. 1990-94, ACPE com. 1990-94), Western Mich. Soc. Health-Sys. Pharmacists (bd. dirs. 1998—), Mich. Pharmacists Assn., Rho Chi Pharm. Soc. Republican. Lutheran. Avocations: aerobics, waterskiing, cross-country skiing, gardening.

CHASE, SEYMOUR M., lawyer; b. N.Y.C., Apr. 14, 1924; s. Harold Chase and Rhoda (Oshrin) Chase Singer; m. Janet Schwartz, Nov. 12, 1960; 1 child, Neil. AB, U. Mich., 1947; MA, Columbia U., 1949, LLB, Columbus U., 1951. Bar: D.C. 1952, N.Y. 1953, U.S. Ct. Appeals (D.C. cir.) 1952, U.S. Supreme Ct. 1956, Colo. 1989. Atty.-adviser FCC, Washington, 1952-53; assoc. Segal, Smith & Hennessey, Washington, 1953-57; sole practice, Washington, 1958-62, 72-88, Colo., 1988—; ptnr. Lyon & Chase, Washington, 1962-63, Philipson, Lyon & Chase, Washington, 1963-67, Smith & Pepper, Washington, 1967-72; mem. D.C. securities adv. com. D.C. Pub. Service Commn., 1965-66. Author: Candidate's Checklist, the Law on Using Radio and Television, 1972, 2d rev. edit., 1976, 3d rev. edit., 1980. Bd. dirs. Washington Home Rule Com., 1963-69, v.p., 1965, chmn. legis. com., 1965; del. Democratic Nat. Conv., 1956, alt. del., 1964; mem. Dem. Central Com., Washington, 1961-68, vice chmn., 1968; field adviser Dem. Nat. Com. Presdl. Campaign, 1968; campaign dir. Dems. United for Johnson, later Dems. United, Washington Primary, 1968; mem. Snowmass Village Election Commn., 1988-89; mem. Pitkin County Fin. Adv. Bd., 1988-94, vice chmn., 1990-92, chmn. 1992-94; bd. dirs. Grass Roots TV, Aspen, Colo., 1988-93, vice chmn. 1990-93; bd. dirs. Aspen-Pitkin Employee Housing, Inc., 1991-94, pres., 1992-94; del. Colo. State Dem. Conv., 1992; mem. Colo. Dem. Ctrl. Com., 1993—, mem. task force on rules, 1993-94, mem. rules com., 1994—; mem. Pitkin County Dem. Ctrl. Com., 1993-95, 1st vice chair, 1993-94, 97—, 2d vice chair, 1995—, mem. exec. com., 1993—; mem. bd. dirs. Balance Colo., 1994—, vice chair 1994—. With U.S. Army, 1943-45; ETO. Mem. ABA, D.C. Bar Assn., Fed. Comm. Bar Assn., Broadcast Pioneers, Clubs: U. Mich. of Washington, Nat. Broadcasters, Nat. Lawyers, Nat. Capital Dem.

CHASE, SYLVIA B., journalist; b. St. Paul, Feb. 23, 1938; d. Kelsey David and Sylvia (Bennett) C. BA, UCLA, 1961. Aide to Calif. State Assembly Com. on Fin. and to Senator Thomas Rees, 1961-65; active polit. campaigns Calif., 1961-68; coord. Kennedy for Pres., 1968; advance person Atty. Gen. Tom Lynch of Calif., 1966; action reporter Sta. KNX, L.A., 1969-71; corr., anchorwoman CBS News, N.Y.C., 1971-77; corr. 20/20 ABC News, N.Y.C., 1978-85, 99—, corr. Primetime Live, 1990-99; anchorwoman Sta. KRON-TV, San Francisco, 1985-90; corr. Primetime Live ABC News, N.Y.C., 1990—. Recipient Emmy award 1978, 80, 86, 87, Headliners award, 1979, 83, 94, Front Page award, 1979, Gainsbrugh award, 1979, consumer award Nat. Press Club, 1982, Pinnacle award, 1983, Award of Courage, NOW, 1987, Peabody award, 1989, Robert F. Kennedy award, 1989, Matrix award Women in Comm., 1992, AWRT award, 1994, UCLA Disting. Alumna award, Cine Golden Eagle award, 1994-96, Nat. Women's Polit. Caucus/Radcliffe Merit award, 1996. Office: ABC 20/20 147 Columbus Ave Fl 3 New York NY 10023-5900

CHASE, THOMAS NEWELL, neurologist, researcher, educator; b. Westfield, N.J., May 23, 1932; s. Newell Adams and Gudrun Margarethe (Eskesen) C.; 1 child, Thomas Newell. BS, MIT, 1954; postgrad., Columbia U., 1957-58; MD, Yale U., 1962; postgrad., Harvard U., 1963-66. Engr. Singer Mfg. Co., Bridgeport, Conn., 1954-55; technician Columbia U. Coll. Phys. and Surgs., 1957-58; intern in internal medicine Yale-New Haven Med. Center, 1962-63; asst. resident in neurology Mass. Gen. Hosp., Boston, 1963-64; resident Mass. Gen. Hosp., 1965-66; fellow in neuropathology Harvard U. Med. Sch., 1964-65; guest worker NIMH, Bethesda, Md., 1966-68; chief unit on neurology NIMH, 1968-70, chief sect. exptl. therapeutics, 1970-74; chief lab. of neuropharmacology Nat. Inst. Neurol. and Communicative Disorders and Stroke, Bethesda, 1974-76; dir. intramural research Nat. Inst. Neurol. and Communicative Disorders and Stroke, 1974-83, chief pharmacology sect., 1976—, chief exptl. therapeutics br., 1983—; clin. assoc. prof. dept. neurology Georgetown U. Sch. Medicine; mem. sci. adv. bd. Nat. Parkinson Found.; mem. adv. bd. ALS Assn., Nat. Ataxia Found., Interneuron Pharms., Polykinetix Inc., Discovery Therapeutics Inc., Athena Neuroscis. Astra-Merck. Assoc. editor Jour. Psychiatry and Neurosci.; mem. editl. bd. Progress in Neuro-Psychopharmacology, Movement Disorders, Drug Devel. Rsch., Acta Neurologica Scandinavica, Parkinsonian and Related Disorders, Contemporary Neurology, Current Treatment Options in Neurology; contbr. articles to med. jours. Served with Signal Corps U.S. Army, 1955-57. Recipient Winternitz prize in pathology, 1960, Ramsay prize for clin. medicine, 1961, diploma of recognition of merit for humanitarian svcs. Govt. of Bolivia, 1974, USPHS Meritorious Svc. medal, 1978, 96, USPHS Outstanding Svc. medal, 1991, Springer prize for Parkinson's disease rsch., 1994; summer fellow, 1960; USPHS summer fellow, 1961; Nat. Inst. Neurol. Diseases and Blindness spl. fellow, 1966-68. Fellow Am. Coll. Neuro-Psychopharmacology; mem. Am. Neurol. Assn., Am. Acad. Neurology, Am. Soc. Exptl. Neurotherapeutics (pres. 1997—), Soc. Neurosci., Internat. Soc. Neurochemistry, Am. Soc. Neurochemistry, Assn. for Rsch. in Nervous and Mental Disease, Internat. Brain Rsch. Orgn., Internat. Basal Ganglia Soc., World Fedn. Neurology, Movement Disorder Soc. Office: NINDS 9000 Rockville Pike Rm 5c103 Bethesda MD 20892-0001

CHASE-DOOLEY, JOHANNA ANNE, medical/surgical and critical care nurse; b. Queens, N.Y., Mar. 30, 1951; d. Edward John I and Bernadette C. (Huggard) Chase; m. Glenn E. Dooley Sr., Oct. 8, 1977; children: Colleen Anne, Glenn Edward, Kaelyn Maureen. Diploma, Creedmoor State Hosp., Queens Village, N.Y., 1972; BSN, C.W. Post Coll./L.I. U., 1075, MPS, 1977; MSN, Russell Sage Coll., 1994, Family Nurse Practitioner, 1995. Cert. in gerontology, med.-surg. nursing. Charge and staff nurse in emergency room/med.-surg. Franklin Gen. Hosp., Valley Stream, N.Y., 1972-76; nurse instr. Bd. Coop. Ednl. Svcs., Mineola, N.Y., 1976-78; staff, charge and head nurse VA Med. Ctr. Hosp., Albany, N.Y., 1978-88; agy. nurse Interim Healthcare formerly Med. Pers. Pool, Albany, 1988-94; part-time critical care staff nurse and home care nurse Around the Clock Care Inc., Albany, 1989-91; adj. nursing instr. Samaritan Hosp. Sch. Nursing, Troy, N.Y., 1990-93; mem. nursing pool Samaritan Hosp., 1991-95; family nurse practitioner Nilofar & Mir MD, Latham, N.Y., 1995-97, Troy (N.Y.) Family Physicians, 1996—, Skidmore Coll. Health Svcs., 1997—; mem. adj. faculty Russell Sage Coll., 1994—. Capt. Nurse Corps., U.S. Army Res., 1977-83. Mem. N.Y. State Nurses Assn., NYSCONP, Sigma Theta Tau. Home and Office: 18 Graffin Dr Latham NY 12110-5609

CHASEK, ARLENE SHATSKY, academic director; b. Newark, N.J., June 1, 1934; d. Herman and Rose (Sporn) Shatsky; m. Marvin B. Chasek, Apr. 10, 1960; children: Pamela S., Laura N., Daniel J. BA, Cornell U., 1956; MA, Columbia U., 1957; postgrad., U. N.D., 1972-74, Rutgers U., 1981-91. Tchr. English and journalism Elizabeth (N.J.) Pub. Schs., 1978-80, Summit (N.J.) Pub. Schs., 1978-80; coord. MA program Fairleigh Dickinson U., Teaneck, N.J., 1979-81; editor AT&T, Murray Hill, N.J., 1980-81; project coord. Consortium for Ednl. Equity, Rutgers U., New Brunswick, N.J., 1981-85, project dir., 1985-88, dir. spl. projects, 1988-93, dir. family involvement programs in math., sci. and tech., 1993-95, dir. Ctr. for Family Involvement in Schs., 1995—; mem. steering com., N.J. coord. Am. Goes Back to Sch. initiative U.S. Dept. Edn., 1997. Author, editor: Rutgers Family Tools and Technology, 1994, Rutgers Family Science, 1993, Mathematics in Art/Art in Mathematics, 1986 (U.S. Dept. Edn. award 1987), From Jumping Genes to Red Giants: A Guide to High School Science Research; author: The Recruitment and Retention Challenge, 1982, Futures Unlimited, 1985 (Curriculum award am. Ednl. Rsch. Assn. 1986). Recipient Golden Apple award for Family Involvement Programs, Working Mother mag., U.S. Dept. Edn., and Tchrs. Coll. Columbia U., 1996. Mem. AAUW, LWV, NSTA, Nat. Assn. Equity Educators, Coop. Learning Assn., Internat. Tech. Edn. Assn., Assn. Math. Tchrs. N.J. Home: 9 Schindler Pl New Providence NJ 07974-1738 Office: Rutgers Univ Consortium for Ednl Equity 4090 Livingston Campus New Brunswick NJ 08903

CHASEMAN, JOEL, media executive; b. Feb. 18, 1926; m. Marlene Meyerson, Sept. 11, 1955; children: Martha Hope, Joanne Amy. BA, Cornell U., 1948. CEO Post-Newsweek Stas., Washington, 1973-90; chmn. NATAS, 1980-82; dir. Advt. Coun., 1986-90; prin. Chaseman Enterprises Internat., Chevy Chase, Md.; dir. Kingworld Prods., 1990—; chmn. Advanced TV Test Ctr., 1987-93; CEO NevadaVision, Inc., 1990—; dir. KingWorld Prodns., 1991-99; CEO Hobby Craft Interactive Network, 1999—. Trustee Mus. Broadcasting, 1988, Nat. Ceramic Mus., 1992-96. Mem. Assn. Maximun Svc. Telecasters (chmn. 1988-91), Nat. Assn. Broadcasters (bd. dirs. 1988-90). Office: Chaseman Enterprises Internat 35 Wisconsin Cir Chevy Chase MD 20815-7015

CHASEN, SYLVAN HERBERT, computer applications consultant, investment advisor; b. Richmond, Va., May 19, 1926; s. Nathan and Hanna (Pass) C.; m. Catherine Hudlow, Mar. 25, 1946; children: Deborah Wyatt, Dianne Lipsey, Jane Morrison, Susan Mazur.. Student, Va. Poly. Inst., 1943-44; B.S. in Engring, Ga. Inst. Tech., 1946, B. Chem. Engring., 1946; M.S., Emory U., 1951. Math. instr. Ga. Inst. Tech., Atlanta, 1946-50; head computer facility Naval Air Test Ctr., Patuxent, Md., 1951-58; dir. advanced computing CAD and interactive graphics Lockheed-Ga. Co., Marietta, 1958-87; pres. Center CAD/CAM Tech., Inc.; cons. Author: Geometric Principles and Procedures for Computer Graphics Applications, 1978, The Guide for the Evaluation and Implementation of CAD/CAM Systems, 1980, 2d edit., 1983. Served as ensign USN, 1944-46. Recipient Outstanding Contbns. award Gov. Md., 1957; recipient Disting. Contbns. award Soc. Mfg. Engrs., 1982. Mem. ASME, Soc. Mfg. Engrs., SIGGRAPH, NCGA. Home: 760 Starlight Ct NE Atlanta GA 30342-2826

CHASEY, JACQUELINE, lawyer. Bar: N.J. 1983, N.Y. 1984. Formerly counsel Bertelsmann, Inc.; sr. counsel Bertelsmann, Inc., 1990-93; v.p., legal affairs, 1994—. Office: Bertelsmann Inc 1540 Broadway New York NY 10036-4039

CHASEZ, ALMA L., federal judge. BA, Sophie Newcomb Coll., 1967; JD, Tulane U., 1969. Law clk. La. Civil Dist. Ct., 1969-70, La. Ct. Appeals (4th cir.), 1970-73; pvt. practice, 1972-80; prof. law, Tulane U., New Orleans, 1974-75; magistrate judge U.S. Dist. Ct. (ea. dist.) La., New Orleans, 1984—. Fax: (504) 589-3781. Office: US Dist Ct (ea dist) La B-347 Hale Boggs Bldg 501 Magazine St New Orleans LA 70130

CHASON, JACOB (LEON CHASON), retired neuropathologist; b. Monroe, Mich., May 19, 1942; s. Ben and Ida (Beiser) C.; m. Helen Pelok, May 19, 1942; children: Steven, Ellen, David. AB, U. Mich., 1937, MD, 1940. Intern Wayne County Gen. Hosp., 1940-41, resident, 1941-42, 46-49, asst. pathologist, 1949-50; fellow in neuropathology Mayo Clinic, 1952; dir. lab. VA Hosp., Allen Park, Mich., 1950-52; asst. prof. neuropathology Wayne State U., 1952-54, asso. prof., 1954-57, prof., 1958-86, chmn. dept. pathology, 1964-78, assoc. dean Sch. Medicine, 1970-72; neuropathologist Henry Ford Hosp., Detroit, 1978-88, cons., 1989-90; cons. in field. Contbr. articles to profl. publs. With U.S. Army, 1942-46. NIH sr. fellow, 1959-60; grantee, 1961-63. Mem. Am. Assn. Neuropathologists, Am. Soc. Clin. Pathologists, Coll. Am. Pathologists, Internat. Acad. Pathology, Am. Acad. Neurology. Home: 4862 Keithdale Ln Bloomfield Hills MI 48302-2422

CHASSAY, ROGER PAUL, JR., engineering executive, project manager; b. Chgo., Aug. 30, 1938; children: Cynthia, Terri, Donald, Dean, Paul, Brett; m. Judith Marie Armstrong, Mar. 1990. BS, La. State U., 1961; postgrad., Ohio State U., 1962. F8U-3 fighter wing designer Dallas, 1958; aerospace engr. Saturn & Skylab Program Offices NASA/Marshall Space Flight Ctr., New Orleans & Huntsville, Ala., 1964-74; SPAR project mgr. NASA/Marshall Space Flight Ctr., Huntsville, 1974-77, mgr. integration/ test office Microgravity Projects Office, 1977-82; mgr. exptl. carriers office Microgravity Projects Office, NASA/Marshall Space Flight Ctr., Huntsville, 1982-86, dep. mgr. Microgravity Projects Office, 1986-88; mgr. space sta. and advanced projects office Microgravity Projects Office NASA/Marshall Space Flight Ctr., Huntsville, 1988-94; chmn. orbiter motion subcom. NASA, 1984-86, ctr. rep. flight assignments working group, Huntsville and Washington, 1985-86, chmn. internat. space sta. microgravity requirements integration group, Huntsville, 1990-94. Author: Application of Mathematics to the XB70 Bomber, 1963, Low-g Measurements by NASA, 1986, Processing Materials in Space: History and Future, 1987, (chpt.) Low Gravity Materials Experiments in Space Sta., 1989, Cooperation Between NASA and ESA for the First Microgravity Materials Science Glovebox, 1992, Microgravity Glovebox Program, 1998; author, editor: (NASA movie) Space Processing Applications Rocket Project, 1979. Sr. arbitrator Better Bus. Bur., Huntsville, 1987-97; pres. Holy Spirit Ch. Coun., Huntsville, 1982, N.E. Ala. Ch. Coun., Huntsville, 1984-85; scoutmaster Boy Scouts Am., Dayton, Ohio,

1963; clarinetist Huntsville Concert Band, 1987-91, 93—. Capt. USAF, 1961-64. Assoc. fellow AIAA. Achievements include management of test program for world's largest turbojet engine, management of first successful levitation experiments in space, management of first materials science glovebox in space, management of first commercial product made in space (monodisperse latex spheres), management of first nuclear detector and beryllium experiments in space, management of first and second lightning detection instruments in space. Office: NASA Marshall Space Flight Ctr SD 30 Huntsville AL 35812

CHASSIN, MARK R., health policy educator. MD, MPP, Harvard U.; MPH, UCLA. Diplomate Am. Bd. Internal Medicine. Dep. dir., med. dir. Office for Profl. Standards Rev. Orgn. Health Care Financing Adminstrn., 1979-81; v.p., co-founder Value Health Sci., 1988-92; sr. project dir. Rand Corp.; commnr. State of N.Y., Dept. Health, 1992-94; prof., chmn. dept. health policy Mt. Sinai Sch. Medicine, 1994—; sr. v.p. clin. quality Mt. Sinai Hosp. and Health Sys., 1994—; co-chmn. Inst. Medicine Nat. Roundtable Health Care Quality. Mem. Inst. Medicine Nat. Acad. Sci. *

CHASSMAN, LEONARD FREDRIC, labor union administrator; b. Detroit, Sept. 30, 1935; s. Joachim and Lillian (Abrams) C.; m. Phyllis Perlman, Aug. 25, 1957; children: Mark, Cheryl, Gregory. B.A., UCLA, 1957. Rep. AFTRA, Los Angeles, 1959-63, Screen Actors Guild, Los Angeles, 1963-65; staff exec. Writers Guild Am., West, Inc., Los Angeles, 1965-77; exec. dir. Writers Guild Am., West, Inc., 1978-82; nat. exec. sec. Screen Extras Guild Inc., 1982-84; Hollywood exec. dir. Screen Actors Guild Inc., 1984—, trustee Screen Actors Guild producers pension and health funds; bd. dirs. Entertainment Industry Found. bd. dirs. L.A. Pvt. Industry Coun. Office: 5757 Wilshire Blvd Los Angeles CA 90036-3635

CHASTAIN, BRANDI DENISE, professional soccer player; b. San Jose, Calif., July 21, 1968. Mem. U.S. Women's Soccer Team; asst. coach women's soccer team Santa Clara U.; Mem. U.S. Women's Nat. Team, 1996, Shiroke Serena, Japan, 1993. Recipient Gold medal Olympic Games, 1996; mem. championship team U.S. Olympic Festival, 1991, CONCACAF Championship, N.Y., 1993. Office: c/o Santa Clara U Athletics Dept 500 El Camino Real Santa Clara CA 95050-4345 also: US Soccer Fedn 1801 S Prairie Ave # 1811 Chicago IL 60616-1357

CHASTAIN, KENNETH DUANE, retired foreign language educator; b. Salem, Ind., July 20, 1934; s. Lloyd Lionel and Cristal Louise (Hoke) C.; m. Mary Janice McFadden, June 14, 1959; children: Kevin Duane, Brian Duane, Michael Allen. BS, Ind. U., 1956; MA, Ball State U., 1962; PhD, Purdue U., 1968. Tchr. Seymour (Ind.) High Sch., 1956-62, Columbus (Ind.) High Sch., 1962-64; grad. instr., prof. Purdue U., Lafayette, Ind., 1964-72; prof. Asbury Coll., Wilmore, Ky., 1972-73; prof. U. Va., Charlottesville, Va., 1973-95, prof. emeritus, 1995—. Author: Developing S-L Skills, 1988, Imaginate, 1991, Spanish Grammar in Review, 1993, Exploraciones en la Literatura Hispanica, 1993. With U.S. Army, 1957-58. Recipient Florence Steiner Leadership in Fgn. Lang. Edn. award Am. Coun. Teaching Fgn. Langs., 1989. Avocations: exercise, gardening, nature, travel. Home: 2674 Bakers Chapel Church Rd Big Sandy TN 38221-5318

CHASTAIN, ROBERT LEE, educational psychologist; b. Olean, N.Y., Aug. 5, 1950; m. Floyd Paul and Patricia Louise (Burroughs) C.; m. Marica Denise Means, July 7, 1973 (div. Sept. 1989); children: Robert Jr., Christy, Michael; m. Susan Lee Frank, Oct. 3, 1992. BA in Religion, Houghton Coll., 1980; MS in Ednl. Psychology, Tex. A&M U., 1983; PhD, Stanford U., 1992, JD, 1997. Bar: Calif. 1997, Nebr. 1998. Diplomate Am. Bd. Psychological Specialties. Inspector Harrison Radiator, Lockport, N.Y., 1968-77, first line supr., 1977-78, inspector, 1978-83; test supr. MCAT, Iowa, 1982-84; grad. asst., research asst. Tex. A&M U., College Station, 1982-83; staff research asst. Behavioral Research Program, College Station, 1983-85; research asst. Stanford U., 1985-89; dir. test devel. Wonderlic Personnel Test, 1991-92; law clerk McCutchen Doyle Brown & Enersen, 1996-97; assoc. Wilson Sonsini Goodrich & Rosati, 1997; pres., CEO Chastain Rsch. Group, Inc., 1983—. Contbr. articles to profl. jours. Served with USMC, 1969-72, Vietnam. N.Y. Regents scholar, 1968, Freshman D scholar, 1973. Mem. ABA, Am. Ednl. Research Assn., Am. Psychol. Assn., Am. Statis. Assn., Internat. Assn. Statis. Computing, Nat. Council on Measurement in Edn., Psychometric Soc., Santa Clara County Bar Assn. Democrat. Avocations: chess, golf, computer programming, writing. Office: Chastain Research Group Inc 310 Ballymore Cir San Jose CA 95136-3932

CHASTAIN-KNIGHT, DENISE JEAN, process engineer; b. Casper, Wyo., Dec. 12, 1961; d. Jerry and Nancy Gayle (Stewart) C. BAChemE, Ga. Inst. Tech., 1986. Registered profl. engr., Ga. Product devel. engr. Ga. Pacific, Atlanta, 1986-89; mgr. engring. process Lockwood Greene Engrs., Atlanta, 1989-94; Ga. Pacific, Atlanta, 1994—. Named Young Engr. of Yr., Ga., 1994, to Coun. of Outstanding Young Alumni, Ga. Inst. Tech., 1995, Ga. Pacific's Women of Achievement, 1997. Mem. AIChE (sec. 1989-90, vice chmn. 1990-91, chmn. 1991-93), Engrs. for Edn. (nat. profl. devel. com. and subcom. for profl. standards). Achievements include patent pending for silicone as water proofing agent in gypsum products.

CHASTANT, LEDOUX J., III, medical clinic administrator; b. New Orleans, Mar. 9, 1956; s. Ledoux J. and Mary Rose (Boscareano) C.; m. Gail White, Apr. 3, 1982; children: Meghan, Adam, Kyle. Student Acctg., La. State U., 1979. Comptroller W. Feliciana Parish Hosp., St. Francisville, La., 1979-82, Baton Rouge (La.) Gen. Hosp., 1982-83; CEO Stanocola Med. Clinic, Baton Rouge, 1983—; bd. dirs., fin. chmn. Bayou Fed. Credit Union, Baton Rouge, 1982—; mem. adv. bd. Stanocola Home Health, Baton Rouge, 1985—. Editor (med. newsletter) Pulse, 1983—. Bd. dirs. Baton Rouge Police Youth Camp, 1984—, pres. 1991; bd. dirs. Rehab. Hosp. of Baton Rouge, 1990—, La. Arthritis Found., 1992-95; chmn. United Way Campaign, Stanocola Med. Clinic, Baton Rouge, 1993—, March of Dimes Campaign, 1993—; Cub Scout den leader, coach Little League, Baton Rouge. Mem. La. Health Care Alliance, Med. Group Mgrs. Assn., La. Med. Group Mgrs. Assn. (bd. dirs., sec., legislative com.), Inst. Mgmt of Accts. Roman Catholic. Avocations: gardening, softball. Office: Stanocola Med Clinic 1401 N Foster Dr Baton Rouge LA 70806-1818*

CHATELIER, PAUL RICHARD, aviation psychologist, training company officer; b. St. Petersburg, Fla., Oct. 1, 1938; s. Paul Andrew and Mary (Knecht) C.; m. Mary Lu Moss, Sept. 26, 1964; children: Michael Andrew, Suzanne Margaret. BS in Biology, Chemistry, Psychology, U. Fla., 1960; MA in Psychology, U. Miss., 1962; postgrad., U. N.Mex., 1967-69. Commd. ensign USN, 1962, advanced through grades to capt., 1986; sr. v.p. strategic planning Perceptronics, Inc., Washington, 1986-93; with Office Sci. and Tech. Policy Exec. Office of President U.S., Washington, 1993-96; dir. for edn. tech. edn. activity Dept. Def., Washington, 1996—; U.S. rep. on human factors NATO, Brussels, 1978-86; mem. task force tng. and wargaming Def. Sci. Bd., 1986-88; U.S. rep. on tng. The Tech. Cooperation Panel, Washington, 1987-86; mem. indsl. adv. com. U. Ctrl. Fla. Inst. for Simulation and Tng.; edn. and tng. cons. Office Sci. and Tech. White Ho., 1993-96; workshop dir. internat. tng. and human factors. Co-author: Psychology of Reality, 1985; editor: Manprint & System Integ, 1988, International Human Factors, 1991, Advanced Technology for Training Design, NATO, 1993, Opening the Classroom Doors...Distance Learning, 1995, Virtual Reality Trainings Future?, 1997. Career advisor Fairfax County Pub. Sch., 1982-88. Mem. Nat. Human Factors Soc. (mem. exec. coun. 1982-85), Va. Human Factors Soc. (pres. 1982-83), Nat. Security Indsl. Assn. (chmn. manpower pers. tng. 1986-89). Avocations: tennis, community activities. Home: 8021 W Point Dr Springfield VA 22153-3023

CHATER, SHIRLEY SEARS, health educator; d. Raymond and Edna Sears; m. Norman Chater, Dec. 5, 1959 (dec. Dec. 1993); children: Cris, Geoffrey. BS, U. Pa., 1956; MS, U. Calif., San Francisco, 1960; PhD, U. Calif., Berkeley, 1964. Asst., assoc., prof. dept. social and behavioral scis. Sch. Nursing U. Calif.-San Francisco, Sch. Edn.-Berkeley, 1964-86; asst. vice chancellor acad. affairs U. Calif., San Francisco, 1974-77, vice chancellor acad. affairs, 1977-82; council assoc. Am. Council Edn., Washington, 1982-84; sr. assoc. Presdl. Search Consultation Svc. Assn. Governing Bds., Washington, 1984-86; pres. Tex. Woman's U., Denton, 1986-93; chair Gov's health policy task force State of Texas, 1992; commr. Social Security Adminstrn., Washington, 1993-97; Regent's prof. Inst. for Health and Aging U. Calif., San Francisco, 1996—; vis. prof. Inst. Health & Aging U. Calif., San Francisco, 1998—. Bd. dirs. Carnegie Found. for Advancement of Teaching, United Educators Ins. Risk Retention Group, Denton United Way, 1986-93; mem. commn. on women Am. Coun. on Edn. Mem. Inst. Medicine, NAS, San Francisco Women's Forum West, Internat. Alliance, Nat. Acad. Pub. Adminstrn., Nat. Acad. Social Ins., Nat. Acad. Nursing.

CHATFIELD, MARY VAN ABSHOVEN, librarian; b. Bay Shore, N.Y.; d. Cornelius and Elma Elizabeth (Sumner) van Abshoven; m. Robert W. Chatfield, June 22, 1963 (div. 1981); 1 child, Robert Warner Jr.; m. Alexander Watts, Jan. 6, 1996. AB, Radcliffe Coll., 1958; SM, Columbia U., 1961; MBA, Harvard U., 1972. With library system Harvard U., Cambridge, Mass., 1961-92, librarian Bus. Sch., 1963-78, head libr., 1978-92; acting head libr. Countway Libr. Harvard Med. Sch., 1988-89; head libr. Angelo State U., San Angelo, Tex., 1992-95; collections care mgr. Fosterfields, Morristown, N.J., 1996-97; mgr. libr. svcs. Montclair (N.J.) Art Mus., 1997; exec. dir. Mendham (N.J.) Free Pub. Libr., 1997—. Mem. Daughters of Brit. Empire, Rotary. Episcopalian. Avocations: reading, embroidery, collecting, museum studies, public art. Home: 95 Ironia Rd Mendham NJ 07945-3130

CHATFIELD, MICHAEL, accounting educator; b. Seattle, June 13, 1934; s. Chester and Thelma (McCormick) C. BA in Bus. Adminstrn., U. Wash., 1957, MBA, 1962; D in Bus. Adminstrn., U. Oreg., 1966. CPA, Wash. Jr. acct. Yergen and Meyer CPAs, Astoria, Oreg., 1957-58; acct. Mill Factors Corp., N.Y.C., 1959; staff acct. R.C. Mounsey and Co. CPAs, Seattle, 1959-61; tchg. asst. acctg. U. Oreg., Eugene, 1962-63; instr. acctg. U. Oreg., 1963-65; asst. prof. acctg. UCLA, 1965-72; sr. lectr. acctg. U. Canterbury, New Zealand, 1972-73; prof. acctg. Calif. State U., Hayward, 1973-82, 84-90, Fresno, 1982-84; prof. acctg. So. Oreg. U., Ashland, 1990—; mem. numerous coms. So. Oreg. U., 1991-96; presenter confs. in field. Author: A History of Accounting Thought, 1974 (rev. edit. 1978, Japanese edit. 1979, Korean edit. 1985, Chinese edit. 1989); co-author: (with Denis Neilson) Cost Accounting, 1983, (with Richard Vangermeersch) The History of Accounting: An International Encyclopedia, 1996; editor: Contemporary Studies in the Evolution of Accounting Thought, 1968 (Spanish edit., 1970, 79), The English View of Accountants' Duties and Responsibilities, 1881-1902, 1978; mem. editl. bd. The Acctg. Rev., 1970-72, 74-75, The Accounting Historians Jour., 1976-95; contbr. articles to profl. jours. Mem. Am. Acctg. Assn., Acad. Acctg. Historians (Hourglass award 1974, 96), Beta Alpha Psi. Office: So Oreg Univ Bus Sch Ashland OR 97520

CHATFIELD-TAYLOR, ADELE, arts administrator, historic preservationist; b. Jan. 29, 1945; d. Hobart and Mary Owen (Lyon) C-T; m. John Guare, May 20, 1981. BA, Manhattanville Coll., 1966; MS in Hist. Preservation, Columbia U., 1974; postgrad., Harvard U., 1978-79; ArtsD (hon.), Lake Forest Coll., 1995. Archtl. historian Hist. Am. Bldg. Survey, Washington, 1967; co-founder, dir. Urban Deadline Archs., Inc., 1968-73; with N.Y.C. Landmarks Preservation Commn., 1973-80; founder, exec. dir. N.Y. Landmarks Preservation Found., 1980-84; dir. design arts pgoram Nat. Endowment for Arts, 1984-88; pres. Am. Acad. in Rome, N.Y.C., 1988—; adj. prof. hist. preservation program Grad. Sch. Arch. and Planning, Columbia U., 1976-84; guest lectr. Harvard U., MIT, Columbia U., NYU, U. Va. Contbr. articles to profl. jours. Bd. dirs. Preservation ACTION, 1976-84, regional v.p., 1978-83, sec., 1983-84; trustee Ctr. for Bldg. Conservation, 1978-84; mem. U.S. del. to China, Women in Arch., 1977, 80, U.S. del. to China, Hist. Preservationists, 1982; mem. exec. com. U.S./Internat Coun. on Monuments and Sites, 1979-84; mem. China adv. com. Nat. Endowment Arts, 1980-84, vice chmn. design arts policy panel, 1978-82; trustee Tiber Island History Mus., 1983—; mem. restoration com. South St. Seaport Mus., 1975-84; mem. Nat. Com. on U.S.-China Rels., 1982—; mem. lawn adv. bd. U. Va., 1982-86; mem. adv. bd. Jeffersonian Restoration, 1989—, Law and the Arts, 1989—; bd. dirs. Greenwich Village Trust for Hist. Preservation, 1983-84, Internat. Design Conf. Aspen, 1986-90, Nat. Bldg. Mus., 1989—; mem. commn. Fine Arts, 1990-94; trustee Nat. Trust for Hist. Preservation, 1999—. Recipient Rome prize Am. Acad. in Rome, 1983-84; Loeb gellow Harvard U, 1978-79; archtl. fellow Ednl. Facilities Lab. Acad. Ednl. Devel., 1982-83, fellow N.Y. Inst. Humanities, 1983-89. Fellow Am. Acad. Arts & Scis.; mem. Nat. Trust Hist. Preservation, Friends of Cast Iron Arch., Preservation League N.Y. State, Met. Mus. Art, Century Assn., Pug Dog Club of Greater N.Y. Office: Am Acad in Rome 7 E 60th St New York NY 10022-1001

CHATIGNY, ROBERT NEIL, judge; b. 1951. AB, Brown U., 1973; JD, Georgetown U., 1978. Atty. Williams & Connolly, Washington, 1981-83; ptnr. Chatigny and Palmer, Hartford, Conn., 1984-86, Chatigny & Cowdery, Hartford, 1991-94; pvt. practice Hartford, 1986-90; dist. judge U.S. Dist. Ct., Hartford, Conn., 1994—. Office: 450 Main St Hartford CT 06103-3022

CHATLOS, WILLIAM EDWARD, management consultant; b. Turtle Creek, Pa., Aug. 28, 1927; s. Rudolph and Elizabeth (Mraz) C.; m. Margaret Eileen Jackson. Student, U. Pitts., 1946-47, Ursinus Coll., 1948-49; BS magna cum laude, Boston U., 1951; postgrad., N.Y. Inst. Fin., 1955-56. With Georgeson & Co., N.Y.C., 1952-81, prin. in charge mgmt. cons. for investor rels., 1957-81; prin. Chatlos & Co. Inc., North Caldwell, N.J., 1981—; bd. dirs. Kelso Inst.; cons. state govts.; lectr. in field. Editor Trends in Mgmt.-Investor Rels., 1957-81; contbr. articles to profl. publs. Mem. Soc. Profl. Mgmt. Cons., Pub. Rels. Soc. Am., Am. Mgmt. Assn., Assn. Corp. Growth, Investor Rels. Assn. (pres. 1966-67), Nat. Investor Rels. Inst. (co-founder, pres. 1974-75). Office: Chatlos & Co Inc 165 Grandview Ave Caldwell NJ 07006-4743

CHATO, JOHN CLARK, mechanical and bioengineering educator; b. Budapest, Hungary, Dec. 28, 1929; s. Joseph Alexander and Elsie (Wasserman) C.; m. Elizabeth Janet Owens, Aug. 1954; children: Christine B., David J., Susan E. ME, U. Cin., 1954; MS, U. Ill., 1955; PhD, MIT, 1960. Co-op student, trainee Frigidaire div. GMC, Dayton, Ohio, 1950-54; grad. fellow U. Ill., Urbana, 1954-55; grad. fellow, inst. MIT, Cambridge, 1955-58, asst. prof., 1958-64; assoc. prof. U. Ill., Urbana, 1964-69, prof., 1969-96, prof. emeritus, 1996—, chmn. exec. com. bioengring. faculty, 1972-78, 82-83, 84-85, asst. dean of engring., 1997-98; cons. Industry and Govt., 1958—; dir., founder Biomed. Engring. Systems Team, Urbana, Ill, 1974-78; assoc. editor Jour. Biomech. Engring., 1976-82. Patentee in field; contbr. articles to profl. jours., chpts. to books. Trustee, elder 1st Presbyn. Ch., Urbana, 1976-78, 82-85, 99—; bd. dirs. Univ. YMCA, Champaign, Ill., 1976-78, 87-90; com. mem. troop 6 Boy Scouts Am., Urbana, 1984-86, Urbana Planning Commn., 1973-78; mem. adv. com. Urbana Park Dist., 1981-84, 2d v.p. Champaign County Izaak Walton League, 1986, 1st v.p., 1987, pres., 1988-92, bd. dirs., state dir., 1992—. Recipient Tobin award Champaign County Izaak Walton League, 1992, Cmty. Svc. award Urbana Park Dist., 1996; named Disting. Engring. Alumnus, U. Cin., 1972, NSF fellow 1961, Fogarty Sr. Internat. fellow 1978-79; Japan Soc. Promotioin of Sci. fellow, 1997. Fellow ASME (exec. com. bioengring. divsn. 1992-96, sec. 1993-94, chmn. 1994-95, Charles Russ Richards Meml. award 1978, N.R. Lissner award 1992), Am. INst. Med. and Biol. Engrs.; mem. ASHRAE (treas. East Ctrl. Ill. chpt. 1984, sec. 1985, 87, 1st v.p. 1988, pres. 1989), IEEE (sr.), Am. Soc. for Engring. Edn., Internat. Inst. Refrigeration (assoc.), Audubon Soc. (bd. dirs. 1988-89, v.p. 1990, 95-96, treas. 1991-93, 98—), Exch. Club (bd. dirs. 1989-91, 95-96, pres.-elect 1996-97, pres. 1997-98). Avocations: tennis, photography, bird watching, hiking, kayaking. Office: U Ill Dept Mech Indsl Engring 1206 W Green St Urbana IL 61801-2906

CHATOFF, MICHAEL ALAN, lawyer; b. N.Y.C., Aug. 18, 1946; s. Alexander Zelig and Leona Rhoda (Weiss) C. BA, CUNY, 1967; JD, Bklyn. Law Sch., 1971; LLM, NYU, 1978. Bar: N.Y. 1971, U.S. Dist. Ct. (so. and ea. dists.) N.Y. 1978, U.S. Ct. Appeals (2d cir.) 1980, U.S. Supreme Ct. 1980. Reader Chgo. Title Ins. Co., N.Y.C., 1972; chief U.S. Code Congl. and Adminstrv. News West Pub. Co., Westbury, N.Y., 1972-97; cons. N.Y. Sch. for Deaf, N.Y.C. Mayor's Office for Disabled, Westchester County Legis.; lectr. N.Y. State Dept. of Edn. Vocat. Ednl. Svcs. for Individuals with Disabilities, N.Y. Sch. Deaf, Lexington Sch. for Deaf, Parents for Deaf Awareness, Am. Profl. Soc. for Deaf, N.Y. Ctr. for Law and the Deaf, Coun. on Jewish Deaf Edn. and Rehab., Nat. Coun. on Deaf People and Deafness, NYU. Assoc. law editor Ency. on Deaf People and Deafness; contbr. articles to Nat. Law Jour., N.Y. Law Jour., Able Adv., Communication Outlook, Deaf Spectrum. Bd. dirs. Westchester Cmty. Svcs. for Hearing Impaired; counsel Conn. African-Am. Deaf Advocate; mem. Supreme Ct. Hist. Soc.; del. nominee Dem. Nat. Conv., 1992. Mem. ABA, Queens County Bar Assn., Assn. of Bar of City of N.Y., Nat. Assn. Deaf, Am. Contract Bridge League. Avocations: bridge, jogging, weight-lifting. Home: 26909T Grand Central Pkwy Floral Park NY 11005-1010

CHATROO, ARTHUR JAY, lawyer; b. N.Y.C., July 1, 1946; s. George and Lillian (Leibowitz) C.; m. Christina Daly, Aug. 6, 1994; 1 child, Alexander. *Wife Christina Daly Chatroo practices anesthesia at the VAMC San Diego, is an ACLS instructor, Sigma Theta Tau Honor Society member, enjoys yoga, playing bridge, growing orchids, and genealogy. She has been a student at the College of New Rochelle, American College in Paris, France, New York Medical College Graduate School, and Case Western Reserve University. Her parents are Dr. Charles and June Daly. She has two brothers, Owen Grant and Douglas Patrick, and a sister, Deborah June.* BChemE, CCNY, 1968; JD cum laude, New York Law Sch., 1979; MBA with distinction, NYU, 1982. Bar: N.Y. 1980, Ohio 1992, Calif. 1993, U.S. Patent Office 1998. Process engr. Std. Oil Co. of Ohio, various locations, 1968-73; process specialist BP Oil, Inc., Marcus Hook, Pa., 1974-75; sr. process engr. Sci. Design Co., Inc., N.Y.C., 1975-78; mgr. spl. projects The Halcon SD Group, N.Y.C., 1978-82; corp. counsel, tax and fin. The Lubrizol Corp., Wickliffe, Ohio, 1982-85; sr. counsel spl. investment projects The Lubrizol Corp., Wickliffe, 1989-90; gen. counsel Lubrizol Enterprises, Inc., Wickliffe, 1985-89; chmn. Correlation Genetics Corp., San Jose, Calif., 1990-91; gen. counsel Agrigenetics Co., Eastlake, Ohio, 1990-92; gen. counsel, dir. comml. contracting Agrigenetics, L.P., San Diego, 1992-93; counsel Agrigenetics, Inc. dba Mycogen Seeds, Mycogen Corp., San Diego, 1994-97; dir. legal affairs Mycogen Corp., San Diego, 1997-98; exec. v.p. bus. devel., legal and regulatory affairs Global Agro, Inc., Encinitas, Calif., 1998—. Mem. Met. Parks Adv. com., Allen County, Ohio, 1973. Mem. ABA, AIChE, Am. Chem. Soc., N.Y. State Bar Assn., San Deigo County Bar Assn., Am. Corp. Counsel Assn., Jaycees (personnel dir. Lima, Ohio chpt. 1972-73), Licensing Execs. Soc., Toastmasters, Omega Chi Epsilon, Beta Gamma Sigma. Club: Toastmasters. Avocations: sailing, photography, skiing. Home: 3525 Del Mar Hts Rd # 285 San Diego CA 92130-2122 Office: Global Agro Inc 12626 High Bluff Dr Ste 250 San Diego CA 92130

CHATT, ALLEN BARRETT, psychologist, neuroscientist; b. Phoenix, July 17, 1949; s. Arthur Beecher Ellis and Helen Berta (Scheidt) Chatt; m. Gail Nancy Anguish, Aug. 21, 1971. *Dr. Chatt is a descendant of Lyman Beecher, Henry Ward Beecher and Harriet Beecher Stowe, clergy, novelists and abolitionists of the early to mid 19th century. He credits his mother, the late Helen Scheidt (Ellis) Chatt, and surrogates Mathew and Doris Kalicki of Stafford, New York with providing the fundamental drive and values necessary to pursue a productive life. Finally, his wife, Gail Nancy Chatt, has provided strength when it was most needed.* BS in Psychology with honors, SUNY, Buffalo, 1971; MS in Psychology, Fla. State U., 1974, PhD in Psychology and Neuroscience, 1978. Rsch. asst. Fla. State U., Tallahassee, 1971-76; predoctoral fellow U. Tex. Med. Br., Galveston, 1977; postdoctoral fellow sch. medicine Yale U., New Haven, Conn., 1978-80; rsch. psychologist VA Med. Ctr., West Haven, Conn., 1978-84, sr. rsch. psychologist, 1985-90; rsch. asst. prof. sch. medicine Yale U., New Haven, Conn., 1981-87; rsch. assoc. prof. Yale U., New Haven, 1988-90; founder, exec. dir., consulting psychologist Phoenix Fund for Neurologically Challenged, Madison and Tallahassee, 1991—; vis. prof. neurosci. Beijing Normal U., 1987, U. Glasgow, 1994-95; grant reviewer NSF, NIH, VA, 1982—; neurosci. reviewer Am. Psychol. Soc. Convs., 1991—; sci.-by-mail scientist Mus. Sci., Boston, 1991—; psychol. cons., case mgr. for neurologically impaired; pvt. funding of neurol. rsch.; adj. prof. movement scis. Fla. State U., 1999—. *Before injuries from an automobile accident forced his disability retirement in 1990, Dr. Chatt was engaged in biomedical research at the Yale University School of Medicine and the Veterans Administration Medical Center in New Haven, Connecticut. Currently, he is founder and executive director of The Phoenix Fund, a privately endowed philanthropic organization committed to the support of neuroscience research, training, education and financial assistance to individuals with special needs. He is also a consulting psychologist for the Fund. He was recently appointed Adjunct Professor of Movement Science at Florida State University and sits on the advisory boards of several non-profit organizations.* Contbr. chpts. and forewards to books, articles to profl. jours.; mem. editorial bd. Brain Rsch., 1983-86, Exptl. Neurology, 1982-86, Quar. Jour. Exptl. Physiology, 1986, Exptl. Brain Rsch., 1984-88. Mem. Rep. Senatorial Inner Circle, Washington, 1985, Rep. Town Com., Guilford, 1992; life mem. Rep. Nat. Com., 1993—, Eisenhower Commn., 1995, Pres. Club, 1994, Chmn.'s Adv. Bd., 1994; sponsor The Phoenix Fund Grad. Rsch. fellowship Dept. of Movement Sci. Fla. State U., 1999—, Jennifer Harrison Meml. Golf Tournament, 1991—, Freedom Scholarship Batavia H.S. Class 1965, 1992—, Bobby Bowden Classic Fellowship Christian Athletes, 1992—, Goodspeed Opera House, 1995—, Bill Campbell Challenge Children's Miracle Network, 1996—, Boy's Town of North Fla., 1999—, Fla. State U. Seminole Classic, 1998—, The Phoenix Fund Grad. Rsch. fellowship Dept. of Movement Scis. of Fla. State U., 1999—, The Phoenix Fund Collegieto Scholarship for Applied Biomed. Undergrad. Study for Leon County, Fla., 1999—, Boy's Town Invitational of North Fla., 1998—, Fla. State U. Seminole Classic, 1998—, Camp Sunshine, 1992—; mem. devel. bd. Coll. Human Scis. Fla. State U., 1998—; bd. dirs. Wal*Mart/Children's Miracle Network, No. Fla., 1998—, Jennifer Harrison Fund, 1995—, The Ellingsworth Press, LLC, 1998—, The Sam Walton Cmty. Leader Scholarship Program, 1999—; judge Sam Walton Cmty. Scholarship Program, The Phoenix Fund Collegiate Scholarship in Human Scis., 1999—; adv. bd. The Ellingsworth Press, 1998—. Merit Review Rsch grantee VA Med. Ctr., 1982-90; RO-1 Rsch. grantee NIH, 1982-87; recipient Most Sr. Benefactor award Children's Miracle Network, 1997—. Mem. Am. Psychol. Soc., AAAS, Epilepsy Found. Am., . for Neurosci., Am. Epilepsy Soc., Yale Neurology Alumni Adv. Assn. (charter). Republican. Methodist. Achievements include the development of a neurosurgical procedure increasing the effectiveness of stellate ganglion blocks for the treatment of reflex sympathetic dystrophy in humans, discovery of differential neuronal circuits involved in focal and secondarily generalized seizure activity in neocortical model of epilepsy, brain cells that become abnormal initially in focal and secondarily generalized seizure activity, mid brain neuronal circuits modulating pain, thermal evoked potential in humans and the localization of cortical cells responsive to pain. Home: PO Box 1449 699 Goose Ln Guilford CT 06437-2114 also: 2949 Golden Eagle Dr E Tallahassee FL 32312-4008

CHATTERJEE, JAYANTA, educator, urban designer; b. Calcutta, India, Mar. 19, 1936; came to U.S., 1959; s. Hari Charan and Asha (Mukherjee) C.; m. Janet Ley Smith, Aug. 31, 1968; children: Eric, Brinda. BArch, Indian Inst. Tech., 1958; M in City and Regional Planning, U. N.C., 1962; MArch in Urban Design, Harvard U., 1965. Asst. prof. U. of Cin., 1967-72, assoc. prof., 1972-77, prof., dept. head, 1977-79, dir., 1979-82, acting dean, 1982-83, dean, 1983—; regional planner Western N.C. Regional Planning Commn., 1962-63; regional designer Met. Area Planning Commn., Boston, 1966-67; cons. OH-KY-IND Council Govt., Cin., 1973-75; urban scholar Cities Recovery Program, Cleve., 1981-82. Co-author: The Planning Partnership, Rebuilding American Cities, Breaking the Boundaries, 1981; co-editor Planning Education and Research Jour., 1981-84. Bd. dirs. Arts Consortium, Cin., 1983-87, Contemporary Arts Ctr., Cin., 1983—, Hillside Trust, Cin., 1983-84, Bethesda Hosp., Cin, 1983—, Total Living Concepts, Cin., 1976-86, Ctr. Mediation of Disputes, Cin., 1989-92, The Emery Ctr., Cin., 1988—, Better Housing League, Cin., 1989-92, Archtl. Found., Cin., 1990-97; mem. Ohio Eminent Scholar Rev. Panel, 1985, Urban Design Rev. Bd., Cin., 1988—. Recipient Apple award Archtl. Fedn. Cin., 1996, Disting. Alumnus award U. N.C., 1996, Disting. Svc. award Assn. Coll. Schs. of Planning, 1991. Mem. AIA (assoc.), Am. Planning Assn. (pres. Ohio chpt. 1970-72, editorial adv. bd. Jour. APA), Am. Inst. Certified Planners (editorial bd. AICP Casebook 1991-93, tech. adv. bd. 1993-96), Ptnrs. of Ams. (Ohio-Parana), Assn. Collegiate Schs. of Planning (pres. 1983-85, Disting. Svc. award 1991), Internat. Coun. Fine Arts Deans. Office: U Cin Coll of Design Architecture Art and Planning PO Box 210016 Cincinnati OH 45221-0016

CHATTERJEE, PAL, electrical engineer, manufacturing executive. BTech, India Inst. Tech., 1972; MS, U. Ill., 1974, PhD in Elec. Engring., 1976. Mem. tech. staff corp. R&D Tex. Instruments, Dallas, 1976-79, sr. mem. tech. staff, 1979-82, fellow and lab. dir., 1982-84, sr. fellow and lab. dir., 1984-86, v.p., 1986-90, v.p. and chief tech. officer semiconductor group, 1990-92, sr. v.p., chief tech. officer semiconductor group, 1992-95, pres.

personal productivity products, 1995-97, chief info. officer, 1997—. Recipient J.J. Ebers award 1986. Fellow IEEE (Keys to Future award 1984), Nat. Acad. Engring., Applied Physics Soc. Office: Tex Instruments Inc PO Box 655303 MS 3665 Dallas TX 75265*

CHATTERJI, DEBAJYOTI, manufacturing company executive; b. Puri, India, Aug. 4, 1944; came to U.S., 1967, naturalized, 1980; s. Kumud Chandra and Mrinmoyee (Mukherji) C.; m. Smee Banerjee, July 11, 1968; children: Ananya, Kooheli, Miabi. BS with honors, Utkal U., India, 1963; B in Metall. Engring., Indian Inst. Tech., Kharagpur, India, 1966; MS, Purdue U., 1968, PhD, 1971. Vis. scientist Wright-Patterson AFB, Ohio, 1971-73; with Research & Devel. Center, Gen. Electric Co., Schenectady, 1973-83; mgr. electrochemistry br. Research & Devel. Center, Gen. Electric Co., 1975-79; mgr. Chem. Systems and Tech. Lab., 1979-80, Inorganic Materials and Structures Lab., 1980-83; v.p. tech. affairs The BOC Group, Inc., Murray Hill, N.J., 1983-89, chef exec. tech. activities, 1990, mng. dir. tech., 1990-99; bd. dirs. The BOC Group, plc., Indsl. Rsch. Inst. Chmn. editl. bd. Rsch. and Tech. Mgmt., mem. R&D Mgmt.; contbr. articles to profl. jours. Bd. dirs. BOC Found. for Environment, Imperial Coll., London. Recipient Disting. Engring. Alumnus award Purdue U., 1987; Disting. fellow Indian Inst. Mgmt., Calcutta, Maurice Holland award Ind. Rsch. Inst. Mem. Internat. Assn. Mgmt. of Tech. (adv. bd.), Am. Soc. for Metals (Geisler award 1979), Electrochem. Soc., Sigma Xi. Patentee in field. Office: The BOC Group 100 Mountain Ave New Providence NJ 07974-2069

CHATTERS, DAVE, member of parliament; b. Westlock, Alberta, Can., 1946. Mem. of parliament, Reform Party House of Commons, Ottawa, 1993—. Office: House of Commons, 258 Wellington Bldg, Ottawa, ON Canada K1A086*

CHATTERTON, ROBERT TREAT, JR., reproductive endocrinology educator; b. Catskill, N.Y., Aug. 9, 1935; s. Robert Treat and Irene (Spoor) C.; m. Patricia A. Holland, June 24, 1956 (div. 1965); children: Ruth Ellen, William Matthew, James Daniel; m. Astrida J. Vanags, June 4, 1966 (div. 1977); 1 child, Derek Scott; m. Carol J. Lewis, May 24, 1985. BS, Cornell U., 1958, PhD, 1963; MS, U. Conn., 1959. Postdoctoral fellow Med. Sch. Harvard U., 1963-65; rsch. assoc. div. oncology Inst. Steroid Rsch. Montefiore Hosp. and Med. Ctr., N.Y.C., 1965-70; asst. prof. Coll. Medicine U. Ill., 1970-72, assoc. prof. Coll. Medicine, 1972-79; prof. Med. Sch. Northwestern U., Chgo., 1979—; mem. sci. adv. com. AID; chairperson Instl. Review Bd. Northwestern U., 1982-83, Intellectual Properties Com., Northwestern U., 1987-95; dir. Immunoassay Facility, R.H. Lurie Cancer Ctr., Northwestern U. Med. Sch., 1997—; dir. Clin. Labs., dept. ob-gyn., Northwestern Med. Faculty Found., 1996—. Contbr. numerous articles to sci. jours.; patents: method of totally suppressing ovarian follicular devel. and method of ovulation detection. Grantee NIH, 1972-90, 95—, NSF, 1975, 95—, AID, 1971-86, Army Office Rsch., 1987-94. Mem. AAAS, N.Y. Acad. Scis., Am. Chem. Soc., Endocrine Soc., Soc. Gynecologic Investigation, Soc. Study Reprodn., Chgo. Assn. Reproductive Endocrinologists (pres. 1987-88), Sigma Xi, Phi Kappa Phi. Presbyterian (deacon). Home: 6001 N Knox Ave Chicago IL 60646-5821 Office: Northwestern U Prentice 1516 333 E Superior St Chicago IL 60611-3056

CHATTIN, GILBERT MARSHALL, financial analyst; b. Decherd, Tenn., Jan. 13, 1914; s. Murrell Emmett and Lena Katherine (Jones) C.; m. Hester Stroud, June 18, 1938; 1 child, Marsha Jane. BA, U South Sewanee, 1937; JD, Blackstone Sch. Law, 1965. Chief credit analyst, mgr. city dept. Dun and Bradstreet, Inc., Knoxville, Tenn., 1938-43; ptnr. A&A Service and Supply Co., Atlanta, 1946-70; chief auditor Ga. Dept. Health, 1963-72; chief auditor, audit mgr. Ga. Dept. Human Resources, 1972-84; corp. auditor Ga. Dept. Revenue, 1955-63; pvt. practice fin. analyst, investor, cons., 1955—. Served with AUS, 1943-46, ETO. Mem. NRA, Am. Assn. Individual Investors, Nat. Assn. Investors, Am. Numismatic Assn., Am. Legion, Phi Gamma Delta. Mem. Ch. of Christ. Avocations: hunting, fishing.

CHATTMAN, RAYMOND CHRISTOPHER, foundation executive; b. San Rafael, Calif., Apr. 11, 1956; s. Raymond Rene Chattman and Virginia Mae (Kirkland) Robinson; m. Patti Lyn Barnard Maxwell, Feb. 14, 1975 (div. 1977); m. Dawn Irene Russell Kilpatrick, Aug. 21, 1993 (div. 1998); children: Christian Paige, Bradley Charles Kilpatrick. BS, SUNY, Albany, 1988; MBA, Averett Coll., 1995. Dir. planning, ops. Comms. Media Group Inc., Alexandria, Va., 1981; comms. mgr. ANPA Found., Reston, Va., 1982-84; graphics editor Times-Herald Record, Middletown, N.Y., 1984-85; editor employee comms. Washington Gas Light Co., 1985-86; exec. dir., CEO Soc. Newspaper Design, Reston, 1986-96; dir. AIAA Found., Reston, 1996—. Asst. coach Herndon (Va.) Optimist Youth Football, 1994, Herndon Youth Soccer, 1992. Served in U.S. Army, 1974-81, Korea, Germany, Res., 1981-90. Recipient Thomas Jefferson award Dept. Def., 1979, Keith L. Ware award Dept. Army, 1978, 83, 86, 87. Mem. Am. Soc. Assn. Execs., Nat. Assn. Govt. Communicators (blue pencil award 1978), Am. Mgmt. Assn., Greater Washington Soc. Assn. Execs. Avocations: travel, reading, softball. Office: AIAA Found 1801 Alexander Bell Dr Ste 500 Reston VA 20191-4344

CHAU, HUNG, engineer, educator; b. Kontum, Vietnam, Aug. 28, 1948; came to U.S., 1978; s. Chuong Van and Tuy Thi (Nguyen) C.; m. Bach-Tuyet Nguyen, Jan. 20, 1979; children: Johann, Johnny, Jeffrey, Jerald. Diploma-engring., U. Hannover, Germany, 1978; MS, Ill. Inst. of Tech., 1983; EdD, U. So. Calif., L.A., 1993. Indsl. engr. Fort Howard Paper Co., Chgo., 1979-84; sr. mgmt. engr. Ind. U. Med. Ctr., Indpls., 1984-86, Straub Clinic and Hosp., Inc., Honolulu, Hawaii, 1986-90; indsl. engr. Dept. of the Army, Honolulu, 1990-97; prof. edn. Troy State U., Pacific Region, Hawaii, 1994—; ltd. ptnr. Neozyme Internat., Inc., Aliso Viejo, Calif., 1996—. Contbr. articles to profl. jours. Pres. Vietnamese Students Assn., Germany, 1974, Inst. of Indsl. Engrs., Honolulu, 1986. Mem. Am. Ednl. Rsch. Assn., U. So. Calif. Gen. Alumni Assn. (life), Phi Delta Kappa. Roman Catholic. Avocations: travel, golf, swimming. Home: 507 Iolani Ave Honolulu HI 96813-1835 Office: Systems Engr Bldg 104 Wright Ave Dir of Pub Works Schofield Barracks HI 96857

CHAUDERLOT, FABIENNE-SOPHIE, foreign language educator; b. Marseilles, France, Aug. 11, 1960; came to U.S., 1985; d. Michel Hubert and Georgia Kalafatides. Maitrise English Lit., U. Scis. Humaines, Aix-en-Provence, France, 1982; MBA in Internat. Adminstrn., Puyricard, France, 1985; PhD, U. Calif., San Diego, 1995. Lectr. U. Calif., Riverside, 1995-96; asst. prof. U. P.R., Mayaguez, 1996-97, Wayne State U., Detroit, 1997—. *Fabienne-Sophie Chauderlot has been teaching in different Universities for over fifteen years. She dedicates her professional life to increasing her students' curiosity for and tolerance of diversity in languages, cultures, mentalities, and world views. In order to offer more students the opportunity to directly experience Differ(e)/(a)nce, she has created and directs Wayne au Soleil, a summer study abroad program in Cannes, France. Personally, she continues her lifelong reflection on ethic and aesthetic philosophy. Fabienne's research focuses on the impact of life affirming philosophers such as Diderot, Nietzsche and Deleuze as well as on the intricate conjunctions between words and images.* V.p. Alliance Francaise, San Diego, 1990-93; founder, pres. Femmes Francaises du Sud Calif., San Diego, 1989-93. Rsch. grantee Humanities Ctr., Detroit, 1997-98. Avocations: painting, piano, cats, aerobics, photography. Office: Wayne State U 487 Manoogian Hall Detroit MI 48202

CHAUDHARI, PRAVEEN, materials physicist; b. Ludhiana, Punjab, India, Nov. 30, 1937; came to U.S., 1961; s. Hans Raj and Ved (Kumari) C.; m. Karin Romhild, June 13, 1964; children: Ashok, Pia. BS with honors, Indian Inst. Tech., Kharagpur, 1961; MS in Phys. Metallurgy, MIT, 1963, ScD in Phys. Metallurgy, 1966. Rsch. assoc. MIT, Cambridge, Mass., 1966; rsch. staff mem. IBM T.J. Watson Rsch. Ctr., Yorktown Heights, N.Y., 1966-70, mgr., 1970-80, dir. phys. scis., 1981-82, v.p. sci., dir. phys. scis., 1982-91, v.p. sci., tech. com., 1988-91, rsch. staff, 1991—; exec. sec. Presdl. Wise Men Com. on Super Conductivity, 1988; mem. Presdl. Commn. on Super Conductivity, 1989; mem. vis. coms. various univs.; co-chmn. Materials Sci. and Engring. Study by NRC; chmn. U.S. Liaison Commn. to Internat. Union of Pure and Applied Physics; mem. com. on Physics for the Next Decade, sponsored by NRC/NAS, Nat. Critical Tech. panel. Author of papers on mechanical properties and defects in crystalline solids, amorphous solids, quantum transport, superconductivity and magnetic monopoles and neutrino mass experiments. Recipient Nat. Medal of Technology, 1995. Fellow Am. Phys. Soc. (George Pake prize 1987); mem. NAS (bd. physics and astronomy, governing bd.), AIME (leadership award 1986), NAE, IEEE (Liebmann prize 1992), Am. Inst. Physics (mem.-at-large of gov. bd.), N.Y. State Inst. of Superconductivity (mem.-at-large), Am. Acad. of Arts and Scis. Office: IBM T J Watson Rsch Ctr PO Box 218 Rte 134 Yorktown Heights NY 10598

CHAUDHARY, SHAUKAT ALI, ecologist, plant taxonomist; b. Sialkot, Punjab, Pakistan, Mar. 1, 1931; s. Allah-Rakha and Raisham Bibi (Din) C.; m. Zahida Sarwar, Oct. 22, 1967; children: Naveed, Naila, Ayesha, Samir. MSc, U. Punjab, Lahore, 1953; PhD, Wash. State U., 1965; DSc (hon.), 1999. Lectr. Gordon Coll., Rawalpindi, Punjab, 1953-54; asst. prof. Agrl. U., Faisalbad, Punjab, 1954-62, reader, head dept., 1965-70; sr. lectr. Am. U. Beirut (Lebanon), 1970-76; assoc. prof. Sana'a (Yemen) U., 1976-78; prof. and sr. scientist Am. U. Beirut on secondment to USDA Team in Saudi Arabia, Riyadh, 1978-89; sr. scientist UN FAO Team in Saudi Arabia, Riyadh, 1989—; dean students Agr. U., Faisalabad, 1966-70; curator Nat. Herbarium Saudi Arabia, Riyadh, 1979—. Author: Weeds of Yemen, 1983, Weeds of Saudi Arabia and Arabian Peninsula, 1987, Weed Control Handbook for Saudi Arabia, 1985, Grasses of Saudi Arabia, 1989, Natural History of Saudi Arabia, 1992, Vegetation of Saudi Arabia, 1999, Flora of the Kingdom of Saudi Arabia I, 1999. Mem. Aril Soc. Internat. (dir. at large 1974-78), Pakistan Bot. Soc. (founding sec.-treas. 1968-69), Sigma Xi. Avocations: study of deserts, photography. Home: 3730 W Lake Dr Martinez GA 30907-9595

CHAUDHRI, AMIN QAMAR, film company executive; b. Gujrat, Punjab, India, Apr. 18, 1942; came to U.S., 1959; s. C.D. and Sardar (Begum) C.; children: Asif Qamar, Asha Noor, Amina Yasmin. Grad., CUNY, 1965. Owner Filmasia Prodns., N.Y.C., 1961-87; pres. Gross Chaudhri Prodns., N.Y.C., 1961-64; film cameraman, editor Francis Thompson, Inc., N.Y.C., 1964-65; music and effect editor Musifex Inc., N.Y.C., 1965-66; pres. Art-scope Ltd., N.Y.C., 1965-78; owner Filmart Internat., Bombay, 1974-97; pres. Filmart Enterprises, Ltd., N.Y.C., 1980-96, Continental Cinema Industries, Inc., Kenilworth, N.J., 1985-87; chmn., chief exec. officer Continental Film Group, Ltd., Sharon, Pa., 1987—; pres. Continental Entertainment Group, Ltd., 1991-97; chief exec. officer, pres. Heron Internat. Pictures, Ltd., 1993-97; pres. Continental Actors/Models Agy., Ltd., 1997; dir. dept. film Jazz Arts Soc., Inc., N.Y.C., 1961-68; pres. Livingston (N.J.) TV 36, 1985. Filmmaker (documentary) Khajuraho Eternal, 1965 (award); dir. photography (TV spl.) Medium is the Message, 1968 (Emmy award); photographer (slides) Pakistan Photography Salon, 1969 (Gold medal), cameraman, editor (film) Right On, 1970 (Cannes Film Festival award 1970); dir., prodr.: (films) An Unremarkable Life, Tiger Warsaw, Once Again, Seventh Veil; prodr. (film) Diary of a Hitman, The Master Mechanic. Mem. Montclair (N.J.) Hist. Soc., 1972, Nat. Assn. for the Blind, Livingston, 1985. Recipient Spl. award City of Sharon, Pa., 1987; Amin Qamar Chaudhri Day proclaimed by City of San Francisco, Amin Qamar Chaudhri Day proclaimed by City of Farell, Pa., 1987, City of Sharon, 1997. Office: Continental Film Group Ltd 1001 Park St Sharon PA 16146-3090

CHAUDHRY, HUMAYUN JAVAID, physician, medical educator, writer; b. Karachi, Sind, Pakistan, Nov. 17, 1965; came to U.S., 1971, naturalized, 1978; s. Hukam Dad and Riffat Sultana (Bhatti) C.; m. Nazli Tabasum Iqbal, June 7, 1992; children: Shaun Hatim, Haris Iqbal. BA, NYU, 1986, MS, 1989; DO, N.Y. Coll. Osteo. Medicine, 1991. Diplomate Nat. Bd. Osteo. Med. Examiners, Am. Bd. Internal Medicine; lic. physician, surgeon, N.Y. Intern St. Barnabas Hosp., Bronx, N.Y., 1991-92; resident in internal medicine Winthrop-U. Hosp., Mineola, N.Y., 1992-95, chief med. resident, 1995-96; clin. asst. prof. medicine N.Y. Coll. Osteo. Medicine, Old Westbury, 1997—; attending physician, dir. med. edn. Long Beach (N.Y.) Med. Ctr., 1996—; attending physician Island Park Med. Care, 1996-98, Family Care Ctr., Long Beach, N.Y., 1996—; adj. instr. anatomy N.Y. Coll. Osteo. medicine, Old Westbury, 1996—; reporter, news editor, TV anchorman Third World Broadcasting Network, N.Y.C., 1986-95, 99—; asst. clin. instr. medicine SUNY Stony Brook Sch. Medicine, 1995-96. Mem. editl. bd. New Physician, Reston, Va., 1991-99; founding editor The NYSSIM Resident newsletter, 1996-97; contbr. articles to profl. jours. Press sec. Pakistan Independence Day Parade N.Y., 1987-88; inaugural spkr. 1st ann. Pakistan Day Festival Bklyn., 1991; founding mem. Pakistan Press Club Am., N.Y.C., 1990-93, v.p., 1992-93. Capt. USAFR, 1999—. Regents Coll. scholar State of N.Y., Albany, 1982; recipient Essay Competition award N.Y.C. Fire Dept., 1979. Fellow ACP, Nassau Acad. of Medicine; mem. AMA, Am. Osteo. Assn., Am. Soc. Internal Medicine, N.Y. State Soc. Internal Medicine (pres. resident physicians sect. 1995-96, bd. dirs. 1996—), Am. Coll. Osteo. Internists (founding pres. N.Y. chpt. 1998—), Islamic Med. Assn. N.Am., Assn. Pakistani Physicians N.Am., Amnesty Internat., Am. Muslim Coun., Kashmiri-Am. Coun., N.Y. Coll. Osteo. Medicine Alumni (sec. bd. dirs. 1995-98, pres. 1998—), Assn. Osteo. Dirs. Med. Educators, N.Y. State Osteo. Med. Soc., Nassau Soc. Internal Medicine (bd. dirs. 1996-98, v.p. 1998-99, pres. 1999—), Islamic Ctr. of L.I., Islamic Soc. N.Am., World Wildlife Fund, Med. Soc. State of N.Y., Am. Acad. Osteopathy. Republican. Muslim. Avocations: tennis, golf, rare books, travel. Home: 1022 Commack Rd Dix Hills NY 11746-8209 Office: Long Beach Med Ctr 455 E Bay Dr Long Beach NY 11561-2301

CHAUHAN, SUNEET BHUSHAN, medical educator; b. Rewa, India, Mar. 28, 1958; came to U.S., 1971; s. Sushila (Singh) C.; m. Laurie Pitchford, Jan. 19, 1985; children: Tara, Kiren. BA in Chemistry/Biology summa cum laude, Beaver Coll., Gleside, Pa., 1979; MD, Thomas Jefferson U., Phila., 1983. Lic. physician, Miss., Ill., Ga. Intern Naval Hosp., Portsmouth, Va., 1983-84, resident, 1986-89; fellow U. Miss., Jackson, 1992-94; asst. prof. U. Ill., Peoria, 1994-95, Med. Coll. Ga., 1995-98. Contbr. articles to Jour. Inorganic Nuclear Chemistry, Am. Jour. Ob/Gyn., Jour. Reproductive Medicine, Jour. Miss. State Med. Assn., Jour. Maternal Fetal Investigation, Perinatol, South Med. Jour. Lt. comdr. USNR, 1979-92. Decorated Navy Commendation medal; Armed Forces Health Professions scholar, 1979-83. Mem. Lambda Delta Alpha, Phi Kappa Phi. Achievements include research in estimate of birth weight among diabetic patients, newborn electrolyte response to amnioinfusion with lactated ringer's versus normal saline, remote umbilical arterial blood pH analysis. Office: Spartanburg Regional Healthcare Sys 853 N Church St Ste 403 Spartanburg SC 30912-0006

CHAUNCEY, BEATRICE ARLENE, music educator; b. Akron, Ohio; d. Joseph Warren Chauncey and Belle E. Chauncey. BS, U. Akron, 1943; MA, Columbia U., 1945, Profl. Diploma, 1948. Prof. flute East Carolina U., Greenville, N.C., 1949-91; ret., 1991. Actress summer stock cos. in Laramie, Wyo., Bar Harbor, Maine, Flat Rock Playhouse, N.C., E. Carolina U. Bd. dirs. Mental Health Assn. Pitt County, N.C., 1978—; Pitt County Family Violence Program, 1985-87, treas., 1986; bd. dirs. Choral Soc., 1989—; tutor Literacy Vols. Am., 1989—. Mem. Nat. Flute Assn., Music Educators Nat. Conf., Sierra Club. Avocations: sailing, walking, traveling. Home: 2005 Quail Ridge Rd Apt A Greenville NC 27858-5540

CHAUVET, GILBERT ANDRÉ, mathematics educator; b. Nueil, France, Oct. 2, 1942; s. Eugene Chauvet and Antonia Mainchain; m. Marie Elizabeth Cottet, June 27, 1940; children: Pierre, Anne, Line. M Maths., Poitiers U., France, 1965; PhD in Molecular Physics, Nantes U., France, 1974; MD, Angers U., France, 1976. Researcher Angers U., 1964-72, assoc. prof., 1972-76; prof. biomath. Angers U., 1976-80; prof. theoretical biology Angers U., 1980—; dir. Med. Computing Dept. Angers Hosp., 1984—; dir., founder Inst. Theoretical Biology/Angers U., 1988—; rsch. prof. U. So. Calif., L.A., 1994—, Pitts. U., 1988-92; dir. Theoretical Biology Svcs., Masson, Paris, 1987—. Author: Theoretical Physiology, 3 vols., 1987-90, La Vie Dans La Matiere, Flammarion, Paris, 1995, Theoretical Systems in Biology: Hierarchical and Functional Integration, 3 vols., 1996; contbr. articles to profl. jours. Avocation: hist. monuments. Office: Inst Biologie Theorique, IBT Physiol Systems Sim Lab, 10 rue A Boquel, Angers 49100, France

CHAUVETTE, CLAUDE R., building materials company administrator; b. Montreal, Que., Can., Mar. 19, 1939; s. Bruno and Germaine (Handfield) C. BA, U. Montreal, 1959; postgrad., Ecole Polytechnique, Montreal, 1959-60; LSc Comm., LSc Compt., Hautes Etudes Comm., Montreal, 1963; CA, Can. Inst. Chartered Accts., Montreal, 1964. Pub. acct. Riddell Stead & Co., Montreal, 1963-67; asst. to v.p. Marine Industries, Montreal, 1967-71; contr. Forano Ltd., Plessisville, Can., 1971-73; sec.-treas. Demix Ltd., Demix (Laval) Ltd., Montreal, 1973-76; mgr. adminstrn. Montreal area St. Lawrence Cement Inc., Montreal, 1977-79, mgr. adminstrn. Que. div., 1979-81, treas., asst. sec., 1981-87, sec.-treas., 1987—. Mem. Can. Inst. Chartered Accts., Risk and Ins. Mgmt. Soc., Cash and Treasurer Mgmt. Inst. Office: St Lawrence Cement Inc, 1945 Graham Blvd, Mount Royal, PQ Canada H3R 1H1

CHAUVIN, CHARLOTTE ANN, computer science educator; b. Idaho Falls, Idaho, Mar. 24, 1960; d. Emil John and Ruth Naomi (Gatewood) Slivka; m. John Arthur Chauvin, Oct. 8, 1983; children: Crystal Dawn, John Arthur II, James Kyle. BS, R.I. Coll., 1982. Mid. sch. tchr. St. Vincent de Paul Sch., Coventry, R.I., 1982-83; instr. computers, tng. coord. CES/Computech, Providence, 1985-92; owner, computer cons. C.C. Computer Instrn., Providence, 1992—; computer instr. Kansas City Mo. Sch. Dist., 1998—; tutor South Providence Tutorial, Providence, 1980, Sylvan Learning, Cranston, R.I., 1990. Co-author: Graphic and Sound, 1989. Office: C C Computer Instrn 22 Myra St Providence RI 02909-6027

CHAUVIN, LEONARD STANLEY, JR., lawyer; b. Franklin, Ky., Feb. 13, 1935; s. Leonard Stanley Sr. C.; m. Cecilia McKay; children: Leonard Stanley III, Jacqueline, McKay. Grad., Castle Heights Mil. Acad., 1953; AB in Polit. Sci., U. Ky., 1957; JD, U. Louisville, 1961, LLD (hon.), 1990; LLD (hon.), Ohio No. U., 1990. Bar: Ky. 1961, U.S. Dist. Ct. (we. dist.) Ky. 1962, U.S. Ct. Appeals (6th cir.) 1964, U.S. Ct. Mil. Appeals 1966, U.S. Ct. Claims 1966, U.S. Supreme Ct. 1966, N.Y. 1983, Ind. 1983, Tenn. 1983, D.C. 1983, U.S. Dist. Ct. (so. and na. dists.) Ind. 1983, U.S. Dist. Ct. D.C. 1983, U.S. Ct. Appeals (7th, D.C. and Fed. cirs.) 1983, U.S. Tax Ct. 1983, U.S. Ct. Internat. Trade 1983, Wis. 1984, U.S. Dist. Ct. (so.and ea. dist.) 1984, U.S. Ct. Appeals (2d cir.) 1984, Fla. 1985, Nebr. 1985, Minn. 1985, Mass. 1986, W.Va. 1986. Assoc. Daniel B. Boone, Louisville, 1962-63, Laurence E. Higgins, Louisville, 1963-68; ptnr. Brown & Chauvin, Louisville, 1968-78, Carroll, Chauvin, Miller & Conliffe, Louisville, 1978-82; sole practice Louisville, 1982-83; ptnr. Barnett & Alagia, Louisville, 1983-92, Chauvin & White, Louisville, 1992-93, Chauvin & Chauvin, 1993—; asst. Commonwealth atty. Jefferson County Commonwealth Attys. Office, Louisville, 1962-63; asst. gen. counsel dept. hwys. Commonwealth of Ky., Louisville; judge pro tem Louisville Police Ct.; master commr. Jefferson Cir. Ct., Louisville, 1992—; asst. county atty. of Jefferson County, 1978-87. Chmn. Registry of Election Fin.; mem. Ky. jud. retirement form system Old Ky. Home Boy Scouts, Frankfort, Ky. Fellow Am. Bar Found. (chmn.); mem. ABA (chmn. ho. of dels. 1982-84, pres. 1989-90), Am. Coll. Tax Counsel, Ky. Bar Assn. (Lawyer of Yr. award), Nat. Jud. Coll., Am. Judicature Soc. (pres. 1986-88, Harley award), Am. Coll. Trust and Estate Counsel. Home: 1648 Cherokee Rd Louisville KY 40205-1369 Office: 1228 Starks Bldg Louisville KY 40202

CHAVARRIA, DOLORES ESPARZA, financial service executive; b. Levelland, Tex., Nov. 13, 1952; d. Thomas Medina and Hermenejilda (Estrada) Esparza; m. Margarito R. Grimaldo (div. Feb. 1975); children: Maurice Patrick, Margarito; m. Frank Sedillo Chavarria; 1 child, Mecca Esparza. AS, South Plains C.C., 1977; student, Tex. Tech U., 1977-78. Notary public, Tex. Supr. cen. supply South Park Med. Ctr., Lubbock, Tex., 1980-84, dir. materials mgmt. dept., 1984-90; buyer City of Lubbock, 1990-94, recruiter, 1994—; prin. D.E.E. Enterprises, Lubbock, 1992—. Chmn. S.W. Voter's Registration, Lubbock, 1988. Mem. Nat. Assn. Purchasing Mgmt. (2d v.p. South Plains chpt.), Am. Bus. Women's Assn., Tex. Purchasing Mgmt. Assn., Hispanic Assn. of Women. Democrat. Roman Catholic. Home: 4502 20th St Lubbock TX 79407 Office: 1625 13th St Lubbock TX 79401-3830

CHAVARRIA, ERNEST MONTES, JR., international trade, business and finance consultant, lecturer; b. Laredo, Tex., May 9, 1955; s. Ernesto M. Sr. and Josefa M. C.; m. Sandra Mercado, Aug. 13, 1978. BBA, U. Tex., 1977, MBA, 1978. Cert. internat. financier. Pres., chief exec. officer ITBR, Inc., Austin, Tex., 1976—; elected del. Nat. White House Conf. on Small Bus., 1986, vice chmn., moderator Tex. del., chmn. internat. trade and investment coms.; issue leader for internat. trade and investment forums; bd. dirs. U.S. SBA Av. Coun. for region 6, 1986—; mem. U.S. SBA, San Antonio Dist. Internat. Trade Task Force, 1987—, U.S. SBA/Hispanic Border Bus. Devel. Com., 1987—, U.S. Congl. Adv. Bd.; mem. steering com. Partnership Tex.-Small and Large Bus. and State Govt. United for Opportunity Gov.'s Task Force, 1987—; co-chmn. membership com. Austin Fgn. Trade Coun., 1986—; ed. appointee to U.S. Dept. Commerce and Industry (sector adv. com. on small and minority bus. for trade policy matters), 1988—; chmn. moderator Tex. conf. Small Bus., 1987, moderator, spkr. confs. in field; lectr. in field; featured in Fortune Mag. April, 1994; apptd. U.S. del. to the Western Hemisphere Trade and Commerce Forum, Denver, 1995. Mem. minority adv. bd. Austin Am. Statesman newspaper, 1987—; author various newsletters; featured in Fortune mag., 1994, Tex. Hispanic mag., 1994, USA Today, also local newspapers, radio and TV talk shows. Participant Austin leadership, 1986-87; vice chmn. extension com. YMCA NW, Austin, 1986—; mem. steering com. Tex. Civil Justice League, Austin, 1987—; bd. dirs. Small Bus. Devel. Com. and Neighborhood Assn., Austin, 1986—, Austin Met. YMCA, 1987—, N.W. Area Coun. Austin, 1986—, Econ. Devel. Assessment Com. and 183 Roadway Plan, Austin, 1986—, Cedar Park (Tex.) Econ. Devel. Com., 1986—, Austin Govtl. Rels. Coun., 1987—, Child Assault Prevention Program, Austin, 1987—, Tex. Civil Justice League, Austin, 1987—; fed. appt. to Industry sector adv. com. on small and minority bus., U.D. Dept. Commerce, 1988; appt. to U.S. del. to the Western Hemisphere Trade and Commerce Forum, Denver, 1995; mem. econ./environment curriculum com. Leadership Austin; chmn., CEO Internat. Latino Found., 1994—; chmn. Internat. Leadership Inst., 1995—. Recipient Am. award for Most Outstanding Bus. Con. Co. in U.S.A., 1986, Internat. Award for Good Svc. and Quality, 1987, 1st Ann. Sanchez to Sanchez Internat. award U.S. Hispanic C. of C., Johnny Canales Internat. award; named Tex. Minority Advocate of Yr., U.S. SBA, 1987, Exporter of Yr., 1987; recognized as one of top 100 most influential in U.S., Hispanic Bus. Mag., 1992, strongest and most outspoken advocate of NAFTA, Hispanic mag., 1994, leadership in successful passage of NAFTA Fortune Mag., 1994; Ernesto Chavarria Day proclaimed by City of Austin, 1986. Mem. Nat. Assn. Profl. Cons., Am. Soc. Profl. Cons. (mem. bd. govs.), Profl. Bus. Cons. Assn. (mem. bd. govs.), Internat. Leadership Inst. (chmn. 1995), U.S. C. of C., U.S. Hispanic C. of C. (bd. dirs., chmn. econ. devel. com. 1988, co-chmn. govt. rels. com. 1988, chmn. region III, chmn. internat. affairs), Tex. C. of C. (keynote speaker Internat. Trade-Investments Conf. 1989), Austin Hispanic C. of C. (cert. appreciation 1987), Am. C. of C. of Mex. (Mem. of Yr. award 1989, various coms. and couns.), Tex. Assn. Mexican-Am. C. of C. (chmn. bd. dirs. 1992—, bd. dirs., exec. com., vice chmn. internat. rels., speaker, moderator Internat. Trade Conf. 1989, 1st vice chmn., chmn. internat. affairs, chief negotiator NAFTA), Internat. Fed. Mex. C. of C. (v.p.), P Internat. Traders Assn., Internat. Latino Found. (chmn.), Tex. Army N.G. Assn., Tex. Bus. Coun. (charter), Tex. Indsl. Devel. Coun. (internat. trade com.), U.S. Hispanic C. of C. (chmn. U.S./Mex./Can. rels., chmn. internat. fin/banking affairs). Avocations: reading, writing, public speaking, travel. Fax: (512) 266-8832. Home: PO Box 160325 Austin TX 78716-0325 Office: ITBR Inc 2 Cielo Ctr 3rd Fl 1250 S Capital Of Texas Hwy Austin TX 78746-6464*

CHAVASSE, PHILIPPE, foreign languages educator; b. Mar. 31, 1968. BA, U. Lyon, France, 1989, MA, 1990; PhD, U. Oreg., 1997. Asst. prof. Marshall U., Huntington, W.Va., 1997-98, So. Ill. U., Carbondale, 1998—. Office: Fgn Langs & Lits So Ill U Carbondale IL 62901-4521

CHAVE, CAROLYN MARGARET, lawyer, arbitrator; b. Chgo., Jan. 30, 1948; d. Grant Carruthers and Priscilla Morrison (Shaw) C.; m. Robert Edmund Hand; children: Joshua, Chloe, Robert, Grant. BA, U. Chgo., 1970; MAT, Oakland U., 1971; JD, Loyola U., Chgo., 1976. Bar: Ill. 1976, N.Y. 1979. Tchr. corps intern Pontiac (Mich.) Pub. Schs., 1970-71; sec., receptionist Grad. Sch. Bus., U. Chgo., 1971; counselor Sonia Shankman Orthogenic Sch., Chgo., 1972; pvt. practice Chgo., 1976-78; asst. v.p., assoc. counsel Bank of Tokyo, N.Y.C., 1978-85; substitute tchr. N.Y.C. Pub. Schs., 1986-88; with Breckenridge Law Offices, 1986-88; sr. v.p., counsel, mgr. human resources Tokai Bank, N.Y.C., 1988-97; dir., counsel Deutsche Bank, N.Y.C., 1997-99; arbitrator Am. Arbitration Assn., N.Y.C., 1986-99. Vol. lawyer Chgo. Vol. Legal Svcs., 1977-78; designer playground PS 41 Parent

Assn., Greenwich Village, N.Y., 1987. Avocations: dancing, skiing, patchwork quilting.

CHAVERS, BLANCHE MARIE, pediatrician, educator, researcher; b. Clarksdale, Miss., Aug. 2, 1949; d. Andrew and Mildred Louise (Cox) C.; m. Gubare Robert Mpambara, May 21, 1982; 1 child, Kaita. B.S. in Zoology, U. Wash., 1971, M.D., 1975. Diplomate Am. Bd. Pediatrics. Intern, U. Wash., Seattle, 1975-76, resident in pediatrics, 1976-78; fellow in pediatric nephrology U. Minn., Mpls., 1978-81, instr., 1981-82, asst. prof. pediatrics, 1983—, assoc. prof. pediatrics, 1990—; attending physician dept. pediatrics, U. Minn. Sch. Medicine, Mpls., 1981—. Contbr. articles to profl. jours. Recipient Clin. Investigator award NIH, 1982. Mem. Am. Acad. Pediatrics, Am. Soc. Nephrology, Am. Soc. Pediatric Nephrology, Internat. Soc. Nephrology, Internat. Soc. Pediatric Nephrology. Democrat. Mem. African Methodist Episcopal Zion Ch. Avocations: tennis, reading, collecting African artifacts, art. Home: 9218 Fawnridge Cir S Bloomington MN 55437-1825 Office: Univ Minn Box 491 Mayo 515 Delaware St SE Minneapolis MN 55455-0348

CHAVERS, KEVIN G., investment company executive; b. Phila.. BA in City Planning, U. Va.; JD, Harvard U. Bar: N.Y., D.C. Majority counsel U.S. Senate Com. Banking, Housing and Urban Affairs, Washington, 1989-93; mem. Pres. Clinton's transition team, Washington, 1992; chief of staff Office Fed. Housing Enterprise Oversight, Washington; sr. v.p., exec. asst. to pres. Govt. nat. Mortgage Assn. (Ginnie Mae), Washington, pres., 1998; v.p. Goldman, Sachs & Co., N.Y.C., 1998—. Office: Goldman Sachs & Co 26th Fl 85 Broad St New York NY 10004*

CHAVES, JOSE MARIA, diplomat, foundation administrator, lawyer, educator; b. Bogotá, Colombia, Aug. 19, 1922; s. Carlos Chaves and María García de C.; m. Elena Gómez y Samperio; children: Cristina María, Tomás José. Bachiller, Bogotá, 1939, cert. in anthropology, 1942, JD, 1945; DSc (hon.), U. Antióquia, 1948; MA, Columbia U., 1951, PhD, 1953; LLD, U. Popayán, Colombia, 1957, Mercy Coll., 1991. Bar: Columbia 1944, Inter-American 1953. Editor in chief Revista Colegio del Rosario (arts and letters mag.), Colombia, 1944; gen. legal duties specializing in public adminstrn. Bogotá, 1942-45; instr. Romance langs. Columbia U., N.Y.C., 1945-48, 50-51; founder, 1st dean faculty U. Andes, Bogotá, 1948-49; head area studies Queens Coll. NYU, 1951-53; counselor Colombian Embassy, Washington, 1953-55; prof. internat. law U. Colombia, 1955-58, U. Paris, 1957; guest prof. internat. law and relations Brit. Council, various univs. Eng., Scotland, 1957; dir., chief exec. Am. Found. for Cultural Popular Action, Inc. (pvt. internat. orgn. for mass edn. by radio), N.Y.C., 1958—; amb. of Kyrgyzstan to UN, 1992—; dir. Center Latin Am. Studies, CUNY; chmn. Hispanic Am. editorial bd. Grolier, Inc., 1971—; ambassador extraordinary, permanent del. Iberoam. Bur. Edn. to UN; A.E. and P., permanent rep. Grenada to OAS; permanent rep. orgn. Iberoam. Countries to UN and OAS, 1986—; alt. gov. World Bank and Internat. Monetary Fund, 1974-77, 94; chmn. C.I.P., 1972—; organizer, dir. tech. assistance mission Unitarian Service Com. in Latin Am.; dir. gen. Nat. Univ. Fund, Colombia, 1955-58; amb. extraordinary Spl. Mission to Brazil, 1995. Editor-in-chief: Grolier Spanish Universal Ency; author: Chaves Plan for settlement religious conflict between Caths. and Protestants in Latin Am; Author: Francisco de Vitoria. Founder International Law, 1945, Intergroup relations in the Spain of Cervantes, 1953, University Reform in Colombia, 1957. Pres. Assn. Latin Am. Unity, 1984; chmn. Summit Coun. World Peace, 1985-92; ambassador extraordinary and plenipotentiary of Kyrgyztan to the UN, 1992-93. Decorated Legion of Honor (France); gran cruz Order of St. Constantine the Great; comdr., knight comdr. Grand Order Isabel La Católica (Spain); knight comdr. Alfonso El Sabio; grand cross Vasco N'nez de Balboa Panama, 1970; grand cross Juan P. Duarte Sanchez y Mella Dominican Republic, 1970, Medal of Jerusalem Israel, 1972; grand cross Order of Malta, 1976; grand cross Order Justice Law and Peace of Mex., 1977, grand cross Order Latin Am. Unity 1986, grand cross Order of St. Michael (Portugal), 1990; grand cross Order of Holy Cross of Jerusalem, 1991, grand cross of Saint Dennis of Zanthe, 1991; recipient medaglia universitaria U. Po Deo, Rome, 1957, medalla de los Andes U., 1958, medaille de Versailles, France, 1990, medalla Universidad, Lima, 1990, Lord Perry World prize for Edn., 1993, Order of Manas of Kyrgyzstan 1995. Mem. Internat. Law Assn., Inter-Am. Bar. Assn., Acad. Polit. Sci., MLA, Academia Hispano Americana, Assn. for Latin Am. Unity (founder, pres. 1984), Summit Coun. for World Peace (dir. 1987), Met. Club, Columbia U. Club (N.Y.C.), Quill Club USA (pres.), Brook Club, Phi Delta Kappa (v.p. Univ. World). Clubs: Metropolitan, Brook, Columbia U. (N.Y.C.), Quill of U.S.A. (pres.). Home: 118 E 60th St New York NY 10022-1103 Office: 401 5th Ave New York NY 10016-3317 *Faith in God is also faith in man. Service of man is also service of God. As we enter a new period of peace in the world, our faith can sustain our peace building efforts and help create a better life for all mankind.*

CHAVEZ, ALBERT BLAS, financial executive; b. L.A., Jan. 1, 1952; s. Albert Blas and Yolanda (Garcia) C.; m. Irma Laura Cavazos, Dec. 21, 1996. BA, U. Tex., El Paso, 1979; MBA, Stanford U., 1985. CPA, Calif. Mem. profl. staff Deloitte Haskins and Sells, L.A., 1980-83; planning analyst corp. fin. planning Boise (Idaho) Cascade Co., 1984; treasury analyst corp. treasury RCA Corp., N.Y.C., 1985; asst. contr. RCA/Ariola Records, Mexico City, 1986; fin. analyst corp. exec. office GE Co., Fairfield, Conn., 1987-90; fin. cons. Entertainment Industry and Litigation Support Svcs., L.A., 1990-91; co-founder, sr. v.p., CFO El Dorado Comm., Inc., L.A., 1991-98; fin. cons. entertainment industry pvt. practice, 1998—. Bd. dirs., treas. L.A. Conservation Corps, 1990—; bd. dirs. Wave Cmty. Newspapers, 1999—. Mem. AICPA, Calif. Soc. CPAs. Democrat. Home: 18744 Strathern St Reseda CA 91335-1221

CHAVEZ, CESAR T., ophthalmologist, cosmetic surgeon; b. Mexicali, Mex., Mexico, Aug. 3, 1952; s. Felipe and Norbertha Chavez; m. Teresa Cardenas, June 1977; children: Elena, Esteban. BA, UCLA, 1973; MD, U. Wash., 1977, MPH, 1977. Diplomate Am. Board Ophthalmology (assoc. examiner), Nat. Bd. Med. Examiners. Intern Kaiser Permanente Hosp., Fontana, Calif., 1977-78; resident Jules Stein Eye Inst.-UCLA Med. Ctr., 1983-85; chief divsn. comprehensive ophthalmology UCLA, 1985-88, asst. prof. ophthalmology, med. dir. Jules Stein Eye Inst., 1985-88; med. dir. Univ. Ophthalmology Assocs., Los Angeles, 1986-88, Camino Coastline Eye Surgeons, Encinitas, Calif., 1988—; qualified med. evaluator State of Calif. Contbr. articles to profl. jours. Bd. dirs. Calif. State U., San Marcos Found. Lt. USPHS, 1978-81. Fellow Am. Acad. Ophthalmology, Am. Acad. Cosmetic Surgery; mem. Med. Group Mgmt. Assn., San Diego County Med. Soc., Calif. Med. Assn. Roman Catholic. Avocation: trout fishing. Office: Camino Coastline Eye Surgeons Ste C200 477 N El Camino Real Encinitas CA 92024-1332

CHAVEZ, EDWARD, police chief; b. Stockton, Calif., Mar. 22, 1943; m. Nancy Ruhr; children: Eric, Jill. AA, San Joaquin Delta Coll., 1971; BA, Calif. State U., 1972; MS, Calif. Polytechnic Pomona, 1990; grad., POST Command Coll., Delinquency Control Inst., Leadership Stockton Program, FBI Nat. Acad. With USAF, 1962-70; officer Stockton Police Dept., 1973, sgt., 1980, lt., 1986, capt., 1990, dep. chief of police, 1990, acting chief of police, 1993, chief of police, 1993—. Bd. dirs. St. Joseph's Med. Ctr., San Joaquin United Way, Lilliput Childrens Svcs., Greater Stockton C. of C.; active Hispanics for Polit. Action; adv. com. Leadership, Stockton. With USAF, 1962-70. Mem. Calif. Peace Officers Assn., Hispanic Am. Police Command Officer's Assn., Mexican Am. C. of C., Stockton E. Rotary, Coun. for Spanish Speaking (past bd. dirs.), Leadership Stockton Alumni Assn. Office: Stockton Police Dept 22 E Market St Stockton CA 95202-2802

CHAVEZ, GILBERT ESPINOZA, bishop; b. Ontario, Calif., May 9, 1932. Student, St. Francis Sem., El Cajon, Calif., Immaculate Heart Sem., San Diego, U. Calif., San Diego. Ordained priest Roman Cath. Ch., 1960; Titular bishop of Magarmel and aux. bishop Diocese of San Diego, 1974—; bishop; b. Ontario, Calif., Mar. 19, 1932; ed. St. Francis Sem., El Cajon, Calif., Immaculate Heart Sem., San Diego, U. Calif., San Diego. Ordained priest Roman Cath. Ch., 1960; titular bishop of Magarmel and aux. bishop Diocese of San Diego, 1974—. Office: St Joseph Cathedral 1535 3rd Ave San Diego CA 92101-3101*

CHAVEZ, JOHN ANTHONY, lawyer; b. Auburn, Calif., Oct. 5, 1955; s. Marco Antonio and Barbara Ann (Lawrence) Chavez-Rivas. BA, U. Calif., Santa Barbara, 1977; JD, Stanford U., 1981. Bar: Calif. 1981, Tex. 1982, U.S. Dist. Ct. (so. and no. dists.) Calif. 1982, (cen. dist.) Calif. 1983, U.S. Dist. Ct. (so. dist.) Tex. 1982, (we. dist.) Tex. 1983, (no. dist.) Tex. 1991, N.Y. 1986, U.S. Dist. Ct. (ea. and so. dists.) N.Y. 1986, U.S. Supreme Ct. 1986. With legal dept. Exxon Co. U.S.A., Houston, 1981-85, N.Y.C., 1985-86; assoc. gen. counsel Sybron Corp., Saddlebrook, N.J., 1986-88, Crown Equipment Corp., New Bremen, Ohio, 1989-90; trial atty. Exxon Co. U.S.A., Houston, 1990-92; counsel complex litigation Exxon Chem. Co., Houston, 1992-95; counsel internat. oil and gas exploration Exxon Exploration Co., Houston, 1995-96; counsel antitrust, mergers and acquisitions Exxon Chem. Co., Houston, 1996—; presenter numerous legal edn. seminars and programs. Contbr. articles to profl. jours. Mentor Ft. Bend Ind. Sch. Dist., 1998, Houston Bar Assn., 1998. Chancellor's scholar U. Calif., 1976; Univ. Svc. award for dist. svc. to campus cmty. U. Calif., Santa Barbara, 1977. Mem. ABA (antitrust, bus. law, criminal justice and litigation sects., joint venture agreements task force of the negotiated acquisitions com. 1998, white collar crime com., criminal litigation com., Sherman Act Sect. 1 com., vice chair corp. counseling com. 1998—), Houston Bar Assn. (chair antitrust and trade regulation sect., 1997-98, vice-chair 1996-97, sec.-treas. 1995-96, coun. 1993-95), Coll. State Bar Tex., Wong Sun Soc.; fellow Houston Bar Found. Republican. Avocations: hiking, theatre, travel. E-mail: anthony.chavez@exxon.com. Home: 7767 Cambridge Houston TX 77054 Office: Exxon Chem Co PO Box 3272 Houston TX 77253-3272

CHAVEZ, JULIO CESAR, professional boxer; b. Ciudad Obregon, Mex., July 12, 1962; s. Rodolfo and Isabelita C.; m. Amalia Carrasco; children: Julio Jr., Omar, Christian. Profl. boxer, 1980—, six time world champion; winner WBC super featherweight championship, 1984; winner WBA lightweight championship, 1987; winner WBC jr. welterweight championship, 1988; world title fight record 31-1-1. Office: World Boxing Coun, Genova 33 Despacho #503, DF 06600 Mexico City Mexico*

CHAVEZ, LLOYD G., automotive executive. CEO Burt on Broadway. Office: Burt Automotive Network 5200 S Broadway Englewood CO 80110-6708*

CHAVEZ, NELBA, federal agency administrator. BA in Sociology and Psychology, U. Ariz.; MSW, UCLA; PhD in Philosophy, U. Denver; student sr. exec. program in state and local govt., Harvard U. From therapist to exec. dir., CEO, COO La Frontera Ctr., Tuscon, 1971-89; prin. Chavez and Assocs., 1989-91; dir. juvenile probation svcs. City and County of San Francisco, 1991-94; adminstr. Substance Abuse and Mental Health Svcs. Adminstrn., U.S. Dept. Health and Human Svcs., Washington, 1994—; bd. dirs. nat. coalition of Hispanic Health and Human Svc. Organs,; mem. U.S. Senate Hispanic Adv. Com., Pres. Nat. Coun. on Handicapped, White House Prevention Com. on Drug-Free Am. Mem. Tuscon Mayor's Task Force on Children. Recipient Outstanding Leadership award Ariz. State U., 1985, Dedication and Commitment award Tenth Ann. Chicano Conf., 1989, Disting. Svc. award Nat. Assn. Profl. Asian Am. Women, 1995, Mujer 95 award League United L.Am. Citizens, 1995, Rafael Tavares, MD, Meml. award Assn. Hispanic Mental Health Profls., 1995, Nat. Health Leadership award Nat. Coalition Hispanic Health and Human Svcs., 1997, Leadership award Fedn. Families for Children's Mental Health, 1997; named to Honor Roll Latino Behavioral Health Inst., 1998. Office: Dept Hlth Human Svcs Subst Abuse & Mental Hlth Svcs Admin 5600 Fishers Ln Rm 12-105 Rockville MD 20857-0002

CHAVEZ, VICTOR EDWIN, judge; b. L.A., Aug. 28, 1930; s. Raymond C. and Sarah (Baca) C.; children: Victoria, Catherine, Stephanie, Christopher, Robert, Elizabeth. BS, Loyola U., L.A., 1953, JD, 1959. Bar: Calif. 1960. Mem. firm Early, Maslach, Foran and Williams, L.A., 1960-69, Pomerantz and Chavez, L.A., 1969-90; judge L.A. Superior Ct., 1990—, mem. exec. com., 1991, 92, 96, asst. presiding judge, 1997-98, presiding judge, 1999—. Mem. com. State Bar Examiners, 1972-76; del. to State Bar, 1971-75; bd. regents Loyola Marymount U., 1973-78. 1st lt. USAF, 1953-55. Mem. ABA (standing com. on fed. judiciary 1979-86), L.A. County Bar Assn., Mex.-Am. Bar Assn. (pres. 1971), Am. Bd. Trial Advocates (pres. L.A. chpt. 1979), Law Soc. Office: Dept I 111 N Hill St Los Angeles CA 90012-3117

CHÁVEZ-SILVERMAN, SUZANNE, Latin American studies educator; b. L.A.; d. Joseph Herman and June Audrey Silverman; 1 child, Etienne Joseph Strauss. BA magna cum laude, U. Calif., Irvine, 1977; MA, Harvard U., 1979; PhD, U. Calif., Davis, 1991. Lectr. U. South Africa, Pretoria, 1982-84; prof. Pomona Coll., Claremont, Calif., 1989—, chair L.Am. studies program, 1997-99. Co-editor: Tropicalizations, 1997, En el Ambiente, 1999; reviewer, editor univ. presses and jours.; contbr. articles to profl. publs. Fellow Harvard U., 1978-79, U. Calif., Davis, 1986; NEH rsch. grantee, 1992-93, 96-98. Mem. MLA, L.Am. Jewish Studies Assn., L.Am. Studies Assn., Am. Studies Assn., Nat. Assn. for Chicano/a Studies. Democrat. Office: Pomona Coll Romance Langs 550 N Harvard Ave Claremont CA 91711

CHAVEZ-THOMPSON, LINDA, labor union administrator; b. Lubbock, Tex., Aug. 3, 1944; m. Robert Thompson (dec.); 2 children. Union sec. Am. Fedn. State, County & Mcpl. Employees, internat. rep., 1971-73, asst. bus. mgr., bus. mgr., exec. dir. local 2399, 1973-95, nat. v.p. labor coun. L.Am. Advancement, 1986-96, v.p., 1988-95, exec. dir. Tex. Coun. 42, 1977-95; v.p. AFL-CIO, Washington, 1993-95, exec. v.p., 1995—. Office: AFL-CIO 815 16th St NW Washington DC 20006-4104

CHAVIN, WALTER, biological science educator and researcher; b. N.Y.C., Dec. 6, 1925; s. Isidor and Fanny (Kesch) C. BS, CCNY, 1946; MS, NYU, 1949, PhD, 1954. Rsch. asst. N.Y. Aquarium, N.Y.C., 1947-48; instr. dept. zoology U. Ariz., Tucson, 1949-51; rsch. specialist dept. fishes Am. Mus. Natural History, N.Y.C., 1951-53; prof. biol. scis. Wayne State U., Detroit, 1953-90, prof. emeritus, 1990—; prof. radiology Wayne State U. Med. Sch., Detroit, 1975-80; dir. Radiation Biology Inst. Wayne State U., Detroit, 1959-71; research assoc. Argonne (Ill.) Nat. Lab., 1955-58. Contbr. 225 articles to profl. jours. NSF Sr. Postdoctoral fellow, 1960-61; Rsch. grantee NSF, AEC, NIH; named Pres. scholar Acad. Scholars Wayne State U., 1980. Fellow AAAS (sec. 1978-85), N.Y. Acad. Scis.; mem. Am. Physiol. Soc., Am. Soc. Zoologists (treas., sec.), Soc. Exptl. Biology and Medicine (com. 1986-90), Endocrine Soc., Am. Orchid Soc., South Fla. Orchid Soc., Pam Orchid Soc., Am. Bonsai Soc., Gold Coast Bonsai Soc. Independent. E-mail: raja@gate.net. Home: 16484 Bridlewood Cir Delray Beach FL 33445-6678

CHAWNER, LUCIA MARTHA, English educator; b. Ithaca, N.Y., Dec. 2, 1933; d. Lowell Jenkins and Lucia Mary (Soule) C.; m. Movses Guichen Andreassian, Mar. 18, 1967 (div. June 1971). Student, Earlham Coll., 1951-53; BA, U. Colo., 1956; MA, So. Meth. U., 1975. Provisional cert. elem., secondary and talented and gifted, Tex.; profl. cert. reading specialist, Tex. Tchr. grade 7 lang. arts and social studies Stonewall Jackson, Dallas Ind. Sch. Dist., 1959-63; reading clinician Reinhardt, Dallas Ind. Sch. Dist., 1963-66; Reading Resource Pilot Project Lakewood, Dallas Ind. Sch. Dist., 1972-74; devel. curriculum specialist El Centro Coll., Dallas County C.C. Dist., Dallas, 1977-78; English tchr. Health Magnet, Dallas Ind. Sch. Dist., 1979-95; univ. supervising tchr. U. Tex. Dallas, Richardson, 1996—; part-time instr. El Centro & Richland Colls., Dallas, 1978-88, Brookhaven Coll., Farmers Branch, Tex., 1996-98; mem. English lit. textbook adoption com. Dallas Ind. Sch. Dist., 1988-89; chmn. English dept. Health Magnet, Dallas Ind. Sch. Dist., 1989-94, mgr. innovative grant, 1994-95. Co-leader child and youth study U. Md., Dallas, 1967-69; pres. English-Speaking Union-Dallas Br., 1992-96; Leadership Arts Dallas Bus. Com. Arts, 1994-95; region 7 chmn., nat. bd. mem. English-Speaking Union of USA, 1996—. Recipient Instrnl. grant Richland Coll., 1980; Advanced Study grantee Dallas Ind. Sch. Dist., 1973; Named Tchr. of the Yr., Health Magnet, 1991, Rotary Tchr. of the Yr., Health Magnet, 1993. Mem. Dallas Mus. Art League (bd. mem. 1997—), New Conservatory of Dallas (bd. mem., 1999), Friends SMU Librs. (bd. mem. 1995-98), Assemblage (pres. 1987-88), Brit. Am. Commerce Assn., Dau. British Empire, Delta Delta Delta, Daughters of British Empire, Phi Delta Kappa, Pi Lambda Theta. Avocations: sculpture, needlepoint, fitness exercise, travel. Office: PO Box 141179 Dallas TX 75214-1179

CHAYES, ABRAM, law educator, lawyer; b. Chgo., July 18, 1922; s. Edward and Kitty (Torch) C.; m. Antonia Handler, Dec. 24, 1947; children: Eve, Abigail, Lincoln, Sarah Prudence, Angelica. AB magna cum laude, Harvard U., 1943, LLB magna cum laude, 1949; LLD (hon.), Syracuse U., 1989. Bar: D.C. 1953, Conn. 1950, Mass. 1958. Legal adviser to Gov. of Conn., 1949-51; assoc. gen. counsel Pres.'s Materials Policy Commn., 1951; law clk. to Justice Felix Frankfurter, 1951-52; assoc. Covington & Burling, Washington, 1952-55; asst. prof. law Harvard U., 1955-58, prof., 1965-93, Felix Frankfurter prof. of law emeritus, 1993—; legal adv. U.S. Dept. State, Washington, 1961-64; with Ginsburg & Feldman, Washington, 1964-65; guest scholar Brookings Inst., 1977-78; chmn. coordinating com. Internat. Nuclear Fuel Cycle Evaluation, 1977-80; mem. fgn. policy and def. task force Carter Presdl. campaign, 1976, nuclear energy policy study, 1976-77; chmn. Georgetown U. Law Ctr. Inst. for Pub. Representation, 1979—; vis. scholar Kistiakowsky Visiting Scholar program Am. Acad. Arts and Scis., 1985-86. Author: (with others) The International Legal Process, 2 vols, 1968, The Cuban Missiles Crisis: International Crises and the Role of Law, 1974, (with Antonia H. Chayes) The New Sovereignty: Compliance with International Regulatory Agreements, 1995; note editor and pres. Harvard U. Law Review; contbr. numerous articles to law jours. Staff dir. Dem. Platform Com., 1960; dir. fgn. policy task forces Dem. campaign, 1972; trustee World Peace Found., 1977; adv. bd. Lawyers Alliance for World Security, 1982—; v.p. Albert Einstein Peace Prize Found., 1980—. Capt. F.A. AUS, 1943-46. Decorated Bronze Star. Named Felix Frankfurter Prof. Law Harvard U., 1976; Rubin fellow Columbia U. Law Sch., 1985. Fellow Am. Acad. Arts and Scis.; mem. U.S. Nat. Group Permanent Ct. Arbitration. Home: 3 Hubbard Park Rd Cambridge MA 02138-4730 Office: Harvard U G-404 Law Sch Cambridge MA 02138*

CHAYKIN, ROBERT LEROY, manufacturing and marketing executive; b. Miami, Fla., May 2, 1944; s. Allan Leroy and Ruth (Levine) C.; m. Patty Jean Patton, Feb. 1971 (div. May 1975); m. Evalyn Marcy Slodzina, Sept. 3, 1989; children: Stephanie Lee, Michelle Alee, Catrina Celia, Ally Sue. BA in Polit. Sci., U. Miami, Fla., 1965, LLB, 1969. Owner, operator Serrating Svcs. Miami, 1969-71, Serrating Svcs. Las Vegas, Nev., 1971-84; pres. Ser-Sharp Mfg., Inc., Las Vegas, 1984—; nat. mktg. dir. Coserco Corp., Las Vegas, 1987—. Patentee in mfg. field. With U.S. Army, 1962. Recipient 2d degree black belt Tae Kwon Do, Profl. Karate Assn., 1954-61. Avocations: travel, camping.

CHAZEN, HARTLEY JAMES, lawyer; b. N.Y.C., Feb. 14, 1932; s. Joseph and Helen (Jacobson) C.; m. Lois Audrey, Dec. 12, 1967; 1 child, Nicole Joanna. AB, CCNY, 1953; LLB, Harvard U., 1958; LLM, NYU, 1959. Bar: N.Y. 1959. Assoc. Hays, St. John, Abramson & Heilbron, 1959-65, Shea & Gould, N.Y.C., 1965-68, Rosenman & Colin, N.Y.C., 1968-70; ptnr. Monasch Chazen & Stream, N.Y.C., 1970-82; pvt. practice, N.Y.C., 1982-88; ptnr. Chazen & Fox, N.Y.C., 1988—; of counsel, McLaughlin & Stern, LLP, 1992—; lectr. in field. Capt. USAR, 1958-68. Mem. Assn. Bar City N.Y. (com. on trademark and unfair competition 1977-80), ABA (subcom. corp. taxation 1987—), Harvard Club. Unitarian. Home: 75 Perkins Rd Greenwich CT 06830-3510 Office: McLaughlin & Stern LLP 260 Madison Ave New York NY 10016-2401

CHAZEN, STEPHEN I., oil company executive; b. Buffalo, N.Y., Aug. 26, 1946; s. Michael M. and Marcia Chazen; m. Patricia L. Orr, Nov. 20, 1971. AB, Rutgers Coll., 1968; PhD, Mich. State U., 1973; MS, U. Houston, 1977. Lab. mgr. Northrop Svcs., Inc., Houston, 1973-77; dir. project evaluation Columbia Gas Devel. Corp., Houston, 1977-81; v.p. Merrill Lynch, Houston, 1982-86; mng. dir. Merrill Lynch, N.Y.C., 1987-93; exec. v.p. Occidental Petroleum Corp., L.A., 1994—; dir. Clark Oil Co., St. Louis, 1996—. Mem. L.A. C. of C. (dir. 1996—). Home: PO Box 427 Pacific Palisades CA 90272-0427 Office: Occidental Petroleum Group 10889 Wilshire Blvd Los Angeles CA 90024-4201

CHCIUK, ZOFIA, women's health nurse, neonatal nurse; b. London, Nov. 9, 1951; d. Wladyslaw W. and Krystyna Maria (Pisarska) C.; 1 child, Veronica Obydzinski. Diploma, Tacoma Gen. Hosp. Sch. Nursing, 1974; BSN, Calif. State U., Dominguez Hills, 1995. Cert. low risk neonatal nursing, neonatal resuscitation, lactation cons. Internat. Bd. Laction Cons. Staff nurse, neonatal ICU Children's Hosp. of San Francisco; clin. neonatal educator Project HOPE-Poland, Millwood, Va.; staff nurse, head nurse in nursery Samuel Merritt Hosp., Oakland, Calif.; staff nurse, asst. mgr. nursery/IICN Community Hosp. of Monterey Peninsula, Monterey, Calif. Author chpt. on car safety. Mem. adv. bd. child passenger car safety Monterey County Health Dept. Named Nurse of Yr. Cmty. Hosp. of Monterey Peninsula, 1990, Nurse of Yr. for low risk neonatal nursing Nat. Cert. Corp., 1994. Mem. ANA, AWHON, Neonatal Nurses No. Calif. (pres. 1978), Nat. Assn. Neonatal Nurses (charter mem.).

CHEATHAM, HAROLD ERNEST, university dean, counselor, educator; b. New Kensington, Pa., Jan. 29, 1937; s. Thomas Greenwood and Elinor Anna (Ross) C.; m. Virginia Arlene Tabb, Aug. 27, 1960; children: Mark R., Brian Ross. BS, Pa. State U., 1961; MA, Colgate U., 1969; PhD, Case Western Res. U., 1973. Prof. edn. Pa. State U., 1981-96, head dept. counselor edn., counseling psychology and rehab., 1991-96; dean Clemson (S.C.) U., 1996—. Office: Clemson U Edwards Hall Clemson SC 29634-0701

CHEATHAM, JOHN BANE, JR., retired mechanical engineering educator; b. Houston, June 29, 1924; s. John Bane and Winnie (Carr) C.; m. Juanita Faye Burns, July 19, 1947; children—Preston, Curtis. B.M.E., So. Methodist U., 1948, M.S., 1953; M.E., M.I.T., 1954; Ph.D., Rice U., 1960. Registered profl. engr. Design engr. Linkbelt Co., Dallas and Houston, 1949-50; rsch. engr. Atlantic Refining Co., Dallas, 1950-53; rsch. assoc., head drilling rschr. Shell Devel. Co., Houston, 1954-63; prof. mech. engring. Rice U., 1963-96; chmn. dept. mech. engring. and materials sci., 1994-96; pres. Cheatham Engring. Inc., Houston, 1977-94, Techaid Corp., Houston, 1978-88; cons. in field. Contbr. to profl. jours.; tech. editor: Jour. Energy Resources Tech, 1979-81. Served to 2d lt. USAAF, 1943-45. Fellow ASME; mem. Am. Inst. Mining and Petroleum Engrs., Am. Soc. Engring. Edn., Sigma Xi. Address: 5671 Longmont Dr Houston TX 77056-2344

CHEATHAM, RICHARD REED, lawyer; b. Pulaski, Tenn., July 14, 1943; s. David Edward and Florence (Abernathy) C.; m. Beverly Paisley, Aug. 7, 1976; 1 child, Richard Reed Jr. BS, U. Va., 1965; LLB, Harvard U., 1968. Bar: Ga. 1970, U.S. Ct. Appeals (5th cir.) 1970, U.S. Ct. Appeals (11th cir.) 1981. Instr. U. Ga., Athens, 1968-69; assoc. Kilpatrick Stockton LLP, Atlanta, 1969-75, 75—; ptnr. Kilpatrick & Cody (now Kilpatrick Stockton), Atlanta, 1975—. Fellow Ga. Bar Found.; mem. ABA, State Bar Ga., Capital City Club, Commerce Club. Democrat. Methodist. Avocations: reading. Office: Kilpatrick Stockton LLP 1100 Peachtree St NE Ste 2800 Atlanta GA 30309-4501

CHEATHAM, ROBERT WILLIAM, lawyer; b. St. Paul, June 4, 1938; s. Robert William and Hildegard Frances Cheatam; m. Kay C. Sarnecki, Mar. 20, 1964; children: Ann Marie, Lynn Marie, Paul William. BCE, U. Minn., 1961, JD, 1966. Bar: Calif. 1967, U.S. Dist. Ct. (no. dist.) Calif. 1967. Assoc. Brobeck, Phleger & Harrison, San Francisco, 1967-74, ptnr., 1974-88; ptnr. Cheatham & Skovronski, San Francisco, 1988-96, Cheatham & Tomlinson, San Francisco, 1996-97, Cassidy, Cheatham, Shimko & Dawson, San Francisco, 1997—; speaker on continuing legal edn., San Francisco. Co-author: Calif. Attorneys Guide to Real Estate Syndicates, 1970, Cheatham and Merritt California Real Estate Forms and Commentaries, 1984-90. Mem. ABA, Calif. Bar Assn., Am. Arbitration Assn. (arbitrator on real estate disputes). Office: Cassidy Cheatham et al 20 California St Ste 500 San Francisco CA 94111-4826

CHEATHAM, VALERIE MEADOR, clinical dietitian; b. Huntington, W.Va., June 17, 1957; d. Phillip Jarrell and Anna Lee (Law) Meador; m. Edward Lee McCallum, May 13, 1978 (div. 1990); children: Shaun Jeffrey, Briana Marie; m. Miles W. Cheatham III, Oct. 26, 1990. BS in Biology, James Madison U., 1979; MS in Nutrition, Clemson U., 1986. Registered dietitian, 1987. Cytotechnologist Roanoke (Va.) Meml. Hosp., 1979-80; greenhouse mgr. Greenwood Nurseries, Princeton, W.Va., 1980-81; vet. technician Lewisburg (W.Va.) Animal Hosp., 1981-82; rsch. asst. Clemson (S.C.) U., 1984-86; clin. dietician Anderson (S.C.) Meml. Hosp., 1986-87, asst. food svc. dir., 1987-91, nutritionist III dept. health and environ. control, 1991-93; program mgr. woman, infant and child health-prenatal svcs. Anderson County Health Dept., 1994-97; dist. dir. nutrition Anderson County Appalachia I Health Dist., 1997—. Mem. Am. Dietetic Assn.,

Piedmont Dist. Dietetics Assn. (sec.), S.C. Dietetics Assn., S.C. Pub. Health Assn. Avocations: practical pistol shooting, Isshinryu karate, sewing, reading. Home: 110 Bobwhite Ln Anderson SC 29625-2521 Office: Dept Health Environ Control 200 McGee Rd Anderson SC 29625-2104

CHEATWOOD, ROY CLIFTON, lawyer; b. Rome, Ga., Aug. 27, 1946; s. Herman Arthur and Dorothy Mary (Griffin) C.; m. Cynthia Morrison, June 27, 1969; children: Clifton, Scott, Dancy. BA, U. South Fla., 1968; JD, Tulane U., 1974. Bar: La. 1974, U.S. Dist. Ct. (ea. dist.) La. 1974, U.S. Dist. Ct. (mid. dist.) La. 1975, U.S. Ct. Appeals (5th cir.) 1975, U.S. Dist. Ct. (we. dist.) La. 1977, U.S. Supreme Ct. 1977, U.S. Ct. Appeals (11th cir.) 1981, U.S. Dist. Ct. (no. dist.) Tex. 1990. Assoc. Jones, Walker, Waechter, Poitevent, Carrere & Denegre, New Orleans, 1974-78, ptnr., 1978-91; ptnr. Phelps Dunbar, New Orleans, 1991—, practice coord., comml. litigation practice group, 1992—, mem. mgmt. com., 1995—; adj. prof. La. State U., Baton Rouge, 1980, Loyola U., New Orleans, 1981, 84-86; faculty mem. Nat. Inst. Trial Advocacy, 1986—; master barrister Tulane Inn of Ct. Co-author: Louisiana Courtroom Evidence, 1993. Firm campaign rep. United Way, New Orleans, 1982, 98, recruiter, 1983-86, 88, acct. exec. area lawyers, 1989; bd. dirs. Children's Bur., New Orleans, 1988, 1st v.p., 1991, pres., 1993-95; mem. session St. Charles Presbyn. Ch., 1988-91. 1st lt. U.S. Army, 1968-71, Vietnam. Mem. ABA (vice chmn. 5th cir. trial practice com. 1975-76, co-chmn. 1976-78, judge regional nat. appellate adv. com. 1978, co-chmn. ann. litigation meeting 1981, judge nat. appellate adv. competition 1978, membership chmn. litigation sect. 1983-86), La. State Bar Assn. (bd. govs. 1998—, bd. legal specialization 1998—). Office: Phelps Dunbar 400 Poydras St New Orleans LA 70130-3245

CHECCHI, ALFRED A., airline company executive; b. 1948; m. BA, Amherst Coll., 1970; MBA, Harvard Univ., 1974. V.p. Marriott Corp., 1975-82; with Bass Bros., 1982-86; pres. Alfred Checchi Assocs., Inc., 1986—; co-chmn., bd. dirs. NWA Inc., -1997, Northwest Airlines Inc., -1997, Wings Holdings Inc., -1997; bd. dirs. Northwest Airlines, Inc., St. Paul, 1997—. Office: NW Airlines Inc 5101 Northwest Dr Saint Paul MN 55111-3034*

CHECCHI, VINCENT VICTOR, economist; b. Calais, Maine, Nov. 25, 1918; s. Arthur R. and Dina I. (Pisani) C.; m. Mary E. Pate, Aug. 2, 1941; children: Dina Ann, Mary Jane, Vincent Arthur. AB, U. Maine, 1940; postgrad., Harvard U., 1941; MA, George Washington U., 1942. Statistician-economist WPB, 1941-45; dep. dir. requirements br. Allied Mil. Govt. in Italy, 1945-46; dir. program coordination UN Relief and Rehab. Adminstrn., Italy; then asst. to chief mission in China UNRRA, 1946-47; loan officer Internat. Bank Reconstrn. and Devel., 1947; dir. China econ. br., later dir. East-West trade br. Econ. Cooperation Adminstrn., 1947; econ. editor Reporter Mag., 1950; spl. rep. in Philippines ECA, 1950-51; founder Checchi and Co., Washington, 1951, CEO, also chmn. bd. dirs., bd. dirs. various subs. Co-author: Honduras, A Problem in Economic Development; author articles on econs. Home: 9206 Watson Rd Silver Spring MD 20910-4136 Office: Checchi and Co 1899 L St NW Ste 800 Washington DC 20036-3812

CHECKETTS, DAVID WAYNE, professional basketball team executive; b. Salt Lake City, Sept. 16, 1955; s. Clyde Alvin and Edith (Jones) C.; m. Deb Leishman, June 2, 1977; children: Spencer, Katie, Nathaniel, Andrew, Benjamin. BS, U. Utah, 1979; MBA, Brigham Young U., 1981. Mgmt. cons. Bain and Co., Boston, 1980-83; exec. v.p. Utah Jazz, NBA, Salt Lake City, 1983-84, pres., 1984-87, pres., gen. mgr., 1987-88, gen. mgr., 1988-89; gen. mgr. N.Y. Knickerbockers, 1991—, pres.; v.p. devel. NBA, N.Y.C.; pres., CEO Madison Sq. Gardens. Trustee Salt Lake Visitor and Conv. Bur., 1986. Mem. LDS Ch. Lodge: Rotary. Avocations: basketball, golf, water sports, photography. Office: NY Knicks Madison Sq Garden 2 Penn Plz New York NY 10121-0091*

CHEDID, JOHN G., bishop; b. Eddid, Lebanon, July 4, 1923. Educated, Sems. in Lebanon and Pontifical Urban Coll., Rome. Ordained priest Roman Cath. Ch., 1951. Titular bishop of Callinico and aux bishop St. Maron of Bklyn., 1981. Office: Our Lady of Lebanon Ch 333 S San Vicente Blvd Los Angeles CA 90048-3313

CHEE, CHEE PIN, neurosurgeon, consultant; b. Georgetown, Penang, Malaysia, June 19, 1953; s. Kim Seong Chee and Hup Inn Ooi; m. Irene Soh Gim Gan, Dec. 25, 1980; children: Oswin Chuan Yinn, Rowena. MB, BS, U. Malaya, Kuala Lumpur, Malaysia, 1979, MD, 1991. House officer Univ. Hosp., Kuala Lumpur, 1979-80, med. officer, 1980-83, lectr. neurosurgery, assoc. prof., 1986-91, head neurosurgery, 1988-91; neurosurg. registrar Inst. Neurol. Scis. Southern Gen. Hosp., Glasgow, Scotland, 1983-84; sr. neurosurg. registrar Royal Victoria Hosp., Belfast, Northern Ireland, 1984-86; cons. neurosurgeon Pantai Med. Ctr., Assunta Hosp., Tung Shin Hosp., Kuala Lumpur, 1991—; vis. cons. neurosurgeon Subang Jaya Med. Ctr., 1996—; cons. neurosurgeon Gleneagles Intan Med. Ctr., Kuala Lumpur, 1996—; staff neurosurgeon Group Health Coop. of Puget Sound, Seattle, 1990; chmn. 50 Med. Specialists Ctr., Kuala Lumpur, 1993-94; convener neurosurgery 7th Congress Asian Surg. Assn., Penang, 1989; neurosurgery organizer 11th Asian Pacific Fedn. Congress, Internat. Coll. Surgeons, Kuala Lumpur, 1996; organizing com. Penang Internat. Tchg. Course in Neurology, 1996. Contbr. over 30 articles to profl. jours. Recipient Penang Best Acad. Student award, 1973. Fellow Royal Coll. Surgeons (Edinburgh), Royal Coll. Physicians and Surgeons (Glasgow), Internat. Coll. Surgeons; mem. Royal Coll. Surgeons, Royal Coll. Physicians (licentiate), Congress Neurol. Surgeons, Malaysian Soc. Neuroscis. (coun. 1994-96, adv. in neurosurgery 1997-98), Asian Congress Neurol. Surgeons (exec. com. 1997—), Chung Ling Alumni Assn. (med. advisor 1995—), Kiwanis (dir. Kidney Found. Bangsar 1994—, v.p. 1991-95, pres. 1995-98, advisor Taman Tun 1997—). Avocations: philatelics, antiques, art collection, music. Office: Gleneagles Intan Med Ctr, Ste 209 2d Fl/Med Ofc Block 282, Kuala Lumpur 50450, Malaysia

CHEE, CHENG-KHEE, artist; b. Xienyou, Fujian, China, Jan. 14, 1934; came to the U.S., 1962, naturalized, 1980; s. Ya-Jie and Xien-chun (Zheng) C.; m. Sing-Bee Ong, Aug. 28, 1965; children: Yi-Hung, Yi-Min, Wan-Ying, Yen-Ying. BA, Nanyang U., Singapore, 1960; MA, U. Minn., 1964. Asst. libr. Nanyang U., 1961-62; tchg. asst. U. Minn., Mpls., 1963-64; libr. U. Minn., Duluth, 1965-68, instr., 1968-80, asst. prof., 1981-88, assoc. prof., 1988—. One-man shows include Zhejiang Acad. Fine Arts, 1984, 87, Tweed Mus. Art, U. Minn., 1982-83, 91-92, Shanghai U. Acad. Fine Arts, China, 1987, Tianjin Acad. Fine Arts, China, 1988, Phipps Ctr. for Arts, Wis., 1991, Cannon Rotunda U.S. Ho. Office Bldg., Washington, 1993, Singapore Nat. Art Mus., 1997, Minn. Mus. Am. Art, 1997; exhibited in group shows Am. Watercolor Soc. Ann., Nat. Acad. and Salmagundi Club, N.Y.C., 1975, 78, 79, 81, 91, 94, 95, 98, Rocky Mountain Nat. Watermedia Exhbn., Foothills Art Ctr., Golden, Colo., 1976, 78, 80, 84, 90, 92, 93, Allied Artists Am. Ann. Exhbn., Nat. Arts Club, N.Y.C., 1980, 82, 91, 92, 93, 94, 95, 96, 97, Adirondacks Nat. Exhbn. Am. Watercolors, Cmty. Arts Ctr., Old Forge, N.Y., 1982, 83, 86, 89, 91, 92, 95, 96, 97, 98, Nat. Watercolor Soc. Ann. Exbhn., 1983, 84, 85, 92, 96, Knickerbocker Artists USA Ann. Exhbn., 1980-81, 89-93, Sumi-e Soc. Am. Ann. Exhbn., 1979-84, 86, Mitchell Mus., Ill., 1983, Mpls. Inst. Arts, 1978, Nat. Taiwan Art Edn. Inst. Watercolor Exhbn. Artist of Taiwan, U.S. and Australia, 1994; author portfolio Cheng-Khee Chee Watercolors, 1984, 87, 91, 94, 96, (book) The Watercolor World of Cheng-Khee Chee, 1997; author exhbn. catalog, 1973-82, Retrospective Exhbn., 1982, China Exhbn. Tour, 1987, Singapore Nat. Art Mus. Exhbn., 1997; contbr. to books: Watercolor Energies, 1983, Learn Watercolor, The Edgar Whitney Way, 1994, Splash 3: Ideas and Inspirations, 1994, The Best of Watercolor, 1995, Splash 4: The Splendor of Light, 1996; illustrator children's book: Old Turtle, 1992 (Abby award, Internat. Reading Assn. award 1993); illustrator: (children's books) Old Turtle, 1992 (AABBY award, Internat. Reading Assn. award 1993), Splash 5: The Glory of Color, 1998. Recipient Gold medal of honor Allied Artists of Am. exhibit, 1980, Knickerbocker Artists Exhbn., 1989, Silver medal of honor Am. Watercolor Soc. Exhbn., 1991, High Winds medal Am. Watercolor Soc. Exhbn., 1994, Grand award Akron Soc. Artists Grant Nat. Exhbn., 1994, Colo. Centennial award Rocky Mountain Nat. Watermedia Exhbn., 1976, Grumbacher Gold medal Midwest Watercolor Soc. Exhbn., 1984, 85, 98, Gold award Ga. Watercolor Soc. Exhbn., 1985, 98, Gold medal and Purchase prize Knickerbocker Artists 43rd Ann. Grand Nat. Open Juried Exhbn., 1993, Chancellor's Disting. Svc. award U. Minn., 1994, Silver award Calif. Watercolor Assn., 1998; named Best in Show Sumi-e Soc. Am., 1984, 86, New Orleans Art Assn. 11th Nat. Art Exhbn., 1986, Western Colo. Watercolor Soc. Ann. Nat. Exhbn., 1993, Red River Watercolor Soc. 1st Nat. Art Exhbn., 1994, La. Watercolor Soc. 26th Ann. Internat. Exhbn., 1996, Duluth's Cultural Amb. to the World, Mayor Doty, 1994. Mem. Am. Watercolor Soc. (Dolphin fellow), Nat. Watercolor Soc., Rocky Mountain Nat. Watermedia Soc., Allied Artists Am., Knickerbocker Artists USA, Midwest Watercolor Soc., Watercolor USA Honor Soc., Sumi-e Soc. Am., others. Home: 1508 Vermilion Rd Duluth MN 55812-1526

CHEE, SHIRLEY, real estate broker; b. Ridley Park, Pa., Dec. 29, 1941; d. Richard E. and Lillian G. (Laudeman) Foehl; married, Nov. 26, 1967 (div. Nov. 1986). BS, Susquehanna U., 1963; grad., Real Estate Inst., 1975, postgrad., 1976-77. Music tchr. Nether Providence (Pa.) Sch. System, 1963-65, Anne Arundel Sch. System, Annapolis, Md., 1965-67; 1st cellist Annapolis Symphony Orch., 1967; bank teller Guaranty Bank & Trust Co., Morgan City, La., 1967-68; real estate agt. Joe J. Relle, Inc., Gretna, La., 1969-71; real estate broker Clyde Casey Real Estate, Inc., Gretna, 1972-75; pres. Chee, Inc. Realtors, Harvey, La., 1976—, Chee St. Tammany Corp., 1996—; pres. West Bank Profl. Real Estate Sch., Inc., Gretna, 1976-87; mem. merger task force New Orleans and Jefferson Bds. Realtors, 1992. Chmn. small bus. Am. Cancer Soc., New Orleans, 1978, 79; pres. West Bank Rep. Women's Club, Gretna, 1976; mem. Harvey Canal Indsl. Assn., 1988. Mem. Jefferson Bd. Realtors (chmn. edn. 1979, dir. 1989-90, chmn. profl. standards 1989, 91), La. Realtors Assn., Nat. Assn. Realtors, ERA-S.E. La. Brokers Coun. (pres. 1990, sec. 1989-90, treas. 1990, Multi-Million Dollar award 1989), New Orleans Met. Assn. Realtors (bd. dirs. 1993-94). Avocations: house renovations, gardening, landscaping, music, fossil hunting. Home: 728 Hickory St Terrytown LA 70056-5113 Office: Chee Inc Realtors 1600 4th St Harvey LA 70058-4410

CHEEGER, JEFF, education educator. Prof. math. Courant Inst. of Math. Scis. N.Y.U. *

CHEEK, ARTHUR LEE, administrative professional; b. Raleigh, N.C., Aug. 6, 1940; s. Arthur Lee Sr. and Margaret Louise (Bradburn) C.; m. Sandra Lee Tigges, July 21, 1958 (wid. Sept. 1971); children: Michael Sidney, Robert Bruce; m. Sheila Ann Waters, June 27, 1987. Comml. pilot. Capt. Air America, Inc., Far East, 1965-66; corp. pilot Am. Enka Corp., Asheville, N.C., 1966-68; capt. TWA/Saudi Arabian Airlines, Jidda, Saudia Arabia, 1968-71; owner Custom Homes, Inc., Asheville, 1971-80; corporate pilot SEU Constrn., Inc., Cape Coral, Fla., 1980-85, contract adminstr., 1985-89, v.p. contract adminstrn and constrn. litigation support svcs., 1989-96; v.p., gen. mgr. Coral Rock, Inc., Punta Gorda, Fla., 1994-96, West Coast Industries, Ft. Myers, Fla., 1990-96, Advantage Transp., Punta Gorda, Fla., 1994-96; ins. sales, 1998—. With USMC, 1957-60, U.S. Army, 1960-65, ETO. Mem. Masons. Republican. Avocations: golf, reading, fishing.

CHEEK, JAMES HOWE, III, lawyer, educator; b. Nashville, Nov. 28, 1942; s. James H. and Anne H. C.; m. Sigourney Woods, June 1, 1968; children—James Howe, IV, Daniel W., Matthew H. A.B., Duke U., 1964; J.D., Vanderbilt U., 1967; LL.M., Harvard U., 1968. Bar: Tenn. 1967. Assoc. firm Shearman & Sterling, N.Y.C., 1967; asst. dean, asst. prof. law Vanderbilt U. Law Sch., 1968-70, adj. prof. law, 1970—; ptnr. Bass, Berry & Sims, PLC, Nashville, 1970—; chmn. legal adv. com. N.Y. Stock Exch., 1989-92; vis. fellow Jesus Coll., Cambridge U., 1985-86; cons. Securities and Investments Bd. U.K., 1985-86; cons. comml. crime unit Commonwealth Secretariat, 1985-86; trustee Elliott E. Cheatham Fund; pres. dean's coun. Vanderbilt U. Law Sch., 1986-89, pres. law alumni bd., 1997-99; mem. exec. and adv. com. San Diego Securities Regulation Inst., 1988—; chmn., legal adv. bd. Nat. Assn. Securities Dealers, Inc., 1996-98; lectr. on CLE at seminars and insts. Contbr. articles to law jours. Recipient Disting. Alumnus award Vanderbilt Univ., 1994. Fellow Tenn. Bar Found. (trustee 1993-97); mem. ABA (chmn. subcom. on 1933 Act 1978-85, sec. com. on corp. law 1980-85, chmn. fed. regulation of securities com. 1987-91, chmn. sect. bus. law 1998-99), Nashville Bar Assn., Am. law Inst., Order of Coif, Belle Meade Country Club, Queen's Club. Home: 4404 Honeywood Ave Nashville TN 37205-3404 Office: Bass Berry & Sims PLC First American Ctr Nashville TN 37238

CHEEK, JAMES RICHARD, ambassador; b. Decatur, Ga., Apr. 27, 1936; s. Woodrow Wilson and Dorothy (Webb) C.; m. Carol Ruth Rozzell, Sept. 1, 1957; children—Leesa Lynn, Forrest Craig, Surya Tamang. B.A., Ark. State Tchrs. Coll., 1959; M. Internat. Service, Am. U., 1961. Dep. chief mission Am. Embassy, Montevideo, Uruguay, 1977-79; dep. asst. sec. state U.S. Dept. State, D.C., 1979-81; dep. chief mission Am. Embassy, Kathmandu, Nepal, 1982-85; charge d'affaires, chief mission Am. Embassy, Addis Ababa, Ethiopia, 1985-88; diplomat-in-residence Howard U., Washington, 1988-89; U.S. amb. to Sudan Am. Embassy, Khartoum, 1989-92; U.S. amb. to Argentina Am. Embassy, Buenos Aires, 1993-96; ambassador in residence U. Ark., Little Rock, 1997—. Served to capt. U.S. Army, 1954-56. Recipient spl. commendation Women's Orgn., Dept. State, 1979, Disting. Alumnus award U. Ark., 1992, U. Ctrl. Ark., 1997. Mem. Am. Fgn. Service Assn. (William R. Rivkin award 1974). Avocations: antique clocks; fishing; trekking; playing squash. Home: 31 Saint Andrews Dr Little Rock AR 72212-2908 Office: U Ark at Little Rock 2801 S University Ave Little Rock AR 72204-1000

CHEEK, JIMMY GEARY, university administrator, agricultural education and communications educator; b. Gorman, Tex., Sept. 7, 1946; s. Geary B. and Mayme (Wright) C.; m. Ileen Griffin, Aug. 23, 1969; children: Jennifer Leigh, Jeffrey Stewart. BS with high honors, Tex. A&M U., 1969, PhD, 1975; MEd, Lamar U., 1972. Agrl. edn. instr. Beaumont (Tex.) High Sch., 1969-73; supr. manpower tng. Beaumont Ind. Sch. Dist., 1971-73; grad. fellow Tex. A&M U., College Station, 1973-74, instr., 1974-75; asst. prof. U. Fla., Gainesville, 1975-80, assoc. prof., 1980-85, prof., 1985—, asst. dean for acad. programs Coll. Agr., 1992-99, dean coll. agr., 1999—; cons., seminar leader Pa. Coop. Extension Svc., 1985, Dept. Agrl. and Extension Edn., Pa. State U., 1985; cons. Gainesville (Fla.) Bd. Realty, Inc., 1988, 89, 90, 91, 92; review team mem. So. Assn. Colls. and Schs., 1977, 78; reviewer various books. Sr. author: (with others) Effective Oral Communication, 2d edit., 2000. Adminstrv. bd. First United Meth. Ch., Gainesville, 1977—, vice chair, 1986, chair, 1987-89, chair libr. com., 1991—, chair evangelism com., 1991—; chair Rawlings Elem. Sch. Adv. Com., 1982-83, 85-86; pres. Rawlings Elem. Sch. PTA, 1985, v.p., 1984; mem. Ft. Clarke Sch. Adv. Com., 1987—; mem. Hidden Oak Elem. Sch. Adv. Com., 1988-90. Recipient Hon. Tex. State Future Farmers Am. degree, 1972, Hon. Fla. State Future Farmers Am. degree, 1978, Hon. Am. Future Farmers Am. degree, 1984, Outstanding Rsch. Paper award So. Agrl. Edn. Rsch. Conf., 1984, 88, 92; Merit award scholar Tex. A&M U., 1967-69. Fellow Nat. Assn. Colls. and Tchrs. Agr. (Ensminger-Interstate Disting. Teaching award 1990); mem. Am. Vocat. Ednl. Rsch. Assn. (pres. 1986), Fla. Vocat. Assn. (pres. 1992), Am. Assn. Agrl. Edn. (v.p. 1991-92, Disting. Svc. award 1998), Am. Vocat. Assn., Nat. Vocat. Agr. Tchrs. Assn. (Outstanding Svc. award so. region 1987), Fla. Vocat. Agr. Tchrs. Assn., Fla. Assn. Vocat. and Adult Tchr. Educators, Nat. Future Farmers Am. Alumni Assn., Assn. Internat. Agrl. Edn., U. Fla. Agrl. Alumni and Friends, Sigma Xi, Phi Kappa Phi, Gamma Sigma Delta, Alpha Zeta, Phi Delta Kappa, Iota Lambda Sigma, Alpha Gamma Rho (hon.). Office: U Fla PO Box 110270 2002 McCarty Gainesville FL 32611

CHEEK, MICHAEL CARROLL, lawyer; b. Fostoria, Ohio, Aug. 28, 1948; s. Carroll Wright and Mabel A. (Smith) C. BA, Hanover Coll., 1970; JD, U. Cin., 1974. Bar: Ohio 1974, Fla. 1974, U.S. Dist. Ct. (mid. dist.) Fla. 1975. Pub. defender Clearwater, Fla., 1974-77, lawyer sole practice, 1977—; vice chmn. bar grievance Clearwater, 1990-94; trustee Pinellas County Law Libr., Clearwater, 1977-92; chmn. Ct. Law Libr., 1982-89. Pres. 1st Step Corp., Clearwater, 1986-93; vice chmn. Long Ctr. Found., Clearwater, 1994-95. Mem. Nat. Assn. Criminal Def. Lawyers, Pinellas Criminal Def. Assn. (v.p. 1987), Am. Inn of Ct. Office: 814 Chestnut St Clearwater FL 33756-5642

CHEELY, DANIEL JOSEPH, lawyer; b. Melrose Park, Ill., Oct. 24, 1949; s. Walter Hubbard and Edith Arlene (Orlandino) C.; m. Patricia Elizabeth Dorsey, May 14, 1977; children: Mary Elizabeth, Daniel, Katherine, Laura, Anne-Marie, Thomas, Susan, Michael, William. AB, Princeton U., 1971; JD, Harvard U., 1974. Bar: Ill. 1974, U.S. Dist. Ct (no. dist.) Ill. 1975, U.S. Ct. Appeals (7th cir.) 1975. With Baker & McKenzie, Chgo., 1974-81, ptnr. litigation, 1981-85, capital ptnr. litigation, 1985-94; ptnr. Mauck, Bellande & Cheely, Chgo., 1994—; liaison counsel Asbestos Claims Facility, Chgo., 1985-88, bus. devel. com., 1987-90, Chgo. assoc. train com., 1988-91, chmn. Chgo. assoc. evaluation; liaison coun. Com. for Claims Resolution, 1988-89. Advisor Midtown Sports and Cultural Ctr., Chgo., 1974—; mem. River Forest Regular Reps., Ill., 1980-88, Ill. Rep. Assembly, Chgo., 1984—; pres. Cath. Evidence Forum, 1984—; pres. Ch. History Forum, 1994—; dir. Cath. Citizens of Ill., 1997—. Mem. ABA (vice chmn. environ. law sect. 1989-97), Ill. Bar Assn., Appellate Lawyers Soc. Ill., Chgo. Bar Assn., Trial Lawyers Club. Chgo., Serra Club (v.p. Chgo. chpt. 1988-89, 92-94, 96-99, treas. 1989-92), Sidney Reilly Soc., United Rep. Fund, Phi Beta Kappa. Roman Catholic. Avocations: history, parent effectiveness training, education. Office: Mauck Bellande & Cheely 19 S La Salle St Ste 1203 Chicago IL 60603-1406

CHEESMAN, FREDERICK S., editor; b. Maple Shade, N.J., Sept. 23, 1945. BA, NYU, 1967, MBA, 1972. Editor Augustus M. Kelley Pubs., N.Y.C., 1982—. Office: Augustus M Kelley Pubs 1140 Broadway Rm 901 New York NY 10001-7504

CHEETHAM, ALAN HERBERT, paleontologist; b. El Paso, Tex., Jan. 30, 1928; s. Herbert and Hildegard Marguerite (Moreton) C.; m. Marjorie Rogers, Apr. 20, 1951; children: Alan Christopher, Jan Alison, Susan Hilarie, Hilary Taber. BS, N.Mex. Inst. Mining & Tech., 1950; MS, La. State U., 1952; PhD, Columbia U., 1959. Instr. paleontology La. State U., Baton Rouge, 1954-60, asst. prof., 1960-63, assoc. prof., 1963-66, cons. prof., 1966-72; assoc. curator Smithsonian Instn., Washington, 1966-69, curator, 1969-87, sr. invertebrate paleontologist, 1987—; guest prof. U. Stockholm, Sweden, 1964-65; adj. prof. U. N.Mex., 1994—. Author: Geological Society of America, Memoir 91, 1963; editor: Animal Colonies, 1973, Fossil Invertebrates, 1987; contbr. articles to profl. jours. Humble Oil Co. fellow, 1951; recipient Raymond C. Moore medal for paleontol., 1997, Disting. Achievement Alumni award N.Mex. Inst. Mining and Tech., 1990; NSF fellow, 1952, 61. Fellow AAAS; mem. Internat. Bryozoology Assn., Paleontol. Soc., Soc. Sedimentary Geology, Sigma Xi. Home: 6215 Winnebago Rd Bethesda MD 20816-3145 Office: Smithsonian Instn MRC NHB 121 Washington DC 20560-0121

CHEEVER, ALLEN WILLIAMS, pathologist; b. Brookings, S.D., June 4, 1932; s. Herbert E. and Margaret Haynes (Williams) C.; m. Jane Ellen Gilkerson, Aug., 1953; children: Carol, Erik, Laura, Angela. BS, Carleton Coll., 1954; MD, Harvard U., 1958. Diplomate Am. Bd. Pathology. Commd. 2d lt. USPHS, 1960, advanced through grades to capt., 1968; researcher NIH, Bethesda, Md., 1960-95; vol. investigator NIH, 1995—, Biomed. Rsch. Inst., Rockville, Md., 1995—. Contbr. articles to profl. jours. Capt. USPHS, 1960-95. Home: 4507 Conifer Ln Bethesda MD 20814-4009 Office: NIH Bldg 4 Rm 126 Bethesda MD 20892-0425

CHEEVER, GEORGE MARTIN, lawyer; b. Boston, Jan. 13, 1947; s. Francis Sargent and Julia Whitney (Martin) C.; m. Mary Margaret Duplain, Feb. 10, 1979; children: Charles Duplain, Frances Sargent, Mary Conner. AB, Harvard U., 1969; JD, U. Pa., 1973. Bar: Pa. 1973, U.S. Dist. Ct. (we dist.) Pa. 1973, U.S. Ct. Appeals (3d cir.) 1978, U.S. Ct. Appeals (4th cir.) 1985, U.S. Supreme Ct. 1992. Law clk. to assoc. justice Pa. Supreme Ct., Pitts., 1973-74; assoc. Kirkpatrick & Lockhart LLP, Pitts., 1974-82, ptnr., 1982—. Mem. ABA, Am. Bankruptcy Inst., Pa. Bar Assn., Allegheny County Bar Assn., Comml. Law League. Office: Kirkpatrick & Lockhart LLP 1500 Oliver Pittsburgh PA 15222-2312

CHEEVER, MEG, non-profit organization administrator; b. Boston, Apr. 10, 1949; d. Charles J. and Mary A. (Malloy) Duplain; m. George M. Cheever, Feb. 10, 1979; children: Charles, Frances, Mary. AB, Wellesley Coll., 1970; JD, Boston U., 1975. Bar: Pa. Assoc. Thorp, Reed & Armstrong, Pitts., 1975-78; gen. counsel QED Comm., Pitts., 1979-89, dir. corp. planning, 1989-91; publisher Pitts. Mag., 1991-97; pres. Pitts. Parks Conservancy, 1997—; pres. bd. Shenley Conservancy, 1996—; bd. mem. Regional Indsl. Devel. Corp., 1995—. Columnist Pitts. mag., 1992. Bd. mem. Pitts. History & Landmarks, 1997—, The Ellis Sch., Pitts., 1995—, Pitts. Ctr. for the Arts, 1994—; adv. bd. The Pitts. Symphony, 1996—; bd. mem. Greater Pitts. C. of C., 1992—. Named Person of Yr. in Comm., Vectors Pitts., 1996; recipient Leadership award in comm. Pitts. YWCA, 1995; recipient Gold medal City and Regional Mag. Assn., 1995. Mem. Mag. Pubs. of Am., Pitts. Women's Forum. Roman Catholic. Office: Pitts Parks Conservancy 3804 Forbes Ave Pittsburgh PA 15213-3506

CHEEVERS, JAMES WILLIAM, museum curator; b. Pittsfield, Mass., Feb. 15, 1942; s. Albert W. and Mildred (Guidi) C. BA, Coll. William and Mary, 1963. Curator 2d Inf. Divsn. Hist. Ctr., Ft. Benning, Ga., 1965-66, U.S. Army Inf. Mus., Ft. Benning, 1966-67; curator of collections U.S. Naval Acad. Mus., Annapolis, Md., 1967-71, sr. curator, 1971—, assoc. dir., 1982—. Bd. dirs. Annapolis Symphony Orch., 1985—, v.p. 1990-91, pres. 1991-94; mem. adv. bd. Md. Commn. on Afro-Am. History and Culture, 1985-90; bd. advisors Hist. Annapolis Found. and Mitchell Gallery, St. John's Coll., 1990—. With U.S. Army, 1964-66. Mem. Am. Assn. Mus., Mid-Atlantic Assn. Mus., Internat. Congress Maritime Mus., Chesapeake Bay Maritime Mus. Forum (chmn. 1979—), Internat. Inst. Conservation of Hist. and Artistic Works, Am. Inst. Conservation, Washington Conservation Guild, Nat. Maritime Hist. Soc., U.S. Naval Inst., Naval Hist. Found., Hist. Naval Ships Assn. N.Am. (exec. sec. 1985—), U.S. Naval Acad. Spkrs. Bur., Hist. Annapolis, Anne Arundel Bird Club (v.p. 1975-76, pres. 1976-78, 80-82, 85-87), Md. Ornithol. Soc. (pres. 1978-80, 82, 85-86, chmn. edn. com. 1984-90, coord. Md. breeding bird atlas project 1983-87), Nat. Audubon Soc., Audubon Naturalist Soc., Am. Birding Assn., N.Am. Bluebird Soc., Hawk Mountain Sanctuary Assn., Cape May Bird Obs., Am. Legion (past post vice-comdr. and adjutant), Friends of Annapolis Symphony, Internat. Club of Annapolis (exec. dir. 1978-81, pres. 1981-83). Democrat. Roman Catholic. Office: US Naval Acad Museum 118 Maryland Ave Annapolis MD 21402-1321*

CHEFITZ, JOEL GERALD, lawyer; b. Boston, Aug. 27, 1951; s. Melvin L. and Bernice L. (Kahn) C.; m. Sharon P. Garfinkel, June 18, 1972; children: Sandra Beth, Miriam Sarah, Michael Hanan. AB cum laude, Boston U., 1972, JD magna cum laude, 1976. Bar: Ill. 1976, U.S. Dist. Ct. (no. dist.) Ill. 1977, U.S. Ct. Appeals (3d cir.) 1981, U.S. Supreme Ct. 1983, U.S. Ct. Appeals (7th cir.) 1984, U.S. Ct. Appeals (9th cir.) 1993, U.S. Ct. Appeals (2d cir.) 1994, U.S. Ct. Appeals (5th cir.) 1996, U.S. Ct. Appeals (4th cir.) 1998. Law clk. to presiding justice U.S. Dist. Ct. Mass., Boston, 1976-77; assoc. Kirkland & Ellis, Chgo., 1977-82, ptnr., 1982-86; ptnr. Katten Muchin & Zavis, Chgo., 1986—. Editor Boston U. Law Rev., 1975-76; contbr. articles to law rev. Dir. Ida Crown Jewish Acad., Chgo., 1982. Am. Jurisprudence scholar Boston U., 1973-76, CJS scholar, 1975, Bigelow scholar, 1976. Mem. ABA, Chgo. Bar Assn., Seventh Cir. Bar Assn., East Bank Club. Office: Katten Muchin & Zavis 525 W Monroe St Ste 1600 Chicago IL 60661-3693

CHEH, HUK YUK, engineering educator, electrochemist; b. Shanghai, China, Oct. 27, 1939; s. Tze Sang and Sue Lan (Che) C.; m. An-li, July 26, 1969; children: Emily, Evelyn. BASc in Chem. Engring., U. Ottawa, Can., 1962; PhD in Chem. Engring., U. Calif., Berkeley, 1967. Mem. tech. staff AT&T Bell Labs., N.J., 1967-70; asst. prof. chem. engring. Columbia U., N.Y.C., 1970-73; assoc. prof. Columbia U., 1973-79, prof., 1979-82, Ruben-Viele prof., 1982—, chmn. dept., 1980-86; program dir. NSF, 1978-79; vis. rsch. prof. Nat. Tsinghua U., Taiwan, 1977. Mem. editorial adv. bd. Ency. of Phys. Sci. Tech.; mem. exec. adv. bd. Dictionary Sci. Tech.; contbr. articles to sci. jours.; patentee in biomaterials and in electrophoresis. Recipient Harold C. Urey award, 1980, sci. achievement award Am. Electroplaters and Surface Finishers Soc., 1989. Fellow Electrochem. Soc. (Electrodeposition Rsch. award 1988); mem. AIChE, Am. Electroplaters Soc., Sigma Xi. Office: Columbia U Dept Chem Engring New York NY 10027

CHEIT, EARL FRANK, economist, educator; b. Mpls., Aug. 5, 1926; s. Morris and Etta (Warshausky) C.; m. June Doris Andrews, Aug. 28, 1950; children: Wendy, David, Ross, Julie. BS, U. Minn., 1947, LLB, 1949, PhD, 1954. Research economist, prof. Sch. Bus. Adminstrn. U. Calif., Berkeley,

1960—; exec. vice chancellor U. Calif., 1965-69, dean Sch. Bus. Adminstrn., 1976-82, 90-91, dean emeritus Sch. Bus. Adminstrn., 1991—; dir. Inst. Indsl. Rels.; program officer in charge higher edn. and rsch. Ford Found., 1972-73; assoc. dir., sr. rsch. fellow Carnegie Coun. on Policy Studies in Higher Edn., 1973-75; sr. adv. con. Asian-Pacific econ. affairs Asia Found.; dir. CNF Transp., Inc., Shaklee Corp., Simpson Mfg. Corp. Author: The Useful Arts and the Liberal Tradition, 1975, The New Depression in Higher Education, 1971, Foundations and Higher Education, 1979; Editor: The Business Establishment, 1964. Trustee Chatham Coll., Pitts., 1975-85, Mills Coll., 1992—, Richmond (Calif.) Unified Sch. Dist., 1961-65, Russell Sage Found., N.Y.C., 1979-89; chmn. State of Calif. Wage Bd. for Agrl. Occupations, 1980—. Office: U Calif Haas Sch Bus Berkeley CA 94720*

CHEITEN, MARVIN HAROLD, writer, hardware manufacturing company executive; b. New Brunswick, N.J., Apr. 24, 1943; s. Samuel and Sarah (Peretzman) C. BA summa cum laude, Rutgers U., 1965; MA, Princeton U., 1967, PhD, 1971, AB (hon.), 1985. Ptnr. The Water Master Co., Highland Park, N.J., 1971-76, v.p., 1976-86, pres., 1986—. *Marvin Harold Cheiten believes that a work of literature is no different from a painting or a piece of music: the beauty and elegance of its form, as much as the importance or power of its subject matter, determine its artistic success. He is at least as interested in the structure of his writing as in his subject. If a piece of writing is not beautifully crafted, it may be informative or cogent but it is not a successful work of art.* Author: (plays) Trial by Fire, 1972, Queen Jane, 1976, The Vault, 1978, The Golden Spy, 1996, Chowder, She Wrote, 1996; (novella) The Long Hello, 1995, (essays) The Fate of Princeton Graduate School, 1991, Touching A Goddess, 1996, Two Voices In The Darkness, 1997, To The Millstone, 1997, Escape from Raritan Prep, 1998, (lyrics) The Inn Cabaret, 1978-80, Deborah, 1996, A Princess In Death, 1998; also short stories; mem. editl. bd. Princeton Alumni Weekly, 1983-87. Bd. dirs. Princeton Rep. Assn., 1972-74; bd. trustees Princeton Chamber Symphony, 1993—; bd. trustees Friends of Theatre Intime, 1996—. Mem. Assn. Princeton Grad. Alumni (gov. bd. 1973-88), Nassau Club, Campus Club, Dramatists Guild, Alliance L.A. Playwrights. Jewish. Office: The Water Master Co PO Box 1186 New Brunswick NJ 08903-1186

CHEITLIN, MELVIN DONALD, physician, educator; b. Wilmington, Del., Mar. 25, 1929; s. James Cheitlin and Mollie Budman; m. Hella Hochschild, July 4, 1952; children: Roger, Kenneth, Julie. AB, Temple U., 1950, MD, 1954. Intern, resident internal medicine Walter Reed Army Med. Ctr., Washington, 1954-59, cardiology fellow, 1959-60, chief cardiology, 1971-74; chief cardiology Madigan Army Med. Ctr., Tacoma, Wash., 1960-64, Tripler Army Med. Ctr., Honolulu, 1964-68, Letterman Army Med. Ctr., San Francisco, 1968-71; assoc. chief cardiology San Francisco Gen. Hosp., 1974-91, chief cardiology, 1991-97; prof. medicine U. Calif., San Francisco, 1974-97, prof. medicine emeritus, 1997—. Author: Clinical Cardiology, 1994; assoc. editor: Cardiology, 1988, rev. edit., 1993. Fellow ACP, Am. Coll. Cardiology. Democrat. Jewish. Home: 224 Castenada Ave San Francisco CA 94116-1445 Office: San Francisco Gen Hosp 1001 Potrero Ave San Francisco CA 94110-3594

CHELARIU, ANA RADU, library director; b. Bucharest, Romania, Nov. 19, 1946; m. Serban H. Chelariu; 1 child, Andrea. MA, U. Bucharest, 1972; MLS, Rutgers U., 1981. Indexer H. W. Wilson Co., N.Y.C., 1981-85; dir. Palisades Pk. (N.J.) Pub. Libr., 1981—. Mem. Soc. Romanian Studies, N.J. Libr. Assn. Christian Orthodox. E-mail: chelariu@bccls.org. Office: Palisades Pk Pub Libr 257 2d St Palisades Park NJ 07650

CHELBERG, BRUCE STANLEY, holding company executive; b. Chgo., Aug. 14, 1934; s. Stanlye Andrew and Josephine Marie (Mohn) C.; children: Stephen E., david M., Kimberly Anne. BS in Commerce, U. Ill., 1956; LL.B., 1958. Bar: Ill. 1958. Atty. Trans Union Corp., Chgo., 1958-64; asst. gen. counsel, 1964-68; pres. Getz Corp., San Francisco, 1968-71; v.p. Trans Union Corp., Chgo., 1971-78; pres., COO, 1978-81; sr. v.p. Whitman Corp. (formerly IC Industries, Inc.), Chgo., 1982-85; exec. v.p., 1985-92, chmn., CEO, 1992—, also bd. dirs.; bd. dirs. First Midwest Bank corp., Northfield Labs, Snap-On-Tools, Inc. Bd. dirs. Arlington Heights Pub. Sch. Dist. 25, Ill., 1974-83, higher edn. State Ill., 1988—. Mem. Ill. State Bar Assn., Chgo., Met. (Chgo.), World Trade (San Francisco). *

CHELBERG, ROBERT DOUGLAS, army officer; b. Ironwood, Mich., Sept. 1, 1938; s. Raymond Rodahl and Marion Dora (Watson) C.; m. Patricia Tobey, Aug. 21, 1962; children: Robert, Kathryn. BS, U.S. Mil. Acad., West Point, N.Y., 1961; MBA, N.Mex. State U., 1973. Commd. 2d lt. U.S. Army, 1961, advanced through grades to lt. gen., 1991, ret., 1993; various assignments in U.S., Europe, 1961-78; student Nat. War Coll., Ft. McNair, Washington, 1978-79; asst. dir. pers. adminstrn. and svcs. Office Asst. Sec. Def. for Mil. Pers. Policy, Washington, 1979-80, staff dir., dep. to dep. asst. sec. def., 1980-81; comdr. 528th Arty. Group, U.S. Army So. Europe Task Force, 1981-83; chief of staff, dep. comdg. gen. Ft. Jackson, S.C., 1983-86; asst. chief of staff, plans and policy Allied Forces So. Europe, 1986; exec. to supreme allied comdr. Europe, 1986-87, chief policy and programs br., policy div. Supreme Hdqrs., 1987-90; spl. asst. to supreme allied comdr. Europe for harmonization and verification Supreme Hdqrs., 1990; spl. advisor to sec.-gen. NATO, 1990-91; chief of staff U.S. European Command, Stuttgart, Germany, 1991-93; dep. dir. George C. Marshall European Ctr. for Security Studies, Garmisch, Germany, 1994-95; mng. dir. European region CUBIC Applications Inc., Stuttgart, Germany, 1995-98. Dist. commr. Transatlantic coun. Boy Scouts Am., Brussels, Belgium, 1987-90. Decorated DEF D.S.M., DEF Superior Svc. medal with oak leaf cluster, Army D.S.M., Legion of Merit, Bronze Star with four oak leaf clusters, 10 Air medals, Meritorious Svc. medal with oak leaf cluster; recipient Vet. of Yr. award VFW Post 3676, 1985, Outstanding Alumnus Svc. award Lake Superior State U., 1986, Army Exceptional Civilian Svc. award. Mem. Fedn. German-Am. Clubs (pres. 1994-96), Phi Eta Sigma, Phi Kappa Phi. Avocations: swimming, horses.

CHELIOS, CHRISTOS K, professional hockey player; b. Chgo., Jan. 25, 1962. Student, U. Wis. With Montreal Canadiens, 1981-90; defenseman Chgo. Blackhawks, 1990-99, Detroit Red Wings, 1999—; mem. NHL All-Rookie team, 1984-85, NHL All-Star 1st team, 1988-89, 92-93, NHL All-Star 2nd team, 1990-91, WCHA All-Star 2nd team, 1982-83. Recipient James Norris Meml. trophy, 1988-89, 92-93; named to NCAA All-Tournament Team, 1982-83, Sporting News All-Star first team, 1988-89, Sporting New All-Star second team, 1990-91, 91-92. Office: Detroit Red Wings 600 Civic Center Dr Detroit MI 48226*

CHELL, BEVERLY C., lawyer; b. Phila., Aug. 12, 1942; d. Max M. and Cecelia (Portney) C.; m. Robert M. Chell, June 21, 1964. BA, U. Pa., 1964; JD, N.Y. Law Sch., 1967; LLM, NYU, 1973. Bar: N.Y. 1967. Assoc. Polur & Polur, N.Y.C., 1967-68, Thomas V. Kingham Esq., N.Y.C., 1968-69; v.p., sec., asst. gen. counsel, dir. Athlone Industries Inc., Parsippany, N.J., 1969-81; asst. v.p., asst. sec., assoc. gen. counsel Macmillan Inc., N.Y.C., 1981-85, v.p., sec., gen. counsel, 1985-90; vice chmn., gen. counsel K-III Holdings, N.Y.C., 1990-92; vice chmn., gen. counsel, sec. Primedia Inc. (formerly K-III Comm. Corp.), N.Y.C., 1992—. Mem. Assn. of Bar of City of N.Y., Am. Soc. Corp. Secs. Home: 1050 5th Ave New York NY 10028-0110 Office: Primedia Inc 745 5th Ave Fl 23 New York NY 10151-0099*

CHELLAS, BRIAN FARRELL, retired philosophy educator, author; b. N.Y.C., Oct. 7, 1941; arrived in Can., 1976; s. Allen Farrell Chellas and Alison Lord (O'Brian) Boylston; m. Merry Elisabeth Morehouse, Dec. 30, 1962; 1 child, Anne Morehouse. BA cum laude with honors, Fla. State U., 1962; PhD in Philosophy, Stanford U., 1969. Instr. philosophy Fla. State U., Tallahassee, 1964-65; asst. prof. U. Pa., Phila., 1968-75; vis. prof. U. Uppsala, 1970; vis assoc. prof. philosophy U. Mich., Ann Arbor, 1975-76; assoc. prof. philosophy U. Calgary, Alta., Can., 1976-81, prof., 1981-97, prof. emeritus, 1997—, dean faculty humanities, 1984-89. Author: Chord Systems for the Guitar, 1968, The Logical Form of Imperatives, 1969, Modal Logic: An Introduction, 1980, Elementary Formal Logic, 1995; reviewer Math. Revs., Ann Arbor, Mich., 1975—; exec. editor Can. Jour. Philosophy, 1977-82; mem. editl. bd. Jour. Philos. Logic, 1981—. Woodrow Wilson fellow Stanford U., 1962-63, Stanford-Wilson dissertation fellow Stanford U., 1967-68; recipient NEH summer stipend U. Pa., 1974; Social Scis. and Humanities Rsch. Coun. Can. fellow, 1982-83. Mem. AAUP, Am. Philos. Assn., Assn. Symbolic Logic, Soc. Exact Philosophy (pres. 1982-840, So. Soc. for Philosophy and Psychology, Am. Fedn. Musicians, Fla. Philos. Assn., Phi Eta Sigma, Phi Kappa Phi, Phi Beta Kappa, Phi Sigma Tau.

CHELLE, ROBERT FREDERICK, electric power industry executive; b. New Brunswick, N.J., July 18, 1948; s. Robert and Frances (Brown) C.; m. Karen Ann Cederburg, Aug. 7, 1971; children: Robert, Pamela. BA, Bethany Coll., 1970; MBA, U. Dayton, 1972. Asst. contr. Tait Mfg. Co., Dayton, Ohio, 1972-73; pres. High Voltage Maintenance Corp., Dayton, Ohio, 1973—; bd. dirs. The Siebenthaler Co., Dayton; adv. bd. U. Dayton Sch. Bus., 1994—. Contbr. articles to profl. jours. Chmn. Dayton C. of C., 1993, County Corp., Dayton, 1995. Recipient Cert. Appreciation Montgomery County Commn., Dayton, 1984-85, Up and Comer award for engrng. City of Dayton, 1988. Mem. Nat. Elect. Testing Assn., Rotary (pres. 1984-85). Presbyterian. Avocations: yachting, fishing.

CHELLGREN, PAUL WILBUR, industrial company executive; b. Tullahoma, Tenn., Jan. 18, 1943; s. Wilbur E. and Kathryn L. (Berquist) C.; m. Sheila Mary McManus, Nov. 21, 1970; children: Sarah, Matthew, Jane. BS, U. Ky., 1964; MBA, Harvard U., 1966; diploma in devel. econ., Univ. Coll., Oxford, Eng., 1967. Assoc. McKinsey & Co., Washington and London, 1967-68; ops. analyst Office Sec. Def., Washington, 1968-70; adminstrv. asst. Boise Cascade Corp., Idaho, 1970-71; div. gen. mgr. Boise Cascade Corp., L.A., 1971-72; pres. Universal Capital Corp., Kansas City, Mo., 1972-74; exec. asst. to chmn. Ashland (Ky.) Inc., 1974-77; adminstrv. v.p. Ashland Chem. Co., Columbus, Ohio, 1977-78, group v.p., 1978-80; sr. v.p., group operating officer Ashland Inc., 1980-88; sr. v.p., CFO Ashland Oil Inc., 1988-92, pres., COO, 1992-96, pres., CEO, 1996-97, chmn., CEO, 1997—; bd. dirs. Ashland Inc., Arch Coal, Inc., PNC Bank Corp., U. Ky., Centre Coll., Medtronic, Inc. Sec.-treas. Am. Friends of Univ. Coll. Oxford, Inc.; bd. dirs., vice chmn. Nat. Found. Advancement in the Arts; bd. dirs. Found. for Tri-State Community, Marshall U. Found.; dir., trustee Taft Mus., Cin., Cin. Mus. Art. 1st lt. U.S. Army, 1968-70. Mem. Am. Petroleum Inst. (bd. dirs.), Nat. Petroleum Refiners Assn., Soc. Chem. Industry, Chem. Mfrs. Assn. (former dir.), Bus. Roundtable (policy com.), Univ. Ky. Fellows, Met. Club (Covington), Rolling Rock Club (Covington), Comml. Club (Cin.), Met. Club, Queen City Club (Cin.). Home: 817 Squire Lake Dr Villa Hills KY 41017-1337 Office: Ashland Inc PO Box 391 50 E Rivercenter Blvd Covington KY 41011-1683

CHELLINE, WARREN HERMAN, English educator, clergy member; b. Jonesport, Maine, Sept. 26, 1923; s. Herman Albert and Olive Viola (Yarwood) C.; m. Bonnibelle Nelson, Jan. 1, 1950 (dec. June 1991); 1 child, Eric Warren; m. Frances Nadine Woodside, Aug. 7, 1993. Student, Brown U., 1941-43; DD, Am. Div. Sch., 1956; BA, MA, U. Mo., 1969, 70; MPhil, PhD, U. Kans., 1979, 82. Cert. secondary education tchr., Mo., Kans. Clergy member Rev. LDS Ch., Independence, Mo., 1942—; prof. English lang. and lit. Mo. We. State U., St. Joseph, 1971-97, prof. emeritus English lang. and lit., 1997—; insp. U.S. Lighthouse Svc., 1997—. Author: John Milton and Roger Williams, 1982; contbg. editor Herald House Pubs., 1940-69; contbr. articles to profl. jours. Chmn. adv. bd. The Salvation Army, 1989—; bd. dirs. Boy Scouts Am., Can. and U.S.A., 1946— (Wood Badge award 1956, Silver Beaver award 1990), St. Joseph Pub. Libr., 1975—, St. Joseph Symphony, 1994—, Allied Arts Coun., 1995—. Chaplain USN, 1941-43. Named James E. West fellow, 1998. Mem. Am. Legion, Moila Shrine, Soc. Profl. Journalists, Milton Soc. Internat., Kiwanis Internat. (disting. lt. gov. 1982—), Am. Mason (32nd degree, chaplain 1988—). Avocations: clowning, lighthouses, circus lore, Scottish bagpipe band. Home: 421 N 25th St Saint Joseph MO 64501-2600 Office: 620 Francis St Saint Joseph MO 64501-1928

CHELSTROM, MARILYN ANN, political education consultant; b. Mpls., Dec. 5; d. Arthur Rudolph and Signe (Johnson) C. BA, U. Minn., 1950; LHD, Oklahoma City U., 1981. Staff asst. Mpls. Citizens Com. Public Edn., 1950-57; coord. policies and procedures Lithium Corp. Am., Inc., Mpls., N.Y.C., 1957-62; exec. dir. The Robert A. Taft Inst. Govt., N.Y.C., 1962-77, exec. v.p., 1977-78, pres., 1978-89, pres. emeritus, 1990—; polit. edn. cons., 1990—; pres. Chelstrom Connection, 1992—. Editor: Teaching the Excitement of Politics in America, 1984, Political Parties, Two Party Goverment and Democracy in United States, 1988. Active LWV, Mpls., 1950-60, N.Y.C., 1972—; charter mem. Citizens League Greater Mpls., 1952-60; del. White House Conf. on Edn., 1955; vice chmn. Minn. Women for Humphrey, 1954; treas. councilman Luth. Ch. Recipient Cert. of Recognition for Svc. to Mpls. Pub. Schs., Mpls. Citizens Com., 1957; named Town Topper, Mpls. Star, 1958. Mem. Am. Polit. Sci. Assn., Minn. Alumni Assn. (gov. N.Y. 1963—, pres. 1971-73, nat. dir. 1971-75), Minn. Alumni Club (Mpls.). Lutheran. Home: 9600 Portland Ave Minneapolis MN 55420-4564 Office: 155 E 38th St New York NY 10016-2660

CHEMA, THOMAS V., government official, lawyer; b. East Liverpool, Ohio, Oct. 31, 1946; s. Stephen T. and Dorothy Grace (McCormack) C.; m. Barbara Burke Orr, Aug. 15, 1970; children: Christine, Stephen. A.B., U. Notre Dame, 1968; J.D., Harvard U., 1971. Bar: Ohio 1971, U.S. Supreme Ct. 1977. Assoc. Arter and Hadden, Cleve., 1971-79, ptnr. 1979-85, 1989—; exec. dir. Ohio Lottery Commn., Cleve., 1983-85, Gateway Econ. Devel. Corp. Greater Cleveland, 1990-95; chmn. Pub. Utilities Commn. Ohio, Columbus, 1985-89; chmn. Ohio Bldg. Authority, 1990-96. Candidate for Ohio Senate, 1980; campaign mgr., Senator Howard M. Metzenbaum, 1976; co-chmn. task force on violent crime, Cleve., 1981-83; trustee Hiram Coll., 1994—, Cleve. Works, Inc., 1995—, Cleve. City Club, 1993-96, Sisters of Charity of St. Augustine Health Sys., 1994—, Historic Gateway Neighborhood, Inc., 1995—; dir. Transtechnology, Inc., 1992—, NuMed Home Health, Inc., 1993—, Fairport Funds, 1994—. Mem. ABA (adv. council), Nat. Assn. Regulatory Utility Commrs., Nat. Assn. State Lotteries (bd. dirs.), Greater Cleve. Bar Assn., Ohio State Bar Assn., Cleve. Legal Aid Soc., Ohio Legal Assistance Found. (chmn. 1996—), Electric Power Research Inst., Sr. Citizens Resources Inc. (trustee), Hospice Council No. Ohio (sec., trustee, legal counsel), Citizens League, NAACP, League Women Voters, Am. Soc. Pub. Adminstrs. Trustee, St. Ignatius High Sch., Prospect Vision, Inc., Downtown Devel. Coordinators Cleve. Found. Arch.. Democrat. Roman Catholic. Club: City (Cleve., trustee 1993—). Avocation: skiing. Home: 18580 Parkland Dr Cleveland OH 44122-3469 Office: Arter & Hadden 1100 Huntington Bldg Cleveland OH 44115

CHEMBERLIN, PEG, clergy, religious organization administrator; Ordained deacon Moravian Ch. of Am., 1982, consecrated presbyter, 1986. BA cum laude, U. Wis., Parkside; grad., United Theol. Sem. Twin Cities, 1982. Formerly dir. campus ministries, tchr., youth min., also outreach min., parish intern pastor; exec. dir. Minn. Coun. Chs., 1995—. Recipient Women of Excellence award Minn. Gov., 1994, NOVA Peace and Justice award, 1985. Office: care Minn Coun Chs 122 W Franklin Ave Minneapolis MN 55404

CHEMERS, ROBERT MARC, lawyer; b. Chgo., July 24, 1951; s. Donald and Florence (Weinberg) C.; m. Lenore Ziemann, Aug. 16, 1975; children: Brandon J., Derek M. BA, U. So. Calif., 1973; JD, Ind. U.-Indpls., 1976. Bar: Ind. 1976, Ill. 1976, U.S. Dist. Ct. (so. dist.) Ind. 1976, U.S. Dist. Ct. (no. and so. dists.) Ill. 1977, U.S. Ct. Appeals 7th cir.) 1977, U.S. Ct. Appeals (5th cir.) 1985. Assoc. Pretzel & Stouffer, Chgo., 1976-79, officer, 1979-81, dir., 1981—. Author: IICLE - Civil Practice, 1978, rev. edit. 1982, 87; IICLE Settlements, 1984. Mem. ABA, Ill. State Bar Assn., Chgo. Bar Assn., Def. Rsch. Inst., Ill. Def. Counsel, Appellate Lawyers Assn. Office: Pretzel & Stouffer One S Wacker Dr Chicago IL 60606

CHEMLA, DANIELS S., director, adult education educator. Dir. materials scis. divsn., advanced light source Lawrence Berkeley Nat. Lab, prof. physics U. Calif., Berkeley.

CHEMSAK, JOHN ANDREW, entomologist; b. Ambridge, Pa., Feb. 19, 1932; s. Andrew and Mary C.; m. Mary Ann McHenry, Sept. 19, 1959 (div. 1980); children: Sheryl, Laurie, John M.; m. Hatsue W. Katsura, Aug. 5, 1985. BS, Penn State U., 1954, MS, 1956; PhD, U. Calif, Berkeley, 1961. Rsch. entomolgist U. Calif., Berkeley, 1961-64, specialist in entomology, 1964-95, ret., 1995; rsch. assoc. Calif. Acad. Scis., San Francisco, 1965—. Editor jour. Pan-Pacific Entomologist, 1984-89. Fellow Calif. Acad. Scis.; mem. Pacific Coast Entomol. Soc. (pres. 1972-73), Coleopterists Soc. (coun. mem.). Avocations: stamp collecting, travel, sports. Office: Essig Mus of Entomol University of Calif Berkeley Berkeley CA 94720

CHEN, BASILIO, engineering executive; b. Panama, Republic of Panama, Mar. 10, 1953. BEE, Calif. State Poly. U., 1974. Engr. Nat. Inst. Tech., Panama, 1974, Wescom, Inc., Santa Clara, Calif., 1978-79; engrng. mgr. Rolm, Corp., Santa Clara, 1979-81; cons. Engrng. Mgmt. cons., Daly City, Calif., 1981—; pres. Evotech, Inc., Burlingame, Calif., 1984—; CEO Grand Battery Techs. Inc., 1984—. Life mem. Gway Sen Assn., San Francisco, 1990—; chmn. Pacific Rim econ. adv. coun. Calif. Rep. Com., 1997—. Mem. IEEE, Asian Am. Mfrs. Assn. (life), Eta Kappa Nu, Tau Beta Pi. Office: Evotech Inc 875 Cowan Rd Ste 203B Burlingame CA 94010-1204

CHEN, CARLSON S., mechanical engineer; b. Orange, N.J., Mar. 17, 1960; s. Kao and May Chen; m. Lynn Duong, Dec. 5, 1992; 1 child, Christopher D. BSME, Brown U., 1982; MBA, U. Pitts., 1987. Engr. Westinghouse Corp., Pitts., 1982-89; sr. engr. Gen. Dynamics, San Diego, 1989-91, GPS Techs., San Diego, 1991-93; sr. mech. engr. Nat. Steel & Shipbuilding, San Diego, 1993—. Contbg. author Standard Handbook of Powerplant Engineering, 1997. Active Brown Cmty. Outreach, 1979-80. Mem. ASME, Soc. Naval Architects & Marine Engrs. (publicity and meetings chmn. San Diego chpt.), Brown Club of San Diego. Office: Nat Steel & Shipbuilding Co Harbor Dr & 28th St San Diego CA 92186

CHEN, CHI (CHEN CHI), artist; b. Wusih, China, May 2, 1912; s. Shih-Pei and Shih Tsai C.; m. Alice Zu Min Huang, Oct. 5, 1962. Mem. faculty St. John's U., Shanghai, China, 1942-46, Pa. State U., 1959-60; artist in residence Ogden, Utah, 1967, Utah State U., 1971. First one-man exhbn. Shanghai, China, 1940; others at various U.S. museums and art galleries in N.Y.C., Boston, N.H., R.I., Conn., Vt., Maine, R.I., Fla., Ariz., Del., Phila., Allentown, Pa., Washington, Chgo., New Orleans, Iowa, Houston, Dallas, Fort Worth, San Antonio, Denver, Boulder, Colo., Seattle, San Francisco, L.A., San Diego, Columbus, Ga., Anchorage, Alaska, Okla., Kans., Mo., S.C., W.Va., Santa Fe, N.Mex., Youngstown, Ohio, Ogden, Utah, Logan, Utah, Wusih, Peking, Shanghai, Taipei, Tai-chung, China; retrospective exhbns. at Allentown Art Mus., 1963, Nat. Mus. History, Tai-Pei, Taiwan Mus. Art, TaiChung, 1988, Columbus Mus., 1989, Blandon Meml. Art Mus., Fordge, Iowa, Butler Inst. Am. Art, Youngstown, 1990, Gilcrease Mus., Tulsa, 1992, Nat. Arts Club, N.Y.C., 1993; group exhbns. include Met. Art Mus., AAAL, Whitney Mus. Am. Art, Bklyn. Mus., Pa. Acad. Fine Arts Phil., Springfield Art Mus., Mo., Contemporary Chinese Am. Artists, San Diego, County Mus. L.A., Corcoran Gallery, Washington, Butler Inst., Am. Art, Ohio, New Brit. Mus. Am. Art, Conn., numerous others; painter series Am. city scenes, Colliers, Olympic Winter Games, Squaw Valley, Sports Illustrated, also other publs.; works represented in permanent collections Met. Mus. Art, Pa. Acad., Nat. Acad., Butler Inst., Cleve., Allentown Mus., Charles & Emma Frye Mus., Washington, New Britain Mus. Conn., Columbus Mus. Ga., Nat. Mus. of History, Taipei, Taiwan Art Mus., Taichun, China Jiangsu Art Mus., Wuxi Art Acad. Shanghai Mus., China, IBM Corp., Ford Motor Co., Gen. Mills, numerous museums, univs., pvt. collections: jury selection and awards Butler Inst. Am. Art, Frye Mus., Seattle, Am. Watercolor Soc., Allied Artists, Audubon Artists, sole judge ann. N.W. Coast Art Exhibit, Seattle, Washington, Pitts., Birmingham, Ala., San Diego, Columbia, S.C., Wilmington, Del., Detroit, Anchorage, N.J., Conn., also others. Author: Watercolors by Chen Chi, 1942, China, Chen Chi Paintings, Switzerland, 1965, Two or Three Lines from Sketchbooks of Chen Chi, 1969, China from the Sketchbooks of Chen Chi, 1974, Chen Chi Watercolors, Drawings, Sketches, 1980, Chen Chi Watercolors, 1981, China, Heaven and Water-Chen Chi, 1983, Chen Chi Nat. Mus. History, Taiwan, 1988 (medal of honor 1988), East Meets West Chen Chi Watercolors, Columbus (Ga.) Mus., 1989; Chen chi retrospective Gilcrease Mus., Tulsa, 1992, Chen Chi retrospective exhbn. The Nat. Arts Club, N.Y.C., 1993, Heart and Chance Chen Chi Watercolor Paintings, 1993. Mem. Nat. Mus. of History, Taiwan, 1988. Recipient numerous awards, gold medals NAD, Am. Watercolor Soc., Nat. Arts Club, Salmagundi Club, Knickerbocker Artists, Audobon Artists, Phila. Watercolor Club; gold medal ann. watercolor exhbn. Nat. Arts Club, 1954, gold medal oil, 1954, Adolph and Clara Obrig prize NAD, 1955, Spl. $1000 award for watercolor 88th Exhbn. Am. Watercolor Soc., 1955; 1st watercolor prize, Butler Inst. Art, 1955, also Chautauqua Art Assn., 1955; Gold medal for Watercolor, 14th ann. Audobon Artists, 1956, spl. $1000 award 21st ann. exhbn.; $1500 grant Nat. Inst. Arts and Letters; gold medal honor, 47th ann. Allied Artists Am., 1960; Samuel Finley Breese Morse medal NAD, 1961; spl. award and medal Audubon Artists, 1963; John Singer Sargent Meml. award Springfield Art Mus.; medal honor Nat. Arts Club, 1966; 99th Ann. $600 Grand award and gold medal of honor Am. Watercolor Soc.; Winslow Homer Meml. award Watercolor U.S.A., Springfield Art Mus.; Gold Medal Honor, Nat. Arts Club, 1967, Audubon Artists, 1968; Thomas Hart Benton award, 1968, Saltus Gold medal or merit NAD, 1969, Silver medal Nat. Arts Club, 1970, Pres.'s award Audubon Artists, 1974, Benjamin West Clinedinst meml. medal, 1976, medal Acad. Western Art, 1990. Mem. NAD (William P. Schweitzer prize 1989), Am. Watercolor Soc. (hon., High Winds award 1972, 74, Bicentennial Gold medal 1976, Dolphin Fellowship medal 1990, Gold medal 1990, 91, inducted in the Cowboy Hall of Fame), Nat. Acad. Western Art, Nat. Arts Club (1st prize 1993), Audubon Artists, Allied Artists, Nat. Acad. Design, Century Club, Dutch Treat Club, Salmagundi Club. Clubs: Century, Dutch Treat, Salmagundi, Nat. Arts. Home: 23 Washington Sq N New York NY 10011-9169 Studio: 15 Gramercy Park S New York NY 10003-1705*

CHEN, CHING-CHIH, information science educator, consultant; b. Foochow, Fukien, China, Sept. 3, 1937; came to U.S, 1959; d. Han-chia and May-ying (Liu) Liu; m. Sow-Hsin Chen, Aug. 19, 1961; children: Anne, Catherine, John. BA, Nat. Taiwan U., Taipei, 1959; MLS, U. Mich., 1961; PhD, Case Western Res. U., 1974. Asst. Sch. Libr. Sci. U. Mich., Ann Arbor, 1960-61, svc. libr., 1961-62; sci. reference libr. McMaster U., Hamilton, Ont., Can., 1962-63, head sci. libr., 1963-64; sr. sci. libr. U. Waterloo, Ont., Can., 1964-65; head engrng., math. and sci. libr. U. Waterloo, Can., 1965-68; assoc. sci. libr. MIT, Cambridge, Mass., 1968-71; asst. prof. Sch. Libr. and Info. Sci. Simmons Coll., Boston, 1971-76, asst. dean for acad. affaris Sch. Libr. and Info. Sci., 1977-79, assoc. dean, prof. Sch. Libr. and Info. Sci., 1979-96, prof. sch. libr. and info. sci., 1979—; cons. Am. Soc. Info. Sci./Cath. U. Am., 1976-77, Chung-Shan Inst. Sci. Rsch., Taiwan, 1977-87, Abt Assocs., Inc., 1980-82, Sci. and Tech. Info. Ctr. Nat. Sci. Coun., Taiwan, 1973-77, S.E. Asia Region WHO, 1980, 81, Engring. Info. Inc., 1982, UNESCO, Paris, 1984, Nat. Geog. Soc., 1985, Norman Bethuen U. Med. Scis. Libr., 1986, Getty Trust, 1988, USIA, 1988, Ont. Coun. Gradual Studies, 1989, FID, 1989, World Bank, 1990, UNESCO, 1991, DataConsult, Mex., 1991, Soros Found., 1992-93, USIA, 1993-95, UN Devel. Program, 1997, Tsinghua U., Taiwan, 1997, Nat. Sci. Coun., Taiwan, 1998—; mem. Pres. Clinton's Presdl. Info. tech. Adv. Com., 1997—. Author, editor 27 books including Biomedical, Scientific and Technical Book Reviewing, 1976, Sourcebook on Health Sciences Librarianship, 1977, Quantitative Measurement and Dynamic Library Service, 1978, Scientific & Technical Information Sources, 2nd edit., 1987, (with others) Numeric Databases, 1984, HyperSource on Hypermedia/Multimedia Technologies, 1989, HyperSource on Optical Technologies, 1989, Optical Technologies in Libraries; Use & Trends, 1991, Planning Global Information Infrastructure, 1995; editor-in-chief: Microcomputers for Information Management, 1983-96; also editor numerous conf. procs.; contbr. over 150 articles to profl. jours. Barbour scholar U. Mich., 1959-61, Case Western Res. U. fellow, 1973-74, NATO fellow, 1975, AAAS fellow, 1985; Emily Hollowell Rsch. grantee, 1972—, Simmons Coll. Fund Rsch. grantee, 1972-81; recipient Disting. Svc. award Chinese-Am. Librs. Assn., 1982, Cert. of Appreciation, Asian-Pacific-Am. Librs. Assn., 1983, Disting. Alumni award U. Mich., 1983, Outstanding Svc. award Nat. Cen. Libr., 1986, Disting. Svc. award Asian-Am. Libr. Assn, 1992, Cindy award Assn. Visual Comm., 1992, Grazella Shepherd Meml. award for Excellence in Edn., Case Western Reserve U. Educator's Forum, 1999. Fellow AAAS; mem. ALA (disting. svc. award 1989, Humphrey award 1996), AAUP, Am. Soc. Info. Sci. (best Info. Sci. Tchr. award 1983), Assn. Am. Libr. Schs., Assn. Coll. and Rsch. Librs., Libr. Info. Tech. Assn. (Gaylord Libr. and Info. Tech. Achievement award 1990, Outstanding Achievement Libr. Hi Tech. award 1994), New Eng. Libr. Assn. (Emerson Greenaway award 1994), Assn. Libr. and Info. Sci. Edn. (1st Alise Pratt-Severn Nat. Faculty award 1997). Avocations: travel, stamp collecting. E-mail: echen@simmons.edu. Home: 1400 Commonwealth Ave Newton MA 02465-2830 Office: Simmons Coll 300 Fenway Boston MA 02115-5820

CHEN, CHUN-FAN, biology educator; b. Taipei, Taiwan, Republic of China, Mar. 20, 1937; came to U.S., 1973; s. Min-mei C.; married, June 20, 1969; children: Edith, Emma. MS, U. Mich., 1967, PhD, 1971. Asst. physiologist U. Mich., Ann Arbor, 1971; asst. scientist Dept. Physiology, U. Mainz, Fed. Republic of Germany, 1971-73; asst. prof. biology Fla. Internat. U., Miami, 1973-77, assoc. prof. biology, 1977—; chmn. state course numbering system Dept. Edn., Tallahassee, 1990—. Author: Oxygen Transport to Tissue, 1988; contbr. articles to Advanced Exptl. Medicine and Biology, Pfluger Archives, Nature. Recipient Excellence in Advising award Fla. Internat U., 1990, Excellence in Svc. award, 1992, Excellence in Teaching award, 1993. Mem. Am. Physiol. Soc., N.Am. Taiwanese Prof. Assn. Office: Fla Internat U Biology Dept University Pk Miami FL 33199

CHEN, CHUNGUANG, cardiologist; b. Fuging, Peoples Republic of China, Dec. 27, 1955; came to the U.S., 1989; s. Xiatong and Surong (Lin) C.; m. Kim Frances Cronin, Dec. 5, 1991; children: Sarah, Catherine. Student, Fujian Med. Coll., 1976-79; diploma, Chongging Med. U., 1981; MD, U. Hamburg, 1984. Resident Hamburg (Germany) U. Hosp., 1983-84; staff physician Hamburg U. Hosp., 1990-92; fellow in cardiology Freiburg (Germany) Univ. Hosp., 1985-86; attending physician, chief Fujian Med. Coll., Fuzhou, Peoples Republic of China, 1987-88; rsch. fellow Mass. Gen. Hosp., Boston, 1989-90, clin. and rsch. fellow, 1992-93; attending cardiologist Hartford (Conn.) Hosp., 1993—; dir. echocardiography Hamburg U. Hosp., 1990-92; assoc. dir. echocardiography Hartford Hosp., 1993—; asst. prof. medicine U. Conn., 1993—; assoc. prof. Fujian Med. Coll., 1988—; dir. echocardigraphy UMDNJ-N.J. Medicine Sch., 1998—. Contbr. articles to profl. jours. Named Best Young Investigator Chinese Assn. Sci. and Tech., 1988; recipient Rsch. awards Ministry of Sci., Peoples Republic of China, 1986, 87; rsch. grantee Alexander-von-Humboldt Found., 1988. Mem. Coun. on Clin. Cardiology, Am. Heart Assn., Am. Soc. Echocardiography. Avocation: table tennis. Office: Newark Beth Israel Med Ctr Cardiac Non-Invasive Lab 201 Lyons Ave Newark NJ 07112-8000

CHEN, DI, electro-optic company executive, consultant; b. Chekiang, China, Mar. 15, 1929; came to U.S., 1954, naturalized, 1972; s. Hsun Yu and chien (Wang) C.; m. Lynn C. Wang, June 14, 1958; children: Andrew A.J., Daniel T.Y. BS, Nat. Taiwan U., 1953; MS, U. Minn., 1956; PhD, Stanford U., 1959. Asst. prof. U. Minn., Mpls., 1959-62; rsch. fellow Honeywell Co., Bloomington, Minn., 1962-80; tech. dir. Optical Peripherals Lab., Colorado Springs, Colo., 1980-84; pres. Chen and Assocs. Cons., 1989—; v.p. tech. and engring. Literal Corp., Colorado Springs, 1990-91; chmn., then co-chmn., advisor, sr. advisor Optical Data Storage, 1983-98. Topical editor Applied Optics Jour., 1991-97; contbr. articles to profl. jours.; patentee in field. Recipient Honeywell Sweatt Scientists and Engrs. award, 1972. Fellow IEEE (chmn. IEEE-MAG Twin Cities chpt. 1974); mem. SPIE, Optical Soc. Am., Sigma Xi, Eta Kappa Nu. E-mail: 71611.3062@compuserve.com.

CHEN, EDEN HSIEN-CHANG, engineering consultant; b. Koachsiung, China, Mar. 1, 1954; came to U.S., 1976; s. Wen-Wu and Wen-Chian (Tien) C.; m. Marilyn L. Haugan, Jan. 18, 1982; children: Jessica, Joshua, Justin, Jerilyn. BS in Indsl. Engring., Chung Yuan U., 1976; MS in Indsl. Engring., N.D. State U., 1980. Sr. engr. Gen. Instruments, Kaohsiung, Taiwan, 1976-78, Litton Industries, Sioux Falls, S.D., 1980-86; engring. mgr. DICKEY-John Corp., Auburn, Ill., 1986-88, TRW, Marshall, Ill., 1988-90; prin. cons. CTI, Springfield, Ill., 1990—; adj. instr. George Washington U., Washington, 1989—, U. Wis., Madison, 1989, U. Dayton, 1996—; instr. Soc. Automotive Engrs., Warrendale, Pa., 1986—, Soc. Mfg. Engrs., Dearborn, Mich., 1989—. Chmn. Springfield Commn. Internat. Visitors, 1995-96, commr., 1992-97; advisor Ill. Staet Treas. Pat Quinn, Chgo., 1992-94, Overseas Chinese Affairs Commn., Taipei, Taiwan, 1995—. Office: CTI PO Box 9302 Springfield IL 62791-9302

CHEN, HSIN-HWA, education educator, researcher; b. Taoyuan, Taiwan, Aug. 19, 1957; d. Shu-Shen and Mei (Cheng) C. BA in English, Fu Jen Cath. U., Taipei, Taiwan, 1981; MA in Applied Linguistics, Ind. U., 1982; MA in Higher Edn., U. Iowa, 1996, PhD in Higher Edn., 1997. Instr. Chien-Hsin Jr. Coll., Chungli, Taiwan, 1983; exec. sec. Chung Shan Inst. Tech., Lungtan, Taiwan, 1983-89; lectr. Fu Jen Cath. U., Taipei, 1983-92, Chung Yuan Christian U., Chungli, 1983-93; rsch. asst. U. Iowa, Iowa City, 1994-96; instr. Yuan Ze U., Chungli, 1989-93, assoc. prof., 1997—. Author: The Big Ten: Activities for Intermediate and advanced EFL Classes, 1993. Recipient Outstanding Tchr. award Taiwan Ministry Edn., 1992, John Leonard Davies Meml. award Coll. Edn., U. Iowa, 1996; Mr. Chi-Ray Huang Found. scholar, 1993-96. Mem. Chinese Coll. Faculty Assn., English Tchrs. Assn. Taiwan, Am. Edn. Rsch. Assn. Avocations: cooking, philately, reading. Home: 30 Chien Kuo N Rd, Chungli 320, Taiwan Office: Yuan Ze U, 135 Yuang Tung Rd, Chungli 320, Taiwan

CHEN, I-WU, pharmaceutical researcher; b. Tainan, Republic of China, Apr. 30, 1943; came to U.S., 1978; s. Chiang Yao and Mei (Hsu) C.; m. Hsin Tsai, July 18, 1970; children: Wei-En, Chia-En. BS in Pharmacy, Taipei Med. Coll., 1970; MS in Clin. Chemistry, West Chester State U., 1984. Pharmacist Jan-Ai Mcpl. Bur., Taipei, 1970-75; reviewer Taipei Health Bur., 1975-78; lab. technician Longacre Poultry, Inc., Franconia, Pa., 1978-80; med. technician chem. and toxicology lab. Pa. Hosp., Phila., 1982-85; med. technologist enzyme lab. St. Christopher's Hosp. for Children, Phila., 1982-83; chemist, biochemist Wyeth Labs., Radnor, Pa., 1984-85; staff chemist Merck Sharp & Dohme Rsch. Labs., West Point, Pa., 1985-88, rsch. chemist, 1988-91, sr. staff rsch. assoc., 1991—. Contbr. articles to profl. publs. Mem. Am. Assn. Pharm. Scientists, Am. Chem. Soc. Office: Merck Rsch Labs Sumneytown Pike West Point PA 19486

CHEN, JAMES PAI-FUN, biology educator, researcher; b. Fengyuan, Taichung, Taiwan, May 1, 1929; came to U.S., 1952; s. Chuan and Su-wuo (Lin) C.; m. Metis Hsiu-chun Lin, Dec. 19, 1964; children: Mark Hsin-tzu, Eunice Hsin-yi, Jeremy Hsin-tao. BS, Houghton (N.Y.) Coll., 1955; MS, St. Lawrence U., 1957; PhD, Pa. State U., 1961. From instr. to assoc. prof. Houghton Coll., 1960-64; rsch. assoc. Coll. of Medicine U. Vt., Burlington, 1964-65; rsch. assoc. Sch. of Medicine SUNY, Buffalo, 1965-68; asst. prof. U. Tex. Med. Br., Galveston, 1968-75; sr. rsch. assoc. NASA/Johnson Space Ctr., Houston, 1975-76; rsch. assoc. prof. U. Tenn. Meml. Rsch. Ctr., Knoxville, 1976-78; assoc. prof. Coll. of Medicine U. Tenn., Knoxville, 1978-84, prof. Grad. Sch. of Medicine, 1984—; mem. rsch. rev. com. Tex. affiliate Am. Heart Assn., Austin, 1974-76; co-investigator Spacelab I project, Johnson Space Ctr., Houston, 1976-83; vis. prof. Trnovo Hosp. Internal Medicine, Ljubljana, Yugoslavia, 1985. Contbr. more than 40 articles to profl. jours. including Thrombosis and Haemostasis. Grantee Robert Welch Found., 1970-74, Ortho Rsch. Found., 1971-75, NIH, 1975-82, Am. Heart Assn. Tex. affiliate, 1969-72, 74-75, Am. Heart Assn. Tenn. affiliate, 1984-85, 89-90, U.S. Army Med. Rsch., 1988-91. Fellow Internat. Soc. Hematology; mem. Am. Assn. Immunologists, Am. Soc. Biochemistry and Molecular Biology, Internat. Soc. Thrombosis and Haemostasis, Internat. Fibrinogen Rsch. Soc., Internat. Soc. Fibrinolysis Proteolysis, Am. Bd. Bioanalysis (clin. lab. dir.). Achievements include research in thrombosis and hemostasis; discovery of additional proteolytic fragmentation in the high temperature trypsin cleavage of human IgM; development of a radioimmunoassay for fragment E-neoantigen and applied it to the clinical assay of hypercoagulable state; discovered evidence of the coagulopathy in Pichinde virus-infected guinea pigs; establishment of blood tests to monitor trauma patients for thromboembolism; recognized that hypercoagulability in preterm infants with intraventricular hemorrhage is associated with fibrinolytic shutdown. Office: U Tenn Med Ctr Dept Med Biology 1924 Alcoa Hwy Knoxville TN 37920-6999

CHEN, JOAN (CHEN CHONG), actress; b. Shanghai, China, Apr. 26, 1961; came to U.S., 1981; Appeared in films including Little Flower, 1978, Awakening, 1980, Dim Sum: A Little Bit of Heart, 1985, Tai-Pan, 1986, The Last Emperor, 1987, Night Stalker, 1987, Blood of Heroes, 1990, Turtle Beach, 1993, Where Sleeping Dogs Lie, 1993, The Joy Luck Club, 1993, On Deadly Ground, 1994, Golden Gate, 1994, Heaven and Earth, 1994, The Hunted, 1995, Judge Dredd, 1995, Wild Side, Precious Find; TV appearances include Twin Peaks, Miami Vice, (TV movie) Shadow of a Stranger; dir., prodr. XIU XIU: The Sent Down Girl, 1998. Office: 2601 Filbert St San Francisco CA 94123-3215*

CHEN, JOHN C., chemical engineering educator; b. Shanghai, China, Feb. 6, 1934; came to U.S., 1945.; s. L.F. and Rena (Tsao) C.; m. Katherine Lee, Oct. 9, 1960; children: Christopher, Lisa, Peter. BS in chem. engring., The Cooper Union, N.Y.C., 1956; MS in chem. engring., Carnegie Inst. of Tech., Pitt., 1959; PhD in chem. engring., U. Mich., 1961. Process engr. Lummus Co., 1956-58; rsch. chem. engr. Brookhaven Nat. Lab, Upton, N.Y., 1960-70; adj. prof. Polytech. Inst. of Bklyn., 1966-70, Stony Brook, N.Y.C., 1965-66; prof. mech. engr. Lehigh U., Bethlehem, Pa., 1970-81, Carl R. Anderson prof., 1981—; nat. chmn. Fluidization & Fluid Particle, 1994-97; exec. com. mem. Particle Tech. Forum. AIChE, 1993-95; dir. Am. Inst. of Chem. engring., 1994—; bd. dirs. Coun. for Chem. Rsch, 1985-88. Recipient Donald Q. Kern award AIChE, 1988, Alexander von Humbolt Sr. Rsch. award Humbolt Found., 1992, Max Planck Rsch. award Max Planck Soc., 1994, Heat Transfer and Energy Conversion Divsn. award AIChE, 1996. Achievements include seminal model for convective boiling, resulting in widely appied "Chen Correlation". Office: Lehigh U Dept of Chemical Engineering 316 Iacocca Hall Bldg 111 Bethlehem PA 18015*

CHEN, JOHN CALVIN, child and adolescent psychiatrist; b. Augusta, Ga., Apr. 30, 1949; s. Calvin H. Chen and Lora L. Liu. BA in History, Pacific Union Coll., 1971; MD, Loma Linda U., 1974; PhD in Philosophy, Claremont Grad. U., 1984; JD, UCLA, 1987. Bar: Calif. 1987, U.S. Dist. Ct. (ctrl. dist.) Calif. 1988; diplomate Am. Bd. Psychiatry and Neurology, Child and Adolescent Psychiatry. Resident in psychiatry Loma Linda U. Med. Ctr., 1975-77; fellow in child and family psychiatry Cedars-Sinai Med. Ctr., L.A., 1977-78; psychiat. cons. San Bernardino (Calif.) County Mental Health Dept., 1979-83; pvt. practice Claremont, Calif., 1980-84; fellow in child and adolescent psychiatry U. So. Calif., L.A., 1983-84; law clk. to Hon. William P. Gray U.S. Dist. Ct., L.A., 1987-88; mental health psychiatrist Los Angeles County Dept. Mental Health, L.A., 1988-94, Alameda County Health Care Svcs. Agy., Fremont, Calif., 1994-97; psychiat. cons. Edgewood Ctr. for Children and Families, San Francisco, 1996-97; physician specialist L.A. County Health Care Svcs. Agy., L.A., 1997—; attending physician Martin Luther King Jr. Hosp., L.A., 1997—; child and adolescent psychiatrist Augustus F. Hawkins Mental Health Ctr., L.A., 1997—, chief psychiatrist, child and adolescent clinic, 1998—; adj. instr. philosophy Fullerton (Calif.) Coll., 1989-90; adj. asst. prof. psychiatry Charles Drew U., 1998—; asst. clin. prof. psychiatry UCLA Sch. of Medicine, 1998—. Recipient Cert. Recognition L.A. County Mental Health Dept., 1993; univ. fellow Claremont Grad. Sch., 1980-81. Mem. ABA, Am. Philos. Assn., Chinese for Affirmative Action, Soc. for Exploration of Psychotherapy Integration, Chinese Hist. Soc. Am., Calif. Hist. Soc., Chinese Hist. Soc. So. Calif., So. Calif. Chinese Lawyers Assn. Office: 745 E Valley Blvd # 120 San Gabriel CA 91776-3549

CHEN, JOHN SHAOMING, architecture educator; b. Tianjin, China, Nov. 8, 1935; came to U.S., 1980; s. Yu Chu and Yu Xian (Mai) C.; m. Hui Fang Mai; children: Bin, Lian. Diploma, Tianjin U., 1962; MArch, U. Calif., Berkeley, 1983. Registered architect, D.C., Md., Va., N.Y. Designer in charge 3d Design Inst., Ministry Peoples Republic of China, Tianjin, 1962-80; architect Clement, Chen & Assoc., San Francisco, 1980-82; sr. designer Group 5 Architects, San Francisco, 1983-84, AEPA Architects, Washington, 1984-86, DNC Architects, Rockville, Md., 1986-87; assoc. prof. Howard U., Washington, 1987—; cons. Harry Weese & Assoc., Washington, 1987, Keyes Condon Florance, Washington, 1995-97; project designer Bryant Assoc., Washington, 1983-85. Author: Architecture in Pen & Ink, 1995, Architectural Perspective Grids, 1996, Architecture in Color Drawings, 1997; prin. works include MCI Ctr. Arena, Washington, Barney Cir. Bridge, Washington, China Cinema City, Shenzhen, Prosperity Metro Ctr., Va., others. Recipient AIA Award of Excellence, 1998, grants for 2 funds for acad. excellence, fall 1997, spring 1998 Howard U.; McGraw Hill grantee, 1994, 95, 96; Howard U. grantee, 1997, 99. Mem. AIA, Design Commn. Assn. (charter mem.), Am. Soc. Architectural Perspectives. Office: Howard Univ Washington DC

CHEN, JOIE, cable news anchor. B of Journalism, Northwestern U., M of Journalism. Reporter Sta. WCIV-TV, Charleston, S.C.; from reporter to anchor Sta. WXIA-TV, Atlanta; host CNNI World News, Atlanta; co-host CNN Saturday Morning News and CNN Sunday Morning News, Atlanta, 1994-96; co-anchor The World Today, CNN. Office: c/o CNN 1 CNN Ctr PO Box 105366 Atlanta GA 30348-5366*

CHEN, JOSEPH TAO, historian, educator; b. Shanghai, China, Jan. 30, 1925; came to U.S., 1951, naturalized, 1964; s. Hung Chun and Wei Tseng (Sze) C.; m. Lucy Zhu; children: Barbara Joanne, Cynthia Anne. B.A., Coll. Emporia, Kans., 1953; M.A., U. Calif., Berkeley, 1958, Ph.D., 1964. Head librarian Center for Chinese Studies U. Calif., Berkeley, 1963-64; asst. prof. history Calif. State U., Northridge, 1964-68; asso. prof. Calif. State U., 1968-71, prof., 1971—; guest lectr. history U. Calif., Santa Barbara, 1970-73, Immaculate Heart Coll., Los Angeles, 1965-79. Author: The May Fourth Movement in Shanghai, 1971, (transl. into Chinese), 1981; contbr. articles to profl. jours. Served with Chinese Navy, 1944-45. Grantee Social Sci. Research Council; Grantee Am. Philos. Soc.; Grantee Calif. State U. Found., Northridge; asso. Danforth Found. Mem. Assn. Asian Studies. Office: Calif State U Dept History Northridge CA 91330 *In this great land of America, with unfailing faith, perseverance and hard work, one has the ability and the power to influence and determine one's own destiny.*

CHEN, KAO, consulting electrical engineer; b. Shanghai, China, Mar. 21, 1919; came to U.S., 1947; s. Chi-son and Wei C. (Hsu) C.; m. May Yee Yoh, Nov. 14, 1948; children: Jennifer H., Arthur B., Carlson s. BSEE, Jiao Tong U., Shanghai, 1942; postgrad., Brit. Industries scholar, Rugby, Eng., 1945-47; MSEE, Harvard U., 1948; postgrad. degree in Elec. Engring., Poly. U., 1953. Registered profl. engr., N.J., N.Y. Relay specialist Am. Gas & Electric Co., N.Y.C., 1950-52; project supr. Ebasco Internat., N.Y.C., 1953-55; sr. project engr. Westinghouse Electric Corp., Bloomfield, N.J., 1956-67, fellow engr., 1968-83; fellow engr., cons. N.Am. Philips Lighting Corp., Bloomfield, N.J., 1983-86; pres. Carlsons Cons. Engrs., San Diego, Calif., 1987—; vis. prof. Fudan U., 1982; cons. in field. Author: Industrial Power Distribution and Illuminating Systems, 1990, Energy Effective Industrial Illuminating Systems, 1994; editor-in-chief Std. Handbook Powerplant Engring., 1997, Energy Management in Illuminating Systems, 1999; contbr. chpts. to 3 engring. handbooks, 6 IEEE stds., over 95 articles and papers to profl. jours.; patentee in field. Exec. PTA, Cedar Grove, N.J., 1960-62; exec. Essex coun. Boy Scouts Am., West Orange, 1966-70; mem. Repub. Presdl. Task Force, 1989—. Recipient Rep. Presdl. award, 1994. Fellow IEEE (life fellow, del. to visit China 1982, vice chmn. indsl. utilization sys. dept. 1981-84, chmn. 1985-87, chmn. prodn. and application of light com. 1983-84, mem. new stds. com. 1985-86, IEEE rep. to IEC TC34 lamps and related equipment 1997—, Soc. best paper awards 1981, 83, Centennial medal 1984, IEEE-IAS award of merit 1985, Richard Harold Kaufmann award 1992, IEEE-IAS Disting. Lectr. 1996-97, IAS Recognition award to disting. lect. 1997, RAB Larry K. Wilson transnational award 1998), Power Engring. Soc. (energy engring. seminar leader 1991), Industry Applications Soc. (mem. transactions adv. bd. 1981-84); mem. NSPE (life), Assn. Energy Engrs., Illuminating Engring. Soc. (emeritus), U.S. Nat. Com. of the Internat. Commn. on Illumination, Am. Biog. Inst. (rsch. bd. advisors, Commemorative Medal of Honor 1987), Energy Svcs. Mktg. Soc. (charter), Jiao Tong Alumni Assn. (v.p. 1962-63), Harvard Club (N.J., sch. com. 1975-83), Harvard Club (San Diego). Achievements include research and development in energy management of industrial power and illuminating systems. Home: 11816 Caminito Corriente San Diego CA 92128-4550 *Honest and hard work is the surest way to success. To be able to leave a small imprint of success on this earth can be the most satisfying life goal.*

CHEN, KEVIN SANGONE, corporate executive, consultant; b. Dover, N.J., Aug. 17, 1960; s. Irving Sangone and Judy (Moy) C.; m. Peggy Eng, June 2, 1990. BS, Stevens Inst. Tech., Hoboken, N.J., 1984, MS, 1988. Purchase parts planning mgr. Rowe Internat. Inc., Whippany, N.J., 1984-86; materials mgr. KDI/Triangle Electronics, Whippany, 1986-90; prodn. control supr. Micron Powder Systems, Summit, N.J., 1990-93; CEO, pres. Business Methods Cons., Cedar Knolls, N.J., 1989—; bd. dirs. Pres. Bus. Methods Corp., Randolph, N.J.; bd. dirs., v.p. CBM Co., 1998—; NBCC registered and cert. profl. cons. to mgmt., 1993—, adv. coun., 1993-97. *With a blend of perseverance and creative use of career experiences, Kevin Chen has had a history of establishing successful ventures in business and in society. Business Methods Consultants, Business Methods Corporation and Custom Scholarship Search were all founded, established and developed under the guidance and leadership of Kevin Chen. Key contributions to society have been in the establishment and development of special first time events and programs for the American Diabetes Association (NJ), Township of Randolph (NJ), Stevens Alumni Association (NJ), County College of Morris (NJ), and Morris Center YMCA (NJ).* Vice chmn., chmn. spl. events, chmn. survey subcom. Randolph Township Environ. Com., 1985-89; pres. Custom Scholarship Search Program, 1991-94; rsch. bd. advisors Am. Biog. Inst., 1992—; C.C.M. instr., 1996—, A.D.A. walk chair, 1993-96, bd. dirs., 1995-97, mem. N.W. regional coun., 1993-97; racquetball events coord. Stevens Alumni Assn., 1994—. Avocations: racquetball, team sports. Home: PO Box 520 Mount Freedom NJ 07970-0520 Office: Business Methods Corp 503 State Route 10 Randolph NJ 07869-2152

CHEN, KUN-MU, electrical engineering educator; b. Taiwan, China, Feb. 3, 1933; came to U.S., 1957, naturalized, 1969; s. Tsa-Mao and Che (Wu) C.; m. Shun-Shun Chen, Feb. 22, 1962; children—Margaret, Katherine, Kenneth, George. B.S., Nat. Taiwan U., 1955; M.S., Harvard, 1958, Ph.D., 1960. Research asso. U. Mich., 1960-64; vis. prof. Chao-Tung U., Taiwan, 1962; asso. prof. elec. engring. Mich. State U., 1964-67, prof., 1967-95; Richard M. Hong Endowed prof. elec. engring. Mich. State U., Lansing, 1995—; dir. elec. engring. grad. program Mich. State U., 1967-70; vis. prof. Tohoku U., Japan, 1989, Nat. Taiwan U., 1989. Author articles on electromagnetic radiation, plasma physics, electromagnetic bioeffects. Recipient Disting. Faculty award Mich. State U., 1976, Outstanding Achievement award in sci. and engring. Taiwanese Am. Found., 1984; Withrow Disting. scholar Coll. Engring., Mich. State U., 1993; C.T. Loo fellow, 1957; Gordon McKay fellow, 1958-60. Fellow IEEE, AAAS; mem. Internat. Union Radio Sci. (commn. A, B and C), AAUP, Sigma Xi, Phi Kappa Phi, Tau Beta Pi. Home: 4433 Comanche Dr Okemos MI 48864-2071 Office: Mich State U Dept Elec Engring East Lansing MI 48824

CHEN, LEILEI, ophthalmologist; b. Jiaxing, Zhejiang, China, July 13, 1972; s. Qibao Chen and Haie Cai; m. Yimin She, Feb. 12, 1998. MD, Shanghai (China) Med. U., 1994; postgrad., Wayne State U. Ophthalmologist Shanghai Eye Inst., 1994-96, Wayne State U., Detroit, 1996—. Cons. Jour. Injuries and Occupl. Diseases of the Eye with Ophthalmia; contbr. articles to profl. jours. Named Outstanding Rschr., Nat. Edn. Commn., China, 1995, Thomas C. Rumble U. Grad. fellow, 1999; recipient Midwest Eye-Banks and Transplantation Ctr. award, 1999. Mem. Assn. for Rsch. in Vision and Ophthalmology, Material Sci. and Chemistry Contact Lenses, Chinese Med. Assn. (sr.). Avocations: travel, swimming, golfing, jogging. E-mail: leichen@med.wayne.edu. Fax: 313-832-6339. Home: PO Box 1692 Warren MI 48090 Office: Wayne State U Sch Medicine Dept Anatomy/Cell Biology 540 E Canfield Detroit MI 48201

CHEN, LI, computer scientist, software engineer; b. Lishui, Jian Su, China, Apr. 23, 1961; came to U.S., 1991; s. Zhengxi and Suqin (Wang) C.; m. Lan Zhang, Apr. 18, 1987; 1 child, Boxi. BS, Wahan (China) U., 1982; MS, Utah State U., 1995. Asst. engr. Rsch. Inst. of Geophys. Prospecting, Nanjing, China, 1982-85; lectr. Nanjing Inst. Tech., 1985-89, Wuhan U., 1989-91; sr. software engr. Spiricon, Inc., Logan, Utah, 1994—; prin. rsch. scientist Sci. and Practical Computing Lab., North Logan, 1997—; adj. assoc. prof. Wuhan U., China, 1997—. Contbr. articles to profl. jours. and internat. confs. Recipient Award Rsch. Fund of Chinese Acad. Sci. for Young Scientists, 1987, 2d Class award Chinese Min. Geology, 1991; named Outstanding Scientist of Wuhan U., 1991. Achievements include definition of gradually varied surfaces and interpolation algorithms; the definition of general discrete manifolds and the classification of digital surface points; optimal algorithm for optimal minimum odd-weigh-column SEC-DED code's check matrix; inventor fuzzy sub-fiber, possibility-based neural networks. Avocation: Chinese flute. Office: Scientific & Practical Computing Lab PO Box 6081 North Logan UT 84341

CHEN, LIPING, molecular biologist, researcher, biochemist; b. Fuzhou, Fujian, China, Jan. 14, 1955; came to U.S., 1989; d. Yueming and Yihua (Ye) C. *Father Yueming Chen was born on October 21, 1909. He studied Traditional Chinese Medicine from 1925-28, and Medicine from 1928-34, received his MD in Medicine from Beiping University in 1934 and a PhD from Kyushu Empire University, Japan, in 1937. He started and edited Beiping Medical Journal, 1931-37. He wrote 2 books: Diagnoses and Treatment in Internal Medicine, 1934, 35 and Emergency Medicine, 1935. From 1938-49, he taught internal medicine in different provinces. From 1949-58 he was the dean and vice president of Fujian Medical College, China. For politcal reason, from 1958-66 he became vice-chairman of the college library. He died June 4, 1966 at the beginning of the Chinese Culture Revolution.* MD, Fujian Med. Coll., Fuzhou, 1983; PhD in Biomed. Scis., Kent State U., 1993. Asst. lectr. in pharmacology Fujian Med. Coll., 1983-88; resh. assoc. in molecular biology NEOUCOM, Rootstown, Ohio, 1991-93; rsch. scientist Gentest Corp., Woburn, Mass., 1993-94; rsch. fellow, immunology, molecular biology NIH, Nat. Inst. Allergy and Infectious Diseases, Bethesda, Md., 1994-97; rsch. fellow biochemistry, molecular biology HIH, Nat. Inst. Diabetes & Digestive & Kidney Diseases, 1997—; cons. NIH Grant, Rootstown, Ohio, 1996—. Contbr. articles to profl. jours. Mem. AAAS, Am. Assn. Cancer Rsch., Am. Chem. Soc. Achievements include: co-developed procedures that identified first P450 with increased expression level in rat hepatic tumors; started new P450 subfamily; patent in process. Developed coexpression of P450 and oxidoreductase in baculovirus sys. by noticing that as a cofactor of P450s, oxidoreductase also degrades P450s; first study of interactions between purine receptor and ligands using surface plasmmon resonance. Avocations: music, reading, sports, collecting. Office: NIH NIDDK Bldg 8 Rm B1A-23 Bethesda MD 20892

CHEN, MEI-QIN, mathematics educator; b. Mar. 26, 1956. BS in Math., Ea. Ill. U., Charleston, 1983; MS in Math., U. Ill., 1985, PhD in Math., 1989. Assoc. prof. math. The Citadel, Charleston, S.C., 1989—. E-mail: chenm@citadel.edu. Office: The Citadel Dept Math 171 Moultrie St MSC 111 Charleston SC 29409-0002

CHEN, MO-SHING, electrical engineering educator; b. Chekiang, China, Aug. 20, 1931; married 1959; 2 children. BS, Nat. Taiwan U., 1954; MS, U. Tex., 1958, PhD in Elec. Engring., 1962. Elec. engr. Taiwan Power Co., 1954-56; from asst. prof. to assoc. prof. U. Tex., Arlington, 1962-69, prof. elec. engring., dir. Energy Sys. Rsch. Ctr., 1969—; cons. in field. Recipient Power Engring. Educator award Edison Elec. Inst., 1976, Halliburton Rsch. award, 1983. Fellow IEEE (Centennial award 1984); mem. Am. Soc. Engring. Edn. (Western Elec. award 1977). Achievements include research in electric power generation, transmission and distribution; system analysis; computer applications; power system load modeling and voltage reduction research. Office: U Tex Arlington Energy System Research Ctr PO Box 19048 Arlington TX 76010*

CHEN, PETER PIN-SHAN, electrical engineering and computer science educator, data processing executive; b. Taishan, Kwangtung, China, Jan. 3, 1947; came to U.S., 1969; s. Man-See and T.T. Chen; m. Li-Chuang Ho; children: Victoria, Angela, Gloria Lily. BSEE, Nat. Taiwan U., Republic of China, 1968; MS, Harvard U., 1970, PhD, 1973. Student assoc. IBM, Yorktown Heights, N.Y., 1970; teaching fellow Harvard U., Cambridge, Mass., 1970-71; prin. engr. Honeywell, Waltham, Mass., 1973-74; vis. researcher Digital Equipment Corp., Maynard, Mass., 1974; asst. prof. MIT, Cambridge, Mass., 1974-78; assoc. prof. UCLA, 1978-82; Sinclair vis. prof. MIT, 1986-87; Foster Disting. Chair prof. La. State U., Baton Rouge, 1983—; vis. prof. Harvard U., Cambridge, 1990, MIT, Cambridge, 1990-92; chmn. Chen & Assocs. Inc., Baton Rouge, 1978—; pres. ER Inst., Baton Rouge, 1980—. Author: ER to Logical DB Design, 1978, ER to Systems Analysis, 1980, ER to Information Modeling, 1983; patentee in field. Tech. officer with Republic of China mil. svcs., 1968-69. Recipient faculty career award UCLA, 1979, Info. Tech. award Data Adminstrn. Mgmt. Assn., 1990; NSF rsch. grantee, 1978—. Fellow IEEE, Assn. for Computing Machinery. Office: La State Univ Computer Sci Dept Baton Rouge LA 70803

CHEN, PETER WEI-TEH, mental health services administrator; b. Fuchow, Fukien, Republic of China, July 20, 1942; came to U.S., 1966; s. Mao-Chuang and Sheu-Lin (Wang) C.; m. Lai-Wah Mui, Nov. 8, 1969; children: Ophelia Mei-Chuang, Audrey Mei-Hui. BA, Nat. Chung Hsing

U., Taipei, Taiwan, Republic of China, 1964; MSW, Calif. State U., Fresno, 1968; D of Social Work, U. So. Calif., 1976. Case worker Cath. Welfare Bur., L.A., 1968-69; psychiat. social worker L.A. County Mental Health Svcs., 1969-78, mental health svcs. coordinator, 1978; sr. rsch. analyst Jud. and Legis. Bur. L.A. County Dept. Mental Health, 1978-79; Forensic In-Patient Program dir. L.A. County Dept. Mental Health, 1979-86, chief Jail Mental Health Svcs., 1986-89, asst. dep. dir. Adult Svc. Bur., 1989, dir. cmty. care programs, 1989—; clin. prof. dept. psychiatry Harbor/UCLA Med. Ctr., 1997—; pres. Orient Social and Health Soc., Los Angeles, 1973-75; bd. dirs. Am. Correctional Health Assn., 1986-87. Author: Chinese-Americans View Their Mental Health, 1976. Bd. dirs. San Marino (Calif.) Cmty. Chest, 1986-87; trustee San Marino Schs. Found., 1987-90; advisor San Marino United Way, 1989-92, AIDS Commn. L.A. County, 1993; founder, chmn. Chinese Sch. of San Marino, 1998—. 2d lt. Chinese Marine Corps, Taiwan, Republic of China, 1964-65. Recipient several cmty. svc. awards, 3 spl. awards Nat. Assn. County Orgn. Mem. Nat. Assn. Social Workers (bd. dirs. Calif. chpt. 1979-80), Nat. Correctional Health Assn., Forensic Mental Health Assn. Calif., L.A. World Affairs Coun., Chinese Am. Profl. Soc. (pres. 1997-98, chmn. bd. dirs. 1998—). Clubs: Chinese of San Marino (pres. 1987-88), San Marino City. Avocations: sports, fishing, bridge. Home: 2161 E California Blvd San Marino CA 91108-1348 Office: LA County Dept Mental Health 155 N Occidental Blvd Los Angeles CA 90026-4641

CHEN, PHILIP MINKANG, investment banker, corporate executive, lawyer, engineer; b. Chungking, Szechuan, China, Oct. 20, 1944; s. Yin Ching and Wansu (Wu) C.; m. Deborah Lynn Carlson, May 7, 1971; children: Martin, Emily. BME with distinction, U. Va., 1968; MS, Stanford U., 1969; JD, U. Minn., 1979. Bar: Minn. 1979, U.S. Dist. Ct. Minn. 1979, N.Y. 1982; registered profl. engr. Va., N.Y.; diplomate Am. Acad. Environ. Engrs., 1996. Copy boy Washington Star Newspaper, 1962-65; mech. engr. Pope, Evans & Robbins, Alex, Va., 1967-68; engr. Westinghouse Orec, Annapolis, Md., 1969-71; sr. environ. engr. Stone & Webster Engring. Corp., Boston, Denver, 1971-78; sr. engr. Dames & Moore, Denver, 1978; assoc. Dorsey & Whitney, Mpls., 1979-82, Mudge, Rose, Guthrie & Alexander, N.Y.C., 1982; mng. dir. Lehman Bros., N.Y.C., 1982-92; pres. Weston Internat., 1992-94; exec. v.p. Roy F. Weston, Inc., West Chester, Pa., 1992-94; investment banker The Chase Manhattan Bank, N.A., N.Y.C., 1995-96; mng. dir. South Africa Infrastructure Fund, Johannesburg, 1996—; editl. adv. bd. American City and County Mag., 1986-87, Project Finance Monthly, 1989-92; mem. environ. technologies trade adv. com., Dept. Commerce, 1995-96, co-chmn. fin. subcom. Patentee for mooring system. Mem. Town Mtg. Winchester, Mass., 1973; past bd. dirs. U.S. Environ. Tech. Export Coun., Greater Phila. Internat. Network, Greater Phila. First Ptnrship. for Econ. Devel.; mem. The Union League of Phila.; participant Presdl. Bus. Devel. mission to Brazil, Argentina, and Chile, 1994. Mem. ABA (vice chmn. elec. power com. natural resources law sect. 1982-85, chmn. spl. com. on energy fin. 1988-89), ASME, Nat. Resource Recovery Assn. (adv. bd. U.S. conf. of mayors 1989), U. Va. Alumni Assn., Phi Sigma Kappa. Avocations: art, writing, fishing. Office: PO Box 61344, Marshalltown 2107, South Africa

CHEN, PHILIP S., JR., government official; b. St. Johns, Mich., July 3, 1932; s. Philip Stanley and Helen Y.C. (Feng) C.; m. Inger Lise Rasmussen, Apr. 2, 1955; children: Bodil Lynn Chen Morris, Iver Allan. B.A., Clark U., 1950; Ph.D., U. Rochester, 1954. Sr. asst. scientist Nat. Heart Inst. NIH, Bethesda, Md., 1956-59; asst. prof. radiation biology, biophysics and pharmacology U. Rochester, N.Y., 1959-67; grants assoc. NIH, 1967-68, spl. asst., br. chief Office Program Planning and Evaluation, 1968-72, assoc. dir. program planning and evaluation Nat. Inst. Gen. Med. Scis., 1972-74, assoc. dir. intramural affairs, 1974-97, sr. advisor to the dep. dir. for intramural rsch., 1997—; bd. dirs. NIH Fed. Credit Union, 1986-92; chmn. Patent Policy Bd., 1987-92; bd. dirs. Brooke Grove Found., Inc. Co-author: Biological Effects of Organic Fluorides, 1963; contbr. articles to profl. jours. Trustee Atlantic Union Coll., South Lancaster, Mass., 1986-92; bd. dirs. Found. for Advanced Edn. in Scis., Bethesda, 1982-91. Served to capt. USPHS, 1956-59. Recipient NIH Dirs. award, 1976, USPHS award, 1978, Disting. Svc. award DHHS, 1993; AEC predoctoral fellow, 1951-53, NSF postdoctoral fellow, 1954-55, Guggenheim Found. fellow, 1966-67. Mem. Am. Physiol. Soc., Am. Chem. Soc., Radiation Research Soc., Sigma Xi. Avocations: music; auto mechanics; skiing; travel. Home: 10093 Dudley Dr Ijamsville MD 21754

CHEN, SHOEI-SHENG, mechanical engineer; b. Taiwan, Jan. 26, 1940; s. Yung-cheng and A-shu (Fang) C.; m. Ruth C. Lee, June 28, 1969; children: Lyrice, Lisa, Steve. B.S., Nat. Taiwan U., 1963; M.S., Princeton U., 1966, M.A., 1967, Ph.D., 1968. Research asst. Princeton U., 1965-68; asst. mech. engr. Argonne (Ill.) Nat. Lab., 1968-71, mech. engr., 1971-80, sr. mech. engr., 1980—; cons. to Internat. Atomic Energy Agy. to assist developing countries in R & D of nuclear reactor systems components, 1977, 79, 80, 94; cons. NASA, NRC, Rockwell Internat., others. Author: Flow-Induced Vibration of Circular Cylinderical Structures, 1987; mem. internat. adv. editorial bd. Acta Mechanica Solida; adv. bd. JSME Internat. Jour.; assoc. editor Applied Mechs. Rev., Jour. of Pressure Vessels Tech.; contbr. articles to profl. jours. Recipient Disting. Performance award U. Chgo., 1986. Fellow ASME (chmn. tech. subcom. on fluid and structure interactions pressure vessels and piping divsn. 1987-90, honors chmn. 1990-94, mem. exec. com. 1990-96, organizer symposia, tech. program chmn. 1994, conf. chair ASME/JSME pressure vessels and piping conf. 1995, pressure vessels and piping divsn., chmn. 1995-96, senate pres. 1997-98, honors and awards chair of materials and structures tech. group 1996—), Instn. Diagnostic Engrs.; mem. Am. Acad. Mechanics, Acoustical Soc. Am., Sigma Xi. Home: 6420 Waterford Ct Hinsdale IL 60521-5438 Office: 9700 Cass Ave Lemont IL 60439-4803

CHEN, SHUANG, computer science professional; b. China, Jan. 29, 1958; m. Hongwen Yan, Aug. 2, 1987; 1 child, Jessica Y. Chen. BSEE, Nanjing Aeronautical U., 1982; MSEE, South China U. Sci. and Tech., Guangzhou, China, 1985; MPH in Computer Engring., Rutgers U., 1990, PhD in Computer Engring., 1991. Mem. faculty South China U. Sci. and Tech., Guangzhou, 1985-86; rsch. asst. Rutgers U., New Brunswick, 1986-91; sr. rsch. engr. Comm. Intelligence Corp., Redwood Shores, Calif., 1991-95; rsch. staff mem. IBM Thomas J. Watson Rsch. Ctr., Yorktown Heights, N.Y., 1995-98; pres. Internat. Interactive Commerce, Ltd., Somers, N.Y., 1999—; reviewer profl. jours.. Author: (with others) Studies in Pattern Recognition, 1997. Grad. Rsch. Assistantship, Rutgers U., 1987-91. Mem. IEEE, Sigma Xi. Office: Internat Interactive Commerce Ltd PO Box 0677 Somers NY 10589

CHEN, SOW-HSIN, nuclear engineering educator, researcher; b. Chia-Yi, Taiwan, Mar. 5, 1935; came to U.S., 1958, naturalized, 1974; s. Pi-Yu Chen and Liang Hsu; m. Ching-Chih Liu, Aug. 19, 1961; children: Anne, Catherine, John. BS in Physics, Nat. Taiwan U., 1956; MS in Physics, Nat. Tsinghua U., 1958; MS in Nuclear Engring., U. Mich., 1962; PhD in Physics, McMaster U., 1964. Postdoctoral fellow AERE Harwell, Berkshire, U.K., 1965; asst. prof. physics U. Waterloo, Ont., Can., 1964-67; research fellow Harvard U., Cambridge, Mass., 1967; asst. prof., then assoc. prof. nuclear engring. MIT, Cambridge, 1968-74, prof. nuc. engring., 1974—; vis. prof. Tsinghua U., Peking, China, 1982, Ecole Superieure de Physique et Chemie, Paris, 1981, Univ. Konstanz, Germany, 1988, Univ. Bayreuth, Germany, 1988, Univ. Bordeaux I, Bordeaux, France, 1991; chmn. Gordon Conf., 1986; co-organizer Conf. Colloid and Interface Sci.: Trends and Applications, 1995; dir. NATO ASI on Scattering Techniques Applied to Supramolecular and Non-Equilibrium Systems, 1980, Structure and Dynamics of Supramolecular Aggregates and Strongly Interacting Colloids, 1991. Author: Spectroscopy in Biology, Chemistry and Physics-Neutron, X-ray and Laser, 1975, Scattering Techniques Applied to Supramolecular and Non-Equilibrium Systems, 1981, Micellar Solutions and Microemulsions: Structure, Dynamics and Statistical Thermodynamics, 1990, Structure and Dynamics of Strongly Interacting Colloids and Supramolecular Aggregates in Solution, 1992, Interaction of Photons and Neutrons with Matter-An Introduction, 1997; contbr. 260 articles to sci. jours. Alexander Von Humboldt U.S. sr. scientist award Govt. of Germany, 1987-88, 95. Fellow AAAS, Am. Phys. Soc., Japan Soc. for the Promotion of Sci. (Rsch. fellow 1995); mem. Sigma Xi. Home: 1400 Commonwealth Ave Newton MA 02465-2830 Office: MIT 24-209 77 Mass Ave Cambridge MA 02139-4307

CHEN, STEPHEN S. F., diplomat; b. Nanking, China, Feb. 11, 1934; m. Rosa Te Chen; three children. BA, U. Santo Tomas, Philippines, 1957, MA, 1959; postgrad., U. Santo Tomas, 1959-60; DBA (hon.), Kensington U. Various positions in field to dir. gen. CCNAA, L.A., 1988-89; dep. rep. CCNAA, Washington, 1989-93; vice-min. fgn. affairs Ministry Fgn. Affairs, Rep. of China, 1993-96; dep. sec.-gen. Office of Pres., China, 1996-97; rep. TECRO, Washington, 1997—. Avocations: fgn. langs. including Chinese, English, Spanish, Portuguese and six Chinese dialects.

CHEN, STEPHEN SHAU-TSI, retired psychiatrist, physiologist; b. Tou-Nan, Yun-Lin, Taiwan, Aug. 18, 1934; s. R-Yue and Pi-Yu (Huang) C.; m. Clara Chin-Chin Liu, Sept. 7, 1936; children: David, Timothy, Hubert. MD, Nat. Taiwan U., Taipei, 1959; PhD, U. Wis., 1968. Diplomate Am. Bd. Psychiatry and Neurology, also sub. bd. Geriatric Psychiatry. Intern Nat. Taiwan U. Hosp., 1959; instr. dept. physiology U. Wis., Madison, 1968-71, asst. prof., 1971-75; resident in psychiatry SUNY, Stony Brook, 1975-78; asst. prof. psychiatry dept. psychiatry U. Pitts., 1978-80; asst. prof. psychiatry dept. psychiatry and behavioral sci. U. Wash., Seattle, 1981-86, clin. asst. prof. psychiatry, 1986-97; chief mental health clinic VA Med. Ctr., Tacoma, 1981-85. Contbr. articles to Am. Jour. Physiol., Jour. Physiology, Can. Jour. Physiology and Pharmacology, Acta Physiol. Fellow Wis. Heart Assn., 1966-68. Mem. APA, North Pacific Soc. Neurology and Psychiatry. Presbyterian. Avocations: tennis, gardening,.

CHEN, STEPHEN SHI-HUA, pathologist, biochemist; b. Taipei, Taiwan, Republic of China, Dec. 25, 1939; came to U.S., 1965; s. Ah-wen and Shun (Pan) C.; m. Hsin-Hsin Yii, July 5, 1969; children: Peter T., Margaret T. MD, Nat. Taiwan U., 1964; PhD, U. Pitts, 1972. Diplomate Am. Bd. of Pathology. Asst. prof. pathology U. Pitts., 1972-76; staff pathologist Presbyn. Hosp., Pitts., 1973-76; asst. prof. pathology dept. Stanford U., Palo Alto, Calif., 1976-80, clin. assoc. prof. pathology dept., 1980-96, clin. prof., 1996—; staff pathologist Veterans Affairs Med. Ctr., Palo Alto, 1976—. Contbr. articles to Jour. Cellular Physiology, Jour. Chromatography, Clinica Chimca Acta. Fellow Coll. Am. Pathologists; mem. Am. Soc. Investigative Pathology, U.S. and Can. Acad. Pathology Inc., Am. Soc. Clin. Pathologists, Am. Soc. Cytopathology. Achievements include chromatography of phospholipids. Office: Vets Affairs Med Ctr (113) 3801 Miranda Ave Palo Alto CA 94304-1207

CHEN, TAK-MING, civil engineer; b. Changning, Hunan, China, July 29, 1936; came to U.S., 1970; s. Jenn-Chiu and Yin (Peng) C.; m. Taining Chou, July 1, 1973; children: Merry, Terry. BS in River/Harbor Engring., Taiwan Provincial Coll. of Marine Sci. and Tech., 1966; MSCE, U. Mo., 1971. Registered profl. engr., N.Y., Md., D.C. Project engr. Chinese Petroleum Corp., Taipei, Taiwan, 1973; structural designer Bellante, Clauss, Miller & Nolan, inc., Scranton, Pa., 1974-76; structural engr. Wayman C. Wings, Cons. Engrs., N.Y.C., 1978-80, Gibbs & Hills, Inc., N.Y.C., 1980-81; civil/structural engr. Bechtel Power Corp., Gaithersburg, Md., 1981-84; structural engr. Hazen & Sawyer, P.C., N.Y.C., 1984-85; civil/structural engr. N.Y.C. Dept. Sanitation, 1985-87; civil engr. N.Y.C. Dept. Bldgs., 1987-94, N.Y.C. Comptroller's Office, 1994—; pres. Chen's Cons. Engrs., Queens, N.Y., 1985-87. Bd. dirs. RFK Dem. Assn., Inc., Forest Hills, N.Y., 1994—. Recipient Cert. of Honor for leadership Dem. Nat. Com. Mem. NSPE, N.Y. State Soc. Profl. Engrs., Chinese Am. Assn. City of N.Y., MSM-UMR Alumni Assn., Comptr. Engrs. Assn. Home: 82-28 255th St Floral Park NY 11004 Office: New York City Comptrollers Office Bur of Engring 2 Lafayette St Rm 204 New York NY 10007-1307

CHEN, TAR TIMOTHY, biostatistician; b. Fuching, China, June 23, 1945; came to U.S., 1967, naturalized, 1979; s. Lin-Tsang and Ai-Ging (Chang) C.; m. Meei-Ming Li, Aug. 9, 1969; children: Stephen, Daniel. BS, Nat. Taiwan U., 1966; MS, U. Chgo., 1969, PhD, 1972; MDiv, Southwestern Bapt. Theol. Sem., 1989. Statistician Ill. Bell Tel., Chgo., 1971-73; asst. prof. Calif. State U., Hayward, 1973-74; vis. assoc. prof. Chung-Hsing U., Taichung, Taiwan, 1974-75; biostatistician The Upjohn Co., Kalamazoo, 1975-79; asst. prof. biometrics M.D. Anderson Cancer Ctr. U. Tex., Houston, 1979-84; sr. biostatistician Alcon Labs., Fort Worth, 1984-89; math. statistician Nat. Cancer Inst., Bethesda, Md., 1989-98; prof., head biostats. sect. U. Md. Greenebaum Cancer Sect., 1998—. Contbr. articles to profl. jours. Deacon, Houston Chinese Ch., 1981-83, McKinney Meml. Bible Ch., Ft. Worth, 1988-89. 2d lt. Republic of China Army, 1966-67. Fellow Am. Statis. Assn., Am. Scientific Affiliation; mem. Biometric Soc., Internat. Chinese Statis. Assn. (pres.). Office: 22 South Green St Rm N9E28 Baltimore MD 21201

CHEN, WAI-FAH, civil engineering educator; b. Chekiang, China, Dec. 23, 1936; m. Lily; children: Eric, Arnold, Brian. BS, Cheng-Kung U., 1959; MS, Lehigh U., 1963; PhD, Brown U., 1966. From asst. prof. to prof. civil engring. Lehigh U., 1966-76; prof. civil engring. Purdue U., Lafayette, Ind., 1976-92, head structural engring., 1980—; cons. Exxon Products, 1979—, Karagozian & Case Structural Engrs., 1985—, Ga. Tech., 1987—, Skidmore, Owings & Merrill, 1987, World Bank, 1988—. Editor-in-chief: The Civil Engineering Handbook, 1995, The Handbook of Structural Engineering, 1997, Bridge Engineering Handbook, 1999. Named George E. Goodwin Disting. prof. Purdue U., 1992. Mem. ASCE (hon.), Internat. Assn. Bridge & Structural Engring., Strucural Stability Rsch. Coun., Am. Acad. Mech., Am. Concrete Inst., Am. Inst. Steel Constrn., Nat. Acad. Engring., Academia Sinica. Office: Purdue U Sch Civil Engring West Lafayette IN 47907

CHEN, WAI-KAI, electrical engineering and computer science educator, consultant; b. Nanking, China, Dec. 23, 1936; came to U.S., 1959; s. You-Chao and Shui-Tan (Shen) C.; m. Shirley Shiao-Ling, Jan. 13, 1939; children—Jerome, Melissa. BS in Elec. Engring., Ohio U., 1960, MS in Elec. Engring., 1961; PhD in Elec. Engring., U. Ill., Urbana, 1964. Asst. prof. Ohio U., 1964-67, assoc. prof., 1967-71, prof., 1971-78, disting. prof., 1978-81; prof., head dept. elec. engring. and computer sci. U. Ill., Chgo., 1981—; vis. assoc. prof. Purdue U., 1970-71; hon. prof. Tianjing U., Peoples Republic of China, 1990, Beijin U. of Posts and Telecomms., Beijing U. of Aeronautics and Astronautics, 1992. Author: Applied Graph Theory, 1970, Theory and Design of Broadband Matching Networks, 1976, Applied Graph Theory: Graphs and Electrical Networks, 1976, Active Network and Feedback Amplifier Theory, 1980, Linear Networks and Systems, 1983, Passive and Active Filters: Theory and Implementations, 1986, The Collected Papers of Professor Wai-Kai Chen, 1987, Broadband Matching: Theory and Implementations, 1988, Theory of Nets, 1990, Linear Networks and Systems: Computer-Aided Solutions and Implementations, 1990, Active Network Analysis, 1991, Modern Network Analysis, 1992; editor: Brooks/Cole Series in Electrical Engineering, 1982-84, Advanced Series in Electrical and Computer Engineering, 1984-86, 98—; editor in chief Advanced Series in Elec. and Computer Engring., World Sci. Pub. Co., Singapore, 1986—, Jour. Circuits, Systems and Computers, 1989—, The Circuits and Filters Handbook, 1995, The VLSI Handbook, 1997—, The Electrical Engineering Handbook, 1998—, Imperial Coll. Press, others; assoc. editor: Jour. Circuits, Systems and Signal Processing, 1981—; editor in charge Advanced Series in Circuits and Systems, World Scientific Publ. Co., 1991—; sect. editor Encyclopedia of Physical Science & Technology, 1998—. Recipient Lester R. Ford award Math. Assn. Am., 1967, Baker Fund award Ohio U., 1974, 78, Disting. Accomplishment award Chinese Acad. & Profl. Assn. in Mid-Am. , 1985, disting. Guest Prof. award Chuo U., Tokyo, 1987, Outstanding Service award Chinese Acad. & Profl. assn. in Mid-Am., 1988, Outstanding Achievement award Mid-Am. Chinese Sci. & Tech. Assn., 1988, disting. alumnus award Electrical and Computer Engring. Dept. Alumni Assn. U. Ill. Urbana-Champaign, 1988, Alexander von Humboldt award Alexander von Humboldt Stiftung, Fed. Republic of Germany, 1985, hon. prof. award Nanjing Inst. of Technology and Zhejing U., Peoples Republic of China, 1985, The Northeast U. Tech., East. China Inst. Tech., Nanjing Inst. of Posts & Telecommunications, AnHui U., Chengdu Inst. Radio Engring., Wuhan Univ.; Research Inst. fellow Ohio U., 1972, Japan Soc. for Promotion of Sci., 1986, Sr. U. Scholar award U. Ill., 1986, Ohio U. Alumni Medal Merit for Disting. Achievement in Engring. Edn., 1987, hon. prof. award Hangzhan U. of Electronic Tech., Peoples Republic of China, 1990, Disting. Prof. award Internat. Technol. U., 1995. Fellow IEEE (Circuits and Sys. Soc. Meritorious Svc. award 1997, Edn. award 1998), AAAS; mem. NSPE, IEEE Cirs. and Sys. Soc. (adminstrv. com. 1985-87, exec. v.p. 1987, assoc. editor Trans. on Cirs. and Sys. 1977-79, editor 1991-93, pres.-elect 1993, pres. 1994), Md.-Am. Chinese Sci. and Tech. Assn. (bd. dirs. 1984-86, 89-93, pres. 1991-92), Chinese Acad. and Profl. Assn. Mid-Am. (advisor to bd. dirs. 1984-89, pres. 1986-87), Soc. Indsl. and Applied Math., Assn. Computing Machinery, Tensor Soc. Gt. Britain, Sigma Xi (sec.-treas. Ohio U. chpt. 1981), Phi Kappa Phi, Eta Kappa Nu. Office: U Ill Dept Elec Engring & Computer Sci 851 S Morgan St Rm 1120 Seo Chicago IL 60607-7042

CHEN, WEI-YIN, chemical engineering educator, researcher; b. Taipei, China, Apr. 5, 1950; came to U.S., 1973; s. Shao-Pong and Fong-Hwa (Tsai) C.; m. Tsuei-Ju Kao, May 18, 1987. BSChemE, Tunghai U., Taichung, Taiwan, 1973; MS in applied math., SUNY, 1975; MSChemE, Poly. Inst. N.Y., 1975; PhDChemE, CUNY, 1981. Sr. rsch. engr. Gulf South Rsch. Inst., New Orleans, La., 1981-85, mgr. fuel rsch., 1985-87; rsch. asst. prof. La. State U., Baton Rouge, 1987-90; asst. prof. U. Miss., 1990-93, assoc. prof., 1993—. Contbr. articles to profl. jours. Recipient numerous grants for rsch. in field. Mem. AIChE, Am. Chem. Soc., Combustion Inst., Sigma Xi. Office: U Miss Dept Chem Engr Anderson Hall University MS 38677

CHEN, WEN, software engineer, researcher; b. Beijing, Nov. 28, 1967; d. Kaihong Chen and Xiangmi Wang; m. Jason Zhao, Nov. 1, 1994. BSCE, Zhejiang (China) U., 1990; MS in Engring., N.C. A&T State U., 1997, MS in Computer Sci., 1998. Registered engr.-in-tng., Ill. Project engr. China Shipbldg. Corp., Beijing, 1990-94; rsch. asst. N.C. A&T State U., Greensboro, 1994-97; software engr. CAM Tech., Inc., Wilmington, N.C., 1997-98, Motorola, Inc., Arlington Heights, Ill., 1998—. Cary rsch. fellow, 1994-97. Home: 1224 E Algonquin Rd Apt 3J Schaumburg IL 60173-4038 Office: 1501 West Shore Dr Arlington Heights IL 60004

CHEN, WESLEY, lawyer; b. N.Y.C., Nov. 29, 1954; s. Tom Y.M. and Mary (Don) C.; m. Vivien Wong, Dec. 10, 1983; 2 children: Marissa, Jocelyn. BA, N.Y. U., 1976, JD, 1980. Bar: N.Y. 1981, U.S. Dist. Ct. (so. and ea. dists.) N.Y. 1981. Lawyer Meissner, Tisch & Kleinberg, N.Y.C., 1980-81; pvt. practice N.Y.C., 1982-85, 89, 91—; of counsel Serchuk, Wolfe & Zelermyer, White Plains, N.Y., 1985-88; ptnr. Cantwell & Chen, N.Y.C., 1988, Kimmelman, Sexter, Warmflash & Leitner, N.Y.C., 1990-91, Krasner & Chen, N.Y.C., 1992-94, Serchuk & Zelermyer, N.Y.C., 1995—; bd. dirs. United Orient Bank, N.Y.C., 1982-92, MFY Legal Svcs., Inc., 1993-96; mem. N.Y. State Banking Bd., 1992—. Mem. ABA, N.Y. State Bar Assn. (mem. banking law com.), N.Y.County Lawyers Assn. (mem. banking law com.), Asian-Am. Bar Assn. of N.Y., Chinese C. of C. (legal adviser 1982—). Office: 641 Lexington Ave Fl 20 New York NY 10022-4503

CHEN, WILLIAM SHAO-CHANG, retired army officer; b. Shanghai, China, Nov. 11, 1939; came to U.S., 1944; s. H. M. and Priscilla (Chang) Ch.; m. Sandra Choy, Dec. 29, 1976; children: William K., Stephen W. BS in Engring. Math., U. Mich., 1960, MS in Aero. and Astronautical Engring., 1961; MBA, Auburn U., 1970. Commd. 2d lt. U.S. Army, 1961, advanced through grades to maj. gen., 1989; various command and staff assignments, 1961-82; chief munitions div. Office Rsch., Devel. and Acquisition, Dept. Army, Washington, 1981-82; project mgr. CHAPARRAL Project Office, U.S. Army Missile Command, Redstone Arsenal, Ala., 1982-84, Div. Air Def. Gun Project Office, Picatinny Arsenal, N.J., 1984-86; dep. dir. weapons systems, dep. chief of staff Office Rsch., Devel. and Acquisition, Washington, 1986-87; dir. program mgmt. oversight, asst. dir. systems mgmt. Office Asst. Sec. Army for Rsch., Devel. and Acquisition, Washington, 1987-89; comdg. gen. U.S. Army Missile Command, Redstone Arsenal, 1989-92; prog. exec. officer Army Global Protection against Limited Strikes, Arlington, Va., 1992-93; div. v.p. Nichols Rsch. Corp., Vienna, Va., 1993-94; v.p., program mgr. Crusader Field Artillery System, Mpls., 1994-95; v.p. army programs United Def. Ltd. Ptnrship, Mpls., 1995-96, v.p. engring. and product devel., 1997—. Decorated Legion of Merit; recipient Disting. Svc. medal U.S. Army Missile Command, 1992, Disting. Svc. Medal PEO Missile Def., 1993. Mem. Assn. U.S. Army. Office: United Def Ltd Ptnrship 4800 E River Rd Ste 200 Minneapolis MN 55421-1402*

CHEN, YU, acupuncturist, Chinese herbologist; b. Beijing, China, Sept. 10, 1942; came to U.S., 1985; d. Hai and Xiu (Wang) C.; m. Paul L. Munson, Feb. 27, 1987; 1 child by previous marriage: Ming Au. MD, Capital Med. Coll., Beijing, 1965; D Traditional Chinese Medicine, Chinese Traditional Med. Sch., Beijing, 1977; MS, Chinese Acad. Med. Sci., Beijing, 1981. Diplomate in acupuncture Nat. Commn. Cert. Acupuncture; cert. Chinese herbologist; lic. acupuncturist, Md. Physician Govt. China, Ching Yang, Gan Su, 1968-73; resident physician dept. ob-gyn. Worker's Hosp., Yen Shan Oil Factory, Beijing, 1974-78; attending physician dept. genetics Nat. Rsch. Inst. Family Planning, Beijing, 1982-83; WHO postdoctoral fellow Karolinska Inst., Stockholm, 1983-85; postdoctoral fellow dept. physiology U. Tex., Houston, 1985-87; postdoctoral fellow dept. pharmacology U. N.C., Chapel Hill, 1987-90; pvt. practice acupuncture and herbology Cmty. Wholistic Health Ctr., Carrboro, N.C., 1989-93; pvt. practice acupuncture, Chinese herbology, magnet therapy Pikesville and Parkville, Md., 1993—. Contbr. articles to profl. jours.; patentee in field; inventor of simple and effective way to treat panic attack by acupuncture. Recipient Best Essay award 1st Internat. Conf. Micro-Acupuncture Therapy, San Francisco, 1995. Democrat. Lutheran. Avocations: painting, photography, travel, classical music, gardening. Office: Beijing Acupuncture Chinese Herb & Magnetic Ctr 1401 Reisterstown Rd Baltimore MD 21208-6502

CHEN, YUAN JAMES, chemical company executive; b. Keelung, Taiwan, China, June 18, 1949; came to U.S., 1975; s. Hong and Shu-chen (Cheng) C.;m. Ruey-chi Shuai, July 8, 1983; children: Eric Yen-Fu, Albert Hsin-Fu. BS in Mech. Engring., Chung-Hsing U., Taichung, Taiwan, 1971; MS in Mech. Engring., Ga. Inst. Tech., 1976, postgrad., 1976-78; postgrad., U. Houston, 1981-83. Registered profl. engr., Ala., Tex. Mech. engr. China Tech. Cons. Inc., Taipei, Taiwan, 1973-75; sr. engr. Monsanto Chems. Co., Guntersville, Ala., 1978-81; engring. specialist Monsanto Chems. Co., Texas City, Tex., 1981-86; engring. technologist Sterling Chems. Inc., Texas City, 1986—; tech. adv. com. Heat Transfer Rsch., Inc., College Station, Tex. 1986—. Mem. ASME. Avocations: tennis, table tennis. Home: 14218 Ridgewood Lake Ct Houston TX 77062-2349 Office: 201 Bay St S Texas City TX 77590-8779

CHEN, ZHANGXIN JOHN, mathematics educator; b. Boying, Jiangxi, China, Oct. 15, 1962; came to the U.S., 1986; s. Furong Chen and Hao-e Fang; m. Aijie Li, Jan. 5, 1986; children: Christina C., Paul Z. BS, U. Jiangxi, Nanchang, 1983; MS, Xi'an (Shaanxi) Jiaotong U., 1985; PhD in Math., Purdue U., 1991. Asst. prof. Xi'an Jiaotong U., 1985-86; rsch. assoc. U. Minn., Mpls., 1991-93; vis. asst. prof. Tex. A&M U., College Station, 1993-95; asst. prof. So. Meth. U., Dallas, 1995-98, assoc. prof., 1999—; cons. Rush Presbyn. St. Luke's Med. Ctr., Chgo., 1994-95; reviewer Math. Revs., Providence, 1994—. Contbr. articles to profl. jours. Grantee NSF, 1996—; univ. fellow Jiangxi U., 1981, 82; David Ross fellow Purdue U., West Lafayette, Ind., 1989, 90. Mem. Am. Math. Soc., Soc. for Indsl. and Applied Math., N.Y. Acad. Scis. Avocations: playing sports. Office: So Meth Univ Dept Math PO Box 750156 Dallas TX 75275-0156

CHEN, ZHENGXIN, computer scientist; b. Nanjing, Jiangsu, China, Oct. 2, 1947; came to U.S. 1983; s. Donald Zhichu and Grace Fang (Chen) C.; m. Mei Zheng, Dec. 19, 1980. BS, East China Normal U., 1982; MS, La. State U., 1985, PhD, 1988. Instr. math. Shanghai Pharm. U., China, 1982-83; asst. prof. computer sci. U. Nebr., Omaha, 1988-94, assoc. prof., 1994—. Author: Computational Intelligence for Decision Making, 1999; referee/reviewer profl. jours.; contbr. numerous articles to profl. jours. UCR grantee U. Nebr., Travel grantee Office of Nava. Rsch.; grantee, co-principle investor, DEPSCOR rsch. project USAF, 1999—. Mem. IEEE, Assn. Computing Machinery, Am. Assn. Artificial Intelligence. Avocations: landscape photography, art appreciation, classical music, stamp collecting. Office: U Nebr at Omaha Dept Computer Sci Omaha NE 68182

CHEN, ZUOHUANG, conductor; b. Shanghai, People's Republic China, Apr. 2, 1947; m. Zaiyi Wang, Sept. 10, 1969; 1 child. MusM, 1982; DMA in Orchtl. Conducting, U. Mich., 1985. Condr. All China Trade Union Music and Dance Troop, 1966-74, China Film Philharm., 1974-76; assoc. prof. conducting U. Kans., Lawrence, 1985-87; condr. Cen. Philharm. Orch. China, 1987-96; music dir. Wichita (Kans.) Symphony, 1990—, R.I. Philharm. Orch., 1992-96; artistic dir./condr China Nat. Symphony Orch., 1996—. Office: Wichita Symphony Orch Century II Concert Hall 225 W Douglas Ave Ste 207 Wichita KS 67202-3181

CHENAULT, KENNETH IRVINE, financial services company executive; b. N.Y.C., June 2, 1951; s. Hortenius and Anne N. (Quick) Ch.; m. Kathryn Cassell, Aug. 20, 1977; children: Kenneth I. Jr., Kevin A. BA, Bowdoin Coll., 1973; JD, Harvard U., 1976; PhD (hon.), Morgan State U., 1990, Stony Brook U., 1996, Bowdoin Coll., 1996, Adelphi U., 1995, Xavier U., 1997, S.C. State U., 1997, Howard U., 1998, U. Notre Dame, 1998. Bar: Mass. 1981. Assoc. Rogers & Wells, N.Y.C., 1977-79; cons. Bain & Co., Boston, 1979-81; dir. strategic planning Am. Express Co., N.Y.C., 1981-83; from v.p. to sr. v.p. Am. Express Travel Related Svcs. Co., Inc., N.Y.C., 1983-96, exec. v.p. platinum card/gold, 1986-88, exec. v.p. personal card divsn., 1988-89, pres. consumer card and fin. svcs. group, 1990-93, pres. U.S.A., 1993-95; vice-chmn. Am. Express Co., N.Y.C., 1995-97, pres., COO, 1997—; bd. dirs. IBM, Am. Express Co., Mt. Sinai-NYU Med. Ctr. & Health Sys., NCAA, CASA, The Ron Brown Award for Corp. Leadership, Arthur Ashe Inst. for Urban Health. Mem. dean's adv. bd. Harvard Law Sch.; mem. Coun. Fgn. Rels., N.Y.C., 1988. Mem. ABA. Congregationalist. Office: Am Express Co Am Express Tower World Fin Ctr 200 Vesey St New York NY 10285-5104

CHENEY, BRIGHAM VERNON, physical chemist; b. Salt Lake City, June 11, 1936; s. Silas Lavell and Klara (Young) C.; m. Marsali McAllister, Aug. 20, 1964; children—Jill, Mark Vernon, Heather, Karin, Brigham McAllister, John David. B.A., U. Utah, 1961, Ph.D., 1966. Research asst. U. Utah, 1964-66; research scientist Upjohn Co., Kalamazoo, 1966-71, scientist, 1971-75, sr. research scientist, 1975-98, vis. scientist, Oxford U., 1986-87. Missonary, Ch. Jesus Ch. Latter-day Saints, Germany, 1956-59; high councilor, Lansing, Mich., 1969-75, Grand Rapids, Mich., 1975-78; bishop, Kalamazoo, 1978-84; leader Boy Scouts Am., 1972—. Served with Army N.G., 1959-67. Mem. Am. Chem. Soc., Sigma Xi, Phi Eta Sigma, Sigma Pi Sigma. Contbr. articles to profl. jours. Home: 3507 Runnymede Dr Kalamazoo MI 49004-3153

CHENEY, DANIEL LAVERN, retired magazine publisher; b. Vernon, N.Y., May 26, 1928; s. Luke Lavern and Estella Mae (Clinch) C.; m. Eleanora Louise Stevenson, Aug. 8, 1959; stepchildren: Patricia Walter, Nancy Fulcher Shannon, Jon Dinsmore (dec.). A.B., Colgate U., 1950. Cost acctg. clk. Gen. Electric Co., Auburn, N.Y., 1955-58; mng. editor, cons. Smith, Kline & French, Phila., 1958-70; founder, pres. Nursing; co-owner Springhouse Corp., Jenkintown, Pa., 1970—; founder, pres. Skillbooks, 1977—; founder, pub. Photobooks.; retired, 1992. Bd. dirs. Meth. Hosp., Phila., 1992—, Robins' Nest, Woodbury, N.J., 1995—; founder Danellie Found., 1990; mem. adminstrv. coun. Haddonfield (N.J.) United Meth. Ch., 1993, 99—. Methodist. Home: 445 Westminster Ave Haddonfield NJ 08033-4024

CHENEY, DICK (RICHARD BRUCE CHENEY), former secretary of defense, former congressman; b. Lincoln, Nebr., Jan. 30, 1941; s. Richard Hebert and Marjorie Lauraine (Dickey) C.; m. Lynne Anne Vincent, Aug. 29, 1964; children: Elizabeth, Mary Claire. B.A., U. Wyo., 1965, M.A., 1966. Asst. to Pres. The White House, Washington, 1975-77; mem. 96th-100th Congresses from Wyo., 1978-89; sec. U.S Dept. of Defense, Washington, 1989-93; sr. fellow Am. Enterprise Inst., Washington, 1993-95; CEO Halliburton Co., Dallas, 1995—. Republican. Office: Halliburton Co 500 N Akard St Ste 3600 Dallas TX 75201-3391

CHENEY, GLENN ALAN, writer, educator; b. Melrose, Mass., Sept. 6, 1951; s. Theodore Albert and Dorothy (Bates) C.; m. Solange Aurora Cavalcante, Apr. 26, 1948; 1 child, Ian Alan. BA in Philosophy, Fairfield U., 1974, MA in Communication, 1982, grad. cert. in profl. writing, 1982; MA in English, Universidade Federal de Minas Gerais, 1990; MFA, Vermont Coll., 1991. Writing cons. Fairfield (Conn.) U., 1980-82, adj. prof., 1988-94; adj. prof. Conn. Coll., 1994—; freelance corp. writer Conn. and N.Y., 1980-84; account exec. Grey Advt., Inc., N.Y.C., 1982-85; pres. English Communications Ltd., Belo Horizonte, Brazil, 1984-98; liaison Fedn. Industries of the State of Miras Gerais, Brazil, 1998—; instr. Inst. for Children's Lit., Redding Ridge, Conn., 1988-91; mktg. cons. Strategies, Stratford, Conn., 1988—; ptnr. Cheney & Assocs.; adj. prof. Albertus Magnus Coll., 1991. Author: El Salvador: Country in Crisis, 1982, rev. edit., 1990, Television in American Society, 1983, Mohandas Ghandi, 1983, The Amazon, 1984, Mineral Resources, 1984, Revolution in Central America, 1985, Responsibility, 1985, Mariana Scouts in the Valley of Spirits, 1986, Drugs, Teens and Recovery, 1993, Chernobyl: The Ongoing Story of the World's Deadliest Nuclear Disaster, 1993, Teens with Physical Disabilities, 1995, Acts of Ineffable Love, Collected Stories, 1995, Journey to Chernobyl: Encounters in a Radioactive Zone, 1995, They Never Know the Victims of Nuclear Testing, 1996, Neclear Proliferation: Problems and Possibilities, 1998; contbr. chpts. to books, short stories to lit. mags. and articles to profl. acctg. and bus. jours.; host Nuclear Safety Issues, 1995-96; host, prodr. Sprague Today!, 1997—. Bd. dirs. Suzuki Music Sch., New Haven, 1988-94; chmn. Sprague Pub. Libr., 1995—; founder Citizen's Regulatory Commn., 1995—; activist Green Party Conn., 1996—. Recipient honorable mention Writers Digest Short Story, Poetry and Articles Contests, 1991, 2d pl. winner arts and entertainment reporting New England Press Assn. Avocations: philosophy, gardening, travel, photography, beekeeping. Home: PO Box 284 Hanover CT 06350-0284

CHENEY, JAMES ADDISON, civil engineering educator; b. Los Angeles, Feb. 2, 1927; s. Burton Howard and Esther Jesse (Dumaresq) C.; m. Frankyee Jane Jackson, June, 23, 1951 (dec. Oct. 1966); children: John Addison, Linanne Dando, Matthew Jackson, Sarah Allan, Sharla Ryan, Jennifer Dumaresq; m. Barbara Louise Chadwick, June 1967 (div. Feb. 1987); children: Michael Chadwick, David Grant; m. Elaine Disbrow Barratt, Apr. 1988. BS, UCLA, 1951, MS, 1953; PhD, Stanford U., 1963. Registered profl. civil engr., Calif. Assoc. engr. L.T. Evans, Foundation Engrs., Los Angeles, 1953-55; staff engr. Lockheed Missile and Space Co., Sunnyvale, Calif., 1955-65; prof. civil engring. U. Calif., Davis, 1962-91, prof. emeritus civil engring., 1991—. Contbr. over 50 articles to scientific jours. Served with USN, 1944-45. Fellow ASCE; mem. Alpha Sigma Phi. Republican. Episcopalian. Home: 418 Anza Ave Davis CA 95616-0404 Office: U Calif Dept Civil Engring Davis CA 95616

CHENEY, LOIS SWEET, infection control nurse; b. Clifton Springs, N.Y., Oct. 26, 1933; d. Merton E. Sr. (dec.) and Jennie M. (Smith) S. (dec.); divorced; children: Linda Cheney Thorpe, Susan Cheney Post, Douglas A. Cheney. Diploma in nursing, Rochester (N.Y.) Gen. Hosp., 1954; BS in Edn. with high honors, Mansfield (Pa.) State Coll., 1973; MS, Columbia Pacific U., Mill Valley, Calif., 1982. RN, N.Y. With Meml. Hosp., Towanda, Pa., 1974-82; coord. infection control and employee health Clifton Springs Hosp. and Clinic, 1982-87; now infection control officer Monroe Cmty. Hosp., Rochester, 1987—; spkr. on mgmt. AIDS in long term care, 1987, 88, 89, 92; spkr. and cons. in infection control. Contbr. articles to profl. jours. Mem. Assn. Profls. in Infection Control and Epidemiology (cert., Rochester-Finger Lakes chpt.), Bus. and Profls. Women's Club, Toastmasters Internat. Intravenous Nurses Soc., N.Y. State Pub. Health Assn.

CHENEY, LYNNE V., humanities educator, writer; b. Casper, Wyo., Aug. 14, 1941; d. Wayne and Edna (Lybyer) Vincent; m. Richard Bruce Cheney, Aug. 29, 1964; children: Elizabeth, Mary. BA, Colo. Coll., 1963; MA, U. Colo., 1964; PhD, U. Wis., 1970. Freelance writer, 1970-83; lectr. George Washington U., Washington, 1972-77, U. Wyo., Casper, 1977-78; researcher, writer Md. Pub. Broadcasting, Owings Mills, 1982-83; sr. editor Washingtonian mag., Washington, 1983-86; chmn. NEH, Washington, 1986-93; W.J. Brady Jr. fellow Am. Enterprise Inst., Washington, 1993-95, sr. fellow, 1996—; commr. U.S. Constitution Bicentennial Commn., Washington, 1985-87. Author: Executive Privilege, 1978, Sisters, 1981, Telling the Truth, 1995; (with others) Kings of the Hill, 1983, 96, The Body Politic, 1988; contbr. articles to profl. jours. Mem. Women's Forum Washington. Mem. Congl. Club, Phi Beta Kappa, Kappa Alpha Theta. Republican. Methodist. Office: Am Enterprise Inst 1150 17th St NW Washington DC 20036-4603*

CHENEY, RICHARD EUGENE, public relations executive, psychoanalyst; b. Pana, Ill., Aug. 30, 1921; s. Royal F. and Nelle E. (Henke) C.; m. Betty L. McCray, Oct. 17, 1943; children: R. Christopher, Elyn G. Cheney MacInnis; m. 2d, Virginia B. Burns, Jan. 23, 1966; children: Benjamin, Anne. AB, Knox Coll., Galesburg, Ill., 1943; MA, Columbia U., 1960; postgrad., Ctr. Modern Psychoa. Studies, 1995. Assoc. editor Tide Mag., 1953; dir. pub. relations Tri Continental Corp., 1953-55; asst. mgr. pub. relations dept. Mobil Corp., 1955-60; chmn. bd., emeritus chmn. Hill & Knowlton, Inc., N.Y.C., 1987-91, 91—, chmn. bd., 1987-91, chmn. emeritus, 1991-93; bd. dirs. Chattem Inc., Chattanooga, Stoneridge, Inc., Warren, Ohio, Rowe Furniture, Salem, Va. Trustee Lown Cardiovascular Found., Ctr. for Modern Psychoanalytic Studies, Ctr. for Advancement of Group Studies. Served to lt. (j.g.) USNR, 1943-47, PTO. Mem. Soc. for Modern Psychoanalysis (trustee), Edgewood Club (Tivoli, N.Y.), Castalia (Ohio) Trout Club, Century Assn. Home: 25 W 81st St Apt 5A New York NY 10024-6023 Office: Eleven Riverside Dr Ste One New York NY 10023

CHENEY, STEPHEN A., career officer; m. Roxanne Lynn Waters. BS in Marine Engring., U.S. Naval Acad., 1971; grad., Arty. Basic, Ft. Sill, 1972, grad., Advanced Course, 1979; MS in Sys. Mgmt., USC, 1978; student, USMC Command Staff Coll., 1985, Nat. War Coll., 1990. Commd. ensign USMC, 1971, advanced through grades to brig. gen., 1997; stationed at Camp Pendleton, Calif., 1972-74, Marine Observation Squadron 6, 1st Marine Aircraft Wing, Okinawa, Japan, 1974-75; stationed at Marine Corps Recruit Depot, San Diego, 1975-78, comd. Recruit Tng. Rgt., 1995-97; various assignments Marine Corps Hdqs., Washington, 1979-83; force arty. officer III Marine Amphibious Force, Okinawa, 1984-85; exec. officer 3d Bn., 11th Marine Rgt., San Diego, 1985-87; commdg. officer Support Bn., Recruit Tng. Rgt., San Diego, 1987-89; ground plans officer Office Sec. Defense, 1990-91; dep. exec. sec. Dept. Defense, 1991-93; mil. fellow Coun. Fgn. Rels., 1993-94; planner, Roles and Missions Coordination Group Hdqs. USMC, 1994-95; insp. gen. USMC, 1997—. Decorated Legion of Merit. Office: USMC Washington DC 20380-0001*

CHENEY, THOMAS WARD, insurance company executive; b. Union, Nebr., Dec. 17, 1914; s. Gilbert Ward and Vernie (Barnum) C.; m. E. Margaret Phillippe, Oct. 15, 1938; children: Patricia Kay Cheney Keim, Thomas Charles. BS, U. Nebr., 1936; student, Life Ins. Mktg. Inst., U. Kans., 1950. With Modern Woodmen of Am., 1935-79; dir., asst. to pres. Modern Woodmen of Am., Rock Island, Ill., 1954-60; pres. Modern Woodmen of Am., 1960-79, also dir.; dir. 1st Nat. Bank of Quad Cities, mem. exec. com., 1974-87. Bd. dirs. Rock Island Community Chest, 1956-58, 65-66, YMCA, Rock Island, 1965-69; v.p. Blackhawk Indsl. Devel. Assn., Rock Island County, 1959; mem. bus. advisory com. Coll. Bus. U. Ill., 1969-81; bd. dirs. Augustana Coll., 1970-78, mem. exec. com., 1972-78, chmn. devel. com., 1972-78; bd. govs. Rock Island Found., 1967-76, Trinity Med. Found., 1994-99; trustee, mem. exec. com. Rock Island Franciscan Med. Center, 1971-78, chmn. bd. trustees, 1974-75; mem. lay advisory bd. St. Anthony's Hosp., Rock Island, 1965-72. Served to lt. col. USAAF, 1941-46. Decorated Legion of Merit.; Recipient Distinguished Service award U.S. Jaycees, 1940. Mem. Fraternal Ins. Counsellors Assn., Life Underwriters Assn., Gen. Agents and Mgrs. Conf., Nat. Fraternal Congress Am. (mem. exec. com. 1961-62, pres. 1967-68), Ill. Fraternal Congress, Ill. (dir. 1966-72), Ill. Fraternal Congress (vice chmn. 1971-72); Ill. C. of C. (bd. dirs. 1966-72, vice chmn. 1970-72), Rock Island C. of C. (pres. 1965), Delta Upsilon. Republican. Presbyterian (elder, trustee, deacon). Club: Rock Island Arsenal Golf (bd. govs. 1975-81, pres. 1979, exec. com.). Home: 3930 38th St Apt H Rock Island IL 61201-7091

CHENG, ALEXANDER HUNG-DARH, engineering educator, consultant; b. Taipei, Taiwan, May 25, 1952; came to U.S., 1976; s. Chia-hua and Yu-Chuen (Chwang) C.; m. Daisy T. Cheng, Nov. 23, 1979; children: Jacqueline, Julia. BS, Nat. Taiwan U., Taipei, 1974; MS, U. Mo., 1978; PhD, Cornell U., 1981. Asst. prof. Cornell U., Ithaca, 1981-82, Columbia U., N.Y.C., 1982-85; assoc. prof. U. Del., Newark, 1985-93, prof., 1993—; vis. scientist Schlumberger Cambridge (U.K.) Rsch., 1991; cons. Dowell Schlumberger Inc., Tulsa, 1985-91. Editor: Engineering Analysis with Boundary Elements, 1996, 6 edited books; editor-in-chief: Progress in Water Resources Series, 1998; assoc. editor Jour. Engring. Mech., 1998—; contbr. over 150 articles to profl. jours. Recipient awards, NSF, 1983, Gas Rsch. Inst., 1987, Agy. for Internat. Devel., 1995, W.L. Huber Civil Engineering prize Am. Soc. of Civil Engineers, 1994, Basic Rsch. award U.S. Nat. Com. Rock Mechics NRC, 1994, 99. Mem. ASCE, Am. Geophysical Union, Internat. Assn. Hydrological Rsch., Internat. Assn. Boundary Element (sec. 1990). Office: U Del Dept Civil Engring Newark DE 19716

CHENG, ALEXANDER LIHDAR, computer scientist, researcher; b. Taichung, Taiwan, Aug. 1, 1956; came to U.S., 1980; s. Pei-Kao and Kuang-Kun (Shiong) C.; m. Wei-Hong Mao, Feb. 16, 1988; children: Alexander Raymond, Bernard King. BS, Nat. Taiwan U., 1978; MS, U. Ky., 1982; PhD, Poly. U., Bklyn., 1992. Rsch. asst. Taiwan Hydraulic Bur., Taichung, 1978; tchg. asst. U. Ky., Lexington, 1981-82; sci. programmer Megadata Corp., Bohemia, N.Y., 1982-83; sr. software engr. Siemens Data Switching, Inc., Hauppauge, N.Y., 1983-87; tech. staff NYNEX S&T, Inc., White Plains, N.Y., 1987-94; pres. C-cation, Inc., 1994—, Zheng Standard Comm. Tech. Co., 1995—; bd. dirs. C&M First Svcs., Inc., N.Y.C.; adj. prof. computer sci., 1992-95; advisor to ministry of post and telecom. UN Devel. Program, China, 1992-96. V.p. Woodcrest Hts. Assn., White Plains, 1991-94. Mem. IEEE, IEEE Computer Soc., Assn. Computing Machinery, Upsilon Pi Epsilon. Avocations: music, stereo, skiing, bicycling, travel. Home: 11 Springdale Ave White Plains NY 10604-2309

CHENG, AMY, artist; b. Gaoshiung, Taiwan, Dec. 8, 1956; came to U.S., 1967; d. Nai Ling and Chai-Ying (Lai) C. BFA, U. Tex., 1978; MFA, Hunter Coll., 1982. Lectr. Hunter Coll., N.Y.C., 1985-86, Princeton (N.J.) U., 1989-90; asst. prof. studio art Bard Coll., Annandale-Hudson, N.Y., 1990-97; asst. prof. art SUNY, New Paltz, N.Y., 1997—. Travel grantee Arts Internat., 1994; grantee Ford Found., 1977-78, N.Y. Found. for the Arts fellow, 1990, 96. Home: 27 Rte 299 West New Paltz NY 12561 Office: SUNY 75 S Manheim Blvd Ste 1 New Paltz NY 12561-2499

CHENG, CHE PING, cardiologist, researcher, educator; b. People's Republic of China, Jan. 24, 1950; came to U.S., 1982; d. Ji and Yu Zhi (Pan) C.; m. Ping Tan, Feb. 23, 1951; 1 child, Xiao Tan. MD, Nanjing (People's Republic of China) Railway Med. U., 1976; PhD, Wayne State U., 1986. Diplomate Am. Bd. Internal Medicine. Attending physician dept. cardiology First Hosp. of Harbin (People's Republic of China) Med. Sch., 1977-81; rsch. assoc. Harbin Cardiovascular Rsch. Inst., 1980-81; teaching asst. dept. pathology Wayne State U., Detroit, 1982-83, teaching asst. dept. physiology, 1983-86; postdoctoral fellow cardiology rsch. Bowman Gray Sch. Medicine, Winston-Salem, N.C., 1986-88, rsch. instr. medicine dept. internal medicine, 1989-91, asst. prof. medicine dept. internal medicine, 1991-95, assoc. prof. medicine dept. internal medicine, 1995—, assoc. physiology and pharmacology, 1991, mem. grad. faculty Ctr. Neurobiol. Investigation Drug Abuse, 1993—; lectr. in field. Author: Novel Pharmacological Interventions for Alcoholism, 1992, Diastolic Relaxation of the Heart: Modulation of Diastolic Dysfunction in the Intact Heart, 1994, Effect of Felodipine on Left Ventricular Performance in Conscious Dogs: Assessment by Left Ventricular Pressure-Volume Analysis, 1994, Left Ventricular Systolic and Diastolic Performance, 1995, Altered Ventricular and Myoyte Response to Antiotensic II in Pacing-induced Heart Failure, 1996, Response of Left Ventricular Filling to Exercise Before and After Heart Failure, 1996; contbr. articles to profl. jours. Established Investigator award Am. Heart Assn., 1997-2000. Travel grantee Internat. Soc. for Biomed. Rsch., Rsch. Soc. on Alcoholism, 1990, grantee Am. Heart Assn., 1988-94, 95-97, NIH, 1986-95, Hassle Pharm., Sweden, 1991-94, travel grantee Nat. Inst. Alcohol Abuse and Alcoholism, 1994; recipient Exptl. Biology Losartan Travel award, 1996. Mem. Am. Heart Assn. (coun.), Am. Fedn. Clin. Rsch., Am. Physiol. Soc., Internat. Soc. Biomed. Rsch. on Alcoholism, Internat. Soc. for Heart Rsch. Avocations: swimming, music, reading, knitting, cooking. Home: 651 Dover Dr Winston Salem NC 27104-1529 Office: Bowman Gray Sch Medicine Cardiology Dept Medical Center Blvd Winston Salem NC 27157-1045

CHENG, CHIACHUN, medical educator; b. Tientsin, Hopei, China, May 5, 1925; came to U.S., 1949; s. Kuo-liang and Chui-yuen (Chien) C.; m. Katherine Cheng, May 30, 1953; children: Amy Yuwei, Anna Yumin, Alice Yuray, Audrey Yuhui. BS, Nat. U. Chekiang, China, 1948; MA, U. Tex., 1951, PhD, 1954. Rsch. assoc. N.Mex. Highlands U., Las Vegas, 1954-57, Princeton (N.J.) U., 1957-59; head med. chemistry sect. Midwest Rsch. Inst., Kansas City, Mo., 1959-78; prof. pharmacology U. Kans.Med. Ctr., Kansas City, 1978—; study sect. mem. med. chemistry NIH, Bethesda, Md., 1973-77; mem. adv. com. on clin. investigation Am. Cancer Soc., N.Y.C., 1983-86; mem. bd. sci. counselors divsn. cancer etiology Nat. Cancer Inst., Bethesda, 1983-86. Contbr. articles to profl. jours. Pres. Chinese Club of greater Kansas City, 1973. Recipient Sci. award Coun. of Prin. Scientists Midwest Rsch. Inst., 1973, Faculty Rsch. award U. Kans. Med. Ctr., 1983, Higuchi/Simons Biomed. Sci. award U. Kans., 1995, Silicon Prairie Tech. Assn. award in bioscis., Kans., 1995. Home: 10301 Overbrook Rd Leawood KS 66206-2652 Office: Univ of Kansas Med Ctr 3901 Rainbow Blvd Kansas City KS 66160-7419

CHENG, CHUEN YAN, biochemist, educator; b. Hong Kong, June 18, 1954; came to the U.S., 1981, naturalized, 1993; s. C. Yin and Tak Ying (Ho) C.; m. Po Lee, Mar. 17, 1978; children; Yan Ho, Chin Ho. BS with honors, Chinese U., Hong Kong, 1978; PhD, U. Newcastle, Australia, 1982. Fellow Population Coun., N.Y.C., 1981-82, rsch. investigator, 1983-84, staff scientist, 1985-87, scientist, 1988-90, sr. scientist, 1991—; assoc. dir. Internat. Consortium on Male Contraception, N.Y.C., 1994-95, dir., 1996—; asst. prof. Rockefeller U., N.Y.C., 1986-90; prof. U. Rome, 1990—; cons. Angelini Pharms., Inc., River Edge, N.J., 1985-91, Angelini Rsch. Inst., Rome, 1992-93, Fidia Pharms., Inc., Italy, 1997. Contbr. numerous articles to profl. jours. Recipient Sea Horse award, Newcastle U., Australia, 1982. Mem. Am. Soc. Andrology (Best Sci. Paper award 1996), Endocrine Soc. (Richard E. Weitzman Meml. award 1988). Achievements include patents for abnormally glycosylated variants of alpha-2-macroglobulin and serum proteins used to detect autoimmune disease, monoclonal antibody specifically detects abbnormal glycosylation site on di-antitrypsin used to detect autoimmunl conditions, testicular protein that regulates androgen production for male fertility control. Office: Population Coun 1230 York Ave New York NY 10021-6307 *Do what is right, not what is popular.*

CHENG, DAVID HONG, mechanical engineering educator; b. I-Shing, China, Apr. 19, 1920; came to U.S., 1945, naturalized, 1956; s. Tze Kuen and Tseng Sun (Sheng) C.; m. Lorraine Hui-Lan Yang, Sept. 4, 1949; children: Kenneth, Gloria. M.S., U. Minn., 1947, Ph.D.; William Richmond Peters, Jr. fellow, Columbia U., 1950; LHD, William Paterson U. N.J., 1997. Instr. Rutgers U., 1949-50; structural engr. Ammann & Whitney, N.Y.C., 1950-52; sr. engr. M.W. Kellogg Co., N.Y.C., 1952-55; lectr. CCNY, 1955, asst. prof. civil engring., 1955-58, assoc. prof., 1959-65, prof., 1966-86, dir. grad. studies and exec. officer Ph.D. programs in engring., 1977-78, dean engring., 1979-86; cons. M.W. Kellogg Co., Inst. Def. Analyses, N.Y.C. Transp. Adminstrn., ASME; pres. Techtran Inc., 1986; dir., v.p. China-Am. Tech. Corp., 1995—. Author: Nuclei of Strain in the Semi-infinite Solid, 1961, Analysis of Piping Flexibility and Components, 1973. Trustee governing bd. William Paterson Coll. N.J., 1990-97, William Paterson U., 1997—. hon. research fellow Harvard, 1967; Recipient 125th Anniversary medal Coll. City N.Y., 1973; Am. Soc. Engring. Edn.-NASA Faculty fellow, 1964-65. Mem. ASCE, ASME, Chinese Inst. Engrs. (Achievement award 1984), Sigma Xi, Tau Beta Pi (Outstanding Tchr. award 1972), Chi Epsilon, Phi Tau Phi. Home: 200 Old Palisade Rd Fort Lee NJ 07024-7056 Office: William Paterson U Wayne NJ 07470

CHENG, DAVID KEUN, engineering educator; b. Kiangsu, China, Jan. 10, 1918; came to U.S., 1943, naturalized, 1955; s. Han J. and Ying H.C.; m. Enid Kwok, Mar. 27, 1948; 1 child, Eugene. B.S. in Elec. Engring., Nat. Chiao Tung U., 1938; S.M., Harvard U., 1944, Sc.D., 1946; D. Engr. (hon.), Nat. Chiao Tung U., 1985; PhD (hon.), Xidian U., China, 1998. Electronics and project engr. research labs. U.S. Air Force, Cambridge, Mass., 1946-48; asst. prof. elec. and computer engring. Syracuse U., N.Y., 1948-51, assoc. prof., 1951-55, prof., 1955—, Centennial prof., 1970—; hon. prof. Beijing Univ. Posts and Telecomm., 1982—, N.W. Inst. Telecomm. Engring., 1982—, Shanghai Jiao Tong U., 1985—, China; exch. scientist NAS, Hungary, 1972, Yugoslavia, 1974, Poland and Romania, 1978; liaison scientist Office of Naval Rsch., London, 1975-76; disting. European lectr. IEEE, 1975-76; pres., chmn., bd. trustees Li Instn. Sci. & Tech., 1992-98; cons. IBM, GE, TRW. Author: Analysis of Linear Systems, 1959, Field and Wave Electromagnetics, 1983, 2d edit., 1989, Fundamentals of Engineering Electromagnetics, 1993; cons. editor elec. sci. Addison-Wesley, 1961-78, elec. engring. monographs Intext Edn. Pubs., 1969-72; mem. editorial bd. Jour. Electromagnetic Waves and Applications, 1987—; mem. internat. adv. bd. book series on Progress in Electromagnetic Rsch., 1989—; contbr. numerous articles to profl. jours. Recipient Disting. Achievement award Chinese Inst. Engrs., 1962, Disting. Engr. award Li Inst. Sci. and Tech., 1979; Guggenheim fellow, 1960-61; Chancellor's citation, 1981. Fellow IEEE, AAAS, Inst. Elec. Engrs. (U.K.); mem. AAUP, Am. Soc. Engring. Edn., N.Y. Acad. Scis., Sigma Xi (7 Best Paper prizes), Eta Kappa Nu, Phi Tau Phi (Disting. Svc. award 1975). Home: 4620 N Park Ave Apt 104E Chevy Chase MD 20815-4550 Office: Syracuse U Link Hall Syracuse NY 13244

CHENG, HERBERT SU-YUEN, mechanical engineering educator; b. Shanghai, China, Jan. 15, 1929; came to U.S., 1949; s. Chung-Mei and Jing-Ming (Xu) C.; m. Lily D. Hsiung, Apr. 11, 1953; children: Elaine, Elise, Edward, Earl. BSME, U. Mich., 1952; MSME, Ill. Inst. Tech., 1956; PhD, U. Pa., 1961. Jr. mech. engr. Internat. Harvester Co., Chgo., 1952-53; project engr. Machine Engring. co., Chgo., 1953-56; instr. Ill. Inst. Tech., Chgo., 1956-57, U. Pa., Phila., 1957-61; asst. prof. Syracuse (N.Y.) U., 1961-62; rsch. engr. Mech. Tech. Inc., Latham, N.Y., 1962-68; assoc. prof. Northwestern U., Evanston, Ill., 1968-74, prof., 1974—, Walter P. Murphy prof., 1987—, dir. Ctr. for Engring. Tribology, 1984-88, 92—; v.p. Gear Rsch. Inst., Naperville, Ill., 1985-90; cons. GM, Chrysler Corp., Deere Co., Nissan, E.T.C., 1970—. Contbr. articles to profl. jours. Deacon South Presbyn. Ch., Syracuse, 1961-62, 1st Presbyn. Ch. Schenectady, N.Y., 1962-68. Named a hon. prof. Nat. Zhejiang (People's Republic of China) U., 1985. Fellow ASME (hon., Mayo D. Hersey award 1990, D.F. Wilcock award 1999), Soc. Tribologists & Lubrication Engrs. (hon., Nat. award 1987, CAP Alfred Hunt award 1997); mem. NAE, Inst. Mech. Engrs. (U.K., Tribology gold medal 1992), Am. Gear Mfrs. Assn. (acad. mem.), Japan Soc. Lubrication Engrs. Avocations: Peking opera, tennis. Office: Northwestern U 219 Catalysis Bldg 2145 Sheridan Rd Evanston IL 60208-0834

CHENG, HSIEN KEI, aeronautics educator; b. Macao, June 13, 1923; came to U.S., 1948; s. Lo Sing and Teresa Sau Kit (Cheng) C.; m. Wai Laan Lee, May 31, 1956; 1 child, Linda Y. H. BS, Chiao-Tung U., China, 1947; MS in Aero. Engring., Cornell U., 1950, PhD in Aero. Engring., 1952. Aerodynamic engr. Bell Aircraft Corp., Niagara Falls, N.Y., 1952-56; rsch. aerodynamicist Cornell Aero. Lab., Buffalo, 1956-59, prin. aerodynamicist, 1959-63; vis. lectr. Stanford (Calif.) U., 1963-64; spl. lectr. U. So. Calif., L.A., 1964-65, prof., 1965-93, prof. emeritus, 1993—; cons. McDonnell Douglas Corp., Santa Monica, Calif., 1963-70, Rand Corp., Santa Monica, 1965-74, Aerospace Corp., El Segundo, Calif., 1969-74, Sci. Applications Inc., El Segundo, 1972-78, TRW Corp., San Bernardino, Calif., 1985-88, Inst. Aero. Astro, Nat. Cheng-Kung Univ., Taiwan, 1994-95, Northwestern Poly. Univ., Xi'an, People's Republic of China, 1993—; proprietor HKC Rsch., 1996—. Contbr. numerous articles to profl. jours. Grantee Office Naval Rsch., 1972-87, NSF, 1977-86, Air Force Office Sci. Rsch., 1985-92, NASA/Dept. Def., 1987-92. Fellow AIAA, Am. Phys. Soc.; mem. NAE (elected), Soc. Indsl. and Applied Math., Acad. Model Aero., Phi Tau Phi. E-mail: cheng@spock.usc.edu. Fax: 213-740-7774. Office: U So Calif Dept Aerospc & Mech Engring University Park Los Angeles CA 90089-1191

CHENG, H(WEI) H(SIEN), soil scientist, agronomic and environmental science educator; b. Shanghai, China, Aug. 13, 1932; came to U.S., 1951, naturalized, 1961; s. Chi-Pao and Anna (Lan) C.; m. Jo Yuan, Dec. 15, 1962; children: Edwin, Antony. BA, Berea Coll., 1956; MS, U. Ill., 1958, PhD, 1961. Rsch. assoc. Iowa State U., Ames, 1962-64, asst. prof. agronomy, 1964-65; asst. prof. agronomy and soils Wash. State U., Pullman, 1965-71, assoc. prof., 1971-77, prof., 1977-89, interim chmn., 1986-87, chmn. program environ. sci. and regional planning, 1977-79, 88-89, assoc. dean Grad. Sch., 1982-86; prof., head dept. soil, water, and climate U. Minn., St. Paul, 1989—; vis. scientist Juelich Nuclear Rsch. Ctr., Fed. Republic Germany, 1971-73, 79-80, Academia Sinica, Taipei, Republic of China, 1978, Fed. Agrl. Rsch. Ctr., Braunschweig, Fed. Republic Germany, 1980; mem. acad. adv. coun. Inst. Soil Sci., Academia Sinica, Nanjing, People's Republic China, 1987—; mem. adv. bd. Inst. Botany, Academia Sinica, Taipei, 1991—; mem. first sci. adv. bd. Dept. Ecology State of Wash., 1988-89. Editor: Pesticides in the Soil Environment: Processes, Impacts, and Modeling, 1990; assoc. editor Jour. Environ. Quality, 1983-89; mem. editorial bd. Bot. bull.

Academia Sinica, 1988—, cons. editor: Pedosphere, 1991—; contbr. articles to profl. jours. Fulbright rsch. scholar State Agrl. U., Ghent, Belgium, 1963-64. Fellow AAAS, Am. Soc. Agronomy (bd. dirs. 1990-93, exec. com. 1994—, pres.-elect 1997-98, pres. 1998—), Soil Sci. Soc. Am. (divsn. chair 1985-86, bd. dirs. 1990-93, exec. com. 1994-97, pres. 1995-96); mem. Am. Chem. Soc., Soc. Environ. Toxicology and Chemistry, Internat. Soc. Chem. Ecology, Internat. Humic Substances Soc., Internat. Soc. Soil Sci., Coun. for Agrl. Sci. and Tech., Soil and Water Conservation Soc., Sigma Xi (pres. U. Minn. chpt. 1995-96), Phi Kappa Phi, Gamma Sigma Delta. Methodist. Office: U Minn Dept Soil Water and Climate 1991 Upper Buford Cir Saint Paul MN 55108-0010

CHENG, KENNETH TAT-CHIU, pharmacy educator; b. Hong Kong, Feb. 24, 1954; came to U.S., 1972; s. Shiu Fun and Alice Shiu-Wing (Leung) C.; m. Ying Hsu, Aug. 11, 1984; children: Jonathan Yee-Hang, Hannah Yee-Shing. BS in Pharmacy, SUNY, Buffalo, 1977; PhD, Purdue U., 1985. Lic. pharmacist N.Y., Ind., Kans., N.Mex., S.C.; diplomate Am. Bd. Sci. in Nuclear Scis.; cert. expert nuclear medicine tng.; cert. nuclear pharmacist. Resident in hosp. pharmacy U. Kans. Med. Ctr., Kansas City, 1978-79; research/teaching asst. Purdue U., West Lafayette, Ind., 1980-84; research fellow Harvard U. Med. Sch., Boston, 1984-85; assoc. prof. U. N.Mex., Albuquerque, 1985-88; dir. nuclear pharmacy and radiology rsch., assoc. prof. Med. U. S.C., Charleston, 1988—, assoc. prof., 1992—, tenured assoc. prof., 1995—; bd. dirs. Am. Bd. of Sci. in Nuclear Medicine, Nat. Assn. Nuclear Pharmacists, chair, APHA APPM, Nuclear Pharm. Practice, 1999—. Recipient Donald E. Francke award Drug Info. Assn., 1981, Glenn E. Jenkins Qualifying Research award Purdue U., 1984; named one of Outstanding Young Men of Am., 1986; David Ross fellow Purdue U., 1982-83, research fellow Am. Cancer Soc., 1984-85. Fellow Am. Pharm. Assn.; mem. AAAS, Soc. Nuclear Medicine, Am. Soc. Hosp. Pharmacists, Am. Chem. Soc., Soc. Magnetic Resonance Imaging, Internat. Assn. Radiopharmacology, Health Physics Soc., Sigma Xi, Rho Chi, Eta Sigma Gamma. Avocations: music, fishing, swimming. Office: Med U SC Nuclear Pharmacy 171 Ashley Ave Charleston SC 29425-0001

CHENG, KWONG MAN, structural engineer; b. Guang Dong, China, Feb. 15, 1952; came to U.S. 1970; s. Kao Chiu and Miu Chun (Koo) C.; m. King-Yu Yeou, Mar. 29, 1984; 1 child, Natalie. BSCE, MIT, 1976; MEng. Civil Engring., Rensselaer Poly. Inst., 1978. Registered profl. engr. 15 states and U.K. Rsch. asst. Rensselaer Poly. Inst., Troy, N.Y., 1976-78; staff engr. T.Y. Lin Internat., San Francisco, 1978-84, sr. bridge engr., 1984-87, dep. chief bridge engr., 1987-89, prin. and chief bridge engr., 1989-90, v.p., chief bridge engr., 1990-91; pres., prin. engr. OPAC Cons. Engrs., San Francisco, 1992—; dir. T.Y. Lin Internat., San Francisco; lectr. in field. Contbr. articles to profl. jours. Recipient Engring. Design award James F. Lincoln Arc Welding Found., Cleve., 1983. Mem. ASCE, Instn. of Structural Engrs. U.K., Internat. Assn. of Bridge and Structural Engring., Chi Epsilon. Achievements include development of complex construction procedures for long span bridges; complex prestressing details in design of long span concrete bridges. Home: 2989 Dolores Way Burlingame CA 94010-5718 Office: OPAC Cons Engrs 315 Bay St San Francisco CA 94133-1923

CHENG, LIANGSHENG, engineer, researcher, educator; b. Chaohu, Anhui, China, Sept. 14, 1962; came to U.S., 1991; s. Shaoda Cheng and Defang Li. BS, Hohai U., Nanjing, Jiangsu, China, 1983, MS, 1986; PhD, U. Minn., 1996. Engr.-in-tng. Asst. prof. Hohai U., 1986-91; rsch. asst. U. Minn., Mpls., 1991-96, rsch. specialist, 1996, rsch. fellow, 1996, rsch. assoc., 1997-99; engr. Worldtrak Co., 1999—. Mem. ASCE, MRS, Phi Kappa Phi.

CHENG, MEI-FANG, psychobiology educator, neuroethology researcher; b. Kee Lung, Taiwan, Republic of China, Nov. 24, 1938; came to U.S., 1959; d. Chao-Chin Hsieh and Ai Tsu; m. Wen-Kwei Cheng; m. June 7, 1963; children: Suzanne, Po-Yuan, Julie. BS summa cum laude, Nat. Taiwan U., Taipei, 1958; PhD, Brywn Mawr Coll., 1965. Postdoctoral fellow U. Pa., Phila., 1965-68; asst. rsch. prof. Inst. Animal Behavior Rutgers U., Newark, 1969-73, assoc. prof., 1973-79, prof., 1979—, acting dir. Inst. Animal Behavior, 1989-91, dir., 1991-95; cons. NIMH, mem. neurosci. study sect., 1991-95; cons., mem. behavioral neurobiology br. NSF; mem. NIH Reviewers Res., 1995—; cons. numerous granting agys. Author: Advance in the Study of Behavior, 1979; co-editor: Reproduction: A Behavioral and Neuroscientific Perspective, 1986; assoc. editor Hormones and Behavior, 1986-96; cons. Brain Rsch., Sci., others; contbr. articles to profl. jours. Fulbright scholar, 1959; recipient Rsch. Scientist Devel. award NIMH, 1974-79, 79-84, Johnson & Johnson Discovery award, 1989, Hoechst-Celanese Innovative award, 1993, award of excellence in rsch. Rutgers Bd. Trustees. Mem. Internat. Conf. Neuroethology, Neurosci. Achievements include discovery that a bird's own songs stimulate the endocrine changes; demonstration of the neutral mechanisms underlying the endocrine changes triggered by biological sounds; proposition of theory that act of vocalization influences one's emotion; discovery that brain lesions in the adult brain can induce active neuronal cell proliferation that raises the possibilty that neurogenesis may mediate social or environmental facilitation of the recovery of function. Office: Rutgers U Inst Animal Behavior 101 Warren St Newark NJ 07102-1811

CHENG, MICHELLE MEI-HSUE, lawyer; b. Camden, N.J., Oct. 12, 1969; d. Richard Sai-Leung and Mary Yee Cheng. BSEE, U. Mich., 1992; JD, U. Tex., 1996. Atty. Whitehurst, Harkness, Ozmun & Archuleta, P.C., Austin, Tex., 1996—. Mem. Tex. Trial Lawyers' Assn., Am. Trial Lawyers' Assn., Austin Young Lawyers' Assn., Travis County Women's Lawyers' Assn. Fax: 512-476-4400. E-mail: mcheng@whoalaw.com. Office: Whitehurst Harkness Ozmun & Archuleta PC PO Box 1802 Austin TX 78767

CHENG, SHARON GOON, lawyer; b. N.Y.C., July 4, 1951; d. Ngookhong Moy and Swey Lan Goon; m. Paul Cheng, Jr., Sept. 2, 1973; children: Christine, Allison, Paula. BS, St. John's U., Jamaica, N.Y., 1978, JD, 1987. Bar: N.Y. 1988, U.S. Supreme Ct. 1997. Assoc. counsel to pub. adminstr. Queen's County Pub. Adminstrn., N.Y.C., 1987-91; assoc. Rocco M. Longo, Esq., Jamaica Estates, N.Y., 1987-92; ptnr. Longo & Cheng, Jamaica Estates, 1993-96; ct. atty., referee King's County Surrogate's Ct., 1996—. Mem. Chinese Ctr. on Long Island, 1990—, prin., jour editor, 1993-98, legal counsel, 1995—. Recipient Svc. award Chinese Ctr. on Long Island, 1998. Mem. N.Y. State Bar Assn., Queen's County Women's Bar Assn., Asian Am. Bar Assn. of N.Y., St. John's Law Sch. Alumni Assn. (edn. com. 1992-98, diversity com. 1992-95, admissions com. 1994-98, co-chair homecoming com. 1995, chair membership com. 1995—, bd. dirs. 1995—, Alumni Achievement award 1997, BALLSA award 1998, v.p. Bklyn. chpt. 1998—. Home: 21744 Stewart Rd Flushing NY 11364-3539

CHENG, STEPHEN ZHENG DI, chemistry educator, polymeric material researcher; b. Shanghai, Aug. 3, 1949; came to U.S., 1981, naturalization, 1992; s. Luzhong and Jingzhi (Zhang) C.; m. Susan Lian Zhi Xue, June 28, 1978; 1 child, Wendy D.W. BS in Math., East China Normal U., 1977; MS in Polymer Engring., China Textile U., 1981; PhD in Polymer Chemistry, Rensselaer Poly. Inst., 1985. Postdoctoral and rsch. assoc. Rensselaer Poly. Inst., Troy, N.Y., 1985-87; asst. prof. polymer sci. U. Akron, Ohio, 1987-91, assoc. prof. polymer sci., 1991-95, prof. polymer sci., trustee, 1995—; faculty rsch. assoc. Maurice Morton Inst. of Polymer Sci., U. Akron, 1987—, faculty rsch. assoc. Inst. Polymer Engring., 1988—; vis. prof. sci, U. of Tokyo, 1994; vis. prof. polymer sci. and engring. Sichun Union U., China, 1994—; fgn. mem. acad. steering com. Nat. Polymer Physics Open Lab., Chinese Acad. Sci., 1994—, guest prof. polymer sci. Guangzhou Inst. Chemistry, 1994—, guest prof. polymer sci. Changchun Inst. Applied Chemistry, 1995—; guest prof. polymer materials and engring. Zhengzhou U., China, 1994—; guest prof. polymer sci. and engring. Peking U., 1996—, Zhejiang U., 1996—; guest prof. U. Sci. and Tech. of China, 1996—; mem. orgn. com. The First Conf. Worldwide Young Chinese Chemists, Beijing, 1995; adv. prof. polymer sci. Chinese Textile U., 1995—, Fudan U., 1996—, Hebei U. of Tech., 1996—; cons., spkr. in field; project dir. thin film optics Sci. and Tech. Ctr. for Advanced Liquid Crystalline Optical Materials, NSF, 1994—, assoc. dir. Ctr. for Molecular and Microstructure of Composites, 1996—; hon. mem. acad. steering com. Nat. Key Lab. of Chem. Fiber Structure Modification, China Textile U., 1995—; internat. lectr. in field. Editor: Jour. Macromolecular Sci. Part B, Physics, 1995—; adv. bd. Polymer Internat. Jour., 1990—, Marcromolecules, 1996—, Trends in Polymer Sci., 1992—; editl. bd. Jour. Macromolecular Sci., Rev. of Macromolecular Chemistry and Physics, 1992—, Thermochemica Acta,, 1992—, Macromolecular Chemistry and Physics, 1994—, Macromolecular Rapid Communications, 1994—, Jour. Polymer Rsch., 1995—, Internat. Jour. Analysis and Characterization, 1995—; vol. editor: Liquid-Crystalline Polymer Systems: Technological Advances, 1996, Handbook of Thermal Analysis and Calorimetry, Vol. 3, 1997; contbr. chpts. to books and more than 180 articles to profl. jours.; patentee in field. Bd. trustees Akron Internat. Inst., 1995—. Grantee in field; recipient Presdl. Young Investigator award NSF and White House, 1991, Appreciation cert. U. Akron Bd. Trustees, 1992, 94, John H. Dillon Medal, Am. Phys. Soc., 1995, Outstanding Rschr. award U. Akron, 1997; named Disting. corp. Inventor, Am. Soc. Patent Holders, Inventure Place and Home of the Nat. Inventors Hall of Fame, 1995. Fellow Am. Phys. Soc., N.Am. Thermal Analysis Soc. (exec. coun. 1991-93, 94-96, awards vice chmn. 1991-92, awards chmn. 1992-93, meeting vice chmn. 1994, meeting chmn. 1995, others); mem. Am. Chem. Soc. (Akron Sect. award 1994), Soc. Plastics Engrs. (awards com. 1991-94), Materials Rsch. Soc., Soc. Advancement Material and Process Engring., Internat. Confedn. for Thermal Analysis (edn. com. 1996—), Material Rsch. Soc., Internat. Liquid Crystal Soc. Achievements include research on solid state of polymeric materials including phase transition thermodynamics, kinetics, molecular motion, crystal structure and morphology, liquid crystal polymers, surface and interface structures, high-performance polymer fibers, films for microelectronic and optical applications, high temperature composites, computer simulation of molecular dynamics and modeling. Office: U Akron Morton Inst Polymer Sci Akron OH 44325-3909

CHENG, THOMAS CLEMENT, parasitologist, immunologist, educator, author; b. Nov. 5, 1930; came to U.S., 1946.; s. James Tsu-Mook and Dorothy (Lee) C.; m. Barbara Ann Schimmel, May 31, 1957 (div. 1982); children: Thomas C., J. Bradford, Allison E.; m. Anne Foos Whitelaw, June 19, 1982 (div. 1985). AB, Wayne State U., 1952; MS, U. Va., 1956, PhD, 1958. Asst. prof. U. Md. Med. Sch., Balt., 1958-59; from asst. prof. to assoc. prof. Lafayette Coll., Easton, Pa., 1959-64; chief immunology and parasitology Northeast Marine Health Sci. Lab USPHS, Narragansett, R.I., 1964-65; from assoc. prof. to prof. U. Hawaii, Honolulu, 1965-69; prof., dir. Ctr. for Health Sci., Lehigh U., Bethlehem, Pa., 1969-80; sr. prof. cell biology Med. U. S.C., Charleston, S.C., 1980-92, dir. Marine Biomed. Research, 1980-91, sr. prof., 1991-92; sr. sci. cons. Atlantic Farms, Folly Beach, S.C., 1993—; dir. Marine Rsch. Inst., Charleston, 1993—; pres. Inventive Marine Enterprises, Charleston, 1996—, Marine Biomed. Rsch. Ctr., Charleston; cons. Acad. Press, San Diego, 1969—, Univ. Park Press, Balt., 1969-80, Divsn. Microbiology FDA, Washington, 1968-72, biomed. rsch. Internat. Copper Rsch. Assn., Inc., N.Y.C., 1970-92, Sandoz Pharm. Co., Winter Park, Fla., 1979—, Xytronyx, Inc., San Diego, 1984—, Atlantic Farms, Folly Beach, S.C., 1993—; mem. USPHS Commn. on Food Protection, Washington, 1965-66, environ. biology and chemistry study sect. NIH, Bethesda, Md., 1969-71, spl. study sect. Marine Environ. Health, Bethesda, 1973-75, planning com. FDA-HHS, Washington, 1969-71; mem. adv. bd. Ctr. for Pathobiology U. Calif.-Irvine, 1969—; mem. rev. panel Div. Ocean Scis., Office of Internat. Decade of Ocean Exploration NSF, Washington, 1977-78, divsn. cell physiology, 1980-83; chmn. molecular biology Office Naval Rsch., Arlington, Va., 1983-92; dir. WHO Collaborative Lab. of Vector Biology, Charleston, S.C., 1982-92, rsch. Centre Nationale de la Recherche, France, 1986-87; prin. lectr. Internat. Soc. Comparative Physiology, Switzerland, 1989; co-chmn. Internat. Congress Parasitology, Paris, 1990; mem. sci. directorate Internat. Orgn. Pathology Marine Aquaculture; adj. marine scientist Marine Resources Rsch. Inst., S.C. Wildlife and Marine Resources Dept., 1993—. Author: The Biology of Animal Parasites (1st prize Phila. Book Show), 1964, 65, Marine Molluscs as Hosts for Symbiosis, 1967, Symbiosis: Organisms Living Together, 1970, General Parasitology, 1973, 2d edit. 1986, Human Parasitology, 1990, 2d edit. 1998; editor, contbr. Some Biochemical and Immunological Aspects of Host-Parasite Relationships, 1963, Aspects of the Biology of Symbiosis, 1971, Molluscicides in Schistosomiasis Control, 1974, Invertebrate Immune Responses, 1977, Invertebrate Models for Biomedical Research, 1978, Structure of Membranes and Receptors, 1984, Invertebrate Blood: Functions of Serum Factors and Cells, 1984; editor: Pathogens of Invertebrates: Application in Biological Control and Transmission Mechanisms, 1984; co-author: Medical and Economic Malacology, 1974, Biology of Microsporidia, 1976, Systematics of the Microsporidia, 1977, Pathology in Marine Science, 1990; editor Jour. Invertebrate Pathology, 1969-91, Exptl. Parasitology jour., 1969-88, Comparative Pathobiology jour., 1975-84; contbr. numerous articles to profl. jours. and revs. Mem. Mayor's Marine Mus. Project, Charleston, 1984-97; regional coord. Nat. Disaster Med. System, Charleston, 1987-94. Capt. USPHS, U.S. Army, 1952-54, 64-65, Korea. Recipient George C. Wheeler Disting. Lectureship award U. N.D., Grand Forks, 1973, Disting. Lectr. Southwestern Assn. Parasitologists, 1973, Disting. Lectureship award Tulane Med. Sch., New Orleans, 1977; Parasitology prin. lectr. award Coll. of Physicians of Phila., 1980; Andrew Fleming Rsch. award U. Va., Charlottesville, 1958, Roy and Ira Jones Superior Tchg. award Lafayette Coll., Easton, Pa., 1962, Disting. Alumnus award Wayne State U., Detroit, 1975, Medal of Honor U. Montpellier, 1992; Fulbright Rsch scholar, France, 1986-87; grantee AEC, 1958-59, 60-62, NSF, 1959-61, 78-83, 82-85, 94-98, NIH 1961-64, 71-76, 75-78, 77-79, Am. Cancer Soc., 1966-69, FDA, 1973-75, Internat. Copper Rsch. Assn., 1971-76, 75-77, 81-84, Nat. Marine Fisheries, NOAA, 1991-93, 95-96, Dept. Agrl. 1995-96, Dept. Commerce, Dept. Energy, WHO, USDA, Am. Cyanamid Co.; Disting Stoll lectr. Rutgers U., 1988; named Hon. Citizen City of Montpellier, France, 1992; inducted Hall of Fame, Greenbrier Alumni Assn., 1998. Fellow Royal Soc. Tropical Medicine and Hygiene, AAAS; mem. Am. Microscopical Soc. (pres. 1980-81), Am. Physiol. Soc., Jefferson Soc. U. Va., Am. Soc. Zoologists (rep. pub. affairs 1982-88), Am. Soc. Parasitologists (exec. council 1974-78), Soc. for Exptl. Biology and Medicine, Soc. Protozoologists, Reticuloendothelial Soc., N.Y. Acad. Scis., Helminthological Soc. Washington, Soc. for Invertebrate Pathology (chmn. publs. bd. 1969-84), N.Y. Soc. Tropical Medicine (sec.-treas. 1975-76), Council of Biology Editors, N.J. Soc. Parasitology (pres. 1977-78), Sigma Xi. Democrat. Episcopalian. Home and Office: 8 Queen St Charleston SC 29401-2111 also: Marine Rsch Inst PO Box 12139 Charleston SC 29422-2139 also: Inventive Marine Enterprises PO Box 13359 Charleston SC 29422-3359 also: Marine Biomed Rsch Ctr PO Box 12139 Charleston SC 29412-2139

CHENG, TSEN-CHUNG, electrical engineering educator; b. Shanghai, Peoples Republic of China, Dec. 24, 1944; s. Yik Yu and Shun Lan (Tsui) C.; m. Doris Tin Gen Lee, Aug. 25, 1974; 1 child, Jason. BS, MIT, 1969, MSEE, 1970, ScD, 1974. Asst. prof. U. So. Calif., Los Angeles, 1974-80, assoc. prof., 1980-84, Lloyd F. Hunt prof., dir. electric power program, 1984—; pres. T.C. Cheng ScD Inc., San Marino, Calif., 1981—; cons. Los Angeles Dept. Water and Power, 1984—, So. Calif. Edison Co., 1982—, Pacific Gas & Electric Co., San Francisco, 1982—. Patentee in field; author over 80 publs. Recipient Outstanding Elec. Engring. faculty award U. So. Calif., 1976, Engring. Service award U. So. Calif., 1981. Fellow IEEE (relay com. award 1986, Best Paper award 1988), Sigma Xi, Eta Kappa Nu, Tau Beta Pi. Office: Univ of So Calif Phe 634 Dept Ee Ep # 634 Los Angeles CA 90089

CHENG, TSUNG O., cardiologist, educator; b. Shanghai, Mar. 30, 1925; came to U.S., 1950, naturalized, 1960; s. Keith S. and Fanny (Wang) C.; m. Marie Ellen Roe, June 18, 1955; children: Mark Dudley, Yvonne Joyce. BS, St. John's U., China, 1945; MD, U. Pa., 1950, MS in Medicine, 1956. Diplomate Am. Bd. Internal Medicine (subsplty. cardiovascular disease), Nat. Bd. Med. Examiners. Intern St. Barnabas Hosp., Newark, 1950-51; resident Cook County Hosp., Chgo., 1952-55; fellow in cardiovascular disease George Washington U., D.C. Gen. Hosp., Washington, 1955-56; instr. cardiology Harvard Med. Sch. Mass. Gen. Hosp., Boston, 1956-57; fellow in cardiorespiratory physiology Johns Hopkins U. Sch. Medicine and Hosp., 1957-59; practice medicine specializing in cardiology Washington, 1970—; asst. prof. medicine SUNY Downstate, 1959-70; assoc. prof. medicine George Washington U., 1970-72; chief cardiology D.C. Gen. Hosp., 1971-72; prof. George Washington U., 1972—; dir. cardiac catheterization lab. George Washington U. Med. Center, 1972-78, assoc. dir. cardiology, 1972-75; asst. physician Cardiac Clinic, Johns Hopkins Hosp., 1957-59, mem. staff cardiac catheterization lab., 1957-59; dir. cardiopulmonary lab. Bklyn. Hosp., 1959-66; co-chief Pediatric Cardiac Clinic, 1959-66; chief Adolescent Cardiac Clinic, 1961-66; attending physician Adult Cardiac Clinic, 1959-66; chief Pediatric Cardiac Clinic Cumberland Hosp., Bkly., 1963-66; asst. chief cardiology VA Hosp., Bklyn., 1966-69; chief Cardiovascular Lab., 1966-70, chief cardiology, 1969-70; asst. vis. physician Kings County Hosp. Med. Center, Bklyn., 1964-70; attending physician Univ. Hosp., SUNY, Bklyn., 1967-70; cons. Beth Israel Med. Ctr., N.Y.C., 1970-82; guest lectr. Chinese Med. Assn., 1972, 73, 75, 77, 79, 83, 86, 89, 92, Chinese Ministry Health, 1990; hon. prof. Shanghai 2d Med. Univ. 1986—, Qingdao Med. Coll., 1989—, Binzhou Med. Coll., 1992—, Taishan Med. Coll., 1992—, Tongji Med. U., Wuhan, China, 1993—, Jiujiang Med. Coll., Jiangxi, China 1994—, U. Cape Town, South Africa, 1995—; hon. dir. Qingdao Cardiovascular Rsch. Inst., 1989—, Guangdong Provincial Cardiovascular Inst., 1990—; hon. pres. Dandong 1st Hosp., Dandong, Liaoning Province, People's Republic of China 1988—, Shanghai St. Luke's Hosp., 1990—, Binzhou Med. Coll. Affiliated Hosp., 1992—, Taishan Med. Coll. Affiliated Hosp., 1992—, Jiujiang Med. Coll. Affiliated Hosp., Jiujiang, Jiangxi, China, 1994—, Second People's Hosp., Jin De Zhen, Jiangxi, 1994—; vis. prof., Peking Union Med. Coll., 1986—; hon. cons. Beijing Hosp., 1989—; vis. prof. Sun Yatsen Med. U., Canton, 1992—, Cairo U., Egypt, 1994—, U. Oxford, Eng., 1995—, U. Witwatersrand Med. Sch., Johannesburg, South Africa, 1995—, U. Paris Hosp., Tenon, France, 1995—, U. Natal, Durban, South Africa, 1995—, Cath. U. Inst. Cardiology, Rome, 1996—, Inst. Clin. Physiology, Nat. Rsch. Coun., U. Pisa, Italy, 1996—, Inst. Clin. Physiology of the Nat. Rsch. Coun., Milan, Inst. of Pathol. Anatomy Med. Sch. U. Milan, 1996—, U. Dusseldorf (Germany), 1997—, U. Hamburg (Germany), 1997—, U. Hannover (Germany), 1997—, U. Melbourne (Australia), 1997—, U. NSW, Sydney, Australia, 1997—, U. Instanbul (Turkey), 1999—, U. Athens (Greece), 1999—; v.p. Am. Ctr. for Chinese Med. Sci., 1982-91; pres. Friends St. Luke's Hosp. Shanghai, 1991—, chmn. bd., 1992—; hon. dir. Inst. Invasive Therapy PLA 150th Ctrl. Hosp., Luoyang, China 1994—; disting. sr. visitor Royal Brompton Hosp./Nat. Heart and Lung Inst., London, 1995—; hon. advisor Guangdong Soc. Interventional Cardiology, Guangzhou, China, 1996—. Sr. editor Vascular Medicine, 1983-88, Angiology, 1986-97; editor: The International Textbook of Cardiology, 1986, 87, Percutaneous Balloon Valvuloplasty, 1992; mem. editl. bd. Catheterization and Cardiovasc. Diagnosis, 1991—, Jour. Noninvasive Cardiology, 1997—; co-editor: Congestive Heart Failure, 1991, Modern Cardiology, 1994, Genetics of Cardiovascular Diseases, 1995, Congestive Heart Failure,em. editl. bd. Catheterization and Cardiovascular Interventions, 1999—; contbg. med. editor: Cortlandt Forum, 1997-98; contbr. numerous articles to sci. and med. jours. Fellow ACP, Am. Coll. Chest Physicians, Am. Coll. Cardiology (ofcl. rep. to standards com. on catheters Assn. Advancement Med. Instrumentation 1971—), Am. Heart Assn., Coun. Clin. Cardiology, Soc. Cardiac Angiography and Interventions, Internat. Coll. Angiology, Am. Coll. Angiology, Soc. Geriatric Cardiology (founding); mem. AAAS, Am. Fedn. Clin. Rsch., Am. Heart Assn., Washington Heart Assn. Home: 7508 Cayuga Ave Bethesda MD 20817-4822 Office: George Washington U Med Ctr 2150 Pennsylvania Ave NW Washington DC 20037-3201 *My goal in life is to serve the people the best way that I know, that is, through medicine which knows no international boundary. Perseverance, patience, hard work and selflessness will always be rewarded by the satisfaction of a job well done.*

CHENG, WAN-LEE, mechanical engineer, industrial technology educator; b. Yi-Hsin, Chaing-Su, Republic of China, Dec. 28, 1945; came to U.S., 1971; s. Teh-Chih and Mei-Nung (Shih) C.; m. Viki Shu-Whei Lu, Dec. 16, 1972; children: Julie Wheichung, Paul Yichung, Lisa Yenchung. BS, Chung Yuan U., Taiwan, 1969; MEd, Sul Ross State U., 1972; PhD, Iowa State U., 1976. Mech. engr. Taiwan Power Co., Taipei, 1970-71; instr. Iowa State U., Ames, 1974-76; asst. prof., then prof. U. N.D., Grand Forks, 1976-85; prof., chmn. dept. design and industry San Francisco State U., 1985—; cons. High-Tech Mobile Lab., N.D. Vocat. Edn. Dept., Bismarck, 1984-85; vis. prof. Nat. Sci. Coun. and Chung Yuan U., Taiwan, Republic of China, 1990-91; chief adminstrv. cons. Coll. of Design, Chung Yuan Christian U., dean, 1994-95. Author computer software; contbr. articles to profl. jours.; mem. rev. bd. Jour. Indsl. Tech., 1986—. Session elder 1st Presbyn. Ch., Grand Forks, 1984-85; session elder Lakeside Presbyn. Ch., 1989-91. Recipient Indsl. Arts Profl. Devel. award N.D. Indsl. Arts Assn., Bismarck, 1985, Outstanding Teaching and Faculty Devel. award Burlington No. Found., Grand Forks, 1985, Outstanging Prof. Indsl. Tech. award Nat. Assn. Indsl. Tech., 1992; 10 grants U. N.D., 1979-85. Mem. Soc. Mfg. Engrs. (sr.), Chinese Inst. Engrs. (v.p. 1993), Chung Yuan Alumni Assn. No. Calif. (pres. San Francisco 1987-88), Chinese Am. Econ. and Tech. Devel. Assn. (pres. 1997—), Joint Alumni Assn. Chinese Univs. and Colls. No. Calif. (pres. San Francisco, 1988-89), Phi Kappa Phi, Epsilon Pi Tau (trustee Gamma Gamma chpt. Grand Forks 1984-85, Laureate award Beta Beta chpt. San Francisco 1991). Office: San Francisco State Univ Dept of Design and Industry 1600 Holloway Ave San Francisco CA 94132-1722

CHENG, WU C., patent examiner; b. Shanghai, China, Aug. 11, 1922; came to U.S., 1948; s. Ting-yih and Wei-chi (Kiang) C.; m. Wenying Liu, 1963; 1 child, Robert C. BS, St. John's U., Shanghai, 1944; MS, Kans. State Coll., 1949; PhD, Ga. Inst. Tech., Atlanta, 1954. Asst. prof. to prof., head chemistry dept. Union U., Jackson, Tenn., 1955-66; assoc. prof. chemistry George Peabody Coll., Nashville, 1966-72; tchr. with rank I Lyman H.S., Longwood, Fla., 1972-75; asst. prof. chemistry to assoc. prof. physics Paine Coll., Augusta, Ga., 1975-89; patent examiner U.S. Dept. Commerce, Washington, 1990-99; vis. instr. chemistry Ga. Inst. Tech., Atlanta, summer 1956; chemist No. Regional Rsch. Ctr., Peoria, Ill., summer 1976, 88; faculty rsch. participant Savannah River Lab., Aiken, S.C., summer 1977, Argonne Nat. Lab., Chgo., summer 1982, Oak Ridge (Tenn.) Nat. Lab., summer 1984; mem. faculty Rockwell Hanford (Wash.) Ops., summer 1979; faculty rsch. fellow USAF Acad., Colorado Springs, Colo., summer 1986. Contbr. articles to profl. jours. Mem. Am. Chem. Soc., Armed Forces Comms. and Electronics Assn., Ga. Acad. Sci., N.Y. Acad. Scis., Sigma Xi. Achievements include patents in field. Address: PO Box 211336 Martinez GA 30917-1336

CHENG, YUHUA, electrical engineer; b. Wudi, Shandong, People's Republic of China, Nov. 2, 1958; s. Jinduo and Wenling (Guo) C.; m. Junhua Li, Aug. 1, 1982; 1 child, Feng. BSEE, Shandong Polytech. U., 1982; MSEE, Tianjin U., 1985; PhDEE, Tsinghua U., 1989. Engr. Acad. of Sci., Jinan, China, 1985-86; rsch. asst. Tsinghua U., Beijing, 1986-89; lectr. Peking U., Beijing, 1990-92, assoc. prof., 1992-96; mem. cons. staff Cadence Design Systems, San Jose, Calif., 1997; sr. staff engr. Conexant Systems, Inc. (formerly Rockwell Semiconductor Sys), Newport Beach, Calif., 1997—; rsch. fellow Norwegian Inst. of Tech., Trondheim, Norway, 1994-95; rsch. scientist U. Calif., Berkeley, 1995-97; cons. BTA Tech., Santa Clara, Calif. Author: MOSFET Compact Modeling and User's Guide to BSIM3, 1999; contbr. articles to profl. publs.; inventor in field. Recipient Award for Outstanding Contbn. Ministry of Electronics in China, 1993. Mem. IEEE. Avocations: fishing, tennis, reading, listening to classic music. Fax: 9494836970. E-mail: chengy@conexant.com. Office: Conexant Systems Inc 4311 Jamboree Rd Newport Beach CA 92660

CHENHALL, DONALD R., airport manager. BA, U. Ariz., 1975. Land surveyor Ketchikan, Alaska, 1981-96; airport mgr. Ketchikan Gateway Borough, 1996—. Mem. ASCE, Am. Soc. Profl. Land Surveyors. Office: Ketchikan Gate Borough Ketchikan Internat Airport 344 Front St Ketchikan AK 99901

CHENHALL, ROBERT GENE, former museum director, consultant, author; b. Maurice, Iowa, Jan. 24, 1923; s. Raymond Ernest and Lillian Georgia (Clark) C.; m. Carol Ann Vandercook, Feb. 26, 1943 (div. 1972); children: Raymond E., Donald R., Doris Chenhall Flenniken; m. Barbara Phyliss Von Lenz, Nov. 16, 1972. BA, San Diego State U., 1946; MA, Ariz. State U., 1965, PhD, 1972. Accountant Price Waterhouse & Co. (C.P.A.'s), Los Angeles, 1951-55, Fisher Contracting Co., Phoenix, 1955-63, Del E. Webb Corp., Phoenix, 1963-66; mem. faculty dept.anthropology U. Ark., Fayetteville, 1969-74; mem. staff Strong Museum, Rochester, N.Y., 1974-79; dir. Buffalo Mus. Sci., 1979-80, N.Mex. Mus. Natural History, Albuquerque, 1980-82; mus. cons., author, 1982—; mem. commn. archaeol. data banks Internat. Union Prehistoric and Protohistoric Scis., 1977-80; mem. trustees vis. com. Internat. Mus. Photography, Rochester, 1978-80; treas. N.E. Museums Conf., 1979-80; mem. mus. aid panel N.Y. State Council Arts, 1979-80; reviewer operating support grants Inst. Mus. Services, 1980-81. Author: Computers in Anthropology and Archeology, 1971, Museum Cataloging in the Computer Age, 1975, Nomenclature for Museum Cataloguing: A System for Classifying Man-Made Objects, 1978, rev. edit. 1988, (with

David Vance) Museum Collections and Today's Computers, 1988, (with Michael Yergin) Wealth Building in the 90s, 1991; also articles, revs., chpts. in books; founder, editor: Newsletter Computer Archaeology, 1965-71; editor: archaeol sect. Computers and the Humanities, 1967-70; corr. editor: archaeol sect. Computers in the Humanities, 1968-71. Served with AUS, 1944-46. Fellow Am. Anthrop. Assn.; mem. Soc. Am. Archaeology, Am. Assn. Museums, Internat. Council Museums (dir. documentation com. 1971-80), Assn. Sci. Mus. Dirs., Council Mus. Anthropology.

CHENHALLS, ANNE MARIE, nurse, educator; b. Detroit, May 26, 1929; d. Peter and Beatrice Mary (Elliston) McLeod; m. Horacio Chenhalls, 1953 (dec.); children: Mark, Anne Marie Chenhalls Delamater. Student Detroit Conservatory Music, 1946-47; grad. Grace Hosp. Sch. Nursing, 1951; B. Vocat. Edn., Calif. State U.-Los Angeles, 1967, B.S. in Nursing, 1968; M.A., Calif. State U.-Long Beach, 1985. R.N., Calif. Nurse, Grace Hosp., Detroit, 1951-52; pvt. duty nurse, Mexico City, 1953-54; nurse St. Francis Hosp., Lynwood, Calif., 1957-63; assoc. prof. nursing Compton Coll. (Calif.), 1964-72; health educator, sch. nurse Santa Ana Unified Sch. Dist. (Calif.), 1972-76, 79—; med. coord., internat. health cons. Agape Movement, San Bernardino, Calif., 1976-79; instr. community health, Uganda, 1982; med. evaluator Athletes in Action, 1979; pub. health nurse Orange County Health Dept., Calif., 1990-95 . Assoc. staff mem. Campus Crusade for Christ. Solo vocalist, Santa Ana, Orange, Seal Beach, Dinner Theater, Calif., Civic Light Opera, Buena Park, Calif.; acting Master's Repertory Theater, 1990-94, Santa Ana. U.S. govt. grantee, 1968. Mem. Calif. Sch. Nurses Assn., Calif. Tchrs. Assn. Democrat. Home: 7 Brisa Del Lago Rancho Santa Margarita CA 92688-1400 Office: Santa Ana Unified Sch Dist 1601 E Chestnut Ave Santa Ana CA 92701-6322

CHENIAE, GEORGE MAURICE, plant biochemist; b. Mounds, Ill., Aug. 27, 1928. BS, U. Ill., 1950; MS, N.C. State Coll., 1957, PhD, 1959. Asst. Oak Ridge Nat. Lab, 1950-52; Nat. Sci. fellow, 1959-60; resident sci. Res. Inst. Advance Study, 1960-75; prof. plant physiol. and biochemistry U. Ky., Lexington, 1975-96. Mem. Am. Soc. Plant Physiologists (Charles F. Kettering award 1990), Am. Soc. Biochemistry and Molecular Biology. Office: U Ky Dept Agronomy Agron Sci Ctr Rm N205 Lexington KY 40546

CHEN NING YANG, physicist, educator; b. Hofei, Anhwei, China, Sept. 22, 1922; naturalized, 1964; s. Ke Chuan and Meng Hwa Lo; m. Chih Li Tu, Aug. 26, 1950; children: Franklin, Gilbert, Eulee. BS, Nat. S.W. Assoc. U., China, 1942; PhD, U. Chgo., 1948; DSc (hon.), Princeton U., 1958, Bklyn. Poly. Inst., 1965, U. Wroclaw, Poland, 1974, Gustavus Adolphus Coll., 1975, U. Md., 1979, U. Durham, Eng., 1979, Fudan U., 1984, Swiss Fed. Inst. Tech., Switzerland, 1987, Moscow State U., 1992, Drexel U., 1995. Instr., U. Chgo., 1948-49; mem. Inst. Advanced Study, Princeton, 1949-55, prof., 1955-66; Albert Einstein prof. SUNY, Stony Brook, 1966-99; dir. Inst. Theoretical Physics SUNY, 1966-99; disting. prof.-at-large Chinese U., Hong Kong, 1986—. Trustee Rockefeller U., 1970-76, Salk Inst., 1978-89, Ben Gurion U., 1980—. Recipient Nobel prize for physics, 1957, Rumford prize, 1980, Nat. Medal of Sci., 1986, Benjamin Franklin medal, 1993, Bower prize, 1994. Mem. AAAS (bd. dirs. 1975-79), NAS, Am. Phys. Soc., Royal Soc. London (fgn.), Chinese Acad. Scis., Academia Sinica, Brazilian Acad. Scis., Venezuelan Acad. Scis., Royal Spanish Soc. Scis., Polish Acad. Scis., Russian Acad. Scis., Korean Acad. Sci. & Tech., Am. Philos. Soc., Pontifical Acad. Scis., Sigma Xi. Office: SUNY Inst Theoretical Physics Stony Brook NY 11794-3840

CHENOWETH, HELEN P., congresswoman; b. Topeka, Kans., Jan. 27, 1938; 2 children. Attended, Whitworth Coll., 1975-79; cert. in law office mgmt., U. Minn., 1974; student, Rep. Nat. Com. Mgmt. Coll., 1977. Bus. mgr. Northside Med. Ctr., 1964-75; state exec. dir. Idaho Rep. Party, 1975-77; chief of staff Congressman Steve Symms, 1977-78; campaign mgr. Symms for Congress Campaign, 1978, Leroy for Gov., 1985-86; v.p. Consulting Assocs., Inc., 1978—; mem. House of Reps., Washington, mem. agriculture com., resources com., vet. affairs com.; mem. agriculture, resources, vets. affairs coms.; bd. dirs. Ctr. Study of Market Alternatives. Deacon Capitol Christian Ctr., Boise. Office: US Ho of Reps 1727 Longworth Bldg Washington DC 20515-1201

CHENOWETH, KRISTIN, actress. Grad., Oklahoma City U. Actress with roles on Broadway including: A New Brain, Steel Pier; Off-Broadway plays include: Scapin, The Fantasticks, Dames at Sea, Strike Up the Band at City Ctr.'s Encores! series; performed leading roles at Goodspeed Opera House, Guthrie Theatre, Paper Mill Playhouse, North Shore Music Theatre; guest soloist West Side Story Suite of Dances, N.Y.C. Ballet; mem. AMC's Paramour TV series, Lateline (NBC), Blind Men (Pilot-NBC). Winner 1999 Tony award for best featured actress in Good Man Charlie Brown, Metropolitan Opera award. Office: c/o SAG 1515 Broadway 44th Flr New York NY 10036*

CHENOWETH, ROSE MARIE, librarian; b. Decatur, Ill., Jan. 22, 1953; d. Harold Everett and Jacqueline Marie (Rhodes) C. BS in Edn., Ill. State U., 1974; MLS, U. Ill., 1979. Librarian Mt. Zion (Ill.) Sch. System, 1974-78; adult services librarian Willard Library, Evansville, Ind., 1979-81; reference librarian River Bend Library System, Coal Valley, Ill., 1981-83; head of extension services Moline (Ill.) Pub. Library, 1983-89; dir. Goshen (Ind.) Pub. Libr., 1989—. Sec. Citizens for Reproductive Choice, Quad Cities, Ill., 1982-88; v.p., archivist Coun. on Community Svcs., Rock Island, 1983-88; mem. planning com. Literacy Coun. Rock Island, Henry and Mercer Counties, Ill., 1983-88; sec., v.p. 23rd Ave. Bus. Assn., Moline, 1985-89; active Goshen Hist. Soc., 1989—, Elkhart County Hist. Soc., 1989—. Mem. ALA, AAUW, NOW (chairperson reproductive rights com. 1982-83), Ill. Libr. Assn. (pub. libr. sect., dir.-at-large 1982-84, chmn. awards com.), Illowa Libr. Assn., Kiwanis (Maple City, Ind.), Beta Phi Mu. Avocation: needlework, politics. Home: 1020 W Lincoln Ave Goshen IN 46526-2127

CHER (CHERILYN SARKISIAN), singer, actress; b. El Centro, Calif., May 20, 1946; d. Gilbert and Georgia LaPiere; m. Sonny Bono, Oct. 27, 1964 (div.); 1 child, Chastity; m. Gregg Allman, June 1975 (div.); 1 child, Elijah Blue. Student drama coach, Jeff Corey. Singer with husband as team, Sonny and Cher, 1964-74; star TV shows: Cher, 1975-76, The Sonny and Cher Show, 1976-77; concert appearances with husband, 1977, numerous recs., TV, concert and benefit appearances with Sonny Bono; TV appearances, ABC-TV, 1978, appearance with Sonny Bono in motion pictures, Good Times, 1966, Chastity, 1969; film appearances include Silkwood, 1983, Mask, 1985 (Best Actress, Cannes Internat. Film Festival), The Witches of Eastwick, 1987, Suspect, 1987, Moonstruck (Golden Globe award 1988, Acad. award for best actress 1988), 1987, Mermaids, 1990, Faithful, 1996, If These Walls Could Talk, 1996; TV movie: The Player, 1992, Pret-a-Porter, 1994; helped form rock band, Black Rose, 1979; recorded albums Black Rose, 1980, Cher, 1987, Heart of Stone, 1989 (Double Platinum and 3 Gold Singles), Love Hurts, 1991, It's A Man's World, 1996, The Casablanca Years, 1996. Office: Bill Sammeth Orgn PO Box 2040 Santa Monica CA 90406-2040 also: Reprise Records 3000 Warner Blvd Burbank CA 19010-4694

CHERAMIE, LESLEY GOYETTE, veterinarian; b. Norwood, Mass., Feb. 26, 1969; d. Robert Ray and Marcia Ann (Bergevine) Goyette; m. Hoyt Stephen Cheramie, Oct. 26, 1996. BS, U. Mass., 1991; DVM, U. Tenn., 1995. Vet. technician Va. Tech., Blacksburg, 1995—. Mem. Am. Vet. Med. Assn. Democrat. Roman Catholic. Avocations: horseback riding, reading. Home: 1412 N Main St Blacksburg VA 24060-2522 Office: Virginia Maryland Regional Coll Vet Medicine Duckpond Dr Phase III Blacksburg VA 24061

CHERCHIGLIA, DEAN KENNETH, lawyer; b. Cold Springs, N.Y., Apr. 11, 1956; s. Patrick Joseph and Bella (Feld) C.; m. Susan Elaine Sonkin, July 5, 1980; children: Brian Alden, Evan James. BBA cum laude, Ohio U., 1977; JD, Case Western Res. U., 1984. Bar: Ohio 1984. Contract specialist NASA Lewis Rsch. Ctr., Cleve., 1980; atty. Hermann, Cahn & Schneider, Cleve., 1984-85; assoc. Schwarzwald, Robiner, Wolf & Rock, Cleve., 1985; asst. counsel HealthAm. Corp., Cleve., 1986-87; atty. TransOhio Savs. Bank, Cleve., 1987-91; asst. v.p., counsel Chase Fin. Corp., Cleve., 1991-97; of counsel Benesch, Friedlander, Coplan & Aronoff, Cleve., 1997—. Mem. Case Western Res. U. Law. Rev., 1982-84. Mem. Ohio Stae Bar Assn., Cleve. Bar Assn., Amnesty Internat. Avocations: photography, scuba diving, weightlifting. Home: 3620 Stoer Rd Shaker Heights OH 44122-5116 Office: Benesch Friedlander Coplan & Aronoff 2300 BP America Bldg 200 Public Sq Cleveland OH 44114-2301

CHERCHI USAI, PAOLO, film curator, film historian; b. Rossiglione, Italy, Nov. 8, 1957; came to U.S., 1989; s. Licinio and Anita (Piccardo) Usai-Cherchi. D in Modern Lit., U. Genoa, Italy, 1981. Editor arts sect. Il Lavoro Newspaper, Genoa, 1982-88; asst. curator George Eastman House, Rochester, N.Y., 1989-92, sr. curator film, 1994—; head preservation projects Royal Film Archive, Brussels, 1993-94; dep. curator Cineteca Del Friuli, Gemona, Italy, 1986-88; dir. Selznick Sch. Film Preservation, Rochester, 1996—. Author: Georges Melies, 1983, Burning Passions: An Introduction to the Study of Silent Cinema, 1994 (Acad. Book Yr. award Choice 1996), Silent Witnesses (Film Book Yr. award Internat. Film Guide 1991); editor: (book) The Griffith Project, 1997; (jour.) Segnocinema, 1986—, Jour. Film Preservation, 1991-95; co-editor Griffithiana, 1984—; adv. bd. Film History, 1993—. Co-dir. Silent Film Festival, Pordenone, Italy, 1982—. Mem. Internat. Fedn. Film Archives (bd. dirs. 1995—), Domitor Assn. Early Cinema Studies (pres. 1995—), Assn. Moving Image Archivists, Nat. Film Preservation Bd. (alt. mem.), Soc. Cinema Studies, Les Amis De Valentin Bru. Avocations: music, art history, studies on creativity, research on artificial intelligence, landscape architecture. Office: George Eastman House 900 East Ave Rochester NY 14607-2298

CHERCOVER, MURRAY, television executive; b. Montreal, Que., Can., Aug. 18, 1929; s. Max M. and Betty (Pomerance) (dec.) C.; m. Barbara Ann Holleran, Aug. 8, 1953; children: Hollis Denny, Sean Peter. Grad., Acad. Radio TV Arts, Toronto, Ont., Can., Neighborhood Playhouse Sch. Theatre, N.Y.C. With Radio Sta. CFPA, Port Arthur, Ont., 1944-46, New Play Soc. Jupiter Theater, Toronto, 1946-48; exec. dir. Equity Library Theatre, N.Y.C., 1948-52; producer, dir. network TV drama Louis G. Cowan Agy., N.Y.C., 1948-52; with Canadian Broadcasting Co., 1952-60; exec. producer all prodn. Sta. CFTO-TV, Toronto, 1960, dir. programming, 1961; exec. v.p., gen. mgr. CTV TV Network Ltd., Toronto, 1966; pres., chief operating officer CTV TV Network Ltd., 1968, pres., mng. dir., 1969—, pres., chief exec. officer, 1987-90, 1990—; pres. Chercover Communications, 1990—; pres., dir. Avanti Mgmt. Ltd.; founding dir., fellow Internat. Coun. Nat. Acat. TV Arts and Scis.; past mem. adv. com. theatre arts George Brown Coll. Applied Arts and Tech.; past mem. adv. coun. film/TV prodn. program Humber Coll. Bd. dirs. Found. for Ocean Rsch. (founding), Can. Satellite Learning Svcs., Inc.; founding, past trustee Ruth Hancock Scholarship Found. Recipient Gold medal Can. Film and TV Assn., 1988, Rockie award Banff TV Festival, 1990, Excellence in Broadcasting Lifetime Achievement award Conestoga Coll., 1990, Achievement award for outstanding contbn. to broadcasting Broadcast Exec. Soc., 1991; named to Can. Broadcasting Hall of Fame, 1994. Fellow NATAS (internat. coun., spl. citation 1989); mem. Acad. Can. Cinema and TV, Internat. Press Inst., Can. Assn. Broadcasters (Disting. Svc. gold ribbon medal 1986), Ctrl. Can. Broadcasters Assn. (past bd. dirs., Broadcaster of Yr. award 1990), Toronto Radio Control Club, Model Aeros. Assn. Can., Giant Scale Club (Oshawa), 400 RC Club, Seaton Valley R/C Flying Club.

CHERENZIA, BRADLEY JAMES, radiologist; b. Niagara Falls, N.Y., Aug. 22, 1931; s. Peter and Myrna (Bradley) C.; m. Paula Joyce, Mar. 9, 1978; children: Kevin, Lori, David, Robert, Lisa. BS in Pharmacy cum laude, U. Buffalo, 1953; MD, SUNY Upstate Med. Ctr., Syracuse, 1957. Cert. Am. Bd. Radiology, Am. Bd. Nuclear Medicine. Intern SUNY Upstate Med. Ctr. Hosps., Syracuse, 1957-58; resident in radiology Wayne State U. Sch. Medicine Hosps., Detroit, 1960-63; practice medicine specializing in radiology Diagnostic Radiology Cons., P.C., Warren, Mich., 1965—, also chmn. bd. dirs.; sr. attending radiologist St. John Macomb Hosp. Corp., med. dir. dept. diagnostic radiology. Served to capt. M.C., U.S. Army, 1958-60. Mem. AMA, Am. Soc. Nuc. Cardiology, Wayne County Med. Soc., Mich. State Med. Soc., Radiol. Soc. N.Am., Mich. Radiol. Soc., Am. Coll. Radiology, Soc. Nuclear Medicine, Am. Coll. Nuclear Medicine, Am. Coll. Physician Execs., Soc. Radiologists in Ultrasound, Am. Heart Assn., Am. Med. Tennis Assn. Republican. Roman Catholic. Avocations: photography, art, music, golfing, tennis.

CHEREWKA, MICHAEL, lawyer; b. Taylor, Pa., July 3, 1955; s. Michael Jr. and Anne (Regan) C.; m. Michele Mary Robinson, Aug. 2, 1980; children: Michael Colin, Matthew Bryan, Meaghan Kelly. Student, U. Bristol, Eng., 1976-77; BSBA cum laude, Bucknell U., 1978; JD cum laude, Dickinson Sch. Law, 1981. Bar: Pa. 1981, U.S. Dist. Ct. (mid. dist.) Pa. 1983, U.S. Tax Ct. 1983, U.S. Ct. Appeals (3d cir.) 1983, U.S. Supreme Ct. 1985. Sr. mem. tax staff Ernst & Whinney, Harrisburg, Pa., 1981-83; assoc. Ball, Skelly, Murren & Connell (formerly Ball & Skelly), Harrisburg, 1983-89; pvt. practice Harrisburg, 1989-96; mng. ptnr. Cherewka & Radcliff, LLP, 1996—. Co-author: Pennsylvania Tax Service, 1987; contbg. editor (legal column) Cen. Penn Bus. Jour., 1985-88; advisor Dauphin County Law Explorers Post, 1982-88. Mem. Country Club Park Civic Assn., 1983-98, pres., 1987-88; mem. Hist. Harrisburg Assn., 1982-84; active Tri-County United Way, 1985-90, cons. planning giving, mem. adv. com., 1988-90; bd. dirs. Capital divsn. Am. Heart Assn., chmn. 1989-91, bd. dirs. Pa. affiliate, 1989-98 , exec. com., 1989-90, 93, treas., 1994-95, incoming chmn. bd., 1995-96, chmn. 1996-97; chmn., bd. dirs. Concertante Chamber Ensemble, 1996-97; mem. planned giving com. Keystone Svc. Sys. Found., 1995—; mem. adv. bd. Found. Caths. United in Svc., Cath. Diocese of Harrisburg, 1991-97. Named Outstanding Young Man Am., U.S. Jaycees, 1983. Mem. Pa. Bar Assn. (tax sect. 1981—, real estate, probate and trust law sect. 1981—, com. state taxation 1984—, chmn. subcom. on compromise tax 1986-97), Dauphin County Bar Assn. (interprofl. rels. com. 1984-89, estate planning sect. 1992—), Estate Planning Coun. Cen. Pa. (chmn. CPA subcom. 1982-83, bd. dirs. 1988-96, treas. 1989-90, v.p. 1990-91, pres. 1991-92), Polit. Info. Com. CPAs Pa. (treas. 1982-83), Greater Harrisburg C. of C. (bus. liaison com. 1984-87, econ. devel. com. 1988-89, 92-93, reaccreditation task force 1996), Nat. Assn. Estate Planners (charter 1988—), Pa. Chamber Bus. and Industry (bus. subcom. 1989), Greater West Shore Area C. of C. (comml.-indsl. devel. com. 1987-89), Alzheimer's Assn. of So. Ctrl. Pa. (bd. dirs. 1998—), Delta Mu Delta, Omicron Delta Kappa. Republican. Orthodox Greek Catholic. Avocations: coin collecting, golf, basketball. Home: 125 Pelham Rd Camp Hill PA 17011-1353 Office: 624 N Front St Wormleysburg PA 17043

CHERIN, AARON SIMON, federal judge; b. 1933. BS, U. Pa., 1955; LLB, NYU, 1962. Bar: N.Y. 1962. Trial atty. Legal Aid Soc., Bklyn. and N.Y.C., 1962-65, with fed. defenders svcs. unit, 1965-76; magistrate judge for ea. dist. N.Y., U.S. Magistrate Ct., Bklyn., 1976-85; chief magistrate judge U.S. Magistrate Ct., 1985—. Office: US Magistrate Ct 225 Cadman Plz E Brooklyn NY 11201-1818

CHERIS, ELAINE GAYLE INGRAM, business owner; b. Ashford, Ala., Jan. 8, 1946; m. Samuel David Cheris, June 8, 1980; 1 child, Zachariah Adam Abraham. BS, Troy State U., 1971. Aquatics dir. Yale U., New Haven, 1976-79; owner, mgr. Cheyenne Fencing Soc., Denver, 1980—; chmn. organizing com. World Fencing Championships, 1989, World Jr./Cadet Fencing Championships, 1993; nat. devel. coord. Modern Pentathlon, 1998. Author: Handbook for Parents - Fencing, 1988, 2d edit., 1992; editor Yofen Mag., 1988-90, 1992—. Mem. Gov.'s Coun. on Sports and Fitness, Colo., 1990—; commr. Colo. State Games-Fencing, 1989—; nat. devel. chmn., nat. chmn. youth and cadet, club coord. Modern Pentathlon, 1998. Mem. U.S. Olympic Foil Team, 1980, 88 (6th place fencing), U.S. Olympic Epee Team, 96 (8th place), 98 (1st place), mem. U.S. Pan-Am. Games Team, 1987 (Gold medal women's foil team), 1991 (Gold medal women's epee team); named Sportswoman of Yr. Fencing, YWCA, 1980, 81, 82, to Sportswoman Hall of Fame, 1982; mem. U.S. World Championship Fencing Team, 1982, 85, 87, 90, 91, 92, 93, U.S. Maccabiah Fencing Team, 1981 (1 gold, 1 silver medal); recipient Gold Medal of Honor from Fedn. Internat. d'Escrime, 1993. Mem. AAPHERD, U.S. Fencing Assn. (youth chmn. 1988-90, editor Youth mag., 1988-90, 92—, chmn. Colo. divsn., 1992-94), Fedn. Internat. d'Escrime (chmn. Atlanta fencing project '96, chmn. World Fencing Day 1994). Jewish. Office: Cheyenne Fencing Soc 5818 E Colfax Ave Denver CO 80220-1507

CHERKEN, HARRY SARKIS, JR., lawyer; b. Phila., Dec. 8, 1949; s. Harry Sarkis and Lorna G. (Demurjian) C. BA, Lafayette Coll., 1971; JD, Villanova U., 1976. Bar: Pa. 1976, U.S. Dist. Ct. (ea. dist.) Pa. 1976, U.S. Supreme Ct. 1983. Assoc. counsel Albert M. Greenfield & Co., Inc., Phila., 1976-79; assoc. Drinker, Biddle & Reath, Phila., 1979-84, ptnr., 1984—, chmn. real estate group, 1991—, mng. ptnr., 1996—; bd. dirs. Urban Outfitters, Inc., H-Technology, Inc.; mem. Phila. adv. bd. Chgo. Title Ins. Co., 1986—; assoc. mem. Wharton Real Estate Rsch. Ctr., U. Pa., 1996—. Trustee The Kulicke Fund, Phila., 1985—, The Balch Inst., 1992—; fellow trustee The Armenian Assembly Am., 1986—, bd. dirs., 1988—, vice-chmn. bd. dirs., 1989-91, 94-95; sec., bd. dirs. Reading Terminal Market Preservation Fund, 1991—. Mem. ABA, Pa. Bar Assn., Phila. Bar Assn., Pa. Land Title Assn. (affiliate), Internt. Coun. Shopping Ctrs. (assoc.). Armenian Apostolic. Home: 106B N 21st St Philadelphia PA 19103-1301 Office: Drinker Biddle & Reath LLP 1345 Chestnut St Ste 1100 Philadelphia PA 19107-3426

CHERKIN, ADINA, interpreter, translator; b. Geneva, Nov. 22, 1921; came to U.S., 1940; d. Herz N. and Genia (Kodriansky) Mantchik; m. Arthur Cherkin, Mar. 14, 1943 (div. Sept. 1980); children: Della Peretti, Daniel Craig. BA in Premed. Studies, UCLA, 1942, MA in Russian Linguistics, 1977. Pvt. practice med. interpreter in 5 langs. L.A., 1942-80; translator UCLA Med. Sch., 1970-79; pres. acad. forum Jewish studies Herz Mantchik Amity Cir., L.A., 1973—. Author: Terse Verse and Oodles of Doodles, 1999; author numerous poems. Active L.A. Internat. Vis. Coun., 1991—; pub. rels. Judge Stanley Mosk's Campaign, L.A., 1960; vol. Senator Cranston's Campaign, 1960. Recipient Community Svc. award L.A. City Coun., 1992. Mem. Am. Soc. for Technion Israel Inst. Tech. (bd. regents). Avocations: dance improvisation, figure skating. Home and Office: 2369 N Vermont Ave Los Angeles CA 90027-1253

CHERKSEY, BRUCE DAVID, physiology educator; b. Phila., Oct. 3, 1946; s. Arthur C. and Jeanne (Braslaw) C. MS, NYU, 1973, PhD, 1980. NIH trainee ophthalmology NYU Med. Ctr., N.Y.C., 1980-81, asst. prof. physiology, 1985-90, assoc. prof. physiology, 1990—, assoc. prof. psychiatry, 1992—; founding scientist, cons. Theracell, Inc., 1993—; co-founder Aegeus, Inc., 1994—; founding scientist, cons. Phytotherapeutics, Inc., 1998—; cons. Titan Pharm. Holdings, Inc., 1993—. Contbr. articles to profl. jours. Mem. Soc. Neuroscis., Assn. for Rsch. in Vision & Ophthalmology, Am. Chem. Soc., N.Y. Acad. Scis., Soc. Exptl. Biology and Medicine. Achievements include patents in membrane channel protein and related therapeutic compounds, pyrones as potassium channel activators, use of pyrones to treat addiction; discovery of the regulation of transport proteins and therapeutic effects in Glaucoma, polyamine toxin in spider venoms; synthetic cacium channel blockers; technology for cell implantation into brain to treat Parkinson's and other diseases, therapeutics to increase lean body mass and to reduce cholestrol. Home: 59 Willow Ter Hoboken NJ 07030-2812 Office: NYU Med Ctr 550 1st Ave New York NY 10016-6497

CHERMAYEFF, IVAN, graphic designer; b. London, June 6, 1932; s. Serge Ivan and Barbara Maitland (May) C.; m. Sara Anne Duffy, July 15, 1956; children: Catherine, Alexandra, Maro; m. Jane Clark, Sept. 24, 1978; 1 son, Sam. Grad., Phillips Acad., Andover, Mass., 1950; student, Harvard, 1950-52, Ill. Inst. Tech., 1952-54; BFA, Yale, 1955; LLD (hon.), Maine Sch. Art, 1981; BFA (hon.), Corcoran Sch. Art, 1988, Maine Coll. Art, 1989, Phila. Coll. Art, 1989, Corcoran Sch. Arts, 1991, U. of Arts, Phila., 1991. Asst. to Alvin Lustig (designer), 1955; asst. art dir. Columbia Records, 1956; partner Brownjohn, Chermayeff & Geismar Assos., 1956-59, Chermayeff & Geismar Inc., N.Y.C., 1959—, Cambridge Seven Assos., 1965—; Bd. dirs. Internat. Design Conf., Aspen, Colo.; bd. dirs. Mcpl. Art Soc. N.Y.; trustee Mus. Modern Art, N.Y.C., 1966-86, Archives of Am. Art, 1987-90, New Sch. Univ., 1988—; bd. overseers Parson's Sch. Design, 1985—; disting. vis. prof. UCLA, 1998. Recipient Awards Art Dirs. Club, N.Y., awards Am. Inst. Graphic Arts, awards Type Dirs. Club, Indsl. Arts, medal AIA, 1967, Gold medal Phla. Coll. Art, 1971, Claude M. Fuess medal Phillips Acad., 1980, Pres.'s award RISD, 1981, Yale Arts medal 1985, Grand Prix Biennale BRNO, 1992; named to N.Y. Art Dirs. Club Hall of Fame, 1981. Mem. SPEE, Am. Inst. Graphic Arts (pres. 1963-66, dir., Gold medal 1979), Nat. Soc. Indsl. Designers, Alliance Graphique Internat., Royal Soc. Arts and Commerce (Benjamin Franklin fellow), Royal Designer for Industry (RDI hon.), Century Assn. Home: 140 E 81st St New York NY 10028-1805 also: Sheep's Hill North Salem NY 10560 Office: 15 E 26th St New York NY 10010-1505

CHERN, SHIING-SHEN, mathematics educator; b. Kashing, Chekiang, China, Oct. 26, 1911; s. Lien Ching and Mei (Han) C.; m. Shih-ning Chern, July 28, 1939; children—Paul, May. B.S., Nankai U., Tientsin, China, 1930; hon. dr., Nankai U., 1985; M.S., Tsing Hua U., Peiping, 1934; D.Sc., U. Hamburg, Germany, 1936, D.Sc. (hon.), 1972; D.Sc. (hon.), U. Chgo., 1969, SUNY-Stony Brook, 1985; LL.D. honoris causa, Chinese U., Hong Kong, 1969; Dr. Math (hon.), Eidgenossische Technische Hochschule, Zurich, Switzerland, 1982; DSc (hon.), U. Notre Dame, 1994. Prof. math. Nat. Tsing Hua U., China, 1937-43; mem. Inst. Advanced Study, Princeton, N.J., 1943-45; acting dir. Inst. Mathematics, Academia Sinica, China, 1946-48; prof. math. U. Chgo., 1949-60, U. Calif., Berkeley, 1960-79; prof. emeritus U. Calif., 1979—; dir. Math. Scis. Rsch. Inst., 1981-84, dir. emeritus, 1984—; dir. Inst. Mathematics, Tianjin, P.R., China. hon. prof. various fgn. univs.; Recipient Chauvenet prize Math. Assn. Am., 1970, Nat. Medal of Sci., 1975, Wolf prize Israel, 1983-84. Fellow Third World Acad. Sci. (founding mem. 1985); mem. NAS, Am. Math. Soc. (Steele prize 1983), Am. Acad. Arts and Scis., N.Y. Acad. Scis. (hon. life), Am. Philos. Soc., Indian Math. Soc. (hon.), Brazilian Acad. Scis. (corr.), Academia Sinica, Royal Soc. London (fgn.), Academia Peloritana (corr. mem. 1986), London Math. Soc. (hon.), Acad. des sciences Paris (fgn. mem.), Acad. der Lincei Rome (stranieri), Russian Acad. Scis. (fgn.). Home: 8336 Kent Ct El Cerrito CA 94530-2548 Office: Univ Calif Berkeley Dept of Mathematics Berkeley CA 94720

CHERNA, MARC KENNETH, human services executive; b. N.Y.C., Jan. 28, 1951; s. Charles H. and Sylvia (Pressman) C.; children: Jessica, Jared, Gabrielle. BA, SUNY, Binghamton, 1972; M in Social Work, Hunter Coll., 1978. Dir. planning, allocations and agy. rels. United Way of Union County, Elizabeth, N.J., 1978-82; pres. Portnoy and Cherna Assoc., Union, N.J., 1982; asst. dir. policy, planning and support State of N.J. Youth and Family Svcs., Trenton, 1982-92, asst. dir. program ops., 1992-95; spl. asst. to dep. commnr. State of N.J. Human Svcs., Trenton, 1995-96; dir. children and youth svcs. Allegheny County, Pa., 1996-97, dir. human svcs., 1997—. Office: Allegheny County Dept Human Svcs 933 Penn Ave Pittsburgh PA 15222-3815

CHERNAK, JERALD LEE, television executive; b. Bklyn., Nov. 7, 1942; s. Jess and Alice Kay (Kosoff) C.; m. Gail Loraine Cooper, March 26, 1967; children: Hope Ann, David. BS in Radio-TV, Indiana State U., 1965. Freelance dir., assoc. dir., asst. dir., stage mgr. N.Y.C., 1965-67; producer, dir., assoc. dir., stage mgr. ABC-TV, N.Y.C., 1967-86; exec. producer, gen. mgr. TV Nat. Shopping Club, Orlando, Fla., 1987-89; v.p., exec. producer U.C. Mktg. Group, Orlando, 1989; v.p., gen. mgr. Channel 7, Orlando, 1989-90; broadcast cons. Orlando, 1990; corp. v.p. Vision Broadcasting, Inc., WHBS, Orlando, 1991-92; v.p., sta. mgr. Stas. WQBN, WHBS, Tampa, Fla., 1992-93; pres. HODA Svcs., Inc., Orlando, Fla., 1993-94; mgr. cellular comms. Radio Shack, Orlando, 1994-97; prodn. mgr. spl. events and entertainment Universal Studios Fla., Orlando, 1997—. Post prodn. (TV news spl.) America Held Hostage ABC-TV, N.Y.C. (Emmy award 1982), 20/20 The Ump ABC-TV, N.Y.C. (Emmy nomination 1980). Bd. dirs. Children Wish Found., Orlando, 1987-88; mem. Mid. Fla. Film Coun., 1988-90. Served with USAR, 1965-70. Recipient Bronze and Silver awards Internat. Film & TV Festival, 1968-71, 82. Mem. NATAS (bd. govs. N.Y. chpt. 1976-80, 82-86), Dirs. Guils Am. (coun. rep. 1968-85, chmn. Fla. coord. com. 1988—), Soc. Profl. Journalists, Sigma Delta Chi. Avocation: amateur radio operator. Home: 136 Margate Mews Longwood FL 32779-5627

CHERNESKY, JOHN JOSEPH, JR., retired naval officer, healthcare executive; b. Hartford, Conn., July 6, 1944; s. John Joseph and Mary (Milewski) C.; m. Patricia Ann Wolf, Oct. 9, 1967 (div. June, 1988); m. Melinda Anne Brown, Aug. 31, 1991; children: Karen Elizabeth, John David. BS, Miami U., 1967. Commd. ensign USN, 1967, advanced through grades to capt., 1985; flag lt., aide Commander Submarines Pacific, Pearl Harbor, Hawaii, 1971-73; engr. officer USS Blueback, Pearl Harbor, 1973-75; exec. officer USS Bonefish, Pearl Harbor, 1975-77; head officer retention Bur.

Naval Personnel, Washington, 1977-79; exec. officer USS Dale, commanding officer USS Patterson Mayport, Fla., 1979-83; exec. officer USS Iowa, Norfolk, Va., 1983-85; dir. navy programs Office of Legisl. Affairs, Washington, 1985-88; commanding officer USS Missouri, Long Beach, Calif., 1988-90; ret., 1990; exec. dir. Cedars-Sinai Comprehensive Cancer Ctr., L.A., 1994-97; sr. v.p., chief info. officer Salick Health Care, Inc., L.A., 1997—, exec. v.p. N.Y. ops., 1998—. Decorated Legion of Merit. Mem. Am. Legion, Delta Tau Delta. Republican. Roman Catholic. Avocation: sailing, golfing. Office: 8201 Beverly Blvd Los Angeles CA 90048-4505

CHERNESKY, RICHARD JOHN, lawyer; b. Scranton, Pa., July 27, 1939; s. Frank Peter and Mary (Stialect) C.; m. Alice Faye Nyfenger, Aug. 1, 1959; children: Christopher John, Joshua James. BA, Ohio St. U., 1963, JD, 1966. Bar: Ohio 1966. Ptnr. Smith & Schnacke, Dayton, Ohio, 1966-88; mng. ptnr. Chernesky, Heyman & Kress P.L.L., Dayton, 1988—; bd. dirs. Am. Indoor Soccer Assn., Inc., 1992-96; pres. Ohio Sports Ctr., Miamisburg, Ohio, 1991—; trustee Hipple Cancer Rsch. Ctr., Kettering, Ohio, 1994-96, Dayton Internat. Aviation Corp., Inc., 1990-92; sec. Iams Co., 1997—. Bd. dirs. Miami Valley Hosp. Found., Dayton, 1987-88, Chapel of the Air, Wheaton, Ill., 1985-91, 94-95, Mike-sell's, Inc., 1994—, Dolly Inc., Tipp City, Ohio, 1989-93; trustee The Luth. Sch. of Dayton, 1988-91, The Waynesville Area Friends of the Parks, 1992—; mem. Luth. Social Svcs. Devel. Com., Dayton, 1987-93; chmn. Wayne Twp. Zoning Bd., Waynesville, 1987-95; bd. dirs. U.S. Soccer Fedn. Found., Inc., 1996—. Mem. Ohio State Bar Assn., Dayton Bar Assn., Dayton Better Bus. Bur. (bd. dirs. 1989-94). Home: 8027 New Burlington Rd Waynesville OH 45068-9705 Office: Chernesky Heyman & Kress PLL PO Box 3808 Ste 1100 10 Courthouse Plz SW Dayton OH 45401-3808

CHERNEV, MELVIN, retired beverage company executive; b. Bklyn., Nov. 29, 1928; s. Irving and Selma (Kulik) C.; m. Noemi Dohnert, May 29, 1955 (dec. July 1, 1985); 1 child, Celia Ann; m. Marlene G. Tonkin, Sept. 4, 1988. A.B., Cornell U., 1950. Chief statistician Eversharp, Inc., N.Y.C., 1951-52; sales adminstr. Eversharp, Inc., 1952-55, asst. gen. sales mgr., 1955-58; sales promotion mgr. Internat. Latex Corp. (Playtex), N.Y.C., 1959-64; product mgr. Internat. Latex Corp. (Playtex), 1964-66; pres. Snow White Corp., San Jose, Calif., 1966-67; dir. planning and research Fromm and Sichel, Inc., distbrs. Christian Bros. wines and brandy, San Francisco, 1967-70; dir. mktg. services Fromm and Sichel, Inc., distbrs. Christian Bros. wines and brandy, 1970-73, v.p. mktg. services, 1973-76, sr. v.p. mktg., 1976-77, exec. v.p., 1977-78, pres., chief operating officer, 1978-83, bd. dirs. Bd. dirs., trustee Cogswell Coll., San Francisco, 1976-86, chmn., 1983-85; bd. govs. City U. Seattle, 1985—; bd. dirs., treas. The Lakes at Northridge Homeowners Assn.; pres. bd. dirs. Albert Einstein Residence Ctr., 1997—. Mem. Commonwealth Club, Cornell Club No. Calif., Cornell Club (N.Y.C.), North Ridge Country Club (Fair Oaks, Calif.). Home: 7529 Pineridge Ln Fair Oaks CA 95628-4858

CHERNEY, JAMES ALAN, lawyer; b. Boston, Mar. 19, 1948; s. Alvin George and Janice (Elaine) Cherney; m. Linda Bienenfeld. BA, Tufts U., 1969; JD, Columbia U., 1973. Bar: Ill. 1973, U.S. Supreme Ct. 1977, U.S. Ct. Appeals (7th cir.) 1979, U.S. Ct. Appeals (3d cir.) 1982, U.S. Ct. Appeals (10th cir.) 1984, U.S. Ct. Appeals (8th and 9th cirs.) 1987. Assoc. Kirkland & Ellis, Chgo., 1973-76; assoc. Hedlund, Hunter & Lynch, Chgo., 1976-79, ptnr., 1979-82; ptnr. Latham & Watkins, Chgo., 1982—. Mem. ABA, Chgo. Bar Assn., Saddle and Cycle Club (sec. 1989, v.p. 1991-92, pres. 1992-94). Office: Latham & Watkins Sears Tower Ste 5800 Chicago IL 60606-6306*

CHERNIACK, NEIL STANLEY, physician, medical educator; b. Bklyn., May 28, 1931; s. Max and Rebecca (Roulnick) C.; m. Sandra Lebowitz, Dec. 31, 1954; children: Evan, Andrew, Emily. AB with honors, Columbia U., 1952; MD, SUNY, 1956; MA, U. Pa., 1972; hon. degree, Karolinska U., 1991. Intern U. Ill., Chgo., 1956-57, resident, 1957-58, 60-62; resident, fellow Columbia Presbyn. Hosp., N.Y.C., 1962-64; practice medicine specializing in pulmonary disease Chgo., 1964-69, Phila., 1969-77, Cleve., 1977—; asst. prof. medicine U. Ill., Chgo., 1964-68, assoc. prof., 1968-69; assoc. prof. U. Pa., Phila., 1969-73, prof., 1973-77; prof. Case Western Res. U., 1977—, chief pulmonary svc., 1977-89, prof. physiology, 1982—, assoc. dean, 1983-90, dean sch. medicine, v.p. med. affairs, 1990-95, vice chmn. div. gen. med. sci., 1986-90, vice chmn. dept. medicine, 1987-90; chief pulmonary svc., sr. attending physician Phila. Gen. Hosp., 1969-77; assoc. dir. pulmonary svc., attending physician U. Pa. Hosp., 1973-77, U. Hosps. of Cleve., Cleve. VA Med. Ctr.; vis. prof. Karolinska U., Stockholm, 1976-77; dir. of clin. svcs., acting chmn. dept. physiology & pharmacology U. Medicine & Dentistry N.J., Newark, 1995-97. Mem. editl. bd. Circulation Rsch., Am. Rev. Respiratory Disease, Respiration; editor Jour. Applied Physiology, Handbook of Physiology; assoc. editor Jour. Lab. Clin. Medicine, Handbooks of Physiology, Respiration. Served to capt. USAF, 1958-60. Mem. Am. Assn. Physicians, Am. Soc. Clin. Investigation, Am. Thoracic Soc., Am. Lung Assn., Am. Physiol. Soc., Bioengrig. Soc., Biomed. Engring. Soc. (bd. dirs. 1984-87), Ctrl. Soc. Clin. Rsch., Neurosci. Soc., Phi Beta Kappa, Alpha Omega Alpha, Beta Sigma Rho. Home: 11 Wood Dr Morris Plains NJ 07950-1509 Office: Univ Med Dental NJ Newark NJ 07103-2714

CHERNIACK, SAUL MARK, retired barrister, solicitor; b. Winnipeg, Man., Can., Jan. 10, 1917; s. Joseph Arthur and Fannie Golden; m. Sybil Claire Zeal, July 10, 1938; children: Howard David, Lawrence Allan. LLB, U. Man., 1939. Queen's Counsel, 1963. Former mem. Security Intelligence Rev. Com. Can.; formerly M.L.A.; Min. Fin. Man., Min. Urban Affairs; Min. for Man. Telephone System; chmn. Man. Hydro-Electric, Winnipeg; Queen's Privy Coun. for Can., 1984; mem. Order of Can., 1994. Past bd. dirs. Cmty. Chest, Welfare Fund Winnipeg, Peretz Folk Sch. Parents' Assn. Capt. Can. Armed Forces, 1943-46. Recipient Queen's Coun. award Lt.-Gov.-in-Coun., 1963, City of Winnipeg Cmty. Svc. award, 1967, Can. Centennial medal, 1967, Queen's Jubilee medal, 1977, 125 Confederation medal, 1992. Mem. New Democratic Party. Jewish. Home: 333 St Johns Ave, Winnipeg, MB Canada R2W 1H2

CHERNICOFF, DAVID PAUL, osteopathic physician, educator; b. N.Y.C., Aug. 3, 1947; s. Harry and Lillian (Dobkin) C. AB, U. Rochester, 1969; DO, Phila. Coll. Osteo. Medicine, 1973. Rotating intern Rocky Mountain Hosp., Denver, 1973-74; resident in internal medicine Cmty. Gen. Osteo. Hosp., Harrisburg, Pa., 1974-76; fell in hematology and med. oncology Cleve. Clinic, 1976-78; asst. prof. medicine sect. hematology-oncology Chgo. Coll. Osteo. Medicine, 1978-82, assoc. prof., 1982-89; co-chmn. tumor task force Chgo. Osteo. Med. Ctr., 1978-89, dir. clin. cancer edn., 1978-89, hematology and oncology; asst. clin. prof. medicine Pa. State U. Coll. Medicine, 1993—; med. dir. Keystone Peer Rev. Orgn., 1997—; chmn. tumor task force Olympia Fields (Ill.) Osteo. Med. Ctr. Trustee, mem. clin. exec. com. Ill. Cancer Coun., 1982-89; bd. dir. Chgo. unit Am. Cancer Soc., 1981-86, chief sec. of Hematology-Oncology Hosp. of Chgo. Coll. Osteo Medicine, 1981-89; med. dir. Keystone Peer Rev. Orgn. Diplomate Nat. Bd. Osteo. Examiners, Am. Osteo. Bd. Internal Medicine, also in Hematology-Oncology. Fellow Am. Coll. Osteo. Internists, Pa. Osteo. Med. Soc., Ea. Coop. Oncology Group (sr. investigator 1981-89), Am. Soc. Clin. Oncology; mem. Am. Osteo. Assn. Contbr. articles to med. jours. Office: 4830 Londonderry Rd Harrisburg PA 17109-5240

CHERNIN, PETER, motion picture company executive. Pres. entertainment group Fox Broadcasting Co., L.A.; former chmn. Twentieth Century Fox Film Corp., Beverly Hills, Calif.; now chmn., CEO The Fox Group, Beverly Hills, Calif.; pres., COO News Corp., 1996—. Office: Fox Inc PO Box 900 Beverly Hills CA 90213-0900*

CHERNISH, LELIA MARGARET, fundraiser; b. Collins, Mo., Mar. 19, 1921; d. Aubra F. and Velta Lelia (Nance) Higgins; m. Stanley M. Chernish, June 19, 1949; 1 child, Dwight Landers. Student, U. Md., 1947-48. Tchr. kindergarten Silver Springs Bethesda, Md., 1945-51; apptd. del. White House Conf. on Aging, 1971, Ind. Health Careers, 1974-84; mem. Ind. Impaired Physicians Com., 1976-79; appointee Ind. Mus. Art, 1976-84; apptd. bd. trustees Ind. Med. Distbn. Loan Fund, 1977-92, Ind. Med. & Nursing Distbn. Loan Fund, 1981-85; mem. Marion County Impaired Physicians Com., 1983-84; liaison to med. student wives, rec. sec., program, publicity and fin. chmn., historian and by-laws chmn. Ind. State Med. Aux.; pres. Marion County Med. Aux., 1965-66, med. student liaison, historian, United Fund chmn., by-laws com., parliamentarian, chmn. cookbook prodn.; mem., fin. chmn., parliamentarian Boys Club Aux. Mem. Winona Meml. Hosp. Aux.; founder Vol. Observer Program, Ind., 1970-71; mem., yearbook chmn. Alliance of Indpls. Mus. of Art; active Women United Against Rape, 1975, Sch. Drop Out Program, Diabetes Detection Dr., drug and internat. health activities; regular ct. watcher Indpls. Anti-Crime Crusade; vol. Ronald McDonald House, 1982-94, trustee, chmn. needle art project, facilities com., chmn. 10th anniversary calendar fund raising project, 1992, bd. dirs., 1999—, sec. to bd. dirs. 1998-99. Recipient Theta Sigma Phi award, 1969, Sagamores of the Wabash award for disting. pub. svc. Gov. Otis R. Bowen, 1977, by Gov. Robert D. Orr, 1981, Ind. Jefferson award, 1982, Lori Kleiman award for svcs. over and above call of duty Ronald McDonald House, 1992; named Ind. Mother of Yr., 1981. Mem. Faculty Women's Club of Ind. U. Sch. Medicine, Hillcrest Garden Club (treas., chmn. flower show), Women in Neighborhood Svc. (WINS), Indpls. chpt. Embroiders Guild of Am. (charter, chmn. nat. embroiders guild exhibit 1989, dean of faculty seminar 1990, co-chmn. nat. seminar 1992, pres. 1997-98), Mag. Club (pres. 1963-65).

CHERNISH, STANLEY MICHAEL, physician; b. N.Y.C., Jan. 27, 1924; s. Michael B. and Veronica (Hodon) C.; m. Lelia M. Higgins, June 19, 1949; 1 child, Dwight. BA, U. N.C., 1945; MD, Georgetown U., 1949. Diplomate Nat. Bd. Med. Examiners, Am. Bd. Internal Medicine. Intern Washington Gen. Hosp., 1949-51; resident Marion County Gen. Hosp., Indpls., 1953-55; with clin. rsch. div. Eli Lilly & Co., Indpls., 1954-85; from asst. to assoc. in medicine Sch. Medicine, Ind. U., 1957-66, asst. prof., 1967-76, clin. assoc. prof., 1977-80, assoc. prof., 1981-94; rsch. cons. Meth. Hosp., Indpls., 1986—; mem. vis. staff Marion County Gen. Hosp., 1965-94. Contbr. more than 115 articles to profl. jours., chpts. to books. Served with USNR, 1943-45, 50-53, ret. comdr. 1984. Fellow ACP, Am. Coll. Gastroenterology; mem. Am. Coll. Clin. Pharmacology and Therapeutics, AMA (Physicians Recognition award in continuing med. edn. 1972—), Ind. State Med. Soc. (mem. subcommn. on accreditation), Marion County Med. Soc., Assn. Am. Physicians and Surgeons, Am. Fedn. Clin. Rsch., Am. Gastroent. Assn., Sci. Rsch. Soc., Sigma Xi. Office: Meth Hosp Ind Dept Med Rsch PO Box 1367 1701 Senate Blvd Indianapolis IN 46202-1239

CHERNO, MELVIN, humanities educator; b. El Paso, Feb. 24, 1929; s. Sol and Deborah (Andes) C.; m. Dolores Ellen Himelstein, Dec. 25, 1950; children—Steven Philip, Paige Elise, Julie Rosanne. AB, Stanford U., 1950; AM, U. Chgo., 1952; PhD, Stanford U., 1955. Instr. Bakersfield Coll., Calif., 1955-60; successively asst. prof., assoc. prof., prof. Oakland U., Rochester, Mich., 1960-80; Vaughan prof. tech., culture and comm. U. Va., Charlottesville, 1980—, prin. second residential coll., 1991-95, co-prin., 1995-96. Co-editor: (4-vol. anthology) Western Society ..., 1967; editor, translator: (essay) Feuerbach on Luther, 1968; contbr. articles on historical topics to profl. jours. Fellow Ford Found., 1953-55, Deutscher Akademische Austauschdienst, 1966, Inst. für Europäische Geschichte, 1966. Mem. Am. Hist. Assn., Am. Soc. Engring. Edn., So. Hist. Assn., Soc. for History of Tech., Soc. for Lit./Sci., Soc. for 19th Century Studies, Phi Beta Kappa. Office: U Va Div Tech Culture Comm Thornton Hall Charlottesville VA 22903-2442

CHERNOFF, AMOZ IMMANUEL, hematologist, consultant; b. Malden, Mass., Mar. 17, 1923; s. Isaiah and Celia (Margolin) C.; m. Renate R. Fisher, Jan. 25, 1953; children: David F., Susan N., Judith A. BS in Chemistry with honors, Yale U., 1944, MD cum laude, 1947. Diplomate Am. Bd. Internal Medicine. Med. intern Mass. Gen. Hosp., Boston, 1947-48; asst. resident in medicine Barnes Hosp., St. Louis, 1948-49; fellow in hematology Michael Reese Hosp., Chgo., 1949-51; asst. dir. hematology research lab. Michael Reese Hosp., 1950-51; A.C.P. fellow Washington U. Sch. Medicine, St. Louis, 1951-52; USPHS spl. research fellow, 1952-53, instr. in medicine, 1952-54, asst. prof., 1954-56; assoc. prof. medicine Duke U., 1956-58; chief sect. hematology VA Hosp., Durham, N.C., 1956-58; rsch. prof. U. Tenn. Meml. Rsch. Ctr., Knoxville, 1958-79, dir., 1964-77; assoc. vice chancellor for acad. affairs Ctr. Health Scis., 1977-79; prof. medicine Coll. Medicine, Memphis, 1966-79; med. dir. Cystic Fibrosis Found., Atlanta, 1975-77; dir. div. blood diseases and resources Nat. Heart Lung and Blood Inst., NIH, Bethesda, Md., 1979-88; assoc. exec. dir. sci. affairs Am. Assn. Blood Banks, Arlington, Va., 1988-90; cons. transfusion medicine programs. Contbr. articles to profl. jours. Served with U.S. Army, 1943-45. Recipient Campbell award Yale U. Sch. Medicine, 1947, Research Career award USPHS, 1962-77. Fellow ACP; mem. Am. Soc. Clin. Investigation, Am. Soc. Hematology, Internat. Soc. Hematology, Cen. Soc. Clin. Rsch., So. Soc. Clin. Investigation, Soc. Exptl. Biology and Medicine, Am. Fedn. Clin. Rsch., Am. Assn. Blood Banks, Sigma Xi, Alpha Omega Alpha.

CHERNOFF, HERMAN, statistics educator; b. N.Y.C., July 1, 1923; s. Max and Pauline (Markowitz) C.; m. Judith Ullman, Sept. 7, 1947; children—Ellen Sue, Miriam Cheryl. B.S., CCNY, 1943; Sc.M., Brown U., 1945, Ph.D., 1948; Sc.D. (hon.), Ohio State U., 1983, Technion, 1984; A.M. (hon.), Harvard U., 1985; laurea (hon.), U. Rome, 1996. Rsch. assoc. U. Chgo., 1948-49; asst. prof. U. Ill., Urbana, 1949-51; assoc. prof. U. Ill., 1951-52; assoc. prof. Stanford (Calif.) U., 1952-56, prof. stats., 1956-74; prof. applied math. MIT, Cambridge, 1974-85, prof. emeritus, 1985—; prof. stats. Harvard U., Cambridge, 1985-97, prof. emeritus, 1997—; researcher in large sample theory, optimal design of expts., sequential analysis, pattern recognition. Author: (with L.E. Moses) Elementary Decision Theory, 1959, Sequential Analysis and Optimal Design, 1972. Recipient Townsend Harris medal CCNY Alumni Soc., 1981. Mem. NAS, Internat. Statis. Inst., Am. Acad. Arts and Scis., Inst. Math. Stats. (pres. 1967-68), Am. Statis. Assn. (Wilks medal 1987, Statistician of Yr. award Boston chpt. 1991). Home: 75 Crowninshield Rd Brookline MA 02446-3177 Office: Harvard U Dept Statistics Cambridge MA 02138

CHERNOW, ANN LEVY, artist, art educator; b. N.Y.C., Feb. 1, 1936; d. Edward P. and Mollie (Citrin) Levy; m. Philip Chenok, Aug. 11, 1957 (div. 1969); children: David Charles, Daniel Joshua; m. Burt Chernow, Dec. 11, 1970. MA, NYU, 1969. Instr. Mus. Modern Art, N.Y.C., 1966-71; prof., head art dept. Norwalk (Conn.) Cmty. Tech. Coll., 1974-96; guest lectr., instr. studio and art history Silvermine Sch. Arts, Silvermine Coll., 1968-80; vis. artist, lectr. Housatonic (Conn.) C.C., 1975-80; guest lectr. Am. Coll. in Paris, 1985, Salem State Coll., 1993, 94, Yale U., 1995, Westport Hist Soc., 1994, Fairfield U., 1993; vis. artist CAP program Wesleyan U., 1979; coord. Bicentennial Exhbn. Norwalk C.C., 1976, Yale U. Art Gallery, 1996. One person shows include Wesleyan U., Middleton, Conn., 1979, Beall/Lambremont Gallery, La., 1980, 81, Gallery Suzanne Maag, Zurich, 1980, Douglass Gallery, Rutgers U., N.J., 1980, Queens Coll., N.Y.C., 1982, Alex Rosenberg Gallery, N.Y.C., 1982, Mattatuck (Conn.) Mus., 1982, Munson Gallery, Conn., 1984, 88, Snug Harbor Cultural Ctr., L.I., 1984, Stamford (Conn.) Mus., 1985, Conn. Fine Arts Mus., 1986, Katonah Gallery, N.Y., 1987, Fairfield U., Conn., 1988, U.F.O. Gallery, Princeton, N.J., 1988, Munson Gallery, New Haven, 1989, Uptown Gallery, 1989, Conn. Gallery, 1989, U.F.O. Gallery, Provincetown, Mass., 1990, 91, 94, Lust Gallery, N.Y.C, 1992, Winfisky Gallery, Salem, 1993, Washington Art Assn., Conn., 1993, NCTC Gallery, Norwalk, Conn., 1994, Uptown Gallery, N.Y.C., 1995, New Rochelle Libr. Gallery, N.Y., 1995, Mcpl. Mus. of St. Paul de Vence, France, 1996, Uptown Gallery, 1997, PMW Gallery, 1997, Westchester C.C., 1997, Albert Merola, Provincetown, Mass., 1998, PMW Gallery, Stamford, Conn., 1998, Stamford Mus., 1999, Uptown Gallery, N.Y.C., 1999; group shows include Alex Rosenberg Gallery, 1980, Mus. Contemporary Art, Sao Paulo, Brazil, 1980, Aldrich Mus., Ridgefield, Conn., 1981, Silvermine Guild, 1982, Print Club, Phila., 1983, Artists Choice Mus., Marisa Del Re Gallery, N.Y.C., 1983, Morris Mus., Morristown, N.J., 1984, John Slade Ely House, New Haven, 1985, Munson Gallery, 1985, Stamford Mus., 1985-86, Katonah Gallery, 1986, Internat. Miniature Print Bienniale, New Canaan, 1987, Uptown Gallery, N.Y.C., Martin Sumers Gallery, N.Y.C., 1994, Nat. Drawings Assn., N.Y.C., 1994, SAGA Prints, N.Y.C. and Fairfield Conn., 1994, Americas 2000, S.D., 1994, Triton Mus., Santa Clara, Calif., 1994, Ctr. for Visual Arts, Oakland, Calif., 1994, Stamford (Conn.) Mus., 1994, 95, Discovery Mus., Conn., 1995, Calif. Soc. Printmakers, San Francisco, 1995, Millennium portfolio Of Time and Place, 1999-01; others pub. collections include Metropolitan Mus. of Art, Rose Art Mus. Brandeis U., Nat. Mus. Women in Arts, Washington, William Benton Mus. Art, Storrs, Conn., New Britain Mus. Am. Art, Conn., Neuberger Mus., Purchase, N.Y., Housatonic Mus. Art, Yale U., Mattatauk Mus., Lehigh U. Art Collection, Pa., Utah Mus. Fine Arts, U. Ariz. Art Collection, Lyman Allyn Mus., Conn., Bruce Mus., Conn., Butler Inst. Am. Art, Ohio, Rutgers U., Hofstra U., Elvejhem Mus., Wis., N.Y. Pub. Libr. Print Collection, Duxbury Mus. Mass., USO of Met. N.Y., Reading (Pa.) Public Mus., Portland (Oreg.) Art Mus., De Cordova Mus., Lincoln, Mass., Yale U. Art Gallery; published poetry in The Cathartic, The New York Times, Heresies, New York Quarterly, Poetry Motel Damaged Wine, Greens, The DeKalb Literary Jour., Alura, Cosmopolitan Magazine, Pegasus Review, Spectrum, Rockford Review, Rhino, The Archer, Parnassus, Writers Voice, others; reviewer art history and appreciation texts Prentice Hall, Harper & Row, 1984; subject bibliographies, art mags., catalogs, jours. Fellow Yale Mellon, 1993-94; named Conn. Woman of Decade in Arts UN Assn., 1987. Mem. Soc. Am. Graphic Artists (mem. coun.), Calif. Soc. Printmakers, Boston Printmakers, L.A. Print Soc., Print Club Phila., Print Club Albany, Nat. Acad. Art (elected), Natl. Acad. of Art (mem. elect), 1999. Studio: 2 Gorham Ave Westport CT 06880-2531

CHERNOW, BART, critical care physician; b. N.Y.C., June 26, 1947. BA, Queens Coll., 1968; MD, SUNY, N.Y.C., 1976. Internal medicine intern Nat. Naval Med. Ctr., Bethesda, Md., 1976-77, internal medicine resident, 1977-79; dir. rsch. dept. critical care medicine Bethesda Naval Hosp., 1981-85, head acad. affairs, 1985-86; assoc. prof. anesthesia Harvard Med. Sch., Boston, 1986-90; assoc. dir. SICU Mass. Gen. Hosp., Boston, 1986-90; prof. medicine, anesthesia and critical care Johns Hopkins U. Sch. Medicine, Balt., 1990-99; physician-in-chief Sinai Hosp., Balt., 1990-97; program dir. John Hopkins U./Sinai Hosp. Program in Internal Medicine, Balt., 1990-97; vice dean for rsch. and tech. Sch. Medicine Johns Hopkins U. Sch. Medicine, Balt., 1997-99; exec. v.p. Global Med. Products, Inc., 1999—. Editor: Pharmacologic Approach to the Critically Ill Patient, 1983, 88, 94; editor-in-chief: Critical Care Medicine, 1990-97. Comdr. med. corps USNR, 1969-86. Recipient Lifetime Achievement award Am. Coll. Nutrition, 1995. Fellow ACP (master), Am. Coll. Critical Care Medicine; mem. Soc. Critical Care Medicine (Presdl. citation 1997), Am. Coll. Chest Physicians (regent 1990-98, pres. 1996-97, CHEST found. pres. 1996-99). Home: 100 Harborview Dr #1802 Baltimore MD 21230

CHERNOW, JAY HOWARD, music industry executive; b. N.Y.C., Dec. 3, 1935; s. Meyer and Gertrude (Simon) C.; m. Eileen Phyllis Messing; children: Michael, Laurie Beth. Tech. degree, RCA Insts., N.Y.C., 1955. Technician N.Y.C. Dept. Hospitals, 1955-58; prodn. mgr. Am. Litho-Craft, N.Y.C., 1958-64; mktg. dir. Mic-Tone Printing Corp., N.Y.C., 1964-72; mktg. dir. San Juan Music Group, N.Y.C., 1972-84, pres., 1984—; pres. bd. dirs. Tring Internat., U.K., 1984—. Mem. B'nai B'rith, Odd Fellows. Jewish. Office: San Juan Music Group 499 Ernston Rd Parlin NJ 08859-1406

CHERNOW, JEFFREY SCOTT, lawyer, educator, author; b. Phila., Mar. 8, 1951; s. William and Sylvia Ann (Rosenberg) C.; m. Debra Sharon Shapiro, Dec. 29, 1974; children: William Ross, Stephanie Lynne. BS, Pa. State U., 1972; JD, U. Balt., 1976. Bar: Md. 1976, U.S. Dist. Ct. Md. 1977, U.S. Supreme Ct. 1980, U.S. Ct. Claims 1991. Assoc. Goodman, Meagher & Enoch, Balt., 1977-79; asst. atty. gen. State of Md., Balt., 1980-85; assoc. Cardin & Cardin, P.A., Balt., 1985-86; pvt. practice law Balt., 1986-89; ptnr. Kandel, Klitenic & Chernow, Owings Mills, Md., 1990—; asst. prof. Towson (Md.) State U., 1978-83, assoc. prof., 1983-86; panel chmn. Md. Health Claims Arbitration Office, 1983-84; lectr. Md. Inst. for Continuing Profl. Edn. of Lawyers, Inc., 1986; dir. Altex Industries, Inc., 1989. Contbr. chpt. to book. Sec., trustee Basic Cancer Rsch. Found., Inc., 1996—; chmn. bldg. com. Congregation Adat Chaim, 1985-86, trustee, 1986-90. Mem. ABA, Md. Bar Assn., Bar Assn. Balt. City, N.Am. Securities Adminstrs. Assn. (mem. various coms. 1980-85, chmn. franchise and bus. opportunities com. 1984-85), Md. State Bar Assn. (sec. bus. law, franchise law com. 1991). Home: 214 Berry Vine Dr Owings Mills MD 21117-4500 Office: Kandel Klitenic & Chernow LLP 1838 Greene Tree Rd Ste 370 Baltimore MD 21208-7102

CHERNOW, RON, writer, columnist; b. Bklyn., Mar. 3, 1949; s. Israel and Ruth (Goldspinner) C.; m. Valerie Stearn, Oct. 22, 1979. BA in English summa cum laude, Yale U., 1970; MA in English, Cambridge (Eng.) U., 1972. Free-lance writer N.Y.C., 1973-82; program officer for fin. policy studies The Twentieth Century Fund, N.Y.C., 1983-86; writer, essayist, lectr., book reviewer N.Y.C., 1988—; occasional columnist The Wall St. Jour., 1990-91; commentator Nat. Pub. Radio, 1994—; guest curator Mus. Am. Fin. History, 1998-99; hist. cons. WGBH Boston. Author: The House of Morgan, 1990, The Warburgs, 1993, The Death of the Banker, 1997, Titan, 1998; also 13 cover stories; contbr. articles to N.Y. Times, N.Y. Mag., Time mag., Bus. Week, Saturday Rev., Vanity Fair, Am. Heritage, Smithsonian and 30 other publs. Vice chmn. Cambridge U. Assn. of N.Y., 1986-87. Recipient Jack London award United Steelworkers, 1980, Nat. Book award Nat. Book Found., 1990, Books to Remember award N.Y. Pub. Libr., 1990, Ambassador Book award English Speaking Union, 1991, George S. Eccles prize Columbia Bus. Sch., 1993, Notable Book citation ALA, 1993, Annual Book award Colonial Dames Am., 1998, Scholar of Yr. award N.Y. Coun. Humanities, 1999. Mem. PEN (chmn. readers and writers com. 1994-98, bd. trustees 1997—, sec. 1999—), Authors Guild, Am. Coun. on Germany, Modern Libr. Bd., Leo Baeck Inst., Wildlife Conservation Soc., The Nature Conservancy, Phi Beta Kappa. Democrat. Jewish. Address: 63 Joralemon St Brooklyn NY 11201-4003

CHERNY, ROBERT WALLACE, history educator; b. Marysville, Kans., Apr. 4, 1943; s. Clarence L. and Lena M. (Hobbs) C.; m. Rebecca Ellen Marshall, June 11, 1967; 1 child, Sarah Catherine. BA with distinction, U. Nebr., 1965; MA, Columbia U., 1967, PhD, 1972. Instr. history San Francisco State U., 1971-72, asst. prof., 1972-77, assoc. prof., 1977-81, prof., 1981—, assoc. dean behavioral and social scis., 1984, acting dean behavioral and social scis., 1985, chair history dept., 1987-92; disting. Fulbright lectr. Moscow State U., 1996; vis. rsch. scholar U. Melbourne, 1997; cons. in field. Author: A Righteous Cause: The Life of William Jennings Bryan, 1985, rev. edit., 1994, Populism, Progressivism and the Transformation of Nebraska Politics, 1981, American Politics in the Gilded Age, 1869-1868, 1997; co-author: (with William Issel) San Francisco, 1865-1932, 1986, San Francisco: Presidio, Port and Pacific Metropolis, 1981, (with Carol Berkin, Christopher L. Miller, James L. Gormly) Making America: A History of the United States, 1995, 2d edit., 1999. Woodrow Wilson fellow, 1965-66, Woodrow Wilson dissertation fellow, 1969, NEH fellow, 1992-93. Mem. Am. Hist. Assn., Orgn. Am. Historians, S.W. Labor Studies Assn. (pres. 1982-86), Calif. Hist. Soc., Soc. Historians of Gilded Age and Progressive Era (pres. 1995), Nebr. State Hist. Soc. Democrat. Office: San Francisco State U Dept of History 1600 Holloway Ave Dept Of San Francisco CA 94132-1722

CHEROUTES, MICHAEL LOUIS, lawyer; b. Chgo., Apr. 27, 1940; s. Louis Samuel Cheroutes and Maria Jane (Zimmerman) Dodd; m. Trisha Flynn, Oct. 30, 1965; children: Michael Louis Jr., Trisha Francesca, Matthew Dodd. BA, Harvard U., 1962; LLB, Stanford U., 1965. Bar: Colo. 1965. Assoc., then ptnr. Sherman & Howard, Denver, 1965-85; chief of staff to Rep. Patricia A. Shroeder U.S. Ho. of Reps., Washington, 1972-74; ptnr. Davis, Graham & Stubbs, Denver, 1985-93, Hogan & Hartson, Denver, 1993—. Contbr. articles to profl. jours. Mem. Colo. Commn. on Higher Edn., 1988-91, chmn., 1989-91; mem. state bd. Gt. Outdoors Colo. Trust Fund, 1996-97. Mem. ABA, Colo. Bar Assn., Nat. Assn. Bond Lawyers. Avocation: sailing. Home: 2625 E Cedar Ave Denver CO 80209-3205 Office: Hogan & Hartson 1200 17th St Ste 1500 Denver CO 80202-5840

CHEROVSKY, ERWIN LOUIS, lawyer, writer; b. Dover, N.J., Dec. 31, 1933; s. Sam and Ida (Bluestein) C.; m. Edith Mayer, June 26, 1966; children: Kim, Karen; children by previous marriage: Debra, Jill. AB, U. Rochester, 1955; LLB, Harvard U., 1958. Bar: N.Y. 1958, U.S. Dist. Ct. (so. dist.) N.Y. 1964, U.S. Ct. Appeals (2d cir.) 1964. Assoc. Stamer & Haft, N.Y.C., 1958-63; assoc. Summit Rovins & Feldesman, N.Y.C., 1963-68, ptnr., 1968-88; ptnr. Proskauer Rose Goetz & Mendelsohn, 1988-89; chmn., legal cost containment cons. WIK Cons. Inc., 1992-97; pres. Old Quarry Devel., 1996—; sec. Space & Leisure Time, Ltd., N.Y.C., 1972-80, Ghiordian Knot, Ltd., N.Y.C., 1978-88, ORS Automation, Inc., Princeton, N.J., 1983-86, Cook United, Inc., Cleve., 1986; chmn. WIK Cons. Inc., legal cost containment cons., 1992-97; pres. Old Quarry Devel., 1996—. Author: The Guide to New York Law Firms, 1991, Competent Counsel: The Business Guide to Hiring Lawyers and Monitoring Their Work, 1992; contbr. articles to profl. jours. Mem. N.Y. State Bar Assn., Assn. of Bar of City of N.Y., Fed. Bar Council (chmn. winter meeting 1980, mem. alternative dispute resolution com. 1984), Phi Beta Kappa. Republican. Jewish. Club:

Canadian (N.Y.C.) (bd. govs. 1988-89, editor The Maple Leaf 1984-89), Metropolitan (N.Y.C.). Author: The Guide to New York Law Firms, 1991, Competent Counsel: The Business Guide to Hiring Lawyers and Monitoring Their Work, 1992; contbr. articles to profl. jours. Fellow Phi Beta Kappa Soc.; mem. N.Y.State Bar Assn., Ass. Bar City of N.Y., Fed. Bar Coun. (chmn. winter meeting 1980, mem. alternative dispute resolution com. 1984). Home: 16 Old Quarry Rd Englewood NJ 07631-5123

CHERRY, ANDREW LAWRENCE, JR., social work educator, researcher; b. Dothan, Ala., Nov. 11, 1943; s. Andrew L. Cherry and Wyalene Cain; m. Mary Elizabeth Dillon, July 16, 1988. MSW, U. Ala., Tuscaloosa, 1974; D Social Work, Columbia U., 1986. Child welfare worker Escambia County Dept. Pensions and Securities, Brewton, Ala., 1968-72; psychiat. social worker Bryce State Hosp., Tuscaloosa, 1974-79; instr. Salisbury (Md.) State Coll., 1981-85; asst. prof. Marywood Coll. Sch. Social Work, Scranton, Pa., 1986-87; prof. Barry U. Sch. Social Work, Miami, Fla., 1987—; conf. Informed Families Dade County, Miami, 1990-98, Miami Coalition for Care to Homeless, 1991-93; cons. to NAACP Minority Media and Telecomm. Coun., 1992—; with drug abuse prevention program Cath. Charities, Miami, 1991—, Broward Children's Svc., Ft. Lauderdale, 1992-94, The Biscayne Inst., 1994—, St. Luke's Addiction Recovery Ctr., 1995—; interim dir. child welfare divsn. Cath. Charities, 1998—. Author: The Socializating Instinct: Individual, Family and Social Bonds, 1994; co-author: Social Bonds and Teen Pregnancy, 1992; series advisor Greenwood Press World View of Social Issues series, 1999; contbr. articles to profl. jours. Scholar NIMH, 1979. Fellow Am. Orthopsychiat. Assn.; mem. NASW, Conf. Social Work Edn., N.Y. Acad. Scis. Democrat. Achievements include research and development of the social bond theory; extensive work and research among the mentally disabled, homeless, at-risk children and the addicted. Office: Barry U Sch Social Work 11300 NE 2nd Ave Miami FL 33161-6628

CHERRY, CAROL JEAN, health educator; b. Altoona, Pa., July 20, 1943; d. Harold Joseph and Vivian Ruth (Moore) Schmittle; m. James Dale Cherry, Jan. 23, 1965, children: Christopher James, Brian Scott,. Diploma in nursing, Altoona Hosp. Sch. of Nursing, 1964; BS in Edn., Indiana U. of Pa., 1975; MEd, St. Francis Coll., 1979. Cert. nurse legal cons. NIPAS. Staff nurse pediatrics Altoona Hosp., Altoona; pediatrics health care instr. Altoona Hosp. Sch. Nursing, Altoona; pediatric nurse clinician Home Nursing Agy. and Vis. Nurse Assn., Altoona, dir. edn., edn. specialist; legal nurse cons., 1999. Vol. ARC, Am. Cancer Soc. Mem. ASTD, ANA (cert. community health nurse).

CHERRY, HAROLD, insurance company executive; b. Bronx, N.Y., June 20, 1931; s. Isidor and Esther C.; m. Maida Welt, Aug. 12, 1961; children—Gina, Joshua. B.S. cum laude, CCNY, 1953. With N.Y. Life Ins. Co., N.Y.C., 1956-89; 2d v.p., actuary N.Y. Life Ins. Co., 1972-78, v .p., actuary, 1978-89; pres. Actuarial Study Materials, Merrick, N.Y., 1983—; cons. in field. Served with U.S. Army, 1954-56. Fellow Soc. Actuaries; mem. Am. Acad. Actuaries, Nat. Assn. Watch and Clock Collectors (past pres. L.I. chpt.). Jewish. Office: Actuarial Study Materials PO Box 522 Merrick NY 11566-0522

CHERRY, JAMES DONALD, physician; b. Summit, N.J., June 10, 1930; s. Robert Newton and Beatrice (Wheeler) C.; m. Jeanne M. Fischer, June 19, 1954; children—James S., Jeffrey D., Susan J., Kenneth C. BS, Springfield (Mass.) Coll., 1953; MD, U. Vt., 1957; MSc in Epidemiology, London Sch. Hygiene and Tropical Medicine, 1983. Diplomate Am. Bd. Pediat., Am. Bd. Pediat. Infectious Diseases. Intern, then resident in pediat. Boston City Hosp., 1957-59; resident in pediat. Kings County Hosp., Bklyn., 1959-60; rsch. fellow in medicine Harvard U. Med. Sch.-Thorndike Meml. Lab., Boston City Hosp., 1961-62; instr. pediatrics U. Vt. Coll. Medicine, also asst. attending physician Mary Fletcher DeGoesbriand Meml. hosps., Burlington, Vt., 1960-61; asst. prof., then assoc. prof. pediat. U. Wis. Med. Sch., Madison, 1963-66; assoc. attending physician Madison Gen., U. Wis. hosps., 1963-66; dir. John A. Hartford Rsch. Lab., Madison Gen. Hosp., 1963-66; mem. faculty St. Louis U. Med. Sch., 1966-73, prof. pediatrics, 1969-73, vice chmn. dept., 1970-73; mem. staff Cardinal Glennon Meml. Hosp. Children, St. Louis U. Hosp., 1966-73; prof. pediatrics, chief divsn. infectious diseases UCLA Med. Ctr. UCLA Sch. Medicine, 1973—; acting chmn. dept. pediatrics UCLA Med. Ctr., 1977-79; attending physician, chmn. infection control com. UCLA Med. Ctr., 1975-93; cons. Project Head Start; vis. worker dept. cmty. medicine Middlesex Hosp. and Med. Sch., London, 1982-83; vis. worker Common Cold Rsch. Unit, 1969-70; mem. immunization adv. com. Los Angeles County Dept. Health Svcs., 1978—. Co-editor Textbook of: Pediatric Infectious Diseases, 1981, 2nd edit., 1987, 4th edit., 1998; assoc. editor: Clin. Infectious Diseases, 1990—; Am. regional editor: Vaccine, 1991—; author numerous papers in field; editl. reviewer profl. jours. Bd. govs. Alexander Graham Bell Internat. Parents Orgn., 1967-69. With USAR, 1958-64. John and Mary R. Markle scholar acad. medicine, 1964. Mem. AAAS, APHA, Am. Acad. Pediat. (mem. exec. com. Calif. chpt. 2 1975-77, mem. com. infectious diseases 1977-83, assoc. editor 19th Red Book 1982), Am. Soc. Microbiology, Am. Fedn. Clin. Rsch., Soc. Pediat. Rsch., Infectious Diseases Soc. Am., Am. Epidemiol. Soc., Am. Pediat. Soc., L.A. Pediat. Soc., Internat. Orgn. Mycoplasmologists, Am. Soc. Virology, Soc. Hosp. Epidemiologists Am., Pediat. Infectious Diseases Soc. (pres. 1989-91), Alpha Omega Alpha. Office: UCLA Sch Medicine Dept Pediatrics Rm 22-442 10833 Le Conte Ave Los Angeles CA 90095-3075

CHERRY, JOHN PAUL, science research association director, researcher; b. Rhinebeck, N.Y., Jan. 31, 1941; s. John and Susan (Borovsky) C.; m. Janet Carrol Day, Aug. 22, 1964; children: Jamie Paulette, Janine Collette. BS, Furman U., 1963; MS, W.Va. U., 1966; PhD, U. Ariz., 1970. NRC postdoctoral rsch. assoc. So. Regional Rsch. Ctr., Agrl. Rsch. Svc., USDA, New Orleans, 1970-72, supervisory rsch. chemist, rsch. leader, lab chief, 1976-82, assoc. dir. Eastern Regional Rsch. Ctr., Phila., 1982-84, dir., 1985—; postdoctoral rsch. assoc. Tex. A&M U., College Station, 1972-73; asst. prof. U. Ga. Exptl. Sta., Griffin, 1973-75; lectr. in field. Editor 3 books; contbr. chpts. to books and more than 130 articles to profl. jours. Recipient Excellence in Govt. Mgr. of Yr. award, Phila. Fed. Exec. Bd., 1991, Presdl. Rank award of Meritorious Exec. for Mgmt. and Rsch., 1991. Fellow Am. Chem. Soc.; mem. Am. Oil Chemists Soc., Assn. Ofcl. Analytical Chemists, Am. Peanut Rsch. Edn. Assn., Inst. Food Technologists, Planetary Soc., Sigma Xi. Methodist. Avocations: travel, gardening, lecturing. Home: 360 Dundee Dr Blue Bell PA 19422-2436*

CHERRY, LEE OTIS, scientific institute administrator; b. Oakland, Calif., Nov. 20, 1944; s. Knorvel and Lucy (Grayson) C.; m. Lauren Michelle Waters, Aug. 30, 1980; children: Aminah L., Jamilah L. AA, Merritt Community Coll., Oakland, Calif., 1965; BSEE, San Jose State U., 1968; cert. Hazardous Material Mgmt., U. Calif., Berkeley, 1995, cert. Site Assessment and Remediation, 1997. Registered Environ. Assessor, Calif. Systems analyst IBM, San Francisco, 1968-69; elec. engr. Pacific Gas & Elec., Oakland, Calif., 1969-79; project mgr. Navy Facility, Dept. Def., Washington, 1979-84; project mgr., environ. engr. NAVFACENGCOM Dept. of Def., San Bruno, Calif., 1984—; co-founder, pres. African Sci. Inst., Oakland, 1967—; sr. cons. Devel. Cons. & Assocs., Oakland, 1972—; proprietor L & L Assocs., Oakland, 1980—. Pubr. mo. mag. "Technology Transfer", 1979-83, quar. newspaper "SciTech", 1988—; developer calendar: Blacks in Science, 1986—. Mem. AAAS, Ghanaian-Am. C. of C. (co-founder, bd. dirs. 1990—), World Affairs Coun. No. Calif. Avocations: reading, futurism studies. Office: African Scientific Inst PO Box 12161 Oakland CA 94604-2161

CHERRY, LINDA LEA, federal agency official; b. Davenport, Iowa, Apr. 6, 1956; d. Francis Eugene and Joan Grace (Rottman) Johnson; m. Bradley Scott Cherry, Mar. 1, 1980; children: Jacob Carl, Lucas Andrew. AA, Des Moines Area Community Coll., 1981; BS, Upper Iowa U., 1992. Cert. peace officer; cert. sex crimes investigator; cert. Iowa/NCIC operator. Cashier Frontier Grocery Store, Polk City, Iowa, 1976; clk. typist Deere Employees Credit Union, Ankeny, Iowa, 1974-76; gas sta. attendant Go-Tane, Ankeny, 1977; radio operator Ankeny Police Dept., 1976-78, detective, 1980-85, 89-90, patrol officer, 1978-80, 85-89; guard U.S. Marshals Svc., Des Moines, 1983-90, dep. U.S. marshal, 1990—, recruiter, pub. info. officer, spl. emphasis program mgr., 1990-95, student intern coord., 1992-95, seized asset specialist, 1994-96; motor vehicle officer Des Moines, 1995-99; witness security contact U.S. Marshals Svc., Des Moines, 1995—, sexual harassment point of contact, 1996—, internal affairs insp., 1996-97, tng. officer, 1999—, health & safety officer, 1999—, worklife program coord., 1999—; instr. Ankeny Police Dept., 1980-90; apptd. mem. coun. Iowa Law Enforcement Acad., 1988-90; apptd. mem. E-911 Commn., 1986-88. Named Officer of Yr., Optimist Club, Ankeny, 1981. Mem. NRA (life), Iowa Assn. Police Women (life, pres. 1982-88, Officer of Yr. 1989, fundraising/publicity officer 1992-95), Iowa State Policemen's Assn. (del. 1989), Iowa Assn. Chiefs and Police Officers (legis. com. 1989-90), Internat. Assn. Women Police (life, regional coord. 1986-88, chmn. membership com. 1991-94, rec. sec. 1992-94, pres. 1994-96, immediate past pres. 1996-97, trustee 1996—, Officer of Yr. award 1989). Republican. Lutheran. Avocations: reading, cross stitching, horseback riding, fishing, golf. Home: RR 2 Box 30 Elkhart IA 50073-9802 Office: US Marshals Svc 208 US Courthouse Des Moines IA 50309

CHERRY, PETER BALLARD, electrical products corporation executive; b. Evanston, Ill., May 25, 1947; s. Walter Lorain and Virginia Ames (Ballard) C.; m. Crissy Hazard, Sept. 6, 1969; children: Serena Ames, Spencer Ballard. B.A., Yale U., 1969; M.B.A., Stanford U., 1972. Analyst Cherry Elec. Products Corp., Waukegan, Ill., 1972-74, data processing and systems mgr., 1974, treas., 1974-77; v.p. fin. and bus. devel. Cherry Elec. Products Corps., Waukegan, Ill., 1977-80; exec. v.p. Cherry Elec. Products Corp., Waukegan, Ill., 1980-82, pres., chief oper. officer, 1982-86; pres., chief exec. officer Cherry Corp., Waukegan, 1986-92, chmn., pres., 1992—. Trustee Lake Forest Coll., Ill., 1982-90; trustee Lake Forest Hosp., 1982—, chmn., 1989-92. Mem. Chgo. Coun. Fgn. Rels., Econ. Club, Comml. Club, Chgo. Club, Commonwealth Club, Onwentsia Club. Office: Cherry Corp 3600 Sunset Ave Waukegan IL 60087-3214

CHERRY, ROBERT NEWTON, JR., army officer, health physicist; b. Bowling Green, Ky., Oct. 6, 1946; s. Robert Newton and Lolita Violet (Tomes) C.; m. Janet Marie Reichenbach, May 31, 1969 (div. Oct. 1983); children: Christopher P., Gregory A.; m. Maria Yolanda Ramirez, Mar. 28, 1984. BS, U. Mich., 1968, MS, 1972, PhD, 1975. Diplomate Am. Bd. Health Physics. Commd. 2d lt. U.S. Army, 1969, advanced through grades to col., 1994; health physicst Army Environ. Hygiene Agy., Aberdeen Proving Ground, Md., 1977-78, 79-80; asst. radiation protection officer Def. Nuclear Agy., Enewetak Atoll, 1978-79; radiation protection officer Brooke Army Med. Ctr., Ft. Sam Houston, Tex., 1980-84; assoc. prof. physics U.S. Mil. Acad., West Point, N.Y., 1984-88; radiation protection staff officer Army Health Svcs. Command, Ft. Sam Houston, 1988-92; dir. radiation and entomology sci. Army Ctr. Health Protection and Pvt. Medicine, Aberdeen Proving Groun, 1992-94; army radiation safety officer U.S. Army Hdqrs., Washington, 1994—; asst. prof. physics Hamilton Coll., Clinton, N.Y., 1975-77. Contbr. articles to profl. jours. Mem. Assn. U.S. Army, Am. Phys. Soc., Health Physics Soc. (bd. dirs. 1996-98). Home: 4523 Butler St Fort George G Meade MD 20755-2103 Office: Dept of the Army 200 Army Pentagon Washington DC 20310-0200

CHERRY, ROBERT STEVEN, III, municipal agency administrator; b. Chgo., Aug. 13, 1951; s. Robert Lee and Jean Louise (Curry) C. BA, Kensington U., 1988. With Chgo. Pk. Dist., 1968—, aquatic supr., 1983—. Asst. capt. 37th precinct, 7th ward, City of Chgo., 1979-80, precinct capt., 1980-83, asst. precinct capt. 2d precinct, 42d ward, 1984-92, capt., 1992—. 1st lt. U.S. Army/Ill. Nat. Guard, 1970-82. Named one of Outstanding Young Men of Am., 1985. Mem. Am. Legion (Post 1976), Young Dems. Am. (Ill. del. 1985), Young Dems. Ill., Young Dems. Cook County, U.S. Water Polo, U.S. Lifesaving Assn., Res. Officers Assn. U.S., Pub. Svc. Employees Union, Lambda Alpha Epsilon. Roman Catholic. Avocations: reading, backgammon, table tennis, swimming. Office: Chgo Park Dist 425 E Mcfetridge Dr Chicago IL 60605-2897

CHERRY, VIVIAN, photographer; b. N.Y.C., Apr. 27, 1920; d. Samuel and Ida (Agranovitch) C.; m. Herb Tank; m. 2d Eric Schmidt; 1 child, Steven Schmidt; m. 3d Louis Finger; m. 4th Alex Redein. Prodr., photographer: (children's film) Hello Halloween, 1970s; one-person shows include 44th St. Gallery, N.Y.C., 1940s, The Gallery, St. Mary's Coll. of Md., St. Mary's City, Md., 1990, Central Fine Arts, Soho, N.Y.C., 1992, 93, 94, Donnell Libr. Ctr., N.Y.C., 1996, 7th and 2d Photo Gallery, N.Y.C., 1997; group exhbns. The N.Y. Pub. Libr., 1998, The Bklyn, Mus. Art, 1996-97, Mus. of Modern Art, 1995, Central Fine Arts, 1991, Art Dir.'s Exhibit, 1950; represented in permanent collections Nat. Portrait Gallery, Smithsonian Instn., Washington, Internat. Mus. Fine Arts, Pretoria, Bergen County Mus. Fine Arts, Paramus, N.J., The N.Y. Pub. Libr., Bklyn. Mus. Art, Mus. Modern Art; photographer: Parents Guide to Child Problems, The Long Loneliness (Dorothy Day); works featured in Popular Photography, Salon Photography, Colliers, Jubilee, Amerika, Pageant, Coronet, numerous others. Home: 343 E 30th St New York NY 10016-6417

CHERRY, WILLIAM ASHLEY, surgeon, state health officer; b. Halls, Tenn., Oct. 25, 1924; s. and Bessie R. C.; m. Jacqueline Guidry, June 2, 1989; children by previous marriage: Neal, Darrell, Philip, Susan. BS, Tulane U., 1946, MD, 1949. Diplomate Am. Bd. Surgery. Rotating intern Phila. Gen. Hosp., 1949-51; resident gen. surgery La. State U. div. Charity Hosp., New Orleans, 1953-56; resident thoracic surgery La. State U. div. Charity Hosp., 1956-57, asst. chief fracture service, 1963-65; practice medicine specializing in gen. and thoracic surgery New Iberia, La., 1957-63; commd. med. officer USPHS, 1963; mem. surg. staff USPHS Hosp., New Orleans, 1963-66; dir. USPHS Hosp., 1966-71, asst. chief surgery dept., 1963-65, dep. chief, 1965-66, dir., 1966-71; regional health dir. Health Services and Mental Health Adminstrn., HEW, USPHS, Region VI, Dallas, 1971-74; sec., state health officer La. Dept. Health and Human Resources, Baton Rouge, 1977-80; commd. ensign USN, 1946, advanced through grades to comdr., 1963; sr. surgeon, comdr. USPHS, 1963; advanced through grades to asst. surgeon gen., admiral; comdg. officer Naval Res. Med. Co. 8-32, 1953-55; ret., 1963; chief med. officer USCG, Washington, 1974-77; pres., CEO, S. La. Health Svcs. Inc., 1987; med. dir. Lallie Kemp Regional Med. Ctr., Independence, La., Div. Mental Retardation and Developmental Disabilities, State of La., Baton Rouge, 1992-93, La. Dept. Health and Hosps., 1992-93; CEO, La. Health Care Authority, 1993-96; staff Met. Health Group, 1996—; asst. clin. dir. surgery Charity Hosp., 1956-57, vis. surgeon, 1963—; chief of surgery Iberia Parish Hosp., 1959-61; chief of staff Dauterive Hosp., New Iberia, 1962-63; clin. asso. instr., surgery dept. La. State U. Sch. Medicine, 1953-57, clin. instr., 1963-66, clin. asst. prof. surgery, 1966-67; clin. asso. prof. surgery Tulane U. Sch. Medicine, 1967-70; adj. assoc. prof. health services adminstrn. Tulane U. Sch. Medicine (Sch. Pub. Health and Tropical Medicine), 1969-70, adj. prof., 1970-73, clin. prof. surgery, 1970—. Contbr. articles to med. jours. Chmn. ofcl. bd. First Methodist Ch., New Iberia, 1960-62; mem. ofcl. bd. Carrollton Meth. Ch., New Orleans, 1964-66; chmn. La. Inter-Agy. Council for Tb, 1966-70; mem. exec. com. New Orleans Poison Control Center, 1966-71; mem. Health Goals Task Force, State of La., 1969-70; mem. Fed. Exec. Bd., New Orleans, 1970-71, Dallas, 1972-73; med. adv. to sec. Dept. Transp., 1974-77; pres. So. Inst. Human Resources, Atlanta, 1979-80; mem. La. Gov.'s Adv. Com. on Edn. of Handicapped Children, 1977-80. Recipient Querens-Rives-Shore award Tulane U. Sch. Medicine, 1949; USPHS Commendation medal, 1969; USPHS Meritorious Service medal, 1974; USPHS Disting. Service award, 1980; USCG Meritorious Service award, 1977; cert. of merit State of La., 1980; Grace A. Goldsmith Disting. Alumnus lectr. Tulane U. Med. Alumni Assn., 1974. Fellow ACS; mem. USPHS Clin. Soc., Nat. Tb Assn., James D. Rives Surg. Soc., Commd. Officers Assn., Mil. Order World Wars, La. Heart Assn., La. Tb and Respiratory Disease Assn. (dir. 1964—), La. Thoracic Soc., La. Pub. Health Assn., Assn. Mil. Surgeons of U.S., Phi Beta Kappa, Alpha Omega Alpha, Delta Omega. Fax: 225-926-3343. Home: 12674 S Highmeadow Ct Baton Rouge LA 70816-2528 Office: 4550 North Blvd Ste 100 Baton Rouge LA 70806

CHERRYH, C. J., writer; b. St. Louis, Sept. 1, 1942; d. Basil L. and Lois Ruth (Van Deventer) C. BA in Latin, U. Okla., 1964; MA in Classics, Johns Hopkins U., 1965. Cert. tchr., Okla. Tchr. Oklahoma City Pub. Schs., 1965-77; lectr. in field. Author: (novels) Gate of Ivrel, 1976, Well of Shiuan, 1978, Brothers of Earth, 1976, Hunter of Worlds, 1976, The Faded Sun: Kesrith, 1977, The Faded Sun: Shon'Jir, 1978, Fires of Azeroth, 1979, The Faded Sun: Kutath, 1979, Hestia, 1979, Sunfall, 1981, Downbelow Station, 1981 (Hugo award for best novel 1982), Wave Without a Shore, 1981, The Pride of Chanur, 1982, Merchanter's Luck, 1982, Port Eternity, 1982, Forty Thousand in Gehenna, 1983, The Dreamstone, 1983, The Tree of Swords and Jewels, 1983, Chanur's Venture, 1984, Cuckoo's Egg, 1985, Visible Light, 1985, The Kif Strike Back, 1985, Angel with the Sword, 1985, Chanur's Homecoming, 1986, Exile's Gate, 1988, Cyteen, 1988 (Hugo award 1988, 89), Smuggler's Gold, 1988, Rimrunners, 1989, Rusalka, 1989, Chernevog, 1990, Yvgenie, 1991, Heavy Time, 1991, Rumrunners, 1991, Hellburner, 1992, Chanur's Legacy, 1992, Goblin Mirror, 1993, Faery in Shadow, 1993, Tripoint, 1994, Foreigner, 1994, Rider at the Gate, 1995, Invader, 1995, Fortress in the Eye of Time, 1995, Inheritor, 1996, Cloud's Rider, 1996, Lois & Clark, 1996, Finity's End, 1997, Fortress of Eagles, 1998; editor: Flood Tide, 1990; translator: Stellar Crusade by Pierre Barbet, 1980, The Green Gods by Nathalie & Charles Henneberg, 1980, The Book of Shai by Daniel Walther, 1982; contbr. short stories to numerous mags. Woodrow Wilson fellow, 1965; recipient John W. Campbell award for best new writer, 1977, Hugo award for short story, 1979, for novel, 1982, 89, Locus award for best sci. fiction novel, 1988. Mem. Sci. Fiction Writers Assn., Alpha Lambda Delta, Phi beta Kappa. Avocations: galactic mapping, guitar and music composition, travel. *

CHERVOKAS, JOHN VINCENT, town supervisor; b. Norwood, Mass., Nov. 14, 1936; s. Bronius John and Anna A. (Kudirka) C.; m. Roseanna Conti, Feb. 23, 1963; children: Jason, Joshua, Jessica. BA, Fordham Coll., 1959. Copywriter Benton & Bowles, N.Y.C., 1961-66; copy group head Grey Advt., N.Y.C., 1966-71; creative dir. McCann-Erickson, N.Y.C., 1971-72, William Esty, N.Y.C., 1972-75; vice chmn., chief creative officer Warwick Advt., N.Y.C., 1975-85; editor-in-chief Madison Ave Mag., N.Y.C., 1985-87; exec. v.p., chief creative officer Sudler & Hennessey Advt., N.Y.C., 1987-94; exec. dir. Greater Ossining (N.Y.) C. of C., 1994-97; supr. Town of Ossining (N.Y.), 1998—. Author: Pinstripe Prayers, 1984, How to Keep God Alive from 9 to 5, 1986, God Lives-In the Suburbs, 1987, Patient Prayers, 1989. Democrat. Roman Catholic. Office: Town of Ossining 16 Croton Ave Ste 4 Ossining NY 10562-4994

CHERWIN, JOEL IRA, lawyer; b. Winthrop, Mass., Apr. 29, 1942; s. Melvin Arthur and Martha C.; m. Sherry Lenore Cherwin, July 5, 1970; children: Alison, Matthew, Joshua. BS in Econs., U. Pa., 1963; JD, Boston U., 1966. Bar: Mass. 1966, U.S. Dist. Ct. Mass. 1968, U.S. Tax Ct. 1969. Ptnr. Cherwin & Glazier, Boston, 1967-77, Cherwin & Glickman, Boston, 1977-96, Cherwin, Glickman & Theise LLP, Boston, 1996—. Mem. ABA, Mass. Bar Assn. Democrat. Jewish. Office: Cherwin Glickman & Theise LLP One International Pl Boston MA 02110

CHERYAN, MUNIR, agricultural studies educator, biochemical engineering educator; b. Cochin, Kerala, India, May 7, 1946; came to U.S., 1968; B. Tech. with honor, Indian Inst. Tech., Kharagpur, 1968; MS, U. Wis., 1970, PhD, 1974. From asst. prof. to assoc. prof. food and biochemical engring. U. Ill., Urbana, 1976-85, prof. food and biochemical engring., 1985—; cons. UN Devel. Program, 1985—. Author: Ultrafiltration Handbook, 1986, Ultrafiltration and Microfiltration Handbook, 1988; mem. editl. bd. Jour. Food Engring., 1985, Jour. Food Process Engring., 1985—, Internat. Dairy Jour., 1989—, Membrane Tech. Newsletter, 1997—; patentee for protein hydrolysis. Recipient Gardners award Assn. Food Scientists and Technologists, India, 1988, A.D.M. award Am. Oil Chemists Soc., 1984, Rsch. Team award Am. Soybean Assn., 1991, Rsch. and Commercialization award Nat. Corn Growers Assn., 1993. Mem. Am. Inst. Chemical Engrs., Inst. Food Technologists, Am. Chemical Soc., N.Am. Membrane Soc. Office: U Ill Agrl Bioprocess Lab 1302 W Pennsylvania Ave Urbana IL 61801-4726

CHESER, KAREN DENISE, school system administrator, writer; b. Bardstown, Ky., Aug. 12, 1963; d. Donald Bruce and Florence Elizabeth (Hutchinson) C.; m. Scott Andrew Richards, Apr. 9, 1996. BA, No. Ky. U., 1988, MA, 1991; postgrad., U. Ky., 1997—. Cert. adminstrn. and tchg., Ky. Elem. tchr. Covington (Ky.) Ind. Schs., 1989-91, Campbell County Schs., Alexandria, Ky., 1991-94; primary program cons. Ky. Dept. Edn., Frankfort, 1994-95, disting. educator, 1995-97; dir. elem. schs. Kenton County Schs., Erlanger, Ky., 1997—; nat. writing project site dir. No. Ky. U., Highland Heights, 1993-95; cons. Ky. Leadership Acad., Frankfort, 1997—. Author: Building the Foundation the Write Way, 1996; co-author: Elementary School Planbook, 1997, (handbook) Connection, 1996; contbr. articles to Regionally Speaking, 1994-96. Pres. coun. St. Paul's United Ch. of Christ, 1992-93; chmn. Soup Kitchen program, Cin., 1991-93; bd. dirs. 10K Run for Missing and Exploited Children, Louisville, 1986; track and field coach Campbell County H.S., Alexandria, 1991-94; mem. edn. com. No. Ky. African-Am. Heritage Task Force, Covington, 1997—. Recipient award of Inspiration Cin. Gas & Elec. Co., 1992; Writing Resource grantee Ky. Dept. Edn., 1992, Ky. Learn and Serve grantee, 1996, Tech. Literacy Challenge grantee, 1998. Mem. Nat. Coun. Social Studies (global edn. spl. interest group 1997), Assn. Suprvision and Curriculum Devel., Nat. Social Studies Suprs. Assn., Nat. Assn. Multicultural Edn. (v.p. Ky. chpt. 1998—), Tchr. Applying Whole Lang. (pres. 1991-95), Covington Women United Against Racism, Phi Delta Kappa. Democrat. Avocations: interior design, water skiing, travel, writing, cooking. Home: 218 E 4th St Newport KY 41071-1641 Office: Kenton County Schs 20 Kenton Lands Rd Erlanger KY 41018-1878

CHESER, RAYMOND NORRIS, III, medical devices company executive; b. Louisville, Oct. 17, 1947; s. Raymond N. II and Martha June Cheser; 1 child, Stephanie Tyukin. BS, Tex. A&M U., 1970, MS, 1976; MBA, U. Conn., 1983; DBA, Nova Southeastern U., 1996. Rsch. chemist The Dow Chem. Co., Freeport, Tex., 1970-76; engring., mfg. mgr. Johnson and Johnson, Skillman, N.J., 1977-80; engring., mfg. mgr. Johnson and Johnson, Southington, Conn., 1980-92, dir. quality assurance, 1995-96; engring. mgr. C.R. Bard, Billerica, Mass., 1992-95; dir. continous improvement U.S. Surg. Corp., North Haven, Conn., 1997—; adj. faculty Boston U., 1994-95; adj. assoc. prof. Albertus Magnus Coll., New Haven, 1996—. Contbr. articles to profl. jours. Bd. dirs. New Britain Symphony, 1989-90. Mem. Acad. of Mgmt., Assn. for Mfg. Excellence, Internat. Assn. of Facilitators. Avocations: music composition, clay sculpture, art collector. E-mail: rayc@ziplink.net.

CHESHIER, STEPHEN ROBERT, former university president, electrical engineer; b. Logan, Ohio, Feb. 21, 1940; s. George Robert Cheshier and Pauline Frazier (Magle) Mason; m. Katherine Joyce Hadley, June 5, 1960; children—David Mark, John Michael. B.S. in Physics, Memphis State U., 1970; M.S. in Elec. Engring., Purdue U., 1972; Ph.D. in Engring. Edn., U. Ill., 1975. Cert. engring. technologist. Prof., head dept. elec. engring. tech. Purdue U., Lafayette, Ind., 1972-80; pres. So. Poly. State U., Marietta, Ga., 1980-97, pres. emeritus, 1997—; cons. Sandia Labs., Albuquerque, 1976—. Contbr. articles to profl. jours. Bd. dirs. Community Symposium Marietta, 1982-97; chmn. U. Ctr. in Ga.; founder Consortium for Polytech. Edn. Recipient James McGraw award McGraw-Hill Pubs., 1984; James G. Dwyer award Purdue U., 1975. Fellow IEEE (sr.), Accreditation Bd. for Engring. and Tech., Am. Soc. Engring. Edn. (chmn. 1981, 92, officer 1985-96), Ga. Soc. Profl. Engrs. (assoc.), Order of the Engr.; mem. Eta Kappa Nu, Tau Alpha Pi, Sigma Pi Sigma, Mensa, Kiwanis (bd. dirs. 1984-88). Mem. Ch. of Christ (elder). Avocations: travel; collecting; music; church work. Office: So Poly State U Pres Office 1100 S Marietta Pky Marietta GA 30060-2855

CHESKY, PAMELA BOSZE, school system administrator; b. Perth Amboy, N.J., June 17, 1942; d. Joseph John and Irene (Konazeski) Bosze; m. Frederick Alan Chesky, Aug. 20, 1966; children: Rick, Scott. BA, Coll. Notre Dame, Balt., 1964; MLS, Rutgers U., 1992. Cert. ednl. media specialist. Tchr. social studies Woodbridge (N.J.) Bd. Edn., 1964-69, ednl. media specialist, 1969-93, supr. librs. guidance and nursing svcs., 1993-95; curriculum specialist for strategic planning Media Ctrs. and Student Assistance Counselors, 1995-97, supr. telecoms. and planning, 1997—; mem. membership com. Infolink, Piscataway, N.J., 1995-96, vice chair, 1996, pres. 97-98; mem. adv. com. Sch. Commn., Info. Libr. Svc. Rutgers U., 1994—. Contbr. articles to profl. jours. Commr. Woodbridge Cultural Arts Commn., 1992-98; vice-chair Middlesex County Dem. Orgn., New Brunswick, N.J., 1992-95; parliamentarian Woodbridge Dem. Orgn., 1993-97; program co-chair Friends Librs. Woodbridge Twp.; mem. Colonia chpt. Hadassah. Mem. ALA (affiliate assembly), Am. Assn. Sch. Librs. (membership com. 1993-95, chair task force on libr. advocacy 1996-98), Edn. Media Assn. N.J. (pres. 1993-94, scholar 1992), Gamma Phi Beta. Democrat. Roman Catholic. Home: 135 Midwood Way Colonia NJ 07067-3116 Office: Woodbridge Bd Edn PO Box 428 Woodbridge NJ 07095-0428

CHESLER, DORIS ADELLE, real estate professional; b. Lincoln, Ill., Sept. 23, 1924; d. Harry and Esther Pearl (Campbell) Schoth; m. Eugene Albert Aughenbaugh, May 23, 1943 (div. Sept. 1970); children: Judith C., Rodney E., Paula Sue; m. Arthur Bernard Chesler, Oct. 16, 1972. Lic. real estate broker, Fla. Realtor, assoc. Kilgore Real Estate, Brandon, Fla., 1969-76; broker Doris A. Chesler, Brandon, 1976—. Den mother Cub Scouts Am., Tampa, 1961-62; leader 4-H Club, Decatur, Ill., 1956. Republican. Presbyterian. Avocations: interior decorating, sewing, gardening, music.

CHESLER, PHYLLIS, psychology educator; b. Oct. 1, 1940; d. Leon Chesler and Lillian Hammer; 1 child, Ariel. BA in Comparative Lit. and Lang., Bard Coll., 1963; MA in Psychology, New Sch. for Social Rsch., 1967, PhD in Psychology, 1969. Instr. in psychology Inst. for Devel. Studies, 1965-66; fellow in neurophysiology N.Y. Med. Coll., 1967-68, clin. rsch. assoc., 1968-69; tchg. fellow in psychology New Sch. for Social Rsch., 1968-69; prof. psychology, sociology, anthropology & women's studies Coll. of S.I./Richmond Coll., CUNY, 1969—; intern dept. psychotherapy Washington Sq. Inst. for Psychotherapy and Mental Health, 1968-69; rsch. asst. New Sch. for Social Rsch., 1966-67; rsch. assoc. grad. dept. physiology Yeshiva U., 1965, Brain Rsch. Lab., N.Y. Med. Coll., 1966-69, Inst. for Devel. Studies, 1965-66; intern. clin. rsch. assoc. N.Y. Med. Coll./Met. Hosp., 1968-69; rsch. scholar Internat. Inst. Rsch. Jewish Women, 1997—; vis. prof. in Psychology and Women's studies, Brandeis U., 1998; lectr., presenter in field. Author: Women and Madness, 1972, 2d edit., 1989, paperback edit., 1972, Eng., 1974, Germany, 1974, The Netherlands, 1974, France, 1975, Italy, 1977, Japan, 1983, Israel, 1987, Women, Money and Power, 1976, paperback edit., 1977, About Men, 1978, 2d edit., 1990, Eng., 1978, Germany, 1979, The Netherlands, 1979, Denmark, 1980, paperback edit., 1980, France, 1982, Sweden, 1983, With Child: A Diary of Motherhood, 1979, paperback edit., 1981, Germany, 1980, The Netherlands, 1981, Sweden, 1982, France, 1983, Mothers on Trial: The Battle for Children and Custody, 1986, 2d edit., 1991, paperback edit., 1987, Sacred Bond: The Legacy of Baby M., 1988, 2d edit., 1989, Eng., 1990, Patriarchy: Notes of an Expert Witness, 1994, With Child: A Diary of Motherhood, 1998; co-editor, contbr.: Feminist Foremothers in Women's Studies, Psychology and Mental Health, 1996, Women & Madness, 25th edit., 1997, Letters to a Young Feminist, 1998; editor-at-large On the Issues mag.; contbr. articles to profl. jours.; mem. adv. bd. Jour. Women and Therapy, Feminism and Psychology, An Internat. Jour. Recipient Medal of Honor, Vet. Feminist Am., 1998. Mem. APA, AAUP, PEN (judge Am. Ctr. 1993 Martha Albrand award), Am. Assn. for Abolition of Involuntary Mental Hospitalization, Assn. for Children of Enforcement of Support (bd. dirs.), Assn. for Women in Psychology (co-founder), Ctr. for Study of Psychiatry (bd. dirs.), Nat. Women's Health Network (co-founder), Vet. Feminists of Am., N.Y. State Psychol. Assn., N.Y. Women's Action Alliance (charter), Women's History Rsch. Ctr. (adv.), N.Y. Women's Forum/Internat. Women's Forum (charter). Home: 732 Carroll St # A Brooklyn NY 11215-2102

CHESLER, STANLEY RICHARD, federal judge; b. Bklyn., June 15, 1947; s. Rubin and Beatrice (Horowitz) C.; m. Francine Richer, June 29, 1969; 1 child, Elizabeth. BA, SUNY, Binghamton, 1968; JD magna cum laude, St. John's U., 1974. Bar: N.Y. 1975, N.J. 1985, U.S. Dist. Ct. (ea. dist., so. dist.) N.Y. 1975, U.S. Dist. Ct. N.J. 1985, U.S. Ct. Appeals (2d cir.) 1975. Asst. dist. atty. Bronx County, N.Y., 1974-80; dep. chief investigations bur. Bronx County, 1976-78, chief investigations bur., 1978-79, chief rackets, narcotics bur., 1979-80; trial atty. U.S. Dept. Justice Organized Crime Strike Force, Newark, 1980-84, deputy chief, 1984-86; asst. U.S. atty. Dist. of N.J., Newark, 1987; U.S. magistrate judge U.S. Dist. Ct. N.J., Newark, 1987—. Fellow Am. Bar Found.; mem. Assn. Fed. Bar State of N.J. (bd. advisors), John J. Gibbons Am. Inn of Ct. (master). Avocations: cross country skiing, biking. Office: US Dist Ct NJ US PO Office & Courthouse Bldg Newark NJ 07101

CHESLEY, STANLEY MORRIS, lawyer; b. Cin., Mar. 26, 1936; s. Frank and Rachel (Kinsburg) C.; children: Richard A., Lauren B. BA, U. Cin., 1958, LLB, 1960. Bar: Ohio 1960, Ky. 1978, W.Va., Tex., Nev. 1981. Ptnr. Waite, Schneider, Bayless & Chesley Co., Cin., 1960; Contbr. articles to profl. jours. Past chmn. bd. commrs. on grievances and discipline Supreme Ct. Ohio; past pres. Jewish Fedn. Cin.; nat. vice chair, bd. govs., trustee, joint distbn. com. United Jewish Appeal; exec. bd., nat. bd. govs. Am.Jewish Com.; nat. bd. govs. Hebrew Union Coll.; exec. com. U.S. Holocaust Meml. Mus. Mem. ABA, ATLA, Am. Judicature Soc., Fed. Bar Assn., Melvin M. Belli Soc., Ohio Bar Assn., Ky. Bar Assn., W.Va. Bar Assn., Tex. Bar Assn., Nev. Bar Assn., Cin. Bar Assn. Office: Waite Schneider Bayless & Chesley 1513 Central Trust Towers Cincinnati OH 45202

CHESLEY-LAHM, DIANE, lawyer; b. Norwood, Mass., Sept. 27, 1942; d. Casimir Peter and Christine (Zabelle) Chesley; m. Wen-hsien Wu, Dec. 26, 1964 (div. July 1973); children: Wendi Ann, Lisa Marie; m. Gunther Karl Lahm, Dec. 14, 1973 (div. Feb. 1993); children: Michael Christopher, Gregory Andrew. AB, Trinity Coll., 1964; postgrad., Temple U., 1973-74; JD, Capital U., 1976. Bar: Ind. 1976, U.S. Dist. Ct. (so. dist.) Ind. 1976, Ohio 1977. Pvt. practice Richmond, Ind., 1976, Columbus, Ohio, 1977; asst. atty. gen. Office Atty. Gen. Ohio, Columbus, 1977; counsel, exec. Ohio Dental Assn., Columbus, 1977-79; dir. Continuing Legal Edn. Capital U. Law Sch., Columbus, 1980-88; sec. to commn. on Continuing Legal Edn. Columbus, 1988—. Leader Green Circle Program, Phila. Human Rels. Com., 1969-71; Brownie leader Girl Scouts U.S., Morgantown (W.Va.) Pub. Schs., 1972-73; leader study group PTA, Morgantown, 1973; panelist Ohio State U. Continuing Edn. Forum, Columbus, 1976; team cons. Ohio Mock Trial Program, Columbus, 1985-86, judge for competition, 1988-93. Mem. ABA, Ohio State Bar Assn., Columbus Bar Assn., Orgn. of Regulatory Adminstrs. for Continuing Legal Edn. Lutheran. Avocations: quilting, cooking, gardening, singing, reading. Office: Supreme Ct Commn Continuing Legal Edn 30 E Broad St Columbus OH 43215-3414

CHESLIK, FRANCIS EDWARD, management consultant; b. Saginaw, Mich., July 26, 1942; s. Wallace Paul and Nellie Elizabeth (Spurbeck) C. BS, Ctrl. Mich. U., 1964; MA, Wayne State U., 1972, PhD, 1977. Cert. tchr. Mich. Gen. mgr. WSUP-FM, Platteville, Wis., 1983-85; comm. rsch. prof. Seton Hall U., South Orange, N.J., 1985-91; dir. Comm. Ctr. Lincoln Meml. U., Harrogate, Tenn., 1991-93; cons. Comm. Mgmt. Rsch. Assn., Emerson, N.J., 1985—; commr. Cable TV Commn., Dubuque, Iowa, 1983-85; regional dir. AERho Nat. Broadcasting Soc., Jonesboro, Ark., 1983; mem. bd. govs. WSOU-FM, South Orange, N.J., 1985-91; media application cons. St. Peters Coll., Jersey City, N.J., 1991. Contbr. articles to profl. jours. Charity contest judge Nabisco, Buffalo, 1995. Mem. Speech Comm. Assn., Internat. Comm. Assn., Tau Kappa Epsilon, Tau Kappa Epsilon (Advisor Recognition 1985, 86, 91, Creation Dr. Cheslik award 1991), Alpha Epsilon Rho (Advisor Recognition 1983, 87). Avocations: computer network evaluation, reading, videography, golf, French cooking. Home: 134 E Ackerman Ave Emerson NJ 07630-1923

CHESNE, EDWARD LEONARD, physician; b. Chgo., June 11, 1931; m. Carol Chesne; children: Lauren, Christopher, Greig. BA, U. Chgo., 1950; MD, Northwestern U. Med. Sch., Chgo., 1955. Lic. phys., Ill., Calif., Hawaii, Guam, Saipan. Capt. U.S. Army, 1957. Fellow Am. Coll. Physicians, Am. Coll. Cardiology, Coun. Clin. Cardiology, Am. Heart Assn. Office: 1380 Lusitana St Ste 1002 Honolulu HI 96813-2461

CHESNEY, LEE ROY, JR., artist; b. Washington, June 1, 1920; s. Lee Roy and Rena Ruth (Beach) C.; m. Betty J. Lamb, Jan. 28, 1943; children: Lee Roy III, Terril Ann Bauer. B.F.A., U. Colo., 1946; M.F.A., U. Iowa, 1948; postgrad., U. Michoacan, Mex., 1950-51. Instr. drawing U. Iowa, 1947-50; prof. art, dir. printmaking, head grad. printmaking and painting U. Ill., Urbana, 1950-67; assoc. dean fine arts U. So. Calif., Los Angeles, 1967-72; prof. art, chmn. grad. art programs U. Hawaii, Honolulu, 1972-84; prof. emeritus U. Hawaii, 1984—; Louis D. Beaumont vis. disting. prof. Washington U.; vis. artist Otis Art Inst., L.A., U. Colo., U. Wash., Mich. State U., Honolulu Acad. Arts Sch., Visual Arts Center, Anchorage, Portland (Oreg.) State U., 1988, U. Fla., 1989, Lacoste Sch. Arts, France, 1989, UCLA, 1989-90 ; mem. com., nat. juror Sr. Fulbright Research Awards, 1968-71, com. chmn., 1969-71; mem. visual arts selection com., Calif. Arts Coun., 1990; juror Hawaii Print Exhbn., 1991; mem. Pacific Rim Lectrs. and Workshops, 1992; artist-in-residence U. Tex., 1993, Pacific Rim Series, 1994. Symposium: Amon Carter Mus., Ft. Worth, 1990, Archer M. Huntington Art Gallery, 1993; one-man shows include: Newman Brown Gallery, Chgo., U. Fla., U. Louisville, U. Mich., U. Wis., Madison, Ohio State U., Ill. State U., Yoseido Gallery, Tokyo, Atrium Gallery, Seattle, Visual Arts Center, Anchorage, Washington U., St. Louis, U. Utah, U. Alaska, Fisher Galleries, U. So. Calif., 1968, Honolulu Acad. Arts, 1973, Comsky Gallery, Beverly Hills, Calif., 1970-76, Downtown Gallery, Honolulu, 1975, BIMC Galerie, Paris, 1979, 81, 83, Galerie Sandoz, Paris, 1979, Cité Internat. des Arts, Paris, 1979, Honolulu Acad. of Arts, Focus Gallery, 1985, Contemporary Arts Center, Honolulu, 1980, 25-yr. retrospective exhbn. of prints circulated by U. Fla., 1977-80, retrospective exhbn. Portland State U., 1988, U. Fla., 1989, Printmaking 1985, Tallahassee, So. Graphics Coun. Emeritus Printmaker Exhbn. Knoxville Mus. Art, 1992; Williams Lamb Gallery, Long Beach, Calif., 1990, 92, West Tex. A&M U., 1993, Oracle (Ariz.) Art Ctr., 1995, Parsons Sch. Design, Paris, 1998; exhibited in group shows including: Am. Fedn. Arts traveling exhbn., Mus. Modern Art traveling exhbn., Am. Cultural Center, Paris, 1964, USIS traveling exhbn., Soc. Am. Graphic artists traveling exhbns., 1973-77, Nihon Sosaku Hanga Kyokai, 1957-84, Contemporary Am. Painting, Bucharest, 1977, Hawaii Nat. Biennial Print Exhbn., Honolulu Acad. Arts, 1971, 73, 75, 77, 78, 80, 83, BIMC Galerie, 1978, 79, 80, 81, 82, 83, 70th Nat. Invitational Drawing Exhbn., Emporia, Kans., 1986, U. West Fla., 1986, Neville-Sargent Gallery, 1986, Northwest Printmakers, 1986, U. Calif., Davis, 1985, Calif. Artists exhbn. at Thomas Ctr. Gallery, Gainesville, Fla., 1987, 25th Anniversary Exhbn. State Found. for Culture and the Arts (reproduction), 1988, Honolulu, 50th Anniversary Exhbn. of Commd. Prints, Honolulu Printmakers, Honolulu Acad. of Arts, 1988, N.W. Print Coun. Exhbn., Australia, 1988, Overreact Gallery, Long Beach, 1989, U. Hawaii, Hilo, 1989, Williams Lamb Gallery, 1990, 91, 92, Worcester (Mass.) Art Mus., 1991, Amon Carter Mus., 1990, Ft. Worth, 1990, Artists Who Teach Exhbn., Champaign, Ill., 1990, Nelson Atkins Mus., Kansas City, 1990, Mona Bismark Found., Paris, 1991, Soc. Am. Graphic Artistd (prize) Nat. Exhbn., N.Y.C., Internat. Exhbn. Artists of Lacoste, France, Paris, 1991, San Diego Art Inst. Invitational, 1991, Williams Lamb Gallery, Long Beach, Calif., 1991, 92, 12th U. Dallas Nat. Print Exhbn., 1991, 92, Nat. Exhbn. Copper Engraving, Portand, Oreg., 1992, Pacific States Biennial Exhbn., Hilo, 1992-94, Northwest Print Coun., Eugene, Oreg., 1993, Indpls. Mus. Art, 1993, Pacific Rim Internat., 1993, 97 (award), Works on Paper, L.A., 1995,96',97',98', Southern Graphics Exhib. of Disting. Print Makers, Tampa,FL, 1997, Los Angeles Print Soc. Exhib. 1997, Portland Art Mus. Intern. Pr. Exhib., 1997: Davis Dominguez Gallery Tucson, 1997, "Exclusively Etchings" Lankersheim Arts, Pacific Rim Internat. Monoprint Exhibition, Hilo, HI, 1998; represented in permanent collections including: Nat. Gallery Art, Washington, Biblioteque Nationale, Paris, Victoria and Albert Mus., London, Tokyo U. Fine Art, Tokyo Mus. Modern Art, Nat. Gallery Art, Stockholm, Tate Gallery, London, USIS, State Dept., Washington, Library of Congress, Washington, Bklyn. Mus., Mus. Modern Art, N.Y.C., Phila. Mus., Denver Mus., Dallas Mus., Pasadena Mus., Honolulu Acad. Arts, Hawaii Council for Arts, Art Inst. Chgo., Oakland Mus., Los Angeles County Mus., Seattle Mus., Worcester Art Mus., Am. Embassy, Bonn, Bank of Am., United Calif. Bank, U. Hawaii, IBM, Litton Industries Corp., Hartford Ins. Co., Fuji Bank Calif., Northrop Corp., 1st Hawaii Trust Bank, Portland (Oreg.) Mus. Art, 1993, Univ. Hawaii, Hilo, 1992, Indpls. Mus. Art, 1991-92, Elvehjem Mus. Art, Wis., West Tex. A&M U., 1993, Wycross Press, Auburn Ala., 1994. Mem. Commn. for Founders' Portfolio for N.W. Printmakers, Portland, 1977. Served to capt. AUS, 1942-45. Recipient Francis G. Logan medal Art Inst. Chgo., 1962, Pauline Palmer award, 1966; Concora Found. prize, 1963; Vera List award Soc. Am. Graphic Artists, Am. Acad., Rome, 1964; appointee Cité Internat. des Arts, Paris, 1970, 78-83; Fondation Gardilanne-Moffat Studio award, 1978-80; purchase award Epinal (France) Biennial Invitational Exhbn., Pacific Rim Internat., 1993, 97; awards Hawaii State Found. for Culture and Arts, 1972, 74, 75, 78, 80; awards Honolulu Acad. Arts, 1973, 78; award San Diego Art Inst., 1991, Fulbright sr. research award, 1956-57; U. Ill. research grantee, 1963-64; Ford Found. faculty enrichment award, 1978, 82, Printmaker Emeritus award So. Graphics Coun., 1992. Mem. Coll. Art Assn. Am., Calif. Soc. Printmakers, N.W. Print Coun. (bd. dirs.), Japan Print Assn., Soc. Am. Graphic Artists, Color Print Soc., World Print Coun., L.A. Printmaking Soc. (hon. dir.), Honolulu Printmakers (past v.p., pres.), Painters and Sculptors League Hawaii, Hawaii Artists League, So. Graphics Coun., Fulbright Assn. Address: 14601 Whitfield Ave Pacific Palisades CA 90272-2645

CHESNEY, MAXINE M., judge; b. 1942. BA, U. Calif., Berkeley, 1964, JD, 1967. Trial atty. Office Dist. Atty., San Francisco, 1968-69, sr. trial atty., 1969-71, prin. trial atty., 1971-76, head atty., 1976, asst. chief dep., 1976-79; judge San Francisco Mcpl. Ct., 1979-83, San Francisco Superior Ct., 1983-95, U.S. Dist. Ct. (no. dist.) Calif., San Francisco, 1995—. Bd. dirs. San Francisco Child Abuse Coun., 1976-79, Hosp. Audiences, 1978-81. Mem. Fed. Judges Assn., Nat. Assn. Women Judges, Edward J. McFetridge Am. Inn of Ct., U.S. Assn. Constl. Law, Queen's Bench, Ninth Jud. Cir. Hist. Soc. Office: US Dist Ct No Dist Calif PO Box 36060 450 Golden Gate Ave San Francisco CA 94102-3661

CHESNEY, ROBERT HENRY, communications executive, consultant; b. Rockville Centre, N.Y., Aug. 12, 1950; s. Robert Lewis and Maureen C. (Oates) C.; m. Donna Marie Mazian, May 1, 1976; 1 child, Alexis Mary. BA in Indsl. Psychology, Hofstra U., 1972, MBA in Quantitative Analysis, 1979. Internal auditor Grumman Aerospace, Bethpage, N.Y., 1974-77, sr. ops. specialist, 1978; sr. systems analyst Sta. WNET, N.Y.C., 1978-79, mgr. mgmt. info. systems and procedures, 1979-81, asst. dir. mgmt. info. systems and procedures, 1981-82; sr. tech. cons. N.Y. Telephone, Melville, 1982-83, AT&T Info. Systems, Melville, 1983-89; from sr. exec. data sales to mgr. territory AT&T Computer Systems, Melville, 1990-94; from sr. client cons. to mng. client cons. AT&T Ops. Cons. Group, Manhasset, N.Y., 1994-95; ptnr. AT&T Bus. Consulting, Manhasset, N.Y., 1995; dist. mgr. AT&T Bus. Cons., Atlanta, Ga., 1996—; dist. mgr. CFO SAP Lucent Technologies Inc., Warren, N.J., 1996—. Mem. IEEE, IEEE Computer Soc., N.Y. Acad. Scis., Hofstra U. Alumni Assn. Republican. Roman Catholic. Office: Lucent Technologies Inc 283 King George Rd Warren NJ 07059

CHESNEY, RUSSELL WALLACE, pediatrician; b. Knoxville, Tenn., Aug. 25, 1941; s. Jack and Helen Wallace (McColl) C.; m. Patricia Joan Cook, June 8, 1968; children: Karen, Christopher, Gillian. AB, Harvard U., 1963; MD, U. Rochester, 1968. Diplomate Am. Bd. Pediatrics. Intern then resident Johns Hopkins U. Hosp., Balt., 1968-70, 72-73; renal fellow NIH, Balt., 1970-72, Montreal Childrens Hosp., Montreal, Que., Can., 1973-75; asst. then prof. U. Wis., Madison, 1975-85; prof., vice chmn. U. Calif., Davis, 1985-88; prof., chmn. pediatrics U. Tenn., Memphis, 1988—; mem. Rsch. Study Sect., NIH, Washington, 1983-88, Nat. Kidney and Urology Diseases Adv. Bd., NIH, 1988-91; sec.-treas., pediat. dept. chmn. Am. Med. Schs., 1993-99, pres.-elect 1999—; editorial com. mem. Am. Pediat. Soc., 1995—; chmn. Fed. Pediat. Orgn., 1995-96; vice chair Task Force on Pediat. Edn., 1996—. Contbr. articles to profl. jours., chpts. to text and med. books. Lt. Comdr. USPHS, 1970-72, Balt. Recipient Founders award in Pediatric Rsch., So. Soc. Pediatric Rsch., 1993; Jour. Pediatrics lectr. U. Rochester, 1985, Paul Gaffney lectr. U. Pitts., 1988. Mem. Am. Acad. Pediats. (pres. Tenn. state chpt. 1995-98, E. Meade Johnson award 1985, Nutrition award 1996), Soc. for Pediat. Rsch. (pres. 1986-87), Midwest Soc. for Pediat. Rsch. (pres. 1984-85), Am. Soc. for Pediat. Nephrology (pres. 1986-87), VA Merit Rev. Bd. (chmn. 1988-90). Office: U Tenn Dept Pediats 50 S Dunlap St Memphis TN 38103-4909

CHESNEY, SUSAN TALMADGE, writer, developer; b. N.Y.C., Aug. 12, 1943; d. Morton and Tillie (Talmadge) Chesney; m. Donald Lewis Freitas, Sept. 17, 1967 (div. May 1976); m. Robert Martin Rosenblatt, Apr. 9, 1980. AB, U. Calif., Berkeley, 1967. Placement interviewer U. Calif., Berkeley, 1972-74, program coord., 1974-79; pers. adminstr. Hewlett-Packard Co., Santa Rosa, Calif., 1982-84; pres. Mgmt. Resources, Santa Rosa, 1984-97; human resources mgr. BioBottoms Inc., Petaluna, Calif., 1990-91; human resources adminstr. Parker Compumotor, Rohnert Park, Calif., 1991-93; writer, developer The E-Myth Acad., Santa Rosa, 1997-98; cons. Kensington Electronics Group, Healdsburg, Calif., 1984-85, Behavioral Medicine Associates, Santa Rosa, 1985-86, M.C.A.I., Santa Rosa, 1986-87, Bowdon Designs, Santa Rosa, 1987-88, Bass & Ingram, Santa Rosa, 1988-96, Eason Tech., Inc., Healdsburg, 1995-96, Interim Svcs., Inc., Santa Rosa, 1995-98, Flex Products, Inc., Santa Rosa, 1996-97, Nev. Prodn. Co., 1998—. Mem. Nat. Soc. Performance Instrn., No. Calif. Human Resources Coun., Pers. Assn. Sonoma County. Avocations: cooking, gardening, music.

CHESNUT, CAROL FITTING, lawyer; b. Pecos, Tex., June 17, 1937; d. Ralph Ulf and Carol (Lowe) Fitting; m Dwayne A. Chesnut, Dec. 27, 1955; children: Carol Marie, Stephanie Michelle, Mark Steven. BA magna cum laude, U. Colo., 1971; JD, U. Calif., San Francisco, 1994. Rsch. asst. U. Colo., 1972; head quality controller Mathematica, Inc., Denver, 1973-74; cons. Mincome Man., Winnipeg, Can., 1974; cons. economist Energy Cons. Assocs. Inc., Denver, 1974-79; exec. v.p. tng. ECA Intercomp, 1980-81; gen. ptnr. Chestnut Consortium, S.F., 1981—; sec., bd. dirs. Critical Resources, Inc., 1981-83. Rep. Lakehurst Civic Assn., 1968; staff aide Senator Gary Hart, 1978; Dem. precinct capt., 1982-88. Mem. ABA, ACLU, AAUW (1st v.p. 1989-90), Am. Mgmt. Assn., Soc. Petroleum Engrs., Am. Nuclear Soc. (chmn. conv. space activities for 1989, chair of spouse activities 1989), Am. Geophys. Union, Assn. Women Geoscientists (treas. Denver 1983-85), Associated Students of Hastings (rep. 1994), Calif. State Bar, Nev. State Bar, Nev. Trial Lawyers Assn., Nat. Acad. Elder Law Attys., Canyon Ranch Homeowners Assn. (sec. bd. dirs. 1994-97), Phi Beta Kappa, Phi Chi Theta, Phi Delta Phi. Unitarian. Office: 2921 N Tenaya Way Ste 201 Las Vegas NV 89128-0454

CHESNUT, DONALD BLAIR, chemistry educator; b. Richmond, Ind., Dec. 27, 1932; s. James Lyons and Naomi Irene (Wright) C.; m. Deborah Berry, Dec. 21, 1954; children—Lauren, Blair, Lynn. B.S., Duke U., 1954; Ph.D., Calif. Inst. Tech., 1958. Postdoctoral fellow, instr. physics Duke U., Durham, N.C., 1957-58, assoc. prof. chemistry, 1965-71, prof. chemistry, 1971—; research chemist E.I. duPont de Nemours, Inc., Wilmington, Del., 1958-65. Mem. Am. Chem. Soc., Am. Phys. Soc., Sigma Xi. Home: 4404 Malvern Rd Durham NC 27707-5646 Office: Duke U Dept Chemistry Durham NC 27706*

CHESNUT, FRANKLIN GILMORE, clergyman; b. Bowling Green, Ky., Mar. 2, 1919; s. Walter Franklin and Fannie (Meador) C.; m. Laurelyn Travillian, Aug. 19, 1950; children: Franklin Gilmore, Kathryn Lynne. Student, W. Ky. State Tchrs. Coll., Bowling Green, 1937-39; BA, Bethel Coll., 1941; BD, Cumberland Presbyn. Theol. Sem., 1943. Ordained to ministry Cumberland Presbyn. Ch., 1940. Pastor in Brunswick, Tenn., 1943-44; denominational youth dir., 1944-53; mgr. Cumberland Presbyn. Book Store, Memphis, 1953-54; pastor Callco Rock, Ark., 1954-58, Russellville, Ark., 1958-75, Booneville, Ark., 1975-90; pastor Gum Springs Ch., Dardanelle, Ark., 1990—; moderator Logan Presbytery, Ky. Synod, 1941, W. Tenn. Synod, 1945, Cumberland Presbyn. Gen. Assembly, 1963, White River Presbytery, 1956, Ewing Presbytery, 1959, 61, 64, Porter Presbytery, 1975; stated clk., Ark. Synod, 1956-86; stated clk. Porter Presbytery, 1977-88; moderator Ark. Synod, 1988, 89; mem. Denominational Commn. on the Ministry, 1975-84, Gen. Bd. Synod of Great Rivers, 1988-92; trustee Cumberland Presbyn. Children's Home, 1962-71. Co-author: Arkansas Cumberland Presbyterians, 1812-1984. Address: 908 N Erie Ave Russellville AR 72801-4009

CHESNUT, NONDIS LORINE, screenwriter, consultant, reading and language arts educator; b. South Daytona, Fla., June 29, 1941; d. Anthony Valentine and Myrtle Marie (Allen) Campbell; m. Raymond Otho Chesnut, Aug. 25, 1962; 1 child, Starlina Mintina Chesnut Kladler. BS in English and Speech, Concord Coll., 1962; postgrad., Frostburg U., 1967; MEd, Shippensburg U., 1972; postgrad., W.Va. U., 1973; Advanced Grad. Specialist Degree, U. Md., 1974, postgrad., Md. State Dept. Edn., 1976-95, Inst. Children's Lit., 1995-97. Cert. adminstr., secondary prin., elem. prin., reading splist., tchr. English and speech, drama. Tchr. English and speech Harpers Ferry (W.Va.) H.S., 1962-64; libr. Great Mills (Md.) H.S., 1968-69; tchr. English and reading North Hagerstown H.S., Hagerstown, Md., 1964-73; tchr. South Hagerstown H.S., Hagerstown, 1974-77; reading resource tchr. Woodland Way Elem. Sch., Hagerstown, 1977-83; adj. instr. grad. sch. Hood Coll., Frederick, Md., 1982-83; reading specialist Fountain Rock Elem. Sch., Hagerstown, 1983-85; tchr. Williamsport (Md.) H.S., 1985-95; reading and lang. arts cons., Md., 1973-95, Fla., 1996-97; adj. reading instr. Daytona Comm. Coll., 1996-97, Galaxy Middle Sch., 1997-98, drama, lang. arts, reading tchr., 1997-98; spkr., presenter local, nat. and internat. workshops, 1973-95; speech and debate coach. Writer for radio programs and advertisements for reading, 1986—, TV programs, 1974-78, 90-91; appeared on TV programs, 1974-78; co-editor column Beckley Post Herald, 1957-59; contbr. articles to newspapers and mags., 1964—; appeared in film Guarding Tess, 1993; screenwriter Heaven on Planet Earth, 1999, Love From Heaven, 1999. Mem. debating team Concord Coll., 1961-62, mem. newspaper staff, 1959-61; mem. Washington County Network of Orgns., 1984-88; co-dir. Billy Bud, 1962; v.p. Women's Ind. Club, 1962, treas., 1961; sec.-treas. Fgn. lang. Club, 1961, Debate Club, 1961-62; treas. Meth. Youth Fellowship, 1961; pres. Tri-Hi-Y, 1959; legis. chairperson State of Md. Reading Coun., 1977-78; active Life in Spirit Group, St. Ann's Roman Cath. Ch., 1994-95, Grace United Meth. Ch., 1995, Lady of Hope Cath. Ch., 1996—; mem. Fla. State Reading Coun. Recipient Pres.'s award State of Md. Reading Coun., 1981, Washington County Reading Coun., 1981, Voice of Democracy award VFW/Ladies Aux., 1992, Am. Heritage Writing award Williamsburg Lions Club, 1995, numerous others; W.Va. Legislature scholar, 1959-62. Mem. AAUW (ednl. chairperson 1983-85, legis. v.p. 1986-87, cmty. chairperson 1987-89), NEA (publicity and scholarship coms., Washington County Tchrs. Assn., bldg. rep. 1989-95, del.), ASCD, VFW (chairperson Voice of Democracy 1989-95, VFW award 1989-95), Md. Dist. Am. Heritage Lions (Region II Lions award, Williamsport Am. Heritage Lions award 1995), State of Md. Tchrs. Assn., Md. State Tchrs. Assn., State of Md. Internat. Reading Assn. Coun. (sec. 1975-79, v.p. elect 1979-80, v.p. 1980-81, pres. 1981-82, nominating chairperson 1982-83), Volusia County Tchrs. Assn., Washington County Tchrs. Assn., Internat. Reading Assn. (sec.-treas. sex differences in reading group 1976-77, 83-85, mem. gender differences in reading group 1985-86, mem. readability interest group, mastery learning interest group, del. convs., internat. rsch. com. 1976-77, 84-85, disabled learners interest group 1975-82), Assn. Rsch. and Enlightenment (Guidance Helping award 1989), Coll. Reading Assn., Md. Assn. English Tchrs., United Dem. Assn., Internat. Platform Assn., Am. Legion (chairperson oratorial contest 1989-95, speech coach), Fla. Devel. Edn. Assn. (mem. com. registration 1996), Screenwriters Unltd. Democrat. Avocations: swimming, dancing, traveling, attending drama prodns., writing. Home: 107 Old Sunbeam Dr Daytona Beach FL 32119-4419

CHESNUTT, JANE, publishing executive; b. Kenedy, Tex., Oct. 10, 1950; m. W. Mallory Rintoul. BJ, U. Tex., 1973. Editorial asst. Am. Jour. Nursing, N.Y.C., 1975-78; asst. editor Woman's Day mag., N.Y.C., 1978-82, health editor, 1982-89, beauty, health, fashion editor, 1989-91, editor-in-chief, 1991—. Mem. bus. adv. coun. Washington Irving H.S., N.Y.C. Mem. Am. Soc. Mag. Editors, Women in Comms., Inc. (Clarion award 1985, Headliner award 1996), YWCA Acad. of Achievers. Office: Woman's Day Mag Hachette Filipacchi Mags Inc 1633 Broadway Ste 4201 New York NY 10019-6742

CHESS, WILLIAM, public relations executive. BS in Mgmt. and Acctg., Fordham U., MBA in Fin. Air traffic controller USAF; with Lever Bros. Co., contr.; fin. v.p. Lever Foods; exec. v.p., CFO Ogilvy & Mather Pub. Rels.; sr. v.p. fin. Ogilvy & Mather; CFO Ogilvy & Mather Worldwide, 1993-95, CFO and COO, 1995; CFO and COO Ogilvy Pub. Rels. Worldwide, N.Y.C. Office: Ogilvy Worldwide 708 Third Ave New York NY 10017*

CHESSER, AL H., union official; b. Pettis County, Mo., Feb. 26, 1914; s. James A. and Mary Pearl (Dirck) C.; m. Rose Burns. Grad. high sch. Brakeman-condr. Santa Fe Ry., Amarillo, Tex., 1941; sec.-treas., legis. rep. Brotherhood R.R. Trainmen, Local 608, 1945-56; sec. Tex. Legis. Bd., 1952-56, legis. dir., 1956-61; nat. legis. rep. Washington, 1961-71, United Transp. Union, 1969-71; pres. United Transp. Union, Cleve., 1971-79; pres. emeritus United Transp. Union, 1979—; v.p., mem. exec. council AFL-CIO; chmn. Congress of Ry. Unions, 1972—; Chmn. Amarillo Civil Svc. Commn., 1950-56, Amarillo Labor Polit. Council, 1954-56; mem. Gov.'s Indsl. Commn., 1957-61, Fed. Task Force on R.R. Safety, 1964-69, Pres.'s Consumers Adv. Council, 1964-68, Greater Cleve. Growth Bd. and Transp. Study Group of Domestic Affairs Task Force, 1973—; mem. adv. panel U.S. Congress Office of Tech. Assessment, 1976; hon. co-chmn. Internat. Guiding Eyes, Inc.,

1976. Author: Transportation and Energy, 1975, Economic Advantages of Transporting Coal by Rail, 1976. Bd. dirs. Dem. Nat. Com., 1973; mem. transp. adv. com. FEA, 1975; co-chmn. R.R. Safety Rsch. Bd., 1975; chmn. bd. CSC; bd. dirs. Amarillo Community Chest, Maverick Boys Club; hon. staff mem. U.S. Army Transp. Sch. Mem. Nat. Def. Execs. Res., Masons, Shriners. Office: United Transp Union 10437 E Dorado Pl Englewood CO 80111-3711

CHESSER, JUDY LEE, federal agency administrator, lawyer; b. Albany, N.Y., May 27, 1948; d. Owen Francis and Sylvia Alice (Tefft) C. BA, Syracuse U., 1970; JD cum laude, Boston Coll., 1977. Bar: D.C. 1977. Legis. asst. Urban Environment Council, Washington, 1973-74, Project on Budget Priorities, Washington, 1974-77; atty. SEC Gen. Counsel's Office, Washington, 1977-78; congl. liaison officer HUD, Washington, 1978-79; spl. asst. to asst. sec. for legislation Health and Human Svcs., Washington, 1979-80; legis. rep. City of N.Y. Washington Office, 1980-83, dir., 1983-94; dep. commr. for legis. Social Security Adminstrn. Congressional and Legis. Affairs, Washington, 1994—. Coordinator Goodell Senate Campaign, N.Y., 1970, McGovern Presdl. Campaign, Pa., 1972. Mem. D.C. Bar. Home: 3901 Alton Pl NW Washington DC 20016-2209 Office: Office of Congl and Legis Affairs Social Security Adminstrn 500 E St SW Ste 800 Washington DC 20024-2796

CHESSER, KERRY ROYCE, financial director; b. Gallipolis, Ohio, July 18, 1956; s. Kenneth LaVerne and Hazel Louise (Steward) C. Student, Mountain State Coll., 1974-76; BA in Acctg., Mt. Vernon Nazarene Coll., 1979; MBA in Fin., Wright State U., 1982. CPA, W.Va., Ohio. Jr. acct. Dayton (Ohio) Tire & Rubber, 1979-80; acct. K-P Acctg., Dayton, 1980-82; chief acct. FMRS Mental Health Council, Beckley, W.Va., 1983-86; acct. Shawnee Hills Community Mental Health/ Retardation Ctr., Charleston, W.Va., 1986-87, auditing supr., 1988-89, mgr. client accounts, 1990-91; dir. fin. and fiscal ops. Health Recovery Svcs., Inc., Athens, Ohio, 1991-95; fiscal officer Franklin County Govt., Columbus, Ohio, 1996—; pres., chief exec. officer Royce Chesser Assoc., Beckley, W.Va., 1984-91. Dir. fin. and audit coms., bd. dirs. Centerville (Ohio) Ch. of the Nazarene, 1979-81; bd. dirs. Athens Ch. of the Nazarene, 1993-95. Mem. AICPA. Avocations: racquetball, tennis, table tennis. Home: PO Box 1025 Athens OH 45701-1025 Office: Franklin County PFM 373 S High St Columbus OH 43215

CHESSER, THELMA JO SYKES, early childhood educator, administrator; b. Hot Springs, Ark., Mar. 8, 1936; d. Harry Freeman and Dorothy Maldana (Bales) Sykes; m. Rev. Zane Leavell Chesser, July 2, 1954 (div. Nov. 1993); children: Michael Zane, Susan Diane C. Branch, Beverly Jo. Student, U. Ctrl. Ark., 1970-72; BS in Edn., Ouachita Bapt. U., 1973, MS in Edn., 1986; postgrad., U. Ark., Little Rock, 1996—. Cert. tchr. K-6, reading specialist K-12, Ark. Kindergarten tchr. Malvern (Ark.) Pub. Schs., 1973-83; kindergarten coord. and tchr. 1st Bapt. Children's Ctr., Malvern, 1983-91; 2d grade tchr. Terry Elem. Sch., Little Rock, 1992—; grad. asst. facilitating Ark.-Okla. Study Circles rsch. U. Ark., Little Rock, 1998—; reading specialist cons., Little Rock, 1987—. Author (prayer guide) State Missions Program Material, 1995; contbr. articles to newsletters. Co-developer North Little Rock Day Care Ctr. for Pike Ave. Bapt. Ch., 1971; asst. and coord. cmty. outreach to needy and transients, various cities and states, 1958-92. Honored Zane and Jo Chesser Day proclamation, City of Malvern/First Bapt. Ch. of Malvern, 1987; Outstanding Tchr. nominee Channel 4, Little Rock, 1995; named Tchr of Yr. Malvern Sch. Dist., 1980, Terry Outstanding Educator, 1994; Edna McGuire Boye Internat. scholar, 1997. Mem. ASCD, NEA, Ark. Edn. Assn., Internat. Reading Assn., The P.E.O. Sisterhood (chpt. pres. 1988-89), Ark. Bapt. Womens Missionary Union (state bd. mem. 1992-97, 5 yr. plaque 1997), Delta Kappa Gamma (Kappa state internat. forum liaison, 1995—, pres. Gamma chpt. 1993-95, mem. adv. bd. to Ark. Friends for Better Schs. 1997—, Dr. Rose Berry State scholar 1996). Baptist. Avocations: music, writing, swimming, travel. Home: 401 Nix Rd Little Rock AR 72211-3278

CHESSLER, RICHARD KENNETH, gastroenterologist, endoscopist; b. N.Y.C., Apr. 6, 1944. BS, Fairleigh Dickinson U., Rutherford, N.J., 1965; MD, Chgo. Med. Sch., 1969. Diplomate Am. Bd. Internal Medicine and Gastroenterology. Asst. chief gastroenterology Englewood Hosp., N.J., 1982—, chief endoscopy, 1992-99; asst. prof. medicine Mt. Sinai Hosp., N.Y.C., 1994-97. Author: Chemical Technicians Ready Reference Book, 1996; mem. editl. bd. Practical Gastroenterology, 1977—. Fellow Am. Coll. Gastroenterology (bd. govs. 1989). Avocations: ski, racquetball, golf. Office: 1555 Center Ave Fort Lee NJ 07024-4612

CHESSON, EUGENE, JR., civil engineering educator, consultant; b. São Paulo, Brazil, Dec. 1, 1928; s. Eugene and Mary Josie (Foy) C.; m. Marilyn Ryder Hershey, Aug. 21, 1954; children—Christopher Eugene, David Anson. B.S.C.E., Duke U., 1950; M.S., U. Ill.-Urbana, 1956, Ph.D., 1959. Registered profl. engr., Ill., Del., Ariz. Refinery engr. Standard Oil Ind., Whiting, 1953; research asst., research assoc. civil engring. dept. U. Ill.-Urbana, 1953-59, asst. prof., 1959-62, assoc. prof., 1962-66; prof. civil engring. U. Del., Newark, 1966-86, dept. chmn., 1966-75; pres. Chesson Engring., Inc., Newark, 1981-85; treas., project mgr. HPR Investors, L.C., Prescott, Ariz., 1992—; treas. Sedona Pinon Woods Partnership, Prescott, 1992—, Hershey Partnership, Prescott, 1993—. Contbr. articles in field to profl. jours. Mem. Nat. Def. Exec. Res., U.S. Dept. Transp., 1973-84. Lt. (j.g.) Civil Engr. Corps, USN, 1950-53. Named Outstanding Young Faculty Mem., Dept. Civil Engring., U. Ill., 1962; Del. Outstanding Engr. Del. Soc. Profl. Engrs., 1981; recipient Teaching award AT&T Found., 1986. Fellow ASCE (pres. local sect. 1982-83); mem. Am. Soc. Engring. Edn. (W.E. Wickenden award 1981), No. Ariz. Geneal. Soc. (v.p., pres. 1989-91). Republican. Presbyterian. Home: 640 Cosmos Way Prescott AZ 86303-5049

CHESSON, MICHAEL BEDOUT, history educator; b. Richmond, Va., Sept. 5, 1947; s. Wesley Earle and Virginia Winborne (Ramsey) C.; A.B. with high honors in History, Coll. William and Mary, 1969; postgrad. (Gilman fellow) Johns Hopkins U., 1972-73; Ph.D. in History (Grad. fellow), Harvard U., 1978. Clk., R.F. & P. R.R., Richmond, 1966-69; park ranger-historian Colonial Nat. Hist. Park, Nat. Park Service, Yorktown and Jamestown, Va., 1969-70, 72, 73; teaching fellow Harvard U., 1975-78; asst. prof. history U. Mass., Boston, 1978-82, assoc. prof., 1982-96; prof. history, 1996—. Served to capt. USNR, 1969—. Mem. Am., So., Va. hist. assns., Orgn. Am. Historians, Naval Res. Assn., Reserve Officer Assn., Fleet Reserve Assn., Navy League. Democrat. Author: Richmond After the War, 1865-1890, 1981.

CHESTER, ARTHUR NOBLE, physicist; b. Seattle, Aug. 5, 1940; s. Arthur Malbridge and Marjorie (Stenberg) C.; m. Cynthia Anne Ashford, Sept. 6, 1961 (div. June 1968); m. Catherine Rogers Buchanan, Aug. 10, 1969. BS in Physics, U. Tex., 1961; PhD in Theoretical Physics, Calif. Inst. Tech., 1965. Mem. tech. staff Bell Labs., Murray Hill, N.J., 1965-69; mem. tech. staff Hughes Research Labs., Malibu, Calif., 1969-73, mgr. laser dept., 1973-75, assoc. dir., 1975-80; program mgr. very high speed integrated circuits Hughes Aircraft Co., El Segundo, Calif., 1980-83, mgr. tactical engring. div., 1984-85; group v.p., mgr. space and strategic systems div. Hughes Aircraft Co., 1985-88; v.p. and dir. research labs. Hughes Aircraft Co., Malibu, Calif., 1988-93; sr. v.p. rsch. and technology Hughes Electronics Corp., L.A., 1993-97; pres. HRL Labs., Malibu, Calif., 1995—; cons. U.S. Dept. Def., Washington, 1975-79; co-dir. Internat. Sch. Quantum Electronics, Erice, Sicily, Italy, 1980—. Co-editor: Integrated Optics: Physics and Applications, 1983, Free Electron Lasers, 1983, Analytical Laser Spectroscopy, 1985, Laser Photobiology and Photomedicine, 1985, Optical Fiber Sensors, 1987, Laser Science and Technology, 1988, Progress in Microemulsions, 1989, Nonlinear Optics and Optical Computing, 1990, Laser Systems for Photobiology and Photomedicine, 1991, Optoelectronics for Environmental Science, 1991, Phase Transitions in Liquid Crystals, 1992, Laser Applications for Mechanical Industry, 1993, Integrated Optics, 1994, Biomedical Optical Instrumentation and Laser-Assisted Biotechnology, 1996, Diffractive Optics and Optical Microsystems, 1997; contbr. articles to jours. Pres. Masterwork Chorus, Morristown, N.J., 1968-69; bd. dirs. Fellows Contemporary Art, Los Angeles. Recipient A.A. Bennett Calculus prize U. Tex., 1959; recipient Nat. Merit scholar, 1957; NSF fellow, 1961; Howard Hughes doctoral fellow, 1963. Fellow IEEE (chmn. com. 1982—, Centennial medal 1984), Optical Soc. Am.; mem. AAAS, IEEE Lasers and Electro-Optics Soc. (pres. 1980), Am. Phys. Soc., Calif. Inst. Tech. (disting. Alumni Svc. award), 1997, UCLA Coun. Rsch. Advisors, Sigma Xi. Office: HRL Labs, LLC 3011 Malibu Canyon Rd Malibu CA 90265-4797*

CHESTER, FRANCIS, political science educator, lawyer; b. Bklyn., Jan. 25, 1936; s. Frank and Mary (DeFrancesco) C.; m. Diane G. Charlson, Oct. 27, 1966; children: Francis Scott, Angelique, Jennifer, Sabrina. BA in Econs., Iona Coll., 1957; JD, St. John's U., Jamaica, N.Y., 1960, MA in Polit. Sci., 1988, cert. in internat. law & diplomacy, 1988. Bar: N.Y. 1961, U.S. Dist. Ct. (ea. and so. dists.) N.Y. 1962, U.S. Ct. Claims 1964, U.S. Supreme Ct. 1964, Va. 1969, U.S. Dist. Ct. (we. dist.) Va. 1994. Sole practice Roslyn Heights, N.Y., 1961-68, East Norwich, N.Y., 1968-69, Gordonsville, Va., 1969-80, Raphine, Va., 1980-88; founder, owner Chester Farms, 1946—; pvt. practice Augusta County, Staunton, Va., 1980-92, 94-97, Churchville, Va., 1997—; asst. prof. polit. sci. So. Sem. Coll., Buena Vista, Va., 1989, faculty, asst. prof. polit. sci. and econs., 1989; lectr. polit. sci. and econs. Piedmont Va. C.C., 1985-87; lectr. in sheep breeding; adj. asst. prof. govt. and econs. Blue Ridge C.C., Weyers Cave, Va., 1986-89; asst. prof. econs. and polit. sci. Christendom Coll., Front Royal, Va., 1989-98, 99—, dir. politics practica program, 1989-94. Mem. Va. Bar Assn., Nat. Columbia Sheep Breeders Assn., KC (4th deg.). Republican. Roman Catholic. Lodge: KC (charter grand knight, co-founder coun. 670). Home: 2490 Little Calf Pasture Hw Swoope VA 24479 Office: 3581 Churchville Ave Churchville VA 24421-2509

CHESTER, JOHN E., III, financial services company executive; b. Newport, R.I., June 21, 1953; s. John E. and Arden C.; m. Debra Chester; children: Paul, Rebecca. BA, U. Conn., 1975; AM, Brown U., 1977; MBA, Wharton Sch./U. Pa., 1980. Asst. treas. JP Morgan & Co., N.Y.C., 1980-83; principal Morgan Stanley & Co., N.Y.C., 1983—. Avocation: golf. Office: 1585 Broadway Lbby 2 New York NY 10036-8200

CHESTER, JOHN JONAS, lawyer; b. Columbus, Ohio, July 13, 1920; s. John J. and Harriet Bonnadine (Rice) C.; m. Cynthia Johnson, Apr. 18, 1959; children: John, James, Joel, Cecily. AB cum laude, Amherst Coll., 1942; JD, Yale U., 1948. Bar: Ohio, 1948. Ptnr., Chester & Chester, Columbus, 1948-57; ptnr. Chester & Rose, Columbus, 1958-70; ptnr. Chester, Hoffman, Willcox and Saxbe (now Chester, Willcox & Saxbe), Columbus, 1971—; spl. counsel Pres. of U.S., 1974. dir. emeritus Grant Riverside Meth. Hosps.; former trustee Columbus Sch. for Girls, Columbus Acad., Shepherd Hill Hosp., Ohio Hist. Found.; trustee emeritus Ohio Hist. Soc.; mem. Ohio Gen. Assembly, 1953-58; Lt. USNR, 1942-46. Mem. ABA, Ohio State Bar Assn., Columbus Bar Assn., Am. Coll. Trial Lawyers. Republican. Episcopalian. Clubs: Columbus, Columbus Athletic, Rocky Fork Hunt and Country, Mason (Columbus). Home: 4906 Riverside Dr Columbus OH 43220-2876 Office: Chester Willcox & Saxbe 17 S High St Ste 900 Columbus OH 43215-3442

CHESTER, LYNNE, foundation executive, artist; b. Fargo, N.D., May 29, 1942. BA in Music, Hillsdale Coll., 1964; MA in Guidance Counseling, Mich. State U., 1965; PhD in Psychology, U. Mich., 1971. Tchr. Warren (Mich.) Consol. Schs., 1965-70; curriculum advisor Royal Oak (Mich.) Pub. Schs., 1974-75; co-founder, exec. dir. Peace Rsch. Found., Carmel, Calif., 1993-98; assoc. Hillsdale Coll., 1989—; guest lectr. ceramics James Milliken U., Decatur, Ill., 1991; guest lectr. creative covergence Carl Cherry Ctr. for Art, Carmel, 1991, Compton lectr., Monterey, Calif., 1996—; co-founder, bd. dirs. Monterey Peninsula Coll. Art Gallery, 1991—; guest juror Monterey County Essay Contest, 1997; cons. Monterey Mus. of Art; guest lectr. Hillsdale (Mich.) Coll., 1997; juror Monterey County Poetry Contest, 1993—; juror photographic show Beauty at the Heart of Things, Carl Cherry Ctr. for Arts, Carmel, 1999. Artist of multiple commd. sculptures for pvt. collections; also ceramics, sculpture and photographs in pvt. and corp. collections; represented in permanent collection at Krammert Art Mus., Champaign, Ill., Fresno (Calif.) Mus. Art; juried show Ctr. for Photographic Art, Carmel, Calif., 1996; art represented at Who's Who in Art, Monterey, 1989—, Christmas Miniatures/Invitational Ctr. for Photographic Art, Carmel, 1996, Holiday Print Show Ctr. for Photographic Art, Carmel, 1996 (Dir.'s Choice 1996); author of poetry; juror essay contest Personal Heroes Monterey County K-12, 1997; juror poetry contest Monterey County 9-12 grades, Carl Cherry Ctr. for the Arts, 1993—; exhibited in photography show at Asilomer Conf. Ctr., Monterey Peninsula Airport, Pacific Grove Art Ctr., Carl Chevry Ctr., Seaside City Hall, Pacific Grove Mus. Natural History, 1995-98, Hillsdale Coll., 1997, Monterey Peninsula Airport, 1998, Calif. State U., Monterey Bay, 1998, Pacific Grove (Calif.) Art Ctr., 1998, Carl Cherry Ctr. for Arts, Carmel, Calif., 1998, Pacific Grove Mus. Nat. History, 1998, Salinas (Calif.) Courthouse, 1998, Asilomar Conf. Ctr., Pacific Grove, 1998, Prints Charming Gallery, Carmel, 1998; represented by Prints Charming Gallery and Carmel Express Internat. Co-founder Southfield (Mich.) Symphony, 1972, World Rhythms Festival, Carmel, 1996—; co-founder, bd. dirs. Monterey Bay Artists Day, Sta. KAZU-FM, 1987-89; pres., bd. dirs. Carl Cherry Ctr. for Arts, Carmel, 1988-94, 95—; bd. dirs. Monterey Peninsula Mus. Art, 1991-93, Carmel Pub. Libr. Found., 1991-93, Monterey Inst. for Rsch. in Astronomy, 1985-95, Cultural Coun. for Monterey County, 1993-98; fundraiser Student Art Gallery, Monterey Peninsula Coll., 1990-97, mem. mentors program Women Helping Women, 1998—. Recipient Citizens Adv. Coun. award City of Royal Oak, 1978-83, Best of Show award for monoprint Monterey Peninsula Coll., 1990, Poetry prizes Carl Cherry Ctr. for Arts, 1990-94, Benefactor of Arts award Monterey County Cultural Coun., 1992, 93, 94, Soccer Mgr./Coach of Yr. 1976-81, 1st pl. award photography contest Monterey Regional Park Dist. Celebration of Open Space, 1998; artist-in-residence Naubinway, Mich., 1997. Mem. AAUW, Internat. Platform Assn., Internat. Sculpture Ctr., Nat. Soc. Fund Raising Execs., Nat. Mus. Women in Art (charter mem.), Am. Crafts Coun., Sigma Alpha Iota (Ruby Sword of Honor 1963). Avocations: reading, playing piano, composing, hiking, photography. Home: 9645 Sandbur Pl Salinas CA 93907-1031

CHESTER, NORMAN CHARLES, bank executive; b. Glen Ridge, N.J., Dec. 7, 1953; s. Norman Harding Chester and Barbara Wanda (Barber) Tessier; m. Vivian Leslie Tarallo, Aug. 15, 1987; children: Alfred Eduardo, Caroline Carmen. BBA, Bucknell U., 1976; MBA, Rutgers U., 1981. Cert. mgmt. acct. Adj. instr. Bergen C.C., Paramus, N.J., 1983-85; rep. Equitable Life, E. Orange, N.J., 1976-77; mgmt. trainee U.S. Life Ins. Co., N.Y.C., 1977-79; from acct. to v.p. Chase Manhattan Bank, N.Y.C., 1979-97; v.p., contr. ABN-AMRO Bank, N.Am. Spcl. Credits, N.Y.C., 1997—; guest speaker Exec. Enterprises, 1993-94. Trustee Westwood (N.J.) United Meth. Ch., 1988-92, fin. chair, 1989-94, sec. adminstrv. coun., 1986-89; publicity chair Hillsdale Vol. Ambulance Svc., 1986—, fin. chair, 1993—, treas., 1994—; dir. Oradell Kids Found., 1996-97. Mem. Inst. of Mgmt. Accts. Methodist. Avocations: triathlons, running, photography. Home: 782 Martin Ave Oradell NJ 07649-2338 Office: ABN-AMRO Bank 10 E 53rd St New York NY 10022-5244

CHESTER, ROBERT SIMON GEORGE, lawyer; b. Chelmsford, Essex, England, Feb. 11, 1949; arrived in Can., 1971.; s. Robert John and Elizabeth Poyitt (Forteath) C.; m. Anna Tharyan, Sept. 18, 1975; 1 child, Rahael Elizabeth Anna. BA, Oxford U., England, 1971, MA, 1979; postgrad., Osgoode Hall Law Sch., Toronto, 1971-72. Bar: Ontario 1982, England and Wales 1988. Vis. lectr. Osgoode Hall Law Sch., Toronto, 1972-74; rsch. staff Ontario Law Reform Commn., Toronto, 1974-77; exec. counsel Dep. Atty. Gen. Ontario, Toronto, 1977-82; counsel policy devel. Ministry Atty. Gen., Ontario, 1982-85; dir. rsch. McMillan Binch, Toronto, 1985—, ptnr., 1988—; counsel Study on Access to Legal Svcs. by Disabled, Ontario, 1982-83; cons. Royal Commn. on Employment Equity, 1983-84, Royal Commn. on Electoral Reform, 1990-91, Royal Commn. on Aboriginal Peoples, 1992. Author: (with others) Environmental Rights in Canada, 1981, Barristers and Solicitors in Practice, 1998; co-editor: Winning with Computers, 1991, 2d vol., 1993; contbr. articles to profl. jours. Can. Rhodes Found. scholar, 1972; trustee fellow Coll. Law Practice Mgmt. Mem. ABA (chmn. New Media and Internet bd., chmn. edn. bd. law practi mgmt. sect. 1994-96, chmn. Techshow 1992-93), Can. Bar Assn. (com. legal opinions 1992—). Anglican. Home: 41 Walmsley Blvd, Toronto, ON Canada M4V 1X7 Office: McMillan Binch, Royal Bank Plz PO Box 38, Toronto, ON Canada M5J 2J7

CHESTER, RUSSELL GILBERT, JR., accountant, auditor; b. Lorain, Ohio, Aug. 6, 1947; s. Russell Gilbert and Elizabeth Jane (Eucker) C.; m. Martha Ann Mamula, Jan. 24, 1970 (div.); children: Sally Ann, Russell Theodore; m. Pamela Jean Huggins, Sept. 26, 1992. BS in Indsl. Mgmt., Purdue U., 1970; grad. with honors, USAF Comm. Analyst Sch., 1971; M Accountancy, Bowling Green State U., 1975; Exec. Mgmt. Program, U. Mich., 1985. CPA, Ohio; cert. systems profl. Staff and sr. acct. Arthur Andersen & Co., Cleve., 1975-77; chief internal auditor lighting fixture div. ITT, Vermilion, Ohio, 1977-78; comptr., dir. pers. lighting fixture div. Lithonia Lighting, Vermilion, Ohio, 1978-80; supr. internal audit indsl. tech. group ITT, Chgo., 1980-81, mgr. internal audit engr. products group, 1981-83; dir. internal audit natural resources group ITT, Stamford, Conn., 1983-84; dir. audit svcs. Parker Hannifin Corp., Cleve., 1984—; cons. Component Repair Tech. Mentor, Ohio, 1984-86, bd. dirs., 1986—; cons. Chester Tax Svcs., Wakeman, Ohio, 1965—, Echo Valley Golf, Wellington, Ohio, 1975-78, Avon Lake (Ohio) Florist, 1975-78, Star Supply, Wadsworth, Ohio, 1984-86; mem. acctg. student adv. bd. Cleve. State U., 1990—, Case Western Res. U., 1994-95. Asst. scoutleader Boy Scouts Am., Cleve., 1985; instr. Jr. Achievement, Cleve., 1986. Sgt. USAF, 1970-73. Mem. AICPA, Inst. Mgmt. Accts., Ohio Soc. CPAs, Inst. Internal Auditors (bd. dirs. Cleve.-Akron chpt. 1991-97, internat. conf. com. 1994-96, chmn. acad. rels. 1991-94, 1st v.p. 1994-95, pres. 1995-96, chmn. attendance and mem. 1996-98, dist. rep. 1997—), Assn. for Sys. Mgmt., Mfrs. Alliance for Productivity and Innovation (gen. auditors coun.), Am. Legion, VFW, Beta Alpha Psi. Republican. Avocations: philately, numismatics, books, yachting, computers. Office: Parker Hannifin Corp 6035 Parkland Blvd Cleveland OH 44124-4141

CHESTER, SHARON ROSE, photographer, natural history educator, writer, illustrator; b. Chgo., July 12, 1942; d. Joseph Thomas and Lucia Barbara (Urban) C. BA, U. Wis., 1964; grad., Coll. San Mateo, 1974, U. Calif., Berkeley, 1977, San Francisco State U., 1989. Flight attendant Pan Am. World Airways Inc., San Francisco, 1965; free lance photographer San Mateo, Calif., 1983—; stock photographer Comstock, N.Y.C., 1987—; lectr. Soc. Expdns., Seattle, 1985-91, Abercrombie & Kent, Chgo., 1992-94, Seven Seas Cruise Line, San Francisco, 1994-95; owner Wandering Albatross, 1993. Author (checklist) Birds of the Antarctic and Sub-Antarctic, 1986, revised, 1994, Antarctic birds and Seals: A Pocket Guide, 1993, South to Antarctica, 1994, The Northwest Passage, 1994; author and illustrator, Birds of Chile, Aves de Chile, 1995; co-author: The Birds of Chile: A Field Guide, 1993, The Arctic Guide, 1996, The Marquesas Islands: Mave Mai, 1997, Ia Orana Tahiti, 1998, Guide to Maritime Britain and The European North Atlantic, 1999; photos featured in Sierra club Book: Mother Earth Through the Eyes of Women Photographers and Writers, 1992; photographer mag. cover King Penguin and Chick for Internat. Wildlife Mag., 1985, Sierra Club Calendar, 1986; exhibited photos at Royal Geographic Soc. London. Mem. Calif. Acad. Sci. Avocations: writing, ice dancing, birdwatching. Home: 724 Laurel Ave Apt 211 San Mateo CA 94401-4131

CHESTER, STEPHANIE ANN, lawyer, banker; b. Oct. 8, 1951; d. Alden Runge and Nina Lavina (Hanson) C.; divorced. BA magna cum laude, Augustana Coll., 1973; JD, U. S.d., 1977; postgrad. C.F.S.C., ABA Nat. Grad. Trust Sch., Evanston, Ill., 1984. Bar: S.D. 1977, Minn. 1979. Asst. counselor Minnehaha County Juvenile Ct. Ctr., Sioux Falls, S.D., 1972-73; child care worker Project Threshold, Sioux Falls, 1973-74; legal intern Davenport, Evans, Hurwitz & Smith, Sioux Falls, 1976; law clk. S.D. Supreme Ct., Pierre, 1977-78; originations dept. buyer Dain Bosworth, Inc., Mpls., 1978-79; v.p., trust officer 1st Bank of S.D., N.A., Sioux Falls, 1979-86; v.p. First Trust Co., Inc., St. Paul, 1986-93; lawyer Westby, Chester & Lees, P.A., 1994-96; pres. Sioux Falls Estate Planning Coun., 1983-85. Projects and rsch. editor S.d. Law Rev., 1977; author law rev. comment. Mem. fund raising coms. S.D. Symphony, Sioux Falls Cmty. Playhouse, Augustana Coll., 1982-83; mem. S.D. divsn. Nat. Women's Polit. Caucus; mem. events com. Augustana Coll. Fellows, Sioux Falls, 1984; bd. dirs. YWCA, Sioux Falls, 1984, Sioux Falls Arena/Coliseum, 1985; mem. Sioux Falls Jr. Svc. League, 1984. Augustana Coll. scholar, 1969-73; Augustana Coll. Bd. Regents scholar, 1973. Mem. ABA, S.D. Bar Assn., Minn. Bar Assn., 2d S.D. Jud. Cir. Bar Assn., Nat. Assn. Bank Women (state conv. com. 1983-85), Mensa, Network Club, Portia Club, Phi Delta Phi, Chi Epsilon. Home: 25 N 4th St # 502 Minneapolis MN 55401-1719

CHESTER, THOMAS JAY, physician; b. Bklyn., Apr. 20, 1947; s. Benjamin J. and Helen (Weltman) C.; m. Dawn C. Bryden, June 2, 1969; children: Janet A., Joyce E. BS in Life Science, MIT, Cambridge, 1968; MD, Stanford U., Palo Alto, Calif., 1973; MPH in Epidemiology, U. Wash., Seattle, 1978. Diplomate Am. Bd. Preventive Medicine. Lt. comdr. USPHS, 1972-78; 0med. dir. urgent care and splty.clinics Fairview Clinics, Mpls., 1999—; med. epidemiologist Ctrs. for Disease Control and Prevention, Atlanta, Ga., 1975-78; chief state epidemiologist Ala. Dept. Pub. Health, Montgomery, 1978-81; dir. health svcs. Conoco, Inc., Houston, 1981-88; v.p. health systems ENSR Health Scis., Alameda, Calif., 1988-90; med. dir. superconducting Super Collider Lab., Waxahatchie, Tex., 1990-95; assoc. prof., acting chmn. Pub. Health & Preventive Medicine U. North Tex. Health Science Ctr., Fort Worth, 1993-95; v.p., med. dir. preventive health Mutual of Omaha, Nebr., 1996; med. dir. occupational health Fairview Clinics, Mpls., 1997—. chmn. editl. com. (CD-ROM) ACOEM Physician's Silver Platter-Occupational Medicine, 1994—. Fellow Am. Coll. Preventive Medicine, Am. Coll. Occupational and Environmentall Medicine, Am. Coll. Epidemiology, Am. Coll. Physicians; mem. Okla. Occupational Medicine Assn. (pres. 1986-87). Office: Fairview Health Works Clinic 3329 University Ave SE Minneapolis MN 55414-3325

CHESTER, TIMOTHY J., museum director. Assoc. dir. for collections La. State Mus., 1985-86; asst. dir. Pub. Mus. of Grand Rapids, Mich., 1986-88, dir., 1988—; pres. Mich. Mus. Assn., Grand Rapids, 1995—. Office: Van Andel Mus Ctr 272 Pearl St NW Grand Rapids MI 49504-5351*

CHESTNOV, RICHARD FRANKLIN, private investor; b. N.Y.C., Mar. 7, 1945; s. Alex and Hannah Chestnov; m. Stephanie Aizer, Aug. 29, 1981; 1 child, Alexis Kyle. BS, Pa. State U., 1966. Jr. sportswear buyer Bloomingdale's, N.Y.C., 1966-72; v.p. Huk-A-Poo Sportswear, N.Y.C., 1972-74; pres. Chego Internat., N.Y.C., 1974-89; chmn. Richarvey Ltd., Hong Kong, 1974-89; bd. dirs. Jaclyn Inc., West New York, N.J. Fellow St. Andrews Country Club. Avocations: tennis, weight training, jogging. Home: 17142 Whitehaven Dr Boca Raton FL 33496

CHESTNUT, HAROLD, foundation administrator, engineering executive; b. Albany, N.Y., Nov. 25, 1917; s. Harry and Dorothy (Schulman) C.; m. Erma Ruth Callaway, Aug. 24, 1944; children: Peter Callaway, Harold Thomas, Andrew Trammell. BSEE, MIT, 1939, MS, 1940; DE (hon.), Case Western Res. U., 1966, Villanova U., 1972. With Gen. Electric Co., 1940-83; cons. systems engr., aeros. and ordnance dept. Advanced Tech. Lab., Schenectady, 1956-66; mgr. Research and Devel. Center, 1966-71; cons. systems engr., 1972-83; pres. SWIIS Found., Inc., 1983—. Editor: Systems Engring. and Analysis, 1965-83, Contributions of Technology to International Conflict Resolution, 1987; author: Servomechanisms and Regulating Systems Design, Vol. I, 1951, Vol. II, 1955, Systems Engineering Tools, 1965, Systems Engineering Methods, 1967; editor: Jour. Automatica, 1961-67. Mem. commn. sociotech. systems NRC, 1975-78. Case Western Res. U. Centennial scholar, 1980. Fellow IEEE (v.p. tech. activities 1970-71, v.p. regional activities 1972, pres. 1973, exec. com. 1967-75, Centennial medal 1984, Richard M. Emberson award 1990), ASME (Rufus Oldenburg award 1990), AAAS, Instrument Soc. Am.; mem. NAE, Internat. Fedn. Automatic Control (pres. 1957-58), World Federalists Assn. (bd. dirs. 1980-92, exec. com. 1984-90), Am. Automatic Control Coun. (pres. 1962-63, Honda prize 1981, Bellman Control Heritage award 1985), Nat. Soc. Profl. Engrs., First Unitarian Soc. (pres. Schenectady chpt. 1983-84), Sigma Xi, Tau Beta Pi, Eta Kappa Nu. Home and Office: 1226 Waverly Pl Schenectady NY 12308-2627

CHESTON, GEORGE MORRIS, lawyer; b. Phila., Aug. 18, 1917; s. Radcliffe and Sydney (Ellis) C.; m. Winifred Dodge Seyburn, May 5, 1955; 1 dau., Sydney. A.B., Harvard U., 1939, LL.B., 1947. Bar: Pa. 1947. Since practiced in Phila.; atty. firm Ballard, Spahr. Andrews & Ingersoll, Phila., 1947-52; farmer Georgetown, S.C., 1968-94; Treas. Nat. Citizens for Eisenhower, 1955-56. Pres. Phila. Soc. to Protect Children, 1959-69; trustee United Fund, Phila., 1958-69; bd. dirs. Phila. Zool. Soc., 1977-86, Saratoga Performing Arts, Am. Fedn. Arts; trustee Phila. Mus. Art, 1962—, pres., 1968-76, Nat. Mus. of Racing. Served to comdr. USNR, 1941-46, PTO. Mem. S.C. Plantation Soc. Home: 229 Spruce St Philadelphia PA 19106-3906 Office: Public Ledger Bldg Philadelphia PA 19106

CHESTON, SHEILA CAROL, lawyer; b. Washington, Nov. 5, 1958; d. Theodore C. and Gabrielle Joan (Hellings) C. BA, Dartmouth Coll., 1980; JD, Columbia U., 1984. Bar: N.Y. 1986, D.C. 1986, U.S. Dist. Ct. D.C. 1987, U.S. Ct. Appeals (D.C. cir.) 1987, U.S. Dist. Ct. (so. and ea. dists.) N.Y. 1989, U.S. Ct. Appeals (2d cir.), U.S. Supreme Ct. 1989. Law clk. to judge U.S. Ct. Appeals for 9th Cir., L.A., 1984-85; assoc. Wilmer, Cutler & Pickering, Washington, 1985-92, ptnr., 1992-93; gen. counsel Def. Base Closure and Realignment Commn., 1993; spl. assoc. counsel to Pres. of U.S., 1994; dep. gen. counsel Dept. Air Force, 1993-95, gen. counsel, 1995-98; ptnr. Wilmer, Cutler & Pickering, Washington, 1998—; adj. prof. in internat. litigation Georgetown Law Sch., 1991—. Mem. ABA, D.C. Bar Assn., Women's Bar Assn., Am. Soc. Internat. Law. Democrat. Episcopalian. Office: Wilmer Cutler & Pickering 2445 M St NW Washington DC 20037*

CHESTON, THEODORE C., electrical engineer; b. Vienna, Austria, May 30, 1922; m. Gabrielle Joan Hellings, Oct. 8, 1956; children—Peter Charles, Sheila Carol. B.Sc., U. Edinburgh, 1947. Engr. Marconi's W.T. Co. Research Lab., Great Baddow, Essex, Eng., 1947-52; sr. engr. Can. Westinghouse Co., Hamilton, Ont., 1952-56; prin. profl. staff Applied Physics Lab. Johns Hopkins U., Laurel, Md., 1956-76; group leader Office of Naval Research NATO, La Spezia, Italy, 1976-79; liaison scientist Office Naval Research, London, 1979-81; br. head Naval Research Lab., Washington, 1981-88; cons., 1988—. Contbr. articles to profl. jours; patentee in field. Served as flying officer RAF, 1942-46. Fellow IEEE, Instn. Elec. Engrs. (Eng.).

CHETIN, HELEN CAMPBELL, writer; b. Chgo., July 6, 1922; d. Guy Edward Campbell and Helen May Collins; m. Adnan Mehmet Chetin, May 1945 (div. 1980); children; Timur Claude, Sara Ruth. BS, U. Tex., 1945. Author: How Far is Berkeley?, 1977, Lady of Strawberries, 1978, Perhans Promise, 1973, 92, Tales From an African Drum, 1970, Angel Island Prisoner, 1982, Chambers of the Heart, 1990, Handles to an Ax, 1999; editor The Wild Iris, 1973-79; editor New Seed Press, 1972-97. Mem. Calif. Writers Assn., Turkish Edn. Found. Independent. Home: 1665 Euclid Ave Berkeley CA 94709

CHETKOVICH, MICHAEL N., accountant; b. Angels Camp, Calif., May 7, 1916; s. Nick M. and Anna (Metkovich) C.; m. Alice Virginia Roosma, Mar. 20, 1947; children: Carol, Mark, John, Kathryn. B.S., U. Calif. at Berkeley, 1939, M.S., 1940. C.P.A., Calif., N.Y. With McLaren, Goode & Co. (C.P.A.'s), San Francisco, 1940-52; ptnr. Deloitte Haskins & Sells, San Francisco and N.Y.C., 1952-78; mng. ptnr. Deloitte Haskins & Sells (now Deloitte & Touche), 1970-78, ret., 1978; dir. Am. Internat. Group Inc., 1980-92, McDonnell Douglas Corp., 1980-88, Phillips Petroleum Co., 1979-87; Regents' prof. Sch. Bus. U. Calif. at Berkeley, 1979, lectr., dir. external affairs, 1980-86. Trustee, chmn. U. Calif. at Berkeley Found., 1981-83. Lt. USNR, 1942-46. Recipient Chancellors award U. Calif. Berkeley, 1986. Mem. AICPA (chmn. 1976-77, Gold medal 1982), Calif. Soc. CPAs (v.p. 1965-66), Am. Acctg. Assn. (v.p. 1975-76), Fgn. Policy Assn., UN Assn. U.S.A., U. Calif. at Berkeley Alumni Assn. (Alumnus of Yr. 1984), Accts. Club Am., Commonwealth Club, Faculty Club, Phi Beta Kappa, Beta Gamma Sigma (chmn. Dirs. Table 1977-93), Beta Alpha Psi. Home: 93 Serrano Dr Atherton CA 94027-3958

CHEUNG, PETER PAK LUN, investment company executive, chemistry educator; b. Shanghai, China, Feb. 2, 1939; came to U.S., 1961; s. Chee Ming and Yik Fan (Chou) C.; m. Evangeline C. Soh, Dec. 19, 1964; children: Wilson, Eric. BS in Chemistry, Colo. State U., 1964; PhD in Chemistry, Okla. State U., 1967. Instr. chemistry Okla. State U., Stillwater, 1967-68; chem. investigator N.J. Zinc Co., Palmerton, Pa., 1968-69; from rsch. chemist to project leader Pennwalt Corp., King of Prussia, Pa., 1969-86; instr. chemistry Del. County Coll., Media, Pa., 1994—; pvt. practice investor Gulph Mills, Pa., 1986—. Inventor dental material, dental varnish, dental porcelain repair. AEC grantee, 1964-66. Mem. Phi Lamda Epsilon. Avocations: music, gardening, investment, basketball. Home and Office: 1011 Jones Rd Conshohocken PA 19428-2617

CHEVALIER, FRANCES SIKOLA, French language educator; b. Paris, Apr. 27, 1947. BS in Med. Tech., Douglass Coll., 1969; MA in French Lang. and Lit., Rutgers U., 1977, PhD in French Lang. and Lit., 1995. Med. technologist, instr. dept. biochemistry Muhlenberg Hosp., Plainfield, N.J., 1969-73; bilingual agt. Coun. of Europe, Strasbourg, France, 1975; tetch. contract rep. E. Merck Diagnostics, Gibbstown, N.J., 1979-83; dir. med. lab. programs Vt. Coll., Montpelier, 1983-86; assoc. prof. French Norwich U., Northfield, Vt., 1987—. E-mail: fchevali@norwich.edu. Office: Norwich U Dept Modern Langs Northfield VT 05663

CHEVALIER, PAUL EDWARD, retired retail executive, lawyer; b. N.Y.C., Jan. 30, 1939; s. Arthur and Grace (Eaton) C.; m. Maggie Helfer, Dec. 29, 1996; 1 child, Marc. BA, Columbia U., 1960, LLB, 1966, MBA, 1966, AMP, Harvard U., 1979. Bar: Ill., 1968, U.S. Supreme Ct. 1974. Dir. labor rels. Carter Hawley Hale Stores, Inc., L.A., 1972-74, v.p. employee relations, 1974-86, sr. v.p. employee relations, 1986-93; pres. Chevalier Cons. Group, 1993-98. Past pres., bd. dirs. Calif. Employment Law Coun. Mem. Nat. Retail Fedn. (chmn. employee rels. com. 1979-82), Calif. Retail Assn., Harvard Bus. Sch. Assn. (bd. dirs. 1980-90, pres. 1984-85), Harvard Bus. Sch. Alumni Coun., 1987-90, Jonathan Art Found. (chmn. emeritus); vice chmn. Western Fed. Credit Union, 1989-93. Lt. USN, 1960.

CHEVALIER, ROBERT LOUIS, pediatric nephrologist, educator, researcher; b. Chgo., Oct. 25, 1946; s. Frank Charles and Marion Helen (Jahnke) C.; m. Janis Julia Slezak, Dec. 23, 1970; 1 child, Juline Arianne. BS, U. Chgo., 1968, MD, 1972. Diplomate Am. Bd. Pediatrics, Bd. Pediatric Nephrology. Pediatric resident U. N.C., Chapel Hill, 1972-75, postdoctoral fellow, 1975-77; nephrology fellow U. Colo., Denver, 1977-78; asst. prof. U. Va., Charlottesville, 1978-83, assoc. prof., 1983-88, prof., 1988—, chief pediatric nephrology, 1978-91, vice chmn. pediatrics, 1988-96, Genentech prof., 1993-97, acting chmn. pediatrics, 1996-97, chmn. pediat., 1997—, Shepherd prof., 1997—; established investigator Am. Heart Assn., 1983-88. Mem. editl. bd. Renal Failure, 1988—, Pediatric Nephrology, 1995-97, Kidney Internat., 1998—; contbr. numerous articles to profl. jours., chpts. to books. Chmn. med. adv. bd. Nat. Kidney Found. Va., Richmond, 1986-89. Fellow Am. Acad. Pediatrics, Am. Heart Assn.; mem. Am. Pediatric Soc., Am. Physiol. Soc., Am. Soc. Nephrology, Am. Soc. Pediatric Nephrology (pres. 1991-92), Am. Bd. Pediatrics, Soc. Pediatric Rsch., So. Soc. Pediatric Rsch. (pres. 1990-91). Office: Univ Va PO Box 386 Charlottesville VA 22902-0386

CHEVALIER, ROGER ALAN, astronomy educator, consultant; b. Rome, Sept. 26, 1949; came to U.S., 1962; s. Frank Charles and Marion Helen (Janhke) C.; m. Margaret Mary With, July 27, 1974.; children: Chase Arthur, Max Toussaint. B.S. in Astronomy, Calif. Inst. Tech., 1970; Ph.D. in Astronomy (Woodrow Wilson and NSF fellow), Princeton U., 1973. Asst. astronomer Kitt Peak Nat. Obs., Tucson, 1973-76, assoc. astronomer, 1976-79; assoc. prof. astronomy U. Va., Charlottesville, 1979-85, prof. astronomy, chmn. dept., 1985-92, W.H. Vanderbilt prof. astronomy, 1990—; dir. Leander McCormick Obs., 1985-92; cons. Lawrence Livermore Nat. Lab., Livermore, Calif., 1981-90. Contbr. numerous research articles to Astrophys. Jour., other astronomy and physics jours. Recipient Heineman prize for astrophysics Am. Astron. Soc./Am. Inst. Physics, 1996; named Va. Outstanding Scientist, Sci. Mus. Va., 1991; Woodrow Wilson Found. fellow Princeton U., 1970-71, NSF fellow, 1970-73; elected to Nat. Acad. Scis., 1996. Mem. NAS, Am. Astron. Soc. (councilor 1988-91), Internat. Astron. Union, Ill. Sci. Lectr. Assn. (v.p. 1975-85). Home: 1891 Westview Rd Charlottesville VA 22903-1632 Office: U Va Dept Astronomy PO Box 3818 Charlottesville VA 22903-0818

CHEVERTON, RICHARD E., newspaper editor. BSJ, Northwestern U., 1964, MSJ, 1965. Reporter Chgo. Today, 1970; editor Sunday Mag. Detroit Free Press, 1970-71; asst. editor Sunday Mag., 1970; editor review & opinion sect. Phila. Inquirer, 1972-75; mng. editor The New Paper, Phila., 1975; freelance Phila., 1975-76; features editor Phila. Daily News, 1976-79; newsfeatures editor Seattle Times, 1979-81; asst. mng. editor, features Orange County Reporter, Santa Ana, Calif., 1982-90, asst. mng. editor strategy and adminstrn., 1990-91, dep. editor strategy and adminstrn., 1991—; pub. Way Point Book, La Palma, Calif.; guest lectr. Poynter Inst., Am. Press Inst. Media mgr. Gray for Cong. campaign; speechwriter Friedman for Mayor campaign, Chgo., 1970. With US Army, 1967-69, Vietnam. Decorated Bronze Star; edited series that won Pulitzer Prize for Spl. Local Reporting, 1982. Mem. Am. Assn. Sunday and Feature Editors. Avocations: painting, sculpture, writing screenplays and short stories, travel. Home: 7211 Monterey Ln La Palma CA 90623-1143 Office: PO Box 11626 Santa Ana CA 92711-1626

CHEVERTON, WILLIAM KEARNS, science corporation executive, consultant; b. Corpus Christi, Tex., 1944; s. Milton Robbins and Pauline (Kearns) C. Student, San Diego State Coll., 1962-65, Chapman Coll., 1965-68; PhD, LaJolla U., 1980. Lic. ins. broker, Calif. Chmn., CEO WYB-SQUIZ Sci., La Jolla, 1980—. Contbr. articles to profl. publs. Cons./vol. YMCA, C. of C., Ednl. Insts.; scoutmaster Boy Scouts Am., 1968-78; dir. Congress Internat. Execs. Named Kiwanian of Yr., Kiwanis Club, 1986. Mem. Camelopard High Intelligence Group, Mensa High Intelligence Group, DRONK Radio Network. Republican. Avocations: sailing, amateur radio, cryptography, amateur TV, teaching. Address: PO Box 2084 La Jolla CA 92038-2084

CHEVES, HARRY LANGDON, JR., physician; b. Birmingham, Ala., Oct. 17, 1924; s. Harry Langdon and Myrtle (Churchill) C.; A.B., Mercer U., 1949; M.D., Med. Coll. Ga., 1953; m. Lois Rebecca Corry, Dec. 25, 1949; children: Rebecca Churchill, Harry Langdon III; m. 2d, Mary Agnes Moon; 1 son, Harry Michael. Intern, Univ. Hosp., Augusta, Ga., 1953-54; practice medicine, East Point, Ga.; mem. staff S. Fulton Hosp., chief of staff, 1980-81; bd. dirs. South Fulton Med. Ctr. Served with USAAF, 1942-46. Fellow Internat., Am. colls. angiology; mem. Royal Soc. Health, AMA, So. Med. Assn., Med. Assn. Atlanta, Atlanta, So. Dist. (past pres.) med. socs., Am. Geriatric Soc., Med. Assn. Ga., Ga. Heart Assn., Phi Delta Theta. Clubs: Am. Antique Automobile, Classic Car Club Am., Packard Automobile Classics, Rolls-Royce Am., Rolls-Royce Owners, Model A, Chrysler Restorers. Home: 333 Plantation Cir Riverdale GA 30296-1106 Office: 1136 Cleveland Ave Ste 400 East Point GA 30344-3618

CHEVINS, ANTHONY CHARLES, retired advertising agency executive; b. Frackville, Pa., Apr. 1, 1921; s. Charles A. and Mary (Swade) C.; m. Margaret Macy, Sept. 18, 1948; children: Cheryl L., Christopher M., Cynthia M. AB in Engl. and Advt. magna cum laude, Syracuse U., 1947; postgrad., Columbia U., 1948-49. Writer Batten, Barton, Durstine & Osborn (advt.), 1948-51; with Cunningham & Walsh, 1951-87, sr. v.p., 1959-61, creative dir., 1958-61, exec. v.p., 1961-68, pres., chief operating officer, 1968-84, chmn., chief exec. officer, 1984-87; chmn., chief exec. officer The C&W Group Inc., 1985-87; vice chmn. N.W Ayer Inc., 1987-90, also bd. dirs. Contbr. articles to mags. Mem. Nat. Advt. Rev. Bd.; mem. dean's adv. coun. Newhouse Sch.; bd. dirs. Medic Alert Found. Internat. Served to lt. USNR, 1941-45. Mem. Phi Beta Kappa, Alpha Delta Sigma. Clubs: Sky, Union League (N.Y.C.); Woodway Country (Darien, Conn.); Nat. Golf Links Am. (Southampton, L.I.); Ocean Reef, Card Sound (Key Largo, Fla.). Home: 10 South Rd Key Largo FL 33037-3729

CHEVIS, CHERYL ANN, lawyer; b. Ann Arbor, Mich., Nov. 9, 1947; d. Peter Paul and Antoinette (Slapinski) C.; m. Edwin Mahaffey Gerow, Nov. 18, 1976. BA, U. Wash., 1969, MA, 1974; postgrad. in Sanskrit, U. Chgo., 1974-77, JD, 1980. Bar: Ill. 1980, U.S. Dist. Ct. (no. dist.) Ill. 1980, U.S. Ct. Appeals (7th cir.) 1982, U.S. Tax Ct. 1982, Oreg. 1986. Tax assoc. Sidley and Austin, Chgo., 1979-80, Mayer Brown and Platt, Chgo., 1981-85; sr. tax atty. Perkins Coie, Portland, 1985-87, tax ptnr., 1987—; mem. faculty Ill. Continuing Legal Edn., Chgo., 1982; vis. lectr. U. B.C., Vancouver, Can., 1983; lectr. Chgo. Tax Club, 1983, Oreg. Securities Lawyers Bar, Bend, 1986, Internat. Employers Seminar, Portland, 1991. Contbr. articles to Jour. Taxation. Vol. atty. Com. Civil Rights Under Law, Chgo., 1982-85. Smithsonian Inst. grantee, 1981. Mem. ABA (tax sect., com. capital recovery and leasing), Oreg. State Bar (sister-bar com. with Lithuanian Lawyers Assn. 1997—). Avocations: music, theater, outdoor sports. Home: 4260 SW Council Crest Dr Portland OR 97201-1531 Office: Perkins Coie LLP 1211 SW 5th Ave Portland OR 97204-3713

CHEVLI, RENATE NAREN, obstetrician, gynecologist; b. Hannover, Germany, 1937; d. Johann and Martha (Bruns) Schmidt; m. Naren A. Chevli, Sept. 18, 1965. MD, SUNY, Syracuse, 1971. Diplomate Am. Bd. Ob-gyn. Intern St. Joseph's Hosp., Syracuse, 1971-72; resident in ob-gyn. SUNY Upstate Med. Ctr., Syracuse, 1972-76; pvt. practice Syracuse, 1976—. Mem. AMA, AAUW, Am. Med. Women's Assn., Med. Soc. of N.Y. State, N.Am. Menopause Soc., Onondoga County Med. Soc., Women's Med. Soc. of N.Y. State. Fax: 315-329-4969. Office: 4117 Med Ctr Dr Fayetteville NY 13066

CHEVRAY, RENE, physics educator; b. Paris, Feb. 6, 1937; came to the U.S., 1962; naturalized U.S. citizen, 1989; s. Robert and Marie-Louise (Fracher) C.; m. Keiko Uesawa, Aug. 9, 1964; children: Pierre-Yves Masaki, Veronique Mie. B.S., U. Toulouse, France, 1962; Dipl. Ing. (French Govt. Highest scholar), Ecole Nationale Supérieure d'Electronique, d'Electrotechnique et d'Hydraulique de Toulouse, 1962; MS (Alliance Française of N.Y. fellow), U. Iowa, 1963, Ph.D., 1967; D.Sc., U. Claude Bernard, Lyon, France, 1978. Product and mfg. engr. Centrifugal Pumps Worthington, Paris, 1963-64; research assoc. Iowa Inst. Hydraulic Research, Iowa City, 1964-67; postdoctoral fellow, lectr. aeronautics Johns Hopkins U., 1967-69; asst. prof. SUNY, Stony Brook, 1969-72; assoc. prof. SUNY, 1972-79, prof., 1979-82; prof. dept. mech. engring. Columbia U., N.Y.C., 1982-87, chmn. dept. mech. engring., 1987-90; cons. physics of fluids and instrumentation; vis. prof. Japan Soc. for Promotion Sci., 1975; vis. prof., von. Humboldt fellow U. Karlsruhe, 1975-76. Author: Topics in Fluid Mechanics, 1993; contbr. articles to profl. jours.; rschr. in transport processes in fluids. Recipient Great Tchr. award Soc. Columbia Grads., 1993; Fulbright scholar, 1962-63; grantee NSF, 1970-73, 73-91, Dept. Energy, 1979-89, Office Naval Rsch., 1985-90, Whitaker Found., 1995—; Rsch. Found. SUNY Faculty Rsch. fellow, 1970-71. Mem. Internat. Assn. Hydraulic Rsch., Am. Phys. Soc., N.Y. Acad. Scis., Sigma Xi. Home: 300 Riverside Dr Apt 10A New York NY 10025-5239 Office: Columbia U Mech Enging New York NY 10027

CHEW, GEOFFREY FOUCAR, physicist; b. Washington, June 5, 1924; s. Arthur Percy and Pauline Lisette (Foucar) C.; m. Ruth Wright, June 10, 1945 (dec. Apr. 1971); children—Berkeley, Beverly; m. Denyse Odette Mettel, Dec. 30, 1971; children—Pierre-Yves, Jean-Francois, Pauline. BS in Physics, George Washington U., 1944; PhD in Physics, U. Chgo., 1948. Research physicist Los Alamos Sci. Lab., N.Mex., 1944-46; research physicist Lawrence Berkeley Lab., Calif., 1948-49; asst. prof. physics U. Calif., Berkeley, 1949-50; asst. prof., assoc. prof. physics U. Ill., Urbana, 1950-56; prof. physics U. Calif., Berkeley, 1957—, chmn. dept. physics, 1974-78, Miller prof., 1981-82, dean physical scis., 1986-92; group leader theoretical physics Lawrence Berkeley Lab., Calif., 1964-83; vis. prof. Princeton U., N.J., 1970-71; sci. assoc. CERN, Geneva, 1978-79; vis. prof. U. Paris, 1983. Author: S-Matrix Theory of Strong Interactions, 1961; Analytic S Matrix, 1966; contbr. articles to profl. jours. Chmn. passport com. Fedn. Am. Scientists, Washington, 1951-56. Recipient E.O. Lawrence award AEC, 1969, Disting. Alumni award George Washington U., 1974, Berkeley citation U. Calif., 1991; Churchill Coll. overseas fellow, 1962. Fellow Am. Phys. Soc. (Hughes prize 1962); mem. Nat. Acad. Scis., Am. Acad. Arts and Scis. Home: 10 Maybeck Twin Dr Berkeley CA 94708-2037 Office: Lawrence Berkeley Lab Berkeley CA 94720

CHEW, KEITH ELVIN, healthcare services administrator; b. Webb City, Mo., Jan. 1, 1957; s. David Elvin and Melinda Lou (Barker) C. BS in Physiology with distinction, U. Ill., 1979, MS in Biol. Sci., 1981, postgrad., 1981-83; MA in Health Svc. Adminstrn., Sangamon State U., Springfield, Ill., 1986. Instr. Sangamon State U., 1985-86; program dir. So. Ill. U. Sch. Medicine, Springfield, 1984-86; dir. bus. and clin. affairs Tex. Tech Health Sci. Ctr., Lubbock, 1986-88; cons. Profl. Cons. Svcs., Long Grove, Ill., 1988-90; adminstr. Primary Care Family Ctr., Libertyville, Ill., 1988-90; instr. Coll. St. Francis, Joliet, Ill., 1991; adminstr. North Suburban Clinic, Skokie, Ill., 1990-91; cons. KEC Healthcare Mgmt. Cons., Forest Lake, Ill., 1991-92; dir. practice mgmt. Contemporary Mgmt. Assocs., Inc., Portsmouth, N.H., 1992-95; exec. dir. Network, Health Mgmt. Ltd. Partnership-Drs. Hosp., Springfield, 1995-96, v.p., 1996-97; CEO Imaging Radiologists, MSO, Inc., Springfield and Chgo, 1998—. Author reports and articles. Mem. Am. Coll. Med. Group Adminstrs. (cert. med. practice exec. 1994), Med. Group Mgmt. Assn., Healthcare Fin. Mgmt. Assn., Chgo. Health Exec. Forum. Avocations: music (aural and vocal), golf, fishing, aviation, gardening. Home: 18 Hawks Nest Chatham IL 62629-2016

CHEW, MARGARET SARAH, geography educator, retired; b. Evanston, Ill., Aug. 20, 1909; d. Nathaniel Durbin and Nettie Jane (Trumbauer) C. BS, Northwestern U., 1930, MS, 1936; PhD with distinction, Clark U., 1960. Maths. and social studies tchr. Iron Belt (Wis.) High Sch., 1930-36; geography tchr. SUNY, Buffalo, 1937-38; social studies tchr. Haven Sch., Evanston, 1938-45; prof. geography U. Wis., La Crosse, 1945-79, chmn. geography dept., 1952-65; emeritus prof. geography U. Wis., 1979—; geography tchr. St. Teresa Coll., Winona, Minn., summer 1939; leader geography credit earning tours U. Wis., La Crosse, summers 1963-80; lectr. in field. Contbr. articles to profl. jours. Recipient fellowships in geog. Clark U., Worcester, 1936-37, 50-51; named fellowship grant presented to outstanding women La Crosse Br. AAUW, 1976. Mem. AAUW, Am. Assn. Geographers, Nat. Coun. Geography (chmn. map com. 1952-54), Wis. Geog. Soc. (founder, several offices), Delta Kappa Gamma (state scholarship chair, summer scholarship award 1951), Philanthropic Ednl. Orgn. (sec., many coms.). Avocations: photography, travel slide talks.

CHEWNING, MARTHA FRANCES MACMILLAN, lawyer; b. Orlando, Fla., Oct. 11, 1951; d. James Francis and Frances Sybil (Es'Dorn) MacMillan; m. John Quinton Chewning, June 3, 1978. BA in Social Work magna cum laude, LaGrange Coll., 1972; JD, Mercer U., 1979. Bar: Ga. Pvt. practice Hamilton, Pine Mountain, Ga., 1979-85; judge probate ct., traffic ct., supt. of elections Harris County, Hamilton, Ga., 1985-98; pvt. practice Hamilton, Ga., 1985—; bd. dirs. First Union Nat. Bank, Pine Mountain. Mem. State Bar Assn. Ga., Pine Mountain C. of C. (pres. 1985), Harris County C. of C. (pres. 1998). Methodist. Avocations: SCUBA diving, motorcycles. Office: PO Box 354 Hamilton GA 31811

CHEWNING, RICHARD CARTER, religious business ethics educator; b. Charlottesville, Va., May 12, 1933; s. Carroll Wills and Vivienne Elizabeth (Akers) C.; m. Shirley Anne Clarke, Nov. 26, 1955; children: Karen Carter Chewning Barnard, John Jeffrey, David Clarke. BSBA, Va. Polytech. Inst., 1956; MBA, U. Va., 1958; PhD in Bus. Adminstrn., U. Wash., 1963. Instr. U. Richmond, Va., 1958-61, from asst. to full prof., 1963-85; part-time instr. U. Wash., Seattle, 1961-63; Chavanne prof. Christian Ethics in Bus. Baylor U., Waco, Tex., 1985—; Chmn. bd. trustees Covenant Coll., Lookout Mountain, Tenn., 1976-88; chmn. bd. dirs. Roger Clarke, Inc., Fredericksburg, Va., 1983-92; bd. dirs. vice-chmn. investment com. Quarryville (Pa.) Presbyn. Home, 1977—; moderator Presbyn Ch. in Am., Atlanta, 1985. Author: Business Ethics In A Changing Culture, 1983, Biblical Principles and Business: The Foundations, 1989, Biblical Principles and Economics: The Foundations, 1989, Biblical Principles and Business: The Practice, 1990, Business Through the Eyes of Faith, 1990, Biblical Principles and Public Policy: The Practice, 1991; also articles. Bd. dirs. Ctr. for Pub. Justice, Washington, 1991-96; trustee LeTourneau U., Longview, Tex., 1993—. Named Disting. Educator, U. Richmond, 1980, Baylor U. Sch. Bus., 1993; The Ann. Richard C. Chewning Award funded by the Service Master Found. in his honor, 1998. Mem. Soc. Bus. Ethics, Assn. Christian Econs., Christian Bus. Faculty Assn. (life), Golden Key, Omicron Delta Kappa, Beta Gamma Sigma. Avocation: traveling, music. Office: Baylor U Hankamer Sch Bus Waco TX 76798-8006

CHEY, WILLIAM YOON, physician; b. Ki Jang, Korea, Jan. 21, 1930; s. Kee Bok and Myungkwon (Lee) C.; m. Fan K. Tang, May 21, 1959; children: William D., Donna C., Richard D., Laura C. M.D., Seoul (Korea) Nat. U., 1953; M.Sc., U. Pa., 1962, D.Sc., 1966. Intern, N.Y.C. Hosp., 1954-55, resident, 1955-56; resident in pathology Mount Sinai Hosp., N.Y.C., 1956-57; fellow in hepatology Seton Hall Med Coll., Jersey City, 1957-58; practice medicine specializing in gastroenterology Phila., 1967-71; attending physician Temple U. Med Center, Phila., 1963—; rsch. fellow in gastroenterology Samuel S. Fels Rsch. Inst., 1959-60; rsch. assoc. Samuel S. Fells Rsch. Inst., 1961, instr. medicine, 1961, assoc., 1963, asst. prof., 1965-68, assoc. prof., 1968-71; prof. medicine U. Rochester, N.Y., 1971-77; clin. prof. U. Rochester, 1977-88, prof. medicine, 1988—; sr. attending physician, founding dir. Isaac Gordon Ctr. for Digestive Diseases and Nutrition, The Genesee Hosp., 1971-91; dir. divsn. gastroenterology and hepatology U. Rochester Sch. Medicine and Dentistry, 1992—; physician Strong Meml. Hosp., Rochester, 1992—; founding dir. William B. and Sheila Konar Ctr. for Digestive Liver Disease, Rochester, 1995—; cons. gastroenterologist Canandaigua (N.Y.) VA Hosp., 1977—; hon. prof. Catholic U. Med. Coll., Seoul, Korea, 1983; clin. prof. medicine Yunsei U. Sch. Medicine, Seoul, Korea, 1984; vis. prof. Peking Union Med. Coll., Beijing, Chinese Acad. Med. Scis., Beijing, 1985, Hallym U. Coll. of Medicine, Choonchun, Korea, 1986, Shanghai (People's Rep. China) Med. U., 1987, Korea U. Coll. Medicine, Seoul, 1991; mem. surgery and bioengrg. study sect. Nat. Inst. of Diabetes, Digestive and Kidney Diseases, NIH, Bethesda, Md., 1982-86. Contbr. articles to profl. and sci. jours and textbooks; mem. editorial bd. The Pancreas, Am. Jour. Physiology. Fellow Am. Coll. Gastroent.; mem. AAAS, Am. Fedn. Clin. Rsch., Am. Gastroent. Assn., Am. Physiol. Soc., Am. Assn. Study Liver Disease, Am. Pancreatic Assn., Internat. Assn. Pancreatology, Am. Motility Soc., Am. Soc. Gastrointestinal Endoscopy, Am. Soc. Acupuncture, Am. Coll. Acupuncture, Sigma Xi. Home: 133 Crescent Hill Rd Pittsford NY 14534-4616 Office: U Rochester Medical Ctr 601 Elmwood Ave Rochester NY 14642-0001

CHI, PETER HOWARD, physicist; b. Hai Ninh, Vietnam, Oct. 19, 1953; came to U.S., 1978; s. Say V. and Kiu (Ho) C.; m. Teresa D. Chi, Dec. 26, 1976; children: Suyin, Irene, Philip, Vincent. BS, SUNY, Albany, 1982; MS, Rensselaer Poly. Inst., Troy, N.Y., 1984. Physicist Nat. Inst. Standards & Technology, Gaithersburg, Md., 1984—. Mem. IEEE, AVS, Sigma Xi. Office: NIST Quince Orchard & Clopper Rd Gaithersburg MD 20899

CHIA, PEI-YUAN, banker; b. Hong Kong, Jan. 27, 1939; came to U.S., 1962, naturalized, 1970; s. Dewey T.H. and Kitty C.; m. Frances T.C. Yen, Feb. 20, 1965; children: Katherine, Douglas, Candice. BA, Tunghai U., Taiwan, 1961; MBA, U. Pa., 1965. Products group mgr. Gen. Foods Corp., White Plains, N.Y., 1965-73; mktg. dir. Citibank (N.A.), N.Y.C., 1974-77; mng. dir. Famibank, Belgium, 1978-80; pres., chief exec. officer Diner Club/Carte Blanche Corp., L.A., 1980, divsn. exec., 1982-84; group exec., mem. policy com. Diner Club/Carte Blanche Corp., 1985-90; sector exec. global consumer banking Citibank, N.Y.C., 1991-92; sr. exec. v.p., mem. mgmt. com. Citicorp, 1992, vice chmn., 1994-96; bd. dirs. Am. Internat. Group, Inc., Baxter Internat., Case Corp. Trustee Mt. Sinai-NYU Med. Ctr. Health Sys., Asia Soc.; mem. grad. exec. bd., sr. fellow SEI Ctr. for Advanced Studies in Mgmt., U. Pa. Wharton Sch.; adv. coun. Rockefeller U. Office: 298 Bedford-Banksville Rd Bedford NY 10506

CHIA, SANDRO, painter; b. Florence, Italy, 1946. Exhibited in one-man shows at Met. Mus. Art, N.Y.C., 1984, Galerie Carola Mosch, Berlin, 1992, Galerie Thaddaeus Ropac, Paris, 1993, Studi d'Arte Raffaeli, 1993, Kohn Abrams Gallery, L.A., 1994, Grand Salon, N.Y.C., 1994, Waddington Galleries, London, 1994; group shows include Bklyn. Mus., Newport Harbor Art Mus., Newport Beach, Calif., Seattle Art Mus., Joslyn Art Mus., Omaha, Phila. Mus. Art, Pa. Acad. Fine Arts, Phila., Storm King Art Ctr., Mountainville, N.Y., Minn. Mus. Art, St. Paul, Sperone Westwater Gallery, N.Y.C., Waddington Galleries, London, Salama-Caro Gallery; subject of numerous articles. Address: care Sperone Westwater 142 Greene St New York NY 10012-3236*

CHIACCHIERE, MARK DOMINIC, lawyer; b. Phila., Dec. 10, 1966; s. Dominic Joseph and Diana (Alosi) C. BSBA, Georgetown U., 1989; JD, Villanova U., 1992. Bar: Pa. 1992, N.J. 1992, U.S. Dist. Ct. (ea. dist.) Pa. 1993, U.S. Ct. Appeals (3d cir.) 1993, U.S. Dist. Ct. N.J. 1992. Assoc. O'Brien & Ryan, Plymouth Meeting, Pa., 1992-94, White & Williams, Phila., 1994-97. Facilitator Parish Coun., Phila., 1996-97. Mem. ABA, Phila. Bar Assn., Savoy Co. (bd. dirs.), Alpha Phi Omega (Mu Alpha alumni sec. 1991-97, bd. dirs. 1995—). Office: 1500 Locust St Ste 3507 Philadelphia PA 19102-4328

CHIANG, ALBERT CHINFA, polymer chemist; b. Pai-ho, Tainan, Taiwan, Jan. 3, 1946; came to U.S., 1973; s. Long and Ping (Su) C.; m. Geraldine Chin, June 4, 1978; 1 child, Scott Jinlong. BS, Nat. Chung-Hsing U., Taichung, Taiwan, 1970; MS, Georgetown U., 1977; PhD, Am. U., 1980. Teaching asst. Georgetown U., Washington, 1974-77, Am. U., Washington, 1977-80; assoc. chemist Pitney Bowes, Stamford, Conn., 1980-81, chemist, 1982-83, staff chemist, 1984-86, sr. chemist, 1987-89, tech. advisor, 1989-92; v.p. R&D Mearthane Products, Cranston, R.I., 1992-97, v.p., 1998—; mem. Chinese Oversea Scholar, Taipei, Taiwan, 1980—. Mem. adv. bd. Am. Security Coun., Washington, 1984. Dissertation fellow Am. U., 1979. Mem. Am. Chem. Soc. (rubber div. 1987—), Soc. Plastics Engring. (sr. mem.), Photography of Sci. and Engring. Achievements include 9 patents and 4 patents pending; development of processes for preparation of polypheynlacetylene and desulfurization of coal; invention of materials for electrophotographic toners, high solid content emulsion formation, flourescent thermal transfer ribbon formation, new dual-step thermal transfer printing; research in rubber, photopolymers, thermal printing, polyurethane manufacturing, conducting polymers including conductive urethane, acrylate, highly conjugated rubber and plastics, and high temperature superconducting material formation, non-impact printing technology and printing materials for postage meter and other mailing system machines; development and production of laser printer rollers including charge roller, developer roller, toner pick-up roller, paper transport roller, in-line skate wheel and live action skate wheel having a breaking mechanism; developed toner for office machine application and medical grade urethane for medical applications. Home: 112 Deerfield Ridge Dr Mystic CT 06355-1150

CHIANG, GEORGE DJIA-CHEE, engineer, educator; b. Shanghai, China, Sept. 29, 1938; came to U.S., 1963; s. Tai Yei and Wai Yui (Lai) C.; m. Betty Theresa Doue, June 11, 1965; children: Andrew H., Audrey H. BS, Harbin (China) Inst. Tech., 1961; MS, U. Calif., Berkeley, 1965; PhD, Ariz. State U., 1971. Registered profl. engr., Tex. Asst. engr. Harbin Steel Co., 1961-62; rsch. asst. U. Calif., 1964-66; sr. project engr. Sperry Rand Corp., Phoenix, 1966-70; faculty assoc. Ariz. State U., Tempe, 1970-71; head, prof. engring dept. U.S. Army Intern Tng. Ctr., Texarkana, Tex., 1971-77; litigation, tech. cons. Nat. Hwy. Traffic Safety Adminstn., Washington, 1977-94; chief trend and analysis divsn. Nat. Hwy. Traffic Safety Adminstrn., 1994—; adj. prof. engring. U. So. Calif., Washington, 1977-89; cons. Sperry Rand Corp., Phoenix, 1970-71, Edgewood (Md.) Arsenal, 1972-77. Contbr. articles to tech. jours. Active local PTA; bd. dirs. Potomac Chinese Sch., 1978-81, CCACC, 1990-92. Active local PTA; bd. dirs. Potomac Chinese Sch., 1978-81; bd. dirs. Chinese Culture and Community Svc. Ctr., 1989-91, pres., 1991-92. Mem. ASME (tech. adv. com. 1980—), Profl. Engring. Soc., Tau Beta Pi. Democrat. Avocations: reading, tennis, travel. Home: 8620 Tuckerman Ln Rockville MD 20854-3159 Office: Nat Hwy Traffic Safety Adminstrn 400 7th St SW Washington DC 20590-0001

CHIANG, HUAI CHANG, entomologist, educator; b. Sunkiang, China, Feb. 15, 1915; came to U.S., 1945, naturalized, 1953; s. Wentse Chiang and Hsiu Hsiu C.; m. Zoh Ing Shen, Sept. 8, 1946; children: Jeanne, Katherine, Robert. B.S., Tsing Hua U., Peking, China, 1938; M.S., U. Minn., 1946, Ph.D., 1948; D.Sc. (hon.), Bowling Green State U., 1979. Asst. instr. entomology Tsing Hua U., Peking, 1938-40, instr., 1940-44; asst. prof. U. Minn., St. Paul and Duluth, 1954-57; assoc. prof. U. Minn., St. Paul, 1957-60, prof., 1960-83, prof. emeritus, 1984—; cons. UNDP FAO, 1970, 72, 75, 76, 80, 82, 85-88, USDA, 1975-83; mem. sci. del. Am. Entomol. Soc., 1974, NAS, 1975, USDA/EPA, 1978, 81, USDA, 1979, 81, FAO, 1980, 82; sci. panel Coun. Environ. Quality, 1977, U.S. Internat. Comm. Agy., 1979, Internat. Centre Insect Physiology and Ecology, Nairobi, Kenya, 1980, Taiwan Coun. Agr., 1979, 84, Chinese Ministry Agr., 1982. Editor 3 publs.; contbr. over 230 rsch. papers to profl. jours. Recipient Cert. Appreciation USDA, 1975, Disting. Svc. award Am. Inst. Biol. Scis., 1979, Regents Cert. Merit U. Minn., 1984, Disting. Svc. award Ministry Agr. and Coops., Thailand, 1988; named Tchr. of yr. Student Assn., U. Minn-Duluth Campus, 1961; Guggenheim fellow, 1955; Phi Kappa Phi nat. scholar, 1983. Mem. Can. Royal London Entomol. Socs., Am. Entomol. Soc. (hon. mem., sect. chmn., chpt. pres., C.V. Riley award, Master Entomologist award), Hungarian Entomol. Soc. (hon. mem.), Japanese Soc. Population Rsch., Internat. Assn. Ecologists, Internat. Orgn. Biol. Control (pres. Western hemisphere, pres., hon. pres. working group), AAAS, Minn. Acad. Scis., Sigma Xi, Gamma Sigma Delta (Merit award 1983), Phi Kappa Phi (scholar of Yr. award 1982, Minn. chpt.). Home: 1896 Carl St Saint Paul MN 55113-5102 Office: Dept Entomology Univ Minn Saint Paul MN 55108-6125

CHIANG, YUNG FRANK, law educator; b. Taichung, Taiwan, Jan. 2, 1936; came to U.S., 1961; s. Ruey-ting and Yueh-yin (Ho) C.; m. Quay-yin Lin, Nov. 1, 1969; children: Amy P., David H. LLB, Nat. Taiwan U., 1958; LLM, Northwestern U., 1962; JD, U. Chgo., 1965. Bar: Taiwan 1960, N.Y. 1974. Assoc. Yen & Lai Law Office, Taipei, Taiwan, 1960-61; editor The Lawyers Co-op Pub. Co., Rochester, N.Y., 1965; rsch. assoc. in law Harvard Law Sch., Cambridge, Mass., 1965-67; asst. prof. law U. Ga. Sch. Law, Athens, 1967-72; assoc. prof. law Fordham U. Sch. Law, N.Y.C., 1972-76, prof. law, 1976—; legal cons., vice chmn. Asia Bank, N.A., Flushing, N.Y., 1983-88; leader N.Y. judge and lawyers del. to China and Hong Kong, People to People Internat., 1994; organizer, moderator 5 Russian delegations to U.S., People to People Amb. Program, 1994-95. *One of the articles published by Professor Chiang titled, The characterization of a vessel as a common private carrier, was cited in Gilmore and Black, the Law Admiralty, and by three federal courts to support their judgements in the following cases: Alamo Chemical Transport Co. v. M/V Overseas Valdea, 469 F.Supp. 203 (EDNY 1985), Larsen v. A.C. Carpenter Inc., 620 F.Supp. 1084, 2 UCC Rep. Serv.2d 433 (EDNY 1985), Shell Oil Co. v. M/T/ Gilda, 790 F.2d 1209 (5th Cir., (La.) 1986). The article was also cited in "Admiralty-International Uniform Law and the Carriage of Goods by Sea," by David M. Collins in 60 Tulane Law Review. His recent publication is Payment By Mistake in English Law.* Contbr. articles to law jours. Organizer, bd. dirs. The Taiwan Mcht. Assn. N.Y., Flushing, 1976-96, pres., 1980-84; pres. N.Y. chpt. Formosan Assn. for Pub. Affairs, Washington, 1991, 92. Mem. N.Y. State Bar Assn., N.Am. Taiwanese Profs. Assn. (bd. dirs. 1994-96, 1997—, v.p. 1997-98, pres. 1998-99), Nat. Assn. of Securities Dealers (arbitrator 1976-98), Order of Coif. Avocations: reading, skiing, archery, swimming. Office: Fordham U Sch Law 140 W 62nd St New York NY 10023-7407

CHIAPELLA, ANNE PAGE, epidemiologist; b. Oakland, Calif., Oct. 12, 1942; d. Karl Josef and Anne Elizabeth (Gorrill) C. BA in Polit. Sci., Stanford U., 1964, PhD in Neurosci., 1982, MS in Stats., 1985; MPH in Epidemiology, Johns Hopkins U., 1986. Med. rschr. Stanford (Calif.) U., 1966-75, postdoctoral fellow, 1983-85; postdoctoral fellow Johns Hopkins U., Balt., 1986-88; program officer Inst. Medicine NAS, Washington, 1989-91; sr. analyst Nat. Inst. on Alcohol and Alcohol Abuse, Rockville, Md., 1991—; statis. and intellectual property cons. various orgns., Washington, 1983—; internat. rsch. on alcohol-related problems, 1993—. Writer humorous, tech. and travel speeches, 1985—; reviewer grants and sci. jours., 1992—; contbr. articles to sci. jours. Pres. Nebr. Ave. Neighborhood Assn., Washington, 1987-91; assoc. Smithsonian Instn., Washington, 1987—; active in Friends of Kennedy Ctr., Washington, 1987—, Friends of Nat. Zoo, Washington, 1987—, Textile Mus., Washington, 1986—, WETA, Pub. Broadcasting Svc., 1997—. Grantee and fellow NIH, 1975, 77, 83, 86; grantee Environ. Health Sci. Ctr., 1986. Mem. AAAS, APHA, Soc. Epidemiologic Rsch., Toastmasters Internat. (officer 1987-89), Am. Statis. Assn. Avocations: travel, writing, photography. Home: 5126 Nebraska Ave NW Washington DC 20008-2047

CHIAPPINELLI, ERIC ANDREW, law educator; b. Santa Monica, Calif., Mar. 22, 1953; s. Bruno Andrea and Evelyn Audrey (Oliver) C.; m. Gail Lorraine Miller, Apr. 18, 1985 (div. Oct. 1992); 1 child, Peter Miller. BA, Claremont (Calif.) Men's Coll., 1975; JD, Columbia U., 1978. Bar: Calif. Law clk. U.S. Dist. Ct., L.A., 1978-80; assoc. Munger, Tolles & Rickershauser, L.A., 1980-83, Jones, Day, Reavis & Pogue, L.A., 1983-84; law clk. Supreme Ct. of Calif., San Francisco, 1984-85; asst. prof. law U. Puget Sound, Tacoma, 1985-88; assoc. prof. law U. Puget Sound, 1988-94; prof. law Seattle U., Tacoma, 1994—. Republican. Episcopalian. Office: Seattle U Sch Law 950 Broadway Tacoma WA 98402-4470

CHIARAMIDA, SALVATORE, cardiologist, educator, health facility adminstrator; b. Manhattan, N.Y., Sept. 15, 1948; s. Joseph and Dina (DiBlasi) C.; m. Susan Postula, June 14, 1970; children: Todd, Tory. BS in Chemistry, Fordham Coll., 1970; MD, N.Y. Med. Coll., 1974. Diplomate Am. Bd. Internal Medicine, Am. Bd. Cardiovasc. Diseases. Intern North Shore Univ. Meml. Hosp., 1974-75, asst. resident in internal medicine, 1975-76, sr. resident in internal medicine, 1976-77, fellow in cardiology, 1977-79; fellow in medicine Cornell U. Med. Coll., 1975-77; chief cardiology Raritan Bay Med. Ctr., 1979-89; chief cardiology Our Lady of Mercy Med. Ctr., Bronx, N.Y., 1989—, assoc. dir. medicine, 1992—; instr. cardiology North Shore Univ. Hosp., 1977-79; clin. instr. medicine U. Medicine and Dentistry N.J., 1981-83, clin. asst. prof., 1983; clin. assoc. prof. N.Y. Med. Coll., 1990—, prof. clin. medicine, 1999—; cons. Woodbridge (N.J.) Devel. Ctr., 1989; v.p., trustee Mercy Care PHO, 1994—; bd. dirs. Cath. Health Care Network, Cath. Health Care Network Physicians Orgn., Servitas IPA, Cath. Healthcare Resources LLC, 1998—, Benefice Health LLC, 1999—. Contbr. articles to profl. jours. Fellow ACP, Am. Coll. Cardiology. Office: Our Lady of Mercy Med Ctr 600 E 233rd St Bronx NY 10466-2697

CHIARCHIARO, FRANK JOHN, lawyer; b. Bklyn., Sept. 11, 1945; s. Joseph Russell and Mary Catherine (Salmieri) C.; m. Judith Ann Penna, July 5, 1970; 1 child, Peter John. BEE, Manhattan Coll., 1967; MSEE, NYU, 1970; JD, Bklyn. Law Sch., 1976. Bar: N.Y. 1977, U.S. Dist. Ct. (ea. and so. dists.) N.Y. 1977, U.S. Ct. Appeals (11th cir.) 1985, U.S. Supreme Ct. 1987, U.S. Ct. Appeals (4th cir.) 1989, U.S. Ct. Appeals (5th cir.) 1991. Engr., USN, Bklyn., 1968-72, USCG, N.Y.C., 1972-77; ptnr. Mendes & Mount, N.Y.C., 1977—. Contbr. articles to profl. jours. Decorated knight of Holy Sepulchre. Mem. ABA, ATLA, N.Y. State Bar Assn., Def. Rsch. Inst. Roman Catholic. Office: Mendes & Mount 750 7th Ave New York NY 10019-6834

CHIARELLA, PETER RALPH, vintner; b. Bklyn., Dec. 6, 1932; s. C. Ralph and Catherine (Zinzi) C.; m. Frances M. Crane, Oct. 10, 1953; children: Ralph, Thomas, John, Karen. B.B.A., St. John's U., 1957. C.P.A., N.Y. Sr. accountant Peat, Marwick, Mitchell & Co., N.Y.C., 1957-61; asst. controller Bonwit Teller, N.Y.C., 1961-62; accounting mgr. plastics div. Celanese Corp., Newark, 1963-67; v.p., controller Clairol, Inc., N.Y.C., 1967-72; pres., dir. Kleinert's, Inc., Kutztown, Pa., 1972-77; v.p., corp. controller United Brands Co., N.Y.C., 1977-79; sr. v.p., chief fin. officer Max Factor & Co., Hollywood, Calif., 1979-83; sr. v.p. fin. and adminstrn. Syncor Internat., Sylmar, Calif., 1983-85; exec. v.p. Doctors' Co., Napa, Calif., 1985-92; pres. Cakebread Cellars, Inc., Rutherford, Calif., 1992-97; bd. dirs. Cakebread Cellars, Inc., Rutherford;. Mem. budget com. United Fund, Stamford, Conn., 1970; bd. dirs. Vis. Nurse Assn., L.A., 1983-90, Napa Valley Opera House, 1991-96, Napa Valley Coll. Found., 1991—, Napa Valley Fair Bd., 1994—. With USN, 1952-54. Mem. AICPA, Fin. Execs. Inst., Delta Mu Delta. Home: 1051 Borrette Ln Napa CA 94558-9702

CHIARELLO, DONALD FREDERICK, lawyer; b. Balt., May 27, 1940; s. Vittorio Joseph and Mary Gertrude (Beall) C.; children: Victoria Lee, Christine Gabrielle. Student, Drexel Inst. Tech., 1959-60; A.A., U. Balt., 1964, J.D., 1967. Bar: Md. 1967. Account exec. Burroughs Corp., 1963-67; assoc. firm Levin & Hochberg, 1968-70; mem. firm Levin, Hochberg & Chiarello, 1970-81, Hochberg, Chiarello, Costello & Dowell, 1982—; v.p. Edna Gardens Lakeside Civic Assn., 1970, Greater Northwood Comty. Coun., 1970-71, 92—; bd. dirs. Rocky Point Sailing Inc. Mem. 3d Dist. Citizens for Good Govt., 1968-72, Md. Polit. Studies Commn., 1969-72; pres. 3d Dist. Young Democratic Club, 1970-71; bd. dirs. Northwood Assn., 1969-71; pres. Federal Hill Neighborhood Assn., 1984-85, Friends of Washington Ballet in Balt., 1987-89; counsel, bd. dirs. Glenmar Community Sailing Ctr., 1995. Mem. ABA, Md. State Bar Assn., Balt. City Bar Assn. (chmn. coms.), Md. Trial Lawyers Assn. (bd. dirs., chmn. coms.), Am. Trial Lawyers Assn., Theta Chi, Sigma Delta Kappa, Balt. Ski Club (treas. 1974-75, pres. 1981-83), Singles on Sailboats (vice commodore 1994, commodore 1995). Home: 33 E Montgomery St Baltimore MD 21230-3808 Office: Hochberg Chiarello & Costello 528 W Joppa Rd Baltimore MD 21204-3832

CHIARENZA, CARL, art historian, critic, artist, educator; b. Rochester, N.Y., Sept. 5, 1935; s. Charles and Mary Rose (Russo) C.; m. Heidi Faith Katz, Aug. 13, 1978; children: Suzanne Mari, Jonah Katz, Gabriella Christine. B.F.A., Rochester Inst. Tech., 1957; M.S., Boston U., 1959; M.A., 1964; Ph.D., Harvard U., 1972. Lectr. Boston U., 1963-64, instr. dept. fine arts, 1964-68, asst. prof., 1968-72, univ. prof., 1972-73, assoc. prof., 1973-80, prof. dept. art history, 1980-86, acting chmn. dept. art history, 1973-74, chmn. dept. art history, 1976-81; Fanny Knapp Allen prof. U. Rochester, N.Y., 1986-98, acting chmn. dept. art history, 1986-87; prof. emeritus, artist-in-residence U. Rochester, 1998—; adj. vis. prof. Visual Studies Workshop, SUNY, 1972-73; vis. prof. Cornell U., 1991; Harnish vis. artist Smith Coll., 1983-84; mem. Artists Adv. Panel, Artists Found., Boston, 1977-81; guest curator Inst. Contemporary Art, Boston, 1980-81; cons. Nat. Endowment for Arts, 1978-80, mem. Artists' Fellowships panel, 1982; bd. dirs. Photographic Resource Ctr.; trustee Visual Studies Workshop. Works represented in permanent collections Mus. Modern Art, N.Y.C., Cleve. Mus. Art, Rose Art Mus., Brandeis, Phila. Mus. Art, Mus. Fine Arts, Boston, Ackland Art Mus., Art Inst. of Chgo., L.A. County Mus. Art, San Francisco Mus. Modern Art, Tampa (Fla.) Mus. of Art, Krannert Art Mus., Exchange Nat. Bank, Chgo., Nat Mus. Am. Art, RISD Mus. Art, Bibliotheque Nationale, Paris, Addison Gallery Am. Art, Mead Mus. Art, New Orleans Mus. Art, Mpls. Inst. Arts, Fogg Art Mus., George Eastman House, Rochester, Ctr. for Creative Photography, Tucson, Princeton (N.J.) U. Mus., Yale U. Art Gallery, New Haven, Mus. Fine Arts, Houston, Worcester Art Mus., Internat. Ctr. Photography, Mus. Art, St. Petersburg, Smith Coll., Mus. Art, others; Author: Aaron Siskind: Pleasures and Terrors, 1982, Standing On the Corner...Reflections upon Winogrand's Gaze, 1992, (with others) Heinecken, 1980; contbg. author: Reading Into Photography: Selected Essays, 1959-80, 1982, Kenneth Josephson, 1983; subject of book Chiarenza: Landscapes of the Mind, 1988; contbr. articles to profl. jours. Served with U.S. Army, 1960-62. Mass. Art and Humanities Found. fellow, 1975-76; Nat. Endowment for Arts fellow, 1977-78, 90-91. Mem. Soc. Photographic Edn., Assn. Historians Am. Art. Office: U Rochester Morey # 424 Rochester NY 14627 *I am a switch-hitter. I have always made, written about, or lectured about pictures. Because I seem to do each best when working in a concentrated spurt, I am often torn between these modes of communication. I work intuitively and in a state of agitation until things find their rightful place on a page or in a picture. It is as if I am reaching for a place of equilibrium or understanding as I move through the world from a position of essential ignorance about the meaning of life.*

CHIARENZA, FRANK JOHN, English language educator; b. New Britain, Conn., Dec. 10, 1926; s. Sebastian X. and Josephine (Spoto) C. A.B., Yale, 1949, Ph.D. in Medieval Lit, 1956; M.A. in English, Rutgers U., 1950; certificate, Inst. for Ednl. Mgmt.; Sloan Found. grantee, Harvard, 1970. Lectr. English U. Conn., 1954-55; instr. English Hillyer Coll., Hartford, Conn., 1955-57; from asst. prof. to prof. Coll. Arts and Scis., U. Hartford, 1958-67, prof. English, 1978-89, emeritus, 1989, chmn. dept., 1958-67, acad. dean Coll. Arts and Scis., 1967-78; Cons., reader English Coll. Entrance Exam. Bd., 1959—; reader advanced placement tests Ednl. Testing Service, Princeton, N.J., 1961—; chmn. for Conn., Nat. Council Coll. Publs. Advisers, 1966-67; adv. council Career Opportunity Program, 1970—; resource cons. Conn. Commn. for Higher Edn., 1972-73; chief reader Coll. Level Exam. Program, Ednl. Testing Service, N.J., 1978—. Author: The Milk Glass Book, 1998; contbr. articles to profl. jours. Corporator Watkinson Sch., West Hartford, Conn.; bd. dirs. Nat. Milk Glass Collectors Soc., 1991—, pres., 1997-99; founder Frank Chiarenza Mus. of Glass, Meriden, Conn. Served with USNR, 1944-46. Fulbright grantee U. Rome, 1953-54. 02084402, AAUP (pres. Hartford 1962-64), NEA, Am. Assn. Higher Edn., Am. Conf. Acad. Deans, Am. Coun. Edn., Nat. Milk Glass Collectors Soc. (bd. dirs. 1991—, v.p. 1994—, v.p., chmn. publs. com. 1994—, pres. 1997—), Yale Club. Home: 80 Crestview Dr Newington CT 06111-2405 Office: Univ Hartford English Dept Hartford CT 06117

CHIARO, A. WILLIAM, management consultant; b. Chgo., July 12, 1928; s. Anthony Joseph and Marie Anne (Bonario) C.; m. Lyne LaVerne Franke, Aug. 27, 1961; children: David Huntington, Caroline Elizabeth. BS, U. Ill., 1954. Cert. profl. bus. cons.; enrolled agent IRS. Acct., IBM, Chgo., 1954-55; with Black & Skaggs Assocs., Chgo., 1955—, pres., 1978—; dir. P.M. Chgo., Inc. Contbr. articles to med. and profl. jours. Served with U.S. Army, 1946-47, USAF, 1950-52. Mem. Soc. Profl. Bus. Cons., Nat. Soc. Public Accts. Presbyterian. Office: PM Chgo Inc 907 Pawnee Rd Wilmette IL 60091-1344

CHIATE, KENNETH REED, lawyer; b. Phoenix, June 24, 1941; s. Mac Arthur and Lillian (Lavin) C.; m. Jeannette Jensen, Aug. 21, 1965; children: Gregory Jensen, Carley McKay. B.A. with honors, Claremont Men's Coll., 1963; J.D., Columbia U., 1966; postgrad. U. So. Calif. Law Sch., 1967. Bar: Calif. 1967, U.S. Dist. Ct. (cen. dist.) Calif. 1967, Ariz. 1971, U.S. Dist. Ct. Ariz. 1971, U.S. dist. (no. dist.) Calif. 1982. Law clk. presiding justice U.S. Dist. Ariz., 1971; ptnr. Lillick McHose & Charles, L.A., 1966-91, Pillsbury Madison & Sutro, L.A., 1991—; arbitrator Los Angeles Superior Ct. Arbitration Panel, 1979-82; mcpl. ct. judge protem Los Angeles, 1979-81; mem. Jury Instrn. Com. Los Angeles County, 1991—. Vice chmn. Los Angeles Open Com., 1969-71. Mem. ABA, Los Angeles County Bar Assn., Calif. State Bar Assn., Ariz. State Bar Assn., Maricopa County Bar Assn., So. Calif. Def. Assn., Am. Trial Lawyers Assn., Maritime Law Assn. of U.S.A., Los Angeles Port Propeller Club, mem. L.A. B.A.J.I. com., 1993-95. Office: Pillsbury Madison 725 S Figueroa St Ste 1200 Los Angeles CA 90017-5443

CHIAVERINI, JOHN EDWARD, construction company executive; b. Providence, Feb. 6, 1924; s. John and Sadie (Ginsberg) C.; m. Cecile Corey, Mar. 31, 1951; children: Caryl Marie, John Michael. Cert. advanced san. engring. U. Ill., 1945; BS in Civil Engring., U. R.I., 1947. Registered profl. engr., Mass., R.I. Project engr. Perini Corp., Hartford, Conn., 1950-51, project mgr., 1951-55, asst. project mgr., Pitts. and Que., 1955-61, v.p., Framingham, Mass., 1965-84, sr. v.p., San Francisco, 1984—; pres., dir. Compania Perini S.A., Colombia, 1961—; v.p., exec. mgr. Perini Yuba Assocs., Marysville, Calif., 1966-70, v.p. Western ops., 1970-78, 79-84, group v.p., 1978-79; sr. v.p. spl. projects Perini Corp., 1984-90, dir., asst. to chmn., 1991—; mem. U.S. com. Internat. Commn. on Large Dams.; bd. dirs. Building Futures Coun., 1990—, vice chmn., 1993, chmn., 1994—; active Civil Engring. Rsch. Found., 1990—, mem. corp. adv. bd., 1992—. Served to 2d lt. USAAF, 1944-46. Recipient Golden Beaver award Supervision, San Francisco Bay Area Coun. Boy Scouts Am., 1989, Good Scout award, 1989; named to U. R.I. Engring. Hall of Fame, 1997. Fellow ASCE (mem. exec. com. constrn. dvsn., vice chmn. 1994-95, chmn. 1995—), Soc. Am. Mil. Engrs., prs. San Francisco post 1991-92, bd. dirs.); mem. NSPE (life), Am. Arbitrators Assn., Calif. Soc. Profl. Engrs., Beavers (bd. dirs.), Moles, Commonwealth Club of Calif., KC, Rotary. Democrat. Roman Catholic. Home: 37 Dutch Valley Ln San Anselmo CA 94960-1045 Office: Perini Corp 101 Spear St Ste 222 San Francisco CA 94105-1554

CHIAZZE, LEONARD, JR., biostatistician, epidemiologist, educator; b. Falconer, N.Y., June 19, 1934; s. Leonard and Jennie (Bondi) C.; m. Ellen Anne Bergman, June 12, 1954; children: Kathleen, Caroline, Michael, Ellen. AA, SUNY, Jamestown, 1953; BS, U. Buffalo, 1955, MBA, 1957; ScD, U. Pitts., 1964. Instr. stats. U. Buffalo, 1955-57; biostatistician Nat. Cancer Inst., Bethesda, Md., 1957-66, acting chief biometry br., 1975-76, dir. div. occupl. health studies, 1994—; dir. div. biostats. and epidemiology Georgetown U. Sch. Medicine, Washington, 1966-94, asst. prof., 1966-69, assoc. prof., 1969-77, prof., 1977—, founder, dir. grad. program in biostats., 1970-94, dir. divsn. occupational health studies, 1994—; mem. subcom. on synthetic vitreous fibers Nat. Acad. Scis./NRC. Contbr. articles to profl. jours. Served with USPHS, 1957-66. Fellow Am. Coll. Epidemiology, Am. Pub. Health Assn.; mem. Am. Statis. Assn., Soc. Occupational and Environ. Health (past pres. governing coun.), Soc. Epidemiologic Rsch., Internat. Epidemiol. Assn., Internat. Assn. Sci. Study Population, Population Assn. Am., Assn. Tchrs. Preventive Medicine, Sigma Xi; mem. Beta Gamma Sigma. Home: 11237 Waycross Way Kensington MD 20895-1034 Office: Georgetown U 3750 Reservoir Rd NW Washington DC 20007-2111

CHICHETTO, JAMES WILLIAM, editor, educator; b. Boston, June 5, 1941; s. Francis Anthony and Christina McInnis C. B of Philosophy, Stonehill Coll., 1964; M of Theology, Holy Cross Coll., 1968; MA, Wesleyan U., 1978. Ordained to ministry, Cath. Ch., 1968. Assoc. editor Gargoyle Mag., Cambridge, Mass., 1975-81, Conn. Poetry Rev., Stonington, 1981-84, 1984-88, asoc. editor, art editor, 1988-89, editor, 1989-91; prof. writing Stonehill Coll., North Easton, Mass., 1991—; art editor East & West Lit. Quar., San Francisco, 1995—. Author of poems, essays, revs. and plays. Mem. Easton Arts Coun., 1994-98. Recipient Sri Chinmoy award, 1986; NEA grantee, 1980, 83. Fellow World Lit. Assn.; mem. Assn. Lit. Scholars. Democrat. Avocations: painting, sketching. Home: 474 Washington St North Easton MA 02357 Office: Stonehill Coll 430 Washington St Easton MA 02357

CHICHILNISKY, GRACIELA, mathematician, economist, educator, consultant; b. Buenos Aires, Mar. 27, 1946; came to U.S., 1968, naturalized citizen, 1992; d. Salomon Chichilnisky and Raquel Gavensky; children: Eduardo Jose, Natasha Sable. Student, MIT, 1967-68; MA, U. Calif., Berkeley, 1970, PhD in Math., 1971, PhD in Econs., 1976. Postdoctoral fellow Harvard U., 1974, lectr. dept. econs., 1975-77, fellow Harvard inst. internat. devel., 1978; assoc. prof. Columbia U., N.Y.C., 1977-80, prof., 1981—; dir. program on info. and resources Columbia U., 1994—; UNESCO chair math. and econs., 1995—; mem. presdl. cabinet Banco Ctrl. Repubica Argentina, 1971-74; co-prin. investigator Urban Inst., Washington, 1975-77; vis. scholar Internat. Inst. Applied Sys, Analysis Laxenburg, Austria, 1975-77; prin. investigator U.S. Dept. Labor, 1977-78, Rockefeller Found. Project Internat. Rels., 1981-83; project dir. UN Inst. Tng. and Rsch., N.Y., 1979-83; chaired prof. econs. U. Essex, 1980-81; vis. prof. inst. math and its applications U. Minn., 1983-84, U. Siena, Italy, summers, 1991-93; vis. prof. Stanford Inst. Theoretical Econs., Stanford U., summers, 1991-93, dept. econs., Inst. Internat. Studies, 1993—, vis. prof. depts., econ. and ops. rsch. Stanford U., 1993-94; prof. missionaire U. des Antilles et de la Guyane, spring 1984-85; NSF prof. dept. math. U. Calif., Berkeley, 1985-86; CEO, chmn. FITEL Ltd., 1985-89; exec. dir. Sci. Internat. Ltd., 1989-90; vis. prof. U. Cath. Buenos Aires, Aug. 1993; cons. in field; UNESCO chair in math. and econs., Columbia U., 1995—; Salinbemi chair U. Siena, Italy, 1994-95. Co-author: Catastrophe or New Society? A Latin American World Model, 1976; author: (with G. Heal) The Evolving International Economy, 1986, Oil in the International Economy, 1991, Sustainability: Dynamics and Uncertainty, 1998, Mathematical Economics, 1998, Topology and Markets, 1998, Markets, Information and Uncertainty, 1998, Environmental Markets, 1999; assoc. editor Jour. Devel. Econs., 1976-86, Advances in Mathematics, 1985, Risk Decision and Policy; mem. various editorial bds.; contbr. articles to profl. jours. Bd. trustees Nat. Resources Def. Coun., N.Y., 1994—. Recipient Internat. Rels. award Rockefeller Found., 1983-84; named Most Disting. Woman Economist, Newcombe Found. and Omega Delta Epsilon, 1991, Leif Johansen award U. Oslo, Norway, 1995; grantee NSF, 1974—; fellow Ford Found., 1967-69, Banco Ctrl. Republica Argentina, 1972-74, spl. fellow UN Inst. Tng. and Rsch., 1977-76. Mem. Coun. Social Choice and Welfare Soc. Office: Columbia U Program Info and Resources 405 Low Libr 116th & Broadway New York NY 10027

CHICK, LAURA, councilwoman. BA, UCLA; MSW, U. So. Calif. Chief field dept. 3rd dist. L.A.; city councilwoman City of L.A., 1993—; chair Pub. Safety Com.; vice chair Pub. Works Commn. Office: LA City Coun 200 N Main St Rm 415 Los Angeles CA 90012-4808

CHICKERING, HOWARD ALLEN, insurance company executive, lawyer; b. San Francisco, Mar. 21, 1942; s. Allen Lawrence and Caroline Cranford (Rogers) C.; m. Elizabeth Douglas Dalton, June 29, 1968; children: Philip Dalton, Caroline Howe. BS in Econs., U. Pa., 1966; JD, Stanford U., 1971. Bar: Calif. 1972. Assoc. Chickering & Gregory, San Francisco, 1971-76; sr. counsel Itel Corp., San Francisco, 1976-79; v.p., gen. counsel, bd. dirs. Clarendon Ins. Co. (Bermuda) Ltd., N.Y.C., 1979-81; pres. Clarendon Group Svcs. Inc., N.Y.C., 1981-85; exec. v.p., bd. dirs. Clarendon Ins. Group, N.Y.C., 1985-88; founder, pres., chief underwriting officer R.V.I. Guaranty Co., Ltd., Hamilton, Bermuda, 1989—; founder, pres. R.V.I. Am. Ins. Co., Stamford, Conn., 1994—. *Mr. Chickering founded the R.V.I. Guaranty Co., Ltd. in 1989, then as now the world's largest residual value insurance company. In 1996, in recognition of its excellent underwriting results, the company was awarded claims-paying ability ratings of "A" by Standard & Poor's and Fitch, and a rating of "AA-" by Duff & Phelps. Ownership of the company has passed from USWest to George Soros' Quantum Fund to the CNA Insurance Companies, but Mr. Chickering continues as President and Chief Underwriting Officer.* Contbr. articles to profl. publs. Co-author, acting campaign chmn. San Francisco Proposition C (Open Space), 1974; campaign sec. Proposition J (Open Space and Park Renovation), 1974; mem. San Francisco Open Space Citizens Adv. Commn., 1976-78; deacon Stanwich Congregational Ch. Lt. (j.g.) USNR, 1966-68, Vietnam. Mem. State Bar Calif., Racquet and Tennis Club, N.Y. Yacht Club, Belle Haven Club (commodore 1996). Republican. Home: 80 Otter Rock Dr Greenwich CT 06830-7029 Office: RVI Am Ins Co 177 Broad St 9th Flr Stamford CT 06901-2048

CHICO, GERY J., lawyer, school system administrator. BA, U. Ill., 1979; JD, Loyola U., Chgo., 1985. Dep. chief of staff Mayor Richard Daley, Chgo., 1991-92; gen. counsel Chgo. Devel. Coun.; chief of staff Mayor Richard Daley, Chgo., 1992-96; ptnr., head govt. and mcpl. fin. group Altheimer & Gray, Chgo.; pub. bldg. commr. City of Chgo.; pres. Sch. Reform Bd. Trustees, Chgo. Active numerous civic groups. Active numerous profl. assns., including Mex.-Am. C. of C. (past pres.). Office: Sch Reform Bd Trustees Chicago Bd Edn 125 S Clark Chicago IL 60603

CHICOINE, ROLAND ALVIN, farmer, state official; b. Rural Elk Point, S.D., Dec. 10, 1922; s. Elmire Joseph and Louise Marie (Ryan) C.; m. Evelyn Marie Lyle, June 18, 1945; children: Jeffrey R., David L., Marcia M. Quinn, Daniel B., Timothy K., Brian Elmire, Ellen Little, Nicole Louise Klein. Owner, farmer Elk Point, 1942-90; state rep. S.D. State Legislature, 1980-86, state Sen., 1987-92, state rep., 1993—. Mem. Elk Point Local Dist. Sch. Bd., 1971-80; bd. dirs. Union County Farmers Home Adminstrn.; 4-H leader (40 yrs.) Sioux Livestock 4-H Club, state past pres.. Named Family of Yr., S.D. State U., 1989, Eminent Farmer of Yr., S.D. State U., 1998. Mem. County Crop Improvement Assn. (past chmn. bd. dirs.), County Livestock Improvement Assn. (past chmn. bd. dirs.), S.D. State Irrigators Assn. (past state chmn. and organizer), S.D. Water Congress (past bd. dirs.), Union County Livestock Assn. (resolutions com. 1980—), Fed. Land Bank Assn. (Sioux Falls area chmn., bd. dirs. 1970-84, Omaha 4 state adv. bd. 1976-80), S.C. State 4-H Leaders Assn. (state chmn.), Lions. Democrat. Roman Catholic. Avocation: golf. Address: RR 2 Box 212 Elk Point SD 57025-9734

CHICOREL, MARIETTA EVA, publisher; b. Vienna, Austria; came to U.S., 1939, naturalized, 1945; d. Paul and Margaret (Gross) Selby. AB, Wayne State U., 1951; MALS, U. Mich., 1961. Asst. chief library acquisitions div. U. Wash., Seattle, 1962-66; project dir. Macmillan Info. Scis., Inc., N.Y.C., 1968-69; pres. Chicorel Library Pub. Corp., N.Y.C., 1969-79, Am. Library Pub. Co., Inc., 1979—; pub. cons. Creative Solutions Co., 1986—; asst. prof. dept. libr. sci. CUNY (Queens Coll.), 1986—; mem. edn. com. Gov.'s Commn. on Status of Women, Wash., 1963-65; instr. libr. scis. No. Ariz. U., Flagstaff, 1990; bd. dirs. Skills Devel. Tng. counseling; pub. cons. creative solutios. Chief editor: Ulrich's International Periodicals Directory, 1966-68; editor, pub.: Chicorel Indexes, 1969—; founding editor: Jour. Reading, Writing and Learning Disabilities International, 1985-90; contbr. chpt. on univs. to Library Statistics: A Handbook of Concepts, Definitions and Terminology, 1966. Mem. ALA (exec. bd. tech. svcs. divsn. 1965-68, chmn. libr. materials price index com. 1968-69, councillor 1969-73), Am. Assn. Profl. Cons., Am. Book Prodrs. Assn., Book League N.Y. (bd. govs. 1975-79), Am. Soc. for Info. Sci., Can. Libr. Assn., Pacific N.W. Libr. Assn., N.Y. Libr. Club, N.Y. Tech. Svcs. Librarians. Home and Office: PO Box 4272 Sedona AZ 86340-4272

CHICOREL, RALPH, composer, lyricist, playwright; b. Detroit, Dec. 4, 1930; s. Jacob and Judith (Louza) C.; m. Phyllis Philko, Feb. 3, 1957 (div. 1979); children: Steven Mitchell, Daniel Adam, Jacob; m. Debra Anne Lisch, Jan. 10, 1981; children: Matthew Aaron, Tyler William, Allison Anne. Grad., Am. Acad. Dramatic Arts, 1955. Performer various groups, Detroit, 1948-51; salesman Stein Ellbogen, Detroit, 1953-57; co-owner, entertainer Kenwood Restaurant and Lounge, Detroit, 1957-66; salesman Music Merchants, Detroit, 1966-67; co-owner Weight Watchers of Wis., Inc., Milw., 1968-92, also advt. spokesperson; pres. Chicorel Music Corp., Milw., 1970-92; co-owner Weight Watchers in Hawaii, Honolulu, 1989-91; pres. Civic Music Assn., Milw., 1990-91. Producer, composer, lyricist 5 albums on Pleasure Records label, 1970-79; composer, lyricist (stage mus., album) Jean, 1973, 85, C. Dickens' Great Expectations, 1995; composer: (songs) Welcome to Wisconsin, Milwaukee (premiere performance Milw. Symphony Orch. Feb. 1988); producer Lynn Redgrave and the World of Weight Watchers, The Milw. Auditorium, 1989; contbg. author: Milwaukee: The Best of All Worlds, 1991. Bd. dirs. Congregation Emanuel Bne Jeshurun Brotherhood, Milw., 1984-86, Comedy Sports, Milw., 1992-98. Served with USMC, 1951-53, Korea. Mem. Nat. Assn. Rec. Arts and Scis., Dramatists Guild, Song Writers Guild Am., ASCAP, Milw. Broadcasters Club. Jewish. Avocation: collecting recordings of musical shows. Office: N64w14660 Poplar Dr Menomonee Falls WI 53051-5197

CHIDESTER, OTIS HOLDEN, retired secondary education educator; b. Mineral City, Ohio, Mar. 22, 1903; s. Harmon Otis and Lillian (Holden) C.; m. Martha Florence Saddlemire, June 28, 1930. Grad., Laurel Hill Acad., 1923; vocat. cert., Buffalo State Tchrs. Coll., 1930; BA, U. Ariz., 1940, MA in Edn., 1948. Editor, pub. Windsor (N.Y.) Standard, 1924-30; established Harpersville-Ninevah Standard, Windsor, 1928; tchr. graphic arts Port Washington Pub. Sch., L.I., N.Y., 1930-33; tchr. Ariz. Sch. for Deaf and Blind, Tucson, 1937-40; dir. graphic arts Tucson High Sch., 1940-68; tchr. tng. summers at various univs. and colls.; Ariz. dir. indsl. arts awards Ford Found., 1955-57; mem. steering com. Printing Industries Tech. Found., Nashville, 1965—. Author: First Year Graphic Arts, 1949, History of Catalina Council, Boy Scouts of America, 1919-55, Fifty Year History of the International Graphic Arts Association, 1975; editor Ariz. State Vocat. Assn. Rev., 1960-61; contbr. articles to profl. jours. Sr. mem. Boy Scouts Am.; historian Catalina Coun., 1963—; nat. dean Scout. Coun. Historians. Recipient Silver Beaver award Boy Scouts Am., 1948, Diamond Vet. Pen and Medallion, 1963, Valley Forge Classroom Tchrs. medal Freedoms Found., 1959, Gold Key Columbia Scholastic Press Assn., 1963, Elmer G. Voigt award Edn. Coun. Graphic Arts Industries, Inc., 1972; named Printer of Yr. Ariz. Interant. Printing House Craftsmen, 1968, Sr. Citizen Man of Yr. Tucson Coun. on Aging, 1970, citation Nat. Retired Tchrs. Assn./Ariz. State Retired Tchrs. Assn., 1974, cert. tech. com. Pima Community Coll., 1977, Vets. citation Boy Scouts Am., 1982, Wood Badge beads Nat. Coun. Boy Scouts Am., 1985, John Leecing Missionary award United meth. Ch., 1987, Diamond Vet. award Nat. Office Boy Scouts Am., 1987; Elmer G. Voigt scholar U. Houston, 1960; The Newspaper Fund, Inc. grantee Western Wash. Coll. Edn., 1961, Lyle Isabell award Tucson Lithographers Assn., 1988, Cmty. Svc. award Am. Assn. Ret. Persons, 1992; inducted Tuscon High Sch. Hall of Fame, 1992. Mem. NEA (life), Trade and Industry Assn. Ariz. (pres. 1960), Am., Ariz. (pres. 1961) vocat. assns., Internat. Graphic Arts Edn. Assn. (S.W. regional v.p. 1951-53, pres. 1956, bd. dirs. 1957, Outstanding Tchrs. award 1941, Fred J. Hartman award 1975, graphic arts/communication merit badge com. 1940-84), Ariz. Archaeol. and Hist. Soc. (pres. 1951-52, Al Merito award 1976, life mem., Victor R. Stoner award), The Westerners Internat. (exec.-sec. 1965, emeritus 1973—, editor The Smoke Signal, award 1960-87), Masons (citations 1975, 90), Alpha Phi Omega (coun. adviser 1949), Phi Delta Kappa, Epsilon Pi Tau (Laurate citation 1955). Avocations: collecting Boy Scout memorabilia for inclusion in Scout Mus. So. Ariz. Home and Office: 1937 E Blacklidge Dr Tucson AZ 85719-2847*

CHIDGEY, TERRI J., educator, principal; b. Toledo, Ohio, Sept. 26, 1955; d. James and Nancy Wassmund; m. Joseph J. Chidgey, June 30, 1974; children: Kristi, Scott. BA in Edn., S.W. Tex. State U., San Marcos, 1976; MEd, Trinity U., San Antonio, 1983. Tchr. N.E. Ind. Sch. Dist., San Antonio, 1976-89, asst. prin., 1989-93, prin., 1993—. Mem. TEPSA, PTA (life). E-mail: tchid133@northeast.isd.tenet.edu. Office: Stone Oak Elem Sch 21045 Crescent Oaks San Antonio TX 78258-3228

CHIECHI, CAROLYN PHYLLIS, federal judge; b. Newark, Dec. 6, 1943. BS magna cum laude, Georgetown U., 1965, JD, 1969, LLM in Taxation, 1971. Bar: D.C. 1969, U.S. Dist. Ct. D.C., U.S. Ct. Fed. Claims, U.S. Tax Ct., U.S. Ct. Appeals (5th, 6th, 9th, D.C. and fed. cirs.), U.S. Supreme Ct. Atty., advisor to Judge Leo H. Irwin U.S. Tax Ct., Washington, 1969-71; assoc. Sutherland, Asbill & Brennan, Washington, 1971-76, ptnr., 1976-92; judge U.S. Tax Ct., 1992—; mem. bd. regents Georgetown U., Washington, 1988-94, 95—, mem. nat. law alumni bd., 1986-93; bd. dirs. Stuart Stiller Meml. Found., Washington, 1986—; prin. Coun. for Excellence in Govt., Washington, 1990-92. Dept. editor Jour. of Taxation, 1986-92; contbr. articles to profl. jours. Fellow Am. Bar Found., Am. Coll. Tax Counsel; mem. ABA, FBA, D.C. Bar Assn., Women's Bar Assn., Am. Judicature Soc., Georgetown U. Alumni Assn. (bd. govs. 1994—). Office: US Tax Ct 400 2nd St NW Washington DC 20217

CHIEFSKY, SUSAN JUSTINE, secondary education educator; b. Bridgeport, Conn., Jan. 9, 1953; d. Walter P. and Frances L. (Ataman) C. BA, U. R.I., 1974, tchr. cert., 1975; MA, Goddard Coll., 1979. 8th grade English and social studies tchr. Woodstock (Vt.) Union Mid. Sch., 1978—; developer faculty workshops in spl. edn. issues and methods of instrn., 1978, 85, yearbook advisor, 1982, 86, class advisor, 1980-86, mem. staff devel. com., 1983-86, new hire tchr. team, 1987-89, culture activities dir., 1987-90, resident rschr., 1987-88, master tchr., 1983-84, adj. prof., 1979; mem. social studies curriculum com. Woodstock Sch. Dist., 1997. Bd. dirs. Pentangle Arts Coun., Woodstock, 1984-87, Woodstock Recreation Ctr., 1980-82; corporator Norman Williams Pub. Libr., Woodstock, 1996—. Recipient Recognition award for curriculum devel. New Eng. League Mid. Schs., 1996. Mem. Nat. Coun. Tchrs. of English. Avocations: outdoor activities, biking, snowshoeing, gardening, reading. Home: 7 Eaton Pl Woodstock VT 05091-1008

CHIEGER, KATHRYN JEAN, recreation company executive; b. Detroit, July 13, 1948; d. George and Goldie Caroline (Payor) C. BA, Purdue U., 1970; MA, U. Mich., 1974; MBA, U. Denver, 1983. Librarian U. Mich., Ann Arbor, 1970-74; staff aide U.S. Senator Gary Hart, Denver, 1974-79; dir. fin. relations Petro-Lewis Corp., Denver, 1979-86, dir. investor rels. Kraft Inc., Glenview, Ill., 1987-89; v.p. corporate affairs Gaylord Container Corp., Deerfield, Ill., 1989-96; v.p. corp. and investor rels. Brunswick Corp., Lake Forest, Ill., 1996—; bd. dirs. Chgo. Fin. Exch. Bd. dirs. North Shore Sr. Ctr., 1994—. Mem. Nat. Investor Rels. Inst. (chpt. bd. dirs. 1979-84, v.p. membership 1982-83, pres. 1983-84, nat. bd. dirs. 1984-88), Chgo. Execs. Club, Investor Rels. Assn. Office: Brunswick Corp 1 N Field Ct Lake Forest IL 60045-4811

CHIEGO, WILLIAM J., museum director; b. Newark, N.J., Sept. 17, 1943; s. William Joseph and Rose Marie (Del Guercio) C.; m. Elizabeth Kimball Lee, July 3, 1971; children: Ruth Katharine, Rose Monica. BA in History with distinction, U. Va., 1965; MA in Art History, Case Western Reserve U., 1968, PhD in Art History, 1974. Asst. curator Toledo (Ohio) Mus. Art, 1973-74, assoc. curator European Paintings, 1974-76; curator Portland Art Mus., 1976-79, chief curator, 1979-82; chief curator N.C. Mus. Art, Raleigh, 1982-86; dir. Allen Meml. Art Mus. Oberlin (Ohio) Coll., 1986-91; dir. Marion Koogler McNay Art Mus., San Antonio, 1991—; regional rep. for N.C. Art Mus. Assn. of Am., 1984; mem. bd. trustees Intermuseum Conservation Assn., Oberlin, 1986-91; mem., co-chmn. mus. liaison com. Midwest Art History Soc., 1987-91; mem. exhbn. adv. com. Am. Fedn. Arts, 1988-94; mem. conservation grant panel Inst. Mus. Svcs., 1991-93; lectr. in field. Co-author, editor exhbn. catalog Sir David Wilkie of Scotland, 1987; co-organizer, author intro. to French Paintings from Tbe Chrysler Museum, 1986; coord. rsch. The N.C. Mus. Art Intro. to the Collections, 1983; author: Master Prints from the Gilkey Collection, 1980, From Oregon Private Collections, 1977; contbr. articles to profl. jours. Resident fellow Yale Ctr. for British Art, New Haven, Conn., 1982, Bingham Travel fellow Art History Case Western Reserve U., 1970-71, Univ. fellow Art History, 1969-70, Nat. Defense Edn. Act fellow Latin Am. History, 1965; Mus. Mgmt. Inst. scholar, 1981. Mem. Assn. of Art Mus. Dirs., Phi Beta Kappa. Office: Marion Koogler McNay Art Museum PO Box 6069 San Antonio TX 78209-0069*

CHIEN, CHIA-LING, physics educator; b. China, Nov. 10, 1942; came to U.S., 1966; s. Ting and An-Hsiu (Wong) C.; m. Christina Yueh Wang, Apr. 15, 1972; children: David, Deborah. BS in Physics, Tunghai U., Taiwan, 1965; MS in Physics, Carnegie-Mellon U., 1968, PhD, 1972. Rsch. assoc. Johns Hopkins U., Balt., 1973-74, assoc. rsch. scientist, 1974-75, asst. prof., 1976-79, assoc. prof., 1979-83, prof., 1983—; vis. prof. Johns Hopkins U., Balt., 1975-76. 2d lt. Air Force, 1965-66, Taiwan. Fellow Am. Phys. Soc.; mem. Materials Rsch. Soc. Office: Johns Hopkins U Dept Physics 3400 N Charles St Baltimore MD 21218*

CHIEN, SHU, physiology and bioengineering educator; b. Beijing, June 23, 1931; came to U.S., 1954; s. Shih-liang and Wan-tu (Chang) C.; m. Kuang-Chung Hu, Apr. 7, 1957; children: May Chien Busch, Ann Chien Guider-a. MB, Nat. Taiwan U., Taipei, Republic of China, 1953; PhD, Columbia U., 1957. Instr. physiology Columbia U. Coll. Physicians & Surgeons, N.Y.C., 1956-58, asst. prof. physiology, 1958-64, assoc. prof. physiology, 1964-69, prof. physiology, 1969-88, dir. div. circulatory physiology and biophysics, 1974-88; dir. Inst. Biomed. Scis. Academia Sinica, Taipei, 1987-88; prof. bioengring and medicine U. Calif.-San Diego, La Jolla, 1988—, bioengring. group coord., 1989-94, dir. Inst. Biomed. Engring., 1991—, chmn. dept. bioengring., 1994—; chmn. adv. com. Am. Bur. for Med. Advancement in China, N.Y.C., 1991—, Inst. Biomed. Scis., Academia Sinica, Taipei, 1991—, Nat. Health Rsch. Inst., Taipei, 1991—. Editor: Vascular Endothelium in Health and Disease, 1988, Molecular Biology in Physiology, 1989, Molecular Biology of Cardiovascular System, 1990; co-editor: Nuclear Magnetic Resonance in Biology and Medicine, 1986, Handbook of Bioengineering, 1986, Clinical Hemorheology, Applications in Cardiovascular and Hematological Disease, Diabetes, Surgery and Gynecology, 1987, Fibrinogen, Thrombosis, Coagulation and Fibrinolysis, 1990, Biochemical and Structural Dynamics of the Cell Nucleus, 1990, others; contbr. more than 300 sci. articles on physiology, bioengrig. and related biomed. rsch. to profl. jours. Recipient Fahraeus award European Soc. for Clin. Haemorheology, London, 1981, Melville award ASME, 1990, 96, Zweifach award World Congress of Microcirculation, Louisville, 1991, Spl. Creativity Grant award NSF, 1985-88, Merit Grant award NIH, 1989-99, Nat. Health medal, Taiwan, 1998. Mem. NAE, Academia Sinica (Taipei), Am. Physiol. Soc. (pres. 1990-91, Daggs award 1999), Biomed. Engring. Soc. (sr., ALZA award 1993), Internat. Soc. Biorheology (v.p. 1983-89), Microcirculatory Soc. (pres. 1980-81, Landis award 1983), N.Am. Soc. Biorheology (chmn. steering com. 1985-86), Fedn. Am. Socs. for Exptl. Biology (pres. 1992-93), Am. Inst. for Med. and Biol. Engring., Inst. of Medicine U.S. NAS. Achievements include elucidation of the mechanism of red cell aggregation in terms of energy balance at cell surface; demonstration of the role of endothelial cell turnover in the transport of protein molecules into the artery wall; research on the molecular basis and physiological implications of blood cell deformability; studies on the effects of mechanicsl forces on endothelial cell gene expression and signal transduction. Office: U Calif San Diego Dept Bioengring Mail Code 0412 La Jolla CA 92093-0412

CHIEN, SUFAN, surgeon, educator; b. Zhejiang Province, China, July 20, 1938; came to U.S., 1982; s. Jiaxing and Julian (You) C.; m. Lorrain Wilson; children: Samson, Lynn. MD, Shanghai 1st Med. Coll., 1962. Resident dept. gen. surgery Zhongshan Hosp. Shanghai 1st Med. Coll., 1962-66, attending gen. surgeon, 1975-79; supr. cardiopulmonary bypass Shanghai Inst. Cardiovasc. Diseases, 1975-82, attending surgeon cardiovascular surgery, 1979-82; vis. scientist cardiovascular divsn. Mayo Clinic, Rochester, Minn., 1982-84; vis. scientist physiology and biophysics La. State U. Med. Ctr., Shreveport, 1984-85; vis. scientist surgery, physiology and biophysics U. Ky. Med. Ctr., Lexington, 1985-87, asst. prof. divsn. cardio-thoracic surgery, 1987-93, assoc. prof., 1993-96; assoc. prof. surgery U. Louisville, 1996—; invited lectr., presenter in field; mem. sci. rev. com. study sect. NIH. Author: Hibernation Induction Trigger for Organ Preservation, 1993; mem. editl. bd. Internat. Medicine Rev., 1979-84; contbr. articles and abstracts to med. jours., chpts. to books. Grantee NIH, VA, U.S. Army, AHA, Univ. Fellow Am. Coll. Angiology; mem. AHA, N.Y. Acad. Scis., Chinese Med. Assn., Chinese Surg. Assn., Chinese Soc. Thoracic Surgeons, Shanghai Med. Soc., Internat. Soc. Heart and Lung Transplantation. Office: U Louisville Sch Medicine Rudd Heart-Lung Ctr 1200 201 Abraham Flexner Way Louisville KY 40202-3841

CHIERICHELLA, JOHN W., lawyer; b. N.Y.C., Mar. 26, 1947; s. Pasquale Joseph and Ruth Cecilia (White) C. AB, Cornell U., 1969; JD, Columbia U., 1972. Bar: N.Y. 1973, D.C., 1975, U.S Dist. Ct. Columbia, 1976, U.S. Claims Ct., 1976, U.S. Ct. Appeals (D.C. cir. 1976, Fed. cir. 1980), U.S. Supreme Ct., 1980. Assoc., Cravath, Swaine & Moore, N.Y.C. 1972-73; assoc., then ptnr. Jones, Day, Reavis & Pogue, Washington, 1975-79, 87-93; ptnr. Crowell & Moring, Washington, 1979-84, Gibson, Dunn & Crutcher, Washington, 1984-87; ptnr. Fried, Frank, Harris, Shriver & Jacobson, 1993—. Contbr. articles to profl. jours. Served to capt. USAF, 1973-75. Harlan Fiske Stone scholar, 1971, James Kent scholar, 1972. Mem. ABA (past chmn. contracts com., contracts clauses and forms com., pub. contracts law sect.), Nat. Contract. Mgmt. Assn., Nat. Security Indsl. Assn. Roman Catholic. Avocation: athletics. Office: Fried Frank Harris Shriver & Jacobson Ste #800 1001 Pennsylvania Ave NW Washington DC 20004-2505*

CHIGIER, NORMAN, mechanical engineering educator; b. Frankfort, South Africa, Aug. 2, 1933; came to U.S., 1981; BSME, U. Witwatersrand, 1952; M.A., U. Cambridge, 1960, Ph.D., 1961, Sc.D., 1977. With Brit. Thompson Houston Co., Rugby, Eng., 1953-56; asst. in research Engring. Labs U. Cambridge, 1956-60; sr. investigator Internat. Flame Research Found., Ijmuiden, Holland, 1961-63; sr. lectr. aero. engring. Technion, Israel, 1964-66; sr. research assoc. NASA-Ames Research Ctr., Calif., 1970-71; lectr. dept. chem. engring. and fuel tech. U. Sheffield, Eng., 1966-68, sr. lectr., 1968-73, reader, 1973-81; Benedum prof. mech. engring. Carnegie-Mellon U., Pitts., 1981-82, William J. Brown prof. mech. engring., 1982—, dir. Spray Syss. Tech. Ctr.; vis. cons. Sandia Labs, Livermore, Calif., 1976; vis. prof. Stanford U., 1977, Ecole Centrale, Lyon, 1977-78, U. Calif.-San Diego, 1979; pres. Internat. Coun. Inst. Liquid Atomization and Spray Systems, 1991—. Author: (with J.M. Beer) Combustion Aerodynamics, 1972, Collective Phenomena, 1975, Energy, Combustion and Environment, 1981, Combustion Measurements, 1991; founding editor: Progress in Energy and Combustion Science, Vols. 1-15, 1974—, Atomization and Sprays, 1989—; assoc. editor Energy-The Internat. Jour., 1979—. Fellow Inst. Fuel (Lubbock-Sambrook award 1968, 75), AIAA (assoc.), ASME (Lewis F. Moody awards Fluids Engring. divsn. 1965); mem. Internat. Coun. Inst. Liquid Atomization and Spray Sys. (pres.). Home: 5284 Northumberland St Pittsburgh PA 15217-1118 Office: Carnegie Mellon U Dept Mech Engring 5000 Forbes Ave Pittsburgh PA 15213-3890

CHIH, CHUNG-YING, physicist, consultant; b. Yuki, Fukien, China, Dec. 11, 1916; s. Lai Sui and Sung-Yee (Lin) C.; BSc, Nat. Tsing Hua U., Peking, China, 1937; PhD, U. Calif., Berkeley, 1954; m. Alice Yuen, Aug. 15, 1955; came to U.S., 1948, naturalized, 1962. Instr. physics Fukien Med. Coll., 1937-40; instr., then asso. prof. Fukien Tchrs. Coll., 1940-44; assoc. prof., then prof. physics Nat. Chi-Nan U., 1944-45; prof. physics Kiang-su Coll., 1945-48; physicist Radiation Lab., U. Calif., Berkeley, 1948-54, summer 1956; mem. faculty Middlebury (Vt.) Coll., 1954-68, prof. physics, 1966-68; sci. cons., Bridgeport, Conn., 1968—. NSF grantee, 1957-60. Mem. Am. Phys. Soc. Address: PO Box 2556 Noble Sta Bridgeport CT 06608

CHIHOREK, JOHN PAUL, electronics company executive; b. Wilkes-Barre, Pa., June 22, 1943; s. Stanley Joseph and Caroline Mary C.; m. Cristina Maria Marroquin, Dec. 28, 1968; children: Jonathan, David, Crista, Daniel. BSEE, Pa. State U., 1965; postgrad., Calif. State U., San Diego, 1970-71; MBA, Calif. State U., Sacramento, 1972. Program officer Hdqrs. Air Force Logistic Command, Dayton, Ohio, 1972-75; sr. engr. Hdqrs. Air Force Space Div., L.A., 1975-78; mgr. software systems dept. Logicon Inc., San Pedro, Calif., 1978; mgr. software product assurance dept. Loral Aeronutronics, Rancho Santa Margarita, Calif., 1978-85, mgr. software engring., 1985—; pres. CMC Sys. Inc. Mem. Congl. Adv. Bd., 1980; active PTA, mem. Republican Nat. com. Served with USN, 1965-70, Vietnam. Decorated Bronze Star. Mem. IEEE (mgmt. bd. Computer Soc., exec. com. on standard), AAAS, Engring. Mgmt. Soc. (v.p. publs.), Air Force Assn., Internat. Platform Assn. Roman Catholic. Clubs: Lions, Odd Fellows. Office: Loral Aeronutronics Ford Rd Newport Beach CA 92633

CHILA, ANTHONY GEORGE, osteopathic educator; b. Youngstown, Ohio, Dec. 14, 1937; s. Paul and Anne (Jurenko) C.; m. Helen Paulick, Oct. 9, 1965; 1 child, Anne Elizabeth. BA, Youngstown State U., 1960; DO, Kansas City Coll. Osteopathy and Surgery, 1965. Assoc. prof. family medicine Mich. State U. Coll. Medicine, East Lansing, 1977-78; assoc. prof. family medicine Ohio U. Coll. Medicine, Athens, 1978-83, prof. family medicine, 1983, chief clin. research, 1982; chmn. instl. rev. bd. Ohio U., Athens, 1986-88; George C. Kozma Meml. lectr. Cleve. Acad. Osteo Medicine, 1979, Andrew Taylor Still Meml. lectr., Chgo., 1990, Sutherland Meml. Lectr., San Francisco, 1992. Contbr. numerous articles to profl. jours. Trustee Saint Vladimir's Orthodox Theol. Sem., Tuckahoe, N.Y., 1975-89; active Kootaga Area coun. Boy Scouts Am. Mem. AAAS, Am. Osteo. Assn. (Louisa M. Burns lectr. Clearwater, Fla. 1987), Am. Coll. Gen. Practitioners, Am. Acad. Osteopathic (pres. 1983-84, 85-86, Scott Meml. lectr. Kirksville, Mo. 1984, Thomas L. Northup lectr. Las Vegas 1986, Gutensohn-Denslow award 1995, Andrew Taylor Still medallion of honor 1997), Cranial Acad., N.Y. Acad. Scis., Am. Assn. Orthopaedic Medicine, Gen. Charles Grosvenor Civil War Round Table. Republican. Avocations: stamp and coin collecting, chess, Am. Civil War history. Office: Ohio U Coll Osteo Medicine Grosvenor Hall Athens OH 45701

CHILCOAT, DALE ALLEN, artist, visual and performing arts educator; b. Phoenix, Ariz., Aug. 16, 1938; s. Robert Polk and Martha Viola (Barton) C.; m. Sharon Fernandez, Dec. 27, 1965; children: Jennifer Lee, Joshua Fernandez. BA, Ariz. State U., 1961; postgrad., U. Florence, 1963; MA, Calif. State U., Northridge, 1967. Cert. tchr., N.Y., Calif. Art tchr. Needles (Calif.) Pub. Schs., 1961-62; chmn. art dept. North Shore Schs., Glen Head, N.Y., 1962-70; chmn. dept. visual arts San Leandro (Calif.) High Sch., 1970-84; dir. collective antiques San Mateo (Calif.) Antique Corp., 1980-81; dir. visual and performing arts San Leandro Schs., 1986—; state mentor tchr. San Leandro Unified, 1984-94; cons. Greater Bay Area, San Mateo, 1981-94; chmn. art curriculum San Leandro Schs., 1988-94; arts dir. North Shore Sch., 1962-70. Author Calif. state art curriculum, 1989. Named Outstanding Artist Operation Democracy Am., 1963. Mem. Calif. Art Educators Assn. (no. state rep. 1994), San Leandro Tchrs. Assn., Nat. Tchrs. Assn. (rep. 1962). Republican. Presbyterian. Home: 62 Broadmoor Blvd San Leandro CA 94577-1818 Office: San Leandro Schs 14735 Juniper St San Leandro CA 94579-1222

CHILCOAT, RICHARD ALLEN, army officer, university president; b. Wilmerding, Pa., Sept. 16, 1938; s. Floyd Donald and Edna Bailey (Moles0 C.; m. Dixie Lowers, June 6, 1964; children: Michael, Sharon A. BS, U.S. Mil. Acad., 1964; MBA, Harvard U., 1974. Commd. 2d lt. U.S. Army, 1964; speechwriter to Gen. John A. Wickham Jr., Office Chief of Staff, U.S. Army, Washington, 1984-87; comdr. Devil Troop Brigade, 5th Inf. Divsn. U.S. Army, Ft. Polk, La., 1987-89; chief of staff, 3d Inf. Divsn. U.S. Army, Germany, 1989-90; exec. asst. to Gen. Colin L. Powell, Joint Chiefs of Staff, Washington, 1990-92; dep. comdg. gen. U.S. Army Tng. Ctr., Ft. Jackson, S.C., 1993-94; comdt. U.S. Army War Coll., Carlisle Barracks, Pa., 1994-97; pres. Nat. Def. U., Washington, 1997—. Decorated DSM, Legion of Merit, Bronze Star with oak leaf cluster, Air medals. Mem. Assn. of U.S. Army, U.S. Mil. Acad. Assn. of Grads. Avocations: tennis, golf. Office: Nat Def U Office of Pres 300 5th Ave Fort Mcnair DC 20319*

CHILCOTE, GARY M., museum director, reporter; b. St. Joseph, Mo., Nov. 2, 1934; s. Merrill and Mary Thelma C.; m. Mary Carolyn Abmeyer, April 2, 1958; children: Douglas A., Carolyn D. BA, Northwest Mo. State U., 1956. News-press spl. corr. St. Joseph News-Press/Gazette, 1954—; mus. dir. Patee House Mus. and Jesse James Home Mus., St. Joseph, 1963—; vocat. tchr. Hillyard Tech. Sch., St. Joseph, 1964-91. Author, editor Pony Express Mail, 1972—. Staff sgt. Mo. Air Guard, 1957-63. Mem. Nat. Pony Express Assn. (nat. dir., nat. v.p. 1990—), Pony Express Hist. Assn. (bd. dirs., co-founder 1963), James-Younger Gang (nat. pres. 1997—, 98-99). Republican. Home: 1910 N 32nd St Saint Joseph MO 64506-2313 Office: Patee Ho Mus/Jesse James Ho Mus 1202 Penn St Saint Joseph MO 64503-2560

CHILCOTE, LUGEAN LESTER, architect; b. Oklahoma City, Jan. 14, 1929; s. Mark H. and Myrita A.J. (Lugeanbeal) C.; m. Clara Bernice Dudis, Dec. 18, 1953; children: Martin L., Frederick M., David L.(dec.), Bradley R. BArch, U. Ark., 1951. Registered architect, Ark., Mo.; cert. Nat. Coun. Archtl. Registration Bds. Designer, draftsman Ken Cole, Jr. (Architect), Little Rock, 1953-54; architect Swaim & Allen Architects, Little Rock, 1954-58; architect, prin. Blass Chilcote Carter Gaskin Bogart Norcross (and predeccessor firms), Little Rock, 1958; gen. chmn. Gulf States Regional Conf., 1966; judge City Beautiful Commn., 1967-68; pres. Ark. State Bd. Architects, 1991-96; apptd. mem. bldg. code bd. of appeals, City of Little Rock, 1986-94. Co-author: 50 Years of Design, 1980; prin. works include First Christian Ch., 1962, Continental bldg., 1969, Main Toll and Dial bldg. Southwestern Bell Telephone Co., 1968, Bapt. Med. Center Complex, 1971-73, U. Ark. Med. Sci. Campus, 1973—, U.S. Postal Svc. Gen. Mail Facility, Conv./Exhibit/Excelsior-Trust Hotel Complex, 1978-96, Ark. Children's Hosp., 1993—, all Little Rock, U.S. Post Office and Courthouse, Pine Bluff, Ark., 1967, Nat. Center for Toxicological Research, Pine Bluff, 1973-90, Jefferson Reg. med. Ctr., Pine Bluff, 1985—, White River Med. Ctr., Batesville, Ark., 1992-95, Drew Meml. Med. Ctr., Monticello, Ark., 1990—. Mem. com. Ark. Art Festival, 1968, West Little Rock YMCA, 1969; mem. Ark. Arts Ctr., 1965—; bd. dirs., treas., mem. exec. com. Ark. Community Found., 1972-85; bd. dirs. Ark. Hall of Fame, 1970—, Quapaw council Boy Scouts Am., Pulaski County, Ark., 1972—; dist. chmn., mem. exec. bd. of council Boy Scouts Am.; mem. Little Rock Bldg. Bd. Appeals, 1986-96; v.p. Ark. Christian Men's Orgn.; mem. exec. com., chmn. bd., elder Ark. Christian Ch. Served to capt. USAF, 1951-53. Recipient Woodbadge Tng. award Boy Scouts Am., Little Rock, 1974, Dist. Award of Merit, 1981, Silver Beaver award, Pulaski County, 1976, Meritorious Service award Ark. Community Found., 1985. Fellow AIA (pres. Ark. chpt. 1966-67, trustee ednl. endowment fund 1970-72, 83-95, gen. chmn. gulf states regional conf. 1966, nat. del. 1967, chmn. nat. profl. interest com. 1982-83, bd. dirs. nat. polit. action com. 1983-85, chmn. legis. affairs, chmn. Nat. Risk Mgmt. Com., chair 1997, profl. adv. bd. U. Ark. 1997, Gold Medal award Ark. chpt. 1996); mem. Pleasant Valley Country Club (Little Rock)(bd. dirs., bd. govs.), Little Rock Club, Capital Club (Little Rock). Avocations: golf, fishing, hunting. Home: 806 Carywood Ln Little Rock AR 72205-2802 Office: Blass Chilcote Carter Gaskin Bogart Norcross PO Box 3019 Little Rock AR 72203-3019

CHILCOTE, SAMUEL DAY, JR., trade association administrator; b. Casper, Wyo., Aug. 24, 1937; s. Sam D. and Juanita C. (Cornelison) C.; m. Ellen Sheridan Spear, Nov. 11, 1966. BS, Idaho State U., 1959. Adminstrv. asst. Continental Oil Co., Glenrock, Wyo., 1960-63; asst. supt. public instrn., dir. Wyo. Surplus Property Agy., Wyo. Sch. Lunch Program, Cheyenne Wyo. Dept. Edn., 1963-67; supr. N. Central region Distilled Spirits Inst., Denver, 1967-71; exec. dir., chief operating officer N. Central region Distilled Spirits Inst., Washington, 1971-73; exec. v.p., chief operating officer Distilled Spirits Council, Inc., Washington, 1973-77, pres., chief exec. officer, 1978-81; pres. Tobacco Inst., Washington, 1981-99; chmn. Chilcote Enterprises, 1999—; mem. industry sect. adv. council consumer goods, Dept. Commerce. Pres. Sky Ranch Found. for Boys, 1975-81, pres. emeritus, 1981—; treas. Ford's Theatre, 1984-88, vice chmn., trustee, 1988—, chmn., 1997—; bd. dirs., exec. com. Art Barn; chmn. Awards Dinner Com., 1989—, USO Met. Washington, past pres. Capt. U.S. Army, 1959-60. Recipient Profl. Achievement award Idaho State U. Coll. Bus., 1986, Man of Yr. award Anti-Defamation league, 1986, Humanitarian of the Yr. award Tobacco and Confectionery Div. Dinner for the UJA-Fedn. 1991 campaign. Mem. U.S. C. of C., Georgetown Club, Congl. Country Club (past pres., exec. com., bd. govs.), Burning Tree Club, Nat. Press Club, Capitol Hill Club, City Club, F St. Club, TPC Avenel (Washington), Jefferson Islands Club (bd. govs.), Masons, Elks, Shriners. Office: Tobacco Inst 1875 I St NW Ste 800 Washington DC 20006-5470

CHILCUTT, DORTHE MARGARET, art educator, artist; b. Fond du Lac, Wis., Jan. 29, 1915; d. John William and Pearl Evelyn (Burnett) Trummer. BS, U. Wis., 1940, MS, 1952; postgrad. NYU, 1975-78, Instituto Allende, Mex., summer 1958, La Romita Sch. Art, Italy, 1978-96, Schohegan Sch. Painting and Sculpture, 1959; m. Booth Chilcutt, Feb. 14, 1942; children: Karen Chilcutt Hulett, Booth, Cindy Jo Chilcutt Underhill, Debra Ann Chilcutt-Flippo. Layout artist DeVry Corp., Chgo., 1941-42; tchr. art St. Louis pub. schs., 1951-53, Monroe County Schs., Key West, Fla., 1957-62, Okeechobee Jr. High Sch. (Fla.), 1963-84, Indian River C.C., 1984-99. One woman shows Little Gallery, Key West, 1960, Martello Gallery, Key West, 1963, Ft. Pierce Art Gallery (Fla.), 1970; exhibited in group shows Jacksonville Art Mus. (Fla.), 1959, Tampa Art Mus., 1960, Norton Art Gallery, West Palm Beach, Fla., 1960, Backus Gallery, Ft. Pierce, 1977-98, St. Louis Art Mus., 1951, Wis. Salon of Art, Madison, 1947, Key West Art and Hist. Soc., 1957-90, Key West Art Ctr., 1959; Lighthouse Gallery, Tequesta, 1998; Court House Cultural Ctr., Stuart, 1998; Schacknow Museum of Fine Art, Coral Springs, 1998; represented in permanent collections Ft. Pierce Art Gallery, Martello Galleries. Recipient Best of Show awards Fla. Fedn. Art, 1974, Ft. Pierce Art Gallery, 1977, Ybor City Ann. Fiesta Day, 1980, Backus Festival, 1992, 1st pl. awards Highlands Art League 8th Ann., 1974, Jensen Beach Ann., Elliot Mus., 1974, 84, Ft. Pierce Scholarship Show, 1972-75, Four-County Art Show, Ft. Pierce, 1972-94, Tchr. of Yr. award Okeechobee County Sch. Bd., 1976, others. Mem. Fla. Watercolor Soc. (sec. 1974-84, bd. dirs. 1984-86), Gold Coast Water Color Soc., Nat. Art Edn. Assn., Fla. Art Edn. Assn. (Career Service award 1986), Miami Watercolor Soc., Treasure Coast Art Soc., Palm Beach Water Color Soc. Democrat. Contbr. articles to profl. jours. Home: 506 SW 15th St Okeechobee FL 34974-5264

CHILD, ABIGAIL, artist, educator. Student, Harvard U. and U. N.Mex., 1966; BA in History and Lit. magna cum laude, Harvard U., 1968; MFA in Graphics with honors, Yale U., 1970; student, Hampshire Coll., 1975. Adj. prof. dept. film and TV N.Y. Sch. Arts, 1980-85; asst. prof. film Mass. Coll. Art, 1985; vis. prof. film San Francisco Art Inst., 1986, 89; adj. prof. Sch. Visual Arts, N.Y.C., 1989-90; assoc. prof. humanities and arts Hampshire Coll., 1990-91; prof. film and video in studio arts Sarah Lawrence Coll., 1991—; instr. Henry Street Movie Club, 1968; artist in residence Huntington Pub. H.S., 1973, SUNY, 1978, Marta Valle Jr. H.S., N.Y.C., 1986; lectr. Inst. Policy Studies, Washington, 1981; sr. narrative critiques R.I. Sch. Design, 1990; vis. artist residency Calif. Inst. Art, L.A., 1990; resident in writing Kootenay Sch. Art, 1992; resident in time-arts Chgo. Art Inst., 1996; judge New England Film Festival, 1975, 86, Black Maria Film and Video Festival, 1989; film judge N.Y. Found. Arts, 1988; BACA film judge Bklyn., 1986; CAPS judge N.Y. State Arts Coun., 1981; mem. Ind. Filmmakers Distribution Network, San Francisco, 1977-78. Dir., editor (films/videos) Tar Garden, 1975, Some Exterior Presence, 1977, Peripeteia I, 1977, Daylight Test Section, 1978, Peripeteia II, 1978, Pacific Far East Line, 1979, Ornamentals, 1979, B/Side, 1996, others; co-dir., co-editor (video) 8 Million, 1993, Through the Looking Glass, 1995, others; one-woman shows include Chgo. Filmmakers, 1990, U. Calif., San Diego, 1990, Millennium, N.Y.C., 1991, Berks Filmmakers, Reading, Pa., 1992, L'Articule Gallery, Montreal, 1992, Concordia U., Montreal, 1992, Pleasure Dome, Toronto, Can., 1995, Vienna Filmmakers Coop, 1995, London Filmmakers Coop, 1995, Mass. Coll. Art Screening Soc., 1996, Cornell U. Film Studies Ctr., 1997, Pfizer Coll., 1997, U. So. Calif., 1997, L.A. Film Forum, 1997, Occidental Coll., 1997, SUNY, Buffalo, 1997, Rocky Mountain Film Ctr., Boulder, Colo., 1998, Utica Coll., 1998, Hampshire Coll., 1998, Ethnicolor, Bordeaux, 1998, Scratch Cinema, Paris, 1998, numerous others; represented in permanent collections; author: From Solids, 1983, Climate/Plus, 1986, A Motive for Mayhem, 1989, (poetry collection) MOB, 1994, Scatter Matrix, 1996, others; contbr. articles to profl. jours.; co-curator Rapp Arts Ctr., 1990, WEBO Gallery, N.Y.C., 1991; curator Loughleton Gallery, 1988, Ear Inn, N.Y.C., 1983, 84; film programmer WPA/Collaborative Projects at Hotel Ritz, Washington, 1983; editor, programmer IDIOLECTS, 1981; co-editor CINEMANEWS, 1978, 79; co-programmer (mid-week screening series) Different Every Viewing. Recipient First prize in photography Radcliffe Coll. Art Show, 1967, Scriptwriting award ITVS Am. Stories, 1997-98; grantee Am. Film Inst. Ind. Filmmakers, 1973; scholar U. Film Studies Summer Inst., 1975; grantee Creative Artists Pub. Svc., 1980; MacDowell Colony fellow, 1983, 86, 88, 91, 94, 96, 98; grantee N.Y. Found. Arts, 1985; grantee Mass. Art Coun., 1986; grantee N.Y. State Arts Coun. Distbn., 1988; Jerome Found. grantee, 1986, 89; Ludwig Vogelstein Found. grantee, 1989; Art Matters grantee, 1989, 90; Electronic Arts Media grantee, 1990; InterArts grantee, Nat. Endowment Arts, 1990; N.Y. Found. Arts grantee, 1985, 89, 95; media grantee N.Y. State Coun. on Arts, 1991, 96; Fulbright fellow to St. Petersburg, 1992-93; John Simon Guggenheim fellow in film, 1995-96; residency fellow Banff Ctr. Arts, 1997. Mem. N.Y. Writers Guild, Canyon Cinema Coop. (film shipper 1978-79), N.Y. Filmmakers Coop., Can. Coop. Film Distbn., London Filmmakers Coop.

CHILD, CARROLL CADELL, research nursing administrator; b. Vicksburg, Miss., Nov. 10, 1949; s. John Clifton and Marie Adelaide (Gerwig) C.; m. Nicole Louise Child, Feb. 11, 1984; children: Dylan Christopher, Brendan Thomas. BA in Philosophy, So. Ill. U., 1972; BSN with honors, U. Calif., San Francisco, 1980; MSc with honors, San Francisco State U., 1994. RN, Calif. Nurse supr. USDA/U. Calif., Berkeley; clin. rsch. supr. drug studies unit U. Calif., San Francisco; rsch. nurse educator Stanford (Calif.) U.; clin. trials coord. Community Consortium U. Calif., San Francisco; participant, co-presenter V Internat. Conf. on AIDS, Montreal, Que., Can., 1989, VI Internat. Conf. on AIDS, San Francisco, 1990, VIII Internat. Conf. on AIDS, Amsterdam, 1992; co-presenter univ.-wide task force on AIDS conf. U. Calif., Berkeley, 1990; chair quality improvement com. Cmty. Programs for Clin. Rsch. on AIDS/NIH, 1993—. Contbr. to profl. jours. Chair quality improvement com. Cmty. Programs for Clin. Rsch. on AIDS (CPCRA)/NIH, 1993—. Mem. Internat. AIDS Soc., Soc. Clin. Trials, Assn. Nurses in AIDS Care, Assn. Rsch. Nurses.

CHILD, IRVIN LONG, psychologist, educator; b. Deming, N.Mex., Mar. 11, 1915; s. Arthur Henry and Martina Avila (Long) C.; m. Alice Dukes Blyth, Mar. 29, 1941 (dec. Nov. 1997); children: Richard Blyth, Pamela Colman (dec.). B.A., UCLA, 1935; Ph.D., Yale U., 1939. Instr. psychology Harvard U. and Radcliffe Coll., 1939-41; with Yale U., 1941—, successively Latin-Am. research fellow, asst. prof., asso. prof., prof. psychology, 1954-85, prof. emeritus, 1985—. Author: Italian or American? The Second Generation in Conflict, 1943, (with J.W.M. Whiting) Child Training and Personality: A Cross-Cultural Study, 1953, Humanistic Psychology and the Research Tradition: Their Several Virtues, 1973, (with Alice B. Child) Religion and Magic in the Life of Traditional Peoples, 1993. Mem. APA, Parapsychol. Assn., Am. Psychol. Soc., Phi Beta Kappa, Sigma Xi. Home: 280 Newtonville Ave Newton MA 02460-2038 Office: 2 Hillhouse Ave New Haven CT 06511-6814

CHILD, JOSEPH ALAN, minister; b. Gary, Ind., Jan. 6, 1959; s. Larry Gene and Dorothy Marcella (Walton) C.; m. Teri Lynn Geil, Nov. 10, 1979; children: Michael, Madison, Mackenzie, Morgan. Diploma, Rhema Bible Tng. Ctr., 1982; BA summa cum laude, Bethel Christian Ctr., 1988, MRE magna cum laude, 1990. Ordained to ministry Rhema Ministerial Assn. Internat., 1989. Assoc. pastor Victory Christian Ctr., Palm Springs, Calif., 1986-93; sr. pastor Impact Christian Ctr., Colorado Springs, Colo., 1996—; prof. grad. sch. theology, Bethel Christian Coll., Riverside, Calif., 1989—. Mem. Western States Ministerial Assn., Rhema Alumni Assn., Rhema Ministerial Assn. Internat. Republican. Home: 5705 Altitude Dr Colorado Springs CO 80918-5247 Office: Impact Christian Ctr 4440 Barnes Rd Ste 100 Colorado Springs CO 80917

CHILD, JUDITH, artist; b. Concord, Mass., June 22, 1948; d. Luther Moore and Virginia (Ellms) C.; m. Alan Leigh Schwartz, June 22, 1974; 1 child, Timothy Child Schwartz. BS, Colby Saywer Coll., 1971; postgrad., Auckland Soc. Arts, New Zealand, 1976; postgrad. program in artistry, Boston U., 1978-80. Artist Boston, 1980-86, St. Louis, 1986—; juror Art St. Louis, 1998. One woman shows include Colby Coll., New London, N.H., 1996; group shows include Art Chgo., 1994, Cedar Rapids Mus. Art, 1997-98; represented in permanent collection Anheuser-Busch Co., Emerson Electric Co. Painting fellow Nat. Endowment Arts, Washington, 1996.

CHILD, JULIA MCWILLIAMS (MRS. PAUL CHILD), cooking expert, television personality, author; b. Pasadena, Calif., Aug. 15, 1912; d. John and Julia Carolyn (Weston) McWilliams; m. Paul Child, Sept. 1, 1945 (dec.). BA, Smith Coll., 1934. With advt. dept. W.&J. Sloane, N.Y.C., 1939-40; with OSS, Washington, Ceylon, China, 1941-45; co-founder Am. Inst. Wine & Food, 1982. Hostess TV program The French Chef, WGBH-TV, Boston, from 1963, Julia Child & Co., 1978-79, Julia Child & More Co., 1980, Dinner at Julia's, PBS, 1983; Cooking with Master Chefs series, PBS, Baking with Julia, PBS; occasional cooking segment Good Morning Am., ABC-TV, 1980—; video cassettes The Way to Cook, 1982; author: (with Simone Beck and Louisette Bertholle) Mastering the Art of French Cooking, 1961, The French Chef Cookbook, 1968, Mastering the Art of French Cooking, Vol. II, 1970, (with Simone Beck) From Julia Child's Kitchen, 1975, Julia Child & Company, 1978, Julia Child & More Company, 1979, Mastering the Art of French Cooking I & II, 1983, The Way to Cook, 1989; columnist McCall's mag., 1975-82, Parade mag., 1982-86. Recipient Peabody award, 1964, Emmy award, 1966, French Ordre de Merite Agricole, 1967, Ordre National de Merite, 1974, Ralph Lowell award, Corp. for Pub. Broadcasting, 1998, TV Cooking Show award James Beard Found. *

CHILDERS, BOB EUGENE, educational association executive; b. Cleveland, Miss., Sept. 16, 1930; s. William Nick and Allie Jeanette (Doty) C.; m. Jo Ann Roberts, May 1, 1953; children: William Frank, Robert Clayton, John Murry, Julia Ann. BA, Union U., 1953; MA, Memphis State U., 1958; EdD, U. Tenn., 1964. Cert. tchr., adminstr., Tenn. Field engr. RCA, El Paso, Tex., 1955-57; instr. USN, Memphis, 1957-60; prin. Halls H.S., Knoxville, Tenn., 1960-61, McMinn County H.S., Athens, Tenn., 1961-64; asst. commr. Tenn. State Dept. Edn., Nashville, 1964-66; regional dir. USOE, Vocat.-Tech. and Adult Edn., Atlanta, 1966-69; exec. dir. Commn. Occupl. Edn., Atlanta, 1969-82, So. Assn. Colls. and Schs., Atlanta, 1982-92; cons. U.S. Dept. Edn., Washington, 1963-79, Fla. State Legislature, Tallahassee, 1979, Md. Values Edn. Commn., Annapolis, 1979-80; founder, pres. Childers-Childress Family Assn., 1982-88, 90-96. Editor SACS Procs., 1982-92. Bd. dirs. Boy Scouts Am., Atlanta, 1990-97, Ctr. for Citizenship Edn., Washington, 1978-81; bd. trustees YMCA, Nashville, 1964-66; v.p. Religious Heritage of Am., St. Louis, 1979-86; active Rotary, Atlanta, 1981-92. With U.S. Army, 1953-55. Mem. Am. Vocat. Assn. (life 1966, cons.), Am. Tech. Edn. Assn. (life 1978, pres.1984, v.p. 1983), Am. Vocat. Rsch. Assn., Am. Soc. Assn. Execs., Phi Delta Kappa (past treas. 1960-61, sec. 1960-61), Iota Lambda Sigma, Sigma Alpha Epsilon (pres. 1952). Democrat. Baptist. Avocations: geneology, vitaculture, gardening. Home and Office: 960 River Rd Woodruff SC 29388-9110

CHILDERS, BUD, university head basketball coach; b. Mar. 18, 1956; m. Judy Childers; children Brad, Brett. BS, Charleston So. U., 1979; MS, Middle Tenn. State U., 1983. Coach Cumberland Jr. Coll., Williamsburg, Ky., 1981-83, Montevallo (Ala.) U., 1983-84, Murray (Ky.) State U., 1984-89; head coach U. Louisville, 1989-97; head coach women's basketball James Madison U., 1997—. Named Conf. USA Coach of Yr., 1993, 95, 97. Fax: 540-568-3703. Office: James Madison U CONC 115A MSC 4702 Harrisonburg VA 22807*

CHILDERS, CHARLES EUGENE, mining company executive; b. West Frankfort, Ill., Oct. 29, 1932; s. Joel Marion and Cora E. (Choate) C.; m. Norma A. Casper, June 8, 1952; children: Joel M., Katrina K. BS, U. Ill., 1955; LLD (hon.), U. Saskatchewan, 1994. With Duval Corp., Carlsbad, N.Mex., 1955-62, Internat. Minerals Corp. (IMC), 1963-77; v.p. Esterhazy oper. IMC, 1977-79; pres. IMC Coal, Lexington, 1979-81; v.p. potash oper. IMC, 1981-82, v.p. expansion and devel., 1982-87; pres., chief exec. officer Potash Corp. of Sask., Inc., Saskatoon, Can., 1987-90, chmn., pres., chief exec. officer, 1990-98, chmn., chief exec. officer, 1998-99, chmn., 1999—; bd. dirs., past chmn. bd. Canpotex Ltd., Sask., Found. for Agronomic Rsch.; past chmn. bd. The Fertilizer Inst.; bd. dirs. Conf. Bd. Can., Battle Mountain Gold Corp.; past chmn. Potash and Phosphate Inst.; mem. fertilizer industry adv. com. to FAO. Dir. at large Jr. Achievement of Can. 1st lt. U.S. Army, 1955-57. Mem. AIME, Can. Inst. Mining and Metallurgy, Sask. Potash Producers Assn. (past. chmn.), Internat. Fertilizer Industry Assn. (past pres.). Republican Baptist. Home: 3835 Placita de Piacho Tucson AZ 85718 Office: Potash Corp of Sask, 122 1st Ave S, Saskatoon, SK Canada S7K 7G3

CHILDERS, JOHN CHARLES, lawyer, engineer; b. Gallipolis, Ohio, Oct. 27, 1950; s. Frank W. and Bernice E. (Ziler) C.; m. Judith Marie Hughes, Jan. 1, 1976; children: Rachel Grace, Benjamin Hughes. BS in Civil Engring. cum laude, Ohio U., 1972; JD cum laude, Capital U., 1978. Bar: Ohio 1978, U.S. Supreme Ct. 1987. Pvt. practice Carrollton, Ohio, 1978—; asst. pros. atty. County of Carroll, Carrollton, Ohio, 1981-89; ptnr. Childers and Smith, Attys., Carrollton, 1982—. Mem. Ohio Bar Assn. (coun. of dels. 1988—), Carroll County Bar Assn. (pres. 1984—). Office: Childers and Smith 70 Public Sq # 252 Carrollton OH 44615-1403

CHILD-OLMSTED, GISÈLE ALEXANDRA, language educator; b. Port-au-Prince, Haiti, Dec. 27, 1946; U.S. citizen by birth; d. Daniel McGuire Child and Alice Dejean Child; m. Hans George Bickel, Sept. 1967 (div. Apr. 1984); children: Anna Kristina Rexrode, Maia Selena Bickel; m. Jerauld Lockwood Olmsted, June 17, 1988. BA in French with honors, U. Md., 1970; MA in French, Johns Hopkins U., 1978, PhD in Romance Langs., 1981; cert. in translation, Georgetown U. Vis. instr. U. Md., College Park, 1980-81; instr. Johns Hopkins U., Balt., 1981-82; lang. instr. Holton-Arms Sch., Bethesda, Md., 1982-83; asst. prof. dept. modern langs. and lit. Loyola Coll., Balt., 1983-89, assoc. prof., 1989-98, chair dept. modern lang. langs. and lit., 1989-94, prof., 1998—; v.p. faculty coun. Loyola Coll., 1998—, mem. steering com. Ctr. for Humanities, 1989-94; organizer, dir. Colloquia on Lang., Lit. and Soc., Balt., 1990, 94, 98. Author: Jean Genet: Criminalité et Transcendance, 1987; contbr. articles to profl. jours. Faculty rsch. grantee Loyola Coll., 1984, 89, study grantee French Embassy, 1986, 89; Gillman Fellow, 1970-73, 79-80; visitor's scholar U. Cape Town, South Africa, 1995. Mem. MLA (del. Mid-Atlantic region 1992-94, 96-98), Am. Assn. Tchrs. French, Soc. Prof. Français et Francophones d'Amérique, Les Amis de Stendhal, Phi Beta Kappa. Avocations: painting, golf, antiques, classical music, flamenco dancing. E-mail: olmsted@loyola.edu. Home: 7735 Arrowood Ct Bethesda MD 20817 Office: Loyola Coll 4501 N Charles St Baltimore MD 21210

CHILDREE, ROBERT L., comptroller. BS in Acctg., U. Ala., 1973. State comptr. Fin. Dept., Ala., 1987—. Mem. Nat. Assn. Comptrs., Auditors, and Treas. (2d v.p.), Nat. Assn. State Comptrs. (pres. 1994, Pres.'s award 1997), Govt. Fin. Officers Assn. of Ala., Assn. Govt. Accts. (pres. Montgomery chpt. 1996-97, Pub. Adminstr. award 1992, Superior Performance award 1996-97, Membership Achievement award 1996-97). Office: Ste 220 100 N Union Montgomery AL 36130

CHILDRESS, DUDLEY STEPHEN, biomedical engineer, educator; b. Cass Co., Mo., Sept. 25, 1934; m., 1959; two children. BS, U. Mo., Columbia, 1957; MS, U. Mo., 1958; PhD in Elec. Engring., Northwestern U., 1967. From instr. to asst. prof. Elec. Engring. U. Mo., Columbia, 1959-63; rsch. asst. Physiology Control Sys. Lab. Northwestern U., Evanston, Ill., 1964-66; from asst. prof. to assoc. prof. Elec. Engring., Ortho. Sur. Northwestern U., 1972-77, co-dir. Rehab. Engring. prog., 1972-85, prof. Elec. Engring., Tech. Inst., 1977-86, prof. biomed. engring., 1986—; prof. Orthopedic Surgery Northwestern Med. Sch., 1977-97, dir. Prosthetics Rsch. Lab., 1971—, dir. Rehab. Engring. prog., 1985—; prof. phys. medicine rehab. Northwestrn Med. Sch., 1997—; elected to Inst. Med. Nat. Acad. Sci., 1995; mem. Com. Prosthetics Rsch. and Devel., Nat. Acad. Sci. Nat. Rsch. Coun., 1969-72. Recipient Nat. Inst. Gen. Med. Sci. rsch. career devel. award, 1970-75, Goldenson award, United Cerebral Palsy Found. Mem. AAAS, Applied Physiology and Bioengring. Study Sec., NIH, 1974-78, Biomed. Engring. Soc., Rehab. Engring. Soc. N. Am., Inst. Soc. Prosthetics and Orthotics, Sigma Xi.

CHILDRESS, ERIC ROGERS, librarian, consultant, metadata specialist; b. Balt., Sept. 11, 1960; s. Bobby B. and Miriam Louise M. Childress. BA in Geography, U. N.C., Greensboro, 1982, MLS, 1987. Serials asst. U. N.C., Greensboro, 1983-84, processing supr., 1985-89; reference libr. Greensboro Coll., Greensboro, 1986; spl. materials cataloger Elon (N.C.) Coll., 1989-96; sr. product support specialist OCLC Online Computer Libr. Ctr., Dublin, Ohio, 1996—; mem. Interactive Multimedia Guidelines Review Task Force, 1993-94; chair Program Coop. Cataloging Core Bibliographic Record Audiovisual Materials Task Group, 1995-96; mem. Program Coop. Cataloging Core Bibliographic Record for Computer Files Task Group, 1997. Mem. editl. bd. Jour. Internet Cataloging, Birghamton, N.Y., 1996—; contbr. articles to profl. jours. Mem. Am. Libr. Assn., U. N.C. Greensboro Libr. & Info. Studies Alumni Assn. (pres. 1993-94), Assn. Libr. Collections & Tech. Svcs. (chair audiovisual com. 1993-94). Office: Online Computer Libr Ctr 6565 Frantz Rd Dublin OH 43017-5308

CHILDRESS, JAMES FRANKLIN, theology and medical educator; b. Mt. Airy, N.C., Oct. 4, 1940; s. Roscoe Franklin and Zella Bessie (Wagoner) C.; m. Georgia Monroe Harrell, Dec. 21, 1958 (dec. Aug. 1994); children: (twins) Albert Franklin, James Frederic. B.A., Guilford Coll., N.C., 1962; B.D. cum laude, Yale Div. Sch, New Haven, 1965; M.A., Yale U., New Haven, 1967, Ph.D., 1968. Asst. prof. dept. religious studies U. Va.-Charlottesville, 1968-71; assoc. prof. dept. religious studies U. Va.-Charlottesville, 1971-75, chmn. dept. religious studies, 1972-75, 86-94, prof. religious studies and med. edn., 1979—; prof. Christian ethics Kennedy Inst. Ethics, Georgetown U., Washington, 1975-79.; vis. prof. U. Chgo. Divinity Sch., 1977, Princeton U., 1978, Coll. Physicians and Surgeons, Columbia U., 1978; cons. and lectr. in field. Author: Priorities in Biomedical Ethics, 1981, Moral Responsibility in Conflicts, 1982, Who Should Decide? Paternalism in Health Care, 1982, Practical Reasoning in Bioethics, 1997; co-author: Principles of Biomedical Ethics, 1979, 4th edit., 1994; co-editor: Westminster Dictionary of Christian Ethics, 1986; contbr. articles to profl. jours., chpts. to books. Trustee Guilford Coll., Greensboro, N.C., 1983-85; mem. subcom. on human gene therapy NIH, Bethesda, Md., 1984-92, mem. NIH recombinant DNA adv. com., 1988-90; mem. Biomed. Ethics Adv. Com., 1988-89; mem. Nat. Bioethics Adv. Commn., 1996—; vice-chmn. Task Force on Organ Transplantation, HHS, 1985-86; bd. dirs. United Network for Organ Sharing, 1987-89. Recipient numerous awards and grants in field including Disting. Prof. award U. Va., 1984, Va. Prof. of Yr. award Coun. for Advancement and Support Edn., 1990; Am. Coun. Learned Socs. fellow, 1972-73, Wilson Ctr. fellow, 1984-85, Guggenheim fellow, 1984-85. Fellow Inst. Social Ethics and Life Scis., Am. Acad. Arts and Scis.; mem. Soc. Christian Ethics (bd. dirs. 1973-76), Am. Acad. Religion, Am. Theol. Soc., Am. Philos. Assn. Democrat. Quaker. Avocations: tennis; reading; music. Office: Dept of Religious Studies University of Virginia Charlottesville VA 22903*

CHILDRESS, JANET LYNN, logistician; b. Knoxville, Tenn., July 24, 1954; d. Albert Lee and Cartha Lynn (Doyle) C. AA, U. Md., 1989; BS, Cameron U., 1996; postgrad., U. Okla., 1997, Embry-Riddle Aeronaut. U., 1998. Logistician Fed. Civil Svc., 1981-99; intern Fed. Civil Svc., 1997-99, facilitator quality mgmt. bd., 1995-97, writer orgn. self-assessment team, 1997; presenter in field. Contbr. articles to profl. jours. With U.S. Army, 1980-84. Mem. Leadership Lawton (Okla.), 1997, Okla. Comm. Status of Women, Oklahoma City, 1996-97; chair Mayor's Commn. Status of Women, Lawton, 1995-97. Mem. Am. Soc. Pub. Adminstrn., Women in Military Svc. for Am., Phi Kappa Phi, LWV (v.p. 1995-97). Democrat. Avocations: volunteering, travel, movies, reading, golf. E-mail: jlchildress@juno.com. Home: 37964 Willowood Ct Harrison Township MI 48045

CHILDRESS, KERRI J., federal agency administrator; b. Sydney, Nebr.; d. Jack L. and Florence (Paris) Lindley; children: Kelly Nicole, Patrick Tyler. BA in History and Polit. Sci. summa cum laude, U. Md., 1983; MA in Pub. Comm., Am. U., 1998. Assoc. editor Navy Times newspaper, Springfield, Va., 1977-80; tchr. history and journalism Dept. Def. High Sch., Wuerzburg, Germany, 1982-84; historian Mt. Vernon Ladies' Assn., Va., 1984-85, Arlington Nat. Cemetery, 1985-89; media rels. officer Mil. Dist. of Washington, Ft. McNair, 1989-91; pub. affairs officer Office Gov. U.S. Soldiers' and Airmen's Home, Washington, 1991—; mem. pub. affairs staff Presdl. Inaugural Com., 1977. Contbr. articles to profl. jours. With USN, 1973-77, lt. Res. Recipient Hon. Tomb Guard ID Badge from sentinels, Tomb of the Unknowns, Arlington Cemetery, Achievement medal, Dept. Army, 1990; named Sailor of Yr., Naval Res. Unit, 1978. Mem. Phi Kappa Phi, Phi Alpha Theta. Avocations: running, writing, photography. Office: Office of the Gov US Soldiers & Airmen's Home Washington DC 20317*

CHILDRESS, MARCIA DAY, humanities educator; b. East Grand Rapids, Mich., June 25, 1948; d. Robert Sheldon Day and Jean Thompson Day Spaanstra; m. Charles Marvin Finney, May 12, 1979 (div. 1988); 1 child, Brendan Day Finney; m. James Franklin Childress, May 10, 1997. BA with high honors, Mich. State U., 1970; MA in English Lit., U. Va., 1976, PhD in English Lit., 1996. Instr., editor dept. medicine U. Va. Sch. Medicine, Charlottesville, 1975-89; spl. asst. to v.p. and provost for health scis. U. Va., Charlottesville, 1989-95; asst. prof. med. edn. (med. humanities) U. Va. Sch. Medicine, 1989—, dir. program of humanities in medicine, 1996—. E-mail: woolf@virginia.edu. Office: Univ Va Sch Medicine Humanities in Medicine HSC # 389 Charlottesville VA 22908

CHILDRESS, SCOTT JULIUS, medicinal chemist; b. Greenville, S.C., Apr. 6, 1926; s. Julius Dunford and Ola Irene (Scott) C.; m. Nelly Araxy Medzadour, Dec. 20, 1975. B.S., Furman U., 1947; Ph.D., U. N.C., 1951. Research chemist Tenn. Eastman, Kingsport, 1951-52; research chemist Wallace & Tiernan, Belleville, N.J., 1952-58; research chemist Wyeth Labs., Radnor, Pa., 1959-62, mgr. medicinal chemistry, 1962-68, asst. to v.p. research and devel., 1968-73, asst. v.p. research and devel., 1973-85. Patentee in field; contbr. articles to profl. jours. Served with AUS, 1944-46. Fellow N.Y. Acad. Scis.; mem. Am. Chem. Soc. (treas. med. div. 1969-71, chmn. nat. med. chem. symposium 1968), Sigma Xi. Home: 604 S Washington Sq Philadelphia PA 19106-4118

CHILDRESS, STEVEN ALAN, law educator; b. Mobile, Ala., Feb. 9, 1959; s. Roy and Mary Helen (Gillion) C.; children: Ani, Steven. BA, U. Ala., 1979; JD, Harvard U., 1982; PhD in Jurisprudence and Social Policy, U. Calif., Berkeley, 1995. Bar: Calif. 1983, U.S. Ct. Appeals (5th cir.) 1984, D.C. 1986, U.S. Ct. Appeals (9th cir.) 1986, U.S. Supreme Ct. 1987. Law clk. to judge U.S. Ct. Appeals (5th cir.), Shreveport, La., 1982-83; assoc. Morrison & Foerster, San Francisco, 1983-84; adj. lectr. law Golden Gate U. Sch. Law, San Francisco, 1984-86; grad. instr. U. Calif., Berkeley, 1985-86; assoc. Brobeck, Phleger & Harrison, San Francisco, 1987-88; assoc. prof. law Tulane U. Law Sch., New Orleans, 1988-96, prof. law, 1996—. Co-author: Federal Standards of Review, 1986, 2d edit., 1992; contbr. articles to profl. jours. Regents fellow U. Calif. at Berkeley, 1985. Mem. Law and Soc. Assn., Phi Beta Kappa. Office: Tulane U School of Law New Orleans LA 70118

CHILDRESS, WALTER DABNEY, III, insurance executive, financial planner; b. Petersburg, Va., Feb. 15, 1943; s. Walter Dabney Jr. and Myrtie Ruth (Braswell) C.; m. Patricia Nan Clark, July 2, 1969; children: Cameron Wyatt, Nora Lynn. AA, Chipola Jr. Coll., 1964; BA, Birmingham (Ala.)-So. Coll., 1969; MEd, U. Montevallo, Ala., 1973. Tchr., coach Curry Sch., Birmingham, Ala., 1969-70; tchr., coach, athletic dir. Birmingham U., 1970-72; tchr., coach Peachtree H.S., DeKalb County, Ga., 1972-74; field rep. Guardian Life Ins. Co. Am., Atlanta, 1974—; rep. Guardian Investors Svcs. Corp., Atlanta, 1976—; owner W.D. Childress & Co., Atlanta, 1982—; investment advisor, pres. Childress Fin. Svcs., Inc., Atlanta, 1989—; owner Childress Leasing, LLC, Atlanta, 1997—; bd. dirs. Atlanta Alumni chpt., Birmingham-So. Coll.; speaker in field. Cubmaster Pack 876 Boy Scouts Am., Stone Mountain, Ga., 1984-85, scoutmaster, 1985-90; deacon Presbyn. Ch. Chipola Jr. Coll. scholar, Birmingham-So. Coll. scholar; recipient Nat. Sales Achievement, Nat. Health Quality and Nat. Quality awards, 1976—. Mem. Nat. Assn. Life Underwriters, Life Underwriters Polit. Action Com., Am. Assn. Chartered Life Underwriters, Internat. Assn. Fin. Planners, Lions (pres. Tucker chpt. 1984-85), Million Dollar Roundtable Internat. (life, honor roll), Million Dollar Roundtable Found. Republican. Avocations: tropical fish, ch. league basketball coach, martial arts (black belt).

CHILDS, BARTON, retired, physician, educator; b. Chgo., Feb. 29, 1916; s. Robert William and Katherine Sayles (Barton) C.; m. Eloise L.B. MacKie, Mar. 29, 1950 (dec. 1980); children—Anne Lloyd, Lucy Barton; m. Ann E. Pulver, Dec. 1986. A.B., Williams Coll., 1938; M.D., Johns Hopkins, 1942. Successively intern, asst. resident, resident pediatrics Johns Hopkins Hosp., 1942-43, 46-48; research fellow Children's Hosp., Boston, 1948-49; Commonwealth Fund fellow Univ. Coll., London, Eng., 1952-53; mem. faculty Johns Hopkins Sch. Medicine, 1949—, prof. pediatrics, 1962—; Mem. NIH Cons. Coms., 1959-63, 63-67, 67-69, 70-74, 78—. Served to capt., M.C. AUS, 1943-46. John and Mary Markle scholar, 1953-58; Grover F. Powers Distinguished scholar, 1960-62; recipient Research Career award NIH, 1962, Meade Johnson award pediatrics, 1959, Allen award human genetics, 1974, Howland award pediatrics, 1989. Mem. Am. Pediatric Soc., Soc. Pediatric Research, Am. Acad. Pediatrics, Am. Soc. Human Genetics, Genetics Soc. Am., Inst. Medicine, Am. Acad. Arts and Scis. Home: 1019 Winding Way Baltimore MD 21210-1232 Address: John Hopkins Sch of Med 600 N Wolfe St Baltimore MD 21287-0005*

CHILDS, BREVARD SPRINGS, religious educator; b. Columbia, S.C., Sept. 2, 1923; s. Richard A. and Reaux (Jones) C.; m. Ann Taylor, Aug. 7, 1954; children—John, Catherine. BA, U. Mich., 1946, MA, 1948; BD, Princeton, 1950; ThD, U. Basel, Switzerland, 1955; DD (hon.), U. Aberdeen, Scotland, 1984, U. Glasgow, Scotland, 1992. Ordained to ministry Presbyn. Ch., 1958. Prof. O.T., Mission House Sem., Plymouth, Wis., 1954-58; prof. religion Yale U., New Haven, 1958—, Sterling prof. div., 1992—. Author: Myth and Reality in the Old Testament, 1960, Memory and Tradition in Israel, 1962, Isaiah and the Assyrian Crisis, 1967, Biblical Theology in Crisis, 1970, The Book of Exodus, 1974, Old Testament Books for Pastor and Teacher, 1977, Introduction to the Old Testament as Scripture, 1979, the New Testament as Canon: An Introduction, 1985, Old Testament Theology in a Canonical Context, 1986, Biblical Theology of the Old and New Testaments, 1992. Served with AUS, 1943-45. Guggenheim fellow, 1963-64; Nat. Endowment for Humanities fellow, 1977-78; Fulbright-Hays fellow, 1981; Deutscher Akademischer Austauschdienst fellow, 1987. Fellow Am. Acad. Arts and Scis. Home and Office: 508 Amity Rd Bethany CT 06524-3015

CHILDS, DONALD RICHARD, pediatric endocrinologist; b. Chgo., Sept. 14, 1945; s. Robert Henry Edward and Dorothy Jane (Mills) C.; m. Diane E. Martin, Apr. 26, 1972 (div. 1981); 1 child, Elena M.; m. Jacquelynne Celeste Bostrom, Aug. 26, 1989; stepchildren: Brandon R. Alexander, Eric T. Alexander. MD, U. Mich., 1970. Diplomate Am. Bd. Pediatrics. Intern Children's Hosp., L.A., 1970-71; resident William Beaumont Hosp., Royal Oak, Mich., 1973-75; fellow U. Calif., Davis, 1975-77; pvt. practice Riverside, Calif., 1977—. Capt. U.S. Army, 1971-73. Fellow Am. Acad. Pediatrics; mem. Am. Diabetes Assn., Calif. Perinatal Assn., Calif. Med. Assn., Endocrine Soc., Juvenile Diabetes Found. Avocations: music, water skiing. Office: Riverside Med Clinic 9041 Magnolia Ave Riverside CA 92503-3900

CHILDS, JAMES WILLIAM, lawyer, legal educator; b. Muncie, Ind., Sept. 20, 1935; s. Dexter William and Marcelle (Mericle) C.; m. Sally Johnston, June 9, 1978; children: Elizabeth, Anne, James William, Dylan Rhys, Karrin Aleen. Student, Denison U., 1953-55; AB, U. Mich., 1957, JD, 1960. Bar: Ohio 1960, Ind. 1980, Pa. 1996. Practiced in Van Wert, Ohio, 1960-84; pres. firm Childs Childs & Fortney Co. (L.P.A.), 1962-83; v.p. Wise Childs & Rice, L.P.A., 1983-85; dir. P.P.A. Inc., 1972-88; adj. prof. Western Ohio br. Wright State U., 1976-80 vis. prof. law U. Akron Sch. Law, 1983-84, prof. law, 1984-89; mem. Starr Commonwealth Adv. Bd., 1962-83, pres., 1970; mem. Van Wert County Hosp. Assn., 1963-83; mem. Alt. Tax Systems Del. to Europe, 1985. Co-author: Estate Planning Idea Book, 1978, Matthew Bender Tax Service, 1993; editor-in-chief CCH Tax Svc., 1994—; cons. writer Farm Jour.; also articles on taxation. Mem., chmn. environ. health com. Ohio Comprehensive Health Planning Adv. Coun., 1976; bd. dirs. Van Wert County Heart Assn. Mem. ABA (chmn. agr. com. sect. taxation 1991-92), Pa. Bar Assn., Ohio State Bar Assn., Ind. State Bar Assn., Northwestern Ohio Bar Assn. (pres. 1976), Van Wert County Bar Assn. (pres. 1969-71), Summit County Bar Assn., Van Wert C. of C. (pres. 1976), Rotary, Kiwanis (pres. Van Wert chpt. 1968, lt. gov. divsn. 2 1972, pres. Bath Richfield chpt. 1998), Shriners. Episcopalian. Home and Office: 3350 Yellow Creek Rd Akron OH 44333-2218 *It has been my goal to try to the very best of my ability over the years to raise the level of knowledge in the very important field of federal taxation as it applies to agricultural enterprises.**

CHILDS, JOHN DAVID, computer hardware and services company executive; b. Washington, Apr. 26, 1939; s. Edwin Carlton and Catherine Dorothea (Angerman) C.; m. Margaret Rae Olsen, Mar. 4, 1966 (div.); 1 child, John-David. Student Principia Coll., 1957-58, 59-60; BA, Am. U., 1963. Jr. adminstr. Page Communications, Washington, 1962-65; account rep. Friden Inc., Washington, 1965-67; Western sales dir. Data Inc., Arlington, Va., 1967-70; v.p. mktg. Rayda, Inc., Los Angeles, 1970-73, pres., 1973-76, chmn. bd., 1976-84; v.p. sales Exec. Bus. Systems, Encino, Calif., 1981-87, sr. v.p. sales and mktg., 1987—; sr. assoc. World Trade Assocs., Inc., 1976—. Pres. Coll. Youth for Nixon-Lodge, 1959-60, dir. state fedn.; mem. OHSHA policy formulation com. Dept. Labor, 1967. Served with USAFR, 1960-66. Mem. Assn. Data Ctr. Owners and Mgrs. (chmn. privacy com. 1975, sec. 1972-74, v.p. 1974). Democrat. Christian Scientist. Office: 3089 Clairemont Dr Ste 213 San Diego CA 92117-6887

CHILDS, JOHN FARNSWORTH, consultant, retired investment banker; b. N.Y.C., Nov. 24, 1909; s. Albert Ewing and Amelia (McGraw) C.; m. Mary Elizabeth Cardozo, Apr. 21, 1950; 1 dau., Susan Elizabeth. BS, Trinity Coll., Hartford, Conn., 1931, MS, 1932; MBA, Harvard, 1933; LLB, Fordham U., 1946. Bar: N.Y. 1946. Analyst Dick & Merle-Smith, N.Y.C., 1935-40; sr. v.p., head corporate services div. Irving Trust Co., N.Y.C., 1941-74; sr. v.p. Kidder-Peabody Inc., 1974-94, Paine Webber Inc., N.Y.C., 1994-97; mem. tech. adv. com. on fin. Fed. Power Commn., 1973-74; adj. prof. Columbia Grad. Bus. Sch.; cons. in field. Author: Long-Term Financing, 1961, Profit Goals and Capital Management, 1968, Earnings Per Share and Management Decisions, 1971, Encyclopedia of Long Term Financing and Capital Management, 1976, Corporate Finance and Capital Management for the Chief Executive Officer and Directors, 1979; Contbr. articles to profl. publs. Past treas., trustee Lenox Sch.; bd. dirs. N.Y. Council on Econ. Edn.; past bd. dirs. Sch. Book Fair Inc., Fla. Power Corp. Served as lt. comdr. USNR, World War II. Mem. Am. Mgmt. Assn. (pres. coun., past dir.), Atomic-Indsl. Forum (past dir.), N.Y. Soc. Security Analysts, Pine Valley Golf Club (Clementin, N.J.). Home: 15 Washington Pl New York NY 10003-6641

CHILDS, K. ROSS, county administrator, consultant; b. London, Ont., Can., June 17, 1937; s. William Ross and Catherine Evelyn (Donaldson) C.; m. Helen Ann Randle, June 28, 1958; children: Mary Elizabeth, Susan Elizabeth. BS in Indsl. Engring., U. Mich., 1960, post-grad. Civil Engr., Bus. Adminstrn.; post-grad. Pub. Adminstrn., Wayne State U. Engring. asst. Washtenaw County, Mich., 1960; tax engr. Washtenaw County, 1960-68, asst. county adminstr., 1968-69, county adminstr., 1970-73; asst. gen. mgr. for Gen. Svcs. S. Ea. Mich. Transportation Authority, 1973-74, acting gen. mgr., 1974-75, dir. adminstrv. svcs., 1975-76; county adminstr. Grand Traverse County, Mich., 1976—; bd. dirs. First of Am. No. Mich.; mem. fin. com. Mich. Mcpl. Risk Mgmt. Pres. Comty. Living Ctr. Endowment; past pres. Washtenaw County Retirement System; trustee Munson Med. Ctr.; past chmn. Grand Traverse County Hosp. Fin. Authority; sec. Grand Traverse County Econ. Devel. Corp.; bd. dirs. Traverse Bay Econ Devel. Corp. Named Mich. Pub. Servant of Yr., Disting. Citizen Traverse City Area C. of C.; elder Presbyn. Ch., Traverse City. Mem. Nat. Assn. County Administrators (past pres.), Mich. Assn. County Adminstrv. Officers, Internat. City and County Mgmt. Assn., Internat. Pers. Mgrs. Assn., Mich. Pub. Risk Ins. Mgmt. Assn., Rotary Club (past pres. Traverse City chpt., asst. dist. gov. 1997-99). Home: 6355 Franklin Woods Dr Traverse City MI 49686-6121 Office: Grand Traverse County 400 Boardman Ave Traverse City MI 49684-2577

CHILDS, RAND HAMPTON, data processing executive; b. Charlotte, N.C., Oct. 20, 1949; s. Wade Hampton and Francis Marion (Rand) C.; m. Anne Elizabeth Turner, Jan. 4, 1986; children: Ian Peter, Ryan Patrick. BS in Chemistry, Ga. Inst. Tech., 1971, MS in Chemistry, 1977; postgrad., Eidgenossische Technische Hochschule, Zurich, Switzerland, 1971-72. Sys. analyst computing svcs. dept. Ga. Inst. Tech., Atlanta, 1974-80, mgr. data processing computing svcs. dept., 1980-83, assoc. dir. office of computing svcs., 1983-87; v.p. software devel. Sirsi Corp., 1987-94, acting mgr. data conversion dept., 1995-97, v.p. R&D, 1994—; cons. in field. Contbr. articles to profl. jours.; compiler: (with Naugle and Sherry) A Concordance to the Poems of Samuel Johnson. World Student Fund scholar G.a inst. Tech. and Swiss Govt., 1971-72. Mem. AAAS, Am. Chem. Soc., Assn. Computing Machinery, Info. Industry Assn., VIM (6000) (Control Data Corp. User Group), Sigma Xi, Alpha Iota Delta of Chi Psi (Atlanta). Home: 12451 N Shawnee Rd SE Huntsville AL 35803 Office: SIRSI Corp 101 Washington St SE Huntsville AL 35801-4827

CHILDS, RHONDA LOUISE, motivational speaker, consultant; b. Albany, N.Y., Sept. 29, 1946; d. David Cornelius and Rhoda Louise (Rodeniser) Curley; m. Lindsay N. Childs, July 22, 1972; children: Ashley Louise, Nathan Shreeve David Curley, Justin David Curley. BA in Sociology and Anthropology, Cath. Convent Coll., Buffalo, 1966; cert. proficiency exam, McGill U., Montreal, Que., Can., 1968; student, Siena Coll., Loudonville, N.Y., Russell Sage Coll. Adminstrv. asst. Hypersonic Lab., McGill U., 1966-68; adminstrv. asst. dept. comparative religions Sir George Williams U., Montreal, 1966-68; with various cmty. svc. orgns., Europe, Can., Africa, 1968-71; recht. N.Y. State Mental Hygiene Dept., Albany, 1971-72; non-teaching profl. SUNY, Albany, 1973-75; cmty. liaison Collins Bay Penitentiary, Kingston, Ont., Can., 1976-77; ct. monitor Family Ct., 1975-78; pres. Concerned Citizens Against Crossgates, Guilderland, N.Y., 1978-80; adminstrv. asst. St. Catherine's Ctr. for Children, Albany, 1980-85; dir. govt. and cmty. affairs Empire Blue Cross and Blue Shield, Albany, 1985-94; devel. counsel St. Peter's Hosp., Albany, 1994-96; prin. New Visions, A Childs Co., Slingerlands, N.Y.; cons. to numerous nonprofit orgns.; founder, coord. Family Agys. Committed to Svc., 1983-86; founder, pres. Corp. Vol. Coun.; lectr. numerous ednl. and exec. seminars; motivational spkr. in field. Author: My Own Telephone Book, 1988. Bd. dirs. Sr. Svc. Ctrs. Found.; grad. Capital Leadership, 1988-94; past pres. adv. bd. Ret. Sr. Vol. Programs; trustee, pres. St. Anne Inst. Recipient Outstanding Svc. award Family Agys. Committed to Svc., 1985, Community Svc. award Cystic Fibrosis Found., 1988, Tribute to Women award, YWCA, 1991, Franklin D. Roosevelt Vol. award March of Dimes, 1991, June A. Bonneau award Sr. Svc. Ctrs. Albany, Citizen of Yr. award Samaritans, 1994, Golden Rule award, 1994, Lifetime Achievement award Women of Excellence, 1994, Outstanding Svc. award St. Anne Inst., 1994. Mem. APHA, Nat. Soc. Fund Raising Execs., Albany-Colonie Regional C. of C. (numerous coms., guest lect.), Corp. Vol. Couns. Am., NAFE, SUNY Women's Club, Enterprising Women's Leadership Inst., Rotary (pres. Albany chpt., coms. Dist. 7190 Citizen of Yr. award 1990, Airport Citizen of Yr. award 1990, Paul Harris fellow 1990). Democrat. Roman Catholic. Office: New Visions A Childs Co 308 Quidor Ct Slingerlands NY 12159-9554

CHILDS, RICHARD FRANCIS, scientist, educator, retired; b. Battle Creek, MI, Sept. 20, 1918; s. Francis Marion and Mary Florence (Crilly) C.; m. Marion R. Avmitage, 1943 (div., 1953), m. Virginia Helen (Ramsdell), Aug. 2, 1958; children: Allen, Bonnie, Kathleen. BA in chem., Olivet, Olivet, MI, 1937-41; BS, MS, U. Wisconsin, Madison, WI, 1954-55; PhD in pharm., U. Arizona, Tucson, AZ, 1962. Cert. Reg. Pharmacist. Indsl. chemist Clover/Brooks, Milwaukee, WI, 1942-43; radio instr. US Army AF, Sioux Falls, SD, 1943-46; chemist ARMOUR, Chicago, IL, 1948-50; assoc. prof. Coll. Pharm., Tucson, AZ, 1955-75; ret., 1975—, 1975; Dir., Southern AZ Sci. Fair, Tucson, 1957-58. assoc. edit. (edit. Homer B. Titton), Lightworks, Pima Community Coll. East, Tucson, AZ, 1998. Served AAF, CPL, 1943-46. Recipient Sci. Faculty, Natl. Sci. Found., U. Arizona, Purdue, Tchg. Fellowship, Natl. SCi. Found., first PhD offered by Coll. of RX, 1962. Democrat. Avocations: theoretical sci. using inductive logic over many topics. Home: 1067 W Miracle Mile #4 Tucson AZ 85705

CHILDS, SALLY JOHNSTON, elementary and secondary education administrator; b. Dover, Ohio, May 22, 1949; d. George W. and Jayne Johnston; m. James William Childs, June 9, 1978; children: Dylan, Karrin. B in Music Edn., Baldwin-Wallace Coll., 1971; MA, Ohio State U., 1973; EdD, U. Akron, 1991. Cert. music tchr., high sch. prin., asst. supt., supervision, Ohio. Dir. band Van Wert (Ohio) Schs., 1973-77, Crestview Schs., Convoy, Ohio, 1977-83, East Holmes Schs., Berlin, Ohio, 1984-85; dir. chorus Green Local Schs., Smithville, Ohio, 1985-88; dir. choir, band, and orch. Akron (Ohio) Pub. Schs., 1988-97, music coord., 1997—. Mem. ASCD, Music Educators Nat. Conf., Ohio Music Edn. Assn., Midwestern Ednl. Rsch. Assn., Kiwanis, Phi Delta Kappa, Pi Lambda Theta, Mu Phi Epsilon, Delta Kappa Gamma. Home: 3350 Yellow Creek Rd Akron OH 44333-2218

CHILDS, TIMOTHY WINSTON, writer; b. N.Y.C., May 28, 1935; s. Starling Winston Jr. and Cynthia Russell (Cheney) C.; m. Hope Stewart Kane, Oct. 4, 1958; children: Katherine Henley, John Davenport. BA, Yale Coll., 1957; MA, Johns Hopkins U., 1961; Phd in European and Middle Eastern Hist., Georgetown U., 1982. Trainee U.S. Dept. State, Washington, 1961-62, jr. officer, 1962-64, econ. officer, 1965-66; polit. officer, aide to ambassador U.S. Embassy, Tehran, Iran, 1966-68; polit., econ. officer U.S. Dept. State, Washington, 1968-70, polit. officer, 1970-72, deputy examiner, 1972-73, resigned, 1973; freelance writer Washington, 1973—; dir. Am. Near East Refugee Aid, Washington; mem. bd. adv. editors Middle East Jour.; bd. govs. Middle East Inst., 1994—. Author: Italo-Turkish Diplomacy and the War Over Libya, 1911-1912, 1990. Trustee Robert Coll., Istanbul, Turkey, 1980—, Yale Lib. Assocs., 1997—; mem. devel. bd. Yale U., New Haven, 1984-87, 92-95; mem. steering com. Friends Music, Smithsonian Inst., 1994—, chmn. steering com., 1993-94. With US Army, 1957-59. Christian Herter fellow Johns Hopkins U., 1960; recipient Meritorious Honor award U.S. Dept. State, 1966. Mem. Soc. of the Cin. (Va.), Co. Mil Historians, Met. Club (Washington), Chevy Chase Club, Yeaman's Hall Club, Century Assn. Republican. Episcopalian. Avocations: military miniatures & wargaming, classical music, golf. Home: 4101 Cathedral Ave NW Ste 705 Washington DC 20016-3585 also: 300 Westside Rd Norfolk CT 06058-1224

CHILES, LAWTON, III, non-profit organization executive; b. Columbia, S.C., Feb. 24, 1953; v.p. HOPE Worldwide, Phila., 1993—.; s. Lawton M. and Rhea Chiles; m. Katherine Orr, Dec. 20, 1975; children: Lawton, Katie, Geoffrey. BA in Comms., Stanford U.; postgrad., Duke U. Asst. prodr. Sta. WTVJ, Miami, 1975; mktg. dir. Citizens Comml. Bank, Tallahassee, 1977; chmn. bd., pres. Chiles Comms., Tallahassee, 1977-93; founder, nat. dir. HOPE for Kids, N.Y.C., 1993-96, nat. chmn., 1996—. Dep. press sec. Presdl. campaign Senator Edwin Muskie, Washington, Fla., Ohio, 1972; prodr., dir. U.S. Senate campaign, Lawton Chiles II, Fla., 1976, gubernatorial campaign Lawton Chiles II, Fla., 1990; Fla. co-chair presdl. campaign Bill Clinton, Fla., 1990. Recipient Proclamation City of N.Y., 1997, City of Phila., 1997; recipient Health Watch honoree Health Watch, 1997, Cmty. Health award Johnson & Johnson, 1996, Growing Healthy Children Procter & Gamble, 1995. Office: HOPE for Kids 100 Hamilton Plz # 1000 Paterson NJ 07505

CHILES, STEPHEN MICHAEL, lawyer; b. Chillicothe, Ohio, July 15, 1942; s. Daniel Duncan and Helen Virginia (Hayes) C.; m. Deborah E. Nash, June 13, 1964; children: Stephen, Abigail. BA, Davidson Coll., 1964; JD, Duke U., 1967. Bar: N.Y. 1970, Pa. 1978, Wis. 1981, U.S. Supreme Ct. 1978, U.S. Ct. Appeals (3d cir.) 1978, U.S. Dist. Ct. (ea. dist.) Pa. 1978, U.S. Tax Ct. 1978, Ill. 1986. Officer trust dept. Irving Trust Co., N.Y.C., 1970-75, v.p., 1975-77; assoc. atty. Stassen Kostos & Mason, Phila., 1978-79, mem., shareholder, 1979-85; ptnr. McDermott, Will & Emery, Chgo., 1986—. Contbr. articles to profl. jours. Served to capt. U.S. Army, 1967-69. Decorated Bronze Star, Army Commendation medal. Mem. ABA, State Bar Wis., Exmoor Country Club (Highland Park, Ill.). Republican. Episcopalian. Office: McDermott Will & Emery 227 W Monroe St Ste 3100 Chicago IL 60606-5096

CHILIVIS, NICKOLAS PETER, lawyer; b. Athens, Ga., Jan. 12, 1931; s. Peter Nickolas and Wessie Mae (Tanner) C.; m. Patricia Kay Tumlin, June 3, 1967; children—Taryn Tumlin, Nicole Tumlin, Nickolas Peter Tumlin. LL.B., U. Ga., Athens, 1953; LL.M., Atlanta Law Sch., Ga., 1955. Bar: Ga. 1952, U.S. Supreme Ct. 1965. Ptnr. Lester & Chilivis, Athens, Ga., 1953-58; ptnr. Erwin, Epting, Gibson & Chilivis, Athens, Ga., 1958-75; commr. of revenue State of Ga., Atlanta, 1975-77; ptnr. Powell, Goldstein, Frazer & Murphy, Atlanta, 1977-84, Chilivis & Grindler, Atlanta, 1984-95, Chilivis, Cochran, Larkins & Bever, Atlanta, 1995—; adj. prof. U. Ga. Sch. Law, Athens, 1965-75. Author: Termination Settlement, 1955. Contbr. chpts. to books, articles to profl. jours. Bd. visitors U. Ga., Athens, 1983-85; trustee Skandalakis Found., Atlanta, 1984, Found. of the Holy Apostles; former trustee U. Ga. Found.; former mem. U. Ga. Rsch. Found. Bd.; pres. and sr. warden Ch. of Apostles. With USAFR, 1953-55. Recipient Archdiocesan medal Archbishop of North and South Am., 1980. Fellow Am. Coll. Trial Lawyers, Am. Acad. Appellate Lawyers; mem. Am. Inns. of Ct. (emeritus, master), Old War Horse Lawyers Club, Lawyers Club Atlanta, Commerce Club, Heritage Club, (Atlanta), Pres.'s Club (U. Ga.), Elks. Avocations: Handball; tennis; writing; lecturing. Home: 855 W Paces Ferry Rd NW Atlanta GA 30327-2655 Office: Chilivis Cochran Larkins & Bever Chilivis Bldg 3127 Maple Dr NE Atlanta GA 30305-2503

CHILLIDA, EDUARDO, sculptor; b. Donostia, Basque Country, Jan. 10; s. Pedro Chillida and Carmen Juantegui Eguren; m. Pilar Belzunce, 1950. Student arch., U. Madrid, 1943-46; degree in arch. (hon.), High Coun. Arch.'s Assn., Spain, 1989; Dr. Honoris Causa, U. Alicante, Spain, 1996. vis. prof. Harvard U., 1971. One-man shows include Clan Gallery, Madrid, 1954, Galerie Maeght, Paris, 1956, 64, McRoberts and Tunnard Gallery, London, 1965, Galeria Iolas Velasco, madrid, 1977, Carpenter Ctr. Visual Arts, Harvard U., Boston, 1977, Nat. Gallery, Washington, Mus. Art, Carnegie Inst., Pitts., 1979, Min. Culture Palacio Cristal, Parque Retiro, Madrid, 1980, Mus. Fine Art, Bilbao, Basque Country, 1981, Hayward Gallery, London, 1990, Tasende Gallery, L.A., 1997; group shows include Mus. Fine Arts, Houston, 1961, Galerie Art Moderne, Basel, Switzerland, 1974, Hastings Gallery Spanish Inst., N.Y.C., 1974, Solomon R. Guggenheim Mus., N.Y.C., 1980, Galerie Beyeler, Basel, 1982, Galerie Herbert MeyerEllinger, Frankfurt, Germany, 1983, Mary-Anne Martin/Fine Art, N.Y.C., 1984, Tasende Gallery, La Jolla, Calif., 1985; represented in permanent collections Kuntmuseaum, Basel, Nationalgalerie, Berlin, Museo Bellas Artes, Bilbao, Art Inst. Chgo., Museo Art, Cuenca, Spain, Mus. Fine Art, Houston, La Jolla Mus. Contemporary Art, Tate Gallery, London, Museo Espanol Arte Contemporaneo, Madrid, Museo Rufino Tamayo, Mexico City, Solomon R. Guggenheim Mus., N.Y.C., Mus. Art, Carnegie Inst., Pitts., Collezione Arte Contemporanea, Musei Vaticani, Rome, Galleria Nazionale Arte Moderna, Rome, Hirshorn Mus., Washington; illustrator Le Chernin des Devins, 1965, Meditation in Kastilien, 1968, Die Kunst und der Raum, 1969, Más Allá, 1973, Voz Acorde: Homenaje a Jorge Guillén, 1982, Ce Maudit Moi, 1983. Recipient Graham Found. prize, 1958, Kandinsky prize, 1960, Wilhelm-Lehmbruck prize, 1966, Nordrhein-Westfalen prize, 1966, Wellington prize, 1970, Critica Arte prize, 1971, Encomienda Ciudad, 1971, Engraving prize Internat. Exhbn. Rijeka, Yugoslavia, 1972, Internat. Biennale Ljubljana, Yugoslavia, 1973, La Taula award Josep Lluis Sert, 1973, Premio Internat. Diano Marino award, 1974, Rembrandt prize, Goethe Found., 1975, First prize Japanese Ministry Fgn. Affairs, 1976, Peace and Truce prize Victor Seix Inst. Polemics, 1978, Gold Merit medal Mus. Fine Art Madrid, 1981, European Fine Arts prize City of Strasbourg, 1983, Gold medal U. Basque Country, 1984, Grand Nat. prize Arts for Sculpture, French Govt., 1984, Internat. Wolf Found. prize, 1985, Imperial Ring, City of Goslar, 1985, Revista Euzkadi prize, 1986, Prince Asturias award, 1987, Lorenzo-il Magnifico prize, 1987, Order Sci. and Art, Fed. German Govt., 1988, Imperial prize Japan Art Assn., 1991, Fundacion Sabino Arana prize, 1992, Gold medal City of Donostia, 1992, Assn. Española Critica Arte, 1995, Cross, Portuguese Order Merit Mario Soares, 1995, Freedom prize, 1995; co-recipient Andrew W. Mellon prize, 1978, Ildefonso Cerda medal Engrs. Coll. Cataluna, 1990. Fellow Hispanic Soc. Am. (hon.); mem. AAAS, Royal Acad. Arts London, Hispanic Soc. N.Y. (hon.), REal Academia Bellas Arts (hon.). Office: Tasende Gallery 8808 Melrose Ave West Hollywood CA 90069

CHILMAN, CATHERINE EARLES STREET, social welfare educator, author; b. Cleve., Sept. 20, 1914; d. Elwood Vickers and Augusta (Jewitt) Street; m. C. William Chilman, Sept. 27, 1936 (dec. 1977); children: Margaret Chilman Carpenter, Jeanne Chilman Klovdahl, Catherine Chilman Brown. AB, Oberlin Coll., 1935; MA, U. Chgo., 1938; PhD, U. Syracuse, 1958. Caseworker United Charities Chgo., 1937-39, Family Svcs., Roanoke, Va., 1939-40; psychiat. cons. ARC, Syracuse, N.Y., 1943-44; tchr. dept. child devel., family rels. Syracuse U., 1947-49, instr., 1949-57, asst. prof., 1957-61; sr. social worker N.Y. State Mental Health Rsch. Unit, Syracuse, 1955-57; parent edn. specialist Children's Bur. HEW, Washington, 1961-64; rsch. adminstr. U.S. Welfare Adminstrn., 1964-69; dean faculty Hood Coll., Frederick, Md., 1969-71; curriculum dir. Internat. Population Planning and Social Work Edn. Project, U. Mich., Ann Arbor, 1971-72; prof. Sch. Social Welfare, U. Wis., Milw., 1972-86; prof. emerita Sch. Social Welfare, U. Wis., 1986—; pres. Nat. Groves Conf. on the Family, 1975-78; speaker, cons. on rsch., family life, pub. policy to univs., fed. govt. and profl. orgns. Author: Your Child: 6 to 12, 1966, Moving into Adolescence, 1966, Growing Up Poor, 1967, Adolescent Sexuality in a Changing American Society, 1983, Families in Trouble, 5 vols., 1988, (with others) Mental Health Crisis and the Nation's Children, 1972, Programs and Policies of National Family Organizations, 1997; mem. editl. bd. Jour. Marriage and Family, 1963-69; contb. articles to profl. jours., chpts. to books. U.S. Office Edn. grantee, 1960-62; Wis. State grantee, 1973-75; Nat. Inst. Child Devel. grantee, 1976-77; recipient Hon. Alumni award Sch. Social Svcs. Adminstrn., U. Chgo., 1978, Honored Scholar award Groves Conf. Marriage and the Family, 1989. Fellow APA; mem. Nat. Coun. on Family Rels. (bd. dirs. 1991-93, sec. 1992-93), Groves Conf. on Marriage and Family (hon. life, bd. dirs., nat. workshop dir. 1992). Home: 1435 4th St SW Washington DC 20024-2200 *Although I have experienced many tragedies and hardships and have lived through tumultuous times, I am continuously surprised and grateful for the many blessings of my life: dear friends and family, the excitement of teaching and research, the marvels of aesthetic creations, and the beauty and wonder of our natural world and most recently, living and writing in our beleaguered but stimulating national capital.*

CHILOW, BARBARA GAIL, social worker; b. Grand Forks, N.D., June 7, 1936; d. Alfred Thomas and Florence (Micken) Seeley; m. Steven Chilow, Aug. 15, 1987; children: John Mark Doss, Timothy Stephen Doss, Elizabeth De La Cruz, David Chilow. BS, UCLA, 1957; MSW, U. So. Calif., 1970; MPA, Calif. State U., Long Beach, 1985. Lic. social worker, Calif., Utah, marriage, family and child counselor, Calif. Social worker Dept. Pub. Welfare, San Diego, 1957, Dep. Pub. Assistance, Whitman, Mass., 1966-68; psychiat. social worker State of Calif., Pomona, 1971-73; clin. social worker Orange County Dept. Mental Health, Santa Ana, Calif., 1973-74, sr. clin. social worker, 1974-79; dep. dir. mental health Orange County Human Svcs. Agy., Santa Ana, 1979-80, dep. regional mgr., 1980-82, adminstrv. mgr. II, 1982-93; clin. coord. Brightway at St. George, Utah, 1993—; pvt. practice clin. social worker Newport Beach, Calif., 1977-93; chmn. So. Calif. Case Mgmt. Coun., 1987-89, Orange County Bd. and Care Quality Com., Santa Ana, 1984-89; owner, mgr. Desert Hills Therapeutic Svcs., Inc., St. George, 1998—. Pres. Winchester Hills Homeowners Assn., St. George, 1995-97; bd. dirs. Southwestern Spl. Svc. Dist., 1997—, Leadership Dixie, 1998—; trustee Music Hall Found. Mem. NASW, AAUW, DAR (Boston Tea Party chpt.), Alliance for Mentally Ill (pres. Orange County chpt. 1994-95), Phi Alpha Alpha, Gamma Phi Beta. Democrat. Presbyterian. Avocations: hiking, piano, reading, travel. Home: 1110 W 5830 N Saint George UT 84770-5944 Office: Brightway at St George 115 W 1470 S Saint George UT 84770-6763 also: Desert Hills Therapeutic Svcs Troon Park Plz 1240 E 100 S Ste 18B Saint George UT 84790

CHILSTROM, ROBERT MEADE, lawyer; b. San Diego, July 1, 1945; s. Arne Oswald and Margaret Myra (Kippax) C.; m. Buena Lelia Hamlin, Aug. 24, 1968; children: Per Benjamin, Mikaela Lynn. BA, Princeton U., 1967; MA, Columbia U., 1969; JD, Yale U., 1973. Bar: N.Y. State 1975, U.S. Dist. Ct. (so. dist., ea. dist.) N.Y. 1975, U.S. Ct. Appeals (2d cir.) 1975. Assoc. Cravath, Swaine & Moore, N.Y.C., Paris, London, 1973-85; assoc. Skadden, Arps, Slate, Meagher & Flom LLP, N.Y.C., 1985-87, ptnr., 1987—. Office: Skadden Arps Slate Meagher & Flom LLP 919 3rd Ave New York NY 10022-3902

CHILTON, ALICE PLEASANCE HUNTER (MRS. ST. JOHN POINDEXTER CHILTON), former state official, vocational counselor; b. Boyce, La., Apr. 16, 1911; d. Albert Eugene and Maggie (Texada) Hunter; BA, La. Coll., 1930; MS, La. State U., 1934, PhD, 1982, Guidance Counselor certificate, 1954; m. St. John Poindexter Chilton, Mar. 2, 1935. Tchr. secondary sch., Glenmora, La., 1931-35; with La. Div. Employment Security and USES, Baton Rouge, 1937-74, employment interviewer and supr., 1937-43, personnel officer, 1943-46, ops. analyst, 1946-55, supr. counseling and tech. svcs., 1955-74. Mem. curriculum study com. East Baton Rouge, Parish Sch. Bd., 1968; rec. sec. Quota Internat., Baton Rouge, 1961-62, 2d v.p., 1963-64. Bd. dirs. YWCO. Recipient certificate of merit La. Acad. Sci., 1960. Mem. Nat. Trust Historic Preservation, La. Geneal. and Hist. Soc. (pres. 1957), La. Landmarks Soc., Found. for Hist. La., Kent Plantation House, Inc. (sec.1979-81), Preservation Resource Ctr., La. Preservation Alliance (dir. 1984-86), Hist. Assn. of Cen. La. (bd. dirs. 1980-86, 89—), Alexandria Hist. and Geneal. Library and Mus. (bd. dirs. 1980-89), Ctrl. La. Geneal. Soc., DAR, Phi Kappa Phi. Methodist. Address: 431 Belgard Bnd Boyce LA 71409-9238

CHILTON, BRADLEY STEWART, law educator; b. Rockford, Ill., Oct. 28, 1955; s. Ermal Rural and Maybelle Rose (McNair) C.; m. Lisa Marie Hartmann, May 21, 1977. BA, Milton Coll., 1977; JD, U. Toledo, Ohio, 1980, MA, 1981; MA, U. Wis., 1982; PhD, U. Ga., 1988; MLS, U. So. Miss., 1989. Instr. S.E. Mo. State U., Cape Girardeau, 1985-86; asst. prof. U. So. Miss., Hattiesburg, 1986-89, Wash. State U., Pullman, 1989-93; assoc. prof. U. Toledo, 1993—, pre-law advisor, 1993—, dir. criminal justice program, 1993-97; pre-law advisor U. Toledo, 1993—. Author: Prisons Under the Gavel, 1991. Mem. Acad. Criminal Justice Scis., Am. Judicature Soc., Am. Polit. Sci. Assn. Congregationalist. Avocations: music, home design and building, religion. Office: U Toledo Dept Polit Sci Pub Adminstr Toledo OH 43606-3390

CHILTON, ELIZABETH EASLEY EARLY, newspaper executive; b. Williamson, W.Va., Dec. 9, 1928; d. Carl Brooks and Susie Mason (Easley) Early; m. William Edwin Chilton III, Apr. 5, 1952 (dec. Feb. 1987); 1 child, Susan Carroll Chilton Shumate. Student, Hollins Coll., Va., 1946-48; AA in Primary Edn., Marjorie Webster Coll., Washington, 1950. Pub. rels. staff The Charleston (W.Va.) Gazette, 1952-87; v.p., treas. Daily Gazette Co., Charleston, 1987-91, pres., 1991—, also dir., 1994—, also bd. dirs.; mgmt. com. The Charleston Newspapers, 1991—; adv. bd. Eberly Coll. Arts and Scis., 1996—. Editl. bd. The Charleston Gazette, 1987—. Chmn. W.Va. Gov.'s Mansion Preservation Found., Charleston, 1989—; bd. trustees U. Charleston, 1989-98, Marshall U.-Yeager Scholars, Huntington, W.Va., 1990-96, W.Va. State Coll. Found., Inst., 1988-96, WSWP-TV Pub. Broadcasting, 1980-94, Faculty Merit Scholars, 1991—, W.Va. Humanities Coun., 1994—; bd. dirs. BIDCO, 1996-98, Advantage Valley, Charleston, 1996-98, Greater Kanawha Valley Found., 1980-86, adv. bd., 1986—; bd. dirs. Childrens Express, 1987—, Charleston Renaissance, 1995—, Washington, 1997—, Gunston Hall Plantation, 1977-92, pres., 1989-92; bd. dirs., exec. com. Worth Bingham Prize Found., 1987—; bd. dirs. Nat. Youth Sci. Camp Found., 1998. Recipient John Marshall Medal for Civic Responsibility Marshall U., 1997. Mem. So. Newspaper Pubs. (journalism edn. com. 1992-94, minority affairs com. 1994—), Nat. Soc. of Colonial Dames of W.Va. (pres.), Internat. Press Inst. (dir. Am. com. 1994—), Newspaper Assn. Am. (com. mem. 1987—), Nat. Trust for Historic Preservation, Garden Club of Am. (chmn. libr., bd. dirs. 1989-92), Jr. League of Charleston, Edgewood Country Club of Charleston, Yale Club of N.Y.C., Sulgrave Club of Washington, Briar Hills Garden Club, Kanawha Garden Club, Sea Pines Country Club of Hilton Head. Democrat. Presbyterian. Avocations: travel, reading, golf, gardening. Home: 806 Cedar Rd Charleston WV 25314 Office: The Charleston Gazette 1001 Virginia St E Charleston WV 25301-2895

CHILTON, HORACE THOMAS, pipeline company executive; b. San Antonio, June 18, 1923; s. Horace Thomas and Lear Isabel (Word) C.; m. Betty Jane Gray, Oct. 18, 1947; children: Thomas G., William D. B.S. in Mech. Engring., U. Tex., 1947, B.A. in Bus. Adminstrn., 1947; grad., Advanced Mgmt. Program, Harvard U., 1958. Engr. Stanolind Pipe Line Co., Tulsa, 1947; div. chief engr. Service Pipe Line Co., Lubbock, 1950-52; supt. maintenance and constrn. Service Pipe Line Co., 1956-60, asst. gen. mgr., 1960; mil. pipe line cons. U.S. Govt., Paris, 1955; mgr. products pipelines, lake tankers and barges Amoco Oil Co., Chgo., 1963-68; mgr. transp. ops., v.p. Amoco Pipeline, 1969-71, gen. mgr. transp., pres., chief exec. officer, 1971-74; pres., chief exec. officer Colonial Pipeline, Atlanta, 1974-88; retired, 1988. Mem. U. Tex. Engring. Advisory Found. Bd., 1977-85. Served with USN, 1944-46. Mem. Assn. Oil Pipe Lines (chmn. 1983-84), Am. Petroleum Inst. (bd. dirs. 1975-88), Nat. Petroleum Coun., Beta Theta Pi. Presbyterian. Club: Cherokee Town and Country (Atlanta). Home: 8920 River Landing Way Atlanta GA 30350-1620

CHILTON, ST. JOHN POINDEXTER, retired plant pathology educator, farm owner; b. Phila., Feb. 3, 1909; s. St. John P. and Helen Frances (McGloin) C.; m. Alice Pleasance Hunter, Mar. 2, 1935. B.S., La. State U., 1935, M.S., 1936; Ph.D., U. Minn., 1938. Agt. plant pathology U.S. Dept. Agr., 1938-40; faculty La. State U., 1940—, prof., 1948—, chmn. dept. botany and plant pathology, 1950-70; plant pathologist, head dept. plant pathology La. Agr. Expt. Sta., 1950-76; rep. div. biology and agr. NRC, 1952-57; pres., dir. LaPlace Enterprises, Inc., 1961-89; pres., mgr. Esperanza Farms, 1974-83; cons. Nicaraque Sugar Estates, Ingenio San Antonio, 1964-86. Fellow AAAS; mem. Am. Phytopath. Soc. (ex-counselor), Internat. Soc. Sugarcane Technologists (vice chmn. 10th congress), Am. Soc. Sugarcane Technologists (past pres.), SAR (past pres. Phil Thomas chpt.), La. Acad. Sci. (past pres.), La. Geneal. and Hist. Soc. (pres. 1972-76), Hist. Assn. Central La. (pres. 1980-82), Am. Sugarcane League U.S. (life). Club: Rotarian. Home: 431 Belgard Bnd Boyce LA 71409-9238

CHILTON, WILLIAM DAVID, architect; b. Tulsa, Jan. 4, 1954; s. Horace Thomas Jr. and Betty Jane (Gray) C.; m. Laura Ann Johnson, Aug. 22, 1981. BA in Architecture, Iowa State U., 1976; MArch, U. Minn., 1980. Registered architect, Minn., Conn. Designer CDG, Tulsa, 1976; assoc. architect Olson & Coffey Architects, Tulsa, 1977-78, Leonard Parker Assocs., Mpls., 1980-81; sr. architect Conoco, Inc., Ponca City, Okla., 1981-89; v.p., project mgr. Ellerbe Becket, Inc., Mpls., 1989, v.p., sr. project mgr., 1990, v.p., project dir., 1991-93, sr. v.p., project dir., 1994-97; dir. The Ellerbe Becket Co., Mpls., 1995-99, pres. arch., mng. prin., 1997-99, mem. mgmt. com., 1997-99; ptnr. Pickard Chilton, New Haven, 1999—; bd. dirs. Rainier Tech., Mpls.; mem. architecture adv. coun. Iowa State U., 1994-99, chair, 1997-98. Prin. works include Milne Point (Alaska) Ops. Complex (award Best of Engring. News Record 1986, Excellence in Architecture award North Ctrl. Okla. chpt. AIA 1987, Honorable Mention Builder mag. 1985), Conoco Corp. Offices, Wilmington, Del. (Excellence in Architecture award North Ctrl. Okla. chpt. AIA 1987), Conoco Office/Housing Facilities, Luanda, Angola, 1985-88, Dow Chem. Corp. Hdqrs. Master Plan, Midland, Mich., 1992, Dow Chem. Global Data Ctr., 1992, Sci. Mus. Minn., St. Paul, 1991-99, Kingdom Centre, Riyadh, Saudi Arabia, 1996—, CalPERS Hdqrs., Sacramento, 1999—, Crawford Long Hosp., Atlanta, 1999—. Bd. dirs. Children's HeartLink, Mpls., 1997-99. Recipient Design Achievement award Iowa State U., 1995. Mem. Minn. Soc. AIA (sec. North Ctrl. Okla. chpt. 1986, v.p. 1987, pres. 1988, bd. dirs. 1986-88, bd. dirs. Okla. Coun. 1987-88), Leadership Mpls., Inst. Dirs. (London), Interlachen Country Club (Edina, Minn.), Mpls. Club. Lutheran. Avocations: fly fishing, golf, reading, music. Home: 452 East River Rd Guilford CT 06437 Office: Pickard Chilton 129 Church St Ste 615 New Haven CT 06510-2014

CHILVERS, DEREK, insurance company executive; b. Torquay, Eng., Feb. 7, 1940; came to U.S., 1962; s. Reginald Charles and Selina Adelaide (Adamson) C.; m. Elizabeth Anne Locke, Aug. 25, 1968 (div. 1983); m. Cheryl Baker, Apr. 14, 1984; children: Justine, Derek Jr. BA, Cambridge U., 1962, MA, 1962. With John Hancock Mut. Life Ins. Co., Boston, 1962—, v.p. internat., 1980-85, sr. v.p. internat., 1985—; bd. dirs. John Hancock Life Ins. (Malaysia) Berhad, Kuala Lumpur, Malaysia, John Hancock Life Assurance Co. Ltd., Singapore, Interlife John Hancock Assurance Pub. Co. Ltd., Bangkok; pres., CEO John Hancock Internat. Holdings Inc., Boston; chmn. bd. John Hancock Internat. Svcs., S.A., Brussels, John Hancock Internat. Svcs. Pte., Ltd., Singapore, John Hancock Life Ins. Corp., Philippines: vice chmn. bd. P.T. Assuransi Jiwa Bumiputera John Hancock, Jakarta. Office: John Hancock Mut Life Ins Co PO Box 111 Boston MA 02117-0111*

CHILVERS, ROBERT MERRITT, lawyer; b. Long Beach, Calif., Oct. 23, 1942; s. James Merritt and Elizabeth Louise (Blackburn) C.; m. Sandra Lee Rigg, Sept. 5, 1969; children: Jeremy Merritt, Jessica Rigg. AB, U. Calif., Berkeley, 1972; JD, Harvard U., 1975. Bar: Calif. 1975, U.S. Dist. Ct. (no. dist.) Calif. 1975, U.S. Ct. Appeals (9th cir.) 1980, U.S. Supreme Ct. 1980, U.S. Dist. Ct. (ctrl. dist.) Calif. 1981, U.S. Ct. Fed. Claims, 1984, U.S. Dist. Ct. (ea. dist.) Calif. 1987, U.S. Ct. Appeals (fed. cir.) 1987. Assoc. Brobeck, Phleger & Harrison, San Francisco, 1975-82, ptnr., 1982-93; spl. master U.S. Dist. Ct. (no. dist.) Calif., 1994—; shareholder Chilvers & Taylor, P.C., 1996—; faculty U. Calif., Hastings Sch. Law, San Francisco, 1983-89, Emory U., Atlanta, 1984-90, fed. practice program U.S. Dist. Ct. (no. dist.) Calif., 1984-86, Nat. Inst. for Trial Advocacy, 1986—, Cardozo Law Sch., Yeshiva U., N.Y.C., 1993—, Stanford U. Law Sch., 1994—, Widener U. Sch. Law, Wilmington, 1994-96, U. San Francisco Sch. Law, 1994—. Mem. Calif. Sch. Bds. Assn, 1985-89; trustee Mill Valley Sch. Dist., Calif., 1985-89, chmn., 1987-89; bd. dirs. Marin County Sch. Bds. Assn., Calif., 1985-86. With USMC, 1964-71. Mem. Calif. Bar Assn. (commendation for Outstanding Contbns. to the delivery of vol. legal svcs. 1984), Marin County Bar Assn., Tau Beta Pi, Sigma Tau. Office: Chilvers & Taylor PC 5801 Christie Ave Ste 590 Emeryville CA 94608-1938

CHIMOSKEY, JOHN EDWARD, physiologist, medical educator; b. Traverse City, Mich., Apr. 15, 1937; s. Edward John and Jane Marie (Langworthy) C.; m. Dianne Marie Dailey, June 1962 (div. 1973); children: Stefan John, David Clifford. Student, U. N.Mex., 1955-56, Cen. Mich. U., 1956-58; MD, U. Mich., 1963. Rsch. fellow in physiology U. Mich., Ann Arbor, 1959-63; intern dept. medicine U. Calif., San Francisco, 1963-64; rsch. fellow in physiology Harvard Med. Sch., Boston, 1964-66; rsch. fellow in muscle rsch. Retina Found., Boston, 1966-67; assoc. prof. in physiology Hahnemann U., Phila., 1969-70; resident, rsch. fellow in dermatology Stanford U., Palo Alto, Calif., 1970-71; asst. prof. in bioengring. U. Wash., Seattle, 1971-74; assoc. prof. in physiology and surgery Baylor Med. Coll., Houston, 1974-78; prof. Mich. State U., East Lansing, 1978-99, chmn. dept. physiology, 1989-93, prof. emeritus, 1999—; guest scientist U.S. Naval Air Devel. Ctr., Johnsville, Pa., 1969-70; adj. assoc. prof. in bioengring. Rice U., Houston, 1974-78; dir. Taub Labs. for Mech. Circulatory Support, 1974-78; physiology cons. Stedman's Med. Dictionary, 1990-97; dir. grad. program Mich. State U., East Lansing, 1986-90, dir. cardiovascular tng. program, 1982-94; del. U.S.-USSR cooperation in artificial heart devel., 1976-77. Contbr. articles to profl. jours. Lt. comdr. USNR, 1967-69. Fulbright fellow, Brazil, 1990. Mem. Am. Physiol. Soc., Kauai (Hawaii) Hist. Soc., Victor Vaughn Soc., Alpha Omega Alpha. Home: 316A Makani Road Kapaa HI 96746-1249

CHIMPLES, GEORGE, lawyer; b. Canton, Ohio, Oct. 8, 1924; s. Mark and Katherine (Hines) C.; m. Margaret Joanna Cavalaris, July 31, 1949; children: Alicia Candace, Mark II, John Hines, Katherine Hines. AB, Princeton U., 1951; LLB, Harvard Coll., 1954. Bar: Pa. 1955, U.S. Dist. Ct. (ea. dist.) Pa. 1955, U.S. Ct. Appeals (3d cir.) 1955, U.S. Ct. Claims, 1965, U.S. Tax Ct., 1965. Assoc. Stradley, Ronon, Stevens & Young, Phila., 1954-61, gen. ptnr., 1961-92; pvt. practice Wayne, Pa., 1993—; adj. prof. law U. Pa., Drexel U. Grad. Sch. Bus.; co-authored establishment of overseas infrastructure for securities mktg. in Europe and the Antilles. Trustee Christ Ch. Preservation Trust; permament assoc. Phila. Mus. Art. Capt. USAAF, 1942-46, ETO. Decorated D.F.C., Air medal with four oak leaf clusters, Air Force Commendation medal, Victory medal, four Battle Stars; recipient Royal Air Force plaque, 1994. Mem. ABA (chmn. subcom. regulated investment cos.), Phila. Bar Assn. (tax sect.), Internat. Bar Assn., Internat. Fiscal Assn. (tax treaty sect.), Mid-Atlantic Coun., Commanderie de Bordeaux aux Etats-Unis d'Amerique (archivist), Newcomen Soc. U.S. (com. chmn., nat. trustee, life mem.) Army and Navy Club (Washington chpt.), Penn Club (life, bd. dirs., historian) Athenaeum of Phila. (life), Libr. Co. of Phila. (life), Phila. Mus. Art (permanent assoc.), Phila. Club, Princeton Club N.Y., Cannon Club (Princeton chpt.), Merion Cricket Club. Home: 1179 Lafayette Rd Wayne PA 19087-2110 Office: 1522 Overington St Philadelphia PA 19124-5808

CHIMSKY, MARK EVAN, publishing consultant; b. Cin., Jan. 24, 1955; s. Matthew and Jean (Berger) C.; life ptnr. Robert Ira Lustig. BA, Carnegie-Mellon U., 1976. Editor Anderson Pub. Co., Cin., 1977-79; copy editor Book-of-the-Month Club, Quality Paperback Book Club, N.Y.C., 1979-85; mng. editor Quality Paperback Book Club, N.Y.C., 1985-89, exec. editor, 1989-91; editor in chief Collier Books Macmillan Co., N.Y.C., 1991-94; dir. trade paperbacks Little, Brown and Co., N.Y.C., 1994-96; from exec. editor to editl. dir. Harper, San Francisco, 1996-98, exec. editor, 1998-99; editl. cons. Mark Chimsky Editl. Plus, Riverdale, N.Y., 1999—; adj. instr. NYU, N.Y.C., 1999—. Contbr. essays and poetry to lit. jours. Recipient New-Emerging Poet/Anna Davidson Rosenberg award, 1997. Office: Mark Chimsky Editorial Plus PO Box 630207 Riverdale NY 10463

CHIN, ALBERT KAE, research physician; b. Spokane, Wash., May 5, 1953; s. Ting H. and Beatrice Y. (Lui) C.; m. Jeanne Yee, Aug. 6, 1977; children: Jennifer, Lisa, Stephanie. BSME, MIT, 1975; MSME, Stanford U., 1976; MD, U. Calif., San Francisco, 1983. Resident in gen. surgery U. Tex. Southwestern, Dallas, 1983-85; dir. rsch. Fogarty Rsch., Portola Valley, Calif., 1985-89; founder, v.p. rsch. Origin Medsystems, Inc., Menlo Park, Calif., 1989—; cardiovascular cons. Baxter Edwards LIS Divsn., Irvine, Calif., 1988; expert witness Advanced Cardiovascular Systems, Santa Clara, Calif., 1989. Contbr. articles to profl. publs.; holder more than 90 patents in field. Bd. dirs. YMCA, Palo Alto, Calif., 1987-89. Mem. AMA, Soc. of Laparoendoscopic Surgeons, Internat. Soc. Endovascular Surgery, FF Fraternity (chmn. San Francisco lodge 1986). Avocations: piano, violin, organ, guitar, weightlifting. Home: 2021 Newell Rd Palo Alto CA 94303-3424 Office: Origin Medsystems Inc 135 Constitution Dr Menlo Park CA 94025-1118

CHIN, ALLEN E., SR., athletic administrator, educator; b. Arlington, Va., Oct. 21, 1950; s. Tung Ock and Hai Ock (Moy) C.; children: Allen Jr., Denise Maria Michelle. BA, George Washington U., 1972, MA, 1974, EdD, 1980. Cert. secondary social studies educator, D.C. Tchr. D.C. Pub. Schs., Washington, 1972-87, 88-91, dir. athletics, 1987-88, 91—; exec. cons. D.C. Coaches Assn., Inc., Washington, 1988—; exec. dir. AEC-10 Found., Inc., Washington, 1988—. Mem. Jefferson Club, Richmond, Va., 1990-91, Dem. Nat. Com., Washington, 1984—, Dem. Senatorial Campaign Com., Washington, 1984—. Recipient Coach of Yr. award 1986, 87, 88, Athletic Dir. of Yr., 1974, Golf Coach of Yr., 1975, Athletic Dir. of Yr. NHSACA Region 2, 1995-98. Mem. D.C. Coaches Assn., D.C. Coun. for Social Studies, Nat. Geog. Soc., Met. Police Boys & Girls Clubs, Nat. Coun. for Social Studies, Nat. Interscholastic Athletic Adminstrs. Assn., Am. Soc. Notaries. Democrat. Avocations: stamp and coin collecting, golf. Home: 6150 Windward Dr Burke VA 22015-3832 Office: Truesdell Elem Sch 800 Ingraham St NW Washington DC 20011-2925

CHIN, CAROLYN SUE, business executive; b. Washington, Nov. 28, 1947; d. Tin Wah and Donna Grace (Ho) C.; m. Gerald Bingham Sweeney, Sept. 18, 1976; 1 child, Patricia Chin-Sweeney. B.S. in Mgmt. Engring, Rensselaer Poly. Inst., 1969; M.B.A., Harvard U., 1971. Buyer R.H. Macy's, N.Y.C., 1971-74; buyer to merchandise adminstr. R.H. Macy's, 1971-74, 74-75; mktg. mgr. AT&T, Morristown, N.J., 1976-78; spl. asst. to sec. HUD, Washington, 1978-79; asst. to sec. and exec. sec. HEW, 1979-80; mgr. strategic planning AT&T, Basking Ridge, N.J., 1980-82; mgr. CIS consumer products Am. Bell, Parsipanny, N.J., 1983; v.p. bus. devel. Citicorp/Citibank, N.Y.C., 1983-86; sr. v.p. Citicorp Retail Services, N.Y.C., 1986—; v.p. strategic planning and bus. devel. Citicorp Quotron, N.Y. and L.A., 1989-91; v.p. pvt. banking Citibank, N.Y.C., 1991-94; dir. strategic devel. IBM, Armonk, N.Y., 1994; gen. mgr. electronic commerce svcs. IBM, Thornwood, N.Y., 1994-95; v.p. corp. strategy IBM, Armonk, N.Y., 1995-98; exec. v.p. mktg. Reuters Am., N.Y.C., 1998-99; CEO The Chin Co., West Orange, N.J., 1999—; Boston Model Cities, 1971, N.Y. State Emergency Fin. Control Bd., 1975; chmn. Task Force on Asian Women Bus. Owners, 1978; mem. South Orange Econ. Devel. Com., 1978; del. bilateral talks U.S.-China, 1987, 92, Dartmouth Conf. on U.S.-USSR, 1988; owner, operator The Island Guest House, Beach Haven, N.J., 1991-95; workshop chair OECD World Forum on Women Entrepreneurs, 1997. Mem. exec. bd. Pacific Asian Coalition, 1978; sec. bd. dirs., exec. com. Albert Einstein Peace Prize Found., Chgo., 1979-90; bd. dirs. Ind. Sector, Washington, 1980-86, Rensselaer Coun., 1982—, White House Fellows Found., 1983-88, N.Y.C. Outward Bound, 1987—, Fund for City of N.Y., 1988-97; participant Renaissance Weekend, 1994—; trustee Com. for Econ. Devel., 1995-; adv. bd. Rensselaer Sch. Humanities and Social Scis., 1996—; trustee James Redford Inst. for Transplant Awareness, 1997—, Children's Orch. Soc., 1997—; adv. bd. Swissotel, 1997—, Horton Internat., 1998—, GAM1999—, Cigna, 1999—; exec. mem. BENS. Named 1 of 10 Outstanding Young Working Women Glamour mag., 1977, Outstanding Young Woman for State of N.J. Outstanding Young Women Am., 1977, Com. of 100 '98, 1998— ('99 Conf. chmn.); White House fellow, 1978-79; recipient Award of Excellence HUD, 1979, Rensselaer Fellows award, 1997; elected to YWCA Acad. of Women Achievers, 1980. Mem. Harvard Bus. Sch. Alumni Assn., Rensselaer Alumni Assn., Orgn. Chinese-Ams., NOW, Alliance for Women, Common Cause. Home: 24 Oak Bend North Llewellyn Park West Orange NJ 07052

CHIN, CECILIA HUI-HSIN, librarian; b. Tientsin, China; came to U.S., 1961; d. Yu-lin and Ti-yu (Fan) C. B.A., Nat. Taiwan U., Taipei, 1961; M.S.L.S., U. Ill., 1963. Cataloger, reference librarian Roosevelt U., Chgo., 1963; reference librarian, indexer Ryerson & Burnham Libraries, Art Inst. Chgo., 1963-70, head reference dept. indexer,, 1970-75; acting dir. libraries Art Inst. Chgo., 1976-77, assoc. librarian, head reference dept., 1975-82; chief librarian Nat. Mus. Am. Art and Nat. Portrait Gallery, Smithsonian Inst., Washington, 1982—. Compiler: The Art Institute of Chicago Index to Art Periodicals, 1975. Reciipient awards Nat. Portrait Gallery, Smithsonian Instn., 1984, 89. Mem. Art Librs. Soc., D.C. Libr. Assn., Washington Rare Book Group. Office: Nat Mus Am Art & Nat Portrait Gallery Smithsonian Instn Washington DC 20560

CHIN, CINDY LAI, accountant; b. Kowloon, Hong Kong, Dec. 2, 1957; came to U.S., 1964; d. Sau Kuen and Koon On C. BS in Acctg., CUNY, 1980; grad., Real Estate Inst., 1990, NYU, 1995. Real estate acct. Milford Mgmt., Inc., N.Y.C., 1980-82; staff acct. Occidental Petroleum Corp., N.Y.C., 1983-85; portfolio acct. Yarmouth Group Inc., N.Y.C., 1985-91; sr. portfolio acct. CPC, N.Y.C., 1993-96; cons. C&M Real Estate Joint Venture, N.Y.C., 1985-89. Mem. China Inst., N.Y.C., 1986. Mem. NAFE, Hunter Coll. Acctg. Alumni Assn. Avocations: travel, poetry, interior designing.

CHIN, DENNY, judge; b. 1954. BA magna cum laude, Princeton U., 1975; JD, Fordham U., 1978. Law clerk Hon. Henry F. Werker, 1978-80; with Davis, Polk & Wardwell, N.Y., 1980-82, Campbell, Patrick & Chin, N.Y., 1986-90, Vladeck, Waldman, Elias & Engelhard, N.Y., 1990-94; dist. judge U.S. Dist. Ct. (so. dist.), N.Y., 1994—; adj. prof. Fordham Law Sch. Mem. ABA, Asian Am. Bar Assn. N.Y. (pres. 1992-94), Assn. Bar of N.Y.C., Fordham Law Review Alumni Assn., N.Y. County Lawyers Assn. Office: U S Dist Ct 500 Pearl St New York NY 10007-1316*

CHIN, DER-TAU, chemical engineer, educator; b. Zhejiang, China, Sept. 14, 1939; came to U.S., 1963, naturalized, 1977; s. Tsu-Kang and Shou-Chen (Chen) C.; BS in Chem. Engring., Chungyuan Coll. Sci. and Engring., 1962; MS in Chem. Engring., Tufts U., 1965; PhD in Chem. Engring., U. Pa., 1969; m. Lorna Fe Gencianeo, July 17, 1971; children: Janet G., Lynn G. Plant engr. Lungyen Sugar Factory, 1962-63; sci. programmer U.S. Air Force Cambridge (Mass.) Research Lab., Lexington, Mass., 1965; sr. research engr. research labs. Gen. Motors Corp., Warren, Mich., 1969-75; prof. Clarkson U., Potsdam, N.Y., 1975—; vis. scientist Brookhaven Nat. Lab., Upton, N.Y., summers 1977, 80, U.S. Army Belvoir Research Devel. Ctr., Ft. Belvoir, Va., summer 1985, U.S. Army Electronics Tech. and Devices Lab., Ft. Mammouth, N.J., summer, 1986, Armstrong Lab. Tyndall Air Force Base, Fla., summer 1995; vis. prof. U. Calif., Berkeley, 1981, Swiss Fed. Inst. Tech., Zurich, 1981, Nat. U. Singapore, 1982, 87, Nat. Tsing Hua UNI, 1989; cons. Centro de Pesquisas do Energia Electrica, Rio de Janeiro, Brazil, summer 1979. Fellow Electrochem. Soc. (Young Authors award 1971); mem. AIChE, Am. Electroplaters Soc., Am. Chem. Soc. Office: Clarkson U Box 5705 Potsdam NY 13699-5705

CHIN, JAMES YING, corporate executive; b. N.Y.C., Nov. 22, 1953; s. Bing Fon and Mung King (Chew) C.; m. Randy-Jo Gensler, June 28, 1981; children: Chelsea Ivy, Madeleine Rose. AAS, Queensborough Community Coll., Queens, N.Y., 1973; BS cum laude, U. Md., 1990. Customer engr. IBM, Bklyn., 1973-83; systems ctr. rep. IBM, Gaithersburg, Md., 1983-86; field mgr. IBM, Reston, Va., 1986-89; area tag mgr. IBM, McLean, Va., 1989-91; adv. info. systems analyst IBM, Bethesda, Md., 1991-92, mgr. billing and shipments devel., 1992-93, svc. billing contract mgr., 1993-94, systems assurance, 1994-95, project exec., 1995-96, mgr. Process, Techniques and Tools Initiative Ctr., 1996-97; mgr. quality assurance, program advisor IBM, Bethesda, 1997-99; quality assurance program mgr. IBM, Gaithersburg, 1999—. Mem. Phi Kappa Phi, Alpha Sigma Lambda. Democrat. Avocations: golf, tennis, literature. Office: IBM 800 N Frederick Ave Gaithersburg MD 20879-3326

CHIN, JANET SAU-YING, data processing executive, consultant; b. Hong Kong, July 27, 1949; came to U.S., 1959; d. Arthur Quock-Ming and Jenny (Loo) C. BS in Math, U. Ill., Chgo., 1970; MS in Computer Sci., U. Ill., Urbana, 1973. Sys. programmer Lawrence Livermore (Calif.) Lab., 1972-79; sect. mgr. Tymshare Inc., Cupertino, Calif., 1979-83, Fortune Systems, Redwood City, Calif., 1983-85; div. mgr. Impell Corp, Berkeley, Calif., 1985; pres. Chin Assocs., Oakland, Calif., 1985-88; bus. devel. mgr. Sun Microsystems, Mountain View, Calif., 1988-92; engring. dir. Cadence Design Systems, San Jose, Calif., 1992-94; quality dir. Cadence Design Sys., San Jose, Calif., 1994-95; asst. to CEO, Avant! Corp., Fremont, Calif., 1995—; provost World Inst. Tech., Fremont, Calif., 1996-98; vice-chmn. Am. Nat. Standards

Inst. X3H3, N.Y.C., 1979-82, internat. rep. X3H3, 1982-88. Co-author: The Computer Graphics Interface, 1991; contbr. tech. papers to profl. publs. Mem. Assn. Computing Machinery, Sigma Xi. Avocations: karate, iaido, science fiction/fantasy.

CHIN, JEAN LAU, health and mental health executive; b. N.Y.C., July 27, 1944; d. Kim Lau and Fung Gor (Jung) Lee; m. Gene S. Chin, Aug. 24, 1968; children: Scott, Stephen. BS in Psychology, Bklyn. Coll., 1966; MA in Psychology, Columbia U., 1969, EdD in Psychology, 1974. Instr. Tchrs. Coll., Columbia U., N.Y.C., 1968; staff psychologist Douglas Thom Clinic, Boston, 1970-73, chief psychologist, 1973-77, co-dir., 1977-85; dir. mental health South Cove Cmty. Health Ctr., Boston, 1986-88, exec. dir., 1988-97; pres. CEO Svcs., 1985—; regional dir. Hass Behavioral Health Partnership, 1998-99; asst. prof. psychiatry Boston U. Sch. of Medicine, Dept. of Child Psychiatry, 1979-87; adj. prof. Mass. Sch. of Profl. Psychology, 1979-82, Boston U., 1977-85; asst. clin. prof. Tufts U. Sch. of Medicine, 1987—; with Ctr. for Mental Health Svcs./Managed Care Workgroup, 1995-97, Office Minority Health Workgroups, 1990, 93; adv. bd. Mass. Dept. of Public Health, Office of Minority Health, 1996—, apptd. blue ribbon panel, 1996-97. Author 4 books in field; contbr. more than 100 articles to profl. jours. Bd. dirs. Newton-Wellesley Multi-Svc. Ctr., 1979-81, Place Runaway, 1977-85, Boston Children's Svcs. Assn., 1984-90, Mass. League of Cmty. Health Ctrs., 1993-98, Mass. Bd. of Registration for Psychologists, 1993-97, Newton Youth Commn., 1995—, Tufts Associated Health Maintenance Orgn., 1994—, Mass. Com. on Children and Youth, 1987-90, Mass. Dept. of Mental Health: Profl. Adv. Com., Children and Adolescent Svcs., 1989-97, Asian Pacific Islander Am. Health Forum, 1989—; Cmty. Edn. Adv. Coun., Commonwealth of Mass. Dept. Edn., 1984-89, industry-edn. subcom., 1984-87; adv. bd. Human Rights Commn., City of Newton, 1984-87; com. Mass. Lt. Govs. Blueprint, 1987-88; bd. pres. Newton Cantonese Sch., 1984-89, bd. dirs. 1982-91; corp. mem. Boston Ptnrs. in Edn., 1986—; active Nat. Asian Pacific Am. Families Against Substance Abuse, 1990-91, chair, 1991-94, exec. bd. 1990—; study group Ctr. for Women Policy Studies, 1993-96. Recipient Women Who Care award Women in Philanthropy, 1991; named Outstanding Exec. Dir. Mass. League of Cmty. Health Ctrs., 1991. Fellow Am. Psychol. Assn. (divsn. of clin. psychology sect. VI program chair 1988-90, pres. 1991-92, newsletter editor 1991—, divsn. psychology of women exec. com. 1991—, com. on ethnic minority affairs appointment to governance 1994-97, chair 1995-96, com. on profl. practice and stds. 1998—). Home: 614 Dedham St Newton MA 02459-2936 Office: CEO Svcs 110 W Squantum St Ste 21 Quincy MA 02171-2122

CHIN, KAI CHI, financial analyst; b. Taipei, Taiwan, May 21, 1966; s. Lee Shan and Li Yu (Hsieh) C. BS in Acctg., Va. Tech., Blacksburg, 1988; MBA, Georgetown U., Washington, 1993. CPA, Md., CMA. Internal auditor Armstrong World Industry, Lancaster, Pa., 1988-89; cost acct. Armstrong World Industry, Macon, Ga., 1989-90; budget analyst Henry Jackson Med. Found., Rockville, Md., 1994-95; sr. auditor Vulcan Materials Co., Birmingham, Ala., 1995, fin. analyst, sr. fin. analyst, 1995-99; audit supr. Vulcan Materials Co., Birmingham, 1999—. Vol. Bus. Presdl. Campaign, Washington, 1991-92, Spl. Olympics, Washington and Blacksburg, 1986-94, Habitat for Humanity, Birmingham, 1997. Mem. Inst. Mgmt. Accts., Asian Am. Soc. Va. Tech. (pres., coord. 19988—), Md. Soc. CPAs, Birmingham C. of C. (project corp. leadership 1997—). Avocations: all major sports, investing, financial, reading. Home: 160 Sheffield Ct Birmingham AL 35226-2100 Office: Vulcan Materials Co 1200 Urban Center Dr Birmingham AL 35242-2545

CHIN, LLEWELLYN PHILIP, lawyer; b. Saigon-Cholon, Vietnam, 1957; s. Thomas and Kim C. AA, Glendale (Calif.) Coll., 1980; BS, U. So. Calif., L.A., 1982; JD, Columbia U., 1986. Bar: Calif. 1988, U.S. Dist. Ct. (cen. dist.) Calif. 1988, U.S. Ct. Appeals (9th cir.) 1988. Sr. counsel Calif. Assn. of Realtors, L.A., 1989—; polit. cons. Robert Kwan for Alhambra Sch. Bd., Monterey Park, Calif., 1988; bus. cons. Larry L. Berg, Inc., L.A., 1986-88; legal advisor L.A. chpt. Chinese Consol. Benevolent Assn., Elderly Indo-Chinese Assn.; adj. prof. Southwestern U. Sch. Law, summer 1995, Loyola Law Sch., 1996; speaker in field. Columnist L.A. County Bar Real Property Newsletter; contbr. articles to profl. jours. Bd. dirs. Chinese-Am. Polit. Action Com., Alhambra, 1986-93, Golden Tours, Alhambra, 1993; candidate Alhambra City Coun., 1992; pres. Chinese Am. Edn. Assn., Monterey Park, 1994-95; bd. dirs. San Gabriel Valley YMCA, 1995-97; planning commr. City of Alhambra, 1995-99; commr. L.A. County Local Govtl. Svcs., 1995-97; commr. State Bd. Dental Examiners, 1998—. Beren Found. scholar, 1983-86, Harlan Fisk Stone scholar, 1986. Mem. ABA (chair home improvements, constrn. and purchase and sale of residential real estate subcom. 1992—, vice chair real estate brokerage subcom. 1998—), L.A. County Bar Assn. (disaster relief com., corp. counsel, elderline, continuing edn. com., gen. real property subsect. steering com.), Calif. Trial Lawyers Assn., So. Calif. Chinese Lawyers Assn., Calif. State Bar (co-chair sales and brokerage subsect. real property sect., 1993-96, 98—, cons. real property sect. 1993-96, continuing edn. of the bar com. 1992-95), Chinese Am. Real Estate Profls. So. Calif. (bd. dirs.), Alhambra C. of C. (legis. com., chair anti-graffiti task force 1993—). Avocations: reading, stamp and coin collecting, organizing political events, hiking. Office: Calif Assn Realtors 525 S Virgil Ave Los Angeles CA 90020-1403

CHIN, MING, state supreme court justice; b. Klamath Falls, Oreg., Aug. 31, 1942; m. Carol Lynn Joe, Dec. 19, 1971; children: Jennifer, Jason. BA in Polit. Sci., U. San Francisco, 1964, JD, 1967. Bar: Calif., 1970, U.S. Fed. Ct., U.S. Tax Ct. Assoc., head trial dept. Aiken, Kramer & Cummings, Oakland, Calif., 1973-76, prin., 1976-88; dep. dist. atty. Alameda County, Calif., 1970-72; judge Alameda County Superior Ct., 1988-90; assoc. justice divsn. 3 Ct. Appeal 1st Dist., 1990-94; presiding justice 1st Dist. Ct. Appeal Divsn. 3, San Francisco, 1994-96; assoc. justice Calif. Supreme Ct., San Francisco, 1996—. Capt. U.S. Army, 1967-69, Vietnam, USAR, 1969-71. Mem. ABA, Calif. Judges Assn., State Bar Calif., Alameda County Bar Assn., San Francisco Dist. Atty.'s Commn. Hate Crimes, Commonwealth Club of Calif. (pres. 1998), Asian Am. Bar Assn., Alpha Sigma Nu. Office: Supreme Court Calif 350 McAllister St San Francisco CA 94102-3600

CHIN, NEE OO WONG, reproductive endocrinologist; b. Hong Kong, Nov. 27, 1955; came to U.S., 1958; s. Bing Leong and Din Sui (Gee) C.; m. Shelly Loraine Crumrine, June 25, 1977; children: Jason Lei, Taryn Mae. BA, U. Cin., 1977; MD, Ohio State U., 1981. Diplomate Am. Bd. Ob-Gyn. Resident Duke U. Med. Ctr., Durham, N.C., 1981-84; chief resident Duke U. Med. Ctr., Durham, 1984-85; fellow Ohio State U. Coll. Medicine, Columbus, Ohio, 1985-87; teaching staff Good Samaritan Hosp., Cin., 1987—; clin. asst. prof. U. Cin. Med. Ctr., 1987—; dir. assisted reproductive techs. The Christ Hosp., Cin., 1992—; mem. High Sch. for the Health Profl. subcom., Cin., 1989—. Author: (with others) Current Therapy in Obstetrics, 1988; contbr. articles to profl. jours. Named to Honorable Order of Ky. Cols., Gov. Martha Collins of Ky., 1987. Fellow Am. Coll. Ob-Gyn.; mem. AAAS, Am. Fertility Soc., Soc. Assisted Reproductive Tech., Soc. for Immunology Repro., Cin. Ob-Gyn. Soc. (med. malpractice com. 1989—), Acad. Medicine Cin. Avocations: tennis, karate. Office: The Christ Hosp Ste 220 11503 Spring Field Pike Cincinnati OH 45246

CHIN, PAUL L., human resources professional; b. July 17, 1949. BA, U. Mass., 1992; MEd, Harvard U., 1981. Pres. P.L. Chin Cons. Co., Newton, Mass., 1976—; supr. Crawford & Co., Waltham, Mass., 1990-92; mgr. Health Pro/United Healthcare, Worcester, Mass., 1982-93; dir. human resources and diversity New England Aquarium, Boston, 1994—. E-mail: plchin@neaq.org.

CHIN, ROBERT ALLEN, engineering graphics educator; b. San Francisco, Oct. 3, 1950; s. Suey Hey and Stella (Yee) C.; m. Susan Curtis Fleming, June 18, 1976. AAS, C.C. Air Force, 1982; BA, U. No. Colo., 1974; MA in Edn., Ball State U., 1975; PhD, U. Md., 1986. Cert. sr. indsl. technologist. Grad. tchg. asst. Ball State U., Muncie, Ind., 1974-75; instr. Sioux Falls (S.D.) Sch. Dist., 1975-79; instr. mech. drawing U. Md., College Park, 1979-86; asst. prof. engrng. graphics, dept. constrn. mgmt. East Carolina U., Greenville, N.C., 1986-92, assoc. prof. engrng. graphics dept. indsl. tech., 1992—, acting chmn. dept. constrn. mgmt., 1989-90; aircraft maintenance officer 113th Logistics Group DCANG Andrews AFB, Md., 1983-95, squadron comdr. 113th Aircraft Generation Squadron, 1995-97, squadron comdr. 113th Logistics Squadron, 1997-99, squadron comdr. 113th Maintenance Squadron, 1999—; faculty advisor Disabled Student Alliance, U. Md., 1982-86. Jour. reviewer; contbr. articles to profl. jours. With USAF, 1968-72, Air N.G., 1977—. Decorated Master Aircraft Munitions and Maintenance badge USAF, Meritorious Svc. medal, Air Res. Forces, Meritorious Svc. medal, Nat. Def. Svc. medal with bronze star, Armed Forces Expeditionary medal, Armed Forces Res. medal. Mem. Air Force Assn. (chpt. sec. 1988-92, chpt. pres. 1992-94), N.G. Assn. U.S., N.G. Assn. D.C., Nat. Assn. Indsl. Tech. (dir. region III 1995-97), Am. Soc. Engrng. Edn. (dir. program, engrng. design graphics divsn. 1998—, chair engrng. graphics divsn. SE sect. 1993-94, vice chair instrnl. unit SE sect. 1994-95, chair 1995-96), Am. Design and Drafting Assn., Nat. Assn. Indsl. and Tech. Tchr. Educators, Coun. Tech. Tchr. Edn., Phi Kappa Phi, Epsilon Pi Tau (citation 1991, trustee Beta Mu chpt. 1995—), Iota Lambda Sigma (v.p. Nu chpt. 1984-85, pres. Nu chpt. 1985-86). Republican. Presbyterian.

CHIN, SUE SOONE MARIAN (SUCHIN CHIN), conceptual artist, portraitist, photographer, community affairs activist; b. San Francisco; d. William W. and Soo-Up (Swebe) C. Grad. Calif. Coll. Art, Mpls. Art Inst., (scholar) Schaeffer Design Ctr.; student, Yasuo Kuniyoshi, Louis Hamon, Rico LeBrun. Photojournalist, All Together Now show, 1973, East-West News, Third World Newscasting, 1975-78, Sta. KNBC Sunday Show, L.A., 1975, 76, Live on 4, 1981, Bay Area Scene, 1981; graphics printer, exhbns. include Kaiser Ctr., Zellerbach Pla., Chinese Culture Ctr. Galleries, Capricorn Asunder Art Commn. Gallery (all San Francisco), Newspace Galleries, New Coll. of Calif., L.A. County Mus. Art, Peace Pla. Japan Ctr., Congress Arts Communication, Washington, 1989; SFWA Galleries, Inner Focus Show, 1989—, Calif. Mus. Sci. and Industry, Lucien Labaudt Gallery, Salon de Medici, Madrid, Salon Renacimento, Madrid, 1995, Life Is a Circus, SFWA Gallery, 1991, 94, UN/50 Exhibit, Bayfront Galleries, 1995, Somar Galleries, 1997, Sacramento State Fair, AFL-CIO Labor Studies Ctr., Washington, Asian Women Artists (1st prize for conceptual painting, 1st prize photography), 1978, Yerba Buena Arts Ctr. for the Arts Festival, 1994; represented in permanent collections L.A. County Fedn. Labor, Calif. Mus. Sci. and Industry, AFL-CIO Labor Studies Ctr., Australian Trades Coun., Hazeland and Co., also pvt. collections; author (poetry) Yuri and Malcolm, The Desert Sun. 1994 (Editors Choice award 1993-94). Del. nat., state convs. Nat. Women's Polit. Caucus, 1977-83, San Francisco chpt. affirmative action chairperson, 1978-82, nat. conv. del., 1978-81, Calif. del., 1976-81. Recipient Honorarium AFL-CIO Labor Studies Ctr., Washington, 1975-76; award Centro Studi Ricerche delle Nazioni, Italy, 1985; bd. advisors Psycho Neurology Found. Bicentennial award L.A. County Mus. Art, 1976, 77, 78. Mem. Asian Women Artists (founding v.p., award 1978-79, 1st award in photography of Orient 1978-79), Calif. Chinese Artists (sec.-treas. 1978-81), Japanese Am. Art Coun. (chairperson 1978-84, dir.), San Francisco Women Artists, San Francisco Graphics Guild, Pacific/Asian Women Coalition Bay Area, Chinatown Coun. Performing and Visual Arts. Chmn., Full Moon Products; pres., bd. dir. Aumni Oracle Inc. Address: PO Box 421415 San Francisco CA 94142-1415

CHIN, SYLVIA FUNG, lawyer; b. N.Y.C., June 27, 1949; d. Thomas and Constance (Yao) Fung; m. Edward G.H. Chin, July 10, 1971; children: Arthur F., Benjamin F. BA, NYU, 1971; JD, Fordham U., 1977. Bar: N.Y. 1978, U.S. Dist. Ct. (so. and ea. dists.) N.Y. 1979, U.S. Supreme Ct. 1990. Law clk. to dist. judge U.S. Dist. Ct. (so. dist.), N.Y.C., 1977-79; assoc. White & Case, N.Y.C., 1979-86, ptnr., 1986—; adj. assoc. prof. law Fordham U., N.Y.C., 1979-81. Co-author (article in book) Negotiating Business Transactions, 1988; mem. editorial bd. Bus. Law Today, 1996—. Mem. ABA, N.Y. County Lawyers Assn., Fordham Law Alumni Assn. (bd. dirs.), Asian Am. Bar Assn. N.Y. (pres. 1994-96, bd. dirs.), Women's World Banking (bd. dirs.), Nat. Asian Pacific ABA (treas. 1997-98). Office: White & Case Bldg Ll 1155 Avenue Of The Americas New York NY 10036-2711

CHIN, TANYA JADE, policy analyst; b. June 12, 1973. BA, Syracuse U., 1995; MPA, Am. U., 1997. Sr. policy analyst Ctr. for Women Policy Studies, Washington, 1997—. E-mail: tjchin@aol.com. and tchin@centerwomenpolicy.org.

CHINARD, FRANCIS PIERRE, physiologist, physician, preventive medicine consultant; b. Berkeley, Calif., June 30, 1918; s. Gilbert and Emma (Blanchard) C.; m. Josephine L. Wise, June 23, 1943; children: Suzanne F., Jeanne M., Marc F. A.B., U. Calif., Berkeley, 1937; M.D., Johns Hopkins U., 1941. Intern, jr. asst. resident in medicine Presbyn. Hosp., N.Y.C., 1941-42; asst. physician Hosp. Rockefeller Inst., N.Y.C., 1945-49; instr. to asso. prof. medicine and physiol. chemistry Johns Hopkins Sch. Med., Balt., 1949-54; asst. prof. medicine U. Md., 1954-62, asso. prof., 1962-63; physician Johns Hopkins Hosp., 1956-63; prof. exptl. medicine, dep. dir. med. clinic McGill U., Can., 1963-64; prof. medicine NYU, 1964-68, adj. prof., 1968-70; career scientist N.Y.C. Health Research Council, 1964-68; prof. medicine, chmn. dept. U. Medicine and Dentistry N.J., Newark, 1968-75, prof. exptl. medicine, 1975-77, prof. research medicine, 1977—, prof. physiology, 1978—, Disting. prof., 1989—, emeritus, 1996; physician-in-chief Balt. City Hosp., 1962-63; acting physician-in-chief Goldwater Meml. Hosp., N.Y.C., 1965-67; dir. med. service Martland Hosp., Newark, 1970-71; cons. physician VA Hosp., East Orange, N.J., 1971-79, 93-95; mem. staff Balt. City Hosps., 1953-63; cons. in field; pres. Faculty Practice Svc. Corp., N.J. Med. Sch., 1986-88; vis. scientist Med. Rsch. Coun. Can., McGill U., Montreal, 1989-90. Author: (With J.W. Bauman Jr.) Renal Function, 1975; editorial com.: Jour. Clin. Investigation, 1954-59, Jour. Applied Physiology, 1959-65, Am. Jour. Physiology, 1959-65, Circulation Research, 1967-72, Microvascular Research, 1981-89, Revue française des Maladies respiratoires, 1979-93, clin. and investigative medicine, 1985-96; contbr. articles on indicator-dilution techniques, membrane permeability and transport, pulmonary, renal function and history of medicine and physiology to med. jours. Mem. profl. adv. com. Martha's Vineyard Guidance Center, 1968-75; mem. pulmonary disease adv. com. Nat. Heart and Lung Inst., 1971-75, chmn., 1974-75, mem. bd. sci. counselors, 1976-80, chmn., 1978-80. Served to maj. M.C. USAAF, 1942-45. Decorated Legion of Merit; recipient Lucian award McGill U., 1989, Sir William Osler Humanitarian award N.J. Thoracic Soc., 1991, Laureate award N.J. chpt. Am. Coll. Physicians, 1993, Charles L. Brown award Alumni Assn. N.J. Med. Sch. Fellow ACP, N.Y. Acad. Scis., AAAS; mem. Am. Chem. Soc., Am. Soc. Biol. Chemists, Am., Canadian socs. clin. investigation, Harvey Soc., Interurban Clin. Club, Soc. Exptl. Biology and Medicine, Assn. Am. Physicians, Am. Physiol. Soc., Peripatetic Soc., Acad. Medicine N.J. (trustee 1972-78), Am. Heart Assn. (research com. N.J. affiliate 1975-81), Inst Français Washington (trustee 1994—), Microcirculatory Soc. (Landis award), Am. Thoracic Soc., Soc. Scholars (Johns Hopkins), Med. History Soc. N.J. (pres. 1984-86), Am. Assn. History of Medicine (councilor), Sigma Xi, Alpha Omega Alpha. Democrat. Club: Century Assn. (N.Y.C.). Office: 40 Warren Pl Montclair NJ 07042-2534

CHING, ANDY KWOK-YEE, minister; b. Shanghai, People's Republic of China, Apr. 12, 1956; arrived in Hong Kong, 1961; arrived in Can., 1973; came to U.S., 1989.; s. Jan Wai and Hon Wah (Kwan) C.; m. Rosita Wai-Mui Tsoi, June 4, 1989; children: Abigail, Aaron. B of Applied Sci., U. Toronto, 1981; M of Theol. Studies, Ontario Theol. Sem., 1982; DD, Internat. Sem., 1988; D in Min., Fuller Theol. Sem., 1996. Ordained to ministry Christian and Missionary Alliance, 1989. Asst. pastor North York Chinese Bapt. Ch., Willowdale, Ont., Can., 1982-83; interim pastor Montreal Chinese Bapt. Ch., Quebec, Can., 1984; lit. coord. Christian Reformed Ch., Toronto, Ont., 1988; gen. sec. Harvester Evangelical Press, Willowdale, 1985-89; pastor Chinese Christian Alliance Ch., Northridge, Calif., 1989-95, The Lord's Grace Christian Ch., Cupertino, Calif., 1996—; guest lectr., Christ Internat. Theol. Sem., Alhambra, Calif., 1990-95; reporter, mem., Evangelical Press. Assn., Canoga Park, 1990—; tchr. trainer, Evangelical Tchr. Tng. Assn., Wheaton, Ill., 1989—; interpreter, Toronto Bd. Edn., 1986-88, instr.m 1986-87. Editor: Onward Christian Soldiers, Toronto, 1982, Three Episodes of Life, 1982; translator (books) Reasons to Believe, 1988, Called to Ministry, 1989; contbr. articles to profl. jours. Vol. Scot's Missions to Native People, Toronto, 1983-84; bd. dirs. China Grad. Sch. Theology Bay Area Coun., 1997—. Mem. Internat. Missions Inc., Cultural Regeneration Rsch. Soc., USA (bd. dirs. 1996—). Office: The Lord's Grace Christian Ch 1101 Saint Antonio Rd Mountain View CA 94040 *The two Josephs in the Old and New Testament teach us one thing: there is a price to pay if we want to actualize the dreams given by God.*

CHING, ERIC SAN HING, health care and insurance administrator; b. Honolulu, Aug. 13, 1951; s. Anthony D.K. and Amy K.C. (Chong) C. BS, Stanford U., 1973, MS, MBA, 1977. Fin. analyst Mid Peninsula Health Service, Palo Alto, Calif., 1977; acting dep. exec. dir. Santa Clara County Health Systems Agy., San Jose, Calif., 1977-78; program officer Henry J. Kaiser Family Found., Menlo Park, Calif., 1978-84; dir. strategic planning Lifeguard Health Maintenance Orgn., Milpitas, Calif., 1984-90; v.p. strategic planning and dir. ops. Found. Life Ins. Co., Milpitas, 1986-90; sr. planning analyst Kaiser Found. Health Plan, Oakland, Calif., 1990-94, coord. product and competition analysis, 1994-95, mgr. ins. ops. and competitive intelligence cons., 1995-97; nat. product leader Kaiser Found. Health Plan, Oakland, 1997—; adj. faculty Am. Pistol Inst., 1991-94. Mem. vol. staff Los Angeles Olympic Organizing Com., 1984; mem. panel United Way of Santa Clara County, 1985, panel chmn., 1986-87, mem. com. priorities and community problem solving, 1987-90, Project Blueprint, 1988-90. Mem. NRA, ACLU, Am. Soc. Law Enforcement Trainers, Internat. Assn. Law Enforcement Firearms Instrs., Internat. Wound Ballistics Assn., Stanford Alumni Assn., Stanford Bus. Sch. Alumni Assn., Stanford Swordmasters (pres. 1980-89), Safari Club Internat., Am. Soc. of Criminology. Avocations: firearms instrn., shoot, photography, travel. Office: Kaiser Found Health Plan Inc One Kaiser Pla 25th Fl Oakland CA 94612

CHING, JAMES MICHAEL, artistic director opera company; b. Honolulu, Hawaii, Sept. 29, 1958. BA summa cum laude, Duke U., 1980. Pianist, composer Houston Opera Studio, 1980-81; music adminstr. Fla. Grand Opera, 1981-85; mus. dir. Triangle Opera Theatre, 1987-88; asst. to gen. dir. Va. Opera, 1989-91, assoc. artistic dir., 1991-92; artistic dir. Opera Memphis, Tenn., 1992—. Mem. Phi Beta Kappa. E-mail: MrBillow@juno.com. Office: U Memphis S Campus Campus Box 526331 Memphis TN 38152

CHING, JULIA, philosophy and religion educator; b. Shanghai, Oct. 15, 1934; came to Can., 1978; d. William Ching and Christina Ching Tsao; m. Willard G. Oxtoby, 1981. PhD, Australian Nat. U., Canberra, 1972; LHD, U. N.C., 1993; DD, Queen's U., 1997. Prof. U. Toronto, Ont., Can., 1978—, univ. prof., 1994—, R.C. and E.Y. Lee chair prof., 1998—. Author: Confucianism and Christianity, 1977 (Outstanding Acad. Book of Yr., Choice), Probing China's Soul, 1990, Chinese Religions, 1993; co-author: Christianity and Chinese Religions, 1989. Trustee United Bd. for Christian Higher Edn. in Asia, N.Y., 1977-86; co-organizer Spirit of Asia Pacific Gala, Toronto, 1990; co-pres. 33d Internat. Congress for Asian and N.African Studies, Toronto, 1990. Fellow Royal Soc. Can.; mem. Am. Soc. for Study of Religion.

CHING, WAI YIM, physics educator, researcher; b. Shaoshing, China, Oct. 18, 1945; came to U.S., 1969; s. Di-Son and Hung-Wong (Sung) C.; m. Mon Yin Lung, Dec. 27, 1975; children: Tianyu, Kunyu. BSc, U. Hong Kong, 1969; MS, La. State U., 1971, PhD, 1974. Rsch. assoc., lectr. U. Wis., Madison, 1974-78; asst. prof. U. Mo., Kansas City, 1978-81, assoc. prof., 1981-84, prof. physics, 1984-88, curators' prof., 1988—, chmn. physics dept., 1990-98; cons. Argonne (Ill.) Nat. Lab., 1978-82, vis. scientist, 1985-86; vis. prof. U. Sci. and Tech., Hefei, China, 1983; guest scientist Max-Planck Inst. für Metallforschung, Stuttgart, Germany, 1997. Contbr. articles to profl. jours. Recipient N.T. Veatch award for disting. rsch., 1985; Trustee fellow U. Mo., 1984, 90. Mem. AAAS, Am. Phys. Soc., Am. Ceramic Soc., Am. Vacuum Soc., Materials Rsch. Soc., Sigma Xi. Achievements include the study of theoretical dondensed matter physics and materials sciences; electronic, magnetic, optical, dynamical structural and superconducting properties of ordered and disordered solids. Home: 2809 W 119th St Leawood KS 66209-1104 Office: U Mo Dept Physics 1110 E 48th St Kansas City MO 64110-1718

CHINITZ, BENJAMIN, economics educator; b. N.Y.C., Aug. 24, 1924; s. Abraham and Mollie (Resnick) C.; m. Ethel Kleinman; children: Adam, Michael. AB, Yeshiva U., 1945, hon. degree, 1969; AM in Econs., Brown U., 1951; PhD in Econs., Harvard U., 1956. Mem. sr. staff N.Y. Met. Region Study Regional Plan Assn., Harvard U., N.Y.C., 1956-59; prof., chair dept. econs., assoc. dir. ctr. regional econ. studies U. Pitts., 1959-65; dep. asst. sec. commerce for econ. devel. Washington, 1965-66; prof., chair dept. econs. Brown U., Providence, 1961-73; prof. econs., dir. ctr. for social analysis SUNY, Binghamton, 1973-81; dean coll. mgmt. sci. U. Mass., Lowell, 1982-87; dir. rsch. Lincoln Inst. of Land Policy, Cambridge, Mass., 1987-91; fellow A. Alfred Taubman Ctr. for State and Local Govt. John F. Kennedy Sch. of Govt., Harvard U., Cambridge, 1992—; faculty assoc. Lincoln Inst. of Land Policy, Cambridge; vis. prof. coll. urban & pub. affairs Fla. Atlantic U., Ft. Lauderdale; vis. mem. faculty dept. urban studies, MIT, 1967; cons. State of Conn., 1961-64, Appalachian Regional Commn., 1963-65, Rand Corp., 1961, 64, 67, U.S. Coun. Econ. Advisors, 1966, The White House, 1970, Resources for The Future, 1970-71, U.S. Econ. Devel. Adminstrn., 1970-72, UN, 1970, 72, NAS, 1970-71, The Brookings Instn., 1972-74, The Ford Found., 1976, Abt Assocs., 1975-81. Author: Freight and The Metropolis, 1960, City and Suburb: The Economics of Metropolitan Growth, 1964, Cities, 1965, The Declining Northeast, 1977, Central City Economic Development, 1979; (with others) Essays in Regional Economics, 1971, Social Responsibility and the Business Predicament, 1974, The Urban Economy, 1976; coord. editor Urban Studies, 1980-92; contbr. articles to profl. jours. Fullbright Vis. scholar U. Glasgow, 1965. Mem. Regional Sci. Assn. (com. urban econs. 1967-75, pres. 1970, 90). *

CHINITZ, DAVID EVAN, literature educator; b. Bklyn., Nov. 19, 1962; s. Wallace and Carol Bette (Brodsky) C.; m. Lisa Gail Gross, June 23, 1991; children: Michael Austin, Raina Joelle. BA, Amherst Coll., 1984; ScM, Brown U., 1985; PhD, Columbia U., 1993. Asst. prof. lit. Loyola U., Chgo., 1993-99, assoc. prof. lit., 1999—. Contbr. articles to profl. jours. Class agt. fundraising Amherst Coll., 1994—. Summer rsch. grantee Nat. Endowment for Humanities, 1997. Mem. MLA, T.S. Eliot Soc., Modernist Studies Assn. (steering com. 1998—). Democrat. Jewish. Avocations: piano, bicycling. Home: 4330 Suffield Ct Skokie IL 60076-1853 Office: Loyola U Dept English Chicago IL 60626

CHINITZ, JODY ANNE KOLB, data processing manager; b. Bay City, Mich., July 8, 1953; d. Adam H. and Evelyn I. (Sylvester) Kolb; m. William A. Chinitz, Feb. 11, 1979. Student Saginaw Valley State Coll., 1972, Bklyn. Coll., 1973-76; BA in Russian Lang. and Lit. summa cum laude, CUNY., 1980. With personnel dept. N.Y. Life Ins. Co., N.Y.C., 1972-77, computer programmer, 1977-80; computer systems cons. Soroban Data Systems, Inc., N.Y.C., 1980-82; project leader Midlantic Nat. Bank, West Orange, N.J., 1982-89, asst. v.p., 1989-96; project leader M&I Data Svcs., Parsippany, N.J., 1996—. Home: 31 Norwood Ave Montclair NJ 07043-1921 Office: M&I Data Svcs One Gatehall Dr Parsippany NJ 07054

CHINN, PEGGY LOIS, nursing educator, editor; b. Columbia, S.C., Feb. 25, 1941; d. Hubert R. and Margaret (Gasteiger) Tatum; m. Philip C. Chinn, June 15, 1964 (div. 1974); children: Kelleth Roger, Jonathan Mark (dec.). AA, Mars Hill Coll., 1960; BS, U. Hawaii, 1964; MS, U. Utah, 1970, PhD, 1971. From instr. to asst. prof. U. Utah, Salt Lake City, 1971-74; assoc. dir., prof. Tex. Woman's U., Denton, 1974-78; prof. Wright State U., Dayton, Ohio, 1978-81, SUNY, Buffalo, 1981-90, U. Colo., Denver, 1990-96; founder, editor Advances in Nursing Sci., Rockville, Md., 1978—; cons., lectr. in field. Author: Child Health Maintenance, 1974, 2d edit. 1978, Theory in Nursing, 1983, 5th edit. 1999, Peace and Power, 4th edit., 1994; contbr. articles to profl. jours. Co-founder Cassandra: Radical Feminist Nurses Network, nationwide 1982, Margaret Daughters Inc., Buffalo, 1984. Fellow Am. Acad. Nursing (governing coun. 1987-90); mem. Am. Nurses Assn., Nat. League for Nursing, Sigma Theta Tau. Office: U Conn Nursing Health Sci Ctr 231 Glenbrook Rd Storrs Mansfield CT 06269-9005

CHINNI, PETER ANTHONY, artist; b. Mt. Kisco, N.Y., Mar. 21, 1928; s. Antonio and Carmella Catherine (Lampo) C.; m. Elisabeth Angela Cott, Aug. 17, 1970 (div. 1986); children—Christine Elizabeth, Megan Margaret. Student, Art Students League N.Y., 1947-49, Accademia di Belle Arti, Rome, 1949-50. One-man shows include Albert Loeb Gallery, N.Y.C., 1966, Loeb-Krugier Gallery, N.Y.C., 1969, A. Monett Gallery, Brussels, 1976, Gallery Bouma, Amsterdam, 1976, Katonah Gallery, N.Y., 1983, Fairlawn Libr. Gallery, N.J., 1993; group exhbns. include Whitney Mus., N.Y.C., 1962, 63, 64, 65, 75, Carnegie Internat., Pitts., 1964-65, Biennale di Roma, 1969, Audubon Artists Ann., 1995 (Gold medal for sculpture);

commd. pub. works, N.Y.C., Columbia, Mo., Yorktown, N.Y.; represented in permanent collections at Whitney Mus., New Orleans Fine Arts Mus., Smithsonian Inst., Washington, City Art Mus., Colo., MIT, Beeckestijn (The Netherlands) Mus., Denver Art Mus., Rockefeller Collection, Boca Raton (Fla.) Mus. Served with U.S. Army, 1951-53. Mem. N.Y. Sculptors Guild, Artists Equity.

CHINNIS, PAMELA P., religion organization administrator; b. Springfield, Mo.; children: Ann, Cabell. BS, Coll. William and Mary, 1946; DHL (hon.), Va. Theol. Sem., 1983, Yale U., 1990, Ch. Divinity Sch. of Pacific, 1992, St. Paul's Coll.; DD, Gen. Theol. Sem., 1992; DHL (hon.), Coll. William and Mary, 1999cre. Sr. warden Ch. Epiphany, Washington, 1972-78, 90-95, v.p. Province III, 1985-91; now pres., House of Deputies Episcopal Church, N.Y.C.; mem. exec. coun., 1979-85; chair stewardship and devel. com., venture in mission process com.; alternate lay del. to Anglican Consultative Coun., 1979-85, lay del., 1985-93; mem. search com. for new Sec. Gen. Anglican Communion, 1992-93; presiding officer 1976 triennial meeting of women of ch., Mpls.; chair Venture in Mission; chair legis. com. on ecumen. rels. Ho. of Deputies 1985 Conv.; chair com. for full participation of women in ch., 1985-88; mem. gen. bd. and exec. coordinating com. Nat. Coun. Chs., 1988—; del. to Anglican Coun. N.Am. and Carribean, 1982-85, sec. exec. com.; del. to World Coun. Chs., Faith and Order Commn., India, 1978, Ptnrs. in Mission Consultation of Nippon Sei Ko Kai, 1980, Internat. Consultation of Community of Women and Men in Ch., Sheffield, Eng., 1980, Anglican Coun. N.Am. and Carribean com. on Refugees, Belize, Ctrl. Am., 1983; mem. ctrl. com. WCC, 1998—. Bd. dirs. Coll. William and Mary Alumni Soc., Am. Friends of Diocese Jerusalem, Washington Theol. Consortium; gov. Va. Bd. Visitors Coll. William and Mary; bd. trustees Gen. Theol. Sem., 1987-90, Bekeley Divinity Sch., Yale U., 1991-93, Greater S.E. Community Hosp., Washington; mem. adv. bd. St. Barnabus Ctr., Wis., Conf. of Deaf, Episc. Radio-TV Found. Recipient Disting. Christian Svc. award Seabury-Western Theol. Sem. Mem. Am. Soc. Order of St. John, Cathedral chpt. Washington Nat. Cathedral. Office: Episcopal Ch 815 2nd Ave Rm 400 New York NY 10017-4503

CHIOGIOJI, MELVIN HIROAKI, government official; b. Hiroshima, Japan, Aug. 21, 1939; came to U.S., 1939; s. Yutaka and Harumi (Yamasaki) C.; m. Eleanor Nobuko Oura, June 4, 1960; children: Wendy A., Alan K. B.S. in Elec. Engring., Purdue U., 1961; M.B.A., U. Hawaii, 1968; D.Bus. Adminstrn., George Washington U., 1972. Registered profl. engr., Hawaii. Head weapons gen. component div. Quality Evaluation Lab., Oahu, Hawaii, 1965-69; dir. weapons evaluation and engring. div. Naval Ordinance Systems Command, Washington, 1969-73; dir. Office Indsl. Analysis Fed. Energy Adminstrn., Washington, 1973-75; asst. dir., div. bldg. and community systems Dept. Energy, Washington, 1975-79, dir. fed. program div., 1980—, dep. asst. sec. state and local assistance program, 1980-85, dir. office of transp. systems, 1985-90; constrn. mgr. Office of New Prodn. Reactors, Washington, 1990-92; pres. EFC, Inc., 1980—, Precision Auto Care, Inc., 1989—, Intemco, 1993—; prof. mgmt. sci. George Washington U., 1972—; bd. dirs. Smith Environ. Techs. Corp. Author: Industrial Energy Conservation, 1979, Energy Conservation in Commercial and Residental Buildings, 1982; contbr. articles to profl. jours. Mem. Md. State Adv. Com. on Civil Rights, 1976—; mem. Nat. Naval Res. Policy Bd., 1977—; vestryman Grace Episcopal Ch., Silver Spring, Md., 1982—; bd. dirs. Japanese Am. Nat. Mus., 1996—; chmn. Nat. Japanese Am. Meml. Found., 1995—. With USN, 1961-65; rear adm. USNR. Decorated Navy Commendation medal, Meritorious Svc. medal, Legion Merit medal. Mem. IEEE (sr.), NSPE, Acad. Mgmt., Naval Res. Assn., Assn. for Sci., Tech. and Innovation (pres. 1979-81), Soc. Am. Mil. Engrs., Armed Forces Mgmt. Assn., Seabee Meml. Scholarship Assn. (bd. dirs. 1973—), Triangle Fraternity Edn. Found. (bd. dirs. 1995—), Purdue U. Alumni Assn., Nat. Japanese Am. Meml. Found. (chmn.), Japanese Am. Nat. Mus. (bd. dirs.). Address: 15702 Thistlebridge Dr Rockville MD 20853 Office: 14660 Rothegeb Rd Rockville MD 20850

CHIPMAN, BRUCE LEWIS, English language educator; b. Phila., June 1, 1946; s. Irvin Lewis and Janet Lydia (Ingerson) C.; m. Pamela Fay Leary, June 15, 1968 (div. 1983); 1 child, Zachary Lewis; m. Robin Sarah Laskey, Mar. 14, 1987; 1 child, Hannah Emily. BA in English, U. Va., 1968; MA in Am. Lit., Tufts U., 1970, PhD in Am. Lit., 1973. Instr. English Tufts U., Medford, Mass., 1970-73; English tchr., dean students Tatnall Sch., Wilmington, Del., 1973-78, head English dept., 1978—; adj. assoc. prof. English U. Del., Newark, 1977—; theatre dir. Tatnall Sch., 1973—, baseball coach, 1977—. Author: Hardening Rock, 1972, America's Dream-Dump, 1999; contbr. articles to popular publs. Trustee Del. Theatre Co., Wilmington, 1985-86. NDEA fellow, 1968-73; Fulbright fellow, Sudan, 1984. Mem. Nat. Coun. Tchrs. English. Democrat. Mem. Universal Life Ch. Avocations: travel, film, music. Home: 39 Tenby Chase Dr Newark DE 19711-2440 Office: Tatnall Sch 1501 Barley Mill Rd Wilmington DE 19807-2299

CHIPMAN, DEBRA DECKER, paralegal; b. Oneonta, N.Y., Sept. 21, 1959; d. Leon Hannibal and Patricia Elizabeth (Ainsworth) Decker; m. Michael A. Chipman, May 24, 1980 (div. Sept. 1990); 1 child, Amanda Michelle. Student, Robert Morris Coll., 1988-94. Sec., receptionist Power Engring. Corp., Binghamton, N.Y., 1977-78; accts. payable clk. Old Dominion U. Rsch. Found., Norfolk, Va., 1978-80; adminstrv. asst. U. Pitts., 1980-81; paralegal Papernick & Gefsky, Attys. at Law, Pitts., 1981-93; mgr. Preferred Settlement Svcs., Inc., Pitts., 1993-97; asst. v.p., agy. rep. First Am. Title Ins. Co., Pitts., 1997—. Recipient award Otsego County Bankers Assn., 1977. Mem. Nat. Assn. Legal Assts, Pitts. Paralegal Assn. (co-chair fundraising com. 1990), Pa. Assn. Notaries, Pa. Land Title Assn. (western Pa. chpt. sec.). Methodist. Avocations: skiing, running, biking. Home: 2593 Hunters Point Ct S Wexford PA 15090-7986 Office: Grant Building Ste 102 Pittsburgh PA 15219-2203

CHIPMAN, JOHN SOMERSET, economist, educator; b. Montreal, Que., Can., June 28, 1926; s. Warwick Fielding and Mary Somerset (Aikins) C.; m. Margaret Ann Ellefson, June 24, 1960; children: Thomas Noel, Timothy Warwick. Student, Universidad de Chile, Santiago, 1943-44; BA, McGill U., Montreal, 1947, MA, 1948; PhD, Johns Hopkins U., 1951; postdoctoral, U. Chgo., 1950-51; Doctor rerum politicarum honoris causa, U. Konstanz, Germany, 1991, U. Würzburg, 1998. Asst. prof. econs. Harvard U., Cambridge, Mass., 1951-55; assoc. prof. econs. U. Minn., Mpls., 1955-60; prof. U. Minn., 1961-81, Regents' prof., 1981—; fellow Ctr. for Advanced Study in Behavioral Scis., Stanford, Calif., 1972-73; Guggenheim fellow, 1980-81; vis. prof. econs. various univs.; permanent guest prof. U. Konstanz, 1985-91; bd. dirs. Leuthold Funds, Inc., 1995—. Author: The Theory of Intersectoral Money Flows and Income Formation, 1951; editor: (with others) Preferences, Utility, and Demand, 1971, Preferences, Uncertainty and Optimality, 1990, (with C.P. Kindleberger) Flexible Exchange Rates and the Balance of Payments, 1980; co-editor Jour. Internat. Econs., 1971-76, editor, 1977-87; assoc. editor Econometrica, 1956-60, Can. Jour. Stats., 1980-82; mem. adv. bd. Jour. Multivariate Analysis, 1988-92. Recipient James Murray Luck award Nat. Acad. Scis., 1981, Humboldt Rsch. award for Sr. U.S. Scientists, 1992. Fellow AAAS, Econometric Soc. (coun. 1971-76, 81-83), Am. Statis. Assn., Am. Acad. Arts and Scis., Am. Econ. Assn. (disting.); mem. NAS (chair sect. econ. scis. 1997—), Internat. Statis. Inst., Inst. Math. Stats., Can Econ. Assn., Royal Econ. Soc., Soc. for Advancement of Econ. Theory, History of Econs. Soc. Home: 2121 W 49th St Minneapolis MN 55409-2229 Office: U Minn Dept Econs 1035 Heller Hall 217 19th Ave S Minneapolis MN 55455-0400

CHIPMAN, MARION WALTER, judge; b. Penokee, Kans., May 5, 1920; s. James Edwin and May Maude (Hatcher) C.; m. Thelma Nadine Clark, Nov. 1, 1941 (div. 1965); m. Nancy Jo Payne, May 28, 1983; children: Clark D., Jill Ellen. AB in Social Sci., Ft. Hays (Kans.) State U., 1942; JD, Washburn U., 1948. Bar: Kans. 1948, U.S. Dist. Ct. Kans. 1948, U.S. Ct. Appeals 1970, U.S. Supreme Ct. 1970. Supt. Prairieview (Kans.) Sch., 1942; atty. County of Graham, Hill City, Kans., 1949-53; counselor County of Johnson, Olathe, Kans., 1967-68; judge 10th Jud. Dist. Kans. Dist. Ct., Olathe, 1980-91, sr. judge, 1996—. Sgt. USAAF, 1942-46. Mem. ABA (life), Johnson County Bar Assn. (life), Kans. Bar Assn. (life), Am. Judicature Soc., Am. Judge's Assn., Am. Arbitration Assn., Am. Legion, Masons, Shriners, Elks. Methodist. Home: 1012 S Stratford Rd Olathe KS 66062-2117 Office: Kans Dist Ct 10 Jud Dist Johnson County Courthouse Olathe KS 66061

CHIPMAN, MARTIN, neurologist, retired army officer; b. Boston, June 16, 1930. AB in History cum laude, Harvard U., 1953, postgrad., 1956; MD, Baylor Coll. Medicine, 1960. Diplomate Am. Bd. Psychiatry and Neurology. Intern Walter Reed Army Med. Ctr., Washington, 1960-61, resident in neurology, 1961-64; assoc. in neurophysiology Walter Reed Army Inst. Rsch., Washington, 1964; neurologist Meml. and Univ. Hosps.; dir. stroke rsch. unit VA Hosp. and SUNY-Upstate Med. Ctr.; chief neurology svcs. VA Hosp.; resident tng. supr. SUNY-Upstate Med. Ctr., assoc. prof. neurology; asst. clin. prof. neurology U. Md., Balt.; chief neurology svc. Eisenhower Med. Ctr., 1980-81; attending neurologist Walter Reed Army Med. Ctr.; prof. neurology Uniformed Svcs. U. of the Health Scis., Bethesda, Md., 1984-86; chief neurology svcs. Womack Army Hosp., 1986-87; attending neurologist Cape Fear Valley Med. Ctr., Highsmith-Rainey Hosp.; dir. sleep disorders lab. Cape Fear Valley Med. Ctr.; rsch. neurologist tropical medicine SEATO Med. Rsch. Lab., 1964-67; cons. neurology Chulalongkorn U. and Prasad Neurol. Inst., Thailand; chief medicine Sioux Valley Hosp.; asst. clin. prof. neurology Sch. Medicine U. S.D.; mem. stroke com. Regional Program for S.D. and Nebr.; cons. neurology Southwestern Mental Health Ctr., VA Hosp., Geneva (N.Y.) Gen. Hosp., Eisenhower Med. Ctr. Svc. Region; neurol. cons. Marion Labs., Kansas City, Kans.; clin. prof. neurology Med. Coll. Ga.; chmn. quality assurance, dept. neurology Walter Reed Army Ctr., Bethesda; vis. prof. neurology Hebrew U., Hadassah Med. Ctr.; sci. exch. officer to Israel, U.S. Army liaison to Israeli Def. Forces; cons., attending neurologist Nat. Naval Med. Ctr., Bethesda; mem. ethics com. Cape Fear Valley Med. Ctr., 1987-88, chmn. therapeutics and pharmacy com., 1988-94, libr. com., 1988-89, ethics com. Southeastern Gen. Hosp.; cons. surveyor Joint Commn. for the Accreditation of Health Care Facilities, 1991-95; mem. exec. com., chmn. medicine Cape Fear Valley Med. Ctr. Contbr. articles to profl. jours. Col. U.S. Army, ret., 1987. Fellow Am. Acad. Neurology; mem. N.C. Med. Soc., N.C. Neurol. Soc., Cumberland County Med. Soc. Office: 4140 Ferncreek Dr #501 Fayetteville NC 28314-2563

CHIPMAN, SUSAN ELIZABETH, psychologist; b. St. Paul, Feb. 12, 1946; d. Robert Louis and Margaret Alice Fitzgerald; m. Eric George Chipman, Aug. 27, 1966. AB in Math., Harvard U., 1966, MBA, 1967, AM in Psychol., 1969, PhD in Exptl. Psychol., 1973. Asst. prof. U. Mich., Ann Arbor, 1974-75; assoc. Nat. Inst. Edn., Washington, 1976-78, asst. dir., 1979-84; sci. officer U.S. Office Naval Rsch., Arlington, Va., 1984-85, cognitive sci. program mgr., 1985—; mem. adv. bd. James S. McDonnell Found., St. Louis, 1987—. Editor, author: Thinking and Learning Skills, 1985, Women and Mathematics, 1985, Foundations of Knowledge Acquisition, 1993, Cognitively Diagnostic Assessment, 1995; contbr. articles to profl. jours. Fellow APA, APS. Avocation: photography. Home: 2606 S Joyce St Arlington VA 22202-2214 Office: Office Naval Rsch 342 800 N Quincy St Arlington VA 22203-1906

CHIQUELIN, DAVID BRYAN, mechanical engineer; b. Warrington, Fla., Apr. 12, 1953; s. William Leonard and Margaret Celeste (Boudreaux) C. BSME, U.S. Naval Acad., 1976. Commd. ensign USN, 1976, advanced through grades to lt., divsn. officer, gunnery officer USS William H. Standley, 1977-78; legal officer, line divsn. officer patrol squadron 56 USN, Jacksonville, Fla., 1980-83; strategic computer models analyst Joint Strategic Target Planning Staff, Omaha, 1983-86; resigned USN, 1986; flight control. tng. guide editor Rockwell Space Ops. Co., Houston, 1988-95; crew on-orbit support sys. lead programmer United Space Alliance, Houston, 1996—. Programmer software in field. Mem. Nat. Mgmt. Assn. (sec. Rockwell-Houston chpt. 1992-93, pub. rels. dir. 1993-94, programs dir. 1994-95, pres. 1995-96). Avocations: golf, reading. Home: 15302 Pleasant Valley Rd Houston TX 77062-3606

CHIRLS, RICHARD, lawyer; b. Newark, 1950. BS, U. Pa., 1973, JD cum laude, 1976; LLM in Taxation, NYU, 1979. Mem. Orrick, Herrington & Sutcliffe LLP, N.Y.C. Mem. ABA (chmn. tax exempt fin.com. 1989-91), Nat. Assn. Bond Lawyers (vice chmn. com. edn. 1985-86, bd. dirs. 1987-92, pres. 1990-91), N.Y. State Bar Assn. (co-chmn. tax exempt fin. com. tax 1984-86). Office: Orrick Herrington & Sutcliffe LLP 666 5th Ave New York NY 10103*

CHIROT, DANIEL, sociology and international studies educator; b. Bélâbre, Indre, France, Nov. 27, 1942; came to U.S., 1949; s. Michel and Hélène C.; m. Cynthia Kenyon, July 19, 1974; children: Claire, Laura. BA in Social Studies, Harvard U., 1964; PhD in Sociology, Columbia U., 1973. Asst. prof. sociology U. N.C. Chapel Hill, 1971-74; asst. prof. to prof. internat. studies and sociology Henry M. Jackson sch. U. Wash., 1975—. Author: Social Change in a Peripheral Society, 1976, Social Change in the Twentieth Century, 1977, translations: Korean, 1984, Italian, 1985, Social Change inthe Modern Era, 1986, translations: Korean, 1984, Chinese, 1991, Modern Tyrants: The Power and Prevalence of Evil in Our Age, 1994, rev. edit., 1996, Polish translation, 1997, How Societies Change, 1994, Romanian translation, 1996; translator: (with Holley Coulter Chirot) Traditional Romanian Villages (Henri H. Stahl), 1980; editor: The Origins of Backwardness in Eastern Europe, 1989, The Crisis of Leninism and the Decline of the Left, 1991, (with Anthony Reid) Essential Outsiders, 1997; founder and editor Ea. European Politics and Socs., 1986-89. John Simon Guggenheim fellow 1991-92. Avocations: skiing, hiking. Office: U Washington Jackson Sch Intl Studies 503 Thompson Hall Seattle WA 98195

CHIROVSKY, NICHOLAS LUDOMIR, economics educator, historian, author; b. West Ukraine, Aug. 5, 1919; came to U.S., 1949, naturalized, 1955; s. Nicholas and Zenobia (Zarycky) Freishyn; adopted son of Leonid Chirovsky; m. Iwanna Smishkewych, Sept. 21, 1947; children: Leo, George, Andrew, John. JSD, MA, U. Graz, Austria; D in Polit. Econs., Ukranian Free U. Instr. Ukranian Grad. Sch. Econs., Munich, Germany, 1947-49; from faculty to prof. econs. Seton Hall U., South Orange, N.J., 1949-85; chmn. dept. Seton Hall U., 1963-74, chmn. MBA program, 1952-62; adj. prof. U. Miami, 1985-91; Ukrainian Cath. U., Rome, 1976—. Author: The Economic Factors in the Growth of Russia, 1957, Old Ukraine, 1963, The Ukrainian Economy, 1965, An Introduction to Russian History, 1967, Philosophy in Economic Thought, 1972, A History of the Russian Empire, Vol. I, 1973, An Introduction to Ukrainian History, Vol. I, 1981, Vol. II, 1984, Vol. III, 1986, Ukraine and the Second World War, 1985; co-author: Ukraine and the European Turmoil, 1973, Philosophical Foundations of Economic Doctrines, 1977, 3d edit., 1981, The Millenium of Ukrainian Christianity, Ukrainian edit. 1988, Aiming for Free Enterprise, Ukrainian, 1994, The Social-Economic Teaching of the Church (in Ukrainian), 1995, An Outline of the Political History of Ukraine (in Ukrainian), 1997; editor: On the Historical Beginnings of Slavic Eastern Europe, 1976, Moscow's Russification of Ukraine, 1987, The Ukrainian Graz-Leoben, 1985, The Ukrainian Heritage in America, 1991; editor jour. The Ukrainian Quar., N .Y.C., 1988-93, The Herald, 1988-93; contbr. articles to profl. jours. Mem. Shevchenko Sci. Soc. (sec.-gen. 1974-80). Home: 8320 Byron Ave Miami FL 33141-1430 *Confidence in God, hard work, responsibility before pleasure, respect for moral values tested by centuries and rooted in Christianity.*

CHISHOLM, DONALD HERBERT, lawyer; b. Kansas City, Mo., Sept. 25, 1917; s. Herbert Charles and Bessie May (Osborne) C.; m. Mildred Ruth Ice, Dec. 1, 1940; children: William L., Nan Elizabeth. AA, Kansas City Jr. Coll., 1935; JD, U. Mo., 1938; LLD (hon.), Park Coll., 1979. Bar: Mo. 1938. Assoc. Wright, Rogers & Margolin, Kansas City, 1938-41; of counsel Stinson, Mag & Fizzell, P.C., Kansas City, 1942—; bd. dirs. Kansas City Bridge Co., Farmers Exch. Bank. Dir., former chmn. Truman Med. Ctr.; trustee Ella C. and Jacob Loose Found., Midwest Rsch. Inst., U. Kans. City, Harry Wilson Loose Trust, Victor E. and Caroline E. Schutte Found., Mag Found., St. Luke Hosp. Found., Harry S. Truman Libr. Inst; past chmn. Children's Mercy Hosp.; trustee emeritus Park Coll.; bd. govs. and bus. coun. Nelson Atkins Mus. Capt. AUS, 1943-46. Recipient Exceptional Merit award U. Mo. Columbia Alumni Assn., 1981. Fellow Am. Coll. Trust and Estate Counsel (regent 1967-73), Am. Bar Found.; mem.ABA, Mo. Bar Assn. (Pres.' award 1977, Spurgeon Smithson award 1981), Kans. City Bar Assn., Mo. Bar Found. (pres. 1984-87, trustee 1988-94), Am. Judicature Soc., Lawyers Assn. of Kans. City, Univ. Club, Mission Hills (Kans.) Country Club, Order of Coif. Republican. Presbyterian. Home: 1015 W 64th Ter Kansas City MO 64113-1533 Office: Stinson Mag & Fizzell PO Box 419251 1201 Walnut St Ste 2800 Kansas City MO 64106-2150

CHISHOLM, GEORGE NICKOLAUS, dentist; b. Pullman, Wash., Sept. 21, 1936; s. Leslie L. and Lila Rene (Cates) C.; D.D.S., U. Nebr., 1960; 1 son, Andrew M. Practice dentistry, Lincoln, Nebr., 1963-83; clin. instr. Coll. Dentistry, U. Nebr., 1976-83. Mem. S.E. Nebr. Health Planning Agy., 1976-82. Served to capt. Dental Corps, USAF, 1960-63. Mem. ADA (del. 1980), Nebr. Dental Assn. (del. 1974-80, trustee 1980-83), Lincoln Dist. Dental Assn. (pres. 1979-80), Sigma Alpha Epsilon, Xi Psi Phi. Mason (32 deg., Shriner). Asst. editor Nebr. State Dental Jour., 1967-69. Home: 1735 S 38th St Lincoln NE 68506-5253

CHISHOLM, MALCOLM HAROLD, chemistry educator; b. Bombay, India, Oct. 15, 1945; came to U.S., 1972; s. Angus MacPhail and Gweneth (Robey) C.; m. Cynthia Ann Truax, May 1, 1982; children: Calum R.I., Selby Scott, Derek Adrian. BS in Chemistry, Queen Mary Coll., London, 1966, PhD in Chemistry, 1969; DSc (hon.), London U., 1981. Postdoctoral fellow U. Western Ont., London, 1969-72; asst. prof. Princeton (N.J.) U., 1972-78; assoc. prof. chemistry Ind. U., Bloomington, 1978-80, prof., 1980-85, Disting. prof. chemistry, 1985—; cons. in field. Editor: Polyhedron, Chem. Comm., Dalton Transactions; mem. editl. bd. Inorganic Chemistry, Organometallics, Inorganic Chimica Acta, Inorganic Syn. Inc., Jour. Cluster Sci., Chem. European Jour., Can. Jour. Chemistry; contbr. over 450 rsch. articles to profl. jours. Fellow AAAS, Ind. Acad. Scis., Royal Soc. (London), Royal Soc. for Chemistry (Corday Morgan medal 1981, award for Transition Metal Chemistry, Centenary Lectr. and medal), Am. Chem. Soc. (Akron sect. award 1982, Buck Whitney award 1987, Inorganic Chemistry award, Disting. Svc. award). Home: 515 S Hawthorne Dr Bloomington IN 47401-5023 also: 38 Norwich St, Cambridge CB2 1NE, England Office: Ind Univ Dept Chemistry Bloomington IN 47405

CHISHOLM, MARGARET ELIZABETH, retired library education administrator; b. Grey Eagle, Minn., July 25, 1921; d. Henry D. and Alice (Thomas) Bergman; children: Nancy Diane, Janice Marie Lane. BA, U. Washington, 1957, MLS, 1958, PhD, 1966. Libr. Everett (Wash.) C.C., 1961-63; from asst. to assoc. prof. edn. U. Oreg., Eugene, 1963-67; assoc. prof. edn. U. N.Mex., Albuquerque, 1967-69; prof., dean U. Md. Coll. Libr. and Info. Svcs., College Park, 1969-75; v.p. univ. rels. and devel. U. Washington, Seattle, 1975-81; dir., prof. Grad. Sch. Libr. and Info. Sci., U. Wash., Seattle, 1981-92; ret., 1992; adv. com. White House Conf. on Libr. and Info. Sci., 1989-91, Pub. Broadcasting Svc. Archive; commr. Western Interstate Commn. Higher Edn., Colo., 1981-85. Author: Information Technology: Design and Applications (with Nancy Lane), 1990. Mem. USIA del. to Mexican-Am. Commn. on Cultural Coop., 1990. Civilian aide U.S. Army, 1978-88. Recipient Ruth Worden award U. Wash., Seattle, 1957, Disting. Alumni award St. Cloud (Minn.) U., 1977, Disting. Alumni award U. Wash., 1979, John Brubaker award Cath. Libr. Assn., 1987, Pres.'s award Wash. Libr. Assn., 1991. Mem. ALA (exec. bd. 1989-90, pres. 1988-89, v.p. 1986-87), Assn. Pub. TV Stas. (trustee 1975-84, 87-93), White House Conf. on Libr. and Info. Svcs. (adv. com. 1989-91), U. Wash. Retirement Assn. (v.p. 1995-96, pres. 1996-98). Home: 5892 NE Park Point Pl Seattle WA 98115-7845

CHISHOLM, MARTHA MARIA, dietitian; b. Havana, Cuba, Nov. 27, 1958; came to U.S., 1961; d. Robert Lester and Martha Clara (Latour) C. BS in Dietetics and Nutrition, Fla. Internat. U., 1983, MS Dietetics/Nutrition magna cum laude, 1995. Lic. dietitian, Fla. Pediat. clin. dietitian Miami (Fla.) Children's Hosp., 1983-86, 92-96, pediat. gastroenterology dietitian, 1986-92, dietitian Ketogenic Diet Ctr., 1994-96, pediat. clin. dietitian, staff relief, 1997; dietitian Pediatric Cystic Fibrosis Ctr., 1993-96, dietitian feeding and swallowing disorder team, 1994-96; clin. dietitian Oncology and Hospice Mercy Cath. Hosp., 1997—; cons. United Cerebral Palsy Assn. Miami, 1989-94, Roche Labs., Miami, 1991-95, Children's Rehab. Network, Miami, 1990-95. Presenter in field. Mem. Homeless Ministry, St. Louis Cath. Ch., Miami, 1991-94, Eucharistic min., 1993-96, young adult ministry co-leader, 1994-96; mem. fgn. mission ministry Amor En Accion, 1995—. Mem. Am. Dietetic Assn. (reg. dietician), Fla. Dietetic Assn. (Disting. Dietitian 1997), Miami Dietetic Assn. (sec. 1988-89, Recognized Young Dietitian award 1988, Hurricane Andrew Relief Fund chair 1992-93, mem. nominating com. 1993-94, Disting. Dietitian 1996), Phi Kappa Phi. Republican. Roman Catholic. Avocations: dog show handling, backpacking, cycling, photography, canoeing. Home: 5935 Turin St Coral Gables FL 33146-3245 Office: Mercy Cath Hosp 3663 S Miami Ave Miami FL 33133-4253

CHISHOLM, ROBERT E., architect; b. Havana, Cuba, Jan. 17, 1950; s. Robert L. and Martha C. (Latour) C.; m. Aug. 9, 1975; children: Robert M., Jacqueline A. BArch, U. Fla., 1973; M.Urban design, U. Miami, Fla., 1977; postgrad., Ga. Inst. Tech., 1992. Architect/planner Metro-Dade County Housing & Urban Devel., Miami, 1974-76; lead prin. planner Metro-Dade County OCED, Miami, 1976-80; v.p. Ramos & Assocs., Inc., Miami, 1980-82; pres. R.E. Chisholm Architects, Inc., Miami, 1982—; design critic UM/MDCC/FIU, Miami. Mem. archtl. adv. com. City of Miami Beach, 1988-89 ad-hoc advisor Dade County Assn. for Retarded Citizens, 1980-83; chmn. design and constrn. CPHI Homeless Assistance Ctr.; architect/planner Moss Plan Hurricane Recovery Master Plan, Fla.; chmn. design/constrn. Cmty. Partnership for Homeless, Inc., Miami, 1993—. Fellow AIA (pres. 1992), Greater Miami C. of C., U. Fla. Alumni Assn. Home: 737 Jeronimo Dr Coral Gables FL 33146-1268 Office: R E Chisholm Architects Inc 7254 SW 48th St Miami FL 33155-5525

CHISHOLM, TAGUE CLEMENT, pediatric surgeon, educator; b. East Millinocket, Maine, Nov. 6, 1915; s. George James and Victoria Mary (Tague) C.; m. Verity Burnett, 1940 (div. 1975); children—Christopher Tague, Penelope Ann, Robin Francis; m. Johanna Lyon Myers, Aug. 9, 1975. A.B. cum laude, Harvard U., 1936, M.D., 1940. Diplomate Am. Bd. Surgery. Intern Peter Bent Brigham Hosp. and Boston Children's Hosp., 1940-41, resident in gen. and pediatric surgery, 1941-46; Arthur Tracy Cabot fellow in surgery Harvard Med. Sch., 1946; practice medicine specializing in pediatric surgery Mpls., 1947—; mem. faculty U. Minn. Sch. Medicine, Mpls., 1947—, clin. prof. surgery, 1965-84; trustee Mpls. Children's Health Ctr. Hosp. Mem. editorial bd. Jour. Pediatric Surgery, 1965-76, Pediatric Digest, 1962-82, Jour. Minn. Med. Assn., 1957-86; contbr. articles in pediatric surgery to profl. jours. and books. Former trustee Bishop Whipple Schs., Faribault, Minn.; bd. dirs. Wells Found., Mpls.; trustee Minn. Internat. Health Vols., Mpls., Surg. Aid to Children of the World, N.Y.C. Recipient Presdl. award Minn. Med. Assn., 1978, merit medal U. Rio Grande Norte, Brazil, 1976, Charles Bowles Rogers award Hennepin County Med. Soc., 1976, Gold Headed Cane award U. Minn., 1992, Harold S. Diehl award U. Minn. Med. Alumni Soc., 1994. Mem. ACS, Am. Acad. Pediat., Am. Pediat. Surg. Assn., Am. Trauma Soc., Am. Mich. Surg. Assn., Western Surg. Assn., N.W. Pediat. Soc. (pres. 1988—). Home: 205 Holly Ln N Plymouth MN 55447-3549 Office: 2545 Chicago Ave Minneapolis MN 55404-4522

CHISHOLM, TOM SHEPHERD, environmental engineer; b. Morristown, N.J., Nov. 28, 1941; s. Charles Fillmore and Eileen Mary (Fenderson) C.; m. Mary Virginia Carrillo, Nov. 7, 1964; children: Mark Fillmore, Elaine Chisholm. Student, Northeastern U., Boston, 1959-61; BS in Agrl. Engring., N.Mex. State U., 1964; MS in Agrl. Engring., S.D. State U., 1967; PhD in Agrl. Engring., Okla. State U., 1970. Registered profl. engr., Ariz., La.; cert. Class A indsl. wastewater operator. Agrl. engr. U.S. Bur. Land Mgmt., St. George, Utah, 1964-65; asst. prof. U. P.R., Mayaguez, 1970-74, La. State U., 1974-77; assoc. prof. S.D. State U., 1977-81; environ. engr. Atlantic Richfield Subsidiary, Sahuarita, Ariz., 1981-86, Ariz. Dept. Environ. Quality, Phoenix, 1986-88; environ. mgr. Galactic Resources, Del Norte, Colo., 1988-91; v.p. M&E Cons., Inc., Phoenix, 1991-94; pres. Chisholm & Assocs., Phoenix, 1991—; v.p. 3R Resources, Tucson, 1994—; cons. various mfrs., Calif., Tex., Ill., Mex., 1980-91. Contbr. articles to profl. jours. NSF fellow, 1965-66, 68-69. Mem. Am. Soc. Agrl. Engrs. (faculty advisor student chpt. 1978-79), Phi Kappa Phi, Sigma Xi, Alpha Epsilon, Beta Gamma Epsilon. Avocations: hiking, running, investing, solar energy. Office: Chisholm & Assocs PO Box 47554 Phoenix AZ 85068-7554

CHISHOLM, TOMMY, lawyer, utility company executive; b. Baldwyn, Miss., Apr. 14, 1941; s. Thomas Vaniver and Rubel (Duncan) C.; m. Janice McClanahan, June 20, 1964; children: Mark Alan (dec.), Andrea, Stephen Thomas, Patrick Ervin. BSCE, Tenn. Tech. U., 1963; JD, Samford U., 1969; MBA, Ga. State U., 1984. Registered profl. engr., Ala., Ark., Del., Ga.,

Fla., Ky., La., N.H., Miss., N.C., Pa., Tenn., S.C., Va., W.Va. Civil engr. TVA, Knoxville, Tenn., 1963-64; design engr. So. Co. Svcs., Birmingham, Ala., 1964-69; coord. spl. projects So. Co. Svcs., Atlanta, 1969-73; sec., house counsel So. Co. Svcs., 1977-82, v.p., sec., house counsel, 1982—; asst. to pres. So. Co., Atlanta, 1973-75; sec., asst. treas. So. Co., 1977—; mgr. adminstrv. svcs. Gulf Power Co., Pensacola, Fla., 1975-77; sec. So. Energy, Inc., Atlanta, 1981-82; v.p., sec. So. Energy Resources Inc., Atlanta, 1982—; sec. So. Co. Energy Solutions Inc., 1985—, So. Energy N.Am. Inc., 1993—, So. Electric R.R. Co., 1993—; Birchwood Devel. Corp., 1992—, SEI Birchwood, Inc., 1992—, So. Energy Inc., 1993—, So. Electric Bahamas Holdings, Ltd., 1993—, So. Electric Bahamas, Ltd., 1993—; asst. sec. Freeport Power Co. Ltd., 1993—. Mem. Am. Bar Assn., State Bar Ala., Am. Soc. Corp. Secs., Am. Corp. Counsel Assn., Phi Alpha Delta, Beta Gamma Sigma. Office: The Southern Co 270 Peachtree St Ste 2200 Atlanta GA 30303

CHISHOLM, WILLIAM DEWAYNE, retired contract manager; b. Everett, Wash., Mar. 1, 1924; s. James Adam and Evelyn May (Iles) C.; m. Esther Troehler, Mar. 10, 1956; children: James Scott, Larry Alan, Brian Duane. *Father Dr. James A. Chisholm received his M.D. and C.M. degree from McGill University in Montreal in 1900 and was a leading physician in Everett, Washington and Snohomish County for thirty-nine years. He then served two years as Medical Director of the Western Washington State Custodial School of Buckley, Washington, retired in 1941. He was a president of the Snohomish County Medical Society and an honorary thirty-third degree Mason.* BSChemE, U. Wash., 1949, BS in Indsl. Engring., 1949; MBA, Harvard U., 1955. Cert. profl. contracts mgr. Chemist, unit leader, tech. rep. The Coca-Cola Co., Atlanta and L.A., 1949-59; contract adminstr. Honeywell Inc., L.A., 1959-61, mktg. adminstr., 1961-64, contracts work dir., 1964-66; contracts mgr. Honeywell Inc., Clearwater, Fla., 1966-73, contracts supr., 1973-75, sr. contract mgmt. rep., 1975-80, prin. contract mgmt. rep., work dir., 1980-82, contracts mgr., 1982-89; ret.; chmn. bd. Creative Attitudes, Inc., 1987-96; adj. faculty Fla. Inst. Tech., 1976-96. Contbr. articles to profl. jours. Trustee John Calvin Found., 1974-82; mem. budget adv. com. City of Clearwater, 1983-85; commr. to 196th gen. assembly Presbyn. Ch. (USA), 1984; sec. bd. trustees, treas. Presbytery of Tampa Bay, 1990-96, sec. coun., 1996-98, mem. rev., evaluation and planning com., 1996-98, treas. 1999—; Clearwater rep. on Long Ctr. bd. dirs., 1991-97, mem. exec. com., 1992-97, treas., 1992-93, v.p., 1993-95. With USN, 1944-46. Recipient Award of Distinction Fla. Inst. Tech. Grad. Ctr., 1987. Fellow Nat. Contract Mgmt. Assn. (chmn. S.E. region fellows 1985-87, past nat. dir., pres., v.p. Suncoast chpt.). Republican. Presbyterian (elder session mem. 1964-65, 73-76, 77-80, 81-84, 86-90, 97—, ch. treas. 1994-96). Home: 1364 S Hercules Ave Clearwater FL 33764-3748 *We can't be too generous in sharing understanding and words of comfort, encouragement, and support to those facing adversity and challenge at various times in their lives.*

CHISHOLM, WILLIAM HARDENBERGH, management consultant; b. N.Y.C., Apr. 24, 1917; s. Hugh J. and Sara Clark (Hardenbergh) C.; m. Alice Jensen, Nov. 7, 1942 (dec. Aug. 5, 1993); children: Barbara Chisholm Young, Margo Jensen; m. Edith E. Griffiths Aug. 13, 1994. A.B., Yale U., 1940. With Oxford Paper Co., N.Y.C., 1940-71, asst. to pres., 1946-50, v.p., dir., 1950-56, pres., 1956-69, chmn., 1969-71; exec. v.p., dir. Ethyl Corp., 1967-71; pres. Boardroom Consultants, Inc., 1975-88; chmn. Boardroom Cons. div. Kenny, Kindler, Hunt & Howe, 1988-90; Dep. dir. pulp and paper div. NPA, Washington, 1951; bd. dirs. Lescarden Inc. Pres. Animal Med. Ctr., 1970-74; bd. dirs. The Dog Mus., 1990-96. Clubs: Westminster Kennel (gov.), Sky, Blind Brook, Round Hill; Yale, Economic (N.Y.C.) Belle Haven. Home: 45 Lismore Ln Greenwich CT 06831-3741 Office: 280 Railroad Ave Greenwich CT 06830-6338

CHISM, JAMES ARTHUR, information systems executive, business consultant; b. Oak Park, Ill., Mar. 6, 1933; s. William Thompson and Arema Eloise (Chadwick) C. AB, DePauw U., 1957; MBA, Ind. U., 1959; postgrad. internat. fin. program, U. pa., 1984; postgrad. sr. exec. devel. program, U. Notre Dame, 1988. Mgmt. engr. consumer and indsl. products divsn. Uniroyal, Inc., Mishawaka, Ind., N.Y.C., 1959-61, sr. mgmt. engr., officer mgr., 1961-63; sys. analyst Miles, Inc. (name now Bayer Corp.), Elkhart, Ind., 1963-64, sr. sys. analyst, 1965-69, project mgr. distbn./logistics sys., 1969-71, mgr. sys. programming for corp. fin. and adminstrv. depts., 1971-73, mgr. adminstrv. sys. and corp. staff svcs., 1973-75, group mgr. consumer products group sys. and programming, 1975-79; dir. corp. orgnl. analysts, adminstrn. and staff svcs. Berkeley, Calif., Elkhart, Ind., London, Toronto, Cutter/Miles, 1979-81; dir. advanced office sys. and corp. adminstrn., 1982-84; dir. advanced office sys. Internat. MIS and Adminstrn., 1984-85, dir. advanced office sys., tng., and adminstrn., 1985-87; exec. dir. fin. and adminstrv. svcs. N.Am. Info. Sys. and Logistics, 1991-92; CFO N.Am. Info. Sys., 1992-95; sr. ptnr. Heartland Consulting Group, 1995—. Bd. dirs. United Way Elkhart County, 1974-78, 91-94, Arts Ind. Inc. State Coun., mem. adv. bd., 1995—; bd. dirs. Ind. Colls. of Ind. Found., 1986-96, devel. comm., 1992-96; bd. dirs. Snite Mus. Art U. Notre Dame, 1990—, v.p., 1993-94, pres., 1994-96, pres. emeritus mus., 1997—; Alliance Roundtable mem. Art Inst. Chgo., 1970— (Ind. Govs. award 1994); mem. Coun. of Sagamores of Wabash, 1993—. with AUS, 1954-56. Mem. No. Ind. Hist. Soc. (life, chmn. fin. com.), Common Dataprocessing Assn., Assn. sys. Mgmt. (chpt., pres. 1969-70, divsn. dir. 1972-77, internat. dir. 1978-80, Merit award 1975, Achievement award 1977, cert. sys. profl. 1984, Disting. Svc. award 1986, 25 Yrs. Leadership award 1988, 30 Yr. Commendation award 1994), Disting. Dean's Assocs. of Ind. U. Kelley Sch. Bus. Bloomington (computer info. sys. adv. coun. 1980—), Ind. U. Alumni Assn. (life), Well House Soc., Assn. Internal Mgmt. Cons. (exec. com., bd. dirs., v.p.), Fin. Execs. Inst., Econ. Club Chgo., Nat. Assn. Bus. Econs., DePauw U. Alumni Assn. (Pres.'s Cir., regents program 1989, nat. ann. fund exec. com. 1990—, bd. frat. affairs 1987-89, bd. visitors 1990-93, alumni assn. bd. dirs. 1994—), Washington C. DePauw Soc. (exec. com. 1993—), DePauw Deke Realty Assn. (past pres. 1988-93), Soc. Info. Mgmt., Morris Park Country Club (South Bend, Ind.), Univ. Club (Notre Dame, Ind.), Yale Club (N.Y.C.), Skyline Club (Indpls.), Ind. Soc. Chgo. Club, Deke Club (N.Y.C.), Delta Kappa Epsilon, Deke Club of N.Y.C., Sigma Delta Chi, Sigma Iota Epsilon, Beta Gamma Sigma, Omicron Delta Epsilon, Alpha Iota Delta. Republican. Episcopalian. Home: 504 Cedar Crest Ln Mishawaka IN 46545-5772 Office: Bayer Corp PO Box 40 1884 Miles Ave Elkhart IN 46514-2291

CHISM, MICHELLE, secondary education educator; b. St. Louis, June 18, 1969; d. John Jefferson and Christine (Stewart) Smith; m. Kevin Lee Chism, Apr. 1, 1995; 1 child, Kevin Lee Jr. BS in Edn., So. Ill. U., Edwardsville, 1993; MEd, U. Mo., St. Louis, 1996. Tchr. mid. sch. lang. arts St. Louis Pub. Schs., 1994-97; tchr. English Riverview H.S., St. Louis, 1997—. Fellow Nat. Coun. Tchrs. of English. Avocations: reading, gymnastics, travel. Home: 11903 Ellens Way Ct Saint Louis MO 63138-1216

CHISOLM, BARBARA WILLE, world affairs organization executive; b. Albany, N.Y., Dec. 8, 1936; d. Edmund James and Marian Virginia (Titter) Bowen; m. Roland Frank Wille, July 2, 1969 (dec. July 1988); children: Serena Bowen, Alison Brevard; m. Oliver Beirne Chisolm, Aug. 10, 1991. BA, Smith Coll., 1958; MA, U. London, 1960. Acting dir. rsch. dept. Met. Mus., N.Y.C., 1966-69; dir. Art Gallery of the China Inst., N.Y.C., 1969-71; N.Y.-New Eng. dir., lectr. Nat. Fine Arts Assocs., Washington, 1974-88; exec. dir., pres. Forum for World Affairs, Stamford, Conn., 1989—; pres. World Affairs Couns. of Am., Washington, 1998—; invited guest NATO, Brussels, 1996, Fgn. Ministry Brazil, 1997, Fgn. Ministry Taiwan, 1999. Mem. Women's Fgn. Policy Group, Fgn. Policy Assn. (bd. dirs.), Republican. Episcopalian. Avocations: classical music, skiing, tennis,fly fishing, travel. Home: 21 Stepping Stone Ln Greenwich CT 06830-4031 Office: Forum for World Affairs 3 Landmark Sq Ste 230 Stamford CT 06901-2585

CHISUM, EMMETT DEWAIN, historian, archeologist, researcher; b. Monroe, La., Mar. 19, 1922. BA in Social Sci., Northwestern State U., 1942; MA in Social Sci., La. State U., 1946; MA in History, U. Wyo., 1952, MA in Polit. Sci. an dAnthropology, 1961. Tchr. sci. Cameron (La.) Parish Sch. System, 1947-51; tchr. English Welsh (La.) High Sch., 1946-47; social sci. librarian U. Wyo., Laramie, 1954-77, prof. rsch. history, archeology, 1977—; mem. faculty senate U. Wyo., 1986—. Author: (books) Guide to Library Research, 1969, Guide to Research in Political Science, 1970, Guide to Research in Education, 1974, Memories: University of Wyoming 1886-1986, 1987; contbr. articles to Ency. of Lir. and Info. Sci. (45 vols.), 1986—, profl. jours. Mem. AAAS, ALA, Am. Archeol. Soc., Western Pol. Sci. Assn., Am. Assn. for State and Local History for Wyo. Publs. (Agnes Milstead award for Disting. Librarianship 1995). Home: 2032 Holliday Dr Laramie WY 82070-4803

CHISUM, MATTHEW EUAL, laboratory manager; b. Amarillo, Tex., Aug. 5, 1953; s. Donzell Eual and Ella Jean (Vincent) C.; m. Elizabeth Kay Neidhardt, Mar. 15, 1980; children: Brett Matthew, Kristen Marie. BS, West Tex. State U., 1975, MS, 1976. Veterinarian asst. High Plains Animal Hosp., Borger, Tex., 1976-77; instr. math. Frank Phillips Jr. Coll., Borger, 1976-77; chem. tech. Mason & Hanger Pantex Plant, Amarillo, 1977-87, sr. scientist, 1987-90; owner Chisum Ranches, Ltd., Stinnett, 1987—, project scientist, 1990-91, sr. project scientist, 1991-96, lab mgr., 1997; project team leader for atomic spectroscopy Pantex Plant, Amarillo, 1994-97; lab. mgr. Engineered Carbons, Inc., Borger, Tex., 1997—; mem. Comm. Task Force-Pantex, Amarillo, 1990-91, Emergency Spill Response-Pantex, Amarillo, 1987-92. Contbr. articles to profl. jours. Mem. Tax Appraisal Rev. Bd., Hutchinson County, 1996-97. Mem. Am. Chem. Soc., ASTM (sec. sect. d 24, 51), Soc. Applied Spectroscopy, Ducks Unltd. (chmn. Canyon chpt. 1985-86), Lions Internat. (sec. Adobe Walls 1988-95), Hutchinson County Pioneers Assn. (pres. 1994-96), Sigma Phi Epsilon (alumni chmn. Tex. Xi chpt. 1976-81, Alumnus of Yr. award 1976, 78, Leadership Borger 1998-99). Avocations: hunting, horse training, ranching. Home: PO Box 3338 400 Lariat St Stinnett TX 79083-3338 Office: Engineered Carbons Inc 1111 Penn St Borger TX 79008-2831

CHISWICK, BARRY RAYMOND, economics educator; b. Feb. 5, 1942. PhD, Columbia U., 1967. Rsch. prof. econs., dept. head U. Ill., Chgo., 1978—.

CHITESTER, ROBERT JOHN, television producer; b. Kane, Pa., Oct. 30, 1937; s. Palmer Rayburn and Ellen Louise (Huffman) C.; m. Carol Beth Lovell, Feb. 28, 1958; children: Cindee Lynn, Kimberly Jo, Mark Kevin, Amy Beth. BA in Radio/TV, U. Mich., 1959, MA in Radio/TV, 1962; D of Lit., Allegheny Coll., 1980. Dir. of TV prodn. Buena Vista H.S., Saginaw, Mich., 1959-61; dir. TV ops. Edinboro (Pa.) State Coll., 1962-66; pres. Public Broadcasting of N.W. Pa., Erie, 1966-82, Amagin Inc., McKean, Pa., 1980-85, Chitester Creative Assocs., McKean, 1984—, Palmer R. Chitester Fund, McKean, 1985—; mng. ptnr. Free to Choose Enterprise, McKean, 1988—; chmn. Share TV, Inc., 1992-98; adv. bd. C. Northcote Parkinson Fund, N.Y.C., 1988—, ACES, Erie, Pa., 1984—. Prodr., dir. writer many prodns. Pres. Planned Parenthood, Erie County, Pa., 1969-73; dir. Erie County Public Libr., 1976-78, Erie County Alcoholism Coun., 1975-78. Republican. Avocations: aquarist, physical fitness, gardening, wood sculpture. Home: 10539 Edinboro Rd Mc Kean PA 16426-1949 Office: Chitester Creative Assocs 9008 Main St # 3 Mc Kean PA 16426-1447

CHITTICK, ARDEN BOONE, steamship agency executive; b. Sunnyside, Wash., Aug. 5, 1936; s. Herbert Boone and Maude Ellen (George) C.; m. Nina Sorensen, Apr. 16, 1960; children: Kyle, Kirsten. BS, Wash. State U., 1964. Ops. mgr. Kerr Steamship Co. Inc., Seattle, 1979-81, marine mgr. PNW, 1981-84; dist. ops. mgr. Merit Steamship Agy. Inc., Seattle, 1984-86, Pacific N.W. ops. mgr., 1986-87; ops. mgr. Internat. Shipping Co. Inc., Seattle, 1987-89, v.p. ops., 1989-91, regional v.p. ops., 1991-96; v.p. Internat. Shipping Co. Inc., Portland, Oreg., 1991-96, bd. dirs., dir., 1996—; v.p. Marine Exch. of Puget Sound, Seattle, 1982-88; pres. Puget Sound Steamship Operators Assn., Seattle, 1987, v.p., 1983, 86, 95. Troop com. mem. Boy Scouts Am., Bainbridge Island, Wash., 1984. Capt. USMCR, 1957-64; comdr. USCG, 1964-79. Mem. Puget Sound Coast Guard Officers Assn. (pres. 1978), Propeller Club of U.S. (gov. Seattle chpt. 1984-87, 89-94). Republican. Methodist. Avocations: fishing, sports, landscape gardening, history. Home: RR 1 Box 57B Porter Hill Rd Bear Lake PA 16402-9622 Office: Internat Shipping Co Inc 1111 3rd Ave Ste 1825 Seattle WA 98101-3207

CHITTICK, ELIZABETH LANCASTER, association executive, women's rights activist; b. Bangor, Pa., Nov. 11, 1918; d. George and Flora Mae (Mann) Lancaster. Student, Columbia U., 1944-45, N.Y. Inst. Fin., 1950-51, Hunter Coll., 1952-56, Upper Iowa U., Fayette, 1976. Adminstrv. asst., chief clk U.S. Naval Air Stas., Seattle and Banana River, Fla., 1941-45; v.p. treas. W.A. Chittick & Co., MAnila, 1945-52; 31062Smith; real estate salesperson La Jolla, Calif., 1949; registered rep. Bache & Co., N.Y. Stock Exch., N.Y.C., 1950-62, Shearson & Hamil, 1962-63; investment adviser, 1962-65; revenue officer IRS, N.Y.C., 1965-72; pres. Nat. Woman's Party, Washington, 1971-89, Woman's Party Corp., 1978-91; commr. Washington Commn. on Status of Women, 1982-86; pres., adminstr. Sewall-Belmont House; bd. dirs. Wexita Corp., N.Y.C., Pan Am. Liason Com. of Women's Orgns. Inc.; 1st v.p., bd. dirs. Nat. Coun. Women U.S. Lectr., TV and radio commentator on Equal Rights Amendment; author: Answers to Questions About the Equal Rights Amendment, 1973, 76. Mem. Coalition for Women in Internat. Devel., Internat. Women's Yr. Continuing Com., 1978-81, Women's Campaign Fund, Washington, 1975-80, Women's Nat. Rep. Club, N.Y.C., Women Govt. Rels., Washington; mem. U.S. com. of cooperation to Inter-Am. Commn. of Women, OAS, 1974-80; del. U.S. World Conf. of Internat. Women's Yr., Mexico City, 1975; mem. women's history ctr. task force Am. Revolution Bicentennial Adminstrn., 1973-76; mem. adv. com. U.S. Ctr. for Internat. Women's Yr., 1973-76; vice convenor com. on law and status of women Internat. Coun. of Women; chmn. UN Drive for war orphans and widows, Manila, 1949;. Mem. Greater Washington Soc. Assn. Execs., Internat. Coun. Women (Paris), Nat. Fedn. Bus. and Profl. Women's Clubs, Gen. Fedn. Women's Clubs, Women's Press Club (N.Y.C.), Am. Newswomen's Club, Nat. Press Club, Order Eastern Star. Home and Office: 3590 S Ocean Blvd Apt 107 Palm Beach FL 33480-5743

CHITTUM, JAMEY EVE, principal; b. Erick, Okla., Mar. 19, 1947; d. James Buford and Etta Eva (Boyd) Mann; divorced; children: Misty Chittum Brower, Gabria Dara. BS in Elem. Edn., U. Sci. and Arts Okla., 1970; M in Elem. Adminstr., Southwestern Okla. State U., 1979; Cert. prin., SWOSU, Weatherford, Okla., 1983. Cert. tchr., adminstr. K-8, Okla. Tchr. Anadarko (Okla.) Pub. Schs., 1970-89, prin., 1989-92; prin. Erick Pub. Schs., 1992—. Mem. Okla. Planning and Coordinating Bd. for Children and Youth, 1994-97; mem. planning com. Progressive Farmer Day Camp, 1997. Mem. ASCD, Nat. Assn. Elem. Sch. Prins., Okla. Assn. Elem. Sch. Prins., Delta Kappa Gamma, Beta Sigma Phi. Democrat. Baptist. Avocations: bridge, reading, sponsoring youth trips. Home: PO Box 94 Erick OK 73645-0094

CHITTY, DENNIS HUBERT, zoology educator; b. Bristol, Eng., Sept. 18, 1912; came to Can., 1930; s. Hubert and Florence Louise (Gwillim) C.; m. Helen Marie Stevens, July 4, 1936 (dec. Apr. 1987); children—Jane Carol, Kathleen Joanna, Stephen Gwilym; m. Sharon Anne Kendall, Aug. 13, 1988. B.A., U. Toronto, 1935; M.A., Oxford U., Eng., 1947, DPhil, 1950; DSc, 1995. Field asst. Ont. Fisheries Research Lab., Toronto, Can., 1932-35; research officer Oxford U., Eng., 1935-61; prof. zoology U. B.C., Vancouver, Can., 1961-78, prof. emeritus, 1978—. Author: Do Lemmings Commit Suicide? Beautiful Hypotheses and Ugly Facts, 1996; contbr. articles to profl. jours. Recipient Master Tchr. award U. B.C., 1973; NSF fellow Smith Coll., 1968-69. Fellow Royal Soc. Can.; mem. Can. Soc. Zoologists (Fry Medalist, 1988). E-mail: chittyinterchange.ubc.ca. Home: 1750 Knox Rd, Vancouver, BC Canada V6T 1S3 Office: U BC, U Brit Col, Dept Zoology, Vancouver, BC Canada V6T 1Z4

CHITTY, (MARY) ELIZABETH NICKINSON, university historian; b. Balt., Apr. 27, 1920; d. Edward Phillips and Em Turner (Merritt) Nickinson; m. Arthur Benjamin Chitty, June 16, 1946; children: Arthur Benjamin, John Abercrombie, Em Turner, Nathan Harsh Brown. BA cum laude, Fla. State U., 1941, MA, 1942; DCL, U. of South, 1988. Tchr. Fla. Indsl. Sch. for Girls, Ocala, 1942-43; psychometrist neuropsychiat. dept. Sch. Aviation Medicine, Pensacola (Fla.) Naval Air Sta., 1943-46; assoc. editor Sewanee (Tenn.) Alumni News, U. of South, 1946-62; bus. mgr., mng. editor Sewanee Rev., 1962-65, dir. fin. aid and career svcs., 1970-80, assoc. univ. historiographer, 1980—; freelance editor. Editor: (with H.A. Petry) Sewanee Centennial Alumni Directory, 1954-62, (with H.A. Petry and R.G. Dudney) Centennial Report of the Registrar of the University of the South, 1959; (with Arthur Ben Chitty) Too Black, Too White (Ely Green), 1970; author: (with Moultrie Guerry and Arthur Ben Chitty) Men Who Made Sewanee, 1981, (with A.B. Chitty and W. Givens) Ninety-Nine Iron, 1992; columnist Sewanee Mountain Messenger, 1985—. Bd. dirs. Sewanee Civic Assn., 1979-80, 86-88; CONTACT-Lifeline of Coffee and Franklin Counties, 1981-84; mem. adv. coun. St. Andrew's Sewanee Sch., 1988—. Recipient Cmty. Svc. award Sewanee Civic Assn., 1996. Mem. Assn. Preservation Tenn. Antiquities (trustee 1985-88), AAUW (pres. Sewanee br. 1975-77), Fla. State U. Alumni Assn. (dir. 1941—, permanent pres. Class of 1941, Commitment to Excellence award, FSU Alumni Emeritus, 1997), Mortar Bd., Phi Beta Kappa, Phi Kappa Phi, Phi Alpha Theta, Kappa Delta. Democrat. Episcopalian. Home: 100 South Carolina Ave Sewanee TN 37375-2045 Office: Univ of South Sewanee TN 37385-1000

CHITWOOD, JULIUS RICHARD, librarian; b. Magazine, Ark., June 1, 1921; s. Hoyt Mozart and Florence (Umfrid) C.; m. Aileen Newsom, Aug. 6, 1944. A.B. cum laude, Ouachita Bapt. Coll., Ark., 1942; M.Mus., Ind. U., 1948; M.A., U. Chgo., 1954. Music supr. Edinburgh (Ind.) Pub. Schs., 1946-47; music and audiovisual librarian Roosevelt Coll., Chgo., 1948-51; humanities librarian Drake U., 1951-53; spl. cataloger Chgo. Tchrs. Coll., 1953; asst. circulation librarian Indpls. Pub. Library, 1954-57, coordinator adult services, 1957-61; dir. Rockford (Ill.) Pub. Library, 1961-79, No. Ill. Library System, Rockford, 1966-76; chmn. subcom. library system devel. Ill. Library Adv. Com., 1965—; adv. com. U. Ill. Grad. Sch. Library Sci., 1964-68; cons. in field, participant workshops. Pres. Rockford Regional Academic Center, 1974-76; Mem. history com. Ill. Sesquicentennial Commn.; mem. Mayor Rockford Com. for UN, 1962-70; sect. chmn. Rockford United Fund, 1966-70; exec. Rockford Civic Orch. Assn., 1962-70. Served to maj., inf. AUS, 1942-45, ETO. Recipient Ill. Librarian of Year award, 1974. Mem. ALA (chmn. subcom. revision standards of materials, pub. library div. 1965-66, pres. bldg. and equipment sect. library adminstrn. div. 1967-68, chmn. staff devel. com. personnel adminstrn. sect., library adminstrv. div. 1964-68, pres. library adminstrn. div. 1969-70), Ill. Library Assn. (v.p. 1964-65, pres. 1965-66), Rockford Area C. of C. Unitarian (pres. 1965-67). Clubs: Rotarian (exec. bd. Rockford 1965-66), Rockford University. Home: 916 Paris Ave Rockford IL 61107-3246 Office: 115 7th St Ste 209 Rockford IL 61104-1224

CHIU, DAVID TAK WAI, surgeon; b. Kwangtung, China, Oct. 23, 1945; s. Bud Yick and Lai Kwai (Lum) C.; m. Lilian Wah-Ying Shen, June 19, 1973; children: Vincent, Edmund, Jerome, Miranda. BA, U. Mo., St. Louis, 1969; MD, Columbia U., 1973. Diplomate Am. Bd. Plastic Surgery. Intern Barnes Hosp., St. Louis, 1973-74, resident in gen. surgery, 1974-77, resident in plastic surgery, 1977-79; fellow NYU Med. Ctr., N.Y.C., 1980, instr. surgery, 1981, asst. prof., 1981-89; supervisory attending Bellevue Hosp. Hand Clinic, N.Y.C., 1981-89; assoc. dir. plastic surgery, chief hand/microsurgery and replantation surgery divsn. plastic surgery Columbia Presbyn. Med. Ctr., N.Y.C., 1989-94, dir. microsurgery ctr., 1993, chief plastic surgery divsn. dept. surgery, 1994-97, prof. clin. surgery, 1990—. Author: Introduction to Microsurgery: A Lab Manual, 1985; mem. editorial bd. Jour. Reconstructive Microsurgery, 1990—. Recipient Alumni Fedn. Columbia U. medal, 1995. Fellow ACS; mem. AMA, Fedn. Chinese Am. and Chinese Can. Med. Socs. (founding pres. 1994-96, chmn. bd. dirs. 1996-98), Chinese Am. Med. Soc. (dir. 1983—, pres. 1985-87), Am. Assn. Plastic Surgeons, Am. Soc. Reconstructive Microsurgery, N.Y. County Med. Soc., N.Y. State Med. Soc., N.Y. Soc. Surgery of Hand (pres. 1996-97), Plastic Surgery Rsch. Council, Coll. Physicians and Surgeons Alumni Assn. (dir. 1984, Bronze medal 1973, Gold medal 1997), N.Y. Regional Soc. Plastic and Reconstructive Plastic Surgery (pres. 1996-97), Am. Soc. Reconstructive Microsurgery (pres.), Am. Soc. Surgery of Hand, Am. Soc. Plastic and Reconstructive Surgeons, Am. Assn. Hand Surgery, Am. Soc. Peripheral Nerve Surgery (founding, pres. 1999—), Royal Soc. Medicine, Northeast Soc. Plastic Surgery, Chinese Am. Med. Soc. (Presdl. medal 1987, Disting. Service award 1988), Internat. Soc. of Reconstructive Microsurgery, Am. Acad. Pediatrics (splty. fellow 1992), Fedn. Chinese Am. and Chinese Can. Med. Socs. (founding pres. 1994-96, outstanding achievement award 1994, chmn. bd. dirs. 1996-98), Sunderland Soc., Tissue Engring. Soc. Office: Columbia Presbyn Med Ctr 161 Fort Washington Ave New York NY 10032-3713

CHIU, DOROTHY, pediatrician; b. Hong Kong, Aug. 8, 1917; came to U.S., 1946; d. Yan Tse Chiu and Connie Kwai-Ching Wan; m. Kitman Au; children: Katherine, Margo, Doris, James, Richard. BS, Lingnan U., 1939; MD, Nat. Shanghai Med. Coll., 1945. Diplomate Am. Bd. Pediats. Sch. physician L.A. Sch. Dist., 1954-55; pvt. practice Burbank, Calif., 1954-55, San Fernando, Calif., 1955—; staff pediatrician Holy Cross Med. Ctr., Mission Hills, Calif., 1961—. Bd. dirs. Burbank Cmty. Concert, 1970-80. Fellow Am. Acad. Pediats.; mem. Calif. Med. Assn., L.A. County Med. Assn. Republican. Avocations: handicrafts, music, travel, reading, photography. Office: 11273 Laurel Canyon Blvd Ste 3 San Fernando CA 91340-4398*

CHIU, HELEN LIENHARD, educator; b. Hartford, Conn., June 10, 1937; d. John B. and Florence Lienhard; m. S.M. Chiu, June 27, 1970. BA, Skidmore Coll., 1959; MA, Am. U., 1964; PhD, Temple U., 1982. Part-time faculty Stockton State Coll., Pomona, N.J., 1979-80, Rutgers U., Camden, N.J., 1980, Drexel U., Phila., 1980-81; asst. prof. Pa. State U., Abington, 1982-87; vis. asst. prof. Temple U.-Japan, Tokyo, 1987-89, Millersville (Pa.) U., 1990-92; pvt. rsch., 1992—; asst. ctr. dir. ARC, Turkey, 1964, France, 1964-66; program dir. Internat. House Phila., 1966-72. Author: Housing Policy in Thailand, 1985; contbr. articles to profl. jours. Del. Internat. Women's Yr. Seminar, N.Y., 1974, 84; v.p. YWCA, Phila., 1975-82; chair Nat. YWCA Planning Com. Asian Study Seminar, 1977; mem. exec. com. Phila. Com. for UNICEF, 1980-86; mem. bd. Phoenix House, Bryn Mawr, Pa., 1981-86; mem. Montgomery County Task Force on Women, 1986-87. Episcopalian. Avocation: travel. Home: 514 Cambridge Rd Bala Cynwyd PA 19004-2252

CHIU, HUNGDAH, lawyer, legal educator; b. Shanghai, China, Mar. 23, 1936; came to U.S., 1960; s. Han-ping and Ming-non (Yang) C.; m. Yuan-yuan Hsieh, May 14, 1966; 1 son, Wei-hsueh. LLB, Nat. Taiwan U., 1958; MA with honors, L.I. U., 1962; LLM, Harvard U., 1962, SJD, 1965. Assoc. in rsch. East Asian Research Center, Harvard U., 1964-65; assoc. prof. internat. law Nat. Taiwan U., 1965-66; rsch. assoc. in law Harvard U., 1966-70, 72-74; vis. prof. law Nat. Chengchi U., Taipei, Taiwan, 1970-72; assoc. prof. law U. Md., Balt., 1974-77, prof., 1977—; min. of state Exec. Yuan (Cabinet), Republic of China, Taiwan, 1993-94; mem. Presdl. Com. on Nat. Unification, Taiwan, 1995—, amb.-at-large, 1998—. Author: The Capacity of International Organizations to Conclude Treaties, 1966, The People's Republic of China and the Law of Treaties, 1972, (with J.A. Cohen) People's China and International Law, 2 vols, 1974 (certificate of merit Am. Soc. Internat. Law 1976), Normalizing Relations with China: Problems, Analysis and Documents, 1978, China and the Taiwan Issue, 1979, Agreements of the People's Republic of China, 1966-80, A Calendar of Events, 1981; (with S.C. Leng) China: 70 years after the 1911 Hsin-Hai Revolution, 1984, Criminal Justice in Post-Mao China, 1985, (with Y.C. Jao and Y.L. Wu) The Future of Hong Kong, 1987, The Draft Basic Law of Hong Kong: Analysis and Documents, 1988, (with G. Knight) International Law of the Sea: Cases, Documents and Readings, 1991; Hsian-t'ai Kuo-chi-fa (Modern International Law), 1995, (with Chun-i Chen) Hsien-tai Kuo-chi-fa Ts'an-kao Wen-chien (Reference Documents of Modern International Law), 1996, 1996 Case and Documentary Supplement for Knight and Chiu's International Law of the Sea, 1997; contbr. numerous articles to profl. jours., chpts. to books; gen. editor: Contemporary Asian Studies, 1976—; editor in chief Chinese Yearbook of Internat. Law and Affairs, 1981—. Del. UN Conf. Law of the Sea, 1976-82 Served to 2d lt. Chinese Army, 1958-60. Named One of 10 Outstanding Young Men, Jr. c. of C. of Republic of China, 1971; Social Sci. Rsch. Coun. fellow, 1968; recipient Cultural award Inst. Chinese Culture, 1980, Toulmin medal Soc. Am. Mil. Engrs., 1982, Nat. Reconstrn. award Chinese Profl. Assn. Mid-Am., 1980, Outstanding Achievement award Mid-Am. Chinese Sci. and Tech. Assn., 1991, 1st class Merit Svc. medal Exec. Yuan (Cabinet), Republic of China, 1994. Mem. Am. Soc. Internat. Law (panel on China and internat. order 1969-74, chmn. interest group on law Pacific region 1987-93), Assn. for Asian Studies (com. on Asian law 1976-89), Am. Assn. for Chinese Studies (v.p. 1982-84, pres. 1985-87), Assn. Am. Law Schs. (chair internat. legal exch. sect. 1986-88), Assn. Chinese Social Scientists, N.A. (pres. 1984-86), Chinese Soc. Internat. Law (pres. 1993—), Internat. Law Assn. (pres. 1998—). Home: 6168 Devon Dr Columbia MD 21044-3821 Office: U Md Law Sch 500 W Baltimore St Baltimore MD 21201-1701

CHIU, JEN-FU, biochemistry educator; b. Tungshi, Taichung, Taiwan, Sept. 30, 1940; came to U.S., 1972; s. Kuo-Feng and Ching-Leon (Yu) C.; m. Lucia Chi-Kai Yin, May 30, 1970; children: Rosaleen I-Hsuen, Cynthia I-Tyng. B Pharmacy, Taipei (Taiwan) Med. Coll., 1964; MS in Biochemistry, Nat. Taiwan U., Taipei, 1967; PhD in Biochemistry, U. B.C., 1972. Asst. biochemist U. Tex. System Cancer Ctr. M.D. Anderson Hosp. & Tumor Inst., Houston, 1974-75; asst. prof. Vanderbilt U., Nashville, 1975-78; assoc. prof. U. Vt., Burlington, 1978-87, prof. biochemistry, 1987—; cons. NIH, Bethesda, Md., 1983-86; dir. grad. studies in biochemistry U. Vt., Burlington, 1982—, dir. cancer biology program, 1983—; rsch. fellow Chinese Nat. Sci. Coun., Taiwan, 1966, Rosalie B Hite Found., Houston, 1972. Author, editor: The Basic of Cancer Molecular Biology, 1989; contbr. numerous sci. papers to publs. Lt. Chinese ROTC, 1966-67, Taiwan. Rsch. grantee NIH, Bethesda, Md., 1975—, March of Dimes, Whiteplain, N.Y., 1978-80. Mem. Am. Soc. Biochemistry and Molecular Biology, Am. Soc. Cell Biology, Am. Assn. Cancer Rsch., Am. Soc. Microbiology, Soc. Chinese Biochemists in Am. (pres. Vt. chpt. 1989—). Office: U Vt Coll Medicine Dept Biochemistry Burlington VT 05405

CHIU, WILLIAM CHIEN-CHEN, surgeon; b. Taipei, Taiwan, Jan. 25, 1963; s. Wu Shung and Hsiu Hui (Kuo) C.; m. Terri-Ann Anthony, May 25, 1991; children: Anthony Kohler, Katherine Anna. MD, U. Md. Sch. Medicine, 1988. Intern in surgery R. W. Johnson Med. Sch. U. Medicine and Dentistry N.J., N.J., 1988-89, res. surgery R.W. Johnson Med. Sch., 1989-94; fellowship trauma surgery, surg. critical care U. Md. Med. Ctr.-RAC Shock Trauma Ctr., Balt., 1994-95; fellowship in surgery rsch. U. Md. Sch. Medicine, 1995-97; attending surgeon U. Md. Med. Ctr.-RAC Shock Trauma Ctr., Balt., 1997—. Mem. ACS, AMA, Internat. Coll. Surgeons., S.C.C.M. Republican.

CHIULLI, MICHAEL RICHARD, laboratory technician; b. Yonkers, N.Y., Aug. 8, 1965; s. Richard Stephen and Gail Doreen (McIntyre) C.; m. Michelle Elizabeth Torrance, Nov. 26, 1992; 1 child, Raymond. BS, SUNY, Geneseo, 1988, MA, 1998. Lab. technician III Med. Ctr. U. Rochester, 1991-93, lab. technician IV, 1993—. Contbr. articles to profl. jours. Mem. Livingston County Hist. Soc., 1993—. Mem. Alpha Chi Rho (Ziegler award 1991, nat. ritual officer 1995-98). Episcopalian. Avocations: genealogy, 18th century U.S. history, Italian history. Home: 27 Lima Rd Geneseo NY 14454-1149 Office: U Rochester Med Ctr Dept Infectious Disease 601 Elmwood Ave # Rochester NY 14642-0001

CHIUSANO, MICHAEL AUGUSTUS, urologic surgeon, mechanical engineer; b. Camden, N.J., Nov. 25, 1960; s. Philip Anthony and Elizabeth Jean (Townsend) C.; m. Rachel Agnes Moffre, May 25, 1985; children: Christina, Caitlin. BS in Mech. Engring., Rensselaer Poly. Inst., 1983; postgrad., Villanova U., 1984-85; DO, Phila. Coll. Osteo. Medicine, 1989. Diplomatic Nat. Bd. Osteo. Med. Examiners. Structural design engr. Boeing-Vertol, Inc., 1983-85; intern Osteo. Med. Ctr., Phila., 1989-90, St. Agnes Med. Ctr., Phila., 1989-90; resident in urology Phila. Coll. Osteo. Medicine, Albert Einstein Med. Ctr., Phila., 1991-95; pvt. practice Whiteville, N.C., 1995-96, Bala Cynwyd, Pa., 1996—; lectr. in field. Mem. ASME, Am. Osteo. Assn., Am. Coll. Osteo. Surgeons (presenter sci. exhibits, Robert Erwin Lit. Achievement award 1993), Am. Coll. Gen. Practitioners, Pa. Osteo. Med. Assn., Soc. Automotive Engrs., Pi Tau Sigma. Office: GSB Bldg Ste 415 Belmont/City Ave Bala Cynwyd PA 19004*

CHIVERS, JAMES LEEDS, lawyer; b. Pitts., Jan. 8, 1939; s. Joseph Hobart and Lorraine Anna (Silhol) C.; m. Patricia Ann Dolan, Sept. 3, 1960; children: Catherine Ann, Christopher John, Matthew Leeds. AB, Colgate U., 1960; LLB cum laude, Union U., Albany, N.Y., 1967. Bar: N.Y. 1967, U.S. Dist. Ct. (no. dist.) N.Y. 1967, U.S. Ct. Appeals (2d cir.) 1982, Fla. 1987, U.S. Dist. Ct. (so. and ea. dists.) N.Y. 1988, U.S. Supreme Ct. 1989, U.S. Dist. Ct. (we. dist.) N.Y. 1993. Assoc. Hinman, Howard & Kattell, Binghamton, N.Y., 1967-75, ptnr., 1975—, ptnr.-in-charge dept. litigation, 1981—; mem. arbitration panel Binghamton City Ct. Past pres. Vol. Am. Binghamton, bd. dirs., 1969-93. Lt. USNR, 1960-64, Vietnam. Mem. ABA (tort and ins. practice sect.), N.Y. State Trial Lawyers Assn., Internat. Def. Counsel, Am. Arbitration Assn. (arbitrator), Def. Rsch. Assn., N.Y. State Bar Assn. (torts, ins. and compensation, trial lawyers exec. com. 1996—, environ., comml. and fed. litigation sects., com. on profl. ethics 1994-98, spl. com. on unlawful practice of law 1998—), Broome County Bar Assn., Broome County C. of C., Broome County YMCA Found., Justinian Soc., Binghamton Club (pres. 1987-89), Harpur Forum, Am. Legion. Republican. Roman Catholic. Avocations: fishing, winemaking, gardening. Office: Hinman Howard & Kattell 700 Security Mutual Bldg Binghamton NY 13901

CHIVERS, LAURIE ALICE, state educational administrator; b. Pittsfield, Mass.; d. John Richard and Julia (Marek) C.; children: Walter Gene, Desiree Lynne. BS in Math., Brigham Young U., 1969; MPA, U. Utah, 1981, PhD in Ednl. Adminstrn., 1982. Cert. tchr., adminstr., Mass., Utah. Tchr. Riverview Jr. H.S., Murray, Utah, 1969-72, chmn. dept. math., 1973-77; tchr. Beverly (Mass.) Jr. H.S., 1972-73; legis. fiscal analyst Utah Legislature, Salt Lake City, 1978-83; dir. planning and budget analysis Govt. Office of Planning and Budget, Salt Lake City, 1983-87; minority edn. policy dir. U.S. Senate, Washington, 1989-92; dir. fin. Utah State Office of Edn., Salt Lake City, 1988-89, dep. supt. schs., 1992—. Office: Utah State Office of Edn 250 E 500 S Salt Lake City UT 84111-3204

CHIVETTA, ANTHONY JOSEPH, architect; b. St. Louis, Dec. 7, 1932; s. Anthony Joseph and Antoinette (Piazza) C.; m. Dolores Krekeler; children: Anthony Joseph III, Victoria, Christopher. BArch, Washington U., St. Louis, 1955. V.p. Hastings & Chivetta Architects, Inc., St. Louis, 1961-95, chmn., 1995—; mem. alumni bd. Washington U. Sch. Architecture, St. Louis, 1987-88. Bd. dirs. Chaminade Coll. Prep., St. Louis, 1975-78, St. Joseph's Inst. for the Deaf, St. Louis, 1993—. Mem. AIA. Club: St. Louis. Office: Hastings & Chivetta Architects Inc 700 Corporate Park Dr # 400 Saint Louis MO 63105-3495*

CHIVIAN, ERIC SETH, psychiatrist, environmental scientist, educator; b. Newark, June 10, 1942; children: Cybele, Dylan C., Judah B. AB, Harvard U., 1964, MD, 1968. Staff psychiatrist MIT, 1980—; asst. clin. prof. psychiatry Harvard Med. Sch., 1987—, dir. Ctr. for Health and the Global Environment, 1996—. Recipient Nobel Peace prize, 1985. Mem. AAAS, Physicians Social Responsibility, Internat. Physicians Prevent Nuclear War (co-founder, treas. 1980-85). Achievements include research on first large scale scientific survey of American and Soviet teenagers' attitudes about the future; US-USSR relations and nuclear war; health implications of species extinction and loss of biodiversity. Home: 136 Carter Pond Rd Petersham MA 01366-9728

CHIZAUSKAS, CATHLEEN JO, manufacturing company executive; b. Little Rock, Dec. 26, 1954; m. Alan Michael Chizauskas, Nov. 11, 1978; children: Marc Alan, Danielle Kelley. Diploma in Mgmt., Simmons Coll., Boston, 1981. Clk. typist to direct materials buyer Gillette Safety Razor Co., Boston, 1972-79, buyer capital equipment, 1979, mgr. MRO and purchasing svcs., 1979-85, adminstrv. asst. to v.p. mktg., 1985-87, exec. asst. to pres., 1987-88, assoc. brand mgr. shave creams, 1988-89, bus. devel. mgr., 1989-91, product mgr., 1991-94, nat. trade mktg. mgr. grooming products, 1994-95; dir. ethnic mktg. Gillette Co., Boston, 1995—, bus. mgr., 1998—; bus. mgr. New Channels, 1998—. Mem. Am. Mgmt. Assn., Simmons Coll. Grad. Sch. Alumnae Assn. Roman Catholic. Office: Gillette Co NAm Comml Ops One Gillette Park Boston MA 02106

CHIZECK, HOWARD JAY, engineering educator. BS, Case Western Res. U., 1974, MS, 1976; DSc, MIT, 1982. From asst. prof. to prof. sys. engring. Case Western Res. U., Cleve., 1981-95, prof., chair, 1995-98; prof., chair elec. engring. U. Wash., Seattle, 1998—. E-mail: chizeck@ee.washington.edu.

CHLAMTAC, IMRICH, computer company executive, educator; b. Zlate Moravce, Czechoslovakia, Mar. 21, 1949; came to U.S., 1977; s. Zoltan and Klara (Csato) C.; children: Eddie, Noga. BS, Tel Aviv U., 1975, MS, 1977; PhD in Computer Sci., U. Minn., 1979. Prin. engr. Digital Equipment Co., Tewksbury, Mass., 1980-82; sr. lectr. Technion, Haifa, Israel, 1987-93; Fulbright prof. U. Mass., Amherst, 1993-94; founder, CEO BCN, Inc., Boston, 1990—, pres.; prof. Boston U., 1995—; disting. chair in telecom. prof. U. Tex., Dallas; cons. Motorola, Austin, Tex., 1983-86, Intel, Haifa, 1982-84, Fibronics, Hyannis, Md., 1984-86, Codex, Mansfield, Mass., 1985-89, GTE, Waltham, Mass., 1991-92, Digital Equipment Co., Littleton, Mass., 1992-93; U.S. del. Internat. Union Radio Sci., 1987, 90; lectr. and presenter in field. Co-author: Local Networks, 1980; editor-in-chief Wireless Networks Jour., 1995—, Jour. Spl. Topics on Mobile Networking and Applications, 1996—; contbr. articles to profl. jours. Recipient New Talents in Simulation award Soc. for Computer Simulation, 1982. Fellow IEEE (IEEE TOC jour. editor 1989-93, founder, chair MobiComm Conf. 1995—), Assn. for Computing Machinery (gen. chmn. Sigcomm conf. 1993—, founder, chair MobiComm Conf. 1995—). Office: Univ of Texas Dallas Engring EC-33 PO Box 830688 Richardson TX 75083

CHMELKA, BRADLEY FLOYD, chemical engineering educator; b. Phoenix, Feb. 23, 1960. BSChemE, Ariz. State U., 1982; PhD in Chem. Engring., U. Calif., Berkeley, 1990. Retort startup engr. Unocal Oil Shale Ops., Parachute, Colo., 1982-84; NSF-chemistry postdoctoral fellow dept. chemistry U. Calif., 1990; NSF-NATO postdoctoral fellow Max-Planck-Institut für Polymerforschung, Mainz, Germany, 1991; asst. prof. dept. chem. engring. U. Calif., Santa Barbara, 1992-95, assoc. prof., 1995-97, prof., 1997—. Recipient Young Investigator award NSF, 1992, Tchr.-Scholar award Camille & Henry Dreyfus Found., 1992; Sci. and Engring. Packard fellow David & Lucile Packard Found., 1993, Rsch. fellow Alfred P. Sloan Found., 1996. Mem. AIChE, Am. Chem. Soc., Am. Phys. Soc., Materials Rsch. Soc. Achievements include devel. and application of nuclear magnetic resonance spectroscopy methods to the characterization of optical, mechanical, adsorption and transport properties of new solid-state materials; correlation of macroscopic material properties and function with molecular structure and dynamics, particularly in heterogeneous macromolecular solids. Office: U Calif Dept Chem Engring Santa Barbara CA 93106

CHMIELARZ, SHARON LEE, writer, educator; b. Mobridge, S.D., Dec. 20, 1940; m. Tadeusz B. Chmielarz, June 27, 1964. BS, U. Minn., 1962, MA, 1976. Tchr. German and English Orono (Minn.) Sch. Dist., 1962-91; editl. work New Rivers Press, Mpls., 1993, 96, Minn. State Bd. Arts, St. Paul, 1992, 96. Author: Different Arrangements, 1982, But I Won't Go Out in a Boat, 1990, Pied Piper of Hamlin, 1990, End of Winter, 1992, Down at Angels, 1994, (chapbook) Stranger in Her House, 1995. Minn. State Arts Bd. fellow, 1991; Jerome Found. travel grantee, 1995. Mem. The Loft/A Place for Writing, S.A.S.E./The Writer Place, Soc. Children's Book Writers and Illustrators. Avocations: driving, swimming, reading.

CHMIELINSKI, EDWARD ALEXANDER, retired electronics company executive; b. Waterbury, Conn., Mar. 25, 1925; s. Stanley ahd Helen Chmielinski; m. Elizabeth Carew, May 30, 1946; children: Nancy, Elizabeth, Susan Jean. BS, Tulane U., 1950; postgrad., Colo. U., 1965. V.p., gen. mgr. Clifton Products, Litton Industries, Colorado Springs, Colo., 1965-67; pres. Memory Products divsn. Litton Industries, Beverly Hills, Calif., 1967-69, Bowmar Instruments Can., Ottawa, Ont., 1969-73; gen. mgr. Leigh Instruments, Carleton Place, Ont., 1973-75; pres., CEO, dir. Lewis Engring. Co., Naugatuck, Conn., 1975-85, Liquidometer Corp., Tampa, Fla., 1975-85; pres. Lewis divsn. Colt Industries, 1985-90; electronics company executive; b. Waterbury, Conn., Mar. 25, 1925; s. Stanley and Helen C.; m. Elizabeth Carew, May 30, 1946; children: Nancy, Elizabeth, Susan Jean. BS, Tulane U., 1950; postgrad. Colo. U., 1965. V.p., gen. mgr. Clifton Products, Litton Industries, Colorado Springs, Colo., 1965-67; pres. Memory Products div. Litton Industries, Beverly Hills, Calif., 1967-69, Bowmar Instruments, Can., Ottawa, Ont., 1969-73; gen. mgr. Leigh Instruments, Carleton Pl., Ont., 1973-75; pres., CEO, dir. Lewis Engring. Co., Naugatuck, Conn., 1975-85; pres., CEO, dir. Liquidometer Corp., Tampa, Fla., 1975-85; pres. Lewis div. Colt Industries, 1985-90, ret., 1990; Pres. Acad. Water Bd., 1963-65; bd. dirs. United Way, Colorado Springs, 1965-67; fellow Tulane U. Served with USN, 1943-46. Mem. Air Force Assn., Navy League. Pres. Acad. Water Bd., 1963-65; bd. dirs. United Way, Colorado Springs, 1965-67;fellow Tulane U. Served with USN, 1943-46. Mem. Air Force Assn., Navy League.

CHMURA, CHRISTINE, economist; b. Cleve., July 3, 1958; d. John Louis and Helen Ann (Rzucidlo) C. BS, Clemson U., 1981, MA in Econs., 1983; PhD in bus., Va. Commonwealth U., 1993. Assoc. economist Fed. Res. Bank, Richmond, Va., 1983-90; regional economist, v.p. Crestar Bank, Richmond, 1990-93, chief economist, sr. v.p., 1993—; adj. faculty Va. Commonwealth U., Richmond, 1991; advisor fund adv. bd. Commonwealth of Va., Employment Commn. Trust, Richmond, 1991—, Gov.'s Econ. Adv. Bd., richmond, 1992—, Am. Bankers Assn. Econ. Adv. Bd., Washington, 1995—. Contbr. articles to profl. jours. Chmn. missions com. West End Presbyn. Ch., Richmond, 1995—. Fellow Va. Assn. Economists (past pres., sec.-treas); mem. Fin. Mgmt. Assn. Republican. Avocations: golf, jogging, reading. Office: Crestar Bank PO Box 26665 Richmond VA 23261-6665

CHO, ALFRED YI, electrical engineer; b. Beijing, China, July 10, 1937; came to U.S., 1955, naturalized, 1962; s. Edward I-Lai and Mildred (Chen) C.; m. Mona Lee Willoughby, June 16, 1968; children: Derek Ming, Deidre Lin, Brynna Ying, Wendy Li. BSEE, U. Ill., 1960, MS, 1961, PhD, 1968. Rsch. physicist Ion Physics Corp., Burlington, Mass., 1961-62; mem. tech. staff TRW-Space Tech. Labs., Redondo Beach, Calif., 1962-65; mem. tech. staff Bell Labs., Murray Hill, N.J., 1968-84, dept. head, 1984-87; dir. Materials Processing Rsch. Lab. AT&T Bell Labs., Murray Hill, 1987-90; dir. semicondr. rsch. lab. Bell Labs. Lucent Techs. (formerly AT&T Bell Labs.), Murray Hill, 1990—; fellow Bell Labs., Lucent Techs. (formerly AT&T Bell Labs.), 1992—; rsch. asst. U. Ill., Urbana, 1965-68; vis. prof. dept. elec. engring., vis. rsch. prof. coordinated sci. lab. U. Ill., Urbana, 1977-78, adj. prof. dept. elec. engring., adj. rsch. prof. coordinated sci. lab., 1978—; bd. dirs. Riber, Edison, N.J.; trustee Coll. of N.J., 1996—. Contbr. over 480 articles to profl. jours.; 51 patents in field; developer molecular beam epitaxy. Recipient Disting. Tech. Staff award AT&T Bell Labs., 1982, Elec. and Computer Engring. Disting. Alumnus award U. Ill., 1985, Disting. Achievement award Chinese Inst. Engrs., U.S.A., 1985, Internat. Gallium Arsenide Symposium award, 1986, Heinrich Welker Gold medal, 1986, The Coll. Engring. Alumni Honor award U. Ill., 1988, World Materials Congress award ASM Internat., 1988, Achievement award Indsl. Rsch. Inst., Inc., 1988, Thomas Alva Edison Sci. award N.J. Gov., 1990, Internat. Crystal Growth award Am. Assn. for Crystal Growth, 1990, Asian Am. Corp. Achievement award, 1992, Chinese Am. Engrs. and Scientists Assn. So. Achievement award, 1993, Nat. Medal of Sci. NSF, 1993, Elliott Cresson medal The Franklin Inst., 1995, Computer and Comm. prize, Japan, 1995; inductee N.J. Inventors Hall of Fame, 1997. Fellow IEEE (Morris N. Liebman award 1982, IEEE Medal of Honor 1994), Am. Phys. Soc. (Internat. prize for new materials 1982); mem. Am. Vacuum Soc. (Gaede-Langmuir award 1988), Electrochem. Soc. (electronic divsn. award 1977, Solid State Sci. and Tech. medal 1987), Materials Rsch. Soc. (Von Hippel award 1994), Academia Sinica (Taiwan), Chinese Acad. Scis., Am. Philos. Soc., Nat. Acad. Engring., Nat. Acad. Scis., Am. Acad. Art & Scis., Sigma Xi, Tau Beta Pi, Eta Kappa Nu, Sigma Tau. Fax: (908) 582-2043. E-mail: ayc@lucent.com. Office: Bell Labs Lucent Tech PO Box 636 New Providence NJ 07974-0636 *I learned early in my life that hard work is a major ingredient for success. We can always do more than we think we are able to do. I drive myself to my utmost capacity so that I will not have regrets later that I did not try my best. My first love is art but I earn my living as an engineer. In my work as a research scientist, the secret for success is that I combine Oriental patience with Western technology. We should always try to enhance the best part of what we have and not be afraid to change.*

CHO, CHENG TSUNG, pediatrician, educator; b. Kaohsiung, Taiwan, Dec. 2, 1937; came to U.S., 1964, naturalized, 1976; s. R.E. and S.M. (Chou) C.; m. Chiou-shya Chen, Dec. 14, 1968; children: Jennifer, Julie. M.D., Kaohsiung Med. Coll., 1962; Ph.D., U. Kans., 1970. Diplomate: Am. Bd. Pediatrics. Intern Norwegian-Am. Hosp., Chgo., 1964-65; resident U. Kans. Med. Center, 1965-67, fellow, 1967-70, asst. prof. pediatrics and microbiology, 1970-74, assoc. prof., 1974-78, prof., 1978—, acting chmn. dept. pediatrics, 1978-79, chief sect. pediatric infectious disease, 1972—; vis. prof. Tri-Service Gen. Hosp. and Nat. Def. Med. Sch., Taiwan, 1980, VA Gen. Hosp., Taiwan, 1984, Nat. Taiwan U. Hosp., 1987, China Med. Coll. Hosp., 1990. Co-author: Pediatric Infectious Diseases; author articles on virology and infectious diseases. Recipient Outstanding Pediatric Teaching award U. Kans. Med. Center, 1975, 80, Chancellor's award for excellence in teaching, U. Kans., 1991. Fellow Am. Acad. Pediatrics, Infectious Disease Soc. Am.; mem. AAAS, Am. Soc. Microbiology, Am. Pediatric Soc., Soc. Pediatric Research, Soc. Exptl. Biology and Medicine, Kans. Med. Soc., Midwest Pediatric Research Soc., Kaohsiung Med. Coll. Alumni Assn. Am. (pres. 1978), Sigma Xi. Home: 10215 Howe Ln Shawnee Mission KS 66206-2420 Office: U Kans Med Ctr Dept Pediatrics Kansas City KS 66103

CHO, EUN-SU, adult education educator; b. Aug. 20, 1958. MA, Seoul (Korea) Nat. U., 1986; PhD, U. Calif., Berkeley, 1997. Asst. prof. U. Mich., Ann Arbor, 1996—. E-mail: eunsucho@umich.edu. Office: 2319 Faye Dr Ann Arbor MI 48103

CHO, HYUN JU, veterinary research scientist; b. Chinju, Korea, June 12, 1939; s. Gil Rae and Sun Gae (Park) C.; m. Kim Bok Mee, June 13, 1967; children—Jae Shin, Elisa, Jane. D.V.M., Gyeongsang Nat. U., 1963; M.Sc., Seoul Nat. U., 1966; Ph.D., U. Guelph, 1973. Vet. research scientist Inst. Vet. Research, Anyang, Korea, 1965-70; vis. scientist Wallaceville Animal Research Center, New Zealand, 1968; research scientist Animal Diseases Research Inst. Can. Food Inspection Agency, Lethbridge, Alta., Can., 1973—. Contbr. articles to profl. jours. Discovered virus of Aleutian disease of mink and developed practical diagnostic test for it. Home: 14 Coachwood Rd W, Lethbridge, AB Canada T1K 6B6 Office: Animal Diseases Rsch Inst, PO Box 640, Lethbridge, AB Canada T1J 3Z4 *A combination of persistent and repeated experimentation, original ideas and thinking and the ambition to succeed where others may have failed, tempered with loyalty and dedication to sound research principles, has been the key to my scientific achievements.*

CHO, JOHN YUNGDO NAGAMICHI, atmospheric research scientist; b. Tokyo, Nov. 24, 1963; s. Joseph Kisun and Lydia (Shoko) C. BS, Stanford U., 1985, MS, 1986; PhD, Cornell U., 1993. With U.S. Peace Corps, Freetown, Sierra Leone, 1986-88; rsch. asst. Cornell U., Ithaca, 1988-93; columnist The San Juan (P.R.) Star, 1996-97; rsch. assoc. Arecibo (P.R.) Obs., 1993-97; rsch. scientist MIT, Cambridge, 1997—; adj. rsch. assoc., U. Colo., 1995—. Author: SPAM-ku: Tranquil Reflections on Luncheon Loaf, 1998; contbr. articles to profl. jours. Recipient CEDAR prize NSF, 1993. Mem. Am. Geophys. Union, Am. Meterol. Soc., Internat. Radio Sci. Union. (young scientist award 1996). Avocations: music, literature, cinema, travel. E-mail: jcho@pemtropics.mit.edu. Office: MIT 77 Massachusetts Ave # 54-1823 Cambridge MA 02139-4307

CHO, KYUNG JAE, physician, radiologist, educator; b. Tokyo, Mar. 26, 1942; s. Bang Kap and Myo Soon (Chai) C.; m. Young Soon Jeung, Sept. 6, 1969; 1 child, Catherine. MD, Cath. Med. Sch., Seoul, 1966. Instr. U. Mich., Ann Arbor, 1973-74, asst. prof., 1975-78, assoc. prof., 1978-82, prof., 1982—, dir. interventional radiology, 1976-96; courtesy prof. U. Fla., Gainesville, 1996—. Co-author: Gastrointestinal Angiography, 1986; contbr. chpt. to book, articles to profl. jours. Fellow Soc. Cardiovascular and Interventional Radiology, Am. Coll. Radiology; mem. AMA, Radiol. Soc. N.Am., Soc. Gastrointestinal Radiology. Home: 413 Dhu Varren Rd Ann Arbor MI 48105-9690 Office: U Mich 1500 E Medical Center Dr Ann Arbor MI 48109-0005

CHO, LEE-JAY, social scientist, demographer; b. Kyoto, Japan, July 5, 1936; came to U.S., 1959; s. Sam-Soo and Kyung-Doo (Park) C.; m. Eun-Ja Chun, May 20, 1973; children: Yun-Kyong Nuy, Sang-Mun Ray, Han-Jae Jeremy. BA, Kookmin Coll., Seoul, Korea, 1959; MA in Govt., George Washington U., 1962; MA in Sociology (Population Council fellow), U. Chgo., 1964, PhD in Sociology, 1965; D in Econs. (hon.), Dong-A U., 1982; DSc in Demography, Tokyo U., 1983; D in Econs., Keio U., Tokyo, 1989. Statistician Korean Census Council, 1958-61; research assoc., asst. prof. sociology Population Research and Tng. Center, U. Chgo., 1965-66; asso. dir. Community and Family Study Center, 1969-70; sr. demographic adv. to Malaysian Govt., 1967-69; assoc. prof. U. Hawaii, 1969-73, prof., 1973-78; asst. dir. East-West Population Inst., East-West Center, Honolulu, 1971-74; dir. East-West Population Inst., East-West Center, 1974-92; pres. pro tem East-West Center, 1980-81, v.p., 1987-98, sr. advisor, 1998—; cons. in field; mem. Nat. Acad. Scis. Com. on Population and Demography; mem. U.S. 1980 Census Adv. Com., Dept. Commerce. Author: (with others) Differential Current Fertility in the United States, 1970; editor: (with others) Introduction to Censuses of Asia and the Pacific: 1970-74, 1976, (with Kazumasa Kobayashi) Fertility Transition in East Asian Populations, 1979, (with Suharto, McNicoll and Mamas) Population Growth of Indonesia, 1980, The OWN Children of Fertility Estimation, 1986, (with Y.H. Kim) Economic Development of Republic of Korea: A Policy Perspective, 1989, (with Kim) Korea's Political Economy: An Institutional Perspective, 1994, (with Yada) Tradition and Change in the Asian Family, 1994, (with Y.H. Kim) Hedging Bets on Groth in a Globalizing Industrial Order, 1997, (with Y.H. Kim) Korea's Choices in Emerging Global Competition and Cooperation, 1998, (with Kim) Ten Paradigms of Market Economies and Land Systems, 1998; contbr. numerous articles on population and econ. devel. to profl. jours. Bd. dirs. Planned Parenthood Assn., Hawaii, 1976-77. Ford Found. grantee, 1977-79; Population Council grantee, 1973-75; Dept. Commerce grantee, 1974-78; recipient Award of Mugunghwa-Jang, govt. Republic of Korea, 1992, 4th N.E. Asia Niigata prize, 1996. Mem. Internat. Statis. Inst. (tech. adv. com. World Fertility Survey), Internat. Union Sci. Study Population, Population Assn. Am., Am. Statis. Assn., Am. Sociol. Assn., N.E. Asia Econ. Forum (founding chmn.). Home: 1718 Halekoa Dr Honolulu HI 96821-1027 Office: 1601 E West Rd Honolulu HI 96848-1601 *The survival and welfare of the future generations will depend largely upon what we do today to plan and manage human population growth and sustainable development.*

CHO, SUNG YOON, law librarian; b. Shinuiju, Pyongan Pukto, Republic of Korea, Sept. 10, 1928; came to U.S., 1955; s. Bong Soon Cho and Yong Soon Kim; m. Won Kyung Bae, Oct. 20, 1962 (dec. Nov. 1982); children: David, Margaret; m. Kyung Soo Kim, Aug. 31, 1985. LLB, Seoul (Republic of Korea) Nat. U., 1953; MA, Tulane U., 1957, PhD, 1963; M in Comparative Law, George Washington U., 1966. Korean atty. Civil Assistance Command UN, Seoul, 1953-55; legal specialist Korean and Japanese law Far Ea. Law div. Libr. of Congress, Washington, 1959-68, sr. legal specialist, 1968-77, asst. to chief, 1977-83, asst. chief, 1983-95, spl. law group leader eastern law divsn., 1995—; cons. Rsch. Analysis Corp., McLean, Va., 1968-71. Author: Asian Survey, 1971, Japanese Writings on Communist Chinese Law, 1977, Law and Legal Literature of North Korea: A Guide, 1988; contbr. articles to profl. jours. Chmn. bd. trustees Korean Ch. Greater Washington, McLean, 1980-82, chmn. adminstrv. bd., 1988-90. Mem. Internat. Assn. Law Librs., Am. Soc. Internat. Law, Am. Assn. Law Librs. (com. fgn. law indexing 1973-79), Assn. Asian Studies (com. Asian law 1982-86), Japanese-Am. Soc. Legal Studies. Methodist. Avocations; music, fishing, reading. Fax no.: (202)707-1820. E-mail: scho@loc.gov. Office: Libr Congress Ea Law Div 101 Independence Ave SE Washington DC 20540-0002

CHO, TAI YONG, lawyer; b. Seoul, Republic of Korea, May 27, 1943; came to U.S., 1966; s. Nam Suck and Sun Yeo (Yoon) C; m. Hea Sun Cho, July 14, 1973; children: Robert, Richard, Susan. BS, Seoul U., 1965; MS, Cooper Union, 1971; CE, Columbia U., 1971; JD, Fordham U., 1981. Bar: N.Y., 1982; registered profl. engr., N.Y., 1973. Engr. Ministry of Constrn., Seoul, 1965-66, Andrews & Clark, N.Y.C., 1967-68, Parsons, Brinckerhoff, Quade & Douglas, N.Y.C., 1969-71; v.p. John R. McCarthy Corp., N.Y.C., 1972-80. Mem. ASCE, ABA, N.Y. State Bar Assn., Am. Arbitration Assn. (panel of arbitrators), Am.-Korean Lawyers Assn. of N.Y. (pres. 1988), Korean TV Broadcasters Assn., Am. (pres. 1990), Internat. Korean Lawyers Assn. (v.p. 1991). Home: 56 Tuttle Rd Briarcliff Manor NY 10510-2233 Office: 309 5th Ave New York NY 10016-6509

CHO, WONHWA, biomedical researcher; b. Seoul, Korea, Apr. 27, 1958. BS in Chemistry, Seoul Nat. U., 1980, MS in Chemistry, 1982; PhD in Chemistry, U. Chgo., 1988. Postdoctoral fellow Calif. Inst. Tech., Pasadena, 1989-90; assoc. prof. chemistry U. Ill., Chgo., 1990—. Mem. Am. Soc. Biochemistry & Molecular Biology, Am. Chem. Soc. Office: U Ill Chgo Dept Chemistry 845 W Taylor St Rm 4500 Chicago IL 60607-7056*

CHO, YOUNG IL, mechanical engineering educator; b. Seoul, Nov. 26, 1949; came to U.S., 1976; s. Sungshik and Keunsook (Oh) C.; m. Sunyoung

Uhm, Oct. 6, 1973; children: Joseph, Daniel. BS, Seoul Nat. U., 1972; MBA, Korea U., 1975; MS, U. Ill., Chgo., 1977, PhD, 1980. Rsch. fellow Energy Resources Ctr., U. Ill., Chgo., 1980-81; mem. tech. staff Jet Propulsion Lab., Calif. Inst. Tech., Pasadena, 1981-85; prof. dept. mech. engring. and mechanics Drexel U., Phila., 1985-91, prof., 1992—. Author: Advances in Heat Transfer, 1982, Handbook of Heat Transfer, 1985; editor Advances in Heat Transfer, 1991—; contbr. articles to profl. jours.; editor Handbook of Heat Transfer, 1996—. Recipient award NASA, 1988, Lindback award of Excellence in Teaching; grantee NSF, 1987, NASA, 1988, Dept. Energy, 1989-92. Fellow ASME, Am. Electrophoresis Soc., Electrochem. Soc. Am., Am. Physics Soc., Korean Scientists and Engrs. in Am. Home: 132 Renaissance Dr Cherry Hill NJ 08003-5102 Office: Drexel U Dept Mech Engring 32d and Chestnut Sts Philadelphia PA 19104

CHOA, WALTER KONG, technical service professional; b. Rangoon, Burma, Aug. 10, 1948; came to U.S., 1974; s. Keng Hong and Kim (Tan) C.; m. Teresa Yeap Myint, Sept. 29, 1979; 1 child, Patricia. BS in Chemistry, Rangoon U., 1967. R & D chemist Diversey Chems., Des Plaines, Ill., 1975-80; mgr. tech. svc. Diversey Wyandotte, Mich., 1980-85, Diversey Wyandotte Metals, 1985-88; western mgr. tech. svc. Henkel Surface Technologies, Atlanta, Ga., 1988—. Mem. Am. Electroplaters and Surface Finishers Assn. (appreciation award L.A. br. 1983), Chem. Coaters Assn. Internat. Home: 3561 Cotter Rim Ln Diamond Bar CA 91765-3763 Office: Henkel Surface Techs 1615 Johnson Rd NW Atlanta GA 30318-8937

CHOATE, BRADFORD EUGENE, foundation executive; b. Anna, Ill., Sept. 17, 1956; s. Robert and Margie (Sloan) C.; m. Julie Durall, Aug. 5, 1978; children: Brent, Lauren, Lindsey. AA, John A. Logan Coll., 1976; BA, So. Ill. U., 1979, MS in Edn., 1984. Dean instnl. advancement Frontier Coll., Fairfield, Ill., 1980-84; dir. corp. & found. rels. Ohio State U., Columbus, 1984-90; assoc. v.p., devel. and alumni rels. Pa. State U., State College, 1990-96; pres., CEO Minn. Med. Found., Mpls., 1996—. Home: 16401 Limerick Ln Minnetonka MN 55345-1842

CHOATE, JEAN MARIE, history educator; b. Syracuse, N.Y., Dec. 17, 1935; d. Max and Betty (Black) Molyneux; m. Woodrow Choate; children: Anne, Mike, Ruth, Susan. BA, Alma Coll., 1958; MA, U. Wis., 1962; MS, St. Cloud State U., 1972; PhD, Iowa State U., 1992. Instr. Open Bible Coll., Des Moines, 1983-85, Des Moines Area Coll., 1985-97; asst. prof. No. Mich. U., Marquette, 1992—; chair women's commn. No. Mich. U., 1996-97. Book reviewer Jour. of the West, 1996-98; contbr. articles to profl. jours. Grantee No. Mich. U., 1993, Iowa Found., 1994; Everett Dirksen grantee, 1995, Franklin and Eleanor Roosevelt grantee, 1996, Carl Albert Libr. grantee, 1998. Mem. AAUW (v.p. 1995-97), Agrl. History, Women Historians of Midwest, Orgn. Am. Historians, Am. Hist. Assn., Social Sci. History Assn., Mich. Barn Preservation Network (bd. dirs.). Office: No Mich Univ Marquette MI 49855

CHOBAN, GLENWOOD T., business owner; b. Avonlea, Sask., Can., Jan. 9, 1948; came to the U.S., 1971; s. Thomas and Betty Mae Choban; m. Jo Ann Lay Konkel, Sept. 1, 1968 (div. Dec. 1979); children: Sandra D. Wolfe, Jani J. Kovach; m. Angela Sue Kelley, May 23, 1982; 1 child, Jonathan T. BA, Walla Walla Coll., 1971; postgrad., Loma Linda U., 1972, Calif. State U., San Bernardino, 1973-74. Lic. nursing home adminstr., Ill., S.D., Calif., Colo. Tchr., prin. SDA Schs., Long Beach, Calif., 1971-73, Winnpeg, Man., Can., 1971-73; adminstr. Beverly Enterprises, Boulder, Colo., San Francisco, Moline, Ill.; regional dir. Beverly Enterprises, Boulder; v.p. Beverly Enterprises, Madison, Milw., 1977-87; pres. Sunbelt Health Care Ctrs., Maitland, Fla., 1987-98; pres., owner Accessible Med. Staffing, Inc., Milw., 1998—; ops. cons. Adventist Living Ctrs., Naperville, Ill., 1987; vice chmn. bd. Sunbelt Health Care Ctrs., Maitland, 1987-98; adv. bd. mem./long-term care degree So. Adventist U., Collegedale, Tenn., 1988-98; bd. mem. Sunbelt Home Health, Sarasota, Fla., 1992-98. Bd. mem., fin. chmn. Markham Woods SDA Ch., Longwood, Fla., 1990-97; bd. chmn., vice chmn. Forest Lake Edn. Ctr., Longwood, 1992-96; bd. mem. Pace Pvt. Sch., Longwood, 1997-98. Mem. Wis. Health Care Assn. (exec. bd. mem. 1984-86), Metro Milw. Assn. Commerce. Avocations: camping, gardening. E-mail: amsi@gateway.net. Office: Accessible Med Staffing Inc 10520 W Bluemound Rd Milwaukee WI 53226

CHOBANIAN, ARAM VAN, medical school dean, cardiologist; b. Pawtucket, R.I., Aug. 10, 1929; s. Van and Marina (Arsenian) C.; m. Jasmine Goorigian, June 5, 1955; children: Karin, Lisa, Aram. BA, Brown U., 1951; MD, Harvard U., 1955. Intern, resident Univ. Hosp., Boston, 1955-59, cardiovasc. rsch. fellow, 1959-62; asst. prof. Boston U. Sch. Medicine, 1964-67, assoc. prof., 1967-70, prof. medicine, 1970—, prof. pharmacology, 1975—, John Sandson disting. prof. health scis., 1992—, dir. U.A. Whitaker Labs. for Blood Vessel Rsch., 1973-88, dir. Hypertension Specialized Ctr. Rsch., 1975-95, dir. Cardiovasc. Inst., 1975-92, dean, 1988—, provost Med. Ctr., 1996—, Univ. prof., 1999—; dir. Nat. Rsch. and Demonstration Ctr. in Hypertension, 1985-90; chmn. FDA Cardiovasc. and Renal Adv. Com., 1978-80, NIH Hypertension and Arteriosclerosis adv. com., 1977-78; chmn. Cardiovasc. Study Sect. B. NIH, 1982-84; chmn. 4th Joint Nat. Com. on Hypertension NIH, 1990-91; Sandoz lectr. Royal Coll. Physicians and Surgeons Can., 1989; mem. NIH Nat. Heart, Lung and Blood Adv. Coun., 1993-96; mem. bd. external advisers NHLBI, 1999—. Author: Heart Risk Book, 1982; mem. editl. bd. New England Jour. Medicine, Hypertension, Jour. Hypertension, Jour. Vascular Biology, Hypertension Rsch., Cardiovasc. Pharmacology. Pres. Am. Heart Assn., Boston, 1974-75; mem. exec. com., trustee Boston Med. Ctr.; bd. dirs. Armenian Culture Soc.; trustee Roger Williams Med. Ctr., Wolfson Found.; fellow trustee Armenian Assembly of Am. Capt. USAF, 1956-57. Recipient Cmty. Edn. and Disting. Svc. award Am. Heart Assn., Boston, 1975, 78, Eastman Kodak award Nat. Acad. Clin. Biochemistry, 1987, Abbott award Am. Soc. Hypertension. Fellow ACP, Am. Heart Assn. (chmn. coun. high blood pressure rsch. 1984-86, Corcoran lectr. 1989, award of merit 1990, Modern Medicine award 1990, Lifetime Achievement award in hypertension Bristol-Myers Squibb), Nat. Heart, Lung and Blood Inst. (Freis award 1997), Am. Soc. Clin. Investigation, Assn. Am. Physicians, Am. Physiol. Soc., New England Cardiovasc. Soc. (pres. 1985-86), Phi Beta Kappa, Sigma Xi, Alpha Omega Alpha. Home: 5 Rathburn Rd Natick MA 01760-1011 Office: Boston U Sch Medicine 80 E Concord St Boston MA 02118-2307

CHOBOT, JOHN CHARLES, lawyer; b. N.Y.C., Feb. 14, 1948; s. Arthur E. and Eleanore L. (Lotito) C.; m. Catherine Anne Moran, Aug. 24, 1974; children: Christine, Keith. BA, Cornell U., 1969; MS in Edn., CCNY, 1971; JD, Fordham U., 1975. Bar: N.Y. 1976, U.S. Dist. Ct. (we. dist.) N.Y. 1976, N.J. 1985, U.S. Dist. Ct. N.J. 1985. Assoc. Phillips, Lytle, Hitchcock, Blaine & Huber, Buffalo, 1975-85; The CIT Group/Sales Financing, Inc., Livingston, N.J., 1985-90; v.p., gen. counsel, sec. AT&T Capital Corp., Morristown, N.J., 1990-98, sr. v.p., chief counsel bus. fin. divsn., 1993-98; v.p. law, asst. gen. counsel Newcourt Credit Group Inc., Parsippany, N.J., 1998—. Contbr. articles on equipment leasing, bankruptcy and secured transactions to legal jours. Mem. ABA, N.Y. State Bar Assn., Am. Bankruptcy Inst., Comml. Law League, Equipment Leasing Assn. of Am., Kappa Alpha Soc. Fax: 973-355-7057. E-mail: johnchobot@newcourt.com. Home: 23 Laurel Hill Dr Randolph NJ 07869-4632 Office: Newcourt Credit Group Inc 2 Gatehall Dr Parsippany NJ 07054-4529

CHOCK, CLIFFORD YET-CHONG, family practice physician; b. Chgo., Oct. 15, 1951; s. Wah Tim and Leatrice (Wong) C. BS in Biology, Purdue U., 1973; MD, U. Hawaii, 1978. Intern in internal medicine Loma Linda (Calif.) Med. Ctr., 1978-79, resident in internal medicine, 1979; resident in internal medicine U. So. Calif.-L.A. County Med. Ctr., L.A., 1980; physician Pettis VA Clinic, Loma Linda, Calif., 1980; pvt. practice Honolulu, 1981—; chmn. Dept. of Family Practice, 1990-98, chmn. utilization rev. com. 1991, 95; physician reviewer St. Francis Med. Ctr., Liliha, Hawaii,, 1985—, chmn. Quality Care for Family Practice, 1990-93, 95-98; chmn. credentials Family Practice, 1990-93, 95-96, acting chmn. credentials com., 1992; physician reviewer Peer Rev. Orgn. Hawaii, Honolulu, 1987-93. Fellow Am. Acad. Family Physicians, Internat. Platform Assn. Avocations: model construction, swimming, Christian ministry, King James Bible study, toy collection. Office: 321 N Kuakini St Ste 513 Honolulu HI 96817-2361

CHODOROW, NANCY JULIA, sociology educator; b. N.Y.C., Jan. 20, 1944; d. Marvin and Leah (Turitz) C.; children: Rachel Esther Chodorow-Reich, Gabriel Issac Chodorow-Reich. BA, Radcliffe Coll., 1966; PhD, Brandeis U., 1975; grad., San Francisco Psychoanalytic, 1993. From lectr. to assoc. prof. U. Calif., Santa Cruz, 1974-86; from asst prof. sociology to prof. U. Calif., Berkeley, 1986—, clin. prof. dept. psychology, 1999—; faculty San Francisco Psychoanalytic Inst., 1994—. Author: The Reproduction of Mothering, 1978 (Jessie Bernard award 1979, named one of Ten Most Influential Books of Past 25 Years, Contemporary Sociology 1996), 2nd edit., 1999, Feminism and Psychoanalytic Theory, 1989, Femininities, Masculinities, Sexualities, 1994, The Power of Feelings: Personal Meaning in Psychoanalysis, Gender, and Culture, 1999; contbr. articles to profl. jours. Fellow Russell Sage Found., NEH, Ctr. Advanced Study Behavioral Scis., ACLS, Guggenheim fellow. Mem. Internat. Psychoanalytic Assn., Am. Psychoanalytic Assn., San Francisco Psychoanalytic Soc. Office: U Calif Dept Sociology 410 Barrows Hall Berkeley CA 94720-1980

CHODOS, DALE DAVID JEROME, physician, consumer advocate; b. Mpls., June 5, 1928; s. John H. and Elvira Isabella (Lundberg) C.; m. Joyce Annette Smith, Sept. 9, 1951; children: John, Julie, David, Jennifer. A.B., Carroll Coll., Helena, Mont., 1950; M.D., St. Louis U., 1954. Diplomate Am. Bd. Pediatrics. Intern U. Utah, Salt Lake City, 1954-55, resident in pediatrics, 1955-57, chief resident in pediatrics, 1957, NIH fellow in endocrinology and metabolism, 1957-58; practice medicine specializing in pediatrics Idaho Falls, Idaho, 1958-62; staff physician Upjohn Co., Kalamazoo, Mich., 1962-64, head clin. pharmacology, 1964-65, research mgr. clin. pharmacology, 1965-68, research mgr. clin. services, 1968-73, group research mgr. med. therapeutics, 1973-81, med. dir. domestic med. affairs, 1981-85, exec. dir. domestic med. affairs, 1985-87; chief pediatrics Latter-day Saints Hosp., Sacred Heart Hosp., Idaho Falls, 1962; cons. to pharm. industry, 1988-91; pres. Am. Health Advocacy, 1991—; chmn. med. rels. oper. com. Nat. Pharm. Coun., 1977-80; mem. med. sect. steering com. Pharm. Mfrs. Assn., 1977-87, chmn., 1984-86; sci. advisor Am. Coun. on Sci. and Health, 1991—. Contbr. articles to med. and pharm. jours. Bd. dirs. Family Service Ctr., Kalamazoo, 1965-71. Served with AUS, 1945-46. Recipient W.E. Upjohn award for excellence, 1969, Physician's Recognition award AMA, 1969, 73, 76, 79, 82, 85, 88. Fellow Am. Acad. Pediats.; mem. Advancement of Sound Sci. Coalition (mem. scientist). Republican. Home: 619 Aquaview Dr Kalamazoo MI 49009-9652

CHODOSH, ROBERT IVAN, retired middle school educator, coach; b. Elizabeth, N.J., May 29, 1946; s. Philip Richard and Jean (Landerman) C.; m. Norman Jean Ries, Feb. 14, 1999. BS in Edn., U. Tenn., Knoxville, 1968; MEd, Fla. Tech. U., Orlando, 1975. Cert. in phys. edn., health edn. Tchr. Old Dixie Elem. Sch., Titusville, Fla., 1968-78, Surfside Elem. Sch., Satellite Beach, Fla., 1978-79; tchr., basketball and track coach Andrew Jackson Middle Sch., Titusville, 1979-98; ret., 1998; mem. comprehensive edn. com. Brevard County Schs., Melbourne, Fla., 1990-91. Com. mem. Brevard County Elementary and Secondary Physical Education Guide, 1977, 82, 85, 88. Gray leader, coach North Brevard YMCA, Titusville, 1968-78; recreation leader North Brevard Recreation Dept., 1968-78, summer program leader, 1970-75, 88; scorer, asst. coach, concession stand mgr. Indian River City Little Leauge, 1987, 89. Recipient Tchr. of Yr. award Old Dixie Elem. Sch., Titusville, 1974, Silver Svc. award Brevard County Sch. System. Mem. U. Tenn. Alumni Assn. Democrat. Jewish. Avocations: walking, watching sports, listening to music, swimming, reading. Home: 7934 Rock Crest Dr Corpus Christi TX 78414-5992

CHOI, JAY LEE, women's apparel executive. Pres. By Design LLC, 1994—. Fax: 201-854-4483. Office: By Design LLC 2400 3rd St North Bergen NJ 07047

CHOI, MAN-DUEN, mathematics educator; b. Nanjing, China, June 13, 1945; came to Can., 1969; m. Pui-Wah Ip, Sept. 1972; children: Winston, Yvonne, Edmond. B.Sc., Chinese U. of Hong Kong, 1967; M.Sc., U. Toronto, 1970, Ph.D., 1973. Lectr. U. Calif.-Berkeley, 1973-76; asst. prof. math. U. Toronto, Ont., Can., 1976-79, assoc. prof., 1979-82, prof., 1982—. invited spkr. for internat. confs. and profl. socs.; invited lectr. for more than 100 univs. in Am., Europe, and Asia. Contbr. articles to profl. jours. Nat. Sci. and Engring. Research Council of Can. grantee, 1977—. Fellow Royal Soc. Can. Acad. Sci.; mem. Am. Math. Soc., Math. Assn. Am., Can. Math. Soc.

CHOI, MICHAEL KAMWAH, aerospace engineer, mechanical engineer, thermal engineer, researcher; b. Aug. 16, 1952; came to U.S., 1972, permanent resident, 1987; s. Ying-Loi and Kan-Hau (Yuen) C.; m. Wendy Liang; 1 child, Natalie. BSc in Engring. magna cum laude, Brown U., 1976; MSME, MIT, 1978. Registered profl. engr., Va. Rsch. asst. dept. mech. engring. MIT, Cambridge, Mass., 1977-79; sr. rsch. engr. Sci. Applications Internat. Corp., McLean, Va., 1979-87; sr. engr. spacecraft thermal control sys. Fairchild Space and Defense Corp., Germantown, Md., 1987-90; project leader, mgr. NASA Goddard Space Flight Ctr., Greenbelt, Md., 1990—; intrument thermal mgr. WIND and POLAR spacecraft Global Geospace Sci. Mission, 1990-92; thermal sys. mgr. Far Ultraviolet Spectroscopic Explorer Project, 1992-94; lead thermal engr. High Energy Solar Imager project, 1994-96; thermal sys. mgr. LANDSAT-7 mission, 1994—; lead thermal mgr. electron reflectometer and magnetometer instruments on Lunar Prospector spacecraft, 1995-97, Next Generation Space Telescope, 1996-97, low energy neutral atom instrument on MIDEX IMAGE spacecraft, 1996—, Solar Probe Study, 1996—, Triana Plasma/Magnetometer instrument, 1999—, Swift Burst Alert Telescope instrument, 1999—; cons. EO-1 Advanced Land Imager, 1997—; reviewer flight assurance office; organizer, chmn. spacecraft and instrument thermal control sessions 32d Intersoc. Energy Conversion Engring. Conf., 1997, 98; contbr. solar heating and cooling program U.S. Dept. Energy; spkr. nat. and internat. confs. Contbr. articles to profl. jours.; reviewer Solar Energy Jour., ASME Solar Energy Divsn., 1983-87. Fellow AIAA (cert. merit 1996); mem. ASME, Soc. Automotive Engring., Sigma Xi, Tau Beta Pi. Home: 2237 Halter Ln Reston VA 20191-5824

CHOI, NAMKEE GANG, educator; b. Korea, Jan. 26, 1955; came to U.S., 1981; s. Heedo Gang and Soon Chung; m. Chong Chul, July 15, 1979; 1 child, Bryan. BA, Ewha Womans U., Seoul, Korea; MA, Ewha Womans U.; MSW, U. Minn., 1983; PhD, U. Calif., Berkeley, 1987. Asst. prof. SUNY, Buffalo, 1987-94, assoc. prof., 1994—. Co-author: Long-Term Care and Ethnicity, 1998. Bd. dirs. Meals in Wheels, Buffalo, 1997—. Mem. Gerontological Soc. Am. Democrat. E-mail: ngchoi@acsu.buffalo.edu. Office: SUNY Sch Social Work 359 Baldy Hall Buffalo NY 14260

CHOI, SANG-IL, physics educator, researcher; b. Gyongbuk, Korea, Sept. 1, 1931; came to U.S., 1956; s. Jeong-ho and Suseon (Hong) C.; m. Etsuyo Itokawa, June 11, 1961; children: Mina N., Don H. BSc., Seoul U., Korea, 1953; Ph.D., Brown U., 1961. Prof. physics U. N.C., Chapel Hill, 1972-91, chmn. dept. physics and astronomy, 1982-88; prof. physics Pohang U. Sci. and Tech., Korea, 1989—, chmn. physics dept., 1989-94, dir. basic scis. rsch. inst., 1993-96, dean Grad. Sch., 1994-96; dir. ctr. for tchg. and learning Pohang U. Sci. and Tech., 1999—; cons. Am. Optical Co., Korea Advanced Inst. Tech. Author research papers in field. Fellow Am. Phys. Soc., Korea Sci. and Tech. Acad.; mem. AAAS, Japanese Phys. Soc., Assn. Korean Scientists and Engrs. in Am. (pres. 1978-79). Avocation: tennis. Office: Pohang U of Sci & Tech, Physics Dept, Pohang 790-784, Republic of Korea

CHOICE, PRISCILLA KATHRYN MEANS (PENNY CHOICE), gifted education educator, international consultant; b. Rockford, Ill., Nov. 8, 1939; d. John Z. and Margaret A. (Haines) Means; m. Jack R. Choice, Nov. 14, 1964; children: William Kenneth, Margaret Meta. BA, U. Wis., 1963; MEd, Nat.-Louis U., 1990; MA, N.E. Ill. U., 1995. Field rsch. dir. Tatham-Laird and Kudner Advt., Chgo., 1964-69; drama specialist Children's Theatre Western Springs (Ill.), 1969-81; gifted teaching asst. Sch. Dist. 181, Hinsdale, Ill., 1980-84; tchr. Sch. Dist. 99, Cicero, Ill., 1984-85; gifted edn. program coord. Community Consolidated Sch. Dist. 93, Carol Stream, Ill., 1985—; drama specialist, cons. Choice Dramatics, Hinsdale and Clarendon Hills, Ill., 1976—; producing dir. Mirror Image Youth Theatre, Hinsdale, 1986-88; adj. prof. Coll. DuPage, Glen Ellyn, Ill., 1990-92, Nat.-Louis U., Evanston, Ill., 1991—, Aurora (Ill.)úU., 1995—, Govs. State U., University Park, Ill., 1992-93; internat. cons. in gifted edn. and drama-in-edn., 1989—. Contbg. author Gifted/Arts Resource Guide, 1990; contbg. editor Ill. Theatre Assn., Followspot News, 1992-95. 96—. Bd. dirs. Ill. Theatre Assn., Chgo., 1983-87; mem. gifted adv. com. Ednl. Svc. Ctr., Wheaton, Ill., 1987-90, 92-95, Regional Office of Edn., Wheaton, 1995—, Northeastern Ill. U., Chgo., 1993-95. Recipient Ill. State Bd. Edn. gifted edn. fellowship, 1988, AAUW continuing edn. scholarship, 1986, 90, Excellence award Ill. Theatre Assn., 1991, Excellence award Ill. Math. and Sci. Acad., 1990, 98, Recognition of Excellence, No. Ill. Planning Commn. Gifted Edn., 1990, Award of Excellence Ill. and Math. Sci. Acad., 1998. Mem. ASCD, World Coun. on Gifted Edn., Nat. Assn. Gifted Children, Ill. Assn. Gifted Children (membership chmn. 1992-94, advocacy com. 1995—), Ill. Coun. Gifted, Am. Assn. Theatre in Edn., Ill. Theatre Assn. (bd. dirs. 1983-87, Outstanding Achievement award 1991), Inst. for Global Ethics, Ill. Alliance Arts Edn., Theatre Western Springs, Phi Delta Kappa. Avocations: swimming, walking, reading. Home: 113 S Prospect Ave Clarendon Hills IL 60514-1422 Office: Cmty Consol Sch Dist 93 Jay Stream Sch 283 El Paso Ln Carol Stream IL 60188-1736

CHOJNACKI, PAUL ERVIN, pharmacist, pharmaceutical company official; b. Chgo., Dec. 29, 1950; s. Ervin Edward and Monica (Jablonski) C.; m. Doris Warenberg, May 26, 1979; children: Brittany, James. BS in Bus., Chgo. State U., 1975; BS in Pharmacy, St. Louis Coll., 1977; MA in Mktg., Webster U., 1982. RPh, Mo., N.C., Ind. Clk. Filmanowicz Drug, Chgo., 1968-70; stock clk. Sears, Roebuck & Co., Chgo., 1974-75; sales rep. Chgo. Motor Club, 1975-76; pharmacist Family Pharmacy, St. Louis, 1977; sales assoc. Eli Lilly & Co., St. Louis, 1977-84; regional mgr. Hosp. Pharmacies Inc., St. Louis, 1984-85; hosp. rep. Glaxo Inc., St. Louis, 1985-91; State of Ind. dist. mgr. Allen & Hanburys/Glaxo Pharms., Fishers, 1991—; assoc. product mgr. Oral Cephaloporins Glaxo, Inc., 1989. Local campaign worker, St. Louis, 1985. Mem. Am. Pharm. Assn., St. Louis Pharmacists Assn., St. Louis Hosp. Pharmacists Assn., Ind. Pharm. Assn., Ind. Pharmacists Assn., St. Joseph County Pharmacist Assn. (officer 1995, continuing edn. coord.), Alpha Zeta Omega (treas. St. Louis 1977-78, pres. 1978-79). Avocation: golf. Home and Office: 10110 Bent Tree Ln Fishers IN 46038-9363

CHOKSY, JAMSHEED KAIRSHASP, historian, religious scholar, language professional, humanities educator; b. Bombay, India, Jan. 8, 1962; arrived in Sri Lanka, 1962; permanent resident, U.S. 1995; s. Kairshasp Nariman and Freny Kairshasp (Cooper) C.; m. Carol Emma Burnside, Sept. 12, 1993; 1 child, Darius Jamsheed. AB in Mid.-Ea. Langs. and Culture, Columbia U., 1985; PhD in History and Religions, Harvard U., 1991. Tchg. fellow dept. anthropology and archaeology Harvard U., 1988, jr. fellow, 1988-91; vis. asst. prof. depts. history and internat. rels. Stanford U., 1991-93; asst. prof. dept. ctrl. Eurasian studies, Indian studies, midieval studies, near eastern lang. and cultures, religious studies Ind. U., Bloomington, 1993-97, assoc. prof., 1997—; dir. undergrad. studies dept. near Ea. langs. and cultures Ind. U., 1995—, chmn. dept. near Ea. langs. and cultures, 1999—, dir. middle ea. studies program, 1999—; mem. Sch. Hist. Studies, Inst. for Advanced Study-Princeton, 1993-94; cons. PBS-TV, 1990, L.A. Times, 1998, Am. Mus. Natural History, 1998; presenter in field. Author: Purity and Pollution in Zoroastrianism, 1989, Conflict and Cooperation, 1997; Contbr. numerous articles to profl. publs. PTO Rsch. fellow Govt. India, Bombay, 1998; John Simon Guggenheim Meml. Found. fellow, 1996-97; resident scholar Ind. U., 1996-97, grantee 1994—, grantee Am. Acad. Religion, 1995-96, Andrew W. Mellon fellow, 1991-93. NEH fellow, Inst. for Advanced Study, Princeton, 1993-94, fellow Royal Asiatic Soc. Great Britain, Ireland. Office: Ind U Dept Near Ea Langs Goodbody Hall 102 1011 E Third St Bloomington IN 47405

CHOLDIN, MARIANNA TAX, librarian, educator; b. Chgo., Feb. 26, 1942; d. Sol and Gertrude (Katz) Tax; m. Harvey Myron Choldin, Aug. 28, 1962; children: Kate and Mary (twins). BA, U. Chgo., 1962, MA, 1967, PhD, 1979. Slavic bibliographer Mich. State U., East Lansing, 1967-69; Slavic bibliographer, instr. U. Ill., Urbana, 1969-73, Slavic bibliographer, asst. prof., 1973-76, Slavic bibliographer, assoc. prof., 1976-84, head Slavic and East European Libr., 1982-89, head, prof., 1984—, dir. Russian and East European Ctr., 1987-89, C. Walter and Gerda B. Mortenson Disting. prof., 1989—, dir. Mortenson Ctr. for Internat. Libr. Programs, 1991—. Author: Fence Around the Empire: Russian Censorship, 1985; editor: Red Pencil: Artists, Scholars and Censors in the USSR, 1989, Books, Libraries and Information in Slavic and East European Studies, 1986. Chair Soros Found. Network Libr. Program Bd., 1997—. Mem. ALA, Am. Assn. for Advancement of Slavic Studies (pres. 1995), Internat. Fedn. Libr. Assns. and Instns., Phi Beta Kappa. Jewish. Home: 1111 S Pine St Champaign IL 61820-6334 Office: U Ill Libr 1408 W Gregory Dr Urbana IL 61801-3607

CHOLE, RICHARD ARTHUR, otolaryngologist, educator; b. Madison, Wis., Oct. 12, 1944; s. Arthur Steven and Wendy Elveyn (Danielczyk) C.; m. Cynthia Beiseker, Dec. 27, 1969; children: Joseph Michael, Timothy Thomas, Katharine, Melinda. Student, U. Calif., Berkeley, 1962-65; MD, U. So. Calif., 1969; PhD in Otolaryngology, U. Minn., 1977. Diplomate Am. Bd. Otolaryngology (sr. bd. examiner). Rotating intern U. So. Calif. Med. Ctr., 1969-70; med. fellow dept. surgery Sch. Medicine U. Minn., 1972-73, med. fellow dept. otolaryngology Sch. Medicine, 1973-77; asst. prof. dept. otolaryngology-head and neck surgery Sch. Medicine U. Calif., Davis, 1977-81, assoc. prof., 1981-84, prof., 1984-98, acting chmn. dept., 1985, chmn., 1985-88; chmn. dept. otolaryngology U. Washington, St. Louis, 1998—; mem. sci. rev. com. Deafness Rsch. Found., 1986—; mem. communicative disorders rev. com. Nat. Inst. Deafness and Communication Disorders, 1989—; staff cons. Dept. Air Force, David Grant USAF Med. Ctr., Travis AFB, Calif., 1981—; keynote speaker 92d Japan Oto-Rhino-Laryngol. Soc. Meeting, Fukuoka City, 1990; faculty mem. 4th Internat. Cholesteatoma Conf., Niigata City, Japan, 1992; lectr. in field. Mem. editorial bd. Laryngoscope, 1985-87; mem. exec. editorial bd. Otolaryngology-Head and Neck Surgery, 1990—; contbr. numerous articles to profl. jours., book chpts., revs.; patentee in field. Mem. profl. edn. com. Am. Cancer Soc., 1977-78, Sacramento Noise Control Hearing Bd., 1977—, Greater Sacramento Profl. Standards Rev. Orgn., 1978-79; deacon 1st Bapt. Ch., Davis, 1979-82, elder, 1983-88. Recipient 1st pl. award Am. Acad. Ophthalmology and Otolaryngology, 1977, care recognition awards U. Calif., Davis, 1988-91; rsch. grantee NIH, Nat. Inst. Aging, Nat. Inst. Neurol. and Communicative Disorders and Stroke, Nat. Inst. on Deafness and Other Communication Disorders, Deafness Rsch. Found., Am. Otol. Soc., U. Calif., 1978-91. Mem. Collegeum Otorhinolaryngologicum Amicitiae Sacrum (U.S. group), Am. Acad. Otolaryngology-Head and Neck Surgery (Honors award 1984, com. on rsch. 1987—, rsch. coordinating coun. 1987—, continuing edn. com. 1991—), Am. Otol. Soc. (trustee rsch. fund 1986—, sec.-treas. 1989—), Assn. for Rsch. in Otolaryngology (pres. 1999-2000, award of merit com. 1988—), Am. Laryngol., Rhinol. and Otol. Soc., Am. Soc. for Bone and Mineral Rsch., Assn. Acad. Depts. Otolaryngology-Head and Neck Surgery (coun. 1986—), Calif. Med. Assn. (sci. adv. panel, sect. on otolaryngology-head and neck surgery 1986—), Sacramento Soc. Otolaryngology and Maxillofacial Surgery, Soc. Univ. Otolaryngologists-Head and Neck Surgeons. Research in experimental cholesteatoma, experimental otosclerosis, the aging auditory system, osteoclast cell biology. Office: Washington U Sch Med CB8115 517 S Euclid Ave Saint Louis MO 63110-1007

CHOLETTE, MAUREEN THERESA, geriatrics nurse, nursing administrator; b. Lakewood, N.J., Feb. 20, 1949; d. I. James and Clare E. (French)

Kress; m. Viateur Cholette; children: Pierre, Paul. AD, Middlesex County Coll., Edison, N.J., 1969. RN, N.J.; cert. in nursing adminstrn. and gerontol. nursing, ANCC. Staff, charge nurse Birchwood Convalescent Ctr., Edison; charge nurse, ADON, DON Burlington Woods Convalescent Ctr., Burlington, N.J.; dir. nursing svcs. Medford (N.J.) Convalescent and Nursing Ctr., 1980—. Fellow Nat. Assn. Dirs. Nursing Adminstrn. in Long Term Care (cert. dir. nursing adminstrn. in long term care, by-laws chmn., NE Region DON of the Yr. 1995); mem. Nat. Gerontol. Nursing Assn., N.J. Assn. Dirs. Nursing Adminstrs./Long Term Care (bd. mem., v.p., DON of the Yr. award 1995). Home: 301 Carrol St Browns Mills NJ 08015-2642

CHOMKO, STEPHEN ALEXANDER, archaeologist; b. Bklyn., Nov. 18, 1948; s. Paul and Lucy Isabella (Bisaccio) C.; m. Leslie M. Howard, Aug. 1972 (div. 1980). BA in Anthropology cum laude, Beloit Coll., 1970; MA in Anthropology, U. Mo., 1976. Mem. rsch. staff Nassau County Mus. Natural History, Glen Cove, N.Y., 1969-71; grad. rsch. asst. U. Mo., Columbia, 1972-74, 75-78; rsch. asst. Ill. State Mus., Springfield, 1974-75; dist. archaeologist Bur. Land Mgmt., Rawlins, Wyo., 1978-80; archaeologist Office of Fed. Inspector, Denver, 1980-82; dir. Paleo Environ. Cons., Wheat Ridge, Colo., 1980-86; archaeologist Interagy. Archaeol. Svcs., Denver, 1982-92; chief rsch. and resource mgmt. Mesa Verde (Colo.) Nat. Park, 1992; chief tng. mgmt. Fort Carson, 1994—. Writer, dir. (video program) Our Past Our Future, 1992; contbr. articles to profl. jours. Grantee Cave Rsch. Found., Yellow Springs, Ohio, 1976; Anthropology scholar U. Mo., Columbia, 1978; recipient Quality Performance award Nat. Park Svc., Denver, 1992, 93, Environ. Quality award Dept. of Army, 1996, Environ. Stewardship award Dept. of Def., 1997. Mem. Soc. Am. Archaeology, Am. Anthropol. Assn., Am. Quaternary Assn., Wyo. Assn. Profl. Archaeologists (exec. com. 1979-82), Mont. Archaeol. Soc., Plains Anthropol. Soc. (v.p. 1988-89, bd. dirs. 1986-89). Home: 1144 Rock Creek Canyon Rd Colorado Springs CO 80926-8710 Office: Decam 801 Tevis St Fort Carson CO 80913-4000

CHOMSKY, AVRAM NOAM, linguistics and philosophy educator; b. Phila., Dec. 7, 1928; s. William and Elsie (Simonofsky) C.; m. Carol Doris Schatz, Dec. 24, 1949; children: Aviva, Diane, Harry Alan. BA, U. Pa., 1949, MA, 1951, PhD, 1955, DHL (hon.), 1984; DHL (hon.), U. Chgo., 1967, Loyola U., Chgo., 1970, Swarthmore Coll., 1970, Bard Coll., 1971, U. Mass., 1973, U. Maine, 1992, Gettysburg Coll., 1992, Amherst Coll., Buenos Aires, 1996, U. Rovira i Virgili, Catalonia, 1998, U. Guelph, Can., 1999, Columbia U., 1999, U. Conn., 1999; LittD (hon.), U. London, 1967, Delhi (India) U., 1972, Visva-Bharati U., Santiniketan, West Bengal, 1980, Cambridge (Eng.) U., 1995. Mem. faculty MIT, 1955—, prof. modern langs., 1961—, Ferrari P. Ward prof. modern lang. and linguistics, 1966—, Inst. prof., 1976—; vis. prof. Columbia U., N.Y.C., 1957-58; mem. Inst. Advanced Study Princeton U., 1958-59, Am. U. of Cairo, 1993; Linguistic Soc. Am. prof. UCLA, summer 1966; Beckman prof. U. Calif.-Berkeley, 1966-67; John Locke lectr. Oxford U., 1969; Bertrand Russell Meml. lectr., Cambridge, 1971; Nehru Meml. lectr., New Delhi, 1972; Huizinga lectr. U. Leiden, 1977; Woodbridge lectr. Columbia U., 1978; Kant lectr. Stanford U., 1979; Jeanette K. Watson disting. vis. prof. Syracuse U., 1982; Pauling Meml. lectr. Oreg. State U., 1995. Author: Syntactic Structures, 1957, Current Issues in Linguistic Theory, 1964, Aspects of the Theory of Syntax, 1965, Cartesian Linguistics, 1966, Topics in the Theory of Generative Grammar, 1966, (with Morris Halle) Sound Pattern of English, 1968, Language and Mind, 1968, American Power and the New Mandarins, 1969, At War with Asia, 1970, Problems of Knowledge and Freedom, 1971, Studies on Semantics in Generative Grammar, 1972, For Reasons of State, 1973, (with Edward Herman) Counterrevolutionary Violence, 1973, Peace in The Middle East, 1974, Logical Structure of Linguistic Theory, 1975, Reflections on Language, 1975, Essays on Form and Interpretation, 1977, Human Rights and American Foreign Policy, 1978, (with Edward Herman) The Political Economy of Human Rights, 2 vols., 1979, Language and Responsibility, 1979, Rules and Representations, 1980, Lectures on Government and Binding, 1981, Concepts and Consequences of the Theory of Government and Binding, 1982, Towards a New Cold War, 1982, Radical Priorities, 1982, Fateful Triangle, 1983, Turning the Tide, 1985, Barriers, 1986, Knowledge of Language, 1986, Pirates and Emperors, 1986, On Power and Ideology, 1987, Language and Problems of Knowledge, 1987, Language in a Psychological Setting, 1987, Generative Grammar, 1987, Culture of Terrorism, 1988, (with Edward Herman) Manufacturing Consent, 1988, Language and Politics, 1988, Necessary Illusions, 1989, Deterring Democracy, 1991, Chronicles of Dissent, 1992, What Uncle Sam Really Wants, 1992, Year 501, 1993, Rethinking Camelot, 1993, Letters from Lexington, 1993, The Prosperous Few and the Restless Many, 1993, Language and Thought, 1994, World Orders, Old and New, 1994, The Minimalist Program, 1995, Powers and Prospects, 1996, The Common Good, 1998, Profits Over People, 1998. Recipient Disting. Sci. Contbn. award APA, 1984, Kyoto prize, 1988, George Orwell award Nat. Coun. Tchrs. English, 1987, 89, James Killian faculty award MIT, 1992, Lannan Lit. award for nonfiction, 1992, Joel Seldin Peace award Psychologists for Social Responsibility, 1993, Homer Smith award NYU Sch. Medicine, 1994, Loyola Mellon Humanities award Loyola U., Chgo., 1994, Helmholtz medal Berlin-Brandenburgische Akademie Wissenschaften, 1996, Benjamin Franklin Inst. award, 1999; jr. fellow Soc. Fellows, Harvard U., 1951-55, rsch. fellow Harvard Cognitive Studies Ctr., 1964-67. Fellow AAAS, Brit. Acad. (corr.), Brit. Psychol. Soc. (hon.), Royal Anthrop. Inst. Gt. Britain, Royal Anthrop. Inst. of Ireland, Utrecht Soc. Arts and Scis. (hon.), Gesellschaft für Sprachwissenschaft (hon.), Am. Acad. Philosophy; mem. APA (William James fellow 1990), NAS, Am. Acad. Arts and Scis., Linguistic Soc. Am., Deutsche Akademie der Naturforscher Leopoldina, Assn. for Edn. in Journalism and Mass Comm. (Profl. Excellence award 1991). Home: 15 Suzanne Rd Lexington MA 02420-1831 Office: MIT 77 Massachusetts Ave Cambridge MA 02139-4307

CHOMSKY, MARTIN S., county executive director; b. N.Y.C., Apr. 15, 1938; s. Nathan and Anna C.; m. Annette Siciliano, Mar. 27, 1960; children: Anita, Ronald, Debra. AA, Monmouth Col., 1962, BS in Biology, 1963; MPH, U. Mich., 1965. cert. health officer, N.J., 1967. Sanitarian N.J. Dept. Health, Trenton, 1963-67; health officer Long Branch (N.J.) Health Dept., 1967-68, Rahway City (N.J.) Health Dept., 1968-72, Asbury Park (N.J.) Regional Health Dept., 1972-85; exec. dir. Monmouth County Mosquito Commn., Eatontown, N.J., 1985—. State committeeman N.J. Dem. State Com., Trenton, 1989-95; mcpl. chmn. Ocean Township (N.J.) Dem. Exec. Com., 1975-87; N. Atlantic regional dir. Am. Mosquito Control Assn., 1997—; chmn. Monmouth County (N.J.) Water Resources Assn., 1990—. Office: Monmouth County MEC PO Box 162 Eatontown NJ 07724-0162

CHONG, ALBERT VALENTINE, artist, educator; b. Kingston, Jamaica, W.I., Nov. 20, 1958; came to U.S., 1977; s. Albert George and Gloria Agnes (Chin) C.; m. Frances Irene Ann Charteris, Nov. 23, 1982; children: Ayinde Jordan, Chinwe Amelia. BFA, Sch. of Visual Arts, N.Y.C., 1981; MFA, U. Calif., San Diego, 1991. Instr. Sch. of Visual Arts, N.Y.C., 1986-88; adjunct faculty Mira Costa Coll., Oceanside, Calif., 1989-90; vis. scholar Mira Costa Coll., Oceanside, 1990-91; asst. prof. art U. Colo., Boulder, 1991—; program auditor, cons. N.Y. State Coun. on the Arts, N.Y.C., 1984-88. Author: (book) Ancestral Dialogues, 1993. Recipient Regional fellowship NEA, Santa Fe, N. Mex., 1991, Artist's fellowship, Washington, 1992. Home: 5155 Santa Clara Pl Apt 1 Boulder CO 80303-4117 Office: Univ Colo Boulder PO Box 318 Boulder CO 80309-0318

CHONG, JOHN KENNETH, plastic surgeon; b. Ipoh, Perak, Malaysia, Apr. 4, 1929; came to U.S., 1967; s. Francis Chong and Catherine Lee; m. Junie Choong, Sept. 4, 1954; children: Lavinia Karen, Kenneth Trevor, Clare Vanessa. BSc, McGill U., Montreal, Que. Can., 1951; BA, Oxford (Eng.) U., 1955, BM, BCh, 1958, MA, 1959. Diplomate Am. Bd. Plastic Surgery (guest examiner 1978, 80). Intern St. Batholomew's Hosp., London, 1959; resident St. Batholomew's and Whipps Cross Hosps., London, 1960, 63-64; sr. resident Queen Victoria Hosp., East Grinstead, Eng., 1964-67; asst. prof. plastic surgery Temple U., Phila., 1967-70, assoc. prof., 1970-72; pvt. practice, Newport Beach, Calif., 1972—; attending plastic surgeon Temple U. Hosp., 1967-72, St. Christopher's Hosp., Phila., 1967-72, Chestnut Hill Hosp., Phila., 1969-72; attending plastic surgeon Hoag Meml. Hosp., Newport Beach. 1972—, chmn. dept., 1976-78; clin. assoc. prof. U. Calif., Irvine, 1973; mem. bd. reviewers internat. abstracts Plastic and Reconstructive Surgery, 1979—; reviewer Med. Bd. Calif., Sacramento, 1990. Fellow ACS (pres. So. Calif. chpt. 1998-99), Royal Coll. Surgeons (Eng.); mem. Am. Soc. Plastic and Reconstructive Surgeons, Am. Soc. for Aesthetic Plastic Surgsons (parliamentarian 1985-86), Internat. Soc. Aesthetic Plastic Surgeons, Brit. Assn. Plastic Surgeons, Pacific Coast Surg. Assn., So. Calif. Chinese Physicians Assn. (chmn. 1974-75). Avocations: deep sea fishing, photography, fine wines, antique silver. Office: 1401 Avocado Ave Ste 803 Newport Beach CA 92660

CHONG, RACHELLE B., lawyer, federal communications commissioner; b. Stockton, Calif., June 22, 1959; d. Edmond and Barbara Mary (Ahtye) C.; m. Kirk E. Del Prete, Oct. 18, 1987. BA in Journalism with high honors, U. Calif., Berkeley, 1981; JD, Hastings Coll. of Law, San Francisco, 1984. Bar: Calif. 1984, D.C. 1985. Assoc. Kadison, Pfaelzer, Woodard & Rossi, Washington and Palo Alto, Calif., 1984-87; assoc. Graham & James, San Francisco, 1987-92, ptnr., 1992-94; commr. FCC, Washington, 1994-97; ptnr. Coudert Bros., San Francisco, 1998—; commr. Legal Svc. Trust Fund Commn. of Calif. State Bar, San Francisco, 1992-94. Editor-in-chief Comm/Ent Law Jour., 1983-85. Finalist for 1994 Woman of Yr., Marketplace Channel 7 KGO-TV, San Francisco, 1994. Mem. ABA (mem. forum fed. comm. bar assn., women in telecomm.), Fed. Comm. Bar Assn. Republican. Methodist. Office: Coudert Bros 4 Embarcadero Ctr Ste #3300 San Francisco CA 94111*

CHONG, RICHARD DAVID, architect; b. Los Angeles, June 1, 1946; s. George and Mabel Dorothy (Chan) C.; m. Roze Gutierrez, July 5, 1969; children: David Gregory, Michelle Elizabeth. BArch, U. So. Calif., 1969; MArch, UCLA, 1974. Registered architect, Utah, Calif., Wyo., Wash. Assoc. Pulliam, Matthews & Assocs., Los Angeles, 1969-76; dir. Asst. Community Design Ctr., Salt Lake City, 1976-77; prin. Richard D. Chong & Assocs., Salt Lake City and L.A., 1977—; planning cons. Los Angeles Harbor Dept., 1974-76; asst. instr. So. Calif. Inst. Architecture, Santa Monica, 1973-74; vis. design critic Calif. State Poly. U., Pamona, 1975, U. Utah, Salt Lake City, 1976-78; design instr. Calif. State Poly. U., 1975-76; adj. asst. prof. urban design, U. Utah, 1980-84; bd. dirs. Utah Housing Coalition, Salt Lake City; Salt Lake City Housing Adv. and Appeals Bd., 1976-80; presenter Rail-Volution Conf., Washington, 1996. Author: Design of Flexible Housing, 1974; prin. works include Airmen's Dining Hall, 1985 (1st Pl. Mil. Facility Air Force Logistics Command, 1986), Oddfellows Hall, 1984 (Heritage Found. award, 1986), Light Rail Sys. for Salt Lake City. Mem. Task Force for the Aged Housing Com. Salt Lake County, Salt Lake City, 1976-77; Salt Lake City Mortgage Loan Instns. Rev. Com., 1978; bd. dirs. Neighborhood Housing Svcs. of Fed. Home Loan Bank Bd., Salt Lake City, 1979-81, devel. com.; vice-chmn. Water Quality Adv. Coun., Salt Lake City, 1981-83; vice-chmn. Salt Lake City Pub. Utilities Bd., 1985-87; mem. adv. bd. Pub. Utilities Commn., Salt Lake City, 1985—; bd. dirs. Kier Mgmt. Corp.; bd. mem. Camp Kostopulos, Altro Nat. Risk Mgmt. Adv. Bd., 1996—, Ft. Douglas Social Adv. Bd., 1996—, Altro Nat. Safety Bd., 1996—. Mem. AIA (jury mem. Am. Soc. Interior Designs Ann. awards 1981-82, treas. Salt Lake chpt. 1988-89, treas. Utah Soc. 1991, sec. 1992, pres.-elect AIA Utah 1993, pres. 1994-95), Am. Inst. Planning (juror Ann. Planning award 1984-85), Am. Planning Assn., Am. Arbitration Assn., Nat. Panel Arbitrators, Ft. Douglas Country Club. Democrat. Avocations: tennis, sailing, fgn. travel. Office: Richard D Chong & Assocs 244 Edison St Salt Lake City UT 84111-2307 also: 714 W Olympic Blvd Ste 732 Los Angeles CA 90015-1439

CHONG, VERNON, surgeon, physician, Air Force officer; b. Fresno, Calif., Nov. 13, 1933; s. Seu Ling and Ruth (Lee) C.; m. Ann Sumiko Kawana, Sept. 7, 1957; children: Christopher Lee, Gerald Scott, Douglas James. BA, Stanford U., 1955, MD, 1958. Diplomate Am. Bd. Surgery. Intern Gen. Hosp. of Fresno (Calif.) County, 1958-59, resident in gen. surgery, 1959-63; capt. USAF, 1963, advanced through ranks to maj. gen., 1987; chief gen. surgery svc. USAF Hosp., Scott AFB, Ill., 1963-65; staff surgeon, dir. edn. USAF Hosp., Tachikawa AFB, Japan, 1965-68; staff surgeon, instr. surgery David Grant USAF Med. Ctr., Travis AFB, Calif., 1968-70, dep. comdr., dir. hosp. svcs., comdr., 1976-81; surgeon, chief surgery, dir. hosp. svcs. USAF Acad. Hosp., Colorado Springs, Colo., 1970-74; dep. comdr. dir. svcs. USAF Acad. Hosp., March AFB, Calif., 1974-76; comdr. Malcolm Grow USAF MEd. Ctr., Andrews AFB, Md., 1981-85; command surgeon Hdqrs., Mil. Airlift Command, Scott AFB, 1985-87; comdr. Wilford Hall USAF Med. Ctr., Lackland AFB, Tex., 1987-90, Joint Mil. Med. Command, San Antonio; command surgeon Hdqrs. Air Tng. Command, Randolph AFB, Tex., 1990-91, Hdqrs. U.S. European Command, 1991-94; ret., 1994; network dir. Vets. Integrated Svc. Network Dept. VA, Grand Prairie, Tex., 1995—. Bd. dirs. Alamo chpt. ARC, San Antonio, 1987-88; trustee Air Force Village Found., 1987-90; bd. dirs. San Antonio chpt. ARC, 1995—. Decorated D.S.M., Legion of Merit with bronze oak leaf cluster; recipient Order of Sword award USAF, 1989. Fellow ACS (gov. 1985-90); mem. Assn. Mil. Surgeons U.S., Aerospace Med. Assocs., Soc. Air Force Clin. Surgeons (bd. govs. 1971-73), Am. Coll. Physician Execs. Methodist. Avocations: physical fitness, running. Home: 2714 Laurel Valley Ln Arlington TX 76006-4020

CHONMAITREE, TASNEE, pediatrician, educator, infectious disease specialist; b. Bangkok, Thailand, Dec. 9, 1949; came to U.S., 1975; d. Surajit and Arporn (Maitong) C.; m. Somkiat Laungthaleong Pong, June 27, 1981; children: Ann L. Pong, Dan L. Pong. BS, Mahidol U., Bangkok, 1971; MD, Siriraj Med. Sch., Bangkok, 1973. Diplomate Am. Bd. Pediatrics, Am. Bd. Pediatric Infectious Diseases. Rotating intern Siriraj Hosp., Bangkok, 1973-74, resident in pediatrics, 1974-75; resident in pediatrics Lloyd Noland Hosp., U. Ala., Birmingham, 1975-78; fellow infectious disease U. Rochester (N.Y.), 1978-81; asst. prof. pediatrics U. Tex. Med. Br., Galveston, 1981-87, asst. prof. pathology, 1985-87, assoc. prof. pediatrics and pathology, 1987-94; prof. pediatrics and pathology, 1994—; assoc. dir. clin. virology lab. U. Tex. Med. Br., Galveston, 1985-92, dir. divsn. pediatric infectious disease, 1985-92. Contbr. 55 articles to profl. jours. Grantee NIH, 1993-99. Fellow Am. Acad. Pediatrics, Pediatric Infectious Diseases Soc., Infectious Diseases Soc. Am.; mem. Soc. Pediatric Rsch., European Soc. for Pediatric Rsch., Tex. Infectious Disease Soc. Buddhist. Avocation: classical music. Home: 1906 Cherrytree Park Cir Houston TX 77062-2327 Office: U Tex Dept Pediatrics Med Br Ninth Street & Market Galveston TX 77555-0371

CHOO, MICHAEL OWEN, executive, consultant; b. L.A., June 14, 1964; s. Herbert Young Ho and Frances C.; m. Laura Kaye Wheeler, Aug. 12, 1995; 1 child, Ashley Leilani. Degree in Respiratory Therapy val., Calif. Paramedical Tech. Coll., 1983. Cert. Respiratory Care Practitioner, Flight and Ground Transport, ABG Interpretion, teaching (Calif.). Respiratory therapy supr. LaMirada (Calif.) Med. Ctr., 1983-92; dir. respiratory Advaned Respiratory Mgmt. Svc., Norwalk, Calif., 1992-94, chief operation officer, 1994-96; v.p. ancillary ops. Midway Hosp. Med. Ctr., L.A., Calif., 1996-98; dir. respiratory Advaned Respiratory Mgmt. Svc., Norwalk, Calif., 1992-94, chief operation officer, 1994-96; v.p. ancillary ops. Midway Hosp. Med. Ctr., L.A., 1996—; v.p. ancillary svcs. City of Angels Med. Ctr., L.A., 1998—; respiratory therapist Anaheim (Calif.) Gen. Hosp., 1983-84, Garden Grove (Calif.) Med. Ctr., 1983-84; clin. instr. Calif. Paramedical Tech. Coll., Long Beach, 1992; sales mgr. Alpine Industries, 1997-98. Mem. Nat. Bd. of Respiratory Care, Am. Assn. of Respiratory Care, Calif. Soc. ofRespiratory Care. Avocations: fishing, surfing, fitness, bicyling, restoration. E-Mail: mochoo@aol.com. Home: 11435 177th Street Artesia CA 90701

CHOOK, EDWARD KONGYEN, university administrator, disaster medicine educator; b. Shanghai, Apr. 15, 1937; s. Shiu-heng and Shuiking (Shek) C.; m. Ping Ping Chew, Oct. 30, 1973; children by previous marriage: Miranda, Bradman. MD, Nat. Def. Med. Ctr., Taiwan, 1959; MPH, U. Calif., Berkeley, 1964, PhD, 1969; ScD, Phila. Coll. Pharmacy & Sci., 1971; JD, La Salle U., 1994. Assoc. prof. U. Calif., Berkeley, 1966-68; dir. higher edn. Bay Area Bilingual Edn. League, Berkeley, 1970-75; prof., chancellor United U. Am., Oakland and Berkeley, Calif., 1975-84; regional adminstr. U. So. Calif., L.A., 1984-90; pres. Pacific Internat. U., Berkeley and Pomona, Calif., and Guam, 1996—, Shanghai Internat. Coll., 1997—; chancellor Bi-Lingual Coll. Zhuhai (China)-Pacific Internat. Joint U., Hong Kong, 1998—; vis. prof. Nat. Def. Med. Ctr., Taiwan Armed Forces U., 1982—, Tongji U., Shanghai, 1992, Foshan U., China, 1992—; cons. specialist Beijing Hosp., 1988—; founder, pres. United Svc. Coun., Inc., 1971—; pres. Pan Internat. Acad., Changchun, China and San Francisco, 1979—, China Gen. Devel. Corp., U.S., 1992—; pub. Unity Jour./Power News, San Francisco, 1979—; sr. cons., Sanye Pharmaceutical Grp., Ltd., Hainan Island, China, 1999—, mem. NAS-NRC, Washington, 1968-71; spl. cons. cultural sensitivity seminars; spl. lectr. KPMG/Peat Warwick Accts., 1996; advisor Ka Wa Bank, Hong Kong, 1986-96. Assoc. editor U.S.-Chinese Times, 1996-98; pub. US-China Times, 1996—, Unity Jour., N.Am. edit., 1996—; contbr. articles to profl. jours. Trustee Rep. Presdl. Task Force, Washington, 1978—; advisor on mainland China affairs Ctrl. Com. Chinese Nationalist party, Taiwan, 1994-97; deacon Am. Bapt. Ch.; sr. advisor U.S. Congl. Adv. Bd.; mem. Presdl. Adv. Commn., 1991—; hon. dep. sec. of state State of Calif., 1990-93; spl. advisor to sec. of state, 1991—; pres. Yuen Kong Found. for Internat. Understanding (aka March Fong EU Found.), 1994-96, 96—; mem. Nat. Heart Coun., 1994—; senatorial commn. Rep. Senatorial Inner Cir., 1996. August 9, 1997 proclaimed Ed Chook Day by City of Oakland. Mem. World Affairs Coun. San Francisco, Rotary (com. chmn. 1971—). Achievements include rsch. on hearing conservation program in U.S. Army, criteria for return to work, principles and practices of nuclear, biol. and chem. weapons. Office: PIU Adminstrn Office 555 Pierce Ste B-2 Albany CA 94706-1044

CHOOK, PAUL HOWARD, publishing executive; b. N.Y.C., Oct. 17, 1929; s. Abraham and Etta (Cohen) C. BBA, CCNY, 1949; MS, Columbia U., 1950. Cons. quality control Philip Morris, Inc., N.Y.C., 1951-55; pres. media studies div. Alfred Politz Rsch., Inc., N.Y.C., 1955-66; v.p. rsch. Young & Rubicam, Inc., N.Y.C., 1966-74; pres. W.R. Simmons Rsch. Assocs., N.Y.C., 1974-75; exec. v.p. mktg. and circulation Ziff Davis Pub. Co., N.Y.C., 1975-84, sr. v.p. mktg., 1986-93; mktg. cons., 1993-95; exec. v.p. CBS Mags., N.Y.C., 1985; ind. mktg. cons., 1995—; instr. CCNY, 1951-63. Sgt. N.Y. NG., 1948-56. Mem. Advt. Rsch. Found. (bd. dirs. 1977-84), Am. Statis. Assn., Am. Mktg. Assn., Am. Assn. Pub. Opinion Rsch., Market Rsch. Coun. Jewish. Avocations: bridge, jogging. Home: 65-65 Wetherole St Flushing NY 11374-4764

CHOOKASZIAN, DENNIS HAIG, financial executive; b. Chgo., Sept. 19, 1943; s. Haig Harold and Annabelle (Kalkanian) C.; m. Karen Margaret Genteman, Mar. 18, 1967; children: Jeffrey, Michael, Kerry. BS in Chem. Engring., Northwestern U., 1965; MBA in Fin., U. Chgo., 1967; MS in Econs., London Sch. of Econs., 1968. CPA, Ill.; cert. mgmt. cons. Mgmt. cons. Touche Ross & Co., Chgo., 1968-75; chief fin. officer CNA Fin. Corp., Chgo., 1975-90; pres., chief operating officer CNA, 1990-92; chmn., CEO CNA Ins., 1992—; bd. dirs. Loews Corp., Mercury Fin. Pres. Found. for Health Enhancement; bd. dirs. Nat. Boy Scouts Am., Northwestern Meml. Hosp., Nat. Merit Scholarship Corp.; mem. adv. coun. U. Chgo. Grad. Sch. of Bus.; mem. adv. bd. Northwestern U. Kellogg Grad. Sch. of Bus., Inroads; trustee Northwestern U., 1996—. Mem. AICPAs, Ill. Soc. CPAs, Westmoreland Country Club (Wilmette), East Bank Club (Chgo.), The Econ. Club of Chgo., The Execs. Club of Chgo. (dirs.' table), Am. Inst. Assn., Am. Coun. of Life Ins., Ins. Svcs. Office, Beta Gamma Sigma. Republican. Avocations: skiing, tennis, triathlons, golf. Home: 1100 Michigan Ave Wilmette IL 60091-1976 Office: CNA CNA Plz Chicago IL 60685

CHOPER, JESSE HERBERT, law educator, university dean; b. Wilkes-Barre, Pa., Sept. 19, 1935; s. Edward and Dorothy (Resnick) C.; m. Mari Smith; children: Marc Steven, Edward Nathaniel. BS, Wilkes U., 1957, DHL, 1967; LLB, U. Pa., 1960. Bar: D.C. 1961. Instr. Wharton Sch. U. Pa., 1957-60; law clk. to Chief Justice Earl Warren U.S. Supreme Ct., 1960-61; asst. prof. U. Minn. Law Sch., 1961-62, assoc. prof., 1962-65; prof. Law Sch. U. Calif., Berkeley, 1965—, dean, 1982-92, Earl Warren prof. Pub. Law, 1991—; vis. prof. Harvard U., 1970-71. Author: Constitutional Law: Cases-Comments-Questions, 8th edit., 1996, The American Constitution, Cases and Materials, 8th edit., 1996, Constitutional Rights and Liberties, Cases and Materials, 8th edit., 1996, Corporations, Cases and Materials, 4th edit., 1995, Judicial Review and the National Political Process, 1980, Securing Religious Liberty, 1995; contbr. articles to profl. jours. Mem. AAUP, Am. Law Inst., Am. Acad. Arts and Scis., Order of Coif. Democrat. Jewish. Office: U Calif Sch Law Berkeley CA 94720

CHOPEY, NICHOLAS P., editor; b. N.Y.C., Dec. 22, 1932; s. Nicholas W. and Alice I. (Keshelak) C.; m. Katherine J. Heaney, Sept. 12, 1959; children: Nicholas, Michael, John, James. BChE, U. Va., 1955; MA in Econs., NYU, 1972. Process engr. Esso Standard Oil Co., Linden, N.J., 1955-56, 58-59; asst. assoc. editor McGraw-Hill, Inc., N.Y.C., 1960-67, sr. assoc. editor, 1967-72, mng. editor, 1972-78, exec. editor, 1978-82, editor-in-chief, 1982-87, exec. editor, 1987—; adv. com. Indsl. Energy Tech. Conf., Houston, 1992—. Editor: Handbook of Chemical Engineering Calculations, 1984, 2d edit., 1994; (reprint books) Environmental Engineering in the Process Plant, 1992, Fluid Movers, 1994. 1st lt. USAF, 1956-58. Mem. AIChE (past chair com.), Am. Soc. Engring. Edn., Knights of Malta, Roselle Golf Club, Tau Beta Pi. Roman Catholic. Office: McGraw Hill Cos 2 Penn Plz New York NY 10121-2298

CHOPIN, L. FRANK, lawyer; b. New Orleans, Apr. 29, 1942; s. Alton Francis and Floretta (Thensted) C.; children: Philip, Alexandra, Christopher. BBA, Loyola U., New Orleans, 1964, JD, 1966; diploma in mil. law, Judge Adv. Gen.'s Sch., U. Va. Sch. Law, 1966; postgrad., Nat. Law Ctr., George Wash. U., 1967-68; LLM in Taxation, U. Miami, Fla., 1976; PhD in Law, Cambridge U., Eng., 1986. Bar: La. 1966, Fla. 1968, Iowa 1980, U.S. Dist. Ct. (so. dist.) Fla. 1968, U.S. Ct. Appeals (5th cir.) 1968. Ptnr. Chopin & Chopin, Miami, 1969-77; assoc. prof. law Drake U., Des Moines, 1979-80; ptnr. Cadwalader, Wickersham & Taft, Palm Beach, Fla., 1980-94, Chopin, Miller & Yudenfreund, Palm Beach, Fla., 1995-98, Chopin & Miller, Palm Beach, Fla., 1999—; adj. prof. law U. Miami, 1982-96, U. Sherbrooke, Can., 1982-94. Author: The New Residency Rules for Canadian Tax Considerations, 1985; also numerous articles in legal jours. Mem. Housing Fin. Authority; trustee Preservation Found., Palm Beach Community Chest, Inc. Served to capt. U.S. Army, 1966-68. Mem. ABA, Internat. Bar Assn., Fed. Bar Assn., Fla. Bar (tax sect.), Loyola U. Alumni Assn., U. Miami Alumni Assn., St. Thomas More Law Soc., Phi Alpha Delta (charter). Republican. Roman Catholic. Office: Chopin & Miller 440 Royal Palm Way Ste 200 Palm Beach FL 33480-4197

CHOPIN, SUSAN GARDINER, lawyer; b. Miami, Fla., Feb. 23, 1947; d. Maurice and Judith (Warden) Gardiner; m. M.S. Rukeyser, Jr. Mar. 10, 1997; children: Philip, Alexandra, Christopher. BBA, Loyola U., New Orleans, 1966; JD cum laude, U. Miami, 1972; MLitt (Law), Oxford U., Eng., 1983. Bar: Fla. 1972, Iowa 1979. Sr. law clk. to judge U.S. Dist. Ct. (so. dist.) Fla., Miami, 1972-73; ptnr. Chopin & Chopin, Miami, 1973-77; assoc. prof. law sch. Drake U., Des Moines, 1979-80; pvt. practice law Palm Beach, Fla., 1981—; ptnr. Chopin & Chopin, 1999—. Mem. editorial bd. Fla. Bar Jour., 1975—; contbr. articles to profl. jours., legal revs. Trustee Preservation Found. of Palm Beach, 1986-89. Mem. ABA, Fla. Bar Assn., Iowa Bar Assn., Fed. Bar Assn., Internat. Bar Assn., Fla. Assn. Women Lawyers, Soc. Wig and Robe, Palm Beach County Bar Assn., English Speaking Union, Phi Kappa Phi, Phi Alpha Delta. Office: Esperante Bldg Ste 1150 222 Lakeview Ave West Palm Beach FL 33401-2328

CHOPKO, MARK E., lawyer; b. Kingston, Pa., Nov. 4, 1953; s. Michael E. and Rose Ann C. (Gavlick) C.; m. Jane F. Kirby; children: Michael, Jessica, Laura. BS summa cum laude, U. Scranton, 1974; JD cum laude, Cornell U., 1977. Bar: Pa. 1977, U.S. Supreme Ct. 1984, D.C. 1987. Gen. counsel Nat. Conf. Cath. Bishops, U.S. Cath. Conf., Washington, 1987—; mem. religious liberty com. Nat. Coun. Chs., N.Y.C., 1987—. Mem. bd. editors Religious Freedom Reporter, N.C., 1987—; contbr. articles to profl. jours. Bd. advisors program on philanthropy and the law Sch. of Law, NYU, 1995-98; bd. dirs. Blessed Sacrament Sch., Alexandria, Va., 1986-88; legal advisor Ams. United for Life, Chgo., 1987-94; mem. legal scholars bd. DePaul Inst. for Ch.-State Studies, Chgo., 1988—; asst. coach basketball Cath. Youth Orgn., Alexandria, 1989-94. Recipient High Quality award U.S. Nuclear Regulatory Commn., 1982. Mem. ABA (vice chmn. religious, charitable and non-profit orgns. tort sect. 1990-92), Cath. Health Assn. (legal affairs com. 1988-96), Am. Corp. Counsel Assn. (com. on non-profit and profl. assn. law). Office: US Cath Conf 3211 4th St NE Washington DC 20017-1194

CHOPLIN, JOHN M., II, lawyer; b. Cedar Rapids, Iowa, Nov. 10, 1945; s. John M. and Joyce G. (Mickelson) C.; m. Linda H. Kutchen, Feb. 14, 1969; children: Julie, John, James. BA, Drake U., 1967; JD, U. Mich., 1974. Bar: Ind. 1974, U.S. Dist. Ct. (so. dist.) Ind. 1974, U.S. Ct. Appeals (7th cir.) 1976, U.S. Supreme Ct. 1977, U.S. Ct. Appeals (6th cir.) 1983, U.S. Dist. Ct. (no. dist.) Ind. 1991. Assoc. Wilson, Tabor & Holland, Indpls., 1974-80;

ptnr. Norris, Choplin & Schroeder, Indpls., 1980—. Committeeman precinct Carmel Reps., Ind., 1982-84. Served to capt. USAF, 1969-73. Mem. ABA, Ind. Bar Assn., Indpls. Bar Assn., 7th Fed. Cir. Bar Assn., Lawyers-Pilots Bar Assn., Ind. Trial Lawyers Assn., Assn. Trial Lawyers Am., Phi Beta Kappa, Omicron Delta Kappa. Baptist. Avocations: water sports, tennis, flying. Home: 8553 Twin Pointe Cir Indianapolis IN 46236-8903 Office: Norris Choplin & Schroeder 101 W Ohio St Ste 900 Indianapolis IN 46204-4213

CHOPORES, JOHN LESLIE, software specialist, educator; b. Centralia, Ill., May 2, 1951; s. Samuel and Mary (Scott) C. AA, Coll. of DuPage, Glen Ellyn, Ill., 1972; AAS, Coll. of DuPage, 1991, Coll. of DuPage, Glen Ellyn, Ill., 1996; spreadsheet proficiency cert., Coll. of DuPage, Glen Ellyn, Ill., 1999; AAS, Coll. DuPage, 1996; cert. Sunday sch. tchr., Berean Coll., 1992. Lic. min. Ch. of God, 1993. Tchr. Coll. DuPage, Glen Ellyn, Ill., 1997, H.S. Dist. 88, Villa Park, Ill., 1997—, MacCormack Jr. Coll., Elmhurst, Ill., 1996—; graphic artist Safeguard Bus. Sys., Addison, Ill., Resource Graphics, Naperville, Ill.; tchr. computer class Wheaton (Ill.) North H.S., 1999; internet founder, tchr. Free Bible Sch., 1998. Composer: Everyday Music, Some Quick Notes, 1997; broadcaster, host Wings of Faith Radio Program WNQM AM, 1993, WJJG AM, 1995. Mem. Nathaniel Hawthorne Soc., Milton Soc. Am., Steinbeck Ctr. Found., Sing Out!, John Donne Soc., Fox Valley Folklore Soc., Henry Wadsworth Longfellow Lit. Soc., Soc. for Pentecostal Studies. Avocations: writing, folk music, writing music, Bible study, singing. Home: 1159 S Grace St Lombard IL 60148-4020

CHOPP, REBECCA S., provost. Dir. grad. studies Inst. for Women's Studies Emory U., dean of faculty and acad. affairs Candler Sch. of Theology, 1993-97, Charles Howard Candler prof. theology Emory's Grad. Divsn., provost, exec. v.p. for acad. affairs, 1998—; chair Commn. on Tchg. Emory U., univ. bd. trustees acad. affairs com.; lectr. in field. Author: The Praxis of Suffering: An Interpretation of Liberation and Political Theologies, 1986, The Power to Speak: Feminism, Language, God, 1989, Reconstructing Christian Theology, 1994, Saving Work: Feminist Practices of Theological Education, 1995; theology editor Religious Studies Rev.; editor-at-large Christian Century; editl. bd. Emory Theol. Studies, REligion and Ideology, Jour. of Religion, Word and World, Internat. Jour. of Practical Theology; contbr. articles to profl. pubs. Recipient Alumna Achievement award Kans. Wesleyan U., 1990, Disting. Alumna award St. Paul Sch. of Theology, 1991, Founder's Day award Baker U., 1995, Alumna of Yr. award U. Chgo. Divinity Sch., 1997. Mem. Am. Acad. of Religion (pres. southeastern divsn.), Am. Theol. Soc. (chair women in leadership project). Office: Emory Univ 1380 S Oxford Rd 404 Administration Bldg Atlanta GA 30322

CHOPPIN, GREGORY ROBERT, chemistry educator; b. Eagle Lake, Tex., Nov. 9, 1927; s. Gilbert P. and Nellie M. (Guidroz) C.; m. Ann M. Warner; children: Denise, Suzanne, Paul, Nadine. BS in Chemistry, Loyola U., New Orleans, 1949, DSc (hon.), 1969; PhD in Chemistry, U. Tex, 1953; DSc Tech. (hon.), Chalmers U., Göteborg, Sweden, 1985. Rsch. scientist Lawrence Radiation Lab., Berkeley, Calif., 1953-56; faculty Fla. State U., Tallahassee, 1956—, now R.O. Lawton Disting. prof. chemistry; vis. scientist Centre d'Etude Nucleaire Mol, Belgium, 1962-63; vis. prof. Sci. U. Tokyo, 1978; vis. scientist European Transuranium Inst., Karlsruhe, Germany, 1979-80, 95; cons. Los Alamos Nat. Lab., N.Mex., Lawrence Livermore Nat. Lab., Calif., Pacific N.W. Nat. Lab., Wash., Sandia Nat. Lab., N.Mex., Mallinckrodt Med. Co., Kaiser-Hill Co., Theragenics, Inc.; served on panels and coms. of Nat. Rsch. Coun., including bd. chem. sci. and tech. Co-author: Nuclear Chemistry: Theory and Applications, 1980, 2d edit., 1995; editor: Plutonium Chemistry, 1983, Actinide-Lanthanide Separations, 1985, Lanthanide Probes in Life, Chemical and Earth Sciences, 1989, Principles and Practice of Solvent Extraction, 1992, Separations of f-Elements, 1995; mem. editl. bd. sci. jours. including Handbook on Physics and Chemistry of Rare Earths; co-discoverer of chemical element 101 Mendelevium; contbr. articles to sci. jours. Served to cpl. U.S. Army, 1946-48. Recipient Alexander von Humboldt Stiftung award, 1979, Chem. Mfrs. Assn. Edn. award, 1979, Seaborg Actinide Separations Sci. award, 1989, Presdl. citation Am. Nuclear Soc., 1991, Scientist of Yr. award Fla. Acad. of Sci., 1992, Spedding award N.Am. Rare Earth Rsch. Conf., 1996, Chem. Pioneer award Am. Inst. Chemistry, 1997. Fellow AAAS; mem. Am. Chem. Soc. (award Fla. sect. 1973, so. chemist award 1971, award in Nuclear Chemistry 1985, OESPER award Cin. sect. 1995), Rare Earth Rsch. Conf. (pres. bd. 1981-83, chmn. 16th conf. 1983), Sigma Xi, Phi Beta Kappa. Avocations: sailing, racquetball. Home: 3290 Longleaf Rd Tallahassee FL 32310-6406 Office: Fla State U Dept Chemistry Dittmer Bldg Tallahassee FL 32306-4390

CHOPPIN, PURNELL WHITTINGTON, research administrator, virology researcher, educator; b. Baton Rouge, July 4, 1929; s. Arthur Richard and Eunice Dolores (Bolin) C.; m. Joan Harriet Macdonald, Oct. 17, 1959; 1 dau., Kathleen Marie. MD, La. State U., 1953; DSc (hon.), Emory U., 1988, La. State U., 1988, Tulane U., 1989, Washington U., 1991, Med. U. S.C., 1995, U. Md., Baltimore County, 1995; MD (hon.), U. Cologne, 1988; DHL (hon.), U. Mass., 1999, Mt. Sinai Sch. Medicine, 1996; D Medicine (hon.), U. Cologne, 1988. Diplomate Am. Bd. Internal Medicine. Intern Barnes Hosp., St. Louis, 1953-54, asst. resident, 1956-57; fellow, rsch. assoc. Rockefeller U., N.Y.C., 1957-60, asst. prof., 1960-64, assoc. prof., 1957-60, prof., sr. physician, 1970-85, Leon Hess prof. virology, 1980-85, v.p. acad. programs, 1983-85; dean grad. studies Rockefeller U., 1985; v.p., chief sci. officer Howard Hughes Med. Inst., 1985-87, pres., 1987—; chmn. sect. 43 microbiology and immunology NAS, 1989-92, chmn. class IV med. scis., 1983-86, mem. com. on reorganization structure, 1985-86; coun. Inst. Medicine, 1987-92, exec. com., 1988-91; mem. virology study sect. NIH, 1968-72, chmn. virology study sect., 1975-78; bd. dirs. Royal Soc. Medicine Found. Inc., N.Y.C., 1978-93; mem. adv. com. fundamental rsch. Nat. Multiple Sclerosis Soc., 1979-84; chmn. adv. com. fundamental rsch., 1983-84; mem. adv. coun. Nat. Inst. Allergy and Infectious Diseases, 1980-83; mem. bd. scis., cons. Meml. Sloan-Kettering Cancer Ctr., N.Y.C., 1981-86; chmn. bd. scis., 1983-84; mem. commn. on life scis. NRC, Washington, 1982-87; mem. sci. rev. com. Scripps Clinic and Rsch. Found., La Jolla, Calif., 1983-85, chmn. sci. rev. com., La Jolla, Calif., 1984; mem. coun. for rsch. and clin. investigation Am. Cancer Soc., N.Y.C., 1983-85; mem. com. priorities for vaccine devel. Inst. Medicine, Washington; mem. governing bd. NRC, 1990-92. Contbr. numerous articles to profl. pubs., chpts. on virology, cell biology, infectious diseases to profl. publs., 1958—; editor: Procs. Soc. Exptl. Biology and Medicine, 1966-69; assoc. editor Virology, 1969-72, editor, 1973-86; assoc. editor: Jour. Immunology, 1968-72, Jour. Supramolecular Structure, 1972-75; mem. editorial bd. Jour. Virology, 1972-85, Comprehensive Virology, 1972; mem. overseas adv. panel Biochem. Jour., 1973-77. Capt. USAF, 1954-56, Japan. Recipient Howard Taylor Ricketts award U. Chgo., 1978; Waksman award for excellence in microbiology Nat. Acad. Scis., 1984; named to alumni Hall of Distinction La. State U., Baton Rouge, 1983, Dean's medal Harvrd Med. Sch., 1992. Fellow AAAS; mem. NAS, Am. Acad. Arts and Scis., Am. Philos. Soc. (coun.), Assn. Am. Physicians, Am. Soc. Clin. Investigation, Am. Soc. Microbiology (chmn. virology div. 1977-79, div. group councilor 1983-85), Harvey Soc., Am. Assn. Immunologists, Soc. Cell Biology, Infectious Diseases Soc. Am., Practitioners Soc. N.Y., Am. Clin. and Climatological Assn., Am. Soc. Virology (pres. 1985-86), Sigma Xi (chpt. pres. 1980-81), Alpha Omega Alpha. Office: Howard Hughes Med Inst 4000 Jones Bridge Rd Chevy Chase MD 20815-6789

CHOPRA, ANIL KUMAR, civil engineering educator; b. Peshawar, India, Feb. 18, 1941; came to U.S., 1961, naturalized, 1977; s. Kasturi Lal and Sushila (Malhotra) C.; m. Hamida Banu, Dec. 7, 1976. B.Sc. in Engring, Banaras Hindu U., Varanasi, India, 1960; M.S., U. Calif., Berkeley, 1963, Ph.D., 1966. Design engr. Standard Vacuum Oil Co., New Delhi, India, 1960-61, Kaiser Engrs. Overseas Corps, India, 1961; asst. prof. civil engr. U. Minn., Mpls., 1966-67; mem. faculty U. Calif., Berkeley, 1967—; prof. civil engring. U. Calif., 1976-92, Johnson prof. engring., 1992—; dir. Applied Tech. Council, Palo Alto, 1972-74; mem. com. natural disasters NRC, 1980-85, chmn., 1982-83; cons. earthquake engring. to govt. and industry. Author: Dynamics of Structures, A Primer, 1981, Dynamics of Structures: Theory and Applications to Earthquake Engineering, 1995; author more than 210 publs. in structural dynamics and earthquake engring.; mem. adv. bd. MIT Press Series in Structural Mechanics. Recipient Gold medal Banaras Hindu U., 1960, Disting. Alumnus award, 1980, certificate of merit for paper Indian Soc. Earthquake Tech., 1974, honor award Assn. Indians in Am., 1985, AT&T Found. award Am. Soc. Engring. Edn., 1987. Mem. ASCE (EMD exec. com. 1981-87, chmn. 1985-86, mem. STD exec. com. 1988-92, chmn. 1990-91, Walter L. Huber prize 1975, Norman medal 1979, 91, Reese rsch. price 1989, Newmark medal 1993), NAE, Seismol. Soc. Am. (bd. dirs. 1982-83), Structural Engrs. Assn. No. Calif. (bd. dirs. 1987-89), Earthquake Engring. Rsch. Inst. (bd. dirs. 1990-93), U.S. Com. on Large Dams. Home: 635 Cross Ter Orinda CA 94563 Office: Univ Calif Dept Civil Engring Dept Civil Engring Berkeley CA 94720*

CHOQUETTE, PAUL JOSEPH, JR., construction company executive; b. Providence, July 24, 1938; s. Paul Joseph and Virginia Josephine (Gilbane) C.; m. Elizabeth Walsh, Aug. 18, 1962; children: Jeanne Marie, Denise Elizabeth, Suzanne, Christine Noell, Paul Joseph III. B.A., Brown U., 1960; LL.B., Harvard U., 1963. Assoc. firm Edwards & Angell, Providence, 1963-65; gov.'s legal counsel State of R.I., Providence, 1965-67; assoc. Edwards & Angell, 1967-69; gen. counsel Gilbane Bldg. Co., Providence, 1969-71, v.p., 1971-75, exec. v.p., 1975-81, CEO, 1981—, dir.; bd. dirs. Fleet Fin. Group, Ea. Utilities Assn., Carbide Corp.; chmn. bd. Gilbane Properties Inc. Nat. Football Found. scholar, 1959; recipient Silver Ann. award NCAA, 1985. Mem. Providence C. of C. (past pres., dir.). Roman Catholic. Clubs: Dunes, Hope, University. Office: Gilbane Bldg Co 7 Jackson Walkway Providence RI 02903-3694*

CHOQUETTE, PHILIP WHEELER, geologist, educator; b. Utica, N.Y., Aug. 16, 1930; s. Charles Auguste and Lucy (Wheeler) C.; m. Jean Henry, July 4, 1959; children: Steven Charles, Janine Tiffany. Cert., Inst. Cath., Paris, 1952; BS in Geology with honors, Allegheny Coll., 1952; MA, Johns Hopkins U., 1954, PhD, 1957. Geologist U.S. Geol. Survey, Washington, 1956-58; rsch. geologist Denver Rsch. Ctr., Marathon Oil Co., Littleton, Colo., 1958-86, ret. as rsch. assoc., 1986; adj. prof. dept. geol. scis. U. Colo., Boulder, Colo., 1987-89, rsch. prof., 1989-92; adj. prof., 1992—; vis. sci. SUNY, Stony Brook, 1987-88. Assoc. editor Geology, 1970-74, Jour. Sedimentary Petrology, 1974-82, GSA Bull.,1974-77, 1990-92; editor: (with P. Roehl) Carbonate Petroleum Reservoirs, 1985, (with N. James) Paleokarst, 1988. Elder United Presbyn. Ch. U.S.A., 1965—; mem. chorus Colo. Symphony Orch., 1984—. Fellow AAAS, Geol. Soc. Am.; mem. Soc. Sedimentary Geology (Coun. for Sedimentology 1981-83), Am. Assn. Petroleum Geologists (co-recipient Levorsen award 1965), Internat. Assn. Sedimentologists, Rocky Mountain Assn. Geologists, Phi Beta Kappa. Avocations: singing, photography, writing. Home: 2191 W Arapahoe Dr Littleton CO 80120-3007*

CHOQUETTE, WILLIAM H., construction company executive; b. Webster, Mass., Jan. 9, 1941; s. Paul J. and Virginia (Gilbane) C.; m. Lynn Devaney, Aug. 12, 1967; children: William, Madeleine. B.A., U. Notre Dame, 1962; M.B.A., Columbia U., 1966. Field supt. Gilbane Bldg. Co., Providence, R.I., 1966-68, asst. adminstrv. mgr., 1968-71, mgr. sales engring., 1971-75, v.p. bus. devel., 1975-79; v.p., regional mgr. Gilbane Bldg. Co., Landover, Md., 1980-82, sr. v.p., regional mgr., 1982—, sr. v.p., dir. federal mktg., 1991—; sr. v.p.. Gilbane Properties, Bethesda, Md., 1993—. Co-chmn. United Way Prince George's County, Md., 1983, 84, Corp. heroes' chmn., 1985; mem. steering com. Greater Washington Bd. Trade, 1983, 84, co-chmn. planning and devel. com., 1986-87; bd. dirs. Wash. area chpt. Boy Scouts Am. Explorers div.; chmn. Nat. Capitol Area; mem. enterprise task force Greater Balt. Com., 1983. Served to 1st lt. Signal Corps, U.S. Army, 1962-64. Mem. Washington Bldg. Congress (bd. govs. 1982-88). Home: 7704 Glendale Rd Bethesda MD 20815-4908 also: Gilbane Bldg Co 7 Jackson Walkway Providence RI 02903-3623*

CHORAZY, ZDZISLAW J., surgeon; b. Gora Mot, Poland, Feb. 25, 1951; came to U.S., 1978; s. Jan and Maria Chorazy; married; children: Christina, Jacqueline. MD, Copernicus Med. Acad., 1975. Physician Allied Urology Assn., Erie, Pa. Fellow ACS; mem. AMA, ANA, Pa. Med. Soc., Erie County Med. Soc. E-mail: chorazyz@worldnet.att.net. Office: Allied Urology Assn 311 West 24th St Erie PA 16502

CHORBA, TIMOTHY A., former ambassador to Singapore; b. Yonkers, N.Y., Sept. 23, 1946. BA magna cum laude, Georgetown U., 1968; JD, Harvard U., 1972. Bar: N.Y. 1973, D.C. 1977. Legis. counsel to Hon. Jonathan B. Bingham U.S. Ho. of Reps., 1972-73; ptnr. Patton, Boggs & Blow, Washington, 1977-94, 98—; amb. to Singapore, 1994-97. Fulbright scholar in Internat. Law and Internat. Rels., U. Heidelberg, West Germany, 1968-69. Mem. D.C. Bar, N.Y. Bar Assn., Phi Beta Kappa. Office: Patton Boggs & Blow 2550 M St NW Washington DC 20037-1301

CHORENGEL, BERND, international hotel corporation executive. Pres. Hyatt Internat. Corp., Chgo. Office: Hyatt Internat Hotels Corp Madison Plz 200 W Madison St Chicago IL 60606-3414*

CHORIN, ALEXANDRE JOEL, mathematician, educator; b. Warsaw, Poland, June 25, 1938; came to U.S., 1962, naturalized, 1971; s. Joseph and Hannah (Judowicz) C.; m. Alice Louise Jones, Aug. 11, 1965; 1 son, Ethan Daniel. Diploma in engring., Swiss Fed. Inst. Tech., Lausanne, 1961; MSc, NYU, 1964, PhD, 1966. Rsch. scientist NYU, 1966-69, asst. prof. math., 1969-71; assoc. prof. U. Calif., Berkeley, 1972-73, prof., 1973—, Miller rsch. prof., 1971-72, 82-83, dir. Ctr. Pure and Applied Math., 1980-82, 95—, Chancellor's prof., 1997—; sr. staff scientist Lawrence Berkeley Lab., 1980—; Disting. vis. prof. Inst. for Advanced Study, Princeton, N.J., 1991-92. Author: (with J. Marsden) A Mathematical Introduction to Fluid Dynamics, 1979, Computational Fluid Mechanics, selected papers, 1989, Vorticity and Turbulence, 1994; contbr. articles to profl. jours. Recipient Nat. Acad. Scis. award in applied math. and numerical analysis, 1989; fellow Sloan Found., 1972-74, Guggenheim Found., 1987-88. Fellow Am. Acad. Arts and Scis.; mem. NAS. Home: 2501 Hawthorne Ter Berkeley CA 94708-1908 Office: U Calif Dept Math Berkeley CA 94720

CHOROMOKOS, JAMES, JR., former government official, consultant; b. Chgo., Dec. 31, 1929; s. James and Harriett (Carayanides) C.; m. Nancy Jane Clarke, (div.); children—Jameson Clarke, Candace Jane; m. Martha Turner (div.). B.S.C.E., U. Miami, 1953; M.S.C.E., U. Wyo., 1963, Ph.D., 1970. Registered profl. engr., Ohio, Ill., Wyo., Vt. Commd. officer U.S. Air Force, 1953, advanced through grades to col., 1973; base engr. Bien Hoa Air Base, South Vietnam, 1970; tech. dir. Def. Nuclear Agy., 1971-73; dir. constrn. USAF Europe, London, 1973-76; ret., 1976; asst. prof. Ill. Inst. Tech., Chgo., 1976-79; dir. research and devel. U.S. Army C.E., Washington, 1979-87; cons. Jaycor, Constrn. Mktg. & Trading Inc., Analytic Svcs. Inc., 1987-96. Contbr. articles to profl. jours. Mem. ASCE, Soc. Am. Mil. Engrs., Permanent Internat. Assn. Navigation Congresses, Am. Arbitration Assn. (arbitrator), Sigma Xi, Sigma Tau, Chi Gamma Iota, Tau Beta Pi. Republican. Greek Orthodox. Club: Army and Navy Country (Arlington, Va.). Avocations: golf; fishing; biking. Home and Office: 650 N Atlantic Ave Apt 711 Cocoa Beach FL 32931-3113*

CHOROSINSKI, EUGENE CONRAD, writer, poet, author; b. Sienno, Poland, Jan. 1, 1930; came to the U.S., 1954, naturalized, 1961; s. Jozef Chorosinski and Weronika Religa; m. Anni Homeier, Mar. 23, 1959; children: Heidi Marie, Ramona Angela, Veronica Ann. LLB, Blackstone Sch. of Law, 1968. Chief field classification AMS, Ehiopia-U.S. Mapping Mission, Addis Ababa, 1965-67; intelligence analyst Combined Intelligence Ctr. Vietnam, 1968-69; sr. intelligence advisor DCAT 70, Lai Khe, South Vietnam, 1970-71; intelligence analyst 1st Armored Divsn., Support Command, Nuremberg, Germany, 1971-73; pvt. investigator Alexandria, Va., 1973-74; chief zoning review Dept. of Consumer and Regulatory Affairs, Govt. D.C., 1974-85; chmn. disaster damage assessment ARC, Ctrl. Fla. chpt., Orlando, Fla., 1995-96; free-lance writer Eustis, Fla., 1996-99; ret., 1999. Author: Through the Years; contbr. articles to profl. publs. Mem. Rep. Nat. com., 1994—; mem. Rep. Presdl. Trust; mem. City of Eustis Parks and Trees Commn., 1996—, chmn., 1998. Decorated Bronze star, Air medal, Joint Svc. Commendation medal, Army Commendation medal, Nat. DSM with bronze svc. star, Vietnam Svc. medal with silver star, others; recipient Editor's Choice award for Outstanding Achievement in Poetry Nat. Libr. of Poetry, Honor Award Spl. Citation for Exceptional Vol. Svc., ARC, 1994; named Best Poet, 1995, 96. Mem. VFW, DAV, Internat. Soc. of Poets (life), Nat. Assn. Ret. Fed. Employees, Acad. Am. Poets. Roman Catholic. Avocations: chess, travel, table tennis. Home: 131 Madrona Dr Eustis FL 32726-2016

CHOTAS, ELIAS NICHOLAS, lawyer; b. Washington, Feb. 8, 1947; s. Nicholas Eli and Georgia (Angel) C.; m. Carla Townsend, Apr. 15, 1984; children: Carl Nicholas Townsend, William Elias Townsend. BS, Duke U., 1969; MS, Ohio State U., 1972; JD, U. Fla., 1976. Bar: Fla. 1976. Ptnr. Carlton, Fields, Ward, Emmanuel, Smith & Cutler, P.A., Tampa, Fla., 1976-84, Dean, Mead, Egerton, Bloodworth, Capouano & Bozarth, P.A., Orlando, Fla., 1984—. Bd. trustees Fla. TaxWatch, Inc., Tallahassee, 1990—; mem. East Ctrl. Fla. Regional Planning Coun., Orlando, 1992—, Econ. Devel. Coun. of Mid-Fla., Orlando, 1988—. Mem. ABA, Fla. Bar Assn. (environ. and land use law sect., real property sect.), Tiger Bay Club of Orlando. Democrat. Presbyterian. Home: 1205 Windsong Rd Orlando FL 32809-3034 Office: Dean Mead Egerton Bloodworth Capouano & Bozarth 800 N Magnolia Ave Ste 1500 Orlando FL 32803-3276

CHOU, CHUNG-KWANG, bio-engineer; b. Chung-King, China, May 11, 1947; came to the U.S., 1969, naturalized, 1979; s. Chin-Chi and Yu-Lien (Hsiao) C.; m. Grace Wong, June 9, 1973; children: Jeffrey, Angela. BSEE, Nat. Taiwan U., 1968; MSEE, Washington U., 1971; PhD, U. Wash., 1975. Postdoctoral fellow U. Wash., Seattle, 1976-77, asst. prof., 1977-81, rsch. assoc. prof., 1981-85; rsch. scientist, head biomed. engring. sect. City of Hope Nat. Med. Ctr., Duarte, Calif., 1985-98; dir. dept. radiation rsch. divsn. radiation oncology City of Hope Nat. Med. Ctr., Duarte, 1985-98; dir. Corp. RF Dosimetry Lab. Motorola, Inc., Plantation, Fla., 1998—. Assoc. editor Jour. Bioelectromagnetics, 1988—; contbr. 140 articles to profl. jours. 2d lt. Army of Taiwan, 1968-69. Fellow IEEE (com. on man and radiation 1990—, vice chmn. 1994-95, chmn. 1996-98, std. coordinating com., subcoms. 1979—, chmn. 1997—, ad hoc task force on health care reform 1993-97, mem. med. tech. policy com. 1995-98), Am. Inst. for Med. and Biol. Engring., Nat. Coun. Radiation Protection and Measurements (subcom. vice chmn. 1995—, IEEE liaison 1997—, coun. mem. 1998—); mem. Internat. Microwave Power Inst. (1st Spl. Decade award 1981, Outstanding Paper award 1985), N.Am. Hyperthermia Soc., Bioelectromagnetics Soc. (bd. dirs. 1981-84, Curtis Carl Johnson Meml. award 1995), Radiation Rsch. Soc., Electromagnetic Acad., Internat. Radio Sci. Union, Commn. K, Sigma Xi, Tau Beta Pi. Mem. Christian Ch. E-mail: ecc017@email.mot.com. Office: Motorola Inc Fla Rsch Lab Plantation FL 33322

CHOU, CLIFFORD CHI FONG, research engineering executive; b. Taipei, Taiwan, Dec. 19, 1940; came to U.S., 1966, naturalized, 1978; s. Ching piao and Yueh li (Huang) C.; m. Chu hwei Lee, Mar. 23, 1968; children: Kelvin Lin yu, Renee Lincy. Ph.D., Mich. State U., 1972. Research asst. Mich. State U., East Lansing, 1967-70; research asst. Wayne State U., Detroit, 1970-72, research assoc., 1972-76; research engr. Ford Motor Co., Dearborn, 1976-81, sr. research engr., 1981-82, prin. research engr. assoc., 1982-89, prin. staff engr., 1989-93; sr. engring. specialist, 1993-95, staff tech. specialist, 1995—; adj. prof. Mich. Technol. U., 1997—; lectr. to China under UN Devel. Program, 1987, 93, 95, lectr. to Taiwan under Automotive Rsch. and Test Ctr., 1991, 97, 98; organizer Safety Test Methodology, SAE session chair, 1997, 98, 99; coord. Detroit Automobile Tech. Conf., 1993, session chair, 1997; mem. safety and environ. systems planning com. IBEC '98, 1997—; indsl. acad. adv. to PhD Coms., U. Mich., 1995-98, U. Va., 1997—, U. W.Va., 1996—, Mich. Tchrs. U., 1997— ; tchr. in field. Five patents in field; contbr. chpts. to books, articles to profl. jours. Recipient Safety Engring. Excellence award Nat. Hwy. Traffic Safety Adminstrn., 1980, Innovation award Engring. and Mfg. Staff Ford Motor Co., 1986, 95, 96, 97, 98, Tech. Accomplishment awards, 1989, 91, 92, 93, 94, Henry Ford Tech. award, 1995, Customer Quality Driven award, 1995, 96; grantee Soc. Automotive Engrs. Mem. ASME, AIAA, Soc. Automotive Engrs., Ford Chinese Club (pres. 1991-92), Mich. Chinese Acad. Profl. Assn. (bd. dirs. 1992-93, pres. 1993-94, advisor 1994—), Detroit Chinese Am. Assn., Sigma Xi. Achievements include patents. Home: 28970 Forest Hill Dr Farmington MI 48331-2439

CHOU, KUO-CHEN, biophysical chemist; b. Guangdong, China, Aug. 14, 1938; came to U.S., 1980; s. Hsiu-Chi Chou and Bi-Kun Luo; m. Wei-Zhu Zhong, Apr. 12, 1968; 1 child, James Jeiwen Chou. BS, Nanking (Peoples Republic China) U., 1960, MS, 1962; PhD equivalent, Shanghai (Peoples Republic China) Inst. Biochemistry, 1976; DSc, Kyoto (Japan) U., 1983. Jr. scientist Shanghai Inst. Biochemistry, Chinese Acad. Sci., 1976-78, assoc. prof., 1978-79; vis. assoc., prof. Chem. Ctr. Lund (Sweden) U., 1979-80; vis. assoc. prof. Max-Planck Inst. Biophys. Chemistry, Göttingen, Fed. Republic Germany, 1979-80; vis. assoc. prof. chemistry Cornell U., Ithaca, N.Y., 1980-83, sr. scientist Baker Lab., 1984-85; vis. prof. biophysics U. Rochester, N.Y., 1985-86; sr. scientist Eastman Kodak Co., Rochester, 1986-87, Upjohn Labs., Kalamazoo, Mich., 1987-94, Pharmacia & Upjohn, Kalamazoo, 1995—. Editor Jour. Molecular Sci., 1983-86, Progress in Physics, 1981-85; contbr. more than 200 rsch. articles and rev. papers to profl. jours. Recipient Sci. and Tech. award Shanghai Com. of Sci. and Tech., 1977, Nat. medal of Sci., Nat. Acad. of Sci., China, 1978, Disting. Leadership award Am. Biog. Inst., N.C., 1989, Commemorative medal of Honor, Am. Biog. Inst., 1991; named for Leadership and Achievement, Internat. Biog. Ctr., Cambridge, U.K., 1990. Fellow Am. Inst. Chemistry; mem. AAAS, N.Y. Acad. Scis., Biophysical Soc., Am. Chem. Soc., Sigma Xi. Achievements include rsch. in protein conformation and folding; graph theory in chem. reaction systems; enzyme kinetics; DNA codon usage analysis; prediction of protein cellular location and structural class; structure and function of antifreeze protein; prediction of HIV protease cleavege site; low-frequency collective motions of biomacromolecules and their biol. functions; structures of growth hormone and membrane proteins, proton-pumping mechanism of membrane proteins, inhibition kinetics of HIV reverse transcriptase, structure and binding site of adhesion proteins, apoptosis, cyclin-dependent kinases, molecular mechanism of Alzheimer's Disease. Home: 7088 Arbor Valley Ave Kalamazoo MI 49009-8540 Office: Pharmacia & Upjohn Labs Computer-Aided Drug Discov 301 Henrietta St Kalamazoo MI 49007-4940

CHOU, SHELLEY NIEN-CHUN, neurosurgeon, university official, educator; b. Chekiang, China, Feb. 6, 1924; s. Shelley P. and Tse-tsun (Chao) C.; m. Jolene Johnson, Nov. 24, 1956 (div. 1977); children: Shelley T., Dana, Kerry; remarried, 1979. B.S., St. John's U., Shanghai, China, 1946; M.D., U. Utah, 1949; M.S., U. Minn., 1954, Ph.D., 1964. Diplomate: Am. Bd. Neurol. Surgery (mem. bd.). Resident U. Minn. Hosps., 1950-55; practice medicine, specializing in neurosurgery Salt Lake City, 1955-58, Bethesda, Md., 1959, Mpls., 1960—; clin. asst. Coll. Medicine U. Utah, 1956-58; vis. scientist Nat. Insts. Neurol. Diseases and Blindness NIH, 1959; mem. faculty U. Minn., 1960—, assoc. prof. neurosurgery, 1965-68, prof. neurosurgery, 1968-92, head dept. neurosurgery, 1974-89, prof. emeritus, 1992, interim dean med. sch., dep. v.p. med. affairs, 1993-95; mem. Am. Bd. Neurol Surg., 1974-79; mem. residency rev. com. ACGME, 1984-90, chmn., 1987-89. Contbr. numerous articles to profl. jours.; Publs. on studies of intracranial lesions using radioactive angiography techniques; malformations of cerebral vasculature; neurol. dysfunctions of urinary bladder. Mem. AMA, ACS (mem. adv. council neurosurgery 1981-87, mem. grad. Med. edn. com. 1984—), Congress Neurol. Surgery, Soc. Neurol. Surgeons (pres. 1978-79), Am. Acad. Neurol. Surgery (pres. elect 1985-86, pres. 1986-87, Disting. Svc. award 1998), Soc. Nuclear Medicine, Am. Assn. Neurol. Surgeons (bd. dirs. 1980-83, v.p. 1984-85, Harvey Cushing medalist 1996), N.Am. Spine Soc. (hon.), Neurosurg. Soc. N.Am. (pres. 1977-78), N.Y. Acad. Medicine, Forum Univ. Neurosurgeons (pres. 1968-69), AAAS, Phi Rho Sigma. Home: 183 Galtier Pl Shoreview MN 55126-2113 Office: Box 96 UMHC 420 Delaware St SE Minneapolis MN 55455-0374

CHOU, TING-CHAO, pharmacology educator; b. Taiwan, Sept. 9, 1938; came to U.S., 1965, naturalized, 1976; s. Chao-Yun and Sheng-Mei (Chen) C.; m. Dorothy Tsui-chin Tseng, June 26, 1965; children: Joseph Hsin-I, Julia Hsin-Ya. BS, Kaohsiung Med. Coll., Taiwan, 1961; MS, Nat. Taiwan U., 1965; PhD, Yale U., 1970. Tchg. asst. pharmacology Nat. Taiwan U., 1964-65; rsch. asst. pharmacology Yale U., 1969; postdoctoral fellow Johns Hopkins U., Balt., 1969-72; assoc. Sloan-Kettering Inst. Cancer Rsch., N.Y.C., 1972-78, assoc. mem., 1978-88, mem., 1988-95, head lab. biochem. pharmacology, 1988-98, dir. preclin. pharmacology core facility, 1995—; asst. prof. Grad. Sch. of Med. Sci. Cornell U., 1972-78, assoc. prof., 1978-88, prof. pharmacology, 1988—; cons. Biogen, 1989, Boehringer Ingelheim Pharm., Inc., 1990-96, Hoffman-La Roche, Inc., 1990-91, U. Tex., Houston, 1991—, Sphinx Pharms., 1992-94, Synaptic Pharms., 1993-95, Virologic, Inc., 1997-99; vis. prof. Chinese Second Mil. Med. U., Shanghai, 1992—, Tonji Med. U., 1993—; hon. prof. Chinese Acad. Med. Scis., Beijing, 1993—, Nanjing Med. U., 1994—, Chinese Acad. Mil. Med. Scis., Beijing,

1995—. Author: (with J. Chou) Dose Effect Analysis with Microcomputers, 1986; co-editor Synergism and Antogonism in Chemotherapy, Acad. Press, 1991, (with M. Hayball) CalcuSyn for Windows, Biosoft, 1996, (with J.H. Chou, M. Hayball) CompuSyn Program by BioSyn, 1999; mem. editl. adv. bd. Cancer Biochemistry Biophysics, 1984—, Jour. of the Nat. Cancer Inst., 1988-92, Kaohsiung Jour. Med. Scis., 1992—; chmn. pub. bd. Bio/Pharma Quarterly, 1995—; contbr. over 340 articles on cancer, and AIDS chemotherapy and theoretical biology to profl. jours.; co-inventor 9 U.S. patents. Rsch. grantee Nat. Cancer Inst., Nat. Inst. of Allergy and Infectious Diseases, Elsa U. Pardee Found. and Am. Cancer Soc., 1975—. Mem. AAAS, Am. Assn. Cancer Rsch., Am. Soc. Pharmacology and Exptl. Therapeutics, Am. Soc. Preventive Oncology (founding mem.), Am. Soc. for Biochem. and Molecular Biol., Am. Bur. Med. Advancement in China (bd. dirs. 1990—, v.p. 1994-98), N.Y. Acad. Sci., Kaohsiung Med. Coll. Alumni Assn. Am. (bd. dir. 1968-91, pres. 1972), Harvey Soc., Sigma Xi. Office: 1275 York Ave New York NY 10021-6007 Address: 599 Mill Run Paramus NJ 07652-1754

CHOU, WUSHOW, computer scientist, educator; b. Shanghai, Kiangsu, China, Feb. 12, 1939; m. Lena Sun, Apr. 17, 1965; children: Warren, Wesley. BEE, Cheng Kung U., Tainan, Taiwan, 1961; MEE, U. N.Mex., 1965; PhD in Elec. Engring. and Computer Sci., U. Calif., Berkeley, 1968. Acting asst. prof. U. Calif., Berkeley, 1968-69; v.p. Network Analysis Corp., Glen Cove, N.Y., 1969-76; vis. prof. SUNY, Stony Brook, 1976; rsch. prof. George Washington U., Washington, 1975-76; prof. computer sci. dept. and elec. and computer engring. dept. N.C. State U., Raleigh, 1976—, dir. computer studies, 1976-88; dep. asst. sec. for info. systems U.S. Dept. Treasury, Washington, 1994-97, chief info. officer, 1996-97; vis. prof. Poly. U., Bklyn., 1988-89; pres. ACK Computer Applications, Cary, N.C., 1978-93; cons. AT&T, IBM, U.S. Govt., Singapore Govt., French Govt, over 40 corp. and other internat. corps. and orgns. Author, editor: Computer Communication, Vol. 1, 1984, Vol. 2, 1985, Advances in Telecommunication, 1985-88; editor in chief Jour. of Telecom., 1982-85, IT Profl., 1998—; contbr. over 70 articles to profl. jours. and confs. Recipient award GSA, Washington, 1988, Treasury Dept., 1997; rsch. grantee NSF, 1978, rsch. grantee Army Rsch. Office, Research Triangle Park, N.C., 1982, rsch grantee AT&T, 1987. Fellow IEEE, Assn. Computing Machines. Office: NC State U Dept Computer Sci PO Box 8206 Raleigh NC 27695-8206

CHOUDHURY, DEO CHAND, physicist, educator; b. Darbhanga, India, Feb. 1, 1926; came to U.S., 1955; s. Kapleshwar and Gutainya Choudhury; BSc, U. Calcutta, 1944, MS., 1946; PhD, UCLA, 1959; m. Annette Patricia DuBois, Aug. 3, 1963; 1 son, Raj. Rsch. fellow Niels Bohr Inst., Cophenhagen, 1952-55; rsch. asst. physics U. Rochester, N.Y., 1955-56; rsch. and teaching asst. physics UCLA, 1956-59; asst. prof. physics U. Conn., Storrs, 1959-62; assoc. prof. Poly. Inst. of N.Y., Bklyn., 1962-67, prof. physics, 1967-97, prof. emeritus, 1997—; vis. asst. physicist Brookhaven Nat. Lab., summer 1960; vis. physicist Oak Ridge Nat. Lab., summer 1962, Niels Bohr Inst., 1978-79. Govt. India Coun. Sci. and Indsl. Rsch. scholar U. Calcutta Coll. Sci., 1947-52. Mem. Am. Phys. Soc., N.Y. Acad. Scis., AAAS, Indian Phys. Soc., Sigma Xi, Sigma Pi Sigma. Contbr. chpt. to book, numerous articles on high energy nuclear scattering, nuclear models, structure and reactions to profl. publs. Home: 90 Gold St New York NY 10038-1833 Office: Poly U Dept Physics 6 Metrotech Ctr Brooklyn NY 11201-3840

CHOUKAS-BRADLEY, MELANIE, writer, photographer; b. Jacksonville, N.C., Aug. 20, 1952; d. Michael Jr. and Juanita May (Crosby) Choukas; m. James Richard Bradley, June 21, 1975; children: Sophia Crane, Jesse Elliott. BA in English, U. Vt., 1974; student, Pierce Coll., Athens, 1971; postgrad., U.S. Dept. Agr. Grad. Sch., Chevy Chase, Md., 1995—. From reporter to news dir. Radio Sta. WBRL, Berlin, N.H., 1975-77; rsch. asst. subcom. on oversight and investigations Commerce Com., U.S. Ho. of Reps., Washington, 1978; writer, 1978—; Earth Day chmn. Sugarloaf Citizens Assn., Barnesville, Md., 1990-92. Author: City of Trees, 1987; contbr. articles to Washington Post, Common Boundary Mag., Washingtonian mag., others. Grantee Am. Forest Inst., Nat. Forest Products Assn., Time Inc., Bendix, Union Camp Corp., 1978-81; grantee Sugarloaf Regional Trails, 1995. Mem. Authors Guild. Democrat. Avocations: hiking, cross-country skiing, running, naturalist activities including botany and birding.

CHOVAN, JOHN DAVID, biomedical engineer; b. Canton, Ohio, Sept. 14, 1958; s. John Jr. and Esther Lee (Baker) C. BS, Ohio State U., 1980, BS in Audio Recording, 1980, BSEE, 1982, MS, 1984, PhD, 1990. Registered profl. engr., Ohio. Evaluation programs assoc. Nat. Bd. Med. Examiners, Phila., 1985-87; rsch. scientist Battelle Meml. Inst., Columbus, 1991-95; grad. rsch. assoc. Ohio State U., Columbus, 1982-84, lead programmer-analyst, 1984-85, grad. rsch. assoc., 1987-90, postdoctoral rschr., 1990-91, sr. tech. specialist, 1995-97, dir. tech. svcs. Coll. Edn., 1997—, adj. asst. prof., 1997—; mem. pres.'s staff adv. com., 1997—. Author: Educom Selected Academic Software, 1990; editor: Preprints of the 1991 IFIP Working Group on Intelligent CAD, 1991; author conf. papers, tech. reports. Mem. Columbus AIDS Task Force, 1985. mem. Ohio State U. AIDS Edn. and Rsch. Com., Columbus, 1987-90, Am. Rose Soc. Recipient Ameritech prize for excellence in telecom., 1998, also. Mem. IEEE, Assn. for Ednl. Comm. and Tech., MAm. Rose Soc., Mensa, Sigma Xi. Home: 135 Arden Rd Columbus OH 43214-3719 Office: Ohio State U 29 W Woodruff Ave Columbus OH 43210-1116

CHOVANES, EUGENE, lawyer; b. Hazleton, Penn., Jan. 1, 1926; s. Michael and Anna (Watro) C.; m. Claire Amelia Puhak, Mar. 27, 1952; children: Michael, George, Nicholas, Joseph, John. BS Engring., Lehigh U., 1950; JD, Villanova U., 1960. Bar: Pa. 1961. Assoc. William Steell Jackson & Sons, Phila., 1957-63; ptnr. Jackson & Chovanes, Phila. and Bala-Cynwyd, Pa., 1963—; lectr. in patent law Villanova U., 1957-80. Served to sgt. U.S. Army, 1943-46, to 1st lt. Ordnance Corps, 1951-52. Mem. ABA, Phila. Intellectual Property Law Assn., Phila. Bar Assn., Soc. Registered Profl. Engrs., Am. Intellectual Property Law Assn. Office: 1 Bala Plz Ste 319 Bala Cynwyd PA 19004-1403

CHOW, AMY, gymnast, Olympic athlete; b. San Jose, Calif., May 15, 1978. Mem. USA Team, Hamamatsu, Japan, 1993, World Championships Team, Dortmund, Germany, 1994, Pan Am. Games Team, Mar del Plata, Argentina, 1995, U.S. Olympic Team, Atlanta, 1996. Placed 1st vault U.S. Gymnastics Championships, Ohio, 1992, 1st all around, vault, uneven bars, balance beam, 2d floor exercise, Mex. Olympic Festival, 1992, 3rd all around, vault, 1st floor exercise, USA/Japan Competition, Hamamatsu, Japan, 1993, 3rd vault Coca-Cola Nat. Championships, Nashville, Tenn., 1994, 1st vault, 2d uneven bars, 3rd all around Pan Am. Games, Mar del Plata, Argentina, 1995; recipient Gold medal Women's Gymnastics Team competition and Silver medal uneven bars, Olympic Games, Atlanta, 1996. Office: care USA Gymnastics Pan American Plaza 201 S Capitol Ave Ste 300 Indianapolis IN 46225-1058*

CHOW, ANTHONY WEI-CHIK, physician; b. Hong Kong, May 9, 1941; s. Bernard Shao-Ta and Julia Chen (Fan) C.; m. Katherine Cue, May 20, 1967; children: Calvin Anthony, Byron Calbert. Student, Brandon (Man., Can.) Coll., 1961-63; MD, U. Man., 1967. Intern Calgary (Atla., Can.) Gen. Hosp., 1967-68; resident in internal medicine Winnipeg (Man.) Gen. Hosp., 1968-70; fellow in infectious disease UCLA Harbor Gen. Hosp., 1970-72, from asst. prof. to assoc. prof., assoc. head div. infectious disease, 1972-78; practice medicine specializing in infectious disease; prof. medicine, head div. infectious disease U. B.C., Vancouver Gen. Hosp., 1979-94; prof. medicine, dir. MD/PhD Program U. B.C., Vancouver, 1995—; mem. Can. Bacterial Disease Network, 1989—, MRC, NIH, FDA coms.; councilor Can. Soc. Clin. Invest., Western Soc. Clin. Invest.; apptd. Can. Inst. Acad. Medicine, 1993. Contbr. articles to profl. jours. Med. Research Council Can. grantee, 1979—. Mem. Am. Soc. Microbiology, Am. Fedn. Clin. Rsch., Western Assn. Physicians, Infectious Disease Soc. Am., Western Soc. Clin. Investigation, Can. Soc. Clin. Investigation, Can. Infectious Disease Soc., Can. Inst. of Acad. Medicine, Can. Bacterial Diseases Network, Nat. Ctr. of Excellence. Roman Catholic. Achievements include rsch. in microbial pathogenesis, cellular and molecular immunology, staphylococcal toxins. Home: 1119 Gilston Rd, West Vancouver, BC Canada V7S 2E7 Office: Vancouver Gen Hosp/Div Infect Dis, 2733 Heather St, Vancouver, BC Canada V5Z 1M9

CHOW, CHI-MING, retired mathematics educator; b. Tai-Yuan, Shansi, Republic of China, Nov. 15, 1931; came to U.S., 1959; s. Wei-Han Chow and Lu-Tsen Hsu. Cert. tech. officer, Chinese Air Force Tech. Inst., Republic of China, 1954; BS in Math., Ch. Coll. Hawaii, 1962; MS in Math., Oreg. State U., 1965. Tech. officer Chinese Air Force, Republic of China, 1954-59; prof. math. Oakland C.C., Mich., 1965-92, ret., 1992. First author of the proof of the theorem, The sight area A of a moving body is inversely proportional to the quare of the distance D between the body and the observing point, i.e. A=C/D2; contbr. articles to profl. jours. including The Math. Tchr. 1st Lt. Air Force of Republic of China, 1954-59. Mem. Pi Mu Epsilon. Avocation: piloting aircraft. Home: PO Box 903 Novi MI 48376-0903

CHOW, GREGORY CHI-CHONG, economist, educator; b. Macau, South China, Dec. 25, 1929; came to U.S., 1948, naturalized, 1963; s. Tin-Pong and Pauline (Law) C.; m. Paula K. Chen, Aug. 27, 1955; children: John S., James S., Jeanne S. BA, Cornell U., 1951; MA, U. Chgo., 1952, PhD, 1955; hon. doctorate, Zhongshan U., 1986; LLD, Lingnan Coll., 1994. Asst. prof. MIT, 1955-59; assoc. prof. Cornell U., 1959-62, vis. prof., 1964-65; staff mem., mgr. econ. models IBM Research Center, Yorktown Heights, N.Y., 1962-70, prof., dir. econometric rsch. program, 1970-97; Class of 1913 prof. polit. economy Princeton U., 1979—; adj. prof. Columbia U., 1965-70; vis. prof. Harvard U., 1967, Rutgers U., 1969; adviser Chinese Natural Sci. Found.; econ. adviser Shandong Provincial Govt. Author: Demand for Automobiles in the United States: A Study in Consumer Durables, 1957, Analysis and Control of Dynamic Economic Systems, 1975, Econometric Analysis by Control Methods, 1981, Econometrics, 1983, The Chinese Economy, 1985, Understanding China's Economy, 1994, Dynamic Economics: Optimization by the Lagrange Method, 1997; co-author: The Demand for Durable Goods, 1960; co-editor: Evaluating the Reliability of Macro-Economic Models, 1982, Asia in the 21st Century, 1997, Sower of Modern Economics in China: Interview of Gregory C. Chow (in Chinese) by Professor Liu Sufen; contbr. articles to profl. jours. Named Hon. Prof., Fudan U., The People's U., Zhongshan U., Shandong U.; hon. pres. Lingnan U. Fellow Econometric Soc., Am. Statis Assn.; mem. Academia Sinica, Am. Philos. Soc., Am. Econ. Assn., Soc. for Econ. Dynamics and Control (pres. 1979-80). Home: 30 Hardy Dr Princeton NJ 08540-1211

CHOW, JOHN LAP HONG, physician, biomedical engineer; b. Bangkok, Thailand, Oct. 20, 1960; arrived in Hong Kong, 1961; came to U.S., 1975; naturalized; s. Pius C. S. and Veronica S. Y. Chow. BS in Cellular and Molecular Biology, U. Wash., 1983, BA in Chemistry, 1983; MS in Biomedical Engring., U. Calif., Davis, 1988; MD, Med. Coll. Wis., 1994. Cert. tchr., Calif. Rsch. assoc. U. Wash. Sch. Medicine, Seattle, 1980-85; rsch. asst. Ctr. for Bioengring., U. Wash., Seattle, 1985; rsch. asst. biomed. engring. U. Calif., Davis, 1985-86, assoc., teaching asst., dept. elec. computer engring., 1986-88; scientific programmer/analyst Genentech, Inc., South San Francisco, 1988-90; summer rsch. fellow neonatology U. So. Calif. Sch. Medicine, L.A., 1991; elected com. mem. admissions com. Med. Coll. Wis., Milw., 1991-94; intern Harbor-UCLA Med. Ctr., 1994-95; resident in anesthesiology Mass. Gen. Hosp.-Harvard Med. Sch., 1995-98, fellow in critical care, 1998-99, instr. dept. anesthesia and critical care, 1999—; biostats. cons. Cyanotech, Corp., Seattle, 1985; com. mem. human subjects review com. U. Calif., Davis, 1986-87. Contbr. articles to profl. jours. including Annals N.Y. Acad. Scis., Annals Biomed. Engring. Lang. interpreter ARC Lang. Bank (King County chpt), Seattle, 1984-85; med. vol. hematology/oncology Milw. County Hosp., 1991; team capt. 1991 fund raising Med. Coll. Wis., Milw., 1991. Scholar Med. Coll. Wis., 1992-93. Mem. AAAS (1st place award for excellence 1989), AMA, Biomed. Engring. Soc., N.Y. Acad. Scis., Sigma Xi. Roman Catholic. Achievements include development of an artificial intelligence expert system for quantification of cardiac metabolites from 31-phosphorus NMR spectroscopy, software systems for biomedical laboratory automations, research in non-invasive hemodynamic monitoring of critical ill patients.

CHOW, POO, wood technologist, scientist; b. Shanghai, China, Apr. 27, 1934; came to U.S., 1960, naturalized, 1971.; s. Kai and Yung-Kwan (Hsieh) C.; m. Ai-Yu Kuo, July 17, 1965; children—Eugenia, Andrew E. M.S. in Forest Products, La. State U., 1961; Ph.D. in Wood Sci. and Tech., Forestry, Mich. State U., 1969. Lab. dir. Pope and Talbot, Inc., Oakridge, Oreg., 1962-67; asst. prof. wood sci. U. Ill., Urbana, 1969-74; assoc. prof. U. Ill., 1974-80, prof., 1980—; sr. Fulbright scholar, Fed. Republic Germany; cons. to industry; external examiner U. Ibadan, Nigeria; expert witness. Contbr. numerous articles to profl. jours.; patentee in field. Mem. ASTM, Forest Products Soc., Am. Chem. Soc., Soc. Wood Sci. and Tech., Am. Ry. Engring. Assn., Internat. Rsch. on Wood Preservation Soc., German Wood Technology Soc., RR Tie Assn., Tropical Forestry Assn., TAPPI, Am. Wood Preservatives Assn., Nat. Forensic Ctr., Sigma Xi, Gamma Sigma Delta, Xi Sigma Pi. Office: Univ Ill 1102 S Goodwin Ave Urbana IL 61801-4730

CHOW, RITA KATHLEEN, nurse consultant; b. San Francisco, Aug. 19, 1926; d. Peter and May (Chan) C. BS, Stanford U., 1950, nursing diploma, 1950; MS, Case Western Res. U., 1955; profl. diploma in nursing edn. adminstrn, Columbia U., 1961, EdD, 1968; B of Individualized Studies, George Mason U., 1983. Asst. in teaching Stanford U., Calif., 1951-52; instr., dir. student health Fresno (Calif.) Gen. Hosp. Sch. Nursing, 1952-54; instr. Wayne State U. Coll. Nursing, Detroit, 1957-58; rsch. assoc., project dir. cardiovascular nursing rsch. Ohio State U., Columbus, 1965-68; commd. officer USPHS, 1968, advanced through grades to nurse dir. (capt.), 1974; spl. asst. to dep. dir. Nat. Ctr. Health Svcs. Rsch., Health Svcs. and Mental Health Adminstrn., HEW, Rockville, Md., 1969-73; dep. dir. manpower utilization br., 1970-73; dep. dir. Office Long Term Care; dep. chief nurse officer USPHS, Rockville, 1973-77; chief quality assurance br. div. long-term care Office of Standards and Certification, Health Standards and Quality Bur., Health Care Fin. Adminstrn., HHS, 1977-82; supervisory clin. nurse and spl. asst. to health systems adminstr. USPHS Indian Hosp., HRSA, HHS, Rosebud, S.D., 1982-83; dir. patient edn., asst. dir. nursing G.W. Long Hansen's Disease Ctr., USPHS, Carville, La., 1984-89; dir. nursing Fed. Med. Ctr., Ft. Worth, 1989-95; pvt. cons., 1995-98. Author: Identifying Nursing Action with the Care of Cardiovascular Patients, 1967, Cardiosurgical Nursing Care: Understandings, Concepts, and Principles for Practice, 1975; mem. editl. bd. Nursing and Health Care, 1983-95; contbr. more than 100 articles to profl. jours. Served with Nurse Corps U.S. Army, 1954-57; U.S. Army Resrves, 1957-68. Recipient Nursing Svc. award Assn. Mil. Surgeons U.S., 1969, Commendation medal USPHS, 1972, citation for outstanding contbn. to cardiovasc. nursing Am. Heart Assn., 1972-79, Nursing Edn. Alumni Assn. award for disting. achievement in nursing rsch. Columbia U. Tchrs. Coll., 1973, Meritorious Svc. medal USPHS, 1977, Disting. Alumnus award Case Western Res. U. Sch. Nursing, 1979, Disting. Svc. medal USPHS, 1987, Artist of Life award Internat. Women's Writing Guild, 1987, Women's Honors in Pub. Svcs. award ANA, 1988, Commendable Svc. medal U.S. Dept. Justice, Bur. Prisons, 1995; AAUW scholar, Nat. League Nursing fellow, 1959-61; rsch. grantee Sigma Theta Tau, 1966.

CHOW, STEPHEN Y(EE), lawyer; b. Cleve., Miss., Sept. 8, 1952; s. Chester H. and June (Eng) C.; children: Astrid Crockett, Augustus Stephen. AB cum laude, SM in Applied Physics, Harvard U., 1975; JD, Columbia U., 1979. Bar: N.Y. 1980, Mass. 1983, U.S. Supreme Ct. 1983, U.S. Patent Office 1984. Assoc. Donovan Leisure Newton & Irvine, N.Y.C., 1979-82, Gaston Snow & Ely Bartlett, Boston, 1982-85, Cesari and McKenna, Boston, 1985-88; ptnr. Nutter, McClennen & Fish, Boston, 1988-90, Cesari and McKenna, Boston, 1990-93, Perkins, Smith & Cohen, Boston, 1993—; adj. faculty Suffolk U. Law Sch., 1995—; mem. Nat. Conf. Mass. Commn. on Uniform State Laws, 1994—; Nat. Conf. Drafting Com. Uniform Comml. Code, 1995—, Drafting Com. Uniform Electronic Transactions Act, 1996—; mem. study com. on taxation of electronic commerce. Bd. editors Mass. Law Rev., 1991-98. Trustee Hawthorne Pl. Condominium Trust, Boston, 1985-92; spl. asst. dist. atty. N.Y. County, 1980-82. Mem. ABA, IEEE, Am. Intellectual Property Law Assn. (chmn. uniform comml. code com. 1997—), Am. Law Inst. (elected), Mass. Bar Assn. (chmn. uniform comml. code project 1990-98, chmn. banking and comml. law com. 1998—), Licensing Execs. Soc. (chmn. uniform comml. code com. 1991-93), Boston Bar Assn. (chmn. intellectual property com. 1991-95, mem. governing coun. 1994-96), N.Y.C. Bar Assn., Boston Patent Law Assn. (chmn. trade secrets law com. 1996—), Assn. Computing Machinery (chmn. ad hoc com. on software patenting 1991-93), Asian Am. Law Assn. Mass. (dir.), Boston Racquet Club. Republican. Avocations: painting, squash, sculling. Home: 9 Hawthorne Pl Boston MA 02114-2344 Office: Perkins Smith & Cohen LLP One Beacon St Boston MA 02108

CHOW, WINSTON, engineering research executive; b. San Francisco, Dec. 21, 1946; s. Raymond and Pearl C.; m. Lilly Fah, Aug. 15, 1971; children: Stephen, Kathryn. BSChemE, U. Calif. Berkeley, 1968; MSChemE, Calif. State U., San Jose, 1972; MBA cum laude, Calif. State U., San Francisco, 1985. Registered profl. chem. and mech. engr.; instr.'s credential Calif. Community Coll. Chem. engr. Sondell Sci. Instruments, Inc., Mountain View, Calif., 1971; mem. R & D staff Raychem Corp., Menlo Park, Calif., 1971-72; supervising engr. Bechtel Power Corp., San Francisco, 1972-79; sr. project mgr. water quality and toxic substances control program Electric Power Rsch. Inst., Palo Alto, Calif., 1979-89, program mgr., 1990-97, product line mgr. environ. market sector, 1997—. Editor: Hazardous Air Pollutants: State-of-the-Art, 1993; co-editor: Clean Water: Factors that Influence Its Availability, Quality and Its Use, 1996; co-author: Water Chlorination, vols. 4, 6; co-editor 1997 Internat. Clean Water Conf.-Today's Sci. for Tomorrows Policies, The Environ. Profl., 1997; contbr. articles to profl. jours. Pres., CEO Directions, Inc., San Francisco, 1985-86, bd. dirs., 1984-87, chmn. strategic planning com., 1984-85; industry com. Am. Power Conf., 1988—; with strategic long-range planning and restructuring com. Sequoia Union H.S. Dist., 1990-93, chmn. dist. ctrl. com., 1992-94. Recipient Grad. Disting. Achievement award, 1985; Calif. Gov.'s Exec. fellow, 1982-83. Mem. ASME, AIChE (profl. devel. recognition award), NSPE, Calif. Soc. Profl. Engrs. (pres. Golden Gate chpt. 1983-84, v.p. 1982-83, state dir.), Water Environ. Fedn., Air and Waste Mgmt. Assn. (mem. electric utility com. 1990—), Calif. State U. Alumni Assn. (bd. dirs., treas. 1989-91), U. Calif. Alumni Assn., Beta Gamma Sigma. Democrat. Presbyterian. Office: Electric Power Rsch Inst 3412 Hillview Ave Palo Alto CA 94304-1344

CHOWDHURI, PRITINDRA, electrical engineer, educator; b. Calcutta, July 12, 1927; came to U.S., 1949, naturalized, 1962; s. Ahindra and Sudhira (Mitra) C.; m. Sharon Elsie Hackebeil, Dec. 28, 1962; children: Naomi, Leslie, Robindro, Rajendro. B.Sc. in Physics with honors, Calcutta U., 1945, M.Sc., 1948; M.S., Ill. Inst. Tech., 1951; D.Eng., Rensselaer Poly. Inst., 1966. Jr. engr. lightning arresters sect. Westinghouse Electric Corp., East Pittsburgh, Pa., 1951-52; elec. engr. high voltage lab. Maschinenfabrik Oerlikon, Zurich, 1952-53; research engr. High Voltage Rsch. Commn., Daeniken, Switzerland, 1953-56; devel. engr. high voltage lab. GE, Pittsfield, Mass., 1956-59; elec. engr. research and devel. ctr. GE, Schenectady, N.Y., 1959-62; engr. elec. investigations transp. systems div. GE, Erie, Pa., 1962-75; staff mem. Los Alamos (N.Mex.) Nat. Lab., 1975-86; prof. elec. engring. Ctr. Elec. Power Tenn. Technol. U., Cookeville, 1986—; lectr. Pa. State U. Behrend Grad. Ctr., Erie, 1969-75. Author: Electromagnetic Transients in Power Systems, 1996. Patentee in field. Fellow AAAS, IEEE, Instn. Elec. Engrs. (U.K.), N.Y. Acad. Scis. Democrat. Unitarian. Home: 690 Valley Forge Rd Cookeville TN 38501-1574 Office: Tenn Technol U Ctr Elec Power PO Box 5032 Cookeville TN 38505

CHOWDHURY, MOHAMMED SHAMSUL, educator; b. Chittagong, Bangladesh; came to U.S., 1982.; MA in Mgmt., Dhaka (Bangladesh) U.; MA in Econs., CUNY, 1988; DBA, Nova Southeastern U., 1997. Lectr. in mgmt. Govt. City Coll., Bangladesh; mgmt. cons. Bangladesh Mgmt. Devel. Ctr.; tchr. N.Y.C. Pub. Schs.; prof. Monroe Coll., Bronx, N.Y. Author: Economic and Commercial Geography, 1982; contbr. articles to profl. jours. Mem. Am. Acad. Mgmt. Avocations: reading, writing, fishing, gardening. Home: 250 22d St Brooklyn NY 11218

CHOWDHURY, SUBIR, business executive, author, researcher; b. Chittagong, Bangladesh, Jan. 12, 1967; came to U.S., 1991; s. Sushil Kumar and Krishna Keshi (Biswas) C.; m. Malina Guha, Feb. 26, 1997. BTech. in Aerospace Engring. with honors, Indian Inst. Tech., Kharagpur, India, 1989; MA in Indsl. Mgmt., Ctrl. Mich. U., 1993. Software and sys. mgr. Ciproco Computers Ltd., Dhaka, Bangladesh, 1989-91; quality mgmt. cons. Gen. Motors Corp., Saginaw, Mich., 1993-97; v.p. bus. devel. Am. Supplier Inst., Livonia, Mich., 1997—. Author: QS-9000 Pioneers, 1996; editor-in-chief Automotive Excellence, 1997—; founding editor Silocon mag., 1990. Fellow Royal Statis. Soc. (U.K.), Quality Soc. Australia; mem. Am. Soc. for Quality (sr.; chair-elect automotive divsn. 1998-99), Soc Mfg. Engrs. (sr.), Inst. Indsl. Engrs. (sr.), Soc. Automotive Engrs. Avocations: photography, music, writing, reading, surfing the Internet. Office: Am Supplier Inst 38701 Seven Mile Rd Ste 355 Livonia MI 48152-1058

CHOWHAN, NAVEED MAHFOOZ, oncologist; b. Pakistan, Oct. 19, 1960; came to U.S., 1979; Student, Mao and Forman Christian Coll., Pakistan, 1979; MD cum laude, U Cetec, Dominican Republic, 1982. Bd. cert. internal medicine, 1986, hematology, 1992, oncology, 1993. Resident internal medicine Georgetown U. Svc., D.C. Gen. Hosp., Washington, 1983-86; fellowship oncology-hematology SUNY, Stony Brook, 1988-91, clin. asst. prof. dept. medicine divsn. oncology, 1992-94; pvt. practice New Albany, Ind., 1994—; pvt. practice, South Bend, Ind., 1986-88; attending physician Meml. Hosp. and St. Joseph Med. Ctr., South Bend, 1987-88, Floyd Meml. Hosp., New Albany, 1994—, Clark Meml. Hosp., Jeffersonville, Ind., 1994—; mem. Com. on Rsch. Involving Human Subjects, 1993-94; pioneer bone marrow transplant program SUNY, Stony Brook, 1994; chair cancer conf. Floyd Meml. Hosp., 1995-97, dir. stem cell transplant unit, 1997, chair cancer com., 1997—; mem. cancer com. Clark Meml. Hosp., 1995—, chair blood transfusion com., 1997—, cancer liaison physician; investigator, rschrs. and presenter in field. Contbr. articles to profl. jours. Fellow ACP; mem. Am. Soc. Clin. Oncology, Am. Soc. Hematology, Am. Soc. Bone Marrow Transplantation. Office: 1919 State St Ste 440 New Albany IN 47150-6809

CHOWNING, ORR-LYDA BROWN, dietitian; b. Cottage Grove, Oreg., Nov. 30, 1920; d. Fred Harrison and Mary Ann (Bartels) Brown; m. Kenneth Bassett Williams, Oct. 23, 1944 (dec. Mar. 1945); m. Eldon Wayne Chowning, Dec. 31, 1959. *Husband and partner, Eldon Wayne Chowning, earned a Bachelors of Architecture from University of Oregon in 1974. One of his design options was creating environments for older Americans. In 1975 they joined Dr. Walter McKain, social gerontologist, from the University of Connecticut on a tour of the Caucasus area in the Soviet Union, to study why people age differently in different societies. Eldon's mother was born in New Denhof, Saratov, in 1908. In 1984, the home they designed and built in 1959 became the Chownings Adult Foster Home, Inc. Their residents enjoyed the experience of living longer in an environment that promoted their varied interests.* BS, Oreg. State Coll., 1943; MA, Columbia U., 1950. Dietetic intern Scripps Metabolic Clinic, LaJolla, Calif., 1944; sr. asst. dietitian Providence Hosp., Portland, Oreg., 1945-49; contact dietitian St. Lukes Hosp., N.Y.C., summer 1949; cafeteria food svc. supr. Met. Life Ins. Co., N.Y.C., 1950-52; set up food svc. and head dietitian McKenzie-Willamette Meml. Hosp., Springfield, Oreg., 1955-59; foods dir. Erb Meml. Student Union, Eugene, Oreg., 1960-63; set up food svc. and head dietitian Cascade Manor Retirement Home, Eugene, 1967-68; owner, operator Veranda Kafe, Inc., Albany, Oreg., 1971-80; owner, operator, sec.-treas. Chownings Adult Foster Home, Albany, 1984-98. Contbr. articles to profl. jours. Lin County Women's chmn. Hatfield for Senator Spaghetti Rally, Albany H.S., 1966; food preparation chmn. Yi for You, Mae Yih for State Senate, Albany Lebanon, Sweet Home, 1982; Silver Clover Club sponsor Oreg. 4-H Found., Oreg. State U., Corvallis, 1994, 95, 96. Recipient coll. scholarship Nat. 4-H Food Preparation Contest, Chgo., 1939. Mem. Am. Dietetic Assn. (registered dietitian, gerontol. nutritionist dietetic practice group 1988—), Oreg. Dietetic Assn. (diet therapy chairperson, newsletter editor 1963-64), Willamette Dietetic Assn., Kappa Delta Pi (Kappa chpt.), Mu Beta Beta. Republican. Mem. Disciples of Christ. Avocations: gardening, genealogy, swimming, traveling, pet therapy. Home and Office: Chownings Adult Foster Home 4440 Woods Rd NE Albany OR 97321-7353

CHOY, CLEMENT KIN-MAN, research scientist; b. Fukien, China, Aug. 4, 1947; came to U.S., 1970.; s. Yick-Chu and Hui-Keng (Sy) C.; m. Anna K. Chan, Oct. 4, 1975; 1 child, Jennifer. Diploma, Hong Kong Baptist Coll., 1970; MS, Cleve. State U., 1972; PhD, Case Western Reserve U., 1976. Technician Univ. Hosps., Cleve., 1974-76; asst. dir. Gen. Med.Labs, Warrensville, Ohio, 1974-76; tech. staff Procter and Gamble, Cin., 1976-80; scientist Clorox, Pleasanton, Calif., 1980-81, sr. scientist, 1981-82, project leader, 1982-89, sr. rsch. assoc., 1989-93; tech. mgr. Asia Pacific region Clorox Internat. Co., Hong Kong, 1993-94; rsch. assoc. Clorox Tech. Ctr.,

1994-97, rsch. fellow, 1997—. Pres. Chinese Assn. of Greater Cleve., 1972-74. Mem. Am. Chem. Soc., Am. Soc. Oil Chemists, Am. Assn. Clin. Chemists. Achievements include U.S. patents in Surfactant Cake Composition, Passive Dosing Dispenser Exhibiting Improved Resistance to Clogging, Poly (ethylene oxide) Compositions with Controlled Solubility Characteristics, Thickened Aqueous Abrasive Scouring Cleanser, Thixotropic Acid-Abrasive Cleaner, Thickened Aqueous Abrasive Scouring Cleanser, Thickened Aqueous Cleanser, Timed-Release Bleach Coated with an Inorganic Salt and an Amine with Reduced Dye Damage, Timed-Release Hypochlorite Bleach Compositions, Hard Surface Acid Cleaner, Polymer Film Composition for Rinse Release of Wash Additives, Aqueous Based Acidic Hard Surface Cleaner, Thickened Liquid Improved Stability Abrasive Cleanser, Isotropic Fabric Softener Composition Containing Fabric Mildewstat, Timed-Release Bleach Coated with an Amine with Reduced Dye Damage, Rinse Release Laundry Additive and Dispenser, Aqueous Based Acidic Hard Surface Cleaner, Rinse Release Laundry Additive and Dispenser; foreign patents in field; patents pending; research in determination of the Si-o-Si Bond Angle common to the shift reagent compounds (CH) SiO (PcSiO) Si(CH) where x=1-5, iron and ruthenium phthalocyanines shift reagents. Home: 1345 Sugarloaf Dr Alamo CA 94507-1238 Office: Clorox Svcs Co 7200 Johnson Dr Pleasanton CA 94588-8004

CHOY, HERBERT YOUNG CHO, federal judge; b. Makaweli, Hawaii, Jan. 6, 1916; s. Doo Wook and Helen (Nahm) C.; m. Dorothy Helen Shular, June 16, 1945. BA, U. Hawaii, 1938; JD, Harvard U., 1941. Bar: Hawaii 1941. Law clk. City and County of Honolulu, 1941; assoc. Fong & Miho, 1947-48; ptnr. Fong, Miho and Choy, 1948-57; atty. gen. Territory of Hawaii, 1957-58; ptnr. Fong, Miho, Choy & Robinson, Honolulu, 1958-71; sr. judge U.S. Ct. Appeals (9th cir.), Honolulu, 1971—; adv. com. on constrn. judiciary bldgs. Chief Justice Hawaii, 1970-71; compilation commn. to compile Revised Laws of Hawaii, 1955, 1953-57; com. to draft Hawaii rules of criminal procedure Supreme Ct., 1958-59; com. on pacific ocean territories Jud. Conf. the U.S., 1976-79. Dir. Legal Aid Soc. Hawaii, 1959-61; trustee Hawaii Loa Coll., 1963-79. Capt. U.S. Army, 1941-46, lt. col. Res. Recipient Order of Civil Merit award Republic of Korea, 1973. Fellow Am. Bar Found.; mem. ABA, Hawaii Bar Assn. (exec. com. 1953, 57, 61, legal ethics and unauthorized practices com. 1953, com. on legis. 1959). Office: US Ct Appeals 300 Ala Moana Blvd Rm C305 Honolulu HI 96850-0305

CHOYKE, PHYLLIS MAY FORD (MRS. ARTHUR DAVIS CHOYKE, JR.), management executive, editor, poet; b. Buffalo, Oct. 25, 1921; d. Thomas Cecil and Vera (Buchanan) Ford; m. Arthur Davis Choyke Jr., Aug. 18, 1945; children: Christopher Ford, Tyler Van. BS summa cum laude, Northwestern U., 1942. Reporter City News Bur., Chgo., 1942-43, Met. sect. Chgo. Tribune, Chgo., 1943-44; feature writer OWI, N.Y.C., 1944-45; sec. corp. Artcrest Products Co., Inc., Chgo., 1958-88, v.p., 1964-88; pres. The Partford Corp., Chgo., 1988-90; founder, dir. Harper Sq. Press div., 1966-90. Author: (under name Phyllis Ford) (with others) (poetry) Apertures to Anywhere, 1979; editor: Gallery Series One, Poets, 1967, Gallery Series Two, Poets—Poems of the Inner World, 1968, Gallery Series Three Poets: Levitations and Observations, 1970, Gallery Series Four, Poets, I am Talking About Revolution, 1973, Gallery Series Five/Poets—To An Aging Nation (with occult overtones), 1977; (manuscripts and papers in Brown U. Library). Bonbright scholar, 1942. Mem. DAR (corr. sec. Gen. Henry Dearborn chpt. 1991-92, treas. 1992—), Soc. Midland Authors (bd. dirs. 1987—, treas. 1988-93, pres. 1993-95, membership dir. 1997-98, corr. sec. 1999—), Mystery Writers Am. (assoc.), Chgo. Press Vets. Assn., Arts Club Chgo., John Evans Club (Northwestern U.), Poetry Soc. Am. (N.Y.C.), Friends of Lit., Acad. Am. Poets (N.Y.C.). Home: 23 Windsor Dr Elmhurst IL 60126-3971

CHOYKE, WOLFGANG JUSTUS, physicist; b. Berlin, Ger., July 24, 1926; s. Frederick Samuel and Alice Sophia Amalia (Dessauer) C.; m. Helen Ruth Rubenfeld, June 19, 1949; children: Alice Mathea, Peter Lyle. BSc, Ohio State U., 1948, PhD, 1952. Rsch. physicist Westinghouse Rsch. Labs., Pitts., 1952-60, fellow physicist, 1960-63, adv. physicist, 1963-78, cons. physicst, 1978-88; adj. prof. physics U. Pitts., 1974-88, rsch. prof. physics, 1988—; cons. Northrup-Grumman and Westinghouse Sci. & Tech. Ctr., Pitts., 1988—; vis. prof. U. Erlangen-Nuremberg, 1990—. Contbr. 320 rsch. articles to profl. jours. With U.S. Army Signal Corps, 1944-46. Recipient Westinghouse Order of Merit, 1983, Humboldt Rsch. prize, Bonn, 1990. Fellow AAAS, Am. Phys. Soc. (mem. com. on aplications physics 1977-86); mem. NRC (chmn. com. on large band gap semiconductor devices 1993-95), Optical Soc. Am., Am. Vacuum Soc., Material Rsch. Soc. Achievements include fundamental studies and development of Silicon Carbide into what is presently the most promising high temperature semiconductor. Office: U Pitts Dept Of Physics Pittsburgh PA 15260

CHOY-KWONG, MARIA, neurologist; b. Lima, Peru, Mar. 14, 1959; came to U.S., 1970; m. David C. Kwong, May 27, 1984; children: Elizabeth, Erika. BA, Boston U., 1984, MD, 1984. Med. intern Harlem Hosp./Columbia U., N.Y.C., 1984-85; acupuncture tng. Am. Coll. Acupuncture, N.Y.C., Beijing, Shanghai, 1985; resident in neurology Albert Einstein Affil. Hosp., Bronx, N.Y., 1985-88; EMG/neuromuscular fellow Hosp. for Spl. Surgery/Cornell U., N.Y.C., 1988-89; dir. CJNI, Morganville, N.J., 1995—. Fellow Am. Coll. of Acupuncture; mem. N.J. Soc. of Acupuncturists (sec., treas.). Office: CJNI 470 Hwy 79 Morganville NJ 07751

CHREBET, WAYNE, professional football player; b. Garfield, N.J., Aug. 14, 1973. Hofstra U. Wide receiver N.Y. Jets, 1995—. Mem. AFC Ea. Championship team, 1998. Office: NY Jets 1000 Fulton Ave Hempstead NY 11550*

CHRENCIK, FRANK, chemical company executive; b. Osage, Iowa, Jan. 6, 1914; s. Tom and Agnes (Walashek) C.; m. Edith Jo Phelps, July 27, 1935; children: Charles Frank, James Phelps (dec.). *Frank Chrencik has a son, Dr. Charles F. Chrencik, who is married to Dr. Bliss Q. Newell. He has four grandchildren: James J. Chrencik, Deborah M. Chrencik, Christina R. Chrencik, and Charlotte P. Chrencik.* B.S. in Chem. Engring, U. Iowa, 1937; grad., Advanced Mgmt. Program, Harvard, 1955. Plant engr., prodn. and constrn. supr. gen. chem. div. Allied Chem. & Dye Corp., 1937-40; mgr. various plants Diamond Shamrock Chem. Co., Cleve., 1946-56; gen. mgr. electrochems. div. Diamond Shamrock Chem. Co., 1956-60, co. v.p., sr. officer, 1960-72; dir., chmn. exec. com. Terra Chem. Internat., Inc., Sioux City, Iowa, 1969-72; exec. v.p. chems. and metals group Vulcan Materials Corp., Birmingham, Ala., 1972-77, also bd. dirs., mem. exec. com.; vice chmn. bd. Vulcan Materials Corp., 1977-79, emeritus dir. and cons., 1979—; bd. govs. Gulf Coast Devel. Co., Pasadena, Tex., 1955; past mem. adv. council Coll. Engring., U. Iowa.; bd. dirs. Chlorine Inst., 1968-72. *Frank Chrencik is multilingual in Slavic and Germanic languages.* Mem. internat. adv. bd.: Ency. of Chem. Processing and Design. Past trustee Nat. Hemophilia Found., N.Y. Served to lt. col. Chem. Corps AUS, 1940-46. Recipient Disting. Alumni Achievement award U. Iowa, 1977; inducted into Acad. of Disting. Engrs., U. Iowa, 1996. Mem. AICE (Outstanding Chem. Engr. award Ala. sect. 1983), U. Iowa Pres.'s Club. Clubs: The Club (Birmingham), Vestavia Country (Birmingham). Home: 3401 Westbury Rd Birmingham AL 35223-1437 Office: PO Box 385014 11200 Urban Center Dr Birmingham AL 35238-5014 also: PO Box 38514 Birmingham AL 35238-5014

CHRETIEN, JANE HENKEL, internist; b. Jersey City, Mar. 24, 1941; m. Paul B. Chretien, Apr. 11, 1970; children: Jean Paul, Yves. AB, Barnard Coll., 1962; MD, N.J. Coll. Medicine, 1966; MPH, Harvard U., 1970. Diplomate Am. Bd. Internal Medicine, Am. Bd. Infectious Disease. Intern Cornell U. Med. Divsn-Bellevue Hosp. Ctr., N.Y.C., 1966-67; resident Meml. Hosp. Sloan Kettering Inst. Med. Ctr., N.Y.C., 1967-69; fellow Georgetown U. Hosp., Washington, 1970-72; clin. instr., staff physician student health svc. Georgetown U. Hosp., 1972-75, asst. dir. student health svc., 1975-87, med. dir., 1987-94, clin. asst. prof., 1975-79, clin. assoc. prof., 1979-94; assoc. prof. George Washington U., 1994-98, clin. assoc. prof., 1998—. Fellow ACP; mem. Am. Pub. Health Assn., Am. Soc. Microbiology, Infectious Diseases Soc. Am., Am. Fedn. Clin. Rsch. Office: Suburban Primary Care Physicians Ste 410 6410 Rockledge Dr Bethesda MD 20817

CHRÉTIEN, (JOSEPH JACQUES) JEAN, prime minister of Canada, lawyer; b. Shawinigan, Que., Can., Jan. 11, 1934; s. Wellie and Marie (Boisvert) C.; m. Aline Chaîné, Sept. 10, 1957; children: France, Hubert, Michel. Law degree, Laval (Que.) U., 1958; LLD (hon.), Wilfred Laurier U., 1981, Laurentian U., 1982, U. Western Ont., 1982, York U., 1986, U. Alta., 1987, Lakehead U., 1988, U. Ottawa, 1994, Meiji U., 1996. Bar: Que. 1958. Former mem. firm Chrétien, Landry, Deschênes, Trudel & Normand; M.P. from St. Maurice Ho. of Commons, 1963-86; Parliamentary sec. to prime min., 1965, Parliamentary sec. to min. of fin., 1966, min. without portfolio, 1967, min. of nat. revenue, 1968, min. of Indian Affairs and No. devel., 1968-74; pres. Treasury Bd. Can., 1974-76; min. of industry, trade and commerce, 1976-77, min. of fin., 1977-79, min. of justice, atty. gen. of Can., min. of state for social devel., min. responsible for Constln. negotiations, 1980-82, min. of energy, mines and resources, 1982-84, deputy prime min., sec. state for external affairs, 1984, external affairs critic for the official opposition, 1984-86; counsel Lang, Michener, Lawrence & Shaw, Toronto, Ottawa and Vancouver, 1986-90; leader Liberal Party of Can., 1990; M.P. from Riding of Beauséjour, 1990-93; M.P. from Riding of St. Maurice Que.; prime min., 1993—. Mem. Can. Bar Assn., Shawinigan Sr. C. of C. (dir. 1962). Office: Parliament Bldgs, Langevin Block, Ottawa, ON Canada K1A 0A6*

CHRETIEN, MARGARET CECILIA, public administrator; b. Tupper Lake, N.Y., Jan. 19, 1953; d. William Lawrence and Catherine Eileen (Dowdle) LaGasse; m. Thomas J. Chretien, Oct. 1, 1977. BA, Siena Coll., 1975; MPA, SUNY, Albany, 1983, postgrad., 1992—. Program coordinator Saratoga County Office for Aging, Ballston Spa, N.Y., 1977-80; crime prevention specialist N.Y. State Div. Criminal Justice Svcs., Albany, 1980-84, pub. info. officer, 1984-86, criminal justice program rep., 1986—; publicity chair Nat. Mus. Dance, Saratoga Springs, N.Y., 1987-90. Mng. editor Crime Prevention Update, 1980-84; mem. editorial rev. bd. Mng. N.Y. State, 1987-89. Bd. dirs. Vol. Ctr. Albany, 1988—, sec., 1992, pres., 1994, 95, 96, 97, 98; fundraising vol. St. Cecilia's Orch., 1992; life mem. Saratoga Performing Arts Ctr. Mem. Women's Press Club N.Y. State, Inc. (v.p. 1984-86). Roman Catholic. Avocations: biking, golf, mountain climbing. Home: 8 Wagner Rd Saratoga Springs NY 12866-3744 Office: NY Div Criminal Justice Svc Executive Pk Albany NY 12203

CHRÉTIEN, RAYMOND A. J., ambassador; b. Shawinigan, Que., Can., May 20, 1942; s. Maurice and Cécile (Marcotte) C.; m. Kay Rousseau; children: Caroline, Louis-François. BA, Sém. de Joliette, 1962; LLL, U. Laval, 1965. Bar: Que. 1966. Mem. legal affairs div. Div. External Affairs Govt. of Can., 1966-67, policy dir. industry, investments and competition, asst. undersec. mfg., tech. and transp., insp. gen., assoc. undersec. state for external affairs, 1988-91; 3rd sec. permanent mission to UN Govt. of Can., N.Y.C., 1967-68; asst. sec. fed. and provincial rels. com. Privy Coun. Office Govt. of Can., 1968-70, exec. asst. to sec., mem. treasury bd. Privy Coun. Office, 1970-71; exec. asst. to pres. Can. Internat. Devel. Agy., 1971-72; 1st sec. Can. Embassy, Beirut, 1972-75; 1st sec., counsellor Can. Embassy, Paris, 1975-78; Can. amb. to Zaïre, 1978-81, Can. amb. to Mexico, 1985-88; Can. amb. to Belgium and Luxembourg Brussels, 1991-94; Can. amb. to U.S. Washington, 1994—. Awarded Order of Aztec Eagle, Mex. Office: Canadian Embassy 501 Pennsylvania Ave NW Washington DC 20001-2111

CHRIEN, ROBERT EDWARD, retired physicist; b. Cleve., Apr. 15, 1930; s. Friedrich and Anna (Goros) C.; m. Susan Varga, June 6, 1953; children: Robert Edward, Katherine, Elizabeth, Thomas. B.S. in Physics, Rensselaer Poly. Inst., 1952; M.S., Case Inst. Tech., 1955, Ph.D., 1958. Research assoc. Brookhaven Nat. Lab., Upton, N.Y., 1957-59, asst. physicist, 1959-61, assoc. physicist, 1961-65, physicist, 1965-72, sr. physicist, 1972-98, group leader medium energy physics, 1976-98; ret., 1998; sci. writer specializing in nuclear physics Grolier, Harper & Rowe, Plenum Press, Pergamon Press, N.Y.C., 1966; chmn. sec. U.S. Nuclear Data Com., 1967-74; mem. European-Am. Nuclear Data Com., 1971-83; chmn. Nuclear Energy Agy. Nuclear Data Com., 1976-79; mem. panel basic nuclear data compilations NRC. Editor Nuclear Sci. and Tech. Series, Pergamon Press; contbr. articles to profl. jours.; patentee fluorescent lamp phosphors. Fellow AAAS, Am. Phys. Soc., N.Y. Acad. Scis.; mem. Am. Chem. Soc. (nuclear chemistry div.), Sigma Xi. Lutheran. Achievements include patents on fluorescent lamp phosphors. Home: 51 S Country Rd Bellport NY 11713-2501 Office: Brookhaven Nat Lab Dept Physics Upton NY 11973

CHRISANT, ROSEMARIE KATHRYN, law library administrator; b. Chgo., Oct. 9, 1946; d. Theodore and Angeline Frances (Pawlik) Layne; m. William C. Chrisant, Mar. 16, 1973; 1 child, Paula Ellen Marie. BS in Edn., No. Ill. U., 1967; MLS, Rosary Coll., 1971. High sch. English tchr. Chgo. Sch. System, 1967-70; asst. libr. Akron (Ohio) Law Libr. Assn., 1971-76, libr. dir., 1976—; cons. law firms, Akron. Contbr. articles to profl. jours. Mem. ABA, Am. Assn. Law Librs., Ohio Regional Assn. Law Librs. (Outstanding Svc. award 1986), Spl. Libr. Assn., Ohio Libr. Assn. E-mail: allarkc@en.com. Office: Akron Law Libr Assn Summit County Courthouse 209 S High St Rm 4 Akron OH 44308-1625

CHRISANTHOPOULOS, PETER, advertising executive; b. N.Y.C.; s. George and Marika Chrisanthopoulos. BBA, Baruch Coll., 1978; MBA, Fordham U., 1982. Media planner, broadcast account exec. Ogilvy & Mather, N.Y.C., 1978-82; broadcast supr. primetime Young & Rubicam, N.Y.C., 1983-84; sr. v.p., dir. broadcast Ohlmeyer Communications, N.Y.C., 1984-86; pres., COO RJR Nabisco Broadcast, N.Y.C., 1986-90; pres., CEO Network TV Assn., 1990-93; exec. v.p. rsch., mktg., and promotion ABC-TV Network Group, 1993-96; pres. broadcast and programming USA, Ogilvy & Mather Advt., 1996—. Office: Ogilvy & Mather Advt Worldwide Plz 309 W 49th St New York NY 10019

CHRISMAN, BRUCE LOWELL, physicist, administrator; b. Stillwater, Okla., Mar. 16, 1943; s. Everett Lowell and Lavinia Evelyn (Roether) C.; m. Barbara JoAnn Karnuth, May 17, 1975; children: Brenden Lowell, Brady Kenneth. SB, MIT, 1964; MS, U. Ill., 1965, PhD, 1971; MBA, U. Chgo., 1975; MA (hon.), Yale U., 1983. With Fermi Nat. Accelerator Lab., Batavia, Ill., 1970-88, physicist, 1970-75, exec. asst., 1975-79, bus. mgr., 1979-83, assoc. dir. adminstrn., 1984-88, 91—; v.p. adminstrn. Yale U., New Haven, 1983-84; assoc. dir. adminstrn. Superconducting Super Collider, Dallas, 1988-89; dir. adminstrn. Wildman, Harrold, Allan & Dixon, Chgo., 1989-91. Bd. dirs. Sch. Dist. 41, Glen Ellyn, Ill., 1986-95. Mem. Sigma Xi (pres. 1981-83). Home: 701 Forest Ave Glen Ellyn IL 60137-3905 Office: Fermi Nat Accelerator Lab PO Box 500 Batavia IL 60510-0500

CHRISMAN, DIANE J., librarian; b. Lackawanna, N.Y., June 20, 1937; d. Floyd R. and Elizabeth R. (Nowakowski) Schutta. B.A., U. Vt., 1959; M.S.L.S., Simmons Coll., 1960. Asst. head Crane br. Buffalo & Erie County Pub. Library, 1961-64, asst. head young adult dept., 1964-65, asst. head order dept., 1965-68, coordinator children div., 1968-79, dep. dir., 1979—; lectr. SUNY-Buffalo, 1966-68, 80, 90-94. Contbr. articles to profl. jours. Mem. ALA, N.Y. Libr. Assn., Rotary, Zonta (past pres.). Avocations: skiing; golf. Home: 78 Rainbow Ter Orchard Park NY 14127-2517 Office: Buffalo & Erie County Pub Libr Lafayette Ct Buffalo NY 14203-1713

CHRISMAN, LILLY BELLE, medical/surgical nurse, educator; b. Alamogordo, N.Mex., Nov. 6, 1951; d. Raymond Zellner and Iona Lillian (Goff) Gormley; m. Michael J. Chrisman, July 5, 1980; children: Stephanie Cox-Chrisman, Sean Chrisman, Tiffani Chrisman, Kayla James. BSN, U. Tex., San Antonio, 1980; MA, Webster U. (St. Louis), San Antonio, 1983; MS in Nursing, Kans. U., 1990. RN, Tex., Kans.; flight nurse; cert. advanced nurse practitioner-clin. nurse specialist; cert. med.-surg. nurse, med.-surg. clin. specialist. Head nurse, gen. med. unit Luth. Gen. Hosp., San Antonio, 1983-84; coord., instr. Barton County Community Coll., Junction City, Kans., 1985-88; head nurse gen. surgery unit Colmery O'Neil VA Med. Ctr., Topeka, 1988-89; nurse clinician, clin. nurse specialist Stormont-Vail Regional Med. Ctr., Topeka, 1989-92; asst. prof. Baker U. Sch. Nursing-Stormont-Vail Campus, Topeka, 1992-94; capt. USAF Nurse Corps, Lackland AFB, Tex., 1994-97; USAF Nurse Corps, Cannon AFB, N.M., 1997—. Mem. ANA, Acad. of Med.-Surg. Nurses, Phi Kappa Phi, Sigma Theta Tau. Home: 2409 Miller St Clovis NM 88101-8671 Office: 27th Medical Group Cannon AFB NM 88103

CHRISMAN, MARLENE SANTIA, special education educator; b. Erie, Pa., Mar. 12, 1946; d. Rudolph Vincent and Angelina Frances (Longo) Santia; children: Bree Elizabeth, Bryn Daniels. BA in English, Gannon U., Erie, 1967, MA in English, 1969; MEd in Spl. Edn., Edinboro (Pa.) U., 1981. Cert. spl. edn. tchr., supr., prin., Pa. Instr. Cathedral Prep. Sch., Erie, 1969-70, Opportunities Industrialization Ctr., Erie, 1970-72; program adminstr. Greater Erie Area Community Action Com., 1972-74; asst. dir., counselor Upward Bound, 1974-75; instr. English Gannon U., Erie, 1976-77; instr. spl. edn. Erie Sch. Dist., 1977—, forensics coach, 1988-90, mem. strategic planning action com., 1993-94, transition facilitator, 1991-98, program mgr. alternative edn. program, 1997—, supr. spl. edn. program. Pres. Leadership Erie Alumni Assn.; mem. adv. bd. L.I.F.E. House, Inc., Erie, 1989-93; bd. dirs. Adolescent Parenting Task Force, Erie, 1988-93; mem. Ctr. for Study Am. Presidency, N.Y.C., 1987; active Leadership Erie, 1992-93; bd. mem., Hamot Wellness Ctr., 1997—, bd. trustees, Boy/Girls Club of Erie, 1997-99; mem. County Task Force for the Elimination for Poverty Among Children; bd. dirs. Leadership Erie. Recipient John C. Tongren award First Ch. of the Covenant, Erie, 1987. Mem. AAUW (nominating com. 1989-90, chair Holly Trail 1989), Pa. Edn. Assn., Erie Edn. Assn., Phi Delta Kappa. Democrat. Home: 316 W 40th St Erie PA 16508-3004 Office: Sch Dist City of Erie 1511 Peach St Erie PA 16501-2193

CHRISMER, RONALD MICHAEL, federal agency administrator; b. Washington, May 4, 1954; s. Michael Joseph and Phyllis Ann (Long) C.; m. Dorothea May Shifflett, Sept. 20, 1986; 1 child, Jeffrey Ronald. BS magna cum laude, Towson State U., 1976; M in Gen. Adminstrn. and MIS, U. Md., 1987. Cert. purchasing mgr. Sr. proofreader Am. Assn. Life Ins., Washington, 1976-77; asst. supr. Coopers & Lybrand, CPAs, Washington, 1978-83, supr., 1983-85; purchasing mgr. APA, Washington, 1985-87; buyer U. Md., Balt., 1988; contract specialist IRS, Washington, 1988—, contracting officer, 1994—; mem. telecom. adv. coun. Bell Atlantic, Washington, 1983-85. Block capt. Neighborhood Watch, Cardinal Forest Devel., 1987—; mem. World Affairs Coun., Washington, 1983-85, Nat. Trust for Hist. Preservation, Washington, 1983-85; asst. den leader Cub troop Boy Scouts Am., 1996-98, scoutmaster Boy Scouts troop, 1998—; mem. sch. bd. St. Mary's Sch., Laurel, Md., 1990-96, chmn., 1992-93, mem. parish coun., 1991-92; min. Children's Liturgy, St. Mary's, 1993—; coach Cath. Youth Orgn., 1994—. Mem. KC (mem. Patuxent coun. 1996—, bd. dirs. club #2203 1996—, sec. 1997—), Nat. Assn. Purchasing Mgmt., Purchasing Mgmt. Assn. Md. (chmn. edn. com. 1988), Purchasing Mgmt. Assn. Washington, Nat. Honor Soc., Psi Chi. Roman Catholic. Avocations: U.S. Civil War history, world history, music, art, literature. Home: 8810 Cardinal Ct Laurel MD 20723-1241

CHRISPEELS, MAARTEN JAN, biology educator; b. Kortenberg, Belgium, Feb. 10, 1938; married, 1966; 2 children. PhD in Agronomy, U. Ill., 1964. Rsch. asst. agronomy U. Ill., La Jolla, 1963-64; rsch. assoc. plant biochemistry Rsch. Inst. Advanced Studies, 1964-65, AEC, 1965-67; rsch. assoc. microbiology Perdue U., 1967, from asst. prof. to assoc. prof., 1967-79; prof. biology U. Calif., San Diego, 1979—; program mgr. competitive rsch. grant office USDA, 1979. John. S. Guggenheim Found. fellow, 1973-74. Mem. AAAS, NAS, Am. Soc. Plant Physiologists (Stephen Hales prize 1996), Am. Soc. Cell Biologists. Office: U Calif at San Diego Dept Biology 9500 Gilman Dr La Jolla CA 92093-5003*

CHRISS, TIMOTHY D. A., lawyer; b. Balt., Oct. 26, 1950; s. Evan Alevizatos and Ceres (Rogokos) C.; m. Karin Elizabeth Jones, Feb. 25, 1978; children: Alexander Wilhelm Alevizatos, Caroline Elizabeth. BA, Washington and Lee U., 1972; JD, Cath. U. Am., 1976. Bar: Md. 1976, U.S. Dist. Ct. Md. 1976. Assoc. Gordon, Feinblatt, Rothman, Hoffberger & Hollander, Balt., 1976-83, ptnr., 1983—; mem. com. on character Ct. Appeals Md., 1991—. Bd. dirs. Citizens Planning and Housing Assn., Balt.,1978-80, Devel. Credit Fund, inc., 1996—, Union Meml. Hosp. Found., 1996—, Greater Homewood Comty. Corp., 1997—; trustee Gilman Sch., 1988-92, Maryvale Prep. Sch., 1997—. Fellow Md. Bar Found.; mem. ABA, Am. Coll. Real Estate Lawyers, Md. Bar Assn. (coun. real property sect. 1988—, sec. 1992-94, chmn.-elect 1994-96, chmn. 1996-98, chmn. real property code revision com. 1988-92), Bar Assn. Balt. City (exec. coun. 1988-90), Balt. City C. of C. (bd. dirs. 1993—), Balt. Country Club, Ctr. Club, Md. Club. Republican. Greek Orthodox. Office: Gordon Feinblatt Rothman Hoffberger & Hollander 233 E Redwood St Baltimore MD 21202-3332

CHRIST, DUANE MARLAND, computer systems engineer; b. Lakota, Iowa, Jan. 5, 1932; s. George Andrew and Esther Gertrude (Franke) C.; m. Lily Esther Shih, Sept. 14, 1963; 1 son, Wesley Anzo. BS, Iowa State U., 1953; MA, U. Minn., 1960; PhD, Rutgers U., 1998. Sci. programmer United Aircraft Corp., Hartford, Conn., 1960-63; computer systems analyst IBM, N.Y.C., 1963-68, staff instr., 1968-76, adv. systems engr., 1976-82, sr. systems engr., 1982-87; prin., 1987—. 1st lt. USAF, 1953-56. IBM Resident Study fellow, 1966-68, .E. Regional Dir. award, 1983; named Area Specialist of Yr., 1986. Mem. Assn. Computing Machinery, Soc. Indsl. and Applied Math., Math. Assn. Am., Inst. Ops. Rsch. and Mgmt. Scis. Home and Office: 15 Tilton Dr Freehold NJ 07728-3359

CHRIST, THOMAS WARREN, electronics research and development company executive, sociologist; b. New Haven, Dec. 16, 1944; s. David Lamar and Wilma Margaret (Zimmerman) C.; m. Patricia Player, Jan. 29, 1967; children: Michael Edward, Tyler Player. AB, Coll. William and Mary, 1966; MS, Cornell U., 1968, PhD, 1973. Asst. prof. sociology Coll. William and Mary, Williamsburg, Va., 1971-78; v.p. HDS, Inc., Reston, Va., 1979-85, chmn., 1985—. Contbr. articles to profl. jours. Mem. Am. Sociol. Assn. Lutheran. Office: HDS Inc 12310 Pinecrest Rd Ste 302 Reston VA 20191-1693

CHRISTALDI, BRIAN, lawyer; b. Passaic, N.J., June 8, 1940; s. Peter Samuel and Helen (O'Brien) C.; m. Amy Edmonds, May 4, 1968; children: Kevin, Justin. BA, Amherst Coll., 1962; LLB, Harvard U., 1965. Bar: D.C. 1966, N.Y. 1967, Calif. 1988. With legal dept. Allied Chem. Corp., N.Y.C., 1967-69; assoc. then ptnr. Kelley, Drye & Warren, N.Y.C., 1969-1995; Counsel Kay, Scholer, Fielderman, Hays & Handler, LLP, New York, NY, 1995-97; sr. comml. counsel Overseas Pvt. Investment Corp., Washington, 1997—. Home: 4031 Oliver St Chevy Chase MD 20815-3432 Office: Overseas Pvt Investment Corp 1100 New York Ave NW Washington DC 20527-0001

CHRISTEN, ARDEN GALE, dental educator, researcher, consultant; b. Lemmon, S.D., Jan. 25, 1932; s. Harold John Christen and Dorothy Elizabeth (Taylor) Deering; m. Joan Ardell Akre, Sept. 10, 1955; children: Barbara, Penny, Rebecca, Sarah. BS, U. Minn., 1954, DDS, 1956; MSD, Ind. U., 1965; MA, Ball State U., 1973. Lic. dentist, Minn., Ind. Commd. 1st lt. USAF, 1956, advanced through grades to col., 1972; base dental surgeon Zaragoza Air Base, Spain, 1970-73; dental surgeon, cons. preventive dentistry RAF Bentwaters, Eng., 1973-75; air force preventive dentistry officer Sch. Aerospace Medicine, Brooks AFB, Tex., 1978-80; prof., chmn. dept. preventive dentistry Ind. U., Indpls., 1981-93, dir. preventive/cmty. dentistry, 1993—, co-dir. nicotine dependence program, 1997—; sr. med. svc. cons. Surgeon Gen., U.S. Air Force, U.S. and Eng., 1974-80; spl. cons. to asst. surgeon gen. for dental svcs., Washington, 1975-80. Co-author: Primary Preventive Dentistry, 4th edit., 1995; contbr. over 250 articles to profl. jours. Bd. dirs. Bexar County chpt. Am. Cancer Soc., San Antonio, 1976-80, Marion County chpt., Indpls., 1980—; mem. Ind. divsn. Pub. Edn. Standing Com., Indpls., 1980. Decorated Service medal with 2 oak leaf clusters, Legion of Merit. Fellow Am. Coll. Dentists; mem. ADA, Am. Acad. Oral Pathology, Internat. Assn. Dental Rsch., Am. Acad. History of Dentistry (v.p. 1984-85, pres. 1986-87). Lutheran. Avocations: photography, classical music, travel, writing. Home: 7112 Sylvan Ridge Rd Indianapolis IN 46240-3541 Office: Ind U Sch Dentistry 1121 W Michigan St Indianapolis IN 46202-5186

CHRISTEN, PAUL RICHERT, financial company executive; b. Mpls., Mar. 11, 1929; s. Philip Gram and Ruby Rose (Richert) C.; m. Donna Lou Starr, Mar. 4, 1951; chidlren: Rebecca Christen Pohlad, Kathryn Christen Mitchell. BA, Dakota Wesleyan U., 1950, D of Bus. Adminstrn., 1971. Pres. Ruby Ann Bake Shops, Inc., Mitchell, S.D., 1950-61, Real Estate Devel., Huron, S.D., 1961-63, Investment Mgmt., Inc., Huron, 1963-65; cons. MEI Corp., Mpls., 1964-67, v.p., 1967-70, pres., 1970-77, vice chmn., 1977-86, chmn. exec. com., 1986—, also bd. dirs.; pres., CEO First Western Bancorp, Hurson, SD; ptnr., bd. dirs. Minn. Twins Baseball Team, Mpls.; chmn., bd. dirs. Bellfonte Co., Mpls., First Western Bank, Wall, S.D., First Western Bank, Sturgis, S.D., State Bank of Mound (Minn.); pres., bd. dirs.

401, Inc., Huron, First Bancorp, Huron, PRC, Inc., Huron, Christen Co., Huron, Skyline Recreation, Inc.; bd. dirs. First Fed. Bank, Huron, Hutchinson (Minn.) Bancorp, First Nat. Bank, Hutchinson, Brooklyn Park (Minn.) State Bank, Huron Ctr., Inc., Midwest Mortgage, Bismark, N.D. Trustee, vice chmn. Dakota Wesleyan U., Mitchell, 1984; pres. Pheasant council Boy Scouts Am., Huron, 1960-66; chmn. Boy Scouts Am. region 10, Mpls., 1964; bd. dirs. Nat. Council Boy Scouts Am., Brunswick., N.J., 1965; mem. north cen. region Boy Scouts Am., Mpls., 1974; bd. dirs. Boys Club, Mpls., 1977; chmn. S.D. govs. Econ. Recruit Com., Pierre, 1987; mem. Mpls. United Way, 1970; bd. dirs. bldg. fund chmn. Meth. Ch., Huron, 1961; trustee, dir. Huron Indsl. Found., 1971. Recipient Silver Beaver award Pheasant Council Boy Scouts Am., 1960, Silver Antelope award Boy Scouts Am., region 10, St. Paul, 1964, Disting. Eagle award Nat. Council Boy Scouts Am., Boston, 1969, Disting. Service award S.D. Jaycees, 1961; named S.D. Businessman of Yr., U. S.D., Vermillion, 1983. Mem. Industry and Commerce Assn. S.D. (bd. dirs. 1987). Republican. Methodist. Lodge: Kiwanis (bd. dirs. 1952-63). *

CHRISTENBURY, EDWARD SAMUEL, lawyer; b. Boone, N.C., May 22, 1941; s. Edward S. Sr. and Frances (Timme) C.; m. Suzanne Bernfeld, Dec. 27, 1971. BS, U. Tenn., 1963, JD, 1965. Bar: Tenn. 1965, U.S. Ct. Appeals (D.C. cir.) 1972, U.S. Ct. Appeals (6th cir.) 1987, U.S. Supreme Ct. 1970. Trial atty., dep. chief edn. sect. civil rights div. Dept. of Justice, Washington, 1968-71, dep. chief appellate and civil litigation sect. internal security div., 1971-73, chief spl. civil litigation unit criminal div., 1973-77, trial atty. civil div., 1977-79; asst. gen. counsel Nuclear Regulatory Commn., Washington, 1979-87; sr. v.p., gen. counsel TVA, Knoxville, 1987—. Lt. U.S. Army, 1966-67. Mem. Tenn. Bar Assn., Knoxville Bar Assn. Presbyterian. Avocation: reading. Office: TVA ET 11A 400 W Summit Hill Dr Knoxville TN 37902-1499

CHRISTENSEN, A(LBERT) KENT, anatomy educator; b. Washington, Dec. 3, 1927; s. Albert Sherman and Lois (Bowen) C.; m. Elizabeth Anne Reynolds Sears, Aug. 26, 1952; children: Anne, Kathleen Martha, Albert David, Jennifer, John Sears. AB, Brigham Young U., 1953; PhD, Harvard U., 1958. Postdoctoral fellow Cornell Med. Coll., 1958-59; postdoctoral fellow Harvard Med. Sch., Boston, 1959-60, instr. dept. anatomy, 1960-61; asst. prof. dept. anatomy Stanford Sch. Medicine, Palo Alto, Calif., 1961-68, assoc. prof., 1968-71; prof., chmn. dept. anatomy Temple U. Sch. Medicine, Phila., 1971-78; prof. anatomy and cell biology U. Mich. Med. Sch., Ann Arbor, 1978—, chmn. dept. anatomy and cell biology, 1978-82. Contbr. articles to profl. jours. With USMC, 1946-47. Mem. AAAS, Am. Soc. Cell Biology, Am. Assn. Anatomists (pres. 1984-85), Microscopy Soc. Am. Office: U Mich Med Sch Dept Anatomy & Cell Biology Med Sci II Bldg Ann Arbor MI 48109-0616

CHRISTENSEN, ALLAN ROBERT, electrical engineer, enrolled agent; b. Newton, Kans., Jan. 5, 1953; s. John Clyde and Margaret Ann (Christensen) Simpson. BSEE cum laude, Wichita (Kans.) State U., 1976; MSEE, So. Meth. U., University Park, Tex., 1981. Registered profl. engr., Tex.; enrolled agt. lic. by U.S. Treasury; accredited tax preparer, accredited tax advisor, by Accreditation Coun. for Accountancy and Taxation, 1996; notary public, Tex.; cert. emergency care attendant, 1995; lic. Tex. Dept. Health; chartered mutual fund counselor Investment Co. Inst. and Nat. Endowment for Fin. Edn. Draftsman, civil engring. asst. Wichita State U. State Architect's Office, 1971-72; chem. lab. asst. Wichita State U., 1973; clerk U.S. Postal Svc., Wichita, 1976; electrical engr., magnetic modulator, defense systems and elec. group, spl. guidance program, harpoon and tomahawk antiship missile projects Tex. Instruments, Inc., Dallas, 1977-96, elec. engr. magnetic modulator, switchmode power supply, radar signal processing, automatic test equipment design, 1977-96, spl. program divsn., 1996-97, jr. engr., 1977-79, engr., 1979-81, lead engr., 1981—; with spl. projects dept. Tex. Instruments, Inc., 1996-97; digital design engr. with spl. equipment/projects Raytheon Systems Company, 1997-98; digital design engr. spl. projects divsn. Raytheon TI Sys., Dallas, 1998—, sr. design engr., level 1, digital and interconnect design, 1998—; emergency care attendant, 1995—; lead engr. spl. projects divsn. Raytheon TI Sys., Dallas, 1997-98, digital design engr. spl. projects divsn., 1998—; co-facilitator semiconductor focus group Tex. Instruments Def. Systems Electronics Group, Dallas, 1993-94; ind. contbr. sr. des. engr. adv. Analog Components QIT, Dallas, 1993-94, core mem. Engring. Sys. Divsn. PWB Adv. Team, 1994-96; core mem. engring. sys. divsn. PWB Adv. Team, 1994-96; cons. engr. to the Nat. Coun. Examiners for Engring. and Surveying, 1996. Inventor in field; cons. engr. and published elec. engring. exam. problem author, 1997 Elec. Engring. Profl. Engrs. Exam, Nat. Coun. Examiners for Engring. and Surveying.; pub. reports in field. Instr., cook Mormon Relief Soc., Rockwall, Tex., 1986; Christmas program com. Tex. Instruments for Hope Cottage, Dallas, 1988-89; vol. tax preparer IRS, Mesquite, Tex., 1990; fundraiser United Way, Dallas, 1990; court-appointed Spl. Advocate, Dallas CASA, 305th Dist. Ct., 1995-97; mem., bd. dirs. Cmty. Restoration Svcs., Inc., Dallas, 1998—. Grantee in field, 1992-94; State of Kans. Hon. scholar, Kans. Engring. Soc. Hungerford Meml. scholar, Martin K. Eby scholar, Western Electric scholar, Ahrens scholar, Nat. Elec. Contractors scholar, Walter H. Beech scholar, 1971; recipient Outstanding Elec. Engring. Project award IEEE, Wichita, 1976, Site Selection Blue Ribbon, Site Mgmt. and People's Choice award Tex. Instruments for Hope Cottage, 1989, Stretch award Tex. Instruments DSE6, 1995, 96, Tex. State Bd. Registration for Profl. Engrs. Continuing Edn. cert. of achievement, 1996, 97, 98; People Assets and Effectiveness award, Systems Group, 1990; "Take-a-Shot" award Tex. Instruments, 1996, Grp. Awd., JC Penny Golden Rule Awd., 1996; 20th Century award for achievement IBC, 1997, Group award Def. Superior Mgmt. award USN, 1997, 98. Mem. NSPE, Nat. Assn. Tax Practitioners (Achievers Club 1992, 93, 94, 95, 96, 97, 98), Tex. Soc. Profl. Engrs., MENSA, Eta Kappa Nu, Tau Beta Pi. Republican. Achievements include investigation cross-talk characteristics of various laminates (FR-4 fiberglass, polyimides, tetraIld) in mixed analog/digital design; designer Taguchi experiements. Avocations: CAD, home remodeling, investing, wood working, weight lifting. Home: 2629 Emberwood Dr Garland TX 75043-6047 *There are no extraordinary men, there are only ordinary men accomplishing extraordinary deeds.*

CHRISTENSEN, BETTY, artist; b. Collingdale, Pa., Apr. 11, 1915; d. Pasquale Grasso and Maria (Santella) Last; widowed, Mar. 1980. Cert., Phila. Coll. Art, 1936. Artist Al Paul Lefton Advt. Agy., Phila., 1940-48, McKee Albright Advt. Agy., 1948-50. Exhibited in group shows at Catherine Lorillard Wolfe Art Club, N.Y., Hudson Valley Art Assn., Conn. Watercolor Soc.; exhibited in permanent collections at Mattatuck Mus., Conn., Hoffman Fuel Co., Conn., Cyrenius Booth Libr., Conn.; illustrator: (book) A Few Thoughts on Trout, 1986. Recipient 1st prize in waterclor Richter Art Assn., 1997, Best in Show award Conn. Classic Arts, 1998, A. F. Harless Landscape award Hudson Valley Art Assn., N.Y., 1998, 1st prize in watercolor Housatonic Art League, 1998. Mem. Am. Watercolor Soc., Allied Artists of Am. (hon.), Conn. Watercolor Soc., Kent Art Assn. Evangelical. Avocation: gardening. Home: 25 West St Newtown CT 06470-2040

CHRISTENSEN, BRADFORD WILLIAM, state official; b. Green Bay, Wis., Feb. 6, 1951; s. William Gordon and Willow Margaret (Humphrey) C.; m. Roxann Mae VanParys, Aug. 4, 1979; children: Matthew, Melanie, Kimberly. BS in Geography, Ariz. State U., 1975, BS in Journalism, 1978. Reporter Ariz. Captol Times, Phoenix, 1978-83, legis. editor, 1983-88, mng. editor, 1988-93; comm. dir. Ariz. Dept. Health Svcs., Phoenix, 1993—; mem. Coalition Against Domestic Violence, Phoenix, 1994—; chmn. Ariz. Pub. Health Week Steering Com., Phoenix, 1994—; mem. ASTHO Drug Resistant Bacteria Com., Austin, Tex., 1996-97, Youth Tobacco Prevention Media Com., Phoenix, 1996—; mem. Ariz. Bioterrorism Task Force, 1998—. Editor Healthlink, 1993—, Pub. Health Week, 1995—; contbg. author Am. Jour. Health Comm., 1995—. Recipient Gov.'s award for excellence Ariz. Gov.'s Office, Phoenix, 1994, Gov.'s recognition award, 1995. Mem. Nat. Pub. Health Info. Coalition (v.p. 1996-97, pres. 1998, 9 awards for excellence in health comm.). Avocations: softball, strat-o-matic baseball league, baseball card collecting, jazz and blues music. Home: 6814 W Sunnyside Dr Peoria AZ 85345-8737 Office: Ariz Dept Health Svcs 1740 W Adams St Rm 407 Phoenix AZ 85007-2602

CHRISTENSEN, BRUCE LEROY, academic administrator, former public broadcasting executive; b. Ogden, Utah, Apr. 26, 1943; s. LeRoy and Wilma (Olsen) C.; m. Barbara Lucelle Decker, June 17, 1965; children—Jennifer, Heather, Holly, Jesse. BA cum laude, U. Utah, 1968; MS, Northwestern U., 1969. Radio and TV news reporter KSL, Inc., Salt Lake City, 1965-68, state house corr., 1969-70; weekend sports writer WGN Radio and TV News, 1968-69; instr. U. Utah, 1969-70, adj. assoc. prof. broadcast regulation, 1980-81, gen. mgr. Sta. KUED-TV and KUER-FM, 1979-82, dir. media svcs., 1981-82; asst. to dir. univ. rels. Brigham Young U., 1970-72, asst. prof., 1971-79, dir. dept. broadcast svcs., 1972-79; pres. Nat. Assn. Pub. TV Stas., Washington, 1982-84; pres., chief exec. officer PBS, Washington, 1984-93; Dean of Fine Arts Cntr. Brigham Young Univ., Provo; bd. govs. Pacific Mt. Network, 1979-82, chmn., 1978-80; vice chmn. (USA) Internat. Coun. Nat. Acad. Arts and Scis., 1990-91, pres. Internat. Coun. NATAS, 1992-93; pres. Prix Italia, 1993; producer, writer Channel 5 Eye-Witness News, 1967-68. Exec. producer numerous TV documentaries including The Great Dinosaur Discovery, 1973, A Time to Dance, 1976, Navajo, 1976, Christmas Snows, Christmas Winds, 1978 (Emmy award 1978). Bd. dirs. Utah Lung Assn., 1976-82, pres., 1978-80. Recipient Disting. Alumnus award U. Utah, 1989; Allen-Heath fellow Medill Sch. Journalism Northwestern U., 1969; recipient Ralph Lowell medal Corp. for Publ. Broadcasting, 1994. Fellow Internat. Coun. NATAS; mem. Rocky Mountain Corp. for Pub. Broadcasting (bd. dirs.), Sigma Delta Chi (pres. U. Utah chpt. 1967-68), Kappa Tau, Phi Kappa Phi. Avocation: photography. Office: Brigham Young Univ A 410 Harris Fne Ctr Provo UT 84602

CHRISTENSEN, CARL ROLAND, business administration educator; b. Tyler, Minn., Aug. 17, 1919; s. Thomas P. and Marie (Dahm) C.; m. Dorothy Isabell Smith, Dec. 26, 1943; children: Philip, Steven, Ann, Joan. AB, U. Iowa, 1941; MBA, Harvard U., 1943, DCS, 1953; DHL (hon.), Babson Coll., 1985; Dr. honoris causa, U. Montreal, Que., Can., 1995. From instr. to assoc. prof. sch. bus. Harvard U., Cambridge, Mass., 1946-58, prof. grad. sch. bus., 1958—, George F. Baker jr. prof. bus. adminstrn., 1963-84, Robert Walmsley univ. prof., 1984—; vis. prof., Stanford, 1955, Imede, Lausanne, Switzerland, 1963-64; vis. prof. Sloan Sch. Mgmt., MIT, 1977-79; bd. dirs. Claflin Capital Mgmt. Inc., Boston. Author: Management Succession in Small and Growing Enterprise, 1953, (with G.A. Smith, Jr.) Policy Formulation and Administration, 1955, 9th edit., 1982, (with A. Zaleznick, F. J. Roethlisberger) Motivation, Productivity and Satisfaction of Workers, 1959, (with E.P. Learned, K.R. Andrews) Problems in General Management, (with others) Business Policy: Text and Cases, 1966, 7th edit., 1990, Teaching and the Case Method, 1987, (with B. Barnes and A. Hansen) Teaching and the Case Method, 3rd edit. 1993, (with D. Carvin and A. Sweet) Education for Judgement, 1991. Served from cpl. to captain AUS, 1943-46. Mem. Am. Soc. Pub. Adminstrn., Acad. Polit. Sci., Phi Beta Kappa. Home: 111 Abbeywood Dr Nashville TN 37215-6145 Office: Harvard U Bus Sch Boston MA 02163

CHRISTENSEN, CAROLINE, vocational educator; b. Lehi, Utah, Oct. 5, 1936; d. Byam Heber and Ruth (Gardner) Curtis; m. Marvin Christensen, June 16, 1961; children: Ronald, Roger, Robert, Corlyn, Richard, Chad. BS, Brigham Young U., 1958, MS, 1964. Sec. Brigham Young U., Provo, Utah, 1954-58; instr. bus. Richfield (Utah) H.S., 1958-61, Sevier Valley Applied Tech. Ctr., Richfield, 1970-92, dept. chairperson, 1988-92. Historian, Sevier Sch. Dist. PTA, 1968, 69; chmn. Heart Fund Dist., 1983, Voting Dist., 1988-90; dist. chmn. Am. Cancer Drive, 1994-95, 98; guide Hist. Cove Fort, Utah, 1996-98, election judge, 1998. Mem. Utah Edn. Assn., Am. Vocat. Assn., Utah Vocat. Assn., Nat. Bus. Edn. Utah Bus. Edn. Assn. (sec. 1986-87), NEA, Western Bus. Edn. Assn., Sevier Valley Tech. Tchrs. Assn. (sec. 1971-92, pres. 1986-87, adv. com. chair 1997—), Delta Pi Epsilon (historian), Delta Kappa Gamma (treas. 1975-90, pres. 1990-92, state nominating com. 1993-97, chmn. 95-97, state treas. 1993-95, state conv. chair 1997-98), Profl. Bus. Leaders (advisor 1988-92).

CHRISTENSEN, C(HARLES) LEWIS, real estate developer; b. Laramie, Wyo., June 3, 1936; s. Raymond H. and Elizabeth C. (Cady) C.; m. Sandra Stadheim, June 11, 1960; children: Kim, Brett. BS in Indsl. Engring., U. Wyo., 1959. Mgmt. trainee Gen. Mills, Chgo., 1959, Mountain Bell, Helena, Mont., 1962-63; data comms. mgr. Mountain Bell, Phoenix, 1964-66, dist. mktg. mgr., so. Colo., 1970-73; seminar leader AT&T Co., Chgo., 1966-68; mktg. supr. AT&T Co., N.Y.C., 1968-70; land planner and developer Village Assocs., Colorado Springs, Colo., 1973, exec. v.p., 1975-77; v.p. Cimarron Corp., Colorado Springs, 1974-75; pres. Lew Christensen & Assocs., Inc.; ptnr., gen. mgr. Briargate Joint Venture, 1977-82; pres. Vintage Comtys., Inc., 1982-95. Bd. dirs. Pikes Peak coun. Boy Scouts Am., Citizens Goals, Colo. Coun. on Econ. Edn., Cheyenne Mountain Zoo; chmn. Colorado Springs Econ. Devel. Coun., 1977, 89; bd. dirs. Penrose St. Francis Hosp., 1996—, U. Wyo. Found., 1993—. Served with USAF, 1959-62. Mem. Colorado Springs Home Builders Assn. (bd. dirs.), Urban Land Inst., Colorado Springs C. of C. (bd. dirs., chmn. bd.), Colorado Springs Country Club (bd. dirs.). Republican. Presbyterian. Achievements include development of 1,000-acre Peregrine planned community, south of USAF Academy; the 7,000 acre planned community of Briargate, just east of the USAF Academy. Office: Lew Christensen & Assocs Inc 2520 Stagsleap Point Colorado Springs CO 80904-1192

CHRISTENSEN, COURTNEY WAIDE, municipal administrator; b. Manhattan, Kans., Dec. 5, 1959; d. R.E. and Janice (Sargent) W.; m. Eric Connet Christensen, Oct. 27, 1990 (div. Feb. 1998); children: Lauren Diane, Connor Waide. B of Social Work, Kans. State U., 1981; MPA, U. Mo., Kansas City, 1988. Cert. govt. fin. mgr. Child care worker St. Vincent Children's Home, Topeka, Kans., 1981-82; social worker Social Rehab. Svcs., State of Kans., 1982-86; budget analyst City of Kansas City, Mo., 1988-93, asst. to fin. dir., 1993-95, asst. to city mgr., 1995—; cons. U.S. AID/ICMA, Lublin, Poland, 1994. Mem. emergency svcs. bd. ARC, Kansas City, 1994-97; bd. dirs. Met. Coun. on Child Care, Kansas City, 1999; v.p. Univ. Assocs., Kansas City, 1996-99, pres., 1999. Named to Outstanding Young Women of Am., 1998; named among 40 Under 40 Up and Coming Leaders, Ingram's Mag., 1998; Rothschild scholar, 1988. Mem. Internat. Assn. City Mgrs., Am. Soc. Pub. Adminstrn. (pres.-elect 1998-99, pres. 1999—), Mo. City Mgr. Assn. (bd. dirs. 1998—), Am. Govtl. Accts., Asst. City Mgrs. of Mo. (chair 1997-98). Office: City of Kansas City Mo 414 E 12th St Kansas City MO 64106

CHRISTENSEN, DAVID ALLEN, manufacturing company executive; b. 1935. BS, S.D. State U., 1957. With John Morrell & Co., 1960-62; with Raven Industries Inc., Sioux Falls, S.D., 1962—, product mgr., 1964-71, pres., chief exec. officer, 1971—. Served with AUS, 1957-60. Office: Raven Industries Inc PO Box 5107 Sioux Falls SD 57117-5107

CHRISTENSEN, DIETER, ethnomusicologist; b. Berlin, Apr. 17, 1932. PhD, Free U., Berlin, 1957. Curator, dir. Berlin Phonogramm Archiv, 1958-72; prof. Columbia U., N.Y.C., 1970—; dir. Ctr. for Ethnomusicology Columbia U., 1971—; lectr. Free U., Berlin, 1962-70, dir. Ctr. for Ethnomusicilogy, 1971—; vis. prof. Hunter Coll.-CUNY, N.Y.C., 1978-80, U. Hamburg (Fed. Republic Germany), 1977; sec. gen. Internat. Coun. for Traditional Music, UNESCO, 1981—; dir. The Universe of Music-A History, UNESCO, 1985-93. Author: Die Musik der Kate, 1957, Die Musik der Ellice-Inseln, 1964; co-author: El Anillo del Tlalocan, 1975, 90, Dictionary of Traditional Music in Oman, 1994; editor Yearbook for Traditional Music, 1981—, (compact discs) UNESCO Collection of Traditional Music, 1995—. Mem. various profl. orgns. in field. Office: Columbia U Music Dept MC 1815 New York NY 10027

CHRISTENSEN, DONN WAYNE, insurance executive; b. Atlantic City, Apr. 9, 1941; s. Donald Frazier and Dorothy (Ewing) C.; BS, U. Santa Clara, 1964; m. Marshella Abraham, Jan. 26, 1963 (div.); children: Donn Wayne, Lisa Shawn; m. Mei Ling Fill, June 18, 1976 (div.); m. Susan Kim, Feb. 14, 1987; stepchildren: Don Kim, Stella Kim. West Coast div. mgr. Ford Motor Co., 1964-65; agt. Conn. Mut. Life Ins. Co., 1965-68; pres. Christensen & Jones, Inc., L.A., 1968—; v.p. Rsch. Devel. Systems Inc. Pres. Duarte Community Drug Abuse Coun., 1972-75; pres. Woodlyn Property Owners Assn., 1972-73; mem. L'Ermitage Found., 1985-90, Instl. Rev. Bd. White Meml. Hosp., L.A., 1975—, Friend's Med. Rsch., 1992—. Recipient Man of Yr. award L.A. Gen. Agts. and Mgrs. Assn., numerous. Mem. Nat. Life Underwriters Assn., Calif. State Life Underwriters Assn., Investment Co. Inst. (assoc.), Soc. Pension Actuaries, Foothill Community Concert Assn. (pres. 1970-73). Registered Investment Advisor, SEC, 1984. Office: 22 Woodlyn Ln Bradbury CA 91010

CHRISTENSEN, DONNA MARIE, congresswoman; b. Teaneck, N.J., Sept. 19, 1945; d. Almeric L. and Virginia (Sterling) Christian; children: Rabiah Green, Karida Green. BS, U. Notre Dame; MD, George Washington U. Pvt. medical practice; cmty. health physician U.S. V.I. Dept. Health; med. dir. Gov. Juan F. Luis Hosp., St. Croix, V.I.; vice chairperson U.S. V.I. Dem. Territorial Com., 1980; mem. U.S. V.I. Bd. Edn., 1984; committeewoman Nat. Dem., 1984; apptd. U.S. V.I. Status Commn., 1988-92; del. Dem. Nat. Conv.; mem. 105th-106th Congress from U.S. V.I., 1996—. Trustee, founding mem. Caribbean Youth Orgn. Mem. Nat. Med. Assn. (trustee), Caribbean Studies Assn., V.I. Med. Inst., V.I. Med. Soc. (pres., sec.), Women's Coalition St. Croix, St. Croix Environ. Assn. Fax: 202-225-5517. E-mail: donna.green@mail.house.gov. Office: 1711 Longworth Ho Office Bldg Washington DC 20515*

CHRISTENSEN, DONNA MARTIN, writer; b. Beaver City, Nebr., July 13, 1932; d. Ray Roy and Mary Eugena (Hollinger) Williams; m. Arlon Fuller, Aug. 12, 1953 (div. 1969); children: Gerald D., Teena M., Richard L., Arlena M., Arlon D.; m. Vernon Arthur Martin, June 3, 1973 (dec. Aug. 12, 1984); m. Aubrey Leigh Christensen, June 4, 1988. Student, U. No. Colo., 1971-73. Nurse's aide Weld County Hosp., Greeley, Colo., 1961-71, Hosp. Long Term Care, Oberlin, Kans.; feature writer Oberlin Herald, 1985-97; freelance writer Superior, Nebr., 1988—; sec. Let Individuals Find Encouragement, Superior, 1991—. Author Reflections weekly column in the Superior Express, 1989—. Recipient Golden Poet award World of Poetry, 1987. Mem. Christian Women's Club (various offices). Republican. Avocations: crafts, walking. Home and Office: 945 E 2nd St Superior NE 68978-2004

CHRISTENSEN, DORIS ANN, antique dealer, researcher, writer; b. Safford, Ariz., Dec. 31, 1938; d. Joseph Solomon Welson and Bernice Beatrice (Blasius) Van Order; m. Donald Edward Christensen, April 22, 1967. Student, Ea. Ariz. Coll., 1961-66. Sec. to dean of admissions Ea. Ariz. Coll., Thatcher, 1963-67; sec. to pres. United Homes Corp., Fed. Way, Wash., 1969-89; office mgr. Heller Co. Realtors, Fed. Way, Wash., 1990-94; antique dealer All That & Everything, Buckley, Wash., 1995—; editor newsletter of Violin Bottle Collectors Assn., U.S. and Canada, 1995—. Author: Violin Bottles, Banjos, Guitars and Other Novelty Glass, 1995. Recipient: DAR Good Citizen's cert., 1957; Outstanding Citizenship award, Am. Legion, Safford, Ariz., 1957; Homemaker award, Betty Crocker, Mpls., 1957; attendee: Ariz. Girls' State, Tucson, 1956. Mem. Violin Bottle Collectors Assn. (editor newsletter U.S. and Can., 1995—). Avocations: collectibles, writing, research. Office: All That & Everything 21815 106th St E Buckley WA 98321-9277

CHRISTENSEN, DOUGLAS, state agency administrator. BA, Midland Luth. Coll., 1965; MA, U. Nebr., 1970, PhD, 1978. Tchr. Holdrege (Nebr.) Sr. H.S., 1965-70; h.s. prin. Bloomfield (Nebr.) Cmty. Schs., 1970-74, supt. of schs., 1974-76; county supt. of schs. Knox County Ctr., Nebr., 1975-76; supt. of schs. Colby Pub. Schs. Unified Sch. Dist. #315, 1978-85, North Platte (Nebr.) Pub. Schs., 1985-90; assoc. commr. of edn. Nebr. Dept. of Edn., Lincoln, 1990-92, dep. commr. of edn., 1992-94, commr. edn., 1994—; presenter, cons. in field. Contbr. articles to profl. jours. Chair North Platte Area Econ. Devel. Task Force, 1986-90, Coun. for Inter-Agy. Cooperation, 1986-90; liturgist First Luth. Ch., 1986-90, chair fin. com., 1988-90; bd. dirs. Mid-Nebr. Cmty. Found., 1989-90; bd. dirs. Mari Sandoz Soc., 1990—; mem. Nebr. Commn. for the Protection of Children, 1994—; advanced planning com. Southwood Luth. Ch., 1994—. Recipient Spirit of PTA award Nebr. PTA, 1997. Mem. ASCD (pres. Kans. affiliate 1984-85), Am. Assn. of Sch. Adminstrs. (Nebr. Supt. of Yr. 1990), Nebr. Coun. of Sch. Adminstrs., Rotary Internat. (pres. 1981-82), Nebr. Ctr. for Ednl. Excellence (chair 1985-90, bd. dirs. 1989-90), Midland Luth. Coll. Alumni Assn. (pres. 1992-93). Office: Commrs Office Dept of Edn PO Box 94987 Lincoln NE 68509-4987

CHRISTENSEN, HANS CHRISTIAN, retired chemist; b. Oslo, Norway, July 26, 1915; s. Haaken Christian and Reidunn (Kaasen) C.; m. Veronica Amorenza Hough, Dec. 2, 1944; children: Reidunn, Therese, Michael Johannes, Bernadette, Jeannette. Engring. chemist, Inst. de Chimie de Univ., Strasbourg, France, 1940, PhD, 1943. Exptl. officer Armament Rsch. Dept./Ministry of Supply, London, 1944-46; liaison officer Norwegian Def. Rsch. Establishment, London, 1946-47; rsch. scientist Norwegian Def. Rsch. Establishment, Kjeller, Norway, 1947-52, head of divsn., 1952-62; tech. cons. to the dir. U.S. Naval Ordinance Test Sta., China Lake, Calif., 1962-65; head of sect. Norwegian Coun. for Scientific and Indsl. Rsch., Oslo, 1965-83; cons. Norwegian Coun. for Scientifc and Indsl. Rsch., Oslo, 1983-92, Norwegian Computing Ctr., 1992-93; founder, mem. STEP Group/Studies in Tech., Innovation and Econ. Policy, Oslo, 1994-98. Patentee in field; contbr. articles to profl. jours.; contbg. author: Evaluation of Technical Research and Development, 1987, Research on Aluminum Particle Combustion, 1965. Pres. Norwegian Astronaut. Soc., 1954-57, Diocesan Lay Coun., Cath. Diocese of Oslo, 1969-77. Maj. Norwegian High Command, 1944-47, London, Oslo. Grantee Norwegian Coun. for Scientific and Indsl. Rsch., 1959-60; decorated Knight of the French Order of Merit, Pres. French Rep., Paris, 1982. Mem. Norwegian Engrs. Assn. (emeritus), Norwegian Polytechnic Assn. (emeritus), Sigma Xi. Roman Catholic. Avocations: mountain hiking, photography, classical music. Home: Hamang Terrace 81, N-1336 Sandvika Norway

CHRISTENSEN, HENRY, III, lawyer; b. Jersey City, Nov. 8, 1944; s. Henry Jr. and M. Louise (Brooke) C.; m. Constance L. Cumpton, July 1, 1967; children: Alexander, Gustavus, Elizabeth, Katherine. BA, Yale U., 1966; JD, Harvard U., 1969. Bar: N.Y. 1970, U.S. Tax Ct. 1973, U.S. Ct. Appeals (2d. cir.) 1973, U.S. Supreme Ct. 1975. Assoc. Sullivan & Cromwell, N.Y.C., 1969-77, ptnr., 1977—; adj. assoc. prof. NYU, N.Y.C., 1985-88, U. of Miami Law Sch., 1997—. Author: International Estate Planning, 1999; contbr. articles to profl. jours. Chmn. Prospect Park Alliance, Bklyn., 1985—; trustee, 1st vice chmn. Peddie Sch., Hightstown, N.J., 1986—; trustee Am. Fund for the Tate Gallery, 1987—, Bklyn. Acad. Music, 1992—, Vincent Astor Found., 1993—; dir., sec. Freedom Inst., N.Y.C., 1980—, The Friends of Jiangnan U., 1987—; dir., v.p. Am. Friends of Whitechapel Art Gallery Found., 1991—; trustee, mem. exec. com. Am. Ctr. Oriental Rsch. in Amman, 1993—. Fellow Am. Coll. Trust and Estate Counsel; mem. N.Y. State Bar Assn. (chmn. estate and gift tax com. 1983-84, chmn. exempt orgn. com. 1986, chmn. income taxation of trusts com. 1984-85, 87-89, exec. com. tax sect. 1983-89), Internat. Acad. Estate and Trust Law (academician). Home: 35 Prospect Park W Apt 8/9B Brooklyn NY 11215-2370 Office: Sullivan & Cromwell 125 Broad St Fl 28 New York NY 10004-2489

CHRISTENSEN, JOHN GARY, urologic surgeon; b. Chgo., Mar. 18, 1957; s. John Gary and Delores Marie Christensen; m. Susan Louise Christensen, June 4, 1983; children: Matthew, Kenneth, Dana. BS in Chemistry summa cum laude, U. Ill., 1979, MD, 1983. Resident in urologic surgery Wake Forrest U., Winston-Salem, N.C., 1983-88; urologist Wheaton (Ill.) Clinic, 1988-90; pvt. practice Wheaton, 1990-94; urologist, pres. DuPage Urol. Cons., Wheaton, 1994—; chmn. dept. urology Cen. DuPage Hosp., Winfield, Ill., 1998, mem. multiple hosp. coms., 1988—, dir. viodynamics lab., 1996—; pres. DuPage Urol. Cons., Wheaton, 1994—; presenter and lectr. in field. Contbr. articles to med. jours. Fellow ACS; mem. Am. Bd. Urology (diplomate), Am. Soc. for Reproductive Medicine, Am. Assn. Clin. Urologists, Am. Endocrinol. Soc., Chgo. Urol. Soc., Phi Beta Kappa. Avocations: boating, golf, skiing. Office: DuPage Urol Cons Ste 106 7 Blanchard Cir Wheaton IL 60187

CHRISTENSEN, JOHN WILLIAM, lawyer; b. Roselawn, Ind., Mar. 14, 1914; s. Henry Julius and Caroline Belle (Conrad) C.; m. Eleanor Schwerak, Sept. 2, 1939; children: William J., Amy Christensen Fox, Martha Christensen Rand, Nancy Christensen Couyoumjian. AB, DePauw U., 1935; JD, U. Ind., 1939. Bar: Ind. 1939, U.S. Supreme Ct., 1945, Ohio 1947. Acct. GE Co., Schnectady, N.Y., 1935-36; atty. SEC, Washington, 1939-44, spl. counsel utilities divsn., 1944-46; assoc., then ptnr. Dargusch, Caren, Greek & King, Columbus, Ohio, 1946-53; ptnr. Gingher & Christensen, Columbus, 1953-86; of counsel Baker & Hostetler, Columbus, 1986—; gen. counsel

Brodhead-Garrett Co., Cleve., 1955-86, also bd. dirs.; v.p., gen. counsel Columbus Mut. Life Ins. Co., 1962-84; v.p., gen. counsel, sec., bd. dirs. O.M. Scott & Sons Co., Marysville, Ohio, 1951-84; chmn., pres., CEO Nat. Extrusion and Mfg., Bellefontaine, Ohio, 1978-87; bd. dirs. State Automobile Mut. Ins. Co., United McGill Corp., Taylor Woodcraft Inc.; adj. prof. law Ohio State U., 1964-72. Trustee DePauw U., Greencastle, Ind., 1962—. With USCGR, 1943-45. Mem. ABA, Ohio Bar Assn., Columbus Bar Assn., Order of Coif, Phi Beta Kappa, Phi Delta Phi. Presbyterian. Home: 8240 Round Hills Cir Las Vegas NV 89113-1230 Office: 65 E State St Columbus OH 43215-4213

CHRISTENSEN, JON, finance company executive, former congressman; b. St. Paul, Nebr., Feb. 20, 1963; s. Harlan and Audrey C.; m. Meredith Stewart Maxfield, 1987. Degrees in biology & bus., Midland Lutheran Coll., 1985; JD, South Tex. Coll. of Law, 1989. V.p. corp. divsn. COMReP, Inc., 1989-91; mktg. dir. Conn. Mutual Ins. Co., 1991; founder The Aquila Group, Inc. (holding co. for Old McDonald's); mem. U.S. Ho. of Reps., Washington, 1994-98; mem. ways & means com., subcoms. health and social security U.S. Ho. of Reps.; sr. v.p. Fin. Continuum, Omaha, 1999—. Mem. Am. Diabetes Assn.'s Celebrity Breakfast. Mem. Nebr. Farm Bureau, Nebr. Cattlemen's Assn. Nat. Fedn. Ind. Bus., Nat. Assn. of Life Underwriters, Omaha Assn. Life Underwriters, ABA (mem real estate, probate & trust divsn.), Nebr. Bar Assn., Omaha Bar Assn., Northwest Rotary Club. Republican. Office: Fin Continuum Lic 1010 S 120th St Omaha NE 68154*

CHRISTENSEN, KENNETH JUSSI, computer science and engineering educator; b. Mpls., Nov. 2, 1960; s. B.A. and Annikki (Hannula) C.; m. Loraine Newman, Oct. 18, 1986; children: Erik, Lukas, Kurt. BSEE, U. Fla., 1981; MSEE, N.C. State U., 1983, PhD, 1991. Engr. IBM Corp., Research Triangle Park, N.C., 1983-95; asst. prof. U. South Fla., Tampa, 1995—; adj. faculty mem. N.C. State U., Raleigh, 1984-85, Campbell U., Butes Creek, N.C., 1993-94; mem. editl. bd. Internat. Jour. Network Mgmt., 1996—. Contbr. articles to profl. jours.; patentee in field. Judge sci. fairs, 1996-97. Mem. IEEE (sr.), Am. Soc. Engring. Educators, Assn. for Computing Machinery. Home: 18211 Cypress Stand Cir Tampa FL 33647-1814 Office: U South Fla 4202 E Fowler Ave # ENB118 Tampa FL 33620-9951

CHRISTENSEN, MARGARET ANNA, nurse, health management educator; b. Nov. 10, 1938; d. John Bernard and Catherine (Scott) Thielen; m. Robert Edwin Christensen, June 24, 1961; children: Marthe Elizabeth Christensen Groves, Katrina Marie Christensen Head, Andrea Susan Christensen Clark. BS, Wichita State U., 1978; EdM, U. Cen. Okla., 1984; EdD, Okla. State U., 1986. Staff devel. supr. St. Joseph Med. Ctr., Wichita, Kans., 1972-79; head nurse Bapt. Med. Ctr., Oklahoma City, 1979-80; clin. supr. Mercy Health Ctr., Oklahoma City, 1980-81, staff devel. coord., 1981-84; pres., sr. cons. Human Resource Cons., Inc., Edmond, Okla., 1982-90; dir. planning and devel. Allied Nursing Care, Inc., Oklahoma City, 1984-85; rehab. specialist LDH Cons., Oklahoma City, 1985-90; pres., CEO Christensen Mgmt. Co., Portsmouth, Ohio, 1990—; adj. faculty U. Cen. Okla., Edmond, 1986-90; asst. prof., coord. health scis. grad. programs Ohio U., 1990-94, coord. health sci. grad. program, 1994-96; coord. health care mgmt. program, assoc. prof. dept. bus. Shawnee State U., Portsmouth, 1996—; dir. Shawnee State Grad. Ctr., 1999—; author performance enhancement plans for long-term care employees, 1995, mgrs. and supr. Health Care, 1992; performance enhancement plans for profl., tech. workers in health care, 1992, performance enhancement plans for office/clerical svc. and maintenance workers Health Care, 1992. Author human resource devel. process, 1984, (booklet) Live-In Companion Guide, 1984, report on hosp. appraisal sys. impact, 1986. Bd. dirs. Dr.'s Hosp., Nelsonville, Hallmark Home Care, Portsmouth, Ohio Presbyn. Retirement Svcs., Columbus, Mt. Pleasant Retirement Ctr., Monroe, Ohio. Mem. Am. Coll. Health Care Execs., Am. Coll. Health Care Adminstrs., Assn. Univ. Programs in Health Adminstrn., Alpha Chi, Kappa Delta Pi, Sigma Kappa, Phi Eta Sigma. Republican. Roman Catholic. Home: 1500 Shady Brook Ln Portsmouth OH 45662-8808 also: 109 Kricker Hall SSU Portsmouth OH 45662

CHRISTENSEN, MARI ALICE, nursing auditor, medicolegal analyst, consultant; b. Omaha, June 13, 1934; d. Benjamin Marion and Alice Minnie (Thompson) Voelte; m. Gerald H. Christensen, Mar. 17, 1956; 1 child, Amy Michaela. Diploma, Nebr. Meth. Coll. Nursing, Omaha, 1955; BSN, U. Nebr., Omaha, 1961; postgrad., Pitts. State U., Ins. Inst. Am., 1992. RN, Nebr.; rehab. nurse certificate, Ga. Nurses Assn. Charge nurse Nebr. Meth. Hosp., Omaha, 1955-56; office nurse Geo. Robertson, M.D., Omaha, 1956-57; surgeon's asst., office nurse Physicians Clinic, Omaha, 1957-74; medicolegal analyst Turner & Boisseau, Chartered, Great Bend, Kans., 1975-82, Schmid, Mooney & Frederick, P.C., Omaha, 1984-89; cons. Mutual of Omaha Ins. Co., 1989-91; nurse auditor, workers compensation case mgr., analyst Mid-Am. Med. Mgmt., Omaha, 1991-92; pvt. nurse auditor, case mgr., medicolegal analyst Omaha, 1992; ret., 1992; rehab. cons. Crawford Rehab., Omaha, 1982. Vol. nurse ARC bloodmobiles, MOBA Clinic for homeless and indigents; mem. Voices of Omaha, Omaha Symphonic Choir and Luth. Ch. of Master; soloist Vets. Hosp. Mem. ANA (exec. com.), Nat. Assn. Legal Assts. (continuing edn. com. 1988), Nebr. Nurses Assn. (sec., bd. dirs. com. mem.), Assn. Oper. Rm. Nurses (sec.), Nat. Disting. Svc. Registry Nursing, Sigma Theta Tau, Gamma Pi Sigma. Home: 11315 Castelar Cir Omaha NE 68144-3085

CHRISTENSEN, MARIA, emergency room nurse; b. Hoboken, N.J., Feb. 13, 1961; d. Pasquale and Gerarda (Tullio) Fallone. Diploma, Englewood (N.J.) Hosp. Sch., 1984; BSN, Fairleigh Dickinson U., 1988; postgrad., Widener U. RN, N.J.; cert. emergency nurse. Staff nurse Englewood Hosp.; trauma program mgr. St. Jospeh's Hosp.& Medical Ctr. Mem. Emergency Nurses Assn.

CHRISTENSEN, MARTHA, mycologist, educator; b. Ames, Iowa, Jan. 4, 1932; d. Leo Martin and Eva (Patterson) C. BS, U. Nebr., 1953; MS, U. Wis., 1956, PhD, 1960. High sch. sci. tchr. Ralston (Nebr.) Pub. Schs., 1953-54; research assoc. U. Wis. Dept. Botany, Madison, 1960-62; asst. prof. U. Wyo. Dept. Botany, 1963-68, assoc. prof., 1968-76, prof., 1976-89, prof. emerita, 1989—. Mem. Ecol. Soc. Am., Brit. Mycol. Soc., Mycol. Soc. Am. (pres. 1987-88). Office: U Wyoming Dept Botany Campus PO 3165 Laramie WY 82071*

CHRISTENSEN, NADIA MARGARET, writer, translator, editor, educator; b. Mpls., July 28, 1937; d. Bernhard Marinus and Lilly Gracia (Gundersen) C. BA, Augsburg Coll., Mpls., 1959; MA, U. Minn., 1964; PhD, U. Wash., 1972. Asst. prof. U. Minn., Mpls., 1972-73; asst. editor Scandinavian Rev., N.Y.C., 1976-78, editor in chief, 1978-82; dir. pub. Am.-Scandinavian Found., N.Y.C., 1980-82; producer Adventure Film Prodns., Paris, 1982-84; exec. dir. Nordic Ctr., Mpls., 1991-96; sr. program devel. officer Augsburg Coll., Mpls., 1997—; freelance writer and translator, 1972—; cons. U.S. & European Pubs., 1970—. Author: (coll. text) The Big Apple, 1985, (non-fiction) Action, Reflection, Celebration, 1988; co-author: (children's book) The Magic Clock, 1979, (non-fiction) Ecuador: Island of the Andes, 1988, Turkestan: Oasis de la Chine, 1991; translator: (poetry) Necropolis, 1977, Selected Poems, 1982, (drama) The Ice Goes Out, 1985, (fiction) Consider the Verdict, 1976, Baby, 1980, Sea-Swell, 1986, Dollar Road, 1989, Dina's Book, 1994, contbr. articles to jours., translations to anthologies and jours. Decorated Knight's Cross of Royal Norwegian Order of Merit, King Harald V of Norway, 1996; recipient Second prize Internat. Poetry Rev., 1979, Pegasus literary prize as translator, 1980, 89; winner Northwind Children's Story competition, 1984; Fulbright scholar U.S. Govt., 1965; George Marshall fellow Am.-Scandinavian Found., 1968, Strong fellow, 1984. Mem. PEN, Poets and Writers, Fulbright Assn. Address: 401 S 1st St Apt 1209 Minneapolis MN 55401-2568

CHRISTENSEN, NIKOLAS IVAN, geophysicist, educator; b. Madison, Wis., Apr. 11, 1937; s. Ivan Rudolph and Alice Evelyn (Ethen) C.; m. Karen Mary Luberg, June 18, 1960; children—Kirk Nathan, Signe Kay. BS, U. Wis., 1959, MS, 1961, PhD, 1963. Rsch. fellow in geophysics Harvard U., Cambridge, Mass., 1963-64; asst. prof. geol. scis. U. So. Calif., 1964-66; prof. U. Wash., Seattle, 1966-83, Purdue U., Lafayette, Ind., 1983-97; Weeks disting. prof. U. Wis., Madison, 1997—; mem. Pacific adv. panel Joint Oceanographic Instns. for Deep Earth Sampling, Seattle, 1973-75, mem. igneous and metamorphic petrology panel, 1973-75, mem. ocean crust panel, 1974-77; mem. adv. panel on oceanography NSF, 1976-78, mem. adv. panel on earth scis. 1994-97; mem. adv. panel on continental lithosphere NRC, 1979-83; mem. adv. panel Internat. Assn. Geodesy, 1980-88. Contbg. author: Geodynamics of Iceland and the North Atlantic Area, 1974; Contbr. numerous articles to profl. jours. NSF grantee, 1968-98. Fellow Geol. Soc. Am. (chmn. geophysics divsn. 1984-86, assoc. editor Geology 1985-89, George P. Woollard award 1996), Am. Geophys. Union (assoc. editor Jour. Geophys. Rsch. 1998—). Research on nature of Earth's interior. Home: 2390 Highway AB McFarland WI 53558 Office: U Wis Dept Earth and Atmospheric Sci Dept Geology and Geophysics Madison WI 53706

CHRISTENSEN, PATRICIA ANNE WATKINS, lawyer; b. Corpus Christi, Tex., June 24, 1947; d. Owen Milton Jr. and Margaret (McFarland) Watkins; m. Steven Ray Christensen, May 28, 1977 (dec. 1985); children: Geoffrey Holland, Jeremy Ladd. BS, U. North Tex., 1971; JD, U. Houston, 1977. Bar: Utah 1977, Tex. 1977, U.S. Dist. Ct. Utah 1977, U.S. Ct. Appeals (10th cir.) 1977, U.S. Supreme Ct. 1990. Assoc. Berman & Giauque, Salt Lake City, 1977-80; ptnr. Parr, Waddoups, Brown, Gee & Loveless, Salt Lake City, 1980—, pres., 1991-93; adj. prof. law U. Utah Law Sch., Salt Lake City, 1979-81; judge pro tem Third Dist. Ct., 1995—. Legislative asst., U.S. Senate, 1970-74, bd. dirs. Comml. Law Affiliate, 1997, co-chair litigation sect., trustee, Rowland Hall St. Mark's Sch., chair devel. com., 1987-90, steering com., comprehensive capital campaig U. Utah Sch. Nursing, steering com., Amer. Elec. Law proj. Named Utah Woman Lawyer of Yr., 1992, recipient, Utah State Bar's Dorothy Merril Brothers Awd., 1996. Mem. ABA, Utah State Bar (Dorothy Merrill Brothers award 1996), State Bar of Tex., Salt Lake County Bar Assn. (exec. com. 1979-87, author editor Utah Lawyers Practice Manual 1986), Women Lawyers Utah (pres. 1988-89, bd. dirs. 1987-90), Phi Delta Phi, Delta Gamma, Alpha Lambda Delta. Avocations: hiking, mountain biking, writing, travel, languages.E-mail: pac@prolaw.com. Office: Parr Waddoups Brown Gee & Loveless 185 S State St Ste 1300 Salt Lake City UT 84111-1537

CHRISTENSEN, PAUL NORMAN, English educator, writer; b. W. Reading, Pa., Mar. 18, 1943; s. Kenneth Serenus and Ann Theresa C.; m. Jane T. Flowers, Apr. 18, 1964 (div. Mar. 1968); 1 child, Sean Oliver; m. Catherine Anne Tensing, Aug. 30, 1969; children: Maxine Elizabeth, Signe Laura, Cedric Owen. BA in English, William and Mary Coll., 1967; MA in English, U. Cin., 1970; PhD in English, U. Pa., 1975. Assoc. editor Stock Car Racing Mag., Alexandria, Va., 1967-68; from asst. prof. to assoc. prof. English Tex. A&M U., College Station, Tex., 1974-83, prof. English, 1983—; editor, pub. Cedarshouse Press, Bryan, Tex., 1977—; dir. Provence Writer's Workshop, Buoux, France, 1998—; Fulbright sr. lectr. Coun. Internet Exchanges, Washington, 1989, 96. Author: Charles Olson: Call Him Ishmael, 1979, Minding the Underworld, 1990, In Love, In Sorrow, 1991. Recipient Chautauqua 2000 award Tulsa Arts Coun., 1999; fellow U. Pa., 1970-72; Writer's grantee Nat. Endowment Arts, 1991. Democrat. Roman Catholic. Avocations: cooking, wine collecting. E-mail: p-christensen@tamu.edu. Office: Tex A&M U Dept English College Station TX 77843

CHRISTENSEN, PAUL WALTER, JR., gear manufacturing company executive; b. Cin., Jan. 31, 1925; s. Paul Walter and Lucy (Sickler) C.; m. Sarah Ernst, Nov. 22, 1947; children: Delle (Mrs. Edmund W. Jones), Sarah (Mrs. William McC. Reynolds), Lucy (Mrs. Craig M. Davis). BS in Mech. Engring., Cornell U., 1945. With Cin. Gear Co., 1946-87, v.p., 1947-58, pres., 1958-78, chmn. bd., 1978-87, ret., 1987; chmn. bd. Cin. Steel Treating Co., 1961-68, 87, pres., 1968-87, ret., 1987. Commr. Hamilton County Park Dist., 1980-93. Mem. Am. Gear Mfrs. Assn. (past pres.), Ohio Mfrs. Assn. (past pres.), Ocean Reef Club, Queen City Club, Commonwealth Club, Camargo Club, Comml. Club. Home: 4660 Drake Rd Cincinnati OH 45243-4118

CHRISTENSEN, RAY RICHARDS, lawyer; b. Salt Lake City, July 7, 1922; s. E.R. and Carrie (Richards) C.; m. Carolyn Crawford, July 9, 1954 (dec. 1986); children: Carlie, Paul Ray, Joan, Eric.; m. Jeanne F. Pyke, June 24, 1989. LL.B., U. Utah, 1944. Bar: Utah 1944. Enforcement atty. OPA, 1946; law clk. to Utah Supreme Ct. Justice Wolfe, 1947-48; practice in Salt Lake City, 1949—; ptnr. Christensen & Jensen, P.C. (and predecessors), 1949—; mem. Utah Bar Commn., 1963-66. Bd. dirs. Salt Lake City Jr. C. of C., 1949-53, v.p., 1950-52. Served with AUS, 1943-46. Fellow Internat. Acad. Trial Lawyers (bd. dirs. 1982-88), Am. Coll. Trial Lawyers (state chmn. 1984-85); mem. ABA (mem. council jr. bar conf. 1952-56, ho. of dels. 1966-68, 73-79, mem. council bar activities sect. 1967-70), Utah State Bar (pres. 1965-66, Utah Lawyer of Yr. 1981, Utah Trial Lawyer of Yr. 1993), Salt Lake County Bar Assn., Western States Bar Conf. (pres. 1969-70), Internat. Assn. Def. Counsel, Fedn. Ins. Counsel, Phi Eta Sigma, Phi Kappa Phi. Home: 992 Oak Hills Way Salt Lake City UT 84108-2022 Office: Christensen & Jensen PC 50 S Main St # 1500 Salt Lake City UT 84144

CHRISTENSEN, RICHARD MONSON, mechanical engineer, materials engineer; b. Idaho Falls, Idaho, July 3, 1932; married, 1958; 2 children. BSc, U. Utah, 1955; ME, Yale U., 1956, DEng, 1961. Structural engr. Convair Divsn., Gen. Dynamics, 1956-58; with technical staff TRW Systems, 1961-64; asst. prof. mech. engring. U. Calif. Berkeley, 1964-67; staff rsch. engr. Shell Devel. Co., 1967-74; prof. mech. engring. Washington U., 1974-76; sr. scientist technical staff Lawrence Livermore (Calif.) Nat. Lab., 1976—; lectr. U. So. Calif., 1962-64, U. Calif. Berkeley, 1969-70, 78, 80, U. Houston, 1973; mem. U.S. Nat. Com. Theoretical and Applied Mechanics, 1980-82, 85-94; mem. Dept. Energy Panel, 1985-87; cons. prof. Stanford U., 1994—, rsch. prof., 1996—; Sir Geoffrey Taylor Meml. lectr. U. Fla., 1991. Assoc. editor Jour. Applied Mechanics, 1984-90. Fellow ASME (chmn. applied mechanics divsn. 1980-81, hon. mem. 1992, William Prager medal); mem. Nat. Acad. Engring. (Worcester Reed Warner Gold medal), Am. Chem. Soc., Soc. Rheology. Achievements include research in properties of polymers, in wave propagation, in failure theories, in crack kinetics, in composite materials. Office: Lawrence Livermore Nat Lab PO Box 355 Livermore CA 94551*

CHRISTENSEN, ROBERT WAYNE, oral maxillofacial surgeon, minister; b. N.Y.C., Apr. 6, 1925; s. Charles Joseph Brophy and Eva Sutherland (Hart) Christensen; m. Ann Forsyth (div.); children: Robert, Joan, Elizabeth, Peter, Mary, Colleen, Patricia, Michelle; m. Lynne Blindbury; children: Andrew, Matthew. DDS, NYU, 1948. Oral surgery tng. L.A. County Gen. Hosp., 1950; oral maxillofacial surgeon, 1950-88; pres. TMJ Implants, Inc., Golden, Colo., 1988—; minister, founder Covenant Marriages Ministry, Golden, 1988—; pres. Design Dynamics Internat., Golden, 1994—; R&D med. adv. bd. mem. Sch. Medicine LLU, Loma Linda, Calif.; pres.'s cabinet mem. Jerry Savelle Ministry, Ft. Worth, 1994—; adj. prof. bioengring. Sch. Engring., Clemson U., 1997; pres. Med. Modeling Corp., 1997. Inventor of 5 U.S. patents. Lt. USNR. Robert W. Christensen fellow TM Joint Surgery, U. Tenn. Sch. Med., 1997. Republican. Avocations: skiing, gardening, photography. Office: TMJ Implants Inc 17301 W Colfax Ave Ste 135 Golden CO 80401-4800

CHRISTENSEN, ROBERT WAYNE, JR., financial and leasing company executive; b. Chester, Calif., Nov. 11, 1948; s. Robert Wayne and Ann (Forsyth) C.; m. Debra Schumann, Dec. 6, 1988; children: Heather, Megan. BA with honors, Coll. Gt. Falls, 1976; MBA, U. Puget Sound, 1978. Cert. flight instr. Corp. pilot Buttrey Food Stores, Gt. Falls, Mont., 1972-74; asst. to pres. Pacific Hide & Fur, Gt. Falls, 1974-76; fin. analyst Olympia Brewing Co., Olympia, Wash., 1977; chmn., CEO Westar Fin. Svcs. Inc., Olympia, 1978—; pres. PacWest Fin. Corp., Olympia, 1984—; bd. dirs. Westar Fin. Svcs., Inc., Olympia, Wash. Independent Bancshares, Olympia, 1982—, PacWest Fin. Corp., Olympia. Trustee CASR Trust, 1993—. Served to sgt. USAF, 1969-72. Mem. Nat. Vehicle Leasing Assn. (bd. dirs. 1978-88, 2d. v.p. 1984, pres. 1986), Western Assn. Equipment Lessors, Western Leasing Conf., Mensa, Rotary (bd. dirs. 1982-89, v.p. 1986-88, pres. 1988-89). Office: Westar Fin Svcs Inc The Republic Bldg PO Box 919 Olympia WA 98507-0919

CHRISTENSEN, STEVEN J., foreign language educator; b. L.A., June 12, 1945; s. Donald Roy and Jocile (Uresenbach) C.; m. Mary Bernice Anderson, Aug. 25, 1967; children: Jennifer, Matthew Alan, Mark Steven. BA, Brigham Young U., Provo, Utah, 1969; MEd, U. Nev., Las Vegas, 1977. Cert. tchr., adminstr., Utah. Camp dir. U.S. Youth Conservation Corps, Las Vegas, Nev., summers 1971-84; tchr. Nebo Sch. Dist., Spanish Fork, Utah, 1969-70; tchr., coach Clark County Sch. Dist., Las Vegas, 1970-78; tchr., coach adminstr. Washington County Sch. Dist., St. George, Utah, 1978—; Comm. specialist Nat. Coun. Tchrs. English, Las Vegas, 1977-78. Author: Population Resources Study Guide, 1975. Mem. S.W. Coun. Fgn. Lang. Tchrs., Utah Fgn. Lang. Assn. Democrat. Mem. Latter-Day Saints Ch. Avocations: hunting, fishing, hiking, river rafting, travel. Home: 236 S 370 W Hurricane UT 84737-3205 Office: Hurricane HS 345 W 100 S Hurricane UT 84737-1927

CHRISTENSEN, WALTER FREDERICK, JR., information, telecommunications and financial systems specialist; b. New Brunswick, N.J., Aug. 2, 1949; s. Walter Frederick Sr. and Alyce Rose (Nomejko) C.; m. Andrea Marie Fay, June 5, 1971; children: Nicole Marie, Daniel Jordan. BS, U. Del., 1971; MS, U. Md., 1973. Dir. GTE, Silver Spring, Md., 1974-79; sr. dir. GTE, Mt. Laurel, N.J., 1979-87, Quotron (subs. Citicorp), N.Y.C., 1987-89; v.p. product engrng. Automatic Data Processing, Mt. Laurel, 1989-91; v.p. systems devel. Dow Jones/Telerate, Jersey City, 1991-98; v.p. infrastructure devel. Bridge Info. Sys., N.Y.C., 1998—; pres. WFC Cons., Mt. Laurel, 1985-90. Author: Optimum Teaching Assembly Language, 1971. Bd. dirs. South Jersey chpt. Am. Cancer Soc., Mt. Laurel, 1990. Capt. USAR, 1973-79. Recipient Excellence award Automatic Data Processing, 1989. Avocations: reading, walking, swimming, children. Office: Bridge Info Sys Harborside Fin Ctr 600 Plaza Two Jersey City NJ 07311-1103

CHRISTENSON, CHARLES JOHN, retired business educator; b. Chgo., Sept. 25, 1930; s. John Edward and Ethel Dagmar (Osterberg) C. B.S., Cornell U., 1952; M.B.A., Harvard, 1954, D.B.A., 1961. Mem. faculty Harvard Grad. Sch. Bus., 1957-58, lectr., 1959-61, asst. prof., 1961-63, assoc. prof., 1963-68, prof., 1968-74, Jesse Isidor Straus prof., 1974-79, Royal Little prof., 1980-96, prof. emeritus, 1996—; prin. Auerbach Christenson Tagiuri, Inc., 1983-92; bd. dirs. Kenetech Corp., Profile Techs., Inc. Author: Strategic Aspects of Competitive Bidding for Corporate Securities, 1965, (with J.L. Bower) Public Management: Cases and Readings, 1978, (with W.L. Berry and J.S. Hammond III) Management Decision Sciences: Cases and Readings, 1979. Bd. dirs. Boston Baroque, 1980—; trustee, chmn. Deep Springs Coll., 1986-94. With AUS, 1955-57. Mem. Am. Econs. Assn. Home: 1 Chauncy Ln Cambridge MA 02138-2401 Office: Harvard Bus Sch Soldiers Fld Boston MA 02163-1317

CHRISTENSON, GARTH NEIL, optometrist; b. River Falls, Wis., Apr. 17, 1959; s. Neil Orvin and Patrica Jo (Hovde) C.; m. Mary Lou Stuesser, July 17, 1993; children: Jessica, Griffin. Student, U. Wis., River Falls, 1980; OD, Ill. Coll. Optometry, 1984; MS in Edn., Calif. State U., Fullerton, 1988. Acting chief vision therapy So. Calif. Coll. Optometry, Fullerton, 1986-90; optometrist pvt. practice, Hudson, Wis., 1990—; cons. in field. Author: (textbook) Optometric Management of Reading Dysfunction, 1997. Bd. dirs. Have a Heart Found., River Falls, 1993-95. Fellow Am. Acad. Optometry (diplomate), Coll. Optometrists in Vision Devel.; mem. Wis. Optometric Assn., Rotary (devel. assets chair 1995—). Lutheran. Avocations: golf, jogging, writing, sporting clays. Home: 556 Stagecoach Trl Hudson WI 54016-7023 Office: Christenson Vision Care 2215 Vine St Hudson WI 54016-5802

CHRISTENSON, GORDON A., law educator; b. Salt Lake City, June 22, 1932; s. Gordon B. and Ruth Arzella (Anderson) C.; m. Katherine Joy deMik, Nov. 2, 1951 (div. 1977); children: Gordon Scott, Marjorie Lynne, Ruth Ann, Nanette; m. Fabienne Fadeley, Sept. 16, 1979. BS in Law, U. Utah, 1955, JD, 1956; SJD, George Washington U., 1961. Bar: Utah 1956, U.S. Supreme Ct. 1971, D.C. 1978. Law clk. to chief justice Utah Supreme Ct., 1956-57; assoc. firm Christenson & Callister, Salt Lake City, 1956-58; atty. Dept. of Army, Nat. Guard Bur., Washington, 1957-58; atty., acting asst. legal adviser Office of Legal Adviser, U.S. Dept. State, Washington, 1958-62; asst. gen. counsel for sci. and tech. U.S. Dept. Commerce, 1962-67, spl. asst. to undersec. of commerce, 1967, counsel to commerce tech. adv. bd., 1962-67, chmn. task force on telecommunications missions and orgn., 1967, counsel to panel on engring. and commodity standards, tech. adv. bd., 1963-65; assoc. prof. law U. Okla., Norman, 1967-70; exec. asst. to pres. U. Okla., 1967-70; univ. dean for ednl. devel., central adminstrn. State U. N.Y., Albany, 1970-71; prof. law Am. U. Law Sch., Washington, 1971-79; dean Am. U. Law Sch., 1971-77; on leave, 1977-79; Charles H. Stockton prof. internat. law U.S. Naval War Coll., Newport, R.I., 1977-79; dean, Nippert prof. law U. Cin. Coll. Law, 1979-85, univ. prof. law, 1985—; assoc. professorial lectr. in internat. affairs George Washington U., 1961-67; vis. scholar Harvard U. Law Sch., 1977-78, Yale Law Sch., 1985-86, Law Sch. U. Maine, Portland, 1997; Wallace S. Fujiyama vis. disting. prof. law Univ. Hawaii Law Sch., 1997; participant summer confs. on internat. law Cornell Law Sch., Ithaca, N.Y., 1962, 64; cons. in internat. law U.S. Naval War Coll., Newport, R.I., 1969; faculty mem., reporter seminars for experienced fed. dist. judges Fed. Jud. Center, Washington, 1972-77. Author: (with Richard B. Lillich) International Claims: Their Preparation and Presentation, 1962, The Future of the University, 1969; Contbr. articles to legal jours. Cons. to Center for Policy Alternatives Mass. Inst. Tech., Cambridge, 1970-81; mem. intergovtl. com. on Internat. Policy on Weather Modification, 1967; Vice pres. Procedural Aspects of Internat. Law Inst., N.Y.C., 1962—. Served with intelligence sect. USAF, 1951-52, Japan. Recipient Silver Medal award Dept. Commerce, 1967; fellow Grad. Sch. U. Cin. Mem. Am. Soc. Internat. Law (mem. panel on state responsibility), Utah Bar Assn., Cin. Bar Assn., Order of Coif, Phi Delta Phi, Kappa Sigma. Clubs: Literary (Cin.); Cosmos (Washington). Home: 3465 Principio Ave Cincinnati OH 45208-4242 Office: U Cin Coll Law 2600 Clifton Ave Cincinnati OH 45221-0040

CHRISTENSON, GREGG ANDREW, bank executive; b. Kalamazoo, Mich., June 11, 1958; s. Elmer J. and Marie E. (Durrstein) C.; m. Karen Peterson. BA, Mich. State U., 1980. CPA. Auditor Price Waterhouse, N.Y.C., 1980-82; with Bankers Trust Co., N.Y.C., 1982-92, v.p., 1987-92; contr., sr. v.p. Huntington Nat. Bank, Columbus, Ohio, 1992—; v.p. ATM. Bd. trustees, v.p. Worthington Pub. Libr.; treas. Far North Columbus Communities Coalition. Mem. Jr. Achievement Alumni Assn. (charter), Mich. State Alumni Assn., Phi Kappa Phi, Beta Gamma Sigma. Republican. Methodist. *

CHRISTENSON, LE ROY HOWARD, insurance company officer; b. Rochester, N.Y., Oct. 28, 1948; s. Howard Le Roy and Sigrid (Anderson) C.; m. Pamala Jean Mattson, Jan. 26, 1974; children: Nathan Lee, David Wayne. BS, Valparaiso U., 1970; MS, Purdue U., 1972. CLU. Corp. actuary Western Life Ins. Co., St. Paul, 1972-84; v.p., reins. actuary Am. United Life Ins. Co., Indpls., 1984—; fin. cons. Mgmt. Assistance Program, Mpls., 1982. Bd. dirs. Lake Wapogasset Bible Camp, Mpls., 1982-83, Christian Businessman's Com., Indpls., 1985-88; age group leader Pioneer Club, Indpls., 1983, 87; mission conf. chmn. Faith Missionary Ch., Indpls., 1987-89, elder, 1991-93, 99—, elder chmn., 1993, mission com. chmn., 1995—; bd. dirs. Interserve, 1996—, chmn. nominating com., 1999—, mem. exec. com., 1999—. Fellow Soc. Actuaries (chmn. audit working group reins. sect. 1985-88, vice chmn. reins. sect. 1988-89, 95-96, chmn. 1989-90, 96-97, sec.-treas. reins. sect. 1994-95); mem. Am. Acad. Actuaries, Tri-State Actuarial Club (Indpls. rep. 1984-90, chmn. 1989-90), Indpls. Actuarial Club (pres. 1987-88). Avocations: tennis, bible study, biking, hiking. Home: 3761 Bridger Dr N Carmel IN 46033-4169 Office: Am United Life Ins Co 1 American Sq Indianapolis IN 46282-0001

CHRISTENSON, RONALD L., military officer; b. Flint, Mich., Nov. 11, 1947; m. Sharon Lee McIntyre; children: Scot, Martin. Grad., U.S. Naval Acad., 1969; degree, Calif. Inst. Tech. Commd. ensign USN, advanced through grades to rear adm.; assigned to Helicopter Antisubmarine Squadron 15, USS Guam, Air Test and Evaluation Squadron 1, Patuxent River, Md., 1975; Sea King pilot 820 and 706 Naval Squadrons, Royal Naval Air Sta., Culdrose, Eng., 1977-79; adminstrv. officer, maintenance officer Helicopter Antisubmarine Squadron 5 USS Dwight D. Eisenhower, 1981; mem. staff Comdr., Sea Based ASW Wings Atlantic, 1982; exec. officer, then comdg. officer Helicopter Antisubmarine Squadron 7, USS John F. Kennedy, 1983-86; aviation enlisted assignment officer Naval Mil. Pers. Command, 1986-88; with Naval Nuc. Power Program, 1988; exec. officer USS Theodore Roosevelt, 1990-91; condr. USS Dubuque, Sasebo, Japan, 1992-94; 5th commdg. officer USS Theodore Roosevelt, 1994-96; head carrier programs and aviation manpower and tng. brs. USN, Washington, 1997—. Office: USN 2000 Navy Pentagon Washington DC 20350-2000*

CHRISTENSON, WILLIAM NEWCOME, retired physician; b. Biltmore Forest, N.C., Dec. 2, 1925; s. William Lambert and Beth (Newcome) C.; BS, U. N.C., 1949; MD, Johns Hopkins U., 1948; m. Elizabeth Chandler White, Aug. 9, 1957; children: Lisa Ann, Laurie E., Susan. Intern, asst. resident Mass. Gen. Hosp., Boston, 1948-50; asst. resident N.Y. Hosp., N.Y.C., 1953-55; dir. personnel health svc., 1960-85, asst. attending physician, 1961-64, assoc. attending physician, 1964-85; attending physician Westchester County Med. Ctr., 1985-95, physician Employee Health Svc., 1985-95; ret., 1995; postgrad. rsch. fellow USPHS; Postgrad. Med. Sch. London, 1955-56; instr. medicine Cornell U. Med. Coll., N.Y.C., 1956-59, asst. prof. medicine, 1959-65, clin. assoc. prof. medicine, 1965-79, assoc. prof. clin. medicine, 1979-85; dir. Office Grad. Med. Advising, N.Y. Med. Coll., 1985-88, 1988-95, prof. clin. medicine, 1986-95, assoc. dean, 1988-95; cons. N.Y. Blood Center, 1976-90; practice medicine specializing in internal medicine and occupational medicine, N.Y.C., 1960-85. With USNR, 1950-52. Fellow ACP, Am. Coll. Occupational and Environ. Medicine; mem. Am. Fedn. Clin. Rsch., Phi Beta Kappa, Alpha Omega Alpha, Delta Kappa Epsilon. Research in hematology and human ecology.

CHRISTIAN, BETTY JO, lawyer; b. Temple, Tex., July 27, 1936; d. Joe and Mattie Manor (Brown) Wiest; m. Ernest S. Christian, Jr., Dec. 24, 1960. B.A. summa cum laude, U. Tex., 1957, LL.B. summa cum laude, 1960. Bar: Tex. 1961, U.S. Supreme Ct. 1964, D.C. 1980. Law clk. Supreme Ct. Tex., 1960-61; atty. ICC, 1961-68; asst. gen. counsel ICC, Washington, 1970-72; assoc. gen. counsel ICC, 1972-76, commr., 1976-79; ptnr. Steptoe & Johnson, Washington, 1980—; atty. Labor Dept., Dallas, 1968-70. Fellow Am. Bar Found.; mem. ABA, FBA (Younger Fed. Lawyer award 1964), Tex. Bar Assn., Am. Law Inst., Am. Acad Appellate Lawyers, Adminstrv. Conf. U.S., City Tavern Club. Office: 1330 Connecticut Ave NW Washington DC 20036-1704

CHRISTIAN, DARRELL L., journalist; b. Henderson, Ky., Dec. 26, 1948; s. James Boyd and Thelma (Todd) C. BA, U. Ky., 1970. Sports writer Gleaner Jour., Henderson, Ky., 1964-65, sports editor, 1965-66; newsman AP, Charleston, W. Va., 1967-68; newsman AP, Indpls., 1972-75, news editor, 1975-80; supervising editor AP, Washington, 1980-81; dep. sports editor AP, N.Y.C., 1981-85, sports editor, 1985-92, mng. editor, 1992-98, dir. MegaSports, 1998—; Pulitzer prize juror, 1995-96. With USN, 1970-73. Avocation: golf. Office: AP 50 Rockefeller Plz New York NY 10020-1605

CHRISTIAN, EDWARD KIEREN, broadcasting station executive; b. Detroit, June 26, 1944; s. William Edward and Dorothy Miriam (Kieren) C.; m. Judith Dallaire, Nov. 25, 1966; children: Eric, Dana. BA, Wayne State U., 1966, postgrad.; MA, Cen. Mich. U., 1980. Mgr. John C. Butler Co., Detroit, 1968-69; nat. sales mgr. WCAR Radio, Detroit, WSUN Radio, St. Petersburg, Fla., 1969-70; v.p., gen. mgr., ptnr. WCER Radio, Charlotte, Mich., 1970-74; pres. Josephson Internat. Broadcast, 1975-86; pres., CEO Saga Comm., Inc., Detroit, 1986—; pres., CEO, bd. dirs. Stas. WSNY-FM, WVKO-FM, Columbus, Ohio, Sta. WNOR-FM, Norfolk, Va., Sta. WAFX, Norfolk, WJO1 AM Norfolk, Stas. WKLH-FM, WLZR-FM, WJYO-AM, WFMR-FM, WMJO-FM Milw., Stas. KRNT, KSTZ-FM, KIOA-AM/FM, KAZR FM, KLTI FM, Des Moines, Stas. WLRW-FM and WIXY-FM, Champaign, Ill., Stas. WYMG-FM, WQQL-FM, WDBR-FM, WYXY-FM, WTAX-AM, WVAX-Am, Springfield, Ill., Stas. WGAN-AM/WMGX, WZAN-AM/WYNZ-FM, WPOR/FM, WBAE-AM Portland, Maine, Sta. WFEA-AM/WZID-FM, WQLL-FM, Manchester, N.H., Sta. WAQY-AM/FM, Springfield, Mass., KOAM TV, Joplin, Mo., WNAX-AM, Yankton, S.D., KCLH-FM, Sioux City, Iowa, KGMI, KISM-FM, Bellingham, Wash., KIXT-AM, KAFE FM, Bellingham, Wash., Victoria Tex., KUNU TV, KAVU TV, KVCT TV, Victoria, WXVT TV, Greenville, Miss., Mich. Radio Network, Ill. Radio Network; Mich. Farm Radio Network; vice-chmn. Mut. Broadcasting Affiliates Coun., 1977-79; chmn. Arbitron Radio Adv. Coun., 1978-79; bd. dirs. All Industry Music Licensing Com. Pres. United Way, Charlotte, 1973-74; del. Rep. State Conv., 1974; bd. dirs. Am. Auto Immune Related Disease Found., 1995—; consul Republic of Iceland for Mich., Ohio and Ind., 1996—. Mem. Alpha Epsilon Rho (nat. adv. coun. 1980—). Home: 21 Newberry Pl Grosse Pointe MI 48236-3749 also: 2055 Lakeshore Rd Applegate MI 48401-9715 also: 3310 Sabal Cove Dr Longboat Key FL 34228-3024 Office: Saga Communications Inc 73 Kercheval Ave Grosse Pointe MI 48236-3603

CHRISTIAN, ERNEST SILSBEE, JR., lawyer; b. Gonzales, Tex., Jan. 15, 1937; s. Ernest Silsbee and Ruby Ruth (Hamon) C.; m. Betty Jo Wiest, Dec. 24, 1960. LL.B. cum laude, U. Tex., 1961. Bar: Tex. bar 1961, D.C. bar 1961, U.S. Supreme Ct. bar 1978. Atty. Treasury Dept., Washington, 1970-72; tax legis. counsel Treasury Dept., 1973-74, dep. asst. sec. treasury (tax policy), 1974-75; ptnr. Patton, Boggs & Blow, Washington, 1975-94, E.S. Christian, 1995—. Mem. Am. Law Inst., Am. Bar Assn. Republican. Clubs: City Tavern (Washington), Met. (Washington). Home: 3750 Fordham Rd NW Washington DC 20016-1934 Office: 800 Connecticut Ave NW Washington DC 20006

CHRISTIAN, FRANCIS JOSEPH, bishop; b. Peterborough, N.H., Oct. 12, 1942; s. Joseph Lucien and Dorothy Mary (Parent) C. BA, PhB, U. Ottawa, Can., 1964; MA in Theology, U. Louvain, Belgium, 1968, PhD in Religious Studies, 1975. Ordained priest Roman Cath. Ch., 1968. Asst. pastor Our Lady of Mercy Parish, Merrimack, N.H., 1968-71, St. Joseph Cathedral Parish, Manchester, N.H., 1971-72; asst. chancellor Diocese of Manchester, 1975-77, chancellor, sec. for administrn. canonical affairs Diocese Manchester, 1978—, vicar gen., 1996—. Named Monsignor (Prelate of Honor), Pope John Paul II, 1986. Home: 145 Lowell St Manchester NH 03104-6121 Office: Diocese of Manchester 153 Ash St Manchester NH 03104-4396*

CHRISTIAN, GARY DALE, chemistry educator; b. Eugene, Oreg., Nov. 25, 1937; s. Roy C. and Edna Alberta (Trout) Gonier; m. Suanne Byrd Coulbourne, June 17, 1961; children: Dale Brian, Carol Jean. BS, U. Oreg., 1959; MS, U. Md., 1962, PhD, 1964. Rsch. analytical chemist Walter Reed Army Inst. Rsch., Washington, 1961-67; asst. prof. U. Md., College Park, 1965-66; asst. prof. U. Ky., Lexington, 1967-70, assoc. prof., 1970-72; prof. chemistry U. Wash., Seattle, 1972—, acting chmn. dept., 1990, assoc. chmn., 1991-92, divisional dean Arts and Scis., 1993—; vis. prof. Free U. Brussels, 1978-79; invited prof. U. Geneva, 1979; cons. Ames Co., 1968-72, Beckman Instruments, Inc., 1972-84, 88, Westinghouse Hanford Co., 1977-83, Tech. Dynamics, 1983-85, Porton Diagnostics, 1990-91, Bend Rsch., 1992-93, E.I. DuPont de Nemours, Inc., 1993; examiner Grad. Record Exam., 1985-90. Author: Analytical Chemistry, 5th edit., 1994, Instrumental Analysis, 1978, 2d edit., 1986, Atomic Absorption Spectroscopy, 1970, Trace Analysis, 1986, Problem Solving in Analytical Chemistry, 1988, Calculations in Pharmaceutical Sciences, 1993; editl. bd. Analytical Letters, 1971—, Can. Jour. Spectroscopy, 1974-96, Analytical Instrumentation, 1974-93, Talanta, 1980-88 (spl. editor USA honor issue, 1989), Analytical Chemistry, 1985-89, Critical Revs. in Analytical Chemistry, 1985—, The Analyst, 1986-90, Jour. Saudi Chem. Soc., 1995—; editor in chief Talanta, 1989—, Electroanalysis, 1988—, Jour. Pharm. and Biochem. Analysis, 1990-97, Fresenius' Z. Analytical Chem., 1991-93, Laborator Automation, 1992—, Quimica Analitica, 1993—; contbr. articles to profl. jours. Recipient Talanta medal Elsevier Sci., 1995; Fulbright Hays scholar, 1978-79. Mem. Am. Chem. Soc. (sect. chmn. 1982-83, chmn. elect divsn. Analytic chemistry 1988-89, chmn. 1989-90, divsn. Analytical Chemistry award for Excellence in Tchg. 1988, Fisher award in analytical chemistry 1996), Soc. Applied Spectroscopy (sect. chmn. 1982), Spectroscopy Soc. Can., Am. Inst. Chemists (cert.), Soc. Electroanalytical Chemistry (bd. dirs. 1993-98). Republican. Home: PO Box 26 Medina WA 98039-0026 Office: U Wash Dept Chemistry Box 351700 Seattle WA 98195-1700

CHRISTIAN, JAMES WAYNE, economist; b. Ft. Worth, Oct. 7, 1934; s. Nap B. and Daphne (Wright) C.; BA, U. Tex., Austin, 1962, MA (univ. fellow), 1964, PhD (NSF fellow), 1965; m. Jo June Maples, June 5, 1952; children: Amy Joella, Nicole Denise. Prof. econs. Iowa State U., 1965-74; dir. internat. div. Fed. Home Loan Bank Bd., Washington, 1972-74; sr. v.p., chief economist Nat. Savs. and Loan League, Washington, 1974-80; sr. v.p., chief economist U.S. League Savs. Inst., Chgo., 1980-91; pres. James Christian Assocs., Fair Oaks Ranch, Tex., 1991—; dir. Real Estate Ctr. at Tex. A & M Univ., 1993-95; dir. Nat. Housing Conf., 1980-84; cons. 23 developing country govts., 1970—. Contbr. articles to fin. and econ. jours. Served with USN, 1952-55, USAF, 1955-59. Recipient Am. Legion award, 1949; Social Sci. Rsch. Coun. grantee, 1968-69. Mem. Am. Econ. Assn., Am. Fin. Assn., So. Econ. Assn., Phi Beta Kappa, Omicron Delta Epsilon, Pi Sigma Alpha, Phi Kappa Phi. Club: Cosmos.

CHRISTIAN, JOE CLARK, medical genetics researcher, educator; b. Marshall, Okla., Sept. 12, 1934; s. Roy John and Katherine Elizabeth (Beeby) C.; m. Shirley Ann Yancey, June 5, 1960; children: Roy Clark, Charles David. BS, Okla. State U., 1956; MS, U. Ky., 1959, PhD, 1960, MD, 1964. Cert. clin. geneticist, Am. Bd. Med. Genetics. Resident internal medicine Vanderbilt U., Nashville, 1964-66; asst. prof. med. genetics Ind. U., Indpls., 1966-69, assoc. prof., 1969-74, prof., 1974—, assoc. dean basic scis. and regional ctrs., 1996-98. Served with USAR, 1953-60. Mem. AMA, Am. Soc. Human Genetics. Democrat. Methodist. Avocations: bicycling, farming. Office: Ind U Dept Med/Molecular Genetics 975 W Walnut St Dept Med Indianapolis IN 46202-5181

CHRISTIAN, JOHN CATLETT, JR., lawyer; b. Springfield, Mo., Sept. 12, 1929; s. John Catlett and Alice Odelle (Milling) C.; m. Peggy Jeanne Cain, Apr. 12, 1953; children: Cathleen Marie, John Catlett, Alice Cain. AB, Drury Coll., 1951; LLB, Tulane U., 1956. Bar: La. 1956, Mo. 1956, U.S. Supreme Ct. 1975. Assoc. Porter & Stewart, Lake Charles, La., 1956-58; assoc. Wilkinson, Lewis, Wilkinson & Madison, Shreveport, La., 1958-62, ptnr., 1962-64; ptnr. Milling, Benson, Woodward, Hillyer, Pierson & Miller, New Orleans, 1964-92, of counsel, 1993-94; pres. Sherburne Land Co., 1974-83; dir. Emerald Land Corp. Pres. Kathleen Elizabeth O'Brien Found., 1963—. Served with USMCR, 1951-53. Fellow Am. Coll. Trial Lawyers; mem. ABA, Fed. Bar Assn., Am. Judicature Soc., Mo. Bar Assn., La. Bar Assn., La. Landowners Assn. (bd.dris. 1983—), Boston Club, Beau Chene Country Club, Kappa Alpha Order, Omicron Delta Kappa, Phi Delta Phi. Home: 807 Tete Lours Dr Mandeville LA 70471-1774 Office: Whitney Bank Bldg PO Box 1317 Mandeville LA 70470-1317

CHRISTIAN, JOHN EDWARD, health science educator; b. Indpls., July 12, 1917; s. George Edward and Okel Kandus (Waltz) C.; m. Catherine Ellen Spooner, July 23, 1948; 1 dau., Linda Kay. BS, Purdue U., 1939, PhD, 1944. Control chemist Upjohn Co., 1939-40; faculty Purdue U., Lafayette, Ind., 1940—; prof. pharm. chemistry Purdue U., 1950-59, head dept. radiol. control, 1956-59, prof. bionucleonics, head dept., 1959-82; chmn. adminstrv. com. Trace Level Research Inst., 1960-88; dir. Inst. for Environmental Health, 1965-88; head Sch. Health Scis., 1979-82, Hovde Disting. prof., 1979-88, Hovde Disting. prof. bionucleonics and health scis. emeritus, 1988—; vis. prof. radiation therapy Ind. U. Sch. Medicine, 1970-88; Harvey Washington Meml. lectr. Purdue U., 1955; Edward-Kremers Meml. lectr. U. Wis., 1956; vis. lectr. U. Tex., 1959, Taylor U. Ann. Sci. Lecture Series, Upton, Ind., 1960; Julius A. Koch Meml. lectr. U. Pitts., 1961. Assoc. editor Radiochem. Letters. Mem. revision com. U.S. Pharmacopeia, 1950-60, mem. adv. panel on radioactive drugs, 1960-70; adv. com. isotope distbn. AEC, 1952-58, mem. med. adv. com., 1967-75; mem. radiation and chem. def. sect. Ind. Dept. Civil Def., 1954—; vice chmn. Radiation Control Adv. Commn., Ind., 1958—; mem. exec. com. Ind. Comprehensive Health Planning Council, 1972-76; mem. adv. com. radiopharms. FDA, 1970-75; mem. Ind. Gov.'s Pesticide Council, 1970-73; Alumni research councilor Purdue Research Found., 1964-88; mem. Ind. Environmental Mgmt. Bd., 1972-87, Nat. Energy Policy Task Force, Dept. Energy, 1981-83; mem. Bd. Grants Am. Found. for Pharm. Edn., 1989—. Recipient award Chilean Iodine Ednl. Bur., 1956, Julius Sturmer award Phila. Coll. Pharmacy and Sci., 1958, Leather medal Purdue U., 1971, Hovde Faculty Purdue U. fellow, 1988. Fellow AAAS (past sec. and chmn. pharm. sci. sect., mem. council), Ind. Acad. Sci.; mem. AMA (spl. affiliate), AAUP, Am. Assn. Colls. Pharmacy (past mem. exec. com., chmn. conf. tchrs., chmn. conf. grad. study and grad. tchrs., chmn. com. study grad. edn. in pharmacy), Am. Chem. Soc. (past chmn. Purdue sect.), Am. Pharm. Assn. (Ebert medal 1957, Justin L. Powers Research Achievement award 1963, past chmn. sci. sect.), Acad. Pharm. Sci. (past v.p.), Ind. Pharm. Assn., Am. Pub. Health Assn., Am. Nuclear Soc., Am. Soc. Bacteriology, Health Phys. Soc., Sigma Xi (past pres. Purdue chpt., research award Purdue chpt. 1950), Rho Chi, Phi Lambda Upsilon, Sigma Pi Sigma., Eta Sigma Gamma, Gamma Sigma Delta. Home: 1301 Woodland Ave West Lafayette IN 47906-2371 Office: Purdue U Sch Health Scis Civil Engring Bldg West Lafayette IN 47907

CHRISTIAN, JOHN KENTON, organization executive, publisher, writer, marketing consultant; b. Pana, Ill., Nov. 6, 1927; s. Ben Ross and Ruth (Stevenson) C.; m. Marjorie Adair Pollock, Nov. 28, 1958; children—Jefrey, Dwane, Kevin. Student, Westminster Coll., 1945, Colo. Coll., 1948, Emerson Coll., 1949; B.S., Boston U., 1951; student, Am. U., 1954-55. Relief editor, rep., columnist St. Louis Daily Record, 1950-51; reporter Commerce Clearing House, Washington, 1952; with U.S. News and World Report, 1953-68; regional sales mgr. U.S. News and World Report, Los Angeles, 1960-63; mktg. mgr. U.S. News and World Report, Washington, 1964-68; pub. Nation's Cities Mag., Washington, 1968-76; mem. U.S. Fed. Preparedness Agy. mission to Iran, 1975-76; pres. Internat. Center for Emergency Preparedness, Washington, 1977-80; also pub. Emergency Preparedness News, 1977-79; v.p. Nat. Radio Broadcasters Assn., 1979-84; pres. Communications Brokers, Inc., 1984-88; author, pub. and mktg. cons., 1988-92; mktg. dir. Marine Corps Assn., 1992—. Served with USAAF, 1945-48. Presbyn. Home: 10867 Deborah Dr Potomac MD 20854-2716

CHRISTIAN, JOHN M., lawyer; b. Wichita, Kans., Sept. 15, 1948. AB with honors, Princeton U., 1970; JD with honors, U. Mich., 1973. Bar: Ill. 1974. Mem. Cahill, Christian & Kunkle, Ltd., Chgo.; adj. prof. law IIT/Chgo.-Kent Coll. Law. Mem. ABA, Chgo. Bar Assn. (mem. spl. task force ins. 1985-86, spl. com. lawyers profl. liability ins. 1987-88, chmn. tort litigation com. 1986-87). Office: Cahill Christian & Kunkle Ltd Santa Fe Bldg 224 S Michigan Ave Ste 1300 Chicago IL 60604-2589*

CHRISTIAN, JOSEPH RALPH, physician; b. Chgo., June 15, 1920; s. Ralph F. and Anna M. (Across) Co; m. Marcia Pomeroy, Sept. 25, 1944; children—Patricia Ann, Joseph Ralph. A.A., U. Chgo., 1941; M.D., Loyola U., Chgo., 1944. Diplomate: Am. Bd. Pediatrics. Intern Cook County Hosp., Chgo., 1944-45; resident Cook County Hosp., 1945-46, 48-49; faculty Stritch Sch. Medicine, Loyola U., Chgo., 1948-61; prof. Stritch Sch. Medicine, Loyola U. (pediatrics), 1957-61, chmn. dept., 1960-61; attending pediatrician Loyola Service at La Rabida Sanitarium, 1948-61; chmn. dept. pediatrics Mercy Hosp., 1960-61; chief pediatrics Lewis Meml. Maternity Hosp., 1951-61; chmn. dept. pediatrics Rush Presbyn.-St. Luke's Med. Center, Chgo., 1961-85; prof. pediatrics U. Ill. Coll. Medicine, Chgo., 1961-70; prof. Rush Med. Coll., Chgo., 1970-85, prof. emeritus, 1985—; chmn. dept. pediatrics Rush Med. Coll., 1970-85; sr. attending pediatrician children's div. Cook County Hosp., 1959-65. Editor: Pediatrics Digest, 1962-78; Mem. editorial bd.: Childcraft, 1963-87; Contbr. articles to med. jours. Chmn. poison control com. Chgo. Bd. Health, 1961-69; chmn. med. com. Infant Welfare Soc., Chgo., 1958-61; chmn. 9th Ill. Congress Maternal and Infant Health, 1962; chmn. bd. trustees Holy Cross Chgo., 1970-75. Served to capt. M.C. AUS, 1946-47. Recipient Clin. Faculty award Stritch Sch. Medicine, 1954, 57. Fellow Am. Coll. Chest Physicians, Am. Acad. Pediatrics (chmn. film rev. com. 1963-73, chmn. com. residency fellowships 1964-67), Am. Pub. Health Assn., A.C.P.; mem. A.M.A., Am. Fedn. Clin. Research, Am. Pediatric Soc., Am. Heart Assn., Ambulatory Pediatric Assn., Am. Assn. Poison Control Centers, Am. Assn. Maternal and Infant Health, Ill. Assn. Maternal and Infant Health (pres. 1964), Am. Pediatric Soc., Chgo. Pediatric Soc. (pres. 1964-65), Midwest Soc. Pediatric Research, Assn. Med. Sch. Pediatric Dept. Chairmen. Home: 3 Oakbrook Club Dr Apt E107 Oak Brook IL 60523-1330

CHRISTIAN, MARY JO DINAN, educator, real estate professional; b. Denver, May 7, 1941; d. Joseph Timothy and Margaret Rose (Ryan) Dinan; m. Ralph Poinsett Christian, Aug. 27, 1966. BA, Loretto Heights Coll., Denver, 1964; MA, George Washington U., 1983. Cert. English educator, adminstrn. and supervision secondary edn. English tchr. Denver Pub. Schs., 1964-67, Prince George's County Pub. Sch., Md., 1967-81; vice-prin. Prince George's County High Sch., Md., 1981-97; ednl. cons., 1997—; presenter gender/ethnic expectations and student achievement Nat. Conf.; Generating Expectations for Student Achievement instr. in-svc. tchrs. and adminstrs. Columnist: WomenSpeak, 1981-91. Rep. Prince George's County Commn. Women UN Fourth World Conf. Women Forum, Beijing, 1995. Md. Ho. of Dels. recognition. Mem. NAFE, ASCD, NEA (chair adminstrs. caucus 1991-93, adminstr.-at-large resolutions com. 1986-92, polit. action com. 1984-86, coord.-at-large women's caucus 1981-91, Creative Leadership award 1989), Md. State Tchrs. Assn. (state coord. Sen. Sarbane campaign 1982, state voter registration coord. 1984, issue coord. Tom McMillen campaign 1986, Women's Rights award 1988), Vail Racquet Club, Capitol Hill Garden Club, Phi Delta Kappa, Alpha Delta Kappa. Home: 504 Independence Ave SE Washington DC 20003-1143

CHRISTIAN, RALPH GORDON, agricultural research administrator; b. Lethbridge, Alta., Can., Apr. 17, 1942; s. Wesley Peel and Mary (Patterson) C.; m. Brenda Esther Kheong, 1976. DVM, U. Guelph, Ont., Can., 1966; vet. pathology diploma, U. Sask., Saskatoon, 1970. Cert. in vet. pathology Am. Coll. Vet. Pathologists. Instr. Vet. Sch. U. Melbourne, Australia, 1977; dir. animal health divsn. Alta. Dept. Agr., Edmonton, 1982-87; acting asst. dep. min. Alta. Agrl. Prodn. Sector, Edmonton, 1987; exec. dir. Alta. Agrl. Rsch. Inst., Edmonton, 1987—; exec. dir. rsch. divsn. Alta. Dept. Agr., Food and Rural Devel., Edmonton, 1987—; br. head pathology br. Alta. Agr. Vet. Lab., Edmonton, 1972-79, 79-82; lab. head Vet. Lab., Fairview, Alta., 1970-72; instr., resident pathology dept. Western Coll. Vet. Medicine, Saskatoon, 1969-70. Mem. Am. Coll. Vet. Pathologists, Can. Vet. Med. Assn. (chmn. specialization com. 1986-88), Alta. Vet. Med. Assn. (pres. 1981-82). Avocations: skiing, equine driving. Home: RR 1, Edmonton, AB Canada T6H 5T6 Office: Alta Agrl Food and Rural De, 7500 113 St, Edmonton, AB Canada T6H-5T6

CHRISTIAN, RICHARD CARLTON, university dean, former advertising agency executive; b. Dayton, Ohio, Nov. 29, 1924; s. Raymond A. and Louise (Gamber) C.; m. Audrey Bongartz, Sept. 10, 1949; children: Ann Christian Carra, Richard Carlton Jr. B.S. in Bus. Adminstrn, Miami U., Oxford, Ohio, 1948; MBA, Northwestern U., 1949; LLD (hon.), Nat.-Louis U., 1986; postgrad., Denison U., The Citadel, Biarritz Am. U. Mktg. analyst Rockwell Mfg. Co., Pitts., 1949-50; exec. v.p. Marsteller Inc., Chgo., 1951-60; pres. Marsteller Inc., 1960-75; bd. dirs., exec. com. Young and Rubicam, Inc., 1979-84; chmn. bd. Marsteller Inc., 1975-84, chmn. emeritus, 1984—; assoc. dean Kellogg Grad. Sch. Mgmt. Northwestern U., 1984-91, assoc. dean Medill Sch. Journalism, 1991—; dir., chmn. Bus. Publs. Audit Circulation, Inc., 1969-75; Speaker, author marketing, sales mgmt., marketing research and advt. Trustee Northwestern U., 1970-74, Nat.-Louis U., Evanston, Ill., 1970-92, James Webb Young Fund for Edn., U. Ill., 1962-95; pres. Nat. Advt. Rev. Coun., 1976-77; bd. adv. coun. mem. Miami U.; mem. adv. coun. J.L. Kellogg Grad. Sch. Mgmt., Northwestern U.; v.p., dir. Mus. Broadcast Comm.; dir. Can. U.S. Ednl. Exch. (Fulbright Found.). With inf. AUS, 1942-46, ETO. Recipient Ohio Gov.'s award 1977, Alumni medal, Alumni, Merit and Svc. awards Northwestern U.; named to the Advt. Hall of Fame, 1991. Mem. Am. Mktg. assn., Indsl. Mktg. Assn. (founder, chmn. 1951), Bus. Profl. Advt. Assn. (life mem. Chgo., pres. Chgo. 1954-55, nat. v.p. 1955-58, G. D. Crain award 1977), U. Ill. Found., Northwestern U. Bus. Sch. Alumni Assn. (founder, pres.), Am. Assn. Advt. Agys. (dir., chmn. 1976-77), Am. Acad. Advt. (1st disting. svc. award 1978), Northwestern U. Alumni Assn. (nat. pres. 1968-70), Mid-Am. Club, Comml. Club, Econ. Club Chgo., Kenilworth Club, Westmoreland Country Club, Alpha Delta Sigma, Beta Gamma Sigma, Delta Sigma Pi, Phi Gamma Delta. Baptist. Office: Northwestern U Medill Sch Journalism Evanston IL 60208

CHRISTIAN, ROBERT HENRY, architect; b. Cin., Feb. 28, 1922; s. Richard Dudley and Lillian Emma (Huber) C.; m. Marjorie Ann Ruff, Apr. 12, 1947; children—Carol Ann, Robert Alan. B.S. in Architecture, U. Cin., 1952. Color matcher Interchem. Corp., Cin., 1945-46; draftsman various cos., 1946-54; asso. architect Sullivan, Isaacs & Sullivan, Cin., 1954-62, L.P. Cotter & Assos., Cin., 1962-67; partner L.P. Cotter & Assos., 1967-72; v.p. devel. D.C. Peterson Co. Inc., Hilton Head Island, S.C., 1972-74; pres. Robert Christian Regimes Inc., 1981-88, Hilton Head/Beaufort Council Architects, 1976. Mem. Hamilton County Regional Planning Commn., Cin., 1963-72; active Boy Scouts Am.; artist and archtl. rep. Cin. Archdiocesan Liturgical Commn., 1970-77 ; tech. adviser to Village Woodlawn, Ohio, 1963-70; mayor Village, 1957-63; Mem. Edgecliff Coll. Acad. Fine Arts Found., 1961-69, chmn., 1963-66. Served with USAAF, 1942-45. Mem. NRA, AIA, U.S. Tennis Assn. Tennis Umpires, Hilton Head Profl. Tennis Umpires Assn. (pres.), Fla. Profl. Tennis Umpires, Scarab, Am. Legion, KC (4th degree). Home and Office: 7211 155th Pl N Palm Beach Gardens FL 33418-7415

CHRISTIAN, ROLAND CARL (BUD CHRISTIAN), retired English language and speech communications educator; b. LaSalle, Colo., June 7, 1938; s. Roland Clyde and Ethel Mae (Lattimer) C.; m. Joyce Ann Kincel, Feb. 15, 1959; children: Kathleen Marie Christian Dunham, Kristine May Christian Sweet. BA in English and Speech, U. No. Colo., 1962, MA, 1966. Cert. tchr., N.Y., Colo. Tchr. Southside Jr. High Sch., Rockeville Ctr., N.Y., 1962-63, Plateau Valley High Sch., Collbran, Colo., 1963-67; prof. English Northeastern Jr. Coll., Sterling, Colo., 1967-93, prof. emeritus, 1993—; presenter seminars, workshops, Sterling, 1967—; emcee/host Town Meeting of Am., Sterling, 1976. Author: Be Bright! Be Brief! Be Gone! A Speaker's Guide, 1983, Potpourrivia, A Digest of Curious Words, Phrases and Trivial Information, 1986, Nicknames in Sports: A Quiz book, 1986; lit. adv. New Voices mag., 1983-93; contbr. Ways We Write, 1964, The Family Treasury of Great Poems, 1982, Our Twentieth Century's Greatest Poems, 1982, Anti-War Poems; vol. II, 1985, Impressions, 1986, World Poetry Anthology, 1986, American Poetry Anthology, 1986, Chasing Rainbows, 1988, The Poetry of Life, 1988, Hearts on Fire, 1988, Wide Open Magazine, 1986, 87, 88; columnist South Platte Sentinel, 1988—. Served with U.S. Army, 1956-59. Recipient Colo. Recognition of Merit scholarship, 1956, Merit cert. Poets Anonymous, 1983, Award of Merit (9), 1985, 86, Golden Poet of Yr. award World of Poetry Press, 1985, 86, 87, 88, Joel Mack Tchr. of Yr. award Northeastern Jr. Coll., 1986; Jr. Coll. Found. grantee, 1986, 87. Avocations: fishing, hunting, sports, trivia, music. Home: 603 Park St Apt 105 Sterling CO 80751-3855

CHRISTIAN, SHERRIL D., chemistry educator, administrator; b. Estherville, Iowa, Sept. 28, 1931; s. Carl B. and Elverna E. (Kuhlman) C.; m. Dolores L. Gabriel, Jan. 7, 1956; children: Dale Warren, Ian Mark, Lani Aloha. BS in math., Iowa State U., 1952, PhD in chemistry, 1956. Asst. prof. chemistry U. Okla., Norman, 1956-60, assoc. prof., 1960-65, asst. dean. Coll. Arts and Scis., 1963-65, prof., 1965-69, chmn. dept. chemistry, 1963, 68-69, George Lynn Cross rsch. prof., 1969—, dir. Inst. for Applied Surfactant Research, 1985—; Fulbright lectr. dept. chemistry U. Ceylon, 1961-62; vis. prof. dept. chemistry U. Oslo, 1966-67, U. Trondheim, 1979-80. Contbr. more than 220 reviewed articles in surface and colloid chemistry, thermodynamics of non-electrolyte solutions, molecular complexes, aqueous solution chemistry and separations and water purification. Postdoc. rsch. fellow Royal Norwegian Coun. Sci. and Indsl. Rsch., 1966-67, 74-75; recipient Okla. Chemist of Yr. award Am. Chem. Soc., 1986. Mem. Am. Chem. Soc., Am. Oil Chemists Soc., Norwegian Acad. Sci. and Letters (fgn.), Phi Lambda Upsilon, Sigma Xi, Phi Kappa Phi, Pi Mu Epsilon. Achievements include patents for ion expulsion ultrafiltration method, 1993, method for removing toxic anions from water, 1994. Home: 2891 Twin Acres Dr Norman OK 73071-7740

CHRISTIANO, MELISSA, artist, educator; b. Jonesboro, Ark.; d. Jimmy and Mary (Moore) Lincoln; m. Richard J. Christiano, June 30, 1990; 1 child, Wes. BFA, Ark. State U., MA; MFA, Memphis State U. Art instr. Jones Sch. Art., Jonesboro, 1985-87; instr., owner Studio Art Gallery, Jonesboro, 1987-88; tchg. asst. printmaking Memphis State U., 1986-90; instr. art Mississippi Coll., Blytheville, Ark., 1988-93, Williams Coll., Walnut Ridge, Ark., 1993—; dir. SAI Gallery, N.Y.C., 1999. Exhbns. include The Forum Gallery, Jonesboro, 1986, Ark. Artist Registry, Little Rock, 1988, Meth. Hosp. Health Sys., Memphis, 1989, U. Memphis Gallery, 1990, U. Ark. Little Rock, 1990, 95, 97, Maddox Fine Art Gallery, Walnut Ridge, 1994, Ark. State U. Gallery, Jonesboro, 1995, 97, Enid Okla Homa Gallery, Chgo., 1995, Chroma Gallery, Little Rock, 1995, B Gallery, Memphis, 1996, Howell Gallery, Jonesboro, 1996, Gallery 479, N.Y.C., 1997, Madison Ave Gallery, Memphis, 1998, Budapest, 1999, Sai Gallery, N.Y.C., 1999, Ark. Artist Register, Little Rock, 1999, Kavehaz Gallery, N.Y.C., 1999, Delta Coomputation, Little Rock, 1999. Home: 509 Jill Dr Jonesboro AR 72404-8559

CHRISTIANO, PAUL P., academic administrator, civil engineering educator; b. Pitts., May 12, 1942; s. Natale Anthony and Ida Stella (Lupori) C.; m. Norene Grace DiBucci, Nov. 11, 1967; 1 child, Beth. B.S.C.E., Carnegie Inst. Tech., 1964, M.S.C.E., 1965; Ph.D. in Civil Engring., Carnegie-Mellon U., 1968. From asst. prof. to assoc. prof. U. Minn., Mpls., 1967-74; assoc. prof., then prof. Carnegie-Mellon U., Pitts., 1974—, assoc. dean of engring., 1982-86, head civil engring., 1986-89, dean engring., 1989-91, provost, 1991—. Co-author: Structural Analysis, 1986; contbr. articles to profl. jours. Mem. ASCE (Prof. of Yr. award Pitts. chpt. 1983). Republican. Roman Catholic. Home: 2176 Truxton Dr Pittsburgh PA 15241-2230 Office: Carnegie Mellon U Schenley Park Pittsburgh PA 15213

CHRISTIANS, CLIFFORD GLENN, communications educator; b. Hull, Iowa, Dec. 22, 1939; s. Arnold and Verbena Janette (Geerdes) C.; m. Priscilla Jean Kreun, June 13, 1961; children: Glenn Clifford, Ted Arnold, Paul Raymond. AB, Calvin Coll., 1961; ThM, Fuller Theol. Sem., 1965; MA, U. So. Calif., 1966; PhD, U. Ill., 1974. Dir. comms. Christian Ref. Home Ministries, Grand Rapids, Mich., 1966-70; rsch. asst. prof. comms. U. Ill., Urbana, 1974-80, rsch. assoc. prof. comms., 1980-87, rsch. prof. comms., 1987—; rsch. fellow Calvin Ctr. for Christian Scholarship, Grand Rapids, 1983-84; vis. scholar in ethics Princeton (N.J.) U., spring, 1979; inst. fellow U. Chgo., 1986-87; Pew Evangel. scholar in ethics Oxford U., spring, 1995; dir. Inst. Rsch. Comms., Urbana, 1987—. Co-author: Jacques Ellul: Interpretive Essays, 1981, Good News: Social Ethics and The Press, 1993, Media Ethics: Cases and Moral Reasoning, 1995, Communication Ethics and Universal Values, 1997; editor: Critical Studies in Mass Communication, 1992-95. Bd. dirs. Empty Tomb, Inc., Champaign, Ill., 1986—; elder Christian Ref. Ch., Champaign, 1974-82; bd. dirs. Univ. YMCA, Champaign, 1974-77, Judah Christian Sch., Champaign, 1984-90. Rsch. fellow Program for Cultural Values and Ethics, 1990. Mem. Soc. for Philosophy and Tech., Assn. for Edn. in Journalism and Mass Comm. (chair qualitative studies divsn. 1980-81), Internat. Assn. Mass Comm. Rsch. (program co-chair 1991-94), Ellul Studies Forum, Speech Comm. Assn. Democrat. Avocations: fishing, travel, reading. Home: U Ill Inst Communications Rsch 1002 W William St Champaign IL 61821 Office: U Ill Communications Dept 505 E Armory Ave Champaign IL 61820-6237

CHRISTIANSEN, ANDREW P., Internet consulting business executive; b. Barre City, Vt., July 9, 1953; s. Stanley Lee and Joyce (Rowland) C.; m. Jennifer Dow Zollner, 1987; 2 children. BA, BM, Lawrence U., 1976. Active Dem. Town Com., 1978-88; justice of peace East Montpelier, Vt., 1980-92; co-chmn. Vt. Rainbow Coalition, 1986-87; state rep. dist. 2 Vt. Ho. of Reps., 1987-97; owner Old Barn Vt. LLC, 1997—; dairy farmer, East Montpelier, 1958-86; rschr. dept. psychology Lawrence U., Appleton, Wis., 1971-76; piano tchr., Ctrl. Vt., 1976—. Mem. Danish Brotherhood Am., Am. Soc. Dowsers, Rural Vt., Vt. Hist. Soc. Address: 470 Hammett Hill Rd East Montpelier VT 05651-4034

CHRISTIANSEN, DAVID K., hospital administrator; b. Logan, Utah, Sept. 10, 1952; s. John R. and Lucele (Kartchner) C.; m. Cynthia Ann Kutsko, July 28, 1982. BS, Brigham Young U., 1977; M of Health Care Adminstrn., U. Ala., 1979. Purchasing asst. McDonald Health Clinic, Provo, Utah, 1975-77; adminstrv. resident Bapt.-Montclair Hosp., Birmingham, Ala., 1978-79, adminstrv. asst., 1979-80; asst. adminstr. Lakeview Cmty. Hosp., Bountiful, Utah, 1980-83; adminstr. Shasta Gen. Hosp., Redding, Calif., 1983-84; chief exec. officer, Knoxville (Iowa) Community Hosp., 1984-89; chief ops. officer Med. Ctr. of Independence, Kansas City, Mo. 1989-92; CEO Newman Regional Hosp., Emporia, Kans., 1992-96; exec. v.p. MED/MAX Health Mgmt., San Diego, 1996—; cons. Ctr. Health Studies, Nashville, 1981-83; mem. faculty Ctr. for Health Studies/Hosp. Corp. Am., Nashville, 1980-82. Explorer advisor Boy Scouts Am., Birmingham, 1977-80; campaign coordinator United Way, Bountiful, 1983; exec. bd. dirs. Boy Scouts Am., Topeka, Kans., 1994-96. Named Outstanding Young Man of Am., U.S. Jaycees, 1982. Fellow Am. Coll. Healthcare Execs.; mem. Knoxville C. of C. (chmn. commerce com. 1986-87), Emporia Kans. C. of C. (bd. dirs. 1994-96). Lodge: Rotary (membership chmn. Redding 1984, knoxville bd. dirs. 87-89). Address: PO Box 520435 Salt Lake City UT 84152-0435 Office: MED/MAX Health Mgmt 968 Emerald St Ste 237 San Diego CA 92109-2709

CHRISTIANSEN, DONALD DAVID, electrical engineer, editor, publishing consultant; b. Plainfield, N.J., June 23, 1927; s. David Carsten and Rita (Holmes) C.; m. Joyce Ifill, Jan. 1, 1951; children: Jacqueline, Jill. BEE, Cornell U., Ithaca, N.Y., 1950; postgrad., Mass. Inst. Tech., 1951, 54, U. Wis., Madison, 1966, 68, 71. Registered profl. engr., Mass. Engr. Philco Corp., Phila., 1948-50, CBS, Danvers, Lowell and Newburyport, Mass., 1950-62; solid-state editor Electronic Design, Hayden Pub. Co., N.Y.C., 1962-63; sr. editor EEE-Circuit Design Engring. Mactier Pub. Co., N.Y.C., 1963-66; sr. assoc. editor Electronics McGraw-Hill Pub. Co., N.Y.C., 1966, sr. editor, 1966-67, assoc. mng. editor, 1967-68, editor-in-chief, 1968-70, mgr. planning, devel. electronics publs., 1970-71; gen. mgr. Electronics in Medicine, 1971; editor and pub. Spectrum jour. of IEEE, N.Y.C., 1971-93, editor emeritus, 1993—, chmn. editorial bd., 1972-93; IEEE rep. to UN, 1974-87; pres. Informatica, Huntington, N.Y., 1993—; lectr. Newark Coll. Engring., 1967, U. Mich., Ann Arbor, 1973, Walla Walla (Wash.) Coll., 1973, Ga. Inst. Tech., 1976, NASA Goddard Space Flight Ctr., 1981, Cornell U., 1982, Disting. lectr. Purdue U., 1986; cons. Bur. of Census, Dept. Commerce, NSF; mem. NRC Com. on Edn. and Utilization of the Engr.; mem. elec. engring. adv. com. Worcester Poly. Inst.; mem. AIP mag. policy com., 1996-98. Editor: Electronics Engineers' Handbook, 4th edit., 1997, Engineering Excellence, 1987; mem. publ. com. Cornell Alumni News mag., 1986-91; contbr. articles to profl. jours. Bd. dirs. YMCA, Newburyport, Mass., 1962, Broadband Info. Svcs., N.Y.C., 1970-87, L.I. Mus. Sci. and Tech., 1993-96. With USN, WWII. Recipient medal and citation for advancement of culture Flanders Acad. Art, Sci. and Lit., citation Folio mag., 1991. Fellow IEEE (co-founder, charter exec. com. chpt. 1958, Centennial medal, Gruenwald award), World Acad. Art and Sci., Radio Club of Am.; mem. Nat. Press Club, N.Y. Acad. Sci., Cornell Soc. Engrs., Council Engring. and Sci. Soc. Execs., Am. Soc. Assn. Execs., Am. Soc. Mag. Editors, Soc. Nat. Assn. Publs. (dir. 1976-79, chmn. editorial com. 1976-79, pres. 1981-83), N.Y. Bus. Press Editors (dir. 1978-79), Cornell Engring. Alumni Council, Delta Club, Union Internationale de la Presse Radiotechnique et Electronique, Deadline Club, Nat. Conf. Electronics in Medicine (chmn. 1971), Soc. for History Tech., Jovians, Antique Wireless Assn., Franklin Inst., Royal Instn., Newcomen Soc., Eta Kappa Nu (chmn., outstanding elec. engr. award 1976-78, dir. 1982-84, eminent mem., chmn. Vladimir Karapetoff award 1991—), Mu Sigma Tau, Sigma Delta Chi. Office: Informatica 434 W Main St Huntington NY 11743-3247

CHRISTIANSEN, JAMES EDWARD, agricultural educator; b. Douglas, Ariz., Sept. 1, 1930; s. Felix Lawrence and Ada Naomi (Squire) C.; m. Jean McInnes, Dec. 25, 1950; children: James Lawrence, Bruce John. BS, U. Ariz., 1951, M Agrl. Edn., 1957; PhD, Ohio State U., 1965. Tchr. vocat. agriculture Tolleson (Ariz.) Union High Sch., 1954-57, Snowflake (Ariz.) Union High Sch., 1957-58, Tempe (Ariz.) Union High Sch., 1958-61; project mgr. Near East Found., Resht, Iran, 1961-63; asst. instr. Ohio State U., Columbus, 1964; cons. ctr. for vocat.-tech. edn. Nat. Ctr. for Rsch. in Vocat.-Tech. Edn., Columbus, 1965; asst. prof. U. Fla., Gainesville, 1966-68; prof. Tex. A&M U., College Station, 1968—; cons. agrl. edn. US/AID, San Jose, Costa Rica, 1967, 86, Asuncion, Paraguay, 1983, Belize, 1990, Malaysia, 1992, El Salvador, 1994. Author: Exploring Agriculture, 6th ed., 1984, 5th ed., 1979; contbr. articles to profl. jours. Elder A&M Presbyn. Ch., College Station, 1969-72, 81-83, 90-92. Mem. Am. Vocat. Assn. (resolutions com. 1988-91), Am. Assn. Tchr. Educators in Agr. (treas. 1977-80, chmn. editing-mng. bd. 1973-76, Disting. Svc. award 1985), Assn. for Internat. Agrl. and Extension Edn. (chmn. constn. and bylaws 1986-87, 96-99), Vocat. Agr. Tchrs. Assn. Tex. (Outstanding tchr. educator award 1979, Disting. Svc. award 1992), Kiwanis (sec. Snowflake chpt. 1957), Phi Beta Delta, Phi Delta Kappa, Phi Kappa Phi. Republican. Avocations: landscape and instructional photography, rifle target shooting, archaeology. Office: Tex A&M U Dept Agrl Edu College Station TX 77843-2116

CHRISTIANSEN, JAY DAVID, lawyer; b. Slayton, Minn., Mar. 22, 1952; s. Holger K. and Dagny (Fjelstad) C.; m. Marilyn Morse, Aug. 10, 1974; children: Tyler, Carrie, Jayne. BA, Luther Coll., 1974; JD, Vanderbilt U., 1977. Ptnr. Faegre & Benson, Mpls., 1977—. Mem. ABA (chair 1997-99, health law sect.), Nat. Health Lawyers Assn., Am. Acad. Hosp. Attys., Order of the Coif. Avocations: golf, canoeing. Office: Faegre & Benson 90 S 7th St Ste 2200 Minneapolis MN 55402-3901

CHRISTIANSEN, JOHN REES, sociologist, educator; b. Wales, Utah, Aug. 17, 1927; s. ElRay Lavar and Lewella (Rees) C.; m. Lucele Kartchner, Sept. 18, 1951; children: David, Steven, ElRay, Carol, Daniel. B.S., Utah State U., 1949, M.S., 1952; Ph.D., U. Wis., 1955. Asst. rural sociologist U. Ky., 1954-55; social sci. analyst Dept. Agr., 1955-57; mem. faculty Brigham Young U., 1957-92, prof. Social work and sociology, 1963-92; ch. svc. missionary Ch. Jesus Christ of Latter-Day Saints, 1993-94; vis. prof. Tex. A & M Univ., 1963-64, Mich. State U., 1969; vis. prof. U. Wis., 1970-71, asst. dir. Sch. of Social Work, 1990-91, prof. emeritus, 1992—; collaborator Dept. Agr., 1963-65; cons. Teamwork Found., 1967-69, Rivkin/Carson, 1973, Center for Planning and Research, 1978, Far West Labs., 1978-83. Author: Introductory Sociology, 1963, Disaster Preparedness, 1984, Emergency Preparedness: A Handbook for Families, 1984; also monographs, articles.; Bull. index editor: Rural Sociology, 1969-76. With USNR, 1945-47. Fellow Am. Sociol. Assn.; mem. Am. Civil Def. Assn., Rural Sociol. Soc., Sigma Xi, Phi Kappa Phi, Pi Kappa Alpha, Alpha Kappa Delta. Home: 1161 Holly Cir Provo UT 84604-3600*

CHRISTIANSEN, KEITH ALLAN, lawyer; b. Madison, Wis., Dec. 14, 1943; s. Herman Louis and Faith Louise (Haase) C.; m. Sheila Irene Stangel, Apr. 11, 1966; children: Douglas, Jeffrey. BS, U. Wis., 1965, JD, 1968. Bar: Wis. 1968, Fla. 1973, U.S. Dist. Ct. (ea. dist.) Wis. 1968. Assoc. Foley & Lardner, Milw., 1968-74, ptnr., 1975—. Co-author: Marital Property Law in Wisconsin, 1984, supplements. Active Potawatomi Coun. Boy Scouts Am. (past pres.), 1975—; v.p. Ctrl. Region Boy Scouts. Am., 1992—. Fellow Am. Coll. Trust & Estate Counselors; mem. Mid-winter Estate Planning Clinic, Estate Counselors Forum. Republican. Office: Foley & Lardner 777 E Wisconsin Ave Ste 3800 Milwaukee WI 53202-5367

CHRISTIANSEN, LARRY K., college president. AA, North Iowa Area C.C.; BA in Bus. Edn., U. Northern Iowa; MS in Ednl. Adminstrn., Drake U.; DEd, U. N.D. Distributive edn. coord., chmn. bus. dept. Perry (Iowa) Cmty. H.S., 1967-74; assoc. prof., chmn. bus. divsn. U. Minn. Tech. Coll., Crookston, 1974-82; dean adminstrv. svc., acting dean of instrn., assoc. dean Glendale C.C.; pres. Mesa C.C.; chair acad. internat. exec. adv. bd. Nat. C.C.; mem. Megacorp Bd.; adv. bd. Nat. Campus Compact Cmty.; spkr. in field. Author: (with others) A Case Approach, 1980; co-author: To the Future and Counselor's Guide to the Future. Pres. East Valley Partnership Bd.; cabinet chair Mesa United Way, 1996; campaign chair Maricopa C.C. Dist. Mem. Mesa C. of C. (nat. campus compact cmty. adv. bd.), Mesa Baseline Rotary, Nat. Assn. of Distributive Edn. Tchrs. Office: 1833 West Southern Ave Mesa AZ 85202

CHRISTIANSEN, MARK D., lawyer; b. Olney, Tex., June 10, 1955; s. Leon H. and Doris J. (Jennings) C.; m. Jane M. Evenson, Mar. 5, 1988. BA, U. Okla., 1977, JD, 1980. Bar: U.S. Dist. Ct. (we. dist.) Okla. 1984, U.S. Dist. Ct. (ea. dist.) Okla. 1993, U.S. Ct. Appeals (10th cir.) 1987. Assoc. Crowe & Dunlevy, Oklahoma City, 1980-85, mem., 1986—. Editor: The Oil and Gas Reporter. Mem. ABA (vice chmn. publs. oil and natural gas exploration and prodn. com. 1985—), Oklahoma City Mineral Lawyers Soc. (pres. 1989-90), Okla. Bar Assn. Home: 7202 Waverly Ave Oklahoma City OK 73120-1214 Office: Crowe & Dunlevy 1800 Mid America Tower 20 N Broadway Ave Ste 1800 Oklahoma City OK 73102-8273

CHRISTIANSEN, NORMAN JUHL, retired newspaper publisher; b. Isle, Minn., Apr. 30, 1923; s. Arthur Theodore and Ingeborg Hansena (Clemensen) C.; m. Margaret Eleanor Whorton, June 13, 1948; children—Gregory Lowell, Susan Joy. B.A. in Journalism, Drake U., Des Moines, 1947. Reporter Bloomington (Ill.) Pantagraph, 1947; spl. agt. FBI, 1948-54; mem. labor relations staff Am. Newspaper Pubs. Assn., 1954-59; with Gannett Newspapers, 1959-67; asst. gen. mgr. Westchester-Rockland Newspaper Group, 1965-67; with Knight-Ridder Newspapers, Inc., 1967-80; group v.p. ops. Knight-Ridder Newspapers, Inc., Miami, Fla., 1975-80; pres., pub. Wichita (Kans.) Eagle and Beacon, 1980-87. Bd. dirs. William Allen White Found. Served with AUS, 1943-45. Home: 1136 Cobblestone Ct Fort Collins CO 80525-2832

CHRISTIANSEN, PATRICK T., lawyer; b. Mpls., 1947. BSEE summa cum laude, U. Notre Dame, 1969; JD, Harvard U., 1972. Bar: Fla. 1972, Minn. 1974, U.S. Tax Ct. 1977, U.S. Supreme Ct. 1980. Mem. Akerman, Senterfitt & Eidson P.A., Orlando, Fla. Chmn. bd. Orlando Mus. Art; mem., bd. dirs. The Greater Orlando C. of C., Jobs and Edn. Partnership; chmn. Orange County Transp. Roundtable; mem. Orange County Blue Ribbon Commn., steering com., chmn. transp. com.; bd. dirs. United Arts Cen. Fla., Orlando Downtown Devel. Bd. Mem. ABA (sects. on bus. law, taxation, real property), Fla. Bar (trial lawyers sect., co-chmn. land trust com. real property, probate and trust law sect. 1978-82, dir. real property divsn. 1982-84, vice chmn. 1984-85, chmn. 1985-86, vice-chmn. UCC subcom. corp., banking and bus. law sect. 1979-84, bd. govs. young lawyers sect. 1981-83), Am. Coll. Real Estate Lawyers, Minn. State Bar Assn., Orange County Bar Assn. Office: Akerman Senterfitt & Eidson PA 17th Fl Citrus Ctr PO Box 231 255 S Orange Ave Orlando FL 32801-3445

CHRISTIANSEN, PEGGY, principal. Prin. Sequoia Elem. Sch., Santa Rosa, Calif., Blinkley Elem. Sch., Santa Rosa, Calif., 1995—. Recipient Elem. Sch. Recognition award U.S. Dept. Edn., 1989-90. Office: Blinkley Elem Sch 4965 Canyon Dr Santa Rosa CA 95409-3204

CHRISTIANSEN, RICHARD DEAN, newspaper editor; b. Berwyn, Ill., Aug. 1, 1931; s. William Edward and Louise Christine (Dethlefs) C. BA, Carleton Coll., Northfield, Minn., 1953; postgrad., Harvard U., 1954; LHD (hon.), DePaul U., 1988. Reporter, critic, editor Chgo. Daily News, 1957-73, 74-78; editor Chicagoan mag., 1973-74; critic-at-large Chgo. Tribune, 1978-83, entertainment editor, 1983-91, chief critic, sr. writer, 1991—. Served to cpl. U.S. Army, 1954-56. Recipient award Chgo. Newspaper Guild, 1969, 74, Joseph Jefferson award, 1996, Excellence in the Arts award DePaul U., 1998; named to Chgo. Journalism hall of Fame, 1998. Mem. Am. Theatre Critics Assn., Chgo. Acad. TV Arts and Scis., Phi Beta Kappa, Sigma Delta Chi. Republican. Lutheran. Clubs: Headline (Chgo.), Arts (Chgo.) (dir.). Office: Chgo Tribune Co 435 N Michigan Ave Chicago IL 60611-4066

CHRISTIANSEN, RICHARD LOUIS, orthodontics educator, research director, former dean; b. Denison, Iowa, Apr. 1, 1935; s. John Cornelius and Rosa Katherine C.; m. Nancy Marie Norman, June 24, 1956; children—Mark Richard, David Norman, Laura Marie. D.D.S., U. Iowa, 1959; M.S.D., Ind. U., Indpls., 1964; Ph.D., U. Minn., 1970. Prin. investigator Nat. Inst. Dental Research NIH, Bethesda, Md., 1970-73, chief craniofacial anomalies program br., 1973-81, dir. extramural Nat. Inst. Dental Research, 1981-82; prof. dept. orthodontics U. Mich., Ann Arbor, 1982-87, dean, Sch. Dentistry and dir. W.K. Kellogg Found. Inst., 1982-87; organizer state-of-the -art workshops in field of craniofacial anomalies and other aspects of oral health; founder Internat. Union Schs. Oral Health, 1985; organizer oral health conf. in Poland, 1989, Jordan, 1995. Contbr. chpts. to books and articles to profl. jours. Chmn. Region III United Way, U. Mich., Ann Arbor, 1984; chmn., v.p. Trinity Luth. Ch., Rockville, Md., 1975; v.p. and chmn. planning task force Trinity Luth. Ch., Ann Arbor, chmn. bd. Sequois Sr. Housing; bd. dirs. Luth. Soc. Svcs. Mich., 1997—. With USPHS, 1959-82. Recipient Commendation medal USPHS, 1980; Cert. of Recognition NIH, 1982, numerous internat. awards. Fellow Internat. Coll. Dentists, Am. Coll. Dentists, Pierre Fauchard Acad.; mem. Am. Assn. Orthodontists, Am. Assn. Dental Sch., ADA (rsch. coun.), Mich. Dental Assn., Am. Assn. Dental Research (dir. craniofacial biology group 1975-79, v.p. 1979-80, pres. 1981-82), Omicron Kappa Upsilon (mem. numerous nat. and internat. coms. and bds.). Avocations: reading, jogging, tennis, sailing, econs. Home: 5612 N Dixboro Rd Ann Arbor MI 48105-9415

CHRISTIANSEN, ROY HVIDKAER, lawyer; b. Detroit, Dec. 24, 1932; s. Rasmus H. and Gudrun (Lohmann-Sorensen) C.; m. Barbara L. Stauffer, June 9, 1956; children: Kathryn G. Hardy, Patricia L. Kalbfleich, Kai H., Karl H. BA, U. Mich., 1954, JD, 1957. Bar: Mich. 1957, U.S. Dist. Ct. (ea. dist.) Mich. 1957, U.S. Supreme Ct. 1962, U.S. Ct. Appeals (6th cir.) 1966, U.S. Dist. Ct. (we. dist.) Mich. 1989. Assoc. Erickson, Dyll, Marentary & Van Alsburg, Detroit, 1958-59; gen. counsel Transam. Freight Lines, Inc., Detroit, 1959-71; of counsel Kerr, Russell and Weber, Detroit, 1972-98. Judge City of Huntington Mcpl. Ct., Huntington Woods, Mich., 1969-76, City of Detroit Recorders Ct., 1971-73; past mayor, councilman City of Huntington Woods. Fielding H. Yost scholar. Fellow Am. Coll. Trial Lawyers, Mich. State Bar Found.; mem. ABA, Mich. Bar Assn., Detroit Bar Assn., Oakland County Bar Assn. Republican. Presbyterian. Avocations: travel, fishing, music, gardening, sports observing. Office: Kerr Russell and Weber 500 Woodward Ave Ste 2500 Detroit MI 48226-3427

CHRISTIANSEN, WALTER HENRY, aeronautics educator; b. McKees Rocks, Pa., Dec. 14, 1934; s. Walter Henry and Elizabeth (Miller) C.; m. Joan Marilyn Swisler, Aug. 5, 1960; children: Walter, Audrey. BS in Mech. Engring., Carnegie Inst. Tech., 1956; MS in Aero. Engring., Calif. Inst. Tech., 1957, PhD, 1961. Sr. scientist Jet Propulsion Lab., Pasadena, Calif., 1961-62, 1963-67; rsch. assoc. prof. aero. and aeronautics U. Wash., Seattle, 1967-70, assoc. prof., 1970-74, prof., 1974—; dept. chmn. U. Wash., 1992—; cons. Boeing Sci. Rsch. Lab., 1967-69, Math. Scis. N.W., 1970-85, Spectra Tech., 1985-88, 91. Contbr. articles to profl. jours.; patentee in field. Com. mem. Directions for 70's Bellevue (Wash.) Sch. Dist., 1970. Served to capt. U.S. Army, 1961-63. Dept. Def. grantee, 1970-91, NSF grantee, 1977, 80, NASA grantee, 1980-89; Mesa Machine fellow, 1952-56, Convair fellow, 1958, Boeing fellow, 1960. Fellow AIAA (Pacific N.W. chpt. Sect. award 1972); mem. Am. Phys. Soc., Sigma Xi, Tau Beta Pi, Pi Tau Sigma, Theta Xi. Home: 1405 Evergreen Point Rd Medina WA 98039-3133 Office: Dept Aero & Astro Box 352400 Univ Wash Seattle WA 98195

CHRISTIANSON, GERYLD B., government relations consultant; b. Boyd, Minn., Dec. 31, 1934; m. Sue Singer, July 9, 1960; children: Stephen, Alexander. BA in Internat. Rels., U. Minn., 1957; postgrad., Johns Hopkins U., 1967-68. Fgn. svc. officer Dept. State, NATO Office, Bur. European Affaira, various fgn. locations, 1958-75; fgn. policy advisor Senator Claiborne Pell, Washington, 1975-81; minority staff dir. Senate Fgn. Rels. Com., Washington, 1981-87, staff dir., 1987-95; sr. counselor The Evans Group, Ltd., Washington, 1995, 97—; v.p. Jefferson Waterman Internat., Washington, 1995-97. Served with USAR, 1957-63. Mem. Coun. on Fgn. Rels., Internat. Inst. for Strategic Studies (London). Democrat. Episcopalian. Avocations: collecting political buttons, tennis. Home: 8716 Mary Lee Ln Annandale VA 22003-3659

CHRISTIANSON, JAMES DUANE, real estate developer; b. Bismarck, N.D., Aug. 18, 1952; s. Adolph M. and Elizabeth M. (Barnes) C.; m. Deborah Jaeger, Oct. 10, 1987. Student, Bismarck Jr. Coll., 1970, 1971-72, U. N.D., 1971. Lic. pvt. pilot; lic. realtor. Gen. mgr. and supr. Nutrition Search, Bismarck, 1974-76; gen. mgr. Home Still, Inc., Bismarck, 1976-78; v.p. Good Heart Assocs., Bismarck, 1978-82; pres. N. W. Devel. Group, Bismarck, 1982—, First Realty Bismark Inc., 1990-93, N.W. Realty Group, Bismarck, 1994—; chmn. bd. Basin State Bank, Stanford, Mont., 1986-94; mem., vice chair Ctr. City Partnership, 1994—; mng. prin. N.W. Lodging Group, LLC. Supr. editor: Nutrition Almanac, 1975. Mem. Bismarck Centennial Com., 1986-89, Bismarck Parking Authority, 1996—. Recipient Outstanding Citizen award Mayor and City Commn., Bismarck, 1982. Mem. Downtown Bus. and Profl. Assn. (bd. dirs. 1989—, pres. 1991). Avocations: traveling, reading, computers, golf. Office: N W Devel Group Inc PO Box 1097 Bismarck ND 58502-1097

CHRISTIANSON, ROGER GORDON, biology educator; b. Santa Monica, Calif., Oct. 31, 1947; s. Kyle C. and Ruby K. (Parker) C.; m. Angela Diane Rey, Mar. 3, 1967; children: Lisa Marie, David Scott, Stephen Peter. BA in Cell and Organismal Biology, U. Calif., Santa Barbara, 1969, MA in Biology, 1971, PhD in Biology, 1976. Faculty assoc. U. Calif., Santa Barbara, 1973-79, staff rsch. assoc., 1979-80; asst. prof. So. Oreg. U., Ashland, 1980-85, assoc. prof., 1985-93, prof., 1993—, coord. gen. biology program, 1980—, chmn. biology dept., 1996, 97—; instr. U. Calif., Santa Barbara, summers 1976, 78, 80. Contbr. articles to profl. jours. Active Oreg. Shakespeare Festival Assn., Ashland, 1983-87; mem. bikeway com. Ashland City Coun., 1986-88; coord. youth program 1st Bapt. Ch., Ashland, 1981-85, mem. ch. life commn., 1982-88, bd. deacons, 1993-95, mem. outreach com., 1994, 95; organizer Bike Oreg., 1982-92, Frontline h.s. staff, 1985—, Mex. Orphanage short-term mission work, 1986—; ofcl. photographer Ashland H.S. Booster Club, 1987-92; youth leader jr. and sr. H.S. students Grace Ch., Santa Barbara, Calif., 1973-80. Mem. AAAS (chair Pacific divsn. edn. sect. 1985—, coun. Pacific divsn. 1985—, chair Pacific divsn. student awards com. 1997—, exec. com. Pacific divsn. 1998—), Am. Mus. Natural History, Oreg. Sci. Tchrs. Assn., Assn. for Biology Lab. Edn., Sigma Xi (chpt. membership com. 1998—), Beta Beta Beta. Republican. Avocations: youth work, sports, photography, multimedia presentations, amateur radio operator. Home: 430 Reiten Dr Ashland OR 97520-8762 Office: Southern Oregon U Dept Biology 1250 Siskiyou Blvd Ashland OR 97520-5010

CHRISTIANSON, STANLEY DAVID, corporate executive; b. Chgo., Dec. 8, 1931; s. Stanley Olai and Emma Josephine (Johnson) D.; m. Elin J. Ballantyne, July 25, 1959; children: Erica Joanna, David Ballantyne. BS, U. Ill., 1954; MBA, U. Chgo., 1960. Auditor Price Waterhouse & Co., Chgo., 1956-58; asst. to controller Miehle-Goss-Dexter, Inc., Chgo., 1960-67, v.p. adminstrn. Goss Div., 1967-69; dir. mgmt. systems MGD Graphics Systems-N.Am. Rockwell (formerly Miehle-Goss-Dexter), Chgo., 1969-70; v.p. fin. Duchossois/Thrall Group (formerly Thrall Car Mfg. Co.), Chicago Heights, Elmhurst, Ill., 1970-83; pres., vice chmn., CEO, bd. dirs. Thrall Enterprises, Inc., Chgo., 1983—; bd. dirs. Midwestern Univ., chmn., 1997-98, mem., 1992—. Chmn., bd. govs. Internat. House, U. Chgo., 1988—; mem. Hobart (Ind.) Plan Commn., 1986-92, pres., 1988-92. Capt. U.S. Army, 1954-56. Home: 141 Beverly Blvd Hobart IN 46342-4346 Office: Thrall Enterprises Inc 181 W Madison St Chicago IL 60602-4510

CHRISTIE, DAVID GEORGE, insurance company executive; b. Glen Ridge, N.J., June 25, 1930; s. Francis Johnston and Catherine Fisher (Somes) C.; student Rutgers U., 1950-52; m. Diane Grace Wettyen, Mar. 23, 1950; children—Lindsey Diane, Mark Wettyen, Meredith Leigh. Asst. U.S. mgr. Union Re-ins. Co., Zurich, Switzerland, U.S. Br., 1956-64; v.p. Am. Re-Ins. Co., N.Y.C., 1964-71; v.p. Towers, Perrin Forster & Crosby Inc., N.Y.C., 1971-78; sr. v.p., dir. Duncanson & Holt Inc., N.Y.C., 1979-83; pres. Fothergill & Hartung Ltd., 1984-89; sr. v.p. Willcox, Inc., Phila., 1989-91; chmn. Reinsurance Cons. Princeton (N.J.), Inc. 1991. With U.S. Army, 1953-54. Republican. Presbyterian. Home: 49 Constitution Hl W Princeton NJ 08540-6774 Office: 371 Nassau St Princeton NJ 08540-4613

CHRISTIE, DONALD MELVIN, JR., physician; b. Lewiston, Maine, May 5, 1942; s. Donald Melvin and Dorothy Carolyn (Doble) C. AB, U. Rochester, 1964, MD, 1968; Diplome de litt. francaise, U. Paris., 1963. Diplomate Am. Bd. Internal Medicine, cert. of added qualifications in sports medicine. Med. intern U. Iowa Hosps. and Clinics, Iowa City, 1968-69, resident, 1969-70, 73, chief med. resident, 1973-74; asst. prof. preventive medicine and medicine U. Rochester (N.Y.) Sch. Medicine, N.Y., 1974-77; univ. physician, dir. clin. svcs. Princeton (N.J.) U. Health Svcs., 1977-83; internist Cmty. Health Plan, Poughkeepsie, N.Y., 1983-98; internist, dir. sports medicine St. Mary's Regional Med. Ctr., Lewiston, Maine, 1999—, St. Mary's Regional med. Ctr., Lewiston, Maine, 1999—; contract escort-interpretor (French), U.S. Dept. State, 1964-70; coord. Robert Wood Johnson Found. grant, primary care tng. evaluation U. Rochester, 1974-77. Trustee Gould Acad., Bethel, Maine, 1984—; coord. internal medicine Hudson Valley Family Practice Residency, St. Francis Hosp., Poughkeepsie, 1989-93, tchg. attending, 1990-98; dir. dept. internal medicine Vassar Bros. Hosp., Poughkeepsie, 1992-98. With M.C. U.S. Army, 1970-72. Decorated Army Commendation medal. Fellow ACP, Am. Coll. Sports Medicine; mem. APHA, Am. Med. Soc. Sports Medicine (bd. dirs. 1999—). Democrat. Home: 7 Fairview Ave Gray ME 04039-9730 Office: St Mary's Regional Med Ctr 99 Campus Ave Lewiston ME 04240

CHRISTIE, GEORGE CUSTIS, lawyer, educator, author; b. N.Y.C., Mar. 3, 1934; s. Custis and Sophie (Velimahitis) C.; m. Susan D. Monserud, Apr. 20, 1965 (div. July 1974); 1 child, Constantine George; m. Deborah D. Carnes, Dec. 20, 1974; children: Rebecca Sophia, Nicholas George. AB, Columbia U., 1955, JD, 1957; diploma in internat. law (Fulbright scholar), Cambridge (Eng.) U., 1962; S.J.D., Harvard U., 1966. Bar: N.Y. 1957, D.C.

1958. Assoc. Covington & Burling, Washington, 1958-60; Ford Found. fellow in law teaching Harvard U., 1960-61; assoc. prof. law U. Minn., Mpls., 1962-65; prof. law U. Minn., 1965-66; asst. gen. counsel for Near E. and S. Asia, AID, Dept. State, 1966-67; prof. law Duke U., 1967-79, James B. Duke prof. law, 1979—; vis. lectr. U. Witwatersrand, South Africa, 1980, Fudan U., China, U. Otago, New Zealand, 1985; fellow Nat. Humanities Center, 1980-81; scholar-in-residence McGuire, Woods & Battle, Richmond, Va., 1983, vis. Freda Alverson prof. law George Washington U., spring 1988; vis. prof. law Northwestern U., 1991-92. Author: Jurisprudence: Text and Readings on the Philosophy of Law, 1973, 2d edit. (with P. Martin), 1995, The Sum and Substance of the Law of Torts, 1980, Law, Norms & Authority, 1982, Cases and Materials on the Law of Torts, 1983, 2d edit. (with J. Meeks), 1990, 3d edit. (with others), 1997. Served with U.S. Army, 1957. Mem. ABA, Am. Law Inst., Am. Soc. Internat. Law, Phi Beta Kappa. Democrat. Greek Orthodox. Home: 17 Stoneridge Cir Durham NC 27705-5510 Office: Duke U Sch Law PO Box 90360 Durham NC 27708-0360

CHRISTIE, HANS FREDERICK, retired utility company subsidiaries executive, consultant; b. Alhambra, Calif., July 10, 1933; s. Andreas B. and Sigrid (Falk-Jorgensen) C.; m. Susan Earley, June 14, 1957; children: Brenda Lynn, Laura Jean. BS in Fin., U. So. Calif., 1957, MBA, 1964. Treas. So. Calif. Edison Co., Rosemead, 1970-75, v.p., 1975-76, sr. v.p., 1976-80, exec. v.p., 1980-84, pres., dir., 1984-87; pres., chief exec. officer The Mission Group (non-utility subs. SCE Corp.), Seal Beach, Calif., 1987-89, ret., 1989, cons., 1989—; bd. dirs. L.A. Ducommun Inc., L.A., UntramarDiamond Shamrock Corp., C.T., Am. Mut. Fund, Inc., AMCAP, Am. Variable Ins., I.H.O.P. Corp., AECom Tech., L.A., Internat. House of Pancakes, Inc., Southwest Water Co., L.A., Smallcap World Fund, L.A., Bond Fund Am., Inc., L.A., Tax-Exempt Bond Fund Am., L.A., Ltd. Term Tax-Exempt Bond Fund Am., Am. High Income Mcpl. Bond Fund, Capital Income Builder, L.A., Capital World Bond Fund, L.A., Capital World Growth Fund, Capital World Growth and Income Fund, Intermediate Bond Fund Am., L.A., Intermediate Tax-Exempt Bond Fund Am., Capital World Growth 2d Income Fund, L.A.; trustee Cash Mgmt. Trust Am., New Economy Fund, L.A., Am. Funds Income Series, L.A., The Am. Funds Tax-Exempt Series II, Am. High Income Trust, L.A., Am. High-Inc Mun. Board Fund, Am. Variable Ins. Trust, U.S. Treasury Fund Am., L.A. Chmn. Nat. History Mus. L.A. County; bd. councillor sch. policy, planning and devel. U. So. Calif.; trustee Occidental Coll., 1984-96. With U.S. Army, 1953-55. Named Outstanding mem. Arthritis Found., L.A., 1975, Outstanding Trustee, Multiple Sclerosis Soc. So. Calif., 1979. Mem. Pacific Coast Elec. Assn. (bd. dirs. 1981-87, treas. 1975-87), L.A. C. of C. (bd. dirs. 1983-87), Calif. Club. Republican. Avocations: swimming; horseback riding; jogging. Home: 548 Paseo Del Mar Palos Verdes Estate CA 90274-1260 Office: PO Box 144 Palos Verdes Peninsula CA 90274-0144

CHRISTIE, JOSEPH FRANCIS, city planner; b. Feb. 5, 1955. BA, Coll. of Charleston, S.C., 1977, MPA, 1981. Tech. assistance mgr. B-C-D Coun. of Govts., Charleston, 1977-82; cmty. svcs. dir. Berkeley County, Moncks Corner, S.C., 1982-84; planning dir. Town of Summerville, S.C., 1984—. Email: jfc@awod.com. Office: 104 Civic Center Summerville SC 29483

CHRISTIE, JULIE, actress; b. Chukua, India, Apr. 14, 1940; d. Frank St. John and Rosemary Ramsden C. Student, Central Sch. Dramatic Art, London, Brighton Coll. Tech. Profl. Debut in Brit. TV series A is for Andromeda, 1962; (TV movies) Dadah is Death, 1988, The Railway Station Man, 1992; (TV miniseries) Karaoke, 1996; (films) Crooks Anonymous, 1962, The Fast Lady, 1963, Billy Liar, 1963, Young Cassidy, 1964, Darling, 1965, Dr. Zhivago, 1965, Farenheit 451, 1966, Far From the Madding Crowd, 1967, Petulia, 1968, In Search of Gregory, 1969, The Go-Between, 1971, McCabe and Mrs. Miller, 1971, Don't Look Now, 1974, Shampoo, 1975, Demon Seed, 1977, Heaven Can Wait, 1978, The Return of the Soldier, 1981, Heat and Dust, 1983, The Gold Diggers, 1984, The Tattoed Memory, 1986, Fathers and Sons, 1988, The Railway Station, 1991, Power, 1986, Miss Mary, 1987, La Memoire tatouél, Fools of Fortune, 1990, Hamlet, 1996, Dragonheart, 1996, Afterglow, 1997; appeared with Birmingham Repertory Co., 1963, Royal Shakespeare Co., 1964; appeared in plays Old Times, Wyndham's, 1995; other TV appearances include: Sins of the Fathers, 1988. Recipient Academy award for best actress in Darling, 1965; N.Y. Film Critics Circle award, 1965; Best Dramatic Actress Laurel award and Herald award, 1967. Office: 23 Linden Gardens, London GB W2, England also: c/o Agents Associes, 201 rue Fauburg St Honore, 75008 Paris France*

CHRISTIE, RICHARD JOEL, studio executive; b. Houston, May 14, 1962; s. Richard Joel and Winnie Jo (Jones) C.; m. Tracy Renee Taylor, Sept. 17, 1988; children: Taylor Jay, Dalton Theadore, KateLyn Renee. BFA, Sam Houston State U., 1984. Sports editor TV Sta. Channel 13, Houston, 1984-85; producer, dir., dir. photography, editor Travelview Internat., Houston, 1985-88; dir. photography, editor, camera operator Studio W, Houston, 1988-92, gen. mgr., owner, 1991—; guest speaker advanced TV prodn. class Sam Houston State U., Huntsville, Tex., 990, career day Northbrook High Sch., Houston, 1982; participant Internat. Film and TV Workshops, Rockport, Maine, 1989, 90, 91. Dir. photography, editor (PBS features) A Teddy Bear Christmas, 1990 (Silver award Houston Internat. Film Festival 1990), The Heart of Things, 1990 (Bronze award Houston Internat. Film Festival 1990), Dickens-On-The-Strand, 1990 (finalist N.Y. Film Festival 1990), New Towns, 1991 (Bronze award Houston Internat. Film Festival 1991), The Joyce Gay Report, 1988—, (local cable series) Hometown Happenings, 1988—; editor (feature films) Haunted, The Hidden Jungle; numerous internat. travel documentaries, promotional videos, indsl. videos. Active Houston Livestock Show and Rodeo, 1991. Recipient Telly award, 1990, Mercury award Nat. Media and Pub. Rels. Forum, 1989, Regional Emmy award, 1998. Mem. Houston Soc. Film and Tape Profls., Tex. Film Commn., Soc. Motion Picture and TV Engrs. Republican. Methodist. Avocations: golf, deep sea fishing, lacross, scuba diving, hunting. Home: 5242 W Bellfort St Houston TX 77035-3030 Office: Studio W 5718 Westheimer Rd Ste 1400 Houston TX 77057-5793

CHRISTIE, THOMAS PHILIP, federal agency administrator, research manager; b. Pensacola, Fla., May 28, 1934; s. Joseph Aloysius and Margaret Gabriel (Donaldson) C.; m. Kathleen Ann Lawson, June 27, 1964; children—Kevin Patrick, Stephanie Marie. BS, Spring Hill Coll., 1955; MS, NYU, 1962. Dir. analysis div. Air Force Armament Lab., Eglin AFB, Fla., 1970-73; dir. Tactical Air Div., Office of Sec. Def., Pentagon, 1973-77, dep. asst. sec. def. for operational test and evaluation, 1977-79, dep. asst. sec. def. for gen. purpose forces, 1979-86; dep. asst. sec. def. for programs and resources, 1986-88, dir. program integration, Under Sec. Def., acquisition, 1988-90; dir. Operational Evaluation Divsn. Inst. for Def. Analyses, Alexandria, Va., 1990—. Recipient Presdl. Merit Rank award, 1980, 88, Def. Disting. Svc. award, 1981, 83, 88, Presdl. Disting. Rank award, 1983. Roman Catholic. Home: 2117 Freda Dr Vienna VA 22181-3259 Office: 1801 N Beauregard St Alexandria VA 22311-1733

CHRISTIE, WALTER SCOTT, retired state official; b. Indpls., 1922; s. Walter Scott and Nina Lillian (Warfel) C.; m. Betty W. Phelps, Dec. 14, 1991 (dec.); stepchildren: Thomas G. Phelps, Judith Phelps Cummings. BS in B.A., Butler U., 1948. CPA, Ind.; cert. fin. examiner. With Roy J. Pile & Co., CPAs, Indpls., 1948-56, Howard E. Nyhart Co., Inc., actuarial cons., Indpls., 1956-62; with Ind. dept. Ind., Indpls., 1962-92, dep. commr., 1966-74, adminstrv. officer, 1974-79, sr. examiner, 1979-81, adminstrv. asst., 1981-82, chief auditor, 1982-91, ret., 1991; bd. dirs., sec., treas. Sr. Enterprises. Treas. Delta Tau/Delta House Corp., 1967—, Butler U. With AUS, 1942-45. Named to Hon. Order Ky. Cols. Mem. Ind. Assn. CPAs, Soc. Fin. Examiners (state chmn.), Indpls. Actuarial Club, Nat. Assn. Ins. Commrs. (chmn. zone IV life and health com. 1970-75), Internat. Platform Assn. Episcopalian (assoc. vestryman 1948-60), Optimist Club Downtown Indpls. (bd. dirs., Outstanding Svc. award 1985-87, Optimist of Yr. 1990). Episcopalian (assoc. vestryman 1948-60).

CHRISTINA, GRETA, book and film critic, writer, editor; b. Chgo., Dec. 31, 1961; d. Richard Hermann and Gretchen Lauranne (Wiant) M.; m. Richard Daniels, Mr. 16, 1985 (div. June 1986); life ptnr. Ingrid Nelson, Jan. 1998. BA, Reed Coll., 1983. News columnist On Our Backs, San Francisco, 1989-91; film critic San Francisco Bay Times, 1993-95, Bay Area Reporter, San Francisco, 1995, Spectator, Berkeley, 1995-99; book critic San Francisco Frontiers, 1996; mng. editor Fishnet (World Wide Web online mag.), 1996-97. Contbr. articles to newspapers, mags., jours. and anthologies. Avocations: reading, dancing.

CHRISTISON, MURIEL BRANHAM, retired art museum director emeritus, fine arts educator; b. Mpls.; d. Harold D. and Helen (Ferguson) Branham; divorced; children: Evelyn, Carolyn. BA, U. Minn., 1933, MA, 1940; diploma, U. Paris, 1936, U. Bruxelles, 1938. Grad. asst. Dept. Fine Arts U. Minn., Mpls., 1933-36; curatorial rsch. asst. Mpls. Inst. Arts, Mpls., 1936-42, head edn., 1944-47; assoc. dir. Va. Mus. Fine Arts, Richmond, 1948-61; oper. and assoc. dir. Krannert Art Mus. U. Ill., Champaign, 1962-74, dir. Krannert Art Mus., 1975-82; ret., 1982; interim dir. Muscarelle Mus., Coll. William and Mary, Williamsburg, Va., 1984-85, 94-96, mem. vis. com., 1982-96, vis. prof. fine arts, 1983-98; head program mus. studies U. Ill., 1974-82; cons. U. Tex., Austin, 1978. V.p. , Midwest Mus. Conf. Am. Assn. Mus., regional rep.; mem. Va. Mus. Fine Arts, Coll. William and Mary Found., Colonial Williamsburg Fund, 1982—. Carnegie scholar Inst. Internat. Edn., 1936; CRB fellow Belgian-Am. Edn. Found., 1938; recipient Disting. Svc. award Midwest Mus. Conf., 1982. Mem. Assn. Art Mus. Dirs. (hon.), Am. Assn. Mus. (coun. 1972-82, surveyor, examiner 1982—), Ohio Arts Coun., S.C. Arts Coun. (examiner 1984, 86), Coll. Art Assn., Soc. Preservation Va. Antiquities, Soc. Archtl. Historians (Williamsburg chpt.), Cosmopolitan Club (N.Y.C.). Home: 257 Littletown Quarter Williamsburg VA 23185-5555

CHRISTISON, WILLIAM HENRY, III, lawyer; b. Moline, Ill., Aug. 30, 1936; s. William Henry and Gladys Evelyn (Matherly) C.; m. Mary Proctor Stone, Sept. 16, 1958; children: William Henry IV, Elizabeth S., Caroline S. BA, Northwestern U., 1958; LLB, U. Iowa, 1961. Bar: Ill., Iowa 1961. Ptnr. Baymiller, Christison & Radley, Peoria, Ill., 1961-93; panel trustee in bankruptcy U.S. Bankruptcy Ct., Cen. Dist. Ill., Peoria, 1967-96; counsel Husch & Eppenberger, Peoria, 1993—; v.p. W.H.C., Inc., Moline, 1958-86, pres., 1987-95; mem. exec. com., trustee investment com. 1st Nat. Bank, Peoria, 1967-92. Mem. Peoria Sesquicentennial Commn., 1968, Peoria Downtown Redevel. Commn., 1993-95; bd. dirs. John C. Proctor Endowment, 1964-96, pres., 1972-96; bd. dirs. Ill. Masonic Youth Found., 1976-82, Meth. Med. Ctr. Found., chmn. bd., 1987-90; bd. dirs. Meth. Med. Ctr. Ill., 1984-97, chmn., 1990-92; bd. dirs. Meth. Health Svcs. Corp., 1985-97, chmn., 1990-92; dir. Great Peoria Family YMCA, 1992-96. Mem. ABA, Ill. Bar Assn. (dist. sec. 1966), Iowa Bar Assn., Peoria Bar Assn. (dir. 1968-69), Greater Peoria Legal Aid Soc. (dir. 1971-74), Peoria Hist. Soc., Peoria Country Club (bd. dirs., sec. 1992-96), Masons (master 1970), Shriners (potentate 1984), Jesters, Rotary (pres. 1979), Phi Gamma Delta, Phi Delta Phi. Home: 7103 N Willow Bend Pt Peoria IL 61614-1190 Office: 800 Central Bldg 101 SW Adams Peoria IL 61602

CHRIST-JANER, ARLAND FREDERICK, college president; b. Garland, Nebr., Jan. 27, 1922; s. William Henry and Bertha Wilhelmina (Beckman) C.-J.; m. Sally Johnson Grice, Sept. 4, 1975. BA, Carleton Coll., 1943; BD, Yale U., 1949; JD, U. Chgo., 1952; LLD (hon.), Coe Coll., 1961, Carleton Coll., 1967, Colo. Coll., 1971; LHD (hon.), Monmouth Coll., 1967, Curry Coll., 1972. Asst. to pres. Lake Erie Coll., Painesville, Ohio, 1952-53; asst. to pres. St. John's Coll., Annapolis, Md., 1953-54; tutor, treas. St. John's Coll., 1954-59, v.p., tutor, 1959-61; pres. Cornell Coll., Mt. Vernon, Iowa, 1961-67, Boston U., 1967-70, Coll. Entrance Exam. Bd., N.Y.C., 1970—73, New Coll., Sarasota, Fla., 1973-75, Stephens Coll., Columbia, Mo., 1975-83, Ringling Sch. Art and Design, Sarasota, Fla., 1984-96; interim pres. Ringling Sch. Art and Design, Sarasota, 1998-99; pres. emeritus Ringling Sch. Art and Design, Sarasota, Fla., 1996—; adv. bd. Sun Bank. Exhibiting artist. Trustee New Coll. Found., U. South Fla., Sarasota, 1973—, Marie Selby Bot. Gardens, 1984—, John and Mable Ringling Mus. Art, 1991-93; bd. dirs. Fla. Ind. Coll. Fund, 1984-96, Fla. Assn. Colls. and Univs., 1984-96. With USAAF, 1943-46. Mem. Am. Acad. Arts and Scis., Assn. Ind. Coll. Art and Design (trustee 1991-96), Nat. Assn. Schs. Art and Design (v.p. 1993-96), Ind. Colls. and Univs. Fla. (bd. dirs. 1984-96), Univ. Club Sarasota, Kiwanis, Phi Beta Kappa (hon.), Phi Delta Theta. Office: Ringling Sch Art and Design 2700 N Tamiami Trl Sarasota FL 34234-5895

CHRISTMAN, ARTHUR CASTNER, JR., scientific advisor; b. North Wales, Pa., May 11, 1922; s. Arthur Castner and Hazel Ivy (Schirmer) C.; m. Marina Ilia Diterichs, Apr. 17, 1945; children: Candace Lee Christman Canto, Tatiana Marina Christman Harvey, Deborah Ann Christman Clark, Arthur C. III, Keith Ilia, Cynthia Ellen Christman Buckwalter. BS in Physics, Pa. State U., 1944, MS, 1950. Teaching asst. dept. physics Pa. State U., State College, 1943-44, grad. asst., 1946-48; instr. dept. physics George Washington U., Washington, 1948-51; cons. U.S. Navy, 1950-51; physicist ops. research office Johns Hopkins U., Chevy Chase, Md., 1951-58; sr. physicist SRI Internat., Menlo Park, Calif., 1958-62, head ops. research group, 1962-64, dept. mgr., 1965-67, dir. dept., 1968-71, dir. tactical weapons systems, 1971-75; sci. advisor to comdg. gen. and dep. chief staff combat devel. U.S. Army tng. and doctrine command Ft. Monroe, Va., 1975-87; cons. in field, 1988—. Author numerous publs. Pres. Valle Verde Continuing Care Retirement Cmty., 1991-93, 94-95, Am. Bapt. Homes of West Assn. of CCRC Resident Presidents, 1991-92; mem. bd. mgrs. fin. com. Valle Verde, 1988—; mem. Valle Verde Adv. Bd., 1997—; bd. dirs. Am. Bapt. Homes of the West, 1997—, Ctrl. Coast Commn. for Sr. Citizens Ara Agy. on Aging, 1993; umpire Palo Alto Little League, Calif., 1962-72. Lt. USNR, 1944-46, PTO. Decorated Meritorious Civilian Service award Dept. Army, 1983, Exceptional Civilian Service award Dept. Army, 1987; recipient Presdl. Rank, 1985. Fellow AAAS; mem. Am. Phys. Soc., Inst. for Ops. Rsch. and the Mgmt. Scis. (U.S. del. internat. confs. Operational Rsch., France 1960, Norway 1963, U.S. 1966, Ireland 1972), Santa Barbara Lawn Bowls Club (bd. dirs. 1990-93), MacKenzie Park Lawn Bowls Club, Sigma Xi, Sigma Pi Sigma, Delta Chi (chpt. pres.). Republican. Baptist (deacon, trustee). Avocations: golf, swimming, tennis, bowling, photography. Home and Office: 900 Calle De Los Amigos Apt W8 Santa Barbara CA 93105-4407

CHRISTMAN, BRUCE LEE, lawyer; b. Bethlehem, Pa., Apr. 1, 1955; s. Raymond J. Jr. and Irene May (Bowman) C.; m. Lynn Eloise Brodt, Oct. 11, 1980; children: Jennifer Lynn, Amy Nicole. BA, Coll. William and Mary, 1977; JD, U. Pa., 1980. Bar: Va. 1980, U.S. Ct. Appeals (4th cir.) 1980, U.S. Dist. Ct. (ea. dist.) Va. 1980. Assoc. Hunton & Williams, Richmond, Va., 1980-84; prin., ptnr. Hazel & Thomas, P.C., Fairfax, Va., 1984—; adj. prof. George Mason Sch. Law; bd. dirs. Luth. Social Svcs. Officer ch. coun., mem. exec. com., trustee St. Andrew Luth. Ch., Centreville, Va., 1988; mem. Leadership Fairfax Class of 1993, bd. dirs. 1997. Mem. Va. State Bar Assn., Phi Beta Kappa, Omicron Delta Kappa, Kappa Sigma. Democrat. Avocations: tennis, basketball, swimming, bicycling, camping. Home: 13610 Flintwood Pl Herndon VA 20171-3331 Office: Hazel & Thomas PC 3110 Fairview Park Dr Falls Church VA 22042-4503

CHRISTMAN, DANIEL WILLIAM, military officer; b. Youngstown, Ohio, May 5, 1943; m. Susan Browning; children: Carin, Catherine. Grad., U.S. Mil. Acad., West Point, N.Y., 1965; M in Civil Engring. and Pub. Affairs, Princeton U., 1969; JD, George Washington U., 1986; grad., Army Command/Gen. Staff Coll., Nat. War Coll. Commd. 2d lt. U.S. Army; co. comdr. 2d Engr. Bn., Changpo-Ri, Korea, 1966, 326th Engr. Bn., Hue, Vietnam, 1969-70; staff asst. Nat. Security Coun. The White House, Washington, 1975-76; staff officer Office of Dep. Chief of Staff for Ops. Dept. of Army, Washington, 1976-78; comdr. Savannah (Ga.) dist. U.S. Army Corps of Engrs., 1984-86; comdg. gen. U.S. Army Engr. Ctr. Ft. Leonard Wood (Mo.) Commandant U.S. Army Engr. Sch., 1991-93; U.S. rep. NATO Mil. Com., Brussels, 1993-94; asst. to chmn. Joint Chiefs of Staff, Washington, 1994-96; supt. U.S. Mil. Acad., West Point, N.Y., 1996—; asst. to atty. gen. of U.S. for Nat. Security Affairs; dir. strategy, plans, and policy Dept. Army Hdqs., Washington. Decorated Def. Disting. Svc. medal, Disting. Svc. medal (2), Def. Superior Svc. medal, Legion of Merit (2), Bronze Star medal (2), Meritorious Svc. medal (2), Air Medal (3). Mem. Coun. Fgn. Rels., Pa. Bar, Wash. Bar, D.C. Bar. Home: Quarters #100 West Point NY 10996 Office: US Military Academy Office of Supt West Point NY 10996-5000*

CHRISTMAN, EDWARD ARTHUR, physicist; b. Lakewood, Ohio, Aug. 3, 1943; s. John N.H. and Mary Elizabeth (Fuller) C.; m. Florence T. Cua, July 21, 1979. MS, Rutgers U., 1975, PhD, 1977. Mech. engr. missile systems div. AVCO Corp., Wilmington, Mass., 1966-72; instr. Rutgers U., New Brunswick, N.J., 1975-77, radiol. physicist, 1977-89, assoc. dir., 1989-91; dir. environ. health and safety Columbia U., N.Y.C., 1991-99; cons. Princeton, N.J., 1999—; cons. in field, 1977—; assoc. faculty Rutgers U., 1978—; faculty Columbia U., 1991—. Mem. Health Physics Soc. N.J. (pres. 1989-90), Health Physics Soc. Office: 443 Sayre Dr Princeton NJ 08540*

CHRISTMAN, LUTHER PARMALEE, retired university dean, consultant; b. Summit Hill, Pa., Feb. 26, 1915; s. Elmer and Elizabeth (Barnicoat) C.; m. Dorothy Mary Black, Dec. 5, 1939; children: Gary, Judith, Lillian. Grad., Pa. Hosp. Sch. Nursing for Men, 1939; BS, Temple U., 1948, EdM, 1952; PhD, Mich. State U., 1965; LHD (hon.), Thomas Jefferson U., 1980; DSc (hon.), Grand Valley State U., 1998. Cons. Mich. Dept. Mental Health, Lansing, 1956-63; assoc. prof. psychiat. nursing U. Mich., 1963-67; rsch. assoc. Inst. Social Rsch., U. Mich., 1963-67; prof. nursing and sociology, dean nursing Vanderbilt U., 1967-72; DON Vanderbilt U. Med. Ctr. Hosp., 1967-72; prof. sociology Rush Coll. Health Scis., Chgo.; sr. scientist Rush-Presbyn.-St. Luke's Med. Center; prof. nursing, v.p. nursing affairs Coll. Nursing Rush U., 1972-87; dean Rush U. Coll. Nursing, 1972-87, dean emeritus, 1987—; sr. advisor to pres. Ctr. of Nursing, Am. Hosp. Assn., 1989; pres. Christman-Cornesky & Assocs., 1990-94; adj. prof. Vanderbilt U., 1991—; cons. cmty. svcs. and rsch. br. NIMH, 1963-66; psychiat. rsch. project So. Regional Edn. Bd., 1964-67; chmn. planning com. 1st Midwest Conf. Psychiat. Nursing, Mpls., 1956; mem. team to survey mental health facilities of Colo. NIMH, 1982, of Ga., 1984; mem., workshop leader White House Conf. on Children, 1970; mem. nursing panel Nat. Commn. for Study Nursing and Nursing Edn., 1968-70; mem. regional med. programs rev. com. Health Svcs. and Mental Health Adminstrn., Dept. Health, Edn. and Welfare, 1968-72; cons. dept. medicine and surgery VA Ctrl. Office, 1968-71, 74-77; mem. panel nurse cons. to com. on nursing AMA, 1968-71; mem. health svcs. adv. com. Am. Assn. Med. Colls., 1968-71; mem. acting com. pub. health Am. Health Found, 1970-72; mem. membership com. Inst. Medicine, NAS, 1972-76, mem. com. on edn. in health professions, 1973-75; participant numerous confs. in field; mem. S.D. Bd. Nursing, Tenn. Bd. Nursing; cons. in field. Contbr. numerous articles to profl. jours. Recipient Old Master Purdue U., 1985, Coun. of Specialists in Psychiat. and Mental Health Nursing award, 1980, Hon. Recognition award Ill. Nurses Assn., 1987, Edith Copeland Founders award for Creativity, 1981, History Makers in Nursing award Ctr. for Advancement of Nursing Practice, Beth Israel Hosp./Mass. Gen. Hosp., 1992, Lifetime Achievement award Sigma Theta Tau, 1992, Disting. Alumnus award Temple U., 1992, Rush U., 1997, Coll. Social Scis. Outstanding Alumnus award Mich. State U., 1999; Hon. Recognition award Nat. Academicians of Practice, 1996, Cert. of Appreciation, Marshall County Adult Edn., 1997. Fellow AAAS, Am. Acad. Nursing (Living Legend award 1995), Inst. Medicine Chgo., Soc. Applied Anthropology; mem. ANA (3d v.p., Jesse M. Scott award 1985), AACN (hon. lifetime membership award 1997), Mich. Nurses' Assn. (pres. 1961-65), Am. Sociol. Assn., Soc. Gen. Sys. Rsch., Inst. Medicine, N.Y. Acad. Scis., Biomed. Engring. Soc., Nat. Acad. Practice (chmn. acad. nursing 1985-92, sec. 1992-96, Disting. Practitioner award 1985, Cert. of Appreciation for Leadership 1995), Alpha Omega Alpha (hon.), Alpha Kappa Delta. Home and Office: 5535 Nashville Hwy Chapel Hill TN 37034-2074

CHRISTMAN, ROBERT ALAN, podiatric radiologist; b. Abington, Pa., July 6, 1955; s. Bertram William and Earlene (Colvin) C.; m. Irene Mary Berberian, Sept. 12, 1982; 1 child, Jessica Lynn. BS, Pa. State U., 1977; D in Podiatric Medicine, Pa. Coll. Podiatric Medicine, 1981. Diplomate Am. Bd. Podiatric Orthopedics & Primary Podiatric Medicine. Resident in podiatric surgery Kensington Hosp., Phila., 1981-82; pvt. practice, Phila., 1982-86; fellow in podiatric radiology Med. Coll. Pa., Phila., 1983-85; fellow in podiatric radiology Pa. Coll. Podiatric Medicine, Phila., 1983-85, instr., 1985-88, asst. prof., 1988-98, assoc. prof., 1998—, dir. radiology, 1986—; group practice, 1986—. Contbg. editor Yearbook of Podiatric Medicine and Surgery, 1986-91, Jour. Podiatric Med. Assn., 1990—; contbr. numerous articles to med. jours. Fellow Am. Coll. Podiatric Radiologists (merit award 1987). Avocation: music.

CHRISTMAS, WILLIAM ANTHONY, internist, educator; b. Montreal, June 5, 1939; came to U.S., 1946; s. William Richard and Marcelle (Hudon) C.; m. Maribeth Hanson, July 14, 1962; children: William, Ann, Gillian, Ira. AB, Bowdoin Coll., 1961; MD, Boston U., 1965. Diplomate Am. Bd. Internal Medicine. Mixed medicine intern Sinai Hosp., Balt., 1965-66; resident in internal medicine Med. Ctrs. Hosps. Vt., Burlington, 1966-68; pvt. practice, Bennington, Vt., 1972-77; med. dir. univ. health svcs., asst. prof. medicine U. Rochester, N.Y., 1977-81; NIH fellow in infectious diseases U. Vt., Burlington, 1968-69, dir. Student Health Ctr., 1981-93, clin. asst. prof. medicine, 1983-89, clin. assoc. prof., 1989-93; assoc. clin. prof. cmty./family medicine/dir. student health Duke U., Durham, N.C., 1994—; sr. assoc. cons. The Spelman & Johnson Group. Cons. editor Jour. Am. Coll. Health, 1985—; contbr. articles to med. jours. Pres., bd. dirs. State Com. Vt. YMCA, Burlington, 1983-91; bd. dirs. Greater Burlington YMCA, 1990-93, Vt. Epilepsy Assn., Rutland, 1990-93; active Vt. Coalition for Disability Rights, 1991-93; chmn. Measles Mumps Rubella Varicella (MMRV) Action Group, Nat. Coalition for Adult Immunizations, 1995-98. Fellow ACP, Am. Coll. Health Assn. (pres. 1987-88, Ruth Boynton award 1989), Infectious Diseases Soc. Am. (emeritus); mem. Am. Coll. Health Found. Bd. (chmn. 1998—), New England Coll. Health Assn. (pres. 1985-86), Vt. Med. Soc., So. Coll. Health Assn. (pres. 1998-99). Avocations: bread baking, medical history. Office: Duke U Duke Family Medicine Ctr PO Box 3886 Durham NC 27710

CHRISTNER, THEODORE CARROLL, architect; b. Quincy, Ill., Oct. 3, 1932; s. Thornton Carroll and Mable Irene (Trogdon) C.; m. Jo Hartmann, 1957 (div. 1980); children: Eric, Kitsy, Caellen, Erin; m. Claudia Trautman, Oct. 4, 1986; 1 child: Adrienne. BArch, Culver-Stockton Coll., 1952, Washington U., St. Louis, 1957. Registered architect, Mo. Staff architect Fischer, Frichtel Design and Constrn., St. Louis, 1961-62; assoc. Gale and Cannon, St. Louis, 1962-63; pres. The Christner Partnership, Inc., St. Louis, 1963-95; chmn. bd. dirs. Christner, Inc., 1995—; bd. dirs. Ecumenical Housing Prodn. Corp., mem exec. com. Bd. dirs., v.p. Ecumenical Housing Corp., St. Louis, 1988—; bd. dirs. Mt. St. Rose Hosp., 1967-75; chmn. bd. St. Joseph's Hosp. Hospice, 1988—; mem. Commn. for Future Washington U., 1988; mem. nat. coun. Wash. U. Sch. Architecture, 1988—. Mem. AIA (dir. 1986), Am. Arbitration Assn. Avocations: golf, tennis, skiing, flying. Home: 6319 San Bonita Ave Saint Louis MO 63105-3115 Office: Christner Inc 7711 Bonhomme Ave Clayton MO 63105-1908

CHRISTO (CHRISTO VLADIMIROV JAVACHEFF), artist; b. Gabrovo, Bulgaria, June 13, 1935; came to U.S., 1964; s. Vladimir Ivan and Tzveta (Dimitrova) C.; m. Jeanne-Claude (de Guillebon); 1 child, Cyril. Student, Fine Arts Acad., Sofia Bulgaria, 1953-56, Vienna (Austria) Fine Arts Acad., 1957. Stacked Oil Barrels, Cologne Harbor (Germany), 1961, Paris, 1962, Storefronts, N.Y.C., 1964, Phila. Mus. Contemporary Art, 1968, Air Package and Wrapped Tree, Stedelijk van Abbemuseum, Eindhoven, Netherlands, 1966, Air Packages, Walker Art Ctr., Mpls. Sch. Art, 1966, Kassel, Germany, 1968; Wrapped Fountain and Tower, Spoleto, Italy, 1968; packaged pub. bldgs., Kunsthalle, Bern, Switzerland, 1968, Mus. Contemporary Art, Chgo., 1969; Stacked Hay, Phila. Inst. Contemporary Art, 1969; wrapped monuments to Vittorio Emanuele and Leonardo da Vinci, Milan, Italy, 1970; Wrapped Coast, Little Bay, Sydney, Australia, 1969, Wrapped Floors and Covered Windows and Wrapped Walk Way, Kaiser Wilhem Haus Lange, Krefeld, Germany, 1971, Valley Curtain, Rifle, Colo., 1970-72; Wrapped Roman Wall Porta Pinciana, Rome; Ocean Front, Newport, R.I., 1974, Running Fence, Sonoma and Marin Counties, Calif., 1972-76; Wrapped Walk Ways, Kansas City, Mo., 1977-78; Surrounded Islands, Biscayne Bay, Miami, Fla., 1980-83; Wrapped Floors and Stairways Arch. Mus., Basel, Switzerland, 1972-85, The Pont Neuf Wrapped, Paris, 1975-85; The Umbrellas, Japan & U.S.A., 1984-91, (with Jeanne-Claude) wrapped the Reichstag, Berlin, Germany, 1995. Address: 48 Howard St New York NY 10013-2514*

CHRISTODOULOU, DEMETRIOS, mathematics educator; b. Athens, Oct. 19, 1951; came to U.S., 1981; s. Lambros Christodoulo and Maria Georgiades; m. Kathleen Kelly, Mar. 8, 1973 (div. May 1995); children: Penelope, Alexandra; m. Nikoleta Sigala, June 12, 1997. MA in Physics, Princeton U., 1970, PhD in Physics, 1971; DSc (hon.) in Math., U. Athens, 1996. Rsch. fellow Calif. Inst. Tech., 1971-72; prof. U. Athens, 1972-73; vis. scientist CERN, 1973-74, Internat. Ctr. for Theoretical Physics, 1974-76;

Humboldt fellow Max Planck Inst., 1976-81; vis. mem. Courant Inst., 1981-83; from assoc. prof. to prof. Syracuse U., 1983-87; prof. math. Courant Inst. NYU, 1988-92; prof. math. Princeton U., 1992—. Author: (with S. Klainerman) The Global Nonlinear Stability of the Minkowski Space, 1993; contbr. articles on gravitational collapse and formation of black holes and singularities to Comms. in Math. Physics, 1984-87, Comms. on Pure and Applied Math., 1991-93, Ann. Math., 1994—, Archtl. Rat. Mech. Anal., 1995—. Recipient Otto Hahn medal for math. physics Max Planck Soc., 1981, Basilis Xanthopoulos award for gen. relativity, 1991, MacArthur Fellowship award MacArthur Found., 1993, Excellence in the Scis. award Acad. of Athens, 1996, Guggenheim fellowship, 1998, Bocher Meml. prize Am. Math. Soc., 1999. Achievements include discovery of nonlinear memory effect of gravitational waves, the formation of unstable naked singularities in gravitational collapse; research in nonlinear partial differential equations, general relativity, fluid dynamics. Office: Princeton U Dept Math Princeton NJ 08544-1000

CHRISTOFFERSEN, RALPH EARL, chemist; b. Elgin, Ill., Dec. 4, 1937; s. Arthur Henry and Mary C.; m. Barbara Hibbard, June 10, 1961; children: Kirk Alan, Rachel Anne. BS, Cornell Coll., 1959, LLD (hon.), 1983; PhD, Ind. U., 1963. Asst. prof. chemistry U. Kans., Lawrence, 1966-69; assoc. prof. U. Kans., 1967-72, prof., 1972-81, asst. vice chancellor for acad. affairs, 1974-75, assoc. vice chancellor for acad. affairs, 1976-79, vice chancellor for acad. affairs, 1979-81; pres. Colo. State U., Ft. Collins, 1981-83; exec. dir. Upjohn Co., 1983-85, v.p. biotech. and basic research support, 1985-87, v.p. discovery research, 1987-89; v.p. rsch. SmithKline Beecham, King of Prussia, Pa., 1989-90, sr. v.p. rsch., 1990-92; CEO, pres. Ribozyme Pharms., Inc., Boulder, Colo., 1992—; bd. dirs. Keystone Symposia, Genomica Corp. Contbr. articles to profl. jours. NIH fellow, 1962-63, 64-66. Fellow Am. Inst. Chemists; mem. Am. Chem. Soc., Am. Phys. Soc. (v.p. theoretical div. 1981), Internat. Soc. Quantum Biology (pres. 1977-79), Pharm. Mfrs. Assn. (chmn. biotech. adv. com. 1983-86, chmn. R&D steering com. 1989-90), Sigma Xi, Phi Lambda Upsilon.

CHRISTOFI, ANDREAS, finance educator; b. Paphos, Cyprus, June 12, 1949; came to U.S., 1975; s. Charalambos and Peraklou Christofi; m. Karen R. Gondek, Mar. 21, 1985; children: Stephen, Michael. BA, Sch. Grad. Indsl. Studies, Thessaloniki, Greece, 1974; MBA, U. New Orleans, 1976; PhD, Pa. State U., 1984. Prof. U. Md., College Park, 1983-88, Pa. State U., Harrisburg, 1988-93, Azusa (Calif.) Pacific U., 1993-97, Monmouth U., West Long Branch, N.J., 1997—. Contbr. articles to profl. publs. Mem. Am. Fin. Assn., Am. Econ. Assn., Fin. Mgmt. Assn. Avocations: fishing, hunting, swimming, travel. Home: 34B Brandywyne Brielle NJ 08730-1322

CHRISTOFOLETTI, ANTONIO, geography educator; b. Rio Claro, Brazil, June 13, 1936; s. Villiariano and Olga (Rovai) C.; m. Aparecida Hebling; children: Antonio Eduardo, Anderson Luis. B in Geography, Cath. U. of Campinas, 1958; DSc, Faculty of Scis. of Rio Clan, 1968. Prof. geography Cath. U., Campinas, Brazil, 1959-71, Sao Paulo State U. (U. Estadual Paulista), Rio Claro, Brazil, 1965-94; prof. emeritus Sao Paulo State U. (U. Estadual Paulista), Rio Claro, 1994-96; dir. Inst. Geociencias e Ciencias Exatas, Rio Claro, 1985-89; supr. Ctr. Environ. Analysis & Planning, 1993-94; titular prof. Inst. of Geoscis. and Exact Scis., Sao Paulo State U., 1979. Author: Geomorfologia, 1974, Análise de sistemas em geografia, 1979, Geomorfologia Fluvial, 1981, Perspectivas da Geografia, 1982, Geografia e Meio ambiente no Brasil, 1995, Sistemas de Informacao Geográ: Dicionário Ilustrado, 1997, Bibliografia en Sistemas de Informação Geográfica, Vol. 1, 1998; chief editor Notícia Geomorfológica, 1966-82, Geografia, 1976-96. Home: Rua 06 #1140, 13500920 Rio Claro Brazil Office: UNESP Caixa Postal 178, Rua 10 # 2527, 13500230 Rio Claro Brazil

CHRISTOFORIDIS, A. JOHN, radiologist, educator; b. Greece, Dec. 24, 1924; s. John P. and Ada A. C.; m. Ann Dimitriadis, Nov. 11, 1961; children: John, Gregory, Alex, Jimmy. M.D. summa cum laude, Nat. U. Athens, Greece, 1949; M.M.Sc., Ohio State U., 1957; Ph.D., Aristotelian U., Greece, 1969. Instr. to prof. Ohio State U., Columbus, 1956-74; clin. prof. Ohio State U., 1974—; chmn. dept. radiology Aristotelian U., Salonika, Greece, 1971; prof., chmn. dept. radiology Med. Coll. Ohio, Toledo, until 1982; prof., chmn. dept. Ohio State U., Columbus, 1982—; researcher in chest and gastrointestinal radiology; cons. Greek Ministry Health, Batelle Meml. Inst., Columbus. Contbr. to textbook Atlas of Axial Sagittal and Coronal Anatomy with Computed Tomography and Magnetic Resonance; author: Radiology for Medical Students, 4th edit., 1988, Diagnostic Radiology-Thorax, 1989; contbr. several chpts. to books, over 100 articles to med. jours. Served to lt. M.C. Greek Army, 1950-52. Recipient Silver award Ohio Med. Assn., 1969, awards Heart Assn., 1960, awards Batelle Meml. Inst., 1965, awards Astra Co., 1967, awards Lung Assn., 1970-71; named Hon. Citizen City of Thessalonike, 1973; Ohio Geriatrics Med. grantee, 1980; NSF grantee, 1980. Fellow Am. Coll. Chest Physicians, Am. Coll. Radiology; mem. AAA, AMA, AAUP, Ohio Radiol. Soc., Assn. Univ. Radiologists, Radiol. Soc. N. Am., Soc. Chmn. Acad. Radiology Depts., Fleishner Soc. (charter), Am. Hellenic Ednl. Progressive Assn., Greek-Am. Progressive Assn., Acad. of Athens (corr. mem.). Greek Orthodox. Office: Ohio State U 410 W 10th Ave Columbus OH 43210-1240

CHRISTOL, CARL Q(UIMBY), lawyer, political science educator; b. Gallup, S.D., June 28, 1913; s. Carl and Winifred (Quimby) C.; m. Jeannette Stearns, Dec. 18, 1949; children: Susan Quimby Christol-Deacon, Richard Stearns (dec.). AB, U. S.D., 1934, LLD (hon.), 1977; AM, Fletcher Sch. Law and Diplomacy, 1936; postgrad., Institut Universitaire des Hautes Etudes Internationales, Geneva, 1937-38, U. Geneva, 1937-38; PhD, U. Chgo., 1941; LLB, Yale U., 1947; postgrad., Acad. Internat. Law, The Hague, 1950. Bar: Calif. 1949, S.D. 1948. Assoc. firm Guthrie, Darling and Shattuck, Los Angeles, 1948-49; of counsel Fizzolio, Fizzolio & McLeod, Sherman Oaks, Calif., 1949-94; assoc. prof. polit. sci. U. So. Calif., 1949-59, prof., 1959-87, prof. emeritus, 1987—, chmn. dept. polit. sci., 1960-64, 75-77; Stockton chair internat. law U.S. Naval War Coll., 1962-63, cons., 1963-70 ; cons. World Law Fund; mem. L.A. Mayor's Adv. Com. Human Rels., Commn. to Study Orgn. of Peace; mem. adv. panel on internat. law Dept. State, 1970-76; v.p. Ct. of Man Found., 1971-77; scholar-in-residence Rockefeller Found. Bellagio Conf. and Study Ctr., Italy, 1980. Author: Transit by Air in International Law, 1941, Introduction to Political Science, 1957, 4th edit., 1982, Readings in International Law, 1959, The International Law of Outer Space, 1966, The International Legal and Institutional Aspects of the Stratosphere Ozone Problem, 1975, The Modern International Law of Outer Space, 1982, Space Law: Past, Present and Future, 1991; bd. editors: Western Polit. Quar, 1970-75, Internat. Lawyer, 1975-84, Space Policy, 1985—, Internat. Legal Materials, 1985—, Australian Internat. Law Jour., 1998—; contbr. articles on legal, polit. and mil. subjects to profl. jours. Bd. dirs. Los Angeles County Heart Assn., 1956-61. Served to lt. col. AUS, 1941-46; col. Res. ret. Decorated Bronze Star medal; recipient Dart award U. So. Calif., 1970, Assos. award for excellence in teaching, 1977, Raubenheimer award, 1982, Disting. Emeritus award, 1990, Rockefeller Found. fellow, 1958-59. Mem. Am., Los Angeles bar assns., Am. Soc. Internat. Law (exec. council 1973-76), Internat. Studies Assn. (chmn. internat. law sect. 1977-78), Internat. Acad. Astronautics, State Bar Calif., UN Assn. Los Angeles (pres. 1961-63), Am. Polit. Sci. Assn., Internat. Inst. Space Law (pres. Am. br. 1973-75), Town Hall, AIAA, Internat. Law Assn., UN Assn. U.S. (dir. 1967-69), Masons, Blue Key, Skull and Dagger, Rotary, Phi Beta Kappa, Phi Kappa Phi (award 1987), Alpha Tau Omega. Republican. Presbyterian. Home: 1041 Anoka Pl Pacific Palisades CA 90272-2414 Office: U So Calif Polit Sci Dept Los Angeles CA 90089-0044

CHRISTOPHE, CLEVELAND ALERIDGE, investment company executive; b. Savannah, Ga., Jan. 1, 1946; s. Cleveland A. and Lucy M. (Hagins) C.; m. Cheryl Delores Smith, Dec. 28, 1966; children: Jean-Paul, Kimberly Diane. BA, Howard U., 1966; MBA, U. Mich., 1967. CFA. Securities analyst Citicorp/Citibank, N.A., N.Y.C., 1967-69, venture capital analyst, 1971-72, investment analyst team head, 1972-75; country ops. head Citicorp/Citibank, N.A., Paris, 1975-79; corp. banking team head Citicorp/Citibank, N.A., San Francisco, 1980-83; country head for Jamaica Citicorp/Citibank, N.A., Kingston, 1983-85; country head for Colombia Citicorp/Citibank, N.A., Bogota, 1985-87; asst. to chmn. Kenton Corp., N.Y.C., 1969; pres. Soul Stop, Inc., N.Y.C., 1970, Banco Internacional de Colombia, Bogota, 1985-87; sr. v.p. TLC Group, L.P., N.Y.C., 1987-88; pres. The Christophe Corp., Stamford, Conn., 1988-89; v.p. Equico Capital Corp., N.Y.C., 1990-92; prin. TSG Ventures, L.P., Stamford, 1992—; mng. ptnr. TSG Capital Group, Stamford, 1995—; bd. dirs. Hayes Lemmerz Internat., Inc., Romulus, Mich., various pvt. cos. Author: Competition in Financial Services, 1973. Trustee King and Low-Heywood Thomas Sch., Stamford; mem. vis. com. Bus. Sch. U. Mich., Ann Arbor; bd. dirs., chmn. bd. dirs. Nat. Conf. for Community and Justice, Fairfield County. Conn. Mem. Nat. Assn. Investment Cos. (chmn. bd. dirs.). Avocations: golf, tennis. Office: TSG Capital Group LLC 177 Broad St Fl 12 Stamford CT 06901-2429

CHRISTOPHE, JOSITA LEJUAN, special education educator; b. New Roads, La., Sept. 2, 1964; d. John Ardel and Adele Rose (Aguillard) C. BS, La. State U., 1987; postgrad., So. U., Baton Rouge, 1988, U. New Orleans, 1989, 91, Northeast La. U., Monroe, 1990, La. U., 1991; MA, La. State U., 1998. Noncategorical presch. handicapped tchr. Point Coupee Parish Sch. Bd., New Roads, 1987-90, primary mild/moderate tchr., 1990-98; tchr. primary moderate/severe/profound/medically fragile Point Coupee Parish Sch. Bd., 1998—; vol. coach Spl. Olympics, La., 1986—, Very Spl. Arts Festival, La., 1986—; paraprofl. trainer La. Dept. Edn., 1990—. Named Morganza Elem. Tchr. of the Yr., Pointe Coupee Parish Sch. Bd., New Roads, 1989-90, Pointe Coupee Parish Spl. Edn. Tchr. of the Yr., Coun. Exceptional Children, Baton Rouge, 1989-90, Pointe Coupee Parish Elem. Tchr. of the Yr., Pointe Coupee Parish Sch. Bd., New Roads, 1990-91. Mem. NEA, Am. Fedn. Tchrs., Coun. Exceptional Children, La. Assn. Educators, La. Fedn. Tchrs., Pointe Coupee Assn. Edn. Democrat. Roman Catholic. Avocations; reading, drawing, arts and crafts, cooking, traveling. Home: 12114 Saint Augustine St New Roads LA 70760-2036 Office: Pointe Coupee Parish Sch Bd PO Box 579 New Roads LA 70760-0579

CHRISTOPHER, ALEXANDER GEORGE, transportation company executive; b. Melrose Park, Ill., Apr. 17, 1941; s. George Alexander and Ann (Gianoulis) C.; m. Susan Bernice Breitweiser, May 12, 1979; children: Anna Bernice, Jason Woodrow. BA in Econs., Elmhurst (Ill.) Coll., 1963, BA in Philosphy, 1963; postgrad., DePaul U., 1963-64. Mgr. Dunn & Bradstreet, Chgo., 1965-67, various Chgo.-area currency exchs., 1967-71; v.p. Ill. Armored Car Corp., River Grove, 1971-82, dir.-in-exile, 1982-83; pres. Ill. Armored Car Corp., Broadview, 1983-95; chmn., CEO Ill. Armored Car Corp., Broadview, Ill., 1995—; CEO, United Armored Svcs,, 1995—; mem. adv. bd. fin. instns. sec. state Ill.. 1983-97; mem. steering com. Security Cos. Organized for Legis. Action, 1988—, treas., 1993—. With USMCR, 1964-70. Mem. Ind. Armored Car Operators Assn. (pres. 1979-80, chmn. bd. 1980-81, chmn. legis. com. 1988—, bd. dirs. 1989-95), Nat. Armored Car Assn. (bd. dirs. 1999—). Greek Orthodox. Office: United Armored Svcs 2100 W 21st St Broadview IL 60153

CHRISTOPHER, CLAUDE, minister; b. Jacksonville, Tex., Oct. 26, 1929; s. William Vanus and Ora (Hancock) C.; m. Mattie Olivia Walker, Aug. 2, 1958; children: Gary J., Sharon D. BA, Prairie View U., 1951; MA, DePaul U., 1958; MDiv, Drew U., 1979. Postal clk. U.S. Post Office, Chgo., 1954-57; tchr. history Manley & Harlan, Chgo., 1957-75; pastor Wallace Chapel, Summit, N.J., 1975-82, Soldiers Meml., Salisbury, N.C., 1982-84, Bethlehem, Gary, Ind., 1984-86, St. Paul, Toledo, Ohio, 1986-96; presiding elder Chgo. Dist., 1996—; pastor St. Matthew-Gordon & Bethlehem, Chgo. and Gary, 1960-75. Author: (poem) Inspiration, 1992, Hope, 1994, Faith, 1996, Charity, 1997. With U.S. Army, 1951-54. Methodist. Avocations: writing poetry, repairing and restoring objects. Home and Office: 243 S Hickory St Glenwood IL 60425-1813

CHRISTOPHER, DANIEL ROY, lawyer; b. Denver, Apr. 10, 1947; s. Gordon Lawrence and Rita Marie (Gaulick) C.; m. Pamela Kay Frangos, Jan. 10, 1970; children: Peter Daniel, Stacy A. BS, U. Colo., 1969; MBA, Idaho State U., 1971; JD, U. Denver, 1974. Bar: Colo. 1974, U.S. Dist. Ct. Colo. 1974, U.S. Ct. Appeals (10th cir.) 1978, U.S. Supreme Ct. 1979. Law clk. Denver Dist. Ct., 1972-73; dep. dist. atty. Office of Dist. Atty., Denver, 1974-79; spl. pros. on police corruption Alamosa, Colo., 1979; asst. U.S. atty. Denver, 1979-81; ptnr. Kennedy & Christopher, P.C., Denver, 1981—; spl. asst. atty. gen. State of Colo., 1991-99; asst. clin. prof. legal medicine U. Colo. Health Scis. Ctr., 1991—. Contbg. editor Dist. Atty. Evidence Manual, 1976; author: Risk Management for Health Care Professionals, 1992. Vol. Rep. party worker Arapahoe County Ct., 1980—; bd. dirs. U. Colo. at Denver, 1986—, Holy Ghost Ch. Foodline for the Homeless, 1997—. Recipient Am. Jurisprudence awrad 1974. Mem. ABA, Colo. Bar Assn., Colo. Def. Lawyers Assn. (pres. 1995), Denver Bar Assn., Def. Rsch. Inst., Cath. Lawyers Guild, Am. Health Lawyer's Assn., U. Colo. Alumni Assn. (bd. dirs. 1989—), Faculty Fed. Advocates. Roman Catholic. Home: 5670 Big Canon Dr Greenwood Village CO 80111-3512 Office: Kennedy & Christopher PC 1660 Wynkoop St Ste 900 Denver CO 80202-1197

CHRISTOPHER, DORIS, consumer products executive. Pres. Pampered Chef Ltd., Addison, Ill. Office: The Pampered Chef 350 S Rohlwing Rd Addison IL 60101-3079*

CHRISTOPHER, JAMES ROY, executive director; b. Fort Worth, Aug. 4, 1942; s. Roy Leslie and Mary Ruth (Hudson) C. Student, U. Tex., 1962-64, UCLA, 1978-79. Program dir. Priority One Outpatient Treatment Ctr., Beverly Hills, Calif., 1987-89; founder, exec. dir. SOS/Secular Orgns. for Sobriety, L.A., 1986—; lectr. in field. Author: How to Stay Sober: Recovery Without Religion, 1988, Unhooked: Staying Sober and Drug Free, 1989, SOS Sobriety: The Proven Alternative to 12 Step Programs, 1992; contbr. articles to profl. jours.; over 300 appearances in radio and TV. Mem. ACA, Am. Coun. on Alcoholism. Unitarian. Avocations: hiking, running, theatre, film. Office: Secular Orgns for Sobriety SOS Internat Clearinghouse 5521 Grosvenor Blvd Los Angeles CA 90066-6915

CHRISTOPHER, JAMES WALKER, architect, educator; b. Phila., Nov. 5, 1930; s. Arthur Bailey and Cornelia (Slater) C.; m. Carolyn Kennard, July 9, 1955; children: William W., Kathryn A., Kimberley, James S., Pamela W. B.A., Rice U., 1953, B.S. in Architecture, 1953; M.Arch., MIT, 1956. Registered architect, Utah, Colo., Nev., Idaho, Wyo. Asst. prof. architecture U. Utah, Salt Lake City, 1956-60, adj. prof. architecture, 1983; archtl. designer various firms, Salt Lake City, 1960-63; founding prin. Brixen & Christopher Architects, Salt Lake City, 1963—. Architect, Phase I, Snowbird, Alta Canyon, Utah (AIA Western Mountain Region award 1971), Numemaker Place Chapel, Salt Lake City (AIA Western Mountain Region award 1977), Congregation Kol Ami, Salt Lake City (AIA Western Mountain Region award 1977), Block 53 Master Plan, Salt Lake City (Utah chpt. AIA award 1979). Mem. Utah Environ. Transp. Council, Salt Lake City, 1970-77, vice chmn., 1970-75; mem. Big Cottonwood Citizens Planning Com., Salt Lake County, Utah, 1975, Salt Lake City Downtown Planning Com., 1981, Utah Transit Authority Transplan, Salt Lake City, 1982. Served to lt. (j.g.) USNR, 1953-55. Fellow AIA (pres. Utah Soc. 1970 12 Utah Soc. Design awards, 12 Western Mountain Region Design awards 1968-83, 8 nat. Design awards 1975-83, Presdl. citation 1982, nat. design and planning com. 1976—, chmn. R/UDAT task group 1987-91, western mountain region Firm of the Yr. award 1987, Silver medal 1991). Episcopalian. Club: Alta. Home: 2954 Millcreek Rd Salt Lake City UT 84109-3108 Office: Brixen & Christopher Architects 252 S 2nd E Salt Lake City UT 84111-2487

CHRISTOPHER, JOE RANDELL, English language educator; b. Bartlesville, Okla., June 27, 1935; s. Ernest Randell and Blanche (Woods) C.; m. Mary Lynn Hayes, June 9, 1958; children: Saralinda Michelle Evans, Vandy Maria, Randell Llewellyn-Hayes. BA, U. Okla., 1957, MA, 1959, PhD, 1969. Instr. Tarleton State U., Stephenville, Tex., 1963-67, asst. prof., 1967-68; vis. prof. Western N.Mex. U., Silver City, summer 1970; assoc. prof. Tarleton State U., Stephenville, Tex., 1968-87, prof., 1987--; invited lecturer Abilene Christian U. Ctr. for Christian Writing, 1990; keynote spkr. C.S. Lewis for 20th Century conf., Oklahoma City U., 1998. Author: (with Dean W. Dickinsheet, Robert E. Briney) A Boucher Bibliography, 1969, (with Joan K. Ostling) C.S. Lewis: An Annotated Checklist of Writings about Him and His Works, 1974; author: (play) A Foretaste of Blood to Come, 1973, (books) C.S. Lewis, 1987, Musings Beneath a Tree of Amalion, 2d edit., 1993; editor: (chapbook) Chad Walsh Reviews C.S. Lewis, 1998; contbg. editor: The Lamp-Post of the Southern California C.S. Lewis Soc.; bd. editors Windhaven: A Journal of Christian Literature, The Mythopoeic Press. Mythopoeic scholar for publ. books, 1976, 88; guest of honor Mythopoeic Conf., N.Y. C.S. Lewis Weekend, Tulsa C.S. Lewis Conf.; papers collected Western History Collections, U. Okla. Librs., Norman. Mem. MLA, South Ctrl. Modern Lang Assn., Conf on Christianity and Literature, Mythopoeic Soc. (bd. advisors), various soc. devoted to authors: C.S. Lewis, Tolkien, Dorothy L. Sayers, Charles Williams, etc. Democrat. Episcopal. Office: Tarleton State U Box T-0300 Stephenville TX 76402-0300

CHRISTOPHER, L. CAROL, communication researcher, freelance writer; b. Dallas; d. Joe R. and S. Lanell Christopher. BA magna cum laude, U. Calif., San Diego, 1991, MA, 1993, Candidate of Philosophy, 1995. Systems editor The Dallas Morning News, 1978-84; systems editor, asst. to editor The Denver Post, 1984-86; tng. and comm. mgr. Newspaper Systems Support and Fngring., San Diego, 1986-88; cons. Christopher Comm., 1988—; tchg./rsch. asst. U. Calif., San Diego, 1991—; corr. The Cole Papers, San Francisco, 1991—; labor organizer Assn. Grad. Student Employees/UAW, Berkeley, 1995. Contbr. articles to profl. jours. Mem. exec. bd. Assn. Grad. Student Employees/UAW, Assn. Student Employees/UAW, Berkeley and San Diego, 1991—; precinct capt. Dukakis campaign, Dem. Nat. Party, San Diego, 1988. Mem. Internat. Comm. Ass., Speech Comm. Assn., Assn. of Educators in Journalism and Mass Comm. Office: 888 Vermont St #212 Oakland CA 94610

CHRISTOPHER, LIN, artist; b. Talladega, Ala., Dec. 23, 1948; d. Newman and Mary Anna (Stewart) White; m. William Jackson Christopher, July 16, 1975. BS, Auburn U., 1971. Artist Roswell, Ga., 1975—; bd. dirs. Roswell Artists' Studio Tour. Represented in permanent collections at IBM, Sunkist, Bell South, Citicorp, Norcom, Hyatt Hotels, Ball Stalker, Ridgeview Inst., United Va. Bank, Price Waterhouse, John Harland Co., Taiyo Elec. Co., Equitable Life Ins. Co., Coopers & Lybrand, Allen & Co., Kinder Care, Hilton Hotels, Crestar Bank, Ala. Power, Ven Der Groen, Sharp Industries, World Carpets, King & Spalding, Workman & Co., Bluff Park Art Assn., Ctrl. Ill. Light Co., SAFE, A.R.T. Sta., Trammel Crowe, Shaw Industries, Perimeter Mall Atlanta, The Landmark Group, Eastman Pharm., James Madison U., Meadows Meml. Hosp., Gainesville Arts Coun., USAF, Bus. Coun. Ga., Albany Mus. Art, Merrill Lynch, Bank of the South, Arthur Anderson, Creative Arts Guild, South Trust Bank, The Marcus Group, Fuqua Industries, North Ga. Coll., So. Engring. Co., Walt Disney World, Springfield (Ill.) Civic Assn., Universal Studios, M G M. Recipient numerous awards. Mem. Nat. Assn. Ind. Artists, Am. Crafts Coun. Avocation: gardening. E-mail: willchristopher@worldnet.att.net. Home: 1534 Jones RD Roswell GA 30075

CHRISTOPHER, LINDA ELLEN, consultant, association executive; b. Flint, Mich., Aug. 26, 1949; d. Junion Homer Christopher and Mildred Ester Dare (Oldham) Burak; mem. Herald René Baxter, Dec. 21, 1994. BA, U. Mich., 1976; MPA, Sonoma State U., Rohnert Park, Calif., 1996. Cert. assn. exec. Med. transcriptionist Delta (Colo.) County Meml. Hosp., 1976-78; vocat. rehab. instr. Svc. Ctr. for Visually Impaired, Flint, Mich., 1978-81; med. record dept. supr. St. Joseph's Hosp., Flint, 1981-85; dir. edn. Am. Assn. Med. Transcription, Modesto, Calif., 1985-90; assoc. exec. dir. Sonoma County Med. Assn., Santa Rosa, Calif., 1990-94; cons. The Christopher Group, Santa Rosa, 1994—; CEO The Christopher Group, San Francisco, 1996—; exec. dir. Hand Therapy Cert. Commn., San Francisco, 1995-96; bd. dirs. Beginning Experience Inc., Flint, 1982-84; key contact Calif. Med. Assn., San Francisco, 1990-94, Am. Heart Assn., Calif., 1994—; exec. dir. Profl. and Personal Coaches Assn., San Francisco, 1996—. Calif. Coaliton of Nurse Practitioners, Sacramento, 1996—; speaker in field. Editor Jour. Sonoma County Med. Assn., 1990-94 (numerous awards); contbr. articles to profl. jours. Pres. Greater Santa Rosa divsn. Am. Heart Assn., 1996-97. Mem. Am. Heart Assn. (pres. elect 1995-96, pres. 1996—), Am. Soc. Assn. Execs. (mem. edn. coun. 1988-91, several awards), No. Calif. Soc. Assn. Execs. (bd. mem. 1993—, profl. recognition scholarships 1984, 89). Avocations: golf, bridge, reading, writing. Office: The Christopher Group 1275 4th St Ste 145 Santa Rosa CA 95404-4049

CHRISTOPHER, MAURINE BROOKS, foundation administrator, writer, editor; b. Three Springs, Tenn.; d. John Davis and Zula (Pangle) Brooks; m. Milbourne Christopher, June 25, 1949. BA, Tusculum Coll., 1941; LittD (hon.), St. John's U., 1984. Reporter, feature writer Balt. Sun, 1943-45; TV radio editor Advt. Age, 1947-51, sr. editor, head broadcast dept., 1951-77; dep. exec. editor Advt. Age, N.Y.C., 1977-84; producer-moderator Adbeat, 1970-78; roving editor, mem. editorial bd. Advt. Age, 1984-91; chmn. Milbourne Christopher Found., 1991—. Author: America's Black Congressmen, 1971, Black Americans in Congress, 1976; co-author: The Milbourne Christopher Library, 1589-1900, The Illustrated History of Magic, 1996, The Milbourne Christopher Library II, 1901-1996, 1998; editor: Howard Thurston's Illusion Show Workbook II, 1992, Houdini's A Magician Among the Spirits-The Original Manuscript, 1996. Mem. Assn. Study Afro-Am. Life and History. Home: 333 Central Park W Apt 25 New York NY 10025-7104

CHRISTOPHER, MICHAEL ANTHONY, township manager; b. Connellsville, Pa., Mar. 18, 1952; s. Anthony Maricondi and Connie (Ringer) Christopher; m. Andrea Dorothy Mavroidis, June 6, 1952; children: Niki K., Michael A. Jr. BS, Pa. State U., 1975. Designer Oliver-Cump Engring., Hagerstown, Md., 1976-77; twp. mgr. Washington Twp. Suprs., Waynesboro, Pa., 1977—. Chmn., treas. Franklin County Crime Solvers, 1982—; sec. Waynesboro Area Drug Edn. Consortium, 1992—; bd. dirs. YMCA, Waynesboro, 1991-96, Cumberland Valley onIce, Inc., 1996—; pres., v.p. Waynesboro C. of C., 1979-92. Recipient Youth Svc. award YMCA, 1995, Pres.'s Leadership award, Pa. State Assn. Township Suprs., 1998, Outstanding Svc. award Frenhlem County, 1998. Mem. Assn. for Pa. Mcpl. Mgrs., KC. Avocations: coaching youth sports, hunting, playing cards, gardening. Office: Washington Twp Suprs 13013 Welty Rd Waynesboro PA 17268-9511

CHRISTOPHER, NICHOLAS, poet, novelist; b. N.Y.C., Feb. 28, 1951; m. Constance Barbara Davidson, Nov. 21, 1980. AB cum laude, Harvard Coll., 1973. Adj. prof. English NYU, 1984—. Author: On Tour with Rita, 1982, A Short History of the Island of Butterflies, 1986, The Soloist, 1986, Desperate Characters, 1988, In the Year of the Comet, 1992, 5 Degrees and Other Poems, 1995, Veronica, 1996, Somewhere in the Night: Film Noir and the American City, 1997, The Creation of the Night Sky, 1998; editor: Under 35: The New Generation of American Poets, 1989, Walk on the Wild Side: Urban American Poetry Since 1975, 1994. Recipient Lavan award Acad. Am. Poets, 1991, Melville Cane award Poetry Soc. Am., 1993; NEA fellow, 1987, Guggenheim fellow, 1993, Amy Lowell fellow. Mem. PEN, Poetry Soc. Am. Office: Janklow & Nesbit Assocs 598 Madison Ave New York NY 10022-1614*

CHRISTOPHER, ROBERT PAUL, physician; b. Cleve., Apr. 27, 1932; s. Walter Matthews and Charity Marie (Roberts) C.; m. Doreen Mary O'Leary, Apr. 28, 1962; children: Robert Jr., Judith, Mark. BS, Northwestern U., 1954; MD, St. Louis U., 1959. Diplomate Am. Bd. Physical Medicine and Rehab. Chief rehab. medicine V.A. Hosp., Ann Arbor, Mich., 1963-67; asst. prof. rehab. medicine U. Mich., Ann Arbor, 1964-67; assoc. prof. rehab. medicine U. Tenn., Memphis, 1967-71, prof. rehab. medicine, 1971—; med. dirs. Les Passees Children's Rehab. Ctr., Memphis, 1976—, Le Bonheur Hosp. Rehab. Svcs., Memphis, 1981—, Regional Med. Ctr. Rehab. Svcs., Memphis, 1967—, assoc. med. dir. St. Joseph Rehab. Ctr., Memphis, 1981—. Contbg. author: Seating the Cerebral Palsey Child, 1983; author: sound/slide program Systems of Physical Therapy in Cerebral Palsy, 1971; contbr. articles to profl. jours. Pres. Mid-South Health Systems Agy., Memphis, 1980; mem. Mayor's Adv. Council for Disabled, Memphis, 1977—. Recipient Disting. Svc. Commn. on Accredited Rehab. Facilities, 1982. Fellow Am. Acad. Phys. Medicine and Rehab. (sec. 1982-88, v.p. 1992—, pres. elect 1993, pres. 1994), Am. Acad. Cerebral Palsy (pres. 1987); mem. AMA, Am. Congress Rehab. Medicine, So. Soc. Phys. Medicine and Rsch. (sec. 1976—), Am. Bd. of Phys. Medicine and Rsch. (vice chmn. 1992—), East Memphis Cath. (bd. dirs. 1969-80), K.C. (Grand Knight 1969-70). Avocations: travel, swimming. Home: 506 Thorn Ridge Cv Memphis TN 38117-3651 Office: U Tenn Coll Med 920 Madison Ave Ste 700 Memphis TN 38103-3446

CHRISTOPHER, RUSSELL LEWIS, baritone; b. Grand Rapids, Mich., Mar. 12, 1930; s. Russell Stewart and Violet (Jurewicz) C.; m. Gail B. Eldredge, Aug. 24, 1963 (div. 1985); 1 son, Russell Frederick. AA, Grand Rapids Jr. Coll., 1950; MusB, U. Mich., 1953, MusM, 1954. Music librarian

NBC, N.Y.C., 1955-58; elected U. Mich. Sch. Music Alumni Bd. Govs., 1997. Prin. artist, N.Y.C. Opera Co., 1958-60, San Francisco Opera Co., 1962, 63, Met. Opera Assn., N.Y.C., 1963-91, soloist, L.A., Montreal, Chgo., Richmond symphony orchs., 1963—; sang role Maecenas in: world premiere Antony and Cleopatra at new, Met. Opera House, 1966; recs.: Carmen (Deutsche Grammophon), 1973, La Traviata (Electra Records), 1982; numerous TV prodns. Live from the Met (Emmy award 1985); Miami Beach Symphony, Hollywood Bowl, Balt. Civic Opera, Central City Opera, Dayton Opera Assn., Phila. Lyric Opera Assn., Met. opera tour, Japan, 1975, 86; concert soloist, Spoleto (Italy) Festival, 1977. mem. U. Mich. Sch. Music Alumni Bd., 1997. Recipient award Martha Baird Rockefeller Fund for Music, 1961; auditions winner Am. Opera, 1962; auditions winner Met. Opera, 1963; Mrs. Frederick K. Weyerhaeuser award, 1963; Disting. Alumni award Grand Rapids Jr. Coll., 1964, Alumnus of Yr. award U. Mich. Club of N.Y., 1978; recipient citation of merit award for outstanding contbns. to field of music, Alumni Bd., Sch. of Music, U. Mich., 1995. Mem. Am. Guild Musical Artists (nat. bd. govs. 1985-91, 94—, exec. com. 1994-99).

CHRISTOPHER, SHARON A. BROWN, bishop; b. Corpus Christi, Tex., July 24, 1944; d. Fred L. and Mavis Lorraine (Krueger) Brown; m. Charles Edmond Logsdon Christopher, June 17, 1973. BA, Southwestern U., Georgetown, Tex., 1966; MDiv, Perkins Sch. Theology, 1969; DD, Southwestern U., 1990; DST, McMurray Coll., 1996. Ordained to ministry United Meth. Ch., 1970; elected bishop 1988. Dir. Christian Edn. First United Meth. Ch., Appleton, Wis., 1969-70, assoc. pastor, 1970-72; pastor Butler United Meth. Ch., Butler, Wis., 1972-76, Calvary United Meth. Ch., Germantown, Wis., 1972-76, Aldersgate United Meth. Ch., Milw., 1976-80; dist. supt. Ea. Dist. Wis. Conf. United Meth. Ch., 1980-85; asst. to bishop Wis. Conf. Wis. Conf. United Meth. Ch., Sun Prairie, Wis., 1986-88; bishop North Cen. jurisdiction United Meth. Ch., Minn., 1988-96; bishop Ill. area United Meth. Ch., Ill. area, 1996—; resident bishop Ill. area United Meth. Ch., Springfield, 1996—. Contbr. articles and papers to religious publs. Bd. dirs. Nat. Coun. Chs. of Christ, 1988—, United Meth. Ch. Bd. of Ch. & Soc., 1988-92, bd. discipleship, 1992—; trustee Hamline U., St. Paul, 1988-96; gen. and jurisdictional conf. del., 1976, 80, 84, 88; mem. N. Cen. Jurisdiction Com. on Episcopacy, 1984-88, Com. on Investigation, 1980-88, Gen. Bd. Global Ministries, 1980-88, chmn. Mission Pers. Resources Program Dept., 1984-88. Named one of Eighty for the Eighties, Milw. Jour., 1980. •

CHRISTOPHER, STEVEN LEE, religious studies educator; b. Long Beach, Calif., May 29, 1956; s. Lehland James and Harriet Ann (Werner) C.; m. Doris Dianne Deterding, Aug. 19, 1978; children: LeAnna Helen, Brett Steven. BS in Edn., Concordia Coll., Seward, Nebr., 1979; MA, U. San Diego, 1989. Cert. tchr. and dir. Christian edn. Min. youth and edn. Bethany Luth. Ch., Long Beach, 1979-85; coord. youth ministries Christ Luth. Ch., La Mesa, Calif., 1985-88; prof., dir. Christian edn. program Concordia U, Calif., 1988-99; asst. to pres. CNH Dist., Luth. Ch. Mo. Synod, 1999—; dir. family ministry Our Savior Luth. Ch., Livermore, Calif., 1999—; chmn. youth com. Pacific SW dist. Luth. Ch.-Mo. Synod, Irvine, 1983-88, mem. extended staff bd. for youth svcs., St. Louis, 1988-91, com. mem. nat. youth gathering, 1986, 89; chmn. 1991 Nat. Dirs. Christian Edn. Conf., River Forest, Ill., 1989-91; mem. youth bd. Abiding Savior Luth. Ch., El Toro, Calif., 1989-94; spkr. various workshops and youth gatherings. Author young adult Bible study and youth Bible study, 1985, 3 devotions for children, 1988, chapel talks for children, 1989; contbr. articles to profl. jours. Mem. Theol. Educators in Assoc. Ministries (pres.-elect 1988-90, pres. 1990-92), Profl. Assn. Christian Educators, Religious Edn. Assn. Office: Concordia U 1530 Concordia Irvine CA 92612-3203

CHRISTOPHER, THOMAS WELDON, legal educator, administrator; b. Duncan, S.C., Oct. 8, 1917; s. William Arthur and Ruby (Thomas) C.; m. Evelyn Montez Hawkins, Oct. 25, 1950 (div.); 1 son, Thomas Heflin; m. Goldie Wood Gambrell, Jan. 6, 1985. AB, Washington and Lee U., 1939; LLB, U. Ala., 1948; LLM, NYU, 1950, JSD, 1957; LLD, U. Ala., 1978. Bar: Ala. 1948, Ga. 1955, N.Y. 1961, N.C. 1963, N.Mex. 1968. From asst. prof. to prof. law Emory U. Law Sch., 1950-61, assoc. dean, 1954-61; atty. Corn Products Co., 1959-60; prof. law U. N.C., 1961-65; dean U. N.Mex. Law Sch., 1965-71; prof. U. Ala. Sch. Law, 1971-88; dean Sch. Law U. Ala., 1971-81, dir. Ctr. Pub. Law and Svc., 1981-85; Mem. nat. adv. food and drug council HEW, 1968-70; v.p. Food and Drug Law Found., 1974-78. Author: Poems from a Carolina Farm, 1948, (with Dunn) Special Federal Food and Drug Laws Annotated, 1951, (with others) Georgia Procedure and Practice, 1957, Constitutional Questions in Food and Drug Law, 1960, Cases and Materials on Food and Drug Law, 1966, (with Goodrich) 2d edit., 1973, Santuc-Poems, 1994. Mem. Am. Bar Assn. Club: North River Yacht. Home: 327 W Prentiss Ave Greenville SC 29605-4035 Office: U Ala Sch Law PO Box 870382 Tuscaloosa AL 35487-0382

CHRISTOPHER, WARREN, lawyer, former government official; b. Scranton, N.D., Oct. 27, 1925; s. Ernest W. and Catharine Anna (Lemen) C.; m. Marie Josephine Wyllis, Dec. 21, 1956; children—Lynn, Scott, Thomas, Kristen. Student, U. Redlands, 1942-43; B.S. magna cum laude, U. So. Calif., 1945; LL.B., Stanford, 1949; LL.D. (hon.), Occidental U., 1977, Bates Coll., 1981, Brown U., 1981, Claremont Coll., 1981. Bar: Calif. 1949, N.Y., U.S. Supreme Ct. 1949. Law clk. U.S. Supreme Ct. Justice William O. Douglas, Washington, 1949-50; practice in Los Angeles, 1950-67, 69-76, 81-93, 97—; mem. firm O'Melveny & Myers, 1950-67, 69, ptnr., 1958-67, 69-76, 81-93, sr. ptnr., 1997—; dep. atty. gen. U.S., Washington, 1967-69; dep. sec. of state Dept. State, Washington, 1977-81; sec. U.S. Dept. of State, Washington, 1993-97; spl. counsel to Gov. Calif., 1959; cons. Office Under Sec. State, 1961-65; mem. bd. bar examiners State Bar Calif., 1966-67; dir. So. Calif. Edison Co., First Interstate Bancorp, Lockheed Corp.; chmn., trustee Carnegie Corp. N.Y.; mem. Calif. Coordinating Coun. for Higher Edn., 1960-67, pres., 1963-65; vice chmn. Gov.'s Commn. on L.A. Riots, 1965-66; chmn. U.S. delegations to U.S.-Japan Cotton Textile Negotiations, 1961, Geneva Conf. on Cotton Textiles, 1961; spl. rep. sec. state for Wool Textile Meetings, London, Rome, Tokyo, 1964-65; mem. Trilateral Commn., 1975-77, 81-88; mem. internat. adv. coun. Inst. Internat. Studies; chmn. Ind. Commn. on L.A. Police Dept., 1991. Author: In the Stream of History, 1998; co-author: American Hostages in Iran: The Conduct of a Crisis, 1985. Trustee Stanford U., 1971-77, 81-93, pres. bd. trustees, 1985-88; bd. dirs., vice chmn. Coun. on Fgn. Rels., 1982-91; bd. dirs. L.A. World Affairs Coun.; mem. exec. com. Am. Agenda, 1988; mem. U.S.-Korea Wisemen Coun., 1991-93. Lt. (j.g.) USNR, 1943-46. Decorated Medal of Freedom 1981; recipient Harold Weill award NYU, 1981, Louis Stein award Fordham U., 1981, Jefferson award Am. Inst. for Pub. Svc., UCLA medal, Thomas Jefferson award in law U. Va. Fellow Am. Bar Found., Am. Coll. Trial Lawyers, AAAS; mem. ABA (ho. dels. 1975-77, chmn. standing com. fed. judiciary 1975-77), Calif. Bar Assn. (gov. 1975-77), L.A. County Bar Assn. (pres. 1974-75), Am. Law Inst., Order of Coif, Calif. Club, Chancery Club, Phi Kappa Phi. Office: O'Melveny & Meyers 1999 Ave Of Stars Fl 7 Los Angeles CA 90067-6022•

CHRISTOPHER, WILFORD SCOTT, public relations consultant; b. Enid, Okla., Feb. 8, 1916; s. W. Scott and Mary Elizabeth (Heaton) C.; m. Marjorie Lois Lester, Dec. 30, 1941; 1 son, Scott Douglas. BA, Phillips U., 1938; MA, U. Iowa, 1941. Cert. chamber exec. Asst. prof. speech Phillips U., 1939, assoc. prof. sociology, 1940-42; clin. psychologist US Med. Adminstrn., 1942-44; chief VA Guidance Ctr U. Miami (Fla.), 1944-45; pub. relations dir. Miami (Fla.) C. of C., 1946-51; gen. mgr. Greater Tampa C. of C., 1951-64, exec. v.p., 1964-76, pres., 1976-78; dir. community relations U. Tampa, Fla., 1978-81; pres. W. Scott Christopher & Assos. (public relations), 1981-96; spl. asst. to chmn. Nat. Exec. Svcs. Corp., N.Y.C., 1980-82, Tampa, Fla.; mem. tech.-occupation adv. com. Hillsborough Jr. Coll., 1969-76, chmn. advanced mgmt. curriculum com., 1958-59; mem. Adv. Group on Continuing Edn. for Urban Leadership, 1967-68; mem. internat. com. C. of C. U.S., 1972-75, sr. adv. coun., 1978—, dir., 1976-78, chmn. nat. adv. coun. urban devel. 1959-60). Author Tampa's People With a Purpose, 1993; contbr. C. of C. Adminstrn. Bd. dirs. Tampa Philharm. Orch. Assn., Tampa Oral Sch. for Deaf, 1971-74; trustee U. South Fla. Found., 1959-65, 87-88, H.B. Plant Mus., 1979-82; mem. pres.'s adv. bd. U. South Fla., 1975-78, mem. pres.'s coun., 1978—; mem. exec. com. Fla. Eye Inst., U. South Fla. Coll. Medicine, 1982-90, bd. dirs., mem. exec. com. Suncoast Gerontology Ctr., 1986-96; v.p. Fla. Found. Eye Rsch.; trustee, mem. exec. com. U. Tampa, 1977-78, mem. bd. fellows, 1974, chmn. bd. fellows, 1976-77, sec.-treas., 1981-82; trustee Berkeley Prep. Sch., 1963-71, v.p., 1967-71. With USAF, 1942-44. Named Tampa Citizen of Year, 1972, Tampa Humanitarian of Year, 1973; elected Phillips U. Hall of Fame, 1988. Mem. Fla. C. of C. Execs. Assn. (pres. 1954), Southeastern Inst. C. of C. Execs. (pres. 1956), So. Assn. C. of C. Execs. (pres. 1972), Inst. Orgn. Mgmt. (bd. regents 1975-77), Am. C. of C. Execs. (sec.-treas., v.p. 1960, pres. 1961-62, chmn. nat. panel on exec. certification 1966). Clubs: Tampa Exchange (pres. 1956), Executive (past pres.), University (dir.), Tampa Yacht and Country, Ye Mystic Krewe of Gasparilla. Home: 10701 Carrollwood Dr Tampa FL 33618-4203

CHRISTOPHER, WILLIAM GARTH, lawyer; b. Beaumont, Tex., Oct. 14, 1940; s. Garth Daugherty and Ollye Mittie (Harkness) C.; m. Kathleen S. Christopher; children: John William, David Noah, Michael O'Hara. BS in Engring., U.S. Mil. Acad., 1962; JD, U. Va., 1970. Bar: Va. 1970, D.C. 1970, U.S. Supreme Ct. 1975, Mich. 1977, Fla. 1988, Tex. 1989. Assoc. Steptoe & Johnson, Washington, 1970-77; ptnr. Honigman Miller Schwartz & Cohn, Detroit, 1977-94, Holland & Knight, Tampa, Fla., 1994-95, Brown Clark, P.A., Sarasota, Fla., 1995—. Contbr. articles to legal publ. Pres. Birmingham (Mich.) Hockey Assn., 1982-84; mem. Episc. Diocese of Mich. Commn. on Ministry, 1983-88, co-chmn. 1987-88, standing com., 1988. Capt. C.E. U.S. Army, 1962-67. Mem. ABA, Va. Bar, D.C. Bar, Fla. Bar (cert. bus. litigation law), Tex. Bar, Sarasota County Bar Assn., Raven Soc., Nat. Bd. of Trial Advocacy (cert. civil trail advocacy), Order of Coif, Phi Delta Phi. Episcopalian. Office: Brown Clark PA 1819 Main St Ste 1100 Sarasota FL 34236-5926

CHRISTOPHERSEN, BILL, editor, writer; b. Bronx, N.Y., Oct. 8, 1949; s. George Wilhelm and Isabel (Thomson) C. BA in English, Columbia Coll., 1971; MA in Tchg. of English, Columbia U., 1976, PhD in Am. Lit., 1980. Bookstore staffer Tchrs. Coll. Bookstore, N.Y.C., 1974-79; adj. English instr. various colls., N.Y. and N.J., 1979-85; letters correspondent Newsweek, N.Y.C., 1985-90, mgr. letters dept., 1990-91, assoc. editor letters, 1991-95; freelance copy editor various mags., N.Y.C., 1996—. Author: The Apparition in the Glass, 1994; contbr. revs., essays to profl. jours., newspapers, mags.; rec. artist with Fly By Night String Band, Lazy Aces String Band. Vol. literacy tutor Jewish Cmty. League, 1995-96; sponsor Save the Children, 1982-96. Nat. Merit scholar, 1967-71. Avocations: traditional musician, fiddle, guitar. Home: 414 W 121st St Apt 58 New York NY 10027-6008

CHRISTOPHERSON, ELIZABETH GOOD, broadcast executive; b. Cin.; d. Walter R. and Jean S. Good; m. Paul C. Christopherson, July 3, 1971; 1 child, Katharine. BA, Wellesley Coll., 1971. Bd. dirs. N.J. State Coun. Arts, 1982—, chmn., CEO, 1989-91; exec. dir., CEO N.J. Network, Trenton, 1994—; pres., CEO NJN Found., 1994—; bd. dirs. McCarter Theater; mem. bus. leadership coun. Wellesly Coll. Pres., bd. dirs. Leadership Am. Assn., Alexandria, Va., 1991-92; bd. dirs. Girl Scouts U.S. Mem. N.J. C. of C. (bd. dirs.), N.J. Women's Forum (pres.). Office: NJ Network CN 777 Trenton NJ 08625

CHRISTOPHERSON, MYRVIN FREDERICK, college president; b. Milltown, Wis., July 21, 1939; s. Fred J. and Inger J. (Haug) C.; m. Anne Christine Marking, June 10, 1967; children: Kirsten, Berit, Bjorn, Nisse. BA, Dana Coll., 1961; MS, Purdue U., 1963, PhD, 1965; DD (hon.), Wartburg Theol. Sem., 1998. Teaching asst., instr. Purdue U., West Lafayette, Ind., 1961-65; asst. prof. speech U. Wis., Madison, 1965-69; assoc. prof. communication U. Wis., Stevens Point, 1969-76, prof. communication, 1976-86, assoc. dean. fine arts and communication, 1970-86; pres. Dana Coll., Blair, Nebr., 1986—; cons. Wis. Telephone, Milw., 1968-78, AT&T, N.Y.C., 1969-71, 1st Fin. Corp., Stevens Point, 1980-86; commr. Nebr. Coordinating Commn. for Post Sec. Edn., 1989-91. Author: Speaker's Trainer's Guide, 1970, The Company Speaker, 1979; editor Jour. of the Wis. Communication Assn., 1978-80. Mem. Nebr. Ednl. Fin. Authority, 1991-99, chmn., 1992-99; mem. adv. bd. The Lutheran, 1987-94, chmn., 1992-94; bd. dirs. Blair Cmty. Found. Bd., Planned Giving Svcs., Nebr., chmn., 1992-94; ann. fund appeal chmn. Meml. Cmty. Hosp., 1994; mem. pastoral call com. First Luth. Ch., 1995, ch. coun. mem., 1999; bd. trustees Palmer Chiropractic U., 1998—. Inducted into Wall of Honor, Unity High Sch., Polk County, Wis.; fellow Palmer Coll. Chiropractic, Palmer Coll. Chiropractic-West; named Knight of The Order of the Dannebrog, Queen Margrethe II of Denmark, 1997. Mem. Nat. Assn. Ind. Colls. and Univs. (bd. dirs. 1997-99), Assn. Ind. Colls. Nebr. (chmn. 1992-93), Nebr. Ind. Coll. Found. (exec. com. 1990-92, vice chmn. 1992-93, chmn. 1994-95), Luth. Edn. Conf. N.Am., (vice chmn. 1994-95, chmn. 1995-96), Nebr. Ednl. TV Coun. for Higher Edn. (chmn. 1990-91), N. Cen. Assn. Colls. and Schs. (cons.-evaluator 1997—). Avocations: international travel, reading, writing, antique collecting, study of theology. Office: Dana Coll Office of Pres Blair NE 68008

CHRISTY, ARTHUR HILL, lawyer; b. Bklyn., July 25, 1923; s. Francis Taggart and Catherine Virginia (Damon) C.; m. Gloria Garvin Osborne, Feb. 14, 1980; children by previous marriage: Duncan Hill, Alexandra. A.B., Yale U., 1945; LL.B., Columbia U., 1949. Bar: N.Y. 1950. Assoc. firm Baldwin, Todd & Lefferts, N.Y.C., 1950-52; spl. asst. atty. gen. Saratoga Investigation, N.Y., 1952-53; asst. U.S. atty. So. Dist. N.Y., 1953-54; chief prosecutor spl. asst. atty. gen. Saratoga and Columbia County Investigations, 1954-55; asst. atty. gen. N.Y., 1955; chief criminal div. U.S. atty.'s Office, So. Dist. N.Y., 1955-57; chief asst. U.S. atty., 1957-58, U.S. atty., 1958-59; partner firm Christy & Viener (and predecessors), N.Y.C., 1959—; spl. asst. to Gov. Rockefeller, 1959-61; apptd. 1st spl. prosecutor Under Ethics in Govt. Act of 1978 to investigate charges against White House Chief of Staff, 1979-80. Artist in scrimshaw. Trustee, vice chmn. Bklyn. Hosp., Cmty. Svc. Soc.; v.p., gen. counsel, mem. coun. N.Y. Heart Assn. Lt. USNR, 1944-46. Mem. ABA, N.Y. State Bar Assn., Fed. Bar Assn., Assn. Bar City N.Y. (chmn. exec. com. 1966-67), Am. Coll. Trial Lawyers, Century Assn., Rockefeller Luncheon Club, Univ. Club (N.Y.C.), Mastigouche Fish and Game Club (Que., Can.). Republican. Episcopalian. Home: 430 E 57th St New York NY 10022-3061 Office: 620 5th Ave New York NY 10020-2402

CHRISTY, CHARLES WESLEY, III, industrial engineering educator; b. Chester County, Pa., Apr. 29, 1942; s. Charles Wesley Jr. and Violet R. (Pierpont) C.; m. D. Jean Cullmann, Jan. 25, 1972; children: Richard Townsend, Charles Wesley IV, Michael Pierpont. BS, Widener U., 1973; MBA, Temple U., 1980. Chmn. indsl. engring. tech. Del. Tech. and C.C., Newark, 1970—; pres. Pierpont Industries, Inc., Wilmington, Del., 1985—; adj. assoc. prof. U. Del., Newark, 1994; examiner Del. Quality Award, Wilmington, 1994. Bd. dirs., past pres. Opportunity Ctr., Inc., Wilmington, 1972—. Mem. Am. Inst. Indsl. Engrs. (bd. dirs. Del. chpt. 1970—, past pres.), Am. Soc. Quality Control. Home: 11 Harlech Dr Wilmington DE 19807-2507 Office: Del Tech & CC 400 Stanton Christiana Rd Newark DE 19713-2111

CHRISTY, DAVID HARDACKER, secondary school educator, music educator; b. El Reno, Okla., Sept. 4, 1955; s. Roy Myron and Mary Kathryn (Collins) C. B of Mus. Edn. summa cum laude, Southwestern Okla. State U., 1977, MEd summa cum laude, 1978. Cert. tchr., Okla., Tex. Dir. of bands Wichita County Pub. Schs., Leoti, Kans., 1978-80, Elk City (Okla.) Pub. Schs., 1980-93, Hale Ctr. Pub. Schs., 1993-95; tchr. Southeastern Okla. State U., 1995—. Mus. dir. Miss Elk City Pageant, 1981-93; dir. Elk City Concert Band Contest, 1981-93, Elk City Cmty. Band, 1981-85, 87-93, Southeastern Okla. State U. Music Festival, 1995—, Hale Ctr. Music Festival, 1993-95; bd. dirs. Elk City Coun. on the Arts, 1980-93, Elk City Pageant, 1986-93, Western Okla. Symphony Soc., 1980-93, Red River Arts Coun., 1997—, Red River Arts Acad., 1997—; site chmn. Southeast Okla. Dist. Band, 1995—; condr. SOSU Cmty. Band, 1995—. Recipient Music Dir.'s award Okla. Secondary Sch. Activities Assn., 1989, 90, 93, award Elk City C. of C., 1989, award of appreciation Denison H.S. Band, 1996, Broken Bow H.S., 1998, faculty senate award for tchg. excellence Southeastern Okla. State U., 1996-97, Ea. Okla. Band Dirs. Assn., 1998. Mem. Western Okla. Symphony soc. (bd. dirs. 1980-93), Okla. Bandmasters Assn. (parliamentarian 1982-83, recording sec. 1983-84, v.p. 1984-85, pres. 1986-87), Okla. Music Educators Assn. (v.p. 1987-89), Okla. Music Adjudicators Assn. (exec. sec. 1986-93), Nat. Band Assn. (state chmn. 1985-86, rep nat. exec. bd. 1990-92, Citation of Excellence 1989, Dir. of Yr. 1989), Southwestern Okla. Band Dirs. Assn. (pres. 1983-84, Bandmaster of Yr. award 1982), Okla. Edn. Assn., Am. Sch. Band Dirs. Assn. (young band dir. of yr. 1986), Nat. Assn. Jazz Educators (Performance Cert. 1977, 78), Assn. Tex. Sml. Sch. Band Dirs. (assoc.), Music Adjudicators Assn. (exec. sec. Okla. 1986-93), Sosu Tchg. Acad., Phi Beta Mu (internat. bd. dirs. 1992-94, state v.p. 1992-93), Durant Lions Club, Phi Mu Alpha (Sinfonia Province Leadership award 1976), Kappa Kappa Psi (hon.). Democrat. Methodist. Avocations: tennis, snow skiing, baseball card collecting. Home: 1101 Melissa Dr Durant OK 74701-1777 Office: Southeastern Okla State U Dept of Music Box 4047 Durant OK 74701

CHRISTY, JOHN GILRAY, financial company executive; b. Silver Creek, N.Y., Aug. 27, 1932; s. John Van Vlack and Ruth (Gilray) C.; m. Helen Llewellyn, 1991; children: Andrew, Jennifer. BA, Dartmouth Coll., 1954; MA in Asian Studies, U. Calif., Berkeley, 1960. Loan officer U.S. Devel. Loan Fund, 1960-61; with AID, New Delhi and Washington, 1961-65; chief extended risk guaranty divsn. AID, 1965; with ITT, N.Y.C., 1965-72, treasury dept., 1965-68, v.p. internat. comm., 1968-69, asst. group exec. internat. comm., 1969-70; pres. ITT World Directories, Inc., N.Y.C., 1970-72; group v.p. land transp. IU Internat., Inc., Phila., 1972-76; exec. v.p. IU Internat., Inc., 1976-78; pres., COO IU Internat. Corp., 1978-80, chmn., pres., CEO, 1982-85, chmn., CEO, 1985-88; chmn. Chestnut Capital Corp., Phila., 1988—, First Fidelity Bank, Phila., 1991; mem. adv. bd.-north First Union Bank, 1995-98; bd. dirs. Echo Bay Mines Ltd., 1838 Bond Debenture Trading Fund, Phila. Contributionship. Chmn. Fgn. Policy Rsch. Inst.; former trustee Colby Coll.; trustee Phila. Orch., Eisenhower Exch. Fellowships Inc. Lt. USNR, 1958. Recipient Disting. Svc. award AID, 1965. Office: Chestnut Capital Corp PO Box 22 Flourtown PA 19031-0022

CHRISTY, LARRY TODD, publisher; b. Tarentum, Pa., July 2, 1946; s. Todd Rowley and Eleanor Fern (Rupert) C.; m. Kathleen Bernadette Braun, Nov. 26, 1976 (div. Feb. 1987); m. Lynn Elwell Sparrow, July 2, 1996. BA in Polit. Sci., Thiel Coll., 1968. Dir. Transact Corp., Geneva, 1972-76; pres. Transact Corp., Pitts., 1976-96, Trendvest Corp., Virginia Beach, Va., 1978—, Thirders Found., Shelocta, Pa., 1989—; dir. Share Found., Inc., Pitts., 1994—; seminar speaker on Hedge Funds, Charles Schwab, Chgo., Phoenix, San Francisco, Pitts. and Columbus, 1989; publisher Internet World Wide Web Svc. for Investors, 1994—. Editor electronic investment svc./ Trendvest Ratings, 1983—; author: Tax Trimmer Manual for Pennsylvania Corporations, 1980. Capt. mil. intelligence U.S. Army, Vietnam, Germany. Decorated Bronze Star. Mem. Thiel Coll. Alumni Assn. (pres. 1992-94, v.p. 1988-92, dir. 1983-95). Republican. Office: Trendvest Corp 1168 First Colonial Rd Ste 12 Virginia Beach VA 23454-2419

CHRISTY, NICHOLAS PIERSON, physician; b. Morristown, N.J., June 18, 1923; s. Leroy and Elizabeth (Baker) C.; m. Beverly Vairin Morris, June 21, 1947 (dec. Mar. 1997); children: Nicholas Pierson, Martha Vairin. A.B., Yale, 1945; M.D., Columbia, 1951. Diplomate: Am. Bd. Internal Medicine. Asst. vis. physician Delafield Hosp., N.Y.C., 1955-66; vis. physician Delafield Hosp., 1966-75; asst. vis. physician 1st med. div. Bellevue Hosp., N.Y.C., 1956-66; assoc. attending physician Presbyn. Hosp., N.Y.C., 1962-78; attending physician Presbyn. Hosp., 1978-93; dir. med. svc. Roosevelt Hosp., N.Y.C., 1965-79; faculty Columbia Coll. Phys. and Surg., N.Y.C., 1956—, assoc. prof. medicine, 1962-65, assoc. clin. prof., 1965-67, clin. prof. medicine, 1967-71, prof. medicine, 1971-79, lectr. in medicine, 1979-88, sr. lectr. medicine, 1988-93, spl. lectr. in medicine, 1993—; mem. Columbia U. Health Scis. adv. coun., 1993—; prof. medicine, assoc. dean vets. affairs Health Sci. Ctr. at Bklyn., SUNY, 1979-88, prof. emeritus, 1988—; chief staff Bklyn. VA Med. Ctr., 1979-88; writer-in-residence, alumni writer Coll. Physicians and Surgeons, Columbia U., 1988—; assoc. Nat. Humanities Ctr., Research Triangle Park, N.C., 1979; cons. FDA, 1966, Bd. of Health, N.Y.C., 1965—, NIH Nat. Inst. Diabetes, Digestive and Kidney Diseases tng. grants divsn., 1969-72, endocrinology study sect., 1975-79; cons., bd. dirs. Royal Soc. Medicine Found., 1984-93. Editor, co-author: The Human Adrenal Cortex, 1971; editor-in-chief: Jour. Clin. Endocrinology and Metabolism, 1963-67; assoc. editor: Beeson-McDermott Textbook of Medicine, 1968-75; cons. editor, 1975-79; cons. Med. Dictionary (Dorland), 1988; adv. editor and contbr. Internat. Dictionary of Medicine and Biology (Endocrinology), 1986; mem. adv. bd.: Am. Jour. Medicine, 1971-88; contbr. numerous papers to profl. publs. Served to lt. (j.g.) USNR, 1943-46, PTO. Recipient Borden award, Joseph Mather Smith prize Columbia; John and Mary R. Markle scholar; NIH tng. grantee, 1959-65, endocrinology study sect. grantee, 1958-69. Fellow Am. Med. Writers Assn. (hon., Swanberg award 1989); mem. Harvey Soc., AAAS, Soc. Exptl. Biology and Medicine, Am. Soc. Clin. Investigation, Am. Fedn. Clin. Rsch., A.C.P., N.Y. Acad. Medicine, Laurentian Hormone Conf., Am. Physiol. Soc., N.Y. State Med. Soc., N.Y. County Med. Soc., Am. Clin. and Climatol. Assn. (recorder 1977-88, pres. 1990), Am. Assn. Study Liver Diseases, Endocrine Soc. (sec.-treas. 1978-89, Ayerst award 1986), N.Y. Clin. Soc., N.Y. Med. and Surg. Soc., Assn. Am. Physicians, Interurban Clin. Club, Hosp. Grads. Club, Peripatetic Soc., Practitioners Soc., Elizabethan (Yale), Colony (Yale), Century Assn. (pres. 1987-90, hon. 1995—). Home: 1260 Palmetto Ct #105 Vero Beach FL 32963-4008

CHRISTY, THOMAS PATRICK, human resources executive, educator; b. Urbana, Ill., May 18, 1943; s. Edward Michael and Iona Theresa (Rogers) C.; m. Marjorie Anne McIntyre, June 1966 (div. May 1973); children: Thomas Patrick Jr., Derek Edward; m. Sandra Allen Stern, May 19, 1984 (div. Aug. 1996); children: Patrick Edward, Margaret Allen. BA in Psychology, Adams State Coll., 1965; MBA, Chapman U., 1997. Tchr. Colorado Springs Pub. Sch., 1965-69; regional personnel dir. Forest Service USDA, Washington, 1969-81; sr. account exec. Mgmt. Recruiters Inc., Costa Mesa, Calif., 1981-84; v.p. Coleman & Assoc. Inc., Santa Monica, Calif., 1984; asst. v.p. Union Bank, Los Angeles, 1984-88; v.p., human resources dir. TOPA Savs. Bank, Los Angeles, 1988-89, Cenfed Bank, Pasadena, Calif., 1989-91; v.p., regional human resources mgr., nat. dir. tng. Tokio Marine Mgmt., Inc., Pasadena, 1991-94, UCLA, 1991—; adj. prof. Coll. Bus. Mgmt., Northrop U., L.A., 1985-91, Coll. Bus. Mgmt., UCLA, 1991-98; bd. dirs. Human Resources Mgmt. Inst., L.A., pres., 1993-95; bd. dirs. The Employers Group; mem. editorial rev. bd. Calif. Labor Letter, L.A. Arbitrator/Bus. and Consumer Arbitrator program Better Bus. Bur., Los Angeles and Orange County; New IOB Dist. Dir. 27th Dist. U.S. Congress, Pasadena, Calif., 1998—; mem. Calif. Lincoln Clubs. Mem. Amer. Assn. Univ. Prof./Calif. Faculty Assn., Pers. and Indsl. Rels. Assn. (pres. 1993), Soc. Human Resources Mgmt. (Calif. state legis. affairs dir.), bd.dirs. Pasadena C. of C. and Civil Assn., Employment Mgmt. Assn., Soc. Profls. in Dispute Resolution, Am. Compensation Assn., Vestry St. Edmund's Episc. Ch., San Marino. Calif., Japanese Am. Soc. So. Calif., Adams State Coll. Alumni Assn. (Calif. state pres.), Town Hall Calif., Valley Hunt Club, L.A. Athletic Club, Beach Club, Sigma Pi Alumni Assn. Episcopalian. Avocations: fly fishing, golf, skiing, collecting antiques, bridge, trapshooting.

CHRITTON, GEORGE A., film producer; b. Chgo., Feb. 25, 1933; s. George A. and Dorothea C.; m. Martha Gilman, Aug. 26, 1956 (div. May 26, 1978); children: Stewart, Andrew, Douglas, Laura, Neil, Lyle. BA, Occidental Coll., 1955; postgrad., Princeton U., 1955-57. With CIA & various U.S. govt. agys., 1960-89; gen. ptnr. Margeo Investment Co., L.A., 1963-76; pres. Wildacre Prodns., Inc., L.A., 1990—; pres., CEO Fin. Svcs. Bancorp, Reno, 1990—; pres. Sycamore Prodns. Ltd., Nev. and Calif., 1994—. Mem. Am. Fgn. Svc. Assn., Washington, 1960—; chmn. bd. Neighborhood Learning Ctr., Capitol Hill, Washington, 1985-87; vol. Options House, Hollywood, Calif.; vol. coord. Rebuild L.A. Maj. USAF, 1957-60. Named Princeton Nat. Fellow, 1955-56, Vis. Fellow & Lectr. U. Calif., 1987-88. Mem. AFTRA, Am. Film Inst., Nat. Assn. Ind. Film & T.V. Prodrs., Phi Beta Kappa, Phi Gamma Delta, Alpha Mu Gamma, Alpha Phi Gamma, Princeton Club (So. Calif.). Office: Wildacre Prodns Inc PO Box 719 Beverly Hills CA 90213-0719

CHROMIZKY, WILLIAM RUDOLPH, accountant; b. Chgo., Jan. 21, 1955; s. Rudolph Joseph and Helen M. (Gniewek) C.; m. Laura Lee Lamoureux, Oct. 24, 1992. BS, No. Ill. U., 1977; M of Mgmt., Northwestern U., 1987. CPA, Ill. Sr. auditor Arthur Andersen & Co., Chgo., 1977-83; supr. internal audit AM Internat., Chgo., 1983-84, mgr. fin. reporting, 1984-85, dir. acctg., 1985; mgr. bus. analysis Premark Internat., Inc., Deerfield, Ill., 1985-87; dir. fin. reporting Premark Internat., Inc., Deerfield, 1987—. Vol. CPAs for the Pub Interest, Chgo., 1990-92; mem. fin. com. Brother Rice H.S., 1995—, bd. dirs., 1999—. Mem. AICPA, Ill. CPA Soc. Avocations: skiing, tennis, bowling, competitive running. Office: Premark Internat 1717 Deerfield Rd Deerfield IL 60015-3977

CHROMOW, SHERI P., lawyer; b. N.Y.C., Aug. 27, 1946; d. Abe and Sara L. Pinsky. BA, Barnard Coll., N.Y.C., 1968; JD, NYU, 1971. Ptnr. Shearman & Sterling, N.Y.C., 1979—; lectr. Omega Enterprises, Practising Law Inst. Mem. Urban Land Isnt., Nat. Realty Com., Women's City Club. Office: Shearman & Sterling 599 Lexington Ave Fl C2 New York NY 10022-6069

CHRONISTER, GREGORY MICHAEL, newspaper editor; b. York, Pa., Nov. 28, 1953; s. Francis Gilbert and Mary Jane (Hamberger) C. AB, Grove City (Pa.) Coll., 1975. Features editor The Ghent Press, Norfolk, Va., 1975, mng. editor, 1976; co-founder, editor Tidewater After Dark, Norfolk, 1977-79; asst. dir. New Va. Rev. Inc., Norfolk, 1979-80; editor univ. publs. Old Dominion U., Norfolk, 1980-85; assoc. editor Edn. Week, Washington, 1985-89, mng. editor, 1989—. Mem. Hist. Soc. Washington, Theodore Roosevelt Assn., Omicron Delta Kappa. Office: Edn Week 6935 Arlington Rd Ste 100 Bethesda MD 20814-5233

CHRONISTER, RICHARD DAVIS, physicist; b. Birmingham, Ala., Aug. 17, 1943; s. Richard D. and Mary Anne (Bealmear) C.; m. Vickie A. Bacon, Apr. 10, 1965; children: Susan K., Karen J. BS in Physics, U. Okla., 1965; MS in Nuclear Engring., Ohio State U., 1968. Cert. electromagnetic compatibility engr. Commd. 2d lt. USAF, 1965; advanced through grades to maj., 1977; Project mgr. USAF Aeropropulsion Lab., Dayton, Ohio, 1965-69; electronics survivability officer Field Command Def. Nuclear Agy., Livermore, Calif., 1969-72; grad. student U. Okla., Norman, 1972-75; mgr., transient radiation effects on electronics USAF Weapons Lab., Albuquerque, 1975-78; chief, radiation analysis lab. USAF Tech. Applications Ctr., Sacramento, Calif., 1979-83; chief aircraft and space sys. USAF Nuclear Criteria Group Secretariat, Albuquerque, 1983-86; prin. engr./physicist BDM Internat., Albuquerque, 1986-97; prin. engr. ops. rsch. TRW, Albuquerque, 1997—. Author, co-author tech. reports. Sr. mem. Am. Inst. Aeronautics and Astronautics; mem. AAAS, Am. Phys. Soc., Nat. Assn. Radio and Telecommunications Engrs. Methodist. Achievements include support of development of Army, Navy, Air Force , NASA and Department of Energy programs in the areas of environmental compliance, integrated electromagnetics, nuclear and natural environmentals, test and evaluation, distributed interactive simulation, verification, validation and accreditation. Home: 13005 Rebonito Rd NE Albuquerque NM 87112-4819 Office: TRW 6001 Indian Sch NE Albuquerque NM 87110

CHRONISTER, VIRGINIA ANN, school nurse, educator; b. York, Pa., Sept. 25, 1940; d. Ernest B. and Mary L. (Anderson) Stokes; m. Burton F. Chronister, June 13, 1964; children: Scott E., Karen A. Student, York Jr. Coll., Millersville (Pa.) Coll.; diploma, Harrisburg (Pa.) Hosp., 1961; BS in Profl. Arts, St. Joseph's Coll., North Windham, Maine, 1985; M. (e-quivalency), Pa. State U., 1989; postgrad., St. Joseph's Coll., North windham, Maine. RN, Pa.; cert. sch. nurse (edn. specialist II), Pa. Charge nurse Harrisburg Hosp., 1961-64; instr., practical nurses York City Sch. Dist., 1964-68; instr., med. secs. Yorktowne Bus. Inst., York, 1985; sch. nurse West York Sch. Dist., York, 1985—; substitute sch. nurse, 1972-85. Recipient Cardiac Nursing award. Mem. NEA, AAUW, Pa. State Edn. Assn. (sch. nurse sect.), Pa. Sch. Health Assn., Nat. Assn. Sch. Nurses, Harrisburg Hosp. Alumnae Assn., York County Sch. Nurse Assn. (pres. 1991-92), United Ostomy Assn. (charter mem.), West York Area Edn. Assn. (pres. 1990-98, chief negotiator 1999—), York County Coord. Coun. (sec. 1998—), Beta Sigma Phi. Home: 2090 Loman Ave York PA 17404-4214

CHRONLEY, JAMES ANDREW, real estate executive; b. Springfield, Mass., July 31, 1930; s. Robert Emmett and Eleanor Agnes (Sullivan) C.; m. Monique Mary Delpech, July 29, 1955; children: Mary Elizabeth, James Michael, Jean Louise, Patricia, Joseph Patrick, John Peter, Robert Emmett. A.B., Brown U., 1952; diploma in real estate, U. R.I., 1963; MBA, Peppderdine U., 1991. With Arco Co., 1954-74, Eastern area mgr., until 1972; nat. real estate dir. Atlantic Richfield Co., Los Angeles, 1972-74; v.p. restaurant real estate Marriott Corp., Washington, 1974-78; exec. v.p. Burger Chef Systems, Inc., Indpls., 1978-82; pres. Burger Chef Systems, Inc., 1982; sr. v.p. devel. Taco Bell, Irvine, Calif., 1983-94. Served with AUS, 1952-54. Mem. Nat. Assn. Corp. Real Estate Execs. (chpt. pres. 1979, chmn. bd. 1985-87, elected trustee 1987-92), Am. Arbitration Assn., Internat. Exec. Svc. Corps, Orange County Assn. Investment Mgrs. Roman Catholic. Office: Taco Bell 19800 Macarthur Blvd Ste 1450 Irvine CA 92612-2421

CHRYSANTHIS, PANOS KYPROS, computer science educator, researcher; b. Nicosia, Cyprus, Feb. 1, 1958; came to U.S., 1983; s. Kypros and Loulla Chrysanthis; m. Areti Papanastasiou, Jan. 7, 1989. BS in Physics and Math., U. Athens, Greece, 1982; MS in Computer and Info. Scis., U. Mass., 1986, PhD in Computer and Info. Scis., 1991. Rsch. scientist U. Athens, Greece, 1983; tchg. asst./assoc. U. Mass., Amherst, 1983-85, rsch. asst., 1984-91, rsch. vis. faculty mem., 1992-94; asst. prof. U. Pitts., 1991-97, assoc. prof. computer sci., 1997—; vis. prof. U. Rome La Sapienta, 1994; hon. rsch. fellow Alba Bus. Adminstrn., Athens, Greece, 1995—; guest editor spl. issue Distributed Sys. Engring. Jour., 1996; co-chair 1998 NSF Info. and Data Mgmt. Workshop Rsch. Agenda for 21st Century; mem. program com., referee, reviewer for numerous confs., orgns. Author: Advances in Concurrency Control and Transaction Processing, 1997; contbr. articles to profl. publs., chpts. to books in field. Recipient award for understanding autonomy in multidatabase NSF, 1992-96, Career award for mobile data mgmt. NSF, 1995—; grantee Rsch. Devel. Fund, U. Pitts., 1992-94, DEC Equipment Allowance, 1991, B-Right Trucking Co., 1994-95. Mem. IEEE, Assn. for Computing Machinery, Hellenic Soc. Computer and Info. Scientists, Sigma Xi. Office: U Pitts Computer Sci Dept Alumni Hall Pittsburgh PA 15260

CHRYSLER, RICHARD R., former congressman; b. St. Paul, Apr. 29, 1942; m. Katie; children: Richard R., Phil, Christie Ann. With Chevrolet divsn. Gen. Motors Corp., 1960-64, Hurst Performance, Inc., Brighton, Mich., 1966-76; founder, chmn. Cars & Concepts, Inc., Brighton, 1976-86, RCI; U.S. congressman Mich. 8th Dist., 1995-96; pres. JPE, Inc., 1998-99; vice chmn. ASCET, Inc., 1999—; bd. dirs. Mich. Nat. Bank. Patentee skylite T-roof. Home: 8485 Hilton Rd Brighton MI 48114*

CHRYSOSTOMOS (GONZÁLEZ-ALEXOPOULOS), archbishop, clergyman, psychologist, educator; b. Apr. 6, 1943. BA, U. Calif.-Riverside, 1964, Calif. State U., San Bernardino, 1971; MA, U. Calif., Davis, 1970, Princeton U., 1974; PhD, Princeton U., 1975. Bishop True Orthodox Ch. of Greece. Preceptor in psychology Princeton U., 1972-75; asst. prof. psychology U. Calif., Riverside, 1975; adj. asst. prof. Christian thought Ashland (Ohio) Theol. Sem., 1981-83; asst., assoc. prof. psychology Ashland U., 1980-83; dir. Ctr. for Traditional Orthodox Studies, Etna, Calif., 1981-85, scholar-in-residence, 1986, acad. dir., from 1986; bishop of Etna; vis. scholar Harvard Divinity Sch., 1981; vis. assoc. prof. Uppsala U., Sweden, from 1987. Marsden research fellow Oxford U., 1985. Greek Orthodox.

CHRYSSAVGIS, JOHN, theology educator, administrator; b. Adelaide, Australia, Apr. 1, 1958; came to U.S., 1995; m. Sophie Antoniadou, Apr. 29, 1959; children: Alexander, Julian. Diploma in Byzantine music, Greek Conservatorium of Music, Athens, 1979; BD with honors, Athens (Greece) U., 1980; DPhil, Oxford (Eng.) U., 1983. Sub-dean St. Andrew's Theol. Coll., Sydney, Australia, 1985-95; lectr. Sydney U., 1986-95; dir. religious studies Hellenic Coll., Boston, 1995—; prof. Holy Cross Sch. of Theology, Boston, 1995—, acting dean, 1997-98; deacon Greek Orthodox Archdiocese of Am., 1995—; protodeacon Greek Orthodox Ch. in Australia, 1984-95; mem. Standing Com. of Liturgical Translations, 1997—, Faith and Sci. Exch., Boston, 1996—. Author: (books) Ascent to Heaven, 1989, Repentance and Confession, 1990, The Desert Is Alive, 1991, Love and Sexuality, 1996; revs. editor: Greek Orthodox Theol. Rev., 1996—; internat. corr.: Pacifica, 1995—. Internat. scholar Ministry of Edn., Greece, 1976-80. Mem. N.Am. Patristics Soc., Inst. for Theology and the Arts (advisor 1990-95). Greek Orthodox. Avocations: reading, walking, traveling. Home: 50 Goddard Ave Brookline MA 02445-7415

CHRYSTAL, WILLIAM GEORGE, minister; b. Seattle, May 22, 1947; s. Francis Homer and Marjorie Isabell (Daubert) C.; m. Mary Frances King, Aug. 24, 1970; children: Shelley, Sarah, John, Philip. BA, U. Wash., 1969, MEd, 1970; MDiv, Eden Theol. Sem., 1978; MA, Johns Hopkins U., 1984. Ordained to ministry, United Ch. of Christ, 1977. Learning resources specialist Seattle C.C. Dist., 1970-71; dir. learning resources ctr. Whatcom C.C., Ferndale, Wash., 1971-73; minister St. Peter's United Ch. of Christ, Granite City, Ill., 1978-79; sr. minister 1st Congl. Ch., Stockton, Calif., 1979-83; minister Trinity United Ch. of Christ, Adamstown, Md., 1983-85; sr. minister Edwards Congl. Ch., Northampton, Mass., 1985-86, 1st Congl. Ch., Reno, Nev., 1991—; hosp. chaplain Washoe Med. Ctr., Reno, 1993—; host Thomas Jefferson Hour, on nat. pub. radio stas. Author: Young Reinhold Niebuhr: His Early Writings, 1911-1931, 1977, 2d edit., 1982, A Father's Mantle: The Legacy of Gustav Niebuhr, 1982, The Fellowship of Prayer, 1987; author monographs; contbr. articles to profl. jours. V.p. Reno-Sparks Met. Ministry, Reno, 1994-97; Chautauqua scholar Great Basin Chautauqua, Reno, 1993, 94, 98. Lt. comdr. USN, 1986-91, maj. Nev. Army N.G., 1992-96. Decorated (2) Meritorious Svc. medal. Mem. Am. Soc. Ch. History, Nev. Soc. Mayflower Descs. (gov.), Am. Legion, Disabled Vets. (life), VFW (life), Rotary Club (Paul Harris fellow 1997). Home: 3820 Bluebird Cir Reno NV 89509-5601 Office: 1st Congl Ch 627 Sunnyside Dr Reno NV 89503-3515

CHRYSTIE, THOMAS LUDLOW, investor; b. N.Y.C., May 24, 1933; s. Thomas Witter and Helen (Duell) C.; m. Eliza S. Balis, June 9, 1955; children: Alice B., Helen S., Adden B., James MacD. BA, Columbia U., 1955; MBA, NYU, 1960. With Merrill Lynch, Pierce, Fenner & Smith, Inc., N.Y.C., 1955-75, dir. investment banking divsn., 1970-75; sr. v.p. Merrill Lynch & Co., 1975-78, CFO, 1976-78; chmn. Merrill Lynch White Weld Capital Markets Group, 1978-81, Merrill Lynch Capital Resources, 1981-83; adv. on strategy Merrill Lynch & Co. Inc., 1983-88; pvt. investor Jackson, Wyo., 1988—; bd. dirs. Consumer Portfolio Svcs., Inc., Eeonyx Corp. Trustee emeritus Columbia U.; trustee Nat. Mus. Wildlife Art, Middleton Place Found. Capt. USAF, 1955-58. Mem. N.Y. Athletic Club, Teton Pines Tennis Club, Columbia Club. Home and Office: PO Box 640 Wilson WY 83014-0640 *Whatever you are involved in, see it as part of a larger picture.*

CHRZANOWSKI, JOSEPH, language educator; b. Providence, Sept. 2, 1941; children: Joseph, Jennifer. AB, Fairfield U., 1966; MA, Pa. State U., 1967, PhD, 1971. Prof. Spanish Calif. State U., L.A., 1969—, chair dept. modern langs. and lit., 1994—; pres. Calif. State U. fgn. lang. coun., 1997-99, SAT II devel. com., 1999. Fordham U. Chilean Program grantee U.S. Dept. State, 1964; NDEA Title IV fellow, 1966-69. Mem. MLA, Am. Coun. on the Teaching of Fgn. Langs., Asociacion Internacional de Hispanistas, Am. Assn. Tchrs. Spanish and Portuguese, Polish Inst. Arts and Scis. Am., Calif. Lang. Tchrs. Assn. (bd. dirs. 1997—), Assn. Depts. Fgn. Lang. (exec. com. 1999—), Phi Kappa Phi (pres. chpt. 1979-80). E-mail: jchrzan@calstatela.edu. Office: Calif State U LA Dept Modern Langs and Lit 5151 State University Dr Los Angeles CA 90032

CHRZANOWSKI, LEYE JEANETTE, publisher; b. Aug. 23, 1946. Pres., founder Excel Networking Group, Inc., Va., 1991-94; v.p., exec. editor EKR Comms., Md., 1993-97; pres. Disability News Svc., Va., 1991-94. E-mail: leye@disabilitynews.com. Home: 13703 Southernwood Ct Chantilly VA 20151-3345

CHRZANOWSKI, WINIFRED HELENE, data management specialist; b. Detroit, Jan. 16, 1944; d. Fred J. Neview and Jacquelyn R. Chuiminatto; m. Daniel D. Deiterick, Feb. 23, 1963 (div. Sept. 1974); children: John, Jill Davies, Jennifer; m. Albert R. Chrzanowski, Aug. 20, 1978. BA, Oakland U., 1992, MA, 1996. Data mgmt. specialist Gen. Dynamics, Sterling Heights, Mich., 1977—; adj. tchr. Oakland C.C., Auburn Hills, Mich., 1997, Dorsey Bus. Sch., Madison Heights, Mich., 1997; ESL tutor Oakland Lit. Coun., Pontiac, Mich., 1997—. Contbr. articles to profl. jours. Tutor Oakland Lit. Coun., Pontiac, 1996—. Mem. Modern Lang. Assn., Midwest Modern Lang. Assn. Avocations: travel, reading, knitting, gardening, fitness. Office: Gen Dynamics Land Systems 38500 Mound Rd Sterling Heights MI 48310

CHU, BENJAMIN THOMAS PENG-NIEN, chemistry educator; b. Shanghai, China, Mar. 3, 1932; came to U.S., 1953; s. Charles C. and Gladys (Chen) C.; m. Louisa King, Mar. 30, 1959; children: Peter, Joanne, Laurence. BS magna cum laude, St. Norbert Coll., 1955; PhD, Cornell U., 1959. Research assoc. Cornell U., Ithaca, N.Y., 1958-62; asst. prof. U. Kans., Lawrence, 1962-65, assoc. prof., 1965-68; prof. chemistry SUNY, Stony Brook, 1968-88, Leading prof. chemistry, 1988-92, Disting. prof., 1992—, chmn. chemistry dept., 1978-85, prof. materials sci. and engring., 1982—; vis. prof. U. New South Wales, Australia, 1974, Australian Nat. U., 1974, Wayne State U., Hokkaido U., 1975, Japan Soc. Promotion Sci., 1975-76, 92-93; vis. scientist Inst. for Theoretical Physics, U. Calif., Santa Barbara, 1982; cons. Calgon, Pitts., 1978-80, E.I. DuPont de Nemours, Wilmington, Del., 1979—, W.L. Gore & Assocs., Inc., Elkton, Md., 1998—, Dow Chem., Freeport, Tex., 1998—, Brookhaven (N.Y.) Instruments, 1981, USRA, Microgravity Sci. and Applications divsn. NASA, 1988, Bristol-Myers Squibb Co., 1990-92; hon. prof. Academia Sinica, China, 1992—, Nankai U., China, 1996—, Xiamen U., China, 1998—. Author: Molecular Forces, 1967, Problems in Chemical Therodynamics, 1967, Laser Light Scattering, 1974; editor: NATO ASI series B: Physics, Vol. 73, 1981, SPIE Milestone series: Selected Papers on Quasielastic Light Scattering by Macromolecular, Supramolecular, and Fluid Systems, Vol. MS 12, 1990, Laser Light Scattering: Basic Principles and Practice, 2d edit., 1991; patentee prism light scattering cells, method and apparatus for determining viscosity, light scattering and spectroscopic detector, magnetic needle rheometer, electrophoretic mobility of fluorophore labeled particles in gels, by fluorophore movement after photo bleaching. Sloan Research fellow, 1966-68, John Simon Guggenheim fellow, 1968-69; recipient Humboldt award 1976-77, 92-93, Disting. Achievement award St. Norbert Coll., 1981, Soc. Polymer Sci. Japan Disting. Svc. in Advancement Polymer Sci. award, 1997, Achievement award Chinese Inst. Engrs., 1998. Fellow Am. Phys. Soc., Am. Inst. Chemists (High Polymer Physics prize 1993); mem. Am. Crystallographic Assn., Am. Chem. Soc. (Langmuir Disting. Lectr. award 1994).

CHU, DAVID S. C., economist; b. N.Y.C., May 28, 1944; s. H.T. and Esther (Briney) C.; m. Laura L. Tosi, Apr. 1, 1978. BA, Yale U., 1964, PhD, 1972. Asst. dir. nat. security and internat. affairs Congl. Budget Office, Washington, 1978-81; dir. then asst. sec. def. for program analysis and evaluation Dept. Def., Washington, 1981-93; economist RAND, Santa Monica, Calif., 1970-78; sr. fellow RAND, Washington, 1993-94, dir. Washington rsch. dept., 1994-96, dir. Washington office, assoc. chmn. of rsch. staff, 1996-98; v.p. army rsch. divsn., dir. Arroyo Ctr., 1998—. Capt. U.S. Army, 1968-70, Vietnam. Decorated Bronze Star, Army Commendation medal. Fellow Nat. Acad. Pub. Adminstrn.; mem. Phi Beta Kappa. Office: Rand 1333 H St NW Washington DC 20005-4707

CHU, DEH-YING, chemist, researcher; b. Shanghai, China, Nov. 13, 1944; came to the U.S., 1981; d. Han Chang Chu and Cai Di Xu; (div. 1995); children: Kevin S. Lu, Xiao Qin Lu. MS, U. Sci. & Tech., Beijing, 1981; PhD, U. Notre Dame, 1986. Asst. faculty fellow U. Notre Dame, South Bend, Ind., 1987-90; R&D chemist Calgon Corp., Pitts., 1990—; symposium presenter Photochemistry and Photophysics, 1996. Contbr. articles to books. Mem. ACS (polymer divsn., analytical chemistry divsn.). Home: 5087 Spring House Ln Bridgeville PA 15017-1549 Office: Calgon Corp PO Box 1346 Pittsburgh PA 15230-1346

CHU, ELLIN RESNICK, librarian, consultant; b. Bklyn., Nov. 23, 1932; d. David and Isobel (Janowitch) Resnick; m. Wallace Chu, Aug. 29, 1960 (div. Sept. 1979); children: Steven, Joshua, Amanda. BA in Modern European Hist. with honors, Ind. U., 1954, MA in Libr. Sci., 1956; postgrad., Columbia U., 1956-57. Young adult libr. Donnell br. N.Y. Pub. Libr., 1956-57; order libr. Nat. Indsl. Conf. Bd., 1957-58; reference libr. Columbia U. Reference Libr., 1958-59; libr. dir. Hillside Hosp., 1959-61, L.I. Jewish-Hillside Med. Ctr., 1972—; adult/young adult libr. Glen Cove (N.Y.) Pub. Libr., 1973-77; young adult cons. Rochester (N.Y.) Pub. Libr. Monroe County Libr. Sys., 1977-93, mgr. lit., religion and philosophy divsn., 1993-98, ret., 1998; mem. nomination com. Glen Cove Interagy. Coun., 1976, chair youth recreation com., 1974-75, chair pre-screening com., info. and referral adv. bd. Nassau Libr. Sys., 1977; mem. libr. planning com. Rochester Sesquicentennial, 1984; mem. cen. libr. planning com. Rochester Pub. Libr., 1985-86; sec. Rochester Area Youth Dirs. Coun., 1980-81, mem. nominating com., 1987, profl. improvement com., 1987-89; presenter programming and svcs. for young adults Mid-Hudson Libr. Sys., Albany, N.Y., 1989-90; mem. On-line pub. catalog planning com. Monroe County Libr. Sys., 1986-92; libr. programming presenter and resource team mem. Learning Odyssey/SUNY Albany and New York State Divsn. Libr. Devel., 1989; active Brighton Cable Commn., 1980-93. Co-author chpt. to book: Our Family, Our Friends, Our World: An Annotated Guide to Significant Multicultural Books for Children and Teenagers, 1991; contbr. articles to profl. jours. Recipient 1st prize N.Y. Libr. Ad Hoc Com. on Women's Concerns, 1975; grantee Young Adult Libr. Instrn. Project, 1982-84; scholar Robert Flaherty Film Seminar, 1976, Lyman Langdon scholar Audubon Ecology Workshop, 1977. Mem. ALA (young adult svcs. divsn., chair high interest/low literacy level materials evaluation com. 1979-81, pub. liaison com. 1988-90, Margaret A. Edwards Author Award com. 1991-93), Ednl. Film Libr. Assn. (juror Am. Film Festival 1976-78, jury chair 1979-88), N.Y. Libr. Assn. (pres. youth svcs. sect. 1984, founding mem./sec. film/video roundtable 1977), Nassau County Libr. Assn. (founding mem. young adult sect. 1976).

CHU, ESTHER BRINEY, retired history educator; b. Bluff City, Ill., Jan. 27, 1911; d. John and Charlotte (Shaw) Briney; m. H.T. Chu, Apr. 19, 1935 (dec. May 1983); children: David S.C., Edna S.C., George S.T. BA, U. Ill., 1935, MA, 1936; PhD, Northwestern U., 1942. Prof. history Hunter Coll., N.Y.C., 1943-45, 55-58; prof. history Jersey City (N.J.) State Coll., 1959-75, prof. emeritus, 1976; pres., faculty assoc. day coun., exec. com. Jersey City State Coll., 1960-75; founder Can. studies program, New Jersey Colls. Author: Briney Families, 1976, Briney Patriots Pioneers and Families, 1979, Briney Families Coast to Coast, 1989. Past pres. YWCA, Mt. Vernon, N.Y.; bd. dirs. Pilgrim Place, Claremont, Calif., 1984-92; chmn. Young People's Dem. Club, Schuyler County, Ill., 1932-33, UN Women's Guild, Westchester County, N.Y., 1951-60. Named Outstanding Educator of Am., 1971, Ill. Coll. scholar, 1931; Northwestern U. fellow, 1938. Mem. Am. Hist. Assn. (life), AAUP (pres. coll. chpt. 1970-72, nat. com. W 1972-75), AAUW, Assn. Can. Studies in U.S., LWV (pres. 1982-83), Phi Alpha Theta. Democrat. Episcopalian. Avocations: theater, music, sports, forums. Home: 2734 Mountain View Dr La Verne CA 91750-4312

CHU, FRANKLIN DEAN, lawyer; b. Hankow, Hubei, China, Apr. 26, 1948; s. Victor Fu Hua and Margaret W.T. (Tsow) C.; m. Christine Park, Sept. 9, 1988; 1 Child; Anthony Tian Ming. AB, Harvard U., 1971; JD, Yale U., 1976; postgrad., Institut d'Etudes Politiques, Paris, 1968-69. Bar: D.C. 1976. Assoc. Shaw, Pittman, Potts & Trowbridge, Washington, 1976-79, Coudert Bros., Hong Kong, 1979-83; ptnr. Kaye, Scholer, Fierman, Hays & Handler, LLP, Hong Kong, 1984—; chmn. Kaye, Scholer Asia Cons., Ltd., 1985—; dir. mental health project Ctr. for Study Responsive Law, Washington, 1969-73. Author: (with others) France: The Events of May-June 1968, 1973, The Madness Establishment, 1974; co-editor: Commercial, Business and Trade Laws: People's Republic of China, 1982; contbr. numerous articles to profl. jours. Henry Russell Shaw fellow Harvard U., 1971. Mem. ABA, D.C. Bar Assn., Am. Arbitration Assn., Internat. Bar Assn., Inter-Pacific Bar Assn., Exec., Comm., Asia Pacific Ctr for the Resolution of Business Disputes, Pacific Basin Econmic Coun., Am. Club. of Hong Kong. Office: Kaye Scholer Fierman et al, 9 Queen's Rd Ctrl 18th Fl, Hong Kong China*

CHU, HORN DEAN, chemical engineer; b. China, Sept. 9, 1933; s. Johnson S.T. and Daisy (Hsia) C.; m. Pik Yu Cheung, June 23, 1962. BS, Waseda U., Tokyo, 1959, MS, 1961; MS, U. Pa., 1963; PhD, U. Ala., 1965. Project engr. Selas Corp., Dresher, Pa., 1965-71; asst. and adj. prof. Rutgers U., New Brunswick, N.J., 1971-79; sr. process engr. MacAndrews & Forbes Co., Camden, N.J., 1979-81; pres. Berkorp, Inc., Haddonfield, N.J., 1981—. Contbr. articles to profl. jours. Fellow Am. Inst. Chemists; mem. AIChE, Am. Chem. Soc., Inst. Food Technologists, AAAS, Sigma Xi. Office: Berkorp Inc 6-10S Haddon Ave Haddonfield NJ 08033-1860

CHU, HSIEN MING, investment company executive; b. Tai-an, Shandon, China, Sept. 17, 1936; came to the U.S., 1965; s. Yung-Bao and I-Ing Chu; m. Anita (Yung) Chu, Sept. 6, 1970; children: Antony, Lawrence, Frederick. BA, Nat. Taiwan U., Taipei, 1964; MA, U. Wis., 1968, PhD, 1978. Acad. staff U. Wis., Madison, 1968-78, rsch. assoc., 1978-84, assoc. rschr., 1984-86; pres. Lanteen Internat. Investment Co., Madison, 1986—; also bd. dirs. Lanteen Internat., Madison. Contbr. articles to profl. jours. Mem. Am. Culinary Fedn., Sigma Xi. Home: 7310 New Washburn Way Madison WI 53719

CHU, HSIEN-KUN, chemist, researcher; b. Shanghai, People's Republic of China, Oct. 14, 1947; came to U.S., 1971; s. Hwei-Teh and Yun-Hsiang (Chang) C.; m. Winnie K.S. Wong, Dec. 23, 1976; children: James C., Jason C. BS, Nat. Taiwan U., Taipei, Republic of China, 1970; PhD, Vanderbilt U., 1976. Vis. instr. U. Tex., Arlington, 1976-77; rsch. assoc. Tex. Christian U., Ft. Worth, 1977-80; rsch. specialist Dow Corning Corp., Midland, Mich., 1980-88; sr. scientist Loctite Corp., Rocky Hill, Conn., 1988—. Contbr. rsch. articles to sci. jours. Mem. Am. Chem. Soc., Sigma Xi. Achievements include patents on silicone sealants; research into mechanistic studies of organic reactions, silicone research. Home: 6 Harvest Hl Wethersfield CT 06109-2422 Office: Loctite Corp 1001 Trout Brook Xing Rocky Hill CT 06067-3910

CHU, JEFFREY CHUAN, business executive, consultant; b. Tianjen, China, July 14, 1919; came to U.S., 1940; s. Yao and Vanyi (Tang) C.; m. Loretta Y. Yung, Feb. 9, 1928; children: Lynnet Helbig, Bambi Rae, Dashie Kocica. BSEE, U. Minn., 1942; MSEE, U. Pa., 1945. Rsch. assoc. Moore Sch., U. Pa., Phila., 1944-48; sr. engr. Reeves Instrument Co., N.Y.C., 1948-50; chief sr. scientist Argonne Nat. Lab., Lemont, Ill., 1950-56; dir engring. Sperry Univac, Phila., 1956-62; v.p. asst., gen. mgr. Honeywell Info. Systems Inc., Waltham, Mass., 1962-72; sr. v.p. Wang Labs., Lowell, Mass., 1972-74; prin. advisor Nat. Sci. Commn., ROC, Taipei, Taiwan, People's Republic China, 1974-77; chmn., chief exec. officer Santec Corp., Amherst, N.H., 1980-85; chmn. Columbia Internat. Corp., Weston, Mass., 1985—; adj. prof. Nankai U., Tanjen, Xinjiang U., Uremaqi; adj. prof., mem. U. Coun., Jiao Tong U., Shanghai; vis. prof. Qingdao U., Peoples Republic of China; advisor Com. for Higher Learning, Shandong U., Jinan; advisor office of pres. SRI Internat., 1986—; bd. dirs. Interproject Corp., BTU Eng. Internat.; prin. cons. DRI/McGraw Hill, 1993—; econ. advisor to Gov. Shandong Province, Peoples Republic of China. Mem. adv. bd. Wharton Sch. in China, U. Pa.; chmn. adv. bd. Far East Bus. Rsch. Ctr., Sloan Sch., MIT.; trustee Moore Sch., U. Pa., Babage Inst., U. Minn.; hon. chmn. Inst. for Soft Sci. Studies, Shandong U., Jinan; bd. dirs. Fairbank Inst. Harvard U. Fellow IEEE (computer pioneer award 1981), Chinese Inst. Engrs.; hon. mem. Chinese Nat. Acad. Social Scis., Chinese Assn. Sci. Studies, Acad. Mil. Med. Sci., Beijing. Avocations: tennis, skiing. Home: 10 Baldwin Cir Weston MA 02493-1520 Office: Columbia Internat Corp PO Box 215 Weston MA 02493-0001

CHU, JOHNSON CHIN SHENG, retired physician; b. Peiping, China, Sept. 25, 1918; came to U.S., 1948, naturalized, 1957; s. Harry S.P. and Florence (Young) C.; m. Sylvia Cheng, June 11, 1949; children—Stephen, Timothy. M.D., St. John's U., 1945. Intern Univ. Hosp., Shanghai, 1944-45; resident, research fellow NYU Hosp., 1948-50; resident physician in charge State Hosp. and Med. Ctr., Weston, W.Va., 1951-56; chief services, clin. dir. State Hosp., Logansport, Ind., 1957-84, ret., 1998; active mem. Meml. Hosp., Logansport, Ind., 1968—. Research in cardiology and pharmacology; contbr. articles to profl. jours. Fellow Am. Psychiat. Assn., Am. Coll. Chest Physicians; mem. AMA, Ind. Med. Assn., Cass County Med. Soc., AAAS. Home: 36 E Lake Shafer Monticello IN 47960 Office: Southeastern Med Ctr Walton IN 46994

CHU, MON-LI HSIUNG, dermatology educator; b. Kwangtung, China, July 27, 1948; came to U.S. 1970; d. Tsun-Shiang and Ah-Wha (Yang) Hsiung; m. Shaw-Chang Chu, Nov. 10, 1972; children: Emily, Andy. BS, Nat. Taiwan U., 1970; PhD, U. Fla., 1975. Adj. asst. prof. U. Med./Dentistry N.J.-Rutgers Med. Sch., Piscataway, N.J., 1979-84, adj. assoc. prof., 1984-86; assoc. prof. Thomas Jefferson U., Phila., 1986-90, prof. molecular biology, 1990-96, prof. dermatology, 1996—. Contbr. over 100 articles to profl. jours. NIH grantee, 1986—. Mem. AAAS, Am. Soc. Biochemistry and Molecular Biology. Achievements include isolation and characterization of cDNAs and genomic DNAs for many human collagens, including Type I, III, VI, XVI collagens; definition of the first deletion mutation in type I collagen in a patient with Osteogenesis Imperfecta. Office: Thomas Jefferson U 233 S 10th St Philadelphia PA 19107-5541

CHU, MORGAN, lawyer; b. N.Y.C., Dec. 27, 1950; m. Helen M. Wong, Dec. 29, 1970. BA, UCLA, 1971, MA, 1972, PhD, 1973; MSL, Yale U., 1974; JD magna cum laude, Harvard U., 1976. Bar: Calif. 1976, U.S. Dist. Ct. (ctrl. dist.) Calif. 1977, U.S. Dist. Ct. (no. dist.) Calif. 1980, U.S. Ct. Appeals (9th cir.) 1980, U.S. Dist. Ct. (so. dist.) Calif. 1984, U.S. Dist. Ct. (ea. dist.) Calif. 1986, U.S. Ct. Appeals (fed. cir.) 1989, U.S. Supreme Ct. 1991. Law clk. to judge U.S. Ct. Appeals (9th cir.), San Francisco, 1976-77; assoc. Irell & Manella, LLP, Los Angeles, 1977-82; ptnr. Irell & Manella, Los Angeles, 1982—, co-mng. ptnr., 1997—, also bd. dirs.; adj. prof. UCLA Sch. Law, 1979-82; judge pro tem L.A. Mcpl. Ct., 1980—. Assoc. editor Litigation News, 1981-84. Recipient Significant Achievement award for excellence and innovation in alternative dispute resolution Ctr. for Pub. Resources, 1987; Postdoctoral fellow Yale U., 1974; named one of 10 New Superstars of 1st ammendment law Legal Times of Washington, 1986, one of 100 Most Influential Lawyers in Am., Nat. Law Jour., 1994, 97, one of Top Ten Trial Lawyers in U.S., 1995, one of top 45 Lawyers in U.S. Under 45 Years Old by Am. Lawyer, 1995; Exec. of Yr. in Law, L.A. Bus. Jour., 1994, one of top 20 lawyers in L.A., Calif. Law and Bus. Mem. ABA (chmn. high tech. intellectual property and patent trials subcom. 1986-90, trial practice com., litigation sect.), Calif. Bar Assn., L.A. County Bar Assn. (judiciary com. 1983—), L.A. Intellectual Property Law Assn. (bd. dirs. 1991-93, bd. dirs. pub. counsel 1993—, exec. com. bd. dirs. pub. counsel 1995—). Office: Irell & Manella LLP 1800 Avenue Of The Stars Los Angeles CA 90067-4276

CHU, PAUL CHING-WU, physicist; b. Hunan, China, Dec. 2, 1941; came to U.S., 1963; m. May P. Chern; children: Claire, Albert. BS, Cheng-Kung U., Taiwan, 1962; MS, Fordham U., 1965; PhD, U. Calif. at San Diego, 1968; PhD (hon.), Fordham U., 1988, Northwestern U., 1988, Chinese U. of Hong Kong, 1988, Fla. Internat. U., 1989, SUNY, 1989, Whittier Coll., 1991. 2d lt. Nationalist Chinese Air Forces, 1962-63; teaching asst. Fordham U., Bronx, N.Y., 1963-65; rsch. asst. U. Calif., San Diego, 1965-68; tech. staff Bell Labs., Murray Hill, N.J., 1968-70; asst. prof. physics Cleve. State U., 1970-73, assoc. prof., 1973-75, prof., 1975-79; prof. physics U. Houston, 1979—, dir. magnetic info. rsch. lab., 1984-88, dir. Space Vacuum Epitaxy Ctr., 1986-88, dir. Tex. Ctr. for Superconductivity, 1987—, dir. NSF/materials rsch. sci. & engring. ctr., 1996-97; dir. Solid State Physics Program NSF, Washington, 1986-87; resident, rsch. assoc. Argonne (Ill.) Nat. Lab., 1972; vis. scientist Hansens Physics Lab., Stanford, 1973; vis. staff mem. Los Alamos (N.Mex.) Sci. Lab., 1975-80; cons. Bell Labs., 1973, 75, 78, NASA Marshall Space Flight Ctr., Hunstsville, Ala., 1982-87, DuPont, 1987-88; chmn. organizing com. Internat. Conf. on High Pressure Low Temperature Physics, 1977; M.D. Anderson chair physics M.D. Anderson Found., 1987-89, T.L.L. Temple chair science T.L.L. Temple Found., 1987—; hon. prof. Zhongshan U., 1988, Chinese Acad. Scis. Physics Inst., 1979, Nankai U., 1991, Chinese U. Sci. and Tech., 1991, Nanjing U., 1996; mem. internat. adv. bd. Materials Chemistry & Physics, 1992-94; bd. dirs. Coun. on Superconductivity for Am. Competitiveness, 1989—, Indsl. Tech. Rsch. Inst., 1988-91; co-chmn. solid state physics symposium Vereschagin Internat. Conf. on High Pressure Physics and Tech., Moscow, 1979; mem. White House ad hoc rev. panel on long-range plan for R & D of superconductivity, 1989; mem. rsch. adv. com. Inst. for Tech. and Strategic Rsch., 1989; adv. bd. Internat. Inst. Cond. Math. Physics Univ. Brasilia, 1993; vis. Miller rsch . prof. U. Calif., Berkeley, 1991; mem. adv. com. to redesign the space sta. The White House, Washington, 1993; mem. sch. adv. bd. Ctr. Nanoscale Sci. & Tech., Rice U., 1995—, internat. adv. com. Hong Kong Bapt. U., 1995—, internat. adv. bd. China-Am. Tech. Corp., 1995—; mem. adv. com. on rsch. planning Higher Edn. Coordinating Bd., State of Tex., 1997-99. Mem. editl. bd. High Tech. Bus., 1988—, Modern Physics Letters B, 1988—, Applied Superconductivity, 1992—, Indian Jour. Pure and Applied Physics, 1992—, News and Reviews of Physics in China Today, 1992—, Internat. Jour. Modern Physics, 1988—, Brazilian Jour. Physics, 1995—, Sci. in China, 1997—, Chinese Sci. Bull., 1997—, Applied Physics Rev. (Korea), 1998—; contbr. numerous articles to profl. jours. Bd. dirs. Houston Mus. Natural Sci., 1988-94; mem. internat. adv. com. World Lab. Pan Am. Ctr. for Collaboration in Sci. and Tech., 1998—. Recipient Phys. and Math. Sci. award N.Y. Acad. Sci., 1987, Leroy Randle Grumman medal Grumman Corp., 1987, Achievement award Chinese Am. Acad. and Profl. Assn., 1987, Disting. Alumnus award U. Calif. at San Diego, 1987, Faculty Rsch. award U. Houston, 1987, Sigma Xi Rsch. Excellence award 1987, Achievement award NASA, 1987, Nat. Medal Sci. Pres. of U.S., 1988, Disting. Alumnus award Cheng-Kung U., 1988, Medal of Sci. Merit World Cultural Coun., 1989, Founders' prize Texas Instruments, 1990, St. Martin de Porres award, 1990, Superconductivity Excellence award in sci. accomplishments World Congress on Superconductivity, 1994, Bernd Matthias prize 4th Internat. Conf. on Materials and Mechanisms of Superconductivity, High Temperature Superconductors, 1994, Disting. Sci. Achievement award Washington Met. Assn. Chinese Am. Profls., 1998; inducted into Houston Hall of Fame, 1988; named hon. citizen State of Tex., 1987, City of Houston, 1987, Best Rschr. in U.S. by U.S. News and World Report, 1990. Fellow Am. Phys. Soc. (Internat. prize for new materials 1988, teller divsn. Sol. St. Physics 1976, internat. materials prize com. 1988-89), Tex. Acad. Scis., Chinese Acad. Scis.; mem. AAAS, NAS (Comstock award 1988, mem. panel on High Temperature Superconductivity 1987, sect. co-chair 1992-95), Royal Soc. Encouragement of Arts Mfrs. and Commerce, Am. Acad. Arts and Scis., Academia Sinica (Taipei, mem. adv. com. Inst. Physics 1997-2000), Third World Acad. Scis., Electromagnetic Acad., State Tex. Sci. and Tech. Coun. Office: U Houston Texas Ctr Superconductivity Houston TX 77204-5932

CHU, RICHARD CHAO-FAN, mechanical engineer; b. Beijing, Hopei, Peoples' Republic China, May 28, 1933; came to U.S., 1958, naturalized, 1968; s. Liang Hsi and Yun Hwa (Wang) C.; m. Theresa Sou-Chin Lee, Aug. 24, 1963; children: Banjamin, Benson, Benedict, Bonita. BSME, Nat. Cheng-Keng U., Tainan, Taiwan, 1958; MSME, Purdue U., 1960. Jr. assoc. engr. IBM Corp., Poughkeepsie, N.Y., 1960-64, sr. assoc. engr., 1964-65, project engr., mgr., 1965-67, devel. engr., mgr., 1967-69, sr. engr., mgr., 1969-75, program mgr., product technology, 1975-79, program mgr., engring. lab., 1979-83, fellow, 1983—; v.p. IBM Acad. Tech., 1990, pres., 1991. Author 2 books; patentee in field; contbr. articles to profl. jours. Pres. Mid-Hudson Chinese-Am. Civic Assn., Poughkeepsie, 1969. Recipient Disting. Alumnus award Purdue U., 1984, Outstanding Alumni award Nat. Cheng-Kung U., 1986. Fellow ASME (Heat Transfer Meml. award 1986), AAAS; mem. N.Y. Acad. Sci., Nat. Acad. Engring. Republican. Roman Catholic. Avocations: swimming, jogging, sailing, skiing, wind surfing. Home: 4 Sun Ln Poughkeepsie NY 12601-5815 Office: IBM Corp P520/003 Poughkeepsie NY 12601

CHU, RODERICK GONG-WAH, educational administrator; b. N.Y.C., Jan. 17, 1949; s. Norton Yuen and Frances (Liang) C. BS, U. Mich., 1969; MBA with honors, Cornell U., 1971. Staff analyst Arthur Andersen and Co., N.Y.C., 1971-75, mgr., 1975-81, ptnr., 1981-83; commr. Taxation and Fin., pres. State Tax Commn. State of N.Y., Albany, 1983-88; ptnr. Andersen Cons., N.Y.C., 1988-95, worldwide mng. ptnr., state and local govt. practice, 1989-91, worldwide mng. ptnr., govt. practice, 1991-92; chancellor Ohio Bd. Regents, Columbus, Ohio, 1998—; bd. dirs. Housing Fin. Agy., Med. Care Facilities Fin. Agy., Project Fin. Agy., Affordable Housing Corp., 1983-86, N.E. States Tax Ofcls. Assn., 1983-88, Fedn. Tax Adminstrs., 1985-88, Nat. Tax Assn.-Tax Inst. Am., 1986-88, mem. adv. bd. Coun. for Excellence in Govt., 1991-93, trustee, 1993-95, mem. N.Y.C. real property tax reform commn., 1993; mem. Ohio Workforce Devel. Bd., 1998—; bd. dirs. BEST (Bldg. Excellent Schs. for Today and the 21st Century), 1998—; mem. Ohio Commn. on African Am. Males, 1998—. Bd. dirs., bd. overseers Jacob's Pillow Dance Festival, Becket, Mass., 1984-97; mem. Cornell U. Coun., 1988-92, 94-98, mem. dean's alumni exec. coun. Johnson Sch. Grad. Mgmt., 1988-90, adv. coun., 1991-98, outdoor edn. adv. coun., 1992-98, strategic planning adv. bd., 1992-96; trustee SUNY, 1990-98, chmn. exec. compensation com., 1993-98; mem. pres.'s adv. coun. China Inst. Am., 1990-94; co-chair pres. circle The Asia Soc., 1994-97; mem. adv. bd. Barnard-Columbia Ctr. for Leadership in Urban Pub. Policy, 1994-98. Recipient Man of Yr. award Chinese-Am. Planning Coun., 1984, N.Y.C. Police Dept., Asian Jade Soc., 1984, Disting. Achievement award United Chinese Am. League, 1985, Spl. Recognition award Asian Ams. for Affirmative Action, 1986, Champion of Excellence award Orgn. Chinese Am., 1986, Outstanding Chinese Entrepreneur award Chinese Mgmt. Assn., 1991; Paul Harris fellow Rotary Internat., 1988, 92. Mem. Am. Soc. Pub. Adminstrn. (hon.), Cornell Club (N.Y.C.), Capital Club (Columbus), New Albany Country Club, Met. Opera Club, Cornell Asian Alumni Assn., Phi Kappa Phi. Democrat. Avocations: skiing, photography, golf, fly fishing. Office: Ohio Bd Regents 30 E Broad St Fl 36 Columbus OH 43266-0417

CHU, SHIH-FAN (GEORGE CHU), economics educator; b. Hubei, China, Dec. 6, 1933; came to U.S., 1959; s. Teh-Chuan and Kuang-Hsin (Chou) C.; m. Li-Ming Kuo, Aug. 18, 1963; children: David Soo-lin, Diana Soo-Yin. BA, Nat. Taiwan U., 1955; MS, U. Ill., 1965, PhD, 1968. Asst. prof. econs. U. Nev., Reno, 1967-70, assoc. prof., 1970-77, prof., 1977—, chmn. dept. econs., 1992—; vis. prof. econs. Huazhong U. Sci. and Tech., Wuhan, China, 1981, Wuhan U., 1984, Nat. Taiwan U., Taipei, 1989. Contbr. numerous articles to econs. jours. Fulbright Travel grantee; Ford Found. Dissertation fellow; Inst. Internat. Edn. grad. scholar. Mem. numerous profl. orgns. in econs. Home: 4490 Gibraltar Dr Reno NV 89509-5620 Office: U Nev Dept Econs Reno NV 89557

CHU, STEVEN, physics educator; b. St. Louis, Feb. 28, 1948; s. Ju Chin and Ching Chen (Li) C.; children: Geoffrey, Michael. BS in Physics, AB in Math., U. Rochester, 1970; PhD in Physics, U. Calif., Berkeley, 1976. Post doctoral fellow U. Calif., Berkeley, 1976-78; mem. tech. staff Bell Labs., Murray Hill, N.J., 1978-83; head quantum electronics rsch. dept. AT&T Bell Labs., Holmdel, N.J., 1983-87; prof. physics and applied physics Stanford (Calif.) U., 1987—, Frances and Theodore Geballe prof. physics and applied physics, 1990—, chmn. physics dept., 1990-93; Morris Loeb lectr. Harvard U., Cambridge, Mass., 1987-88; vis. prof. Coll. de France, fall 1990; Richtmeyer Meml. lectr., 1990. Contbr. papers in laser spectroscopy and atomic physics, especially laser cooling and trapping, and precision spectroscopy of leptonic atoms, polymer and biophysics. Recipient Humboldt sr. scientist award, Sci. for Art prize, 1995; co-recipient King Faisal prize for sci., 1993, Nobel prize for physics, 1997; Woodrow Wilson fellow 1970, doctoral fellow NSF, 1970-74, postdoctoral fellow 1977-78, Guggenheim fellow, 1996. Fellow Am. Phys. Soc. (Herbert P. Broida prize for laser spectroscopy 1987, chair laser sci. topical group 1989, A.L. Schawlow prize 1994), Optical Soc. Am. (William F. Meggars award 1994), Am. Acad. Arts and Scis.; mem. NAS, Academica Sinica, Am. Philos. Soc., Chinese Acad. Sci. (fgn.), Korean Acad. Sci. and Tech. (fgn.).

CHU, SUNG NEE GEORGE, materials scientist; b. Shanghai, China, Sept. 11, 1947; came to U.S., 1971; m. Teresa T. Yang, Sept. 10, 1974; children: Karen, Eric. BS, Nat. Taiwan U., Taipei, 1970; MS, U. Rochester, 1974, PhD, 1978. Jr. physicist Microelectronic Ltd., Hong Kong, 1970-71; rsch. assoc. U. Rochester, N.Y., 1977-80; tech. staff AT&T Bell Labs., Murray Hill, N.J., 1980-86, disting. mem. tech. staff, 1986-96; disting. mem. tech. staff Bell Labs., Lucent Techs., Murray Hill, N.J., 1996—. Fellow Electrochem. Soc. (vice chmn. compound semiconductor subcom. 1989—); mem. Am. Phys. Soc., The Minerals, Metals & Materials Soc. Home: 55 Murray Hill Blvd Murray Hill NJ 07974 Office: Bell Labs Lucent Techs 600 Mountain Ave # 7c-221 Murray Hill NJ 07974-2008

CHU, TSANN MING, immunochemist, educator; b. Kaohsiung, Taiwan, Apr. 18, 1938; came to U.S., 1963, naturalized, 1971; s. Tsi Fa and Su Lian (Sun) C.; m. Bonnie Diane Covert, Sept. 28, 1967; children: Nancy, Daniel. BS, Nat. Taiwan U., 1961; MS, N.C. State U., 1965; PhD, Pa. State U., 1967. Fellow Med. Found. Buffalo, 1967-69, Buffalo Gen. Hosp., 1969-70; assoc. chief cancer rsch. scientist, dir. diagnostic immunology and clin. chemistry Roswell Park Meml. Inst., Buffalo, 1970-76, dir. cancer rsch. in diagnostic immunology research and biochemistry, 1976-98; asst. prof. exptl. pathology SUNY, Buffalo, 1970-74, assoc. prof., 1974-77, prof., 1977-98; cons. nat. prostatic cancer project Nat. Cancer Inst., NIH, 1973-84, mem. com. cancer immunodiagnosis, 1978-79, mem. tumor immunology com., 1979-81; mem. immunology and immunotherapy com. Am. Cancer Soc., 1979-81; rsch. cons. Nat. Sci. Coun., Taiwan, 1976-94, vis. prof., 1986; adv. coun. Internat. Soc. Oncodevel. Biology and Medicine, 1978-94; mem. sci. rev. panel N.J. Commn. on Cancer Rsch., 1983-85, 87—; cons. Merit Rev. Bd., VA, 1980-85, 94-98; mem. cancer therapeutic program rev. com. Nat. Cancer Inst., 1985-88; reviewers reserve NIH, 1988-92, 94-98; mem. scientific adv. coun. Internat. Acad. Tumor Marker Oncology, 1986—; mem. sci. coun. Swedish Cancer Found., 1988—; adv. com. Nat. Def. Med. Ctr. Cancer Rsch. Group, 1993-97. Mem. editorial bd. Tumor Biology, 1983-92, Jour. Clin. Lab. Analysis, 1985—, Jour. Tumor Marker Oncology, 1988—, Cancer Investigation, 1989—; contbr. articles to profl. jours. United Health Found. Western N.Y. fellow, 1968-69; recipient Presdl. Citation award Am. Urol. Assn., 1993, Am. Found. for Urologic Disease, 1993, Dornier Innovative Rsch. award, 1993, Roswell Park Cancer Inst. and Geritourinary Cancer Symposium award, 1993, Disting. Alumni award Pa. State U., 1994, N.C. State U., 1995, Abbott award Internat. Soc. Oncodevel. Biology and Medicine, 1996, Achievement in Health Care award D'Youville Coll., 1998, Honors award Pres. U.S., 1999; Alumni fellow Pa. State U., 1997. Mem. Am. Chem. Soc. (Jacob F. Schoellkopf medal 1997), Am. Assn. Clin. Chemists (Van Slyke award 1997), Am. Assn. Cancer Rsch. (cancer rsch. cover legend 1998), Am. Assn. Immunologists, Am. Soc. Biochem. and Molecular Biology, Am. Assn. Investigative Pathology, Phi Lambda Upsilon. Home: 117 Old Orchard St Buffalo NY 14221-2136 Office: Roswell Park Cancer Inst Elm And Carlton St Buffalo NY 14263-0001

CHU, VALENTIN YUAN-LING, author; b. Shanghai, Republic of China, Feb. 14, 1919; came to U.S., 1956, naturalized, 1961; s. Thomas V.D. and Rowena S.N. (Zee) Tsu; m. Victoria Chao-yu Tsao, Sept. 25, 1954; 1 child, Douglas Chi-hua. BA, St. John's U, Shanghai, 1940. Asst. Shanghai Mcpl. Coun., 1940-42; asst. mgr., pub., printer Thomas Chu & Sons, Shanghai, 1943-45; chief reporter China Press, Shanghai, 1945-49; pub. rels. officer Cen. Air Transport Corp., Hong Kong, 1949; Hong Kong corr. Time & Life mags., Hong Kong, 1949-56; with Time, Inc., N.Y.C., 1956-76; writer, asst. editor Time-Life Books, N.Y.C., 1968-76; assoc. editor Reader's Digest Gen. Books, N.Y.C., 1978-83; lectr. on China. Author: Ta Ta, Tan Tan---Fight Fight, Talk Talk, 1963, Thailand Today, 1968, (with others) U.S.A., A Visitor's Handbook, 1969, The Yin-Yang Butterfly---Ancient Chinese Sexual Secrets for Western Lovers, 1993; contbr. articles to popular mags. Recipient spl. award UN Internat. Essay Contest, 1948. Mem. Authors League Am., Authors Guild, China Inst. in Am., Inst. Noetic Scis. Presbyterian. Home: 4520 Wildcat Cir Antioch CA 94509-7149

CHU, WEI-KAN, physicist, educator; b. Kunming, China, Apr. 1, 1940; came to the U.S., 1963; s. Din Yuan and Y.C. (Wong) C.; m. Agnes Kuen, May 28, 1966; 1 child, Lawrence D. BS in Physics, Cheng-Kung U., 1962; MS, Baylor U., 1965, PhD, 1969. Postdoctoral fellow Baylor U., Waco, Tex., 1969-72; rsch. fellow, sr. rsch. fellow Calif. Inst. Tech., Pasadena, 1972-75; staff advisor, sr. engr. IBM, Hopewell Junction, N.Y., 1975-81; rsch. prof. physics U. N.C., Chapel Hill, 1981-88; disting. prof. physics U. Houston, 1989—; panel mem. NSF, Washington, 1992, U.S. Dept. Energy, Washington, 1992, 93, 94, 97. Co-author: Backscattering Spectrometry, 1978; editor: HTS Materials, Bulk Processing and Bulk Applications, 1992, Proceedings of the 6th U.S.-Japan Workshop on High Tc Superconductors, 1994, Proceedings of the 10th Anniversary High Temperature Superconductors Workshop on Physics, Materials and Applications, 1996; contbr. chpts. to books and numerous articles to profl. jours.; holder 15 U.S. patents in field. Recipient Disting. Achievement award Baylor U., Waco, 1991, Assn. Am.-Chinese Profls., 1994, Superconductivity award of excellence for outstanding individual accomplishment World Congress on Superconductivity, 1994, Outstanding Alumni of Yr. Nat. Cheng-Kung U., 1997, 98. Fellow Am. Phys. Soc.; mem. Materials Rsch. Soc. Office: Tex Ctr Superconductivity U Houston Houston TX 77204-5932

CHUA, NAM-HAI, plant molecular biologist, educator; b. Singapore, Apr. 8, 1944; came to U.S., 1971; m. Suat-choo Pearl, 1970; children: Lu-leng Felicia, Lu-san Clarissa. BSc, U. Singapore, 1965; AM, Harvard U., 1967, PhD, 1969. Andrew W. Mellon prof., head lab. plant molecular biology Rockefeller U., N.Y.C., 1988—, head lab. plant plant molecular biology, 1988—; bd. dirs. DNAP Holdings, Oakland, Calif.; cons., dir. Delta and Pine Land Co., Scott, Mich.; cons. Global Tech. Ctr. and Nutrition, Monsanto Co., St. Louis, 1997—, Shanghai Rsch. Ctr. Life Scis., Chinese Acad. Sci., 1996—; dir. exec. com., bd. dirs. Singapore BioInnovators of Am., Redwood City, Calif., 1991—; advisor World Sci. Pub. Co. Pte. Ltd., Singapore, 1996—; mem. Nat. Biotech. Com., Singapore, 1988—; chmn. mgmt. bd. and sci. adv. bd. Inst. Molecular Agrobiology, Nat. U. Singapore, 1995—; hon. rsch. prof. biotech. Chinese Acad. Agrl. Sci., 1987—; Sir Edward Youde vis. prof. U. Hong Kong, 1996; cons. in field. Contbr. articles to profl. jours. Gadsby Flying fellow Sainsbury Lab., John Innes Inst., 1992. Fellow Royal Soc. U.K.; mem. AAAS, Internat. Assn. for Plant Tissue Culture, Internat. Soc. Plant Molecular Biologists, Am. Soc. Biol. Chemists, Am Soc. Cell. Biologists, Am. Soc. Plant Physiologists, Am. Soc. for Microbiology, Soc. Chinese Biioscientists in Am., Japanese Biochem. Soc. (hon. mem.), N.Y. Acad. Scis. Office: The Rockefeller U 1230 York Ave New York NY 10021-6399

CHUANG, FRANK SHIUNN-JEA, engineering executive, consultant; b. Taiwan, China, Sept. 5, 1942; came to U.S., 1966, naturalized, 1974; s. Swiss S. and Chin-May C.; m. Lily L. Chuang, Aug. 14, 1971; 1 child, Eugene. BS, Nat. Taiwan U., 1964; MS, U. Mass., 1968, PhD, 1971. Instr. engring. U. Conn., 1971-72; dept. mgr. C.E. Maguire; cons. engrs. New Britain, Conn., 1972-78; v.p., cons. engrs. Hayden, Harding & Buchanan, Inc., East Hartford, Conn., 1978-82; pres., cons. engrs. L-C Assocs., Inc., Rocky Hills, Conn., 1982—; bd. dirs. Equity Bank, Wethersfield Conn.; mem. Conn. State Bd. Examiners for Profl. Engrs. and Land Surveyors. Chmn. Wethersfield Flood Encroachment Control Bd. U. Mass. Water Resource Rsch. Ctr. grantee, 1966-71. Mem. ASCE, Nat. Soc. Profl. Engrs., Water Pollution Control Fedn., Wethersfield Country Club. Home: 38 Stonegate Dr Wethersfield CT 06109-3652 Office: L-C Assocs Inc 1960 Silas Deane Hwy Rocky Hill CT 06067-1310

CHUANG, HAROLD HWA-MING, banker; b. Hong Kong, Feb. 13, 1941; s. Hung-Chuan and Chih-Chuan (Wu) C.; MBA, UCLA, 1969; CPA, Calif.; m. Christina Chu, Apr. 1974; children: Harrison, William. Sr. in charge Touche Ross & Co., L.A., 1970-75; ptnr.-in-charge Chuang, Chen & Lau Acctcy. Corp., 1978-85; chmn. bd. Am. Internat. Bank, 1985-94; asst. prof. Calif. State U., L.A., 1994-98; 1st v.p. Prudential Securities, Rolling Hills Estate, Calif., 1998—; acting sec. State of Calif., 1988. Del. Rep. Nat. Conv., Calif., 1992; pres. Monterey Park and Yung Ho Sister City Assn., 1983-85; co-chair Asians for Bush-Quayle, 1992. Recipient Ann. award of excellence Calif. State U.-L.A. Found., 1989, Asian Bus. Owner of the Yr. award, 1987. Mem. AICPA, Calif. Soc. CPAs, Nat. Assn. Chinese Am. Bankers (chmn.), Calif. State L.A. U. Found. (del. republican nat. conv. 1992), Tamkang U. Alumni Assn. (pres.), Chinese U. Alumni Assn. Am. (chmn.). Avocations: tennis, swimming, weight lifting. Office: Prudential Securities 501 Deep Valley Dr 4th Flr Rolling Hills Estates CA 90275

CHUANG, TSU-YI, dermatologist, epidemiologist, educator; b. Amoy, China, May 21, 1946; s. Hsi and Kia-Ling (Hwang) C.; m. Lydia Ling-Chuan Lee, Dec. 22, 1973; children: Chester, Nancy. B of Medicine, Nat. Taiwan U., Taipei, 1971; MPH, U. Wash., 1978. Diplomate Am. Bd. Dermatology, Am. Bd. Preventive Medicine. From asst. prof. to assoc. prof. dermatology U. Wis., Madison, 1984-92; chief dermatology svc. Middleton VA Med. Ctr., Madison, 1984-90; assoc. prof. dermatology Wright State U., Dayton, Ohio, 1990-95, dir. immunopathology lab., 1994-95; dir. dermatology clinic Frederick A. White Health Ctr., Dayton, 1995; prof. dermatology Ind. U., Indpls., 1995—, med. dir. melanoma program, 1996—; vis. prof. Nat. Taiwan U., Taipei, 1991-95. Co-author: Conn's Current Therapy, 1992, The Challenge of Dermato-Epidemiology, 1997; editl. cons. Arch Dermatol., Chg., 1990-97; editor Dermatologica Sinica, Taipei, 1994-96; contbr. over 90 articles to profl. jours. Pres. Rochester (Minn.) Chinese Culture Assn., 1980-82; v.p. Orgn. of Chinese Ams., Madison, 1986-90; pres. Midwest Chinese Christian Assn., Dayton, 1993-94, Indpls., 1996-97. Rsch. grantee U. Wis., 1985-89, VA merit rev. bd. grantee Dept. Vets. Affairs, 1986-88, 90-94; recipient Burdette-Kunkel award Mary Margaret Walther Program for Cancer Care Rsch., 1996-97. Fellow Am. Acad. Dermatology (editl. cons. Am. Acad. Dermatology jour. 1996-98), Am. Soc. for Dermatol. Surgery; mem. Soc. for Investigative Dermatology, Ind. Chinese Profls. Assn. (pres. 1998). Achievements include first historical cohort study of human papilloma virus infection in U.S. in a defined population, first historical cohort study of genital herpes virus infection in U.S. in a defined population, first incidence study of polymyalgia rheumatica in the U.S. in a defined population, first population-based incidence study of skin cancer in U.S. in two well-defined populations. Home: 7314 Chestnut Hills Blvd Indianapolis IN 46278-1793 Office: Ind U 550 University Blvd Indianapolis IN 46202-5149

CHUBB, PERCY, III, insurance company executive; b. N.Y.C., Oct. 14, 1934; s. Percy, 2d and Corinne Roosevelt (Alsop) C.; m. Sally Gilady, Dec. 29, 1956; children—Percy Lee, Sarah Caldecot, Lucy Alsop. BA, Yale U., 1956. With Chubb & Son Inc., N.Y.C., 1957-97, dir., 1965-97; sr. v.p., dir. Chubb Corp., Warren, N.J., 1979-81, exec. v.p., dir., 1981-86, vice chmn., 1986-97, also bd. dirs.; bd. dirs. Fed. Ins. Co. Bd. dirs. N.J. Performing Arts Ctr.; trustee Mystic Seaport Mus.; pres., trustee Victoria Found. Inc. With U.S. Army, 1956-58. Office: Chubb Corp PO Box 1615 15 Mountain View Rd Warren NJ 07059-6795

CHUBB, STEPHEN DARROW, medical corporation executive; b. Newton, Mass., Mar. 16, 1944; s. Phillip Darrow and Clarissa Stoddard (Nye) C.; m. Kathleen Alice Zimmerman, 1973. BS, U.S. Naval Acad., 1965; MBA, Northwestern U., 1974. CPA, Ill. With Am. Can Co., 1970-73, Baxter Labs., Deerfield, Ill., 1974-81; pres. Hyland Diagnostics, 1978-81; pres., chief exec. officer, dir. Cytogen Corp., 1981-84, T Cell Scis., Inc., 1984-86, Matritech Inc., 1987—; dir. Charles River Labs., 1994—, Compucyte, Cambridge, Mass., 1992—, I-Stat, Princeton, N.J., 1999—; alumni adv. bd. Northwestern U., 1998. Bd. dirs. Sherwood Cmty. Assn., 1978-79, v.p., 1979-80; trustee Huntington Theatre Co., Boston, 1991-95, treas., 1992-95; trustee Mt. Auburn Hosp., Cambridge, 1995—; mem. Literacy Vols. Mass. With USN, 1965-70; capt., USNR (ret.). Recipient Meritorious Svc. medal, Combat Action Ribbon, U.S. Navy. Mem. AICPA, John Evans Club Northwestern U., U.S. Naval Acad. Alumni Assn. Avocation: deep sea diving. Home: 282 Beacon St # 9 Boston MA 02116-1101 Office: Matritech Inc 330 Nevada St Newton MA 02460-1458

CHUBB, TALBOT ALBERT, physicist; b. Pitts., Nov. 5, 1923; s. Charles F. and Mary Clare (Albert) C.; m. Martha Capps, Oct. 24, 1947 (dec. June 1990); children: Mary Carroll, Nancy Henderson, Talbot Spence, Constance Lamont. A.B., Princeton U., 1944; Ph.D., U. N.C., 1950. Physicist, U.S. Naval Research Lab., 1950-58, head upper air physics br., 1958-82; pres. Research Systems, Inc., Oxon Hill, Md., 1982—. Recipient Elisha Mitchell Soc. award U. N.C., 1951, E.O. Hulbert award Naval Research Lab., 1963, Pure Sci. award Naval. Research Lab.-Research Soc. Am., 1970, Disting. Civilian Service award Dept. Navy, 1978. Fellow Am. Geophys. Union, Am. Phys. Soc.; mem. Am. Astron. Soc. Achievements include rsch. on solar flare x-rays, x-ray stars, UV aurora, cosmology, solar thermal power, cold fusion theory. Home: 5023 38th St N Arlington VA 22207-2845 Office: Code 7620 Naval Rsch Lab Washington DC 20375*

CHUCK, LEON, materials scientist; b. Balt., Mar. 7, 1955; s. Billy and Yuk Yin C. BSME, U. Md., 1978, MSME, 1984. Ceramic engr. Naval Rsch. Lab., Washington, 1976-79; rsch. engr. Nat. Bur. Stds., Gaithersburg, Md., 1979-86; sr. rsch. engr. Norton Co. High Performance Ceramics Div., Northboro, Mass., 1986-88; owner Advanced Structural Materials Consulting, Auburn, Mass., 1988-89; assoc. materials scientist U. Dayton (Ohio) Rsch. Inst., 1989—; part-time prof. dept. mech. and aerospace engring. U. Dayton, 1990—, faculty advisor, coach men's volleyball, 1991-96; instr. Women in Engring. Program, 1994, 96; NSF proposal reviewer, 1996. Judge Montgomery County Sci. Day. Mem. ASME, ASTM (task group leader 1991-96), Am. Ceramic Soc., Am. Soc. Materials, Soc. Automotive Engrs., Soc. Exptl. Mechanics, Soc. Application and Materials Processing Engrs., Nat. Inst. Ceramic Engrs. Achievements include invention of high temperature ceramic instruments; research of failure and degradation mechanisms of structural ceramics for high temperature applications (turbine engine blades & combustion chambers) for long term reliability; developed testing and analysis methodology for enhanced life prediction theory. Home: 612 Acorn Dr Dayton OH 45419-3928 Office: U Dayton Rsch Inst 300 College Park Ave Dayton OH 45469-0001

CHUCK, WALTER G(OONSUN), lawyer; b. Wailuku, Maui, Hawaii, Sept. 10, 1920; s. Hong Yee and Aoe (Ting) C.; m. Marian Chun, Sept. 11, 1943; children: Jamie Allison, Walter Gregory, Meredith Jayne. Ed.B., U. Hawaii,

1941; J.D., Harvard U., 1948. Bar: Hawaii 1948. Navy auditor Pearl Harbor, 1941; field agt. Social Security Bd., 1942; labor law insp. Terr. Dept. Labor, 1943; law clk. firm Ropes, Gray, Best, Coolidge & Rugg, 1948; asst. pub. prosecutor City and County of Honolulu, 1949; with Fong, Miho & Choy, 1950-53; ptnr. Fong, Miho, Choy & Chuck, 1953-58; pvt. practice law Honolulu, 1958-65, 78-80; ptnr. Chuck & Fujiyama, Honolulu, 1965-74; ptnr. firm Chuck, Wong & Tonaki, Honolulu, 1974-76, Chuck & Pai, Honolulu, 1976-78; pres. Walter G. Chuck Law Corp., Honolulu, 1980-94; pvt. practice Honolulu, 1994—; dist. magistrate Dist. Ct. Honolulu, 1956-63; gen. ptnr. M & W Assocs., Kapalama Investment Co.; bd. dirs. Aloha Airlines, Inc., Honolulu Painting Co., Ltd. Chmn. Hawaii Employment Rels. Bd., 1955-59; bd. dirs. Nat. Assn. State Labor Rels. Bds., 1957-58, Honolulu Theatre for Youth, 1977-80; chief clk. Hawaii Ho. of Reps., 1951, 53, Hawaii Senate, 1959-61; govt. appeal agt. SSS, 1953-72; former mem. jud. coun. State of Hawaii; mem. exec. com. Hawaiian Open; former dir. Friends of Judiciary History Ctr. Inc., 1983-94; former mem. bd. dirs. YMCA. Capt. inf. Hawaii Terr. Guard. Recipient Ha'Aheo award for cmty. svc. Hawaii chpt. Am. Bd. Trial Advocates, 1995. Fellow Internat. Acad. Trial Lawyers (founder, dean, bd. dirs., state rep.), Am. Coll. Trial Lawyers; mem. ABA (former chmn. Hawaii sr. lawyers divsn., former mem. ho. of dels.), Hawaii Bar Assn. (pres. 1963), ATLA (former editor), U. Hawaii Alumni Assn. (Disting. Svc. award 1967, former dir., bd. govs.), Law Sci. Inst., Assoc. Students U. Hawaii (pres.), Am. Judicature Soc., Internat. Soc. Barristers, Am. Inst. Banking, Chinese C. of C., U. Hawaii Founders Alumni Assn. (v.p., bd. dirs., Lifetime Achievement award 1994), Harvard Club of Hawaii, Waialae Country Club (pres. 1975), Oahu Country Club. Republican. Home: 2691 Aaliamanu Pl Honolulu HI 96813-1216 Office: Pacific Tower 1001 Bishop St Ste 2750 Honolulu HI 96813-3410

CHUDZINSKI, MARK ADAM, lawyer; b. Chgo., Oct. 13, 1956; s. Brunon and Maria (Chmielinski) C.; m. Barbara Podkul, July 31, 1993; 1 child, Anna. BA, Northwestern U., 1977, MBA, 1981, JD, 1981; Diplome d'Etudes Approfondies, U. Paris, 1982. Bar: N.Y. 1982, Ill. 1990, U.S. Supreme Ct. 1994. Assoc. Coudert Bros., N.Y.C., 1982-85, London, 1985-88, Sydney, Australia, 1988-89; sr. assoc. Winston & Strawn, Chgo., 1990-95, ptnr., 1995-96; gen. counsel Ameritech Internat., 1996—. Articles editor Northwestern Jour. Internat. Law and Bus., 1981. Trustee Window To The World Comm., Inc. (Stas. WTTW-TV and WFMT-FM), Chgo.; mem. adv. bd. Sta. WBEZ-FM, Chgo.; bd. dirs. Chgo. Legal Clinic, Inc., Polish Mus. Am., 1991-98, Polish Am. Congress, 1992-96. Austin scholar 1978; fellow Leadership Greater Chgo., 1990; U.S. Champ Jessup Moot Ct., 1979. Mem. ABA, N.Y. State Bar Assn., Am. Soc. Internat. Law, French-Am. C. of C., German-Am. C. of C., U.S.-Poland C. of C. (founder, chmn. 1991-95). Roman Catholic. Home: 6005 N Oconto Ave Chicago IL 60631-3620 Office: Ameritech Internat 225 W Randolph St Fl 18 Chicago IL 60606-1824

CHUGH, RAM L., economics educator; b. Leiah, Panjab, India, Feb. 5, 1935; came to U.S., 1966; s. Ishwar Das and Hari (Dhingra) C.; m. Seema Gandhi, May 7, 1966; 1 child, Pooja H. BA, Panjab U., 1960, MA in Econs., 1962; PhD in Econs., Wayne State U., 1970. Asst. prof. econs. SUNY, Potsdam, 1970-73, assoc. prof., 1973-79, prof., 1979-91, disting. svc. prof., 1991—, spl. asst. to the pres. for pub. affairs, dir. rural svc., 1990—. Co-author: Black Economy in India, 1986; author: Higher Education and Regional Development, 1992; contbr. articles to profl. jours. Recipient Commr. Outstanding Svc. award N.Y. Dept. Social Svcs., 1993, Cert. Merit N.Y. State Gov.'s award for excellence in rural svc., 1994, Pres.'s award Excellence in Pub. Svc., 1994; sr. rsch. fellow Rockefeller Inst. Govt., Albany, N.Y., 1986. Mem. Am. Econ. Assn., So. Regional Sci. Assn., Adirondack North Country Assn. (bd. dirs. Sarnac Lake, N.Y. chpt. 1984-88), Phi Kappa Phi. Avocations: music, travel, reading, current events. Office: SUNY Potsdam Dept of Economics Potsdam NY 13676

CHUI, CHARLES K., mathematics educator; b. Macau, May 7, 1940; m. Margaret K. Lee, Aug. 22, 1964; children: Herman, Carie. BS, U. Wis., 1962, MS, 1963, PhD, 1967. Asts. prof. math. SUNY, Buffalo, 1967-70; assoc. prof. math. Tex. A&M U., College Station, 1970-74, prof. math., 1974-89, disting. prof. math., 1989—; dir. Ctr. for Approximation Theory Tex. A&M U., 1988—, joint appointment in stats., computer sci. and electrical engring. Author: Multivariate Splines, 1988 (translated into Japanese and Chinese), An Introduction to Wavelets, 1992 (translated into Japanese and Chinese), Wavelets, A Mathematical Tool for Signal Analysis, 1997 (translated into Japanese); co-author: Elements of Calculus, 1983, 2nd edit., 1988, Kalman Filtering with Real-Time Applications, 1987, 2nd edit., 1991, Linear Systems and Optimal Control, 1988, Signal Processing and Systems Theory, Selected Topics, 1992; editor: Approximation Theory and Functional Analysis, 1991, Wavelets: A Tutorial in Theory and Applications, 1992 (translated into Japanese), (series) Wavelet Analysis and Its Applications, Approximations and Decompositions; co-editor: Approximation Theory II, 1976, Approximation Theory IV, 1983, Approxiamtion Theory V, 1986, Topics in Multivariate Approximation, 1987, Approximation Theory VI, vols. 1 and II, 1989, Multivariate Approximation Theory IV, 1989, Approximation Theory VII, 1992, Approximation Theory VIII, 1995; editor-in-chief Applied and Computational Harmonic Analysis: Wavelets, Signal Processing and Applications; editor: Wavelets: Theory, Algorithms, and Applications, Approximation Theory and Its Applications, Jour. Approximation Theory, Advances in Computational Math., Annals Numerical Math., Electronic Jour. Differential Equations, Advances in Computational Math., Neurocomputing; assoc. editor Jour. Math. Rsch. and Exposition, Revista de Matemáticas Aplicadas; patentee spline-wavelet signal analyses and methods for processing signals; patent pending method and apparatus for video image compression and decompression using boundary-spline-wavelets. Named. Hon. Prof., Ningxia U., China, 1987; Erskine fellow U. Canterbury, New Zealand, 1987; fellow Houston Advanced Rsch. Ctr., 1994. Fellow IEEE; mem. Am. Math. Soc., Math. Assn. Am., Soc. for Indsl. and Applied Math., Assn. Former Students Tex. A&M U. (Disting. Rsch. Achievement award 1981, 94). Roman Catholic. Avocations: music, fishing. Office: Tex A&M U 623 Blocker Univ Ave College Station TX 77843*

CHUMBLEY, ROBERT EDWARD, artistic director; b. Miami, Fla., Oct. 22, 1954; s. Robert Edward and Nanette (Gibbons) C.; m. Shirley Irek, Dec. 31, 1978; 1 child, Vanessa Irene. MusB, Temple U., 1975; MusM, Juilliard Sch., 1977. Exec. dir. Chopin Found. of the U.S., Miami, 1981-84; dir. cultural affairs Appalachian State U. (U. N.C.), Boone, N.C., 1984-90; artistic dir. Lied Ctr. for Performing Arts, U. Nebr., Lincoln, 1990-97, Charles Bethea exec. dir., 1997—; exec. music dir. Atlanta Ballet Inc., 1997—; composer-in-residence Entrecasteaux Festival, Nice, France, 1985, N.C. Symphony, Raleigh, 1987-91; concert tours U.S., 1980-90, Europe, 1980, 85, 86, Japan, 1986, Africa, 1982. Composer (opera) Ordinary People, 1990, (symphonies) Reflections on a Tropical Evening, 1989, Violin Concerto, 1988, Songs of Persuasion, 1989, (chamber music) Odyssey of Reminiscence, 1985 (N.C. Arts Coun. Composer fellow), Homage to Wordsworth, 1986, (solo) Homage to Keats, 1986. Vice-chair Tourism Devel. Authority, N.C., 1988-90; bd. dirs. Arts Coun., Lincoln, 1990—. Mem. Chamber Music Am., Broadcast Music, Inc., Am. Compoers Alliance, Internat. Soc. of Performing Arts Presenters, Assn. Performing Arts Presenters, Am. Music Ctr., N.C. Arts Coun. (Composer Fellowship award). Republican. Avocations: golf, gem collecting. Office: Atlanta Ballet Inc 1400 W Peachtree St NW Atlanta GA 30309-2906 Address: Lied Center PO Box 880151 Lincoln NE 68588-0151*

CHUN, ARLENE DONNELLY, special education educator; b. Maspeth, N.Y., Dec. 10, 1952; d. William James Jr. and Marguerite Anna (Miller) Donnelly; m. Edward Howard Chun, Aug. 9, 1975; children: Christine, Jennifer, Scott. AA, Luther Coll., 1972; BA, Marymount Manhattan Coll., 1974; MA, C.W Post Coll., 1979; postgrad., Bklyn. Coll., 1989-91. Rsch. asst., adminstrv. asst. LaGuardia C.C., L.I. City, N.Y., 1975-77; substitute tchr. various sch. dists., Nassau County, N.Y., 1978-88; family day care provider, 1983-88; speech lang. therapist Sch. for Lang. and Comm. Devel., Glen Cove, N.Y., 1988—. C.W. Post Coll. fellow, 1978-79. Mem. N.Y. State Speech Hearing Lang. Assn., L.I. Speech Hearing Lang. Assn., N.Y. State Day Care Assn., Nassau County Day Care Assn., L.I. U. Alumni Assn. Lutheran. Avocations: crafts, camping, sewing, reading, plate collecting. Home: 95 Rhodes Dr New Hyde Park NY 11040-3527 Office: Sch for Lang and Communication Devel 100 Glen Cove Rd Glen Cove NY 11542

CHUN, WENDY SAU WAN, investment company executive; b. China, Oct. 17, 1951; came to U.S., 1975, naturalized, 1988; d. Siu Kee and Lai Ching (Wong) C.; m. Tan Ng Wong, Jan. 1992; children: Sze Ho, Sze Man. BS, Hong Kong Bapt. Coll., 1973; postgrad. U. Hawaii-Manoa, 1975-77. Real estate saleswoman Tropic Shores Realty Co., Honolulu, 1977-80; pres., prin., broker Advance Realty Investment Co., Honolulu, 1980—; owner Video Fun Centre, Honolulu, 1981-83; pres. Asia-Am. Bus Cons., Inc., Can., 1983—; bd. dirs., exec. dir. B.P.D. Internat., Ltd., Hong Kong; exec. dir. Asia-Am. Bus. Cons., Inc., Hong Kong br., 1985—; pres. Asia-Am. Internat., Ltd., Honolulu, 1989; pres. Maurey Internat., Ltd., Hong Kong, 1990, Century 21 G & W Holdings Ltd., Hong Kong, 1994. Mem. Nat. Assn. Realtors. Avocations: singing, dancing, swimming, dramatic performances. Home: 38th Flr Flat G Robinson Pl 1, 70 Robinson Rd, Hong Kong China

CHUNG, BONGKIL, Asian studies educator; b. Yongqwang, Chonnam, Korea, May 20, 1936; came to U.S., 1967; s. Nam-do Chung and Inuk Lee; married; children: Andrew, Daniel. BA, Wongkwang U., Iri, Korea, 1959; MA, Ohio State U., 1972; PhD, Mich. State U., 1979. Tchr. English Wongkwang Girls High, Iksan City, Chonbuk, Korea, 1961-67; adj. asst. prof. Mich. State U., East Lansing, 1979; instr. Towson (Md.) State U., 1980-81; asst. prof. Fla. Internat. U., Miami, 1979-80, assoc. prof., 1986-98, prof., 1999—. Author: Introduction to Won Buddhism, 1993. Mem. Am. Philos. Assn., Internat. Soc. for Chinese Philosophy, Internat. Soc. for Asian Comparative Philosophy. Home: 16021 SW 81st Ave Miami FL 33157 Office: Fla Internat U University Park Campus Miami FL 33199

CHUNG, CAROLINE, airline executive, aerobics instructor; b. Washington, Apr. 27, 1970; d. Jae Wan and Soojun Chung. BS, U. Wis., 1992; MBA, Vanderbilt U., 1997. Cert. mad dogg spinning Aerobics and Fitness Assn. Am. Mgr. US Airways, Washington. Roman Catholic. Avocations: exercise, travel, reading, world maps, music. E-mail: cchung@usairways.com. Home: 8380 Greensboro Dr # 125 McLean VA 22102 Office: US Airways 2345 Crystal Dr Arlington VA 22227

CHUNG, CONNIE (CONSTANCE YU-HWA CHUNG), broadcast journalist; b. Washington, Aug. 20, 1946; d. William Ling and Margaret Chung; m. Maurice Richard Povich. BS, U. Md., 1969; DJ (hon.), Norwich U., 1974, Providence Coll., 1988; LHD, Brown U., 1987; LLD (hon.), Wheaton Coll., 1989. News copyperson, writer, reporter Sta. WTTG-TV, Metromedia, Washington, 1969-71; corr. CBS News, Washington, 1971-76; TV news anchor Sta. KNXT-TV, CBS, L.A., 1976-83; anchor NBC News, NBC News at Sunrise, NBC Nightly News (Saturday), NBC News Digests, NBC News Mag. 1986, NBC News Spls., N.Y.C., 1983-89, Saturday Night with Connie Chung, CBS-TV, 1989-90, CBS Evening News (Sunday edit.), 1989-93, Face to Face, 1990-91, Eye to Eye, 1993-95; co-anchor CBS Evening News, 1993-95; achor, corres. 20/20, ABC, N.Y.C., 1995—. Recipient Achievement cert. for series of broadcasts U.S. Humane Soc., 1969, Metro Area Mass Media award AAUW, 1971, Outstanding Young Woman of Am. award, 1971, Atlanta chpt. Nat. Assn. Media Women award, 1973, Outstanding Excellence in News Reporting and Pub. Svc. award Chinese-Am. Citizens Alliance, 1973, Hon. award for news reporting Chinese YMCA Boston, 1974, Woman of Distinction award Golden Slipper Club-Phila., 1975, Best TV Reporting award Sta. KNXT-TV and L.A. Press Club, 1977, Outstanding TV Broadcasting award Valley Press Club, 1977, Golden Mike award for best documentary, 1978, Emmy award for individual achievement L.A. chpt. NATAS, 1978, 80, Mark Twain trophy Calif. Associated Press. TV and Radio Assn., 1979, Best News Broadcast 4:30 p.m., 1980, Women in Comm. award Calif. State U. at L.A., 1979, George Foster Peabody award for programs on environ. Md. Ctr. Pub. Broadcasting, 1980, Portraits of Excellence award Pacific S.W. Region B'nai B'rith, 1980, Newscaster of Yr. award Temple Emanuel Brotherhood, 1981, First Amendment award Anti-Defamation League of B'nai B'rith, 1981, Best Newscast 6:00 p.m. award AP, 1981, Calif. Associated Press TV and Radio Assn., 1981, Golden Mike award for best news broadcast, 1981, Disting. Contbns. in area of Comm. Media award L.A. Basin Equal Opportunity League, 1983, Women in Bus. award, 1983, L.A. Press Club award for 4:30 p.m. broadcast, 1983, L.A. Press Club award for 6:00 p.m. broadcast, 1983, Emmy award, 1986, Emmy award for outstanding interview, 1989, 90, Silver Gavel award ABA, 1991, Ohio State of Achievement of Merit award, 1991, Nat. Headliner award NCCJ, 1991, Clarion award Women in Comm., 1991, Commendation award for AIDS and rape Am. Women in Radio and TV, Commendation award for breast implants, 1991. Office: ABC 147 Columbus Ave New York NY 10023*

CHUNG, CYNTHIA NORTON, communications specialist; b. Milton, Mass., Apr. 14, 1955; d. Ralph Arnold and Mary Elizabeth (McDonald) N.; m. Chinsoo Chung; children: Sara Jane, Steven Joonmok. BFA in Archtl. and Graphic Design, U. Mass., 1977. Graphic designer Garber Travel, Inc., Brookline, Mass., 1977-78; graphic and exhibit designer Rust Craft, Inc., Dedham, Mass., 1978-80; corp. advt. artist Morse, Inc., Canton, Mass., 1980-83; pvt. practice designer Boston, 1983-84; asst. art dir. Cahners Pub. Co., Newton, Mass., 1984-86, art dir., 1986-87; art dir. Knapp, Inc., Brockton, Mass., 1987-89; customer svc. rep. TWA, Boston, 1990; communications specialist Boston Fin. Data Svcs., Quincy, Mass., 1992—. Designer graphs and charts for Vols. I and II State Budget Commonwealth of Mass., 1982; art dir. Mini Micro Systems, 1984-87. Mem. Kappa Kappa Gamma (pres. 1975-76). Roman Catholic. Avocations: photography, real estate, travel. Home: 134 Samoset Ave Quincy MA 02169-2452 Office: Boston Fin Data Svcs Inc Two Heritage Dr Quincy MA 02170

CHUNG, DAE HYUN, retired geophysicist; b. Jeongup, Korea, Dec. 6, 1933; came to U.S., 1955, naturalized, 1974; s. Mynn and Mockdaan (Rhee) C.; m. Inhan Choi, Oct. 19, 1963 (dec. Aug. 1993); children: Henry H., Gene H. AB, Alfred U., 1959, MSc, 1961; PhD, Pa. State U., 1966. Postgrad. rsch. fellow MIT, Cambridge, 1967-68, rsch. assoc. geophysics, 1968-74; prof. geophysics, dir. Weston (Mass.) Obs., 1972-74; geophysicist, coordinator geophysics programs, dept. applied sci. U. Calif. and Lawrence Livermore Nat. Lab., 1974-80; program mgr., staff geophysicist Lawrence Livermore Nat. Lab., 1980-89, sr. scientist, 1990-96, dir. Nuc. Safety Info. Ctr., 1996-97; pres. Livermore Associated Rsch. Group, 1982-90, chmn., 1990-96, ret., 1997; sr. fellow and Inst. prof. Internat. Ctr. Peace Studies, Internat. Assn. Univ. Pres., 1980-95; hon. prof. Inter-Cultural Inst. Calif., San Francisco, 1994—; bd. dirs. Am. Inst. Ednl. Leadership and Devel., 1987-89; instr., rschr. Pa. State U., MIT, U. Calif.; cons. MIT Lincoln Lab.; staff councillor to Min. Sci. and Tech. Republic of Korea, 1969-70; mem. seismic expert panel IAEA, Vienna, 1982-96; mem. field mission to Turkish govt., Ankara and Istanbul, 1982; cons. Atomic Energy Bd., Pretoria, South Africa, 1982; seismic cons. Korea Advanced Energy Rsch. Inst., Seoul, 1984-90, Korea Inst. Nuc. Safety, Daeduk, 1990-96. Contbr. articles to profl. jours. and chpts. to textbooks. Liaison mem. com. on seismology U.S. NAS, 1990-95, com. on earthquake engring. U.S. NAS and NAE, 1989-95; mem. exec. bd. com. for Korean art De Young Mus. San Francisco, 1989-96. Recipient Maj. Edward Holmes award SUNY-Alfred, 1959; recipient achievement citation Geol. Survey, Korea, 1970; decorated Order of Confrerie des Vignerons de St. Vincent, 1977. Fellow Geol. Soc. Am.; mem. AAAS, Am. Geophys. Union, Am. Acad. Mechanics, N.Y. Acad. Scis., MIT Faculty Club, Castlewood Country Club (bd. dirs. 1996-97), Sigma Xi. Home: 16 Golden Gate Cir Napa CA 94558-6190

CHUNG, EDWARD KOOYOUNG, cardiologist, educator, author; b. Seoul, Korea, Mar. 3, 1931; came to U.S., 1958, naturalized, 1971; s. Il-Chun C.; m. Lisa Sang-In Lee, May 28, 1958; children: Linda, Christopher. B.S., Seoul Nat. U., 1953, M.D., 1957. Intern St. Louis City Hosp., 1958-59; resident in medicine St. Louis County Hosp., 1959-60, St. John's Hosp., St. Louis, 1960-62; fellow in cardiology Washington U. Sch. Medicine, Barnes Hosp., St. Louis, 1962-64; asst. prof. medicine, dir. heart sta. Meharry Med. Coll., Nashville, 1964-66; assoc. prof. Meharry Med. Coll., 1966-68; vis. investigator in cardiology Vanderbilt U. Sch. Medicine, Nashville, 1965-68; asso. prof. W.Va. U. Sch. Medicine, Morgantown, 1968-70; prof. medicine W.Va. U. Sch. Medicine, 1970-73, dir. heart sta., 1968-73; prof. medicine, dir. heart sta. Jefferson Med. Coll., Thomas Jefferson U., Phila., 1973—. Author: 90 med. textbooks including Non-Invasive Cardiology, 1976, Controversy in Cardiology, 1976, Principles of Cardiac Arrhythmias, 3d edit., 1983, 4th edit., 1989, Electrocardiography - Practical Applications with Vectorial Principles, 3d edit, 1985, Artificial Cardiac Pacing - Practical Approach, 1979, 2d edit., 1984, Exercise Electrocardiography - Practical Approach, 1979, Ambulatory Electrocardiography, 1979, 2d edit., 1983, Cardiac Emergency Care, 4th edit., 1991, One Heart . . . One Life, 1982, Heart Attack . . . Health Guide for Executives, 1982, Cardiac Arrhythmias: Self Assessment, Vol. II, 1982, Introduction to Clinical Cardiology, 1983, Quick Reference to Cardiovascular Diseases, 3d edit., 1987, Complex Arrhythmias: Self Assessment, 1985, Cardiac Arrhythmias: Self Learning, 1986, Manual of Cardiac Arrhythmias, 1986, Cardiovascular Emergencies, 1986, Complex Arrhythmias: Self Assessment, 1986, Manual of Exercise ECC Testing, 1986, Cardiac Arrhythmias: Self Assessment, vol. 3, 1987, Electrocardiography: Self Assessment, 1988, Manual of Acute Cardiac Disorders, 1988, Pocket Guide to ECG Diagnosis, 1996, Pocket Guide to Stress Testing, 1997, (CD-Rom) ECG Diagnosis and Self-Assessment, 1997, A Pocket Guide To Cardiovascular Diseases, 1999; editorial cons., Williams & Wilkins Co., 1969—, Harper & Row Pubs., 1971—, Lea & Febiger Pubs., Springer-Verlag Pubs., 1974—, J.B. Lippincott Co., 1975—, Medcom, Inc., 1972—, AMA Jour. Questions and Answers, 1973—; book reviewer: Annals of Internal Medicine, 1969—; contbr. numerous articles to profl. jours., Am. Jour. Cardiology, 1971—, New Eng. Jour. Medicine, 1971—, Cardiology, 1975—; manuscript reviewer: Am. Heart Jour, 1972— , Heart and Lung, Chest, 1973—, Cardiology (Switzerland), 1973—, J.A.M.A, 1974—, Circulation, 1978—; editorial bd.: Heart and Lung, 1973—, Jour. Electrocardiology, Cardiology, 1975—, Primary Cardiology, Drug Therapy, 1976—, Hosp. Physician, 1978—. Edward K. Chung Distng. Lectr. established in honor Thomas Jefferson U., 1990. Fellow Am. Coll. Cardiology (gov. W.Va. 1970-73), A.C.P., Philippine Heart Assn. (hon.), Philippine Coll. Cardiology (hon.); mem. AMA, Am. Heart Assn., Am. Fedn. for Clin. Research, Pa. Med. Soc., Philadelphia County Med. Soc. Home: 777 Woodleave Rd Bryn Mawr PA 19010-1708 Office: Thomas Jefferson U Hosp 1025 Walnut St # 410 Philadelphia PA 19107-5001

CHUNG, JOSEPH SANG-HOON, economics educator; b. Unmun-myon, Chongdo-kun, Kyongbuk, Korea, Oct. 11, 1929; came to U.S., 1953; s. Anthony Doseng and Martha (Cho) C.; m. Louise Carol Guenther, Aug. 17, 1957; children: Vincent, Sara, Melissa. Student, Seoul Nat. U., Korea, 1949-51; BS in Econs., Marquette U., 1956, MA, 1958; PhD, Wayne State U., 1964. Lectr. in econs. Marquette U., Milw., 1958-60; from instr. to asst. prof. Kalamazoo Coll., 1962-63, 63-64; asst. prof. Ill. Inst. Tech., Chgo., 1964-68, chmn. dept. econs., 1975-82, assoc. prof., 1968-73, prof. econs., 1973-95, prof. emeritus, 1996—; Fulbright prof. Seoul Nat. U. Korea, 1966-68; cons. Hoover Instn., 1964-66, Def. Dept., 1969; assoc. Asia Sci. Rsch. Assocs., Menlo Park, Calif., 1968-85. Author: Evolution of the Japanese Electronics Industry, 1980, The North Korean Economy: Structure and Development, 1974; editor: Patterns of Economic Development: Korea, 1966. Social Sci. Rsch. Coun. fellow, 1962; Stanford U. Hoover Instn. grantee, 1964-65; Fulbright lectr. Dept. State, 1966-68; Gen. Electric Found. grantee, 1975. Mem. Am. Econs. Assn., Assn. Asian Studies, Midwest Econs. Assn. Roman Catholic. Home: 22 W County Line Rd Barrington IL 60010-2611

CHUNG, KING-THOM, microbiologist, educator; b. Tou Fen, Taiwan, Apr. 25, 1943; came to U.S., 1966; s. Aa-Yuan and Yi-Ing (Buu) C.; m. Lan-Seng Fang, Oct. 27, 1973; children: Theodore, Serena. MA, U. Calif., Santa Cruz, 1967; PhD, U. Calif., Davis, 1972. Scientist Frederick (Md.) Cancer Rsch. Ctr., 1972-77; vis. asst. prof. Food Sci. Inst. Purdue U., West Lafayette, Ind., 1977-78; assoc. prof. Tunghai U., Taichung, Taiwan, 1978-80; prof., chmn. dept. Soochow U., Taipei, Taiwan, 1980-87, dean, 1983-87; vis. scientist U.S. Meat Animal Rsch. Ctr., Clay Center, Nebr., 1987-88; assoc. prof. biology U. Memphis, 1988-93, prof., 1993—; mem. adv. bd. Dept. Agr. and Forestry, Taiwan Provincial Govt., Taichung, 1982-87; exec. sec. Internat. Symposium on Biogas, Microalgae and Livestock Wastes, Taipei, 1980. Author: (in Chinese) Environment and Pollution, 1987, Intellectuals and Academic Education, 1987, Stories of 25 World Leading Microbiologists, 1996; contbr. articles to profl. jours. Grantee Am. Inst. Cancer Rsch., 1992. Fellow Am. Acad. Microbiology; mem. Am. Soc. Microbiology, Am. Acad. Microbiology, Inst. Food Technologists, Sigma Xi. Achievements include the illustration of the significance of azo reduction in the azo dye mutagenesis and carcinogenesis, quantitative structure activity relationships (QSAR) of aromatic amines, tannins and health, food safety, and history of microbiology. Office: U Memphis Dept Microbiology and Molecular Cell Scis Memphis TN 38152

CHUNG, KYUNG CHO, Korean specialist, scholar, educator, author; b. Seoul, Korea, Nov. 13, 1921; s. Yang Sun and Kyung Ok (Peng) C.; m. Yosi S. Chung, Oct. 10, 1958; children: In Kyung, In Ja. Student, Waseda U., Tokyo, 1941-43; B.A., Seoul Nat. U., 1947; postgrad., Columbia U., 1948-49; M.A., N.Y. U., 1951; LL.D., Pusan Nat. U., 1965; Litt.D., Sungkyunkwan U., 1968; M.A., Monterey Inst. Fgn. Studies, 1974. Mem. faculty U.S. Def. Lang. Inst., Monterey, Calif., 1951-92, Monterey Inst. Fgn. Studies, 1973-74, Hartnell Coll., Salinas, Calif., 1974-93; pres. Korean Rsch. Coun.; adviser Korean Assn., Monterey, 1974—, Am.-Korean Found., Crossroads, Inc., 1992, Asia Devel. Inc.; treas. Korean Rsch. Bull.; hon. prof. Kunkuk U.; pres. South Carmel Hills Assn., 1962-93; hon. chmn. Inst. Far Eastern Studies Joint Rsch. Program U.S.-Russia-Korea-Japan-China, 1993—; chmn. Korea-Am. Assn. Author: Korea Tomorrow, 1957, New Korea, 1962, Seoul (Ency. Americana), 1965, Naeil Hankuk, 1965, Sae Hankuk, 1968, Korea: The Third Republic, 1972, Korean Unification, 1973, Korea Reunion and Reunification, 1974, Hankuk Gaido, 1988, The Korea Guidebook: North and South Korea, 6th edit., 1997, Korea edit., 1995, Hankuk-chongran, 1995, East and West 1000 Munsun, 1995, Japanese Kangoku Gaizobuk, 1997. Recipient Superior Performance award U.S. Govt., 1964, Korean Prime Min. citation, 1965, cert. of achievement U.S. Def. Lang. Inst., 1976, Outstanding Performance award U.S. Def. Lang. Inst., 1980, Olympic-svc. Gold medal Korean Pres., 1989, Spl. Commendation award Korean Pres., 1990, Commendation award U.S. Def. Lang. Inst., 1991, Recognition award of 40 Yrs. Svc., U.S. Govt., 1991, Excellency medal U.S. Govt., 1992, Nobel Peace prize candidate, 1999. Mem. AAUP, Am. Assn. Asian Studies, Am. Assn. Modern Langs., Am.-Korean Polit. Assn. Democrat. Mem. Korean Ch. Home and Office: 25845 S Carmel Hills Dr Carmel CA 93923-8310 *Dedicate and contribute toward better relations among the nations and the lasting peace in the world, teaching other languages to meet the other nations half way by speaking the same language.*

CHUNG, PAUL MYUNGHA, mechanical engineer, educator; b. Seoul, Dec. 1, 1929; came to U.S., 1947, naturalized, 1956; s. Robert N. and Kyungsook (Kim) C.; m. E. Jean Judy, Mar. 8, 1952; children: Maurice W., Tamara P. BSME, U. Ky., 1952, MS, 1954; Ph.D., U. Minn., 1957. Asst. prof. mech. engring. U. Minn., 1957-58; aero. research scientist Ames Research Center, NASA, Calif., 1958-61; head fluid physics dept. Aerospace Corp., San Bernardino, Calif., 1961-66; prof. mech. engring. U. Ill., Chgo., 1966-95, head dept. energy engring., 1974-79, dean engring., 1979-94, prof., dean emeritus, 1995—; mem. tech. adv. com. Ill. Inst. Environ. Quality, 1975-77; corp. mem. Underwriters Lab., 1983-95; cons. to industry, 1966—. Author numerous papers in field; author: Electric Probes in Stationary and Flowing Plasmas, 1975, Russian edit., 1978; contbr. chpt. to Advances in Heat Transfer, 1965, to Dynamics of Ionized Gases, 1973. Bd. govs. Redlands (Calif.) YMCA, 1965-67. Fellow AIAA (nat. tech. com. on plasmadynamics 1972-74, com. on propellants and combustion 1976-80); mem. AIChE (nat. com. on internat. activities 1992-94), Am. Soc. Engring. Edn. (exec. bd. engring. dean's coun. 1983-84), Sigma Xi, Tau Beta Pi, Pi Tau Sigma, Phi Kappa Phi. Home: 2003 E Lillian Ln Arlington Heights IL 60004-4215 Office: Univ Ill Off of Dean Chicago IL 60680

CHUNG, ROBERT, dentist, educator; b. Canton, China, Aug. 10, 1966; came to the U.S., 1982; s. Kwok Wah Chung and Yuen Ying Kwan. DDS, Northwestern U., 1992; MA, Columbia U., 1995, specialty cert. in periodontics, 1995. Pvt. practice Diamond Spring Dental Assocs., Denville, N.J., 1995—; clin. instr. Columbia U., N.Y.C., 1995—. Mem. Internat. Congress Oral Implantology, Internat. Assn. Dental Rsch., Am. Acad. Periodontology, Sigma Xi, Omicron Kappa Upsilon. Office: Diamond Spring Dental Assocs 16 Pocono Rd #117 Denville NJ 07834

CHUNG, TAE-SOO, physician; b. Tae-Gu, Korea, Feb. 1, 1937; came to U.S., 1964, naturalized, 1975; s. Sang-Taik and Chuwan (Ha) C.; m. Kwangja Park, Apr. 3, 1965; children: Peter, Alexander. MD, Yonsei U., Seoul, 1963. Chief resident rehab. medicine N.Y.U. Med. Ctr., 1967; fellow in rehab. medicine N.Y. Med. Coll., 1968; clin. dir. Children's Rehab. Ctr., St. John's, Nfld., Can., 1969-71; chief spinal cord injury svc., chief children's rehab. unit N.Y. Med. Coll., 1971-75, clin. asst. prof., 1971-80; dir. phys. medicine and rehab. dept. Northwest Covenant Med. Ctr., N.J., 1975—; dir. rehab. unit Newton (N.J.) Meml. Hosp., 1981—; clin. asst. prof. U. Medicine and Dentistry N.J., Newark, 1976—; mem. N.J. State Phys. Therapy Bd., 1995—; cons. to Sussex County Edn. Commn., 1980—, Kessler Inst. Rehab., 1998—. Mem. N.J. Soc. Phys. Medicine and Rehab. (sec. 1979-80, pres. 1983-84), Am. Korean Med. Soc. (v.p. N.Y. met. area 1979-80, news editor 1989-90), Am. Acad. Phys. Medicine and Rehab., N.J. Acad. Medicine, N.J. State Physical Therapy Bd. Office: 400 W Blackwell St Dover NJ 07801-2525

CHUNG, TCHANG-IL, engineer; b. Seoul, Dec. 12, 1932; came to U.S., 1954; s. In-Taek and Yang-Rae (Rhee) C.; m. Pauline Lamarche, Sept. 16, 1958; children: Daniel, Christopher. BS, Seoul Nat. U., 1955; postgrad., Santa Rosa Jr. Coll., 1956; MS, U. Mass., Lowell, 1958; postdoctoral, MIT, 1958-59; PhD, Calif. Western U., 1982. Mgr. mfg. engring div. Unitrode Corp., Salem, Mass., 1966-69, mgr. quality reliability assurance, 1969-72; product mgr. Unitrode Corp., Watertown, Mass., 1972-77, product line mgr., 1977-81; mgr. subcontract Unitrode Corp., Watertown, 5, 1981-88; purchasing cons. Digital Equipment Corp., Marlboro, Mass., 1988-90; tech. purchasing agt. Picturetel Corp., Andover, Mass., 1992—; mem. adv. bd. Electronics Internat. Adv. Panel, 1974-75. Mem. IEEE (sr.), Cert. Mfg. Engrs., Electrochem. Soc. Home: 35 Sonning Rd Beverly MA 01915-1743 Office: Picturetel Corp 100 Minuteman Rd Andover MA 01810-1012

CHUNG-WELCH, NANCY YUEN MING, biologist; b. N.Y.C., July 28, 1960; d. Thomas Richard and Jennie Kan Fee (Lew) Semler; m. James Michael Welch, June 29, 1985. BS, Northea. U., Boston, 1982; PhD, Boston U., 1990. Rsch. technician dept. biology Boston U., 1983-85, tchg. fellow dept. biology, 1987-89; rsch. fellow surgery Mass. Gen. Hosp., Harvard Med. Sch., Boston, 1989-94, instr. surgery, 1994-95; instr. in surgery Harvard Med. Sci., 1994-95; rsch. assoc. prof. Boston U., 1996-97; product mgr. Oncogene Rsch. Products, Cambridge, Mass., 1997-99, Becton Dickinson, Bedford, Mass., 1999—. Contbr. articles to profl. jours. including Jour. Cellular Physiology, Differentiation, Analytical Biochemistry, Surg. Forum, Microvascular Rsch., Biotechniques, Jour. Electrophoresis. Boston U. Grad. Sch. grad. rsch. award, 1987, Biology Dept. grad. travel award, 1988-89, Grega-Zacharkow Young Investigator award Microcirculatory Soc., 1988; named Outstanding Young Woman of Mass., 1988; Repligen Corp fellow, 1993-95. Mem. AAAS, Am. Soc. Cell Biology, Tissue Culture Assn., Electrophoresis Soc. Achievements include devel. of tissue culture technique for the isolation and culture of pulmonary microvascular endothelial cells human omental microvascular endothelial cells and mesothelial cells in vitro; demonstrated presence of simple epithelial keratins in endothelial cells; rsch. on the phenotypic properties between endothelial and mesothelial cells using histochemical and biochemical criteria and in vitro assays of angiogenic potential, vascular smooth muscle interactions with extracellular matrices as it relates to intimal hyperplasia. Office: Becton Dickinson Labware 2 Oak Park Bedford MA 01730

CHUN OAKLAND, SUZANNE NYUK JUN, state legislator; b. Honolulu, June 27, 1961; d. Philip Sing and Mei-Chih (Chung) Chun; m. Michael Sands Chun Oakland, June 11, 1994; children: Mailene Nohea Pua Oakland, Christopher Michael Sing Kamakakiu Oakland, Lauren Suzanne LeRong Kemelenohea Oakland. BAs in Psychology and Comm., U. Hawaii, 1983. Adminstrv. asst. Au's Plumbing and Metal Works, Hawaii, 1979-90; community svc. specialist Senator Anthony Chang, Hawaii, 1984; adminstrv. asst. Smolenski and Woodell, Hawaii, 1984-86; rsch. asst., office mgr. City Coun. Mem. Gary Gill, Hawaii, 1987-90; mem. Hawaii Ho. of Reps., 1990-96; mem. Hawaii State Senate, 1997—, chair com. health and human svcs., 1999—. Named Legis. of Yr. Hawaii Long Term Care Assn., 1993, Healthcare Assn. Hawaii, 1993, 95, Hawaii Psychiat. Med. Assn., 1994, Autism Soc. Hawaii, 1994; recipient Friend of Social Workers award NASW, 1995, Outstanding Govt. Svc. award Hawaii Pacific Gerontol. Soc., 1996, Outstanding Legislator award Hawaii Med. Assn., 1996, Na Lima Kokua Ma Waema O Makua award pacific Gerontol. Soc. Democrat. Episcopalian. Avocations: raising animals, gardening, swimming. Office: State Senate Rm 228 415 S Beretania St Honolulu HI 96813-2437*

CHUPKA, WILLIAM ANDREW, chemical physicist, educator; b. Pittston, Pa., Feb. 12, 1923; s. William and Antoinette C.; m. Olive Augusta Pirani, May 21, 1955; children: Jocelyn Terese, Marc William. B.S., U. Scranton, 1943; M.S., U. Chgo., 1949, Ph.D., 1951. Instr. Harvard U., 1951-54; asso. physicist Argonne (Ill.) Nat. Lab., 1954-67; sr. physicist, 1967-75; prof. chemistry Yale U., 1975-96, prof. emeritus, 1996—. Research, numerous publs. in chem. physics. Served with U.S. Army, 1943-46. Guggenheim fellow, 1961-62. Mem. Am. Chem. Soc. Office: PO Box 208107 New Haven CT 06520-8107

CHUPP, TIMOTHY EDWARD, physicist, educator, nuclear scientist, academic administrator; b. Berkeley, Calif., Nov. 30, 1954. AB, Princeton U., 1977; PhD in Physics, U. Wash., 1983. Instr., asst. prof. physics Princeton U., 1983-85; from asst. prof. to assoc. prof. physics Harvard U., 1985-91; assoc. prof U. Mich., Ann Arbor, 1991-94, prof. physics, 1994—; fellow Alfred P. Sloan Found., 1987. Recipient Presdl. Young Investor award NSF, 1987. Fellow Am. Phys. Soc. (I.I. Rabi prize 1993). Achievements include research in low energy particle physics particularly by study of symmetries accessible with polarization; weak interactions: CP violation and time reversal violation; fundamentals of quantum mechanics; structure of nucleons; biomedical and technological applications of optical pumping. Office: U Mich Dept Physics Ann Arbor MI 48109

CHURCH, AVERY GRENFELL, retired anthropology educator, poet; b. North Wilkesboro, N.C., Feb. 21, 1937; s. Avery Milton and Eulah May (Lowe) C.; m. Joyce Elaine Riggs, Jan. 29, 1965 (div. Oct. 1968); m. Dora Ann Creed, Oct. 5, 1991; 1 stepchild, Mark Donald Burney. Student, U. N.C., 1959-60, 61; BA cum laude, Baylor U., 1962; MA, U. Colo., Boulder, 1965. Tchg. asst. U. Colo., Denver, 1965; asst. prof. anthropology Memphis State U., 1965-66, 69-72; lectr. U. So. Ala., Mobile, 1972-83; various positions with businesses, ednl. and humanitarian orgns., 1984-95; interviewer Navaho urban relocation project U. Colo., Boulder, 1964, rschr. Indian edn. project, 1966-69; mem. rsch. staff, bd. dirs. Sociol. and Anthrop. Svcs. Inst., Inc., Mobile, 1974-79. Author: (poetry) Rainbows of the Mind, 1982, Patterns of Thought, 1986, Waves of Life, 1995; contbr. over 200 articles, hist. sketches and poems to books, lit. mags., profl. and lit. jours., including Dan River Anthology, New Dawn Poetry, Yearbook Modern Poetry, Am. Bd., Bardic Echoes, Hoosier Challenger, Orphic Lute, Parnassus Lit. Jour., Pasque Petals, San Fernando Poetry Jour., Jour. Ala. Acad. Sci., So. Jour. Ednl. Rsch., Symposium on Drug Use for PTA Leaders, others. Hon. trustee Am. Indian Relief Coun., 1997-99; active Project Independence, campaign fin. reform Common Cause, Washington, 1997; freedom writer Amnesty Internat., N.Y.C., 1997-98. With USN, 1955-57. Woodrow Wilson fellow, 1962-63, Univ. fellow U. Colo., Boulder, 1964-65; recipient various lit. awards. Fellow Am. Anthrop. Assn.; mem. Poetry Soc. Am., Ala. Acad. Sci. (vice chmn. anthropology 1975-76, exec. com. 1975-77, v.p. 1976-77), Nature Conservancy, USN Meml. Found., Pres.'s Club U. Colo. (Silver Circle award 1994-95), Alpha Chi, Alpha Kappa Delta (vice chmn. anthropology 1975-76, exec. com. 1975-77, v.p. 1976-77). Democrat. Unitarian. Avocations: hiking, golf. Home: 2749 Park Oak Dr Clemmons NC 27012

CHURCH, BARBARA RYAN, organizational psychologist; b. Vallejo, Calif.; d. William Russell and Geraldine Hall (Hatcher) Ryan; divorced; children: Gabrielle Church Russell, Elizabeth Broward McGhie. BA, U. Fla., 1974; MA in Psychology, West Ga. Coll., 1981; EdD in Applied Psychology and Adult Edn., U. Ga., 1985. Pub. svc. dir., news editor, anchorwoman WJKS-TV, Jacksonville, Fla., 1969-71; dir. cmty. rels. Atlanta Assn. Ret. Citizens, 1977-78; coord. pub. info. Mental Health Assn., Atlanta, 1978-80; edn./testing specialist Federal Law Enforcement Tng. Ctr., Glynco, Ga., 1984-86; dir. evening coll., asst. prof. psychology Brewton-Parker Coll., Mt. Vernon, Ga., 1986-88; tng. rsch. analyst Federal Law Enforcement Tng. Ctr., 1988-90; researcher, edn. specialist U.S. Dept. Justice, Immigration & Naturalization Svc., Glynco, 1990-98, chief rsch. and evaluation, 1998—; tchr., cons. adult edn. courses Ga. State U., Atlanta, 1978, Brunswick (Ga.) Coll., 1993; adj. prof. orgnl. behavior and Leadership, MBA Program, Sch. Bus. Adminstrn., Brenau U., 1997—. Convenor, cons. Kettering Found., 1987-88; mem. adv. bd. HRD degree, dept. adult edn. U. Ga. Recipient award for best campaign of non-profit orgn. Am. Mktg. Assn., 1978, ann. award for innovative programming Ga. Adult Edn. Assn., 1983; named communicator of yr. United Way, 1980. Mem. U. Ga. Lifelong Learning Assn., Ga. Adult Edn. Assn. (bd. dirs. 1989-91), Soc. Police & Criminal Psychology, Commn. Profs. of Adult Edn. Episcopal. Avocations: writing non-fiction, painting, travel, photography. Home: 257 Charlemagne Cir Ponte Vedra Beach FL 32082-2907 Office: US Dept Justice Immigration & Naturalization Svc Federal Law Enforcement Tng Ctr Bldg T-706 Glynco GA 31522

CHURCH, DALE WALKER, lawyer; b. Portland, Oreg., Dec. 17, 1939; s. Floyd Walker and Lydia Belle (Barnette) C.; m. Mollie Ann Harper, Apr. 11, 1964; 1 child, Forrest Gregory. BS, Oreg. State U., 1961; JD, George Washington U., 1967. Bar: D.C. 1968, Calif. 1971. Contracting officer, exec. sec. contract rev. bd. CIA, Langley, Va., 1963-69; corp. gen. counsel, asst. sec. directory of contracts ESL, Inc., Sunnyvale, Calif., 1969-77; dep. under sec. research and engring. U.S. Dept. Def., Washington, 1977-80; ptnr. Surrey and Morse, Washington, 1980-84, Seyfarth, Shaw, Fairweather & Geraldson, Washington, 1984-88, Pillsbury, Madison & Sutro, Washington, 1988-93, McDermott, Will & Emery, Washington, 1993-97; chmn., CEO Ventures & Solutions, LLC, Williamsburg, Va., 1998—; counsel def. mgmt. to pres.'s Blue Ribbon Commn.; cons. Def. Sci. Bd., Washington, 1980—; lectr. profl. orgns. and colls. Mem. task force on Industry-to-Industry Coop.; active Ctr. Strategic and Internat. Studies Def. Orgn. Project; trustee Oratorio Soc. Washington; co-founder, counsel, treas. Youth Engaged in Svc. Am. Mem. ABA, Am. Electronics Assn. (former gen. counsel, chmn. def. conversion com.), Nat. Security Indsl. Assn. (trustee, chmn. acquisition reform task force), Nat. Contracts Mgmt. Assn., Def. Sci. Bd. Acquisition Reform Task Force, Calif. Bar Assn., D.C. Bar Assn., Fed. Bar Assn., Soc. Logistics Engrs. (hon.), Delta Theta Phi, Sigma Phi Epsilon. Home: 9 Franklin St Alexandria VA 22314-3828 Office: Ventures & Solutions LLC 704 Fairfax Way Williamsburg VA 23185-8202

CHURCH, EUGENE LENT, physicist, consulting scientist; b. Yonkers, N.Y., July 30, 1925; s. Wallace L. and Wilhelmina L. (Binger) C.; m. Anne Richardson Meirs, May 15, 1948; children—Rebecca Meirs, David Lent. A.B., Princeton U., 1948; Ph.D., Harvard U., 1953. With U.S. Dept. Def., 1952-94; sr. phys. scientist Picatinny Arsenal, Dover, N.J., 1977-94; sr. physicist Frankford Arsenal, Phila., 1971-77; guest physicist Argonne (Ill.) Nat. Lab., 1952-55, Brookhaven Nat. Lab., 1955-59, 61-71, 81—; vis. scientist Niels Bohr Inst., Copenhagen, 1959-61. Contbr. numerous articles to profl. jours. Served with USN, 1944-46. Recipient R&D-100 award, U.S. Army Achievement awards. Fellow Am. Phys. Soc., AAAS, Am. Optical Soc., Soc. Photo-Optical, Instrumentation Engrs.; mem. IEEE (life sr.). Republican. Presbyterian. Club: Princeton (N.Y.C.). Achievements include research in nuclear physics, electromagnetic scattering, surface metrology and signal processing.

CHURCH, FRANK FORRESTER, minister, author, columnist; b. Boise, Idaho, Sept. 23, 1948; s. Frank Forrester and Bethine (Clark) C.; m. Amy Furth, May 30, 1970 (div. 1991); children: Frank Forrester, Nina Wynne; m. Carolyn Buck Luce, July 25, 1992. AB, Stanford U., 1970; MDiv, Harvard U., 1974, PhD, 1978. Sr. min. All Souls Unitarian Ch., N.Y.C., 1978—; columnist The Chicago Tribune, 1987-88, The New York Post, 1989; vis. prof. Dartmouth Coll., Hanover, N.H., 1989. Author: Father and Son: A Personal Biography of Senator Frank Church of Idaho, 1985, The Devil and Dr. Church, 1985, Entertaining Angels, 1987, The Seven Deadly Virtues, 1988, Everyday Miracles, 1988, Our Chosen Faith: An Introduction to Unitarian Universalism, 1989, God and Other Famous Liberals, 1991, Life Lines, 1996, A Chosen Faith, 1998; translator: Greek Word-Building (Matthias Stehle), 1976; editor: Continuity and Discontinuity in Church History, 1978, The Essential Tillich, 1987, 2d edit., 1999, The Macmillan Book of Earliest Christian Prayers, 1988, The Macmillan Book of Earliest Christian Hymns, 1988, The MacMillan Book of Earliest Christian Meditations, 1989, One Prayer at a Time: A 12 Step Anthology, 1989, The Jefferson Bible, 1989, Without Apology: The Liberal Faith of A. Powell Davies, 1998; contbr. articles to Harvard Theol. Rev., Church and State Quar., Vigiliae Christianae, Bill Moyer's World of Ideas, Philip Berman's The Search for Meaning, others; contbr. speeches to Rep. Am. Speeches, 1983-84, 86-87, 87-88, 89-90, 92-93, 95-96, 97-98. Bd. dirs. Union Theol. Sem., N.Y.C., Coun. on Econ. Priorities, N.Y.C., 1984-91, Religion in Am. Life, Christianity in Christ, 1991, Franklin and Eleanor Roosevelt Found., N.Y.C., 1990—, N.Y. Correctional Assn., Osborne Inst., 1991-94, Enterprise Found., N.Y.C. HIV Planning Coun.; chmn. Coun. on Environment N.Y.C., 1995—; mem. svc. com. Unitarian Universalist Ch., 1978—. Montgomery fellow Dartmouth Coll., 1989. Mem. Am. Acad. Religion, Unitarian Universalist Mins. Assn., Soc. Bibl. Lit., Citizens United for Separation of Church and State. Democrat. Home: 201 E 80th St New York NY 10021-0511 Office: All Souls Unitarian Church 1157 Lexington Ave New York NY 10021-0440

CHURCH, GAIL GRAHAM, former television producer, consultant; b. Providence, May 10, 1924; d. Harry Jackson and Gertrude (Connors) Graham; m. Thomas William Rice Gerber, Jan. 20, 1951 (div. Jan. 1971); children: Cheryl Ann Gerber, Linda Lee Gerber; m. Herbert Church Jr., July 6, 1974. BS, R.I. State Coll., 1945; M of Nursing, Yale U., 1948. Nurse, instr. Mary Hitchcock Hosp., Hanover, N.H., 1948-49; head nurse rooming-in unit Grace New Haven (Conn.) Hosp., 1949-51; nurse, instr. Home Health Agy., Chicopee, Mass., 1951; educator, pub. health nurse N.H. Divsn. Pub. Health, Concord, N.H., 1972-74; ednl. advisor communicable diseases N.H. Dept. Edn., Concord, 1980; founder, prodr. pub. affairs TV series Life: Living It and Loving It, Concord, 1985-89; advisor Hospice Adv. Com., Concord, 1985; pres. Life: Living It and Loving It, Inc., Concord, 1985—. Founder, pres. Concord Area Drug Action Com., 1968; initiator first HELP-Line in N.H., Concord, 1969; organizer Reps. for Clinton/Gore, N.H. Dem. Party, Concord, 1992; mem. Task Force Against Racism, Concord, 1997—; mem. adv. bd. Internat. Health Found., 1998—. Recipient Leadership award YMCA, 1969, Dedicated Svc. to N.H. award Gov. Walter Peterson, 1970, Vol. Svc. award Gov.'s Coun. on Volunteerism, 1987. Mem. AAUW (membership chair Concord 1997, pres. Concord br. 1997—), N.H. Women's Lobby, Concord Hosp. Assocs., Concord Garden Club, UN Assn., Coalition for Am. Leadership Abroad. Republican. Episcopalian. Avocations: watercoloring, biking, reading, walking, art and music appreciation. Home: 1 Pleasant View Ave Concord NH 03301-2555

CHURCH, GEORGE JOHN, journalist; b. Union City, N.J., Aug. 19, 1931; s. John Andrew and Julia (Abraham) C.; m. Lucille Anne Nardone, Feb. 6, 1954; 1 child, Frederick G. BA, Manhattan Coll., 1952; postgrad., Syracuse U., 1952-53. Copyboy, news clk. N.Y. Times, N.Y.C., 1953-54; reporter Wall St. Jour., N.Y.C., 1954-59; mgr. Pitts. Bur. Wall St. Jour., 1959-61; news editor Wall St. Jour., N.Y.C., 1961-69; contbg. editor Time Mag., N.Y.C., 1969-70, assoc. editor, 1970-74, sr. editor, 1974-78, sr. writer, 1978-94, contbr., 1995—. Recipient award for excellence in fin. writing John Hancock Life Ins., 1970, 77, Page One award N.Y. Newspaper Guild, 1977. Achievements include writing most cover stories in history of Time Mag. Avocations: fishing, golf, swimming. Home: 1042 Commack Rd Dix Hills NY 11746-8210 Office: Time Mag Time-Life Bldg Rockefeller Ctr New York NY 10020

CHURCH, GEORGE MILLORD, real estate executive; b. Philadelphia, Miss., Sept. 21, 1924; s. George W. and Maggie (Smith) C.; m. Ruth Green, Nov. 12, 1948; children: Ray, Gary. Diploma in acctg., So. Bus. Coll., 1947; AA with honors, Meridian (Miss.) Jr. Coll., 1954; BA in History and Polit. Sci., Coll. of Ozarks, 1957; disting. grad., U.S. Army Noncommd. Officer's Acad., 1961; grad., Realtor's Inst., 1971; postgrad., U. Miss., 1976. Boatswain's mate 1st class USN, South Pacific, Aleutian's, 1942-46; shipfitter Ala. Dry Dock and Ship Bldg., Mobile, 1946; acct. Milton Supply Co., Meridian, 1948-50; staff sgt. USMC, Camp Pendelton, Calif., 1950-51, Meridian, 1953-54; chief acct. Meridian Grain and Elevator Co., 1951-52; cost acct. Flintkote Co., Meridian, 1952-53; enlisted U.S. Army, 1954, advanced through grades to command sgt. maj., 1968, served in Vietnam, retired, 1969; pres. Church Realty Co., Meridian, 1969—; instr. real estate, real estate math Meridain Jr. Coll. Chmn. Toys for Tots, Meridian, 1954; active Lauderdale County Planning Commn., 1980-84, past chmn.; active VFW Home for Children: charter mem. Rep. Presdl. Task Force, Washington, 1982—. Decorated 3 Bronze Star medals, Air medal, Gallantry Cross with Palm (Republic of South Vietnam), Gallantry Cross with Silver Star. Mem. Miss. Assn. Realtors (bd. dirs. 1972-73, 91, past chmn. profl. stds. com., FHA and VA liason officer), Meridian Bd. Realtors (pres. 1972-73, 91, bd. dirs. 1972-73, 91, chmn. legis. and polit. action com., bd. congl. coord., Realtor of Yr. 1973, 89), Realtors Polit. Action Com. (life), Navy League U.S. (life commodore), VFW (life, Nat. Home for Children), Am. Legion (life), NRA, Sons of Confederate Vets., (life, gen. exec. coun., comdr. Camp 1221, 1992, 93, chief of staff Miss. divsn. 1993, 94, comdr./founder Camp 1649, 1994, brigade comdr., life, Miss. divsn. 1995, gen. exec. coun. svc., 1998), The Jefferson Davis Soc. (co-founder, sec.-treas. 1994-96, dir. 1997—), Order of So. Cross (life). Baptist. Avocations: hunting, fishing, traveling, golf. Home: 4200 Pineview Dr Meridian MS 39305-3345 Office: Church Realty Co PO Box 224 Meridian MS 39302-0224

CHURCH, HERBERT STEPHEN, JR., retired construction company executive; b. Framingham, Mass., July 24, 1920; s. Herbert Stephen and Edith L. (Shaw) C.; m. Carol S. Orzech, Apr. 2, 1945; children: Carolyn, David, Kathryn, Patricia, Virginia. B.S. in Civil Engring, Northeastern U., Boston, 1943. Constrn. insp. N.Y., New Haven & Hartford R.R., 1940-43; with Turner Constrn. Co., 1943; from gen. supt. to v.p., gen. mgr. Chgo. terr., 1965-73; sr. v.p. Western region Chgo., 1974-80, sr. v.p. Central region, 1980-85; dir., 1972-85. Trustee Nat. Commn. for Coop. Edn., 1981-90. Mem. Contractors Mut. Assn. (dir. 1974-84), Builders Assn. Chgo. (dir. 1969-74), Chgo. Club, Inverness Golf Club. Roman Catholic. Home: 811 W George St Arlington Heights IL 60005-1751

CHURCH, IRENE ZABOLY, personnel services company executive; b. Cleve., Feb. 18, 1947; d. Bela Paul and Irene Elizabeth (Chandas) Zaboly; children: Irene Elizabeth, Elizabeth Anne, Lauren Alexandria Gadd, John Dale Gadd II. Grad. high sch. Pers. cons., recruiter, Cleve., 1965-70; chief exec. officer, pres. Oxford Pers., Pepper Pike, Ohio, 1973-89, Oxford Temporaries, Pepper Pike, 1979—, Oxford Group Ltd., Inc., 1989—; guest lectr. in field, 1974—; expert witness for ct. testimony, 1982—. Troop leader Lake Erie coun. Girl Scouts U.S., 1980-81; mem. Christian action com. Federated Ch., United Ch. Christ, 1981-85, sub-com. to study violence in rels. to women, 1983, creator, presenter programs How Work Affects Family Life and Re-entering the Job Market, 1981, mem. Women's Fellowship Martha-Mary Circle, 1980—, program dir., 1982-84, 87—; chpt. leader Nat. Coalition on TV Violence, 1983—; mem. The Federated Ch., United Ch. of Christ, Chagrin Falls, Ohio, program dir Mary-Martha Circle, 1982—, christian action com. 1981-85, mem. Mary-Martha Circle, Women's fellowship, 1980—; mem Better Bus. Bur., 1973-82. Mem. Nat. Assn. Pers. Cons. (cert., mem. ethics com. 1976-77, co-chairperson ethics com. 1977-78, mem. bus. practices and ethics com. 1980-82, mem. cert. pers. cons. soc. 1980-82, regional leader for membership 1987—, Pres.'s award 1988), Ohio Assn. Pers. Cons. (trustee 1975-80, 85—, sec. 1976-77, 85-87, chairperson bus. practices and ethics com. 1976-77, 81-82, 1st v.p., chairperson resolutions com. 1981-82, chairperson membership com. 1985-89, 2d v.p. 1987—, Outstanding Svc. award 1987, pres. 1988-89), Greater Cleve. Assn. Pers. Cons. (2nd then 1st v.p., 1974-76, state trustee 1975-80, pres. 1976-77, bd. advisor 1977-78, chairperson bus. practices and ethics com. 1974-76, chmn. nominating com., 1983-88, membership com. 1987-87, arbitration com., 1980, 85-87, fundraising, 1980-89, bd. dirs. 1980-89, trustee 1985-89, program chair 1987-89, Vi Pender Outstanding Svc. award 1977), Euclid C. of C. (small bus. com. 1981, chairperson task force com. evaluating funding in social security and vet.'s benefits 1981), Internat. Platform Assn., Am. Bus. Women's Assn., Nat. Assn. Temp. Svcs., Chagrin Valley C. of C. (leader Chagrin Blvd./East chpt. 1987—, Pres.'s award for Outstanding Contbns. 1988, pres. bd. dirs 1990—), Greater Cleve. Growth Assn. Coun. Small Enterprises, Rotary (vocat. svc. chairperson, program com. 1987—, membership chairperson 1988-89). Home: 8 Ridgecrest Dr Chagrin Falls OH 44022-4218

CHURCH, JAY KAY, psychologist, educator; b. Wichita, Kans., Jan. 18, 1927; s. Kay Iverson and Gertrude (Parrish) C.; BA, David Lipscomb Coll., 1948; MA, Ball State U., 1961; PhD, Purdue U., 1963; m. Dorothy Agnes Fellerhoff, May 21, 1976; children: Karen Patrice Turnbull, Caryn Annice Church Casey, Rex Warren, Max Roger. Chemist, Auburn Rubber Corp., 1948-49; salesman Midwestern United Life Ins. Co., 1949-52; owner, operator Tour-Rest Motel, Waterloo, Ind., 1952-66; tchr., guidance dir., public schs., Hamilton, Ind., 1955-61; counselor Washington Twp. (Ind.) Schs., Indpls., 1961-62; asst. prof. psychology Ball State U., 1963-67, assoc. prof., 1967-71, prof., 1971-88, prof. emeritus, 1988—, chmn. dept. ednl. psychology, 1970-74, dir. advanced grad. programs in ednl. psychology, 1978-81; pvt. practice psychology, 1963—. Mem. Am. Psychol. Assn., Nat. Assn. Sch. Psychologists. Home: 8501 N Ravenwood Dr Muncie IN 47303-9029

CHURCH, JO HALL, educator; b. Bryan, Tex., Nov. 8, 1931; d. Dan and Inez (Etheridge) Hall; m. Donald Roussel Church, May 7, 1954; children: Lynn Church Jordan, Carol Church Wood, Donald Roussel Church Jr., John Hall Church, Joseph Cornay Church. BA, Sam Houston State U., 1953; MA, Tex. Woman's U., 1978, PhD, 1985. Tchr. Manvel (Tex.) Ind. Sch. Dist., 1953-55; substitute tchr. Mary Immaculate Sch., Dallas, 1965-70; staff and dir. writing lab. Tex. Woman's U., Denton, 1983-84, teaching fellow, 1980-84, teaching ESL Japanese, 1986, 87; asst. prof. Cameron U., Lawton, Okla., 1988; instr. N. Ctrl. Tex. Coll., Lewisville, Tex., 1989—; adj. prof. U. North Tex., 1987, Tex. Woman's U., 1985-87, 88-89, coord. grad. student symposium in rhetoric, 1979. Dir. ch. choir St. Thomas Ch., Pilot Point, Tex., 1976—. Mem. MLA, South Cen. Modern Lang. Assn. (sec. rhetoric sect. 1989, chmn. rhetoric sect. 1990), New Chaucer Soc., Rhetoric Soc. Am. (panel organizer 1988), Conf. of Coll. Tchrs. of English, Conf. on Coll. Composition and Communication, Nat. Coun. of Tchrs. of English, Tex. Coun. of Tchrs. of English, Phi Delta Gamma. Roman Catholic. Office: North Ctrl Tex Coll Corinth Campus 1500 N Corinth Corinth TX 76208

CHURCH, JOHN W., quality engineer; b. Aug. 5, 1946. AAS in Mech. Engring., CPCC, 1975; BSBA in Mgmt. Sci., Limestone Coll., 1982. Quality engr. Allied-Signal, Charlotte, N.C., 1980-97, BE Aerospace, Winston-Salem, N.C., 1997-99; quality assurance mgr. Duff-Norton, Charlotte, 1999—. Address: 15926 Woodcote Dr Huntersville NC 28078

CHURCH, KERN EVERIDGE, engineer, consultant; b. North Wilkesboro, N.C., July 22, 1926; s. Wilford Albert and Rosa Bell (Everidge) C.; m. Agnes Elouise Pardue, Dec. 25, 1947; children: Ronald Kern, David Albert, Deborah Jean, Stephen Sherwood, Anne Michele. BS in Gen. Engring., N.C. State U., Raleigh, 1949. Registered profl. engr., N.C. Plan rev. engr. State Bldg. Codes Div., Raleigh, N.C., 1949-67; dir. bldg. codes State of N.C., Raleigh, 1967-82; cons. engr. W.H. Gardner and Assocs., PA, Durham, N.C., 1983-85; consulting engr. pvt. practice, Raleigh, 1985—; mem. constrn. panel Am. Arbitration Assn., N.Y.C., 1984—; mem. safety to life com. Nat. Fire Protection Assn., Boston, 1954-68; mem. bldg. code com. So. Bldg Code Congress, Birmingham, 1965-80; bd. dirs. Nat. Conf. of States on Bldg. Codes, Herndon, Va., 1967-82, pres. 1971-72; mem. fire coun. Underwriters Labs., Chgo., 1970-82. Editor N.C. State Building Code, 1967. Recipient Frank Turner award, N.C. chpt. AIA, Profl. Engrs. and Associated Contractors, 1983. Mem. N.C. chpt. AIA (hon.), Nat. Soc. of Profl. Engrs. (life), Nat. Soc. Fire Protection Engrs. Democrat. Address: 1217 Trailwood Dr Raleigh NC 27606-3714

CHURCH, MARTHA ELEANOR, retired academic administrator, scholar; b. Pitts., Nov. 17, 1930; d. Walter Seward and Eleanor (Boyer) C. BA, Wellesley Coll., 1952; MA, U. Pitts., 1954; PhD, U. Chgo., 1960; DSc (hon.), Lake Erie Coll., 1975; LittD (hon.), Houghton Coll., 1980; LHD (hon.), Queens Coll., 1981, Ursinus Coll., 1981, St. Joseph Coll., 1982, Towson State U., 1983, Dickinson Coll., 1987, Coll. Notre Dame Md., 1995; LLD (hon.), Hood Coll., 1995. Instr. geography Mt. Holyoke Coll., South Hadley, Mass., 1953-57; lectr. geography Ind. U. Gary Ctr., 1958; instr., then asst. prof. geography Wellesley Coll., 1958-59; dean coll., prof. geography Wilson Coll., 1965-71; assoc. exec. sec. Commn. Higher Edn., Middle States Assn. Coll. and Secondary Sch., 1971-75; pres. Hood Coll., Frederick, Md., 1975-95, pres. emerita, 1995—; sr. scholar Carnegie Found. for Advancement of Tchg., Princeton, 1995-97; bd. dirs. Farmers and Mechanics Nat. Bank, 1982—, Montgomery Mut. Ins. Co., 1989-90; cons. for Choice: Books for Coll. Librs.; co-chmn. nat. adv. panel nat. Ctr. for Rsch. to Improve Post-secondary Teaching and Learning, U. Mich., 1985-90; mem. bd. vis. Def.

Intelligence Coll., 1988-91; mem. adv. bd. dirs. Automobile Club Md., 1991—; bd. dirs. AAA Mid-Atlantic, 1997—; mem. adv. bd. The Boyer Ctr. Messiah Coll., Grantham, Pa., 1997—. Author: The Spatial Organization of Electric Power Territories in Massachusetts, 1960; Co-editor: A Basic Geographical Library: A Selected and Annotated Book List for Am. Colls, 1966; cons. editor, Change mag., 1980—. Bd. dirs. Coun. for Internat. Exch. of Scholars, 1979-80, Japan Internat. Christian U. Found., 1977-91, Nat. Ctr. for Higher Edn. Mgmt. Sys., 1980-83; bd. dirs. Am. Coun. on Edn., 1976-79, vice chmn., 1978-79, mem. nat. identification panel, 1977-95, Nat. Rsch. Com., 1993-96; bd. advisors Fund for Improvement of Postsecondary Edn., HEW, 1976-79; mem. Sec. of Navy's Adv. Bd. on Edn. and Tng., 1976-80; chmn. Md. Commn. on Civil Rights, 1981-82; trustee Bradford Coll., Mass., 1982-87, Peddie Sch., N.J., 1982-98, chair acad. affairs com., 1996-97, adv. trustee, 1998—; trustee Carnegie Found. for the Advancement of Tchg., 1986-96, vice chair, 1990-92, chair, 1992-94, immediate past chair, 1994-96; trustee Nat. Geog. Soc., 1989—, mem. com. on rsch. and exploration, 1998—, chair audit rev. com., 1993—, mem. exec. and compensation coms.; trustee Nat. Geog. Soc. Edn. Found., 1989-96, 99—; chmn. bd. dirs. Medici Found., Princeton, N.J., 1985—; trustee United Bd. for Christian Higher Edn. in Asia, 1995—, sec. bd. trustees, 1998—, chmn. East and Intra-Asia program subcom., 1996-97, sec., exec. com., 1998—; mem. Md. Humanities Coun., 1985-86, Md. Jud. Disabilities Commn., 1985-94; commr. Edn. Commn. States, Md., 1981—; exec. com. Campus Compact: Project for Pub. and Cmty. Svc., 1986-89—; trustee Internat. Partnership for Svc. Learning, 1999—. Mem. AAUW, Am. Assn. Advancement of Humanities (bd. dirs. 1979-81), Am. Assn. Higher Edn. (chmn. 1980-81, bd. dirs. 1979-83), Assn. Am. Geographers, Nat. Assn. Ind. Colls. and Univs. (bd. dirs. 1983-86), Md. Ind. Colls. and Univs. Assn. (pres. 1979-81, mem. exec. com. 1988-92), Assn. Am. Colls. and Univs. (mem. adv. com. project on status and edn. of women 1980-85), Women's Coll. Coalition (mem. exec. com. 1976-80, 87-89), Am. Conf. Acad. Deans (sec., editor 1969-71), Coun. Protestant Colls. and Univs. (bd. dirs. 1969-71), Soc. Coll. and Univ. Planning (mem. editl. bd. 1979-95), Cosmos Club (mem. jour. editl. bd. 1990-94), Inst. Ednl. Leadership (bd. dirs. 1982-87), Sigma Delta Epsilon, Delta Kappa Gamma (hon.). Fax: (301) 663-3018. Home: 104 Mercer Ct Apt 15-6 Frederick MD 21701-4033

CHURCH, PHILIP THROOP, mathematician, educator; b. Conn., Mar. 18, 1931; s. Russell Frank and Margaret C.; m. Patricia Ethel Flynn, Sept. 1, 1954; children—Peter Thomas, Susan Elisabeth, Daniel Russell. B.A., Wesleyan U., 1953; M.A., Harvard U., 1954; Ph.D., U. Mich., 1959. Asst. prof. Syracuse (N.Y.) U., 1958-62, assoc. prof., 1962-65; prof. Syracuse (N.Y.) U., N.Y., 1965-76; Francis H. Root prof. math. Syracuse (N.Y.) U., 1976—; mathematician Inst. for Def. Analyses, Princeton, N.J., 1962-63; mem. Inst. for Advanced Study, Princeton, N.J., 1961, 65-66, summer 1977, summer 1978; vis. fellow Princeton U., N.J., spring 1976; disting. vis. prof. U. Alberta, fall, 1987;. Contbr. articles to profl. jours. Fellow NSF, 1965-66, Danforth Found., 1953-57. Mem. Am. Math. Soc. (council 1973-77, 80, com. to monitor problems in communication, 1978-80, chmn. 1980, editor Trans. 1973-77, chmn. 1977); mem. Math. Assn. Am., AAUP, Sigma Xi, Phi Beta Kappa. Methodist. Office: Syracuse U Dept Math Syracuse NY 13244

CHURCH, RANDOLPH WARNER, JR., lawyer; b. Richmond, Va., Nov. 6, 1934; s. Randolph Warner and Elizabeth Lewis (Gochnauer) C.; m. Lucy Ann Canary, July 4, 1970; children: Leslie R. Pennell, L. Weeks Kerr. BA with honors, U. Va., 1957, LLB, 1960. Bar: Va. 1960, U.S. Dist. Ct. (ea. dist.) Va. 1962, U.S. Ct. Appeals (4th cir.) 1981. Assoc. McCandlish, Lillard & Marsh, Fairfax, Va., 1960-63; ptnr. McCandlish, Lillard, Rust & Church, Fairfax, 1963-75; city atty. Fairfax, 1968-72; mng. ptnr. McCandlish, Lillard, Rust & Church, Fairfax, 1975-83; mng. ptnr. Hunton & Williams, Fairfax, 1984—, mem. exec. com., 1988-94; bd. dirs. George Mason Bank, George Mason Bankshares, Inc., George Mason Mortgage Co., 1991-98, Va. Found. for Rsch. and Econ. Edn., Inc., 1994—. Author: Appellate Civil Litigation, 1984; panelist: Lawyer Professionalism: Is Change in Order? 1988, Marketing Legal Services: What's Hot and What's Not, 1990. Active Fairfax Com. of 100, 1988—, bd. dirs., 1989-92; bd. visitors George Mason U., Fairfax, 1982-90, rector, 1983-86; bd. dirs. George Mason Fund for Arts, 1987-96, Fairfax Symphony, 1991—, gen. counsel, exec. com., 1996—; bd. dirs. Va. Found. for Humanities and Pub. Policy, 1999; vice pres., exec. com. Va. Found. for Rsch. and Econ. Edn., 1996—; lectr., author Va. Continuing Edn. Program Appellate Litigation, 1985, Equity Practice, 1987-90; panelist Va. Continuing Edn. Programs; trustee George Mason U. Edn. Found., 1986-95, trustee emeritus, 1995—. Fellow Va. Law Found., Am. Bar Found.; mem. ABA, Am. Judicature Soc., Va. Bar Assn. (v.p. 1975), Tower Club, Country Club Fairfax County, U. Va. Club, Phi Beta Kappa. Episcopalian. Home: 5114 Forsgate Pl Fairfax VA 22030-4507 Office: Hunton & Williams 1751 Pinnacle Dr Ste 1700 Mc Lean VA 22102-3836

CHURCH, RICHARD DWIGHT, electrical engineer, scientist; b. Ogdensburg, N.Y., June 27, 1936; s. Dwight Perry and Carmeta Elizabeth (Walters) C.; m. Vernice Naomi Ives, Aug. 26, 1961; children: Joel, Benjamin. BEE, Clarkson Coll. Tech., 1963. Electronic design engr. IBM, Owego, N.Y., 1963-69; prin. engr., pres. ASL Systems, Inc., Afton, N.Y., 1969-94, chmn. bd. dirs.; sr. electronic design engr. Magnetic Labs., Inc., Apalachin, N.Y., 1980-82; power supply engring. cons., 1982—; sci. Two Forty-Eight Co., Afton, N.Y., 1994—; guest lectr. Afton Sch., Clarkson U. Co-author: Career Oriented Problems for Secondary Mathematics, 1974; contbr. articles to profl. jours.; patentee in field. Treas., trustee Candor Congregational Ch., 1972-84; vice chmn. Town Planning Bd. Candor, 1975-82; rep., mem. Candor Fire Co., 1972-87; bd. dirs., treas. Candor Community Club, 1970-72. With USAF, 1955-59. Recipient Dr. Carl Michel award Clarkson Coll. Tech., 1960. Mem. IEEE (sr. mem.), Assn. Energy Engrs. (sr.), Afton Bd. Fire Commrs., Candor Coin Club (pres. 1978-81), Union of Concerned Scientists. Avocations: maple syrup production, maple tree farm development, pyramid geometry, bicycling. Home: 1249 County Road 30 Afton NY 13730-2181 Office: PO Box 235 Afton NY 13730-0235

CHURCH, RUSSELL MILLER, psychology educator; b. N.Y.C., Dec. 24, 1930; s. Donald E. and Dee (Friedman) C.; m. Ruth Kutz, Apr. 4, 1954; children—Kenneth, Emily. B.A., U. Mich., 1952; M.A., Harvard U., 1954, Ph.D., 1956. Mem. faculty Brown U., 1955—, prof. psychology, 1965—, chmn. dept. psychology, 1980-83; chair faculty exec. com. Brown U., 1995-96. Editor: (with E.E. Boe) Punishment: Issues and Experiments, 1968; editor (with B.A. Campbell) Punishment and Aversive Behavior, 1969. Fellow AAAS, Am. Psychol. Assn. (pres. div. exptl. psychology 1987-88, comparative and physiol. psychology 1991-92); mem. Ea. Psychol. Assn. (pres. 1991-92). Office: Brown U Dept of Psychology 89 Waterman St Providence RI 02912-9079

CHURCH, THOMAS TROWBRIDGE, former steel company executive; b. N.Y.C., Nov. 21, 1919; s. William Bowen and Agnes Mansfield (Curtis) C.; m. Sylvina Williams, Sept. 20, 1943; children: Daniel C., Martha C., Thomas N., Sara C., Warren B., Minette C. B.A., Yale U., 1941. With Bethlehem Steel Corp. (Pa.), 1941-82, gen. traffic mgr., 1968-71, asst. v.p., 1971-75, v.p. transp., 1975-82. Pres. Bach Choir of Bethlehem, 1981-91. Served with USAAF, 1942-44, to capt. Transp. Corps., 1944-46. Mem. Am. Iron and Steel Inst. (chmn. traffic com. 1978-80), Nat. Freight Transp. Assn., Transp. Assn. Am. (dir., chmn., user panel, chmn. transp. data coordinating com.). Episcopalian. Club: Saucon Valley Country (Bethlehem). Address: 438 High St Bethlehem PA 18018-6134

CHURCHILL, DANIEL WAYNE, management and marketing educator; b. Bloomington, Ind., Dec. 2, 1947; s. Warren L. and Mary Ellen (Boynton) C.; m. Jean F. McEnroe, Nov. 11, 1972. BBA, U. Mass., 1970, MBA, 1972. Lic. real estate broker, Mass. Internal auditor Liberty Mut. Ins. Co., Boston, 1972-73; site location analyst, mktg. rschr. Zayre, Framingham, Mass., 1974-75; pres. Daniel W. Churchill Real Estate, South Easton, Mass., 1976-83; prof. mgmt. and mktg. Mt. Ida Coll., Newton, Mass., 1984—. Exec. bd. Easton Field Authority, 1981-85, supt. screening com., 1988; mem. Easton Continuing Sch. Bldg and Site Com., 1993-99; exec. bd. Easton Softball League, 1975-85, Camp Yomechas, Middleboro, Mass., 1978-82; chmn. Cable 2 Auction, Easton, 1980, Easton Walkathon, 1979-81; chmn. C.A.R.E.S., 1989; selectman Town of Easton, 1994-97; adv. bd. Mass. Faculty Devel. Consortium, 1997-99; steering team Mass. All-Acad. Two-Year Coll., 1996-99; bd. dirs. Ames Free Libr., 1997—. Mem. Easton Jaycees (pres. 1981, Jaycee of Yr. award), Lions (pres. Easton chpt. 1988, Lion of Yr. award), Phi Theta Kappa (hon.). Avocations: sports, games, reading, computers. Home: 16 Summer St North Easton MA 02356-2132 Office: Mt Ida Coll 777 Dedham St Newton MA 02459-3323

CHURCHILL, JAMES ALLEN, lawyer; b. Kingsport, Tenn., Sept. 13, 1935; s. Robert Lang and Jamie Louise (Hill) C.; m. Jackeen Kelleher, Aug. 9, 1958; children: James Allen Jr., Courtney Bartlett. AB, Princeton U., 1957; LLB, Harvard U., 1960; M in Civil Law, Tulane U., 1963. Bar: La. 1961, U.S. Dist. Ct. (ea. dist.) La. 1962, U.S. Ct. Appeals (5th cir.) 1965; admitted as Gaikokuho Jimu Bengoshi, Japan, 1992. Ptnr. Lemle, Kelleher, Kohlmeyer & Matthews, New Orleans, 1960-79; dir. Barham & Churchill, New Orleans, 1979-88; ptnr. Pillsbury Madison & Sutro, L.A. and Tokyo, 1988-95; sr. v.p., gen. counsel, corp. sec. Ventura Foods, LLC, City of Industry, Calif., 1995—. Mem. ABA, Am. Law Inst., Calif. Bar Assn., La. Bar Assn., Calif. Club (L.A.), Boston Club (New Orleans), Annandale Golf Club. Democrat. Office: Ventura Foods LLC 14840 Don Julian Rd City of Industry CA 91746-3109*

CHURCHILL, LARRY RAYMOND, ethics educator; b. Russellville, Ark., June 24, 1945; s. Olen Raymond and Mary Josephine (Cheek) C.; m. Sandra Wade; children: Shelley, Blair Naylor. BA, Rhodes Coll., 1967; MDiv, Duke U., 1970, PhD, 1973. Asst. prof. U. N.C., Chapel Hill, 1976-82, assoc. prof., 1982-88, prof., 1988—, chmn. dept. social medicine, 1988-98; cons. med. schs. and orgns. in bioethics, 1976—. Author: Rationing Health Care in America, 1987; co-author: Professional Ethics of Primary Care, 1986, The Physician As Captain of the Ship, 1988, Self-Interest and Universal Health Care, 1994, The Social Medicine Reader, 1997. Charles E. Culpeper scholar in med. humanities, 1991-94. Mem. Soc. for Health and Human Values (pres. 1980-81), Inst. of Medicine, The Hastings Ctr., The Hume Soc. Office: Univ of NC Dept Soc Medicine Campus Box 7240 Wing D Chapel Hill NC 27599

CHURCHILL, MAIR ELISA ANNABELLE, medical educator; b. Liverpool, Eng., Nov. 28, 1959. BA in Chemistry, Swarthmore (Pa.) Coll., 1981; PhD in Chemistry, Johns Hopkins U., 1987. Lab. asst. Swarthmore Coll., 1979-81; teaching asst. Johns Hopkins U., Balt., 1981-83; non-clin. sci. staff grade I MRC Lab. Molecular Biology, Cambridge, Eng., 1987-93; asst. prof. biophysics U. Ill., Urbana, 1993-97, U. Colo., Denver, 1997—. Contbr. numerous articles to profl. jours. Am. Cancer Soc. fellow, 1987-89, Cambridge U. fellow, 1988-91. Mem. Am. Chem. Soc., Sigma Xi (assoc.). Office: U Colo Health Scis Dept Pharm Campus Box C236 4200 E 9th Ave Denver CO 80220-3706

CHURCHILL, ROBERT WILSON, state legislator, lawyer; b. Waukegan, Ill., Apr. 10, 1947; s. George Oliver and Helga C. (Carlson) C.; m. Sandra Lee Bartlett, Aug. 5, 1985; children: Abigail Lee, Julia Aubrey, Christine Lizbeth. BA, Northwestern U., Evanston, Ill., 1969; JD, U. Iowa, 1972. Elected del. Rep. Nat. Conv., 1980, 92, 96, alt. del., 1984; trustee Lake Villa (Ill.) Township, 1981-83; rep. Ill. Ho. Reps., 1983-99; minority whip Ill. Gen. Assembly, 1987-89, asst. minority leader, 1989-91, dep. minority leader, 1991-94, 97-99; majority leader, 1995-97; chmn. Rep. Ctrl. Com. for Lake County, Ill., 1990-94; co-chmn. Ill. Econ. and Fiscal Commn., Springfield, 1991-95, Space Needs Commn., 1997-99. Mem. ABA, Lake County, Ill. Bar Assn., Ducks Unlimited, Lake Villa Lions, Exchange Club, Moose. Republican.

CHURCHILL, STEVEN WAYNE, former state legislator, marketing professional; b. Akron, Ohio, May 8, 1963; s. Wayne Stevenson and Susan (Gurney) C. BA, Iowa State U., 1985. Fin. asst. The Governor Branstad Com., Des Moines, 1986, fin. dir., 1988-90; mktg. mgr. Iowa Dept. Econ. Devel., Des Moines, 1987; devel. officer Simpson Coll., Indianola, Iowa, 1990-93; fundraising cons. The Churchill Group, Johnston, Iowa, 1993-97; mktg. mgr. Mid-Am. Group, West Des Moines, Iowa, 1997—. Elected State Rep., Johnston, Iowa, 1993-99; commr. Iowa Civil Rights Commn., Des Moines, 1991-92; deacon Plymouth Congl. Ch., 1988-91, 96—; admissions amb. Iowa State U., 1990-92; mem. Greater Des Moines Leadership Inst., 1998-99. Recipient Comdr.'s Award for Pub. Svc., Dept. of the Army, 1991; named one of 10 Outstanding Young Iowans, Iowa Jaycees, 1995. Mem. Bull Moose Club (pres. 1990-91), Rotary of Des Moines (pres. 1991-92), Sigma Alpha Epsilon (pres. 1989-90, Order of the Lion 1990, 96, 99). Avocations: politics, tennis, reading, travel. Home: 6140 Nottingham Johnston IA 50131-8713 Office: Mid-Am Group 4700 Westown Pkwy Ste 303 West Des Moines IA 50266-6718

CHURCHILL, STUART WINSTON, chemical engineering educator; b. Imlay City, Mich., June 13, 1920; s. Howard Heenan and Faye Erma (Shurte) C.; m. Donna Belle Lewis, Feb. 22, 1946 (div.); children: Stuart Lewis, Diana Gail, Cathy Marie, Emily Elizabeth; m. Renate Ursula Treibmann, Aug. 3, 1974. BS in Math, U. Mich., 1942, BSChemE, 1942, MS, 1948, PhD, 1952; MA (hon.), U. Pa., 1972. Technologist Shell Oil Co., 1942-46; tech. supr. Frontier Chem. Co., 1946-47; mem. faculty U. Mich., 1949-67, prof. chem. engring., 1957-67, chmn. dept. chem. and metall. engring., 1962-67; mem. faculty U. Pa., 1967—, Carl V.S. Patterson prof. chem. engring., 1967-90, Carl V.S. Patterson prof. emeritus, 1990—; chmn. region 2 edn. and accreditation com. Engrs. Council Profl. Devel., 1961-65, mem. nat. council, 1965-71, exec. com., 1968-71; mem. bd. trustees Chemical Heritage Found., 1983-99; mem. fin. com., 1987—; cons. heat transfer and combustion. Recipient S. Reid Warren, Jr. award for disting. teaching U. Pa., 1976, Max Jakob Meml. award for heat transfer ASME/Am. Inst. Chem. Engrs., 1979, medal for disting. achievement U. Pa., 1993; Japan Soc. for Promotion of Sci. grantee, 1977. Fellow AIChe (nat. coun. 1962-64, pres. 1966, Profl. Progress award 1964, William H. Walker award 1969, Warren K. Lewis award 1978, Founders award 1980, eminent chmn. engr. Diamond Jubilee 1983, heat transfer and energy conversion divsn. award 1997, inst. lectr. 1998); mem. Nat. Acad. Engring., Combustion Inst., Am. Chem. Soc., Am. Soc. for Engring. Edn. (Corcoran award for best paper 1993), Verein Deutscher Ingenieure (corr. mem.), Sigma Xi, Phi Kappa Phi, Phi Lambda Upsilon (award U. Mich. chpt. 1961), Tau Beta Pi. Unitarian. Home: 137 Pole Cat Rd Glen Mills PA 19342-1301

CHURCHILL, WINSTON JOHN, lawyer, investment firm executive; b. Phila., Aug. 12, 1940; s. Winston and Virginia (Kelly) C.; m. Barbara D. Gerner, June 1, 1983; 1 child, John Justin. BS, Fordham U., 1962; MA, Oxford U., 1964; JD, Yale U., 1967. Bar: Pa. 1967, N.Y. 1983. Investigator Civil Rights div. Dept. Justice, 1962-63; assoc. Saul, Ewing, Remick & Saul, Phila., 1967-72, ptnr., 1972-83, mem. exec. com., 1975-83; ptnr. Bradford Assocs., Princeton, N.J., 1984-88; pres. Churchill Investment Ptnrs., Inc., 1989—; chmn. Churchill Investment Ptnrs., Malvern, 1990-96; mng. gen. ptnr. SCP Pvt. Equity Ptnrs. L.P., Malvern, 1996—; adj. prof. law Temple U., Phila., 1978-82; bd. dirs. Freedom Securities, Inc., Amkor Tech., Inc., Griffin Land Nurseries Inc. Author (novel): Running in Place, 1973; contbr. articles to profl. publs. Adminstrv. judge Southeastern Pa. Transit Authority, 1981-82; chmn. Gesu Sch., 1990—; co-chmn. Phila. chpt. NCCJ, 1981-83; trustee Am. Friends of New Coll., Oxford U., 1975—, Briarcliff Coll., 1976-78, Georgetown U., 1987—, Fordham U., 1993—, Pa. Pub. Sch. Employees' Retirement Sys., 1989-93. Rhodes scholar Oxford U., Eng., 1962-64. Mem. ABA, N.Y. State Bar Assn., Pa. Bar Assn., Links Club, Stonewall Links Golf Club. Home: 197 Mine Rd Malvern PA 19355-9656 Office: 435 Devon Park Dr Ste 300 Wayne PA 19087-1937

CHURCHWELL, EDWARD BRUCE, astronomer, educator; b. Sylva, N.C., July 9, 1940; s. Doris L. Churchwell; m. Dorothy S. Churchwell, June 24, 1964; children: Steven T., Beth M. BS, Earlham Coll., 1963; PhD, Ind. U., 1970. NASA fellow Ind. U., Bloomington, 1963; postdoctoral fellow Nat. Radio Astronomy Obs., Charlottesville, Va., 1970; Heinrich Hertz postdoctoral fellow Max Planck Inst. Radioastronomie, Bonn, Fed. Republic Germany, 1970-72, staff scientist, 1972-77; asst. prof. U. Wis., Madison, 1977-79, assoc. prof., 1979-83, prof. of astronomy, 1983—. Fellow NASA, 1985, Fulbright rsch. fellow, 1988-89. Mem. Am. Astron. Soc., Internat. Astron. Union, Union Concerned Scientists. Office: U Wis Washburn Observatory 475 N Charter St Madison WI 53706-1507

CHURG, JACOB, pathologist; b. Dolhinow, Poland, July 16, 1910; came to U.S., 1936, naturalized, 1943; s. Wolf and Gita (Ravich) C.; m. Vivian Gelb, Oct. 18, 1942; children: Andrew Marc, Warren Bernard. MD, U. Wilno, Poland, 1933, MD in Pathology, 1936. Diplomate Am. Bd. Pathology. Intern City Hosp., Wilno and State Hosp., Wilejka, Poland, 1933-34; asst. in gen. and exptl. pathology U. Wilno, 1934-36; asst. in bacteriology Mt. Sinai Hosp., N.Y.C., 1938; fellow in pathology Mt. Sinai Hosp., 1941-43, rsch. asst., 1946-61, attending physician, 1962-81, cons., 1982—; resident in pathology Beth Israel Hosp., Newark, 1939-40; pathologist Barnert Meml. Hosp., Paterson, N.J., 1946-96; prof. pathology and community med. Mt. Sinai Sch. Med., N.Y.C., 1966-81, prof. emeritus, 1982—; cons. pathologist VA Hosp., Bronx, N.Y., Nassau County Med. Ctr., East Meadow, N.Y., St. Barnabas Med. Ctr., Livingston, N.J., Valley Hosp., Ridgewood, N.J., St. Joseph's Hosp., Paterson, Englewood Hosp.; chmn. mesothelioma reference panel Internat. Union Against Cancer, 1965-81, mem., 1982-96; chmn. com. for histologic classification renal diseases WHO, 1975-98; Lady Davis vis. prof. pathology, Jerusalem, 1975; past mem. sci. adv. group NIH, Bethesda, Md.; clin. prof. pathology U. Medicine and Dentistry N.J. Author: Histological Classification of Renal Diseases, 1979, Renal Disease—Present Status, 1979, Glomerular Diseases, 1985, 2d edit., 1995, Tubulo-Interstitial Diseases, 1985, 2nd edit., 1999, Tumors of Serosal Surfaces, 1985, Vascular Diseases of the Kidney, 1987, 2nd edit., 1999, Developmental and Hereditary Diseases of the Kidney, 1987, Infections and Tropical Diseases of the Kidney, 1988, Systemic Vasculitides, 1991, Urinary Tract Pathology, 1992, The Kidney in Collagen-Vascular Diseases, 1993, Renal Disease: Classification and Atlas of Tubulo-Interstitial and Vascular Diseases, 1999; mem. editl. bd. Nephron., Contbns. to Nephrology, Histopathology, Lab Investigation, Modern Pathology; contbr. numerous articles to sci. jours.; discovered Churg-Strauss Syndrome, 1951. Served to capt., M.C. AUS, 1943-46. Mem. Am. Assn. Pathologists, Am. Soc. Nephrology (John P. Peters award 1987), N.Y. Acad. Medicine, Internat. Acad. Pathology, Harvey Soc., Internat. Soc. Nephrology, Alpha Omega Alpha. Achievements include research in vascular diseases, renal structure and pneumokonioses. Address: 100 Coast Blvd Apt 304 La Jolla CA 92037-4604

CHURGIN, AMY, publishing executive. Pub. K III Mag. Corp. (now Primedia Corp.--N.Y. Mag.), N.Y.C., 1993—. Office: K III Mag Corp 717 5th Ave New York NY 10022-8101 Office: New York Mag 444 Madison Ave Fl 14 New York NY 10022-6999*

CHURGIN, MICHAEL JAY, law educator; b. N.Y.C., Feb. 25, 1948; s. Raphael B. and Sylvia (Nussbaum) C. AB magna cum laude, Brown U., Providence, 1970; JD, Yale U., 1973. Bar: Conn. 1974, Tex. 1975. Supervising atty., teaching fellow Yale Law Sch., New Haven, 1973-75; asst. prof. U. Tex. Sch. Law, Austin, 1975-79, assoc. prof., 1979-81, prof., 1981-90, Raybourne Thompson prof., 1990—; bd. dirs. Legal Aid Soc. Cen. Tex., Austin; mem. adv. bd. Advocacy, Inc., Austin, 1985-90; vis. fellow Clare Hall, Cambridge, Eng., 1996; vis. fellow Wolfson Coll., Cambridge, Eng., 1992. Co-author: Toward a Just and Effective Sentencing System, 1977; author: (monograph) Analysis of the Texas Mental Health Code, 1988, 2d edit., 1994; contbr. articles to profl. jours. Mem. pub. responsibility com. Austin Travis County MHMR, 1979-85. Fellow W.K. Kellogg Nat. Found., 1980-83. Mem. Am. Soc. for Legal History (chair com. 1987—), Phi Beta Kappa. Jewish. Home: 3203 Oakmont Blvd Austin TX 78703-1345 Office: U Tex Sch Law 727 E Dean Keeton Austin TX 78705-3224

CHUSED, RICHARD HARRIS, law educator; b. St. Louis, Jan. 31, 1943; s. Joseph and Marie Irene (Steinberg) C.; m. Elizabeth Langer, May 11, 1974; children: Benjamin Langer, Samuel Jacob. BA, Brown U., 1965; JD, U. Chgo., 1968. Asst. prof. Sch. of Law, Rutgers U., Newark, 1968-71, assoc. prof., 1971-73; assoc. prof. Georgetown U. Law Ctr., Washington, 1973-85, prof., 1985—. Author: Modern Approach to Property, 1978, Cases, Materials and Problems in Property, 1988, 2d edit., 1999, A Property Anthology, 1993, 2nd edit., 1997, Private Acts in Public Places: A Social History of Divorce in the Formative Era of American Family Law, 1994, A Copyright Anthology: The Technology Frontier, 1998; topic and comments editor U. Chgo. Law Rev., 1967-68; contbr. numerous articles to profl. jours. Brown U. Nat. Honor scholar, 1965-68, Bowman C. Lingle fellow, 1966-67. Mem. Soc. Am. Law Tchrs. (bd. govs. 1983-94), Am. Soc. Legal History, Am. Hist. Assn. Democrat. Jewish. Home: 3712 Ingomar St NW Washington DC 20015-1820 Office: Georgetown U Law Ctr 600 New Jersey Ave NW Washington DC 20001-2022

CHUTE, HAROLD LEROY, veterinary pathologist, former chemical company executive; b. Winnipeg, Man., Can., Sept. 4, 1921; came to U.S., 1949; naturalized, 1955; s. Kenneth Karl and Hilda Mae (Stoddart) C.; m. Marion B. Baker, Aug. 9, 1947; children: Pamela D., Hazel Lee., Cameron C. Student, N.S. Agrl. Coll., 1942-44, hon. assoc., 1976; DVM, Ont. Vet. Coll., U. Guelph, 1949; MS, Ohio State U., 1953; DVSc, U. Toronto, 1955; LLD (hon.), Dalhousie U., 1998. Poultry pathologist U. Maine, Orono, 1950-80, prof., 1949-76; treas., dir. MeBio Labs Inc., 1958-66; dir. pullorum typhoid testing U. Maine, Orono, 1958-68, dir. devel., 1967-76; pres. Chute Chem. Co., Bangor, Maine, 1977-95; bd. dirs. Blue Cross Blue Shield, Maine, 1988-99, dir. Key Bank of Eastern Maine. Contbr. over 200 articles to profl. jours. Mem. cmty. rels. Coun. of Job Corps; mem. EMTEC, 1990—; dir. Machigonne Agy.,; pres., CEO Margaret Villa Inc.; bd. dirs. U. Maine Found.; trustee Grand Lodge Charity Fund, 1969—; mem. Orono Town Coun., 1963-72; pres. Pine Tree 4-H Found., 1986-93; mem., trustee, deacon Ch. Univ. Fellowship, U. Maine. Mem. Am. Assn. Avian Pathologists (past pres.), Am. Assn. Vet. Lab. Diagnosticians (past pres., Pope award 1990), AVMA (del.), Maine Vet. Med. Assn. (past pres.), Shriners (potentate Anah Shrine Temple, Bangor 1981), Order of DeMolay (exec. officer Maine 1971-80, grand master grand lodge of Maine 1968-70), Mason (33 degree). Republican. Home: 432 Main St Orono ME 04473-1325

CHUTE, ROBERT MAURICE, retired biologist, educator, poet; b. Bridgton, Maine, Feb. 13, 1926; s. James Cleveland and Elizabeth Ellen (Davis) C.; m. Virginia Hinds, June 24, 1946; children: David Christopher, Dian Leslie. B.A. in Zoology, U. Maine, Orono, 1950; Sc.D., Johns Hopkins U., 1953. Asst. prof. biology Middlebury (Vt.) Coll., 1953-59, San Fernando Valley State Coll., Northridge, Calif., 1959-61; asso. prof. Lincoln (Pa.) U., 1961-62; prof. biology Bates Coll., Lewiston, Maine, 1962-92; Dana prof. Bates Coll., 1975-92, chmn. dept., 1962-83, chmn. div. natural scis., 1983-85, prof. emeritus, 1992—. Author: Environmental Insight, 1971, Introduction to Biology, 1975; (poetry) Quiet Thunder, 1975, Uncle George Poems, 1977, Voices Great and Small, 1977, Thirteen Moons, 1978, French-English bilingual edit., 1981, Sanku Kisultsok (Passamaguoddy translation), 1991, Samuel Sewall Sails for Home, 1986, When Grandmother Decides to Die, 1989, Woodshed on Moon: Thoreau Poems, 1991, Barely Time to Study Jesus, 1996, Androscoggin Too, 1997; also more than 600 poems in jours.; founder, editor lit. mag. The Small Pond, 1963; contbr. articles to profl. jours. Served with USAAF, 1944-46. NIH grantee. Fellow AAAS; mem. Maine Biologists Assn. (hon. life), Phi Beta Kappa, Sigma Xi, Phi Kappa Phi. Office: Bates Coll Dept Biology Lewiston ME 04240

CHUTKOW, JERRY GRANT, neurologist, educator; b. Denver, June 14, 1933; s. Samuel and Yvette (Robinson) C.; m. Melicent Kratz Rupp, June 14, 1957 (dec.); children: Dawn Michelle, Cyanne Tamar, Mark Daniel Rupp, William Alexander; m. Edith A. Murray, Nov. 24, 1992. A.B., U. Chgo., 1952, B.S., 1954, M.D., 1958. Diplomate Am. Bd. Internal Medicine, Am. Bd. Psychiatry and Neurology. Intern Columbia-Presbyn. Hosp., N.Y.C., 1958-59; resident in internal medicine U. Chgo., 1959-62, resident in neurology, 1964-67, instr. internal medicine, 1962-64, asst. prof., 1967-69; research asst. Argonne Cancer research Hosp., 1961-63; cons. neurology Mayo Clinic, 1969-77; asst. prof. Mayo Med. Sch., 1970-74, asso. prof., 1974-77; prof. dept. neurology SUNY-Buffalo, 1977—, chmn. dept., 1977-83, dep. chmn. dept. neurology, 1987-88, dir. Neuromuscular Clinics and Labs., 1984-92; dir. dept. neurology Erie County Med. Center, N.Y., 1979-82, 90-92; chief neurology service VA Med. Center, Buffalo, 1979-84; cons. in field. Contbr. chpts. to books and articles in field. Served with U.S. Army, 1967-69. Nat. Insts. Neurologic Disease spl. fellow, 1965-67; Schweppe found. fellow, 1967-69. Mem. Am. Neurologic Assn., Am. Acad. Neurology, A.C.P., Assn. Univ. Profs. Neurology, Am. Coll. nutrition, Am. Psychiat. Assn., Soc. Neurosci., Central Soc. Neurologic Research, Phi Beta Kappa, Sigma Xi, Alpha Omega Alpha. Office: SUNY at Buffalo Sch Medicine 462 Grider St Buffalo NY 14215-3021

CHVALA, KATHLEEN ANN, administrative assistant; b. Vandergrift, Pa., June 17, 1947; d. George Anthony and Madeline Adeline (Biagioni) Troilo; m. Paul Ronald Chvala Jr., Nov. 4, 1967; children: Keith Michael, Jacqueline Christine. Student, U. Pitts., 1965-66, Pa. State U., 1977. Engring. asst.

NUMEC, Leechburg, Pa., 1966-68; tchr. substitute St. Gertrude Sch., Vandergrift, 1969-70; adminstrv. asst. Oberg Industries, Freeport, Pa., 1974—; bd. dirs. Allegheny Valley Fed. Credit Union, Pitts. Mem. Vandergrift Coun., 1990—, chmn. police and pub. safety, 1990—, chmn. negotiations boro contracts, 1990—; chmn. Vandergrift Cmty. Pool, 1990—. Democrat. Roman Catholic. Avocations: golf, nautilus and aerobics, car cruises and shows. Home: 222 Emerson St Vandergrift PA 15690-1516 Office: Oberg Industries Ind Tool and Die Divsn 604 Oberg Dr Freeport PA 16229

CHWAST, SEYMOUR, graphic artist; b. N.Y.C., Aug. 18, 1931. Student, Cooper Union Sch., N.Y.C.; PhD (hon.), Parsons Sch. Design, 1992. Co-founder Push Pin Studios, 1954; dir., pres. The Pushpin Group Inc.; instr. Parsons Sch. of Design. One-man exhbns. include Royal Palm Gallery, Palm Beach, Fla., 1982, Galerie Delpire, Paris, 1974, Gutenburg Mus., Mainz, Germany, 1984, 35 yr. retrospective exhibition Cooper Union, 1986, Jack Gallery, N.Y., 1987, Mus. of Art, Sao Paulo, Brazil, 1989, Lustrare Gallery, N.Y., 1991, Ginza Graphic Gallery, Tokyo, 1992, Kunstschalter Gallery, N.Y.C., 1994; various group shows; work in permanent collections Mus. Modern Art, N.Y.C., Library of Congress, Washington, Met. Mus. Art, N.Y.C., Whitney Mus. Am. Art, N.Y. Recipient numerous awards including Saint-Gaudens medal, 1972; named to Art Dir.'s Hall of Fame, 1984. Mem. Am. Inst. Graphic Artists (former v.p., medal 1986), Art Dirs.' Club (v.p.), Alliance Graphique Internationale. Office: Pushpin Group 18 E 16th St New York NY 10003-3111

CHWATSKY, ANN, photographer, educator; b. Phila., Jan. 11, 1942; BS in Art Edn., Hofstra U., 1965, MS, 1971; postgrad. L.I. U., 1973-74. Cert. tchr. Photography editor L.I. mag., 1976-80; instr. Internat. Ctr. Photography, N.Y.C., 1979-80, Parrish Art Mus., Southampton, N.Y., 1984—; former dir. master art workshop Southampton Coll., 1985-96; mem. art faculty NYU, 1991—. Author, photgrapher The Man In The Street, 1989; photographer The Four Seasons of Shaker Life; photographs featured in Time, Newsweek, Newsday, Manchete, N.Y. Times, MD Medical Times; one person shows include Photographers Gallery, London, 1985, Shakers, Nassau County Mus. Fine Arts, 1987, Greater Lafayette (Ind.) Mus. Art, 1988, Brooklyn Coll., 1990, Kiev, USSR Exhibition Hall, 1991, Brooklyn Coll., Lincoln Ctr., Buenos Aires, 1993; group shows include The Other, Houston Ctr. Photography, 1988, L.I. Fine Arts Mus., 1984, Women's Interart Ctr., N.Y.C., 1976, 80, Parrish Art Mus., Southampton, 1979, Internat. Ctr. Photography, N.Y.C., 1980, 82, Nassau County Mus. Fine Arts, 1983, Soho 20 Gallery, N.Y.C., 1984, New Orleans World's Fair, 1984, Southampton Gallery, 1988, 89, Lizan Tops Gallery, L.I., 1994, Apex Art, N.Y.C., 1995, Am. Mus., Prague, 1997, First Seoul Internatl. Tribunal, 1998; represented in permanent collections: Forbes N.Y.C. Midtown YWCA, Nassau County Mus. Fine Arts, Susan Rothenberg, others. Recipient Estabrook Disting. Alumni award Hofstra U., 1984; Kodak Profl. Photographers award, 1984; Eastman Found. grantee, 1981-82; Polaroid grantee, 1980. Mem. Assn. Am. Mag. Profls., Picture Profls. Am., Profl. Women Photographers N.Y.C. Democrat. Jewish. Avocations: tennis, gardening. Home & Studio: 29 E 22nd St Apt 3N New York NY 10010-5305

CHYNOWETH, ALAN GERALD, retired telecommunications research executive, consultant; b. Harrow, Eng., Nov. 18, 1927; came to U.S. 1952; s. James Charles and Marjorie (Fairhurst) C.; m. Betty Freda Edith Boyce, Sept. 22, 1950; children: Trevor Alan, Kevin Ray. BS in physics, U. London Kings Coll., 1948, PhD, 1950. Demonstrator U. London Kings Coll., 1948-50; post doctoral fellow Nat. Research Council, Ottawa, Can., 1950-52; mem. tech. staff Bell Labs., Murray Hill, N.J., 1953-60, dept. head, 1960-65, dir., 1965-76, exec. dir., 1976-83; v.p. applied rsch. Bellcore, Morristown, N.J., 1984-92; cons. R/D Strategy and Mgmt., 1993—; cons. advanced study inst. and rsch. workshops com. NATO, Brussels, 1982-90; lectr. Electrochem. Soc., 1983; alt. dir. Microelectronics and Computer Tech. Corp., Austin, Tex., 1984-92; mem. The Conf. Bd. Internat. Coun. on Mgmt. of Innovation and Tech., 1990-97, mgr., 1995; dir. Optoelectronic Industry Devel. Assn., 1991-92; mem. adv. bd. dept. elec. engring. and computer sci. U. Calif., Berkeley, 1987-93; mem. natural sci. adv. bd. U. Pa., 1988-93; mem. adv. bd. dept. elec. engring. U. So. Calif., 1988-93; mem. Indsl. Rsch. Inst., 1980-92, dir., 1990-92, emeritus, 1993—; mem. indsl. and profl. adv. coun. elec. engring. dept. Pa. State U., 1993—, chmn., 1995; mem. adv. task force on U.S. indsl. competitiveness U.S. Ho. of Reps., 1987; cons. European Commn. Telecom. Directorate, 1995; advisor to panel on high performance computing and comm. Office Sci. and Tech. Policy, The White House, 1991-92. Assoc. editor Solid State Communications, 1975-83; co-editor: Optical Fiber Telecommunications, 1979; contbr. articles to profl. jours.; patentee in field. Mem. vis. com. Cornell U. Materials Sci. Ctr., 1973-76, Am. Mgmt. Assn. R & D Coun., 1989-93; chmn. tech. transfer merit program N.J. Commn. on Sci. and Tech., 1992-98. Fellow IEEE (chmn. device rsch. conf. 1963, mem. com. on U.S. competitiveness 1988-89, bd. adv. task force on new initiatives 1989-90, chmn. Marconi award com. 1987, mem. Alexander Graham Bell prize com. 1990-94, chmn. 1992-94, mem. Frederik Philips award com. 1998—, W.R.G. Baker prize, 1967, Frederik Philips award 1992, engring. leadership recognition 1996, mem. corp. achievement award com. 1999—), Am. Phys. Soc. (indsl. affiliates com. 1984-87, editl. bd. Physics Today 1985-88, George E. Pake prize 1992), Inst. Physics and Phys. Soc. (London); mem. AAAS, NRC (survey dir. com. on survey of materials sci. and engring. 1970-74, panel chmn. com. on mineral resources and environ. 1973-75, panel chmn. materials sci. engring. study com. 1986-88, nat. materials adv. bd. 1976-80), Metall. Soc. of AIME (chmn. John Bardeen prize com. 1993-95), Materials Rsch. Soc., N.Y. Acad. Scis. Avocations: travel, boating. Home: 6 Londonderry Way Summit NJ 07901-2914 Office: Telecordia Techs Box 7040 331 Newman Springs Rd Red Bank NJ 07701-5699 also: 17 Mill Close Fishbourne, Chichester West Sussex PO19 3JW, England

CHYTIL, FRANK, biochemist; b. Prague, Czechoslovakia, Aug. 28, 1924; came to U.S., 1965, naturalized, 1971; s. Frantisek and Ruzena (Vitouskova) C.; m. Lucie Scheinost, Nov. 26, 1949; children: Frank, Anna, Helena. M.S., Sch. Chem. Tech., Prague, 1949, Ph.D., 1952; C.Sc., Czechoslovak Acad. Sci., Prague, 1956. Rsch. biochemist Charles U., Prague, 1949-51; rsch. fellow Inst. Human Rsch., Prague, 1952-63; sr. scientist Czechoslovak Acad. Sci., Prague, 1956-64; sr. rsch. fellow Brandeis U., Waltham, Mass., 1964; sr. rsch. assoc. Brandeis U., 1965-66; head sect. enzymology S.W. Found. Rsch. and Edn., San Antonio, 1966-69; mem. faculty Vanderbilt U., 1969—, prof. biochemistry, 1975—, Gen. Foods Disting. prof. nutrition, 1984-89, Harvie Branscomb disting. prof., 1993-94; adj. assoc. prof. U. Tex., San Antonio, 1968-69. Editor: Vitamins and Hormones, 1983; mem. editl. bd. Analytical Biochemistry, 1980-87, Jour. Biol. Chemistry, 1982-88, 96—, Am. Jour. Clin. Nutrition, 1993-95; contbr. articles to profl. jours. Recipient Osborne-Mendel and Lederle awards; USPHS grantee, 1967-99. Fellow Am. Soc. Nutritional Scis.; mem. Am. Soc. Biochemistry and Molecular Biology, Endocrine Soc., Sigma Xi. Home: 914 Lynnwood Blvd Nashville TN 37205-4527 Office: Vanderbilt U Sch Medicine Dept Biochemistry Nashville TN 37232

CHYUNG, CHI HAN, management consultant; b. Seoul, Korea, Jan. 27, 1933; s. Do Soon and Boksoon (Kim) C.; came to U.S., 1954, naturalized, 1963, BS, Kans. Wesleyan U., 1958; M.BA, Mich. State U., 1960; postgrad. Mass. Inst. Tech.; m. Alice Yvonne Whorley, Dec. 23, 1961; children: Eric, Diana. Ops. analyst Chevrolet div. Gen. Motors Corp., Detroit and Flint, Mich., 1959-61; economist Internat. Harvester Co., Chgo., 1961-63; sr. analyst market div. Internat. Minerals & Chem. Corp., Skokie, Ill., 1963-66; mgr. market info. and planning Gulf & Western Industries, N.Y.C., 1966-68; dir. market planning and devel. Am. Standard, Inc., N.Y.C., 1968-71; pres. Oxytech Corp., Medcraft Industries, Inc.; mgmt. cons., internat. market devel., Darien, Conn., 1971—; dir. Korea Hapsum Co.; cons. Govt. of Korea, Taisei Constrn. Co., Tokyo. Served with Korean Army, 1951-53. Mem. Inst. Mgmt. Scis., Am. Mktg. Assn., Ops. Research Soc., Am. Chem., N.Am. Corp. Planning Soc., Beta Gamma Sigma. Contbr. papers to profl. lit. Office: Oxytech Corp 433 Post Rd Darien CT 06820-3606

CIA, MANUEL LOPEZ, artist; b. Las Cruces, N.Mex., Jan. 4, 1937; s. Anastacio Cea Lopez and Mercedes Rivera. Student, Am. Acad. Art, Chgo., 1958-61, Art Inst. San Francisco, 1962, L.A. Trade Tech., 1963-64, U. N.Mex., 1990. Author: Color Quest, 1991, Theory of Sophisticism, 1993; Exhibited in group shows at The Fundacion Teleton de Honduras, Tegucigalpa, 1989, France-USA, Paris, 1991, Arts and the Quincentennial, Albuquerque, 1992, U.S. Artists, Phila., 1993, State of the Art, Boston, 1993, Miniatures 1993, Albuquerque, 1993, Montserrat Gallery, N.Y.C., 1995; one man shows include El Prado Galleries, Sedonia, Ariz. and Santa Fe, N.Mex., 1989, 90, 95. With USAF, 1954-57. Recipient Outstanding Individual award Youth Devel., Albuquerque, 1991. Mem. Internat. Assn. Contemporary Art, Soc. Am. Impressionists. Avocations: study and writing of aesthetics. Home: PO Box 7332 Albuquerque NM 87194-7332

CIALLELLA, EMIL ANTHONY, library director, consultant; b. Fall River, Iowa, July 1, 1943; s. Emil Anthony Ciallella and Italia Carmela DiBiase; m. Carol Ann Cunniff, Nov. 24, 1974. BA, Providence Coll., 1965; MA, Assumption Coll., 1967; MLS, U. R.I., 1971. Cert. tchr., Ariz., county libr. Libr. dir. Ctrl. Falls (R.I.) Free Pub. Libr., 1974-84, Richard Salter Storrs Libr., Longmeadow, Mass., 1984-86, Gila County Libr. Dist., Miami, Ariz., 1989-93, Ector County Libr., Odessa, Tex., 1996—; pres., libr. cons. Cal-Em Assocs., Globe, Ariz., Odessa, 1976—; bd. dirs. Ptnrs. in Learning. With U.S. Army, 1967-69. Mem. ALA (mem. numerous ALA assns. and programs), Tex. Libr. Assn., Am. Legion. E-mail: ect@apex2000.net. Home: PO Box 2853 Odessa TX 79760-2853 Office: Ector County Libr 321 West Fifth St Odessa TX 79761-5066

CIAMPAGLIO, JEFF WILLIAM, sculptor; b. N.Y.C., July 6, 1968; s. Joseph Anthony and Pauline Elizabeth (Bartels) C. Diploma, Calvert Hall Coll., 1987; BA in Art and Comms., Towson State U., 1992; postgrad., U. Md. Balt. County, 1998—. Tchr. Great Bay Sch., Dover, N.H., 1992-93; counselor Jewish Family Svcs., Park Heights, Md., 1993-95; foreman Finishing Touch Painting, Balt., 1995-97; tutor Towson State U., 1996—; tchr. painting, Balt., 1996—. Artist: (sculptures) Circle of Life, 1992 (grant 1992), untitled piece for Towson U. campus, 1992 (scholarship 1992), other untitled works, 92, 96, (painting) Light House, 1993, others. Grantee Towson State U., 1992; recipient Jack F. Tolbert scholarship Towson U., 1992, Wood Guild award Wood Guild Soc. of Md., 1992. Democrat. Roman Catholic. Avocations: Tai Chi, Kung Fu, drawing, exercising. Home: 30A Owens Landing Ct Perryville MD 21903

CIANCHETTE, ALTON E., construction company executive; b. 1930; married. Chmn., CEO Cianbro Corp., Pittsfield, Maine. Office: Cianbro Corp Hunnewell Sq Pittsfield ME 04967*

CIANCIO, SEBASTIAN GENE, periodontist, educator; b. Jamestown, N.Y., June 21, 1937; m. Marilyn Bonfiglio; children: Michele Ann, Sebastian. DDS, SUNY, Buffalo, 1961. Diplomate Am. Bd. Periodontology; cert. periodontist, 1965. Postdoctoral fellow depts. pharmacology and periodontology SUNY, Buffalo, 1963-65, instr., 1964-65, asst. clin. prof. pharmacology, asst. prof. periodontology, 1966, acting co-chmn. dept. periodontology, 1967-68, acting chmn., 1968, chmn. dept. periodontology, 1969-72, prof., chmn. dept. periodontics-endodontics, 1972-80, chmn. dept. periodontics, 1980—, clin. prof. dept. pharmacology, 1973—, dir. Ctr. for Dental Studies, 1988—; mem. vis. faculty Sch. Dentistry, U. Zurich, Switzerland, 1976; dental chmn. com. on revision U.S. Pharmacopeia, 1981—. Author: Clinical Pharmacology for Dental Professionals, 1980, 3rd edit., 1989; editor Biological Therapies in Dentistry, ADA Guide to Dental Therapeutics, 1998, Periodontal Insights; contbr. numerous articles to profl. jours., chpts. to books. Bd. dirs. Internat. Health Care Found., 1993—. Capt. U.S. Army Dental Corps, 1961-63. Recipient George B. Snow prize in Prosthetic dentistry, 1961, hon. citation U. Chile, 1980, Gies. Found. award in Periodontics, 1988, Sch. of Dental Medicine Dean's award, 1992; named Alpha Omega Dental Educator of Yr., 1971, Buffalo Dental Man of Yr., 1987. Fellow Internat. Coll. Dentist, Am. Acad. Periodontology (exec. com. 1981—, spl. citation 1983, v.p. 1989-90, pres. 1991-92, v.p. found. bd. 1996-98, Clin. Rsch. award 1996); mem. ADA (chmn., cons. coun. on dental therapeutics, 1976-78, cons. coun. on dental edn. 1982—, coun. on scientific affairs 1995—), Internat. Assn. Dental Rsch., Nat. Soc. Dental Rsch. (bd. dirs. 1981-84), Royal Soc. Health (London), Dental Soc. State N.Y. (Jarvie-Burkhardt award 1997), 8th Dist. Dental Soc., Erie County Dental Soc., Fedn. Dentaire Internationale, Omicron Kappa Upsilon. Office: SUNY at Buffalo Dept of Periodontology Buffalo NY 14214

CIANGIO, SISTER DONNA LENORE, religious organization administrator; b. Newark, Feb. 2, 1949; d. Nicholas Gabriel and Elizabeth Helen (Cwikla) C. BA, Caldwell (N.J.) Coll., 1971, 82; MA, NYU, 1980. Joined Sisters of St. Dominic of Caldwell, N.J., Roman Catholic Ch., 1967. Tchr. Blessed Sacrament Sch., Bridgeport, Conn., 1971-73, St. Ann Sch., Newark, 1973; chairperson art dept. St. Dominic Acad., Jersey City, 1974-78; art instr., gallery dir. Caldwell Coll., 1978-80; art dept. chairperson St. Cecilia High Sch., Englewood, N.J., 1979-81; assoc. dir. internat. office RENEW, Plainfield, N.J., 1981-94, also coord. for internat. tng. and planning; project dir. Nat. Pastoral Life Ctr., N.Y.C., 1994—; cons. in art for secondary schs. Archdiocese of Newark, 1976-79. Recipient awards for paintings and drawings. Office: Nat Pastoral Life Ctr 18 Bleecker St New York NY 10012-2404

CIANI, ALFRED JOSEPH, language professional, associate dean; b. N.Y.C., June 29, 1946; s. Joseph Alfred and Aurora Smiles (VanOver) C.; m. Sharon Skolkey, Aug. 16, 1968 (div. 1979); children: Mieke Jo, Gabriel Wolf; m. Lesley Lockwood, Aug. 9, 1980; children: Joseph Alfred, Clinton Lockwood. BA, U. Albany, 1969; MA, Coll. of St. Rose, 1972; EdD, Ind. U., 1974. Tchr. Greater Amsterdam (N.Y.) Schs., 1969-72; rsch. asst. Ind. U., Bloomington, 1972-73; assoc. instr. Ind. U., 1973-74; asst. prof. U. Cin., 1974-79, assoc. prof., 1979—; vis. prof. U. Wis., Milw., 1980; assoc. dean, info. officer U. Cin., 1988-92; pres. Ohio Internat. Reading Assn., Columbus, 1981-82; outside cons. State of Miss., Jackson, 1982-84, State of Ky., 1996—, State of W.Va., 1972-74, 97-98, City of N.Y. Pub. Schs.; cons., U. Oreg. Profl. Devel., Eugene, 1979-80, Nashville Schs., 1982-83, State of W.Va., N.Y.C. Pub. Schs.; mem. Dean's Cabinet. Author: Motivating Reluctant Readers, 1981; editor: (book series) Reading in Content Areas, 1979-81; rev. editor: Rsch. in Mid. Level Edn., 1995—. Grantee Ford Found., 1990, IBM, 1990. Mem. AAUP, Internat. Reading Assn., Am. Ednl. Rsch. Assn. Assn. Tchr. Educators (nat. com.), Nat. Coun. Tchrs. English (nat. coms.), , Nat. Mid. Sch. Assn. (nat. coms.), Nat. Reading Coun., YMCA, Phi Delta Kappa, Kappa Delta Pi. Democrat. Roman Catholic. Avocations: reading, walking, family oriented activities. Office: U Cin Mail Location 02 Cincinnati OH 45221

CIANNELLA, JOEEN MOORE, legislative staff member, small business owner; b. Warren, Ohio, Mar. 20, 1948; d. Joseph Alvie and Elizabeth Dorthea Moore; m. Christopher M. Ciannella, July 31, 1976 (div. Jan. 1987); children: Bryce C., Tara E. BA in French, Denison U., 1970. Profl. staff U.S. Senate Rep. Policy Com., Washington, 1971-75; owner Jo Moore-Sophisticated Country, Park Ridge, N.J., 1984—; dir. cmty. affairs Congresswoman Marge Roukema U.S. Ho. Reps., Ridgewood, N.J., 1985—. Elected mem. Park Ridge County Com., 1983—, mcpl. chairperson, 1986-96; active Bergen County (N.J.) Rep. County Com., 1983—, Park Ridge Rep. Orgn., 1983—, v.p., 1988-89; active N.E. Rep. Orgn. Dist. 39, State N.J., 1984—, sec., 1990-91, treas., 1991-92, chairperson, 1992-93; active Bush for Pres. Campaign, 1988, 92, Dole for Pres. Campaign, 1996; ofcl. com. mem. N.J. GOP Conv., 1991; charter mem. Women Leadership Summit, Rep. Network to Elect Women, 1996-97; trustee Greater Roles and Opportunities for Women, N.J. GOP, 1997—; mem. Park Ridge Bd. Health, 1984-86; founding mem. Pioneer Women Bergen County, 1992—; mem. exec. bd. Bergen Coun.-Boy Scouts Am., 1991-98, co-chairperson Pascack Valley Dist. Luncheon, 1991-92, chairperson spl. events fin., 1993-94, mem. exec. com., 1993-98, vice chmn. fin., 1995-98; mem. Nat. Coun.-Boy Scouts Am., 1995-98; mem. exec. bd. No. N.J. Coun.-Boy Scouts Am., 1999— (Silver Beaver award), Northern N.J. Coun. Boy Scouts Am., 1999; mem. exec. bd. Ramapo Coll. Found., 1991—, theme chairperson fundraiser, 1991-94, disting. citizen dinner com., 1991—, bus. network com., 1994-97, chmn. pub. rels. and mktg. com., 1996—, mem. exec. com., 1996—. Recipient Silver Beaver award No. N.J. Coun. Boy Scouts Am., 1999. Mem. N.J. Fedn. Rep. Women, Rep. Women of the 90's State N.J., Bergen County Women's Rep. Club, Ridgewood Unit Rep. Women, Jr. League Bergen County (com. mem. Festival of Trees 1988), Park Ridge Rotary Club (com. mem. annual auction 1990-98, chairperson holiday party 1991-98). Republican. Avocations: gardening, antiquing, sports, travel. E-mail: joeen.ciannella@mail.house.gov. Home: 34 Spring Valley Rd Park Ridge NJ 07656 Office: Congresswoman Marge Roukema US Ho of Reps 1200 E Ridgewood Ave Ridgewood NJ 07450

CIAO, FREDERICK J., educational administrator, educator; b. Phila.; married; 3 children. BA, LaSalle U., 1962; MEd, Temple U., 1965; MA, Villanova U., 1972; PhD, Southwest U., 1990. From tchr. to counselor to dept. chmn. N.E. Cath. High Sch., Phila., 1962-73; vice prin. Archibishop Wood High Sch., Warminster, Pa., 1973-85; prin. Bishop McDevitt H.S., Wyncote, Pa., 1985-93, pres., 1993—; mem. adj. faculty St. Agnes Hosp. Nursing Sch., Phila., 1963-71, Spring Garden Coll., Phila., 1971-73, Gwynedd Mercy Coll., Gwynedd Valley, Pa., 1976-84, LaSalle U., 1980—; presentor Nat. Diffusion Network, 1992—. Mem. edn. advisor Phila. Orch., 1993—. Named Man of the Yr., N.E. Cath. Alumni Assn., 1972, Educator of the Yr., Millay Club, 1986; named to Legion of Honor, Chapel of Four Chaplains, 1980; recipient John Neumann medal St. John Neumann High Sch., 1985. Mem. Nat. Assn. Secondary Sch. Prins., Nat. Cath. Edn. Assn., Nat. Coun. Tchrs. of Maths., Maths. Assn. Am., Nat. Assn. Curriculum Devel., Nat. Coun. for Self Esteem, Mid. States Assn. of Colls. (chair). Office: Bishop McDevitt High Sch 125 Royal Ave Wyncote PA 19095-1198

CIBBARELLI, PAMELA RUTH, information executive; b. Odessa, Tex., Mar. 26, 1946; d. Everett M. and Geneva (Hill) Johnson; 1 child, Shawn Edward. A.A., Orange Coast Coll., 1966; B.A., Calif. State U.-Long Beach, 1971; M.S.L.S., Calif. State U.-Fullerton, 1973. Library clk. Golden West Coll., Huntington Beach, Calif., 1967-70; pres., founder Cibbarelli & Assocs., Huntington Beach, 1973-82; dir. research Korn-Ferry Internat., Los Angeles, 1982; Western regional mgr. Battelle Software Products Ctr., Costa Mesa, Calif., 1983-85; v.p. mktg. INLEX, Inc., Monterey, Calif., 1985-86; pres. Cibbarelli's, Huntington Beach, 1986—; ref. coord. City of Commerce (Calif.) Pub. Libr., 1995—; lectr., assoc. prof. UCLA Grad. Sch. Libr. Sci., Calif. State U., San Jose, Fullerton, San Bernardino; mem. organizing com. Integrated Online Libr. Sys. Meeting, 1994, 95, 96, 97, 98, 99, Computers in Libr. Meeting, 1996, 97, 98, 99, Internet Libr., 1997, 98. Editor: Directory of Information Management Software, 1983, 85, 87, 89, 91, Proceedings of the Integrated Online Library Systems Meeting, 1994, 95, 96, 97, 98, 99, Directory of Library Automation Software, Systems, and Services, 1994, 96. 98; compiler: Cibbarelli's Surveys: User Ratings of Library Automation Software and Systems, 1997; contbr. numerous articles to profl. jours. Mem. adv. com. UCLA Grad. Sch. Library Info. Scis., Los Angeles. Mem. Am. Soc. Info. Sci., ALA, Spl. Libraries Assn., Calif. Libr. Assn.

CIBES, WILLIAM JOSEPH, JR., chancellor, educator; b. Newton, Kans., Aug. 25, 1943; s. William Joseph and Dorothy Beulah (Revell) C.; m. Margaret Ann Collins, Sept. 2, 1967; 1 child, Julia Katherine. BA, U. Kans., 1965; PhD, Princeton (N.J.) U., 1975. Instr. to prof. Conn. Coll., New London, 1969-91; sec. Office of Policy and Mgmt., State of Conn., Hartford, 1991-94; chancellor Conn. State U. System, Hartford, 1994—. state rep. Conn. Gen. Assembly, Hartford, 1979-91. Democrat. Roman Catholic. E-mail: cibesw@sysoff.ctstateu.edu. Office: Conn State Univ System 39 Woodland St Hartford CT 06105

CIBOROWSKI, PAUL JOHN, counseling psychology educator; b. N.Y.C., Jan. 15, 1943; s. Paul J. and Mary (Deptuch) C.; m. Doris E. Carlo, June 24, 1973; children: Philip Alan, Kevin Michael. BA, U. Dayton, 1965; MA, NYU, 1969; PhD, Fordham U., 1979. Cert. counselor. Counselor Christ the King H.S., Queens, N.Y., 1967-70; coord. drug edn. Sachem Sch. Dist., Holbrook, N.Y., 1971-73; sr. counselor, grant coord. Sachem Schs., Holbrook, N.Y., 1973-89; mental health counselor, 1980—; assoc. prof. counseling and psychology L.I. U., 1989—, coord. Brentwood campus; pres. Stratmar Ednl. Systems; pvt. practice marriage and family therapy; coord. Dept. Counseling and Devel., Brentwood, N.Y.; cons., trainer Family Life Bur., Diocese of Rockville Centre. Author: The Changing Family I, 1984, 2d edit., 1986, Survival Skills for Single Parents, 1987; contbr. articles to profl. jours. Mem. parish coun. St. Mark's Roman Cath. Ch., also chmn. fin. com.; bd. dirs. Soundview Civic Assn.; fellow Ctr. for Study of the Changing Family, Port Chester, N.Y.; chair Brookhaven; mem. Brookhaven Anti-Bias Coalition; mem. exec. com. Suffolk County Anti-Bias Task Force; chair N.Y. Youth Bd., Western Suffolk Coalition on Child Abuse and Neglect. Grantee in field. Mem. AACD (com. on children, youth and families), N.Y. State Assn. for Counseling and Devel. (legis. chmn. 1989-92, v.p., state curriculum com. 1981-82), Am. Mental Health Counselors Assn. (chmn. spl. interest network on children and adolescents, coord. Child Adv. Network, exec. bd., nat. com. for the rights of children 1992-96), Western Suffolk Counselors Assn. (past treas., past v.p.), Phi Delta Kappa. Home: 38 Mary Pitkin Path PO Box 284 Shoreham NY 11786-0284

CICALA, JAC, soccer coach; married; 3 children. BA in Polit. Sci., George Mason U., 1975, M.Sec. Sch. Adminstrn., 1988. Asst. coach women's soccer George Mason U., Fairfax, Va., 1982-83, 90-91, head coach, 1992—; head coach boys soccer Lake Braddock Sec. Sch., 1982-90; head coach Region I Girls Olympic Devel. Program, 1986—; asst. coach Women's Nat. Under-20 team, 1993; head coach East team U.S. Olympic Festival, 1993, Nat. under-16 girls, 1990-92; asst. coach Olympic Sports Festival, 1989-90. Office: George Mason Univ MS3A5 Sports Info 4400 University Dr Fairfax VA 22030-4444

CICALA, ROGER STEPHEN, physician, educator; b. Parkersburg, W.Va., Aug. 21, 1956; s. Edmond D. and Ann (Pettit) C.; m. Shari Lee Miller, Mar. 17, 1982 (div. Dec. 1989); children: Kristin Pettit, Paul Andrew. BS in Biology, Christian Bros. Coll., Memphis, 1978; MD, U. Tenn., Memphis, 1982. Diploamte Am. Bd. Anesthesiology, Am. Bd. Med. Examiners. Intern dept. surgery U. Tenn., 1982-83, chief resident, 1985, from instr. to asst. prof., 1987-90, assoc. prof. anesthesiology, 1990-94, dir. pain ctr., 1988-94; pvt. practice Memphis, 1986-87; med. author, illustrator, 1994—; anesthesiology staff Memphis Neurosci. Ctr., 1986-87; dir. trauma anesthesia Elvis Presley Trauma Ctr., Memphis, 1988-92, mem. staff, 1987-94; mem. staff Meth. Hosp. Memphis, 1986-94, Eastwood Med. Ctr., Memphis, 1991-94; dir. Meth. Hosps. Comprehensive Pain Treatment Ctr., 1998; presenter in field. Author: (with others) Courtroom Medicine: Pain and Suffering, 1991, Geriatric Anesthesiology, 1992, Textbook of Trauma Anesthesia and Critical Care, 1992, Headache: Diagnosis and Interdisciplinary Treatment, 1992, Refresher Course in Anesthesiology, vol. 20, 1992, Handbook of Trauma Surgery, 1993, Manual of Trauma Anesthesia, 1993, The Heart Disease Handbook, 1996; editor: (with others) Textbook of Trauma Anesthesia and Critical Care, 1992, and others. Mem. AAAS, AMA, Am. Soc. Anesthesiologists, Am. Pain Soc., Internat. Soc. Study of Pain, Internat. Trauma Anesthesia and Critical Care Soc. (co-chmn. task force 1991-93), Internat. Anesthesia Rsch. Soc., Tenn. Med. Assn., Tenn. Soc. Anesthesiologists, Shely County Med. Soc., Shelby County Anesthesia Soc., Soc. Cardiovascular Anesthesiologists, Soc. Pain Practice Mgmt. (bd. dirs. 1991-94), Assn. U. Anesthesists. Avocation: computer programming. Home: 2577 Copperfield Dr Memphis TN 38119-8204

CICARELLI, JAMES S., college dean; b. New Haven, Aug. 24, 1941; s. Pasquale Cicarelli and Jelsumina Passarelli; m. Julianne Marie Bellmore, June 12, 1966; children: Jill, David. BA in Econs., U. Conn., 1963, MA in Econs., 1964, PhD in Econs., 1968. Econs. instr. Lewis & Clark Coll., Portland, Oreg., 1966-70; prof. econs., chair dept. SUNY, Oswego, 1970-83; dean Sch. Bus. St. Bonaventure U., Olean, N.Y., 1983-84; chair dept. bus. SUNY, Fredonia, 1984-88; dean Williamson Coll. Bus. Youngstown (Ohio) U., 1988-94; dean Heller Coll. Bus. Roosevelt U., Chgo./Schaumburg, Ill., 1994—; participant mgmt. devel. program Harvard U., Cambridge, Mass., summer 1997; mem. bus. adv. bd. Malcolm X Coll., Harold Washington Coll., Chgo., 1996—. Co-author: Joan Robinson: A Bio-Bibliography, 1996. Pres. N.Y. State Econs. Assn., 1983-85. Mem. Am. Mgmt. Assn., Fin. Execs. Inst. (bd. dirs. Chgo. chpt. 1997—), Arlington Econ. Alliance (bd. dirs. 1997—), Coun. Ill. Bus. Deans, Execs.' Club of Chgo. Democrat. Avocations: basketball, tennis, writing, walking. E-mail: jcicarel@roosevelt.edu. Home: 1220 E Vargo Ln Arlington Heights IL 60004 Office: Roosevelt U 1400 N Roosevelt Blvd Schaumburg IL 60173

CICCARELLI, DINO, professional hockey player; b. Sarnia, Ont., Canada, Feb. 8, 1960. With Detroit Red Wings, 1992-96; right wing Tampa Bay Lightning, 1996-97, Fla. Panthers, 1997—. Recipient Jim Mahon Meml. Trophy, 1977-78; named to OMJHL All-Star second team, 1977-78; played in NHL All-Star Game, 1982, 83, 89. Achievements include NHL single-season playoff records for most points by rookie (21) and most goals by rookie (14) in 1981. Office: Fla Panthers 100 NE 3rd Ave 2d Fl Fort Lauderdale FL 33301*

CICCARIELLO, PRISCILLA CHLOE, librarian; b. Ann Arbor, Mich., Oct. 27, 1925; d. Oakley Calvin and Mary Charity (Olmsted) Johnson; m. Gerard Ciccariello (dec. May 1974); children: Stephen (dec.), Peter, Thomas, Michael, William, Daniel, John. BA, Queens Coll., 1973; MLS, 1974; cert. in Advanced Librarianship, Columbia U., 1981; cert. in Not for Profit Mgmt., 1986. Clk. typist Port Washington (N.Y.) Pub. Libr., 1968-70; sr. libr. clk., 1970-73, libr. trainee, 1973-75, reference libr., 1975-82, dir. Info. Svcs., 1982-93; chmn. of bd. Nat. Marfan Found., 1993—; vol. exec. dir., 1984-93, chmn. bd., 1993—, Nat. Marfan Found.; com. Reference Adult Membership Com. Am. ALA, Chgo., 1981-85; sec., bd. mem. Nat. Orgn. for Rare Disorders, New Fairfield, Conn., 1987-95; mem. nat. adv. coun. Nat. Inst. Arthritis, Musculoskeletal and Skin Diseases, 1998—. Author (chpt.) Proceedings/Genetic Support Groups, 1987, Proceedings/Genetics Services for Underserved Populations. Pres. Coalition of Heritable Disorders of Connective Tissue, Port Washington, N.Y., 1989—. Recipient 3 month stipendiate for study Internat. Youth Libr., Munich, Germany, 1974, 1990 Congl. Achievement award House Reps., Washington, 1990, Pub. Health Svc. award Orphan Product/U.S. Dept. Health and Human Svcs., Washington, 1991. Mem. LWV. Home: 30 Laurel Ln Sag Harbor NY 11963-3816 Office: National Marfan Found 382 Main St Port Washington NY 11050-3136

CICCARONE, RICHARD ANTHONY, financial executive; b. Akron, Ohio, June 15, 1952; s. Andrew and Marie Antoinette (Danzi) C.; m. Marilyn Douglas DeBorde, May 26, 1984. BA, Miami U., Oxford, Ohio, 1974; MA, U. Akron, 1978. Mcpl. bond analyst Harris Bank, Chgo., 1977-82, mcpl. rsch. mgr., 1982-83; v.p., dir. rsch., sr. analyst Van Kampen Merritt Investment Adv. Corp. (formerly Am. Portfolio), Lisle, Ill., 1983-89; sr. v.p., dir. fixed income rsch. Blunt Ellis & Loewi, Inc., Chgo., 1989-90; exec. v.p., dir. tax exempt fixed income rsch. Everen Securities Inc. (formerly Kemper Securities), Chgo., 1990-96; sr. v.p., co-dir. mcpl. investments, dir. mcpl. rsch. Van Kampen Inv. Adv. Corp., Oakbrook Terrace, Ill., 1996—. Contbr. articles to profl. jours. and fin. pubs. Mem. exec. com., bd. dirs. Civic Fedn. Chgo.; mem. Village of Hinsdale Plan Commn., 1995-99; trustee Village Hinsdale, 1999—. Named All-Am Mcpl. Analyst (2d team), Global Guaranty, 1990, 91, The Bond Buyer, 1993, All-Am. Mcpls. Analyst, Generalist (2d team), 1993, Institutional Investor Mag., 1992, 94, Mcpl. Analyst Generalist (1st team), Institutional Investor Mag., 1995, 1st Team All-Star Smith's Rsch. and Ratings, 1995, 96, 97, 98, 1st Team All-Star Buyside Mcpl. Rsch. Dir., 1997, 98. Mem. Nat. Fedn. Mcpl. Analysts (nat. chmn. 1984-85, Disting. Svc. award 1988, Standards and Practices chair 1991-92, Long Term Planning Chair 1993-94, govt. acctg. standards adv. coun. 1996—), Soc. Mcpl. Analysts, Chgo. Mcpl. Analysts Soc. (pres. 1984), So. Mcpl. Fin. Soc., Miami (Ohio) U. Alumni Assn. (pres. Chgo. chpt. 1988-89), Com. of One Hundred (Hinsdale, Ill., pres. 1998-99), Omicron Delta Kappa. Roman Catholic. Home: 733 S Bodin St Hinsdale IL 60521-4316 Office: Van Kampan Investments Inc One Parkview Plaza Oakbrook Terrace IL 60181

CICCHELLI, JOSEPH VINCENT, secondary education educator; b. Jersey City, Sept. 14, 1953; s. Anthony Charles and Julia Marie (Libri) C.; m. Joanne Savino, July 11, 1981; children: Jaime Michele, Jason Michael. AA, Bergen C.C., 1973; BA, William Paterson Coll. of N.J., 1975; MA, Seton Hall U., 1981. Tchr.'s aide Bergen County Spl. Svcs. Sch. Dist., Paramus, 1975-76; tchr. Hackensack High Sch., 1976—; asst. prin. Fairmount Elem. Sch., Hackensack, 1976-97; educator Hackensack Adult Edn. Ctr., Hackensack, N.J., 1978-92; supr. Hasbrouck Heights Adult Edn. Ctr., Hackensack, N.J., 1987-92, Hackensack Adult Edn. Ctr., 1992-94; tchr. Hackensack High Sch., 1976—; cons. Belville (N.J.) Pub. Sch. Dist., 1987. Active Fairmount Creative Playground Com., Hackensack. Mem. AAHPERD, N.J. Assn. Health, Phys. Edn., Recreation and Dance, Calif. Alliance Sch. Health Educators, Kappa Delta Pi. Roman Catholic. Avocations: photography, fishing, woodcrafting, automobile restoration and shows. Office: Hackensack High Sch First & Beech St Hackensack NJ 07601

CICCIARELLI, JAMES CARL, immunology educator; b. Toluca, Ill., May 26, 1947; s. Maurice Cicciarelli and Helen Ippolito; 1 daughter: Nicola. BS, Tulane U., 1969; PhD, So. Ill. U., 1977. Lic. clin. lab. dir., Calif. Fellow dept. surgery UCLA, 1977-79, asst. prof. immunology, 1980-87, assoc. prof., 1987-91; prof. urology and microbiology U. So. Calif., L.A., 1992—; lab. dir. Metic Transplant Lab., Inc., L.A., 1984—; bd. dirs.. So. Calif. Organ Procurement Agy.; clin. lab. dir. Am. Bd. Bioanalysis, 1991—; mem. histocompatibility com. United Network Organ Sharing, 1991-94; mem. scientific adv. com. United Network for Organ Sharing, 1997—; lab. dir. Sharp Hosp. and Clinic, San Diego. Contbr. articles to profl. jours., chpts. to books. Rsch. grant NIH, 1985-88. Mem. Am. Soc. Histocompatibility and Immunogenetics, Internat. Transplant Soc., Am. Soc. Transplant Physicians, Internat. Soc. Heart Lung Transplantation. Libertarian. Roman Catholic. Avocations: boating, biking, skiing, tennis, running. Home: 5 W Ringbit Rd Rolling Hills CA 90274 Office: USC Dept Urology Metic Transplant Lab 2100 W 3rd St Ste 280 Los Angeles CA 90057-1922

CICCONE, AMY NAVRATIL, art librarian; b. Detroit, Sept. 19, 1950; d. Gerald R. and Ruth C. (Kauer) Navratil. BA, Wayne State U., 1972; AM in Library Sci., U. Mich., 1973. Rsch. libr. Norton Simon Mus., Pasadena, Calif., 1974-81; chief libr. Chrysler Mus., Norfolk, Va., 1981-88; head libr. Architecture and Fine Arts Libr. U. So. Calif., L.A., 1988-97, acting asst. univ. libr. pub. svcs., 1993-95, ref. libr., 1997—. Contbr. articles to profl. jours.; cons. editor Art Reference Svcs., 1990—. Mem. Art Libraries Soc. N.Am. (moderator Decorative Arts Roundtable, 1991-93, facilities standards com. 1986-91, chmn. strategic planning task force 1994-96, vice-chmn. So. Calif. chpt. 1989, chmn. 1990) Rsch. Librs. Group, Art & Architecture Group (steering com. 1992-94). Office: U So Calif Libr Los Angeles CA 90089-0182

CICCONE, F. RICHARD, retired newspaper editor; b. Sewickley, Pa., Feb. 23, 1940; s. Samuel C. and Mary (Thomas) C.; m. Joan M. Garrity, Nov. 18, 1967; children: Cristin, Richard. Reporter Chgo. Bur. AP, 1962-63, 66-74, news editor, 1974-76; reporter Chgo. Tribune, 1976-77, polit. editor, from 1976, mng. editor, assoc. editor, 1995-98; ret., 1998. Co-author: Who's Running Chicago, 1979. With USMC, 1963-66, Vietnam. Decorated Bronze star. *

CICCONE, JOSEPH LEE, criminal justice educator; b. Teaneck, N.J., Jan. 21, 1960; s. Joseph D. and Catherine (Mazzone) C. BS in Police Sci., Jersey City State Coll., 1983, MS in Criminal Justice, 1987; postgrad., Seton Hall U., 1992-93; EdD, Nova Southeastern U., 1996. Supr. N.J. Meadow Lands, East Rutherford, 1978-80; police officer Cliffside Park (N.J.) Police Dept., 1980-83; police sgt. Fairview (N.J.) Police Dept., 1983—; tchr., coach Lincoln Sch., Fairview, N.J., 1987-89; jr. H.S. tchr. Our Lady of Grace Sch., Fairview, 1989-91; prof. sociology, chairperson dept. social sci. Berkeley Coll., Paterson/Waldwick, N.J., 1991-98; dean instrnl. tech. Berkeley Coll., 1998—; prof. criminal justice Monmouth Univ., West Long Branch, N.J., 1991—; sheriff Bergen County Sheriff's Dept., Hackensack, N.J., 1999—; 1st v.p. N.J. State Police Benevolent Assn., East Bergen County, 1983—; instr. Drug Abuse Resistance Edn., Bergen City, N.J., 1989—; chairperson N.J. Gov. Alliance, Fairview, 1990—; acad. trainer Bergen County Police Acad., Mahwah, N.J., 1990—. Author: The Evaluation and Implementation of DARE, 1993, Police Staff Development in Minority Issues; contbr. articles to profl. jours. Mem. Young Dem. Club, Fairview, 1983—, PTA, Fairview, 1989—, Holy Trinity Ch. Choir, 1994, Bd. of Edn., Fairview; exec. bd. N.J. Honor Legion, Hudson City, N.J., 1990—; spkr. in field; sheriff Bergen County, N.J., 1998. Named Police Office of Yr., D.A.R.E. Am., 1990, 93. Mem. Acad. Criminal Justice Sci., Officers Action League, Police Benevolent Assn., Lambda Alpha Epsilon, Phi Delta Kappa. Democrat. Roman Catholic. Avocations: gourmet cooking, bicycling, running, photography, civil rights activist. Home: 373 Park Ave Fairview NJ 07022-1116 Office: Bergen County Sheriff's Dept Justice Ctr 10 Main St Hackensack NJ 07601

CICCONE, MADONNA LOUISE VERONICA See MADONNA

CICCONE, MARGARET, mayor; d. Norman and Bernice Rose; m. Fred Ciccone; children: Nicholas, Anthony. A in Acctg., Wis. Indianhead Tech. Coll.; Cert. Mcpl. Clk., U. Wis., Green Bay, Internat. Inst. Mcpl. Clks., 1991; Cert., U. Wis., Madison, U. Wis., Superior. Electronic assembler Duluth (Minn.) Avionics; acctg. clerk WDSM-TV; office mgr. Amsoil, Inc.; clerk, stenographer City of Superior (Wis.), 1976-80, dep. city clerk, 1980-88, city clerk, 1988-95, mayor, 1995—; mem. numerous coms. City of Superior, including Bd. of Estimates, City Plan Commn., Cmty. Devel. Block Grant Bd., Heritage Com., Mayor's Bus. Adv. Com., Spirit of Superior, others; mem. League of Wis. Municipalities, Wis. Alliance of Cities, No. Networks Trade Conf., Internat. Great Lakes Mayor's Conf., others. Exec. bd. Superior Days Legis. Efforts; panel, govt. chair United Way; active LWV, Salvation Army, Superior-Douglas County Task Force on Drug and Alcohol Abuse, Am. Cancer Soc., Cathedral of Christ the King. Named Woman of the Yr., Douglas County Hist. Soc., 1996, nominee 1993, 96; recipient Outstanding Vol. Svc. award Superior-Douglas County C. of C., 1994, Disting. Alumni award Wis. Indianhead Tech. Coll., 1997. Mem. Internat. Inst. Mcpl. Clks., Wis. Mcpl. Clks., Am. Fedn. of State, County and Mcpl. Employees (past pres., sec.), Toastmasters. Office: Mayor/City of Superior 1407 Hammond Ave Superior WI 54880-4517

CICCONI, JAMES WILLIAM, lawyer; b. Elmira, N.Y., June 8, 1952; s. Raymond Joseph and Doris Arlene (Strong) C.; m. Patricia Olivia Burgess, Aug. 10, 1974; children: Jill, Sara, Rachel. BA, U. Tex., 1974, JD, 1977. Bar: Tex. 1977, D.C. 1985. Issues dir. Jim Baker for Atty. Gen. campaign, Austin, Tex., 1977-78; adminstrv. asst. to the gov. State of Tex., Austin, 1979-80, gen. counsel to the sec. of state, 1980-81; spl. asst. to the pres., to the chief of staff The White House, Washington, 1981-85; sr. issues advisor Bush-Quayle '88 campaign, Washington, 1987-88; asst. to the pres., dep. to the chief of staff The White House, Washington, 1989-90; atty. Akin Gump Strauss Hauer & Feld, Washington, 1985-88, 91—, ptnr., 1991—; bd. dirs. Found. for Nat. Archives, Washington, Tex. Pub. Policy Found., San Antonio; issues dir. Bush-Quayle '92 Campaign; dep. dir. strategy Dole-Kemp '96 Campaign. V.p. George Bush Presdl. Libr. Found., College Station, Tex., 1991—; legal adv. bd. Defenders of Property Rights, Washington. Republican. Roman Catholic. Avocations: baseball, tennis. Office: Akin Gump Strauss Hauer & Feld Ste 400 1333 New Hampshire Ave NW Washington DC 20036-1564*

CICERCHI, ELEANOR ANN TOMB, fundraising executive; b. Sayre, Pa., Dec. 11, 1944; d. William Horton and Brinton Elizabeth (Cauffiel) Tomb; m. Robert A. Weskerna, Nov. 19, 1966 (div. Feb. 1981); children: Amy Marie, Robert Campbell; m. Philip J. Cicerchi, July 1982. AB with great distinction, Mt. Holyoke Coll., 1966; MS, New Sch. Social Rsch., 1992. Cert. fundraising exec. Sr. mktg. rep. Group Health Plan, Guttenberg, N.J., 1976-79; dir. comty. rels. Burke Rehab. Ctr., White Plains, N.Y., 1979-84; exec. dir. Bergen comty. Coll. Fedn., Paramus, N.J., 1984-86; campaign counsel Brakeley John Price Jones, Inc., Stanford, Conn., 1986-88; v.p. instnl. advancement Marymount Coll., Tarrytown, N.Y., 1988-93; dir. maj. gifts Am. Found. for AIDS Rsch., N.Y.C., 1993-95, chief devel. officer, 1995-96; v.p. devel. and external affairs ORBIS Internat., Inc., N.Y.C., 1996—; faculty mem. Fundraising Sch., Ctr. Philanthropy, Ind. U., Indpls., 1989—; adj. grad. faculty mem. NYU, N.Y.C., 1990-97, New Sch. for Social Rsch., N.Y.C., 1995—, chmn. task force for Vision 2000: The Right to Sight, Geneva, 1998—; chair PR Group, Internat. Assn. Prevention of Blindness, 1998-99. Author: Raid!, 1978, Anonymous Giving, 1991; co-author: The Earth Shook and the Sky Was Red, 1976, The Flower of the Virginian, 1980. Pres. Dem. Club, River Vale, N.J., 1978-81; bd. dirs., immediate past chmn. Philharmonia Virtuosi, Dobbs Ferry, N.Y., 1985—; bd. dirs., sec. Am. Anorexia-Bulimia Assn., N.Y.C., 1984—. Woodrow Wilson fellow, 1966; Sarah Williston scholar, 1964, Mt. Holyoke scholar, 1963. Mem. Nat. Soc. Fundraising Execs. (Greater N.Y. chpt. v.p. 1993-95), Women in Fin. Devel., Phi Beta Kappa. Home: 385 Sunset Rd River Vale NJ 07675-5704 Office: ORBIS Internat Inc 330 W 42nd St New York NY 10036-6902

CICHELLO, SAMUEL JOSEPH, architect; b. Syracuse, N.Y., June 19, 1931; s. Anthony John and Margaret (Stanziana) C.; m. Eileen Agnes O'Toole, Feb. 13, 1960; children: Mary, Teresa, Claire, Anthony, John, Michael, Paul. BArch, Syracuse U., 1954. Lic. architect, N.Y. Draftsman Pederson & Hueber, Syracuse, 1951-53, Hawley E. McAfee, Fayetteville. N.Y., 1954-55; project adminstr. Hueber Hares & Glavin, Syracuse, 1959-63; pvt. practice Weedsport, N.Y., 1963—. Editor: Environment of Educational Facilities, 1966. Town assessor Town of Brutus, 1972-95. With U.S. Army, 1955-56. Mem. AIA (award of merit 1967), N.Y. State Assn. Architects, Weedsport C. of C. (pres. 1965-68), Lions Club (pres. 1968-70). Republican. Roman Catholic. Avocation: woodworking. Office: 2714 Franklin St # 326 Weedsport NY 13166

CICHOKE, ANTHONY JOSEPH, JR., chiropractor, writer, health consultant, researcher, lecturer; b. Peoria, Ill., Nov. 23, 1931; s. Anthony Joseph Sr. and Margaret Mary (Conwell) C.; m. Margaret A. Kovner, Feb. 24, 1962; children: Anthony Joseph III, Michael David, William F., Margaret Kathleen. BS in Social Sci., John Carroll U., 1954; student, Army Lang. Sch., Monterey, Calif., 1955; MA in Speech and Theater, St. Louis U., 1964; MA in Speech Sci. Pathology and Audiology, U. Minn., 1967; postgrad., Case Western Res. U., 1969; D. Chiropractic, Nat. Coll. Chiropractic, Lombard, Ill., 1973; postgrad., Western States Chiropractic Coll., 1975. Diplomate Am. Chiropractic Bd. Nutrition. Actor, promoter Schubert Orgn., N.Y.C., 1960-61; entertainment dir., producer U.S. Army and 2d Army, Ft. Eustis, Va., 1961-62; actor, tchr. radio announcer U. Minn., Mpls., 1964-67; tchr., researcher Eastman Dental Ctr., Rochester, N.Y., 1967-68; team physician Portland State U. Amateur Athletic Union, 1975-84; instr. and lectr. on sports medicine, nutrition, and chiropractic medicine at seminars, convs. and various colls. and univs; researcher. Author: Enzymes and Enzyme Therapy: How to Jumpstart Your Way to Lifelong Good Health, Introduction to Chiropractic Health, Enzymes: Nature's Energizers, Nutrition to Give Your Athlete the Winning Edge, Acute Trauma and Systemic Enzyme Therapy, A New Look at Chronic Disorders and Systemic Enzyme Therapy, A New Look at Enzyme Therapy, AIDS and Metabolic Therapy, New Hope for AIDS, Neurologic Considerations in Toxic, Metabolic and Nutritional Disorders, The Complete Book of Enzyme Therapy; contbr. over 300 articles to profl. journals; editor Nutritional Prospectives mag, 1979; producer Blockheads, London, 1984-85, This was Burlesque, L.A., 1985. Chmn. sports medicine com. Amateur Athletic Union, 1975—; mem. postgrad. faculty numerous chiropractic colls. 1st lt. U.S. Army, 1955-59. Grantee U.S. Office Edn., 1965-67, Case We. Res. U., 1968-69, U. Minn., 1965-67, NIH, 1968-69. Fellow Internat. Assn. Study of Pain (diplomate), Internat. Coll. Chiropractic; mem. Am. Chiropractic Assn. (coun. orthopedics, 3 man posture com., coun. sports injuries, past pres. and v.p. coun. nutrition), N.Y. Acad. Scis., Orthomolecular Med. Soc., Acad. Orthomolecular Psychiatry, Acad. Sports Medicine, U.S. Sports Acad., Found. Chiropractic Edn. and Rsch., Metabolic Rsch. Found. Republican. Roman Catholic. Avocation: writing. Office: PO Box 92094 Portland OR 97292-2094

CICILLINE, J. CLEMENT, state legislator; b. Providence, Feb. 7, 1940; m. Kathleen Arnau, Sept. 8, 1967; 6 children. AB, Providence Coll., 1962; MS, U. R.I., 1967. Mem. Newport (R.I.) Sch. Com., 1979-91, 92—; mem., majority policy leader R.I. State Senate, 1992—; pres., CEO Newport County Cmty. Mental Health Ctr., 1986—. Mem. Vols. in Newport Edn. Mem. R.I. Assn. of Cmty. Mental Health Ctr., R.I. State Senate, 1992—, Senate Majority Pol. Leader; Forum Lodge Sons of Italy, Newport County Psychol. Soc. Democrat. Address: PO Box 3383 Newport RI 02840-0992

CICIRELLI, VICTOR GEORGE, psychologist; b. Miami, Fla., Oct. 1, 1926; s. Felix and Rene (DeMaria) C.; m. Jean Alice Solveson, Aug. 9, 1953; children: Ann Victoria, Michael Felix, Gregory Sheldon. B.S., Notre Dame U., 1947; M.A., U. Ill., Urbana, 1950; M.Ed., U. Miami, 1956; Ph.D. (Univ. fellow), U. Mich., 1964; Ph.D., Mich. State U., 1971. Asst. prof. ednl. psychology U. Mich., 1963-65; dir. student teaching for elem., secondary and M.A.T. programs U. Pa., 1965-67; assoc. prof. early childhood edn. Ohio U., 1967-68; dir. research Nat. Evaluation of Head Start Westinghouse Learning Corp. at Ohio U., 1968-69; Office Edn. postdoctoral fellow U. Wis. Inst. Cognitive Learning, 1969-70; prof. human devel. Purdue U., 1970-73, prof. devel./aging psychology, 1974—, dir. devel. psychology program, 1977-78, 80-81, 82-83, 92-93, 96, 99—; vis. sci. fellow Max Planck Inst. for Human Devel. and Edn., Berlin, 1991; fellow Ctr. for Health Policy Rsch., J. Hillis Miller Health Sci. Ctr., Sch. Medicine, U. Fla., Gainesville, summer 1991; cons. in field; mem. research adv. bd. Calif. Commn. for Tchr. Preparation and Licensing, 1973-78; scholar NSF Inst., Ohio U., 1956, Am. U., 1958, U. Fla., 1960. Author: Helping Elderly Parents: Role of Adult Children, 1981, Family Caregiving: Autonomous and Paternalistic Decision Making, 1992, Sibling Relationships Across the Life Span, 1995; mem. editl. bd. Jour. Marriage and the Family, 1990—; contbr. articles to profl. publs. Bd. dirs. Nat. Com. on Prevention of Elder Abuse, 1988-91; mem. adv. com. Ind. Geriatric Edn. Ctr., U. Ind., 1991. Grantee OEO, 1968-69, 71-73, U.S. Office Edn., 1971-73; Nat. Inst. Edn., 1973-74, NIH, 1973-74, Office Child Devel., 1973-74, Nat. Ret. Tchrs. Assn./Am. Assn. Ret. Persons Andrus Found., 1978-82, 90-91, 92, 95, Retirement Rsch. Found., 1984-85, 87-89; fellow Andrew Norman Inst. Advanced Study, Andrus Gerontology Ctr., U. So. Calif., 1984, Gerontology Soc., 1983, 84. Fellow APA, Gerontol. Soc.; mem. Internat. Soc. Study Behavioral Deve., Am. Psychol. Soc., Am. Assn. Aging, Nat. Coun. on Family Rels. Soc. for Chaos Theory, Phi Kappa Phi. Roman Catholic. Home: 1221 N Salisbury St West Lafayette IN 47906-2415 Office: Purdue U Dept Psychol Sci West Lafayette IN 47907

CICOLANI, ANGELO GEORGE, research company executive, operating engineer; b. Norwood, Mass., Mar. 4, 1933; s. Luigi and Maria (Fossa) C.; m. Marilyn Adell Griffith, June 4, 1955 (div. 1968); children: George, Susanne, Diana; m. Patricia Anne Kirsch, Nov. 1, 1979 (dec. July 1995). *Father born in Brazil 1902; family moved back to Italy in 1906. After four years as a Carabinieri (Rome), he emigrated 1927 from Poggio Moiano (near Reiti) and settled near Boston. Mother born 1901, emigrated in 1919 from Cassano Magnago (near Varese, Italy). Settled with an Uncle's family in Boston. Introduced by friends, they married in 1932. Completing grade school was not an option for either. However, they instilled the quintessential immigrant educational ambitions in their two children. A thorough science background was provided by their Westwood (Massachusetts) science teacher, Christos Sarris. Angelo graduated from the Naval Academy and Luigi from MIT.* Student, Northeastern U., 1950; BS, U.S. Naval Acad., Annapolis, Md., 1955; profl. cert., Advanced Nuclear Power Sch., 1960; BS, Naval Postgrad. Sch., 1969. Commd. ensign U.S. Navy, 1955, advanced through grades to lt. comdr., 1975, chief reactor operator, 1958-62, exec. officer, 1963-67; systems analyst for startegic sys. project office U.S. Navy, Arlington, Va., 1969-75; cons. Arlington, 1975-77; sr. rschr. R&D Assocs., Arlington, 1977-82, program mgr., 1977-88, sr. scientist, 1982-87, tech. dir. Sprinfield rsch. facility, 1988—. Author: The Role of Systems Analysis, 1974; author, editor Mineral Minutes Jour., 1972-74; author numerous reports on command and control survivability rsch., 1978-86, numerous reports on underground mil. facilities rsch., 1987—; developer installation vulnerability assessment techniques and courses of instrn., 1987—; designer Low Speed Ram-Jet, 1954 (Inst. Aero. Scis. 1st Pl. award). Pres. emeritus bd. dirs. Dumbarton Concert Series, Washington, 1982—. Mem. Ops. Rsch. Soc. Am., Naval Inst., Mineral Soc. D.C. (pres. 1972-77), Naval Submarine League, Ret. Officers Assn., Nature Conservancy. Office: Springfield Rsch Facility 6801 Telegraph Rd Alexandria VA 22310-3398

CICOTELLO, THOMAS MATTHEW, property manager; b. Altoona, Pa., May 2, 1970; s. Guy Michael and Elaine Ann C. BSBA, Am. U., 1992. Registered rep. Minn. Mutual Life Ins. Co., Rockville, Md., 1992; office mgr. MRC Mortgage, Annandale, Va., 1993; property mgr. Insignia/ESG, Inc., Washington, 1994—. Roman Cath. Fax: 202-842-9106. E-mail: tomcic@iesg.com. Home: 3701 Connecticut Ave NW 339 Washington DC 20008 Office: Insignia/ESG Inc 1015 15th St NW Washington DC 20005

CIENFUEGOS, MAURICIO, professional soccer player; b. San Salvador, El Salvador, Feb. 12, 1968. Profl. soccer player El Salvador's First Divsn., 1988-91, 93-95, Mex. Nat. Team, 1991-93; midfielder L.A. Galaxy, 1996—. Three time MLS All-Star; named Galaxy's Most Valuable Player, 1997; one of six Galaxy players selected to 1996 All-Star game. Office: Los Angeles Galaxy 1010 Rose Bowl Dr Pasadena CA 90025*

CIERESZKO, LEON STANLEY, SR., chemistry educator; b. Holyoke, Mass., July 31, 1917; s. Albert Wojciech and Valeria Ann (Keller) C.; married; 1 child, Leon Stanley. BS in Chemistry, U. Mass., 1939; PhD in Physiol. Chemistry, Yale U., 1942. Rsch. chemist Sharp & Dohme, Glenolden, Pa., 1942-45; instr. biochemistry U. Utah, Salt LakeCity, 1945-46; instr. chemistry U. Ill., Urbana, 1946-48; prof. biochemistry U. Okla., Norman, 1948-90; rschr. in thalassobiogeochemistry. Office: U Okla Dept Chemistry Norman OK 73019

CIESLAK, WILLIAM, academic administrator; b. East Chgo., Sept. 12, 1946; s. Walter Bernard and Irene Joan (Koziol) C. BA in Philosophy, St. Joseph Coll., Rennasalear, Ind., 1969, BA in Theology, 1969; MDiv., Franciscan Sch. Theology, Berkeley, Calif., 1973; PhD, Grad. Theol. Union, Berkeley, Calif., 1979. Prof. Franciscan Sch. Theology, Berkeley, 1980—, pres., 1993—. Mem. Soc. Liturgica, N. Am. Acad. Liturgy, Cath. Theol. Soc. Am. Democrat. Office: Franciscan Sch Theology 1712 Euclid Ave Berkeley CA 94709-1294

CIESZKOWSKI, EDWARD D., marketing and management professional; b. Warsaw, Poland, Feb. 22, 1941; s. Alexander and Maria Cieszkowski; m. Diana Mignon, 1975; children: Duncan, Robert, Alistair, Hamish, Andrew, Konrad. B of Commerce, Stafford Poly., Eng., 1963; MBA, Newcastle U., Eng., 1965; diploma in behavioral sci., Rutherford Coll., Eng., 1966. Mng. dir. Grandmet Indsl., U.K., 1970-78; exec. v.p., COO VS Svcs., Can. and Europe, 1978-84; pres. Eastwood Svcs. Inc., Can., 1984-88; mng. ptnr. Delisser Romanoff Assocs., Toronto, Ont., Can., 1988—. Author: (book) Food for Thought, 1976; author, editor: (book) Cooking Success, 1985; pub.: (newsletter) Asia Pacific Update, 1993—. Avocations: traveling, reading, writing, business mentoring. E-mail: edc3@ix.netcom.com. Home: 2006 Aviation Way Redondo Beach CA 90278 Office: Delisser Romanoff Inc, 115 Winchester St, Toronto, ON Canada M4X ITI

CIFELLI, JOHN LOUIS, lawyer; b. Chicago Heights, Ill., Aug. 19, 1923; s. Antonio and Domenica (Liberatore) C.; m. Irene Romandine, Jan. 4, 1948; children—Carla, David, John L., Bruce, Thomas, Carol. Student, Bowdoin Coll., 1943, Norwick Mil. Acad., 1943, Mt. Pilar Acad., 1943, U. Ill. Extension Ctr., 1946-47; LLB, DePaul U., 1950, JD (hon.), 1975. Bar: Ill. 1950, U.S. Supreme Ct. 1960. Ptnr. Piacenti, Cifelli & Sims, Chicago Heights, 1950-78; pres. John L. Cifelli & Assocs., Chicago Heights, 1978-85; sr. ptnr. Cifelli Baczynski & Scrementi Ltd. (now Cifelli & Scrementi), Chicago Heights, 1985—; spl. counsel City of Chicago Heights, 1961-72; village atty. Village of Richton Park, Ill., 1962-77, Village of Ford Heights, Ill., 1984-89; counsel Maj. League Umpires Assn., 1973-78, Ill. High Sch. Baseball Coaches Assn., 1975-89. Sec. Bd. Fire and Police, Chicago Heights, 1959-65; co-founder Small Fry Internat. Basketball, 1969, pres., 1969—; coach, baseball coordinator Chicago Heights Park Dist., 1970-75; coach Babe Ruth League Baseball, 1972, 74, 75, asst. Ill. dir., 1973; dir. Ill. tournament, 1973. Served to 2d lt. USAAF, 1942-45, ETO. Mem. ABA, Ill. Bar Assn., Ill. Trial Lawyers Assn., Asns. Trial Lawyers Am., Justinian Soc. Lawyers, Isaac Walton League, Italo Am. Vets. Group, VFW (judge adv. 1951-72), Cath. War Vets. (judge adv. 1951-70), Am. Legion. Republican. Clubs: Chicago Heights Country (bd. dirs. 1972-76), Mt. Carmel; Pike Lake Fishing (Wis.). Lodges: Moose, Amaseno. Avocations: hunting, fishing, golf. Home: 879 Amico Dr Chicago Heights IL 60411 Office: Cifelli & Scrementi 100 1st National Plz Chicago Heights IL 60411-3555

CIHAK, ERWIN FRANK, retired securities trader, real estate developer; b. Chgo., Mar. 22, 1915; s. Louis V. and Mary Anna (Petrak) C.; m. Irene R. Wiktor, Nov. 1, 1943; children: Sandra I., Alan W. Swinger, Pamela R. Paul Maksinovic, Bernadette. BS in Agrl. Edn., U. Ill., 1939. Mktg. mgr. Midwest Grocery, Chgo., 1942-49; owner, pres. Miracle Ham Co., Chgo., 1950-57; owner Custom Beef Co., Chgo., 1957-60; meat broker, buyer P.B.S. Enterprise Inc., Oak Brook, Ill., 1960-70; real estate developer P.B.S. Enterprise Inc., 1971—. Capt. USAF, ret. Decorated DFC, Purple Heart, Air medal, Presdl. Citiation, Two oak leaf clusters, Pearl Habor survivors medal. Mem. Am. Legion, Disabled Am. Vets., VFW, Pearl Habor Survivors Assn., 19th Bomb Group-38th Rescue Squad. Avocations: historian, writer, organic gardening, golf. Home: 2600 S Finley Rd Lombard IL 60148

CIKOVSKY, NICOLAI, JR., curator, art history educator; b. N.Y.C., Feb. 11, 1933; s. Nicolai and Hortense (Hilbert) C.; m. Sarah Eden Greenough, June 17, 1978; children—Emily Hilbert, Sophia Greenough. A.B. magna cum laude, Harvard Coll., 1955; A.M., Harvard U., 1958, Ph.D., 1965. Asst. prof. Skidmore Coll., Saratoga Springs, N.Y., 1961-63; chmn., assoc. prof. Pomona Coll., Claremont, Calif., 1964-68; vis. assoc. prof. U. Tex., Austin, 1969-70; dir. art gallery, assoc. prof. Vassar Coll., Poughkeepsie, N.Y., 1971-74; prof., chmn. dept. art U. N.Mex., Albuquerque, 1974-83; curator Am. & British painting Nat. Gallery Art, Washington, 1983—, sr. curator Am. and Brit. painting, 1998—. Author: Sanford Robinson Gifford, exhbn. catalogue, 1970; editor: Lectures on the Affinity of Painting with the Other Fine Arts (Samuel F.B. Morse), 1983; George Inness, 1971, The Life and Work of George Inness, 1977, Winslow Homer, 1990, Winslow Homer Watercolors, 1991, George Inness, 1993; contbg. author: exhbn. catalogues George Inness, 1985, Ansel Adams: Classic Images, 1985, William Merritt Chase: Summers at Shinnecock, 1987, Raphaelle Peale Still Lifes, 1988, William M. Harnett, 1992, James McNeill Whistler, 1994, Winslow Homer, 1995; also articles on William Merritt Chase, George Inness, Winslow Homer, Thomas Eakins, Am. landscape painting. Am. Council Learned Socs.-Smithsonian Instn. postdoctoral research fellow, 1968-69; Guggenheim fellow, 1978-79; Kress sr. fellow Nat. Gallery Art, 1983. Mem. Phi Beta Kappa. Club: Harvard (N.Y.C.). Office: Nat Gallery Art Off of Curator Paintings Washington DC 20565

CILELLA, MARY WINIFRED, director; b. Oak Park, Ill., Aug. 24, 1943; d. Charles William Sr. and Theresa Mary (Gilligan) Broucek; m. Salvatore G. Cilella Jr., Aug. 29, 1970; children: Salvatore George III, Peter Dominic. BA, Dominican U., 1965; MAT, U. Notre Dame, 1966; grad. The Prin.'s Inst., Harvard U., 1993; postgrad., U. S.C., 1994-97. Tchr. Miner Jr. H.S., Arlington Heights, Ill., 1966-67; sec. White House, Washington, 1969-70; devel. officer Textile Mus., Washington, 1982-83; dir. meetings and continuing edn. Am. Assn. Mus., Washington, 1983-87; interim lower sch. head, lower sch. head Heathwood Hall Episc. Sch., Columbia, S.C., 1989-94; dir. acad. adminstrn. Heathwood Hall Episc. Sch., Columbia, 1994-95, dir. fin. and adminstrn., 1995-96, asst. head, 1996-98, assoc. head fin. and ops., 1998—; mem. profl. edn. unit adv. com. U. S.C., 1996—; mem. U.S. Dept. of Edn.'s Blue Ribbon Schs. Planning Group, 1996; examiner Malcolm Baldrige Nat. Quality award bd. U.S. Dept. Commerce and Nat. Inst. Stds. and Tech., 1999. Mem. ASCD, S.C. Assn. Sch. Librs., Rotary Internat., Phi Delta Kappa. Roman Catholic. Avocations: gardening, collecting antiques, music, aerobics. Home: 48 Old Still Rd Columbia SC 29223-3040 Office: Heathwood Hill Episc Sch 3000 S Beltline Blvd Columbia SC 29201-5130

CILELLA, SALVATORE GEORGE, JR., museum director; b. Chgo., Oct. 19, 1941; s. Salvatore G. and Mary Genevieve (LaRocque) C.; m. Mary Winifred Broucek, Aug. 29, 1970; children: Salvatore G. III, Peter Dominic. BA, U. Notre Dame, 1963, MA in Am. History, 1966; MA in museum adminstrn., Univ. N.Y., Oneonta, 1971. Community amb. Experiment in Internat. Living, Iran, 1965; exec. dir. No. Ind. Hist. Soc., South Bend, 1970-72; registrar, asst. dir. N.Y. State Hist. Assn., Cooperstown, 1973-76; exec. dir. Historic Bethlehem (Pa.) Inc., 1976-79; dir. devel. and membership Old Sturbridge (Mass.) Village, 1979-81; devel. officer Smithsonian Instn., Washington, 1981-87; exec. dir. Columbia (S.C.) Mus. Art, 1987—; cons. various mus., 1979—; overseer Old Sturbridge Village, 1982-89; lectr. Seminar for Hist. Adminstrn., Williamsburg, Va., 1983—, Mus. Mgmt. Program, Boulder, Colo., 1993. Editor Collections mag.; contbr. articles to profl. jours. Co-chmn. United black Fund, 1999; chmn. search com. Hist. Columbia. 1st lt. U.S. Army, 1966-69. Decorated Army commendation medal, 1969. Mem. Am. Assn. Mus. (chmn. devel. and membership com. 1984-89, bd. dirs. 1989-92), Am. Hist. Print Collectors Assn., Assn. Art Mus. Dirs., Rotary. Roman Catholic. Avocations: collecting 18th and 19th century American prints and maps, antiques, tribal art and rugs. Office: Columbia Mus Art PO Box 2068 Columbia SC 29202-2068

CIMA, GAY GIBSON, English educator; b. Falls City, Nebr., Nov. 18, 1948; s. Richard Marion and Geraldine Smith Gibson; m. Ronald Jerry Cima, July 3, 1976; children: Gibson Alessandro, Anna Francesca. BS, U. Nebr., 1970; MA, Northwestern U., 1971; PhD, Cornell U., 1978. Instr. Clayton Jr. Coll., Atlanta, 1971-73; grad. asst. Cornell U., Ithaca, N.Y., 1973-76; ast. prof. Blackburn Coll., Carlinville, Ill., 1976-77; adj. instr. Georgetown U., George Washington U., No. Va. C.C., Washington, Manassas, Va., 1978-80; asst. prof. Georgetown U., Washington, 1980-86, assoc. prof., 1986-94, prof., 1994—; reader, evaluator Cornell U. Press, U. Mich. Press, Ind. U. Press, 1981—; project dir. Internat. Voices and Bicentennial Voices Poetry Series, Georgetown U., 1989. Author: Performing Women, 1993; co-author: Theatre Studies in Higher Education, 1996; assoc. editor Ibsen News and Comment, 1988-90; actor, dir. cmty. theatre. Canvasser Clean Water Action Project, McLean, Va., 1989-90; neighborhood coord. March of Dimes, Am. Heart Assn., Am. Cancer Soc., McLean, 1991-93; vol. Girl Scouts Am., McLean, 1991—. Summer Rsch. grantee Georgetown U., Washington, 1984, 90, 93, 98. Mem. Am. Soc. for Theatre Rsch. (conf. devel. task force, rationales task force, chambers playwriting award panel, Kahan prize com. 1995-98, exec. bd. 1996-98, Kahan Scholar's prize 1984), Assn. for Theatre in Higher Edn. (chair program com. 1987-89, activism facilitator Women and Theatre Forum 1992-94, mem. program com. 1995-97, mem. rsch. and publs. com. 1998—). Democrat. Unitarian. Avocations: swimming, acting, reading, writing about women's history, playing guitar. E-mail: cima@gusun. Office: Georgetown Univ Dept English 37th and O Sts NW Washington DC 20057

CIMBOLO See GIMBOLO, ALEKSEI FRANK CHARLES

CIMENT, MELVYN, mathematician; b. Bronx, Sept. 23, 1941; s. Jack and Regina (Moskowitz) C.; m. Barbara Ann Kagan, July 3, 1966; children: Ethan J., Daniel I. BS, U. Miami, 1962; MS, NYU, 1964, PhD in Math., 1968; JD, Am. U., 1978. Mathematician Denver Rsch. Ctr., Marathon Oil Co., 1968-69; asst. prof. math. U. Mich., Tel-Aviv U. and NYU, 1967-72; applied mathematician Naval Surface Weapons Ctr., 1972-77; sr. applied mathematician Nat. Bur. Stds., Gaithersburg, Md., 1977-83; prog. analyst Nat. Bur. Stds., 1981-82; Dept. Commerce, Sci. and Tech. congl. fellow U.S. Senate Com. on Commerce, Sci. and Transp., Washington, 1980-81; prog. dir. applied math. DMS, NSF, 1983-86, prog. dir. computational math., 1986; dep. dir. div. Adv. Sci. Computing, Computer, Info. Scis. NSF, Washington, 1986-90, coord. high performance computing and communications program, 1991, exec. officer Computer Info. Sci. and Engring., 1992-93, acting asst. dir., 1993-94, dep. asst. dir., 1993-99; dir. info. techs. Potomac Inst. for Policy Studies, Arlington, Va., 1999—; mem. FCCSET Working Group on High Performance Computing, 1986-92, exec. com. high performance computing and comm. info. tech. subcom., 1993-94; vice chmn. com. info. and comm. Nat. Sci. and Tech. Coun., 1994, co-chmn. fed. info. svcs. and applications coun., com. computing, info. and comm., 1996-98; acting chmn. Fed. Networking Coun., 1993-94; vis. scientist U. Md., 1994-95; cons. Coun. on Competitiveness, 1994-95. Courant Inst. Math. Scis. fellow, 1962-66, others. Mem. AAAS, Am. Math. Soc., Soc. for Indsl. and Applied Math. (mem. coun. 1988-90), D.C. Bar Assn., Fla. Bar Assn., Md. Bar Assn. Jewish. Avocations: reading, music, biking. Email: mel@ciment.com. Home: 11712 Kemp Mill Rd Silver Spring MD 20902-1720 Office: Potomac Inst Policy Studies 1600 Wilson Blvd Ste 1200 Arlington VA 22209

CIMINI, JOSEPH FEDELE, law educator, lawyer, former magistrate; b. Scranton, Pa., Sept. 8, 1948; s. Frank Anthony and Dorothy Theresa (Musso) C. AB in German and Polit. Sci., U. Scranton, 1970; JD, Columbus Sch. Law, Cath. U. Am., 1973. Bar: Pa. 1973, U.S. Dist. Ct. (mid. dist.) Pa. 1973, D.C. 1976, U.S. Ct. Appeals (3d cir.) 1978, U.S. Supreme Ct. 1978. Law clk. to judge Ct. Common Pleas Lackawanna County (Pa.), 1973-75; asst. U.S. atty. Middle Dist. Pa., Dept. Justice, 1975-80, spl. asst. to U.S. Atty. Middle Dist. Pa., 1980-81; asst. prof. sociology/criminal justice U. Scranton, 1980-94, assoc. prof., 1994—; U.S. magistrate judge U.S. Dist. Ct. (mid. dist.) Pa., 1981-92; spl. trial master Lackawanna County Ct. Common Pleas, 1995—. Past pres. Lackawanna Hist. Soc.; v.p. adv. bd. Holy Family Residence, Scranton, Pa., 1997—; v.p. pastoral coun. St. Francis Ch., 1994-96. Recipient Meritorious award Dept. Justice; German Acad. Exchange Service fgn. study travel grantee, W.Ger., 1981. Mem. ABA, Fed. Bar Assn. (past v.p. mid. dist. Pa. chpt.), Am. Judges Assn., Fed. Magistrate Judges Assn., Acad. Criminal Justice Scis., Pa. Bar Assn., Northeastern Assn. Criminal Justice Scis. (pres. 1987-88), Lackawanna Bar Assn., U. Scranton Alumni (nat. sec. 1997-99), Cath. U. Law Alumni, Purple Club, Victor Alfieri Lit. Soc., UNICO Nat. Republican. Roman Catholic. Address: Univ Scranton Dept Sociology/Criminal Justice Scranton PA 18510-4605

CIMINO, ANN M., education educator; b. Easton, Pa.; d. John and Melina (Castelluzzo) C. BS, Pa. State U., 1955, MEd, 1958; student cert., Lehigh U. Cert. reading specialist. Instr. Sonoma State U., Santa Rosa, Calif., U. Md.; asst. prof. Muhlenberg Coll., Allentown, Pa., Towson (Md.) State U.; assoc. prof. Kutztown (Pa.) U.; bd. dirs. Alumni Coun., Coll. Edn.-Pa. State U., mem. Lehigh Valley adv. bd.

CIMINO, JAMES ERNEST, physician; b. N.Y.C., July 7, 1928; s. Ernest S. and Rose (Gorga) C.; m. Dorothy Hilary Naperkoski, June 5, 1954; children: James, Ernest, Christopher, Peter, Paul, Maria. Student, Syracuse U., 1946-48; AB, NYU, 1950, MD, 1954. Diplomate Am. Bd. Internal Medicine, Am. Bd. Nephrology. Intern, then resident E.J. Meyer Meml. Hosp., Buffalo, 1954-58; rsch. fellow in physiology U. Buffalo, 1957-58; internal medicine physician, dir. renal svc. VA Hosp., Bronx, N.Y., 1960-68; attending physician Calvary Hosp., Bronx, N.Y., 1961—, chief medicine, med. dir., 1963-80, co-med. dir., 1994, dir. Palliative Care Inst., 1994—; cons. medicine St. Joseph's Hosp., Yonkers, N.Y., Holy Name Hosp., Teaneck, N.J., cons. medicine VA Hosp., Bronx, 1970-77, dir. hemodialysis unit, 1960-70; asst. clin. prof. medicine Mt. Sinai Sch. Medicine, N.Y.C., 1970-73; clin. prof. medicine N.Y. Med. Coll., 1980—; adj. prof., cons. nutrition NYU, 1972-93; cons. internal medicine N.Y.C. Dept. Health, 1971-74, also chmn. com. advanced cancer, 1971-74; mem. instnl. biohazards com. Albert Einstein Coll. Medicine, 1980-92. Mem. edit. bd. N.Y. Med. Quar.; mem. edit. review bd. Am. Jour. of Hospice and Palliative Care; contbr. articles to med. jours. Bd. dirs. N.Y.C. chpt. Am. Cancer Soc. With USAF, 1958-60. Recipient commendation VA, 1968, Ann. Merit award N.Y.C. Pub. Health Assn., 1979, 1st ann. Catherine McParlan Humanitarian award, 1980, Dialysis Pioneering award Nat. Kidney Disease Found., 1982, Il Leone di San Marco award in medicine, 1991; co-recipient Good Samaritan award Nat. Cath. Devel. Conf., 1981; included in The Best Drs. in N.Y., N.Y. Mag., 1996, Best Drs. in Am. North East Region Woodward White, 1996-97. Fellow ACP (Laureate award 1992); mem. AMA, Am. Heart Assn., Internat. Soc. Nephrology, Am. Soc. Nephrology, Am. Dietetic Assn. (Hon. Membership award 1995), Greater N.Y. Dietetic Assn. (hon.). Achievements include development of arterio-venous fistula in hemodialysis and pioneering work in field of palliative care for cancer patients and in the field of nutritional education.

CIMINO, JAY, automotive company executive. CEO Phil Long Dealerships, Colorado Springs, Colo. Office: Phil Long Ford 1212 Motor City Dr Colorado Springs CO 80906-1392*

CIMINO, JOSEPH ANTHONY, physician, educator; b. N.Y.C., Jan. 1, 1934; m. Margaret Langan; children—Andrea, Laura, Lisa, Joseph, Linda, Margaret, John. B.A. in Am. History, Harvard U., 1956, M.I.H., 1964, M.P.H., 1965; M.S. in Biology, Fordham U., 1958; M.D., U. Buffalo, 1962. Diplomate: Am. Bd. Preventive Medicine. Intern Grasslands Hosp., Valhalla, N.Y., 1962-63; AEC fellow in environ. medicine Harvard U. Sch. Public Health, 1963-65; research asso., health officer N.Y.C. Dept. Health, 1965-66; dir. Bur. Community Safety and Occupational Health, 1968-71, dep. commr. health, 1971-72, commr. health, 1972-74; chief med. officer N.Y.C. Dept. Sanitation, 1966-69; med. dir. N.Y.C. Poison Control Center, 1966-72; dir. health and safety N.Y.C. Environ. Protection Adminstrn., 1968-71; commr. hosps. Westchester County, N.Y., 1974-78; pres., chief exec. officer N.Y. Med. Coll., 1978-81, prof. preventive medicine, 1976—, chmn. dept. preventive medicine, 1980—; pres. Occupational Medicine Assocs., 1978—; assoc. prof. environ. medicine and pub. health NYU, 1971-76; prof. comty. dynamics Pace U., 1977-78; adj. prof. pub. health and tropical medicine Tulane U., 1972-76; lectr. in pub. health Columbia U., 1973-76; vis. prof. comty. health Albert Einstein Coll. Medicine, 1973-76, N.Y. State Pub. Health Coun.; pres. bd. Dominican Sisters Family Health Svcs., Inc.; bd. dirs. Westchester Artificial Kidney Ctr. Author: Safety: Protection from Injury, 1969, Medical Service Manual, 1971, Drug Abuse Treatment Agencies in New York City, 1972; author numerous profl. monographs; contbr. articles to profl. publs. Chmn. Cath. Interracial Coun. of Westchester County; chief med. cons. N.Y.C. CSC, 1966-71. Civilian U.S. Army, 1964-65. Fellow Am. Coll. Preventive Medicine, N.Y. Acad. Medicine, Am. Coll. Occupational Medicine, N.Y. Acad. Sci.; mem. Am. Pub. Health Assn., N.Y.C. Pub. Health Assn., Indsl. Med. Assn., Assn. Govtl. Hygienists, Aerospace Med. Assn., Westchester County Med. Soc., N.Y. State Med. Assn., AMA, Am. Soc. Clin. Nutrition. Home: 50 Willard Ave Pocantico Hills NY 10591-1210 Office: NY Med Coll Dept Preventive Med Valhalla NY 10595

CIMINO, MICHAEL, film director, writer; b. N.Y.C., 1948. BFA, MFA, Yale U. Screenwriter Silent Running, 1972, Magnum Force, 1973; screenwriter dir. Thunderbolt and Lightfoot, 1974; producer, writer, dir. The Deer Hunter, 1978 (Acad. awards for Best Dir. and Best Producer); writer, dir. Heaven's Gate, 1980, Year of the Dragon, 1985, The Sicilian, 1987, Desperate Hours, 1990. *

CIMINO, RICHARD DENNIS, lawyer; b. Omaha, Nebr., June 6, 1947; s. Lewis Raymond and Louise (Monaco) C.; m. Mary Scott Reins, Feb. 12, 1977; children: John Damon, Mary Drusilla, Robert Andrew, Ann Marie. BBA, U. Notre Dame, 1969; JD, St. Louis U., 1974. Bar: Nebr. 1975, U.S. Dist. Ct. Nebr. 1975, Kans. 1989, U.S. Dist. Ct. Kans. 1989, Fla. 1995. Assoc. Kutak, Rock & Campbell, Omaha, 1975-78, ptnr., 1979; v.p., gen. counsel Silvey Refrigerated Carriers, Omaha, 1980-86, pres., 1987; ptnr. Dwyer, Pohren, Wood, Heavey & Grimm, Omaha, 1988-89; sole practice St. Marys, Kans., 1989-93; ptnr. Treadwell, Stetler, Erickson, Cimino & McElrath, Naples, Fla., 1993—. Editor St. Louis U. Law Jour., 1972-74. Bd. dirs. Bergan Mercy Hosp. Found., Omaha, 1986-87. With U.S. Army, 1969-71, Vietnam. Mem. Fla. Bar Assn., Kans. Bar Assn., Nebr. Bar Assn., Notre Dame Alumni Club (pres. Omaha chpt. 1980), Alpha Sigma Nu. Republican. Roman Catholic. Avocations: golf, family activities. Office: 4001 Tamiami Trl N Naples FL 34103-3556

CINADER, BERNHARD, immunologist, gerontologist, scientist, educator; b. Vienna, Austria, Mar. 30, 1919; s. Leon and Adele (Schwarz) C.; 1 child, Agatha. B.Sc., U. London, 1945, Ph.D., 1948, D.Sc., 1958. Research asst. Jenner Meml. student Lister Inst. Preventive Medicine, London, 1945-46; Beit Meml. fellow Jenner Meml. student Lister Inst. Preventive Medicine, 1949-53; fellow immunochemistry Inst. Pathology, Western Res. U., Cleve., 1948-49; prin. sci. officer, dept. exptl. pathology Inst. Animal Physiology, Babraham Hall, Cambridge; also hon. lectr. biochemistry dept. U. Coll., London, 1955-58; head subdiv. immunochemistry, div. biol. research Ont. (Can.) Cancer Inst., Toronto, 1958-69; assoc. prof. depts. med. biophysics and pathol. chemistry U. Toronto, 1958-67, prof. dept. med. biophysics, 1967-89, prof. dept. med. cell biology, 1969-82, prof. dept. clin. biochemistry, 1970-92, prof. dept. immunology, 1981-92; dir. Inst. Immunology, 1971-81; mem. governing body U. Toronto, 1980-89, prof. emeritus, 1992—; vis. prof. U. Man., 1967, U. Alta., 1968, U. Sask, 1970, U. Western Ont., 1972, U. Bombay, 1981, Rockfeller Found. vis. prof. Mahidol U., Bangkok, Thailand, 1982, 91; guest lectr. Chinese Acad. Med. Scis., Beijing, People's Republic China, 1990; chmn. immunology com. Biol. Coun. Can., 1967-90; mem. expert adv. panel on immunology WHO, 1970—, mem. sci. and tech. adv. group to Spl. Programme Research and Research Tng. in Human Reprodn., WHO, Geneva, 1985, steering com. task force on vaccine for fertility regulation, 1991—; chmn. adv. bd. Internat. Immunology Tng. and Rsch. Ctr., Amsterdam, 1975-80; chmn. nomenclature com. WHO/Internat. Union Immunol. Socs., 1980-83; chmn. organizing com. 6th Internat. Congress of Immunology, 1986. Editor: Antibody to Enzymes - A Three Component System, 1964, Antibodies to Biologically Active Molecules, 1967, Regulation of the Antibody Response, 1968, Immunological Response of the Female Reproductive Tract, 1976, Immunology of Receptors, 1976-77, Imunology in Canada, 1986, Immunology To-day, 1986; series editor: Receptors and Ligands in Intercellular Communication, 1983—; editorial bd. Immunochemistry, 1965-70; editorial bd. Immunology, Serology, Transplantation sect., Excerpta Medica Found., 1966-76; editorial bd. Can. Jour. Biochemistry, 1967-71, Immunol. Methods, 1970-74, Bolletino dell'istituto sieroterapico Milanese, 1972-90, Immunol. Communication, 1973—, Jour. Immunogenetics, 1973-90, Immunology Letters, 1978—, Jour. Receptor Research, 1979-83, Asian Pacific Jour. Allergy and Immunology, 1983—, Immunol. Investigations, 1985—; contbr. articles to numerous profl. publs.; also catalogues and articles on Canadian Indian art. Recipient Old Student prize London, 1944; medal Société de Chimie Biologique, Paris, 1954; Pfizer fellow Institut de Recherches Cliniques de Montreal, 1972; Jubilee medal Can., 1977; Ignác Semmelweis medal Budapest, 1978; Hardi Cinader prize set up by U. Toronto for best student in immunology, 1985; Karl Landsteiner medal for contbns. to immunology, 1986; decorated Officer Order of Can., 1985; Annual B. Cinader lectr. set up by Can. Soc. Immunology, 1986; Jan E. Purkyne medal, Pilsen, Czechoslovakia, 1988; Commemorative medal 125th Anniversary Confedn. Can., 1992. Fellow Royal Inst. Chemistry (U.K.), Royal Soc. Can., N.Y. Acad. Scis.; mem. Internat. Union Immunol. Socs. (chmn. 1970—, pres. 1969-74), Can. Soc. Immunology (pres. 1967-69, 79-81), Nat. Com. Immunology (chmn. 1981-90), Royal Can. Inst. (pres. 1988-89), Can. Fedn. Biol. Socs. (chmn. 1976-77), Internat. Council of Sci. Unions (mem. council and assembly 1980-85). Research: characterization of two distinct isotypes of immunoglobulins; hypothesis of tolerance-steered specificity; analysis of the effect of antibody on catalysis by biologically active molecules; 1st description of a murine allotype; analysis of polymorphic gerontological changes in different classes of suppressor cells thymus precursors; isotypes, interleukins, Th1 and Th2 cells, H1 histones, repair capacity, dopamine receptors, insulin receptors and adrenoceptors; development of strategies to alter progression of age-related changes by dietary and pharmacological interventions. Home: 73 Langley Ave, Toronto, ON Canada M4K 1B4 Office: U Toronto-Dept Immunology, 73 Langley Ave, Toronto, ON Canada M4K 1B4

CINDRICH, ROBERT JAMES, judge; b. Avella, Pa., Sept. 22, 1943; s. Anthony Joseph and Stella Dolores Cindrich; m. Bonnie Alice Jones, June 25, 1966; children: Stephen, Scott, Amanda. AB in Polit. Sci., Wittenberg U., 1965; JD magna cum laude, U. Pitts., 1968. Bar: Pa. 1968, U.S. Supreme Ct. 1968, U.S. Dist. Ct. (we. dist.) Pa. 1968, U.S. Ct. Appeals (3d cir.) 1974, U.S. Supreme Ct. 1980, U.S. Tax Ct. 1982. Law clk. to presiding judge U.S. Ct. Appeals (3d cir.), Pitts., 1968-69; asst. trial defender Pub. Defender of Allegheny County, Pitts., 1969-70; asst. dist. atty. Allegheny County, Pitts., 1970-71; ptnr. McVerry, Baxter, Cindrich & Mansmann, Pitts., 1972-78; U.S. Atty. Western Dist. Ct. Pa., Pitts., 1978-81; ptnr. Gondelman, Baxter, Mansmann, McVerry & Cindrich, Pitts., 1981, Mansmann, Cindrich & Titus, Pitts., 1981-94; judge U.S. Dist. Ct. (we. dist.) Pa., 1994—; mem. Pa. Supreme Ct. Procedural Rules Com., Pitts., 1987—. Author: (with others) Criminal Courts Manual, 1975; contbr. articles, revs. to profl. jours. Former chmn. South Side Hosp., Pitts.; bd. dirs. U. Pitts. Med. Ctr. Sgt. USAR, 1968-75. Named Man of Yr. in Law and Govt., Pitts. Jaycees, 1981. Fellow ABA; mem. Pa. Bar Assn., Allegheny County Bar Assn., Assn. Former U.S. Attys., Allegheny Acad. of Trial Lawyers, Order of Coif, U. Pitts. Law Sch. Alumni Assn. (pres. bd. govs. 1984). Democrat. Roman Catholic. Avocations: fishing, hunting. Office: US PO & Courthouse Courtroom #11 Rm 1014 700 Grant St Pittsburgh PA 15219*

CINQUE, THOMAS JOSEPH, dean. Dean Creighton U. Sch. Medicine, Omaha, Nebr., 1992-97; med. dir. edn. Sierra Health Svcs., Inc., Las Vegas, Nev., 1997—; prof. medicine U. Nev. Sch. Medicine. Office: Sierra Health Svcs Inc Med Edn Dept Bldg 2716-326 PO Box 15645 Las Vegas NV 89114-5645

CIOBANU, NICULAE, oncologist, researcher; b. Bucharest, Romania, Feb. 7, 1947; came to U.S., 1978; s. Niculae and Maria (Dimitriu) C.; m. Ellen J. Ferranti, Sept. 7, 1985; children: Christian, Alexandra. Baccalaureat degree, Lyceum Balcescu, Bucharest, 1965; MD, Bucharest Sch. Medicine, 1971. Diplomate Am. Bd. Internal Medicine, Am. Bd. Med. Oncology, Am. Bd. Hematology. Asst. prof. medicine Albert Einstein Sch. Medicine, Bronx, N.Y., 1983-88, assoc. prof. medicine, 1988—; dir. bone marrow transplant program Montefiore Med. Ctr. Albert Einstein Cancer Ctr., Bronx, 1986-92; dir. bone marrow transplant program St. Vincent's Hosp. and Med. Ctr., N.Y.C., 1993-97; med. dir. stem cell transplant program L.I. Coll. Hosp., Bklyn., 1994-98; dir. bone marrow transplant svc. Schneider Children's Hosp., L.I. Jewish Med. Ctr., 1997-98. Contbr. chpts. to books and numerous articles to profl. jours. in field of bone marrow transplantation, immunotherapy with interleukin-2/LAK, infection in immunocompromised host. Recipient Rep. scholarship of Romania Ministry Edn., 1966-71, nat. rsch. award U.S. Dept. Health, 1982-83, spl. fellowship Leukemia Soc. Am., 1983-85. Fellow ACP; mem. Internat. Soc. Exptl. Hematology, Am. Soc. Clin. Oncology, Am. Soc. Hematology, Am. Radium Soc., Am. Assn. Cancer Rsch. Internat. Soc. Hematotherapy and Graft Engring. (founding mem.). Achievements include initiation of bone marrow transplant programs for British Hosp., Montevideo, Uruguay, Instituto De Criopreservacion Y Transplante Medula Osea, Buenos Aires. Office: 10 E 38th St Fl 7 New York NY 10016-0004

CIOC, CHARLES GREGORY, information systems executive; b. Scottsbluff, Nebr., Apr. 16, 1951; s. Charles John and Beatrice Devona C.; children: Christopher, Connor. AA in Bus. Adminstrn., Casper (Wyo.) Coll., 1971; BA in Bus. Adminstrn., Wash. State U., 1973; M in Urban Planning, U. Wash., 1990. Indsl. engr. Boeing, Seattle, 1974-77, database adminstr., 1980-81; database analyst Transp. Sys. Ctr., Cambridge, Mass., 1978-80; systems officer Seafirst Bank, Seattle, 1981-83; airport planner TRA-Arch Engr., Seattle, 1986-90; sr. transp. planner King County Dept. Transp., Seattle, 1990-96, data devel. mgr. Puget Sound Regional Coun., 1997—. Avocations: choral music, archaeology, coaching soccer. Home: 7534 NE Emerald Way Bainbridge Island WA 98110-4054

CIOCIOLA, CECILIA MARY, science education specialist; b. Chester, Pa., Feb. 9, 1946; d. Donato Francis Pasqual and Mary Theresa (Dugan) C. BA, Immaculata Coll., 1975; MA, West Chester U., 1984. Tchr. Archdiocese of Phila., 1964-72, Harrisburg (Pa.) Diocese, 1972-74, Camden (N.J.) Diocese, 1974-76; tchr., elem. sci. chairperson Archdiocese of Phila., 1976-86; ednl. cons. Macmillan Pub. Co., Delran, N.J., 1986-88; program officer PATHS/PRISM, Phila., 1988-90; mgr. spl. programs minority engring., math., sci. program Prime, Inc., Phila., 1988-99; founder, CEO Rubicon Ednl. Asocs.: Sci. Edn. and Info. Tech. Cons., 1998—; dir. partnership and cmty. devel. FOUNDATIONS, Inc.; instr. edn. dept. Chestnut Hill Coll., Phila; mem. tchr. cert. adv. com. Phila. Coll. Pharmacy and Sci.; cons. Delaware County Intermediate Unit, Media, Pa.; chairperson elem. (grades 1-8), sci. com. Phila. Archdiocese, 1985-86, mem., 1984-86; coord. Chester County Cath. Schs.: Computer Edn., Pa., 1982-84, Fed. Nutrition Program, St. Agnes Sch., West Chester, Pa., 1982-84, Justice Edn. Teaching Strategies, St. Agnes Sch., West Chester, 1983-84; mem. Mayor's Telecom. Policy Adv. Com., Phila., 1998—, Phila. 4-H Program Devel. Com., 1998—. Author, editor: (curriculum) Elementary Life and Earth Science, 1984. Mem. adv. com. environ. edn. program Fairmount Pk. Commn., 1998. NSF grantee Operation Primary Phys. Sci., La. State U., 1997—, Project GLOBE, 1997. Mem. AAUW, ASCD, Nat. Sci. Tchrs. Assn., Pa. Biotech. Assn. (edn. coun.), U. of the Scis. in Phila. (sci. edn. adv. com.), Pa. Sci. Tchrs. Assn. Avocations: poetry, country music, reading, photography, fitness. Office: FOUNDATIONS Inc 1st Flr 821 East Gate Dr Mount Laurel NJ 08054

CIOCZEK, HENRYK ANTONI, medical oncologist, internist; b. Lublin, Poland, May 27, 1961; came to U.S., 1987; s. Jan and Marianna (Szyszkowska) C.; m. Anna Wlaz, June 11, 1988. MD, Med. Acad., Lublin, 1985. Surgical intern Teaching Hosp. nr 1, Lublin, 1985-86, resident in neurosurgery, 1986-87; rsch. worker NYU Med. Ctr., N.Y.C., 1987-89, intern in surgery, 1991-92; intern in medicine Flushing (N.Y.) Hosp. Med. Ctr., 1992-93, resident in medicine, 1993-95; fellow in oncology Albert Einstein Cancer Ctr./Montefiore Med. Ctr., 1995-97; physician pvt. practice, 1997—; rsch. coord. Montefiore Med. Ctr./Albert Einstein Cancer Ctr., 1996-97, attending physician, 1997—; attending physician Maimonides Med. Ctr., 1997—, Flushing Hosp. Med. Ctr., 1997—; rsch. coord. Flushing Hosp., 1996-97, del. com. interns and residents, 1993-94; rsch. coord. Harvard U., 1993-94. Author: (in Polish) Intern of Bellevue Hospital N.Y., 1994, Bishop in Stripes - The Life and Martyrdom of God's Servant Wladyslaw Goral 1898-1945, 1998; contbr. articles to profl. jours. Active Student Orgn. Solidarity, Lublin, 1980-85. Recipient Rectors award and Sci. scholar Med. Acad., Lublin, 1982, 84, 85. Mem. ACP, Polish Med. Soc. Club. Avocations: sports, travel, movies, music, history of medicine.

CIOFFI, EUGENE EDWARD, III, educational administrator; b. Somerville, N.J., July 26, 1948; s. Eugene E. and Carmela Agnus (Montenegro) C.; m. Ellen Gertrude Coolbaugh, Sept. 12, 1969; children: Christopher, Daniel. BS in Edn., Bloomsburg U., 1970; MEd, Trenton State Coll., 1973. Cert. sch. adminstr., prin., elem. and secondary tchr., N.J. Chief sch. adminstr. Frelinghuysen Twp. Bd. Edn., Johnsonburg, N.J.; chief sch. adminstr., prin. Frelinghuysen (N.J.) Twp. Bd. Edn., 1994—. Pres. Warren County Spl. Svcs. Sch. Dist. Bd. Edn. Mem. ASCD, Warren County Assn. Sch. Adminstrs., N.J. Assn. Sch. Adminstrs., Warren County Prins. and Suprs. Assn., N.J. Sch. Bds. Assn., Phi Delta Kappa. Office: Frelinghuysen Twp Bd Edn PO Box 421 780 Rt 94 Johnsonburg NJ 07846

CIOFFI, MICHAEL LAWRENCE, lawyer; b. Cin., Feb. 2, 1953; s. Patrick Anthony and Patricia (Schroeder) C.; children: Michael A., David P., Gina M. BA magna cum laude, U. Notre Dame, 1975; JD, U. Cin., 1979. Bar: Ohio 1979, U.S. Dist. Ct. (so. dist.) Ohio 1980, U.S. Dist. Ct. (no. dist.) Ohio 1983, U.S. Ct. Appeals (6th cir.) 1985. Asst. atty. gen. Ohio Atty. Gen., Columbus, 1979-81; from assoc. to ptnr. Frost & Jacobs, Cin., 1981-87; staff v.p., asst. gen. counsel Penn Cen. Corp., Cin., 1988-93; v.p., asst. gen. counsel Am. Fin. Group, Cin., 1993—; adj. prof. law U. Cin. Coll. Law, 1983—. Author: Ohio Pretrial Litigation, 1991; co-author: Sixth Circuit Federal Practice Manual, 1993. Bd. dirs. Charter Com. of Greater Cin., 1985-88. Recipient Goldman Prize for Tchg. Excellence U. Cin. Coll. Law, 1995, Nicholas Longworth Disting. Alumni award, 1996. Mem. ABA, Fed. Bar Assn. (mem. exec. com., pres.1994), Ohio Bar Assn., Cin. Bar Assn. Avocations: tennis, travel. Office: Am Fin Group 1 E 4th St Cincinnati OH 45202-3717

CIOFFI, PATRIZIA, soprano, voice educator, arts consultant; b. Bloomfield, N.J., Feb. 9, 1946; d. Raphael and Musette (Recchia) C.; children: Regina, Jennifer. BA cum laude, Mt. Holyoke, 1998; cert. lang. proficiency, Inst. Lorenzo de Medici, Florence, Italy. Bus. mgr. Whole Theatre Co., Montclair, N.J., 1972-75; founder, exec. dir. New Sch. for Arts/N.J. Opera Inst., Montclair, 1975-92; pvt. tchr. voice, Montclair, 1987—; artistic dir. le voci internazionali, Montclair, 1998—; freelance on-site evaluator, writer, panel mem., cons. Nat. Endowment for Arts, Washington, 1983—; freelance writer, arts cons. to several artists and orgns., N.Y.C., 1991—; tchr. voice Mt. Holyoke Coll., South Hadley, Mass., 1996; career devel. cons. Pro Arte Internat., N.Y.C., 1997—, others; author: le donne che non sorridono mai, the Women Who Never Smile, 1997. Well-known for high vocal range and rendering of heroic Puccini, Verdi, Wagner music, In Questa Reggia, Turandot, Brunhilde's Battle Cry; recorded Petit Messe Solenelle, 1993. Mem. Nat. Italian-Am. Found., leader in preservation of the indigenous style in Italian singing. Fellow Nat. Endowment for Arts, 1982; Mary Vance Young and Frances Perkins scholar Mt. Holyoke Coll., 1995-97; various vocal study grants for study La Scala, Milan, Covent Garden, London, Mrs. Franco Corelli, N.Y.C., 1986—; scholar Lee Strasberg Theatre Inst. Mem. Nat. Assn. Tchrs. Singing, Nat. Opera Assn. Roman Catholic. Avocations: swimming, horseback riding, bike riding, advocate for singer over 35. Fax: 973-744-2292. Office: le voci internazionali 197 Grove St Montclair NJ

CIONGOLI, ALFRED KENNETH, neurologist; b. Phila., Jan. 11, 1943; s. Alfred Anthony and Antoinette Marie (Ragano) C.; m. Barbara, Nov. 22, 1966; children: Adam, Happy, Gregory, Alessandra, Antonio. AB, U. Pa., 1964; DO, Phila. Coll. Osteopathic Med., 1968. Diplomate Am. Bd. Psychiatry & Neurology. Resident in neurology, chief resident neurology unit U. Vt. Coll. Medicine, 1968-73; attending neurologist U. Pa. Med. Sch., Phila., 1974-75; rsch. fellow in neuroimmunology Danish Muscular Sclerosis Soc., Copenhagen, 1973-74, Hosp. U. Pa., Phila., 1975-77; pres. Neurol. Assocs. Vt., Burlington, 1977—; attending neurologist Hosp. U. Pa. Med. Sch., 1975-77; clin. asst. prof. neurology U. Vt. Coll. Medicine, Burlington, 1977-87, clin. assoc. prof., 1987—, dir. Multiple Sclerosis clinic, 1975; pres. Bd. Alumni Dirs. Phila. Coll. Osteopathic Med., 1994—, chmn. internat. fellowship com., 1990—; chmn. com. NIH, 1990—. Apptd. boxing commr. State of Vt., 1982; sr. med. officer U.S. Olympics team, 1986. Recipient Ellis Island Medal of Honor, 1997, Grand Officiale Order Merit Republic Italy, Italian Pres. Scalfaro, 1998. Mem. AMA, Am. Assn. Neurology, Phila. Neurol. Soc., Ethan Allan Club (bd. govs.), Nat. Italian-Am. Found. (sr. v.p. 1992-95, pres. 1996—). Office: Neurol Assn Vt 89 S Williams St Burlington VT 05401-3405

CIPARELLI, PETER FRANCIS, library director; b. Hartford, Conn., Sept. 10, 1951; s. Francis Joseph and Irene Janet (Manning) C.; m. Wendy Jean Jolly, June 28, 1975; children: Jessica, Christopher, Gregory, Angela. BS in Edn., Ctrl. Conn. State U., 1973; MLA, U. R.I., 1980. Libr. II East Hartford (Conn.) Pub. Libr., 1980-82, asst. libr. dir., 1982-85; asst. libr. dir. Manchester (Conn.) Pub. Libr., 1986-93; libr. dir. Rockville (Conn.) Pub. Libr., 1994—. Mem. libr. bd. dirs. Town of Ellington, 1999—. Mem. Eastern Conn. Librs. (treas. 1997—), Bibliomation (bd. dirs. 1996—), Elks. Avocations: videotapes, sports, baseball card collecting, camping. E-mail: rockville.pub.lib@snet.net. Office: Rockville Pub Libr 52 Union St Rockville CT 06066

CIPARICK, CARMEN BEAUCHAMP, state judge; b. N.Y.C., 1942. Grad., Hunter Coll., 1963; JD, St. John's U., 1967; LLD (hon.), CUNY, Queens Coll., 1994. Staff atty. Legal Aid Soc., N.Y.C.; asst. counsel Office of the Judicial Conf., 1969-72; chief law asst. N.Y.C. Criminal Ct., 1972-74; counsel Office of N.Y.C. Adminstrv. Judge, 1974-78; judge N.Y.C. Criminal Ct., 1978-82, N.Y. Supreme Ct, 1982-94; assoc. judge N.Y. State Ct. Appeals, N.Y.C., 1994—; former mem. N.Y. State Commn. Judicial Conduct. Trustee Boricua Coll.; bd. dirs. St. John's U. Sch. of Law Alumni Assn. Named to Hunter Coll. Hall of Fame, 1991. Office: 122 E 42nd St New York NY 10168-0002*

CIPFL, JOSEPH JOHN, JR., university administrator; b. East St. Louis, Ill., Jan. 23, 1945; s. Joseph John and Marguerite (Vogt) C.; m. Linda Louise Williams, June 16, 1967; children Joseph John III, Jennifer Lynn. BS, Ill. State U., 1967; MS, So. Ill. U., 1968, Edn. specialist, 1976; PhD, St. Louis U., 1982. Cert tchr., sch. adminstr., Ill. Tchr. East St. Louis (Ill.) Sch. Dist. 189, 1967-68; tchr. Belleville (Ill.) Sch. Dist. 118, 1968-70, prin., 1970-76, supt., 1976-88; coll. pres. Belleville Area Coll., 1988-97; pres., CEO Ill. Comty. Coll. Bd., Springfield, Ill., 1997—; instr. So. Ill. U., Carbondale, 1976-88, St. Louis (Mo.) U., 1979-82; cons. Il. Adminstrs. Acad., Springfield, 1980-88. Disting. pres. Optimist Club, Belleville, 1981; chmn. of the bd. United Way of Ill., Belleville, 1983, Belleville Econ. Progress, 1985, Bi-county YMCA, 1987. Named Outstanding Educator, Nat. PTA, 1986; recipient Disting. Citizen award Boy Scouts of Am., 1996; named to Coll. of Edn. Hall of Fame, Ill. State U., Normal, 1997. Mem. Am. Assn. C.C.s, Am. Assn. Sch. Adminstrs., Ill. PTA (bd. dirs. 1976-88, life mem. 1980), Ill. Coun. C.C. Pres. (pres. 1988-97), Phi Theta Kappa (life, Shirley B. Gordon award 1997), Phi Delta Kappa. Roman Catholic. Avocations: boating, water skiing, racquetball, antique collector. Office: Ill Comty Coll Bd 401 E Capitol Ave Springfield IL 62701-1711

CIPINKO, SCOTT J., lawyer, general counsel, secretary; b. Chgo., Aug. 24, 1960; s. Morris and Lillian (Gomberg) C.; m. Karen Mandel, May 17, 1987; 1 child, Adam. BA, DePaul U., 1982; JD, Ill. Inst. Technology-Chgo., 1987. Bar: Ill. 1987, U.S. Dist. Ct. (no. dist.) Ill. 1989. Assoc. gen. counsel Office Spl. Dep. Receiver, Chgo., 1987-88; assoc. Garofalo, Hanson, Schreiber & Vandlik, Ltd., Chgo., 1988-89; sec. and gen. counsel Consumer Credit Ins. Assn., Chgo., 1989—. Committeeman Lake County (Ill.) Dem. Party, 1989—. Mem. ABA, Chgo. Bar Assn., Conf. on Consumer Fin., Decalogue Soc. Lawyers, Am. Trial Lawyers Assn., Ill. Bar Assn. Avocation: semi-profession baseball player. Office: Consumer Credit Ins Assn 542 S Dearborn St Ste 400 Chicago IL 60605-1592

CIPLIJAUSKAITE, BIRUTE, humanities educator; b. Kaunas, Lithuania, Apr. 11, 1929; came to U.S., 1957; d. Juozas and Elena (Stelmokaite) C. B.A., Lycee Lituanien Tubingen, 1947; M.A., U. Montreal, 1956; Ph.D., Bryn Mawr Coll., 1960. Permanent mem. Inst. Rsch. in Humanities U. Wis., Madison, 1974, asst. prof., 1961-65, assoc. prof., 1965-68, prof., 1968-73, John Bascom prof., 1973—. Author: La Soledad y la poesia española contemporánea, 1962, El poeta y la poesia, 1966, Baroja, un estilo, 1972, Deber de plenitud: La poesia de Jorge Guillén, 1973, Los noventayochistas y la historia, 1981, La mujer insatisfecha, 1984, La novela femenina contemporánea (1970-85), 1988, Literaturos eskizai, 1992, De signos y significaciones. I: Juegos con a vanguardia, 1999; editor: Luis de Gongora, Sonetos completos, 1969, critical edit., 1981, Jorge Guillén, 1975, (with C. Maurer) La voluntad de humanismo: Homenaje a Juan Marichal, 1990, Novisimos, postnovisimos, clásicos: la poesia de los 80 en España, 1991; translator: Juan Ramón Jiménez, Sidabrinukas ir as, 1982, María Victoria Atencia, Svenciausios Karalienes Ekstazes, 1989, Voces en el silencio: Poesia lituana contemporánea, 1991, Birute Pukeleviciute, Planto, 1994, (with Nicole Laurent-Catrice) Vingt poètes lituaniens d'aujourd'hui, 1997. Guggenheim fellow, 1968. Mem. Assn. For Advancement Baltic Studies (v.p. 1981), Asociación Internacional de Hispanistas. Office: U Wis Inst Rsch in Humanities 1401 Observatory Dr Madison WI 53706-1209

CIPOREN, FRED, publishing executive. V.p., group pub., pub. Pubs. Weekly, N.Y.C.; v.p., group pub. Pubs. Weekly, Lib. Jour., Sch. Lib. Jour., N.Y.C., 1988—. Office: Library Journal 249 W 17th St New York NY 10011-5300*

CIPPARONE, JOSEPHINE MAGNINO, medical/surgical and community health nurse; b. Mason, Mich., Oct. 18, 1931; d. Joseph John and Amelia Mary (Masini) Magnino (dec.); m. Joseph Robert Cipparone, Sept. 12, 1953 (dec.); children: Lori, Teresa, Joseph, Vincent (dec.), Albert. Diploma, Misericordia Sch. Nursing, Milw., 1953; student, Mich. State U. Cert. phlebotemist; cert. in colostomy care. Nurse Phys. Measurements Inc., Lansing, Mich.; staff nurse Roselawn Manor Nursing Ctr., Lansing; sch. nurse, clinic supr. East Lansing (Mich.) Sch. Dist.; nurse Upjohn Healthcare Svcs., East Lansing; mem. hospice care Shoreline Health Care Svcs., Lansing.

CIPRIANI, FRANK ANTHONY, college president; b. N.Y.C., Sept. 28, 1933; s. Domenico and Maria (DiGiesi) C.; m. Judith Pellathay, Aug. 9, 1959; children: Maria, Frank, Michael, Dominique. A.B. in Polit. Sci., Queens Coll., 1955; M.A. in Edn., NYU, 1961, Ph.D., 1969. Adminstrv. asst. to v.p. bus. affairs NYU, 1961-64; prof. history SUNY Farmingdale, 1964, asst. dean, 1964-67, asst. to pres., 1966-69, v.p. adminstrn., 1969-78, pres. coll., 1978—. Chmn. L.I. Regional Adv. Coun. on Higher Edn.; chmn. bd. dirs. Regional Indsl. Tech. Edn. Coun.; chmn. L.I. Regional Ashfill Bd.; trustee L.I. Power Authority; mem. L.I. Bi-County Planning Bd, L.I. Regional Econ. Devel. Coun. Capt. USAF, 1955-57. Mem. Middle States Assn. Colls. and Secondary Schs., Consortium L.I. Italian Ams., Italian Order Merit. Roman Catholic. Office: SUNY Farmingdale Off of Pres Melville Rd Farmingdale NY 11735*

CIPRIANO, PATRICIA ANN, secondary education educator, consultant; b. San Francisco, Apr. 24, 1946; d. Ernest Peter and Claire Patricia (Croak) C. BA in English, Holy Names Coll., Oakland, Calif., 1967; MA in Edn. of Gifted, Calif. State U.-L.A., 1980. Cert. tchr., tchr. gifted, adminstrv. svc., lang. devel. specialist, Calif. Tchr. English, math. Bancroft Jr. High Sch., San Leandro, Calif., 1968-79, 83-85, coord. gifted edn., 1971-79; tchr. English, math., computers San Leandro High Sch., 1979-83, 85-96, mentor tchr., 1991-94, chmn. English dept., 1992-96, coord. gifted and talented edn., 1981-83; tchr. English, social studies, ELD, math. Los Cerritos Mid. Sch., Thousand Oaks, Calif., 1996—, chmn. English dept., 1996—; cons. Calif. State Dept. Edn., various Calif. sch. dists.; dir. Calif. Reading and Lit. Project Policy Bd. Recipient Hon. Svc. award Tchr. of Yr., Bancroft Jr. High Sch. PTA, 1973; bd. dirs. Calif. Curriculum Correlating Coun. Mem. NEA, ASCD, Calif. Assn. for Gifted, World Coun. Gifted and Talented, Cen. Calif. Coun. Tchrs. English (past pres.), Southland Coun. Tchrs. English, Calif. Assn. Tchrs. English (bd. dirs., past pres., disting. svc. award 1996), Nat. Coun. Tchrs. English (bd. dirs.), Unified Assn. Conejo Tchrs., Calif. Tchrs. Assn., Computer Using Educators, Curriculum Study Commn. (bd. dirs.), Delta Kappa Gamma (past pres.). Roman Catholic. Avocations: reading, piano, calligraphy, tennis, photography. Contbr. articles to profl. jours. Office: Los Cerritos Mid Sch 2100 E Avenida De Las Flores Thousand Oaks CA 91362-1530

CIRAFESI, ROBERT J., lawyer; b. Bklyn., Apr. 14, 1942; s. James Vincent and Mildred (McKay) C.; m. Jo-Anne Danek, Aug. 20, 1966; children: Chad, Craig. BA, Rutgers U., 1964, JD, 1967. Bar: N.J. 1967, U.S. Ct. Appeals (3d cir.) 1968. Law clerk to Hon. David Furman Superior Ct., New Brunswick, N.J., 1967-68; asst. U.S. dist. atty. U.S. Atty.'s office, Newark, 1968-70; with Wilentz, Goldman & Spitzer, Woodbridge, N.J., 1970—, ptnr., 1975—. Office: Wilentz Goldman & Spitzer PO Box 10 90 Woodbridge Center Dr Woodbridge NJ 07095-1146

CIRANDO, JOHN ANTHONY, lawyer; b. Syracuse, N.Y., June 25, 1942; s. Daniel John and Anne Marie (Farone) C.; m. Carolyn Joyce Lace, Sept. 17, 1966; children: Lisa Marie, Julie Lynn, Jennifer Mary. BA in History, St. Bonaventure (N.Y.) U., 1963; JD, SUNY, Buffalo, 1966. Bar: N.Y. 1966, U.S. Dist. Ct. (no. dist.) N.Y. 1966, U.S. Dist. Ct. (we. dist.) N.Y. 1994, U.S. Claims Ct. 1991, U.S. Ct. Mil. Appeals 1967, U.S. Ct. Appeals (2d cir.) 1985, U.S. Supreme Ct. 1974. Chief asst. dist. atty. Onondaga County Dist. Atty.'s Office, Syracuse, N.Y., 1971-87; atty. D.J. & J.A. Cirando, Syracuse, 1966—; treas. N.Y. State Dist. Atty.'s Office, 1977-87; chair Govs. Jud. Screening Com. 4th Jud. Dept., 1997—. Pres. bd. dirs. Vera House, Shelter for Women and Children in Crisis, Syracuse, 1988-90; bd. trustees Leukemia Soc. Am., 1995—, asst. sec., 1995-96, sec., 1996—. Capt. JAG, U.S. Army, 1967-71. Mem. N.Y. State Bar Assn. (chair com. on county cts. 1975-78, chair com. on pub. rels. 1979-83), Onondaga County Bar Assn. (bd. dirs. 1974-77, sec. 1979). Office: DJ & JA Cirando 101 S Salina St Ste 1010 Syracuse NY 13202-1357

CIRAULO, STEPHEN JOSEPH, nurse, anesthetist; b. Danville, Pa., Feb. 25, 1960; s. Leonard Joseph and Mary Louise (Purpuri) C. Diploma, Geisinger Med. Ctr. Sch. Nursing, Danville, 1980; cert., Sch of Anesthesia for Nurses Univ. Health Ctr. Pitts., 1983; BA Mgmt. Health Scis., Ottawa U., Kansas City, 1997. Nursing asst. Geisinger Med. Ctr., Danville, 1978-80; staff RN, part time charge RN cardiac care unit Williamsport (Pa.) Hosp., 1980-81; asst. gastroenterology research group Presbyn. Univ. Hosp., Pitts., 1982-83; staff nurse anesthetist dept. anesthesia Duke U. Med. Ctr., Durham, N.C., 1983-90; with Anesthesia Anytime, Winston-Salem, N.C., 1990, Nash Gen. Hosp., Rocky Mount, N.C., 1991-92; staff nurse anesthetist, mem. epidural analgesia svc. Nash Gen. Hosp., 1991-92; staff nurse anesthetist Wake Anesthesiology Assocs., Inc., Raleigh, N.C., 1992—; mem. coun. for nurse anesthetists dept. anesthesia Duke U. Med. Ctr., Durham, 1985-89; Wake Anesthesiology Assocs., Inc., 1992—. Charter mem. Outstanding Young Ams., 1988; mem. Duke U. Artists Series Adv. Bd., 1994-97, Friends of Duke artist series devel. com. 1997—; bd. dirs. Whitehall Homeowners Assn., Raleigh, N.C., 1995—, sec., 1996—. Mem. Am. Assn. Nurse Anesthetists, N.C. Assn. Nurse Anesthetists (bylaws com. 1984-86, chmn. fin. com. 1986-88, mem. fin. com. 1988-95, fall program com. 1988, spring program speaker 1990, treas. 1991-93, pres. 1994-95, chmn. history com. 1995-97, mem. strategic planning com. 1995-97), Triangle Transplant Recipient Internat. Orgn. (charter), Triangle Bus. and Profl. Guild, Internat. Platform Assn., Am. Assn. Nurse Anesthetists. Republican. Avocations: music, art, weight lifting, traveling, gardening. Home and Office: 1710 Falls Church Rd Raleigh NC 27609-3531

CIRELLO, JOHN, utility and engineering company executive; b. Bound Brook, N.J., Apr. 17, 1943; s. Fiore Avanti and Assunta C.; m. Sherron Anne Thomas, July 31, 1965; children: Assunta Anne, Elizabeth Rose, Sherron Marie. BS, Rutgers U., 1965, MS, 1971, PhD, 1975. Registered profl. engr., N.J., Pa. Engr. Calif. Dept. Water, L.A., 1965-66, U.S. Army Corps of Engrs., Ft. Belvoir, Va., 1966-68, Balt. Gas and Elec., 1968-69; rschr. Rutgers Water Resources Inst., New Brunswick, N.J., 1969-71; asst. prof. Rutgers U., New Brunswick, 1971-80; pres. Princeton Aqua Sci., Edison, N.J., 1980-85; v.p. IT Corp., Edison, N.J., 1985-88; v.p. ea. region Chem. Waste Mgmt., Inc., Princeton, N.J., 1988-92; pres. Metcalf & Eddy Svcs., Inc., Branchburg, N.J., 1992-95; Environ. Engring. Svcs. Inc., 1995-96; pres., CEO Fla. Water Svcs. Corp., 1995—; exec. v.p. Minn. P&L, Duluth, Minn., 1995—; pres.'s coun. U. Fla.; mem. dean's exec. coun. U. Ctrl. Fla. Editor (tng. manuals) Land Application of Effluents & Sludges, 1976, Ultimate Disposal of Organic and Inorganic Sludges, 1976, Water and Wastewater Polishing and Rennovation Techniques, 1976; co-editor (tng. manual) Construction and Environmental Inspectors Training Manual, 1977; contbr. articles to profl. jours. Mem. Bd. Adjustment, Bound Brook, N.J., 1976-81; councilman, pres., Bound Brook Town Coun., 1981-87; chmn. Dem. com. Bound Brook, 1982-86; Grad. Leadership Fla. Class XVI. Capt. U.S. Army Engr. Corps, 1966-68. Recipient award N.J. Water Pollution Control Assn., 1990. Mem. ASCE, Water Environ. Fedn., Am. Chem. Soc., Fla. Water Works Assn., Nat. Assn. Water Cos., Water Utilities Exec. Coun., Fla. State C. of C. (bd. dirs. 1997—). Roman Catholic. Avocations: antique and classic cars, golf. Home: 540 Winding Creek Pl Longwood FL 32779-6119 Office: Fla Water Svcs Corp PO Box 609520 Orlando FL 32860-9520

CIRESI, MICHAEL VINCENT, lawyer; b. St. Paul, Apr. 18, 1946; s. Samuel Vincent and Selena Marie (Bloom) C.; m. Ann Ciresi; children: Dominic, Adam. BBA, U. St. Thomas; JD, U. Minn. Bar: Minn. 1971, U.S. Dist. Ct. Minn. 1974, U.S. Ct. Appeals (8th cir.) 1971, U.S. Supreme Ct. 1981, U.S. Ct. Appeals (2d cir.) 1986, U.S. Ct. Appeals (9th cir.) 1987, U.S. Ct. Appeals (10th cir.) 1990, N.Y. 1995, fed. cir., 1998, U.S. Ct. Appeals (5th cir.) 1999. Assoc. Robins, Kaplan, Miller & Ciresi, Mpls., 1971-78, ptnr., 1978—, exec. bd., 1983—, chmn. exec. bd., 1995—; adv. bd. Ctr. Advanced Litigation, Nottingham (Eng.) Law Sch. Trustee U. St. Thomas. Named Product Liability Lawyer of Yr., Australian Nat. Consumer Law Assn., 1989, Trial Lawyer of Yr. Trial Lawyers for Public Justice Found., 1998. Mem. ABA, Minn. State Bar Assn., Hennepin County Bar Assn., Ramsey County Bar Assn., Assn. Trial Lawyers Am., Am. Bd. Trial Advocates, Internat. Bar. Assn., Inner Circle of Advocates, Trial Lawyers for Pub. Justice (bd. dirs.). Roman Catholic. Avocation: sports, U.S. history. Home: 1247 Culligan Ln Saint Paul MN 55118-4151 Office: Robins Kaplan Miller & Ciresi 2800 Lasalle Plz Minneapolis MN 55402

CIRKER, HAYWARD, publisher; b. N.Y.C., June 1, 1917; s. Solomon and Sadie (Goodman) C.; m. Blanche Brodsky, Aug. 11, 1939; children: Steven, Victoria Cirker Fremont. B.S. in Social Studies, Coll. City N.Y., 1936. Salesman Crown Pubs., N.Y.C., 1936-43; pres. Dover Publs. Inc., N.Y.C., 1943—. Served with USN, 1945. Home: 199 Woodside Dr Hewlett NY 11557-2417 Office: Dover Publications Inc 31 E 2nd St Mineola NY 11501-3582

CIRONE, WILLIAM JOSEPH, educational administrator; b. Bklyn., Dec. 27, 1937; s. Joseph Nicholas and Marie Ann (Basile) C.; m. Barbara Jane Skirkie, Dec. 22, 1962; 1 child, Peter Craig. BA, Providence Coll., 1959; MA, NYU, 1960; adminstrv. cert., U. Calif., Santa Barbara, 1977. Tchr. N.Y.C. Pub. Schs., 1960-68; dir. product devel. ednl. divsn. Mead Corp., Atlanta, 1968-70, dir. mktg., 1970-73; founder, dir. Ctr. Cmty. Edn. and Citizen Participation, Santa Barbara, Calif., 1973-82; supt. schs. Santa Barbara County, 1983—; vis. fellow Chisholm Inst. Tech., Melbourne, Australia, 1986; vis. scholar Ctr. for xcellence Tenn. State U., 1986. Contbg. editor New Designs for Youth Development, 1984-97. Bd. dirs. S.B. Cmty. Found., Cmty. Action Commn., 1973-81, Cmty. Resource Info. Svc., 1978-82, Nat. Partnership in Edn., 1998—; bd. dirs., sec. Pvt. Industry Coun., Santa Barbara, 1983-89; bd. dirs. Industry Edn. Coun. Santa Barbara, 1983—, pres., 1990; bd. dirs. Coun. of Alcoholism and Drug Abuse, 1998—, Santa Barbara Lung Assn., 1983-87, Philip Francis Siff Ednl. Found., 1986—; bd. dirs. Impact II, 1989—, pres., 1993—; bd. dirs. Nat. Comm. Edn. Assn., 1989-92, pres., 1990; regional chair Calif. County Supt. Assn., 1990—, bd. dirs. media and values, 1989-92; hon. bd. dirs. So. Coast Spl. Olympics; mem. Gov.'s Commn. on Earthquake Hazards, 1981; mem. state bd. Common Cause, 1974-77, organizer and 1st state chmn., Ga., 1970-73; mem. voter accessibility adv. bd. Santa Barbara County, 1986—; mem. adv. bd. CALM, Peace Resource Ctr., Marymount Sch., Women's Cmty. Bldg., Jodi House, Girl Scouts U.S.; comdrs. cmty. liaison com. Vandenberg AFB; mem. Access Theatre; mem. Hon. Commn. for Goleta Hosp.; mem. campaign cabinet Santa Barbara United Way, 1991, 98. Recipient Smallheiser award United Fedn. Tchrs., 1968, Hon. Svc. award 15th Dist. PTA, 1979, 81, Intercongregation Orgn. Project Action award, 1995, Anti-Defamation League Santa Barbara Disting. Svc. award, 1996, Meritorious Svc. award Cmty. Action Com., Santa Barbara, 1981, Ind. Living Resource Ctr., 1985, Hon. Svc. award Calif. State PTA, 1995, 99 for '99 award, Santa Barbara C. of C., 1999; named Calif. Cmty. Educator of Yr., Calif. Cmty. Edn. Assn., 1984, Pub. Servant of Yr., Santa Barbara County, 1987. Mem. World Future Soc. (life), Am. Assn. Sch. Adminstrs., Assn. Calif. Sch. Adminstrs., So. Coast Coord. Coun. (past chmn., past exec. com.), Nat. Soc. Fundraising Execs., Automobile Assn. Am. (So. Calif. adv. bd.), Phi Delta Kappa. Democrat. Unitarian. Home: 953 Elk Grove Ln Solvang CA 93463-9608 Office: PO Box 6307 Santa Barbara CA 93160-6307

CIROU, JOSEPH PHILIP, priest, organist, educator; b. Chgo., Nov. 3, 1943; s. Ernest Henry and Virginia (Milord) C. BA, St. Mary of the Lake Sem., Mundelein, Ill., 1965, STB, 1967, Sacred Theology Licentiate, 1969; MA, Govs. State U., 1985. Ordained to ministry Byzantine-Bielarusian Cath. Ch. as deacon, 1968, as priest, 1969. Deacon St. John Berchmans' Ch., Chgo., 1968-69; asst. pastor St. Mary of the Assumption Ch., Chgo., 1969-76, St. Gerald Majella Ch., Markham, Ill., 1976-81, St. Irenaeus Ch., Park Forest, Ill., 1981-87, St. Florian Ch., Chgo., 1987-92; adminstr. Christ the Redeemer Ch., Chgo., 1987-94; pastor St. Aelred Ecumenical Cath. Ch., Atlanta, 1997—; ch. musician, Chgo. and Atlanta, 1957—; tchr. music Cath. Sch. System, Chgo., 1980-82, 89—; mem. Cons. on Ecumenical Hymnody, 1970-80. Editor Johannine Hymnal, 1970; contbr. articles to profl. jours. Mem. Ea. Cath. Clergy Assn. (sec. Chgo. chpt. 1972-76, 88-90, treas. 1976-80, pres. 1990-94), Am. Cath. Press (bd. dirs. 1989—). Democrat. Home: 1111 Clairemont Ave Apt K6 Decatur GA 30030-1216

CIRUTI, JOAN ESTELLE, Spanish language and literature educator; b. Ponchatouia, La., Aug. 8, 1930; d. Joseph Aloysius and Olga (Jordan) C. B.A., Southeastern La. Coll., 1950; M.A., U. Okla, 1954; Ph.D., Tulane U., 1959. Instr. modern langs U. Okla., Norman, 1957-59; asst. prof. U. Okla, Norman, 1959-63; research asst. U.S. Office Edn., Washington, 1959-60; asst. prof. Spanish Mt. Holyoke Coll., South Hadley, Mass., 1963-66; assoc. prof. Mt Holyoke Coll., South Hadley, Mass., 1966-71; chmn. dept. Spanish Mt. Holyoke Coll., South Hadley, Mass., 1965-71; prof. Mt. Holyoke Coll., South Hadley, Mass., 1971-77; Helen Day Gould prof. Spanish Mt. Holyoke Coll., South Hadley, Mass., 1977-92, prof. emeritus Spanish, 1992—, dean studies, 1971-74, chmn. dept. Spanish and Italian, 1975-81, 85-86; cons. Ednl. Testing Service, 1968-79. Co-author: Modern Spanish, 2d edit., 1966, Continuing Spanish, 1967; contbg. editor, Handbook of Latin-American Studies, vol. 28, 1966, Handbook of Latin-American Studies vol. 30, 1968, Handbook of Latin-American Studies, vol. 32, 1970. Ciruti Ctr. for Fgn. Langs. classroom bldg. named in her honor, Mt. Holyoke Coll., 1992; named Disting. Alumnus Southeastern La. Coll., 1973. Mem. Am. Council on Teaching Fgn. Langs., MLA (nomination adv. com. 1962-64, nominating com. 1979-80, acad. freedom com. 1980-83), Latin Am. Studies Assn. (mem. steering com. consortium Latin Am. studies programs 1969-72, com. on women 1973-74, nominating com. 1975), New Eng. Council Latin Am. Studies, Am. Assn. Tchrs. Spanish and Portuguese, AAUW. Home: 111 Spencer Dr Amherst MA 01002

CISKI, LESLIE A., government official; b. Elizabethon, Tenn., Mar. 1, 1945; d. Robert P. and Goldie Carie (Phipps) C.; children: Monti Ciski, Heather Henderson. A in Law, U. Md., 1981, B in Bus. and Mgmt., 1983; MPA, Troy State U., 1998; cmty. bldg. exec. leadership cert., Harvard U., 1998. Resident initiatives coord. HUD, Atlanta, 1989-95, urban revitalization specialist, 1995-96, cmty. rels. and involvement specialist, 1996-98; cmty. builder HUD, Las Vegas, 1998—. Editor (newsletter) HUD newsletters and circulars, 1989-92. Rep. Assisted Nat. Assn. Neighborhoods Nat. conf., Atlanta, 1994. Mem. ASPA, Fed. Emergency Mgmt. Agy., Habitat for Humanity. Avocations: reading, traveling, community, politics. E-mail: LACiski914@aol.com. Office: HUD 333 N Rancho Dr Las Vegas NV 89106

CISNEROS, HENRY G., former federal official, broadcast executive; b. San Antonio, June 11, 1947; s. J. George and Elvira (Munguia) C.; m. Mary Alice Perez; children: Teresa Angelica, Mercedes Christina, John Paul. BA, Tex. A&M U., 1969, M. Urban and Regional Planning, 1970; MPA, Harvard U., 1973; D.Public Adminstrn., George Washington U., 1975. Adminstrv. asst. to city mgr. San Antonio, 1968, Bryan, Tex., 1969-70; asst. dir. dept. model cities San Antonio, 1969-70; asst. to exec. v.p. Nat. League Cities, Washington, 1970-71; White House fellow asst. Sec. of HEW, Washington, 1971-72; teaching asst. dept. urban studies and planning M.I.T., 1972; mem. City Coun., San Antonio, 1975-81; mayor City of San Antonio, 1981-89; sec. U.S. Dept. HUD, Washington, 1993-97; pres., COO, Univision

Comm., Inc., L.A., 1997—. Trustee City Pub. Service Bd., City Water Bd., San Antonio; chmn. Fire and Police Pension Fund; mem. strategy council Nat. Democratic Party; mem. Twentieth Century Fund Ednl. Task Force, Eisenhower Found., com. on visual arts Tex. A & M U., bus. adv. com. Trinity U.; tri-chmn. United San Antonio; bd. dirs. San Antonio Symphony Soc., 1974-75. Recipient Thomas Jefferson award for pub. architecture AIA, 1995. Office: Univision Comm Inc 1999 Ave Of Stars Ste 6050 Los Angeles CA 90067-6022*

CISNEROS, JOSE A., historical site administrator. Supt. Gettysburg National Military Park, Gettysburg, Pa. Office: Gettysburg Nat Mil Pk PO Box 1080 Gettysburg PA 17325-1080

CISNEROS, SANDRA, poet, short story writer, essayist; b. Chgo., Dec. 20, 1954. BA, Loyola U., 1976. Author: (books) The House On Mango Street, 1983 (Am. Book award Columbus Found. 1985), Woman Hollering Creek and Other Stories, 1991, (children's) Hairs=Pelitos, 1994, (poetry) Bad Boys, 1980, The Rodrigo Poems, 1985, My Wicked, Wicked Ways, 1987, Loose Women, 1994, Hist Story, La Casa en Mango Street, 1994, El Arroyo de la Llorona, 1996. Fellow NEA, 1982, 87, MacArthur fellow, 1995; recipient Lannan Found. Lit. award, 1991. Office: Ramdom House Pub 201 E 50th St Fl 22D New York NY 10022-7703 Home: Susan Bergholz Agy 17 W 10th St # 5 New York NY 10011-8746*

CISSELL, JAMES CHARLES, lawyer; b. Cleve., May 29, 1940; s. Robert Francis and Helen Cecelia (Freeman) C; children: Denise, Helene-Marie, Suzanne, James. Student, Sophia U., Tokyo, 1961; AB, Xavier U., 1962; JD, U. Cin., 1966; postgrad., Ohio State U., 1973-74; D. Tech. Letters, Cin. Tech. Coll., 1979. Bar: Ohio 1966, U.S. Dist. Ct. (so. dist.) Ohio 1967, U.S. Ct. Appeals (6th cir.) 1978, U.S. Supreme Ct. 1980, U.S. Dist. Ct. (ea. dist.) Ky. 1981. Pvt. practice law, 1966-78, 82—; asst. atty. gen. State of Ohio, 1971-74; first v.p. Cin. Bd. Park Commrs., 1973-74; vice mayor City of Cin., 1976-77; U.S. atty. So. Dist. Ohio, Cin., 1978-82; adj. instr. law No. Ky. U., 1982-86; sec. Nat. Assn. Former U.S. attys., 1998-99. Author: Oil and Gas Law in Ohio, 1964, Federal Criminal Trials, 4th edit., 1996; editor Proving Federal Crimes. Gen. chmn. amateur pub. links championship U.S. Golf Assn., 1987; mem. coun. City of Cin., 1974-78, 85-87, 89-92; clk of cts., Hamilton County, 1992—, commr. Recreation Bd. Cin., 1974, Planning Bd. Cin., 1977; pres. Ohio Clk. of Cts. Assn., 1998; mem. Ohio Bicentennial Commn., 1998—; mem. Ohio Cts. Futures Commn., 1998—. Ford Found. fellow Ohio State U., 1973-74. Mem. Ohio Bar Assn., Cin. Bar Assn., Fed. Bar Assn., Former U.S. Attys. Assn. (sec. 1998-99). Avocations: golf, jogging. Home: 201B Belvedere 3900 Rose Hl Cincinnati OH 45229 Office: 602 Main St Ste 320 Cincinnati OH 45202-2521

CISSELL, WILLIAM BERNARD, health studies educator; b. Fancy Farm, Ky., Apr. 21, 1941; s. James S. and Lucille Marie C.; m. Mary Ellen Siebe, Aug. 26, 1967; 1 child, Lisa Kyung Mi. BS, So. Ill. U., Carbondale, 1967; MS in Pub. Health, UCLA, 1970; PhD, So. Ill. U., 1977. Cert. health edn. specialist. Curriculum coord. Dept. Def. Schs., 1972-75; asst. prin. Teagu (Korea) Am. Sch., 1975-77; asst. prof. U. Tex., Austin, 1977-79, East Tenn. State U., Johnson City, 1979-84; assoc. prof. East Tenn. State U., 1984-89; prof., chmn. health studies Tex. Woman's U., Denton, 1989-98, prof., 1997—; co-dir. Tex. Statewide Coordinated Statement of Need Project, 1997—; assoc. dir. Prairie Area Health Edn. Ctr.; mem. joint com. on grad. standards Am. Assn. for Health Edn. and Soc. for Pub. Health Edn., 1993-96; treas. Commn. Nat. Com. for Health Edn. Credentialing, 1989-91; mem. Nat. Task Force for Prep. and Practice of Health Educators, 1986-88; pres. Tenn./Amazonas Ptnrs. of the Ams., 1987-88, Tenn./Amazonas Venezuela Ptnrs. of the Ams., 1981-82. Co-editor: Community Orgn., 1990, (newsletter) SHESIGN, 1989-92, Tenn. So. Pub. Health Edn., 1985-88. Chmn. sch. health com. Am. Lung Assn., Dallas, 1990-92; mem. evaluation com. Smoke Free Class 2000, 1991-93; mem. school site task force Am. Heart Assn., 1985-90. Served with USMC, 1961-64. Mem. Tex. Assn. Health, Phys. Edn., Recreation and Dance (chair cmty. health sect. 1993), Soc. Pub. Health Edn. (historian 1990-92, chair nominating and leadership devel. com. 1991-92, trustee 1995-97, disting. fellow award 1996), Soc. Pub. Health Edn. and Am. Assn. for Health Edn. (baccalaureate approval process com. 1993—), Tenn. Soc. Pub. Health Edn. (pres. 1987-88), Tex. Soc. Pub. Health Edn. (pres. 1995-96, Helen Hill Disting. Svc. award 1994, Past Pres. award 1995, Dorothy Huskey Disting. Career award 1997), Golden Key Honor Soc. (co-advisor 1992-97), Phi Kappa Phi, Eta Sigma Gamma (co-advisor Alpha Phi chpt. 1992—, disting. fellow 1997), Denton Breakfast Club (pres.-elect 1999), Kiwanis Internat. (sponsor, U. North Tex. Cir. K 1995-98), Divsn. 39, Tex./Okla. Dist. Kiwanis Internat. (sec. 1993-94), TAMS Key Club (sponsor 1998—). Office: Tex Woman's U Dept of Health Studies PO Box 425499 Denton TX 76204-5499

CISZAK, LYNN MARIE, city planner; b. Dec. 21, 1967; d. James E. and Jane M. (Clarke) C. BA, SUNY, Geneseo, 1990; MS, So. Conn. State U., 1995. Dept. head Staples, Inc., Westchester County, N.Y., 1990-93; city planner City of Bridgeport, Conn., 1993—; sec. bd. dirs. Bridgeport Neighborhood Housing and Comml. Svcs., Inc., 1995—. Docent Beardsley Zoo, Bridgeport, 1996—. Mem. Am. Planning Assn., Planners Network, Leadership Greater Bridgeport (alumni). Office: City of Bridgeport 45 Lyon Ter Rm 212 Bridgeport CT 06604-4060

CITARDI, MATTIO H., business analyst, project manager, researcher; b. N.Y.C., Jan. 20, 1966; s. Mattio and Timotea G. Citardi; m. Ann Marie Delli Pizzi, June 27, 1993; 1 child, Daniel James. BS in Biology, Manhattan Coll., 1989; MS in Computer Sci., Pace U., 1992; postgrad., L.I. U., 1996—. Chemist Pepsico Inc., Valhalla, N.Y., 1985-88, Gen. Foods Corp., Tarrytown, N.Y., 1988-89; analytical chemist, system mgr., lab. automation specialist Am. Cyanamid Co., Pearl River, N.Y., 1989-94; bus. project mgr. IT Barr Labs., Blauvelt, N.Y., 1994—. Co-author: Validation of Two Zymark Batch Dissolution System in a QC Lab, Managing a Robotics Laboratory in a QC Environment; contbr. articles to profl. jours. Mem. ACM, Am. Assn. Pharm. Scientists, Am. Chem. Soc., Am. Mgmt. Assn., Project Mgmt. Inst. Republican. Roman Catholic. Achievements include research in new technologies, networking and analytical method development; robotics automation systems and Laboratory Information Management System; co-development of the algorithm to find longest up sequence (LUP) in a series of data points. Office: Barr Labs Inc Bradely Corp Park 300 Corporate Dr Blauvelt NY 10913-1144

CITINO, SCOTT BRADLEY, wildlife veterinarian; b. Oct. 13, 1956. MS, U. Notre Dame, 1979; DVM, Ohio State U., 1983. Head dept. vet. scis. Miami (Fla.) Metro Zoo, 1984-90; resident in zool. medicine Nat. Zool. Pk., Smithsonian Instn., Washington, 1983-84, staff veterinarian, hosp. adminstr., 1990-93; staff veterinarian White Oak Conservation Ctr., Yulee, Fla., 1993—. E-mail: scottc@wo.gilman.com. Office: White Oak Conservation Ctr 3823 Owens Rd Yulee FL 32097-2145

CITRON, DAVID SANFORD, physician; b. Atlanta, Jan. 8, 1920; s. Morris and Ida (Levine) C.; m. Doris Berman, Feb. 14, 1946; children: Michael, Dennis, Lynn, Steven. A.B., U.N.C.-Chapel Hill, 1941, cert. in medicine, 1943; M.D., Washington U., St. Louis, 1944. Lic. physician, N.C. cert. Am. Bd. Internal Medicine, Am. Bd. Family Practice. Intern Barnes Hosp., St. Louis, 1944-45; resident USPHS Hosp., Kirkwood, Mo., 1946-49, Boston, 1949-52; gen. practice medicine Charlotte, N.C., 1952-73; dir. family practice residency Charlotte Meml. Hosp. & Med. Ctr., 1973-84, dir. med. edn., 1984-87; mem. N.C. Bd. Med. Examiners, 1974-81, 1984-87; bd. dirs. Nat. Bd. Med. Examiners, 1981-95. Served with USPHS, 1946-52. Recipient Disting. Service award U.N.C. Sch. Medicine, 1975. Fellow ACP; mem. Nat. Acad. Sci., Inst. Medicine, AMA, N.C. Med. Soc., Mecklenburg County Med. Soc. (pres. 1972-73). Democrat. Jewish. Home: 6363 E Placita Divina Tucson AZ 85750-0954

CITTONE, HENRY ARON, hotel and restaurant management educator; b. Istanbul, Turkey, May 15, 1937; s. Joseph and Debrah (Benbanaste) C.; m. Liliane Robert, Oct. 2, 1965; children: Henry Joseph, Marc Ely. BA, Coll. St. Michel, 1956; student, Trade and Tech. Coll., L.A., 1971; MS, U. Houston, 1990; postgrad. in edn., Fla. Atlantic U., Boca Raton, 1993-94. Food svc. mgr. U. So. Calif., L.A., 1971; mgr. food and beverage Sheraton Poste Inn, Cherry Hill, N.J., 1972-73; resident mgr. Aruba Caribbean Hotel, Netherlands, Antilles, 1973-74, Lima (Peru) Sheraton Hotel, 1974-76; dir. food and beverage Bahia Mar Hotel, Ft. Lauderdale, Fla., 1978-79, Maison Dupuy, New Orleans, 1979-81, Virgin Isle Hotel, St. Thomas, 1981-84; asst. prof. hotel and restaurant mgmt. Galveston Coll. (Tex.), 1984-90; prof. Morehead (Ky.) State U., 1990-92; instr. Coll. V.I., 1983-84, Houston C.C., 1985-90; mem. adj. faculty North Miami (Fla.) Johnson & Wales U., 1994. With Israeli Army, 1956-59. Recipient Cert. Hotal Adminstr. Designation award Ednl. Inst. AH & MA, 1986. Mem. Nat. Restaurant Assn., Am. Hotel and Motel Assn., Internat. Hotel Sales Mgmt. Assn., Internat. Soc. Food and Beverage Execs., Coun. on Hotel, Restaurant, and Instnl. Edn., CHRIE (internat. exch. com.), Conrad Hilton Coll. Alumni Assn. (Disting. Hospitality Educator of Yr. 1988). Address: PO Box 3208 Alpine WY 83128-3208

CIULLA, JOANNE BRIDGETT, business ethics educator; b. Rochester, N.Y., June 16, 1952; d. Andrew Joseph and Corrine Margaret (Christiano) C.; m. René Petrus Franciscus Kanters, Dec. 15, 1990. BA in Philosophy, U. Md., 1973; MA in Philosophy, U. Del., 1975; PhD in Philosophy, Temple U., 1985. Adj. asst. prof. La Salle U., Phila., 1975-84; fellow in bus. and ethics Harvard U., Cambridge, Mass., 1984-86; sr. fellow Wharton Sch. U. Pa., Phila., 1986-71; Coston Family chair in leadership and ethics Jepson Sch. of Leadership Studies U. Richmond, Va., 1991—; cons. bus. ethics and leadership, pvt. practice, Cambridge, Phila. Richmond, 1984—. Editor (books) Jour. of Bus. Ethics, 1992—, Ethics, the Heart of Leadership, 1998; mem. editl. bd. Bus. Ethics Quarterly, Bus. Ethics: A European Quarterly, 1991—. Mem. Soc. for Bus. Ethics, Acad. Mgmt. Office: U Richmond Jepson Sch Richmond VA 23173

CIULLO, ROSEMARY, psychologist; b. Chgo.. BA, U. Ill., Chgo., 1974; MA, Gov.'s State U., University Park, Ill., 1977; PsyD with high distinction, Forest Inst. Profl. Psychology, 1986. Pvt. practice Ill. Mem. APA, Ill. Psychol. Assn., Orthopsychiatry.

CIURCZAK, ALEXIS, librarian; b. Long Island, N.Y., Feb. 13, 1950; d. Alexander Daniel and Catherine Ann (Frangipane) C. BA Art History magna cum laude, U. Calif., L.A., 1971; MA Libr. Sci., San Jose State U., 1975; cert. tchr. ESL, U. Calif., Irvine, 1985. Intern IBM Rsch. Libr., San Jose, Calif., 1974-75; tech. asst. San Bernardino Valley Coll. Libr., Calif., 1975; tech. svcs. librarian Palomar Coll., San Marcos, Calif., 1975-78, pub. svcs. librarian, 1978-81, libr. dir., 1981-86, pub. svcs. librarian, 1987—, instr. Libr. Technology Cert. Program, 1975—; exchange librarian Fulham Pub. Libr., London, 1986-87; coord. San Diego C.C. Consortium Semester-in-London Am. Inst. Fgn. Study, 1988-89. Mem. ALA, San Diego Libr. Svcs. com., Calif. Libr. Media Educators Assn., Patronato por Niños, Kosciuszko Found., So. Calif. Tech. Processes Group, Pacific Coast Coun. Latin Am. Studies, Libros, Reforma, Libr. Assn. (British), Calif. Libr. Assn., Calif. Tchrs. Assn., Phi Beta Kappa, Beta Phi Mu. Office: Palomar CC 1140 W Mission Rd San Marcos CA 92069-1415

CIVELLO, ANTHONY NED, retail drug company executive, pharmacist; b. Pitts., Aug. 27, 1944; s. Joseph N. and Rose (Calbone) C.; m. Colleen M. McCarthy, July 26, 1969; 1 child, Erin Rose. BS, U. Pitts., 1967. Lic. pharmacist, Pa. Asst. store mgr. Thrift Drug Co., Pitts., 1968, store mgr., 1968-75, dist. mgr., 1975-80, v.p. loss prevention and security, 1980-85, v.p. facilities planning and constrn., 1985, sr. v.p. adminstrn., 1985-86, sr. v.p. ops., 1986-87, exec. v.p. retail ops., 1987—, pres. of stores, 1993—; pres., CEO, chmn. Kerr Drug, Inc., Pitts., N.C., 1997—; bd. dirs. Kerr Drug Inc. Account exec. United Way, Pitts., 1982-85, chmn. retail sect., 1988; bd. visitors U. N.C. Sch. Pharmacy; mem. grad. sch. bus. U. Pitts. Assoc. Program, 1985—; bd. visitors Sch. Pharmacy U. Pitts., 1988; mem. Corp. Leadership Coun. St. Margaret Meml. Hosp.; mem. program com. Allegheny County Spl. Olympics; bd. dirs. Family House, Inc., Oakland Cath. H.S., 1999 Spl. Olympic Workd Games, N.C. Mem. Am. Mgmt. Assn., Nat. Assn. Chain Drug Stores. Republican. Roman Catholic. Avocation: jogging. Office: Kerr Drug Inc 2522 S Tricenter Blvd Durham NC 27713-1852

CIVITELLO-JOY, LINDA JOAN, association executive; b. Sacramento, Jan. 21, 1951; d. Theodore Edward and Dorothy Mae (McCarnes) Civitello; m. David Franklin Joy, Nov. 14, 1981; children: Aileen F. Joy, Nicholas E. Joy. BA, Antioch West U., 1976; MA in Polit. Sci., San Francisco State U., 1985. Exec. dir. Tri-Cities Child Devel., Fremont, Calif., 1974-76; cmty. svcs. liaison U. Calif., San Francisco, 1976-91; sr. v.p. McClaughlin Young, San Francisco, 1991-93; exec. dir. Am. Lung Assn. San Francisco and San Mateo, Daly City, Calif., 1993—; bd. dirs. Am. Lung Assn. Contbr. articles to profl. jours. Mem. Am. Soc. Assn. Execs. Roman Catholic. E-mail: LindaCJ@alafsm.Org. Home: 3455 Sacramento St San Francisco CA 94118-1913 Office: Am Lung Assn 2171 Junipero Serra Blvd Daly City CA 94014-1906

CIZEK, DAVID JOHN, sales engineer, small business owner; b. Chgo., Sept. 29, 1959; s. John Jacob and Cecelia Ursula (Shway) C.; m. Kimberly Ann Kral, May 12, 1984. BSEE, U. Ill., 1981. Asst. sales engr. control divsn. Westinghouse Electric Co., Chgo., 1981-83; product line engr. control divsn. Westinghouse Electric Co., Fayetteville, N.C., 1983-85; sales engr. field sales divsn. Westinghouse Electric Co., Chgo., 1985-86, aerospace and def. automation specialist, 1987-88, engr. distbn. support sales, 1988-94; field sales divsn. sales engr. Cutler-Hammer, 1994-95; pres., owner Lakeridge Electric Supply Co., Inc., Romeoville, Ill., 1995—. Mem. U. Ill. Alumni Assn., Girl Scouts of Am., Kappa Sigma Alumni Assn. Republican. Presbyterian. Avocations: real estate investing, fishing, hunting, tennis. Home: 8409 Willow West Dr Willow Springs IL 60480-1139 Office: Lakeridge Electric Supply 734 Oakridge Dr Romeoville IL 60446

CIZEK, JOHN GARY, safety and fire engineer; b. St. Louis, Sept. 16, 1948; s. John Ernst and Ann Margaret (Seith) C.; m. Carolyn Marie Haas, Dec. 4, 1971; children: Laura Suzanne, John David. BSCE, U. Mo., 1971. Registered profl. engr.; cert. safety profl. Loss prevention engr. Factory Mutual Engring. Assn., St. Louis, 1971-76; safety engr. Diamond Shamrock Corp., Cleve., 1977-80; from corp. safety specialist to mgr. safety Diamond Shamrock Corp., Dallas, 1980-87; cons. safety and fire protection, asst. v.p. M&M Protection Cons., Houston, 1987-90, v.p., 1990—, energy and chem. industry practice leader, 1997-98; mem. risk control strategies group Marsh Inc., Houston, 1997-98. Mem. AIChE, Am. Soc. Safety Engrs., Soc. Fire Protection Engr. Lutheran. Office: Marsh Inc Risk Control Strategies Group 1000 Louisiana St Ste 4000 Houston TX 77002-5021

CIZIK, ROBERT, manufacturing company executive; b. Scranton, Pa., Apr. 4, 1931; s. John and Anna (Paraska) C.; m. Jane Morin, Oct. 3, 1953; children: Robert Morin, Jan Catherine, Paula Jane, Gregory Alan, Peter Nicholas. BS, U. Conn., 1953; MBA, Harvard U., 1958; LLD (hon.), Kenyon Coll., 1983. Acct. Price Waterhouse & Co. (CPAs), N.Y.C., 1953-54, 56; fin. analyst Exxon U.S.A., N.J., 1958-61; exec. asst. Cooper Industries, Inc., Houston, 1961-63, treas., 1963-64, contr., 1964-67, v.p. planning, 1967-69, exec. v.p., 1969-73, pres., 1973-92, COO, 1973-75, CEO, 1975-95, chmn., 1983-96; propr. Cizik Interests, Houston, 1996—; dir. Am. Indsl. Ptnrs., 1996-98; adv. dir. Wingate Ptnrs., 1994—; chmn. bd. dirs. Easco, Inc., 1997-98; chmn. bd. dirs. Stanadyne Automotive, Koppers Industries; bd. dirs. Harris Corp., Temple Inland, Air Products and Chems., Inc.; mem. Bus. Roundtable, 1978-95; mem. host com. Houston Econ. Summit Meeting, 1990. Bd. dirs. Assocs. Harvard Bus. Sch., Boston, 1984-96; mem. Tex. Bus. and Edn. Coalition, 1991-94; chmn. Heartstrings Benefit, Design Industries Found. for AIDS, 1991-92; mem. nat. adv. coun., trustee Tex. Heart Inst.; mem. devel. bd. U. Tex. Houston Health Sci. Ctr.; campaign co-chair Wortham Theater Ctr., 1981-83, United Way of Tex., Gulf Coast, 1994-95. 1st lt. USAF, 1954-56. Recipient Gen. Maurice Hirsch award Bus. Com. for Arts, 1984, CEO of Yr. bronze award Fin. World Mag., 1987, CEO of Decade bronze award in Indsl. Equipment Cos., 1988, Masterson award Houston Grand Opera, 1998; named Best CEO in Machinery Industry, Wall St. Transcript, 1980, 81, 83, 86, 87, 88, 89, 90-91, Internat. Exec. of Yr., Greater Houston Partnership and Houston World Trade Assn., 1990. Mem. NAM (chmn. 1992-93), Elec. Mfrs. Club (bd. govs. 1984—, pres. 1990-92), River Oaks Country Club, Forum Club Houston (founding), Houston Ctr. Office: Cizik Interests Chase Tower 600 Travis St Ste 3628 Houston TX 77002-2910

CIZZA, JOHN ANTHONY, insurance executive; b. Utica, N.Y., Oct. 22, 1952; s. Louis Pasquale and Dolores Prudence (Dieglio) C.; m. Barbara Ellen Hansen, Nov. 27, 1982. BS, Clarkson U., 1974; A in Risk Mgmt., Ins. Inst., 1979. Underwriter Utica Nat. Ins. Group, New Hartford, N.Y., 1974-77, supr. underwriter, 1977-78, supr. nat. accts., 1978-79; casualty mgr. Providence (R.I.) Wash. Ins., 1979-81, regional casualty mgr., 1981-82; underwriter Am. Re-Ins. Co., Chgo., 1982-84, sr. underwriter, 1984-86, dir. unit mgr., 1986-89, asst. v.p., 1989-92; v.p. Am-Re Mgrs., Chgo., 1992-94; v.p., regional mgr. Am.-Re Mgrs., Dallas, 1994-97; ctrl. regional mgr. Am.-Re Mgrs., Chgo., 1997-98, Munich Am. RiskPtnrs., 1998—. Roman Catholic. Avocations: photography, cooking, music, motorcycling. Office: Munich Am Risk Ptnrs 10 S Wacker Dr Ste 1800 Chicago IL 60606-7407

CLAAR, VICTOR VYRON, economics educator; s. Herbert Ellsworth and Marcille Elaine (Staton) C.; m. Elizabeth Greer Oswalt. BA in Bus. Adminstrn., Houghton Coll., 1987, postgrad. math., 1991; MA in Econs., W.Va. U., 1995. Grad. tchg. asst. W.Va. U., Morgantown, 1994-98, grad. rsch. asst., 1997-98; vis. prof. econs. Houghton (N.Y.) Coll., 1999—; referee Jour. Pub. Econs.; pres. Thompson's Econs. Club, Morgantown, 1995-96; discussant Allied Social Sci. Assns., Chgo., 1998. Author: survey report for Regional Rsch. Inst., 1998; contbr. articles to profl. jours. Cantor, mem. choir Trinity Episcopal Ch., Morgantown, 1996-98; mem. evangelism com. Trinity Episcopal Ch., 1998; charter mem. Brotherhood St. Andrew, Trinity Episcopal Ch., 1998-99. Presidential scholar Houghton Coll.; Swiger Supplemental fellow W.Va. U. Mem. Am. Econs. Assn., Econometric Soc., So. Econ. Assn. (presenter, discussant), Ea. Econ. Assn., Assn. Christian Economists, Omicron Delta Epsilon (grad.). Office: W Va U Coll Business and Econs Morgantown WV 26506-6025

CLAASSEN, W(ALTER) MARSHALL, employment company executive; b. St. Paul, Jan. 16, 1943; s. Walter Marshall and Marie Christine (Petersen) C.; m. Nancy Rector Alcock, Mar. 2, 1974; children: Katherine, Walter. BA, U. Mo., 1966, BJ, 1966. Sr. adminstr. Honeywell, Inc., Chgo., 1968-74; pers. dir. Lyon-Healy, div. of CBS, Inc., Chgo., 1974-78; mgr., corp. placement CF Industries, Long Grove, Ill., 1978-82; mgr. of recruiting Newark Electronics, Chgo., 1983-84; dir. human resources Swift, div. of Reichold Chem., Downers Grove, Ill., 1984-86, ECM, Inc., Schaumburg, Ill., 1986-87; pres. GBX, Inc., dba Express Personnel Svcs. of Vernon Hills, Ill. and Express Pers. Svcs. of Palatine,, Ill., 1988—. Bd. dirs. Elk Grove-Schaumburg Mental Health Ctr., 1975-77, Pvt. Industry Coun. of Lake County, Waukegan, Ill., 1990-96, chmn., 1994-96; bd. dirs. Pvt. Industry Coun. Found., 1992—. Lt.(j.g.) USNR, 1966-68. Recipient Circle of Excellence award, 1992—. Mem. No. Ill. Bus. Assn., Libertyville-Vernon Hills C. of C., Lake County C. of C., Lincolnshire C. of C., Arlington Heights C. of C., Univ. Mo. Alumni Assn., Phi Delta Theta. Republican. Quaker. Avocations: skiing, fly fishing, scuba diving. Home: 25030 N Pawnee Rd Barrington IL 60010-1380 Office: Express Personnel Svcs 977 Lakeview Pkwy Ste 190 Vernon Hills IL 60061

CLABAUGH, ELMER EUGENE, JR., lawyer; b. Anaheim, Calif., Sept. 18, 1927; s. Elmer Eugene and Eleanor Margaret (Heitshusen) C.; m. Donna Marie Organ, Dec. 19, 1960 (div.); children: Christopher C., Matthew M. BBA cum laude, Woodbury U.; BA summa cum laude, Claremont McKenna Coll., 1958; JD, Stanford U., 1961. Bar: Calif. 1961, U.S. Dist. Ct. (cen. dist.) Calif., U.S. Ct. Appeals (9th cir.) 1961, U.S. Supreme Ct. 1971. With fgn. svc. U.S. Dept. State, Jerusalem and Tel Aviv, 1951-53, Pub. Adminstrn. Svc., El Salvador, Ethiopia, U.S., 1953-57; dep. dist. atty. Ventura County, Calif., 1961-62; pvt. practice, Ventura, Calif., 1962-97; mem. Hathaway, Clabaugh, Perrett and Webster and predecessors, 1962-79, Clabaugh & Perloff, Ventura, 1979-97; state inheritance tax referee, 1968-78, ret. Bd. dirs. San Antonio Water Conservation Dist., Ventura Community Meml. Hosp., 1964-80; trustee Ojai Unified Sch. Dist., 1974-79; bd. dirs. Ventura County Found. for Parks and Harbors, 1982-96, Ventura County Maritime Mus., 1982-94. With USCGR, 1944-46, USMCR, 1946-48. Mem. NRA, Calif. Bar Assn., Safari Club Internat., Mason, Shriners, Phi Alpha Delta. Republican.

CLACK, JERRY, classics educator; b. N.Y.C., July 22, 1926; s. Christopher Thrower and Mildred Taylor (VanDyke) C. AB, Princeton U., 1946, MA, 1958; PhD, U. Pitts., 1962; MA, Duquesne U., Pitts., 1977. Documents officer U.S. Nat. Commn. for UNESCO, 1946-52; exec. dir. Allegheny County chpt. Nat. Found., Pitts., 1953-68; asst. prof. dept. classics Duquesne U., Pitts., 1968-71, assoc. prof., 1971-75, prof., 1975—, chmn. dept., 1973-75, 80-83, mem. preprofl. health com., 1970-76, mem. univ. library com., 1979-93, mem. univ. due process, core curriculum, arts and scis. curriculum coms., 1986-94, mem. univ. promotion and tenure com., 1988-90. Editor: The Classical World, 1977-93, Anthology of Hellenistic Poetry, 1982, Meleager: The Poems, 1992, Asclepiades of Samos and Leonidas of Tarentum: The Poems, 1999; mem. editl. bd. Duquesne Univ. Press, 1991-94; author books, articles, revs. in field. Pres. Western Pa. Pub. Health Council, 1967; v.p. Western Pa. Council World Federalists, 1965-88, treas., 1987—; mem. U.S. del. to 3d UNESCO Gen. Conf., Florence, Italy, 4th UNESCO Gen. Conf., Paris. Mem. Classical Assn. Pitts. and Vicinity (treas. 1970-78, sec. 1988—), Pa. Classical Assn. (treas. 1977—), Classical Assn. Atlantic States (pres. 1987, exec. com. 1974—, 2d v.p. 1975, 1st v.p. 1976, exec. dir. 1993—), Am. Philol. Assn. (chmn. working group editors classical jours. 1982-93, chmn. com. regional classical orgns. 1986-95), Vergilian Soc. Am. (trustee 1985-87), Phi Sigma Iota, Delta Phi Alpha, Alpha Epsilon Delta, Phi Alpha Theta. Home: 5920 Kentucky Ave Pittsburgh PA 15232-2824 Office: Duquesne U Department of Classics Pittsburgh PA 15282-1741

CLAES, DANIEL JOHN, physician; b. Glendale, Calif., Dec. 3, 1931; s. John Vernon and Claribel (Fleming) C.; AB magna cum laude, Harvard U., 1953, MD cum laude, 1957; m. Gayla Christine Blasdel, Jan. 19, 1974. Intern, UCLA, 1957-58; Bowyer Found. fellow for rsch. in medicine, L.A., 1958-61; pvt. practice specializing in diabetes, L.A., 1962—; biotech. cons. SIRA Techs., 1995—; v.p. Am. Eye Bank Found., 1978-83, pres., 1983—, dir. rsch., 1980—, chmn., CEO 1995—; pres. Heuristic Corp., 1981—. Mem. L.A. Mus. Art, 1960—. Mem. AMA, AAAS, Calif. Med. Assn., L.A. County Med. Assn., Am. Diabetes Assn. (profl. coun. on immunology, immunogenetics and transplantation), Internat. Diabetes Fedn., Internat. Pancreas & Islet Transplant Assn. Clubs: Harvard and Harvard Med. Sch. of So. Calif.; Royal Commonwealth (London). Contbr. papers on diabetes mellitus, computers in medicine to profl. lit. Office: Am Eyebank Found 15237 W Sunset Blvd Ste 108 Pacific Palisades CA 90272-3690

CLAES, GAYLA CHRISTINE, writer, editorial consultant; b. L.A., Oct. 17, 1946; d. Henry George and Glorya Desiree (Curran) Blasdel; m. Daniel John Claes, Jan. 19, 1974. AB magna cum laude, Harvard U., 1968; postgrad., Oxford (Eng.) U., 1971; MA, McGill U., Montreal, 1975. Adminstrv. asst. U. So. Calif., L.A., 1968-70; teaching asst. English lit. McGill U., Montreal, 1970-71; editorial dir. Internat. Cons. Group, L.A., 1972-78; v.p. Gaylee Corp., L.A., 1978-81, CEO, 1981-88; writer, cons. L.A. and Paris, 1988—; dir. pub. rels. Centre Internat. for the Performing Arts, Paris and L.A., 1991—. Author: (play) Berta of Hungary, 1972, (novel) Christopher Derring, 1990; contbr. articles to lit. and sci. jours. Mem. Harvard-Radcliffe Club of So. Calif., Royal Commonwealth Soc. (London).

CLAFLIN, ARTHUR CARY, lawyer; b. Bowling Green, Ohio, July 7, 1950; s. Edward Scott and Mona Sophia (Cretney) C.; m. Gretchen Elaine Anders, May 31, 1975; children: Rachel Anders, Emily Anders. BA magna cum laude, Wesleyan U., 1972; JD, Yale U., 1975. Bar: Wash. 1975, U.S. Dist. Ct. (we. dist.) Wash. 1975, U.S. Dist. Ct. (ea. dist.) Wash. 1981, U.S. Ct. Appeals (9th cir.) 1979, U.S. Ct. Appeals (5th cir.) 1982. Assoc. Bogle & Gates, Seattle, 1975-81, ptnr., 1981-99; ptnr. Claflin & Christensen, Seattle, 1999—. Mem. Phi Beta Kappa. Presbyterian. Office: Claflin & Christensen 1200 5th Ave Ste 1902 Seattle WA 98101

CLAFLIN, JAMES ROBERT, pediatrician, allergist; b. Apr. 30, 1946; m. Marcee Claflin; children: James Sean (dec.), Brian Scott (dec.), Susan Nicole, Timothy Lynn. Student, Northwestern State Coll.; MD, U. Okla., 1971. Diplomate Am. Bd. Pediatrics, Am. Bd. Allergy Immunology. Intern U. Tex. Med. Br., Galveston, 1971-72; advanced through grades to lt. col. USAF, 1969-84, chief pediatric svcs. Goodfellow AFB, 1972-73, 75-77; chief pediatric svcs. and hosp. svcs. RAF Upper Heyford USAF, Eng., 1977-80; chief allergy and clin. immunology USAF, Carswell AFB, 1982-84; fellow allergy/immunology Willford Hall USAF Med. Ctr., Lackland AFB, Tex., 1980-82; ret. USAF, 1984; clin. asst. prof. pediatrics, Oklahoma U.; presenter in field. Contbr. articles to profl. jours. advisor child welfare com. Tom

Green County, 1976-77; mem. child welfare com. RAF, Upper Heyford, Eng., 1978-80; mem. sch. and pub. health com. Tarrant County Med. Soc., 1984-85, chmn., 1986-87, publs. com., 1988-89, religion and meml. com., 1989; mem. quality assurance and infectious disease coms. Cook-Ft. Worth Children's Hosp., 1986-89; v.p. Brenham State Sch. Parent Assn., 1987-88; pres. Parents Assn. for the Retarded of Tex., 1987-88; chmn. cmty. conscience com. Wedgwood Bapt. Ch. Recipient Svc. award Am. Diabetes Assn., 1976. Fellow Am. Acad. Pediatrics, Am. Coll. Allergy (mem. com. on allergic rhinitis, mem. com. on adverse reactions to food 1991-96), Am. Acad. Allergy; mem. AMA, Am. Coll. Allergy, Asthma and Immunology (adverse reaction to food com., bylaws com. 1998—), Okla. County Med. Soc. (pub. rels. com. 1991-95, ad hoc com. RBRVS conversion 1991, grievance com. 1991-94, quality of care com. 1991—), Okla. State Med. Assn. (medicare carrier adv. com. 1992-95, coun. on med. svcs. 1998—), Okla. Allergy and Asthma Soc. (pres. 1998—). Home: 750 NE 13th St Oklahoma City OK 73104-5051

CLAFLIN, ROBERT MALDEN, retired veterinary educator, university dean; b. Flint, Mich., Nov. 11, 1921; s. Robert Hugh and Kathryn Elizabeth (Ruhl) C.; m. Barbara Ellen Garrison, June 21, 1957; children—Deborah Ann, Blair Lawrence, Kathryn Elizabeth. D.V.M., Mich. State U., 1952; M.S., Purdue U., 1956, Ph.D., 1958. Mem. faculty Purdue U., Lafayette, Ind., 1952—, prof. vet. pathology Sch. Vet. Sci. and Medicine, 1959—; prof. emeritus Purdue U., 1988—; head dept. vet. microbiology, pathology and pub. health Purdue U., Lafayette, Ind., 1959-86, assoc. dean Sch. Vet. Medicine, 1986-88; assoc. dean emeritus Purdue U., 1988-89. Mem. AVMA, Internat. Acad. Pathology, Conf. Research Workers Animal Diseases N.A., Sigma Xi, Phi Zeta, Phi Kappa Phi. Office: Purdue U Dean Sch Vet Med Lafayette IN 47907*

CLAGETT, ARTHUR F(RANK), psychologist, sociologist, qualitative research writer, retired sociology educator; b. Little Rock, Dec. 3, 1916; s. A.F. and Mary Gertrude (Bell) C.; m. Dorothy Ruth Pinckard, Dec. 23, 1954. BA in Chemistry, Baylor U., 1943; MA in Psychology, U. Ark., 1957; PhD in Sociology, La. State U., 1968. Shift chemist Celanese Corp., Cumberland, Md., 1942-44; shift supr. penicillin prodn. Comml. Solvents Corp., Terre Haute, Ind., 1944-45; rsch. supr. streptomycin pilot plant Schenley Labs., Lawrenceburg, Ind., 1945-48; asst. mgr. Clagett's Feed and Seed Store, Donna, Tex., 1948-50; med. svc. rep. Blue Line Chem. Co., St. Louis, 1952-56; prison classification officer La. State Penitentiary, 1956-59, classification supr. new admissions, 1959-60; instl. sponsor inmate Sober Alcohol Anonymous Group; organizer Hew Hope Alcohol Anonymous Group; condr. group counseling studies; counseling psychologist Baker, La., 1960-64; asst. prof. sociology Lamar State Coll. Tech., Beaumont, Tex., 1964-66; assoc. prof. sociology Stephen F. Austin State U., 1968-83, prof., 1983-85, prof. emeritus, 1986—; consulting sociologist, social psychologist, criminologist, Nacogdoches, Tex., 1986-91; qualitative rsch. writer, 1992—. Mem. editl. bd. Quar. Jour. Ideology, 1982-93; contbr. numerous articles to profl. jours. including Jour. Offender Counseling, Internat. Rev. Mod. Sociol., Jour. Offender Rehab., Criminal Justice Policy Rev. Mem. univ. rsch. coun., 1973-75, Sch. Liberal Arts coun., 1970-71. Mem. Am. Assn. Individual Investors, Internat. Platform Assn., So. Sociol. Soc., Am. Soc. Criminology, Am. Acad. Criminal Justice Scis., Am. Sociol. Assn. (chaired annual meetings, presented 33 papers). Methodist. Avocations: reading, internet, classical music. Home and Office: 619 E Oak Ln Nacogdoches TX 75961-4771

CLAGETT, BRICE MCADOO, lawyer, writer; b. Washington, July 6, 1933; s. Brice and Sarah Fleming (McAdoo) C.; m. Virginia Lawrence Parker, Sept. 18, 1965; children: John Brice, Ann Calvert Brooke; m. Diana Wharton Sinkler Knop, July 26, 1987. AB summa cum laude, Princeton U., 1954; postgrad. U. Allahabad (India), 1954-55; JD magna cum laude, Harvard U., 1958. Bar: D.C. 1958, U.S. Supreme Ct. 1962. Assoc., Covington & Burling, Washington, 1958-67, ptnr., 1967—; jud. counsellor Cambodian delegation to Internat. Ct. Justice, 1960-62; legal adviser Transition Team U.S. Dept. State, 1980-81; mem. nat. steering com. U.S. Iran Claimants Com., 1982—; adv. bd. Inst. for Transnat. Arbitration, 1989—; mem. lawyers com. Ctr. Individual Rights, 1992—; mem. records preservation access com. Fedn. Geneal. Socs., 1993-97. Bd. advisors Nat. Trust for Hist. Preservation 1978-81; Clagett family com. Chesapeake Bay Found., 1982—; trustee Md. Hist. Trust, 1971-78, chmn., 1972-78, Md. State House Trust, 1972-76, Md. Environ. Trust, 1978—, vice chmn., 1981-85, chmn. 1985-89; mem. Internat. Human Rights Law Group del. to Romania, 1990; bd. dirs. Chester-Sassafras Found., 1985-89; trustee New Eng. Hist. Geneal. Soc., 1989-92, 1995-98, Tudor Place Found., 1992-96; counsellor to the Pres. Gen., Soc. of the Cin., 1988-98, solicitor, 1998—; mem. adv. coun. Accokeek Found., 1989-91, trustee, 1991-94; mem. arbitration com. U.S. Coun. Internat. Bus., 1989—. Commdr. Royal Order Cambodia, 1962. Recipient Cert. Disting. Citizens State of Md., 1978. Mem. Am. Soc. Internat. Law, Am. Law Inst., Am. Arbitration Assn. (panel of arbitrators 1990—, large complex case panel arbitrators 1993—, internat. panel arbitrators 1997—), Internat. Law Assn., Washington Inst. Fgn. Affairs, Federalist Soc., Sons Confederate Vets., Mil. Order Stars and Bars, So. Md. Soc., Phi Beta Kappa. Republican. Episcopalian. Clubs: Met., City Tavern, Harvard (N.Y.C.), Soc. Cin. Md., Marlborough Hunt (Upper Marlboro, Md.), Radnor (Pa.) Hunt. Co-author: The Valuation of Property in International Law, vol. 4, 1987, An Illustrated History of St. Albans School, 1981; bd. editors: Harvard Law Review, 1956-58; contbr. numerous articles to legal, geneal. and hist. jours. Home: Holly Hill PO Box 86 Friendship MD 20758-0086 also: 3331 O St NW Washington DC 20007-2814 Office: Covington & Burling PO Box 7566 1201 Pennsylvania Ave NW Washington DC 20044

CLAGETT, DIANA WHARTON SINKLER, museum docent; b. Phila., Aug. 24, 1943; d. James Mauran Rhodes and Sarah Brinton (Wentz) Sinkler; m. Peter John Knop, Nov. 23, 1966 (div.); children: Alexandra Brinton, Peter Rhodes Quast, William James Wharton; m. Brice McAdoo Clagett, July 26, 1987. BA, George Wash. U., 1966. Rsch. asst. Nat. Investigations Com. on Aerial Phenomena, Washington, 1966-69; docent Asia Hall Smithsonian Instn., Washington, 1982-83, docent Sackler Gallery, 1989—, docent Freer Gallery, 1993—; propr. Georgian Antiques and Decorative Arts, Washington, 1983—; bd. dirs. Sinkler Corp., Wentz Corp.; mem. Smithsonian Ednl. Vol. Adv. Bd., 1990-93. Mem. bd. devel. Hosp. for Sick Children, Washington, 1980—, vice chmn. bd. devel., 1985-86, co-chmn. flower and garden festival, 1988-90; mem. bd. devel. Children's Hearing and Speech Ctr., Washington, 1988—; mem. women's com. Phila. Acad. Fine Arts, 1980—; mem. alumni bd. Foxcroft Sch., Middleburg, Va., 1983-86; trustee The McLean Sch., 1993-96. Mem. City Tavern Club (bd. govs. 1990-98), Radnor Hunt Club (racing com.), Acorn Club, Evermay Club Georgetown, New Scotland Garden Club (pres. 1993-94). Avocations: gardening, Asian art. Home: Holly Hill PO Box 86 Friendship MD 20758 also: 3331 O St NW Washington DC 20007-2814

CLAGUE, CHRISTOPHER K(ARRAN), economics educator; b. Washington, May 28, 1938; s. Ewan and Dorothy Clague; m. Monique Weston, June 9, 1960 (div. 1982); children: Holly Weston, Heather Whipple. BA, Swarthmore Coll., 1960; PhD, Harvard U., 1966. Instr. Harvard U., Cambridge, Mass., 1965-67; sr. staff economist Coun. Econ. Advisers, Washington, 1967-68; asst. prof. U. Md., College Park, 1968-71, assoc. prof., 1971-79, prof. econs., 1979-98; dept. chmn., 1980-82; cons. World Bank, Washington, 1977-80, 83, 95-96; dir. rsch. IRIS, 1990-97. Co-author: Capital Utilization, 1981; editor: Institutions and Economic Development, 1997; co-editor: The Emergence of Market Economics in Eastern Europe, 1992; bd. editors So. Econ. Jour., 1977-79. Mem. Am. Econ. Assn., Conf. on Income and Wealth (exec. com. 1983-87). Democrat. Home: 2647 Ocean Front Walk San Diego CA 92109-8242 Office: San Diego State U San Diego CA 92182-4485

CLAGUE, DAVID A., geologist; b. Phila., Aug. 3, 1948; married; 1 child. PhD in Earth Sci., Scripps Inst. Oceanography, 1974. With nat. rsch. coun. U.S. Geol. Survey, 1974-75, rsch. geologist, 1979-96; asst. prof. geology Middleberry Coll., 1975-79; scientist-in-charge Hawaiian Volcano Obs., 1991-96; dir. rsch. an devel. Monetary Bay Aquarium Rsch. Inst., 1996—. Fellow Geol. Soc. Am., Am. Geophysical Union. Office: Monterey Bay Aquarium PO Box 628 7700 Sandholdt Rd Moss Landing CA 95039-0628*

CLAIBORNE, LIZ (ELISABETH CLAIBORNE ORTENBERG), fashion designer; b. Brussels, Mar. 31, 1929; came to U.S., 1939; d. Omer Villere and Louise Carol (Fenner) C.; m. Arthur Ortenberg, July 5, 1954; 1 son by previous marriage, Alexander G. Schultz. Student, Art Sch., Brussels, 1948-49, Academie, Nice, France, 1950; DFA, R.I. Sch. Design, 1991. Asst. Tina Lesser, N.Y.C., 1951-52, Omar Khayam, Ben Reig, Inc., N.Y.C., 1953; designer Juniorite, N.Y.C., 1954-60, Dan Keller, N.Y.C., 1960-76, Youth Guild Inc., N.Y.C., 1976-89; designer, pres., chmn. Liz Claiborne Inc., N.Y.C., 1985-89, pres., 1976-89, chmn., chief oper. officer, until 1989; chmn. Liz Claiborne Cosmetics, 1985-89, cons.; guest lectr. Fashion Inst. Tech., Parsons Sch. Design; bd. dirs. Coun. of Am. Fashion Designers, Fire Island Lighthouse Restoration Com. Recipient Designer of Yr. award Palciode Hierro, Mexico City, 1976, Designer of Yr. award Dayton Co., Mpls., 1978, Ann. Disting. in Design award Marshall Field's, 1985, One Co. Makes a Difference award Fashion Inst. Tech., 1985, award Coun. Fashion Designers, 1986, Gordon Grand Fellowship award Yale U., 1989, Jr. Achievement award Nat. Bus. Hall of Fame, 1990, Frederick A.P. Barnard award Barnard Coll., 1991, Hon. Doctorate, R.I. Sch. of Design, 1991; named to Nat. Sales Hall of Fame, 1991. Mem. Fashion Group. Roman Catholic. *

CLAIBORNE, WILLIAM, journalist; b. N.Y.C., 1936. Diploma in English, Hobart Coll., 1959. Reporter Rochester Democrat & Chronicle, 1959-66; city editor L.I. Suffolk Sun, 1966-69; nat. corr. The Washington Post, Washington, 1969-74, N.Y.C. bur. chief, 1974-77, Jerusalem corr., 1978-82, New Delhi corr., 1982-85, Johannesburg corr., 1986-90, Toronto corr., 1990-92, nat. corr., 1992-94, L.A. corr., 1994-97, Chgo. bur. chief, 1997—. Office: The Washington Post 1150 15th St NW Washington DC 20071-0001

CLAIR, THEODORE NAT, educational psychologist; b. Stockton, Calif., Apr. 19, 1929; s. Peter David and Sara Renee (Silverman) C.; A.A., U. Calif. at Berkeley, 1949, A.B., 1950; M.S., U. So. Calif., 1953, M.Ed., 1963, Ed.D., 1969; m. Laura Gold, June 19, 1961; children: Shari, Judith. Tchr., counselor Los Angeles City Schs., 1957-63; psychologist Alamitos Sch. Dist., Garden Grove, Calif., 1963-64, Arcadia (Calif.) Unified Sch. Dist., 1964-65; head psychologist Wiseburn Sch. Dist., Hawthorne, Calif., 1966-69; asst. prof. spl. edn., coordinator sch. psychology program U. Iowa, Iowa City, 1969-72; dir. pupil personnel services Orcutt (Calif.) Union Sch. Dist., 1972-73; adminstr. Mt. Diablo Unified Sch. Dist., 1973-77; program dir., psychologist San Mateo County Office of Edn., Redwood City, 1977-91; assoc. prof. John F. Kennedy U. Sch. Mgmt., 1975-77; pvt. practice as ednl. psychologist and marriage and family counselor, Menlo Park, Calif., 1978—, Menlo Park, Calif., 1977-93, dir. Peninsula Vocat. Rehab. Inst., 1978—; psychologist Coll. Counseling Svc., Menlo Pk., 1992—, Calif. Pacific Hosp., San Francisco, 1993—. Served with USNR, 1952-54. Mem. APA, Nat. Assn. Sch. Psychologists, Calif. Assn. Marriage and Family Counselors, Nat. Rehab. Assn, Palo Alto B'nai B'rith Club (pres.). Author: Phenylketonuria and Some Other Inborn Errors of Amino Acid Metabolism, 1971; editor Jour. Calif. Ednl. Psychologists, 1992-94; contbr. articles to profl. jours. Home and Office: 56 Willow Rd Menlo Park CA 94025-3654

CLAIRMONT, WILLIAM EDWARD, developer; b. Walhalla, N.D., Jan. 2, 1926; s. Emil O. and Mae E. (Bisenius) C.; student N.D. State U., 1948-49; m. Patricia Ann Filben, Oct. 7, 1950; children: Stephen, Julie, Cynthia, Nancy. Founder, William Clairmont, Inc., Bismarck, N.D., 1949, owner, 1949—; chmn. bd. First Southwest Bank (N.D.), 1975-89, Grant County State Bank, Carson, N.D., 1981-85; land developer, Bismarck; owner farm, N.D. Mem. City Council, Walhalla, 1955-56; owner ranch, irrigation farm, Costa Rica, 1975-83; owner, pres. Country West Real Estate, 1978—; mem. exec. com. bd. regents U. Mary, Bismarck, chmn. bd., 1980-81; trustee Bismarck State Coll. Found.. Served with USMCR, 1944-46. Mem. N.D. Assoc. Gen. Contractors (dir. 1964-72, pres. 1971). Home: 1938 Santa Gertrudis Dr Bismarck ND 58501-0865 Office: 1720 Burnt Boat Dr Bismarck ND 58501-0806

CLAMME, MARVIN LESLIE, recording engineer, electronic engineer; b. Hartford City, Ind., May 28, 1953. BSEET, Purdue U., 1976. Electronic technician engr. Holzer Audio Engring. Co., Van Nuys, Calif., 1976-77; electronic technician Audio Industries Corp., L.A., 1977-85; maintenance technician, rec. engr. Britannia Studios, Hollywood, Calif., 1985-90, The Way Internat., Knoxville, Ohio, 1985-90; svc. mgr. Carlin Audio and Video, Dayton, Ohio, 1990—. Inventor in field. Office: Carlin Audio & Video 930 E Dorothy Ln Dayton OH 45419-2000

CLAMPITT, SUSAN, federal agency administrator; b. Perth Amboy, N.J., Oct. 15, 1940. BA, Rutgers U., 1962; MS, Bank St. Coll. Edn., 1972; postgrad., Radcliffe Coll., 1998. Curator edn. Corcoran Gallery Art, Washington, 1962; curator Montclair (N.J.) Art Mus., 1965-67; assoc. dir. pub. info. Mus. Modern Art, N.Y.C., 1967-70; elem., middle sch. tchr. Little Red Sch. House, N.Y.C., 1971-75; dir. grad. programs in mus. edn. Bank St. Coll. Edn., N.Y.C., 1973-81; exec. prodr. children's programming WNYC Radio and TV, N.Y.C., 1986-88; owner Clampitt Assocs.: Planning/Mgmt./Exec. Search, N.Y.C., Washington, 1981-93; dir. women's appts. and arts and humanities appts. The White House-Exec. Office Pres., Washington, 1993, 97; dep. chmn. for program Nat. Endowment for the Arts, Washington, 1993-97; assoc. adminstr. for mgmt. and workplace programs U.S. Gen. Svcs. Adminstrn., Washington, 1997-98, assoc. adminstr. child care, 1998—. Bd. dirs., mem. adv. com. Arena Stage, Children's Def. Fund, INFORM, Internat. Youth Found., WETA Radio and TV, Smithsonian Instn.; vice chmn. Children's Express; conf. bd. mem., mem. Worklife Leadership Coun. Woodrow Wilson vis. fellow, 1999; co-chair board devel., nominating com. Ms. Found. Women, 1999. Office: US Gen Svcs Adminstrn 1800 F St NW Washington DC 20405

CLANCY, JOHN PATRICK, real estate company executive; b. N.Y.C., Aug. 4, 1942; s. Joseph Edward and Rita Gertrude (Hass) C.; m. Carol Ann Furnari, May 26, 1962 (div. 1982); children: Laureen, Lisa, Janine; m. Maureen Kearney Rose, Oct. 1, 1988; 1 child, Kim. BBA, St. John's U., 1965. CPA, N.Y. Acct. McGrath, Doyle & Phair, N.Y.C., 1965-66; mgr. Ernst & Young, N.Y.C., 1966-81; exec. v.p., CFO Douglas Elliman Gibbons & Ives, Inc., N.Y.C., 1981-97; CFO, sr. v.p. Julien J. Studley, Inc., N.Y.C., 1997—. Mem. Am. Inst. CPAs, N.Y. State Soc. CPAs. Office: Julien J Studley Inc 300 Park Ave New York NY 10022-7402

CLANCY, KEVIN F., cardiologist; b. Rahway, N.Y., May 23, 1953; s. Francis R. and Corinne V. (Vitarius) C.; m. Deborah Y. Quirk, July 15, 198; children: Michael, Erin, Heather. AB, Princeton U., 1975, MS, 1977; MD, U. Medicine and Dentistry N.J., 1981. Intern and resident Hahneman U. Hosp., Phila., 1981-84; cardiology fellow Grad. Hosp., Phila., 1985-87; postdoctoral fellow cardiology U. Pa., Phila., 1985-87; attending cardiologist Cmty. Med. Ctr., Toms River, N.J., 1987—, chmn. sect. cardiology, assoc. chmn. dept. medicine, 1995—. Contbr. articles to profl. jours. Coach Toms River Basketball Assn., 1993-96. Fellow Am. Coll. Cardiology; mem. AMA, Ocean Count Med. Soc., Med. Soc. N.J. Avocations: charity basketball, home computers. Office: Cardiology Cons Toms River 9 Hospital Dr Toms River NJ 08755-6425*

CLANCY, LOUIS JOHN, newspaper editor, journalist; b. Utrecht, The Netherlands, Aug. 10, 1946; emigrated to Can., 1946, naturalized, 1946; s. John Joseph and Maria Wilhelmina (Van Dommelen) C.; m. Rhonda Darlene Jackson, Apr. 7, 1969; children—Robin, Jamie. Student, Centennial Coll., Can., 1967-69. Copy boy Toronto (Ont.) Star, 1964-65; sports editor Simcoe (Ont.) Reformer, 1965-66; reporter, news editor Owen Sound (Ont.) Sun-Times, 1969-71; copy editor Kitchener-Waterloo (Ont.) Record, 1971-73; mem. staff Toronto Star, 1974—, asst. nat. editor, asst. city editor, then week in rev. editor, 1975-78, nat. editor, 1978-81, Sunday editor, 1981-83, city editor, 1983-89, dep. mng. editor, 1989-93, mng. editor, 1993-97; editor The Record, Kitchener, Ont., 1998—; dir. Torstar Electronic Pub., 1996, Nat. Newspapers Awards, 1997—. Home: 121 Belmont Ave, Waterloo, ON Canada N2L2A6 Office: 1 Yonge St, Toronto, ON Canada M5E 1E6

CLANCY, MICHAEL NEVILLE, military officer; b. Bronx, N.Y., Aug. 25, 1971; s. William Gerald and Mary Anne Clancy. BS in Engring. Mgmt., U.S. Mil. Acad., 1993; MS in Engring. Mgmt., U. Mo., Rolla, 1997. Registered profl. engr., Mo. Commd. 2d lt. U.S. Army, 1993, advanced through grades to capt., 1997; combat engr. officer 12th Engr. Battalion, Mannheim, Germany, 1993-94, 168th Engr. Battalion, Ft. Lewis, Wash., 1994-97, 41st Engr. Battalion, Ft. Drum, N.Y., 1998—. Mem. NSPE, Assn. U.S. Army, Am. Legion, Army Engr. Assn., West Point Soc. N.Y., Nat. Eagle Scout Assn. Roman Catholic. Home: 348 Brady Rd Sackets Harbor NY 13685

CLANCY, THOMAS HANLEY, seminary administrator; b. Helena, Ark., Aug. 8, 1923; s. Thomas Hornor and Ruth (Lewis) C. AB, Spring Hill Coll., 1948; MA, Fordham U., 1950; STL, Facultes S.J., Louvain, Belgium, 1956; PhD, U. London, 1960. Joined S.J., Roman Cath. Ch., 1942, ordained priest, 1955. Instr. Spring Hill Coll., Mobile, Ala., 1950-52; assoc. editor America mag., N.Y.C., 1970-71; provincial supr. New Orleans Province S.J., 1971-77, archivist, 1977—; asst. prof. history and polit. sci. Loyola U., New Orleans, 1960-68, chmn. dept., 1966-69, v.p. acad. affairs, 1968-70, v.p. communications, 1978-89, trustee, 1968-72, 78-89; dir. Jesuit Sem. and Mission Bur., New Orleans, 1989—; lectr. on constns. and history of S.J., 1970—. Author: English Catholic Books 1641-1700: A Bibliography, 1974, 2d edit., 1996, An Introduction to Jesuit Life, 1976, Our Friends, 1978, 2d edit., 1989, The Conversational Word of God, 1978 (Japanese edit. 1986), A Literary History of the English Jesuits 1615-1714, 1996; contbr. articles and book revs. to profl. jours. Trustee Spring Hill Coll., 1980-89, Loyola Marymount U., L.A., 1989-94; chmn. Inst. Politics, New Orleans, 1968—. Folger Shakespeare Libr. fellow, 1961. Mem. Cath. Record Soc. Democrat. Avocation: golf. Office: 500 S Jefferson Davis Pkwy New Orleans LA 70119-7128 Home: Loyola U New Orleans LA 70118

CLANCY, THOMAS L., JR., novelist; b. Balt., Mar. 12, 1947; m. Wanda Thomas, Aug. 1969; children: Michelle, Christine, Tom, Kathleen. Grad., Loyola Coll., 1969. Ins. agent Balt., Hartford, until 1973; ins. agent O. F. Bowen Agy., Owings, Md., 1973-80, owner, from 1980; writer. Author: (novels) The Hunt for Red October, 1984, Red Storm Rising, 1986, Patriot Games, 1987, The Cardinal of the Kremlin, 1988, Clear and Present Danger, 1989, The Sum of All Fears, 1991, Without Remorse, 1993, Debt of Honor, 1994, Executive Orders, 1996, Balance of Power, 1998, Rainbow Six, 1998; (non-fiction) Submarine, 1993, Armored Cav, 1994, Fighter Wing, 1995, Marine, 1996, Airborne, 1997, Into the Storm, 1997, Every Man a Tiger, 1999; creator: (with Steve Pieczenik) Tom Clancy's OP Center, 1995-97. Roman Cath. Address: PO Box 800 Huntingtown MD 20639-0800 also: care Putnam Pub 200 Madison Ave New York NY 10016-3903*

CLAPMAN, PETER CARLYLE, lawyer, insurance company executive; b. N.Y.C., Mar. 11, 1936; s. Jack and Evelyn (Clapman); m. Barbara Posen, May 8, 1966; children: Leah, Alice. AB, Princeton U., 1957; JD, Harvard U., 1960. Bar: N.Y. 1961, Conn. 1972. Assoc. Sage, Gray, Todd & Sims, N.Y.C., 1961-63; asst. counsel Stichman Commn., N.Y.C., 1964; legal cons. OEO, Washington, 1965; assoc. counsel Equitable Life, N.Y.C., 1965-72; sr. v.p., chief counsel investments Tchrs. Ins. and Annuity of Am., Coll. Ret. Equities Fund, N.Y.C., 1972—. Author: Fiduciary Responsibilities of Institutional Managers on Proxy Issues, Iowa Law Jour., 1994, SEC Market 2000 Report; co-author: Notre Dame U. Law Rev., 1981. Mem. ABA, Assn. Bar City N.Y. (com. on securities regulation special com. on mergers), Am. Law Inst., Assn. Life Ins. Counsel (bd. govs., chmn. investment sect.), Am. Coll. Investment Counsel (trustee), Am. Coun. Life Ins. (chmn. securities investment commn.). Home: 3 Valley Rd Scarsdale NY 10583-1123 Office: Tchrs Ins & Annuity Assn Am 730 3rd Ave New York NY 10017-3206

CLAPP, BEVERLY BOOKER, accountant; b. Savannah, Ga., Oct. 26, 1954; d. Herschel Ray and Ida Marie (Bove) Beville; m. William L. Clapp III; 1 child, Matthew Anthony. BS in Med. Tech., Med. Coll. Ga., 1976; MS in Clin. Lab. Sci., U. Ala., Birmingham, 1977, BS in Acctg., 1989. CPA, Ala. Blood bank technologist U. Ala. Hosp., Birmingham, 1976-77; asst. supr. physiology Bapt. Med. Ctr., Montclair, Birmingham, 1977-79; rsch. chemist Nephrology Rsch. and Tng. Ctr. U. Ala., Birmingham, 1979-91; med. technologist VA Med. Ctr., Gainesville, Fla., 1991-92; acct., mgr. J.J. Lucky & Co., Gainesville, 1992; sr. grants specialist U. Fla., Gainesville, 1992-93; acct. Beverly Booker Clapp Acctg. Svc., 1993—. Mem. AICPA, Ala. Soc. CPAs, Am. Soc. Clin. Pathology, Fla. Inst. CPAs, Fla. Soc. Med. Tech., Alpha Aeta, Phi Kappa Phi. Roman Catholic.

CLAPP, CHARLES E., II, senior judge; b. Newton, Mass., Dec. 25, 1923; m. Elinor L. Jones, 1951. BA, Williams Coll., 1945; LLB, Harvard U., 1949. Bar: Mass. 1949, R.I. 1956, Fla. 1982. Pvt. practice Boston, 1949-50; law clk. Hon. J. Edgar Murdock U.S. Tax Ct., 1952-55; pvt. practice Providence, 1955-83; sr. judge U.S. Tax Ct., Washington, 1983-98; ret., 1998. Exec. com. Fed. Tax Inst. New England; co-founder Fed. Tax Forum R.I.; adv. com. U. R.I. Inst. on Fed. Taxation; past pres. Barrington R.I. Town Coun., Narragansett Coun. Boy Scouts Am.; mem. United Way Bd. Campaign. Lt. USN, PTO. Mem. ABA (taxation com.), R.I. Bar Assn. (chmn. tax com. 1966-69, 79-82), Mass. Bar Assn. Office: US Tax Ct 400 2nd St NW Washington DC 20217

CLAPP, C(HARLES) EDWARD, research chemist, soil biochemistry educator; b. Holden, Mass., Aug. 29, 1930; s. Charles Edward and Natalie (Shepard) C.; m. Betty Joyce Huff, June 13, 1953; children: David L., Duane E., Jonathan C., Jay J. BS, U. Mass., 1952; MS, Cornell U., 1954, PhD, 1957. Asst. soil chemist Cornell U., Ithaca, N.Y., 1952-56; organic chemist Agrl. Rsch. Svc., USDA, Beltsville, Md., 1956-61; rsch. chemist Agrl. Rsch. Svc., St. Paul, 1961—; from asst. prof. to prof. U. Minn., St. Paul, 1961—. Author: (with others) Utilization of Municipal Wastewater and Sludge on Land, 1983, Role of Organic Matter in Modern Agriculture, 1986, Humic Substances II: In Search of Structure, 1989, Rhizosphere Dynamics, 1990, Interactions at the Soil Colloid-Soil Solution Interface, 1991, Organic Substances in Soil and Water: Natural Constituents and Their Influences on Contaminant Behaviour, 1991, Humic Substances in the Global Environment and Implications on Human Health, 1994, Advances in Soil Science: Soil Management and Greenhouse Effect, 1995, Nutrient Cycling in Agroecosystems, 1997, Soil Processes and the Carbon Cycle, 1997, Biosolids and Their Effects on Soil Properties, 1997, Humic Substances, Peats and SludgesL: Health and Environmental Aspects, 1997, Humic Substances: Structures, Properties and Uses, 1998; editor, author (with others): Humic Substances in Soil and Crop Sciences: Selected Readings, 1990, Sewage Sludge: Land Utilization and the Environment, 1994, Humic Substances and Organic Matter in Soil and Water Environment: Characterization, Transformation and Interaction, 1996. Y's men officer YMCA, Roseville, Minn., 1965-70; boy and cub scout leader Boy Scouts Am., Roseville, 1965-75. Hon. Sr. Rsch. fellow U. Birmingham, Edgbaston, Eng., 1988-89, Hebrew U. Jerusalem, Rehovot, Israel, 1989. Fellow Soil Sci. Soc. Am. (rep. to Internat. Humic Substance Soc. 1990—), Am. Soc. Agronomy, Am. Inst. Chemists; mem. Internat. Soil Sci. Soc., Internat. Humic Substances Soc. (chair nominating com. 1986-90, treas. 1993—), Sigma XI, Gamma Sigma Delta. Mem. United Ch. of Christ. Achievements include research in chemistry of soil organic matter; in clay-organic complexes; in electrophoresis; in polysaccharide chemistry; in ethylenimine chemistry; in viscosity of naturally occurring polysaccharides; in soil structure; in sewage sludge and waste water chemistry; in soil nitrogen transformations and modeling; in humic substance chemistry; in pesticide-organic matter complexes; in ground water quality; in N-15 and C-13 stable isotope analysis, in plant-humic substances interactions. Office: USDA Agrl Rsch Svc/U Minn 1991 Upper Buford Cir Saint Paul MN 55108-6010

CLAPP, DAVID FOSTER, library administrator; b. Birmingham, Ala., July 17, 1952; s. Merwin Bailey and Katherine Lorraine (Aderholt) C.; m. Sara Louise Stephan, Sept. 18, 1982. BA in Classical Langs., Tulane U., 1975; MS in LS, U. Ill., 1980; cert. advanced study in info. mgmt., U. Chgo., 1987. Asst. mgr. Kroch's & Brentano's Bookstore, Chgo., 1976-79; libr. I acquisitions dept. Chgo. Pub. Libr., 1980-82, libr. II, 1st asst. Walker br., 1982-83, libr. II, head Clearing br., 1983-84, libr. III, head Rogers Park br., 1984-89; asst. dir. extension svcs. Chattanooga Pub. Libr., 1989—. Recipient Outstanding Pub. Svc. award Friends Chgo. Pub. Libr., 1987; Josie B. Houchens fellow U. Ill., 1979. Mem. ALA, Pub. Libr. Assn., Libr. Adminstrn. and Mgmt. Assn., Tenn. Libr. Assn. (exec. bd. 1991-92), Chattanooga Area Libr. Assn. (pres. 1991-92), Mensa, Beta Phi Mu. Avocations: genealogy, history, development and philosophy of religions, ancient history. Office: Chattanooga Pub Libr 1001 Broad St Chattanooga TN 37402-2620

CLAPP, MARTIN, university co-head women's basketball coach; b. Mayfield, Ky., Apr. 10, 1963; m. Sara White, Aug. 9; 1 child, Chelsea. B in Phys. Edn., Mgmt., Admission, Murray State U., 1989. Asst. coach women's program Ark. Coll., 1983; scouting coord. Murray State U.; co-head coach women's basketball U. Louisville, 1992—. Office: Univ of Louisville Womens Athletic Dept Student Activities Ctr Louisville KY 40292*

CLAPP, NEAL KEITH, experimental pathologist; b. Waldron, Ind., Oct. 14, 1928; s. Worrill Groven and Dora M. (Hurst) C.; m. Dorothy Louise Stockwell, Dec. 19, 1953; children: Cheryl Lynne, Mark Allen, Stephen Neal. BS, Purdue U., 1950; DVM, Ohio State U., 1960; MS, Colo. State U., 1962, PhD, 1964. NIH postdoctoral fellow Colo. State Univ., Ft. Collins, 1961-64; experimental pathologist Oak Ridge (Tenn.) Nat. Lab., 1964-81; dir. Marmoset Rsch. Ctr. Oak Ridge (Tenn.) Assoc. U., 1981-92; dir. MARCOR U. Tenn. Med. Ctr., Oak Ridge, 1992—. Editor: A Model for Colon Diseases, 1993; contbr. over 150 articles to profl. jours. Min. Clinton (Tenn.) Christian Ch., 1972-94. With USAF, 1951-55. Mem. Am. Assn. Cancer Rsch., Am. Vet. Med. Assn., Inflammation Rsch. Assn., Am. Assn. Lab. Animal Sci., Am. Primatology Assn., Radiation Rsch. Soc., Optimist Club, Masons. Republican. Avocations: golfing, fishing, baseball, football. Home: PO Box 88 628 Riverbend Rd Clinton TN 37716-3413 Office: U Tenn Marmoset Rsch Ctr 110 Badger Rd Oak Ridge TN 37830-6218

CLAPP, ROGER HOWLAND, retired newspaper executive; b. Scarsdale, N.Y., May 11, 1928; s. Kenneth John and Louise (Allen) C.; m. Patricia Anne Townshend, June 26, 1954; children: Roger Howland Jr., Georgia Louise, Sarah Townshend. BA cum laude, Amherst Coll., 1954. V.p. Benton & Bowles, Inc., N.Y.C., 1954-67, Rumrill-Hoyt, Inc., N.Y.C., 1967-72; v.p., advt. dir. Richmond (Va.) Newspapers, Inc., 1972-93. Bd. dirs. Richmond chpt. Better Bus. Bur., 1986-88, ARC, 1987-93. With USN, 1948-52, Korea. Recipient Silver medal Am. Advt. Fedn., 1980. Mem. Internat. Newspaper Advt. and Mktg. Execs. (pres. 1988). Home: 15470 Cedarwood Ln # 103 Naples FL 34110-8638

CLAPP, STEPHEN CASWELL, journalist; b. Lawrence, Mass., Dec. 25, 1938; s. Edward Theodore and Ruth Elinor (Caswell) C.; m. Sara Victoria Sarfati, June 17, 1967 (div. Nov. 1995); children: Emilia, Melissa. BA, Harvard Coll., 1960; MS, Columbia U., 1966. H.s. tchr. U.S. Peace Corps, Yola, Nigeria, 1963-65; field program evaluator Office Econ. Opportunity, Washington, 1966-69; reporter Nat. Jour., Washington, 1969-70; investigative reporter Pub. Info. Ctr., Washington, 1970-71; pubs. dir. Cmty. Nutrition Inst., Washington, 1971-83; comms. dir. Interfaith Action for Econ. Justice, Washington, 1983-88; freelance journalist Washington, 1988-93, 95—; European editor World Food Chem. News, Brussels, Belgium, 1993-95; cons. Consultative Group on Internat. Agrl. Rsch., Washington, 1996; conf. organizer European Food Law Update Conf., Washington, 1996-98; columnist Meat & Poultry Mag., Kansas City, Mo., 1996-99, Road Runners Club Am., Alexandria, Va., 1978-90. Mem. Washington Ind. Writers. Democrat. Unitarian. Avocations: running, choral singing, photography. Home: 11171 Lake Chapel Ln Reston VA 20191-4308

CLAPPER, GEORGE RAYMOND, retired accountant, computer consultant; b. New Palestine, Ind., June 29, 1931; s. Raymond Henry and Magdalene Barbara (Niedenthall) C.; m. Mary Vaneta Shine, June 29, 1957 (div. 1978); children: Christine M. Dux, Joseph W., Ann T. Wendling, Michael R. BS in Acctg., Ind. U., 1956. With The Upjohn Co., 1956-81; distbn. ctr. mgr. The Upjohn Co., Cin., 1956-57, N.Y.C., 1957-62, Kalamazoo, Mich., 1962-66, 68-69, New Orleans, 1966-68, Mpls., 1969; mgr., controller Lab. Procedures, Inc. (name now SmithKline Clin. Labs), King of Prussia, Pa., 1969-72, v.p., gen. mgr., 1972-81; exec. v.p. Lab. Procedures, Inc. (name now SmithKline Clin. Labs), Kalamazoo, 1981; v.p., gen. mgr. SmithKline Clin. Labs., St. Louis, 1981-82, MDS Labs., Inc., Buffalo, N.Y., 1982-84; COO Specialty Svcs. Group, Phila., 1985-86; pub. acct., computer cons. Indpls., 1987-96. With USMCR, 1947-60. Mem. Am. Legion, KC, Moose. Republican. Roman Catholic. Avocations: music, sports, crafts, cooking. Home and Office: 2041 Ticen Ct Beech Grove IN 46107-1474

CLAPPER, LYLE NIELSEN, magazine publisher; b. Evanston, Ill., Apr. 24, 1941; s. John Marion and Edna (Nielsen) C.; m. Lynn Dewey, Sept. 1, 1962 (div. June 1978); children: John Scott, Susan Louise; m. Marie Petersen, Jan. 1, 1980; children: Jeffrey Leland, Anne Reinke. Student, Cornell U., 1959-60; BS in Quantative Econs., U. Ill., 1964. Chief exec. officer Clapper Communications (pubs. Crafts 'N Things mag., Pack-O-Fun mag., Decorative Arts Painting mag., Cross Stitcher Mag., Bridal Crafts mag.), Des Plaines, Ill., 1960—. Avocations: teaching flying, photography, computer programming.

CLAPPER, MARIE ANNE, magazine publisher; b. Chgo., Nov. 21, 1942; d. Chester William and Hazel Alice (Gilso) Reinke; m. William Neil Petersen, Aug. 17, 1963 (div. 1975); children: Elaine Myrtice, Edward William; m. Lyle N. Clapper, Jan. 1, 1980; children: Jeffrey Leland, Anne Reinke; stepchildren: John Scott, Susan Louise. Student, Augustana Coll., Rock Island, Ill., 1960-63; EdB, Northeastern U., 1964. Writer Pack-o-Fun mag., Park Ridge, Ill., 1976-77; editor Pack-o-Fun mag., Des Plaines, Ill., 1977-78, pub., 1990—; asst. to pub., circulation dir. Crafts 'n Things mag., Des Plaines, Ill., 1978-82, pub., 1982—; pub. Decorative Arts Painting mag., Des Plaines, Ill., 1990—, The Cross Stitcher Mag., Des Plaines, 1991—, Bridal Crafts mag., Des Plaines, 1991—; pub., pres. Clapper pub. Host TV show The Crafts 'n Things Show, 1984-86, Crafting for the 90s, 1990-94; author: EveryDay Matters, 1996. Mem. TEC, Mag. Pubs. Am. (bd. dirs.), Hobby Industry Am. (bd. dirs., treas. 1998-99), Soc. Craft Designers. Office: Crafts 'n Things 2400 E Devon Ave Ste 375 Des Plaines IL 60018-4618

CLAPTON, ERIC, musician; b. Ripley, Surrey, Eng., Mar. 30, 1945; m. Patricia Anne Boyd, 1979 (div. 1988); 1 son, Conor (dec.). Student, Kingston Art Sch. Former mem. rock music groups Yardbirds, John Mayall's Bluesbreakers, Cream, Blind Faith, Delaney & Bonnie & Friends, Derek & the Dominos; now solo performer; films: A Concert for Bangladesh, 1972, Tommy, 1975, Music Communion, 1989; composer: Badge, Let It Rain, Layla; albums include Eric Clapton, 1970, Rainbow Concert, 1973, 461 Ocean Boulevard, 1974, There's One in Every Crowd, 1974, EC Was Here, 1975, No Reason to Cry, 1976, Slowhand, 1977, Backless, 1978, Just One Night, 1980, Another Ticket, 1981, Money and Cigarettes, 1983, Behind the Sun, 1985, Lethal Weapon, 1986, August, 1987, Crossroads (retrospective), 1988, Time Pieces/Best of Eric Clapton, 1988, Time Pieces II/Live in the Seventies, 1988, One Moment in Time, 1988, Journeyman, 1989, 24 Nights, 1991, Unplugged, 1992, From the Cradle, 1994 (Grammy award Best Traditional Blues Album), Crossroads II: Live in the 70's, 1996, EC Was Here, 1996, Eric Clapton, 1996, 461 Ocean Boulevard, 1996, There's One in Every Crowd, 1996, Pilgrim, 1998; wrote songs for BBC miniseries Edge of Darkness, 1986; composer film scores Homeboy, 1988, Lethal Weapon 2, 1989, The Van, 1996, Nil by Mouth, 1997; co-composer film score Lethal Weapon 3, 1992. Recipient 2 Grammys, 1989, 1 Grammy, 1991, 6 Grammies, 1993, Grammy nomination (Best Rock Duo or Group Performance, 1994) for "My Back Pages" (with Bob Dylan, Roger McGuinn, Tom Petty, Neil Young, and George Harrison); inducted into Rock and Roll Hall of Fame, 1993. Office: care Polygram Records Inc 825 8th Ave Fl 23 New York NY 10019-7416*

CLARDY, JON CHRISTEL, chemistry educator, consultant; b. Washington, May 16, 1943; s. Warren Davenport and Elisabeth (Christel) C.; m. Andrea Emily Fleck, Dec. 30, 1966; children: Peter Fleck, Benjamin Christopher. BS, Yale U., 1964; PhD, Harvard U., 1969. Instr. Iowa State U., Ames, 1969-70, asst. prof. chemistry, 1970-72, assoc. prof., 1972-75, prof., 1975-77; prof. Cornell U., Ithaca, N.Y., 1978—, chmn. dept. chemistry, 1988-93, Horace White prof., 1990—. Contbr. numerous articles to profl. jours. Camille and Henry Dreyfus fellow, 1972-77, J.S. Guggenheim fellow, 1984-85. Fellow AAAS, Am. Acad. Arts and Scis.; mem. Am. Chem. Soc. (Akron sect. award 1987, Ernest Guenther award 1995, Arthur C. Cope scholar award 1997), Am. Crystallographic Assn., Am. Acad. Arts and Scis. Avocations: travel, reading, cooking. Office: Cornell U Dept Chemistry & Chem Biol Baker Lab Ithaca NY 14853-1301*

CLARDY, THELMA SANDERS, lawyer; b. Okemah, Okla., Jan. 11, 1955; d. Hobart Curtis and Maurine Yvonne (Lee) Sanders; m. James E. Clardy, June 28, 1980; 1 child, Michelle Elizabeth. BS cum laude, Tenn. State U., 1976; JD, Tex. So. U., 1979. Bar: Tex. Staff atty. U.S. Dept. Edn., Dallas, 1979-87; assoc. Law Offices Earl Luna, Dallas, 1987-88; staff atty. Legal Svcs. North Tex., Dallas, 1988-91; assoc. Robinson & West, P.C., Dallas, 1992-94; pvt. practice Dallas, 1995—. Pres. Oak Tree Colony Neighborhood Assn., Dallas, 1984-85, North Meadows Community Improvement Assn., DeSoto, Tex., 1992-94; bd. dirs. Women's Ctr. Dallas, Child Care Partnership, Dallas; with Nat. Assn. Negro Bus. and Profl. Women, Dallas, 1984-86. Recipient Juanita Craft award NAACP, Dallas, 1985; named Member of Yr. United for Action, Dallas, 1982. Fellow Tex. Bar Found.; mem. State Bar Tex. (bd. dirs.), Dallas Bar Assn. (sec.-treas. 1991), Dallas Assn. Black Women Attys. (founder, 1st pres. 1982-84), Vis. Nurse Assn. Tex. (bd. dirs. 1989-94), Alpha Kappa Alpha. Baptist. Avocations: education, health care, reading, tennis. Home: 1117 Bluffview Dr De Soto TX 75115-3519 Office: Ste # 950 1845 Woodall Fwy Ste 1200 Dallas TX 75201

CLARE, FRANK BRIAN, neurosurgeon, neurologist; b. Southport, Eng., June 27, 1919; came to U.S., 1920; s. Joseph and Nellie Elam C.; m. Shirley Edmondson, June 28, 1950 (dec. Apr. 1992); children: Frank Brian Jr., Shelley Jo Williamson, Merr Loucales, William Thomas Clare. BS, U. Ill., Chgo., MS, PhD. Diplomate Am. Bd. Neurosurgery. Chief neurosurgeon U.S. Naval Hosp., Stalbans, N.Y., 1946-48, Portsmouth, Va., 1950-60, San Diego, 1960-63; neurosurgeon Portsmouth Gen., 1963-98; staff neurosurgeon Meryvie Hosp., Portsmouth, 1963-99, Norfolk (Va.) Gen., 1963-99; pres. Neurosurg. Soc. Va., 1965-67. Contbr. articles to profl. jours. Commr. sister city City Gov., Portsmouth, 1990-96. Capt. USN, 1942-43. Mem. Portsmouth Med. Soc. (pres. 1968), Rotary Internat. (bd. dirs. 1964). Republican. Episcopalian. Avocations: sailing, airplane pilot. Home: 3201 High Point Dr Portsmouth VA 23703

CLARE, GEORGE, safety engineer, system safety consultant; b. N.Y.C., Apr. 8, 1930; s. George Washington and Hildegard Marie (Sommer) C.; student U. So. Calif., 1961, U. Tex., Arlington, 1963-71, U. Wash., 1980; m. Catherine Saidee Hamel, Jan. 12, 1956; children: George Christopher, Kristine René. Enlisted man U.S. Navy, 1948, advanced through grades to comdr., 1968; naval aviator, 1951-70; served in Korea; comdr. Res., 1963-70; ret., 1970; mgr. system safety LTV Missiles and Electronics Group, Missiles div., Dallas, 1963-90. Mem. Nat. Republican Com., Rep. Senatorial Com., Rep. Congl. Com., Tex. Rep. Com., Citizens for Republic. Decorated Air medal with gold star, others; cert. product safety mgr. Mem. AIAA, Am. Security Council, Internat. Soc. Air Safety Investigators, System Safety Soc., Am. Def. Preparedness Assn., Assn. Naval Aviation, Ret. Officers Assn., Air Group 7 Assn. (pres.). Roman Catholic. Home and Office: 825 Bayshore Dr Apt 500 Pensacola FL 32507-3463

CLARENS, JOHN GASTON, investment executive; b. Bordeaux, France, July 16, 1924; s. Pierre Maurice and Cecile (Dupreuilh) C.; m. Francoise Legrand, Aug. 7, 1948. Engr., Ecole Polytechnique, Paris, 1948; MBA (Am. Field Service scholar), Harvard U., 1950. Chartered fin. analyst, N.Y. Vice-pres. Lepercq, de Neuflize & Co., Inc., N.Y.C., 1970-75; pres., chief exec. officer Lepercq, de Neuflize & Co., Inc., 1975-76; pres. Istel Fund, N.Y.C., 1975-76; chmn., pres. Clarens Assocs., Inc., N.Y.C., 1976—. Served to lt. French Army. Club: Knickerbocker. Avocations: tennis, skiing. Home: 51 Fox Run Rd West Redding CT 06896-2802 Office: Clarens Assocs Inc 730 5th Ave Ste 900 New York NY 10019-4105*

CLAREY, DONALD ALEXANDER, government affairs consultant; b. Johnson City, N.Y., Feb. 8, 1950; s. James Roger and Dorothy (Wait) C. B.A., Union Coll., Schenectady, 1972; M.P.A., Harvard U., Cambridge, Mass., 1977. Exec. asst. to dir. for Congl. affairs FEA, Washington, 1973-76; program assoc. to majority leader N.Y. State Senate, Albany, 1977-79, adminstrv. asst. to majority leader, 1979-82; cons. Dept. State, Washington, 1983; assoc. dir. cabinet affairs The White House, Washington, 1983-85, spl. asst. to Pres. of U.S., 1985-87; dep. adminstr. SBA, 1987-88; cons. govt. affairs, v.p. Strategic Mgmt. Assocs., Washington, 1989-96; pres. Minerva Group, 1996—. Republican candidate for N.Y. State Assembly, 1980, 82. Roman Catholic. Avocations: skiing; golf. Home: 234 Lenox Ave Albany NY 12208 Office: PO Box 459 Albany NY 12201-0459

CLAREY, JOHN ROBERT, executive search consultant; b. Waterloo, Iowa, June 5, 1942; s. Robert J. and Norma (Knox) C.; m. Kathleen Ann Kingsley, June 5, 1965; children: Sharon Diane, Suzanne Marie. BSBA, Iowa State U., 1965; MBA, U. Pa., 1972. Fin. analyst Ford Motor Co., Dearborn, Mich., 1972-74; cons. Price Waterhouse, Chgo., 1974-75, mgr., 1975-76; assoc. Heidrick & Struggles, 1976-81, v.p., ptnr., 1981-82; pres. Clarey & Andrews Inc., Northbrook, Ill. Served to lt. USN, 1965-70, Vietnam. Mem. Stick and Rudder, Assn. Exec. Search Cons., Lifeline Pilots. Republican. Roman Catholic. Clubs: Mid-Am. (Chgo.), Sunset Ridge Country (Northbrook). Avocations: flying, microcomputers, tennis. Home: 1347 Hillside Rd Northbrook IL 60062-4612 Office: Clarey & Andrews Inc 1200 Shermer Rd Ste 108 Northbrook IL 60062-4563

CLARIDGE, ELMOND LOWELL, retired engineering educator, consultant; b. Delaplaine, Ark., June 5, 1917; s. Elmond Lee and Irene Cynthia Gates (Compton) C.; m. Zola Ruth McDowell, Jan. 1, 1939 (dec. Oct. 9, 1990); children: David Elmond, Jonathan McDowell; m. Mary Lasley Moore, Feb. 11, 1995 (dec. Feb. 16, 1999). BS in Chem. Engring., U. Mo., Rolla, 1939, MS in Chem. Engring., 1941; PhD in Chem. Engring., U. Houston, 1979. Registered profl. engr., Tex. Rsch. chemist Shell Oil Co., Wood River, Ill., 1941-43, technologist, 1943-48; sr. technologist Shell Oil Co., Houston, 1948-55, 57-60; sr. technologist head office Shell Oil Co., N.Y.C., 1960-64; group leader Royal Dutch Shell, Amsterdam, 1955-57; sr. rsch. assoc. Shell Devel. Co., Houston, 1964-79; assoc. prof. chem. engring. dept. U. Houston, 1979-91; cons. Gulf Univs. Rsch. Consortium, Houston, 1979-85, TCA Reservoir Engring. Svcs., Houston, 1979—. Author: PE 506, Miscible Processes, 1992; contbr. articles to profl. jours. Recipient Disting. Life award St. Luke's United Meth. Ch., 1990. Mem. AIChE, Am. Chem. Soc. (mem., chmn. sub com. petroleum res. fund adv. com. 1985-88), AAAS, Am. Petroleum Inst. (mem. rsch. adv. bd. prodn. divsn. 1978-81), Petroleum Soc./Can. Inst. Mining, Metallurgy and Petroleum, Soc. Petroleum Engrs. (editor reprint book Surfactant/Polymer Chemical Flooding vols. I, II, 1982, Enhanced Oil Recovery Pioneer 1980), Sigma Xi, Alpha Chi Sigma. Achievements include ten patents. Home and Office: 5439 Paisley St Houston TX 77096-4025

CLARIDGE, RICHARD, structural engineer; b. Chgo., Feb. 22, 1932; s. Dalbert Otis and Lucille Alma (Lindquist) C.; m. Joan Elaine Powell, June 12, 1952; children: Cathy L. Jansen, Richard Allen Jr., Jaylynn P. Cook. BSBA, Fla. State U., Tallahassee, 1953; BCE, U. Fla., 1959; postgrad., U. Cen. Fla., 1972-75. Registered profl. engr. Fla., S.C. Structures engr. Douglas Aircraft Co., 1959-63, McDonnell Douglas Astro, 1963-89; ground supt. equipment, design engr. McDonnell Douglas Astro, Cape Canaveral, Fla., 1974-81; stress analyst McDonnell Douglas Astro, Titusville, Fla., 1982-89; structural cons., analyst Atlantic CADD Assocs., Titusville, 1989—; group engr. McDonnell Douglas Astro, Kennedy Space Ctr., 1963-74; sect. chief stress McDonnell Douglas Missile Sys., Titusville, 1983-89; structural analyst, designer Lockheed Martin Astronautics, Cape Canaveral, Fla., 1989-97. Mem. Titusville Shoreline Authority, 1965. Lt. (j.g.) USNR, 1953-57. Mem. NSPE, ASCE (computer practices reviewer), AIAA, Am. Welding Soc., Fla. Engring. Soc., U.S. Naval Inst. (life), Internat. Soc. Allied Weight Engrs. Avocations: woodworking, photography, volleyball, surfing. Office: Atlantic CADD Assocs PO Box 386 New Smyrna Beach FL 32170-0386

CLARIZIO, JOSEPHINE DELORES, corporate services executive, former manufacturing and engineering company executive, foundation executive; b. Montclair, N.J., Dec. 15, 1922; d. Thomas and Raffaela (Caruso) D'Andrea; m. Robert Clarizio, June 3, 1951. Cert., Katharine Gibbs Sch., 1942; B.S., Seton Hall U., 1947; postgrad., Fordham U. Sch. Law, 1947-48, N.Y. Inst. Fin., 1964. Registered rep. Drexel, Burnham & Co., N.Y.C., 1965-70; asst. to pres. Wheelabrator-Frye Inc., Hampton, N.H., 1970-78, corp. sec., 1981-83; pres. Wheelabrator Found. Inc., Hampton, 1978-83; cons. Signal Cos. Inc., N.Y.C., N.H., 1983-85. Mem. Seton Hall U. Alumni Assn. Republican. Roman Catholic.

CLARK, A. JAMES, real estate company executive; b. 1927. BCE, U. Md. CEO, chmn. Clark Enterprises, Bethesda, Md., 1951—. Office: Clark Enterprises Inc 7500 Old Georgetown Rd Bethesda MD 20814-6133*

CLARK, ALAN FRED, physicist; b. Milwaukee, June 29, 1936. B.S. in Physics, U. Wis., Madison, 1958, M.S. in Nuclear Engrin., 1959; Ph.D. in Nuclear Sci., U. Mich., Ann Arbor, 1964. NAS-NRC postdoctoral assoc. Nat. Bur. Standards, Boulder, Colo., 1964-66, physicist, 1966-78, chief cryogenic properties of solids, 1978-80, group leader supercondr. and magnetic measurements, 1981-87; liaison scientist Office Naval Rsch., London and Europe, 1987-89; group leader fundamental elec. measurements Nat. Inst. Stds., Gaithersburg, Md., 1989-92, 95-98, sr. scientist electricity divsn., 1992-94; dep. chief optoelectronics divsn. Nat. Inst. Stds., Boulder, Colo., 1998—; chmn., founder Internat. Cryogenic Materials Conf. Bd., Boulder, Colo., 1975—; mem. Internat. Cryogenic Engring. Conf. Bd., 1982—. Contbr. over 150 articles to profl. jours.; editor Cryogenics Jour., 1982-94, IEEE Trans. Applied Superconductivity, 1994-98, 8 conf. proceedings, 4 books. Recipient Superior Rsch. Nat. Bur. Standards, 1967, 74, 82, 83, 84, 85, 86, 93-97. Fellow IEEE, Am. Phys. Soc.; mem. ASTM (chmn. superconductor com. 1980-89), IEEE Superconductivity Com. (chmn. 1989-94), Internat. Acad. Electrotech. Scis. Office: Nat Inst Standards & Tech MS 815.00 325 Broadway Boulder CO 80303

CLARK, ALAN MARSHALL, umpire; b. Trenton, N.J., Jan. 9, 1948. Student, Ea. Ky. U. Former umpire Midwest League, Tex. League, Am. Assn., Venezuela Winter League; umpire maj. league baseball Am. League, N.Y.C., 1976—; with Umpires Union, Phila.; with World Wide Mktg. Inc. Avocations: financial planning, marketing, golfing. Office: Am League 350 Park Ave New York NY 10022 also: Umpires Union 1735 Market St Philadelphia PA 19103

CLARK, ANN BLAKENEY, educational administrator; b. Greensboro, N.C., May 21, 1958; d. Blake Campbell and Nancy (Hamel) C. BA in English, Davidson (N.C.) Coll., 1980; MEd, U. Va., 1982; postgrad., U. N.C., 1985—. Spl. edn. tchr. Virginia Beach (Va.) Pub. Schs., 1982-83, Devonshire Elem. Sch., 1983-87; asst. prin. Montclare Elem. Sch., 1987-88; prin. Shamrock Gardens Elem. Sch., 1988-90, Alexander Graham Mid. Sch., Charlotte, N.C., 1990-96, Vans H.S., 1996—. Vice pres. Jr. League of Charlotte, 1988-89; mem. bd. mgrs. Johnston YMCA, Charlotte, 1987—; chmn. bd. A Child's Place, Charlotte, 1989—. Named Nat. Principal of Yr. 1994; named Tchr. of Yr., Devonshire Elem., 1987-88. Mem. ASCD, NAESP, Coun. for Exceptional Children, Coun. for Children, Phi Delta Kappa. Republican. Episcopalian. Avocations: golf, tennis. Home: 7920 Neal Rd Charlotte NC 28262-3226*

CLARK, ARTHUR BRYAN, engineer; b. St. Paul, Aug. 26, 1964; s. Arthur Bryan and Frankie Lucy (Cartier) C.; m. Candace Lee Stutsman, Oct. 19, 1984; 1 child, Courtney Marie. Sr. engr. Eldyne, Inc., San Diego, 1987-99. With USN, 1981-87, USNR, 1987—. Mem. Navy League (bd. dirs. 1995-96), Naval Inst., Loyal Order Moose. Avocations: computers, photography. Home: 603 Elaine Ave Oceanside CA 92057-3538

CLARK, ARTHUR WATTS, insurance company executive; b. Seattle, Nov. 28, 1922; s. Irving Marshall and Nell (Watts) C.; m. Mary Dick Cannon, Nov. 21, 1942; children: Arthur Watts, Claiborne Marshall, Johnston Jewell. AB, U. N.C., 1943; MA, U. Calif., 1948. With Home Security Life Ins. Co., Durham, N.C., 1948-50, 52-85; pres. Home Security Life Ins. Co., 1967-75, chmn., chief exec. officer, 1975-85, also dir.; chmn., chief exec. officer Peoples Life Ins. Co. of Washington, D.C., 1983-85; chmn., pres., chief exec. officer Peoples Security Life Ins. Co., 1985-86, chmn. bd., 1986-88; mem. Res. Forces Policy Bd., Office Sec. Def., 1975-78. Treas. Research Triangle Regional Planning Commn., 1959-63; mem. N.C. Health Ins. Adv. Bd., 1966-70; chmn. bd. dirs. N.C. Ctrl. U. Found.; vice-chmn. bd. dirs. N.C. Med. Found.; chmn. bd. dirs. Zool. Coun., 1994—, chmn., 1996—; chmn. Greater Triangle Cmty. Found., 1992-94, The Explorer's Club, 1999—. With USAAF, 1942-46, USAF, 1952, maj. gen. USAF, ret. Decorated D.S.M., Legion of Merit with oak leaf cluster, Bronze Star. Mem. Am. Life Conv. (dir. 1972), Am. Life Ins. Assn. (dir. 1973-75), Life Office Mgmt. Assn. (dir. 1973-76), Am. Council Life Ins. (dir. 1976), Life Insurers Conf. (exec. com. 1972-75, 1983-86), Assn. N.C. Life Ins. Cos. (chmn. 1986-87), Phi Beta Kappa, Sigma Xi. Home: 3540 Rugby Rd Durham NC 27707-5434 Office: PO Box 61 Durham NC 27702-0061

CLARK, BARBARA WALSH, nurse educator, administrator, clinical specialist; b. Phila., Sept. 24, 1948; d. James and Pauline Walsh; m. James W. Clark, July 2, 1977; children: Shannon, Jim. BSN, Pa. State U., 1971; MS in Nursing, U. Pa., Phila., 1975; postgrad., U. Ky. Staff nurse Nazareth Hosp., Phila., 1971-73, Bucks County Hosp., Bristol, Pa., 1973-78; assoc. prof. Bucks County C.C., Newtown, Pa., 1972-80; asst. prof. U. Ky., Lexington C.C., 1986-88; prof. nursing Midway (Ky.) Coll., 1988—, chair BSN completion program; clin. nurse specialist Ea. State Hosp., Lexington, 1998—; speaker in field. Contrb. articles to profl. jours. Mem. ANA, Ky. Nurses Assn., Ctrl. Area Psychiat. Nurses Group, Assn. Edn. Comm. Tech., Sigma Theta Tau. Home: 504 Retrac Rd Lexington KY 40503-4324

CLARK, BETH, minister; b. Bradford, N.H., Apr. 15, 1914; d. John Scott and Bessie (Murdock) Pendleton; m. John Guill Clark, June 20, 1940 (dec. 1955); children: John Guill Jr., Beverly Estelle Clark Daggett. *Beverly Clark Daggett, daughter of Beth Clark, was elected to the State Senate in Maine in November, 1996. Previously, she had been a member of the State Legislature for nine years. She was sponsored by George Mitchell, former Senate Majority Leader in the Federal Government.* BA, Colby Coll., 1935; BD, Andover Newton Theol. Sch., 1938; MDiv, Ea. Bapt. Theol. Sem., 1967; D Ministry, Lancaster Theol. Sem., 1981; postgrad., U. Athens, 1970, Jungian Inst., Zurich, 1980, Mansfield Coll., Oxford, Eng., 1982, 85, Caribbean Inst., 1989. Ordained to ministry United Ch. of Christ, 1967. Exec. dir. YWCA, Bristol, Tenn., 1955-59, Asheville, N.C., 1959-60; dean of women Anderson (S.C.) Coll., 1960-61, Eastern Coll., St. Davids, Pa., 1961-65; vol. rsch. coord. Selinsgrove (Pa.) State Sch., 1965-78; interim min. various chs. Pa. Ctrl. Conf., United Ch. of Christ, Harrisburg, Pa., 1968-96. Author: Grief in the Loss of a Pastor, 1981; editor: Meditations on the Lord's Supper (John G. Clark), 1958. Bd. mgr. Bethany Children's Home, Womelsdorf, Pa., 1982-88; mem. adv. com. Sun Home Nursing Svcs., Northumberland, Pa., 1982-95, sec. bd. dirs., 1989-96; mem. stewardship coun. United Ch. of Christ, 1997—. Mem. Interim Network (steering com. 1978-80), Assn. Ret. State Employees, Alban Inst., Interagy. Club (pres. 1966-68), Triangle Club (v.p. 1970-74, pres. 1996-98), Phi Mu. Democrat. Home: 709 9th St Selinsgrove PA 17870-1707 *Our world is crying out for honesty, for absolute truth. Communication is impossible without belief and trust in the sincerity of the other person. Better the bitter truth than favor catering deception.*

CLARK, BILLY PAT, physicist; b. Bartlesville, Okla., May 15, 1939; s. Lloyd A. and Ruby Laura (Holcomb) C. BS, Okla. State U., 1961, MS, 1964, PhD, 1968. Grad. asst. dept. physics Okla. State U., 1961-68; postdoctoral rsch. fellow dept. theoretical physics U. Warwick, Coventry, Eng., 1968-69; sr. mem. tech. staff Booz-Allen Applied Rsch., 1969-70; sr. mem. tech. staff field svcs. div. Computer Scis. Corp., Leavenworth, Kans., 1970-73, sr. mem. tech. staff field svcs. div., Hampton, Va., 1973-76, head quality assurance engring. Landsat project Goddard Space Flight Center, NASA, Greenbelt, Md., 1976-77, quality assurance sect. mgr., 1977-79, sr. staff scientist engring. dept., 1979-80, sr. staff scientist image processing ops., 1980-82, sr. prin. engr./scientist GSFC sci. and application operation, system scis. div., 1982-83, sr. adv. staff CSC/NOAA Landsat Operation, 1983-91; sr. scientist Computer Scis. Corp. Ctr. Excellence in Geographic Info., 1991—; tech. rep. internat. Landsat Tech. Working Group (representing USA Landsat operation). Author tech. publs. Recipient undergrad. scholarships Phillips Petroleum Co., 1957-61, Am. Legion, 1957-58, Okla. State U., 1957-58. Mem. AAAS, IEEE, Am. Acad. Polit. and Social Sci., Internat. Platform Assn., Am. Phys. Soc., N.Y. Acad. Scis., Soc. Photo Optical Instrumentation Engrs. (organizer 1st GIS conf.), Internat. Soc. for Photogrammetry and Remote Sensing (organizer and dir. plenary sessions XVII congress meeting 1992), Am. Soc. for Photogrammetry and Remote Sensing, Victory Hills Golf and Country Club, Crofton Country Club, Pi Mu Epsilon, Sigma Pi Sigma. Home: 5811 Barnwood Pl Columbia MD 21044-2811

CLARK, BRANDI M., veterinary technician; b. Aug. 13, 1970. Assoc. degree, U. Minn., 1991. Vet. technician Jordahl Animal Hosp., Minot, N.D., 1991-92, Roosevelt Park Zoo, Minot, 1992—. E-mail: bclark@ndak.net. Office: 1219 Burdick Expy E Minot ND 58701

CLARK, BRIAN THOMAS, mathematical statistician, operations research analyst; b. Rockford, Ill., Apr. 7, 1951; s. Paul Herbert and Martha Lou (Schlensker) C.; m. Suzanne Drake, Nov. 21, 1992; 1 child, Branden Ward. BS cum laude, No. Ariz. U., 1973; postgrad. Ariz. State U., 1980-82. Math. aide Center for Disease Control, Phoenix, 1973-74, math. statistician, 1979-83; math. Statistician Ctrs. for Disease Control, Atlanta, 1983-84 ops. research analyst U.S. Army Info. Systems Command, Ft. Huachuca, Ariz., 1984—; math. statistician U.S. Navy Metrology Engring. Center, Pomona, Calif., 1974-79. Republican. Mormon. Office: US Army Signal Command Dep Chief Staff Resource Mgmt G8 Managerial Acctg Pricing Fort Huachuca AZ 85613

CLARK, BRUCE BUDGE, humanities educator; b. Georgetown, Idaho, Apr. 9, 1918; s. Marvin E. and Alice (Budge) C.; m. Ouida Raphiel, Nov. 7, 1946; children—Lorraine, Bradley, Robert, Jeffrey, Shawn, Sandra. B.A., U. Utah, 1943, Ph.D., 1951; M.A., Brigham Young U., 1948. Teaching fellow Brigham Young U., 1946-47, U. Utah, 1947-50; asst. prof. Brigham Young U., 1950-55, assoc. prof., 1955-58, prof., 1959—, dir. humanities program, 1958-60, chmn. dept. English, 1960-65; dean Coll. Humanities, 1965-81. Author: The Spectrum of Faith in Victorian Literature, 1966, The Challenge of Teaching, 1966, Romanticism through Modern Eyes, 1968, Oscar Wilde, A Study in Genius and Tragedy, 1970, Brigham Young on Education, 1970, Idealists in Revolt, 1975, History of the Brigham Young U. Coll. Humanities, 3 vols., 1984, Family History, 3 vols., 1998, Selected Essays and Other Writings, 1998; Editor: Richard Evans Quote Book, 1971; anthology (Out of the Best Books, vol. 1, 1964, vol. II, 1966, vol. III, 1967, vol. IV, 1968, vol. V, 1969, Great Short Stories for Discussion and Delight, 1979; Contbr. articles to profl. jours. Served with AUS, 1944-46. Recipient Karl G. Maeser Teaching Excellence award, 1972, David O. McKay Humanities award, 1983, Brigham Young U. Presdl. citation for disting. svc., 1994. Mem. MLA, Nat. Coun. Tchrs. English, Rocky Mountain Modern Lang. Assn., Coll. Conf. on Composition and Communications, Phi Kappa Phi. Mormon. Home: 365 E 1655 S Orem UT 84058-7903 Office: Brigham Young U Dept of Humanities Provo UT 84602

CLARK, BRUCE ROBERT, geology consultant; b. Pitts., June 17, 1941; s. Harold Thomas and Florence (Miller) C.; m. Karen Pelton Heath, Dec. 30, 1967; children: Adam, Andrea. BS, Yale U., 1963; PhD, Stanford U., 1967. Asst. prof. U. Mich., Ann Arbor, 1968-73, assoc. prof., 1973-77; v.p. Leighton and Assocs., Inc., Irvine, Calif., 1977-85, pres., 1986—, chief exec. officer, 1988—. Contbr. articles to profl. jours. Chmn. bd. YMCA Orange County, Calif., 1999—. Fellow Geological Soc. Am.; mem. Earthquake Engring. Rsch. Inst., Am. Geophysical Union, Assn. Engring. Geologists, Seismological Soc. Am., Sigma Xi. Office: Leighton & Assocs Inc 17781 Cowan Irvine CA 92614-6009

CLARK, BURTON ROBERT, sociologist, educator; b. Pleasantville, N.J., Sept. 6, 1921; s, Burton H. and Cornelia (Amole) C.; m. Adele Halitsky, Aug. 31, 1949; children: Philip Neil (dec.), Adrienne. B.A., UCLA, 1949, PhD, 1954; PhD (hon.), U. Strathclyde, 1998. Asst. prof. sociology Stanford U., 1953-56; research asso., asst. prof. edn. Harvard U., 1956-58; asso. prof., then prof. edn. and asso. research sociologist, then research sociologist U. Calif. at Berkeley, 1958-66; prof. sociology Yale U., 1966-80, chmn. dept., 1969-72, chmn. higher edn. rsch. group, 1973-80; Allan M. Cartter prof. higher edn. UCLA, 1980-91, chmn., prof. emeritus, 1982-91. Author: Adult Education in Transition, 1956, The Open Door College, 1960, Educating the Expert Society, 1962, The Distinctive College, 1970, The Problems of American Education, 1975, Academic Power in Italy, 1977, The Higher Education System, 1983, The Academic Life, 1987, Places of Inquiry, 1995, Creating Entrepreneurial Universities, 1998; co-author: Students and Colleges, 1972, Youth: Transition to Adulthood, 1973, Academic Power in the United States, 1976, Academic Power: Patterns of Authority in Seven National Systems of Higher Education, 1978; editor: Perspectives on Higher Education, 1984, The School and The University, 1985, The Academic Profession, 1987, The Research Foundations of Graduate education, 1993; co-senior editor: Encyclopedia of Higher Education, 1992. Served with AUS, 1942-46. Recipient Comenius medal UNESCO, 1998. Fellow Brit. Soc. for Rsch. in Higher Edn.; mem. Am. Sociol. Assn., Am. Ednl. Rsch. Assn. (Am. Coll. Testing award 1979, Divsn. J. Disting. Rsch. award 1988, Outstanding Book award 1989), Assn. Study Higher Edn. (pres. 1979-80, Rsch. Achievement award 1985, Howard Bowen Distinguished Svc. award 1997), Am. Assn. Higher Edn., Nat. Acad. Edn. (v.p. 1989-93), Consortium Higher Edn. Rschrs., European Assn. for Instnl. Rsch. (disting. mem.). Home: 201 Ocean Ave Apt 1710B Santa Monica CA 90402 Office: UCLA Dept Edn Los Angeles CA 90095

CLARK, CANDY, actress; b. Norman, Okla.; d. Thomas Prest and Ella Lee (Padberg) C. Student public schs., Ft. Worth. Appeared in movies Fat City, 1971, American Graffiti, 1973 (nominated for best supporting actress), The Man Who Fell to Earth, 1975, Citizens Band, 1976, The Big Sleep, 1977, When Ya' Coming Back Red Ryder, 1978, More American Graffiti, 1978, National Lampoon Goes to the Movies, 1981, Blue Thunder, 1981, Amityville 3-D, 1983, Stephen King's Cat's Eye, 1984, At Close Range, 1986, The Blob, 1988, Cool-As-Ice, 1991, Buffy the Vampire Slayer, 1992, Radioland Murders, 1994, Niagara, Niagara, 1996, Cherry Falls, 1999; appeared in TV movies Amateur Night at the Dixie Bar and Grill, 1978, Where The Ladies Go, 1980, Rodeo Girl, 1980, Popeye Doyle, 1986, Plan of attack, 1992; appeared in off-Broadway show A Coupla White Chicks Sitting Around Talking, 1981, (play) It's Raining on Hope Street, 1988, Loose Lips, 1995.

CLARK, CARLETON EARL, tax consultant; b. North Easton, Mass., Apr. 5, 1942; s. Carleton Earl and Amy Ella (Toner) C.; m. Judy Carol Johnson (div. 1983); children: Amy Laura, Carla Elaine; m. Janice E. Dutra, Apr. 30, 1989. BS in Acctg., Bentley Coll., 1980. Asst. v.p. BayBank Norfolk, Dedham, Mass., 1967-89; tax cons. E.W. Costa, Pub. Acct., Brockton, Mass., 1989-93; pres. Costa & Clark, Inc., Brockton, 1993-96; tax preparer H&R Block, 1997—; pvt. practice tax cons., Brockton, Mass., 1985—. Mem. Nat. Assn. Accts., Nat. Soc. Pub. Accts., Mass. Soc. Ind. Accts. Democrat. Congregationalist. Home: 670 Pearl St Brockton MA 02301-4527

CLARK, CAROLYN ARCHER, aerospace technologist, life scientist; b. Leon County, Tex., Feb. 16, 1944; d. Ray Brooks and Dena Mae (Green) Archer; m. Frank Ray Clark, Nov. 20, 1960 (div. Oct. 1979); children: Frank Ray, Valerie Lynn, Bruce Layne; m. Jack G. Simpson, May 1993. BA, Sam Houston State U., 1961; MS, Tex. A&M U., 1973, PhD, 1977. Supr., bookkeeper Rep. Sewing Machine Distbrs., Dallas, 1961-65; door-to-door sales rep. Avon Products, Inc., Bryan, Tex., 1965-72; lectr. Tex. A&M U., College Station, 1977, rsch. assoc., 1977-79; sr. scientist Lockheed Emsco, Houston, 1979-82, prin. scientist, 1983-85, staff scientist, 1987-88; aerospace technologist, phys. scientist NASA Stennis Space Ctr., Miss., 1985-87; sr. project mgr., office mgr. Ctr. for Space and Advanced Tech., Houston, 1988-91; staff scientist Lockheed Engring. and Scis. Co., Houston, 1991-94; pres. Archer, Clark & Assocs., The Woodlands, Tex., 1994—; adj. prof. Montgomery Coll., Conroe, Tex.; cons. in field. Contbr. articles to profl. publs. Recipient Commendation for Outstanding Contbns. Lockheed, 1979-80, 91, Commendation for Excellence, 1984; Cert. of Merit U.S. Dept. Agr. 1980; Grad. Rsch. fellow Tex. A&M, 1975-76; NSF co-grantee Tex. A&M, 1976-77. Mem. Am. Soc. Plant Taxonomists, Bot. Soc. Am., Sigma Xi, Phi Sigma, Alpha Chi, Kappa Delta Pi. Republican. Avocations: sailing, scuba diving, tennis, piano.

CLARK, CAROLYN CHAMBERS, nurse, author, educator; b. Superior, Wis., Mar. 25, 1941; d. John and Phyllis (Olsen) Stark. BS, U. Wis., 1964; MS, Rutgers U., Newark, 1966; EdD, Columbia U., 1976. RN, Fla.; cert. advanced registered nurse practitioner, Fla. Instr. Bergen Community Coll., Paramus, N.J., 1972-74; pvt. practice wellness nursing, 1972—; found, dir. The Wellness Inst., Sloatsburg, 1979-84; assoc. prof. Pace U., Pleasantville, N.Y., 1983-84; prof., wellness coord. U. Tampa, Fla., 1984-85; cons. VA Med. Ctr., Bay Pines, Fla., 1988-89, provider continuing programs for nurses, 1990—; nurse practitioner/cons. Bay Area Psychol. Svcs., 1994—; dir. Women's Wellness Ctr. of the Resource Ctr. for Women, 1994—; mem. grad. faculty Walden U., 1999—, Schiller Internat. U., 1998—. Author: Nursing Concepts and Processes, 1977, The Nurse as Group Leader, 1977, 3rd edit., 1994 (also pub. in Swedish, German), Mental Health Aspects of Community Health Nursing, 1978, Classroom Skills for Nurse Educators, 1978, Assertive Skills for Nurses, 1978, Management in Nursing, 1979, The Nurse as Continuing Educator, 1979, Enhancing Wellness: A Guide for Self-Care, 1981, Wellness Nursing: Concepts, Theory, Research and Practice, 1986, Deadlier than Death, 1993, Dangerous Alibis, Cast Into The Fire, 1994, Wellness Practitioner, 1996, Creating a Climate for Power Learning, 1997; editor, pub. The Wellness Newsletter, 1980-94; editor Alternative Health Practitioner: The Jour. of Complimentary and Natural Care, 1995—; pres. Wellness Resources, 1992—; editor-in-chief Ency. Complementary Health Practices, 1999; contbr. articles to profl. jours.; mem. editl. bd. Am. Jour. Holistic Nursing, 1985-88, Women's Health Care Internat., 1985—. Recipient award Fla. Free Lance Writers Assn., 1988, 92, comm. and media award Fla. Nurses Assn., 1997. Fellow Am. Acad. Nursing. Office: 3451 Central Ave Saint Petersburg FL 33713-8522

CLARK, CAROLYN COCHRAN, lawyer; b. Kansas City, Mo., Oct. 30, 1941; d. John Rogers and Betty Charleton (Holmes) Cochran; m. L. David Clark, Jr., Dec. 29, 1967; children: Gregory David, Timothy Rogers. BA, U. Mo., 1963; LLB, Harvard U., 1968. Bar: N.Y. 1968, Fla. 1979. Assoc. Milbank, Tweed, Hadley & McCloy, N.Y.C., 1968-76, ptnr., 1977—. Mem. deferred giving com., former regional chmn. major gifts com. Harvard Law Sch. Fund; mem. vis. com. Harvard Law Sch., 1982-88; mem. com. on trust and estate gift plans Rockefeller U.; trustee Madison Ave. Presbyn. Ch., 1984-86, N.Y. Bot. Garden, 1993-96, Vis. Nurse Assn. N.Y. and Vis. Nurse Health Care, 1991-96, Riverdale Country Sch., 1994-98, Milbank Meml. Fund, 1996—; del. John D. Rockefeller Conf. Philanthropy in the 21st Century, N.Y., 1989; bd. advisors NYU program Philanthropy and the Law; chmn. program taxation exempt orgns. NYU Tax Inst. Recipient Disting. Alumna award U. Mo., 1989. Fellow Am. Coll. Trust and Estate Counsel (regent, chmn. com. on charitable giving and exempt orgns.), N.Y. Bar Found., Am. Bar Found.; mem. ABA (chmn. subcom. income taxation of charitable trusts 1976-78, chmn. com. charitable instns. 1989-94), Assn. Bar City of N.Y. (chmn. com. on non-profit orgns. 1986-89, sec. com. philanthropic orgns. 1976-82, mem. com. trusts, estates and surrogates cts. 1977-80, 85-86), N.Y. State Bar Assn. (com. estate planning, trusts and estates sect. 1978-89), Am. Law Inst., Practising Law Inst. (lectr.), Harvard U. Law Sch., Assn. Greater N.Y. (trustee 1978-80, v.p. 1980-81, pres. 1981-82), NYU Tax Inst. (chmn. conf. tax planning charitable orgns. 1993-95), Nat. Harvard Law Sch. Alumni Assn. (exec. com. 1978-80, v.p. 1986-90, pres. 1990-92), Soc. Colonial Dames Am. in Mo., Maidstone Club. Home: 161 E 79th St New York NY 10021-0421 Office: Milbank Tweed Hadley Et Al 54th Fl 1 Chase Manhattan Plz New York NY 10005-1401

CLARK, CATHERINE KAY, human recources specialist; b. Eaton, Ind., July 21, 1930; d. Sidney Clarence and Ora Matteson Crawley; m. Richard C. Clark, Jr., June 2, 1951; children: Richard C., Steven Crawley, Mary. BS, Ball State U., 1962, MA, 1973. Cert. tchr. (life) English, speech, journalism, libr. sci., audio/visual, Ind. Tchr./libr. Daleville H.S., Ind., 1962-66; tchr. Yorktown H.S., Ind., 1966-67; head libr. loan svc. Ball State U., Muncie, Ind., 1967-71; employment specialist E. Cen. Pvt. Industry Coun., Muncie, Ind., 1995-99. Author: (book) Verbs, Nouns, Kings and Clowns, 1972. Recipient Svc. in Edn. award, Daleville Cmty. Schs., 1997. Avocations: martial arts, cycling. Office: ECPIC 201 E Charles Muncie IN 47305

CLARK, CATHY ANN, mathematician; b. Paterson, N.J., June 2, 1948; d. Donald Bradway and Susan Johns (Latham) C.; children: Julianne Jones, Jared Jones, Jessica Jones. BS in Math., Morehead State U., 1970; MS in Math., U. Conn., 1976, postgrad., 1975-77, 92-95, doctoral, 1993-96; student in Elec. Engring., U. R.I., 1996—. Systems analyst Western Union Corp., Mahwah, N.J., 1969-73; tchr., rsch. asst. U. Conn., Storrs, 1973-77; lectr. Conn. Community Colls., Manchester, Danielson and, Norwich, 1975-78; mathematician Sonalysts, Inc., Waterford, Conn., 1979-97, Naval Undersea Warfare Ctr., Newport, R.I., 1997—. Mem. Susila Buddhi Dharma Internat. Mem. Am. Math. Soc., Soc. for Indsl. and Applied Math., Mensa. Avocations: writing, painting, music, lit.; E-mail address: clark-ca@mot.nuwc.navy.mil. Office: Naval Undersea Warfare Ctr Submarine Sonar Dept Code 2111 1176 Howell St Newport RI 02841-1708

CLARK, CELIA RUE, lawyer; b. N.Y.C., Aug. 16, 1951; d. Edward Frank and Rosemary (Reddick) Clark, Jr.; m. Edgar Crawford Gentry, Jr., Aug. 11, 1979; children: Diana Marron, Carl Edgar. B.A. with distinction, U. Wis., 1974; J.D., U. Chgo., 1979, LLM, NYU, 1988. Bar: N.Y. 1980. Mng. editor Heldref Publs., Washington, 1974-78; assoc. Rogers & Wells, N.Y.C., 1979-84; adj. asst. prof. law Yeshiva U., 1985; assoc. Weitzner, Levine & Hamburg, N.Y.C., 1988-92; counsel Pirro, Collier, Cohen, Crystal & Block, White Plains, N.Y., 1992-96; ptnr. Smith, Buss & Jacobs, L.L.P., Yonkers, N.Y., 1996—. Contbg. author: Asset-Based Financing, 1984, Jour. Taxation, 1998. Mem. ABA, Westchester County Bar Assn. Democrat. Office: Smith Buss & Jacobs LLP 733 Yonkers Ave Yonkers NY 10704-2635

CLARK, CHAPIN DEWITT, law educator; b. Lawrence, Kans., Dec. 27, 1930; s. Carroll DeWitt and Pearl (Holl) C.; m. Dorothy L. Becker, May 25, 1952; children—Julia Kay, Jeffrey Becker. A.B., U. Kans., 1952, LL.B., 1954; LL.M., Columbia U., 1959. Bar: Kans. 1954, Oreg. 1965. Asst. prof. law U. S.D., 1959-62; assoc. prof. law U. Oreg., 1962-67, prof., 1967-91, prof. emeritus, 1991—, dean Sch. Law, 1974-80; vice chmn. Oreg. Water Policy Rev. Bd., 1975-77, chmn., 1977-79; vis. prof. U.S. Mil. Acad., West Point, N.Y., 1980-81, 86-87; pres. Pacific 10 Athletic Conf., 1984-85; vis. prof. Wash. U. Law Sch., 1992. Contbr. articles to profl. jours. Pres. Planned Parenthood Lane County, 1975-76; mem. Gov.'s Commn. on Oceanography, 1967-68. Served with JAGC U.S. Army, 1954-58; col. USAR. Mem. Am. Bar Assn., AAUP (pres. U. Oreg. chpt. 1970-71, pres. Oreg. State conf. 1985-86), Am. Alpine Club. Home: 3565 Knob Hill Ln Eugene OR 97405-4738 Office: U Oreg Sch of Law Eugene OR 97403

CLARK, CHARLES ALAN, financial analyst; b. Wichita, Kans., July 17, 1951; s. Marvin Daniel and Doris Marie (Huson) C.; m. Barbara Annemarie Schmelz, May 18, 1985. BSEE, U. Colo., 1977, MS in Fin., 1988. New product devel. engr. Hewlett-Packard Co., Loveland, Colo., 1977-83, regional sales engr., 1983-85; investment adv. cons. Palo Alto, Calif., 1988-92; equity analyst ValueLine, Inc., N.Y.C., 1992—. Office: ValueLine Inc 220 E 42nd St New York NY 10017-5806

CLARK, CHARLES EDWARD, arbitrator; b. Cleve., Feb. 27, 1921; s. Douglas James and Mae (Egermayer) C.; m. Nancy Jane Hilt, Mar. 11, 1942; children: Annette S. (Mrs. Paul Gernhardt), Charles Edward, John A., Nancy P. Gonzalez, Paul R., Stephen C., David G. Student, Berea Coll., 1939-40, King Coll., 1945; JD, U. Tex., 1948. Bar: Tex. 1948, Mass. 1956, U.S. Supreme Ct. 1959. Sole practice San Antonio, 1948-55; writer legal articles, editor NACCA Law Jour., Boston, 1955-58; legal asst. to vice chmn., chief voting sect. U.S. Commn. on Civil Rights, Washington, 1958-61; spl. counsel Pres.'s Com. on Equal Employment Opportunity, Washington, 1961-65; sr. compliance officer Office Fed. Contract Compliance, Washington, 1965-66; regional dir. Equal Employment Opportunity Commn., Kansas City, Mo., 1966-79, arbitrator, 1979—; prof. law, asst. dean St. Mary's U. Sch. Law, 1948-55; lectr. Rockhurst Coll., 1980-91, Longview Coll., 1988—. Contbr. articles to legal jours. Active Boy Scouts Am. Served with AUS, 1943-44. Mem. VFW, Soc. Profls. in Dispute Resolution, State Bar Tex., Tex. Law Rev. Assn., Am. GI Forum (D.C. vice chmn. 1962-63), Indsl. Rels. Rsch. Assn. (exec. bd. Kansas City 1976-91, pres. chpt. 1986), Phi Delta Phi (province pres. 1951-55). Home and Office: 6418 Washington St Kansas City MO 64113-1732

CLARK, CHARLES M., JR., research institution adminstrator; b. Greensburg, Ind., Mar. 12, 1938; s. Charles Malcolm and Mary Louise (Christian) C.; m. Julia Berg Freeman, Jan 27, 1963 (div. 1982); children: Margaret Louise, Brian Alexander; m. Eleanor DeArman Kinney, June 25, 1983; 1 child, Janet Marie Clark. BA, Ind. U., 1960, MD, 1963. From asst. prof. to prof. medicine Ind. U., Indpls., 1969—, from asst. prof. to prof. pharmacology, 1970—; assoc. chief staff rsch. and devel. VA Hosp., Indpls., 1988—; dir. Diabetes Rsch. and Tng. Ctr., Indpls., 1977—; co-dir. Regenstrief Inst., Indpls., 1993-97; chmn. Safety and Quality com. DCCT, 1982-93, Nat. Diabetes adv. bd., 1987-88; chair Nat. Diabetes Edn. Program, 1995—. Editor Diabetes Care, 1996—; contbr. numerous articles to profl. jours. Lt comdr. USPHS, 1967-69. Mem. ACP, Am. Soc. Clin. Investigation, Internat. Diabetes Fedn., Am. Diabetes Assn. (Banting award 1989). Office: Regenstrief Inst 1001 W 10th St Fl 5 Indianapolis IN 46202-2859

CLARK, CHARLES SUTTER, interior designer; b. Venice, Calif., Dec. 21, 1927; s. William Sutter and Lodema Ersell (Fleeman) C. Student Chouinard Art Inst., Los Angeles, 1950-51. Interior designer LM.H. Co., Gt. Falls, Mont., 1956-62, Andreason's Interiors, Oakland, Calif., 1962-66, Western Contact Furnishers Internat., Oakland, 1966-70, Design Five Assocs., Lafayette, Calif., 1972-73; owner, interior designer Charles Sutter Clark Interiors, Greenbrae, Calif., 1973-91, San Rafael, Calif., 1991—. Served with USAF, 1951-55. Recipient prizes Mont. State Fair, 1953-55. Mem. Am. Soc. Interior Designers. Home: 429 El Faisan Dr San Rafael CA 94903-4517

CLARK, CHARLES T(ALIFERRO), retired business statistics educator; b. Danville, Ill., Mar. 18, 1917; s. Charles A. and Kathryn S. (Gentry) C.; m. Pearl W. DuBose, Oct. 6, 1943; children: Charles A., Mary D., Robert S. B.B.A., U. Tex., 1938, M.B.A., 1939, Ph.D., 1956. Asst. mgr. Austin C. of C., Tex., 1940-41; dir. personnel U. Tex., Austin, 1946-59, asst. prof. bus. stats., 1959-60, assoc. prof., 1961-79, prof., 1979-91, Mary Lee Harkins Sweeney Centennial prof. emeritus in bus., 1991—; bd. dirs. Tex. Student Publs., Austin, 1964-69, Tex. Union, Austin, 1969-83, Univ. Fed. Credit Union, Austin, 1976-84 , Univ. Coop. Soc., Austin, 1980-84. Author numerous text books; (with L.L. Schkade) textbooks Statistical Analysis for Adminstrative Decision, 1969, 4th edit., 1983, (with John R. Stockton) Introduction to Business and Economic Statistics, 1971, 3d edit., 1980; contbr. articles to profl. jours. Served to 2d lt. USAAC, 1941-46, PTO. Recipient 11 teaching awards U. Tex., 1960-80. Mem. Coll. and Univ. Personnel Assn. (pres. 1959), Austin Personnel Assn. (pres. 1950), Austin Stat. Assn. (pres. 1975). Home: 4106 Farhills Dr Austin TX 78731-2812 Office: U Tex Dept of Business Austin TX 78712

CLARK, CHRISTINE MAY, editor, author; b. Peoria, Ill., Apr. 25, 1957; d. Darrell Ronald and Alice Venita (Burkitt) French; m. Terry Randolph Clark, Aug. 28, 1982. BA, Judson Coll., 1978. Assoc. editor David C. Cook Pub., Elgin, Ill., 1978-80; editor Humpty Dumpty, 1980-94; editor Children's Digest, 1980-83, Jack and Jill , 1983-86, Turtle mag., 1990—; editorial dir. Children's Better Health Inst., Indpls.; assoc. editor Highlights for Children, Honesdale, Pa., 1994-96; mng. editor Highlights for Children, 1996—; v.p. editl. Highlights for Children, 1997—; bd. dirs. Highlights for Children, Inc. Author: (religious curriculum) Come, Follow Me, 1983, Living in Covenant, 1985. Contbr. articles and stories to children's and adult religious mags., also to Indpls. Monthly, Indpls. Woman, This Is Indianapolis, Key Horizons. Asst. scout leader Fox Valley Council Girl Scouts U.S., 1972; vol. Elgin Mental Health Ctr., 1975-76; big sister Big Sister-Little Sister Program, Elgin, 1980. Recipient journalism award EDPRESS, 1986, 87, 88, 89, 90, 92, Outstanding Reporting award Soc. Profl. Journalists, 1990; Aurora Found. scholar, 1975. Mem. Am. Soc. Mag. Editors, Soc. Children's Book Writers and Illustrators, Ednl. Press Assn., Judson Coll. Alumni Assn. Reorganized Ch. of Jesus Christ of Latter-day Saints. Avocations: Piano; travel. Office: Highlights for Children 803 Church St Honesdale PA 18431-1895*

CLARK, CLAUDIA PIA, preschool administrator; b. Stamford, Conn., Dec. 20, 1950; d. Albert James and Patricia Romme (de Vitalis) Pia; (div. 1990); children: Jason Matthew, Justin Michael. BS in Psychology, U. Bridgeport, 1974; MS in Edn. in Guidance/Sch. Psychology, So. Conn. State U., 1979; postgrad., Fla. Atlantic U. Cert. behavior analysis, Fla.; cert. tchr., Fla. Pvt. practice cons. intensive behavioral and autism Broward County, Fla.; coord. presch. program/autism St. Mary's Hosp., West Palm Beach, Fla., 1996—; cons. behavior analysis Subcontract-HRS Devel. Svcs., Ft. Lauderdale, Fla., 1991-95; tchr. autism primary and elem. edn. Broward County Bd. Edn., Ft. Lauderdale, 1990-95; presenter in field. Mem. Coun. for Exceptional Children, Assn. for Behavior Analysis, Phi Kappa Phi. Episcopalian. Avocations: stained glass artist, martial arts, music (vocal, guitar and harp). Office: St Marys Hosp Preschool for Autism 5313 Greenwood Ave West Palm Beach FL 33407-2440

CLARK, CLIFFORD EDWARD, JR., history educator; b. BayShore, N.Y., July 13, 1941; s. Clifford Edward and Helen C.; m. Grace Williams, Aug. 20, 1966; children: Cynthia Williams, Christopher Allen, Susan McGrath. BA, Yale U., 1963; MA, Harvard U., 1964, PhD in Am. Civilization, 1968. History tutor Harvard U., Cambridge, Mass., 1966-67; instr. Amherst (Mass.) Coll., 1968-69, asst. prof., 1969-70; from asst. to assoc. prof. Carleton Coll., Northfield, Minn., 1970-80, prof. history, 1980—, M.A. & A.D. Hulings Prof. of Am. Studies, 1982—, dir. summer acad. programs, 1984—, chmn. history dept., 1986-89; cons. Minn. Humanities Commn., Mpls., 1976—, Minn. Hist. Soc., Mpls., 1982—; Northfield Sch. Bd., 1978-87; editl. cons. Winterthur Portfolio, Del., 1983-92. Author: Henry Ward Beecher, Spokesman for a Middle-Class America, 1978, The American Family Home, 1800-1960, 1986, (with others) The Enduring Tradition, 1996; editor: Minnesota in a Century of Change: The State and Its People Since 1900, 1989. Mem. Northfield Heritage Preservation Commn., 1986. Fellow Woodrow Wilson Found., 1964, 67; Demonstration grantee NEH, 1978, sr. fellow NEH, 1980; recipient Younger Humanist Summer Stipend, NEH, 1973. Mem. Am. Studies Assn., Am. Hist. Assn., Orgn. Am. Historians, Northfield Hist. Soc. Episcopalian. Avocations: tennis, squash. Home: 718 4th St E Northfield MN 55057-2316 Office: Carleton Coll Dept History One N College St Northfield MN 55057

CLARK, CLIFTON BOB, physicist; b. nr. Fort Smith, Ark., July 8, 1927; s. Clifton Breckenridge and Coly (Stroud) C.; m. Sue Magruder, Sept. 1, 1950; children—Carol Jane, Charles Brian, Richard Thomas. B.A., U. Ark., 1949, M.A., 1950; Ph.D., U. Md., 1957. Asst. prof. sci. Florence State Tchrs. Coll., 1950-51; asst. prof. physics U.S. Naval Acad., 1951-55; asso. prof., 1956-57; physicist U.S. Naval Research Lab., 1955-56; asso. prof. physics So. Meth. U., Dallas, 1957-61; prof. So. Meth. U., 1961-65, head dept., 1962-65; physicist, head dept. U. N.C., Greensboro, 1965-75, prof., 1965-94, prof. emeritus, 1994—; vis. prof. physics Fla. State U., 1975-76. Served with USNR, 1945-46. Mem. Am. Assn. Physics Tchrs. (pres. South Atlantic Coast sect. 1974-75, 77-78, pres. N.C. sect. 1996-97), Am. Phys. Soc. (treas. S.E. sect. 1973-91), N.C. Acad. Sci., Phi Beta Kappa, Sigma Xi, Sigma Pi Sigma, Pi Mu Epsilon, Kappa Mu Epsilon, Omicron Delta Kappa. Home: 800 Montrose Dr Greensboro NC 27410-5428 Office: U NC Dept Physics and Astronomy PO Box 26170 Greensboro NC 27402-6170 *I believe people who are happy are those who accept doing things they do not enjoy as the price they pay for getting to do the things they enjoy. The most pleasant of experiences is the completion of a task which demanded extremely hard work. The most unhappy people I have known are those who cheated themselves of this satisfaction, because they tired of hard work and quit before they completed an endeavor.*

CLARK, COLIN WHITCOMB, mathematics educator; b. Vancouver, B.C., Can., June 18, 1931; s. George Savage and Irene (Stewart) C.; m. Janet Arlene Davidson, Sept. 17, 1955; children: Jennifer Kathleen, Karen Elizabeth, Graeme David. BA, U. B.C., 1953; PhD, U. Wash., 1958. Instr. math. U. Calif., Berkeley, 1958-60; asst. prof. math. U. B.C., 1960-65, assoc. prof., 1965-68, prof., 1968-94, acting dir. Inst. Applied Math., 1983-86, prof. emeritus, 1994—; vis. prof. math. N.Mex. State U., 1970-71; vis. scientist Fisheries and Oceanography div. C.S.I.R.O., Cronulla, Australia, 1975-76, Ecology and Evolutionary Biology, U. Ariz., 1992; Regents lectr. U. Calif., Davis, 1986; vis. prof. Biol. Scis. Cornell U., 1987; vis. prof. Princeton U., 1997. Author: The Theoretical Side of Calculus, 1972, Mathematical Bioeconomics, 1976, 2d edit., 1990, Elementary Mathematical Analysis, 1982, Bioeconomic Modelling and Fisheries Management, 1985, (with J. Conrad) Resource Economics: Notes and Problems, 1987, (with M. Mangel) Dynamic Modeling in Behavioral Ecology, 1988, (with J. Yoshimura, eds.) Adaption in Stochastic Environments, 1993; contbr. articles to profl. jours. Fellow Royal Soc. Can., Royal Soc. (U.K.); mem. Can. Applied Math. Soc. (pres. 1981-83), Soc. Indsl. and Applied Math., Resource Modeling Assn. (pres. 1988-90), Internat. Soc. for Ecol. Econ. Office: Univ BC, Dept Math, Vancouver, BC Canada V6T 1Z2

CLARK, DAVID LEIGH, marine geologist, educator; b. Albuquerque, N.Mex., June 15, 1931; s. Leigh William and Sadie (Ollerton) C.; m. Louise Boley, Aug. 31, 1951; children: Steven, Douglas, Julee, Linda. BS, Brigham Young U., 1953, MS, 1954; PhD in Geology, U. Iowa, 1957. Geologist Standard Oil Calif., Albuquerque, 1954; asst. geologist Columbia U., 1954-

55; asst. U. Iowa, 1955-57; asst. prof. So. Meth. U., Dallas, 1957-59; asst. to assoc. prof. Brigham Young U., Provo, Utah, 1959-63; assoc. prof. U. Wis., Madison, 1963-68; prof. geology and geophysics U. Wis.-Madison, 1968—, chmn. dept. geology and geophysics, 1971-74, assoc. dean natural scis., 1986-91; chmn. polar rsch. bd. NAS, 1995—. Author Fossils, Paleontology, Evolution, 1968,72; author and coordinator: Treatise on Invertebrate Paleontology-Conodonts, 1981. Recipient Fulbright award Bonn, W.Ger., 1965-66; Disting. Professorship U. Wis., 1974. Fellow Geol. Soc. Am.; mem. Paleontol. Soc., Am. Assn. Petroleum Geologists, Soc. Econ. Paleontologists and Mineralogists, Am. Geophys. Union, Pander Soc., Paleontol. Assn., N.Am. Micropaleontology Soc., AAAS. Mem. LDS Ch. Home: 2812 Oxford Rd Madison WI 53705-2218

CLARK, DAVID MCKENZIE, lawyer; b. Greenville, N.C., Sept. 1, 1929; s. David McKenzie and Myrtle Estelle (Brogdon) C.; m. Martha McKellar Early; children: David, Martha Dockery, Marietta Brogdon, Carolyn Elizabeth; m. Susan Summers Mullally; 1 child, McKenzie Lawrence. BA, Wake Forest Coll., 1951; LLD, NYU, 1957. Law clerk Chambers of Justice Black U.S. Supreme Court, Washington, D.C., 1957-59; assoc. Smith, Moore, Smith, Schell & Hunter, Greensboro, N.C., 1959-63; ptnr. Stern Rendleman & Clark, Greensboro, N.C., 1964-68, Clark & Wharton, Greensboro, N.C., 1968-98, Clark Bloss & McIver, Greensboro, 1999—. Mem. bd. dirs. Legal Svcs. of N.C., Raleigh, 1976-82; pres. Summit Rotary Club, Greensboro, 1967; mem. bd. trustees W. Market Street Methodist Ch., Greensboro; chmn., co-founder Greensboro Legal Aid Found., 1965-68. Mem. ABA, Am. Trial Lawyers Assn., Am. Bd. Trial Advocates, N.C. Bar Assn. (bd. govs. 1982-85), N.C. Acad. Trial Lawyers, Greensboro Bar Assn. (bd. dirs.). Avocations: golf, tennis. Home: 328 E Greenway Dr N Greensboro NC 27403-1560 Office: Clark & Wharton 125 S Elm St Ste 600 Greensboro NC 27401-2644

CLARK, DAVID RANDOLPH, wholesale grocer; b. Columbia, S.C., Mar. 25, 1943; s. Joseph Wilbur and Josephine (Timberlake) C.; m. Carole Jane Cooper, Aug. 21, 1965; 1 dau., Catherine. BA, Wofford Coll., 1965; MBA, U. S.C., 1966. V.p., gen. mgr. Thomas & Howard Co., Spartanburg, S.C., 1969-77; pres., CEO Thomas & Howard Co., Columbia, S.C., 1977—; chmn. T&H Ins. Agy.; bd. dirs. Timberlake Grocery Co., Macon, Ga.; Columbia regional adv. bd. SCANA Corp.; sec. Flint Lake, Inc. 1993—; mng. ptnr. Timber Lands Co.; mng. gen. ptnr. Tanglewood Co., L.P., 1995-98; pres. WDM Co., Inc., 1998—. Mem. campaign cabinet United Way, 1975; Eagle Scout, Boy Scouts Am., bd. dirs. Indian Waters coun.; trustee S.C. Found. Ind. Colls., S.C. Coll. Coun. Lt. U.S. Army, Vietnam. Mem. Nat. Am. Wholesale Grocers Assn., So. Food Dealers Assn. (sec.-treas. 1988-90, pres. 1998—), S.C. Assn. Convenience Food Stores (bd. dirs.), Wofford Coll. Alumni Assn. (bd. dirs. 1984-87, 89-92, pres. 1990-91, v.p. 1991-92), Sapphire Valley Country Club, Wofford Club Greater Columbia (bd. dirs. 1979—), Forest Lake Club (mng. com. 1998—), Flamenco Club, Tarantella Club, Camellia Ball (treas. 1992-95, pres. 1995), Rotary (pres. Columbia 1989-90), Scabbard & Blade, Phi Beta Kappa, Pi Gamma Mu, Pi Kappa Alpha. Episcopalian. Office: Thomas & Howard Co P O Box 23659 Columbia SC 29224-3659

CLARK, DAVID WILLIAM, lawyer, councilman; b. Manchester, Eng., Jan. 27, 1954; s. Chandler Kinney and May Clark; m. Debra Solseng, June 10, 1980 (div. Sept. 1986); m. Sally Catherine Grigg, June 27, 1987; children: Hilary Alexandra, Gillian Noelle. AB in History, Princeton U., 1975; JD, Duke U., 1978. Bar: Calif. 1978, Colo. 1990, Fla. 1992. Assoc. Thelen, Marrin, Johnson & Bridges, L.A., 1978-84; counsel Ultrasys. Inc. (later Hadson Corp.), Irvine, Calif., 1984-89, Oxbow Corp., West Palm Beach, Fla., 1989—. Councilman City of Palm Beach Gardens, Fla., 1993—, mayor, 1994-95; bd. dirs. Palm Beach County chpt. ARC, West Palm Beach, 1998—. Mem. State Bar Calif., Colo. Bar Assn., Fla. Bar Assn. Republican. Avocations: reading, history, ships and the sea. Home: 134 Satinwood Ln Palm Beach Gardens FL 33410 Office: Oxbow Corp 1601 Forum Pl Ste P-2 West Palm Beach FL 33401

CLARK, DAVID WRIGHT, lawyer; b. West Point, Miss., May 19, 1948; s. Douglas Earl and Sarah Evelyn (Wright) C.; m. Victoria Baugher, Oct. 16, 1976; children: Alexander, Nicholas, Peter. BA with high honors, Millsaps Coll., 1970; MA, Harvard U., 1971; JD, U. Mich., 1974. Bar: Ill. 1974, Miss. 1978, U.S. Dist. Ct. (no. dist.) Ill. 1974, U.S. Ct. Appeals (7th cir.) 1974, U.S. Dist. Ct. (so. and no. dists.) Miss. 1978, U.S. Ct. Appeals (5th cir.) 1978. Adj. prof. Miss. Coll. Sch. Law, Jackson, 1978-82; assoc. Wildman, Harrold, Allen & Dixon, Chgo., Friedman & Koven, Chgo., 1974-78; shareholder Wise Carter Child & Caraway, P.A., Jackson, 1978-96; ptnr. Lake Tindall, LLP, Jackson, 1996—; bd. dirs. Ctrl. Miss. Legal Svcs., Jackson, 1989-97; pres. Miss. Bar Rev., 1979—. Mem. Miss. Constitution Study Commn., Jackson, 1985-87; bd. dirs. Miss. First, Inc., Jackson, 1983-87; pres. U.S.A. Internat. Ballet Competition, Jackson, 1990-98; mem. Leadership Jackson, 1989-90. Mem. ABA (dir. sect. litigation divsn., com. chmn. and task force chmn. 1987-95, chmn. gun violence coord. com. 1998—), Miss. Bar Assn. (chmn. litigation sect. 1994-95), Am. Law Inst., Charles Clark Am. Inn of Ct. Avocations: musicals, opera. E-mail: dlark@laketindall.com. Home: 110 Olympia Fields Jackson MS 39211-2509 Office: Lake Tindall LLP One Jackson Pl Ste 450 Jackson MS 39201

CLARK, DAYLE MERITT, civil engineer; b. Lubbock, Tex., Sept. 5, 1933; s. Frank Meritt and Mamie Jewel (Huff) C.; BS, Tex. Tech. U., 1955; MS, So. Meth. U., 1967; m. Betty Ann Maples, Apr. 11, 1968; 1 dau., Alison. Registered profl. engr., registered profl. land surveyor. Field engr. Chgo. Bridge & Iron Co., 1955; mgr. L.K. Long Constrn. Co., 1958-64; faculty U. Tex., Arlington, 1964—; cons. AID, 1966, NSF, 1967-68; expert witness in court cases. Served to capt. USAF, 1955-57. Recipient Achievement award in Civil Engring., Tex. Soc. Profl. Engrs., Dallas chpt., 1995. Fellow ASCE (pres. Dallas br. 1987, pres. Tex. sect. 1992-93, Profl. Svcs. award 1991, Award of Honor, 1998); Club: Rotary (pres. Arlington-West 1986, Paul Harris fellow, Rotarian of Yr. 1987). Editor Tex. Civil Engr., 1967-71. Contbr. papers, reports to profl. jours. Office: PO Box 185 Arlington TX 76004-0185

CLARK, DEANNA DEE, civic leader and volunteer; b. Cedar Rapids, Iowa, June 1, 1944; d. Cyrus Dean and Isabelle Esther Thomas; m. Glen Edward Clark, July 16, 1966; children: Andrew Curtis, Carissa Jane. AA, Coll. of the Desert, 1964; BA, Coe Coll., 1966. Fund. devel. chmn. Nat. Assistance League, 1992-94, nationwide resource devel. writer and trainer, 1992—; pres. Provo-Jordan River Pky. Found., 1993-95; sustaining mem. Jr. League Salt Lake City, 1976—, Assistance League Salt Lake City, 1986—; mem. info. practices com. Utah Legislature, 1990; elder Presbyn. Ch., 1983—; bd. dirs. Friends of Libr., U. Utah, 1991-94, vice moderator, 1999—; convenor U.S. Internat. Youth Exch. Initiative Cmty. Network, Utah, 1984-94; mem. coun. Presbytery of Utah, 1985-98; mem. human svcs. subcom. child advocacy project, social justice and peacemaking ministry unit Presbyn. Ch. U.S.A., 1992-93, exec. com., pers. subcom., adv. com. on news, nat. ministries div. com., advocacy com. racial ethnic concerns, worldwide ministries divsn. com., 1993-98; bd. dirs. Westminster Coll. Found., 1993-96; co-chmn. Utah chpt. NCCJ, 1988-94, hon. co-chmn. 1994—; mem. Utah Riverway Enhancement com., 1993-96; bd. govs. Salt Lake Cmty. Found., 1995—; moderator Salt Lake Tribune Common Carrier, 1983-85, pres. Cottonwood H.S. PTS Assn., 1991-92. Mem. LWV (Utah pres. 1981-83), P.E.O. (historian Utah chpt. 1992-95, chpt. H 1990-92, pres. 1995-97, Utah chmn. Gump & Agers Scholarship Com. 1998-99). Home: 2102 Pheasant Way Salt Lake City UT 84121-1311

CLARK, DICK, former senator, ambassador, foreign affairs specialist; b. Central City, Iowa, Sept. 14, 1928; s. Clarence and Bernice C.; m. Jean Gross, 1954 (div. 1976); children—Thomas Richard, Julie Ann; m. Julie Kennett, 1977. Student, U. Md., Wiesbaden, Germany, 1950-52; B.A., Upper Iowa U., Fayette, 1953, LL.D. (hon.), 1973; M.A., U. Iowa, Iowa City, 1956; L.H.D. (hon.), Parsons Coll., 1973, Mt. Mercy Coll., Drake U., Cornell Coll., Haverford Coll., St. Ambrose Coll., Loras Coll.; LLD (hon.), Elizabethtown Coll., 1986. Instr. U. Iowa, Iowa City, 1956-59; asst. prof. history Upper Iowa U., 1959-64, pres. faculty; chmn. Office Emergency Planning, Iowa, 1963-64; adminstrv. asst. Congressman John C. Culver, 1965-72; nat. polit. organizer Presdl. campaign staff Robert F. Kennedy, 1968; mem. U.S. Senate from Iowa, 1973-79, chmn. African affairs sub-com. of fgn. relations Com., mem. rules com., fgn. relations com., agr. com., com. on aging, Democratic steering com.; dir. Congl. Program Aspen Inst., Washington, 1980—; pres. Members of Congress for Peace through Law, 1975-76; ambassador-at-large U.S. Dept. of State in charge of Am. Refugee Program, 1979; dep. campaign mgr. for Presdl. campaign Edward M. Kennedy, 1980. Bd. dirs. Ctr. Responsive Politics. Recipient Congl. Common Cause award, 1978. Fellow Woodrow Wilson Fellowship Found. (sr.); Coun. Fgn. Rels. Avocations: tennis, reading, music, theater. Address: Aspen Inst One Dupont Cir NW 7th Fl Washington DC 20036-1511*

CLARK, DON ALAN, journalist, reporter; b. June 6, 1953. BA in English, UCLA, 1975; MA, U. Minn., 1983. Reporter St. Paul Pioneer Press, 1980-86, San Francisco Chronicle, 1986-93; reporter, dep. bur. chief Wall St. Jour., San Francisco, 1993—. E-mail: dclark@well.com.

CLARK, DONALD MALIN, professional association executive; b. Buffalo, Feb. 11, 1929; s. Jack Merritt Malin and Louise Mary C.; m. Joan Marie Coyle, Dec. 27, 1958; children—Kevin Malin, Michael John, Elizabeth Anne. B.S. magna cum laude, Canisius Coll., Buffalo, 1950, M.A., 1952; Ed.D., SUNY, Buffalo, 1961; grad., U.S. Army Advanced Armor Sch., Ft. Knox, Ky., 1964, U.S. Army Command and Gen. Staff Coll., 1969, U.S. Army War Coll., 1975. Administrv. asst. Traveler's Ins. Co., Buffalo, N.Y., 1950-57; mem. faculty Orchard Park (N.Y.) Sr. High Sch., 1957-66; dir. Ctr. Econ. Edn. SUNY, Buffalo, 1966-70; exec. dir. Industry-Edn. Coun., Niagara Falls, N.Y., 1970-79; pres., CEO, Nat. Assn. Industry-Edn. Cooperation, Buffalo, 1979—; radio and TV pub. info. news commentator, 1962-78; adj. prof. Canisius Coll. Grad. Sch., Buffalo, 1962-63, Lemoyne Coll. Sch. Mgmt., Syracuse, N.Y., 1973-79, Rochester Inst. Tech., 1983-84; adj. prof. Mt. Carmel Coll., Niagra Falls, Ont., Can., 1966; summer faculty Nat. War Coll., Washington, 1967-68; pres. Consumer Credit Counseling Svc., Buffalo, 1973, edn. chmn.; dir. Industry Edn. Coun. Calif., 1992-94; mem. Econ. Forum, Buffalo, 1994—; mem. editl. adv. bd. for Business Ethics, 1988-92; selected by People to People Internat.'s Citizen Amb. Program as del. leader for industry and edn. leaders in U.S. to visit Russia, Latvia, 1993, to China, 1995, South Africa, 1996, U.K., 1997, Australia/New Zealand, 1998, China, 1999; cons. (on site) to Ministry of Ed., Koror, Rep. of Palau, Micronesia, 1996; profl. pianist pvt. functions, spl. occasions for agencies and orgns., 1986—. Author: Meeting the Challenge of a Free Society, 1965, United Kingdom, 1997; writer editls. Buffalo News and Business First; also newsletters handbooks, articles, guides; prodr. film on industry-edn. cooperation; author over 100 articles to nat. and Can. publs. Apptd. by Pres. Reagan to Nat. Adv. Coun. on Ednl. Rsch. and Improvement, 1988-90; lectr. St. Michael's Roman Cath. Ch., Buffalo; mem. cmty. adv. coun. SUNY, Buffalo, 1981—; mem. adv. bd. Erie C.C., Williamsville, N.Y., 1995-97. With U.S. ANG, col. USAR, 1948-83; held position of chief of the Western/East European Divsn., Directorate of Fgn. Intelligence, Dept. Army, 1980-83; bd. dirs. Amherst (N.Y.) Symphony Orch., 1997-98. Recipient Kazanjian Found. Coll. Econs. Tchg. award, 1968, Freedoms Found. medal, 1965, Presdl. Citation for Pvt. Sector Initiatives, 1985, Cert. of Recognition, U.S. Dept. Edn. for contbns. of time and talent toward adult literacy, 1984, Canisius Coll. Disting. Alumni award 1996; fellow NAM, 1965. Mem. Am. Soc. Tng. and Devel., Western N.Y. Export Coun. (assoc.), U.S. Dept. Commerce, Active Corps Execs., U.S. SBA, Ret. Officers Assn., Amherst Dance Club (pres. 1987-88), Phi Delta Kappa (rsch. award 1996). Republican. Roman Catholic. Avocations: piano, travel, reading, theatre, tennis, ballroom dancing. Home: 235 Hendricks Blvd Amherst NY 14226-3304 *Being in the vanguard of change has been the most exciting aspect of my professional career. To participate in effecting change, particularly in education and human resources, economic development requires risk taking and the determination to gain support for one's ideas.*

CLARK, DONALD ROBERT, retired insurance company executive; b. Chgo., Jan. 19, 1924; s. Sherman Fred and Frieda (Grossklags) C.; m. Lora Marie Steiner, Aug. 11, 1945; children: Gregory Wayne, Sharon Louise. Student, Northwestern U., 1941-43, U. Wis., 1943-44. With Kemper Nat. Ins. Cos., 1941-89; ret., 1989; exec. v.p. , dir. Am. Mfrs. Mut. Ins. Co., Am. Motorists Ins. Co., Kemper Corp., Lumbermen's Mut Casualty Co.; former v.p., dir. Am. Protection Ins. Co., Economy Fire & Casualty Co., Fed. Kemper Ins. Co., Fed. Kemper Life Assurance Co., Fidelity Life Assn., Kemper Internat. Corp., Kemper Europe Reassurances, Belgium, Kemper S.A., Belgium, Kemper Ins. Co., Australia, Kemper Reins. Co., Long Grove, Ill.; former dir. Kemper Reins. Co. London Ltd., Kemper Fin. Services, Inc., Kemper Fin. Cos., Inc., Kemper Investors Life Ins. Co. Chgo. Contbr. to: Insurance Accounting Fire and Casualty, 2d edit, 1965, Property-Liability Insurance Accounting, 1974. Mem. Ins. Acctg. and Systems Assn. (pres. 1968-69), Fin. Execs. Inst. Lutheran (past chmn. congregation and fin. com.). Home: 689 Glasgow Ln Prospect Heights IL 60070-2588

CLARK, DONALD SCOTT, federal official. B of Econs., Stanford U., 1974, M in Econs., 1976; JD, UCLA, 1977. Bar: Calif., D.C. Staff atty. Bur. Consumer Protection, Washington, 1977-80, Planning Office Bur. Competition, Washington, 1980-83; atty. advisor Commr. George Douglas, Washington, 1983-85, Chmn. James C. Miller III, Washington, 1985, Acting Chmn. Terry Calvani, Washington, 1985-86; staff atty. Appellate Sect. Antitrust Divsn., Dept. Justice, Washington, 1986-87; atty advisor Chmn. Daniel Oliver, Washington, 1987-88; sec. of the commn. Fed. Trade Commn., Washington, 1988—. Office: FTC 600 Pennsylvania Ave NW Washington DC 20580

CLARK, DWIGHT EDWARD, sports team executive, former professional football player; b. Kinston, N.C., Jan. 8, 1957. B.A., Clemson U., 1979. Wide receiver San Francisco 49ers, NFL, 1979-87, exec. v.p., dir. football ops., 1995-98, played in Super Bowl, 1981, 84; v.p., dir of football ops. Cleveland Browns, 1998—. Mem. NFL All-Star Team, 1981, 82. Office: c/o Cleveland Browns Cleveland Browns Stadium 1085 W 3rd St Cleveland OH 44114*

CLARK, EARNEST HUBERT, JR., tool company executive; b. Birmingham, Ala., Sept. 8, 1926; s. Earnest Hubert and Grace May (Smith) C.; m. Patricia Margaret Hamilton, June 22, 1947; children: Stephen D., Kenneth A., Timothy R., Daniel S., Scott H., Rebecca G. BS in Mech. Engring, Calif. Inst. Tech., 1946, MS, 1947. Chmn., chief exec. officer Friendship Group, Baker Hughes, Inc. (formerly Baker Oil Tools, Inc.), L.A., 1947-89, v.p., asst. gen. mgr., 1958-62, pres., chief exec. officer, 1962-69, 75-79, chmn. bd., 1969-75, 79-87, 87-89, ret., 1989; chmn. The Friendship Group, Newport Beach, Calif., 1989—; bd. dirs. Regenesis Inc., Am. Mut. Fund. Past chmn., bd. dirs. YMCA of U.S.A.; past chmn. bd. YMCA for Met. L.A.; mem. nat. coun. YMCA; trustee Harvey Mudd Coll. With USNR, 1944-46, 51-52. Mem. AIME, Am. Petroleum Inst., Petroleum Equipment Suppliers Assn. (bd. dirs.), Tau Beta Pi. Office: Friendship Group 3822 Calle Ariana San Clemente CA 92672-4502

CLARK, EDGAR SANDERFORD, insurance broker, consultant; b. N.Y.C., Nov. 17, 1933; s. Edgar Edmund, Jr., and Katharine Lee (Jarman) C.; student U. Pa., 1952-54; BS, Georgetown U., 1956, JD, 1958; postgrad. INSEAD, Fountainbleau, France, 1969, Golden Gate Coll., 1973, U. Calif., Berkeley, 1974; m. Nancy E. Hill, Sept. 13, 1975; 1 child, Schuyler; children by previous marriage: Colin, Alexandra, Pamela. Staff asst. U.S. Senate select com. to investigate improper activities in labor and mgmt. field, Washington, 1958-59; underwriter Ocean Marine Dept., Fireman's Fund Ins. Co., San Francisco, 1959-62; mgr. Am. Fgn. Ins. Assn., San Francisco, 1962-66; with Marsh & McLennan, 1966-72, mgr. for Europe, resident dir. Brussels, Belgium, 1966-70, asst. v.p., mgr. captive and internat. div., San Francisco, 1970-72; v.p., dir. Risk Planning Group, Inc., San Francisco, 1972-75; v.p., dir. global constrn. group Alexander & Alexander Inc., San Francisco, 1975-94; exec. dir. The Surplus Line Assn. of Calif., 1995-97; CEO Risk Solutions Corp., 1997—; lectr. in field; guest lectr. U. Calif., Berkeley, 1973, Am. Grad. Sch. Internat. Mgmt., 1981-82, Golden Gate U., annually 1985-91; dir. Soc. Ins. Brokers, 1991-94; del. Calif. Agts. and Brokers Legis. Coun., 1992-95; pres. Ins. Forums San Francisco. With USAF, 1956-58. Mem. Am. Mgmt. Assn., Am. Risk and Ins. Assn., Internat. Insurance Soc., Chartered Ins. Inst., Am. Soc. Internat. Law, Soc. Calif. Pioneers San Francisco, Meadow Club, Fairfax, Calif., World Trade San Francisco. Republican. Episcopalian. Mem. editl. bd. Risk Mgmt. Reports, 1973-76. Office: Risk Solutions Corp c/o 72 Millay Pl Mill Valley CA 94941-1501

CLARK, EDWARD FERDNAND, lawyer; b. Delaware, Ohio, May 10, 1921; s. Daniel John and Lillian (Holdgreve) C.; m. Helen Ruth Swick, Feb. 10, 1945; children—Pamela Ann (Mrs. James R. Hanser), Michael E., Steven J., Philip J., Joseph W., Edward C., Nicholas J. J.D., Ohio No. U., 1953. Bar: Ohio bar 1953. Claims examiner Central Mut. Ins. Co., Van Wert, Ohio, 1954-63; asso. firm Lindeman-Shenk-Clark, Delphos, 1963—; Sec., treas. M.I. Clark, Inc. Past pres. Citizens for Delphos Com.; mem. exec. com. Mental Health and Retardation Bd., Van Wert, Mercer and Paulding Counties; pres. St. John's Parochial Sch. Bd. Served to capt. AUS, 1942-47. Mem. Van Wert County (sec.-treas., pres.), Allen County, Ohio, N.W. Dist. bar assns., Delphos C. of C., V.F.W., Am. Legion, Am. Fedn. Musicians (v.p. local 1949-50), Home and Sch. Assn. (pres. 1959). Democrat. Roman Catholic. Clubs: Kiwanian (pres. Delphos 1964-65), K.C. (4 deg.). Home: 425 N Clay St Delphos OH 45833-1453 Office: 214 W 2nd St Delphos OH 45833-1603*

CLARK, ELIAS, law educator; b. New Haven, Aug. 19, 1921. B.A., Yale U., 1943, LL.B., 1947, M.A., 1957. Bar: N.Y. 1948, Conn. 1950. Assoc. Cleary, Gottlieb, Friendly & Cox, N.Y.C., 1947-49; mem. faculty Law Sch., Yale U., New Haven, 1949—, prof., 1958—, Lafayette S. Foster prof., 1968—; master Silliman Coll., 1962-81. Co-author: Gratuitous Transfers, 1985, Cases and Materials on Federal Estate and Gift Taxation, 1996; contbr. articles to legal jours. Bd. dirs. Mental Health Conn., 1957-67; bd. dirs. New Haven Found., 1969-76. Mem. Conn. Bar Assn. (Disting. Pub. Service 1959). Home: 1179 Whitney Ave # B Hamden CT 06517-3434 Office: Yale U Sch Law 127 Wall St New Haven CT 06511-6636*

CLARK, ELIZABETH ADAMS (LIZ CLARK), genealogy educator; b. Arcadia, Fla., Jan. 16, 1944; d. Calvin Emmett and Ruth Gertrude (Paxton) Adams; m. Eugene Corry Clark, Apr. 27, 1963; children: Mary Corry, Walter Emmett. BS in History, Ga. Coll., 1971. Tchr. spl. reading Washington County Schs., Sandersville, Ga., 1971-72; tchr. spl. needs Adairsville (Ga.) Sch., 1973-75; instr. genealogy Blue Ridge Community Coll., Flat Rock, N.C., 1977-85; property mistress, set decorator Flat Rock Playhouse, State Theatre N.C., 1979-85; software specialist, computer cons. Fonda Corp., St. Albans, Vt., 1985-87; pub., editor Cane Break Pub., Spartanburg, S.C., 1985—; cons. in arts State Theatre N.C., 1984. Author: Cane Break Cooking, 1990; contbr. articles to profl. jours. Organizing corr. sec. Henderson County Dem. Women, 1978-80, bd. dirs.: bd. dirs. Henderson Little Theatre, 1977-85, exec. v.p., 1985; bd. dirs. Spartanburg Coalition for Choice, 1989-96; active NOW, 1992—, coord. Spartanburg chpt., 1992-93, 98—, treas., 1996-98, sporting coord., 1998—, coord. S.C., 1993-95, S.C. legis. coord., 1996—; chair Fight the Right; active Voters United for Equality, 1993-98, Spartanburg Nat. Women's Polit. Caucus, 1992-98, Fair Share, Human Rights Campa ign Fund, County Dem. Party Golden Donkey Group; participant MS Mag. Forum on Women's Reproductive Rights, 1995-97; co-chair Clark Family Reunion, 1995—, website designer Clark Family Homepage and Geneal. Repository; S.C. chair Fight The Right, 1992—, MS Found. Dialog on Religion and Reproductive Choice, 1998. Recipient S.C. NOW award, 1994, Geraldine Ferraro Woman of Yr. award, 1994; named Woman of Yr., DAR, 1974, Spartanburg NOW award 1998 for work with disadvantaged and spl. abled. Mem. AAUW, ACLU, VOICES (organizing mem. 1996), Carolina Alliance for Fair Employment, 1994—, Corry Family Soc., Clark Family Soc. (bd. dirs., editor newsletter 1989-93). Episcopalian. Avocations: computing, photography. Home and Office: 1009 Oak Creek Dr Spartanburg SC 29302-2981

CLARK, ELIZABETH ANNETTE, retired insurance company administrator; b. Mpls., Oct. 6, 1934; d. Walter Burdette and Daveda Marguerite (Hansen) Garver; m. Forrest Halter, May 17, 1958 (div. Feb. 1973); children: Gregory, Linda Halter Balsiger; m. Leslie Matthew Clark, Sept. 28, 1976 (dec. Oct. 1997). AA, Montgomery Coll., 1954; AAS, Greenville (S.C.) Tech. Coll., 1973; B in Gen. Studies, Furman U., 1979; MBA, Clemson (S.C.) U., 1987. CLU. Data processor Liberty Life Ins. Co., Greenville, 1973-84, mgr. quality improvement dept., 1984-88, dir. project mgmt., 1989, asst. v.p. policy forms, 1989-95; ind. policy forms contractor, 1998—; instr. computer programming part-time Greenville Tech. Coll., 1980-81. Sec. S.C./Piedmont chpt. Nat. Multiple Sclerosis Soc., Greenville, 1974-76; bd. dirs. Greenville Little Theatre, 1974-76; chmn. invitation com. Bicentennial Ball, Greenville, 1976; mem. Spkrs.' Bur., Family Counseling Ctr., 1991-95; docent Greenville County Mus. Art, 1996—; v.p. Centre Stage-S.C.!, 1997-98, bd. dirs., 1997-99; house mgr. Orcas Ctr., Eastsound, Wash., 1998—; bd. dirs. Furman Univ. Learning in Retirement, newsletter editor, 1998-99. Fellow Life Mgmt. Inst.; mem. Life Office Mgmt. Assn. (rep. so. systems devel. commn. 1985-90, program chmn. 1987-88, sec. 1988-89, chmn. 1989-90), EFS Users (v.p. 1992-95), Life and Health Compliance Assn. (mem. exec. com.), Am. Coun. Life Ins. (task force on policy forms filing 1994-95), Mensa, Beta Sigma Phi (pres. Greenville chpt. 1975-76, 93-94, v.p. coun. 1975-76, Woman of Yr. 1975, 89, 90, 93, Alpha-Omega award 1977). Unitarian. Home: 121 Rockwood Dr Greenville SC 29605-1942 also: 172 Lovers Ln PO Box 524 Eastsound WA 98245-0524

CLARK, ELOISE ELIZABETH, biologist, educator; b. Grundy, Va., Jan. 20, 1931; d. J. Francis Emmett and Ava Clayton (Harris) C. BA, Mary Washington Coll., 1951; PhD in Zoology, U. N.C., 1958; DSc, King Coll., 1976; postdoctoral rsch., Washington U., St. Louis, 1957-58, U. Calif. at Berkeley, 1958-59. Rsch. asst., then instr. U. N.C., 1952-55; instr. physiology Marine Biol. Lab., Woods Hole, Mass., 1958-62; asst. prof. Columbia U., 1960-65, assoc. prof. biol. sci., 1966-69; with NSF, Washington, 1969-83; head molecular biology NSF, 1971-73, div. dir. biol. and med. scis., 1973-75, dep. asst. dir. biol., behavioral and social scis., 1975-76, asst. dir. biol., behavioral and social scis., 1976-83; v.p. acad. affairs, prof. biol. sci. Bowling Green (Ohio) State U., 1983-96, acting pres., 1992; trustee prof. Biol. Sci., 1996—. Contbr. articles to profl. jours. Mem. alumnae bd. Mary Washington Coll., U. Va., 1967-70; bd. regents Nat. Libr. of Medicine, 1973-83; mem. policy group competitive grants program U.S. Dept. Agr.; mem. White House interdepartmental task force on women, 1978-80, task force for conf. on families, 1980, mem. com. on health and medicine, 1976-80, vice chmn. com. on food and renewable resources, 1977-80; mem. selective excellence task force Ohio Bd. Regents, 1984-85; mem. Ohio Adv. Coun. Coll. Prep. Edn., 1983-84; mem. Ohio Inter-Univ. Coun. for Provosts, 1983-96, chmn., 1984-85, 95-96; nat. adv. rsch. resources coun. NIH, 1987-89; mem. informal sci. edn. panel NSF, 1986-88, adv. com., social, behavioral and econ. scis., 1997—; program adv. coun. sci., tech. and pub. policy Harvard U., 1988-90; mem. governing bd. OhioLink, 1990-96, vice chair, 1992, chair, 1993-94. Named Disting. Alumnus Mary Washington Coll., 1975; Wilson scholar, 1956; E.C. Drew scholar, 1956; USPHS postdoctoral fellow, 1957-59; recipient Disting. Service award NSF, 1978. Mem. AAAS (coun. 1969-71, bd. dirs. 1978-82, pres.-elect, 1992, pres., 1993, chmn. bd. 1994), Soc. Gen. Physiology (sec. 1965-67, coun. 1969-71), Biophys. Soc. (coun. 1975-76), Am. Soc. Cell Biology (coun. 1972-75), Am. Inst. Biol. Scientists, Marine biol. Lab. (trustee 1993), NASULGC (higher edn. and tech. com. 1988-93, com. on info. tech. 1994-96), Consortium of Social Sci. Assn. (bd. dirs. 1993-96), Ohio Coun. rsch. and Econ. Devel., Assn. Women in Sci. (bd. dirs. 1998—), Phi Beta Kappa (com. on qualifications 1985—, chair 1998—, senate 1996—), Sigma Xi, Omicron Delta Kappa. Home: 1222 Brownwood Dr Bowling Green OH 43402-3503 Office: Bowling Green State U Dept Biol Scis Bowling Green OH 43403

CLARK, EMORY EUGENE, financial planning executive; b. Opelika, Ala., Jan. 24, 1931; s. Bunk Henry and Dorothy (Bolt) C.; m. Jean F. Reed, Sept. 30, 1951; children: Steven E., Michael E. Grad. pubs. schs. CLU, CFP. With Mgrs. Life Ins. Co., 1956-74; agt. supr. Mgrs. Life Ins. Co., L.A., 1956-60; mgr. Hawaii br. Mgrs. Life Ins. Co., 1960-65, mgr. Pitts. br., 1965-68, mgr. Houston br., 1968-74; with Jefferson Std. Life Ins. Co., Fort Worth, 1974-82; fin. planner E.F. Hutton & Co., Inc., 1983-90; v.p. investments A.G. Edwards & Sons, Inc., Ft. Worth, 1990-99, sr. v.p. investments, 1999—. 1st lt. Inf. AUS, 1950-56. Mem. Fort Worth Life Underwriters Assn., Am. Soc. Life Underwriters, Fort Worth Soc. Life Underwriters, Ft. Worth Securities Dealers Assn., Inst. Cert. Fin. Planners (cert., registered practitioner). Home: 8109 Meadowbrook Dr Fort Worth TX 76120-5309 Office: AG Edwards & Sons Inc 777 Main St Ste C-50 Fort Worth TX 76102-5333

CLARK, ERIC C., state official; b. Smith County, Miss.; s. Mr. and Mrs. John S. C.; m. Karan C.; children: Charles, Catherine. BA, Millsaps Coll.;

MA, U. Miss.; PhD in History, Miss. State U. Prof. history and govt. Miss. Coll., 1989-95; mgr. family tree farm Smith County; mem. Miss. Ho. of Reps., 1980-96; sec. of state State of Miss., 1996—. Mem. Baptist Ch. Address: PO Box 136 Jackson MS 39205-0136

CLARK, ESTHER FRANCES, law educator; b. Phila., Aug. 29, 1929; d. John and Lucy (Scapula) Giaccio; m. John H. Clark, Jr., June 12, 1954; 1 child, Jacqueline. B.A., Temple U., 1950; J.D., Rutgers U., 1955. Bar: Pa. 1956. Pvt. practice law Chester, 1976; prof. Widener U. Sch. Law, Wilmington, Del., 1976-98; disting. vis. prof. law Roger Williams U., Bristol, R.I., 1994—. Assoc. editor: Rutgers U. Law Rev, 1954-55. Bd. dirs. Lindsay Law Libr. Fellow Am. Bar Found.; mem. ABA, Pa. Bar Assn., Delaware County Bar Assn. (pres. 1982), Delaware County Legal Assistance Assn. (dir. 1972-77, pres. bd. dirs. 1974-76). Roman Catholic. Home: 207 Knoll Rd Wallingford PA 19086-6009 Office: PO Box 7474 Wilmington DE 19803-0474

CLARK, EUGENIE, zoologist, educator; b. N.Y.C., May 4, 1922; m. Hideo Umaki, 1942; m. Ilias Konstantinou, 1949; 4 children; m. Chandler Brossard, 1966; m. Igor Klatzo, 1969; m. Henry Yoshinobu Kon, 1997. BA, Hunter Coll., 1942; MA, NYU, 1946, PhD (Pacific Sci. Bd. fellow 1949), 1950; DSc (hon.), U. Mass., Dartmouth, 1990, U. Guelph, 1995, U. South Hampton, 1995. Rsch. asst. in ichthyology Scripps Instn. Oceanography, 1946-47; with N.Y. Zool. Soc., 1947-48; research asst. in animal behavior Am. Museum Nat. History, N.Y.C., 1948-49; research assoc. Am. Museum Nat. History, 1950-80; instr. Hunter Coll., 1954; exec. dir. Cape Haze Marine Lab., Sarasota, Fla., 1955-67; asso. prof. biology City U. N.Y., 1966-67; asso. prof. zoology U. Md., 1968-73, prof. zoology, 1973-92, prof. emerita, sr. rsch. scientist, 1992—; vis. prof. Hebrew U., 1972. Author: Lady with a Spear, 1953, The Lady and the Sharks, 1969, Desert Beneath the Sea, 1991; subject of biographies Shark Lady (Ann McGovern), 1978, Adventures of the Shark Lady (Ann McGovern), 1998. Recipient Myrtle Wreath award in sci. Hadassah, 1964, Nogi award in art Underwater Soc. Am., 1965, Dugan award in aquatic sci. Am. Littoral Soc., 1969, Diver of Yr. award Boston Sea Rovers, 1978, David Stone medal, 1984, Stoneman Conservation award, 1982, Gov. of S. Sinai medal, 1985, Lowell Thomas award Explorers Club, 1986, Wildscreen Internat. Film Festival award, 1986, medal Gov. Red Sea, Egypt, 1988, Nogi award in Sci., 1988, Women's Hall of Fame award State of Md., 1989, Women Educators award, 1990, Alumnae award, Franklin Burr award Nat. Geographic Soc., 1993; named to Hunter Coll. Hall of Fame, 1990, DEMA Hall of Fame, 1993; Fellow AEC, 1950; Saxton Fellow, 1952; Breadloaf Writer's fellow; Fulbright scholar Egypt, 1951 . Fellow AAAS; mem. Am. Soc. Ichthyology and Herpetology (life), Soc. Woman Geographers (Gold medal 1975, U. Md. Pres.'s medal 1993), Internat. Soc. Profl. Diving Scientists, Nat. Pks. and Conservation Assn. (vice chmn. 1976), Am. Littoral Soc. (v.p. 1970-89), Am. Elasmobranch Soc. (distinguished fellow 1999). Spl. rsch.: ecology and behavior of tropical sand fishes, morphology and taxonomy marine fishes, isolating mechanisms poecillid fishes and behavior deep sea sharks. Home: Bay Plz No 503 1255 Gulf-stream Ave Sarasota FL 34236 Office: Univ Md Dept Biology College Park MD 20742

CLARK, FAYE LOUISE, drama and speech educator; b. La., Oct. 9, 1936; m. Warren James Clark, Aug. 8, 1969; children: Roy, Kay Natalie. Student, Centennary Coll., 1954-55; BA with honors, U. Southwestern La., 1962; MA, U. Ga., 1966; PhD, Ga. State U., 1992. Tchr. Nova Exptl. Schs., Ft. Lauderdale, Fla., 1963-65; faculty dept. drama and speech Ga. Perimeter Coll. (formerly DeKalb C.C.), Atlanta, 1967—; chmn. dept., 1977-81. Pres. Hawthorne Sch. PTA, 1983-84. Mem. Nat. Comm. Assn., Ga. Theatre Conf. (sec. 1968-69, rep. to Southeastern Theatre Conf. 1969), Ga. Psychol. Assn., Ga. Comm. Assn., Friends of the Atlanta Artists Club (sec. 1981-83, dir. 1983-89), Atlanta Press Club, , Friends of Atlanta Opera, Oglethorpe Mus., Southeastern Theatre Conf., Atlanta Hist. Soc., Atlanta Artists Club (sec. 1981-83, dir. 1983-89), Thalian-Blackfriars, Lake Lanier Sailing Club, Phi Kappa Phi, Pi Kappa Delta, Sigma Delta Pi, Kappa Delta Pi. Home: 2521 Melinda Dr NE Atlanta GA 30345-1918 Office: Ga Perimeter Coll Humanities Divsn Dunwoody Campus Dunwoody GA 30338

CLARK, FRED, legal writer, editor; b. Limón, Costa Rica, Dec. 12, 1930; came to U.S., 1968; s. Thomas and Irene (Penney) C.; m. Dorothy Hyacinth James, Aug. 4, 1956; children: Paul, Fred Jr., Lydia Ramona. Student, Ctrl. Am. Acad., 1944-49; BLitt, U. Costa Rica, 1951; postgrad., Stafford Coll., 1956-57; barrister-at-law, Inner Temple, London, 1960. Bar: Eng., 1960, Jamaica, 1960; cert. in law Coun. Legal Edn. Master of langs. Merl Grove Sch., 1951-55; trust officer Govt. of Jamaica, 1960-61; individual practice of law Kingston, Jamaica, 1961-67; legal editor Corp. Trust Co., N.Y.C., 1968-69; sr. legal editor Prentice-Hall, Inc., Englewood Cliffs, N.J., 1969-91; cons. commonwealth law. Editor The Corp. Jour., 1968-69. Trustee United Ch. of Christ, 1970-78; spl. advisor U.S. Congl. Adv. Bd.; mem. nat. adv. bd. Am. Security Coun. Recipient Disting. Leadership award, 1984, Presdl. medal of merit, 1986. Mem. Am. Mgmt. Assn., Internat. Platform Assn., Internat. Commn. Jurists, Am. Mus. Natural History, Nat. Geog. Soc., N.Y. Acad. Scis., Am. Ballet Theater, Met. Opera Guild, U.S. Naval Inst., Freeport Bus. Promotion (bd. dirs.), U.S. Power Squadron (asst. sec.), Inter-Am. Soc., Rosicrucians. Home: PO Box 291 Bergenfield NJ 07621-0291

CLARK, GAIL THEROUX, artist; b. Framingham, Mass., Aug. 27, 1954; d. William Henry Theroux and Francis Regina La Salle; m. Gordon Hostetter Clark Jr., July 23, 1988; 1 child, Adam Arthur. BFA in Painting, U. Mass., 1976; MA in Painting, Edinboro U. Pa., 1994. Art tchr. King Philip Regional Sch. Dist., Wrentham, Mass., 1977-78, Holliston (Mass.) Pub. Schs., 1978-81, 87-88; dir. children's programs, adminstrv. asst. Newport Harbor Art Mus., Newport Beach, Calif., 1981-83; art tchr. Millis (Mass.) Pub. Schs., 1984-87; co-owner N.H. Artists Guild Gallery, Laconia, 1988-90; artist, owner Royal River Art Studio, Yarmouth, Maine, 1995—; juror Fort Williams Arts Festival, New Eng. Exhibit, South Portland, Maine, 1996, 97. Bd. mem. Erie (Pa.) Art Mus., 1991-93, Florence Krittenon Home, Erie, 1991-92; vice chair Yarmouth Sch. Bd., 1997-99. Works exhibited at U. Ctrl. Fla., Orlando, 1989 (1st place award 1989), Lakes Region Festival of the Arts, Laconia, 1990 (1st place award 1990), So. Vt. Art Ctr., 1992, Chantauque (N.Y.) Arts Nat., 1993, Westmoreland Arts Nats., Latrobe, Pa., 1993, 94 (Heritage award 1994), Kennebeck Valley Art Assn., 1998. Democrat. Avocations: running, tennis, mountain climbing, gardening. E-mail: RyeRvrArt@aol.com. Home: 10 Park St Yarmouth ME 04096 Office: Royal River Art Studio 161 E Elm St Yarmouth ME 04096

CLARK, GARY CARL, lawyer; b. Flippin, Ark., Mar. 4, 1947; m. Jane W. Clark; children: Ross, Lauren. BS in Agrl. Edn., Okla. State U., 1969, MS, 1972; JD with honors, U. Tex., 1975. Bar: Okla. 1975, U.S. Dist. Ct. (no. dist.) Okla. 1975, U.S. Ct. Appeals (10th cir.) 1979. Tchr. Laverne H.S., Okla., 1969-70; assoc. Conner, Winters, Ballaine, Barry & McGowen, 1975-81, ptnr., 1981; ptnr. Baker & Hoster, Tulsa, 1981-97; dir. Crowe & Dunlevy, PC, Tulsa, 1997—; lawyer-staffed Panel of Ct. Appeals, 1991; speaker in field. Vol. Legal Svcs. Ea. Okla., 1993—; trustee Okla. State Univ., Tulsa, 1999—; mem. bd. regents Okla. State Univ. and A&M Colls., 1993—; past v.p. Jane Addams Elem. Sch. PTA, sch. vol.; chair site adv. Recipient Silver Beaver award Boy Scouts Am., 1996. Fellow Am. Bar Found., Okla. Bar Found.; mem. Okla. Bar Assn. (chair estate planning and probate sect. 1988-89, vice chair probate code com. 1991, bd. dirs. young lawyers divsn., mem. real property sect., bd. govs. 1997—), Tulsa County Bar Assn. (pres. 1993-94, Golden Rule award 1993, Outstanding Sr. Lawyer 1996), Tulsa County Bar Found. (pres. 1994-95, treas. 1995-99, charter fellow), Tulsa Title and Probate Lawyers Assn. (pres. 1989-90), Okla. State U. Alumni Assn. (life), FFA Alumni Assn. (life), Order of Coif, Alpha Gamma Rho Alumni Assn. (Okla. chpt. dir., past pres.), Phi Delta Phi. Home: 5505 S 97th West Ave Sand Springs OK 74063-4726 Office: Crowe & Dunlevy 500 Kennedy Bldg Tulsa OK 74103

CLARK, GARY R., newspaper editor; b. Cleve., June 27, 1946; s. Dale Francis and Mary Louise (Rozeski) C.; m. Caryn Elaine Helm, Dec. 18, 1976; children: Jessica Lynn, Brian Michael. BA, Ohio State U., 1973, MA, 1978. Reporter Chronicle-Telegram, Elyria, Ohio, 1973-77; reporter The Plain Dealer, Cleve., 1978-88, state editor, 1988-89, nat. editor, 1989, city editor, 1989-90, mng. editor, 1990—; tchg. assoc. Ohio State U., Columbus, 1977-78. Sgt. USMC, 1966-69, Vietnam. Mem. AP Mng. Editors, Am. Soc. Newspaper Editors, Investigative Reporters and Editors, Cleve. City Club. Office: The Plain Dealer 1801 Superior Ave E Cleveland OH 44114-2198*

CLARK, GARY RAY, licensing board executive; b. Keokuk, Iowa, Jan. 18, 1944; s. G. Raymond and M. Lucille (Logsdon) C.; m. Mala S. Clark; children: Mary Ellen Shimmens, Kelley Barnard. BS, Quincy U., 1967. Pharmaceutical detail man Merck & Co., Jefferson City, Mo., 1968-71, Hoffmann La Roche, Jefferson City, 1971-75; lic. bd. adminstr. Mo. Bd. Healing Arts, Jefferson City, Mo., 1975-90; exec. dir. Okla. Bd. Osteo. Med. Examiners, Okla. City, 1990—; cons. Nat. Bd. Osteo. Medicine, Des Plaines, Ill.; mem. Coun. on Licensure Enforcement and Regulation. Mem. Coun. Licensure Enforcement and Regulation (past pres.), Adminstrs. in Medicine (pres. 1996), Willow Creek Country Club (Okla. City, bd. dirs.). Avocations: golf, writing, cooking. Office: Okla Bd Osteopatic Exam 4848 N Lincoln Blvd Ste 100 Oklahoma City OK 73105-3321

CLARK, GEORGE WHIPPLE, physics educator; b. Evanston, Ill., Aug. 31, 1928; s. Robert Keep and Margaret (Whipple) C.; m. Elizabeth Kister, Dec. 1956 (div. 1972); children: Katherine, Jacqueline; m. Charlotte Huston Reischer, Jan. 1988. BA, Harvard U., 1949; PhD, MIT, 1952. Instr. MIT, Cambridge, 1952-54, asst. prof., 1954-60, assoc. prof., 1960-65, prof., 1965-98, Breene M. Kerr prof. physics, 1984-95, prof. emeritus, 1998—; cons., dir. Am. Sci. and Engring., Inc., Cambridge, 1958-69; dir. Assn. Univs. for Rsch. in Astronomy, Washington, 1982-90. Contbr. numerous articles to profl. jours. Fellow Am. Phys. Soc., Am. Astronomy Soc.; mem. NAS, Am. Acad. Arts and Scis. Office: MIT 37-611 77 Massachusetts Ave Cambridge MA 02139-4301

CLARK, GLEN EDWARD, judge; b. Cedar Rapids, Iowa, Nov. 23, 1943; s. Robert M. and Georgia L. (Welch) C.; m. Deanna D. Thomas, July 16, 1966; children: Andrew Curtis, Carissa Jane. BA, U. Iowa, 1966; JD, U. Utah, 1971. Bar: Utah 1971, U.S. Dist. Ct. Utah 1971, U.S. Ct. Appeals (10th cir.) 1972. Assoc. Fabian & Clendenin, 1971-74, ptnr., 1975-81, dir., chmn. banking and comml. law sect., 1981-82; judge U.S. Bankruptcy Ct. Dist. Utah, Salt Lake City, 1982-86, chief judge, 1986—; bd. govs. nat. Conf. Bankruptcy Judges, 1988-94; mem. com. on bankruptcy edn. Fed. Jud. Ctr., 1989-92; vis. prof. U. Utah, Salt Lake City, 1977-79, 83; pres. Nat. Conf. Bankruptcy Judges, 1992-93; chair bd. trustees Nat. Conf. Bankruptcy Judges Endowment for Edn., 1990-92. vis. assoc. prof. law Univ. Utah; instr. adv. bus. law Univ. Utah. Articles editor: Utah Law Review. With U.S. Army, 1966-68. Finkbine fellow U. Iowa. Fellow Am. Coll. Bankruptcy (charter, mem. bd. regents 1995—); mem. Jud. Conf. U.S. (mem. com. jud. br. 1992—, 10th cir. bankruptcy appellate panel 1996—), Utah Bar Assn., Order of Coif. Presbyterian. Office: 365 US Courthouse 350 S Main St Salt Lake City UT 84101-2106

CLARK, GORDON HOSTETTER, JR., physician; b. New Haven, Aug. 5, 1947; s. Gordon Hostetter and Elizabeth Master (Mapes) C.; m. Gail Marie Theroux, July 23, 1988; children: Emily Blakeslee Clark Ehl, Christopher Robert, Heather Mays Richmond, Adam Arthur. BA, Yale U., 1970; MDiv, Pacific Sch. Religion, 1973; MD, George Washington U., 1977. Diplomate Am. Bd. Psychiatry and Neurology, Am. Bd. Med. Mgmt., Am. Coll. Physician Execs.; cert. in adminstrv. psychiatry, APA, 1992; cert. physician exec. Commn. in Med. Mgmt., 1998. Intern, then resident, then fellow Dartmouth-Hitchcock Med. Ctr., Hanover, N.H., 1977-81; staff psychiatrist Lakes Region Med. Health Ctr., Laconia, N.H., 1981-82, med. dir., 1982-86; dir. psychiat. unit Lakes Region Gen. Hosp., Laconia, 1986-89; med. dir. behavioral svcs. St. Vincent Health Ctr., Erie, Pa., 1990-93; dir. med./profl. adminstrn. Deerfield Mgmt. Group, Erie, Pa., 1991-94; pres. Deerfield Profl. Assocs., 1992-94; med. advisor Deerfield Behavioral Health Network, 1994-95; sr. psychiat. cons. Med. Groups Divsn. Maine Harvard Cmty. Health Plan, Portland, Maine, 1995-96; pres., med. dir. Integrated Behavioral Healthcare, Portland, Maine, 1995—; med. dir. Behavioral Health Network of Maine, 1995—, Augusta (Maine) Mental Health Inst., 1995-96; assoc. med. dir. Maine Dept. Mental Health and Mental Retardation, Augusta, 1995-96; med. dir. med.-psychiat. program Westbrook (Maine) Comty. Hosp., 1996-97; sr. physician advisor CMG Healthsource Maine, Maine, 1996-97; adj. asst. prof. clin. psychiatry Dartmouth Med. Sch., Hanover, 1983-90; clin. asst. prof. psychiatry U. Pitts. Sch. Medicine, 1990-96; clin. assoc. prof. psychiatry U. Vt. Med. Sch., 1996—; chmn. com. psychiatrists in N.H. Comty. Mental Health Ctrs., Concord, 1982-86; med. liaison to Pa. Office of Mental Health and Mental Retardation and Erie County Office of Mental Health and Mental Retardation, 1991-94. Exec. v.p. Erie Phiharm., 1991-92. Recipient Exemplary Psychiatrist award Nat. Alliance for Mentally Ill, 1992; recipient Benjamin Manchester award George Washington U., 1977. Fellow Am. Psychiat. Assn. (task force to develop guidelines for psychiat. practice in cmty. mental health ctrs., com. on state and cmty. psychiatry systems, com. chronically mentally ill, Falk fellow 1979-81, examiner oral part of exams. cert. adminstrn. psychiatry 1993-96, com. on stds. and survey procedures 1998—), Am. Coll. Mental Health Adminstrn., Am. Assn. Social Psychiatry (mem. coun.), Am. Coll. Physician Execs.; mem. AMA, Am. Assn. Cmty. Psychiatrists (com. to develop guidelines for psychiat. practice in cmty. mental health ctrs., founding pres. 1984-90, bd. dirs. 1984—, Disting. Svc. award 1990), Am. Assn. Psychiat. Adminstrs. (mem. coun. 1996—, pres.-elect 1997—), Am. Coll. Psychiatrists, Nat. Psychiatric Alliance (chmn. med. staff com. 1992-94, exec. com. 1992-95), Psychiat. Physicians Pa. (coun., govt. rels. com., fed. legis. rep. pub. psychiatry com. 1993-94, treas. 1994), Western Pa. Psychiat. Soc. (pres. elect 1992-94), Maine Psychiat. Assn. (chair program com. 1996-97). Avocations: hockey, tennis, biking, hiking, camping. Home: 10 Park St Yarmouth ME 04096-7757 Office: Integrated Behavioral Healthcare 1 Forest Ave Portland ME 04101-2810

CLARK, HANLEY C., state insurance commissioner; b. West Hamlin, W. Va.; m. Holly Hoback; 3 children. BA in History, English, Bus., Marshall U., 1972; MA in History, U. W. Va., 1974. Spl. asst. to gov. State of W. Va., Charleston, 1980-81, asst. to ins. commr., 1981-85, dep. ins. commr., 1985-88, acting ins. commr., 1988-89, ins. commr., 1989—. Mem. Nat. Assn. Ins. Commrs. (former chmn s.e. zone). Office: WV Insurance Comm PO Box 50540 Charleston WV 25305-0540*

CLARK, HARRY WARREN, public policy consultant; b. South Bend, Ind., Mar. 9, 1949; s. Harry Warren Jr. and Jacquelyn Milgram Clark; m. Katherine Knight, Apr. 30, 1987; children: Abigail, Taylor, Caitlin. Student, George Washington U., 1974-75; BS, Cornell U., 1992. Exec. asst. U.S. Congressman Jack N.Y., Washington, 1972-75; mng. dir. Young & Rubicam, N.Y.C., 1977-80; pres., prodr. One Eleven Com., N.Y.c., 1980-83; sr. v.p., sr. cons. Burson Marsteller, N.Y.C., 1983-85; sr. v.p., group dir. Bozell Inc., N.Y.c., 1985-87; pres., mng. ptnr. Clark & Weinstock Inc., N.Y.C., 1987—. Prodr. TV documentaries: Countdown to the White House: The Reagan Transition, 1981, Admiral William Crowe's the Future of Military Power, 1989. Trustee Greenwich (Conn.) Acad., 1987-93, Greenwich Pub. Libr., 1997—; trustee, mem. exec. com. U.S. Ski and Snowboard Team, Park City, Utah, 1994—. Republican. Avocations: skiing, tennis, squash. E-mail: hwc@cwnye.com. Office: Clark & Weinstock 52 Vanderbilt Ave New York NY 10017

CLARK, HOWARD LONGSTRETH, JR., finance company executive; b. N.Y.C., Feb. 1, 1944; s. Howard Longstreth and Elsie (Dancaster) C.; m. Karen K. Burke, July 25, 1992; 1 child by previous marriage, Howard Longstreth III. BSBA, Boston U., 1967; MBA, Columbia U., 1968. Exec. v.p., chief fin. officer Am. Express Co., N.Y.C., 1981-90; vice chmn. Lehman Bros., Inc.; bd. dirs. The Maytag Co., Compass Internat. Svcs. Corp., Fund Am. Cos. Inc., Walter Industries, Inc. Episcopalian. Clubs: River, Racquet and Tennis, Round Hill, Blind Brook, Links, Seminole, Jupiter Island, Nantucket Golf. Home: 404 Round Hill Rd Greenwich CT 06831-2637 Office: Lehman Bros Inc 3 World Fin Ctr New York NY 10285-1600

CLARK, IRA C., hospital association administrator, educator. BA Gen. Sci., U. Iowa, 1959, MA honors Health and Hosp. Adminstrn., 1966; grad. Bus. Adminstrn., Rider Coll., 1963. Adminstrv. asst. divsn. Hosps. Iowa State Dept. Health, Des Moines, 1964; spl. asst. dir. planning and devel. Montefiore Hosp. and Med. Ctr., Bronx, N.Y., 1970; asst. dir. Montefiore Hosp. and Med. Ctr., Bronx, 1965-70; assoc. dir. Jersey City Med. Ctr., 1970-71, exec. dir., 1971-75; CEO Woodhull Hosp. and Mental Health Ctr., 1982-84; exec. dir. Bellevue Hosp. Ctr., 1984-85; CEO, regional adminstr. Kings County Hosp. Ctr., Bklyn., 1976-87; pres. & ceo Pub. Health Trust Jackson Meml. Hosp., 1987—; bd. dirs. Fla. Hosp. Assn., So. Fla. Hosp. Assn.; panelist Robert Wood Johnson Found. Symposium, Princeton, N.J., 1986; chmn. Coun. Exec. dirs. N.Y.C. Health and Hosps. Corp., 1978-82; chmn. com. strategic planning Coun. Exec. dirs. Counterpart com. bd. dirs.; spl. adv. panel Emergency Svcs. Act, Advanced Para-medic Tng. N.J.; adj. faculty, lectr. various Univs.; spkr. in field. Author: The History and Development of Continuing Physical Education, 1966. Recipient Disting. Svc. award Commr. Mental Health, N.Y., 1981. Mem. Am. Hosp. Assn. (house dels., charter mem. pub. gen. hosps. sect., com. nominations bd. trustees pub.-gen. hosp. sect.), Assn. Am. Med. Colls. (gen. assembly coun. teaching hosps.), N.J. Hosp. Assn. (vice chmn., chmn. coun. govt. ops. of bd. trustees, spl. com. polit. strategy). Office: Jackson Meml Hosp 1611 NW 12th Ave Miami FL 33136-1096*

CLARK, JACI, women's collegiate basketball coach; b. Milw., July 6, 1961. Grad., U. Wis., 1984; MA, U. Ind., 1986. Grad. asst. coach Ind. U., 1985-86; asst. coach Bowling Green (Ohio) State U., 1986-91, head coach, 1991-99; head coach women's basketball U. Dayton, Ohio, 1999—. Inducted hall of fame U. Wis., Milw., 1995. Mem. Women's Basketball Coaches Assn. (legis. com. rep., Kodak All-Am. com.). Office: Bowling Green State U Athletic Dept Stadium East Bowling Green OH 43403-0030*

CLARK, JACK, retired hospital company executive, accountant; b. Munford, Ala., Feb. 23, 1932; s. Raymond E. and Ora (Camp) C.; m. Louise Omega Lackey, Jan. 30, 1951; 1 son, Terry Wayne. BS, Springhill Coll., Mobile, Ala., 1960. Staff acct. Max E. Miller, C.P.A., Mobile, 1960-62; comptr. Mobile Gen. Hosp., 1962-67; assoc. adminstr. fin. Univ. Med. Ctr., Mobile, 1967-74; regional mgr. Humana Inc., Mobile, 1974-75, v.p., 1975-80, sr. v.p., 1980-84, exec. v.p., 1984-93; exec. v.p. Galen Health Care, Mobile, 1993-94; ret. Columbia-HCA Healthcare, 1994; trustee Mid-South region Humana hosps., 1974-87, Southwestern region, 1987-89, region IV, 1989-91, region 2, 1991-93, Regional Hosps., Columbia/HCA, 1994—. Bd. dirs. Agape S. Ala., Mobile, 1983; trustee Faulkner U., Montgomery, Ala., 1993—. Served in USAF, 1952-56, Korea. Mem. Hosp. Fin. Mgmt. Assn. (assoc.), Am. Hosp. Assn., Ala. Hosp. Assn., Ala. Hosp. Assn. Accts. (pres. so. council, dir. 1967-68), Mobile C. of C. Democrat. Mem. Ch. of Christ. Home: 6449 Cane Brake Dr Mobile AL 36695-3817

CLARK, JACK I., civil engineer, researcher. Grad., Acadia U., Tech. U. N.S., Can.; DEng (hon.), Tech. U. N.S., Can.; grad., U. Alta., Can.; DSc (hon.), Laurentian U., 1998. With major civil engring. projects, 1957—; dir. Ctr. for Cold Ocean Resources Engring. Meml. U. Nfld., St. John's, Can, 1984-91, 1st pres., CEO, Ctr. for Cold Ocean Resources Engring., 1991-97, prin. cons. Ctr. for Cold Odean Resources Engring., 1997—. Past editor Can. Geotech. Jour. Recipient R.M. Hardy keynote address, 1996, Roger J.E. Brown award, 1996; Karl Terzaghi fellow Norwegian Tech. Inst., 1997. Fellow Engring. Inst. Can. (Julian C. Smith medal 1987), Can. Soc. Civil Engrs.; mem. Can. Acad. Engring., Nat. Scis. and Engring. Coun. (v.p., exec. com. for coun. 1988-94), Can. Geotech. Rsch. Bd. (chmn. 1991-94), Founds. for Offshore Structures (chmn. Can. Stds. Assn. Com. S472), Can. Geotech. Soc. (G. Geoffrey Meyerhof award 1995). Office: Meml U Nfld, C-CORE, Saint John's, NF Canada A1B 3X5

CLARK, JAMES ALLEN, lawyer, educator; b. Canton, Ill., Nov. 13, 1948; s. Howard R. and Helen (McElwain) C. BS in Edn., Miami U., Oxford, Ohio, 1971, BA in Polit. Sci., 1971; MS in Urban Studies, Cleve. State U., 1974; JD, Case Western Res. U., 1977. Bar: U.S. Dist. Ct. (no. dist.) Ohio 1977, U.S. Ct. Appeals (6th cir.) 1978, U.S. Dist. Ct. (no. dist.) Ill. 1979, U.S. Ct. Appeals (7th cir.) 1980, U.S. Supreme Ct. 1981, U.S. Ct. Appeals (D.C. cir.) 1985, U.S. Dist. Ct. (ea. dist.) Wis. 1986, U.S. Ct. Appeals (8th cir.) 1994. Law clk. U.S. Dist. Ct., Cleve., 1977-79; assoc. Schiff Hardin & Waite, Chgo., 1979-85, ptnr., 1985—; prof. De Paul U. Law Sch., Chgo., 1985-98. Mem. Order of the Coif. Office: Schiff Hardin & Waite 7200 Sears Tower Chicago IL 60606*

CLARK, JAMES BENTON, railroad industry consultant, former executive; b. Sweetwater, Tenn., Jan. 3, 1914; s. John Edgar and Nancy Ella (Webster) C.; m. Maxine Jeanette Butcher, Oct. 14, 1939; children—Diana Clark Hudgens, Sylvia Clark Pulliam. B.S., U. Tenn., 1937; grad. transport course, Northwestern U., 1959. Registered profl. engr. Ky. Coop. student Bur. Pub. Rds., 1934-36; with Louisville & Nashville R.R., 1937-74, asst. dir. personnel, 1955-59, chief engr., 1959-69, asst. v.p. personnel and labor relations, 1969-73, v.p. personnel and labor relations, 1973-74; v.p. ops. Seaboard Coast Line R.R., Jacksonville, Fla., 1974-76, v.p. exec. dept., 1976; cons. Louisville, 1976-81, Franklin, Ky., 1982—; mem. pvt. industry council Barren River Area Devel. Dist., 1985-91; mem. Nat. Ry. Labor Conf., Southeastern Carriers Conf. Com., 1969-73. Chmn. bd. trustees Simpson County Libr. Dist., 1989-92; mem. Simpson County (Ky.) Solid Waste Mgmt. Bd., 1990-93, chmn., 1993. Mem. Am. Ry. Engring. Assn. (life, bd. dirs. 1965-68, v.p. 1969), Franklin-Simpson County C. of C. (pres. 1986), Chi Epsilon. Baptist. Home: 305 Hillcrest St Franklin KY 42134-2374

CLARK, JAMES COVINGTON, journalist, historian; b. Washington, May 22, 1947; s. William Edward and Louise (Covington) C.; children: Randall Healy, Kevin Healy. BA, Lenoir-Rhyne Coll., 1975; MA, Stetson U., 1986; PhD, U. Fla., 1998. Reporter UPI, Washington, 1967, Columbia (S.C.) Record, 1968; reporter AP, Charlotte, N.C., 1969-70, Phila., 1972-73; reporter Hickory (N.C.) Daily Record, 1974-75; regional editor Tampa (Fla.) Tribune, 1976-77; asst. exec. editor The Orlando (Fla.) Sentinel, 1977-98, syndicated columnist, 1997—; adj. prof. U. Ctrl. Fla., Orlando, 1986—. Author: Last Train South, 1984, Faded Glory: Presidents Out of Power, 1985, The Murder of James Garfield, 1994. Recipient George Polk award L.I. U., 1983, Gerald Loeb award, L.A., 1983, Arthur Thompson prize Fla. Hist. Soc., Gainesville, 1989. Mem. Authors Guild, Orgn. Am. Historians, Am. Hist. Assn.

CLARK, JAMES MILFORD, college president, retired; b. Mich., Apr. 11, 1930; s. Roy Wesley and Florence (Grice) C.; m. Patricia Ann Haynes, Mar. 11, 1960; children—Pamela, Matthew, Timothy. B.A., U. Mich., 1952, Ph.D. (Horace H. Rackham fellow), 1962; M.A., U. Philippines, 1955; Doctor (hon.), U. North London, 1993; Dr. (hon.), Capital Normal U., Beijing, 1994. Fulbright travel grantee France, 1955-56; teaching fellow U. Mich., 1957-59; asst. prof. polit. sci. U. Maine, Orono, 1960-64; asso. prof. U. Maine, 1964-79, asst. to pres., 1966-68, v.p. for acad. affairs, 1968-79; pres. SUNY Coll., Cortland, 1979-95; ret., 1995; Fulbright lectr. U. Toulouse (France), 1965-66; mem. Com. on Internat. Exchange Scholars, 1988-92. Author: Teachers and Politics in France, 1967. Chmn. Maine Health Planning Coun., 1970-72, mem. exec. com., 1972-76; bd. dirs. Penobscot Valley United Fund, 1972-77, Cortland County United Way, 1979-85; bd. overseers Rockefeller Inst. Govt., 1988-91; mem. N.Y. State Citizens com. on Bicentennial of French Revolution, 1988-90. With U.S. Army, 1952-55. Mem. Nat. Assn. State Univs. and Land-Grant Colls. (exec. com. council for acad. affairs 1971-76, sec. council 1974-76), Am. Assn. State Colls. and Univs. (N.Y. rep. 1979-81), Phi Beta Kappa, Phi Kappa Phi, Phi Eta Sigma, Pi Sigma Alpha, Sigma Phi Epsilon.

CLARK, JAMES NORMAN, insurance executive; b. Decatur, Ill., Jan. 30, 1932; s. John W. and Pearl (Allen) C.; m. Marlene F. Geason, Oct. 10, 1953; children—Paul R., Donald A., Robert S., Christine A. Tax and acctg. mgr. Caterpillar Tractor Co., 1957-66; mgr. tax dept. Towmotor Corp., 1966-68; with Western & So. Life Ins. Co., Cin., 1968—, exec. v.p., 1980—, also bd. dirs.; dir. Columbus (Ohio) Life Ins. Co. Former trustee Good Samaritan Hosp. Found. Capt. USAF, 1954-57. Mem. Life Office Mgmt. Assn. (prin. rep.), Fin. Exec. Inst. (former nat. chmn.), Tax Execs. Inst. Office: Western & So Life Ins Co 400 Broadway St Cincinnati OH 45202-3312

CLARK, JAMES RICHARD, lawyer; b. Madison, Wis., Mar. 30, 1946; s. James F. and Gloria J. C.; m. Martha C. Conrad, Mar. 18, 1950; children: Lindsey Kelley, Chad. BA Ripon Coll., 1968; JD, U. Wis., 1971. Bar: Wis. 1971, U.S. Dist. Ct. (we. dist.) Wis. 1972, U.S. Dist. Ct. (ea. dist.) Wis. 1972, U.S. Ct. Appeals (7th cir.) 1973, U.S. Dist. Ct. (no. dist.) Ill. 1974, U.S. Supreme Ct. 1976. Assoc. Foley & Lardner, Milw., 1971-78, ptnr., 1978—. Trustee Ripon Coll., 1985—. Served to 1st lt. U.S. Army, 1971. Mem. Am. Coll. Trial Lawyers, Wis. Bar Assn., ABA, 7th Cir. Bar Assn., Ripon Coll. Alumni Assn. (past pres.), Order of Coif, Phi Beta Kappa. Clubs: Milw.

Athletic, Tripoli Country. Editor-in-chief Wis. Law Rev., 1971. Home: 9719 N Dalewood Ln Mequon WI 53092-6210 Office: Foley & Lardner Firstar Ctr 777 E Wisc Ave Milwaukee WI 53202

CLARK, JAMIE RAPPAPORT, fish and wildlife service administrator; m. Jim Clark. BS in Wildlife Biology, Towson State U.; MS in Wildlife Ecology, U. Md.; postgrad. in Environ. Planning, Towson State U. Wildlife biologist Nat. Inst. for Urban Wildlife, 1979-81; rsch. biologist U.S. Army Med. Rsch. Inst.; natural/cultural resources program mgr. N.G. Bur.; fish and wildlife adminstr. Dept. of Army, 1988-89; sr. staff biologist endangered species divsn. U.S. Fish and Wildlife Svc., Dept. of Interior, Washington, 1989, chief endangered species, asst. dir. ecol. svcs., dir. Office: Fish and Wildlife Svc 1849 C St NW Washington DC 20240-0001

CLARK, JANET, retired health services executive; b. Detroit, Oct. 3, 1941; d. John Francis Bullock and Martha Barbara (Bauer) Clark; m. Donald Bruce Tyson, Feb. 29, 1964; children: William John, Barbara June; m. Herman John Husmann, Nov. 11, 1988. AAS in Dental Hygiene, Broome C.C., 1961; BS in Health Edn., SUNY, Cortland, 1963; MPA in Mgmt., SUNY, Albany, 1993. Dental hygiene tchr. West Genessee Ctrl. Schs., Camillus, N.Y., 1964-65; health educator N.Y. State Dept. of Health, Syracuse, 1965-70; sr. sanitarian N.Y. State Dept. of Health, Monticello, 1977-80; prin. sanitarian N.Y. State Dept. of Health, N.Y.C., 1980-86; field ops. rep. N.Y. State Dept. of Health, Albany, 1986-89, mgr. Indian health, 1990-95, ret., 1995; sanitarian, health educator Onondaga County Health Dept., Syracuse, 1970-77; chmn., CEO Ha'awi Found. for Econ. Deve. in Indigenous Nations, 1994—; office mgr. Latham Area C. of C., 1995-97; CEO, CFO Workplace Safety Svcs. LLC, 1998—, Alpha Strike Computers, 1998—. Mem. AAUW, NAFE, Am. Legion Aux., Nat. Environ. Health Assn., N.Y. Soc. Profl. Sanitarians (sec. 1970-84), N.Y. State Registry of Sanitarians (treas. 1987-90, pres. 1990-95, Meritorious Svc. award 1986), Hawaii C. of C., Elks. Avocations: reading, real estate, music, snorkeling, cards. Office: PO Box 6190 Hilo HI 96720

CLARK, JANET EILEEN, political scientist, educator; b. Kansas City, Kans., June 5, 1940; d. Edward Francis and Mildred Lois (Mack) Morrissey; m. Caleb M. Clark, Sept. 28, 1968; children: Emily Claire, Grace Ellen, Evelyn Adair. AA, Kansas City Jr. Coll., 1960; AB, George Washington U., 1962, MA, 1964; PhD, U. Ill., 1973. Staff U.S. Dept. Labor, Washington, 1962-64; instr. social sci. Kansas City (Kans.) Jr. Coll., 1964-67; instr. polit. sci. Parkland Coll., 1970-71; asst. prof. govt. N.Mex. State U., Las Cruces, 1971-77, assoc. prof., 1977-80; assoc. prof. polit. sci. U. Wyo., 1981-84, prof., 1984-94; prof. polit. sci., head dept. State U. West Ga., Carrollton, 1994—. Co-author: Women, Elections and Representation, 1987, The Equality State, 1988, Women in Taiwan Politics: Overcoming Barriers to Women's Participation in a Modernizing Society, 1990; editor Women and Politics, 1991—; contbr. articles to profl. jours. Wolcott fellow, 1963-64, NDEA Title IV fellow, 1967-69. Mem. Internat. Soc. Polit. Psychology (gov. coun., 1987-89), NEA (pres. chpt. 1978-79), Am. Polit. Sci. Assn., We. Polit. Sci. Assn. (exec. coun. 1984-87), Western Social Sci. Assn. (exec. coun. 1978-81, v.p. 1982, pres. 1985), Women's Caucus for Polit. Sci. (treas. 1982, pres. 1987), LWV (exec. bd. 1980-83, treas. 1986-90, pres. 1991-93), Women's Polit. Caucus, Beta Sigma Phi (v.p. chpt. 1978-79, sec. 1987-88, treas. 1988-89, v.p. 1989-90, pres. 1990-91), Phi Beta Kappa Chi Omega (prize 1962), Phi Kappa Phi. Home: 2507 Waterford Rd Auburn AL 36832-2873 Offiice: State University of West Georgia Dept Polit Sci Carrollton GA 30118

CLARK, JEANENNE FRANCES, community health nurse specialist; b. St. Louis, Oct. 1, 1954; d. Pete Jr. and Marie (Risch) Stoplos; m. Richard Edward Clark, June 9, 1974; childen: Richard Paul, Jason Nicholas. Diploma, Jewish Hosp. Sch. Nursing, St. Louis, 1975; BSN cum laude, U. Mo., St. Louis, 1992; MPH, MSN, St. Louis U., 1996. Staff nurse, acute medicine Jewish Hosp., St. Louis, 1975-77; critical care nurse, med.-coronary ICU St. Anthony's Med. Ctr., St. Louis, 1977-88; staff nurse level III burn/trauma, respiratory ICU Barnes Hosp., St. Louis, 1988-91; staff nurse trauma ICU St. Louis U. Hosp., 1991-94; pub. health nurse Family Care Health Ctrs., 1994, community health supr., 1994-96, acting health svcs. dir., 1995-96; quality improvement coord. women and infants BJC Health Sys., 1999—; amb., mem. Critical Care Nursing Delegation, Russia, Hungary, 1992; program coord. Immunization Info. Sys., St. Louis U., 1996; spl. programs coord. Care Ptnrs. Medicaid Managed Care HMO, BJC Health Sys., St. Louis, 1997-99; presenter in field. Contbr. articles to profl. jours. Mem. Citizens for Mo.'s Children; elected B.O.D. Teen Prevention Partnership, St. Louis, 1999. Recipient St. Anthony's Star of Excellence award, 1986, Recognition award Barnes Hosp. Nursing Svc., 1990, Dean's Disting. Nurse award U. Mo., St. Louis, 1992; AACN scholar. Mem. ANA (inst. constituent mems. on nursing practice 1991-94), APHA, AACN (clin. practice spl. interest cons. region 14 1990-92, pres. St. Louis chpt. 1991-92, chmn. pub. rels. 1988-90, health care policy and legis. editor St. Louis chpt. 1989-95; cert. corp., exam. writer 1990-92), Assn. Women's Health, Obstet. and Neonatal Nurses, Mo. Nurses Assn. (2 v.p. 3d dist. 1994-96, coun. nursing practice 1987-91, med.-surg. chmn. 1989-91), Mo. Pub. Health Assn. (2d v.p. St. Louis chpt. 1995-96), LWV, Sigma Theta Tau. Home: 9939 Affton Pl Saint Louis MO 63123-4305

CLARK, JEFF RAY, economist; b. Waynesboro, Va., Nov. 6, 1947; s. Jefferson Davis and Mildred (Cameron) C.; m. Arlene Donowitz, Dec. 17, 1988. BS, Va. Commonwealth U., 1970; MA, Va. Tech. U., Blacksburg, 1972, PhD, 1974. Assoc. dir. Joint Coun. Econ. Edn., N.Y.C., 1974-78, dir., 1978-80; chmn. econ./fin. Fairleigh Dickinson U., Madison, N.J., 1980-87; rsch. fellow Princeton (N.J.) U., 1987; Hendrix chair econs. U. Tenn., Martin, 1987-92; Probasco chair econs. U. Tenn., Chattanooga, 1992—; cons. Pew Charitable Trusts, Phila., 1987—, IT&T, Nutley, N.J., 1985, Fed. Res. Bank N.Y., N.Y.C., 1980, The Johns Hopkins U., Balt., 1984-86; disting. teaching fellow NSF, Washington, 1977, 78. Author: The Science of Cost, Benefit and Choice, 1988, 93, 96, Essentials of Economics, 1982, 86, Economics Cost and Choice, 1987, Macroeconomics for Managers, 1990, Survey of Economics, 1997. Bd. dirs. The William B. Cockroft Found., The Palmer Chitester Fund. Mem. Assn. for Pvt. Enterprise (v.p. 1991, pres. 1992, sec.-treas.), Am. Econ. Assn., Ea. Econ. Assn. (bd. dirs. 1980-85), Mont Pelerin Soc., Western Econ. Assn., So. Econ. Assn. Avocations: aviation, skiing, boating, scuba diving. Home: 1623 Ashley Mill Dr Chattanooga TN 37421-3259 Office: U Tenn 615 Mccallie Ave Chattanooga TN 37403-2504

CLARK, JEFFREY RAPHIEL, research and development company executive; b. Provo, Utah, Sept. 29, 1953; s. Bruce Budge and Ouida (Raphiel) C.; m. Anne Margaret Eberhardt, Mar. 15, 1985; children: Jeffrey Raphiel, Mary Anne Elizabeth, Edward William Eberhardt. BS, Brigham Young U., 1977, MBA, 1979. CPA, Tex. Fin. analyst Exxon Coal USA, Inc., Houston, 1979-83; constrn. mgr. Gen. Homes, Inc., Houston, 1983-84; controller Liberty Data Products, Houston, 1984-86; v.p. Tech. Rsch. Assocs., Inc., Salt Lake City, 1987—; also dir. Tech. Rsch. Assocs., Inc. Scoutmaster Boy Scouts Am., Salt Lake City, 1989-91. Mem. AICPA, Utah Inst. CPAs, Salt Lake C. of C. (legis. action com.), Salt Lake Country Club. Republican. Mormon. Avocations: snow skiing, golf, mountain climbing. Home: 1428 Michigan Ave Salt Lake City UT 84105-1609 Office: Technical Rsch Assocs 2257 S 1100 E Salt Lake City UT 84106-2379

CLARK, JEFFREY RAY, surgeon; b. Sioux Falls, S.D., Feb. 28, 1945; s. Ray Walter and June Marie (Kleespies) C.; m. Constance Jean Ranek, July 1, 1947; children: Jason, Aaron, Amy. BS in Zoology, S.D. State U., 1967; MD, Creighton U., 1971. Diplomate Am. Bd. Surgery. Resident in gen. surgery Fitzsimons Army Hosp., Denver, 1976; surgeon Ft. Carson Army Hosp., Colorado Springs, 1976-78; from asst. chief surgery to program dir. surgery residency Fitzsimons Army Hosp., 1978-93; dir. surgery edn., program dir. surgery residency St. Joseph Hosp., Denver, 1993—. Fellow Am. Coll. Surgeons; mem. Western Surg. Assn., Denver Acad. Surgery. Avocations: outdoor activities. *

CLARK, JIM, communications executive; b. Plainview, Tex., 1945. M in Physics, La. State U., 1971; PhD in Computer Sci., U. Utah, 1974. Asst. prof. U. Calif., Santa Cruz, 1974-78; assoc. prof. Stanford (Calif.) U., 1979-82; founder, chmn. Silicon Graphics, 1982-94; chmn. Netscape Comms. Corp., Mountain View, Calif., 1994—. Office: Netscape Comms Corp 501 E Middlefield Rd Mountain View CA 94043-4042*

CLARK, JOAN HARDY, retired journalist; b. Toronto, Ont., Can., Apr. 17, 1934; came to the U.S., 1960; d. Henry Hardy and Irene Elsie Stevens; m. James McConnell Clark; children from previous marriage: Lisa Anne Hanson, Anthony David Stuart Hanson. BA, Carleton U., Ottawa, Can., 1954; postgrad., Sarah Lawrence Coll., 1973-75. Bd. mem. Whitney Mus., N.Y.C., 1983—; chmn. coun. conservators N.Y. Pub. Libr., N.Y.C., 1986—, bd. mem., 1996—. Mem. Cosmopolitan Club. Home: 1 Gracie Sq New York NY 10028

CLARK, JOHN ARTHUR, lawyer; b. Glen Ridge, N.J., Dec. 22, 1920; s. Franklin Jones and Eleanor Newhall (Moss) C.; m. Dorothy Winton Bateson (dec.), Apr. 21, 1945; children: William F., Margaret W., John R. BA, Haverford Coll., 1942; JD, U. Pa., 1948. Bar: Pa. 1949, N.Y. 1954. Assoc. Moss, Rieser & Bingaman, Reading, Pa., 1948-51; special atty. IRS Regional Counsel, N.Y.C., 1951-53; assoc. Davies, Hardy, Ives & Lawther, N.Y.C., 1953-58, ptnr., 1958-70; ptnr. Duane, Morris & Heckscher, Phila., 1970-88, of counsel, 1989—. Author: How To Save Time and Taxes Handling Estates, 1965; contbr. articles to profl. jours. Treas. Met. Christian Coun. Phila., 1980-93; trustee Upper Moreland Free Pub. Libr., 1995-97. 1st lt. AUS, 1942-46, PTO. Mem. ABA, Pa. Bar Assn., Phila. Bar Assn. (vice chmn. com. on income of estates and trusts, ABA tax sect. 1987-89, chair 1989-91), Order of Coif. Office: Duane Morris & Heckscher One Liberty Pl Philadelphia PA 19103

CLARK, JOHN DESMOND, anthropology educator; b. London, Eng., Apr. 10, 1916; came to U.S., 1961, naturalized 1993; s. Thomas John Chown and Catherine (Wynne) C.; m. Betty Cable Baume, Apr. 30, 1938; children: Elizabeth Ann (Mrs. David Miall Winterbottom), John Wynne Desmond. B.A. Hons, Cambridge U., 1937, M.A., 1942, Ph.D., 1950, Sc.D., 1974; Sc.D. (hon.), U. Witwatersrand, Johannesburg, 1985, U. Cape Town, 1985. Dir. Rhodes-Livingstone Mus., No. Rhodesia, 1938-61; prof. anthropology U. Calif., Berkeley, 1961-86; prof. emeritus U. Calif., 1986—; faculty rsch. lectr. U. Calif., 1979; Raymond Dart lectr. Inst. for Study of Man, Africa, 1979; Sir Mortimer Wheeler lectr. Brit. Acad., 1981; J.D. Mulvaney lectr. Australian Nat. U., 1990. Author: The Stone Age Cultures of Northern Rhodesia, 1950, The Prehistoric Cultures of the Horn of Africa, 1954, The Prehistory of Southern Africa, 1959, Prehistoric Cultures of Northeast Angola, 1963, Distribution of Prehistoric Culture in Angola, 1966, The Atlas of African Prehistory, 1967, Kalambo Falls Prehistoric Site, Vol. I, 1969, Vol. II, 1974, The Prehistory of Africa, 1970; editor: Cambridge History of Africa, Vol. I, 1982, (with G.R. Sharma) Palaeo environment and Prehistory in the Middle Son Valley Madhya Pradesh, North Central India, 1983, (with S.A. Brandt) The Causes and Consequences of Food Production in Africa, 1984, Cultural Beginnings: Approaches to Understanding Early Hominid Life-ways in the African Savanna, 1991; contbr. articles to profl. jours. Served with Brit. Army, 1941-46. Decorated comdr. Order Brit. Empire; comdr. Nat. Order Senegal; recipient Huxley medal Royal Anthrop. Inst., London, 1974, Ad personam internat. Gold Mercury award Addis Ababa, 1982, Berkeley citation U. Calif., 1986, Fellows medal Calif. Acad. Scis., 1987, Gold medal of Am. Archaeol. Inst., 1989. Fellow AAAS, Brit. Acad. (Grahame Clark medal for prehistory 1997), Royal Soc. South Africa, Soc. Antiquaries London (Gold medal 1985); mem. NAS, Am. Anthropol. Assn. (disting. lectr. 1992, emeritus prof. of yr. 1996, L.S.B. Leakey Found. prize, 1996), Pan-African Congress Prehistory, Geog. Soc. Lisbon, Instituto Italiano di Preistoria e Protostoria, Body Corporate Livingstone Mus., Deuschen Archaologischen Instituts (corr. mem.). Office: U Calif Dept Anthropology Berkeley CA 94720

CLARK, JOHN F., aerospace research and engineering educator; b. Reading, Pa., Dec. 12, 1920; s. John F. Clark and Edith Dix (Long) Guenther; m. June Teubner Schweiger, July 14, 1974; children from previous marriage: Linda J. Marks, James C. BSEE with honors, Lehigh U., 1942, EE, 1947; MS in Math., George Washington U., 1946; PhD in Physics, U. Md., 1956. Registered profl. engr., N.J. Electronic engr. Naval Rsch. Lab., 1942-47, physicist, atmospheric electricity br. head, 1948-58; asst. prof. elec. engrng. Lehigh U., 1947-48; dir. physics and astronomy programs NASA, 1958-63, dep. assoc. adminstr. space sci. and applications (scis.), 1963-65, chmn. space sci. steering com., 1963-65; dir. Goddard Space Flight Center, 1965-76; dir. space applications and tech. RCA Corp., Princeton, N.J., 1976-86; part-time cons. Gen. Electric Astro Space Div., 1987-88; NAVSPACE rsch. prof. U.S. Naval Acad. aerospace engring. dept., Annapolis, Md., 1988-90; dir. grad. studies, prof. space sytems Fla. Inst. Tech., 1990—; part-time lectr. math. George Washington U., 1956-58; part-time cons. rsch. Grad. Coun., 1960-66; part-time lectr. physics U. Md., 1958; mem. indsl. and profl. adv. coun. Pa. State U., 1963-65; mem. vis. com. physics Lehigh U., 1966-74; mem. Com. on Fed. Labs., 1971-75, Md. Gov.'s Sci. Adv. Coun., 1972-76, N.J. Gov.'s Sci. Adv. Com., 1980-86, Am. Geophys. Union-URSI Bd. Radio Sci., 1974-78; mem. study panel Office Telecommunications, Nat. Assembly Engring., 1976-77; chmn. adv. com. FCC, 1981-83; mem. U.S. del. to Internat. Telecommunication Union Conf., Regional Adminstrv. Radio Conf., 1983, World Adminstrv. Radio Conf., 1985; chmn. Direct Broadcast Satellite Assn., 1986; mem. spectrum planning adv. com. U.S. Dept. Commerce, 1986-92; bd. dirs. ECON Inc.; mem. Calif. Inst. Tech. Jet Propulsion Lab.'s Mars Observer Program Rev. Bd., 1986-93. Contbr. numerous articles to profl. jours.; cons. editor space tech. McGraw-Hill Ency. Sci. and Tech. 1977—. Recipient NASA medals for Disting. Service, Outstanding Leadership, Exceptional Service, Collier trophy Nat. Aero. Assn. Fellow Am. Astron. Soc., AIAA (gen. chmn. Communications Satellite System Conf. 1984, v.p. pub. policy 1986-90), IEEE, Explorers Club; mem. Am. Geophys. Union, Am. Meterol. Soc., Satellite Broadcasting and Communications Assn. (chmn. 1987, chmn.'s coun. 1989-90, 1st Pres.'s award 1993), Internat. Soc. Satellite Profls. (bd. dirs. 1985-89), Internat. Acad. Astronautics, Phi Beta Kappa, Sigma Xi, Pi Mu Epsilon, Tau Beta Pi, Sigma Phi Epsilon, Sigma Pi Sigma. Patentee electronic circuits and systems. Home: 947 Loggerhead Island Dr Satellite Beach FL 32937-3863

CLARK, JOHN FRANKLIN, lawyer; b. Salt Lake City, June 22, 1948; s. John Fabian and Margaret Estelle (Johnson) C.; m. Carole Ann Ramme, Jan. 8, 1982; children: Lauren, Jonathan, Timothy. BA, Yale U., 1970; JD, U. Utah, 1974; MPA, Harvard U., 1996. Bar: Utah 1974. Dep. county atty. Salt Lake County, 1974-82; mng. ptnr. Sessions & Moore Law Firm, Salt Lake City, 1982-89; counsel to atty. gen. Utah Atty. Gen.'s Office, Salt Lake City, 1989-95; atty. advisor, dep. divsn. chief FCC/Wireless Telecomm. Bur., Washington, 1996—. Campaign mgr. Bobbie Coray for Congress, Layton, Utah, 1994; chmn. Kennedy Sch. D.C. Alumni Coun., 1997; nat. committeeman Dem. Nat. Com., Washington, 1995-96; bd. dirs., counsel Ronald McDonald House, Salt Lake City, 1987-88; mem. bd. govs. Assn. of Yale Alumni, 1979-82. Littauer fellow Kennedy Sch. Govt., Harvard U., 1996. Mem. Utah State Bar, Fed. Comm. Bar Assn. Democrat. Unitarian. Avocations: U.S. civil war history, golf. Office: 445 12th St SW Washington DC 20554

CLARK, JOHN GRAHAM, III, lawyer; b. Greenville, N.C., Dec. 28, 1950; s. John Graham Jr. and Ariane (Downarowicz) C. BA, U. N.C., 1973; MA, E. Carolina U., 1977; JD, Campbell U., 1984. Bar: N.C. 1984, U.S. Dist. Ct. N.C. 1988, U.S. Supreme Ct. 1988; cert. specialist criminal law N.C. State Bar. Assoc. Nelson Taylor, III, Morehead City, N.C., 1985; asst. dist. atty. State of N.C., 1985-87; ptnr. Clark & James law firm, Greenville, 1987—. Named to Internat. Law Moot Ct. Assn. Student Internat. Law Socs., 1983. Mem. N.C. Bar Assn., N.C. Acad. Trial Lawyers, Phi Alpha Delta, Pi Sigma Alpha, Phi Alpha Theta. Avocations: golf, travel, tennis. Office: 315 S Evans St Greenville NC 27858-1832

CLARK, JOHN HALLETT, III, consulting engineering executive; b. Bristol, Va., Oct. 31, 1918; s. John Hallett, Jr. and Shirley (Winston) C.; m. Suzanne North Hazelet, Sept. 19, 1942; children: Craig Winston, John Hallett IV, Philip Winston. Student, Williams Coll., 1937-38, Colo. Coll., 1938-42; B.S. in Civil Engring, U. Ky., 1948. Registered profl. engr., Ky. Jr. engr. Austin Co., 1942; with Hazelet & Erdal, Louisville, 1942-43, 47—; partner Hazelet & Erdal, 1956—, mng. partner, 1973-82, pres., 1982-86, chmn., 1986-87, retired, 1987; co-designer major hwy. and bridge projects. Mem. Louisville and Jefferson County Planning and Zoning Commn., 1957-64, vice chmn., 1962-64; bd. dirs. Better Bus. Bur. Louisville, 1965-68; mem. town coun., Anchorage, Ky., 1969-71. With C.E., U.S. Army, 1943-46, PTO. Fellow ASCE (pres. Ky. 1954); mem. Am. Inst. Cons. Engrs. (councilor 1970-73), Nat., Ky. socs. profl. engrs., Cons. Engrs. Council U.S. (dir. Ky. 1968-70, pres. Ky. 1967), Tau Beta Pi, Delta Kappa Epsilon. Episcopalian. Clubs: Red Lantern (Colo. Coll.), Harmony Landing Country (Goshen, Ky.). Home: 520 Old Stone Ln Louisville KY 40207-2336

CLARK, JOHN J., economics and finance educator; b. N.Y.C., June 21, 1924; s. John J. and Mary E. (Taylor) C.; m. Margaret T. Norton, July 1, 1965; 1 dau., Patricia Ann. B.B.A. magna cum laude, St. John's U., 1948; M.B.A., CCNY, 1950; Ph.D., NYU, 1959. Prof. econs. Coll. Bus. Adminstrn., St. John's U., 1950-69, chmn. dept., 1959-62, dean, 1962-70; Royal H. Gibson Sr. prof. bus. adminstrn. Drexel U., Phila., 1971-90, prof. emeritus; lectr. econs. Bklyn. Poly. Inst., 1954-58. Co-author: The Impact of the Foundation Reports on Business Eudcation, 1963, Business Fluctuations, Growth and Economic Stabilization, 1963, Professional Education for Business, 1964, The New Economics of National Defense, 1966, Financial Management: A Capital Market Approach, 1976, Management of Capital Expenditures, 1979, 3rd rev. edit., 1989, Lease/Buy Decision, 1980, A Statistics Primer for Managers, 1980, Business Mergers and Acquisition Strategies, 1985, Restructuring Corporate America, 1996; also numerous articles; editor: Business and the Liberal Arts, 1962; contbg. editor: Fin. Mgmt. Jour., 1972-82. Mem. Borough Pres.'s Planning Com., Queens County, N.Y.C., 1964-69; economist joint legislative com. banking law N.Y. State Legislature, 1965-68. Recipient Mil. Rev. award U.S. Army Command and Gen. Staff Coll., 1964. Mem. Am. Econ. Assn., Eastern Fin. Assn. (exec. dir. 1974-77), U.S. Naval Inst. (medal 1969), Royal United Service Inst. for Def. Studies, Phila. Maritime Mus. (advisor), Beta Gamma Sigma, Delta Mu Delta, Omicron Delta Epsilon. Home: White Horse Village 535 Gradyville Rd # V101 Newtown Square PA 19073-2815 Office: Coll Bus Adminstrn Drexel U Philadelphia PA 19104

CLARK, JOHN PETER, III, engineering consultant; b. Phila., May 6, 1942; s. John Peter Jr. and Victoria Mary (McQuaide) C.; m. Nancy Ann Lapin, June 22, 1968; children: Shannon John, Hannah Marie. BSChemE, Notre Dame U., 1964; PhD, U. Calif., 1968. Registered profl. engr., Va., Ill. Rsch. engr. Agrl. Rsch. Svc., USDA, Berkeley, Calif., Washington, 1968-72; from asst. to assoc. prof. Va. Poly. Inst. and State U., Blacksburg, 1972-78; dir. rsch. and devel. ITT Continental Baking, Rye, N.Y., 1978-81; pres. Epstein Process Engring. Inc., Chgo., 1981-94; pvt. practice, engring. cons., Oak Park, Ill., 1994-95, v.p. Tech. Fluor Daniel, Inc., 1995-98. Co-author: Food Processing Operations and Scale-up, 1991; editor: Exercises in Process Simulation, 1977; contbr. articles to profl. jours; patentee (with C.J. King) in field for System for Freeze Drying. Fellow AIChE (div. chmn. 1982), Inst. Food Technologists (div. chmn. 1984). Roman Catholic. Avocations: reading, running, golf, Indian art. Home: 644 Linden Ave Oak Park IL 60302-1661

CLARK, JOHN RUSSELL, marine biologist; b. Seattle, Apr. 11, 1927; s. Donald Hathaway and Mildred (Taylor) C.; m. Catherine Lochner; children: John M., Jeffry R., George K., Linda J., Kerry S., Karen M. B.S., U. Wash., Seattle, 1949. Research biologist Woods Hole (Mass.) Fishery Lab., Dept. Interior, 1950-59; asst. dir. Sandy Hook (N.J.) Marine Lab., Dept. Interior, 1960-70; dir. Narragansett (R.I.) Marine Lab., Dept. Interior, 1971; dir. water programs Conservation Found., Washington, 1972-81; mgr. coastal programs internat. affairs office Nat. Park Svc., Washington, 1982-87; sr. rsch. assoc. U. Miami Sch. Marine Sci., Fla., 1988—; adj. scientist Mote Marine Lab., Sarasota, Fla., 1994—. Author: Through the Fish's Eye, 1973, Shark Watch, 1975, Coastal Ecosystems Management, 1977, The Sanibel Report, 1977, Wetland Functions and Values, 1979, Coastal Environment Management, 1980, Wetlands of Bottomland Hardwood Forests, 1981, Marine and Coastal Protected Areas, 1984, Snorkeling: A Complete Guide, 1985, Integrated Management of Coastal Zones, 1992, Coastal Zone Management Handbook, 1996, Coastal Seas, 1998. Served with USNR, 1945-46. Named Conservationist of Year Am. Motors Corp., 1968; recipient Meritorious Publ. award U.S. Fish and Wildlife Service, 1969. Mem. Am. Littoral Soc. (founder, dir., past pres.). Office: Mote Marine Lab Field Office 281 W Indies Dr Ramrod Key FL 33042-5462

CLARK, JOHN W., lawyer; b. Dallas, Nov. 7, 1938; s. John W. and Grace Lillian (Hobgood) C.; m. Ann burnett, Feb. 16, 1991 (dec. Jan. 1993); children: Catherine Kimball, Sue Harralson; m. Barbara Priddy, Mar. 9, 1996. BA, So. Meth. U., 1960, JD, 1963. Assoc. Douglas Bergman, Dallas, 1963-68; ptnr. Turner, Hitchins, McInerney, Webb & Hartnett, Dallas, 1968-88; founding ptnr. Clark, Wiley & Goodall, Dallas, 1988-92; pvt. practice, Dallas, 1992—. Fellow Am. Bar Found.; mem. ABA (bd. govs. 1971-75, 1998-99, Outstanding Solo Practitioner award 1996), State Bar Assn. Tex. (bd. dirs. 1978-83), Royal Oaks Country Club, Dallas Petroleum Club. Methodist. Avocations: golf, sport fishing. Home: 3637 Roseale Dallas TX 75205

CLARK, JOHN WALTER, JR., shipping company executive; b. Mobile, Ala., Oct. 21, 1919; s. John Walter and Mae (Kappner) C.; m. Evelyn Ruth Hamilton, Aug. 29, 1941 (dec.); children: Ann Clark Morgan (dec.), Ruth Clark Day, Susan Clark Wells; m. Sandra L. Sharp, June 21, 1977; stepchildren: Kirsten J. Acomb, Heidi G. Qualey. Grad., U.S. Mcht. Marine Acad., 1940; postgrad., Tulane U., 1950-55. Served as officer, master mariner U.S. Mcht. Marine, 1940-46; mgr. Argentina, Brazil, West Africa and Europe Delta Steamship Lines, Inc., 1946-50; asst. to pres. Delta Steamship Lines, Inc., New Orleans, 1950-53, v.p., 1953-59, pres., 1959-79, chmn. bd., 1979-80; pres. Clark Maritime Assocs., Inc., 1979—; bd. dirs. Panama Canal Commn., 1978-82; past pres., mem. exec. com., bd. dirs. World Trade Ctr. of New Orleans; maritime arbitrator New Orleans Bd. of Trade; commr., pres. Port of New Orleans, 1978-82; exec. dir. Miss. State Port Authority, 1982-85; nat. vice chmn. Coun.of Ams., 1974-80. Decorated Order of Crown of Belgium; Order of Star of Africa Liberia; Order of So. Cross Brazil; comendador de la Orden de Mayo Argentina; Order de Isabel La Catolica Spain; named Maritime Man of Year Port of New Orleans, 1965. Mem. U.S. Mcht. Marine Acad. Alumni Assn. (Alumnus of Yr. 1975, named to Hall of Fame 1998). Methodist. Clubs: Plimsoll, So. Yacht, Pickwick, Pass Christian Yacht, Pass Christian Isles Golf. Office: Clark Maritime Assocs Inc 23322 Woodland Way Pass Christian MS 39571-5711

CLARK, JOHN WHITCOMB, diagnostic radiologist; b. Walkerton, Ind., Aug. 14, 1918; s. John and Minnie (Whitcomb) C.; m. Mary Louise Dormady, Apr. 15, 1961. Student, U. Chgo., 1936-39; M.D., Harvard, 1943. Diplomate: Am. Bd. Radiology. Intern Presbyn. Hosp., Chgo., 1943-44; resident radiology Presbyn. Hosp., 1946-49, asst. attending radiologist, 1949-50, asso. attending, 1950-55; attending radiologist div. radiology and nuclear medicine Presbyn.-St. Luke's Hosp., Chgo., 1955-70; attending radiologist Presbyn.-St. Luke's Hosp., 1970-86, head radioisotope dept., 1955-65, chmn. radioisotope com., 1956-70; mem. faculty U. Ill. Sch. Medicine, Chgo., 1948-70; prof. radiology U. Ill. Sch. Medicine, 1963-70; prof. radiology Rush Med. Coll., Chgo., 1970-89, dir. computed tomography and nuclear magnetic resonance, 1982-86; assoc. scientist div. biol. and med. research Argonne Nat. Lab., Lemont, Ill., 1952-56, cons. scientist, 1956-62; mem. radiation study sect. NIH, 1962-66; mem. com. community health Inst. Medicine, Chgo., 1968-80; cons. in field. Mem. editorial bd. Radiology Jour., 1966-86; contbr. numerous articles to profl. jours. Served to capt. AUS, 1944-46. Fellow Am. Coll. Radiology; mem. Radiol. Soc. N.Am., Chgo. Roentgen Soc. (pres. 1963-64), AMA, Am. Roentgen Ray Soc. Patentee ultrasonic rapid sector scan imaging system. Home: 3740 N Lake Shore Dr Chicago IL 60613-4237 Office: 1753 W Congress Pky Chicago IL 60612-3809

CLARK, JOHN WILLIAM, JR., electrical engineer, educator; b. Rochester, N.Y., Dec. 24, 1936; s. John William and Dorothy Louise (Springett) C.; m. Betty Faye Stovall, Dec. 29, 1955; children: John William III, Nan Ellen, Adrienne Anne, Michael Christian. BS, Christian Bros. U., Memphis, 1962; MS, Case Inst. Tech., 1965; PhD, Case Western Res. U., 1967. Rsch. assoc. Case Western Res. U., Cleve., 1967-68; asst. prof. dept. elec. and computer engring. Rice U., Houston, 1968-73, assoc. prof. dept. elec. and computer engring., 1973-79, prof. dept. elec. and computer engring., 1979—. Assoc. editor: IEEE Transactions on Biomed. Engring., 1979-85; contbr. articles to CRC Critical Revs. on Bioengring., Am. Jour. Physiology, IEEE Trans. on Biomed. Engring., Jour. Physiology (London), and others; contbr. chpts. to books. Recipient Disting. Svc. award Alliance for

Engring. in Medicine and Biology, 1988. Fellow Am. Inst. Med. and Biol. Engring. (founding); mem. IEEE (sr.), Biomed. Engring. Soc. (sr.), Biophys. Soc., Houston Soc. for Engring. in Medicine and Biology (chmn. 1986—). Republican. Roman Catholic. Home: 3020 Locke Ln Houston TX 77019-6202 Office: Rice U PO Box 1892 6100 Main St Houston TX 77005-1892

CLARK, JONATHAN L., photographer, printer, publisher; b. Ottawa, Ill., Mar. 24, 1952; s. Keith S. and Harriet S. Clark. BA in Photography, U. Calif., Santa Cruz, 1974. Self employed artist, 1975—; founder, propr. The Artichoke Press, Mountain View, Calif., 1975—. Editor The Hedgehog arts rev., San Francisco, 1997—; exhibited 16 one-man shows in U.S., Japan and Europe; exhibited in more than 60 group shows. Mem. visual arts com. City of Mountain View, Calif. Photography fellow Arts Coun. Santa Clara County, 1997, Book Club of Calif. grantee, 1997; USIS travel grantee, Poland, 1994; travel grantee, Barcelona, 1994. Avocation: bicycling. Home: 550 Mountain View Ave Mountain View CA 94041-1941

CLARK, JOYCE LAVONNE, receptionist; b. Ashland, Oreg., Jan. 1, 1931; d. John Arthur and Minnie Lucille (Wisecarver) Freeman; m. Robert Glines, 1948 (div. Aug. 1958); children: Judy Cabe, Jari Evelund, Cynthia Glines, Kevin Glines; m. L. A. Clark, June 1972 (div. 1983); children: Peter Clark, John Freeman, Drew Freeman. BA in History, So. Oreg. State Coll., 1989, BA in Edn., 1989. Mgr. R/V trailer and laundromat, Soldotna, Alaska, 1981-84; substitute tchr. Kenai Peninsula Sch. Borough, Soldotna, 1989-91; receptionist Women in Crisis, Fairbanks, Alaska, 1991-95, Adult Learning Programs, Fairbanks, 1995—. Contbr. poem, articles to profl. publs. Sec. Lit. Arts Com., 1994-96. Democrat. Mem. Assembly of God. Avocations: writing, reading, music, walking.

CLARK, JOYCE NAOMI JOHNSON, nurse; b. Corpus Christi, Tex., Oct. 4, 1936; d. Chester Fletcher and Ermal Olita (Bailey) Johnson; m. William Boyd Clark, Jan. 4, 1958; (div. 1967); 1 child, Sherene Joyce. Student, Corpus Christi State U., 1975-77. RN, CNOR, ACLS, TNCC; cert. instrument flight instr.; cert. core trauma nurse. Staff nurse Van Nuys (Calif.) Cmty. Hosp., 1963-64, U.S. Naval Hosp., Corpus Christi, 1964-68; patient care coord. Spohn Meml. Hosp. (formerly Meml. Med. Ctr.), Corpus Christi, 1968—. Leader Paisano Coun. Girl Scouts U.S.A., Corpus Christi, 1968-74; past comdr. 3rd group USAF Aux., CAP Air Search and Rescue, wing chief pilot, ret. lt. col. 1993. Recipient Charles A. Mella award Meml. Med. ctr., 1981, Paul E. Garbert award CAP, 1986, cert. of appreciation in recognition of Support Child Guard Missing Children Edn. Program Nat. Assn. Chiefs of Police, Washington, 1987, Charles E. Yeager Aerospace Edn. Achievement award, 1985, Grover Loenig Aerospace award, 1986, Cert. of World Leadership Internat. Biographical Ctr., Cambridge, Eng., 1987, Gill Robb Wilson award #1021, 1988, Merit award Drug Free Am. Through Enforcement, Edn., Intelligence Nat. Assn. Chiefs of Police, Sr. Mem. of Yr. USAF Aux., CAP Air Search and Rescue, 1986. Mem. USAF Aux., CAP Air Search and Rescue (past comdr. 3rd group, wing chief pilot, ret. lt. col., Sr. Mem. of Yr. 1986), Am. Assn. Oper. Rm. Nurses (v.p. 1969), Aircraft Owners and Pilots Assn. Avocation: flying. Home: 625 Gregory Dr Apt 67 Corpus Christi TX 78412-3051 Office: Spohn Meml Hosp 4606 Hospital Blvd Corpus Christi TX 78405-1818

CLARK, JUDITH REDMOND, editor, writer; b. Mansfield, Ohio, Feb. 21, 1939; d. William Earl and Frances Marie (Frassrand) Redmond; m. Jack Palmer Clark, June 8, 1957 (div. Oct. 1996); children: Robert Cornell, Julie Elizabeth, April Kelly, Stephanie Rachelle. Student, U. Houston, 1964-68. Assoc. editor Universal News, Houston, 1977-90, editor, 1990-92; assoc. editor/writer Pipeline Digest, 1977-90, editor, 1990-94. Mem. Roseate-Pres.'s Adv. Bd., 1989, Greater Houston Area Women's Found., Literacy Advance, 1988—, also bd. dirs., 1998—; freelance writer Ideal Images, 1994; sr. staff editor, technical writer and tng. developer Daniel Follette, Inc., 1994—. Recipient Bell Ringer's award Literacy Advance, 1989. Mem. Assn. Women in Communications, Inc. (pres.-elect 1987-88, pres. Houston profl. chpt. 1988-89, v.p. 1985-86, treas. 1986-87, nat. and regional del. 1988, Pres. award 1990, Headliner's award 1996), Soc. Profl. Journalists (pres.-elect/membership v.p. Houston profl. chpt. 1993-94, pres. Houston profl. chpt. 1994-95, treas. 1996-99), Altrusa Internat. (sec. Houston chpt. 1993-94), 1960 Photog. Soc. (editor newsletter 1987), Fedn. Houston Profl. Women (del. 1988-92, Woman of Excellence 1997). Home: 15823 Cutten Rd Houston TX 77070-2078 Office: Daniel Follette Inc 1937 W Gray St Ste 110 Houston TX 77019-4809

CLARK, KAREN HEATH, lawyer; b. Pasadena, Calif., Dec. 17, 1944; d. Wesley Pelton and Lois (Ellenberger) Heath; m. Bruce Robert Clark,Dec. 30, 1967; children: Adam Heath, Andrea Pelton. Student, Pomona Coll., Claremont, Calif., 1962-64; BA, Stanford U., 1964-66; MA in History, U. Wash., 1968; JD, U. Mich., 1977. Bar: Calif. 1978. Instr. Henry Ford Community Coll., Dearborn, Mich., 1968-72; assoc. Gibson, Dunn & Crutcher LLP, Irvine, Calif., 1977-86, ptnr., 1986—. Bd. dirs. Dem. Found. Orange County, 1989-91, 94—, Planned Parenthood Orange County, Santa Ana, Calif., 1979-82, New Directions for Women, Newport Beach, 1986-91, Women in Leadership, chair, 1995—. Recipient 1996 Choice award Planned Parenthood of Orange & San Bernardino Counties. Mem. Women in Leadership (founder 1993), Comml. Real Estate Women, Bldg. Industries Assn. So. Calif., Internat. Coun. Shopping Ctrs., Calif. Mortgage Bankers Assn. Office: Gibson Dunn & Crutcher LLP 4 Park Plz Ste 1400 Irvine CA 92614-8557

CLARK, KATHLEEN VERNON, special education educator; b. Nashville, Apr. 16, 1939; d. Walter Newton Jr. and E. Ruth (Mason) Vernon; m. Stanley Prentiss Clark, Apr. 16, 1962; children: Stanley Martin, Jennifer Kathleen Clark. BA, So. Meth. U., 1961; postgrad., George Peabody Coll., 1975; MA, U. Ala., Tuscaloosa, 1977; EdS, Jacksonville State U., 1986; EdD, U. Ala., Tuscaloosa, 1991. Cert. spl. edn. tchr., Ala. Tchr., spl. olympics coach Piedmont (Ala.) City Schs., 1975-86, testing coord., 1982-86; tchr. Tuscaloosa City Schs., 1986-90, 97, continuing edn. presenter, 1989; tchr. Lauderdale County Schs., Florence, Ala., 1990-97; chairperson SPE dept. Tuscaloosa Mid. Sch., 1987-89; mem. grad. adv. coun. area of spl. edn. U. Ala., Tuscaloosa, 1989-90; adj. prof. spl. edn. U. No. Ala., 1991-96; spl. edn. tchr. Etowah County Schs.; mem. steering com. So. Assn. Colls. and Schs., sponsor Leo Club. Dir. Meth. Elem. Camps, Sumatanga, Ala., Southeastern Meth. Assembly Grounds; bd. dirs. Lake Junaluska, N.C., 1988-96; pres. Ch. Women United, Decatur, Ala., 1971-72; v.p. United Meth. Women, Northport, Ala., 1988-90; mem. Meth. Commn. on Status and Role of Women, Birmingham, Ala., 1990-92; mem. N. Ala. Meth. Bd. Social Concerns. Mem. NEA, Coun. for Exceptional Children (Tchr. of Yr. 1978), Assn. for Retarded Citizens, Ala. Edn. Assn. (rep. 1988-90), Kappa Delta Pi, Phi Kappa Phi, Psi Chi. Avocations: reading, traveling. Home: PO Box 175 Centre AL 35960-0296

CLARK, KEITH COLLAR, musician, educator; b. Grand Rapids, Mich., Nov. 21, 1927; s. Harry Holt and Bethyl June (Collar) C.; m. Marjorie Ruth Park, Dec. 8, 1951; children: Nancy Joy McColley, Sandra Lynn Masse, Karen Jean Moore, Beth Anne Barnard. Student of trumpet, Nat. Music Camp, Interlochen, Mich., 1943. 44, 45; studied under Lloyd Geisler, 1947-48, studied under Armando Ghitalla, 1974. Trumpet player Grand Rapids Symphony Orch., 1943-46; with U.S. Army, 1946, advanced through grades to master sgt., 1966; trumpet player U.S. Army Band, Washington, 1946-66; ret., 1966; assoc. prof. brass Houghton (N.Y.) Coll., 1966-80; cons., asst. project dir. Dictionary Am. Hymnology, Bethesda, Md., 1980-81; prin. trumpet S.W. Fla. Symphony Orch., Ft. Myers, 1982-86, Treasure Coast Symphony Orch., Ft. Pierce, Fla., 1989-94, Atlantic Classical Orch., Vero Beach, Fla., 1991—; adj. prof. Edison C.C., Ft. Myers, 1984-89, Indian River C.C., Ft. Pierce, 1989-94; instr. Montgomery Coll., Bethesda, 1964-66, Roberts Wesleyan Coll., Rochester, N.Y., 1969-70; condr. Houghton Coll. Symphony Orch., 1966-78, Concert Band, 1975-80; lectr. Inst. Musica Suera Mexicana, Pueblo, 1973; guest condr. Buffalo Philharm. Orch., 1969, Treasure Coast Symphony Orch., 1990. Author: A Selective Bibliography for the Study of Hymns, 1980; assoc. editor The Instrumentalist mag., 1974-76; contbr. articles to profl. publs. Music dir. Maryland Avenue Bapt. Ch., Washington, 1947-51, Cherrydale Bapt. Ch., Arlington, Va., 1953-60, Christ Meth. Ch., Arlington, 1961-65, Vero Beach Alliance Ch., 1990-93. Recipient honor awards Nat. Sch. Orch. Assn., 1976, 80. Mem. Internat. Trumpet Guild (charter, project dir. 1978-80), Hymn Soc. Am. (life, grantee 1980-81), Ch. Music Soc. (Eng.) (life), Hymn Soc. Gt. Britain and Ireland (life), Nat. Ch. Music Fellowship (pres. 1967-69), Sonneck Soc. Avocations: collecting books and early records, jogging. Home: 801 Linnaen Ter NW Pt Charlotte FL 33948-3616

CLARK, KENNETH COURTRIGHT, retired physics and geophysics educator; b. Austin, Tex., Sept. 30, 1919; s. Evert Mordecai and Grace (Courtright) C.; m. Eleanor Lorraine McKenna, June 10, 1947; children: David Templeton, Gracia Courtright. B.A., U. Tex., 1940; A.M., Harvard U., 1941, Ph.D., 1947. Spl. research assoc. nat. def. research project Electro-Acoustic Lab., Harvard, 1942-45, instr. physics, 1947-48; mem. faculty U. Wash., Seattle, 1948—, asso. prof., 1955-60, prof., 1960-90; prof. emeritus U. Wash., 1990—, chmn. geophysics, 1967-69; research asso. prof. Geophys. Inst., U. Alaska, Fairbanks, 1957-58; mem. sci. adv. bd. Geophys. Inst., U. Alaska, 1972-76; vis. prof. div. theoretical and space physics LaTrobe U., Melbourne, Australia, 1979-80; cons. AID, State Dept. and Ministry Edn. India, Varanasi, 1964, Udaipur, 1966; dir. aeronomy program NSF, Washington, 1969-70. Fellow Am. Phys. Soc., Optical Soc. Am.; mem. Am. Geophys. Union, Am. Assn. Physics Tchrs., Phi Beta Kappa, Sigma Xi. Methodist. Home: 4739 University View Pl NE Seattle WA 98105-4035

CLARK, KENNETH EDWIN, psychologist, former university dean; b. New Madison, Ohio, Dec. 18, 1914; s. Harry H. and Nellie B. (Tremps) C.; m. Helen Titelmaier, June 29, 1942 (div. 1983); children: Patricia Hill, Virginia, Joyce Marie; m. Miriam B. Rock, May 25, 1983. B.S., Ohio State U., 1935, M.A., 1937, Ph.D., 1940. Tchr. Ashtabula County (Ohio) Schs., 1935-37; asst. dept. psychology Ohio State U., 1937-40; instr. U. Minn., 1940-42, asst. prof., 1946-60, chmn. dept. psychology, 1957-60; assoc. dean Grad. Sch., 1960; dean U. Colo. Coll. Arts and Scis., Boulder, 1961-63; prof. psychology U. Rochester, N.Y., 1963-83, dean Coll. Arts and Sci., 1963-80; Smith Richardson sr. scientist Ctr. Creative Leadership, 1985—; Mem. Pres.'s Com. on Nat. Medal of Sci., 1962-64; cons. Office Sci. and Tech., 1961-69; mem. Army Sci. Bd., 1966-82. Author: America's Psychologists, 1957, Vocational Interests of Nonprofessional Men, 1961 (with G.A. Miller) Psychology, 1970 (with M.B. Clark) Measures of Leadership, 1990, (with M.B. Clark and D.P. Campbell) Impact of Leadership, 1992, (with M.B. Clark) Choosing to Lead, 1994; editor Jour. Applied Psychology, 1961-70. Trustee Am. Psychol. Found., 1966-73; chmn. bd. govs. Center for Creative Leadership, 1974-81, pres., 1981-85; chmn. Am. Conf. Acad. Deans, 1976-77. Served with USAAF, 1942-44; lt. (j.g.) USNR, 1944-46. Recipient Psychol. Gold medal Am. Psychol. Found., 1986. Fellow AAAS, Am. Psychol. Assn., Am. Psychol. Soc.; mem. Assn. Advancement Psychology (trustee 1974-78, chmn. 1974-75), Am. Bd. Examiners in Profl. Psychology (pres. 1959-63), Psi Chi, Phi Delta Kappa, Phi Beta Kappa. Home: 4551 Gulf Shore Blvd N Naples FL 34103-3459

CLARK, KENNETH WILLIAM, mechanical engineer; b. Royal Oak, Mich., July 6, 1960; s. Ralph Waldo and Shirley Anne (Cutright) C. BS in Mech. Engring., Mich. Tech. U., 1983. Engr.-in-tng. status, Mich. Design engr. Troy (Mich.) Design Svcs., 1983-84; application engr. NOK, Inc., Bloomfield Hills, Mich., 1984-86, supr. application engring., 1986-88; asst. mgr. application engring. Freudenberg-NOK, Plymouth, Mich., 1988-92, mgr. application engring., 1992-94; mgr. air/fuel systems Auttocom, Plymouth, Mich., 1995-96; mgr. engine sealing Freudenberg-NOK, Plymouth, Mich., 1986-98; exec. engring. staff Freudenberg-NOK, Plymouth, 1998—. Mem. Soc. Automotive Engrs. Avocations: comml. aircraft pilot, auto racing, fishing, hunting, backpacking. Office: Freudenberg-NOK 47690 E Anchor Ct Plymouth MI 48170-2400

CLARK, KEVIN ANTHONY, marketing executive, communications executive; b. Kansas City, Mo., Dec. 10, 1956; s. Harley Leon and Virginia Lee (Magee) C.; m. Heidi Jean Sawyer. BS, U. Tulsa, 1978. Producer, announcer Sta. KWGS-FM, Tulsa, 1976-78; assoc. communications specialist IBM Corp., Charlotte, N.C., 1979-80; communications specialist IBM Corp., Tarrytown, N.Y., 1981-82; staff communications specialist IBM Corp., White Plains, N.Y., 1983-84; corp. speak up adminstr., sr. communications specialist IBM Corp., Armonk, N.Y., 1985-87; info. rep., program adminstr. IBM Corp., White Plains, 1988-90, mgr. svcs. and mktg. media rels., 1991-93; mgr. U.S. pub. rels. IBM, 1993-94; mgr. Global Multimedia Comms., 1994-95; product mgr. global strategic mktg. mobile computing IBM PC Co., Research Triangle Park, N.C., 1995-96; program dir. strategic mktg. IBM Mobile Computing, 1997-98; program dir. brand stewardship IBM ThinkPad, 1997-98; program dir. brand mgmt. IBM Think and IBM Work Pad, 1999—; dir. corp. comms. Okla. Intercollegiate Legislature, Oklahoma City, 1977; mem. steering com. MIT Media Lab. Author: IBM Speak Up Manual, 1986; editor: (brochure) IBM in Real Estate and Construction, 1984 (Excellence award IBM 1984, cert. Merit Printing Industries Am. 1984); author: (with others) Strategic Public Relations and Integrated Communications. Named one of Outstanding Young Men of Am., 1985. Mem. Nat. Spkrs. Assn. Avocations: alpine skiing, reading, writing, public speaking. Home: 907 Linden Rd Chapel Hill NC 27514-8046 Office: IBM Corp 3039 Cornwallis Rd Research Triangle Park NC 27709

CLARK, KIM BRYCE, business educator; b. Salt Lake City, Mar. 20, 1949; s. Merlin and Helen Mar (Hickman) C.; m. Sue Lorraine Hunt, June 14, 1971; children: Bryce, Erin, Jonathan, Andrew, Michael, Julia, Jennifer. BA, Harvard U., 1974, MA, 1977, PhD, 1978. From asst. prof. to prof. Bus. Sch. Harvard U., Boston, 1978-89, Harry E. Figgie prof. bus. adminstrn. Bus. Sch., 1989-95, dean Grad. Sch. Bus. Adminstrn., 1995—; bd. dirs. Ceramics Process System Corp., Milford, Mass., Analysis Group, Belmont, Mass., Automotive Industries, Inc. Author: (with others) Industrial Renaissance, 1983, Dynamic Manufacturing, 1988, (with T. Fujimoto) Product Development Performance, 1991, (with S. Wheelwright) Revolutionizing Product Development, 1992; editor: The Uneasy Alliance, 1985; contbr. articles to profl. jours. Coord. Belmont Youth Basketball, 1983—. Mem. IEEE (assoc. mem.), Am. Econ. Assn., Inst. Mgmt. Sci. Avocations: golf, jogging. Office: Harvard Bus Sch Soldiers Fld Boston MA 02163-1317

CLARK, LADY ELLEN MARIE, occupational health nurse, consultant; b. Jennings, La., Jan. 12, 1944; d. Henry A. and Marie Kathryn (Werner) Winters; m. Gerald L. Clark, May 12, 1990; 1 child, Eric Paul Cone; 1 foster child, Jerri Lynn Jacobs; stepchildren: Lisa Lynn Barroso, Julie Ann Rothschild. Diploma, Bapt. Hosp. Sch. Nursing, 1966; student, Lamar U., 1961-64. RN, Tex.; cert. occupational health nurse specialist, cert. case mgr. Coord. infection control dept. Beaumont (Tex.) Med./Surg. Hosp., 1980; occupational health coord. The Goodyear Tire & Rubber Co., Beaumont Chem. Plant, Beaumont, 1980-89; supr. health svcs. Sea World of Tex., San Antonio, 1989; occupational health cons. Rehab. Ctr. of South Tex., San Antonio, 1990-91; corp. dir. C.H. Guenther & Son, Inc., San Antonio, 1991—; v.p. adv. coun. Park Place Hosp., 1986-87, pres., 1987-89. Mem. steering com. and parish coun. St. Jude Thaddeus Cath. Ch., 1974-84, St. Jude's Cath. Ch., San Antonio; commn. Tex. div. Am. Cancer Soc., 1986-94. Recipient Don't Get Burned award Am. Cancer Soc., 1986, Tex. State Occupational Health Schering award, 1989. Mem. Am. Assn. Occupational Health Nurses (chmn. com. local chpt. Am. Occupational Health conf. 1990), Tex. State Assn. Occupational Health Nursing (pres. 1986-90, treas. 1990-94, Sabine area chpt. 1981-84, treas. 1984, pres. 1984-87, State Occupational Health Nursing Achievement award 1986), S.E. Tex. Safety Coun. (treas. 1987-89), Sigma Theta Tau (Nat. Nursing Imagemaker award Delta Alpha chpt. 1989). Fax: 210-444-7326. E-mail: lclark@c.h.guenther.com. Home: 310 Clubhill Dr San Antonio TX 78228-1905 Office: CH Guenther & Son Inc PO Box 118 San Antonio TX 78291-0118

CLARK, LARRY, photographer; b. Tulsa, Jan. 19, 1943. Artist, photographer N.Y.C. Author: (book of photographs) Tulsa, 1971, (photographs and text) Teenage Lust, 1983, (book of photographs) Larry Clark, 1992, 1992 (book of collages, photographs and text) The Perfect Childhood, 1993, (book of photographs and text) Heroin, 1999; filmmaker: Kids, 1995, Another Day in Paradise, 1998. Served with U.S. Army, 1965-66. Nat. Endowment for Arts photographers fellow, 1973; Creative Arts Pub. Service grantee N.Y.C., 1980.

CLARK, LAUREL JAN, adult education educator, author, editor, minister; b. Denver, Jan. 29, 1957; d. Clyde C. Dale and Ethelyn (Goldberg) Fuller; m. John Gordon Clark, May 29, 1994. BA with honors, U. Mich., 1978; PsD, Sch. Metaphysics, 1987; DD, Coll. Metaphysics, 1992, DM, 1994. Cert. tchr., Mo.; ordained min. Interfaith Ch. Metaphysics. Tchr. adult edn. Sch. Metaphysics, 1979—; dir., teaching supr. Sch. Metaphysics, St. Louis, Ann Arbor, Mich., 1979-82; v.p. Sch. Metaphysics, Windyville, 1988—; cert. counselor Interfaith Ch. Metaphysics, Windyville, Mo., 1987—; author SOM Pub., Windyville, Mo., 1981—; mng. editor Thresholds Quarterly, Windyville, Mo., 1990—; field dir. Sch. Metaphysics, 1984-94, sec., 1990—; internat. adv. bd. Unity and Diversity World Coun., L.A., 1995—; bd. dirs. Sch. Metaphysics; spkr. U. Mo., St. Louis, U. Mo., Columbia, Am. Bus. Women's Assn., Boulder (Colo.) Sheriff's Dept., Penn Valley C.C., U. Colo., Ft. Collins. Author: Shaping Your Life, 1994, Concentration, 1995, Vital Ingredient, 1998, Vital Ingredient, 1998; co-author: Power of Structure, 1987, Total Recall, 1993; contbg. author: First Opinion, 1997; contbr. articles to profl. jours. Mem. Am. Holistic Health Assn., Interfaith Alliance, Inst. Noetic Scis., World Peace Prayer Soc., Spiritual Frontiers Fellowship Internat., Phi Beta Kappa. Avocations: writing, music, composing, broadcasting, children's books. Home and Office: Sch Metaphysics HC 1 Box 15 Windyville MO 65783-9703

CLARK, LEIF MICHAEL, federal judge; b. Washington, Nov. 12, 1947; s. Charles G. and Gertrude Lyda (Zimmer) C. BA cum laude, U. Md., 1968; MDiv, Trinity Luth. Sem., Columbus, Ohio, 1972; JD cum laude, U. Houston, 1980. Bar: Tex. 1980, U.S. Dist. Ct. (we. dist.) Tex. 1981, U.S. Dist. Ct. (so. dist.) Tex. 1983, U.S. Ct. Appeals (5th cir.). 1984. Dir. Housing for Exceptional People, Detroit, 1974-75; ptnr. Cox & Smith, Inc., San Antonio, 1980-87; judge for western dist. Tex. U.S. Bankruptcy Ct., San Antonio, 1987—; prof. McGeorge Internat. Law Program, Salzburg, Austria, 1989-99; mem. adv. group U.S. Del. Working Group UNCITRAL, 1995-96; mem. adv. bd. ALI-ABA Cross Border Insolvency Project, 1995-96, USAID Jud. Tng. Project, 1995-98. Adv. bd. Insol Internat. Project, 1995. Mem. ABA, Am. Coll. Bankruptcy, Am. Bankruptcy Inst. (dir. 1991—, exec. com. 1995—, v.p. rsch. 1998—), Nat. Conf. Bankruptcy Judges (planning com. 1992 ann. meeting), Comml. Law League, State Bar Tex. Lutheran. Avocations: photography, choral singing, running, traveling. Office: PO Box 2676 San Antonio TX 78299-2676

CLARK, LELAND CHARLES, JR., biochemist, medical products executive; b. Rochester, N.Y., Dec. 4, 1918; married, 1939; 4 children. BS, Antioch Coll., 1941; PhD in Biochemistry, U. Rochester, 1944. Chmn. biochem. dept. Fels Rsch. Inst., 1944-58; asst. prof. biochem. Antioch coll., 1944-56, prof., 1956-58; from assoc. prof. to prof. surg. Med. Ctr. Univ. Ala., 1958-68; prof. rsch. pediats. Children's Hosp. Rsch. Found. Med. Coll., U. Cin., 1968—; sr. rsch. assoc. surg. and pediats. U. Cin., 1955-58; cons. Wright-Patterson AFB, 1956-58, NIH, 1961—; vis. prof. Cardiovasc. Rsch. Inst., San Francisco, 1967. Editor: Symp. Oxygen Transport. Recipient Disting. Lectr. award Am. Coll. chest Physicians, 1975, Rsch. Career award NIH, 1962-68. Mem. AAAS, Am. Heart Assn. (fellow coun. cerebrovasc. disease 1967—), Artificial Organs Soc., N.Y. Acad. Sci., Sigma Xi. Achievements include research in vitamin, steroid and oxygen metabolism; polarography; cardiovascular disease; hydrogen and oxygen electrodes in diagnosis; ion exchange resins in biology; glucose electrodes. Office: Synthetic Blood Internat Inc 2685 Culver Ave Kettering OH 45429-3755*

CLARK, LEROY D., legal educator, lawyer; b. 1934. B.A., CCNY, 1956; LL.B., Columbia U., 1961. Bar: N.Y. 1961. Staff atty. Office N.Y. Atty. Gen., 1961-62; asst. counsel NAACP Legal Def. and Edn. Fund, Inc., N.Y.C., 1962-68; prof. law NYU Law Sch., N.Y.C., 1969-79, Cath. U., 1981—; gen. counsel EEOC, 1979-81; arbitrator Am. Arbitration Assn., Fed. Mediation and Conciliation Svc.; mem. Pub. Employee Rels. Bd. Author: The Grand Jury: The Use and Abuse of Political Power, 1975, Employment Discrimination Law-Cases and Materials, 4th edit., 1997. Office: Law School Catholic Univ Am 3600 John McCormack Rd NE Washington DC 20064

CLARK, LETITIA Z., federal judge; b. 1945. BA, Rice U., 1967; MA, Rutgers U., 1970; JD, Syracuse U., 1973. Atty. EPA, Dallas, 1974-76; asst. U.S. atty. Southern District of Texas, 1982-85; bankruptcy judge Southern District of Texas, Houston, 1985—. Office: US Bankruptcy Ct PO Box 61010 515 Rusk St Houston TX 77002-2600

CLARK, LLOYD, historian, educator; b. Belton, Tex., Aug. 4, 1923; s. Lloyd C. and Hattie May (Taylor) C.; m. Jean Reeves, June 17, 1950; children: Roger, Cynthia, Candyce. BSJ, So. Meth. U., 1948; B in Fgn. Trade, Am. Grad. Sch. Internat. Mgmt., 1949; MPA, Ariz. State U., 1972. String corr. A.P., Dallas, 1941-42; reporter Dallas Morning News, 1947; editor, pub. Ex-Press, Arlington, Tex., 1945-48; publicity mgr. Advt. Counselors Ariz., Phoenix, 1949; reporter Phoenix Gazette, 1949-65; asst. pub. Ariz. Weekly Gazette, 1965-66; founder Council on Abandoned Mil. Posts-U.S.A., 1966; project cons. City of Prescott, Ariz., 1971-72; dep. dir. adminstrv. svcs. No. Ariz. Coun. Govts., Flagstaff, 1972-73; regional adminstr. South Eastern Ariz. Govts. Orgn., Bisbee, 1973-75; local govt. assistance coordinator Ariz. Dept. Transp., Phoenix, 1975-80, program adminstr., 1980-83; history instr. Rio Salado Community Coll., Phoenix, 1983-89, Ariz. State U.-West, Sun City, 1995-98; proprietor LC Enterprises, 1993—; editor and pub. Clark Biog. Reference, 1956-62; mem. spkrs. bur. Ariz. Humanities Coun., 1998-99. Bd. dirs. Friends of Channel 8, 1984-86; mem. transit planning com. Regional Pub. Transit Authority, 1988; bd. dirs. Friends of Ariz. Highways Mag., 1989-92; mem. Ariz. State Geographic and Historic Names Bd., 1994—. Served to lt. AUS, 1942-46; maj., 1966-70; col. Res. Recipient Ariz. Press Club's exemplary gen. news coverage award, 1960, outstanding news reporting, 1961; Lloyd Clark Journalism scholarship named in honor U. Tex. at Arlington Alumni Assn., 1992. Mem. Am. Grad. Sch. Internat. Mgmt. Alumni Assn. (pres. Phoenix chpt. 1965), Ariz. Hist. Soc. (bd. dirs. cen. Ariz. chpt. 1992-93, state bd. dirs. 1993-95), Sharlot Hall Hist. Soc. (life), Res. Officers Assn. (life), Ex-Students Assn. No. Tex. Agrl. Coll. Arlington (pres. 1946-48), U. Tex. Arlington Alumni Assn. (life, bd. dir. 1994—, Disting. Alumni Svc. award 1997, Mil. Sci. Dept. Hall of Honor 1998), The Westerners (sheriff Phoenix Corral 1986-88), Sigma Delta Chi (pres. Valley of Sun chpt. 1964). Club: University (Phoenix). Author: Lloyd Clark's Scrapbook, Vol. 1, 1958, Vol. 2, 1960, Here's Looking at You, 1997, The Usual Suspects, 1998, You Must Remember This, 1999. Address: PO Box 1537 Surprise AZ 85378-1537

CLARK, LORI DEVITO, environmental scientist; b. Elizabeth, N.J., Apr. 25, 1954; d. Carmin John and Marie Casciano DeVito; m. Arthur Franklin Clark, Jan. 8, 1992; children: Derek, Theodore, Hayley. BA, Cornell U., 1976; MA, Columbia U., 1979; PhD, CUNY, 1994. Instr. Berkeley Coll., N.Y.C., 1979-85; estimator Geo-Tech. Assocs., Fanwood, N.J., 1986-92; pres. AET/Source Environ., Denver, 1993—; adj. prof. Borough of Manhattan C.C., N.Y.C., 1984-92, Hunter Coll., N.Y.C., 1989. Mem. Colo. Hazardous Waste Mgmt. Assn. Roman Catholic. Avocations: European and American intellectual history, literature. E-mail: AETenvic@ix.netcom.com. Home: 25835 Buffalo Ln Golden CO 80401 Office: AET/Source Environ 4785 Tejon St Denver CO 80401

CLARK, LUTHER THEOPOLIS, physician, educator, researcher; b. Bradenton, Fla., Oct. 21, 1949; m. Camille C. Jackson; children: Jason Myles, Monica Marie. AB, Harvard U., 1971, MD, 1975. Intern, resident, chief residency internal medicine Roosevelt Hosp., N.Y.C., 1975-79, fellow cardiology, 1978-80; dir. preventive cardiology Health Sci. Ctr. SUNY, Bklyn., 1992-95, chief divsn. cardiovascular medicine Health Sci. Ctr., 1995—, prof. clin. medicine Health Sci. Ctr. Fellow ACP, Am. Coll. Cardiology; mem. Nat. Med. Assn. Avocations: tennis, jogging. Office: SUNY Health Sci Ctr Box 1199 450 Clarkson Ave Brooklyn NY 11203-2056

CLARK, MARCIA RACHEL, prosecutor; b. Berkeley, Calif., 1954; d. Abraham I. Kleks; m. Gabriel Horowitz, 1976 (div. 1980); m. Gordon Clark (div. 1994); 2 children. BA in Polit. Sci., UCLA, 1974; JD, Southwestern U., 1979. Atty. Brodey and Price, L.A., 1979-81, L.A. County Dist. Attys. Office, 1981-97. Author (with Teresa Carpenter) Without a Doubt, 1997. Office: William Morris Agy 151 S El Camino Dr Beverly Hills CA 90212-2704*

CLARK, MARGARET PRUITT, education and advocacy executive administrator; b. Eau Claire, Wis., May 9, 1946; d. Robert Earl and Gladys (Taylor) Pruitt; m. Kenneth Hall Clark, Aug. 14, 1966; children: Deborah Margaret, Robert James (dec.). BA in Sociology, Beloit Coll., 1966; MA in Sociology, U. Ill., Chgo., 1970; PhD in Sociology, U. Tex., 1976. Instr. U. Md., 1977-79, George Mason U., Fairfax, Va., 1979-80; asst. prof. sociology

Bowdoin Coll., Brunswick, Maine, 1980-83; instr. U. Maine, Augusta, 1983; mediator Maine Ct. Mediation Svc., Brunswick, 1985-87; mem. Maine Ho. of Reps., Augusta, 1986-92; exec. dir. Adolescent Pregnancy Coalition, 1988-90, Advocates for Youth (formerly Ctr. for Population Options), Washington, 1992-97; pvt. cons. in field Surprise, Ariz., 1997—. Vol. coord. steering com. ERA, 1984; coord. Maine chpt. NOW, 1984-86; mem. Gov. Brennen's Task Force on Adolescent Pregnancy and Parenting, 1985-86, Commn. to Study Health Svcs. in Pub. Schs., 1987-88, Blue Ribbon Commn. on Health Care Expenditures, 1987-89, Commn. to Study Status of Nursing and Health Care Professions in Maine, 1988-89; bd. dirs. Family Planning Assn. Maine, 1980-88, chmn. nominating com. 1985-86, v.p., 1987; bd. dirs. pub. policy com. Nat. Coun. on Alcoholism, 1985-88, others. Mem. Northeast Network Progressive Elected Ofcls., Nat. Order Women Legislators, Am. Sociol. Assn., Assn. Clin. Sociologists, Sociologists for Women in Soc., NOW.

CLARK, MARK ANTHONY, electrical engineer; b. Fayetteville, Tenn., Jan. 23, 1961; s. Henry Harwell and Mary Marjorie (Milam) C.; m. Kemberly Carol Pate, Aug. 20, 1983 (div. 1991); children: Megan Amberly, Travis Logan; m. Laura Leanne Young, Dec. 10, 1994. BSEE, Tenn. Tech. U., 1983; MSEE, So. Meth. U., 1986; postgrad., Auburn U., 1987-88. EIT, Tenn. Electronic engr. Tex. Instruments, Dallas, 1983-85, Electrospace Sys., Inc., Richardson, Tex., 1985-86; elec. engr. Def. Intelligence Agy., Huntsville, Ala., 1988—; tchg. asst. Auburn (Ala.) U., 1987-88. Bd. dirs. Indsl. Devel. Bd., Fayetteville-Lincoln County, Tenn., 1989-94; alderman City of Fayetteville, 1994-98, mayor 1998—; bd. dirs. Bd. Edn. Fayetteville, 1994-98—; youth baseball coach. Mem. IEEE. Mem. Ch. of Christ. Avocations: amateur radio, guitar. Home: 1853 Dunroamin Ln Fayetteville TN 37334-3728 Office: Def Intelligence Agy Martin Rd Redstone Arsenal AL 35898

CLARK, MARK JEFFREY, paralegal, researcher; b. Alton, Ill., Nov. 2, 1953; s. William Alfred and Winifred May (Young) C.; m. Patricia Ann Newell, July 29, 1989; children: Jason William, Brandi Leigh. AS in Bus. Adminstrn., Lewis & Clark Coll., 1978; cert. paralegal, Paralegal Inst., Atlanta, 1994, diploma in civil lit. and bus. law, 1994. Commd. spl. officer Lake Ozark (Mo.) Police Dept., 1975-78; ind. paralegal J & B Enterprises, Woodriver, Ill., 1994—; criminal rschr. Pinkerton Svcs. Group, Charlotte, N.C., 1998—; cons., rschr. Nationwide Corps., 1994—. With USN, 1972-75, Vietnam. Mem. Nat. Paralegal Assn., KC (4th degree), Am. Legion. Democrat. Roman Catholic. Avocations: scuba diving, golf, bowling. Home: Rt # 71 Box 272 Camdenton MO 65020

CLARK, MARK WILLIAM, dean, educator; b. Jacksonville, N.C., July 19, 1945; s. Herbert P. and Elsa M. Clark; m. Reiko Watanabe, Jan. 10, 1969; children: Midori, Saori. BA, U. Calif., Berkeley, 1973, MA, 1976; PhD, Stanford (Calif.) U., 1980. Asst. prof. Hofstra U., Hempstead, N.Y., 1977-81; assoc. prof. U. Mont., Missoula, 1981-86; asst. dean grad. sch., assoc. prof. U. Northern Colo., Greeley, 1986-92; asst. v.p. acad., dean grad. sch. affairs Adams State Coll., Alamosa, Colo., 1992-96; dean edn. Northeastern State U., Tahlequah, Okla., 1996—. Author: (with others) Minorities in History Education, 1994, Cooperstown Symposium on Baseball and American culture, 1990, 91, Comparative Physical and Education and Sport, 1986, 88; contbr. articles to profl. jours. Bd. dirs. Great Expectations Found., Tahbquah, Okla., 1996—. Recipient Outstanding Adminstr. award Okla. Assn. of Helath, Phys. Edn. Recreation and Dance, 1997. Mem. Am. Assn. of Colls. for Tchrs. Edn., Am. Edn. Rsch. Assn., Soc. for Am. Baseball Rsch., Kappa Delta Pi (Educators Who Make a Difference award 1998), Phi Delta Kappa. Avocations: blues music, Japanese wood block prints. E-mail: clarkmn@cherokee.nsuok.edu. Office: Coll Edn Northeastern State U 600 N Grand Ave Tahlequah OK 74464

CLARK, MARY ELLEN, Olympic athlete; b. Abington, Pa., Dec. 25, 1962; d. Gene and Carolyn Clark. BS, Pa. State U.; MS, Ohio State U. Bronze medalist, Platform Diving Barcelona Olympic Games, 1992; bd. dirs. U.S. Diving; pub. rels. rep. Yellow Strawberry Hair Salons; exec. distbr. NuSkin Internat./Interior Design Nutritionals; nat. spokesperson Speedo Corp. Recipient Silver medal Goodwill Games, 1994, Bronze medal Women's Platform Diving Atlanta Olympics, 1996, Phillips Performance award, 1993-94, 96; 5 time U.S. platform champion, 2 time U.S. springboard champion; winner Alam Challenge, 1992, New Zealand Internat., 1993, HTH Classic, 1993, U.S. Olympic Festival 3 meter, 1993. Address: Internat Swimming Hall of Fame 501 Seabreeze Blvd Fort Lauderdale FL 33316-1623*

CLARK, MARY HIGGINS, author, business executive; b. N.Y.C., Dec. 24, 1931; d. Luke J. and Nora C. (Durkin) Higgins; m. Warren Clark, Dec. 26, 1949 (dec. Sept. 1964); children: Marilyn, Warren, David, Carol, Patricia. BA, Fordham U., 1979; hon. doctorate, Villanova U., 1983, Rider Coll., 1986, Stonehill Coll., 1992, Marymount Manhattan Coll., 1992, Chestnut Hill, 1993, Manhattan Coll., 1993, St. Peter's Coll., 1993. Advt. asst. Remington Rand, 1946; stewardess Pan Am., 1949-50; radio scriptwriter, prodr. Robert G. Jennings, 1965-70; v.p., ptnr., creative dir., prodr. radio programming Aerial Communications, N.Y.C., 1970-80; chmn. bd., creative dir. D. J. Clark Enterprises, N.Y.C., 1980—. Author: Silent Night, Aspire to the Heavens, A Biography of George Washington, 1969 (N.J. Author award 1969), Where Are the Children?, 1976 (N.J. Author award 1977), A Stranger Is Watching, 1978 (N.J. Author award 1978), The Cradle Will Fall, 1980, A Cry in the Night, 1982, Stillwatch, 1984, Weep No More, My Lady, 1987, While My Pretty One Sleeps, 1989, The Anastasia Syndrome and Other Stories, 1989, Loves Music, Loves to Dance, 1991, All Around the Town, 1992, I'll Be Seeing You, 1993, Remember Me, 1994, The Lottery Winner, 1994, Bad Behavior, 1995, Let Me Call You Sweetheart, 1995, Moonlight Becomes You, 1996, Pretend You Don't See Her, 1997, The Plot Thickens, 1997, You Belong to Me, 1998, All Through the Night, 1998; (with Thomas Chastain and others) Murder in Manhattan, 1986; editor: Murder on the Aisle: The 1987 Mystery Writers Anthology, 1987. Recipient Grand Prix de Litterature Policiere, France, 1980. Mem. Mystery Writers Am. (pres. 1987, dir.), Authors League, Am. Soc. Journalists and Authors, Acad. Arts and Scis. Republican. Roman Catholic. *

CLARK, MARY MACHEN, community health nurse; b. LeCompte, La., Jan. 13, 1940; d. Isaac and Louella (Snowden) Machen; m. Johnnie L. Clark, Nov. 5, 1961; 1 child, Roxane M. ADN, La. State U., 1969; BS in Nursing, Northwestern State U., 1985. Cert. med-surg. nurse, ACLS and CPR instr. Staff nurse VA Med. Ctr., Alexandria, La., 1973-90; staff nurse ob-gyn. ICU Rapids Gen. Hosp., Alexandria, 1969-73; med. nurse VA Med. Ctr., Alexandria, 1990—, community health nursing coord., 1990—; reporter Monitor Alexandria VA Med. Ctr. Newsletter, 1988-90. Mem. Rapides Parish Libr. Bd. of Control, 1989-94. Recipient Svc. award Girl Scouts U.S., 1982, Spl. Advancement for Performance award Alexandria VA Med. Ctr., 1982, 86, 91, Cert. of Appreciation Profl. Image award Dept. Veterans Affairs, 1993, Performance award, 1996, 97, James MacGregor Burns Leadership award from Senator Bill Bradley, 1998. Mem. ANA, La. State Nurses Assn., Alexandria Dist. Nurses Assn. (bd. dirs. 1997-98), Nurses Orgn. Vets. Affairs, Am. Heart Assn., Sigma Theta Tau (Nu Tau chpt.). Home: PO Box 101 Lecompte LA 71346-0101

CLARK, MATT, science writer; b. Chgo., Feb. 3, 1930; s. Matthew and Kathryn Clark; m. Ellen Ann Mitchell, Aug. 23, 1952 (dec. 1978); children: Thomasin, Geoffrey Beach, Douglas Mitchell; m. Phyllis Malamud, Nov. 9, 1986. Grad., Hill Sch., 1947; A.B., Wesleyan U., Middletown, Conn., 1951. Reporter Boston Traveler, 1953-56, sci. editor, 1956-58; writer Med. News, N.Y.C., 1958- 61; medicine editor Newsweek mag., 1961-88; free-lance sci. writer, 1958—. Served with USNR, 1951-53. Recipient Albert Lasker Med. Journalism award, 1964, 67, Howard W. Blakeslee award Am. Heart Assn., 1965, 68, 73, 83, Penney-Mo. mag. award in health, 1967, 71, 75, med. journalism award AMA, 1969, Claude Bernard Sci. Journalism award Nat. Soc. Med. Rsch., 1971, Page One award Newspaper Guild N.Y., 1974, 83, Media award (mag.) Am. Cancer Soc., 1976, N.Y. Deadline Club award 1977, James T. Grady award Am. Chem. Soc., 1983, Am. Med. Writers Assn.-Searle Labs. journalism award, 1983. Fellow AAAS; mem. Am. Med. Writers Assn., Nat. Assn. Sci. Writers, Century Assn., Coffee House Club (N.Y.C.). Home: 1199 Park Ave Apt 15D New York NY 10128-1791

CLARK, MATTHEW HARVEY, bishop; b. Troy, N.Y., July 15, 1937; s. M. Harvey and Grace (Bills) C. Student, Coll. Holy Cross, Worcester, Mass.; BA, St. Bernard's Sem., Rochester, N.Y.; STL, N. Am. Coll., Rome; JCL, Gregorian U., Rome. Ordained priest Roman Catholic Ch., 1962—; vice chancellor Diocese of Albany, N.Y.; Cath. chaplain Albany Law Sch.; mem. faculty Vincentian Inst.; chmn. personnel bd. Diocese of Albany; spiritual dir. N. Am. Coll.; bishop Diocese of Rochester, 1979—. Office: Chancery Office 1150 Buffalo Rd Rochester NY 14624-1823*

CLARK, MAXINE, retail executive; b. Miami, Fla., Mar. 6, 1949; d. Kenneth and Anne (Lerch) Kasselman; m. Robert Fox, Sept. 1984. B.A. in Journalism, U. Ga., 1971. Exec. trainee Hecht Co., Washington, 1971, hosiery buyer, 1971-72, misses sportswear buyer, 1972-76; mgr. mdse. planning and research May Dept. Stores Co., St. Louis, 1976-78, dir. mdse. devel., 1978-80, v.p. mktg. and sales promotion Venture Stores div., 1980-81, sr. v.p. mktg. and sales promotion Venture Stores div., 1981-83, exec. v.p. mktg. and softlines, 1983-85; exec. v.p. apparel Famous-Barr, St. Louis, 1985-86; v.p. mdsing. Lerner Shops div. Limited Inc., N.Y.C., 1986-88; exec. v.p. Venture Stores, St. Louis, 1988-92; pres. Payless ShoeSource, Topeka, 1992-96; founder, CEO Smart Stuff, Inc. children's retail concept devel. firm and the Build-A-Bear Workshop, 1996—; bd. dirs. Earthgrains Co., Tandy Brands Accessories Co., Wave Techs., Inc., Dept. 56. Sec., Lafayette Sq. Restoration Com., 1978-79; mem. Com. 200 Nat. Coun. Coll. Arts and Scis. Washington U., St. Louis; trustee U. Ga. Found., 1995—; mem. nat. adv. coun. Girl Scouts U.S.A., 1995-97.*

CLARK, MAYNARD STEPHEN, vegetarian resource center administrator; b. Reidsville, N.C., Aug. 26, 1949. AB, Wheaton U., 1969; BA in Philosophy, Calif. State U., 1973; MDiv, Harvard U., 1979. Adminstrv. sec. Fidelity Data Svcs., Boston, 1980-82; sec. Coopers & Lybrand, Boston, 1982-84; with elec. engring. dept. Tufts U., Medford, Mass., 1984-91; health policy and mgmt. profl. Harvard Sch. Pub. Health, Boston, 1991-92; space planning analyst John Hancock Fin. Svcs., Boston, 1992-93; with news office/office of curriculum devel. Harvard Med. Sch., Boston, 1992-93; statistician, assoc. adminstrv. asst. Filene's, Boston, 1993-98; exec. dir. Vegetarian Resource Ctr., Cambridge, Mass., 1993—; regional coord. FARM, Bethesda, Md., 1985-92, nat. coord., 1989-90; developer Internet topical and local discussion lists, 1995—; publicist regional vegetarian projects, 1995—. Author numerous fact sheets on nutrition, philosophy, and vegetarianism. Bd. dirs. New Hippocrates Health Inst., Medford, Mass., 1992-94; 1st v.p. Tufts U. Staff Assn., Medford, 1989-91; mem. steering com. for recycling City of Somerville, Mass. and City of Medford, Mass., Tufts U., 1988-91; mem. pub. info. com. Assn. for Pub. Transp., Boston, 1992-97; mem. fundraising com. EarthWorks, Boston, 1994-95; vol. soup kitchen, musician recruiter Bread and Jams, Cambridge, 1992-94. Lt. Army ROTC, 1966-68. Channing fellow Unitarian Universalist Assn., 1974-78. Mem. Vegans Internat. (conf. program planner 1993-95), N.Am. Vegetarian Soc. (life, affiliate, lectr.), Am. Vegan Soc. (conf. program planner 1993-95), Vegetarian Union of N.Am. (life, v.p., regional coun., pres. 1989-95, conf. program planner 1991-95), Boston Vegetarian Soc., Inc. (founder, pres. 1985—), Boston Vegetarian Food Festival (planner, publicist, CORE com. 1995—), UUMA. Avocations: Bible study, philosophy, traveling, Internet, vegan cooking. Office: Vegetarian Resource Ctr PO Box 38-1068 Cambridge MA 02238-1068

CLARK, MELVILLE, JR., physicist, electrical engineer; b. Syracuse, N.Y., Dec. 19, 1921; s. Melville and Dorothy Drew (Speich) C. S.B., M.I.T., 1943, postgrad., 1943-44; postgrad. U. N.Mex., 1945-46, Princeton U., 1946; A.M., Harvard U., 1947, Ph.D., 1949. Mem. staff Radiation Lab., M.I.T., Cambridge, 1942-45; mem. staff Manhattan dist. U. Calif., Los Alamos, N.Mex., 1945-46; physicist Brookhaven Nat. Lab., Upton, N.Y., 1949-53; mem. staff Radiation Lab., U. Calif., Livermore, 1953-55; dir. Clark Music Co., Syracuse, N.Y., 1948-60, v.p., 1957-60; pres. Meldor Corp., Cazenovia, N.Y., 1960-66; sr. engring. specialist Sylvania Electric Products, Waltham, Mass., 1962-64; sr. cons. scientist Avco, Wilmington, Mass., 1964-67; sr. scientist NASA, Cambridge, 1967-70; sr. devel. engr. Thermo Electron, Waltham, 1970-73; sr. cons. engr., sr. tech. strategist Combustion Engring., Windsor, Conn., 1973-83; pres. Melville Clark Assocs., Wayland, Mass., 1949—; bd. dirs. 416 South Salina St. Corp., Syracuse, 1957-60; cons. Raytheon Mfg. Co., Waltham, 1955-58, United Shoe Machinery Co., Beverly, Mass., 1956, Arthur D. Little, Cambridge, 1957-58, Aerodyne Research, Inc., Billerica, Mass., 1983-84; tech. expert witness Pennie and Edmonds, N.Y.C., 1984—; trustee Inst. for Sci. Rsch. in Music, Wayland, Mass., 1990—; assoc. prof. nuclear engring. M.I.T., Cambridge, 1955-62; adviser to Congressman Robert Drinan. Author: (with Rose) Plasmas and Controlled Fusion, 1961; (with Hansen) Numerical Methods of Reactor Analysis, 1964; translator, editor (with B. Daniel) Introduction to the Theory of Ionized Gases, 1960; contbr. articles to profl. jours. MIT Scholar, 1939-43; NRC predoctoral fellow Harvard U., 1946-49, NRC predoctoral and Hercules Powder Co. fellow Princeton U., 1946. Registered profl. engr., Mass. Mem. Am. Phys. Soc., Am. Inst. Physics, Fusion Power Assocs., AAAS, Acoustical Soc. Am., IEEE, Assn. Computing Machinery (Greater Boston chpt.), Soc. Music Perception and Cognition, Sigma Xi. Patentee in field. *All of the biographees efforts, resources, present research, and development are focused on a commercially attractive musical instrument that enables thefaithful performance of any kind of musical instrument composition (songs, hymns, symphonies, marches, popular music, etc.) by one person (or very few persons) with little training, little practicing, and little or no artistic compromise. The goal is to raise the standard of appreciation and excitement of playing musicby making it possible for an amateur to express himself with great artistry. Entirely new man-machine interfaces, algorithms, and paradigms are used. High performance electronic digital microprocessing is exploited* Home and Office: 8 Richard Rd Wayland MA 01778-4010

CLARK, MELVIN EUGENE, chemical company executive; b. Ord, Nebr., Oct. 2, 1916; s. Ansel B. and Ruth Joy (Bullock) C.; m. Virginia May Hiller, Sept. 16, 1938; children—John Robert, Walter Clayton, Dale Eugene, Merry Sue. BSChemE cum laude, U. Colo., 1937; grad. exec. program, Columbia U., 1952; grad. advanced mgmt. program, Harvard U., 1961. Asst. editor Chem. Engring., McGraw-Hill, N.Y.C., 1937-41; mktg. staff Wyandotte Chem. Corp., Mich., 1941-53; chief program br. War Prodn. Bd., Washington, 1942-44; v.p. mktg. Frontier Chem. Co., Wichita, 1953-69; exec. v.p. chems. div. Vulcan Materials Co., Birmingham, Ala., 1969-81; v.p. planning, chems. and metals group Vulcan Materials Co., 1981-82; cons., 1982—; pres. Chlorine Inst., 1977-80. Contbr. numerous articles to profl. jours. Recipient U. Colo. Alumni Recognition award, 1972; named Chem. Market Rsch. Assn. Man of Year, 1963, Disting. Engring. Alumnus, U. Colo., 1985, Centennial medallist Coll. of Engring., U. Colo., 1994. Mem. AIChE, Chem. Mgmt. and Resources Assn., Am. Chem. Soc., Boulder Country Club, Tau Beta Pi, Pi Mu Epsilon. Republican. Mem. Christian Ch. Home and Office: 7145 Cedarwood Cir Boulder CO 80301-3716

CLARK, MERRELL EDWARD, JR., lawyer; b. Bklyn., Apr. 30, 1922; s. Merrell Edward and Eleanor Everest (Wild) C.; m. Hollis Logan, May 22, 1943; children—Julie Clark Goodyear, Kenyon Wild. B.A., Yale U., 1943, LL.B., 1948. Bar: N.Y. 1948, U.S. Dist. Ct. (so. dist.) 1949, U.S. Ct. Appeals (2d cir.) 1949, U.S. Tax Ct. 1951, Conn. 1952, U.S. Dist. Ct. (ea. dist.) N.Y. 1952, U.S. Supreme Ct. 1956, U.S. Ct. Appeals (5th cir.) 1963, U.S. Ct. Appeals (6th cir.) 1965, U.S. Ct. Appeals (8th cir.) 1973, U.S. Ct. Appeals (4th cir.) 1974, U.S. Dist. Ct. (no. dist.) N.Y. 1982, U.S. Dist. Ct. (we. dist.) N.Y. 1982. Assoc., Winthrop, Stimson, Putnam & Roberts, N.Y.C., 1948-55, ptnr., 1956-91. Editor Yale LAw Sch. Jour., 1947-48. Mem. Town Meeting, Greenwich, Conn., 1953-56, com. on jud. appointments (Appelate Div. 1st Dept.), 1978-82, 2d cir. jud. conf. evaluation com., 1980-87; dir.; trustee Perrot Meml. Library, Old Greenwich, Conn., 1956-63, Pomfret (Conn.) Sch., 1966-74, Richard Found., N.Y.C., 1965—, William Nelson Cromwell Found., N.Y.C., 1979—, Steep Rock Assn., Washinton, Conn., 1993—, Internat. Coll. Hospitality Mgmt., 1994—; adviser women's rights project ACLU, 1976-90; mem. N.Y.C Bd. Ethics, 1987-89; chair N.Y.C. Conflicts of Interest Bd., 1989-90, N.Y.C. Hardship Appeals Bd., 1993—; bd. dirs. N.Y. Legal Aid Soc., 1985-88. Served to capt. AUS, 1943-46. Decorated Bronze Star with two battle stars. Mem. ABA (ho. of dels. 1985-89), Assn. Bar City N.Y. (pres. 1978-80), Am. Law Inst. Am. Coll. Trial Lawyers, Conn. Bar Assn., N.Y. State Bar Assn. (ho. of dels. 1978-80). Clubs: River (N.Y.C.), India House (N.Y.C.); Washington (Conn.). Office: Winthrop Stimson Putnam Roberts 1 Battery Park Plz Fl 31 New York NY 10004-1490

CLARK, MICHAEL EARL, psychologist; b. Berea, Ohio, July 20, 1951; s. William Gray and Marguerite Jane (Charles) C.; m. Laura Lynn Putt, June 19, 1976 (div. Nov. 1987); 1 child, Brian Gray. BA, Kent State U., 1974, PhD, 1978. Asst. dir. chem. dependency unit N.D. State Hosp., Jamestown, N.D., 1978-79; staff psychologist VA Med. Ctr., Chillicothe, Ohio, 1979-84, Bay Pines, Fla., 1984-89; clin. dir., pain program James A. Haley Vets. Hosp., Tampa, Fla., 1989—; assoc. prof. dept. psychology U. South Fla., Tampa, 1986—, clin. asst. prof. dept. neurology Sch. Medicine, Tampa, 1991—; adj. psychologist, counseling ctr. U. South Fla.; cons. to the correctional med. authority, State of Fla., 1993—; adv. bd. Pain Program Accreditation and Nat. Pain Data Bank; mem. nat. pain edn. com. Dept. Vets. Affairs; cons. in field. Contbr. chpts. to Innovations in Clinical Practice, 1991, Social Psychology: A Sourcebook, 1983; contbr. articles to Biofeedback and Self-Regulation, Jour. Personality Assessment, Jour. Clin. Psychology, Jour. Dental Rsch., The Va. Practitioners, Psychol. Assessment, Pain Forum, Am. Jour. Pain Mgmt.; ad hoc reviewer Biofeedback and Self-Regulation, Psychol. Assessment, Jour. Personality Assessment. Vice-chmn. Paint Valley Mental Health Bd., Chillicothe, 1980-84. Mem. APA, Am. Psychol. Soc. (charter), Am. Pain Soc., Am. Acad. Pain Mgmt., N.Y. Acad. Scis., Internat. Assn. for Study of Pain, Soc. for Personality Assessment, So. Pain Soc. Democrat. Home: 9645 Fox Hearst Rd Tampa FL 33647-1829 Office: Psychology Svc (116B) VAMC 13000 Bruce B Downs Blvd Tampa FL 33612-4745

CLARK, MICHAEL PHILLIP, English educator; b. Marlin, Tex., May 27, 1950; s. Burton Francis and Nelda (Blount) C.; m. Kathleen Mack, 1971 (div. 1973); m. Katherine Weber, May 26, 1977. BA magna cum laude, Rice U., 1972; MA, U. Calif., Irvine, 1973, PhD, 1977. Asst. prof. U. Mich., Ann Arbor, 1977-83; prof. in English and comparative lit. U. Calif., Irvine, 1983—. Author: Michael Foucault, 1983, Jacques Lacan, 1989; contbr. articles to profl. publs. Mem. MLA, Soc. Early Americanists. Office: U Calif Dept English & Comparative Lit Irvine CA 92697-2650*

CLARK, MORTON HUTCHINSON, lawyer; b. Norfolk, Va., Apr. 21, 1933; s. David Henderson and Catharine Angelica (Hutchinson) C.; m. Lynn Harrison Adams, Aug. 12, 1961; children: Allison Adams, David Henderson, Susan West, Julia Dixon. BA in English, U. Va., 1954, LLB, 1960. Bar: Va. 1960, U.S. Dist. Ct. (ea. dist.) Va. 1960, U.S. Ct. Appeals (4th cir.) 1976, U.S. Ct. Appeals (1st cir.) 1993, U.S. Supreme Ct. 1993. Assoc. Vandeventer Black LLP, Norfolk, 1960-65, ptnr., 1965—. Co-editor: The Virginia Lawyer, 1991-93. Chmn. Va. Commn. for Children and Youth, Richmond. Fellow Am. Coll. Trial Lawyers, Va. Law Found.; mem. Maritime Law Assn. (exec. com. 1984-87), Hoffman I'Anson Am. Inns of Ct. (exec. com. 1993-95), The Harbor Club (pres.), Town Point Club, Princess Anne Country Club, Farmington Country Club. Episcopalian. Avocations: off shore racing, cruising. Home: 103 Rivers Edge, Kingsmill Williamsburg VA 23185-8930 Office: Vandeventer Black LLP 500 World Trade Ctr Norfolk VA 23510-1679

CLARK, NOREEN MORRISON, behavioral science educator, researcher; b. Glasgow, Scotland, Jan. 12, 1943; came to U.S., 1948; d. Angus Watt and Anne (Murphy) Morrison; m. George Robert Pitt, Dec. 3, 1982; 1 child, Alexander Robert. BS, U. Utah, 1965; MA, Columbia U., 1972, MPhil, 1975, PhD, 1976. Rsch. coord. World Edn. Inc., N.Y.C., 1972-73; asst. prof. Sch. Pub. Health Columbia U., N.Y.C., 1973-80, assoc. prof., 1980-81; assoc. prof. Sch. Pub. Health U. Mich., Ann Arbor, 1981-85, prof., chmn. dept. health behavior and health edn., 1985-95, Marshall H. Becker prof. of pub. health, 1995—, dean, 1995—; adj. prof. health adminstrn. Sch. Pub. Health Columbia U., 1988—; prin. investigator NIH, 1977—; mem. adv. com. pulmonary diseases Nat. Heart, Lung & Blood Inst., Rockville, Md., 1983-87, mem. adv. com. for prevention, edn. and control, 1987-91, coordinating com. Nat. Asthma Edn. Program, 1991—; assoc. Synergos Inst., N.Y.C., 1987—. Co-author: Evaluation of Health Promotion, 1984; editor Health Edn. and Behavior, 1985-97; mem. editorial bd. Women in Health, Advances in Health Edn. and Promotion, Home Health Care Services Quarterly; contbr. articles to profl. jours. Hon. dir. Freedom from Hunger Found., Davis, Calif., 1980-94; bd. dirs. Aaron Diamond Found., 1990-97, Family Care Internat., N.Y.C., 1987—, Internat. Asthma Coun., Am. Lung Assn., N.Y.C., 1988—, World Edn., Inc., The Healthtrak Found. Prize. Fellow Soc. Pub. Health Edn. (pres. 1985-86, Disting. Fellow award 1987); mem. APHA (chair health edn. sect. 1982-83, Derryberry award in behavioral sci. 1985, Disting. Career award 1994), Am. Thoracic Soc. (Health Edn. Rsch. award Nat. Asthma Edn. Program 1992, Healthtrak Edn. prize 1997), Internat. Union Health Edn., Soc. Behavioral Medicine, Coun. Fgn. Rels., Overseas Devel. Coun., Pi Sigma Alpha. Office: U Mich Sch Pub Health 109 Observatory St Ann Arbor MI 48109-2029

CLARK, OLIVE IOLA, retired secondary and elementary education educator; b. Stratford, Wis., Apr. 2, 1917; d. Irving Zestel and Esther Sigrid (Eckerson) C. BS, U. Wis., 1937; diploma, Moody Bible Inst., 1944; MA, McCormick Theol. Sem., 1952. Tchr. Amasa (Mich.) H.S., 1937-38, Bruce (Wis.) H.S., 1938-42; tchr. weekday religious edn. Taft, Calif., 1944-49, Waynesboro, Va., 1952-87; state coord. weekday religious edn. Va. Coun. Chs., Richmond, 1982-90; staff writer Scripture Press, Chgo., 1950; ret. Author: Along the Way, 1997; contbr. articles to profl. jours. Pres. Guilders Cir., Meth. Ch., 1997-98. Inducted into Internat. Poetry Hall of Fame, 1996. Mem. Va. Weekday Religious Edn. Tchrs. Fellowship (pres. 1980-82), Waynesboro Ch. Women United (pres. 1989-98). Avocations: writing, traveling. Home: 501 Oak Ave # 22 Waynesboro VA 22980-4426

CLARK, OUIDA OUIJELLA, public relations executive, educator; b. Birmingham, Ala., Dec. 7, 1949; d. Fred and Johnnie (Norrington) C. BA in Spanish Edn., Dillard U., 1971; grad. cert. pub. rels., Am. U., 1973, U. Valencia (Spain), 1974; cert. journalism, NYU, 1972; postgrad., U. Chgo., 1980. Intern Fgn. Svc. USIA, 1971; freelance pub. rels. cons., 1972-76; tchr. English as a 2nd lang. Arlington (Va.) Pub. Schs., 1976-78; founder, pres. Global Pub. Rels., Inc., Washington, 1976-, pres., founder, 1976; pres., founder Global Pub. Rels., Inc., Little Rock, 1981-95, Clark Prodns., Ltd., Inc., Little Rock, 1981—, Am. Remodeling Century 21 Home Improvement, L.A., 1996; multilingual free-lance pub. rels. cons.; rsch. assoc. Philander Smith Coll., 1980-81, 96—; Sears contractor Am. Remodeling, Little Rock and L.A., 1994-95. Author: (radio play) Bon Voyage, Everything Has Its Place, You Just Can't Drift, Culture is Never Tasteless, Royal Blood, 1995, Strange Twist of Fate, 1996; other dramas for Horizons of Success series include Everything Has Its Place, On Life of James Weldon Johnson, You Just Can't Drift, Culture Is Never Tasteless, It Comes from Within Life of J.C. Penny, Controlled by the Stars of Life of the Founders of Sears and Roebuck, You Must Make a Decision Life of Mahalia Jackson, A Mixed Blessing Life of W.C. Handy, A Passion to Succeed-A Story on the Life of Milton Hershey, A Vision of Tomorrow-A Story of Ralph Bunche; contbr. articles to profl. jours.; project dir. radio programs; composer, dir. Children of the 21st Century; patent for Nat. Dir. Music and Dance Studios, 1978, rev. edit., 1980. Active Africare Project, Senegal, Upper Volta, Mauritania, Niger, Chad, Sierra Leone, 1973; founder Internat. Ptnr. Sch., Vienna. Grantee Ark. Endowment Humanities, 1982; recipient Pub. Rels. award Nat. Powderly Alumni Assn., 1997, NEA Support Funds, 1987. Mem. Pub. Rels. Soc. Am., Am. Film Inst., Capital Press Club, Dillard U. Alumni Assn. (co-founder Ark. chpt.). Baptist. Office: PO Box 583 Little Rock AR 72203-0583

CLARK, PAT ENGLISH, lawyer; b. Austin, Tex., Feb. 26, 1940; s. Pat Wheeler and Jennie Bell (Lagrone) C.; m. Maren Louise Westerfeldt, June 1, 1961; 1 child, Susan Louise Beisert. BA, U. Tex., JD. Bar: Tex. 1963, U.S. Ct. Mil. Appeals 1964, U.S. Dist. Ct. (so. and no. dists.) Tex.; cert. in oil, gas and mineral law Tex. Bd. Legal Specialization. Staff atty. Phillips Petroleum Co., Houston, 1967-69; atty. Amoco Production Co., Houston, 1969-75; ptnr. Vinson & Elkins, Houston, 1975-95, Borrego & Clark, 1996—. Served to capt. JAGC, U.S. Army, 1964-67. Methodist. Office: 19 S Briar Hollow Ln Ste 236 Houston TX 77027-2820

CLARK, PATRICIA, molecular biologist; b. Lake Village, Ark., Mar. 21, 1928; d. Cleburn Clem and Helen Miller (Baker) C. BA, Washington U., St. Louis, 1950, MA, 1955; PhD, Purdue U., 1962. Microanalyst Washington U., St. Louis, 1950-51; rsch. chemist The Chemstrand Corp., Decatur, Ala., 1953-55; assoc. chemist So. Rsch. Inst., Birmingham, Ala., 1955-56; grad. asst. Purdue U., West Lafayette, Ind., 1956-61; biochemist Gerontology Rsch. Ctr. Child Health and Human Devel. NIH, Balt., 1961-78, Nat. Inst. on Aging NIH, Balt., 1978-96; ret.; vis. rschr. Gerontology Rsch. Ctr., NIA, NIH, 1997. Hon. mention Westinghouse Talent Search, 1946. Fellow Am. Inst. Chemists; mem. AAAS, Am. Chem. Soc., Gerontol. Soc., N.Y. Acad.

Scis., Sigma Xi, Pi Mu Epsilon, Alpha Lambda Delta. Home: Dulaney Towers 1 Smeton Pl Apt 1206 Baltimore MD 21204-2737

CLARK, PATRICIA ANN, federal judge; b. Buffalo, July 26, 1936; d. Andrew A. and Mary (Gardner) Zacher; m. James A. Clark, Mar. 25, 1960; B.A., Goucher Coll., Towson, Md., 1958; postgrad. Duke U., 1958-60; LL.B., U. Colo., 1961. Bar: Colo. 1961, U.S. Dist. Ct. D.C. 1961. With Transamerica Title Ins. Co., 1962-65; assoc. Holme, Roberts and Owen, 1965-70, ptnr., 1970-74; judge U.S. Bankruptcy Ct., Denver, 1974—. Commr., Colo. Civil Rights Commn., 1969-72; trustee Waterman Fund, 1978—; mem. transition adv. com. U.S. Cts., 1980-84, com. jud. resources, 1987-91. Recipient Disting. Alumni award U. Colo. Sch. Law, 1984. Mem. Colo. Bar Assn., Denver Bar Assn. Office: US Bankruptcy Ct US Custom House 721 19th St Denver CO 80202-2500

CLARK, PATRICIA RYAN, crisis intervention specialist; b. Waterloo, N.Y., Nov. 26, 1947; d. Thomas Harold and Ellen (Browne) Ryan; m. Richard Lewis Clark, Sr., Jan. 24, 1966; children: Rick, Michael, Theresa, Catherine, Elisabeth. AAS, Empire State Coll., 1992, BA in History, 1998. Tchr. aide, tchr. asst., clk., crisis intervention asst. Sodus (N.Y.) Ctrl. Sch., 1977—. Vol. medic Sodus Town Ambulance, 1982—, CPR instr., 1995, 96, 97. Roman Catholic. Avocations: swimming, jogging, water and snow skiing, canoeing, camping.

CLARK, PAUL BUDDY, management information systems educator, consultant; b. Pitts., Dec. 30, 1944; s. Cecil Conrad and Joyce Agnes (Scott) C.; m. Joann Mariano, Mar. 1, 1969 (div. Mar. 1993); 1 child, Scott. BSBA, Duquesne U., 1968; MBA, Kent State U., 1979, PhD, 1992. Food svc. dir. U. Pitts., 1970, Drew U., Madison, N.J., 1970-74, Kent (Ohio) State U., 1974-80; food svc. dir. Cleve. City Sch. Dist., 1980-85, purchasing dir., 1985-86, dir. mgmt. info. sys., 1986-93; asst. prof. S.C. State U., Orangeburg, 1993-98, assoc. prof., 1998—, interim chair dept. bus. adminstrn., 1997—; bd. trustees Nutrition for Greater Cleve., 1980-84, pres., 1984; mgmt. seminar presenter Food Svc. Assoc., Inc., Dunkirk, N.Y., 1982-86. Developer Problem Decision Support Sys. Info. sys. developer, cons. Spears for Adj. Gen. Campaign, Columbia, S.C., 1994. Sgt. U.S. Army, 1969-70, Vietnam, officer Army Nat. Guard, 1976-95. Decorated Bronze Star; recipient Rsch. grant S.C. State U., 1995. Mem. Internat. Info. Sys. Mgmt. Assn., Internat. Sch. Bus. Computing Assn., So. Mgmt. Assn., Beta Gamma Sigma. Avocations: tennis, reading, gourmet cooking. Home: 501 Pelham Dr Apt D-103 Columbia SC 29209-1360 Office: SC State Univ Sch of Bus Orangeburg SC 29117

CLARK, PAUL J., management consultant. Treas. Towers, Perrin, N.Y.C. Office: Towers Perrin 1500 Market St Philadelphia PA 19102*

CLARK, PETER BRUCE, newspaper executive; b. Detroit, Oct. 23, 1928; s. Rex Scripps and Marian (Peters) C.; m. Lianne Schroeder, Dec. 21, 1952 (dec. Jan. 1996); children: Ellen Clark Brown, James. B.A., Pomona Coll., 1952, LL.D. (hon.), 1972; M.P.A., Syracuse U., 1953; Ph.D., U. Chgo., 1959; H.H.D., Mich. State U., 1973, Lawrence Inst. Tech., 1982; LL.D. (hon.), U. Mich., 1977. Research assoc., then instr. polit. sci. U. Chgo., 1957-59; asst. prof. polit. sci. Yale U., 1959-61; with Evening News Assn., Detroit, 1960-86, corp. sec., 1960-61, v.p., 1961-63, pres., 1963-86, chmn. bd., chief exec. officer, dir., 1969-86; pub. Detroit News, 1963-81, also dir.; Regent's prof. UCLA Grad. Sch. Mgmt., 1987; chmn. Fed. Res. Bank Chgo., 1975-77, former chmn. br. Fed. Res. Bank Detroit; bd. dirs. Gannett Co., Inc. Served with AUS, 1953-55. Mem. Am. Newspaper Pubs. Assn. (dir. 1966-74), Am. Soc. Newspaper Editors, Detroit Club, Ironwood Country Club.

CLARK, R. BRADBURY, lawyer; b. Des Moines, May 11, 1924; s. Rufus Bradbury and Gertrude Martha (Burns) C.; m. Polly Ann King, Sept. 6, 1949; children: Cynthia Clark Maxwell, Rufus Bradbury, John Atherton. BA, Harvard U., 1948, JD, 1951; diploma in law, Oxford U., Eng., 1952; D.H.L., Ch. Div. Sch. Pacific, San Francisco, 1983. Bar: Calif. 1952. Assoc. O'Melveny & Myers, L.A., 1952-62, sr. ptnr., 1961-93; mem. mgmt. com., 1983-90; of counsel O'Melveny & Myers LLP, L.A., 1993—; bd. dirs. Golden State Water Co., Econ. Resources Corp., Brown Internat. Corp., Automatic Machinery & Electronics Corp., John Tracy Clinic, also pres. 1982-88, Tracy Family Hearing Ctrs. Editor: California Corporation Laws, 6 vols, 1976—. Chancellor Prot. Episcopal Ch. in the Diocese of L.A., 1967—, hon. canon, 1983—. Capt. U.S. Army, 1943-46. Decorated Bronze Star with oak leaf cluster, Purple Heart with oak leaf cluster; Fulbright grantee, 1952. Mem. ABA (com. law and acctg., task force on audit letters 1976-93, com. on opinions 1988-92), State Bar Calif. (chmn. drafting com. on gen. corp. law 1973-81, drafting com. on nonprofit corp. law 1980-84, mem. exec. com. bus. law sect. 1977-78, 84-87, sec. 1986-87, mem. com. nonprofit orgns. 1991—), L.A. County Bar Assn., Harvard Club, Chancery Club, Alamitos Bay Yacht Club (Long Beach, Calif.). Republican. Office: O'Melveny & Myers LLP 400 S Hope St Los Angeles CA 90071-2899

CLARK, RAYMOND JOHN, Academic Administrator; b. Highland Park, Mich., May 10, 1951; s. John Harold and Mima Jean (Baker) C.; m. Sally Ann Narhi, June 14, 1975; 1 child, Arvid John. AA, Oakland Community Coll., 1971; BS in Animal Husbandry, Mich. State U., 1973, BS Agribus. and Natural Resources Edn., 1974, MA in Agrl. Edn., 1976, PhD in Agrl. and Ext. Edn., 1991. Tchr. Grand Ledge (Mich.) High Sch., 1974-76; instr. Mich. State U., East Lansing, 1976-80; dir. coop. edn. Soumi Coll., Hancock, 1980-81; county extension dir. Mich. State U., Hancock, 1981-84; dist. farm mgmt. agt. Mich. State U., Marquette, 1984-88, acting regional extension supr., 1988-90; county extension dir. Mich. State U., Ontonagon, 1990—; extension advisor Armenian/Am. Extension Project, Stepanavan Region Republic of Armenia, 1993, Stepanavan and Tumanian Regions, 1994, Agrl. Support Ctr. Extension advisor Gyumri Region, Armenia, 1999—; presenter in field; inbound coord. 4-H/Japanese Exch., 1996, outbound coord., 1997. Chmn. agrl. bus. com. Houghton (Mich.) C. of C., 1972-74; bd. dirs. Copper Country Farm Bur., Houghton, 1978-80; bd. dirs., mem. exec. com. Vol. Action Ctr. of the Keeweensaw, 1992—; chair Cmty. Cares Coalition, 1995; treas., pres. Ontonegon County Habitat for Humanity, bd. dirs., 1995—. Mem. Nat. Assn. Agrl. Extension Agts., Mich. Assn. Agrl. Extension Agts., Mich. 4-H Internat. Assn., Ontonagon County C. of C. (bd. dirs. 1992—), Phi Delta Kappa, Epsilon Sigma Phi (v.p., pres., chair chpt. internat. com. and nat. internat com.). Lutheran. Avocations: farming, hunting, fishing, travel. Home: RR 1 Box 54 Pelkie MI 49958-9714 Office: Mich State U 725 Greenland Rd Ontonagon MI 49953-1423

CLARK, RAYMOND LEROY, singer; b. Springfield, Mass., Dec. 11, 1917; s. Mary Ann (Horrigan) C.; m. Celia Jo Roberson, 1943 (div. 1969); children: Wilf Carter, Jewell La-Verne; m. Kathleen Marie Pigeon, Feb. 20, 1982. Self-employed recording artist, entertainer. Recording artist over 100 albums and cassettes, 1945-97; composer over 50 songs; art works represented in pvt. collections. Named to Country Music Hall of Fame, 1996, Hall of Fame, Maine, 1980, Mass., 1989, R.I., 1996; recipient Pioneer award Maine Country Music Assn., 1981, Solo Artist of Yr. award Maine Country Music Assn., 1996. Roman Catholic. Avocations: fishing, hunting, golf. Home: 91 Finson Rd Saint Albans ME 04971-7312

CLARK, RAYMOND OAKES, banker; b. Ft. Bragg, N.C., Nov. 9, 1944; s. Raymond Shelton and Nancy Lee (McCormick) C.; m. Patricia Taylor Slaughter; children: Matthew Patrick, Geoffry Charles. BBA, U. Ariz., 1966; postgrad., U. Wash., 1984-86. Mgmt. trainee First Interstate Bank, Phoenix, 1966, credit analyst, 1968-69, asst. br. mgr., Scottsdale, Ariz., 1969-72, asst. v.p., br. mgr., Tempe, Ariz., 1972-90, v.p. br. mgr. Scottsdale, 1990-92, v.p. mgr. main office Phoenix, 1992—. Pres., bd. dirs. Sun Devil Club, Tempe, 1975-98; bd. dirs. Valley Big Brothers/Big Sisters, 1994-98; pres. Tempe Diplomats, 1979-89; pres. Tempe Diablos, 1975—; major chmn. Fiesta Bowl, Tempe, 1975-79, mem. com., 1996—; bd. dirs. Maricopa County Bd. Mgrs., Phoenix, 1973, YMCA, Tempe, 1974, Tempe Design Rev. Bd., 1983-87. Named one of Outstanding Young Men of Am., 1978. Bd. dirs., treas. East Valley divsn. Am. Heart Assn., 1989-92. Served with U.S. Army, 1966-68. Mem. Tempe C. of C. (pres. 1979-80), Kiwanis (dist. lt. gov. 1972-87). Republican. Episcopalian.

CLARK, RICHARD PAUL, electronics company executive; b. Lewistown, Pa., Aug. 24, 1947; s. Harry E. and Alma E. (Koons) C.; m. Beth Millington, Oct. 23, 1971; children: Brian R., Steven M. BSEE, U. Pitts., 1969. Product engr. AMP Inc., Harrisburg, Pa., 1970-72, product engring. supr., 1972-76, product engring. mgr., 1976-79, mgr. devel. engring., 1979-82, mgr. electronic divsn., 1982-83, mgr. connector products, 1983-87, dir. ops., 1987-89, dir. engring., 1989, assoc. dir. corp. devel., 1989-95; pres., CEO M/A-COM a div. of AMP Inc., Lowell, Mass., 1995—; bd. dirs. BroadBand Techs. Inc., Durham, N.C., ADFlex Solutions, Inc., Chandler, Ariz. Mem. Pitt vis. com. U. Pitts., 1993—; coach Highland Baseball, Camp Hill, Pa., 1981-91; booster Cedar Cliff Baseball, Camp Hill, 1989-94, Cedar Cliff Football, Camp Hill, 1991-95; session mem. Christ Presbyn. Ch., Camp Hill, 1984-87, 93-95. Recipient Disting. Alumnus award in Elec. Engring., U. Pitts., 1996. Office: M/A-COM a div of AMP Inc 1011 Pawtucket Blvd Lowell MA 01854-1089

CLARK, RICHARD WARD, trust company executive, consultant; b. N.Y.C., Oct. 23, 1938; s. Richard Leal and Dorothy Jane (Whittaker) C. BA with distinction, U. Rochester, N.Y., 1960; MBA in Fin., U. Pa., 1962. Corp. planning analyst Campbell Soup Co., Camden, N.J., 1965-67; asst. product mgr. Gen. Mills, Inc., Mpls., 1967-70; sr. fin. analyst McKesson Corp., San Francisco, 1970-71, asst. div. controller, 1971-72, div. controller, 1972-78, gen. mgr. grocery products devel., 1978-79; v.p., controller McKesson Foods Group/McKesson Corp., 1979-85, dir. strategic planning, 1985-87; v.p. fin., CFO, Provigo Corp., San Rafael, Calif., 1987-90; cons. on hotel devel., Napa Valley Assocs., S.A., San Francisco, 1990-92, health care cons., 1993-97; exec. trust dir. Park Trust, Ltd., San Francisco, 1998—; bd. dirs. Taylor Cuisine, Inc., San Francisco. Author: Some Factors Affecting Dividend Payout Ratios, 1962; musician (albums) Dick Clark at the Keyboard, I Love a Piano, 1990, I Play the Songs, 1993, On My Way to You, 1997. Adv. bd. Salvation Army, San Francisco, 1984—, chmn., 1993—; bd. dirs. Svcs. for Srs., San Francisco, 1990-93. Lt. (j.g.) USNR, 1962-64, PTO. Sherman fellow U. Rochester, 1960. Mem. Bohemian Club, Beta Gamma Sigma. Republican. Presbyterian. Avocations: piano, skiing, tennis, singing, jogging. Home: 2201 Sacramento St Apt 401 San Francisco CA 94115-2314

CLARK, ROBERT ARTHUR, mathematician, educator; b. Melrose, Mass., May 3, 1923; s. Arthur Henry and Persis (Kidder) C.; m. Jane Burr Crofut Kinder, June 25, 1966. Student, Colo. Coll., 1940-42; BA, Duke, 1944; MA, MIT, 1946, Ph.D., 1949. Instr., research asso. MIT, 1946-50, vis. asst. prof., 1956-57; faculty Case Inst. Tech. (now Case Western Res. U.), Cleve., 1950—; prof. math. Case Inst. Tech. (now Case Western Res. U.), 1964-85, prof. emeritus, 1985—, acting head dept. math., 1960-61, assoc. chmn. dept. math., 1974-79, 82-84, exec. officer, 1981-82; vis. mem. U.S. Army Math. Research Center, Madison, Wis., 1961-62. Mem. AAAS, Am. Math. Soc., Math. Assn. Am., Soc. Indsl. and Applied Math., Phi Beta Kappa, Sigma Xi. Spl. research asymptotic integration theory of differential equations and theory thin elastic shells. Home: 7469 Sherman Rd Gates Mills OH 44040-9769 Office: Case Western Res Univ Dept Math Cleveland OH 44106

CLARK, ROBERT CHARLES, law educator, dean; b. New Orleans, Feb. 26, 1944; s. William Vernon and Edwina Ellen (Nuessly) C.; m. Kathleen Margaret Tighe, June 1, 1968; children—Alexander Ian, Matthew Tighe. BA, Maryknoll Sem., 1966; PhD, Columbia U., 1971; JD, Harvard U., 1972. Bar: Mass. 1972. Assoc. firm Ropes & Gray, Boston, 1972-74; asst. prof. Yale U. Law Sch., New Haven, 1974-76, assoc. prof., 1976-77, prof., 1977-78; prof. law Harvard U., Cambridge, Mass., 1978—, dean of Law Sch., 1989—. Contbr. articles to profl. jours. Mem. Am. Bar Assn. Office: Harvard Law Sch Office of Dean 200 Griswold Hall 1525 Massachusetts Ave Cambridge MA 02138-2903*

CLARK, ROBERT HENRY, JR., holding company executive; b. Manchester, N.H., Mar. 4, 1941; s. Robert Henry and Elva C. (Stearns) C.; m. Rosalie Foster Case, Dec. 21, 1963; children: Robert Henry III, Hilary Eagan, Hadley Case. BSBA, Boston U., 1964. Mcpl. bond underwriter Merrill Lynch, Pierce, Fenner & Smith, N.Y.C., 1964-70; v.p. Case, Pomeroy & Co., Inc., N.Y.C., 1971-75, exec. v.p., 1975-83; pres. Case, Pomeroy & Co., Inc., 1983—, CEO, 1993—, also dir.; v.p. fin. Felmont Oil Corp., 1972-79, exec. v.p., 1979-84; bd. dirs. Homestake Mining Co., FINOVA Group, Inc. Trustee Boston U., 1984-87. Mem. Sigma Alpha Epsilon. Office: Case Pomeroy & Co Inc 529 5th Ave Fl 16 New York NY 10017-4684

CLARK, ROBERT KING, communications educator emeritus, lecturer, consultant, actor, model; b. Springfield, Mass., Apr. 12, 1934; s. Harry Robert and Alice (McClure) C.; m. Suzanne Chapin, Apr. 9, 1966; children—Jennifer, Jeffrey, Anne Elizabeth. B.A., U. Wyo., 1956; M.A., U. Tenn., 1960; Ph.D., Ohio State U., 1971. Instr. journalism U. Tenn., Knoxville, 1958; instr. speech Westminster Coll., New Wilmington, Pa., 1959-61; faculty Bowling Green State U., Ohio, 1963—; prof. radio-TV film Bowling Green State U., 1980-84, prof. emeritus, 1985—; gen. mgr. Sta. WBGU-FM, 1976-85; cons. in field; lectr. in field; seminar leader in field. Contbr. articles to profl. jours. Mem. Broadcast Edn. Assn., Ohio Assn. Broadcasters. Presbyterian. Office: 1064 Village Dr Bowling Green OH 43402-1231

CLARK, ROBERT LLOYD, JR., librarian; b. McAlester, Okla., Sept. 12, 1945; s. Robert Lloyd and Ruth Fairel (Nelson) C.; children: Roberta, Johnathan, Kathryn; m. Audrey Lynn Wolfe, 1987. B.A., U. Okla., 1968, M.L.S., 1969. Dir. div. archives and records Okla. Dept. Librs., Oklahoma City, 1968-72; data processing coord. Okla. Dept. Librs., 1972-73, dir., 1976—; asst. dir. pub. services Jackson (Miss.) Met. Library System, 1973-74; dir. Mid-Miss. Regional Library, Kosciusko, 1974-76; sec. Okla. Archives and Records Commn., 1976—; ex officio sec. Okla. Arts and Humanities Council, 1976-81; sec. adv. council Library Services and Constrn. Act., 1976—; adv. bd. Okla. Hist. Records, 1979—; adv. council U. Okla. Sch. Library and Info. Sci., 1985-88, 95—; adv. council State regents for Higher Edn. on Ednl. Outreach, 1985-88; cons. in field. Author: Archive-Library Relations, 1976; contbr. articles to library pubs. Mem. adv. com. State Regents for Higher Edn., 1984-88. Robert L. Clark, Jr. Day proclaimed by Gov. of Okla., Nov. 15, 1982. Mem. ALA (chmn. pub. library assn. interlibrary coop. com. 1974-77, mem. standards com. 1979-82), Okla. Library Assn., Southwestern Library Assn. (pres. 1980-82), Amigos Bibliog. Council (exec. bd. 1977-80), Assn. State Libraries (bd. dirs. 1977-80), Assn. Chief Officers of State Library Agys. (chmn. legis. com. 1979-81, chmn. 1982-84). Office: Librs Dept 200 NE 18th St Oklahoma City OK 73105-3205

CLARK, ROBERT MUREL, JR., lawyer; b. Dallas, Mar. 7, 1948; s. Robert M. Sr. and Dorrace Helen (Schaerdel) C.; m. Kimberly Anne Kerss, Oct. 25, 1986; 1 child, Ashley Pendleton. BBA, U. Tex., 1972; MBA, So. Meth. U., 1978; JD, Oklahoma City U., 1982. Bar: Tex. 1982, U.S. Dist. Ct. (no. dist.) Tex. 1982, U.S. Ct. Appeals (5th cir.) 1982, U.S. Supreme Ct. 1988; cert. in civil trial law Tex. Bd. Legal Specialization; cert. trial specialist Nat. Bd. Trial Advocacy. Ptnr. Eddleman, Clark & Rosen, Dallas, 1989—. Contbr. articles to profl. jours. Del. state conv. Tex. Rep. Party, 1970, 72, 74, 82, 90; bd. dirs. Haile Selassie Fund for Ethiopian Children in Need; sec., bd. dirs. Dallas Goethe Ctr. Decorated grand officer Order of Ethiopian Lion, hon. knight Order of Vitez (Hungary), knight Order of St. John (Brandenburg). Fellow Tex. Bar Found. (life), Soc. Antiquaries (Scotland); mem. State Bar Tex., Am. Bd. Trial Advs. (Dallas chpt.), Oak Cliff Bar Assn. (pres. 1990), Am. Soc. Legal History, Soc. of the Cin., Aztec Club, Sons Republic of Tex., Founders and Patriots Am., Nat. Huguenot Soc. (former coun. gen. and 3d v.p. gen.), St. Nicholas Soc., Johanniterorden-Bailiwick of Brandenburg, Johanniter Hilfsgemeinschaften (bd. dirs., Washington), Army and Navy Club (Washington), City Tavern Club (Washington), Phi Delta Phi, Phi Delta Theta. Episcopalian. Office: 4627 N Central Expy Dallas TX 75205-4022

CLARK, ROBERT NEWHALL, electrical and aeronautical engineering educator; b. Ann Arbor, Mich., Apr. 17, 1925; s. Ellef S. and Esther (Baker) C.; m. Mary Quiatt, Aug. 20, 1949; children: Charles W., John R., Timothy J., Franklin T. B.S. in Elec. Engring., U. Mich., 1950, M.S. in Elec. Engring., 1951; Ph.D., Stanford U., 1969. Registered profl. engr., Wash., Minn. Research engr. Honeywell, Inc., Mpls., 1951-57; lectr. Stanford U., 1968; prof. elec. engring. U. Wash., Seattle, 1957—, prof. aeronautics and astronautics, 1986-94; prof. emeritus, 1994—; vis. scientist Fraunhofer Gesellschaft, Karlsruhe, W.Ger., 1976-77; guest prof. U. Duisburg, W.Ger., 1983-84; cons. analyst Boeing Aerospace Co., Seattle, 1971-92. Author: Introduction to Automatic Control Systems, 1962, Fault Diagnosis in Dynamic Systems, 1989, Control System Dynamics, 1996. Served with USMC, 1943-46. NSF fellow, 1966-68. Fellow IEEE (life), AIAA (assoc.). Home: 3900 50th Ave NE Seattle WA 98105-5238 Office: U Wash PO Box 352500 Seattle WA 98195-2500

CLARK, ROBERT PHILLIPS, newspaper editor, consultant; b. Randolph, Vt., Dec. 3, 1921; s. James S. and Gladys M. (Phillips) C.; m. Jeanne Orr Rice, Dec. 14, 1949; children: Patricia Orr Clark Blackstone, Elizabeth Phillips Clark Christiansen. AB, Tufts U., 1942; MA, U. Mo., 1948. Reporter Owensboro (Ky.) Messenger & Inquirer, 1948-49; reporter, sci. writer Courier-Jour., Louisville, 1949-62; Washington corr. Courier-Jour., 1958; mng. editor Louisville Times, 1962-71; exec. editor Courier-Jour. and Louisville Times, 1971-79; editor Fla. Times-Union and Jacksonville Jour., 1979-82; v.p news Harte-Hanks Newspapers, 1983-86; co-chmn. rsch. com. Newspaper Readership Project, 1982-83; news, editorial cons., 1987—; disting. vis. prof. Baylor U., 1990-92, Slippery Rock U., 1990; mem. accrediting com. Accrediting Coun. on Edn. in Journalism and Mass Comm., 1986-89. Author: Success Stories: What 28 Newspapers Are Doing to Gain and Retain Readers, 1988, Keys to Success: Strategies for Newspaper Marketing in the '90s, 1989; also numerous articles. Bd. dirs. Louisville Presbyn. Theol. Sem., 1968-73, past sec.; trustee S.W. Sch. of Art and Craft, 1993-96; bd. dirs. San Antonio Bot. Soc., 1996—; Pulitzer Prize juror, 1968, 69, 88, 89. Served to capt. U.S. Army, WWII, PTO. Decorated Bronze Star, Purple Heart; Nieman fellow Harvard U., 1960-61; named Editor of Yr., Nat. Press Photographers Assn., 1967. Mem. Am. Soc. Newspaper Editors (pres. 1985-86, v.p. found. 1980-81, 85-86, contbr. Bull.), Soc. Profl. Journalists (contbr. Quill Jour.), AP Mng. Editors Assn. (pres. 1974-75, chmn. regents 1979-80), Internat. Press Inst. (bd. dirs. Am. com. 1981-87), Soc. Mayflower Descendants, Club Giraud, Torch Club (San Antonio, pres. 1997-98), Harvard Club, Delta Tau Delta. Democrat. Presbyterian. Home: 3506 Elm Knoll San Antonio TX 78230-2706

CLARK, ROBERT STOKES, lawyer; b. Bogota, Colombia, Aug. 6, 1954; came to U.S., 1956; s. Robert Sevy and Verna (Stokes) C.; m. Wendy K. Williams, July 9, 1976; children: Robert, Joseph, Christopher, Kathleen, Callie, Margaret, Rebecca. BS, Brigham Young U., 1977, JD magna cum laude, 1980. Bar: Calif. 1980, Utah 1983, U.S. Supreme Ct. 1987. Assoc. O'Melveny & Myers, L.A., 1980-83; shareholder Parr, Waddoups, Brown, Gee, & Loveless, Salt Lake City, 1983—. Editor Brigham Young U. Law Rev., 1979-80. Joseph Fielding Smith scholar Brigham Young U., 1972-77, J. Reuben Clark scholar, 1980. Office: Parr Waddoups Brown Gee & Loveless Ste 1300 185 S State St Salt Lake City UT 84111-1537

CLARK, ROBERT T., career officer; b. Aug. 28, 1948. Commd. U.S. Army, advanced through grades to maj. gen., 1998; comdg. gen. 101st airborne div. air assault U.S. Army, Ft. Campbell, Ky., 1998—. Office: 101st Airborne Div Air Assault Fort Campbell KY 42223

CLARK, ROBERT WESLEY, neurologist; b. Jamestown, N.Y., Apr. 16, 1946; s. Robert Wesley and Dorothy (Depue) C.; m. Linda Gray, June 15, 1968 (div. Jan. 1982); 1 child, Jennifer Marie; m. Marcia Ramm, June 10, 1983; 1 child, Robert Scott. BS in Biology, John Carroll U., 1968; MD, Ohio State U., 1972. Diplomate Am. Bd. Psychiatry and Neurology, Am. Bd. Med. Examiners, Am. Bd. Sleep Medicine. Intern Barnes Hosp., St. Louis, 1972-73, resident, 1973-74; resident in neurology Ohio State U. Coll. Medicine, Columbus, 1974-77, clin. instr. neurology and psychiatry, 1977-78, asst. prof., 1978-81; med. dir. clin. sleep lab. St. Anthony Med. Ctr., Columbus, 1981-85, dir. clin. sleep and electroencephalography labs., 1985-90; med. dir. Mt. Carmel East Sleep Disorders Ctr., Columbus, 1990-97, Columbus Cmty. Hosp. Regional Sleep Disorders Ctr., 1997—; cons. neurology Columbus Children's Hosp., Columbus, 1982—, Doctor's Hosp., Columbus, 1984—; med. advisor Ohio Narcolepsy Assn., Akron, Ohio, 1983—; cons. Nat. Insts. Health Gen. Clin. Research Com., Bethesda, Md., 1979. Contbr. articles on neurology, other topics; also reviewer. Recipient Nu Sigma Nu award Ohio State U. Coll. Medicine, 1969, John Edwin Brown award Ohio State U. Coll. Medicine, 1972. Mem. Am. Acad. Neurology (Weir Mitchell award 1977), Am. Narcolepsy Assn. (bd. dirs. 1986-91), Sociedade Latinoamericano do Sono (mem.-at-large 1989-90), Ohio Narcolepsy Assn., Assn. Profl. Sleep Socs. (accredited clin. polysomnographer), Epilepsy Found. Ohio, Epilepsy Found. Franklin County, Jaleistas Club (San Diego chpt.). Roman Catholic. Avocations: flamenco guitar, photography. Office: Columbus Cmty Hosp 1430 S High St Columbus OH 43207

CLARK, ROBERT WILLIAM, III, lawyer; b. Chgo., May 21, 1945; s. Robert William Jr. and Marjorie (Kimball) C.; m. Toni K. Allen, July 22, 1985; children: William Thomas, Marjorie Kimball. BA, Brown U., 1968; JD, U. Chgo., 1973. Bar: D.C. 1973. Assoc. Sutherland, Asbill & Brennan, Washington, 1973-79, ptnr., 1979—. Mem. ABA (chmn. natural resources, energy and environ. law sect. 1991-92, chmn. natural gas com. 1985-87), Fed. Energy Bar Assn., D.C. Bar Assn. Home: 5640 Bent Branch Rd Bethesda MD 20816-1048 Office: Sutherland Asbill & Brennan 1275 Pennsylvania Ave NW Ste 1 Washington DC 20004-2415

CLARK, ROGER GORDON, educational administrator; b. St. Louis, Nov. 1, 1937; s. Frank E. and Bernice A. (Ervin) C.; m. Jane F. Carfagno, Sept. 6, 1968 (div. 1976); m. Janet Gaye Wong, Jan. 3, 1994. BA, U. Mo., 1959, MA, 1961; PhD, U. Colo., 1969. Project mgr. Nat. Council Tchrs. English Ednl. Resources Info. Clearinghouse, Champaign, Ill., 1967-69; asst. prof. English U. Ill., Urbana, 1969-80, asst., then assoc. dean Grad. Coll., 1969-75, 76-80, acting dir. Sch. Library Sci., 1978-79; assoc. dir. U. Ill. Press, Champaign, 1980-85; dir. Com. Instl. Cooperation between Big Ten Univs. and U. Chgo., Champaign, 1985—. Club: University (Chgo.). Home: 507 G H Baker Dr Urbana IL 61801-1162 Office: Com Instl Coop 302 E John St Ste 1705 Champaign IL 61820-5613

CLARK, RON D(EAN), cosmetologist; b. Wagga Wagga, NSW, Australia, Nov. 4, 1947; came to U.S., 1976; s. J. D. and Lura A. (Bennington) C. M Internat. Cosmetology, U. Geneva, Switzerland; ed., Eng., France, Belgium, Fed. Republic Germany, The Netherlands. Registered cosmetologist, Tex. Free-lance cosmetologist Houston and L.A.; cosmetologist N.Y.C. Make-up and hair stylist for feature films, TV, commls. and Broadway musicals, 1977—. Decorated Order of Svc. to the Empire (Eng.); Emmy nomination for spl. effects, 1989, 91. Home and Office: 1227 W Clay St Houston TX 77019-4153

CLARK, RONALD DEAN, newspaper editor; b. Millersburg, Ohio, Aug. 29, 1943; s. Dean Eli and Lavaun Lurline (Glasgo) C.; m. Carole Ann Smith, Oct. 15, 1983; children from previous marriage—Kelly Jay, Carrie Anne, Courtney Erin. B.A., Kent State U., 1965; M.S. in Journalism, Northwestern U.-Evanston, Ill., 1966; MPA, Humphrey Inst. of Pub. Affairs, U. Minn., 1999. Reporter Akron Beacon Jour., Ohio, 1966-67, asst. city editor, 1967-68, city editor, 1968-70, met. editor, 1970-71, statehouse bur. chief, 1971-76, chief editorial writer, 1976-81; editorial page editor St. Paul Pioneer Press, 1981—. past pres. Minn. Newspaper Found. Recipient Pulitzer Prize (shared) Columbia U., 1971. Mem. Soc. Profl. Journalists, Nat. Conf. Editorial Writers, World Press Inst. (bd. dirs.), COMPAS (bd. dirs.). Lutheran. Club: Minnesota, Informal (St. Paul). Avocations: cycling, music. Home: 13823 Tomahawk Dr S Afton MN 55001-9706 Office: Saint Paul Pioneer Press 345 Cedar St Saint Paul MN 55101-1004

CLARK, ROY THOMAS, JR., chemistry educator, administrator; b. Lockhart, Tex., Feb. 22, 1922; s. Roy Thomas and Ada Louise (Masur) C.; B.S. in Chemistry, S.W. Tex. State Coll., 1947, M.A. in Chemistry, 1950; m. Lavanie Anne Busby, Jan. 3, 1948; 1 son, Thomas David. Commd. 2d lt. USAAF, 1943; advanced through grades to lt. col. USAF, 1966; various assignments U.S., 1943-59; project officer propulsion br. Agena div. Directorate Space Systems, Air Force Ballistic Missile Div., Los Angeles, 1959-60; chief propulsion sect., astrovehicle br. Agena div. Office Dep. Comdr. Satellite Systems, Space Systems Div., Los Angeles, 1960-61; asst. prof. chemistry USAF Acad., Colo., 1961-63, assoc. prof., 1963-64; student Air Force Inst. Tech., Edn.-with-Industry Program, Aerojet Gen. Corp., Sacramento, 1964-65; project officer 6595th Aerospace Test Wing, Vandenberg AFB, Calif., 1965-66; chief Titan Launched Satellite Systems Office, 1966-69; ret., 1969; adminstrv. officer dept. chemistry U. Tex. at

Austin, 1969-84. Decorated Air medal, Air Force Commendation medal, Meritorious Service medal. Mem. Am. Chem. Soc. Episcopalian. Home: 7711 Shadyrock Dr Austin TX 78731-1432

CLARK, RUSSELL GENTRY, federal judge; b. Myrtle, Mo., July 27, 1925; s. William B. and Grace Frances (Jenkins) C.; m. Jerry Elaine Burrows, Apr. 30, 1959; children: Vincent A., Viki F. LLB, U. Mo., 1952. Bar: Mo. 1952. Mem. firm Woolsey, Fisher, Clark, Whiteaker & Stenger, Springfield, Mo., 1952-77; judge U.S. Dist. Ct. (we. dist.) Mo., Kansas City, 1977-91, sr. judge, 1991—. 2d lt. U.S. Army, 1944-46. Fellow Am. Bar Found.; mem. ABA, Internat. Platform Soc., Mo. Bar Assn. (continuing legal edn. com. 1969), Greene County Bar Assn. (dir. 1968-71), Kiwanis (past pres. Springfield chpt.). Democrat. Methodist. Club: Kiwanis (past pres. Springfield chpt.). Office: US Dist Ct 3100 US Courthouse 222 N John Q Hammons Pkwy Springfield MO 65806-2541 *Notable cases include: Jenkins vs. State of Mo., which involved the desegregation of the Kansas City, Mo. Schs.; Bauer vs. Kincaid, et al, which resolved whether news media were entitled to S.W. Mo. State's criminal activity reports; U.S. vs. Nepacco, which established liability for cost of cleaning up toxic waste.*

CLARK, SAMUEL DELBERT, sociology educator; b. Lloydminster, Alta., Canada, Feb. 24, 1910; s. Samuel David and Mary Alice (Curry) C.; m. Rosemary Josephine Landry, Dec. 26, 1939; children—Ellen Margaret, Samuel David, William Edmund. BA, U. Sask., 1930, MA, 1931; MA, McGill U., 1935; PhD, U. Toronto, 1938; LLD (hon.), U. Calgary, 1978, Dalhousie U., 1979, U. Western, Ont., 1984, U. Man., 1985, U. Toronto, 1988; DLitt (hon.), St. Mary's U., 1979, Lakehead U., 1982. Lectr. sociology U. Man., 1937-38; lectr. U. Toronto, 1938-44, asst. prof., 1944-48, asso. prof., 1948-53, prof., 1953-76; vis. prof. U. Calif., Berkeley, 1960-61, U. Sussex, 1970-71; McCulloch prof. Dalhousie U., 1972-74; vis. prof. U. Guelph, 1976-78, Lakehead U., Thunder Bay, Ont., 1978-80, Tsukuba U., Japan, spring 1980, U. Edinburgh, 1980-81. Author: Canadian Manufacturers' Association, 1939, The Social Development of Canada, 1942, Church and Sect in Canada, 1948, Movements Political Protest in Canada, 1957, The Suburban Society, 1963, The Developing Canadian Community, 1968, The Canadian Society in Historical Perspective, 1976, The New Urban Poor, 1978. Guggenheim fellow, 1943-44; officer Order of Can., 1978. Fellow Royal Soc. Can. (pres. 1975-76); mem. Am. Acad. Arts and Scis., Can. Polit. Sci. Assn. (pres. 1958-59), Can. Assn. Sociology and Anthropology (hon. pres.). Home: 61 St Clair Ave W # 302, Toronto, ON Canada M4V 2Y8

CLARK, SANDRA ANN, clinical social worker; b. Long Branch, N.J., Dec. 4, 1942; d. Richard Marshall and Margaret (Novak) C.; m. John Jacob Hoffman, May 4, 1969 (div. 1987); children: Rebecca L., Benjamin C., Rachael A.; m. William E. Wilbur, June 25, 1989. BA, Valparaiso U., 1966; MSW, SUNY, Albany, 1968. Lic. clin. social worker, Maine. Pvt. practice psychotherapy Kittery, Maine, 1982—; asst. exec. dir., coord. children's program N.H. Parents Anonymous, Portsmouth, 1985-86; mental health cons. Strafford County Head Start, Somersworth, N.H., 1985-88; interim exec. dir. N.H. Parents Anonymous, Portsmouth, 1986-87; home sch. coord. Portsmouth Sch. System, 1986-87; clin. social worker Rackingham Counseling Ctr., Exeter, N.H., 1986-89, York County Counseling Svcs., Kittery, 1989-90; exec. dir. Growing Consciousness Assn., Saco, Maine, 1995-96; mem. faculty U. Conn., Concord, N.H., 1987. Mem. NASW, Acad. Cert. Social Workers. Democrat. Home and Office: 25 Old Ferry Ln Kittery ME 03904

CLARK, SANDRA MARIE, school administrator; b. Hanover, Pa., Feb. 17, 1942; d. Charles Raymond Clark and Mary Josephine (Snyder) Clark Wierman. BS in Elem. Edn., Chestnut Hill Coll., 1980; MS in Child Care Adminstrn., Nova U., 1985; MS in Ednl. Adminstrn., Western Md. Coll., 1992. Cert. elem. tchr., elem. prin., Pa. Tchr. various elem. schs., Pa., 1962-75; asst. vocation directress Mt. St. Joseph Motherhouse, Chestnut Hill, Pa., 1975-76; tchr. St. Catharine's Sch., Spring Lake, N.J., 1976-77; asst. mgr. Jim's Truck Stop, New Oxford, Pa., 1977-81; adminstr. Little People Day Care Sch., Hanover, 1981-88, sec., treas. bd. dirs., 1985-86; coord. regional resource Magic Yrs. Child Care & Learning Ctrs., Inc., Hanover, 1987-88; prin. St. Vincent de Paul Sch., Hanover, Pa., 1988—; presenter Hanover Area Seminar for Day Care Employees, 1983-86. coord. sch. safety patrols St. Vincent's Sch., Hanover, 1969-75, vice-chmn. bd., 1982-84; multi-media instr. first aid ARC, Hanover, 1983-86, bd. dirs., 1984-88; exec. sec. of bd. of dirs. ARC, Hanover, 1988; 1st v.p. Hanover Area Coun. of Chs., 1988, pres., 1989; validator accredidation program Nat. Acad. Early Childhood Programs, Washington, 1987—; bd. dirs. Life Skills Unltd. Handicapped Adults, 1988—; facilitator Harrisburg Diocesan Synod, Hanover, 1985-88, parish del., 1988. Pa. Dept. Pub. Welfare tng. grantee, 1986. Mem. NAFE, Nat. Cath. Ednl. Assn. Democrat. Roman Catholic. Club: Internat. Assn. Turtles (London). Avocations: swimming, reading, writing children's stories. Home: 348 Barberry Dr Hanover PA 17331-1302 Office: St Vincent De Paul Sch Hanover PA 17331

CLARK, SCOTT, newspaper editor. Tech. editor Houston Chronicle, asst. mng. editor, 1999—. Office: Houston Chronicle Pub Co 801 Texas Ave Houston TX 77002-2996*

CLARK, SCOTT H., lawyer; b. Logan, Utah, Jan. 7, 1946. BA with honors, U. Utah, 1970; JD, U. Chgo., 1973. Bar: Utah 1973. Ptnr. Ray, Quinney & Nebeker P.C., Salt Lake City, 1980—. Mem. ABA, Utah State Bar, Salt Lake County Bar Assn., Phi Kappa Phi, Pi Sigma Alpha. Office: Ray Quinney & Nebek PC PO Box 45385 Salt Lake City UT 84145-0385

CLARK, SHARON JACKSON, private school administrator; b. Istanbul, Turkey, Feb. 3, 1939; d. John Warren and Maxine Jett (Brient) Jackson; m. Ronald Eugene Clark, June 6, 1959; children: Kristen Anne, Kevin Brooks, Jeffrey Kimball. BFA, Calif. Coll. Arts and Crafts, 1968; MS in Edn., Wheelock Coll., 1978; student, Moore Coll. Art. Co-founder Jowanio, Syracuse, N.Y., The Thoreau Sch., Salt Lake City, Glen Urquhart Sch., Beverly, Mass.; head, founder Clark Sch. Creative Learning, Danvers, Mass. Mem. Gifted/Talented Educators North Shore (bd. dirs.).

CLARK, STANFORD E., accountant; b. Farmington, Utah, Sept. 21, 1917; m. Merrial Jane Knight Mackay, Nov. 16, 1942 (dec. July 1993); m. Evelyn Harrow, Nov. 3, 1995. Student, LDS Bus. Coll., Salt Lake City, 1935. With Utah Constrn. Co., Riverton, Wyo., 1955-57; rancher Riverton, 1948-55; office mgr. Superior Bit Svc., Riverton, 1958-68; v.p., sec., treas. Allied Nuclear Corp., Riverton, 1957-69; v.p., sec., treas. Western Std. Corp., Riverton, 1957-83, pres., treas., dir., 1989—; also bd. dirs.; treas., v.p., sec., bd. dirs. Snow King Resort Mgmt. Inc., Jackson, 1992-99, Jackson Hole Springs Water Co., 1995—; treas. S.K. Land Ltd. Liability Co., 1992—; v.p., treas., bd. dirs. Snow King Resort Ctr., Inc., 1999—, Snow King Resort, Inc., 1999—; sec., treas., bd. dirs., 1991-99; pres. Western Recreation Corp., 1957—. With USCG, 1942-45. Republican. Office: Western Standard Corp 205 S Broadway Ave Riverton WY 82501-4331

CLARK, STEVEN MARSTON, film producer, real estate licensee; b. Pasadena, Calif., Aug. 26, 1947; s. Howard Marston and Lucille (Woods) C. AA, Pasadena City Coll., 1967; student, Lincoln U., 1971, U. Calif., Berkeley, 1972; film studies stud., U. of Calif. Irvine, 1995. V.p. Nimrod River Park Co., Sprague River, Oreg., 1967-68, Nordland Inc., San Gabriel, Calif., 1969-70; real estate developer Morro Strand, Inc., Morro Bay, Calif., 1976-80; v.p. Morro Rock View Co., Morro Bay, 1980-85; pres. Clark Prodns., Inc., Hollywood, Calif., 1985—. Actor in stage prodns. MacBeth, Merry Wives Windsor, Merchant of Venice, King John, Hamlet. Active Calif. Rep. Assembly (editor mag. 1988—). Mem. SAG, Harkness Foundation of Commonwealth of N.Y. (life), direct descendant of Founders of the Harkness Found. for Dance.

CLARK, SUE JANET, business owner; b. Vancouver, Wash., Oct. 17, 1929; d. Day Walter and Dorothy Janet (White) Hilborn; children: Leslie Lora, Kyle Scott, Sidne Suzanne, Brian Casey. AA, Stephens Coll., 1949; student, Northwestern U., 1949-51; BA, U. Wash., 1952. Continuity dir. KING-TV, Seattle, 1952-54; traffic mgr. KTNT-TV, Tacoma, 1954; freelance pub. rels. cons., 1966-70; continuity dir. KTIM, San Rafael, Calif., 1966-68; coord. vol. svcs. Sunny Hills Residential Treatment Ctr. for Teenagers, San Anselmo, Calif., 1968-73; adminstr. asst. tech. publs. Bechtel Power Corp., San Francisco, 1973; dir. unv. rels. U. Calif., San Francisco, 1973-77; real estate agt. Home & Land Co., San Rafael, 1977-80; pres. Lindberg-Clark, Inc., Mokelumne Hill, Calif., 1978-82; owner, ptnr. Travel Cons., San Francisco, 1985-94; writer, 1966—; propr. SJ Clark Lit. Agy., 1982—; writing instr., 1993—; owner, ptnr. Light Age Pub. House; guest spkr. numerous confs., workshops, seminars. Contbg. writer articles and poetry Terra Linda News, Pacific Sun, Ind. Jour., various anthologies, others; contbr. articles on fundraising and pub. rels. to profl. jours. Bd. dirs. Vol. Bur. Marin County, 1978-80, San Francisco Easter Seal Soc., 1974-77. Mem. Nat. Soc. fund Raisers (charter; bd. dirs. 1969-77), Lions Internat., Phi Beta, Alpha Delta Pi. Republican. Presbyterian.

CLARK, SUSAN (NORA GOULDING), actress; b. Sarnia, Ont., Can., Mar. 8, 1943; d. George Raymond and Eleanor Almond (McNaughton) C. Student, Toronto (Ont.) Children's Players, 1956-59; student (Acad. scholar), Royal Acad. Dramatic Art, London. partner Georgian Bay Prodns. Producer: Jimmy B. and Andre, 1979, Word of Honor, 1980, Maid in America, 1982; star Webster, ABC-TV, 1983-89; appeared in Brit. TV prodns., repertory theatre; appeared in Brit. premiere of play Poor Bitos; appeared in Can. TV prodns., including Heloise and Abelard, Hedda Gabler, Emily of New Moon (series 1996-97); starred in Taming of the Shrew; appeared in Sherlock Holmes, Williamstown Theatre Festival, (taped for HBO), 1981, Meetin's on the Porch, Canon Theater, Beverly Hills, 1990, Lion in Winter, Walnut St. Theater, Phila., 1992; Getting Out, Mark Taper Forum, Los Angeles, 1978, The Vortex, Walnut Street Theatre, 1994; films include The Apple Dumpling Gang, Night Moves, The North Avenue Irregulars, Airport '75, Midnight Man, Porky's, Murder by Decree, Tell Them Willie Boy is Here, Skin Game, City on Fire, Madigan, Coogan's Bluff, Skullduggery, Promises in the Dark, Valdez is Coming, Showdown, Double Negative, Nobody's Perfekt, The Canadian Conspiracy; appeared in segments of TV series Columbo, Marcus Welby, Barnaby Jones, Webster; appeared in Double Solitaire, Pub. Broadcasting System, Emily of New Moon, 1996-97; TV films include: Something for a Lonely Man, 1968, The Astronaut, 1972, Trapped, 1973, Babe, 1975 (Emmy award), McNaughton's Daughter, 1976, Amelia Earhart, 1976 (Emmy nom.), Jimmy B. & Andre, 1980 (also co-prodr.), The Choice, 1981, Maid in America, 1982 (also co-prodr.), Snowbound, The Jim and Jennifer Stolpa Story, 1993, Tonya and Nancy, The Inside Story, 1994, The Butterbox Babies, 1994 (Gemini nomination), (play) After-Play, 1997, 98. Mem. ACLU, Am. Film Inst. Office: care Georgian Bay Prodns 13400 Riverside Dr Ste 308 Sherman Oaks CA 91423

CLARK, SUSAN MATTHEWS, psychologist; b. Newton, Kans., Aug. 5, 1950; d. Glenn Wesley Matthews and Jane Buckles; m. S. Bruce Clark, Aug. 14, 1971; children: Casandra Jane, Ryan Matthews. BME, Wichita State U., 1971, MME, 1975, MA, 1982; PhD, North Tex. State U., 1985. Elem. tchr. Derby (Kans.) Pub. Schs., 1972-74; profl. musician Amarillo (Tex.) Symphony, 1974-77; psychol. cons. Achenbach Ctr., Hardtner, Kans., 1983-85; psychologist intern VA Med. Ctr., Wichita, Kans., 1984-85; psychologist St. Francis Acad., Inc., Salina, Kans., 1986-89, Psychiat. Clinic Wichita, 1989-93; gen. mgr. Affiliated Psychiat. Svcs., Wichita, 1993-95; psychologist Charter Clinic, Wichita, Kans., 1995-99; bd. dirs. Salina Coalition for the Prevention of Child Abuse, 1986-87. Author: Grant, 1987. Bd. deacons Plymouth Congl. Ch., Wichita, 1989-92. Recipient: Phi Kappa Phi, Mu Phi Epsilon, Psi Chi. Mem. APA, Nat. Acad. Neuropsychology, Kans. Psychol. Assn., Children with Attention Deficit Disorder. Republican. Congregationalist. Avocations: stained glass, photography, bridge, tennis, reading. Office: 242 Courtleigh St Wichita KS 67218-1712

CLARK, TERESA WATKINS, psychotherapist, clinical counselor; b. Hobart, Okla., Dec. 18, 1953; d. Aaron Jack Watkins and Patricia Ann (Flurry) Greer and Ralph Gordon Greer; m. Philip Winston Clark, Dec. 29, 1979; children: Philip Aaron, Alisa Lauren. BA in Psychology, U. N.Mex., 1979, MA in Counseling and Family Studies, 1989. Lic. profl. clin. counselor, N.Mex. Child care worker social svcs. divsn. Family Resource Ctr., Albuquerque, 1978-79; head tchr., asst. dir. Kinder Care Learning Ctr., Albuquerque, 1979-80; psychiat. asst. Vista Sandia Psychiat. Hosp., Albuquerque, 1980-87; psychotherapist outpatient clinic Bernalillo County Mental Health Ctr.-Heights, 1989-91; therapist adolescent program Charter/Heights Behavioral Health Sys., Albuquerque, 1991—; travel agt. Travel Navigator. Mem. ACA, Am. Assn. Multicultural Counseling and Devel., N.Mex. Health Counselors Assn. (former cen. regional rep., ethics chair, bd. dirs.), Mental Health Councelor's Assn., Billy The Kid Outlaw Gang Hist. Soc. Democrat. Avocations: music, camping, horseback riding, reading. Office: Charter/Hlth Behav Hlth Sys 103 Hospital Loop NE Albuquerque NM 87109-2115

CLARK, THOMAS ALONZO, federal judge; b. Atlanta, Dec. 20, 1920; s. Fred and Prudence (Sprayberry) C.; m. Betty Medlock, July 16, 1978; children: Thomas Alonzo, Christopher S., Julia M.; stepchildren: Allen L. Carter, Rosalyn Lackey Howell. BS, Washington and Lee U., 1942; LLB, U. Ga., 1949. Pvt. practice law Bainbridge, Ga., 1949-55; ptnr. Dykes, Marshall & Clark, Americus, Ga., 1955-57, Fowler, White et al, Tampa, Fla., 1957-61; sr. ptnr. Carlton, Fields, et al, Tampa, 1961-79; judge U.S. Ct. Appeals (5th cir.), 1979-81; judge U.S. Ct. of Appeals (11th cir.), Atlanta, 1981-99, sr. judge, 1991-99; ret., 1999. Mem. Ga. Ho. of Reps., 1951-52; pres. Fla. Assn. for Retarded Citizens, 1974-75, Served to lt. comdr. USN, 1942-46. Fellow Am. Coll. Trial Lawyers; mem. ABA, Ga. Bar Assn., Fla. Bar Assn.

CLARK, THOMAS CARLYLE, banker; b. Barbourville, Ky., Dec. 1, 1947; s. Buford Thomas and Eleanor Randolph (Owens) C. AB, Duke U., 1969; MBA, Harvard U., 1971; LLD, Cumberland Coll., 1991. Officer Chem. Bank, N.Y.C., 1975-78; mng. dir. U.S. Trust Co. N.Y., N.Y.C., 1978—; bd. dirs. U.S. Trust N.J., U.S. Trust, N.A., U.S. Trust Conn. Pres. bd. dirs. Concert Artists Guild, Lubovitch Dance Co.; vice chmn. bd. trustees Union Coll., Ky.; bd. dirs. Am. Composers Orch. With USN, 1971-75; comdr. USNR ret. Mem. Robert Morris Assn. (chmn. pvt. lending com.), Lincoln's Inn Soc. (alumni coun.), Duke U. Met. Alumni Assn. (pres. 1984), Am. Banking Assn. (past chair exec. com. for pvt. banking, alumni coun.), Kentuckians N.Y. Club, Met. Opera Club (bd. dirs., treas.). Republican. Methodist. Office: US Trust Co NY 11 W 54th St New York NY 10019-5404

CLARK, THOMAS P., JR., lawyer; b. N.Y.C., Sept. 16, 1943. AB, U. Notre Dame, 1965; JD, U. Mo., Kansas City, 1973. Bar: Calif. 1973. Ptnr. Stradling, Yocca, Carlson & Rauth P.C., Newport Beach, Calif., 1978—. Editor-in-chief The Urban Lawyer, 1972-73; contbr. articles to profl. jours. Capt. USMC, 1966-70. Mem. State Bar Calif., Orange County Bar Assn., Phi Kappa Phi, Bench and Robe. Office: Stradling Yocca Carlson & Rauth PC 660 Newport Center Dr Newport Beach CA 92660-6401

CLARK, THOMAS RYAN, retired federal agency executive, business and technical consultant; b. Aberdeen, Wash., Sept. 16, 1925; s. George O. and Gladys (Ryan) C.; m. Barbara Ann Thiele, June 14, 1948; children: Thomas R. III, Kathleen Clark Sandberg, Christopher J.T. Student, U. Kans., 1943-44; BS, U.S. Mil. Acad., 1948; MSEE, Purdue U., 1955; cert., U.S. Army Command and Gen. Staff Coll., 1960, Harvard U., 1979. Commd. C.E., U.S. Army, 1948, advanced through grades to col., 1968; ret. U.S. Army, 1968; program mgr. U.S. AEC, Washington, 1968-75; dep. mgr. Dept. of Energy, Albuquerque, 1976-83; sr. exec. svc., 1977; mgr. Nev. ops. Dept. of Energy, Las Vegas, 1983-87, ret., 1987; cons. in field Las Vegas and Albuquerque, 1987—; mem. adv. bd. Dept. Chem. and Nuclear Engring., U. N.Mex., 1984—; mem. statewide adv. bd. Desert Research Inst., U. Nev., 1985-88. Editor, co-author: Nuclear Fuel Cycle, 1975. Trustee Nev. Devel. Authority, Las Vegas, 1984-88, Nat. Atomic Mus. Found., 1993—, pres., 1997—. Decorated Legion of Merit, Bronze Star; named Disting. Exec., Pres. of U.S., 1982. Mem. Las Vegas C. of C. (bd. dirs. 1983-87), Sigma Xi, Tau Beta Pi, Eta Kappa Nu, Rotary Club of Albuquerque (pres. 1993-94). Episcopalian. Lodge: Rotary.

CLARK, THOMAS SULLIVAN, lawyer; b. Bakersfield, Calif., Dec. 12, 1947; s. Walter J. and Ruth Virginia (Sullivan) C. BA in History, U. So. Calif., 1969, JD, 1973. Gen. counsel Income Equities Corp., Los Angeles, 1972-74; campaign cons. Huntington Beach, Calif., 1974-75; prosecutor Office of Kern County Dist. Atty., Bakersfield, 1975-78; ptnr. Arrache, Clark & Potter (formerly Rudnick, Arrache & Clark), Bakersfield, 1978—; cons. Vol. Attys. Program, Bakersfield, 1985—. Bd. dirs. Kern Bridges Youth Found., pres. 1987-89; bd. dirs. Bakersfield City Sch. Dist. Ednl. Found. Mem. Calif. Bar Assn., Kern County Bar Assn. (bd. dirs., chmn. jud. qualifications com.), Community Assns. Inst., Kern County Hist. Soc., Kern County U. So. Calif. Alumni Assn. (bd. dirs., v.p. 1985-88, pres. 1988-95), Rotary (bd. dirs. Bakersfield), Seven Oaks Country Club. Republican. Roman Catholic. Avocations: skiing, history. Office: Arrache Clark & Potter 4800 Easton Dr #114 Bakersfield CA 93309

CLARK, THREESE ANNE, occupational therapist, disability analyst; b. Bath, N.Y., Jan. 16, 1946; d. Frank George and Beulah Irene (Harris) Brown; m. Jacob Clark, Mar. 11, 1966 (div. Mar. 1977); 1 child, Jayson Todd. BS in Occupational Therapy, U. N.D., 1967, MS in Counseling and Guidance, 1977. Lic. occupational therapist, Pa., Md.; diplomate Am. Bd. Disability Analysts (charter adv. bd. mem. 1995—). Occupational therapist U. N.D. Med. Ctr., 1968; chief occupational therapist, program developer Corning (N.Y.) Hosp., 1968-69, Arnot-Ogden Hosp., Elmira, N.Y., 1969-71; staff occupational therapist VA Ctr., Bath, N.Y., 1971-74; instr. occupational therapy U. N.D., Grand Forks, 1974-77; prin. investigator occupational therapy Ohio State U., 1977-79; occupational therapist Regional Ednl. Assessment and Cons. Team, Hillsboro, Ohio, 1979-81; occupational therapist, phys. medicine and rehab. Saint Mary's Hosp., West Palm Beach, Fla., 1981-82; chief occupational therapist Mercy Med. Ctr., Oshkosh, Wis., 1982-87; dir. occupational/recreational therapy HealthSouth Rehab. Hosp., Altoona, 1987-95, clin. dir. spinal injury program, 1987-95; pres., owner Life Care Planning and Mgmt. Inc., Altoona, 1993—; assoc. prof., program dir. BS occupl. therapy program Mt. Aloysius Coll., Cresson, Pa., 1995—; co-owner, sec.-treas. Shears-a-GoGo, Inc., Altoona, 1996—; cons. Founders Pavillion, Corning, 1969, Grafton (N.D.) State Sch. for the Retarded, 1975-76, Heart of Am. Rehab. Ctr., Rugby, N.D., 1976-77, Andrea Clifford program, 1978; guest lectr. support groups, community groups, ednl. programs, 1987—; presenter in field. Contbr. articles to profl. jours. Charter mem. profl. adv. coun. Am. Bd. Disability Analysts; pres. adv. bd. Occupational Therapy Asst. Program, Mt. Aloysius Jr. Coll., 1988-92, 94-96; mem. adv. profl. com. Home Nursing Agy., Altoona, 1988-93; mem. Com. Health Care Adv. Com., 1994—; bd. dirs. Ctr. for Internat. Living of South Cen. Pa., 1992-95; mem. med. svc. com. Evergreen Manor, Oshkosh, 1985-87; chair home/family life and human rels. Northtowne Elem. Sch. PTA, Columbus, Ohio, 1978, others. Mem. Am. Occupational Therapy Assn. (coun. edn. 1974-76, coun. affiliate pres. 1976), Nat. Rehab. Assn., Ohio Occupational Therapy Assn., Columbus Dist. Occupational Therapy Assn., Pa. Occupational Therapy Assn., Am. Assn. Hand Therapists. Baptist. Avocations: volksports, needlecrafts, signing, reading, dog obedience trials. Home and Office: Life Care Planning Mgmt Inc 5300 5th Ave Altoona PA 16602-1312 Office: Mt Aloysius Coll 7373 Adm Peary Hwy Cresson PA 16630

CLARK, TONY, state agency administrator. Student, Mich. State U., 1990-91; BS in Polit. Sci., N.D. State U., 1994, BS in History Edn., 1996. Mem. Dist. 44 N.D. Ho. of Reps., 1994-97, mem. edn., govt. and vet. affairs coms.; adminstrv. officer N.D. Tax Dept., 1997—; mem. legis. audit & fiscal rev. com., mem. info. tech. com. N.D./S.D. Commn. Sec. Dist. 44 Rep. Com.; adult leader Boy Scouts Am. Named Eagle Scout Boy Scouts Am. Mem. Elks, Phi Kappa Phi. Office: 600 E Boulevard Ave Bismarck ND 58505-0660

CLARK, TRENT L., federal affairs manager; b. Jackson Hole, Wyo., July 12, 1961; s. Richard L. and Carolyn T. Clark; m. Rebecca L. Lee, May 23, 1986; children: Brittany, Kathleen, Christin, Alexander. AS, Ricks Coll., 1980; BA, Brigham Young U., 1984; cert. pub. health, Harvard U., 1995. Legis. staff U.S. Senate, Washington, 1983-90; chief environ. economist Joint Econ. Com. Congress, Washington, 1990-91; state dir. Idaho Farm Svcs. Adminstrn., Boise, 1991-93; sr. comms. specialist Monsanto Co., Soda Springs, Idaho, 1993-98; fed. affairs mgr. Solutia, Inc., Soda Springs, Idaho, 1998—. Dir. Get the Waste Out, Soda Springs, 1996; vice chmn. Idaho Rep. Orgn., Region 6, Pocatello, 1998; chmn. Idaho Rural Devel. Coun., Boise, 1997. Recipient Merit award USDA, 1992, Gov.'s Safety Conf. award Gov. Idaho, 1998. Mem. Idaho Assn. Commerce and Industry (dir. 1993—), Idaho Coun. on Industry and the Environment (dir. 1998—), Soda Springs C. of C. (pres. 1998). Republican. Mem. LDS Ch. Avocations: fencing, backcountry horsepacking. E-mail: tlclar@solutia.com. Office: Solutia Inc 1853 Hwy 34 Soda Springs ID 83276-0816

CLARK, VERONICA ANN WILDS (RONNI PATRIQUIN CLARK), journalist; b. St. Louis, May 22, 1943; d. Charles Ernest, Jr. and Marie Elizabeth (Perabo) Wilds; m. Guy Albert Luno, Jr., Aug. 10, 1961 (div. Nov. 1967); children: Judith Wilds Luno Adams, Guy Albert Luno III; m. Francis David Patriquin, Dec. 23, 1972 (dec. Apr. 1982); m. Farris Laray Clark, Jr., Nov. 25, 1995. Student, La. State U., 1961, N.E. La. U., 1964-1967. Soc. editor The Monroe (La.) News Star, 1964; news reporter The Monroe Morning World, 1967; news dir. Televisual News, Baton Rouge, 1972-73; capital corr. The Clarion Ledger, Jackson, Miss., 1974-76; capital bur. chief capital bur. The Shreveport Jour., Baton Rouge, 1976-91; polit. writer Gannett News Svc., Tallahassee, 1991-92; sr. reporter The Mobile (Ala.) Register, 1992—; pres. Capital Corrs. Assn., Baton Rouge, 1979-80, Mobile Gridiron, 1993; judge Loyola U. Silver Scribe Competition, New Orleans, 1985-90. Pres. Hist. Spanish Town Civic Assn., Baton Rouge, 1982-85; mem. Hist. Dist. Commn., Baton Rouge, 1984-85. Recipient numerous 1st Pl. AP awards Miss., Ala., La., 1974-97, Best Coverage Gov. award La. Press Assn., 1986, 88, Media Environ. award Organized Fisherman Fla., 1992, Edward J. Meeman Nat. Journalism award Scripps Howard Found, 1993. Mem. Mobile Press Club (News & Excellence award 1992, 98, Gen. Excellence/Cmty. Svc. award 1998), Soc. Profl. Journalists (pres. 1993-94). Roman Catholic. Avocations: canoeing, biking, gardening, reading, traveling. E-mail: rpatriquin@mobileregister.com. Office: The Mobile Register 304 Government St Mobile AL 36602

CLARK, WENDEL, hockey player; b. Kelvington, Sask., Can., Oct. 25, 1966. Hockey player Toronto Maple Leafs Nat. Hockey League, 1985-94, hockey player Quebec Nordiques, 1994-96, hockey player Toronto Maple Leafs, 1996-98, hockey player Tampa Bay Lightning, 1998-99, hockey player Detroit Red Wings, 1999—; capt. Toronto Maple Leafs, 1991-94; played All-Star Game, 1986. Named Rookie of Yr. Sporting News, 1985-86, All Rookie team, 1985-86. Office: Detroit Red Wings, Joe Louis Arena, 600 Civic Ctr, Detroit, MI Canada M5B 1L1*

CLARK, WENDELL W., lawyer; b. Tulsa, Okla., June 10, 1944; s. Wesley D. and M. Janice (Ford) C.; children from previous marriage: Lanette C., Ashley A.; m. Kimberly G. Finch, Dec. 2, 1978; stepchildren: James W., Amanda G. Simmons. BA in History and Polit. Sci., U. Tulsa, 1966, JD, 1968. Assoc. VanCleave, Thomas, Liebler & Gresham, Tulsa, 1968-73, Gresham, Bivens, Clark and Bennett, Tulsa, 1973-74; ptnr. Wendell W. Clark & Assoc., Tulsa, 1974-77, Clark & Williams, Tulsa, 1977—. Pres. Minshall Park Homeowners, Tulsa, 1996-98; pub. defender, Tulsa, 1969-70; pres. Philcrest Hills Tennis Club, 1991. Capt. Okla. Air N.G., 1971-78. Mem. Okla. Bar Assn., Tulsa County Bar Assn. (sec. 1984, bd. dirs. 1985-86, Meritorious Svc. award 1984, 86, chmn. fee arbitration 1982-83), Tulsa Apartment Assn., Bldg. Owners and Mgrs. Assn. (bd. dirs. 1999), City of Tulsa Sales Tax Overview Com., pres., Philcrest Tennis Club, 1991. Democrat. Methodist. Office: 5416 S Yale Ave Ste 600 Tulsa OK 74135-6244

CLARK, WILL (WILLIAM NUSCHLER CLARK, JR.), professional baseball player; b. New Orleans, Mar. 13, 1964. Student, Miss. State U. Baseball player San Francisco Giants, 1986-93, Texas Rangers, 1994-99; infielder Balt. Orioles, 1999—; mem. U.S. Olympic baseball team, 1984. Recipient Golden Spikes award USA Baseball, 1985, Gold Glove award Nat. League, 1991, Silver Slugger, 1989, 91; named to Sporting News Nat. League All-Star team, 1988-89, 91, Coll. All-Am. Team Sporting News, 1984-85, Nat. League All-Star team, 1988-92, 4, Am. League All-Star team, 1994; Nat. RBI leader, 1988. Player in World Series, 1989. Office: Balt Orioles Oriole Park at Camden Yards 333 W Camden St Baltimore MD 21201*

CLARK, WILLIAM, JR., political advisor; b. Oakland, Calif., Oct. 12, 1930; s. William and Mary Edith (Coady) C.; m. Judith Lee Riley, Sept. 11,

1954; 1 child, Jared Riley. BA, San Jose State U., 1955; postgrad., Columbia U., 1967-68; diploma with distinction, Nat. War Coll., 1977; LittD (hon.), Calif. State U., 1992. Dir. liaison dept. U.S. Civil Adminstrn., Naha, Japan, 1970-72; U.S.-Japan Trade Officer Am. Embassy, Tokyo, 1972-74, minister, 1981-85; polit. counselor Am. Embassy, Seoul, Republic of Korea, 1977-80; minister Am. Embassy, Cairo, 1985-86, charge d'affaires, 1986; dir. spl. trade activities Dept. of State, Washington, 1974-76, dir. Japanese Affairs, 1980-81, dep. asst. sec. state, 1986-89; ambassador to India, 1989-92; asst. sec. of state East Asian and Pacific affairs Dept. of State, Washington, 1992-93; Japan chair, sr. advisor Ctr. for Strategic and Internat. Studies, Washington, 1993-95; pres. Japan Soc., N.Y.C., 1996—; sr. advisor Ctr. for Strategic and Internat. Studies, Washington, 1996—. Lt. (j.g.) USN, 1950-53. Recipient Superior Svc. award Dept. Army, 1971, Outstanding Svc. award Dept. Army, 1972, Disting. Svc. award Pres. U.S., 1985, Meritorious Svc. award Pres. U.S., 1987, 89, Disting. Honor award Dept. State, 1989, Charles E. Cobb award Dept. State, 1991, Disting. lectr. Fgn. Svc. Inst., 1995. Mem. Am. Fgn. Svc. Assn., Asian Soc., Japan Am. Soc. (bd. dirs. 1994—), Am. Japan Soc. (bd. dirs. 1981-85), Am. C. of C. (hon. mem. Tokyo 1981-85, Cairo 1985-86), Gizira Club (Cairo), Tokyo Am. Club, Pres.'s Estate Polo Club (New Delhi), Chevy Chase Club (Washington). Episcopalian. Avocations: tennis, riding, skiing, golf. Home: 420 E 54th St Apt 5J New York NY 10022-5150

CLARK, WILLIAM ALFRED, federal judge; b. Dayton, Ohio, Aug. 27, 1928; s. Webb Rufus and Dora Lee (Weddle) C.; m. Catherine C. Clark, Apr. 5, 1952; children: Mary Clark Youra, Jennifer Clark Kinder, Cynthia Clark Regan, Andrea G. Bell. AB, U. Mich., 1950, JD, 1952. Bar: Ohio 1952, Mich. 1953. Pvt. practice Dayton, 1954-57; assoc. Frank J. Svoboda, Dayton, 1957-73; ptnr. Legler, Lang & Kuhns, Dayton, 1973-82, Pickrel, Schaeffer & Ebeling, Dayton, 1982-85; chief judge so. dist. Ohio U.S. Bankruptcy Ct., Dayton, 1985-99, recall judge, 1999—; apptd. recalled bankruptcy judge, 1999—; judge Montgomery County Ct., Dayton, 1958-63; trial counsel in eminent domain Asst. Atty. Gen. Ohio, Dayton, 1963-70; tchr. bus. law Dayton chpt. Cert. Property and Casualty Underwriters, 1963-83; arbitrator Montgomery County Common Pleas Ct., Am. Arbitration Assn., Better Bus. Bur. Contbr. to Ohio Practice and Procedure Handbook, 1962. Lt. USAF, 1952-54. Named Alumnus of Yr., U. Mich. Club, Dayton, 1965. Mem. ABA, Ohio State Bar Assn. (chmn. eminent domain 1979-82), Dayton Bar Assn. (treas. 1964-65), Nat. Conf. Bankruptcy Judges, Lawyers Club. Republican. Methodist. Avocations: tennis, other sports, reading, travel. Office: US Bankruptcy Ct Federal Bldg 120 W 3rd St Dayton OH 45402-1872

CLARK, WILLIAM ARTHUR V., geographer, demographer; b. Christchurch, N.Z., Mar. 21, 1938; came to U.S., 1961; s. Edward Arthur and Gertrude Rita (MacDonald) C.; m. Valmai Ruth Kirklam, July 1, 1961 (div. Oct. 1971); m. Irene Stephanee Borah, Mar. 25, 1978; children: Elisa, Louisa, Clifton, Justin. BA, U. N.Z., 1960; MA, U. Canterbury, N.Z., 1961; PhD, U. Ill., 1964; Doctorem Honoris Causa, U. Utrecht, The Netherlands, 1992; DSc, U. Auckland, N.Z., 1994. Lectr. U. Canterbury, 1964-66; asst./assoc. prof. U. Wis., Madison, 1966-70; prof. geography UCLA, 1970—, chmn. dept. geography, 1987-92, 95-97, assoc. dir. Inst. Social Sci. Rsch., 1984-87; vis. prof. U. Amsterdam, 1981; Belle Van Zuylen prof. U. Utrecht, 1989; cons. state atty. gens. Mo., Calif., Wis., Minn. Author: Human Migration, 1986, Households and Housing, 1996, The California Cauldron: Immigration and the Fortunes of Local Communities, 1998; author/editor: Residential Mobility and Public Policy, 1980, Rediscovering Geography: New Relevance for Science and Society, 1997. Fellow-in-residence Netherlands Inst. Advanced Studies, The Hague, 1993, Guggenheim fellow, 1994-95. Fellow Royal Soc. New Zealand (elected hon. 1997); mem. Assn. Am. Geographers (Honors award 1986), Population Assn. Am. Anglican Ch. Achievements include research in district and appellate court rulings on demographic change and school desegregation. Avocations: skiing, scuba diving, sailing, music. Office: UCLA Dept Geography 405 Hilgard Ave Los Angeles CA 90095-9000

CLARK, WILLIAM FREDERICK, lawyer; b. Denver, Aug. 2, 1941. Student, Am. Univ., 1960, U. Colo., 1963; JD, San Francisco Law Sch., 1967. Bar: Calif. 1969, U.S. Supreme Ct. 1975. Mng. ptnr. William Clark and Assocs., San Jose, 1979-97; sr. dep. city atty. City San Jose, 1997—; judge pro-tem Worker's Compensation Appeals Bd., 1982—; lectr. Continuing Edn. of Bar Def. Attys. Assn., 1988—, Indsl. Claims Assn., 1988—. Mem. ABA, Calif. Bar Assn., Santa Clara County Bar Assn. (worker's compensation com.). Office: City Attys Office City San Jose 151 W Mission St San Jose CA 95110-1710

CLARK, WILLIAM H., JR., lawyer; b. Phila., Apr. 10, 1951; s. William H. and Alice Kimes (Metts) C.; m. Cristine D. Merkel, Aug. 18, 1973; children: Matthew, Alison, Daniel. BA summa cum laude, Amherst Coll., 1973; MA in Religion, Westminster Sem., 1979; JD magna cum laude, Temple U., 1983. Bar: Pa. 1983. Assoc. Morgan, Lewis & Bockius, Phila., 1983-89; ptnr. Klett Lieber Rooney & Schorling, Pitts., 1989-98, Phila., 1998—; chmn. corp. bur. advisory com. Pa. Dept of State, 1991—; cons. rules disciplinary bd. Supreme Ct. Pa., Harrisburg, 1983—. Fellow Am. Bar Found.; mem. ABA (com. on corp. laws, com. on bus. courts), Pa. Bar Assn. (draftsman, lobbyist, corp. law com. 1984—, coun. sect. corp. banking and bus. law 1989-93, officer 1993—), Allegheny County Bar Assn. (coun. sect. corp. banking and bus. law 1991-97, officer 1997-98), Phila. Bar Assn. (coun. bus. law sect. 1998—), Am. Law Inst., Phi Beta Kappa. Republican. Presbyterian. Office: Klett Lieber Rooney & Schlorling Two Logan Sq Philadelphia PA 19103

CLARK, WILLIAM HARTLEY, political science educator; b. Pitts., Apr. 29, 1930; s. Arthur Tillotson and Ruthanna Frame (Anderson) C.; m. Barbara Jean Rockne, June 27, 1953; children—Heather Anderson, Jill Eleanor, Robert Hartley, Edward Kirtland. B.A., Carleton Coll., 1952; M.A., N.Y. U., 1955, Ph.D., 1960. Researcher for Carnegie Endowment for Internat. Peace, Brookings Instn., N.Y. U., 1953-54; instr. polit. sci. Western Coll., Oxford, Ohio, 1954-55; instr. internat. relations Carleton Coll., 1955-60, asst. prof., 1960-66, assoc. prof., 1966-70, prof., 1970-92, prof. emeritus, 1992—, chmn. dept. polit. sci., 1972-76, Frank B. Kellogg prof. internat. rels., 1973-92; lectr. U. Minn., 1970; dir. Geneva Seminar on Internat. Instns., 1975-91; pres. Clark Assocs., 1992—. Author: The Politics of the Common Market, 1967; contbr. articles and revs. to profl. publs. Fulbright research fellow, 1961-62; Ford Found. research fellow, 1967; NSF research fellow, 1970, 71, 79; von Humbolt-Stiftung fellow, 1961. Mem. Coun. Fgn. Rels. (St. Paul-Mpls. com. fgn. rels.), UN Assn. Home: 216 Nevada St Northfield MN 55057-2343

CLARK, WILLIAM JAMES, retired insurance company executive; b. Kansas City, Mo., Oct. 1, 1923; s. William LeRoy and Margaret (Theobald) C.; children: Holly Clark, Jane Clark, Nancy Clark Mundel, Patricia Clark Midura; m. Elizabeth A. Smith, May 1, 1984. Student, Kansas City Jr. Coll., 1941-42; BS, U. Mo., 1947. With Mass. Mut. Life Ins. Co., Springfield, 1947-96, v.p. sales, 1967-70, sr. v.p., 1971-74, pres., 1974-86, chief exec. officer, 1980-88, chmn., 1988-96; ret., 1996. Served to 1st lt. USAAF, 1943-45. Mem. Audubon Country Club, Longmeadow Country Club. Home: 577 Portsmouth Ct Naples FL 34110-8687 Office: Mass Mut Life Ins Co 1295 State St Springfield MA 01111-0001

CLARKE, ALLEN BRUCE, mathematics educator, retired academic administrator; b. Saskatoon, Sask., Can., Sept. 8, 1927; came to U.S., 1947, naturalized, 1953; s. Arthur Roy and Florence (Clarke) C.; m. Florence Myres, Sept. 14, 1949; children—David John, Richard Neil, Deborah Lynn. B.A. with Honours, U. Sask., 1947; M.Sc., Brown U., 1949, Ph.D., 1951. From instr. to prof. U. Mich., 1951-67; Fulbright lectr. U. Turku and U. Abo, Finland, 1959-60; prof., chmn. dept. math. Western Mich. U., Kalamazoo, 1967-78, dean Coll. Arts and Sci., 1978-88, assoc. v.p., 1988-90, provost, 1990-91; cons., lectr. probability and random processes. Author: Elementary Statistics, 1961; (with R.L. Disney) Probability and Random Processes for Engineers and Scientists, 1970, Probability and Random Processes, 1985; contbr. articles to profl. jours. Mem. Math. Assn. Am. (sect. chmn. 1969-70), Inst. Math. Statistics, ACLU. Home: 3745 Tartan Cir Portage MI 49024-7890 Office: Western Mich U Dept Math And Statistics Kalamazoo MI 49008*

CLARKE, SIR ARTHUR CHARLES, author; b. Minehead, Somerset, Eng., Dec. 16, 1917; s. Charles Wright and Norah (Willis) C.; m. Marilyn Mayfield, June 15, 1953 (div. 1964). B.Sc. in Physics and Math. with 1st class honors, King's Coll., London, 1948; D.Sc. (hon.), Beaver Coll., 1971, U. Moratuwa, 1979; D.Litt. (hon.), U. Bath, Eng., 1988, U. Liverpool, Eng., 1995, U. Hong Kong, Beijing, 1996. Auditor British Civil Service, His Majesty's Exchequer and Audit Dept., London, 1936-41; asst. editor Science Abstracts Inst. of Elec. Engineers, London, 1949-50; lectr., author, 1951—; chancellor U. Moratuwa, Sri Lanka, 1979—; Vikram Sarabhai prof. Phys. Research Lab., Ahmedabad, India, 1980; underwater explorer, photographer Great Barrier Reef of Australia and coast of Ceylon, 1954-64; commentator with Walter Cronkite Apollo missions, 1968-70; dir. Rocket Pub. Co., Underwater Safaris, Sri Lanka; founder Arthur C. Clarke Centre for Modern Technologies, Sri Lanka, 1984—; trustee Inst. Integral Edn.; fellow Franklin Inst., 1971, King's Coll., 1977, Inst. of Robotics, Carnegie-Mellon U., 1981; lectr. U.S. and Britain, 1957-74; bd. dirs. Nat. Space Soc., Space Generation Found., Internat. Astronomical Union, Planetary Soc., Rocket Pub. Co., Eng., Underwater Safaris, Sri Lanka; chmn. Second Internat. Astronautics Congress, London, 1951; moderator "Space Flight Report to the Nation", N.Y., 1961; fgn. assoc. Nat. Acad. Engring. (U.S.); mem. adv. coun. Internat. Sci. Policy Found., Fauna Internat., Sri Lanka, Earth Trust. Author: (non-fiction) Interplanetary Flight, 1950, The Exploration of Space, 1951 (Internat. Fantasy award 1952), The Young Traveller in Space, 1953 (pub. as Going Into Space, 1954), (with R.A. Smith) The Exploration of the Moon, 1955, The Coast of Coral, 1956, The Making of a Moon, 1957, The Reefs of Taprobane, 1957, The Scottie Book of Space Travel, 1957, (with Mike Wilson) Boy Beneath the Sea, 1958, Voice Across the Sea, 1958, The Challenge of the Spaceship, 1959, The Challenge of the Sea, 1960, (with Wilson) The First Five Fathoms, 1960, (with Wilson) Indian Ocean Adventure, 1961, Profiles of the Future, 1962, The Treasure of the Great Reef, 1964, (with Wilson) Indian Ocean Treasure, 1964, (with editors of Life mag.) Man and Space, 1964, Voices from the Sky, 1965, The Promise of Space, 1968, (with astronauts) First on the Moon, 1970, Report on Planet Three, 1972, (with Chesley Bonestell) Beyond Jupiter, 1972, The View from Serendip, 1977, (with Simon Welfare and John Fairley) Arthur C. Clarke's Mysterious World, 1980, Ascent to Orbit, 1984, 1984: Spring-A Choice of Futures, 1984, (with Welfare and Fairley) Arthur C. Clarke's World of Strange Powers, 1984, (with Peter Hyams) The Odyssey File, 1985, Arthur C. Clarke's July 20, 2019: Life in the 21st Century, 1986, Arthur C. Clarke's Chronicles of the Strange and Mysterious, 1987, Astounding Days, 1989, Opus 700, 1990, How the World Was One, 1992, (with Welfare and Fairley) Arthur C. Clarke's A-Z of Mysteries, 1993, By Space Possessed, 1993, The Snows of Olympus, 1994, Front Line of Discovery: Science on the Brink of Tomorrow, 1994, Greetings, Carbon-based Bipeds, 1999; (fiction) The Sands of Mars, 1951, Prelude to Space, 1951, Islands in the Sky, 1952, Against the Fall of Night, 1953, Childhood's End, 1953, Expedition to Earth, 1953, Earthlight, 1955, Reach For Tomorrow, 1956, The City and the Stars, 1956, Tales from the White Hart, 1957, The Deep Range, 1957, The Other Side of the Sky, 1958, Across the Sea of Stars, 1959, A Fall of Moondust, 1961, From the Oceans, from the Stars, 1962, Tales of Ten Worlds, 1962, Dolphin Island, 1963, Glide Path, 1963, Prelude to Mars, 1965, The Nine Billion Names of God, 1967, (with Stanley Kubrick) 2001: A Space Odyssey, 1968, The Final Odyssey, 1997, The Lion of Comarre and Against the Fall of Night, 1968, The Wind from the Sun, 1972, Of Time and Stars, 1972, The Lost Worlds of 2001, 1972, Rendezvous with Rama, 1973 (Nebula award Sci. Fiction Writers Am. 1973, Hugo award World Sci. Fiction Conv. 1974, John W. Campbell Meml. award Sci. Fiction Rsch. Assn. 1974, Jupiter award Instructors of Sci. Fiction in Higher Edn. 1974), The Best of Arthur C. Clarke, 1973, Imperial Earth, 1975, The Fountains of Paradise, 1979 (Nebula award Sci. Fiction Writers Am. 1980, Hugo award World Sci. Fiction Conv. 1980), 2010: Odyssey Two, 1982, The Sentinel, 1983, Selected Works, 1985, The Songs of Distant Earth, 1986, 2061: Odyssey Three, 1988, (with Gentry Lee) Cradle, 1988, A Meeting with Medusa, 1988, (with Lee) Rama II, 1989, Tales from Planet Earth, 1989, (with Gregory Benford) Beyond the Fall of Night, 1990, Ghost from the Grand Banks, 1990, (with Lee) Garden of Rama, 1991, More Than One Universe, 1991, The Hammer of God, 1993, (with Lee) Rama Revealed: The Ultimate Encounter, 1994, (with Mike McQuay) Richter 10, 1996, 3001: The Final Odyssey, 1997, (with Mike-Kube-McDowell) Trigger, 1999; screenwriter: (films) (with Stanley Kubrick) 2001: A Space Odyssey, 1968 (Academy award nomination best original screenplay 1968, Second Internat. Film Festival Spl. award 1969); writer, host: (TV series) Arthur C. Clarke's Mysterious World, 1980, Arthur C. Clarke's World of Strange Powers, 1984, Mysterious Universe, 1994; actor: (films) Beddagama, 1979; editor: Time Probe: The Science in Science Fiction, 1966, The Coming of the Space Age, 1967, Three for Tomorrow, 1972, The Science Fiction Hall of Fame Vol. III, 1982. With Lindbergh Award Noms. Com. Served to flight lt. RAF, 1941-46. Recipient Presdl. award U. Ill., 1997. Fellow Royal Astron. Soc., Royal Soc. Arts; mem. Brit. Interplanetary Soc. (chmn. 1947-50, 53), Internat. Council Integrative Studies, AIAA, Inst. Engrs. Sri Lanka (named hon. fellow 1983), Sri Lanka Astron. Soc., Royal Astron. Soc., Assn. Brit. Sci. Writers (life), Internat. Acad. Astronautics, World Acad. Art and Sci., Nat. Space Inst. (dir.), Brit. Sci. Fiction Assn. (pres.), Royal Soc. Arts, Brit. Sub-Aqua Club, Brit. Astron. Assn., H.G. Wells Soc. (hon. v.p.), Sci. Fiction Writers Am., Internat. Sci. Writers Assn., Sci. Fiction Found., Soc. Authors (mem. coun.), Am. Astronautical Assn., Am. Assn. for Advancement of Sci., Nat. Acad. Engring., Third World Acad. of Scis. (assoc. fellow), Sri Lanka Animal Welfare Assn., Sri Lanka Assn. Advancement Sci., Sri Lanka Nat. Inst. Paraplegics, Astron. Soc. Haringey, Soc. Satellite Profls. (hon. chmn., Hall of Fame 1987), Nat. Space Soc. (bd. dirs., R.A. Heinlein Meml. award 1990), Royal Asiatic Soc., Astron. Soc. Pacific, Nat. Acad. Engring. (fgn. assoc.), U.N. Assn. Sri Lanka (hon. life pres.). Office: David Higham Assocs 5 Lower John St Golden Sq London W1R 4HA, England

CLARKE, CHARLES FENTON, lawyer; b. Hillsboro, Ohio, July 25, 1916; s. Charles F. and Margaret (Patton) C.; m. Virginia Schoppenhorst, Apr. 3, 1945 (dec. July 1989); children: Elizabeth, Margaret, Jane, Charles Fenton, IV; m. Lesley Wells, Nov. 13, 1998. AB summa cum laude, Washington and Lee U., Lexington, Va., 1938; LLB, U. Mich., 1940; LLD (hon.), Cleve. State U., 1971. Bar: Mich. 1940, Ohio 1946. Pvt. practice Detroit, 1942, Cleve., 1946—; ptnr. firm Squire, Sanders & Dempsey, 1957—, adminstr. litigation dept., 1979-85; trustee Cleve. Legal Aid Soc., 1959-67; pres. Nat. Assn. R.R. Trial Counsel, 1966-68; life mem. 6th Circuit Jud. Conf.; chmn. legis. com. Cleve. Welfare Fedn., 1961-68; master bencher Celebrezze Inn of Ct., 1991—; bd. dirs. Wheeling and Lake Erie R.R. Co. Pres. alumni bd. dirs. Washington and Lee U., 1970-72; pres. bd. dirs. Free Med. Clinic Greater Cleve., 1970-86; trustee Cleve. Citizens League, 1956-62, Cleve. chpt. ACLU, 1986-93, Cleve. Works Inc., 1995—; bd. dirs. citizens adv. bd. Cuyahoga County (Ohio) Juvenile Ct., 1970-73; bd. dirs. George Jr. Republic, Greenville, Pa., 1970-73, Bowman Tech. Sch., Cleve., 1970-91; vice chmn. Cleve. Crime Commn., 1973-75; exec. com. Cuyahoga County Rep. Orgn., 1950—; councilman Bay Village, Ohio, 1948-53; pres., trustee Cleve. Hearing and Speech Ctr., 1957-62, Laurel Sch., 1962-72, Fedn. Cmty. Progress, 1984-90; mem. planning commn. Cleveland Heights, 1994—. Fellow Am. Coll. Trial Lawyers; mem. Greater Cleve. Bar Assn. (trustee 1983-86), Cleve. Civil War Round Table (pres. 1968), Cleve. Zool. Soc. (dir. 1970), Phi Beta Kappa. Presbyterian. Clubs: Skating, Union (Cleve.); Tavern, Rowfant. Home: 4566 Tangleberry Ln NE Bainbridge Is WA 98110-2057 Office: Squire Sanders & Dempsey 4900 Key Tower 127 Public Sq Cleveland OH 44114-1304

CLARKE, CORDELIA KAY KNIGHT MAZUY, managment executive, consultant; b. Springfield, Mo., Nov. 22, 1938; d. William Horace and Charline (Bentley) Knight; m. Logan Clarke, Jr., July 22, 1978; children by previous marriage—Katharine Michelle Mazuy, Christopher Knight Mazuy. AB with honors in English, U. N.C., 1960; MS in Statistics, N.C. State U., 1962. Statistician Research Triangle Inst., Durham, N.C., 1960-63; statis. cons. Arthur D. Little, Inc., Cambridge, Mass., 1963-67; dir. mktg. planning and analysis Polaroid Corp., Cambridge, 1967-70; dir. mktg. and bus. planning Transaction Tech. Inc., Cambridge, 1970-72; pres. Mazuy Assocs., Boston, 1972-73; v.p. Nat. Shawmut Bank, Boston, 1973-74; sr. v.p., dir. mktg. Shawmut Corp., 1974-78; sr. v.p., dir. retail banking Shawmut Bank, 1976-78; v.p. corp. devel. Arthur D. Little, Inc., 1978-79; v.p. Conn. Gen. Life Ins. Co., 1979-85; pres. CIGNA Securities, 1983-85; chmn. Templeton, Inc., 1985-92, 95—; exec. v.p. McGraw-Hill Inc., 1988-90; pres. micromarketing divsn. ADVO, 1990-95; faculty Williams Sch. Banking; adv. com. Bur. of Census, 1978-84; bd. dirs. Guardian Life Ins. Co., Providence Jour. Co., Age Wave, Inc., Cybex, Inc.; tchr. Amos Tuck Grad. Sch. Bus., Dartmouth Coll., 1964-65, exec.-in-residence, 1978, 80; bd. overseers, 1979-85; exec.-in-residence Wheaton Coll., 1978; vis. prof. Simmons Grad. Sch. Mgmt., 1978; mem. schs. adv. coun. Bank Mktg. Assn., 1976-78; mem. corp. adv. bd. Hartford Nat. Bank & Trust Co., 1980-87. Columnist Am. Banker, 1976-78. Mem. Mass. Gov.'s Commn. on Status of Women, 1977-79; bd. corporators Babson Coll., 1977-80; adv. bd. Boston Mayor's Office Cultural Affairs, 1977-79; bd. dirs. McGraw-Hill, Inc., 1976-88, Blue Shield of Mass., 1976-79, Greater Hartford Arts Coun., 1979-93; trustee Children's Mus. Hartford, 1980-82; corporator Inst. of Living, 1981-92; regent U. Hartford, 1982—; bd. dirs. Hartford Art Sch., 1982-94, Hartford Stage Co., 1985—, Manhattan Theatre Club, 1988-91, Inst. for Future, 1988-92, N.Y. Internat. Festival of Arts, 1988-91, Goodspeed Opera, 1990—, Inst. Design, 1990-98, Aeroflex Found., 1972—. Mem. Internat. Womens Forum, Power 10, Phi Beta Kappa, Phi Kappa Phi, Kappa Alpha Theta. Home and Office: 89 River Rd East Haddam CT 06423-1462

CLARKE, CORNELIUS WILDER, religious organization administrator, minister; b. White Plains, N.Y., May 11, 1935; s. Cornelius Wilder and Margaret (Sutherland) C. BS, Nyack Coll., 1957; B of Div., Gordon Divinity Sch., 1960; MDiv, Gordon Conwell Theol. Sem., 1978. Ordained minister 1964. Pastor Missionary Alliance Ch., Bennington, Vt., 1960-65, Rock Hill Alliance Ch., Boston, 1965-73; sr. pastor Cranford (N.J.) Alliance Ch., 1973-76; dir. personnel Christian & Missionary Alliance, Nyack, N.Y., 1976-78; sr. pastor Simpson Meml. Ch., Nyack, N.Y., 1978-89; dist. supt. New Eng. Dist. of Christian & Missionary Alliance, South Easton, Mass., 1989-97; interim pastor Hillside Chapel, Beaver Creek, Ohio, 1997-99, sr. pastor, 1999—; trustee Nyack Coll., 1989—. Avocations: golf, sailing, backpacking, fishing, travel. Office: Hillside Chapel 3515 Shakertown Rd Beaver Creek OH 45430-1423*

CLARKE, DAVID H., industrial products executive; b. 1941; married. Vice chmn. bd. Hanson Pub. Ltd. Co., 1965-83; dep. chmn., pres., CEO Hanson Industries N.Am. (subs. Hanson Trust PLC, London), 1978-95, also bd. dirs.; chmn., pres., CEO US Industries Inc., 1995—. Office: US Industries Inc 101 Wood Ave S Iselin NJ 08830-2703*

CLARKE, EDWARD NIELSEN, engineering science educator; b. Providence, Apr. 25, 1925; s. Edward O.A. and Edith (Nielsen) C.; m. Vivian Constance Bergquist, July 23, 1949; children—Sandra J., David E., Allan R., Jeffrey B. BS, Brown U., 1945, PhD, 1951; MS, Harvard, 1947, M.Engring. Sci., 1948. Mem. tech. staff, sect. head for semiconductors, physics lab. Sylvania Electric Products Co., Bayside, N.Y., 1950-56; group head for research Sperry Semiconductor div. Sperry Rand Corp., Norwalk, Conn., 1956-59; v.p. ops. and dir. Nat. Semiconductor Corp., Danbury, Conn., 1959-65; assoc. dean faculty, assoc. dean grad. studies, dir. research Worcester Poly. Inst., 1965-86, prof. engring. scis., 1968-94, dir. Ctr. Solar Electrification, 1986-94, prof. emeritus, 1995—; tri-coll. coordinator research Clark U.-Holy Cross Coll.-Worcester Poly. Inst., 1974-85; co-founder Nat. Semiconductor Corp.; founder solar electrification ctr. Worcester Poly. Inst. Trustee Upsala Coll., East Orange, N.J., 1971-74. Served with USNR, 1943-46. Recipient Brown U. Engring. Alumni medal, 1998. IEEE, Am. Phys. Soc., Sigma Xi (past chpt. pres.), Tau Beta Pi. Lutheran. Clubs: Rotarian (Worcester), Torch (Worcester). Achievements include patents and inventions in semiconductor technology; pioneering development of solar powered racing car. Home: 85 Richards Ave Paxton MA 01612-1123 Office: Worcester Poly Inst Dept Interdisciplinary and Global Studies Worcester MA 01609 *Helping others to achieve has been my own principal achievement. Retain mobility and be willing to use one's skills wherever they are needed. Do not become too comfortable and secure. Move on to find new challenges. Stay young with variety in one's life and a healthy use of the out-of-doors.*

CLARKE, EDWARD OWEN, JR., lawyer; b. Balt., Dec. 19, 1929; s. Edward Owen and Agnes Oakford C.; m. P. Rhea Parker, Dec. 18, 1954; children: Deborah Jeanne, Catherine Ann, Carolyn Agnes, Edward Owen III. AB magna cum laude, Loyola Coll., Balt., 1950; JD with honors, U. Md., 1956. Bar: Md. 1956, U.S. Dist. Ct. Md. 1956. Law clk. U.S. Dist. Ct. Md., 1956-57; assoc. Smith, Somerville & Case, Balt., 1957-62, ptnr., 1962-71; ptnr. Piper & Marbury, Balt., 1971-94, mem. policy and mgmt. com., 1981-94, mng. ptnr., 1987-90, co-chmn. bus. div., 1991-94; mem. Gov.'s Com. to Study Blue Sky Law, 1961; mem. Md. Commn. on Revision Corp. Law, 1965-66. Bd. dirs. Bon Secours Hosp., 1964-73, sec., 1968-73; bd. dirs. Hosp. Cost Analysis Svc., 1966-81; bd. pres. mem. exec. coun. Md. Hosp. Assn., 1968-74, chmn. com. on legislation, 1971-73, treas., 1973; trustee St. Mary's Coll. Md., 1983-94, chmn. bd., 1988-94; trustee St. Mary's Sem., U. Balt., 1986-89, Loyola H.S., Balt., 1984-90, Hannah More Ctr., 1980-83; bd. dirs. Helix Health Sys., Inc., 1995-98, Med Star Health, 1998—; mem. Md. Higher Edn. Commn., 1994—, chmn. 1995—. Lt. USNR, 1952-55. Mem. ABA, Md. State Bar Assn. (mem. sect. coun. corp., banking and bus. law sect. 1968-71, chmn. 1970-71), Wednesday Law Club (sec., treas. 1984-88, v.p. 1988-89, pres. 1990), Center Club (Balt., bd. govs. 1988-94), Order of Coif, Order of the Ark and the Dove, Phi Beta Kappa, Alpha Sigma Nu, Tau Kappa Alpha.

CLARKE, FRANK WILLIAM, advertising agency executive; b. Quebec, Que., Can., Apr. 16, 1942; came to U.S., 1946; s. William Frank Clarke and Tolly (English) Wing; m. Barbara Jean Dreher, Mar. 1966 (div. Sept. 1975); children: Kathleen Julienne Clarke Smith, Lori Christine Clarke Genovese; m. Vera Gretel Thol, Nov. 14, 1977; stepchildren: Teo Capriles, Gretel Capriles. Student, U. Va., 1958-61; BS in Commerce, NYU, 1964; MS in Journalism, Northwestern U., 1965. Staff asst., then asst. account exec. Grey Advt. Inc., N.Y.C., 1969-70, account exec., 1970-73; account dir. Grey Advt. Inc., Caracas, Venezuela, 1973-75, v.p. account svcs., 1975-78, v.p., area dir., 1978-82; v.p., area dir. Grey Advt. Inc., N.Y.C., 1982-88, sr. v.p., area dir., 1988-93, exec. v.p., area dir., 1993—. Mem. product mktg. com. U.S. Com. for UNICEF, N.Y.C., 1989-93, nat. adv. coun., 1991-93, bd. dirs., 1994—, mem. exec. com., 1996—. Capt. U.S. Army, 1966-69. Mem. Am. Assn. Advt. Agys. (internat. com. 1990—, chmn. 1993-95), Internat. Advt. Assn. (bd. dirs. N.Y. chpt. 1987-92), Racquet and Tennis Club N.Y. Republican. Avocations: gardening, cross-country skiing. Office: Grey Advt Inc 777 3rd Ave New York NY 10017-1401

CLARKE, FRED W., III, architect, architectural firm executive; b. Houston, Feb. 24, 1947. Grad. with honors, U. Tex., 1970. Registered architect, Conn., Calif., Del., Fla., Iowa, Ill., La., N.Y., N.C., Ohio, Tex., Washington, Wyo.; 1st class registered architect, Japan. With Gruen Assocs., L.A., 1970-77; project prin., collaborating designer, co-founder, mgr. Cesar Pelli & Assocs., New Haven, Conn., 1977—; instr. Sch. Architecture UCLA, 1972-76, Sch. Architecture Rice U., Houston, 1976; vis. critic arch. Yale U., 1977-82; keynote spkr. VIII Bienal de Arquitectura de Quito; guest lectr., spkr. Iberian-Am. Forum of Architecture and Urbanism of São Paulo, Profl. Design-Build Conf., Asia Soc.; guest critic Colegio Arquitecos de Chile, others; chmn. design juries, profl. panels Urban Land Inst. Prin. works include Mus. Modern Art expansion and renovation, U.S. Embassy in Toyko, Herring Hall Rice U., Carnegie Hall Tower in N.Y.C., World Financial Ctr. in N.Y.C., terminal at Wash. Nat. Airport, Petronas Towers in Kuala Lumpur, corp. hdqrs., hosps., rsch. labs., acad. bldgs., mus., performing arts ctrs., office towers, airports. MacDowell Colony fellow, 1998. Fellow AIA (chmn. design juries, profl. panels, Firm award 1989). Office: Cesar Pelli & Assocs Inc care Jillian Brown 1056 Chapel St New Haven CT 06510-2402

CLARKE, FREDERIC B., III, risk analysis consultant; b. Portsmouth, N.H., Aug. 31, 1942; s. Fredric B. and Elizabeth Jane (Leach) C.; m. Dorothy Hoff; children by previous marriage: Frederic B., Claire Buchner; stepchildren: Peter Edward Stambaugh, Elisabeth Marie Stambaugh. Student, U. Mo., 1960-62; A.B., Washington U., 1966; A.M., Harvard U., 1968, Ph.D., 1971. Research chemist Monsanto Co., 1971-73; mktg. supr., 1973-74; asst. to dir. Center for Fire Research, Nat. Bur. Standards, Dept. Commerce, 1974-76, dep. dir., 1977-78; dir. Center for Fire Research, Nat. Engring. Lab., 1978-81; pres. Benjamin/Clarke Assocs. Inc., 1981—; chmn. U.S.-Japan Joint Panel on Fire Research and Safety, 1979-80; mem. com. on fire toxicology Nat. Acad. Scis., 1985-86; U.S. expert Internat. Standards Orgn. Com. on Fire Safety, Internat. Electrotech. Commn., com. on fire hazard testing. Contbr. articles to profl. jours. Legis. asst. to Sen. John C. Culver, 1976-77, also to Congressman Jim Wright. NSF fellow, 1966-69; Congl. fellow, 1976-77. Mem. ASTM (com. on rsch. and tech.

planning 1986-88, chmn. 1987-89, bd. dirs. 1990-93), Am. Chem. Soc., Nat. Fire Protection Assn., Congl. Fellows Assn. (pres. 1981), Phi Beta Kappa, Sigma Xi. Patentee in field. Office: Benjamin/Clarke Assocs PO Box 10624 Arlington VA 22210-1624

CLARKE, FREDERICK JAMES, civil engineer; b. Little Falls, N.Y., Mar. 1, 1915; s. Edward James and Grace Ellen (Zoller) C.; m. Isabel Morrison Van Slyke, Sept. 15, 1938; children—Warren E., Isabel V., Nancy S. B.S., U.S. Mil. Acad., 1937; M.S.C.E., Cornell U., 1940; postgrad., Harvard U. Bus. Sch., 1954; grad., Nat. War Coll., 1957. Commd. 2d lt. U.S. Army, 1937, advanced through grades to lt. gen., 1969; mgr. Hanford Ops., Richland, Wash., 1945-47; dist. engr. Pakistan, 1957-59; engr. commr. D.C., 1960-63; comdt. U.S. Army Engring. Sch., Ft. Belvoir, Va., 1965-66; chief engr. U.S. Army, Washington, 1969-73; ret., 1973; exec. dir. Nat. Commn. on Water Quality, Washington, 1973-76; cons. engr. Tippetts-Abbett-McCarthy-Stratton, Washington, 1973-79. Decorated Legion of Merit, D.S.M. with oak leaf cluster. Mem. Nat. Acad. Engring., Nat. Soc. Profl. Engrs., ASCE, Am. Acad. Environ. Engrs., Am. Public Works Assn. (hon.), Am. Water Resources Assn. (hon.), U.S. Com. on Large Dams, Soc. Am. Mil. Engrs. (hon.), Assn. U.S. Army, AIA (hon.), Permanent Internat. Assn. Navigational Congresses. Clubs: Chevy Chase, Cosmos. Home: 9110 Belvoir Woods Pky Apt 116 Fort Belvoir VA 22060-2717

CLARKE, GARRY EVANS, composer, educator, musician, administrator; b. Moline, Ill., Mar. 19, 1943; s. Clarence Henderson and Gladys Arlene (Hokinson) C.; m. Melissa Jane Naul, May 24, 1975; children: Catharine van Gelder, Margaret Elizabeth Jane. MusB summa cum laude, Cornell Coll., Mount Vernon, Iowa, 1965; MusM, Yale U., 1968; LittD (hon.), Washington Coll., 1988. Asst. prof. music Washington Coll., Chestertown, Md., 1968-73; assoc. prof., 1973-79; prof. Washington Coll., Chestertown, 1979—, dean coll., 1977-83, acting pres., 1981-82; Am. liaison Harrison & Harrison Ltd., Durham, Eng. Composer symphonic, chamber, vocal, piano and organ music and opera; lectr. and recitalist (U.S., Europe): Am. music; condr. piano workshops; opera coach; organist and choir master, St. Paul's Episcopal Parish, Centerville, Md., 1975-88; Chester Parish, Chestertown, Md., 1988—; author: Essays on American Music, 1977; contbr. articles, revs. to profl. jours.; co-editor: Varied Air and Variations (Ives), 1971; editor: Charles Ives. Soc. publs. Trustee Coun. Econ. Edn. Md.; bd. dirs. Talbot Chamber Orch. Ford Found. fellow, 1965, Woodrow Wilson fellow, 1965; Carnegie Found. rsch. grantee, 1964, NEH rsch. grantee, 1970; recipient Bronze medal Coun. for Advancement and Support of Edn., 1993. Mem. AAUP, Soc. Music Theory, Assn. Anglican Musicians, Sonneck Soc., Council Higher Edn. in Music, Am. Conf. Acad. Deans, Nat. Assn. Schs. Music, Am. Assn. Higher Edn., Yale Sch. Music Alumni Assn. (exec. com. 1975-80), Assn. Yale Alumni, Yale Club (N.Y.C.), Pi Kappa Lambda, Omicron Delta Kappa, Phi Delta Theta (adviser). Episcopalian. E-mail: garry.clarke@washcoll.edu. Home: Fairways 7775 Waterview Ln Chestertown MD 21620-9507 Office: Washington Coll 300 Washington Ave Chestertown MD 21620-1197

CLARKE, GARRY KENNETH CONNAL, geophysics educator; b. Hamilton, Ont., Can., Oct. 6, 1941; s. Kenneth Andrew Connal and Elna Marie (Skarin) C.; m. Julia Cruikshank, July 30, 1994; 1 child from previous marriage, Julian. BS, U. Alta., 1963; MA, U. Toronto, 1964, PhD, 1967. Cert. profl. geoscientist, 1992. Asst. prof. U. B.C., Vancouver, 1967-71, assoc. prof., 1971-77, prof., 1977—. Sci. editor Annals Glaciology jour., 1980; assoc. editor Jour. Geophys. Rsch., 1989-92; contbr. numerous articles to profl. jours. Fellow Royal Astron. Soc., Royal Soc. Can., Arctic Inst. N.Am. (chmn. 1979), Am. Geophys. Union; mem. Can. Geophys. Union (v.p. 1991-93, pres. 1993-95), Internat. Glaciological Soc. (v.p. 1987-90, pres. 1990-93, Richardson Medal 1998). Avocations: jazz piano, hiking, skiing. Office: U BC, Dept Earth & Ocean Scis, Vancouver, BC Canada V6T 1Z4

CLARKE, GARVEY ELLIOTT, educational association administrator, lawyer; b. Christ Church, Barbados, May 13, 1935; came to U.S., 1941; s. Elliott and Marion (Gibbs) C.; m. Yvonne E. Hayling, 1961; children: Wendy Y., Garvey H. AB, Dartmouth Coll., 1957; JD, N.Y. Law Sch., 1961. Bar: N.Y. 1963. Attorney legal dept. NBC, N.Y.C., 1963-65; v.p. A Better Chance, Inc., N.Y.C., 1965-75; pres. Nat. Fund for Minority Engring. Students, N.Y.C., 1975-82; v.p. Nat. Action Coun. for Minorities in Engring., N.Y.C., 1982-83; sr. assoc. Right Assocs., N.Y.C., 1983-85; dir. Morehouse Coll. Campaign The Oram Group, Inc., N.Y.C., 1985-86; dir. devel. Project Orbis, N.Y.C., 1986-87; dir. capital campaign United Negro Coll. Fund, N.Y.C., 1987-89; pres. Leadership Edn. and Devel. Program in Bus., Inc., N.Y.C., 1989—; cons. Edn. Assoc., Washington, 1968-70, Frantzreb and Pray, N.Y.C., 1968-71. Pres. Stuyford Action Coun., Bklyn., 1963-70, Black Alumni of Dartmouth Assn., Hanover, N.H., 1976-78; mem. Dartmouth Alumni Coun., Hanover, 1977-79; bd. dirs. Boys Club of N.Y., N.Y.C., 1970-92; active Greater Centennial A.M.E. Zion Ch. Mem. New York County Lawyers Assn., Dartmouth Lawyers Assn. Home: 33 Jordan Rd Hastings Hdsn NY 10706-3919 Office: LEAD Program in Bus Inc Ste 443 420 Lexington Ave Rm 443 New York NY 10170-0439

CLARKE, GEORGE ALTON, chemist, academic administrator, retired; b. N.Y.C., Apr. 4, 1933; s. Cecil Malcolm and Linda Clarke; m. Janice E. Avery, July 16, 1966; children: Jill Romy, Kristin Lynne. BS, CCNY, 1955; PhD, Penn. State U., 1960. Postdoctoral rschr. Columbia U., N.Y.C., 1960-62; asst. prof. SUNY, Buffalo, 1962-68; assoc. prof. Drexel U., Phila., 1968-71; assoc. prof. U. Miami, 1971-84, assoc. dean, 1978-84; dean Sch. Arts and Scis., Ctrl. Conn. State U., New Britain, 1984-97, spl. asst. to pres., 1997-98, emeritus, 1998—. Contbr. articles to profl. jours. Bd. dirs., v.p. New Britain C. of C., 1985-92; bd. dirs., pres. Human Resources Agy., New Britain, 1991-96; bd. dirs. Am. Savs. Bank, New Britain, 1994-98; bd. dirs., v.p. Substance Abuse Action Coun., New Britain, 1992-97. Mem. Am. Phys. Soc., Am. Chem. Soc., Sigma Xi. Avocations: swimming, gardening, hiking, tinkering, computers. Home: 88 Lincklaen St Cazenovia NY 13035-1031

CLARKE, HENRY LEE, foreign service officer, former ambassador; b. Ft. Benning, Ga., Nov. 15, 1941; s. Edwin Lee and Jane Iredell (Jones) C.; m. Kathleen Ann Smith, May 19, 1973 (div. 1996); children: Ann Marie, Edwin Lee; m. Elena Anatolyevna Fedyai, Jan. 8, 1997; children: Julia Chikerenda, Christopher Lee. AB, Dartmouth Coll., 1962; MPA, Harvard U., 1967. U.S. fgn. svc. officer Dept. State, 1967—; econ. counselor Am. Embassy, Moscow, 1982-85; dep. chief Am. Embassy, Bucharest, Romania, 1985-89; econ. counselor Am. Embassy, Tel Aviv, 1989-92; amb. to Uzbekistan, Am. Embassy, Tashkent, 1992-95; internat. affairs advisor Nat. War Coll., Washington, 1995-98; sr. advisor for property restituion in Europe, Dept. State, Washington, 1998—. Chmn. bd. Am. Sch., Bucharest, 1985-89, Tashkent Internat. Sch., 1994-95.

CLARKE, J. CALVITT, JR., federal judge; b. Harrisburg, Pa., Aug. 9, 1920; s. Joseph Calvitt and Helen Caroline (Mattson) C.; m. Mary Jane Cromer, Feb. 1, 1943 (dec.1985); children: Joseph Calvitt III, Martha Tiffany; m. Betty Ann Holladay, May 29, 1986. BS in Commerce, U. Va., 1945, JD, 1945. Bar: Va. 1944. Practiced in Richmond, Va., 1944-74; partner firm Bowles, Anderson, Boyd, Clarke & Herod, 1944-60; firm Sands Anderson, Marks and Clarke, 1960-74; judge U.S. Dist. Ct. (ea. dist.) Va., 1975-91, sr. judge, 1991—; mem. 4th Circuit Judicial Conf., 1963; hon. consul for Republic of Bolivia, 1959-75. Chmn. Citizen's Advisory Com. on Joint Water System for Henrico and Hanover counties, Va., 1968-69; mem. Mayor's Freedom Train Com., 1948-50; del. Young Republican Nat. Conv., Salt Lake City, 1949, Boston, 1951; chmn. Richmond (Va.) Republican Com., 1952-54; candidate for Congress, 1954; chmn. Va. 3d Dist. Rep. Com., 1955-58, 74-75, Va. State Rep. Conv., 1958—; co-founder Young Rep. Fedn. of Va., 1950, nat. committeeman, 1950-54, chmn., 1955; chmn. 3d dist. Speakers Bur., Nixon-Lodge campaign, 1960, mem. fin. com., 1960-74; chmn. Henrico County Republican Com., 1956-58; fin. chmn. 1956; pres. Couples Sunday Sch. class Second Presbyn. Ch., Richmond, Va., 1948-50, mem. bd. deacons, 1948-61, elder, 1964—; bd. dirs. Family Service Children's Aid Soc., 1948-61, Gambles Hill Community Center, 1950-60, Christian Children's Fund, Inc., 1960-67, Children, Inc., 1967-75, Norfolk Forum, 1978-83; mem. bd. of chancellors Internat. Consular Acad., 1965-75; trustee Henrico County Pub. Library, chmn., 1971-73. Fellow Va. Law Found.; mem. Va. State Bar (mem. 3rd dist. com. 1967-70, chmn. 1969-70), Richmond Bar Assn., Norfolk-Portsmouth Bar Assn., Va. Bar Assn., Thomas Jefferson Soc. of Alumni U. Va. Lile Law Soc., McGuires U. Sch. Alumni (pres. 1995-96), Am. Judicature Soc., ABA, Va. Bar Assn. (vice chmn. com. on cooperation with fgn. bars 1960-61), Richmond Jr. C. of C. (dir. 1946-50), Windmill Point Yacht Club, Westwood Racquet Club (pres. 1961-62), Commonwealth Club, Delta Theta Phi. Office: US Dist Ct 420 US Courthouse 600 Granby St Norfolk VA 23510-1915

CLARKE, JAMES WESTON, political science educator, writer; b. Elizabeth, Pa., Feb. 16, 1937; s. Alonzo Peterson and Beatrice (Weston) C.; m. Jeanne Nienaber; children—Julianne, Michael. BA, Washington and Jefferson Coll., 1962; MA, Pa. State U., 1964, PhD, 1968. Asst. prof. Fla. State U., 1967-71; assoc. prof. U. Ariz., Tucson, 1971-76, prof. polit. sci., 1976—; chmn. dept. U. Ariz., 1973-78. Author: American Assassins: The Darker Side of Politics, 1982, Last Rampage: The Escape of Gary Tison, 1988, On Being Mad or Merely Angry: John W. Hinckley Jr. and Other Dangerous People, 1990,l The Lineaments of Wrath: Race, Violent Crime, and American Culture, 1998. Served with USMC, 1955-58. Recipient James Gillespie Blaine prize Washington and Jefferson Coll., 1962, Matthew Brown Ringland prize, 1962, Burlington Northern Found. award for excellence in tchg., 1987, Golden Key Nat. Honor Soc. award for tchg., 1989, Social and Behavioral Scis. award for outstanding tchg., 1991, 96; Udall fellow, 1993; Fulbright scholar, Ireland, 1999. Mem. Am. Polit. Sci. Assn., Authors Guild Am. Home: 855 E Placita Leslie Tucson AZ 85718-1960 Office: U Ariz 315 Social Sci Bldg Tucson AZ 85721

CLARKE, JAY A., art historian, curator; b. Lake Forest, Ill., May 16, 1966. BA, Coll. of Holy Cross, 1988; MA, Brown U., 1991, PhD, 1999. NEA intern Art Inst. Chgo., 1991-92, rsch. asst., 1992-95, asst. curator, 1997—. Grantee Ferdinand Möller Found., Germany, 1996, Brown U. Rsch. & Travel grantee, 1996. Mem. Coll. Art Assn., Historians German and Ctrl. European Art, Historians 19th Century Art, NOW, German Am. C. of C. Office: Art Inst Chgo 111 S Michigan Ave Chicago IL 60603

CLARKE, JAY MARION, editor, author; b. Jacksonville, Fla., Oct. 6, 1927; s. Charles Williamson and Gabrielle Jeanne (Creusot) C.; m. Patricia Lee Hughes, Nov. 2, 1963; children: Anne Patrice Clarke-Eriksson, Dougan Hughes, Paul Creusot. BA, U. Miami, 1950. Copy editor Fairchild Pub., N.Y.C., 1951-55; Sunday, travel editor Miami (Fla.) Herald, 1955—. Contbr. articles to newspaper and mags. Mem. Soc. Am. Travel Writers (trustee Found. 1995—). Home: 1001 Sunset Dr Coral Gables FL 33143-6129 Office: Miami Herald 1 Herald Plz Miami FL 33132-1693

CLARKE, JEFF, television station executive. BA, U. N.C., Greensboro; MA, U. Wis. CEO, gen. mgr. KUHT, Houston, 1992—. Home: KUHT 4513 Cullen Blvd Houston TX 77004*

CLARKE, JERROLD, architect; b. N.Y.C., Apr. 29, 1942; s. Fred and Gussie (Cohen) C.; m. Dianne Sawyer, Dec. 27, 1995; children: Michael, David, Steven; stepchildren: Kim, Caryn. BS, Pratt Inst., N.Y.C., 1966. Registered architect, N.Y. Asst. architect N.Y.C. Bd. Edn., 1964-67; architect Schuman, Lichtenstein, Claman & Efron, N.Y.C., 1969—, ptnr., 1985—. Coach L.I. Jr. Soccer League, 1977-90, Jericho Athletic Assn., 1978, 79; bd. dirs. Birchwood Civic Assn., Jericho, 1981-83; bd. dirs. Temple Or Elohim, Jericho, 1982-84, pres., 1985-87, chmn. bd. dirs., 1987-95; bd. trustees Queens (N.Y.) Museum of Art. Served to capt. U.S. Army, 1967-69, Vietnam. Decorated Bronze Star with combat V and one oak leaf cluster; honoree United Jewish Appeal, 1988. Mem. AIA, Constrn. Specifications Inst. Avocations: skiing, tennis, coaching soccer. Home: 9 Pony Cir Roslyn Heights NY 11577-1958 Office: Schuman Lichtenstein Claman 841 Broadway Fl 7 New York NY 10003-4785

CLARKE, JOHN, physics educator; b. Cambridge, Eng., Feb. 10, 1942; came to U.S., 1968; s. Victor Patrick and Ethel May (Blowers) C.; m. Grethe Fog Pedersen, Sept. 15, 1979; 1 child, Elizabeth Jane. BA, Cambridge U., 1964, MA, 1968, PhD, 1968. Postdoctoral scholar U. Calif.-Berkeley, 1968-69, asst. prof. physics, 1969-71, assoc. prof., 1971-73, prof., 1973—; chair experimental physics Luis W. Alvarez Meml., 1994-99. Contbr. numerous articles to profl. jours. Recipient Charles Vernon Boys prize Brit. Inst. Physics, 1977, award Soc. Exploration Geophysics, 1979, Outstanding Teaching award U. Calif., 1983, Fritz London award for low temperature physics, 1987, Fed. Lab. Consortium award for excellence in technology transfer, 1992, div. materials scis. award in solid state physics Dept. Energy, 1986, 92, IEEE U.S. Activities Bd. Electrotechnology Transfer award, 1995, Comstock prize Physics NAS, 1999; fellow Sloan Found., 1970-72, Miller Inst. for Basic Rsch., 1975-76, 94-95; Guggenheim fellow, 1977-78; named Calif. Scientist of Yr., 1987. Fellow AAAS, Royal Soc. London, Am. Phys. Soc. (Joseph F. Keithley Advances in Measurement Sci. award 1998). Office: U Calif Dept Physics Berkeley CA 94720-7300

CLARKE, JOHN CLEM, artist; b. Bend, Oreg., June 6, 1937; s. Eugene and Wilma Mary (Owen) C.; m. Jane Dee Purucker. B.S., U. Oreg., 1960; student, Oreg. State U., U. Mexico, Mexico City Coll. Exhbns. include Whitney Mus., N.Y.C., 1967-73, Realism Now, N.Y. Cultural Center, Tokyo Biennale, Mus. Modern Art, N.Y.C., USA Bicentennial, U.S. Dept. Interior; represented in permanent collections, Whitney Mus. Am. Art, Met. Mus., Mus. Modern Art, Dallas Mus. Fine Arts, Va. Mus. Fine Arts, William Rockhill Nelson Gallery Art, Kansas City, Mo., Balt. Mus. Fine Arts, Hirshorn Mus., Washington, Utrecht Mus., The Netherlands, Bklyn. Mus., Milw. Arts Ctr., Indpls. Mus. Art, Fort Worth Art Ctr., Fogg Mus., Boston, L.A. County Mus. Art, Akron (Ohio) Art Inst., U. Calif., Berkeley, Flint (Mich.) Inst., Sch. of Art, Syracuse (N.Y) U., U. Ga. at Atlanta, Security Pacific Nat. Bank, N.Y.C., Security Pacific Nat. Bank, World Hdqrs., L.A., Chase Manhattan Bank, N.Y.C., Post Keyes Garner, Inc., Chgo., Wichita State U., Westmoreland County Mus., Greenburg, Pa., Kresge Co., Detroit, Am. Republic Ins. Co., Des Moines, Lewis and Clark Coll., Portland, Oreg. *

CLARKE, JOHN M., lawyer. BS, Rutgers U., 1963; JD, NYU, 1968. Bar: Ill. 1968, Wis. 1971, N.Y. 1975. Atty. AT&T, 1968-71, Wis. Telephone Co., 1971-74, N.Y. Telephone Co., 1974-78, AT&T, 1978-79; gen. atty. N.Y. Telephone Co., 1979-83, v.p. and gen. couns., 1983-94; v.p. Law NYNEX Corp., 1994-97; of counsel Winthrop, Stimson, Putnam & Roberts, N.Y.C., 1998—. Office: Winthrop Stimson Putnam & Roberts 1 Battery Park Plz Fl 31 New York NY 10004-1490*

CLARKE, JOHN PATRICK, retired newspaper publisher; b. Mattoon, Ill., Oct. 29, 1930; s. Patrick Joseph Clarke and Lucille (Hennebry) Stoeckinger; m. Roberta June Steiner, July 25, 1959 (div. 1984); children: Shannon, Dana; m. Sheila Cordill, June 24, 1995. BS, Ind. U., 1958; MBA, Harvard U., 1962. With contr.'s staff Ethyl Corp., N.Y.C., 1958-60; bus. mgr. State Jour.-Register, Springfield, Ill., 1962-68, pub., 1968-96; ret., 1996. Sec., bd. dirs. Ill. Ambassadors, 1986—; mem. Atty. Registration and Disciplinary Commn., 1987—; chmn bd. dirs. State Farm Rail Classic (LPGA tour). With USN, 1949-50, 52-54. Mem. Am. Newspaper Pubs. Assn., Inland Daily Press Assn., Kensington Golf and Country Club, Sangamo Club (pres. 1978-79). Avocations: sailing, golf. Address: 4255 Gulf Shore Blvd N Naples FL 34103-2225

CLARKE, JOHN RODNEY, surgeon; b. Ft. Riley, Kans., Apr. 24, 1943; s. Alfred Nelson and Kathryn Helen (Brossard) C. BA, Wesleyan U., Middletown, Conn., 1965; MD, U. Pa., 1968. Diplomate Am. Bd. Surgery. Intern and resident Presbyn.-St. Luke's Hosp., Chgo., 1968-70; resident St. Joseph Mercy Hosp., Ann Arbor, Mich., 1972-75; trauma fellow Boston City Hosp., 1975-76; instr. in surgery Med. Coll. Pa./Hahnemann U., Phila., 1976-77, asst. prof. surgery, 1977-80, assoc. prof., 1980-84, prof., 1984—; adj. prof. computer and info. sci. U. Pa., Phila., 1991—; mem. health care tech. study sect. U.S. Agy. for Health Care Policy and Rsch., Washington, 1990-92. Author: Surgical Judgment Using Decision Sciences, 1984; assoc. editor Theoretical Surgery, 1991-94; contbr. articles to profl. publs., chpt. to books. Maj. Med. Corps, U.S. Army, 1970-72. Recipient Resident Tour award Frederick A. Coller Surg. Soc., 1975, Samuel D. Gross prize for rsch. in surgery, 1983; Wellcome rsch. travel grantee Burroughs Wellcome Fund, 1984. Fellow ACS, Phila. Acad. Surgery (pres. elect 1999); mem. Am. Assn. Surgery of Trauma, Am. Med. Informatics Assn., Soc. for Medical Decision Making (v.p. 1989-90), Soc. Univ. Surgeons, Am. Assn. Artificial Intelligence, Internat. Soc. Surgery. Avocation: philosophy. Office: Med Coll Pa Hosp/Hahnemann U 3300 Henry Ave Philadelphia PA 19129-1121

CLARKE, JOHN TERREL, astrophysicist; b. Chgo., Mar. 4, 1952; s. Terrel Edward and Catherine Evelyn (Carr) C.; m. Cleda Elisabeth Clarke, 1997. BS in Physics, Denison U., 1974; MA in Physics, Johns Hopkins U., 1978, PhD in Physics, 1980. Rsch. physicist U. Calif., Berkeley, 1980-84; assoc. project scientist, Hubble Space Telescope NASA Marshall Space Flight Ctr., Huntsville, Ala., 1984-85; advanced instruments, project scientist NASA Goddard Space Flight Ctr., Greenbelt, Md., 1985-87; rsch. scientist U. Mich., Ann Arbor, 1987—; mem. Hubble Space Telescope user's com., NASA, 1996—. Assoc. editor: Jour. of Geophys. Rsch., 1997—, Icarus, 1997—; contbr. articles to profl. jours. Mem. Internat. Astron. Union, Am. Geophysical Union, Am. Astron. Soc. (div. planetary sci. com. 1997—), Sigma Pi Sigma. Home: 1078 Ferdon Rd Ann Arbor MI 48104-3631 Office: Dept Atmospheric Oceanic & Space Sci U Mich Ann Arbor MI 48109-2143

CLARKE, J(OSEPH) HENRY, dental educator, dentist; b. Salt Lake City, July 19, 1930; s. Emanuel Henry and Bertha Clara (Langton) C.; m. Linda Louise Maxfield, Apr. 8, 1953; children: Linda, Candice, Susan. Student U. Utah, 1948-50; M.S., Portland State Coll., 1989. D.M.D., U. Oreg., 1961. Practice gen. dentistry, Portland, Oreg., 1961-71, part time 1971—; mem. med. staff Woodland Park Hosp., Portland, 1963-74, chief dental service, 1970-71; supervising dentist Dental Hygiene Clinic, Oreg. Health Scis. U., Portland, 1971—, chair dept. behavioral sci., 1973—. Author videocassette and workbook: Dental Treatment of Family Members, 1977; contbr. chpt. to book. Served with U.S. Army, 1953-55. Recipient Hayden-Harris Contribution to Dental History award, 1992, Milton H. Erickson Sci. Excellence award, 1992. Fellow Am. Soc. Clin. Hypnosis; mem. AAAS, Am. Acad. History of Dentistry (pres. 1974-75), ADA, Soc. Clin. and Exptl. Hypnosis (ADA liaison 1984—), Portland Acad. Hypnosis (pres. 1983-84), Omicron Kappa Upsilon. Mormon. Office: Oregon Health Scis U 611 SW Campus Dr Portland OR 97201-3001*

CLARKE, JUANITA M. WAITERS, education educator; b. Forkland, Ala., Sept. 29, 1923; d. James Walter and Mary Ellen (McAlpine) Waiters; m. Charles Henry Clarke, Aug. 20, 1946; children: Charles Henry Jr., Charlotte Jean, Jacquelin Marie, Victoria Teresa, Carol Evangeline. BS cum laude, Xavier U., 1944; MA, U. Ala., 1967, EdS, 1974, PhD, 1979. Cert. secondary edn. tchr., Ala.; lic. profl. counselor. English tchr., counselor Holy Family High Sch., Birmingham, Ala., 1954-69; English tchr. Miles Coll., Birmingham, 1969-73, from asst. prof. edn. to assoc. prof., coord. secondary edn., 1974-86; English tchr. Lawson State Community Coll., Birmingham, 1973-74; assoc. prof. edn. Talladega (Ala.) Coll., 1987-89; asst. prof. English Ala. State U., Montgomery, 1989-91; coord. title III, dir. instl. rsch. and planning Miles Coll., Birmingham, Ala., 1992-96, dir. counseling and testing, 1996-97; asst. prof. English Miles Coll., Birmingham, 1997—. Author: The Right Writer, 1990. Mem. Ala. Counseling Assn., Am. Assn. Individual Investors, Alpha Kappa Mu, Delta Sigma Theta. Avocations: sewing, knitting. Home: 1752 Brookfield Ln Birmingham AL 35214-4820 also: PO Box 3800 Birmingham AL 35208-0800

CLARKE, KENNETH KINGSLEY, electrical equipment company executive; b. Miami, Fla., June 7, 1924; s. Kenneth Kingsley and Mary (Coffin) C.; m. Nona Nelme, Sept. 15, 1945; 1 son, Kenneth Stephen. Student, Cornell U., 1941-43; MSEE, Stanford, 1948; DEE, Bklyn. Poly. Inst., 1959. Rsch. fellow Bklyn. Poly. Inst., 1949-50; asst. prof. Madras (India) Inst. Tech., 1950-52; lectr. U. Ceylon, Colombo, 1952-54; asst. prof. Clarkson Coll. Tech., Potsdam, N.Y., 1954-55; faculty Bklyn. Poly. Inst., 1955-69, prof. elec. engring., 1965-69, dir. grad. elec. engring. divsn., 1967-69; pres. Clarke-Hess Comm. Rsch. Corp., N.Y.C., 1969—; Cons. in field; vis. prof. Middle East Tech. U., Ankara, Turkey, 1961-62; dir. Julie Research Labs., 1966-71. Author: (with M.V. Joyce) Transistor Circuit Analysis, 1961; (with D.T. Hess) Communication Circuit Analysis, 1971; co-inventor frequency locked loop. 2d lt. USAAF, 1943-46. Recipient Svc. award Parlar Found., 1992. Fellow IEEE (life), Instrument and Measurement Soc. (adminstrv. com. 1993-96, visitor for accreditation bd. engring. and tech. 1983-88, bd. dirs. Instrumentation/Measurement Tech. Conf., tech. program chmn. Instrumentation/Measurement Tech. Conf. 1995); mem. AAUP, AAAS, Sigma Xi, Tau Beta Pi. Home: 300 Riverside Dr New York NY 10025-5279 Office: Clarke-Hess Communication Res 220 W 19th St New York NY 10011-4035

CLARKE, KENNETH STEVENS, insurance company executive; b. South Bend, Ind., Aug. 18, 1931; s. Walter Robert and Mattie Marie (Boley) C.; m. Vivian Elizabeth Long, July 5, 1958; children—Patrick Stevens, Mary Elizabeth, Margaret Christine, Daniel Whitman. M.S., U. Ill., 1957, Ph.D., 1963. Program cons. Chgo. Heart Assn., 1957-59; supr. recreation and athletics U. Ill. div. rehab.-edn., 1959-63; cons. health and fitness AMA, Chgo., 1963-68; coordinator continuing edn. Am. Acad. Orthopedic Surgeons, 1968-70; prof. health scis. Mankato (Minn.) State U., 1970-73; prof., chmn. health edn. Pa. State U., 1973-77; dean Coll. Applied Life Studies U. Ill., Urbana, 1977-81; assoc. sec. gen. U.S. Olympic Com., Colorado Springs, Colo., 1981-89; sr. v.p. risk analysis SLE Worldwide, Inc., Ft. Wayne, Ind., 1989—; cons. athletic injury prevention; founder Nat. Athletic Injury/Illness Reporting System; active Pa. Emergency Med. Svcs. Coun., 1974-77; chmn. NCAA Med. Aspects of Sports, 1974-79; v.p. Nat. Safety Coun., 1987-89. Editor: Standard Nomenclature of Athletic Injuries, 1966, (with J.C. Hughston) Bibliography of Sports Medicine, 1970, Fundamentals of Athletic Training, 1971, Drugs and the Coach, 1972, 2d edit., 1976; contbr. profl. articles to ednl. and med. jours. Served with CIC U.S. Army, 1953-55. Recipient Spl. citation Nat. Fedn. State High Sch. Assns., Achievement award U.S. Baseball Fedn., Disting. Service to Safety award Nat. Safety Council; named to Nat. Wheelchair Athletic Assn. Hall of Fame; named Safefy Profl. of Yr., Hoosier Safety Coun.. Fellow Am. Coll. Sports Medicine (past chair ethics com.); mem. AAHPER, Am. Acad. Phys. Edn., Assn. for Advancement Health Edn., Am. Orthopedic Soc. for Sports Medicine (hon.), U. Ill. Alumni Assn. (Merit award), Rotary Internat. Roman Catholic. Home: 27751 Calle Rabano Sun City CA 92585-3949 Office: 1712 Magnavox Way Fort Wayne IN 46804-1538

CLARKE, LAMBUTH MCGEEHEE, retired college president; b. Salisbury, Md., Oct. 4, 1923; s. Hawes Palmore and Jessie Lee (Ham) C.; m. Alice Royall Acree, July 16, 1955; children: Leighton Krips, Palmore, Jessica, Virginia Hitch. BA, Randolph-Macon Coll., 1944, LLD (hon.), 1969; MA, Johns Hopkins U., 1948; postgrad., U. Birmingham, 1948, Harvard U., 1982. English instr. Randolph-Macon Coll., Ashland, Va., 1948-51, asst. to pres., 1951-58, v.p. devel., 1958-66; pres. Va. Wesleyan Coll., Norfolk, 1966-92, pres. emeritus, 1992—, also trustee; acting pres. Randolph-Macon Womans' Coll., 1993-94. Bd. dirs. Va. Symphony, Norfolk, 1970-88, trustee, 1990—; bd. dirs. Leigh Meml. Hosp., later Med. Ctr. Hosps., 1970-82, Norfolk Forum, 1970-80, World Affairs Coun., 1972-76, YMCA, Norfolk, 1972-78, Sta. WHRO-TV, 1972-76, Greater Norfolk Corp., 1978-92, Com. of 101-Future of Hampton Rds., Norfolk, 1983-92, Order of Cape Henry 1607, Norfolk, Va. Eye Found., Norfolk, 1973-92, Va. Coun. Chs., 1978-82; trustee Va. Found. Ind. Colls., Richmond, 1982-92, vice-chmn., 1990-92, assoc., 1992-97; trustee Randolph-Macon Womans Coll., 1992-97, hon. trustee, 1998—; mem. univ. senate United Meth. Ch., Nashville, 1988-92, bd. dirs., gen. bd. higher edn., 1980-88, del. jurisdictional conf., 1976-96, gen. conf., 1980-92; adv. bd. DePaul Med. Ctr., Norfolk, 1988-96; bd. dirs. Lee's Friends, 1993-99, adv. bd., 1999—; bd. dirs. Tidewater Scholarship Found., Westminster-Canterbury of Hampton Rds., Portsmouth Mus. Found., Inc., Norfolk Bot. Gardens Found.; chmn. adminstrv. bd. Larchmont United Meth. Ch., 1993, 97. Lt. (j.g.) USNR, 1943-46. Recipient Brotherhood citation NCCJ, 1991, John Wesley Disting. Educator award, 1991, Francis Asbury Educator award, 1995, Jerry G. Bray Dist. Svc. medal Va. Wesleyan Coll., 1997. Mem. Soc. Alumni Randolph-Macon Coll. (bd. dirs. 1993-99), Soc. of the Cin., Phi Beta Kappa, Omicron Delta Kappa, Phi Kappa Phi, Lambda Chi Alpha. Methodist. Avocations: volunteerism, reading, music, art and church architecture, philately.

CLARKE, LEWIS JAMES, landscape architect; b. Eng., Mar. 10, 1927; s. Roland and May (Pringle) C.; children: Lewis Nigel, Jennifer Kay, Rachel May, Lisa Elaine. Dip. Arch., Sch. Architecture, Leicester, Eng., 1950; Dip. L.D., Kings Coll, U. Durham, 1951; M.L.A., Harvard U., 1952. Prof. Sch. Design N.C. State Univ., Raleigh, 1952-68; sr. partner Lewis Clarke Assos., Raleigh, 1952—. Served with Corps Royal Engrs., 1946-49. Smith Mundt fellow, Fulbright fellow, 1951-52. Fellow Inst. Landscape Architects, Am. Soc. Landscape Architects; mem. Royal Inst. Brit. Architects. Office: Lewis Clarke Assocs 1701 Glen Eden Dr Raleigh NC 27612-4335

CLARKE, LOGAN, JR., management consultant; b. Atlanta, May 28, 1927; s. Leonard Warner Moore and Marion (Ray) C.; children: Logan III, Jeffrey Reed, Jonathan, Lisa Beth; m. Cordelia Kay Knight Mazuy. Student, U. Okla., 1944; La. State U., 1945; Stonier Grad., Sch. Banking, 1960; B.A., U. Pa., 1949; M.S., Hartford Grad. Center, 1981. Salesman Liberty Mut. Ins. Co., Boston, 1949-52; with Nat. Shawmut Bank Boston, 1952-70, asst. v.p., 1955-58, v.p., 1958-70; exec. v.p. County Bank NA, Cambridge, Mass., 1970-71; pres., dir. County Bank NA, 1971—, Shawmut Corp., 1975-78; alt. dir. Atlantic Internat. Bank Ltd., London; alt. rep. Internat. Monetary Conf., 1976-78; lectr. Hartford (Conn.) Grad. Center, 1979-86, dean Sch. Mgmt., 1983-85; exec. v.p. Soc. for Savings, Hartford, 1986-90; acting pres. Hartford Coll. for Women, 1990-91; pres. Templeton Inc., 1991—; cons. Arthur D. Little, Inc., 1979-85 ; dir. Scan-Optics, Inc., 1981—. Mem. Town Meeting Lexington, Mass., 1961-70, appropriations com., 1960-66, sch. com., 1966-70; bd. overseers Children's Hosp. Med. Ctr., Boston, 1967-87; trustee Lesley Coll., Cambridge, 1971-86, Hartford Coll. for Women, 1985-92; chmn. bd. Govs. Higher Edn., Conn., 1992-97, chmn., 1994-97; corporator Northeastern U., Boston, 1976-85. Recipient Outstanding Young Man award Boston Jr. C. of C. Mem. Masons. Episcopalian. Home: 89 River Rd East Haddam CT 06423-1462

CLARKE, MARJORIE JANE, environmental consultant, author, researcher; b. Miami, Fla., July 14, 1953; d. Garnet Winston Clarke and Janice Marie (Platt) Johnson. BA in Geology, Smith Coll., 1975; MA in Environ. Sci., Johns Hopkins U., 1978; MS in Energy Tech., NYU, 1982; MPhil, CUNY, 1996. Cert. qualified environ. profl. Intern EPA, Washington, 1974-75, 76; phys. scientist U.S. EPA, N.Y.C., 1978; sr. economist Tri-State Regional Planning Commn., N.Y.C., 1979-81; policy coord. N.Y. Power Authority, N.Y.C., 1981-83; environ. scientist N.Y.C. Dept. Sanitation, 1984-88; dir. solid waste rsch. INFORM, Inc., N.Y.C., 1988-90; tech. rsch. cons. for four PBS Videos WNET-Channel 13, N.Y.C., 1990; environ. cons. Natural Resources Def. Coun., N.Y.C., 1990—; sr. solid waste cons. INFORM, 1990-94; cons. Air & Waste Mgmt. Assn./Solid Waste Mgmt., 1993-94; rsch. fellow Ctr. for Applied Studies of the Environment, CUNY, 1992—; adj. lectr. Hunter Coll., 1996, 98, 99; cons. Hampshire County (Eng.) Coun., 1994-95; cons. to Commonweal, 1996; mem. steering com. Citywide Recycling Adv. Bd., N.Y.C., 1991—; mem. Camden County Environ. Tech. Adv. Com., 1993-95; mem. N.J. Dept. Environ. Protection and Energy, Mercury Emission Standard-Setting Task Force, 1992-95; mem. N.Y. State Adv. Bd. on Operating Requirements, Albany, 1988-92; examiner Qualified Environ. Profls. Program, 1995—; peer reviewer Environ. Def. Fund, N.Y.C., 1988—, Nat. Resources Def. Coun., N.Y.C., 1988-90; mem. Manhatt an Citizens' Solid Waste Adv. Bd., 1990—, chair, 1992-94, vice chair, 1994-96, chair waste prevention com., 1991—. Contbr. articles to profl. confs. and jours., 1983—; webmaster. Mem. USEPA/Nat. Recycling Coaliton's Nat. Task Force to develop and promote a source reduction procurement strategy, 1996-98; founder, pres. Riverside-Inwood Neighborhood Gardens, 1984—. Recipient citation Dartmouth Coll., 1974, Roy F. Weston award Jour. Solid Waste Tech. and Mgmt., 1997, Cert. of Merit for Best Film by NGO category Environment India's 1998 Internat. Film Festival; featured on cover Money Mag., 1981; U.S. EPA grantee, 1991-95; Gilleece fellow CUNY, 1991-95. Mem. ASME (indsl. and mcpl. waste rsch. com. 1986—, operator cert. com. 1988-98), Nat. Acad. Scis. (nat. rsch. coun. com. health effects waste incineration 1995—), Air and Waste Mgmt. Assn. (sec. 1988-89, session chair annual meeting 1988—, vice chair 1989-90, chmn. solid waste and thermal treatment com. 1990-92, vice chair solid waste intercom. task force 1992-94, chair integrated waste mgmt. com. 1994—, tech. dir. video 1993-94), N.Y. Cycle Club (ride leader 1982—). Democrat. Avocations: bicycling, photography, guitar, gardening. Home and Office: 1795 Riverside Dr Apt 5F New York NY 10034-5334

CLARKE, MERCER KAYE, lawyer; b. N.Y.C., Sept. 27, 1944; s. Fred Wylly and Helen Frances (Kaye) C.; m. Elizabeth Koebel (div. 1987); 1 child, James Wylly. BA in Econs., Washington and Lee U., 1966; JD, U. Fla., 1970. Bar: Fla. 1971, U.S. Dist. Ct. (so. dist.) Fla. 1971, U.S. Ct. Appeals (5th cir.) 1971, U.S. Supreme Ct. 1977, U.S. Dist. Ct. (mid. dist.) Fla. 1978, U.S. Ct. Appeals (11th cir.) 1981, U.S. Dist. Ct. (no. dist.) Fla. 1986. Assoc. Smathers & Thompson (now Kelley, Drye & Warren), Miami, Fla., 1970-75, ptnr., 1975-83, proprietary ptnr., 1983-93; ptnr. Clarke & Silverglate, 1993—. Bd. govs. Better Bus. Bur. S. Fla., Miami; trustee Beacon Council, Miami. Recipient Golden Key award City of North Miami Beach, 1988. Mem. ABA, Fla. Bar Assn., Dade County Bar Assn., Internat. Assn. Def. Counsel, Miami C. of C. (trustee), Miami City Club. Republican. Episcopalian. Home: 4880 Hammock Lake Dr Miami FL 33156-2218 Office: Clarke & Silverglate 100 Biscayne Blvd Ste 2401 Miami FL 33132-2399*

CLARKE, MILTON CHARLES, lawyer; b. Chgo., Jan. 31, 1929; s. Gordon Robert and Senoria Josephine (Carlisa) C.; m. Dorothy Jane Brodie, Feb. 19, 1955; children: Laura, Virginia, Senoria K. BS, Northwestern U., 1950, JD, 1953. Bar: Ill. 1953, Mo. 1956, U.S. Dist. Ct. (we. dist.) Mo. 1961, U.S. Ct. Appeals (8th cir.) 1961. Assoc. Swanson, Midgley, Gangwere, Clarke & Kitchin, Kansas City, Mo., 1955-61, ptnr., 1961-91; of counsel Olsen & Talpers, P.C., Kansas City, 1994—. Served with U.S. Army, 1953-55. Mem. Rotary. Office: Olsen and Talpers PC 1500 City Center Square 1100 Main St Ste 1500 Kansas City MO 64105-2125

CLARKE, OSCAR WITHERS, physician; b. Petersburg, Va., Jan. 29, 1919; s. Oscar Withers and Mary (Reese) C.; m. Susan Frances King, June 18, 1949; children—Susan Frances, Mary Elizabeth, Jennifer Ann. BS, Randolph Macon Coll., 1941; MD, Med. Coll. Va., 1944. Intern Boston City Hosp., 1944-45; resident internal medicine Med. Coll. Va., 1945-46, 48-49, fellow in cardiology, 1949-50; pvt. practice specializing in internal medicine and cardiology Gallipolis Holzer Med. Ctr., Ohio, 1950—; pres., bd. dirs. Holzer Clinic Inc., 1981-89; bd. dirs. Ohio Valley Devel. Co., Gallipolis, Cmty. Improvement Corp.; pres. Ohio State Med. Bd.; chmn. Ohio Med. Edn. and Rsch. Found., Commn. Heart Attack Alert Program NIH, 1995-96; pres. Gallipolis City Bd. Helath, 1955—, Gallia County Heart Coun., 1955—. Contbr. articles to med. jours. V.p. Tri-State Regional coun. Boy Scouts Am., 1957; pres. Tri-State Community Concert Assn., 1957-59; trustee Med. Meml. Found., Holzer Hosp. Found. Capt. M.C., AUS, 1946-48, ETO. Recipient John Stewart Bryant pathology award Med. Coll. Va., 1943. Fellow ACP (Laurate award 1997), Royal Soc. Medicine; mem. AMA (chmn. coun. on ethics and jud. affairs 1991—), Am. Heart Assn., Gallia County Med. Soc. (pres. 1953), Cen. Ohio Heart Assn. (Merit medal 1960, trustee), Ohio Med. Assn. (pres. 1973-74, Disting. Svc. citation 1988, Physician of Century 1996), Am. Soc. Internal Medicine (Disting. Internist award 1992), Alpha Omega Alpha, Sigma Zeta, Chi Beta Phi. Presbyterian. Club: Rotary (pres. 1953-54). Home: 108 Spruce Knls Gallipolis OH 45631-1066 Office: Holzer Med Ctr Hosp 90 Jackson Pike Gallipolis OH 45631-0344

CLARKE, PETER, communications and health educator; b. Evanston, Ill., Sept. 19, 1936; s. Clarence Leon and Dorothy (Whitcomb) C.; m. Karen Storey, June 4, 1962 (div. 1984); 1 child, Christopher Michael. BA, U. Wash., 1959; MA, U. Minn., 1961, PhD, 1963. Dir., asst. prof. Comm. Rsch. Ctr. U. Wash., Seattle, 1965-68, assoc. prof. sch. comm., 1967-72, dir. sch. comm., 1971-72; prof. dept. journalism U. Mich., Ann Arbor, 1973-74, chmn., prof. dept. journalism, 1975-78, chmn., prof. dept. comm., 1979-80; dean, prof. Annenberg Sch. Comm., U. So. Calif., L.A., 1981-92, prof., 1993—; prof. preventive medicine U. So. Calif. Sch. Medicine, L.A., 1985—; co-dir. From the Wholesaler to the Hungry, 1991—; dir. Ctr. for Health and Med. Comm., 1997—; cons. for various fed. and state govt. commns. on mass media and social problems. Co-author: (with Susan H. Evans) Covering Campaigns: Journalism in Congressional Elections, 1983, Surviving Modern Medicine: How to Get the Best from Doctors, Family and Friends, 1998; editor: New Models for Communication Research, 1973; co-editor: (with Susan H. Evans) The Computer Culture, 1985; contbr. articles to profl. jours. Numerous Fed., corp., pvt. founds. grants. Office: U So Calif Annenberg Sch Comm 3502 Watts Way Los Angeles CA 90089-0011

CLARKE, PETER RANDOLPH HASCHE, neurologist; b. Richmond, Va., July 3, 1951; s. Richard Penfield and Geraldine (Hasche) C.; m. Laurence Tatiana Rimsky, Aug. 4, 1957; children: Rebecca, Maxim, Hervé, Rémy. AB, Princeton U., 1974; PhD, Mich. State U., 1981; MD, U. Mich., 1983. Diplomate Am. Bd. Psychiatry and Neurology. Intern in medicine Duke U. Med. Ctr., Durham, N.C., 1983-84, resident in neurology, 1984-87, neurology fellow, 1987-88, assoc. in medicine, 1988-89, assoc. in medicine, neuromuscular fellow, 1989-90; neurologist Kernodle Clinic, Burlington, N.C., 1990—, hed dept. neurology, 1994, also shareholder, 1994. Contbr. articles to profl. jours. Soccer coach YMCA, Durham, 1998. Mem. AAAS, Am. Acad. Neurology, Am. Assn. Electrodiagnostic Medicine (cert. 1995), Nat. Stroke Assn., N.Y. Acad. Sci. Episcopalian. Avocations: travel, skiing, camping, tennis, soccer. Home: 3822 Hillgrand Dr Durham NC 27705 Office: Kernodle Clinic 1234 Huffman Mill Rd Burlington NC 27215

CLARKE, PHILIP REAM, JR., investment banker; b. Chgo., Feb. 10, 1914; s. Philip Ream and Louise (Hildebr) C.; m. Valerie Mead, Oct. 20, 1939 (dec. Sept. 1965); children: Barbara Foster, Philip Ream III; m. Jan Finan, Dec. 2, 1967; m. Barbara Schroeder, Apr. 15, 1977. AB, U. Chgo., 1937. With Glore, Forgan & Co., Chgo., 1937-42, City Nat. Bank & Trust Co., Chgo., 1946-57; asst. v.p. City Nat. Bank & Trust Co., 1947-51, v.p., 1951-57; with Lehman Bros., Chgo., 1957-65; mgr. indsl. dept. Lehman Bros., 1957-62, dir. new bus., 1962-65; v.p., treas., dir. Hinsdale Cemetery Co., 1946-66; from sr. v.p. to vice-chmn Chgo. Corp., 1965-86, vice-chmn. emeritus, 1986-96, vice chmn. emeritus, 1997—, dir., 1965-86; pres., CEO Hollymatic Corp., 1978-79, chmn., CEO, 1979-81, dir., 1969-81; mem. Midwest Stock Exchange, 1954-56; pres., treas., dir. Bronswood Cemetery, Inc., 1966-89, chmn., 1990—; vice-chmn. emeritus ABN Amro Inc. Bd. dirs., exec. com. Cook County Sch. of Nursing, 1958-68, v.p., 1965-68; treas., dir. Chgo. Com. on Alcoholism, 1952-56, v.p., 1957, exec. v.p., 1958, pres., 1959, chmn., 1960-61; charter mem. bd. assocs., Chgo. Theol. Sem., 1980-84; vice chmn. Chgo. Non Partisan Com. to Bring Rep. Nat. Conv. to Chgo.; Mem. Rep. Nat. Conv., 1959-60; treas. Citizens Com. to Bring Rep. and Dem. convs. to Chgo., 1952, 56; bd. govs. Hinsdale Community House, 1968-70, vice chmn., 1969, chmn., 1970, life trustee 1993—; trustee, chmn. fin. com., 1951-55, Village of Clarendon Hills, Ill., 1956-60, pres., 1961-65; bd. govs. United Rep. Fund of Ill., 1948-74, treas., 1948-62, v.p., exec. com., 1955-69; bd. dirs. Ill. council Trout Unltd., 1972-75; trustee U. Chgo. Alumni Found., 1958-61, citizens bd., 1955-80; mem. exec. com. Citizens of Greater Chgo., 1960-61. Lt. comdr. USNR, 1942-46. Mem. Chgo. Assn. Commerce and Industry (dir., treas. 1952-53), Chgo. Zool. Soc. (governing mem. 1956-69, 79—), Nat. Council on Alcoholism (v.p. 1959-62), Alpha Delta Phi. Republican. Episcopalian. Clubs: Chicago (Chgo.), Monroe (Chgo.), Bond (Chgo.); Hinsdale Golf; Coleman Lake (dir. 1972-84, v.p. 1982) (Wis.); Plaza (Chgo.). Home: 404 Burr Ridge Clb Burr Ridge IL 60521-5207 Office: 208 S La Salle St Chicago IL 60604-1000

CLARKE, RICHARD ALAN, electric and gas utility company executive, lawyer; b. San Francisco, May 18, 1930; s. Chauncey Frederick and Carolyn (Shannon) C.; m. Mary Dell Fisher, Feb. 5, 1955; children: Suzanne, Nancy C. Stephen, Douglas Alan. AB Polit. Sci. cum laude, U. Calif., Berkeley, 1952, JD, 1955. Bar: Calif. 1955. V.p., asst. to chmn. Pacific Gas and Electric Co., San Francisco, 1979-82, exec. v.p., gen. mgr. utility ops., 1982-85, pres., 1985-86, chmn. bd., CEO, 1986-94, chmn. bd., 1994-95; ptnr. Rockwell, Fulkerson and Clarke, San Rafael, Calif., 1960-69; bd. dirs. Pacific Gas & Electric Co., Potlach Corp., CNF TransInc.; mem. Bus. Coun. Pres.' Coun. on Sustainable Devel. Bd. dirs., past chmn. Bay Area Coun.; trustee Boalt Hall Trust, Sch. Law U. Calif., Berkeley; mem. adv. bd. Walter A. Haas Sch. Bus., U. Calif., Berkeley; chmn. adv. bd. Ctr. for Orgnl. and Human Resource Effectiveness, U. Calif., Berkeley;bd. dirs. Nature Conservancy of Calif.; co-chair U. Calif. Regents Outreach Task Force. Mem. Calif. C. of C. (past dir.), San Francisco C. of C. (past dir., v.p. econ. devel.), Edison Elect. Inst. Office: Pacific Gas & Electric Co H17F 123 Mission St San Francisco CA 94105-1551

CLARKE, RICHARD LEWIS, health science association administrator; b. Indpls., Sept. 9, 1948; s. John Richard and Opal (Emmons) C.; m. Linda DeMattia, Aug. 12, 1972; children: John, Laura, R. Bradley. BS, Bradley U., 1971; MBA, U. Miami, 1972. Bus. mgr. Jackson Meml. Hosp., Miami, 1973-76; controller Palmetto Gen. Hosp., Hialeah, Fla., 1976-80; sr. v.p. fin. Swedish Med. Ctr., Englewood, Colo., 1980-86; pres. Healthcare Fin. Mgmt. Assn., Westchester, Ill., 1986—; bd. dirs., treas. Colo. Hosp. Assn. Trust, Denver. Fellow Healthcare Fin. Mgmt. Assn.; mem. Am. Soc. Assn. Execs., Econ. Club of Chgo. Avocations: sailboat racing, skiing. Office: Healthcare Fin Mgmt Assn 2 Westbrook Corp Ctr Ste 700 Westchester IL 60154

CLARKE, ROBERT EARLE (BOBBY CLARKE), hockey executive; b. Flin Flon, Manitoba, Can., Aug. 13, 1949; m. Sandy Clarke; children: Wade, Lucas, Jody, Jakki. Player Phila. Flyers, NHL, 1969-84, gen. mgr., 1984-90; gen. mgr., v.p. Minn. North Stars, NHL, 1990-92; now pres., gen. mgr. Phila. Flyers. Winner West Divsn. Rookie of Yr., 1970, Player of Yr. West Divsn. Sporting News, 1972-73, Bill Masterton Meml. trophy, 1972, Hart Meml. trophy, 1973, 75, 76, Player of Yr. Comp. Conf. Sporting News, 1974-75, Player of Yr. Sporting News, 1975-76, NHL Exec. of Yr. Sporting News, 1993-94, 94-95; co-winner Lester Patrick award, 1981; named to NHL Hall of Fame, 1987. Office: Phila Flyers Core States Spectrum 1 Corestates Complex Philadelphia PA 19148-5250*

CLARKE, ROBERT F., utilities company executive; b. Oakland, Calif.. BA, U. Calif., Berkeley, 1965, MBA, 1966. Pres., CEO Hawaiian Electric, 1991—. Office: Hawaiian Electric Industries Inc 900 Richards St Honolulu HI 96813-2919

CLARKE, ROBERT LOGAN, lawyer; b. Tulsa, Okla., June 29, 1942; s. Ralph Logan and Faye Louise (Todd) C.; m. Jean Puddin Barrow Talbert, Sept. 23, 1967; 1 child, Robert Logan Jr. BA Econs., Rice U., 1963; LLB, Harvard U., 1966. Bar: N.Mex. 1966, Tex. 1967. Legis. asst. to U.S. Senator Edwin L. Mechem Washington, 1964; assoc. Hinkle, Bondurant, Cox, Eaton & Hensley, Roswell, N.Mex., 1966; assoc. Bracewell & Patterson, Houston, 1968-73, ptnr., 1973-85, ptnr., head fin. svcs. sect., 1992—; comptr. of currency Washington, 1985-92; dir. FDIC, Washington, 1985-92, Resolution Trust Corp., Washington, 1989-92; bd. dirs. Cmty. Bancorp. N.Mex., Inc., Centex Constrn. Products, Inc., First Investors Fin. Svcs., Inc.; sr. advisor to pres. Nat. Bank Poland, 1992—; advisor to bank suprs. in Ea. Europe, Mexico, Argentina, Brazil and Kazakhstan. Precinct chmn. Harris County Reps., 1970-74, 76-85, legal counsel, 1984-85; trustee Mus. N.Mex. Found., 1992—, Southwestern Grad. Sch. Banking Found., 1993—, Internat. Folk Art Found., 1995—; dist. chmn. Senatorial Dist. 15, 1978-80; del. numerous state and dist. Rep. convs., 1970-84; founding dir. Houston Rep. Club, 1982-85; bd. dirs. Houston Polit. Action Com., 1983-85; mem. adv. com. Harris County Reagan-Bush campaign, 1984; asst. scoutmaster Boy Scouts Am., Houston, 1980-85; deacon 1st Presbyn. Ch. Houston. Capt. U.S. Army, 1966-68. Recipient Disting. Svc. medal U.S. Treasury Dept., 1992, Banking Leadership award Western States Sch. Banking, Albuquerque, 1993. Mem. ABA, Houston Bar Assn., Houston Bar Found., State Bar Tex., State Bar N.Mex., Rice U. Alumni Assn. (chmn. area club com. 1984-85, mem. exec. bd. dirs. 1987-89, Disting. Alumnus award 1992), River Oaks Country Club, Chevy Chase Club, Houston Club, Coronado Club, Houston City Club, Sangre de Cristo Racquet Club (Santa Fe), Rotary (trustee student's ednl. fund), Trout Unltd. (trustee 1997—). Avocations: tennis, fishing, hiking. Office: Bracewell & Patterson Pennzoil South Tower 711 Louisiana St Ste 2900 Houston TX 77002-2781

CLARKE, S. BRUCE, paper company executive; b. Wheeling, W.Va., Oct. 28, 1940; s. W. Russell and Eugenia Marie (O'Connor) C.; m. Nancy McCleary, Dec. 29, 1962 (div. Sept. 1983); children: R. Scott, S. Carter, Karen M.; stepchildren: Christine M., J. Mark; m. Marie Weaver, June 25, 1988. BA, W.Va. U., 1962. Sales mgr. Clarke Paper Co., Wheeling, 1962-72, pres., 1972-87; pres. Paper Shack, Inc., Wheeling, 1982—, Proven Papers, Inc., Wheeling, 1988-97. Bd. dirs. Easter Seals Soc., Wheeling, 1980, pres., 1998-2000; pres. Wheeling Symphony Soc., 1983-85, mem., 1975—; pres. Symposiarchs Soc., Wheeling, 1984-85, mem., 1968—; bd. dirs. W.Va. Independence Hall Fedn., 1989—. Mem. Wheeling C. of C. (bd. dirs. 1983-85). Republican. Presbyterian. Home: 102 Park Pl Wheeling WV 26003-5441 Office: Paper Shack Inc 3900 Wood St Wheeling WV 26003-4360

CLARKE, S. GORDON, clergyman; b. Charleston, W.Va., Mar. 3, 1931; s. Leonard Gordon and Marguerite (Lyons) C.; m. Martha Thompson, Nov. 3, 1950; children: Daniel Gordon, David Allen. AB in Religion, Marion (Ind.) Coll., 1959, ThM, 1962; DD (hon.), Colo. Theol. Sem. Ordained to ministry Friends Ch., 1959. Dir. Creative Ministries, Indpls., 1959-69; regional exec. sec. Am. Bible Soc., Chgo., 1959-77; pastor Forsyth Friends Ch. Winston-Salem, N.C., 1977-79; sr. pastor Garden Grove (Calif.) Friends Ch., 1979—; vol. chaplain Wayne County Sheriff Office, 1996—; chaplain Garden Grove Police Dept.; chmn. Bd. Spiritual Life Friends United Meeting, chmn. program meeting 1987, mem. meeting ministries commn.; mem. exec. com. bd. adminstrn. S.W. Yearly Meeting, chmn. spiritual life com.; pres. bd. trustees Calif. Friends Homes; founder Chaplain-on-Call. Mem. Spl. Task Force of Religious Well Being for White House Conf. on Aging; mem. Gov.'s Commn. on Aging, Gov.'s Commn. on Tourism, Gov.'s Com. on Migrant Labor. Sgt. USAF, 1950-55. Mem. Coll. Chaplains Am. Protestant Hosp. Assn., Correctional Chaplains Assn., Internat. Platform Assn., Nat. Assn. Religious Broadcasters, Leisure Fellowship Ministry. Home: 102 Woods Mill Rd Goldsboro NC 27534-9122 Office: Garden Grove Friends Ch 12211 Magnolia St Garden Grove CA 92841-3318

CLARKE, TERENCE MICHAEL, public relations and advertising executive; b. Altoona, Pa., Apr. 9, 1937; s. Robert Ewing and Louise Mercedes (Eckley) C.; m. Judith Ann Lawson, Oct. 15, 1966; children: Lawson Robert, Penn Terence. Student, U. Pitts., 1955-57; cert., Inst. Far Ea. Langs., Yale U., 1958; BS, Boston U., 1963, MS, 1989. Pub. rels. mgr. Pepsi-Cola Co., N.Y.C., 1963, H.P. Hood & Sons, Boston, 1964-66; pres. The Taggart Co., Chgo., 1966-70; dir. pub. rels. Creamer, Trowbridge, Case & Basford, Boston, 1970; v.p., dir. Johnson, Raffin & Clarke Inc., Boston, 1971-76; assoc. prof. Boston U., 1976-77; chmn. Clarke Goward Advt. Inc., Boston, 1977—; chmn., CEO Clarke & Co. Inc., Boston, 1997—; bd. dirs. Liberty Bank & Trust, Boston, Sentry Tech., Inc. Chmn. planning, site, constrn. com. Hingham (Mass.) Sch., 1971-86; exec. com. Coll. Comm., Boston U., 1987—; bd. dirs. Mass. Soc. for Prevention of Cruelty to Children, 1980-94; mem. Hingham Police Sta. Constrn. Com., 1987-90; trustee Belmont (Mass.) Hill Sch., 1988—, Boston U.; bd. overseers Huntington Theatre Co., Boston, 1992—. With USAF, 1957-60. Recipient L.E. Sissman award Greater Boston Advt. Club, 1984. Mem. Greater Boston Advt. Club (bd. dirs. 1980-83), Soc. for Preservation of Barber Shop Quartet Singing in Am. (internat. quartet champions 1980), Boston U. Alumni (pres. 1995—, Disting. Alumni award 1984), Algonquin Club, Univ. Club. Republican. Presbyterian. Avocations: barber shop quartet singing. Office: Clarke & Company PR Clarke Goward Advt 535 Boylston St Boston MA 02116-3720*

CLARKE, THOMAS HAL, lawyer; b. Atlanta, Aug. 10, 1914; s. James Caleb and Mary Cox (DeSaussure) C.; m. Mary Louise Hastings, July 12, 1951; children: Thomas Hal Jr., Katie Clarke Hamilton, Rebecca DeSaussure Morrison. LLB, Washington and Lee U., 1938. Bar: Ga. 1939, U.S. Dist. Ct. (no. dist.) Ga., U.S. Ct. Appeals (5th cir.), U.S. Supreme Ct., 1973. Ptnr. Clarke & Anderson, Atlanta, 1948-60, Mitchell, Clarke, Pate & Anderson, Atlanta, 1960-69, 73-85; of counsel Gambrell, Clarke, Anderson & Stolz, Atlanta, 1985-92; copyright trustee Gone With the Wind and sequels, 1983—. Mem. Fed. Home Loan Bank Bd., Washington, 1969-73; past pres., bd. dirs. Atlanta Hist. Soc.; past bd. visitors Emory U.; trustee emeritus Washington and Lee U.; mem. Hibernian United Service Club, Dublin, Ireland. Served with USNR, 1942-46, ETO, PTO. Mem. Internat. Bar Assn. (past chmn. savs. and bldg. socs. com.), ABA (chmn. savs. and loan com. 1970-73, chmn. corp. banking and bus. law sect. 1973-74, mem. ho. of dels. 1974-80, editor The Business Lawyer 1972), Ga. Bar Assn., Atlanta Bar Assn., Am. Law Inst., Atlanta Lawyers Club (past pres.), Selden Soc., English Speaking Union (past pres., chmn. bd.), Metropolitan Club (Washington D.C.), Commerce Club, Piedmont Driving Club (Atlanta). Presbyterian. Home: 186 15th St NE Atlanta GA 30309-3511 Office: 600 W Peachtree St NW Ste 1580 Atlanta GA 30308-3603

CLARKE, UNA, city official; married; two children. BS, L.I. U.; MEd, NYU, Columbia U. City councilwoman dist. #40 N.Y. City Coun., 1992—, mem. youth, health and gen. welfare coms., mem. mental health subcom., mem. aging. com., mem. econ. devel. com.; past sr. cons. early edn. N.Y. C. Agy. Child Devel.; past adj. prof. Medgar Evans Coll. Revson fellow, Columbia U., 1984. *

CLARKE, URANA, writer, musician, educator; b. Wickliffe-on-the-Lake, Ohio, Sept. 8, 1902; d. Graham Warren and Grace Urana (Olsaver) C.; artists and tchrs. diploma Mannes Music Sch., N.Y.C., 1925; cert. Dalcroze Sch. Music, N.Y.C., 1950; student Pembroke Coll., Brown U.; BS, Mont. State U., 1967, M of Applied Sci., 1970. Mem. faculty Mannes Music Sch., 1922-49, Dalcroze Sch. Music, 1949-54; adv. editor in music The Book of Knowledge, 1949-65; v.p., dir. Saugatuck Circle Housing Devel.; guest lectr. Hayden Planetarium, 1945; guest lectr., bd. dirs. Roger Williams Park Planetarium, Providence; radio show New Eng. Skies, Providence, 1961-64, Skies Over the Big Sky Country, Livingston, Mont., 1964-79, Birds of the Big Sky Country, 1972-79, Great Music of Religion, 1974-79; mem. adv. com. Nat. Rivers and Harbors Congress, 1947-58; instr. continuing edn. Mont. State U. Chmn. Park County chpt. ARC, 1967-92, chmn. emeritus 1992-99, co-chmn. county blood program, first aid instr. trainer, 1941-93; instr. ARC cardio-pulmonary resuscitation, 1976-84; mem. Mont. Commn. Nursing and Nursing Edn., 1974-76; mem. Park County Local Govt. Study Com., 1974-76, chmn., 1984-86, vice-chair, 94-96. Mem. Am. Acad. Polit. Sci., Am. Musicol. Soc., Royal Astron. Soc. Can., Inst. Nav., Maria Mitchell Soc. Nantucket, N.Am. Yacht Racing Union, AAAS, Meteoritical Soc., Internat. Soc. Mus. Research, Skyscrapers (sec.-treas. 1960-63), Am. Guild Organists, Park County Wilderness Assn. (treas.), Trout Unlimited, Nature Conservancy, Big Sky Astron. Soc. (dir. 1965-99), Sierra Club. Lutheran. Club: Cedar Point Yacht. Author: The Heavens are Telling (astronomy), 1951; Skies Over the Big Sky Country, 1965; also astron. news-letter, View It Yourself, weekly column Big Skies, 1981-98; contbr. to mags, on music, nav. and astronomy. Pub. Five Chorale Preludes for Organ, 1975; also elem. two-piano pieces. Inventor, builder of Clarke Adjustable Piano Stool. Died May 18, 1999. Address: Log-A-Rhythm 9th St Island Livingston MT 59047

CLARKE, WALTER SHELDON, military consultant, educator; b. Washington, Dec. 28, 1934; s. Walter Clowes and Lena Phoebe (Lovejoy) C.; m. Chantal Aubert, Dec. 26, 1974; children: Philippe, Quentin, Aurélie; 1 stepson, Nicolas Lance. B.A., Yale U., 1957; cert. African studies, Northwestern U., 1968. Joined Fgn. Svc., Dept. State, 1958; served in Ruanda-Urundi (Later Kingdom of Burundi), 1960-62; served in Am. embassy, San Jose, Costa Rica, 1963-65, Bogota, Colombia, 1965-67; desk officer West African affairs Dept. State, 1968-70; chief polit. sect. Am. embassy, Abidjan, Ivory Coast, 1970-72; consul Am. consulate Douala, Cameroon, 1972-74; desk officer Latin Am. affairs Dept. State, 1974-76; info. programmer A/OASIS, 1976-77; consul gen. Djibouti, French Ter. of Afars and Issas, 1977; became charge d'Affaires upon independence of Djibouti, 1977-80; polit. counselor Am. embassy Lagos, Nigeria, 1980-83; dir. intelligence liaison U.S. Dept. State, Washington, 1983-87; instr. Strategy U.S. Naval War Coll., Newport, R.I., 1987, State Dept. advisor to Pres., prof. Dept. Strategy and Policy, 1987-89; counselor of embassy for polit. affairs Am. Embassy, Madrid, 1989-92; prof. internat. rels. U.S. Army War Coll., Carlisle, Pa., 1992-94; ret. State Dept., 1994; instr. U. Alcala-Henares, 1991-92; dep. chief of mission U.S. Liaison Office, Mogadishu, Somalia, 1993; cons. U.S. Army Peace Keeping Inst., 1994—; adj. prof. peace ops. U.S. Army Peacekeeping Inst., Carlisle, Pa.; cons. various mil. commands on peacekeeping, humanitarian ops. Contbr. bibliog. and hist. research articles to profl. jours.; co-editor: (with Jeffrey Herbst) Learning from Somalia: Lessons of an Armed Humanitarian Intervention, 1997. Recipient Superior Honor awards Dept. State, 1980, 85, 92, 93, Meritorious Honor award, 1983, U.S. Army Comdr. Pub. Svc. award, 1994. Mem. African Studies Assn. (life), U.S. Naval Inst. (life), U.S. Army War Coll. Alumni Assn. (faculty, life).

CLARKIN, JOHN FRANCIS, health care management executive; b. Atlantic City, Dec. 30, 1936; s. John Francis and Agnes (Winterholer) C.; BSBA, Rider Coll., 1959; postgrad. Temple U.; m. Dorothy Louise Piffath; 1 son, John F. Mktg. rep. Scott Paper Co., Indpls., 1960-62; systems and mktg. rep. Burroughs Corp., Phila., 1962-67; dir. Mid-Atlantic health care ops. mgmt. practice Coopers & Lybrand, Phila., 1967-92; v.p. corp. fin. svcs. Crozer-Keystone Health System, Upland, Pa., 1992-97, pres. The Clarkin

Group, West Chester, Pa., 1997-98, v.p. bus. svcs. Thomas Jefferson U. Hosp., Phila., 1998—; lead instr. speaker numerous meetings and seminars. Mem. Grand Oak Run Civic Assn., 1970—. With U.S. Army, 1959. Rotary Club grantee, 1955-59; cert. mgmt. cons. Mem. Inst. Mgmt. Cons., Hosp. Mgmt. Systems Soc., Hosp. Fin. Mgmt. Assn., Med. Group Mgmt. Assn., Am. Hosp. Assn. Republican. Roman Catholic. Clubs: Vesper, Pickering Racquet. Author: Topics in Health Care Financing, 1982; (with others) Handbook of Health Care Accounting and Finance, 1982, 89, Billing Systems, 2 vols., 1982, 89, Managing Accounts Receivable, 1990; contbr. articles to profl. jours. Home: 1421 Grand Oak Ln West Chester PA 19380-5951 Office: Thomas Jefferson Univ Hosp 925 Chestnut St Philadelphia PA 19107-4216

CLARK-JOHNSON, SUSAN, publishing executive. Pres., pub. Reno Gazette-Jour., 1985—; sr. group pres. Pacific Newspaper Group, Gannett, 1985—; bd. dirs. Harrah's Entertainment, Inc.; bd. visitors John S. Knight Fellowships for Profl. Journalists, Stanford U. Office: Gannett Co Inc Box 22000 955 Kuenzli St Reno NV 89502-1160

CLARKSON, CHERYL LEE, healthcare executive; b. Chgo., Apr. 14, 1953; d. George Mendenhall and Carol Ann (Fertig) C.; m. Daniel J. Townsend; children: Drew Scott Clarkson-Townsend, Danielle Ann Clarkson-Townsend. BA in Sociology, Ariz. State U., 1975; MS in Mgmt., MIT, 1990. Sales rep. Am. Hosp. Supply, Inc., Phoenix, 1975-78; area sales mgr. Am. Hosp. Supply, Inc., Dallas, 1978-79, Edison, N.J., 1979-81; regional mgr. Am. Hosp. Supply, Inc., Boston, 1981-83; dir. sales Am. Hosp. Supply, Inc., Evanston, Ill., 1983-85; v.p. sales, mktg. Rudolph Beaver, Inc., Waltham, Mass., 1985-88; pres. Beaver Steriseal, Inc., Waltham, 1987-88, Clarkson and Assocs., 1988-90, Abiodent, Inc., Danvers, Mass., 1990-92; CEO, COO, bd. dirs. Peer Review Analysis, Inc., Boston, 1992-95; bd. overseers Boston U. Med. Ctr. Hosp., 1993—; bd. dirs. Visualization Tech., Inc., Andover, Mass., 1995—; ceo, pres. SkinHealth, Inc., Newton, Mass., 1997—. Trustee Kingsley Montessori Sch., Boston, 1996—; bd. mem. Northeastern U. Sch. of Bus., 1998—; bd. trustees Mass. Eye and Ear Infirmary, Boston, 1998—, bd. mem., Visulaization Tech., 1996—. Mem. Algonquin Club (Boston). Avocations: travel, golf, horseback riding. Office: SkinHealth Inc 233 Needham St Ste 300 Newton MA 02116-1002

CLARKSON, ELISABETH ANN HUDNUT, civic worker; b. Youngstown, Ohio, Apr. 20, 1925; d. Herbert Beecher and Edith (Schaaf) Hudnut;. AB, Wilson Coll., 1947; MA, State U. N.Y., 1973, also postgrad; LHD, Wilson Coll., 1985. m. William M.E. Clarkson, Sept. 23, 1950; children: Alison H., David B., Andrew E. With J.L. Hudson Co., Detroit, 1947-50; writer The Minute Parade daily Sta. WGR, Detroit, 1948-50. Author: You Can Always Tell a Freshman, 1949, An Adirondack Archive: The Trail to Windover, 1993; author articles, dramatic presentations, archival materials Adirondack Mus., 1950-77. Trustee Wilson Coll., Chambersburg, Pa., 1970-83, chmn. bd. trustees, 1979-82; bd. dirs. Buffalo Mus. Sci., 1972-87, 90-96; mem. Trinity Episcopal Ch., 1950—, Trinity Vestry, 1996-99, mem. cultural leadership group, 1994-96, 98—; mem. racism commn. Episcopal Diocese of Western N.Y., 1989-92; bd. dirs., companion-in-charge soc. Companion of the Holy Cross, 1986-90, N.Y. State Mus., 1985-90; pst chmn. jr. group Albright Knox Art Gallery; collector, curator Graphic Controls Corp. art collection, 1976-83; bd. dirs. Bischoff Clarkson Hudnut corp., North Creek, N.Y., 1973-83; bd. dirs. windover corp., 1997—, pres., 1998—; trustee Clarkson Ctr. for Human Svcs., 1995—, Irish Classical Theatre, 1998—; mem. Buffalo Art Commn., 1983—, chmn., 1990-96; mem. cmty. adv. panel Niagara Fronotier Transp. Authority, 1991-94; mem. exec. bd. arts adv. coun. SUNY at Buffalo, 1985-95; bd. dirs. N.Y. State Mus. Assn., Albany, 1985-90; sustainer Jr. League, 1983—. Recipient Trustee award for disting. svc. Wilson Coll., 1983, award in the Arts, NCCJ, 1998. Mem. Garret Club, Buffalo Tennis and Squash Club, Sloane Club (London). Episcopalian. Home: 156 Bryant St Buffalo NY 14222-2003

CLARKSON, GEORGE EDWARD, theology educator, minister; b. Skaneateles, N.Y., Sept. 3, 1917; s. George Henry and Ingeborg Regina Thorkildsen) C.; m. Elizabeth Rachel Hutton, July 5, 1941; children: Ellen Regina Emery, Evelyn Ann Zumaya, Kathleen Elaine Clarkson. AB, Drew U., 1939; MA, Haverford Coll., 1940; MDiv, Union Theol. Sem., N.Y.C., 1943; PhD, U. Wales, Lampeter, 1980. Ordained Meth. Min., Friends Coun. on Edn. Asst. Madison Ave. Presbyn. Ch., N.Y.C., 1940-41; pastor Cmty. Ch., Island Park, N.Y., 1941-45, Dresden (N.Y.)-Milo Parish, 1945-57, Danby Fedn. Ch., Ithaca, N.Y., 1945-62; prof. theology Ithaca Coll., 1962-82, Wells Coll., Aurora, N.Y., 1978-98; pastor Poplar Ridge (N.Y.) Friends, 1978—; hon. advisor Brit. Univ. Summer Schs., London, 1960-75; coord. off-campus study, Wells Coll., 1984-93. Author: Grounds for Belief, Life After Death, 1988, Mysticism of William Law, 1992, George Whitefield and Welsh Calvinistic Methodism, 1996. Chair transit com. Ithaca Schs., 1962-65; co-founder Ithaca Suicide Prevention, 1965; pres. Danby Fire Co., Ithaca, 1970, fire commr., 1965-72. Recipient Oberlin award N.Y. State Coun. Chs., 1965. Mem. Am. Acad. Religion, Sigma Phi. Democrat. Mem. Soc. of Friends. Avocations: beekeeping, carving, ship models, gardening, skiing. Home: 650 Nelson Rd Ithaca NY 14850-9437

CLARKSON, JOHN G., academic administrator, ophthalmologist; m. Diana Teasdale; children: Paige Black, David. BS, Princeton U.; MD, Miami Sch. Medicine, 1968. Intern U. Hosp., Boston; resident ophthalmology U. Miami/Jackson Meml. Med. Ctr., Fla.; opthalmic pathology, retinal and vitreous surgery fellow Johns Hopkins U., Balt.; chmn. dept. ophthalmology, dir. Bascom Palmer Eye Inst., 1991-96; sr. v.p. med. affairs, dean Sch. Medicine U. Miami, 1995—. Mem. Am. Bd. Ophthalmology (bd. dirs.), Am. Acad. Ophthalmology, Retina Soc., Club Jules Gonin, Macula Soc. Office: U Miami Sch Medicine PO Box 016099 (R699) 1600 NW 10th Ave Miami FL 33136-1090*

CLARKSON, JULIAN DERIEUX, lawyer; b. Coral Gables, Fla., Mar. 12, 1929; s. Julian Livingston and Hazel (Lamar) C.; m. Joan Combs, Dec. 24, 1950, children—James L., Julian L., Joanna D., Melinda C.; m. 2d, Shirley Lazonby, Nov. 8, 1979; 1 child, Shirley Lamar. B.A., U. Fla., 1950, LL.B., 1955, J.D., 1967. Bar: Fla. 1955, U.S. Ct. Appeals (5th cir.) 1961, U.S. Supreme Ct. 1964, U.S. Ct. Appeals (11th cir.) 1981, D.C. 1983. Ptnr., Henderson, Franklin, Starnes & Holt, Ft. Myers, Fla., 1955-76; sole practice, Ft. Myers, 1976-77; ptnr. Holland & Knight, Ft. Myers, 1977-79, Tampa, 1979-82, Tallahassee, 1982—; lectr. in field. Chmn. Fla. Supreme Ct. Jud. Nominating Commn., 1976-78. Served to 1st lt. U.S. Army, 1950-53. Decorated Purple Heart, 1951; named Outstanding Grad. Province V Phi Delta Phi, 1955. Mem. Am. Coll. Trial Lawyers, Am. Acad. Appellate Lawyers, Fla. Blue Key, Order of Coif, Phi Beta Kappa. Democrat. Episcopalian. Author: Let No Man Put Asunder—Story of a Football Rivalry, 1968, Golden Era II, 1994. Home: 1826 NW 26th Way Gainesville FL 32605-3861 Office: Holland & Knight PO Box 810 315 S Calhoun St Ste 600 Tallahassee FL 32301-1897*

CLARKSON, LAWRENCE WILLIAM, airplane company executive; b. Grove City, Pa., Apr. 29, 1938; s. Harold William and Jean Henrietta (Jaxtheimer) C.; m. Barbara Louise Stevenson, Aug. 20, 1960; children: Michael, Elizabeth, Jennifer. BA, DePauw U., 1960; JD, U. Fla., 1962. Counsel Pratt & Whitney, West Palm Beach, Fla., 1967-72, program dep. dir., 1972-75, program mgr., 1974-75; v.p., mng. dir. Pratt & Whitney, Brussels, Belgium, 1975-78; v.p. mktg. Pratt & Whitney, West Palm Beach, 1978-80; v.p. contracts Pratt & Whitney, Hartford, Conn., 1980-82, pres. comml. products div., 1982-87; sr. v.p. Boeing Comml. Airplanes Group, Seattle, 1988-91; corp. v.p. planning and internat. devel. Boeing Co., Seattle, 1992-93, sr. v.p., 1994-99; pres. Boeing Enterprises, Seattle, 1997-99; dir. Partnership for Improved Air Travel, Washington, 1988-91. Trustee DePauw U., Greencastle, Ind., 1987—; overseer Tuck Sch. Dartmouth, Hanover, N.H., 1993—; corp. coun. Interlochen (Mich.) Ctr. for Arts, 1987, trustee, 1988—, chmn., 1996—; trustee Seattle Opera, 1990—, chmn., 1991—; pres. Japan-Am. Soc., Wash., 1993, pres. Wash. State China Rels. com., 1992-93; chmn. Nat. Bur. of Asia Rsch., Coun. Fgn. Rels.; chmn. U.S. Pacific Econ. Corp. Coun., 1993—. Mem. Nat. Assn. Mfrs. (bd. dirs.), N.Y. Yacht Club, Seattle Yacht Club, Met. Opera Club, Wings Club (bd. govs. 1987-91, Order of St. John (commdr. 1994—), Met. Club D.C., Am. Inst. Contemporary German Studies (bd. dirs.). Episcopalian. Home: 10127 NE 66th Lane Kirkland WA 98033

CLARKSON, THOMAS BOSTON, comparative medicine educator; b. Decatur, Ga., June 13, 1931. DVM, U. Ga., 1954; Diploma, Am. Coll. Lab. Animal Medicine, 1963. Rsch. assoc. pharmacology and exptl. therapeutics sect. S. E. Massengill Co., 1954-57; from asst. to assoc. prof. exptl. medicine, dir. vivarium Wake Forest U., Winston-Salem, N.C., 1957-64, assoc. prof. lab. animal medicine, head dept., 1964-65, prof., chmn. dept. Bowman Gray sch. medicine, 1965-97, dir. arteriosclerosis rsch. ctr., 1971-91, dir. comparative medicine clin. rsch. ctr., 1989-97; prof. Wake Forest U. Sch. of Medicine, 1997—; mem. sci. adv. com. regional primate rsch. ctr. U. Wash., 1971—; mem. adv. com. Cerbrovascular Rsch. Ctr., 1973—; mem. com. vet. med. sci. NAS-Nat. Rsch. Coun., 1975—; chmn. arteriosclerosis, hypertension and lipid metabolism adv. com. Nat. Heart Lung & Blood Inst., 1983-85. Recipient Griffin award Am. Assn. Lab. Animal Sci., 1977, Albion O. Bernstein award N.Y. State Med. Soc., 1992; Duphar lectr. British Menopause Soc., 1993; Joseph Price orator Am. Ob-Gyn. Soc., 1993. Fellow Am. Soc. Primatology, Acad. Behavioral Med. Rsch., Soc. Behavioral Medicine; mem. NAS (mem. clin. sci. panel study nat. needs biomedical and behavioral rsch. pers. com. and task force animal models atherosclerosis 1976—), Am. Heart Assn. (mem. com. coronary artery lesions and myocardial infarctions 1970—, chmn. task force rsch. animal use, vice-chmn. coun. arteriosclerosis 1979-81, chmn. 1981-83, G. Lyman Duff Meml. lectr. 1985, Award of Merit 1987, Lewis A. Conner Meml. lectr. 1991), Am. Assn. Advancement Lab. Animal Sci., Am. Assn. Pathologists, Am. Soc. Exptl. Pathology, Am. Vet. Medicine Assn. (Charles River prize 1978), Sigma Xi. Achievements include research in comparative and experimental atherosclerosis, particularly factors affecting susceptibility and resistance to the disease and the mechanisms by which risk factors affect the pathogenesis. Office: Wake Forest U Dept Pathology Medical Center Blvd Winston Salem NC 27157*

CLARKSON, THOMAS WILLIAM, toxicologist, educator; b. Eng., Aug. 1, 1932; came to U.S., 1957; s. William and Olive (Jackson) C.; m. Winifred Browne, Mar. 4, 1957; children: Ian, Jean, Ann. BSc, U. Manchester, 1953, PhD, 1956; Dr Medicine (hon.), U. Umea, Sweden, 1986. Sci. officer tox research unit Med. Research Council U.K., Carshalton, Surrey, 1962-64; sr. fellow polymer sci. Weizmann Inst. Sci., Rehovot, Israel, 1964-65; mem. faculty U. Rochester (N.Y.) Med. Sch., 1958—, prof. toxicology, 1971—, head div., 1980-86, J. Lowell Orbison Disting. Svc. Alumni prof., 1983—, dir. Environ. Health Scis. Ctr., 1986-98; chmn. Dept. Environ. Medicine, 1992-98; dir. NASA Ctr. Rsch. and Tng. in Space Environ. Health, 1991-95. Mem. editorial bds. profl. jours.; author articles in field. Recipient Founders' award CIIT, 1997. Mem. Inst. Medicine of NAS, Permanent Commn. Internat. Assn. Occupational Health, Soc. Toxicology (Arnold J. Lehman award 1993, merit award 1999), Brit. Pharm. Soc., Am. Soc. Pharmacology and Exptl. Therapeutics, Internat. Soc. for Trace Element Rsch. in Humans, Ramazzini Collegium, Polish Toxicology Soc. (hon.), La Academia Nacional de Medicina de Buenos Aires (hon. mem.). Office: Dept Environ Medicine U Rochester Med Sch Rochester NY 14642

CLARKSON, WILLIAM MORRIS, children's pastor; b. Newport, R.I., Feb. 23, 1954; s. George and Lois Ruth (Terwilligar) C.; m. Janice Aiko Enoki, June 16, 1978; children: Kyle Hideo, Keith Hiroshi. BA, Muhlenberg Coll., Allentown, Pa., 1976; MPA, Ball State U., Muncie, Ind., 1977. Advanced cert. in Employee Relations Law, Mich., Ind.; cert. Rev., Assemblies of God, Springfield, Mo., 1997. Research asst. Ball State U. Bur. Govtl. Research, Muncie, Ind., 1977; field staff cons. Ind. U., Div. Pub. Service, Indpls., 1977-78; adminstrv. asst. City of Midland, Mich., 1978-81, pers. dir., 1981-91; asst. city mgr. for pers. and risk mgmt., 1991-96; children's pastor Christian Celebration Ctr., Midland, 1996—; adj. instr. pub. adminstrn. Ctrl. Mich. U., Mt. Pleasant, 1982-91, mem. MPA program adv. bd., 1988-91; mem. planning and evaluation com. Mich. Inst. for Pub. Adminstrn., 1989-91; dir. apptd. com. on act 312/PERA Det., Mich. Employment Rels. Commn., 1987-91; chmn. edn. and tng. com. Mich. Mcpl. League, 1991-95; mem., govtl. sector chmn. Midland Area Chamber Quality Coun., 1992-96; mem. Dow Chem. Cmty. Adv. Panel, 1994-98; dir. Mid-Mich. Royal Family Kids Camp, 1996—. Co-author: Manual Indiana Counties Model Personnel Policies, 1978. Bd. dirs. Salvation Army Adv. Bd., Midland Mich., 1978-81, trustee Meml. Presbyn. Ch., Midland Mich., 1984-87, Loaned Exec. United Way Midland Mich., 1985; vice-chair Midland County Drug Abuse Resistance Edn. Project, 1989-95. Recipient Mcpl. Achievement award Mich. Mcpl. League 1984; named one of Outstanding Young Men of Am., 1981. Mem. Midland Area Soccer League Club Mich. Mem. Assembly of God. Avocations: guitar, soccer, Bible study, religious retreat leadership, directing children's church camp. Home: 3806 Westbrier Ter Midland MI 48642-6658 Office: Christian Celebration Ctr 6100 Swede Ave Midland MI 48642-7144

CLARY, BRADLEY G., lawyer, educator; b. Richmond, Va., Sept. 7, 1950; s. Sidney G. and Jean B. Clary; m. Mary-Louise Hunt, July 31, 1982; children: Benjamin, Samuel. BA magna cum laude, Carleton Coll., 1972; JD cum laude, U. Minn., 1975. Bar: Minn. 1975, U.S. Dist. Ct. Minn. 1975, U.S. Ct. Appeals (10th cir.) 1977, U.S. Ct. Appeals (8th cir.) 1979, U.S. Ct. Appeals (6th cir.) 1980, U.S. Ct. Appeals (7th cir.) 1981, U.S. Supreme Ct. 1986, U.S. Ct. Appeals (4th cir.) 1989, U.S. Ct. Appeals (9th cir.) 1991. Assoc. Oppenheimer Wolff & Donnelly, St. Paul, 1975-81, ptnr., 1982—; legal writing dir. Law Sch. U. Minn., 1999—; adj. prof. Law Sch. U. Minn., Mpls., 1985-99; adj. instr. William Mitchell Coll. Law, St. Paul, 1995-96, 98, adj. prof., 1997, 99. Author: Primer on the Analysis and Presentation of Legal Argument, 1992. Vestryman St. John Evangelist Ch., St. Paul, 1978-81, 98—, pledge drive co-chmn. 1989-90; mem. alumni bd. Breck Sch., Mpls., 1981-85, 89-96, exec. com., 1991-96, dir. emeritus, 1996—; mem. adv. bd. Glass Theatre Co., West St. Paul, Minn., 1982-87; mem. antitrust adv. panel dept. health State of Minn., 1992-93. Mem. ABA (adv. group antitrust sect. 1987-89, corp. counseling com.), Minn. Bar Assn. (program chmn. antitrust sect. 1986-87, treas. 1987-88, vice-chmn. 1989-90, co-chmn. 1990-92), Phi Beta Kappa. Avocations: tennis, sailing. Office: U Minn Law Sch Rm 444 229 19th Ave S Minneapolis MN 55455

CLARY, KEITH UHL, retired industrial relations executive; b. Logansport, Ind., Mar. 7, 1921; s. Glen Uhl and Lucile (Billman) C. BSBA, Ind. U., 1943, MBA, 1948. Asst. dir. personnel and placement bur. Ind. U., Bloomington, 1947-48; mgr. personnel RCA plant, Monticello, Ind., 1948-54, Indpls. RCA plants, 1954-57; mgr. orgn. devel., corp. hdqrs. RCA, Camden, N.J., 1957-59; mgr. personnel EDP div. RCA, Cherry Hill, N.J., 1959-64; v.p. indsl. rels. RCA Consumer Electronics World Hdqs., Indpls., 1964-86; ret., 1987; asst. prof. Military Sci. and Tactics Howe Military Acad., Howe, Ind., 1945-46; adv. bd. Ind. Exec. program, Ind. U., 1970-71. Trustee, Indpls. Mus. Art, 1970—. Capt. inf., U.S. Army, 1943-46, ETO. Mem. Indpls. Urban League (founding mem., bd. dirs. 1972-76), Ind. State C. of C. (labor rels. com. 1964-74), Ind. Pers. Assn. (bd. dirs.), Ind. Hist. Soc. (libr. com. 1990), Oriental Art Soc., Indpls. Mus. Art (pres. 1991, human resources com. 1990—, donated numerous pieces of Chinese art and other objects to Indpls. Mus. of Art and Evansville Mus. of Art), Phi Eta Sigma, Beta Gamma Sigma. Republican. Methodist. Avocations: gardening, art collecting, travel. Home: 6407 Landborough South Dr Indianapolis IN 46220-4356

CLARY, RICHARD WAYLAND, lawyer; b. Tarboro, N.C., Oct. 10, 1953; s. S. Grayson and Jean (Beazley) C.; m. Suzanne Clerkin, July 21, 1991; children: Grayson Edward, Taryn Fenner. BA magna cum laude, Amherst Coll., 1975; JD magna cum laude, Harvard U., 1978. Bar: N.Y. 1981, U.S. Dist. Ct. (so. and ea. dists.) N.Y. 1981, U.S. Dist. Ct. (no. dist.) Calif., 1982, U.S. Ct. Appeals (9th cir.) 1983, U.S. Supreme Ct. 1989, U.S. Ct. Appeals (3d cir.) 1990, U.S. Ct. Appeals (2d cir.) 1994, U.S. Ct. Appeals (fed. cir.) 1995. Law clk. to judge U.S. Ct. Appeals (2d cir.), N.Y.C., 1978-79; law clk. to Justice Thurgood Marshall U.S. Supreme Ct., Washington, 1979-80; assoc. Cravath, Swaine & Moore, N.Y.C., 1980-85, ptnr., 1985—, mng. ptnr. litigation, 1997—. Bd. dirs. Legal Aid Soc., 1998—. John Woodruff Simpson fellow Amherst Coll., 1975-76. Mem. ABA, Fed. Bar Found. (bd. dirs. 1998—), N.Y. State Bar Assn., Assn. Bar City N.Y., Fed. Bar Coun., Phi Beta Kappa. Episcopalian. Office: Cravath Swaine & Moore Worldwide Pla 825 8th Ave New York NY 10019-7475

CLARY, RONALD GORDON, insurance agency executive; b. Moultrie, Ga., May 2, 1940; s. Ronald Ward and Hazel (Collins) C.; m. Adrian Irene Baker; children: Lynn, Beth, Lindsay, Baker. Student, Young Harris Coll., 1958-60; BBA in Ins., U. Ga., 1963; LLB, Woodrow Wilson Coll. Law, 1966. Registered rep. fin. planner. Field rep. Comml. Union Ins. Cos., 1962-67; ind. ins. agt., 1967—; ins. agt., sec. of agy. Day, Reynolds & Parks, Gainesville, Ga., 1970-93, pres., 1993—; fin. planner, registered rep. Am. Express Fin. Advisors, Inc. Mem. Profl. Ins. Agts. Am., Ga. Assn. Ind. Ins. Agts., Gainesville Assn. Ind. Ins. Agts. (past pres.), Young Agts. Com. Ga. (past chmn.), Am. Legion, Elks, Rotary. Republican. Baptist. Avocations: tennis, sailing. Fax: 770-754-9690. Home: 730 Lindsay Baker Ct NW Gainesville GA 30506 Office: 2475 Northwinds Pky Ste 100 Alpharetta GA 30004-4800

CLARY, ROSALIE BRANDON STANTON, timber farm executive, civic worker; b. Evanston, Ill., Aug. 3, 1928; d. Frederick Chase Hite-Smith and Rose Cecile (Liebich) Stanton; BS, Northwestern U., 1950, MA, 1954; m. Virgil Vincent Clary, Oct. 17, 1959; children: Rosalie Marian Hawley, Frederick Stanton, Virgil Vincent, Kathleen Elizabeth. Tchr., Chgo. Public Schs., 1951-55, adjustment tchr., 1956-61; faculty Loyola U., Chgo., 1963; v.p. Stanton Enterprises, Inc., Adams County, Miss., 1971-89; author Family History Record, genealogy record book, Kenilworth, Ill., 1977—. also lectr. Leader Girl Scouts U.S., Winnetka, Ill., 1969-71, 78-86, Cub Scouts, 1972-77; badge counselor Boy Scouts Am., 1978-87; election judge Rep. Com., 1977—; vol. Winnetka Libr. Genealogy Projects Com., 1995—. Mem. Nat. Soc. DAR (Ill. rec. sec. 1979-81, nat. vice chmn. program com. 1980-83, state vice regent 1986-88, state regent 1989-91, rec. sec. gen., 1992-95), Am. Forestry Assn., Forest Farmers Assn., North Suburban Geneal. Soc. (governing bd. 1979-86, pres. 1997-99), Winnetka Hist. Soc. (governing bd. 1978-90, 95—), Internat. Platform Assn., Delta Gamma (mem. nat. cabinet 1985-89). Roman Catholic. Home: 509 Elder Ln Winnetka IL 60093-4122 Office: PO Box 401 Kenilworth IL 60043-0401

CLARY, ROY, hospital administration executive; b. Winnipeg, Man., Can., Aug. 20, 1939; s. Omar LeRoy and Lois Ruth (Corey) C.; m. Marlene Alice Kogan; children: Megan Jennifer, Evan Samuel. BA, Ohio State U., 1961; BFA/MFA, Art Inst. Chgo., 1964. Actor Seattle Repertory Theatre, 1964-66, Barter Theatre, Abingdon, Va., 1969-70, Great Lakes Shakespeare Festival, Lakewood, Ohio, 1970-71; campaign dir. USO of Metro. N.Y.C., 1973-78; assoc. dir. devel. NYU, 1978-87; exec. v.p. Calvary Hosp. Fund, Bronx, 1987—. Mem. Rotary (pres. Bronx club 1996-97). Avocations: chess, golf, theatre. Office: Calvary Hosp Fund 1740 Eastchester Rd Bronx NY 10461-2322

CLARY, WARREN UPTON, neurosurgeon; b. Byronville, Ga., Feb. 8, 1920; s. George Esmond Clary and Ruby Mottweiler-Clary; m. Ruth Orleana Brown, June 10, 1948; children: Carolyn, Patricia. BS, Emory U., 1942, MD, 1944. Intern U.S. Naval Hosp., Portsmouth, Va., 1944-45; med. officer, lt. (j.g.) USNR, Portsmouth, 1944-46; resident in gen. surgery VA Hosp., Atlanta, 1946-47; resident in neurosurgery Lawson VA Hosp., Emory U. Hosp., Atlanta, 1947-50; resident in neurology and neuropathology Phila. Gen. Hosp., 1950-51; pvt. practice neurosurgery Neurol. Inst. Savannah, Ga., 1951—; chief-of-staff Candler Gen. Hosp., Savannah, 1970, Meml. Med. Ctr., Savannah, 1972. Contbr. articles to med. jours. Pres. Ga. Neurosurg. Soc., 1971-72. Fellow ACS; mem. Med. Assn. Ga. (cert. distinction 1994), Congress Neurol. Surgery, So. Neurosurg. Soc. (Disting. So. Neurosurgeon 1989), Am. Assn. Neurol. Surgery, Rotary. Methodist. Avocations: gardening, hiking, reading. Home: 22 Chatuachee Crossing Savannah GA 31411 Office: Neurol Inst Savannah 4 Jackson Blvd Savannah GA 31405

CLARY, WILLIAM VICTOR, minister; b. Baraboo, Wis., May 27, 1946; s. Harry Theone and Ruth Margaret (Harris) C.; m. F. Marie Bush, Aug. 12, 1966; children: Donna, Vicki, William. AA, Rochester Coll., 1966; BA, Okla. Christian U., 1968; postgrad., Abilene Christian U., 1972, No. Ill. U., 1973. Ordained to ministry Ch. of Christ, 1966. Min. Clinton, Ill., 1974-78, Lincoln, Ill., 1978-84, Anchorage, 1984—. v.p. Ill. Christian Camp, Decatur, 1978-84, dir., 1976-84; dir. Ill. Ch. of Christ Exhibit, Springfield, Ill., 1977-84; chaplain Abraham Lincoln Hosp., Lincoln, 1978-84, Logan County Jail, Lincoln, 1983-84; host-parent Am. Field Svcs., 1988-90, 92-94, chpt. pres., 1988-92. Republican. Avocations: reading, athletics, fishing, photography, traveling. Home: 1031 W 73rd Ave Anchorage AK 99518-2139 Office: 7800 Stanley Dr Anchorage AK 99518-2645 *No matter at what stage one is in life, the best is yet to come. Live each day joyfully knowing that a victory is certain for those in Christ!.*

CLASTER, JILL NADELL, university administrator, history educator; d. Harry K. and Edith Lillian Nadell; m. Millard L. Midonick, May 24, 1979; 1 child from previous marriage, Elizabeth Claster (dec.). B.A., NYU, 1952, M.A., 1954; Ph.D., U. Pa., 1959. Instr. history U. Pa., 1956-58; instr. ancient and medieval history U. Ky., Lexington, 1959-61; asst. prof. U. Ky., 1961-64; asst. prof. classics NYU, N.Y.C., 1964-65; asst. prof. history NYU, 1965-68, assoc. prof., 1968-84, prof., 1984—, acting undergrad. chmn. history, 1972-73, dir. M.A. in liberal studies program, 1976-78; assoc. dean Washington Sq. and Univ. Coll., 1978, acting dean, 1978-79, dean, 1979-86; dir. Hagop Kevorkian Ctr. for Near Eastern Studies, NYU, 1991-96; Appointee N.Y.C. Commn. on Status of Women. Author: Athenian Democracy: Triumph or Travesty, 1967, The Medieval Experience, 1982; Contbr. articles to profl. jours. Danforth grantee, 1966-68; Fulbright grantee, 1958-59. Mem. Am. Hist. Assn., Medieval Acad. Am., Archaeol. Inst. Am., Medieval Club N.Y. Home: 161 W 15th St New York NY 10011-6720 Office: NYU Dept History 53 Washington Sq S Dept History New York NY 10012-1098

CLAUS, CAROL JEAN, small business owner; b. Uniondale, N.Y., Dec. 17, 1959; d. Charles Joseph and Frances Meta (Fichter) C.; m. Armand Joseph Gasperetti, Jr., July 7, 1985. Student pub. schs., Uniondale. Asst. mgr. Record World, L.I., N.Y., 1977-82, mgr. Info. Builders Inc., N.Y.C., 1982-92; pres. Carol's Creations, Belen, N.Mex. Mem. NAFE, Nat. Organization for Women. Democrat. Roman Catholic.

CLAUSEL, NANCY KAREN, minister; b. Jackson, Tenn., Jan. 1, 1948; s. Clinton Prentice and Martha Juanita (Felker) C.; children: Richard D. Harwood Jr., Kara Harwood Fricke. Student Lambuth Coll., 1966-67, George Peabody Coll. for Tchrs.; BSE, Memphis State U., 1971; MDiv summa cum laude, Memphis Theol. Sem., 1980. Ordained to ministry United Meth.; cert. counselor Tenn. Ch. Dir. Christian edn. Grimes United Meth. Ch., Memphis, 1977-79, Wesleyan Hills United Meth. Ch., Memphis, 1979-80; assoc. minister St. James United Meth. Ch., Memphis, 1981-82; dir. Wesley Pastoral Counseling Ctr., Memphis, 1982-85; co-dir. Connection: Holistic Counseling Ctr., Memphis, 1985-87; co-founder, co-min. The Connection Ch., 1986-87; founder, min., Ch. in the Round; chaplain Addiction Recovery Sys., 1993-95; pastor Stevenson United Meth. Ch., 1995-98; pastor Montesano (Wash.) United Meth. Ch., 1998—; bd. dirs. Wesley Found.-Memphis State, 1979-80, 82-84; vice chmn. commn. on status and role of women Memphis Ann. Conf., 1980-86; mem. work area on worship McKendree Dist. Memphis Ann. Conf., 1980-84; mem. Bd. Pensions Memphis Ann. Conf., 1983-84; supervising pastor Candidacy for Min. program Memphis Ann. Conf., 1984-86. Vol. Johnson Aux. City of Memphis Hosp., 1975; sec. Peacemakers Memphis, 1979; clergy rep. adv. bd. Memphis chpt. Parents Without Ptnrs., 1984-85; mem. Network, Memphis, 1984-87; chmn. Pacific N.W. ann. conf. UMC Episcopal Task Force on Children and Poverty; chmn. bd. discipleship sect. on worship and spirituality PNWAC; bd. dirs. Greater Columbia Regional Adv. Network. Mem. Internat. Transactional Analysis Assn. (clin. mem. 1981—, provisional teaching mem. 1982—), Assn. for Specialists in Group Work, Memphis Mins. Assn. (treas. 1985-86), Altrusa Internat., Skamania County Ministers Assn. (pres. 1997-98), Pacific N.W. Conf. Coun. Ministry, Phi Kappa Phi. Columnist: The Light (newspaper). Avocations: hiking, music. Home: 415 Spruce Ave East Montesano WA 98563

CLAUSELL, DEBORAH DELORIS, artist, songwriter; b. Mobile, Ala., July 16, 1951; d. Stephen Joseph and Estell Abney Clausell. *Great-great-great grandfather, General Count Bertrand Clausel, was one of the Bonpartists that fled to America. He was one of the most important officers. He was an officer of merit throughout Napoleon's campaigns. He had commanded at Bordeaux during the Hundred Days, having made the Duchess of Anguleme prisoner (granddaughter of the executed Louis XVI of France). He released her for reasons which were never known. He did not occupy his grant on the Tombigbee but in 1821, settled on the bay near Mobile. In 1825, he was allowed to return to France and was made governor.* BA in Sociology, U.

Mobile, 1976; cert., Barbizon Modeling Sch., 1984. Movie extra Century Casting, Santa Monica, Calif., 1984-85; libr. Mobile Pub. Libr., 1996-97. Exhibited in group shows Greater Gulf State Fair, Mobile, 1990, 96 (3d, 2d and 1st prize ribbons), 97 (3rd prize ribbon), Mercy Med. Gallery, Daphne, Ala., 1993, Mus. of City of Mobile, 1993, Fine Art Mus. of the South, Mobile, 1993, Spring Hill Art, Mobile, 1993; pvt. collection The White House. 2d lt. USAFR. Recipient Gold Eagles and Stars Letters from U.S. President. Mem. VFW, U.S. Naval Inst., Libr. Congress Assn., Nat. Trust for Hist. Preservation, Civil War Trust. Democrat. Roman Catholic. Avocations: classic guitarist, harmonica, swimming, vocal singing, reading. Home and Studio: 5859 Reams Dr N Mobile AL 36608-3652

CLAUSEN, BRET MARK, industrial hygienist, safety professional; b. Hayward, Calif., Aug. 1, 1958; s. Norman E. and Barbara Ann (Wagner) C.; m. Cheryl Elaine Carlson, May 24, 1980; children: Kathrine, Eric, Emily. BS, Colo. State U., 1980, MS, 1983. Cert. indsl. hygienist, safety profl., hazard control mgr., hazardous materials mgr.; cert. in comprehensive practice Am. Bd. Inds. Hygiene; cert. in comprehensive practice and mgmt. aspects Bd. Cert. Safety Profls. Assoc. risk mgmt., indsl. hygienist, safety rep. Samsonite Corp., Denver, 1980-83, mgr. loss prevention, 1984-88; health, safety and environment rep. Storage Tech., Longmont, Colo., 1984; sr. project cons. Occusafe Inc., Denver, 1988; numerous indsl. hygiene and safety mgmt./tech. assignments Rocky Flats Environ. Tech. Site, Golden, Colo., 1988—; mem. radiol. assistance program team U.S. Dept. Energy, Region VI, 1994—. Local emergency planning com. Weld County, Colo., 1996—. Mem. Am. Indsl. Hygiene Assn. (pres. Rocky Mountain sect. 1988-89), Am. Soc. Safety Engrs. (prof., acad. accreditation/site evaluator 1998—, profl. and ednl. stds. com. 1998—), Inst. Hazardous Materials Mgmt. (cert. sr. level), Ins. Inst. Am. (assoc. in risk mgmt.), Am. Nat. Stds. Inst. (com. on confined spaces 1993—), Am. Acad. Indsl. Hygiene (diplomate, acad. accreditation com. site evaluator 1994—). Republican. Lutheran. Avocations: hunting, backpacking, snowshoeing. Home: 16794 Weld County Rd # 44 La Salle CO 80645 Office: Safe Sites of Colo PO Box 464 Mail Stop B750 Golden CO 80402-0464

CLAUSEN, HUGH JOSEPH, retired army officer; b. Mobile, Ala., Dec. 25, 1926; s. Hugh Martin and Elizabeth Hazel (Orrell) C.; m. Betty Sue Richards, June 7, 1949; children: Melinda, Joseph. LL.B., U. Ala., 1950; grad., Advanced Mgmt. Program, Harvard U., 1970. Bar: Ala. 1950, U.S. Supreme Ct. 1959, U.S. Ct. Mil. Appeals 1959. Commd. 1st lt. U.S. Army, 1951; advanced through grades to maj. gen.; various assignments U.S. Army, U.S. and Europe, 1951-62; asst. staff judge adv. (8th Army), Korea, 1962-64; judge adv. U.S. Disciplinary Barracks, Fort Leavenworth, Kans., 1964-66; instr. U.S. Army Command and Gen. Staff Coll., 1966-68; staff judge adv. 1st Inf. Div., Vietnam, 1968-69; assigned Office Legis. Liaison, Dept. Army, Washington, 1969-71; chief mil. justice div. Office JAG, 1971-72, exec. officer, 1972-73; staff judge adv. III Corps and Ft. Hood, Tex., 1973-76; chief judge U.S. Army Ct. Mil. Rev., Falls Church, Va., 1976-78; asst. judge adv. gen. for mil. law Dept. Army., 1978-79, asst. judge adv. gen., 1979-81, judge adv. gen., 1981-85. Vice pres. for adminstrn., sec. bd. trustees Clemson U., S.C., 1985-92, v.p. emeritus, 1992—. Decorated Disting. Service Medal, Bronze Star with 3 oak leaf clusters, Meritorious Service medal, Legion of Merit with oak leaf cluster, Air medal with oak leaf cluster, Army Commendation medal with oak leaf cluster; RVN Honor medal; RVN Gallantry Cross with palm; RVN Civic Action Honor medal with palm. Mem. Ala. Bar Assn., Phi Alpha Delta. Address: 107 Hermitage Mooring Dr Seneca SC 29672-9138

CLAUSEN, JERRY LEE, psychiatrist; b. Wausau, Wis., Nov. 5, 1939; s. Douglas William and Florence Jean (Amidon) C.; m. Nancy Eileen Longdon, Aug. 3, 1962; children: Keith Russell, Pamela Dawn. BA, Wesleyan U., Middletown, Conn., 1961; MD, Albany Med. Coll., N.Y., 1965. Dilomate Am. Bd. Psychiatry and Neurology with qualification in Addiction Psychiatry; cert. Am. Soc. Addiction Medicine, N.Y. State Alcoholism Counselor. Psychiatry intern Upstate Med. Ctr., Syracuse, N.Y., 1965-66; psychiatric resident Upstate Med. Ctr., 1966-67, 69-71, asst. attending, 1971-72, attending, 1972-80; staff psychiatrist Onondaga Mental Health Clinic, Syracuse, 1971-72; courtesy staff Benjamin Rush Psychiatric Ctr., Syracuse, 1971-84, active staff, 1984—; pvt. practice psychiatry Syracuse, 1971—; clin. asst. prof. SUNY, 1972—; staff psychiatrist Onondaga Pastoral Counseling Ctr., Syracuse, 1971-73, 81-97, psychiatric dir., 1973-81; cons. psychiatrist Loretto Rest Geriatric Ctr., Syracuse, 1972-74. Tchr. First Universalist Ch., Syracuse, 1966—. Lt. comdr. USN, 1967-69. Fellow Am. Psychiat. Assn. (chmn. ins. mktg. com. 1979-88); mem. Onondaga County Med. Soc., N.Y. State Med. Soc. Universalist-Unitarian. Avocations: walking, tennis, cross-country skiing. Office: 300 Burnet Ave Syracuse NY 13203-2302

CLAUSEN, WENDELL VERNON, classics educator; b. Coquille, Oreg., Apr. 2, 1923; s. George R. and Gertrude (Johnson) C.; m. Corinna Slice, Aug. 20, 1947; children: John, Raymond, Thomas; m. Margaret W. Woodman, June 19, 1970. A.B., U. Wash., 1945; Ph.D., U. Chgo., 1948; A.M. (hon.), Harvard U., 1959. Mem. faculty Amherst Coll., 1948-59, assoc. prof. classics, 1955-59; prof. Greek and Latin Harvard U., 1959-82, Victor S. Thomas prof. Greek and Latin, 1982-88, Pope prof. Latin lang. and lit., 1988-93, prof. comparative lit., 1984-93, prof. emeritus, 1993—, chmn. dept. classics, 1966-71; vis. prof. Univ. Coll., London, 1971; Sather prof. U. Calif., Berkeley, 1982; vis. prof. I Tatti, Florence, Italy, 1989. Author: Virgil's Aeneid and the Tradition of Hellenistic Poetry, 1987, A Commentary on Virgil's Eclogues, 1994; editor: Persius, 1956, Persius and Juvenal, 1959, rev. edit., 1992, Appendix Vergiliana, 1966; editor, contbr.: The Cambridge History of Latin Literature, 1982, Premio Internazionale Virgilio, 1994; assoc. editor: Am. Jour. Philology, 1976-81, Style and Tradition: Studies in Honor of Wendell Clausen, 1998; editor Harvard Studies in Classical Philology, 1990-92; author articles in classical philology. Fellow Am. Acad. in Rome, 1952-53, Am. Council Learned Socs., 1962-63; fellow commoner Peterhouse, Cambridge. Fellow Am. Acad. Arts and Sciences; mem. Am. Philol. Assn., Cambridge Philol. Soc., Phi Beta Kappa. Home: 8 Kenway St Cambridge MA 02138-4724 Office: Harvard U 319 Boylston Hall Cambridge MA 02138

CLAUSER, ANGELA FRANCES, medical surgical, pediatrics and geriatrics nurse; b. Leavenworth, Kans., June 25, 1955; d. Donald F. Sr. and Agnes Angela (Forge) C. AA, Kansas City (Kans.) Jr. Coll., 1984; BSN, Pitts. State U., 1986. RN, Kans.; cert. provider CPR, Am. Heart Assn. Sec. U.S. Army, Ft. Leavenworth, Kans., 1978, 79-80, USAF Acad., Colorado Springs, Colo., 1981-82, VA, Leavenworth, 1982-84; staff nurse St. John's Hosp., Leavenworth, 1989-96, unit edn. coord., 1995-96; oncology prn nurse U. Kans. Hosp., Kansas City, 1997—; clin. nurse Gentry Clinic, Ft. Leavenworth, Kans., 1998—, instr. pediatric asthma class, 1998-99; substitute sch. nurse Ft. Leavenworth, Kans., 1997—. Mem. Nurses Svc. Orgn., Pitts. State U. Alumni Assn., Kans. City Jr. Coll. Alumni Assn.

CLAUSER, DONALD ROBERDEAU, musician; b. Fort Worth, Mar. 2, 1941; s. Donald Milton and Selina Almira (Sizer) C. B.F.A., U. N.M., 1962; Mus.M., Boston U., 1964; diploma, Curtis Inst. Music, 1967. Mem. viola sect., Phila. Orch., 1966—. Home: 1609 Chanticleer Cherry Hill NJ 08003-4820 *It is my conviction that music is a universal medium of communication—a factor which is surely of distinct value in these troubled times. Keeping this in mind has constantly been uppermost in the pursuit of my career, wherever this may have led me.*

CLAUSER, KENNETH ALTON, professional photographer, banjo player; b. Cementon, Pa., May 24, 1932; s. Alton L.R. Clauser and Margaret M. (Nagel) Lansky; m. Alma Ellen Kunkel, Sept. 24, 1955; children: Mark W., John T. Grad., Eastman Kodak Sch. Photography, 1952. Staff photographer Call-Chronicle Newspapers, Allentown, Pa., 1952-79; photog. supr. Pa. Power and Light Co., Allentown, 1979-92; owner Ken Clauser Photography Studio, Allentown, 1952—; bd. dirs. W.K.&S. R.R., Kempton, Pa. Advisor Muhlenberg Coll., Photography Explorer Post 35, Allentown, 1981—; asst. scoutmaster Boy Scouts Am., Orefield, Pa., 1970—; charter mem. adv. bd. Marine Band, Allentown, 1991—. Mem. Profl. Photographers Am., Eastman Kodak Pro Passport Assn., Fretted Instrument Guild Am., Am. Newspaper Guild (treas. local 49 1952-79, 25 yr. award). Republican. Mem. United Ch. of Christ. Avocations: banjo player (with The Keystone String Band, Dixieland Five), stamp collecting, camera collecting.

CLAUSING, ARTHUR MARVIN, mechanical engineering educator; b. Palatine, Ill., Aug. 17, 1936; s. Arthur Fred and Emma Marie (Opfer) C.; m. Willa Louise Spence, Dec. 19, 1964; children—Erin, Kimberly. B.S. in Mech. Engring., Valparaiso U., 1958; M.S. in Mech. Engring., U. Ill., 1960, Ph.D. in Mech. Engring., 1963. Research asst. U. Ill., Urbana, 1962-63, asst. prof., 1963-68, assoc. prof., 1968-84, asst. dean coll. engring., 1982—, prof. mech. engring., 1984-98, assoc. head dept. mech. and indsl. engring., 1987-98; prof. emeritus mech. and indsl. engring. U. Ill., 1998—; cons. Solar Energy Research Inst., 1984-86, M.A.N. Neve Technologie, Munich, Fed. Republic Germany, 1980-87, Ill. Power Co., 1979-81. Author: Numerical Methods in Heat Transfer, 1969; editor Am. Soc. Mech. Engrs. Jour. of Solar Energy Engring., 1984-88; contbr. articles to profl. jours. Recipient Instructional award U. Ill., 1967; Standard Oil award for devel. of heat transfer lab., 1968; Fulbright scholar, 1983; Valparaiso U. Disting. Alumnus award, 1985; ASME fellow, 1997. Mem. ASME, ASHRAE, Am. Soc. Engring. Edn., Internat. Solar Energy Soc. Lutheran. Avocations: running; bicycling; photography; music. Home: 613 Hessel Blvd Champaign IL 61820-6328 Office: Univ Ill Dept Mech Engring Room 152 1206 W Green St Urbana IL 61801-2906*

CLAUSMAN, GILBERT JOSEPH, medical librarian; b. Los Angeles, Nov. 8, 1921; s. Peter Joseph and Lila (Mason) C. A.B., Willamette U., 1947; B.S., Columbia U., 1948, M.S., 1952. Med. librarian N.Y. Acad. Medicine, N.Y.C., 1948-55; med. librarian NYU Med. Ctr., N.Y.C., 1955-86, librarian emeritus, 1987—; cons. Milton Helpern Library Legal Medicine, 1963-88. Served with USN, 1942-45. Mem. Med. Libr. Assn. (pres. 1977-78), Archons of Colophon, N.Y. Acad. Medicine, Acad. Health Info. Profls. (Disting. mem. emeritus). Home: 6 Cobble Hill Rd Westport CT 06880-2915

CLAUSON, GARY LEWIS, chemist; b. Peoria, Ill., Feb. 25, 1952; s. Cecil Lewis and Virgie Grace (Shryock) C. AAS, Ill. Cen. Coll., East Peoria, 1974; BA in Chemistry, U. Calif., San Diego, 1977; MS in Chem., Bradley U., Peoria, 1981; PhD in Organic Chemistry, U. Ill., 1987. Engring. technician U.S. Naval Sta., San Diego, 1974-75; lab. analyst Lehn & Fink Products Co., Lincoln, Ill., 1978-79; part-time faculty Bradley U., Peoria, 1980-81; sci. asst. Ill. State Geol. Survey, Urbana, 1986-87; sr. chemist Ciba-Geigy Corp., McIntosh, Ala., 1987-92; rsch. scientist Gensia, Inc., San Diego, 1992-95, cons., 1995-96; prin. scientist Alliance Pharm. Corp., San Diego, 1996—. Mem. Am. Chem. Soc., Assn. Ofcl. Analytical Chemists. Avocations: paleontology, tennis, basketball, softball, bicycling. Home: 3277 Berger Ave Apt 20 San Diego CA 92123-1933

CLAUSON, SHARYN FERNE, consulting company executive, educator; b. Phila., Oct. 4, 1946; d. Eugene and Gertrud Jayn (Besser) C. BA in English, Temple U., 1968; MEd in Psychology, Beaver Coll., 1979; MBA in Marketing, Drexel U., 1982; postgrad. in law, Temple U., 1987. Market analyst Epstein Rsch., Bala, Pa., 1967-69; cons. Ednl. Testing Svc., Princeton, N.J., 1979-80; CEO CCX, Narberth, Pa., 1978-79; mem. faculty Cheltenham Twp. Sch. Dist., Elkins Park, Pa., 1969—; dir. Sharyn Clauson Bus. Comm., Narberth, Pa., 1975-85; pres. S. Clauson & Assocs., Inc., King of Prussia, Pa., 1985—; dir. Execuwriter, King of Prussia, 1985—; mem. adj. faculty Drexel U., Phila., 1979-96, Phila. Coll. Textiles and Sci., 1985-89, St. Joseph's U., Phila., 1986-92, Phila. Ctr. of Gt. lakes Coll. Assn., 1988; mem. adv. bd. Ergodyne, Inc., 1995-96; talk show host Sta. WDVT-AM, Phila., 1985; bd. dirs. Site Selex, Inc., Doylestown, Pa., dir. comm. and pub. rels., 1988-95. Editor: Curriculum for Optacon Music Reading, 1984; mem. editorial adv. bd. Bus. Communications and Concepts, 2d edit., 1985. Mem. com. Women's Polit. Caucus, Phila.; mem. Phila. Art Alliance; mem. exec. bd., arts and scis. alumni bd. Temple U. Women's Law Caucus. Golden Hearts honoree, 1999. Mem. ASCD, AAUW, Am. Mktg. Assn., Nat. Spkrs. Assn. (chairperson 1985), Nat. Assn. Profl. Saleswomen (honoree 1982—), Nat. Coun. Tchrs. of English, Delaware Valley Writing Coun., Wallenberg Communicators, Phi Delta Kappa. Office: 21036 Valley Forge Cir Ste 1 King Of Prussia PA 19406

CLAUSSEN, LISA RENEE, engineering executive; b. Cedar Grove, Wis., Mar. 28, 1964; d. Erwin John and Shirley Ann (Winkelhorst) C. BS in Indsl. Engring., U. Wis., Platteville, 1987; MS in Ops. Mgmt., U. Ark., Fayetteville, 1990. Registered profl. engr., Wis. Quality engring. process coord. Speed Queen Co., Ripon, Wis., 1987-88; plant quality control engr. Speed Queen Co., Searcy, Ark., 1988-90; quality engring. rep. Snap-on Inc., Kenosha, Wis., 1990-92, quality engr. med. products divsn., 1992-94; quality assurance supr. Snap-on Inc., Elizabethton, Tenn., 1994—. Active Nat. Kidney Found. Wis., Milw., 1994—. Mem. NAFE, Am. Soc. for Quality (sr., cert. quality engr., cert. quality auditor, SMP coord. Racine-Kenosha sect. 1992-94, membership chair N.E. Tenn. 1995-96, chair elect 1996-97, chair 1997-98, past chmn. 1998-99, dir. 1999—), Inst. Indsl. Engrs. (sr., bd. dirs. Ctrl. Ark. 1989-90, dir. support Tri-Cities Tenn. 1995-97, pres.-elect 1998-99, pres. 1999—). Avocations: music, literature, travel, science/science fiction. Office: Snap On Inc 2195 State Line Rd Elizabethton TN 37643-4636

CLAVER, ROBERT EARL, television director, producer; b. Chgo., May 22, 1928; s. Louis E. and Sara M. (Sosna) C.; 1 child, Nancy Beth. BS in Journalism, U. Ill., 1950. Prodr.-writer: first 1000 Captain Kangaroo shows (Sylvania award, Peabody award); prodr., dir.: (TV shows) Here Comes the Brides, 1968-70, The Interns, 1970-71, Partridge Family, 1970-74, Gloria, CBS-TV, 1982-83, Small Wonder, 1985, New Love American Style, 1985, New Leave It to Beaver, 1986-87, Charles in Charge, 1987, Out of This World, 1987-91, numerous other series; dir.: (TV shows) Welcome Back Kotter, ABC-TV, 1977-78, All's Fair, CBS-TV, Housecalls, CBS-TV, 1979-80, Mork and Mindy, ABC-TV, 1981-82. With U.S. Army, 1951-53. Mem. Dirs. Guild Am.

CLAVERIE, PHILIP DEVILLIERS, lawyer; b. New Orleans, June 29, 1941; s. Louis Barbot and Viola Aimee (Schlegel) C.; m. Laura Lynn McCampbell, Apr. 27, 1974; children: Philip deVilliers Jr., Stephanie McCampbell. A.B., Princeton U., 1963; J.D., Tulane U., 1966. Bar: La. 1966. Assoc. Phelps Dunbar, New Orleans, 1966-70, ptnr., 1970—. Contbr. articles to profl. jours. Pres. bd. trustees Children's Hosp. New Orleans, 1978-80; chmn. bd. govs. Isidore Newman Sch., 1995-98; mem. exec. bd. New Orleans Police Found. Served to lt. comdr., JAGC, USNR, 1973-79. Fellow Am. Bar Found., La. Bar Found.; mem. ABA, La. State Bar Assn., New Orleans Bar Assn., Assn. Bar City N.Y., Am. Law Inst., Am. Judicature Soc., La. State Law Inst. Clubs: Pickwick, Stratford. Home: 14 Versailles Blvd New Orleans LA 70125-4114 Office: Phelps Dunbar 30th Fl Texaco Ctr 400 Poydras St New Orleans LA 70130-3245*

CLAVERIE, ROY E., water transportation executive, transportation exec. Chmn., CEO Ingram Industries, Nashville. Office: Ingram Industries Inc 1 Belle Meade Pl 4000 Harding Rd Nashville TN 37205-1901

CLAWSON, DAVID KAY, orthopedic surgeon; b. Salt Lake City, Aug. 8, 1927; s. David J. and Elva (Gundry) C.; m. Janet Dorothy Smith, June 1, 1952; children: Kim Debra, David Roger. Student, U. Utah, 1944-45, 47-48; M.D., Harvard U., 1952. Diplomate: Am. Bd. Orthopedic Surgery. Intern Stanford U. Hosp., 1952-53, resident gen. surgery, 1953-54; resident orthopedic surgery Stanford U. Hosp., also San Francisco City and County Hosp., 1954-57; fellow in orthopedics Nat. Found. Infantile Paralysis, 1955-58; hon. sr. registrar Royal Nat. Orthopedic Hosp., London, Eng., 1957-58; asst. prof. UCLA Med. Sch., 1958; asst. prof. surgery, head div. orthopedic surgery U. Wash. Med. Sch., 1958-61, assoc. prof. surgery, head div. orthopedic surgery, 1961-65, prof., 1964-83, chmn. dept. orthopedics, 1964-75; dean Coll. Medicine, U. Ky., 1975-83, vice chancellor for clin. profl. services, 1982-83; exec. vice chancellor U. Kans. Med. Ctr., Kansas City, 1983-94, cons. to chancellor, 1994; prof. surgery/orthopaedics U. Ky., 1994—; mem. Accreditation Coun. for Grad. Med. Edn., 1977-88; chmn. residency rev. com. on structure and functions, 1987-88; chmn. coun. of deans Assn. Am. Med. Coll., 1985-86, chmn. of the assembly, 1988-89, immediate past chmn., 1989-90, disting. svc. rep. to exec. coun., 1992-95; active Am. Orthopaedic Soc. for Sports Medicine, 1972-87, founder, 1972; active Assn. Orthopaedic Chmn., 1971-73, founder, 1971. Contbr. med. jours.; mem. editorial bd.: Clin. Orthopedics and Related Research, 1964—. Mem. Heart of Am. coun. Boy Scouts Am., 1989—, mem. adv. bd., 1989-92, Regional Task Force and Edn. Found., 1972—. With USNR, 1945-46. Exchange fellow Am. Orthopedic Assn., 1967. Mem. AMA (coun. for med. affairs 1988—), Am. Acad. Ortho. Surgeons (coun. on health policy 1990-95), Am. Orthopaedic Assn., Assn. Acad. Health Ctrs., Assn. Am. Univs., Assn. Bone and Joint Surgeons (pres. 1977), Ky. Med. Assn., Fayette County Med. Soc., Harvard Med. Sch. Alumni Assn. (pres. 1984-85). Home: 3785 Jamaica Ct Lexington KY 40509-9506 also: 10 E Roanoke St Seattle WA 98102-3257 *Look to the past only for the lessons we can learn, live today for the joy of being alive, plan to the future to insure that what should be, will be.*

CLAWSON, JOHN ADDISON, financier, investor; b. Monaco, Pa., June 4, 1922; s. Ralph S. and Elsie (Winnett) C.; m. Patricia Harmon, July 5, 1947; children: Christine Brandwie, Hunter Winnett. BS, Miami U., 1943, LLD, 1979; postgrad., Harvard U., 1968. Vice pres., nat. mgr. bus. and labor reports div. Prentice-Hall, N.Y.C., 1948-55; with DuBois Chems. div. Chemed Corp., Cin., 1955-78; dist. mgr. DuBois Chems. div. Chemed Corp., N.Y.C., 1955-60; regional mgr. Ea. div. DuBois Chems. div. Chemed Corp., 1960-64, divisional mgrs. v.p., 1964-66, exec. v.p., dir. sales, 1966-70, gen. mgr., 1968-70, pres., chief exec. officer, 1970-79, group exec., 1975-79; v.p. Chemed Corp., 1971-77, exec. v.p., 1978-79, ret., 1979; chmn. Whitehall Mgmt. Corp., Cin.; bd. dirs. Suburban Fed. Savs. & Loan Assn. Trustee Providence Hosp., 1974-76; dean's assoc. Miami U., 1973—. Lt. (j.g.) USNR, 1943-46. Mem. Cin. C. of C. (city and county planning com. 1971-74), Soap and Detergent Assn. (vice-chmn. bd. 1971-73, chmn. bd., chief exec. officer 1974-75, mem. exec. com., bd. dirs. 1976-79), Delta Sigma Phi, Sigma Alpha Epsilon. Presbyterian. Clubs: Queen City (Cin.), Kenwood Country (Cin.); John's Island (Fla.), Cat Cay, Ltd., Commodore (Bahamas). Home: Johns Island 301 Island Creek Dr Vero Beach FL 32963-3306

CLAWSON, JOHN THOMAS, government relations professional; b. St. Paul, Aug. 7, 1945; s. Eugene Woodrow and Lila Lavonne (Christensen) C.; m. Annette Helene Roth, 1998; children: Jennifer Susan, Amanda Jennifer. BA, Augsburg Coll., 1967; MDiv, Northwestern Luth. Theol. Sem., 1971. Staff chaplain Hazelden Found., Center City, Minn., 1971-84; state rep. Minn. Legis., St. Paul, 1975-84; asst. commr. Minn. Dept. Human Svcs., St. Paul, 1984-86; exec. dir. Minn. Coun. on Disability, St. Paul, 1986-87; pvt. practice lobbyist St. Paul, 1987-89; exec. dir. Cmty. Clinic Consortium, St. Paul, 1989-92; dir. pub. policy and advocacy Luth. Social Svc. Minn., St. Paul, 1992—; pub. policy com. Minn. AIDS Project, Mpls., 1991—; health adv. com. Urban Coalition, St. Paul, 1992—; pub. policy cabinet Minn. Coun. Non-Profit, St. Paul, 1995—. Pres. bd. dirs. St. Croix Valley Heritage Coalition, Taylors Falls, Minn., 1993—; judge of elections City Mpls., 1994—. Recipient Dwight V. Dixon award Minn. Mental Health Assn., 1982, Svc. award Minn. Dept. Health, 1984. Mem. Minn. Govt. Rels. Coun., Minn. Social Svcs. Assn. (legis. com. 1995—). Avocations: history of Minnesota's U.S. senators, travel, cooking, gardening, antiques. Home: 3226 19th Ave S Minneapolis MN 55407-2402 Office: Luth Social Svc Minn 2485 Como Ave Saint Paul MN 55108-1445

CLAWSON, ROXANN ELOISE, college administrator, computer company executive; b. Dallas, Oct. 15, 1945; d. Robert Wellington Clawson and Jeannette Irene (Rodenhauser) Clawson Clayton. BFA, Mich. State U., 1968. Library asst. Cooper Union, N.Y.C., 1970-75, asst. librarian, 1976-82, assoc. to dean, 1985—; computer cons., 1986—. Acting appearance in The Dragon's Nest, La MaMa Theatre, 1989. Mem. NAFE, N.Y. Personal Computer Group. Democrat. Lutheran. Avocation: administration.

CLAXTON, HARRIETT MAROY JONES, retired English language educator; b. Dublin, Ga., Aug. 27, 1930; d. Paul Jackson and Maroy Athalia (Chappell) Jones; m. Edward B. Claxton, Jr., May 27, 1953; children: E. B. III, Paula Jones. AA with honors, Bethel Woman's Coll., 1949; AB magna cum laude, Mercer U., 1951; MEd, Ga. Coll., 1965. Social worker Laurens County Welfare Bd., Dublin, 1951-56; H.S. tchr. Dublin, 1961-66; instr. Middle Ga. Coll., Cochran, 1966-71, asst. prof. English, lit. and speech, 1971-85, assoc. prof., 1985-86; rsch. tchr. Trinity Christian Sch., 1986, 92, sr. English tchr., 1986-87; tchr. Ga. Coll., 1987, , E. Ga. Coll., 1988-99, Middle Ga. Coll., 1985-99. Weekly columnist Dublin Courier Herald, 1993—; contbr. articles to profl. jours. and newspapers; editor Laurens County History, II, 1987; author: History of Laurens Superior Court. Pres., chmn. bd. Mensea/Laurens unit Am. Cancer Soc.; bd. dirs. Friends of Vets., Heart of Ga. Altamaha Regional Devel. Ctr.; pres. bd. Dublin Assn. Fine Arts, 1974-76, 82-84, 90-98, Dublin Hist. Soc., 1976-78, 95-98; mem. Laurens County Libr. Bd., 1960-68; chmn. Dublin Hist. Rev. Bd., 1980—; sec. Am. Assn. Ret. Persons, 1987-90; v.p. Dublin Cmty. Concert, 1991-98. Named Woman of Yr., St. Patrick's Festival, Dublin, 1979, Most Popular Tchr., Dublin Ctr., 1985, Olympic Torch Bearer, 1996; recipient Outstanding Svc. award CAncer Soc., Dublin, 1985, 93, 98, Ga. Coll. Outstanding Alumni award for cmty. svc., 1996. Mem. DAR (regent, vice regent, historian, state, dist., nat. awards), Woman's Study Club (pres.), Erin Garden Club (pres.), Sigma Mu, Alpha Delta Pi (scholarship plaque 1950), Phi Theta Kappa (treas.), Chi Delta Phi (sec.), Delta Kappa Gamma. Democrat. Baptist. Home: 101 Rosewood Dr Dublin GA 31021-4129

CLAY, CAROL ANN, family nurse practitioner; b. South Hill, Va., Sept. 21, 1967; d. Arthur Lee and Helen Irene Bottoms; m. Edward Alan Clay, Oct. 1, 1996. BSN, Radford U., 1990; MSN, Old Dominion U., 1995. RN, Va.; Clin. Specialist, Am. Nurse's Credentialing Ctr.; cert. family nurse practitioner Am. Acad. Nurse Practitioners. RN charge nurse Southside Regional Med. Ctr., Petersburg, Va., 1990; RN staff nurse Culpeper (Va.) Meml. Hosp., 1990-91; RN charge nurse W.S. Hundley Annex, South Hill, Va., 1991; charge nurse, house supr. Brian's Ctr., Lawrenceville, Va., 1991-92; PN, NA instr. Southside Va. C.C., Alberta, 1991-95; RN PRN pool Cmty. Meml. Health Ctr., South Hill, 1993-97, family nurse practitioner urgent care, 1997-98, family nurse practitioner occupl. health svcs., 1998—. Mem. APHA, Am. Acad. Nurse Practitioners, VA Nurse Practitioner Coun., Sigma Theta Tau. Avocation: reading. Home: 19491 Highway One Brodnax VA 23920-2247 Office: Cmty Meml Health Ctr PO Box 90 125 Buena Vista Cir South Hill VA 23970-1431

CLAY, CASSIUS MARCELLUS See ALI, MUHAMMAD

CLAY, CLARENCE SAMUEL, acoustical oceanographer; b. Kansas City, Mo., Nov. 2, 1923; s. Clarence Samuel and Mary Else (Hall) C.; m. Andre Jane Edwards, Mar. 27, 1945; children: Arnold, Jo, David, Michael. BS, Kans. State U., 1947, MS, 1948; PhD in Physics, U. Wis., 1951. Asst. prof. U. Wyo., Laramie, 1950-51; physicist Carter Oil Co., Tulsa, 1951-55; rsch. scientist Columbia U., Dobbs Ferry, N.Y., 1955-67; prof. dept. geol. geophysics U. Wis., Madison, 1967-89, emeritus prof., 1989—. Author: Elementary Exploration Seismology, 1990, (with I. Tolstoy) Ocean Acoustics, 1966, (with H. Medwin) Acoustical Oceanography, 1977, Fundamentals of Acoustical Oceanography, 1997; (with I. Tolstoy) Ocean Acoustics, 1987. Fellow Acoustical Soc. Am. (Silver medal in Acoustical Oceanography, 1993); mem. Sigma Xi. Home: 5033 Saint Cyr Rd Middleton WI 53562-2424 Office: U Wis Weeks Hall 1215 W Dayton St Madison WI 53706-1600

CLAY, DON RICHARD, environmental consulting firm executive; b. Washington Court House, Ohio, June 26, 1937; s. Chester T. and Margaret Louise Clay; m. JoAnn Elizabeth Smith, Sept. 21, 1958; children: Rebecca Ann, Jeffrey Markham. B Chem. Engring., MSc, Ohio State U., 1960. Registered profl. engr., Ohio. Project engr. plastics div. Monsanto Co., 1963; staff assoc. Ops. Rsch. Inc., 1963-65; project mgr. Davidson, Talbird & McLynn Inc., 1965-68; program dir. Resource Mgmt. Corp., 1968-70; exec. v.p. Resource Allocations, Arlington, Va., 1970-71; sr. systems analyst Nelsen Commn., Washington, 1971-72; program analysis officer Bur. Drugs, FDA, Washington, 1972; supr. ops., rsch. analyst Asst. Commr. for Planning and Evaluation, Washington, 1972-74; supr. ops., rsch. analyst Consumer Product Safety Commn., Washington, 1974-77, dep. assoc. exec. dir. for engring. and scis., 1977-81; dir. Office Toxic Substances, EPA, Washington, 1981-86, dep. asst. adminstr. Office Air and Radiation, 1986-89, asst. adminstr. Office Solid Waste and Emergency Response, 1989-93; pres. Don Clay Assocs. Inc., Washington, 1993—; environ. gen. mgr. Koch Industries, Washington, 1998—. Recipient award for excellence Office Adminstr., EPA, 1984, Pres.'s Meritorious Exec. Rank award, 1987, Pres.'s Disting. Exec. Rank award, 1988, Fed. Women's program Achievement award, 1992. Mem. Air Pollution Control Officers Assn., Am. Indsl. Chem. Engrs. Assn., Am. Inst. Chem. Engrs., Sr. Execs. Assn., Univ. Club, Am. Running and

Fitness Club. Home: 5305 Albemarle St Bethesda MD 20816-1826 Office: Koch Industries Inc 1450 G St NW Ste 445 Washington DC 20005-2001*

CLAY, ERIC L., judge; b. Durham, N.C., Jan. 18, 1948. BA, U. N.C., 1969; JD, Yale U., 1972. Bar: Mich. 1972, U.S. Dist. Ct. (ea. dist.) Mich. 1972, U.S. Supreme Ct. 1977, U.S. Ct. Appeals (6th cir.) 1978, U.S. Dist. Ct. (we. dist.) Mich. 1987, U.S. Ct. Appeals (D.C. cir.) 1994. Law clk. to Judge Damon J. Keith U.S. Dist. Ct. (ea. dist.) Mich., 1973-97; shareholder, dir. Lewis, White & Clay, P.C., Detroit, 1997; now judge U.S. Ct. Appeals (6th cir.), Detroit, 1997—. John Hay Whitney fellow Yale U. Mem. ABA, Nat. Bar Assn., Nat. Assn. Railroad Trial Counsel, U.S. Sixth Jud. Conf. (life), Detroit Bar Assn., Wolverine Bar Assn., Phi Beta Kappa. Office: US Courthouse 231 W Lafayette Blvd Detroit MI 48226-2702*

CLAY, JUANITA LOUNDMON, mental health consultant; b. Charleston, W.Va., Aug. 11; d. Albert D. and Mattie L. (Collins) L.; children: Pamela Clay-Mitchell, Kimberly Clay-Clay, Dana Clay-Braddock. BA, W.Va. State U.; MSW, W.Va. U.; MA, Ind. U.; PhD, Fla. State U., 1978. Psychologist Navistar Corp., Indpls., 1978-80; pvt. practice psychology, Indpls., 1980-84; clin. psychologist Lakeview Mental Health Ctr., Pensacola, Fla., 1984-85; pvt. practice A Better Way Christian Counseling Ministry, Tallahassee, Fla., 1985-88; prof. Regent U., Virginia Beach, Va., 1988-89; assoc. prof. Am. U. of Les Cayes, Haiti, 1989-91; mental cons. to Christian Orgns., Ft. Wayne, Ind.; pres., CEO A Better Way Counseling and Cons. Agy., Ft. Wayne; cons. Washington Project, 1989—, Haiti Mins. Conf., Port-Au-Prince, 1989; founder, dir. first group treatment home for girls in State of Ind.; founder A Better Way. Prodr. Black-on-Black Pub. Svc. TV Program. Precinct chmn. Rep. Exec. Com., Tallahassee, 1987-88; bd. mem. City Coun. EEO Commn., Tallahassee, 1987-89; pres. Ind. Conf. Social Welfare, Indpls., 1970-73; bd. dirs. Cmty. Action of N.E. Ind., Ft. Wayne Ballet, Old Fort br. YMCA; life mem., mem. cmty. access network TV NAACP, Martin Luther King Breakfast Club Inc.; vol. docent Lincoln Mus. Fla. U. Systems grantee, 1976; named one of Outstanding Young Women Am., 1968; recipient Cmty. Svc. award City of Pensacola, 1974, YMCA, C. of C., Ft. Wayne, Ind., 1970, Ebony in Excellence award, 1997. Mem. Am. Assn. Counseling and Devel., Va. Assn. Counseling and Devel., Ind. Psychology Assn. (life). Office: PO Box 12642 Fort Wayne IN 46864-2642

CLAY, ORSON C., insurance company executive; b. Bountiful, Utah, July 26, 1930; s. George Phillips and Dorothy (Cliff) C.; m. Dianne Jones, June 13, 1961; children: Orson Cliff, Charles Kenneth, Elizabeth Temple. BS, Brigham Young U., 1955; MBA with distinction, Harvard U., 1959. With Continental Oil Co., various locations in, U.S.; mng. dir. Conoco A.G., Zug, Switzerland, 1962-63; dir. econs. divsn. Continental Oil Co. Ltd., London, Eng., 1964-65; gen. mgr. adminstrn. and ops. Continental Oil (U.K.) Ltd., London, 1965-66; asst. mgr. marine transp. Continental Oil, N.Y.C., 1966-68; exec. asst. fin. Pennzoil United, Inc., Houston, 1968-70; exec. v.p. fin., treas. Am. Nat. Ins. Co., Galveston, Tex., 1970-73, sr. exec. v.p., treas., 1973-76, pres., 1977-95, CEO, 1978-91, also bd. dirs., ret., 1995; past mem. nat. adv. coun. mgmt. Brigham Young U. Past trustee United Way Galveston; past bd. dirs. Tex. Rsch. League; active LDS Ch., missionary in Can., 1951-53. 1st lt. USMCR, 1955-57. Donald Kirk David fellow Harvard U., 1959. Mem. Life Officers Mgmt. Assn. (bd. dirs. 1993-95). Home: 5682 169th Pl SE Bellevue WA 98006-5514

CLAY, RICKY PERRY, plastic surgeon, consultant, medical educator; b. Dec. 30, 1953. BS, Sanford U., 1976; MD, U. Ala. Sch. of Medicine, 1980. Dir., cons. plastic surgery Mayo Craniofacial Clinic and Cutaneous Ctr., Rochester, Minn., 1989—; asst. prof. plastic surgery Mayo Med. Sch., Rochester, Minn., 1989—. E-mail: rclay@mayo.edu. Office: Mayo Clinic 200 First St SW Rochester MN 55905

CLAY, RYBURN GLOVER, JR., resort executive; b. Atlanta, Oct. 15, 1928; s. Ryburn Glover and Catherine (Sanders) S.; m. Patricia Markwell, Nov. 10, 1951; children: Ryburn Clover III, Thomas Markwell, Zaida Sanders. BS, U.S. Mil. Acad., 1951. Commd. 2d lt. U.S. Army, 1951, advanced through grades to capt., 1955, resigned, 1955; pres. St. Simons Co., St. Simons Island, Ga., 1971-73, Sea Gate Inn, Inc., St. Simons Island, 1973—. Pres. ARC, Glynn County, Ga., 1974; vestryman Christ Ch. Frederica, St. Simons Island, 1987, sr. warden, 1988—. Decorated Silver Star, Purple Heart. Mem. St. Simons C. of C. (pres. 1972). Episcopalian. Clubs: Piedmont Driving (Atlanta), Sea Island Beach. Office: Sea Gate Inn 1014 Ocean Blvd Saint Simons GA 31522

CLAY, WILLIAM LACY, congressman; b. St. Louis, Mo., Apr. 30, 1931; s. Irving C. and Luella (Hyatt) C.; m. Carol A. Johnson, Oct. 10, 1953; children: Vicki, Lacy, Michelle. B.S. in Polit. Sci, St. Louis U., 1953. Real estate broker, from 1964, mgr. life ins. co., 1959-61; alderman 26th Ward, St. Louis, 1959-64; bus. rep. state, county and municipal employees union, 1961-64; edn. coord. Steamfitters local 562, 1966-67; mem. 91st-105th Congresses from 1st Mo. dist. U.S. Ho. of Reps., Washington, 1969—, ranking minority mem. edn. and the workforce. Served with AUS, 1953-55. Mem. NAACP (past exec. bd. mem. St. Louis), CORE, St. Louis Jr. C. of C. Democrat. Office: US Ho of Reps 2306 Rayburn Bldg Washington DC 20515-2501

CLAY, WILLIAM LACY, JR., state legislator; b. St. Louis, July 27, 1956; s. William L. and Carol Ann (Johnson) C.; m. Ivie Lewellen, Jan. 24, 1992. BS in Polit. Sci., U. Md., Coll. Park, 1983. Cert. paralegal; lic. real estate salesman, Mo. State senator Mo. Gen. Assembly, Jefferson City, 1983—. Chmn. Mo. Jesse Jackson 1988 Presdl. Campaign; Jackson del. to 1988 Dem. Nat. Conv.; committeeman to Dem. Nat. Com.; bd. dirs. William L. Clay Scholarship and Rsch. Fund. Mem. Ams. Dem. Action (Outstanding Legis. Mo. chpt. 1985, 86), Roman Catholic. Office: Mo State Senate Capitol Building Jefferson City MO 65101-1556

CLAYBURGH, JILL, actress; b. N.Y.C., Apr. 30, 1944; d. Albert Henry and Julia (Door) C.; m. David Rabe, Mar., 1979. BA, Sarah Lawrence Coll., 1966. Former mem., Charles Playhouse, Boston; Off-Broadway plays include The Nest; Broadway debut in The Rothschilds, 1970; stage appearances include In the Boom Boom Room (David Rabe), Design for Living (Noel Coward); film appearances include The Wedding Party, 1969, The Telephone Book, 1971, Portnoy's Complaint, 1972, The Thief Who Came to Dinner, 1973, The Terminal Man, 1974, Gable and Lombard, 1976, Silver Streak, 1976, Gable and Lombard, 1976, Semi-Tough, 1977, An Unmarried Woman, 1978, Luna, 1979, Starting Over, 1979, It's My Turn, 1980, First Monday in October, 1981, I'm Dancing as Fast as I Can, 1982, Hannah K, 1983, In Our Hands, 1984, Where Are The Children, 1986, Shy People, 1987, Beyond the Ocean, 1990, Whispers in the Dark, 1992, Le Grand Pardon II, 1992, Rich in Love, 1993, Naked in New York, 1994, Fools Rush In, 1997, Going All the Way, 1997; appeared in TV films Snoop Sisters, 1972, The Art of Crime, 1975, Hustling, 1975, Griffin and Phoenix, 1976, Miles to Go..., 1986, Who Gets the Friends?, 1988, Fear Stalk, 1989, Unspeakable Acts, 1990, Reason for Living: the Jill Ireland Story, 1991, Trial: The Price of Passion, 1993, Firestorm: A Catastrophe in Oakland, 1993, For the Love of Nancy, 1994, Honor Thy Father and Mother: The True Story of the Menendez Brothers, 1994, The Face on the Milk Carton, 1995, When Innocence is Lost, 1997, Sins of the Mind, 1997, Crowned and Dangerous, 1998; TV documentary: Ask Me Anything: How to Talk to Kids About Sex, 1989; TV series Trinity, 1998, Everything's Relative, 1999. Recipient Best Actress award for An Unmarried Woman, Cannes Film Festival; Golden Apple award for best film actress in An Unmarried Woman. Office: care William Morris Agy c/o John Kimble 151 S El Camino Dr Beverly Hills CA 90212-2704*

CLAYCOMB, CECIL KEITH, biochemist, educator; b. Twin Falls, Idaho, Oct. 19, 1920; s. Cecil R. and Frilla E. (Reams) C.; m. Elizabeth Jane Gregg, Mar. 10, 1943; children: John K., Mary E. B.S., U. Oreg., 1947, M.S., 1948, Ph.D., 1951. Prof., head dept. biochemistry Dental Sch. U. Oreg., Portland, 1951-82, dir. minority recruitment, 1971-74, asst. to pres./dir. minority student affairs, 1974-84, coordinator basic sci. curriculum, 1951-77, chmn. admissions com., 1959-69, emeritus, 1985—; emeritus prof. biochemistry Oreg. Health Scis. U., 1986—. Contbr. articles to sci. jours. Served to 1st lt. AUS, 1943-46. Scholar dental bd. New South Wales, Sydney, Australia, 1970. Mem. Am. Chem. Soc., Internat. Assn. Dental Research, AAAS, Res. Officers Assn., Sigma Xi. Home: 3326 SW 13th Ave Portland OR 97201-2922

CLAYCOMB, HUGH MURRAY, lawyer, author; b. Joplin, Mo., May 19, 1931; s. Hugh and Fern (Murray) C.; m. Jeanne Cavin, May 6, 1956; children: Stephen H., Scott C. BS in Bus., U. Mo., 1953, JD, 1955; LLM, U. Miss., 1969. Bar: Mo. 1955, Ark. 1957, U.S. Tax Ct. 1956, U.S. Dist. Ct. (ea. dist.) Ark. 1957, U.S. Supreme Ct. 1979. Asst. staff judge advocate USAF, 1955-57; law clerk Ark. Supreme Ct., Little Rock, 1957-58; ptnr. Gregory & Claycomb, Pine Bluff, Ark., 1958-69; partner Haley, Claycomb, Roper & Anderson, Warren, Ark., 1969—; dir. Strong Systems, Inc., Pine Bluff, Ark., 1967—. Author: Arkansas Corporations, 1967, 82, 92. Pres. Jefferson County Bar Assn., Pine Bluff, 1969, Warren YMCA, 1973-75, S.E. Ark. Legal Inst., 1980-81, Ctrl. Ark. Estate Planning Coun., 1963-64; trustee Bradley County YMCA Found.; spl. assoc. justice Ark. Supreme Ct., 1978, 87. Lt. USAF, 1955-57. Recipient Pres.'s award Ark. Trial Lawyers Assn., 1985. Mem. Ark. Bar Found. (pres. 1990), Ark. Bar Assn. (sec.-treas. 1998—, C.E. Ransick award 1996), Warren Rotary (pres. 1972). Episcopalian. Home: 619 E Cedar St Warren AR 71671-3001

CLAYPOOL, DAVID L., lawyer; b. Springfield, Ill., 1946. BA in History, Ill. Coll., 1968; JD with high distinction, U. Iowa, 1975. Bar: Iowa 1975. Ptnr. Dorsey & Whitney, LLP, Des Moines. Editor notes and comments Iowa Law Review, 1974-75. Capt. U.S. Army, 1968-72. Mem. Iowa State Bar Assn., Pol County Bar Assn., Nat. Assn. Bond Lawyers, Iowa Mcpl. Attys. Assn., Order of Coif. Office: Dorsey & Whitney LLP 801 Grand Ave Ste 3900 Des Moines IA 50309-2790

CLAYPOOL, ROBERT T., military career officer; b. Oak Park, Ill., Sept. 28, 1939; m. Nancy Claypool; children: Elizabeth, Stephen, Mark, Candace. B in Chemistry, Northwestern U., MD; grad., U.S. Army War Coll., Nat. Def. U. Diplomate Am. Bd. Internal Medicine subspecialty cert. in rheumatology. Commd. officer U.S. Army, 1965, advanced through grades to maj. gen., 1997; preventive medicine officer U.S. Army, Ft. Benning, Ga.; internal medicine resident Walter Reed Army Med. Ctr., Washington; rheumatology fellow Letterman Army Med. Ctr., San Francisco; commdg. gen. Great Plans Regional Med. Command and Brooke Army Med. Ctr., Ft. Sam Houston, Tex.; chief dept. medicine Ftzsimons Army Med. Ctr., Aurora, Colo.; program dir. internal medicine residency Ftzsimons Army Med. Ctr., Aurora; comdr. 98th Gen. Hosp., Nuremberg, Germany, Darnall Army Cmty. Hosp. and III Corps Surgeon, Ft. Hood, Tex.; various positions including dir. profl. svcs. Office of the Army Surgeon Gen., chief med. corps affairs; dep. asst. sec. of def. (health ops. policy) Office of the Sec. of Def., Washington, 1997—; assoc. clin. prof. medicine U. Colo. Sch. Medicine, Denver; clin. assoc. prof. medicine Uniformed Svcs. U. Health Scis., Bethesda, Md. Decorated Legion of Merit with two oak leaf clusters, Meritorious Svc. medal with one oak leaf cluster. Fellow ACP, Am. Coll. Rheumatology. Office: Office of Sec of Def Washington DC 20301

CLAYSON, SUSAN HOLLIS, art historian, educator; b. Dec. 26, 1946. BA, Wellesley Coll., 1968; MA, UCLA, 1975, PhD, 1984. Asst. prof. art history Northwestern U., Evanston, Ill., 1985-91; assoc. prof. art history Northwestern U., Evanston, 1991—, assoc. dean Grad. Sch., 1995-98; asst. prof. art history U. Ill., Chgo., 1994-95. E-mail: shc@nwu.edu.

CLAYTON, BRUCE DAVID, pharmacology educator; b. Grand Island, Nebr., Mar. 9, 1947; s. John David and Eloise Regnier (Camp) C.; m. Francine Evelyn Purdy, June 19, 1971; children: Sarah Elizabeth, Beth Anne. Student, Hastings Coll., 1965-67; BS, U. Nebr., 1970; D Pharmacy, U. Mich., 1973. Resident U. Mich., 1972-74; asst. prof. clin. pharmacy Creighton U., Omaha, 1974-77; assoc. prof. Coll. Pharmacy, U. Nebr. Med. Ctr., Omaha, 1978-85, vice chmn. dept. pharmacy practice, 1978-84, interim chmn., 1984-85; prof., chmn. dept. pharmacy practice U. Ark. for Med. Scis., Little Rock, 1985-87, prof. pharmacy practice, 1985-89; prof., assoc. dean Coll. Pharmacy, Butler U., Indpls., 1989-99, acting dean, 1999—; unit coord. perinatal pharmacy svcs. Univ. Hosps., Omaha, 1978-80; clin. pharmacist pediatrics Ark. Children's Hosp., Little Rock, 1986-89; Ciba-Geigy vis. prof., Australia and N.Z., 1979; S.E. Wright traveling fellow Pharm. Soc. Australia, 1983; lectr. in field. Author: (with S.A. Ryan) Handbook of Practical Pharmacology, 1977, 2d edit., 1980, (with J.E. Squire) Basic Pharmacology for Nurses, 7th edit., 1981, Handbook of Pharmacology in Nursing, 1984, Handbook of Pharmacology, 1987, (with Yvonne Stock) Basic Pharmacology for Nurses, 11th edit., 1997; contbr. articles to profl. jours. Recipient Bristol award for professionalism, 1970; named Nebr. Hosp. Pharmacist of Yr., 1978. Mem. Nebr. Soc. Hosp. Pharmacists (dir. 1977-80, pres. 1978-79), Ind. Soc. Hosp. Pharmacists, Am. Soc. Hosp. Pharmacists (coun. on orgnl. affairs 1979-82, com. on nominations 1980-85, chmn. 1985, ho. of dels. 1980-88, coun. on ednl. affairs 1987-89, chmn. 1989), Am. Pharm. Assn. (APHA-PAC bd. govs. 1994-96), Ind. Pharm. Assn. (bd. dirs. 1991-97, 98—, v.p. 1995-96, pres.-elect 1996-97, pres. 1997-98), Indian Pharmacists Alliance (pres. 1998), Am. Assn. Colls. Pharmacy, Rho Chi.

CLAYTON, DAVID A(LVIN), biology educator; b. Joliet, Ill., Feb. 5, 1944; m. Lauretta Swanson, 1965; children: Lindsay, Ryan, Megan. BS, No. Ill. U., 1965; PhD in Biophysics and Chemistry, Calif. Inst. Tech., 1970. Asst. prof. pathology Stanford U., 1970-76, assoc. prof., 1976-82, prof., 1982-89, prof. devel. biology, 1989—; sr. sci. officer Howard Hughes Med. Inst., 1996—; mem. adv. com. nucleic acids and protein synthesis, Am. Cancer Soc., 1976-80; mem. molecular biology study sect., NIH, 1982-86, chmn., 1984-86; mem. sci. rev. bd. Howard Hughes Med. Inst., 1993-96; mem. nat. adv. bd. Gen. Med. Sci. Coun., 1996—; Fisher lectr. So. Ill. U., 1989.. Recipient Warner-Lambert/Parke Davis award, 1982. Mem. Inst. Medicine Nat. Acad. Sci., Am. Soc. Biochemistry and Molecular Biology.

CLAYTON, DONALD DELBERT, astrophysicist, nuclear physicist, educator; b. Shenandoah, Iowa, Mar. 18, 1935; s. Delbert Homer and Avis (Kembery) C.; children: Donald, Devon, Alia, Andrew; m. Nancy McBride. BS, So. Meth. U., 1956; PhD, Calif. Inst. Tech., 1962. Rsch. fellow in physics Calif. Inst. Tech., 1961-63; staff scientist Aerospace Corp., El Segundo, Calif., 1961-63; faculty Rice U., Houston, 1963-65; assoc. prof. physics and space sci. Rice U., 1965-69; prof. physics and space sci., faculty assoc. Wiess Coll., 1969-77, Andrew Hays Buchanan prof. astrophysics, 1975-89; prof. physics and astronomy Clemson (S.C.) U., S.C., 1989—; centennial prof. Clemson (S.C.) U., 1996—; vis. assoc. physics Calif. Inst. Tech., 1966-67; vis. fellow Inst. Theoretical Astronomy, Cambridge, summers 1967-72. Author: Principles of Stellar Evolution and Nucleosynthesis, 1968, The Dark Night Sky, 1975, The Joshua Factor, 1986; contbr. over 175 articles to profl. jours. Recipient Humboldt award Max Planck Inst., Heidelberg, 1977, 82, Exceptional Sci. Achievement medal NASA, 1992, Disting. Alumni award So. Meth. U., 1993, S.C. Gov.'s award for sci. excellence, 1994, Jesse Beams award, 1998; Sloan fellow, 1966-70, Fulbright fellow, Heidelberg, 1979-80. Fellow Am. Phys. Soc. (Jesse W. Beams medal 1998), Meteoritical Soc. (Leonard medal 1991); mem. AAAS, Am. Astron. Soc., Royal Astron. Soc. (G.H. Darwin lectr. 1981), Cosmos Club (Washington), Phi Beta Kappa, Sigma Xi. Office: Clemson U Dept Physics Astronomy Clemson SC 29634-1911 *My life centers on love of nature. As a cosmologist studying the universe, I find the truth to be stranger than fiction, and the commonplace to be the spectacular. To share this joy with laymen, I wrote a personal memoir, The Dark Night Sky, and a scientific novel, The Joshua Factor.*

CLAYTON, EVA M., congresswoman, former county commissioner; b. Savannah, Ga., Sept. 16, 1934; m. Theaoseus T. Clayton; children: Theaoseus Jr., Martin, Reuben, Joanne. BS, Johnson C. Smith U.; MS, North Carolina Central U. Former commr. Warren County, N.C.; mem. 103rd Congress from 1st N.C. dist., Washington, D.C., 1993—; mem. agriculture com. resource conservation, rsch. and forestry 103rd Congress from 1st N.C. dist., mem. house democratic policy com., mem. com. on budget. Democrat. Office: US Ho of Reps 2440 Rayburn Bldg Washington DC 20515-3301

CLAYTON, JAMES A., broadcast executive. BA, Ctrl. Mich. U., 1971. V.p., gen. mgr. Sta. WJBK, Southfield, Mich., 1997—. Mem. Detroit C. of C. Office: Sta WJBK PO Box 2000 16550 W Nine Mile Rd Southfield MI 48037*

CLAYTON, JAMES EDWIN, journalist; b. Johnston City, Ill., Nov. 14, 1929; s. John Herman and Vinnie Ethel (Black) C.; m. Elise Brookfield Heinz, June 3, 1961; children—Jonathan Brown, David Lake. BS, U. Ill., 1953; MPA, Princeton, 1956. Reporter So. Illinoisan, Carbondale, Ill., 1951-52; reporter Washington Post, 1956-64, asst. mng. editor, 1964-67, 72-74, editorial writer, 1967-72, assoc. editor, 1974-82; assoc. dir. Reporter's Com. for Freedom of Press, 1984; sr. fellow Airlie Found., 1984-94; vis. lectr. Northwestern U., 1966-67, Johns Hopkins, 1970. Author: The Making of Justice, 1964; editor: The Rights of Free Men, 1984. Pres. Sofia Am. Schs., Inc. Served to 1st lt. AUS, 1951-52. Recipient Interpretive Reporting awards Washington Newspaper Guild, 1959, 62, 63, Distinguished Washington Correspondence award Sigma Delta Chi, 1960, Worth Bingham prize, 1970, George Polk Meml. award for editorial writing, 1970. Baptist. Club: Princeton (Washington). Home: 2728 N Fillmore St Arlington VA 22207-4936

CLAYTON, JOE DON, lawyer; b. Sentinel, Okla., Sept. 3, 1934; s. Elam Basil and Addie (Armstrong) C.; m. Denise Crimmins, Feb. 19, 1966; children: Thomas, Katherine, Andrew. BA, Yale U., 1957, LLB, 1964; DPhil, Oxford U., 1961. Bar: N.Y. 1966, D.C. 1971. Assoc. Davis, Polk & Wardwell, N.Y.C., 1964-69; assoc. Mudge, Rose, Guthrie, Alexander & Ferdon, N.Y.C., 1969-70, ptnr., 1971-90; ptnr. White & Case, N.Y.C., 1990—. chmn. St. Ann Ctr. for Restoration and the Arts, Bklyn., 1983-86. Democrat. Home: 151 Willow St Brooklyn NY 11201-2201 Office: White & Case LLP 1155 Avenue Of The Americas New York NY 10036-2711*

CLAYTON, JOHN, retired engineering executive and consultant; b. Marlboro, Mass., Aug. 16, 1930; s. John and Esther Elizabeth (Gray) C.; m. Carol Ann Kopp, Feb. 19, 1954; children: Susan A., Dianne G., Jacqueline. Various positions, 1948-52; with Tech. Instrument Corp., Acton, Mass., 1952-56; engring. mgr. R&D Waters Mfg. Inc., Wayland, Mass., 1956-94; ret., 1994; cons. in field. Active Stow Bd. Selectmen; clk. Stow Zoning Bd. Appeals; pres. Stow Cmty. Housing Corp., Stow Elderly Housing Corp.; radio officer Mass. Emergency Mgmt. Agy., Stow, 1995—. Mem. IEEE (life), Amateur Radio Relay League. Republican. Achievements include 9 patents in electro-mechanical transducers and conductive plastics. Home: 15 Walnut Ridge Rd Stow MA 01775-1109 Office: Data Instruments Waters Products 100 Discovery Way Acton MA 01778-1890

CLAYTON, JOHN CHARLES, scientist, researcher; b. Pittston, Pa., June 15, 1924; s. Charles Conrad and Madeline Eleanor (Hastings) C.; m. Mary Catherine Mulvaney, Aug. 9, 1968. B.S., St. Joseph's U., 1949; M.S., U. Pa., 1950, Ph.D., 1953. Postdoctoral fellow U. Pa., Phila., 1953-55; sr. scientist Westinghouse Electric Corp., Pitts., 1954-81, fellow, scientist, 1981—; sec., dir. Mulvaney Corp., Pitts. Contbr. chpts. to books. Patentee in field. Cpl. U.S. Army, 1943-45, ETO. Fellow AAAS, Am. Inst. Chemists; mem. N.Y. Acad. Scis., Am. Chem. Soc., Am. Ceramic Soc., Am. Nuclear Soc., Am. Soc. Metals, Pitts. Chemists Club (officer 1990—), Toastmasters Internat. Club (area gov. Western Pa. br. 1981-83, officer Pitts. br. 1976—). Am. Youth Hostels Club (officer Pitts. br. 1960-68), Pitts. Ski Club (officer 1960-70), South Hills Cotillion Club (officer 1983-85), Alpha Chi Sigma, Phi Lambda Upsilon. Roman Catholic. Avocations: skiing, ice skating, hiking, sailing, gardening. Home: 1663 Citation Dr Library PA 15129-8832 Office: Westinghouse Electric Corp Bettis Atomic Power Lab PO Box 79 West Mifflin PA 15122-0079

CLAYTON, JONATHAN ALAN, banker; b. New Brunswick, N.J., Jan. 20, 1937; s. Llewellyn H. and Florence E. (Denton) C.; m. Carole Elaine Jolly, Sept. 23, 1961; children—David Alan, Susan Beth. B.A. in History, Lafayette Coll., 1959; postgrad., N.Y. U. Law Sch., 1959, N.Y. U. Grad. Sch. Bus. Adminstrn., 1961-64; grad., Robert Morris Loan Mgmt. Seminar, 1973. Trainee mgmt. program Mfrs. Hanover Trust Co., N.Y.C., 1961-64; asst. sec. Mfrs. Hanover Trust Co., 1966-69, asst. v.p., 1969-71, v.p., 1971-80, officer in charge credit and fin. group, 1972-74, officer in charge hdqrs. br., 1974-76; dep. officer in charge Mfrs. Hanover Trust Co., Upper Manhattan, Westchester, Bronx and Orange counties, 1976-78; dep. mgr. Mfrs. Hanover Trust Co., Bklyn. and S.I. brs., 1978-80, sr. v.p. Bklyn. and S.I. comml. and retail banking, 1980-83; sr. v.p. comml. and retail banking Mfrs. Hanover Trust Co., N.Y., 1983-85, sr. v.p. comml. ctrs. and brs., 1986-87; sr. v.p., mgr. Bus. Banking Group Mfrs. Hanover Trust Co., 1987-90, mng. dir., gen. mgr. profl. credit unit, 1990-92; mng. dir., middle market banking group, asset mgmt. Chem. Bank, N.Y.C., 1992; ret., 1992; instr. comml. banking Stonier Grad. Sch. Banking Rutgers U., New Brunswick, N.J., 1973-84; instr. comml. banking N.Y. State Bankers Assn. Exec. Devel. Schs., West Point, 1973-81, Syracuse, 1979-81; mem. bd. govs. N.Y. chpt. Robert Morris Associates, 1979-81. Vice pres. bd. trustees, treas., chmn. fin. com. Rutgers Preparatory Sch., Somerset, N.J., 1975-78; bd. regents St. Francis Coll., Bklyn., 1981—; elder First Presbyn. Ch., Cranbury, N.J., 1981-83; v.p. Men's Fellowship, 1981-83; bd. dirs. Bklyn. Borough Hall Restoration Found. Served from 2d. lt. to capt. U.S. Army, 1959-66. Mem. N.Y. State Bankers Assn. (mem. edn. com. 1975-81), Downtown Bklyn. Devel. Assn. (vice chmn., dir. 1981-83), N.Y.C. C. of C., Bklyn. C. of C. (dir. 1980-82), Am. Arbitration Assn. (arbitrator 1971—). Republican. Clubs: Bklyn, Mcpl. of Bklyn, Marco Polo, Candy Execs. and Affiliated Industries. Lodge: Lions (Cranbury) (dir. 1981-82). Office: 270 Park Ave New York NY 10017-2014

CLAYTON, MACK LOUIS, surgery professor, educator; b. Round Mountain, Ala., Nov. 25, 1921; s. James Euclid and Alma (Longshore) C.; m. Sara Elizabeth Lee, June 3, 1948; children: James Lee, Lee Alison. BS, U. Ariz., 1942; MD, Columbia U., 1945. Diplomate Am. Bd. Orthop. Surgery. Founder Denver Orthop. Clinic, 1952-90; doctor Denver Broncos, 1969-73, U.S. Ski Team, 1971; clin. prof. orthop. surgery U. Colo., 1985-95; asst. chief orthop. surgery USVA Med. Ctr., Denver, 1990—. Author, editor: Surgery for Rheumatoid Arthritis, 1992; contbr. numerous articles to profl. jours. Elder Presbyn. Ch., Denver, 1958; with armed forces, 1946-48. Recipient Best Clinical Rsch. award U. Colo Med. Sch., 1958, 25 yrs. svc. award Arthritis Found., 1982. Mem. Am. Orthop. Assn., Am. Soc. for Surg. of Hand, Clin. Orthop. Soc. (pres. 1978). Avocations: skiing, golf, fishing, hunting. Home: 2552 E Alameda Ave Unit 18 Denver CO 80209-3324 Office: USVA Med Ctr 1055 Clermont St Denver CO 80220-3808

CLAYTON, MARVIN COURTLAND, engineering, manufacturing sourcing and health wellness consultant; b. Norwich, Conn., Feb. 19, 1938; s. Marvin C. and Peggy (Farmer) C.; children: Cheryll, Michelle, Deborah. BS in Indsl. Engring., Purdue U., 1963; MBA, U. Louisville, 1971; MPA, Penn. State U., 1986; grad., U.S. Army War Coll., 1986. Registered profl. engr., Calif., Ky., Mo., Pa.; cert. purchasing mgr., mfg. engr., mfg. mgr., profl. mgmt. cons., logistician, exec. in logistics. Mgr. shop ops. GE Appliances, Louisville, 1968-69, prog. mgr. mfg. engring., 1969-71, contracting agt. material handling and computer systems, 1973-76, program mgr., material resource systems, 1976-80, mgr., advance and indirect material purchasing, 1980-82, program mgr., purchasing programs, 1982-87, program mgr., sourcing integration, 1987-89, mgr. supplier productivity engring., 1989-93, puchasing mgr. range products bus., 1993; prin. The Clayton Group, Louisville, 1993-94; mgr. range bus. purchasing GE Appliances, Louisville, 1992-94; mgr. Strategic Sourcing, Louisville, 1994; mgr. mfg. engring. Emerson Electric Co., St. Louis, 1971-72; corp. engring. and mfg. cons. AMEDCO, Springfield, Mo., 1972-73; pres. Clayton Cons., Louisville, Ky., 1994—; prin. The Clayton Group, Global Cons., Exec. Distbrs., NuSkin, Pharmanex, Internat., Phamanex, Big Planet, 1992—; pres. CC Global, Louisville, Queretaro, Mex., 1996—. Patentee in field. Chmn. bd. deacons Bapt. Ch., Louisville, 1975; dir. ch. choir Bapt. Ch., Arkansas City, Kans., 1963. Col. USAR, 1963-93. Named to Honorable Order of Ky. Cols. Mem. Res. Officers Assn. (exec. bd., pres. 1984, nat. councilman 1990-94), Ky. Res. Officers Assn., Inst. Indsl. Engrs., Assn. Internal Mgmt. Cons., Assn. of U.S. Army, Purdue Alumni Assn., U. Louisville Alumni Assn., Pa. State Alumni Assn., Army War Coll. Alumni Assn. Republican. Avocations: piano, gardening, sports. Home and Office: 8215 Camberley Dr Louisville KY 40222-5534

CLAYTON, ORVILLE WOOLFORD, surgeon; b. Ft. Payne, Ala., May 30, 1921; s. Olney Walker Clayton and Flora Pauline Wheeler; m. Dorothy Nell Meadows, June 20, 1944; children: Stephen W., Kathy L. Stockham, Shelley E. BA, U. Ala., Tuscaloosa, 1943; B in Medicine, Northwestern U., 1945, MD, 1946. Post surgeon U.S. Army, Huntsville, Ala., 1946-48; chief resident surgery Univ. Hosp., Birmingham, Ala., 1948; chief surgery Bapt. Med. Montclair, Birmingham, 1969-74, pres. staff, 1982; clin. assoc. prof. surgery U. Ala., Birmingham, 1973-91; bd. dirs. Am. Pulmonary Unit, Birmingham, 1996-99. Capt. U.S. Army, 1946-48. Fellow ACS, So.

Thoracic Soc. Avocations: gardening, genealogy. Home: 3133 Ryecroft Rd Birmingham AL 35223

CLAYTON, PAUL DOUGLAS, medical facility director; b. Salt Lake City, Mar. 9, 1943. PhD in Physics, U. Ariz. Dir. Ctr. for Advanced Tech., Columbia Presbyn. Med. Ctr., 1994—, dir. clin. info. svcs., 1992—; chmn. Med Informat, 1989—. Mem. Inst. Medicine of Nat. Acad. Sci. *

CLAYTON, RAYMOND EDWARD, government official; b. Saskatoon, Sask., Can., Nov. 6, 1942; m. Joan Ann Snodgrass, Sept. 21, 1963; children: Grant, Sheila, Matthew, Daniel. B. of Commerce, U. Sask., 1964; MA in Econs., 1965. Dir. rsch. Dept. Mcpl. Affars, Govt. Sask., Regina, 1965-67; dir. rsch. Dept. Edn., Govt. Sask., Regina, 1967-69, dir. ednl. adminstrn., 1969-77, dep. minister, 1979-84; dir. taxation and fiscal policy Dept. Fin., Govt. Sask., Regina, 1977-78; dep. minister Dept. Urban Affairs, Govt. Sask., Regina, 1978-79; chmn. Govt. Fin. Commn., Regina, 1984-86; asst. dep. minister Dept. Energy & Mines, Govt. Sask., Regina, 1986-94, dep. minister, 1994—. Office: Dept Energy and Mines, 2101 Scarth St, Regina, SK Canada S4P 3V7

CLAYTON, RICHARD REESE, retired holding company executive; b. St. Louis, Aug. 26, 1938; s. Lester Cox and Gladys Caroline (Reese) C.; m. Leigh Ila Smith, Feb. 25, 1961; children: Mark, Catherine, Christine. B.S. in Indsl. Econs., Purdue U., 1960. With Trane Co., 1960-73; mng. dir. Trane Co., Sydney, Australia, 1970-73; pres. Hallowell div. Standard Pressed Steel Co., Hatfield, Pa., 1973-77; exec. v.p. domestic ops., dir. SPS Technologies Inc., Jenkintown, Pa., 1977-84; pres., CEO, dir. Vermont Castings, Inc., Randolph, Vt., 1984-87; exec. v.p., chief adminstrv. officer Ea. Enterprises (formerly Ea. Gas & Fuel Assocs.), Weston, Mass., 1987-89, exec. v.p., COO, 1990-91, pres., COO, 1991-98. Baptist.

CLAYTON, ROBERT NORMAN, chemist, educator; b. Hamilton, Ont., Can., Mar. 20, 1930; came to U.S., 1952, naturalized, 1995; s. Norman and Gwenda (Twist) C.; m. Cathleen Shelburne, Jan. 30, 1971; 1 dau., Elizabeth Jane. B.Sc., Queens U., 1951, M.Sc., 1952; Ph.D., Calif. Inst. Tech., 1955. Research fellow Calif. Inst. Tech., 1955-56; mem. faculty Pa. State U., 1956-58; mem. faculty U. Chgo., 1958—, prof. chemistry and geochemistry, 1966—. Fellow AAAS, NAS, Royal Soc. (London), Royal Soc. Can., Am. Acad. Arts Scis., Am. Geophys Union, Meteoritical Soc. Research distbn. stable isotopes of light elements in nature, application to problems in geology. Home: 5201 S Cornell Ave Chicago IL 60615-4207

CLAYTON, THOMAS SWOVERLAND, English educator; b. New Ulm, Minn., Dec. 15, 1932; s. Robert Schoomaker and Vida Virginia (Swoverland) C.; m. Ruth Barbara Madison, Sept. 24, 1955 (dec. Dec. 1989); children: Pamela Alison, Katherine Anne, John Robert, David Montgomery. BA, U. Minn., 1954; DPhil, Oxford U., England, 1960. Instr. English Yale U., New Haven, Conn., 1960-62; asst., assoc. prof. English UCLA, L.A., 1962-68; assoc. prof., prof. English, classical studies U. Minn., Mpls., 1968—. Editor Shakespeare's Hand in The Book of Sir Thomas Moore, 1969, The Non-Dramatic Worls of Sir John Suckling, 1971, Cavalier Poets, 1977. Sgt. U.S. Army, 1955-57. Am. Coun. Learned Studies grantee, 1962, NEH grantee, 1988; Guggenheim fellow, 1976; Rhodes scholar, 1954. Mem. Am. Assn. Rhodes Scholars. Democrat. Episcopalian. Home: 1866 Portland Ave Saint Paul MN 55104-5953 Office: U Minn Classical Civilization Prog 9 Pleasant St SE Minneapolis MN 55455-0125

CLAYTON, VERNA LEWIS, retired state legislator; b. Hamden, Ohio, Feb. 28, 1937; d. Matthews L. and Yail (Miller) Lewis; m. Frank R. Clayton, Feb. 4, 1956; children: children: Valerie S., Barry L. Office mgr. Village of Buffalo Grove, Ill., 1972-78; village clk. Village of Buffalo Grove, 1971-79, village pres., 1979-91; mem. Ill. Ho. of Reps., Springfield, 1993-99. Mem. Lake County Solid Waste Planning Agy., chmn. tech. com., chmn. agy., Nat. League of Cities, chmn. transp. and comms. steering com. Recipient Disting. Svc. award Amvets, 1981; named Libr. Legislator of the Yr. 1997. Mem. N.W. Mcpl. Conf. (pres. 1983-84), Chgo. Area Transp. Study Coun. Mayors (vice chmn. 1981-83, chmn. 1985-91), Mcpl. Clks. Ill. (treas. 1978-79), Mcpl. Clks. Lake County (pres. 1977-78), Ill. Mcpl. League (bd. dirs., v.p. 1985-90, pres. 1989-90), Buffalo Grove Rotary Club (hon. mem.), Buffalo Grove C. of C. (bd. dirs.). Republican. Methodist. Home: 11 Overlook Dr Mc Cormick SC 29835-2850

CLAYTON, WILLIAM E., naval officer; b. Phila., Aug. 9, 1938; s. William E. and Harriet E. (Martin) C.; m. Dorothy Rems Sapoch, June 30, 1962; children: Amy E., Troy C. BS in Chemistry, Coll. william & Mary, 1961; MD, U. Va., 1965. Diplomate Am. Bd. Urology. Intern U. Fla., 1965-66, resident in urology, 1966-70; commd. ensign USN, 1970, advance through grades to capt., 1979; chief urology Naval Hosp., Key West, Fla., 1970-73, Camp Lejenne, N.C., 1973-75; officer in charge PA programs USAF Sch. Healthcare Sci., Wichita Falls, Tex., 1975-77; dir. urology residency Naval Regional Med. Ctr., Oakland, Calif., 1977-83; comdg. officer U.S. Naval Hosp., Subic Bay, The Philippines, 1983-85; dir. officer pers. Naval Med. Command, Washington, 1985-86; comdg. officer Naval Hosp. Millington, Tenn., 1986-87, U.S. Naval Hosp., Naples, Italy, 1987-91; sr. mem. phys. disability evaluation bd. Naval Coun. Pers. Bds., Ballston, Va., 1991-96; health care expert Troy Systems, Inc., Fairfax, Va., 1996—; asst. clin. prof. urol. dept. U. San Francisco, 1977-83; chmn. No. Calif. Urol. Competition, Oakland, 1982; cons. Navy Surgeon Gen. in Urology, Washington, 1981-83; bd. dirs. Nat. Choral Found. Author, editor Videotapes to Teach Gen. Surg. Urol., PPx, 1977; editor, producerMovie to Teach Surgical Technique, 1982; contbr. articles to profl. jours. Chmn., mem. coun. and exec. com. United Svc. Orgn. Gala, Naples, 1989-91; mem. Protestant Chapel Coun., 1988-91. Fellow ACS; mem. AMA, Am. Acad. Med. Dirs., Am. coll. Physician Execs., Omicron Delta Kappa, Lambda Chi Alpha. Republican. Avocations: reading, traveling. Home: 4000 Kloman St Annandale VA 22003-2227

CLAYTON, WILLIAM HOWARD, retired university president; b. Dallas, Aug. 16, 1927; s. William Howard and Blanche (Phillips) C.; children: Jill, Gregory. B.S., Bucknell U., 1949; Ph.D., Tex. A & M U., 1956. Instr. Bucknell U., 1949; grad. asst. Ohio State U., 1949, U. N.Mex., 1949-50; research asst. oceanography and meteorology Tex. A&M U., College Station, 1950-51; asst. oceanography Tex. A. and M. U., 1951-54; assoc. oceanography, instr. math. Tex. A&M U., 1954-56, micrometeorologist U. Research Found., instr. math., 1956-58, faculty oceanography, meteorology, 1958—, prof. oceanography, 1965—, prin. investigator Research Found., 1956-65; asso. dean Coll. Geoscis. Tex. A & M U., 1970-71; pres. Tex. A&M U., Galveston, 1977-87, pres. emeritus, 1987—; sec.-treas. Tex. Coastal Higher Edn. Authority, 1981-88; dean Moody Coll., Galveston, 1971-74; provost Moody Coll., 1974-77, pres. coll., 1977-79; bd. dirs. Bank of West; vis. prof. U. Hawaii, 1963-64; tech. dir. Project Themis, U.S. Army Electronics Command, 1967-74; chmn. field observing facility adv. panel Nat. Center for Atmospheric Research, 1973-74. Contbr. articles to profl. lit., chpts. to books. Commr. Galveston Police and Fire Dept. CSC; mem. Galveston City Coun., 1990—, Galveston Marine Affairs Coun.; trustee Gulf Univs. Rsch. Consortium, 1971-84, chmn., 1977-79. Served with RCAF, 1940-44; Served with USAAF, 1944-45; rear admiral U.S. Maritime Service. Mem. Am. Geophys. Union, Am. Meteorol. Soc. (dir.), Galveston C. of C., Sigma Xi, Pi Mu Epsilon, Sigma Pi Sigma, Phi Kappa Phi, Sigma Phi Epsilon. Home: 5222 Denver Dr Galveston TX 77551-5943 Office: Tex A&M U PO Box 1675 Galveston TX 77553-1675

CLAYTON, WILLIAM L., investment banking executive; b. Tenafly, N.J., Oct. 27, 1929; s. Walter I. and Emily A. (Caverly) C.; m. Carol L. Farmer, June 23, 1951; children: Andrew L., Robin L., Kathleen L., Kevin L., Susan L., Christopher L. BS, Lehigh U., 1951, LLD (hon.), 1987; postgrad. in Bus., NYU, 1953-56. Asst. portfolio mgr. Marine Midland, N.Y.C., 1953-54; account exec. E.F. Hutton, N.Y.C., 1954-64, v.p., 1964-71, sr. v.p., 1971-81, exec. v.p., 1981-87; sr. v.p. Smith Barney, N.Y.C., 1988—; bd. dirs. Stabler Cos., Harrisburg, Pa., Eastern Industries, Harrisburg, Pa. Trustee Lehigh U., 1980—, Blair Acad., 1984—, New Eyes for Needy, 1984-90. Recipient Nat. Mktg. Club, 1980; named Outstanding Alumnus Lehigh U., 1971. Mem. Lehigh U. Alumni Assn. (pres. 1980-82), Baltusrol Club (Springfield, N.J.), Univ. Club, Short Hills Club, Orchid Island Golf Club (Vero Beach, Fla.), Knights of Malta, Beta Gamma Sigma, Chi Phi. Home: 5 Carriage Hill Dr Morristown NJ 07960-6994 Office: Smith Barney 325 Columbia Tpke Florham Park NJ 07932-1212*

CLAYTON-TOWNSEND, JOANN, aerospace analyst; b. Ft. Smith, Ark., Dec. 8, 1935; d. James Wooley and Rachel (McLaughlin) C.; m. John David Clayton (dec.); children: Rachel Diana, David Edward; m. John W. Townsend, Sept. 17, 1996. BA, U. Tulsa, 1958; MA, George Washington U., 1990. Chief legis. asst. U.S. Ho. Reps., Washington, 1974-79; analyst NRC/NAS, Washington, 1979—; dir. aeronautics and space engring. bd. NRC, 1990—. Pres. Turkish-Am. Cultural Soc., Ankara, Turkey, 1972-73. Recipient Disting. Profl. Staff award NRC, 1990; McClure scholar U. Tulsa, 1955. Fellow AIAA (assoc.); mem. AAAS, Am. Astron. Soc., Internat. Inst. Space Law (proceedings editor 1998—), Women in Aerospace (v.p. 1990, Outstanding Achievement award 1991, Outstanding Mem. 1997,), Internat. Acad. Astronautics (elected 1992), Kappa Alpha Theta. Avocations: oil painting, sailing.

CLAYTOR, RICHARD ANDERSON, retired federal agency executive, consultant; b. Roanoke, Va., Sept. 4, 1927; s. William Graham and Gertrude (Boatwright) C.; m. Mary Lee Leary, June 18, 1949; children: Gale Catherine, Douglas Gordon, Richard Anderson Jr. BS, U.S. Naval Acad., 1949; BS in Marine Engring., Webb Inst. Naval Architecture, 1956, MS in Naval Architecture, 1956. Registered profl. engr., N.J., Calif. Commd. ensign USN, 1949, advanced through grades to capt., 1969; served in various ships, 1949-53; project mgr. nuclear power div. USN Bur. Ships, Washington, 1956-63; asst. mgr. Pitts. Naval Reactors Office, AEC, 1963-73; ret., 1973; v.p., asst. to pres. Burns and Roe, Inc., Oradell, N.J., 1973-79; pres. Burns and Roe-Humphreys & Glasgow Synthetic Fuels, Inc., Oradell, 1979-81, Burns and Roe Pacific Co., L.A., 1981-90; asst. sec. for def. programs U.S. Dept. Energy, Washington, 1990-93; ind. cons. Decorated Legion of Merit. Mem. ASME, Soc. Naval Engrs., Am. Nuclear Soc., Army-Navy Club. Republican. Episcopalian. Avocations: tennis, bridge, hiking, canoeing, oil painting.

CLEAR, ALBERT F., JR., retired hardware manufacturing company executive; b. N.Y.C., June 9, 1920; s. Albert F. and Edna (Coyle) C.; m. Jeanne Posselt, Aug. 7, 1947; children: Geoffrey Posselt, Gregory Stuart. BS, MIT, 1942; MBA, Harvard U., 1948. V.p., mgr. Mallory div. John B. Stetson Co., Danbury, Conn., 1948-57; mng. assoc. Booz-Allen & Hamilton, N.Y.C., 1957-65; v.p., gen. mgr. hardware div. Stanley Works, New Britain, Conn., 1965-69, v.p. consumer group, chmn. European ops., 1967-69, exec. v.p., 1969-76, pres., 1977-80, vice chmn., 1980-82; vice chmn. Ansonia (Conn.) Copper & Brass, 1999—; bd. dirs. The Stanley Works, New Britain, Stanley Home Products, Westfield, Mass., Barden Corp., Danbury, Curtis Corp., Sandy Hook, Constructive Workshop, Inc., New Britain, D&L Corp., Danbury; adv. dir. Conn. Nat. Bank. Vice chmn. MIT Ctr. N.Y., 1965; bd. dirs. Danbury chpt. ARC, 1953; trustee Hartford Grad. Ctr., Hartford Coll. for Women, Housatonic Valley Assn., 1976-80. Capt. AUS, 1942-46. Mem. Builders Hardware Mfrs. Assn. (exec. com.), Danbury C. of C. (pres. 1954), New Britain C. of C. (dir. 1967-69, 72-80, pres. 1977). Home: 344 Westmont St Hartford CT 06117-2938

CLEAR, JOHN MICHAEL, lawyer; b. St. Louis, Dec. 16, 1948; s. Raymond H. and Marian (Clark) C.; m. Isabel Marie Bone, May 10, 1980. BA summa cum laude, Washington U., St. Louis, 1971; JD with honors, U. Chgo., 1974. Bar: Mo. 1974, D.C. 1975, U.S. Ct. Appeals (5th and D.C. cirs.) 1975, U.S. Supreme Ct. 1977, U.S. Ct. Appeals (3d cir.) 1978, U.S. Ct. Appeals (8th cir.) 1980, U.S. Ct. Appeals (9th cir.) 1990, U.S. Dist. Ct. (so. dist.) Ill. 1995, U.S. Ct. Appeals (7th cir.) 1997. Law clk. to judge U.S. Ct. Appeals (5th cir.), Atlanta, 1974-75; assoc. Covington & Burling, Washington, 1975-80; jr. ptnr. Bryan, Cave, McPheeters & McRoberts, St. Louis, 1980-81, ptnr., 1982—. Mem. ABA, Mo. Bar Assn., D.C. Bar Assn., St. Louis Met. Bar Assn., Am. Law Inst., Order of Coif., Racquet Club, Noonday Club, Fox Run Golf Club, Phi Beta Kappa. Office: Bryan Cave LLP One Metropolitan Sq Saint Louis MO 63102-2750

CLEAR, TODD, criminal justice educator. BA, Anderson Coll., 1971; MA, SUNY, Albany, 1972, PhD, 1977. Tchg. asst. criminal justice, vis. lectr. sociology SUNY, Albany, 1973-75; instr. sociology DePaul U., Chgo., 1975-76; prof. criminal justice Ball State U., Muncie, Ind., 1976-78, Rutgers U., Newark, 1978-96; assoc. dean, prof. criminology Fla. State U., Tallahassee, 1996-99; disting. prof. John Jay Coll. Criminal Justice CUNY, 1999—; v.p. Nat. Coun. Crime and Delinquency, San Francisco, 1991-93; cons. in field. Author: Harm in American Penology: Offenders, Victims and Their Communities, 1995; co-author: The Pre-Sentence Investigation Report: Information for Sentencing and Corrections, 1988, American Corrections, 1986, Controlling the Offender in the Community Reform of Community Supervision, 1983, The Impact of Sentencing Reform, 1983, Sentencing by Mathematics, 1982, Corrections: An Issues Approach, 1980, 3d edit., 1989, The Community Justice Ideal, 1999; contbr. chpts. to books, articles to profl. jours. Recipient Vincent O'Leary award Internat. Assn. Paroling Authorities, 1993, disting. faculty award Nat. Coun. Juvenile & Family Ct. Judges, 1993, Valorous B. Clear award Ind. Jud. Ctr., 1993. Mem. Acad. Criminal Justice Scis. (pres. elect 1998—), Am. Soc. Criminology, Am. Mgmt. Assn., Orgnl. Devel. Network. Office: John Jay Coll Criminal Justice Dept Law and Police Sci 899 10th Ave New York NY 10019

CLEARFIELD, HARRIS REYNOLD, physician; b. Phila., Aug. 8, 1933; s. Samuel and Rae (Lewis) C.; m. Louise Libby, June 30, 1957; children: Andrea, Jonathan. BS, Franklin and Marshall Coll., 1955; MD, Jefferson Med. Coll., 1959. Intern Grad. Hosp. U. Pa., Phila., 1959-60, resident in internal medicine, 1960-62, resident in gastroenterology, 1962-63, mem. staff, 1963-72; mem. staff Episcopalian Hosp., Phila., 1967-72, head sect. gastroenterology, until 1972; sr. attending physician Phila. Gen Hosp., 1972-77; mem. faculty U. Pa. Med. Sch., Phila., 1963-72; clin. asst. prof. medicine Temple U. Med. Sch., Phila., 1967-72; dir. div. gastroenterology Hahnemann Hosp., Phila., 1972—, prof. medicine, 1972—; lectr., cons. Naval Regional Med. Ctr., Phila., 1976-78; sr. cons. Phila. Gen. Hosp., 1972-74; mem. gov.'s adv. com. of ACP, 1980-88; dir. Krancer Ctr. for Inflamatory Bowel Disease Rsch., 1985—. Author: (with Dinoso) Gastrointestinal Emergencies, 1979, (with Borowsky) Case Studies in Gastroenterology, 1989; editorial cons. Am. Jour. Proctology, 1976-86; contbr. articles to profl. jours. Chmn. sci. adv. bd. Nat. Found. Ileitis and Colitis, 1976-80, trustee, 1990—. Recipient Lindback award Phila. chpt. Nat. Found. Ileitis and Colitis, 1979, named Physician of Yr., 1980, Janssen award, 1998. Fellow ACP (mem. bd. regents 1999), Phila. Coll. Physicians; mem. Am. Gastroenterologic Assn., Bockus Internat. Soc. Gastroenterology (trustee, v.p., pres. 1993-95), Phila. Gastroenterology Group (pres. 1974-75), Am. Soc. Gastrointestinal Endoscopy, Am. Coll. Gastroenterology (gov. Ea. Pa. 1990-92, bd. trustees 1992-96), Pa. Soc. Gastroenterology (pres. 1993-95), Delaware Valley Soc. Gastrointestinal Rsch. Forum, Pa. Med. Soc. (commn. on accreditation 1986-92), Phila. Med. Soc. (bd. dirs. 1996—, sec. 1998—, v.p. 1999—). Home: 720 Oxford Rd Bala Cynwyd PA 19004-2112 Office: 230 N Broad St Philadelphia PA 19102-1121

CLEARFIELD, SIDNEY, religious organization executive; b. Phila.; m. Lois Goodman; 2 children. BA, Temple U., 1961; MSW, U. Pa., 1963; PhD, Cath. U., Washington, 1973. Assoc. prof., asst. dean Sch. Social Work, Va. Commonwealth U., 1967-76; internat. dir. B'nai B'rith Youth Orgn., Washington, 1977-91; exec. v.p. B'nai B'rith Internat., Washington, 1991—. Mem. Assn. Nat. Dirs. of Jewish Youth Orgns. (past chmn.), Internat. Assn. Jewish Communal Svc. Workers, Assn. Jewish Cmty. Orgn. Profls., World Jewish Restitution Orgn. Office: B'nai B'rith Internat 1640 Rhode Island Ave NW Washington DC 20036-3279*

CLEARY, BEVERLY ATLEE (MRS. CLARENCE T. CLEARY), author; b. McMinnville, Oreg., 1916; d. Chester Lloyd and Mable (Atlee) Bunn; m. Clarence T. Cleary, Oct. 6, 1940; children: Marianne Elisabeth, Malcolm James. BA, U. Calif., 1938; BA in Librarianship, U. Wash., 1939; LHD (hon.), Cornell Coll., 1993. Children's librarian Pub. Libr., Yakima, Wash., 1939-40; post librarian U.S. Army Regional Hosp., Oakland, Calif., 1942-45. Author: Henry Huggins, 1950, Ellen Tebbits, 1951, Henry and Beezus, 1952, Otis Spofford, 1953, Henry and Ribsy, 1954, Beezus and Ramona, 1955, Fifteen, 1956, Henry and the Paper Route, 1957, The Luckiest Girl, 1958, Jean and Johnny, 1959, The Real Hole, 1960, Hullabaloo ABC, 1960, 98, Two Dog Biscuits, 1961, Emily's Runaway Imagination, 1961, Henry and the Clubhouse, 1962, Sister of the Bride, 1963, Ribsy, 1964, The Mouse and the Motorcycle, 1965, Mitch and Amy, 1967, Ramona the Pest, 1968, Runaway Ralph, 1970, Socks, 1973, (play) The Sausage at the End of the Nose, 1974, Ramona the Brave, 1975, Ramona and Her Father, 1977 (Newbery Honor Book award ALA 1978), Ramona and Her Mother, 1979, Ramona Quimby, Age 8, 1981 (Newbery Honor Book award ALA 1982), Ralph S. Mouse, 1982, Dear Mr. Henshaw, 1983 (ALA Notable Book citation 1984, John Newbery medal 1984), Ramona Forever, 1984, Lucky Chuck, 1984, The Ramona Quimby Diary, 1984, Beezus and Ramona Diary, 1986, Janet's Thingamajigs, 1987, The Growing Up Feet, 1987, A Girl from Yamhill: A Memoir, 1988, Muggie Maggie, 1990, Strider, 1991, Petey's Bedtime Story, 1993, My Own Two Feet: A Memoir, 1995, Ramona's World, 1999. Recipient Disting. Alumna award U. Wash., 1975, Laura Ingalls Wilder award ALA, 1975, Regina medal Cath. Libr. Assn., 1980, De Grummond award U. Miss., 1982, U. So. Miss. medallion, 1982, Hans Christian Andersen medal nominee, 1984. Mem. Authors Guild of Authors League Am. Office: William Morrow & Co 1350 Ave of Americas New York NY 10019-4702

CLEARY, DAVID MICHAEL, composer, library assistant; b. Chelsea, Mass., Nov. 11, 1954; s. Robert Joseph and Sally Ann (Deuker) C. MusB, New Eng. Conservatory Music, 1976; MusM, U. Hartford, 1978; MusD, U. Cin., 1982. Asst. to composition dept. New Eng. Conservatory Music, Boston, 1974-76; teaching asst. in music theory U. Hartford (Conn.), 1976-78; teaching asst. in music theory U. Cin., 1978-80, rotating instr. in music theory, 1980-81; libr. asst. Harvard U., Cambridge, Mass., 1984—; assoc. prodr. The Composers Show, Sta. WGBH-FM, Boston, 1974-75; co-dir. Composers in Red Sneakers, 1994—, pres., 1997—. Compositions include Five Character Studies, 1979, A Gathering of Quokkas, 1985 (commd. Dinosaur Annex Ensemble), Lake George Overture, 1988, String Quartet no. 1, 1988, Gryllus, 1988-89, Cruikshank Fantasy, 1989 (commd. Alea III), Woodwind Quintet no. 2, 1990 (commd. Arcadian Winds), String Quartet no. 2, 1991 (commd. Artaria Quartet Boston), Linsner Sextet, 1992 (commd. Northwestern U. Trombone Ensemble), Western Wind Fragments, 1993-94 (commd. Eos Ensemble), Fanfares for Teddy Roosevelt, 1994-95, The Deeper Magic, 1995-96 (commd. Duo Renard), Fourteen Movie Characters, 1996-97 (commd. Am. Composers Forum Boston Area chpt.); contbg. music writer (website) All-Music Guide, 1997—, (book) All Music Guide to Rock, 2d edit.; contbr. articles, revs., chpts. to profl. publs., books and websites; recordings on Centaur, Vienna Modern Masters CD labels. Recipient 1st pl. Rosenberger Meml. Comm. Competition, Cin., 1989, Harvey Gaul Composition Competition, 1990; ASCAP grantee U. Hartford, 1978, grantee Somerville Arts Coun., 1987, 90, Meet the Composer, 1990, ASTRAL grantee Nat. Found. for Advancement in Arts, 1994; rsch. fellow U. Cin., 1980, Douglas W. Bryant fellow, 1988, fellow Va. Ctr. for Creative Arts, 1988, 89, Yaddo fellow, 1988, Cummington fellow, 1989, Millay fellow, 1990, fellow Ella Lyman Cabot Trust, 1990, Ragdale fellow, 1992, MacDowell fellow, 1995, Tyrone Guthrie Ctr. fellow, 1998. Mem. BMI, Am. Music Ctr., Am. Composers Forum, Soc. Composers. Home: 7 Arlington St Apt 34 Cambridge MA 02140-2736 Office: Harvard U Biolabs Libr 16 Divinity Ave Cambridge MA 02138-2020

CLEARY, EDWARD WILLIAM, retired diversified forest products company executive; b. Sergeant Bluff, Iowa, May 21, 1919; s. Edward D. and Laura Helen (Rich) C.; m. Arita Louise Hefferan, June 12, 1946; children: John William, Kathryn Louise, Patricia Jane. BA, DePauw U., 1941; BSC, Ohio State U., 1947. Sr. acct. Price Waterhouse & Co., Portland, Oreg., 1947-53; treas., contr. Nat. Hosp. Assn., Portland, 1953-55, Valsetz Lumber Co., Portland, 1955-60; asst. compt. Boise Cascade (Idaho) Corp., 1960-63, compt., 1963-68, v.p., compt., 1968, v.p., treas., 1968-80, v.p., 1980-82, ret., 1982; bd. dirs. Farmers & Merchants State Bank. Mem. Pacific N.W. Area coun. YMCA, 1967-70; mem. exec. com. Boise United Fund, 1966-69, chmn. budget com., 1966-69; pres., bd. dirs. YMCA, 1967-69; bd. dirs. Idaho Blue Cross Hosp. Assn., 1969-75; bd. dirs., past pres. Bogus Basin Recreation Assn., bd. dirs. 1973-91. With AUS, 1941-42, USNR, 1942-46. Mem. AICPA, Nat. Assn. Accts. (past pres. Boise chpt., past nat. dir.), Idaho Soc. C.P.A.'s, Hillcrest Country Club (past dir., past v.p.). Home: 2018 N Beach St Boise ID 83706-1004

CLEARY, JAMES C., JR., audio-visual producer; b. N.Y.C., Mar. 15, 1921; s. James Charles and Elizabeth Adelaide (Anglin) C.; grad. Scarsdale (N.Y.) High Sch., 1940; m. Adele Lillian Coe, Nov. 28, 1954. Lithographer, cameraman Advt. Lit. Inc., N.Y.C., 1940-41; advt. copy writer Grosset & Dunlap, book pubs., N.Y.C., 1942-44; advt. copy writer, editor Baker & Taylor, book wholesalers, N.Y.C., 1945-46; asst. mgr. sales Camera Craft Inc., retail photog. sales, White Plains, N.Y., 1946-50, Colortone Camera Inc., White Plains, 1950-57; producer, lectr. Ansco div. Gen. Aniline & Film Corp., Binghamton, N.Y., 1959-61; lab. photographer Nevis Lab. Nuclear Research, Columbia U., 1959-75; audio-visual specialist Edgemont Sch. Dist., Scarsdale, 1975-83; owner-producer Cleary Sound-Slides, New Rochelle, N.Y., 1950—. Mem. Scarsdale Camera Club (pres. 1948-49), Color Camera Club Westchester N.Y. (dir. 1958-59), Am. Security Council (advisory bd. 1970—), U.S. Air Force Assn., Am. Def. Preparedness Assn., Westchester County Grand Jurors Assn., The Baker Street Irregulars, Three Garridebs, Sherlock Holmes Socs., Thomas Wolfe Soc. Patentee of complete sound-synchronized, dissolving slide projection control system, 1966; pioneer in use of dissolve projection and synchronized sound in presentation of color slide continuities. Address: Cleary Sound-Slides 28 Pengilly Dr New Rochelle NY 10804-3016

CLEARY, JOHN WASHINGTON, lawyer; b. Milw., Feb. 22, 1911; s. Peter A. and Mathilda A. (Borning) C.; m. Alice M. Shinners, Jan. 15, 1938; children: Terrence P., Mary E., Peter J., Margaret A., John T., Catherine A. J.D., Marquette U., 1933. Bar: Wis. 1933. Since practiced in Milw.; partner Erbstoeszer, Cleary & Misey, 1936-82, Fiorenza & Hayes, 1982—; sec. Hopkins Savs. & Loan Assn., Milw., 1936-65, pres., 1965—; faculty Savs. and Loan Inst., Milw., 1961-63. Vice chmn. Milw. Commn. Community Relations, 1959-63; savs. and loan commr., Wis., 1963-65; mem. pres.'s senate Marquette U., 1977—; bd. dirs. Greater Milw. chpt. ARC, pres., 1961-63; trustee Marquette U. High Sch.; gov. nat. ARC. Mem. Wis. Legis. Council, Milw. Savs. and Loan Council (pres. 1948-50), Wis. Savs. and Loan League (pres. 1954-55), U.S. Savs. and Loan League (dir. 1962-63). Home: 2728 N 98th St Milwaukee WI 53222-4513 Office: 7901 W Burleigh St Milwaukee WI 53222-4916

CLEARY, LYNDA WOODS, financial advisor, consultant; b. Birmingham, Ala., June 18, 1950; d. Eugene and Elizabeth (Wright) Woods; m. George Cassius Riley, Nov. 29, 1975 (div. 1979); m. Richard Charles Cleary, Dec. 12, 1987. Student, Dartmouth Coll., 1970-71; BA, Tougaloo (Miss.) Coll., 1972; postgrad., Rutgers U., 1981-83; MBA, N.Y. Inst. Tech., 1992. Comml. underwriter Continental Ins. Co., N.Y.C., 1973-74; lectr. John Ericson Sch., Ostersund, Sweden, 1974; asst. underwriting cons. Prudential Property and Casualty, Holmdel, N.J., 1975-80; market rsch. analyst Continental Ins. Co., Piscataway, N.J., 1981-86; bus. systems analyst Am. International Group, N.Y.C., 1986-87; ins. agt. Equitable Fin. Cos., N.Y.C., 1988; spl. agt. Northwestern Mut. Life, Princeton, N.J., 1988-89; cons. Cleary Woods Cons., Princeton, 1989—; account exec. Dean Witter, N.Y.C., 1992-93; fin. cons. Fahnestock & Co., Inc., Red Bank, N.J., 1993-95, Securities Am., Inc., Princeton, N.J., 1995—; cons. Nat. Torque Tech. Labs., Piscataway, 1989—. Mem. fin. com. Princeton Walk Homeowners Assn., 1988-95; fundraiser Crossroads Theatre, New Brunswick, N.J., 1988—; asst. troop leader Girl Scouts U.S., West Windsor. Recipient Cert. of Appreciation Concerned Community Women of Jersey City, Inc., 1990. Mem. Nat. Assn. Securities Profls., Coalition Black Investors. Democrat. Baptist. Avocations: macrame, gardening, playing word games, birdwatching, tennis. Office: 22 Springwood Ct Princeton NJ 08540-9403

CLEARY, MANON CATHERINE, artist, educator; b. St. Louis, Nov. 14, 1942; d. Frank and Crystal (Maret) C. BFA, Washington U., St. Louis, 1964; MFA, Tyler Sch. Art, Temple U., 1968. Instr. fine arts SUNY, Oswego, 1968-70; from instr. to assoc. prof. D.C. Tchrs. Coll., Washington, 1970-78; from assoc. prof. to prof. art U. D.C., Washington, 1978—, acting chmn. dept., 1985-86, 90-91; assoc. dean Coll. Liberal and Fine Arts U. D.C., 1992-94, acting coord. art program, 1994—. One woman shows include Mus. Modern Art Gulbenkian Found., Lisbon, Portugal, 1985, Iolas/Jackson Gallery, N.Y.C., 1982, Osuna Gallery, Washington, 1974, 77, 80, 84, 89, Univ. D.C., 1987, Tyler Gallery SUNY at Oswego, 1987, J. Rosenthal Fine Arts, Washington, 1991, Addison/Ripley Gallery, Washington, 1994, 99, Md. Arts Pl., 1997, Kramer Book Afterwords, 1998, others; group exhibits include Twentieth Century Am. Drawings: The Figure in Context, Traveled Nat. Acad. Design, 1984-85, Butler Inst. Am. Art, Youngstown, Ohio, 1987, Huntsville (Ala.) Mus., 1987, Boca Raton (Fla.) Mus. Art, 1987, Corcoran Gallery Art, Washington, 1987, 96, Dimock Gallery, Washington, 1987, Tretyakov Gallery, Moscow, 1990, Nohra Haime Gallery, 1994, Holter Mus., Helena, Mont., 1996, Gallery Stendahl, N.Y.C., 1996, Alt. Mus., N.Y.C., 1996, Kasteyev Mus., Almaty, Kazakstan, 1996, Alouan Gallery, Almaty, 1997, others. Artist-in-residence Herning Hojskole, Denmark, 1980, Ucross Found., Wyo., 1984, Bridge Assn., Creative Lab. Project, Almaty, 1996, 97. Recipient Faculty Rsch. award, U. D.C., 1984, 89, Mayor's 14th ann. award for excellence in an artistic discipline, 1998. Mem. Coll. Art Assn., Pi Beta Phi. Democrat. Presbyterian. Home: 1736 Columbia Rd NW Washington DC 20009-2833 Office: UDC Dept Mass Media Vis & Performing Arts Rm A-08 Bldg 42 4200 Connecticut Ave NW Bldg 48 Washington DC 20008-1176

CLEARY, MARTIN JOSEPH, real estate company executive; b. N.Y.C., July 27, 1935; s. Patrick Joseph and Kathleen Theresa (Costello) C.; m. Peggy Elizabeth McIntyre, June 22, 1957; children: Patrick Francis, Eileen Ann, Michael Thomas, Kathleen Marie, Maureen Elizabeth. B.S., Fordham U., 1960; M.B.A., N.Y. U., 1963. With Tchrs. Ins. and Annuity Assn. and Coll. Retirement Equities Fund, N.Y.C., 1953-81; pres. Jacobs, Visconsi, Jacobs, Westlake, Ohio, 1981—; bd. dirs. Guardian Life Ins. Co., Lamson & Sessions, Cleveland Indians. Mem. Internat. Coun. Shopping Ctrs. (trustee 1980—, pres. 1983-84). Office: The Richard David & Jacobs Group 25425 Center Ridge Rd Cleveland OH 44145-4122

CLEARY, MICHAEL J., educational administrator. Exec. dir. Nat. Assn. Collegiate Dirs. Athletics. Office: NACDA PO Box 16428 Cleveland OH 44116-0428

CLEARY, ROBERT EMMET, gynecologist, infertility specialist; b. Evanston, Ill., July 17, 1937; s. John J. and Brigid (O'Grady) C.; M.D., U. Ill., 1962; m. June 10, 1961; children—William Joseph, Theresa Marie, John Thomas. Intern, St. Francis Hosp., Evanston, 1962-63, resident, 1963-66; practice medicine specializing in gynecology and infertility, Indpls., 1970—; head Sect. of Reproductive Endocrinology and Infertility, Chgo. Lying-In Hosp., U. Chgo., 1968-70; head Sect. of Reproductive Endocrinology and Infertility, Ind. U. Med. Center, Indpls., 1970-80; prof. ob-gyn Ind. U., Indpls., 1976-80, clin. prof. ob-gyn, 1980—. Recipient Meml. award Pacific Coast Obstetrical and Gynecol. Soc., 1968; diplomate Am. Bd. Ob-Gyn, Am. Bd. Reproductive Endocrinology and Infertility. Fellow Am. Coll. Ob-Gyn, Am. Fertility Soc.; mem. Endocrine Soc.,Soc. Gynecol. Investigation, Pacific Coast Fertility Soc., Soc. Reproductive Endocrinologists, Soc. Reproductive Surgeons, N.Y. Acad. Scis., Sigma Xi. Roman Catholic. Contbr. articles in field to med. jours. Home: 7036 Dubonnet Ct Indianapolis IN 46278-1541 Office: 8091 Township Line Rd Indianapolis IN 46260-2495

CLEARY, SUE ELLEN, secondary school educator; b. Normal, Ill., Aug. 21, 1948; d. Towner E. and Helen L. (Coe) Jacobus; m. Paul G. Cleary, Aug. 11, 1979; 1 child, Sean David. BS in English/Journalism, Ill. State U., 1970; MA in Journalism, No. Ill. U., 1976. Cert. tchr., Ill. Adj. instr. U. Ill., Chgo., 1981-83; tchr. English James B. Conant H.S., Hoffman Estates, Ill., 1970—. Reporter-intern news, features Daily Pantagraph, 1976, 77. Named Outstanding Tchr., U. Chgo., 1983, Inspirational Tchr., Western Ill. U., 1997. Mem. Nat. Coun. Tchrs. English, Ill. Assn. Tchrs. English, Jane Austen Soc. N.Am. Avocations: reading, needlework, travel.

CLEARY, THOMAS CHARLES, technology company executive; b. Chgo., Nov. 15, 1921; s. Thomas Harold and Mary Margaret (Russell) C.; m. Barbara Winnifred Johnson, Dec. 18, 1948; children: Thomas Robert, Margaret Mary Cleary Nurmia, Mary Ann Cleary Robitaille. BS in Mech. Engring., UCLA, 1949. Pres., gen. mgr. Whittaker Corp., Denver, 1950-63; dir. program mgmt. Litton Industries, Woodland Hills, Calif., 1963-65; asst. gen. mgr. Teledyne Sys., Inc., 1965-66; v.p., CEO Viking Industries, Chatsworth, Calif., 1966-67; v.p. Power Conversion, Inc., Long Beach, Calif., 1967-68; chmn. bd. dirs., mng. dir TRW Electronic Comp. Co., Taiwan, Republic of China, 1968-69; pres., CEO Deutsch Relays, Inc., East Northport, N.Y., 1969-89, Struthers Dunn-Hi G, Pitman, N.J., 1989-91; chmn., CEO G&H Tech., Inc., Camarillo, Calif., 1992—. Author: Dynamic Management System, 1990, Management By Intent, 1991. Fundraiser Meml. Sloan-Kettering Cancer Ctr., N.Y., 1989—; mem. chancellor's assocs. UCLA, 1992—, mem. exec. com., dean's coun., sch. engring., 1992—; mem. bd. councillors UCLA Found., 1997. Capt. inf. U.S. Army, 1942-50, PTO. Named Entrepreneur of Yr. in mfg. Greater L.A. Area, 1997. Republican. Roman Catholic. Achievements include patents in the gyroscope and relay areas. Office: G&H Tech Inc 750 W Ventura Blvd Camarillo CA 93010-8382

CLEARY, THOMAS J., social worker, administrator; b. Indpls., May 28, 1942; s. Douglas L. and June Rose (McCalip) C.; m. Kathryn Anne Beuby, Aug. 31, 1968; children: Mary Kathryn, Stephen Michael; m. Yvonne Edith Perkins, Mar. 18, 1989. BA, Marian Coll., 1964; MA, Ind. U., 1966, Midwestern State U., 1992. Cert. social worker, Tex. Psychiat. social worker Ind. State Welfare, Indpls.; psychiat. social worker U.S. Army, Ft. Riley, Kans., Ft. Sam Houston, Tex.; psychiat. social worker C.F. Menninger Meml. Hosp., Topeka; chief social work svcs. USAF, Wichita Falls, Tex.; clin. social worker Red River Hosp., Tex.; clin. social worker psychology dept. Wichita Falls Rehab. Hosp., 1995-96; pvt. practice, 1993; clin. social worker Saratoga Med. Ctr., Sheppard AFB, Tex., 1996—. Contbr. articles to various publs. Lt. col. USAF, 1972—. Mem. Nat. Assn. Social Workers, Wichita County Mental Health Assn. (pres. 1986-87, bd. dirs. 1995—). Office: North TexasNTNS 1722 1/2 9th St Wichita Falls TX 76301-5003

CLEARY, TIMOTHY FINBAR, professional society administrator; b. Cork, Ireland, Sept. 30, 1925; s. John Francis and Nora (Riordan) C.; m. Patricia Agnes Hanley, June 21, 1947; children: Timothy F. X., Maureen P., Therese A., Richard S., Gail P., Eileen P. B.S., Fordham U., 1955, J.D., 1959. Bar: N.Y. 1959, D.C. 1980. Atty. N.Y.C. Police Dept., 1959-67; asst. counsel Fair Labor Standards div. U.S. Dept. Labor, Washington, 1967-71, chief counsel, 1971-73, mem., 1973-85; cons. in occupational safety and health, 1985—; exec. dir. Nat. Trust for Tng., Edn. and Research in Constrn., 1987-1991; internal campaign contbn. administrator Internat. Brotherhood Elec. Workers; chmn. U.S. Occupational Safety and Health Rev. Commn., Washington, 1977-81; mem. Adminstrv. Conf. U.S.; cert. arbitrator Nat. Mediation Bd.; lectr. labor law Practising Law Inst., U. Wis., Washington and Lee U., Cumberland Sch. Law, Ohio No. U., Brookings Instn., AFL-CIO Center for Labor Studies, Gompers-Murray Inst.Trade Assc., numerous others. Contbr. articles to profl. jours. Served with USN, 1943-45. Mem. Friendly Sons St. Patrick, D.C. Friends of Ireland. Home and Office: 5709 Cheshire Dr Bethesda MD 20814-2207

CLEARY, WILLIAM JOSEPH, JR., lawyer; b. Wilmington, N.C., Aug. 14, 1942; s. William Joseph and Eileen Ada (Gannon) C. AB in History, St. Joseph's U., 1964; JD, Villanova U., 1967. Bar: N.J., 1967, Calif. 1982, U.S. Ct. Appeals (3d cir.) 1969, U.S. Ct. Appeals (9th cir.) 1983, U.S. Dist. Ct. (ctrl. dist.) Calif. 1983, U.S. Supreme Ct. 1992. Law sec. to judge N.J. Superior Ct., Jersey City, 1967-68; assoc. Lamb, Blake, H&D, Jersey City, 1968-72; dep. pub. defender State of N.J., Newark, 1972-73; 1st asst. city corp. counsel Newark, 1973-76; assoc. Robert Wasserwald, Inc., Hollywood, Claif., 1984-86, 86-89, Gould & Burke, L.A., Hollywood, 1986-87; pvt. practice Hollywood, 1989—. Mem. ABA, FBA, N.J. State Bar Assn., Calif. Bar Assn., L.A. County Bar Assn., Nat. Jesuit Hon. Soc., Alpha Sigma Nu. Democrat. Roman Catholic. Office: 1853 1/2 Canyon Dr Los Angeles CA 90028-5607

CLEARY, WILLIAM T., marketing executive. BS in History, SUNY, Buffalo, MS in Anthropology. Various advertising positions N.Y.C.; sr. level mgr. ActiVision, Apple Computer; founder, mng. ptnr. CKS Ptnrs., 1987-1998, pres. and CEO, 1987-1990. Mem. adv. bd. Leavey Sch. Bus. and Adminstrn., Santa Clara U. Fullbright scholar. Office: CKS Ptnrs 10260 Bandley Dr Cupertino CA 95014-1911*

CLEASBY, JOHN LEROY, civil engineer, educator; b. Madison, Wis., Mar. 1, 1928; s. Clarence Allen and Othelia Amanda (Swanson) C.; m. Donna Jean Haugh, Sept. 2, 1950; children: Teresa, Richard, Lynne. B.S., U. Wis., 1950, M.S., 1951; Ph.D., Iowa State U., 1960. Diplomate: Am. Acad. Environ. Engrs.; registered profl. engr., Iowa. Inspection engr. Standard Oil Co. Ind., Whiting, 1951-52; project engr. Consoer Townsend & Assocs., Chgo., 1952-54; instr. Iowa State U., Ames, 1954-56, asst. prof., 1956-61, assoc. prof., 1961-65, prof., 1965-93, disting. prof., 1983-93, disting. prof. emeritus, 1994—; vis. prof. Univ. Coll. London, 1975-76; cons. World Bank, Washington, Pan Am. Health Orgn., WHO, U. Sao Paulo. Co-author: Water Supply Engineering, 1962; contbr. articles to profl. jours. Served with USN, 1945-46. Recipient Outstanding Tchr. award Iowa State U., 1977, David R. Boyan Eminent Faculty award for rsch. Iowa State U., 1989. Mem. ASCE (sec. Environ. Engring. divsn. 1969-73, pres. Iowa sect. 1966, Hering medal 1968, 70, 83, Norman medal 1980), Nat. Acad. Engring., Am. Water Works Assn. (trustee Water Quality divsn. 1981-87, chmn. 1985, chmn. Iowa sect. 1982, hon., Publs. awards 1962, 80, Divsn. Best Paper awards 1970, 92, 95, Rsch. award 1982, Abel Wolman award 1997), Kiwanis. Am. Baptist. Home: 4805 Dover Dr Ames IA 50014-4586 Office: Iowa State U 487 Town Engring Ames IA 50011

CLEAVER, EMANUEL, II, former mayor, minister; b. Waxahachie, Tex., Oct. 26, 1944; s. Lucky and Marie (McKnight) Cl; m. Dianne Donaldson, June 1970; children: Evan Donaldson, Emanuel III and Emiel Davenport (twins), Marissa Dianne. BA, Prairie View (Tex.) A&M Coll.; ThM, St. Paul Sch. Theology, Kansas City, Mo.; DD (hon.), Baker U., 1988. Ordained to ministry United Meth. Ch. Pastor St. James-Paseo United Meth. Ch.; mayor pro-tem City of Kansas City, 1987-91, mayor, 1991-98; Lectr. to chs., schs., civic and social orgns. nationwide. Councilman Fifth Dist. City, 1979-91; chmn. City Coun. Plans and Zoning Com., 1984-87, Policy and Rules Com., 1987-91; mid-cen. regional v.p. So. Christian Leadership Conf., Drum Major for Justice award, 1991; founder, co-chair Kansas City Harmony In A World of Difference. Recipient Centurions Leadership award Greater Kansas City C. of C., 1987, William Yates Disting. Svc. Medallion William Jewel Coll., 1987, Pub. Svc. award Am.-Jewish Com., 1991, Junteenth Man of Yr. award Black Archives of Mid-Am. Inc., 1991, Disting. Citizen award Greater Kansas City Urban Affairs Coun., 1991, Community Svc./Leadership award Webster U., 1991, Disting. Svc. award Park Coll., 1991, Drum Major of Justice award Nat. SCLC, 1991, Friend of Youth award Boys & Girls Clubs, 1991, Outstanding Contbns. to Black Cmty. award Concerned Citizens Black Clergy of Atlanta, 1991, Rainbow award, 1992, 100 Most Influential Kansas Citians award Kansas City Globe, 1991, 92, 93, Bridge Builders award Kansas City Globem 1992, Harold L. Holiday Sr. Civil Rights award NAACP, 1992, Disting. Grad. award St. Paul Sch. Theology, 1993, Kansas City Anti-Apartheid award, 1993, James C. Kirkpatrick Excellence for Govt. award, 1993, Disting. Citizen of Midwest award NCCJ, 1993, Gov. award for local elected ofcl. of yr. State of Mo., 1994. Mem. NAACP, Greater Kansas City C. of C. (Centurions Leadership award 1987), Alpha Phi Alpha. Founder and co-chmn., Harmony In A World of Difference program. *

CLEAVER, JAMES EDWARD, radiologist, educator; b. Portsmouth, England, May 17, 1938; came to the U.S., 1964; s. Edward Alfred and Kathleen Florence (Cleveley) C.; m. Christine J. Cleaver, Aug. 8, 1964; children: Jonathan, Alison. BA, St. Catharine's Coll., 1961; PhD, U. Cambridge, 1964. Rsch. fellow Mass. Gen. Hosp., Boston, 1964-66; asst. rsch. biophysicist lab. radiobiology environ. health U. Calif., San Francisco, 1966-68, asst. prof. radiology, 1968-70, assoc. prof. radiology, 1970-74, prof. radiology, 1974—; vis. prof. Imperial Cancer Rsch. Fund, London, 1973-74, prof. radiology, 1975-96, prof. dermatology, 1996—. Contbr. over 300 articles to profl. jours. Recipient Lila Gruber award Am. Acad. Dermatology, 1976, Sr. Investigator award Am. Soc. Photobiology, 1995, Luigi Provasoli Awd., 1992, Phycol. Soc. Am. Mem. NAS, Nat. Coun. on Radiation Protection, Radiation Rsch. Soc. (councillor 1982-84, rsch. award 1973).

CLEAVER, WILLIAM LEHN, lawyer; b. Harrisburg, Pa., Dec. 7, 1949; s. Gene Franklin and Goldie Jean (Haldeman) C.; children: Benjamin Neville, Valerie Anne. BA, Augustana Coll., 1971; JD, U. Iowa, 1974. Bar: Iowa 1974, Ill. 1975, U.S. Dist. Ct. (so. dist.) Iowa 1975, U.S. Dist. Ct. (so. dist.) Ill. 1975. Ptnr. Bozeman, Neighbour, Patton & Noe, Moline, Ill., 1991—; chmn. bd. govs. BBB Ctrl. Ea. Iowa. Mem. adv. coun. Luth. Social Svcs. of Ill. Adult Day Care Ctr., Rock Island; v.p., bd. dirs. United Way of Quad Cities, Rock Island; pres. adv. coun. Ret. Sr. Vol. Program, Moline; bd. govs. Rock Island Cmty. Found.; commr., chmn. Rock Island Preservation Commn.; mem. Citizen's Adv. Com.; bd. dirs. Quad Cities chpt. ARC; mem. Rock Island/Milan Dist. 41 Sch. Bd. Col. USAR. Mem. ABA, Ill. State Bar Assn., Iowa State Bar Assn., Rock Island County Bar Assn., Scott County Bar Assn. Lutheran. Lodge: Kiwanis (pres. 1983-84, bd. dirs. 1984-85). Avocations: fine arts, racquet sports. Home: 8806 Ridgewood Rd Rock Island IL 61201-7655 Office: Bozeman Neighbour Patton & Noe 1630 5th Ave Moline IL 61265-7910

CLEAVER, WILLIAM PENNINGTON, retired sugar refining company executive, consultant; b. Newark, Nov. 13, 1914; s. Chester H. and Mildred (Day) C.; m. Virginia Whaley, Apr. 15, 1938; 1 dau., Jane P. A.B., Princeton U., 1937. With Domino Sugar (formerly Amstar Corp.), N.Y.C., 1937-79; raw sugar buyer Amstar Corp., 1954-57, v.p., 1957-79, pres. Am. Sugar divsn., 1975-79; cons., 1979—. Presbyterian. Home: 38 Manor Ave Cranford NJ 07016-2330

CLEAVES, PETER SHURTLEFF, university and foundation official; b. Washington, Dec. 4, 1943; s. Richard Delaplane and Margaret Grant (Shurtleff) C.; m. Dorothy Barcham, Aug. 31, 1968; children: Geoffrey, Rachel. AB, Dartmouth Coll., 1966; MA, Vanderbilt U., 1968; PhD, U. Calif., Berkeley, 1972. Escort interpreter U.S. Dept. State, Washington, 1966-68; assoc. rep. for Peru, Ecuador and Bolivia, Ford Found., Lima, Peru, 1972-76; rep. for Mex. and C.Am., Ford Found., Mexico City, 1977-82; vis. scholar Yale U., New Haven, 1976-77; v.p. 1st Nat. Bank Chgo., 1982-90; prof. U. Tex., Austin, 1990—, dir. Inst. Latin Am. Studies,, 1990-95; dir. Ctr. for Study Western Hemisphere Trade U. Tex., 1995-97; sr. adviser Avina Found., Hurden, Switzerland, 1997—; cons. UN U., Tokyo, 1977, various corp. and non-profit orgns. in Latin Am., 1990—. Author: Bureaucratic Politics and Administration in Chile, 1974, Agriculture, Bureaucracy and Military Government in Peru, 1980, Profession and the State, The Mexican Case, 1987; also numerous articles. Chmn., trustee Internat. Sch. Panama, Panama City, 1984-86; advisor on L.Am. policy position papers Nat. Dem. Com., Washington, 1988, 92, 96. William Hill Meml. fellow Dartmouth Coll., 1966, NDEA Title VI fellow U. Calif., 1968, Doherty rsch. fellow Doherty Found., 1970, Fulbright-Hays fellow, 1971. Mem. L.Am. Studies Assn., Barton Creek Country Club. Episcopalian. Avocations: tennis, languages. Fax: 512-471-1061. E-mail: pcleaves@uts.cc.utexas.edu. Office: U Tex Govt Dept Ste A1800 Mail Code A1800 Austin TX 78712*

CLEBERG, HARRY C., food products company executive. Pres., CEO Farmland Foods, Inc., Kansas City, Mo., 1991—; v.p. fertilizer/agriculture chems. Farmland Industries, Inc., Kansas City, 1991. Office: Farmland Industries Inc 3315 N Oak Traffic Way PO Box 7305 Kansas City MO 64116-0005*

CLECAK, DVERA VIVIAN BOZMAN, psychotherapist; b. Denver, Jan. 15, 1944; d. Joseph Shalom and Annette Rose (Dveirin) Bozman; m. Pete Emmett Clecak, Feb. 26, 1966 (div. 1993); children: Aimée, Lisa; m. John Pricz, Sept. 12, 1998. BA, Stanford U., 1965; postgrad., U. Chgo., 1965; MSW, UCLA, 1969. Lic. clin. social worker, Calif.; lic. marriage, family and child counselor, Calif. Social work supr. Harbor City (Calif.) Parent Child Ctr., 1969-71; therapist Orange County Mental Health Dept., Laguna Beach, Calif., 1971-75, area coordinator, 1975-79; pvt. practice psychotherapy Mission Viejo, Calif., 1979—; founder, exec. dir. Human Options, Laguna Beach, 1981—; mem, co-chmn. domestic violence com. Orange County Commn. on Status of Women, 1979-81; mem. mental health adv. com. extension U. Calif., Irvine, 1983, counseling psychologist, 1980, lectr., 1984-85; lectr. Saddleback Community Coll., Mission Viejo, 1981-82, Chapman Coll., Orange, 1979; field instr. UCLA, 1970-71, 77-78. Co-chair Nat. Philanthropy Day, Orange County, 1996. Recipient Women Helping Women award Saddleback C.C., 1987, Cert. for child abuse prevention Commendation State of Calif. Dept. Social Svcs., 1988, Comty. Svc. award Irvine Valley Coll. Found., 1989, Disting. Svc. award in field of domestic violence Nicole Brown Simpson Found., 1996, Amelia Earhart award for svc. to women Women's Opportunity Ctr., U. Calif.-Irvine, 1997, Lee Steelman award South Orange County Cmty. Svcs., 1998; named Orange County Non-profit Exec. of Yr., 1994, Humanitarian of Yr., Alexis de Tocqueville Soc., 1997, Woman of Distinction, Laguna Beach Soroptimists, 1998, Desert Dist. Soroptimists, 1998. Mem. NASW, Calif. Marriage Family and Child Counselors' Assn., Phi Beta Kappa.

CLECH, JEAN PAUL MARIE, mechanical engineer; b. Morlaix, France, Sept. 16, 1958; s. Edouard Marie and Marie Guillemette (Lozach) C. A in Econs., Sorbonne, Paris, 1980; diploma engr., Ecole Cen. of Paris, 1981; MSME, Northwestern U., 1982, PhD, 1985. Rsch. asst., lectr. Northwestern U., Evanston, Ill., 1982-85; tech. staff mem. AT&T Bell Labs., Whippany, N.J., 1985-90; mgr. Advanced Computer Rsch. Inst., Lyon, France, 1990-92; cons. Electronic Packaging, Bridgewater, N.J., 1992-93; sr. cons. electronic packaging & reliability The Kohl Group, Inc., Montclair, N.J., 1993-95; pres., CEO Electronics Packaging Solutions Internat. Inc., 1995—; expert in design and reliability of electronic assemblies and solder interconnects. Contbr. chpts. in book and articles to profl. jours. Mem. IEEE (tech. com. mem. and reviewer), ASME (tech. com. mem. and reviewer), Internat. Electronic Packaging Soc. Avocations: sailing, bicycling. Home: 101 Gates Ave Apt H10 Montclair NJ 07042-2520 Office: EPSI Inc PO Box 1522 Montclair NJ 07042-1522

CLECKLEY, FRANKLIN D., law educator. Justice W.Va. Supreme Ct., Charleston, 1994-96; prof. law W.Va. U. Coll. Law, Morgantown, 1996—. Office: WVa U Coll Law PO Box 6130 Morgantown WV 26506-6130*

CLEEK, CLIFFORD R., power assembly company executive; b. Guthrie, Okla., Jan. 2, 1949; s. Eulin R. Cleek and Alice Pamela Cleek-Farrar; m. Deborah L. Brouchoud, Aug. 12, 1972; children: Kenneth, Kari, Travis. BA in Sociology, U. Ctrl. Okla., 1975; M Religious Edn., Southwestern Bapt. Theol. Sem., 1975. Min. youth and edn. First Bapt. Ch., Tuttle, Okla., 1976-78; religious edn. dir. First Bapt. Ch., Billingt, Mont., 1979-81; welder Autoquip, Guthrie, Okla., 1981-97, power assembly specialist, 1997—. Pres., fin. sec. local union United Steelworkers Am.; pres. Logan County Reps., Guthrie, 1997—; mem. gov.'s task force on edn. Okla. State Bd. Employment, Oklahoma City, 1998—; supt. schs. Logan County, Guthrie, 1988; Sunday sch. dir., vacation Bible sch. dir., head usher, Sunday sch. tchr., ch. tng. dir. First So. Bapt. Ch. Republican. Baptist. Avocations: religion, politics. Address: 5824 E Charter Oak Rd Guthrie OK 73044-9267

CLEESE, JOHN MARWOOD, writer, businessman, comedian; b. Weston-super-Mare, Eng., Oct. 27, 1939; s. Reginald and Muriel C.; m. Connie Booth, 1968 (div. 1978); 1 child, Cynthia; m. Barbara Trentham, 1981 (div. 1990); 1 child, Camilla; m. Alyce Faye Eichelberger, 1992. Student, Clifton Coll., Bristol, Eng.; M.A., Downing Coll., Cambridge U., Eng.; LL.D., St. Andrews U. Profl. writer, comedian, 1963—. First appearance on Brit. TV as writer, performer on The Frost Report, 1966; other TV series include At Last the 48 Show; co-author, actor Monty Python's Flying Circus, Fawlty Towers; guest TV appearance Cheers (Emmy award); appeared in BBC prodn. The Taming of the Shrew, 1981; guest TV appearance Third Rock from the Sun, 1998 (Emmy nom.); film appearances include Interlude, 1968, The Magic Christian, 1970, The Rise and Rise of Michael Rimmer, 1970, And Now for Something Completely Different, 1972, Monty Python and the Holy Grail, 1975, Romance with a Double Bass, 1975, Life of Brian, 1979, The Secret Policeman's Ball, 1979, Time Bandits, 1981, Monty Python Live at the Hollywood Bowl, 1982, The Secret Policeman's Other Ball, 1982, Privates on Parade, Yellowbeard, 1983, The Meaning of Life, 1983, Silverado, 1984, Clockwise, 1986, A Fish Called Wanda (author screenplay, Best Actor Brit. Acad. Film and TV Arts), 1988, Erik the Viking, 1988, Splitting Heirs, 1992, Mary Shelley's Frankenstein, 1994, Jungle Book, 1994, (voice) The Swan Princess, 1994, Fierce Creatures, 1997, The Out of Towners, Isn't She Great, 1998, ; founder, former dir. Video Arts Ltd., London, 1979—, also created series of TV & radio commls. for products advertised internationally; co-author: Monty Python's Big Red Book, 1975, The Strange Case of the End of Civilization as We Know It, 1977, Families and How to Survive Them, 1983, Life and How to Survive It, 1993. Recipient Queen's award for Exports (awarded to Video Arts Ltd.), 1982. Office: care David Wilkinson, 115 Hazlebury Rd, London SW6 2LX, England

CLEGG, JAMES STANDISH, physiologist, biochemist, educator; b. Aspinwall, Pa., July 27, 1933; divorced; 3 children; m. Eileen Clegg; 1 stepchild. BS, Pa. State U., 1958; PhD in Biology, Johns Hopkins U., 1961. Rsch. assoc. biologist Johns Hopkins U., 1961-62; asst. prof. zoology U. Miami, 1962-64, from assoc. prof. biology to prof., 1964-86; prof. sect. molecular and cellular biology U. Calif., Davis, 1986—, dir. Bodega Marine Lab., 1986—; with CNRS Thias France, 1983; pres. Nat. Assn. Marine Labs., 1992-94. Recipient Fulbright Sr. Rsch. award U. London, 1978, U. Ghent, 1999; Wilson fellow, 1958-59. Fellow AAAS; mem. Am. Soc. Zoologists, Am. Soc. Cell Biology, Biophys. Soc., Soc. Cryobiology, Sigma Xi. Achievements include research in comparative biochemistry and biophysics; mechanisms of cryptobiosis; properties and role of water in cellular metabolism; cytoplasmic organization. Office: U Calif Bodega Marine Lab PO Box 247 Bodega Bay CA 94923-0247

CLEGG, MICHAEL TRAN, genetics educator, researcher; b. Pasadena, Calif., Aug. 1, 1941. AA, Sacramento City Coll., 1967; BS, U. Calif., Davis, 1969, PhD, 1972. chmn. biology bd., NRC, mem. commn. on life scis., NRC, 1990-96. Asst. prof. Brown U., Providence, 1972-76; assoc. prof. U. Ga., Athens, 1976-82, prof., 1982-84; prof. U. Calif., Riverside, 1984—, acting dean Coll. Natural and Agrl. Scis., 1994-97, dean Coll. Natural and Agrl. Scis., 1997—; mem. biology bd., NRC, mem. commn. on life scis., NRC, 1990—. Co-author: Principles of Genetics, 1988; co-editor: Plant Population Genetics, 1989, Molecular Evolution, 1990. Sgt. U.S. Army, 1960-63. Guggenheim Found. fellow, 1981-82. Fellow Am. Acad. Arts and Scis.; mem. NAS, Am. Soc. Naturalists (v.p. 1986), Am. Genetics Assn. (pres. 1987), Soc. for the Study of Evolution (v.p. 1986), Genetics Soc. Am. Avocations: skiing, flying. Office: U Calif Dept Botany And Plant Sci Riverside CA 92521*

CLEGG, ROGER BURTON, lawyer; b. Odessa, Tex., Apr. 18, 1955; s. Joe Dunn and Margaret Elisabeth (Blau) C.; m. Joann Ruth Catalfamo, June 15, 1985; 1 child, Paul. B.A. magna cum laude, Rice U., 1977; J.D., Yale U., 1981. Bar: D.C. 1981. Grad. fellow Office Gen. Counsel, CIA, Langley, Va.; mem. staff editorial and research div. Republican Nat. Com., Washington, 1980; law clk. to presiding judge U.S. Ct. Appeals, Washington, 1981-82; atty.- adviser office of legal policy U.S. Dept. Justice, Washington, 1982, spl. asst. to atty. gen., 1982-83, dep. asst. atty. gen., 1983-84, acting asst. atty. gen., office legal policy, 1984, assoc. dep. atty. gen., 1984-85, spl. litigation counsel, civil div., 1985, asst. to solicitor gen., 1985-87, dep. asst. atty. gen. civil rights div., 1987-91, dep. asst. atty. gen. env. div., 1991-93; v.p., gen. counsel Nat. Legal Ctr. for Pub. Interest, Washington, 1993-97; gen. counsel Ctr. for Equal Opportunity, Washington, 1997—. Editor-in-chief Yale Studies in World Public Order, 1979-80. Mem. D.C. Bar, Federalist Soc., Phi Beta Kappa. Republican. Methodist. Home: 9703 Flintridge Ct Fairfax VA 22032-1712 Office: 815 15th St NW Ste 928 Washington DC 20005-2253

CLEGHORN, JOHN EDWARD, bank executive; b. Montreal, July 7, 1941; m. Pattie E. Hart; children: Charles, Ian, Andrea. B in Commerce, McGill U., Montreal, 1962; DCL (hon.), Bishop's U., 1989; LLD (hon.), Wilfrid Laurier U., 1991; DCL (hon.), Acadia U., 1996. Chartered acct. Articled with Clarkson Gordon, chartered Accts., Montreal, 1962-64; sugar and futures trader St. Lawrence Sugar Ltd., Montreal, 1964-66; with assignments Citibank, NY, Montreal, Winnipeg & Vancouver, 1966-74; various posts Royal Bank of Canada, Montreal, Toronto & Vancouver, 1974-86; pres. Royal Bank of Canada, 1986-90; pres. and COO RBC, 1990-94; CEO Royal Bankof Can., Montreal, 1994-95; chmn., CEO, 1995—; bd. dirs. Royal Bank of Canada; bd. dirs. RBC Dominion Securities, Ltd., Inc., Royal Trust; chmn. Conf. Bd. of Can.; vice chmn. Bus. Coun. on Nat. Issues, Gov. McGill U.; chmn. McGill Fund Coun.; dir. Can. Spl. Olympics Found.,

Royal Trust; chancellor Wilfrid Laurier Univ.; dir. Internat. Monetary Conf. Fellow Order of Chartered Accts. Quebec, Inst. Chartered Accts. Ont.; mem. Can. Inst. Chartered Accts., Inst. Chartered Accts. Brit. Columbia. Office: Royal Bank Can, 200 Bay St Royal Bank Plz, Toronto, ON Canada M5J 2J5

CLELAND, CHARLES CARR, psychologist, educator; b. Murphysboro, Ill., May 15, 1924; s. Homer W. and Stella (Carr) C.; m. Betty Lou Woodburn, July 18, 1948. B.S., So. Ill. U., 1950, M.S., 1951; Ph.D., U. Tex., 1957. Lic. psychologist, Tex. Chief psychologist Lincoln State Sch., Ill., 1956-57; chief psychologist Austin State Sch., 1957-59; supt. Abilene State Sch. Tex., 1959-63; prof. spl. edn. and ednl. psychology U. Tex.-Austin, 1963—. Author: Mental Retardation, 1969, 2d edit., 1978, Handbook for Widowers, 1997, Profound Retardation, 1979, Exceptionalities, 1982; contbr. articles to profl. jours.; patentee in field. Bd. dirs. Child Guidance Ctr., Austin, 1966-67. Served with USAAF, 1943-46, PTO. Recipient Disting. Psychologist award Tex. Psychol. Assn., 1980, Edn. award Am. Assn. Mental Deficiency, 1978. Fellow AAAS, Am. Psychol. Assn., Am. Assn. for Mental Deficiency (v.p. psychology div. 1973); mem. Tex. Psychol. Assn. (pres. 1962-63). Republican. Presbyterian. Office: U Tex E Db408A Austin TX 78712

CLELAND, JOSEPH MAXWELL (MAX CLELAND), state official; b. Atlanta, Ga., Aug. 24, 1942; s. Joseph Hugh and Juanita (Kesler) C. BA, Stetson U., Deland, Fla., 1964, LLD (hon.), 1979; MA, Emory U., 1968, hon. degree. Mem. Ga. Senate, Atlanta, 1971-75; cons. Com. on Vets. Affairs, U.S. Senate, Washington, 1975; profl. staff mem. Com. on Vets. Affairs, U.S. Senate, 1975-77; adminstr. VA, Washington, 1977-81; sec. of state State of Ga., Atlanta, 1982-95; U.S. senator, mem. armed svcs. com., govtl. affairs com., small bus. com.; mem. commerce com. U.S. Senate, 1999—. Candidate U.S. Senate, Ga., 1996. Capt. U.S. Army, 1965-68, Vietnam. Decorated Bronze Star, Silver Star; recipient Disting. Alumnus award Stetson U., 1972, Gt. Georgian award WSB Radio, award for gallantry Easter Seal Soc., 1973, Outstanding Handicapped Citizen in Ga. award, 1973, Jefferson award for greatest pub. service by individual under 35 Am. Inst. Pub. Service, 1977, Inspiration award Assn. U.S. Army, Atlanta, 1978, AMP of Yr. award, 1978, Life Inspiration award Religious Heritage Am., 1978, Golden Key award Am. Assn. Sch. Adminstrs., 1978, Gold medallion Chapel of Four Chaplains, 1979, Am. Patriot's medal Valley Forge Freedom's Found., 1979, J.O. Wright award, 1979, Neal Pike award, 1979, Citizen of Yr. award Nat. Conf. Citizenship, 1986; named One of Five Outstanding Young Men in Ga. Ga. Jaycees, Outstanding Disabled Vet. DAV, one of 100 most influential people in Ga. by Ga. Trend mag. Democrat. Office: US Senate 461 Dirksen Sen Office Bldg Washington DC 20510-1001*

CLELAND, MAX, senator; b. Atlanta, 1942. BA, Stetson U., doctorate (hon.); MA in Am. History, Emory U., doctorate (hon.). Mem. Ga. State Senate, 1971-75, sec. of state, 1983-96; U.S. senator from Ga., 1996—; head U.S. VA, 1977-81, mgr. GI Bill, VA Home Loan Guaranty program, VA Hosp. program; founder First Stop Bus. Info. Ctr.; mem. Senate Armed Svcs. com., 1997—, com. on commerce, sci. and transp., 1999—, com. on govtl. affairs, 1997—, com. in small bus., 1997—. Author: (autobiography) Strong at the Broken Places. Capt. U.S. Army, 1967, Vietnam. Decorated Bronze Star, Silver Star; named One of Rising Democrats, Time Mag.; recipient Victory award Nat. Rehab. Hosp., Washington, 1996, Nat. award U.S. Small Bus. Adminstrn. Office: 461 Dirksen Sen Office Bldg Washington DC 20510-1001*

CLELAND, ROBERT ERKSINE, plant physiologist, educator; b. Balt., Apr. 30, 1932; s. Ralph Erskine and Elizabeth (Shoyer) C.; m. Mary Love, Sept. 2, 1957; children: Thomas Andrew, Alison Anne. B.A., Oberlin Coll., 1953; Ph.D., Calif. Inst. Tech., 1957. Postdoctoral fellow U. Lund, Sweden, 1957-58, King's Coll., London, 1958-59; asst. prof. botany U. Calif.-Berkeley, 1959-64; assoc. prof. botany U. Wash., Seattle, 1964-68, prof., 1968—, dir. biology program, 1987-92. Mem. editorial bd. Plant Physiology, 1966-92, Planta, 1977-90, Plant Sci., 1981—, Ann. Rev. Plant Physiology, 1985-89; contbr. articles to profl. jours. Fellow AAAS; mem. Am. Soc. Plant Physiologists (pres. 1974-75). Methodist. Office: U Wash Botany Dept PO Box 355325 Seattle WA 98195-5325*

CLELAND, ROBERT HARDY, federal judge; b. 1947. BA, Mich. State U., 1969; JD, U. N.C., 1972. Pvt. practice Port Huron, Mich., 1972-75; chief trial atty. County Prosecuting Atty's. Office, Port Huron, 1975-80; prosecuting atty. St. Clair County, 1981-90; judge U.S. Dist. Ct. (ea. dist.) Mich., Bay City, 1990—. Positions with Port Huron Hosp., 1989-91, United Way of St. Clair County, 1988-90, Civic Theater of Port Huron, Blue Water YMCA, First Congl. Ch. of Port Huron, MADD, St. Clair Rep. Party. Mem. ABA, Mich. Bar Assn., St. Clair County Bar Assn., Prosecuting Atty's. Assn. Mich. (pres. 1988-89). Office: US Dist Ct 214 US Courthouse Bay City MI 48708-5749*

CLELAND, SHERRILL, college president; b. Galion, Ohio, Sept. 21, 1924; s. Fred Burr and Doris Louise (Gregg) C.; m. Betty Irene Chorpenning, July 6, 1946 (dec. June 1986); children: Ann Denise Cleland Feldmeier, Douglas Stewart, Sarah McDermott Cleland Allen, Scott Cameron; m. Diana Ashley Drake, Sept. 3, 1988; stepchildren: Cynthia Rush, Allison Abizaid, Linda Wiener, Carol Abizaid, Amanda Abizaid, Richard Abizaid. A.B., Oberlin Coll., 1949; M.A., Princeton U., 1951, Ph.D. in Econs., 1957; LLD (hon.), Marietta Coll., 1989. Instr. econs. Princeton U., 1951-55; asst. prof. U. Richmond, 1955-56; mem. faculty Kalamazoo Coll., 1956-73, acad. v.p., 1964-67; prof. econs., pres. Marietta Coll., Ohio, from 1973, now prof. emeritus; econs. adviser Hashemite Kingdom Jordan, 1963-64; Ford Found. vis. prof. econs. and devel. adminstrn. Am. U. Beirut, Lebanon, 1967-69, hon. prof. Southwestern U. Fin. and Econs., Chengdu Peoples Republic China, 1985; cons. examiner North Ctrl. Assn. Colls., 1960-90; dir. Cleve. Fed. Res. Bank, Cin. br., 1980-85. Co-editor, author: Continuity and Change in the World Oil Industry, 1970; contbg. author: Linear Programming and Theory of Firm, 1962; contbr. to profl. jours. Pres. Kalamazoo chpt. Human Rels. Coun., 1958-60; bd. dirs. Tuition Exch., Inc.; chmn. Student Loan Funding Corp., 1991-97; bd. dirs. AHEAD Corp., Coll. and Univ. Resource Inst., Amideast, Inc.; past pres. Ohio Coll. Assn.; chmn. East Ctrl. Coll. Consortium, Ind. Colls., Univs. Ohio; trustee Oberlin Coll., 1976-82, Mt. Vernon Coll., 1992-97; Trustee Thomas L. Conlan Edn. Found., Cin., 1997—. With AUS, 1944-46. Decorated Bronze Star, Purple Heart.; recipient Kazanjian Found. teaching award econs., 1971; Leadership tng. fellow N. Central Assn. Colls., 1959. Fellow Middle East Studies Assn.; mem. Am. Econ. Assn., UN Assn. (past pres. Kalamazoo chpt.), Ohio Assn. for Freedom to Die. Presbyterian. Home: 416 Park Ave Falls Church VA 22046-3304

CLELAND, THOMAS EDWARD, JR., secondary school educator; b. Holyoke, Mass., Nov. 4, 1943; s. Thomas Edward and Hazel (Mitchell) C.; m. Patricia Helen Deitz, Apr. 10, 1965; children: David T., Donna J., Todd R. BA in Liberal Arts, U. Mass., 1965; MS in Guidance, Troy State U., 1976. Cert. tchr. Ark., Mass., USAF. Commd. 2d lt. USAF, 1965, advanced through grades to col., 1986, ret., 1991; dir. aerospace sci. Pine Bluff (Ark.) H.S., 1991-93; chmn. aerospace sci. dept. Ctrl. H.S., Springfield, Mass., 1993—. Author: (manual) Guide for Instructor Supervisors, 1978, AFJROTC Cadet Guide, 1992. Deacon, trustee United Congl. Ch., Holyoke, 1994—; mem. Vets. Activities Com., Sprinfield, 1996, pastoral search com., Holyoke, 1994—. Recipient 13 Air medals, Letter of Appreciation Pres. Bush, 1991. Mem. Air Force Assn., Am. Legion, Retired Officers Assn., Aircraft Owners & Pilots Assn., Red River Valley Fighter Pilots Assn., Springfield Tchrs. Assn., Order of Daedalians (flight capt.). Avocations: aviation history, running. Home: 36 Roosevelt Ave South Hadley MA 01075-2337 Office: Springfield Ctrl HS 1840 Roosevelt Ave Springfield MA 01109-2437

CLELAND, W(ILLIAM) WALLACE, biochemistry educator; b. Balt., Jan. 6, 1930; s. Ralph E. and Elizabeth P. (Shoyer) C.; m. Joan K. Hookanson, June 18, 1967 (div. Mar. 1999); children: Elsa Eleanor, Erica Elizabeth. A.B. summa cum laude, Oberlin Coll., 1950; M.S., U. Wis., 1953, Ph.D., 1955. Postdoctoral fellow U. Chgo., 1957-59; asst. prof. U. Wis., Madison, 1959-62, assoc. prof., 1962-66, prof., 1966—, M.J. Johnson prof. biochemistry, 1978—, Steenbock prof. chem. sci., 1982—. Contbr. articles to profl. biochem. and chem. jours. Served with U.S. Army, 1957-59. Grantee NIH, 1960—, NSF, 1960-94; recipient Stein and Moore award Protein Soc., 1999. Mem. NAS, Am. Acad. Arts and Scis., Am. Soc. Biochemistry and Molecular Biology (Merck award 1990), Am. Chem. Soc. (Alfred R. Bader Bioinorganic or Bioorganic Chem. award 1993, Repligen award 1995). Achievements include development of dithiothreitol (Cleland's Reagent) as reducing agent for thiol groups; development of application of kinetic methods for determining enzyme mechanism. Office: Enzyme Inst 1710 University Ave Madison WI 53705-4087

CLEM, ALAN LELAND, political scientist; b. Lincoln, Nebr., Mar. 4, 1929; s. Remey Leland and Bernice (Thompson) C.; m. Mary Louise Burke, Oct. 24, 1953; children: Andrew, Christopher, Constance, John, Daniel. BA, U. Nebr., 1950; MA, Am. U., 1957, PhD, 1960. Copywriter, research dir. Ayres Advt. Agy., Lincoln, 1950-52; press sec. to Congressman Carl Curtis of Nebr., 1953-54, Congressman R. D. Harrison of Nebr., 1955-58; info. specialist Fgn. Agrl. Service, Dept. Agr., 1959-60; asst. prof. polit. sci. U. S.D., Vermillion, 1960-62; assoc. prof. U. S.D., 1962-64, prof., 1965—; assoc. dir. Govtl. Research Bur., 1962-76, chmn. dept. polit. sci., 1976-78; ptnr. Opinion Survey Assocs., 1964-88; state analyst Comparative State Elections Project, U. N.C., 1968-73; dir. Mt. Rushmore Presdl. Inst., 1970-71; mem. U.S. Census Bur. Adv. Com. on State and Local Govt. Stats., 1970-74. Author: several books, including Prairie State Politics: Popular Democracy in South Dakota, 1967, The Making of Congressmen: Seven Campaigns of 1974, 1976, American Electoral Politics: Strategies for Renewal, 1981, Law Enforcement: The South Dakota Experience, 1982, The Government We Deserve, 1985, 5th edit., 1995, Congress: Powers, Processes and Politics, 1989; contbr. articles to profl. jours.; editor: Contemporary Approaches to State Constitutional Revision, 1969. Mem. Vermillion City Coun., 1965-69; sr. warden St. Paul's Episcopal Ch., Vermillion, 1971-73, treas., 1996—. Named Outstanding Alumnus, U. Nebr. Coll. Arts and Scis., 1998; Nat. Conv. faculty fellow, 1964. Mem. Mensa, Midwest Polit. Sci. Assn. (exec. council 1970-72, editorial bd. Am. Jour. Polit. Sci. 1971-72), Am. Polit. Sci. Assn., Phi Beta Kappa, Phi Alpha Theta, Pi Sigma Alpha (nat. coun. 1986-89), Sigma Delta Chi. Republican. Club: Vermillion Golf Assn. (pres. 1986-87). Home: 608 Colonial Ct Vermillion SD 57069-3424 Office: U SD Dept Polit Sci Vermillion SD 57069 *Avoid haste, anxiety, contentiousness, and self-centeredness. Care, clarity, persistence, honesty, and grace will prevail in the long run.*

CLEM, HARRIET FRANCES, library director; b. Akron, Ohio, Nov. 8, 1940; d. Paul Milton and Mary Eva (Koppes) Miller; m. Ross Lynn Clem, June 23, 1979. BA cum laude, Kent State U., 1963, MLS, 1965. Teletype operator Babcock & Wilcox Co., Barberton, Ohio, 1958-59; bookmobile libr. Wadsworth (Ohio) Pub. Libr., 1963-64; head ext. dept. Rodman Pub. Libr., Alliance, Ohio, 1965-68, libr. dir., 1969—; instr. children's lit. Mt. Union Coll., Alliance, 1970-71; instr. libr. sci. Kent (Ohio) State U., 1975-7. Trustee YMCA, Alliance, 1974-84; pres. ARC, Alliance, 1975-77; bd. dirs. Leadership Stark County, Canton, Ohio, 1997—. Named Boss of Yr., Assn. Secs., Alliance, 1982. Mem. Ohio Libr. Coun. (founder accrg. divsn.), Alliance C. of C. (pres. 1983, 93, Athena award 1990), Beatrix Potter Soc., C.S. Lewis Soc., Alliance Women's Club (pres. 1977), Alliance Country Club, Coterie, Sorosis, Beta Phi Mu (nat. coun. 1978-80). Episcopalian. Avocations: travel, cooking. Home: 13484 Louisville St NE Paris OH 44669-9713 Office: Rodman Pub Libr 215 E Broadway St Alliance OH 44601-2650

CLEM, JOHN RICHARD, physicist, educator; b. Waukegan, Ill., Apr. 24, 1938; s. Gilbert D. and Bernelda May (Moyer) C.; m. Judith Ann Paulsen, Aug. 27, 1960; children—Paul Gilbert, Jean Ann. BS, . Ill., 1960; MS, U. Ill., 1962, PhD, 1965. Rsch. assoc. U. Md., College Park, 1965-66; vis. rsch. fellow Tech. U., Munich, Ger., 1966-67; asst. prof. physics Iowa State U., Ames, 1967-70, assoc. prof., 1970-75, prof. physics, 1975—, chmn. dept. physics, 1982-85, disting. prof. in liberal arts and scis., 1989—; vis. staff mem. Los Alamos Nat. Lab., 1971-83; cons. Argonne Nat. Lab., Ill., 1971-76, Oak Ridge (Tenn.) Nat. Lab., 1981, Brookhaven Nat. Lab., Upton, N.Y., 1980-81, Allied-Signal, Torrance, Calif., 1990-92, Am. Superconductor Corp., Westborough, Mass., 1996-97,, Pirelli Cable Corp., Lexington, S.C., 1996-97, Los Alamos Nat. Lab., 1997-99; guest prof. U. Tuebingen, Fed. Republic Germany, 1978; cons. IBM Watson Rsch. Ctr., Yorktown Hts., N.Y., 1982-85, vis. scientist, 1985-86; vis. scientist Electric Power Rsch. Inst., Palo Alto, Calif., 1992-93; vis. prof. applied physics Stanford U., 1992-93. Sci. editor newsletter High-Tc Update; contbr. articles to profl. jours.; patentee in field. Recipient award for sustained outstanding rsch. in solid state physics, U.S. Dept. Energy; Fulbright sr. rsch. fellow, 1974-75; NATO grantee, 1979-82. Fellow Am. Phys. Soc. (chair divsn. condensed matter physics 1994-95); mem. AAUP, Iowa Acad. Sci., Sigma Xi, Tau Beta Pi, Phi Kappa Phi. Democrat. Presbyterian. Avocation: singing. Home: 2307 Timberland Rd Ames IA 50014-8251 Office: Iowa State Univ A517 Physics Ames IA 50011

CLEM, RALPH S., career officer. BA in Geography with honors, San Diego State Coll., 1965; MA in Geography and Soviet Studies, Columbia U., 1972, PhD in Geography and Soviet Studies with distinction, 1976; student, Air Command and Staff Coll., 1987, Air War Coll., 1989. Commd. 2d lt. USAF, 1965, advanced through grades to brig. gen., 1996; spl. agt. detachment 101 Office Spl. Investigations, Hartford, 1965-68; spl. agt. dist. 51 Office Spl. Investigations, Bangkok, 1968-69; supervising case officer hdqs. Office Spl. Investigations, Washington, 1969-70; chief intelligence 915th Airborne Early Warning and Control Group, Homestead AFB, Fla., 1976-78, 93rd Tactical Fighter Squadron, Homestead AFB, 1978-83, 482d Tactical Fighter Wing, Homestead AFB, 1983-90; intelligence staff officer, sr. strategic air ops. analyst Office Mil. Forces, Nat. Security Agy., Ft. George G. Meade, Md., 1990-93; mobilization asst. to asst. dep. dir. ops. Nat. Security Agy., Ft. George G. Meade, 1993-96; mobilization asst. to comdr. Hdqs. Air Intelligence Agy., Kelly AFB, Tex., 1996-98; dep. chief Air Force Res. Hdqs. USAF, Washington, 1998—. Contbr. articles to profl. jours. Decorated Rep. Vietnam Campaign medal. Office: HQ USAF/RE 1150 Air Force Pentagon Washington DC 20330-1150

CLEMA, JOE KOTOUC, computer scientist; b. Omaha, Sept. 23, 1938; s. Joseph Arthur and Sylva Marie (Kotouc) C.; m. Maria Estela Cobos, Apr. 1, 1960; children: Jennifer, Arta. Student, U.S. Mil. Acad., 1957-60; BS, U. Nebr., 1963; MS, U. Miami, 1969; PhD, Colo. State U., 1973. Systems analyst Gen. Electric, Louisville, 1969-70; head sci. applications Colo. State U., Ft. Collins, 1970-73; project engr. Gen. Dynamics, Ft. Worth, 1973-77; sr. mgr. Simulation Tech., Inc., Dayton, Ohio, 1977-79; program mgr. Pratt and Whitney, West Palm Beach, Fla., 1979-82; dept. mgr. CACI, Dayton, 1982-83; dir. spl. projects Systems and Applied Scis., Vienna, Va., 1983-85; chief software engr. IIT Rsch. Inst., Annapolis, Md., 1985-90; cons. to IBM with Neurosystems, Inc., Bethesda, Md., 1991-98; cons. on IRS tax system modernization TRW, Merrifield, Va., 1993-95, cons. simplified tax & wage sys., 1995-96; mgr. Sys. Resources Corp., 1997-98, Houston Assocs., Inc., 1998—. Contbr. articles to profl. jours. Sustaining mem. Rep. Nat. Com., Washington, 1983—. Served to capt. U.S. Army, 1963-67. First Ann. Simulation Symposium Rsch. grantee, 1972; recipient Outstanding Svc. award Ann. Simulation Symposium Bd. Dirs., 1980. Mem. IEEE (sr.), ACM (nat. lectr. 1978-83), Soc. Computer Simulation (bd. dirs. , program chmn. 1988-96), Mid Atlantic Electronic Commerce Network (bd. dirs. 1995-98), Spl. Interest Group on Simulation (chmn. 1979-81), Ann. Simulation Symposium (chmn. bd. dirs. 1979), Internat. Platform Assn., Armed Forces Comms. and Elec. Assn., Herndon C. of C., Hidden Creek Country Club, Worldgate Athletic Club. Republican. Avocations: bridge, tennis. Home: 301 Missouri Ave Herndon VA 20170-5426 Office: Houston Assocs Inc 4601 N Fairfax Dr Arlington VA 22203

CLEMEN, JOHN DOUGLAS, lawyer; b. Mineola, N.Y., Dec. 18, 1944; s. John Douglas and Amy Gertrude (Ackerson) C.; m. Judith Anne Davis, June 3, 1967; children: Elizabeth, Jennifer. BA, Hobart Coll., 1966; JD, Seton Hall U., 1974. Bar: N.J. 1974, U.S. Dist. Ct. N.J. 1974, U.S. Ct. Appeals (3d cir.) 1980, U.S. Supreme Ct. 1982, N.Y. 1984, U.S. Dist. Ct. (so. dist.) N.Y. 1985, U.S. Dist. Ct. (ea. dist.) N.Y. 1989, U.S. Ct. Appeals (2d cir.) 1989. Law sec. to assoc. justice N.J. Supreme Ct., Trenton, 1974-75; assoc. Shanley & Fisher, P.C., Newark, 1975-83, ptnr., 1983—; arbitrator U.S. Dist. Ct. N.J., 1985—, N.J. Superior Ct., Morristown, 1986—; guest lectr. Acad. Medicine N.J., 1980-82. Contbg. editor Seton Hall Law Rev., 1973-74. Bd. dirs. Acad. Decathalon of N.J., 1997—; mem. Mass Disaster Response Team, ARC, 1997—. Capt. USAF, 1966-71, Vietnam. Decorated Air medal. Mem. ABA, N.J. Bar Assn. (chmn. aviation sect. 1992-94), N.Y. State Bar Assn., Trial Attys. N.J., Bergen County Bar Assn., Morris County Bar Assn. (chmn. continuing legal edn.), Commerce & Industry Assn. N.J. (bd. dirs., counsel 1988-92), Morristown Club. Home: 574 Colonial Rd River Vale NJ 07675-6107 Office: Shanley & Fisher PC 89th Fl One Worl Trade Ctr New York NY 10048

CLEMENCE, BONNIE J., pediatrics nurse; b. McKeesport, Pa., Jan. 8, 1953; d. Lester Jack Sr. and Betty Ann (Carrberry) Arthur; m. Ronald D. Clemence, Oct. 12, 1974. Diploma, Butler County Meml. Hosp. Sch. Nursing, Butler, Pa., 1971-73; cert. enterostomal therapist, Harrisburg (Pa.) Sch. Enterostomal Therapy, 1977; BSN, Pa. State U., 1980; MS in Nursing, U. Pitts., 1983. RN, Pa. Pediatric staff nurse Allegheny Valley Hosp., Natrona Heights, Pa., 1973-75, asst. head nurse pediatrics, staff devel. instr., 1978-80, head nurse pediatrics, 1980-82, staff nurse med./surg. unit, 1983-84; office nurse Freeport (Pa.) Med. Assn., 1982-83; asst. prof. nursing Community Coll. Allegheny County, Monroeville, Pa., 1984; pvt. duty nurse Pitts. Nursing Specialists, 1984-86; pvt. duty nurse, cons. pediatric patients Norelle Nursing Agy., Mars, Pa., 1987-88; head nurse pediatric/adult orthopedic unit, cons. enterostomal therapy Butler (Pa.) Meml. Hosp., 1985-88; emergency rm. staff nurse Children's Hosp. Pitts., 1988-90, asst. head nurse emergency rm., 1990—. Contbr. articles to profl. jours. (writing award for article 1980). Mem. Pa. State U. Alumnae Assn., U. Pitts. Alumnae Assn., Butler County Alumnae Assn. Home: 371 Collins Dr Pittsburgh PA 15235-3839 Office: Children's Hosp Pitts 1 Childrens Way Pittsburgh PA 15212-5250

CLEMENCE, ROGER DAVIDSON, landscape architect, educator; b. Worcester, Mass., Jan. 20, 1936; s. Luther Davidson and Dorothy (Kay) C.; m. Margaret Ann Weinandy, Aug. 19, 1961; children: Peter, Benjamin, Ellsabeth. AB, Amherst Coll., 1957; MArch, U. Pa., 1960, M in Landscape Architecture, 1962. Registered landscape architect, Minn. Instr., asst. prof. Coll. Architecture and Design U. Mich., Ann Arbor, 1962-66; assoc. prof. Sch. Architecture and Landscape Architecture U. Minn., Mpls., 1966-73, dir. Urban Edn. Ctr., Sch. Architecture and Landscape Architecture, 1970-77, interim head Sch. Architecture and Landscape Architecture, 1984, mem. urban studies faculty Coll. Liberal Arts, 1973—, mem. Am. studies faculty Coll. Liberal Arts, 1986—, dir. grad. studies in architecture Sch. Architecture and Landscape Architecture, 1978-85, prof. dept. architecture, 1973, assoc. dean Coll. of Architecture and Landscape Architecture, 1989-95, acting dean, spring 1993, interim dean, 1995-96; landscape arch., planner, Mpls., 1963; collegiate program leader Minn. Ext. Svc., 1993-97, prof. emeritus, summer 1997. Co-creator 10-part TV series The Meanings of Place, 1986. Mem. Minn. Com. on Urban Environment, 1979-88, Designer Selection Bd., 1980-85, chmn., 1983-84; mem. Mpls. Fed. Cts. Master Plan Com., 1991-92. Recipient Morse-Alumni Disting. Tchg. award, 1974, Pub. Svc. award Minn. Soc. Landscape Architects, 1982, Lob Pine award, 1996, CALA Disting. Svc. award, 1995; T.P. Chandler fellow U. Pa. Grad. Sch. Fine Arts, 1960-62. Fellow Am. Soc. Landscape Architects; mem. AIA (prof. affiliate Minn. chapt. 1979), MASLA, Tau Sigma Delta. Democrat. Mem. Unitarian Universalist Assn. Avocations: photography, writing, golf, reading, gardening. Office: U Minn CALA 89 Church St SE Minneapolis MN 55455-0109

CLEMENCEAU, PAUL B., lawyer; b. Bordeaux, France, Aug. 8, 1940. BA, Washington & Lee U., 1962; LLB, Tulane U., 1965. Bar: La. 1965, U.S. Dist. Ct. (ea. dist.) La. 1969, Tex. 1982, U.S. Dist. Ct. (so. dist.) Tex. 1982, Conseil Juridique 1971; cert. avocat (France) 1992. Ptnr. Mayer, Brown & Platt, Houston. Adv. bd. Houston Jour. Internat. Law, 1986—. Pres. French Am. C. of C., Houston, 1985-89. Mem. ABA, La. State Bar Assn., State Bar Tex. (chmn. internat. law sect. 1985-86), Tex. Bar Found. Office: Mayer Brown & Platt 700 Louisiana St Ste 3600 Houston TX 77002-2700*

CLEMENDOR, ANTHONY ARNOLD, obstetrician, gynecologist, educator; b. Port-of-Spain, Trinidad, West Indies, Nov. 8, 1933; s. Anthony Arnold and Beatrice Helen (Stewart) C.; came to U.S., 1954, naturalized, 1959; A.B., NYU, 1959; M.D., Howard U., 1963; m. Elaine Browne, May 31, 1958 (dec. May, 1991); children: Anthony Arnold, David Alan; m. Janet Jenkins, Sept. 23, 1993. Intern, USPHS, S.I., N.Y., 1963-64; resident Met. Hosp. Ctr., N.Y.C., 1964-68, chief outpatient dept. ob-gyn, 1969-73; med. dir. family planning Human Resources Adminstrn., N.Y.C., 1973-74; assoc. dean student affairs, dir. office of minority affairs N.Y. Med. Coll., Valhalla, N.Y., 1974-97, assoc. clin. prof. dept. ob-gyn., 1978-90, prof. clin. ob-gyn, 1990—. Bd. dirs. Elmcor, Caribbean-Am. Ctr. N.Y.C., Nat. Assn. of Minority Med. Educators, Inc., 1978-88, Empire State Med. Sci. and Ednl. Found., Inc., Caribbean Am. Ctr. of N.Y., 1988-91; mem. Nat. Urban League, N.Y. Urban League; life mem. NAACP. Diplomate Am. Bd. Ob-Gyn. Fellow Am. Coll. Ob-Gyn, Am. Pub. Health Assn.; mem. AMA, Royal Soc. Medicine, Nat. Med. Assn., N.Y. State Med. Soc., N.Y. County Med. Soc. (sec. 1989, v.p. 1990, pres. elect 1991, pres. 1992-93, bd. trustees, chmn. bd. trustees 1997-98), N.Y. Acad. Medicine, N.Y. Gynecol. Soc. (v.p. 1996, pres. 1988), N.Y. Acad. Medicine.

CLEMENS, ALVIN HONEY, insurance company executive; b. Pa., July 10, 1937; m. Valerie Crooker, Aug. 26, 1989; children: Kelli, Julie, Tracy, Wendy, Amy, Alvin H. Jr., Conner. BA, Pa. State U., 1959; postgrad. in ins., San Diego State U. Supr. sales assn. group dept. Ins. Co. Am., 1959-63; founder, ptnr. Butera, Clemens & Beyer Ins. Cons., Norristown, Pa., 1963-67; founder, dir., pres., chmn. Ex. Commn. Acad. Ins. Group, Valley Forge, Pa., 1967-85; dir., chmn., CEO Acad. Ins. Group (formerly Unicom Ins. Group), 1984-85; founder, dir., chmn. CEO Exec. Internat. Life, Bermuda, 1981-89; chmn., CEO Maine Nat. Life Ins. Co., Portland, 1985-96; chmn., CEO, pres. Provident Am. Corp., Norristown, 1989—, Provident Indemnity Life Ins. Co., Norristown, 1989—; mem. exec. com. bd. dirs. Ins. Fedn. Pa. trustee Pa. State U., mem. bd. visitors bus. sch.; apptd. to Banking and Ins. Transistion Team, Pa., 1995—; co-chmn. Ins. Task Force of Pa. IMPACCT Commn. on Banking and Ins. trustee Pa. State U., mem. bd. visitors bus. sch. Mem. Young Pres. Orgn., Phila. Pres. Orgn., World Pres. Orgn., Aronimink Golf Club, Pyramid Club. Office: Provident Am Corp PO Box 511 Norristown PA 19404-0511*

CLEMENS, DAVID ALLEN, lawyer; b. Cleve., Jan. 3, 1946; s. Peter John and Betty Jane (Slavik) C.; m. Jane Lucille Friou, June 14, 1969; children: David Allen Jr., Amy Jane. BA with high honors, Oberlin Coll., 1968; JD summa cum laude, Ohio State U., 1974. Bar: N.Y. 1975, U.S. Dist. Ct. (we. dist.) 1975. Assoc. Phillips, Lytle, Hitchcock, Blaine & Huber, Buffalo, 1974-81, ptnr., 1982—. mem. fin. com. Wesleyan Ch. of Hamburg (N.Y.), 1984—. Mem. ABA, N.Y.S. Bar Assn., Erie County Bar Assn., Eden C. of C., HoliMont Ski Club, Clarksburg Country Club. Avocations: skiing, running, tennis, golf, reading. Office: Phillips Lytle Hitchcock Blaine & Huber 3400 Marine Midland Ctr Buffalo NY 14203-2887*

CLEMENS, DAVID ALLEN, minister; b. Camden, N.J., Aug. 8, 1941; s. Arleigh Allen and Mae Elizabeth (Browne) C.; m. Janice Ruth Bonino, Feb. 13, 1965; children: Stephen David, Daniel Lee. *Wife Janice teaches sixth grade. She is also responsible for all scheduling of David's international Bible teaching ministry. Summers, she accompanies him to Europe, assisting in ministry there. She is an invaluable, God-given, absolutely essential part of David's life and ministry. Son Stephen is married to Paula and father of Samantha Jo. With two partners, he started and now manages Quaker Mechanical, Inc., "the fourth fastest growing company in eastern Pennsylvania," Philadelphia Inquirer. He and Paula are active in church/missionary ministries. Son Daniel, married to Jill and father of Juliana, is a mechanical engineer specializing in medical equipment design. Both are active in church/missionary ministry.* BA magna cum laude, Houghton Coll., 1963; MA, Nat. Christian U., 1972; ThD, Clarksville Sch. Theology, 1980; PhD, Christian Bible Coll., 1990. Ordained to ministry Ind. Bapt. Ch., 1963. Missionary Pocket Testament League, Chile, Peru, Bolivia, 1963-66; min. Richfield (Pa.) Mennonite Ch., 1966-67; itinerant Bible tchr. Bible Club Movement Inc., Upper Darby, Pa., 1968-71, nat. rep., 1971-77, dir. family adult ministries dept., 1977-80, min. at large, 1980-99, missionary, Bible tchr., 1999—; preaching and teaching tours Eng., Scotland, The Netherlands, Belgium, Sweden, Spain, Ireland, Can., Middle East, The Philippines, Zimbabwe, Poland, Cuba. Author: Steps to Maturity, Vols. I-III, 1973-79. Mem. Nat. Home Missions Fellowship. Home: 72 Knox Blvd Marlton NJ 08053-2921 Office: 237 Fairfield Ave Upper Darby PA 19082-2206 *To know,* *love, and serve God (as revealed in Jesus Christ) is the highest privilege of life.*

CLEMENS, DONALD FAULL, chemistry educator; b. Dover, Ohio, Aug. 14, 1929; s. John William and Ruth (Faull) C.; m. Martha Kay Lemmon, July 2, 1950; children: Richard, Nancy, Barbara, Rebecca, Margaret. BS, Fla. Southern, 1961; MS, U. Fla., 1963, PhD, 1965. Prof. chemistry East Carolina U., Greenville, N.C., 1965-95, prof. emeritus, 1995—; v.p. Whitehurst Assocs., New Bern, N.C., 1982—. Co-inventor, patentee processes for making chelating agents for metal ions from saccharides, wet process phosphoric acid brightening reagent for alumninum. Bd. dirs. Kiwanis Club, Greenville, 1986-89; chmn. bd. St. James Meth. Ch., Greenville, 1989-90. Mem. Am. Chem. Soc. (councilor ea. N.C. sect. 1985-94, nat. com. on chem. safety 1988-94), N.C. Acad. Sci., Masons, Sigma Xi. Avocations: woodworking, birdwatching, ham radio operator. Home: 405 Walnut Ridge Dr Floyd VA 24091

CLEMENS, RICHARD GLENN, lawyer; b. Chgo., Oct. 8, 1940; s. James Ralston and Jeanette Louise (Moellering) C.; m. Judith B. Clemens, Aug. 19, 1967; 1 child, Kathleen. BA, U. Va., 1962, JD, 1965. Bar: Ill. 1965. Assoc. Sidley & Austin, Chgo., 1965-66, Washington, 1968-71, Brussels, 1972-73; ptnr. Sidley & Austin, Chgo., 1973—. Served to capt. U.S. Army, 1966-68. Mem. ABA, Chgo. Bar Assn., Legal Club, Mid-Day Club. Office: Sidley & Austin 1 First Natl Plz Chicago IL 60603-2003

CLEMENS, ROBERT, violin maker; b. Kitchener, Ont., Can., Mar. 22, 1963; s. Adam Alphonse and Carolyn Mary (Weber) C.; m. Julia Hodgson, July 17, 1984. Diploma, Chgo. Sch. Violin Making, 1986; postgrad. study with, Zenon W W. Petesh, 1987-89. Profl. violin maker supplying instruments to Kenneth Warren and Son, Ltd., Chgo., William Moennig and Son, ltd., Phila., Gengakki Duo Co., Tokyo, 1987-91; founder, ptnr. Clemens Violins, Violas and Violoncellos, St. Louis, 1991—. Can. Arts Coun. grantee, 1984-85, 85-86. Address: 6353 Clayton Rd Saint Louis MO 63117-1808

CLEMENS, T. PAT, manufacturing company executive; b. Hibbing, Minn., July 26, 1944; s. Jack LeRoy and Mildred (Coss) C.; m. 1966 (div. 1992); children: Patrick Michael, Heather Kristen. BS in Econs. and Mgmt., St. Cloud State U., 1968; student of theology, Coll. St. Thomas, 1985-87. Sales adminstr. Transistor Electronics Co., Eden Prarie, Minn., 1969; head instnl. sales Chiquita Brands, Edina, Minn., 1970; dist. sales mgr. Menley & James Labs., Phila., 1971-75; owner, pres. T.P. Clemens Labs., Eagan, Minn., 1975—; instr community edn. Rosemount, Minn., 1977-78; bd. dirs. Rosemount Hockey, 1977-78, Relocation Assistance Assn. Am., 1984-85; v.p. Sch. Dist. #196 Booster Club, 1984-85; lectr. econs. to corps., high schs. and colls. in U.S., Scotland, Ireland, and Jamaica, 1979—. *The concern of one man and many students helped a four and a half year old deaf boy hear. T. Pat Clemens, an Eagan businessman, figured out the insurance arrangements and took charge of the fundraising for the deaf boy. He obtained donations from the high schools in Rosemount, Apple Valley, and Burnsville. A carwash was held by Clemens' nieces and nephew (Tiff & Jamie Elj, Nicole & Peter Raukar, and Marica & Casey Cox).* Author, editor: How Prejudice and Narcissism Control Economics of the United States and the World, 1979. Mem. Rosemont Cmty. Edn. Bd., 1985, chmn., 1986-87; chmn. speakers bur. Citizens Steering Com., 1984-85; coach Little League, 1970-82, 88-91; coach high sch. weight lifting team, 1975-95; vol. worker with comatose children, 1975-96, 97—. Recipient letter of recognition for stopping armed robbery Dakota County Atty.'s Dept., 1979, 93. Mem. Internat. Platform Assn., Kids-N-Kinship Program 1988-92. Home and Office: 1276 Vildmark Dr Eagan MN 55123-2801

CLEMENS, TAMMY LEAH, geriatrics nurse; b. Roaring Spring, Pa., Apr. 2, 1958; d. Ronald Robert and Doris Marie (Ott) Ferry; 1 child, Jamie Marie. Diploma, Altoona Hosp. Sch. Nursing, 1979. RN, Pa.; cert. in CPR. Charge nurse, staff nurse Nason Hosp., Roaring Spring, 1979-83; nursing supr. Morrison's Cove Home for Aged, Martinsburg, Pa., 1983—. Substitute organist, ch. sch. pianist Trinity United Meth. Ch., Roaring Spring, Pa., 1974-79; asst. troop leader Girl Scouts U.S.A., 1988-92; mem. Friendship Fire Co. 1 Inc., Ctrl. H.S. Alumni Band, Ctrl. H.S. Alumni Chorus. Mem. NAFE, Altoona Hosp. Sch. Nursing Alumni Assn. Republican. Methodist. Avocations: traveling, baking, reading, walking. Home: 430 Locust St Roaring Spring PA 16673-1734 Office: Morrison's Cove Home for Aged 429 S Market St Martinsburg PA 16662-1098

CLEMENS, WILLIAM ROGER, professional baseball player; b. Dayton, Ohio, Aug. 4, 1962; m. Debbie Lynn Godfrey, May 27, 1963; children: Koby Aaron, Kory Allen.. Student, San Jacinto North Jr. Coll., Houston, 1980-81, U. Tex., 1981-83. Baseball player Boston Red Sox, 1984-96, Toronto Blue Jays, 1997-98, N.Y. Yankees, 1998—. Recipient Cy Young award Am. League, 1986, 87, 91, Most Valuable Player award Am. League, 1986, Most Valuable Player award All-Star Game, 1986; named to Am. League All-Star Team, 1986, 88, 90-92; named Major League Player of Yr., Sporting News, 1986, Am. League Pitcher of Yr., 1986, 91. Office: New York Yankees, Yankee Stadium, E 161 St & River Ave, Bronx, NY Canada M5V 1J1*

CLEMENT, ALAIN GÉRARD, photographer; b. Balesmes, France, Mar. 17, 1945; came to U.S., 1978; s. Gabriel P. and Anne E. (Beuret) C. Lic. en Droit, U. Dijon, France, 1968. photographer: one-man exhbns. include Alain Clement, N.Y.C., Galerie Jacques Bosser, Paris, 1977, 91, Galerie L'Orange Le Havre, 1978, Danny Clayton, Houston, 1979, Pools, D. Clayton & Co., Houston, 1979, at W.A. Graham Gallery, Houston, 198, 83, 86, 87, 89, 92, Houston Photographs by Alain Clement, 1981, New Photographs, 1983, Alain Clement Photographs, 1986, Photoworks, 1989, Passage, 1992, Large Photograms: Recent Recollections, Allan Frumkin Gallery, N.Y.C., 1987, Alain Clement New Work James Gallery, Houston, 1996, 98, Weil Gallery, Tex. A&M U. Ctr. Arts, Corpus Christi, 1997; group exhbns. include Art from Houston in Norway, Stavenger (Norway) Art Mus., 1982, Constructions/Photographs, San Antonio Art Inst., 1984, Intersections: Artists View the City, Laguna Gloria Mus., Austin, Tex., 1986, Focus 87 Art Gallery of Ont., Toronto, Can., 1987, Photography, the 80's: Discovery and Invention, spl. exhbn., Basel (Switzerland) Art Fair, 1990, Fantastic Voyages, Houston Ctr. for Photography, 1992, Out of This World, Contemporary Arts Mus., Houston, 1994, Images from Space, Glassel Sch., Mus. of Fine Arts, Houston, 1998; represented in pub. collections: Menil Collection, The Mus. of Fine Arts, Houston, Bibliotheque Nationale, Paris, Dallas Mus. of Fine Arts, Musee Nicephore Niepce Chalons/Saone, France, McNeese State U., La., Houston Light and Power Collection. Recipient Creative Artist award Cultural Arts Coun. of Houston, 1987; grantee Nat. Endowment of the Arts, 1988. Mem. The William A. Graham Artists Emergency Fund in Houston (founder, pres.). *

CLEMENT, BARBARA KOLTES SADTLER, academic administrator; b. Hutchinson, Kans., Mar. 1, 1940; d. Edwin Michael and Rose Marie (Meyers) Koltes; m. David R. Sadtler, Aug. 24, 1963 (div. June 1974); m. Charles F. Clement III, Mar. 7, 1987. BA, U. Minn., 1961. Analyst Nat. Security Agy., Ft. Meade, Md., 1961-63; journalist Newhouse Nat. News Svc., N.Y.C., 1966-71; v.p. advt., pub. rels. Leslie Fay, Inc., N.Y.C., 1971-79; v.p. internat. pub. rels. Estee Lauder Internat. Cos., N.Y.C., 1979-94; asst. v.p., dir. pub. rels. Villanova (Pa.) U., 1994—. Author: Orbits of Venus, 1994; editor Villanova Mag., 1994—. Republican. Office: Villanova Univ 800 Lancaster Ave Villanova PA 19085-1478

CLEMENT, BETTY WAIDLICH, literacy educator, consultant; b. Honolulu, Aug. 1, 1937; d. William G. Waidlich and Audrey Antoinette (Roberson) Malone; m. Tom Morris, Jan. 16, 1982; 1 child, Karen A. Bratesani. BA in Elem. Edn., Sacramento State U., 1960; MA in Elem. Reading, U. No. Colo., 1973, MA in Adminstrn., EdD in Edn. & Reading, 1980. Elem. sch. tchr. pub schs., Colo., Calif., 1960-66; reading specialist, title I European area U.S. Dependent Schs., various locations, 1966-75; grad. practicum supr. U. No. Colo. Reading Clinic, Greeley, 1976-77; grant cons. Colo. Dept. Edn., Denver, 1978-81; adult edn. tutor, cons. various orgns., Boulder, Colo., 1983-87; student tchr. supr. U. San Diego, 1989-90; adult literacy trainer for vols. San Diego Coun. on Literacy, 1988—; adj. prof. U. Colo., Denver, 1981-82, U. San Diego, 1994—; adj. prof. comm. arts Southwestern Coll., Chula Vista, Calif., 1990-99; presenter various confs. Co-author, editor: Adult Literacy Tutor Training Handbook, 1990, author rev. edit., 1998. Grantee Fed. Right-to-Read Office Colo. Dept. Edn., 1979, curriculum writing Southwestern Coll., 1992. Fellow San Diego Coun. on Literacy (chair coop. tutor tng. com. 1991-93); mem. Whole Lang. Coun. San Diego, Calif. Reading Assn. Avocation: psychology. Office: U San Diego Olin Hall Alcala Park San Diego CA 92110

CLEMENT, BOB, congressman; b. Nashville, Sept. 23, 1943; m. Mary Carson; children: Greg, Jeff, Elizabeth, Rachel. BS, U. Tenn., 1967; MBA, Memphis State U., 1968. Founder, owner Bob Clement and Assocs., 1979—; with Ctr. for Govt. Tng. U. Tenn., 1971-72; commr. Tenn. Pub. Svc., 1973-79; dir. TVA, 1979-81; ptnr., owner Charter Equities, 1981-83; pres. Cumberland U., 1983-87; mem. 100th-105th Congresses from 5th Tenn. dist., Washington, 1988—; mem. transp. & infrastructure com., mem. internat. rels. com. With U.S. Army, 1969-71, with USNG, 1971—. Office: US Ho of Reps 2229 Rayburn Bldg Washington DC 20515-4205*

CLEMENT, EDITH BROWN, federal judge; b. Birmingham, Ala., Apr. 29, 1948; d. Erskine John and Edith (Burrus) Brown; m. Rutledge Carter Clement Jr., Sept. 3, 1972; children: Rutledge Carter III, Catherine Lanier. BA, U. Ala., 1969; JD, Tulane U., 1972. Bar: La. 1973. Law clk. to Hon. Herbert W. Christenberry U.S. Dist. Ct., New Orleans, 1973-75; ptnr. Jones, Walker, Waechter, Poitevent, Carrere & Denegre, New Orleans, 1975-91; judge U.S. Dist. Ct. (ea. dist.) La., New Orleans, 1991—. Fellow La. Bar Found. (life); mem. Am. Law Inst., La. Bar Assn., Federalist Soc., Maritime Law Assn. U.S., Fed. Bar Assn. Office: US Dist Ct 500 Camp St Rm C-455 New Orleans LA 70130-3313

CLEMENT, ELIZABETH STEWART, artist; b. Chattanooga, Sept. 24, 1928; d. Thomas Hill Sr. and Emma Owen (Wallace) Stewart; m. Coleman Clay Clement Jr., June 19, 1948; children: Catherine, Clare, Richard. Grad. art sch., High Mus. Art, Atlanta, 1948. Represented by Sotto Galleries, Pensacola, Fla., 1996, Soho Galleries, Foley, Ala.; condr. workshops on abstract painting, orgns. including Studio 1212, Clearwater, Fla., BIG Arts, Sanibel, Fla., Eloise (Fla.) Elem. Sch., Elem. Sch. of Spring Valley Bruderhof, Farmington, Pa., St. Petersburg (Fla.) Ctr. for Arts, All Sts. Acad., Winter Haven, Fla., Fla. Sheriff Youth Ranches, Bartow, Maitland (Fla.) Art Ctr., Donne Bitner Workshops, Cocoa Beach, Fla., others. One-woman show at Lee County Alliance of Arts, Ft. Myers, Fla., 1993; exhibited in group shows at Arts on the Park, Lakeland, Fla., Capital Gallery, Tallahassee, Lemoyne Ctr., Tallahassee, Phillips Gallery of Barrier Island Group for Arts, Sanibel, Soc. of Four Arts, Palm Beach, Fla., Atlanta Coll. Art (formerly High Mus. Art), Polk Mus., Lakeland, Daytona (Fla.) Mus., Boca Raton (Fla.) Mus., Winston-Salem (N.C.) Art Assn., Melvin Gallery, Fla. So. Coll., Lakeland, Abney Gallery Internat., N.Y.C., Fla. chpt. Nat. Assn. Women Artists, others (various awards). Mem. Polk Mus. Art. Mem. Fla. Artist Group Inc. (pres. 1996—), Ridge Art Assn. Inc. (v.p. 1996—), Art League (Alexandria, Va.). Republican. Episcopalian. E-mail: cccesc1150@aol.com. Home: 1150 W Lake Hamilton Dr Winter Haven FL 33881-9268

CLEMENT, FRANCES ROBERTS, lawyer, nurse, consultant; b. Columbia, S.C., Oct. 1, 1945; d. Ralph Winfred and Frances Lucille (Harter) Roberts; m. Tom F. Clement; children: Everett Hudson Smith, Armenta Harter Smith. BS in Biology, U. Ala., 1967; MS in Counseling, Fla. State U, 1970; AA in Nursing, Victoria Coll., Tex., 1978; JD with honors, Jones Sch. Law, Montgomery, Ala., 1986. Bar: Ala. 1987, U.S. Supreme Ct. 1997. Staff nurse Citizen's Meml. Hosp., Victoria, Tex., 1978-81, DeTar Hosp., Victoria, Tex., 1981, Bapt. Med. Ctr., Montgomery, 1982-84; adminstr sch. nurse Bloomington (Tex.) Sch. Dist., Montgomery, 1981-82; supr. Humana Hosp., Montgomery, 1985; legal asst. Kaufman, Rothfeder & Blitz, Montgomery, 1985-87; assoc. Powers & Willis, Montgomery, 1987-88; pvt. practice Montgomery, 1988-90; with Office of Atty. Gen., 1990—; adj. prof. U. Houston, Victoria, 1980, Auburn U., Montgomery, 1988-90, facilitator, mediator, 1999—. Mem. Montgomery County Bar Assn. Methodist. Avocation: computers. Home: 3502 Bankhead Ave Montgomery AL 36111-2018 Office: Criminal Appeals Divsn 11 S Union St Montgomery AL 36130-2102

CLEMENT, HENRY JOSEPH, JR., diversified building products executive; b. New Orleans, May 14, 1942; s. Henry Joseph Sr. and Margaret (Dowd) C.; m. Kathleen Erin Shean; children: Colleen and Collette (twins). BS, Loyola U., 1973. Sales rep. GE, New Orleans, 1972-77; mgr. product planning GE, Louisville, Ky., 1977-79; mgr. internat. market GE, Tyler, Tex., 1979-83; v.p. internat. sales Phillips Industries, Inc., Dayton, Ohio, 1983-84, pres. internat. div., 1984-88; pres. internat. group Tomkins Industries, Dayton, 1988-94; pres. Crescent Group, Inc., Dublin, Ohio, 1994—; vice chmn., bd. dirs. Shaanxi-Hytec, Ltd., Xian, Chila, 1988-89. Loan exec. United Way, New Orleans, 1974, Tyler, 1979. Mem. Miami Valley (Ohio) Internat. Trade Assn. (trustee), Blue Key (Cross Key Svc. award 1973). Republican. Roman Catholic. Home: 4666 Chatham Ct Dublin OH 43017-8607

CLEMENT, HOPE ELIZABETH ANNA, librarian; b. North Sydney, N.S., Can., Dec. 29, 1930; d. Harry Wells and Lana (Perkins) C. BA, U. of King's Coll., 1951; MA, Dalhousie U., 1953; BLS, U. Toronto, 1955; D of Civil Law (hon.), U. King's Coll., 1992. With Nat. Library of Can., Ottawa, Ont., 1955-92; chief nat. bibliography div. Nat. Library of Can., 1966-70, asst. dir. research and planning br., 1970-73, dir. research and planning br., 1973-77, assoc. nat. librarian, 1977-92. Editor: Canadiana, 1966-69. Mem. Can. Libr. Assn. (Outstanding Svc. to Librarianship award 1992), Internat. Fedn. Libr. Assns. (medal 1991).

CLEMENT, JOHN EDWARD STRAUSZ, minister, religious organization administrator; b. Enid, Okla., Jan. 9, 1934; s. Joseph Alvis and Sarah Evelyn (Brown) C.; m. Judith A. Strausz-Clement; children: Stephen W., Paul E., Catherine K., Stephanie L. Taylor, Christopher S. Clark, Karen L. Clark. BA, Oberlin Coll., 1956; MDiv, Union Theol. Sem., 1960. Ordained to ministry Presbyn. Ch., 1960. Pastor Williamsport, Pa., 1960-65, Wilmington, Del., 1965-69; project leader S. Cen. Ministry, Minn., 1969-74; mission enabler Los Ranchos Presbytery, Long Beach, Calif., 1974-78; exec. presbyter Cayuca-Syracuse Presbytery, Syracuse, N.Y., 1978-91, Pitts. Presbytery, 1991-95; interim exec. presbyter Carlisle Presbytery, Camp Hill, Pa., 1995-96; gen. presbyter Blackhawk Presbytery, Oregon, Ill., 1996—. organizing mem. Habitat for Humanity, Syracuse, N.Y.; chmn. ecumenical exec. cabinet and v.p. Syracuse Interreligious Coun., 1985-87; ch.-wide adminstrv. coord. cabinet Presbyn. Ch. (USA), 1986-88, 91-92; chmn. pers. com. N.Y. State Coun. of Chs., 1989-91; chmn. Synod of N.E. Ecumenical Cabinet, 1987-91; mem. AIDS Task Force of Ctrl. N.Y.; mem. nat. com. Bicentennial Fund Campaign, Presbyn. Ch. (USA), 1988-92; organizing mem. Christian Leaders Fellowship, Pitts., 1991-95; exec. com. Coun. of Christian Assocs. of Western Pa., 1991-95; mem. coun. judicatory execs. Ill. Conf. Chs., 1996—. Office: Blackhawk Presbytery Box 157 Oregon IL 61061-0157 *I believe God loves our world and has become one of us to redeem us and guide us toward a new humanity. I see our ministry standing on the side of the poor and oppressed as well as loving the oppressor.*

CLEMENT, MEREDITH OWEN, economist, educator; b. Colusa, Calif., June 7, 1926; s. Eldon Wilford and Lillian (Ohm) C.; m. Jacqueline Parker, Apr. 10, 1955; children—William, Christopher. Student, Yuba Coll., Marysville, Calif., 1946-48; B.S., U. Calif. at Berkeley, 1950, Ph.D., 1958. Rsch. economist CIA, 1954-56; mem. faculty Dartmouth Coll., Hanover, N.H., 1956—, prof., 1967-96, prof. emeritus, 1996—; vis. asst. prof. U. Calif. at Berkeley, 1961-62; Brookings research prof. Brookings Instn., 1964-65; Fulbright lectr. Robert Coll., Istanbul, Turkey, 1969-70; vis. scholar U. New S. Wales, 1988-89. Author: (with others) Theoretical Issues in International Economics, 1967, An Economic Evaluation of the Federal Grant-in-Aid Programs in New England, 1961, also articles. Served with USMCR, 1944-46. Mem. Am., So. econ. assns., Royal Econ. Soc., Econometric Soc. Unitarian. Home: PO Box 247 Etna NH 03750-0247 Office: Dartmouth Coll Dept Econs Hanover NH 03755

CLEMENT, PAUL PLATTS, JR., performance technologist, educator; b. Geneva, Ill., Aug. 30, 1935; s. Paul P. and Vera Elizabeth (Dahlquist) C.; BA in Math., Coe Coll., 1957; m. Susan Alice Aikins, June 7, 1958; children: Paul P. IV, Kathleen Elizabeth. Sales tech. rep. Burroughs Corp., Chgo., 1960-63; mgr. EDP, Harding-Williams Corp., Chgo., 1963-65; edn. coordinator Standard Oil Co., Chgo., 1965-69; mgr. product planning Edutronics Systems Internat., Chgo., 1969-71; interactive video instrn. specialist Advanced Systems Inc., Chgo., 1971-88; ind. cons. in tng., media use (animated film, videotape, interactive videodiscs), computers, Downers Grove, Ill., 1988; prin. instr., developer UNISYS Corp., Lisle, Ill., 1988-89; mgr. employee devel. CNA Ins. Cos., Chgo., 1990-91; cons. media, tng. Internet Systems Corp., Chgo., 1990-93; prin. Clement Consulting Group, Downers Grove, Ill., 1993—; part-time data processing faculty Coll. of DuPage and Coll. extension, Harper Coll., Ill., DeVry Inst.; invited speaker numerous computer and tng. confs., nat. and internat. assns.; developer, presenter workshops in field; mem. adv. bd. Northeastern Ill. U., Chgo. Served to capt. USAF, 1958-60. Developer and pub. 12 animated films with supplementary texts, 84 videotapes, 17 interactive videodiscs and over 7000 pages of expository texts; collaborator 100 other videotapes with supplementary texts; prin. developer micro-computer based People Compatability System, 1983; developer Decision Table Algorithms,1986, 94th Inf. Div. Assn. Info. System, 1977, Basic Computer Programmer Tng. Curriculum for Eng. Govt., 1979, Computerized Data Processing Curricula Devel. System, 1973, Early COBOL Lang. precompiler, 1967, Automagic Glossary, 1992; contbr. articles to Datamation mag., Data Training Mag. Mem. Nat. Soc. Performance and Instrn. (contbr. to jour.). Recipient Silver award WPC, 1996, Gold award, 1998. Fax: (630 969-7957. E-mail: PaulClementJr@IBM.net. Home and Office: 4942 Linscott Ave Downers Grove IL 60515-3537

CLEMENT, RICHARD WILLIAM, plastic and reconstructive surgeon; b. Pontiac, Mich., Nov. 10, 1953; s. William Henry and Jean Elizabeth (Girst) C.; m. Phyllis Jean Hobson, Aug. 15, 1981; children: Nicholas William, Kimberly Ashley, Christopher Richard. BS, Alma Coll., 1975; MD, U. Va., 1979. Diplomate Am. Bd. Plastic Surgery; fellow Am. Coll. Surgeons. Asst. prof. surgery Washington U., St. Louis, 1984-88; dir. Southwest Plastic Surgeons, Paradise Valley, Ariz., 1988—. Contbr. articles to profl. jours.; co-author: Essentials of Plastic Surgery, 1987. Fellow Am. Coll. Surgeons; mem. AMA, Am. Soc. Plastic and Reconstructive Surgeons., Bellerive Country Club. Republican. Presbyterian. Office: 9220 E Mountain View Rd Ste 214 Scottsdale AZ 85258-5136*

CLEMENT, ROBERT ALTON, retired chemist; b. Rockland, Mass., Aug. 12, 1929; s. Chester Alfred and Gertrude Louella (Beal) C.; m. Noriko Chiwaki, May 1, 1955; children: Brian, Colin, Nathan, Justin. SB, MIT, 1950; PhD, UCLA, 1954. Postgrad. rschr. U. Wis., Madison, 1953-55; from instr. to asst. prof. U. Chgo., 1955-62; rsch. scientist E.I. Dupont Co., Wilmington, Del., 1962-92; ret., 1992. Contbr. 21 articles to sci. jours.; 9 patents in field. Mem. Am. Chem. Soc. Avocations: photography, birding.

CLEMENT, ROBERT LEBBY, JR., lawyer; b. Charleston, S.C., Dec. 14, 1928; s. Robert Lebby and Julia Axson (Thayer) C.; m. Helen Mathilda Lewis, Nov. 26, 1954; children: Jeanne Marie, Robert Lebby III, Thomas L.T. AB, The Citadel, 1948; JD, Duke U., 1951. Bar: N.C. 1951, S.C. 1954. Practiced in Charlotte N.C., 1951-53; ptnr. Cornish, Clement & Horlbeck, Charleston, 1955-60, Hagood, Rivers & Young, 1960-65; ptnr. Young, Clement, Rivers & Tisdale, LLP, 1965-93, of counsel, 1994—; pres. Charleston Automotive Parts, Inc., 1969-84, Charleston Mus., 1980-83; mem. adv. bd. NationsBank, 1960—; asst. city atty., Charleston, 1960; judge Mcpl. Ct., Charleston, 1961-63. Mem. Charleston County Coun., 1983-86, chmn., 1985-86. With JAGC, USAF, 1953-55. Mem. ABA, N.C. Bar Assn., S.C. Bar Assn., Charleston County Bar Assn. (pres. 1990-91), Rotary. Presbyterian. Office: Young Clement Rivers & Tisdale PO Box 993 Charleston SC 29402-0993

CLEMENT, ROBERT WILLIAM, retired air force officer; b. Columbus, Ohio, Aug. 8, 1927; s. Coleman Clay and Leola Marie (Barnett) C.; m. Leila Ann Cameron, Dec. 27, 1950 (dec. Nov. 1998); children: Susan Lee, Robert William, Sandra Gay, Randall Clay. Student, Yale U., 1945-46; BS, U.S. Mil. Acad., 1950; MS in Aero. Engring., U. Colo., 1957; postgrad., Army War Coll., 1966-67. Commd. 2d lt. USAF, 1950, advanced through grades to maj. gen., 1978; vice comdr. 12th Air Force, Tactical Air Command, Bergstrom AFB, Tex., 1976; dep. chief staff for ops. and intelligence USAF in Europe Ramstein Air Base, Federal Republic of Germany, 1978-80; comdr. 16th Air Force, Torrejon AB, Spain, 1980-84; ret., 1984; asst. prof. math U.S. Air Force Acad., 1956-59. Decorated Air Force DSM, Legion of Merit with 3 oak leaf clusters, DFC with one oak leaf cluster, Bronze Star, Air medal with 9 oak leaf clusters. Mem. Haines City Citrus Growers Assn. (pres. 1990-92). Home: PO Box 2207 Haines City FL 33845-2207

CLEMENT, THOMAS EARL, lawyer; b. Watertown, N.Y., Sept. 9, 1932; s. Andrew W. and Dorothy L. (Martin) C.; m. Marion Jeanne Flotow, May 7, 1955; children—Christopher M., Thomas M., Peter J., Martha E. B.A., St. Lawrence U., Canton, N.Y., 1954; LL.B., Cornell Law Sch., 1959. Bar: N.Y., D.C., U.S. Supreme Ct. Assoc. Nixon, Hargrave, Devans & Doyle, Rochester, N.Y., 1959-64, ptnr., 1965—; bd. dirs. The Genesee Corp., Rochester. Trustee Genesee County Mus., Mumford, N.Y.; bd. dirs. St. Joseph's Villa. 1st lt. U.S. Army, 1955-57. Mem. ABA, N.Y. State Bar Assn., Monroe County Bar Assn., Cornell Law Assn., Country Club Rochester, Omicron Delta Kappa. Avocations: squash; platform tennis; golf; bird-watching. Home: 421 Cobbs Hill Dr Rochester NY 14610-2825 Office: Nixon Hargrave Devans & Doyle Clinton Sq Rochester NY 14604 also: One Thomas Cir Washington DC 20005

CLEMENTE, CARMINE DOMENIC, anatomist, educator; b. Penns Grove, N.J., Apr. 29, 1928; s. Ermanno and Caroline (Friozzi) C.; m. Juliette Vance, Sept. 19, 1968. AB, U. Pa., 1948, MS, 1950, PhD, 1952; postdoctoral fellow, U. London, 1953-54. Asst. instr. anatomy U. Pa., 1950-52; mem. faculty UCLA, 1952—, prof., 1963-95, chmn. dept. anatomy, 1963-73, dir. brain rsch. inst., 1976-87; prof. surg. anatomy Charles R. Drew U. Medicine and Sci., L.A., 1974—; prof. neurobiology UCLA, 1995—; hon. rsch. assoc. Univ. Coll., U. London, 1953-54; vis. scientist Nat. Inst. Med. Rsch., Mill Hill, London, 1988-89, 91; cons. VA Hosp., Sepulveda, Calif., NIH; mem. med. adv. panel bank Am.-Giannini Found.; chmn. sci. adv. com., bd. dirs. Nat. Paraplegia Found.; bd. dirs. Charles R. Drew U., 1985-94. Author: Aggression and Defense: Neurol Mechanisms and Social Patterns, 1967, Physiological Correlates of Dreaming, 1967, Sleep and the Maturing Nervous System, 1972, Anatomy: An Atlas of the Human Body, 1975, 4th edit., 1997; editor: Gray's Anatomy, 1973, 30th Am. edit., 1985, also Exptl. Neurology; assoc. editor Neurol. Rsch.; contbr. articles to sci. jours;. Recipient award for merit in sci. Nat. Paraplegia Found., 1973; 23d Ann. Rehfuss Lectr. and recipient Rehfuss medal Jefferson Med. Coll., 1986, award for excellence in med. edn., UCLA, 1996, Award of Extraordinary merit UCLA Med. Alumni Assn., 1997; John Simon Guggenheim Meml. Found. fellow, 1988-89. Mem. NAS (mem. com. on neuropathology, mem. BEAR coms.), Inst. Medicine of NAS (mem. sci. adv. bd.), Pavlovian Soc. N.Am. (Ann. award 1968, pres. 1972), Brain Rsch. Inst. (dir. 1976-87), Am. Physiol. Soc., Am. Assn. Anatomists (v.p. 1970-72, pres. 1976-77, Henry Gray award 1993), Am. Acad. Neurology, Am. Assn. Clin. Anatomists (Honored Mem. of Yr. 1993), Am. Acad. Cerebral Palsy (hon.), Am. Neurol. Assn., Assn. Am. Med. Colls. (mem. exec. com. 1978-81, disting. svc. mem. 1982), Coun. Acad. Socs. (mem. adminstrv. bd. 1973-81, chmn. 1979-80), Nat. Bd. Med. Examiners (bd. dirs. 1978-84, mem. anatomy test com. 1980-84), Assn. Anatomy Chairmen (pres. 1972), Biol. Stain Commn., Internat. Brain Rsch. Orgn., AMA-Assn. Am. Med. Colls. (mem. liaison com. on med. edn. 1981-87), Med. Rsch. Assn. Calif. (bd. dirs. 1976—), N.Y. Acad. Scis., Japan Soc. Promotion of Sci. (Rsch. award 1978), Soc. for Neurosci., Penn Club (N.Y.C.), Sigma Xi, Alpha Omega Alpha. (hon.). Democrat. Home: 11737 Bellagio Rd Los Angeles CA 90049-2158 Office: UCLA Sch Medicine Dept Neurobiology Los Angeles CA 90095

CLEMENTE, CELESTINO, physician, surgeon; b. Penns Grove, N.J., June 11, 1922; s. Ermanno and Caroline (Friozzi) C.; m. Marie Ann Strangio, Nov. 16, 1946; children: Jeffrey, Roderick, Mark, Laurie Ann, Jonathan. BS, Rutgers U., 1942; MD, U. Pa., 1945. Diplomate Am. Bd. Surgery. Intern Jersey City Med. Ctr., 1945-46; resident in gen. surgery Martland Med. Ctr., 1950-53; practice medicine specializing in gen. surgery Newark, 1953—; dir. surgery Children's Hosp., Newark, 1962-70, St. Vincent's Hosp., Montclair, N.J., 1972-83; trustee United Hosps. Med. Ctr., Newark, 1972-88, v.p. med. affairs, 1975-88; assoc. clinic prof. surgery N.J. Med. Sch., Newark, 1975—; dir. surgery Roseland (N.J) Surg. Ctr., 1983—, also chmn. bd. Rep. candidate for U.S. Ho. of Reps, N.J., 1968; active Nat. Ad Council/HEW, 1970-74. Served to lt. USNR, 1946-48. Fellow ACS,

Internat. Coll. Surgeons; mem. AMA, AAAS. Club: Essex (Newark). Home and Office: 364 Ridgewood Ave Glen Ridge NJ 07028-1513 Office: 556 Eagle Rock Ave Roseland NJ 07068-1500

CLEMENTE, FRANCESCO, artist; b. Naples, Italy, 1952. One-man shows include James Corcoran Gallery, L.A., 1983, Mezzanine Gallery and Met. Mus. Art, N.Y., 1985, Ringling Mus. Art, Sarasota, Fla., 1985-87, Mus. Modern Art, N.Y., 1986, Art Inst. Chgo., 1987, Milw. Art Mus., 1988, Phila. Mus. Art, 1990-91, Solomon R. Guggenheim Mus., N.Y., 1983, San Francisco Mus. Modern Art, 1984, Walker Art Ctr., Mpls., 1984-85, Seattle Art Mus., 1985, Joslyn Art Mus., Omaha, 1985-86, Phila. Mus. Art, 1988, L.A. County Mus., 1987, Minn. Mus. Art, St. Paul, 1987-88, Milw. Art Mus., 1988, Dolan/Maxwell, Phila., 1990-91, Sidney Mishkin Gallery, Baruch Coll., N.Y., 1994, Luhring Augustine, N.Y., 1994, Galerie Graff, Montreal, 1994, Anthony D'Offay Gallery, London, 1994, U. Mo., 1994, others; exhibited works at Mus. Modern Art Paris, 1981, 89, Aldrich Mus. Contemporary Art, Ridgefield, Conn., 1983, others. Office: care Sperone Westwater 142 Greene St New York NY 10012-3236 Office: care Gagosian Gallery 980 Madison Ave New York NY 10021-1848*

CLEMENTE, PATROCINIO ABLOLA, psychology educator; b. Manila, Philippines, Apr. 23, 1941; s. Elpidio San Jose and Amparo (Ablola) C.; came to U.S., 1965; BSE, U. Philippines, 1960; postgrad. Nat. U., Manila, 1961-64; MA, Ball State U., 1966, EdD, 1969; postgrad. U. Calif., Riverside, 1970, Calif. State Coll., Fullerton, 1971-72. High sch. tchr. gen. sci. and biology, div. city schs., Quezon City, Philippines, 1960-65; doctoral fellow dept. psychology Ball State U., Muncie, Ind., 1966-67, dept. spl. edn., 1967-68, grad. asst. dept. gen. and exptl. psychology, 1968-69; tchr. educable mentally retarded high sch. level Fontana (Calif.) Unified Sch. Dist., 1969-70, intermediate level, 1970-73, dist. sch. psychologist, 1973-79, bilingual edn. counselor, 1979-81; resource specialist Morongo (Calif.) Unified Sch. Dist., 1981-83, spl. day class tchr., 1983-90, tchr. math, sci., Spanish, English, 1990—; adj. assoc. prof. Chapman Coll., Orange, Calif., 1982-91. Adult leader Girl Scouts of Philippines, 1963-65; mem. sch. bd. Blessed Sacrament Sch., Twentynine Palms, Calif. State bd. scholar Ball State U., 1965-66. Fellow Am. Biographical Inst. (hon. mem. research bd. advisors, life); mem. ASCD, NEA, Coun. for Exceptional Children, Am. Assn. on Mental Deficiency, Nat. Assn. of Sch. Psychologists, Found. Exceptional Children, Assn. for Children with Learning Disabilities, Nat. Geographic Soc., Calif. Tchrs. Assn., Morongo Tchrs. Assn., Smithsonian Inst. Roman Catholic. Home: PO Box 637 Twentynine Palms CA 92277

CLEMENTE, ROBERT STEPHEN, lawyer; b. Bklyn., May 5, 1956; s. Hugo and Mildred (Wilinsky) C.; m. Mary Martin, June 8, 1985. AA, St. John's U., 1976; BFA, NYU, 1978; JD, Southwestern U., 1981. Bar: N.Y. 1982, U.S. Dist. Ct. (ea. and so. dists.) N.Y. 1982, U.S. Supreme Ct. 1988, Calif. 1997, U.S. Dist. Ct. (ctrl. dist.) Calif. 1997. Counsel Composto & Longo, Bklyn., 1981-86; arbitration counsel N.Y. Stock Exch., N.Y.C., 1986-88, mgr. arbitration, 1988-91, dir. arbitration, 1991—; arbitrator N.Y.C. Civil Ct., 1988—; adj. prof. securities arbitration NYU, 1999—. Mem. ABA, Am. Arbitration Assn., Am. Judges Assn., N.Y. Bar Assn., Assn. of Arbitrators, Phi Alpha Delta. Avocations: reading, exercising, golf. Office: NY Stock Exch Inc 20 Broad St 5th Fl New York NY 10005-1974

CLEMENTI, MARK ANTHONY, clinical and sport psychologist, educator; b. Milw., Oct. 11, 1955; s. Anthony Clementi and Liz (Coffman) Schmidt; m. Christina Masterson-Clementi, Oct. 26, 1988. BA, Humboldt State U., 1977; MA, Sonoma State U., 1988; PhD, Fla. State U., 1991. Clin. and sport psychologist pvt. practice pvt. practice, San Francisco, Santa Rosa, Calif., 1991-95; psychology editor, columnist GOLFWEEK Mag., Winter Haven, Fla., 1991-92, Inside Golf, Port Orchard, Wash., 1992; clin. psychologist, dual diagnosis coord. Drug Abuse Alternatives Ctr., Santa Rosa, 1992-95; adj. prof. John F. Kennedy U., Orinda, Calif., 1994-95; psychol. cons. Fla. State U. Track Team, Tallahassee, 1989-91; cons. Sauer Golf Sch., 1991, S.W. Athletic Clin., 1990, Seminole Jr. Golf Camp, 1990. Author: (audio tapes) INSIDE GAME-Golf, INSIDE GAME-Tennis, 1991; co-author: The Parachute Games, 1995. Featured speaker Rotary Internat., Terra Linda, Calif., 1992, Marin Breakfast Club, San Rafael, Calif., 1992, Lion's Internat., San Rafael, Calif., 1992; community columnist Ind. Jour., Novato, Calif., 1992, Golf Expo '92, Seattle, 1992; featured guest on KNBR radio's Sports Phone 68, San Francisco, 1992. Recipient Cert. Appreciation award Lion's Internat., San Rafael, Calif., 1992. Mem. Am. Psychol. Assn., Ctr. for Performance Enhancement, Assn. Advancement of Applied Sport Psychology, Internat. Assn. Sport Psychology. Avocations: golf, gardening, fishing, travel, songwriting/music. Office: Soma Health Ctr 862 Folsom St San Francisco CA 94107-1123 Also: 515 Webster St # A Petaluma CA 94952-2455

CLEMENTS, ALLEN, JR., lawyer; b. Macon, Ga., Jan. 15, 1924; s. Allen C. and Mamie F. (Vinson) C.; children: Mary, Jill, Byng, Allen. BBA, U. Miami, 1948, JD cum laude, 1951. Bar: Fla. 1951, U.S. Tax Ct. 1951, U.S. Dist. Ct. (so. dist.) Fla. 1951, U.S. Ct. Appeals (5th cir.) 1952, U.S. Ct. Appeals (11th cir.) 1981. Sr. assoc. Claude Pepper Law Offices, Miami Beach, Fla., 1953-72; ptnr. Pepper, Clements, Hopkins & Weaver, Miami Beach, 1972-79; of counsel Tew, Critchlow, Sonberg, Traum & Friedbauer, Miami, Fla., 1979-82, Finley, Kumble, Wagner, Heinz, Underberg & Casey, Miami, 1982-87; pros. atty. City of West Miami, Fla., 1954-56, city atty., 1956-83; legal advisor Dade County Coun. Mayors, 1964-72; cons. atty. Dade County League of Cities, 1966-77; city atty. City of South Miami, 1969-72; atty. Miami Beach Tourist Devel. Authority, 1970-78, Village of Biscayne Park, 1972-75. Mem. West Miami Town Coun., 1952-53; bd. dirs. Claude Pepper Found., Tallahassee, 1992—, sec., 1994—. Served with U.S. Army, 1943-45. Decorated Bronze Star. Mem. ABA, Lake County Bar Assn., Dade County Bar Assn. (bd. dirs. 1984-86, grievance com., ethics com.). Democrat. Methodist. Fax: 352-753-7785. Home and Office: 1004 Aloha Way Lady Lake FL 32159-1304

CLEMENTS, JAMES DAVID, retired psychiatry educator, physician; b. Pineview, Ga., May 7, 1931; s. Marcus Monroe and Dewey Thelma (Gammage) C.; m. Janet Collier Swan, Aug. 25, 1952; children—Leiliar Ann, David Marcus. B.A., Emory U., 1952; M.D., Med. Coll. Ga., 1956. Intern Temple U., Phila., 1956-57; resident in pediatrics Temple U., 1957-59; fellow mental retardation Sch. Medicine, Yale U., 1959-60; med. dir. Gracewood (Ga.) State Sch. Hosp., 1960-62, asst. supt., 1963-64; dir. planning mental retardation Ga. Dept. Pub. Health, Atlanta, 1964-65; dir. Ga. Retardation Center, Atlanta, 1964-79; med. cons. mental retardation Ga. Dept. Human Resources, 1979-81; resident in psychiatry Emory U., Sch. Medicine, Atlanta, 1983-86; clin. asst. prof. pediatrics and psychiatry Emory U. Sch. Medicine, Atlanta, from 1964, asst. prof. psychiatry, 1985-95; ret., 1995; assoc. clin. prof. neurology, asst. clin. prof. pediatrics Med. Coll. Ga., Augusta, 1970—; spl. cons. neurology mental retardation dept. pediatrics Ga. Bapt. Hosp., 1965—; mem. adv. com. program exceptional children Ga. Dept. Edn., 1968-70; mem. adv. bd. Sch. Allied Health Sci., Ga. State U., 1971-76; mem. accreditation council mental retardation council Joint Commn. on Accreditation Hosps., Chgo., 1975-79; del. White House conf. Ga. com. children youth, 1970; mem. Pres.'s Com. on Mental Retardation, 1975-78; chmn. Willowbrook rev. panel Fed. Ct. Eastern Dist. N.Y.; reviewer NSF; cons. Inst. Society, Ethics and Life Scis., Hastings Center; commr. Am. Bar Assn., 1976-80. Contbr. articles to profl. jours., anthologies, seminars. Mem. adv. bd. Arbor Acad., DeKalb County (Ga.) Dept. Edn., 1973-75; mem. bd. founders, adv. com. Ashdun Hall, 1965-70; trustee Gatchell Sch., Mental Health Law Project (now Bazelon Ctr. for Mental Health Law); adv. com. Kennedy Center, Johns Hopkins U. Recipient Leadership award Am. Assn. Mental Deficiency, 1980. Fellow Am. Acad. Pediatrics (cons. head start med. cons. service), Am. Assn. Mental Deficiency (pres. 1974-75), Pan Am. Med. Assn., Am. Geriatrics Soc.; mem. Ga. Pediatric Soc., Nat. Assn. Supts. Pub. Residential Facilities Mentally Retarded, Nat. Assn. Retarded Citizens (legal advocacy adv. com. 1975), Internat. Assn. Sci. Study Mental Deficiency (chmn. local organizing com. 4th internat. congress, mem. council 1976-78), Am. Psychiatric Assocs. Home: 475 Grant St SE Atlanta GA 30312-3154

CLEMENTS, JOHN ROBERT, real estate professional; b. Richmond, Ind., Nov. 2, 1950; s. George Howard and Mary Amanda (McKown) C. Grad. high sch., Phoenix. Sales assoc. Clements Realty, Inc., Phoenix, 1973-75; office mgr. Clements Realty, Inc., Mesa, Ariz., 1975-78; v.p., co-owner Clements Realty, Inc., Phoenix, 1978-80; broker, assoc. Ben Brooks & Assocs., Phoenix, 1980-88; pres. John R. Clements, P.C., 1984—; broker Keller Williams Realty, Phoenix and Mesa, Ariz., 1994-96; facilities dir. Outdoor Sys., Phoenix, 1996—. Real estate dir. Circle K Corp., Western Region, 1989-92; bd. dirs., v.p. Big Sisters Ariz., Phoenix, 1974-80; trustee Ariz. Realtors Polit. Action Com., 1975-85, Realtors Polit. Action Com., Ill., 1985-88; appointee Govtl. Mall Co., Ariz., 1986—, commr. chair, 1991-95. Mem. Ariz. Assn. Realtors (bd. dirs., pres. 1981), Mesa-Chandler-Tempe Bd. Realtors (past bd. dirs., pres., 1978), Nat. Assn. Realtors (past bd. dirs., exec. com.), Residential Sales Coun. Realtors, Nat. Mktg. Inst. (bd. govs. 1986—, v.p. 1990, pres. 1991), Ariz. Country Club. Republican. Presbyterian. Home: 3618 N 60th St Phoenix AZ 85018-6708 Office: Outdoor Sys 2502 N Black Canyon Hwy Phoenix AZ 85009-1800

CLEMENTS, LYNNE FLEMING, family therapist, programmer; b. Bklyn., Aug. 8, 1945; d. Daniel Gillies and Dorothy Frances (Zitzmann) Fleming; m. Louis Myrick Clements, Feb. 19, 1972; children: Ryan Louis, Glenn Fleming. BA in Sociology, Bradley U., 1967; MSW, Fordham U., 1973; postgrad. studies, Columbia U., 1970-71; cert. family therapy, Inst. for Mental Health Edn., 1990. Lic. clin. social worker, N.J.; cert. social work mgr. Computer programmer Employer's Comml. Union Group Ins. Cos., Boston, 1967-69, Harvard Bus. Sch., Cambridge, Mass., 1969-70, Volkswagon of Am., Englewood Cliffs, N.J., 1971; psychiat. social worker Associated Cath. Charities Family and Children's Svcs., Paramus, N.J., 1973-74, Christian Health Ctr., Wyckoff, N.J., 1976; owner, mgr. Wicker Wagon, Bergenfield, N.J., 1977-85; psychotherapist The Psychotherapy Counseling Ctr., Bergenfield, N.J., 1982-89; programmer analyst Atlas Computing Svcs., Secaucus, N.J., 1984-86; program coord., family therapist Divsn. Family Guidance, Hackensack, N.J., 1986-91; pres. Corp. Family Resources, Ridgewood, N.J., 1989—; family therapist cons. Family Recovery of Valley View, White Plains, N.Y., 1992-94, Furman Clinic, Fair Lawn, N.J., 1995-96, Van Ost Inst. for Family Living, Englewood, N.J., 1996; cert. social work mgr., 1997—; part-time family therapist N.J. Ctr. for Psychotherapy Inc., Ridgefield Park, 1990. Sunday sch. tchr. All Saints Ch., 1982-89, 94—, chmn. bd. cmty. play ctr., 1977-78; mem. Twin-Boro Youth Ministry Coun., 1989—, Bergen County Family Day Care Coalition, 1989—; apptd. sec. Mayor's Beautify Bergenfield Com., 1991-95; chmn. entertainment Bergen County Children's Festival, 1993; apptd. chmn., designer Bergenfield's Coun. for Arts, 1993—; chmn. curriculum enhancement com. Bergen County Acad. for Advancement of Sci. and Tech., 1992-96. Recipient 1st and 2nd pl. awards Bergenfield 1980 Art Contest; NIMH grantee, 1973. Mem. AAUW, Gifted Child Soc. (parent workshop coord. 1989—, bd. dirs. 1991—), NASW, Acad. Cert. Social Workers, Am. Orthopsychiat. Assn., Fordham U. Alumni Assn., N.J. Commerce and Industry Assn. (mem. child care com. 1990—, mem. human resources com. 1990—), N.J. Soc. Clin. Social Workers, Zonta (Amelia Earhart chmn. 1987-88, mem. literacy com. 1995—, chmn. status of women com. 1993-94), Women of Accomplishment (founder, pres. 1990—, chmn. women's coalition conf. 1993—). Episcopalian. Avocations: walking, art, music, crafts, boating. Home: 148 Harcourt Ave Bergenfield NJ 07621-1917 Office: Corp Family Resources 15 Godwin Ave Ste 1 Ridgewood NJ 07450-3705

CLEMENTS, MICHAEL CRAIG, health services consulting executive, retired renal dialysis technician; b. Cin., Sept. 17, 1945; s. Marvin Hubert and Mildred Helen (Rabe) C.; m. Minnie Faye Pospisil, Dec. 1, 1972; children: Melissa Ayn, Michael Aaron. Student, U. Cin., 1968-70; EMT/paramedic, Good Samaritan Health Ctr., 1980. Cert. renal dialysis technician. Hemodialysis technician Christ Hosp., Cin., 1968-79; tech. svcs. dir. Dialysis Clinic, Inc., Cin., 1980-91; pres. Critical Care Svcs., Inc., Mason, Ohio, 1987—; firefighter/paramedic Mason Vol. Fire Co., 1978-85, EMS tng. officer, 1984, EMS capt., 1985; coop employers environ. and sci. lab. tech. programs Cin. State Coll. Contbr. articles to profl. jours. Mem. Mason Environ. Adv. Commn., 1990—, vice chmn., 1992-93, bus. and parent curriculum review com. Mason City Schs., 1992; employer advisor coop. program Cin. Tech. Coll. Biomed. Engring. Tech., 1986-91. With USN, 1964-70. Mem. Assn. for Advancement of Med. Instrumentation, Ohio Acad. Sci. Mem. Ch. of Christ. Office: Critical Care Svcs Inc PO Box 252 1091 A Reading Rd Mason OH 45040-1345

CLEMENTS, ROBERT, insurance executive; b. Chgo., Sept. 7, 1932; s. John and Mildred L. (Chapman) C.; m. Marilyn Trexler, Dec. 27, 1955; children: Paula J., John, Jeffrey, Ben T. BA, Dartmouth Coll., 1954. Underwriter Royal Ins. Co., N.Y.C., 1956-59; sr. v.p. Marsh & McLennan, Ltd., Toronto, Ont., Can., 1959-75; chmn. Marsh & McLennan Inc., N.Y.C., 1975-92; pres. Marsh & McLennan Cos., Inc., N.Y.C., 1992-94; chmn. Marsh & LcLennan Risk Capital Corp., 1994-96, Risk Capital Holdings, Inc., 1996—, Risk Capital Reins., 1996—; bd. dirs. EXEL Ltd., Hiscox PLC, Annuity Reins Corp., Stockton Holdings, Affinity, Inc.; chmn. bd. trustees Coll. of Ins.; mem. RAND Corp. adv. coun. Bd. overseers Inst. for Civil Justice. With U.S. Army, 1954-56. Mem. Nat. Assn. Ins. Brokers, Am. Risk and Ins. Assn. Democrat. Office: Risk Capital Holdings 20 Horseneck Ln Greenwich CT 06830-6327

CLEMENTS, ROBERT DONALD, sculptor; b. Pitts., Dec. 24, 1937; s. Clyde Clifford and Rosa Theresa Clements; m. Claire Brown, June 24, 1961; children: David Cal, Megan Lynn Tyler. BFA in Painting and Design, Carnegie Mellon U., 1959; MA in Art, Pa. State U., 1962, PhD, 1964. Tchr. art Pitts. Pub. Schs., 1961-62; asst. prof. art Ball State U., Muncie, Ind., 1964-68; assoc. prof. art U. Ga., Athens, 1969-81, prof. art, 1981-94; design cons. Corp. for Olympic Devel. in Atlanta, 1993-96. Initiator, designer outdoor sculpture park Folk Art Park, 1994-96 (award 1997); sculptor S.E. Natatorium, 1994 (award 1995), Indian Creek Marta Sta. Mural, 1993 (award 1994), Marietta Bollard, CODA, 1996; author: Emphasis Art, 5th edit. 1991, 6th edit. 1997. Recipient Indsl. Artists awards Ga. Coun. for the Arts, 1987, 91, Reg. Site Sculpture award Arts Festival of Atlanta, 1987, Recognition award Urban Design Commn., Atlanta, 1995, 97, Outstanding Rsch. and Tchg. awards U. Ga., 1991, 93. Mem. Internat. Sculpture Ctr. Unitarian. Home: 155 Bar H Ct Athens GA 30605-4702

CLEMENTS, ROBERT W., lawyer; b. Lake Charles, La., Oct. 2, 1934; s. Arthur Joseph and Ruth (Lewis) C.; m. Gay Nell McDonnold, Apr. 14, 1960; children: Robert Scott, Shannon Ruth, Jennifer Gay. BBA, LLB, Tulane U., 1959. Bar: La. 1959, U.S. Dist. Ct. (we. dist.) La. 1959, U.S. Ct. Appeals (5th cir.) 1967, U.S. Dist. Ct. (ea. dist.) La. 1977, U.S. Dist. Ct. (mid. dist.) La. 1984, U.S. Ct. Appeals (11th cir.) 1987, U.S. Dist. Ct. (ea. dist.) Tex. 1992. Law clk. to Hon. E.F. Hunter, Jr., U.S. Dist. Ct. for Western Dist. La., Lake Charles, 1962; assoc. Stockwell, Sievert, Viccellio, Clements & Shaddock, Lake Charles, 1963-66, ptnr., then sr. ptnr., 1967—. Pres., bd. dirs. Lake Charles YMCA, 1973-74. 1st lt. U.S. Army, 1960-61. Mem. ABA, S.W. La. Bar Assn. (pres. 1985), La. Assn. Def. Counsel (bd. dirs. 1973), La. Assn. Hosp. Attys. (pres. 1989), Maritime Law Assn. U.S. Democrat. Presbyterian. Avocations: golf, hunting, photography. Home: 2301 Barbe Ct Lake Charles LA 70601-9015 Office: Stockwell Sievert Viccellio Clements & Shaddock One Lakeside Plz Ste 400 Lake Charles LA 70601

CLEMENTS, RONALD FRANCIS, animation director; b. Sioux City, Iowa, Apr. 25, 1953; s. Joseph and Gertrude (Gereau) C.; m. Tamara Lee Glumace, Feb. 25, 1989; 1 stepchild, Marc Wilhite. Grad high sch., Sioux City, Iowa. Artist KCAU-TV, Sioux City, 1969-73; animation asst. Hanna Barbera Prodns., North Hollywood, Calif., 1973-74; animation asst. Walt Disney Prodns., Burbank, Calif., 1974-76, animator, 1976-84, writer, dir., 1984-90; writer, dir., producer Walt Disney Prodns., Glendale, Calif., 1990—. Writer, dir. (motion picture) The Great Mouse Detective, 1986, The Little Mermaid, 1989 (L.A. Film Critics Best Animation 1989); writer, dir., prodr.: Aladdin, 1992 (L.A. Film Critics Best Animation, 1992, ASIFA Individual Achievement 1992, Golden Globe nominee Best Picture 1992), Hercules, 1997 (L.A. Film Critics Best Animation 1997, ASIFA Best Dir. and Best Prodr. of Animated Feature 1997). Mem. Acad. Motion Picture Arts & Scis. Avocations: reading, horseback riding, skiing. Office: care Walt Disney Productions 500 S Buena Vista St Burbank CA 91521-0001

CLEMETSON, CHARLES ALAN BLAKE, physician; b. Canterbury, Eng., Oct. 31, 1923; came to U.S., 1961, naturalized, 1972; s. Charles Harold and Gwendoline Maude Winefred (Blake) C.; m. Helen Cowan Forster, Mar. 29, 1947; children: Claudia, Charles, David, Andrew. B.M.,B.Ch., Oxford (Eng.) U., 1948. Lic. physician, La., U.K. Research asst. Obstetric Hosp., Univ. Coll. Hosp., London, 1950-52; Nichols research fellow Royal Soc. Medicine, 1951-52; house surgeon obstetrics W. Middlesex Hosp., 1952-53; resident med. officer obstetrics Queen Charlotte's Hosp., 1953; house surgeon gynecology Hammersmith Hosp., 1953-54; obstetric and gynecol. registrar Lake Hosp., Ashton-under-Lyne, Lancashire, Eng., 1954-56; lectr. ob-gyn. Univ. Coll. Hosp., London, 1956-58; asst. prof. Univ. Hosp., Saskatoon, Sask., Can., 1958-61, U. Calif., San Francisco, 1961-67; dir. dept. ob-gyn. Meth. Hosp., Bklyn., 1967-81, Huey P. Long Meml. Hosp., Pineville, La., 1981-91; assoc. prof. SUNY, Bklyn., 1967-72; prof. Downstate Med. Ctr., SUNY, 1972-81; prof. Tulane U., 1981-91, prof. emeritus, 1991; mem. obstetric adv. com. N.Y.C. Dept. Health, 1968; cons. in field; mem. med. adv. com. Planned Parenthood N.Y.C., 1971; mem. physicians rev. com. Blue Cross-Blue Shield N.Y.C., 1975; lectr. maternal health U. Calif., Berkeley, 1964-65. Author: Vitamin C, 3 vols., 1989; contbr. articles to med. jours. Served in RAF, 1948-50. Recipient Rsch. Career Devel. award NIH, 1965-67. Fellow ACOG, Royal Coll. Obstetricians and Gynecologists, Royal Coll. Physicians and Surgeons Can.; mem. Bklyn. Gynecol. Soc. (pres. 1977-78). *Certainty of knowledge is the antithesis of progress.*

CLEMINS, ARCHIE R., naval career officer; b. Mt. Vernon, Ill., Nov. 18, 1943; m. Marilyn Clemins; children: Becky, Travis. BS in Elec. Engring., U. Ill., 1966, MS, 1972. Commd. ensign USN, 1972, advanced through grades to adm., 1997; exec. officer USS Parche; command officer USS Pogy; commdr. Submarine Group 7; chief staff to commdr. 7th Fleet; commdr. Tng. Command U.S. Pacific Fleet; dep., chief staff to commdr. U.S. Atlantic Fleet; comdr. 7th Fleet; comdr.-in-chief U.S. Pacific Fleet. Office: US Pacific Fleet 250 Makalapa Dr Pearl Harbor HI 96860-3131

CLEMMER, DAN ORR, librarian; b. Etowah, Tenn., Dec. 28, 1938; s. Dan Orr and Nancy Elizabeth (Haney) C.; m. Elizabeth Louise Campbell, Aug. 25, 1962; children: Nancy Day, Helen, Stephen. BA, Davidson Coll., 1961; MA Teaching, Brown U., 1964; MS Libr. Svc., Columbia U., 1967. Intern Libr. of Congress, Washington, 1967-68, asst. head African-Asian exchange, 1968-70; asst. to librarian Smithsonian Inst. Libr., Washington, 1970-72, asst. chief access svc., 1972-73; chief, reader svcs. U.S. Dept. State Libr., Washington, 1973-92, chief librarian, 1992—; mem. Depository Libr. Coun., 1994-98. Contbr. articles to profl. jours. em. ALA (pres. Fed. Librs. Roundtable 1993-94, exec. bd. of Fed. Libr. and Info. Ctr. com.); mem. D.C. Libr. Assn. (pres. 1995-96). Home: 5527 Trent St Chevy Chase MD 20815-5511 Office: US Dept of State Library 2201 C St NW Washington DC 20520-0001*

CLEMMER, LEON, architect, planner; b. Phila., Feb. 11, 1926; s. Leon and Mary Colton (Steele) C.; m. Mary Jane Bertolet, 1955, Nov. 19, 1955; children: Catherine C. Pickell, Leon Jr. BArch, U. Pa., 1951. Registered architect, Pa., N.J., Fla. Architect Vincent G. Kling, FAIA, Phila., 1951-56, Nolen & Swineburne, Phila., 1957-58, Gleeson & Mulrooney, Phila., 1958-62; pvt. practice Leon Clemmer Arch., Phila./Jenkintown, 1962-. Author: One God, 16 Homes. Vice-chmn. Abington Township Planning Comm.; mem. Phila., Glenside, Jenkintown C. of C., Independence Hall Assn.; mem. bd. of mgrs. Abington YMCA; bd. dirs. Friends of Historic Rittenhouse Town, Historic Bartram Gardens. With USN, 1943-46, PTO. Recipient Disting. Bldg. award Pa. Soc. Architects, MacArthur award Carpenters' Co. of Phila., 1988, Juvenile Justices Penna/'s Best, 1990, Juvenile Justices Nation's Best, 1991. Mem. AIA, Pa. Soc. Architects (bd. dirs.), Engrs. Club, Found. for Architecture, Carpenters Co. City and County Phila. (pres.), Am. Soc. Planning Ofcls., Am. Soc. Ch. Architecture, Nat. Trust for Hist. Preservation, Soc. for Indsl. Archaeology (bd. dirs.), Pa. Hist. Soc., Old York Road Hist. Soc. (bd. dirs., pres.), Victorian Soc., Union League Phila. (bd. dirs.), Mennonite Historians Ea. Pa., Clinkers Club, Athenaeum of Phila., Seaview Country Club, Mfrs.' Country Club, Huntingdon Valley Kennel Club (pres.), Rotary. Republican. Episcopalian. Avocations: watercolorist, historian. Home: 160 Woodpecker Rd Jenkintown PA 19046-3922*

CLEMMONS, DAVID ROBERT, internist, educator; b. Nashville, May 19, 1947; s. Robert Starr and Beatrice (Winter) C.; m. Kathy Silverman, Nov. 27, 1971; children: Amy Elizabeth, Anna Katherine. Student, Vanderbilt U., 1965-66; BS, Davidson Coll., 1969; MD, U. N.C., 1974. Diplomate Am. Bd. Internal Medicine. Intern in medicine Mass. Gen. Hosp., Boston, 1974-75, jr. and sr. resident in medicine, 1975-77; fellow in endocrinology Harvard U., Boston, 1977-79; asst. prof. medicine U. N.C., Chapel Hill, 1979-83, assoc. prof., 1983-87, prof. medicine, 1987—, div. chief endocrinology and metabolism, 1990—, assoc. chmn. dept. medicine, 1997—, Kenan prof. medicine, 1999—; assoc. dir. clin. rsch. unit N.C. Meml. Hosp., Chapel Hill, 1979—; cons. Monsanto Inc., St. Louis, 1982—, Celltrix Inc., Santa Clara, Calif., 1991—, Genentech, Inc., So. San Francisco, 1991—; mem. cell biology and Physiology study sect. NIH, 1986-90. Contbr. articles to profl. jours. Chmn. adminstrv. bd. Univ. Meth. Ch., Chapel Hill, 1986, lay leader, 1987. Research grantee Nat. Inst. Aging, 1980, 83, 87, 92, 97, Nat. Heart, Lung and Blood Inst., 1980, 84, 86, 91, 96, Am. Heart Assn. Fellow ACP; mem. Am. Soc. Clin. Investigation, Am. Fedn. Clin. Research, Assn. Am. Physicians (young investigator award 1986), Endocrine Soc. Democrat. Office: U NC Dept Medicine CB # 7170 Thurston-Bowles Chapel Hill NC 27599-7170

CLEMMONS, NANCY WASHINGTON, library administrator; b. Sept. 6, 1947; m. Ronald Clemmons. BS in Chemistry, Birmingham So. Coll., 1968; MLS, U. Ala., 1973. Grad. sci. libr. Samford U., Birmingham, Ala., 1973-76; sr. libr. govt. docs. La. State U., Baton Rouge, 1976-77; reference libr. Lister Hill Libr. U. Ala., Birmingham, 1977-81, vision sci. libr., 1981-82, head reference svcs., 1983-89, head info. and instrnl. svc., 1989-92, acting dir., assoc. prof., 1992-95, dep. dir., 1995—; mem. regional adv. coun. Southeastern Atlantic Med. Library Svcs., Balt., 1994-96; mentor Acad. Health Info. Profls., 1995—. Author: (with others) Reference and Information Services Quarterly, 1994; mem. edtl. bd. Med. Ref. Svcs. Quar., 1990—; various book reviews; contbr. articles to profl. jours. Mem. adopt a troop com. Boy Scouts Am., 1988-92; alt. rep. Faculty Senate U. Ala., 1996-98. Mem. Acad. Health Info. Profls. (distinguished mem., Med. Lib. Assn. (chair so. chpt. 1997-98, chpt. coun. rep. 1994-97, chair pub. svcs. sect. 1988-89, chair mem. com. 1988-89, chair awards com. 1993-94), Ala. Health Librs. Assn. (pres. 1983-84), Beta Phi Mu. Office: Lister Libr Health Scis U Ala 1700 University Blvd Birmingham AL 35233-1816

CLEMON, U. W., federal judge; b. Birmingham, Ala., Apr. 9, 1943; m. Barbara Lang; children: Herman Issac, Addine Michele. Bar: Ala. Ptnr. Adams and Clemon and predecessor, Birmingham, 1969-80; fed. judge U.S. Dist. Ct. (no. dist.) Ala., Birmingham, 1980—. Mem. Ala. Senate, 1974-80. Recipient Law and Justice award SCLC, 1980. Mem. ABA (exec. coun. 1976-79, C. Francis Stratford award 1986), Alpha Phi Alpha. Office: US Dist Ct US Courthouse 1729 5th Ave N Ste 519 Birmingham AL 35203-2049*

CLEMONS, JOHN ROBERT, lawyer; b. Oak Park, Ill., June 9, 1948; s. Robert N. and Arline (Flatland) C.; m. Susan Morrison, June 19, 1971; children: Jason, David, Joseph. BA, U. Iowa, 1970; JD, DePaul U., 1975. Bar: Ill. 1975, U.S. Dist. Ct. (so. dist.) Ill. 1978, U.S. Ct. Appeals (7th cir.) 1989, U.S. Supreme Ct. 1989. Asst. village mgr. Village of Riverside, Ill., 1970-72; co-dir. dist. 208 Youth Ctr., Riverside, 1970-73; area dir. S.W. area Cook County OEO, 1972-73; clk., legal researcher Klein, Thorpe & Jenkins, attys., Chgo., 1974-75; asst. state's atty. Jackson County, Murphysboro, Ill., 1975-80, state's atty., 1980-88; asst. prof. So. Ill. U., Carbondale, 1977-79, lectr., 1987—; pvt. practice law, Carbondale, 1988-91; ptnr. Clemons & Hood, Carbondale, 1991—. Mem. Jackson County Youth Svc. Program, Carbondale, 1975-78, chmn., 1978-80; mem. Criminal Justice Standards Project, So. Ill., 1978; mem. Suspected Child Abuse and Neglect Team, Carbondale, 1978-88, Gov.'s Task Force on Detention Standards, 1986-87, State Coordinated Systems Response Project for Child Abuse, 1987-90, Atty. Gen.'s Task Force on Domestic Violence, 1989; bd. dirs. Good Samaritan House, 1989-94; pres. Jackson County Dem. Booster Club; chair pub. rels. Covenant Christian Sch. Mem. Jackson County Bar Assn. Democrat. Lutheran. Home: 375 Mount Joy Rd Murphysboro IL 62966-4464 Office: 813 W Main St Carbondale IL 62901-2537

CLEMONS, JULIE PAYNE, telephone company manager; b. Attleboro, Mass., June 13, 1948; d. John Gordon and Claire (Paquin) P.; m. W.

Richard Johnson, Oct. 10, 1970 (div. Oct. 1980); m. E.L. Clemons, Apr. 23, 1988. BBA, U. R.I., 1970. Svc. rep. New England Telephone, East Greenwich, R.I., 1970-71; svc. rep. So. Bell, Jacksonville, Fla., 1971-73, bus. office supr., 1973-77, bus. office mgr., 1978-84, staff mgr. assessment, 1984-86, mgr. assessment ctr., 1987-89; dir. human resource assessment State of Fla., Jacksonville, Fla., 1987-89; dir. human resource assessment Customer Svcs. Revenue Recovery Ctr., 1989-93, mgr. small bus. sales and svc., 1994-95, br. mgr. small bus. No. Fla., 1995-97; product support mgr. Sm. Bus. Mktg., 1997-98, sr. product support mgr., 1998—. Vol. Learn to Read; bd. dirs. Duval Assn. Retarded Citizens, Jacksonville, 1981-86, treas., 1983-84; mem. Leadership Jacksonville, Class of '97. Mem. NAFE, Am. Mgmt. Assn., Pioneers of Am., Jacksonville C. of C. Roman Catholic. Avocations: gardening, water and snow skiing. Office: BellSouth Ctr 675 W Peachtree St NW Atlanta GA 30375-0001

CLEMONS, LYNN ALLAN, land use planner; b. New Orleans, Oct. 23, 1946; s. Gaylord Wilson and Jessica Monica (McDonald) C. BS, Colo. State U., 1973. Planner outdoor recreation Bur. Outdoor Recreation, Denver, 1974-75; planner outdoor recreation Bur. Land Mgmt., Golden, Co., 1975-77, Winnemucca, Nev., 1977—; pub. affairs officer Bur. Land Mgmt., Winnemucca, 1989-93. Co-author environ. impact statements. With USN, 1968-69, Vietnam. Recipient Spl. Achievement award Dept. of Interior, 1988, 91. Mem. Am. Radio Relay League, U.S. Chess Fedn., No. Nev. Amateur Radio Club (sec.-treas. 1992), Winnemucca Amateur Trap Assn. (sec.-treas. 1981), Assn. for Preservation Tech., Wilderness Soc., One Moccasin Toastmasters Club (officer, Competent Toastmaster award 1988). Roman Catholic. Avocations: woodworking, backpacking, gourmet cooking, reading for the blind, guitar. Office: Bur Land Mgmt 5100 E Winnemucca Blvd Winnemucca NV 89445-2921

CLENDENEN, CORINNA PAKENHAM, art critic, writer, auctioneer; b. Bellefonte, Pa., June 29, 1953; d. Gordon Ross and Jane Kendrick (Pakenham) Smith; m. William Herbert Clendenen Jr., May 7, 1994; children: Allison, Derek, Luke. BA in Art History, Ohio State U., 1975; MA in Cinema Studies, NYU, 1976. Free-lance writer on art and art news various arts mags., N.Y.C., Boston and Conn., 1975—; head speakers bur. Sotheby's, N.Y.C., 1980-82; art and antiques auction adminstr. Pub. Broadcast Sta. Channel 13, N.Y.C., 1979-80; front counter asst. Christie's, N.Y.C., 1977-79; auctioneer Auction 393, N.Y.C., 1976-77. Auctioneer for non-profit fundraising auctions, Conn. and Mass., 1992—; bd. dirs. Projects for a New Millenium, New Haven, Conn., 1996—. Mem. Shoreline Alliance for Arts (co-chair visual arts com. 1997—). Avocations: horsemanship, SCUBA diving, travel. Home and Office: 102 River Edge Farms Rd Madison CT 06443-2756

CLENDENEN, WILLIAM HERBERT, JR., lawyer; b. New London, Conn., Dec. 2, 1942; s. William H. and Ethel L. (Clifford) C.; children: William, Patrick, Allison, Derek, Luke; m. Corinna P. Smith. BA, Providence Coll., 1964; JD, Cath. U. Am., 1967. Bar: Conn. 1967, U.S. Dist. Ct. Conn. 1971, U.S. Dist. Ct. (so. dist.) N.Y. 1977, U.S. Dist. Ct. R.I. 1977, U.S. Ct. Clms. 1977, U.S. Ct. Appeals. (2d cir.) 1971, U.S. Sup. Ct. 1976. Reginald Heber Smith Cmty. Lawyer fellow U. Pa. 1967-68; staff atty. New Haven Legal Assistance Assn., Inc., 1968-73; prin. William H. Clendenen Jr., P.C., New Haven, 1973—; supervising atty. Yale Law Sch., 1981; alt. pub. mem. Conn. State Bd. Mediation and Arbitration, 1976-78; co-chmn. U.S. Dist. Ct. Conn. Spcl. Masters Com., New Haven, 1985-89. Fellow Am. Coll. Trial Lawyers, Conn. Bar Found. (life, dir. 1991—, treas. 1992—); mem. ABA, ATLA, Conn. Bar Assn. (chmn. consumer law sect. 1974-78, chmn. lawyer referral com. 1987-89, jud. independence task force 1998—), New Haven County Bar Assn. (sec. 1986-87, treas. 1987-88, v.p. 1988-89, pres. 1989-90), Conn. Trial Lawyers Assn., New Haven County Bar Found. (dir. 1993—). Home: 102 River Edge Farms Rd Madison CT 06443-2756 Office: PO Box 1729 New Haven CT 06507-1729

CLENDENNING, WILLIAM EDMUND, dermatologist; b. Waynesburg, Pa., June 23, 1931; s. William Burdette and Anna Marie (Schellhase) C.; m. Elizabeth Woodbury Bennett, Sept. 6, 1958; children—William Alan, Joy Marie, Bruce Bennett, Sarah Elizabeth. B.S., Allegheny Coll., Meadville, Pa., 1952; M.D., Jefferson Med. Coll., Phila., 1956. Diplomate Am. Bd. Dermatology, Am. Bd. Dermatopathology. Intern St. Luke's Hosp., Cleve., 1956-57; resident in dermatology Univ. Hosps. of Cleve., 1957-60; sr. investigator dermatology br. Nat. Cancer Inst., USPHS, 1961-63; asst. prof. dermatology Western Res. U. Med. Sch., 1963-67; prof. medicine (dermatology) Dartmouth Coll. Med.; prof. emeritus, 1996—; also mem. staff Mary Hitchcock Meml. Hosp., Hitchcock Clinic, 1967-94; mem. Nat. Mycosis Fungoides Coop. Group, N.Am. Contact Dermatitis Group; Prosser White Orator St. John's Hosp. Dermatol. Soc., London, 1985. Author articles in field, chpts. in books. Nat. Cancer Inst. grantee, 1963-67. Mem. Am. Acad. Dermatology, Soc. Investigative Dermatology, Am. Dermatol. Assn., Am. Soc. Dermatopathology, New Eng. Dermatol. Soc., Am. Fedn. Clin. Research, N.H. Med. Assn., AMA. Home: 7 Pleasant St Hanover NH 03755-2008 Office: 1 Medical Center Dr Lebanon NH 03756-0001

CLERGUE, LUCIEN GEORGES, photographer; b. Arles, France, Aug. 14, 1934; s. Etienne and Jeanne (Grangeon) C.; m. Yolande Wartel, Jan. 10, 1963; children: Anne, Olivia. Dr. es Letters in Photography, U. Provence, 1979. tchr. workshops New Sch., N.Y.C., Art Ctr., Pasadena, Osaka U., Japan, other U.S. univs. and colls. Freelance photographer, 1959—; artistic dir. Arles Festival, 1971-75, 86-88; founder, Rencontres Internationales de la Photographie, Arles, 1969, art dir. XXVth anniversary, 1994; one-man exhbns. include Kunstgewerbe Mus., Zurich, 1958, 63, Mus. Modern Art, N.Y.C., 1961—, Musée d'Arts Decoratifs, Paris, 1962—, Moderna Museet, Stockholm, 1969—, Art Inst. Chgo., 1970—, Kunsthalle, Düsseldorf, Fed. Republic Germany, 1970—, Gallery Witkin, N.Y.C., 1972-79, Bruxelles Musee d'Ixelles, 1974—, Israel Mus., Jerusalem, 1974—, Ctr. Pompidou, Paris, 1980—, Musée d'Art Moderne Paris, 1984, George Eastman House, Rochester, 1985, ICP, N.Y.,1986, Amos Anderson Mus., Helsinki, 1987, Real Maestranza Sevilla, 1991, Houston Photo Fest, 1992, Milw. Art Mus., 1993, Calif. Mus. Photography, Riverside, 1997, Centro de la Imagen, Mexico, 1997; works rep. books, movies; represented in permanent collection Fogg Mus., Harvard U., Cambridge, Mass.; films include Picasso War Love and Peace; books include Footprints of the Gods, 1988, Picasso my friend, 1993; author of 50 publs. Decorated chevalier Nat. Order Merit, 1980; recipient Louis Lumière prize, 1966, Grand Prix of Higashikawa Photo Fest, 1986, 3rd prize World Press Photo Internat., Amsterdam, 1997, Prix Polyedre, Aix, France, 1998. Mem. Assn. Nat. Photographers Createurs, Parc Regional Camargue, Ste. des Amis de Jean Cocteau, Ste des Amis de La Fond, St. J. Perse, Aix en Pr., Rencontres Internat. de la Photographie Arles, Memoire 2000. Roman Catholic. Home: 17 Rue Aristide Briand, BP 84, 13632 Arles France

CLERKIN, EUGENE PATRICK, physician; b. N.Y.C., Feb. 22, 1931; s. Eugene and Nance (Fitzsimmons) C.; m. Nancy Lucille Oshirak, Aug. 16, 1958; children: Eugene J., Brian A., Lucille A., Kathryn M. BS, Manhattan Coll., 1952; MD, NYU, 1956. Diplomate Am. Bd. Internal Medicine. Physician Lahey Clinic Found., Burlington, Mass., 1963—, chmn. dept. internal medicine, 1970-91, also bd. govs., 1981-91; asst. clin. prof. medicine Harvard Med. Sch., Boston, 1976—; mem. corp. N.E. Deaconess Hosp., 1980-93. Lt. USNR, 1958-60. Fellow ACP; mem. Endocrine Soc., Am. Diabetes Assn. Roman Catholic. Avocations: tennis, hiking. Office: Lahey Clinic Med Ctr 41 Mall Rd Burlington MA 01805-3406*

CLERMONT, YVES WILFRID, anatomy educator, researcher; b. Montreal, Que., Can., Aug. 14, 1926; s. Rodolphe and Fernande (Primeau) C.; m. Madeleine Bonneau, June 30, 1950; children—Suzanne, Martin, Stephane. B.Sc., U. Montreal, 1949; Ph.D., McGill U., 1953. Lectr. anatomy McGill U., Montreal, 1953-56, asst. prof., 1956-60, assoc. prof., 1960-63, prof., 1963-97, prof. emeritus, 1997—, chmn. dept., 1975-85; mem. Nat. Bd. Med. Examiners, Phila., 1979-82; mem. rsch. grant com. Med. Rsch. Coun., Ottawa, 1970-97; cons. WHO, NIH, Ford Found., Fonds pour la formation de chercheurs et l'aide à la recherché, Quebec; sec. Artur Lucian Award Com. for Rsch. in Circulatory Diseases, 1983-97, hon. mem., 1997—. Contbr. chpts. to books, numerous articles to profl. jours. Recipient Ortho prize Can. Soc. Study Fertility, 1958, Prix Scientifique Govt. of Que., 1963, S.L. Siegler award Am. Soc. Study Fertility, 1966, Van Campenhout award Can. Fertility and Andrology Soc., 1986, Osler Teaching award McGill U., 1990. Fellow Royal Soc. Can.; mem. Am. Assn. Anatomists (v.p. 1970-73), Soc. Study of Reprodn., Am. Assn. Andrology (Disting. Andrologist award 1988, Serono award lectureship 1992), Can. Assn. Anatomists (hon., J.C.B. Grant award 1986), Can. Assn. Microscopy (v.p. 1982-83). Home: 567 Townshend St, Saint Lambert, PQ Canada J4R 1M4 Office: McGill U Dept Anatomy Cell Biol, 3640 University St, Montreal, PQ Canada H3A 2B2

CLEVELAND, ASHLEY, musician; b. Knoxville, Tenn., Feb. 2, 1957; m. Kenny Greenberg. Recs. include Big Town, 1991, Bus Named Desire, 1993, Lesson of Love (Grammy award for Best Rock Gospel Album, 1996, Nashville Music award, 1996), You Are There, 1998 (Grammy award for Best Rock Gospel Album 1999); singer on over 200 albums; TV appearances include Austin City Limits, Saturday Night Live, TNN Country News, American Music Shop, 1991, CCM-TV, 1993, Gospel Music Assn. Dove Awards, 1994, 96, 98, The Road, 1994, Prime Time Country, 1996, Peace In The Valley, 1997, CeCe's Place, 1997, Stone Country: A Tribute To The Rolling Stones, 1997, Profiles in Praise, 1999. Recipient Dove award for Praise and Worship Album of Yr., 1994; Big Town named one of 1991's Ten Most Overlooked Albums, Billboard. *

CLEVELAND, CHARLENE S., community health nurse; b. Haverhill, N.H., Aug. 20, 1945; d. Thomas D. and Willie E. (Smith) Sargent; children: Laura, Mary Ann. Diploma, Sylacauga Hosp. Sch. Nursing, 1967; student, Gadsden State Jr. C.C., 1979-82; BSN magna cum laude, Jacksonville State U., 1995. Staff nurse Sylacauga (Ala.) Hosp.; pub. health nurse Ala. Dept. Pub. Health, Sylacauga; staff nurse TCRC Child Devel. Ctr., Talladega, Ala.; homebound nurse Ala. Dept. Rehab., Anniston. Mem. Ala. State Nurses Assn., ARA, ASEA.

CLEVELAND, CHARLES SIDNEY, secondary education educator; b. Portland, Oreg., Apr. 8, 1951; s. Sidney Charles and Virginia May (Seitzinger) C.; m. Joyce Kristine Nofziger, Nov. 5, 1972; children: Justin Charles, Christpher Joseph Sidney. BS, Portland State U., 1974; MAT, Lewis and Clark Coll., 1980. Geography tchr. Hillsboro (Oreg.) Union High Dist., 1976-98, Hillsborough (Oreg.) H.S., 1998—. Pres. Hillsboro (Oreg.) Active 20-30 Club, 1989, Oreg. Soccer Coaches Assn., 1983-84; asst. scoutmaster Boy Scouts Am., Hillsboro, 1991—; bd. dirs. Oreg. Geog. Alliance, 1987-93, Hillsboro Edn. Assn., 1983-86, 92—. Recipient Instructional Leadership Inst. award Nat. Geog. Soc., 1989; named Oreg. and Region IV Soccer Coach of Yr. by Nat. High Sch. Athletic Coaches Assn., 1984, Outstanding Young Man by Hillsboro C. of C., 1976. Mem. Assn. Am. Geographers, Nat. Coun. Geog. Edn. (Disting. Teaching Achievement award 1992), Nat. Coun. Social Studies, Oreg. Coun. Social Studies (bd. dirs.), Active 20-30 Internat. (life), Elks. Avocations: photography, coaching soccer, scout leader. Office: Hillsborough HS 3285 SE Roodridge Dr Hillsboro OR 97123*

CLEVELAND, CLYDE, city official; b. Detroit, May 22, 1935; m. Mary; 1 child. Student, Wayne State U. Pub. aid worker City of Detroit, 1958, 60-64; supervisor cmty. svc. Mayor's Com. Human Resources Devel., Detroit, 1965-68; cmty. planner Inner City Bus. Improvement Forum, 1968-71; city councilman City of Detroit, 1974—. Del. Dem. Nat. Conv., 1980; former vice chair Mich. State Dem. Party; co-campaign mgr. Jesse Jackson Victory in Mich., 1988; vice chair Southeastern Mich. Coun. Govts.; cmty. orgn. specialist New Detroit, Inc., 1971-73. Served in U.S. Army, Korea. Mem. NAACP, Elks, People's Cmty. & Civic League, Assn. Study Negro Life & History, Booker T. Washington Bus. Assn., Shriners, Masons. Baptist. Office: 1340 City County Bldg Detroit MI 48226*

CLEVELAND, ELBIN L., theatre design and technology educator; b. Cedar Rapids, Iowa, Dec. 18, 1940; s. Loras L. and Helen Beatrice (Miller) C. BA, U. Northern Iowa, 1962; MA, U. Iowa, 1969, MFA, 1972. Cert. profl. tchr. Tchr. Belmond & Cedar Rapids (Iowa) Pub. Schs., 1962-67; instr. U. Iowa, Iowa City, 1969-72; asst. prof. U. Wis., LaCrosse, 1972-75; assoc. prof. theatre design and tech. U. S.C., Columbia, 1975-90, full prof., 1990—; Fulbright lectr. Traditional Opera Acad., Beijing, China, 1994; guest lectr. Shanghai Theatre Acad., 1994, Nat. Inst. for Arts, Taipei, Taiwan, 1994, Nat. Acad. Scenography, Seoul, 1993. Scene designer of over 165 stage plays including Hamlet, Crucible, Coctail Hour, Peer Gynt; tech. dir. over 220 stage plays; lighting designer over 40 stage plays; theatre architecture 13 bldgs.; author: SC Guidelines for Identification of Artistically Gifted and Talented Students, 1985, SC Curriculum Framework for Theatre/Drama Education, 1988, Bibliographic and Supplier Listing for Scenic Modelers, 1990, rev. edit., 1992; contbg. writer Stage Directions Mag., 1996—; contbr. more than 100 articles to profl. jours.; assoc. editor for edn. Theatre Design and Tech., new products editor, 1988—; assoc. editor for scenography So. Theatre Mag., 1995—, Sightlines, Tech. Resource Guide; new products editor Quar. Rev., 1997—; inventor Clevair Lift, 1997, Clevair Chair, 1997. Mem. Arts in Basic Curriculum Steering Com., S.C., 1988—, Samsung Found. Grantee S.C. Arts Commn., 1989, S.C. Humanities Coun., 1989, U. S.C. Venture Fund, 1989, Instrnl. Innovation, 1996, R&D, 1996, USITT, 1998. Mem. S.C. Theatre Assn. (past pres., Founders award 1988, 94), U.S. Inst. Theatre Tech. (nat. chmn. publs. 1990-92, vice commr. edn. 1990-92, edn. editor 1990-96, ex-officio officer,bd. dirs. 1988—), U.S. Inst. Theatre Tech.-SE (life, commr. new products, commr. archives, Founder's award 1995), S.C. Alliance for Arts Edn. (chmn.-elect 1989-90), Southeastern Theatre Conf. (life; bd. dirs. 1989-91, S.C. rep. 1990-92), Assn. Theatre in Higher Edn, MAMPIST (U.S. dir. interns in theatre arts). Avocations: films, sailing, travel. Office: U SC Dept Theatre and Speech Columbia SC 29208

CLEVELAND, MARY LOUISE, librarian, media specialist; b. Clarksdale, Miss., Dec. 4, 1922; d. George Washington and Beatrice (Orange) Jones; m. Chester Lloyd Cleveland, June 5, 1950 (div. 1973); 1 child, Ann. BS, Ala. State U., 1947; MLS, Case-Western Res. U., 1957; EdD, East Tex. State Coll., 1991. Asst. prof. libr. edn. Ala. State U., Montgomery, 1957-65; head libr. Talladaga (Ala.) Coll., 1965-66; asst. prof. Atlanta U., 1966-71; head libr. Wiley Coll., Marshall, Tex., 1971-77; assoc. prof. Ala. A&M U., Huntsville, 1977-83; dir. libr. Tex. Coll., Tyler, 1985—. So. Edn. Found. fellow, 1963, East Tex. State U. fellow, 1982-83. Democrat. Methodist. Avocations: writing, preparation of audio-visual materials. Home: 2508 Fieldcrest Dr NW Huntsville AL 35810-2122 Office: Tex Coll 2404 N Grand Ave Tyler TX 75702-1962

CLEVELAND, SUSAN ELIZABETH, library administrator, researcher; b. Plainfield, N.J., Mar. 14, 1946; d. Robert Astbury and Grace Ann (Long) Williamson; m. Stuart Craig Cleveland, Aug. 21, 1971; children: Heather Elizabeth, Catherine Elisa. BA, Douglass Coll., Rutgers U., 1968; MLS, Rutgers U., 1969. Acquisitions libr. Jefferson U., Phila., 1970-71; biomed. libr. VA Hosp., Hines, Ill., 1972; med. cataloger U. Ariz., Tucson, 1973-74; dir. U. Pa. Hosp. Libr., Phila., 1974-87; exec. dir. Cleveland, Lamb, Urban Assocs., 1987-89; libr. dir. Mt. Sinai Hosp., Phila., 1989, West Jersey Health System (now Virtua Health Sys.), Voorhees, N.J., 1990—; cons. in field, Phila. USPHS fellow, Detroit, 1969-70; recipient Chapel of 4 Chaplains Legion of Honor. Mem. Med. Libr. Assn. (Phila. chpt.), Spl. Libr. Assn., Basic Health Sci. Libr. Consortium, S.W. N.J. Consortium for Health Info. Svcs., Health Scis. Libr. Assn. N.J., Acad. Health Info. Profls., Caravan Club. Home: 9 Sylvan Ct Laurel Spgs NJ 08021-4883

CLEVEN, CAROL CHAPMAN, state legislator; b. Hanover, Ill., Nov. 2, 1928; d. Edward William and Vivian (Strasser) Chapman; m. Walter Arnold Cleven; children: Kern W., Jeffrey P. BS, U. Ill., 1950, postgrad., 1950-56. Elem. sch. tchr. Derinda Ctr., Ill., 1946-47; with rsch. staff U. Ill., Urbana, 1950-56; exec. dir. Crittenton Hasting House, Brighton, Mass., 1975-86; mem. Mass. Ho. of Reps., Boston, 1987—; mem. edn. com., mem. human svcs. com., mem. election laws com. Mass. Ho. Reps.; mem. Rep. Task Force on Pediatric AIDS, Mass. Caucus of Women Legislators, Gov.'s Adolescent Health Adv. Coun., Spl. Commn. on Pub. Assiatance, Spl. Com. on Women and the Criminal Justice System; co-chair Legis. Caucus on Older Citizens' Concerns, Dept. Social Svcs. Working Group; mem. steering com. Mass. Legis. Children's Caucus. Mem. Chelmsford (Mass.) Sch. Com., 1969-87, mem. elem. needs com., 1969-71, mem. sch. bldg. com., 1971-76; bd. dirs. Camp Paul for Exceptional Children, 1987—; past pres. Lowell (Mass.) YWCA, Lowell Coll. Club; mem. Merrimack River Watershed Coun., Mass. Coalition for Pregnant and Parenting Teens, Alliance for Young Families; treas. Boston Ctr. Blind Children; bd. dirs. Chelmsford Ednl. Found.; bd. dirs. Greater Lowell Alzheimers Assn., Ea. Mass. Alzheimers Assn.; mem. spl. adv. bd. Cmty. Teamwork, Inc. Mem. Mass. Assn. Sch. Coms. (life), Friends of the Library, Chelmsford Hist. Soc., Chelmsford LWV, Florence Crittenton League of Lowell, Phi Sigma, Sigma Delta Epsilon. Congregationalist. Home: 4 Arbutus Ave Chelmsford MA 01824-1113 Office: State House Rm 167 State Capitol Boston MA 02133

CLEVENGER, JEFFREY GRISWOLD, mining company executive; b. Boston, Sept. 1, 1949; s. Galen William and Cynthia (Jones) C. BS in Mining Engring., N.Mex. Inst. Mining and Tech., Socorro, 1973; grad. advanced mgmt. program, Harvard U., 1996. Engr. Phelps Dodge, Tyrone, N.Mex., 1973-78, gen. mine foreman, 1979-81, mine supt., 1981-86; mine supt. Phelps Dodge, Morenci, Ariz., 1986, gen. supt., 1987; asst. gen. mgr. Chino Mines Co., Hurley, N.Mex., 1987-88; asst. gen. mgr. Phelps Dodge, Morenci, 1988-89, gen. mgr., 1989-92; pres. Phelps Dodge Morenci, Inc., 1989-92, Morenci Water & Electric Co., 1989-92; sr. v.p. Cyprus Copper Co., Tempe, 1992-93; pres. Cyprus Climax Metals Co., Tempe, 1993—; sr. v.p. Cyprus Amax Minerals Co., Littleton, Colo., 1993-97, exec. v.p., 1998—. Contbr. articles to profl. jours. Bd. dirs. Valley of the Sun YMCA, Mining Hall of Fame; chmn. Copper Devel. Assn. Recipient Disting. Achievement award N.Mex. Inst. Mining & Tech., 1988. Mem. AIME (chmn. S.W. N.Mex. chpt. 1982), Soc. Mining Engrs. (Robert Peele award 1984), Mining and Metall. Soc. Am., Coppr Devel. Assn. (chmn.), Elks. Home: 4575 N Launfal Ave Phoenix AZ 85018-2961 Office: Cyprus Climax Metals Co PO Box 22015 1501 W Fountainhead Pkwy Tempe AZ 85282-1868

CLEVENGER, MARK THOMAS, communications executive, writer; b. L.A., Aug. 21, 1928; s. John Thomas Clevenger and Alice Laura (Wilburn) Gable; m. Ann Marie Kelley, Oct. 27, 1957; children: Kelley Patricia, Maura Theresa, Sean, Kate Clevenger Westerlund. BS in Agronomy, U. Calif., Davis; MA in Journalism, U. So. Calif.; PhC in Higher Edn., U. Wash. USAF, 1951-55; Pub. rels. rep. Lockheed Corp., Burbank, Calif., 1959-70; dir. pub. rels. Lockheed Shipbldg., Seattle, 1970-72; cons. Lockheed Shipbldg., 1974-82; dir. info. svcs. U. Wash., Seattle, 1972-73; instr. bus. comm. U. Wash., 1974-91; pres. Interface Comm., Kirkland, Wash., 1976—, Polychite Corp., Redmond, Wash., 1985-91. Editor various newspapers, Calif., 1955-59. Trustee Group Health Coop., Seattle, 1979-82. Various awards Calif. Newspaper Pubs. Assn.

CLEVENGER, PENELOPE, international business consultant; b. Denver, Dec. 6, 1940; d. Harold Friedland and Charlotte (Glatt) Friedland Beskin; m. Willie K. Clevenger, Oct. 15, 1961 (div.). AA, Stephens Coll., 1960. Office mgr. Malcolm S. Gerald, Chgo., 1977-79; pers. mgr. Rolm/Midwest, Chgo., 1979-82; office adminstr. Nutech Engrs., Chgo., 1982-83; office mgr. Am. Acad. Orthopaedic Surgeons, Chgo., 1983-85; dir. adminstrn. Telecommunications Industry Assn. (formerly U.S. Telecommunications Suppliers Assn.), Chgo., 1985-88; pres. InterWorld Svcs., Ltd., 1988—. Bd. dirs. Ctr. Tng. and Rehab. of Disabled, Chgo., 1981-84; vol. Northwestern Meml. Hosp., 1985-87, Christian Industrial League, 1992-97. Mem. Meeting Profls. Internat. (Chgo. chpt.), Meeting Profls. Internat. (nat. orgn.), Chgo. Coun. on Fgn. Rels., U.S. China Friendship Assn. Democrat. Jewish. Home and Office: 233 E Wacker Dr Apt 3910 Chicago IL 60601-5116

CLEVENGER, RAYMOND C., III, federal judge; b. Topeka, Kans., Aug. 27, 1937; s. Raymond C. and Mary Margaret (Ramsey) C.; m. Celia Faulkner, Sept. 9, 1961 (dic. Mar. 1987); children: Winthrop, Peter. BA, Yale U., 1959, LLB, 1966. Ptnr. Wilmer Cutler & Pickering, Washington, 1975-90; judge U.S. Ct. Appeals (Fed. Cir.), Washington, 1990—. Mem. ABA, D.C. Bar Assn. Office: Fed Cir Ct 717 Madison Pl NW Washington DC 20439-0002*

CLEVENGER, SARAH, botanist, computer consultant; b. Indpls., Dec. 19, 1926; d. Cyrus Raymond and Mary Beth (Stevens) C. A.B., Miami U., 1947; Ph.D., Ind. U., 1957. Tchr sci. Radford Sch., El Paso, Tex., 1949-51, Hillsdale Sch., Cin., 1951-52; asst. prof. Berea (Ky.) Coll., 1957-59, 61-63, Wittenberg U., Springfield, Ohio, 1959-60, Eastern Ill. U., 1960-61, Ind. State U., Terre Haute, 1963-66; assoc. prof. Ind. State U., 1966-78, prof., 1978-85, prof. emerita, 1985—. Mem. Am. Inst. Biol. Sci., Am. Soc. Plant Taxonomists, Bot. Soc. Am., Internat. Assn. Plant Taxonomy, Phytochem. Soc. N.Am. (past sec.). Home: 717 S Henderson St Bloomington IN 47401-4838

CLEVER, LINDA HAWES, physician; b. Seattle; d. Nathan Harrison and Evelyn Lorraine (Johnson) Hawes; m. James Alexander Clever, Aug. 20, 1960; 1 child, Sarah Lou. AB with distinction, Stanford U., 1962, MD, 1965. Diplomate Am. Bd. Internal Medicine, Am. Bd. Preventive Medicine in Occupational Medicine. Intern Stanford U. Hosp., Palo Alto, Calif., 1965-66; resident Stanford U. Hosp., Palo Alto, 1966-67, fellow in infectious disease, 1967-68; fellow in community medicine U. Calif., San Francisco, 1968-69, resident, 1969-70; med. dir. Sister Mary Philippa Diagonostic and Treatment Ctr. St. Mary's Hosp., San Francisco, 1970-77; chmn. dept. occupational health Calif. Pacific Med. Ctr., San Francisco, 1977—; clin. prof. medicine Med. Sch., U. Calif., San Francisco; NIH rsch. fellow Sch. Medicine, Stanford U., 1967-68, mem. nat. adv. panel Inst. Rsch. on Women and Gender, 1990—, chair panel, 1998—; mem. San Francisco Comprehensive Health Planning Coun., 1971-76, bd. dirs.; mem. Calif.-OSHA Adv. Com. on Hazard Evaluation System and Info. Svc., 1979-85, Calif. Statewide Profl. Stds. Rev. Coun., 1977-81, San Francisco Regional Commn. on White House Fellows, 1979-81, 83-89, 92, 95, chmn., 1979-81, bd. sci. counselors Nat. Inst. of Occupl. Safety and Health, 1995—. Editor Western Jour. Medicine, 1990-98; contbr. articles to profl. jours. Trustee Stanford U., 1972-76, 81-91, v.p. 1985-91; trustee Marin Country Day Sch., 1978-85; bd. dirs. Sta. KQED, 1976-83, chmn., 1979-81; bd. dirs. Ind. Sector, 1980-86, vice chmn. 1985-86; bd. dirs. San Francisco U. H.S., 1983-90, chmn. 1987-88; active Womens Forum West, 1980—, bd. dirs. 1992, 93; mem. Lucile Packard Children's Hosp. Bd., 1993-97, Lucile Packard Found. Children, 1997-99; mem., chair policy adv. com. U. Calif. Berkeley Sch. of Pub. Health. Master ACP (gov. No. Calif. region 1984-89, chmn. bd. govs. 1989-90, regent 1990-96, vice chair bd. regents 1994-95)); Fellow Am. Coll. Occupl. and Environ. Medicine; mem. Inst. Medicine NAS, Calif. Med. Assn., Calif. Acad. Medicine, Am. Pub. Health Assn., Western Occupl. Medicine Assn., Western Assn. Physicians, Stanford U. Women's Club (bd. dirs. 1971-80), Chi Omega. Office: 2351 Clay St San Francisco CA 94115-1931

CLEVER, W(ARREN) GLENN, editor, publishing executive, poet, writer, educator; b. Champion, Alta., Can., Feb. 10, 1918; s. Martin George and Florence (Anderson) C.; m. Elizabeth Hall, June 13, 1942; 1 child, Christine Susan. MA, U. Ottawa, Ont., Can., 1964, U. Ottawa, Ont., Can., 1966; PhD, U. Ottawa, Ont., Can., 1969. Joined Canadian Army, 1939, advanced through grades to maj., 1955; served Canadian Army, U.K., Sicily, Italy, Netherlands; staff Surgeon Gen. of Can. Forces, 1952-55, 61-66, ret., 1966; lectr. U. Ottawa, 1967-70, asst. prof. English lit., 1970-72, assoc. prof., 1972-80, prof., 1980-83, adj. prof., 1986—, gen. editor U. Ottawa Short Story Series, 1971-81, chnm. dept. English, 1972-75, coordinator symposia series, 1977-83; v.p. Borealis Press Ltd., Ottawa, 1972—; pres. Techumseh Press Ltd., Ottawa, 1972—. Co-editor Jour. Can. Poetry, Ottawa, 1978-85; editor: books including Selected Short Stories of Duncan Campbell Scott, 1972, 75, 87, Selected Poetry of Duncan Campbell Scott, 1974, 75, The E.J. Pratt Symposium, 1977, Index to Canadian Literature, 1985-97, The Sir Charles G.D. Roberts Symposium, 1984; author 5 vols. of poetry including Alberta Days, 1974 (Ont. Arts Coun. award 1976), on E.J. Pratt, 1977. Past bd. dirs. Can. Writers' Found., Ottawa, 1974—, v.p., Can. Writers' Found., Ottawa, 1976—. Can. Coun. grantee, 1974-75; founder David Clever Meml. award, dept. English, U. Ottawa, 1993—, Glenn Clever Scholarship Fund, 1996. Home: 110 Bloomingdale, Nepean, ON Canada K2C 4A4 Office: Dept English U Ottawa, Arts Bldg, Ottawa, ON Canada K1N 6N5

CLEWETT, KENNETH VAUGHN, college official; b. Pomona, Calif., June 3, 1923; s. Heber Hovey and Thelma Lela (Sikes) C.; m. Margery Marie Haas, July 10, 1949; children: Richard A., Bruce D., Curtis L., Janet M. AA, Pomona Jr. Coll., 1943; student naval tng., U. Redlands, 1943-44, Columbia U., 1944; BA, Stanford U., 1947. Gen. clk. So. Counties Gas Co., Pomona, 1947; pers. examiner Calif. Pers. Bd., Sacramento, 1947-50; asst. pers. officer Calif. Dept. Mental Hygiene, Sacramento, 1950-52; pers. dir. Sonoma State Hosp., Eldridge, Calif., 1952-60; hosp. adminstr. Sonoma State Hosp., 1960-72, Fairview State Hosp., Costa Mesa, Calif., 1972-75, 76;

acting exec. dir. Patton (Calif.) State Hosp., 1975-76, exec. dir., 1976-78; bus. mgr. So. Calif. Coll., 1978-82, dir. planning and corp. rels., 1982-84; v.p. adminstrn., dir. external affairs Kona campus U. of the Nations (formerly Pacific and Asia Christian U.), 1985—; preceptor George Washington U., Grad. Sch. Health Care Adminstrn., 1962-78, Northwestern U. Grad. Sch. Mgmt., 1975-78, U. Minn. Program Mental Health Adminstrn., 1976-78. Pres. Sonoma Valley C. of C., 1964; v.p. Sonoma-Mendocino coun. Boy Scouts Am., 1968-71, bd. dirs., 1965-72; v.p. Sonoma County United Crusade, 1969-70; chmn. Sonoma Valley Coun. Edn. Com., 1969-71; founding chmn. bd. dirs. Sonoma Valley United Crusade, 1969-70, bd. dirs., 1969-72; vice chmn. bd. dirs. Big Sisters Orange County, Calif., 1975-77; bd. dirs. So. Calif. Coll., 1977-78, Goodwill Industries Ctrl. Calif., 1951-52, Goodwill Industries Inland Counties, 1978; bd. dirs. West Hawaii Housing Found., 1988—, vice-chmn. 1994—; vice-chmn. Cmty. Orgn. for Edn. Devel., 1995—, Bridge House Rehab. Ctr., 1997—, Kona Pacific Condo Owners Assn., 1990—, pres., 1992-93, 98—; mem. sch./cmty. -based mgmt. coun. Konawaena High Sch., 1992-95, Kealakehe High Sch., 1998—; mem. adv. bd. Orange County Rescue Ctr., 1980-84, Hawaii County Decisions, 1988-91, West Hawaii ARC Svc. Ctr., 1988-98; mem. adv. bd. Salvation Army Kona, 1991—, chmn. 1995-98; West Hawaii Food Bank, 1994—, vice chair, 1998—, Kona Hosp., 1996—; mem. Hawaii Health Sys. Corp.'s West Hawaii Adv. Com., 1997—; trustee Sonoma Valley Unified Sch. Dist., 1971-72; pres. Redwood Empire Hosp. Conf., 1967, bd. dirs., 1966-68; elder United Presbyn. Ch. in U.S.A., 1949-74; deacon Newport-Mesa Christian Ctr., Costa Mesa, Calif., 1975-76, 79-84; founding co-chair West Hawaii Coalition on Homeless Concerns, 1991-92; founding chair Meet 'N Eat feeding program, 1992—, Kona-Area Coun. of Svc. Clubs, 1993—; bd. dirs. Greater Kona Cmty. Coun., 1991-92, vice chmn., 1992. Lt. (j.g.) USNR, 1943-46, PTO. Recipient Citizens award of Year Valley Moon Tchrs. Assn., 1970, Outstanding Svc. award Redwood Empire Hosp. Conf., 1972, Clara Barton vol. award ARC. Fellow Royal Soc. Health, Assn. Mental Health Adminstrs. (pres. 1976, bd. dirs. 1967-72, 74-77); mem. Am. Assn. Mental Retardation, Christian Mgmt. Assn., Kona-Kohala C. of C., Rotary (pres. Kona 1993-94, bd. dirs. 1989-95), Alpha Gamma Sigma (hon. life). Home: 75-5787 Kakalina St Kailua Kona HI 96740-1909 *Each additional personal achievement further confirms the weakness of depending upon myself alone and that real success is dependent upon truly following the leading of God, our heavenly Father.*

CLEWETT, RAYMOND WINFRED, mechanical design engineer; b. Upland, Calif., Nov. 7, 1917; s. Howard Jasper and Pansy Gertrude (Macy) C.; m. Hazel Royer, June 11, 1938; children: Alan Eugene, Patricia Gail, Charles Raymond, Richard Howard, Beverly Lynn. Student, Chaffey Jr. Coll., 1937. Exptl. mechanic Douglas Aircraft Co., Santa Monica, Calif., 1937-51; shop foreman, exptl. designer Lear, Inc., Los Angeles, 1945-51; design engr., shop mgr. The RAND Corp., Santa Monica, Calif., 1951-83, also design cons.; owner, mgr. HY-TECH Engring. and Devel. Lab., Malibu, Calif., 1983—; design cons. Pacific-Sierra Research Corp. Exhbns. include Malibu Art Festival, 1998, Art Affair XIII, Pacific Palisades, Calif., 1998; works include mech. design of JOHNNIAC early model electronic computer on permanent display Comp. Mus., Boston; designer various computer input/output devices, 1953-70; developer low vision reading aids for the blind, 1970-75; design and constrn. spl. equipment for sci. and research, 1983—; stone sculptor, 1994—; patentee in field. Mem. AAAS, Soc. Mfg. Engrs., Am. Soc. Metals. Republican. Office: HY-TECH Engring & Devel Lab 7069 Fernhill Dr Malibu CA 90265-4240

CLEWIS, CHARLOTTE WRIGHT STAUB, mathematics educator; b. Pitts., Aug. 20, 1935; d. Schirmer Chalfant and Charlotte Wright (Rodgers) Staub; student Memphis State Coll., 1953-54, U. Wis., 1957-59; BA, Newark State Coll., 1963; MAT, Loyola Marymount U., 1974; m. John Edward Clewis, Aug. 11, 1954; 1 dau., Charlotte Wright. Asst. to dir., housemother Leota Sch. and Camp, Evansville, Wis., 1957-59; tchr. math. Rahway Jr. H.S. (N.J.), 1963-70; tchr. math. Torrance (Calif.) Unified Sch. Dist., 1970-95, coord. math. dept., 1977-95; mem. instrnl. materials rev. panel State of Calif., 1986; instr. Weekend Coll. Marymount-Palos Verdes, 1992-94; coach math. teams. Sec., pres. Larga Vista Property Owners Assn., 1975-84; mem. Rolling Hills Estates City Celebration Com., 1975-81; treas. adult leaders YMCA, Metuchen, N.J., 1967-69; bd. dirs. Peninsula Symphony Assn., 1978-84, sec., 1993-97; commr. Rolling Hills Estates Parks and Activities, 1981—, chmn., 1985, 90, 96. Named Tchr. of Yr., Rahway Jr. H.S., 1966; recipient appreciation award PTA, 1984, hon. svc. award PTA, 1986. Mem. Nat. Coun. Tchrs. Math., Calif. Math. Coun. Avocations: bicycling, camping, reading, horseback riding, computers. Home: 1 Gaucho Dr Rolling Hills Estates CA 90274

CLEWS, WILLIAM VINCENT, producer, writer; b. Richmond, Va., Sept. 5, 1943; s. Charles Gordon and Eleanora Maria (Marciano) C.; children: Christopher William, Ashleigh Elizabeth; m. Carol Ann Peterson, May 30, 1986; stepchild, Todd Clinton. BS, Frostburg State Coll., 1966; MS, Ind. State U., 1969. Tchr. pub. schs. Rivera Beach, Md., 1966-67; writer Md. Pub. TV, Balt., 1968-70, producer, 1970-78; pres. Vince Clews & Assocs., Balt., 1979—; CEO VcAnet, Inc.; drama dir. Md. Pub. Schs., 1966-67; tchr. Am. U., Washington, 1977, Western Md. Coll., 1978; lectr. Internat. TV Assn., San Francisco, 1980-90, Internat. Quorum of Film and Video Producers, Rio de Janeiro. Writer (TV show) Inventory, 1971 (Golden Gate award 1971), (video prodn.) Medical 12 (N.Y. Film Festival award 1980); producer (TV shows) Consumer Survival Kit, 1973 (Emmy nominee 1973), 1974 (Emmy nominee 1974), Scepter of Violence, 1981 (Gold Cindy 1981), Fight for Freedom, 1988 (Telly 1988), (tng. video) Salesability, 1982 (Silver Screen 1982), (corp. image video) The Rouse Co., 1986 (N.Y. Film Festival 1986); producer, dir. (pub. rels. video) Safe and Sound, 1989 (Telly 1989). Mem. Balt. County Cable Commn., 1981-83. Named one of Outstanding Young Men in Am., U.S. C. of C., 1975, for Excellence in Consumer Reporting, Nat Press Club, 1974; recipient Gavel award ABA, 1977, 78. Mem. Internat. Quorum Film & Video Producers (v.p. North Am. 1988-90), Internat. TV Assn. Republican. Avocations: tennis, travel. Home: 1205 Nicodemus Rd Reisterstown MD 21136-5823

CLIBURN, VAN (HARVEY LAVAN CLIBURN, JR.), concert pianist; b. Shreveport, La., July 12, 1934; s. Harvey Lavan and Rildia Bee (O'Bryan) C. Studied music with, mother, 1937-51; studied with, Mme. Rosina Lhevinne; grad. with highest honors; grad. (Frank Damrosch scholar), Juilliard Sch. Music, 1954; HHD (hon.), Baylor U., 1958; MFA, Moscow Conservatory, 1989; D (hon.), The Juilliard Sch. of Music, 1998. Pub. appearances, Shreveport, 1940, debut, Houston Symphony Orch., 1947; appeared with Dallas Symphony Orch., 1952, N.Y. Philharm. Orch., Carnegie Hall, 1954, 58; concert pianist on tour, U.S., 1955-56, Soviet Union, 1958, recs. RCA Victor; guest TV shows, concert with Symphony of the Air, Carnegie Hall, 1958, concert Brussels Fair, Belgium, 1958, other appearances: Phila., Chgo., Hollywood, Denver, London, Amsterdam, Paris, Athens, Monaco, The Hague, Copenhagen, Stockholm, Bucharest, Oslo, La Scala, Moscow, Leningrad, Kiev, Boston, Washington, Dallas, Rio de Janeiro, Mexico City, Tokyo, Berlin, Munich, Zurich, Geneva, Madrid, Barcelona, Lisbon, Vienna, Tel Aviv; nation-wide tour U.S., 1958—; extensive recs. of works by Rachmaninoff, Chopin, Beethoven, others; composer classical music; recordings include My Favorite Encores-Works by Chopin, et. al., A Romantic Collection, World's Favorite Piano Music. Recipient Tex. State prize, 1947; Nat. Music Festival award, 1948; G.B. Dealy award Dallas, 1952; Kosciuszko Found. Chopin award, 1952; grantee Olga Samaroff Found., 1953; 1st place Juilliard Concerto concert, 1953; Edgar M. Leventritt Found. award, 1954; Carl M. Roeder Meml. award Juilliard Sch. Music, 1954; 1st prize Internat. Tchaikovsky Piano Competition Moscow, 1958; citation Am. Assn. Sch. Adminstrs., 1959; U. Mich. Musical Soc. First Disting. Artist award, 1996; Arturo Toscanini award, Classical Music Broadcaster's Assn., 1998; named number one in classical field Top Artists on Campus Poll (album sales), 1968. Mem. Am. Guild Mus. Artists. Baptist. Clubs: Thespian (Kilgore, Tex.) (pres.), Rotary (hon.), Lotos (life), Shreveport, Ft. Worth. Office: care Ann Hilton PO Box 470217 Fort Worth TX 76147-0217 Office: Van Cliburn /Foundation 2525 Ridgmar Blvd Ste 307 Fort Worth TX 76116-4583*

CLICK, BENNIE R., protective services official; married; 4 children. BS in Criminal Justice summa cum laude, Ariz. State U., postgrad. With Phoenix Police Dept.; chief of police Dallas Police Dept., 1993—. Active Boy Scouts Am., Greater Dallas Crime Commn., Jr. League of Dallas, Southwestern Law Enforcement Inst., Dallas Blue Found.; mem. criminal justice policy devel. com. North Ctrl. Coun. Govts.; vol. Children's Med. Ctr. of Dallas/ Dallas Cowboys in multi-facted campaign to discourage possession of firearms by area youth. Mem. Internat. Assn. Chiefs of Police, Tex. Police Chiefs Assn., Nat. Law Enforcement Exec. Inst. Office: Office of Police Chief 2014 Main St Rm 506 Dallas TX 75201-4426*

CLICK, DAVID FORREST, lawyer; b. Miami Beach, Fla., Dec. 17, 1947; s. David Gorman and Helen Margaret (McPhail) C.; m. Helaine London, June 2, 1974; children: Kenneth Randall, Adam Elliott. BA, Yale U., 1969, JD, 1973, MA, 1974. Bar: Conn. 1973, Md. 1983, U.S. Supreme Ct. 1983, Fla. 1984, Maine 1984. Asst. prof. Western New England Sch. Law, Springfield, Mass., 1974-77; assoc. prof. Ind. U., 1977-78, U. Md., Balt., 1978-84; assoc. Nixon, Hargrave, Devans and Doyle, Jupiter, Fla., 1984-86; sole practice Jupiter, 1986—; pres., dir. Click Farms, Inc., Clewiston, Fla.; vice chmn. adv. com. Palm Beach County Coop. Ext. Svc. Contbr. articles to profl. jours. Mem. Christmas Cove (Maine) Improvement Assn., Palm Beach-Martin County Estate Planning Coun., pres. 1988-89; participant Leadership Palm Beach County, 1991-92. Mem. ABA, Fla. Bar Assn., Palm Beach County Bar Assn. (cultural activities award 1992), Nat. Soc. Arts and Letters, Yale Club of the Palm Beaches (pres.), Kiwanis. Presbyterian. Home: 19216 Pinetree Dr Jupiter FL 33469-2002 Office: 810 Saturn St Ste 15 Jupiter FL 33477-4456

CLICK, JAMES H., automotive executive. Co-CEO Tuttle-Click Automotive Group. Office: 14 Auto Center Dr Irvine CA 92618-2802*

CLICK, JOHN WILLIAM, communication educator; b. Huntington, Ind., Apr. 22, 1936; s. Eric Alger and Ethel (McKenzie) C.; m. Dixie Darlene Brown, Nov. 27, 1960; children: Reid William, Kevin Leon. AB, Ball State U., 1958; MS, Ohio U., 1959; PhD, Ohio State U., 1977. Dir. pub. rels. Findlay (Ohio) Coll., 1959-60; instr. journalism Cen. Mich. U., Mt. Pleasant, Mich., 1960-65; from asst. prof. to prof. Ohio U., Athens, 1965-83; prof., dir. Sch. Journalism La. State U., Baton Rouge, 1983-87; chmn., prof. dept. mass communication Winthrop U., Rock Hill, S.C., 1987—; cons. Motorola Inc., Franklin Park, Ill., 1968, Portland (Oreg.) State U., 1988, Lenoir-Rhyne Coll., N.C., 1990, U. Tenn. Chattanooga, 1990, Otterbein Coll., 1992; mem. Accrediting Coun. Edn. in Journalism and Mass Comm., 1989-95; 1998-2001. Author: Magazine Editing and Production, 1974—, Governing College Student Publs., 1980, 93, monograph Ethics and Responsibilities of Advising College Student Publs., 1978, 87, 93; mng. editor: Journalism Quarterly, 1982-91. Recipient Meritorious Course award, 1980, Faculty Svc. award Nat. U. Continuing Edn. Assn., 1983; Medal of Merit, Soc. for Collegiate Journalists, 1979; named to Journalism Hall of Fame, Ball State U., 1987, named Magbazine Educator of the Year, 1999. Mem. Soc. Profl. Journalists, Assn. for Edn. in Journalism (Magazine Educator of Yr. 1999), Coll. Media Advisers (pres. 1971-75, Hall of Fame 1994), Soc. for Collegiate Journalists (pres. 1977-79), S.C. Press Assn., Assn. Schs. of Journalism and Mass Comms. (bd. dirs. 1993-95, v.p. 1995-96, pres.-elect 1996-97, pres. 1997-98), Coun. of Comm. Assn. (rep. 1997-98). Office: Winthrop Univ Dept Mass Communication Rock Hill SC 29733

CLICK, MARIANNE JANE, credit manager; b. Marion, Ohio, Aug. 2, 1949; d. Raymond E. and Martha C. (Robinson) C. BS in Edn., Ohio State U., 1971. Various positions Western Auto Supply, Delaware, Ohio, 1973-87; dept. mgr. Western Auto Supply, Kansas City, Mo., 1988-89, dir. revolving ops., 1989; mgr. credit/collections Yellow Freight Sys., Kansas City, MO, 1998. Bd. dirs. Consumer Credit Counseling Svcs., Kansas City, 1992—, sec., 1995-96, treas., 1996-97. Mem. Internat. Credit Assn. (cert. consumer credit exec.), Credit Assn. Greater Kansas City (bd. dirs. 1991—, 2nd v.p. 1995-96, 1st v.p. 1996-97, pres. 1997-98), Internat. Assn. Credit Card Investigators, Mchts. Rsch. Coun., Alpha Lambda Delta. Avocations: swimming, reading, spectator sports, travel, music. Office: Yellow Freight Sys 10990 Roe Ave Overland Park KS 66207

CLIETT, CHARLES BUREN, aeronautical engineer, educator, academic administrator; b. Montpelier, Miss., July 10, 1924; s. James Thomas and Sallie Lou (Saul) C.; m. Grace Holland Campbell, Dec. 25, 1946; children—Susan Marie, Charles Buren. B.S. in Aero. Engring, Ga. Inst. Tech., 1945, M.S. in Aero. Engring, 1950. Registered profl. engr., Miss. Faculty Miss. State U., 1947—, prof. aero. engring., 1957-91, prof. emeritus, 1991—, chmn. dept., 1960-91. Served to lt. (j.g.) USNR, 1943-46. Recipient Spl. Achievement award Miss. State U. Alumni Assn., 1987, Faculty award for Career Achievement Faculty of Coll. Engring., Miss. State U., 1988. Mem. Am. Soc. Engring. Edn., AIAA, Am. Legion, Nat. Soc. Profl. Engrs., Miss. Engring. Soc., Aerospace Dept. Chairpersons Assn. (pres. 1979), Tau Beta Pi, Sigma Gamma Tau. Mem. Christian Ch. Home: 638 Commerce St West Point MS 39773-3016 Office: Engring Rsch Ctr Miss State PO Box 6176 Mississippi State MS 39762-6176

CLIFF, JOHNNIE MARIE, mathematics and chemistry educator; b. Lamkin, Miss., May 10, 1935; d. John and Modest Alma (Lewis) Walton; m. William Henry Cliff, Apr. 1, 1961 (dec. 1983); 1 child, Karen Marie. BA in Chemistry, Math., U. Indpls., 1956; postgrad., NSF Inst., Butler U., 1960; MA in Chemistry, Ind. U., 1964; MS in Math., U. Notre Dame, 1980. Cert. tchr., Ind. Rsch. chemist Ind. U. Med. Ctr., Indpls., 1956-59; tchr. sci. and math. Indpls. Pub. Schs., 1960-88; tchr. chemistry, math. Martin U., Indpls., 1989—, chmn. math. dept., 1990—, divsn. chmn. depts. sci. and math., 1993—; adj. instr. math. U. Indpls., 1991. Contbr. rsch. papers to sci. jours. Grantee NSF, 1961-64, 73-76, 78-79, Woodrow Wilson Found., 1987-88; scholarship U. Indpls., 1952-56, NSF Inst. Reed Coll., 1961, C. of C., 1963. Mem. AAUW, NAACP, NEA, Assn. Women in Sci., Urban League, N.Y. Acad. Scis., Am. Chem. Soc., Nat. Coun. Math. Tchrs., Am. Assn. Physics Tchrs., Nat. Sci. Tchrs. Assn., Am. Statis. Assn., Am. Assn. Ret. Persons, Neal-Marshall-Ind. U. Alumni Assn., U. Indpls. Alumni Assn., U. Notre Dame Alumni Assn., Ind. U. Chemist Assn., Notre Dame Club Indpls., Kappa Delta Pi, Delta Sigma Theta. Democrat. Baptist. Avocations: gardening, sewing. Home: 405 Golf Ln Indianapolis IN 46260-4108 Office: Martin U 2171 Avondale Pl Indianapolis IN 46218-3878

CLIFF, STEVEN BURRIS, engineering executive; b. Knoxville, Tenn., Mar. 30, 1952; s. Edgar Burris and Otella (Patterson) C.; m. Sharon Grace Davis, Sept. 11, 1971 ; children: Sarah Elizabeth, Susan Rebecca, Steven John. BS in Engring. Sci., U. Tenn., 1974, MS in Engring. Sci., 1976; postgrad., So. Sem., 1974-75. Rsch. asst. U. Tenn., Knoxville, 1972-75, asst. rsch. prof., 1975-76; program analyst Oak Ridge (Tenn.) Nat. Lab., 1976-77, rsch. engr., 1977-79; chief tech. officer Computer Concepts Corp., Knoxville, 1979-81; pres. Productive Programming Inc., Knoxville, 1981-82; v.p. R&D Control Tech. Inc., Knoxville, 1982-98, sr. v.p. R&D, 1998—, corp. sec., 1991—; ptnr. Middlebrook Indsl. Properties, 1985—, Cliff Bros. Investments, 1988—. Contbr. articles to profl. jours. Exec. bd. Rocky Hill Parent-Tchr. Orgn., Knoxville, 1987, 91-97, pres. 1994-95; deacon West Knoxville Bapt. Ch., 1984-87, Loveland Bapt. Ch., Knoxville, 1976-82; tech. com. Bearden (Tenn.) Mid. Sch., 1996-97; bd. dirs. Rocky Hill Baseball League, 1995—. U. Tenn. scholar, 1970. Mem. Soc. Mfgs. Engrs. (sr.), Nat. Electronic Mfg. Assn. (chmn. com. 1987-94, seminar spkr. 1988-94), Am. Assn. for Artificial Intelligence, Instrument Soc. Am., Open DeviceNet Vendors Assn. (com. chair 1998—). Avocations: photography, home improvement projects, fishing, bluegrass guitar. Home: 8210 Northshore Dr SW Knoxville TN 37919-8711

CLIFF, WALTER CONWAY, lawyer; b. Detroit, Jan. 2, 1932; s. Frank V. and Virginia L. (Conway) C.; m. Ursula McHugh, Nov. 5, 1960; children: Walter C., Mary F., Catherine C. B.S., U. Detroit, 1955, LL.B., 1955; LL.M., NYU, 1956. Bar: Mich. 1956, N.Y. 1958. Assoc. firm Cahill Gordon & Reindel, N.Y.C., 1958-66, ptnr., 1966—; pres. Walter C. Cliff, P.C., N.Y.C., 1982—. Bd. dirs. Florence Gould Found., N.Y.C., 1983—; bd. dirs. Austen Riggs Center, Stockbridge, Mass., 1983-89, Geoffrey Hughes Found., 1992—; mem. Collections com. Harvard U. Art Mus., 1992—. Served with U.S. Army, 1956-58. J.K. Lasser fellow NYU, 1955-56. Mem. ABA, Assn. of Bar of City of N.Y., N.Y. Bar Assn. Democrat. Roman Catholic. Clubs: Down Town, Stockbridge Golf. Office: Cahill Gordon & Reindel 80 Pine St Fl 17 New York NY 10005-1790

CLIFFORD, EDWARD R., municipal official; b. Nov. 30, 1962. BA, U. Dayton (Ohio), 1985; MPA, U. Maine, 1989. Asst. twp. mgr. Lower Gwynedd Twp., Spring House, Pa., 1990-93; twp. mgr. Lower Gwynedd Twp., Spring House, 1993-97; asst. city mgr. City of Norwich (Conn.), 1997—. E-mail: eclifford@cityofnorwich.org.

CLIFFORD, EUGENE THOMAS, lawyer; b. Utica, N.Y., July 15, 1941; s. James Anthony and Mary Margaret (Ellard) C.; m. Joyce Victoria Siwinski, Sept. 4, 1965; children: Michael Sean, Elizabeth Joyce, Thomas More. BA, Boston Coll., 1963, LLB, 1966. Bar: N.Y. 1967, U.S. Dist. Ct. (we. dist.) N.Y. 1967. Assoc. Chamberlain, D'Amanda, Bauman, Chatman & Oppenheimer, Rochester, N.Y., 1967-72, Lamb, Webster, Walz, Telesca & Donovan, Rochester, 1972-76; ptnr. Webster, Sullivan, Santoro & Clifford, Rochester, 1976-86, Fulreader, Rosenthal, Sullivan, Clifford, Santoro & Kaul, Rochester, 1986—. Bd. dirs. N.Y. state divsn. Am. Cancer Soc., Syracuse, 1972-78, 82-88, 90-97, chmn. bd. dirs., 1982-83, nat. bd. dirs., 1991-97; bd. dirs. Urban League of Rochester, 1988-91. Recipient Nat. Bronze award N.Y. state divsn. Am. Cancer Soc., 1984, Hope award Monroe County unit, 1983. Office: 1350 Midtown Tower Rochester NY 14604-2010

CLIFFORD, GEORGE W., college administrator; b. Rome, N.Y., Aug. 18, 1952; s. George William Clifford and M. Elizabeth Wheeler. BS, SUNY, Oneonta, 1974; MPA, SUNY, Albany, 1978, PhD with distinction, 1992. Dir. grants mgmt. AIDS program N.Y. Dept. Health, N.Y.C., 1987; dir. contracts and grants N.Y.C. Human Resources Adminstrn., 1987-89; AIDS coord. N.Y. OMB, N.Y.C., 1989-90; adminstr. AIDS program Albany (N.Y.) Med. Ctr., 1991—; cons. HIV Health and Human Svc. Planning Coun., N.Y.C., 1990-91. Author: The AIDS Epidemic: 1980-1989, 1991. Bd. dirs. Support Ministries, Waterford, N.Y., 1992-94, Names Project of the Capital, Albany, 1997—; co-chmn. bd. dirs. N.E. N.Y. Ryan White Steering Com., Albany, 1995-97. Grantee N.Y. State Dept. Health, 1996, 97,98, Health Rsch., Inc., 1997, 98, 99, U.s. HHS/HRSA, 1998. Mem. APHA, ASPA, Am. Polit. Sci. Assn. Home: 1 North St Delmar NY 12054 Office: Albany Med Coll 47 New Scotland Ave Albany NY 12208

CLIFFORD, JAY, artist; b. Worcester, Mass., Sept. 22, 1954; s. James L. and Lois (Brown) C. Student, Worcester Art Mus. Sch., 1990, Boston Mus. Sch., 1979, Boston Mus. Sch.; BA in English, Conn. Coll., 1998; postgrad., Mass. Coll. Art. Case worker Devereaux Sch., Rutland, Mass., 1988-98; represented by Rotenberg Gallery, Boston, Copley Soc. and Greiger Assocs., Boston; residential counselor CASCAP, Inc., Cambridge, Mass., 1998-99. One man shows include Montserrat Coll. Art, 1994, AS 220, Providence, R.I., 1995, Bromfield Gallery, Boston, 1995, Heywood Gallery, Worcester, 1996, Zeitgeist Gallery, Cambridge, Mass., 1996, Anna Maria Coll., Paxton, Mass., 1997, Copley Soc., Boston, 1997, San Francisco State U., 1998, Quansigamond C.C., Worcester, 1998, Zeitgeist Gallery, Cambridge, Mass., 1999; exhibited in group shows at Artworks Gallery, Hartford, 1992, 96, Slater Meml. Mus., Norwich, Conn., 1992, 93, Arts Worcester, 1993, 95, Hera Gallery, Wakefield, R.I., 1993, Nat. Arts Club, N.Y.C., 1994, 95, Berkshire Mus., Pittsfield, Mass., 1994, Contemporary Artist Ctr., North Adams, Mass., 1994, Copely Soc., Boston, 1994, 95, 97, 98, N.E. Mo. State U., 1995, Springfield (Mass.) Art Mus., 1995, Brown U. Sarah Doyle Gallery, 1995, Providence Art Club, 1995, Fitchburg (Mass.) Art Mus., 1992, 93, 94, 95, 99, Concord (Mass.) Art Assn., 1995, Pleides Gallery, N.Y.C., 1995, Ward-Nasse Gallery, N.Y.C., 1995, Ctrl. Mo. State U., 1996, Ceres Gallery, N.Y.C., 1996, U. Hartford, 1996, Stamford Mus., 1996, Ea. Conn. State U., 1996, Faber Birren Nat. Colar Show, Stamford, 1994, 96, 97, Chuck Levitan Gallery, N.Y.C., 1996, 97, Viridian Artists, N.Y.C., 1997, Gallery 84, N.Y.C., 1997, Judi Rotenberg Gallery, Boston, 1998, Truman State U., 1998, Nebr. Wesleyan U., 1998, Lamar U., Tex., 1998, Pleides Gallery, N.Y.C., 1998, No Bias Gallery, North Benington, Vt., 1998, Barrett House Galleries, Poughkeepsie, NY, 1998, Mass. Coll. Art, Boston, 1998, Heywood Gallery, Worcester, Mass., 1998, Worcester Cmty. Found., 1999, others. Recipient Juror's award Cape Cod Art Assn., 1993, Copley Soc., 1995, Providence Art Club, 1995, Conn. Acad. Fine Arts, 1996, Outstanding Merit award Art Ctr. No. N.J., 1999. Mem. Copley Soc., Conn. Acad. Fine Arts, Arts Worcester, Heywood Galley, Cambridge Art Assn. Home: 51 Hollywood St Worcester MA 01610-1346

CLIFFORD, LAWRENCE M., real estate company executive; b. Bronxville, N.Y., 1955. Grad., St. Lawrence U., 1977; MBA, Babson Coll., 1979. Pres., CEO Clifford Property Co./DBA Coldwell Banker Preferred Realty, Longmont, Colo. Home: 7282 Augusta Dr Boulder CO 80301-3795

CLIFFORD, MARGARET LOUISE, psychologist; b. Lakeland, Fla., Dec. 13, 1920; d. Thomas Saxon and Beatrice (Tillie) C.; m. Charles Robert Davis, Apr. 4, 1950; children: Daniel Thomas Davis, Kelly Owen Davis. BA in Edn., Chapman Coll., Orange, Calif., 1950; MS in Cons. & Sch. Psycho, San Diego State U., Calif., 1972; PhD Psychology, The Union Inst., Cin., 1976. Tchr. Elem. schs., Blythe, San Diego., Calif., 1950-68; columnist Daily Midway Driller, Taft, Calif., 1955; owner, operator Marge Davis Sch. Dance, Blythe, Calif., 1961-64; psychologist U.S. Peace Corps, Kingston, Jamaica, 1973-76, Apalachee Community Mental Health Ctr., Talahassee, Fla., 1977-80; coordinator of elderly services Beth Johnson Community Mental Health Ctr., Orlando, Fla., 1980-83; crisis support counselor Mental Health Services of Orange County, Orlando, 1983-88; supr. therapist Peace River Ctr. for Personal Devel., Bartow, Fla., 1988-89; therapist pvt. practice, Winter Garden, Fla., 1989—; guest speaker Fla. So. Coll., Orlando, 1981-82, Rollins Coll., Winter Park, Fla. Organizer, bd. pres. Widowed Person Svc. Orange County, Orlando; bd. dirs. Coun. on Aging, sec., 1982-85; mem. adv. bd. Cmty. Care for the Elderly, Orange County, Fla., 1992-95. Mem. Fla. Coun. Community Mental Health (pres. 1978-81), Am. Psychol. Assn. Avocations: traveling, scuba diving, drawing. Home: 223 N Central Ave Winter Garden FL 34787-2761 *When life deals out it's hardest and most painful experiences, I have finally learned to take several deep breathes and face up to what has to be done. The pain and hardship is a small price to pay for the insights and knowledge that can surely grow from every difficult experience.*

CLIFFORD, MAURICE CECIL, physician, former college president, foundation executive; b. Washington, Aug. 9, 1920; s. Maurice C. and Rosa P. (Linberry) C.; m. Patricia Marie Johnson, June 15, 1945; children: Maurice Cecil III, Jay P.L., Rosemary Clifford McDaniel. AB, Hamilton Coll., 1941, ScD, 1982; AM, U. Chgo., 1942; MD, Meharry Med. Coll., 1947; LHD, LaSalle Coll., 1981, Hamilton Coll., 1982, Hahnemann U., 1985, Meharry Med. Coll., 1992; LLD, Med. Coll. Pa., 1986. Diplomate Am. Bd. Ob-Gyn. Intern Phila. Gen. Hosp., 1947-48, resident in ob-gyn, 1948-51, asst. chief service ob-gyn, 1951-60; mem. faculty Med. Coll. Pa., Phila., 1955—, prof. ob-gyn., 1975-91, prof. emeritus, 1992—, v.p. for med. affairs, 1978-80, pres., 1980-86, trustee, 1980-96, pres. emeritus, 1992—; commr. pub. health City of Phila., 1986-92; chmn. HMA Found., Phila., 1991-93; exec. v.p. The Lomax Co., Chalfont, Pa., 1993-96; pres. The Lomax Companies, Chalfont, Pa., 1996-98. Contbr. articles to profl. jours. Former trustee Phila. Award, Phila. Art Mus., 1982-93; hon. trustee Phila. Coll. Textiles and Sci., 1982-94; trustee emeritus Phila. Acad. Natural Scis.; life trustee Meharry Med. Coll.; trustee Allegheny U. Health Scis., 1996-98; former alumnus trustee Hamilton Coll.; mem. nat. med. com. Planned Parenthood, 1975-78; mem. adv. com. on arts John F. Kennedy Ctr. for Performing Arts, 1978-80. Capt. M.C., U.S. Army, 1952-54. Recipient Dr. Martin Luther King, Jr. award PUSH, 1981, Dr. William H. Gray, Jr. award Educators Roundtable Assn., 1981, Ann. award Phila. Tribune Charities, 1981, Disting. Am. award Edn. and Rsch. Fund Am. Found. for Negro Affairs, 1980; Outstanding Svc. award Phila. br. NAACP, 1965, others. Fellow Am. Coll. Obstetricians and Gynecologists (life); mem. Nat. Med. Assn., Pa. Med. Soc., Med. Soc. Eastern Pa., Philadelphia County Med. Soc., Phi Beta Kappa, Alpha Omega Alpha.

CLIFFORD, BROTHER PETER, academic administrator, religious educator; b. N.Y.C., Feb. 17, 1925; s. Peter and Mary (Lynch) C. AB, Manhattan Coll., 1950; MA, Fordham U., 1957; EdD, Harvard U., 1970; EdD (hon.), St. Mary's Coll., Winona, Minn., 1987. Cert. sch. supt., N.Y. Tchr., prin. Cath. schs., N.Y.C., 1947-57; dean De La Salle Coll., Manila, 1957-61; asst. prin. Bishop Loughlin High Sch., Bklyn., 1962-64; assoc. supt. schs. Diocese Bklyn., 1968-71; exec. sec. Nat. Cath. Edn. Assn., Washington, 1971-74; assoc. dean edn. St. John U., N.Y.C., 1974-76; pres. St. Mary's Coll., Winona, Minn., 1976-84; provincial Bros. Christian Schs., Narragansett, R.I., 1984-87; staff asst. higher edn. U.S. Cath. Conf., Washington, 1987-89; pres. St. Mary Coll., Leavenworth, Kans., 1989-94; dir. fin. Narragansett Christian Bros. Ctr., 1994—. Mem. Leavenworth Area Devel., 1989-94; trustee Christian Bros. Investment Svcs., 1994—, Christian Bros. Svcs.,

1994—; mem. bd. regents La Salle Acad., Providence, 1994-96; mem. diocesan sch. bd. Diocese of Providence, 1994—. Recipient Avila award Coll. St. Teresa, Winona. Mem. Kans. Ind. Coll. Assn., Kans. Ind. Coll. Fund, Bros. of the Christian Schs (Christian Bro. 1943—).

CLIFFORD, ROBERT WILLIAM, state supreme court justice; b. Lewiston, Maine, May 2, 1937; s. William H. and Alice (Sughrue) C.; m. Clementina Radillo, Jan. 18, 1964; children: Laurence M., Matthew P. BA, Bowdoin Coll., 1959; LLB, Boston Coll., 1962; LLM in Jud. Process, U. Va., 1998. Bar: Maine 1962, U.S. Dist. Ct. Maine 1965. Ptnr. Clifford & Clifford, Lewiston, 1964-79; justice Maine Superior Ct., Auburn, 1979-83, chief justice, 1984-86; assoc. justice Maine Supreme Jud. Ct., Auburn, 1986—. Mem. Lewiston City Coun., 1968-70, mayor, 1971-72; mem. Maine State Senate, 1973-76; chmn. Lewiston Charter Commn., 1978-79; mem. Maine Probate Law Revision Commn., 1973-79. Mem. Maine Bar Assn., Androscoggin County Bar Assn., Am. Judicature Soc. Roman Catholic. Home: 14 Nelke Pl Lewiston ME 04240-5318 Office: Maine Supreme Jud Ct PO Box 3488 Auburn ME 04212-3488

CLIFFORD, STEVEN FRANCIS, science research director; b. Boston, Jan. 4, 1943; s. Joseph Nelson and Margaret Dorothy (Savage) C.; children from previous marriage: Cheryl Ann, Michelle Lynn, David Arthur; m. Theresa Kavanagh, Aug. 1996. BSEE, Northeastern U., Boston, 1965; PhD, Dartmouth Coll., 1969. Postdoctoral fellow NRC, Boulder, Colo., 1969-70; physicist Wave Propagation Lab., NOAA, Boulder, 1970-82, program chief, 1982-87, dir. environ. tech. lab., 1987—; mem. electromagnetic propagation panel, NATO, 1989-93; vis. sci. closed acad. city Tomsk, Siberia, USSR. Author: (with others) Remote Sensing of the Troposhpere, 1978; contbr. 125 articles to profl. jours.; patentee in acoustic scintillation liquid flow measurement, single-ended optical spatial filter. Recipient 5 Outstanding publs. awards Dept. Commerce, 1972, 75, 89, 96, Outstanding Career Performance, U.S. Presidential award, 1998. Fellow Optical Soc. Am. (editor atmospheric optics 1978-84, advisor atmospheric optics 1982-84), Acoustical Soc. Am.; mem. IEEE (sr.), Nat. Acad. Engring., Internat. Radio Sci. Union, Am. Geophys. Union; inducted NAE. Avocations: running, cross country skiing. Office: NOAA Environ Tech Lab 325 Broadway St Boulder CO 80303-3337

CLIFFORD, STEWART BURNETT, banker; b. Boston, Feb. 17, 1929; s. Stewart Hilton and Ellinor (Burnett) C.; m. Cornelia Park Woolley, Apr. 26, 1952; children: Cornelia Lee Wareham, Rebecca Lyn Mailer-Howat, Jennifer Leggett Danner, Stewart Burnett. AB, Harvard U., 1951, MBA, 1956. Asst. cashier Citibank, N.A., N.Y.C., 1958-60, asst. v.p., 1960-63; exec. v.p., gen. mgr. Merc Bank, Montreal, Que., Can., 1963-67, v.p. planning Overseas div., 1967-68; v.p., adminstr. comml. banking group Citibank, N.Y.C., 1969-72; v.p. head world corp. dept. Citibank, London, 1973-75; sr. v.p. domestic energy Citibank, N.Y.C., 1975-80, sr. v.p., head pvt. banking and investment div., 1981-87, div. exec., head investment div., 1987-93; sr. banker Pvt. Bank U.S., 1993-94; cons. Munn Bernhard & Assocs., N.Y.C., 1995—; dir. Monumental Corp., Balt., 1974-89. Pres. 120 East End Ave. Corp., Woolley-Clifford Found.; life trustee Spence Sch.; vice chmn. Neighborhood Com. for Asphalt Green; elder and trustee Brick Ch.; trustee YWCA, N.Y.C., Princeton Theol. Seminary, Presbyn. Ch. (USA) Found.; mem. com. univ. resources Harvard Coll. Republican. Clubs: Pilgrims, Union, University (N.Y.C.); Duxbury Yacht (Mass.), Bath & Tennis (Palm Beach). Avocations: squash, tennis. Home: 120 E End Ave New York NY 10028-7552 Office: Munn Bernhard & Assocs 6 E 43rd St New York NY 10017-4609

CLIFFORD, WALTER JESS, microbiologist, immunologist; b. Safford, Ariz., July 18, 1944; s. Walter Elijah, Jr. and Helen (Taylor) C.; m. Laura Bigler Clifford, Dec. 15, 1967; children: Jess. A., Terri L., Vera L., Jerald G., Joseph L. Rachel D., Jason C., Eva R. Student, Eastern Ariz. Coll., Thatcher, 1963, 65; BS, U. Ariz., Tucson, 1968, MS, 1975. Registered Microbiologist (Am. Acad. of Microbiology). Officer U.S. Army, 1968-72; staff microbiologist Tucson Med. Ctr., Tucson, 1972-73; tech. dir. Cochise Pathology Cons., Sierra Vista, Ariz., 1973-75; lab supr./dir. S.E. Svcs., Inc., Sierra Vista, Ariz., 1975-77, Benson Health Svc., Benson, Ariz., 1977-78; dir. of tech. svc. AID Lab., Richardson, Tex., 1978-80; v.p., tech. Bio Med Labs., N. Hollywood, Calif., 1980-83; dir. of rsch. Toxic Element Rsch. Found., Colorado Springs, Colo/, 1986-88; pres. and dir. Clifford Consulting and Rsch., Colorado Springs, Colo., 1982—; instr. Cochise Coll., Douglas, Ariz., 1977-78; UT Tech. Coll., Provo, UT, 1985-86. Author: Biomaterials Microbiology, 1980, 86, 90. Sch. Bd. Mem. Westside Union Sch. Dist., Rotary Club Mem. Rotary, Internat., Ad hoc steering com. Nat. Registry for Microbiologists. Recipient Phillip Hoekstra Memorial Lecture, Great Lakes Assn. for Alternative Medicine, Provisional Approval Materials Reactivity Testing Protocol, Internat. Acad. of Oral Medicine and Toxicology. Fellow Internat. Acad. Oral Medicine and Toxicology; mem. Am. Soc. for Microbiology, Am. Assn. for the Advancement of Sci., Am. Chemical Soc., N.Y. Acad. of Sci., Nat. Registry for Microbiologists, Am. Assn. for Clin. Chemistry. Republican. Mem LDS Ch. Avocations: aviation, gardening, music, photography. Office: Clifford Consulting & Rsch 2275 Waynoka Rd Ste J Colorado Springs CO 80915-1635

CLIFT, ELEANOR, magazine correspondent; b. Bklyn., July 7, 1940; d. Erk and Inna Roeloffs; m. Brooks Clift, 1964-1981; children: Edward, Woodbury, Robert; m. Tom Brazaitis, 1989. Student, Hofstra U., Hunter Coll. Former White House corr. now contbg. editor Newsweek; commentator The McLaughlin Group, also Fox News Channel. Co-author: War Without Bloodshed: The Art of Politics, 1996. Office: Newsweek Washington Bur 1750 Pennsylvania Ave NW Washington DC 20006-4502

CLIFT, G. W., critic; b. Winfield, Kansas, May 27, 1952; s. W.S. Clift and Jane Lee Marsh; m. D. Cheryl Collins, May 26, 1975; 1 child, John Wesley. BS in History, Kans. St. U., Manhattan, 1974, MA in English, 1979. Instr. Kans. St. U. English Dept., Manhattan, 1976-95; editor Kans. Quar., Manhattan, 1991-95, Lit. Mag. Rev., Cedar Falls, Iowa, 1979—; critic Manhattan Mercury, Manhattan, 1987—. Author: Britain 101, 1989, Mustaches, 1996. Recipient Seaton award, 1984. Methodist. E-mail: gwclift@ksu.edu. Home: 1724 Fairchild Ave Manhattan KS 66502-4038 Office: Lit Mag Review English Dept UNI Cedar Falls IA 50613

CLIFT, WILLIAM BROOKS, III, photographer; b. Boston, Jan. 5, 1944; s. William Brooks C. and Anne (Pearmain) Thomson; m. Vida Regina Chesnulis, Aug. 8, 1970; children: Charis, Carola, William. Free lance comml. photographer in partnership with Steve Gersh under name Helios, 1963-71; pres. William Clift Ltd., Santa Fe, 1980-85; cons. Polaroid Corp., 1965-67. Photographer one-man shows, Carl Siembab Gallery, Boston, 1969, Mus. Art, U. Oreg., Eugene, 1969, New Boston City Hall Gallery, 1970, U. Mass., Berkshire Mus., Pittsfield, Mass., William Coll., Addison Gallery of Am. Art, Wheaton Coll., Mass., Worcester Art Mus., 1971, Creative Photography Gallery, MIT, 1972, St. John's Coll. Art Gallery, Santa Fe, 1973, Wiggin Gallery, Boston Pub. Library, 1974, Australian Ctr. for Photography, Sydney, 1978, Susan Spiritus Gallery, Newport Beach, Calif., 1979, MIT Creative Photography Gallery, 1980, William Lyons Gallery, Coconut Grove, Fla., 1980, Eclipse Gallery, Boulder, Colo., 1980, Atlanta Gallery of Photography, 1980, Phoenix Art Mus., 1981, Jeb Gallery, Providence, 1981, Portfolio Gallery, 1981, Images Gallery, Cin., 1982, Boston Atheneum, 1983, Bank of Santa Fe, 1984, Susan Harder Gallery, N.Y.C., 1984, Cleve. Art Mus., 1985, Art Inst. Chgo., 1987, Amon Carter Mus., Ft. Worth, 1987, Clarence Kennedy Gallery, Cambridge, Mass., 1988, Equitable Gallery, N.Y.C., 1993, Vassar Coll. Art Mus., N.Y., 1994, Vassar Coll. Art Gallery, N.Y., 1995; exhibited in group shows Gallery 216, N.Y., N.Y. Grover Cronin Gallery, Waltham, Mass., 1964, Carl Seimbab Gallery, Boston, 1966, Lassall Jr. Coll., 1967, Hill's Gallery, Santa Fe, Tyler Mus. Art, Austin, Tex., Dupree Gallery, Dallas, 1974, Quindacqua Gallery, Washington, 1978, Zabriskie Gallery, Paris, 1978, Am. Cultural Ctr., Paris, 1978; photographer AT&T Project-Am. Images, 1978, Seagram's Bicentennial Project, Courthouse, 1975-77, Readers Digest Assn. Project, 1984, Hudson River Project, 1985-92; author: Photography Portfolios, Old Boston City Hall, 1971, Photography Portfolios, Courthouse, 1979, Photography Portfolios, New Mexico, 1975, Certain Places, Photographs, 1987, A Hudson Landscape, Photographs, 1993. Nat. Endowment for Arts photography fellow, 1972, 79; Guggenheim fellow, 1974, 80, N.Mex. Gov.'s Excellence in The Arts award, 1987. Home and Office: PO Box 6035 Santa Fe NM 87502-6035

CLIFTON, ANNE RUTENBER, psychotherapist; b. New Haven, Dec. 11, 1938; d. Ralph Dudley and Cleminette (Downing) Rutenber; 1 dau., Dawn Anne. BA, Smith Coll., 1960, MSW, 1962. Diplomate in Clin. Social Work. Psychiat. case worker adult psychiatry unit Tufts-New Eng. Med. Ctr., Boston, 1962-68, supr. students, 1967-68; pvt. practice psychotherapy, Cambridge, Mass., 1966—; supr. med. students, staff social workers outpatient psychiatry Tufts New Eng. Med. Ctr., 1973—, also mem. exec. bd. Women's Resource Ctr., interim co-dir., 1986-88. Lic. clin. social worker, Mass. asst. clin. prof. psychiatry Tufts U. Med. Sch., 1974—, research dept. psychiatry, 1966-68, 73, 77—. Mem. Acad. Cert. Social Workers, Nat. Assn. Social Workers, Phi Beta Kappa, Sigma Xi. Clubs: Cambridge Tennis, Mt. Auburn Tennis. Contbr. articles to profl. jours. Home: 126 Homer St Newton MA 02459-1518 Office: 59 Church St Ste 4 Cambridge MA 02138-3724

CLIFTON, DAVID SAMUEL, JR., research executive, economist; b. Raleigh, N.C., Nov. 15, 1943; s. David Samuel and Ruth Centelle (Paker) C.; m. Karen Lisette Buhrer (div. June 1980); children: Derek Scott, Mark David; m. Eileen Lois Cooley, July 30, 1983; children: Dana Cooley, Michael Cooley. B in Indsl. Engring., Ga. Inst. Tech., 1966; MBA in Econs., Ga. State U., 1970, PhD in Econs., 1980. Customer facilities engr. Lockheed Ga. Co., Marietta, 1966-70; prin. rsch. scientist Ga. Tech. Rsch. Inst., Atlanta, 1970-93, dir. econ. devel. lab., 1979-90, dir. econ. devel. and tech. transfer, 1990-93, dir. Ctr. for Internat. Stds. and Quality, 1991-99; acting exec. assoc. dir. Ga. Tech. Econ. Devel. Inst., Atlanta, 1993-94, group dir. ctrs. Econ. Devel. Inst.,, 1998-99, group dir. bus. and industry, 1999—; bd. dirs. Sea Adventure Unltd., Inc., Atlanta; cons. UN Indsl. Devel. Orgn., Vienna, 1982, Inst. de Adminstn. Cientifica de los Empreos, Mexico City, 1978; apptd. by gov. So. Tech. Coun., Rsch. Triangle Park, N.C., 1992—. Coauthor: Project Feasibility Analysis, 1977; contbr. articles to profl. jours. Mem. Am. Econs. Assn., Atlanta Power Squadron Club, Sigma Xi. Avocation: sailing, navigating. Home: 2486 Williamswood Ct Decatur GA 30033-2810 Office: Ga Tech Ctr Internat Stds & Quality Atlanta GA 30332-0640

CLIFTON, DOUGLAS C., newspaper editor; b. Bklyn., July 14, 1943; s. Norman Stanton and Anne Frances (Montesano) C.; m. Margaret E. Clifton, Dec. 18, 1965; children: Amy Elizabeth Clifton Gallup, Clay Norman. BA Polit. Sci., Dowling Coll., 1965. Reporter, editor Miami Herald, 1970-87; news editor Knight Ridder, Washington, 1987-89; mng. editor Charlotte (N.C.) Observer, 1989-91; sr. v.p., exec. editor Miami Herald, 1991-99; exec. editor Plain Dealer, Cleve., 1999—. Lt. U.S. Army, 1966-69, Vietnam. Home: 4085 Battersea Rd Coconut Grove FL 33133-6601 Office: Plain Dealer 1801 Superior Ave NE Cleveland OH 44114*

CLIFTON, JAMES ALBERT, physician, educator; b. Fayetteville, N.C., Sept. 18, 1923; s. James Albert, Jr. and Flora M. (McNair) C.; m. Katherine Rathe, June 25, 1949; children—Susan M. (dec.), Katherine Y., Caroline M. B.A., Vanderbilt U., 1944, M.D., 1947. Diplomate: Am. Bd. Internal Medicine (mem. 1972-81, mem. subsplty. bd. gastroenterology 1968-75, chmn. 1972-75, mem. exec. com. 1978-81, chmn. 1980-81). Intern U. Hosps., Iowa City, Iowa, 1947-48; resident dept. medicine U. Hosps., 1948-51; staff dept. medicine Thayer VA Hosp., Nashville, 1952-53; asst. clin. medicine Vanderbilt Hosp., Nashville, 1952-53; cons. physician VA Hosp., Iowa City, 1965-93; assoc. medicine dept. internal medicine Coll. Medicine, U. Iowa, 1953-54, chief div. gastroenterology, 1953-71, asst. prof. medicine, 1954-58, assoc. prof., 1958-63, prof., 1963-91, prof. emeritus, 1991—, traveling fellow, 1964, vis. prof. dept. physiology, 1964, vice chmn. dept. medicine, 1967-70, chmn. dept. medicine Coll. Medicine, 1970-76, Roy J. Carver prof. medicine, 1974-91, Roy J. Carver prof. emeritus, 1991—, dir. James A. Clifton Ctr. Digestive Diseases, 1985-90, interim dean, 1991-93; investigator Mt. Desert Isle Biol. Lab., Salisbury Cove, Maine, 1964; vis. faculty mem. Mayo Found. and Mayo Clinic, 1966; vis. prof. dept. medicine U. N.C., Chapel Hill, 1970; cons. gastroenrology and nutrition tng. grants com. Nat. Inst. Arthritis and Metabolic Diseases, NIH, 1964-68, chmn., 1965-68; mem. Nat. Adv. Arthritis and Metabolic Diseases Coun., 1970-73; mem. gastroenterology tng. com. VA, Washington, 1967-71, chmn. tng. grants com., 1971-73; mem. med. adv. bd. Digestive Disease Found., 1969-73; vis. prof. gastroenterology U. London (St. Marks Hosp.), 1984-85; mem. sci. adv. com. Ludwig Inst. Cancer Rsch., Zurich, Switzerland, 1984-95. Mem. internat. editorial bd.: Italian Jour. Gastroenterology, 1970-90, Gastroenterology, 1964-68. Recipient Disting. Alumnus of Yr. award Vanderbilt U. Sch. Medicine, 1984; Phi Connell scholar Vanderbilt U., 1943-44; spl. rsch. fellow NIH, USPHS, 1955-56, fellow in medicine Evans Meml. Hosp., Mass. Meml. Hosps., also Boston U. Sch. Medicine, 1955-56. Fellow ACP (bd. regents 1972-79, pres. 1977-78 Alfred Stengel award 1984, Laureate award 1989); mem. Inst. Medicine of Nat. Acad. Scis., Am. Gastroent. Assn. (pres. 1970-71), AMA (liaison com. grad. med. edn. 1976-77), Am. Heart Assn., Am. Assn. Study Liver Disease, Am. Soc. Internal Medicine (Internist of Yr. award Iowa chpt. 1986), AAAS, Am. Fedn. Clin. Research, Am. Clin. and Climatol. Assn. (v.p. 1984), Assn. Am. Physicians, AAUP, Soc. Exptl. Biology and Medicine, Am. Physiol. Soc., Assn. Am. Med. Colls., Assn. Profs. Medicine (councillor 1972-73, sec.-treas. 1973-75), Internat. Soc. Internal Medicine (exec. com. 1978-80), U. Iowa Retirees Assn. (pres.-elect). Home: 2620 Newport Rd NE Iowa City IA 52240-7852 Office: U Iowa Hosp and Clinics 4 JCP Hawkins Dr Iowa City IA 52242

CLIFTON, JAMES K., market research company executive. CEO mktg. Gallup, Inc., Lincoln, Nebr. Office: Gallup Inc 300 S 68th Street Pl Lincoln NE 68510-2449*

CLIFTON, JUDY RAELENE, association administrator; b. Safford, Ariz., Nov. 8, 1946; d. Ralph Newton and Fayrene (Goodner) Johnson; student Biola Coll., 1964-65; BA in Christian Edn., Southwestern Coll., 1970; married. Editl. asst. Accent Publications, Denver, 1970-73; expediter Phelps Dodge Corp., Douglas, Ariz., 1974-78; exec. asst. So. Ariz. Internat. Livestock Assn., Inc., Tucson, 1978-81; adminstrv. asst. Phelps Dodge Corp., 1981—; sec. exec. bd. PAC, Phelps Dodge, 1985-90. Mem. adv. bd. Ariz. Lung Assn.; mem. Silver City Arts Coun., 1986-90; mem. Am. Security Council, 1979-85; leader 4-H, Douglas; mem. Rep. Nat. Com., 1978—, Conservative Caucus, 1979-85; del. Quadrennial N.Mex. State Rep. Con., 1988, 92. Recipient Am. Legion Good Citizen award, 1964, DAR award, 1964. Mem. NAFE, DAR, Nat. Assn. Evangelicals, U.S. Tennis Assn., Nat. Right to Life, So. Ariz. Internat. Livestock Assn., AAUW, Eagle Forum, Freedom Found., N.Mex. Eagle Forum, Mus. N.Mex. Found., Lordsburg/Hidalgo County C. of C. (1st v.p bd. dirs. 1990-97), Concerned Women of Am., Sigma Lambda Delta. Baptist. Clubs: Trunk & Tusk, Pima County Republican, Centre Ct., Westerners Internat., So. Ariz. Depression Glass, Tucson Tennis, Rep. Senatorial. Home: Drawer M Playas NM 88009

CLIFTON, LUCILLE THELMA, author; b. Depew, N.Y., June 27, 1936; d. Samuel Louis and Thelma (Moore) Sayles; m. Fred James Clifton, May 10, 1958 (dec. Nov. 1984); children—Sidney, Fredrica, Channing, Gillian, Graham, Alexia. Student, Howard U., 1953-55, Fredonia (N.Y.) State Tchrs. Coll., 1955. Prof. literature and creative writing U. Calif., Santa Cruz, 1985—. Poet-in-residence, Coppin State Coll., Balt., 1972-76, Jenny Moore vis. writer, George Washington U., 1982-83. Author: Good Times, 1969, Good News About The Earth, 1972, An Ordinary Woman, 1974, Generations, 1976, Two-Headed Woman, 1980, Sonora Beautiful, 1981, Next, 1987, Good Woman, 1987; Everett Anderson books and other books for children; co-author: Free to Be You and Me, 1974 (Emmy award), Free To Be A Family. Named Poet Laureate, State of Md., 1979; Recipient Discovery award Poetry Center, 1969; YMHA grantee, 1969; Nat. Endowment Arts grantee, 1970, 72. Mem. Authors League, Author Guild, P.E.N.

CLIFTON, MARK STEPHEN, administrator; b. San Diego, May 25, 1955; s. Paul Clifford and Dorothy Jean (Gross) C.; m. Margaret Eileen Hower, July 20, 1985; 1 child, Casey Mariah. Student, Grossmont Coll., 1973-74, San Diego City Coll., 1981. Oper. supr. San Diego Unified Sch. Dist., 1979—; owner A Home Touch Housecleaning, San Diego, 1985—; speaker in field. Author: There Goes the Neighborhood, 1993; contbr. articles to profl. jours. Mem. Ocean Beach Town Coun., San Diego, 1993—. Recipient Hon. Svc. award PTA, Point Loma High Sch., 1989. Mem. San Diego Writers and Editor's Guild, Christian Writers Guild, Adminstrs. Assn., Maranatha Surfing Assn. (founder, pres. 1983-86), Christian Surfing Assn. (co-founder 1982-83). Republican. Avocations: surfing, golf, walking, exercise, Aikido-martial arts. Office: San Diego Unified Sch Dist 8460 Ruffner St San Diego CA 92111

CLIFTON, NELIDA, social worker; b. Buenos Aires, Argentina, Aug. 16, 1944; came to the U.S., 1968; d. Juan Antonio and Zaira Elizabeth (Vera) Tovar; m. Mark Earl Jolls, Nov. 8, 1968 (div. July 1984); children: Patricia Elizabeth, Michael Thomas, Diana Marie Kathleen; m. Anthony Gene Clifton, June 19, 1993. BA in Bus. Adminstrn., Nat. Sch. Commerce, Tucuman, Argentina; BA in Psychology magna cum laude, Fairleigh Dickinson U., 1986; postgrad., William Paterson Coll., 1988-89. Diplomate Am. Psychotherapy Assn.; lic. cert. social worker Bd. Social Work Examiners, N.J.; cert. bilingual. Social worker Bergen County Bd. Social Svcs., Rochelle Park, N.J., 1987—; Solid Rock Prison Ministry pen pal, crisi intervention vol., phone counsellor, cmty. resources referral profl. Prison ministry pen pal; church mem. Hawthorne Gospel Ch. Mem. APA, NASW, Phi Zeta Kappa, Phi Omega Epsilon, Psi Chi Nat. Honor Socs. Republican. Avocations: reading, chess, tennis, gardening. Home and Office: PO Box 8581 Saddle Brook NJ 07663-8581

CLIFTON, RODNEY JAMES, engineering educator, civil engineer, consultant; b. Orchard, Nebr., July 10, 1937; s. James Edward and Minnie Gertrude (Williamson) C.; m. Mercedes Bonde, Dec. 28, 1958; children: Mark Bradford, Jeffrey John, Gregg Andrew, Anne Michelle. B.S.C.E., U. Nebr., 1959; M.S.C.E., Carnegie Inst. Tech., 1961, Ph.D. in Civil Engring., 1964. Registered profl. engr., R.I. Interdisciplinary fellow Brown U., Providence, 1964-65, asst. prof. engring., 1965-68, assoc. prof., 1968-71, prof., 1971—, chmn. exec. com. div. engring., 1974-79, Rush C. Hawkins Univ. Prof., 1988—; dean engring., 1998—; vis. prof. materials sci. and engring. Stanford U., Calif., 1979-80; cons. in field; mem. Nat. Materials Adv. Bd. Commn. on Personnel Armor, 1968, Nat. Materials Adv. Bd. Commn. on Material Response to Ultra-High Loading Rates, 1978. Research, numerous publs. in solid mechanics with emphasis on dynamic plasticity, plate impact expts., hydraulic fracturing; assoc. editor: Jour. Applied Mechanics, 1980-86; editorial advisor Jour. of the Mechanics and Physics of Solids, 1982—. NSF sci. faculty fellow Southampton, Eng., 1971; NDEA fellow, 1960-63. Fellow Am. Acad. Mechanics; mem. NAE, ASCE, ASME (Melville medal 1981), Soc. Engring. Sci. (prs. 1982-83, Prager medal 1986), SPE, APS, MRS, SIAM, Sigma Xi, Phi Kappa Phi, Pi Mu Epsilon, Sigma Tau. Presbyterian. Fax: (401) 863-9983. E-mail: clifton@engin.brown.edu. Home: 18 Starbrook Dr Barrington RI 02806-3718 Office: Brown U Divsn Engring Box D Providence RI 02912

CLIFTON, RUSSELL B., banking and mortgage lending consultant, retired mortgage company executive; b. Maroa, Ill., Jan. 16, 1930; s. Russell Thomas and Clara Leoda (Luckenbill) C.; m. Mary Joyce Hartline, Oct. 10, 1948; 1 son, Steven Shawn. BA, Mich. State U., 1957. Bank auditor Arthur Andersen & Co., Detroit, 1957-59; v.p. Mich. Nat. Bank, Lansing, 1959-65; sr. v.p. Assoc. Mortgages Co., Kansas City, Mo., 1965-69; v.p. Fed. Nat. Mortgage Assn., Washington, 1969-85, ret., 1985; pres., chief exec. officer First Chesapeake Mortgage, Inc., Beltsville, Md., 1985-86, also bd. dirs.; cons. banking and mortgage lending, 1986—; mem. adv. com. Home Owner's Warranty Corp., Washington, 1978-81; bd. dirs., mem. exec. com., treas. Nat. Acad. Conciliators, Washington, 1979-91; bd. dirs. Lincoln Savs. & Loan (now Seasons Savs. Bank), Richmond, Va., 1987-89; bd. dirs., treas. Nat. Ctr. for Dispute Settlements, Washington, 1987-91. Served with U.S. Army, 1952-54. Named disting. fellow Nat. Assn. Cert. Mortgages Bankers, 1975. Mem. Phi Kappa Phi, Beta Alpha Psi, Beta Gamma Sigma, Tau Sigma. Methodist.

CLIFTON, THOMAS E., seminary president, minister; m. Audrey Vought; children: Sandra, Jill Clifton Mallard. Student, Duke Divinity Sch.; M in Divinity, Crozer Theol. Sem., Rochester, N.Y.; MS in Personnel Counseling, Wright State U., Dayton; D in Ministry, Princeton Theol. Sem. Pastor First Bapt. Ch., Perry, Ohio, 1967-70, Sidney, Ohio, 1970-73; assoc. pastor Binkley Bapt. Ch., Chapel Hill, N.C., 1973-77; pastor First Bapt. Ch., Lafayette, Ind., 1977-85, Penifield, N.Y., 1985-93; pres. Ctrl. Bapt. Theol. Sch., Kansas City, Kans., 1993—. Writer: Bapt. Leader, Capitol Report; (curriculum) Judson Press. Office: Ctrl Bapt Theol Sem 741 N 31st St Kansas City KS 66102-3964*

CLIFTON-SMITH, RHONDA DARLEEN, art center director; b. Dyersburg, Tenn., Mar. 19, 1954; d. Charles Burton Clifton and Mary Opal (Carter) Harris; m. Michael Frederick Smith, Feb. 14, 1980 (dec. Sept. 1981). BS in Art Edn., Columbus Coll., 1977; MA in Hist. Adminstrn., Eastern Ill. U., 1986. Asst. cataloging libr. Lawton (Okla.) Pub. Libr., 1978-79; registrar Mus. of the Great Plains, Lawton, 1979-82; curator Boot Hill Mus., Dodge City, Kans., 1982-94; exec. dir. Carnegie Ctr. for Arts, Dodge City, 1994—. Author: (booklet) Dodge City: The Early Years, 1985; co-author: (booklet) Cattle and Wheat: Agricultural Growth in 19th Century Dodge City, 1985. Mem. Am. Assn. Mus., Am. Assn. State & Local History (c-chair mem. com. 1990-92), Kan. Mus. Assn. (treas. 1989—, area rep. 1982-85), Mt. Plains Mus. Assn., Soroptimists Internat. Avocations: painting and drawing, theater. Office: Carnegie Ctr for Arts 701 2d Ave Dodge City KS 67801

CLIMAN, RICHARD ELLIOT, lawyer; b. N.Y.C., July 19, 1953; s. David Arthur and Mary (Vitale) C. AB cum laude, Harvard U., 1974, JD cum laude, 1977. Bar: Calif. 1977. Assoc. Pettit & Martin, San Francisco, 1977-83, ptnr., 1984-94; ptnr., head mergers and acquisitions group Cooley Godward LLP, Palo Alto, San Francisco, Calif., 1994—. Contbr. articles to profl. jours. Mem. ABA (sect. bus. law, vice chair com. on negotiated acquisitions). Home: 1 Tulip Ln San Carlos CA 94070-1551 Office: Cooley Godward LLP 5 Palo Alto Sq 3000 El Camino Real Palo Alto CA 94306-2120

CLINARD, JOSEPH HIRAM, JR., securities company executive; b. N.Y.C., Jan. 29, 1938; s. Joseph Sr. and Bertha (Feins) C.; m. Marcia Blyer, Sept. 1, 1958; children: Susan Clinard Jacobs, Robert. Cert., N.Y. Inst. Fin., 1962, Am. Coll., 1976, Adelphi U., 1980. Cert. fin. planner. Account exec. Merrill Lynch, N.Y.C., 1964-68; v.p. Shearson Lehman, N.Y.C., 1968-73; nat. dir. fin. planning Herzfeld & Stern, N.Y.C., 1974-78; v.p. Chem. Bank, N.Y.C., 1978-83; pres. DESCAP Securities, Inc., Hauppauge, N.Y., 1983-90; chmn. CEO North Shore Capital Mgmt. Corp., Melville, N.Y., 1990—; adj. prof. Adelphi U., Garden City, N.Y., 1980-90, asst. to dean, 1983-87; chief cons. Clinard Mgmt. Assocs., Hungington, N.Y., 1985-91; exec. dir. L.I. Ctr. Fin. Studies, Hauppauge, 1986-90; instr. C.W. Post U., 1991-98. Author: Increasing Your Worth Through Personal Financial Planning, 1987. Bd. dirs. L.I. div. Am. Cancer Soc., 1992—. With USAF, 1956-59. Mem. L.I. Internat. Assn. Fin. Planning (pres. 1980-83, chmn. bd. dirs. 1983-88) (Appreciation award 1988), Adelphi Soc. Fin. Planners (v.p. 1985-86), Kiwanis (bd. dirs. Huntington chpt. 1997—). Republican. Avocations: boating, skiing. Home: 3 Colyer Pl Greenlawn NY 11740-3004 Office: North Shore Capital Mgmt 1895 Walt Whitman Rd Melville NY 11747-3031

CLINARD, MARSHALL BARRON, sociologist, educator; b. Boston, Nov. 12, 1911; s. Andrew Marshall and Gladys (Barron) C.; m. Ruth Blackburn, Aug. 28, 1937; children: Marsha Clinard, Stephen Andrew. BA, Stanford U., 1932, MA, 1934; PhD, U. Chgo., 1941; LLD (hon.), U. Lausanne, Switzerland, 1985. Instr. U. Iowa, 1937-41; chief criminal stats. U.S. Bur. Census, 1941-43; chief analysis report, enforcement dept. OPA, 1943-45; assoc. prof. Vanderbilt U., 1945-46; mem. faculty U. Wis., 1946—, prof. sociology, 1951-79, prof. emeritus, 1979—; Fulbright rsch. prof. U. Stockholm, 1954-55; vis. prof. Makerere U. Coll., Kampala, Uganda, 1968-69; cons. urban cmty. devel. Ford Found., India, 1958-60, 62-63; UN expert Asian Seminar Urban Cmty. Devel., Singapore, 1962; rapporteur 3rd UN Congress Prevention Crime and Treatment Offenders, Stockholm, 1965; panel expert 4th UN Congress, Kyoto, 1970; cons. 5th UN Congress, Geneva, 1975, Dept. Labor, 1966-67. Author: The Black Market: A Study of White Collar Crime, 1952; (with Robert F. Meier) Sociology of Deviant Behavior, 1957, 10th edit., 1998; editor, contbr.: Anomie and Deviant Behavior: A Discussion and Critique, 1964, Slums and Community Development: Experiments in Self-Help, 1966; (with Richard Quinney and John Wildeman) Criminal Behavior Systems: A Typology, 1967, 3rd edit., 1994; (with Daniel J. Abbott) Crime in Developing Countries: A Comparative Perspective, 1973, Cities with Little Crime: The Case of Switzerland, 1978, Illegal Corporate Behavior, 1979; (with Peter C. Yeager) Corporate

Crime, 1980, Corporate Ethics and Crime: The Role of Middle Management, 1983, Corporate Corruption: The Abuse of Power, 1990. Recipient Sutherland award Am. Soc. Criminology, 1970, Cressey award Assn. Cert. Fraud Examiners, 1994; NSF rsch. grantee, Switzerland, 1973, U.S. Dept. Justice grantee, 1977, 81. Mem. Soc. Study Social Problems (exec. com. 1959-60, 62-63, 65-67, pres. 1961-62), Midwest Sociol. Soc. (pres. 1965-66), Am. Sociol. Assn. (coun. mem. at large 1966-68). Home: Apt B-205 900 Calle De Los Amigos Santa Barbara CA 93105-4486

CLINARD, ROBERT NOEL, lawyer; b. Welch, W.Va., Nov. 1, 1946; s. Vernon Carlos and Mary Elizabeth (Noel) C.; m. Margaret Hawthorne Higgins, May 21, 1977; children: Elizabeth Kercheval, Edward Noel, Margaret Graham Robinson, Kathryn Moir. BA, Washington & Lee U., 1968, JD, 1976. Bar: N.Y. 1977, Va. 1978, U.S. Dist. Ct. (so. dist.) N.Y. 1977, U.S. Dist. Ct. (ea. dist.) Va. 1978, U.S. Ct. Appeals (4th cir.) 1986, U.S. Supreme Ct. 1990. Assoc. Winthrop, Stimson, Putnam & Roberts, N.Y.C., 1976-78; assoc. Hunton & Williams, Richmond, Va., 1978-86, ptnr., 1986—. Sec. Va. Cultural Laureate Soc., Richmond, 1981-86, bd. dirs., 1981-90. Served to lt. USNR, 1969-72. Mem. ABA (antitrust sect., franchising and healthcare coms.), Va. State Bar (vice chmn. antitrust com. health law sect. 1985-86, chmn. 1986-87, bd. govs. antitrust sect. 1989—, vice chmn. antitrust sect. 1992, chmn. 1993), Nat. Health Lawyers Assn., Coun. of Franchise Suppliers, Internat. Franchise Assn., Order of Coif, Phi Beta Kappa, Omicron Delta Kappa. Republican. Episcopalian. Avocations: boating, saltwater fishing, house renovation. Home: 6010 York Rd Richmond VA 23226-2737 Office: Hunton & Williams Riverfront Plaza East Tower 951 E Byrd St Richmond VA 23219-4074

CLINCH, NICHOLAS BAYARD, III, business executive; b. Evanston, Ill., Nov. 9, 1930; s. Nicholas Bayard Jr. and Virginia Lee (Campbell) C.; m. Elizabeth Wallace Campbell, July 11, 1964; children: Virginia Lee, Alison Campbell. Student, N.Mex. Mil. Inst., Roswell, 1948-49; AB, Stanford U., 1952, LLB, 1955. Bar: Calif. 1959. Expedition leader First Ascent, Gasherbrum I (26,470 ft.), Pakistan, 1958, First Ascent, Masherbrum (25, 660 ft.), Pakistan, 1959-60; assoc. Voegelin, Barton, Harris & Callister, L.A., 1961-68; pvt. practice Washington, 1968-70; v.p., counsel Lincoln Savs. & Loan Assn., L.A., 1970-74; exec. dir. Sierra Club Found., San Francisco, 1975-81; environ. cons. Fluor Corp., Grass Valley, Calif., 1981-84; v.p., sec. CCA, Inc., Denver, 1984—; bd. dirs. Growth Stock Outlook Inc., Potomac, Md., Recreational Equipment Inc., Seattle. Author: A Walk in the Sky, 1982. Leader Am. Antarctic Mountaineering Expdn., Sentinel Range, 1966-67; co-leader Chinese Am. Ulugh Muztagh Expdn., Kun Lun Range, Xinjiang, 1985, Am. Expdns. to Kang Karpo Range, Yunnan-Tibet border, 1988, 89, 92, 93; co-founder, trustee Calif. League Conservation Voters, San Francisco, 1972-97. 1st lt. USAF, 1956-57. Recipient John Oliver La Gorce medal Nat. Geog. Soc., Washington, 1967. Fellow Royal Geog. Soc., Explorers Club; mem. ABA, Am. Alpine Club (hon., pres. 1967-70), Appalachian Mountain Club (hon.), State Bar Calif., Alpine Club (hon. London), Chinese Assn. Sci. Expdns. (hon.). Republican. Episcopalian. Avocations: mountaineering, skiing, book collecting. Home: 2001 Bryant St Palo Alto CA 94301-3714 Office: CCA Inc 4100 E Mississippi Ave Ste 1750 Denver CO 80246-3067

CLINE, ANDREW HALEY, lawyer; b. Fountain Hill, Pa., Nov. 30, 1951; s. William Matthew and Eleanor Mary (Bosich) C.; m. Eileen Louise Feher, Mar. 2., 1986; children: Haley Andrea, Catherine Anne. BA, Guilford Coll., 1973; JD, U. Ala., 1978. Bar: Pa. 1978, U.S. Dist. Ct. (mid. dist.) Pa. 1982, U.S. Dist. Ct. (ea. dist.) 1989, U.S. Ct. Appeals (3rd cir.) 1988, U.S. Supreme Ct. 1990. Law clk. Commonwealth Ct. Pa., Harrisburg, 1978-80; asst. counsel Dept. Transportation, Harrisburg, 1980-86; assoc. dep. gen. counsel Gov's. Office, Harrisburg, 1986-87, dep. gen. counsel, 1987-89; with Kirkpatrick & Lockhart, LLP, Harrisburg, 1989—. Editor-in-chief Ala. Law Rev., 1978. Named one of Outstanding Young Men Am. Jaycees, 1978. Mem. Fed. Bar Assn. (pres. Ctrl. Pa. chpt. 1994-95, nat. del. 1995-97), Pa. Bar Assn., Dauphin County Bar Assn. (chmn. continuing legal edn. com. 1992-95, bd. dirs. 1993-95, chmn. govt. law sect. 1994, sec. 1996), Bench and Bar Soc., Am. Inns of Ct. (master emeritus J.S. Bowman chpt.), St. Thomas More Soc. (bd. dirs. 1997-98), Omicron Delta Kappa. Avocation: photography. Office: Kirkpatrick & Lockhart 240 N 3rd St Harrisburg PA 17101-1503

CLINE, SISTER BARBARA JEAN, educational administrator; b. Ft. Dodge, Iowa; d. Kenneth Hicks and Catherine Gertrude (Riney) C. BA, Viterbo Coll., La Crosse, Wis., 1966; MA, Mich. State U., 1974, PhD, 1977. Joined Franciscan Sisters of Eucharist, Roman Cath. Ch., 1959; cert. family life tchr.; cert. dir. spl. edn., Mich. Tchr. pub. schs., Wis., Ohio, 1962-69; supr. Misericordia Home, Chgo., 1969-71; dir. Respite Care-Life Process Presch., Lowell, Mich., 1971-75, Hawthorne Learning Ctr., Pontiac, Mich., 1975-78; asst. prof. U. N.H., Durham, 1978-79; supr. E.D.I.T., Early Devel. Intervention Tng., 1979-80; child devel. specialist, proj. mgr. Cath. Relief Svcs., Jerusalem, Israel, 1980-84; dir. for Near East Cath. Relief Svcs., Jerusalem and Amman, Jordan, 1984-87; coord. spl. edn. and early childhood edn. Kent Intermediate Sch. Dist., Grand Rapids, Mich., 1988-93; tech. assistance coord. for S.W. Mich. EarlyOn Pers. Devel. Sys., 1993-96; EOPDS coach for Western Mich., 1996—; adminstr. Franciscan Life Process Child Devel. Ctr., Lowell, 1987—; cons. Life Ctr. Network, Meriden, Conn., 1989-92; co-chmn. Mich. Com. on Interagy. Affairs, Lansing, 1989—; chmn. policy and legis. com. State Interagy. Coord. Coun., 1993—; mem. Sys. Reform tech. Assistance Com., 1995—; state trainer in infant-toddler devel. assessment; presenter in field. Author: Child Development: Birth to Five Years, 1981, Hygiene: Changing Behavior through Education, 1982, Fundamentals of Health Edn., 1986. Mem. task force, bd. dirs. Project Harmony, Grand Rapids, 1989-92; mem. gov.'s task force drug exposed infants, 1992; appointee gov.'s State Interagency Coordinating Coun., 1992, reapptd., 1996, 99. Recipient Outstanding Adminstr. award Pontiac Sch. System, 1978. Mem. ASCD, Nat. Coun. Family Rels., Coun. for Exceptional Children (divsn. early childhhod edn.), Nat. Assn. for Edn. Young Children, Assn. for Childhood Edn. Internat., Am. Assn. for Protecting Young Children, Mich. Assn. for Infant Mental Health (bd. dirs., sec. 1989-96, Selma Freiburg award 1998, Jane Scandry award DEC/CEC 1999), Kent County Assn. for Prevention Child Abuse and Neglect (bd. dirs. 1988-94), Phi Delta Kappa, Omicron Nu. Home: 11761 Downes St Lowell MI 49331-9761 Office: Kent Intermediate Sch Dist 2930 Knapp St NE Grand Rapids MI 49525-7006

CLINE, BETH MARIE, school psychologist; b. San Diego, Apr. 21, 1959; d. Roy Donald and Betty Ruth (Gainey) Hendricks. AAS in Police Sci., Hinds Community Coll., 1979; BS in Criminal Justice, Delta State U., 1981, MEd in Sch. Psychology, 1984, EdS in Sch. Psychology, 1988, D in Edn., 1995. Sch. psychometrist Chattahoochee Flint Regional Edn. Svc. Agy., Americus, Ga., 1984-85; sch. psychometrist Clarksdale (Miss.) Mcpl. Sch. Dist., 1985-88, sch. psychologist, 1988—; coord. crisis mgmt. team, positive behavioral specialist, sch. psychologist Clarksdale Screening Team, 1988-93; cons. trainer Miss. Dept. Edn., Jackson, 1988—, cons., portfolio reviewer, 1990—. Mem. adult and handbell choirs Clarksdale Bapt. Ch., 1989—, asst. Sunday sch. dir. and tchr., 1990-92, mem. Ladies Ensemble, 1994—, Sunday sch. dir., 1992-94. Mem. Nat. Assn. Sch. Psychologists, Miss. Assn. for Psychology in the Schs. (sec. 1985-87, northern mem.-at-large 1989-91, pres.-elect 1991-92, pres. 1992-93, past pres. 1993-94), Ga. Assn. Sch. Psychologists (chairperson nominations com. 1985, rsch. com. 1985), Miss. Profl. Educators, Learning Disabilities Assn., Phi Delta Kappa. Baptist. Office: Clarksdale Mcpl Sch Dist PO Box 1088 Clarksdale MS 38614-1088

CLINE, BOBBY JAMES, insurance company executive; b. Floydada, Tex., Mar. 12, 1932; s. Howard O. and Carrie (Tomlinson) C.; m. Martha Nolen, May 29, 1954; children: Carolyn, Pamela, Millie, Robert, Sean. BBA, U. Tex., Austin, 1954. Casualty underwriter Ins. Co. N.Am., Dallas, 1956-59; account exec./ptnr. Munger-Moore & Assocs., Dallas, 1959-68; ptnr. Harris-Moore & Assocs., Dallas, 1968-70; sr. v.p. Alexander & Alexander Inc., Dallas, 1970-72, exec. v.p., 1972-77, pres., 1977-96; vice chmn. bd. Alexander & Alexander Inc.; exec. v.p. Aon Risk Svcs. Tex., Dallas, 1997—. Served with USN, 1954-56. Mem. Soc. CPCUs (dir.), Dallas Assn. Ins. Agts., U. Tex. Ex-Students Assn. (past pres.), Salesmanship Club, Preston Trails Golf Club, Dallas Club, Dallas Athletic Club, Garland Toastmasters, Riverhill Country Club. Baptist. Avocations: golfing, hunting. Office: Aon Risk Svcs Tex 2711 N Haskell Ave Ste 800 Dallas TX 75204-2932*

CLINE, CAROLYN JOAN, plastic and reconstructive surgeon; b. Boston; d. Paul S. and Elizabeth (Flom) Cline. BA, Wellesley Coll., 1962; MA, U. Cin., 1966; PhD, Washington U., 1970; diploma Washington Sch. Psychiatry, 1972; MD, U. Miami (Fla.) 1975. Diplomate Am. Bd. Plastic and Reconstructive Surgery. Rsch. asst. Harvard Dental Sch., Boston, 1962-64; rsch. asst. physiology Laser Lab., Children's Hosp. Research Found., Cin., 1964, psychology dept. U. Cin., 1964-65; intern in clin. psychology St. Elizabeth's Hosp., Washington, 1966-67; psychologist Alexandria (Va.) Community Mental Health Ctr., 1967-68; research fellow NIH, Washington, 1968-69; chief psychologist Kingsbury Ctr. for Children, Washington, 1969-73; sole practice clin. psychology, Washington, 1970-73; intern internal medicine U. Wis. Hosps., Ctr. for Health Sci., Madison, 1975-76; resident in surgery Stanford U. Med. Ctr., 1976-78; fellow microvascular surgery dept. surgery U. Calif.-San Francisco, 1978-79; resident in plastic surgery St. Francis Hosp., San Francisco, 1979-82; practice medicine, specializing in plastic and reconstructive surgery, San Francisco, 1982—. Contbr. chpt. to plastic surgery textbook, articles to profl. jours. Mem. Am. Soc. Plastic and Reconstructive Surgeons, Royal Soc. Medicine, Calif. Medicine Assn., Calif. Soc. Plastic and Reconstructive Surgeons, San Francisco Med. Soc.

CLINE, CHARLES WILLIAM, poet, pianist, rhetoric and literature educator; b. Waleska, Ga., Mar. 1, 1937; s. Paul Ardell and Mary Montarie (Pittman) C.; m. Sandra Lee Williamson, June 11, 1966 (div. 1996); 1 son, Jeffrey Charles. Student, U. Cin. Conservatory of Music, 1957-58; AA, Reinhardt Coll., 1957; BA, George Peabody Coll. for Tchrs., 1960; MA, Vanderbilt U., 1963; LittD, World U., 1981; DFA (hon.), Australian Inst. Coordinated Rsch., 1996. Asst. prof. English Shorter Coll., Rome, Ga., 1963-64; instr. English West Ga. Coll., Carrollton, 1964-68; manuscript procurement editor Fideler Co., Grand Rapids, Mich, 1968; assoc. prof. English Kellogg Community Coll., Battle Creek, Mich., 1969-75, prof. English and resident poet, 1975—; chmn. creative writing sect. Midwest Conf. on English, 1976; condr. poetry readings and workshops. Piano recitals at Internat. Congress on Arts and Comm., 1992, 93, 94, 95, 96; author: Crossing the Ohio, 1976, Questions for the Snow, 1979, Ultima Thule, 1984, (with Amal Ghose and others) Wholeness of Dream, 1989; editor: Forty Salutes to Mich. Poets, 1975; contbr. Gifts of Music, 1994; contbr. poems to jours. and anthologies. Decorated knight comdr. Lofsensischen Unsiniusordens, 1991, knight Order of Knights Templars of Jerusalem, 1991, knight Order of Circulo Nobilario de los Caballeros Universales, 1993, knight Order of Holy Grail, 1996, baron Royal Order of the Bohemian Crown, 1996, count Order of San Ciriaco, 1996; recipient Poetry awards Modus Operandi, 1975, Internat. Belles-Lettres Soc., 1975, Poetry Soc. Mich., 1975, N. Am. Mentor, 1977, 78, Lit. Prize World Inst. Achievement, 1986, 88, Star of Distinction, 19th Internat. Congress on Art and Comm., St. John's Coll., U. Cambridge, 1992, Disting. Participation medallion 20th Congress, Cambridge, Mass., 1993, Diplôme d'Honneur en Littèrature et Musique, Inst. des Affaires Internats., 1996; resolutions recognition Kalamazoo City Commn., Mich. Ho. of Reps. and Senate, 1981, others. Fellow World Literary Acad. (founding, prize 1983), Internat. Soc. Lit. (life), Am. Biog. Inst. (life, World Fellowship award 1987, Internat. Hall of Leaders 1988, hon. advisor rsch. bd. advisors nat. divsn. 1994); mem. Tagore Inst. Creative Writing Internat. (life), World Poetry Soc. Intercontinental, Centro Studi e Scambi Internazionali (Poet Laureate award, Diploma di Benemerenza, Diploma d'Onore), Accademia Leonardo da Vinci, Poetry Soc. Am., Poets and Writers Inc., Acad. Am. Poets, Am. Biog. Inst. Rsch. Assn. (dep. gov.), Internat. Biog. Assn. (life patron), World U. Roundtable, Internat. Biog. Ctr. (dep. dir. gen. 1991, 20th Century award for achievement 1992, World Intellectual 1993), Accademia Internationale di Pontzen (distintivo palmato 1991, lauro d'oro for literary merit 1991, grande medaglia Aurata della fondazione 1997; scettro d'argento 1998), Maison Internat. des Intellectuels, Acad. M.I.D.I., Wordsworth-Coleridge Assn., Assn. Lit. Scholars and Critics. Presbyterian. Office: Kellogg Community Coll 450 North Ave Battle Creek MI 49017-3306 *The creative urge seems natural; each practitioner surrenders to what demands utterance: not so much a gift, as viewed by others, but a need for humane survival.*

CLINE, HARVEY ELLIS, metallurgist; b. Cambridge, Mass., Aug. 15, 1940; married; two children. BS, MIT, 1962, MS, 1964, PhD in Metallurgy, 1965. Rsch. physicist Gen. Electric Rsch. and Devel. Ctr., Schenectady, N.Y., 1965—, physicist, 1984—. Fellow Am. Physics Soc.; mem. NAE, IEEE, Am. Inst. Physics, Internat. Soc. Magnetic Resonance in Medicine, Sigma Xi. Office: Gen Electric Corp Rsch & Devel Ctr Bldg K1 Rm IC32 1 Research Cir Schenectady NY 12309-1027

CLINE, JOHN CARROLL, clinical psychologist; b. Staunton, Va., Sept. 6, 1955; s. Carroll Hubert and Naomi Edith (Hevener) C.; m. Diane Jeannette Goudreau, May 21, 1983; 1 child, Virginia Goudreau Cline. BA, U. Va., 1977; PhD, U. Toledo, 1984. Lic. psychologist, Conn.; cert. biofeedback; clin. assoc. Am. Bd. Med. Psychotherapists; diplomate Am. Acad. Pain Mgmt. Psychology intern U. Toledo, 1980-81; predoctoral intern VA Med. Ctr., West Haven, Conn., 1981-82, attending psychologist, 1984-85; clinician Alcohol Svcs. Orgn., New Haven, 1982-85; team leader, staff psychologist Elmcrest Hosp., Portland, Conn., 1985-86, asst. unit chief, 1986, dir. behavioral medicine svc., 1986-90; pvt. practice psychologist Hamden, Conn., 1986-94; dir. adult outpatient svcs. Inst. of Living, Hartford, Conn., 1990-93; psychol. svcs. cons. Hamden, Conn., 1994—; clin. dir. dept. counseling and psychiat. svcs. Grove Hill Med. Ctr., New Britain, Conn., 1994—, chair quality assurance & outcomes mgmt. dept. psychiat. svcs., 1995—; clin. affiliate Yale Psychol. Svcs. Clinic, Yale U., New Haven, 1985—; cons. psychologist VA Med. Ctr., West Haven, 1985-91; asst. prof. clin. psychiatry U. Conn. Med. Sch., Farmington, Conn., 1991-94; instr. orthopaedic phys. therapy program Sch. Grad. and Continuing Edn. Quinnipiac Coll., Hamden, Conn., 1992—; sr. cons. network devel. Inst. of Living, Hartford, 1993-94. Mem. mission study com. 1st Presbyn. Ch., New Haven, 1990-91; mem. Conn. Coun. Mental Health Providers, 1993-96, chair, 1993-94. Mem. AAAS, APA (coun. rep. 1997—), Conn. Psychol. Assn. (chair hosp. practice com. 1990-92, practice directorate coord. 1993, pres.-elect 1994, pres. 1995-96, past pres. 1997), Conn. Behavior Therapy Assn. (mem. exec. com. 1992—), N.Y. Acad. Scis., Soc. for Psychotherapy Rsch., Assn. Psychiat. Clinics of Conn. (mem. polit. com. 1993-94, mem. edn. com. 1993-94), Assn. for Applied Psychophysiology and Biofeedback, Soc. Behavioral Medicine. Avocations: microcomputers, fitness walking, fatherhood. Home: 4 Lamkin St Hamden CT 06517-3309 Office: Grove Hill Med Ctr 300 Kensington Ave New Britain CT 06051-3916

CLINE, JUDY BUTLER, human resources executive; b. Kodiak, Alaska, Jan. 9, 1952; d. James Rucious and Elizabeth (Strong) Butler; m. James Carter Cline, Aug. 17, 1973; children: John Wesley, James Andrew. BS in Mktg., Middle Tenn. State U., 1974; postgrad., U. Tenn., Nashville, 1974, 76. Cert. employee benefit specialist; cert career mgmt. profl.; sr. profl. in human resources. Benefits mgmt. Aladdin Industries, Inc., Nashville, 1974-83; mgr. human resources Kusan, Inc., Brentwood, Tenn., 1983-89; transition cons. Stolle Corp./Alcoa, Sidney, Ohio, 1989-90; dir. human resources Datrek, Inc., Springfield, Tenn., 1990-91; v.p. Schroeder, Flynn & Co., Brentwood, Tenn., 1991-92; prin., part owner BenchMark Group, Inc., Brentwood, 1992-95; sr. v.p., gen. mgr. Lee Hecht Harrison, Inc., Brentwood, Tenn., 1995—; mem. Outplacement Inst. bd. dirs., bd. chair Nashville Area ARC, 1994—; classroom cons. Jr. Achievement, 1993-94. Mem. Soc. for Human Resource Mgmt. (state coun. 1995—, bd. dirs. area II 1989-99, nat. coll. rels. com. 1987-92), Mid-Tenn. Employee Benefits Coun. (exec. com. 1981-89), Springfield-Robertson County C. of C. (bd. dirs.), Nashville Area C. of C. (subcom. chair employers coun. 1996—), Internat. Assn. Career Mgmt. Profls., Rotary Club of Nashville, Exec. Com. for Davidson County Pvt. Industry Coun. Republican. Presbyterian. Avocations: reading, snow skiing, piano. Office: Lee Hecht Harrison 155 Franklin Rd Ste 140 Brentwood TN 37027-4646

CLINE, MICHAEL ROBERT, lawyer; b. Parkersburg, W.Va., Oct. 13, 1949; s. Robert Rader and Hazel Mae (Boice) C.; m. Carole R. Davis, Aug. 28, 1972. A.B., Morris Harvey Coll., 1972; J.D., Wake Forest U., 1975. Project coordinator Gov.'s Office Fed.-State Relations, Charleston, W.Va., 1970-72; spl. asst. W.Va. Office Econ. Opportunity, 1973; spl. asst. W.Va.-Dept. Labor, Charleston, 1974; staff asst., hearing officer, 1975-77; sole practice, Charleston, 1977—. Mem. ABA, Assn. Trial Lawyers Am., Comml. Law League Am., So. Mems. Assn. (bd. dirs.), Nat. Assn. Criminal Defense Lawyers, W.Va. Trial Lawyers Assn. (bd. dirs. 1982—, treas. 1984, v.p. 1985-86, Outstanding Mem. 1983), W.Va. State Bar (chmn. com. on econs. of law practice 1986, 91-92), Pi Kappa Delta, Phi Alpha Delta. Republican. Methodist. Lodge: Elks, Rotary. Home: 1531 Dixie St Charleston WV 25311-1903 Office: 323 Morrison Bldg Charleston WV 25301

CLINE, PAULINE M., educational administrator; b. Seattle, Aug. 25, 1947; d. Paul A. and Margaret R. Cline. BA in Edn., Seattle U., 1969, MEd, 1975, EdD, 1983. Cert. tchr., prin., supt., Wash. Tchr. Marysville High Sch., Wash., 1969-70; tchr., adminstr. Blanchet High Sch., Seattle, 1970-78; asst. prin. Edmonds High Sch., Wash., 1978-84; prin. College Place Middle Sch., Edmonds, 1984-85, Mountlake Terrace High Sch., Wash., 1985-93; asst. supt. Mount Vernon Sch. Dist., 1993—. Recipient Washington award for excellence in edn. Gov. and Supt. Pub. Instruction, 1992, IDEA Kettering fellow, 1984, 86-87, 90-95, 97. Mem. ASCD, Am. Assn. Sch. Adminstr., Rotary (charter mem., past pres. Alderwood club), Phi Delta Kappa. Roman Catholic. Avocations: skiing, kayaking, backpacking. Office: Mount Vernon Sch Dist 124 E Lawrence St Mount Vernon WA 98273-6110

CLINE, PLATT HERRICK, author; b. Mancos, Colo., Feb. 7, 1911; s. Gilbert T. and Jessie (Baker) C.; m. Barbara Decker, Sept. 11, 1934. Grad., N.Mex. Mil. Inst., 1930; student, Colo. U., 1930-31; LittD, No. Ariz. U., 1966, BS, 1982. Advt. solicitor Denver Post, 1931; with Civilian Conservation Corps., 1934-36; Nat. Monument ranger, 1936; pub. Norwood (Colo.) Post, 1937-38; advt. mgr. Coconino Sun, Flagstaff, Ariz., 1938-41; mng. editor Holbrook Tribune-News, 1941-45; editor Coconino Sun, 1945-46; mng. editor Ariz. Daily Sun, 1946-53, pub., 1953-69, pres., 1969-76, v.p., 1976-96; rsch. assoc. Mus. No. Ariz., 1976—; adj. prof. history No. Ariz. U., 1983—. Author: They Came to the Mountain, 1976, Mountain Campus, 1983, The View From Mountain Campus, 1990, Mountain Town, Flagstaff in the 20th Century, 1994. Mountain Campus Centennial, 1999. Mem. Ariz. Commn. Indian Affairs, 1952-55, Norwood (Colo) Town Coun., 1937-38; chmn. Flagstaff Citizen of Yr. Com., 1976-96; bd. dirs., past pres. Raymond Edn. Found., No. Ariz. U. Found.; bd. dirs. Transition Found; trustee Flagstaff Community Hosp., 1954-58. Recipient Ariz. Master Editor-Pub. award, 1969, El-Merito award Ariz. Hist. Soc., 1976; named Flagstaff Citizen of Yr., 1976, Disting. Citizen, No. Ariz. U. Alumni, 1983, Outstanding Flagstaff Citizen of Century award, 1994; dedicatee No. Ariz. U. Libr., 1988. Mem. Ariz. Newspapers Assn. (past pres., Golden Svc. award 1989), No. Ariz. Pioneers Hist. Soc. (trustee 1972-75), Odd Fellows, Sigma Delta Chi, Phi Alpha Theta, Phi Kappa Phi, Masons. Home: PO Box 578 Flagstaff AZ 86002-0578

CLINE, RICHARD ALLEN, lawyer; b. Columbus, Ohio, Oct. 1, 1955; s. Ralph S. and Myrtle O. (Harrison) C.; m. Nora Jean Arth, Oct. 2. 1982; children: Caitlin, Patrick. BA in Polit. Sci., Kent State U., 1977, BS in Criminal Justice, 1977; JD, Ohio State U., 1981. Bar: Ohio 1981, U.S. Dist. Ct. (so. dist.) Ohio 1981, U.S. Ct. Appeals (6th cir.) 1983, U.S. Supreme Ct. 1985. Assoc. David Riebel, Columbus, 1981-84; ptnr. Riebel & Cline, Columbus, 1984-85; ptnr., pres. Durkin, Cline and Co. L.P.A., Columbus, 1985-88; pres. Richard Cline & Co. L.P.A., Columbus, 1988-92; mem. Mitchell Allen Catalano & Boda Co. LPA, Columbus, 1992—, ptnr., 1996—; prosecutor City of Whitehall, Ohio, 1980-81, Village of Powell, Ohio, 1983-85, Powell Village Coun., 1996—; instr. Ohio Peace Officers Tng. Counsel, Columbus, 1985. Bd. dirs. Woodbridge Village Assn., Columbus, 1983-86. Served with JAGC, Ohio Nat. Guard, 1983—. Mem. Ohio Bar Assn., Jaycees (named one of Outstanding Young Men of Am., 1979), Phi Alpha Delta, Omicron Delta Kappa. Republican. Baptist. Avocations: martial arts, military history. Home: 290 Weatherburn Ct Powell OH 43065-9103 Office: Mitchell Allen Catalano & Boda 490 S High St Columbus OH 43215-5603

CLINE, ROBERT STANLEY, air freight company executive; b. Urbana, Ill., July 17, 1937; s. Lyle Stanley and Mary Elizabeth (Prettyman) C.; m. Judith Lee Stucker, July 7, 1979; children: Lisa Andre, Nicole Lesley, Christina Elaine, Leslie Jane. BA, Dartmouth Coll., 1959. Asst. treas. Chase Manhattan Bank, N.Y.C., 1960-65; v.p. fin. Pacific Air Freight Co., Seattle, 1965-68; exec. v.p. fin. Airborne Express (formerly Airborne Freight Corp.), Seattle, 1968-78, vice chmn., CFO, dir., 1978-84, chmn., CEO, dir., 1984—; bd. dirs. Metricom Corp., Safeco Corp. Trustee Seattle Repertory Theatre, 1974-90, chmn. bd., 1979-83; trustee Children's Hosp. Found., 1983-91, 96—, Corp. Coun. of Arts, 1983—; bd. dirs. Washington Roundtable, 1985—, chmn. 1995-96; chmn. bd. dirs. Children's Hosp. Found., 1987-89; trustee United Way of King County, 1991-93. With U.S. Army, 1959-60. Home: 1209 39th Ave E Seattle WA 98112-4403 Office: Airborne Express PO Box 662 Seattle WA 98111-0662

CLINE, ROBERT THOMAS, retired land developer; b. McClave, Colo., May 31, 1925; s. John Howard and Goldie Gladys (Hiltabidel) C.; m. Martha Carolyn Erwin, Mar. 6, 1946; children: Carolyn Cline Price, Roberta Cline Colquitt. Student, Pueblo (Colo.) Jr. Coll., 1943, Wofford Coll., 1944. Real estate salesperson George H. Williams Co., Arlington, Va., 1946; real estate broker Lyon Pk. Realty Co., Arlington, 1946-48; cartographic rep. Hearne Bros. Map Co., Detroit, 1949-58; owner Aero Surveys Map Co., Marietta, Ga., 1958-65, Imperial Builders, Marietta, 1965-69; sec., treas. Personality Homes, Landmark Realty, Smyrna, Ga., 1969-78, Landmark Bldg. & Devel., Inc./Landmark Realty Co., Smyrna, 1978-96; ret., 1996. State sec. Christian Men's Fellowship Christian Ch., Ga., 1962-64; bd. dirs. Campbellstone Apts. for Elderly, Atlanta, 1980-86. With USAF, 1943-46. Republican. Avocations: collecting and flying radio controlled aircraft. Home: 2665 Cold Springs Trl SW Marietta GA 30064-4461

CLINE, THOMAS WARREN, molecular biologist, educator; b. Oakland, Calif., May 6, 1946; married, 1986. AB, U. Calif. Berkeley, 1968; PhD in Biochemistry, Harvard U., 1973. Fellow devel. genetics Helen Hay Whitney Found., U. Calif. Irvine, 1973-76; from asst. to prof. biology Princeton U., 1976-90; prof. genetics U. Calif. Berkeley, 1990—. Recipient Molecular Biology award NAS, 1992. Fellow Am. Acad. Arts and Scis.; mem. AAAS, Genetics Soc. Am., Soc. Devel. Biology. Achievements include research in development regulation of gene expression and pattern formation in Drosophila melanogaster with emphasis on oogenesis, sex determination, and X-chromosome dosage compensation. Office: U Calif 401 Baker Hall #3204 Berkeley CA 94720

CLINE, THOMAS WILLIAM, real estate leasing company executive, management consultant; b. Flint, Mich., Oct. 17, 1932; s. Leo D. and Helen (Wolohan) C.; m. Joanne Greiner, July 18, 1959; children: Robert Arthur, Thomas John, Mary Elizabeth. BS, U. Detroit, 1954, JD, 1956. Bar: Mich. 1957. Gen. atty. Wickes Corp., Saginaw, Mich., 1958-61, sec., gen. counsel, 1961-69, sr. v.p., gen. counsel, 1969-71, sr. v.p., sec., 1971-80, dir., 1964-70, 74-80; sr. v.p., group officer, dir. Wickes Cos. Inc., Saginaw, 1980-83; pres. Cline Mgmt. Co., Saginaw, 1983—; pres., chief oper. officer Signature Corp., Chgo., 1984-85; exec. v.p., chief oper. officer Seitner Bros. Inc., Saginaw, 1986—; bd. dirs. Mid-Am. Life Assurance Co., Mich. Nat. Bank, Saginaw, Can. West Fin. Svcs.(U.S.) Inc., Aristar Inc. Chmn. fin. com. Diocese of Saginaw, 1970-72; chmn. Saginaw Cath. Schs. Study Com., 1969, Nat. assn. Boys Clubs Am.; bd. dirs. San Diego Symphony Assn., 1975-78, Econ. devel. Corp. San Diego County, 1975-78, Saginaw Japanese Cultural Ctr. and Tea House; vice chmn. Boys Clubs San Diego, 1975-77; trustee Saginaw Gen. Hosp. Assn., 1971-72, 73-75; trustee, fin. chmn. Saginaw Coop. Hosp. Inc., 1972; trustee, v.p. United Way of Saginaw County; bd. fellows Saginaw Valley Coll., 1973-75, chmn. bus. fund dr., 1978; mem. adv. bd. Delta Coll., U. San Diego, 1975-78, San Diego State U. Bus. Sch., 1975-78, Saginaw Art Mus., 1986-94; mem. fin. com. Diocese San Diego, 1975-78; bd. dirs. Mich. State C. of C., 1973-75; chmn. Saginaw Met. Area Nat. Alliance of Bus., 1979-80; bd. dirs. San Diego C. of C., 1976-77. With U.S. Army, 1956-58. Mem. Mich. Bar Assn., Mich. Mfrs. Assn. (bd. dirs. 1980-88), U.S. C. of C. (adv. com.), Saginaw Club (bd. dirs., v.p. 1991), Serra Club Saginaw County (pres., bd. dirs.), Rotary (pres. Saginaw 1990-91, dist. gov. 1994-95, chair dist. found.1996, del. coun. on legis. 1998), Blue Key Soc., Delta Sigma Pi, Beta Alpha Psi, Delta Theta Pi. Home and Office: 4640 Ashland Dr Saginaw MI 48603-4605

CLINE, WILLIAM RICHARD, economist, educator; b. Denver, Oct. 30, 1941; s. John Russell and Marian Alice (Franklin) C.; m. Ruth Eleanor Harwood, June 10, 1967; children: Alison Margaret, Marian Harwood. AB Pub Affairs summa cum laude, Princeton U., Princeton U., 1963; MA in

Econs., Yale U., 1964, PhD, 1969. Lectr. Princeton U., 1967-69, asst. prof., 1969-70; Ford Found. vis. prof. Brazilian Planning Ministry and U. Sao Paulo, 1970-71; dep. dir. trade and devel. research U.S. Treasury Dept., Washington, 1971-73; sr. fellow Brookings Instn., Washington, 1973-81, Inst. for Internat. Econs., Washington, 1982—; pres. Econs. Internat., Inc., Washington, 1981—; dep. mng. dir., chief economist Inst. Internat. Fin., Washington, 1996—; professorial lectr. Johns Hopkins Sch. Internat. Studies, 1981-82, 84; vis. lectr. Princeton U., 1983, 85; vis. prof. Aoyama Gakuin U., Tokyo, 1992-94; adv. bd. U.S. Export-Import Bank, 1986-87. Author: Economic Consequences of a Land Reform in Brazil, 1970, Potential Effects of Income Redistribution, 1972, Trade Negotiations in the Tokyo Round, 1978, World Inflation and the Developing Countries, 1981, International Debt: Systemic Risk and Policy Response, 1984, The U.S.-Japan Economic Problem, 1985, Exports of Manufactures From Developing Countries, 1984, The Future of World Trade in Textiles and Apparel, 1987, Informatics and Development, 1987, United States External Adjustment and the World Economy, 1989, The Economics of Global Warming, 1992, International Economic Policy in the 1990s, 1994, International Debt Reexamined, 1995, Trade and Income Distribution, 1997. Woodrow Wilson fellow, 1964, Ford Found. fellow, 1965; recipient Harold and Margaret Sprout award Internat. Studies Assn., 1993. Mem. Am. Econ. Assn., Council Fgn. Relations. Episcopalian. Home: 5315 Oakland Rd Bethesda MD 20815-6638 Office: Inst Internat Finance Ste 8500 2000 Pennsylvania Ave NW Washington DC 20006-1852

CLINESMITH, FREDERICK CLINTON, business executive; b. Altus, Okla., Dec. 29, 1959; s. Troy Clennard and Alice Mallard Clinesmith; m. Janet Dawn Tharp, Dec. 27, 1996. BBA, Baylor U., 1982; M in Internat. Mgmt., Am. Grad. Sch., 1997. Internat. bus. mgr. Dyno Nobel, Inc., Salt Lake City; ptnr. Clinesmith Properties, Jamaica Free Zone Mfg. Assn.; dir. Clinesmith Fund, Free Trade Assn. Avocations: golf, scuba diving, flying. Office: Dyno Nobel Inc Crossroad Tower 11th Fl Salt Lake City UT 84144-0103

CLINGAN, CHARLES EDMUND, historian; b. N.Y.C., Oct. 12, 1962; s. Eldon Ray and JoAnn Kay (McNamara) C. BA, CUNY, Queens, 1985; MA, U. Wis., 1987, PhD, 1991. Vis. asst. prof. Montclair State Coll., Upper Montclair, N.J., 1991-92, CUNY, 1992-95, NYU, 1994-95; asst. prof. history U. N.D., Grand Forks, 1995—. Author: From the General Manager's Files, 1993. Vice pres. Broadway Dem. Club, N.Y.C., 1994-95. Fulbright scholar, 1988-89. Mem. Am. Hist. Assn., German Studies Assn., Austrian Studies Ctr., Conf. Group on Ctrl. European History, Soc. for French Hist. Studies, Fulbright Assn. (pres. No. Prairie chpt. 1995—), Phi Beta Kappa. Office: Univ of North dakota PO Box 8096 Grand Forks ND 58202-8096

CLINGER, WILLIAM FLOYD, JR., former congressman; b. Warren, Pa., Apr. 4, 1929; s. William Floyd and Lella May C.; m. Julia Whitla, Aug. 2, 1952; children: Eleanore, William Floyd, James, Julia. BA, Johns Hopkins U., 1951; LLB, U. Va., 1965. Bar: Pa. 1965, U.S. Supreme Ct. 1975. Advt. exec. New Process Co., Warren, 1955-62; ptnr. Stone and Harper, and successor firm Harper, Clinger & Eberly, Warren, 1965-78; mem. 96th-104th Congresses from 5th (formerly 23d) Pa. dist., Washington, 1979-96; mem. govt. ops. com., vice chmn. transp. and infrastructure com., chmn. govt. reform and oversight com.; sr. fellow John Hopkins U., 1996—; chief counsel Econ. Devel. Adminstrn., 1975-77; del. Pa. Constl. Conv., 1968; chmn., bd. dirs. Ripon Ednl. Fund, Inc. Editorial bd.: U. Va. Law Rev, 1964-65. Chmn. Kinzua Dam Dedication Com., 1966; del. Republican Nat. Conv., 1972, 88, 96; pres. Warren Library Assn., 1957-62, 67-70, Warren Hosp. Bd., 1971-75. Served to lt. USN, 1951-55. Decorated Spirit of Honor medal; named Man of Year Pa. Jaycees, 1960. Mem. ABA, Pa. Bar Assn., Warren County Bar Assn., Warren Jaycees (pres. 1959-60), House Wednesday Group (former chmn.). Presbyterian. Office: Johns Hopkins U Sch Arts and Scis/Polit Sci 3400 N Charles St Baltimore MD 21218

CLINGERMAN, EDGAR ALLEN, SR., financial services executive; b. Wolf Lake, Ind., Dec. 27, 1934; s. Virgil Wilson and Jessie Pauline (Miller) C.; children: Tammie, Sarha, Johnny, Edgar Allen Jr. BS in Bus. Adminstrn., Ball State U., 1960; AMP, Harvard U., 1974. Mgr. Coopers & Lybrand, Fort Wayne, Ind., 1960-64; controller Joy Mfg. Co., Michigan City, Ind., 1964-67; exec. v.p. Milton Roy Co., St. Petersburg, Fla., 1967-85; sr. v.p. The Geneva Cos., Clearwater, Fla., 1985—. With USN, 1952-56. Mem. Nat. Assn. Accts., Assn. Corp. Growth, Fin. Execs. Inst. Home: 2192 Feather Sound Dr Clearwater FL 33762-5502 Office: The Geneva Cos 13535 Feather Sound Dr Clearwater FL 33762-2259

CLINKENBEARD, JAMES HOWARD, principal; b. Alexandria, Va., Apr. 1, 1950; s. Howard Samuel and Ethel Jane (Schwager) C.; m. Janelle Darlene Turner, May 27, 1972; children: Adam James, Nathan Linton, Evan Joel. BS, Murray State U., 1977; MEd, Xavier U., 1985, postgrad., 1986-87, 89-92. Cert. tchr. and adminstr., Ky. Tchr. art Newport (Ky.) Ind. Schs., 1978-88, chief negotiator, 1985-88, asst. prin., 1988-91, 92-96, dir. Title V, 1991-92, acting prin., 1992, 94-95, prin., 1996—; freelance artist, designer Bellevue, Ky., 1977—; juror various sch. and profl. art shows; speaker pub. sch. in-service programs. Featured in Kentucky Artist and Craftsman mag., 1977; author various documents, ednl. reports. State advisor Ky. Imagination Celebration, 1984-85; bd. dirs. Kt. Citizens for the Arts in Edn., 1983-85; advisor Ky. Task Force for Comprehensive Arts, 1984, Ky. Task Force on Acad. Competition, 1985; active Ft. Thomas and Newport PTAs, Bellevue Civic Assn.; chmn. Citizens for Bellevue Schs., 1980-81, Arts Subcom., Coun. on Higher Edn., 1985-86, Ky. Foster Care Rev. Bd., 1991-97; deacon First Christian Ch., Ft. Thomas, 1976—, chmn. bd., 1982-83, Sunday Sch. tchr., 1976-97; mem. select panel Ky. Disting. Educators Program; chmn. Sch. Based Decision Making Coun., 1996—. Recipient commendation Ky. Supt. Pub. Instrn., 1984. Mem. NEA, Nat. Art Edn. Assn. (Ky. del. 1976-77, 81), Ky. Art Edn. Assn. (various offices including pres. 1983-84, Project Art Tchr. award 1980), Ky. Edn. Assn. (svcs. com. 1985-87, del. 1986-88, mem. task force 1987-88), Newport Tchrs. Assn. (sec. 1982-83, treas. 1985-88, pres. 1988, vice chmn. polit. action com. 1984), Newport Adminstrs. Assn. (pres. 1994-97), Washington Evening Star Cartoonists Guild, Ft. Thomas Swim Club (bd. dirs. 1994—, pres. 1995—), Alpha Tau Omega (chpt. advisor 1987-91, chpt. housing corp. pres. 1993—, chpt. bd. trustees 1995—). Republican. Mem. Christian Ch. (Disciples of Christ). Avocations: reading, sports, working with children. E-mail: jclink.nky@fuse.net. Home: 30 Kathy Ln Fort Thomas KY 41075-1914 Office: Newport Ind Schs 101 E 4th St Newport KY 41071-1615

CLINTON, BARBARA MARIE, university health services director, social worker; b. Bklyn., May 21, 1947; d. Lawrence Joseph and Kathleen Byrne C.; m. James Edward Selin, Sept. 12, 1981; children: Greta Maureen, Caitlin Carol. Auditor's cert., U. Tunis, Tunisia, 1968; BS, State U. Coll., Buffalo, 1971; student, SUNY, Buffalo, 1970-71; MSW, U. Ga., 1979. Child care worker Gateway United Meth. Youth Ctr., Williamsville, N.Y., 1970; caseworker Erie County Dept. Social Svcs., Buffalo, 1975-76; social worker Orchard Park (N.Y.) Nursing Home, 1976-77; group counselor Erie Med. Ctr., Buffalo, 1976-77; therapist Buffalo Children's Hosp., 1977-78; intern N.E. Ga. Community Mental Health Ctr., Athens, 1980-81; assoc. dir. ctr. health svcs. Vanderbilt U., Nashville, 1981-87, acting dir. ctr. health svcs., 1987-88, dir. ctr. health svcs., 1988—; lectr. sch. medicine SUNY, Buffalo, 1977-78; gov.'s intern State of Ga., 1978, 79; dir. Maternal Infant Health Outreach Worker Project, 1982-90; adj. lectr. community health sch. nursing Vanderbilt U., 1986—; expert panelist Nat. Resource Ctr. Children Poverty Columbia U., 1987-89, Save The Children Fedn., Westport, Conn., 1992-93, cons.; evaluation advisor Tenn. Comm. Aging, 1991-92; mem. adv. bd. Vanderbilt U. Women's Ctr., 1992-94; presenter in field. Author: (with Mary Porter) Postnatal Home Visit Guide: The Second Year of Life, 1986, (with Toby Barnett) The Emotional Development of Infants: A Discussion Guide for Outreach Workers, 1987; contbr. articles to profl. jours. Active Bring Urban Recycling Nashville Today, Woodbine Community Orgn.; mem. steering com. S.E. Women's Employment Coalition, Lexington, Ky., 1988-91, bd. dirs., 1989-91; bd. dirs. Tenn. Coalition Def. Battered Women, 1990—, Vanderbilt Women's Ctr., 1992—, U. Ky. Coalition on Cancer, Lexington, 1992—. Regents scholar State of N.Y., 1965, 66, 68, 69; grantee Ford Found., 1982-88, J.C. Penny Found., 1983, Robert Wood Johnson Found., 1983-89, van Leer Found., 1986-93, Pub. Welfare Found., 1989-93, Unitarian Universalist Veatch Fund, 1988-93. Mem. APHA, NASW, Nat. Women's Health Network, Internat. Childbirth Edn. Assn., Tenn. Primary Care Assn., Acad. Cert. Social Workers. Home: 313 Peachtree St Nashville TN 37210-4925 Office: Vanderbilt U Ctr Health Svcs Sta 17 Nashville TN 37232

CLINTON, EDWARD XAVIER, lawyer; b. Chgo., July 13, 1930; s. Michael Xavier and Mary Agnes (Joyce) C.; m. Margaret Mary Clinton, May 1, 1965 (div. Oct. 1978); 1 child, Edward Xavier Jr. Student, DePaul U., 1949-50; JD, John Marshall U., 1953. Bar: Ill. 1953, U.S. Dist. Ct. (no. dist.) Ill. 1955, U.S. Ct. Appeals (7th cir.) 1955. Assoc. Schultz & Biro, Chgo., 1955-56; with securities dept. Ill. State Dept., Springfield, 1956-57; assoc. Hough, Young & Coale, Chgo., 1957-65, Keck, Mahin & Cate, Chgo., 1965-92; pvt. practice Chgo., 1992—; spl. counsel Bullrinkel Ptnrs., Ltd.; instr. John Marshall Law Sch., Chgo., 1965-74; arbitrator N.Y. Stock Exch. Contbr. articles to profl. jours.; speaker in field. Bd. dirs. Chgo. Opera Theatre, 1983-88, Children's Care Found., Records Mgmt. Svcs., 1966-97; pastoral coun. Holy Name Cathedral, 1989-94; mem. adv. bd. Steppenwolf Theatre, Chgo., 1988-89. With U.S. Army, 1953-55. Postgrad. scholar John Marshall Law Sch., 1953, John Jewell scholar, 1953. Mem. ABA, Ill. Bar Assn., Chgo. Bar Assn., Bar. Assn. of 7th Cir., Rotary, Law Club, Union League Club, Execs. Club of Chgo. (bd. dirs. 1985-95), Evanston Golf Club, Am. Legion. Roman Catholic. Avocations: golf, prisoner appeals (pro bono). Home: 990 N Lake Shore Dr Chicago IL 60611-1366 Office: 19 S La Salle St Ste 1300 Chicago IL 60603-1406

CLINTON, GORDON STANLEY, lawyer; b. Medicine Hat, Alta., Can., Apr. 13, 1920; s. John H. and Gladys (Hall) C.; m. Florence H. Vayhinger, Dec. 19, 1942; children: Barbara H. Clinton Tompkins, Gordon Stanley Jr., Deborah Ruth. AB in Polit. Sci. with honors, U. Wash., 1942, JD, 1947; postgrad., Naval Fin. Sch., 1944-45, Harvard U., 1945; LLD (hon.), U. Puget Sound, 1957, Seattle Pacific U., 1960. Bar: Wash. 1947. Spl. agt. FBI, 1942-44; pvt. practice law Seattle, 1949—; ptnr. Clinton, Fleck, P.S., 1949-98; dep. pros. atty. King County, 1947-49; judge pro-tem Mcpl. Ct., Seattle, 1949-52; spl. atty. City Coun. of Seattle; mayor City of Seattle, 1956-64; chmn. exec. com. Japan-Am. Conf. Mayors; adv. bd. U.S. Conf. Mayors, 1956-64; mem. Presdl. Commn. Intergovtl. Rels., 1959-60, chmn. adv. bd. Pacific Ctr. Internat. Studies, Edmonds Community Coll.; v.p. Western region, civic com. People to People; founder, chmn. Kobe-Seattle Affiliation Com., Marine Employees Commn. Mem. Wash. Bd. Edn., 1966-70; trustee Seattle Pacific Coll., 1964-70, Alaska Meth. U., 1979-84; bd. dirs. YMCA, Wesley Found., Town Affiliation Assn.; pres. First Meth. Home, Inc., 1969-72; mem. bd. missions Meth. Ch.; del. Gen. Conf. Meth. Ch.; pres., chief Seattle coun. Boy Scouts Am., 1988-90. Lt. (j.g.) USNR, 1944-46. Decorated Order of Sikatunah, Philippines, 3rd Class Order of Rising Sun, Japan; recipient Silver Beaver award Disting. Svc. award Chief Seattle Coun. Boy Scouts Am., 1983, Disting. Grad. award Roosevelt High Sch., 1960, Newsmakers of Tomorrow award Time Mag. and Seattle C. of C., 1953, citation of honor Wash. State chpt. AIA, 1957, Human Rels. award Seattle Civic Unity Commn., 1963, citation NCCJ, 1964, Outstanding Pub. Ofcl. award Mcpl. League, 1964, Eisenhower award Sister Cities Internat., 1985. Mem. ABA, Am. Mcpl. Assn. (exec. com. 1957—, pres. 1962), Wash. State Bar Assn., Seattle Bar Assn., NCCJ (citation 1964), Japan-Am. Soc. Seattle (pres. 1973), Phillipine-Am. Soc. Pacific N.W. (pres. 1988-98), Phi Delta Phi, Shriners. Republican. Methodist. Home: 6650 Park Point Way NE Seattle WA 98115-7860 Office: Third-Lenora Bldg 2112 3rd Ave Ste 500 Seattle WA 98121-2326

CLINTON, HILLARY RODHAM, First Lady of United States, lawyer; b. Chgo., Oct. 26, 1947; d. Hugh Ellsworth and Dorothy (Howell) Rodham; m. William J. Clinton, Oct. 11, 1975; 1 child, Chelsea Victoria. BA with high honors, Wellesley Coll., 1969; JD, Yale U., 1973; LLD (hon.), U. Ark., Little Rock, 1985, Ark. Coll., 1988, Hendrix Coll., 1992, U. Sunderland, 1993, U. Pa., 1993, U. Mich., 1993, U. Ill., 1994, U. Minn., 1995, San Francisco State U., 1995; D Pub. Svc. (hon.), George Washington U., 1994, U. Md., College Park, 1996; DHL (hon.), Drew U., 1996, Ohio U., 1997. Bar: Ark. 1973, U.S. Dist. Ct. (ea. and we. dists.) Ark. 1973, U.S. Ct. Appeals (8th cir.) 1973, U.S. Supreme Ct. 1975. Atty. Children's Def. Fund, Cambridge, Mass. and Washington, 1973-74; legal cons. Carnegie Coun. on Children, New Haven, 1973-74; counsel, impeachment inquiry staff Judiciary Com. U.S. Ho. of Reps., Washington, 1974; asst. prof. law, dir. Legal Aid Clinic U. Ark. Sch. Law, Fayetteville, 1974-77; asst. prof. law U. Ark. Sch. Law, Little Rock, 1979-80; ptnr. Rose Law Firm, Little Rock, 1977-92; chair Presdl. Task Force on Nat. Health Care Reform, 1993. Author: Handbook on Legal Rights for Arkansas Women, 1977, 87, It Takes a Village: And Other Lessons Children Teach Us, 1996; syndicated columnist Talking It Over, 1995—; contbr. articles to profl. jours. Bd. dirs. Childrens Def. Fund, Washington, 1976-92, chair, 1986-91, Legal Svcs. Corp., Washington, 1977-81, chair, 1978-80; founder, pres., bd. dirs. Ark. Advs. for Children and Families, 1977-84; bd. dirs. Child Care Action Campaign, 1986-92, Nat. Ctr. on Edn. and the Economy, 1987-92, Ark. Children's Hosp., 1988-92, Franklin and Eleanor Roosevelt Inst., 1988-92, Children's TV Workshop, 1989-92, Pub./Pvt. Ventures, 1990-92; chmn. Ark. Edn. Stds. Com., 1983-84; mem. commn. on quality edn. So. Regional Edn. Bd., 1984-92; chair ABA Commn. on Women in the Profession, 1987-91; hon. pres. Girl Scouts of Am., 1993—; mem. adv. bd. HIPPY, 1988-92, bd. dirs.; hon. chair Pres.' Com. on the Arts and Humanities, 1993—, U.S. Del., UN Fourth World Conf. on Women, 1995; hon. mem. The Pen and Brush, 1996—. Named Outstanding Layman of Yr. Phi Delta Kappa, 1984, Health Educator of Yr., Ryan White Found., 1995; recipient Lewis Hine award Nat. Child Labor Law Com., 1993, Albert Schweitzer Leadership award Hugh O'Brian Youth Found., 1993, Iris Cantor Humanitarian award UCLA Med. Ctr., 1993, Friend of Family award Am. Home Econs. Assn., 1993, Charles Wilson Lee Citizen Svc. award Com. for Edn. Funding, 1993, Claude D. Pepper award Nat. Assn. for Home Care, 1993, Commitment to Life award AIDS Project L.A., 1994, Disting. Svc., Health Edn. and Prevention award Nat. Ctr. for Health Edn., 1994, First Ann. Eleanor Roosevelt Freedom Fighter award, 1994, Brandeis award U. Louisville Sch. of Law, 1994, Social Justice award United Auto Workers, 1994, Ernie Banks Positivism trophy Emil Verban Meml. Soc., 1994, Humanitarian award Alzheimer's Assn., 1994, Elie Wiesel Found., 1994, Internat. Broadcasting award Hollywood Radio and TV Soc., 1994, Ellen Browning Scripps medal Scripps Coll., 1994, Disting. Pro Bono Svc. award San Diego Vol. Lawyer Program, 1994, HIPPY U.S.A. award, 1994, C. Everett Koop medal Am. Diabetes Assn., 1994, Women's Legal Def. Fund award, 1994, Martin Luther King, Jr. award Progressive Nat. Bapt. Conv., 1994, 30th Anniversary Women at Work award in Pub. Policy, Nat. Commn. on Working Women, 1994, Greater Washington Urban League award, 1995, Servant of Justice award N.Y. Legal Aid Soc., 1995, Presdl. award Bklyn. Coll., 1995, Outstanding Mother award Nat. Mother's Day Com., 1995, Dedication, Annual Survey Am. Law, NYU, 1995, Nat. Breast Cancer Coalition Leadership award, 1995, Faith in Humanity award Nat. Coun. Jewish Women, 1996, NICHE Humanitarian award, 1996, Nat. Assn. Elem. Sch. Prins. Dist. Svc. award, 1996, Grammy award, 1997, Bully Pulpit award Nat. Coun. for Adoption, 1997, Nat. Family Advocate award Parents' Plus Newspaper, 1997, Disting. Svc. to Edn. award Coll. Bd., 1997, Disting. Svc. award Columbia U. Ctr. of Addiction and Substance Abuse, 1997, Commitment to Children award The Elizabeth Glaser Pediat. AIDS Found., 1997, Eleanor Roosevelt Living World award Peace Links, 1997; Paul Harris fellow Rotary Found., 1996. Fellow Am. Bar Found.; mem. Ark. Bar Assn., Ark. Trial Lawyers Assn., Ark. Women Lawyers Assn., Am. Trial Lawyers Assn., Pulaski County Bar Assn. Home and Office: The White House 1600 Pennsylvania Ave NW Washington DC 20500-0005*

CLINTON, JOHN PHILIP MARTIN, communications executive; b. Sheffield, Eng., Apr. 30, 1935; came to U.S., 1967; s. John A.T. and Phyllis Mary (Fowler) C.; m. Margaret Rosemary Morgan, Aug. 26, 1961; children: Alaric, Ivan, James. BA, Oxford U., 1959, MA, 1962. Mgr. computer systems Stanford (Calif.) U., 1967-70; v.p. systems devel. Computer Curriculum Corp., Palo Alto, Calif., 1970-79; exec. v.p. Captec, Inc., Santa Clara, Calif., 1979-80; mgr. product devel. Siltec Corp., Menlo Park, Calif., 1980-82; cons. Instructive Tech., Palo Alto, 1982-83; mgr. software devel. Voicemail Internat., Inc., Santa Clara, 1983-85, v.p. engring., 1985-87, sr. v.p. engring., 1987-88; pres. In-Gate Tech., Sunnyvale, Calif., 1988-99, OST Corp., Mountain View, Calif., 1999—. Author: Begin Algol, 1966; editor (newsletter) Flat Tyre, 1982. Adv. com. Sunnyvale City Coun., 1994-98, chmn., 1996-97; mem. adv. com. Palo Alto City Coun., 1998. Hastings scholar Queens Coll., Oxford U., 1955-59. Mem. Oxford Soc. (No. Calif. com. 1993—), Western Wheelers Bicycle Club (pres. 1983), Oxford and Cambridge Club (London), Tandem Club Am., Folding (Bicycle) Soc. Avocations: calligraphy, bicycling. Home: 2420 Olympia Dr Santa Rosa CA 95405-8131 Office: OST Corporation 480 Mariposa Ave Unit B Mountain View CA 94041

CLINTON, KATHLEEN ANN, sales executive; b. N.Y.C.; d. Lawrence and Kathleen C.; children: Kathryn, Alexa. BA, SUNY Buffalo, 1975; postgrad., Hunter Coll. Acct. mgr. Fieldd Spot Sales, N.Y.C., 1976-78; v.p. sales Petry TV, N.Y.C., 1978-86; sr. v.p. Discovery Channel, N.Y.C., 1986-91; sales mgr. TV Food Network, N.Y.C., 1995-97; v.p. regional mgr. Weather Channel, N.Y.C., 1997—. Recipient Pres. award Cable Advt. Bur., 1990. Mem. Advt. Club. Office: Weather Channel 845 3rd Ave New York NY 10022-6601

CLINTON, MARIANN HANCOCK, educational association administrator; b. Dyersburg, Tenn., Dec. 7, 1933; d. John Bowen and Nell Maurine (Johnson) Hancock; m. Harry Everett Clinton, Aug. 25, 1956; children—Carol, John Everett. BMus, Cin. Conservatory Music, 1956; BS, U. Cin., 1956; MMus, Miami U., Oxford, Ohio, 1971. Tchr. music public schs. Hamilton County, Ohio, 1956-57; tchr. voice and piano Butler County, Ohio, 1964—; instr. music Miami U., 1972-75; exec. dir. Music Tchrs. Nat. Assn., Cin., 1977-86; mng. dir. Am. Music Tchr., 1977-86. Mem. adminstrv. bd. Middletown (Ohio) 1st United Methodist Ch., 1968-72; bd. dirs. Friends of the Sorg Opera House; concert presenter Friends of Music of Charlotte County (Fla.). Mem. Music Educators Nat. Conf., Am. Ednl. Research Assn., Am. Soc. Assn. Execs., Nat. Fedn. Music Clubs, Pi Kappa Lambda, Kappa Delta Pi, Mu Phi Epsilon, Phi Mu. Republican. Home: 714 Macedonia Dr Punta Gorda FL 33950-8013 *I have found that a consideration for the interrelatedness of all parts so necessary in the presentation of music and a warm regard for the feelings of others which is implicit in the practice of good manners in daily observance create success in one's personal and professional lives.*

CLINTON, RICHARD M., lawyer; b. Milw., June 25, 1941; s. William J. and Idella (Loftis) C.; m. Barbara Lynch, June 14, 1969; children: Amanda, Camille, Rebecca. BS, U. Wis., 1963, JD, 1967; LLM, George Washington U., 1971. Bar: Wis. 1967, Wash. 1971, U.S. Dist. Ct. (ea. dist.) Wash. 1975, U.S. Ct. Appeals (9th cir.) 1972. Instr. legal writing U. Wis. Law Sch., Madison, 1966-67; trial atty. antitrust div. U.S. Dept. Justice, Washington, 1967-71; assoc. Bogle & Gates, Seattle, 1971-75, mem., 1975—. Fellow Am. Coll. Trial Lawyers; mem. ABA, Wash. Bar Assn. (pres. antitrust sect. 1982-83), Fed. Bar Assn. (pres. 1986-87), Am. Arbitration Assn. (corp. counsel com., mem. CPR Inst. for Dispute Resolution), Wash. Athletic Club, Columbia Tower Club. Roman Catholic. Avocations: sailing, skiing, fishing, hiking, travel. Home: 3863 50th Ave NE Seattle WA 98105 Office: Dorsey & Whitney LLP US Bank Centre 1420 Fifth Ave Seattle WA 98101

CLINTON, STEPHEN MICHAEL, academic administrator; b. Wichita, Kans., Aug. 21, 1944; s. Thomas Francis and Bettie Lee (Harrison) C.; m. Virginia Ann Schoonover, Aug. 30, 1964; children: Matthew, Michael, Shanna. MA in Philosophy, Trinity Evang. Div. Sch., Deerfield, Ill., 1969, MDiv, 1970; PhD in Theology, Calif. Grad. Sch. Theology, 1979; MA in Counseling, Internat. Sch. Theology, San Bernardino, Calif., 1987; MA in Edn., Calif. State U., San Bernardino, 1988; PhD in Edn., U. Calif., Riverside, 1997. Ordained to ministry Evang. Free Ch. Am., 1973; cert. gifted edn. tchr., Calif. Pastor Lake Zurich (Ill.) EFC, 1967-69, Faith Presbyn. Ch., Wichita, Kans., 1972-74, East Cmty. Ch., Orlando, Fla., 1993-94, First Bapt. Ch., St. Cloud, Fla., 1999—; dir. extension degree programs Internat. Sch. Theology, 1974-86, assoc. prof., 1978-86; dir. Internat. Leadership Coun., 1986-96; pres. Orlando (Fla.) Inst., 1991—, prof., 1992—; pres. Ministry Devel., Inc., San Bernardino, 1978-86; dir. EdD program Internat. Leadership U., Miami, 1998—. Author: The Doctrine of the Christian Life, 1981, Cultural Apologetics, 1983, Calvinism and Arminianism, 1985, The Everlasting God, 1989, Movements Which Changed History, 1993, Theistic Realism, 1998; also 40 articles. Pres. Advs. for Gifted and Talented Edn., San Bernardino, 1979-85; chmn. state parent coun. Calif. Assn. for Gifted, 1978-83; mem. adv. bd. for gifted and talented edn. San Bernardino Unified Sch. Dist., 1984-87; chmn. bd. dirs. Ctr. for Individuals with Disabilities, San Bernardino, 1984-88. Mem. Evang. Philos. Soc. (editor 1979-81, 84-98, pres. 1983), Evang. Free Ch. Ministerial Assn., Evang. Theol. Soc. (chmn. 1982), John Dewey Soc. E-mail: sclinton@toi.edu. Office: The Orlando Inst 100 Sunport Ln Ste 3000 Orlando FL 32809-7892

CLINTON, TRACY PETER, SR., financial executive, systems analyst; b. Laconia, N.H., Jan. 10, 1948; s. Francis Arthur and Jane Audrey (Ely) C.; m. Sally Carol Dedmon, Apr. 27, 1969 (div. Dec. 1975); children: Tracy Peter Jr., Christopher Mathew; m. Sheryl Ann McPherson, May 6, 1982. BBA in Banking and Fin., U. Ark., 1971. Controller Superior Air Parts, Inc., Addison, Tex., 1971-74; supr., mgr. Levi Strauss & Co., Little Rock, 1975-76; salesperson Levi Strauss & Co., Columbus, Ohio, 1977; supr. Walter E. Heller Co., Dallas, 1978-79; supr., mgr. Mary Kay Cosmetics, Inc., Dallas, 1980-92; gen. agt. Alt. Fin. Solutions, Inc., 1993; sr. bus. analyst, Tax Outsourcing Project Coord., state coord., audit mgr. 1st Am. Real Estate Tax Svc., Irving, Tex., 1993—. Co-chmn. Citizens for Organized Growth, Lewisville, Tex., 1983; mem. Lewisville Zoning Bd. Adjusters, 1984-86; vice chmn. Lewisville Planning and Zoning Commn., 1984-86; mem. Lewisville City Coun., 1986-92; dir. adult ministries, bd. dirs. 1st Ch. of Nazarene, Lewisville; mem. SSS Bd.; bd. dirs. Denton Ctrl. Appraisal Dist., 1992-97, chmn. Mem. Am. Prodn. and Inventory Control Soc., Am. Mgmt. Assn. Home: 2509 Vail Ln Flower Mound TX 75028-7188 Office: 1st Am Real Estate Tax Svc 1400 Corporate Dr Irving TX 75038-2499

CLINTON, WILLIAM JEFFERSON, President of the United States; b. Hope, Ark., Aug. 19, 1946; m. Hillary Rodham, Oct. 11, 1975; 1 child, Chelsea Victoria. BS in Internat. Affairs, Georgetown U., 1968; postgrad., Oxford U., 1968-70; JD, Yale U., 1973. Prof. U. Ark. Sch. Law, Fayetteville, 1973-76; pvt. practice law, 1973-76; atty. gen. State of Ark., Little Rock, 1977-79; gov. State of Ark., 1979-81, 83-92; of counsel Wright, Lindsey & Jennings, Little Rock, 1981-82; President of the United States, 1993—; chmn. So. Growth Policies Bd., 1985-86. Chmn. Edn. Commn. of the States, 1986-87, mem. steering com.; mem. Task Force on Adolescent Edn., Carnegie Found.; chmn. Dem. Leadership Coun., 1990-91. Rhodes scholar Univ. Coll., Oxford U., 1968-70. Mem. ABA, Ark. Bar Assn., Nat. Govs. Assn. (vice chmn. 1986, chmn. 1986-87, exec. com., fin. com., com. on human resources, com. on internat. trade and fgn. rels., task force on rural devel., co-chmn. task force for edn. 1990-92). Home and Office: The White House 1600 Pennsylvania Ave NW Washington DC 20500-0005*

CLIPPERT, CHARLES FREDERICK, lawyer; b. Detroit, May 21, 1931; s. Harrison Frank and Ethelyn (Reuss) C.; m. Lynne Davison, June 6, 1959; children: Martha G. Shannon, Charles Frederick III, Thomas Harrison. BA, U. Mich., 1953, LLB, 1959. Bar: Mich. 1959. Assoc. Dickinson, Wright, Moon, Van Dusen & Freeman, Bloomfield Hills, Mich., 1959-67, ptnr., 1967-97, mem. exec. com., 1986-89; mem. Dickinson Wright PLLC, Bloomfield Hills, Mich., 1998—. Commr. City of Birmingham, Mich., 1964-70, mayor, 1969-70; gov. Cranbrook Schs., Bloomfield Hills, 1978—; trustee Cranbrook Ednl. Community, Bloomfield Hills, 1980-98, sec., 1989-93. Lt. (j.g.) USNR, 1953-56; mem. endowment com. The Consortium of Endowed Episcopal Parishes, 1998—. Fellow Am. Bar Found., Mich. Bar Found.; mem. ABA, State Bar Mich. (real property law coun. 1980-85, mem. select com. on professionalism 1992—), Oakland County Bar Assn. (bd. dirs. 1985-91, pres. 1990-91), Orchard Lake Country Club (gov. 1986-92, pres. 1991-92), Pi Sigma Alpha. Office: Dickinson Wright PLLC 525 N Woodward Ave Bloomfield Hills MI 48304-2971

CLITHERO, MONTE PAUL, lawyer; b. Vandalia, Mo., Dec. 18, 1953; s. Paul L. and Patsy S. (Bland) CL.; m. Marilyn V. Easterly, Nov. 1, 1980; children: Ryan P., Lauren A. BA, Culver Stockton Coll., Canton, Mo., 1975; JD, U. Mo., 1978. Bar: Mo. 1978, U.S. Dist. Ct. (we. dist.) Mo. 1978, U.S. Ct. Appeals (8th cir.) 1993. Assoc. Taylor, Stafford et al, Springfield, Mo., 1978-82; ptnr. Taylor, Stafford, Woody, Clithero & FitzGerald LLP, 1983—. Mem. ABA, Mo. Bar Assn., Internat. Assn. Def. Counsel, Def. Rsch. Inst. Home: 1478 S Summer Pl Springfield MO 65809-2246 Office: Taylor Stafford et al 3315 E Ridgeview St Ste 1000 Springfield MO 65804-4083

CLIVE, CRAIG N., compensation executive; b. Waltham, Mass., June 10, 1947; s. Craig Clive and Marie Hope (Smith) Hodge; m. Charlotte Cranford, Aug. 23, 1970; children: Sarah Putnam, Andrew Ross. BSBA with high honors, Northeastern U., 1974; MBA, Babson Coll., 1975. Cert. compensation profl. Compensation staff analyst Mitre Corp., Bedford, Mass., 1971-74; pers. mgr. High Voltage Engring. Corp., Burlington, Mass., 1974-78; employment mgr. CompuGraphic Corp., Wilmington, Mass., 1978-80; compensation and benefits mgr. TRW Fasteners Divsn., Cambridge, Mass., 1981-84; corp. compensation mgr. TRW Inc., Cleve., 1984-87; v.p. U.S. compensation Alexander & Alexander Inc., Owings Mills, Md., 1987-96; mng. ptnr. Baylights Compensation Cons., LLC, Ellicott City, Md., 1996—, futures chair, 1996—. Lay leader Bethany United Meth. Ch., Elliott City, Md., 1992-95; bd. dirs. Grey Rock Homeowner's Assn., Elliott City, 1992; asst. den leader Cub Scouts Pack 944, Elliott City, 1992-95, asst. scoutmaster Troop 794 Boy Scouts Am., Ellicott City, 1995—, unit commr. Nat. Pike Dist., 1998—; cert. lay speaker Balt.-Washington Conf., 1993. 1st lt. U.S. Army, 1967-69, Vietnam. Mem. Am. Compensation Assn. (instr. sales compensation 1990—), Soc. for Human Resource Mgmt. (compensation and benefits com.), Ctrl. Md. Compensation Assn. (compensation benefits com., steering com.), An Comunn Gaidhealach Am., Mackenzie's Co. 71st Regiment of Highland Foot-Hist. Reenactment, DAV (life), Cons. Forum. Methodist. Avocations: hist. reenactment, computing, reading, travel. Home: 3748 Dorsey Search Cir Ellicott City MD 21042-3753 Office: Baylights Compensation Cons LLC 3748 Dorsey Search Cir Ellicott City MD 21042-3753

CLIVER, DEAN OTIS, microbiologist, educator; b. Oak Park, Ill., Mar. 2, 1935; s. Milton Clarence and Ivy Ada (Erb) C.; m. Carolyn Elaine Parker, Aug. 13, 1960; children—Blanche Irena, Frederick Lajos, Carl Milan, Marguerite Estelle. B.S., Purdue U., 1956, M.S., 1957; Ph.D., Ohio State U., 1960. Postdoctoral rsch. assoc. Ohio State U., 1960; resident rsch. assoc. NAS-NRC, U.S. Army Biol. Labs., Ft. Detrick, Md., 1961-62; rsch. assoc., instr. Food Rsch. Inst., U. Chgo., 1962-66; asst. prof. dept. food microbiology and toxicology, dept. bacteriology Food Rsch. Inst., U. Wis., Madison, 1966—; assoc. prof. Food Rsch. Inst., U. Wis., 1967-76; prof. Food Rsch. Inst. U. Wis., 1976-95, Dept. Animal Health and Biomed. Scis. U. Wis., 1992-95; prof. dept. population health and reprodn. Sch. Vet. Medicine, U. Calif., Davis, 1995—; prin. investigator, head WHO Collaborating Centre for Food Virology, Davis. Contbr. articles to profl. jours. and chpts. to books; editor 4 books in field. Served as 2d lt. U.S. Army Res., 1957. Recipient Borden undergrad. award Purdue U., 1956; Ralston-Purina grad. fellow, 1956-57. Mem. Am. Soc. Microbiology, Inst. Food Technologists (food sci. communicator 1991—), Internat. Assn. Milk, Food and Environ. Sanitarians, Internat. Assn. Water Quality, Sigma Xi. Home: 920 Villanova Dr Davis CA 95616-1749 Office: U Calif Sch Vet Medicine Dept Population Health/ Rep Davis CA 95616-8743

CLIVER, JEFFREY G., career officer. B in Econ., Rutgers U., 1965; student undergrad. pilot tng., Moody AFB, Ga., 1965-66; student F-105 tng., Nellis AFB, Nev., 1966-67; student F-4 tng., George AFB, Calif., 1970; student, Fighter Weapons Sch., 1972, Air Command and Staff Coll., 1978, Air War Coll., 1985. Commd. 2d lt. USAF, 1965, advanced through grades to maj. gen., 1994; pilot 18th Tactical Fighter Wing, Kadena Air Base, Japan, 1967-70; various assignments 469th Tactical Fighter Squadron and 388th Fighter Wing, Korat Royal Thai AFB, Thailand, 1971-72; fighter weapons instr. 414th Fighter Weapons Squadron, Nellis AFB, 1972-74; various pilot assignments, 1974-78; weapons and tactics officer then ops. officer 32d Tactical Fighter Squadron, Soesterberg Air Base, The Netherlands, 1978-81; various assignments USAF, 1981-89; asst. dir. ops. Hdqs. USAF Europe, Ramstein Air Base, Germany, 1989-91; dir. ops. plans and intelligence Hdqs. USAF Europe, Ramstein Air Base, 1994, dir. ops., 1994-96; vice comdr. 7th Air Force, chief staff Combined Rep. Korea/U.S. Air Component Command, Osan Air Base, S. Korea, 1991-92; comdr. 18th Wing, Kadena Air Base, Japan, 1992-94; dep. asst. sec. def. res. affairs Office Sec. Def., Washington, 1996-97; comdr. Air Force Operational Test and Evaluation Ctr., Kirtland AFB, N.Mex., 1997—. Decorated D.S.M., Legion of Merit, D.F.C. with oak leaf cluster, Air medal with 12 oak leaf clusters, Rep. Vietnam Gallantry Cross, Rep. Vietnam Campaign medal, Chonsu medal Rep. Korea, Japanese Order Rising Sun. Office: AFOTEC/CC 8500 Gibson Blvd SE Kirtland AFB NM 87117-5558

CLIZBE, JOHN ANTHONY, psychologist, organization administrator; b. Council Bluffs, Iowa, June 28, 1942; s. Harold George and Margaret Jane (Fariday) C.; m. Rebecca Rose Maddox, Jan. 30, 1965; children: Mark Andrew, Diane Christine. BA, William Jewell Coll., Liberty, Mo., 1964; PhD, Washington U., St. Louis, 1967. Clin. psychology resident Norfolk (Nebr.) State Hosp. and Northeast Mental Health Clinic, 1967-68; cons. psychologist Nordli, Wilson Assocs., Worcester, Mass., 1968-97, gen. ptnr., 1975-97, resident mgr., 1978—, mng. ptnr., 1983-93; sr. ptnr. Nordli, Wilson Assocs., 1993-97; v.p. disaster svcs. ARC, Falls Church, Va., 1997—; pres. PCMS, Inc., 1984-97; dir., treas. PSI, Inc., 1983-97, Human Interface Group, Inc., 1986-97; dir., v.p., treas. Student Achievement Inst., Worcester, 1973-97. Columnist Bus. Times. Dir., treas., pres. Nat. Psychol. Cons. to Mgmt.; mem. bd. edn. Town of Madison, Conn., 1980-86; trustee Calvin K. Kazanjian Econ. Found., Inc., 1986—; dist. chmn. 101st Assembly Dist., 1992-97, Conn. Party, 1992—; chmn. Conn. Red Cross Disaster Mental Health Com., 1992-97, Nat. Bd. Emergency Ford and Shelter Program, 1997—; facilitator Vision Project City of New Haven, 1994; coord. Mental Health Svcs., 1995, Spl. Olympics World Games; mem. exec. com. Nat. Hurrican Conf., 1997—; chmn. waterfront com. City of New Haven Vision Project; others; nat. chmn. disaster svcs. ARC, 1995-97. NDEA fellow Washington U., 1967. Mem. APA (membership com. div. 14), Mass. Psychol. Assn., Am. Mgmt. Assn. (faculty President's Assn. 1987-97), New Haven C. of C. (bd. dirs. 1989-95), Sigma Xi, Pi Gamma Mu, Pi Kappa Delta. Home: 607 Queen St Alexandria VA 22314-2514 Office: ARC 8111 Gatehouse Rd Falls Church VA 22042-1203

CLODFELTER, MARK A., air force officer, educator; b. Asheboro, N.C., Dec. 16, 1954; s. Walter Allen and Joan Lee (Cross) C.; m. Donna Marie Mac Isaac, June 21, 1986. BS, USAF Acad., 1977; MA, U. Nebr., 1983; PhD, U. N.C., 1987. Commd. 2d lt. USAF, 1977, advanced through grades to lt. col.; air weapons contr. 73d Tactical Control Flight, Myrtle Beach AFB, S.C., 1978-80; group tng. officer 5th Tactical Air Control Group, Osan Air Base, Republic of Korea, 1980-81; instr. history USAF Acad., Colorado Springs, Colo., 1983-84, assoc. prof., 1987-91; prof. airpower history Sch. Advanced Airpower Studies, Montgomery, Ala., 1991-94; prof. aerospace studies U. N.C., Chapel Hill, 1994-97; prof. mil. strategy Nat. War Coll., Washington, 1997—. Author: The Limits of Air Power: The American Bombing North Vietnam, 1989; contbr. articles to profl. mil. jours. Mem. Soc. Mil. Historians (trustee 1994—), Air Force Assn., Air Force Acad. Assn. Grads., U. N.C. Alumni Assn. Avocations: watching North Carolina basketball and football and Air Force football, listening to classical music. Office: Nat War Coll 300 D St Fort Mcnair DC 20319-5078

CLODIUS, ALBERT HOWARD, history educator; b. Spokane, Wash., Mar. 26, 1911; s. William Sr. and Mary Hebner (Brown) C.; m. Wilma Charlene Candler, June 3, 1961; children: Helen Lou Namikas, John Charles Parker. BA in Edn., Ea. Wash. State U., 1937; postgrad., Stanford U.; MA in History, Claremont (Calif.) Grad. U., 1948, PhD in History, 1953. Cert. secondary edn. tchr., Calif. Editorial asst. Pacific N.W. Quarterly, U. Wash., Seattle, 1938-40; reader Stanford U., Palo Alto, Calif., 1940-42; instr. Claremont-McKenna Coll., 1946-50; asst. prof. Pepperdine U., L.A., 1952-53; instr. Ventura (Calif.) Community Coll., 1953-76; adj. prof. Northrop U., L.A., 1977-85; prof. Nat. U., San Diego, 1987-88; ret., 1988. English conversation tchr., vol. internat. student ctr. U. Calif., L.A., 1979—. John R. and Dora F. Haynes Found. fellow, 1950-52; Clarence D. Martin scholar Ea. Wash. State U., 1936-37. Mem. Plato Soc. U. Calif. Democrat. Unitarian. Avocations: classical music, swimming. Home: 4832 Salem Village Pl Culver City CA 90230-4324

CLODIUS, ROBERT LEROY, economist, educator; b. Walla Walla, Wash., Mar. 10, 1921; s. Hans Friedrich and Emma (Wellman) C.; m. Joan Elizabeth Coyle, Aug. 27, 1949; children: Catherine, Mark. Student, Whitman Coll., 1938-40, LLD, 1970; BS, U. Calif., Berkeley, 1942, PhD, 1950. Lectr. econs. U. Calif., 1949-50; mem. faculty U. Wis., 1950-90, prof. agrl. econs., 1958-90, chmn. dept., 1960-62, v.p. univ., 1962-71, acting pres., 1970, prof. agrl. econs. emeritus, 1990—, prof. econs., 1971-90, prof. econs. emeritus, 1990—, prof. ednl. adminstrn., 1971-90, prof. ednl. administr. emeritus, 1990—, prof. univ., 1971-90, prof. univ. emeritus, 1990—, v.p. univ. emeritus, 1990—; pres. Nat. Assn. State Univs. and Land Grant Colls., 1979-91; pres. emeritus, 1992—; vis. assoc. Harvard Bus. Sch., 1954; lectr. Am. Coun. Edn., Inst. Coll. and Univ. Adminstrs.; State Dept. specialist in South Am., 1961; cons. Dept. Agr., 1961; mem. com. agr. scis. to Sec. Agr., 1961-69; cons. Rockefeller Found., 1963-67; adviser U. East Africa, 1963-67; chmn. Com. Instnl. Coop., 1968; cons. Ford Found., Philippines, 1970; chmn. exec. bd. commn. instns. higher edn. North Ctrl. Assn., 1972-74; v.p. Midwest Univs. Consortium Internat. Activities, Inc., 1964-70, chmn. bd., 1970-71; mem. Commn. on Higher Edn., Govt. Sierra Leone, 1969; adminstr. Indonesian Higher Agr. Edn. Project, 1971-77; adv. commr. Edn. Commn. of the States, 1980-91; mem. Nat. Commn. on Higher Edn. Issues, 1981-82, chmn. adv. com. Nat. Ctr. Food and Agrl. Policy, Resources for the Future, 1984-89; nat. adv. com. Adult Learning Svc. PBS, 1987-91, Debt for Devel. Coalition, Inc., 1988-92, chmn., 1988-91, chmn. adv. com., 1992-97; cons. U.S. Info. Agy., 1991-94; v.p. WM Acad. Search Consultants Internat. Inc., 1991-94. Author articles, monographs, chpts. in books; editor: Jour. Farm Econs, 1958-60. bd. dirs. Univ. Corp. Atmospheric Rsch., 1962-67, Ctr. for Rsch. Librs., 1969-71, Argonne Univ. Assocs., 1978-84, USN Meml. Found., 1995—, sec., 1998—; docent Navy Mus., Washington Navy Yard, 1997—. Lt. USNR, 1942-46. Decorated Commendation medal; recipient Kiekhofer Teaching award U. Wis., 1953. Mem. AAUP (pres. U. Wis. 1957), Am. Econ. Assn., Am. Agrl. Econs. Assn. (v.p. 1960), U.S.-Indonesian Soc. Washington, Phi Beta Kappa, Alpha Zeta, Phi Kappa Phi. Home: 3828 Klingle Pl NW Washington DC 20016-5433

CLOGAN, PAUL MAURICE, English language and literature educator; b. Boston, July 9, 1934; s. Michael J. and Agnes J. (Murphy) C.; m. Julie Sydney Davis, July 27, 1972 (div. 1982); children: Michael Rodger, Patrick Terence, Margaret Murphy. BA, Boston Coll., 1956, MA, 1957; PhD, U. Ill., 1961; F.A.A.R., Am. Acad. in Rome, 1966. Asst. prof. Duke U., 1961-65; assoc. prof. Case Western Res. U., Cleve., 1965-72; prof. English U. North Tex., Denton, 1972—; vis. prof. U. Keele, Eng., 1965, U. Pisa, Italy, 1966, U. Tours, France, 1978; vis. mem. Inst. Advanced Study, Princeton, N.J., 1970, 77; cons. Library of Congress, Ednl. Testing Service, NEH, Nat. Acad. Scis., NRC Commn. Human Resources, Nation Rsch. Council Com. for the Study of Rsch.-Doctorate-Programs in the U.S., Am. Council Learned Socs., Nat. Enquiry into Scholarly Communication, Chilton Research Services; mem. Am. Arts Assn., Inst. Internat. Edn., nat. screening com. 1984-88. Author: The Medieval Achilleid of Statius, 1968, Social Dimensions in Medieval and Renaissance Studies, 1972, In Honor of S. Harrison Thomson, 1970, Medieval and Renaissance Studies in Review, 1971, Medieval and Renaissance Spirituality, 1973, Medieval Historiography, 1974, Medieval Hagiography and Romance, 1975, Medieval Poetics, 1976, Transformation and Continuity, 1977, Byzantine and Western Studies, 1984, Fourteenth and Fifteenth Centuries, 1986, The Early Renaissance, 1987, Literary Theory, 1988, Spectrum, 1992, Columbian Quincentenary, 1992, Renaissance and Discovery, 1993, Breaching the Boundaries, 1994, Convergences, 1994, Diversity, 1995, Historical Inquiries, 1997, Transitions, 1998; editor: Medievalia et Humanistica, Studies in Medieval and Renaissance Culture, 1970—; contbr. articles to profl. jours. Grantee Duke Endowment 1961-62, Am. Coun. Learned Socs., 1963-64, 70-71, 88, Am. Philos. Soc., 1964-69, U. North Tex., 1972-75, 80-81, 89; sr. Fulbright-Hays postdoctoral rsch. fellow, Italy, 1965-66, France, 1978, fellow Prix de Rome, 1966-67, Bollingen Found., 1966, NEH, 1969-70, 86, 90-91. Mem. Internat. Assn. Univ. Profs. English, MLA (exec. com. 1980-86, del. assembly 1981-86), Internat. Comparative Lit. Assn., Internat. Arthurian Soc., Modern Humanities Research Assn., Medieval Acad. Am. (nominating com. 1975-76, John Nicholas Brown Prize com. 1981-83), Internat. Assn. for Neo-Latin Studies, The New Chaucer Soc., Fulbright Assn. Democrat. Roman Catholic. Office: PO Box 5074 Wayland MA 01778-6074

CLOHESY, WILLIAM WARREN, philosophy educator; b. Chgo., July 31, 1946; s. John Cecil and Mary Evelyn (Ahern) C.; m. Stephanie June Jagucki, June 19, 1971. BS, Loyola U., Chgo., 1964-68; MA, So. Ill. U., 1968-71; PhD, New Sch. for Social Rsch., N.Y.C., 1981. Instr. Loyola U., Chgo., 1967, asst. prof., 1982-83; teaching asst. So. Ill. U., Carbondale, 1969; adj. prof. Montclair State Coll., Upper Montclair, N.J., 1981-82; asst. prof. Rochester (N.Y.) Inst. Tech., 1983-86, rsch. assoc., 1986-87; lectr. U. Belgrano, Buenos Aires, 1987; asst. prof. U. No. Iowa, Cedar Falls, 1987-93, assoc. prof., 1993—; mem. BSN adv. com. Allen Coll., Waterloo, Iowa, 1991—. Editor: Ethics at Work, 1992; contbr. articles to profl. jours. Rsch. and faculty devel. grantee W.K. Kellogg Found., 1995—, Symposium grant Iowa Humanities Bd., 1991-92, Symposium grant NEH, 1991-92, Fulbright fellowship to Argentina, 1987, Kurt Riezler Meml. awar New Sch. for Social Rsch., 1982. Mem. Internat. Soc. for 3d Sector Rsch., Am. Philos. Assn., Hume Soc., N.Am. Soc. for Social Philosophy, N.Am. Kant Soc., Soc. for the Advancement of Am. Philosophy. Democrat. Roman Catholic. Avocations: Irish lang., lit. and music. Office: U No Iowa Dept Philosophy & Religion Cedar Falls IA 50614-0501

CLONINGER, CLAUDE ROBERT, psychiatric researcher, educator, genetic epidemiologist; b. Beaumont, Tex., Apr. 4, 1944; s. Morris Sheppard and Marie Concetta (Mazzagatti) C.; m. Sharon Lee Rogan, July 11, 1969; children: Bryan Joseph, Kevin Michael. BA U. Tex., 1966; MD, Washington U., St. Louis, 1970, (hon.) U. Umea, Sweden, 1983. Diplomate Am. Bd. Psychiatry and Neurology. Instr. psychiatry Washington U., St. Louis, 1973-74, asst. prof. 1974-78, assoc. prof., 1978-81, prof., 1981—, prof. genetics, 1978—, prof. psychology, 1989—, Wallace Renard prof. psychiatry, 1991—, head dept. psychiatry, 1989-94, dir. ctr. psychobiology personality, 1994—; psychiatrist-in-chief Barnes and Renard Hosps., St. Louis, 1989-94; vis. prof. U. Hawaii, Honolulu, 1978-79, U. Umea, Sweden, 1980; chmn. NIMH Psychopathology Review Com., Washington, 1980-84; cons. WHO, Geneva, 1981—, Am. Psychiatric Assn., Washington, 1978—, Nat. Inst. on Alcohol Abuse and Alcoholism, 1984—, Inst. Medicine, 1986; chmn. genetics initiative schizophrenia NIMH, 1989-97; mental health commr. State of Mo., 1990-95. Author 6 books; editor: Jour. Behavior Genetics, 1980-86, Am. Jour. Human Genetics, 1980-83; assoc. editor Genetic Epidemiology, 1983-92, Human Heredity, 1989—; mem. editl. bd. Arch. Gen. Psychiatry, Comprehensive Psychiatry, Neuropsychopharmacology, Jour. Comprehensive Psychiatry, Jour. Psychiat. Rsch., Jour. Med. Genetics; contbr. articles to profl. jours. Recipient Rsch. Scientist award NIMH, 1975, 80, 85, Strecker award Inst. Pa. Hosp., 1988, James B. Isaacson award, ISBRA, 1992. Fellow AAAS, Am. Psychiat. Assn. (Adolph Meyer award, 1993), Am. Psychopathol. Assn. (treas. 1984-89, v.p. 1990, pres. 1991-93, sec. 1994-96, Samuel Hamilton award 1993); mem. Am. Soc. Human Genetics (editl. bd. 1980-83), Behavior Genetics Assn. (editl. bd. 1980—), Inst. Medicine of NAS, Rsch. Soc. Alcoholism (bd. dirs. 1987-90). Avocations: gardening, reading, travel. Home: 7100 Delmar Blvd University Heights MO 63130-4303 Office: Washington U Dept of Psychiatry 4940 Childrens Pl Dept Of Saint Louis MO 63110-1002

CLONINGER, KRISS, III, insurance company executive; b. Houston, Oct. 21, 1947; s. Kriss and Jewel JoAnn (Jones) C.; children: Laura Kay, Kriss Alan. B.B.A., U. Tex, 1969, M.B.A., 1971. Actuary KPMG Peat Marwick, Dallas, 1973-74, Atlanta, 1977-92; actuary Rudd & Wisdom, Austin, Tex., 1974-77; exec. v.p., chief fin. officer AFLAC Inc., Columbus, Ga., 1992—. Served to 1st lt. USAF, 1971-73. Fellow Soc. Actuaries; mem. Am. Acad. Actuaries. Home: 5 Odom Dr Hamilton GA 31811 Office: AFLAC Ctr 1932 Wynnton Rd Columbus GA 31999-0001

CLONTZ, JERRY MICHAEL, sales administrator; b. Charlottesville, Va., Apr. 22, 1960; s. Billy Gerald and Sandys Gray Clontz; m. Mary Louise Touchette, Jan. 2, 1988. B of Indsl. Engring., Ga. Inst. Tech., 1984. Sr. engr. Charleston (S.C.) Naval Shipyard, 1984-88; plant supt. Baker Material Handling, Summerville, S.C., 1988-89; ops./engring. mgr. Diesel Recon Charleston, 1990-93; co. mgr. Recon Gas Engines, 1994-97; factory mgr. Yale Security, Wingate, N.C., 1997; bus. mgr. Frigidaire Home Products, Nashville, Ark., 1998-99. *Author of the following published poems: "C.S. Lewis' Grief After the Death of Joy," Lamp-Post, Spring 1998; "Karl Barth's Moment," Candelabrum Poetry Magazine, April 1997; "At Midnight a Cloud," Frogpond, May 1997; "Karl Barth's Pontius Pilate," HRAFNHOH XXIX; "An Outdoor Cafe," Haiku Headlines, May 1997; "The Party," Night Roses, 1996.* Author: New Psalms, 1996, Women and the Cross, 1997; pub. PFPA, 1995—. Mem. Inst. Indsl. Engring., Internat. Assn. Women Ministers, Pubs. Mktg. Assn., Small Pubs. Assn. N.Am., Southeastern Regional Poetry Soc. (pres. 1996-97), Poetica X. Avocations: writing poetry, oil painting, jet skiing, soccer, praying. E-mail: ClontzJM@AOL.com. Home: 310 Kleinshore Rd Ste C-15 Hot Springs National Park AR 71913

CLOONAN, CLIFFORD B., electrical engineer, educator; b. Chugwater, Wyo., Aug. 28, 1928; s. Clifford Brokaw and Jessie Fern (Dowler) C.; m. Ann Jean Worstell, Mar. 23, 1951; children: Clifford Cameron, Alison Ann, Kevin Allen. Student, S.D. State Coll., 1945-46; B.S., U. Colo., 1955; M.S., Mont. State Coll., 1961; postgrad., Utah State U., 1964, Colo. U., 1967-69; Ph.D., Colo. U., 1975. Systems engr. Collins Radio Co., Cedar Rapids, Iowa, 1955-57; asst. prof. Calif. Poly. State U., San Luis Obispo, 1957-62, assoc. prof., 1962-67, prof. elec. engring., 1967-90, prof. emeritus, 1990—; rsch. assoc. Mont. State Coll., 1960-61; electronic scientist Environ. Sci. Services Adminstrn., Boulder, Colo., 1966-68; cons. McDonnell Aircraft Co., St. Louis, TRW, Redondo Beach, Calif., Hewlett-Packard, Santa Rosa, Calif. Served with inf. AUS, 1946-47; Served with Signal Corps, 1951-53. NSF fellow, 1968-69. Mem. IEEE, Am. Radio Relay League, Sigma Xi, Phi Kappa Phi. Republican. Baptist.

CLOONAN, JAMES BRIAN, investment executive; b. Chgo., Jan. 28, 1931; s. Bernard V. and Lauretta D. (Maloney) C.; m. Edythe Adrianne Ratner, Mar. 26, 1970; children: Michele, Christine, Mia; stepchildren: Carrie Madorin, Harry Madorin. Prof. Sch. Bus. Loyola U., Chgo., 1966-71; pres. Quantitative Decision Sys., Inc., Chgo., 1972-73; chmn. bd. Heinold Securities, Inc., Chgo., 1974-77; prof. grad. sch. bus. DePaul U., Chgo., 1978-82; chmn. Investment Info. Svcs., 1981-86; pres. Mktg. Sys. Internat. Inc., 1985-87, Analytics Sys. Inc., 1987—; bd. dirs., chmn. Mktg. Svcs. Internat., Inc., Wizeup.com, Inc. Author: Estimates of the Impact of Sign and Billboard Removal Under the Highway Beautification Act of 1965, 1966, Stock Options-The Application of Decision Theory to Basic and Advanced Strategies, 1973, An Introduction to Decision Making for the Individual Investor, 1980, Expanding Your Investment Horizons, 1983, A Lifetime Strategy for Investing in Common Stocks, 1988. Mem. Am. Fin. Assn., Am. Mktg. Assn., Am. Assn. Individual Investors (pres. 1979-92, chmn. 1992—). Home: 1242 N Lake Shore Dr Chicago IL 60610-2361 Office: Am Assn Individual Investors 625 N Michigan Ave Chicago IL 60611-3110

CLOONAN, PATRICK MICHAEL, radio news producer, writer; b. Pitts., Oct. 13, 1954; s. Joseph Patrick and Margaret (Leister) C. BA in Journalism, Pa. State U., 1976. Freelance journalist AP, 1975-82, 89—; news dir. WNCC-AM, Barnesboro, Pa., 1976-82; assignment editor WTAJ-TV, Altoona, Pa., 1982-83; editor, reporter News Publishing Co., Homestead, Pa., 1984-85; cashier's clk. Legg Mason Masten Inc., Pitts., 1986-87; columnist Expression, Pitts., 1986—; freelance corr. Post-Gazette, Pitts., 1989-92; freelance journalist CBS Radio Network, N.Y.C., 1989—; prodr. KQV-AM, Pitts., 1989—; commentator WPLW-AM, Pitts., 1996-97; news writer WPXI-TV, Pitts., 1997-98. Editor The Keystone State Times Newsletter, Munhall, Pa., 1997—; contbr. articles to newspapers. Vol. Bush-Quayle '88, Pitts., 1988, Robertson for Pres., Pitts., 1987; Munhall, Pa., Mayor's adv. bd. rep. Salvation Army, Homestead, Pa., 1985-87. Mem. Soc. Profl. Journalists, Am. Fedn. TV and Radio Artists, Pa. State Alumni Assn., South Hills Coin Club (newsletter writer 1988), KC. Roman Catholic. Avocations: reading, travel, shortwave radio, dogs, lay ministry.

CLOONEY, GEORGE, actor; b. Lexington, Kentucky, May 6, 1961; s. Nick C.; m. Talia Blasam (div.). Actor: (TV series) E/R, 1984-85, The Facts of Life, 1985-86, Roseanne, 1988-89, Sunset Beat, 1990, Baby Talk, 1991, Sisters, 1992-94, ER, 1994-99, (films) Return of the Killer Tomatoes, 1988, Red Surf, 1990, Unbecoming Age, 1993, One Fine Day, 1996, Batman & Robin, 1997, From Dusk Till Dawn, 1997, The Peacemaker, 1997, The Thin Red Line, 1998, Out of Sight, 1998, Three Kings, 1999. Office: William Morris Agency 151 S El Camino Dr Beverly Hills CA 90212-2775*

CLOPTON, KAREN VALENTIA, lawyer, president civil services commission. BA with hons., Vassar Coll., 1980; JD, Antioch U., 1983. Bar: Calif. Maguire fellow internat. and comparative labor studies London, 1984; trial atty NLRB, Washington, San Francisco; counsel Leland, Parachini, Steinberg, Matzger & Melnick LLP, San Francisco, 1998—; lectr. mgmt. tng. programs emphasizing preventive labor rels.; mem. faculty San Francisco State U. Coll. Extended Learning. Past mem. L.A. Dist. Atty.'s Office Youth Adv. Bd; pres. San Francisco City and County Civil Service Commn. Mem. Lawyers Club of San Francisco (bd. govs.), Calif. Young Lawyers Assn. (Jack Berman Individual award of achievement 1994). Office: San Francisco Civil Svc 25 Van Ness Ave Rm 304 San Francisco CA 94102-6033 Other Office: Leland Parachini et al 333 Market St Fl 27 San Francisco CA 94105-1701*

CLORE, LAWRENCE HUBERT, lawyer; b. Tulsa, July 31, 1944; s. Hubert Charles and Jessie Louada (Fowler) C.; m. Carol Jean Roegelein, June 3, 1967 (div. 1981); children: Robert William, James Lawrence; m. Martha Jo Lawyer; children: Kathryn Denise, Michael Hubert. BBA, Tex. Christian U., 1966; JD, U. Tex., 1969. Bar: Tex. 1969. Assoc. Fulbright & Jaworski, Houston, 1971-77, ptnr., 1977—. Capt. U.S. Army, 1969-71, Vietnam. Mem. ABA, Tex. Bar Assn. (labor and employment sect., coun. 1990-93, vice chair 1993-94, chair 1994-95), Indsl. Rels. Rsch. Assn., Houston Mgmt. Lawyers Forum (chmn. 1976-77). Republican. Methodist. Avocations: hunting, fishing, golf. Office: Fulbright & Jaworski 1301 Mckinney St Ste 5100 Houston TX 77010-3031

CLOSE, DAVID PALMER, lawyer; b. N.Y.C., Mar. 16, 1915; s. Walter Harvey and Louise De Arango (Palmer) C.; m. Margaret Howell Gordon, June 26, 1954 (dec. July 1992); children: Louise, Peter, Katharine, Barbara. B.A., Williams Coll., 1938; JD, Columbia U., 1942; LHD, Mount Vernon Coll., 1998. Bar: N.Y. State bar 1942. Practice law Washington, 1946—; ptnr. Dahlgren & Close. Mem. adv. council Nat. Capital area Boy Scouts Am., 1961—; bd. dirs. Nat. Soc. Prevention Blindness, 1961-63, Internat. Eye Found., 1965—, chmn., 1985-89; bd. dirs. D.C. Soc. Prevention of Blindness, 1957-63, pres., 1961-63; bd. dirs. Internat. Humanities, Inc., 1960—, pres., 1989—; bd. dirs. Marjorie Merriweather Post Found., 1974—, sec.-treas., 1974-76, sec., 1991—; trustee Williams Coll., 1963-68; trustee Hill Sch., 1965-85, chmn., 1973-85 ; trustee Mount Vernon Coll., 1963-75 , pres., 1971-74; mem. am. coun. UN U., 1980—. Served with O.N.I., USN, 1942-46. Mem. ABA, Inter-Am. Bar Assn., D.C. Bar Assn., Assn. Bar City of N.Y., Assn. Trial Lawyers Am., World Jurist Assn. of World Peace Through Law Ctr., Pilgrims, Order of St. John, Chevy Chase (Md.) Club, Fauquier Springs Country Club (Warrenton, Va.), Univ. Club (Washington). Home: 40 Hungry Run Farm Ln Amissville VA 20106-4017 Office: Dahlgren & Close 1000 Connecticut Ave NW Ste 204 Washington DC 20036-5395

CLOSE, DONALD PEMBROKE, management consultant; b. Orange, N.J., July 11, 1920; s. Charles Mollison and Simah Close; BS in Econs., U. Pa., 1942; m. L. Carolyn Reck, Apr. 22, 1950 (dec. Mar. 1983); children: Geoffrey Stuart, Cynthia Leigh, Sara Carolyn; m. Diane M. Wisdo Kendzor, Dec. 31, 1996. Sales rep. IBM, Newark, 1946-47; asst. budget dir. L. Bamberger & Co., Newark, 1947-53; staff exec. Am. Express, N.Y.C., 1953; controller, sec. Ciba Co., Inc., N.Y.C., 1953-59; dir. fin. and control Avon Products Inc., N.Y.C., 1960-72; pres. Corp. Fin. Assos., Inc., N.Y.C., 1973-76; v.p. Nelson Walker Assos., N.Y.C., 1973-76, Internat. Mgmt. Advisors, Inc., N.Y.C., 1976-86, prin. Deven Assocs. Internat. Inc., 1986-91, The Pembroke Close Mgmt. Group, 1991—; mem. Pvt. Sector Study on Cost Control in Fed. Govt., 1982. Trustee, Morristown (N.J.) Beard Sch., 1974-77; pres. Jr. Essex Troop Cavalry, 1964-68. With AUS, 1942-46. Decorated Bronze Star with oak leaf cluster, Letter of Commendation. Mem. Fin. Execs. Inst., Am. Soc. Corp. Secs., Systems and Procedures Assn., Internat. Assn. Accts., Human Resources Planning Soc., Group for Strategic Organizational Effectiveness, St. Andrews Soc. of N.Y., St. George's Soc. N.Y., Navy League U.S., 102nd Inf. Divsn. Assn., U.S. Naval Inst., Campbell Soc., Internat. Assn. Corp. and Profl. Recruiters, Human Resources Exch. Assn., Phi Sigma Kappa (past sec.). Republican. Episcopalian. Clubs: University (N.Y.C.); Morristown; Wharton, Essex Hunt, Burnt Mills Polo. Home: 6 Ridge Rd Gladstone NJ 07934-2000 Office: The Pembroke Close Mgmt Group PO Box 226 Gladstone NJ 07934-0226

CLOSE, EDWARD ROY, hydrogeologist, environmental engineer, physicist; b. Pilot Knob, Mo., Oct. 7, 1936; s. Edward Theodore and Bernice Marie (Tyndall) C.; m. Roberta Jane Lamb, June 20, 1959 (div. 1978); children: Edward M., Christiana J.; m. Jacquelyn Ann Hill, July 7, 1979; 1 child, Joshua J. BA in Math. and Physics, Cen. Meth. Coll., Fayette, Mo., 1962; postgrad., U. Calif., Davis, 1968, Johns Hopkins U., 1972; PhD in Environ. Engring., Pacific Western U., L.A., 1988. Registered environ. assessor, Calif. Hydrologist U.S. Geol. Survey, Iowa City and Rolla, Mo., 1974-67; rsch. hydrologist U.S. Geol. Survey, Arlington, Va., 1967-72; project hydrologist U.S. Geol. Survey, San Juan, P.R., 1972-74; supr. hydrologist U.S. Geol. Survey, Tampa, Fla., 1974-78; environ. engr. Ralph M. Parsons/S.A.P. Ltd., Pasadena and Yanbu, Saudi Arabia, 1979-85; sr. environ. scientist Amartech, Ltd., Jeddah, Saudi Arabia, 1985-87; hydrology project mgr. W.W. Irwin, Inc., Long Beach, Calif., 1987-90; sr. hydrologist, mgr. R.L. Stollar & Assocs., Palo Alto, Calif., 1990-92; assoc. engr. hydrogeologist Dames & Moore Environ. Svcs., Cape Girardeau, Mo., 1992-95; owner, mgr. Close Environ. Cons., Jackson, Mo., 1995—; sons. sr. scientist Tetratech, Pasadena, Calif., 1987-88. Author: The Book of ATMA, 1978, Infinite Continuity, 1990, Transcendental Physics, 1997, Proof of the Existence of Non-Quantum Receptors, Toward a Science of Consciousness, Tucson II, 1996; contbr. articles to profl. jours. Asst. scoutmaster Boy Scouts Am., North Liberty, Iowa, 1966. Recipient 10-yr. svc. award U.S. Geol. Survey, 1975, outstanding performance award, 1976. Mem. Am. Math. Soc., Am. Inst. Hydrology (cert. profl. hydrologist), Nat. Water Well Assn., Groundwater Scientists and Engrs., Mensa N.Am., Cape Girardeau Area Engrs. Club (bd. dirs.), Kappa Mu Epsilon. Mem. Self-Realization Fellowship. Achievements include development of calculus of distinctions with applications to theoretical physics, of theory of infinite continuity unified field concept, of method for indirect determination of aquifer characteristics in shallow alluvial aquifers. Office: Close Environ Cons 129 Court St Jackson MO 63755-1807

CLOSE, ELIZABETH SCHEU, architect; b. Vienna, Austria, June 4, 1912; came to U.S., 1932, naturalized, 1938; d. Gustav and Helene (Riesz) Scheu; m. Winston A. Close, 1938; children: Anne Miriam Close Ulmer, Roy Michel, Robert Arthur. Student, Technische Hochschule, Vienna, 1931-32; B.Arch., MIT, 1934, M.Arch., 1935. Draftsman Oscar Stonorov, Architect, Phila., 1935-36; designer Magney & Tusler, Mpls., 1936-38; ptnr., architect Elizabeth and Winston Close (changed to Close Assos., Inc., 1969), Mpls., 1938-92; instr. Mpls. Sch. Art, 1936-37; instr. design U. Minn. Sch. Architecture, 1938-39. Prin. works include Garden City Devel, Brooklyn Center, Minn., 1957, Duff House, variety structures Met. Med. Center Complex, 1960-75, Golden Age Homes, 1960, Peavey Tech. Center, Chaska, Minn., 1970, Gray Freshwater Biol. Inst., Orono, Minn., 1974, U. Minn. Music Bldg., Mpls., 1985, Internat. Sch. Minn., Eden Prairie, 1988. Bd. dirs. Civic Orch. Mpls., 1951-68; bd. dirs. Minn. Opera Co.; past pres. New Friends Chamber Music; mem. Commn. on Minn.'s Future. Recipient Honor award Pub. Housing Adminstrn., 1964; hon. mention F.D. Roosevelt Meml. competition, 1960, 25 Yr. award MSAIA, 1988; named Outstanding Woman of Yr., YWCA, 1983. Fellow AIA (dir. Mpls. chpt. 1964-69, jury of Fellows 1986-87); mem. Minn. Soc. Architects (pres., Honor award 1975), Minn. Hist. Soc. (jury bldg. competition 1986). Home: 1588 Fulham Ave Saint Paul MN 55108-1312

CLOSE, GEORGE F., JR., career officer; b. Mass., Nov. 27, 1946. Commd. U.S. Army, advanced through grades to maj. gen., 1997; dir. operational plans and interoperability Joint Staff U.S. Army, Washington, 1997—. Office: The Joint Staff 7000 Joint Staff Pentagon Washington DC 20318-7000

CLOSE, GLENN, actress; b. Greenwich, Conn., Mar. 19, 1947; d. William and Bettine Close; m. Cabot Wade (div.); m. James Marlas, 1984 (div.); 1 child, Annie Maude Starke. B.A., Coll. William and Mary, 1974. Profl. actress, also accomplished mus. performer (lyric soprano); co-owner The Leaf and Bean Coffee House, Bozeman, Montana, 1991—. Joined New Phoenix Repertory Co., 1974; made Broadway debut in Love for Love; other Broadway appearences include The Rules of the Game, The Member of the Wedding, 1974-75, Rex, Barnum, 1980-81 (Tony award nominee), The Real Thing, 1984-85 (Tony award for Best Actress in Drama), Benefactors, 1986, Wine Untouched, Death and the Maiden, 1992 (Drama League N.Y. Distinguished Performance award, 1992, Tony award for Best Actress in Drama, 1992), Sunset Boulevard, 1994-95 (Tony award Lead Actress in a Musical, 1995); other theatre appearences include Uncommon Women and Others, The Singular Life of Albert Nobbs, 1982 (Obie award), Childhood, 1985, one performance oratorio Joan of Arc at the Stake, 1985, Sunset Boulevard (L.A.), 1993-94, and other repertory and regional theatres; films include The World According to Garp, 1982 (Acad. award nominee), The Big Chill, 1983 (Acad. award nominee), The Natural, 1984 (Acad. award nominee), Greystoke: The Legend of Tarzan, Lord of the Apes (voice), 1984, The Stone Boy, 1984, Maxie, 1985, Jagged Edge, 1985, Fatal Attraction, 1987, Light Years (voice), 1988, Dangerous Liaisons, 1988, Immediate Family, 1989, Reversal of Fortune, 1990, Hamlet, 1990, Hook (cameo), 1991, Meeting Venus, 1991, The House of the Spirits, 1994, The Paper, 1994, 101 Dalmations, Mars Attacks!, 1996, Air Force One, 1997, Paradise Road, 1997; TV films include Too Far To Go, 1979, Orphan Train, 1979, The Elephant Man, 1982, Something about Amelia, 1984 (Emmy award nominee), The Elephant's Child (host), 1987, The Emperor's New Clothes (host), 1987, The Legend of Sleepy Hollow (narrator), 1988, Stones for Ibarra, 1988, (also exec. prodr.) Sarah, Plain and Tall, 1991, Skylark, 1993 (Emmy award nomine for Lead Actress in a Miniseries, 1993), Serving in Silence: The Margarethe Cammermeyer Story, 1995 (Emmy award), In the Gloaming, 1997, The Vagina Monologues, 1998. Recipient Woman of Yr. award Hasty Pudding Theatricals, 1990, Dartmouth Film Soc. award, 1990. Mem. Phi Beta Kappa. Office: CAA 9830 Wilshire Blvd Beverly Hills CA 90212-1804*

CLOSE, JACK DEAN, SR., physical therapist; b. Provo, Utah, Apr. 21, 1943; s. Melvin D. Sr. and Hope (Coleman) C.; m. Gaylee King, Dec. 7, 1962; children: Jack Dean Jr., Tiffany Lee, Kristina Louise, Stephen William. BS in Zoology, Brigham Young U., 1967; MA in Phys. Therapy, U. So. Calif., 1970; postgrad., U. Nev. Las Vegas, 1978-87. Registered phys. therapist, Calif. and Nev. Staff phys. therapist Glendale (Calif.) Meml. Hosp., 1969-70; phys. and respiratory therapist So. Nev. Meml. Hosp., Las Vegas, 1970-71; pres. Phys. Therapy Svcs., Las Vegas, 1971-74, Close and Kleven, Ltd., Las Vegas, 1974-96; pres./CEO Jack D. Close and Assocs., Phys. Therapy & Rehab. Ctr., Las Vegas, 1996—; clin. instr. 14 major univs.; adv. com. respiratory therapy Clark County Community Coll., 1980; adv. bd. phys. therapy U. Nev. Las Vegas, 1988—, instr. U. Nev., mem adv. bd. Phys. Therapy Asst. Program C.C. of So. Nev., 1982—; presenter various confs., profl. meetings. Contbr. articles to profl. jours. Chmn. reunions Las Vegas High Sch. Class 1961; numerous leadership positions LDS Ch.; mem. exec. com. Nev. Friendship Force; past mgr., coach Little League Baseball; past mem. profl. adv. staff Easter Seal, cons. staff Muscular Dystrophy, med. adv. bd. Multiple Sclerosis, adv. coun. and gov. bd. Health Systems Agy. adv. com. Clark County Community Devel., 1981-83; mem. Nev. State Assemblyman Dist. 15 (Las Vegas), mem. ways & means, election/procedures and ethics, and commerce coms., 1995, 1997—. Allied Health Profession scholar; named one of Outstanding Young Men of Am. Brigham Young U. Alumni Assn., 1979; recipient Bachelor Commr. Sci. award Boulder Dam area coun. Boy Scouts Am., 1989, Master Commr. Sci. award, 1990, Merit award, 1991, Silver Beaver award. Fellow Am. Phys. Therapy Assn. (v.p., chmn. joint task force, trustee and exec. com. Found. Phys. Therapy 1990, pres. APT Svcs. Corp. 1989, Lucy Blair Svc. award); mem. AACD, Nat. Athletic Trainers Assn. (assoc.), Am. Running and Fitness Assn., Nat. Strength and Conditioning Assn., Nat. Wellness Assn., Aquatic Exercise Assn., Nev. Athletic Trainers Assn. Avocations: politics, sports, antique auto restoration, coin collecting, travel. Office: Jack D Close and Assocs Phys Therapy & Rehab Ctr 3650 So Eastern Ave Ste 100 Las Vegas NV 89109

CLOSE, LANNY GARTH, otolaryngologist, educator; b. San Antonio, Aug. 13, 1946; s. James Garth and Nona Lee (Galbraith) C.; m. Sharron Maredith Smith, Nov. 22, 1980; children: Hunter, Maredith. BA summa cum laude, Tex. Tech. U., 1968; MD cum laude, Baylor Coll. Medicine, 1972. Diplomate Am. Bd. Otolaryngology. Resident in surgery Johns Hopkins Hosp., Balt., 1972-74; resident in otolaryngology Baylor Affiliated Hosps., Houston, 1974-77; asst/assoc. prof. otolaryngology U. Tex., Houston, 1977-82; asst. surgeon dept. head & neck surgery M.D. Anderson Hosp., Houston, 1978-79; from assoc. prof. to prof. otolaryngology U. Tex. Southwestern Med. Sch., Dallas, 1982-94; prof., chmn. dept. otolaryngology/head and neck surgery Columbia U., N.Y.C., 1994—; guest examiner Am. Bd. Otolaryngology, 1993, 94, 96, 97; pres.-elect Columbia-Presbyn. Med. Bd. Contbr. numerous articles to profl. jours. Fellow ACS, Am. Laryngological Assn., The Triological Soc., Am. Rhinological Assn., Am. Broncho Esophageal Assn., Am. Soc. for Head & Neck Surgery, Soc. of Head and Neck Surgery; mem. Johns Hopkins Soc. Scholars, Alpha Omega Alpha. Office: Coll Physicians & Surgeons Columbia U 630 W 168th St New York NY 10032-3702

CLOSE, MICHAEL JOHN, lawyer; b. Sandusky, Ohio, Jan. 24, 1943; s. Robert J. and Mary Lee (Graefe) C.; m. Nancy L. Schelp, June 18, 1995; children: Christina C., Karen L. AB in History, Lafayette Coll., Easton, Pa., 1965; JD cum laude, U. Mich., 1968. Assoc. Dewey, Ballantine, Bushby, Palmer & Wood, N.Y.C., 1968-76; ptnr. Dewey Ballantine, N.Y.C., 1976-96; pvt. practice Greenwich, Conn., 1996-98, Sarasota, Fla., 1998—; mem. Tax Exempt Bond Group, NYU Tax Study Group; chmn. Tax Rev., N.Y.C. Author: Tax Aspects of Oil and Gas Drilling Funds, 1972, Drilling Funds: The 1977 Perspective, 1977, Special Allocations in Oil and Gas Ventures, 1982, The Final Section 704 (b) Regulations: Special Allocations Reach New Heights of Complexity, 1986, Fringe Benefit Regulation and the New York Law Firm Culture: A New Era, 1989, Off Balance Sheet Financings, 1994; contbr. articles to profl. jours. Bd. dirs., adminstrv. vice-chmn. Conn. Swimming, Inc., 1992-99; bd. dirs. Sharks Swim Team, Inc., 1991-94, pres., 1992-94. Mem. ABA (mem. tax sect. com. on partnerships), Assn. of Bar of City of N.Y., N.Y. Law Inst. (life mem.), N.Y. State Bar Assn. (mem. tax sect. com. partnerships, com. tax exempt financings), Ohio State Bar Assn., India House (N.Y.C.), Burning Tree Country Club (Greenwich), Theta Chi (Alpha Omega chpt.). Republican. Congregationalist. Home and Office: 4951 Windsor Pk Sarasota FL 34235-2610

CLOSE, SANDY, journalist; b. N.Y.C., Jan. 25, 1943. BA, U. Calif., Berkeley, 1964. Exec. dir., editor Pacific News Svc., San Francisco. MacArthur fellow, 1995. Office: Pacific News Service 660 Market St Ste 210 San Francisco CA 94104

CLOSEN, MICHAEL LEE, law educator; b. Peoria, Ill., Jan. 25, 1949; s. Stanley Paul and Dorothy Mae (Kendall) C. BS, MA, Bradley U., 1971. Bar: Ill. 1974; notary pub., Ill. Instr. U. Ill., Champaign, 1974; jud. clk. Ill. Appellate Ct., Springfield, 1974-76, 77-78; asst. states atty. Cook County, Chgo., 1978; prof. law John Marshall Law Sch., Chgo., 1976—; vis. prof. No. Ill. U., 1985-86, adj. prof., 1990; adj. prof. St. Thomas U., 1991; vis. prof. U. Ark, 1993, 96; reporter Ill. Jud. Conf., Chgo., 1981—; arbitrator Am. Arbitration Assn., Chgo., 1981—; arbitrator Cook County Cir. Ct. Mandatory Arbitration Program, 1990—, Will County Cir. Ct. Mandatory Arbitration Program, 1996—; lectr. Ill. Inst. Continuing Legal Edn., Chgo., 1981—; dir. Ctr. for Legal Edn., Ltd., 1995-96. Author: (casebooks) Agency and Partnership Law, 1984, 2d edit., 1992, (with others) Contracts, 1984, 3d edit., 1992, AIDS Cases and Materials, 1989, 2d edit., 1995, Notary Law and Practice, 1997, Contract Law and Practice, 1998; co-author: The Shopping Bag: Portable Art, 1986, AIDS Law in a Nutshell, 1991, 2d edit., 1996, Legal Aspects of AIDS, 1991; contbr. articles to profl. jours. Recipient Svc. award Am. Arbitration Assn., 1984, 5-Yr. Comty. Achievement award Ill. Politics Mag., 1998; named one of Outstanding Young Men in Am., 1981. Mem. ABA, Ill. Bar Assn., Appellate Lawyers Assn., Chgo. Coun. Lawyers, Nat. Notary Assn. (Achievement award 1998), Am. Soc. Notaries, Notary Law Inst. Home: 17640 S Mccarron Rd Lockport IL 60441-9774 Office: John Marshall Law Sch 315 S Plymouth Ct Chicago IL 60604-3968

CLOSSER, PATRICK DENTON, radio evangelist, artist; b. San Diego, Apr. 27, 1945; s. Edward and Helen Thompson. AA in Psychology, Brookhaven Coll., 1986; Diploma, Am. Schs. of Cinema, 1970; Dr of Cultural Arts, World U., Tucson, 1985. Artist Sta. KBFI-TV, Dallas, 1972-73; with Stas. KVTT and KDTX, Dallas, 1976-81, Stas. KTER and KTXO, Dallas, 1980-83; broadcaster Radio Newspaper, Panama, 1989-91; prodr., editor broadcasts Dallas Cmty. TV, TCI Cablevision Network, 1996—; prodr. AM-FM and shortwave broadcsts, including Religious Broadcasts for Pan Am. Broadcasting worldwide, 1983-95. *If it weren't for God and Jesus, I wouldn't be here. Patrick Closser is a pioneer of religious radio and TV. He helped lay the foundation for independent religious radio and TV stations in America and throughout the world for 23 years. He worked with religious radio pioneer J.C. Bishop of XERF-AM for 15 years (1980-1995). From 1980-93, he helped build, install and operate equipment for U.S. and foreign religious broadcasts. In 1985, he filed official record of invention and copyrighted theory of the arc/xenon transmitting tube. In 1997, he filed and copyrighted theory of linear final audio-consoles and linear final equalizers.* Worked on TV commls. for Dr. Pepper, Am. Chiropractic Assn., feature movies, show Comment on Our Times, Bible's Forecast; evangelist Stas. KDTX-FM, KVTT-FM; worked on theatre trailers, network TV shows, Nelson Golf Classic, Operation Entertainment; radio evangelist Sta. Radio Africa, KXVI, WINB-shortwave, Radio Caroline, Sta. Radio East Africa Broadcasts, 1990-92, Sta. Radio Africa 2, 1991-93; spl. broadcasts Sta. Radio KSKY-AM, Radio Africa Shortwave, 1985-90; art exhbns. St. Luke's Ch. Art Exhibit, 1987, 89, DEA Art Exhibit, 1992 (winner 1st prize, 2d prize 1991), Bachman Ctr. Art Exhibit, 1992, Dorothy Michaelsen Art Exhibit, 1998; art display/exhibit Ch. of the Ascention, 1995; contbr. articles on evangelism and learning disabilities to various mags.; prodr. TV documentary Turner Falls: Niagara of the Southwest, 19997; broadcaster Pan Am. Broadcasting, 1983-96; prodr., cinematographer documentary Chickasaw National Park; prodr., sponsor of broadcasts at Radio Newspaper, Panama, 1986-96; prodr., sponsor of religious music spl. Pan Am. Broadcasting, Radio Newspaper, 1996; prodr., editor, mem. DCTV Dallas Cmty. TV, 1997—; prodr. of religious radio AM/FM, shortwave broadcasts, 1974-97; prodr., cinematographer, editor, narrator (cable TV) Turner Falls, 1996-97, Niagara of the Southwest, Chickasaw National Park, 1997, Americans with Disabilities, 1997, Anderson Bonner Park, 1997, Bachman Creek, By the Day and Night, 1997-98; prodr. (cable TV documentary) The Trinity River and its Tributaries, 1998; prodr. (cable TV) Save the Land, Save the Senery, Save the River, 1998, St. Luke's Episcopal Svc., 1999. Mem. Coalition for Better TV CBTV, Tupelo, Miss.; mem. So. Poverty Law Ctr., Birmingham, Ala., 1981-84. Named to Life History Ctr., Conroe, Tex., Internat. Hall of Leaders, 1988, Artist of Month, Reach Inc., Dallas, 1997; recipient award Republican Com., 1962, 1st place award Dallas Epilepsy Assn. Art Exhibit Contest, 1991; named hon. reverend doctor by several Tasmanian ofcls., 1985. Mem. Am. Family Assn. Avocation: amateur radio operator. Home: 3875 Dunhaven Rd Dallas TX 75220-3733

CLOSSON, WALTER FRANKLIN, prosecutor; b. Phila., Dec. 24, 1944; s. David Mayard Jr. and Florence Louise (Anderson) C.; m. Irene Veronica Jones, Aug. 10, 1968; children: Forrest Troy, Carey-Walter Franklin. BS in Music Edn., West Chester U., 1967; JD, Potomac Sch. Law, Washington, 1981. Bar: Ga. 1983, Md. 1985. Tchr. music D.C. Pub. Schs., Washington, 1967-77; tchr. woodwinds D.C. Youth Orch. Program, Washington, 1969-71; dist. ct. commr. Dist. Ct. of Md., Ellicott City, 1978-89; supervising dist. ct. commr. Dist. Ct. of Howard County, Ellicott City, 1984-89; asst. state's atty. State's Atty.'s Office, Ellicott City, 1989-99; chief child support divn. State's Atty.'s Office, 1999—. Mem.. Howard County Bar Assn., Waring-Mitchell Law Soc. (pres. 1992-94, Man of Yr. 1990), Masons (sr. deacon 1996-97, sr. warden 1997-98, worshipful master, 1998-99), Delta Theta Phi (v.p. 1979-80). Office: Howard County States Atty 3565 A-1 Ellicott Mills Dr Ellicott City MD 21043

CLOSTER, SIDNEY HOWARD, international service organization administrator; b. Bklyn., July 7, 1917; s. Harry and Mollie (Ginsburg) C.; m. Rose May Closter, Nov. 9, 1941; children: Gale Hilary, Harold Alan. BA, NYU, 1938; JD, George Washington U., 1949. Asst. chief reports sect. War Assets Adminstrn., Washington, 1946-48; exec. dir. B'nai B'rith Found. of the U.S., Washington, 1948-96; trustee B'nai B'rith Retirement Plan, Washington, 1978-85, Assn. Jewish Cmty. Orgn. Pers., Columbus, Ohio, 1986-90. Contbr. articles to profl. jours. Mem., com. chair Rosemary Hills Civic Assn., Silver Spring, Md., 1954-60; mem. adv. bd. Cmty. Sch. Bd., Silver Spring, 1975—; bd. dirs. Inst. on Global Aging; active vol. charitable orgns. Warrant officer U.S. Army, 1942-45, Pacific Theatre of Operations. Decorated Bronze Star medal General Headquarters; recipient Resolution and Commendation, Senate of State of Md., 1995. Mem. Nat. Soc. Fund Raising Execs. (com. chair), Planned Giving Com., Alumni Assn. N.Y. and George Washington U. Democrat. Jewish. Home: 3330 N Leisure World Blvd Silver Spring MD 20906-5622

CLOTHIAUX, EUGENE EDMUND, climate research scientist, meteorology educator; b. Las Cruces, N.Mex., Oct. 13, 1961; s. Eugene John and Clara Ann Clothiaux; m. Jessica Rhoda Staley, Aug. 11, 1990; children: Daniel Blair, Joshua David. BS, Auburn (Ala.) U., 1983; ScM, Brown U., 1986, PhD, 1990. Tchg. asst. Brown U., Providence, 1984-85, rsch. asst., 1985-90; postdoctoral fellow Pa. State U., University Park, 1991-93, rsch. assoc., 1993-99, asst. prof. meteorology, 1999—; sci. field expts. to study clouds and their impact on climate -- Fire Cirrus II, Coffeyville, Kans., 1991, ASTEX, Santa Maria, Azores, 1992, MCTEX, Darwin, Australia, 1995, U.S. Dept. Energy, Lamont, Okla., 1995—. Contbr. articles to profl. jours. Univ. scholar, 1983; U.S. Dept. Energy Global Change Disting. Postdoctoral fellow, 1991-93. Mem. Am. Geophys. Union, Am. Meteorol. Soc. Office: Pa State U Dept Meteorology 503 Walker Bldg University Park PA 16802

CLOTHIER, ISAAC H., IV, lawyer; b. Phila., July 14, 1932; s. Isaac H. and Emily (Bartow) C.; m. Barbara K. Massey, June 25, 1955; children: Isaac H. Clothier V, Melinda C. Biddle, Rebecca C. Case. BA, Princeton U., 1954; JD, U. Pa., 1957. Assoc. Dechert Price & Rhoads, Phila., 1957-66, ptnr., 1966-97; bd. dirs. Bryn Mawr (Pa.) Hosp. Found., Boettner Inst. chmn., former companion Diocese Com.-Episcopal Ch. Diocese Pa.; mem. Phila. Estate Planning Coun.; trustee emeritus Shipley Sch.; former bd. dirs. Melmark House, ARC Southeastern Pa. chpt. Fellow Am. Coll. Trusts and Estates Coun.; mem. ABA, Pa. Bar Assn., Phila. Bar Assn., Estate Planning Coun., Merion Cricket Club, Mill Dam Club, Phila. Club, Soc. War 1812. Office: Dechert Price & Rhoads 4000 Bell Atlantic Towers 1717 Arch St Ste 3 Philadelphia PA 19103-2793

CLOTWORTHY, JOHN HARRIS, oceanographic consultant; b. Balt., Mar. 23, 1924; s. Harris A. and Violet (Klein) C.; m. Martha D. Wilson, Mar. 22, 1947; 1 son, John S. B.E.E., U. Va., 1946; certificate, Harvard Bus. Sch., 1956. Registered profl. engr., Md. With Westinghouse Electric Corp., 1948-67, v.p. def. and space center, gen. mgr. underseas div., 1963-67; chmn. div. ocean engring. U. Miami, Fla., 1967-68; cons. to oceanographic industry, 1967-68; founder, pres. Oceans Gen., Inc., Miami, 1968-71; dir. office congl. and legislative affairs NOAA, Washington, 1971-78; v.p., gen. mgr. Joint Oceanographic Instns. Inc., Washington, 1978-88, cons., 1988—; Sec., v.p. Oak Bldg. & Savs. Assn., 1946-56; Bd. govs. Va. Engring. Found., 1965-68, 72-78. Trustee, co-chmn., bd. advisors Mare Nostrum Found., 1986-88. Fellow Marine Tech. Soc. (founding mem., bd. dirs. 1966-69, chmn. silver anniversary com. 1986-88, Lockheed award for ocean sci. and enging. 1992); mem. AAAS, Am. Geophys. Union, Nat. Oceanography Assn. (pres. 1966-69), Internat. Club of Annapolis (pres. 1995-96), Annapolis Yacht Club, Atlantic City Convention Hall Organ Soc. (sec., treas. 1998—), Alpha Tau Omega. Home: 1270 Log Canoe Ct Annapolis MD 21403-4333

CLOUD, BARBARA LEE, adult education educator; b. Tulare, Calif., June 12, 1938; d. Virgil R. and Nina N. Hicks; m. Stanley Donovan Cloud, 1960. BA, Stanford U., 1960; MA, U. Oreg., 1967; PhD, U. Wash., 1979. News editor Springfield (Oreg.) News, 1961-65; info. officer Australian Nat. U., Canberra, 1968-70; pub. rels. cons. Eric White Assoc., Perth, Australia, 1970-76; asst., assoc. and prof. U. Nev., Las Vegas, 1979—, assoc. provost, 1998—. Author: The Business of Newspapers on the Western Frontier, 1992 (Nev. Humanities award); co-author: Media Law in Nevada, 1992; editor Journalism History, 1992—; contbr. articles to profl. jours. Mem. Nev. Humanities Com., 1994—, N.W. Commn. on Colls., 1997—. Mem. Am. Journalism Historians Assn. (pres. 1984-85), Assn. Edn. Journalism and Mass Comm. (head history divsn. 1992-93, History Svc. award 1995), Soc. Profl. Jounalists, Conf. Hist. Jours., Phi Kappa Phi. Avocations: hiking, weaving, photography. Office: U Nev 4505 S Maryland Pkwy Las Vegas NV 89154-1002

CLOUD, BRUCE BENJAMIN, SR., construction company executive; b. Thomas, Okla., Feb. 15, 1920; s. Dudley R. and Lillian (Sanders) C.; m. Virginia Dugan, June 5, 1944; children: Sheila Marie Cloud Kiselis, Karen Susan, Bruce Benjamin, Deborah Ann Cloud McKenzie, Virginia Ann Cloud Treadwell. BCE, Tex. A. and M. U., 1940. Registered profl. engr., Tex. With H.B. Zachry Co., San Antonio, 1940-42, 55-99, exec. v.p., 1963-87, pres., 1987-93, vice chmn., 1993-94, sr. corp. advisor, 1995-99, adv. dir., 1999—; ptnr., bd. dirs. Dudley R. Cloud & Son, Constrn., San Antonio, 1946-55; owner Cloud Enterprises, San Antonio; mem. adv. bd. dirs. Capitol Cement Co./Aggregate Co., 1999—. Mem. adv. coun. Boysville Inc., 1978-79; bd. dirs. Tex. State Tech. Coll. Found., 1983-97, 98—, hon. life bd. mem.; mem. adv. bd. Tex. Engring. Extension Svc., 1995—. Lt. col. C.E. AUS, 1942-46, ETO. Recipient Pro Deo Et Juventute award Nat. Council Catholic Youth. Mem. AIM, NSPE, KC (3d degree), Tex. Assn. Gen. Contractors (life, dir. hwy. and heavy br. 1947-48, 72-76, pres. 1974, chmn. corps engrs. joint com. 1989-90), Am. Concrete Paving Assn. (v.p. 1970-74, bd. dirs., 1st v.p. 1975, pres. 1976), Nat. Asphalt Paving Assn., Tex. Hotmix Paving Assn. (bd. dirs. 1972), Nat. Assn. Gen. Contractors (bd. dirs. 1976-88, life dir., exec. com. 1978-79, bur. reclamaton com. 1977-97, corps engrs. com. 1986-97, equipment mgmt. com. 1978-97, chmn. heavy divsn. 1979), San Antonio Livestock Assn. (life), Tex. Soc. Profl. Engrs., Tex. Good Rds.-Transp. Assn. (dir. 1974-79, exec. com. 1975-81, 85-89), Am. Mgmt. Assn., San Antonio C. of C. (chmn. better rds. task force 1978-79, 85-93, bd. dirs. 1993-94), Tex. Transp. Inst. (adv. bd. 1993-97), Tex. Ext. Svc. (adv. bd. 1995-97), Cons. Contractors Coun. Am. (chmn. 1989), Holy Name Soc. (v.p. 1962-63), Nocturnal Adoration Soc., Alpha Epsilon Chi. Home: 127 Cave Ln San Antonio TX 78209-2208 Office: Cloud Enterprises 127 Cave Ln San Antonio TX 78209

CLOUD, GARY LYNN, food and nutrition services administrator; b. Knoxville, Tenn., July 14, 1945; d. Henry Kelso Cloud. BS in Home Econs., Food and Nutrition, U. Tenn., 1966; MPH, U. N.C., 1972; postgrad., SUNY, Albany, 1988—. Lic. dietitian and pub. health nutritionist, Tenn.; registered Am. Dietetic Assn. Dietetic technician Fort Sander's Presbyn. Hosp., Knoxville, Tenn., 1966; dietetic internship N.Y. State Dept. Mental Hygiene Hudson River State Hosp., Poughkeepsie, N.Y., 1966-67; svc. systems corp. Del Monte, Inc., Bennington, Vt., 1967-70; sr. nutritionist, apprentice nutrition svc. cons. to nutrition svcs. cons. N.Y. State Dept. Health, 1970-73; assoc. nutritionist N.Y. State Bd. Social Welfare, Albany, 1973-76; playground supr. Knox County Dept. Recreation, Knoxville, 1980; chief clin. dietitian II, asst. dietary dept. dir. N.C. Dept. Human Resources, O'Berry Ctr., Goldsboro, N.C., 1980-82; nursing asst. Hillcrest North Nursing Home, Knox County, Tenn., 1988; libr. asst. U. Tenn. Libr.-Reserve Book Rm., 1990; shared facility registered dietitian Hillhaven Corp., Loudon Health Care, Tenn., 1990; auditor RQA Inc. Nat. Retail Quality Evaluators, Darion, Ill., 1994—; regional supervising dietitian Svc. Sys. Corp., Del Monte Inc., 1967-70; dir. Bur. Nutrition Svcs. Mem. Am. Dietetic Assn., Tenn. Dietetic Assn., Knoxville Dist. Dietetic Assn., Knoxville Nutrition Coun. Home: 8500 Millertown Pike Knoxville TN 37924-1105

CLOUD, LINDA BEAL, retired secondary school educator; b. Jay, Fla., Dec. 4, 1937; d. Charles Rockwood and Agnes (Diamond) Beal; m. Robert Vincent Cloud (Aug. 15, 1959 (dec. 1985). BA, Miss. Coll., 1959; MEd, U. So. Fla., 1976; EdS, Nova U., 1982; postgrad., Walden U., 1983. Cert. tchr., Fla. Tchr. Ft. Meade (Fla.) Jr.-Sr. H.S., 1959-67, 80-89, Lake Wales (Fla.) H.S., 1967-80; pres. Cloud Aero Svcs., Inc., Babson Park, Fla., 1992—; part-time tchr. Spanish, English, Polk County Adult Schs., 1960-76; instr. Spanish Warner So. Coll., Lake Wales, 1974; instr. vocal music, drama, composition Webber Coll., Babson Park, Fla.; cons. Fla. Assn. Student Couns. Workshops, 1968-81; pvt. tutor in field. Contbr. articles to profl. and equine publs.; author, dir. numerous pageants for schs.; poetry in The Nat. Libr. of Poetry. Charter mem., bd. dirs. Lake Wales Little Theatre, Inc., 1976; dir. Four Sq. swing choir; entertainer for various local orgns.; ring announcer Fla. State Fair, 1987-88; judge poetry and essay contests; mem. Defenders of Crooked Lake; mem., soloist Babson Pk. Cmty. Ch.; vol., dir. Candy Stripers, Lake Wales Hosp., 1973-79. Recipient Best Actress award Lake Wales Little Theatre, Inc., 1978-79. Mem. AAUW, Nat. Coun. Tchrs. English, Fla. Coun. Tchrs. English, Polk Coun. Tchrs. English, Polk Fgn. Lang. Assn., Babson Park Womans Club, Sassy Singers, Southeastern Peruvian Horse Club (life). Republican. Baptist. Avocations: singing, acting, costume design, horseback riding, Peruvian horse exhibitions and parades. Home: Diamond Firefox Peruvians 4405 Hwy 197-A Jacksonville FL 32565

CLOUD, ROBERT ROYCE, surgeon; b. Houston, Feb. 12, 1954; s. Albert Hadden and Emily Ann (Royce); m. Karen Sue Mooneyham, June 5, 1982; children: Kyle, Ashley, Tyler. BS, Northeast La. U., 1976; MD, Tulane, 1980. Intern gen. surgery Baylor Med. Ctr., Dallas, 1980-81, resident gen. surgery, 1981-85, fellow colon rectal surgery, 1985-86; private practice Dallas, 1986—; mem. staff Med. City Hosp., Dallas, 1986—, Baylor Hosp., 1986—, Presbyn. Hosp., Dallas, 1988—. Bd. dirs. Wednesday's Child, Am. Cancer Soc. Fellow ACS, Am. Soc. Colon Rectal Surgeons; mem. Tex. Surgical Soc., Tex. Med. Assn., Tex. Soc. Colon Rectal Surgeons, Dallas County Med. Soc. Avocations: golf, tennis. Office: 12200 Park Central Dr Ste 100 Dallas TX 75251-2107*

CLOUD, STANLEY WILLS, journalist, editor, writer; b. Los Angeles, Nov. 4, 1936; s. Wade and Esther Maxine (Sowers) C.; m. Nancy Jean Fuller, June 22, 1962 (div. 1979); children: Michael Sean, David Stanley, Matthew Wade; m. Christina Lynne Olson, Jan. 5, 1980; 1 child, Caroline Wills. B.A., Pepperdine Coll., Los Angeles, 1958; postgrad. in Russian lang., Def. Lang. Inst., Monterey, Calif., 1961-62. Editorial clk. Los Angeles Times Mirror Syndicate, 1954-58; reporter Monterey Peninsula Herald, Calif., 1964-66; editor The Advocate, Monterey, 1966-68; corr. Time Mag., San Francisco, 1968-69, Moscow, USSR, 1969-70; bur. chief Time Mag., Bangkok, Thailand, 1970-71, Saigon, Vietnam, 1971-72; Senate corr. Time Mag., Washington, 1972-74, polit. corr., 1974-76, White House corr., 1976-78, news services editor, 1978-79, dep. Washington bur. chief, 1987-89, Washington bur. chief, 1989-93, Washington contbg. editor, 1993-94; contbributor, 1994; asst. mng. editor Washington Star, 1979-80, mng. editor, 1980-81; exec. editor Los Angeles Herald Examiner, 1982-86; freelance journalist Alexandria, Va., 1986-87; writer, author, 1995—. Co-author: The Murrow Boys, 1996. Exec. dir. The Citizens Election Project, 1995-96. Served to lt. USNR, 1958-64. Mem. Coun. on Fgn. Rels., The Cosmos Club.

CLOUDSLEY, DONALD HUGH, library administrator; b. Buffalo, Jan. 11, 1925; s. James Rowland and Helen Margaret (Macgregor) C. BA, Bethany Coll., W.Va., 1948; MLS, Carnegie Inst. Tech., 1949. Jr. librarian Buffalo Pub. Library, 1949-52; sr. librarian I Erie County Pub. Library, Buffalo, 1952-58; sr. librarian II Buffalo and Erie County Pub. Library, 1958-59, dep. dir., 1974-83, dir., 1983-95; reference librarian Grosvenor Library, Buffalo, 1959-61; head Brighton br. Tonawanda Library, N.Y., 1961-65; dir. Tonawanda Library, 1965-73; trustee West N.Y. Libr. Resources Coun., Buffalo, 1983-93, treas., 1976-89; mem. N.Y. State Regent's Adv. Coun. on Librs., 1988-93, chmn., 1990-91; mem. adv. com. on pub. librs. Online Computer Libr. Ctr., 1991-94. Mem. citizens adv. coun. SUNY-Buffalo, 1983—. Named Boss of Yr., Am. Bus. Women's Assn., Buffalo, 1984; recipient Alumni Achievement award Bethany Coll., 1991, Buffalo (N.Y.) News Citizen of Yr. award, 1992. Mem. ALA, N.Y. Libr. Assn., N.Y. State Pub. Librs. Assn. (cert. com. 1971-75), Rotary (treas. Kenmore, N.Y. club 1975-76), Beta Theta Pi. Methodist. Home: 152 Hidden Ridge Cmn Williamsville NY 14221-5765

CLOUES, EDWARD BLANCHARD, II, lawyer; b. Concord, N.H., Dec. 28, 1947; s. Alfred Samuel and H. Jeannette (Callas) C.; m. Mary Anne Matthews, Aug. 21, 1971; children: E. Matthew, M. Elizabeth. BA, Harvard U., 1969; JD, NYU, 1972. Bar: Pa. 1972, U.S. Dist. Ct. (ea. dist.) Pa. 1973. Law clk. to hon. judge James Hunter III U.S. Ct. Appeals (3d cir.), Phila. and Camden, N.J., 1972-73; assoc. Morgan, Lewis & Bockius, LLP, Phila., 1973-79, ptnr., 1979-98; chmn., CEO K-Tron Internat., Inc., Pitman, N.J., 1998—; bd. dirs. K-Tron Internat., Pitman, N.J., vice chmn. bd., 1987-94; bd. dirs. Amrep Corp., chmn., 1995—; bd. dirs. AmeriQuest Tech., Inc. Republican. Lutheran. Avocations: travel, reading. Office: K-Tron Internat Inc PO Box 888 Rtes 55 & 553 Pitman NJ 08071

CLOUGH, BARRY, marketing executive; b. June 19, 1941; married; 3 children. BS in Bus. Adminstrn., BS in Applied Math. Engring., U. Colo., 1964; M in Computer Sci., Bradley U., 1970. Mgr. sales, customer svc. engine divsn. Caterpillar, Inc., Peoria, Ill.; chmn. bd. WTVP-Channel 47, Peoria; bd. trustees Mt. Hawley C.C.; bd. trustees., chmn. bd. Advanced Filter Sys. Inc. Mem. parents bd. Internat. Sch. Brussels. Office: Caterpillar Inc 100 NE Adams St Peoria IL 61629-0002*

CLOUGH, GERALD WAYNE, academic administrator; b. Douglas, Ga., Sept. 24, 1941; married; 2 children. BS in Civil Engring., Ga. Inst. Tech., 1964, MSCE, 1965; PhD, U. Calif., Berkeley, 1969. Registered profl. engr., Calif., Va. Assoc. prof. to prof. civil engring. Stanford (Calif.) U., 1974-82; prof. civil engring., coord. geotech. program Va. Polytechnic Inst. and State U., 1982-83, prof. civil engring., head dept. civil engring., 1983-90, dean Coll. Engring., 1990-93; provost, prof. civil engring. U. Wash., Seattle, 1993-94; pres. Ga. Inst. Tech., Atlanta, 1994—. Office: Ga Inst Tech Office of the Pres 225 North Avae NW Carnegie Bldg Atlanta GA 30332*

CLOUGH, LAUREN C., retired special education educator; b. Canton, N.Y., Mar. 17, 1924; s. Hiram William and Lena May (Ladison) C.; m. Margaret Ellen Williamson, June 8, 1951; children: David Wayne, Carol Canty (dec.). BA, U. Ala., 1947; MA in Teaching, U. Jacksonville, 1969; cert. mental retardation, U. Fla.; cert. specific LDEH, U. North Fla. Tchr. Duval County Bd. Pub. Instrn., Jacksonville, Fla., 1964-70; tchr. history Nassau County Bd. Pub. Instrn., Fernandina Beach, Fla., 1970-71, tchr. mentally retarded, 1971-73, specific learning disabled and emotionally handicapped resource tchr., 1973-98; tchr. Hilliard (Fla.) Elem. Sch., 1973-98; ret., 1998; mem. Hilliard Elem. Sch. improvement co., 1991-98, chmn. sch. pub. rels. com., 1993-95, mem. comm. com., 1994-98, Title I com., 1994-97; mem. SACS Sch. Accreditation com., 1995-96, mem. student svcs. com., 1997-98.

CLOUGH, RAY WILLIAM, JR., civil engineering educator; b. Seattle, July 23, 1920; s. Ray William and Mildred (Nelson) C.; m. Shirley Claire Potter, Oct. 30, 1942; children—Douglas Potter, Allison Justine, Meredith Anne. B.S. in Civil Engring, U. Wash., 1942; M.S., Calif. Inst. Tech., 1943; S.M., MIT, 1947, Sc.D., 1949; D.Tech. (hon.), Chalmers U., Goteborg, Sweden, 1979, U. Trondheim, (Norway), 1982. Registered profl. engr., Wash. Faculty U. Calif.-Berkeley, 1949—, prof. civil engring., 1959—, chmn. div. structural engring. and structural mechanics, 1967-70, dir. Earthquake Engring. Research Ctr., 1973-76, Nishkian prof. structural engring., 1983-87, emeritus, 1987—; cons. in field, 1953—; mem. NAS-NAE adv. com. Environ. Sci. Svcs. Adminstrn., 1967-70; mem. dynamics panel NAS adv. bd. on hardened electric power system, 1964-70; mem. U.S. C.E. Structural Design Adv. Bd., 1967-79. Served to capt. USAAF, 1942-46. Recipient Sr. Rsch. award Am. Soc. for Engring. Edn., 1986, Congress medal Internat. Assn. Computer Mechanics, 1986, citation U. Calif. at Berkeley, 1987, A.C. Eringen medal soc. of Engring. Sci., 1992, U.S. Nat. Medal of Sci. presented by Pres. William J. Clinton, 1994, Prince Philip medal Royal Acad. Engring., 1997; Fulbright fellow Ship Rsch. Inst. Trondheim, Norway, 1956-57, Tech. U. Norway, 1972-73, Overseas fellow Churchill Coll., Cambridge (Eng.) U., 1963-64; hon. rschr. Lab. Nacional De Engenharia Civil Lisbon, Portugal, 1972. Fellow ASCE (chmn. engring. mechanics divsn. 1964-65, Rsch. award 1960, Howard award 1970, Newmark medal 1979, Moissieff medal 1980, hon. mem. 1989, T. VonKarman medal 1995), Inst. Water Conservation and Hydroelectric Power Rsch. (hon. mem. People's Republic of China 1992); mem. NAS, NAE, Structural Engrs. Assn. No. Calif. (bd. dirs. 1967-70), Earthquake Engring. Rsch. Inst. (bd. dirs. 1957-60, 70-73, George W. Housner medal 1996), Seismol. Soc. Am. (bd. dirs. 1970-73). Home: PO Box 4625 Sunriver OR 97707-1625

CLOUS, JAMES M., electrical equipment company executive, engineer; b. Traverse City, Mich., July 22, 1959; s. August J. and Beverly J. (Kroetsch) C.; m. Mimi M. O'Connell, June 28, 1979 (div. July 1983). AS, Northwestern Mich. Coll., 1979; BSME, Mich. Tech. U., 1981. Sales engr. Louis Allis-Litton, Houston, 1981-83; dist. mgr. Louis Allis-Magnetek, Baton Rouge, 1984-85, GEC Automation Projects, Houston, 1986-88; regional mgr. Ross Hill Controls, Houston, 1989-91; nat. sales mgr. ABB Indsl. Systems, New Berlin, Wis., 1991-94; v.p. sales and mktg. Ideal Electric, Mansfield, Ohio, 1994-96; pres. Clous Cons., Traverse City, MI, 1996—; pvt. practice mktg. cons., Houston, 1987-91. Mem. Nat. Rep. Com., Washington, 1988. Mem. IEEE. Republican. Roman Catholic. Home and Office: 4062 Waterview Grawn MI 49637-9503

CLOUSE, JOHN DANIEL, lawyer; b. Evansville, Ind., Sept. 4, 1925; s. Frank Paul and Anna Lucille (Frank) C.; m. Georgia L. Ross, Dec. 7, 1978; 1 child, George Chauncey. AB, U. Evansville, 1950; JD, Ind. U., 1952. Bar: Ind. 1952, U.S. Supreme Ct. 1962, U.S. Ct. Appeals (7th cir.) 1965. Assoc. Firm of James D. Lopp, Evansville, 1952-56; pvt. practice law James D. Lopp, Evansville, 1956—; guest editorialist Viewpoint, Evansville Courier, 1978-86, Evansville Press, 1986-98, Focus, Radio Sta. WGBF, 1978-84; 2d asst. city atty. Evansville, 1954-55; mem. appellate rules sub-com. Ind. Supreme Ct. Com. on Rules of Practice and Procedure, 1980.. Pres. Civil Svc. Commn. Evansville Police Dept., 1961-62, v.p., 1988; pres. Ind. War Memls. Com., 1963-69; mem. jud. nominating com. Vanderburgh County, Ind., 1976-80; dir. Ind. Fed. Cmty. Defender Project, Inc., 1993-98. With inf. U.S. Army, 1943-46. Decorated Bronze Star; named one of World's Most travelled Man Guinness Book of Records, 1993, Most Travelled Man, 1995-99. Fellow Ind. Bar Found.; mem. Evansville Bar Assn. (v.p. 1972, James Bethel Gresham Freedom award 1997), Ind. Bar Assn. (chmn. com. on civil rights 1991-92), Travelers Century Club (L.A.), Pi Gamma Mu. Republican. Methodist. Office: 123 NW 4th St Ste 317 Evansville IN 47708

CLOUSE, MELVIN E., radiologist; b. Vinita, Okla., June 6, 1934; s. Clifford Powell and Agnes Elizabeth (Betcher) C.; m. Marian Upton, Feb. 16, 1966; children: Graydon Melville, Thomas Philip. BS, Tex. Christian U., 1967; MD, U. Tex., 1960. Diplomate Am. Bd. Radiology; lic. physician, Mass., Tex. Intern Phila. Gen. Hosp., 1960-61; resident in radiology Mass. Gen. Hosp., Boston, 1962-64, fellow radiology, 1964-65, radiologist, 1966-69; fellow radiology Armed Forces Inst. Pathology, Washington, 1965; from asst. in radiology to prof. Harvard Med. Sch., 1966-87; radiologist New Eng. Deaconess Hosp., Boston, 1969-96; chmn. dept. radiology Deaconess Hosp., Boston, 1975-96; vice chmn. dept radiology Beth Israel Deaconess Med. Ctr., Boston, 1996—; vis. prof. radiology U. Conn. Med. Sch., 1980, U. Va. Med. Sch., 1980, Loyola U., Maywood, Ill., 1981; examiner Am. Bd. Radiology, various yrs., question devel. written exam., 1994; staff dept. radiology Dana Farber Cancer Inst., 1989—; mem. various coms. New Eng. Deaconess Hosp., 1975—, ex-officio mem. bd. dirs., 1979-81; clin. assoc. Cancer Rsch. Inst./New Eng. Deaconess Hosp., 1978-90; chief radiology svc. Quigley meml. Hosp./Soldiers Home, 1985-87; pres. Deaconess Profl. Practice Group/New Eng. Deaconess Hosp. Mem. reviewer Cardiovascular and Interventional Radiology, 1980—, Transplantation, 1981—, Radiology, 1982—, Radiographics, 1988—, Investigative Radiology, 1990—, assoc. editor Liver Transplantation and Surgery, 1994—, Gastroenterology, 1994—; contbr. articles to profl. jours. Trustee Beaver Country Day Sch., Chestnut Hill, Mass., 1988-91, v.p., trustee, 1991. Grantee Nat. Inst. Arthritis, Diabetes, Digestive and Kidney Diseases, Nat. Inst. Neurol. Diseases and Blindness, Am. Cancer Soc., USPH; U. Tex. fellow, 1958; recipient 4th Pl. award Soc. Nuclear Medicine, 1983; named Hon. Prof. Xi'an Med. U., China, 1989. Fellow Am. Coll. Radiology (councillor 1971-75), Soc. Cardiovascular and Interventional Radiology; mem. AMA, Am. Roentgen Ray Soc., Radiol. Soc. N.Am. (councillor, program com. cardiovascular radiology 1983), Mass. Radiologic Soc. (exec. com. 1971-75, councillor 1973-76, tribunal com. 1980, com. on standards in radiol. practice 1984-85, standards on radiologistical practice com., others, 1992), Mass. Med. Soc., New Eng. Roentgen Ray Soc. (sec. 1974-77, pres. 1980-81, exec. com. 1981-82, chmn. exec. com. 1983-84, nominating com., profl. ethics com. 1984-85, chmn. nominating com. 1986-87), New Eng. Cardiovascular and Interventional Roentgen Soc. (pres. 1982-83), Soc. for Magnetic Resonance in Medicine, Assn. Univ. Radiologists (membership com. 1985-87), Am. Heart Assn. Home: 59 Monmouth St Brookline MA 02446-5606 Office: Beth Israel Hosp 1 Deaconess Rd Boston MA 02215-5321

CLOUSE, R. WILBURN, education educator; b. Manchester, Tenn., May 13, 1937. BA in Chemistry, David Lipscomb U., 1959; postgrad., U. Tenn., 1960-63; MA in Econs., Mid. Tenn. State U., Murfreesboro, 1968; PhD in Ednl. Adminstrn., Vanderbilt U., 1977; postgrad., U. N.C., 1981. Rsch. asst. dept. biochemistry Vanderbilt U., Nashville, 1959-63; assoc. prof. dept. libr. and info. sci. Vanderbilt U., 1977-89, assoc. prof. dept. ednl. leadership Peabody Coll. Edn. and H, 1977—; founder, dir. ctr. entrepreneurship Vanderbilt U., Nashville, 1997—; chemist process and product devel. systems E.I. DuPont, Old Hickory, Tenn., 1963-65; experimental test supr. Dacron mfg. E.I. DuPont, Old Hickory, 1965-66, internat. tng. coord., 1966-67; part-time instr. econs. Mid. Tenn. State U., Murfreesboro, 1966-67; acting dir. computer ctr., acting chmn. dept. computer sci. Columbia (Tenn.) State C.C., 1966-67; instr. libr. sci., dir. Kennedy Ctr. Rsch. and Instrnl. Comp George Peabody Coll. for Tchrs., 1969-70, asst. dir. for adminstrn., 1969-81, asst. prof. edn., 1970-77, 1976-77; part-time spl. lectr. in bus. mgmt. David Lipscomb U., Nashville, 1967-73; co-dir. Kennedy Ctr. Rsch. and Instrnl. Computer Ctr., George Peabody Coll. for Tchrs., 1973-74, chmn. libr. sci. faculty, 1977-79; sr. rsch. assoc. Inst. for Pub. Policy Studies, Vanderbilt U., 1981-86, assoc. dir. Corp. Learning Inst., 1984-87, rsch. assoc. Learning Tech. Ctr., 1984-88, dir. program libr. and info. sci., 1988-89, dir. Ctr. for Entrepreneurship Edn., 1997—; spl. asst. IBM Edn. Industry Nat. Mktg. Hdqs., Atlanta, 1982; grants reviewer Social Scis. and Humanities Rsch. Coun. of Can., 1989—; policy reviewer Nat. Ctr. for Rsch. in Vocat. Edn., 1983-86; presenter, cons. in field. Author: A Comparison of a Manual Library Reclassification Project With a Computer Automated Library Reclassification Project, 1975, A Planning Strategy for an Information Network for the University of Costa Rica, 1978, The Expected Role of Beginning Librarians: A Comparative Analysis from Administrators, Educators and Young Professionals, 1979, A Review of Educational Role Theory: A Teaching Guide for Administrative Theory, 1990; co-author: (tchr. manual) (with Darlene McDowell, Noel McDowell, Marshal Williams, J.B. Hill and Steven Baum) The LOGO Classroom, 1985, (student workbook) The LOGO Classroom, 1985, (with Larry Garrett) A Review of Selected Literacy Related Programs, 1988, (with Leslie McLean) Stress and Burnout: An Organizational Synthesis, 1992; contbr. articles to profl. jours.; editor: Research Management Systems for Mental Retardation Research Centers: Proceedings of a Conference, 1974, Adminstrators as Educators: Proceedings of a National Conference for Administrators of University Affiliated Facilities, 1976; co-editor: Education of Health Service Administrators in an Interdisciplinary Model, University of Oregon Health Sciences Center, 1975; mem. editl. rev. bd. Psychology—A Jour. of Human Behavior, 1996—; mem. editl adv. bd. The Inst. for Memetric Rsch., 1990—; editl. advisor Operational Rsch. Quar., Birmingham, Eng., 1974—. Grantee Nat. Inst. Child Health and Human Devel., 1970-81, 73-74, NIH, 1970-80, Tenn. Dept. Mental Health and Mental Retardation, 1974-81, 75-76, U. Oreg./Human Svcs. Mental Health Adminstrn., 1975-76, UCLA/Am. Assn. Mental Deficiency, 1975-76, Joseph P. Kennedy Jr. Found. Fellowship Program in Edn. and Pub. Policy, Tanzania, 1980-81, Tenn. Dept. Vocat. Edn., 1970-71; Sam Walton Free Enterprise fellow, 1997; recipient honor Peabody Round Table, 1988, 92, Peabody Outstanding Faculty award, 1983. Fax: (615) 343-7094. E-mail: clouserw@ctrvax.vanderbilt.edu. Office: Peabody Coll Dept Leadership & Orgn 202 Payne Hall Box 514 Peabody Vanderbilt U Nashville TN 37203

CLOUSE, VICKIE RAE, biology and paleontology educator; b. Havre, Mont., Mar. 28, 1956; d. Olaf Raymond and Betty Lou (Reed) Nelson; m. Gregory Scott Clouse, Mar. 22, 1980; 1 child, Kristopher Nelson. BS in Secondary Sci. Edn., Mont. State U. No., Havre, 1989; postgrad., Mont. State U., Bozeman, 1991-94. Teaching asst. biology and paleontology Mont. State U.-No., Havre, 1986-90; rsch. asst. dinosaur eggs and embryos Mus. of the Rockies, Bozeman, 1992-95; instr. biology and paleontology Mont. State U.-No., Havre, 1990—; dir. Dinosaur Rsch. Expdns. Bd. trustees H.E. Clack Mus., Havre, 1991-97, H.E. Clack Mus. Found., Havre, 1991-97, Mont. Bd. Regents of Higher Edn., Helena, 1989-90, Mont. Higher Edn. Student Fin. Assistance Corp., Helena, 1989-90; mem. Ea. Mont. Hist. Soc., 1993—. Named Young Career Woman of Yr., Bus. and Profl. Woman's Club, 1986. Mem. AAAS, Soc. Vertebrate Paleontologists, Mont. Geol. Soc. Avocations: collecting vertebrate fossils, dir. dinosaur excavations for laypersons, boating. E-mail: ClouseV@yahoo.com. Office: Mont State U-No Hagener Sci Ctr Havre MT 59501

CLOUSHER, FRED EUGENE (FREDDIE CEE CLOUSHER), entertainment producer, booking agent, musician; b. Hanover, Pa., May 6, 1941; s. Raymond Samuel and Helena Elizabeth (Geiman) C.; m. Vicky S. Sumile, Dec. 18, 1967; 1 child, Michelle Marie Clousher Lively. Student, USN Sch. Music, Little Creek, Va., 1964. Music instr. various music stores Pa., 1958-63, 68-72; owner, pres. Clousher Prodns., Mechanicsburg, Pa., 1972—; leader Freddie & The Hy-Lites, Hanover, Pa., 1959-63, Tremors rock band, Norfolk, Va., 1964-65, Hawaiian Revue Show Band, Harrisburg, Pa., 1974-90. Performer (recording ABS Records) Five Minutes More b/w Foolish Love, 1960; co-writer (with Slim Anderson, K-Ark Records), Navy Wings of Gold, 1966; guitarist, musician USO shows, Vietnam and far East, 1966, navy unit band, Europe, 1967. With USN, 1963-67, Vietnam. Mem. Nat. Assn. Orch. Leaders (dist. adminstr. 1981-91), Pa. State Assn. County Fairs, Md. Assn. Agrl. Fairs and Shows, Inc., Am. Legion, VFW. Avocations: fitness walking, football, concerts, music. Home and Office: Clousher Prodns PO Box 1191 Mechanicsburg PA 17055-1191

CLOUSTON, ROSS NEAL, retired food and related products company executive; b. Montreal, Que., Can., Sept. 13, 1922; came to U.S., 1965, naturalized, 1973; s. Alan Roy and Maude (Neal) C.; m. Brenda Kerson, Feb. 12, 1944; children: Robert, Brendan. B.Sc., McGill U., 1949; M.B.A., Harvard U., 1951. With fisheries plant N.S., Can., from 1940; founder LaSalle Foods Ltd., 1953, Blue Water Sea Food Ltd., Montreal, 1959, Blue Water Sea Food Ltd. (merged into Gorton Corp., 1963, merged into Gen. Mills, Inc. 1968); pres. Gorton Group div. Gen. Mills, Inc., 1969-86, chmn., 1986-87, corp. v.p. parent co., 1970-87; v.p. Gen. Mills Can. Ltd.; pres. Nat. Fisheries Inst., 1975, Fisheries Council Can., 1962. Served with RCAF, 1941-45. Decorated Royal Norwegian Order of Merit; recipient Man of Yr. award Nat. Fisheries Inst., 1985. Mem. The Oaks.

CLOUTHIER, HECTOR, member of Canadian parliament; b. Pembroke, Ont., Can., Oct. 18, 1949; m. Deborah Ruth Mason; children: Geoffrey, Nicholas, Tyler. Student, Pembroke Collegiate Inst., Loyola Coll., Montreal, Que., Can., Harvard U., Oxford (Eng.) U. V.p. Hec Clouthier & Sons, Ltd.; v.p., sec.-treas. Clouthier Bros. Farms Ltd.; bd. mem. Rideau Carleton Raceway; M.P. from Renfrew-Nipissing-Pembroke Ho. of Commons, Can., 1997—; mem. standing com. on nat. def. and vets. affairs, 1997—, standing com. on Libr. of Parliament, 1997—; vice chair No. Ont. Liberal Caucus, 1997—; mem. Can.-Japan Inter-Parliamentary Group, Can. NATO Parliamentary Assn. Past pres. Pembroke & Area C. of C.; past campaign chair United Way, Upper Ottawa Valley; past bd. mem. St. Joseph's Food Bank, St. Joseph's Non-Profit Housing, Pembroke Gen. Hosp.; past v.p. Ottawa Valley Lumbering Mus.; past dir. Ottawa Valley Harness Horseman's Assn.; past pres. Renfrew-Nipissing-Pembroke Riding Assn.; ind. candidate Renfrew-Nipissing-Pembroke, 1993. Avocations: licensed harness driver, golfing, skiing, hockey, jogging. Fax: (613) 995-2561. Office: House of Commons, Rm 413, Confederation Bldg, Ottawa, ON Canada K1A 0A6 and: 541 Pembroke St E, Pembroke Ont Canada K8A 3L5

CLOUTIER, GILLES GEORGES, academic administrator, research executive; b. Quebec, Que., Can., June 27, 1928; m. Colette Michaud, May 1954; children: Hélène, Suzanne, Pierre, Benoit, Nathalie. BA, Laval U., 1949, BScA, 1953; PhD in Physics, McGill U., 1956, PhD, 1959; PhD (hon.), U. de Montréal, 1982, U. Alta., 1983, McGill U., 1986, U. Lyon II, France, 1987, U. Toronto, 1991. With RCA Research Lab., 1959-63; assoc. prof. U. Montreal, 1963-67, prof., 1967-68; dir basic. scis., then dir. rsch. and asst. dir. the inst. Hydro Que. Inst. Rsch., 1968-78; pres. Alta. Rsch. Coun., 1978-83; exec. v.p. technology and internat. affairs Hydro-Quebec, 1983-85; rector U. Montreal, 1985-93; dep. chair Prime Min.'s Adv. Coun. on Sci. and Tech., 1998—; cons., 1993—; bd. dirs. Bechtel Can., Gentec Inc.; mem. Nat. Rsch. Coun., Can., 1973-77; conseil de la politique scientifique de Que., 1975-77. Bd. govs. U. Montreal, 1976-80, 83-85; bd. dirs. Asia Pacific Found. of Can., 1990. Decorated Companion, Order of Can., 1994, Officer Order of Que., 1989; chevalier de la Légion D'Honneur (France), 1991. Mem. IEEE (sr.), Can. Assn. of Physicists (pres. 1971-72), Order of Engrs. of the Province of Que., Am. Phys. Soc., Can. Acad. Engring., Assn. Univs. and Colls. Can. (bd. dirs. 1986-89), C. of C. of Greater Montreal, Corp.-Higher Edn. forum (chmn. 1992-93), Royal Soc. Can. Roman Catholic. Home: Apt 1208, 4500 Promenade Paton, Laval, PQ Canada H7W 4Y6 Office: U de Montréal, PO Box 6128 Sta A, Montreal, PQ Canada H3C 3J7 Office: U Montreal, 2910 Edouard-Montpetit Rm 6, Montreal, PQ Canada H3C 3J7

CLOUTIER, WILFRID AMÉDÉE, retired surgeon; b. Lewiston, Maine, Dec. 5, 1921; s. Amedee and Fedora (Bisson) C.; m. Rolande Jean d'Arc Lanoue, June 23, 1949; children: Louise, Pauline, Gisele, Suzanne, Marie, Lisa, Robert. BA, Coll. Montreal, Can.; MD, Laval U., Quebec City, Can. Diplomate Am. Bd. Surgery. Intern Laval U. Hosp., Quebec City, resident in surgery; resident in surgery Bellevue Hosp./NYU Med. Ctr., N.Y.C., asst. resident, chief resident, chief resident surgery, 1953-57; resident in chest surgery Tokyo Army Hosp., 1951-53; surg. practice St. Mary's Hosp., Lewiston, 1957-90, chief of surgery, 1962-75; ret., 1990. Capt. Med. Corps U.S. Army, 1951-58. Fellow ACS. Home: 29 W Woods Keys Way Yarmouth Port MA

CLOVIS, DONNA LUCILLE, journalist, editor; b. East Orange, N.J., Aug. 22, 1957; d. Clarence M. and Annye Brown; m. James R. Clovis III; children: Justin, Matthian, Michaela. BA, Trenton (N.J.) State Coll., 1978, LittD (hon.), 1991; MA in Jouralism, Columbia U. Cert. in ESL, elem. edn. Tchr. New Brunswick (N.J.) Bd. Edn., 1981-86, North Brunswick (N.J.) Bd. Edn., 1986-88, Voorhees (N.J.) Bd. Edn., 1989-91, Princeton Regional Schs., Princeton (N.J.) Bd. of Edn., 1991-96; journalist, editor Scholastic Inc., N.Y.C., 1996—; presenter ESL workshop, Burlington City, N.J., 1990, N.J. Fedn. Program Adminstrs., Atlantic City, TESOL Conv., N.Y.C., Cen. Jersey African Am. Bookfair, 1991, Borders Bookshop, Marten, 1992. Author: Metamorphosis, 1988 (N.J. Inst. Tech. 1990), Survival Through These Hard Times, 1990, A Kid's Guide to Getting Published, 1993, Struggles for Freedom, 1994, Native American Wisdom Book of Stories, 1997; author numerous poems. Presenter Voorhees Women's Club, 1990, Echelson Towers Assn., Vorhees, 1990; mem. Princeton Arts Coun. Recipient 3rd place award Poet's Press, Tex., 1987, Success award Scholastic Mag., N.Y.C., 1990, Southern Poetry Blue Ribbon award Southern Poetry Soc., 1989, Citation award-writer's N.J. Inst. Tech., 1990, N.J. Author award 1991, 94, N.J. Edn. award, 1995, A for Kids award, 1995, Law Related award, 1996, Tchr. of Yr. award, 1996, MasterTchr. award PBS/Thirteen, 1996, Unsung Heroes award, 1996, English Educator of Yr. award, 1997, Puffin Grant award, 1997, Albert Einstein award, 1997, career award, 1997, award Soc. Profl. Journalists, 1998, achievement award Cosmopolitan mag., 1998. Mem. TESOL, Poet's and Writer's Guild, Soc. for Poet's and Writer's Guild, Soc. for Poets So. N.J., World Acad. Arts and Culture, World Congress Poets, Conservatory Am. Letters, N.J./Penn TESOL, N.J. Poetry Soc., IPA Washington, Nat. Coun. Tchrs. English (membership com. for publishing, storytelling com., Mrs. D.C., 1994), Internat. Women's Writers Guild (N.J. bilingual/ESL state com.). Avocations: ballet/jazz dance, piano, flute, guitar. Home: PO Box 0741 Princeton Junction NJ 08550-0741 Office: Scholastic Inc New York NY 10000

CLOW, LEE, advertising agency executive. Formerly exec. v.p., creative dir. Chiat/Day, L.A., now pres., chief creative officer, chmn, cco, 1995. Office: TBWA Chiat/Day 5353 Grosvenor Blvd Playa Del Rey CA 90296*

CLOWARD, RICHARD ANDREW, social work educator; b. Rochester, N.Y., Dec. 25, 1926; s. Donald Bernard and Esther (Fleming) C.; m. Ethelmarie McGaffin, Mar. 25, 1951 (div. 1979); children—Leslie Anne, Mark, Kevin, Keith. B.A., U. Rochester, 1948; M.S.W., Columbia, 1950, Ph.D., 1958; D.H.L., Adelphi U., 1985, Hunter Coll., 1999. Mem. faculty Columbia U., 1954—, prof. social work, 1961—; dir. research Moblzn. for Youth, N.Y.C., 1958-65. Author: Social Perspectives on Behavior, 1958, Delinquency and Opportunity, 1960 (Dennis Carroll award Internat. Soc. Criminology 1965), Regulating the Poor: The Functions of Public Welfare, 1971 (C. Wright Mills award Soc. Study Social Problems 1972), The Politics of Turmoil: Essays on Race, Poverty and the Urban Crisis, 1974, Poor People's Movements: Why They Succeed, How They Fail, 1977, The New Class War, 1982, The Mean Season, 1987, Why Americans Don't Vote, 1988; updated edition: Regulating the Poor, 1993, The Breaking of the American Social Compact, 1997. Trustee Abbott House for Children, N.Y.C., 1965-69, Northside Center Child Devel., 1964-68, Citizens Crusade Against Poverty, Washington, 1964-68, Poverty/Rights Action Center, 1966—; bd. dirs. N.Y. Civil Liberties Union, 1968-80. Served with USNR, 1944-46; as officer AUS, 1951-54. Recipient Bryan Spann award Eugene V. Debs Found., 1986, Lee

Founders award Soc. for Study Social Problems, 1991, Excellence in Social Work Edn. award Mandel Sch. Applied Social Sci., Case Western Res. U., 1992, Jim Waltermire award Nat. Assn. Secs. of State, 1994, Lifetime Achievement award Assn. Cmty. Orgn. and Social Adminstrn., 1995. Mem. NASW (Lifetime Achievement award 1999), AAUP, Am. Sociol. Assn. (Lifetime Achievement award in Polit. Sociology 1995). Home: 35 Claremont Ave New York NY 10027-6802 Office: 622 W 113th St New York NY 10025-7982

CLOWER, WILLIAM DEWEY, trade association executive; b. Salem, Va., Oct. 9, 1935; s. Alton Oliver and Addie Vane (Young) C.; m. Shirley Carol Tuttle, Sept. 1, 1956; children—Candice Denise, Michael DeWayne, Catherine Dione. BS, U. Va., 1958, MS, 1958. Applications engr. ITT, Nutley, N.J., 1958-60; regional mktg. mgr. Litton Industries, Washington, 1960-61; propr. W.D. Clower Co., Gt. Falls, Va., 1961-70; spl. asst. to Pres. of U.S., 1970-75; exec. v.p. CISPI, Washington, 1975-76; pres. Food Processing Machinery and Supplies Assn., Washington, 1976-86; dir. Food Processors Inst., 1977-80; propr. Clower Assocs., Great Falls, Va., 1986-88; pres., CEO NATSO, Inc., Alexandria, Va., 1988—. Dir. Small Bus. Legis. Coun., 1991-92; chmn. Found. for Internat. Meetings, 1993; mem. campaign svcs. steering com. Rep. Nat. Com., 1977; mem. President's adv. coun. Peace Corps, 1982-85; mem. Industry Policy Adv. Coun. for Export Policy, 1982-86; pres. The NATSO Found., 1991—. With USAF, 1959-60. Va. Gen. Assembly scholar, 1954-58. Mem. Am. Soc. Assn. Execs., Aircraft Owners and Pilots Assn., Sertoma (pres. 1963-64), Capitol Hill Club, Belle Haven Country Club, Country Club at Two Rivers, Gamma Delta Epsilon. Presbyterian. Home: 1098 Fairbank St Great Falls VA 22066-1804 Office: 1199 N Fairfax St Alexandria VA 22314-1437

CLOWES, GARTH ANTHONY, electronics executive, consultant; b. Didsbury, Eng., Aug. 30, 1926; came to U.S., 1957; s. Eric and Doris Gladys (Worthington) C.; m. Katharine Allman Crewdson, July 29, 1950; children: John Howard Brett, Peter Miles, Vicki Anne. BSc, Stockport Coll., Cheshire, Eng., 1953; postgrad., UCLA, 1965-66; higher nat. cert., Birmingham (Eng.) Coll. Tech., 1955-56. Gen. mgr., v.p., dir. Eldon Industries, Inc., El Segundo, Calif., 1962-69; CEO, founder Entex Industries, Inc., Compton, Calif., 1969-83; pres., founder Entex Electronics, Inc., Valley Ford, Calif., 1983—; pres., founder TTC, Inc., Carson, Calif., 1984-86; pres. Universal Telesis Electronics, Inc., Carson, 1986-87; gen. mgr. Matchbox Toys (U.S.A.) Ltd., Moonachie, N.J., 1987-88; dir. gen. Matchbox Spain, S.A., Valencia, 1988-89; cons. Matchbox Internat. Ltd., worldwide, 1986-89. Inventor electronic voice recognition devices, numerous others. Mem. pres.'s com. UNICEF, N.Y., 1972-74, Senate Adv. Bd., Washington, 1982-83; cons. Interracial Coun., L.A., 1967-69. Decorated Knight of Malta. Avocations: antiques, gardening, art. Home: 13950 Coast Hwy 1 Valley Ford CA 94972

CLOYD, BONITA GAIL LARGENT, rehabilitation nurse, educator; b. Paducah, Ky., Oct. 1, 1952; d. Thomas Edward and Melodean (Keeling) Largent; m. Richard Frank Cloyd, June 8, 1974; 1 child, Lawrence. ADN, Paducah C.C., 1972; BSN, Bellarmine Coll., Louisville, 1991; MSN, U. Evansville, 1994; FNP, Belmont U., 1996. RN, Ky.; cert. in enterostomal therapy. Nurse, team leader Lourdes Hosp., Paducah, 1972-74; nurse, med.-surg. team leader Suburban Hosp., Louisville, 1974-76; enterostomal therapist Western Bapt. Hosp., Paducah, 1976—. Speakers Bur. Am. Cancer Soc.; helpline vol. Chosen Children Adoption Svcs., Inc. Mem. Wound, Ostomy and Continence Nurses Soc., United Ostomy Assn. (program planner), Belmont Nurses Honor Soc. (charter), Sigma Theta Tau, Phi Theta Kappa. Home: 247 Seminole Dr Paducah KY 42001-5425

CLOYD, HELEN MARY, accountant, educator; b. Austria-Hungary, 1918; d. Valentine and Elizabeth (Kretschmar von Kienbusch) Yuhasz; came to U.S. 1922, naturalized, 1928; BS, Eastern Mich. U., 1953; MA, Wayne State U., 1956; PhD, Mich. State U., 1963; m. George S. Smith, Mar. 4, 1939 (dec.); children: George, Nora; m. Chester L. Cloyd, Apr. 16, 1960 (dec.). Pub. accounting Haskins & Sells, Detroit, 1945-53; tchr. Marine City (Mich.) High Sch., 1954-59; instr. acctg. Central Mich. U., Mt. Pleasant, 1959-60; asst. prof. Wayne State U., Detroit, 1960-61; tchr. Grosse Pointe (Mich.) High Sch., 1961-64; assoc. prof. acctg. Ball State U., Muncie, Ind., 1964-71; prof. Shepherd Coll., Shepherdstown, W.Va., 1971-76; assoc. prof. George Mason U., Fairfax, Va. Recipient McClintock Writing award CPA, Mich., Ind., W.Va. Mem. AICPA, Am. Acctg. Assn., Am. Econs. Assn., AAAS, Assn. Sch. Bus. Ofcls., Delta Pi Epsilon, Pi Omega Pi, Pi Gamma Mu. Clubs: Order Eastern Star, White Shrine. Contbr. numerous articles to publs. Home: PO Box 186 Inwood WV 25428-0186

CLOYD, THOMAS EARL, broadcast designer, consultant; b. Washington, Sept. 1, 1944; s. Buford Thomas Cloyd and Florence Elizabeth (Green) Paterson; m. Linda Oblak, Apr. 17, 1968 (div. Mar. 1989); 1 child from previous marriage, Lisa; 1 child, Tobey. Broadcast designer Sta KYW-TV/CBS, Phila., 1965-90; owner Barboza Assocs., Blackwood, N.J., 1970—; cons. emerging techs. Broadcast Designers Assn., San Francisco, 1981-89. Designer: (TV show) Mike Douglas Show, 1965-76, Sta. WWL-TV News Set, 1974, Shattered Dreams, 1985 (Emmy nomination 1985), (TV show logo) Steve Allen Show, 1971, and corp. trade exhibits. With U.S. Army, 1962-65, ETO. Home: 590 Lower Landing Rd Apt 183 Blackwood NJ 08012-4125

CLUBB, BRUCE EDWIN, retired lawyer; b. Blackduck, Minn., Feb. 6, 1931; s. Ernest and Abigail (Gordy) C.; m. Martha Lucia Trapp, Dec. 19, 1954; children: Bruce Allen, Christopher Wade. B.B.A., U. Minn., 1955, LL.B. cum laude, 1958. Bar: D.C. 1959. Atty. Covington & Burling, 1958-61, Devel. Loan Fund, 1961-62, Chapman, DiSalle and Friedman, 1962-67; commr. U.S. Tariff Commn., 1967-71; ptnr. firm Baker & McKenzie, Washington, 1971-96; disting. lawyer in residence U. Minn. Law Sch., 1981-82; chmn. bd. dirs. Sunrise Properties, Inc., 1989—. Author: (treatise) United States Foreign Trade Law (2 vols.), 1991; contbr. law revs. Served with AUS, 1952-54. Mem. D.C. Bar Assn., Am. Arbitration Assn. (arbitrator 1994—), Order of Coif. Republican. Clubs: Cosmos (pres. 1986), Metropolitan, Army Navy. Home: 100 Quay St Alexandria VA 22314-2609

CLUFF, LEIGHTON EGGERTSEN, physician; b. Salt Lake City, June 10, 1923; s. Lehi Eggertsen and Lottie (Brain) C.; m. Beth Allen, Aug. 19, 1944; children: Claudia Beth, Patricia Leigh. BS, U. Utah, 1944, ScD (hon.), 1989; MD with distinction, George Washington U., 1949; ScD (hon.), Hahnemann Med. Sch., 1979, LI. U., 1988, St. Louis U., George Washington U., 1990, U. Utah, 1990. Intern Johns Hopkins Hosp., Balt., 1949-50, asst. resident, 1951-52; asst. resident physician Duke Hosp., Durham, N.C., 1950-51; vis. investigator, asst. physician Rockefeller Inst. Med. Research, 1952-54; fellow Nat. Found. Infantile Paralysis, 1952-54; mem. faculty Johns Hopkins Sch. Medicine, Balt.; staff Johns Hopkins Hosp., Balt., 1954-66, prof. medicine, 1964-66, physician, head div. clin. immunology, allergy and infectious diseases, 1958-66; prof., chmn. dept. medicine U. Fla., Gainesville, 1966-76; VA disting. physician U. Fla., 1990-95, prof. emeritus dept. medicine, 1990—; exec. v.p. Robert Wood Johnson Found., Princeton, N.J., 1976-86, pres., 1986-90, trustee emeritus, 1990—; U.S. del. U.S.-Japan Coop. Med. Sci. Program, 1972-81; mem. council drugs AMA, 1965-67; mem. NRC-NAS Drug Research Bd., 1965-71; mem. expert adv. panel bacterial diseases (coccal infection) WHO; mem. council Nat. Inst. Allergy and Infectious Diseases, 1968-72; cons. FDA; mem. tng. grant com. NIH, 1964-68. Author, editor books on internal medicine, infectious diseases, clin. pharmacology, long-term care; contbr. articles to profl. jours. Bd. dirs. Nat. Coun. on Aging, 1995-98. Recipient Ordronaux award for med. scholarship, 1949, Career Rsch. award NIH, 1962, Edward Jill award Acad. Medicine N.J., 1990, Disting. Alumnus award Duke U. Sch. Medicine, 1978, Disting. Alumnus award Johns Hopkins Sch. Med., 1992, Theobald Smith award Albany Med. Coll., 1988, Outstanding Contbn. to Health and Health Care, Am. Acad. Nursing, 1996; Markle scholar, 1955-62; Mead-Johnson Postgrad. scholar, 1954-55. Mem. ACP (master, Fla. gov. 1975-76), Inst. Medicine of NAS, Assembly Life Scis. of NAS, Am. Soc. Clin. Investigation, Assn. Am. Physicians, Soc. Exptl. Biology and Medicine, Am. Assn. Immunologists, Am. Fedn. Clin. Rsch., Harvey Soc., Infectious Diseases Soc. Am. (pres. 1975-76), N.Y. Acad. Scis., So. Soc. Clin. Investigation, Am. Clin. and Climatol. Assn., Am. Social Health Assn. (bd. dirs. 1991—, chair 1997-99), Bd. Inst. for Child Health Policy (bd. dirs. 1991—), Johns Hopkins U. Soc. Scholars, Alpha Omega Alpha, Sigma Theta Tau (Archon award 1992). Home: 8851 SW 45th Blvd Gainesville FL 32608-4138

CLUFF, LLOYD STERLING, earthquake geologist; b. Provo, Utah, Sept. 29, 1933; s. Colvin Sterling and Melba (Walker) C.; m. Anne Provstgard, Aug. 28, 1958 (div. June 1974); m. Janet L. Peterson, Dec. 21, 1976; children: Tanya, Sasha, Branden. BS in Geology, U. Utah, 1960. Registered profl. geologist, Calif.; cert. engrng. geologist, Calif. Jr. geologist El Paso Natural Gas Co., Salt Lake City, 1957-59; teaching asst. dept. geology U. Utah, Salt Lake City, 1958-60; geologist Lottridge Thomas & Assocs., Salt Lake City, 1960; v.p., prin. geologist, bd. dirs. Woodward-Clyde Cons., San Francisco, 1960-85; assoc. prof. U. Nev., Reno, 1967-73; mgr. dept. geoscis. Pacific Gas and Electric Co., San Francisco, 1985—; Cons. Trans-Alaska Pipeline Siting Study, 1972-74, Aswan High Dam, Govt. of Egypt, 1982-86; mem. com. Nat. Earthquake Hazards Reduction Program, Washington, 1987, Decade for Natural Disaster Reduction, Washington, 1989; advisor Venezuela Pres.'s Earthquake Safety Com., 1967-72; advisor Joint Legis. Com. on Seismic Safety, State of Calif., 1970-74; chmn. seismic rev. panel Calif. Pub. Utilities Commn., San Francisco, 1980-81; mem. Calif. Seismic Safety Commn., 1985—, chmn., 1988-90, 95-97; mem. Bd. on Natural Disasters NRC, 1996—; mem. adv. coun. So. Calif. Earthquake Ctr., 1996—; chmn. Tech. Adv. Bd. on Earthquake Risk, Israel, 1996—; bd. dirs. Calif. Inst. for Energy Efficiency, 1997-98; mem. organizing com. for Pub. Policy Partnership 2000-White House Confs. on Natural Disaster Loss Reduction, 1997-98; mem. NAS com. on assessing costs of natural disasters, 1998—; mem. FEMA nat. pre-disaster mitigation program adv. panel, 1998—; mem. external adv. panel for Pacific Earthquake Engrg. Ctr., 1998—. Recipient Hogentagler award ASTM, 1968; Woodward lectr., San Francisco, 1979. Fellow Calif. Acad. Scis.; mem. NAE, NSF (adv. panel on earth scis. 1992-95), NAS (chmn. com. Practical Lessons from the Loma Prieta Earthquake 1994), Seismol. Soc. Am. (pres. 1982-83), Assn. Engrng. Geologists (pres. 1968-69), Earthquake Engrng. Rsch. Inst. (hon., pres. 1993-95, chmn. Internat. Conf. on Seismic Zonation, Nice, France 1995), Geol. Soc. Am., Structural Engrs. Assn. No. Calif. Republican. Avocations: photography, skiing, mountain climbing, hiking, bicycling. Office: Pacific Gas and Elec Co 245 Market St San Francisco CA 94105-1797

CLUM, DEBRA SUE, elementary education educator; b. Bowling Green, Ohio, Feb. 24, 1955; d. James and Carol (Moor) Durliat; m. Daniel Ray Clum, June 10, 1977; two children. BS, Bowling Green State U., 1976; MS, Defiance Coll., 1999. Learning disabilities tutor Stryker (Ohio) Schs., 1977, Bryan (Ohio) City Schs., 1977-78; learning disabilities tchr. Montpelier (Ohio) Extn. Village Sch., 1979-89; elem. tchr. Bryan City Schs., 1989—. Mem. Bryan Edn. Assn., Concerns Com.

CLUM, GERARD W., academic administrator. D in Chiropractic, Palmer Coll. Chiropractic, 1973. Instr. Palmer Coll. Chiropractic, Davenport, Iowa, 1974; assoc. prof. Life Chiropractic Coll., Atlanta, 1978-81; pres. Life Chiropractic Coll. W., San Lorenzo, Calif., 1981—. E-mail: GCLUM@LIFEWEST.EDU. Office: 2005 Via Barrett San Lorenzo CA 94580

CLUNEY, J(OHN) C(HARLES) (JACK CLUNEY), minister; b. Buffalo, Aug. 16, 1948; s. Edward Cecil and Edna Mary (Kinley) C.; m. Evelyn Mae Chapman, July 11, 1970; children: John C. Jr., Carrie Lynn. PhD in Counseling Psychology, Carolina Christian U., 1993; ThD, Bibl. Life Coll. and Sem., 1995. Ordained to ministry So. Bapt. Conv., 1983. Assoc. pastor Starlight Park Bapt. Ch., Phoenix, 1982-83; pastor Rainbow Valley Bapt. Ch., Buckeye, Ariz., 1983-85, Hopewell Bapt. Ch., Pana, Ill., 1985-89, Forsyth (Ill.) Bapt. Ch., 1989-93; CEO J.C. Cluney and Assocs., Decatur, Ill., 1993—; pres. Health Source, Inc., Springfield. Author: Satanism and the Occult A Rational Look, 1989, Eclipse of Reason, 1997. Mem. Optimist Internat. (dist. gov. 1999—), Am. Assn. Christian Counselors, Decatur Noon Optimist Club (past pres.). Fax: 217-546-6554; e-mail: docjack@midwest.net. Office: Health Source Inc 145 A S Veterans Pkwy Springfield IL 62704 *Every man has lodged in his Being, the very purpose of God for his life. It remains his mission to discover it and use it to serve mankind. Know God, and enjoy the peace that only the manifest will of God can bring.*

CLURFELD, ANDREA, editor, food critic; b. N.Y.C., Mar. 13, 1954; d. Jerome and Geraldine R. Clurfeld. BA in Art History, Wells Coll., 1976. Reporter, arts editor Hunterdon County Democrat, Flemington, N.J., 1977-82; night and Sunday editor New Jersey Herald, Newton, N.J., 1982-86; restaurant critic/food editor Asbury Park Press, Neptune, N.J, 1986—; editor The Guide to The Jersey Shore; columnist Gannett News Svc. Editor N.J. Zagat Survey 2000; wine-food columnist Gannett News Svc. Mem., judge Beard Found. Restaurants Awards Com. Recipient award N.J. Press Assn., 1978-99, Nat. Newspaper Assn., 1981, Soc. Profl. Journalists, 1991, 94, First Place award for criticism N.J. Press Assn., 1997. Mem. Internat. Assn. Culinary Profls., Assn. Food Journalists, James Beard Found., Monmouth County Cooks Coop. (founding), Field Spanish Soc. Am., Radcliffe Culinary Friends. Avocations: fine American crafts, travel, gardening. Home: 65 Old Tavern Rd Howell NJ 07731-8729 Office: Asbury Park Press Inc PO Box 1550 3601 Highway 66 Neptune NJ 07753-2694

CLURMAN, MICHAEL, newspaper publishing executive; b. N.Y.C., June 23, 1952. BA, U. Md.; PMD, Harvard Bus. Sch. Apprentice printer The Washington Post, 1971-76, mgmt. trainee prodn. staff, 1976-79, asst. v.p. ops., 1979-81; plant mgr. The Washington Post, Springfield, Va., 1981-89; dir. prodn. The Washington Post, 1989-90, v.p. prodn., 1990—. Office: The Washington Post 1150 15th St NW Washington DC 20071-0002

CLUTE, ROBERT EUGENE, political and social science educator; b. Earlville, Iowa, July 12, 1924; s. Henry and Leta (Allen) C.; m. Doris Reams, 1947; children: Robert Eugene, Andrea Reams. BA, U. Ala., 1947; MA, George Washington U., 1948; PhD, Duke U., 1957. Selector U.S. Displaced Persons Commn., Frankfurt, Fed. Republic Germany, 1948-50; analyst USAF, Austria, 1950-54; rsch. assoc. Duke U., Durham, N.C., 1957-58; vis. asst. prof. Tulane U. La., New Orleans, 1958-59; asst. prof. U. Nev., 1959-62; assoc. prof. U. Ga., Athens, 1962-68, prof. polit. sci., 1968—, head dept. polit. sci., 1972-75, grad. coord., 1975-88, chmn. social scis. div., 1982-93, prof. emeritus, 1993—; Am. specialist to Anglophone Africa, Cultural Affairs div. U.S. Dept. State, 1977. Author: The International Legal Status of Austria, 1962; (with others) The International Law Standard and Commonwealth Developments, 1966, De lege pactorum, 1970, Law and Justice, 1970; contbr. articles to polit. jours. With U.S. Army, 1943-46. Fulbright scholar 1967-68; Danforth assoc. 1972. Mem. Am. Soc. Internat. Law, Am. Polit. Sci. Assn., Ga. Polit. Sci. Assn., So. Polit. Sci. Assn., Internat. Studies Assn., African Studies Assn., Phi Kappa Phi, Phi Alpha Theta, Pi Sigma Alpha, Phi Beta Delta. Democrat. Episcopalian. Home: 180 Sunny Brook Dr Athens GA 30605-3348 Office: U Ga Dept Polit Sci Athens GA 30602 *It is important for me to have career opportunities which help people. The preservation, analysis and dissemination of the knowledge of the past is as essential as the creation of new knowledge. Practical application of knowledge is extremely important. One must be loyal to one's colleagues and the institutions in which one participates.*

CLUTTER, BERTLEY ALLEN, III, management company executive; b. Oskaloosa, Iowa, Oct. 21, 1942; s. Bertley Allen and Dorothy A. (Martin) C.; divorced; children: Allen, Julie. Student, Macalester Coll., 1960-62, 64-66, BA, 1966; MA, Eastern Mich. U., 1973. Mem. Peace Corps, Iran, 1962-64; asst. prof. USAF Acad., Colo., 1973-76; exec. dir. Minn. Ethical Practices Bd., St. Paul, 1976-80; staff dir. Fed. Election Commn., Washington, 1980-83; v.p., gen. mgr. Owners Mgmt. Co., Cleve., 1983-98; pres., CEO Wilder Richman Mgmt. Corp., Elmsford, N.Y., 1999—. Contbr. articles to profl. jours. Pres. North End Homeowners Assn., Colorado Springs, Colo., 1975-76, Blvd. Cmty. Assn., Shaker Heights, Ohio; v.p. Lowry Hill Residents Assn., Mpls., 1977-80; chmn. Shaker Heights Recreation Bd., 1985-87; bd. dirs. Am. Field Svc.-U.S.A., N.Y.C., 1986-95; trustee AFS Intercultural Programs, Inc., N.Y.C., 1991-96; bd. govs. Human Rights Campaign, Washington, 1996-98. Decorated Bronze Star; recipient Commendation medal; USAF scholar Eastern Mich. U., 1972; endowed scholar Macalester Coll., 1961, 65, 66. Mem. N.E. Ohio Apt. Assn. (bd. dirs., mem. exec. com., pres. 1996, 97, Karl M. Duldner Meml. award 1994), Ohio Apt. Assn. (pres.-elect 1997, pres. 1998). Home: 341 Monmouth St Jersey City NJ 07302 Office: Wilder Richman Mgmt Corp 570 Taxter Rd Elmsford NY 10523*

CLUTTER, MARY ELIZABETH, federal official; b. Charleroi, Pa.; BS, Allegheny Coll., 1953, DSc., 1986, MS, U. Pitts., 1957, PhD in Botany, 1960; Rsch. assoc. Yale U., 1961-73, lectr. biology, 1965-78, sr. rsch. assoc., 1973-78; program dir. NSF, Washington, 1976-81, sect. head, 1981-84, div. dir., 1984-85, 87-88, sr. sci. advisor, 1985-87, asst. dir., 1989—. Mem. AAAS (bd. dirs. 1986-90), Human Frontiers Sci. Program (trustee), Internat. Soc. Plant Molecular Biology, Am. Soc. Cell Biology, Am. Soc. Plant Physiologists, Soc. Devel. Biology, Assn. Women in Sci. Office: Nat Sci Found Biological Sciences 4201 Wilson Blvd Arlington VA 22203-1859*

CLUTZ, CHARLES NESBITT, architect; b. Rochester, N.Y., July 8, 1937; s. Charles Wendell and Lois Katherine (Rumberger) C.; m. Lela Kay Lowe, Dec. 26, 1964; 1 child, Lisa Anne Eskola. BArch, U. Kans., 1960, B in Music, Organ and Theory, 1964. Registered arch., Mass.; cert. Nat. Coun. Archl. Registration Bds. Designer Aeolian-Skinner Organ Co., Boston, 1964-68; draftsman Shepley Bulfinch Richardson & Abbott, Boston, 1968-78; project mgr. Profl. Designs, Inc., Boston, 1978-79; assoc. Perry Dean Stahl & Rogers, Boston, 1979-83; project mgr. Bergmeyer Assocs., Boston, 1983-85; prin. Charles N. Clutz Assocs., Hyde Park, Mass., 1985—. Prins. works include St. Paul's Ch., Natick, Mass., 1993, Grace Chapel, Dover, Mass., 1999. Mem. sub-com. on liturgy Episcopal Diocese, Mass., 1975-81, mem. music commn., 1982-88; jr. warden All Saints Paris, Brookline, Mass., 1982-83. Recipient citation/altar hangings Interfaith Forum on Religion, Art and Arch., All Saints Parish, Brookline, 1987. Mem. AIA, Am. Guild Organists (exec. com. 1994-96), Boston Soc. Archs., Illuminating Engrng. Soc. (pres. new engrng. sect. 1989-92, Disting. Svc. award 1993), Pi Kappa Lambda. Avocations: perennnial gardens, stage design, trains, carousels, reading. Home: 296 Georgetowne Dr Hyde Park MA 02136

CLUTZ, WILLIAM (HARTMAN CLUTZ), artist, educator; b. Gettysburg, Pa., Mar. 19, 1933; s. Paul Alexander and Catherine (Hartman) C. BA, U. Iowa, 1955. Instr. drawing, painting Parsons Sch. Design, N.Y.C., 1969-96. One-man shows include Condon Riley Gallery, N.Y.C., 1959, David Herbert Gallery, N.Y.C., 1962, Triangle Gallery, San Francisco, 1967, Bertha Schaefer Gallery, N.Y.C., 1963, 64, 66, 69, Bklyn. Coll., 1969, Graham Gallery, N.Y.C., 1972, Mercersburg (Pa.) Acad., 1972, Lamont Gallery, Phillips Exeter (N.H.) Acad., 1973, Addison Gallery Am. Art, Phillips Acad., Andover, Mass., 1973, Moravian Coll., Bethlehem, Pa., 1977, Brooke Alexander Gallery, N.Y.C., 1973, Alonzo Gallery, N.Y.C., 1977, 78, 79, Walther-Rathenau-Saal, Rathaus Kunstamt Wedding, Berlin, 1978, Mellon Art Center, Wallingford, Conn., 1979, Gallery 333, Dayton, Ohio, 1980, Tatistcheff & Co., N.Y.C., 1981, 82, 84, John C. Stoller & Co., Mpls., 1983, 87, Gallery van Voorst van Beest, The Hague, 1984, Tweed Mus., Duluth, 1986, Tatistcheff Gallery, L.A., 1988, Washington County Mus., Hagerstown, Md., 1991, Tatistcheff Gallery, L.A., 1992, Nicholas Davies Gallery, N.Y.C., 1997; exhibited in group shows including Mus. Modern Art, N.Y.C., 1956, 62, Am. Fedn. Arts Traveling Exhbn., 1961-62, Contemporary Arts Mus., Houston, 1961, Am. Fedn. Fine Arts Traveling Exhbn., 1963-64, Pa. Acad. Fine Arts, Phila., 1964, 65, 66, U. Wis., 1967, Purdue U., 1968, Tweed Gallery, U. Minn., Duluth, 1968, Ringling Mus. Art, Sarasota, Fla., 1969, Columbus (Ohio) Gallery Fine Arts, 1970, Hall Gallery, Miami, Fla., 1972, Brooke Alexander Gallery, 1973, Smithsonian Traveling Exhbn., 1976-79, Westmoreland County Mus., Greensburg, Pa., 1979, Hirschl & Adler, N.Y.C. and L.A., 1980, Aaron Berman Gallery, N.Y.C., 1980, Stoller Gallery, 1980, 81, 83, 85, 88, Tatistcheff & Co., 1980, 81, 82, 84, 87, 89, 90, Corcoran Gallery Art, Washington, 1982, Bklyn. Mus., 1983, Mus. Modern Art, San Francisco, 1985, Chem. Bank, N.Y.C., 1987, Montclair (N.J.) Mus., 1989; represented in permanent collections, Addison Gallery Am. Art, Ball State U. Art Gallery, Muncie, Ind., Bklyn. Mus., Fogg Art Mus., Harvard U., Cambridge, Mass., Guggenheim Mus., N.Y.C., Hirshhorn Mus. and Sculpture Garden, Washington, Dayton Art Inst. (Ohio), Mercersburg Acad., Miles Coll., Atlanta, Milw. Art Center, Mus. Modern Art, N.Y.C., Met. Mus. Art, N.Y.C., N.Y. Sch. Interior Design, N.Y.C., N.Y. U. Art Collection, Newark Mus., Minn. Mus., St. Paul, Sheldon Meml. Art Gallery, Lincoln, Nebr., U. Mass., Amherst, Tweed Mus., Duluth, Washington County Mus. Fine Arts, Hagerstown, Md., also, AT&T, Ashland Oil, Inc., Chase Manhattan Bank, Schroder Bank, Topseal Corp., Wausaw Ins. Co., Lehman Bros., Milbank Tweed, Minn. Mut. Ins. Co., Simpson Thatcher & Bartlett, Solomon Bros., Third Nat. Bank, Dayton, Chem. Bank, McKinsey & Co., Mobil Corp., Mpls. Star Tribune, and many others. Address: Katharina Rich Perlow Gallery 41 E 57th St New York NY 10022

CLUXTON, JOANNE GENEVIEVE, elementary school educator; b. Omaha, May 2, 1936; d. Joseph Emil and Anna (Nespesny) Sabacky; m. William Wayne Cluxton, Aug. 2, 1959; 1 child, Edsel Ross. BS in Edn., U. Nebr., Omaha, 1959; postgrad., Pepperdine U., L.A., 1975-77, San Diego U., L.A., 1987-88, Evangel Coll., 1989, UCLA, 1997. Cert. gen. elem. and lang. devel. specialist. Tchr. Graham Elem. Sch., L.A., 1969-83; kindergarten and resource tchr. 92d St. Sch., L.A., 1983-88; kindergarten mentor tchr. San Gabriel Ave. Sch., South Gate, Calif., 1988—; presenter insvc. workshops and new tchr. orientation workshops, L.A. Unified Sch. Dist., 1990-99. Organist Bell (Calif.) Friends Ch., 1975-83; pianist 1st So. Bapt. Ch., Downey, Calif., 1993-99. Mem. NEA (life), Calif. Tchrs. Assn., United Tchrs. L.A. Republican. Avocations: piano, organ, sewing, reading, handicrafts.

CLYATT, ROBERT LEE, executive distance learning firm; b. Sept. 17, 1958. AB in Econs., U. Calif., Berkeley, 1980; SM in Mgmt., MIT, 1985. Mktg. dir. Japan equities Reuter, Tokyo, 1988-90; regional dir. midwest Reuters Am., Farmington Hills, Mich., 1990-93; CEO, founder I/O 360 Digital, N.Y.C., 1994-98, Horizon Live Distance Learning, N.Y.C., 1998—. E-mail: bob@horizonlive.com. Home: 189 Milton Rd Rye NY 10580-3812

CLYBURN, JAMES E., congressman; b. Sumter, S.C., 1940; m. Emily England; children: Mignon, Jennifer, Angela. Grad., S.C. State Coll.; LHD (hon.), Winthrop Coll., 1987; DSc (hon.), Coll. of Charleston, 1992, Med. U. S.C., 1993; LHD (hon.), St. Augustine Coll., 1994; LLD (hon.), Claflin Coll., 1995; LHD (hon.), S.C. State U., 1995; LLD (hon.), Voorhees Coll., 1996. Teacher Charleston County Pub. Sch. System; counselor S.C. Employment Security Commn.; dir. Charleston County Neighborhood Youth Corps/New Careers Projects; exec. dir. S.C. Commn. Farmworkers Inc.; staffer for Gov. John C. West, Charleston, S.C., 1971-74; commr. S.C. Human Affairs Commn., Columbia, 1974-92; mem. 103rd Congress from 6th S.C. dist., D.C., 1993—; transp. & infrastructure com. 105th Congress; pres. Nat. Assn. Human Rights Workers, 1980-81, Internat. Assn. Official Human Rights Agys., 1985-87. Active Southern Regional Coun., Atlanta; bd. dirs. Wofford Coll., Spartanburg, Allen U., Columbia, Brookgreen Gardens Murrell's inlet, James R. Clark Sickle Cell Anemia Found., Ctr. for Cancer Treatment and Rsch., S.C. Literacy Assn. Recipient ann. award for disting. svc. to state gov. Nat. Govs. Assn.; named Pub. Adminstr. of Yr. Am. Soc. Pub. Adminstrn. S.C. chpt. Mem. NAACP (life), Masons, Shriners, Omega Psi Phi. Democrat. Office: US Ho of Reps 319 Cannon HOB Washington DC 20515*

CLYBURN, LUTHER LINN, real estate broker, appraiser, ship captain; b. Evansville, Ind., May 17, 1942; s. Luther and Robbie (Cobb) C.; children: Lisa Michelle, Luther Brent. Grad., Am. Savs. and Loan Inst., 1970; ABA, Pontiac (Mich.) Bus. Inst., 1972; BS, Detroit Coll. Bus., 1972; M of Bus. Mgmt., Ctrl. Mich. U., 1983. Lic. merchant marine. Chief loan officer First Fed. Savs. and Loan Assn. Oakland, Pontiac, 1964-74; assoc. broker Bateman Real Estate Corp., Pontiac, 1975-77; regional rep. United Guaranty Residential Ins., Troy, Mich., 1977-83; sr. account mgr. Investors Mortgage Ins. Co., Boston, 1983-87; real estate broker, appraiser White Lake, Mich., 1977—, Clyburn Appraisal Svcs., White Lake, 1987—. Project dir., capt.: (documentary film) Angels of the Sea, 1982 (N.Y. Film Festival award 1983); photographer for Tundra Tours 25th anniversary of Alaska's Iditarod dog sled race, 1997. Capt., comdr. "Noble Odyssey" Tng. Ship, Mt. Clemens, Mich., 1977-89; dir., comdr. U.S. Naval Sea Cadet Corps Great Lakes div., Mt. Clemens, Mich., 1973—; nat. bd. dirs. U.S. Naval Sea Cadet Corps, 1988; project dir. Interseas Inc., Pontiac, 1982; ship capt. Great Lakes Botanical Island research project for Cranbrook Inst. Sci. (Thunder Bay Islands, Lake Huron, 1987, Islands of Green Bay, 1989, 90); dir. of Underwater Cinitofu; capt. Pride of Mich., 1989—; capt. Great Lakes Island Rsch. Project for Oakland U., Fox Islands, 1996; project dir. In Search of the Griffin, Great Lakes Rsch. Bd., Pride of Mich., 1998—; founder/pres. Inter-Seas Exploration Ltd., 1999—. Recipient Cert. Appreciation award Southfield Bicentennial Commn., 1976, Letter of Commendation award Sec.

of Navy, 1983, Quality People award Meritorious Cmty. Svc., 1993, Oakland County Q2 award, 1993, Unsung Hero award Mich. Ho. of Reps., 1994. Mem. Internat. Ship Masters Assn., Navy League of U.S., Am. Soc. Appraisers, Mich. Assn. Real Estate Appraisers. Home and Office: 9000 Gale Rd White Lake MI 48386-1411

CLYDE, LARRY FORBES, banker; b. Heber, Utah, Nov. 19, 1941; s. Don and Kathryn (Forbes) C.; m. Barbara Eliason, Dec. 23, 1963 (div. Jan. 1985); children: Lynne, Karen Lee; m. Katharyn L. Decker, July 3, 1986. BA, Utah State U., 1963, MS, 1965. With Pitts. Nat. Bank, 1965-68; with Crocker Nat. Bank, San Francisco, 1968-86, mgr. investment banking, 1973-75, mgr. capital markets divsn., 1975-86, sr. v.p., 1976-78, exec. v.p., mem. policy com., 1978-86; mng. dir., chief exec. U.S. capital markets activities Midland Bank Group, N.Y.C., 1986-87; CEO Midland Montagu Govt. Securities, Midland Montagu Mcpl. Securities, and Midland Montagu Trust Co., 1986-87; exec. v.p., mgr. global fin. institutions mktg. Am. Express Bank, 1987-88; exec. v.p., mgr. global securities, mem. sr. mgmt. com. Mellon Bank N.A., Pitts., 1988—; bd. dirs. Pub. Securities Assn., 1976-83, mem. govt. borrowing com., 1981-87, vice chmn., 1981, chmn., 1982; treas., dir. No. Calif. chpt. Invest-In-Am., 1975-87; dir. ABA Securities Assn., 1995—. Mem. Am. Bankers Assn. (vice chmn. bank investment and funds mgmt. divsn. exec. com. 1982, chmn. exec. com. 1983), Dealer Bank Assn. (bd. dirs. 1986-87), San Francisco Bond Club, Duquesne Club, Allegheny Country Club. Office: Mellon Bank NA 2 Mellon Bank Ctr Rm 0675 Pittsburgh PA 15259-0001

CLYMER, ADAM, newspaper editor; b. N.Y.C., Apr. 27, 1937; s. Kinsey and Eleanor (Lowenton) C.; m. Ann Wood Fessenden, June 3, 1961; 1 child, Jane Emily (dec.). BA, Harvard U., 1958; postgrad., U. Cape Town, South Africa, 1959. Reporter Virginian-Pilot, Norfolk, Va., 1960-62, Balt. Sun, 1963-76, N.Y. Daily News, Washington, 1977; reporter, editor N.Y. Times, N.Y.C. and Washington, 1977-90; asst. Washington editor N.Y. Times, 1991-97, Washington editor, 1997-99, chief Washington corr., 1999—. Co-author: Reagan: The Man, The President, 1981; editor: N.Y. Times Year in Review-1986, 1987. Mem. Harvard Crimson Grad. Bd., Cambridge, Mass., 1958—. With U.S. Army, 1961-62. Recipient Everett Dirksen award Dirksen Congl. Rsch. Ctr., 1994. Mem. Delhi Golf Club (India) (life mem.). Avocation: fly-fishing. Office: New York Times 1627 I St NW Ste 700 Washington DC 20006-4085

CLYMER, BRIAN WILLIAM, insurance company executive, former state official; b. Camden, N.J., May 16, 1947; s. Howard Young and Jean (Hatch) C.; children: Kathleen Norris, Richard Hatch. AA in Bus., Mitchell Coll., 1968; BS in Bus. and Econs., Lehigh U., 1969. CPA, Pa. Ptnr. Clymer, Merves & Amon, CPAs, Media, Pa., 1982-89; adminstr. Fed. Transit Adminstrn., Dept. Transp., Washington, 1989-93; pres., CEO Railway Systems Designs Inc., 1993-94; treas. State of N.J., Trenton, 1994-97; v.p. mkting and planning Prudential Ins. Co., 1997—; vice chmn. Southeastern Pa. Transp. Authority, Phila., 1981-89; bd. dirs. exec. com. Am. Pub. Transit Assn., 1993-95; bd. dirs. N.J. Sports Exposition Authority, Casino Reinvestment Devel. Authority, N.J. Performing Arts Ctr., 1994-97. With Pa. N.G., 1970-76. Mem. AICPA, Pa. Inst. CPA, N.J. Soc. CPA. Republican. Presbyterian. Avocations: fishing, golf. Home: 1111 Beach Haven West Blvd Manahawkin NJ 08050-3814 Office: Prudential Ins Co Am 751 Broad St Newark NJ 07102-3714

CLYMER, JAY PHAON, III, science educator; b. Lancaster, Pa., June 23, 1951; s. Jay Phaon Jr. and Jeannette (Armold) C.; m. Elizabeth Teresa Ruddy, June 4, 1988; children: Candace Rose, Colin Jay. BS in Zoology, U. R.I., 1973; MS in Biology, Lehigh U., 1975, PhD in Biology, 1978. Teaching asst. Lehigh U., Bethlehem, Pa., 1973-75, rsch. asst., 1975-78; asst. prof. Marywood U., Scranton, Pa., 1978-83, assoc. prof., 1983—, chmn. sci. dept., 1987-90, v.p. Faculty Senate; tech. advisor Lackawanna River Corridor Assn., Scranton, 1985—; dir. Riverwatch program, Scranton, 1985—; chmn. edn. com. County Conservation Dist., Clarks-Summit, Pa., 1990—; cons. to environ. firms; rsch. fish survey Wetlands Inst., Stone Harbor, N.J. Author: (booklets) Perspectives on Matter Energy Technology - Study Guide, vol. I, 1987, vol. II, 1991, Ecology - The Science of Nature, vol. I, 1988, vol. II, 1993, Biology - The Study of Life, 1995, Life Science, 1995; contbr. articles to sci. jours. Bd. dirs., v.p. Lackawanna County Conservation Dist., Clarks-Summit, 1990—; coord. fundraising March of Dimes. Mem. Atlantic Estaurine Rsch. Soc. (Grad. award 1979), Internat. Ctr. Environ. Mgmt. Enclosed Coastal Seas, Register of Pa. Biologists, Register of Estaurine Scientists, Lackawanna Fedn. of Sportsmen (officer 1990—), Phi Kappa Phi, Sigma Xi. Avocations: fishing, hunting, woodworking, gardening, softball. Home: 210 Melrose Ave Clarks Summit PA 18411-1440 Office: Marywood U 2300 Adams Ave Scranton PA 18509-1598

CLYMER, JERRY ALAN, educational administrator; b. Easton, Pa., Nov. 3, 1946; s. Wilbur L. and Dorothy M. (Cutsler) C.; m. Theresa M. Merlo, July 26, 1969; children: Shane A., Marc A., Adam T. BA, Moravian Coll., Bethlehem, Pa., 1969; MA, Rider Coll., Lawrenceville, N.J., 1976; postgrad., Trenton (N.J.) State Coll., 1976-80, East Stroudsburg U., 1976-80. Cert. elem. tchr., prin., supr., sch. adminstr., student pers. svcs., N.J. Elem. tchr. Pohatcong Twp. Bd. Edn., Bloomsbury, N.J., 1969-77, asst. prin., 1977-89, chief sch. adminstr., 1989—, dir. child study team, grants coord., testing coord., 1977-89, supr. summer sch., 1978-79, affirmative action officer, drug free liaison person, 1987-89, chief sch. adminstr., 1989-99, supt., 1999—; coord. N.J. instrnl. child study team dir. for mini grant dist. award FHA and N.J. Dept. Edn., 1989-90. Mem., coach Pohatcong Recreation Assn., 1969—; mem. Pohatcong Centennial Incorporation, 1980-81; chmn. Pohatcong Twp. Sch. Dist. Staff Scholarship Fund, 1971-77. Mem. Am. Soc. Sch. Admin. (N.J. chpt.), N.J. Prins. and Suprs. Assn., Warren Coun. Sch. Adminstrs., Warren County Elem. Sch. and Mid. Sch. Prins. (v.p. 1981-82, 85-86). Avocations: camping, swimming, hiking, tennis, basketball. Home: 100 Falmer St Phillipsburg NJ 08865-4810 Office: Pohatcong Twp Bd Edn 45 County Road 519 Bloomsbury NJ 08804-3409

CLYMER, WAYNE KENTON, bishop; b. Napoleon, Ohio, Sept. 24, 1917; s. George Arnold and Sallie Grace (Hulvey) C.; m. Helen Eloise Graves, Sept. 3, 1939; children: Kenton James, Richard George. AB, Asbury Coll., 1939; MA, Columbia U., 1942; BD, Union Theol. Sem., 1944; PhD, NYU, 1950; LLD, Westmar Coll., 1969; DLitt, Hamline U., 1975; DD, Iowa Wesleyan Coll., Rust Coll., Garrett-Evang. Theol. Sem. Ordained to ministry Evang. Ch., 1942; pastor Emanuel Ch., Ozone Park, N.Y.C., 1939-41, St. Paul's Ch., Forest Hills, N.Y.C., 1941-46; prof. Evang. Theol. Sem., Naperville, Ill., 1946-57; dean Evang. Theol. Sem., 1957-67, pres., 1967-72; bishop United Meth. Ch., Mpls., 1972-80, Des Moines, 1980-84; lectr. St. Andrews Theol. Coll., Manila, 1966, Trinity Coll., Singapore, 1967, U. Dubuque, 1985, Ill. Coll., 1990, United Theol. Sem. in Twin Cities, 1990; pres. United Meth. Com. on Relief, 1976-84; mem. del. UN Conf. Refugee, 1979; liaison to theol. sems. Coun. of Bishops, 1984-87; chair Grannis-Martin Found., 1984-98. Author: Affirmation, 1971, Membership Means Discipleship, 1976; Contbr. to: Ency. Religious Edn. Pres. Naperville Sch. Bd., 1959-63; Mem. bd. Naperville Community Fund, 1966; pres. Chgo. Pastoral Counseling Center. Mem. Soc. Sci. Study Religion, Kappa Delta Pi. Club: Kiwanian.

CLYNCH, EDWARD JOHN, political science educator, researcher; b. South Bend, Ind., Nov. 30, 1942; s. James Harpster and June May (Roberts) C.; m. Barbara Meadow, Aug. 22, 1970; children: Barnaby Patrick, Jennifer Sarah. BA, Hillsdale (Mich.) Coll., 1965; MA, Ball State U., 1968; PhD, Purdue U., 1975. Tchr. Penn H.S., Mishawaka, Ind., 1967; instr. Elizabethtown (Ky.) C.C., 1968-70; asst. prof. polit. sci. U. New Orleans, 1974-78, Kans. State U., 1978-81; assoc. prof. Miss. State U., Mississippi State, 1981-87, prof., 1987—, head. dept. polit. sci., 1983-94, grad. coord., 1995—. Co-author: (with Tom Lauth) Governors, Legislators and Budgets: Diversity Across the American States, 1991; contbr. articles to profl. jours. Pres. Miss. Pub. Mgmt. Grad. Edn. Coun., 1985—; mem. Oktibbeha County Dem. Conv., 1984. Mem. Nat. Assn. Schs. Pub. Affairs and Adminstrn. (mem. exec. coun. 1984-86, chair polit. sci. based program of nation sect. 1987-89, mem. commn. on peer rev. and accreditation 1988-91), S.E. Conf. Pub. Adminstrn. (chair 1989 meeting), Am. Soc. Pub. Adminstrn. (pres. Miss. chpt. 1984-85, mem. pub. adminstrn. edn. nat. coun. sect. 1988—, pub. adminstrn. program evaluator 1990—, pres. pub. adminstrn. edn. sect. 1992-94), Am. Poli. Sci. Assn., So. Polit. Sci. Assn., Starkville C. of C. (mem. govtl. affairs com. 1987—), Rotary, Epsilon Delta Alpha, Omicron Delta Kappa, Pi Alpha Alpha, Pi Sigma Alpha, Phi Kappa Phi. Democrat. Presbyterian. Home: 401 Colonial Cir Starkville MS 39759-4213 Office: Miss State U Dept Polit Sci PO Drawer PC Mississippi State MS 39762

CLYNE, DIANNA MARIE, psychiatrist; b. Lincoln, Nebr., Mar. 16, 1959; d. John Clayton Clyne and Marilynn Paula (Matt) Hoenig; m. Jerry Lee Govier, Oct., 1981 (div. Sept. 1984); 1 child, Chanda Marie; m. Jerry Lee Smith, Sept. 9, 1991; children: Cassandra Lee, Crystal Renee, Catrina Diane, Corrin Pauline. Student, U. Nebr., 1977, 80, Southeast C.C., Lincoln, Nebr., 1978, 79-80; BS in Comprehensive Biology summa cum laude, Kearney State Coll., 1983; MD, U. Nebr. Med. Ctr., 1989. Diplomate Am. Bd. Forensic Examiners (bd. cert.). Intern, then resident in psychiatry Maricopa Med. Ctr., Phoenix, Ariz., 1989-93; adult sr. med. investigator Cmty. Care Network/Maricopa Clin. Mgmt./ComCare, Phoenix, 1991-95, Urgent Care Ctr. Southwest Behavioral Health, Phoenix, 1995; adult sr. med. investigator rehab. Chemical Dependency Unit Hastings (Nebr.) Regional Ctr., 1996; pvt. practice Lincoln Psychiat. Group, 1996—; provider psychiat. svcs. St. Monicas Drug and Alcohol Rehab., 1998—, Outpatient Ctr., Drug and Alcohol Rehab., 1997—, O.U.R. Residential Home. With USNG, 1977-85, capt. Res. Mem. AMA, NAFE, Am. Psychiat. Assn., Am. Neuropsychiat. Assn., Am. Soc. Clin. Psychopharmacology, Am. Profl. Practice Assn., Am. Med. Women's Assn., Am. Assocs. Suicidology, Am. Field Svc., Assn. Am. Physicians and Surgeons, Nat. Assn. Residents and Interns, Nat. Assn. of Drs., Nat. Found. Depressive Illness, Inc., Nat. Family Assn., Nebr. Psychiat. Soc., Nebr. Med. Assn., Ariz. Med. Assn., Ariz. Psychiat. Assn., Ariz. Med. Polit. Action Com., Lancaster County Med. Soc., Phoenix Psychiat. Coun., Physicians Planning Svc. Corp., Women in the Arts, U. Nebr. Alumni, Kearney State Alumni, Southeast C.C. Alumni Assn. Roman Catholic. Avocations: jogging, biking aerobics, swimming, traveling, cooking. Home: 8211 Knoll View Ct Lincoln NE 68506-4152 Office: Lincoln Psychiat Group 2221 S 17th St Ste 110 Lincoln NE 68502-3763

COAD, DENNIS LAWRENCE, real estate broker; b. St. Louis, Mar. 16, 1959; s. Stanley Meredith and Olga Martha (Salarano) C.; m. Linda Marie Kasmarzik, June 20, 1980 (div. May, 1982): 1 child, Jason Christopher. AA, Jefferson Coll., Pevely, Mo., 1979; BS, S.W. Mo. State U., 1988, MBA, 1990. Systems engr. Computer Task Group, St. Louis, 1981-84; owner, mng. dir. Sci. Resources Cons. Group, La Mirada, Calif., 1990-97; dir. bus. devel. AGCT Inc., Irvine, Calif., 1993-97; real estate broker, owner Home Town Realty, Hemet, Calif., 1997—. Author: Nature, 1994—, Genetic Engring News, 1993—, Biotechniques, 1996. Active United We Stand, Calif., 1992. With U.S. Army, 1984-87. Boatmen's Bank scholar, 1977. Mem. AAAS, Am. Mgmt. Assn., Smithsonian Inst., Regulatory Profl. Soc. Roman Catholic. Avocations: computer programming, camping, hiking, cycling, boating. Home: 2070 Rosemary Ct Hemet CA 92545-5614 Office: Home Town Realty PO Box 4471 Hemet CA 92546-4471

COADY, PHILIP JAMES, JR., retired naval officer; b. Boston, Aug. 25, 1941; s. Philip James and Helen (Mowles) C.; m. Judith Mary Greene, July 11, 1964; children: Meredith, Philip, Adrienne. AB, Tufts U., 1963; MS, Naval Postgrad. Sch., 1972. Commd. ensign USN, 1963, advanced through grades to rear adm., comdg. officer USS Conolly, 1981-83; dir. command and tactics dept. USN, Newport, R.I., 1983-86; comdg. officer USS Antietam USN, 1986-89; dir. polit. and mil. policy and current plans div. Chief of Naval Ops. Washington, 1989-91; comdr. Cruiser-Destroyer Group Five, 1991-93; dir. surf warfare divsn. Chief of Naval Ops., 1994-95; pres. Navy Mutual Aid Assoc., Arlington, VA, 1995; ret., 1995. Author: (monograph) Shipbuilding: Perspective for the '80s, 1980. Nat. v.p. Surface Navy Assn., 1998-99. Decorated D.S.M., Legion of Merit with 5 gold stars. Roman Catholic. Office: Henderson Hall 29 Carpenter Rd Arlington VA 22204-4596

COAKER, GEORGE MACK, minister; b. McLain, Miss., Jan. 9, 1927; s. George Mack and Kate Dean (Leeke) C.; m. Catherine Sabina Pennington, Mar. 19, 1948; children: Carol Dean Coaker Brewer, JoaAnn Coaker Littlejohn, Cathy Kay Coaker Vickers. BA, Howard Coll., Birmingham, Ala., 1948; MTh, New Orleans Bapt. Theol. Sem., 1951; MA, U. Miss., 1955; PhD, Vanderbilt U., 1962. Ordained to ministry, So. Bapt. Conv., 1948. Pastor Chunchula (Ala.) Bapt. Ch., 1948-51, Ecru (Miss.) Bapt. Ch., 1951-53; chaplain USAF and VA, various locations, 1953-83; pastor Milton (Tenn.) Bapt. Ch., 1983-91, Greenvale (Tenn.) Bapt. Ch., 1991—; exec. bd. Tenn. Bapt. Conv., Nashville, 1983-90. Lt. col. chaplain corps USAF, 1953-57. Mem. Res. Officers Assn., Ret. Officers Assn., Am. Legion, DAV. Home and Office: 2535 Oregon Rd Milton TN 37118

COAKER, JAMES WHITFIELD, mechanical engineer; b. Boston, Nov. 12, 1946; s. George W. and Margaret N. Coaker; m. Ruth Johnson, May 17, 1969; children—James W., John A., Stephen D. BSME, Lafayette Coll., 1968; MSB, Va. Commonwealth U., 1976. Registered profl. engr., Va. Application engr. pump and condenser div. Ingersoll-Rand Co., Richmond, Va., 1972-76; project mgr. Reco Industries, Inc., Richmond, Va., 1976-77; asst. mgr. engring. Reco Industries, Inc., Richmond, 1977-79, mgr. engring., 1979-83; systems engr., program mgr. Advanced Tech., Inc., Arlington, Va., 1983-87; program mgr. Boiler and Elevator Safety U.S. Postal Svc., Washington, 1987—; lectr. and educator in field. With USN, 1969-72; capt. (ED) USNR, ret. Mem. ASME (vice chmn. Coun. Codes & Standards, vice chmn. Elevator and Escalator Safety Code Com., mem. Bd. Profl. Devel. 1990-96, past national chmn. Plant Engring. & Maintenance Divsn.), Nat Coun. Examiners for Engring. and Surveying (affiliate), Naval Res. Assn. (life). Home: 11675 Captain Rhett Ln Fairfax Station VA 22039-1236

COAKLEY, JANET MARIE, English educator, consultant creative arts theater; b. Louisville, Ky., Mar. 15, 1949; d. John David and Clara Elizabeth Sames; children: Amy, Susan, Laura, Sara. BA in English Edn., Morehead (Ky.) State U., Morehead, Ky., 1972; MA in English, Morehead (Ky.) State U., 1976. Tchr. Blanchester (Ohio) H.S., 1973-74, So. Hills Joint Vocat., Georgetown, Ohio, 1976-77; tchr. dept English William Henry Harrison H.S., Harrison, Ohio, 1977—; chmn. William Henry Harrison H.S., Harrison, 1995—; presenter in field. Founder Citizens Against Poor Planning, Harrison, 1986; precinct capt. Citizens for Better Schs., Harrison. Grantee Cin. Found. 1984; S.W. Local Classroom Tchrs. Assn. scholar, 1990. Mem. Nat. Coun. Tchrs. English, Morehead State U. Alumni Assn. (pres. bd. dirs. 1998—). Office: William Henry Harrison H S 9860 West Rd Harrison OH 45030-1929

COAKLEY, JOHN WAYLAND, theological historian, educator; b. Washington, Apr. 5, 1949; s. James Treakle and Mable Esther (Farwell) C.; m. Margaret Cadman Brown, June 26, 1976; children: Mary Rachel, Philip Wayland. AB, Wesleyan U., 1971; MDiv, Harvard U., 1974, ThD, 1980. Ordained to ministry United Ch. of Christ, 1974. Assoc. pastor Congl. Ch. West Medford, Mass., 1974-80; pastor Union Congl. Ch., East Walpole, Mass., 1980-84; assoc. prof. ch. history New Brunswick (N.J.) Theol. Sem., 1984-90, prof. ch. history, 1990-95, L. Russell Feakes Meml. Prof. Ch. History, 1995—; gen. synod prof. Reformed Ch. in Am., 1995—. Co-editor: Creative Women in Late Medieval and Reformation Italy, 1994. NEH fellow, 1997-98. Mem. Reformed Ch. in Am. Office: New Brunswick Seminary 17 Seminary Pl New Brunswick NJ 08901-1107

COAKLEY, MICHAEL JAMES, university administrator; b. Chgo., Mar. 26, 1954; s. William James and Jane (Wallace) C. BS, U. Ill., 1976; MS in Higher Edn., So. Ill. U., 1978; postgrad., Western Mich. U. Resident dir., instr. health edn. U. Ill., Urbana, 1978-79; complex dir. Western Mich. U., Kalamazoo, 1979-81, asst. dir. residence hall life, 1981-85; dir. residence svcs. Wright State U., Dayton, Ohio, 1985—; NIV, Dekalb, Ill.; founder, developer The Clark Experiment, a residence hall based on Burns Crookston's Intentional Dem. Cmty., U. Ill., 1974; cons., owner Midwest Cons., 1983-85; lectr. in field. Contbr. articles to profl. jours. Chmn. bd. trustees AIDS Found. Miami Valley, Dayton, 1987—; mem. City Priority Bd., Dayton, 1992; bd. dirs. Dayton Art Inst. Guild, 1990-91; mem. cmty. action com. Regional Transp. Authority, 1993—; mem. Friends of Wesleyan Nature Ctr., Dayton, 1992; mem. Dayton AIDS Consortium, 1990-93; mem. City of Kalamazoo Awareness Com., 1982-85. named Advisor of the Yr., Great Lakes affiliate Nat. Assn. Coll. and Univ. Residence Halls, 1983, Western Mich. U., 1983; recipient Disting. Svc. award Kalamazoo Alcohol and Drug Abuse Coun., 1984, Outstanding Svc. award Great Lakes Assn. Coll. and Univ. Housing Officers, 1984, Disting. Svc. award, 1988, Good Neighbor of the Wk. award EDTN-TV, Dayton, 1990; Coakley scholarship Western Mich. U. Mem. Assn. Coll. and Univ. Housing Officers (chair task force on regional relationships 1990-92, program chair internat. Automation of Housing workshop 1987), Great Lakes Assn. Coll. and Univ. Housing Officers (mem. visioning com. 1993—, past pres., sec.-treas. 1983-88, editor Trends newsmag. 1981-83), Nat. Assn. Student Pers. Adminstrs., Ohio Housing Officers, Southwestern Ohio Housing Officers, Omicron Delta Kappa. Avocations: music, cooking, speculative fiction. Home: 1181 Golf Ct Dekalb IL 60115 Office: Wright State Univ NIV Student Housing and Svcs Dekalb IL 60115

COAKLEY, WILLIAM THOMAS, utilities executive; b. Dubuque, Iowa, Oct. 18, 1946; s. Harold Leo and Mary Margaret (Schwartz) C.; m. Deborah Dixon Leach, Nov. 25, 1971; children: Matthew David, Kenneth William. BA, Loras Coll., 1968; postgrad., Drake U., 1968-69, 71. Commd. U.S. Army, 1970, advanced through grades to capt.; co. exec. officer U.S. Army, Fort Bragg, N.C., 1971-73; brigade staff officer U.S. Army, Stuttgart, Fed. Republic of Germany, 1973-75; budget analyst U.S. Army Corps of Engrs., Frankfurt, Fed. Republic of Germany, 1975-77; budget officer U.S. Army Corps of Engrs., Riyadh, Saudi Arabia, 1977-80; resigned U.S. Army Corps of Engrs., 1980; budget and fin. officer Western Area Power Adminstrn., Billings, Mont., 1980-85, fin. mgr., 1985-95; fin. sys. mgr. Western Area Power Adminstrn., Golden, Colo., 1996—, co-project mgr. Oracle U.S. Fed. Fins.,, 1997—. Author, editor Fiscal Procedures and Control of Funds, 1975. Chmn. divsn. United Way Fundraiser of Yellowstone County, 1992, 93, mem. bd. dirs., 1994-96; mem. St. Patrick's Co-Cathedral Parish Coun., 1990-92, pres., 1991-92. Mem. Internat. Soc. Am. Mil. Engrs. (sec., treas. Frankfurt chpt. 1974-75), Yellowstone Country Club (bd. dirs. 1984-86, 95-96), Rotary, Pacific Northwest Golf Assn. (Mont. rep. 1995-96), Colo. Golf Assn. (rules ofcl. 1997—). Republican. Roman Catholic. Home: 2164 S Parfet Ct Lakewood CO 80227-1913 Office: Western Area Power Adminstrn PO Box 3402 1627 Cole Blvd Golden CO 80401-3398

COALE, ANSLEY JOHNSON, economics educator; b. Balt., Nov. 14, 1917; s. James Johnson and Nellie Ansley (Johnson) C.; m. Sarah Hamilton Campbell, Oct. 18, 1941; children: Ansley Johnson, Robert Campbell. BA, Princeton U., 1939, MA, 1941, PhD, 1947; D (hon.), U. Louvain, Belgium, 1979; D.honoris causa, U. Liege, Belgium, 1983; LL.D. (hon.), U. Pa., 1983; DHL (hon.), Princeton (N.J.) U., 1994. Research asst. Office Population Research, Princeton, 1941-42; instr. elec. communications M.I.T., 1943-44; sec. com. social implications atomic energy Social Sci. Research Council, 1946-47; faculty Princeton, 1947-86, prof. econs., 1959-86; dir. Princeton (Office Population Research), 1959-75; vis. prof. demography U. Calif., Berkeley, 1987; U.S. rep. UN Population Commn., 1961-67; Social Sci. Research Council-Nat. Sci. Research Council fellow Inst. Advanced Study, 1947-49; chmn. com. on population and demography Nat. Acad. Scis., 1977-82; fellow Ctr. Advanced Study Behavioral Scis., 1982-83. Author: The Problems of Reducing Vulnerability to Atomic Bombs, 1947, (with Edgar M. Hoover) Population Growth and Economic Development in Low Income Countries, 1958, (with Melvin Zelnik) New Estimates of Population and Births in the United States, 1963, (with Paul Demeny) Regional Model Life Tables and Stable Populations, 1966, The Growth and Structure of Human Populations, 1972, (with B. Anderson and E. Härm) Human Fertility in Russia Since the Nineteenth Century, 1979, (with S. Watkins et al) The Decline of Fertility In Europe, 1986; also articles. Served with USNR, 1942-46. Recipient Mindel Sheps prize in math. demography, 1974, Irene Taeuber prize in population rsch., 1988. Fellow AAAS, Am. Statis. Assn., Brit. Acad. (corr.); mem. Population Assn. Am. (pres. 1967-68), Am. Econ. Assn., Am. Philos. Soc., Internat. Population Union (pres. 1977-81), Am. Acad. Arts and Scis., Nat. Acad. Scis. Home: 1382 Langhorne Newtown Rd Newtown PA 18940-2401 Address: F113 Pennswood Village Newtown PA 18940

COALE, SHERRI, university women's basketball coach. B in Edn. summa cum laude, Okla. Christian U. Sci./Arts, 1987. Asst. coach Edmond Meml. H.S., 1987-89; head varisty coach Norman H.S., 1989-96; head coach women's basketball U. Okla., 1996—. Bd. dirs. Am. Cancer Soc.; mem. Coaches vs. Cancer, Westside Ch. of Christ, Norman; vol. Children's Miracle Network. Named All-State Coach, 1993, Regional Coach of Yr., 1993, Big All-City Coach of Yr., 1993. Mem. NEA, Women's Basketball Coaches Assn., Okla. Girls Basketball Coaches Assn., Okal. Coaches Assn., Fellowship of Christian Athletes, Norman Optimists, Okla. Edn. Assn., Profl. Educators of Norman. Fax: 405-325-7623. Office: U Okla 180 W Brooks St Rm 235 Norman OK 73019-6010*

COALTER, MILTON J, JR., library director, educator; b. Memphis, July 5, 1949; s. Milton J. and Jewel (Mitchel) C.; m. Linda M. Block, May 20, 1973; children: Martha Claire, Siram Jacob. BA, Davidson Coll., 1971; MDiv, Princeton Theol. Sem., 1975, ThM, 1977; PhD in Religion, Princeton U., 1982. Asst. prof. Am. Religion N.C. State U., Raleigh, 1981-82; pub. svcs. libr. The Iliff Sch. Theology, Denver, 1982-84, acting libr. dir., 1984-85; libr. dir., prof. bibliography and rsch. Louisville Presbyn. Theol. Sem., 1985—; bd. dirs. Louisville Inst. for Study Protestantism and Am. Culture, Scholars Press; mem. Gen. Assembly Coun. Task Force on Ch. Membership Growth, Presbyn. Ch., Louisville, 1989-91. Author: (with John M. Mulder) The Letters of David Avery, 1979, Gilbert Tennent, Son of Thunder, 1986; (with John M. Mulder and Louis B. Weeks) The Presbyterian Presence in the Twentieth Century, 7 vols., 1989-92, Vital Signs, 1996; editor: (with Virgil Cruz) How Shall We Witness?, 1995; contbr. articles to profl. jours. Recipient Jonathan Edwards award Princeton U., 1977-80, Tchg. award Assn. Princeton Grad. Alumni, 1979-80, Francis Makemie award Presbyn. Ch. Dept. History; Lily Endowment grantee, 1987-90, 99—, N.J. Hist. Commn. grantee, 1979-80, Pew Charitable Trust grantee, 1990-93; Princeton U. Whiting fellow, 1980-81. Mem. Am. Theol. Libr. Assn. (bd. dirs. 1997—, pres. 1998—), Am. Soc. Ch. History, Am. Acad. Religion. Presbyterian. Office: Louisville Presbyn Theol Sem 1044 Alta Vista Rd Louisville KY 40205-1758

COANE, JAMES EDWIN, III, information technology executive; b. N.Y.C., July 21, 1940; s. James Edwin and Mary Elizabeth (Brown) Bromwell; m. JoAnn Sabasteanski, Mar. 23, 1968; children: James Edwin IV, Mary Ashley. BBA, Duke U., 1963. V.p. sales Am. Flagpole Equipment Co., Setauket, N.Y., 1964-68; dir. mktg./sales Bldg. Products-Kearney Nat., Setauket, 1968-70, pres., gen. mgr., 1970-79; v.p. ops. Kearney Nat., Inc., N.Y.C., 1979-81, group v.p., 1981-84; pres., bd. dirs. Morris Decision Systems, Inc., N.Y.C., 1984-86; chmn., pres., CEO, bd. dirs. Telebase Systems, Inc., Wayne, Pa., 1987-96; pres., bd. dirs. N2K Inc., N.Y.C. and Wayne, Pa., 1996—; bd. dirs., exec. com. Ben Franklin Tech. Ctr., Phila., 1993—, Nat. Coun. Growing Cos., Bethesda, Md.; chmn., bd. dirs., CEO coun. PENJERDEL chpt., Phila.; dir. CD Now, Inc., 1999. Co-author: Specialty Elements of Architecture, 1982; contbr. articles to The Fisherman. Bd. dirs. BBB, Conn., 1984-85; mem. adv. com. on admissions Duke U., Durham, N.C., 1968-72; mem. devel. com. Stony Brook (N.Y.) Sch., 1974-78, class rep., 1964—; past bd. dirs., v.p., chmn. industry divsn. Nat. Assn. Archtl. Metal Mfrs., 1970's. With U.S. Army, 1964-70. Recipient Creative Tech. award IBM, 1998. Mem. Info. Industry Assn. (vice chmn., bd. dirs., exec. com., treas. 1993—, Appreciation awards 1990, 91, 92), Software Info. Industry Assn. (dir. 1999), Phi Beta Kappa. Avocations: skiing, fishing, golf. Office: N2K Inc 55 Broad St Fl 26 New York NY 10004-2501

COAR, DAVID H., federal judge; b. Birmingham, Ala., Aug. 11, 1943; s. Robert and Lorayne C.; children: Chinyelu, Kamau, Jamila. BA, Syracuse U., 1964; JD, Loyola U., 1969; LLM, Harvard U., 1970. Bar: Ill. 1969, Ala. 1971. Atty.-extern NAACP Legal Def. and Edn. Fund, Inc., N.Y.C., 1970-71, Crawford & Cooper, Mobile, Ala., 1971-72, Adams, Baker & Clemon, Birmingham, 1972-74; prof. DePaul U. Law Sch., Chgo., 1974-79, 82-86; U.S. trustee U.S. Justice Dept., Chgo., 1979-82; bankruptcy judge U.S. Bankruptcy Ct., Chgo., 1986-94; dist. ct. judge U.S. Dist. Ct., Chgo., 1994—. Bd. dirs. Boys and Girls Club, Chgo. Mem. ABA, Am. Coll. Bankruptcy, Law Club, Legal Club Chgo., Chgo. Inns of Ct. Office: US Dist Ct 219 S Dearborn St Ste 1478 Chicago IL 60604-1705*

COAR, RICHARD JOHN, mechanical engineer, aerospace consultant; b. Hanover, N.H., May 2, 1921; s. Herbert Greenleaf and Anne (Langill) C.; m. Cecilie Berle, 1942 (dec. 1971); children—Gregory, Candace, Andrea, Kenneth; m. Lucille Hicks, 1972. B.S. in Mech. Engring., Tufts U., 1942. Engr. Pratt & Whitney Aircraft, East Hartford, Conn., 1942-56; chief engr. Fla. Research and Devel Ctr Pratt & Whitney Aircraft, 1956-70, asst. gen. mgr., 1970-71; v.p. engring. Pratt & Whitney Aircraft, East Hartford, 1971-76, exec. v.p., 1976-83, pres., 1983-84; sr. v.p. United Techs., Hartford, 1983-84, exec. v.p., 1984-86. Patentee aircraft engines and controls. Corporator Hartford Hosp., 1983; bd. dirs. Hartford Symphony, 1985-87, 98. Recipient Daniel Guggenheim medal for contbns. to aeronautic and space propulsion sys. Mem. ASME (George Westinghouse Gold medal 1986), Nat. Acad. Engring., Soc. Automotive Engrs., Tau Beta Pi, Water's Edge Country Club. Avocations: sailing; golf. Home and Office: 2842 Summit Ridge Rd NE Roanoke VA 24012-6944

COASE, RONALD HARRY, economics educator; b. Willesden, Eng., Dec. 29, 1910; came to U.S., 1951; s. Henry Joseph and Rosalie (Giles) C.; m. Marian Ruth Hartung, Aug. 7, 1937. B of Commerce, London Sch. Econs., 1932, DSc, 1951; Dr. Rer. Pol. honoris causa, Cologne U., Fed. Republic Germany, 1988; D of Social Sci. (hon.), Yale U., 1989; LLD (hon.), Washington U., St. Louis, 1991, U. Dundee, Scotland, 1992; DSc (hon.), U. Buckingham, Eng., 1995; DHL (hon.), Beloit Coll., 1996; docteur honoris causa, U. Paris, 1996. Sir Ernest Cassel Travelling scholar, 1931-32; asst. lectr. Dundee Sch. Econs., 1932-34, U. Liverpool, Eng., 1934-35; from asst. lectr. to reader London Sch. Econs., 1935-51; prof. U. Buffalo, 1951-58, U. Va., Charlottsville, 1958-64; prof. U. Chgo., 1964—, now Clifton R. Musser prof. emeritus, sr. fellow in law and econs. Law Sch.; statistician, then chief statistician Central Statis. Office, Offices War Cabinet, Eng., 1941-46. Author: British Broadcasting, A Study in Monopoly, 1950, The Firm, the Market and the Law, 1988, Essays on Economics and Economists, 1994; editor Jour. Law and Econs., 1964-92. Rockefeller fellow, 1948; fellow Center for Advanced Study Behavioral Scis., 1958-59; sr. research fellow Hoover Instn., Stanford U., 1977; recipient Nobel Prize in econ., 1991. Fellow Am. Acad. Arts and Scis., Am. Econ. Assn. (disting.), The Brit. Acad. (corr.), European Acad.; mem. Royal Econ. Soc., Mont Pelerin Soc. Home: 1515 N Astor St Chicago IL 60610-1627 Office: U Chgo Laird Bell Law Quadrangle 1111 E 60th St Chicago IL 60637-2776

COATES, BEN TERRENCE, professional football player; b. Greenwood, S.C., Aug. 16, 1969. BS in Sports Mgmt., Livingstone Coll. Tight end New Eng. Patriots, Foxboro, Mass., 1991—. Named to Sporting News NFL All-Pro Team, 1994, 95, to NFl Pro Bowl Team, 1994-96. Office: New Eng Patriots Foxboro Stadium 60 Washington St Foxboro MA 02035-1388*

COATES, CLARENCE LEROY, JR., research engineer, educator; b. Hastings, Nebr., Nov. 5, 1923; s. Clarence Leroy and Mildred (Creighton) C.; m. Henrietta Hoff, Jan. 1, 1943; children: Catherine Anne, Christopher John; m. Lila M. Mustola, Mar. 5, 1969; 1 son, Randall Lee; m. Henrietta Coates, July 17, 1972. B.S. in Elec. Engring, U. Kans., 1944, M.S., 1948; Ph.D., U. Ill., 1954. Instr. elec. engring. U. Kans., 1946-48; instr., then asso. prof. elec. engring. U. Ill., 1948-56; research scientist Gen. Electric Research Labs., 1956-63; prof. elec. engring. U. Tex., 1963-71, chmn. dept., 1964-66, dir. electronics rsch ctr., 1967-71; dir. coord. sci. lab., prof. elec. engring. U. Ill., 1971-72; prof. sch. elec. engring. Purdue U., 1973-88, head, 1972-83; cons. NSF, 1969-70, mem. sci. info. coun., 1972-75; mem. research adv. com. NASA, 1971-76. Author: Threshold Logic; Cons. editor, Blaisdell Pub. Co., 1968-70; Contbr. articles in field to profl. jours. Served as officer USNR, 1944- 46. Fellow IEEE (v.p. publ. activities, dir. 1971-72), AAAS; mem. Sigma Xi, Phi Kappa Phi, Tau Beta Pi, Eta Kappa Nu, Sigma Tau. Home: 280 Woods Point Rd Osprey FL 34229-9264

COATES, DIANNE KAY, social worker; b. Adrian, Mich., Jan. 4, 1945. Student, Jackson Bus. U., 1962-63; AA with honors, Macomb C.C., Warren, Mich., 1977; BA with high distinction, Madonna Coll., 1979; MSW, Wayne State U., 1982, cert. devel. disabilities, 1999; postgrad., Internat. Grad. Sch., 1984, Ea. Mich. U., 1989. Cert. social worker, Mich. Nat. svc. officer Mil. Order of the Purple Heart, Detroit, 1973-80; psychology technician VA Med. Ctr., Allen Park, Mich., 1980-84; clin. cons. HOMEBASE, Detroit, 1983-85; clin. social worker Cmty. Counseling Assocs., Adrian, 1983, Roseville, Mich., 1983-87; clin. social worker Ypsilanti (Mich.) Regional Psychiat. Hosp., 1987-90, Southgate (Mich.) Regional Ctr. for the Developmentally Disabled, 1990-92, 92-96, Lafayette Clinic, 1992; intake/admissions/discharge coord. Southgate Ctr., 1996—; group counselor Survivors of Homicide, Detroit, 1981-82; vol. HAVEN, Pontiac, Mich., 1986-87; internat. exch. counselor Edn. Found. Fgn. Study, 1987-92; field instr. Wayne State U., 1988—; ind. contract therapist Renaissance West Cmty. Mental Health Svcs. Clinic, Detroit, 1988-89, Caknipe-Kovach Assocs., 1988-92; area rep. Ednl. Resource Devel. Trust, 1991-94;. Recipient Ann. Disting. Svc. award LA MOPH Dept. of Mich., 1992. Mem. NASW (bd. cert. diplomate), Nat. Acad. Cert. Social Workers, Assn. State Employed Mental Social Work (v.p. 1991-93), Mich. Mental Health Assn., Mich. Assn. Mental Health Profls., Social Work Assn. Madonna Coll. (co-founder), Mich. Alcohol and Addiction Assn., Wayne State U. Alumni Assn., Bus. and Profl. Women, Vietnam Vets. Am. (hon. life assoc. mem.), Met. Svc. Officers Assn. (pres. 1990-92), Ladies Aux. Mil. Order of Purple Heart (region 2 v.p. 1985-86, nat. membership officer 1995-96), Ladies Aux. VFW, DAV Aux. Home: 1502 Elias St Westland MI 48186-4919

COATES, DONALD ROBERT, geology educator, scientist; b. Grand Island, Neb., July 23, 1922; s. Frank Jefferson and Harriet (Ferris) C.; m. Jeanne Louise Grandison, Mar. 18, 1944 (dec. Jan. 1993); children: Cheryl D., Donald Eric, Lark J.; m. Marilyn Hilton Williams, Jan. 12, 1998. BA, Coll. Wooster, 1944; MA, Columbia U., 1948, PhD, 1956. Faculty Earlham Coll., Richmond, Ind., 1948-51; geologist, project chief U.S. Geol. Survey, Tucson, 1951-54; faculty Harpur Coll. (now Binghamton U./SUNY), Binghamton, N.Y., 1954-90, chmn. dept. geology, 1954-63, prof., 1963-90; prof. emeritus Binghamton U. SUNY, Binghamton, 1990—; research geologist U.S. Geol. Survey, Vestal, N.Y., 1958-61; vis. geoscientist Am. Geol. Inst., 1963-65; cons. C.E. U.S. Army, 1965-66; cons. Empire State Electric Energy Research Corp., Consol. Edison N.Y., Niagara Mohawk Power Corp., Mohonk Preserve Corp., Protector Pine Oak Woods Inc., U.S. Army C.E., Town of Islip, N.Y. State Dept. Environ. Conservation, N.Y. State Electric & Gas Corp., N.Y. State Dept. Transp., N.Y. State Atty. Gen., N.Y. State Power Authority, N.Y. Low Level Nuclear Waste Siting Commn., Town of Vernon, N.Y., Broome County, Chemung County, Town of Vestal, N.Y., Town of Trenton, N.Y., Town of Deerfield, N.Y., Town of Norwich, also pvt. cos.; assoc. program dir. NSF Found., 1963-64. Editor: Geology of South-Central New York, 1963, Environmental Geomorphology and Landscape Conservation, 3 vols., Coastal Geomorphology, Glacial Geomorphology, Geomorphology and Engineering, Landslides, (with John Vitek) Threshholds in Geomorphology, Urban Geomorphology, Environmental Geomorphology, 1971, Environmental Science Workbook, 1972, (with Charles Higgins) Ground Water Geomorphology, 1990; editor, author: Environmental Geology; author: Geology and Society; contbr. to Science - A Process Approach, 1965; also articles, reports. Lt. U.S. Navy, 1943-46, USNR, 1946-54. Recipient award for Sustained Superior Performance NSF, 1964; Rsch. grantee NSF, U.S. Dept. Commerce, U.S. Geol. Survey, N.Y. State Atomic and Space Devel. Authority, Rsch. Found. SUNY, 1958-61. Fellow AAAS, Geol. Soc. Am. (Merit cert. engring. geology divsn. 1980, E.B. Burwell Jr. award 1995); mem. Assn. Engring. Geologists, Nat. Assn. Geology Tchrs. (pres. Eastern sect. 1962, Ralph Digman award 1972, Coll. Tchr. of Yr. award 1971), Am. Inst. Profl. Geologists, N.Y. State Geol. Assn. (pres. 1963, 81), Phi Beta Kappa. Home: 11306 Olde Turnbury Ct Charlotte NC 28277-6519 Office: Binghamton U SUNY Dept Geol Scis Binghamton NY 13902

COATES, FREDERICK ROSS, lawyer; b. Madison, Va., June 27, 1933; s. Fred Icer and Sarah (Hale) C.; m. Rebecca White, Nov. 25, 1959; children: Stephanie Renee Piper, Susan C. McCoy. BA, U. Richmond, 1954, JD, 1959. Bar: Va., U.S. Dist. Ct. (we. dist.) Va. 1959. Vice chmn. Madison County Rep. party, 1968-88; mem. Rescue Squad Madison County, Madison County Planning com.; commr. accounts Madison County; asst. commr. accounts Greene County, Va. Served with U.S. Army, 1954-57. Recpient Key Man award Madison Jaycees, 1962-64. Mem. ABA, Va. State Bar Assn., Madison-Greene Bar Assn., Red Land Club, Greene Hills Club, Masons, Boosters Club, Lions, Shriners. Baptist. Avocation: golf. Home and Office: PO Box 328 Madison VA 22727-0328

COATES, GLENN RICHARD, lawyer; b. Thorp, Wis., June 8, 1923; s. Richard and Alma (Borck) C.; m. Dolores Milburn, June 24, 1944; children—Richard Ward, Cristie Joan. Student, Milw. State Tchrs. Coll., 1940-42, N.M.A. and M.A., 1943-44; LL.B., U. Wis., 1949, S.J.D., 1953. Bar: Wis. 1949. Atty. Mil. Sea Transp. Service, Dept. Navy, 1951-52; pvt. practice law Racine, Wis., 1952—; of counsel Dye, Foley, Krohn, Shannon, S.E.; sec., gen. counsel Racine Federated Inc.; lectr. U. Wis. Law Sch., 1955-56. Author: Chattel Secured Farm Credit, 1953; contbr. articles to profl. publs. Chmn. bd. St. Luke's Meml. Hosp., 1973-76, bd. dirs., 1990-91; pres. Racine Area United Way, 1979-81; bd. curators State Hist. Soc. Wis., 1986—, pres., 1995-97; bd. dirs. Racine County Area Found., 1983-89; bd. dirs. Wis. History Found., Inc., 1983-99, Hist. Sites Found., Inc., 1987-89, St. Luke's Hosp./St. Mary's Med. Ctr. Healthcare Found., 1992-96. With U.S. Army, 1943-46. Fellow Am. Bar Found. (life); mem. ABA, State Bar Wis. (bd. govs. 1969-74, chmn. bd. 1973-74), Wis. Jud. Coun. (chmn. 1969-72), Am. Law Inst. (life), Order of Coif. Methodist (chmn. fin. com. 1961-67). Club: Racine Country. Lodge: Masons. Home: 2830 Michigan Blvd Racine WI 53402-4254 Office: 1300 S Green Bay Rd Racine WI 53406-4469

COATES, JOHN PETER, technical executive; b. Coventry, Eng., Apr. 4, 1946; came to U.S., 1978; s. Harry and Barbara Joan (Snape) C.; m. Laura Frances Curran, July 28, 1979; children: Jonathan Edmund, Kristen Elizabeth, Ross James. BS/MS in Chemistry, Slough Coll. of Tech. now Thames Valley Univ., Eng., 1972; PhD in Chemistry, Brunel U., London, 1987. Analytical chemist Castrol Oil Co., Bracknell, Eng., 1964-73; sr. chromatographer Burmah Oil, Bromboro, Eng., 1973-74; sr., chief chemist Perkin-Elmer Ltd., Beaconsfield, Eng., 1974-78; sr. staff scientist Perkin-Elmer Corp., Norwalk, Conn., 1978-85; dir. mktg. Spectra-Tech Inc., Stamford, Conn., 1985-88; dir. analyzer div. Nicolet Instrument Corp., Madison, Wis., 1988-92; dir. mktg. real time systems divsn. (PAI) Perkin-Elmer, Norwalk, Conn., 1992-96; prin. cons. Coates Cons., Newtown, Conn., 1996—; dir. techs. Top Source Instruments, Atlanta, Ga., 1998—; dir. indsl. rels. MCEC, U. Tenn., Knoxville, 1999—. Co-author: (with L.C. Setti) Oils, Lubricants and Petroleum Products--Characterization by Infrared Spectra, 1985; patentee in field; contbr. chpts. to books and articles to profl. jours. Fellow Royal Soc. Chemistry; mem. Am. Chem. Soc., Instrument Soc. Am., Soc. Automotive Engrs., Soc. Applied Spectroscopy. Avocations: writing, photography, music, computers. Office: Coates Cons PO Box 3176 Newtown CT 06470-3176

COATES, ROBERT JAY, retired electronic scientist; b. Lansing, Mich., May 8, 1922; s. Archie Louis and Ruth Agnes (Hutchings) C.; m. Gladys Buchhorn, Aug. 17, 1946; 1 child, Bonnie. B.S.E.E., Mich. State U., 1943; M.S.E.E., U. Md., 1948; Ph.D., Johns Hopkins U., 1957. Electronic scientist U.S. Naval Research Lab., Washington, 1943-49, 52-59; instr. physics Johns Hopkins U., Balt., 1949-52; asso. chief tracking systems div., chief space data acquisition div., chief advanced devel. div., chief advanced data systems div. Goddard Space Flight Center, Greenbelt, Md., 1959-79; mgr. crustal dynamics project Goddard Space Flight Center, 1979-89; cons., 1989—. Home constrn. vol. Habitat for Humanity, 1996—. Served with USN, 1944-45. Recipient Group Achievement award NASA, 1973, 1968, 1986, Apollo Achievement award, 1969, Exceptional Performance award Goddard Space Flight Center, 1971, Exceptional Service medal, 1986; Outstanding Performance award NRL, 1959, Outstanding Leadership medal NASA, 1989. Fellow IEEE; mem. Am. Phys. Soc., Am. Geophys. Union, AAAS, Sigma Xi, Phi Kappa Phi, Tau Beta Pi. Home: 529 Whitingham Dr Silver Spring MD 20904-6330

COATES, TIMOTHY JOEL, historian; b. Tucson, Ariz., July 2, 1952; s. Charles Kedron Coates and Barbara Bernice Batchelor. BA, U. Ariz., 1974; MA, U. Minn., 1976, PhD, 1993. Vis. asst. prof. Brown U., Providence, 1993-95; asst. prof. Coll. of Charleston, S.C., 1995—. Author: Degredados e Orfas, 1998; assoc., book rev. editor Portuguese Studies Rev., 1997—. Calouste Gulbenkian Found. fellow, Portugal, 1990, Fundação Oriente fellow, Macau, 1997; grantee Am. Inst. Indian Studies, India, 1991, Luso-Am. Devel. Found., Portugal, 1997. Mem. Am. Hist. Assn., Soc. for Spanish and Portuguese Hist. Studies, Soc. for the History of Discoveries, Hakluyt Soc., James Ford Bell Libr. E-mail: coatest@cofc.edu. Office: Coll of Charleston Dept History 66 George St Charleston SC 29424

COATES, WAYNE EVAN, agricultural engineer; b. Edmonton, Alta., Can., Nov. 28, 1947; came to U.S., 1981; s. Orval Bruce Wright and Leora (Raeseler) C.; m. Patricia Louise Williams, Aug. 28, 1970. BS in Agr., U. Alta., 1969, MS in Agrl. Engring., 1970; PhD in Agrl. Engring., Okla. State U., 1973. Registered profl. engr., Ariz., Sask. Forage systems engr. Agr. Can., Melfort, Sask., 1973-75; project engr., tech. advisor, asst. sta. mgr. Prairie Agrl. Machinery Inst., Humboldt, Sask., 1975-81; cattle, grain farmer pvt. practice, Humboldt, 1975-81; assoc. prof. U. Ariz., Tucson, 1981-91, prof., 1991—; prof. titular ad honorem U. Nat. de Catamarca, Argentina, 1993—; cons. Vols. in Coop. Assts. and Ptnrs. of Ams., 1991—, Paraguayan Govt. UN Devel. Program, 1987-90, Argentine Govt., univs. and pvt. industry, 1991—, govt., univ. and agrl. orgns., Mid East agrl. projects, 1986-89, 98—; spkr. at internat. confs., Australia, Paraguay, Argentina, Peru, Chile, U.S.; expert witness in field. Designer farm equipment primarily for alternative crops and tillage; patentee in field; contbr. articles to profl. jours. Pres. Sunrise Ter. Village Townhomes Homeowners Assn., Tucson, 1990-92, 98—. Grantee USDA, Washington, 1981—, Ariz. Dept. Environ. Quality, Phoenix, 1989—, U.S. Dept. of Energy, Washington, 1991-98, agrl. industries western U.S., 1982—. Mem. AAAS, NSPE, Am. Soc. Agrl. Engrs. (chmn. Ariz. sect. 1984-85, vice-chmn. Pacific region 1988-89, dir. dist. 4 1991-93, rep. to AAAS Consortium of Affiliates for Internat. Programs 1992-97, internat. dir. 1994-96), Assn. for Advancement of Indsl. Crops (pres. 1994-95, Outstanding Rschr. award 1997), Soc. Automotive Engrs., Air and Waste Mgmt. Assn., Coun. for Agrl. Sci. and Tech., Can. Soc. Agrl. Engring., Australian Soc. for Agrl. Engring., Asian Assn. for Agrl. Engring., Asociacion Latinoamericana de Ingenieria Agricola, Sigma Xi. Avocations: jogging, hiking. Office: U Ariz Office Arid Lands Studies 250 E Valencia Rd Tucson AZ 85706-6800

COATES-SHRIDER, LISA NICOLE, psychology educator; b. Cleve., Jan. 24, 1967; d. Joel D. Coates and Margaret E. Schweitzer; m. Scott R. Schweitzer; 1 child, Jordan. BA in Psychology, U. Cin., 1989; MA in Psychology, N.Mex. State U., 1992, PhD in Social Psychology, 1996. Instr. psychology U. Tex., El Paso, 1995-96; asst. prof. psychology McMurry U., Abilene, Tex., 1997—; vis. asst. prof. psychology U. Tex., 1996-97. Co-author: (chpt.) Enhancing Education in Heterogeneous Environments, 1996. Coach YMCA Tee-Ball League, Abilene, 1998. Mem. AAAS, APA, Am. Psychol. Soc., Soc. Psychol Study Social Issues, Soc. Teaching Psychology, Phi Beta Kappa. E-mail: shriderl@mcmurryadm.mcm.edu.

COATS, ANDREW MONTGOMERY, lawyer, former mayor, dean; b. Oklahoma City, Okla., Jan. 19, 1935; s. Sanford Clarence and Mary Ola (Young) C.; m. Linda M. Zimmerman; children—Andrew, Michael, Jennifer, Sanford. B.A., U. Okla., 1957, J.D., 1963. Assoc. Crowe and Dunlevy, Oklahoma City, Okla., 1963-67, ptnr., 1967-76, sr. trial ptnr., 1980—; dist. atty. Oklahoma County, Oklahoma City, Okla., 1976-80; mayor City of Oklahoma City, 1983-87; dean U. Okla. Coll. Law; vis. prof. law U. Okla., 1969-71; pres. Okla. Young Lawyers Conf., 1968-69; dir. Meml. Bank, N.A., Oklahoma City, Federal Bank. Democratic nominee U.S. Senate, 1980; pres. Oklahoma County Legal Aid Soc., 1972-73 Served to lt. USN, 1960-63. Named Outstanding Lawyer in Okla., Oklahoma City U., 1977. Fellow Am. Coll. Trial Lawyers (pres. 1996-97, pres.-elect 1995-96), Am. Bd. Trial Advocates (charter pres. Okla. 1986); mem. ABA, Okla. Bar Assn. (pres. 1992-93), Oklahoma County Bar Assn. (pres. 1976-77), Order of Coif, Oklahoma City Golf and Country Club (bd. dirs. 1977-80, 93-96), Beacon Club, Petroleum Club (pres. 1995), Phi Beta Kappa (pres. 1975), Pi Kappa Alpha (pres. 1956), Phi Delta Phi (pres. 1962). Democrat. Episcopalian. Clubs: Oklahoma City Golf and Country (bd. dirs. 1977-80), Beacon, Petroleum. Avocations: music; golf. Office: Crowe and Dunlevy 1800 Mid-Am Tower 20 N Broadway Ave Ste 1800 Oklahoma City OK 73102-8273*

COATS, DANIEL RAY, former senator; b. Jackson, Mich., May 16, 1943; s. Edward R. and Vera E. C.; m. Marcia Crawford, Sept. 4, 1965; children: Laura, Lisa, Andrew. B.A., Wheaton (Ill.) Coll., 1965; J.D. cum laude, Ind. U., 1971. Bar: Ind. 1972. Mem. 97th-100th Congresses from 4th Dist. Ind., Washington, 1981-89; Dist. rep. U.S. Congressman Dan Quayle, 1976-80; U.S. senator from Ind., 1989-99; bd. dirs. IPALCO; mem. armed svcs. com., labor and human resources com., intelligence com. Pres., Big Bros./Big Sisters, Ft. Wayne, Ind. Served with U.S. Army, 1966-68. Office: 901 15th St NW Washington DC 20005-2301*

COATS, WILLIAM SLOAN, III, lawyer; b. Fresno, Calif., Mar. 31, 1950; s. William Sloan Jr. and Willa (Macdonell) C.; m. Sherri Lee Young, Aug. 3, 1980; children: Devin Roseanne, Allyn Elizabeth. AB, U. San Francisco, 1972; JD, U. Calif., San Francisco, 1980. Bar: Calif. 1980, U.S. Dist. Ct. (no. dist.) Calif. 1980, U.S. Dist. Ct. (cen. and so. dists.) Calif. 1982. Assoc. Bancroft, Avery & McAlister, San Francisco, 1980-82, Hopkins, Mitchell & Carley, San Jose, Calif., 1982-84, Gibson, Dunn & Crutcher, San Francisco, 1984-93; ptnr. Brown & Bain, Palo Alto, Calif., 1993-96, Howrey & Simon, Menlo Park, Calif., 1996—. Nat. Merit scholar, 1968. Mem. ABA (vice chair program com., sect. on sci. and tech.), Calif. Bar Assn. (co-chair copyright com. intellectual property sect., co-chair edn. com.), Green and Gold Club, Univ. Club. Republican. Roman Catholic. Office: Howrey & Simon 301 Ravenswood Ave Menlo Park CA 94025

COATSWORTH, JOHN HENRY, history educator; b. N.Y.C., Sept. 27, 1940; s. Joseph Samuel Coatsworth and Janet Whedon (Bell) Barr; m. Patricia Ann Sopiak, June 13, 1964; 1 child, Anna Catherine. BA, Wesleyan U., 1963; MA, U. Wis., 1967, PhD, 1972; MA, Harvard U., 1993. From asst. to full prof. dept. history U. Chgo., 1969-92; prof. history, Monroe Gutman prof. L.Am. affairs Harvard U., Cambridge, Mass., 1992—; cons. Ford Found., John D. and Catherine T. McArthur Found., Social Sci. Rsch. Coun. Author: Growth Against Development, 1981, The United States and Central America, 1994; co-editor: Images of Mexico in the United States, 1989, Latin America and the World Economy Since 1800, 1998. John Simon Guggenheim fellow Guggenheim Found., 1986-87. Mem. Am. Hist. Assn. (pres. 1995), L.Am. Studies Assn., Econ. History Assn., Conf. on L.Am. History. Home: 2 Scott St Cambridge MA 02138-2016

COBB, BRIAN ERIC, broadcasting executive; b. Berlin, N.H., Jan. 3, 1945; s. Everett Bryan and Eleanore (Bouchard) C.; m. Denise Leclair, Sept. 20, 1986; children: Jennifer, Heather. BS, U. Nev., 1967. Gen. sales mgr. Sta. WNGE-TV, Nashville, 1972; mktg. mgr. Sta. WNGE-TV, 1973-76, v.p., gen. mgr., 1977; v.p., gen. mgr. Sta. WSIX AM/FM, Nashville, 1977, Gen. Electric Broadcasting of Colo., stas. KOA-AM, KOAQ, KOA-TV, Denver, 1978-81; v.p. TV Chapman Assocs., Washington, 1982-87; ptnr. Media Venture Ptnrs., Naples, Fla., 1987—; cons. Denver Broncos, 1982—; pres. Media Venture Mgmt., Biltmore Broadcasting. Comml. chmn. Mile-Hi United Way, 1980; bd. dirs. Vanderbilt Children's Hosp., 1973-76. Named an Outstanding Young Man of Yr., Nashville Jaycees, 1978. Mem. Nat. Assn. Broadcasters, Nat. Assn. TV Program Execs., Tenn. Assn. Broadcasters (bd. dirs. 1975-77), Nat. Assn. Media Brokers (pres. 1993-95), Rotary. Republican. Roman Catholic. Avocations: golfing, reading. Office: Media Venture Ptnrs Ste 500 8889 Pelican Bay Blvd Naples FL 34108

COBB, CALVIN HAYES, JR., lawyer; b. San Diego, Aug. 2, 1924; s. Calvin Hayes and Frances King (Halm) C.; m. Olive Latimer Watson, Mar. 19, 1955; children: Alice Cobb Parte, Joan Cobb Pettit, Calvin Hayes III, Robert Watson, Olive Latimer Waxter. BS with distinction, U.S. Naval Acad., 1944; LLB, Georgetown U., 1950. Bar: D.C. 1950, Md. 1950, U.S. Supreme Ct. 1953. Assoc. Law Offices of Elisha Hanson, Washington, 1950-55; ptnr. Hanson, Cobb & O'Brien, Washington, 1955-69, Steptoe & Johnson, Washington, 1969—. Leading article editor Georgetown Law Jour., 1949; contbr. articles to law revs. and profl. jours. Trustee Naval Hist. Found., 1983-98, Found. Mid. East Peace, 1969—. Lt. (j.g.) USN, 1944-47. Recipient Disting. Pub. Svc. award Sec. of Navy, 1979, 91, Pub. Svc. award USCG, 1991. Mem. USN League (sr. v.p. 1988-89, pres. 1989-91, nat. judge adv. 1975-89, bd. dirs. 1975—, Nat. Pres.'s award 1976, 83, 86), U.S. Naval Acad. Alumni Assn. (trustee 1955-58), Soc. of Cin., Lawyers Club, Chevy Chase Club (pres. 1974-75), Gibson Island Club, Royal Poinciana Golf Club (Fla.), Naples Bath and Tennis Club, Barristers Club (pres. 1974), Naples Athletic Club. Republican. Roman Catholic. Avocations: tennis, golf. Home: 3571 Hamlet Pl Chevy Chase MD 20815-4822 Office: 1330 Connecticut Ave NW Washington DC 20036-1704

COBB, DAVID KEITH, business executive; b. Calhoun City, Miss., Mar. 2, 1941; s. Bayne and Frances (Clements) C.; m. Dorothy Hill, June 15, 1963; children: Paul J., John D., Mark F. BS, U. So. Miss., 1963. Nat. mng. ptnr. fin. svcs. KPMG Peat Marwick, N.Y.C., 1963-95; CEO, vice chmn. Alamo Rent A Car, Inc., 1995-97; chmn. Laundromax, Inc., 1999—; bd. dirs. Miami Br. Fed. Res. Bank of Atlanta, RHR Internat., Inc., First Fleet Corp., Laundromax, Inc., Rennaisance Cruises, Inc., Capitol Ins. Co., Dispatch Mgmt. Svcs. Corp., CRS Investment Fund. Bd. dirs. Broward Cmty. Found.; chmn. United Way of Broward County. Republican. Presbyterian. Home and Office: 2521 Del Lago Dr Fort Lauderdale FL 33316-2303

COBB, G. ELLIOTT, JR., lawyer; b. Franklin, Va., July 11, 1939; s. Gardner E. and Thelma L. (Whitley) C.; m. Betty Minor, July 15, 1961; children: Polly, Susan, Gardner. B.S., U. Va., 1960, LL.B., 1966. Bar: Va. 1966, Supreme Ct. U.S 1974. Asso. counsel Union Camp Corp., Wayne, N.J., 1967-74; counsel, mgr. adminstrn. Union Camp Corp., 1974-76, gen. counsel, asst. sec., 1976, v.p., gen. counsel, sec., 1976-78; ptnr. Moyler, Moyler, Rainey & Cobb, Franklin, 1978—; mem. adv. bd. Crestar Bank, Franklin;. Mem. Franklin City Council, 1980-88; vice mayor of Franklin, 1982-84, mayor, 1984-88; bd. dirs. Southampton Meml. Hosp. Served with USMC, 1960-61. Mem. ABA, Va., Southampton-Franklin bar assns. Episcopalian. Clubs: Cypress Cove Country, Rotary. Home: 913 Clay St Franklin VA 23851-1306 Office: Moyler Moyler Rainey & Cobb 506 N Main St Franklin VA 23851-1438

COBB, HENRY NICHOLS, architect; b. Boston, Apr. 8, 1926; s. Charles Kane and Elsie Quincy (Nichols) C.; m. Joan Stewart Spaulding, June 5, 1953; children: Sara Quincy, Emma Trow, Pamela Codman. AB, Harvard, 1947, MArch, 1949; DFA (hon.), Bowdoin Coll., 1985; D Tech. Scis. (hon.), Swiss Fed. Inst. Tech., 1990. Designer in office Hugh Stubbins, 1949-50; mem. archtl. div. Webb & Knapp, Inc., 1950-60; ptnr. Pei Cobb Freed & Ptnrs. (formerly I.M. Pei & Ptnrs.), N.Y.C., 1960—; vis. critic Yale U., 1963-66, Bishop vis. prof. architecture, 1973, 78, Davenport vis. prof., 1975; studio prof., chmn. dept. architecture Harvard U. Grad. Sch. Design, Cambridge, Mass., 1980-85. Prin. works include Pl. Ville Marie, Montreal, Can., 1962; acad. ctr. and residence halls State U. Coll., Fredonia, N.Y., 1967, John Hancock Tower, Boston, 1972, Collins Place, Melbourne, Australia, 1976, Wilson Commons, U. Rochester, 1976, World Trade Ctr., Balt., 1977, Dallas Ctr., 1979, Johnson & Johnson World Hdqrs., New Brunswick, N.J., 1981, 16th St. Mall, Denver, 1982, Mobil Rsch. Lab., Farmers Branch, Tex., 1983, Portland (Maine) Mus. Art, 1983, Arco Tower, Dallas, 1984, hdqrs. Pitney Bowes Corp., Stamford, Conn., 1985, Fountain Place, Dallas, 1986, Columbia Sq., Washington, 1986, Commerce Sq., Phila., 1987, First Interstate World Ctr., L.A., 1989, Anderson Grad. Sch. Mgmt. UCLA, 1994, AAAS Hdqrs., Washington, 1997, U.S. Courthouse, Boston, 1998, World Trade Ctr., Barcelona, 1999, Head Office ABN-AMRO Bank, Amsterdam, 1999, Coll.-Conservatory of Music, U. Cin., 1999. Trustee Am. Acad. in Rome, 1972-90, Brearley Sch., 1975-80. Served with USNR, 1944-46. Recipient Topaz medallion for excellence in archtl. edn. Assn. Collegiate Schs. of Architecture/AIA, 1995. Fellow AIA (medal of honor N.Y. chpt. 1982), Am. Acad. Arts and Scis.; mem. Am. Acad. Arts and Letters (Arnold W. Brunner Meml. prize in architecture 1977), Nat. Acad. Design. Office: Pei Cobb Freed & Ptnrs 600 Madison Ave Fl 9 New York NY 10022-1615

COBB, HOWELL, federal judge; b. Atlanta, Dec. 7, 1922; s. Howell and Dorothy (Hart) C.; m. Torrance Chalmers (dec. 1963); children: Catherine Cobb Cook, Howell III, Mary Ann Cobb Walton; m. Amelie Suberbielle, July 3, 1965; children: Caroline Cobb Ervin, Thomas H., John L. Student, St. John's Coll., Annapolis, Md., 1940-42; LLB, U. Va., 1948. Assoc. Kelley & Ryan, Houston, 1949-51, Fountain, Cox & Gaines, Houston, 1951-54; assoc. Orgain, Bell & Tucker, Beaumont, 1954-57, ptnr., 1957-85; judge U.S. Dist. Ct. (ea. dist.) Tex., Beaumont, 1985—; mem. jud. coun. U.S. Ct. Appeals (5th cir.), 1994-97; mem. adv. com. East Tex. Legal Svcs., Beaumont. Pres. Beaumont Art Mus., 1969, bd. dirs., 1967-68; mem. vestry St. Stephens Episcopal Ch., Beaumont, 1973; mem. bd. adjustment City of Beaumont, 1972-82; trustee All Saints Episcopal Sch., Beaumont, 1972-76. 1st lt. USMC, 1942-45, PTO. Mem. ABA, State Bar Tex. (grievance com.

1970-72, chmn. 1972, admissions com. 1974—, bd. dirs. 1993-94, adv. mem.), Jefferson County Bar Assn. (sec. 1960, bd. dirs. 1960-61, 67-68), Am. Judicature Soc., Am. Bd. Trial Advs., Maritime Law Assn. U.S., Beaumont Country Club. Office: US Dist Ct 118 US Courthouse PO Box 632 Beaumont TX 77704-0632

COBB, HUBBARD HANFORD, magazine editor, writer; b. N.Y.C., Aug. 5, 1917; s. Frank I. and Margaret Hubbard (Ayer) C.; m. Elizabeth Youngblood Simon, Feb. 6, 1954. Grad., Avon Old Farms Sch., Conn., 1936. Bldg. editor Am. Home mag., 1952-61, editor, 1961-69; author syndicated column home problems, 1946-60, condr. radio program home bldg., 1947-54; contbg. editor Woman's Day mag., 1972-84. Author: How to Build Your Dream House, 1948, Home Handyman's Guide, 1949, Homeowners Guide to Remodeling, 1950, Complete Homeowner, 1965, The Dream House Encyclopedia, 1970, How to Buy and Remodel the Older House, 1972, How to Paint Anything, 1972; (with Betsy Cobb) Vacation Houses--All You Should Know Before You Buy or Build, 1973, City People's Guide to Country Living, 1973, Preventive Maintenance for Your House or Apartment, 1975, Improvements That Increase the Value of Your House, 1976, Woman's Day Homeowners Handbook, 1976, (with Betsy Cobb) Your Barn House, 1991, American Battlefields, 1995. With USAAF, World War II. Mem. Authors Guild. Home: PO Box 498 Chester CT 06412-0498

COBB, JANE OVERTON, legislative staff member; b. Charleston, S.C., July 23, 1962; d. Dolphin Dunnaha and Sue (Hagood) Overton; m. Robert Watson Cobb, July 15, 1989; children: Robert Watson, Jr., Johnson Hagood, Calvin Hayes. BA, Vanderbilt U., 1984, MEd, 1985. Cert. secondary tchr., Ga. Tchr. English Columbia High Sch., Atlanta, 1985-86; tchr. ESL Hangzhou, China, 1986-87; govt. affairs sect. Hewlett Packard Co., Washington, 1987-89; mem. congrl. staff U.S. Ho. Reps., Washington, 1989—. Office: US Ho Reps Govt Reform & Oversight Com 2157 Rayburn Ho Office Bldg Washington DC 20515

COBB, JEANNE BECK, education educator, researcher, consultant; b. Thomasville, N.C., Apr. 5, 1948; d. Howard Paul and Thelma Lorene (Clanton) Beck; m. James Paul Cobb, June 10, 1974; children: James Alexander, Rebecca Jeanne. BS in Elem. Edn., West Carolina U., 1970; MS in Elem. Edn. and Reading, U. Tenn., 1971, EdD in Reading and Lang. arts, 1992. Cert. tchr., Tex.; cert. reading specialist, Tex. Title one tchr. Decatur (Ga.) City Schs., 1976-80; grad. tchg. asst. U. Tenn., Knoxvlle, 1989-92, asst. dir. Reading Ctr., 1991-92; adj. prof. U. North Tex., Denton, 1992-93, 1992-93, lectr., 1993-97, lectr., site coord. Evers Park Profl. Devel. Sch., 1995—, asst. prof., 1997—, TAMS selection com., 1995-96; adj. prof. Tex. Weslayen U., Ft. Worth, 1992-93; cons. Greenhill Sch., Dallas, 1995; reviewer Multicultural Edn., 1995—. Contbr. articles to profl. jours. Dir. Sat. sch. scholars First Christian Ch., Ft. Worth, 1997—; teams vol. L.D. Bell H.S., Hurst, Tex., 1996-97; mem. PTA Ga., Tenn., Tex., 1985-96; band boosters fundraiser HEB Parent Assn., Hurst, 1996—. Mem. Internat. Reading, Assn. (corr. sect. 1971—), Assn. Childhood Edn. Internat. (pres. 1975-80, v.p. 1993—), Internat. Listening Assn. (edn. task force 1994—), Phi Kappa Phi, Pi Lambda Theta, Alpha Delta Kappa. Democrat. Avocations: reading, hiking, camping, collecting children's china and old basal readers. Home: 460 Shade Tree Cir Hurst TX 76054-2942 Office: U North Tex PO Box 31137 Denton TX 76203-1337

COBB, JOHN BOSWELL, JR., clergyman, educator; b. Kobe, Japan, Feb. 9, 1925; s. John Boswell and Theodora Cook (Atkinson) C.; m. Jean Olmstead Loftin, June 18, 1947; children: Theodore, Clifford, Andrew, Richard. MA, U. Chgo. Div. Sch., 1949, PhD, 1952. Ordained to ministry United Meth. Ch., 1950. Pastor Towns County Circuit, N.Ga. Conf., 1950-51; faculty Young Harris Coll., Ga., 1950-53, Candler Sch. Theology and Emory U., 1953-58, Sch. Theology, Claremont, Calif., 1958-90; Avery prof. Claremont Grad. Sch., 1973-90; ret., 1990; mem. commn. on doctrine and doctrinal standard United Meth. Ch., 1968-72; mem. commn. on mission, 1984-88. Author: A Christian Natural Theology, 1965, The Structure of Christian Existence, 1967, Christ in a Pluralistic Age, 1975, (with Herman Daly) For the Common Good, 1989. Dir. Center for Process Studies. Fulbright prof. U. Mainz, 1965-66; fellow Woodrow Wilson Internat. Ctr. for Scholars, 1976. Mem. Am. Acad. Religion, Am. Metaphys. Soc.

COBB, JOHN CANDLER, medical educator; b. Boston, July 8, 1919; s. Stanley and Elizabeth Mason (Almy) C.; m. Helen Imlay-Franchot, July 27, 1946; children: Loren, Nathaniel, Bethany, Julianne. BS in Astronomy cum laude, Harvard U., 1941, MD, 1948; MPH, Johns Hopkins U., 1954. Diplomate Nat. Bd. Med. Examiners, Am. Bd. Preventive Medicine and Pub. Health; lic. physician, Conn., Md., N.Mex. Intern Yale New Haven Hosp., 1948-49, fellow in pediatrics, 1949-50; jr. asst. resident Yale Psychiatric Clinic, 1950-51; instr. pediatrics Johns Hopkins U., 1951-56, asst. prof. hygiene, 1954-56; cons. Indian Health divsn. USPHS, Albuquerque, 1956-60; prof. preventive medicine U. Colo., Denver, 1965—, chmn. dept., 1966-73; dir. med. social rsch. project on population Govt. of Pakistan, 1960-64; exch. prof. Guangxi Med. Coll., Nanning, China, 1985-86; coord. ethics seminars U. Health Scis. Ctr., 1980-85; cons. in field. Contbr. numerous articles to profl. jours. Chmn. Task Force for Preparing 314(b) Agy. Grant Application, 1969; mem. Gov.'s Task Force on Health Effects of Air Pollution, 1978-79; commr. Air Pollution Control Commn. of Colo., 1976-79; mem. air quality policy com. Denver Regional Coun. of Govts., 1978-80; bd. dirs. ROMCOE Ctr. for Environ. Problem Solving, 1978-81, Colo. Coalition for Full Employment, 1978-80; mem. Am. Friends Svc. Com. Adv. Group on Rocky Flats/Nuclear Weapons Project, 1979-85. Recipient Florence Sabin award Colo. Pub. Health Assn., 1979, Jack Gore Meml. Peace award Am. Friends Svc. Com., 1980; U.S. EPA grantee, 1975-82. Mem. AAAS, WHO, Internat. Solar Energy Soc., Am. Solar Energy Soc., Internat. Physicians for Prevention of Nuclear War (del. to Congresses in Moscow and Montreal), Appropriate Rural Tech. Assn. (bd. dirs. 1987—, v.p. 1991-92), Nat. Resources Def. Coun. (bd. advisors 1991-92), N.Mex. Solar Energy Assn. (bd. dirs.), Physicians for Human Rights, Physicians for Social Reponsibility. Home and Office: # 4320 10501 Lagrima De Oro NE Albuquerque NM 87111

COBB, MILES ALAN, retired lawyer; b. Salt Lake City, May 8, 1930; s. Miles Cobb and June (Ray) Cobb Wilson; children: Jennifer, Melissa, Mary. B.S., U. Calif.-Berkeley, 1953, LL.B., 1958. Bar: Calif. 1958. Assoc. Bronson, Bronson & McKinnon, San Francisco, 1958-65, ptnr., 1965-76, 78-84; gen. counsel FDIC, Washington, 1976-78; pres. Bell Savs & Loan Assn., San Mateo, Calif., 1984-85. Author: Federal Regulation of Depository Institutions, 1984. Served to 1st lt. U.S. Army, 1953-55; Korea. Democrat. Avocations: photography; golf; gardening.

COBB, ROWENA NOELANI BLAKE, real estate broker; b. Kauai, Hawaii, May 1, 1939; d. Bernard K. Blake and Hattie Kanui Yuen; m. James Jackson Cobb, Dec. 22, 1962; children: Shelly Ranelle Noelani, Bret Kimo Jackson. BS in Edn., Bob Jones U., 1961; broker's lic., Vitousek Sch. Real Estate, Honolulu, 1981. Lic. real estate broker, Honolulu; cert. residential broker. Med. supr. Hawaii Med. Svc. Assn., 1964-65, 66-68; bus. mgr. Micronesian Occupl. Ctr., Koror Palau, 1968-70; prin. broker Cobb Realty, Lihue, Hawaii, 1983—; sec. Neighbor Island MLS Svc., Honolulu, 1985-87, vice chmn., 1987-88; chmn. MLS Hawaii, Inc., Honolulu, 1988-90. Assoc. editor Jour Entymology, 1965-66. Sec. Koloa Cmty. Assn., 1981-98, pres., 1989; mem. Kauai Humane Soc., YWCA, Kauai Mus., Kauai Visitors Bur.; bd. dirs. Wong Care Home, Hoi'Ke Pub. TV, 1998—, v.p., treas., 1999; vice chairperson Kauai Schs. Adv. Coun., 1995-98. Mem. Nat. Assn. Realtors (grad. Realtors Inst., cert. residential specialist), Hawaii Assn. Realtors (cert. tchr., state bd. dirs. 1984, v.p. 1985, dir. 1995-96), Kauai Bd. Realtors (v.p. 1984, pres. 1985, bd. dirs. 1995-97, treas. 1999, Realtor Assoc. of Yr. award 1983, Realtor of Yr. award 1986), Kauai C. of C., Soroptomists (bd. dirs. Lihue chpt. 1986-89, treas. 1989). Avocations: reading, music, travel. E-mail: rcobb@hawaiian.net. Office: PO Box 157 Koloa HI 96756-0157

COBB, ROY LAMPKIN, JR., retired computer sciences corporation executive; b. Oklahoma City, Sept. 23, 1934; s. Roy Lampkin and Alice Maxine Cobb; m. Shirley Ann Dodson, June 21, 1958; children: Kendra Leigh, Cary William, Paul Alan. BA, U. Okla., 1972; postgrad., U. Calif., Northridge, 1976-77. Naval aviation cadet USN, 1955, advanced through grades to comdr., 1970, ret., 1978; mktg./project staff engr. Gen. Dynamics, Pomona, Calif., 1978-80; mgr. dept. support svcs. Computer Scis. Corp., Point Mugu, Calif., 1980-97; ret. Decorated Navy Commendation medal, Air medal (13). Mem. Assn. Naval Aviators, Soc. Logistic Engrs. (editor Launchings 1990-98), Las Posas Country Club, Spanish Hills Country Club. Republican. Home: 2481 Brookhill Dr Camarillo CA 93010-2112

COBB, RUTH, artist; b. Boston, Feb. 20, 1914; d. Charles Edward and Bessie (Cohen) C.; m. Lawrence Kupferman, Apr. 29, 1937; children: Nancy Rose, David. Diploma, Mass. Coll. Art, 1935. One-woman shows include Shore Galery, Boston, 1958, 60, 63, 65, 70, DeCordova Mus., Lincoln, Mass., 1955, Art Unlimited Gallery, San Francisco, 1961, Cober Gallery, N.Y.C., 1962, 65, 67, McNay Mus., San Antonio, 1966, Phila. Art Alliance, 1962, Galerie Moos, Montreal, Que., Can., 1969, Witte Mus., San Antonio, 1967, Harold Ernst Gallery, Boston, 1974, 75, 76, Midtown Gallery, N.Y.C., 1981, 82, Foster Harmon Gallery, Sarasota, 1984, Francesca Anderson Gallery, Boston, 1984, 87, Cen. Pl. Galleries, Bangor, Maine, 1988, Thayer Acad., Braintree, Mass., 1994, Cataumet (Mass.) Art Ctr., 1997, A.R.A. Gallery, Hamilton, Mass., 1999; featured in exhbn. Boston's Honored Artists, Danforth Mus., Framingham, Mass., 1995; represented in permanent collections Boston Mus. Fine Arts, Brandeis U., Butler Inst. Am. Art, Munson-Williams-Proctor Inst., Addison Gallery Am. Art, Va. Mus. Fine Arts, DeCordova Mus., Tufts U.; featured in TV program Artist At Work, 1981; work featured in Am. Artist mag., 1979. Recipient awards Pa. Acad. Fine Arts, 1967, awards Allied Artists N.Y.C., 1966. Mem. Am. Watercolor Soc. (award), New Eng. Watercolor Soc., Allied Artists Am. (award), NAD (award).

COBB, SHIRLEY ANN, public relations specialist, journalist; b. Oklahoma City, Jan. 1, 1936; d. William Ray and Irene Dodson; m. Roy Lampkin Cobb, Jr., June 21, 1958; children: Kendra Leigh, Cary William, Paul Alan. BA in Journalism with distinction, U. Okla., 1958, postgrad., 1972; postgrad., Jacksonville U., 1962. Info. specialist Pacific Missile Test Ctr., Point Mugu, Calif., 1975-76; corr. Religious News Chronicle, 1977-81; pub. rels. cons. Camarillo, Calif., 1977—; media mgr. pub. info. League of Calif. Cities City of Thousand Oaks, Calif., 1983—; telecomm. project City of Thousand Oaks. Contbr. articles to profl. jours. Pres. Point Mugu Officers' Wives Club, 1975-76; trustee Ocean View Sch. Bd., 1976-79; bd. dirs. Camarillo Hospice, 1983-85; sec. Conejo Valley Hist. Soc., 1993-96; sec. Ednl. TV for Conejo, 1997-98, pres., 1998—. Recipient Spot News award San Fernando Valley Press Club, 1979, First Pl. Calif. Assn. Lublie Info. Offcls., 1985, Helen Putnam award League of Calif. Cities, 1997. Mem. Pub. Rels. Soc. Am. (L.A. chpt. liaison 1991), Calif. Assn. Pub. Info. Ofcls. (pres. 1989-90, Paul Clark Lifetime Achievement award 1993), Las Posas Country Club, Spanish Hills Country Club, Town Hall of Calif. Club. Republican. Home: 2481 Brookhill Dr Camarillo CA 93010-2112 Office: 2100 E Thousand Oaks Blvd Thousand Oaks CA 91362-7610

COBB, STEPHEN A., lawyer; b. Moline, Ill., Jan. 27, 1944; s. Archibald William and Lucile Bates C.; m. Nancy L. Hendrix, Dec. 18, 1972. AB cum laude, Harvard U., 1966; MA in Sociology, Vanderbilt U., 1968, PhD in Sociology, 1971, JD, 1977. Bar: Tenn. 1978, U.S. Dist. Ct. (mid. dist.) Tenn. 1978. Asst. prof. Tenn. State U., Nashville, 1970-74, dept. head, 1972-74; mem., chair edn. oversight com. Tenn. Ho. Reps., Nashville, 1974-86; pvt. practice law Nashville, 1978-86; with Waller Lansden Dortch & Davis, Nashville, 1986-90, ptnr., 1990—; Fullbright Jr. lectr. U. Caen, France, 1977-78; lectr. dept. sociology Fisk U., 1981-86. Former pres. Sister Cities of Nashville, Inc.; former vice chmn. commn. ednl. quality So. Regional Edn. Bd. Recipient Paul Simon Internat. award, 1990, Edwin Cudeki Internat. Bus. award, 1992; fellow NDEA, NIMH, 1966-70; officer l'Ordre des Palmes Academiques, Govt. France. Mem. ABA, Am. Immigration Lawyers Assn., Am. Sociol. Assn., So. Sociol. Soc., Tenn. Bar Assn., Tenn Fgn. Lang. Inst., Nashville Bar Assn., Fedn. Alliances Francaises (former pres.), Order of Coif. Home: 1929 Castleman Dr Nashville TN 37215-3901 Office: 511 Union St Ste 2100 Nashville TN 37219-1760

COBB, TERRI REAMER (CECI COBB), film and video producer; b. N.Y.C., Feb. 18, 1934; d. Leo Odell and Jean (Wister) Gruber; m. Ira Reamer, July 4, 1954 (div. May 1975); children: Jeff, David, Ellen; m. David G. Cobb, Aug. 2, 1975. Student, U. Miami, 1953-54, Miami Dade C.C., 1970-72. Vocalist The Girlfriends, N.Y.C., 1952-53; dental asst. Miami, Fla., 1953-56, med. asst., 1956-58; prodr., host TV talk show People and Places, Tampa, Fla., 1981—; freelance film and video prodr., prodn. coord. Encore Film & Video Prodn., Tampa, 1984—; freelance model, actress, Fla.; seminar leader Tom Kirby Assocs., Fla., 1986—; cons. U. South Fla. Dept. Edn., Tampa, 1980—; location scout, coord. films and commls.; freelance TV prodr., tech. dir. Health educator, fund raiser, speaker Fla. March of Dimes, 1964-91; planning commr. Tampa/Hillsborough; bd. dirs. Fla. Healthy Mother-Healthy Baby Coalition, Hillsborough County Fair. Recipient Jone Intercable Golden Cassette award, 1989, Crystal Reel award Fla. Motion Picture & TV Assn., 1990. Mem. Fla. Perinatal Assn. (bd. dirs.), Fla. Womens' Alliance, Fla. Motion Picture and TV Assn. (bd. dirs.), Fla. Soc. Assn. Execs. (bd. dirs.). Avocations: tennis, boating, walking. E-mail: terricobb@aol.com. Home: 16612 Hutchinson Rd Odessa FL 33556-2327

COBB, VICKI, writer; b. Bklyn., Aug. 19, 1938; d. Benjamin H. and Paula (Davis) Wolf; m. Edward S. Cobb, Jan. 31, 1960 (div. Oct. 1975); children: Theodore Davis, Joshua Monroe; m. Richard Trachtenberg, May 11, 1996. Cancer rschr. Pfizer & Sloan Kettering, N.Y., 1959-61; sci. tchr. Rye (N.Y.) H.S., 1961-66; tv host, creator Telprompter, N.Y.C., 1971-72; network staff writer Good Morning Am., ABC, N.Y.C., 1975-76; pub. rels. dir. Scott Pub. Co., N.Y.C., 1978-83; spkr. in field. Author: Science Experiments You Can Eat, 1972, Supersuits, 1975, More Science Experiments You Can Eat, 1979, Truth on Trial: The Story of Galileo Galilei, 1979, with Kathy Darling) Bet You Can't! Science Impossibilities to Fool You, 1980, How To Really Fool Yourself: Illusions for All Your Senses, 1981, Lots of Rot, 1981, (with Kathy Darling) Bet You Can! Science Possibilities To Fool You, 1983, Chemically Active!, 1985, The Place is Cold (Alaska), 1989, This Place is Dry (Sonoran Desert), 1989, This Place is High (Andes), 1989, This Place is Wet (Amazon Basin), 1989, This Place is Lonely (Australia), 1991, This Place is Crowded (Japan), 1992, Why Can't You Unscramble an Egg? And Other Not Such Dumb Questions About Matter, 1990, Why Doesn't the Sun Burn Out? And Other Not Such Dumb Questions About Energy, 1990, (with Kathy Darling) Wanna Bet! Science Challenges Bound to Fool You, 1993, paperback edit., 1994, (with Josh Cobb) Light Action! Amazing Experiments with Optics, 1993, Why Can't I Live Forever? And Other Not Such Dumb Questions About Life, 1996This Place is Wild: East Africa, 1997, Blood and Gore Like You've Never Seen, 1997, Dirt and Grime Like You've Never Seen, 1998, Don't Try This at Home, 1998, You Gotta Try This, 1999, many others. Presenter Asian Cultural Ctr. for UNESCO, Tokyo, 1992. Recipient Children's Sci. Book award N.Y. Acad. Scis., N.Y.C., 1981, Washington Irving Childrens Book Choice award Westchester Libr. Sys., 1986, 94, Eva L. Gordon award Am. Nature Study Soc., 1988. Mem. Am. Soc. Journalists and Authors, Soc. Childrens Book Writers and Illustrators, Authors Guild. Avocations: skiing, tennis, piano, crewel embroidery, travel. E-mail: vickie@idt.net. Home: 302 Pondside Dr White Plains NY 10607-1365

COBB, VIRGINIA HORTON, artist, educator; b. Oklahoma City, Nov. 23, 1933; d. Wayne and Ruth (Goodale) Horton; m. Bruce L. Cobb, Dec. 30, 1951 (div. 1985); children: Bruce Wayne, Julliann, William Stuart, M. Jerrold Friedman, 1988. Student, U. Colo., 1966-67, Community Coll., Denver, 1967; student of, William Schimmel, Ariz., 1965-66, Edgar Whitney, N.Y.C., 1966, Chen Chi, N.Y.C., 1974. Comml. artist and designer Ruth Horton Studios, Oklahoma City, 1954-63; instr. seminars, 1974—, N.Mex. Watercolor Soc., Albuquerque, 1976, Okla. Mus. Art, Oklahoma City, 1976, Upstairs Gallery Workshops, Arlington, Tex., 1977, 78, 79, 80, St. Louis Art Guild, 1980, Alaska Water Color Soc., Anchorage, 1981, Needham (Mass.) Art Center, 1981, N.C. Watercolor Soc., Charlotte, 1981, San Diego Watercolor Soc., 1981, S.C. Water Color Soc., Florence, 1981, Hawaii Water Color Soc., 1989; instr. seminars Trillium Workshops, Toronto, 1989, 90, Baffin Island, 1992, Maui, Hawaii, 1993; instr. seminars Vancouver Island, 1990, 91; guest instr. Crafton Hills Coll. Master Seminars, Yucaipa, Calif., 1979, 80, 81, U. Alaska, Anchorage, 1981, Master Class/Santa Fe Painting Workshops/Friedman Cobb Studios, 1989—; lectr. Sta. KRDO-TV, 1977, Francis Marion Coll., Florence, 1981, Sta. KAKM, Anchorage, 1981. Author: Discovering The Inner Eye, 1988; author (with Jerrold Friedman) Alice...on bristol, 1996; contbr. articles to art publs.; one-woman shows of watercolor paintings, Jack Meier Galleries, Houston, 1979-81, 83-85, One Artist: San Juan Coll., 1995, Art Resources, St. Paul, 1988, Sturh Mus., Grand Island, Nebr., 1982, group shows include recent acquisitions of the Nat. Acad., 1982, layering, an art of time and space, 1985, NAD, N.Y.C., 1978, 79-81, San Bernardino (Calif.) County Mus., 1978, Nat. Watercolor Invitational, Rochester, N.Y., 1981, Rocky Mountain Nat. Watermedia Exhbt., Golden, Colo., 1978, 79, 81, Albuquerque Mus. Art, 1985, Am. Watercolor Soc., 1985; invitational exhibitions include Internat. Waters: A Touring Exhibit, Canada, 1991, USA, 1992, Great Britain, 1992, Scotland, 1993; represented in permanent collections, NAD, Jefferson County (Colo.) Public Library, Foothills Art Center, Golden, Colo., St. Lawrence U., Canton, N.Y., N.Mex. Watercolor Soc., Albuquerque, Santa Fe Mus. Fine Arts. Recipient Foothills Art Ctr. award, 1976, Edgar Fox award Watercolor U.S.A., 1973, Denver award Rocky Mountain Nat. Exhbn., 1981, Am. Artist Achievement award, 1994. Mem. NAD (Walter Biggs Meml. award 1978, 81), Nat. Watercolor Soc. (Strathmore Paper Co. award 1975), Am. Watercolor Soc. (Paul B. Remmey Meml. award 1974,. Arches Paper Co. award 1977, Edgar Whitney award 1978, Mary Pleishner Meml. award 1980, High Winds medal 1981, Silver medal of Honor 1983, guest demonstrator 1980, nat. juror 1981, Dolphin fellow 1982, juror Watercolor West 1990, Juror award 1999), N.Mex. Watercolor Soc. (hon.), Rocky Mountain Watermedia Soc.

COBBAN, WILLIAM AUBREY, paleontologist; b. Anaconda, Mont., Dec. 31, 1916; s. Ray Aubrey and Anastacia (McNulty) C.; m. Ruth Georgina Loucks, Apr. 15, 1942; children: Georgina, William, Robert. BA, U. Mont., 1940; PhD, Johns Hopkins U., 1949. Geologist Carter Oil Co., Tulsa, 1940-46; paleontologist U.S. Geol. Survey, Washington, 1948-92, emeritus scientist, 1992—. Contbr. numerous articles to profl. jours. Recipient Meritorious Svc. award Dept. Interior, 1974, Paleontol. medal Paleontol. Soc. Am., 1985, Disting. Svc. award U.S. Dept. Interior, 1986. Fellow AAAS, Geol. Soc. Am.; mem. Soc. Econ. Paleontologists and Mineralogists (hon.; Disting. Pioneer Geologist award 1985, Raymond C. Moore Paleontology medal 1990), Rocky Mountain Assn. Geologists (hon.), Mont. Geol. Soc. (hon.), Wyo. Geol Assn. (hon.), Paleontol. Soc., Am. Assn. Petroleum Geologists, Paleontol. Rsch. Inst. (Gilbert Harris award 1996), Phi Beta Kappa, Sigma Xi. Republican. Mem. United Ch. of Christ. Office: U S Geol Survey Federal Ctr PO Box 25046 # 913 Denver CO 80225

COBBLE, JAMES WIKLE, chemistry educator; b. Kansas City, Mo., Mar. 15, 1926; s. Ray and Crystal Edith (Wikle) C.; m. Margaret Ann Zumwalt, June 9, 1949; children—Catherine Ann, Richard James. Student, San Diego State Coll., 1942-44; BA, No. Ariz. U., 1946; MS, U. So. Calif., 1949; PhD, U. Tenn., 1952. Chemist Oak Ridge Nat. Lab., 1949-52; postdoctoral research asso. U. Calif., Berkeley, 1952-55; instr. dept. chemistry U. Calif., 1954; asst. prof. dept. chemistry Purdue U., Lafayette, Ind., 1955-58; asso. prof. Purdue U., 1958-61, prof., 1961-73; prof., dean Grad. div. San Diego State U., 1973—; v.p. rsch., dean Grad. divsn. San Diego State U., 1997—; cons. in field. Contbr. articles to sci. publs. Mem. bd. visitors USAF Air U., 1984-92, chmn., 1988-90; v.p. San Diego State U. Found., 1975—; trustee Calif. We. Law Sch., 1987-93; mem. Joint Grad. Bd., 1973—. Lt. (j.g.) USNR, 1945-46. Recipient E.O. Lawrence award U.S. AEC, 1970, Disting. Svc. award USAF, 1992; Guggenheim fellow, 1966; Robert A. Welch Found. lectr., 1971. Fellow Am. Inst. Chemists, Am. Phys. Soc.; mem. Am. Chem. Soc., Sigma Xi, Phi Kappa Phi, Alpha Chi Sigma, Phi Lambda Upsilon. Home: 1380 Park Row La Jolla CA 92037-3709 Office: San Diego State Univ Dept Chemistry Grad Divsn and Rsch San Diego CA 92182*

COBBLE, STEVEN BRUCE, political consultant, strategist; b. Perrysburg, Ohio, July 7, 1951; s. Milan H. and Nancy L. (Musselman) C.; m. Molly E. Smith, July 3, 1983; children: Elizabeth A., Julia S. BS in Math., N.Mex. State U., 1974, BA in Govt., 1974. Speechwriter, spl. asst. Office of Gov., Santa Fe, N.Mex., 1982-86; nat. del. selection dir. Jesse Jackson for Pres., Chgo. and Washington, 1987, 88; exec. dir. Keep Hope Alive Polit. Action Com., Washington, 1988-90; advisor Ron Brown for Dem. Nat. Com. Chair Campaign, Washington, 1988, 89; democracy reform cons. Ctr. for New Democracy, Grinnell, Iowa, 1991-93; polit. and fin. dir. Carol Moseley-Braun for U.S. Senate Campaign, Chgo., 1992; speechwriter, policy analyst Office of Mayor, Albuquerque, 1994, 95; speech writer, polit. dir. Nat. Rainbow Coalition, Washington, 1996, 97; exec. dir. Arca Found., 1998; pub. spkr. numerous groups, meetings, 1970-98; panelist, presenter numerous polit. forums/panels, 1970-98; adv. bd. Hotline Index, Campaign Hotline newsletter, Washington, 1995, 96. Editor Nat. Rainbow Coalition Jax Fax, 1996, 97; contbr. articles to profl. jours.; guest appearance CNN's Inside Politics TV show, Washington, 1995. Nat. conv. del. Dem. Nat. Conv., Miami, 1972; democracy trainer Nat. Dem. Inst./African Nat. Congress, South Africa, 1991; mem. nat. rules com. Nat. Dem. Party, Washington, 1992; polit. party trainer Nat. Dem. Inst., Panama, 1993. Fellow LBJ Sch. Pub. Affairs, Austin, Tex., 1974, Inst. Politics, Harvard U., Cambridge, Mass., 1990; named Young Polit. Leader Am. Coun. Young Polit. Leaders, Washington, 1986. Methodist. Avocations: travel, Beatles music, reading, baseball, basketball, camping. Home: 6909 Williamsburg Blvd Arlington VA 22213-1812 Office: Arca Found 2040 S St NW Ste 200 Washington DC 20009

COBBS, ALFRED LEON, German language educator; b. Sept. 12, 1943. BA in German, Berea Coll., 1966; MA in German, U. Mo., 1968; PhD in German, U. Cin., 1974. Asst. prof. Germanic langs. and lits. U. Va., Charlottesville, 1973-79; assoc. prof. Romance and Germanic langs. Wayne State U., Detroit, 1979-89, assoc. prof. German and Slavic studies, 1989—. E-mail: a.cobbs@wayne.edu. Home: 14030 Faust Detroit MI 48223-3540 Office: Wayne State U Dept German-Slavic Studies Wayne MI 48202

COBBS, CHARLENE RENE', parent educator; b. Trenton, N.J., Oct. 31, 1972; d. Andy and Charlotte M. Cobbs. BA in Sociology, Claflin Coll., 1994; postgrad., Midlands Tech. Coll. Adminstrv. specialist Claflin Coll., Orangeburg, S.C., 1990-93; salesperson Seven Dollar Store, Inc., Columbia, S.C., 1993-94; substitute tchr., tutor Joseph Keels Elem. Sch., Columbia, 1994-97; educator parent and family literacy program Hyatt Park Elem. Sch., Columbia, 1997—; group facilitator Boys Transitional Group, Columbia, Fathers Are Parents Too, Columbia. Author: Talking From Experience, 1998. Democrat. Avocations: writing poetry, reading, family, internet. Fax: (803) 691-3391. E-mail: ccobbs9840@aol.com. Home: 3630 Ranch Rd Apt 4-4 Columbia SC 29206-5274 Office: Hyatt Park Elem Sch 4200 Main St Columbia SC 29203-5888

COBBS, JAMES HAROLD, engineer, consultant; b. Bristow, Okla., Aug. 25, 1928; s. Harold Martin and Ella A. (Rountree) C.; m. Charlotte Marie Fisher, Aug. 16, 1953 (dec. June 1990); m. Mary J. Armer, May 28, 1994; children: James Harold, David Charles, Gregory Lee, Matthew Louis. BS in Petroleum Engring., U. Okla., 1949, postgrad., 1949-51; postgrad. U. Tulsa, 1955-68. Assoc. engr. Tidewater Oil Co., Midland, Tex., 1951-52; reservoir engr., Houston, 1952-55, div. reservoir engr., Tulsa, 1955-59; pvt. practice cons. engr., 1959-63; sr. engr. Fenix & Scisson Inc., Tulsa, 1963-69; pres. Cobbs Engring., Inc., cons. engrs., Tulsa, 1969—; faculty U. Wis. Extension. Various positions including scoutmaster Indian Nations coun. Boy Scouts Am., 1962-81; instr. first aid ARC, 1969-81; active Vols. in Tech. Assistance, 1978—. Registered profl. engr., 8 states; cert. of qualification Nat. Council Engring. Examiners. Mem. Petroleum Engrs., Nat. Soc. Profl. Engrs., Okla. Soc. Profl. Engrs., Inst. Shaft Drilling Tech., Nat. Acad. Forensic Engrs., World Rock Boring Assn. Republican. Mem. Christian Ch. (elder, chmn. bd. elders 1971, 79). Contbr. articles to profl. jours.; patentee in field. Home: 4620 E 55th Pl Tulsa OK 74135-4306 Office: 5350 E 46th St Tulsa OK 74135-6612

COBBS, NICHOLAS HAMMER, lawyer; b. N.Y.C., June 28, 1946; s. John Lewis and Phyllis Cobbs; m. Louise Bertram Stolman, Mar. 26, 1983; children: Robert White, Rebecca Ann. AB cum laude, Amherst (Mass.) Coll., 1968; JD, U. Pa., 1974. Bar: N.Y. 1975, D.C. 1982, Md. 1984, Va. 1990, U.S. Dist. Ct. (so. dist.) N.Y. 1975, U.S. Dist. Ct. D.C. 1982, U.S. Dist. Ct. (ea. dist.) Va. 1990, U.S. Dist. Ct. (we. dist.) Va. 1990, U.S. Dist. Ct. Md. 1989, U.S. Supreme Ct. 1984. Assoc. Burlingham Underwood & Lord, N.Y.C., 1974-77, Haight, Gardner, Poor & Havens, N.Y.C., 1977-83; ptnr., of counsel Tigert & Roberts, Washington, 1984-89; Law Offices of Nicholas H. Cobbs, Washington, 1989—; of counsel Harris Beach & Wilcox, LLP, N.Y.C. and Rochester, 1995—. Contbr. articles to profl. jours. Arbitrator, mediator D.C. Superior Ct., Washington, 1990—; instr. D.C. Bar Continuing Legal Edn., 1993—. Lt. USNR, 1969-73. Mem. ABA, Fed. Bar Assn., Lawyer-Pilot's Bar Assn., Maritime Law Assn. of the U.S. Episcopalian. Address: Law Offices of Nicholas H Cobbs 1776 K St Ste 300 Washington DC 20006-2304

COBBS, PRICE MASHAW, social psychiatrist; b. L.A., Nov. 2, 1928; s. Peter Price and Rosa (Mashaw) C.; m. Evadne Priester, May 30, 1957 (dec. Oct. 1973); children—Price Priester, Marion Renata; m. Frederica Maxwell, May 26, 1985. A.B., U. Calif.-Berkeley, 1953; M.D., Meharry Med. Coll., 1958. Intern San Francisco Gen. Hosp., 1958-59; psychiat. resident Mendocino State Hosp., Talmage, Calif., 1959-61, Langley Porter Neuro-Psychiat. Inst., San Francisco, 1961-62; pres. Pacific Mgmt. Systems, San Francisco, 1967—; CEO Cobbs, Inc.; mgmt. cons. in workforce diversity numerous cos., govt. agys. and community projects; conducted seminars UN, Dept. State; guest lectr. leading colls. and univs.; chair 1st Ann. Nat. Diversity Conf., San Francisco, 1991; speaker 1st Internat. Diversity Conf., Johannesburg, South Africa, 1991; vis. cons., lectr. workforce diversity, South Africa, 1993; co-founder, pres. Renaissance Books, Inc.; adv. bd. Black Scholar. Author: (with William H. Grier) Black Rage, 1968, The Jesus Bag, 1971; contbr. State of Black America 1988, 89; pub. Mother Jones Mag. Bd. dirs. Found. for Nat. Progress; Served to cpl. U.S. Army, 1951-53. Recipient Pathfinder award Assn. Humanistic Psychology, 1993. Fellow Am. Psychiat. Assn.; mem. Nat. Med. Assn., NAACP (life), Nat. Acad. Scis.; charter mem. Nat. Urban League. Pioneer in discipline of ethnotherapy to understand differences in race, culture and ethnicity. Avocations: bicycling; walking; reading; blues singing. Office: Pacific Mgmt System 3528 Sacramento St San Francisco CA 94118-1850

COBER, KAY ANN, secondary school educator; b. Meyersdale, Pa., Sept. 30, 1948; d. John and Christine Lucille (Lowry) Lichvar; m. William Raymond Cober Jr., June 6, 1970; children: Elizabeth, Christa, William John. BS, California U. of Pa., 1970. Tchr. elem. sch. Berlin (Pa.) Brothersvalley Schs., 1970-73; tchr. English Meyersdale Area H.S., 1987—; track coach, Meyersdale Area H.S., 1991—, basketball coach, 1997-98. Vol. Am. Cancer Soc.; active Top of the Mountain Dem. Club, Berlin, Holy Trinity Luth. Ch. Mem. NEA, Nat. Coun. Tchrs. English, Pa. Edn. Assn., Meyersdale Area Edn. Assn., Am. Legion Aux., VFW Aux. Avocations: golf, needlework, the theater, Broadway shows. Office: Meyersdale Area HS Meyersdale PA 15552

COBERLY, PATRICIA GAIL, elementary education educator, adult education educator; b. Fort Smith, Ark., Jan. 7, 1962; d. Charles Joe and Marie Opal Stracener; m. Mark Windfield Coberly, Nov. 6, 1990; children: Laura Kendrick, Christy Gail. BS with honors, Ark. Tech. U., 1987; MEd, U. Ark., 1993, EdD, 1995. Cert. tchr., Ark. Tchr. Ozark (Ark.) Sch. Dist., 1988-96; asst. prof. Armstrong Atlantic State U., Savannah, Ga., 1996—, adminstrv. dept. head middle and secondary edn., 1997—; cons. in field. Contbr. articles to profl. jours. Mem. Effingham County Family Connection Collaborative. Mem. AAUW, Ga. Prof. Mid. Edn., Ga. Middle Grades Assn., Nat. Sci. Tchrs. Assn., Southern Futurists, World Futures Soc., Nat. Sci. Tchrs. Assn., Profs. Mid. Level Edn., Phi Delta Kappa, Phi Kappa Phi, Alphi Chi. Home: 718 Plantation Dr Rincon GA 31326-9708 Office: Armstong Atlantic State U 11935 Abercorn St Savannah GA 31419-1909

COBEY, JOHN GEOFFREY, lawyer; b. Cleve., Aug. 16, 1943; s. Herbert Todd and Phyllis Jean (Weston) C.; m. Jan M. Frankel, 1983; children: Max Todd, David William. BS, Cornell U., 1966; postgrad. U. de Deusto, Balboa, Spain, 1968, Exeter U. (Eng.), 1969; JD, U. Cin., 1969. Bar: Ohio 1969, U.S. Dist. Ct. (so. dist.) Ohio 1969, U.S. Ct. Appeals (6th cir.) 1970, Ky. 1978, U.S. Dist. Ct. (no. dist.) Ky. 1978. Mem. Cohen, Todd, Kite and Stanford LLC, 1969—; bd. dirs. 1st Nat. Bank No. Ky., C&W Equipment Repair, Armstrong Coffee Co.; sec. bd. dirs. Elegant Fare; bd. dirs., sec. Apt. Assn. Title Co.; bd. dirs. Real Time Syss., Inc.; counsel coop. housing City of Cin. Founder, pres. Young Men's Wing, Mercantile Library, 1971; regional amb. Cornell U., 1998, 99; trustee Ohio chpt. Nature Conservancy, 1974-82, Hillel of Cin., 1980-86, Women's Def. Fund, 1977, Holmes House, 1978-80; sec. Arts Consortium, Cin., 1975-77, trustee, 1975-78; mem. exec. com. Cin. chpt. Am. Jewish Com., 1981—; trustee Hillel House, Better Housing League; chmn. bd. Friends Cin. Parks, 1982-84, pres., 1977-79; chmn. bd. dirs. Washington Park Housing Co., 1997—; bd. dirs. Greater Cin./No. Ky. apt. Assn., 1975-94, Chinese Music Festival, 1996-98, United Jewish Cemetary, 1999, Opn. Smile, 1998. Mem. Ohio State Bar Assn., Ky. Bar Assn., Cin. Bar Assn., No. Ky. Bar Assn., Fed. Bar Assn., Lawyers Club, Cornell U. Coll. Life Scis. and Agr. Alumni Assn. (dist. dir.), Ohio Apt. Assn. (bd. dirs.), Cin. Apt. Assn. (bd. dirs., v.p. 1986-87), U. Cin. Law Sch. Alumni Assn. (bd. dirs 1973-76). Home: 231 Oliver Rd Cincinnati OH 45215-2638 Office: Cohen Todd Kite and Stanford 525 Vine St Ste 16 Cincinnati OH 45202-3121

COBEY, RALPH, industrialist; b. Sycamore, Ohio, Aug. 15, 1909; m. Hortense Kohn, Feb. 28, 1944; children: Minnie, Susanne. ME, Carnegie Inst. Tech., 1932; D.Sc. (hon.), Findlay Coll., 1958. Pres. Perfection Steel Body Co., Galion, Ohio, 1945-70, Perfection-Cobey, Co., Galion, Ohio, 1949-70; pres. Eagle Crusher Co., 1954-90, chmn. bd., 1990—; pres. Philips-Davies Co., 1965-70, Cobey Co., 1946-70, Diamond Iron Works, 1972-90, Austin-Western Crusher Co., 1974-90, Scoopmobile Co., 1978-90, Madsen Co., 1979-90, World Wide Investment Co., 1950—; aide in preparation of prodn. and design of Army tanks OPM, 1939-42. Mem. contbg. com. NCCJ, 1951-55, now area chmn. spl. gifts com.; founder, pres. Harry Cobey Found.; area chmn. U.S. Savs. Bonds; mem. pres.'s adv. coun. for devel. Ashland Coll., Ohio, mem. Ohio Gov.'s Citizens' Task Force on Environ. Protection, 1971-72, Pres.'s Tax Com., 1962-66; pioneer chaplain svcs. in indsl. plants; mem. Ohio Expns. Commn., 1964, Radio Free Europe Com.; chmn. Cmty. Heart Fund Campaign, 1971-72; pres., spl. gifts chmn. Crawford County Heart Fund, 1972-78; mem. Ohio fin. bd. Heart Fund, 1973—; mem. Ohio Rep. Fin. Com.; mounted dep. sheriff, Morrow County (Ohio), 1974-84; bd. dirs., chmn. long range planning com. Johnny Appleseed Area coun. Boy Scouts of Am.; hon. life mem. Galion Cmty. Ctr.; trustee Galion City Hosp. Found. Bd.; mem. pres.'s coun. Ohio State U.; chmn., founder Minnie Cobey Meml. Libr.; founder, chmn. bd. trustees Louis Bromfield Malabar Farm Found.; bd. dirs. Morrow County United Appeals; State of Ohio amb. of natural resources; numerous other civic activities. Capt. USAAF, 1942-46, 51, Korea. Recipient Disting. Citizen of Yr. award Heart of Ohio Coun., Boy Scouts Am., 1995, Lifetime Commitment to Humanitarianism award from Rep. Joan Lawrence, Ohio Ho. Reps., 1996. Mem. NAM, Nat. Assn. 4-H Clubs, Future Farmers Am., U.S. C. of C. (mem. taxation, fgn. affairs, labor rels. coms.), Masons (32 degree), Shriners (sec.-treas.). Home: 4270 State Route 309 Galion OH 44833-9618 Office: Eagle Crusher Co Inc PO Box 537 Galion OH 44833-0537

COBIANCHI, THOMAS THEODORE, engineering and marketing executive, educator; b. Paterson, N.J., July 7, 1941; s. Thomas and Violet Emily (Bazzar) C.; m. Phyllis Linda Asch, Feb. 6, 1964; 1 child, Michael. Student, Clemson U., 1963; BS, Monmouth Coll., 1968, MBA, 1972; postgrad., U. Pa., 1987; D Bus. Adminstrn., U.S. Internat. U., 1994. Sales mgr. Westinghouse Electric Corp., Balt., 1968-74; sr. internat. sales engr. Westinghouse Electric Corp., Lima, Ohio, 1975-77; program mgr. Westinghouse Electric Corp., Pitts., 1977-78, mgr. bus. devel., 1978-82; dir. mktg. Westinghouse Electric Corp., Arlington, Va., 1982-86; acting dir., engring. mgr. General Dynamics Corp., San Diego, 1986-89; dir. bus. devel. RPV Programs Teledyne Ryan Aero., San Diego, 1989-90; pres. Cobianchi & Assocs., San Diego, 1990; v.p. strategic planning and program devel. S-Cubed div. Maxwell Labs., Inc., San Diego, 1991; v.p. corp. devel. Orincon Corp., San Diego, 1995-98; mgr. client bus. AT&T, Irvine, Calif., 1998—; instr., lectr. various ednl. instns. Active various polit. and ednl. orgns.; mem. bus. adv. coun. U.S. Internat. U.; bd. dirs. Cath. Charities San Diego; vol. exec., sect. chmn. United Way San Diego. Mem. Armed Forces Communications and Electronics Assn. (acting chmn. 1988), Princeton Club of Washington, Nat. Aviation Club, General Dynamics Health Club, Delta Sigma Pi. Home: PO Box 500027 San Diego CA 92150-0027

COBLE, G. DREW, umpire; b. Burlington, N.C., Dec. 18, 1947; m. Kim Coble; children: Bryant, Kiersten. BS in Phys. Edn., Elon Coll.; grad., Bill Kinnamon Sch. Umpiring. Former umpire We. Carolina League, Carolina League, Am. Assn.; umpire maj. league baseball Am. League, N.Y.C., 1982—; with Umpires Union, Phila. With USAF. Avocation: woodworking, golfing, working out, reading novels. Office: Am League 350 Park Ave New York NY 10022 also: Umpires Union 1735 Market St Philadelphia PA 19103

COBLE, HOWARD, congressman, lawyer; b. Greensboro, N.C., Mar. 18, 1931; s. Joseph Howard and Johnnie (Holt) C. Student, Appalachian State U., 1949-50; AB in History, Guilford Coll., 1958; JD, U. N.C., 1962. Bar: N.C. 1966. Field claim rep., supt. State Farm Mut. Ins., 1961-67; asst. county atty. Guilford County, N.C., 1967-69; mem. N.C. Ho. of Reps., Raleigh, 1969, 79, 81, 83; asst. U.S. atty. U.S. Dist. Ct. (mid. dist.) N.C., 1969-73; sec. N.C. Dept. Revenue, Raleigh, 1973-77; atty. Turner, Enochs & Sparrow, Greensboro, 1979-84; mem. 99th-105th Congresses from 6th N.C. dist., Washington, D.C., 1984—; mem. cts. & intellectual property, crime, Coast Guard & maritime transp., surface transp. coms. Served to capt. USCG, 1952-80, comdg. officer USCGR. Mem. N.C. State Bar Assn., Greensboro Bar Assn., Masons (master mason Guilford lodge # 656), Am. Legion, VFW, Lions. Republican. Presbyterian. *

COBLE, HUGH KENNETH, engineering and construction company executive; b. Rochester, Pa., Sept. 26; s. John L. and Victoria (Neilson) C.; m. Constance Stratton, June 2, 1956; children: Keith Allen, Kimberly Ann, Jon Arthur, Scott Arnold, Neal Stewart. BSChemE, Carnegie Mellon U., 1956; postgrad., UCLA, 1966, U. Houston, 1963-65, Stanford U., 1981. Engr. Standard Oil Calif., El Segundo, 1956-61; sales mgr. Turco Products, Houston, 1961-63; sales dir. W.R. Grace, Houston, 1963-65; vice chmn. emeritus Fluor Corp., Irvine, Calif., 1966-97, 1997—; bd. dirs. Beckman Instruments, Inc., Flowserve Corp., ICO Global Comm. Bd. dirs. John Henry Found., Orange, Calif., 1992-96, Sedona Cultural Park, Sedona Med. Ctr.; trustee Scripps U., Claremont, Calif., 1991-93, Fluor Found.; mem. adv. bd. Thunderbird U., Phoenix, 1992—; exec. engring. adv. com. U. Calif.-Irvine. Mem. Am. Petroleum Inst., Am. Inst. Chem. Engrs. (bd. dirs. 1983-88). Presbyterian. Avocation: golf, piano, organ.

COBLE, PAUL ISHLER, advertising agency executive; b. Indpls., Mar. 17, 1926; s. Earl and Agnes Elizabeth (Roberts) C.; A.B., Wittenberg U., 1950; postgrad. Case-Western Res. U., 1950-53; m. Marjorie M. Trentanelli, Jan. 27, 1951; children—Jeffery Mansfield, Sarah Anne Davis, Douglass Paul Coble. Reporter, Springfield (Ohio) Daily News, 1944; reporter, feature writer Rockford (Ill.) Register-Republic, 1947-48; account exec. Fuller & Smith & Ross, Inc., Cleve., 1949-57; dir. sales promotion McCann Erickson, 1957-63; dir. sales devel. Marschalk Co., 1963-65, v.p., 1965-70, sr. v.p., 1970-73; pres. Coble Group, 1973—; chmn. bd., sec.-treas. Hahn & Coble, Inc., advt., mktg. and pub. relations, 1977—; pub. Islander mag., Hilton Head Island, S.C., 1973-83; asst. prof. advt. W.Va. U., 1982-83. Chief instr. Cleve. Advt. Club Sch., 1961-73. Active fund raising drives for various charitable and youth orgns. Served with AUS, 1944-46. Mem. Sales and Marketing Internat., Assn. Indsl. Advertisers, Cleve. Advt. Club, Newcomen Soc., River Oaks Racquet Club, Sea Pines Country Club, Cleve. Rotary. Contbr. articles to profl. pubs. Home: 37 Club Course Dr Hilton Head Island SC 29928-3137

COBOS, JOSÈ MANUEL, Spanish language educator; b. Sabinas Hgo, Nuevo Leon, Mex., Feb. 13, 1957; came to U.S., 1972; s. Juan and Olga (Flores) C.; m. Susan Ojeda, Aug. 19, 1989; 1 child, Aracely Susan. BA, U. Calif., Berkeley, 1978; MA, U. Calif., Santa Barbara, 1980; JD, U. Calif., San Francisco, 1984. Spanish tchr. Vista Coll., Berkeley, 1980-82; substitute tchr. Hayward (Calif.) Unified Sch. Dist., 1984, 88-89, San Francisco Unified Sch. Dist., 1984-87; paralegal San Francisco, 1987-88; Am. govt. tchr. Merritt Coll., Oakland, Calif., 1988-90; Spanish tchr. James Logan H.S., Union City, Calif., 1990—. Vol. Pelosi for Congress, San Francisco, 1987. Summer fellow Govt. of Mex., 1979. Mem. NEA, Fgn. Lang. Assn., Calif. Tchrs. Assn., Hastings Alumni Assn. Democrat. Roman Catholic. Avocations: camping, reading, traveling. Office: James Logan HS 1800 H St Union City CA 94587-3321

COBURN, D(ONALD) L(EE), playwright; b. Balt., Aug. 4, 1938; s. Guy Dabney and Ruth Margaret (Somers) C.; m. Nazlee Joyce French, Oct. 24, 1964 (div. Sept. 1971); children: Donn Christopher, Kimberly; m. Marsha Woodruff Maher, Feb. 22, 1975. Student pub. schs., Balt. Propr. Don Coburn & Assocs., Balt., 1966-70; with Stanford Agy., Dallas, 1970-73; propr. Donald L. Coburn Corp. Cons., Dallas, 1973-75; ind. playwright, 1975—. Playwright: The Gin Game, 1977 (Pulitzer prize in drama 1978, Tony award nomination 1978, Golden Apple 1978), Bluewater Cottage, 1979, The Corporation Man, 1981, Currents Turned Awry, 1982, Guy, 1983, Noble Adjustment, 1986, Anna-Weston, 1988, Return to Blue Fin, 1991; (screenplays) Flights of Angels, 1987, A Virgin Year, 1992. Served with USNR, 1958-60. Mem. Authors League Am., Writers Guild Am., Tex. Inst. Letters, Soc. des Auteurs et Compositeurs Dramatiques.

COBURN, HORACE HUNTER, retired physics educator; b. Cambridge, Mass., May 10, 1922; s. Charles A. and Viola M. (Hunter) C.; m. Hope Pleyl, Dec. 24, 1947; children: Lynn L., Carol A., James H. BS, Ohio State U., 1943; MS, U. Ill., 1947; PhD, U. Pa., 1956. Physicist Manhattan Dist., Oak Ridge, Tenn., 1944-46; assoc. prof. physics Moravian Coll., Bethlehem, Pa., 1950-51; prof., ret. N.Mex. State U., Las Cruces, 1954-93; sci. advisor Las Cruces (N.Mex.) Sch. Sys., 1994—; lectr. U.S. AID, India, 1966, 69. Mem. Optical Soc. Am., Am. Assn. Physics Tchrs., Nat. Sci. Tchrs. Assn. Mem. Christian Ch. Avocations: bicycling, gardening. Home: PO Box 928 Mesilla Park NM 88047-0928 Office: NMex State U Physics Dept Las Cruces NM 88003

COBURN, JAMES, actor; b. Laurel, Nebr., Aug. 31, 1928; children: James IV, Lisa; m. Paula Murad, Oct. 22, 1993. BA, L.A. City Coll. Owner Panpiper Prodns., Hollywood, Calif. Appeared in movies Ride Lonesome, 1959, Face of A Fugitive, 1959, The Magnificent Seven, 1960, Hell Is For Heroes, 1962, The Great Escape, 1963, Charade, 1964, The Americanization of Emily, 1964, Major Dundee, 1965, Our Man Flint, 1966, What Did You Do in the War, Daddy?, 1966, In Like Flint, 1967, Pat Garrett and Billy the Kid, 1973, The Last of Sheila, 1973, Bite the Bullet, 1975, Hard Times, 1975, Sky Riders, 1976, The Last Hard Men, 1976, Midway, 1976, The Muppet Movie, 1979, Fire Power, 1979, Cross of Iron, 1977, Golden Girl, 1979, Loving Couples, 1980, The Baltimore Bullet, 1980, High Risk, 1981, Looker, 1981, Martin's Day, 1985, Death of a Soldier, 1986, Young Guns II, 1990, Hudson Hawk, 1991, The Player, 1992, (narrator) Hugh Hefner: Once Upon a Time, 1992, Sister Act 2, 1993, Maverick, 1994, Eraser, 1996, Nutty Professor, 1996, Skeletons, 1996, The Disappearance of Kevin Johnson, 1996, Ben Johnson: Third Cowboy on the Right, 1996, Affliction, 1997, Keys to Tulsa, 1997, Payback, 1999, Atticus, 1999; TV mini-series The Dain Curse, 1978, Malibu, 1983, Draw, 1984; TV films The Dain Curse, 1978, Malibu, 1983, Draw!, 1984, Sins of the Father, 1985, Crash Landing: The Rescue of Flight 232, 1992, The Hit List, 1993, Greyhounds, 1994, The Set Up, 1995, Ray Alexander: A Menu for Murder, 1995, The Avenging Angel, 1995, The Cherokee Kid, 1996, The Second Civil War, 1997, Mr. Murder, 1998, Atticus, 1999, Noah's Ark, 1999; producer The President's Analyst, 1967, Waterhole No. 3, 1967; writer Circle of Iron, 1979; numerous TV guest appearances including Perry Mason, Profiler. Won Best Supporting Actor, American Academy Awards, Affliction, 1999. *

COBURN, JAMES LEROY, educational administrator; b. Oak Park, Ill., Nov. 21, 1933; s. Forest Edward and Myrtle Emmaline (Clarke) C.; m. Julianne Whitty, Sept. 3, 1955; children: James, Gregory, Julie, Cheryl. BA, North Cen. Coll., Naperville, Ill., 1956; MS, No. Ill. U., 1965; EdD, Vanderbilt U., 1983. Cert. tchr., guidance counselor, supt., Ill. Tchr. Luther South High Sch., Chgo., 1956-58; tchr. Maine Township High Sch. East, Park Ridge, Ill., 1958-61, dean, counselor, 1961-64; dir. student pers. svcs. Maine Twp. High Sch. South, Park Ridge, 1964-67; asst. prin. for staff Maine Twp. High Sch. West, Des Plaines, Ill., 1967-73, prin., 1973-97; ret., 1997; cons. Pitts. Pub. Schs., 1965; chmn. Ill. Blue Ribbon Com. on Edn., Bloomington, 1988; spkr. Internat. Ednl. Symposium, South Korea, 1996. Editor: Growth through Reading, 1960, 61. Pres. Inter-Suburban Assn.; chmn. judges 4th of July Parade, Des Plaines, 1980-86; mem. Des Plaines Beautification Com., 1987, Des Plaines Mayor's Adv. Com., 1989—; Ill. state commr. North Ctrl. Assn., 1992-95; pres. Des Plaines chpt. United Way, 1997—. Recipient Those Who Excel award Ill. Bd. Edn., 1977, Disting. Educator's award Idea Inst., 1984. Mem. Nat. Assn. Secondary Sch. Prins., Am. Assn. Sch. Adminstrs., Ill. Prins. Assn., Intersuburban Assn. Prins. (pres. 1986—), Des Plaines C. of C. (bd. dirs 1980-85, 92-95), Rotary (pres. Des Plaines 1976-77, Most Valuable Mem. award 1979, Paul Harris fellow 1989, John Vaughin excellence in edn. award 1997). Lutheran. Avocations: reading, travel, recreational sports, gardening. Home: 1843 Locust St Des Plaines IL 60018-2326

COBURN, JOHN G., career officer; b. Oct. 9, 1941. Commd. U.S. Army, advanced through grades to gen., 1999. Office: US Army Material Command 5001 Eisenhower Ave Alexandria VA 22333-0001

COBURN, LEWIS ALAN, mathematics educator; b. Austin, Tex., Aug. 16, 1940; s. Nathaniel and Ann (Block) C.; m. Charlaine Elizabeth Ackerman, June 19, 1966; 1 child, Elinor Nadia. BS, U. Mich., 1961, MS, 1962, PhD, 1964. Asst. prof. NYU, N.Y.C., 1964-65, Purdue U., West Lafayette, Ind., 1965-66; asst. prof. Yeshiva U., N.Y.C., 1966-68, assoc. prof., 1968-72, prof. math., 1972-79; prof. SUNY, Buffalo, 1979—, chmn. dept. math., 1979-97. Mem. editorial bd. Jour. Integral Equations and Operator Theory, 1978—; contbr. over 35 articles to math. rsch. jours. NSF grantee, 1966—. Mem. Am. Math. Soc. Office: SUNY Dept of Math Buffalo NY 14214

COBURN, MARJORIE FOSTER, psychologist, educator; b. Salt Lake City, Feb. 28, 1939; d. Harlan A. and Alma (Ballinger) Polk; m. Robert Byron Coburn, July 2, 1977; children: Polly Klea Foster, Matthew Ryan Foster, Robert Scott Coburn, Kelly Anne Coburn. B.A. in Sociology, UCLA, 1960; Montessori Internat. Diploma honor grad. Washington Montessori Inst., 1968; M.A. in Psychology, U. No. Colo., 1979; Ph.D. in Counseling Psychology, U. Denver, 1983. Licensed clin. psychologist. Probation officer Alameda County (Calif.), Oakland, 1960-62, Contra Costa County (Calif.), El Cerrito, 1966, Fairfax County (Va.), Fairfax, 1967; dir. Friendship Club, Orlando, Fla., 1963-65; tchr. Va. Montessori Sch., Fairfax, 1968-70; spl. edn. tchr. Leary Sch., Falls Church, Va., 1970-72, sch. administr., 1973-76; tchr. Aseltine Sch., San Diego, 1976-77, Coburn Montessori Sch., Colorado Springs, Colo., 1977-79; pvt. practice psychotherapy, Colorado Springs, 1979-82, San Diego, 1982—; cons. spl. edn., agoraphobia, women in transition. Mem. Am. Psychol. Assn., Am. Orthopsychiat. Assn., Phobia Soc., Council Exceptional Children, Calif. Psychol. Assn., San Diego Psychological Assn., The Charter 100, Mensa. Episcopalian. Lodge: Rotary. Contbr. articles to profl. jours.; author: (with R.C. Orem) Montessori: Prescription for Children with Learning Disabilities, 1977. Office: 826 Prospect St Ste 101 La Jolla CA 92037-4206

COBURN, ROBERT CRAIG, philosopher; b. Mpls., Jan. 25, 1930; s. William Carl and Esther Therice (Rudd) C.; m. Martha Louise Means, July 12, 1974. B.A., Yale U., 1951; B.D., U. Chgo., 1954; M.A., Harvard U., 1958, Ph.D., 1958. Asst. prof. philosophy U. Chgo., 1960-65, assoc. prof., 1965-68, prof., 1968-71; prof. philosophy U. Wash., Seattle, 1971—; vis. assoc. prof. philosophy Cornell U., 1966, U. Bergen, Norway, spring 1986; condr. NEH summer seminar, 1983; cons. ERDA. Author: The Strangeness of the Ordinary: Issues and Problems in Contemporary Metaphysics, 1989; contbr. articles to philos. jours., chpts. to books. Ordained elder Rocky Mountain Conf. United Methodist Ch. Andrew Mellon postdoctoral fellow in philosophy U. Pitts., 1961-62; NSF grantee, 1968-69. Mem. Am. Philos. Assn. (exec. com. Pacific div. 1973-74), AAUP, Soc. Values in Higher Edn., Phi Beta Kappa. Home: 6852 28th Ave NE Seattle WA 98115-7145 Office: Univ Wash Dept Philosophy Seattle WA 98195

COBURN, RONALD MURRAY, ophthalmic surgeon, researcher; b. Detroit, Aug. 25, 1943; s. Sidney and Jean (Goldberg) C.; m. Barbara Joan Levy, Feb. 21, 1969; children: Nicholas Scott, Lauren Joy. BS, Wayne State U., 1965, MD, 1969. Diplomate Am. Bd. Ophthalmology, Am. Bd. Eye Surgery (surg. examiner). Dir. The Coburn Clinic, Dearborn, Mich., 1976—; chief ophthalmology Straith Hosp. for Spl. Surgery, Southfield, Mich., 1985—; cons. CooperVision, Inc., Bellevue, Wash., 1985-88, Alcon Surg., Inc., Ft. Worth, 1988—. Co-author: Lens-Stat Intraocular Lens Modeling System; editorial advisor Phaco and Foldables, 1990. Trustee Straith Hosp. for Spl. Surgery, 1986—. Capt. Mich. N.G., 1969-76. Fellow ACS, Internat. Coll. Surgeons, Soc. Eye Surgeons, Royal Soc. Medicine (London), Leadership Soc. ACS; mem. AAAS, Am. Soc. Cataract and Refractive Surgery, Am. Diabetes Assn., Mich. Ophthal. Soc., Wayne County Med. Soc., Rsch. To Prevent Blindness, N.Y. Acad. Scis., Internat. Assn. Ocular Surgeons, Internat. Eye Found., Soc. Geriatric Ophthalmology, Soc. for Excellence in Eye Cre, Internat. Glaucoma Congress, Phi Beta Kappa. Achievements include design of Am. Med. Optics PC19LB intraocular lens, CILCO CPLU CP20 intraocular lenses, CooperVision CP10BG posterior chamber intraocular lens, Alcon CZ20BD intraocular lens. Home: 1490 W Long Lake Rd Bloomfield Hills MI 48302-1340 Office: The Coburn Clinic 19855 Outer Dr Dearborn MI 48124-2022

COBURN, TOM A., congressman; b. Casper, Wyo., Mar. 14, 1948; m. Carolyn Coburn; 3 children. BS in Acctg., Okla. State U., 1970; MD, U. Okla., 1983. Mfg. mgr. ophthalmic divsn. Coburn Optical Industries, 1970-78; resident surgery St. Anthony's Hosp., 1983-84; resident in family practice U. Ark. Area Health and Edn. Ctr., 1984-86; family practice physician, obstetrician, 1986—; mem. 104th Congress from 2d Okla. dist., 1995—; commerce and sci. com. 105th Congress; mem. energy & power, health & environment, oversight & investigations coms. Republican. Office: US House Reps 429 Cannon Bldg Ofc Bldg Washington DC 20515-3602*

COCANOUGHER, ARTHUR BENTON, university dean, former business administration educator; b. Lubbock, Tex., July 6, 1938; s. Arthur Clifton and Bonnie Odell (Ford) C.; m. Dianne Esther Reisenauer, May 27, 1967; children: Carolyn, David. Mgr. Gen. Electric Co., N.Y.C., 1962-67; asst. prof. U. So. Calif., Los Angeles, 1970-72; assoc. prof. So. Meth. U., Dallas, 1972-73; prof. mktg. U. Houston, 1973-75, chmn. dept., 1975-76, dean Coll. Bus., 1976-85, sr. v.p., provost, 1985-87; dean Coll. Bus. Tex. A&M U., College Station, 1987—; trustee Concert Investment series Smith Barney; bd. dirs. Randall's Food Co.; dir. First Am. Bank; cons. in field. Contbr. articles to profl. jours. Bd. dirs. Better Bus. Bur., Houston, 1979-87, West Houston Assn., 1984-87. Served to 1st lt. U.S. Army, 1960-62. Recipient Nicholas Salgo award So. Meth. U., 1973, Outstanding Service award U. Houston Alumni Assn., 1982, Disting. Alumnus award Coll. Bus. U. Tex.-Austin, 1981. Mem. Am. Mktg. Assn., Am. Acctg. Assn. Home: 4409 Nottingham Ln Bryan TX 77802-5904 Office: Tex A&M U Coll Bus Adminstrn 413 Wehner Bldg College Station TX 77843

COCCO, KAREN JEAN, school psychologist; b. Erie, Pa., Sept. 30, 1952; d. Donald Wilson and Cecelia Ida (Patchen) Clark; m. James Michael Cocco, Dec. 26, 1970 (div. Feb. 1984); 1 child, Carolyn Marie Cocco. BS, Gannon U., Erie, 1982; MEd, Edinboro (Pa.) U., 1986, postgrad., 1988. Cert. sch. psychologist; lic. psychologist. Substitute tchr. Gertrude A. Barber Ctr., Erie, 1982, Millcreek (Pa.) Sch. Dist., 1983-84; tchr. Iroquois Sch. Dist., Wesleyville, Pa., 1984-87; substitute tchr. N.W. Tri-County Intermediate Unit, Edinboro, 1987-88, Erie Sch. Dist., 1987-88; psychologist Harcourt Brace Jovanovich, Inc., Erie, 1987-89, Sarah A. Reed Children's Ctr., Erie, 1988-90, N.W Tri-County Intermediate Unit, Edinboro, 1990—; tchr. parenting class N.W Tri-County Intermediate Unit, Erie, 1997—, cons. to Head Start staff and other preschool, 1997—. Mem. scuba team Erie County Sheriff's Dept., Erie, 1977-87; vol. United Cerebral Palsy, Erie, 1965-68; vol., co-leader ARC, Girl Scouts, Erie, 1976-88; tchr., mem. coun. and numerous coms. Mt. Calvary Luth. Ch., Erie, 1968—. Recipient Letter of Commendation, Millcreek Police Dept., 1978. Mem. Nat. Assn. Sch. Psychologists, Assn. Sch. Psychologists of Pa., N.W. Pa. Psychologists Assn., Pa. State Edn. Assn., Phi Delta Kappa (sec.). Republican. Lutheran. Avocations: boating, skiing, whitewater rafting, birdwatching, travel. Office: NW Tri-County Intermed Unit 670 W 36th St Erie PA 16508-2645

COCCO, MARIE ELIZABETH, journalist; b. Malden, Mass., Jan. 15, 1956; d. Morris Alfred and Dorothy Anne (Colameta) C.; m. Thomas Neal Burrows, Sept. 4, 1982; children: Matthew C. Burrows, Michael C. Burrows. BA, Tufts U., 1978; MS, Columbia U., 1979. Journalist Daily Register, Shrewsbury, N.J., 1979-80, Newsday, L.I., N.Y., 1980—. Recipient Excellence in Editorial Writing award N.Y. State Pubs. Assn., 1992, Nat. Reporting award Sigma Delta Chi, 1991, N.Y. State AP award, 1997. Mem. White House Corrs. Assn. (Barnet Nover award 1991), Nat. Press Club

(Washington Corr. award 1991). Office: Newsday Washington Bur 1730 Pennsylvania Ave NW Washington DC 20006-4706

COCH, NICHOLAS KYROS, geologist, educator; b. N.Y.C., Mar. 30, 1938. BS, CCNY, 1959; MS, U. Rochester, 1961; PhD, Yale U., 1965. Cert. profl. geologist, Am. Inst. Profl. Geologists. Asst. prof. geology L.I. U., Southampton (N.Y.) Coll., 1965-67; from asst. prof. to prof. geology CUNY, Flushing, 1967-76, prof. geology, 1976—. Author: Geohazards, 1995; co-author: Physical Geology, 1982, 91. Fellow Geol. Soc. Am.; mem. Am. Assn. Petroleum Geologists (Meritorious Contbn. in Environ. Geoscis. award, ea. sect., 1996), Am. Meteorology Soc., Soc. Sedimentary Geology. Avocations: photography, scale modeling, cooking, computer graphics, model railroads. Office: Queens Coll CUNY Sch Earth and Environ Sci Flushing NY 11367

COCHÉ, JUDITH, psychologist, educator; b. Phila., Sept. 2, 1942; d. Louis and Miriam (Nerenberg) Milner; m. Erich Coché, Oct. 16, 1966 (dec.); 1 child, Juliette Laura; m. John Anderson, Jan. 1, 1994. BA, Colby Coll., 1964; MA, Temple U., 1966; PhD, Bryn Mawr Coll., 1975. Diplomate Am. Bd. Profl. Psychology; lic. Psychologist, Pa., Md., N.J.; cert. in group psychotherapy Nat. Registry Group Psychotherapists. Rsch. asst. Jefferson Med. Coll., 1965-66; diagnostician Law Ct., Aachen, Germany, 1967-68; staff psychologist N.E. Community Mental Health Ctr., Phila., 1969-74; family clinician Inst. Pa. Hosp., 1974-76; instr. psychology Drexel U., 1976-77; lectr. Med. Coll. Pa., 1977-78; asst. clin. prof. Hahnemann Med. Coll., Phila., 1979—; pvt. practice Phila., 1974—, N.J., 1985—; assoc. prof. psychiatry U. Pa., 1985—; assoc. clin. prof. psychology in psychiatry U. Pa. Med. Coll., 1986—; mem. faculty Family Inst. of Phila., 1990—; sr. cons. Phila. Child Guidance Clinic, 1992-96; assoc. clin. prof. psychology in psychiatry U. Pa. Med. Coll., 1986—; clin. cons. Hilltop Prep Sch., 1977-86; clin. supr. Am. Assn. Marriage and Family Therapy. Co-author: Couples Group Psychotherapy, A Clinical Practice Model, 1990, Co. author Powerful Wisdom: Voices of Distinguished Women Psychotherapists, (1993); contbr. chpts. to books, articles to profl. jours. Bd. dirs. Whitemarsh Art Ctr., 1977-78, Please Touch Museum, 1982-89; mem. prof. adv. bd. Parents Without Ptnrs., 1977-86; mem. adv. com. Pa. Ballet/Shirley Rock. Grantee Del. Children's Bur. Bryn Mawr Coll., 1974-75, Pa. Hosp., 1975-77. Fellow Am. Group Psychotherapy Assn.; mem. APA, Am. Assn. Marriage and Family Therapy (approved supr.), Am. Family Therapy Assn., Phila. Soc. Clin. Psychologists (pres. 1980-81), Family Inst. Phila., Pa. Psychol. Assn. (chmn. legis. com. 1982), Soc. Rsch. in Psychotherapy. Address: Acad House 1420 Locust St Ste 410 Philadelphia PA 19102-4201

COCHIN, RITA R., nurse; b. Chgo., Feb. 13, 1936; d. Louis and Mary (Nims) Gang; m. Alan Cochin, Dec. 31, 1960; 1 child, Gayle Lynn. Diploma in Nursing, Michael Reese Hosp., Chgo., 1961; diploma in employee rels., Cornell U., Ithaca, N.Y., 1963. RN, Ill., N.Y.; cert NAACOG; cert. neonatal advanced life support. Asst. head nurse oper. rm. Michael Reese Hosp., 1961; head nurse labor & delivery Brookdale Hosp., Bklyn., 1962-63; staff nurse labor & delivery Michael Reese Hosp., 1963-64, phlebotomist-blood bank, 1965-69; staff nurse labor & delivery Luth. Gen. Hosp., Park Ridge, Ill., 1973-77, NST/OCT testing program, 1977-86, staff nurse perinatal unit, 1986—; coord. unit based quality assurance of perinatal unit. active Immunization Clinic, Health Dept., Hoffman Estates, Ill., 1978. Mem. AWHONN (cert.), Nurses Assn. Ob-Gyn., Nurses' Coun., Hadassah (Chgo. chpt.). Avocations: travel, needlework, photography. Home: 1595 W Oakmont Rd Hoffman Est IL 60194-1241 Office: Luth Gen Hosp 3 W Perinatal Unit Park Ridge IL 60068

COCHRAN, ANNE WESTFALL, public relations executive; b. Cairo, Ill., Sept. 16, 1954; d. Howard Thurston and Flora Isabelle (Stone) Westfall; m. Charles Eugene Cochran, June 14, 1975; 2 children. BA in Advt., So. Ill. U., 1974; MA in Communications, U. Wis., Milw., 1975. Dir. advt. Sight and Sound Systems Inc., Milw., 1975-76; nat. publicity/promotions mgr. 20th Century Fox Classics, L.A., 1981-85; nat. publicity dir. Cannon Films Inc., L.A., 1985-86; publicist, staff writer Warner Bros. Inc., Burbank, Calif., 1986-87; v.p. mktg. Cinetel Films, Inc., L.A., 1987; v.p. publicity and promotion U.S. U.S. Cineplex Odeon Films, Inc., L.A., 1987-89; ptnr. Jones Cochran Assocs., Beverly Hills, Calif., 1989-92; sr. v.p. corp. and motion picture divsns. Bender, Goldman & Helper, L.A., 1992-95; ptnr. Mission Appraisal Group, L.A., 1995—; mktg. cons., L.A., 1976-81. Bd. dirs. Casa de Rosas Sunshine Mission, L.A., 1990. Mem. Publicists Guild. Republican. Mem. Christian Sci. Ch. Home: 13935 Hatteras St Van Nuys CA 91401-4342

COCHRAN, CAROLYN, library director; b. Tyler, Tex., July 13, 1934; d. Sidney Allen and Eudelle (Frazier) C.; m. Guy Milford Eley, June 1, 1963 (div.). BA, Beaver Coll., 1956; MA, U. Tex., 1960; MLS, Tex. Woman's U., 1970. Libr., Canadian (Tex.) High Sch., 1970-71; rep. United Food Co., Amarillo, Tex., 1971-72; libr. Bishop Coll., Dallas, 1972-74; interviewer Tex. Employment Commn., Dallas, 1975-76; libr. St. Mary's Dominican, New Orleans, 1976-77, DeVry Inst. Tech., Irving, Tex., 1978-98, libr. dir. emeritus, 1998—; with Database Searching Handicapped Individuals, Irving, 1983—; vol. bibliographer Assn. Individuals with Disabilities, Dallas, 1982-85. Mem. Am. Coalition of Citizens with Disabilities, 1982-85, Assn. Individuals with Disabilities, 1982-86, Vols. in Tech. Assistance, 1985—, Radio Amateur Satellite Corp., 1985-86; sponsor 500, Inc., 1988-95. HEW fellow, 1967; honored Black History Collection, Dallas Morning News, Bishop Coll., Dallas, 1973. Mem. ALA, Spl. Libr. Assn., Am. Coun. of Blind (sec. Dallas chpt. 1997—). Club: Toastmistress (pres. 1982-83) (Irving). Reviewer Library Jour., 1974, Dallas Morning News, 1972-74, Amarillo Globe-News, 1970-71. E-mail: Boeldesuet@aol.com.

COCHRAN, DALE M., state agency administrator; b. Ft. Dodge, Iowa, Nov. 20, 1928; s. Melvin and Gladys C.; m. Jeannene Hirsch, 1952; children: Deborah, Cynthia, Tamara. BS, Iowa State U., 1950. Rep. Iowa State Rep. Dist. 14, 1965-86; spkr. of house Iowa Ho. of Reps., 1975-78, exec. com. mem. nat. conf. state legis. and coun. state govt.; sec. agrl. Iowa, 1987—; owner of farm; pres. Midwestern Assn. State Depts. Agrl. and Mid-Am. Int. Agrl. Trade Coun. Farm editor: Ft. Dodge Messenger. Recipient Altig award Nat. Fedn. Blind, Sweepstakes award Friends of Agrl. Mem. Iowa Assn. Soil (hon. life), Iowa Soybean Assn. (bd. dirs. 1969-75), Lions, Pi Kappa Phi, Gamma Sigma Delta. Office: Agr & Land Stewardship Dept Wallace Bldg 9th and Grand Des Moines IA 50319

COCHRAN, DAVID MACDUFFIE, management consultant; b. Greenwich, Conn., Aug. 6, 1942; s. James J. and Dorothy Goff (MacDuffie) C.; children: David M. Cochran Jr., Michele T. Cochran. BA, Columbia U., 1968; MBA, NYU, 1971. Product mgr. Colgate Palmolive Co., Inc., N.Y.C., 1968-71; group product mgr. Colgate Palmolive Co.-Can., Toronto, 1971-72; v.p. mktg. and sales Colgate Palmolive Co.-Portugal, Lisbon, 1972-74, pres., gen. mgr., 1974-76; exec. v.p. Colgate Palmolive Co.-Brazil, Sao Paulo, 1976-77; pres. Latin Am. Joseph E. Seagram & Sons, Inc., N.Y.C., 1977-82; pres. internat. The Mennen Co., Morristown, N.J., 1982-85; ptnr. Barry Persky & Co., Westport, Conn., 1986-92; pres., owner Cochran & Co. Internat., Stamford, Conn., 1992—; bd. dirs. New Canaan Inn, chmn. nominating com., 1998—. Pres. New Canaan (Conn.) Lacrosse Asn., 1987—; bd. dirs. Conn. Lacrosse Found., 1995—, Conn.-N.Y. Lacrosse Assn., New Haven, 1989—. With U.S. Army, 1962-65. Mem. Country Club New Canaan (bd. govs. 1990-93, 96—, chmn. nominating com. 1996—, chmn. tennis com. 1996—). Republican. Presbyterian. Avocations: tennis, scuba diving, reading, photography, biking. Home: 155 Thurton Dr New Canaan CT 06840-6013 Office: Cochran & Co Internat PO Box 4095 Stamford CT 06907-0095

COCHRAN, GEORGE CALLOWAY, III, retired bank executive, lawyer; b. Dallas, Aug. 29, 1932; s. George Calloway and Miriam (Welty) C.; m. Jerry Bywaters, Dec. 9, 1961; children—Mary, Robert. BA, So. Meth. U., 1954; JD, Harvard U., 1957; cert., La. State U. Sch. Banking, 1969. Bar: Tex. 1957. Assoc. Leachman, Gardere, Akin and Porter, Dallas, 1960-62; with Fed. Res. Bank of Dallas, 1962-76, sr. v.p., 1976-92, ret., 1992; adv. com. Bank Ops. Inst., Tex. A&M U., Commerce, 1982—; mem. task force on truth in lending regulation Bd. Govs. of Fed. Res. System, Washington, 1968-69; bd. dirs. Am. Inst. Banking., Dallas, 1986-90. Hist. landmark survey task force City of Dallas, 1974-78. Capt. USAF, 1958-60. Mem. State Bar Tex., Phi Beta Kappa (pres. North Tex. Assn. 1998—), Harvard Club. Methodist. Home: 3541 Villanova St Dallas TX 75225-5008

COCHRAN, GEORGE MOFFETT, retired judge; b. Staunton, Va., Apr. 20, 1912; s. Peyton and Susie (Robertson) C.; m. Marion Lee Stuart, May 1, 1948; children—George Moffett, Harry Carter Stuart. BA, U. Va., 1934, LLB, 1936; LLD (hon.), James Madison U., 1991. Bar: Va. 1935, Md. 1936. Asso. law firm Balt., 1936-38; partner firm Peyton Cochran and George M. Cochran, Staunton, 1938-64, Cochran, Lotz & Black, Staunton, 1964-69; justice Supreme Ct., Richmond, Va., 1969-87; Pres. Planters Bank & Trust Co., Staunton, 1963-69. Chmn. Woodrow Wilson Centennial Commn. Va., 1952-58, Va. Cultural Devel. Study Commn., 1966-68, Frontier Culture Mus. Va., 1986-98; mem. Va. Commn. Constl. Revisi on, 1968-69, Jud. Coun. Va., 1963-69, Va. Ho. Dels., 1948-66, Va. Senate, 1966-68; chmn. bd. dirs. Stuart Hall, 1971-86; mem. bd. visitors Va. Poly. Inst., 1960-68; trustee Mary Baldwin Coll., 1967-81, U. Va. Law Sch. Found., 1975-89, Woodrow Wilson Birthplace Found., 1955-93. Lt. comdr. USNR, 1942-46. Recipient Algernon Sydney Sullivan award Mary Baldwin Coll., 1981. Mem. ABA, Va. Bar Assn. (pres. 1965-66), Raven Soc., Soc. of Cin., Phi Beta Kappa, Phi Delta Phi, Beta Theta Pi. Episcopalian.

COCHRAN, GLORIA GRIMES, pediatrician, retired; b. Washington, June 24, 1924; d. Paul DeWitt and Muriel Ann (Quackenbush) Grimes; m. Winston Earle Cochran, June 10, 1950; children: Edith Ann, Winston Earle, Jr., Donald Lee, Robert Edward. BS in Zoology, Duke U., 1945; MD, 1949; MPH, Johns Hopkins Sch. Hygiene, Balt., 1979. Diplomate Nat. Bd. Med. Examiners, 1950, Am. Bd. Pediatrics, 1958. Clinic pediatrician, sch. med. advisor health dept. Montgomery County, 1955-65; fellow in pediat. habilitation St. Christopher Hosp. for Children, Phila., 1965-66; assoc. dir. Child Development Clinic Baylor Med. Sch., Tex. Children's Hosp., 1966-72; dir. Northern Va. Child Devel. Field Svcs. Bur. Child Health State Health Dept. Commonwealth Va., 1972-76; coord. Handicapped Svcs. Children's Hosp. Nat. Med. Ctr., Washington, 1976-78; acting chief Divsn. of Svcs. to Children with Spl. Needs Bur. Sch. Health Svcs., Washington, 1982-89; retired, 1989; cons. Head Start Program, Md., Va., Tex., Pa., D.C., 1965-89; bd. mem. Ctrs. for Handicapped, Silver Spring, Md., 1982-89; Child Health com. Med. Soc. D.C., Washington, 1976-91. Producer, editor: (teaching film) Challenge for Habilitation: The Child with Congenital Rubella Syndrome, 1976. Steering com. Rock Days Inter-Church Camp, Washington, 1978-82; bd. mem. Open Door Cmty. Ctr., Columbus, Ga., 1993-94; co-chair curriculum com. Columbus Coll. Acad. of Life Long Learning, Columbus, 1994. Mem. Am. Assn. Mental Retardation, Am. Med. Women's Assn., Assn. for Retarded Citizens, Am. Acad. Cerebral Palsy, Am. Acad. Pediatrics, Phi Beta Kappa, Delta Omega. Democrat. Methodist. Avocation: travel. Home: 1605 Greenbriar Dr Norman OK 73072-6717

COCHRAN, JACQUELINE LOUISE, management executive; b. Franklin, Ind., Mar. 12, 1953; d. Charles Morris and Marjorie Elizabeth (Rohrbaugh) C. BA, DePauw U., 1975; MBA, U. Chgo., 1977. Fin. analyst Pan Am World Airways, N.Y.C., 1977-79, Gen. Bus. Group W. R. Grace & Co., N.Y.C., 1979-80; sr. fin. analyst Gen. Bus. Group div. W. R. Grace & Co., N.Y.C., 1980-81, mgr. fin. analysis, 1981-82; dir. fin. planning and analysis Gen. Bus. Group div. W. R. Grace & Co., N.Y.C., 1982-85; v.p. fin. Am. Breeders Svc. div. W. R. Grace & Co., DeForest, Wis., 1985-87, v.p. feed ops. Grace Animal Svc. div., 1987-89; gen. mgr., chief ops. officer SoftKat div. W. R. Grace & Co., Chatsworth, Calif., 1990; pres. SoftKat div. W.R. Grace & Co., Chatsworth, Calif., 1990-92; vice-chmn., chief adminstrv. officer Baker & Taylor, Inc., Chatsworth, Calif., 1992, pres. SoftKat div., 1992; exec. cons. Jacqueline Cochran Cons., Westlake Village, Calif., 1993, 94; gen. mgr. Attica Cybernetics, Inc., Chatsworth, Calif., 1995; pres., owner CorporateLinks, Westlake Village, Calif., 1996—. Bd. visitors DePauw U., 1993-96. Recipient Women of Distinction award Madison (Wis.) YWCA, 1987; named to Acad. Women Achievers YWCA N.Y., 1984. Mem. Omicron Delta Epsilon, Phi Beta Kappa, Alpha Lambda Delta, Delta Delta Delta (advisor scholarship com. Madison chpt. 1985-89, treas. 1986-89, ho. corp. bd. dirs. 1986-89, fin. advisor 1986-89). Republican. Methodist. Avocations: reading, golf.

COCHRAN, JAMES ALAN, mathematics educator; b. San Francisco, May 12, 1936; s. Commodore Shelton and Gwendolyn Audrey (Rosenau) C.; m. Katherine Koehler Kern, Sept. 6, 1958; children: Cynthia Royal, Sarah Lynn. BS in Physics, Stanford U., 1956, MS in Physics, 1957; PhD in Math., Stanford U., 1962. Mem. tech. staff, supr. applied math. Bell Telephone Labs. Inc, Whippany, N.J., 1962-72; prof. math. Va. Poly. Inst. and State U., Blacksburg, 1972-78; prof., chmn. dept. math. Wash. State U., Pullman, 1978-84, prof., 1978-89; campus exec. officer and founding dean tri-cities Wash. State U., Richland, Wash., 1989-98, prof. math., 1999—; vis. prof. math. Stanford U., 1968-69, Wash. State U., 1977, U. NSW, Sydney, Australia, 1985, Southeast U., Nanjing, China, 1994; fgn. scholar math. and mechanics Nanjing Inst. Tech., 1984; vis. fellow Deakin U., Victoria, Australia, 1985, 87. Author: Analysis of Linear Integral Equations, 1972, Applied Mathematics: Principles, Techniques, and Applications, 1982, Advanced Engineering Mathematics, 1987; also articles. Mem. nat. coun. Boy Scout Am., 1973-76, 99—, mem. local coun., 1974-77, 82-84, 93—, coun. pres., 1999—, mem. western region, 1996—; chmn. bd. commrs. Morris County (N.J.) Area Libr. Sys., 1971-72; mem. bd. dirs. Tri-Cities Sci. and Tech. Park Assn., 1990—, chmn., 1990-93; bd. dirs. Wash. Environ. Industry Assn., 1990-95, TRIDEC, 1996—; dir. state bd. Math. Engring. Sci. Achievement, 1992—; mem. Am. Pub. TV Stas. Bd., 1992-96; exec. com. Tri-Cities Commercialization Partnership, 1993-97; mem. Hanford Adv. Bd., 1994—; sr. advisor Tri-Cities Corp. Coun. for the Arts, 1991—. Recipient Silver Beaver award Boy Scouts Am., 1997, disting. Eagle Scout award, 1997; Gordon vis. fellow, Deakin U., Victoria, Australia, 1985. Mem. Am. Math. Soc., Math. Assn. Am., Soc. Indsl. Applied Math., Nat. Eagle Scout Assn. (young man pres. 1957-58, adviser 1958-71, Disting. Service award 1976), Phi Beta Kappa, Sigma Xi, Golden Key, Alpha Phi Omega. Republican. Presbyterian. Home: 1927 Cypress Pl Richland WA 99352-2414 Office: Wash State U Tri-Cities 2710 University Dr Richland WA 99352-7271

COCHRAN, JAMES KIRK, dean, oceanographer, geochemist, educator. BS summa cum laude, Fla. State U., 1973; M in Philosophy, Yale U., 1975, PhD in Geochemistry, 1979. Rsch. staff geochemist Yale U. dept. geology and geophysics, New Haven, Conn., 1979-81; asst. scientist dept. chemistry Woods Hole (Mass.) Oceanographic Instn., 1981-83; asst. prof. marine scis. SUNY, Stony Brook, 1985-90, assoc. prof., 1985-90, prof., 1990—, assoc dir. for rsch., 1990-92; assoc. dean for rsch. Marine Scis. Rsch. Ctr., SUNY, Stony Brook, 1992-94, dean, dir., 1994-98; rsch. assoc. dept. invertebrates Am. Mus. Natural History, N.Y.C., 1986—; invited lectr., UCLA, 1979, vis. scholar, Dept. Oceanography, U. Wash., Seattle, 1982, vis. scientist Ctr. des Faibles Radioactivités CNRS, Gif sur Yvette, France, 1989; vis. fellow Program in Oceanic and Atmospheric Scis., Princeton (N.J.) U., 1990, vis. prof. Inst. di Geol. Marina, Bologna, Italy, 1992, 98; assoc. rschr. European Ctr. for Environ. Geoscis., Aix-en-Provence, France, 1998, vis. scientist Internat. Atomic Engr. Agency, Monaco, 1999; mem. Group of Experts on Sci. Aspects of Marine Pollution and Internat. Atomic Energy Agy. working group to formulate an oceanographic model for dispersion of wastes disposed in the deep sea, 1980-82; sci. rep. to Phys. Oceanography Task Group of the Internat. Seabed Working Group, 1983-87; mem. Alvin Rev. Com., 1984-87, Joint Global Ocean Flux Steering Com., 1990-93. Contbr. over 70 articles to profl. jours. Mem. Am. Geophys. Union, Geochem. Soc., Oceanography Soc., Sigma Xi. Office: SUNY at Stony Brook Marine Sciences Rsch Ctr Stony Brook NY 11794-5000

COCHRAN, JOHN EUELL, JR., aerospace engineer, educator, lawyer; b. Dawson, Ala., May 22, 1944; s. John Euell and Beatrice Ann (Raley) C.; m. Gladys Carol Holdbrooks, Dec. 26, 1965; children: Christopher, Jonathan. B.A.E., Auburn U., 1966, M.S., 1967; Ph.D., U. Tex.-Austin, 1970; J.D., Jones Law Inst., 1976. Bar: Ala. 1977; registered profl. engr., Ala. Asst. prof. aerospace engring. Auburn (Ala.) U., 1970-75, assoc. prof., 1975-78, alumni assoc. prof., 1978-80, alumni prof., 1980-81, prof., 1981—, assoc. athletic dir., 1981-84, interim head aerospace engring., 1992-93, head aerospace engring., 1993—; cons. Northrup Svcs., Huntsville, Ala., 1970-71, U.S. Army Missile Command, Redstone Arsenal, Ala., 1975-82, various law firms, 1977—, Accident Prevention, Investigation and Analysis, Daleville, Ala., 1983-87, SRS Tech., Huntsville, 1984-89; pres. Eaglemark, Inc.; legal cons. Sigmatech, Inc. Contbr. articles to profl. jours.; assoc. editor Jour. Guidance Control and Dynamics, 1989-91. Tau Beta Pi fellow, 1965; Nat. Coll. Athletic Assn. fellow, 1965; NSF fellow, 1968. Fellow AIAA (assoc.), Am. Astronautical Soc.; mem. ABA, NSPE, Am. Helicopter Soc., Ala. Soc. Profl. Engrs. (Young Engr. of Yr. 1980, v.p. Auburn chpt. 1985, pres. 1986). Methodist. Achievements include (with others) simulation and reconstruction of aircraft accidents; rsch. in areas of dynamics and control, spacecraft attitude dynamics and control, dual-spin, tethered satellites; on the stability and control of aircraft (including towed vehicles); on missile launcher dynamics; and on the simulation of aerospace systems; short courses/seminars on engring. law and ethics. Home: 1887 Prim Dr Auburn AL 36830-7545 Office: Auburn U 211 Aerospace Engring Buil Auburn AL 36849

COCHRAN, JOHN THOMAS, professional association executive; b. Butler, Ga., Sept. 30, 1941; s. Robert T. and Marion (Payne) C.; m. Caroline Mansour, July 31, 1961 (div. Sept. 81); children: John Thomas, John Stuart, John Alexander; m. Carlotta Pye, July 26, 1988; stepchildren: Ansleigh Riddle, Harold Riddle, Havalynn Riddle. BA, U. Ga., 1964, JD, 1977. Dir. congl. rels. Job Corps, Washington, 1966-69; legis. rep. Nat. League Cities/U.S. Conf. Mayors, Washington, 1969-71; dep. exec. dir. U.S. Conf. Mayors, Washington, 1971-87, exec. dir., 1987—; editor in chief, pub. U.S. Mayor. Recipient Disting. Svc. award Job Corps, 1978, Luther J. Roberts Jr. Meml. award Nat. Community Devel. Assn., 1991. Mem. Am. Soc. Assn. Execs., Interam. Found. Cities (bd. dirs.), Fed. City Club. Home: 3801 Center Way Fairfax VA 22033-2645 Office: US Conf Mayors 1620 I St NW Washington DC 20006-4005*

COCHRAN, JOHNIE FAYE, registrar; b. Greensboro, Ala., Dec. 3, 1939; d. Johnie Alvin and Faye Thomas (Fowler) Christian; m. Ernest Evans, Dec. 31, 1956; children: Michael Evans, Mona Rae McPherson. BS in Edn. cum laude, U. Ala., 1980. Cert. tchr., Ala. Social worker Hale County, Greensboro, 1983-85, tax assessor, 1989-91; tchr. So. Acad., Greensboro, 1992-94; receptionist Hale County Hosp., Greensboro, 1994-95; registrar Hale County Bd. Registrars, Greensboro, 1987-88, 95—. Co-organizer, chmn. Hale County Reps., Greensboro, 1988-98; mem. Ala. Reunion Celebration, Greensboro, 1987-88, Juvenile Justice Coordinating Coun., Greensboro, 1989-92, Hale County Rural Devel. Com., Greensboro, 1989-92; chmn. Hale County Vets. War Meml., Greensboro, 1989-92, 5-Yr. Celebration of Bicentennial of U.S. Constitution, Greensboro, 1987-92. Mem. Bds. of Registrars Assn. (mem. legis. com. 1995-99), Phi Theta Kappa, Kappa Delta Pi. Republican. Baptist. Avocations: piano, singing, traveling, history, sewing.

COCHRAN, JOHNNIE L., JR., lawyer; b. Shreveport, La., Oct. 2, 1937. BS, UCLA, 1959; JD, Loyola U., 1962; postgrad., U. So. Calif. Bar: Calif. 1963, U.S. Dist. Ct. (we. dist.) Tex. 1966, U.S. Supreme Ct. 1968. Dep. city atty. criminal divsn. City of L.A., 1963-65; asst. dist. atty. L.A. County, 1978-82; now pvt. practice atty. L.A.; former adj. prof. law UCLA Sch. Law, Loyola U. Sch. Law; lawyer rep. U.S. Dist .Ct. (ctrl. dist.) Calif., 1990, U.S. Ct. Appeals (9th cir.) Judicial Conf., 1990; bd. dirs. L.A. Family Housing Corp., Lawyers Mut. Ins. Co. Spl. counsel, chmn. rules com. Dem. Nat. Convention, 1984; spl. counsel com. on standard ofcl. conduct, ethics com. 99th congress U.S. Ho. Reps.; bd. dirs. L.A. Urban League, Oscar Joel Bryant Found., 28th St. YMCA, ACLU Found. So. Calif. Fellow Am. Bar Found.; mem. Am. Coll. Trial Lawyers, State Bar Calif. (co-chair bd. legal svc. corps 1993), L.A. African Am. C. of C. (bd. dirs.), Airport Commrs. City of L.A., Black Bus. Assn. L.A. (pres. 1989). Office: 4929 Wilshire Blvd Ste 1010 Los Angeles CA 90010-3825*

COCHRAN, JOSEPH WESLEY, law librarian, educator; b. Jeanerette, La., July 11, 1954; s. Joseph Reeves Jr. and Mary Jane (Neill) C.; children: Brandon Reeves, Joseph Pierson. BA, Austin Coll., 1976; JD, U. Houston, 1978; M in Law Librarianship, U. Wash., 1980. Bar: Tex. 1979, U.S. Ct. Appeals (5th cir.) 1979, U.S. Ct. Appeals (11th cir.) 1981. Reference libr. Loyola U. Law Libr., New Orleans, 1980-81, head pub. svcs., 1981-83; assoc. law libr. U. Wash. Law Libr., Seattle, 1983-85; law libr., asst. prof. law U. Miss., University, 1985-91; assoc. prof. law Tex. Tech. U., Lubbock, 1991-94, prof. law, 1994—; chmn. bd. Consortium Southeastern Law Librs., 1987-89; libr. cons. Mitchell, McNutt, Bush, Lagrone & Sams, Tupelo, Miss., 1986-87. Author: Time Management Handbook for Librarians, 1991, (with Nancy Johnson) Legal Research Exercises, 5th edit., 1996. Mem. ABA, Tex. Bar Assn., Am. Assn. Law Librs. (pres. southeastern chpt. 1989-90), Southwestern Assn. Law Librs. Democrat. Presbyterian. Office: Tex Tech U Law Libr Lubbock TX 79409*

COCHRAN, KENNETH WILLIAM, toxicologist; b. Chgo., Nov. 2, 1923; m. Martha Louise Wells, May 10, 1945; children: Kenneth W. III, Kimberley W. Cochran Nelson. SB, U. Chgo., 1947, PhD, 1950. Rsch. asst. to instr., toxicity lab. and dept. pharmacology U. Chgo., 1946-52; from rsch. assoc., instr. to prof. emeritus U. Mich., Ann Arbor, 1952—. Contbr. articles to profl. jours. 1st lt. U.S. Army, 1943-46. Fellow AAAS; mem. Am. Soc. for Microbiology, Soc. for Exptl. Biology and Medicine, Am. Soc. for Pharmacology and Exptl. Therapeutics, Mycol. Soc. of Am., N.Am. Mycol. Assn. (exec. sec. 1988-97). Home: 3556 Oakwood St Ann Arbor MI 48104-5213

COCHRAN, LESLIE HERSCHEL, university administrator; b. Valparaiso, Ind., Apr. 24, 1939; s. Robert H. and Dellcena (Marquart) C.; m. Linda Stockman, May 20, 1978; children: Troy, Kirt, Leslee. B.S., Western Mich. U., 1961, M.A., 1962; Ed.D., Wayne State U., 1968. Mem. faculty Central Mich. U., Mt. Pleasant, 1968-80, assoc. dean, 1970-75, dean fine and applied arts, 1975-76, vice provost, 1976-80; provost S.E. Mo. State U., Cape Girardeau, 1980-92; pres. Youngstown (Ohio) State U., 1992—; mem. accreditation team North Ctrl. Assn., Chgo., 1982—. Author: Advisory Committee in Action, 1980, Innovative Program in Industrial Education, 1970, Administrative Commitment to Teaching, 1989, Publish or Perish: The Wrong Issue, 1992. Trustee Butler Inst. Am. Art, Western Res. Health Care System, N.E. Ohio Med. Coll. Japan Soc. Promotion of Sci. fellow Tokyo, 1976. Mem. Nat. Assn. Indsl. and Tech. Tchr. Edn. (pres. 1976), Rotary. Office: Youngstown State U Office of Pres Youngstown OH 44555*

COCHRAN, MARY ANN, nurse educator; b. Chgo., Dec. 12, 1951; d. Lawrence Donovan and Mary Gracz (Capizzi) Lee; m. Thomas Lee Cochran, Mar. 12, 1971; 1 child, Nathan Edgar. Diploma in nursing, St. Joseph's Hosp., Joliet, Ill., 1973. RN, Ill.; cert. post anesthesia nurse; cert. ambulatory perianesthesia. Staff nurse Silver Cross Hosp., Joliet, 1973—, stafff nurse ICU, 1979—, in-svc. educator post anesthesia care unit, 1987-92, BLS instr., 1987—, postanesthesia care unit charge nurse, 1994—. Mem. AACN, Am. Soc. Post Anesthesia Nurses, Ill. Soc. Post Anesthesia Nurses (membership chair 1990-92, ways & means chair 1992-95, Ill. dist. 1 dir. 1995—). Avocations: camping, fishing, boating, water skiing. Office: Silver Cross Hosp 1200 Maple Rd Joliet IL 60432-1497

COCHRAN, RAYMOND MARTIN, university financial administrator; b. Passaic, N.J., Aug. 10, 1943; s. Mark and Catherine (Brown) C.; m. Dorothy Parcells; children: Tamara, Tania. BS, Farleigh Dickinson U., 1966; MBA, NYU, 1968. CPA, N.Y., N.J. Mgr. audit KPMG, N.Y.C., 1968-79, Engelhard Minerals and Chems. Corp., N.Y.C., 1979-81; dir. internal audit Columbia U., N.Y.C., 1981—; founder, coord. N.Y. Metro Region Coll. and Univ. Audit Dirs., 1993—. Bd. dirs., treas. Japan Internat. Christian U. Found., Inc., 1985—. 1st lt. U.S. Army, 1969-71. Mem. AICPA, Assn. Coll. and Univ. Auditors (pres. 1999—), N.J. Soc. CPAs, Inst. Internal Auditors (v.p. N.Y. chpt.). Home: 818 E Ridgewood Ave Ridgewood NJ 07450-3911 Office: Columbia U 475 Riverside Dr Ste 510 New York NY 10115-0510

COCHRAN, ROBERT GLENN, nuclear engineering educator; b. Indpls., July 12, 1919; s. Lucian Glenn and Daisy P. (Wachstetter) C.; m. Mary Olive Worland, Mar. 1945; 1 son, Robert Glenn. B.A., Ind. U., 1948, M.S., 1950; Ph.D., Pa. State U., 1957. Registered profl. engr. Physicist Ohio State Health Dept., 1950; physicist, group leader Oak Ridge Nat. Lab., 1950-55; dir. research reactor, asso. prof. Pa. State U., 1955-59; prof., head dept. nuclear engring. Tex. A&M U., College Station, 1959-83; prof. Tex. A&M U., 1983—; vis. prof. nuclear engring. Tex. A&M U., 1985—; cons. USAF, U.S. AEC, NRC. Author: (textbook) The Nuclear Fuel Cycle: Analysis and Management, 1989; contbr. articles to profl. jours. and textbooks. Served with USNR, 1942-45. Fellow Am. Nuclear Soc.; mem. Am. Phys. Soc., Am.

Soc. Engring. Edn. (life), Sigma Xi, Phi Kappa Phi. Lodge: Mason. Home: 12305 Hopes Creek Rd College Station TX 77845-9241 Office: Tex A&M U Dept Nuclear Engring College Station TX 77843

COCHRAN, SAMUEL M., protective services official; b. Mobile, Ala., Nov. 16, 1954. BA, U. Southern Ala., 1980, MA, 1990. Police cadet Mobile (Ala.) Police Dept., 1975-77, patrolman, 1977-87, sgt., 1987-90, lt., 1990-95, dep. chief, 1995-96, chief of police, 1996—. Office: Mobile Police Dept 2460 Government Blvd Mobile AL 36101*

COCHRAN, SUSAN MILLS, librarian; b. Grinnell, Iowa, Nov. 21, 1949; d. Lawrence Omen and Louise Jane (Morgan) Mills; m. Stephen E. Cochran, July 1, 1972; children: Bryan, Jeremy. Libr. Iowa Geneal. Soc., Des Moines, 1987-96; asst. to dir. Local History Ctr., Canon City (Colo.) Pub. Libr., 1997—. Editor: Mingo, Iowa 1884-1984, 1984; contbr. articles to profl. jours. Past bd. dirs. Jasper County Libr., Newton, Iowa; past mem. Jasper County Cemetery Commn., Newton; mem. Jasper County His. Soc. Mem. Iowa Geneal. Soc., Jasper County Geneal. Soc., State Assn. for the Preservation of Iowa Cemeteries (charter). Avocations: genealogy, history, birding. Office: Canon City Pub Libr 516 Macon Ave Canon City CO 81212-3310

COCHRAN, THAD, senator; b. Pontotoc, Miss., Dec. 7, 1937; s. William Holmes and Emma Grace (Berry) C.; m. Rose Clayton, June 6, 1964; children: Thaddeus Clayton, Katherine Holmes. BA, U. Miss., 1959, JD cum laude, 1965; postgrad. (Rotary Found. fellow), U. Dublin, Ireland, 1963-64. Bar: Miss. 1965. Practiced in Jackson, 1965-72; assoc. firm Watkins & Eager, 1965-72; mem. 93d-95th congresses from Miss., 1973-79; U.S. senator from Miss., 1979—, chmn. Rep. conf. 104th Congress, 1995; mem. agr. nutrition and forestry com., appropriations com., govtl. affairs com., rules and adminstrn. com., senate Rep. conf. com. Mem. exec. bd. Andrew Jackson council Boy Scouts Am., from 1973. Served to lt. USNR, 1959-61. Named Outstanding Young Man of Jackson, 1971, One of Three Outstanding Young Men of Miss., 1971. Mem. ABA, Miss. Bar Assn. (pres. young lawyers sect. 1972-73), Omicron Delta Kappa, Phi Kappa Phi, Pi Kappa Alpha. Republican. Baptist. Club: Rotarian.

COCHRAN, WILLIAM JOHN, physician, pediatrician, gastroenterologist, nutritionist, consultant; b. Binghamton, N.Y., Apr. 22, 1953; s. John Joseph and Natalie Jane (King) C.; m. Deborah Janaskie, May 26, 1979; children: Shawn Patrick, Shelby St. John. BA in Biology, Franklin and Marshall Coll., 1975; MD, Pa. State U., 1979. Diplomate Am. Bd. Pediats., Am. Bd. Nutrition, Am. Bd. Pediats. in Pediatric Gastroenterology. Intern U. Rochester, N.Y., 1979-80, resident pediats., 1979-82, fellow pediat. GI/Nutrition, 1982-83; fellow sects. gastroenterology and nutrition Dept. Pediats. Baylor Coll. Medicine, Houston, 1983-84, instr. sects. gastroenterology and nutrition dept. pediats., 1984-85, asst. prof. sects. gastroenterology and nutrition USDA/ARS Childrens Nutrition Rsch. Ctr., 1985-87; assoc. in pediat. gastroenterology and nutrition Geisinger Clinic, Danville, Pa., 1987—; clin. assoc. prof. dept. pediats. Jefferson Med. Coll., Phila., 1988-98; clin. assoc. prof. dept. pediats. Pa. State U. Coll. Medicine, Hershey, 1998—, assoc. prof. clin. pediat., 1998—; mem. infant formula expert panel FDA, 1997. Active FDA expert panel on infant formulas, 1997; mem. editl. bd. Healthy Kids mag., 1998—. Soccer coach Am. Youth Soccer Assn., Danville, Pa., 1988-89. Travel grantee IV Internat. Congress of Auxology, Montreal, 1985, XIII Internat. Congress of Nutrition, Brighton, Eng., 1985; recipient Jr. Investigator award Internat. Congress Auxology, Montreal, 1985. Mem. Am. Soc. Parenteral and Enteral Nutrition (mem. Ctrl. Pa. chpt.), Am. Acad. Pediats. (gastroenterology sect., nutrition com., exec. com. gastroenterology and nutrition sect.), Am. Gastroenterological Assn., Am. Coll. Nutrition, Pa. Soc. Gastroenterology, Pa. Nutrition Coun., N. Am. Soc. Pediat. Gastroenterology. Roman Catholic. Avocations: scuba diving, tennis, cross country skiing. Office: Geisinger Clinic Dept Pediats GI and Nutrition 100 N Academy Ave Danville PA 17821-1203

COCHRAN, WILLIAM MICHAEL, librarian; b. Nevada, Iowa, May 6, 1952; s. Joseph Charles and Inez (Larson) C.; m. Diane Marie Ohm, July 24, 1971. BLS, U. Iowa, 1979, MA with distinction in Libr. Sci., 1983; MA in Pub. Adminstrn., Drake U., 1989. Dir. Red Oak (Iowa) Pub. Libr., 1984; patron svcs. libr. Pub. Libr. of Des Moines, 1984-87; LSCA program coord. State Libr. of Iowa, Des Moines, 1987-88, dir. libr. devel., 1988-89, asst. state libr., 1989-90; dir. Parmly Billings Libr., 1990-99, Aurora Pub. Libr., 1999—. Contbr. articles to profl. jours. Bd. dirs. Billings Cmty. Cable Corp., 1994-97. Mem. ALA, Mont. Libr. Assn. (pub. libr. divsn., chair 1991-92, legis. com. chair 1992-93, pres. 1998-99; named Libr. of Yr., 1998), Mont. Gov.'s Blue Ribbon Telecommunications Task Force, White House Conf. on Libr. and Info. Svcs., Libr. Adminstrn. and Mgmt. Assn., Pub. Libr. Assn., U. Iowa Alumni Assn. (life), Rotary, Beta Phi Mu. Office: Aurora Pub Libr One E. Benton St Aurora IL 60505

COCHRANE, BETSY LANE, state senator; b. Asheboro, N.C.; d. William Jennings and Bobbie (Campbell) Lane; m. Joe Kenneth Cochrane, 1958; children: Lisa, Craig. BA cum laude, Meredith Coll., 1958. Tchr. for eleven yrs.; mem. N.C. Ho. of Reps., Raleigh, 1980-88; house minority leader N.C. Ho. of Reps., Raleigh, N.C., 1985-88; mem. N.C. Senate, Raleigh, 1988—, chmn. Commn. on Aging, 1989—, vice chmn. higher edn. com., 1991-92; senate minority whip, 1993-94, senate minority leader, 1995-96; tchr. Winston-Salem Sch. System, Highland Presbyn. Ch. Sch.; mem. Nat. Rep. Platform Com., So. Regional Edn. Bd., 1987—; chmn. Joint Legis. Ethics Com., 1989, N.C. Parks Com., 1986-90. Trustee Davie County Hosp.; bd. advisors Z. Smith Reynolds, 1995—, Meredith Coll., 1995. Recipient Woman in Govt. award N.C. Jaycees, 1985; named One of 10 Outstanding Legislators in Nation, 1987, Disting. Citizen of Yr. N.C. Libr. Dirs., 1991, Legislator of Yr. N.C. Divsn. Aging, 1991, N.C. Assn. for Home Care, 1992, Citizen of Yr. N.C. Health Facilities Assn., 1993, Legislator of Yr. award N.C. Wildlife Fedn., 1995, Legislator of Yr. award Austism Found., 1995, Myers-Honeycutt award for excellence in pub. svc., 1996, Disting. Alumnae of the Yr. Meredith Coll., 1996, Dr. Ewald W. Busse award Aging Advocates of N.C., 1997. Baptist. Home and Office: 122 Azalea Cir Advance NC 27006-9582 Office: NC Senate 1119 Legislative Bldg Raleigh NC 27601

COCHRANE, JAMES LOUIS, economist; b. Nyack, N.Y., Aug. 31, 1942; s. Thomas and Anna (Yaroscak) C.; m. Katherine Prince Schirmer, Mar. 24, 1984; 1 child. BA, Wittenberg U., 1964; PhD, Tulane U., 1968. Instr. Tulane U., New Orleans, 1967-68; asst. prof. U. S.C., Columbia, 1968-70, assoc. prof., 1970-72, prof., 1972-77; sr. staff mem. NSC, Washington, 1978-79; directorate of intelligence CIA, Washington, 1980-83; sr. v.p., chief economist Tex. Commerce Bancshares Inc., Houston, 1984-88, N.Y. Stock Exch., 1988—; assoc. staff Brookings Instn., Washington, 1972-76, 76-78; 1st v.p. So. Econ. Assn., U. N.C., 1976-77; vis. prof. U. Melbourne, Australia, 1972, U. Tex., Austin, 1973-74; mem. adv. bd. White Ctr. Fin. Rsch., U. Pa., Fin. Markets Rsch. Ctr., Vanderbilt U.; mem. bd. advisors N.Y. Assembly; bd. dirs. Catalyst Inst., Columbia U. Ctr. Law and Econ. Studies; mem. emerging econs. program bd. U. Pa. Wharton Sch.; mem. deans adv. bd. Hofstra U. Sch. Bus.; mem. study equities markets Pace U.; mem. internat. adv. com. Ctr. for Internat. Affairs, Harvard U., U.S. Nat. Com. for Pacific Econ. Cooperation. Author: Macroeconomics Before Keynes, 1970, Macroeconomics Analysis and Policy, 1974, Industrialism and Industrial Man in Retrospect, 1977; editor: Multiple Criteria Decision Making, 1975; mem. editl. bd. History Polit. Economy, Duke U., 1974-80, So. Econ. Jour., U. N.C., 1976-79. Mem. History of Econs. Soc. (treas. 1974-80), Asia Soc. (adv. dir. 1986), Am. Econ. Assn., Western Fin. Assn. Avocations: tennis, singing, writing. Office: NY Stock Exch 11 Wall St Fl 7 New York NY 10005-1974

COCHRANE, ROBERT LOWE, biologist; b. Morgantown, W.Va., Feb. 10, 1931; s. Thomas Joseph and Isabelle Durston (Lowe) C. *His father was Thomas J. (Tim) Cochrane, BS, MS in Chemical Engineering. He was born in Belfast on August 17, 1894 and died June 30, 1988. He was head of the West Virginia State Road Commission Test Laboratories from the middle 1940s to 1961. His mother was Isabelle Durston (Lowe) Cochrane, BS in Home Economics, member of the home economics faculty of West Virginia University, 1922 to 1925, was born August 28, 1897 and died June 16, 1993. She was a member of the home economics faculty at West Virginia University, 1922-1925.* BA, W.Va. U., 1953; MS, U. Wis., 1954, PhD, 1961. Rsch. asst. genetics U. Wis., Madison, 1953-55; with Fur Animal Exptl. Sta., Petersburg, Alaska, 1955; rsch. asst. zoology U. Wis., Madison, 1957-60; agt. in animal husbandry U.S. Dept. Agr., Madison, Wis., 1955-61; biologist FDA, Washington, 1961-62; sr. research fellow dept. anatomy U. Birmingham (Eng.), 1962-65; project assoc. dept. physiology U. Pitts., 1965-66; sr. endocrinologist Eli Lilly & Co., Indpls., 1966-80; rsch. assoc. G.D. Searle & Co., Skokie, Ill., 1980-81; with Short's Fur Farm, Granton, Wis., 1981-83; rsch. assoc. Marshfield (Wis.) Med. Found., 1983-84; biologist Northwood Fur Farms, Inc., Cary, Ill., 1984; cons. for FAO to Wildlife Inst. India, Dehara Dun, 1985; adj prof. div. animal and vet. sci., W.Va. U., Morgantown, 1987—. *He was a student of Dr. R.M. Shackleford with a minor in zoology with Dr. R.K. Meyer. Dr. L.E. Casida also played a major role in his PhD Thesis work. He has been an unofficial advisor to the West Virginia University Block and Bridle Club since 1987 and is presently working to develop a means for raising ruffed grouse commercially in captivity.* Ad hoc reviewer various sci. jours.; ad hoc reviewer U.S. Dept. of Agr. Competitive Rsch. Grants; participant Internat. Mink Show, Wis., 1976-99, W. Va. State Fox Show, Morgantown, 1989. Rsch. bd. advisors The Am. Biog. Inst., 1988-98; mem. adv. coun. Internat. Biog. Centre, 1989-98; mem. Golden Horseshoe Reunion Com., W.Va. Homecoming '96. Recipient Knight of Golden Horse Shoe award W.Va. Pub. Sch. System, 1945, W.Va. Boy's State, 1948; U. Birmingham (Eng.) sr. rsch. fellow, 1962-65. Mem. AAAS, Am. Inst. Biol. Scis., Soc. Exptl. Biology and Medicine, Soc. for Study of Fertility, Soc. Study of Reproduction, Am. Soc. Animal Sci., Endocrine Soc., N.Y. Acad. Sci., Soc. Endocrinology, Coun. Agrl. Sci. and Tech., Internat. Platform Assn., NRA (life), Sigma Xi, Pi Kappa Alpha, Gamma Sigma Delta. Presbyterian. Achievements include major contributions to the establishment of the hormonal requirements for ova-implantation and embryonic diapause in the rat, the elucidation of the role played by prostaglandins in corpus luteum function, parturition and ductus arteriosus closure in the rat; the development of steroid synthesis inhibitors for controlling reproduction in mammals; the documentation of the timing, duration and pattern of reproductive cycles in martens; the dissemination of scientific information on fur farming to the commercial fur trade and public. Home: 404 Junior Ave Morgantown WV 26505

COCHRANE, THOMAS THURSTON, tropical soil scientist, agronomist; b. Gisborne, N.Z., Mar. 18, 1936; came to U.S., 1990; s. Thomas Nicholson and Muriel Hope (Morrison) C.; m. Rosa Elena Fajardo de las Muñecas, Mar. 18, 1970; 1 child, Thomas Arey. B Agrl. Sci., U. N.Z., 1960; Assoc., Imperial Coll. Tropical Agr., Trinidad, B.W.I., 1962; PhD, U. W.I., Trinidad, W.I., 1969. Agronomist U. W.I., Trinidad, 1962; soil scientist Ministry Overseas Devel., U.K., Bolivia, 1963-74; cons. Tate and Lyle, U.K., Bolivia and Mex., 1974-77; land resource specialist Centro Internacional de Agricultura Tropical, Colombia, 1977-81; soil scientist S.E. Consortium for Internat. Devel., Washington, 1981-82; land resource specialist Inter-Am. Inst. for Agrl. Cooperation, Brazil, 1982-85; cons. West Lafayette, Ind., 1986—. Author: The Land Use Potential of Bolivia, 1973, Land in Tropical America, 1985; contbr. over 50 articles to sci. publs. Decorated El Condor de los Andes, Bolivia, 1973. Mem. Internat. Soil Sci. Soc., Soil Sci. Soc. Am., Am. Soc. Agronomy. Achievements include development of an equation for liming acid soils to compensate aluminum toxicity, a differential equation for predicting crop fertilizer response, an equation for calculating the contribution of the separate ions and molecules of water solutions to osmotic pressure; research showing that the Amazonian forests depend on both climate and soils. Home: 623 N Salisbury St West Lafayette IN 47906-2711

COCHRANE, TIM, landmark administrator; b. St. Paul, Sept. 1, 1954. BS, U. Mont., 1967; MS, Western Ky. U., 1982; PhD, Ind. U., 1986. Anthropologist Alaska Region Nat. Pk. Svc., 1991-97; supt. Grand Portage Nat. Monument, Grand Marais, Minn., 1997—. Mem. Am. Anthropol. Assn., Am. Folklore Soc., Cultural Survival. Office: Grand Portage Nat Monument 315 S Broadway PO Box 668 Grand Marais MN 55604*

COCHRANE, WALTER E., education administrator, writer; b. Phila.; s. Earl and Martha (Binder) C. BS, U. Pa., Phila., MS; grad. study, Columbia U., 1959-60. Cert. adminstr., N.Y., Pa., Mass., N.J., Maine; supt. schs., N.Y., Mass.; sch. prin., N.Y., Pa., Mass. Dist. dir. Sch. Dist. II, L.I., N.Y., 1958-60; supr. music N.Y. State Edn. Dept., Albany, 1960-67, v.p. Found. Am. Art Song, 1965-70; supr. music Hartford (Conn.) City Schs., 1967-69; asst. supt. Sch. Dist. 5, L.I., N.Y., 1970-78; supt. schs. Maine Sch. Adm. Dist. 19, Lubec, Maine, 1978-80; v.p. and dean Inst. Security and Tech., Phila., 1980-87; corp. dir. edn. PTC Career Insts., Phila., 1987; pres. Career Guidance Corp., 1988-91, dir. GED home study program N.Y. State, 1992—. Author: GED Home Study Program, Meet The Great Composers, The Gulf War, Science Mastery Manual, Understand Music, Women Composers, Literature Mastery Manual, Who Was the Killer Composer?. Recipient Humanitarian award Chgo. PTC. Mem. ASCD, NEA, MENC, SAR, NYSSMA (adjudicator, all-state conductor), NASSP, Am. Assn. Sch. Adminstrs., N.Y. Assn. Supr. and Curriculum Devel., Phila. Musical Soc.

COCHRANE, WILLIAM HENRY, municipal administration executive; b. Norfolk, Va., Apr. 3, 1912; s. William F. and Gretchen (Schneider) C.; m. Elizabeth J. Ballantine, Aug. 3, 1935 (dec. July 1977); children: William Henry, Elizabeth J., Susan B., Peter B.; m. Deborah E. Collyer, June 14, 1978; stepchildren, Nancy Havecotte, George Shepard, Debbie Van Felter, Elizabeth Shepard, Alexander Shepard. Student, Princeton, 1931-32. Successively chemist, salesman, dist. mgr., mgr. market and sales analysis, mgr. detergent project U.S. Indsl. Chems. Co., 1932-52; gen. mgr. indsl. div. Lever Bros. Co., 1952-57; exec. v.p. Neptune Internat. Corp., 1957-58, pres., 1958-69, chmn., 1966-72; also bd. dirs.; bd. dirs. Los Angeles Soap Co.; v.p. Mountain Lake Corp., 1975-77, pres., 1978-81; pres. Indian River Lands Inc., 1987—, also bd. dirs. Mem. Vero Beach (Fla.) City Coun., 1980-87, vice mayor, 1980-82, mayor, 1982-87, chmn. fin. commn., 1987—; bd. dirs. Vero Beach Civic Assn., Humane Soc., Coun. of Aging; trustee Vero Beach Ctr. Arts, 1983-90, pres., 1984-89; mem. Fla. Arts Coun., 1990-91. Lt. USNR, 1944-46. Mem. Newcomen Soc., Princeton Club N.Y., Nassau Club, Riomar Bay Yacht Club, Mountain Lake Club, Riomar Country Club. Home: 2320 Club Dr Vero Beach FL 32963-2158 Office: City Hall Vero Beach FL 32960

COCHRUN, JOHN WESLEY, financial consultant; b. Spencerville, Ohio, May 4, 1918; s. Paul Wesley and Laura Edna (McClure) C.; m. Shirley Bunnell Stephens, June 7, 1942; children: Timothea Jourdan, David Wesley. BS, Purdue U., 1940; diploma, U.S. Army Command and Gen. Staff Coll., 1944; MS in Fin. Svcs., Am. Coll., 1985. CLU, chartered fin. cons. Spl. apprentice Bendix-Westinghouse A.A.B. Co., Pitts., 1940-41; asst. svc. mgr. Bendix-Westinghouse A.A.B. Co., Elyria, Ohio, 1945-50; mgr. customer svc. DeVilbiss Co., Toledo, 1950-58; exec. v.p. Elec. Products R & D Co., Toledo, 1958-60; spl. agt. Northwestern Mut. and other ins. cos., Toledo, 1961-81, St. Petersburg, Fla., 1981-87, Las Cruces, N.Mex., 1987-97; registered investment adviser SEC, State of N.Mex., 1989-95; pres. Cochrun Inc., Sylvania, Ohio, 1976-81, Seminole, Fla., 1981-87. Author: Service of the Piece, 1945, Avoid Financial Shocks in Your Family's Future, 1976, Wills, Trusts, and Life Insurance Settlement Options, 1995. Pres. Community League Sylvania, 1954; lobbyist Ohio Pub. Expenditure Coun., Sylvania, 1955, Fed. Transp. Commn., Washington, 1947-50. Lt. col. U.S. Army, 1941-45. Mem. Am. Soc. CLU and ChFC, Million Dollar Round Table (life), Res. Officers Assn., Phi Kappa Psi. Republican. Avocations: gardening, canoeing. Home and Office: 3045 Buena Vida Cir Apt 204E Las Cruces NM 88011-9123

COCKBURN, JOHN F., retired banker; b. Everett, Wash., Apr. 8, 1928; s. Charles G. and Florence S. Cockburn; m. Lynn F. Pierson, June 29, 1960; children: Steven, Matthew, Teresa, Patrick. BBA, U. Wash., Seattle, 1950. With Rainier Nat. Bank (now Seafirst Bank), Seattle, 1948-88, exec. v.p., 1975-88, mgr. pvt. banking, 1987-88; pres. Pacific Coast Banking Sch., 1977-79; fin. chmn. Wash. Coun. Econ. Edn., 1980-81, also bd. dirs. Trustee Forest Ridge Sch., Bellevue, Wash., 1983-89, chmn., 1988-89; trustee, fin. chmn. Horizon House, Seattle, 1988-91; exec. bd. Wash. Pub. Power Supply System, 1989-93, apptd. by gov., 1995—, apptd. by bd., chmn. audit, legal, fin. com., 1995—. Mem. Rainier Club (trustee 1987-90), Seattle Tennis Club, Broadmoor Golf Club (trustee, pres. 1994-95). Congregationalist. Home: 1524 Shenandoah Dr E Seattle WA 98112-3732

COCKE, ERLE, JR., international business consultant; b. Dawson, Ga., May 10, 1921; s. Erle and Elise (Meadows) C., Sr.; m. Madelyn Alice Grotnes, May 28, 1955; children: Elise Carol, Jennifer Cocke Carpenter, Carolyn Cocke Whitsett. A.B., U. Ga., 1942; M.B.A., Harvard, 1947; LL.D., Mercer U., 1951; L.H.D., Mo. Valley Coll., 1960; D.B.A., Presbyn. Coll., 1979. Asst. gen. mgr. Cinderella Foods, Dawson, 1946-47; exec. dir. Agrl. and Indsl. Devel. Bd. of the State of Ga., 1947-48; gen. indsl. agt. central Ga.; with Ry. Co., Atlanta, 1948-50; asst. to pres. Delta Air Lines, Atlanta, 1950-54; v.p. Delta Air Lines, Inc., Atlanta, 1954-61; alt. exec. dir. World Bank, Washington, 1961-64; v.p. Peruvian Airlines, Inc., Washington, 1964-66; now cons.; chmn. bd. Cocke and Phillips Inc.; dir. State Mut. Ins. Co., Rome, Ga.; Toured 39 countries as mem. Def. Dept's Spl. Civilian Adv. Com. on Armed Forces Installations, 1951-52; civilian aide to sec. of Army, 1952-60; co-chmn. Nat. Conf. Fgn. Aspects of U.S. Nat. Security, 1958; U.S. alt. rep. to 14th gen. assembly UN, 1959-60. Entered U.S. Army as lt., Inf. 1941; disch. as major, Inf. 1946; brig. gen. N.G.; ret. Decorated Silver Star, Bronze Star with cluster; Purple Heart with 3 clusters; Croix de Guerre; Chevalier Legion of honor France; awarded Medal of Honor Republic of the Philippines; Star of Solidarity; Comdr. Knight of Malta. Italy; Diploma and Medal Cruz Roja Red Cross, Spain; Hon. Comrd. Nationalist Chinese Air Force, 1951; Recipient Ga. Jr. C. of C. award for Outstanding Young Man of the Year, 1949; U.S. Jr. C. of C. for one of ten Outstanding Young Men of Year, 1950. Mem. U. Ga. Alumni Soc. (past v.p.), Am. Legion (nat. comdr. 1950-51, hon. pres. Soc. Am. Legion Founders 1983), Sphinx Soc., Kappa Alpha. Baptist. Clubs: Masons, Shriners, Army and Navy (Washington), City Tavern (Washington). Wounded 3 times; prisoner of war 3 times (actually 'executed' by German firing squad and delivered the coup de grace but survived, 1945). Home: 5610 Wisconsin Ave Apt 403 Chevy Chase MD 20815-4429 also: 139 W Lee St Dawson GA 31742-0350 Office: 1629 K St NW Ste 1250 Washington DC 20006-1602*

COCKE, WILLIAM MARVIN, JR., plastic surgeon, educator; b. Balt., Aug. 2, 1934; s. William M. and Clara E. (Bosley) C.; m. Sue Ann Harris, Apr. 25, 1981; children: Gregory William, Laura Marie, Julie Ann; children by previous marriage: William Marvin III, Catherine Lynn, Deborah Kay, Brian Thomas. B.S. with honors in Biology, Tex. A&M U., 1956; M.D., Baylor U., 1960. Diplomate: Am. Bd. Plastic Surgery (guest examiner 1978). Intern surgery Vanderbilt U. Hosp., Nashville, 1960-61; fellow gen. surgery Ochsner Clinic and Found. Hosp., New Orleans, 1961-64; chief resident surgery Monroe (La.) Charity Hosp., 1963-64; resident reconstructive surgery Roswell Park Meml. Inst., Buffalo, 1965-66; chief resident plastic surgery VA Hosp., Bronx, N.Y., 1966; practice medicine specializing in plastic surgery Nashville, 1968-75, Sacramento, 1976-79; pvt. practice medicine specializing in plastic surgery Bryan, Tex., 1980-92; prof. surgery, head div. plastic/reconstructive surgery Marshall U. Sch. of Medicine, Huntington, W.Va., 1992—; mem. staff St. Mary's Hosp., Cabell-Huntington Hosp., Huntington Vets. Med. Ctr.; asst. prof. plastic surgery Vanderbilt U. Sch. Medicine, Nashville, 1968-69, asst. clin. prof. plastic surgery, 1969-75; assoc. prof. plastic surgery Ind. U. Sch. Medicine, Indpls., 1975-76; chief plastic surgery service Wishard Meml. Hosp., Ind. U., 1975-76; assoc. prof. surgery U. Calif. Sch. Medicine, Davis, 1976-79, chmn. dept. plastic surgery, 1976-79; prof. surgery, chief div. plastic surgery Tex. Tech. U. Sch. Medicine, Lubbock, 1979-80, dir. Microsurg. Research Lab., 1979-80; clin. prof. surgery Tex. A&M U. Sch. Medicine, 1983-92; prof. plastic surgery, 1986-89; chief plastic surgery svc., dept. surgery, Olin Teague VA Med. Ctr., Temple, Tex., 1986-92; prof. head surgery divsn. plastic and reconstruction Marshall U. Sch. Medicine, 1992—. Author textbooks on plastic surgery; contbr. articles to profl. jours. Served with M.C. USAF, 1966-68. Recipient Dean Echols award Ochsner Hosp. Found., 1963. Mem. ACS, Am. Assn. Plastic Surgeons, Soc. Head and Neck Surgeons, Assn. for Acad. Surgery, Alton Ochsner Surg. Soc. Episcopalian. Home: 45 Olde Farm Rd Ona WV 25545-9747 Office: Marshall U Sch Medicine Dept Surgery 1600 Medical Center Dr Huntington WV 25701-3656

COCKERHAM, KIMBERLY PEELE, ophthalmologist; b. Bellevue, Wash., Apr. 10, 1961; d. Fred Arthur and Dorothy Anne (Cooper) Piontkowski; m. Glenn Cooper Cockerham, Feb. 22, 1997. BA in Biology, U. Calif., San Diego, 1983; MD, George Washington U., 1987. Commd. 2d lt. U.S. Army, 1983, advanced through grades to maj.; surg. intern Letterman Army Ctr., San Francisco, 1987-88; chief emergency svcs. McDonald Army Hosp., Newport News, Va., 1988-89; resident in ophthalmology Walter Reed Army Med. Ctr., Washington, 1989-92, neuro-ophthalmology fellow, 1992-93, mem. neuro-ophthlamology staff, 1993-94, 95—; orbital disease fellow Allegheny Gen. Hosp., Pitts., 1994-95; dir. orbital disease and oculoplastics Walter Reed Army Med. Ctr., Washington, 1995-98; ophthalmologist Cockerham Eye Cons., Lock Haven, Pa., 1997—; dir. oculoplastics, orbital disease and reconstruction Allegheny Ophthalmic and Oribital Assocs., Pitts.; neuro-ophthalmology cons. Fitzsimons Army Med. Ctr., Denver, 1993-94; asst. clin. prof. Uniformed U. Health Scis., Bethesda, Md.; instr. neuro-ophthalmology Harvard's Lancaster and Stanford basic ophthalmology courses, 1994—; oral bd. examiner Acad. Ophthalmology, 1998—. Contbr. articles to profl. jours., chpts. to books. Eye camp doctor Charitable Trust, New Delhi, India, 1996; mem. Surg. Eye Expedition Internat., 1997-99. Fellow Am. Acad. Ophthalmology; mem. N.Am. Soc. Neuro-Ophthalmology, Assn. Rsch. in Vision and Ophthalmology, Rotary Club, Alpha Omega Alpha. Avocations: running, rollerblading, writing. Office: Allegheny Gen Hosp Office Ophthalmis Plastics and Reconstrn Pittsburgh PA also: Cockerham Eye Cons 930 Bellefonte Ave Lock Haven PA 17745 also: Allegheny Ophthalmic & Orbital Assocs 420 East North Gate #116 Pittsburgh PA 15212

COCKERHAM, SIDNEY JOE, professional society administrator; b. Waxahachie, Tex., Aug. 17, 1951; s. Sidney Julius and Joan (Barlow) C. BS in Biology, U. Tex., Arlington, 1973. Cert. tchr., Tex. Tchr. Tex. Pub. Schs., Waxahachie, 1973-77; dir., founder U.S. Nat. Tennis Acad., Waxahachie, 1982—. Lt. USN, 1977-82. Avocation: tennis. Home: 2200 Brown St Waxahachie TX 75165-5127 Office: US Nat Tennis Acad 1014 Ferris Ave Waxahachie TX 75165-2599

COCKREL, SHEILA M., councilwoman; b. Corktown, Mich.; d. Lou Murphy and Justine M.; m. Ken Cockrel, 1978 (dec.); 1 child, Kathy. Founder Ad-Hoc Action Group, 1968; mem. Labor Def. Coalition; city councilwoman City of Detroit, 1994—; contract and grant adminstr. Mich. Modernization Svc.; pres. Cockrel Polit. Cons. Co-mng. editor Modern Mich. Recipient Mademoiselle award, 1968. Office: Detroit City Coun City County Bldg 2 Woodward Ave Detroit MI 48226-3437*

COCKRELL, RICHARD CARTER, lawyer; b. Denver, Oct. 9, 1925; s. Harold Arthur Sweet and Mary Lynne Cockrell. AB, U. Denver, 1949, JD cum laude, 1950. Bar: Colo. 1950, U.S. Supreme Ct. 1954. Supr. real estate, tax and claims Standard Oil, Denver, 1950-52; from assoc. to ptnr. Cockrell, Quinn & Creighton and predecessor firms, Denver, 1952-91; of counsel Cockrell, Quinn & Creighton, Denver, 1992-99, ret., 1999. Mem. law com. Colo. State Bd. Law Examiners, Denver, 1958-79; mem. bd. mgrs. Nat. Conf. Bar Examiners, Chgo., 1965-69. With U.S. Army, 1943-46, USAR, 1946-51, maj. USAFR, 1951-67, ret. 1985. Mem. Denver Bar Assn., Colo. Bar Assn., Denver Law Club (pres. 1963-64, Svc. to Bar and Cmty. Lifetime Achievement award 1996), University Club (bd. dirs. 1982-88), Phi Beta Kappa, Beta Theta Pi, Phi Delta Phi. Episcopalian. Home: 1155 Ash St Apt 1504 Denver CO 80220-3727

COCKRELL-FLEMING, SHELIA YVETTE, public health nurse; b. Houston, July 20, 1961; d. Morgan O. and Alma (Wheeler) Cockrell; m. Wesley T. Fleming, May 25, 1991; 1 child, Khelli E. BSN, U. Tex. Health Sci. Ctr., Houston, 1983. RN; cert. pub. health nurse. Asst. head nurse Harris County Hosp. Dist., Houston, 1988-89; perinatal nurse HealthMark, Houston, 1989-90, Meml. N.W. Hosp., Houston, 1990-91, Lompoc (Calif.) Hosp. Dist., 1991-92; pub. health nurse Santa Barbara County, Lompoc, 1992-94; perinatal nurse Spectrum Health Care, Vendenberg AFB, Calif., 1994-96; dir. health promotion/disease prevention Am. Indian Health and Svcs., Santa Barbara, Calif., 1996-99; pres., CEO Sojourner Nurse Cons., Lompoc, Calif., 1999—; mem. adv. bd. Healthy Start, Lompoc, 1992-93; mem. cmty. adv. bd. Santa Barbara Health Initiative, 1997—; mem. Breast Cancer Early Detection Partnership Santa Barbara County, 1996—. Author poems. CPR, first aid instr. ARC. 1st lt. USAF, 1985-88. Mem. Nat. Coun. Nurse Adminstrs., Am. Diabetes Assn. Baptist. Avocations: reading, writing. Office: Sojourner Nurse Cons Lompoc CA 93436

COCKRILLE, STEPHEN, art director, business owner; b. Washington, Jan. 19, 1945; s. Donald Herbert and Dorothy Charolette (Hoover) C.; m. Éva Vágréti, May 17, 1987; children: Christopher Lewis, Micki Lee. BA, W.Va. State Coll., 1968; MA, U. N.D., 1972. Grad. tchg. asst. U. N.D., Grand Forks, 1971; design asst. Thomas Clayton Printing, N.Y.C., 1974-75; art dir. West Side Printing & Graphics, N.Y.C., 1975-76; studio mgr. Graphic Concern, Inc., N.Y.C., 1976-78; ind. art dir. N.Y.C., 1978-84; pres. Textart, Inc., N.Y.C., 1984-97; ret., 1997; judge New Eng. Book Show, Boston, 1987; selected for presentation to the Jordanian Min. of Edn. and staff on the U.S. textbook industry, N.Y.C., 1995. Prodr. numerous basal ednl. programs for nat. distbn., 1984-97. With U.S. Army, 1968-70, Vietnam. Recipient hon. mention New Eng. Book Show, Boston, 1992, Pupil's Edit. and Theme Posters, Boston, 1992, bronze award Dimensional Illustrators Awards Show, N.Y.C., 1992, 1st place award Ednl. Sch. Divsn. N.Y. Book Show, N.Y.C., 1994. Republican. Avocations: painting, reading, skiing, investing. Home: 1150 Kings Crown Rd Woodland Park CO 80863-7731

COCKROFT, JEANNETTE WIMMER, historian educator; b. Bad-Hersfeld, Germany, Mar. 17, 1957; d. Charles Samuel and Elaine D. (Bouchard) Wimmer; m. Ronald D. Cockroft, Nov. 26, 1986. Student, U. Maine, Orono, 1975-78; BA in East Asian Langs. & Cultures, U. Pa., 1980; MA in Polit. Sci., U. Kans., 1989; PhD, Tex. A&M U. Adminstrv. asst. Christian Assn., U. Pa., 1978-80; tutor Supportive Ednl. Svcs., U. Kans., 1981; part-time faculty Blinn Coll., Bryan, Tex., 1992-96; grad. tchg. asst. dept. history Tex. A&M U., College Station, 1995-98. *From March 1986 to March 1987, Jeannette was with VISTA as Food Solicitation Coordinator at Capitol Area Food Bank, Austin, Texas. She designed a program to facilitate public solicitation of surplus food and to provide public education on hunger issues. She then went on to teach U.S. government and Texas government at Blinn College and to teach East Asian and American History while pursuing a Ph.D. in history at Texas A&M University. Her dissertation research deals with the political career development of former U.S. Senator Margaret Chase Smith, Republican from Maine.* Vol. VISTA Capitol Area Food Bank, Austin, Tex., 1986-87; nursing home visitor, Bryan, Tex., 1991—. Mem. Phi Kappa Phi, Phi Alpha Theta, Pi Sigma Alpha, Alpha Lambda Delta. Avocations: knitting, reading, collecting books. Office: Tex A&M U Dept History College Station TX 77840

COCKRUM, BOB, city official; b. Jeffersonville, Ind., Sept. 8, 1933; m. Mary Louise; children: Michael Alan, Karen Sue, Barry Lee, Robert. BSEE, Purdue U., 1955. Airport lighting engr. FAA, 1957-59; engring. project adminstr. Hazeltine Elec. Corp., 1959-64; from program adminstr. to supervisor Allison Gas Turbine, 1964-81; from chief program adminstr. to adminstr. Allison Transmission, 1981-91; city coun. Indpls., 1996—. Pres. Decatur Sch. Bd., 1970-78; mem. Marion County Tax Adjustment Bd., 1984-86, chair, 1985-86; v.p. Decatur Civic Coun., 1987-88, 89-92, pres., 1988-89, 92-94; pres. Decatur Rep. Club, 1985-86. Served in Army Signal Corps, 1955-57. Recipient outstanding neighborhood leader award City of Indpls., 1994. *

COCKRUM, WILLIAM MONROE, III, investment banker, consultant, educator; b. Indpls., July 18, 1937; s. William Monroe C. II and Katherine J. (Jaqua) Moore; m. Andrea Lee Deering, Mar. 8, 1975; children: Catherine Anne, William Monroe IV. AB with distinction, DePauw U., 1959; MBA with distinction, Harvard U., 1961. With A.G. Becker Paribas Inc., L.A., 1961-84, mgr. nat. corp. fin. div., 1968-71, mgr. pvt. investments, 1971-74, fin. and adminstrv. officer, 1974-80, sr. v.p., 1975-78, vice chmn., 1978-84, also bd. dirs.; prin. William M. Cockrum & Assocs., L.A., 1984—; mem. faculty Northwestern U., 1961-63; vis. lectr. grad. sch. mgmt. UCLA, 1984-88, adj. prof., 1988—. Mem. Monterey Club (Palm Desert, Calif.), Deke Club (N.Y.C.), UCLA Faculty Club, Alisal Golf Club (Solvang, Calif.), Bel-Air Country Club (L.A.), Delta Kappa Epsilon.

COCKS, FRANKLIN HADLEY, materials scientist; b. S.I., N.Y., Oct. 1, 1941; s. Charles Franklin and Ruth (Hadley) C.; m. Pamela Kay Pfaff, Aug. 6, 1966; children—Elijah Eugene, Josiah Charles. B.S., MIT, 1963, M.S., 1964, Sc.D., 1965; postgrad. (Fulbright fellow), Imperial Coll. Sci. and Tech., London, 1965-66. Registered patent agt. Staff scientist Tyco Labs., Waltham, Mass., 1966-67; sr. scientist Tyco Labs., 1967-70, asst. head materials sci. dept., 1970-72; assoc. prof. Duke U., Durham, N.C., 1972-76; prof. dept. mech. engring. and materials sci. Duke U., 1976—, chmn. dept. mech. engring. and materials sci., 1994—, dir. M of Engring. mgmt. program, 1997—; cons. Los Alamos Sci. Lab., 1979—. Author: (with M.L. Shepard, J.B. Chaddock, C.M. Harman) Introduction to Energy Technology, 1976, Manual of Industrial Corrosion Standards and Control; Editor ASTM spl. tech. publ., 1973. NSF fellow, 1964-65; recipient NASA award, 1974. Mem. Nat. Assn. Corrosion Engrs., AIME, Instn. Metallurgists (Brit.), Sigma Xi, Tau Beta Pi. Club: London House (life). Patentee in field. Office: Duke U Dept Mech Engring & Materials Sci Durham NC 27708-0300

COCKS, GEORGE GOSSON, retired chemical microscopy educator; b. Sioux City, Iowa, Mar. 22, 1919; s. George Green and Nellie Patricia (Gosson) C.; m. Marian L. Singer, May 11, 1942; children: Gary, Kathleen (Mrs. Thomas Sadlowski), Francis, Kenneth. B.S. in Chemistry, Iowa State U., 1941; Ph.D. in Chem. Microscopy, Cornell, 1949. Researcher Battelle Meml. Inst., Columbus, Ohio, 1949-64; prof. chem. microscopy Cornell U., 1964-81, prof. emeritus, 1981—; cons. Los Alamos (N.Mex.) Nat. Lab., 1980-81, staff mem., 1981-90; ret., 1990. Scoutmaster Central Ohio council Boy Scouts Am., 1956-64. Served to lt. comdr. USNR, 1942-45. NSF grantee to study crystallization inorganic materials in polymers, 1966-68, to study biomed. uses collagen, 1972—, DOE grantee in hot dry rock geothermal energy project, 1981-90. Fellow AAAS (coun. 1970-75); mem. Am. Optical Soc., Am. Chem. Soc., Microscopy Soc. Am. (exec. sec. 1964-76), Sigma Xi, Phi Kappa Phi. Patentee in field. Home: 1719 Hyland St Bayside CA 95524-9302

COCKSHUTT, E(RIC) PHILIP, engineering executive, research scientist, energy consultant; b. Brantford, Ont., Can., May 30, 1929; s. Eric Morton and Kathleen Isobel (Buck) C.; m. Julia Ann Fink, Sept. 11, 1954; children: Martha Jane, Catherine Margaret, Eric William, Amanda Mary, Paul Edmund. BASc in Mech. Engring, U. Toronto, 1950; MS, MIT, 1951, ScD, 1954. Research officer Engine Lab., NRC, Ottawa, Ont., 1953-67; sect. head Engine Lab., NRC, 1967-75, dir. energy research, 1975-86, exec. dir. engring. programs, 1986-90; exec. dir. Energy Coun. Can., 1991-97; prin. E.P. Cockshutt & Assocs., Ottawa, 1991—; sessional lectr. Carleton U., Ottawa, 1959-73. Mem. Engring. Alumni Hall of Distinction, U. Toronto; Ethyl Corp. fellow, 1952-54. Fellow Can. Aero. and Space Inst. (Casey Baldwin award 1960, 64), Engring. Inst. can., Can. Soc. Mech. Engring., Can. Acad. of Engring. Anglican. Home: 120 Dorothea Dr, Ottawa, ON Canada K1V 7C7

COCKWELL, JACK LYNN, financial executive; b. East London, South Africa, Jan. 12, 1941; s. William Henry and Daphne (Cound) C.; children: Linda, Lorie, Leslie, Tessa, Malcolm, Gareth. M.Com., U. Cape Town, 1964, postgrad. with distinction, 1966. Chartered Acct. Mgr. Touche Ross & Co., Montreal, Que., Can., 1959-67; exec. v.p., chief oper. officer Edper Enterprises Ltd., Toronto, Ont., Can., 1968-90; exec. v.p., chief oper. officer Brascan Ltd., Toronto, 1979-91, pres. and CEO, 1991-97, also bd. dirs.; pres., CEO EdperBrascan Corp., Toronto, 1997—, also bd. dirs.; bd. dirs. CBOC Continental Inc., Brascade Resources Inc., Falconbridge Inc., Noranda Inc., Nexfor Inc., Trilon Fin. Corp., Can. Hunter Exploration Ltd., Great Lakes Power, Inc., Brookfield Properties, Inc., World Fin. Properties Inc., Astral Comm. Inc. Bd. govs. Ryerson Poly. U., Royal Ont. Mus. Found.; bd. dirs. C.D. Howe Inst. Office: EdperBrascan Corp Ste 4400, 181 Bay St PO Box 762, Toronto, ON Canada M5J 2T3

COCO, SAMUEL BARBIN, venture consultant; b. Cottonport, La., Nov. 6, 1927; s. Samuel Barbin and Hattie (Smith) C.; m. Hannalou John, June 25, 1957; children: Harvey Samuel, Caroline Shannon. B.S. in Mech. Engring., La. State U., 1950; postgrad., MIT, 1964. Plant engr. Cabot Corp., Ville Platte, La., 1950-52; with mfg. dept. Cabot Corp., Pampa, Tex., 1952-56; sales rep. Cabot Corp., Akron, Ohio, 1956-60; exec. asst. Cabot Corp., Boston, 1960-64, asst. gen. mgr. carbon black div., 1964-70, v.p., gen. mgr. carbon black div., 1970-77, sr. v.p., 1977-85, exec. v.p., 1985-89, pres., 1989-91, also bd. dirs., 1992; pres. Barbin Corp., Wellesley Hills, Mass., 1992—; bd. dirs. Thermal Conversion Tech., Sarasota, Fla. Vis. com. Spaulding Rehab. Hosp.; active Mass. Gen. Hosp. Corp., Boston; overseer Newton-Wellesley Hosp.; chmn. Wellesley (Mass.) Cmty. Ctr. Avocations: golf, running, cooking. Office: Barbin Corp 30 Sawyer Rd Wellesley Hills MA 02481-2936

COCOLIS, PETER KONSTANTINE, business development executive; b. Stamford, Conn., Sept. 22, 1942; s. Gus and Agnes (Vender) C.; m. Lorraine Patricia Marut, July 2, 1966; children: Peter Konstantine Jr., William Jonathan. BS in Engring., Boston U., 1964; MBA, Auburn U., 1976; cert., Def. Sys. Mgmt. Coll., 1973; cert. in nat. and internat. security mgmt., Harvard U., 1996. Commd. 2nd lt. USAF, 1964, advanced through grades to lt. col., 1980, ret., 1984; mktg. mgr. N.Am. Aircraft Rockwell Internat., Washington, 1984-87, dir. mktg. and govt. affairs, 1987-89; dir. bus. devel. and govt. affairs Rocketdyne divsn. Rockwell Internat., Washington, 1989-95; sr. dir. bus. and govt. affairs N.Am. Aircraft divsn. Rockwell Internat., Washignton, 1995-96; sr. dir. bus. and govt. affairs The Boeing Co., Washington, 1996—. Contbr. articles to profl. jours. Bd. dirs. Lakeforest Home Owners Assn., Springfield, Va., 1985-88; v.p. Morwood Estates Home Owners Assn.; swimming ofcl. U.S. Swimming Orgn., No. Va., 1981-91. Decorated DFC, Air medals. Mem. AIAA (sr., coun. mem., com. chmn., bd. dirs.), Am. Mgmt. Assn., Nat. Space Club, Air Force Assn., Navy League, Emeritus Found. (bd. dirs., com. chmn.), Clifton Lions. Avocations: racquetball sailing, reading, swimming. Office: The Boeing Co 1200 Wilson Blvd Arlington VA 22209-2305

CODD, RICHARD TRENT, JR., computer scientist, educator; b. Norfolk, Va., June 1, 1945; s. Richard Trent and Mildred Joyce C.; m. Celine Marie Morisset, Aug. 10, 1968; children: Richard Trent, III, Patrick Timothy, Matthew Paul, Kevin Andrew. A.A., Miami-Dade Community Coll., 1967; B.S., U. Miami, 1970, M.A., 1974; B.S., Fla. Internat. U., 1985. Lic. tchr., ednl. adminstr. Fla. Audio technician U. Miami, Coral Gables, Fla., 1968-71; tchr. Archbishop Curley High Sch., Miami, Fla., 1972-74; tchr. St. Brendan High Sch., Miami, 1974-80, adminstr., 1980-87, asst. prin., 1981-87, dir. computer services, 1981-87; instr. St. Thomas U., Opa Locka, Fla., 1980-87, St. John Vianney Coll. Sem., Miami, 1985-87, A.C. Reynolds High Sch., Asheville, 1988-90, U. N.C., Asheville, 1988—, Advanced Edn. Ctr., Asheville, 1990-92; math. instr., computer applications programmer Haywood C.C., Clyde, N.C., 1991—; bus. ptnr. Raintree House, 1992—; software systems developer Archdiocese of Miami, 1984-87; bd. dirs. Archdiocese of Miami Credit Union, 1979-80. Developer Master Acad. Record/Scheduling ADP System, Univ./C.C. Class Scheduling ADP System. Mem. Math. Assn. Am. Republican. Roman Catholic. Avocations: music, hiking, boating. Office: Haywood CC 185 Freedlander Dr Clyde NC 28721-9441

CODDING, FREDERICK HAYDEN, lawyer; b. Hopewell, Va., Dec. 13, 1938; s. Francis Chadwick and Ruthcille Sharon (Craven) C.; m. Judith Willis Hawkins, Apr. 30, 1966; children: Forrest Hayden, Judith Chadwick, Cally Willis, Clare Catharine. A.B., Coll. William and Mary, 1962; J.D., Georgetown U., 1966. Bar: Va. 1966, D.C. 1968, U.S. Supreme Ct. 1979. Legal asst. VA, Washington, 1963-65; Capitol Hill reporter, editor Congressional Monitor, Washington, 1966; law clk. to chief judge D.C. Ct. Appeals, 1966-68; individual practice law Va. and Washington; v.p., counsel Nat. Assn. Miscellaneous, Ornamental and Archtl. Products Contractors, Fairfax, Va., 1970—; counsel, dir. Nat. Assn. Reinforcing Steel Contractors, Fairfax, 1970—. Editor pub. legis., adminstrv., bldg. and constrn. industry newsletters, reports. Mem. federally established rev. bds. for constrn., OSHA and industry; counsel, pres. Fairfax Police Youth Club; appointee Fairfax City Sch. Bd., 1983-88. Mem. ABA, D.C. Bar Assn., Va. Bar Assn., Fairfax Bar Assn., Nat. Council Erectors, Fabricators and Riggers, Sigma Nu. Office: 10382 Main St Fairfax VA 22030-2412

CODDING, MITCHELL A., cultural organization administrator; b. Bartlesville, Okla., Sept. 20, 1954; m. Amparo Gonzalez, Aug. 10, 1983. BA in Spanish, U. Okla., 1954; PhD in Spanish, U. Ky., 1998. Vis. asst. prof. U. Calif., Riverside, 1983-84; asst. dir. The Hispanic Soc. Am., N.Y.C., 1984-95, dir., 1995—; lectr. in field. Co-author: Maps, Charts, Globes: Five Centruies of Exploration, 1992, Defining the Americas: Accounts and Images of Latin America fromthe European Encounter through Independence, 1997; co-editor: Coastal Charts of the Americas and West Africa from the School of Luis Teixeira, circa 1585, 1993, Facsimiles from an Illuminated Hebrew Bible of the Fifteenth Century at The Hispanic Society of America, 1993. Edward Larocque Tinker fellow The Hispanic Soc. Am., 1982, John Carter Brown Libr. fellow Brown U., 1982. Office: Hispanic Soc Am 613 W 155th St New York NY 10032-7501*

CODE, ARTHUR DODD, astrophysics educator; b. Bklyn., Aug. 13, 1923; 4 children. MS, U. Chgo., 1947, PhD, 1950. Asst. Yerkes Obs. U. Chgo., 1946-49; instr. U. Va., Charlottesville, 1950; instr. then asst. prof. astronomy U. Wis., Madison, 1951-56, prof., 1969-92, prof. emeritus, 1992—; mem. staff Mt. Wilson and Palomar Obs. Calif. Inst. Tech., Pasadena, 1956-58, prof., 1958-69; adj. prof. U. Ariz., Tucson, 1992—; Hilldale prof., dir. Space Astronomy Lab. U. Wis. Recipient Disting. Pub. Svc. medal and Pub. Svc. award NASA, Profl. Achievement award U. Chgo. Mem. NAS, Am. Acad. Arts and Scis., Internat. Acad. Astronautics, Assn. of Univs. for Rsch. in Astronomy (chmn. bd. dirs. 1977-80.), Am. Astonomical Soc. (pres. 1982-84). Home: U Wis Washburn Obs 250 N Arcadia Ave Tucson AZ 85711*

CODELL, JULIE FRANCIA, university administrator; b. Chgo., Sept. 19, 1945; d. Seymour and Rosalie Codell; 1 child, Ethan Granger. AB in English, Vassar Coll., 1967; MA in English, U. Mich., 1968; MA in Art History, Ind. U., 1975, PhD in Comparative Lit., 1978. Instr. English Western Ill. U., Macomb, 1968-71; prof., dept. chair art dept. U. Mont., Missoula, 1979-90; dir. sch. of art Ariz. State U., Tempe, 1991—. Co-editor, author: Orientalism Transposed, 1998; author: (with others) Reframing Pre-Raphaelites, 1995, Collecting Pre-Raphaelites, 1997; editl. bd. Victorian Periodicals Rev., 1992—; contbr. articles to profl. publs. Fellowship Nat. Endowment for Humanities, 1992-93, travel grant, 1986, 90; fellowship Yale U., 1994; recipient summer stipend NEH, 1988. Mem. Coll. Art Assn., Historians of British Air (exec. bd. 1993-97), Rsch. Soc. for Victorian Periodicals (v.p. 1997—), Assn. for Art Historians. Office: Sch of Art Ariz State U Tempe AZ 85287-1505

CODERE, HELEN FRANCES, anthropologist, educator, university dean; b. Winnipeg, Man., Can., Sept. 10, 1917; came to U.S., 1919, naturalized, 1924; d. Charles Francis and Mabelle (Prosser) C. B.A. summa cum laude, U. Minn., 1939; Ph.D., Columbia, 1950. Instr. Vassar Coll, 1946-50, asst. prof., 1951-53, asso. prof., 1955-57, prof., 1958-63; vis. lectr. anthropology U. B.C., 1954-55, Northwestern U., winter 1963; mem. faculty Bennington Coll., 1963-64; prof. anthropology Brandeis U., 1964-82; dean Brandeis U. (Grad. Sch. Arts and Scis.), 1975-77, retired, 1982; anthrop. fieldwork Kwakiutl Indians of, B.C., 1951-55, Rwanda, Africa, 1959-60; Mem. adv. panel on anthropology Nat. Sci. Found., 1968-71. Author: Fighting with Property: A Study of Kwakiutl Potlatching and Warfare, 1792-1930, 1950, The Biography of an African Society, Rwanda 1900-1960; also articles.; Editor: Kawkiutl Ethnography (Franz Boas), 1966. Faculty fellow Vassar Coll., 1956; Social Sci. Research Council fellow, 1956, 62-63; Guggenheim fellow, 1959-60. Fellow Am. Anthrop. Assn. (exec. council 1966-69), AAAS; mem. Am. Ethnol. Soc. (pres. 1972-73), Northeastern Anthrop. Assn. (pres. 1970-71), Phi Beta Kappa. Home: 22 Concord Greene Apt 5 Concord MA 01742-3138

CODESPOTI, DANIEL JOSEPH, computer science educator; b. Charleston, S.C., Jan. 18, 1941; s. Peter J. Sr. and Eula Lee (Pellum) C.; m. Sandra Lynn Huey, Mar. 16, 1963; 1 child, Daniel J. Jr. BA, Auburn U., 1964; MS, U. Mo., Rolla, 1974; PhD, Kans. State U., 1977. Computer programmer Auburn (Ala.) U., 1964-66; computer programmer, instr. S.E. Mo. State U., Cape Girardeau, 1969-73; grad. tchg. asst. Kans. State U., Manhattan, 1974-77; asst. prof. U. S.C., Columbia, 1977-79; asst. prof. U. S.C., Spartanburg, 1980-82, assoc. prof., 1982-90, prof. computer sci., 1990—; propr. So. Computer Svcs., Mayo, S.C., 1981—. Pres. Spartanburg PC Users Group, 1989-90; v.p. chpt. S.C. State Employees, Spartanburg, 1993-94, pres., 1994-95, 98—. Lt. USNR, 1966-69. Mem. IEEE, Assn. Computing Machinery, S.C. Acad. Sci. Avocation: fishing. Office: U SC Spartanburg 800 University Way Spartanburg SC 29303-4999

CODISPOTI, ANDRE JOHN, allergist, immunologist; b. Bklyn., Apr. 27, 1938; s. Bruno Mario and Antoinette (Savarese) C.; m. Miranda Babini, June 14, 1967; children: Rita, Elisa, Andrew. BA, Coll. of Holy Cross, 1959; MD, U. Bologna, Italy, 1965. Diplomate Am. Bd. Pediatrics, Am. Bd. Allergy and Immunology. Rotating intern Long Island Coll. Hosp., Bklyn., 1966, resident in pediatrics, 1967-69, fellow in allergy and immunology, 1971-73; pvt. practice Suffern, N.Y., 1972—. Maj. M.C., U.S. Army, 1969-71. Fellow Am. Coll. Allergy, Asthma and Immunology, Am. Acad. Allergy, Asthma and Immunology. Republican. Roman Catholic. Avocations: reading, music, travel, tennis, skiing. Office: 7 Hemion Rd Suffern NY 10901-4903 also: 70 Gilbert St Monroe NY 10950-1538

CODON, DENNIS P., lawyer. V.p., gen. counsel, corp. sec. Unocal Corp., L.A. Office: Unocal Corp 2141 Rosecrans Ave Ste 4000 El Segundo CA 90245*

CODONI, FREDERICK PETER, editor; b. San Rafael, Calif., Dec. 22, 1934; s. Frederick Q. and Ruth A. (Steinkellner) C.; m. Sheila Ann Kane, Feb. 4, 1961 (div. Aug. 1986); m. Denyce Vogler, July 7, 1989; children: Frederick Jr., James, Michael, Charles. BA, U. San Francisco, 1956. Mgr. loading svcs. So. Pacific R.R., San Francisco, 1963-88; editor The Native Son, The Headlight, The Northwesterner; cons. transp., Fairfax, Calif., 1988—. Sgt. U.S. Army, 1958-60, Korea. Mem. Native Sons of Golden West (grand pres. 1994-95), Northwestern Pacific R.R. Hist. Soc. (editor 1986—), Fairfax Hist. Soc., Marin County Hist. Soc., Bay Area Electric R.R. Assn. Republican. Roman Catholic. Avocations: history, railroads, big bands. Home and Office: 162 Porteous Ave Fairfax CA 94930-2036

CODRON, MICHAEL VICTOR, theatrical producer; b. June 8, 1930; s. I.A. and Lily (Morganstern) C. Ed., St. Paul's Sch.; BA, Worcester Coll., Oxford U. Dir. Hampstead Theatre; adminstr. Aldwych Theatre; Cameron Mackintosh prof. contemporary theatre Oxford U., Eng., 1993. Prodns. include: Breath of Spring, 1957; The Birthday Party, 1958; Pieces of Eight, 1959; The Caretaker, 1960; The Tenth Man, 1961; Rattle of a Simple Man, 1962; Next Time I'll Sing to You, Private Lives, The Lovers and the Dwarfs, Cockade, 1963; Poor Bitos, The Formation Dancers, Entertaining Mr. Sloane, 1964; Loot, The Killing of Sister George, Ride a Cock Horse, 1965; Little Malcolm and His Struggle Against the Eunuchs, The Anniversary, There's a Girl in My Soup, Big Bad Mouse, 1966; The Judge, The Flip Side, Wise Child, The Boy Friend, 1967; Not Now Darling, The Real Inspector Hound, 1968; The Contractor, Slag, The Two of Us, The Philanthropist, 1970; The Foursome, Butley, A Voyage Round My Father, The Changing Room, 1971; Veterans, Time and Time Again, Crown Matrimonial, My Fat Friend, 1972; Collaborators, Savages, Habeas Corpus, Absurd Person Singular, 1973; Knuckle, Flowers, Golden Pathway Annual, The Norman Conquests, John Paul George Ringo...and Bert, 1974; A Family and a Fortune, Alphabetical Order, A Far Better Husband, Ashes, Absent Friends, Otherwise Engaged, Stripwell, 1975; Funny Peculiar, Treats, Donkey's Years, Confusions, Teeth 'n' Smiles, Yahoo, 1976; Dusa Stas, Fish & Vi, Just Between Ourselves, Oh, Mr. Porter, Breezeblock Park, The Bells of Hell, The Old Country, 1977; The Rear Column, Ten Times Table, The Unvarnished Truth, The Homecoming, Alice's Boys, Night and Day, 1978; Joking Apart, Tishoo, Stage Struck, 1979; Dr. Faustus, Make and Break, The Dresser, Taking Steps, Enjoy, 1980; Hinge & Bracket, Rowan Atkinson in Revue, House Guest, Quartermaine's Terms, 1981; Season's Greetings, Noises Off, Funny Turns, 1982, The Real Thing, 1982; The Hard Shoulder, 1983; Look, No Hans!, Benefactors, 1984; Jumpers, Who Plays Wins, Clockwise (film), 1985, Made in Bangkok, 1986, Woman in Mind, 1986; Hapgood, Uncle Vanya, Re Joyce!, The Sneeze, Henceforward, 1988; The Cherry Orchard, 1989; Man of the Moment, Look, Look, Hidden Laughter, Private Lives, 1990, What the Butler Saw, 70 Girls 70, The Revengers Comedies, 1991, The Rise and Fall of Little Voice, 1992, Time of My Life, 1993, Jamais Vu, 1993, Dead Funny, 1994, Arcadia, 1994, The Sisters Rosensweig, 1994, Indian Ink, 1995, The Killing of Sister George, 1995, Dealer's Choice, 1995, The Shakespeare Revue, 1995, A Talent to Amuse, 1996, Tom and Clem, 1997, Silhouette Heritage, 1997, Things We Do For Love, 1998, Elton John's Glasses, 1998, Alarms and Excursions, 1998, The Invention of Love, 1998, Copenhagen, 1999, Quartet, 1999. Recipient Michael Victor Codron CBE. Mem. Garrick Club. Office: Aldwych Theatre, Aldwych, London WC2B 4DF, England

CODY, AELRED JOSEPH, editor, priest; b. Oklahoma City, Feb. 3, 1932; s. Joseph Francis Cody and Frances Margaret Tucker. BA, St. Meinrad Coll., 1956; Sacrae Theologiae Licentiatus, U. Ottawa, Ont., Can., 1958, Sacrae Theologiae Doctor summa cum laude, 1960; Sacrae Scripturae Licentiatus, Pontifical Bibl. Inst./Commn., Rome, 1962, Sacrae Scripturae Doctor summa cum laude, 1968; diploma, French Bib. and Archaeol. Sch., Jerusalem. Ordained priest, 1957; professed Benedictine, 1952. Prof. Old Testament and ancient Near East studies S. Anselmo, Pontifical Biblical Inst., Rome, 1968-78; organist Abbazia di S. Anselmo, Rome, 1968-76; procurator gen. in Roman Curia Am.-Cassinese & Swiss-Am. Benedictine Congregations, Rome, 1975-78; master of novices and juniors St. Meinrad (Ind.) Archabbey, 1978-92; mem. pres.'s coun. Swiss-Am. Benedictine Cong., 1981-96, mem. legal com., 1984—, chmn. legal com., 1990—; assoc. editor Cath. Bib. Quar., Washington, 1987-92; gen. editor Cath. Bib. Quar., St. Meinrad, 1993—; mem. ofcl. Oriental Orthodox-Roman Catholic Consultation in U.S., Nat. Conf. of Cath. Bishops and Standing Conf. of Oriental Orthodox Bishops, 1981—; consultor for Holy See, Mixed Commn. Roman Cath. Ch. and World Alliance Ref. Chs., 1970. Author: Heavenly Sanctuary and Liturgy in the Epistle to the Hebrews, 1960 (prize of Christian Rsch. Found. Harvard U. 1960), A History of Old Testament Priesthood, 1969, Ezekiel, 1984; contbr. to profl. jours. and encycs.; mem. editl. bd. Biblica, Rome, 1968-73; mem. editl. com., consultative com. Concilium, Nijmegen, 1969-91. Mem. Royal Coll. Music (assoc., London), Royal Coll. Organists (assoc., London), Internat. Orgn. for Study of Old Testament, Internat. Assn. for Coptic Studies, Am. Oriental Soc., Soc. Bib. Lit., Cath. Bib. Assn. Am. (life, trustee 1984-87, exec. bd. 1993—). Avocations: reading, hiking, Renaissance and baroque keyboard music. Home: St Meinrad Archabbey Saint Meinrad IN 47577 Office: The Cath Bib Quar St Meinrad Archabbey Saint Meinrad IN 47577

CODY, ALDUS MORRILL, journalist, retired editor, typographer; b. Somerville, Mass., Jan. 11, 1915; s. Luther Morrill and Josephine Belle (Morrill) C.; m. Dorothy Gifford, Dec. 25, 1936; 1 child, Raymond Gifford. BA in Journalism, U. Fla., 1936. Editor Suwannee Dem., Live Oak, Fla., 1936-37, Williamson County News, Franklin, Tenn., 1937, Marion County News, Ocala, Fla., 1938-39; Kissimmee (Fla.) Gazette, 1939-41, Share Your Knowledge Rev. (later Rev. Graphic Arts), Cin., 1970-80, The High Twelvan, St. Louis, 1989-95; mng. editor Ocala Morning Banner, 1937-38; editor, pub. The Fla. Cattleman, Kissimmee, 1940-45; founder, CEO, Cody Publs., Kissimmee, 1946-77; editor News of Masonic Cmty., Kissimmee, 1989-96; ret., 1996. Author: (with Robert Cody) Osceola County—First 100 Years, 1996. Former commr. and mayor City of Kissimmee. Mem. Internat. Assn. Printing House Craftsmen (dist. gov. 1968-70, nat. editor 1970-80), Fla. Assn. Square Dancers (founder, pres.), Masons (past master), Shriners, Rotary (past pres. Kissimmee). Democrat. Methodist. Avocation: genealogy. Fax: 407-870-8266. E-mail: aldus-cody@kua.net. Address: 3610 North Gate Dr Apt T-2 Kissimmee FL 34746

CODY, FRANK JOSEPH, secondary school administrator, education educator; b. Detroit, Sept. 13, 1940; s. Burns J. and Margaret (Dowley) C.; m. Shirley Black, May 16, 1992. AB, Loyola U., 1962, MA, 1966, MDiv, 1975; PhD, Ohio State U., 1980. Cert. tchr., prin., supr., Ohio, Mich. Headmaster St. Ignatius H.S., Cleve., 1977-81; dir. Chapel Sch., Sao Paulo, Brazil, 1981-83, U. Detroit Ctr. Econ. Edn., 1988-91; assoc. prof., tchr. adminstrv. edn. U. Detroit, 1983-91; adminstr. Grand Rapids Cath. Secondary Schs., 1991-95; headmaster Woodside Priory Sch., Portola Valley, Calif., 1995-97; tchr. Kalamazoo Ctrl. H.S., 1997, asst. prin., 1998—; trustee Wheeling Coll., 1980-82, mem. Coun. Entrance Svcs. Coll. Bd., 1978-81; mem. Mich. Supt.'s Com. on Accreditation, 1984-88; commr. Nat. Assn. Secondary Sch. Prins./Carnegie Found. Commn. on Future of Am. H.S., 1994-96. Co-author: Manual of Educational Risk Management, Escola e Communidade: Uma Parceria Necessaria; contbr. articles to profl. jours. Trustee Trinity Sch., Menlo Park, Calif., 1996-97. Mem. ASCD (assoc.), ACSA (bd. dirs. Region V 1995-97), Nat. Assn. Secondary Sch. Prins. (nonpub. schs. com. 1993-96),

Am. Ednl. Rsch. Assn., Nat. Cath. Edn. Assn. (regional assoc. 1991-97). Roman Catholic. Office: Kalamazoo Ctrl High Sch 2432 N Drake Rd Kalamazoo MI 49006-1361

CODY, HIRAM SEDGWICK, JR., retired telephone company executive; b. Evanston, Ill., Nov. 1, 1915; s. Hiram Sedgwick and Harriett Mary (Collins) C.; m. Mary Vaughn Jacoby, Oct. 4, 1941; children: Margaret Vaughn, Harriett Mary, Hiram Sedgwick III, Henry Jacoby, William Collins. BS cum laude, Yale U., 1937, LLB, 1940. Bar: N.C., 1940. With Western Electric Co., Inc., 1946-71, regional mgr. engring. and installation, Chgo., 1961-64, dir. orgn. planning, N.Y.C., 1964-65, sec., treas., 1965-71; asst. treas. AT&T, N.Y.C., 1971-80. Vice pres. Morris-Sussex council Boy Scouts Am., 1970-80; vice chmn. Zoning Bd. Adjustment Mountain Lakes, 1968-80; boro councilman, Mountain Lakes, N.J., 1960-61; trustee, treas. Asheville (N.C.) Sch., 1974-84; trustee Asheville Symphony Orch., 1981-91, Asheville Community Concert Assn., 1981-91; bd. advisors Warren Wilson Coll., 1983—, chmn. 1987-90. Served USN, 1941-45, MTO, comdr. USNR 1946. N.C. State Bar, Tel. Pioneers Am. (v.p. 1969-71, treas. 1971-78), Tau Beta Pi. Home: 64 Wagon Trl Black Mountain NC 28711-2563

CODY, JAMES PATRICK, writing educator; b. Bklyn., Sept. 25, 1960; s. Daniel G. and Eileen A. (Blackburn) C.; m. Anne M. Crane, Dec. 7, 1985; children: Melissa, Thomas, Emily. BA, Boston Coll., 1983; MA, Montclair State U., 1995. Cert. tchr. English, N.J. Tchr. English Paterson (N.J.) Cath. H.S., 1995, Columbia H.S., Maplewood, N.J., 1996-97; writing instr. Brookdale C.C., Lincroft, N.J., 1997—; cons. Martin Kane Assn., Inc., Dover, N.J., 1993-96. Contbr. articles to profl. jours. Mem. Nat. Coun. Tchrs. of English, N.J. Edn. Assn. Avocations: writing, reading, literary criticism. Home: 275 S Washington Ave Dunellen NJ 08812-1644 Office: Brookdale C C 765 Newman Springs Rd Lincroft NJ 07738-1543

CODY, PETER MALCOLM, economics, development, management consultant; b. Paris, France, July 30, 1925; s. Edward Morrill C. and Frances (Ryan) Millington; m. Rosa Maria Alatorre, Jan. 28, 1957; children: Cornelia Francisca, Cecilia Leonor, Michael Peter, William Ryan, Peter Malcolm. BA in Internat. Rels., Yale U., 1947, MA in Econs., 1948, postgrad., 1949. Instr. econs. Yale U., 1948-50; economist Fed. Res. Bd., Washington, 1950-54; economist U.S. Agy. Internat. Devel., Mex., El Salvador, 1954-80, program officer, 1954-59; Laos affairs officer U.S. Agy. Internat. Devel., 1959-61; dep. mission dir. U.S. Agy. Internat. Devel., Cambodia, 1961-64; dir. office Vietnam affairs U.S. Agy. Internat. Devel., 1964-65; dep. mission dir. U.S. Agy. Internat. Devel., Laos, 1965-67; mission dir. U.S. Agy. Internat. Devel., Paraguay, Ecuador, The Philippines, Lebanon, 1967-80; economic and soc. devel. and mgmt. cons. D.C., Haiti, Mauritania, Zaire, Sudan, Kenya, Guatamala, ElSalvador, 1981—. Mem. sch. bd. Am. Sch. Laos, Vientiane, Laos, 1965-67, Am. Sch. Paraguay, Asunción, Paraguay, 1967-71, Paraguay Nat. Cultural Ctr., Asunción, 1964-71. Recipient Orden Nacional del Merito Pres. of Paraguay, 1971, Meritorious Svc. award US AID, 1981. Mem. Am. Econ. Assn., 1947-85, Am. Fgn. Svc. Assn., 1960—, Cosmos Club, Washington, 1994—. Avocations: computers, reading, tennis, skiing, hiking. Home: 5600 Wisconsin Ave Apt 609 Chevy Chase MD 20815-4410

CODY, RICHARD A., army officer; b. Montpelier, Vt., Aug. 20, 1950; m. Vicki Lyn Cody; children: Clint, Tyler. BS, U.S. Mil. Acad., 1972. Master army aviator. Commd. 2d lt. U.S. Army, 1972, advanced through grades to brig. gen.; comdr. 1st bn., 101st aviation regt. 101stAairborne Divsn., Operation Desert Storm; bn. exec. officer, co. comdr. Attack Helicopter Bns.; asst. divsn. comdr. for maneuver 4th Inf. Divsn. (Mechanized), 1998—. Decorated Legion of Merit with 2 oak leaf clusters, DFC, Bronze Star medal, Air medals, others. Office: 4th Infantry Divsn Mechanized Fort Hood TX 76544-5200

CODY, THOMAS GERALD, management consultant, writer; b. Holyoke, Mass., Feb. 18, 1929; s. John Francis and Mary Gertrude (Scanlon) C.; m. Kathleen Mary Maguire, Nov. 17, 1956; children—Kathleen, Joseph. AB, Coll. of Holy Cross, 1950; postgrad., Boston Coll., 1950-52; MBA, Harvard U., 1957. Various corporate mgmt. positions, 1955-62; cons., prin., v.p. Fry Cons., Inc., Chgo., L.A., Washington, 1962-72; exec. dir. U.S. Equal Employment Opportunity Commn., Washington, 1972-74; asst. sec. for adminstrn. HUD, Washington, 1974-76; v.p., Washington mgr. L.B. Knight & Assos., Inc., 1976-79; pres. Lester B. Knight Mgmt. Cons. Group, 1979-81, Thomas Cody & Assocs., Annapolis, Md. and Washington, 1981-84; v.p. human resources Baxter Travenol Labs. Inc., Deerfield, Ill., 1984-86, corp. v.p., 1985-87; exec. v.p., Chgo. office Jannotta Bray & Assoc. Inc., 1987—, ptnr. Washington office, 1989-96; ptnr. The Washington Group, 1996—. Author: Management Consulting: A Game Without Chips, 1986, Strategy of a Megamerger, 1990, Innovating For Health, 1994. Mem. U.S. Archtl. and Transp. Barriers Compliance Bd., 1974-76, Anne Arundel Commn. on Women, 1977-79, U.S. Comptr. Gens. Cons. Adv. Panel, 1983-88; bd. dirs. Found. for Jr. Blind, L.A., 1968-70, Baxter Am. Found., 1986-88, Chgo. Tokyo Group, 1988—, Suburban Cook County Area Agy. on Aging, 1988-89; trustee St. Mary of the Woods Coll., Terre Haute, Ind., 1987-90; mem. panel on employers and working families NAS. 1st lt. USMC, 1953-55. Mem. Harvard Club of N.Y.C. Home: 5450 Whitley Park Ter Apt 303 Bethesda MD 20814-2054

CODY, THOMAS GERALD, lawyer; b. N.Y.C., Nov. 4, 1941; s. Thomas J. Cody and Esther Mary Courtney; m. Mary Ellen Palmer, Nov. 26, 1966; children: Thomas Jr., Mark, Amy, Anne. BA in Philosophy, Maryknoll Coll., 1963; JD, St. John's U., 1967; LLD (hon.), Cen. State U., Wilberforce, Ohio, 1985. Bar: N.Y. 1967. Assoc. Simpson Thacher & Bartlett, N.Y., 1967-72; asst. prof. law sch. St. John's U., N.Y., 1972-76; sr. v.p., gen. counsel, sec. Pan Am. Airways, N.Y., 1976-82; sr. v.p. law and pub. affairs Federated Dept. Stores, Cin., 1982-88, exec. v.p. legal & human resources, 1989—. Trustee Xavier U., Cin., Children's Hosp. Med. Ctr., Cin. Mem. ABA, Bankers Club, Queen City Club, Hyde Park Country Club, Commonwealth Club of Cin. Roman Catholic. Office: Federated Dept Stores Inc 7 W 7th St Cincinnati OH 45202-2424*

CODY, WALTER JAMES MICHAEL, lawyer, former state official; b. Memphis, Mar. 13, 1936; s. Walter James and Bess Lou (Hill) C.; m. Suzanna Marten; children; Jane BArton, Michael, Mia. BA, SouthwesternU., Memphis, 1958; JD, U. Va., 1961; LLD, Rhodes Coll., Memphis, 1989. Bar: Tenn. 1961. Ptnr. Burch, Porter & Johnson, Memphis, 1961-77, 81-84, 89—; U.S. atty. Western Dist. Tenn., Memphis, 1977-81; atty. gen. State of Tenn., 1984-88; ptnr. Bass, Berry and Sims, Nashville, 1988-89; lectr. LeMoyne-Owen Coll., Memphis State U. Law Sch.; instr. polit. sci. Southwestern U., Memphis; adj. prof. law Vanderbilt U.; mem. bd. profl. responsibility Tenn. Supreme Ct., 1990-92; bd. dirs. Nat. Civil Rights Mus. Contbr. to: You Can't Eat Magnolias, 1972. Pres. L.Q.C. Lamar Soc., 1970-71; chmn. Shelby County Dem. Party, 1972-74; mem.-at-large Memphis City Coun., 1975-77; trustee, mem. exec. com. Memphis Acad. Arts; chmn. Tenn. Sports Festivals, 1989-92. 1st lt. U.S. Army Res., 1961-67. Recipient Sam A. Myer Meml. award, 1976. Fellow Am. Coll. Trial Lawyers, Am. Bar Found.; mem. ABA, Fed. Bar Assn., Tenn. Bar Assn., Memphis and Shelby County Bar Assn. (co-founder neighborhood legal service project), Nat. Assn. Former U.S. Attys., Memphis and Shelby County Legal Services Assn. (dir.). Democrat. Episcopalian. Office: Burch Porter & Johnson 130 Court Ave Memphis TN 38103-2288*

CODY, WILLIAM BERMOND, political science educator; b. Brunswick, Ga., Jan. 15, 1949; s. Bermond Hamp and Dorothy Jane (Satterfield) C.; m. Mildred Ann McInnis, Sept. 5, 1970; children: Margaret Jae, Elizabeth Joelle. AB, U. Ga., 1971, MA, 1973, JD, 1986; PhD, New Sch. Social Rsch., 1980. Bar: Ga. 1986. Student advisor New Sch. Social Rsch., N.Y.C., 1978-79; asst. to pres. Robeal Mgmt. Co., Charleston, S.C., 1983-85; assoc. Carr, Tabb & Pope, Atlanta, 1987; legal asst. Ga. Ct. Appeals, Atlanta, 1987-89; asst. prof. polit. sci. U. Ga., Athens, 1989-90; asst. prof. Oxford (Ga.) Coll. Emory U., 1990-93; assoc. prof. Oxford (Ga.) Coll. Emory U., 1993—; adj. instr. Coll. New Rochelle, N.Y., 1978-79; vis. asst. prof. Clemson (S.C.) U., 1980-83; mem. Emory U. Senate, 1995-97, pres.-elect, 1996-97, pres., 1997-98. Vestryman St. Bede's Episcopal Ch., Atlanta, 1988-92, jr. warden, 1990, sr. warden, 1991; bd. dirs. Interfaith, Inc., Atlanta, 1989-90. Mem. ABA, Am. Polit. Sci. Assn., Ga. Polit. Sci. Assn., So. Polit. Sci. Assn., Am. Hist. Assn., Acad. Polit. Sci., Ga. Bar Assn. Democrat. Office: Polit Sci Dept Oxford Coll Emory U Oxford GA 30054

CODY, WILMER ST. CLAIR, educational administrator; b. Mobile, Ala., Jan. 1, 1937; s. Wilmer St. Clair and Madeline (Maygarden) C.; m. Caroline Marie Burns, Aug. 16, 1958; children: David Marshall, Alison Marie. AB, Harvard U., 1959, EdM, 1960, EdD, 1968. Tchr. Newton (Mass.) Schs., 1960; tchr. Mobile County Schs., 1960-62, prin., 1962-64; dir. tchr. edn. Atlanta Schs., 1966-67; supt. Chapel Hill (N.C.) Schs., 1967-71; sr. research assoc. Nat. Inst. Edn., 1971-73; supt. Birmingham (Ala.) City Schs., 1973-83, Montgomery County Schs., Rockville, Md., 1983-87; dir. nat. assessment project Council Chief State Sch. Officers, 1987-88; supt. edn. State of La., 1988-92; exec. dir. Nat. Edn. Goals Panel, Washington, 1992-93; dir. Nat. Faculty/So. Region, New Orleans, 1993-95; commr. edn. State of Ky., Frankfort, 1995—; mem. Nat. Assesment Governing Bd., 1998—. Contbr. articles to ednl. jours. Mem. Nat. Adv. Com. on Juvenile Justice and Delinquency Prevention, 1976-78; bd. dirs. Comty. Chest, Campfire Girls; trustee Nat. Coun. Econ. Edn., So. Assn. Colls. and Schs., 1990-92; chmn. Nat. Assessment Edn. Policy Com., 1983-87; dir. S.W. Edn. Devel. Lab., 1988-92; steering com. Edn. Commn. of the States, 1990-92, So. Region Edn. Bd., 1990-92, 96—; exec. bd. Nat. Coun. for Accreditation of Tchr. Edn., 1990-92, 1996—, chair 1998; pres. Coun. Chief State Officers, 1997-98. Named Educator of Yr. ALA, 1977. Mem. Am. Assn. Sch. Adminstrs., Am. Edn. Research Assn., Phi Delta Kappa. Methodist. Home: 415 Mill Road Pl Midway KY 40347-1009 Office: State Dept of Edn 500 Mero St Frankfort KY 40601-1957

COE, ANNE ELIZABETH, artist; b. Henderson, Nev., Feb. 27, 1949; d. Percy Ellis and Mary Ernest (Jackson) Coe; m. Dennis Neal Barr, Sept. 13, 1970 (div. May 1973); 1 child, Laurye; m. Robert Patrick Horvath, Apr. 11, 1992. BA cum laude, Ariz. State U., Tempe, 1970, MFA cum laude, 1980. Artist in residence Ariz. Commn. for the Arts, Phoenix, 1982. Illustrator: (children's book) Here is the Southwestern Desert, 1995; exhibited in solo shows at Harry Wood Gallery/Ariz. State U., 1980, Elaine Horwitch Galleries, 1987, 89, 92, 94, Anne Reed Gallery, Sun Valley, Idaho, 1991, 92, Horwitch Newman Gallery, Scottsdale, 1995, 96, Joseph Gross Gallery/ U. Ariz., 1998, Moynihan Gallery, Jackson, Wyo., 1995, others; group shows include Suzanne Brown Gallery, Scottsdale, The White House, Washington, Segal Gallery, N.Y.C., Bruce Mus., Greenwich, Conn., White Tops Gallery, Palm Desert, Calif., Elaine Horwitch Galleries, Soho West, Denver, Americana Mus., El Paso, Ariz. Mus. for Youth, MARS Artspace, Phoenix, Martin Harris, Jackson, Wyo., numerous others; included in collections at Eiteljorg Mus., Indpls., Whitney Mus. Western Art, Cody, Wyo., Centro de Arte Moderna, Guadalajara, Mex., Mus. of N.D., Grand Forks, Sky Harbor Internat. Airport, Phoenix, Smithsonian Instn., Washington, Ariz. State U., Tempe, Scottsdale Ctr. for the Arts, numerous others; subject of numerous articles. Mem. adv. bd. Ctrl. Ariz. Land Trust, 1994—; chmn. superstition area land trust Apache Junction Sch. Dsit., 1995-96; mem. Gov.'s Exec. Task Force for the Ariz. Preserve Initiative, 1995; mem. State Land Conservation Adv. Com., 1996-99. Avocations: land use issues, hiking, the environment. Home: 5776 E Forest St Apache Junction AZ 85219-9506

COE, BENJAMIN PLAISTED, retired state official; b. Long Beach, Calif., Aug. 24, 1930; s. Benjamin and Mary Plaisted (Ricker) C.; m. Margaret Jane Butler, Sept. 5, 1953; children: Benjamin B., Elizabeth C., Mary Susan, Margaret Jane. A.B., Bowdoin Coll., 1953; B.S., Ch.E., MIT, 1953. Lic. profl. engr., N.Y. With silicone products dept. Gen. Electric Co., Waterford, N.Y., 1953-65; process econs. engr. Gen. Electric Co., 1963-65; exec. dir. Vols. for Internat. Tech. Assistance, Schenectady, 1965-68; exec. dir. U.S.A. div. Vols. for Internat. Tech. Assistance, 1969-73, v.p., 1971-73; exec. dir. Tug Hill Commn., N.Y. State, 1973-93; ret. Tug Hill Commn., 1993. Vestryman Trinity Episcopal Ch., 1978-81, warden, 1981-86, 93-96; bd. dirs. Schenectady Symphony, 1969, Adirondack North Country Assn., 1985-88; chmn. pub. svc. divsn. Jefferson County United Way, 1982-84, bd. dirs., 1985-88, 2d v.p., 1988-89, 1st v.p., 1990-91, pres., 1992-94; pres. Vol. Ctr. Jefferson County, 1994-96, 98—. Named Exec. of Yr. Watertown Profl. Secs. Internat., 1978-79. Mem. AIChE (chmn. N.E. N.Y. sect. 1965), ASPA, Rotary (pres. Watertown 1989-90, dist. gov. 1996-97), Phi Beta Kappa, Sigma Xi, Tau Beta Pi. Home: 314 Paddock St Watertown NY 13601-3943 *I have come to think that success should be measured internally, between man and his maker, rather than by external signs. My goals are to involve myself with mankind in a worthwile way and at the same time keep my family fed, healthy, and in a position to work toward their own goals.*

COE, DONALD KIRK, university official; b. Tuscaloosa, Ala., Nov. 21, 1934; s. Glen Dale and Hazel Mae (Coley) C.; m. Frances Ellen Truman, May 31, 1958; children: Mark William, Sandra Elizabeth, Bonnie Lee. BA, U. Ala., 1957. Wire editor Xenia (Ohio) Daily Gazette, 1958-59; reporter, county editor Sharon (Pa.) Herald, 1959-61; asst. wire editor Pitts. Press, 1961-66; in public relations and fund raising Carnegie-Mellon U., Pitts., 1966-70; editorial writer St. Petersburg (Fla.) Times, 1970-75; chief editorial writer Chgo. Sun-Times, 1975-84; univ. dir. pub. affairs U. Ill., 1984-98, spl. asst. to pres., 1998—. Pres. Nat. Conf. Editorial Writers Found., 1989-91. Capt. USAR, 1958-68. Recipient Ill. UPI award, 1977. Mem. Sigma Delta Chi (pres. coll. chpt. 1957). Presbyterian. Home: 723 Bonnie Brae Pl River Forest IL 60305-1930 Office: 1737 W Polk St # 971 Chicago IL 60612-7224 also: 305 Henry Adminstrn Bldg MC-370 506 S Wright St Urbana IL 61801-3620

COE, FELIX GILMORE, science educator; b. Bluefields, Nicaragua, Apr. 30, 1953; s. Sturdee Beatty and Lilia Alberta (Hodgson) C.; m. Irene Lucy Nowak, Oct. 11, 1978; children: Darda, Christopher. PhD, U. Conn., 1994. Mgr. environ. affairs Atlantic Aerospace/Textron, Newington, Conn., 1979-90; rschr. U. Conn., Storrs, 1994-96; asst. prof. Tenn. Technol. U., Cookeville, 1996—. Contbr. articles to profl. jours. Mem. Lion Club, Cookeville, 1998. Recipient grant NSF, 1992, U. Conn., 1993, 94, Tenn. Dept. Environ. and Conservation, 1997. Mem. AAAS, Soc. Econ. Botany (membership com. 1998-99), Bot. Soc. Am., Am. Soc. Plant Taxonomists. Avocations: hiking, tennis. FAX: 931-372-6257. E-mail: fcoe@tntech.edu. Home: PO Box 5137 Cookeville TN 38505 Office: Tenn Technol Univ PO Box 5063 Cookeville TN 38505

COE, FREDRIC L., physician, educator, researcher; b. Chgo., Dec. 25, 1936; s. Lester J. and Lillian (Chaitlen) C.; m. Eleanor Joyce Brodny, May 5, 1965; children: Brian, Laura. A.B., U. Chgo., 1955; M.S., U. Chgo., 1957; M.D., U. Chgo., 1961. Diplomate Am. Bd. Internal Medicine. Intern Michael Reese Hosp., Chgo., 1961-62, resident, 1962-65; resident U. Tex. S.W. Med. Sch., 1967-69; chmn. nephrology Michael Reese Hosp., 1972-82; prof. medicine U. Chgo., 1977—, prof. physiology, 1979—; chmn. nephrology A.M. Billings Hosp., Chgo., 1982—; founder, pres. Litholink Corp., 1995. Author: Nephrolithiasis, 1978, 2d edit. (with J. Parks), 1987, (with B. Brenner and F.C. Rector) Renal Physiology, 1986, Clinical Nephrology; editor: Renal Therapeutics, 1978, Nephrolithiasis, 1980, Hypercalciuric States, 1983, (with M. Favus) Disorders of Bone and Mineral Metabolism, 1993; editor-in-chief Yearbook of Nephrology, 1991-96; editor: (with others) Kidney Stones: Medical and Surgical Management, 1996. Served to capt. USAF, 1961-67. Grantee NIH, 1977—. Fellow ACP; mem. Am. Soc. Clin. Investigation, Am. Physiol. Soc., Assn. Am. Physicians. Jewish. Achievements include first evidence for hyperuricosuria as cause of calcium renal stones; discovery of nephro calcin a protien inhibitor of crystal growth; first demonstration that human idiopathic hypercalciuris is hereditary. Home: 5490 S South Shore Dr Chicago IL 60615-5984 Office: U Chgo Med Ctr 5841 S Maryland Ave Chicago IL 60637-1463

COE, JOHN WILLIAM, management consultant; b. Highland Park, Mich., Oct. 2, 1924; s. C. Leroy and Grace Lamont C.; m. Sally Childs, Oct. 24, 1953; children: John Childs, Daniel William. BS in Indsl. Mech. Engring., U. Mich., 1949. Acct. Charles L. Coe and Assocs., 1949; buyer J.L. Hudson Co., Detroit, 1950-58, divsn. mdse. mgr., 1959-81; v.p., gen. mgr. stores, 1981-83; dir. Champion Enterprises Inc., 1970-91; v.p. mktg., 1982-84; pres. Coe and Assocs., 1984—. Dist. chmn. United Found.; bd. dirs. Planned Parenthood League, Inc. Lt. (j.g.) USNR, 1943-46. Mem. Am. Mus. Fly-Fishing, Northland-Eastland Mchts. Assn. (dir., past pres.), Mensa, Country Club Detroit, Econ. Club Detroit, Pere Marquette Rod and Gun Club, Rotary (past pres.), Trout Unltd., U. Mich. Alumni Club, Psi Upsilon Alumni Assn. Republican. Episcopalian. Home: 393 Notre Dame Ave Grosse Pointe Park MI 48230

COE, MICHAEL DOUGLAS, anthropologist, educator; b. N.Y.C., May 14, 1929; s. William Rogers and Clover (Simonton) C.; m. Sophie Dobzhansky, June 5, 1955; children: Nicholas, Andrew, Sarah, Peter, Natalie. AB, Harvard, 1950, PhD, 1959. Asst. prof. U. Tenn., 1958-60; mem. faculty Yale U., 1960—, prof. anthropology, 1968-90, Charles J. MacCurdy prof. anthropology, 1990-94, prof. emeritus, 1994—; adviser Robert Woods Bliss Collection Pre-Columbian Art, Dumbarton Oaks, Harvard, 1963-80. Author: La Victoria, An Early Site on the Pacific Coast of Guatemala, 1961, Mexico, 1962, The Jaguar's Children: Pre-Classic Art of Central Mexico, 1965, The Maya, 1966, (with Kent V. Flannery) Early Cultures and Human Ecology in South Coastal Guatemala, 1967, America's First Civilization, 1968, The Maya Scribe and His World, 1973, Classic Maya Pottery at Dumbarton Oaks, 1975, Lords of the Underworld, 1978, (with Richard A. Diehl) In the Land of the Olmec, 1980, Young Lords and Old Gods, 1982, (with Dean R. Snow and Elizabeth P. Benson) Atlas of Ancient America, 1986, Breaking the Maya Code, 1992, (with Sophie D. Coe) The True History of Chocolate, 1996, (with Justin Kerr) The Art of the Maya Scribe, 1998; contbr. articles to profl. jours. Pres., chmn. bd. Planting Fields Found., 1985—; pres. Heath Hist. Soc., Mass., 1984-90. Fellow Royal Anthrop. Soc.; mem. NAS, Mex. Soc. Anthropology, Am. Anthrop. Assn., Soc. for Hist. Archaeology, Conn. Acad. Arts and Scis., Conn. Acad. Scis. and Engring., Limestone Trout Club, Sigma Xi. Home: 376 St Ronan St New Haven CT 06511-2251

COE, MICHUAL WILLIAM, physical therapist; b. Emporia, Kans., Aug. 31, 1950. EdD; JCB, EdD, Cath. U., 1983; BS in Phys. Therapy, Ind. U., Indpls., 1985. Lic. phys. therapist, Ill., Ind. Rehab. supr. Healthmark, Indpls., 1985-88, v.p., 1987-89; dir. phys. therapy Vermillion County Hosp., Clinton, Ind., 1988-91, Valley Rehab., Terre Haute, Ind., 1991-96; clinic mgr. Novacare/Valley Rehab., Terre Haute, 1996—; pres., sec., treas. Rehab. Svcs., Inc., Terre Haute, 1991. Mem. Am. Phys. Therapy Assn. (Mary McMillan scholar 1985, pvt. practice sect., Ind. chpt.), Nat. Assn. Rehab. Agys. Home: 1353 Linwood Ct Terre Haute IN 47802 Office: Novacare/ Valley Rehab 1212 S Third St Terre Haute IN 47802

COE, ROBERT CAMPBELL, retired surgeon; b. Seattle, Nov. 14, 1918; s. Herbert Everett and Lucy Jane (Campbell) C.; m. Josephine Austin Weiner, Mar. 24, 1942; children: Bruce Everett, Virginia Austin, Matthew Daniel. BS, U. Wash., 1940; MD, Harvard U., 1950. Diplomate: Am. Bd. Thoracic Surgery, Am. Bd. Surgery. Intern Mass. Gen. Hosp., Boston, 1950-51; asst. resident Mass. Gen. Hosp., 1951-54, chief surg. resident, 1955, chief surg. clinics, 1956; instr. surgery Med. Sch. Harvard U., 1956; pvt. practice medicine specializing in thoracic and vascular surgery Seattle, 1957-84; hon. mem. staff Children's Hosp.; attending surgeon Swedish Hosp.; cons. thoracic surgeon Firland Sanitarium, Seattle, 1957-68, Children's Hosp. Tumor Clinic, 1968-84; mng. ptnr. Invex & Inpark med. offices, Seattle, 1970-88; clin. prof. U. Wash., 1973—; mem. Wash. State Med. Disciplinary Bd., 1981-86; chmn. med. adv. bd. Physio-control. div. Eli Lilly, 1979-85; pres. 1st Mercer (Wash.) Corp., 1969-73, 80-91, treas., 1973-80; owner, operator Hidden Valley Guest Ranch Cle Elum, Wash., 1969-93; developer Kula Estate, Maui, Hawaii; treas. 13th Internat. Cancer Congress. Editor: King County Med. Soc. Bull, 1964-70; mem. adv. bd. Pacific N.W. Mag. 1968-85; contbr. articles to profl. jours. Mem. Mayor's Harbor Adv. Com., 1958-61; chmn. bd. N.W. Seaport, Inc., hist. mus. Seattle, 1974-75; mem. Mercer Island City Coun., 1988-92. With USNR, 1941-46. Decorated Bronze Star, Presdl. Unit citation. Fellow ACS; mem. North Pacific Surg. Assn. (sr. mem.), Pacific Coast Surg. Assn. (sr. mem.), King County Med. Soc. (jud. coun. 1972-78, chmn. 1976-78), Seattle Surg. Soc. (pres. 1969), Psi Upsilon, Seattle Yacht Club, Cruising of Am. Club (bd. govs. 1992-95). Episcopalian. Home and Office: 7260 N Mercer Way Mercer Island WA 98040-2132

COE, ROBERT STANFORD, retired management educator; b. Cin., July 9, 1919; s. Louis Herman and Alma Mary (Jenkins) C.; children: Carolyn Lee, William Ayres, Jon Bruce; m. Dorothy June Harris, Nov. 25, 1977. B.S., Miami U., Oxford, Ohio, 1941; M.S., U. Houston, 1948, Ph.D., 1957. Asst. to v.p. Dresser Industries, Dallas, 1956-58; personnel adminstr. Ling-Temco-Vought, Dallas, 1958-64; prof., grad. adviser Stephen F. Austin State U. (Tex.), 1964-69, chmn. dept. bus. adminstrn., 1969-74; mgmt. prof. Angelo State U., San Angelo, Tex., 1969-87; pres. Mgmt. Resources Assocs., San Angelo, 1970-87; lectr. U. Tex.-Arlington, 1960-64. Contbr. articles to profl. jours. Mem. Gov.'s Com. on Goals for Tex., 1970; bd. dirs. YMCA, 1970-72, West Tex. Lighthouse for Blind, 1985-87. Served with USN, 1941-45. Mem. Am. Psychol. Assn., Acad. Mgmt., AAUP, Am. Inst. Decision Scis., Alpha Kappa Psi, Phi Kappa Phi, Pi Kappa Alpha. Presbyterian. Clubs: San Angelo Country, Rolling Hills Country. Lodge: Rotary. Home: 3917 Driftwood Dr San Angelo TX 76904-5975 *Since my high school days, my life has been guided by the principle expressed by the Latin phrase, "Esse Quam Videre", which means, to be, rather than to appear to be.*

COE, RODNEY MICHAEL, medical educator; b. Marquette, Mich., Nov. 10, 1933; s. Roy Arthur and Renee Adelaide (Reeder) C.; m. Elaine Elwell, Sept. 6, 1954; children: Kevin Elwell, Curtis Daniel, Andrea, Douglas Arthur. BS, Iowa State Coll., 1955, MA, So. Ill. U., 1959; PhD, Wash. U., 1962. From asst. to assoc. prof. Wash. U., St. Louis, 1962-70; from assoc. prof. to prof. St. Louis U., 1970—, chmn. cmty. and family medicine, 1989—; exec. dir. Med. Care Rsch. Ctr., St. Louis, 1963-73; vis. prof. L.Am. Faculty Social Scis., Santiago, Chile, 1969-70; cons. Chilton Rsch. Svcs., Radnor, Pa., 1970-79, NIH, Bethesda, Md., 1976—. Author: Sociology of Medicine, 1970, and eighteen others; contbr. articles to profl. jours. Mem. Health Care for the Homeless, St. Louis, 1985—; mem., past pres. SSM Rehab. Inst., St. Louis, 1968—. Capt. U.S. Army, 1956-58. Recipient Geriatric Leadership Acad. award NIH, 1986-92; grantee NIH, Dept. Vets. Affairs, pvt. founds. Avocations: swimming, golfing. Office: Saint Louis U Sch Medicine Dono Bldg Comm Family Med 1320 S Grand Blvd Saint Louis MO 63104-1019

COE, THOMAS R., police chief; m. Patty Coe, 1975; 2 children. B in Criminology, Fla. State U., M in Pub. Adminstrn.; grad., FBI Nat. Acad., Fla. Dept. Law Enforcement Chief Exec. Inst., Sr. Mgmt. Inst. Police. Cert. assessor Commn. Accreditation for Law Enforcement. Various positions Tallahassee (Fla.) Police Dept., 1972-94, chief, 1994-97; asst. city mgr. City Mgrs. Office, Tallahassee, 1997—; chmn. criminal justice adv. bd. Tallahassee C.C.; mem. criminal justice adv. panel Fla. State U.; mem. Gov.'s Violent Crime Coun. Mem. FBI Nat. Acad. Assocs., Internat. Assn. Chiefs of Police, Fla. Police Chiefs Assn. (legis. and edn. coms.), Police Exec. Rsch. Forum. Office: 300 S Adams St Tallahassee FL 32301-1731*

COELHO, ANTHONY MENDES, JR., health science administrator; b. Danbury, Conn., May 26, 1947; s. Anthony Mendes and Angela (Fernandes) C.; m. Linda Straw, Jan. 12, 1974. BS in Social Scis., Western Conn. State U., 1970; MA in Phys.-Biol. Anthropology, U. Tex., 1973, PhD in Phys.-Biol. Anthropology, 1975. Cert. social scis. secondary tchr., Conn. Asst. prof. anthropology Tex. Tech U., Lubbock, 1974-75; instr. social-cultural anthropology U. Tex., Austin, 1971-72, teaching asst. phys.-biol. anthropology, 1972-74; asst. scientist S.W. Found. for Biomed. Rsch., San Antonio, 1975-76, assoc. scientist, 1976-86, scientist, 1986-92, head Behavioral Medicine Lab., 1975-92; health sci./sci. rev. adminstr., leader clin. studies SRG, NHLBP/NIH, Bethesda, Md., 1992—; adj. asst. prof. pediatrics U. Tex. Health Scis. Ctr., San Antonio, 1976-84, adj. assoc. prof., 1984-92, adj. assoc. prof. dental diagnostic scis., 1984-90, adj. prof. surgery and neurosurgery, 1989-92; lectr. social and behavioral scis. U. Tex., San Antonio, 1977-82; mem. rsch. manpower rev. com. NIH, Bethesda, Md., 1988-92; grant reviewer NSF, Nat. Geog. Soc., NIMH, Alcohol Drug Abuse and Mental Health Adminstrn., Nat. Scis. and Engring. Rsch. Coun., Can. Wenner-Gren Found. for Anthrop. Rsch. Contbr. articles to sci. jours.. Active Am. Heart Assn. Epidemiology and Prevention Coun. Scholar Command Security Corp., 1970, U. Tex., 1972-74; grantee NIH, 1983, 85, 89. Mem. Am. Soc. Primatologists (exec. sec., bd. dirs. 1982-84, cons. editor Am. Jour. Primatol., 1986—, editor book reviews 1989-91), Am. Assn. Phys. Anthropologists, Soc. Behavioral Medicine, Nat. Coun. U. Rsch. Adminstrs., Animal Behavior Soc., Human Biology Coun., Inst. for Advancement Health, Internat. Primatol. Soc., Latin Am. Soc. Primatology, Soc. Rsch.

Adminstrs., Sigma Xi, Phi Kappa Phi, Delta Tau Kappa. Home: 6 Canterfield Ct Germantown MD 20876-4374 Office: NIH-NHLBI Rev Br 6701 Rockledge Dr Bethesda MD 20892

COELHO, TONY, former congressman; b. Los Banos, Calif., June 15, 1942; s. Otto and Alice (Branco) C.; m. Phyllis Butler, June 10, 1967; children: Nicole, Kristin. B.A., Loyola U., Los Angeles, 1964. Agr. asst. to Rep. B.F. Sisk, 1965-70, adminstrv. asst., 1970-78; mem. 96th-101st Congresses from 15th Calif. Dist., 1979-89; chmn. Dem. Congl. Campaign Com., 1981-87; majority whip 100th, 101st Congress, 1987-89; resigned, 1989; mng. dir. Wertheim Schroder & Co., Inc.; pres., CEO Wertheim Schroder Investment Svcs., Inc., 1989-95; chmn., CEO Coelho Assocs., LLC, 1996-98; chmn., president's comm. on employment of people with disabilities Dept. of Labor, 1994—; bd. dirs. ITT Edn. Tech., Svc. Corps. Internat., Tanknology Environ. Inc., Kistler Aerospace, Kaleidoscope, Inc.; bd. dirs. ICF Kaiser Internat., Inc., chmn. bd. dirs.; chmn. Internat. Thoroughbred Breeders, Inc., Cyberonics, Inc.; amb. U.S. Pavillion-Expo, Lisbon, Portugal, 1998; chmn. U.S. Census Bd., 1998—; vice chair disability task force The White House, Washington, 1998—; mem. adv. bd. Fleishman Hillard Internat.; mem. Nat. Coun. for Political Mgmt. George Washington U. V.p., bd. dirs. Epilepsy Found. Am. Roman Catholic. Fax: 202-682-3983. Office: Coelho Assocs LLC 1225 I St NW Ste 600 Washington DC 20005 also: Pres Comm Employment People Dis 1331 F St NW Washington DC 20004-1107

COELING, HARRIET V., nursing educator, editor; b. Grand Rapids, Mich., Dec. 3, 1943; d. Louis and Helen Angeline (DeGraff) Van Ess; m. Kenneth J. Coeling, June 27, 1970; children: Valerie Coeling Nandor, Beverly Coeling Corder. BSN, U. Mich., 1966, MS, 1968; PhD, Bowling Green State U., 1987. RN, Ohio; cert. nurse specialist. Head nurse, clin. specialist Presbyn. Univ. Hosp., Pitts., 1968-70; instr. U. Pitts. Sch. Nursing, 1970-72; staff devel. instr. Braddoch (Pa.) Hosp., 1976-78, Med. Coll. Ohio, Toledo, 1978-83; asst. prof. U. Mich. Sch. Nursing, Ann Arbor, 1987-88; asst. prof. Kent (Ohio) State U. Sch. Nursing, 1988-93, asoc. prof., 1994—. Editor, Online Jour. Issues in Nursing, ANA/Kent State U., 1997—; contbr. articles to profl. jours. Coord. St. Malachi Healthcare Clinic, Cleve., 1993—. Tchr. and Nonsvc. fellow Bowling Green State U., 1983-87. Mem. Nat. Assn. Clin. Specialists, Ohio Assn. Advanced Practice Nurses, Ohio Nurses Assn. (chair human rights com. 1998), Greater Cleve. Nurses Assn., Midwest Nursing Rsch. Assn., Christian Assn. Psychol. Studies, Sigma Theta Tau (Excellence in Use of Tehc. award 1997). Christian. Avocations: travel, swimming. Office: Kent State U 1743 Settlers Reserve Westlake OH 44145

COEN, ADRI STECKLING See ADRI

COEN, CHERYL LYNN, secretary; b. Houston, Mo., Aug. 17, 1953; d. Willard Clark Coen and Verona Evelyn Pirkl. BS in Art/Psychology, S.W. Bapt. U., 1979. Sec./aide Bolivar (Mo.) R-1 Spl. Edn., 1980—; tutor art, Bolivar, 1986—. One-person shows include Bolivar (Mo.) Family Care Ctr., 1995; exhibited in group shows at Jordan Creek Gallery, Springfield, Mo., 1986-87, Artsfest on Walnut St., Springfield, 1989-93, artCentral, Carthage, Mo., 1992-93, New Coast Gallery, Reed Springs, Mo., 1993, Factory Merchants Mall, Osage Beach, Mo., 1993, Unitarian Ch., Springfield, 1994, SBU Art Dept., Bolivar, 1997, Ozark Pastel Soc., Neosho, Mo., 1997, 98, Sugar Creek Art Spring Competition, Siloam Springs, Ark., 1998, 99. Vol. Mo. chpt. Nature Conservancy, Springfield, 1998-99. Recipient Merit award SBU Walkway Gallery Show, Bolivar, 1986, Ozark Empire Fair Fine Arts, Springfield, 1986, Hon. Mention, Fescue Funfest, Clinton, Mo., 1987, others. Mem. Ozark Pastel Soc. (sec. 1998-99). Avocations: hiking, bicycling, camping, photography, traveling. E-mail: coench@bolivar.r1.k12.mo.us. Office: Bolivar R-1 Spl Edn Coop 316 W Jackson Bolivar MO 65613

COEN, JOEL, film director, writer; b. Saint Louis Park, Minn., 1955; s. Ed and Rena C.; divorced. Student, Simon's Rock Coll.; student in film, NYU. asst. editor Fear No Evil, Evil Dead,; worked with rock video crews; screenwriter: (with Ethan Coen) Crime Wave (formerly XYZ Murders); dir., screenwriter Blood Simple, 1984, Raising Arizona, 1987, Miller's Crossing, 1990, Barton Fink (Palme D'Or and Best Dir. awards, Cannes Internat. Film Festival), 1991, The Hudsucker Proxy, 1994, Fargo (Best Dir. award, Cannes Internat. Film Festival, 1996), The Big Lebowski, 1998. Office: United Talent Agy 9560 Wilshire Blvd Fl 5 Beverly Hills CA 90212-2400*

COERPER, MILO GEORGE, lawyer, priest; b. Milw., May 8, 1925; s. Milo Wilson and Rose (Schubert) C.; m. Lois Hicks, Apr. 11, 1953; children: Milo Wilson, Allison Lee, Lois Paddock. BS, U.S. Naval Acad., 1946; LLB, U. Mich., 1954; MA, Georgetown U., 1957, PhD, 1960. Bar: D.C. 1954, Md. 1960, N.Y. 1980. Since practiced in Washington; asso. firm Wilmer & Broun, 1954-60; firm Coudert Bros., 1961-63, mem. firm, 1964-96, retired ptnr., 1996—; ordained deacon Episcopal Ch., 1978, priest, 1979; Cathedral chaplain Washington Nat. Cathedral, 1986—. Contbr. articles to profl. jours. Trustee, vice chmn. for U.S., Canterbury Cathedral Trust in Am., 1982-97, acting chmn., 1991, 97. Ensign USN, 1946-49; to lt. 1951-53. Mem. Bar Assn. D.C., ABA, Md. State Bar Assn., Am. Law Inst., Am. SOc. Internat. Law, Internat. Law Assn. Clubs: Army and Navy, Metropolitan (pres. 1986), Chevy Chase; Union League (N.Y.C.). Home: 7315 Brookville Rd Chevy Chase MD 20815-4057 Office: Coudert Bros 1627 I St NW Washington DC 20006-4007

COFER, BERDETTE HENRY, public management consulting company executive; b. Las Flores, Calif.; s. William Walter and Violet Ellen (Elam) C.; m. Ann McGarva, June 27, 1954 (dec. Feb. 20, 1990); children: Sandra Lea Cofer-Oberle, Ronald William; m. Sally Ann Shepherd, June 12, 1993. AB, Calif. State U., Chico, 1950; MA, U. Calif., Berkeley, 1960. Tchr. Westwood (Calif.) Jr.-Sr. High Sch., 1953-54, Alhambra High Sch., Martinez, Calif., 1954-59; prin. adult and summer sch. Hanford (Calif.) High Sch., 1959-60, asst. supt. bus., 1960-67; dean bus. svcs. West Hills Coll., Coalinga, 1967-76; vice chancellor Yosemite Community Coll. Dist., Modesto, 1976-88; pres. BHC Assocs., Inc., Modesto, 1988—; chmn. Valley Ins. Program Joint Powers Agy., Modesto, 1986-88. Contbr. articles to profl. publs. Pres. Coalinga Indsl. Devel. Corp., 1972-74, Assn. for Retarded Citizens, Modesto, 1985; mayor City of Coalinga, 1974-76; foreman Stanislaus County Grand Jury, Modesto, 1987-88. 1st lt. USAF, 1951-53. Recipient Outstanding Citizen award Coalinga C. of C., 1976, Walter Starr Robie Outstanding Bus. Officer award Assn. Chief Bus. Officers Calif. Community Colls., 1988. Mem. Assn. Calif. C.C. Adminstrs. (life), Lions (dist. gov. 1965-66), Phi Delta Kappa (pres. Kings-Tulare chpt. 1962-63), Am. Legion, 40 and 8, Sons in Retirement. Democrat. Avocation: bowling. Home and Office: 291 Leveland Ln # D Modesto CA 95350-6806

COFER, JOHN ISAAC, IV, mechanical engineer; b. Balt., Oct. 15, 1950; s. John Isaac III and Eliza Moore (Beck) C.; m. Sharon Nazzaro, July 29, 1972; children: Emily E., John I. V. BS, U. Va., 1972; MS, MIT, 1974; ME, Northeastern U., 1980. Engr. thermo design GE Marine Turbine & Gear Dept., Lynn, Mass., 1974-76; from engr. thermo devel. to mgr. fluid mechs. GE Medium Steam Turbine Dept., Lynn, 1976-85; tech. leader fluid mechs. GE Naval & Drive Turbine Dept., Fitchburg, Mass., 1986-90; from tech. leader adv. design to mgr. aerodynamics engring. GE Power Sys., Schenectady, N.Y., 1990-96; from mgr. fluid mech. engring. to mgr. R&D Demag Delaval Turbomachinery Corp., Trenton, N.J., 1996-98; dir. aerospace and turbomachinery industries Engineous Software Inc., Morrisville, N.C., 1999—. Mem. ASME, Sigma Xi. Democrat. Episcopal. Achievements include patents in field. Office: Engineous Software Inc Ste 275 1800 Perimeter Park W Morrisville NC 27560

COFER, JONATHAN H., career officer; b. Pa., July 13, 1950. Commd. 2d lt. U.S. Army, 1972, advanced through grades to brig. gen., 1998; dir. joint rear area coord. U.S. Ctrl. Command, MacDill AFB, Fla., 1998—. Office: US Ctrl Command MacDill AFB FL 33621

COFFEE, JOHN COLLINS, JR., legal educator; b. Albany, N.Y., Nov. 15, 1944; s. John Collins and Mary E. (Morse) C.; m. Jane Purcell, July 1, 1970; 1 dau., Megan Purcell. BA, Amherst Coll., 1966; LLB, Yale U., 1969; LLM in Taxation, NYU, 1976. Bar: N.Y. 1970, U.S. Dist. Cts. (so. and ea. dists.) N.Y. 1974, U.S. Ct. Appeals (2d cir.) 1974, D.C. 1980. Assoc. Cravath, Swaine & Moore, N.Y.C., 1970-76; assoc. prof. law Georgetown U. Law Ctr., Washington, 1976-79; vis. prof. U. Va. Law Sch., Charlottesville, 1979; Adolf A. Berle prof. law Columbia U. Law Sch., N.Y.C., 1980—. vis. prof. Stanford U. Law Sch., Palo Alto, Calif., 1987. Mem. panel on sentencing research Nat. Acad. Scis., 1980-83; mem SEC Adv. Com. on Capital Formation, 1995-96, Subcoun. on Capital Markets, U.S. Competitiveness Policy Coun., 1994, Standing Com. On Law and Justice Nat. Rsch. Coun., 1992-95; legal adv. com. N.Y. Stock Exch., NASD, 1996—; gen. coun. Am. Econ. Assn.; mem. legal adv. bd. NASD; mem. market regulation com. NASD Regulation, Inc.; mem. adv. bd. LENS, Inc.; mem. standing com. on law and justice NAS. Reginald Heber Smith fellow, 1969-70. Fellow AAAS, Am. Bar Found.; mem. Am. Law Inst. (reporter project on corp. governance), ABA (reporter minimum standards for criminal justice), Am. Assn. Law Sch. (chmn. sect. on bus. assns. 1981-82, chmn. com. on sects. 1984-85, chmn. audit com.), Assn. Bar City of N.Y. (com. on securities laws 1981-92). Author: (with others) Knights, Raiders, and Targets: The Impact of the Hostle Takeover, 1988, Business Organization and Finance, 5th edit., 1995, Cases and Materials on Securities Regulation 8th edit., 1998, Cases and Materials on Corporations, 4th edit., 1995. Contbr. articles to legal jours. Office: Columbia U Sch Law 435 W 116th St New York NY 10027-7201*

COFFEE, JOSEPH DENIS, JR., retired college chancellor; b. Glens Falls, N.Y., Dec. 8, 1918; s. Joseph Denis and Kathryne Grace (Dwyer) C.; m. Margaret Mary Jennings, Oct. 7, 1941 (dec. Aug. 1998); children: John Allan (dec.), James Jennings, Mary Joyce Coffee Dies, Barbara Grace Coffee Wolf, Matthew Brian, Margaret Erin Coffee Giovannini, Ann Ellen Coffee Beach. A.B., Columbia U., 1941. Asst. to gen. sec. Columbia U., N.Y.C., 1946-50, dir. devel., 1950-60, founder corp. matching gift program of alumni support, 1953, assoc. dean, 1959-60, asst. to pres. for alumni affairs, 1960-66; v.p. Eisenhower Coll., Seneca Falls, N.Y., 1966-69, exec. v.p., 1969-76, acting pres., 1975-76, pres., 1976-80, chancellor, 1980-81, chancellor emeritus, 1981—; dir. scholarship program Joint Industry Bd., Elec. Industry of N.Y., 1947-81; exec. sec. Com. for Corporate Support Am. Univs., 1962-64. Chmn. March Dimes campaign, Closter, N.J., 1953; active Boy Scouts Am.; former treas., dir. Anglo-Am. Hellenic Bur. Edn.; pres. Seneca County United Way, 1973-75; Chmn. Teaneck Polit. Assembly, 1967-68; Trustee Teaneck Bd. Edn., 1961-64, 65-68, Columbia U., 1978-84; bd. dirs. Nat. Women's Hall of Fame. Served from ensign to lt. comdr. USNR, 1941-46. Mem. Seneca Falls Hist. Soc. (past trustee), Rotary (past pres. Senaca Falls, Paul Harris fellow 1988), Psi Upsilon. Roman Catholic.

COFFEE, RICHARD JEROME, II, lawyer; b. Chgo., Nov. 12, 1954; s. James F. and Jean Marie (Hackman) C.; children: David Patrick Coffee, Brent William Coffee; m. Sue Heberlie, Dec. 12, 1997. BS, So. Ill. U., 1975; JD, U. Ill., 1978. Bar: Ill. 1978, U.S. Dist. Ct. (no. dist.) Ill. 1978, U.S. Dist. Ct. (ctrl. dist.) Ill. 1980, U.S. Dist. Ct. (so. dist.) Ill. 1998. Staff atty. Ill. Dept. Ins., Springfield, 1979-80; counsel Ill. State Employees Assn., Springfield, 1980-84; staff counsel Ill. Bd. Regents, Springfield, 1984-87, legal counsel Chancellor's Office, 1987-89; univ. legal counsel Sangamon State U., Springfield, 1989-90; chief legal advisor Ill. State Bd. Edn., Springfield, 1990-96; assoc. Rau & Rau Attys., Waterloo, Ill., 1997—. Mem. Chgo. Bar Assn. Avocations: licensed pilot, licensed amateur radio operator. Office: 119 E Mill St Waterloo IL 62298-1518

COFFEE, VIRGINIA CLAIRE, civic worker, former mayor; b. Alliance, Nebr., Dec. 8, 1920; D. James Maddigan and Adelaide Mary (Forde) Kennedy; M. Bill Brown Coffee, June 21, 1942; children: Claire, Sara, Virginia Anne, Sue. BS, Chadron State Coll., 1942. H.s. prin. Whitman (Nebr.) High Sch., 1942; bookkeeper Coffee & Son, Inc., Harrison, Nebr., 1965—; officer Coffee & Son, Inc., Harrison, 1967, pres., 1987-97, v.p., 1998—; dir. Friends of Agate Fossill Beds, Inc., Harrison, 1988, v.p., 1988-98. Chmn. compilation com. book Sioux County Memoirs of Its Pioneers, 1967; coordinator Harrison sect. book Nebraska Our Towns, 1988. Mayor City of Harrison, 1978-80; leader Girl Scouts U.S.A., 1953-63; mem. Harrison Elem. Sch. bd., 1958-64, liason com. Chadron State Coll., 1975, pub. rels. chmn Nebr. Cowbelles, 1968; hon gov. Nebr. Centennial, 1967; sec. NW Stock Growers, 1971-73; corp. officer Ft. Robinson Centennial, 1973-88; officer Gov's Ft. Robinson Centennial Commn., 1973-74; chmn. Sioux County Bicentennial, 1973-77; trustee Nebr. State Hist. Soc. Found., 1975—, Village of Harrison, 1973-80, Chadron State Coll. Found., 1995—, bd. dirs. 1996—; bd. dirs. Harrison Cmty. Club, Inc., 1983-86, officer, 1984-86; apptd. Sioux County Vis. com. 1989—, adm. Nebr. Navy, 1992; mem. Nebr. State Hist. Soc. (life, dir. 1979-85, 2d v.p. 1982-84, 1st v.p. 1984-85, com. for marker to honor Harrison centennial 1985-86), Wyo. State Hist. Soc., Sioux County Hist. Soc. (bd. dirs. 1975-81, 83-84, 87-90, 97—, pres. 1988-90, co-pres., sec. v.p.) Sioux County history book com. 1985-86. Recipient Disting. Svc. award Chadron State Coll., 1994. Mem. Nebr. Cattle Women, Harrison Cmty. Inc. Roman Catholic. Address: PO Box 336 Harrison NE 69346-0336

COFFEL, PATRICIA K., retired clinical social worker; b. Bismarck, N.D., Sept. 14, 1934; m. Raymond A. Kobe, 1956; children: Anne, Elizabeth, Colleen, Denise, Tim, Heidi; m. Mitchel D. Coffel, 1983. Student, U. N.D., 1954-55; BA in Sociology, Coll. St. Benedict, 1956; MSW, Wayne State U., 1981. Diplomate in clin. social work; cert. social worker, Mich. Dir. social svcs. dept. Pontiac Nursing Ctr., 1978-84; dir. of med. social work dept. Advanced Profl. Home Health Care, Troy, Mich., 1985-86; med. social worker Visiting Nurses of Met. Detroit, 1987; family worker, therapist Camp Oakland Youth Svcs., Oxford, Mich., 1987-89; client svcs. case mgr. Macomb-Oakland Regional Ctr., Mt. Clemens, Mich., 1989-90; clin. social worker, case mgr. Oakdale Regional Ctr., Lapeer, Mich., 1990-91; clin. social worker Clinton Valley Ctr., Pontiac, Mich., 1991-96; retired, 1996; counselor Suicide Prevention, Inc., St. Louis, 1971-72, Macomb County Crisis Ctr., Warren, Mich., 1973-74; geriatric counselor Beverly Enterprises, Pontiac and Novi, Mich., 1981-83; grief and loss counselor Hospice SE Mich., Southfield, 1982-83. Grad. profl. scholar Wayne State U. Sch. Social Work, 1980. Mem. NASW (qualified clin. social worker), Acad. Cert. Social Workers. Avocations: antique silver collecting, board games. Home: 645 Oakwood Rd Ortonville MI 48462-8589

COFFELT, JANICE LITHERLAND, contracting officer; b. Fargo, N.D., May 9, 1953; d. Robert Norris and Phyllis (Chilcott) Litherland; m. James Frederick Coffelt, Aug. 27, 1988; 1 child, Laura. BS in Hotel Mgmt., Moorhead State U., 1976; MS in Tech. Comm., U. Colo., Denver, 1993. Purchasing agt. VA Med. Ctr., Denver, 1983-85, Nat. Oceanic and Atmospheric Ad., Boulder, Colo., 1985-88; from chief small purchases to contract specialist U.S. Bur. Mines, Denver, 1988-96; analyst procurement sys. U.S. Geol. Survey, Denver, 1996—, contract specialist, 1997-99. Mem. Nat. Contract Mgmt. Assn. (cert. profl. contract mgr.), Fed. Acquisition Coun. Home: 2359 S Holland Ct Lakewood CO 80227-2229 Office: US Geol Survey Denver Fed Ctr MS-204 B 53 Denver CO 80225

COFFEY, C(HARLES) EDWARD, physician; b. May 11, 1952. BS, Wofford Coll., 1974; MD, Duke U., 1979. Diplomate Am. Bd. Psychiatry and Neurology. Intern Duke U. Med. Ctr., Durham, N.C., 1980-81, resident in psychiatry, 1979-80, 83-84, resident in neurology, 1981-83, dir. neuropsychiatry, 1984-90; dir. Allegheny Neuropsychiat. Inst., Pitts., 1991-96; v.p. Henry Ford Behavioral Health, Detroit, 1996—. E-mail: ecoffey1@hfhs.org. Office: Henry Ford Health Sys 1 Ford Pl Detroit MI 48202-3450

COFFEY, CHARLES MOORE, communication research professional, writer; b. Chgo., July 8, 1941; s. Charles Adams and Helen Marie (Moore) C. BA in Econs., Beloit Coll., 1963; postgrad., Purdue U., 1980. WDBJ radio and TV reporter Times-World Corp., Roanoke, Va., 1964-65; reporter, anchor, prodr. WHAS AM FM TV, Louisville, 1967-72; asst. to chancellor Ind. U. S.E., New Albany, 1972-77; dir. spl. events Ind. U., Bloomington, 1977-82; dir. alumni affairs Ind. U.-Purdue U., Indpls., 1982-88; comm. advisor Bayh-O'Bannon Campaign, Indpls., 1988; comm. asst. Lt. Gov. of Ind., Indpls., 1989-97; dir. comm. rsch. Ind. Dept. Adminstrn., Indpls., 1997—; lt. gov.'s rep. INTELENET Commn., Indpls., 1990-97, gov.'s rep., 1997—; gov.'s rep. Enhanced Data Access Rev. Com., Indpls., 1997—. Contbr. articles to profl. jours. Pres. Coun. for Retarded Children, Clark County, Ind., 1975-76, Bloomington Restorations, 1982; founding chmn. Clark-Floyd Conv. Bur., Jeffersonville, Ind., 1977; bd. dirs. YMCA Greater Indpls., 1989-95, 97—, sec. bd. 1998—. With USAF, 1963. Recipient AP award for comprehensive reporting Va. AP Broadcasters, 1964-65. Mem. Rotary Club Indpls. Democrat. Home: 3922 Alsace Pl Indianapolis IN 46226-5413 Office: Ind Dept Adminstrn 402 W Washington St Indianapolis IN 46204-2739

COFFEY, CLARENCE W., treasurer; b. New Orleans, July 10, 1946; s. Clarence W. and Kathryn (Robinson) C.; m. Saundra Louise Goodson, Feb. 1, 1969; children: Brian, Kimberly. BBA, U. Tex., 1968; MBA, Our Lady of the Lake U., 1994. CPA, Tex. Staff acct. Freeport Sulphur Co., New Orleans, 1968-70, Tenneco Inc., Houston, 1970-73; corp. acct. First City Bankcorp., Houston, 1973-75; v.p., controller ATCO Drilling Ltd., Calgary, Alberta, Canada, 1975-81; controller Goldrus Drilling Co., Houston, 1981-86; sec. treas. Barwil Agys. NA, Inc., Houston, 1986-98; treas. Merichem Co. and Merichem Chems. & Refinery Svcs., Houston, 1998—. Coach Meml. Ashford Little League, Houston, 1981-89, Katy (Tex.) Little Dribblers Little League, 1985-89. Named one of Outstanding Young Men Am., 1977. Mem. AICPA, Delta Mu Delta. Home: 1106 Daria Dr Houston TX 77079-5026 Office: Merichem Co 5455 Old Spanish Trail Houston TX 77023

COFFEY, DARREN KEMPER, planner; b. Waynesboro, Va., Apr. 4, 1970; s. Glenn Robert and Peggy Ann (Hawpe) C. BS in econs. & geography, James Madison, 1992; MA in geography, Rutgers Univ., 1993. Park planner Mecklenburg County Park & Rec., Charlotte, N.C., 1995—. Cartographer: City of Harrisonburg Map, 1991-93; contbr. articles to profl. jours. Mem. Am. Planning Assn., Phi Chi Theta (parlamentarian 1990-92), Gamma Theta Upsilon (co-founder), Omicron Delta Epsilon, Golden Key Nat. Honor Soc. Avocations: reading, music, movies, hiking, travel. Home: 4522 Avalon Forest Ln Charlotte NC 28269-8195

COFFEY, DENNIS JAMES, performance technology consultant; b. Detroit, Nov. 11, 1940; s. James Patrick Coffey and Gertrude Viola Rinne Coffey Schultz; m. Joyce Crim (div. 1967); children: Jordan Collard, Denise Van Patten, Dennis Michael; m. Kathryn Osborne (div. 1988); children: James Donald, Andrew Joseph. BA, Wayne State U., 1990, MEd, 1992. Artist, writer, producer Maverick/MGM Records, Detroit, 1964-68, Sussex/Buddah Records, L.A., 1970-74, West Bound/Atlantic Records, Detroit, 1974-78; studio guitarist Motown Records, Detroit, 1968-76; v.p., co-owner Theocoff Prodns., Detroit, 1978-80, Glen Ridge, N.J., 1980-82; free-lance guitarist Farmington Hills, Mich., 1982-85; instrnl. technologist GM, Warren, Mich., 1985-89, Detroit Art Svcs., Troy, Mich., 1989-92; tng. cons. Farmington Hills, Mich., 1993-94; tng. mgr. ISI Robotics Inc., Warren, 1994-95. Artist, writer and producer record albums including Hair and Thangs, 1969, Evolution, 1971, Going For Myself, 1972, Electric Coffey, 1973, Instant Coffey, 1974, Finger Lickin Good, 1975, Back Home, 1976, A Sweet Taste of Sin, 1978, Motor City Magic, 1988, Under the Moonlight, 1990, Flight of the Phoenix, 1999; author: (book) Guitars, Cars and Motown Super Stars, 1999; contbr. articles to Discoveries Mag. and Tech. Skills and Tng. Mag. With U.S. Army, 1959-61. Recipient 3 cert. gold singles Rec. Industry Assn. Am., cert. gold album, Australia, award for best instrumental record NATRA, 1972, Alumni Acad. Achievement award Wayne State U. Coll. Lifelong Learning, 1995; named top instrumentalist and outstanding prodr. Record World, 1978; featured on cover Cashbox mag., 1972. Mem. ASTD, Nat. Soc. Performance and Instrn., Am. Fedn. Musicians, Mich. Soc. Instructional Tech. (hon. Achievement award 1991, Recognition award 1992), Broadcast Music Inc. (Citation Achievement award), Soc. for Tech. Communication (award 1991). Lutheran. Guitar featured in Motown exhibit, Henry Ford Mus., Greenfield Village, Dearborn, Mich., 1995-97.

COFFEY, JEAN SHEERIN, pediatric nurse, educator; b. Bklyn., May 27, 1957; d. William Raymond and Theodora Julia (Woitazek) Sheerin; m. Jay W. Coffey, Aug. 6, 1977; 3 children. AS, U. Vt., Burlington, 1977; BS, Norwich U., 1992; MSN, U. Vt., 1996. RN, Vt.; cert. pediatric nurse, ANA. Staff nurse Med. Ctr. Hosp. Vt., Burlington, 1977-82, Courville at Nashua, N.H., 1982-86, Med. Ctr. Hosp. Vt., Burlington, 1986-91, Pediatric Medicine, South Burlington, Vt., 1989-95; care coord., program dir. pediatric high tech. home care Profl. Nurses Svc., Burlington, 1988-89; clin. instr. U. Vt., Burlington, 1992-95; nurse adminstr. pediatrics Fletcher Allen Health Care, Burlington, 1995—; adj. prof. U. Vt., 1995—. Co-creator asthma edn. for asthma camp and workshops, 1986—. Pres. Am. Lung Assn. of Vt., bd. dirs., vol., chair Christmas Seal, 1988; BCLS instr. Am. Heart Assn. of Vt., Williston, 1986—; youth coach Essex Recreation/Nashua Recreation, 1985—; religious educator St. Pius X Parish, Essex, 1988-92. Presdl. fellow Norwich U., 1991-92; Comolli scholar, 1988-92; recipient Women in Sports award Essex Sch. Dist., 1993; named Outstanding Young Vermonter Jaycees, 1988. Mem. AACN, ANA, Soc. Pediatric Nurses, Sigma Theta Tau. Roman CAtholic. Avocations: basketball, soccer, coaching, nordic skiing. Home: 260 Browns River Rd Essex Junction VT 05452-2221

COFFEY, JOANNE CHRISTINE, dietitian; b. Cambridge, Mass., Aug. 18, 1942; d. Timothy Patrick and Helen (Stevens) C. BS in Nutrition, Simmons Coll., 1964, M in Libr. and Info. Sci., 1994; MPH, U. Calif., Berkeley, 1966. Registered dietitian. Dietitian, clin. sect. chief VA Med. Ctr., Manchester, N.H., 1976-80; chief dietetic svc. VA Med. Ctr., Altoona, Pa., 1980-82, Providence, 1982-89; asst. chief dietetic svc. VA Med. Ctr., Boston, 1989-96, supervisory dietitian, 1996-97. Mem. Nature Conservancy, Smithsonian. Mem. Am. Dietetic Assn. Democrat. Roman Catholic. Avocations: cooking, music, reading, walking.

COFFEY, JOHN LOUIS, federal judge; b. Milw., Apr. 15, 1922; s. William Leo and Elizabeth Ann (Walsh) C.; m. Marion Kunzelmann, Feb. 3, 1951; children: Peter, Elizabeth Mary Coffey Robbins. BA, Marquette U., 1943, JD, 1948; MBA (hon.), Spencerian Coll., 1964. Bar: Wis. 1948, U.S. Dist. Ct. 1948, U.S. Supreme Ct. 1980. Asst. city atty. City of Milw., 1949-54; judge Civil Ct., Milw. County, 1954-60, Milw. County Mcpl. Ct., 1960-62; judge criminal divsn. Cir. Ct., Milw. County, 1962-72, sr. judge criminal divsn., 1972-75, chief presiding judge criminal divsn., 1976, judge civil divsn., 1976-78; justice Wis. Supreme Ct., Madison, 1978-82; cir. judge U.S. Ct. Appeals (7th cir.), Chgo., 1982—; mem. Wis. Bd. Criminal Ct. Judges, 1960-78, Wis. Bd. Circuit Ct. Judges, 1962-78. Chmn. adv. bd. St. Joseph's Home for Children, 1958-65; mem. adv. bd. St. Mary's Hosp., 1964-70; past bd. dirs., mem. exec. bd. Milw.-Waukesha chpt. ARC; past mem. Milwaukee County council Boy Scouts Am.; chmn. St. Eugene's Sch. Bd., 1967-70; pres. St. Eugene's Ch. Coun., 1974; mem. vol. svcs. adv. com. Milwaukee County Dept. Pub. Welfare. Served with USNR, 1943-46. Named Outstanding Man of Yr., Milw. Jr. C. of C., 1951, One of 5 Outstanding Men in the State, 1957, Outstanding Law Alumnus of Yr., Marquette U., 1980. Fellow Am. Bar Found.; mem. Wis. Bar Assn., 7th Cir. Bar Assn., Ill. State Bar Assn., Nat. Lawyers Club, Am. Legion (Disting. Svc. award 1973), Marquette U. Law Alumni Assn. (Disting. Profl. Achievement Merit award 1985), Marquette U. M Club (former dir.), Alpha Sigma Nu, Phi Alpha Delta (hon.). Roman Catholic. *I have tried to the best of my ability to render justice to all and remember that "We are a country of laws, not of men" and while protecting the individual's rights I have not lost sight of the common good of all mankind and cautioned each and every one who appeared before me that with every right there is a corresponding obligation.*

COFFEY, JOSEPH IRVING, international affairs educator; b. St. Louis, Feb. 13, 1916; s. Joseph Aloysius and Catherine Elizabeth (Burns) C.; m. Marjorie Ann Strode, Nov. 15, 1939 (div. 1963); m. Rosemary Klineberg, June 28, 1963 (div. 1976); m. Maryann Bishop, May 13, 1978; children: John Patrick, Catherine Elizabeth, Judith Ann, Megan Forbes, Susan Fox, James Odell; 1 stepchild, Janet Lynn Bishop. B.S., U.S. Mil. Acad., 1939; postgrad., Columbia U., 1943-45; Ph.D. in Internat. Relations, Georgetown U., 1954. Asst. dir. programs, spl. studies project Rockefeller Bros. Fund, 1956-57; exec. asst. to spl. asst. to Pres. for security ops. coordination, Washington, 1958-60; mem. staff Pres.'s Com. on Info. Activities Abroad, White House, 1960; research analyst Inst. for Def. Analyses, Washington, 1960-63; chief office of nat. security studies Bendix Systems div., Ann Arbor, Mich., 1963-67; prof. public and internat. affairs U. Pitts., 1967-80, Disting. Service prof., 1980-82, prof. emeritus, 1982—, dir. Ctr. for Internat. Security Studies, 1975-81; sr. research fellow Ctr. Internat. Studies Univ. Ctr. Internat. Studies, 1981-90; vis. prof. internat. peace and security studies Carnegie-Mellon U., 1986-91; adj. prof. Carnegie Mellon U., 1991-92; sr. vis. fellow Ctr. for Internat. Studies, Princeton U., 1990-91; vis. lectr. Woodrow Wilson Sch., Princeton U., 1992; cons. AID, ACDA, Dept. Def. Dept. State, Internat. Comm. Agy. Author/editor books in field including Strategic Power and National Security, 1971, Arms Control and European Security, 1977, Allied Perceptions of Threat, 1983, Deterrence and Arms Control: American and West German Perspectives on INF, 1985, The Atlantic Alliance and the Middle East, 1989, Defense and Détente: U.S. and West German Perspectives on Defense Policy, 1989, Germany, the EU and the Future of Europe, 1995, The Future Rule of NATO, 1997. Served to col. U.S. Army, 1939-60. Internat. Inst. Strategic Studies rsch. assoc., 1972-73; Stockholm Internat. Peace Rsch. Inst. fellow, 1977, NATO rsch. fellow, 1981, 89. Mem. Coun. Fgn. Rels., Fgn. Policy Assn., Internat. Inst. Strategic Studies, Internat. Studies Assn., European Cmty. Studies Assn., Atlantic Coun. U.S., Istituto Affari Internat. Home: 89 Castle Howard Ct Princeton NJ 08540-4025 Office: Princeton U Bendheim Hall Princeton NJ 08544

COFFEY, LARRY B(RUCE), lawyer. BA, Wabash Coll., Crawfordsville, Ind., 1962; JD with honors, Ind. U., 1965; M of Comparative Law, U. Chgo., 1967. Bar: Ind. 1965, U.S. Dist. Ct. (so. dist.) Ind. 1965, N.Y. 1975, N.C. 1989, U.S. Dist. Ct. (we. dist.) N.C., 1989. Atty. European Cmty. Commn., Brussels, 1967; assoc. Dewey Ballantine, N.Y.C. and Brussels, 1968-71; atty. GM, N.Y.C. and London, 1971-78; v.p. Revlon, Europe, Mid. East and Africa, Paris, 1978-83; pvt. practice Paris, 1983-89; counsel Womble, Carlyle, Sandridge & Rice, Charlotte, N.C., 1989-91; pvt. practice, 1991—. Editor: The Common Market and Common Law, 1967. Wabash Coll. scholar 1958-62, Ind. U. Law Sch. fellow, 1962-65, U. Chgo. Law Sch. fellow, 1965-67. Mem. ABA, N.Y. State Bar Assn., N.C. Bar Assn. Office: 2449 Ardmore Manor Winston Salem NC 27103-4866

COFFEY, MARGARET TOBIN, education educator, county official; b. Binghamton, N.Y., Mar. 30, 1940; d. Henry L. and Mary Margaret (Keenan) Tobin; m. Joseph M. Coffey, Aug. 20, 1968; children: Timothy, Erin, David, Tobin. BA, Manhatten Coll. Sacred Heart, 1962; Cert. Edn., SUNY, Cortland, 1967. Cert. tchr., N.Y. Tchr. Binghamton Sch., 1963-69; early childhood coord. Broome Community Coll., Binghamton, 1971-72; staff caseworker U.S. Rep. Matthew F. McHugh, Washington and Binghamton, 1974-79; dir. Bur. of Census, Binghamton, 1979-80; tchr. adult edn. PROBE Local CBO, Binghamton, 1980-81; tchr. Binghamton City Sch. Dist., 1981-86, coord. VEA, 1986-90, prog. mgr. BCSD adult edn. programs, 1990—. Bd. dirs. Inner City Nursery Sch., Local Devel. Corp., Binghamton; bd. pres. Broome County Coun. Alcoholism, 1986-90; del. N.Y. Dem. Com., Albany, 1970-74; legislator Broome County, 1982—; mem. Children Youth Svcs. Coun., Youth Bur. Bd. Mem. Am. Vocat. Assn., Adult Continuing Edn. Assn., Phi Delta Kappa. Roman Catholic. Home: 30 Davis St Binghamton NY 13905-4318 Office: Binghamton City Sch Dist 98 Oak St Binghamton NY 13905-3717*

COFFEY, MATTHEW B., trade association executive; b. Cumberland, Md., Jan. 20, 1941; s. Francis Wade and Mary Agnes (Stegmaier) C.; m. Sharon Harriet West, May 20, 1971; children—Julia Katherine West, Francis Matthew West. A.A., Potomac State Coll., 1960; B.S., W.Va. U., 1962, M.B.A., 1969. Investigator U.S. CSC, Washington, 1964-65; staff asst. to Pres. Johnson The White House, Washington, 1965-69; dir. planning Corp. for Pub. Broadcasting, Washington, 1969-73; dir. recruiting Carter-Mondale Transition, Washington, 1976-77; pres. Assn. of Pub. Radio Stas., Washington, 1973-77; sr. v.p. Nat. Pub. Radio, Washington, 1977; exec. v.p. Nat. Alliance of Bus., Washington, 1977-78; dir. Washington Office Textron, Inc., Washington, 1978-79; v.p., chief fin. officer Bridgeport-Textron, Bridgeport, Conn., 1979-83; exec. dir. Nat. Assn. Counties, Washington, 1983-85; pres. Nat. Tooling and Machining Assn., 1985—; bd. dirs. Coun. for Adult and Experiential Learning, 1996-97; co-chmn. Commn. on Workforce Skills in Indsl. Found. Firms, 1992-94; mem. Nat. Alliance Bus. Coun. on Work Force Excellence, 1992-97; mem. industry adv. bd. D.O.E. Labs., 1993-96. Author: Toward a Clinical Method of Executive Selection, 1969; pub. Precision Mag., 1992-96; contbr. articles to profl. jours. Chmn., bd. dirs. Pub. Interest Groups, Washington, 1985; bd. dirs. Bridgeport (Conn.) Econ. Devel. Corp., 1981-83, Naugatuck Valley Indsl. Devel. Com., 1980-83; chmn. Pvt. Industry Coun., Bridgeport, 1981-83; bd. govs. Nat. Cathedral Sch., 1988; mem. bldg. com. Washington Nat. Cathedral, 1989—, co-chair long range planning task group, 1994-98, chmn. bldg. com., 1998—, mem. Cathedral chpt. 1998—; prin. Ctr. for Excellence in Govt., 1988-98. Fellow Nat. Acad. Pub. Adminstrn., Congl. Country Club, Univ. Club. Roman Catholic. Avocation: sailing. Home: 3602 Massachusetts Ave NW Washington DC 20007-1449 Office: Nat Tooling & Machining Assn 9300 Livingston Rd Fort Washington MD 20744-4998

COFFEY, NANCY ANN, commercial real estate broker; b. Palm Springs, Calif.; d. Arthur Johnson and Joan (Hunter) C. BA, Stanford U., MS in Engring. Indsl. real estate broker Coldwell Banker, Houston, 1977-79; comml. broker Coldwell Banker, San Francisco, 1980-87, Cushman & Wakefield, N.Y.C., 1987-90; model Gilla Roos, N.Y.C., 1991-96; self-employed real estate broker, 1990-96; comml. real estate broker The Rolfe Group, N.Y.C., 1997-98, Cushman & Wakefield, Inc., N.Y.C., 1998—. Active Jr. League, San Francisco, 1981-87, N.Y.C., 1987-92; mem. exec. com. spl. projects bd. Meml. Sloan Kettering Cancer Ctr., N.Y.C.; mem. parish life com. St. James Ch.; v.p. Class of 1967, Stanford U. Mem. Rockaway Hunting Club.

COFFEY, THOMAS FRANCIS, JR., writer; b. Walthourville, Ga., Feb. 14, 1923; s. Thomas Francis and Julian (Bacon) C.; m. Mary Corley, Apr. 6, 1946 (dec. July 1988); 1 child, Mary Cynthia Smith; m. Marjorie Kinsner Guice, Nov. 11, 1989. Student Am. Press Inst., Columbia U., 1964; student program for urban execs., MIT, 1970. Reporter Savannah (Ga.) Eve. Press, 1940-42, asst. city editor, sports editor, 1945-55, city editor, 1960-64, mng. editor, 1964-67; dir. civilian pub. relations U.S. Army, Camp Stewart, Ga., 1942; news dir. Sta. WSAV-TV, Savannah, 1955-57; sports editor Savannah Morning News, 1957-60, mng. editor, 1967-69, assoc. editor, 1974-87, editor, 1987-89, columnist, 1989-98; commentator WJCL-TV, Savannah, 1990—. Author: Working for God, 1992, Only in Savannah, 1995, Savannah Lore and More, 1997. Asst. city mgr., City of Savannah, 1969-74; Bd. dirs. United Way of Savannah. Served with AUS, 1943-45. Decorated Bronze Star, Purple Heart. Mem. Ga. A.P. News Coun., Greater Savannah Hall Fame Assn. (pres. 1969), Internat. City Mgmt. Assn., Nat. Conf. Edit. Writers, Nat. Soc. Newspaper Columnists, Midway Soc. Ga. (pres. 1985), SR (pres. Ga.), Am. Legion, Sigma Delta Chi. Republican. Episcopalian (lic. lay reader). Club: Am. Business (past pres. Savannah chpt.). Home: 209 Kensington Dr Savannah GA 31405-5422 Office: Savannah News Bldg 111 W Bay St Savannah GA 31401-1108 *Dedication to the task at hand/Compassion and concern for others/Gratitude to those who have built this nation/Faith in God.*

COFFEY, THOMAS WILLIAM, lawyer; b. Cin., Jan. 19, 1959; s. Joseph Paul and Doris June (Adams) C.; m. Shirley Ann Strode, July 24, 1982. MusB, U. Cin., 1981, JD, 1987. Bar: Pa. 1987, U.S. Dist. Ct. (we. dist.) Pa. 1987, U.S. Ct. Appeals (3d cir.) 1988, Ohio 1990, U.S. Dist. Ct. (so. dist.) Ohio 1990, U.S. Ct. Appeals (6th cir.) 1990. Dir. band Ea. Local Sch., Brown County, Ohio, 1981-83, Goshen (Ohio) High Sch., 1983-84; assoc. Buchanan Ingersoll, P.C., Pitts., 1987-90; chmn. bankruptcy group Cors & Bassett, Cin., 1990—. Mem. ABA, Ohio Bar Assn., Cin. Bar Assn., Am. Fedn. Musicians, Masons, Shriners. Avocations: symphonic and Dixieland jazz. Home: 933 Monastery St Cincinnati OH 45202-1510 Office: Cors & Bassett 537 E Pete Rose Way Ste 400 Cincinnati OH 45202

COFFEY, TIMOTHY, physicist, think-tank executive; b. Washington, June 27, 1941; s. Timothy and Helen (Stevens) C.; m. Paula Marie Smith, Aug. 24, 1963; children: Timothy, Donna, Marie. B.S. in Elec. Engring. (Cambridge scholar 1958), MIT, 1962; M.S. in Physics, U. Mich., 1963, Evening News Assn. fellow, 1964, Ph.D., 1967. Rsch. physicist Air Force Cambridge Rsch. Lab., 1964; theoretical physicist EGG, Inc., Boston, 1966-71; head plasma dynamics br., then supt. plasma physics div. Naval Rsch. Lab., Washington, 1971-80; assoc. dir. rsch. for gen. sci. and tech. Naval Rsch. Lab., 1980-83; dir. rsch. Naval Research Lab., 1983—. Recipient award Naval Rsch. Lab., 1974, 75, Disting. Civilian award Dept. Defense, 1991. Fellow Am. Phys. Soc., Washington Acad. Scis.; mem. AAAS, Franklin Inst. (Delmar S. Fahrney medal 1991 com. for sci. and arts), Am. Inst. Physics. Office: Naval Research Lab Code 1001 4555 Overlook Ave SW Washington DC 20375-0001

COFFIELD, CONRAD EUGENE, lawyer; b. Hot Springs, S.D., Nov. 26, 1930; s. Eugene M. and Alice (Hotvet) C.; children: Conrad Eugene, Michael, Megan, Edward, Philip; m. Mona L. Enfield, May 2, 1992. Student S.D. Sch. Mines and Tech., 1948-49; BBA, Washington U., St. Louis, 1952; LLB, U. Tex., 1959. Bar: Tex. 1959, N.Mex. 1959. Mem. Hervey, Dow & Hinkle, Roswell, N.Mex., 1959-64; gen. ptnr. Hinkle, Cox, Eaton, Coffield & Hensley, Roswell, 1964-66, resident ptnr., Midland, 1966-94, resident ptnr., Santa Fe, N.Mex., 1994—. Trustee Petroleum Mus., Library and Hall of Fame; bd. govs. Midland Community Theatre; bd. dirs. Santa Fe Pro Musica. Served with USCGR, 1952-56. Fellow Tex. Bar Found.; mem. ABA, Tex. Bar Assn., N.Mex. Bar Assn. (mem. bd. dirs. sr. lawyers), Santa Fe County Bar Assn., N.Mex. Oil and Gas Assn. Episcopalian. Office: Hinkle Cox Eaton Coffield Hensley 218 Montezuma Ave Santa Fe NM 87501-2625

COFFIELD, MARY ELEANOR, speech clinician, educator; b. Ft. Smith, Ark., July 28, 1921; d. Willard M. and Edith Isabel (Stemmons) C. Student, No. Ariz. State U., 1941-42; BE, Cen. Mo. State U., 1948; MA in Speech Pathology, U. Denver, 1960. Lic. speech pathologist, Mo. Tchr. music pvt. kindergarten Carthage, Mo., 1940-41; tchr. Columbian Elem. Sch., Carthage, 1943-47; fellowship tchr. Lab. Sch. Cen. Mo., Warrensburg, 1947-48; elem. tchr. Roswell (N.Mex.) Schs., 1948-49, Kansas City (Mo.) Sch., 1949-50; speech clinician Carthage Schs., 156-59, 60-86. Editor Jasper County Jour., 1983—. Pres. Rep. Women, Carthage, Carthage Social Agys.; hon. mem. United Presbyn. Ch., mem. choir, commr. synod; treas. McCune-Brooks Hosp. Aux.; mem. Presbytery Com., Profl. Devel. and Support Com., Presbytery Nominating Com.; moderator, enabler Gathering of Presbyn. Women in Carthage; mem. com. planning World Day of Prayer, Jasper County Sheltered Facilities Bd.; past pres., v.p., sec. Jasper County Crisis Intervention Bd.; past sec.-treas. Hard of Hearing Parents and Friends Group; instr. home nursing, chmn. water safety, staff aide ARC; pres. Friends of Libr., 1994—. Named Citizen of Yr. Carthage Lions, 1985, Citizen of the Yr., C. of C., 1999; recipient citation Future Farmers Am., 1985, Recognition Outstanding Svc. award Region V Coun. Devel. Disabilities, 1989. Mem. AAUW (pres., Woman of Distinction 1990), Internat. Platform Assn., Coun. Exceptional Children (state treas. 1969, 89, Merit award 1982, Mo. Tchr. of Yr. 1986, Nat. Tchr. of Yr. 1987, participant ann. meeting 1992, 93, 94), Am. Speech and Hearing Assn. (life), Mo. Assn. Social Welfare (life, chmn. state membership), Four State Stroke Club (sec. 1975—), Joplin Area Assn. Retarded Citizens (pres. 1978-81, 87-89, bd. dirs.), Carthage Tchrs. (Outstanding Ret. Mem.), Jasper County Hist. Soc., Ret. Tchrs. Assn. (pres. 1992-98). Avocations: photography, singing, collecting angels, bells, elephants. Home: 1718 S Garrison Ave Carthage MO 64836-3045

COFFIELD, SHIRLEY ANN, lawyer, educator; b. Portland, Oreg., Mar. 31, 1945. BA, Willamette U., 1967; MA, U. Wisc.-Madison, 1969; JD, George Washington U., 1974. Bar: D.C. 1975. Clk. Stitt, Hemmendinger and Kennedy, Washington, 1973-74; asst. gen. counsel Office U.S. Trade Rep., Washington, 1975-79; ptnr. Reaves & Coffield, Washington, 1979-82; sr. counsel to dep. asst. sect. textiles and apparel U.S. Dept. Commerce, Washington, 1982-85; spl. counsel Skadden, Arps, Slate, Meagher and Flom, Washington, 1985-87; ptnr. Piper & Marbury, Washington and Balt., 1987-90, Baker & Hostetler, Washington, 1990-94, Keller and Heckman, L.L.P., Washington, 1994-98, Duane, Morris & Heckscher, 1998—; adj. prof. internat. econ. law Georgetown U. Law Sch., 1982—. Mem. ABA, Fed. Bar Assn., Am. Soc. Internat. Law, D.C. Bar, Pi Gamma Mu, Phi Delta Phi. Office: Duane Morris & Heckscher 1667 K St NW Ste 700 Washington DC 20006-1608

COFFIN, BERTHA LOUISE, telephone company executive; b. Atlanta, Aug. 19, 1919; d. William Wesley and Bertha Louise (Marsh) Mendenhall; m. J. Donald Coffin, Feb. 14, 1943 (dec. Sept. 1978). BA, U. Kans., 1940. Med. technologist Midwest Research Lab., Emporia, Kans., 1940-43; ins. agt. Coffin Ins. Agy., Council Grove, Kans., 1943—, sole owner, mgr., 1978-82; treas. Council Grove Telephone Co., 1947-50, sec.-treas., 1950-78, pres., chmn. bd., 1978-98, gen. mgr., 1978-99; del. legis. confs. Nat. Tel. Coop. Assn., 1986, 88, 91-92, 94, 97, comem. comml. co. com., 1987-91, mem. govt. affairs com., 1991-98, exec. com., 1996-98; founder, pres., chmn. bd. Kans. Personal Comm. Svcs. Ltd., 1995—. Copy preparation for book The Story of the Santa Fe Trail, 1982; author: History of Council Grove Telephone Company, 1991; ann. civic sects. tel. directory. Pres. various lit. clubs, Council Grove, 1945-72; speaker various civic, polit. and religious groups, 1962—; mem. adv. coun. Manhattan Christian Coll., 1983-86, trustee, 1986-92, 93-99, chmn., 1991-92. Mem. Kans. Telecomm. Assn. (bd. dirs. 1992-95), Ind. Tel. Pioneers (dir. 1984-92). Democrat. Avocations: travelling, ch. related activities, speaking. Office: PO Box 272 Council Grove KS 66846-0272

COFFIN, CHARLSA LEE, Montessori school educator, writer, artist; b. Dallas, Nov. 23, 1940; d. Charles Thomas and Zena Madora (Hall) Gaskin; m. Dwight Clay Coffin, June 23, 1964 (div. 1980); 1 child, John Charles. BA, Lawrence U., Appleton, Wis., 1962; postgrad., U. Pitts., 1962-64; Am. Montessori Soc. cert., Rosary Coll., Chgo., 1964. Cert. primary tchr., Am. Montessori Soc., 1984. Asst. to dean of women U. Pitts., 1962-64; directress The Parkside Montessori Sch., Upper Montclair, N.J., 1967—; collaborator (with Dr. James J. Strain) on chem. imbalance Mt. Sinai Hosp., N.Y.C., 1980—. Author: The State of Focus, 1992, 250 Poems and 250 Songs for Newborn to 8-year old Children, 1993, A Christmas Book: Thoughts of Mother to Son with 2-year old Child, 1996; one-woman show Montclair Libr., 1991. Home: The Rockcliff 10 Crestmont Rd Montclair NJ 07042-1930

COFFIN, CHRIS, managing editor; b. Portland, Oreg., Sept. 19, 1960. BA, Univ. Oreg., 1983. Mng. editor Grapevine Publs. Inc., Corvallis, Oreg., 1983—. Office: Grapevine Publ Inc PO Box 2449 Corvallis OR 97339-2449

COFFIN, DAVID ROBBINS, art historian, educator; b. N.Y.C., Mar. 20, 1918; s. H. Errol and Lois (Robbins) C.; m. Nancy Merritt Nesbit, June 10, 1947; children—Elizabeth, David Tristram, Lois, Peter. A.B., Princeton, 1940, M.F.A., 1947, Ph.D., 1954; postgrad., Yale U., 1940-41. Instr. fine arts U. Mich., 1947-49; lectr. art and archaeology Princeton, 1949-54, asst. prof., 1954-56, assoc. prof., 1956-60, prof. art and archaeology, 1960-66, Marquand prof. art and archaeology, 1966-70, Howard Crosby Butler Meml. prof. history architecture, 1970-88, prof. emeritus, 1988—, chmn. dept. art and archaeology, 1964-70; editor-in-chief Art Bull., 1959-62; Kress prof. CASVA Nat. Gallery Art, 1995-96. Author: Villa d'Este at Tivoli, 1960, The Villa in the Life of Renaissance Rome, 1979, Gardens and Gardening in Papal Rome, 1991, The English Garden: Meditation and Memorial, 1994; editor: The Italian Garden, 1st Dumbarton Oaks Colloquium on History of Landscape Architecture, 1972. Recipient Howard R. Marraro book award Am. Cath. Hist. Assn., 1979; Fulbright research award to Italy, 1951-52; McCosh Faculty fellow, also Am. Council of Learned Socs. fellow, 1963-64; Guggenheim Meml. Found. fellow, 1972-73; recipient Alice Davis Hitchcock book award Soc. Archtl. Historians, 1960; Howard T. Behrman award for disting. achievement in humanities, 1982. Mem. Coll. Art Assn. Am. (dir. 1957-61), Soc. Archtl. Historians (dir. 1968-70, treas. 1970-71), Renaissance Soc., Phi Beta Kappa. Office: Princeton U Dept Art and Archaeology Princeton NJ 08544

COFFIN, DWIGHT CLAY, grain company executive; b. Evansville, Ind., Aug. 21, 1938; s. Dwight DeWitt and Ruth Robertson (Clay) C.; m. Carol Ann Elsaesser, Dec. 27, 1986; 1 child by previous marriage, John Charles. Student, DePauw U., 1959-61; BA, U. Pitts., 1963; MBA, NYU, 1970; postgrad. in bus., Harvard U., 1976. With Chase Manhattan Bank, N.Y.C., 1964-72, employee rels. officer, 1968-70, mgmt. svcs. officer, 1970-72; dir. employment and tng. Continental Grain Co., N.Y.C., 1972-73; dir. internat. pers. Continental Grain Co., Paris, 1973-75; v.p. pers. Continental Grain Co., N.Y.C., 1975-85, v.p., sec., 1985-86, v.p. human resources, 1986—; mem. Am. Grad. Sch. Internat. Mgmt., Global Adv. Coun., 1986—. Mem. candidates com. Citizens Union, N.Y.C., 1976—: bd. dirs. St. Luke's Life Works, Stamford, 1989—; warden St. Barnabas Episcopal Ch., 1992—; v.p. Bishop's Fund for Children. Mem. SAR (treas. Capt. Matthew Mead chpt.), Orgn. Devel. Network, Indsl. Rels. Rsch. Assn., Mgmt. Devel. Forum, Nat. Fgn. Trade Coun. (chmn. mgmt. resources com. 1984), N.Y. Pers. Mgmt. Assn., Human Resource Planning Soc., Innis Arden Golf Club. Republican. Home: 40 Ettl Ln Greenwich CT 06831-4160 Office: Continental Grain Co 277 Park Ave New York NY 10172

COFFIN, FRANK MOREY, federal judge; b. Lewiston, Maine, July 11, 1919; s. Herbert Rice and Ruth (Morey) C.; m. Ruth Ulrich, Dec. 19, 1942; children: Nancy, Douglas, Meredith, Susan. A.B., Bates Coll., 1940, LL.D., 1959; postgrad. indsl. adminstrn., Harvard U., 1943, LL.B., 1947; LL.D., Bates Coll., 1959, U. Maine, 1967, Bowdoin Coll., 1969; degree (hon.), Colby Coll., 1975. Bar: Maine 1947. Law clk. to fed. judge Dist. of Maine, 1947-49; engaged in practice Lewiston, 1947-52; Verrill, Dana, Walker, Philbrick & Whitehouse, Portland, Maine, 1952-56; mem. 85th-86th Congresses from 2d Dist. Maine, House Com. Fgn. Affairs; mng. dir. Devel. Loan Fund, Dept. State, Washington, 1961; dep. adminstr. AID, 1961-64; U.S. rep. devel. assistance com. Orgn. Econ. Coop. and Devel., 1964-65; judge 1st circuit U.S. Ct. Appeals, 1965—, chief judge, 1972-83, sr. judge, 1989—; chmn. com. jud. br. U.S. Jud. Conf., 1984-90; adj. prof. U. Maine Sch. Law, 1986-89. Author: Witness for Aid, 1964, The Ways of a Judge-Reflections from the Federal Appellate Bench, 1980, A Lexicon of Oral Advocacy, 1984, On Appeal, 1994. 25798620emeritus Bates Coll.; dir. The Governance Inst., 1987—; mem. emeritus The Examiner; chair Maine Justice Action Group, 1996—. Lt. USNR, 1943-46. Mem. Am. Acad. Arts and Scis. Office: US Ct Appeals 156 Federal St Portland ME 04101-4152

COFFIN, JOHN MILLER, molecular biologist, educator; b. Boston, Apr. 20, 1944; s. Louis Fussell and Mary Elizabeth (McCarthy) C.; m. Marion Clair Szurek, June 22, 1968; children: Erica Mary, Heather Rachel. BA, Wesleyan U., 1967; PhD, U. Wis., 1972. Fellow U. Zurich, 1972-75, Switzerland; from asst. prof. molecular biology to assoc. prof. Tufts U., Boston, 1975-82, prof., 1982—, spl. asst. to dir. Nat. Cancer Inst. for HIV and AIDS, 1997—; mem. virology study sect. NIH, Bethesda, Md., 1980-84; mem. scientific adv. bd. Viagene, Inc., San Diego, 1988; Am. Cancer Soc. rsch. prof., 1994. Editor: RNA Tumor Viruses, 2 vols., 1985, Retroviruses, 1997; mem. editl. bd. Jour. Virol, Virology, Oncogene, Oncogene Res., Leukemia; editor Jour. Virol, 1991-97; contbr. articles to profl. jours. Trustee Leukemia Soc. Am., N.Y., 1987. Recipient Outstanding Investigator award Nat. Cancer Inst., 1987; Am. Cancer Soc. Rsch. Professorship, 1994. Mem. AAAS, Am. Soc. Microbiology, Nat. Acad. Sci. Office: Tufts Med Sch 136 Harrison Ave Boston MA 02111-1817

COFFIN, JUDY SUE, lawyer; b. Beaumont, Tex., Aug. 17, 1953; d. Richard Wilson and Genie (Mouton) C.; m. Gary P. Scholick, Nov. 10, 1983; children: Jennie Sue, Kate Frances. BA, U. Tex., 1974; JD, So. Meth. U., 1976. Bar: Tex. 1977, Calif. 1982. Atty. NLRB, Tex., 1977-80; shareholder Littler Mendelson, San Francisco, 1980—, also bd. dirs. Office: Littler Mendelson 20th Fl 650 California St Fl 20 San Francisco CA 94108-2702

COFFIN, LAURENCE EDMONDSTON, JR., landscape architect, urban planner; b. Toronto, Ont., Can., May 28, 1928; came to U.S., 1930; s. Laurence Edmondston and Josephine (Hewitt) C.; m. Beatriz de Winthuysen, Jan. 4, 1958; children: Thomas Amory, Alisa Winthuysen. B.S. in Hort., Va. Poly. Inst. and State U., 1952; M.L.A., Harvard U., 1957. Ptnr. Coffin & Winthuysen, East Lansing, Mich., 1962-65; asst. prof. Mich. State U., East Lansing, 1960-65; adj. assoc. prof. Cath. U. Am., Washington, 1966-81; ptnr. Coffin & Coffin, Washington, 1966—; sr. landscape architect Nat. Capital Devel. Commn., Canberra, Australia, 1985-86; mem. architect/engr. select bd. Pennsylvania Ave. Devel. Corp., Washington, 1978-90; mem. design adv. panel Dept. of Housing and Community Devel., Balt., 1978-87; sec. Internat. Inst. Site Planning, Washington, 1980—; lectr. city planning Georgetown U., 1968, George Washington U., 1973, U. Md., 1982; vis. evaluator Landscape Archtl. Accreditation Bd., 1979-85. Elder Presbyterian Ch., Washington, 1977—. Fellow Am. Soc. Landscape Architects; mem. Am. Inst. Cert. Planners, Cosmos Club Washington. Democrat. Home: 510 C St NE Washington DC 20002-5810 Office: 715 G St SE Washington DC 20003-2853

COFFIN, LOUIS FUSSELL, JR., mechanical engineer; b. Schenectady, Aug. 30, 1917; s. Louis Fussell and Laura C. (Glen) C.; m. Mary Elizabeth McCarthy, Apr. 24, 1943; children—John, Sarah (Mrs. Joseph Fitzgerald), Laura (Mrs. Thomas Koch), Robert, Patricia (Mrs. Jeffrey Mullen), Deborah (Mrs. Patrick Higgins), Louis Fussell III, Margaret (Mrs. Neil Sharkey). B.S., Swarthmore (Pa.) Coll., 1939; Sc.D., Mass. Inst. Tech., 1949. From asst. to asst. prof. mech. engring. Mass. Inst. Tech., 1939-49; research asso., then supr. mech. metallurgy Knolls Atomic Power Lab., Gen. Electric Co., 1949-54; mech. engr. Corp. Research and Devel. Gen. Electric Co., Schenectady, 1954-86; adj. prof. mech. engring. Rensselaer Poly. Inst., Troy, N.Y., 1955-60, disting. rsch. prof., 1986-96; adj. prof. Union Coll., Schenectady, 1965-86; vis. fellow Clare Hall, Cambridge (Eng.) U., 1976; cons. in field. Author. Recipient Alfred E. Hunt award Am. Soc. Lubrication Engrs., 1958; award excellence Carborundum Co., 1974; Francis Clamer medal Franklin Inst., 1984 Clayton lectr. Inst. Mech. Engrs., London, 1974; Coolidge fellow, 1974. Fellow ASME (Nadai award 1979), Am. Soc. Metals (Albert Sauveur Achievement award 1980), ASTM (chmn. E9 com. on fatigue 1974-78, Dudley award 1975, award of merit 1978, Kroll zirconium medal 1991); mem. Nat. Acad. Engring., Am. Inst. Metall. Engrs. (Disting. Career award 1978), Sigma Xi, Pi Tau Sigma, Sigma Tau. Patentee in field. Home: 235 Walker St Apt 172 Lenox MA 01240-2747

COFFIN, RICHARD KEITH, lawyer; b. St. Louis, Apr. 6, 1940; s. Kenneth and Agnes (Ryan) C.; m. June Springmeyer, Apr. 8, 1972; children: Jennifer, Joanna. B.S., U. Notre Dame, 1962; MBA, St. Louis U., 1967, JD, 1971. Engr., Nooter Corp., St. Louis, 1962-72; spl. prosecutor U.S. Dept. Justice, St. Louis, 1972-74; ptnr. Coffin & Torrence, P.C., St. Louis; gen. counsel Southwestern Linen & Indsl. Supply Assn., St. Louis; gen. counsel Mission Industries, Las Vegas, Nev., 1996. Mem. Citizens Adv. Com., Parkway Sch. Bd., Chesterfield, Mo., 1980-82; treas. PSO Com., Parkway Sch., 1982-83. Mem. ABA, Mo. Bar Assn., Met. Bar Assn. St. Louis, Assn. Trial Lawyers Am., Mo. Assn. Trial Attys., Phi Alpha Delta. Roman Catholic. Club: Optimist (sec. 1981). Home: 1748 Orchard Hill Dr Chesterfield MO 63017-5127

COFFIN, THOMAS M., federal magistrate judge; b. St. Louis, May 30, 1945; s. Kenneth C. and Agnes M. (Ryan) C.; m. Penelope Teaff, Aug. 25, 1973; children: Kimberly, Laura, Colleen, Corey, Mary, Brendan, T.J. BA, St. Benedict's Coll., 1967; JD, Harvard, 1970. Bar: Mo. 1970, Calif. 1972, Oreg. 1982, U.S. Dist. Ct. (so. dist.) Calif. 1971, U.S. Dist. Ct. Oreg. 1980, U.S. Ct. Appeals (9th cir.) 1971. Asst. U.S. atty., chief criminal divsn. U.S. Attys. Office, San Diego, 1971-80; asst. U.S. atty., supr. asst. U.S. atty. U.S. Attys. Office, Eugene, Oreg., 1980-92; U.S. Magistrate judge U.S. Dist. Ct., Eugene, Oreg., 1992—; sr. litigation counsel U.S. Dept. Justice, 1984. Mem. Oreg. Bar Assn. Avocations: soccer, jogging. Office: US Dist Ct 211 E 7th Ave Eugene OR 97401-2774

COFFIN, TRISTRAM POTTER, retired English educator, writer; b. San Marino, Calif., Feb. 13, 1922; s. Tristram Roberts Coffin and Elsie Potter Robinson; m. Ruth Anne Hendrickson, Feb. 15, 1944; children: Patricia, Mark, Priscilla, Jonathan. MS, Haverford Coll., 1943; MA, U. Pa., 1947, PhD, 1949. From instr. to assoc. prof. English and folklore Denison U., Granville, Ohio, 1949-58; from assoc. prof. to prof. U. Pa., Phila., 1958-84, emeritus prof., 1984—, vice dean grad. arts and scis., 1965-68; vis. prof. UCLA, 1955, U.S. Mil. Acad., West Point, N.Y., 1962-63, U. R.I., Kingston, summers 1968-70, Providence Coll., 1985-93. Author: Uncertain Glory: Folklore and the American Revolution, 1971, The Old Ball Game: Baseball in Folklore and Fiction, 1971, illustrated edit., 1972, the Book of Christmas Folklore, 1973, illustrated edit., 1974, The Female Hero, 1975, paperback edit., 1978, The Proper Book of Sexual Folklore, 1978, Great Game for a Girl, 1980, How to Play Tennis with What You Already Have, 1997; co-editor: (with Helen Flanders and Bruno Nettl) Ancient Ballads Traditionally Sung in New England, 4 vols., 1960, (with MacEdward Leach) Critics and the Ballad, 1961, (with Hennig Cohen) Folklore in America, 1966, Folklore from the Working Folk, 1974, the Folklore of the American Holidays, 1987, 3d edit., 1998, America Celebrates, 1991; editor: Our Living Traditions, 1968; contbr. over 100 articles and revs. to profl. publs. Coord. Voice of Am. Forum, 1966-67; chmn. Athletic Coun. U. Pa., 1965-72; soccer ofcl. USSFA, Phila., 1959-74; chief cons. Time-Life Enchanted World series, 1982-87. Recipient Citation for Outstanding Reference Work ALA, 1988; Guggenheim fellow, 1953; ACLS grantee, 1963. Fellow Am. Folklore Soc. (sec.-treas. 1961-65, editor spl. series and supplements 1961-65); mem. Dunes Club (bd. dirs.), Point Judith Country Club (tennis pro 1954-76), Merion

Cricket Club, Phi Beta Kappa. Episcopalian. Avocations: tennis, bowling. Home: 94 Edgewood Farm Rd Wakefield RI 02879

COFFMAN, BARBARA LEANN, environmentalist, state official; b. Conrad, Mont., Nov. 21, 1968; d. Walter Lloyd and Loretta Louise (Tomsha) C. AS in Agrl. Tech., Mont. State U.-No., 1990, AS in Environ. Health, 1991, BS in Water Quality and Chemistry, 1993. Cert. backflow assembly tester and proctor. Indsl. waste technician No. Mont. Coll., City of Havre (Mont.), Burlington No., 1990; rsch. technician No. Mont. Coll., Mont. Salinity Control Assn., 1990-93; EPA grant asst., tng. asst. No. Mont. Coll. (now Mont. State U.-No.), 1989-93, lab. technician, 1991-93, lab. tchg. asst., 1992; hydrotechnician, rsch. asst. Mont. Bur. Mines and Geology, Butte, 1993-94; tng. specialist Mont. Environ. Tng. Ctr., Gt. Falls, 1994—; mem. continuing edn. credit rev. com. for Mont. water and wastewater cert., 1996; adv. bd. Mont. State U. No. Sci., 1997—. Bd. dirs. Collins (Mont.) Cmty. Hall, 1994—. Recipient Earth Team Vol. award Soil Conservation Svc., Havre, 1989, cert. of achievement Dept. Energy, Richland, Wash., 1991. Mem. Am. Backflow Prevention Assn., Christian Women's After 5 Club. Avocations: family farming, stamp and rock collecting, fly fishing, horseback riding, playing basketball. Office: Mont Environ Tng Ctr 1211 Northwest Byp Great Falls MT 59404-1756

COFFMAN, DALLAS WHITNEY, financial consultant; b. Louisville, Sept. 18, 1957; s. Lawrence DuWaine and Jean (Smith) C.; m. Deborah Joan Schneider, May 18, 1980 (div. July 1987); 1 child, Robert Smith; m. Francine R. Chaput, Dec. 26, 1987 (div. Jan. 1995); m. Diana E. Pivo, May 28, 1995. AS in Bus. Mgmt., No. Essex Community Coll., Haverhill, Mass., 1977; BS in Mktg. Mgmt., Bentley Coll., 1979. CLU, CFP; chartered fin. cons.; registered investment adviser; lic. ins. adviser, Mass. Mgr. McDonalds Corp., Westwood, Mass., 1975-79; fin. salesman Gold Assocs., Chestnut Hill, Mass., 1979-84; propr., fin. planner Whitman Fin. Svcs., Wakefield, Mass., 1984—; prin. gen. securities N.Y. Stock Exchange, 1987; adj. faculty Am. Coll., Bryn Mawr, Pa., 1986—, Northeastern U., Boston, 1986—, Coll. for Fin. Planning, Denver, 1986—; enrolled agt. IRS, 1989; gen. securities prin. br. mgr. Office of Supervisory Jurisdiction for LINSCO/Pvt. Ledger, 1990—; former mem. Boston chpt. Am. Soc. CLUs and ChFCs, Mass. and Boston chpts. Nat. Assn. Life Underwriters. Pub. Who's Who in Life Ins., 1982-84; contbr. articles to profl. jours. Test participant Project PIPER IRS, 1990-92; sponsor Wakefield Little League. Mem. HALT, Am. Arbitration Assn. (panel arbitrators), Nat. Assn. Securities Dealers (bd. arbitrators large and complex case pool 1990), Internat. Assn. for Fin. Planning, Registry Fin. Planning Practitioners, Boston Estate Planning Coun., Bentley Coll. Reps. for Admissions Vol. Orgn., Inst. of Cert. Fin. Planners. Avocations: frustrated carpenter, music, skiing, motorcycles. Office: Whitman Fin Svcs 233 Albion St Wakefield MA 01880-3122

COFFMAN, DAVID ERVIN, accountant, valuation analyst; b. Hershey, Pa., Sept. 20, 1954; s. Ervin H. and Mary E. (Geib) C.; m. Joan Leathers, Sept. 7, 1983 (div. Dec. 1993); m. Georgia Geise, July 19, 1997. BSBA, Bloomsburg (Pa.) U., 1976. CPA; cert. valuation analyst; diplomate Am. Bd. Forensic Accts.; cert. forensic examiner Am. Coll. Forensic Examiners. Mem. econ. devel. staff Susquehanna Econ. Devel. Assn., Lewisburg, Pa., 1984-86; acct. Harold Witmer CPA, Montoursville, Pa., 1986-97; pvt. practice Danville, Pa., 1997—; instr. Pa. Coll. Tech., Williamsport, Pa., 1996—. Mem. AICPA, Nat. Assn. Cert. Valuation Analysts, Pa. Inst. CPAs, Nat. Assn. Bus. Coaches. Home: 119 W Market St Danville PA 17821-1818 Office: PO Box 428 Danville PA 17821-0428

COFFMAN, EDWARD MCKENZIE, history educator; b. Hopkinsville, Ky., Jan. 27, 1929; s. Howard Beverly and Mada (Wright) C.; m. Anne Nelson Rouse, June 30, 1955; children: Anne Wright, Lucia Page, Edward McKenzie. A.B., U. Ky., 1951, M.A., 1955, Ph.D. (So. Faculty fellow), 1959. Instr., asst. prof. Memphis State U., 1957-61; research asso. George C. Marshall Research Found., 1960-61; asst. prof., assoc. prof., prof. history U. Wis., Madison, 1961-92, prof. emeritus, 1992—; Dwight D. Eisenhower vis. prof. Kans. State U., 1969-70; vis. prof. mil. history U.S. Mil. Acad., 1977-78; disting. vis. prof. USAF Acad., 1982-83; Harold K. Johnson vis. prof. U.S. Army Mil. History Inst., 1986-87; mem. adv. com. Dept. Army Mil. History Program, 1971-76, 87-89, chair, 1989-93; mem. Nat. Hist. Publs. and Records Commn., 1972-76; John F. Morrison vis. prof. U.S. Army Command and Gen. Staff Coll., 1990-91. Author: The Hilt of the Sword: The Career of Peyton C. March, 1966, The War to End All Wars: The American Military Experience in World War I, 1968, The Old Army: A Portrait of the American Army in Peacetime, 1784-1898, 1986; mem. editorial bd. Mil. Affairs, 1974-77, Arno Press series The American Military Experience and The George C. Marshall Papers; chmn. editorial bd. Jour. Mil. History, 1995-99. Served with U.S. Army, 1951-53. Recipient Outstanding Civilian Svc. medal Dept. Army, 1978, Comdr.'s Pub. Svc. award, 1987, Disting. Civilian Svc. medal, 1991; Guggenheim fellow, 1973-74; Harmon Lectr. USAF Acad., 1976; Am. Philos. Soc. grantee, 1960; named U. Ky. Disting. Alumnus, 1995. Mem. Soc. for Mil. History (pres. 1983-85, Samuel Eliot Morison prize 1990, Moncado prize 1995), U.S. Commn. Mil. History, So. Hist. Soc., Phi Beta Kappa. Democrat. Home: 1089 Lakewood Dr Lexington KY 40502-2523

COFFMAN, JAMES RICHARD, academic administrator, veterinarian; b. Lyndon, Kans., July 19, 1938; s. Harry Thomas and Eleanor Louise (Lowe) C.; m. Sharon Sue Neill, June 10, 1960; children: David Neill, Michael James, Scott Thomas. BS, Kans. State U., 1960, DVM, 1962, MS, 1969. Pvt. practice equine vet. Wichita, Kans., 1962-65, Oklahoma City, 1969-71; inst. vet. medicine Kans. State U., Manhattan, 1965-69, prof., head dept. surgery and medicine, vet. medicine, 1981-84, prof. vet. medicine, dean, 1984-87, provost, 1987—; assoc. prof. vet. medicine and surgery U. Mo., Columbia, 1971-75, prof., 1975-81, dir. Equine Ctr., 1973-78; prof., head dept. surgery and medicine Sch. Vet. Medicine Kans. State U., Manhattan, 1981-84, prof., dean, 1984-87, provost, 1987—. Author: Equine Chemistry and Pathophysiology, 1991; equine editor Compendium on Continuing Edn. 1980-83, mem. editorial bd., 1980-85; editor in chief Equine Sportsmedicine, 1981-85; mem. editorial bd. Jour. Equine Medicine and Surgery, 1979-80; adv. bd. Equine Vet. Jour., 1980—; contbr. numerous articles to profl. jours. Bd. dirs. St. Mary Hosp., Manhattan, 1989—. Recipient Disting. Tchr. award Norden Labs., 1969. Mem. Am. Coll. Vet. Internal Medicine (diplomate, pres. 1978-79, chmn. bd. regents 1979-80), Am. Assn. Equine Practitioners (dir. at large 1982-83, v.p. 1984, pres. 1986-87), Am. Vet. Med. Assn. (trustee profl. liability ins. trust 1978-85, chmn. 1980-82), Nat. Acads. Practice Vet. Medicine (exec. bd. 1985-87, founding com. mem. 1985—), Kans. Vet. Med. Assn., Nat. Assn. State Univs. and Land Grant Colls. (coun. chief acad. officers 1987—), Kans. Livestock Assn., Am. Quarter Horse Assn., Rotary (bd. dirs. 1989-90), Phi Kappa Phi, Gamma Sigma Delta, Phi Zeta. Avocation: oil painting. Home: 3727 Anderson Ave Manhattan KS 66503-2512*

COFFMAN, JAY DENTON, physician, educator; b. Quincy, Mass., Nov. 17, 1928; s. Frank David and Etta (Kline) C.; m. Louise G. Peters, June 29, 1955; children: Geoffrey J., Joanne K., Linda J., Robert B. A.B., Harvard U., 1950; M.D., Boston U., 1954. Med. intern Univ. Hosp., Boston, 1954-55; asst. resident in medicine Univ. Hosp., 1955-56, chief resident in medicine, 1957-58, fellow in cardiovascular disease, 1956-57, sect. head peripheral vascular dept., 1960—; asso. in medicine Boston U. Med. Sch., 1960-65, mem. faculty, 1965—, prof. medicine, 1970—. Author: Raynaud's Phenomenon, 1989; co-author: Ischemic Limbs, 1973. Trustee Solomon Carter Fuller Mental Health Center, Boston, 1975-81. Served to capt. M.C. USAR, 1958-60. Diplomate Am. Bd. Internal Medicine.; Mem. Am. Soc. Clin. Investigation, Am. Fedn. Clin. Research, Am. Heart Assn., A.C.P., Begg's Soc., Phi Beta Kappa, Alpha Omega Alpha. Office: 88 E Newton St Boston MA 02118-2308

COFFMAN, JENNIFER B., federal judge; b. 1948. BA, U. Ky., 1969, MA, 1971, JD, 1978. Ref. libr. Newport News (Va.) Pub. Libr., 1972-74, U. Ky., 1974-76; atty. Law Offices Arthur L. Brooks, Lexington, Ky., 1978-82; ptnr. Brooks, Coffman and Fitzpatrick, Lexington, 1982-92, Newberry, Hargrove & Rambicure, Lexington, 1992-93; judge U.S. Dist. Ct. (ea. dist. and we. dist.) Ky., London, 1993—; adj. prof. Coll. Law, U. Ky., 1979-81. Bd. dirs. YWCA Lexington, 1986-92; elder Second Presbyn. Ch., 1993. Mem. Ky. Bar Assn., Fayette County Bar Assn., U. Ky. Law Sch. Alumni Assn. Office: 207 US Courthouse 300 S Main St London KY 40741-1924

COFFMAN, ORENE BURTON, hotel executive; b. Fluvanna, Va., Mar. 13, 1938; d. John C. and Adele (Melton) Burton; m. John H. Emerson, Aug. 5, 1955 (div. 1972); 1 child, Norman Jay; m. Mack H. Coffman, Oct. 26, 1986. Degree in hotel and motel mgmt., Michigan State U., 1966-70. Cert. hotel mgr., Mich. State U., 1970. Telephone operator Colonial Williamsburg (Va.) Hotel, 1962-64; room clk. Colonial Williamsburg (Va.) Hotel, 1964-68; mgr. front office Colonial Williamsburg (Va.) Hotel, 1968-83; asst. mgr. Williamsburg Inn, 1983—; pres. Colonial Williamsburg Employees Fed. Credit Union, 1980-85; owner Scavengers Paradise, Inc., 1995—. Mem. Am. Hotel Motel Assn. (nat. acctg. award 1970). Democrat. Baptist. Office: Williamsburg Inn PO Box 1776 Williamsburg VA 23187-1776

COFFMAN, PATRICIA JOANNE, school nurse, counselor; b. Hagerstown, Md., Sept. 7, 1944; d. Glen Franklin and Hope LouEmma (Mellott) Smith; m. James Lee Coffman Sr., June 17, 1962; children: James Lee, Joel, Daniel, Julie. ADN, Hagerstown Jr. Coll., 1973; BS in Health Care Adminstrn., St. Joseph's Coll., North Windham, Maine, 1983; MS in Psychology, Shippensburg (Pa.) U., 1993; PhD in Counseling summa cum laude, LaSalle U., Mandeville, La., 1995. RN, Pa. Staff nurse Fulton County Med. Ctr., McConnellsburg, Pa., 1973-75; sch.nurse Tuscarora Sch. Dist., Mercersburg, Pa., 1975—, dept. head of nursing; sec. Nursing Home Bd. Dirs., Coshocton, Ohio, 1973-94, Jacob's Dwelling Nursing Home; chmn. Ctrl. Banking Sys., Hagerstown, 1989-95, Supreme Coun. of the House of Jacob; part-time tchr. Hagerstown Bus. Coll. Author policy manual and articles. Co-facilitator victims group, 1994-95, children of divorce, 1994-95, others; developer "at risk" program Caring for Kids vol. tutoring program and classes. Mem. Psi Chi. Avocations: travel, reading, family activities, church activities, crocheting. Home: 10809 Etter Ave Mercersburg PA 17236

COFFMAN, ROY WALTER, III, publishing company executive; b. Detroit, May 27, 1943; s. Roy Walter and Adele Ruth (Carlson) C.; m. Brenda Lynn Spies, June 27, 1964; children: Christa Ruth, Eric Ross. Student, U. Okla., 1967-70. Enlisted USAF, 1960, advanced through grades to tech. sgt., 1968, resigned; sales mgr. Christian Sci. Monitor, Boston, 1968-75; v.p. Logos Internat., Plainfield, N.J., 1975-77; promotion mgr. Aspen Systems Corp., Germantown, Md., 1977-78; v.p. Christianity Today, Inc., Carol Stream, Ill., 1978-85, sr. v.p., 1985-96, pub. Campus Life mag., 1989-95; dir. internat. tng. The Upper Room, 1996-98; bd. dirs. Evang. Christian Pubs. Outreach; dir. internat. ministries The Upper Rm., 1998. Trustee Wheaton (Ill.) Christian High Sch., 1987-90. Mem. Evang. Christian Pubs. Assn. (bd. dirs. 1986-92). Home: 13673 N Pima Spring Way Tucson AZ 85737-7199*

COFFMAN, STANLEY KNIGHT, JR., English educator, former college president; b. Huntington, W. Va., Dec. 30, 1916; s. Stanley Knight and Werneth (Brockmeyer) C.; m. Ann Channing Wrentmore, Dec. 27, 1942; children: Ann Channing, Stanley Knight III, Eric Ewing. A.B., Haverford Coll., 1939; M.A., Ohio State U., 1940, Ph.D., 1948. Part-time instr. English Ohio State U., 1946-48; faculty U. Okla., 1948-62, prof. English, 1956-62; asst. dean Univ. Coll., 1954-62; prof. English, chmn. dept. Bowling Green (Ohio) State, 1962-68; acting dean Grad. Sch., 1967-68, v.p. acad. affairs, 1968-70, provost, 1970; pres. SUNY, New Paltz, 1972-79; prof. English SUNY, Albany, 1979-83. Author: Imagism, 1951, 2d rev. edition 1972, translated to Japanese 1995; contbr. articles to profl. jours. Served with AUS, 1942-46; lt. col. Res. Mem. MLA, Phi Beta Kappa, Omicron Delta Kappa. Presbyterian. (past elder).

COFFMAN, TERRENCE J., academic administrator. Pres. Milw. Inst. Art & Design. Office: Milw Inst Art & Design 273 E Erie St Milwaukee WI 53202-6003

COFFMAN, VANCE D., aerospace company executive; b. Kinross, Iowa, Apr. 3, 1944. BS in Aerospace Engring., Iowa State U.; MS in Aeronautics/Astronautics, Stanford U., PhD in Aeronautics and Astronautics. Guidance and control sys. analyst Space Sys. divsn. Lockheed Martin, 1967, v.p., 1985-87, divsn. v.p., asst. gen. mgr., 1987-88, pres. Space Sys. divsn., 1988, exec. v.p.; pres., COO Missiles sector Lockheed Martin, Bethesda, Md., CEO and vice chmn. bd. dirs., 1997-98, chmn., CEO, 1998—; bd. dirs. Bristol-Myers Squibb. Recipient Profl. Progress in Engring. award Iowa State U., 1989. Fellow AIAA, Am. Astron. Soc.; mem. Nat. Acad. Engring., Am. Def. Preparedness Assn., Nat. Security Indsl. Assn., Security Affairs Support Assn. Office: Lockheed Martin 6801 Rockledge Dr Bethesda MD 20817-1877*

COFFMAN, WILMA MARTIN, women's health nurse, educator; b. Washington County, Tenn., Dec. 29, 1939; d. Oval Earnest and Buena (Light) Martin; m. Niles Lee Coffman, Aug. 26, 1961; children: Stephen Lee, Ruth Marie, Andrew William. BSN, East Tenn. State U., 1962; MS, U. Tenn., Knoxville, 1987. RN, Tenn. Staff nurse in maternal-child health Holston Valley Hosp. and Med. Ctr., Kingsport, Tenn.; instr. Kingsport City Schs., Johnson City Schs. Organist, pianist Beulah Bapt. Ch., Jonesborough, Tenn., Greenvale Bapt. Ch.; pianist First Bapt. Ch., Jonesborough, Tenn. Mem. Toonie Cash Evangelist Assn., Pi Lambda Theta. Home: 410 Lakeridge St Kingsport TN 37663-3770

COFIELD, PHILIP THOMAS, educational association administrator; b. Monmouth, Ill., July 3, 1951; s. Earl Crescant and Vera (Shunick) C.; divorced; children: Calla, Megan. BA in English, St. Ambrose U., 1973. Dir. Jr. Achievment of Quad Cities, Davenport, Moline, Iowa, Ill., 1980-83; account exec. Jr. Achievment Inc., 1983-85; pres., CEO Jr. Achievment of Utah, Salt Lake City, 1985—. Established Utah Bus. Hall of Fame, 1991; bd. dirs. Utah Partnership for Edn1. and Econ. Devel. Mem. Utah Coun. on Economic Edn. (bd. dirs.), Salt Lake area C. of C., Rotary Club, (com. co-chmn. Salt Lake City). Office: Jr Achievment of Utah 182 S 600 E Salt Lake City UT 84102-1909

COFIELD, SHERDENA DORSEY, education director; b. Pitts., Aug. 19, 1944; d. Cornelius H. (dec.) and Clara Walker (dec.) Dorsey; (div. Aug. 1992); children: Elissa Mittie, Alexis Johanna. BA, Ashland Coll., 1967; MSW, Mich. State U., 1969; EdD, Boston U., 1999. Social worker Bridgeport (Conn.) Hosp., 1969-70; sr. social worker SUNY-Downstate Med. Ctr., Bklyn., 1970-75; chief clin. social worker J.J. Putnam Children's Ctr., Boston, 1975-78; asst. dean continuing edn. Boston U. Sch. Social Work, 1979-95, student program coord., 1995-99; part-time project cons. Levine-Brickman Assocs., Brookline, Mass., 1992-94; part-time rsch. assoc. U. Mass./Boston Trotter Inst., 1993-94. Profl. Devel. grantee AAUW, 1994-95. Mem. Phi Delta Kappa, Pi Lambda Theta. E-mail: sherdena@bu.edu. Home: 728 Boylston St Brookline MA 02467

COFRAN, GEORGE LEE, telecommunication consultant; b. Buffalo, Sept. 30, 1945; s. Louis Lee and Virginia Carolyn Cofran; divorced; children: Jeffrey Todd, Jennifer Renee. BSEE, Purdue U., 1967; MBA, Dartmouth Coll., 1969. CPA, Tex. Sys. analyst Burlington Mgmt. Svcs., Greensboro, N.C., 1969-70; mgmt. cons. Arthur Young & Co., Houston, 1971-77; pres. Cofran & Assoc., Inc., Houston, 1977—; comml. arbitrator Am. Arbitration Assn.; spkr., lectr. in field. Bd. dirs., pres. Huntwick Civic Assn., Houston; charter v.p. Active Corps of Execs., SBA, 1974, 75. 1st lt. AUS, 1970-71. Decorated Army Commendation medal. Mem. AICPA, IEEE, Assn. Sys. Mgmt. (past pres., dir. Houston chpt., Outstanding Svc. award 1978-79), Data Processing Mgmt. Assn. (cert.), Olde Oaks Racquet Club, Huntwick Racquet Club (Houston), Tau Beta Pi. E-mail: georgecofran@cofran.com. Office: Cofran & Assoc Inc 14611 Benfer Rd Houston TX 77069-2807

COFRANCESCO, DONALD GEORGE, health facility administrator; b. New Haven, May 29, 1953; s. George William and Marie Teresa (Marra) C. BS with distinction in Chemistry and Life Scis., Worcester Poly. Inst., 1975; MA in Gerontology, U. New Haven, 1979; MPH, Yale U., 1992. Lic. nursing home adminstr., Conn. Dir. biostats. and health planning Dept. of Health, New Haven, 1980; adminstr. Golden Manor Convalescent Home, New Haven, 1980-81, West Haven (Conn.) Nursing Ctr., 1981-85, Independence Manor, Meriden, Conn., 1986-87, Hillside Manor, Hartford, Conn., 1987-88; asst. in rsch. Yale U. Sch. Medicine, New Haven, 1975-77; asst. adminstr., fin. analyst, lectr., clin. practice specialist Yale U. Sch. Medicine, New Haven, 1990—; cons. Hospice: Project Care, Inc., Watertown, Conn., 1989-90; v.p., CFO Environ. Health Corp., Hamden, Conn., 1991-98. Bd. dirs. Partnerships Ctr. for Adult Day Care, Inc., Hamden, 1991—, pres., 1997-98, treas., 1998—; mem. Health Systems Agy. South Cen. Conn., Inc., Woodbridge, 1982-87; commr. human svcs. Town of Hamden, 1998—. Named one of Outstanding Young Men of Am., 1983. Mem. APHA, Am. Chem. Soc., Conn. Pub. Health Assn., Planetary Soc. Roman Catholic. Home: 104 Hillfield Rd Hamden CT 06518-1852 Office: Yale U Sch Medicine PO Box 208041 333 Cedar St New Haven CT 06510-3289

COGAN, JOHN DENNIS, artist; b. Wichita Falls, Tex., Feb. 24, 1953; s. John Patrick and Thrasilla Barbara (Forster) C.; m. Karen Elizabeth Smith, May 15, 1976; children: Jennifer, Tiffany, Kimberly, Courtney. BS in Physics, Tex. A&M U., 1975; MA in Physics, Rice U., 1978, PhD in Physics, 1981. Geophysicist Shell Oil Co., Houston, 1980-82; artist pvt. practice, Houston, Farmington, N.Mex, 1982—. Artist: one man show San Juan Coll., Farmington, N. Mex., 1994. Recipient Landscape award of merit Nat. Park Acad. Arts, Jackson, Wyo., 1994, Collectors award, 1995.

COGAN, JOHN FRANCIS, JR., lawyer; b. Boston, June 13, 1926; s. John Francis and Mary (Galligan) C.; m. Mary T. Hart, May 1, 1951 (div.); m. Mary L. Cornille, June 24, 1989; children: Peter G., Pamela E., Jonathan C., Gregory M. AB cum laude, Harvard U., 1949, JD, 1952. Bar: Mass. 1953. Since practiced in Boston; ptnr. firm Hale and Dorr, 1957-80, mng. ptnr., 1976-84, chmn., 1984-96; pres. The Pioneer Group, Inc., Boston, 1996—; trustee various Pioneer Funds, Inc., Boston, 1963—; pres. Pioneer Group, Inc., Boston, 1963—, Pioneering Mgmt. Corp., Boston, 1963; chmn. bd. dirs. Teberebie Goldfields, Inc., 1986—, chmn. bd. dirs. ICI Mutual Ins. Co., 1987-94, dir. 1994—; dir. Seatrain Lines, Inc., 1959-65; sec. Cabot, Cabot & Forbes Co., 1963-72, Ritz-Carlton Hotel Co., Boston, 1964-79; corporator Boston 5 Savs. Bank, 1961-79; chmn. exec. com., bd. dirs. Pioneer Western Corp., 1968-79; sr. v.p., bd. dirs. Western Res. Life Assurance Co., Ohio, 1968-79. Treas. Lexington (Mass.) Counseling Svc., 1964-69; trustee U. Hosp., Boston, 1965-95, chmn. bd., 1972-89; trustee Boston Med. Ctr., 1995—; treas. Friends of Harvard Track, 1964—; mem. Mass. Dem. State Com., 1968-80; bd. dirs. Wendell P. Clark Meml. Assn., Walker Home for Children, Brigham Surg. Group, Inc., 1981-95, The Med. Found., 1986-90; trustee Boston U. Med. Ctr., 1973-90; bd. govs. Investment Co. Inst., 1971-74, 75, 81, 82, chmn. bd. govs. 1978-80, 82-85, 86-89, 91—; trustee Boston Symphony Orch., 1989—, overseer, 1984-92, chmn., 1989-92; overseer Mus. Fine Arts, 1989-90, trustee 1990—, chmn., 1994—; trustee Boston Ballet, 1986-89. USNR, 1944-46. Mem. ABA, Internat. Bar Assn., Mass. Bar Assn. (chmn. corp. banking and bus. law com. 1973-76), Boston Bar Assn. (past chmn. profl. svcs. sect., mem. bench-bar com.), Boston Estate and Bus. Planning Coun. (past pres.), Boston Probate and Estate Planning Forum (sec. 1958-73), Nat. Assn. Security Dealers (bd. dirs. 1983-86, legal adv. bd. 1988-94). Home: 975 Memorial Dr Apt 802 Cambridge MA 02138-5755 Office: The Pioneer Group Inc 60 State St Ste 3 Boston MA 02109-1820*

COGAN, KAREN ELIZABETH, author, educator; b. Houston, Sept. 24, 1954; d. Hugh and Kathryn (DeGaugh) Smith; m. John Cogan, May 15, 1976; children: Jennifer, Tiffany, Kimberly, Courtney. BS in Elem. Edn., U. Houston, 1976. Kindergarten tchr. Houston Ind. Sch. Dist., 1976-79; writer Farmington, N.Mex., 1981—. Contbr. to anthology; author articles and short stories. Mem. Nat. Writers Assn. (profl. mem.), Soc. Children's Book Writers and Illustrators. Avocations: reading, gardening.

COGAN, MARSHALL S., entrepreneur; b. Boston, 1937. Grad., Harvard U., 1959, MBA, 1962. With Carter Berlind Weill, 1962-67; vice chmn. Cogan Weill & Levitt, 1968-71, CBWL Hayden-Stone, 1973; chmn., chief exec. officer Knoll Internat. Holdings Inc., N.Y.C., 1989-90, Trace Internat. Holdings, Inc., N.Y.C., 1989—. Office: Trace Internat Holdings Inc 375 Park Ave New York NY 10152-0002*

COGBURN, MAX OLIVER, lawyer; b. Canton, N.C., Mar. 21, 1927; s. Chester Amberg and Ruby Elizabeth (Davis) C.; m. Mary Heidt, Oct. 15, 1949; children: Max O. Jr., Michael David, Steven Douglas, Cynthia Diane, Christine Cogburn (Babb), (deceased). AB, U. N.C., 1948, LLB, 1950; LLM, Harvard U., 1951. Bar: N.C. 1950, U.S. Dist. Ct. (we. dist.) N.C. 1953, U.S. Ct. Appeals (4th cir.) 1984. Asst. dir. Inst. Govt., Chapel-Hill, N.C., 1951-52; staff mem. Atty. Gen. N.C., Raleigh, 1952-54; adminstr. asst. Chief Justice N.C., Raleigh, 1954-55; judge Gen. County Ct. Buncombe County, Asheville, N.C., 1968-70; sole practice Canton, Asheville, N.C., 1968, 1971—; ptnr. Roberts, Stevens & Cogburn, P.A., Asheville, 1986-95, Cogburn, Cogburn, Goosmann & Brazil, P.A., Asheville, 1995—. Chmn. Buncombe County Dem. Exec. Com., Asheville, 1974-76; mem. State Dem. Exec. Com., Raleigh, 1974-76. Mem. ABA, N.C. State Bar Assn., N.C. Bar Assn. (Gen. Practice Hall of Fame 1997), 28th Jud. Dist. Bar State of N.C., Buncombe County Bar Assn. (past pres.). Roman Catholic. Home: RR 1 Candler NC 28715-9801 Office: 77 Central Ave Ste H Asheville NC 28801

COGGESHALL, BRUCE AMSDEN, lawyer; b. Brattleboro, Vt., Sept. 24, 1941; s. Theodore Ronna and Katherine (Emery) C.; m. Phyllis Conroy, June 22, 1963; children: Bruce Jr., John P. AB, Dartmouth Coll., 1963; LLB, Cornell U., 1967. Bar: Me. 1967, U.S. Dist. Ct. Me. 1967, U.S. Tax Ct. 1970, U.S. Ct. Appeals (1st cir.) 1972, U.S. Supreme Ct. 1972. Mng. ptnr. Pierce Atwood, Portland, Maine, 1967—; commr. Nat. Commn. Uniform State Laws, Chgo., 1987—; mem. Maine Small Bus. Econ. Growth Bd., 1997—. Chmn. Cape Elizabeth (Maine) Charter Rev. Commn., 1986-87, Cape Elizabeth Harbor Commn., 1987-89; mem. Maine Econ. Devel. Incentive Commn., 1998—. Mem. Am. Law Inst., ABA, Nat. Assn. Bond Lawyers, Maine Bar Assn., Cumberland County Bar Assn. (pres. 1976-77). Avocations: skiing, running. Home: 336 Ocean House Rd Cape Elizabeth ME 04107-2615 Office: Pierce Atwood 1 Monument Sq Portland ME 04101-1110

COGGIN, CHARLOTTE JOAN, cardiologist, educator; b. Takoma Park, Md., Aug. 6, 1928; d. Charles Benjamin and Nanette (McDonald) Coggin; BA, Columbia Union Coll., 1948; MD, Loma Linda U., 1952, MPH, 1987; DSc (hon.), Andrews U., 1994. Intern, L.A. County Gen. Hosp., L.A., 1952-53, resident in medicine, 1953-55; fellow in cardiology Children's Hosp., L.A., 1955-56, White Meml. Hosp., L.A., 1955-56; rsch. assoc. in cardiology, house physician Hammersmith Hosp., London, 1956-57; resident in pediatrics and pediatric cardiology Hosp. for Sick Children, Toronto, Ont., Can., 1965-67; cardiologist, co-dir. heart surgery team Loma Linda (Calif.) U., asst. prof. medicine , 1961-73, assoc. prof., 1973-91, prof. medicine, 1991—, asst. dean Sch. Medicine Internat. Programs, 1973-75, assoc. dean, 1975—, spl. asst. to univ. pres. for internat. affairs, 1991, co-dir., cardiologist heart surgery team missions to Pakistan and Asia, 1963, Greece, 67, 69, Saigon, Vietnam, 1974, 75, to Saudi Arabia, 1976-87, People's Republic China, 1984, 89-91, Hong Kong, 1985, Zimbabwe, 1988, Kenya, 1988, Nepal, 1992, 93, China, 1992, Zimbabwe, 1993, Myanmar, 1995, North Korea, 1996, Penang, Malaysia, 1999; mem. Pres's. Advisory Panel on Heart Disease, 1972—; hon. prof. U. Manchuria, Harbin, People's Republic China, 1989, hon. dir. 1st People's Hosp. of Mundanjiang, Heilongjiang Province, 1989. Apptd. mem. Med. Quality Rev. Com.-Dist. 12, 1976-80. Recipient award for service to people of Pakistan City of Karachi, 1963, Medallion award Evangelismos Hosp., Athens, Greece, 1967, Gold medal of health South Vietnam Ministry of Health, 1974, Charles Elliott Weinger award for excellence, 1976, Wall Street Jour. Achievement award, 1987, Disting. Univ. Svc. award Loma Linda U., 1990; named Honored Alumnus Loma Linda U. Sch. Medicine, 1973, Outstanding Women in Gen. Conf. Seventh-day Adventists, 1975, Alumnus of Yr., Columbia Union Coll., 1984, Outstanding Achievement in Edn., Adventist Alumni Achievement award, 1999. Diplomate Am. Bd. Pediatrics. Mem. Am. Coll. Cardiology, AMA (physicians adv. com. 1969—) Calif. Med. Assn. (com. on med. schs., com. on member services), San Bernardino County Med. Soc. (chmn. communications com. 1975-77, mem. communications com. 1987-88, editor bull. 1975-76, William L. Cover, M.D. Outstanding Contbn. to Medicine award 1995), Am. Heart Assn., AAUP, Med. Research Assn. Calif., Calif. Heart Assn., AAUW, Am. Acad. Pediatrics, World Affairs Council, Internat. Platform Assn., Calif. Museum Sci. and Industry MUSES (Outstanding Woman of Year in Sci. 1969), Am. Med. Women's Assn., Loma Linda Sch. Medicine Alumni Assn. (pres. 1978), Alpha Omega Alpha, Delta Omega. Author: Atrial Septal Defects, motion picture (Golden Eagle Cine award and 1st prize Venice Film Festival 1964); contbr. articles to med. jours. Democrat. Home: 11495 Benton St Loma Linda CA 92354-3682 Office: Loma Linda U Magan Hall Rm 105 11060 Anderson St Loma Linda CA 92350

COGGIN, MICHAEL WRIGHT, insurance marketing and training executive; b. New Bern, N.C., Oct. 12, 1955; s. Garland Wright and Ava Gray (Evans) C.; m. Jean Anise Walker, Feb. 12, 1978; children: Christina Michelle, Michael Wright Jr. Student, U. N.C., 1975-76, N.C. Wesleyan Coll., 1973-75, Am. Coll., Bryn Mawr, Pa., 1988-91, Regents Coll., 1994. CLU, ChFC; cert. life underwriter tng. coun. fellow; assoc. customer svc. Life Office Mgmt. Assn. Dist. mgr., staff mgr., agent Durham Life Ins. Co., Durham/Wilmington, N.C., Morehead City, N.C.; sales mgr./agt. Durham Life Ins. Co., Conway, S.C., Rocky Mount, N.C.; regional supr. Durham Life Ins. Co., Raleigh, N.C.; regional tng. and advt. mktg. cons. Durham Life Ins. Co., Raleigh, 1977-88; agy. dir. Cen. Am. Life Ins. Co., Monroe, La., 1988-89; asst. v.p., gen. mgr. Durco agy. Durham Life Ins. Col., Raleigh, 1989-92, asst. v.p. dist. agy., 1989-92; dir. mgmt. devel. and tng. Capital Holding Agency Group, 1993-94; asst. v.p. new product devel. and tng. PennCorp Fin., Inc., Raleigh, 1994-96; v.p. field ops. Imperial Tng. Svcs., Raleigh, N.C., 1996-97; v.p. agy. ops. Imperial Ins. Group, Raleigh, N.C., 1996-97; owner Michael W. Coggin, Ins. Svcs., Zebulon, N.C., 1996—. Advisor N.C. Continuing Edn. Com., Raleigh, 1990—; pastor Corinth Bapt. Ch., Nashville, N.C., 1997—. Mem. Am. Soc. CLU and ChFC, Raleigh Chpt. of Am. Soc. CLU and ChFC, Nat. Assn. Life Underwriters. Baptist. Avocations: golf, traveling. Office: Corinth Bapt Ch 2883 North NC 58 Nashville NC 27856

COGGINS, PAUL EDWARD, JR., prosecutor; b. Hugo, Okla., May 21, 1951; s. Paul E. and Rebecca (Cates) C.; m. Regina T. Montoya, June 12, 1976; 1 child, Jessica Chandler. BA in Polit. Sci. summa cum laude, Yale U., 1973; BA with honors, Oxford U., 1975; JD cum laude, Harvard U., 1978. Bar: Tex. 1978. Tchr. Project New Gate N.Mex. State Penitentiary, 1973; law clk. Mass. Ct. Appeals, 1978-79; fed. prosecutor U.S. Attys. Office, Dallas, 1980-83; assoc. Johnson & Swanson, Dallas, 1979-80, ptnr., 1983-86; ptnr. Meadows, Owens, Collier, Reed & Coggins, Dallas, 1986-93; U.S. atty. U.S. Dept. of Justice, Dallas, 1993—; mem. adv. com. Magnet Sch. in Dallas, 1984—. Author: The Lady is the Tiger, 1987; co-author: Out of Bounds, 1992. Pres. bd. dirs. Dem. Forum, Dallas, 1985—. Rhodes scholar, 1973-76. Mem. ABA, Dallas Bar Assn. (mem. pro bono panel), Harvard Club (v.p. 1987—), Yale Club. Office: US Attys Office Earle Cabell Federal Bldg 1100 Commerce St Fl 3 Dallas TX 75242-1027

COGHILL, WILLIAM THOMAS, JR., lawyer; b. St. Louis, July 20, 1927; s. William Thomas and Mildred Mary (Crenshaw) C.; m. Patricia Lee Hughes, Aug. 7, 1948; children: James Prentiss, Victoria Lynn, Cathryn Anne. JD, U. Mo., 1950. Bar: Mo. 1950, Ill. 1958. Pvt. practice Farmington, Mo., 1950-51; spl. agt. FBI, 1951-52; ptnr. Smith, Smith & Coghill, Farmington, 1952-57; assoc. Coburn & Croft, St. Louis, 1957-58; ptnr. Thompson Coburn (formerly Thompson & Mitchell and predecessor firm), Belleville, Ill., 1958—. Co-author: Illinois Products Liability, 1991, Cavaliers, 1999. With USN, 1945-46. Fellow Am. Coll. Trial Lawyers; mem. ABA, Ill. State Bar Assn., Mo. State Bar Assn., Trial Attys. Am., Product Liability Adv. Coun. (sustaining mem.), Def. Rsch. Inst., Inc., Ill. Assn. Def. Counsel, Nat. Assn. R.R. Trial Counsel, Media Club, Elks. Home: 715 W Moon Valley Dr Phoenix AZ 85023-6234 Office: Thompson Coburn 525 W Main St Belleville IL 62220-1534

COGHLAN, KELLY JACK, lawyer; b. Longview, Tex., Sept. 3, 1952; s. Howard and Peggy Coghlan. BBA with honors, So. Meth. U., 1975, JD cum laude, 1978. Bar: Tex. 1978, U.S. Dist. Ct. (so. dist.) Tex. 1979, U.S. Tax Ct. 1981, U.S. Ct. Appeals (5th cir.) 1981, U.S. Supreme Ct. 1984. Law clk. to presiding judge Finis E. Cowan U.S. Dist. Ct. (so. dist.) Tex., 1978-79; assoc. Vinson & Elkins, Houston, 1979-84; equity ptnr. Dotson, Babcock & Scofield, Houston, 1984-88, chmn. risk mgmt. com., head gen. litigation group, 1987-88; pvt. practice, Houston, 1988—; bd. dirs. Sta. KSBJ, Houston, sec., 1990-93, chmn. long range planning com., 1989-93, mem. exec. com., 1990-97, v.p., 1994-97. Mem. So. Meth. U. Law Sch. Southwestern Law Jour. Mem. steering com. Palmer Drug Abuse Program, Houston, 1980-82; vol. jr. high and H.S. youth programs, 1990—, 2d Bapt. Ch., Houston, 1990—. Recipient So. Meth. U. M award, 1975, Russell Baker Moot Ct. 1st pl. award So. Meth. U. Law Sch., 1976. Fellow Houston Bar Found., Coll. State Bar Tex.; mem. ABA, Tex. Bar Assn., Houston Bar Assn., Houston Young Lawyers Assn. (chmn. com. on consumer rights 1981-82), Nat. Eagle Scout Assn. (life), So. Meth. U. Student Found. (hon.), Order of Coif (hon.), Am. Mensa, Gulf Coast Mensa, Blue Key Soc. (hon., pres. 1974-75), Beta Gamma Sigma (hon.), Phi Delta Phi (hon.), Lambda Chi Alpha. Avocations: druming, singing, youth work, working out. E-mail: www.christianattorney.com. Office: Ste One 505 Lanecrest Ln Houston TX 77024-6716

COGNATA, JOSEPH ANTHONY, retired football commissioner; b. Ashtabula, Ohio, Feb. 11, 1946; s. Joseph and Ella Jane (Dispense) C.; m. Betty Jean Jacobs, Dec. 17, 1978; children: Joseph Anthony Jr., Susan, Diana. Student, Kent State U., 1964-66. Sales rep. Endicott Buick, Pompano Beach, Fla., 1977-80; sales mgr. Fla. Chrysler Plymouth, West Palm Beach, Fla., 1980-82; owner, CEO So. States Football Club, Tequesta, Fla., 1982-85; backfield/spl. teams coach San Jose (Calif.) Bandits Minor League Football Sys., 1987-90; asst. head coach Calif. Outlaws Minor League Football Sys., Hayward, Calif., 1990-91; asst. to dir. football ops. Profl. Spring Football League, Meadowlands, N.J., 1991-92; co-founder Golden West Football League, Sacramento, 1991-96; commr. West Coast Amateur Football League, Mountain View, Calif., 1992-96; pres., CEO, commr. Pacific Western Football Alliance, Sacramento, 1992-96; pres. CEO U.S. Amateur Football Fedn., 1994—; ret., 1996; pres., CEO West Coast Football Conf., 1994-95. Author: Complete Football Playbook, 1969. Lutheran. Avocations: reading, sporting events, concerts, theater, dog. Home and Office: Barefoot Bay 1276 N Barefoot Cir Micco FL 32976-7039

COGSWELL, FREDERICK WILLIAM, English language educator, poet, editor, publisher; b. East Centreville, N.B., Can., Nov. 8, 1917; s. Walter Scott and Florence (White) C.; m. Margaret Hynes, July 3, 1944 (dec. May 1985); children: Carmen Patricia Cogswell Robinson (dec.), Kathleen Mary Cogswell Forsythe; m. Gail Fox, Nov. 6, 1985 (div. Aug. 1997); m. Adele Bartlett, Sept. 20, 1997. BA with honors, U. N.B., 1949, MA, 1950; PhD (Imperial Order Daus. Empire fellow), U. Edinburgh, Scotland, 1952; LLD (hon.), St. Francis Xavier U., 1982; DCL (hon.), King's Coll., 1985; LLD (hon.), Mt. Allison U., 1988. From asst. to assoc. prof. dept. English U. N.B., Fredericton, 1952-64; prof. U. N.B., 1964-83, prof. emeritus, 1983—; exchange writer in residence, Scottish Arts Council, 1983-84. Editor: The Fiddlehead, 1952-66, Humanities Assn. Bull, 1967-72; publisher: Fiddlehead Poetry Books, 1956-87; Author: prose Charles G.D. Roberts, 1983, Charles Mair, 1986; poetry The Stunted Strong, 1954, The Haloed Tree, 1957, Descent From Eden, 1959, Lost Dimension, 1960, Star People, 1968, Immortal Plowman, 1969, In Praise of Chastity, 1970, The Chains of Liliput, 1971, The House Without A Door, 1973, Light Bird of Life, 1974, Against Perspectives, 1977; collected poems A Long Apprenticeship, 1980, Selected Poems, 1982, Pearls, 1983; Meditations: 50 Sestinas, 1986, An Edge To Life, 1987, The Best Notes Merge, 1988, Black and White Tapestry, 1989, Watching an Eagle, 1991 When the Right Light Shines, 1992, In Praise of Old Music, 1992, In My Own Growing, 1993, As I See It, 1994, The Trouble With Light, 1996, Folds, 1997; translator: The Testament of Cresseid, 1958, One Hundred Poems of Modern Quebec, 1970, 71, A Second Hundred Poems of Modern Quebec, 1971, The Poetry of Modern Quebec, 1976, Confrontation, 1973, The Complete Poems of Emile Nelligan, 1983, (with Jo-Anne Elder) Unfinished Dreams: Contemporary Poetry of Acadie, 1991, anthologies Five New Brunswick Poets, 1961, (with W.S. MacNutt and Robert Tweedie) The Arts in New Brunswick, 1967, (with Thelma Reid Lower) The Enchanted Land, 1968, One Hundred Poems of Modern Quebec, A Second Hundred Poems of Modern Quebec, The Poetry of Modern Quebec; Atlantic Anthology, Vol. 1 (prose), 1983, Vol. 2 (poetry) 1985, A Double Question, 1999, Climates by Hermeéneé Chiasson; contbr. poems, articles to profl. jours. Mem. sr. arts fellowship awards com. Can. Council, 1972, mem. centennial poetry awards com., 1968; mem. Leave fellowship awards bd. humanities sect., 1973, 74; mem. poetry sect. Gov. Gen.'s award bd., 1973, chmn., 1974; bd. dirs. Can. Found., 1983—. Served with Canadian Army, 1940-45. Decorated mem. Order of Can., 1981; recipient Bliss Carman medal for poetry, 1945, 47, Douglas Gold medal, 1949, Gold medal for svc. to poetry as mag. editor Republic of Philippines, 1956, Gold medal as disting. poet, 1956, medal for 125 Can. anniversary, 1992, Aiden Nowlan award for excellence in the arts N.B. Gov., 1995; Nuffield fellow, 1959-60, Can. Coun. Sr. fellow, 1967-68. Mem. League Canadian Poets (regional exec. 1973-80, 1st v.p. 1985-86 , hon. life mem.), Canadian Authors Assn., Internat. P.E.N., Assn. Can. Pubs. (hon. life), Ind. Pubs. Assn., Atlantic Pubs. Assn. (pres. 1979-80), Assn. Can. and Que. Lits. (pres. 1978-80), N.B. Writers' Fedn. (hon. life.; pres. 1983-85). Home: 31 Island View Dr, Douglas, NB Canada E3A 7R7 *Anything I have accomplished has come about because it has been very easy for me to work hard at anything in which I have been interested and I have been interested in a good many things.*

COGSWELL, JOHN HEYLAND, retired telecommunications executive, financial consultant; b. Southampton, N.Y., Oct. 18, 1933; s. John W. and Lucy A. (McCurdy) C.; m. Patricia A. Morrissey, June 18, 1955; children: Julie A., Catherine J. AB, Dartmouth Coll., 1955, MS, 1956. Registered profl. engr., Mass. Engr. New Eng. Telephone Co., Boston, 1956-61, planning engr., Pittsfield, Mass., 1961-63, staff acct., Boston, 1963-65, constrn. program engr., 1969-71, div. mgr. fin., 1971-83, sec.-treas., 1983-90; engr. Am. Telephone Co., N.Y.C., 1965-68, mgr. econs., 1968-69; treas., bd. dirs. Neighborhood Health Plan, Boston, 1986-88, 90-98, pres. 1988-90. Pres., bd. dirs. Health Action Forum, Greater Boston, 1992-97, treas. 1983-92, 97-98; treas., bd. dirs. Muscular Dystrophy Assn., Greater Boston, 1978-91, Needham (Mass.) Hist. Soc., Inc., 1975-95, trustee, 1995—, Cmty. Health Ctr. Capital Fund, 1992—; mem., chmn. Needham Planning Bd., 1977-87; mem. Needham Bd. Appeals, 1987-91, Needham Bd. Selectmen, 1996—; bd. dirs. Pathway Health Networks, 1995-96, Care Group, 1996—, Health Agys. of Mass., 1996-99, Cmty Health Charities, 1999—; bd. dirs. Combined Health Appeal of Mass., 1991-96, pres. 1993-95; bd. dirs. Ctr. Comty. Responsive Care, 1994-98, treas.. 1994-95; trustee Deaconess-Glover Hosp., 1991—, vice chmn. 1992-94, chmn. 1994—; bd. dirs. Mass. Health Data Consortium, 1991-96, treas., 1994-96, New Eng. Health Care Found., 1992-96; mem. Needham Town Meeting, 1975—. Named Vol. of the Yr., Combined Health Appeal of Am., 1992. Mem. Fin. Mgmt. Assn. (bd. dirs. 1977-79), Fin. Exec. Inst. (bd. dirs. 1988-90), Treas.'s Club Greater Boston (pres. 1987-88), Republican Club (New Providence, N.J.; pres. 1966-68). Episcopalian. Avocations: gardening, golf. Home and Office: 1479 Great Plain Ave Needham MA 02492-1217

COGUT, THEODORE LOUIS, environmental specialist, meteorologist; b. Royal Oak Twp., Mich., Jan. 3, 1928; s. Louis and Mary Agnes (Evanish) C.; m. Martha Marie Nordstrom, Nov. 1, 1945; children: Leta Marie Cogut Mach, Willa Lynette Cogut Swartz, Pamela Anne Cogut Bryant. Grad. several meteorol. schs., USAF and U.S. Army; BA with honors, U. Md., 1965; MA in Teaching, Wayne State U., 1970. Weather forecaster USAF, 1948-53, 56-62; environ. analyst Climatology Ctr. USAF, Washington, 1962-64; instr. U.S. Army Arty. Meteorology Sch., Ft. Sill, Okla., 1965; grad. rsch. asst. in meteorology U. Okla., 1972-73; chief meteorologist Phelps Dodge Corp., Morenci, Ariz., 1974-79; environ. svcs. supr. Phelps Dodge Morenci, Inc., 1979-93; environ. cons. Tucson, Ariz., 1993—; mem. SKYWARN Spotter Network of Nat. Weather Svc., 1991-93; Citizen Amb. Environ. Del. to China, 1988; editor-in-chief Morenci Copper Rev., 1985-98. Author: (programmed text) Ballistic Wind Plotting, 1968; author meteorol. newsletters, 1968-69; co-author: History of Arizona's Clifton-Morenci Mining District, 2 Vols., 1998; inventor computerized air quality and weather prediction system MCAPS, 1975. Pres. Greenlee County Hist. Soc., Clifton, Ariz., 1990. Chief warrant officer arty. U.S. Army, 1965-69, Vietnam. Decorated Bronze Star, Legion of Merit; Gallantry Cross (Vietnam). Mem. AIME (chmn. Morenci chpt. 1989), Am. Meteorol. Soc. (pres. So. Ariz. chpt. 1980), Nat. Weather Assn. (mem. indsl. meteorology com. 1980), Air and Waste Mgmt. Assn., Greenlee County C. of C. (pres. 1992-93), Rotary Internat. (sec. Clifton-Morenci chpt. 1979), Phi Kappa Phi (U. Md. chpt.). Avocations: writing, painting, gardening, designing brochures. Home and Office: 5810 E Paseo San Valentine Tucson AZ 85750-1722

COHAN, CHRISTOPHER, professional sports team executive; b. Salinas, Calif., 1951; s. Helen C.; m. Angela; three children. BA, Ariz. State U., 1973. With Feather River Cable TV Corp., Orinda, Calif., 1973-77; owner Sonic Comms., Alaska, 1977; owner, CEO Golden State Warriors, Calif.; bd. dirs. Calif. TV Assn. Office: c/o Golden State Warriers 1011 Broadway Oakland CA 94607-4019 also: Golden State Warriors 1221 Broadway Fl 20 Oakland CA 94612-1822*

COHAN, GEORGE SHELDON, advertising and public relations executive; b. Oak Park, Ill., May 30, 1924; s. Charles and Ann (Holt) C.; m. Natalie Holmes, Dec. 14, 1974; children—Barry, Gail, Charles, Victoria. Student, Colo. Sch. Mines, 1941-42, Ind. U., 1942-43; BS in Mech. Engring, U. Cin., 1948; postgrad., John Marshall Law Sch., 1954-56. Certified bus. communicator. Field engr. Indsl. Erectors, Inc., Chgo., 1948-50; sales engr. Fairbanks-Morse & Co., Chgo., 1950-56; v.p., account supr. Hoffman & York Advt. Agy., Milw., 1956-62, Tobias & Olendorf, Chgo., 1962-65; sr. v.p., gen. mgr. Bozell & Jacobs, Inc., Chgo., 1965-74; chmn. bd., pres. Cohan & Paul, Inc., Chgo., 1975-84; pres. Fletcher, Mayo & Assocs., Chgo., 1984-87, Doremus & Co., Chgo., 1987-89, George Cohan Co., Chgo., 1989—; chmn. Cohan Seafood Co., San Francisco, 1988—; bd. dir. Forest Labs., N.Y.C., Universal Gift Cert., Inc. Author: (play) Black Mutiny, 1948; contbr. articles to profl. jours. Mem. Cen. Ind. coun. Boy Scouts Am., 1965-69; mem. exec. com. March of Dimes, 1965-69, ANTA, 1948-51. 1st lt. C.E. AUS, 1943-45, CBI. Recipient Outstanding Merit award 8th Pan Am. Ry. Congress, 1954, 1st pl. Nat. Lithographic Soc., 1955, 15th ann. G.D. Crain award, 1981, gold award Chgo. Assn. Direct Mktg., 1979, 80, Pres.'s Cup award, 1986; named to Advt. Hall of Fame, 1981. Mem. ASME, Bus. and Profl. Advertisers Assn. (internat. pres. 1976-77, Best Seller award 1954, Best of Show 1962, Best of Show Indpls. 1966-67, ABP award 1971, Addy Gold award 1979, Profl. Excellence award 1978, Gold medal 1979, 80, Pro-Com. Gold award, 1981, 83, 84, Career of Excellence Spl. award 1989, Lifetime Career of Excellence award 1989), Pub. Rels. Soc. Am., Screen Actors Guild. Unitarian. Avocations: flying, cooking, fishing, opera, acting. Home: 2048 Foxfire Ct Henderson NV 89012-2190

COHAN, JOHN ROBERT, retired lawyer; b. Arnhem, Netherlands, Feb. 10, 1931; came to U.S., 1940, naturalized, 1945; s. Max and Ann (deWinter) C.; m. Joan B. Gollob, Sept. 6, 1954; children: Deborah Joyce, Steven Mark, Judson Seth; m. Patricia S. Cohan, Nov. 8, 1970; m. Roberta Cohan, Nov. 23, 1980; 1 child, Alexis Marissa Muffin. B.S. in Bus. Adminstrn, U. Ariz., 1952; LL.B., Stanford U., 1955. Bar: Calif. 1956; cert. specialist in taxation. Assoc. firm Irell & Manella, Los Angeles, 1955-61, ptnr., 1961-95; ret., 1995; adj. prof. U. Miami Sch. Law, 1975-85, Ventura/Santa Barbara Coll. Law, 1996—; lectr. fed. income taxation U. So. Calif. Sch. Law, 1961-63; lectr., writer Calif. Continuing Edn. Bar Program, 1959, Practicing Law Inst., 1968—, also various tax and probate insts. Editor: Drafting California Revocable Trusts, 1972, 2d edit., 1984, Drafting California Irrevocable Trusts, 1973, 3d edit., 1997, Inter Vivos Trusts, Shephard's Citations, 1975; mem. supervisory bd. Thesaurus of World Tax Data, 1987—; contbr. articles on tax, estate planning, probate law to profl. jours. Pres. Portals House, Inc., 1966-69; chmn. Jewish Big Bros., Los Angeles, 1963-65; trustee Hope for Hearing Research Found., 1979-81, pres., 1972-75; chmn. charitable founds. com. Big Bros. Big Sisters Am., 1965-67, chmn. internat. expansion, 1967—, pres. western region, 1977-78, also bd. dirs.; bd. dirs. Jewish Community Found., 1979—, v.p., chmn. legal com., 1978—; mem. planning com. U. So. Calif. Tax Inst., 1969—, chmn., 1983—; mem. planning com. U. Miami Estate Planning Inst., 1971-86; bd. dirs. Los Angeles Campus Hebrew Union Coll., 1974-77; mem. Mayor's Commn. on Ethics in Charitable Giving, L.A., 1991-93. Fellow Am. Coll. Probate Counsel (mem. planning com. 1986—); mem. ABA (chmn. com. on estate planning for closely held bus. 1979-80, vice chmn. estate and gift tax com. of sect. on taxation), Los Angeles Bar Assn. (com. on fed. and Calif. death and gift taxation 1965-67, co-chmn. com. on bioethics 1979-80, Outstanding Tax Lawyers of the Year Dana Latham award 1987), Beverly Hills Bar Assn. (past chmn., lawyer placement com. and probate com.), Calif. State Bar (probate and trust com. 1971-74), Internat. Acad. Probate and Trust Law (exec. com.), Town Hall of Los Angeles (exec. com., past pres. Western div.), Beta Gamma Sigma, Alpha Kappa Psi, Phi Alpha Delta. Home: 79 Daily Dr # 199 Camarillo CA 93010-5807 Office: Irell & Manella 1800 Avenue Of The Stars Los Angeles CA 90067-4276 *I have tried to make my life a quest for excellence, not only in my career, but in serving others through charitable and educational organizations.*

COHAN, LEON SUMNER, lawyer, retired electric company executive; b. Detroit, June 24, 1929; s. Maurice and Lillian (Rosenfeld) C.; m. Heidi Ruth Seelmann, Jan. 22, 1956; children: Nicole, Timothy David, Jonathan Daniel. B.A., Wayne State U., 1949, J.D., 1952. Bar: Mich. 1953. Pvt. practice Detroit, 1954-58; asst. atty. gen. State of Mich., Lansing, 1958-61, dep. atty. gen., 1961-72; v.p. legal affairs Detroit Edison Co., 1973-75, v.p., 1975-79, sr. v.p., gen. counsel, 1979-93; counsel Barris, Sott, Denn & Driker, Detroit, 1993—; bd. dirs. Oakland Commerce Bank. Trustee Mich. Cancer Found.; bd. dirs. Orch. Hall., Concerned Citizens for Arts in Mich., U. Mich. Musical Soc.; mem. arts commn. Detroit Inst. Arts; mem. exec. bd. Friends Detroit Pub. Libr.; mem. Race Rels. Coun. Met. Detroit; pres. Arts Action Alilance. With U.S. Army, 1952-54. Recipient Disting. Alumni award Wayne State U. Law Sch., 1972, Disting. Svc. award Bd. Govs., Wayne State U., 1973, Judge Ira W. Jayne award NAACP, 1987, Israel Histadrut Menorah award, 1987, Knights of Charity award Pontifical Inst. for Fgn. Missions, 1989, Fellowship award Am. Arabic and Jewish Friends of Met. Detroit, Judge Learned Hand Human Rels. award, 1991, Gov.'s Arts award for Civic Leadership in the Arts, Michiganian of Yr. award Detroit News, 1993. Mem. ABA, Detroit Bar Assn., State Bar Mich. (Champion of Justice award 1993), Mich. Gen. Counsel Assn., Detroit Club. Democrat. Jewish. Home: 17 Eastbury Ct Ann Arbor MI 48105-1402 Office: Barris Sott Denn & Driker 15th Fl 211 W Fort St Lbby 15 Detroit MI 48226-3211

COHANE, HEATHER CHRISTINA, magazine publisher, editor; b. Camberley, Surrey, Eng.; came to U.S., 1982; d. William Willoughby and Naomi Mary (Winder) Fausset; m. John Philip Cohane, May 13, 1961 (dec. Dec. 1981); children: Alexander, Candida, Ondine; m. Ossian Kare Berga, Nov. 2, 1985. Student pvt. schs., Isle of Wight, Eng. and Neuchatel, Switzerland. Founding editor, pub. Quest mag., N.Y.C., 1987—. Office: Quest Mags Inc 100 Avenue Of The Americas New York NY 10013-1689

COHEN, AARON, aerospace engineer; b. Tex., Jan. 31, 1931; s. Charles and Ida (Moloff) C.; m. Ruth Carolyn Goldberg, Feb. 7, 1953; children—Nancy Ann Santana, David Blair, Daniel Louis. BS, Tex. A&M U., 1952; MS in Applied Math., Stevens Inst. Tech, 1958, D Engring. (hon.), 1982. Microwave tube design engr. RCA, Camden, N.J., 1954-58; sr. research engr. Gen. Dynamics, San Diego, 1958-62; mgr. Apollo command and service module lunar module guidance nav. and control NASA, Houston, 1962-70, mgr. command and service module project, 1970-72, mgr. shuttle orbiter project, 1972-82, dir. research and engring., 1982-86, dir. Johnson Space Ctr., 1986-93; prof. Tex. A&M U., College Station, 1993—. Editor Astronautics sect. Marks Mechanical Engineer's Handbook, 9th edit.; contbr. articles to profl. jours. Vice chmn. engring. task force Target 2000 Tex. A&M U., College Station, 1981-83. Served to lt. C.E., U.S. Army, 1952-54, Korea. Recipient Exceptional Service medal NASA, Houston, 1969, Disting. Service medal, 1973, 81, 88, 93—, Goddard Meml. trophy, 1988; Presdl. Rank of Meritorious Exec., U.S. Govt., Washington, 1981, Presdl. Rank of Disting. Exec., 1982, 88; Named NASA Engr. of Yr., Washington, 1982, Engr. of Yr. Nat. Acad. Engring., 1988. Fellow Am. Astron. Soc. (W. Randolph Lovelace II award 1982), AIAA (Von Karman lectureship 1984, Von Braun award 1993, Hon. Fellow, 1995, Robert H. Goddard Astronautics award 1996), ASME (medal 1984), AJAA, Tau Beta Pi. Jewish. Avocation: tennis. Office: Texas A&M University Dept Mech Engineering College Station TX 77843-3123

COHEN, AARON MITCHELL, producer, publisher, writer; b. West Palm Beach, Fla., Aug. 12, 1948; s. Seymour Benjamin and Frances Rhoda (Bachman) Cole. BA, Boston U., 1970, MEd, 1974. Psychiat. milieu therapist Human Resource Inst. Boston, 1970-73; dir. prodn. Videograf Inc., Needham, Mass., 1972-74; assoc. prodr., asst. to founder Regional Arts Found., West Palm Beach, Fla., 1977-81; adj. instr. Palm Beach Atlantic Coll., West Palm Beach, 1980-82; exec. v.p., exec. prodr., artistic dir. Leonard Davis Ctr. for Arts CUNY, N.Y.C., 1982-90; instnl. advancement cons. Aaron M. Cohen, West Stockbridge, Mass., N.Y.C., 1990-93; project dir. model libr. of future project Lenox (Mass.) Libr. Assn., 1993-95; program dir. Peter F. Drucker Found. Nonprofit Mgmt., N.Y.C., 1997-98; pres. Kiosk 2000, Palm Beach, Fla., 1998—; exec. prodr., cons., Boston, West Palm Beach, N.Y.C., 1974-82, 90-96; columnist Palm Beach Post, Palm Beach Daily News, West Palm Beach, 1976-78, 81-82; co-exec. prodr. Nat. Town Meeting with Nelson Mandela ABC-TV Ted Koppel Prodns., 1990; program dir. Peter F. Drucker Live by Satellite, 1997. Author: The Golden Anniversary Book of Congregation Beth El, 1976; author, dir. (documentary) And the Wilderness Shall Bloom: The Story of Henry Morrison Flagler and the East Coast of Florida, 1980; contbr. writer Handbook of Children and Media,1999; pub. Kiosk2000.com, 1998—. Exec. com. N.Y.C. Arts Coalition, 1988-90; bd. dirs. Lenox Libr. Assn., 1992-94. Winner internat. poster design competition Palm Beach Festival, 1981; Joseph Laffan Morse Found. scholar, 1966-70; Nat. Endowment Arts and NEH project grantee, 1980-90, 94. Mem. Dramatists Guild. Avocations: writing, art, musical composition, teaching. E-mail: aaron@kiosk.2000.com. Office: Kiosk2000 PO Box 47 Palm Beach FL 33480

COHEN, ABBY JOSEPH, investment strategist; b. N.Y.C., Feb. 29, 1952; d. Raymond and Shirley (Silverstein) Joseph; m. David M. Cohen. AB in Econs., Cornell U., 1973; MA in Econs., George Washington U., Washington, 1976. CFA. Economist Fed. Res. Bd., Washington, 1973-76; economist/analyst T. Rowe Price Assocs., Balt., 1976-83; investment strategist Drexel Burnham Lambert, N.Y.C., 1983-90; investment strategist Goldman, Sachs & Co., N.Y.C., 1990—, mng. ptnr., 1998—. Trustee/fellow Cornell U.; bd. overseers Cornell Med. Sch. Recipient Woman Achiever (Woman of Yr.) award YWCA, N.Y.C., 1989; named to top 50 in Global Fin., 1996, Wall St. Week Hall of Fame, 1997. Mem. Nat. Assn. Bus. Economists, Inst. Chartered Fin. Analysts (chair), N.Y. Soc. Security Analysts (mem. bd. govs.), Nat. Economists Club (bd. govs.), Assn. for Investment Mgmt. and Rsch. (chair bd. govs. 1997-98). Office: Goldman Sachs & Co 85 Broad St New York NY 10004-2456*

COHEN, ABRAHAM J. (AL COHEN), educational administrator; b. Chelsea, Mass., Mar. 19, 1932; s. Samuel and Sarah (Liskofsky) C.; m. Isabel M. Reardon, Aug. 23, 1959; children: David Joseph, Jonathan William, Jennifer Eve. B.S., Salem State Coll., 1959; M.Edn., Boston U., 1960; postgrad., U. Calif. at Santa Barbara, 1968, Fordham U., 1965; Ed.D., Columbia U., 1974; grad., U.S. Army Command and Gen. Staff Coll., 1975, Indsl. Coll. Armed Forces, 1976, Air Force War Coll., 1977. Tchr. social studies Chelsea jr. high schs., 1959-61; coord. instructional materials and svc. North Reading (Mass.) Pub. Schs., 1961-64; supr. instructional materials and sch. libraries White Plains (N.Y.) Pub. Schs., 1964-92, coord. health edn., 1974-88; pres. Ednl. Film Libr. Assn. and Am. Film Festival, N.Y.C., 1971-73; lectr. Sch. Continuing Edn., NYU, 1965-68, Sch. Libr. Svc., Columbia U., 1972-92; dir. audiovisual ctr. Salem (Mass.) State Coll., 1961-62; adj. prof. Westchester C.C., 1988-93; mem. adv. bd. Ednl. Products Info. Exch. Inst., N.Y.C., 1972-78; instr. U.S. Army Command Gen. Staff Coll.; comdt. 1150th USARF Sch., Ft. Hamilton, N.Y., 1983-87; dir. Sta. Cable 36-TV, White Plains, N.Y., 1982-92. Contbr. articles to profl. jours. Scoutmaster, instnl. rep. Muscoot-Westchester coun. Boy Scouts Am., 1971-72; pres. Westchester Libr. Assn., 1972-74; mem. expansion com. J.C. Hart Libr., Yorktown, NY., 1969-71; pres. Westchester County Ednl. Comm. Assn., 1968-69; chmn. bd. dirs., pres. Yorktown Jewish Ctr., 1969-70; bd. dirs. Westchester divsn. Am. Cancer Soc., chmn. pub. edn., 1981-83; mem. N.Y. State Employer Guard and Res. Com., 1987; exec. officer, duty officer, tng. officer, mem. Sheriff's Armed Posse Sun City West, Ariz., 1993—, bd. dirs., 1996-97; trustee Temple Beth Emeth. With U.S. Army, 1952-54; col. USAR ret. Decorated Legion of Merit; recipient Gen. John J. Pershing award U.S. Army Command and Gen. Staff Coll., 1975, Educator of Yr. award Am. Cancer Soc., 1983; named to U.S. Army Disting. Med. Rgt. Hall of Fame, 1987; Col. Cohen Day proclaimed by County of Westchester and Town of Yorktown, 1987. Mem. Mass. Audio Visual Assn. (bd. dirs. 1962-64), Ednl. Media Coun. (bd. dirs. 1971-73, exec. com. 1972-73), N.Y. State Edn. Comm. Assn. (bd. dirs. 1968-69), Assn. Edn. Comm. and Tech., Masons (32d degree, master Yorktown 1992-93), Shriners, Phi Delta Kappa. Home: 16014 W Sentinel Dr Sun City West AZ 85375-6681

COHEN, ALAN NORMAN, business executive; b. Clifton, N.J., Dec. 19, 1930; s. Samuel and Ida (Phillips) C.; m. Joan Meryl Fields, Nov. 25, 1953 (dec.); children: Laurie Elizabeth, Gordon Geoffrey; m. Carol F. Vasil, June 21, 1992; 1 child, Rebecca Samantha. Student, Dartmouth, 1948-49; AB,

Columbia U., 1952, LLB, 1954. Bar: N.Y. 1954. Assoc. Cahill, Gordon, Reindel & Ohl, N.Y.C., 1954-55; assoc. Paul, Weiss, Goldberg, Rifkind, Wharton & Garrison, N.Y.C., 1957-63, ptnr., 1964-70, 78-80; pres. Andal Corp., N.Y.C., 1980—, also bd. dirs.; chmn. ANC Sports Enterprises, LLC, 1997—; co-chmn. Sportsco. Internat. L.P., Toronto; exec. v.p., dir., mem. exec. com. Warner Comms., Inc., N.Y.C., 1970-74; pres., CEO, dir., mem. exec. com. Madison Sq. Garden Corp., N.Y.C., 1974-77; chmn. N.J. Nets, 1978-83; vice chmn., treas., dir. Boston Celtics Ltd. Partnership, 1986-93; co-chmn., pres. dir. Boston Celtics Comms. Partnership, 1990-92; mem. bd. visitors Columbia Coll., 1988-94; mem. bd. visitors Columbia Law Sch., 1994-96, chmn. ann. fund, 1994-98. Bd. overseers Grad. Sch. Mgmt. and Urban Professions; mem. bd. govs. NBA, 1978-93, chmn., 1986-88; trustee Am. Friends of Tel Aviv U., 1999—. With AUS, 1955-57. Named to Jewish Sports Hall of Fame, 1988; recipient John Jay award Columbia Coll., 1988. Office: 2500 Westchester Ave Purchase NY 10577-2515

COHEN, ALAN SEYMOUR, internist; b. Boston, Apr. 9, 1926; s. George I. and Jennie (Laskin) C.; m. Joan Elizabeth Prince, Sept. 12, 1954; children: Evan Bruce, Andrew Hollis, Robert Adam. AB magna cum laude, Harvard Coll., 1947; MD magna cum laude, Boston U., 1952. Intern Harvard Med. Svc., Boston City Hosp., 1952-53, resident, 1953-55; exch. registrar in medicine Dundee Royal Infirmary and U. St. Andrews, Scotland, 1955-56; rsch. and clin. fellow in rheumatology Mass. Gen. Hosp., Boston, 1956-58; instr. Med. Sch. Harvard Coll. and Mass. Gen. Hosp., 1958-60; head arthritis and connective tissue disease sect. Evans dept. clin. rsch. Mass. U. Hosp., Boston, 1960-72; Conrad Wesselhoeft prof. medicine Sch. Medicine Boston U., 1972-93, prof. pharmacology, 1974-92, disting. prof. medicine in rheumatology, 1993—; dir. Arthritis Ctr., 1977-94; dir. divsn. medicine Boston City Hosp., 1973-93; dir. Thorndike Meml. lab., 1973-93; bd. dirs. Hemagen Diagnostics Inc.; scientific bd. Neurochem. Inc., Can., 1997—. Editor: Laboratory Diagnostic Procedures in the Rheumatic Diseases, 1967, rev. edit., 1975, 3d edit., 1985, (with others) Symposium on Amyloidosis, 1968, (With R. Friedin and M. Samuels) Medical Emergencies: Diagnostic and Management Procedures from Boston City Hospital, 1977, (with J. Combes and H. Koh) 2d edit., 1983, Rheumatology and Immunology, 1979, (with J.C. Bennett) 2d edit., 1986, Progress in Clinical Rheumatology, 1984, (with D. Goldenberg) Drugs in the Rheumatic Diseases, 1986, Amyloidosis, 1986, Clinical Problems in Acute Care Medicine (J.J. Heffernan, R.A. Witzburg, A.S. Cohen), 1989; founder, editor-in-chief Amyloid: The Internat. Jour. of Exptl. and Clin. Investigation, 1994—; contbr. over 700 articles to profl. jours. Trustee Arthritis Found., Atlanta, 1976-82, trustee Mass. chpt., 1966-85, vice chmn., 1971-84, pres., 1981-94; vice sec. for N.Am., mem. exec. com. Pan Am. League Against Rheumatism, 1982-85; chmn. Boston City Hosp. Physician Alumni Reunion Com., 1992; pres. Boston City Hosp. Fund for Excellence, 1992. Served to surg. USPHS, 1953-55. Recipient Outstanding Alumnus award Boston U. Sch. Medicine, 1975, Purdue Frederic Arthritis award, 1979, James H. Fairclough Jr. award for disting. svc. to Mass. chpt. Arthritis Found., 1981, Alumni award for spl. distinction Boston U., 1981, Jan Van Bremeen Gold medal Dutch Rheumatism Soc., 1990, Commrs. Disting. Physician award Boston City Hosp., 1991, Gold medal Am. Coll. Rheumatology, 1994, Dr. Marian Ropes award Arthritis Found., 1995. Master Am. Coll. Rheumatology; fellow ACP; mem. Am. Coll. Rheumatology (pres. 1978-79), Am. Soc. Clin. Investigation, Assn. Am. Physicians, Am. Fedn. Clin. Research, Am. Soc. Exptl. Pathology, Interurban Clin. Club, Soc. Exptl. Biology and Medicine, Electron Microscopy Soc. Am., New Eng. Soc. for Electron Microscopy, Am. Soc. Cell Biology, N.Y. Acad. Sci., AMA, Mass. Med. Soc., New Eng. Rheumatism Assn. (past pres.), Italian Rheumatism Soc. (hon.), Spanish Rheumatism Soc. (hon.), Finnish Rheumatism Soc. (hon.), Brazilian Rheumatism Soc. (hon.), Irish Soc. Rheumatism and Rehab. (hon.), Italian Soc. Amyloidosis (hon.), Boston U. Sch. Medicine Alumni Assn. (past pres.), Phi Beta Kappa, Alpha Omega Alpha. Jewish. Clubs: Harvard (Boston); Wightman Tennis Center (Weston, Mass.). Office: Boston U Sch Medicine Amyloid Program 80 E Concord St # F-113 Boston MA 02118-2307

COHEN, ALBERT, musician, educator; b. N.Y.C., Nov. 16, 1929; s. Sol A. and Dora C.; m. Betty Joan Berg, Aug. 28, 1952; children—Eva Denise, Stefan Berg. B.S., Juilliard Sch. Music, 1951; M.A., NYU, 1953, Ph.D. (Fulbright fellow), 1959; postgrad., U. Paris, 1956-57. Mem. faculty U. Mich., Ann Arbor, 1960-70, assoc. prof. music, 1964-67, prof., 1967-70; prof. music, chmn. dept. SUNY-Buffalo, 1970-73; prof. music, chmn. dept. Stanford U., Calif., 1973-87, William H. Bonsall prof. music, 1974—; editor Broude Bros. Ltd., N.Y.C., Info. Coordinators, Detroit. Author: Treatise on the Composition of Music, 1962, Elements or Principles of Music, 1965; (with J.D. White) Anthology of Music for Analysis, 1965; (with L.E. Miller) Music in the Paris Academy of Sciences, 1666-1793, An Index, 1979, Music in the French Royal Academy of Sciences, 1981, Music in the Royal Society of London 1660-1806, 1987; contbr. articles to profl. jours. Guggenheim fellow, 1968-69; NEH fellow, 1975-76, 82-83, 85-89. Mem. Internat., Am., French musicol. socs., Galpin Soc. (Eng.), Music Library Assn. Office: Stanford U Dept Music Stanford CA 94305

COHEN, ALBERT DIAMOND, retail executive; b. Winnipeg, Man., Can., Jan. 20, 1914; s. Alexander and Rose (Diamond) C.; m. Irena Kankova, Nov. 6, 1953; children: Anthony Jan, James Eduard, Anna-Lisa. LLD (hon.), U. Man., 1987. Pres. Gendis Inc., Winnipeg, 1953-87; chmn., chief exec. officer Winnipeg, 1987-99, chmn., 1999—; chmn. exec. com. Gendis Realty Inc., Winnipeg, 1961—, also bd. dirs.; chmn., CEO Saan Stores Ltd. Author: The Entrepreneurs (Cert. of Merit Nat. Bus. Book award 1986). Past pres. Winnipeg Clin. Rsch. Inst., 1975-80, Paul H.T. Thorlakson Rsch. Found., 1978-80, Man. Theatre Ctr., 1968-71, 76-81; past hon. chmn. St. John's Ravenscourt Sch., 1984-94; commr. Metric Bd. Ottawa, 1978. Named mem. Order of Can., 1983, promoted to officer, 1995; recipient Internat. Disting. Entrepreneur award U. Man., 1983, Man. of Yr. award Sales and Advt. Club, Winnipeg, 1974, Commemorative medal 125th Ann. Can. Fedn., 1992; inducted into Can. Bus. Hall of Fame, 1994. Office: Gendis Inc, 1370 Sony Pl, Winnipeg, MB Canada R3T 1N5

COHEN, ALEX, retired publisher; b. N.Y.C., Jan. 1, 1927; s. Henry and Fanny (Menche) C.; m. Audrey Joan Katz, Dec. 23, 1950; children—Elynn Ruth, Laura Susan, Philip Henry. B.B.A. cum laude, Coll. City, N.Y., 1950; J.D., Bklyn. Law Sch., 1958; LL.M., N.Y. U., 1963. Bar: N.Y. 1958; C.P.A., N.Y. Engaged as pub. accountant, 1950-62, pvt. practice as pub. accountant, 1962-75, tax atty., 1958—; lectr. taxation Bernard Baruch Grad. Sch., 1968-69; spl. investigator N.Y. State Elections Frauds Bur., 1958. Pub.: Client's Monthly Alert; founder, publisher: Practical Accountant mag, N.Y.C., 1968—, Computers in Accounting mag.; editor: Practical Accountant Alert; tech. editor: Jour. Taxation, 1963-68; author: Accounting Shortcuts and Workpaper Techniques, 1970; contbr. articles to profl. jours.; editor: Tulane Tax Institute, 1974, Tactics and Strategies in Handling A Tax Audit, 1973. Founder, treas. North Jersey Operetta Guild, 1968. Served with AUS, 1945-46. Mem. Am. Inst. C.P.A.'s, N.Y. State Soc. C.P.A.'s, N.Y. County Bar Assn. Home: 2000 Island Blvd Aventura FL 33160-4957

COHEN, ALEXANDER H., theatrical and television producer; b. N.Y.C., July 24, 1920; s. Alexander H. and Laura (Tarantous) C.; m. Jocelyn Newmark, Jan. 12, 1942; 1 child, Barbara Ann; m. Hildy Parks, Feb. 24, 1956; children: Gerald Parks, Christopher Alexander. Student, NYU, Columbia U. Conceived and administered First Am. Congress of Theatre, Princeton U. Producer plays, 1941—; starting with Angel Street, other prodns. include At the Drop of a Hat, An Evening with Yves Montand, Victor Borge's Comedy in Music, An Evening with Mike Nichols and Elaine May, Beyond the Fringe, Maurice Chevalier at 77, Hamlet (Richard Burton), The Homecoming, Baker Street, Marlene Dietrich, Home, Little Murders, La Tragedie de Carmen, Dear World, Ulysses in Nighttown, The Devils, The School for Scandal, Ivanov, The First Gentleman, King Lear, Black Comedy, At the Drop of Another Hat, Dear World, The Madwoman of Chaillot, 6 Rms Riv Vu, Words and Music, 1974, Who's Who in Hell, 1974, Good Evening, 1974, Comedians, Hellzapoppin, 1976, Anna Christie, 1977, I Remember Mama, 1979, A Day in Hollywood/A Night in the Ukraine, 1980, 84 Charing Cross Road, 1982, Ben Kingsley as Edmund Kean, Peter Brook's Carmen, 1983, Play Memory, 1984, Dario Fo's Accidental Death of an Anarchist, 1985, Accomplice, 1990, Comedy Tonight, 1994, Sacrilege, 1995, Taking Sides, 1996; also numerous plays presented in West End of London, including Come as You Are, 1776, The Happy Apple, Who Killed Santa Claus?, Harvey, The Price, Plaza Suite, Halfway Up the Tree, Man and Boy, Merchant of Venice, The Rivals, Applause, The Unknown Soldier and His Wife, The Herbal Bed, 1997, Life Support, 1997; for TV has produced ann. Antoinette Perry (Tony) Awards Show, 1967-86; other TV prodns. include A World of Love; CBS-TV Spl. for UNICEF, 1970, Marlene Dietrich's I Wish You Love, 1972, CBS: On the Air, A Celebration of Fifty Years, 1978, Emmy awards, 1978, 85, 86, Night of 100 Stars, 1982, Parade of Stars, 1983, The Best of Everything, 1983, The Placido Domingo Special, 1985, Night of 100 Stars II, 1985, NBC's 60th Anniversary Special, 1986, Happy Birthday Hollywood, 1987, ACE Awards, 1987, Classical Music Awards show, 1988, Sam Found Out: A Triple Play starring Liza Minnelli, 1988; Disney MGM Studio Opening Spl., 1989, Night of 100 Stars III, 1990; supervised design and redesign and operation of numerous theatres including O'Keefe Ctr., Toronto, Can., New Mechanic Theatre, Balt., Erlanger Theatre, Phila., Locust St. Theatres, Phila., Rich Forum, Stamford, Conn., Palace Theatre, Stamford, Conn.; dir., writer, star (play) Star Billing, 1998. Named to Theater Hall of Fame, 1999. *

COHEN, ALLAN RICHARD, broadcasting executive; b. Bklyn., Dec. 27, 1947; s. Ike and Fae C.; m. Roberta Segal, July 12, 1970; children: Evan, Stacie. BS, Hofstra U., 1970; MM, Poly. Inst. Bklyn., 1976. Electronics engr. Sperry Systems Mgmt. Div., Great Neck, N.Y., 1970-74; with CBS/Viacom, 1974—; dir. planning and adminstrn. WCBS-TV, 1977-79; v.p. personnel CBS Broadcast Group, 1979-80; v.p., gen. mgr. Sta. KMOX-TV, St. Louis, 1980-86, Sta. KMOV-TV, St. Louis, 1986—; lectr. in comm. and journalism Washington U., St. Louis; mem. affiliates adv. bd. CBS. Restaurant critic, travel editor St. Louis Bus. Jour. Vice chmn. bd. dirs. St. Louis Symphony; bd. dirs. Paraquad, Jewish Hosp., United Way, Variety Club; mem. adv. bd. Nat. Coun. Jewish Women, St. Louis. Recipient Flair awards, Emmy awards. Mem. NATAS (v.p. St. Louis chpt. 1987-88, pres. 1989-91), Mo. Broadcasters Assn. (bd. dirs.), Ill. Broadcasters Assn., Nat. Assn. Broadcasters, St. Louis Jr. League (adv. bd.), Westwood Club, St. Louis Variety Club (bd. dirs.).

COHEN, ARMOND E., rabbi; b. Canton, Ohio, June 5, 1909; s. Samuel and Rebecca (Lipkowitz) C.; m. Anne Lederman; children: Rebecca Long, Deborah (dec.), Samuel. *Deborah Josepha Cohen was 22 years old when she died in the art colony in Alicante, Spain in January 21, 1963. She was a young artist in sculpture and oil painting. She was a graduate of Brandeis University.* BA, NYU, 1931; rabbi, Jewish Theol Sem. Am., 1934, M Hebrew Lit., 1945, DD (hon.), 1966; LLD (hon.), Cleve. State U., 1969; LHD (hon.), Baldwin-Wallace Coll., 1989. Ordained rabbi, 1934. Rabbi Pk. Synagogue, Cleve., 1934—; adj. prof. psychiatry Jewish Theol. Sem. Am., N.Y.C., 1970-75; bd. dirs. Inst. Religion and Health, N.Y.C. *On December 2, 1998, the Jewish Theological Seminary, at a general convocation, recognized Rabbi Cohen as the longest serving rabbi in the United States. For sixty-five years The Park Synagogue has been his only pulpit where he serves as Distinguished Service Rabbi. In 1983, he was named Humanitarian of the Year by the National Conference of Christians and Jews. In 1969, he was the first American rabbi to be named honorary fellow of the Hebrew University of Jerusalem. He is the founder of the Cleveland Board of Rabbis, and was Adjunct Professor of Pastoral Psychiatry at the Jewish Theological Seminary of America.* Author: All God's Children, Selected Readings on Zionism, Outline of Jewish History, Readings in Medieval Jewish Literature; mem. editorial bd. Jour. Religion and Health, 1943-67; contbr. articles to profl. jours. Bd. govs. Hebrew U., Jerusalem; trustee Am. Friends of Hebrew U., 1969—; bd. dirs. consumers League Ohio, Cleve., Jewish Community Fedn., Cleve., Coun. World Affairs, Cleve.; hon. v.p. Zionist Orgn. Am. Mem. Rabbinical Assembly Am., Cleve. Bd. Rabbis (founder), Lotos Club (N.Y.C.), Oakwood Club (Cleve.). Home: 8 Sherwood Ct Cleveland OH 44122-7592 Office: The Park Synagogue 3300 Mayfield Rd Cleveland OH 44118-1899 *Anyone can struggle through life without faith but everyone needs faith if he would confront life's inevitable challenges and sorrows and stand erect. It is easier to go through this life with faith than without it.*

COHEN, ARNOLD A., electrical engineer; b. Duluth, Minn., Aug. 1, 1914; s. Julius Ben Cohen and Nellie Harriet (Friedman) Laskin; m. Annette Goldberg, Jan. 18, 1942 (dec. Feb. 1989); children: Judith Cohen Libman, Melissa Cohen Silberman; m. Leah Davis, Dec. 17, 1989. BEE with high distinction, U. Minn., 1935, MS in Physics, 1938, PhD in Physics, 1947. Registered profl. engr., Minn. Devel. engr. electron tubes RCA Corp., Lancaster, Pa., 1942-46; computer devel. engr., tech. dir. Engring. Rsch. Assocs., Inc. and successor cos. through Sperry Rand Corp., St. Paul, 1946-71; asst. dean industry and profl. rels. U. Minn. Inst. Tech., Mpls., 1971-79, sr. fellow Charles Babbage Inst. for the History of Computing, 1980-92; mem. sci. adv. bd. Nat. Security Agy., Ft. Meade, Md., 1960-74; adv. coun. Chem. Abstracts Svc., Columbus, Ohio, 1969-72; founding mem. bd. dirs. Am. Fedn. Info. Processing Socs., 1960-65. Contbg. author: High-Speed Computing Devices, 1950, editor rev. edit., 1983; contbr. numerous articles to profl. jours.; patentee in field. Founding mem. bd. dirs. Charles Babbage Found., 1980—. Recipient Valuable Invention citation Am. Patent Law Assn., 1962. Fellow IEEE (Centennial medal 1984); mem. IEEE Computer Soc. (formerly Profl. Group on Electronic Computers, nat. chair 1960-62), B'nai B'rith, Sigma Xi, Tau Beta Pi, Eta Kappa Nu. Jewish. Home: 6051 Laurel Ave Minneapolis MN 55416-1044

COHEN, ARNOLD NORMAN, gastroenterologist; b. N.Y.C., Nov. 5, 1949; s. Norman and Edna Clara (Arnold) C.; m. Colleen Ruth Carey; children: Eric Arnold, Leslie Carey. BA summa cum laude, Hobart Coll., 1971; MD, Harvard U., 1975. Diplomate Am. Bd. Internal Medicine, Am. Bd. Gastroenterology. Resident internal medicine U. Pa., Phila., 1975-78, asst. instr. medicine, 1977-78; fellow gastroenterology, instr. medicine Northwestern U., Chgo., 1978-80; asst. clin. prof. medicine U. Wash. Med. Sch., Seattle, 1980—; mem. faculty Spokane (Wash.) Family Medicine Residency, 1980—; pvt. practice gastroenterology Spokane, 1980—; mem. various coms. St. Lukes-Deaconess Hosp., Spokane, 1980—; pres. med. staff St. Lukes Hosp., 1985-86. Contbr. articles to profl. jours. and textbooks. Fellow ACP, Am. Coll. Gastroenterology; mem. Am. Soc. Gastrointestinal Endoscopy, Am. Gastroent. Soc., Wash. Med. Soc., Spokane Internal Med. Soc., Phi Beta Kappa, Alpha Omega Alpha. Avocations: shooting sports, martial arts, swimming. Home: 3514 S Jefferson St Spokane WA 99203-1441 Office: Spokane Digestive Disease Ctr 801 W 5th Ave Spokane WA 99204-2823

COHEN, ARTHUR M., education educator; b. Caldwell, N.J., June 14, 1927; s. Harry Cohen and Rae Berke; m. Florence Brawer; children: Bill, Wendy, Andrew, Nancy. BA, U. Miami, 1949, MA, 1955; PhD, Fla. State U., 1964. Prof. higher edn. UCLA, 1964—. Author: The American Community College, 1996. Avocation: tournament bridge. Office: U Calif 405 Hilgard Ave Los Angeles CA 90095-1521

COHEN, ARTHUR MORRIS, artist; b. N.Y.C., Jan. 2, 1928; s. Morris Aaron and Flora (Hasson) C.; m. Elizabeth Copstein, Jan. 15, 1972; 1 son, Ezekiel. Student, Cooper Union, 1947-49, Art Student's League, N.Y.C., 1951, 60. mem. faculty Studio Art Sch. of the Agean, Greece, 1987. Represented in permanent collections Met. Mus. Art, N.Y.C., Hirshhorn Mus., Washington, Bklyn. Mus., N.Y.C., Boston Mus., Mus. City N.Y., N.Y. Hist. Soc., Everson Mus., Syracuse, Cooper Hewitt Mus., N.Y.C.; group shows include Everson Mus., Syracuse, Nat. Acad. Design, N.Y.C., 1976, 82, 83, David Findlay Gallery, N.Y.C., 1983, Hirshhorn Mus., Washington, 1979-80, Bklyn. Mus., N.Y.C., 1983, Cooper Hewitt Mus., N.Y.C., 1983, Albany Inst. History and Art, N.Y., 1985-86, East End Gallery, Provincetown, 1986, Lillian Kornbluth Gallery, 1987, Provincetown (Mass.) Art Assn., 1987, Forum Gallery, 1993; one-man shows at Blue Mountain Gallery, N.Y.C., 1980, 83, 85, Swansborough Gallery, Wellfleet, Mass., 1980, 83, Peter Rose Gallery, N.Y.C., 1982, Munson Gallery, Chatham, Mass., 1981, 85, 89, 90, East End Gallery, Provincetown, 1986, 87, Forum Gallery, N.Y.C., 1976, 90, Roko Gallery, N.Y.C., 1970, Ellen Harris Gallery, Provincetown, 1985, Lillian Kornbluth Gallery, Fairlawn, N.J., 1986, Phoenix Gallery, Provincetown, 1988, New East End Gallery, Provincetown, 1989, Forum Gallery, N.Y.C., 1990, East End Gallery, Provincetown, Mass., 1991, 92, Munson Gallery, Chatham, Mass., 1990, Wellfleet (Mass.) Fine Arts Gallery, 1990, Ease End Gallery, Provincetown, Mass., 1991, New East End. Gallery, Provincetown. 1993; contbr. articles to various periodicals. Served with U.S. Army, 1946-47. Named N.Y. State grantee, 1977, Ingram Merill grantee, 1979, Guggenheim grantee, 1981, Pollack Krasner grantee, 1993; recipient Pollock-Krasner award, 1986, 93, Adolf Gottlieb award, 1987, William Palmer prize Nat. Acad. Design, 1993. Jewish. Home: 55 Tiemann Pl New York NY 10027-3332

COHEN, BARBARA L., clinical neuropsychologist; b. June 22, 1956. Cert. in Sch. Psychology, Bryn Mawr Coll., 1991; D of Psychology, Widener U., 1993. Intern in neuropsychology Grad. Hosp., Phila., 1993-94; postdoctoral fellow in clin. neuropsychology Foote Meml. Hosp., Jackson, Mich., 1993-94; child psychologist Divsn. Child Mental Health Svcs., State of Del., Wilmington, Pa., 1995-96; clin. neuropsychologist Psychol. Assn. Bethlehem (Pa.), PC, 1996—.

COHEN, BARRY MENDEL, financial executive, educator; b. Dallas, Feb. 1, 1939; s. Ben and Marjorie Joyce (Novich) C.; BA, Rice U., 1960; MA, U. Tex., 1964, PhD, 1980; postgrad. (fellow) U. Ill., summer 1974; MLS North Tex. State U., 1987; m. Rosalee Valent-Torres, July 30, 1967. Instr. history Tex. Arts and Industries U., Kingsville, 1965-67; prof. social sci. Chowan Coll., Murfreesboro, N.C., 1969-73; exec. Cohen Candy Co., Dallas, 1973-83; asso. sales mgr. McCraw Candy, 1981-83; owner BMC Brokerage, 1983—; pub. svcs. libr. Tex. Southmost Coll., 1987-90; fed. programs tutor to migrant students Porter High Sch., Brownsville, Tex., 1991-96; lectr. Richland Coll., Dallas, 1976-77, Mountain View Coll., Dallas, 1977-84, U. Tex. at Dallas, summer 1977, South Tex. C.C., McAllen, 1996—; stringer UPI, Rio Grande Valley, 1990—; symposium speaker 14th Internat. Genetics Congress, Moscow, 1978; invited speaker John Innes Inst., Norwich, Eng., 1984; adj. prof. So. Tex. Cmty. Coll., 1996. Mem. nat. bd. advisers Ad Hoc Com. for Intellectual Freedom; mem. Cameron County Hist. Commn., 1989; bd. dirs. Kleberg County Community Action, 1966-67, Chowanoke Area Devel. Assn., 1971, City of Brownsville Pub. Libr., 1992—. Recipient Vavilov Century Bronze medallion Lenin Acad. Agrl. Scis., 1987. Mem. Am. Hist. Assn., Am. Assn. for Advancement Slavic Studies, AAUP. Democrat. Jewish. Contbr. articles to profl. jours. and newspapers. Home and Office: 239 Hibiscus Ct Brownsville TX 78520-8034

COHEN, BENJAMIN, federal judge. Judge Ala. Bankruptcy Ct., Birmingham, 1993—. Office: Robert S Vance Fed Bldg Rm 311 1800 5th Ave North Birmingham AL 35203

COHEN, BERNARD CECIL, political scientist, educator; b. Northampton, Mass., Feb. 22, 1926; s. Louis Mark and Lena (Slotnick) C.; m. Laura Mae Propper, Sept. 1, 1947; children: Barbara Ellen, Janie Louise. BA, Yale U., 1948, MA, 1950, PhD, 1952. Rsch. asst. Yale U., New Haven, 1950-51; rsch. asst., then rsch. assoc. Princeton (N.J.) U., 1951-59, asst. prof., 1957-59; mem. faculty U. Wis., Madison, 1959—, prof. polit. sci., 1963-73, Quincy Wright prof. polit. sci., 1973-90, prof. emeritus, 1990—, chmn. dept., 1966-69, assoc. dean Grad. Sch., 1971-75, vice chancellor acad. affairs, 1984-86, 88-89, acting chancellor, 1987, vice chancellor emeritus, 1990—; vis. rsch. scholar Carnegie Endowment Internat. Peace, 1965-66; mng. editor World Politics, 1956-59, mem. bd. editors, 1959-60, 72-78; mem. bd. editors Internat. Studies Quar., 1966-78; bd. dirs. Nat. Register Health Svcs. Providers in Psychology. Author: The Political Process and Foreign Policy, 1957, The Press and Foreign Policy, 1963, The Public's Impact on Foreign Policy, 1973, Democracies and Foreign Policy, 1995; editor: Foreign Policy in American Government, 1965. Served with AUS, 1944-46. Ford Found. Faculty Research fellow, 1969-70; fellow Center Advanced Study Behavioral Scis., 1961-62, 69-70; Fulbright-Hays research scholar Netherlands, 1975-76; Guggenheim fellow, 1981-82. Mem. Am. Polit. Sci. Assn. Home: 87 Oak Creek Trl Madison WI 53717-1509

COHEN, BERNARD S., lawyer; b. Bklyn., Jan. 17, 1934; s. Benjamin and Fannie Linda (Davis) C.; m. Rae Rose, Dec. 21, 1958; children: Bennett Alan, Karen Linda. BBA, CCNY, 1956; JD, Georgetown U., 1960. Cert. civil trial advocate, Nat. Bd. Trial Advocacy; bar: Va. 1961. Labor economist and labor law advisor U.S. Dept. Labor, Washington, 1956-61; ptnr. Cohen, Dunn, Curcio, Keating & Rohrstaff, PC, Alexandria, Va., 1961—; mem. Va. Ho. of Dels., Richmond, 1980-95. co-author: Environmental Rights and Remedies, 1971. Chmn. Alexandria (Va.) Dem. Com., 1967; alt. del. Nat. Dem. Conv., N.Y.C., 1980. Mem. ABA, Va. State Bar Assn. Trial Lawyers of Am., Va. Trial Lawyers Assn., B'nai B'rith. Democrat. Jewish. Office: Cohen Dunn et al PC 221 S Alfred St Alexandria VA 22314-3647*

COHEN, BETH ANN, neurologist; b. N.Y.C., Dec. 1, 1960; d. Steven S. and Marian Diane C.; m. Eric A. Goehl, June 11, 1995. MD, 1990. Diplomate Am. Acad. Psychiatry and Neurology. Intern Med. Coll. Pa.; fellow Cleve. Clinic; pvt. practice E. Stroudsburg, Pa. Mem. AMA, Am. Acad. Neurology, Am. Acad. Electrodiagnostic Medicine, Pa. Med. Soc., Monroe County Med. Soc., Alpha Epsilon Delta, Psi Chi, Sigma Psi. Avocations: exercise, gardening, traveling. Home: 4 White Haven Lake East Stroudsburg PA 18301 Office: East Brown St RR 5 Box 5186B East Stroudsburg PA 18301

COHEN, BETSY Z., bank executive; m. Edward C. Cohen; children: Daniel, Jonathan, Abigail. BA cum laude, Bryn Mawr Coll.; JD cum laude, U. Pa. Law clk. hon. John Biggs chief judge U.S. Ct. Appeals 3rd Cir.; law prof. Rutgers U. Law Sch.; co-founder Spector, Cohen, Gadon & Rosen, Phila.; founder, chmn., CEO Jefferson Bank, Downingtown, Pa., 1974—; founder Jefferson Bank N.J., 1992; chmn., CEO JeffBanks, Inc., 1993—; founder Resource Asset Investment Trust; bd. dirs. Aetna US Healthcare, The Opera Co. Phila., WHYY-TV; trustee Phila. Mus. Art, Jewish Theol. Sem.; vice chair Bryn Mawr Coll., chair fin. com.; chair Phila. Mus. Art Corp. Ptnrs. Article editor The Law Rev. Recipient Paradigm award Greater Phila. C. of C., 1997, Elizabeth Dole Glass Ceiling award Southeastern Pa. ARC, 1998; named Delaware Valley Master Entrepreneur of the Yr., 1994, one to Top 50 Bus. Women in Commonwealth of Pa., 1996, one of 50 Leading Female Entrepreneurs of the World, Nat. Found. for Women Bus. Owners, 1997, A Woman of Distinction, Cmty. Women's Edn. Project, 1998; ranked 103 Working Woman Mags. Top 500 Bus. Women, 1998. Mem. Order of the Coif. E-mail: bcohen@jeffbanks.com. Office: Jefferson Bank 1607 Walnut St Philadelphia PA 19103

COHEN, BONNIE R., government official; b. Brockton, Mass., Dec. 11, 1942; d. Harold I. and Irma (Sims) Rubenstein; m. Louis R. Cohen, Sept. 29, 1965; children: Amanda, Eli. BA, Smith Coll., 1964; EdM, Harvard U., 1965; MBA, Harvard Bus. Sch., 1967. Analyst RMC, Inc., Washington, 1967-71; asst. to vice supt. Washington Pub. Schs., 1971-72; sr. cons. Levin & Assocs., Washington, 1972-76; treas. UMWA Funds, Washington, 1976-81; advisor Stanford U. Treas., Palo Alto, Calif., 1981; sr. v.p. Nat. Trust for Historic Preservation, Washington, 1981-93; asst. sec. of interior Dept. of the Interior, Washington, 1993—; trustee ARC Retirement System, Washington, 1986-89; investment chair DC Retirement System, 1984-87. Bd. dirs. Beauvoir Sch., Washington, 1985-88, Nat. Cathedral Sch., Washington, 1985-88, Environ. Defense Fund, Washington, 1982-86, Ctr. for Marine Conservation, Washington, 1987-93. Mem. City Club. Democrat. Avocations: sports, antiques, basketball refereeing. Home: 1824 Phelps Pl NW # 1810 Washington DC 20008-1850 Office: Dept of the Interior Management 2201 C St NW Washington DC 20520-0001

COHEN, BRETT I., health products executive; b. Bronx, N.Y., Aug. 13, 1962; s. Gilbert Victor and Phyllis C. (Strassberg) C.; m. Elissa Bloom, Aug. 23, 1986; children: Harley Lennon, Jake Aaron. BS, SUNY, Albany, 1984, PhD in Chemistry, 1987. Postdoctoral fellow Rutgers U., New Brunswick, N.J., 1988; CEO, v.p. dental rsch. Essential Dental Systems, South Hackensack, N.J., 1989—; mem. dental magnets subcom. Am. Dental Assn./ISO Specification No. 81 Magnets and Keepers, 1993—. Contbr. articles to profl. jours.; patentee in field. Mem. Am. Chem. Soc., Soc. for Dental Materials, Soc. for Lasers, Am. Soc. Quality Control. Avocations: reading, running, movies. Office: Essential Dental Systems 89 Leuning St South Hackensack NJ 07606-1308

COHEN, BRIAN S., public relations executive. Chmn. bd., CEO Technology Solutions, Inc., N.Y.C. Office: Technology Solutions Inc 136 Madison Ave Fl 14 New York NY 10016-6901*

COHEN, BRUCE MICHAEL, psychiatrist, educator, scientist; b. Cleve. Heights, Ohio, Sept. 1, 1947; s. Herschel and Natalie (Marshall) C.; m.

Marian A. Oliner, July 11, 1970; children: Matthew, Laura. BS, MIT, 1969; MD, Case Western Res. U., 1975, PhD, 1975. Diplomate Am. Bd. Psychiatry and Neurology, Am. Bd. Med. Examiners. Resident in psychiatry McLean Hosp., Belmont, Mass., 1975-78, chief resident in psychiatry, 1977-78; instr. in psychiatry Harvard Med. Sch., Boston, 1978-81, asst. prof. psychiatry, 1981-85; chief clin. biochem. lab. Mailman Rsch. Ctr. McLean Hosp., Belmont, Mass., 1981-85, assoc. dir. mental health clin. rsch. ctr., 1981-85, chief clin. and molecular pharmacology lab., Mailman Rsch. Ctr., 1985—; assoc. prof. psychiatry Harvard Med. Sch., Boston, 1985-95, prof. psychiatry, 1995—; assoc. gen. dir. McLean Hosp., Belmont, Mass., 1988-94; dir. Brain Imaging Ctr. McLean Hosp., Belmont, 1993-97; sr. v.p. Rsch. and Tng. McLean Hosp., Belmont, Mass., 1994-97; pres., psychiatrist in chief McLean Hosp., Belmont, 1997—, head dept. psychiatry Med. Sch. Harvard U., 1997—, dir. Brain Imaging Program, 1997—; vis. physician Clin. Rsch. Ctr., MIT, 1979-88, 93—; cons. psychiatrist Westwood (Mass.) Lodge, 1986-88; dir. Brain Imaging Ctr., McLean Hosp., 1993—. Contbr. numerous sci. articles and abstracts to peer-reviewed jours.; author 20 book chpts. Laureate investigator Nat. Alliance for Rsch. on Schizophrenia and Depression, 1989. Predoctoral fellow NSF, Case Western Res. U., 1971-73, Ethel duPont Warren fellow in psychiatry Harvard Med. Sch., McLean Hosp. 1977-78; recipient 6 grants NIMH, 3 grants Scottish Rite Schizophrenia Program, 7 projects program grants NIMH. Fellow Mass. Psychiatric Soc., Soc. Magnetic Resonance, Am. Psychiat. Assn., Am. Coll. Neuropsychpharmacology; mem. AAAS, AMA. Office: McLean Hosp 115 Mill St Belmont MA 02478-1048

COHEN, BURTON DAVID, franchising executive, lawyer; b. Chgo., Feb. 12, 1940; s. Allan and Gussy (Katz) C.; BS in Bus. and Econs., Ill. Inst. Tech., 1960; JD, Northwestern U., 1963; m. Linda Rochelle Kaine, Jan. 19, 1969; children: David, Jordana. Bar: Ill., 1963. Staff atty. McDonald's Corp., Oak Brook, Ill., 1964-69, asst. sec., 1969-70, asst. gen. counsel, 1970-76, asst. v.p., 1976-78, dep. dir. legal dept., 1978-80, v.p. franchising, asst. gen. counsel, asst. sec., 1980-89, sr. v.p., chief franchising officer, 1989—; adv. dir., 1992-93, McDonald's Corp., 1992—; lectr. Practising Law Inst.; guest lectr. grad. sch. of bus. U. Chgo., Northwestern U.; adv. bd. La. State U. Franchise U.; dir. Goodwill Enterprises Devel. Corp. With AUS, 1963-64. Mem. Am. Bar Assn., Ill. Bar Assn., Chgo. Bar Assn., Internat. Franchise Assn. (lectr.), Assn. Nat. Advertisers, Chgo. Coun. Fgn. Rels., Tau Epsilon Phi, Phi Delta Phi. Club: Execs. (Chgo.). Author: Franchising: Second Generation Problems, 1969. Office: McDonalds Corp 1 Mcdonalds Plz Hinsdale IL 60523-1928

COHEN, BURTON JOSEPH, state senator; b. Boston, Dec. 6, 1950; s. Martin Erwin and Alice Florence (Wander) C.; m. Patty Scholz, 1991. BA, Windham Coll., 1972; MS, Boston U., 1978. In real estate, 1978-56; mem. N.H. Senate, 1991—, mem. jud., environ., capital budget coms., chmn. exec. depts. and adminstrn., chmn. energy and econ. devel., edn., rules and facilites, chief environment, majority leader; talk show host, 1985-90; instr. history and govt. N.H. Coll., 1987-95; mem. faculty Coll. Lifelong Learning, 1997—. Polit. columnist, 1986-90. Bd. govs. Abraham Lincoln Brigade Archives; bd. dirs. ACLU, 1989-90, Campaign for Ratepayer Rights, 1988-90. Named Favorite Columnist, Seacoast Life Mag., 1989, Favorite Politician, 1994. Office: PO Box 208 New Castle NH 03854-0208

COHEN, CARLA LYNN, publisher; b. N.Y.C., Feb. 27, 1937; d. Barnet and Florence (Skolnick) Ellowis; children—Beth Diane, Jeffrey. Student Clark U., Adelphi U. Editor, Oceanside (N.Y.) Beacon, 1975-77; adminstrv. asst. pub. relations Bd. Suprs. Nassau County, 1977-78; pres. Carla Cohen Communications, Oceanside, N.Y., pres. Cotar Publs., Nassau Borders Papers, Floral Park, N.Y., 1981—; editor Voters Guide, Lawrence, N.Y., 1979-80. Grand Marshall Meml. Day parade, 1986; panelist weekly Town Meeting radio talk show Sta. WGBB, panelist Davidson and Co., TV talk show; founding mem. Resident Referral Network, 1995. Recipient Patriotic Service award VFW, 1976; Outstanding Achievement award Am. Cancer Soc., 1976-77; Pub. Service award USAF, 1983; named Woman of Yr., B'nai B'rith, 1985, Sons of Italy, 1985, Businessperson of the Yr. Nassau County Coun. C. of C., 1989-90. Mem. C. of C. (v.p. 1982—), LWV (v.p. 1979), Woodbury Republican Club (pres. syosset), Internat. Platform Assn. Republican. Jewish. Office: PO Box 155 Franklin Square NY 11010

COHEN, CAROLYN ALTA, health educator; b. Boston, Aug. 25, 1943; d. Haskell Mark and Sarah (Siegal) Cohen. BS, Boston U., 1965; postgrad., Boston State Coll., U. Mass., 1978, Boston Leadership Acad., 1989, Boston Leadership Inst., 1997. Health and phys. edn. tchr., coach, girls athletic coord. Roslindale H.S., Boston, 1965-76; health and phys. edn. tchr., coach, athletic coord. West Roxbury H.S., Boston, 1976-87; asst. dir. health phys. edn. athletics Madison Park Campus, Boston, 1979-87; health educator dept. phys. edn./athletics West Roxbury H.S., Boston, 1989-90, 90—; commr. girls' basketball Boston Pub. Schs., 1979—; cheerleading judge various orgns., 1963, 64, 65, 70, 74, 80, 69-74; coach recreational programs N.E. Deaconess Hosp. Sch. Nursing, 1962-64, Beth Israel Hosp. Sch. Nursing, 1961-64; basketball ofcl. Bay State League, Pvt. Sch. League, Cath. H.S., 1961-80; coach phys. edn. dept. Boston U., 1962-65, 65-68; ofcl. Boston Park and Recreation Dept., 1962-75, summer playgrounds instr., 1961-65; instr. garening, athletic specialist agr. dept. Boston Schs., 1965-76. Instr. ARC, 1965—; trustee Adaptic Environ. Ctr., Boston, 1986—, treas., mem. exec. bd., 1990—; rep. Office Children-Area IV, Roslindale, Boston, 1974-76; liaison West Roxbury H.S. and Cmty. Sch. New Move Unltd. Theatre, Boston, 1981-84; liaison spl. arts project West Roxbury H.S., Boston, 1993-94; trustee Friends of Boston Harbor Islands Inc.; inducted Boston Harbor Scarlet Key Soc., 1998. Recipient Spl. Citation Boston U. Sargent Coll. Alumni Assn., Boston, 1980, Cert. of Appreciation ARC Mass Bay, 1986, Disting. Svc. to Alma Mater award Boston U., 1994, New Agenda award Boston Salute to Women in Sport, 1993. Mem. AAHPERD (bus. mgr. nat. conv. 1988-89, Presdl. medallion Ea. Dist. 1976), Mass. Assn. Health, Phys. Edn. Recreation and Dance (state and exec. com. 1969-94, treas. 1981-94, coord. registration ann. state conv. 1975-94, Honor award recognition 1978, Presdl Citation 1988), Boston U. Alumni Assn. (v.p. 1980-82, 87-89, v.p. cmty. 1995-97, sec. 1997—), Boston U. Nat. Alumni Coun (v.p. scholarships 1981-83, 88—), Sargent Coll. Alumni Assn. (class sec., editor class newsletter 1965—, Spl. Citation 1980, Black Gold award, 1995), Boston U. Women's Grad. Club. Home: 100 Corey St West Roxbury MA 02132-2330

COHEN, CHERYL DENISE, municipal official; b. Ft. Bragg, N.C., Mar. 23, 1955. BA, Princeton U., 1977; MBA, Columbia U., 1983. Treas. internat. divsn. commodity import-export financing Bank of N.Y., N.Y.C., 1977-81; v.p. City Corp. Securities Markets, Inc. City Corp., N.Y.C., 1983-90; v.p. Weldon, Sullivan, Carmichael & Co., 1990-92; asst. v.p. Kirkpatrick Pattis, 1993-95; mgr. revenue dept. City of Denver, 1996—. Bd. dirs. Mile High chpt. ARC; trustee The Gathering Pl.; treas. The Place Ministries. Recipient Consortium of Grad. Mgmt. Edn. fellowship, 1981-83, Recognition of Achievement award Five Points Bus. Assn., Inc., 1995, Leadership Denver award Denver C. of C., 1994; honored in Living Portraits of African-Am. Women Nat. Coun. Negro Women, 1997. Mem. Govt. Finance Officers Assn. Office: Revenue Dept City of Denver Annex III Rm 300 144 W Colfax Ave Denver CO 80202-5391

COHEN, CHRISTOPHER B., lawyer; b. Washington, July 10, 1942; m. Judith Calder; 2 children. BA, U. Mich., 1964, JD, 1967. Bar: Ill. 1968, Wis. 1986, D.C. 1972, U.S. Dist. Ct. D.C. 1969, U.S. Dist Ct. (no. dist.) Ill. 1968, U.S. Ct. Mil. Appeals 1977, U.S. Supreme Ct. 1974; lic. real estate broker, cert. real estate continuing edn. instr., Ill. Clerk, lawyer Legal Aid Bur.-United Charities of Chgo., 1967-68; adminstrv. asst. to pres. Cook County Bd. Commrs., 1969-71; hearing officer Liquor Commn. Cook County, Chgo., 1970-71; alderman 46th ward Chgo. City Coun., 1971-77; atty. Schwartzberg, Barnett & Cohen, Chgo., 1973-77; midwest regional dir. U.S. Dept. HHS, Chgo., 1977-81; atty. Hinshaw, Culbertson, Moelmann, Hoban & Fuller, Chgo., 1981-82, Cassiday, Shade & Gloor, Chgo., 1982-85; ptnr. Holleb & Coff, Chgo., 1985-98; of counsel Buyer & Rubin, Chgo., 1998—; lectr. Northwestern U., 1973, DePaul U., Chgo., 1981, U. Ill., Chgo., 1981, 82; adult edn. tchr. Francis Parker Sch., Chgo., 1979, 80, 81; bd. dirs. Ill. Hosp. Licensing Bd., 1987-97; mem. fed. regional coun. and nursing home adv. coun. Office of Ill. Atty. Gen., 1988-94. Contbr. articles to profl. jours. and nat. newspapers. field organizer Humphrey for Pres., Chgo., 1968; asst. to Ill. field dir. Jimmy Carter for Pres., Chgo., 1976; active spl. projects, polit. unit Clinton/Gore Campaign, Little Rock, 1992; mem. govt. affairs com. Jewish Fedn. Met. Chgo., 1988—; mem. U. Mich. Law Sch. Alumni Fund; fin. chair New Trier Township Dem. Orgn., 1993—; bd. dirs. UNICEF Chgo., 1996—. Mem. ABA (adminstrv. law and regulatory practice sect.), Ill. State Bar Assn. (founding mem., chair health care sect. coun. 1986-87, mem. legis. com. 1988-90, assembly 1991-97, local govt. sect.), Chgo. Bar Assn. (vice chair urban affairs com. 1991, chair health law com. 1983, mem. real estate tax com.), D.C. Bar Assn., State Bar Wis. Office: Buyer & Rubin 205 W Wacker # 701 Chicago IL 60606-1212

COHEN, CLAIRE GORHAM, investors service company executive; b. St. Johnsbury, Vt., May 9, 1934; d. John David and Muriel (Somers) Gorham; m. Richard D. Cohen, Nov. 26, 1959; 1 son, James H. BA, Radcliffe Coll., 1956; student, U. Vt., 1953-54. Proofreader Dun & Bradstreet, Inc., 1956, mcpl. bond analyst, 1957-64, sr. state analyst, 1965-66, sr. analyst, 1970-71; sr. analyst Moody's Investors Svc. Inc., N.Y.C., 1971-75; v.p., assoc. dir. rsch. Mcpl. Bond Rsch. Divsn., N.Y.C., 1975-86, v.p. mng. dir. state ratings, 1986-89; exec. mng. dir. govtl. fin. Fitch Investors Svc., Inc., N.Y.C., 1989-91, exec. v.p., 1991-94, vice chmn., 1994-97; vice chmn. Fitch IBCA, 1997—; mem. Govt. Acctg. Stds. Adv. Coun., 1999—. Mem. Task Force on N.Y. State Pub. Authorities, 1974-75. Mem. N.Y. Harvard-Radcliffe Schs. Com.; 1952 class agt. St. Johnsbury Acad. , 1981-86; 1956 class agt. Radcliffe Coll., 1981-86. Mem. Mcpl. Forum N.Y., Mcpl. Analysts Group N.Y. (treas. 1983-84, chmn. 1984-85), Nat. Fedn. Mcpl. Analysts (bd. govs. 1984-86, chmn. awards com. 1984-85, Career Achievement award 1991), Soc. Mcpl. Analysts, Radcliffe of N.Y. Club, India House Club. Office: Fitch IBCA One State St Plz New York NY 10004-2614

COHEN, CLARENCE BUDD, aerospace engineer; b. Monticello, N.Y., Feb. 7, 1925; s. Isidor and Dora Cohen; m. Beatrice Sholofsky, Jan. 1, 1947; children: William David, Deborah Ann. BAE, Rensselaer Poly. Inst., 1945, MAE, 1947; MA, Princeton U., 1952, PhD, 1954. Aerospace research scientist NASA, Cleve., 1947-56; assoc. chief. spl. projects br. TRW Electronics and Def., Redondo Beach, Calif., 1957-87, head hypersonics research section, 1957-61; mgr. aerodynamics dept. TRW Electronics and Defense, Redondo Beach, Calif., 1961-63, mgr. aero scis. lab., 1966-69, dir. tech. application, 1970-80, dir. technology, 1980-87; cons. in field. Contbr. articles to profl. jours; patentee manned spacecraft with staged reentry. Trustee, vice chmn. Northrup U., 1991-99. With USNR, 1943-46. Recipient Class of 1902 Rsch. Prize, Rensselaer Poly. Inst., 1945; Guggenheim fellow Princeton U., 1950-52. Fellow AIAA; mem. Licensing Execs. Soc., Research Soc. Am. (past pres.), Indsl. Research Inst. (emeritus), TRW Retirees Assn. (dir. 1997-98, v.p. 1999), Sigma Xi. Club: King Harbor Yacht. Achievements include development of now-classical solutions to equations of viscous compressible flow with heat transfer; technical direction for aerothermodynamic aspects of USAF ICBM programs; 1 patent. Home: 332 Via El Chico Redondo Beach CA 90277-6756

COHEN, CLAUDIA, journalist, television personality; b. Englewood, N.J., Dec. 16, 1950; d. Robert B. and Harriet (Brandwein) C.; 1 child, Samantha. BA, U. Pa., 1972. Mng. editor The Daily Pennsylvanian; with More Mag., N.Y.C., 1973-76, mng. editor, 1976-77; reporter N.Y. Post, N.Y.C., 1977-78, editor, author Page Six column, 1978-80; daily columnist I, Claudia/N.Y. Daily News, N.Y.C., 1980-81; TV entertainment reporter Live with Regis and Kathie Lee, 1983—; reporter Eyewitness News, WABC 1984-89. Bd. overseers Sch. of Arts and Scis. U. Pa.; mem. adv. bd. N.Y. Hosp. Cornell Med. Ctr.; mem. steering com. Alzheimer's Assn. Rita Hayworth Gala. Honoree Sarah Herzog Meml. Hosp. Centennial, 1995. Office: Sta WABC 7 Lincoln Square Plz New York NY 10023-7101

COHEN, CORA, artist; b. N.Y.C., Oct. 19, 1943; d. George and Anne (Lenarsky) C. BA, Bennington Coll., 1964, MA, 1972. Vis. artist U. Pa., 1969-70, U. Chgo., 1983-95, Boston Mus. Sch. Fine Arts, 1994-95, U. Minn., 1996, Kunsthögskolan, Stokholm, 1996, Sch. of Art Inst., Chgo., 1997; vis. artist Art Inst. Chgo., 1983-85, vis. prof., 1992-93; mem. adj. faculty NYU, 1990-98; assoc. prof. of art, U. North Carolina, Greensboro, 1998—, Vt. Studio Ctr., 1999. Exhibited paintings in one-person shows at Everson Mus. Art, Syracuse, N.Y., 1974, Max Hutchinson Gallery, N.Y.C., 1979, 80, 84, Wolff Gallery, 1988, Holly Solomon Gallery, 1990, New Arts Program, Kutztown, Pa., 1993, Jason McCoy Gallery, N.Y.C., 1993, 94, David Beitzel Gallery, N.Y.C., 1994, Sarah Moody Gallery Art, Tuscaloosa, Ala., 1996, Joslyn Art Museum, Omaha, 1996, Hering Raum, Bonn, Germany, 1997, Rena Bransten Gallery, San Francisco, 1997, Jason McCoy Gallery, N.Y.C., 1997, Hering Raum Bonn, Germany, 1998, Belvedere Strasse, 1999, Bentley Gallery, Scottsdale, Ariz., 1999; exhibited in groups including Baxter Art Gallery, Pasadena, Calif., 1985, Am. Acad. and Inst. Arts and Letters, N.Y.C., 1987, Barbara Krakow Gallery, Boston, 1987, Pamela Auchincloss Gallery, Contemporary Surfaces, N.Y.C., 1992, A/C Project Room, An Esemplastic Shift, N.Y.C., 1992, Sandra Gering Gallery, 1992, Piccolo Spoleto Festival, Charleston, S.C., 1992, The Fetish of Knowledge, A/C Project Room, N.Y.C., 1992, Daniel Weinberg Gallery, L.A., 1989, Wolff Gallery, N.Y.C., 1991, Feigen Gallery, 1991, Sytsema Galleries, Baarn, Holland, 1992, Jason McCoy Gallery, N.Y.C., 1993, The Painting Ctr., N.Y.C., 1993, White Columns, N.Y.C., 1993, Bill Maynes Contemporary Art, N.Y.C., 1994, Penine Hart Gallery, N.Y., 1994, Trans Hudson Gallery, Jersey City, Out of the Blue Gallery, Edinburgh, Scotland, 1994, CEPA Gallery, Buffalo, 1995, the Smart Fair, Stockholm, 1995, NYU, N.Y.C., 1995, Newhouse Ctr. Contemporary Art, S.I., N.Y., 1997, Galleri Mariann Ahnlund Umea, Sweden, 1996, Accrochage, Hering Raum Bonn, Bonn, Germany, 1996, Galerie Brigitte Schenk, Köln, Germany, Köln Art Fair, 1997, Cepa Gallery, Buffalo, N.Y., Galleri Mariann Ahnlund, Stockholm, Sweden, Hering Raum Bonn, Germany, Stalke Out of Space, Copenhagen, Denmark, Barbara Davis Gallery, Houston, Tex., 1998,Oppenhoff & Rädler, Leipzig, Galerie Mariann Ahnlund, Stockholm Art Fair, Stockholm, Hunter Coll., Times Square Gallery, N.Y., Jason McCoy Gallery, The Art Fair, The 69th Regiment Armory, N.Y., 1999. Recipient N.Y. Found. Arts Gottlieb Found. award, 1990, Pollock Krasner award, 1998, Kohler Fund award U. N.C., 1999; Painting fellow Nat. Endowment for the Arts, 1987; Yaddo Residence grantee, 1982, 95, New Faculty grantee U. N.C., 1999. Mem. Simon Wiesenthal Ctr., Coll. Art Assn. Jewish. Home: 287 Broadway New York NY 10007-2004

COHEN, CYNTHIA MARYLYN, lawyer; b. Bklyn., Sept. 5, 1945. AB, Cornell U., 1967; JD cum laude, NYU, 1970. Bar: N.Y. 1971, U.S. Ct. Appeals (2nd cir.) 1972, U.S. Dist. Ct. (so. and ea. dists.) N.Y. 1972, U.S. Supreme Ct. 1975, U.S. Dist. Ct. (cen. and no. dists.) Calif. 1980, U.S. Ct. Appeals (9th cir.) 1980, U.S. Dist. Ct. (so. dist.) Calif. 1981, U.S. Dist. Ct. (ea. dist.) Calif. 1986. Assoc. Simpson Thacher & Bartlett, N.Y.C., 1970-76, Kaye, Scholer, Fierman, Hayes & Handler, N.Y.C., 1976-80; assoc. Stutman, Treister & Glatt, P.C., L.A., 1980-81, ptnr., 1981-87; ptnr. Hughes Hubbard & Reed, N.Y.C. and L.A., 1987-93, Morgan, Lewis & Bockius, LLP, L.A., Phila., N.Y.C., 1993-98, Jeffer, Mangels, Butler & Marmaro LLP, L.A. and San Francisco, 1998—. Bd. dirs. N.Y. chpt. Am. Cancer Soc., 1977-80. Recipient Am. Jurisprudence award for evidence, torts and legal instns., 1968-69; John Norton Pomeroy scholar NYU, 1968-70, Founders Day Cert., 1969. Mem. ABA, Assn. Bar City N.Y. (trade regulation com. 1976-79), Assn. Bus. Trial Lawyers, Fin. Lawyers Conf., N.Y. State Bar Assn. (chmn. class-action com. 1979), State Bar Calif., Los Angeles County Bar Assn., Order of Coif, Delta Gamma. Avocations: tennis, bridge, rare books, wines. Home: 4531 Dundee Dr Los Angeles CA 90027-1213 Office: Jeffer Mangels Butler Marmaro LLP 2121 Ave Of Stars Fl 10 Los Angeles CA 90067-5010

COHEN, CYNTHIA PRICE, institute administrator; b. Washington, Aug. 20, 1933; d. Duncan and Rachael (Wiley) Price; m. Joseph Cohen, Oct. 24, 1954; children: James Stirling, Andrew Lindsay. BA, CCNY, 1975; JD, N.Y. Law Sch., 1979; MA, CUNY, 1988; JSD, Polish Acad. Sci., 1994. Co-dir. child ambassador program ABA Ctr. Children and Law, Washington, 1992-93; exec. dir. Child Rights Internat. Rsch. Inst., N.Y.C., 1992—; co-dir. best interests of children program Internat. League for Human Rights, N.Y.C., 1997; adj. prof. Tulsa U. Coll. Law, 1996, 97, 98, Washington Coll. of Law Am. U., Washington, 1998; mem. exec. bd. Nat. Com. for Rights of the Child; mem. adv. bd. Coun. on Econ. Priorities. Editor: Human Rights of Indigenous Peoples, 1998, (jour.) Transnat. Law and Contemporary Problems, 1996; contbr. articles to profl. jours. Judge Campaign to End Violence, N.Y.C., 1998, ASIC Temp. Moot Ct., 1997; mem. observer NGO Group for Conv. of Rights of Child, 1989—. Mem. ABA, Okla. Bar Assn., Am. Soc. Internat. Law, Okla. Indian Bar Assn. Democrat. Avocations: skiing, tennis, music, cooking, entertaining. Home: 35 W 83rd St New York NY 10024-5201 Office: Child Rights Internat Rsch Inst 35 W 83d St New York NY 10024

COHEN, D. ASHLEY, clinical neuropsychologist; b. Omaha, Oct. 2, 1952; d. Cenek and Dorothy A. (Bilek) Hrabik; m. Donald I. Cohen, 1968 (div. 1976); m. Lyn J. Mangiameli, June 12, 1985. BA in Psychology, U. Nebr., Omaha, 1975, MA in Psychology, 1979; PhD in Clin. Psychology, Calif. Coast U., 1988. Lic. psychologist, Calif.; lic. marriage and family therapist, Nev. Family specialist Ea. Nebr. Human Svcs. Agy. Consultation & Edn., 1979-80; psychotherapist Washoe Tribe, Gardnerville, Nev., 1980; therapist Family Counseling Svc., Carson City, Nev., 1980-93; psychotherapist Alpine County Mental Health, Markleeville, Calif., 1981-89, dir., 1990-93; psychologist Golden Gate Med. Examiners, San Francisco, San Jose, Calif., 1993-97; pvt. practice assessment and neuropsychology CogniMetrix, San Jose, 1997—; conf. presenter and spkr. in field; presenter rsch. findings 7th European Conf. Personality, Madrid, 1994, Oxford (Eng.) U. ISSID Conf., 1991; site coord. nat. standardization Kaufmann brief intelligence test A.G.S., 1988-90. Vol. EMT, Alpine County, 1983-93. Recipient Svc. to Youth award Office Edn., 1991. Mem. APA, Internat. Neuropsychol. Soc., Internat. Soc. Study Individual Differences, Am. Psychol. Soc., Nat. Acad. Neuropsychology. Avocation: astronomy, adventure travel, dog training. Office: 320 S 3d St # 201 San Jose CA 95112

COHEN, DANIEL EDWARD, writer; b. Chgo., Mar. 12, 1936; s. Milton M. and Sue Greenberg C.; m. Susan Lois Handler, Feb. 2, 1958; 1 child, Theodora (dec.). BA in Journalism, U. Ill., 1958. Mng. editor Sci. Digest mag., N.Y.C., 1959-70; writer N.Y.C., 1970—. Author: Myths of the Space Age, 1967, Secrets from Ancient Graves, 1968, Vaccination and You, 1968, The Age of Giant Mammals, 1969, Animals of the City, 1969, Mysterious Places, 1969, A Modern Look at Monsters, 1970, Night Animals, 1970, Conquerors on Horseback, 1970, Talking with Animals, 1971, Superstition, 1971, A Natural History of Unnatural Things, 1971, Ancient Monuments and How They Were Built, 1971, Masters of the Occult, 1971, Voodoo, Devils, and the New Invisible World, 1972, Watchers in the Wild, 1972, In Search of Ghosts, 1972, The Magic Art of Foreseeing the Future, 1973, How Did Life Get There?, 1973, Magicians, Wizards and Sorcerers, 1973, How the World Will End, 1973, reissued as Waiting for the Apocalypse, 1983, Shaka: King of the Zulus, 1973, ESP: The Search Beyond the Senses, 1973, The Black Death, 1974, The Magic of the Little People, 1974, Curses, Hexes, and Spells, 1974, Intelligence: What Is It?, 1974, Not of the World, 1974, Human Nature, Animal Nature, 1974, The Far Side of Consciousness, 1974, The Mysteries of Reincarnation, 1975, The Greatest Monsters in the World, 1975, The Body Snatchers, 1975, The Human Side of Computers, 1975, Monsters, Giants, and Little Men from Mars, 1975, The New Believers, 1975, The Spirit of Lord, 1975, Animal Territories, 1975, Mysterious Disappearances, 1976, The Ancient Visitors, 1976, Dreams, Visions, and Drugs, 1976, Gold, 1976, Biorhythms in Your Life, 1976, Supermonsters, 1977, Ghostly Animals, 1977, The Science of Spying, 1977, Real Ghosts, 1977, Meditation, 1977, What Really Happened to the Dinosaurs?, 1977, Creativity: What Is It?, 1977, Ceremonial Magic, 1978, The World of UFO's, 1978, The World's Most Famous Ghosts, 1978, Young Ghosts, 1978, rev. edit., 1994, Frauds, Hoaxes, and Swindles, 1979, Missing, 1979, Mysteries of the World, 1979, What's Happening to Our Weather, 1979, Dealing with the Devil, 1979, Famous Curses, 1979, Great Mistakes, 1979, Close Encounters with God, 1979, The Monsters of "Star Trek", 1980, Monsters You Never Heard Of, 1980, The Tomb Robbers, 1980, Bigfoot: America's Number One Monster, 1980, Everything You Need to Know about Monsters and Still Be Able to Sleep, 1981, Ghostly Terrors, 1981, The Headless Roommate and Other Tales of Terror, 1981, The Last Hundred Years' Medicine, 1981, The Great Airship Mystery, 1981, Re-Thinking, 1982, America's Very Own Monsters, 1982, How to Buy a Car, 1982, Horror in the Movies, 1982, How to Test Your ESP, 1982, Real Magic, 1982, The Last Hundred Years' Household Technology, 1982, Monster Hunting Today, 1983, The Encyclopedia of Monsters, 1983, The Simon and Schuster Question and Answer Book on Computers, 1983, Southern Fried Rat and Other Gruesome Tales, 1983, Monster Dinosaur, 1983, The Restless Dead, 1983, The Encyclopedia of Ghosts, 1984, Musicals, 1984, Horror Movies, 1984, Hiram Bingham and the Dream of Gold, 1984, Masters of Horror, 1984, America's Very Own Ghosts, 1985, Henry Stanley and the Quest for the Source of the Nile, 1985, The Encyclopedia of the Strange, 1985; (with Susan Cohen) The Kids' Guide to Home Computers, 1983, Teenage Stress, 1984, The Kids' Guide to Home Video, 1984, Screen Goddesses, 1984, Hollywood Hunks and Heroes, 1985, Rock Video Superstars, 1985, Wrestling Superstars, Vol. 1, 1985, Vol. 2, 1986, Heroes of the Challenger, 1986, A Six-Pack and a Fake ID, 1986, The Encyclopedia of Movie Stars, 1986, A History of the Oscars, 1986, ESP: The New Technology, 1986, Strange and Amazing Facts About Star Trek, 1986, (with Susan Cohen) Wrestling Superstars II, 1986, Teenage Competition, 1986, Hollywood's Newest Superstars, 1987, The Encyclopedia of Unsolved Crimes, 1988, UFO's: The Third Wave, 1988, (with Susan Cohen) What Kind of Dog is That, 1989, Zoo Superstars, 1989, When Someone You Know is Gay, 1989, Ancient Egypt, 1990, The Ghosts of War, 1990, Ancient Greece, 1990, The Magical World of Monsters, 1991, Beverly Hills 90210: Meet the Stars, 1991, (with Susan Cohen) Going for the Gold: Medal Hopefuls for Winter '92, 1991, Zoos, 1992, Where to Find Dinosaurs Today, 1992, Ancient Rome, 1992, Ghostly Tales of Love and Revenge, 1992, Prophets of Doom, 1992, Ghosts of the Deep, 1993, Ghost in the House, 1993, Animal Rights, 1993, Dinosaur Discovery, 1993, The Beheaded Freshman and Other Nasty Rumors, 1993, The Ghost of Elvis and other Celebrity Spirits, 1994, Cults, 1994, 101 of the World's Strangest Mysteries, 1994, Into The Darkness, 1994, Real Vampires, 1995, The Phantom Hitchhiker, 1995, Riddle of the Stones, 1995, Prohibition, 1995, The Modern Ark, 1995, Gus the Bear, The Flying Cat and the Lovesick Moose, 1995, Allosaurus and Other Jurassic Meat Eaters, 1995, Stegosaurus and Other Jurassic Plant Eaters, 1995, Tyrannosaurus Rex and Other Cretaceous Meat Eaters, 1995, Triceratops and Other Cretaceous Plant Eaters, 1995, Werewolves, 1996, The Alaska Purchase, 1996, Joseph McCarthy: The Misuse of Political Power, 1996, Ghostly Warnings, 1996, Dangerous Ghosts, 1996, Screaming Skulls: 101 of the World's Great Ghost Stories, 1996, (with Susan Cohen) Gold Medal Glory: The Story of America's 1996 Women's Gymnastics Team, 1996, Hollywood Dinosaur, 1997, Great Conspiracies and Elaborate Cover-ups., 1997, Raising the Dead, 1997, The Millennium, 1997, Watergate: Deception in the White House, 1998, Cloning, 1998, The Alien Files 1, 1998, Contact, 1998, The Alien Files 2, Conspiracy, 1998, Are You Ready, The Best and Worst Predictions for the Millennium, 1998, The Manhattan Project, 1999, Prophets of Doom, The Millennium Edition, 1999, Wrestling Renegades. Mem. Authors Guild, Watson's Erroneous Deductions Club, The Wodehouse Soc., Chapter One, The Capers of Sherlock Holmes Club, Clumber Spaniel Club Am. Avocation: dogs. Home and Office: 877 W Hand Ave Cape May Court House NJ 08210-1865

COHEN, DANIEL MORRIS, museum administrator, marine biology researcher; b. Chgo., July 6, 1930; s. Leonard U. and Myrtle (Gertz) C.; m. Anne Carolyn Constant, Nov. 4, 1955; children—Carolyn A., Cynthia S. BA, Stanford U., 1952, MA, 1953, PhD, 1958. Asst. prof., curator fishes U. Fla., Gainesville, 1957-58; systematic zoologist Bur. Comml. Fisheries, Washington, 1958-60; dir. systematics lab. Nat. Marine Fisheries Service, Washington, 1960-81; sr. scientist Nat. Marine Fisheries Service, Seattle, 1981-82; chief curator life scis. Los Angeles County Mus. of Natural History, 1982-93, dep. dir. rsch. and collections, 1993-95; emeritus, 1995—; adj. prof. biology U. So. Calif., 1982-98. Contbr. numerous articles to profl. jours. Fellow AAAS, Calif. Acad. Sci.; mem. Am. Soc. Ichthyologists and Herpetologists (v.p. 1969, 70, pres. 1985, Gibbs award 1997), Biol. Soc. Washington (pres. 1971-72), Soc. Systematic Biology (mem. coun. 1976-78). Avocation: gardening, cooking, reading. E-mail: acohen@neteze.com. Home: PO Box 192 Bodega Bay CA 94923-0192

COHEN, DAVID, councilman; m. Florence; children: Mark B., Denis, Sherrie, Judy. Student, U. Pa. City councilman dist. 8 City of Phila., 1968-71, city councilman-at-large, 1979—; atty.-at-large; chmn. Law and Govt. Com.; vice chmn. Streets and Svc. Com.; mem. Pub. Safety, Transp. and Pub. Utilities, Rules, Labor and Civil Svc. Com., Edn. and Ethics Com. Sgt. U.S. Army. Gowen Meml. fellow U. Pa. Mem. Pa. Bar Assn., Phila. Bar Assn., Jewish War Vets, Pannonia Beneficial Assn., Urban League. Office: Phila City Coun Rm 588 City Hall Philadelphia PA 19107-3290*

COHEN, DAVID, public affairs specialist, educator; b. Philadelphia, Pa., Oct. 10, 1936; s. Joseph and Gertrude (Schwalb) C.; m. Carla Furstenberg, Sept. 7, 1958; children: Aaron, Eve. B.A., Temple U., 1957. Researcher, adminstr. contracts Upholsterers Internat. Union, Washington, 1958-63; legis. rep. Ams. for Democratic Action, Washington, 1963-67; legis. rep. indsl. union dept. AFL-CIO, Washington, 1967-68; assoc. legis. dir. Council for Community Action, Washington; program mgr. Center for Community Change, Washington, 1968-71; legis. cons. Common Cause, Washington, 1971; dir. field orgn. Common Cause, 1971-73, v.p. ops., dir. ops., 1973-74, exec. v.p., 1974-75, acting pres., 1975, pres., COO, 1975—, CEO, 1975-81; pres. Social Devel. Corp., 1981-84; sr. fellow Roosevelt Ctr. Study Am. Policy, 1982-83; lectr. Coe Coll., 1964-71, Wharton Sch., U. Pa., spring 1975; adj. prof. Washington Ctr. Pub. Affairs, U. So. Calif., 1981-86; pres., co-dir. Advocacy Inst., 1985—; pres. Profls. Coalition for Nuclear Arms Control, 1984-91. Author book chpt., forward to book. Contbr. articles to jours., newspapers, mags. Bd. dirs. Nuclear Control Inst., 1993—, Poverty Race and Rsch. Action Coun., 1996—. Mem. Nat. Acad. Pub. Adminstrn. Jewish. Office: Advocacy Inst 1707 L St NW Ste 400 Washington DC 20036-4213

COHEN, DAVID B., optical company executive; b. Bklyn., Apr. 22, 1943; s. Noah and Sylvia (Naimark) C.; 1 child, Ronald; m. Madeleine Goldman, Dec. 21, 1975; children: Lawrence, Louis, Linda. BA in Philosophy, SUNY, Buffalo, 1960-64; student, CUNY, Long Island U., Bklyn. Coll., St. John's U., Hofstra U., 1964-70; AS in Opticianry, Interboro Inst., 1972-74. Lic. ophthalmic dispenser, N.Y.; cert. optician. Educator N.Y.C. Bd. Edn., 1966-90; v.p. dir. ops. London Optical, Long Island, 1990—; pres. Quick 'n Easy Convenience Stores, L.I., 1972-74, Eyesite, L.I., 1982—; chmn. Optical Adv. Bd. Coun. to Interboro Inst., N.Y., 1993-96; mem. NYSSO Conv. Com., N.Y., 1993-97, sec. 1996—, dir. L.I. chpt., 1994-96, chpt. pres. 1996-98, state sec. 1995-96, 96-97, state treas., 1998—. Trustee, pres. Temple Beth El Men's Club, Cedarhurst, N.Y., 1992-94; trustee, L.I. regional Met. N.Y. Fedn. Jewish Men's Clubs, 1995-96, Nassau City liaison 1996-97; pres. Cedarhurst Bus. Assn., 1993-97; mem. Cmty. Chest Fair Com., Cedarhurst, 1992—; Ann. CBA Mayoral Program Golf and Tennis Charity Tournament, 1993-95; chmn. revitalization com. BID; bd. govs. North Woodmere Civic Assn. and Park Found.; mem. 5 Towns Jewish Cmty. Coun. Mem. Kiwanis Internat., Rep. Club (committeeman, poll watcher). Republican. Jewish. Avocations: video photography, travel, reading. Home: 33 Captains Rd N Woodmere NY 11581-2806 Office: London Optical 494 Central Ave Cedarhurst NY 11516-2007

COHEN, DAVID HARRIS, neurobiology educator, university official; b. Springfield, Mass., Aug. 26, 1938; s. Nathan Edward and Sylvia (Golden) C.; m. Arline Wyler, June 17, 1960 (div. Aug. 1980); children: Bonnie, Daniel, Ian; m. Anne Helena Remmes, Jan. 17, 1981; 1 child, Kaitlin. BA, Harvard U., 1960; PhD, U. Calif., Berkeley, 1963. Postdoctoral fellow UCLA, 1963-64; asst. prof. physiology Western Res. U., Cleve., 1964-68; assoc. prof. to prof. physiology U. Va. Med. Sch., Charlottesville, 1968-79; prof., chmn. neurobiology SUNY, Stony Brook, 1979-86; v.p. research, dean grad. sch. Northwestern U., Evanston, Ill., 1986-91, provost, 1992-95, prof. neurobiology and physiology, 1986-95; v.p. arts and scis., dean of faculty Columbia U., N.Y.C., 1995—, prof. biol. scis. and psychiatry, 1995—; mem. adv. com. directorate biol., behavioral and social scis. NSF, 1982-89; mem. life scis. rsch. adv. bd. Air Force Office Sci. Rsch., 1985-91; mem. bd. govs. Argonne Nat. Lab., 1986-92; bd. dirs. Rsch. Librs. Group, 1993-97, Zenith Electronics, Inc., 1990-95, Columbia U. Press, 1996—. Mem. various edit. bds. profl. jours.; contbr. articles to profl. jours. Bd. overseers Fermi Nat. Accelerator Lab., Batavia, Ill., 1987-94; exec. com. Ill. Gov.'s Sci. Adv. Com., 1989-95; mem. Liaison Com. MEd Edn., 1987-89. Mem. Soc. Neurosci. (pres. 1981-82), Pavlovian Soc. (pres. 1978-79), Assn. Neurosci. Depts. and Programs (pres. 1981-82), Nat. Soc. Med. Rsch. (v.p. 1984-85), Nat. Assn. Biomed. Rsch. (bd. dirs. 1985-87), Coun. Acad. Socs. (adminstrv. bd. 1982-87, chmn. 1985-86), Assn. Am. Med. Colls. (exec. coun. 1984-91, chmn. 1989-90), Internat. Brain Rsch. Orgn. (cen. coun. 1978-82). Jewish. Home: 445 Riverside Dr Apt 72 New York NY 10027-6801 Office: Columbia Univ Low Meml Library 208 New York NY 10027

COHEN, DAVID JOEL, medical educator; b. New Haven, Conn., Nov. 2, 1960. AB summa cum laude, Harvard U., 1982, MD, 1986, MSc, 1994. Diplomate Am. Bd. Internal Medicine; lic. physician, Mass. Intern then resident Brigham and Women's Hosp., Boston, 1986-89; clin. rsch. fellow Beth Israel Hosp., Boston, 1989-94, now asst. dir. interventional cardiology; fellow Harvard Sch. Pub. Health, Boston, 1992-94, instr. health policy and mgmt., 1995—; instr. medicine Harvard Med. Sch., Boston, 1993-96, asst. prof., 1996—; asst. dir. invasive cardiology sect. Beth Israel Hosp., 1994—. Contbr. chpts. to books and numerous articles to profl. jours. Grantee Johnson and Johnson, 1993-94, Am. Heart Assn., 1995—. Mem. Phi Beta Kappa. Home: 29 Reservoir Ave Chestnut Hill MA 02467-1329 Address: 29 Reservoir Ave Chestnut Hill MA 02467-1329*

COHEN, DAVID JOHN, cardiothoracic surgeon; b. San Antonio, Jan. 13, 1947; s. Melvin David and Betty (Brown) C.; m. Deborah Milton, May 29, 1976; children: John, Christopher, Scott, Joshua, Benjamin. BA in Biochemistry, Rice U., 1968; MD, Washington U., 1972; student in Mech. Engring., U. Tex., San Antonio, 1998—. Intern Johns Hopkins Hosp., Balt., 1972-73, resident in gen. surgery, 1973-74; resident in gen. surgery U. Wash. Affiliated Hosps., Seattle, 1976-79; resident in cardiothoracic surgery Hosp. of U. Pa., Phila., 1979-81; chief dept. cardiovasc. physiology Walter Reed Army Inst. of Rsch., Washington, 1981-83; staff Brooke Army Med. Ctr., Ft. Sam Houston, Tex., 1983-84, U. Wis. Hosp., Madison, 1984-87; staff William S. Middleton VA Hosp., Madison, 1984-87, chief thoracic surgery svc., 1986-87; staff Med. Ctr. Hosp., San Antonio, 1987-92; staff Audie L. Murphy VA Hosp., San Antonio, 1987-92, chief cardiothroacic surgery, 1991-92, dir. surg. ICU, 1988-92; asst. chief cardiothoracic surgery Brooke Army Med. Ctr., San Antonio, 1992-93, dir. heart transplant program, 1994—, chief cardiothroacic surgery, 1993—; bd. dirs. Tex. Organ Sharing Alliance, San Antonio; cardiac transplant fellow Tex. Heart Inst., Houston, 1993—; cons. thoracic and cardiovascular surgery U.S. Army Surgeon Gen., 1999—. Asst scoutmaster Boy Scouts Am., San Antonio, 1990—, Weblos den leader, 1988-90. Col. U.S. Army. Decorated Bronze Star, Meritorious Svc. medal (2), Army Commendation medal (4), Order of Mil. Med. Merit; recipient Nat. Collegiate Engring. award U.S. Achievement Acad., 1998. Fellow ACS, Am. Coll. Cardiology, Am. Coll. Chest Physicians; mem. Am. Assn. Thoracic Surgeons, Soc. Thoracic Surgeons, Soc. Univ. Surgeons, San Antonio Cardiology Soc. (sec.-treas. 1997-98, pres. 1998—), Golden Key, Tau Beta Pi. Jewish. Avocations: horseback riding, camping, skiing. Office: Cardiothoracic Surgery Svc BAMC 3851 Roger Brooke Dr Fort Sam Houston TX 78234-4500

COHEN, DAVID LEON, physician; b. St. Louis, Feb. 2, 1947; s. Benjamin David and Hannah (Finfer) C.; m. Sheila Zeisel, July 2, 1974; children: Robin, Lori, Jonathan, Jennifer. BS, Roosevelt U., 1967; MS, Chgo. Med. Sch., 1972; MD, Mt. Sinai Sch. Medicine, 1976. Diplomate Am. Bd. Dermatology. Intern in internal medicine Michael Reese Hosp., Chgo., 1976-77; resident Mt. Sinai Hosp., N.Y.C., 1977-80; pvt. practice Hewlett and Jamaica, N.Y., 1980—. Office: 1800 Rockaway Ave Ste 208 Hewlett NY 11557-1645 also: 86-75 Midland Pkwy Jamaica NY 11432

COHEN, DAVID LOUIS, lawyer; b. N.Y.C., Apr. 11, 1955; s. Arthur Stanley and Barbara (Cohen) C.; m. Rhonda Resnick, Aug. 14, 1977; children: Benjamin Jeffrey, Joshua Scott. BA, Swarthmore Coll., 1977; JD cum laude, U. Pa., 1981; LLD (hon.), Drexel U., 1997. Bar: Pa. 1981, U.S. Dist. Ct. (ea. dist.) Pa. 1982, U.S. Ct. Appeals (3rd cir.) 1982, U.S. Supreme Ct. 1983. Press sec. U.S. Rep. James H. Scheuer, Washington, 1976, adminstrv. asst./chief of staff, 1977-78; law clk. to Hon. Joseph S. Lord III U.S. Dist. Ct., Phila., 1981-82; from assoc. to ptnr. Ballard Spahr Andrews & Ingersoll, LLP., Phila., 1982-92; ptnr. Ballard Spahr Andrews & Ingersoll, Phila., 1997—, chmn., 1998—. Co-author: Continuing Care Retirement Communities: An Empirical, Financial and Legal Analysis, 1984; contbr. articles to profl. jours. Dir. comms. Rendell for Mayor, Phila., 1987, campaign mgr., 1991; chief of staff Hon. Edward G. Rendell, Mayor, Phila., 1992-97; bd. dirs. Wistar Inst., Phila., 1994—, Stratford Friends Sch., Phila., 1993—, Regional Performing Arts Ctr., 1997—, United Way of Southeastern Pa., Phila., 1993—, first vice chair, 1997-98, chair 1998—; bd. dirs. Greater Phila. C. of C., 1998—; bd. dirs., exec. com. Port Wardens of the Ind. Seaport Mus., 1998—; trustee Phila. Bar Found., 1999—, Hosp. U. Pa., 1999, Overseers Sch. Medicine U. Pa., 1999; mem. health sys. trustee bd. U. Pa., 1999; co-chair Phila. 2000, 1998. Recipient Hatikvah award Jewish Nat. Fund, 1993, Americanism award Anti-Defamation League, 1993, Cmty. Leader of Yr. award Arthritis Found., 1994, Citizen of the Yr. award March of Dimes, 1994, ARC, 1999, Outstanding Young Leader award Jaycees, 1995, Jerusalem Covenant award State of Israel Bonds, 1996, Clarence Farmer Service award Phila. Commn. Human Rels., 1997, Phila. Bar medal, 1997, Champions award Cmty. Legal Svcs., 1997, Cora Svcs. award, 1997, Cmty. Svc. award Episcopal Hosp., 1997, Golden Heart Humanitarian award Variety Club, 1998, Cmty. Svcs. Recognition award Phila. Tribune Charities, 1998, Success award March of Dimes Found., 1999, Cmty. Svc. award Operation Understanding, 1999, Vision for Phila. award Phila. Hospitality, 1999, Dr. John Kearsley award, 1999. Mem. ABA, Pa. Bar Assn., Phila. Bar Assn. Dem. Home: 7 W Sunset Ave Philadelphia PA 19118-3621 Office: Ballard Spahr Andrews & Ingersoll LLP 1735 Market St Ste 5100 Philadelphia PA 19103-7599

COHEN, DAVID MICHAEL, newspaper editor, journalist; b. Phila., Feb. 20, 1963; s. Albert Franklin and Lenore (Trainor) C.; m. Debbie Bodin. BA, Northwestern U., Evanston, Ill., 1985. Editor Virginian-Pilot, Norfolk, Va., 1985-86, Courier-Post, Cherry Hill, N.J., 1986-89; wire editor Bergen Record, Hackensack, N.J., 1989-97; mng. editor Nando Times, Raleigh, N.C., 1997—. Recipient 1st pl. award for sports writing Phila. Press Assn., 1989. Jewish. Home: 108 Long Shadow Ln Cary NC 27511-9703 Office: Nando 127 W Hargett St Raleigh NC 27601-1351

COHEN, DAVID MICHAEL, federal magistrate judge; b. Manchester, N.H., Nov. 8, 1942; s. Alexander and Bertha (Michaelson) C. AB, Bowdoin Coll., 1964; LLB, Boston Coll., 1967. Bar: Maine 1967, U.S. Dist. Ct. Maine 1968, Mass. 1967. Law clk. Hon. Frank M. Coffin, U.S. Ct. Appeals, 1st Cir., Portland, Maine, 1967-68; assoc. Berman, Berman, Wernick & Flaherty, Portland, Maine, 1968-71; assoc., ptnr. Preti & Flaherty, Portland, Maine, 1971-77; ptnr. Preti, Flaherty & Beliveau, Portland, Maine, 1978-80, Petruccelli, Cohen, Erler & Cox, Portland, Maine, 1980-88; U.S. magistrate judge Dist. of Maine, Portland, 1988—. Exec. com. alumni coun. Bowdoin Coll., Brunswick, Maine, 1990—, pres., 1993-94. Mem. Maine Bar Assn., Cumberland County Bar Assn. (gen. com. 1976-78, nominating com. 1985), Fed. Magistrate Judges Assn. (dir. 1991—). Jewish. Office: US Dist Ct 156 Federal St Portland ME 04101-4152

COHEN, DAVID WALTER, academic administrator, periodontist, educator; b. Phila., Dec. 15, 1926; s. Abram and Goldie (Schlein) C.; m. Betty Axelrod, Dec. 19, 1948 (dec. Mar. 1992); children: Jane Ellen, Amy Sue, Joanne Louise. DDS, U. Pa., 1950; DSc (hon.), Boston U., 1975; PhD (hon.), Hebrew U., Jerusalem, 1977, U. Athens, 1979; Dr Honoris Causa, U. Louis Pasteur, Strasbourg, France, 1986; DHL (hon.), U. Detroit, 1989. Diplomate: Am. Bd. Periodontology (chmn. 1972). Research fellow pathology and periodontia Beth Israel Hosp., Boston, 1950-51; mem. faculty U. Pa. Sch. Dentistry, Phila., 1951—, prof. periodontics, 1962-86, chmn. dept., 1962-73; dean Sch. Dental Medicine U. Pa., Phila., 1972-83; dean emeritus U. Pa. Sch. Dentistry, Phila., 1983—; pres. Med. Coll. Pa., 1986-93; chancellor Allegheny U. of Health Scis., 1993-98, chancellor emeritus, 1998—; mem. staff Albert Einstein Med. Center, Phila., Children's Hosp., Phila.; pres. Jewish Publ. Soc., 1993-96; vis. prof. Boston U. Sch. Grad Dentistry, 1972—; nat. cons. periodontics USAF, 1965-70; bd. govs. Hebrew U., Jerusalem, Betty and Walter Cohen chair in periodontal rsch., 1986; D. Walter Cohen endowed chair in periodontics U. Pa., 1995. Author: (with H.M. Goldman) Periodontia, 1957, (with others) An Introduction to Periodontia, 1959, Periodontal Therapy, 1960, (with R. Genco and Goldman) Contemporary Periodontics, 1990; also numerous articles and chpts. V.p. Jewish Publ. Soc., 1985-89, pres., 1993-96; pres. Nat. Mus. Am. Jewish History, Phila., 1996—. Served with USN, 1944-45. First Presdl. scholar U. Calif., San Francisco, 1985-86; named for him Hebrew U. Betty and D. Walter Cohen Chair in Periodontal Rsch., 1986, U. Pa. D. Walter Cohen Endowed Chair in Periodontics, 1995; D. Walter Cohen Mid. East Ctr. for Dental Edn. dedicated by Hebrew U. of Jerusalem, 1997. Fellow AAAS, Am. Acad. Oral Pathology, Am. Acad. Periodontology, Inst. of Medicine of Nat. Acad. Scis.; mem. Am. Soc. Periodontists (pres. 1967), Friends of Nat. Inst. Dental Rsch. (pres. 1998—). Office: Med Coll Pa 3300 Henry Ave Philadelphia PA 19129-1191

COHEN, DIANA LOUISE, private practice, consultation, psychology, educator, psychotherapist, consultant; b. Phila., Apr. 8, 1942; d. Nathan and Dorothy (Rubin) Blasberg; 1 child, Jennifer. BA, Temple U., 1964, MEd, 1969, PhD, 1996. Lic. psychologist, Pa., N.J.; lic. profl. counselor, N.J.; cert. mental health counselor. Caseworker Phila. Gen. Hosp., 1964-69, staff psychologist, 1969-70; staff psychologist Atlantic Mental Health Ctr., McKee City, N.J., 1970-80, unit dir., 1980-87, v.p. profl. svcs., 1987-91; pvt. practice Pa., N.J., 1991—; adj. faculty Glassboro (N.J.) State Coll., 1988—; cmty. & family mediator Cmty. Justice Inst., Atlantic County, N.J., 1990—. Com. chmn. Atlantic County Commn. for Missing and Abused Children, 1984-89. Grantee N.J. Dept. Edn., 1988-89, N.J. Job Tng. Partnership Act, 1990. Mem. APA (assoc.), N.J. Counseling Assn., N.J. Mental Health Counselors Assn. (pres.-elect 1996, pres. 1997), South Shore Region Mental Health Counselors Assn. (sec. 1994-97). Avocations: painting, tennis, cross-country skiing. Home: 569 Gravelly Run Rd Mays Landing NJ 08330-1654 Office: 2106 New Rd Ste E 1 Linwood NJ 08221

COHEN, DONALD JAY, pediatrics, psychiatry and psychology educator, administrator; b. Chgo., Sept. 5, 1940; m. Phyllis Cohen, 1964; children—Matthew, Rebecca, Rachel, Joseph. B.A. in Philosophy and Psychology summa cum laude, Brandeis U., 1961; Student in philosophy and psychology, U. Cambridge, 1961-62; M.D., Yale U., 1966. Diplomate Am. Bd. Psychiatry and Neurology, Am. Bd. Child Psychiatry. Intern in pediatric medicine Children's Hosp. Med. Ctr., Boston, 1966-67; resident in child psychiatry Judge Baker Guidance Ctr., Children's Hosp. Med. Ctr., Boston, 1969-70; resident in psychiatry Mass. Mental Health Ctr., Boston, 1967-69; fellow in child psychiatry Hillcrest Children's Ctr. and Children's Hosp., Washington, 1970-72; asst. in medicine Children's Hosp., Boston, 1967-69; asst. to dir. child devel. Dept. Health, Washington, 1970-72; assoc. prof. pediatrics, psychiatry, and psychology Yale U., New Haven, Conn., 1972-79; prof. pediatrics, psychiatry, psychology Yale U., New Haven, 1979—; Irving B. Harris prof. child psychiatry, pediatrics and psychology Yale U., New Haven, Conn., 1987—, dir. Child Study Ctr., 1983—; clin. assoc. adult psychiatry br. NIMH Sect. on Twin and Sibling Studies, 1970-72; vis. prof. Hebrew U. Hadassah Med. Ctr., summer 1982; mem. Nat. Commn. on Children, 1988; tng. and supervising analyst Western New Eng. Psychoanalytic Inst., 1992—; trustee Anna Freud Ctr., London, 1992; pres. pubsls. com. Yale U. Press, 1995—. Contbr. numerous articles to profl. jours., chpts. to books; author monographs: Serving Sch. Age Children, 1972, Serving Presch. Children, 1974; editor monographs: Schizophrenia Bull., Vol. 8, No. 2, 1982, Jour. Autism and Devel. Disorders, 1982; co-editor monographs: (with A. Donnellan) Handbook of Autism and Pervasive Developmental Disorders, 1985; (with A.J. Solnit, J.E. Schowalter) Psychiatry, 1985, 91; author of book revs.; mem. editl. bd. Jour. Am. Acad. of Child Psychiatry, 1972-76, 80—, Israel Jour. Psychiatry, 1983—, Am. Jour. Psychiatry, 1996—; mem. adv. bd. Jour. Child Psychology and Psychiatry, 1977. Chmn. profl. adv. bd. Nat. Soc. for Autistic Children, 1981—; mem. med. adv. bd. Tourette Syndrome Assn., 1980—, mem. profl. adv. bd. Benhaven, New Haven, Conn., 1972—; bd. dirs. NIMH Treatment Devel. and Assessment Study Sect., 1979-82, Psychoanalytic Research and Devel. Fund, 1982—, Found.'s Fund for Research in Psychiatry, 1977-81, Spl. Citizens, Futures Unlimited, Inc., 1983—, Ounce of Prevention Fund Nat. Adv. Com., 1983—, B'nai B'rith Hillel Found., Yale U., 1984—; trustee Brandeis U., 1982—, Western New Eng. Inst. for Psychoanalysis, 1984—. Served with USPHS, 1970-72. Recipient Ann. Pub. Svc. award Nat. Soc. for Autistic Children, 1972, Spl. Recognition, Hofheimer prize Am. Psychiatric Assn., 1977, Ittleson award Am. Psychiat. Assn., 1981, Strecker award Inst. of Pa. Hosp., U. Pa., 1990; Woodrow Wilson fellow, 1961, Falk fellow Am. Psychiat. Assn., 1970-71; Fulbright scholar Trinity Coll., U. Cambridge, 1961-62. Fellow Am. Acad. Child Psychiatry (chmn. com. on rsch. 1975-81), Am. Pediatric Soc., Am. Acad. Pediatrics; mem. Inst. Medicine of NAS, Soc. for Rsch. in Child Devel., Internat. Assn. Child and Adolescent Psychiatry and Allied Professions (pres. 1992—), Internat. Psychoanalytic Soc., Am. Psychoanalytic Assn., Israel Psychoanalytic Soc. (corr.), Western New Eng. Psychoanalytic Soc., Phi Beta Kappa, Sigma Xi, Alpha Omega Alpha. Office: Yale Child Study Ctr 230 S Frontage Rd New Haven CT 06520-7900*

COHEN, EARL HARDING, lawyer; b. St. Paul, Mar. 24, 1948; s. Samuel W. and Sylvia S. (Peters) C.; m. Phyllis S. Bruzonsky; children: Melissa Anne, Amy Beth. BS, U. Minn., 1970, JD, 1973. Bar: Minn. 1973, D.C. 1980, U.S. Tax Ct. 1981. Trust officer Norwest Bank Mpls., 1973-76; atty. Halpern & Halpern, Mpls., 1976-77; prin. Halpern & Cohen, Mpls., 1977-80, Cohen & Bialick, Mpls., 1980-84, Cohen & Cohen, Mpls., 1984-90; pres. Kensington Properties, Inc., Mpls., 1978-90; of counsel Mansfield & Tanick, Mpls., 1990-92; CEO, dir. Mansfield, Tanick & Cohen, P.A., Mpls., 1992—; counsel, bd. cons. No. Computer Sys., Inc., Mpls., 1987-92; dir. United Sys. Techn., Inc., 1995—. Bd. trustees Torah Acad. of Mpls., St. Louis Park, Minn., 1973-91, Talmud Torah of Mpls., 1988. Mem. ABA, Minn. State Bar Assn., Am. Bankruptcy Inst., St. Pauls Boys and Girls Club. Avocations: skiing, golf, travel. Home: 6700 Field Way Minneapolis MN 55436-1719 Office: Mansfield Tanick & Cohen PA 900 2nd Ave S Ste 1560 Minneapolis MN 55402-3333

COHEN, EDMUND STEPHEN, lawyer; b. Newark, June 25, 1946; s. Louis William and Edna (Medresch) C.; m. Lisa Beth Sonenthal, June 30, 1968; children: Ellen Paige, Paul Lawrence. BA cum laude, Dartmouth Coll., 1968; JD cum laude, Harvard U., 1971; LLM in Taxation, NYU, 1975. Bar: N.Y. 1972, U.S. Ct. Appeals (2d cir.) 1972, U.S. Ct. Claims, 1973, U.S. Tax Ct. 1973, U.S. Dist. Ct. (so. dist.) N.Y. 1975. Assoc. Davis Polk & Wardwell, N.Y.C., 1971-78; ptnr. Cole & Deitz, N.Y.C., 1978-81, Coudert Bros., 1981—; adj. prof. law grad. tax program NYU Law Sch., 1977-86; chmn. seminars World Trade Inst., N.Y.C., 1977—, Practicing Law Inst., N.Y.C., 1977—, NYU Fed. Tax Inst. Mem. ABA, N.Y. State Bar Assn., Assn. Bar City N.Y., Internat. Fiscal Assn. Office: Coudert Bros 1114 Avenue Of The Americas New York NY 10036-7703

COHEN, EDWARD, civil engineer; b. Glastonbury, Conn., Jan. 6, 1921; s. Samuel and Ida (Tanewitz) C.; m. Elizabeth Belle Cohen, Dec. 19, 1948 (dec. June 1979); children: Samuel, Libby M. Wallace, James; m. Carol Simon Kalb, Jan. 11, 1981; stepchildren: Anne Kalb Bronner, Paul Kalb. BS in Engring., Columbia U., 1945, MS in Civil Engring., 1954. Registered profl. engr., N.Y., Conn., Fla., Ga., Md., N.J., La., Mass., Mich., Pa., D.C., Okla., Va., Wis., Del., Nat. Council Engring. Examiners; chartered civil engr., Gt. Britain; cert. Eur ING (FEANI Europe); lic. land surveyor, N.Y., Conn., Mass., N.J. Engring. aide Conn. Hwy. Dept., 1941-42; asst. engr. East Hartford Dept. Pub. Works, 1942-44; structural engr. Hardesty & Hanover, N.Y.C., 1945-47, Sanderson & Porter, N.Y.C., 1947-49; lectr. architecture Columbia U., 1948-51; with Ammann & Whitney, N.Y.C., 1949-96, assoc. engr., 1954-63; ptnr. Ammann & Whitney, 1963-74, sr. ptnr., 1974-77, mng. ptnr., 1977-95, dir. co. work as engrs. of record restoration of Statue of Liberty, West Face and Olmsted Ters. of U.S. Capitol Bldg. and Roebling Del. Canal Bridge; exec. v.p. Ammann & Whitney, Inc., 1974-77, in charge bldg., transp., communications, mil. and hist. preservation projects, chmn., CEO, 1977-96; v.p. Ammann & Whitney Internat. Ltd., 1963-73; pres. Safeguard Constrn. Mgmt. Corp., 1973-77, chmn., CEO, 1977-95; pvt. practice as civil engr. ECCE Internat., 1996—; cons. RAND Corp., Santa Monica, Calif., 1958-72, Dept. Def., 1962-63, Hudson Inst., Croton-on-Hudson, N.Y., 1967-71, World Bank, 1984, TVA, 1987, Nat. Trust for Hist. Preservation, Drayton Hall Restoration, 1990; Stanton Walker lectr. U. Md., 1973, Henry M. Shaw lectr. N.C. State U., 1987; deptl. adv. com. Urban and Civil Engring. U. Pa., 1978-84, Rutgers U., 1982-90; mem. engring. coun. Columbia U., 1975—, vice chmn., 1985-86; chmn. Bldg. Rsch. Bd. Com. on Fed. Construction Stds. to control building life-cycle costs, 1989-91; mem. Planning Group Nat. Consortium for infrastructure rsch. and tech. tranfer, 1987-90, Na. Rsch. Coun. Com. for Infrastructure and Rsch. Agenda, 1992-94; commr. Bklyn. Bridge Centennial Commn., 1981-83; spl. adv. N.Y. State Centennial Commn. Statue of Liberty, 1985; chmn. engring. com. NEA first U.S. Presdl. awards for design excellence, 1985, mem., 1991, 95. Mem. adv. bd. Jour. Resource Mgmt. and Tech., 1981-91; co-editor: Handbook of Structural Concrete, 1983; contbr. more than 100 papers and articles to profl. jours. and govt. manuals on bridge, structural, siesmic, and hardened design, wind forces, dynamic analysis, ultimate strength and plastic design, restoration of bridges and aesthetics, guyed towers and shell structures. Bd. dirs. Cejwin Youth Camps, 1972-92; mem. com. of 100 Trailblazer Summer Camp for Underprivileged Children, 1985-89; trustee Hall of Sci., N.Y.C., 1976-99; mem. com. March of Dimes Transp. Award Luncheon, 1983-99; mem. exec. com. Architects/Engrs. divsn. United Jewish Appeal-Fedn., 1985-93; mentor in engring. N.Y. Alliance for Pub. Schs., 1986-91; N.Y. area chmn. engring. divsn. Orgn. for Rehab. Through Training, 1983-98, nat. dir., 1989-95. Recipient Illig medal in Applied Sci. Columbia U., 1946, Patriotic Civilian Svc. award Dept. of Army, 1973, Egleston medal Columbia U., 1981, Goethals medal for Engring. Achievement Soc. Am. Mil. Engrs., 1985, Mayor's Award of Honor for Sci. and Tech., N.Y., 1988, U.S. Presdl. Design Excellence award for Roebling Del. Aqueduct Bridge Restoration, NEA, 1988, Prize Bridge award Am. Inst. of Steel Contrn. for Engring. Trinity Ch. Pedestrian Bridge, 1989; Best of Program award for Achievement in Arc Welded Design Engring. and Fabrication for Trinity Ch. Pedestrian Bridge, Bronze award Roebling (Del.) Aqueduct Bridge James F. Lincoln Arc Welding Found., 1988, Nat. Historic Preservation award for engring. U.S. Capitol restoration U.S. Dept. Interior and Adv. Coun. Historic Preservation, 1988. Fellow Am. Cons. Engr. Coun. (life, Grand award for Engring. Excellence 1986), Inst. Civil Engrs. (Gt. Britain), N.Y. Acad. Scis. (hon. life fellow, Laskowitz Aerospace Rsch. Gold medal 1970, chmn. engring. sect. 1977-79, N.Y. Acad. Scis. award 1989, mem. bd. govs. 1991-97, v.p. 1991-95, Charles Darwin Assocs. inagural mem. 1992-98), ASCE (hon. fellow, chmn. com. design loads for bldgs. and other structures A7 (ANSI A58), 1968-88, chmn. reinforced concrete rsch. coun. 1980-89, Civil Engring. State of the Art award 1974, Outstanding Civil Engring. Achievement award 1987, Raymond Reese award 1976, Ernest Howard Gold Medal 1983, Svc. to People award 1987, met. sect. v.p. 1978-79, pres. 1980, Ridgeway award 1946, Met. Civil Engr. of Yr. 1986), Am. Concrete Inst. (hon. fellow, dir. 1966-76, v.p. 1970-72, pres. 1972-73, chmn. com. bldg. code requirements for reinforced concrete 1963-71, Wason medal 1956, Delmar Bloem award 1973); mem. Nat. Acad. Engring., N.Y. Assn. Cons. Engrs. (bldg. code adv. com., bd. dirs. 1981-82, 85-89, emeritus mem. 1997—), N.Y. Concrete Industry Bd. (bd. dirs. 1976—, pres. 1978-79, Leader of Industry award 1997, emeritus mem. 1998—), Columbia U. Sch. Engring. Alumni Assn. (bd. dirs. 1985-86), N.Y. Concrete Constrn. Design Inst. (pres. tall bldgs. coun. 1975-80), NSPE (Outstanding Engring. Achievement award 1987, N.Y. State/NSPE Engr. of Yr. 1986), Soc. Am. Mil. Engrs., Internat. Bridge and Turnpike Assn., Internat. Assn. Bridge and Structural Engrs., Am. Welding Soc. (life), Mcpl. Engrs. City of N.Y., Comite Europeen de Beton (specialist), Moles (emeritus mem. 1996), Century Assn., Sigma Xi, Chi Epsilon, Tau Beta Pi. Clubs: Engrs. N.Y.C. (dir. 1974-75), Wings, Club at World Trade Ctr. Lodge: B'nai Brith. Avocation: golf. Home: 4702 Carlton Golf Dr Lake Worth FL 33467 *Do not give up personal integrity for any apparent "practical" advantage . . . Strive for successful projects rather than personal credit. Make no adverse judgments of people unless it is an active consideration in a necessary decision. Judge people by their actions, not their words.*

COHEN, EDWARD, state official. Commr. Dept. Correction, Indpls. Office: IGCS Rm E334 302 W Washington St Indianapolis IN 46204-2738*

COHEN, EDWARD BARTH, lawyer; b. Washington, Oct. 13, 1949; s. Stanley Edward and Marjorie (Barth) C.; m. Charlene Barshefsky, Jan. 25, 1976; two children. BA with acad. honors, U. Wis., 1971; JD, Georgetown U., 1974. Bar: D.C. 1975, U.S. Ct. Appeals (D.C. and 9th cirs.) 1981, U.S. Supreme Ct. 1981, U.S. Ct. Internat. Trade 1982, U.S. Tax Ct. 1983. Mem. profl. staff, counsel commerce com. U.S. Senate, Washington, 1971-77; gen. counsel U.S. Office Consumer Affairs, Washington, 1977-79; dep. spl. asst. Pres. Jimmy Carter, Washington, 1979-81; assoc. Davis, Wright & Jones, Washington, 1981-83; ptnr. Davis Wright Tremaine (and predecessor firm Davis, Wright & Jones), Washington, 1983-94; counselor to Sec. of Interior U.S. Dept. Interior, Washington, 1994-95, dep. solicitor, 1995—. Mem. Bar of D.C. Democrat. Jewish. Office: US Dept Interior 1849 C St NW Washington DC 20240-0001

COHEN, EDWARD HERSCHEL, lawyer; b. Lewistown, Pa., Sept. 30, 1938; s. Saul Allen and Barbara (Getz) C.; m. Arlene Greenbaum, Aug. 12, 1962; children: Fredrick, James, Paul. AB, U. Mich., 1960; JD, Harvard U.,

1963. Bar: N.Y. 1964. Assoc. Rosenman and Colin, N.Y.C., 1963-72, ptnr., 1972-86, 88—, counsel, 1987; v.p., gen. counsel, sec. Phillips-Van Heusen Corp., N.Y.C., 1987. Republican. Jewish. Club: Fenway Golf (Scarsdale, N.Y.). Avocations: golf, travel. Home: 21 Sycamore Rd Scarsdale NY 10583-7322 Office: Rosenman & Colin 575 Madison Ave Fl 26 New York NY 10022-2585

COHEN, EDWARD PHILIP, microbiology and immunology educator, physician; b. Glen Ridge, N.J., Sept. 28, 1932; s. Harry and Rae (Berke) C.; m. Toba Joy Gold, Mar. 24, 1963; children—Mark L., Lauren L., Jennifer L., Jonathan M. Tuition scholarship student, U., Miami (Fla.), 1950-53; M.D., Washington U., St. Louis, 1957. Diplomate: Am. Bd. Allergy and Immunology, Nat. Bd. Med. Examiners. Intern. U. Chgo. Hosps., 1957-58; research asso. Nat. Inst. Allergy and Infectious Diseases, NIH, 1958-60; resident in medicine U. Colo. Med. Center, 1960-61, instr. dept. medicine, 1962-74; instr., then asst. prof. microbiology U. Colo., 1963-65; asso. prof. Inst. Microbiology, Rutgers U., 1965-67; asso. prof. microbiology and medicine Rutgers Med. Sch., 1967-68; asso. prof. La Rabida-U. Chgo. Inst. and dept. medicine U. Chgo. Sch. Medicine, 1968-69, asso. prof. depts. medicine and microbiology, 1969-77, prof. microbiology, 1977-79, asst. dean, 1971-73; prof. microbiology and immunology, dean Sch. Basic Med. Scis., Coll. Medicine U. Ill., 1979-82, also prof. Ctr. Edn. and Research in Genetics, 1979-82, dir. Office of Research and Devel., 1982-84, prof. dept. microbiology and immunology, 1985—, research prof. dept. medicine, 1986—; dir. MD/PhD program U. Ill. Coll. Medicine, 1993—. Editor: Immune RNA, 1976, Medicine in Transition: The Centennial of the University of Illinois College of Medicine, 1981; co-editor: Membranes, Receptors and the Immune Response, 1980; contbr. over 200 articles and revs. to profl. jours. Sci. adv. bd. Leukemia Research Found., 1978-83 ; chmn. Biotech. Contact Group City of Chgo., 1982-83 . Served with USPHS, 1958-60. Spl. postdoctoral fellow USPHS, 1961-63; Research Career Devel. grantee, 1963-65. Mem. Am. Assn. Immunologists, Am. Soc. Cell Biology, Am. Acad. Allergy, Acad. Medicine N.J., Am. Soc. Microbiology, Central Soc. Clin. Research, Chgo. Assn. Immunologists (pres. 1974-75), Chgo. Soc. Allergy, Inst. Medicine Chgo., Reticuloendothelial Soc. Home: 4737 S Kimbark Ave Chicago IL 60615-1901 Office: 835 S Wolcott Ave Chicago IL 60612-7340

COHEN, EDWIN ROBERT, financial executive; b. St. Louis, Apr. 13, 1939; s. Harry W. and Sally (Robinson) C.; m. Sheilah Renee Aron, Aug. 20, 1961; children: David Brian, Golda, Scott Alan, Craig Aron, Rebecca Leah, Adam Jacob. BS, Washington U., St. Louis, 1966; CLU, 1973. Chartered fin. cons., 1985. Pres. Edwin R. Cohen & Assocs., St. Louis, 1966—; gen. agt. Amer US Life Ins. Co., Des Moines, 1969—; with Fin. Network Investment Corp.; mem. 21st Jud. Cir. Bar Com. Author: The New Agents Survival Manual, 1987, Spanish edit., 1994, How to Recognize a Professional, 1988, So You Want to be a Financial Planner, 1988. Arbitrator Better Bus. Bur. St. Louis, 1976-89, NASD, 1990—; chmn. local SSS, 1982—. Recipient Appreciation certs. Better Bus. Bur. St. Louis, 1979-89. Mem. Am. Soc. CLUs, Million Dollar Round Table (life), Nat. Assn. Life Underwriters (27 years Nat. Quality awards 1982, 12 years Nat. Sales Achievement award 1988), Nat. Assn. Securities Dealers (bd. arbitrators, registered rep.), Gen. Agts. and Mgrs. Assn. (past pres.), St. Louis Life Underwriters Assn. (dir. 1978-88), Am. Legion, St. Louis Jaycees (v.p. 1965-66). Jewish. Home: 10256 Lylewood Dr Saint Louis MO 63124-1283 Office: Bellerive Office Park 1023 Executive Pkwy Saint Louis MO 63141-6323

COHEN, EDWIN SAMUEL, lawyer, educator; b. Richmond, Va., Sept. 27, 1914; s. LeRoy S. and Miriam (Rosenheim) C.; m. Carlyn Labenberg, June 27, 1936 (dec. 1942); m. Helen Herz, Aug. 31, 1944; children: Edwin C., Roger, Wendy. B.A., U. Richmond, 1933; J.D., U. Va., 1936. Bar: Va. 1935, N.Y. 1937, D.C. 1973. Assoc. firm Sullivan & Cromwell, N.Y.C., 1936-49; ptnr. Root, Barrett, Cohen, Knapp & Smith (and predecessor firm), N.Y.C., 1949-65; counsel Root, Barrett, Cohen, Knapp & Smith, 1965-69; prof. law U. Va., Charlottesville, 1965-68, Joseph M. Hartfield prof., 1968-69, 73-85, prof. emeritus, 1985—, Professorial Lectr. in Law, 1994—; asst. sec. treasury for tax policy, 1969-72, under sec. treasury, 1972-73; of counsel Covington & Burling, Washington, 1973-77, ptnr., 1977-86, sr. counsel, 1986—; vis. prof. Benjamin N. Cardozo Sch. Law, Yeshiva U., 1987-92, U. Miami Law Sch., 1993, 95, 99, chmn. grad. program in taxation and estate planning, 1995-98; mem., counsel adv. group on corp. taxes ways and means com. U.S. Ho. of Reps., 1956-58; spl. cons. on corps. fed. income tax project Am. Law Inst., 1949-54; mem. adv. group Fed. Estate and Gift Tax Project, 1964-68; mem. Va. Income Tax Conformity Study Commn., 1970-71; cons. Va. Income Tax Conformity Study Commn., 1966-68; mem. adv. group to commr. IRS, 1967-68. Author: A Lawyer's Life Deep in the Heart of Texas, 1994. Recipient Alexander Hamilton award Treasury Dept. Mem. Am. Judicature Soc., ABA (chmn. com. on corporate stockholder relationships 1956-58, mem. council 1958-61, chmn. spl. com. on substantive tax reform 1962-63, chmn. spl. com. on formation tax policy 1977-80, Disting. Svc. award taxation sect. 1997), Va. Bar Assn., D.C. Bar Assn., N.Y. State Bar Assn., Va. Tax Conf. (planning com. 1965-68, 85-95, trustee emeritus 1995—), C. of C. of U.S. (bd. dirs., chmn. taxation com. 1979-84), Assn. Bar City N.Y., N.Y. County Lawyers Assn., Am. Law Inst., Am. Coll. Tax Counsel, Order Coif, Raven Soc., Colonnade Club, Boar's Head Club, Farmington Club, City Club, Phi Beta Kappa, Omicron Delta Kappa, Pi Delta Epsilon, Phi Epsilon Pi (Nat. Achievement award). Home: 104 Stuart Pl Ednam Forest Charlottesville VA 22903

COHEN, ELAINE HELENA, pediatrician, pediatric cardiologist; b. Boston, Oct. 14, 1941; d. Samuel Clive and Lillian (Stocklan) C.; m. Marvin Leon Gale, May 7, 1972; 1 child, Pamela Beth Gale. AB, Conn. Coll., 1963; postgrad., Tufts U., 1963-64; MD, Woman's Med. Coll. Pa., 1969. Diplomate Am. Bd. Pediats. Intern in pediats. Children's Hosp. of L.A., 1969-70, resident in pediats., 1970-71; fellow in pediat. cardiology UCLA Ctr. Health Scis., 1971-72, L.A. County/U. So. Calif. Med. Ctr., L.A., 1972-74; pediatrician Children's Med. Group of South Bay, Chula Vista, Calif., 1974—; clin. instr. dept. pediats. UCLA Sch. Medicine, 1971-72, U. So. Calif., L.A., 1972-74; clin. asst. prof. dept. pediats. U. Calif., San Diego, 1974—, preceptor dept. pediats., 1992—. Fellow Am. Acad. Pediats.; mem. Calif. Med. Assn., San Diego County Med. Soc. Avocations: sketching, design. Office: Children's Med Group South Bay 280 E St Chula Vista CA 91910-2945*

COHEN, ELLIOT L., urologist, educator; b. Bklyn., Aug. 13, 1941; m. Eileen Cohen, Aug. 12, 1979; children: Seth, Dina. BA, NYU, 1963; MD, Chgo. Med. Sch., 1967. Diplomate Am. Bd. Urology. Chief dept. urology USPHS Hosp., S.I., N.Y., 1975-81; asst. prof. urology Mt. Sinai Sch. Med., N.Y.C., 1981—; attending urologist Mt. Sinai Hosp., N.Y.C., 1981—. Contbr. articles to med. jours. Maj. M.C., USAF, 1969-71. Fellow ACS; mem. Am. Urol. Assn., Soc. Univ. Urologists, N.Y. Sect. Am. Urol. Assn. Avocations: skiing, sailing, bicycling. Office: 103 E 80th St New York NY 10021

COHEN, ELLIS AVRUM, producer, author, investigative journalist; b. Balt., Sept. 15, 1945; s. Leonard Howard and Selma Jean (Lattin) C. AA in Comm., C.C. of Balt., 1965; cert. in law, U. West Los Angeles, 1992. Dir. pub. rels. The Camera Mart, Inc., N.Y.C., 1971-72; editor-in-chief TV/New York mag., N.Y.C., 1972-74; dir. worldwide pub. rels., advt. and mktg. William Morris Agy., N.Y.C., 1974-77; sr. publicist Solters, Roskin & Friedman, L.A., 1977-78; sr. v.p. creative affairs Don King Prodns., N.Y.C., 1978; TV-movie prodr. (staff) CBS Entertainment Prodns., Studio City, Calif., 1979-88; CEO/pres. Hennessey Entertainment, Ltd., L.A., 1983—; film cons. Assn. Film Commrs., 1987—. Author: Dangerous Evidence, 1995, Avenue of the Stars, 1991; prodr. (Lifetime Cable Network movie) Dangerous Evidence: The Lori Jackson Story, 1999, (CBS-TV) Love, Mary, 1985 (Luminas award 1986), (network TV movies) First Steps, 1985 (Film Adv. Bd. award 1985), Aunt Mary, 1979 (Grand prize winner MIFED film festival, Milan, Italy 1980); on-camera spokesperson for Web TV and Sony Infomercials; movie and book cons. Polit. cons. Mayor Tom Bradley re-election campaign, L.A., 1977; mayoral appointee Com. in the Pub. Interest, N.Y.C., 1973-77; prodr., dir., cons. Dem. Nat. Conv., N.Y.C., 1975-76. With U.S. Army, 1965-67. Recipient Gov.'s award for employment of the handicapped, L.A., 1980, Christopher award, 1980, Humanities cert. Human Family Cultural & Ednl. Inst., L.A., 1986, Key-to-City mayor of Balt., 1979. Mem. AARP, Academy of Television Arts and Sciences, Prodrs. Guild of Am., Caucus for Producers, Writers and Directors, Writers Guild of Am., West (nominated Outstanding TV Movie Story 1979), The Authors Guild of Am. , Investigative Reporters and Editors, The Reporters Networks, Nat. Writers Union, Soc. of Profl. Journalist, Internat. Fedn. Journalists, HTML Writers Guild., Producers Guild Am., Acad. TV Arts and Scis., Caucus for Producers, Dirs. and Writers, Amnesty Internat.,(USA). Democrat. Jewish. Avocations: photography, hat collecting, exploring islands of the world, trail riding, volunteering. Office: Hennessey Entertainment Ltd PO Box 481164 Los Angeles CA 90048-9319

COHEN, EUGENE ERWIN, university health institute administrator, accounting educator emeritus; b. Johnstown, Pa., Nov. 1, 1917; s. Leroy Samuel and Ann (Aronson) C.; m. Lee Woodard Edmundson, Dec. 31, 1944; children: William Palmer, Margaret Gene, Ann Woodard. B.B.A., U. Miami, Fla., 1941, M.B.A., 1951; postgrad., Wayne State U., 1944-45, U. N.C., 1951-52. Mem. faculty U. Miami, 1945—, asso. prof. accounting, 1954-67, prof. accounting, 1967-79, prof. emeritus, 1979—, treas., 1957-79, v.p., 1958-79, v.p. emeritus, 1979—; also treas. Univ. Research Found.; treas., CFO Howard Hughes Med. Inst., 1979-88; co-founder U. Miami Sch. Medicine; v.p., bd. dirs. Dormitory Housing Assn., Inc.; chmn., pres. Laurel Corp., 1971-73; dir., chmn. Fed. Res. br. Bank, Miami, Fla., Am. Laser Corp., Garrett & Co., Fla. Fed. Savs. & Loan Assn.; bd. dirs. Am. Bankers Ins. Co., Fla.; pres., sec. Investors Forum; mem. adv. bd. Tech. Systems, Inc.; cons. Greyhound Corp., Plastetics, Inc., Reynolds & Co., NSF, NIH; U.S. Office Edn.; pres., dir. So. Assn. Colls. and Schs., J.L. Mailman Found., A.L. Mailman Family Found.; stockholders agt. Garrett Trust; rep. Univ. Corp. for Atmospheric Research, 1969-73; mem. com. taxation Am. Council Edn. Cons. editor Coll. and Univ. Bus. Mag, 1963-68; author articles in field. Bd. dirs. Miami Goodwill Industries, Dade County Citizens Safety Council, Greater Miami Indsl. Com., Heart Learning Resource Center; pres. Orange Bowl Com., mem., 1950—; chmn. Dade County Higher Edn. Facilities Authority, 1969-81, Jackson Found., 1972-83; vice chmn., dir. Nat. Childrens Cardiac Hosp.; trustee United Way Dade County, White Belt Found., J. Parker Mickle Research Found., Robert Z. Greene Found., John G. Du Puis Found.; asso. mem. Internat. Center Coral Gables, 1973-79, New World Center, Miami; mem. Health Systems Agy., South Fla.; bd. dirs. Family Services, Miami, 1968-74; mem. Miami Mayor's Spl. Adv. Com. on Interama, 1969-72; 1st chmn. Anat. Bd. State of Fla. Served to maj. U.S. Army, 1941-45. Recipient Distinguished Alumni award U. Miami, 1961, Distinguished Grad. Alumnus award, 1963. Mem. Dade County C. of C., Am. Mgmt. Assn., The Miamians, Nat. Assn. Coll. and Univ. Bus. Officers (dir.), So. Assn. Coll. and Univ. Bus. Officers (pres. 1963), Coll. and Univ. Personnel Assn., Coll. and Univ. Housing Officers Assn., Nat. Assn. Cost Accts., Fin. Execs. Inst. (founder mem. Fla. chpt., chpt. pres. 1963), Fin. Analysts Soc. Miami, Econ. Soc. South Fla., Miami Beach Com. of 100, Hist. Assn. So. Fla. (dir.), Coral Gables Com. of 21, Friends of Univ. Library, Newcomen Soc., Iron Arrow, Omicron Delta Kappa, Alpha Phi Omega, Phi Mu Alpha, Beta Gamma Sigma, Alpha Kappa Psi. Clubs: Univ. Yacht, Miami; Ocean Reef Yacht and Country (Key Largo, Fla.). Home: 6700 SW 117th St Miami FL 33156-4750

COHEN, EVELYN L., nursing educator, author; b. N.Y.C.; d. Solomon and Rebecca (Schwam) Leeds; m. Seymour Cohen; children: Robert, Sandra. Diploma, Jewish Hosp., Bklyn.; BS, SUNY, Oneonta, 1973; MEd, Hofstra U., 1976. RN; health writer. Sch. nurse Merrick and Levittown Sch. Dists.; pub. health nurse N.Y.C. Dept. Health; pvt. duty nurse Jewish Hosp. Bklyn., asst. charge nurse.

COHEN, EZECHIEL GODERT DAVID, physicist, educator; b. Amsterdam, Holland, Jan. 16, 1923; came to U.S., 1963; s. David Ezechiel and Sophia Louisa (de Sterke) C.; m. Marina Arnoldina Linnekamp, Apr. 19, 1950; children: Michael Benjamin, Andrea Margaret. BS in Math., Physics and Astronomy, U. Amsterdam, 1947, PhD, 1957. First asst. U. Amsterdam, 1950-61, asso. prof., 1961-63; research asso. U. Mich., 1957-58, Johns Hopkins, 1958-59; prof. Rockefeller U., 1963-93, prof. emeritus, 1993—; Vander Waals prof. U. Amsterdam, 1969; Lorentz prof. U. Leiden, 1979; vis. prof. Coll. de France, 1969, 72, 79, 83, 90, Inst. for Advanced Studies, Australian Nat. U., Canberra,1982, 88, 92, 96; Donders prof. U. Utrecht, 1988; Francqai prof. interuniversitaire U. Brussels and U. Leuven, 1997. Editor: Fundamental Problems in Statistical Mechanics, Vol. I, 1961, Vol. II, 1968, Vol. III, 1975, Vol. IV, 1978, Vol. V, 1980, Vol. VI, 1985, Statistical Mechanics at the Turn of the Decade, 1971, The Boltzmann Equation, Theory and Applications, 1973. Fellow Am. Phys. Soc.; mem. Royal Dutch Acad. Scis., Johns Hopkins Soc. of Scholars. Home: 450 E 63rd St New York NY 10021-7957 Office: Rockefeller U 1230 York Ave New York NY 10021-6399

COHEN, EZRA HARRY, lawyer; b. Macon, Ga., Mar. 13, 1942; s. Harry M. and Rena C. Cohen; m. Bonnie E. Cohen, Feb. 1, 1969 (div. Mar. 1988); children: Aaron M., Eileen R.; m. Katherine C. Meyers, June 18, 1989. BA, Columbia U., 1964; JD, Emory U., 1969. Bar: Ga. 1969. Ptnr. Troutman, Sanders, Lockerman & Ashmore, Atlanta, 1969-76, 79—; judge U.S. Bankruptcy Ct., U.S. Dist. Ct. (no. dist.) Ga., Atlanta, 1976-79; dir. S.E. Bankruptcy Law Inst., Atlanta. Contbg. author: Cowan's Bankruptcy Laws & Practices, 1979. Mem. Emory U. Law Sch. Coun., Atlanta, 1988—. With U.S. Army, 1964-66, ETO. Fellow Am. Coll. Bankruptcy; mem. Ga. Bar Assn. (chmn. bankruptcy law sect.), Assn. Former Bankruptcy Judges (bd. dirs.), Nat. Assn. Bank Judges (assoc.), Atlanta Bar Assn. (bd. dirs. 1988-90), Lawyers Club of Atlanta. Home: 546 W Wesley Rd Atlanta GA 30305-3534 Office: Troutman Sanders 600 Peachtree St NE Ste 5200 Atlanta GA 30308-2216

COHEN, FELIX ASHER, lawyer; b. Pitts., Aug. 11, 1943; s. Alex Harry and Audrey Gwen (Williams) C.; m. Nancy Ann Wills, July 24, 1971; children: Timothy Asher, Blair Wills Lavey. A.B., Princeton U., 1965; J.D., U. Pitts., 1971. Bar: Pa. 1972, U.S. Dist. Ct. (we. dist.) Pa. 1972, U.S. Tax Ct. 1972. Systems engr. IBM Corp., Pitts., 1965-68; law clk. U.S. Dist. Ct., Pitts., 1971-72; assoc. Buchanan Ingersoll, Pitts., 1972-75; sr. v.p., sec., counsel, bd. dirs. Signal Fin. Corp., Pitts., 1975-92; counsel CoreStates Fin. Corp., Phila., 1994-98; ptnr. Wolf Block Schorr & Solis-Cohen, Phila., 1999—. Mem. ABA, Pa. Bar Assn., Allegheny County Bar Assn., Phila. Bar Assn., Del. State Bar Assn. Home: 3 Black Rock Rd Chadds Ford PA 19317-9271

COHEN, FLORENCE EMERY, financial services executive; b. Paterson, N.J., Mar. 6, 1944; d. Claude John and Esther (Belber) Emery; m. Harvey H. Cohen, Sept. 5, 1965; children—John Aaron, Jason Matthew. A.B. in History, Temple U., 1965; M.A. in Social Scis., U. Chgo., 1970. Product planning mgr. Penn Mut. Ins. Co., Phila., 1970-77; dir. mktg. systems Prudential Co., Newark, 1978-80, v.p. mktg. analysis, 1980-82, v.p. tax administrn., 1983-84, v.p. market devel., 1984-88, v.p. enterprise planning, 1988-90; sr. v.p. individual pensions Pruco Life Co., 1990-93, v.p., prudential annuity svcs. exec., 1993—, ret.; lectr. numerous industry assns.; Exec. coun. Jersey City (N.J.) State Coll., 1985; mem. bd. visitors St. Andrews Presbyn. Coll., N.C. Grad. Study fellow U. Del., 1965, Temple U., 1965, U. Chgo. 1970; republican committeewoman, West Windsor; elder First Presbyn. Ch. Dutch Neck, mission com.; bd. dirs. Project Freedom; mem. Affordable Housing Com., West Windsor. Fellow Life Office Mgmt. Assn., Limra Life Inst.; mem. Am. Soc. CLUs, Soc. for Advancement of Mgmt. (N.J. chpt., Exec. of Yr. 1986), Rotary (Princeton Corridor). Republican. Avocations: cooking, gardening, swimming. Home: 3 Stonelea Dr Princeton Junction NJ 08550-1907

COHEN, FRANK BURTON, wholesale novelty company executive; b. Miami, Fla., Dec. 18, 1927; s. Herman and Helen Florence (Rudich) C.; BS, Emory U., 1948; m. Janis E. Stewart, Sept. 19, 1971; children: Ilene Michele, Mona Helene, Randy Stewart. With Tampa Novelty Co., Inc. (Fla.), 1948—, ptnr., 1953-72, owner, pres., 1972—. Officer Rodeph Sholom Synagogue, Tampa; mem. Am. Jewish Com.; pres. React Hillsborough County Team #4909. With USNR. Mem. Tampa C. of C., Fla. C. of C., Eagle Squadron CB Club, Classic Cadillac Convertible Club Am., Classic Thunderbird Club Am., Jewish War Vets., Nat. Fedn. Ind. Bus., Internat. Platform Assn., Fla. Sheriffs Assn., Fla. Assn. State Troopers, Internat. Buckskin Horse Assn., Am. Buckskin Horse Assn., B'nai B'rith, Masons, Moose, Appaloosa Horse, Rodeph Sholom Men's (officer), BMW Car Am., Appaloosa Cover, Cen. Fla. Appaloosa Horse. Democrat. Recipient Who's Who Worldwide Men of Achievement award; patentee center seat car tray. Home: 4934 W San Rafael St Tampa FL 33629-5404 Office: 501 S Florida Ave Tampa FL 33602-5419

COHEN, FRED HOWARD, lawyer, investment company executive; b. Pitts., Mar. 22, 1948; s. Morris and Sylvia (Kalickman) C.; m. Katherine Jane Litman, July 12, 1970; children: Julia Jackson, Joseph Litman. BA, Stanford U., 1970; MA, York U., Toronto, Can., 1971; postgrad., Princeton U., 1971-72; JD, Harvard U., 1976. Bar: Calif. 1976. Assoc. Latham & Watkins, L.A., 1976-82; ptnr. Latham & Watkins, 1983-85; v.p. Salomon Bros. Inc., N.Y.C., 1985-86; dir. Salomon Bros. Inc., 1986-88; v.p. Goldman Sachs & Co., N.Y.C., 1988-89; ptnr. Shearman & Sterling, N.Y.C., 1989-94; mng. dir. Salomon Bros. Inc., N.Y.C., 1994—. Mem. Phi Beta Kappa. Home: 86 Kellogg Hill Rd Weston CT 06883-2640

COHEN, GABRIEL MURREL, editor, publisher; b. Louisville, Aug. 31, 1908; s. Isaac and Jenny (Rosenbaum) C.; m. Helen Aronovitz, Sept. 22, 1938; children: Lawrence, Theodore, Miriam, Debbie, Ben-Zion, Jennie, Hermine, Rena. A.B., U. N.C., 1930. Reporter Louisville Herald-Post, 1927-28, 30-31; founder, editor, pub. Ky. Jewish Chronicle (now Ky. Jewish Post and Opinion), Louisville, 1931—, Ind. Jewish Post, Indpls., 1935—, Mo. Jewish Post and Opinion, St. Louis, 1948-92, Nat. Jewish Post (now Nat. Jewish Post and Opinion), Indpls., 1948—. Founding chmn. Am. Jewish Press Assn., 1944—. Home: 7984 Lieber Rd Indianapolis IN 46260-2835 Office: Nat Jewish Post & Opinion 238 S Meridian St Indianapolis IN 46225-1032

COHEN, GEORGE LEON, lawyer; b. Covington, Ga., June 20, 1930; s. Leon and Callie (Harrison) C.; m. Jacqueline Lanier Edwards, Nov. 17, 1951; children—George Leon, Gardner Edwards. AB, Va. Mil. Inst., 1951; LLB, U. Va., 1956. Bar: Va. 1956, Ga. 1957, D.C. 1964, U.S. Ct. Appeals (11th cir.). Assoc. Sutherland, Asbill & Brennan, Atlanta, 1956-62, ptnr., 1962—. Editorial bd. Va. Law Rev., 1954-56. Mem. ABA (various coms.), Ga. State Bar (chmn. corp. and banking law sect. 1968-69, Ga. bus. corp. code revision com. 1986-89, various coms.), Atlanta Bar Assn., Lawyers Club Atlanta, Am. Law Inst. (advisor to corp. governance project), Peachtree Club, Order of Coif, Omicron Delta Kappa. Office: Sutherland Asbill & Brennan 999 Peachtree St NE Ste 2300 Atlanta GA 30309-3996

COHEN, GERALD LEONARD, foreign language educator; b. N.Y.C., Mar. 22, 1941; s. Irving Alexander Cohen; m. Brigitte Helga Cohen, Aug. 11, 1968; children: Sharon, Michael. BA, Dartmouth Coll., 1962; diploma in Slavonic Studies, Oxford (Eng.) U., 1963; PhD in Slavic Linguistics, Columbia U., 1971. Prof. fgn. langs. U. Mo., Rolla, 1968—. Author: Origin of the Term Shyster, 2 vols., 1982, 84, Studies in Slang, 5 vols., 1985-97, Origins of NYC's Nickname, The Big Apple, 1991; editor: Comments on Etymology, 1971—. Mem. Am. Dialect Soc., Am. Name Soc. Office: Dept Fgn Langs Univ Mo Rolla Rolla MO 65401

COHEN, GORDON S., health products executive; b. N.Y.C., May 18, 1937; s. Leon Lewis and Irene (Lipton) C.; m. Marjorie Rennick, June 12, 1960; children: Terri Susan, Lisa Michelle, Bonnie Lynne. AB, Brown U., 1959; MD, Yale U., 1963. Diplomate Am. Bd. Pathology, Anatomic Pathology and Clin. Pathology. Instr. dept. pathology Yale U., New Haven, 1967-70, asst. prof. pathology, 1970-71, asst. clin. prof. pathology, 1971-76; pres. Jeneric Industries, Wallingford, Conn., 1975-86; chmn. Pentron Corp., Wallingford, 1977-87; pres. Jeneric/Pentron, Inc., Wallingford, 1987—; chmn. Customedix Corp., Wallingford, 1987—; attending pathologist Yale-New Haven Hosp., 1970-71, Hosp. St. Raphael, New Haven, 1971-76; pathologist The Charlotte Hungerford Hosp., Torrington, Conn., 1967-70. Author numerous articles in field. Sr. edn. officer Milford (Conn.) U.S. Power Squadron, 1987; mem. Congressman DeNardis's Small Bus. Adv. Com., 1982. Capt. (M.C.) USAR, 1964-70. Mem. Internat. Acad. Pathology, N.Y. Acad. Scis., Phi Beta Kappa, Sigma Xi, Alpha Omega Alpha. Avocations: sailing, shooting, book collecting. Office: Jeneric Pentron Inc 53 N Plains Industrial Rd Wallingford CT 06492-5841

COHEN, GREGORY LEIGHTON, computer operations executive; b. Marlton, N.J., Aug. 28, 1982; s. Mark N. and Rhoda P. (Posner) C. Dir. computer ops. Nat. Recall Alert Ctr., N.J., 1995—, Slim Scents, Inc., N.J., 1996—, Thin Scents, Inc., N.J., 1996—, Coast to Coast Advt., Inc., N.J., 1996—; pres., chmn. Myriad Techs., Inc., Voorhees, N.J., 1996—; Dir. computer animation Eastern H.S. Robotics Team, 1998—. Mem. Aircraft Owners and Pilots Assn., Sigma Alpha Rho (treas. 1997-98). Jewish. Avocations: airplant piloting, computers, tennis, racquetball. Office: Myriad Techs Inc 6 Alluvium Lakes Dr Voorhees NJ 08043-4816

COHEN, HARRIS L., diagnostic radiologist, consultant; b. Bklyn., Sept. 18, 1951; s. Samuel G. and Lola Estera (Altman) C.; m. Sandra Wilensky, Oct. 18, 1979; children: David Matthew, Lauren Elizabeth, Benjamin Adam. BA, CUNY, Bklyn., 1973; MD, SUNY, Bklyn., 1976. Diplomate Am. Bd. Radiology, Nat. Bd. Med. Examiners; cert. added qualifications in pediatric radiology Am. Bd. Radiology. Asst. prof. radiology SUNY Health Sci. Ctr., Bklyn., 1981-88, prof. radiology, 1993—; med. dir. diagnostic med. imaging program Coll. Helth Related Professions, SUNY Health Sci. Ctr., Bklyn., 1985-88, 94—; assoc. chmn. clin. rsch. SUNY Health Sci. Ctr., Bklyn., 1998—; asst. chief of imaging Brookdale Hosp. Med. Ctr., Bklyn., 1983-85; assoc. prof. radiology Cornell U. Med. Coll., N.Y.C., 1988-93; chief pediatric CT and ultrasound North Shore U. Hosp.-Cornell, Manhasset, N.Y., 1988-93, assoc. dir. divsn. CT/ultrasound/magnetic resonance imaging, 1988-93; assoc. dir. radiology Kings County Hosp., Bklyn., 1993—; dir. divsn. ultrasound U. and Kings County Hosps., Bklyn., 1985-88, 93—; cons. ultrasound and pediatric imaging Brookdale Hosp. Med. Ctr., Bklyn., 1988—; cons. diagnostic radiology Med. Mut. Liability, N.Y.C., 1992—. Article reviewer: Am. Jour. Roentgenology, 1988—, Radiographics, 1991— (Editor's Recognition award); co-editor: (textbook) Ultrasonography of the Prenatal and Neonatal Brain, 1996, Obstetrics & Gynecology (Ultrasound), 1997; mem. editl. bd. Jour. Diagnostic Med. Sonography, 1985—; contbr. articles to sci. jours. and chpts. to med. texts. Recipient Master Tchr. award in radiology SUNY Health Sci. Ctr. at Bklyn. Alumni Assn., 1996. Fellow Soc. Radiologists in Ultrasound (chmn. constitution com. 1996-98), Am. Coll. Radiology (stds. and accreditation com. 1992-98, commn. ultrasound edn. com. 1998—), Am. Acad. Pediatrics (chmn. radiology sect. 1992-94), Am. Inst. Ultrasound in Medicine (chmn. ctrl. program com. 1995-97, chmn. pediatrics sect. 1994-95, bd. dirs. 1999—); mem. Soc. Pediatric Radiology (liaison to Am. Acad. Pediatrics 1993-94, liaison to Am. Inst. Ultrasound in Medicine 1995), Radiologic Soc. N.Am. (audiovisual com. 1992-96), SUNY-Downtown Alumni Assn. (councillor, bd. mgrs. 1998-2000), Alpha Omega Alpha. Avocations: computers and computer education, basketball, Little League coaching, movies, American Jewish history. Home: 78 Grove Ave Cedarhurst NY 11516-2311

COHEN, HARRIS SAUL, dean; b. Neptune, N.J., Aug. 29, 1941; s. Meyer and Henrietta (Gershman) C.; m. Zipora Milner, June 21, 1964; children: Aaron M., Miriam S., David P., Hannah E. BA, Bklyn. Coll., 1962; postgrad., Kollel Gur Aryeh Inst., Bklyn., 1963-65; MA, New Sch. Social Rsch., 1965; PhD, NYU, 1970. Lectr. in polit. sci. Bklyn. Coll., 1967-68; rsch. assoc. dept. psychiatry Georgetown U., 1968-70; analyst Nat. Ctr. for Health Svcs. Rsch./HEW, Rockville, Md., 1970-72; chief polit. and legal analysis br. HEW, Rockville, 1972-74; chief, health resources branch, office policy devel. Office Asst. Sec. Health U.S. Dept. Health Human Svcs., Washington, 1974-82; v.p. Brochers Trading Corp., N.Y.C., 1982-89; sr. exec. L & B Industries, N.Y.C., 1989-94; assoc. dean, sch. career and applied studies Touro Coll., Bklyn., 1994-96, dean, 1996—; lectr. in Talmud Woodside Synagogue, Silver Spring, Md., 1969-82. Co-author: Developments in Health Manpower Licensure, 1973, Credentialing Health Manpower, 1977, Safer Maadanci Chain: Analytical Notes and Essays on the Talmud, 1959; mem. editl. bd. Jour. Health Politics, Policy and Law, 1976-82; author numerous articles on health care, public policy, Talmudic law. Recipient Meritorious Svc. award HEW, 1972, Spl. Recognition award, 1977. Mem. Phi Beta Kappa. Home: 43 Stevens Pl Lawrence NY 11559-1328 Office: Touro Coll 1870-86 Stillwell Ave Brooklyn NY 11223

COHEN, HARVEY, lawyer; b. Far Rockaway, N.Y., Sept. 20, 1918; s. Theodore Bernard and Gertrude (Gottlieb) C.; m. Norma Ruth Boiles, Nov. 2, 1947; children: Douglas Lee, Beth Cohen DeGrasse, Barry Scott. BA, Lafayette Coll., Easton, Pa., 1940; JD, Harvard U., 1947. Bar: N.Y. 1948.

Atty. Bernhardt, Sahn, Shapiro & Epstein, N.Y.C., 1947-49; ptnr. Murtagh, Cohen & Byrne, N.Y.C., 1950-77, Garden City, N.Y., 1977—; bd. dirs., officer L.K. Comstock Co., Inc., N.Y.C., 1965-88, Electrospace Corp., Glen Cove, N.Y., 1963-81, Radiation Dynamics, Inc., Westbury, N.Y., 1958-83, Med. Sterilization, Inc., Syosset, N.Y., 1983-97. Mem. housing bd. dirs. Unitarian Universalist Congregation at Shelter Rock, 1970-72, chmn. bd. govs., 1978, trustee, 1966-75, 95-98, pres., 1974-75; trustee Mental Health Assn. Nassau County, 1984—, pres., 1990-91; active Port Washington Youth Activities. Recipient Wittelsburger award Heros, Inc., 1984, Good Guy award Nassau County Lacrosse Ofcls. Assn., 1985, Man of Yr. award Nassau County Lacrosse Coaches Assn., 1988, Bernie Ullman award Nat. Collegiate Lacrosse Ofcls. Assn., 1996, others; named to L.I. Met. Lacrosse Hall of Fame, 1986, Nat. Lacrosse Hall of Fame, 1988, Pt. Washington Youth Activities Hall of Fame, 1991. Mem. Nassau County Bar Assn., Phi Beta Kappa. Democrat. Avocations: youth sports, lacrosse, charitable work. Home: 125 Woodhill Ln Manhasset NY 11030 Office: Murtagh Cohen & Byrne 1100 Franklin Ave Ste 303 Garden City NY 11530

COHEN, HARVEY JAY, physician, educator; b. Bklyn., Oct. 21, 1940; s. Joseph and Anne (Margolin) C.; m. Sandra Helen Levine, June 1964; children: Ian Mitchell, Pamela Robin. BS, Bklyn. Coll., 1961; MD, Downstate Med. Coll., Bklyn., 1965. Diplomate Am. Bd. Internal Medicine, Am. Bd. Hematology. Intern, then resident internal medicine Duke U. Med. Ctr., Durham, N.C., 1965-67, fellow hematology and oncology, 1969-71; chief hematology-oncology VA Med. Ctr., Durham, N.C., 1975-76, chief med. service, 1976-82, assoc. chief of staff-edn., 1982-84, now dir. geriatric research, edn. and clin. ctr.; assoc. prof. medicine Duke U. Med. Ctr., Durham, 1976-80, now prof. medicine, chief geriatric div., also dir. Ctr. for Study of Aging. Author: Medical Immunology, 1977; editor: Cancer I and II, 1987, Jour. Gerontology: Med. Scis., 1988-92, Geriatric Medicine, 1997; contbr. numerous articles to profl. jours. Served as surgeon USPHS, 1967-69. Fellow ACP, Am. Geriatrics Soc. (bd. dirs. 1987-96, chair bd. dirs. 1995-96, sec. 1991-93, ethics com. 1992-96, pres. 1994-95), Gerontology Soc. Am. (clin. sec., rsch. com. 1987-92, chair publs. com. 1996—, program chair 1994); mem. Am. Soc. Clin. Oncology, Am. Soc. Hematology, Am. Assn. Cancer Rsch. (cancer and acute leukemia group B, chair cancer in the elderly com.), Assn. Am. Physicians. Home: 2811 Friendship Cir Durham NC 27705-5521 Office: Duke U Med Ctr for Study Aging & Human Devel Box 3003 Durham NC 27710-3003

COHEN, HARVEY JOEL, pediatric hematology and oncology educator; b. N.Y.C., July 4, 1943; s. Phillip and Ida (Teitel) C.; m. Ilene Verne Bookseger, Aug. 15, 1965; children: Philip Jason, Jonathan Todd. BS, CUNY, 1964; MD, PhD, Duke U., 1970. Intern Children's Hosp., Boston, 1970-71, resident, 1973-74; instr. pediatrics Harvard U. Med. Sch., Boston, 1974-76, asst. prof., 1976-79, assoc. prof., 1979-81; assoc. prof. pediatrics U. Rochester (N.Y.) Med. Ctr., 1981-84, prof., 1984-93, assoc. chmn. dept., 1987-93, chief pediatric hematology and oncology, 1981-93; prof., chmn. dept. pediatrics Stanford (Calif.) U. Sch. Medicine, 1993—; chief staff Lucile Salter Packard Children's Hosp. at Stanford, 1993-98; med. advisor Montgomery Med. Ventures, San Francisco, 1984-97; sci. advisor St. Jude Children's Rsch. Hosp., Memphis, 1985-90; chmn. hematology study sect. NIH, Washington, 1986-88. Editor: Hematology: Basic Principles and Practice, 1991, 94, 99. Med. dir. Camp Good Days and Spl. Times, Rochester, 1981-93, Monroe County chpt. Am. Cancer Soc., Rochester, 1983-93, Rochester br. Cooley's Anemia Found., 1984-93; bd. dirs. Lucile Packard Children's Hosp., 1993-97, Ronald McDonald House of Palo Alto, Calif., 1995—, Children's Health Coun., 1996—, Lucile Packard Found. for Children's Health, 1997—. Tng. grantee Nat. Inst. Gen. Med. Scis., 1983-90, Nat. Inst. Child Health and Human Devel., 1990-94. Mem. Soc. for Pediatric Rsch. (pres. 1988-89), Am. Soc. for Clin. Investigation, Am. Pediatric Soc. Democrat. Jewish. Achievements include research on continuous assay for superoxide production, effect of selenium on synthesis of glutathione peroxidase, relationship of in vitro and in vivo killing of leukemic cells by asparagase. Office: Stanford U Sch Medicine Dept Pediatrics Rm H-310 Stanford CA 94305

COHEN, HENRY, historian, retired educator; b. Bklyn.; s. Sam and Lily Cohen. BA, Columbia Coll., 1955; PhD, Cornell U., 1965. Asst. prof. Calif. State Coll., Long Beach, 1964-69; from asst. prof. to prof. Loyola U., Chgo., 1969-94. Author: Business and Politics in America to the Civil War, 1971, Brutal Justice, 1981; founder, editor Criminal Justice History: An International Annual 1980-83; editor The Public Enemy, 1981. Social Sci. Rsch. Coun. fellow, 1960-62. Mem. Group for Use of Psychoanalysis in History, Internat. Soc. for Polit. Psychology. Avocations: the arts, travel, wine.

COHEN, HENRY BRUCE, mathematics educator; b. Newark, Oct. 12, 1937; s. Benjamin and Dora Cohen; m. Deanna Harrington (div.); children: Jennifer, Jeffrey, Andrew; m. Reva Leah Balk, Apr. 22, 1969; children: Abby, Stuart Polonsky. BS, Columbia Coll., N.Y.C., 1959; MA, Brandeis U., 1961; PhD, N.Mex. State U., 1963. Tenure Stream faculty math. dept. U. Pitts., 1963—; pres. product devel. Play Power Inc., Pitts., 1995—. Creator Pitt's Coll. in H.S. Program, 1981, Puzzle Play, 1994; author children's games, books and puzzles; author math. rsch. papers on isomorphisms of continuous function spaces. Recipient tchr. tng. grant NSF, Pitts., 1981, cmty. of scholar grant NSF, Pitts., 1984-87, chancelors disting. pub. svc. award U. Pitts., 1987. Democrat. Jewish. Avocations: tennis, birdwatching. Home: 626 Gettysburg St Pittsburgh PA 15206-4550

COHEN, HENRY C., lawyer; b. Pitts., Mar. 12, 1945. BS, Miami U., 1967; JD, Cornell U., 1971. Bar: Maine 1972, Pa. 1973; CPA Ohio, Pa. 1975. Ptnr. Cohen & Grigsby P.C., Pitts.; adj. prof. Duquesne U. Sch. of Law, 1976-88. Bd. Dirs. Estate Planning Coun. of Pitts. 1984-87. Mem. Pa. Inst. of CPA. Office: Cohen & Grigsby PC 11 Starwix St 15th Fl Pittsburgh PA 15222-3110*

COHEN, HENRY RODGIN, lawyer; b. Charleston, W.Va, May 7, 1944; s. Louis W. and Bertie (Rodgin) C.; m. Barbara Latz, Aug. 31, 1969; children: Sarah Abigail, Jonathan David. BA, Harvard U., 1965, LLB, 1968. Bar: W.Va. 1968, N.Y. 1970. Assoc. Sullivan & Cromwell, N.Y.C., 1970-77, ptnr., 1977—. Contbg. editor Fin. Svcs. Regulation Newsletter, 1985; bd. advisors Banking Law Rev.; mem. editorial adv. bd. Banking Expansion Reporter; mem. nat. bd. contbrs. Am. Lawyers Newspaper Group. Served with U.S. Army, 1968-70. Office: Sullivan & Cromwell 125 Broad St Fl 28 New York NY 10004-2489

COHEN, HERBERT JESSE, physician, educator; b. N.Y.C., Apr. 27, 1935; s. Barnet and Edith (Lepolstat) C.; m. Marion E. Finger, Aug. 29, 1960; children—Linda Elizabeth, Gerald Daniel, Seth Michael. B.A. (Ford Found. scholar), Columbia, 1955; M.D., State U. N.Y., 1959. Intern Bellevue Hosp., N.Y.C., 1959-60; resident N.Y. Hosp., N.Y.C., 1960-62; asst. instr. Cornell Med. Sch., 1961-62; instr. Tulane Med. Sch., 1962-64; NIH fellow Albert Einstein Coll. Medicine, 1964-66, asst. prof. pediatrics and rehab. medicine, 1966-71, assoc. prof., 1971-76, prof., 1976—; dir. Children's Evaluation and Rehab. Ctr., Rose F. Kennedy Center for Mental Retardation and Human Devel., Bronx, N.Y., 1968-74, 78—, Bronx Developmental Services, N.Y. State Dept. Mental Hygiene, 1971-80; dir. Rose F. Kennedy Univ. Affiliated Facility Program, 1974—, dir. div. child devel. and devel. disabilities, dept. pediatrics, 1981—; vice chmn. Pres.'s Com. on Mental Retardation, 1978-81; mem. study sect. human devel. NIH, 1978-82; mem. profl. adv. bd. various founds. and profl. orgns. Author 4 books; also contbr. over 70 articles to profl. pubs. Served with USPHS, 1962-64. Recipient Disting. Humanitarian Research and Devel. awards Mental Retardation Service Orgns.; United Cerebral Palsy Research and Edn. Found. fellow, 1966-68. Fellow Am. Acad. Pediatrics (chmn. child devel. sect., chmn. com. on children with disabilities); mem. AAAS, Am. Acad. Cerebral Palsy, Am. Assn. Univ. Affiliated Facilities (pres. 1980-81, dir. 1977-84), Am. Assn. Mental Retardation (Leadership award 1996). Office: R F Kennedy Center 1410 Pelham Pky S Bronx NY 10461-1101

COHEN, HERMAN NATHAN, private investigator; b. Bklyn., June 3, 1949; s. Stanley and Hannah (Persky) C.; m. Carolyn P. Grillo, Jan. 8, 1989. BA, Bklyn. Coll., 1970; MS in Ednl. Adminstrn., Hofstra U., 1975. Investigator IRS, N.Y.C., 1970-72; adminstrv. intern IRS, Washington, 1972-73; employee devel. specialist IRS, Uniondale, N.Y., 1973-75; br. chief IRS, Bklyn., 1975-79; pers. officer Home Ins. Co., N.Y.C., 1979-81; asst. v.p. City Investing Co., N.Y.C., 1981-85; prin. H.N. Cohen Enterprises, Inc., N.Y.C., 1985-86; human resources dir. Empire Blue Cross Blue Shield, N.Y.C., 1986-89; v.p. adminstrn. ASPCA, N.Y.C., 1989-90, sr. v.p., 1990, exec. v.p., 1990-91, chief adminstrv. officer, 1991-92, chief law enforcement, 1992-94; CEO, pvt. investigator Due Diligence Plus, Amherst, N.Y., 1994—; pvt. investigator Due Diligence Plus, West Hartford, Conn., 1994—; arbitrator Am. Arbitration Assn., 1986—; bd. dirs. Ashfield Corp.; adj. faculty Conn. Criminal Law Found. Bd. dirs. Owen Sch., Centennial Legion of Hist. Mil. Commands; mem. amb.'s coun. Wadsworth Atheneum, Conn., 1st co. Gov. Foot Guard, Conn. Mem. Internat. Assn. Chiefs of Police (chmn. pvt. security com.), Conn. Police Chiefs Assn., Vet. Corps. Arty., Nat. Assn. Investigative Specialists, World Affairs Coun., Mensa, Ancient Free and Accepted Masons, Am. Soc. Indsl. Security. Democrat. Jewish. Office: Due Diligence Plus 3940 Harlem Rd Amherst NY 14226-4704 also Office: Due Diligence Plus 1028 Boulevard Ste 226 West Hartford CT 06119-1801

COHEN, IRA, legislative staff member; b. Chgo., Sept. 6, 1947. With Rep. Danny K. Davis, Washington, 1979—, issues and comm. dir., 1996—. Office: Office of Rep Danny K Davis Ste 130 333 W Arthington St Chicago IL 60624*

COHEN, IRA MYRON, aeronautical and mechanical engineering educator; b. Chgo., July 18, 1937; s. Harry Nathan and Esther (Lenchner) C.; m. Linda Barbara Einstein, June 12, 1960; children: Susan Ellen Bolstad, Nancy Beth Cavanaugh. B. in Aero. Engring., Poly. Univ., Bklyn., 1958; MA, Princeton U., 1961, PhD in Aero. Engring., 1963; MA (hon.), U. Pa., 1971. Mem. tech. staff Sandia Labs., Albuquerque, summers 1971, 74, 77; asst. prof. engring. Brown U., Providence, 1963-66; asst. prof. mech. engring. U. Pa., Phila., 1966-67, assoc. prof., 1967-76, prof., 1976—, chmn. dept., 1992-97; guest prof. Technische Hochschule Aachen, W. Ger., 1966; cons. fluid mechanics related problems to industry, 1966—, attys., 1966—; Mem. bd. The Sch. in Rose Valley, Moylan, Pa., 1969-74. Contbr. articles to various publs. Recipient Fulbright Travel grant, 1966. Fellow AIAA (sect. sec. 1977-80, 85—); mem. AAUP, ASME, Am. Phys. Soc., Internat. Microelectronics and Packaging Soc., Sigma Xi. Office: U Pa Dept Mech Engrng & Applied Mechanics 297 Towne Bldg Philadelphia PA 19104-6315 *Persistant hard work and uncompromising high standards will eventually overcome greed, corruption, and evil. Never forget to treat every human being with dignity, respect, kindness, and compassion. A loving mate is a lifelong inspiration.*

COHEN, IRWIN, economist; b. Bronx, N.Y., Feb. 29, 1936; s. Samuel and Gertrude (Levy) C.; B.S. in Accounting, N.Y. U., 1956, M.B.A. in Finance, 1964, M.A. in Econs., 1969; B.S. in Math., CCNY, 1970. Financial analyst U.S. SEC, N.Y.C., 1965-67, Fed. Res. Bank N.Y., N.Y.C., 1967-72, Prudential Ins. Co. Am., 1973-74, SEC, N.Y.C., 1974—. Life Fellow Internat. Biog. Assn., Am. Biog. Inst. Research Assn. (dep. gov.), World Acad. Scholars, World Literary Acad., World Inst. Achievement; mem. Internat. Biographical Ctr. (dep. dir. gen.), Internat. Platform Assn (life), Math. Assn. Am., Am. Finance Assn., Econ. History Assn. Home: 372 Central Park Ave Apt 2K Scarsdale NY 10583-1308

COHEN, ISAAC LOUIS (IKE COHEN), financial consultant; b. N.Y.C., Sept. 15, 1948; s. Louis and Dora (Dostis) C.; divorced; children: Janice, Matthew. AAS in Bus. Adminstrn., Kingsborough Community Coll., 1977. Asst. v.p. Mfrs. Hanover Trust Co., N.Y.C., 1966-87; data processing ops. mgr. First Boston Corp., Princeton, N.J., 1987—; owner ILC Liquidators Co., High Bridge, N.J., 1990—, ILC Vending Co., High Bridge, 1991—, ILC 900 Co., High Bridge, 1991—, ILC Fin. Mgmt. Co., High Bridge, 1991—; co-owner, sr. tech. support and shift mgr. M&I Interactive Svcs., 1995—. Editor booklet: Annadale Memorial Day Parade, 1985, 86, 87. Asst. v.p. Annadale Community Assn., 1982-89; umpire S.I. High Sch. League & Semi-Pro Baseball, 1985—; assoc. scout Kansas City Royals Profl. Baseball Team, 1988—. With USNR, 1967-75. Mem. U.S. Submarine Vets., Am. Legion, Jewish War Vets., Vietnam Vets. Avocations: baseball, motorcycle riding, skiing, roller skating, stamp and coin collecting. Home: 137 Fairview Ave High Bridge NJ 08829-1214 Office: CS First Boston 700 College Rd E Princeton NJ 08540-6617

COHEN, JACQUELINE, university researcher, sociology educator; b. N.Y.C., Nov. 30, 1945; d. John William and Veronica Loretta McNulty; m. Stuart Louis Cohen, Aug. 27, 1965. BS in Math., U. Pitts., 1966, MA in Sociology, 1970; PhD in Urban and Pub. Affairs, Carnegie Mellon U., 1982. Rsch. asst. Learning Rsch. and Devel. Ctr., U. Pitts., 1967-68; rsch. asst. Carnegie Mellon U., Pitts., 1971-79, rsch. assoc., 1979-82, assoc. dir. Urban Sys. Inst., 1982-89, sr. rsch. scientist, 1989-93, prin. rsch. scientist, 1993—; cons. various panels NRC, Washington, 1975-76, 81-82, 83-85, 89-91. Contbr. articles to Law and Society, Criminology, Jour. Quantitative Criminology, Jour. Rsch. in Crime and Delinquency, Jour. Criminal Law and Criminology, others. Bd. dirs. Health Sys. Agy. Southwestern Pa. Nat. Inst. Justice grantee, 1979—; Alfred P. Sloan Found. rsch. grantee, 1995-98. Mem. Am. Soc. Criminology, Acad. Criminal Justice Scis., Law and Society Assn., Am. Sociol. Assn. Office: Carnegie Mellon U Heinz Sch 5000 Forbes Ave Pittsburgh PA 15213-3890

COHEN, JAMES ROBERT, oncologist, hematologist. *Grandfather A.J. Cohen, M.D., founded the first TB sanitorium in Philadelphia. Father Robert V. Cohen, M.D., was a distinguished professor of medicine at Temple University Medical School for many years.Brother Richard S. Cohen danced professionally with the Martha Graham dance troupe. Developerd new techniques in kinetic therapy and practiced and taught such therapy in Monterey, California. Brother Thomas V. Cohen, tenured professor of early modern European History, York University, Toronto, Canada.* BA in English Lit., Cornell U., 1967, MD, 1971. Diplomate Am. Bd. Internal Medicine, Am. Bd. Oncology. Intern N.Y. Hosp./Meml. Sloan Kettering Cancer Ctr., N.Y.C., 1971-72, resident in medicine, 1972-73; sr. resident in medicine U. Calif., San Francisco, 1973-74; postdoctoral fellow in hematology, oncology Stanford (Calif.) U. Sch. Medicine, 1976-78, clin. instr., 1978-85, clin. asst. prof., then clin. assoc. prof., 1986-93; pvt. practice San Jose, Calif., 1978—; clin. assoc. in medicine U. Nebr. Sch. Medicine, 1975-76; chmn. divsn. oncology Good Samaritan Hosp., 1981-83, dir. med. oncology, 1983—; bd. dirs. Hospice of the Valley, 1979-85, v.p. profl. svcs., 1981-83, pres. bd., 1983-85; clin. investigator No. Calif. Oncology Group, 1977-88; mem. regional steering com. Calif. Cancer Registry, 1987-92, chmn., 1990-92; prin. investigator S.W. Oncology Group, 1992—; mem. adv. bd. Saratoga Subacute Hosp., Los Gatos Health Care Ctr., 1994-96. Contbr. articles to profl. jours. Maj. USAF, 1974-76. Fellow ACP; mem. ACS (liaison assoc. in cancer), AAAS, Santa Clara County Med. Soc., Calif. Med. Assn., Calif. Soc. Internal Medicine, Am. Soc. Internal Medicine, Am. Soc. Clin. Oncology, N.Y. Acad. Scis., Am. Acad. Med. Adminstrs., Am. Coll. Oncology Adminstrs., Alpha Omega Alpha. Home: 5931 Kyburz Pl San Jose CA 95120-1711 Office: 15400 National Ave Los Gatos CA 95032-2433

COHEN, JEFF, media critic, columnist; b. Detroit, Nov. 10, 1951. Student U. Mich.; grad., Peoples Coll. Law. Bar: Calif. 1981. Investigative reporter Rolling Stone, New Times, Mother Jones, L.A. Weekly, others; atty. ACLU Found. So. Calif.; founder, exec. dir. Fairness & Accuracy in Reporting (FAIR), N.Y.C., 1986—; lectr. media Harvard, Princeton, Columbia, Dartmouth, Johns Hopkins, Augusta Coll., others. Syndicated columnist (co-written with Norman Solomon) USA Today, L.A. Times, Newsday, Boston Globe, St. Louis Post-Dispatch, others; co-author: Adventures in Media: Behind the News, Beyond the Pundits; appeared TV and radio including Larry King Live, Pozner & Donahue, C-Span, Crossfire; quoted in TV Guide, N.Y. Times, Washington Post, Newsweek. Past bd. dirs. So. Christian Leadership Conf., L.A., So. Calif. ACLU. Office: Fairness and Accuracy In Reporting 130 W 25th St New York NY 10001-7406*

COHEN, JEFFREY MICHAEL, lawyer; b. Dayton, Ohio, Nov. 13, 1940; s. H. Mort and Evelyn (Friedlob) C.; m. Betsy Z. Zimmerman, July 3, 1966; children: Meredith Sue, Seth Alan. AB, Colgate U., 1962; JD, Columbia U., 1965. Bar: Fla. 1965, U.S. Supreme Ct. 1969; cert. civil trial lawyer Fla. Bar Bd. Cert., diplomate Nat. Bd. Trial Advocacy. Asst. pub. defender Dade County (Fla.), 1968-70, asst. state's atty., 1970-72, spl. asst. state's atty., 1973; ptnr. Fromberg Fromberg Gross Cohen Shore & Berke, P.A., 1972-84, Cohen, Berke, Bernstein, Brodie & Kondell, P.A., Miami, Fla., 1984—; adj. prof. litigation skills U. Miami Sch. Law, 1989—, chmn. Fla. bar com. on civil trial cert. Mem. ABA, Dade County Bar Assn. (bd. dirs.), Acad. Fla. Trial Lawyers, Assn. Trial Lawyers Am., Am. Judicature Soc., Nat. Inst. Trial Advocacy (chair and faculty mem.), Fla. Criminal Def. Attys. Assn. Home: 3628 Saint Gaudens Rd Miami FL 33133-6533 Office: Cohen Berke Bernstein Brodie & Kondell PA 2601 S Bayshore Dr Fl 19 Miami FL 33133-5419

COHEN, JEROME, psychology educator, electrophysiologist; b. Pitts., May 27, 1925; s. Abraham Wolfe and Dorothy (Middleman) C.; m. Florence A. Chanock, Oct. 28, 1945; children—Marcus, Mara, Aaron. AA, Princeton U., 1943; BA, U. Pitts., 1947; MA, Cornell U., 1949; PhD, U. Pitts., 1951. Instr. U. Pitts., 1950-51; asst. prof., assoc. prof. Antioch Coll., Yellow Springs, Ohio, 1951-57; prof. psychiatry and behavioral sci. and neurology Northwestern U. Med. Sch., Chgo., 1957—; dir. Electroencephalography Lab. Presbyn.-St. Lukes Hosp., Chgo., 1967-72, Cook County Hosp., Chgo., 1973—; vis. scientist Neurol. Inst., U. London, 1963-64; vis. prof. Hebrew U., 1972-73. Lt. (j.g.) USNR, 1943-46. Commonwealth Fund fellow, 1963-64. Mem. Am. EEG Soc., Am. Psychol. Assn., Psychophysiol. Research Soc., Internat. Brain Research Soc., AAUP, AAAS, Am. Soc. for Applied Psychophysiology and Biofeedback, Sigma Xi. Office: Northwestern U Med Sch 303 E Chicago Ave Ward 9217 Chicago IL 60611-3072*

COHEN, JEROME BERNARD, materials science educator; b. Bklyn., July 16, 1932; s. David I. and Shirley Anne C.; m. Lois Nesson, Sept. 15, 1957; children: Elissa Diane, Andrew Neil. BS, MIT, 1954, ScD, 1957; DSc (hon.), Linköping U., Sweden, 1991. Sr. scientist materials AVCO Corp., Wilmington, Mass., 1958-59; mem. faculty Northwestern U., 1959—, prof. materials sci. and engring., 1965—, chmn. dept. materials sci. and engring., 1973-78, Frank C. Engelhart prof., 1974—, fellow Ctr. for Tchg. Professions, 1971—, prof. McCormick Sch. Engring., 1983—, dean McCormick Sch. Engring., 1986-99; sci. liaison officer Office Naval Rsch., London, 1966-67; cons. to govt. and industry. Author: Diffraction Methods in Materials Science, 1966; co-author: Diffraction from Materials, 1978, 2d edit., 1987; co-author Residual Stress: Measurement by Diffraction and Interpretation, 1987; co-editor: Local Atomic Arrangements Studied by X-Ray Diffraction, 1967, Jour. Applied Crystallography, Modulated Structures, 1979; patentee in field. All-Star coach Glencoe (Ill.) Hockey Assn., 1974-77. Served as 1st lt. AUS, 1959. Fulbright fellow U. Paris, 1957-58; recipient Tech. Inst. Tchg. award Northwestern U., 1976, C.S. Barrett Diffraction award, 1989, Gold medal Acta Metallurgica, 1992. Fellow AIME (Hardy gold medal 1960, R.F. Mehl and Inst. of Metals lectr. 1992, Educator award 1997), Am. Soc. Metals (Henry Marion Howe medal 1981), Japan Inst. Metals; mem. AAUP, NAE, Am. Soc. for Engring. Edn. (George C. Westinghouse award 1976), Am. Ceramic Soc., Am. Crystallographic Assn., Royal Instn. Gt. Britain, Econ. Club Chgo., Sigma Xi (nat. lectr. 1989-90), Tau Beta Pi, Alpha Sigma Mu, Phi Lambda Upsilon. Jewish. Home: 574 Woodlawn Ave Glencoe IL 60022-2040 Office: Nothwestern U McCormick Sch Engring 2145 Sheridan Rd Evanston IL 60208-0834

COHEN, JOEL EPHRAIM, scientist, educator; b. Washington, Feb. 10, 1944; s. Hymen Ezra and Alice. C.; m. Audrey Jane Biller, June 14, 1970; children: Zoe, Adam. BA, Harvard U., 1965, MA, 1967, MPH, 1970, PhD, 1970, DrPH, 1973; MA (hon.), Cambridge U., 1974. Fellow in math. biology and sociology Soc. of Fellows Harvard U., 1967-71, asst. prof. biology, 1971-72, assoc. prof., 1972-75; prof. populations Rockefeller U., N.Y.C., 1975—, Abby Rockefeller Mauzé prof., 1996—; prof. populations Columbia U., N.Y.C., 1995—; dir.'s visitor Inst. for Advanced Study, Princeton, 1989-90; chmn. bd. Societal Inst. of Math. Scis., 1973-88, bd. dirs., 1988-91; mem. ednl. adv. bd. John Simon Guggenheim Meml. Found., 1985—, mem. com. on selection of fellows, 1990—; mem. Mayor's Commn. for Sci. and Tech., City of N.Y., 1984-90; mem. sci. adv. bd. Inst. for Sci. Interchange, Torino, Italy, 1991—; bd. dirs. Nat. Ctr. for Health Edn., N.Y.C., 1991-96; mem. bd. math. scis. NRC, 1991-92. Author: A Model of Simple Competition, 1967, Casual Groups of Monkeys and Men, 1971, Food Webs and Niche Space, 1978, Community Food Webs, 1990, Absolute Zero Gravity, 1992, How Many People Can the Earth Support?, 1995, Comparisons of Stochastic Matrices, 1998; edtl. bd. American Scholar, 1994—. Trustee Russell Sage Found., 1989—, Black Rock Forest Preserve, 1989—. Recipient Mercer award Ecol. Soc. Am., 1972, disting. statis. ecologist award 6th Internat. Congress of Ecology, 1994, Olivia Nordberg award for excellence in writing on population scis. Population Coun., N.Y.C., 1997, Fred L. Soper award Pan Am. Health & Edn. Found., Washington, 1998; fellow Ctr. for Advanced Study in Behavioral Scis., Stanford, 1981-82, John Simon Guggenheim Meml. fellow, 1981-82, MacArthur Found. fellow, 1981-86. Fellow AAAS, Am. Acad. Arts and Scis., Am. Statis. Assn.; mem. Population Assn. Am. (Mindel Sheps award for math. demography 1992), Cambridge Philos. Soc., Am. Statis. Assn., Am. Soc. Naturalists, Am. Philos. Soc., U.S. Nat. Acad. Scis. Office: Rockefeller U 1230 York Ave Ste 20 New York NY 10021-6399

COHEN, JOEL J., lawyer, investment banker; b. N.Y.C., Feb. 8, 1938; s. David M. and Eva (Weinstein) C.; m. Lillian Zeisel, June 30, 1963; children: Peter, Andrew Daniel, Nancy Elizabeth. BBA, CCNY, 1959; JD, Harvard U., 1962. Bar: N.Y. 1963. Assoc. Davis, Polk & Wardwell, N.Y.C., 1963-69, ptnr., 1969-87; mng. dir. investment banking, dir. mergers and acquisitions Donaldson, Lufkin & Jenrette Securities Corp., N.Y.C., 1989—; bd. dirs. Maersk Inc., Madison, N.J., Chubb Corp., Warren, N.J., Fed. Ins. Co., Warren, Vigilant Ins. Co., Warren, gen. counsel Presdl. Task Force on Market Mechanisms, 1987-88; cons., 1988-89. Served with USAR, 1962-68. Mem. ABA, Assn. of Bar of City of N.Y. Office: Donaldson Lufkin & Jenrette Securities Corp 277 Park Ave Fl 7 New York NY 10172-3400

COHEN, JON STEPHAN, lawyer; b. Omaha, Nov. 9, 1943; s. Louis H. and Bertha N. (Goldstein) C.; m. Maxine B. Turetsky, Dec. 1, 1968 (div. Dec. 1992); children: Carolyn, Sherri, Barbara; m. Cheryl A. Jiroux, Oct. 7, 1994. Student, London Sch. Econs., 1963-64; BA, Claremont Men's Coll. (now Claremont McKenna Coll.), 1965; JD, Harvard U., 1968. Bar: Ariz. 1968. Assoc. Snell & Wilmer, Phoenix, 1968-73, ptnr., 1973—; bd. dirs. Vika Corp., Phoenix, Enterprise Network, Phoenix, Ariz. Software Assn., Phoenix, Ariz. Sci. Ctr., Phoenix. Fellow Ariz. Bar Found.; mem. ABA, Ariz. Bar Assn., Maricopa County Bar Assn., Village Athletic Club, City Sq. Athletic Club. Avocations: record collecting, skiing, racquetball. Home: 3500 E Lincoln Dr Phoenix AZ 85018-1010 Office: Snell & Wilmer One Arizona Ctr Phoenix AZ 85004-0001

COHEN, JONATHAN BREWER, molecular neurobiologist, biochemist; b. Akron, Ohio, Dec. 17, 1944; s. Saul G. and Doris E. (Brewer) C.; m. Victoria Ann Rhoden, July 20, 1981; children: Deborah Karen, Samuel Max. AB, Harvard U., 1966, MA, 1967, PhD, 1972. Postdoctoral fellow Pasteur Inst., Paris, 1971-74; asst. prof. pharmacology Harvard Med. Sch., Boston, 1975-80, assoc. prof., 1980-82; prof. neurobiology Washington U. Med. Sch., St. Louis, 1982-92, prof. biol. chemistry, 1982-92; prof. neurobiology Harvard Med. Sch., Boston, 1992—; head neuroscis. grad. program Washington U., 1987-92, Harvard Med. Sch., 1993—; mem. pharm. scis. rev. com. NIH, 1988-92. Mem. editorial bd. Jour. Biol. Chemistry, 1986-91, 94-98. Mem. Am. Chem. Soc., Soc. Neurosci., Am. Soc. Pharmacology and Exptl. Therapeutics, Am. Soc. Biochemistry and Molecular Biology, Phi Beta Kappa. Office: Harvard Med Sch Dept Neurobiology 220 Longwood Ave Boston MA 02115-5701

COHEN, JONATHAN LITTLE, investment banker; b. N.Y.C., Feb. 18, 1939; s. Reuben and Marjorie (Little) C.; children: Gregory David, Suzanne Elizabeth; m. Allison B. Morrow, 1998. AB, Dartmouth Coll., 1960, MBA, 1961. Asst. v.p. Irving Trust Co., N.Y.C., 1963-68; assoc. Goldman, Sachs & Co., N.Y.C., 1969-73, v.p., 1973-84, gen. ptnr., 1984-96; ltd. ptnr. The Goldman Sachs Group, L.P., N.Y.C., 1996-99, adv. dir., 1999—. Trustee The First Presbyn. Ch., N.Y.C., The Pa. Acad. of the Fine Arts; former trustee Oberlin Coll.; chmn. bd. overseers Amos Tuck Sch. Bus. Adminstrn., Dartmouth Coll.; former mem. coun. alumni Dartmouth Coll., 1983-86; former mem. sch. com. Friends Sem., N.Y.C., 1985-91; mem. bd. advisors Wildlife Conservation Soc., N.Y.C., 1997—. Lt. USN, 1961-63. Mem. India House (N.Y.C.), Bellport Bay Yacht Club, Bond Club (N.Y.C.), Downtown Athletic Club (N.Y.C.). Office: Goldman Sachs & Co 85 Broad St New York NY 10004-2456

COHEN, JORDAN JAY, medical association executive; b. St. Louis, June 18, 1934; s. Bernard and Gladys (Brauer) C.; m. Carole Goldstein, Aug. 26, 1956; children: Deborah, Joel, David. BA, Yale U., 1956; MD, Harvard U., 1960; LHD, Chgo. Med. Sch., 1988; DSc, George Washington U. Sch. Med., and Health Scis., 1995, SUNY Health Sci. Ctr., Syracuse, 1996, Wake Forest U., 1997, U. Med. and Dental, N.J., 1998. Diplomate Am. Bd. Internal Medicine (mem. critical care medicine test and policy com. 1985-87, chmn. 1987-89, mem. subspecialty com. on nephrology 1981-86, chmn. 1986-88, chmn. com. on evaluation of clin. competency 1987-92, bd. dirs. 1986-94, mem. exec. com. 1990-94, chmn. 1993-94). Intern, asst. resident Boston City Hosp., 1960-62, sr. resident, 1964-65; rsch. fellow in renal medicine New Eng. Med. Ctr. Hosp., Boston, 1962-64; tchg. fellow Harvard U. Med. Sch., Boston, 1964-65, instr. in medicine, 1968-74, lectr. in medicine, 1974-82; asst. prof. med. scis. Brown U., Providence, 1965-68, assoc. prof. med. scis., 1968-71; assoc. prof. medicine Tufts U. Sch. Medicine, Boston, 1971-75, prof. medicine, 1976-82; prof., assoc. chmn. medicine Pritzker Sch. Medicine, U. Chgo., 1982-88; dean sch. medicine, prof. medicine SUNY, Stony Brook, 1988-94; dir. Univ. Med. Ctr., Stony Brook, 1993-94; pres. Assn. Am. Med. Colls., Washington, 1994—; dir. divsn. renal disease R.I. Hosp., Providence, 1965-71; chief renal svc. New Eng. Med. Ctr. Hosp., Boston, 1971-82, pres. med. staff, 1975-76, physician-in-chief and chmn., dept. medicine Michael Reese Hosp. and Med. Ctr., Chgo., 1982-88; pres. med. staff Univ. Hosp., Stony Brook, N.Y., 1988-94. Co-author: (textbooks) Acid-Base, 1982, Nephrology Forum, 1983, Repairing Bodily Fluids, 1989; author chpts. to books; editor Nephrology Forum, 1978—, Tufts Family Health Guides, 1979-82; manuscript reviewer Am. Jour. Physiology, Annals Internal Medicine, Jour. Clin. Investigation, Kidney Internat., New England Jour. Medicine; contbr. articles to profl. jours. Lt. col. M.C., U.S. Army, 1969-71. Recipient Scroll of Merit, Nat. Med. Assn., 1997. Master ACP (mem. coun. on subsplty. socs. 1979-84, chmn. edn. policy com. 1983-89, bd. regents 1983-89, chmn. search com. for assoc. exec. v.p. for edn., mem. nephrology com. med. knowledge self-assessment program, chmn., com., rep. to Coun. Med. Splty. Socs. 1991-94, vice chmn. 1988-89), Dept. Vet. Affairs, Spl. Med. Adv. Group, 1995-98; fellow Royal Soc. Medicine; mem. Inst. Medicine of NAS, Am. Clin. and Climatol. Assn., Am. Fedn. Clin. Rsch. (chmn. Ea. sect. 1975), Am. Geriat. Soc. (mem. program com. 1985-88), Am. Heart Assn., Am. Soc. Clin. Investigation, Am. Soc. Nephrology (rep. to CSS 1978-82, chmn. manpower task force 1980), Nat. Kidney Found. (mem. task force on nephrology manpower 1987-89), Soc. Med. Adminstrs., Assn. Am. Physicians, Assn. Program Dirs. in Internal Medicine (mem. coun. 1984-90, pres. 1988-89), Ctrl. Soc. Clin. Rsch., Internat. Soc. Nephrology, Midwest Salt and Water Club, Cosmos Club, Phi Beta Kappa, Sigma Xi. Home: 1819 Kalorama Sq NW Washington DC 20008-4021 Office: Assn Am Med Colls 2450 N St NW Washington DC 20037-1167

COHEN, JOSEPH M., investment company executive. Chmn. bd. SG Cowen, N.Y.C. Office: SG Cowen 712 5th Ave New York NY 10019-4108*

COHEN, JOSEPH MICHAEL, communications executive; b. Holyoke, Mass., June 1, 1950; s. Samuel and Lillian Mae (Margolis) C. BA, U. Mass., 1972; MBA, Rensselaer Poly. Inst., 1983. Newspaper reporter Springfield (Mass.) Union, 1969-72, Hartford (Conn.) Courant, 1974-84; exec. sec. New Eng. Daily Newspaper Survey, Southbridge, Mass., 1972-73; commodities futures trader Chgo. Mercantile Exch., 1985-87; east coast editor Soundings Boating Newspaper, Essex, Conn., 1987-88; mgr. pub. and govt. affairs Conn. Hazardous Waste Mgmt. Svcs., Hartford, 1989-92; dir. comms. State of Conn. Dept. Econ. Devel., Rocky Hill, 1992-95; comms. mgr. IBM, White Plains, N.Y., 1996—. Recipient Bellringer award Publicity Club of New Eng., 1993, Effie award Am. Mktg. Assn., 1994. Jewish. Home: PO Box 126 Chester CT 06412-0126 Office: IBM 1133 Westchester Ave White Plains NY 10604-3599

COHEN, JULES, physician, educator, former academic dean; b. Bklyn., Aug. 26, 1931; s. Samuel S. and Dora (Goldstein) C.; m. Doris Eidlin, Mar. 25, 1956; children: Stephen E., David E., Sharon E. AB, U. Rochester, 1953, MD, 1957. Intern Beth Israel Hosp., Boston, 1957-58; resident, fellow in medicine U. Rochester (N.Y.) Strong Meml. Hosp., 1958-60, mem. faculty, 1963—, prof. medicine, 1973—; NIH research asso. Bethesda, Md., 1960-62; research fellow Postgrad. Med. Sch., London, 1962-63; physician in chief Rochester Gen. Hosp., 1976-82; sr. asso. dean med. edn. U. Rochester Sch. Medicine, 1982-97. USPHS research grantee, 1963-69; USPHS research grantee, 74-77; recipient USPHS Research Career Devel. award, 1970-75; Am. Heart Assn. grantee-in-aid, 1969-71. Fellow ACP, Am. Coll. Cardiology; mem. Am. Physiol. Soc., Am. Heart Assn. (fellow coun. on clin. cardiology), Monroe County Med. Soc., N.Y. State Med. Soc., Rochester Acad. Medicine. Jewish. Home: 152 Burkedale Cres Rochester NY 14625-1704 Office: U Rochester Sch Medicine and Dentistry 601 Elmwood Ave Rochester NY 14642-0001

COHEN, KARL PALEY, nuclear energy consultant; b. N.Y.C., Feb. 5, 1913; s. Joseph M. and Ray (Paley) C.; m. Marthe H. Malartre, Sept. 20, 1938; children: Martine-Claude Leboue, Elisabeth M. Brown, Beatrix Josephine Cashmore. A.B., Columbia U., 1933, M.A., 1934, PhD in Phys. Chemistry, 1937; postgrad., U. Paris, 1936-37. Research asst. to Prof. H. C. Urey Columbia U., 1937-40; dir. theoretical div., SAM Manhattan project, 1940-44; physicist Standard Oil Devel. Co., 1944-48; tech. dir. H.K. Ferguson Co., 1948-52; v.p. Walter Kidde Nuclear Lab., 1952-55; cons. AEC, sr. sci. Columbia U., 1955; mgr. advance engring. atomic power equipment dept. Gen. Electric Co., 1955-65, gen. mgr. breeder reactor devel. dept., 1965-71, mgr. strategic planning, nuclear energy div., 1971-73, chief scientist, nuclear energy group, 1973-78; cons. prof. Stanford U., 1978-81. Author: The Theory of Isotope Separation as Applied to Large Scale Production of U-235, 1951; contbr. articles to profl. jours. Recipient Energy Research prize Alfried Krupp Found., 1977; Chem. Pioneer award Am. Inst. Chemists, 1979. Fellow AAAS, Am. Nuclear Soc. (pres. 1968-69, bd. dirs.), Am. Inst. Chemists; mem. NAE, IEEE, Am. Phys. Soc., Cactus and Succulent Soc., Phi Beta Kappa, Sigma Xi, Phi Lambda Upsilon. Home and Office: 928 N California Ave Palo Alto CA 94303-3405

COHEN, LARRY, film director, producer, screenwriter; b. Chgo., Apr. 20, 1947. TV writer: (series) Kraft Mystery Theatre, The Defenders, Arrest and Trial, NYPD Blue, 87th Precinct Ice, Heatwave; (movies) Cool Million, 1972, Shootout in a One-Dog Town, 1974, Man on the Outside, 1975, Desperado: Avalanche at Devil's Ridge, 1988; creator: Branded, 1965-66, The Invaders, 1967-68; film writer: The Return of the Seven, 1966, Daddy's Gone A-Hunting, 1969, El Condor, 1970, I, The Jury, 1982, Best Seller, 1987, Deadly Illusion, 1987, Guilty as Sin, 1993; dir., prodr., writer: Bone, 1972, Black Caesar, 1973, Hell in Harlem, 1973, It's Alive, 1974, Demon, 1976, The Private Files of J. Edgar Hoover, 1978, It Lives Again, 1978, Full Moon High, 1982, Q, 1982, Perfect Strangers, 1984; story: Success, 1979, The Man Who Wasn't There, 1983, Scandalous, 1984, Body Snatchers, 1984; dir., writer: Special Effects, 1984, The Ambulance, 1990; exec. prodr., dir., writer: The Stuff, 1985, It's Alive III: Island of the Alive, 1987, Return to Salem's Lot, 1987, Wicked Stepmother, 1989; prodr., writer: Maniac Cop II, 1990.; writer, dir.: As Good As Dead, 1996; dir.: Original Gangstas. 1997.

COHEN, LAWRENCE ALAN, health facility administrator; b. N.Y.C., Nov. 29, 1953; s. Irwin Wolf Cohen and Ernestine Jacqueline (Rosenbloom) Breiner; m. Ilene Beth Rosen, May 27, 1979; children: Bari, Kerri, Andrew. BBA in Acctg., George Washington U., 1975; JD, St. Johns U., 1979; LLM in Taxation, NYU, 1982. Bar: N.Y.; CPA. Assoc. Rogers & Wells, N.Y.C., 1979-82, Battle Fowler, N.Y.C., 1982-84; 1st v.p. VMS Realty Ptnrs., N.Y.C., 1984-88; exec. v.p. PaineWebber Properties Inc., N.Y.C., 1989-90, pres., CEO, 1991-96; vice-chmn., CFO Capital Sr. Living Corp., N.Y.C., 1996-98, CEO, 1999—. Mem. Nat. Realty Com. (exec. com. 1990—), Nat. Multi Housing Coun. (exec. com. 1992—), Am. Srs. Housing Assn. (exec. bd. dirs. 1992—). Jewish. Home: 41 Willow Rd Woodmere NY 11598-2228

COHEN, LAWRENCE BARUCH, neurobiologist, educator; b. Indpls., June 18, 1939; s. Gabriel Murel and Helen (Aronovitz) C.; children: Daniel, Avrum; m. Barbara Ellen Ehrlich; 1 child, Lily Rachel. BS, U. Chgo., 1961; PhD, Columbia U., 1965. Asst. prof. Yale U., New Haven, 1968-71, assoc. prof., 1971-79, prof. physiology, 1979—. Recipient Elizabeth R. Cole award, Biophys. Soc., 1987, McMaster Award, Columbia U., 1965; named Dist. Lectr., Am. Psychol. Soc., 1998. Office: Yale U Sch Medicine 333 Cedar St New Haven CT 06510-3289

COHEN, LAWRENCE EDWARD, sociology educator, criminologist; b. L.A., July 20, 1945; s. Louis and Florence (White) C. BA, U. Calif., Berkeley, 1969; MA, Calif. State U., 1971; PhD, U. Wash., 1974; postdoctorate study, SUNY, Albany, 1973-75. Rsch. assoc. Sch. of Criminal Justice, SUNY, Albany, 1973-76; asst. prof. U. Ill., Urbana, 1976-80; assoc. prof. U. Tex., Austin, 1980-85; prof. Ind. U., Bloomington, 1985-88, U. Calif., Davis, 1988—. Cons. editor Social Forces, 1981-84, Jour. Criminal Law and Criminology, 1982-98, Am. Sociol. Rev., 1982-84, Am. Jour. Sociology, 1990-98, Criminology, 1996-98; contbr. numerous articles to profl. jours. Sgt. USMC, 1963-66, Vietnam. Grantee NIMH, 1978-80, NSF, 1983-89. Mem. Am. Sociol. Assn., Am. Soc. Criminology, Acad. Criminal Justice Scis., Soc. for Study Social Problems. Office: U Calif Dept Sociology Davis CA 95616

COHEN, LAWRENCE N., health care management consultant; b. Woodmere, N.Y., June 30, 1932; s. Irving and Helen (Spiegel) C.; m. Ilene R. Lang, Nov. 1968; children by previous marriage: Randall, Douglas, Pamela. BA in Econs., Cornell U., 1954; PhD (hon.) in Commercial Sci., Dowling Coll., 1993. With Lumex, Inc., Bay Shore, N.Y., 1966-94, contr., 1966-72, treas., 1972-81; sec. Lumex, Inc., Bay Shore, 1975-81, pres. divsn., 1981-86, v.p., 1975-86, chmn., pres., CEO, 1986-94; mem. exec. com., past chmn. Medmarc; mem. adv. bd. Liberty Mut. N.Y.; sr. cons. Corp. Performance Cons.; mgmt. cons. LARC Strategic Concepts LLC, Syosset, N.Y., 1999—. Chmn., gen. chairperson Southside Hosp. annual ball, 1990; former mem. bd. dirs., former vice chmn. L.I. Assn. former co-chair Helen Keller Svcs. Sound and Light Ball; hon. bd. dirs. L.I. Edn. Conf. Bd.; hon. co-chair Alzheimers Assn. 3d ann. Memory Walk; vice chmn. fin. leadership com. L.I. chpt. NCCJ; trustee, dep. mayor, police commr. Village of Brookville, rd. commr.; former mem. Pres. Coun. Dowling Coll. Lt. (j.g.) USNR, 1954-56. Decorated Korean Svc. medal; recipient Disting. Citizen award Dowling Coll., 1993; honoree United Cerebral Palsy, 1991. Avocation: piloting. Home: 9 Hemlock Dr Brookville NY 11545-3324 Office: LN Cohen & Assocs 9 Hemlock Dr Glen Head NY 11545-3324 also: LARC Strategic Concepts LLC 115 Eileen Way Ste 103 Syosset NY 11791-5314

COHEN, LAWRENCE P., federal judge; b. 1939. LLM, U. Ala., 1966. Bar: Mass. Trial atty. U.S. Dept. Justice, Washington, 1966-69; asst. atty. gen. for dist. Mass., U.S. Dept. Justice, Boston, 1969-70, asst. U.S. atty., chief criminal divsn., 1970-76; magistrate judge for Mass., U.S. Magistrate Ct., Boston, 1976—. Office: McCormack PO and Courthouse 1 Courthouse Way Ste 7420 Boston MA 02210-3009

COHEN, LAWRENCE SOREL, physician, educator; b. N.Y.C., Mar. 27, 1933; s. Max and Fannie (Cooper) C.; m. Jane Abramson, Aug. 5, 1961; children: Melanie, Wendy. A.B., Harvard U., 1954; M.D., N.Y. U., 1958; M.A. (hon.), Yale U., 1970. Diplomate: Am. Bd. Internal Medicine, Sub Bd. Cardiovascular Diseases. Intern, then resident in medicine Yale-New Haven Hosp., 1958-60, 64-65; asst. in medicine Harvard U. Med. Sch., 1962-64; sr. investigator Nat. Heart, Lung and Blood Inst., 1965-68, mem. task force on arteriosclerosis, 1978-80, chmn. clin. trials rev. com., 1984-85, 87-89; assoc. prof. medicine U. Tex. Med. Sch., Dallas, 1968-70; prof. medicine Yale U. Med. Sch., 1970-81, Ebenezer K. Hunt prof. medicine, 1981—, dep. dean, 1991-95, spl. advisor to dean, 1995—. Mem. editorial bd. Circulation, Am. Jour. Cardiology, Am. Heart Jour.; contbr. over 160 articles to med. jours. Active Am. Heart Assn., chpt. pres., 1980-81, affiliate pres. Conn. chpt., 1984-86. With USPHS, 1960-62. Recipient Francis Gilman Blake award for Teaching of Med. Scis., 1973. Fellow ACP, Am. Coll. Cardiology (trustee 1978-83, mem. editorial bd. jour.); mem. Assn. Univ. Cardiologists (pres.-elect 1990, pres. 1991), Interurban Clin. Club (pres. 1988), Alpha Omega Alpha. Home: 633 Whitney Ave New Haven CT 06511-2218 Office: Yale U Sch Medicine 333 Cedar St New Haven CT 06510-3289

COHEN, LEONARD (NORMAN COHEN), poet, novelist, musician, songwriter; b. Montreal, Que., Can., Sept. 21, 1934; s. Nathan B. and Marsha (Klinitsky) C. B.A., McGill U., 1955; postgrad., Columbia.; LLB (hon.), Dalhousie U., 1971; LLD (hon.), McGill U., 1992. Author: (poetry) Let Us Compare Mythologies, 1956, The Spice Box of Earth, 1961, Flowers for Hitler, 1964, Parasites of Heaven, 1966, Selected Poems, 1956-68, 1968, The Energy of Slaves, 1972, Death of a Lady's Man, 1979, Book of Mercy, 1984, Stranger Music: Selected Music and Songs, 1993, Dance Me to the End of Love, 1995, (novels) The Favorite Game, 1963, Beautiful Losers, 1966, also articles, songs including music for McCabe and Mrs. Miller, 1971, Natural Born Killers, 1994; rec. artist for Sony Music; albums include I'm Your Man, 1988, The Future, 1992, Cohen Live, 1993, More Best Of, 1997. Decorated Order of Can., 1992; recipient McGill Lit. award, 1956, Que. Lit. award, 1964, Gov. Gen.'s Performing Arts award, Can., 1993; Can. Coun. grantee, 1960-61. Office: c/o Kelley Lynch Stranger Mgmt Inc 419 N Larchmont Blvd Ste 88 Los Angeles CA 90004-3013

COHEN, LEWIS ISAAC, lawyer; b. N.Y.C., July 27, 1932; s. Benjamin and Jeannette (Klotzko) C.; m. Sheila Lipman, Sept. 8, 1957; children—Leslie, Bruce, Wendy. B.A., U. Calif. at Los Angeles, 1953; LL.B., Columbia, 1958. Bar: N.Y. State bar 1959, D.C. bar 1964, U.S. Supreme Ct. bar 1966. Atty. FCC, Washington, 1959-64; practiced in Washington, 1964—; ptnr. Cohen & Berfield, 1964-95. Served with AUS, 1954-56. Mem. Fed. D.C. bar assns., FCC Bar Assn. Home: PO Box 126 Mount Jackson VA 22842-0126

COHEN, LITA INDZEL, state legislator; m. Stanley S. Cohen; children: Reuven, Shoshana. AB in Polit. Sci. cum laude, U. Pa., 1962, postgrad., JD, 1965. Bar: Pa. 1965. Clk. Henderson, Wetherill & O'Hey, Norristown, 1964, Levi, Mandel & Miller, Phila., 1965; asst. regional counsel HUD, 1966-67; asst. counsel Sch. Dist. Phila., 1967-71; pvt. practice Merion, Pa., 1971-76; exec. v.p., gen. counsel, COO Ind. Broadcasting Co., Inc. and Banks Broadcasting Co., 1976-82; pres. Orange Prodns., Inc.-Nat. Radio Syndication Co., 1983-87, Lita Cohen Radio Svcs., Merion, Pa., 1987-93; mem. Ho. of Reps., Conshohocken, Pa., 1992—. Bd. dirs. Merion Civic Assn.; mem. citizens fire prevention com. Phila. Fire Dept.; active Lower Merion/ Narberth Watershed Assn., Lower Merion Twp. Police Pension Assn., Har Zion Temple; v.p. bd. dirs. Phila. Child Guidance Ctr.; Lower Merion Twp. commr., 1986-93; capt. Heart Fund Block; mem. women's adv. com. Montemery County C.C.; hon. pres. Golda Meir Profl. Women's Hadassah; past bd. dirs. Kaiserman JYC, Atwater Kent Mus. Mem. Pa. Bar Assn., Phila. Bar Assn., Montgomery County Bar Assn. Office: Pa Ho of Reps PO Box 202020 Harrisburg PA 17120-2020 also: 1010 Fayette St Conshohocken PA 19428-1562*

COHEN, LOUIS RICHARD, lawyer; b. Washington, Nov. 28, 1940; s. Milton Howard and Rowna (Chaffetz) C.; m. Bonnie Rubenstein, Aug. 29, 1965; children: Amanda Carroll, Eli Augustus. AB, Harvard U., 1962, LLB, 1966; student, Wadham Coll., Oxford, Eng., 1962-63. Bar: D.C. Law clk. to Hon. John M. Harlan U.S. Supreme Ct., Washington, 1967-68; assoc. Wilmer, Cutler & Pickering, Washington, 1968-74, ptnr., 1974-86, 88—; dep. solicitor gen. U.S. Dept. Justice, Washington, 1986-88; ptnr. Wilmer, Cutler & Pickering, Wash., 1988—; vis. prof. Stanford (Calif.) Law Sch., 1981; lectr. law Harvard Law Sch., Cambridge, Mass., 1986. Author: Book Review Michigan Law Review, 1993. Chair Harvard Law Sch. Fund, 1993-96; mem. overseers com. to Visit Harvard Law Sch., 1986-92; bd. dirs. Woolly Mammoth Theatre Co., Washington, 1988-91, 96—. Mem. Supreme Ct. Hist. Soc., Am. Acad. Appellate Lawyers, The Met. Club (Washington). Jewish. Avocation: hiking. Office: Wilmer Cutler & Pickering 2445 M St NW Ste 500 Washington DC 20037-1487

COHEN, MALCOLM MARTIN, psychologist, researcher; b. New Brunswick, N.J., May 13, 1937; s. Nathan and Esther (Greenhaus) C.; m. Marilyn Jerrow, Jan. 2, 1959 (dec. 1967); m. Eleanor Johnson, June 30, 1969 (div. 1988); m. Suzana Gal, Feb. 14, 1988. BA, Brandeis U., 1959; MA, U. Pa., 1961, PhD, 1965. Lic. psychologist, Pa. Asst. instr. U. Pa., Phila., 1961-63; rsch. psychologist Naval Air Engring. Ctr., Phila., 1963-67; supervisory rsch. psychologist Naval Air Devel. Ctr., Warminster, Pa., 1967-82; asst. chief biomed. rsch. div. NASA-Ames Rsch Ctr., Moffett Field, Calif., 1982-85, chief neurosci. br., 1985-88, rsch. scientist, 1988—; lectr. dept. aeros. and astronautics Stanford (Calif.) U., 1982-92, lectr. human biology program, 1994-95, consulting assoc. prof. human biology program, 1995-98, cons. prof. human biology program, 1998—; mem. aerospace med. adv. panel Am. Inst. Biol. Scis., Washington, 1984-92; v.p. Nat. Hand Rehab. Fund, Washington, 1975—. Contbr. numerous articles to profl. jours. Patentee light bar to monitor human acceleration tolerance. Founding mem. Common Cause of Phila., 1973. Recipient Exceptional Sci. Achievement medal NASA, 1994. Fellow Aerospace Med. Assn. (editorial bd. Aviation Space and Environ. Medicine 1985-93, Environ. Sci. award 1985, William F. Longacre award 1989), Aerospace Human Factors Assn. (pres. 1992); mem. AAAS, AIAA, N.Y. Acad. Scis., Psychonomics Soc., Sigma Xi. Jewish. Avocation: scuba diving. Office: NASA Ames Rsch Ctr Mail Stop 239-11 Moffett Field CA 94035

COHEN, MALCOLM STUART, economist, research institute director; b. Mpls., Jan. 17, 1942; s. Jack Alvin and Lorraine Ethel (Hill) C.; m. Judith Ann Arenson, Sept. 25, 1965; children: Laura, Randall, Ilona. BA in Econs. summa cum laude, U. Minn., 1963; PhD in Econs., MIT, 1967. Labor economist U.S. Bur. Labor Stats., Washington, 1967-68; lectr. U. Md., College Park, 1968; asst. to v.p. state rels. and planning U. Mich., Ann Arbor, 1968-70, various tchr. positions, 1968-85; co-rsch. dir. U. Mich. Inst. of Labor and Indsl. Rels., Ann Arbor, 1973-80, dir., 1980-93; cons. Corp. Pub. Broadcasting, 1994-97; vis. prof. indsl. rels. ctr. U. Minn., 1994-96; pres. Employment Rsch. Corp., Ann Arbor, 1997—; cons. U.S. Dept. Labor, 1995—, EEOC, 1996—, Money Mag., 1995—, Mich. Senate Fiscal Agy., Lansing, 1988; project dir. various projects Washington, 1968-92; expert witness discrimination and econs. various clients, 1982—. Author: Labor Shortages: As America Approaches the 21st Century, 1995; co-author: A Micro Model of Labor Supply, 1970; mem. edil. bd. Worklife, 1992—; contbr. articles to profl. jours. Pres. Jewish Community Ctr., Ann Arbor, 1991-93. Mem. Nat. Assn. Forensic Economists, Indsl. Rels. Rsch. Assn. (mem. stats. com. 1988—), Internat. Indsl. Rels. Assn., N.Am. Econs. and Fin. Assn. Avocations: jogging, geneology. Office: Employment Rsch Corp 305 E Eisenhower Pkwy Ste 110 Ann Arbor MI 48108-3348 also: U Mich Inst Labor and Indsl Rels Ann Arbor MI 48109-2054

COHEN, MARC, cardiologist; b. Cairo, Egypt, Mar. 3, 1953; came to U.S., 1958; BA, U. Chgo., 1973; MD, NYU Sch. Medicine, 1977. Prof. medicine, dir. cardiac cath lab. MCP Hahnemann Sch. Medicine, Phila., 1995—. Fellow ACP, Am. Coll. Cardiology; mem. Am. Heart Assn. Office: Hahnemann U Hosp Broad & Vine Philadelphia PA 19102

COHEN, MARC JACOB, researcher; b. Indpls., July 17, 1952; s. Louis Alexander and Barbara Baylah (Zucrow) C.; m. Linda Marla Hoffman, May 5, 1978; children: Amy Victoria, Michael Louis. BA magna cum laude, Carleton Coll., 1974; MA, U. Wis., 1977, PhD, 1983. News editor Blue Earth (Minn.) Post, 1974-75; rsch. asst. USDA, Washington, 1980-82; rschr. Bus. Environ. Risk Info., S.A., Washington, 1983-84; staff assoc. Formosan Assn. for Pub. Affairs, Washington, 1984-86; assoc. dir. Asia Resource Ctr., Washington, 1986-90; policy analyst Bread for the World, Washington, 1990-91; sr. rsch. assoc. Bread for the World, Silver Spring, Md., 1991-98; special asst. to dir. gen. Internat. Food Policy Rsch. Inst., Washington, 1998—; cons. in field; bd. dirs. Asia Pacific Ctr., Washington, 1995—, Asia Resource Ctr., Washington, 1986-97, Trees for the Future, 1989—. Author: Taiwan at the Crossroads, 1988; editor, contbr. Ann. Report on the State of World Hunger, 1991-98 (award); author monograph. Pres. Teaching Assts. Assn., Madison, 1978-79, Share, Inc., McLean, Va., 1995-98; del. Va. State Dem. Convention, 1985, 88; co-chair social action com. Temple Rodef Shalom, Falls Church, Va., 1997—. Wis. Alumni Rsch. Found. fellow, 1976-77, Fgn. Lang. and Area Studies fellow, 1977-80, Inst. for Study of World Politics fellow Fund for Peace, 1980-81. Mem. Assn. for Asian Studies, Soc. for Internat. Devel., Results, Phi Beta Kappa. Jewish. Avocations: swimming, bicycling, gardening. Home: 7808 Falstaff Rd Mc Lean VA 22102-2725 Office: Internat Food Policy Rsch Inst 2033 K St N.W. Washington DC 20006

COHEN, MARCIA ALICE, special education administrator; b. New Haven, Dec. 25, 1951; d. Seymour A. and Phyllis T. (Feinberg) C. BA, Am. U., 1972; MA, Columbia U., 1974, MEd, 1980; EdD, Nova Southea. U., 1999. Cert. spl. edn. elem. tchr., N.Y., Conn., adminstr., supr., Conn. Tchr. spl. edn. Celentano Sch., New Haven, 1974-77; tchr. spl. edn. Wilbur Cross H.S., New Haven, 1978-82, program coord., 1982-89; dir. edn. Klingberg Family Ctr., New Britain, Conn., 1989-99; mgr. pvt. sch. approval project U. Conn., Storrs, 1998—. Mem. Vol. for Israel, New Haven, 1983—. Mem. ASCD, Coun. Exceptional Children, Conn. Assn. Pvt. Spl. Edn. Facilities (treas. 1991-93), Assn. Retarded Citizens, Conn. Assn. for Children with Learning Disabilities. Jewish. Avocations: tennis, skiing, travel, computers. Home: 165 Promenade Dr Hamden CT 06514-2377 Office: AJ Pappanikou Ctr 249 Glenbrook Rd U-64 Storrs Mansfield CT 06269

COHEN, MARCUS, allergist, immunologist; b. Appleton, Wis., June 8, 1937; s. Frank and Hannah (Weinstein) C.; m. Sheila Terman, July 14, 1963; children: Kimberly Ellyn, Louis Jeffrey. BA, U. Wis., Madison, 1959, MD, 1962. Rotating intern San Francisco Gen. Hosp., U. Calif. San Francisco, 1962-63; resident in pediat. U. Calif., San Francisco, 1962-65; fellow in allergy and immunology U. Wis., Madison, 1965-66; pvt. practice allergy and immunology Madison, 1966—; pres. Madison Gen. Hosp. Med.-Surg. Found., 1986-91; pres. Quisling Clinic S.C., 1973-86; vice chair Physicans Plus Med. Group, 1987; vice chair, mem. exec. com. Physicians Plus Ins. Co., 1993-98, bd. chair, 1996-98; chair dept. pediat. Madison Gen. Hosp., 1969-70; sr. med. flight examiner FAA, 1981—; mng. ptnr. Quisling Clinic Real Estate Partnership; clin. asst. prof. dept. pediat. U. Wis. Med. Sch. Bd. dirs. Meriter Found., 1994-95; mem. U. Wis. Med. Found., 1998-99. Fellow Am. Acad. Pediat., Am. Acad. Allergy, Asthma & Immunology, Am. Coll. Allergy, Asthma and Immunology, Wis. Allergy Soc. (pres. 1993-95), Bascom Hill Soc., Univ. Wis. Found. Jewish. Avocations: skiing, bicycling, sailing, fishing, photography. Office: 1 S Park St Ste 440 Madison WI 53715-1374

COHEN, MARK D., social service administrator; b. Des Plaines, Ill., Dec. 5, 1973; s. Alan Joel and Karen Lee (Schiff) C. BA in Polit. Sci., Washington U., St. Louis, 1995, BA in English Lit., 1995; M in Mass Comm., Ariz. State U., Tempe, 1998. In refugee job devel. Cath. Social Svc. of Phoenix, 1997—. Pub. info. officer ARC, Phoenix, 1996—; Democratic committeeman, Phoenix, 1996. Mem. Soc. Profl. Journalists, Pi Sigma Alpha. Avocations: reading, travel, gardening, movies.

COHEN, MARK HERBERT, broadcasting company executive; b. Boston, Mar. 27, 1932; s. Henry I. and Francis C.; m. Mary Jane Pitman, July 30, 1961; children: Patricia Beth, H. Jonathan, Cathy Ann. B.A. in Bus. Adminstrn., U. Maine, 1954; M.S. in TV Prodn, Syracuse U., 1958. Announcer Sta. WGUY-AM-FM, Bangor, Maine, 1954, Sta. WGAN-AM-TV, Portland, Maine, 1954-55; various positions in sales, planning and station clearance ABC-TV network, N.Y.C., 1958-68, v.p. sales planning, 1967-70, v.p., assoc. dir. planning, bus. and fin. analysis, 1970-76, sr. v.p. fin. and planning, 1976-77, sr. v.p., 1977-85; v.p. Am. Broadcasting Cos. Inc., 1981-83, sr. v.p., 1983-85, exec. v.p. broadcast group, 1985-86; exec. v.p. ABC Network Div., 1986-88; v.p. Capital Cities/ABC, 1986-88; pres. distbn. and prodn. co. D.L. Taffner Ltd., Armonk, N.Y., 1990-91; broadcasting cons., 1991—. Mem. exec. com. of alumni coun. U. Maine, 1980-86. Mem. adv. bd. Newhouse Sch., Syracuse U., 1985-88; mem. exec. com. of pres.'s coun. U. Maine, 1988, vice chmn. of pres.'s coun., 1992-93, chmn., 1993-95, vice chmn. Campaign for Maine, 1991-96. Fellow Nat. Acad. Arts and Scis. (pres. internat. coun. 1984-85, exec. com. 1986-92); mem. Internat. Radio and TV Soc. (gov. 1980-81, v.p. 1983-85), Whipporwill Club.

COHEN, MARK N., business executive; b. Camden, N.J., July 14, 1947; s. Morris and Esther (Sobel) C.; m. Rhoda Posner, Dec. 19, 1971; children: Michele Rebecca, Gregory Leighton. BS, U. Mo., Kansas City, 1969; postgrad., N.Y. Med. Coll., 1969-70; MS, Am. Western U., Tulsa, 1972, PhD, 1976. Cert. state advisor U.S. Congl. Adv. Bd. Founder, pres., chmn. Nat. Recall Alert Ctr., Marlton, N.J., 1973—; founder Acad. Guidance Svcs., Marlton, 1975-88; founder, pres., chmn. Nat. Corp. Svcs., Marlton, 1977—, Nat. Pub. Corp., Marlton, 1979—; pres. Am. Bus. Opportunity Commn., N.J., 1975; bd. dirs., chmn. Health Sytems Agy., Bellmawr, N.J., 1982; treas., bd. dirs. Perinatal Coop./South N.J., Camden, 1983; mem. bd. advisors Free Enterprise, Marlton, 1985; pres. Cohenterprises, Inc., Marlton, 1986, Am. Profl. Copy-Quick Printing Corp., Marlton, 1985, Nationwide

Wats Telephone Answering Service, Inc., Marlton, 1985-88, Slim Scents, Inc., 1993, On Air-Everywhere, Inc., 1994, In-Press Express, Inc., 1994. Author: 100 Best Spare Time Business Opportunities Today, 1990, Win Your Weight, Loss War, 1998, Mindstrings and How to Pull Them, 1998. Bd. dirs. Beth Israel Synagogue; trustee Cooper Found./Cooper Hosp. U. Med. Ctr.; assoc. advisor post 65 Explorer Scouts. Recipient Young Exec. of Yr. award Jim Walter Corp., Tampa, Fla., 1972, Disting. Leadership award Am. Security Council Found., 1984, Annual Register award Esquire mag.; named one of 50 Bus. People to Watch, N.J. Bus. Jour. Mem. Am. Hosp. Assn., U.S. C. of C., Am. Assn. Fin. Profls., Nat. Council on Patient Info. and Edn., Nat. Health Lawyers Assn., N.J. Assn. Commerce and Industry (chmn. 1974), Am. Assn. Sch. Adminstrs., Am. Assn. Univ. Adminstrs., Am. Assn. Indiv. Investors, Internat. Coun. Computers Edn., MENSA. Republican. Jewish. Home: 6 Alluvium Lakes Dr Kirkwood Voorhees NJ 08043-4816

COHEN, MARK STEVEN, dentist; b. N.Y.C., Dec. 10, 1948; s. Lawrence and Yetta (Grossman) C.; m. Arlene Debbie Deutsch, Aug. 23, 1970 (div. May 1984); 1 child, Aaron Philip; m. Donna Lynn Poissonnier, Nov. 27, 1985. BS, CCNY, 1971; DDS, Columbia U., 1975, cert. in Pedodontics, 1976. Practice dentistry Yonkers, N.Y., 1975-76, Bristol, Conn., 1976-79, Brookfield, Conn., 1977—; dir. dental service N.Y. Inst. for the Edn. Blind, Bronx, 1976-78; assoc. attending dentist Danbury (Conn.) Hosp., 1976-82, Blythdale Children's Hosp., Valhalla, N.Y., 1986-87; assoc. clin. prof. dentistry Columbia U., N.Y.C., 1976—, mem. quality assurance com., 1982-85. Patentee in field. Active Dental Guidance Council for Cerebral Palsy, N.Y.C., 1976-81. Chemistry fellow NSF, Washington, 1969-71, research fellow NIH, 1971, United Cerebral Palsy, 1975-76. Mem. ADA, Conn. State Dental Assn., Greater Danbury Dental Soc., Am. Dental Vols. for Israel, OKU Dental Honor Soc. Democrat. Jewish. Avocations: travel, photography, biking, collecting antiques. Office: Mark S Cohen 940 Federal Rd Brookfield CT 06804-2418

COHEN, MARSHALL HARRIS, astronomer, educator; b. Manchester, N.H., July 5, 1926; s. Solomon and Mollie Lee (Epstein) C.; m. Shirley Kekst, Sept. 19, 1948; children: Thelma, Linda, Sara. BEE, Ohio State U., 1948, MS, 1949, PhD, 1952. Rsch. assoc. Ohio State U., Columbus, 1950-54; asst. prof. elec. engring. Cornell U., Ithaca, N.Y., 1954-58, assoc. prof., 1958-63, assoc. prof. astronomy, 1963-66; prof. applied electro-physics U. Calif., San Diego, 1966-68; prof. radio astronomy Calif. Inst. Tech., Pasadena, 1968-90, prof. astronomy, 1990-96, exec. officer for astronomy, 1981-84, prof. emeritus, 1996; prof. associé U. Paris VI, 1989; mem. numerous coms. NSF, NRC, vis. coms. various obs. in U.S., Fed. Republic Germany. Contbr. articles, book revs. to profl. jours.; patentee radio astronomy. With U.S. Army, 1943-46. Co-recipient Rumford medal Am. Acad. Arts and Scis., 1971; Guggenheim Found. fellow Paris Obs., 1960-61, MIT/Inst. Astronomy, Cambridge, Eng., 1980-81; Morrison fellow Lick Obs., 1988. Fellow AAAS; mem. NAS (chmn. sect. astronomy 1989-92), Am. Astron. Soc. (publ. bd. 1980-83), Astron. Soc. Pacific (bd. dirs. 1969-72), Am. Acad. Arts and Scis., Internat. Union for Sci. Radio (chmn. commn. V of U.S. nat. com. 1970-73), Internat. Astron. Union (U.S. nat. com. 1989-92). Avocation: mountain hiking. Office: Calif Inst Tech Dept Astronomy Pasadena CA 91125

COHEN, MARVIN LOU, physics educator; b. Montreal, Que., Can., Mar. 3, 1935; came to U.S., 1947, naturalized, 1953; s. Elmo and Molly (Zaritsky) C.; m. Merrill L. Gardner, Aug. 31, 1958 (dec. Apr. 1994); children: Mark, Susan; m. Suzy R. Locke, Sept. 8, 1996. AB, U. Calif., 1957; MS, U. Chgo., 1958, PhD, 1964. Mem. tech. staff Bell Telephone Labs., Murray Hill, N.J., 1963-64; asst. prof. physics U. Calif., Berkeley, 1964-66, assoc. prof., 1966-69, prof. physics, 1969-95, univ. prof., 1995—, prof. Miller Inst. Basic Resch. in Sci., 1969-70, 76-77, 88, chmn., 1977-81, univ. prof., 1995—; U. Calif. Faculty Rsch. lectr. U. Calif.,, 1997; chmn. Gordon Rsch. Conf. Chemistry and Physics of Solids, 1972; U.S. rep. to Semicondr. Commn., Internat. Union Pure and Applied Physics, 1975-81; Alfred P. Sloan fellow Cambridge U., Eng., 1965-67; vis. prof. Cambridge U., Eng., 1966, U. Paris, France, 1972-73, summers 68, 75, 87, 88, U. Hawaii, Honolulu, 1978-79, Technion, Haifa, Israel, 1987-88; chmn. planning com. Pure and Applied Sci. Inst. U. Hawaii, 1980—; mem. selection com. Presdl. Young Investigator Awards, 1983; mem. Com. on Nat. Synchrotron Radiation Facilities, 1983-84; chmn. 17th Internat. Conf. on Physics of Semicondrs., 1984; mem. exec. com. Govt.-Univ.-Industry Research Roundtable, 1984—; vice chmn. Govt.-U. Industry Research Roundtable Working Group on Sci. and Engring. Talent, 1984—; mem. rev. bd. for Ctr. for Advanced Materials Lawrence Berkeley Lab., 1986-87; mem. panel on Implications for Mechanisms of Support and Panel on High Temperature Superconductivity, NAS, NSF, 1987; mem. adv. bd. Tex. Ctr. for Superconductivity, 1988-90, vice chair, 1991—; mem. U.S. del. to Bilateral Dialog R&D in the U.S. and Japan, NRC, 1989; mem. sci. policy bd. Stanford Synchrotron Rad. Lab., 1990-92. Editorial bd. Perspectives in Condensed Matter Physics, 1987—; adv. bd. Internat. Jour. Modern Physics B, 1987—, Modern Physics Letters B, 1987—; assoc. editor Materials Sci. and Engring., 1987—; contbr. more than 600 articles to tech. jours. Mem. vis. com. Ginzton Lab., Stanford U., 1991; mem. sci. policy com. Stanford Linear Accelerator, 1993-95. Recipient Outstanding Accomplishment in Solid State Physics award U.S. Dept. Energy, 1981, Sustained Outstanding Rsch. in Solid State Physics award U.S. Dept. Energy, 1990, Cert.of Merit, Lawrence Berkeley Lab., 1991; A.P. Sloan fellow, 1965-67, Guggenheim fellow, 1978-79, 90-91. Fellow AAAS, Am. Phys. Soc. (exec. coun. divsn. solid state physics 1975-79, chmn. 1977-78, Oliver E. Buckley prize for solid state physics 1979, Buckley prize com. 1980-81, chmn. 1981, Julius Edgar Lilienfeld prize 1994, Lilienfeld prize com. 1994—, Isakson Prize com. 1995-98, chmn. 1999); mem. NAS (chmn. condensed matter physics search/screening com. 1981-82, chmn. Comstock prize com. 1988, nominating com. for selection of pres., v.p., councilors 1992-93), Am. Acad. Arts and Scis., Nat. Acad. Scis. Home: 201 Estates Dr Piedmont CA 94611-3315 Office: U Calif Dept Physics Berkeley CA 94720 *Make decisions only when things go well and stick to them when things go badly.*

COHEN, MARY ANN, judge; b. Albuquerque, July 16, 1943; d. Gus R. and Mary Carolyn (Avriette) C. BS, UCLA, 1964; JD, U. So. Calif., 1967. Bar: Calif. 1967. Ptnr. Abbott & Cohen, P.C. and predecessors, Los Angeles, 1967-82; judge U.S. Tax Ct., Washington 1982—, chief judge 1996—. Mem. ABA (sect. taxation), Legion Lex. Republican. Office: US Tax Ct 400 2nd St NW Washington DC 20217

COHEN, MELANIE ROVNER, lawyer; b. Chgo., Aug. 9, 1944; d. Millard Jack and Sheila (Fox) Rovner; m. Arthur Wieber Cohen, Feb. 17, 1968; children: Mitchell Jay, Jennifer Sue. AB, Brandeis U., 1965; JD, DePaul U., 1977. Bar: Ill. 1977, U.S. Dist. Ct. (no. dist.) Ill., U.S. Ct. Appeals (7th cir.). Law clk. to Justice F.J. Hertz U.S. Bankruptcy Ct., 1976-77; ptnr. Altheimer & Gray, Chgo., 1977-89, 89—, Antonow & Fink, Chgo., 1977-89; mem. Supreme Ct. of Ill. Atty. Registration and Disciplinary Commn. Inquiry Bd., 1982-86, hearing bd., 1986-94; instr. secured and consumer transactions creditor-debtor law DePaul U., Chgo., 1980-90; bd. dirs. Bankruptcy Arbitration and Mediation Svcs., 1994—; instr. real estate and bankruptcy law John Marshall Law Sch., Chgo., 1996-98. Contbr. articles to profl. jours. Panelist, spkr., bd. dirs., v.p., fellow Brandeis U. Nat. Alumni Assn., 1981—; life mem. Nat. Women's Com., 1975—, pres. Chgo. chpt., 1975-82; mem. Glencoe (Ill.) Caucus, 1977-80; chair lawyers com. Ravinia Festival, 1990-91, chmn. sustaining com., 1991—, chair sustaining fund subcom., 1992—. Mem. ABA (co-chair com. on enforcement of creditors' rights and bankruptcy), Ill. State Bar Assn., Chgo. Bar Assn. (chmn. bankruptcy reorganization com. 1983-85), Comml. Law League, Ill. Trial Lawyers Assn., Comml. Fin. Assn. Edn. Found. (bd. govs.), Turnaround Mgmt. Assn. (pres. Chgo./midwest chpt. 1990-92, nat. bd. dirs. 1990—, mem. mgmt. com. 1995—, pres. nat. bd. dirs. 1999—). Home: 167 Park Ave Glencoe IL 60022-1351 Office: Altheimer & Gray 10 S Wacker Dr Ste 4000 Chicago IL 60606-7407

COHEN, MELVIN IRWIN, communications systems and technology executive; b. N.Y.C., June 25, 1936; s. Alexander and Fannie (Becker) C.; m. Elaine Chesin; children: Daniel Marc, Martha Rachel. SB, MIT, 1957, SM, 1958; PhD, Rensselaer Poly. Inst., 1965. Engr. Pratt & Whitney Aircraft, East Hartford, Conn., 1958-61; mem. tech. staff, supr. Bell Telephone Labs., Murray Hill, N.J., 1964-72; asst. dir. Western Elec. Co., Princeton, N.J., 1972-79; dept. head AT&T Bell Labs., Murray Hill, 1979-82; dir. AT&T Bell Labs., Whippany, N.J., 1982-87, Murray Hill, 1987; v.p. mfg. R&D AT&T Bell Labs., Princeton, 1987-88, exec. dir., 1988-90; exec. dir. electronics and photonics div. AT&T Bell Labs., Breinigsville, Pa., 1990-93; v.p. rsch. effectiveness AT&T Bell Labs., Murray Hill, N.J., 1993-96, Bell Labs/Lucent Techs., Murray Hill, 1996—; mem. panel on assessment of Nat. Inst. Standards and Tech. Programs, NRC, 1990-96; trustee AT&T Found., 1993-96; mem. sci. policy bd. Rutgers U., Newark, 1993-96. Patentee in laser tech. Trustee Temple Sinai Summit, N.J., 1977-79, N.J. Prison Complex, Trenton, 1975-83; bd. advisors Rahway Lifers Program, 1979-83; mem. deptl. adv. bd. Rensselaer Poly. Inst., 1988-92, mem. exec. bd. Anderson Ctr. for Innovation in Undergrad. Edn., 1992—. Named Key Exec., Rensselaer Poly. Inst., 1986—, chmn. Key Exec. Program, 1994-95; recipient Clarence E. Davies medal for engring. achievement, 1993, Fellow award Rensselaer Poly. Inst. Alumni Assn., 1993. Fellow IEEE, Optical Soc. Am.; mem. AAAS, IEEE Lasers and Electrooptics Soc. (pres. 1989). Home: 188 High Tor Dr Watchung NJ 07060-5412 Office: Bell Labs/Lucent Techs 600 Mountain Ave New Providence NJ 07974-2008

COHEN, MELVIN R., physician, educator; b. Chgo., May 24, 1911; s. Louis M. and Anna S. (Friedman) C.; m. Miriam, May 19, 1946; children: Nancy, Alan. B.S., U. Ill., 1931, M.S. in Pathology, 1933, MD, 1934. Diplomate: Am. Bd. Ob-Gyn. Practice medicine specializing in infertility Chgo.; sr. attending physician Michael Reese Med. Ctr., Chgo., Northwestern Meml. Hosp., Chgo.; founder, dir. Fertility Inst. Ltd., Chgo.; prof. Northwestern U. Med. Sch., Chgo., prof. emeritus; guest vis. prof. first Martin Clyman postgrad. course in infertility Mount Sinai Hosp., N.Y.C., 1982. Author: Laparoscopy, Culdoscopy and Gynecography: Technique and Atlas, 1970; contbr. numerous chpts. in med. books and articles in med. jours. on infertility, endometriosis and Spinnbarkeit. Dir., producer: 8 teaching films on infertility; video films during surgery; ektochrome slides established world-wide technique. Pioneer use of Pergonal for stimulating ovulation. Served with MC, AUS, 1942-45. Co-recipient Gold Medal for Infertility exhibit AMA, 1951; recipient award for film on endometriosis 10th World Congress of Fertility and Sterility, Madrid, Spain, 1980, Lifetime Achievement award for contbns. to gynecologic endoscopy and women's health care Internat. Congress of Gynecologic Endoscopy, 1994; named honoree Internat. Soc. Gynecologic Endoscopy for pioneering work in laparoscopy, 1996. Fellow Chgo. Gynecol. Soc. (life); mem. AMA, Am. Fertility Soc., Am. Coll. Ob-Gyn., Am. Assn. Gynecol. Laparoscopists (Lifetime Achievement award Internat. Congress 1994), Internat. Fertility Assn., Internat. Family Planning Research Assn., Ill. State Med. Soc., Chgo. Gynecol. Soc., Kansas City Gynecol. Soc. (hon.), Los Angeles Gynecol. Soc., Inst. Medicine Chgo., Midwest Bio-Laser Inst., Indian Assn. Gynecol. Endoscopists (hon.), Soc. Reproductive Surgeons, Chgo. Assn. Reproductive Endocrinologists (pres. 1984-85), Sigma Xi, Alpha Omega Alpha. Named Father of Modern Am. Laparoscopy, 1974. Address: 990 N Lake Shore Dr Chicago IL 60611-1366

COHEN, MELVYN DOUGLAS, securities company executive; b. Newtonards, Northern Ireland, Nov. 29, 1943; came to U.S., 1972; s. Arnold Ernest and Clara (Praeger Bethune) C.; m. Rosita Nahum, May 9, 1974; children: Andrew, Suzanne, Cary. AA, Miami Dade Community Coll., 1975; BBA, Fla. Internat. U., 1977, MS in Mgmt., 1981. Cert. fin. planner. With Merrill Lynch, Miami, 1977-91; v.p., mgr. sales Merrill Lynch, N.Y.C., 1986-88; v.p., resident mgr. Merrill Lynch, Coral Springs, Fla., 1988-91; divisional v.p., br. mgr. Paine Webber, Plantation, Fla., 1991-92; divsn. v.p. investments Paine Webber, Boca Raton, Fla., 1992-94; 1st v.p. Prudential Securities, Boca Raton, 1994—; fin. mgr. Donald Regan Sch. Fin. Planning. Pres. City of Parkland Homeowners Assn., 1991—; chmn. charter rev. bd. dirs. Assn. Faternal Order of Police, City of Parkland, 1990; pres. Concerned Citizens of Cypress Head, 1990-91. Mem. Jaycees (pres. Miami chpt. 1982), Parkland Optimist Club (dir. 1990). Jewish. Avocations: music, creative writing, poetry. Office: Prudential Securities 5355 Town Center Rd Ste 600 Boca Raton FL 33486-1097

COHEN, MERRILL, chemist; b. Boston, Feb. 5, 1926; s. Alfred and Goldie (Baitler) C.; m. Eleanor Barbara Goldstein, Sept. 10, 1950; children: Mark Allen, Steven, Linda Lee Cohen Ben-Ezra. BA, Boston U., 1948; MS, U. Chgo., 1949, PhD, 1951. Devel. chemist Gen. Electric, Schenectady, Lynn, N.Y., Mass, 1951-56; mgr. Gen. Electric, Lynn, Mass., 1956-87; owner, mgr. Chemco Consulting, Marblehead, Mass., 1987—. Contbr. articles to profl. jours.; patentee in field. Sgt. U.S. Army, 1944-46, with Res. 1946-49. Mem. Am. Chem. Soc., Geothermal Rsch. Soc., Soc. Plastics Engrs., Soc. for Advancement of Materials and Process Engring. Avocations: gardening, fishing. Office: Chemco Consulting Inc 8 May St Marblehead MA 01945-1708

COHEN, MICHAEL, psychologist; b. Yonkers, N.Y., Mar. 14, 1950; s. Joseph and Mary (Harris) C.; m. Amy Beth Siskind, Nov. 1, 1987; 1 child, Laura Reneé. BA, SUNY, Binghamton, 1972; MA, PhD, CUNY, N.Y.C., 1992. Pvt. practice psychotherapist N.Y.C., 1973-89; rsch. cons. N.Y.C. Bd. Edn., 1986-87; sr. rsch. analyst Kennan Rsch. and Cons., N.Y.C., 1987-90; dir. qualitive rsch. KRC Rsch. and Cons., N.Y.C., 1990-91, pres., 1992-95; prin., founding ptnr. ARC Cons. LLC, N.Y.C., 1995—; mem. adv. bd. Handprints Prodns., N.Y.C., 1990—. Editor: The Einstein Connection, 1979. Avocation; poet. Office: ARC Cons LLC 295 Lafayette St New York NY 10012-2701*

COHEN, MICHAEL I., pediatrician; b. Bklyn., Feb. 9, 1935; s. Nat L. and Fannie (Wechsler) C.; m. Nancy Ann Wood, Oct. 28, 1963; children—Adam Wood, Amy Melissa, Meg Rebecca. B.A., Columbia U., 1956, M.D., 1960. Intern Mary Imogene Bassett Hosp., 1960-61; resident Babies Hosp., N.Y.C., 1961-63; USPHS postdoctoral fellow in gastroenterology Albert Einstein Coll. Medicine, 1965-67, mem. faculty, 1967—, prof. pediatrics, 1976—, chmn. dept., 1980—; pres., chief exec. officer Montefiore Med. Ctr., 1985-86; dir. div. adolescent medicine Montefiore Hosp., N.Y.C., 1967-80. Author numerous papers in field; contbr. chpts. to books. Served with M.C. USAF, 1963-65. Decorated Air Force Commendation medal. Mem. Inst. Medicine of NAS, Am. Acad. Pediatrics (chmn. com. adolescence 1977-80, award sect. adolescence 1980), Soc. Adolescent Medicine, Am. Fedn. Clin. Research, Ambulatory Pediatrics Assn., Soc. Pediatric Research, Am. Psychosomatic Soc., Am. Pediatrics Soc., Am. Gastrointestinal Assn., Alpha Omega Alpha. Office: Montefiore Med Ctr 111 E 210th St Bronx NY 10467-2401

COHEN, MICHAEL WAYNE, physician; b. San Francisco, Nov. 11, 1956. BA, U. Calif., Berkeley, 1978; MPH, U. Tex., 1993; MD, U. Calif., Irvine, 1983. Diplomate Am. Bd. Occupl. Medicine, Am. Bd. Aerospace Medicine, Am. Bd. Preventive Medicine. Intern in surgery U. So. Calif., 1983-84, resident in orthopedic surg., 1984-86; resident in aerospace medicine USAF Sch. Aerospace Medicine, San Antonio, Tex., 1993-94, resident in occupl. medicine, 1994-95; commd. 2d lt. USAF, 1986, flight surgeon, 1986-95, advanced through grades to maj., ret., 1995; med. dir. Sutter Occupl. Health, Roseville, Calif., 1995—; lectr. Sch. Pub. Health, U. Calif., 1996—. Mem. Am. Coll. Preventive Medicine, Am. Coll. Occupl. and Environ. Medicine. Avocations: mountain biking, skiing, scuba diving. Office: Sutter Occupl Health 2 Medical Plz # 105 Roseville CA 95661

COHEN, MILDRED THALER, art gallery director; b. N.Y.C., Oct. 30, 1921; d. William and Dora (Snow) Intner; m. Seymour R. Thaler, June 17, 1945 (dec. 1976); children: Frederic I., Joan Thaler Zimmer; m. Sidney Cohen, Mar. 20, 1982. BA, Hunter Coll., 1942; BLS, Pratt Inst., 1943. Librarian Queens Borough Pub. Libr., N.Y.C., 1943-44, Mus. of French Art, French Inst., N.Y.C., 1944-46; dir. Marbella Gallery, Inc., N.Y.C., 1971—. Author: (catalogues) Women Students of William Merritt Chase, 1973, Robert Hallowell, 1983, Eliot Clark, 1990, Tonalism, America's Gift to Landscape Painting, 1993, (brochures) Ethel Paxson, 1976, Three Generations of Wiggins, 1981, Samuel Rothbart, 1989, Rachel V. Hartley, 1991, Frank Kleinholz, 1992, Anthony Springer, 1996, Joseph Margulies, 1997, Allen Blagden, 1998, Hildegarde Hamilton, 1999. Bd. dirs. Lenox Hill Settlement House, N.Y.C., 1955-77. Mem. Appraisers Assn. Am., Hunter Coll. Alumni (pres. Queens chpt. 1951-54, past bd. dirs., pres. scholarship and welfare fund 1958-60, mem. coll. art adv. com., named to Hall of Fame 1973). Democrat. Jewish. Home and Office: 28 E 72nd St New York NY 10021-4234

COHEN, MORREL HERMAN, physicist, biologist, educator; b. Boston, Sept. 10, 1927; s. David and Rose (Kemler) C.; m. Sylvia Zwein, June 18, 1950; children: Julie, Robert, Daniel, Lisa. BS in Physics, Worcester Poly. Inst., 1947, DSc (hon.), 1973; MA in Physics, Dartmouth Coll., 1948; PhD in Physics, U. Calif., Berkeley, 1952. Faculty U. Chgo., 1952-57, assoc. prof. physics, 1957-60, prof., 1960-72, prof. theoretical biology, 1968-72, Louis Block prof. physics and theoretical biology, 1972-81, com. developmental biology, 1973-74, publs. bd., 1969-70; acting dir. James Franck Inst., 1965-66, dir., 1968-71; dir. materials rsch. lab. NSF, 1977-81; sr. sci. advisor Corp. Rsch. Lab. Exxon Rsch. and Engring. Co., 1981-96; cons. govt. and industry, 1953-81, 96—; vis. scientist NRC, Can., 1960, Xerox Corp., 1975, 78; dist. vis. scientist Rutgers U., 1998—; vis. fellow Clare Hall U., Cambridge, 1972-73; Shrum lectr. Simon Fraser U., 1973; assoc. Clare Hall U. Cambridge, Eng., 1973-85; vis. prof. U. Va., 1976, Kyoto U., 1979; mem. adv. panel electrophysics NASA, 1962-66; mem. adv. com. Nat. Magnet Lab., 1963-66; mem. rev. com. solid state sci. and metallurgy div. Argonne Nat. Lab., 1964-67, chmn., 1966, bd. govs., 1982-89, sci. & tech. adv. com., 1983-91; chmn. Gordon Conf., 1968, 4th Internat. Conf. Armorphous and Liquid Semicondrs., 1971; mem. adv. com. Inst. Amorphous Studies, 1982—; mem. Army Basic Research Com., 1979-85, mem. steering com., 1980-85; adv. com. dept. physics U. Tex., Austin, 1982-91; chmn. vis. com. dept. Physics Colo. Sch. of Mines, 1987-94; vice chmn. IUPAP commn. on stats. mechanics, 1987-93; van der Waals prof. U. Amsterdam, 1991-92. Contbr. articles on physics of solids, liquids, gases, theoretical and developmental biology, geophysics, materials sci., chem. physics, and chem. engring.; assoc. editor Jour. Chem. Physics, 1960-63; mem. editorial bd. advanced physics monograph series McGraw-Hill Co., 1963-70; mem. editorial bd. The Physics of Condensed Matter, 1962-74, Advances in Chem. Physics, 1960-93; mem. publs. bd. U. Chgo., 1969-70; bd. editors Jour. Statis. Physics, 1970-75. AEC fellow, 1951-52, Guggenheim fellow, 1957-58, NSF sr. postdoctoral fellow Rome, 1964-65, Spl. fellow NIH, 1972-73. Fellow AAAS, Am. Phys. Soc. (divsn. coun. 1978-82, exec. com. solid state physics divsn. 1968-71, chmn. 1970); mem. AAUP, Am. Inst. Physics, Nat. Acad. Scis., N.Y. Acad. Scis., Sigma Xi (nat. lectr. 1966). Home: 1100 Crim Rd Bridgewater NJ 08807-1872 Office: Exxon Rsch & Engring Co Corp Rsch Sci Labs Rt 22 E Clinton Township Annandale NJ 08801

COHEN, MORRIS LEO, retired law librarian and educator; b. N.Y.C., Nov. 2, 1927; s. Emanuel and Anna (Frank) C.; m. Gloria Weitzner, Feb. 1, 1953; children—Havi, Daniel Asher. BA, U. Chgo., 1947; LLB, Columbia U., 1951; MLS, Pratt Inst., 1959. Bar: N.Y. bar 1951. Pvt. practice N.Y.C., 1951-58; asst. law librarian Rutgers U. Law Sch., 1958-59, Columbia Law Sch., 1959-61; law librarian, assoc. prof. law State U. N.Y. at, Buffalo, 1961-63; Biddle law librarian, prof. law U. Pa. Law Sch., Phila., 1963-71; law librarian, prof. law Harvard U. Law Sch., 1971-81, Yale U. Law Sch., New Haven, 1981-91; prof. emeritus, 1991—; lectr. Drexel Inst. Sch. Libr. Sci., 1964-70, Columbia Sch. Libr. Svc., 1965-70; vis. prof. Simmons Coll. Libr. Sch., 1977-80; mem. exec. bd. Phila. chpt. ACLU; bd. visitors Columbia U. Law Sch., 1977-95. Author: Legal Research in a Nutshell, 1968, 6th edit., 1996, How to Find the Law, 9th edit., 1989, Law and Science: A Selected Bibliography, 1980, Finding the Law, 2d edit., 1989, Law: The Art of Justice, 1992, A Guide to the Early Reports of the Supreme Court of the United States, 1995, The Bench and Bar: Great Legal Caricatures from Vanity Fair, 1997, Bibliography of Early American Law, 1998. NEH grantee. Mem. ABA, ALA (chmn. law and polit. sci. sect. 1967-69), AAUP (pres. U. Pa. chpt. 1966-67), Am. Assn. Law Librs. (pres. 1970-71), Jewish Publs. Soc. (v.p. 1975-80), Bibliog. Soc. Am., Internat. Assn. Law Librs., Grolier Club, Yale Club of N.Y.C. Jewish. Office: Yale U Sch Law PO Box 208215 New Haven CT 06520-8215

COHEN, MORTON NORTON, English educator, writer; b. Calgary, Alberta, Can., Feb. 27, 1921; came to U.S., 1934; s. Samuel Cohen and Zelda Jenny Miller. AB, Tufts U., 1949; MA, Columbia U., 1950, PhD, 1958. Instr. English W.Va. U., 1950-51; lectr. English Rutgers U., N.J., 1952-53; vis. prof. Syracuse U., N.Y., 1965-66, 67-68; prof. CUNY, prof. emeritus, 1982—; mem. faculty advisory coun. CUNY Rsch. Found., 1976-80; lectr. in field. Author: Lewis Carroll, Photographer of Children: Four Nude Studies, 1979, Lewis Carroll's Photographs of Nude Children, 1978, Lewis Carroll and Alice 1832-1982, 1982, 2d edit., 1990, 3rd edit., 1996, Lewis Carroll: A Biography, 1995, 2d edit., 1996, Reflections in a Looking Glass, 1998; co-author: A Brief Guide to Better Writing, 1960, Rider Haggard: His Life and Works, 1960, 61, 2d rev. edit., 1968, An Exhibition from the Jon A. Lindseth Collection of C. L. Dodgson and Lewis Carroll, 1998, The World of Interiors, 1998, numerous others; editor: Rudyard Kipling to Rider Haggard: The Record of a Friendship, 1965, 68, The Russian Jour.-II, 1979, Lewis Carroll and the Kitchins, 1980, The Selected Letters of Lewis Carroll, 1982, 2d edit., 1990, 3rd edit., 1996, Lewis Carroll: Interviews and Recollections, 1989; co-editor: The Letters of Lewis Carroll, 1979, Lewis Carroll and the House of Macmillan, 1987; contbr. articles to profl. jours.; book reviewer; appeared in TV and radio programs, U.K., U.S.A.; guest curator Pierpont Morgan Libr., N.Y.C., 1982; reader, cons. maj. univ. and comml. presses; contbr. Cambridge Bibliography of English Literature, 3rd edit.; author children's books under pseudonym. Sgt. U.S. Army, 1943-45. Faculty fellow Ford Found., 1951-52; Fulbright fellow at U. Leeds, 1954-55; grantee Am. Philos. Soc., summers 1962, 64; grant-in-aid Am. Coun. Learned Socs., summer 1963; Guggenheim fellow, 1966-67; Sr. fellow NEH, 1970-71, 78-79; Fulbright Sr. Rsch. fellow at Christ Church, Oxford, Eng., 1974-75; Rsch. grantee NEH, 1974-75; Guggenheim Found. Publ. grantee, 1979. Fellow Royal Soc. Lit.; mem. Lewis Carroll Soc. N.Am., Lewis Carroll Soc. Japan, Lewis Carroll Soc., Am. Trust Brit. Libr. (mem. adv. coun. 1980), Century Assn. Democrat. Jewish. Avocations: travel, theater, antiques, watercolors. Home: 55 East 9th St Apt 10-D New York NY 10003 also: Condo Miramar Plz Apt 21-E 954 Ponce de Léon Ave San Juan PR 00907 also: 28 Pembridge Villas, London W11 3EL, England

COHEN, MYRON, lawyer, educator; b. Paterson, N.J., Feb. 4, 1927; s. Jacob B. and Rose (Stone) C.; m. Nancy Kamin, Nov. 4, 1951 (div. 1960); m. Barbara Levitov, May 12, 1963; children: Peter Fredric, Lee Susan. BEE, Cornell U., 1948; LLB, Columbia U., 1951. Bar: N.Y. 1951, U.S. Dist. Ct. (so., ea. dists.) N.Y. 1955, U.S. Ct. Appeals (2nd cir.) 1960, U.S. Ct. Appeals (Fed. cir.) 1984, U.S. Supreme Ct. 1974. Staff atty. Union Switch and Signal, Swissvale, Pa., 1952-54; assoc. Levisohn, Niner & Cohen, N.Y.C., 1954-56; sr. ptnr. Hubbell, Cohen, Stiefel & Gross, N.Y.C., 1956-85, Cohen, Pontani, Lieberman & Pavane, N.Y.C., 1985—; adj. prof. N.Y. Law Sch., 1970—; bd. dirs. Tri Magna Corp.; sec. Medallion Funding Corp., N.Y.C., 1979-86, 86-96. Author: U.S. Patent Law and Practice, 1976, Recent Developments in U.S. Law of Intellectual Property, 1985. Chmn. Mayor's Subway Watchdog Commn., N.Y.C., 1974-76. Lt. j.g. USNR, 1944-57. Mem. ABA, N.Y. State Bar Assn., Assn. Bar City N.Y., N.Y. Intellectual Property Law Assn., Internat. Trademark Assn. Democrat. Jewish. Avocation: skiing. Home: Two Fifth Ave New York NY 10011 Office: Cohen Pontani Lieberman & Pavane 551 5th Ave New York NY 10176

COHEN, MYRON LESLIE, business executive; mechanical engineer; b. N.Y.C., Mar. 7, 1934; s. Henry and Minnie (Pechenik) C.; B.S.M.E., Purdue U., 1955; M.S.E., U. Ala., 1958; Ph.D., Poly. Inst. Bklyn., 1966; m. Sally Claire Gilman, June 19, 1955; children—Amy Beth, David Lawrence, Hilary Ann. Research engr. Allegany Ballistics Lab., Hercules, Inc., Cumberland, Md., 1955-56; sr. thermodynamics engr. Republic Aviation Corp., Farmingdale, N.Y., 1958-60; instr. mech. engring. Poly. Inst. Bklyn., 1960-66; asst. prof. mech. engring. Stevens Inst. Tech., 1966-69, assoc. prof., 1969-77, prof., 1977-78, dir. Med. Engring. Lab., 1975-78; prof. Institut fur Biokybernetik und Biomedizinische Technik, Universitat Karlsruhe (W.Ger.), 1974-75; dir. research and devel. hosp. products, Chesebrough-Ponds's Inc., Trumbull, Conn., 1978-83; pres. CAS Med. Systems, Inc., Branford, Conn., 1983-91, chmn. bd., exec. v.p., 1991—; v.p. Freshet Press, Rockville Centre, N.Y., 1970-78; pres. C.A.S., Inc., Upper Montclair, N.J., 1975-78; adj. assoc. prof. surgery Coll. Medicine and Dentistry N.J., Newark, 1978-92. V.p. Temple Beth Tikvah, Madison, Conn., 1980-82. Lt. U.S. Army, 1956-58. Recipient Humboldt prize, Sr. U.S. Scientist award Govt. W.Ger., 1974, old master Purdue U., 1996; Outstanding Mech. Eng., Purdue U., 1998; registered profl. engr., N.J. Fellow N.Y. Acad. Medicine; mem. ASME (chmn. standards com. on med. devices 1982), Assn. Advancement Med. Instrumentation, AAUP, Soc. Biomaterials, Cardiovascular System Dynamics Soc., AIAA (chmn. N.Y. sect. 1971-72), N.Y. Acad. Sci. Sigma Xi, Pi Tau Sigma. Club: Theodore Gordon Flyfishers, Conn. River Salmon Assn. (bd. dirs. 1987—). Contbr. articles on heat transfer, thermodynamics, tech. applied to medicine, phys. properties human skin, biomed. engring. to profl. jours.; research in rocket propulsion, biomed. engring. Home: 401 Three Corners Rd Guilford CT 06437-2523 Office: 21 Business Park Dr Branford CT 06405-2935

COHEN, N. JEROLD, lawyer; b. Pine Bluff, Ark., June 13, 1935; s. Maurice and Gertrude L. Cohen; children: Pamela, Lindsey L., Giles T. BBA, Tulane U., 1957; LLB magna cum laude, Harvard U., 1961. Bar: N.Y. 1962, Ga. 1966, D.C. 1966. Assoc. Cleary, Gottlieb, Steen and Hamilton, N.Y.C., 1961-65; assoc. Sutherland, Asbill, and Brennan, Atlanta, Washington, 1965, ptnr., 1968-79, 81—; chiefe counsel IRS, 1979-81, adv. coun., 1999—. Former pres., former mem. nat. bd. dirs. ACLU Ga.; chmn. Atlanta Cmty. Rels. Commn., 1976-79. 1st lt. U.S. Army, 1958. Recipient Gen. Counsel's award U.S. Dept. Treasury, Commrs. award IRS. Fellow Am. Bar Found.; mem. ABA (past chair tax sect.), FBA, Am. Law Inst., Am. Coll. Tax Counsel (regent, vice chair). Office: Sutherland Asbill & Brennan 999 Peachtree St NE Ste 2300 Atlanta GA 30309-3996

COHEN, NANCY L., high school teacher; b. Rhinelander, Wis., Apr. 13, 1950; d. Luke Louis and Rose Margaret (Schroeder) Kuczmarski; m. Leonard M. Cohen, June 4, 1976; children: Leonard, Nicholas, Julia, Andrew. BA in English, Purdue U., 1972; MS in Edn. Adminstrn., Northern Ill. U., 1975. Cert. in Secondary English Edn. Team tchr. Woodstock (Ill.) School, 1972-75; h.s. English tchr. La Crosse (Wis.) Sch. Dist., 1975-80, Rhinelander (Wis.) Sch. Dist., 1984—; advisor La Crosse (Wis.) Ctrl. H.S. yearbook, 1975-80, Rhinelander (Wis.) H.S., 1984-92; head debate coach Rhinelander H.S., 1992-97. Mem. Historical Preservation Commn., Rhinelander, Wis., 1996—. Recipient numerous yearbook awards Columbia Press Assn., N.Y.C., 1978, 79, 84-92, Wis. Yearbook Assn., 1978-79; coach of first place debate team in Intervarsity Tournament of Champions, Sheboygan, Wis., 1996. Mem. AAUW, Purdue Alumni Assn., Northern Arts Council, Rhinelander Sch. Booster Club, Cmty. Concert Assn. Avocations: historical preservation, natural resource conservation, travel. Home: 105 E Frederick St Rhinelander WI 54501-3147 Office: Rhinelander Sch Dist 665 Coolidge Ave Rhinelander WI 54501-2814

COHEN, NELSON CRAIG, lawyer; b. Harrisburg, Pa., Nov. 8, 1947; s. Raymond and Rhea (Jaschik) C. BS in Acctg., Pa. State U., 1969; JD, George Washington U., 1973. Bar: Md. 1973, D.C. 1974. Assoc., ptnr. Levitan Ezrin West & Kerxton, Bethesda, Md., 1973-84; ptnr. Kerxton & Cohen Chartered, Bethesda, 1984-87, Zuckerman, Spaeder, Goldstein, Taylor & Kolker, Washington, 1987—; speaker on bankruptcy matters. Mem. ABA (bus. banking sec.), Bankruptcy Bar Assn. Md., Montgomery County Bar Assn., Md. State Bar Assn. Republican. Jewish. Avocation: golf. Office: Zuckerman Spaeder et al 1201 Connecticut Ave NW Washington DC 20036-2605

COHEN, NICHOLAS, immunologist, educator; b. N.Y.C., Nov. 20, 1938; s. Saris and Frances (Pakett) C.; m. Jayne Sevin Rogal, July 1, 1962 (div. 1972); children: Jaime Anne, Jessica Sevin; m. Catharina Johanna van der Harst, Oct. 23, 1974; children: Misha Thomas, Mark Sebastian. AB, Princeton U., 1959; PhD, U. Rochester, 1965. Asst. prof. microbiology and immunology Sch. Medicine and Dentistry U. Rochester, N.Y., 1967-73, assoc. prof., 1973-80, prof. microbiology, immunology and psychiatry, 1980—, prof. oncology, 1997—, dir. divsn. immunology, 1980—; assoc. dir. Ctr. for Psychoneuroimmunology Rsch., Rochester; vis. prof. Agrl. U., Wageningen, The Netherlands, 1982-83; mem. Basel Inst. for Immunology, Switzerland, 1975-76; mem. peer rev. bds. NIH, 1976-80; cons. NIH study sects., NIMH study sects., NSF. Co-author: Monograph; assoc. editor Brain, Behavior and Immunity Jour., Devel. Comparative Immunology; editor 4 books; contbr. articles to profl. jours. Postdoctoral scholar in immunology UCLA, 1965-67, Fulbright scholar, 1982-83; grantee NIH, NIMH, NSF, 1967—; recipient Rsch. Career Devel. award NIH, 1974-78, NIH Merit award, 1987-97. Mem. Am. Soc. Zoologists (chmn. divsn. comparative immunology 1977-79), Transplantation Soc., Am. Soc. Immunologists, Brit. Soc. Immunology, Internat. Soc. Devel. and Comparative Immunology (v.p. the Americas 1994—), Psychoneuroimmunology Rsch. Soc. (councilor 1993-97). Democrat. Avocations: music, travel. Home: 211 Highland Pkwy Rochester NY 14620-2544

COHEN, NICKI SANDRA, music educator, music therapist; b. Easton, Pa., Mar. 16, 1955; d. Merton Emil and Claire Sybil (Reichlin) C.; m. Bruce Cline Bond, June 16, 1984. BS in Mus. Edn., Duquesne U., 1977; MA in Voice, U. Denver, 1983; PhD in Music Edn., U. Kans., 1991. Bd. cert. music therapist. Clin. music therapist Colo. State Home, Wheat Ridge, 1980-81; pvt. practice Roundup, Bethpage, Ctr. Pines, Susqueview, Denver and Lock Haven, Pa., 1981-91, Cmty. MT Svcs., Waterloo, Ont., Can., 1991-92; instr. Lock Haven U., 1991; asst. prof. Wilfrid Laurier U., Waterloo, 1991-92; pvt. practice in guided imagry and music therapy Denton, Tex., 1992—; from asst. to assoc. prof. Tex. Woman's U., Denton, 1992—; music therapy cons., Denton, 1992—. Author: (book chpt.) Case Studies in Music Therapy, 1991; contbr. rsch. and clin. articles to profl. jours. Mus. dir. Denton Cmty. Chorus, 1994-98; vol. AIDS Denton, 1996-97, Ann's Haven Hospice, Denton, 1998—. Rsch. grantee Tex. Woman's U., 1992, 93, 95, 97, 99, Wilfried Laurier U., 1991; student fellow/assistantships U. Denver and U. Kans., 1981-83, 87-90. Fellow Pi Kappa Lambda; mem. Am. Music Therapy Assn., Nat. Assn. Tchrs. Singing, Assn. for Music and Imagery, Phi Delta Kappa, Sigma Alpha Iota (patroness). Democrat. Jewish. Avocations: hiking, gardening, reading, book groups. E-mail: ncohen@twu.edu. Office: Tex Woman's U PO Box 425768 Denton TX 76204

COHEN, NOEL LEE, otolaryngologist, educator; b. N.Y.C., Sept. 20, 1930; s. Victor Max and Esther Lily (Schonfeld) C.; m. Baukje Philippina Boersma, June 1, 1957; 1 child, Mark Bennett. AB, NYU, 1951; MD, U. Utrecht, The Netherlands, 1957. Intern Stads-en Aacademish Ziekenhuis, Utrecht, 1955-57; resident in otolargyngology Bellevue Med. Ctr. NYU, N.Y.C., 1959-62, instr. Sch. Medicine, 1962-64, asst. prof., 1964-69, assoc. prof., 1969-73, clin. prof., 1973-80, prof. otolaryngology, 1980—, chmn. dept. otolaryngology, 1981—, interim dean, provost Sch. Medicine, 1997-98, vice dean for clin. affairs, 1998—; bd. dirs. League for Hard of Hearing, Am. Auditory Soc.; mem. rsch. adv. bd. EAR Found., Nashville, 1987—; mem. adv. bd. Self Help for Hard of Hearing People, 1995. Mem. editl. bd. Am. Jour. Otology, 1986—, Otolaryngology-Head and Neck Surgery; reviewer articles and books for profl. jours.; contbr. numerous articles to profl. jours.; author chpts. in books. Lt. USNR, 1957-59. Fellow ACS; mem. Am. Acad. Otolaryngology-Head-Neck Surgery (Honor award 1985), Am. Laryngol., Rhinol. and Otol. Soc., Am. Soc. Head and Neck Surgery, Am. Bronchoesophagol. Assn., Am. Otol. Soc., N.Y. Acad. Medicine, N.Y. State Soc. Otolaryngology-Head and Neck Surgery (pres. 1988-89), N.Y. Head and Neck Soc. (charter mem., pres. 1984), N.Am. Skull Base Soc., Am. Neuro-Otol. Soc., Soc. Univ. Otolaryngologists, Soc. Acad. Depts. Otolaryngology, N.Y. Otol. Soc. (pres. 1998—), N.Y. Acad. Scis., Acoustic Neuroma Soc., Alexander Graham Bell Assn. (med. adv. bd.). Democrat. Jewish. Avocations: tennis, skiing, gardening, carpentry. Office: NYU Med Ctr 530 1st Ave New York NY 10016-6481

COHEN, NORM, chemist; b. N.Y.C., Dec. 13, 1936; s. Moshe and Yetta (Pickman) C.; m. Anne Elizabeth Billings, July 11, 1959 (div. 1987); children: Alexandra Elizabeth Rachel, Carson Benjamin; m. Verni Greenfield, Feb. 6, 1987; 1 child, Matthew Jonathan Greenfield. BA in Chemistry, Reed Coll., 1958; MA in Math., U. Calif., Berkeley, 1960, PhD in Chemistry, 1963. Mem. tech. staff Aerospace Corp., El Segundo, Calif., 1963-72, head dept. chem. kinetics, 1972-84, sr. scientist, 1984-94; adj. asst. prof. chemistry U. Portland, 1995—, Portland C.C., 1995—; exec. sec. John Edwards Mem. Forum, L.A., 1969-94. Author: Long Steel Rail, 1981 (Chgo. Folklore prize 1982, Deems Taylor award ASCAP 1982, Botkin prize Am. Folklore Soc. 1983), Traditional Anglo-American Folk Music: An Annotated Disography of Published Recordings, 1994; editor: Ozark Folk Songs, 1982, John Edwards Meml. Forum Quar., 1966-83, 85-86; asst. editor Internat. Jour. Chem. Kinetics, 1977-83, editor, prodr. album Minstrels and Tunesmiths, 1982 (Grammy nomination 1982); contbr. articles and revs. to chemistry and folk, music jours. Grantee NEA, NEH, DOE, EPA, NIST. Mem. Am. Chem. Soc., Am. Folklore Soc., Sigma Xi. Democrat. Jewish. Achievements include research and publications in combustion chemistry, atmospheric chemistry, thermochemistry, chemistry of high energy chemical lasers. Home: 6507 SE 31st Ave Portland OR 97202-8627

COHEN, PERRY D., management consultant; b. Atlanta, May 27, 1946; s. Bernard W. and Rae Alice Cohen; m. Rosalie Mandelbaum, Aug. 16, 1975; children: Shayna K., Jonah B. BS, Carnegie-Mellon U., 1968; MS, MIT, 1971, PhD, 1979. Assoc. engr. Lockheed Ga. Co., Marietta, 1968-69; rsch. analyst Blue Cross-Blue Shield of Mass., Boston, 1971-72; instr. bus. MIT, Cambridge, 1972-75; rsch. assoc. Assn. Am. Med. Colls., Washington, 1975-77; sr. assoc. Urban Systems Rsch., Washington, 1977-79; pres. Perry Cohen Assocs., Washington, 1979—, Unison Corp., Bethesda, 1987-89; adj. assoc. prof. U. Md., 1991—; dir. health svcs. rsch. Parkinsons Disease Found., 1998—. Contbr. articles to profl. jours. Trustee Group Health Assn., Washington, 1986-92, Consumer Health Found., 1995-96, Medlantic Rsch. Inst., 1998—; trustee Nat. Capital chpt., Am. Parkinson's Disease Assn., 1996-98, v.p., 1997-98. MIT Spl. Rsch. fellow, 1972-75; grantee NIH, 1986-87, Nat. Cancer Inst., 1985-86. Mem. Am. Pub. Health Assn., Manpower Analysis and Planning Soc. (from v.p. to prs. 1981-83), Assn. Health Svcs. Rsch., Acad. Mgmt., Soc. for Health Care Planning and Mktg. Home: 3914 Harrison St NW Washington DC 20015-1938

COHEN, PHILIP, retired hydrogeologist; b. N.Y.C., Dec. 13, 1931; s. Isadore and Anna (Katz) C.; m. Barbara Sandler, Dec. 26, 1954; 1 son, Jeffery. B.S. cum laude, CCNY, 1954; M.S., U. Rochester, 1956. Cert. profl. geologist, Va. With U.S. Geol. Survey, 1956-94, chief Long Island program, 1968-72; assoc. chief land info. and analysis office U.S. Geol. Survey, Reston, Va., 1975-78, asst. chief hydrologist water resources div., 1978-79, chief hydrologist water resources div., 1979-94; ret., 1994. Contbr. numerous articles on geology and hydrology to profl. jours. Recipient Ward medal Coll. City, N.Y., 1954; Meritorious Ser. award Dept. Interior, 1975, Disting. Ser. award, 1979, Presdl. Meritorious Exec. Rank award, 1986, Presdl. Disting. Exec. Rank award, 1988. Fellow Geol. Soc. Am.; mem. Am. Water Resources Assn., Am. Inst. Hydrology (C.V. Theis award 1993), Sigma Xi.

COHEN, PHILIP D., book publishing executive. Pres. Chelsea Pub., Broomall, Pa. Office: Chelsea House Pubs 1974 Sproul Rd Ste 400 Broomall PA 19008-3402*

COHEN, PHILIP HERMAN, accountant; b. Bklyn., Dec. 4, 1936; s. David J. and Toby (Jaeger) C.; m. Susan Rudd; children: Davina Ellen, Tobias Samuel Dory. BS, NYU, 1957. From acct. to ptnr. Touche Ross & Co., N.Y.C., 1957-81; exec. v.p. fin., CFO Integrated Resources, Inc., N.Y.C., 1981-86, sr. exec. v.p. fin., CFO, 1986-90; fin. and real estate cons. Philip H. Cohen & Co., Cedarhurst, N.Y., 1990—; chmn. bd. dirs., pres., CEO FRMT Ltd. (A Bermuda Mut. Ins. Co.), 1996—; bd. dirs. Diwal Corp., Mitcor Corp., Odin Mgmt. Corp., Sy Sims Sch. Bus. Yeshiva U.; chmn. bd. dirs. Fraternity Risk Mgmt. Trust, 1994—; lectr. in field. Bd. dirs. Alpha Epsilon Pi Found., Inc., 1976—, Nat. Interfrat. Conf., 1975-86, Nat. Interfrat. Found., 1996—, State of Israel Bonds, N.Y.; bd. dirs. Sutton Pl. Synagogue, 1984—, v.p., 1993—; bd. dirs. joint purchasing com. Fedn. Jewish Philanthropies, 1977-78; mem. Cmty. Bd. Manhattan, N.Y., 1992—. Recipient State of Israel Bond Peace award 1983, Accts. Bankers and Fin. award Am. Jewish Congress, Gold medal Nat. Interfraternity Conf., 1994. Mem. Found. Acctg. Edn., Am. Inst. CPA's (real estate com. 1987-90), N.Y. State Soc. CPA's (admissions com. 1968-69, chmn. fin. and leasing com. 1972-74, com. on rels. with the bar 1974-76, com. on real estate acctg. 1976-79, com. ins. 1980-81, fin. acctg. standards com. 1983-86, chmn. mem.-in-industry com. 1981-83, chief fin. officers com. 1984-86, furtherance com. 1986, annual conf. com. 1985-87, com. on ops. 1987-88, bd. dirs. 1983-86, v.p. 1985-86, Outstanding CPA in Industry award 1986), Fin. Execs. Inst., Am. Acctg. Assn., Nat. Assn. Accts., Soc. Ins. Accts., Alpha Epsilon Pi (supreme gov. 1966-73, nat. pres. 1974-76, mem. fiscal control bd. 1977-81, vice chmn. 1981-92, chmn. 1992—), Beta Alpha Psi, Areopagus. Jewish. Club: N.Y. Alumni of Alpha Epsilon Pi. Lodge: Masons. Home: 30 Beekman Pl New York NY 10022-8060 Office: 123 Grove Ave Cedarhurst NY 11516-2302

COHEN, PHYLLIS JOANNE, nurse; b. Freeport, Ill., May 18, 1935; d. Leonard Lawrence and Elsie Hedwig (Schmoldt) Dickman; m. Ralph Cohen, May 17, 1953 (div. 1967); children: Jeffry Alan, Douglas Neil. AS with honors, Highland Community Coll., Freeport, Ill., 1980. LPN, Ill.; RN, Ill., Fla., Ga. Nurse Freeport Meml., Ill., 1977-81; traveling nurse Holy Cross Hosp., Ft. Lauderdale, Fla., 1981-82, Palms of Pasadena, St. Petersberg, Fla., 1982-83, West Paces Ferry, Atlanta, 1983-86, Md. Gen. Hosp., Balt., 1986-87, Chandler Gen. Hosp., Atlanta, 1987—; nurse Eggleston Hosp., Atlanta, 1987, St. Francis Med. Ctr., Honolulu, 1990-91; staff nurse Swedish Am. Hosp., Rockford, Ill., 1988-90; staff nurse Rockford Meml. Hosp., 1992-94, nurse psychiat. unit, 1994—; bd. dirs. Freeport Meml. Hosp., Ill. Artist: Oil Painting Empty Rooms (Blue Ribbon award 1968); Poet: Poetry, Contemplation (Golden Poets award 1986, 88); Before It's Gone (Golden Poets award 1987), Change of Seasons (Golden Poets award 1988), A Letter From Dad (Golden Poets award) 1989. Vol. St. Anthony Aux., Rockford, 1960-61, Contact, 1974-75; mem. YWCA. Mem. Nat. Assoc. Smithsonian Inst., Alumni Assn. of Nurses, Phi Theta Kappa. Republican. Home: 1393 Us Highway 20 E Freeport IL 61032-9699 Office: Rockford Meml Hosp 2400 N Rockton Ave Rockford IL 61103-3681

COHEN, RACHELLE SHARON, journalist; b. Phila., Oct. 21, 1946; d. Hyman and Diane Doris (Schultz) Goldberg; m. Stanley Martin Cohen, June 22, 1968; 1 dau., Avril Heather. BS, Temple U., 1968. Editor, Somerville Jour. (Mass.), 1968-70; reporter Lowell Sun (Mass.), 1970-72, AP, Boston, 1972-79; state house bur. chief Boston Herald Am., 1979-80, editorial page editor, 1980-82; editorial page editor, columnist Boston Herald, 1982—. Mem. Mass. Bar Assn. (bench, bar, press com.), Mass. Assn. Mental Health (bd. dirs. 1993—). Office: Boston Herald 1 Herald St Boston MA 02118-2200

COHEN, RAYMOND, mechanical engineer, educator; b. St. Louis, Nov. 30, 1923; s. Benjamin and Leah (Lewis) C.; m. Katherine Elise Silverman, Feb. 1, 1948 (dec. May 1985); children—Richard Samuel, Deborah, Barbara Beth; m. Lila Lakin Cagen, Nov. 30, 1986. B.S., Purdue U., 1947, M.S., 1950, Ph.D., 1955. Instr. mech. engring. Purdue U., 1948-55, asst. prof., 1955-58, assoc. prof., 1958-60, prof., 1960—, asst. dir. Ray W. Herrick Labs., 1970-71, dir., 1971-93, acting head Sch. Mech. Engring., 1988-89, Herrick prof. engring., 1994—; cons. to industry. Departmental editor: Ency. Brit., 1957-62; editorial bd. Jour. Sound and Vibration, 1971-87; editor Internat. Jour. of Heating, Ventilating, Air Conditioning and Refrigerating Rsch., 1994-98. Served as sgt. inf. AUS, 1943-46. Recipient Kamerlingh Onnes gold medal, 1995; NATO sr. fellow in sci., 1971. Fellow ASME, ASHRAE; mem. NSPE, Am. Soc. Engring. Edn., Soc. Exptl. Mechanics, Internat. Inst. Refrigeration (chmn. U.S. nat. com. 1992-95, U.S. del. 1992-98), Acoustical Soc. Am., Inst. Noise Control Engring. (pres. 1990), Sigma Xi, Pi Tau Sigma, Tau Beta Pi. Home: 316 Leslie Ave West Lafayette IN 47906-2412 Office: Purdue U Ray W Herrick Labs Sch Mechanical Engring West Lafayette IN 47907-1077

COHEN, RICHARD B., grocery company executive; b. Worcester, Mass., July 25, 1952; s. Lester and Norma (Russem) C.; m. Janet Lee, May 26, 1974; children: Perry, Jill, Rachel. BA in Econs., U. Pa., 1974. V.p. fin. C&S Wholesale, Worcester, Mass., 1977-81; gen. mgr. C&S Wholesale, Brattleboro, Vt., 1981-83, pres., chief exec. officer, 1983—, chmn. bd., dir. Jewish. Avocations: fishing, tennis, travel. Office: C & S Wholesale Grocers Inc Old Ferry Rd PO Box 821 Brattleboro VT 05302-0821*

COHEN, RICHARD EDWARD, journalist; b. Northampton, Mass., 1948. AB, Brown U., 1969; JD, Georgetown U., 1972. Corr. Nat. Jour., Washington, 1973—. Author: Washington at Work: Back Rooms and Clean Air, 1992. Office: Nat Jour 1501 M St NW Ste 300 Washington DC 20005-1700*

COHEN, RICHARD GERARD, lawyer; b. N.Y.C., June 11, 1931; m. Evelyn Streit, June 22, 1952; Children: Frances, Andrew Steven, Emilie, Sarah Jane Grossbard. B.S. in Econs, U. Pa., 1952; LL.B., Columbia U., 1955. Bar: N.Y. 1956. With Office Chief Counsel, IRS, Treasury Dept., 1957-64, tech. asst. to chief counsel, 1961-64; with Lord, Day & Lord, N.Y.C., 1964-86, ptnr., 1966-86; ptnr. Winthrop Stimson Putnam & Roberts, N.Y.C., 1986—; chmn. adv. bd. NYU Inst. Fed. Taxation, 1991; lectr. in field. Contbr. articles to profl. jours. Served with Audit Agy. U.S. Army, 1955-57. Mem. ABA, N.Y. State Bar Assn. (chmn. tax sect. 1986-87), Assn. Bar City N.Y. (chmn. coun. on taxation 1989-93), Am. Law Inst. (cons. fed. income tax project 1974—, reporter ptnrship tax issues 1976-84). Jewish. Office: Winthrop Stimson Putnam & Roberts One Battery Park Plaza New York NY 10004

COHEN, RICHARD MARTIN, journalist; b. N.Y.C., Feb. 6, 1941; s. Harry Louis and Pearl (Rosenberg) C.; m. Barbara Stubbs, May 3, 1969 (div.); m. Leslie Feely, July 17, 1992; 1 son, Alexander Prescott. B.S., N.Y. U., 1967; M.S. in Journalism, Columbia U., 1968. With UPI, 1967-68; gen. assignment reporter Washington Post, 1968-76, syndicated columnist, 1976—. Author: A Heartbeat Away, 1973. Office: Washington Post Co 251 W 57th St New York NY 10019-1802

COHEN, RICHARD NORMAN, insurance executive; b. N.Y.C., Oct. 28, 1923; s. Norman M. and Janet (Goldsmith) C.; m. Ann Robertson, Oct. 25, 1975; children: Daniel Hays, James Matthew; 1 stepchild, Mark Thompson. Grad., Phillips Exeter Acad., 1941; BA, Yale U., 1945. CLU. Salesman Cohen, Goldman & Co., N.Y.C., 1947-50; mens fashion editor Fawcett Publs., N.Y.C., 1951-52; life ins. broker Mass. Mut. Life Ins. Co., N.Y.C., 1954—; account exec. John M. Riehle, Inc., N.Y.C., 1961-63, v.p., 1963-83; v.p. Leonard Newman Agy. Inc., White Plains, N.Y., 1984-94, Artur Gallagher & Co., White Plains, 1994—. Dir. Silver Hill Hosp., New Canaan, Conn. Served to 2d lt. USAAF, 1943-45. Mem. Am. Coll. Life Underwriters, Million Dollar Round Table, Country Club of New Canaan, Beta Theta Pi. Republican. Jewish. Clubs: Yale (N.Y.C.); Century Country (White Plains, N.Y.). Home: 1062 Ponus Rdg New Canaan CT 06840-3420

COHEN, ROBERT, medical device manufacturing-marketing executive; b. Glen Cove, N.Y., Sept. 23, 1957; s. Alan and Selma (Grossman) C.; m. Nancy A. Arey, Jan. 17, 1981. BA, Bates Coll., 1979; JD, U. Maine, 1982. Bar: N.Y. 1983, U.S. Dist. Ct. (so. and ea.) N.Y. 1983. Atty. Pfizer Inc., N.Y.C., 1982-86; asst. corp. counsel, asst. sec. Pfizer Hosp. Products Group, Inc., N.Y.C., 1986-88; v.p. bus. devel., dir. for med. device mfr. and marketer Deknatel Inc., Fall River, Mass., 1988-92; pres., CEO GCI Med., Braintree, Mass., 1992-93; v.p. bus. devel. Sulzermedica USA, Inc., Angleton, Tex., 1993-94, group v.p., 1994-98; v.p. bus. & tech. devel. St. Jude Med., Inc., St. Paul, Minn., 1998—; dir. Horizon Med. Products, Inc., Atlanta, 1998—, CardioFocus, Inc., Atlanta, Mass., 1999—; bd. dirs. Horizon Med. Products, Inc., CardioFocus, Inc. Author: 19th Century Maine Authors, 1978. Mem. ABA, Am. Corp. Counsel Assn., Am. Mgmt. Assn., Licensing Execs. Soc. Republican. Home: 18683 Bearpath Tr Eden Prairie MN 55347 Office: St Jude Med Inc One Lillehei Plz Saint Paul MN 55117

COHEN, ROBERT ABRAHAM, retired physician; b. Chgo., Nov. 13, 1909; s. Ezra Harry and Catherine (Kurzon) C.; m. Mabel Jean Blake, Mar. 21, 1933 (dec. Oct. 1972); children—Donald Edward, Margery Jean; m. Alice L. Muth, Mar. 31, 1974. B.S., U. Chgo., 1930, Ph.D., M.D., 1935. Intern Michael Reese Hosp., Chgo., 1936-37; resident Henry Phipps Psychiat. Clinic Johns Hopkins U., 1937-38; resident Sheppard-Pratt Hosp., Towson, Md., 1938-39, 40-41; sr. fellow Inst. Juvenile Research, Chgo, 1939-40; pvt. practice psychiatry Washington, 1946-48; clin. dir. Chestnut Lodge, Rockville, Md., 1948-53, dir. psychotherapy, 1981-91; dir. clin. investigations NIMH, Bethesda, Md., 1953-69; dir. div. clin. and behavioral research NIMH, 1969-81, dep. dir. intramural research program, 1969-81; pres. Washington Sch. Psychiatry, 1973-82; Bd. dirs. Founds. Fund for Research in Psychiatry, 1960-63, chmn. bd., 1962-63; trustee William Alanson White Psychiat. Found. Served from lt. (j.g.) to comdr. M.C. USNR, 1941-46. Recipient Salmon medal N.Y. Acad. Scis., 1978, Fromm-Reichmann award Am. Acad. Psychoanylsis, 1979, HEW Disting. Service award, 1970. Fellow Am. Psychiat. Assn. (life); mem. Am. Psychoanalytical Assn., Am. Psychopathol. Assn., Assn. Research in Nervous and Mental Disease, Washington Psychoanalytic Soc. (pres. 1951-53), Washington Psychiat. Soc. (pres. 1958-59), Washington Psychoanalytic Inst. (chmn. edn. com. 1955-59), Washington Acad. Medicine. Home: 5216 Elsmere Ave Bethesda MD 20814-5734

COHEN, ROBERT EDWARD, chemical engineering educator, consultant; b. Oil City, Pa., Jan. 21, 1947; s. David M. and Minnie E. (Magdovitz) C.; m. D. Jane Woodman, Nov. 18, 1978; children: Genevieve Elizabeth, Eliot Lee. BS with distinction, Cornell U., 1968; MS, Calif. Inst. Tech., 1970, PhD, 1972. Postdoctoral rsch. fellow Calif. Inst. Tech., Pasadena, 1972; ICI rsch. fellow Oxford (Eng.) U., 1972-73; asst. prof. chem. engring. MIT, Cambridge, 1973-75, Harold and Esther Edgerton asst. prof., 1975-77, assoc. prof., 1977-82, prof., 1982—, founding dir. program in polymer sci. and tech., 1985-88, Bayer prof. chem. engring., 1988-95, St. Laurent prof. chem. engring., 1995—, assoc. chmn. of faculty, 1989-91; vis. appointment Sandia Nat. Labs., Albuquerque, summer 1979, Istituto Guido Donegani, Novara, Italy, 1981-82; vis. prof. dept. chemistry Harvard U., 1989; co-founder, bd. dirs., cons. MatTek Corp., Ashland, Mass., 1985—; bd. dirs. Kiser Rsch., Inc., Washington, 1992-94; chmn. sci. adv. bd. William and Mary Greve Found., N.Y.C., 1988—, bd. dirs., 1997—. Co-editor: Jour. Polymer Engring.; mem. editorial adv. bd. Jour. Applied Polymer Sci., 1989—, Chemistry of Materials, 1989-93; cons. editor AIP Series on Polymers and Complex Fluids, 1992-97; contbr. articles to profl. jours.; patentee in field. Bd. trustees The Advent Sch., Boston, 1996—. Recipient DuPont Young Faculty award MIT, 1974, Camille and Henry Dreyfus Tchr. Scholar award Dreyfus Found., 1977; Shell Disting. lectr. dept. materials sci. Northwestern U., 1996. Mem. AIChE (program chair materials divsn. polymer sect. 1993-97, dir. materials divsn. 1998—), Am. Chem. Soc., Am. Phys. Soc., Materials Rsch. Soc., Soc. Rheology, N.Y. Acad. Scis. Jewish. Avocation: golf. Office: MIT Dept Chem Engring Bldg 66 Rm 554 Cambridge MA 02139

COHEN, ROBERT SONNÉ, physicist, philosopher, educator; b. N.Y.C., Feb. 18, 1923; m. Robin Gertrude Hirshhorn, June 18, 1944; children: Michael, Daniel, Deborah. BA, Wesleyan U., Middletown, Conn., 1943, LHD, 1986; MS, Yale U., 1943, PhD (NRC fellow), 1948. Instr. physics Yale U., 1943-44, instr. philosophy, 1949-51; sci. staff, war research div. Columbia U. and Communications Bd., U.S. Joint Chiefs Staff, 1944-46; asst. prof. physics and philosophy Wesleyan U., 1949-57; assoc. prof. physics Boston U., 1957-59, prof. physics and philosophy, 1959-93, chmn. dept. physics, 1959-73, chmn. dept. philosophy, 1986-88, prof. emeritus, 1993—; acting dean Coll. Liberal Arts, 1971-72; chmn. Boston U. Center for Philosophy and History Sci., 1970-93, chmn. emeritus, 1993—; vis. lectr. humanities and philosophy of sci. Mass. Inst. Tech., 1958-59, 61-62; vis. prof. history of ideas Brandeis U., 1959-60; lectr. history and philosophy of sci. Am. U., Washington, summers 1958-68; vis. fellow Polish and Yugoslav Acad. Sci., 1963, Hungarian Acad. Sci., 1964; vis. prof. philosophy U. Calif., San Diego, 1969, Yale U., 1973; rsch. fellow history of sci. Harvard U., 1974; mem., chmn. U.S. Nat. Com. for Internat. Union History and Philosophy of Sci., 1969-75; trustee Wesleyan U., 1968-84, emeritus, 1984—; trustee Tufts U., 1984-93, emeritus, 1993—. Author, editor articles, books and jours. in field.; Editor: Boston Studies in Philosophy of Sci., Vienna Circle Collection, Sci. in Context. Trustee Bill of Rights Found. Am. Council Learned Soc. fellow philosophy and sci., 1948-49; Ford faculty fellow Cambridge, Eng., 1955-56; fellow Wissenschaftskolleg zu Berlin, 1983-84, Inst. fur Wissenschaften dem Menschen, Vienna, 1994. Fellow AAAS (chmn. sect. L history and philosophy of sci. 1978-79); mem. AAUP, Am. Phys. Soc., Am. Assn. Physics Tchrs., Am. Philos. Assn. (exec. com. 1988-91), History Sci. Soc., Philosophy Sci. Assn. (v.p. 1972-75, pres. 1982-84), Nat. Emergency Civil Liberties Com. (mem. nat. coun.), Am. Inst. Marxist Studies (chmn. 1964-82), Fedn. Am. Scientists (nat. coun. 1967-70), Inst. for Unity of Sci. (exec. com. 1960-74). Home: 44 Adams Ave Watertown MA 02472-1391 Office: Boston U Dept Philosophy 745 Commonwealth Ave Boston MA 02215-1401

COHEN, ROBERT STEPHAN, lawyer; b. N.Y.C., Jan. 14, 1939; s. Abraham and Florence C.; children: Christopher, Ian, Nicholas. BA, Alfred U., 1959; LLB, Fordham U., 1962. Bar: N.Y. 1963, U.S. Dist. Ct. (so. and ea. dists.) N.Y 1964, U.S. Ct. Appeals (2nd cir.) 1965. Assoc. Saxe, Bacon & O'Shea, N.Y.C., 1963-68; mng. ptnr. Morrison, Cohen, Singer & Weinstein and predecessor firms, N.Y.C., 1968—; lectr. in field; mem. faculty Am Acad. Psychiatry and the Law, 1984—. Bd. dirs. N.Y. Pops, 1983—. 1st lt. JAG, USAR, 1965-67. Fellow Am. Coll. Family Trial Lawyers; mem. ABA, FBA, ATLA, N.Y. State Bar Assn., N.Y.C. Bar Assn., N.Y. Acad. Matrimonial Lawyers, Univ. Club (N.Y.C.). Contbr. articles to legal jours. Home: 920 5th Ave New York NY 10021-4160 Office: 750 Lexington Ave New York NY 10022-1200

COHEN, ROBERT STEPHEN, drama educator; b. Washington, July 14, 1938; s. Lester Ellis and Lydia Rita (Goldblatt) C.; m. Lorna Lee Buck, Nov. 13, 1972; children: Michael Geoffrey, Whitney. Student, Dartmouth Coll., 1956-58; BA, U. Calif., Berkeley, 1961; DFA, Yale U., 1965. Prof. drama U. Calif., Irvine, 1965—, chmn. drama dept., 1970-91; acting dean fine arts, 1994-95; stage dir. Colo. Shakespeare Festival, Boulder, 1982—, Utah Shakespearean Festival, Cedar City, 1985—, FRP in Medieval Drama, Irvine, 1985-91. Author: Giraudoux, 1968, Acting Professionally, 1972, 97, Creative Play Direction, 1974, Acting Power, 1978, Theater, 1981, 99, Acting One, 1984, 97, Acting in Shakespeare, 1990. NEH grantee, 1989. Mem. Actors Equity Assn., Am. Theatre Critics Assn., Phi Beta Kappa. Office: U Calif Irvine Dept Drama Irvine CA 92697

COHEN, ROBERTA JANE, government executive; b. N.Y.C., Feb. 5, 1940; d. George H. and Ethel (Israel) C.; m. David A. Korn, Apr. 8, 1981; stepchildren: Marie, David, Philip, Stephen. BA, Barnard Coll., 1960; MA, Johns Hopkins U., 1963. Exec. dir. Internat. League for Human Rights, N.Y.C., 1971-78; sr. adviser to U.S. del. to UN and human rights officer Dept. of State, Washington, 1978-80, dep. asst. sec. state for human rights, 1980-81; head pub. affairs office U.S. Embassy, Addis Ababa, 1982-85; hon. sec. Parliamentary Human Rights Group, London, 1985-86; sr. adviser to refugee policy group Washington, 1989-96; sr. advisor NAS Com. on Human Rights, Washington, 1991-95; sr. advisor to rep. of sec.-gen. on internally displaced UN, 1994—; co-dir. project on internal. displacement, guest scholar Brookings Instn., Washington, 1994—; chmn. task force on human rights UN Assn., Washington, 1993-94; chair task force on China of Internat. Human Rights Law Group, Washington, 1997—; vice chair Internat. Human Rights Law Group, Washington, 1992-96; bd. dirs. Jacob Blaustein Inst. for Advancement Human Rights, Women's Commn. for Refugee Women and Children; mem. adv. com. Human Rights Watch/Africa. Author: People's Republic of China: The Human Rights Exception, 1987; co-author: Masses in Flight: The Global Crisis of Internal Displacement, 1998; co-editor: The Forsaken People, 1998. Pub. mem. U.S. Del. to UN Commn. on Human Rights, 1998. Recipient Superior Honor award U.S. Info. Agy., Addis Ababa, 1985, Human Rights award UN Assn., 1994. Mem. Coun. on Fgn. Rels., Women's Fgn. Policy Group.

COHEN, RONALD S., accountant; b. Lafayette, Ind., July 13, 1937; s. William and Stella (Fleischman) C.; m. Nancy Ann Plotkin, May 29, 1960; children: Philip, Douglas. BS in Acctg., Ind. U., 1958. CPA, Ind. Staff acct. Crowe, Chizek & Co., South Bend, Ind., 1958-65, ptnr., 1965-82, mng. ptnr., 1982-94, chmn. bd. dirs., 1994—; mem. Dean's adv. coun. Ind. U. Sch. Bus., 1996—. Commr. Housing Authority of South Bend, 1976-85, also vice-chmn.; pres. Jewish Fedn., 1979-82; bd. dirs. United Way of South Bend, 1987-90. Served to lt. USAR, 1958-66. Mem. AICPA (bd. dirs. 1990-97, vice-chmn. 1994, chmn. 1995), Ind. Soc. CPAs, Ind. U. Sch. Bus. Alumni Assn. (bd. dirs. 1992-95). Democrat. Jewish. Office: Crowe Chizek & Co PO Box 7 330 E Jefferson Blvd South Bend IN 46601-2366

COHEN, ROSALIE, civic worker; b. New Orleans, May 27, 1910; d. Leon and Fannie (Brener) Palter; m. Joseph Johen, July 7, 1929 (dec. Oct. 1979); children: Carmel Jonathan, Sharon Cohen Leviton. BA, Tulane U., 1940. Chmn. women's divsn. campaign New Orleans Jewish Welfare Fund, 1945; chmn. family svc. New Orleans Jewish Fedn., 1950-56, pres., 1959-61; vice chmn. women's divsn. Heart Campaign, 1950; pres. New Orleans B'nai B'rith Hillel Corp., 1954—, pres. New Orleans B'nai B'rith Hillel Found., 1954-59, Isidore Newman Sch. PTA, 1950-51; nat. vice chmn. women's divsn. United Jewish Appeal, 1954-60, mem. adv. bd., 1960—; mem. regional bd. Anti-Defamation League, 1956—; mem. B'nai B'rith Adult Jewish Edn. Commn., 1960-66; bd. dirs. Nat. Found. Jewish Culture, 1960—; founder Willow Wood Home for Jewish Aged, New Orleans, 1962-97; mem. Orleans Parish Bd. Welfare, 1958-66, New Orleans Bd. Wefare, 1958, Citizens Com. for Juvenile Ct., 1963-66; organizer year-round women's divsn. Jewish Welfare Fedn., New Orleans, 1965, hon. pres., 1966—; organizer citizens steering com. Orleans Parish Welfare Dept., 1966; v.p. Coun. Jewish Fedns. and Welfare Funds, 1963-66, sec., 1966—; bd. overseers Philip Lown Ctr. Judaic Studies, Brandeis U., Waltham, Mass., 1966—; sec. Fgn. Rels. Assn., 1966-67, bd. dirs., 1967—; chpt. pres. Hadassah, 1932-36, 40-42, 47, hon. v.p., 1950; founder Am.-Christian Palestine Com., New Orleans, 1945-48, Hillel chpt., Tulane U., New Orleans, Lemann-Stern Young Leadership, New Orleans; founding mem. Nat. Found. for Jewish Culture, N.Y.C. Recipient svc. award United Jewish Appeal, award of honor Govt. of Israel Bonds, 1954, citation Orleans Parish Bd. Welfare, 1966, cert. of merit U.S. Office Censorship, 1944, hon. award Tulane U. Sch. Social Work, Hebrew U. Mem. Am. Assn. for Jewish Edn. (v.p. 1965—), Jewish Publs. Soc. Am. (bd. dirs.). Democrat. Home: 241 Audubon Blvd New Orleans LA 70125-4123

COHEN, SAMUEL ISRAEL, clergyman, organization executive; b. Asbury Park, N.J., Apr. 17, 1933; s. Meyer and Henrietta (Gershman) C.; m. Mira Hager, Sept. 5, 1960; children: Baruch Chaim and Adina, Michael Nachum and Yocheved, Miriam Rachel and Chaim Silberberg. BA, Bklyn. Coll., 1955; MRE, Yeshiva U., 1959, EdD, 1967. Ordained rabbi, 1956. Exec. dir. L.I. Zionist Youth Commn., Queens, N.Y., 1957-61; regional dir. Supreme Lodge B'nai B'rith, Queens, 1961-66; dir. membership dept. dist. 1 Supreme Lodge B'nai B'rith, N.Y.C., 1966-72; nat. dir. orgn. Am. Jewish Congress, N.Y.C., 1972-74; exec. dir. Am. Zionist Fedn., N.Y.C., 1974-77; exec. v.p. Jewish Nat. Fund, N.Y.C., 1977-96, sr. exec. v.p., 1997-98; sr. cons. Influence, 1998—; adj. asst. prof. sociology L.I. U., 1967; lectr. sociology Queensborough Community Coll., 1968, adj. asst. prof., 1971-74; lectr. Borough of Manhattan Community Coll., 1968, adj. asst. prof., 1970-72; adj. asst. prof. John Jay Coll. Criminal Justice, 1973—; lectr. Herzl Inst., N.Y.C., 1974-78. Contbr. articles to nat. publs. Chmn. edn. adv. bd. Yeshiva Toras Chaim, Woodmere, N.Y., 1971-74; mem. Religious Zionists Am., 1960—, Zionist Orgn. Am., 1960—, Nat. Coun. Jewish Edn., 1970—; mem. Conf. Jewish Communal Svc., 1970—; mem. Congregation Shaarei Tephila, Lawrence, N.Y., 1983—, Congregation Kneseth Israel, 1983—; sec. Olam Chadash, 1980—; bd. dirs. Union Orthodox Jewish Congregations Am., 1973—, United Israel Appeal, 1984-90; founding chmn. Assn. of Orthodox Jewish Communal Execs., 1998—; chmn. N.Y. State Israel Cultural Exch. Commn., 1998. Co-recipient Boneh Israel award Mercaz Horav Kook; named one of four Winner's Cir. for Fund Raiser of Yr. award Non-Profit Times, 1994, Herman J. Quitman award as Outstanding Profl. in Jewish Communal Svc. B'nai Zion, 1996, Jewish Communal Leadership award Be'er Hagolah Inst., 1997. Mem. Adult Edn. Assn. (nat. com. on goals and objectives religious edn. sect. 1967-68), Educators Council Am., Young Israel of Wavecrest and Bayswater (v.p. 1973-75), Assn. Jewish Community Orgn. Profls., Nat. Council for Adult Jewish Edn., Nat. Soc. Fund Raising Execs, B'nai B'rith (v.p. Briarwood Lodge 1964), Assn. Orthodox Jewish Communal Execs. Home: 112 Rand Pl Lawrence NY 11559-1327 Office: Influence 80 8th Ave New York NY 10011-5126

COHEN, SANFORD IRWIN, physician, educator; b. N.Y.C., Sept. 5, 1928; s. George A. and Gertrude (Slater) C.; m. Jean Steinbruecker, Nov. 30, 1952; children—Jeffrey, Debra, John, Robert. A.B. magna cum laude, N.Y. U., 1948; M.B., M.D., Chgo. Med. Sch., 1952. Intern Jackson Meml. Hosp., Miami, Fla., 1952-53; resident psychiatry U. Colo. Med. Center, 1953-54; resident Duke Med. Center, 1954-55, 57-58, mem. faculty, 1956-68, prof. psychiatry, 1964-68, head div. psychosomatic medicine and psychophysiol. research, 1964-68, lectr. psychology, 1960-68; instr. Washington Psychoanalytic Inst., 1964-68; cons. VA Hosp., Durham, N.C., 1957-65, NIMH, 1963-66; prof. psychiatry Boston U. Med. Sch., 1970-86, chmn. dept., 1970-86; vis. research scientist health and behavior br., div. basic scis. NIMH, 1986-88; prof. psychiatry U. Miami (Fla.) Sch. Medicine, 1988—, vice chmn. dept., 1990—; Markle scholar med. sci., 1957-62; Commonwealth fellow, Czech Republic and USSR, 1996. Contbr. articles to profl. jours., chpts. to books. Recipient Robert Morse award excellence in sci. writing, 1965. Fellow Am. Psychiat. Assn. (life), Am. Coll. Clin. Pharmacology (life); mem. AAAS, Am. Psychosomatic Soc., Acad. Behavioral Medicine Rsch. Home: 808 Brickell Key Dr #1601 Miami FL 33131

COHEN, SANFORD NED, pediatrics educator, academics administrator; b. N.Y.C., June 12, 1935; s. George M. and Fannie Leah (Epstein) C.; m. Judith Luskind, June 22, 1958 (div. 1984); 1 child, Andrew B.; m. Elizabeth Prevot, Aug. 19, 1984 (div. 1991); m. Sandra Hoffmann, June 13, 1992. AB, The Johns Hopkins U., 1956, MD, 1960. Diplomate Am. Bd. Pediatrics. Intern in pediatrics Johns Hopkins Hosp., 1960-61, resident, 1961-63; instr. to assoc. prof. NYU Sch. Medicine, N.Y.C., 1965-74; chmn., prof. pediatrics Wayne State U. Sch. Med., Detroit, 1974-81, assoc. dean, 1981-86, sr. v.p. for acad. affairs, provost, 1986-91, prof. pediatrics, 1991-98, prof. emeritus, 1998—, dir. Wayne State U. Devel. Disability Inst., 1983-86, Child Research Ctr., Detroit, 1975-81; pediatrician-in-chief Children's Hosp. Mich., Detroit, 1974-81; adj. faculty U. Mich. Sch. Pub. Health, Ann Arbor, 1980-90; chair steering com. NIH Network of Pediat. Pharmacology Rsch. Units, 1994-98, mem. adv. com., 1999—. John and Mary R. Markle scholar acad. medicine, 1968-74. Editor: Progress in Drug Therapy in Children, 1981. Contbr. articles to profl. jours. Mem. bd. health, Leonia, N.J., 1972-74; mem. Bd. Police Commrs., Detroit, 1995—, chmn., 1997-98. Mem. Am. Pediat. Soc., Midwest Soc. Pediatric Rsch. (pres. 1979-80), Soc. Pediatric Rsch. (v.p. 1980-81). Avocations: reading, golf. Office: Children's Hosp Mich 3901 Beaubien St Detroit MI 48201-2119

COHEN, SAUL BERNARD, former college president, geographer; b. Malden, Mass., July 28, 1925; s. Barnett and Anna (Kaplinsky) C.; m. Miriam Friederman, June 11, 1950; children: Deborah Fae, Louise Esther. AB, Harvard U., 1947, AM, 1949, PhD, 1955; DSc (hon.), CUNY, 1986, LLD (hon.), 1986; DSc (hon.), Clark U., 1991. From instr. to prof. geography Boston U., 1952-65; vis. prof. U.S. Naval War Coll., 1957; prof. geography, dir. Grad. Sch. Geography, Clark U., Worcester, Mass., 1965-78; dean Grad. Sch. Geography, Clark U. (Grad. Sch.), 1967-70, chmn. faculty, 1973-76, 77-78; pres. Queens Coll., Flushing, N.Y., 1978-85; univ. prof. geography Hunter Coll., N.Y., 1986-96, univ. prof. emeritus, 1996—; vis. prof. Hebrew U., Jerusalem, 1971, 74, 75; adj. prof. Haifa U., 1977; cons. social sci. div. NSF, 1966-74, U.S. Office Edn., 1966-77; mem. U.S. nat. delegation Internat. Geog. Union, 1966-69; chmn. com. geography Nat. Acad. of Scis.-NRC, 1966-69. Author: Geography and Politics in a World Divided, 1963, rev. edit., 1973, Problems and Trends in American Geography, 1967, Experiencing the Environment, 1976, Resources and Human Networks, 1977, Jerusalem-Bridging the Four Walls, 1977, Jerusalem Undivided, 1983, Israel's Defensible Borders: A Geopolitical Map, 1987, The Geopolitics of Israel's Border Question; also articles; geog. editor The Oxford World Atlas, 1973; geog. advisor New Columbia Ency., 1991, 93; editor-in-chief Columbia Gazetteer of the World, 1998. Chmn. N.Y.C. Early Childhood Commn., 1985-86; co-chmn. N.Y. State Sch. and Bus. Alliance, 1986-94; mem. Temp. State Commn. on N.Y.C. Sch. Governance, 1989-91; at-large mem. N.Y. State Bd. Regents, 1993—, chmn. Regents Telecom. Policy Commn., 1994-97, Regents Elem., Secondary and Continuing Edn. Com., 1995-98, Regents Higher Edn. and Profession com., 1999—; mem. N.Y. State Archives Partnership Trust, 1994—; chmn. vis. com. N.Y. State Mus., 1997—. Mem. Consortium Profl. Assns. (chmn. 1965-71), Assn. Am. Geographers (exec. officer 1964-65, del. Am. Coun. Learned Socs. 1964-66, mem. coun. 1966-70, chmn. commn. coll. geography 1965-67, v.p. 1988-89, pres. 1989-90, past pres. 1990-91, chmn. com. on geog. curriculum internat. exch. 1990-96), Am. Geog. Soc. (coun. 1970-79). Home: 82 Taymil Rd New Rochelle NY 10804-2802 Office: Hunter Coll Geography & Geology Dept 695 Park Ave New York NY 10021-5024

COHEN, SAUL G., chemist, educator; b. Boston, May 10, 1916; s. Barnet M. and Ida (Levine) C.; m. Doris E. Brewer, Nov. 27, 1941 (dec. July 1971); children—Jonathan Brewer, Elisabeth Jane; m. Anneliese F. Kissinger, June 1, 1973. AB summa cum laude, Harvard U., 1937, MA, 1938, PhD, 1940; ScD, Brandeis U., 1986. Research fellow Harvard, 1939-40, 41-43, instr., 1940-41; NRC fellow, lectr. U. Calif. at Los Angeles, 1943-44; research chemist Pitts. Plate Glass Co., 1944-45; research chemist Polaroid Corp., 1945-50, cons., 1950—; with Brandeis U., 1950—, prof. chemistry, 1952—, Univ. prof., 1974-86, prof. emeritus, 1986—, chmn. Sch. Sci., 1950-55, dean faculty, 1955-59, chmn. dept. chemistry, 1959-66, 68-72; vis. prof. Havard Med. Sch., 1965, Hebrew U., Jerusalem, 1972. Contbr. articles on reaction mechanisms, free radicals, photochemistry, enzymology to profl. jours. Bd. overseers Harvard U., 1983-89; mem. Joint Com. on Appointments, 1984-89. Fulbright sr. scholar, 1958-59; Guggenheim fellow, 1958-59; Centennial medalist Harvard Grad. Sch. Arts and Scis., 1992. Fellow Am. Acad. Arts and Scis. (council), AAAS; mem. Am. Soc. Biol. Chemists, Am. Chem. Soc. (James F. Norris award 1972, trustee Northeastern sect. 1976-84), Chem. Soc. London, AAUP, Fedn. Am. Scientists, Phi Beta Kappa, Sigma Xi. Achievements include patents in polymers, hyroxylamines as photographic developers, heterocyclic silver solvents, dye-developers, diagnostic assays. Home: 90 Commonwealth Ave Boston MA 02116-3040 Office: Brandeis U Dept Chem Waltham MA 02254

COHEN, SELMA, reference librarian, researcher; b. N.Y.C., Mar. 14, 1930; d. George and Rose (Cohen) Unger; m. Irwin H. Cohen, Nov. 19, 1950; children: Barbara Katzeff, Joel. Grad. high sch., William Howard Taft High Sch., 1948. Asst. bookkeeper acctg. dept. Severud, Perrone et al, N.Y.C., 1970-75; asst. bookkeeper acctg. dept. Russell Reynolds Assocs., Inc., N.Y.C., 1976-77, rsch. asst., 1977—, reference libr., 1985—. Chairwoman Scott Tower Charity Com., Bronx, 1976-84, Scott Tower Property Improvement Com., Bronx, 1983-84. Home: 3400C Paul Ave Bronx NY 10468-1042 Office: Russell Reynolds Assocs 200 Park Ave New York NY 10166-0005

COHEN, SELMA JEANNE, dance historian; b. Chgo., Sept. 18, 1920; d. Frank A. and Minna (Skud) C. A.B., U. Chgo., 1941, M.A., 1942, Ph.D., 1946. Free lance writer, 1949—; editor Dance Perspectives, N.Y.C., 1959-76; founder, dir. Dance Critics Conf., Am. Dance Festival, 1970-72, U. Chgo. Seminars in Dance History, 1974-76; disting. vis. prof. Five Colls., Inc., 1976-77; editor Internat. Ency. Dance, N.Y.C., 1998; dance editor World Ency. Contemporary Theatre, 1985—; adj. prof. U. Calif., Riverside, 1983-89, disting. scholar, 1990—. Author: The Modern Dance: Seven Statements of Belief, 1966, Doris Humphrey, An Artist First, 1972, Dance as a Theatre Art, 1974, Next Week, Swan Lake: Reflections on Dance and Dances, 1982. Rockefeller Found. grantee, 1969; Am. Dance Guild award, 1976; Guggenheim fellow, 1980; recipient Profl. Achievement award U. Chgo., 1974; award Dance mag., 1981. Mem. Am. Soc. Aesthetics, Am. Soc. Theatre Rsch., Dance History Scholars, Am. Coun. Learned Socs., Internat. Fedn. for Theatre Rsch., World Dance Alliance. Home and Office: 29 E 9th St New York NY 10003-6301

COHEN, SEYMOUR, lawyer; b. Chgo., Sept. 27, 1917; s. Sol and Sophie (Norinsky) C.; m. Marcia Meltzer, Aug. 10, 1952; children: Susan Ruth, James Burton. BS, Ind. U., 1939, JD, 1941. Bar: Ind. 1941, Ill. 1948, U.S. Supreme Ct. 1971. Atty. NLRB, Washington, 1946-47; practice law Chgo., 1947—; mem. firm Dorfman, Cohen, Laner & Muchin, Ltd. (and predecessor), 1953-86. Mem. Northbrook (Ill.) Library Bd., 1963-69, pres., 1965-67. Served to lt. comdr. USNR, 1941-45. Mem. ABA, Chgo. Bar Assn. (chmn. com. labor law 1961-63). *A belief in one's own abilities is not enough. There must be a need by others for what those abilities can provide. The utilization of those abilities then will produce rewards both for the provider and the receiver.*

COHEN, SEYMOUR STANLEY, biochemist, educator; b. N.Y.C., Apr. 30, 1917; s. Herman and Lena (Tanz) C.; m. Elaine Pear, July 12, 1940; children: Michael, Sara. B.S., CCNY, 1936; PhD. in Biol. Chemistry, Columbia U., 1941; Dr.h.c., U. Louvain, Belgium, 1972, U. Kuopio, Finland, 1982. NRC fellow Rockefeller Inst., 1941-42; mem. faculty U. Pa., 1943-71, prof. biochemistry in pediatrics, 1954-71, Charles Hayden-Am. Cancer Soc. prof. biochemistry, 1957-71, Hartzell prof., chmn. dept. therapeutic research Sch. Medicine, 1963-71; Am. Cancer Soc. prof. microbiology U. Colo. Sch. Medicine, Denver, 1971-76; distinguished prof., Am. Cancer Soc. prof. pharm. scis. State U. N.Y., Stony Brook, 1976-85, prof. emeritus, 1985—; chmn. council analysis and projection Am. Cancer Soc., 1972-74, adviser research, 1974-76; Guggenheim fellow Pasteur Inst., Paris, 1947-48; Jesup lectr. Columbia U., 1967; guest investigator Institut du Radium, Paris, 1967-68; vis. prof. Collège de France, Paris, 1970; vis. fellow Smithsonian Instn., 1973-74, 86; vis. prof. U. Tokyo, 1974, Hadassah Med. Sch., 1974, Zuckerman lectr. tropical disease, 1979; Guggenheim and Lady Davis fellow Faculty Agr., Israel, 1983; fellow Nat. Humanities Ctr., N.C., 1982-83, 85; research assoc. history of sci., Smithsonian Inst., 1986; presdl. scholar U. Calif., San Francisco, 1988; lectr. Academia Sinica, R.O.C., 1989; trustee Marine Biol. Lab., Woods Hole, Mass.; bd. sci. cons. Sloan-Kettering Inst. Author: Virus-Induced Enzymes, 1968, Introduction to the Polyamines, 1971, Guide to the Polyamines, 1998, Biography of Thomas Cooper, 1999; editorial bd.: Virology, 1954-59, Jour. Biol. Chemistry, 1959-65, Jour. Cell Physiology, 1966-71, Bacteriol. Revs, 1969-73, Hist., Philos. Life Scis., 1985—. Recipient cert. for war research OSRD, 1945, War Manpower Commn., 1945; War Research medal Columbia U., 1943; Eli Lilly award and medal Am. Soc. Bacteriology, Immunology and Pathology, 1951; 1st Mead Johnson award Am. Acad. Pediatrics, 1952; medal Soc. de Chimie Biologique France, 1964; Borden award Am. Assn. Med. Colls., 1967; Passano award, 1974; Townsend Harris medal CCNY Alumni Assn., 1978; Forster award German Acad. Sci. and Letters, Mainz, 1978; Fogarty scholar NIH, 1973-74. Fellow AAAS (Newcomb Cleveland award 1955), Am. Acad. of Microbiology; mem. NAS, Am. Acad. Arts and Scis., Soc. Gen. Physiologists (councilor, pres. 1967-88), Serbian Acad. Scis. and Art, Inst. Medicine, Am. Assn. Cancer Rsch. (hon., bd. dirs. 1974-77), French Soc. Microbiology, Phi Beta Kappa. Home: 10 Carrot Hill Rd Woods Hole MA 02543-1206

COHEN, SHARLEEN COOPER, interior designer, writer; b. L.A., June 11, 1940; d. Sam and Claretta (Ellis) White; m. R. Gary Cooper, Dec. 18, 1960 (dec. Feb., 1971); m. Martin L. Cohen, M.D., Aug. 27, 1972; children: Cami Gordon, Dalisa Cooper Cohen. Student, U. Calif., Berkeley, 1957-58, UCLA, 1958-60, L.A. Valley Film Sch., 1976-78. Owner, mgr. Designs on You, L.A., 1965-77; writer L.A., 1977—; prodr. Jewish Repertory Theatre, N.Y.C., 1996. Author: (books) The Day After Tomorrow, 1979, Regina's Song, 1980, The Ladies of Beverly Hills, 1983, Marital Affairs, 1985, Love, Sex and Money, 1988, Lives of Value, 1991, Innocent Gestures, 1994; (play) Solomon and Sheba, 1990; (musical) Sheba, 1996; assoc. prodr. Broadway show Street Corner Symphony; prodr. Cookin' At The Cookery, The Best of Times; assoc. prodr. Duet. Mem. exec. com. Women of Distinction United Jewish Appeal, 1990-95; chair L.A. chpt. Nat. Gaucher Found., 1991-95; bd. dirs., mem. com. chair Calif. Coun. for the Humanities, San Francisco, 1992-98. Recipient Hon. Mention, Santa Barbara Writers Conf., 1978. Mem. PEN, Writers Guild of Am.

COHEN, SHELDON GILBERT, physician, historian, immunology educator; b. Pittston, Pa., Sept. 21, 1918; s. Samuel H. and Dorthy (Goldberg) C. Grad., Wyo. Sem., 1936; student, Syracuse U., 1936-37; BA, Ohio State U., 1940; MD, NYU, 1943; DSc (hon.), Wilkes U., 1976. Diplomate Am. Bd. Allergy and Immunology. Intern Bellevue Hosp., N.Y.C., 1944; resident internal medicine Ft. Howard VA Hosp., Balt., 1947-48; resident in allergy VA Hosp., Aspinwall, Pa., 1948-49, U. Pitts. Med. Ctr., 1948-49; rsch. fellow U. Pitts. Sch. Medicine, 1949-50; practice medicine specializing in allergy Wilkes-Barre, Pa., 1951-72; rsch. assoc. U. Pitts., 1950-51; attending physician Allergy Clinic, Falk Clinics, 1950-51; chief of allergy Mercy Hosp., Wilkes-Barre, 1951-72; attending physician in allergy VA Hosp., Wilkes-Barre, 1951-60; cons. in internal medicine and rsch. VA Hosp., 1960-72; assoc. prof. biol. rsch. Wilkes U., Wilkes-Barre, 1952-62, prof. biol. rsch., 1962-68, prof. exptl. biology, 1968-72, adj. prof. immunology, 1991—; cons. extramural programs Nat. Inst. Allergy and Infectious Diseases, 1972-73, chief allergy and immunology br., 1973-76, dir. immunology, allergic and immunologic diseases program, 1977-88, sci. advisor div. of intramural rsch. office of dir., 1988—; bd. sci. advisors Allergy and Immunology Inst. of Internat. Life Scis. Inst., 1989-97; adj. prof. medicine Northwestern U., 1988—; scholar Nat. Libr. Medicine, 1988—; regional med. cons. Children's Asthma Research Inst. and Hosp., Denver, 1969-72; mem. medico adv. bd. CARE, 1977-89; cons. to Ministry Public Health, State of Kuwait, 1981-83; mem. expert adv. panel on immunology WHO, Geneva, Switzerland, 1979—, dir. WHO Collaborating Ctr. for Allergy, 1985-89; bd. dirs. Asthma and Allergy Found. Am., 1969-81, mem. com. public edn., 1976-81; bd. dirs. Lupus Found. Am., 1978-85, exec. v.p., 1981-85, mem. med. council, 1978-93; mem. aeroallergens com. NRC, 1976-80. Author: Excerpts from Classics in Allergy, 1992, Asthma Among the Famous, 1995-99; mem. editl. bd. Jour. Devel. and Comparative Immunology, 1976-81, Allergy Proc., 1983-93; editor Hist. Notes, Allergy Proc., 1988-93; cons. editor Am. Jour. Rhinology, 1986-93; contbr. articles to profl. jours., chpts. to books. Trustee Marywood Coll., Scranton, Pa., 1983-89; bd. govs. adv. coun. Wilkes U., Wilkes-Barre, 1991-92. Capt. M.C., USAF, 1944-46. Recipient Disting. Svc. award Wyo. Sem., 1978, Asthma and Allergy Found. Am., 1981, Clemens von Pirquet award Georgetown U., 1981, NIH Centennial award, Terri Gottheif Lupus Rsch. Inst., 1987, NYU Med. Alumni Achievement award in health sci., 1988, Achievement award Internat. Assn. Allergology and Clin. Immunology, 1988, Spl. Recognition award Am. Acad Allergy and Immunology, 1989, recognition citation ILSI Allergy and Immunology Inst., 1992. Fellow ACP, Am. Acad. Allergy (chmn. rsch. coun. 1963-66, historian 1963-69, v.p. 1979-80, Disting. Svc. award 1971), Am. Coll. Allergists; mem. Coll. Physicians Phila., Am. Assn. Immunologists, Assn. Am. Physicians, Clin. Immunology Soc., Am. Thoracic Soc., Am. Coll. Rheumatology, Soc. for Exptl. Biology and Medicine, Collegium Internat. Allergologicum, Am. Fedn. Clin. Rsch., Am. Assn. for History of Medicine, Washington Soc. for History of Medicine (v.p. 1993-94, pres. 1994-96), Cosmos Club, Sigma Xi, Alpha Omega Alpha (NYU alumni). Home: 5500 Friendship Blvd Apt 1927N Chevy Chase MD 20815-7272 Office: NIH NIAID MSC 7600 Rockledge Bldg Rm 3125 Bethesda MD 20892

COHEN, SHELDON HERSH, chemistry educator, university official; b. Milw., May 21, 1934; s. Louis and Tabitha (Kaiser) C.; m. Virginia D. Yeatts, Aug. 22, 1962; children—Alexander P., William E., Gerald Y. B.S., U. Wis., 1956; Ph.D., U. Kans., 1962. Asst. prof. chemistry Washburn U., Topeka, 1960-65, assoc. prof., 1965-67, prof., 1967—, chmn. dept., 1967-82, provost, v.p., 1982-84, exec. dir. planning, 1991—. Contbr. articles to profl. jours. Bd. dirs. ARC, Topeka, 1982-84; mem. adv. bd. Stormont-Vail Hosp., Topeka, 1980-84. Mem. Am. Chem. Soc., Kans. Wildflower Assn. (dir. 1984—, pres. 1987-91), Phi Lambda Upsilon (nat. editor 1972-81, nat. sec. 1981-87, nat. pres. 1987-91), Phi Kappa Phi. Avocations: wildflower photography, tennis, growing orchids. Home: 1612 SW Mulvane St Topeka KS 66604-2746 Office: Washburn U Planning Ofc Topeka KS 66621

COHEN, SHERRY SUIB, writer; b. Bklyn., Oct. 17, 1934; d. David and Jane (Goldman) Suib; m. Lawrence A. Cohen, Nov. 25, 1956; children: Jennifer Goldstein, Adam Cohen. BS, Syracuse U., 1955. Cert. tchr., N.Y. Tchr. various schs., N.Y., 1956-76; writer N.Y.C., 1976—; lectr. in field. Author: 17 books, including The Magic of Touch, 1990, Decorating for Comfort, 1995, Secrets of a Very Good Marriage, 1993, Looking For the Other Side, 1997, Big City Look, 1998; contbg. editor New Woman, McCall's; contbr. articles to mags. Mem. Am. Soc. Journalists Authors (bd. dirs., Best First Person Article award 1997).

COHEN, SHIRLEY MASON, educator, writer, civic worker; b. Jersey City, June 24, 1924; d. Herman and Esther (Vinik) Mason; m. Herbert Leonard Cohen, June 24, 1951; children: Bruce Mason, Annette Pauline, Carol Elyse, Debra Tamara. BA, Rutgers U., 1945; MA, Columbia U., 1946; postgrad., U. Calif., Berkeley, 1946-51. Instr. U. Calif., Berkeley, 1946-51, Am. River Coll., Sacramento, 1962; tchr. various H.S., Sacramento, 1975-92; mentor tchr. Sacramento City Unified Sch. Dist., 1987-88. Author: Yearning to Breathe Free: The Story of the Vinik, Mason, and Gatkin Families, 1997. Bd. dirs. Sacramento Cmty. Concerts, 1965—. Mem. Phi Beta Kappa. Avocations: theatre, music, tennis, writing, literature.

COHEN, SIDNEY, medical educator; b. N.J., Feb. 5, 1939; m. Lois Cohen, 1961; children: Caryn, Michael, Douglas. BA, Rutgers U., 1960; MD, SUNY, Albany, 1964. Diplomate Am. Bd. Internal Medicine, Am. Bd. Gastroenterology. Teaching fellow in medicine Tufts U., Boston, 1966-68; teaching asst. Boston U., 1968-69; assoc. in medicine U. Pa., Phila., 1969-71, asst. prof., 1971-72, assoc. prof., 1972-77, T. Grier Miller prof., 1977-86; prof., chmn. dept. medicine Temple U., Phila., 1986-94; asst. v.p. for Health Scis. Ctr. Temple U., 1994—. Office: Temple U Medicine Dept Broad And Ontario St Philadelphia PA 19140*

COHEN, STANLEY, pathologist, educator; b. N.Y.C., June 4, 1937; s. Herman Joseph and Eva (Lapidus) C.; m. Marion Doris Cantor, Aug. 30, 1959; children: Laurie Ellen, Ronald Nelson, Kenneth Stuart. A.B., Columbia U., 1957, M.D., 1961. Diplomate Am. Bd. Pathology (mem. immunopathology com.). Intern Albert Einstein Med. Ctr., Bronx, N.Y., 1961-62; resident Mass. Gen. Hosp., 1962-64; fellow NYU Med. Ctr., 1964-66; prof. pathology SUNY, Buffalo, 1968-74; acting dir. Ctr. for Immunology, Buffalo, 1973-74; prof. pathology U. Conn. Health Ctr., Farmington, 1974-87; assoc. chmn. U. Conn. Health Ctr., 1976-80; prof., chmn. bd. Hahnemann U., Phila., 1987-94; prof., chmn. U. Medicine Dentistry-N.J. Med. Ctr., 1994—; mem. study sect. allergy and immunology, 1981-85; chair study sect. tumor immunology ahd therapy TRORP, 1992-94; co-chmn. 3d, 4th and 5th Internat. Lymphokine Workshops, 1982, 84, Congress on Cytokines, 1987, UCLA colloquium: molecular pathways of cytokines, 1990—, Keystone Symposium, 1992. Author: Mechanisms of Cell-Mediated Immunity, 1974, Mechanisms of Tumor Immunity, 1976, Mechanisms of Immunopathology, 1978, Biology of the Lymphokines, 1979, Interleukins, Lymphokines and Cytokines, 1983, Molecular Basis of Lymphokine Action, 1987, Role of Lymphokines in the Immune Response, 1989; assoc. editor-in-chief Clin. Immunology and Immunopathology; mem. editorial bds. 8 profl. jours.; contbr. more than 195 articles to profl. jours. Served to capt. U.S. Army, 1966-68. Recipient Kinne award, 1954, Borden award, 1961, Parke-Davis award in Exptl. Pathology, 1977, Outstanding Investigator award Nat. Cancer, Inst., 1986; Witobsky Meml. lectr., 1995. Mem. Am. Assn. Pathologists, Am. Assn. Immunologists, Clin. Immunol. Soc. (councilor), Pluto Soc. Home: 600 Hudson St Apt 3A Hoboken NJ 07030-5925 Office: UMDNJ Med Sch Newark NJ 07103

COHEN, STANLEY, biochemistry educator; b. Brooklyn, N.Y., Nov. 17, 1922; s. Louis and Fannie (Feitel) C.; m. Olivia Larson, 1951 (div.); children: Burt Bishop, Kenneth Larson, Cary; m. Jan Elizabeth Jordan, 1981. BA, Bklyn. Coll., 1943; MA, Oberlin Coll., 1945, PhD, 1989; PhD in Biochemistry, U. Mich., 1948; PhD, U. Chgo., 1985, Washington U., 1993. Instr. dept. biochemistry and pediatrics U. Colo., Denver, 1948-52; Am. Cancer Soc. fellow in radiology Washington U., St. Louis, 1952-53, assoc. prof. dept. zoology, 1953-59; asst. prof. biochemistry, sch. medicine Vanderbilt U., Nashville, 1959-62, assoc. prof., 1962-67, prof. biochemistry, 1967-86, disting. prof., 1986—; rsch. prof. biochemistry Am. Cancer Soc., Nashville, 1976—; Charles B. Smith vis. rsch. prof. Sloan Kettering, 1984; Feodor Lynen lectr. U. Miami, 1986, Steenbock lectr. U. Wis., 1986. Mem. editorial bd. Abstracts of Human Developmental Biology, Jour. of Cellular Physiology. Cons. Minority Rsch. Ctr. for Excellence. Recipient Research Career Devel. award NIH, 1959-69, William Thomson Wakeman award Nat. Paraplegia Found., Earl Sutherland Research Prize Vanderbilt U., 1977, Albion O. Bernstein MD award Med. Soc. State N.Y., 1978, H.P. Robertson Meml. award Nat. Acad. Sci., 1981, Lewis S. Rosentiel award Brandeis U., 1982, Alfred P. Sloan award Gen. Motors Cancer Research Found., 1982, Louisa Gross Horwitz prize Columbia U., 1983, Disting. Achievement award UCLA Lab. Biomed. and Environ. Scis., 1983, Lila Gruber Meml. Cancer Research award Am. Acad. Dermatology, 1983, Bertner award MD Anderson Hosp. U. Tex., 1983, Gairdner Found. Internat. award, 1985, Fred Conrad Koch award Endocrine Soc., 1986, Nat. Medal Sci., 1986, 89, Albert and Mary Lasker Found. Basic Med. Research award, 1986, Nobel Prize in physiology or medicine, 1986, Tennessean of Yr. award Tenn. Sports Hall of Fame, 1987, Franklin Medal, 1987, Albert A. Michaelson award Mus. Sci. and Industry, 1987. Fellow Jewish Acad. Arts and Sci.; mem. Nat. Acad. Sci., Am. Soc. Biol. Chemists, Am. Chem. Soc., AAAS, Internat. Inst. Embryology, Internat. Acad. Sci. (hon. internat. coun. for sci. devel.). Office: Vanderbilt U Sch Medicine Dept Biochemistry 607 LH Nashville TN 37232-0146*

COHEN, STANLEY NORMAN, geneticist, educator; b. Perth Amboy, N.J., Feb. 17, 1935; s. Bernard and Ida (Stolz) C.; m. Joanna Lucy Wolter, June 27, 1961; children: Anne, Geoffrey. B.A., Rutgers U., 1956; M.D., U. Pa., 1960, ScD (hon.), 1995; ScD (hon.), Rutgers U., 1994. Intern Mt. Sinai Hosp., N.Y.C., 1960-61; resident Univ. Hosp., Ann Arbor, Mich., 1961-62; clin. assoc. arthritis and rheumatism br. Nat. Inst. Arthritis and Metabolic Diseases, Bethesda, Md., 1962-64; sr. resident in medicine Duke U. Hosp., Durham, N.C., 1964-65; Am. Cancer Soc. postdoctoral rsch. fellow Albert Einstein Coll. Medicine, Bronx, 1965-67, asst. prof. devel. biology and cancer, 1967-68; mem. faculty Stanford (Calif.) U., 1968—, prof. medicine, 1975—, prof. genetics, 1977, chmn. dept. genetics, 1978-86, K.-T Li Prof., 1993—; mem. com. recombinant DNA molecules NAS-NRC, 1974; mem. com. on genetic experimentation Internat. Council Sci. Unions, 1977-96. Mem. editorial bd. Jour. Bacteriology, 1973-79, Molecular Microbiology, 1986—, Proceedings Nat. Acad. Sci., 1996—; assoc. editor Plasmid, 1977-86. Trustee, mem. bd. overseers U. Pa. Med. Ctr. With USPHS, 1962-64. Recipient Burroughs Wellcome Scholar award, 1970, Mattia award Roche Inst. Molecular Biology, 1977, Albert Lasker basic med. rsch. award, 1980, Wolf prize, 1981, Marvin J. Johnson award, 1981, Disting. Grad. award U. Pa. Sch. Medicine, 1986, Disting. Svc. award Miami Winter Symposium, 1986, Nat. Biotech. award, 1989, LVMH Inst. de la Vie prize, 1988, Nat. Medal Sci., 1988, City of Medicine award, 1988, Nat. Medal of Tech., 1989, Am. Chem. Soc. Spl. award 1992, Helmut Horten Rsch. award, 1993, Jerome H. Lemelson MIT prize for excellence in invention and innovation, 1996; Guggenheim fellow, 1975; Josiah Macy Jr. Found. faculty scholar, 1975-76. Fellow AAAS; mem. NAS (chmn. genetics sect. 1988-91), Am. Acad. Microbiology, Am. Soc. Biol. Chemists, Genetics Soc. Am., Am. Soc. Microbiology (Cetus award 1988), Am. Soc. Pharmacology and Exptl. Therapeutics, Am. Soc. Clin. Investigation, Assn. Am. Physicians, Inst. Medicine, Sigma Xi, Phi Beta Kappa, Alpha Omega Alpha. Office: Stanford U Sch Med Dept Genetics # M-320 Stanford CA 94305

COHEN, STEPHEN FRAND, political scientist, historian, educator, author, broadcaster; b. Indpls., Nov. 25, 1938; s. Marvin Stafford and Ruth (Frand) C.; m. Katrina vanden Heuvel; children: Andrew, Alexandra, Nicola. B.S., Ind. U., 1960, M.A., 1962; Ph.D., Columbia U., 1969; cert., Russian Inst., 1969. Instr. Columbia U., N.Y.C., 1965-68; asst. prof. politics Princeton (N.J.) U., N.J., 1968-73; assoc. prof. Princeton U., N.J., 1973-80, prof., 1980-98; prof. emeritus Princeton U., 1998—; dir. Russian studies Princeton U., N.J., 1973-80, 88-94; prof. Russian studies and History NYU, 1998—; cons. on Russia, CBS news TV commentator, 1989—; corr. and chief cons. PBS WNET films on Russia, 1994—; mem. adv. coun. U.S. Acad. Scis., Washington, 1979-82. Author: Bukharin and the Bolshevik Revolution, 1973 (Bukharin prize 1989), Rethinking the Soviet Experience, 1985, Sovieticus: American Perceptions and Soviet Realities, 1985 (Page One award 1985); editor: (with Robert C. Tucker) The Great Purge Trial, 1965, (with Rabinowitch and Sharlet) The Soviet Union Since Stalin, 1980, An End to Silence, 1982, (with Katrina vanden Heuvel) Voices of Glasnost: Interviews with Gorbachev's Reformers, 1989; mem. editl. bd. Slavic Rev., 1977-82, Post-Soviet Affairs, 1992—; assoc. editor World Politics, 1972-88; columnist The Nation Mag., 1982-87; contbg. editor, 1994—. Bd. dirs. NYU Ctr. for the Media. Fellow Am. Council Learned Socs., 1971, 72-73; fellow John Simon Guggenheim Found., 1976-77, 88-89, Rockefeller Found., 1980-81; NEH fellow, 1985-86; Fulbright-Hays fellow, 1988-89. Mem. Council Fgn. Relations, Am. Polit. Sci. Assn., Am. Hist. Assn., Am. Assn. for Advancement Slavic Studies. Home: 340 Riverside Dr Apt 8B New York NY 10025-3436

COHEN, S(TEPHEN) MARSHALL, philosophy educator; b. N.Y.C., Sept. 27, 1929; s. Harry and Fanny (Marshall) C.; m. Margaret Dennes, Feb. 15, 1964; children: Matthew, Megan. B.A., Dartmouth Coll., Hanover, N.H., 1951; postgrad., Harvard U., 1953; M.A., Oxford U., Eng., 1977. Jr. fellow, Soc. of Fellows Harvard U., 1955-58, asst. prof. philosophy and gen. edn., 1958-62; asst. prof. U. Chgo., 1962-64, assoc. prof., 1964-67; assoc. prof. Rockefeller U., N.Y.C., 1967-70; prof. philosophy CUNY, 1970-83, exec. officer program in philosophy Grad. Ctr., 1975-83; prof. philosophy and law U. So. Calif., L.A., 1983-97, dean div. humanities, 1983-94, interim dean Coll. Letters, Arts and Scis., 1993-94; univ. prof. emeritus philosophy and law, dean emeritus Coll. Letters, Arts and Scis., U. So. Calif., L.A., 1998—; lectr. Lowell Inst., Boston, 1957-58; vis. fellow All Souls Coll., Oxford, Eng., 1976-77; mem. Inst. for Advanced Study, Princeton, N.J., 1981-82. Editor: The Philosophy of John Stuart Mill, 1961, Philosophy and Public Affairs, 1970—, Philosophy and Society series, 1977-83, Ethical, Legal and Political Philosophy series, 1983-99; co-editor: Film Theory and Criticism, 1974, 79, 85, 92, 98, War and Moral Responsibility, 1974, The Rights and Wrongs of Abortion, 1974, Equality and Preferential Treatment, 1977, Marx, Justice and History, 1980, Medicine and Moral Philosophy, 1982, What Is Dance?, 1983, International Ethics, 1985, Punishment, 1995. Rockefeller Found. humanities fellow, 1977, Guggenheim fellow, 1976-77. Mem. Am. Philos. Assn., Am. Coun. Learned Socs. (bd. dirs. 1987-91, 93—), Coun. on Internat. Edn. Exch. (bd. dirs. 1991-94). Democrat. Jewish. Office: U So Calif Law Sch Los Angeles CA 90089-0071

COHEN, STEPHEN PHILIP, political science and history educator; b. Chgo., Mar. 9, 1936; s. Saul and Bess (Passovoy) C.; m. Roberta Sue Brosilow, June 22, 1958; children: Edward, Jeffrey, Peter, Benjamin, Tamara, Susan. B.A., U. Chgo., 1958, M.A., 1959; Ph.D., U. Wis., 1967. Prof. emeritus history and polit. sci. U. Ill., Urbana, 1998—; sr. fellow Brookings Instn., Washington, 1998—; mem. policy planning staff for South Asia, Dept. State, 1985-87; vis. prof. Keio U., Tokyo, 1974, Andhra U., India, 1977-78; co-founder Program Arms Control, Disarmament and Internat. Security, U. Ill., 1978-85 cons. U.S. State Dept. Arms Control Agy., Ford Found., Lawrence Livermore Nuclear Lab., Dept. State, Rand Corp., Asia Soc.; dir. Program in Arms Control, U. Ill., 1994-98. Author: The Indian Army, 2d edit., 1990; co-author: (with Richard L. Park) India: Emergent Power?, 1979, (with C.V. Raghavulu) The Andhra Cyclone of 1977, 1980, The Pakistan Army, 1984, (with others) Brasstacks and Beyond: Perception and Management of Crisis in South Asia, 1995; editor: The Security of South Asia, American and Asian Perspectives, 1987, Nuclear Proliferation in South Asia: The Prospects for Arms Control, 1991, South Asia After the Cold War, 1993. Ford Found. scholar in residence, India, 1992-93. Mem. Am. Polit. Sci. Assn., Internat. Inst. Strategic Studies, Inter-Univ. Seminar on Armed Forces and Soc., Psi Upsilon. Jewish. Home: Apt 912N 2501 Virginia Ave NW Washington DC 20037-2829 Office: Brookings Instn 1775 Massachusetts Ave NW Washington DC 20036-2188 *The central challenge facing mankind is a competition between self-destructive violence and reasoned restraint. My professional activities as a researcher, teacher, consultant and government official are devoted to understanding— and ameliorating— the institutions and forces which now have us racing along the edge of catastrophe.*

COHEN, SUSAN LOIS, author; b. Chgo., Mar. 27, 1938; d. Martin and Ida Handler; m. Daniel E. Cohen, Feb. 2, 1958; 1 child, Theodora (dec.). BA, New Sch. for Social Rsch., 1960; MA in Social Work, Adelphi U., 1962. Social worker N.Y.C., 1962-67; various social work positions in N.Y.C., 1962-68. Author: The Liberated Couple, 1969, reassued under title Liberated Marriage, 1973; (under name Elizabeth St. Clair) Stonehaven, 1974, The Singing Harp, 1975, Secret of the Locket, 1975, Provenance House, 1976, Mansion in Miniature, 1977, Dewitt Manor, 1977, The Jeweled Secret, 1978, Murder in the Act, 1978, Sandcastle Murder, 1979, Trek or Treat, 1980, Sealed with a Kiss, 1981; (with Daniel Cohen) The Kids' Guide to Home Computers, 1983, The Kids' Guide to Home Video, 1984, Teenage Stress, 1984, Screen Goddesses, 1984, Rock Video Superstars, 1985, Wrestling Superstars, Vol. 1, 1985, Vol. 2, 1986, Hollywood Hunks and Heroes, 1985, Heroes of the Challenger, 1986, A Six-Pack and a Fake ID, 1986, The Encyclopedia of Movie Stars, 1986, A History of the Oscars, 1986, Teenage Competition: A Survival Guide, 1987, Young and Famous: Hollywood's Newest Superstars, 1987, Going for the Gold, 1987, What You Can Believe about Drugs, 1988, What Kind of Dog is That, 1989, When Someone You Know Is Gay, 1989, Zoo Superstars, 1989, Zoos, 1992, Where to Find Dinosaurs Today, 1992, Going for the Gold: Medal Hopefuls for Winter '92, 1992, Gold Medal Glow: The Story of America's Women's Gymnastic Team, 1996. Mem. Wodehouse Soc., Watson's Erroneous Deductions, Chapter One, The Capers of Sherlock Holmes, Clumber Spaniel Club of Am. Avocation: cats. Address: 877 W Hand Ave Cape May Court House NJ 08210-1865

COHEN, SYLVAN M., lawyer; b. Phila., July 28, 1914; m. Alma Orlowitz, Sept. 5, 1943; children: Stephen B., Marc Alan. BA, U. Pa., 1935, JD, 1938. Bar: Pa., U.S. Dist. Ct. (ea. dist.) Pa. 1939, U.S. Ct. Appeals (3rd cir.) 1939. Chmn., ptnr. Cohen, Shapiro, Polisher, Shiekman & Cohen, Phila., 1939-95; of counsel Drinker, Biddle & Reath, Phila., 1995—; chmn., CEO Pa. Real Estate Investment Trust, Ft. Washington, Pa., 1960—; bd. dirs. Fidelity Bank, Phila., FPA Corp., Pompano Beach, Fla. Editor law revs. Trustee United Way; mem. com. Albert Einstein Med. Ctr.; bd. dirs., trustee Hosp. U. Pa., Zool. Soc. Phila., NCCJ, Police Athletic League Phila., Pop Warner Little Scholars, Jr. Baseball Fedn., Fedn. Jewish Agys. Greater Phila., Lawrence J. Gibbons Teenage Achievement Award. 1st lt. USAAF, 1943-46, PTO. Recipient Svc. award NCCJ-Human Rels. award of Honor United Jewish Appeal, Community award Fedn. of Jewish Agys., Disting. Svc. award Motion Picture Assocs. Found., Appreciation award Bicentennial Commn. Pa., Disting. Svc. award Irish Bicentennial, Communal award Brith Sholom; named Man of Yr. Blue Mountain Camp Alumni. Mem. ABA, Phila. Bar Assn., Pa. Bar Assn., Locust, Squires Golf, Variety (disting. svc. award), Meadowlands Country, University clubs, Emile Zola Lodge (Man of Yr. award). Home: 1820 Rittenhouse Sq Apt 17W Philadelphia PA 19103-5833 Office: 1345 Chestnut St Philadelphia PA 19107-3426

COHEN, TED, philosophy educator; b. Danville, Ill., Dec. 13, 1939; s. Sam and Shirley E. (Nimz) C.; m. Julie Simon, Apr. 18, 1940 (div. 1992); children: Shoshannah, Amos; m. Ann Rutherfurd Collier Austin, 1994. AB, U. Chgo., 1962; MA, Harvard U., 1965, PhD, 1972. Prof. philosophy U. Chgo., 1967—, chmn. dept. philosophy, 1974-79. Author: Jokes, 1999; editor: Essays in Kant's Aesthetics, 1982, Pursuits of Reason, 1993; contbr. articles to profl. jours. in German, Polish, Italian, French, Norwegian, Spanish, Finnish, Russian, and Dutch, 1972—. Bd. dirs. Ctr. for Rehab. and Tng. of Disabled, B'nai Brith Hillel Found. of U. Chgo., KAM Isaiah Israel Congregation, Chgo., 1980—, mem. faculty religious sch.; chmn. com. on gen. studies in humanities U. Chgo., 1991—. Named William R. Kenan Jr. Disting. Prof. Humanities Coll. of William and Mary, 1986-87; grantee Am. Council Learned Socs., 1980, 85. Mem. Am. Soc. Aesthetics (v.p., pres.-elect, pres. 1997—). Avocation: baseball theory and practice. Home: 4950 S Chicago Beach Dr Apt 3B Chicago IL 60615-3207 Office: U Chgo Dept Philosophy 1050 E 59th St Chicago IL 60637-1512

COHEN, TOM F., critic; b. N.Y.C., Aug. 13, 1953; s. Martin A. and Mary McCann Cohen. BA, Bennington Coll., 1974; MA, U. Chgo., 1978; PhD, Yale U., 1986. Prof. U. N.C., Chapel Hill, 1989-98; prof., chair English depts. U. Albany, SUNY, 1998—. Author: Anti-Mimesis, 1994, Heology and Inscription, 1998. Fulbright scholar Fulbright Commn., 1980-81. Mem. MLA (exec. com. philos. and approach divsn.). Office: English Dept SUNY/Albany Albany NY 12222

COHEN, TRUDY ORNSTEIN, adult nurse practitioner, educator; b. N.Y.C., Nov. 24, 1943; d. Daniel and Phyllis (Rosenglick) O.; div.; children: Lisa, Jonathan, Matthew. BSN, Hunter Coll., 1965; MS in Nursing, Cath. U. Am., 1980; Adult Nurse Practitioner cert., George Washington U., 1998. Cert. med.-surg. clin. specialist. Prof. nursing sci. Montgomery Coll., Takoma Park, Md. Mem. NLN, ANA, Md. Nurses Assn., D.C. Nurses Assn., Sigma Theta Tau, Alpha Eta. Home: 11200 Angus Pl Potomac MD 20854-3248

COHEN, WALTER STANLEY, accountant, financial consultant; b. Bklyn., Oct. 24, 1936; s. Harry and Ruth (Spitz) C.; m. Barbara Lee Cooper, June 18, 1960; children: Howard H., Andrea Sue. BS, U. Buffalo, 1958; postgrad., NYU, 1960-64. Jr. acct. Morris, Sherwood & May (CPAs), N.Y.C., 1958-59; semi-sr. acct. H. Merdinger & Co. (CPAs), 1960-61; sr. acct. Skillman & Michaels (CPAs), N.Y.C., 1961-62; with Blessings Corp., N.Y.C., 1962-84, sr. acct., 1962-66, asst. contr., 1966-69, asst. sec., 1969-70, sec., 1970-79, sec.-treas., 1979-84; v.p. fin. Sketchley Am., Inc., 1984-86; fin. cons. Thomson-McKinnon Securities, 1987-89; assoc. v.p. investments Prudential Securities, Bridgewater, N.J., 1989-94; assoc. v.p. Morgan Stanley Dean Witter, Somerville, N.J., 1994—. With AUS, 1959-60. Mem. B'nai B'rith, Kappa Nu (treas. 1955-56, v.p. 1956-57). Republican. Jewish. Home: 1 Bryant Dr Morganville NJ 07751-1502 Office: Morgan Stanley Dean Witter 166 W Main St Somerville NJ 08876-2204

COHEN, WARREN I., history educator; b. Bklyn., June 20, 1934; s. Murray and Fay (Phillips) C.; m. Janice Prichard, June 22, 1957 (div. Mar. 1986); children: Geoffrey Scott, Anne Leslie; m. Nancy Bernkopf Tucker, June 12, 1988. A.B., Columbia U., 1955; A.M., Fletcher Sch. Law and Diplomacy, Tufts U., 1956; Ph.D., U. Wash., 1962. Lectr. U. Calif.-Riverside, 1962-63, asst. prof., 1963-67, assoc. prof., 1967-71; prof. history Mich. State U., East Lansing, 1971-93, disting. univ. prof., 1990-93, dir. Asian Studies Ctr., 1979-89; disting. univ. prof. U. Md., Baltimore County, 1992—; vis. prof. Nat. Taiwan U., Taipei, 1964-66, Columbia U., N.Y.C., 1971, Fgn. Affairs Coll., Beijing, 1986; mem. Com. on Am.-East Asian Rels., Balt., 1973—; mem. adv. com. on hist. diplomatic documentation Dept. State, 1986-90, chmn., 1988-90; scholar-in-residence Assn. for Diplomatic Studies and Tng., 1994-95; acting dir. Asia program Wilson Ctr., 1995-99. Author: The American Revisionists, 1967, America's Response to China, 1971, The Chinese Connection, 1978, Dean Rusk, 1980, Empire without Tears, 1987, East Asian Art and American Culture, 1992, America in the Age of Soviet Power, 1945-1991, 1993; editor Diplomatic History, 1979-82, New Frontiers in American-East Asian Relations, 1983, (with Akira Iriye) Japan and the United States in the Postwar World, 1988, Great Powers in East Asia, 1953-60, 1990, (with Nancy Bernkopf Tucker) Lyndon Johnson Confronts the World, 1994, Pacific Passage, 1996, (with Li Zhao) Hong Kong Under Chinese Rule, 1997. Bd. dirs. Mich. China Council, East Lansing, 1978-92; exec. sec. Gov's Mich. and China Com., Lansing, 1982-84; mem. Gov's Commn. on China, 1984-88; bd. dirs. Japan Council, 1979-92. Served to lt. (j.g.) USNR, 1956-59, PTO. Fulbright lectr. Tokyo, 1969-70; research grantee Am. Council Learned Socs., 1968, Ford Found., 1976-77, Henry Luce Found., 1983-84; recipient Disting. Faculty award Mich. State U., 1988; Wilson Ctr. fellow, 1990-91. Mem. ACLU, Coun. on Fgn. Rels., Orgn. Am. Historians, Soc. for Historians of Am. Fgn. Rels. (v.p. 1983, pres. 1984). Democrat. Jewish. Office: U Md Balt County Dept History Baltimore MD 21250 also: 11500 S Glen Rd Potomac MD 20854-1852

COHEN, WILLIAM, law educator; b. Scranton, Pa., June 1, 1933; s. Maurice M. and Nellie (Rubin) C.; m. Betty C. Stein, Sept. 13, 1952 (div. 1976); children: Barbara Jean, David Alan (dec. 1995), Rebecca Anne; m. Nancy M. Mahoney, Aug. 8, 1976; 1 dau., Margaret Emily. BA, UCLA, 1953, LLB, 1956. Bar: Calif. 1961. Law clk. to U.S. Supreme Ct. Justice William O. Douglas, 1956-57; from asst. prof. to assoc. prof. U. Minn. Law Sch., 1957-60; vis. asso. prof. UCLA Law Sch., 1959-60, mem. faculty, 1960-70, prof., 1962-70; prof. Stanford (Calif.) Law Sch., 1970—, C. Wendell and Edith M. Carlsmith prof. law, 1983-99, Carlsmith prof. emeritus, 1999—; vis. prof. law European U. Inst., Florence, Italy, fall 1977; Merriam vis. prof. Ariz. State U. Law Sch., Spring 1981. Co-author: The Bill of Rights, a Source Book, 1968, Comparative Constitutional Law, 1978, Constitutional Law Cases and Materials, 1981, 2d edit., 1985, 3d edit., 1989, 4th edit., 1993, 5th edit. 1997, Constitutional Law: The Structure of Government, 1981, Constitutional Law: Civil Liberty and Individual Rights, 1982, 2d edit., 1994, 3rd edit., 1997. Home: 698 Maybell Ave Palo Alto CA 94306-3819 Office: Stanford Law Sch Nathan Abbott Way Stanford CA 94305

COHEN, WILLIAM ALAN, marketing educator, author, consultant; b. Balt., June 25, 1937; s. Sidney Oliver and Theresa (Bachman) C.; m. Janice Dawn Stults, Jan. 3, 1963 (div. Jan. 1966); 1 child, William Alan II; m. Nurit Kovnator, May 28, 1967; children—Barak, Nimrod. BS, U.S. Mil. Acad., 1959; MBA, U. Chgo., 1967; MA, Claremont Grad. Sch., 1978; PhD, Indsl. Coll. of the Armed Forces, 1989. Registered profl. engr., Israel. Project mgr. Israel Aircraft Industries, 1970-73; mgr. rsch. and devel. Sierra Engring. Co., Sierra Madre, Calif., 1973-76; pres. Global Assocs., 1973—; mgr. advanced tech. mktg. McDonnell-Douglas Co., Huntington Beach, Calif., 1976-78; prof. mktg. Calif. State U., L.A., 1979—, dir. bur. bus. and econ. rsch., 1979-83, chmn. mktg. dept., 1986—; bd. dir. Inst. Bus. Devel.; cons. Fortune 500 cos. Author: The Executives Guide to Finding a Superior Job, 1978, 83, Principles of Technical Management, 1980, Successful Marketing for Small Business, 1981, How to Sell to Government, 1981, The Entrepreneur and Small Business Problem Solver, 1983, 89, Direct Response Marketing, 1984, Building a Mail Order Business, 1982, 85, 91, 96, Making It Big as a Consultant, 1985, 90, Winning on the Marketing Front, 1986, High Tech Management, 1986, Developing a Winning Marketing Plan, 1987, The Students Guide to Finding a Superior Job, 1987, 93, The Practice of Marketing Management, 1988, 91, The Entrepreneur and Small Business Financial Problem Solver, 1989, The Art of Leader, 1990, The Entrepreneur and Small Business Marketing Problem Solver, 1991, Get a Great Job Fast, 1993, The Paranoid Corporation and Eight Other Ways Your Company Can Be Crazy, 1993, The Marketing Plan, 1994, 98, Making It!, 1994, Model Business Plans for Service Businesses, 1995, Model Business Plans for Product Businesses, 1995, The Stuff of Heroes: The 8 Universal Laws of Leadership, 1998; contbr. numerous articles to profl. jours. Maj. USAF, 1959-70, maj.-gen. USAFR, ret. Decorated Disting. Svc. Medal, Legion of Merit, D.F.C. with 3 oak leaf clusters, Meritorious Svc. medal with 2 oak leaf clusters, Air medal with 11 oak leaf clusters, numerous other U.S. and fgn. awards; named Disting. Grad. Indsl. Coll. Armed Forces, 1989; recipient Ministry Def. award State of Israel, 1976, Outstanding Svc. award Nat. Mgmt. Assn., 1979, Pres.'s award West Point Soc., 1982, Outstanding Prof. awd., 1983, Chgo. Tribune Gold medal, George Washington medal Freedoms Found. at Valley Forge, 1986, CSULA Statewide Outstanding Prof., 1996; numerous grants. Fellow Acad. Mktg. Sci.; mem. Direct Mktg. Assn. (fellow 1980, 83), World Mktg. Congress (del. N.S. 1983), Direct Mktg. Club So. Calif. (bd. dirs., grantee 1981), Am. Mktg. Assn. (award 1982), West Point Soc. (pres., bd. dirs. 1981-82), Beta Gamma Sigma, Phi Sigma Phi. Republican. Jewish. Office: Sch Bus and Econs Calif State U Los Angeles CA 90032

COHEN, WILLIAM BENJAMIN, historian, educator; b. Jakobstad, Finland, May 2, 1941; came to U.S., 1957; s. Walter Israel and Rosi (Hirschberg) C.; m. Christine Matheu; children: Natalie, Leslie, Laurel. B.A., Pomona Coll., 1962; M.A., Stanford U., 1963, Ph.D., 1968. Vis. lectr. Northwestern U., Evanston, Ill., 1966-67; instr. history Ind. U., Bloomington, 1966-68, asst. prof., 1968-71, assoc. prof., 1971-80, prof., 1980—, chmn. West European studies, 1978-80, chmn. dept. history, 1980-87. Author: Rulers of Empire, 1971, Robert Delavignette, 1977, French Encounter, 1980, European Empire Building, 1980, (with Thomas F. Noble et al) Western Civilization: The Continuing Experiment, 1994, 2d edit., 1998, Urban Government and the Rise of the French City, 1998, The Transformation of Modern France, 1997. NEH fellow, 1972, Fulbright fellow, 1983-84. Mem. Am. Hist. Assn. (mem. nominating com. 1987-90, George Louis prize com. 1997—), Coun. for European Studies, Soc. French Hist. Studies (pres. 1980-81, exec. com. 1980-83). Democrat. Home: 1016 S Highland Ave Bloomington IN 47401-6016 Office: Ind Univ History Dept Ballantine Hall Bloomington IN 47405

COHEN, WILLIAM MARK, publisher; b. N.Y.C., Aug. 23, 1949; s. Abraham and Florence C. B.A., Columbia U., 1971. Dir. mktg. Human Sci. Press, Inc., N.Y.C., 1972-75; pub., pres., owner The Haworth Press, Inc., N.Y.C., 1975—. Conceptualization, founder numerous profl. jours. in medicine and sci.; editor-in-chief profl. book program. Mem. Am. Soc. Info. Sci., Spl. Libraries Assn., ALA, Soc. Scholarly Pub., Am. Mktg. Assn., Med. Library Assn. Democrat. Jewish. Office: The Haworth Press Inc 10 Alice St Binghamton NY 13904-1503*

COHEN, WILLIAM NATHAN, radiologist; b. Balt., Dec. 10, 1935; s. Herbert and Lillian (Goldberg) C.; m. Sylvia Weinstein, Feb. 9, 1964; children: Elaine, Shirah, Jonathan. Student, Johns Hopkins U., 1952-55; M.D., U. Md., 1959. Intern U. Mich. Hosp., Ann Arbor, 1959-60; resident in radiology Mallinckrodt Inst., Washington U., St. Louis, 1960-63; chief radiology sect. Gallup Indian Hosp., USPHS, 1963-65; asst. prof. radiology U. Iowa, Iowa City, 1965-69; asso. prof. U. Iowa, 1969-73, prof., 1973-76; prof. radiology SUNY Health Sci. Ctr., Syracuse, 1976-83, clin. prof. radiology, 1983—; attending radiologist Crouse-Irving Meml. Hosp., Syracuse; vis. prof. radiology Hebrew U., Jerusalem, 1971-72; examiner Am. Bd. Radiology, 1981-87. Contbr. articles in field to med. jours. Fellow Am. Coll. Radiology; mem. Radiol. Soc. N. Am., Am. Roentgen Ray Soc., Am. Inst. Ultrasound in Medicine (sr.), Alpha Omega Alpha. Office: Crouse Irving Meml Hosp 736 Irving Ave Syracuse NY 13210-1687

COHEN, WILLIAM SEBASTIAN, federal official, former senator; b. Bangor, Maine, Aug. 28, 1940; s. Reuben and Clara (Hartley) C.; children: Kevin, Christopher. AB cum laude, Bowdoin Coll., 1962; LLB cum laude, Boston U., 1965; LLD, St. Joseph's Coll., Windham, Maine, 1974; LL.D., U. Maine, 1975, Western New Eng. Coll., 1975, Bowdoin Coll., 1975, Nasson Coll., 1975, Thomas Coll., 1988, Colby Coll., 1988. Bar: Maine, Mass., D.C. Ptnr. Paine, Cohen, Lynch, Weatherbee & Kobritz, Bangor, 1966-72; instr. U. Maine, 1968-72; asst. county atty. Penobscot County, Maine, 1968-70; U.S. Senator from Maine, 1979-96; sec. defense The Pentagon, 1997—; Mem. Bangor Sch. Com., 1970-71, Bangor City Council, 1969-72, mayor, Bangor, 1972; Trustee Unity Coll.; bd. overseers Bowdoin Coll., 1973-85. Author: Of Sons and Seasons, 1978, Roll Call, 1981, Getting the Most Out of Washington, 1982, A Baker's Nickel, 1986, One-Eyed Kings, 1991, (with Gary Hart) The Double Man, 1985, (with George Mitchell) Men of Zeal, 1988, (with Thomas B. Allen) Murder in the Senate, 1993. Recipient Alumni award for disting. pub. service Boston U., 1976; named to N.E. Hall of Fame Basketball Team, 1962, Silver Anniversary award Nat. Collegiate Athletic Assn., 1987; Outstanding Young Man of Yr. Nat. Jaycees, 1975; James

Bowdoin scholar, 1961-62; Alumni Fund scholar, 1962, selected for Balfour Silver Anniversary All-Am. Team, Nat. Assn. Basketball Coaches U.S., 1987. Office: Sec of Def 1000 Defense Pentagon Washington DC 20301-1000*

COHEN-SABBAN, NESSIM, auditor, accountant; b. Cairo, Aug. 4, 1930; came to U.S., 1984; s. Haim and Zakia (Baredes) C.-S.; m. Klemy Rodriguez, Apr. 7, 1960 (div. Mar. 1988); children: Haim, Nava, Shimon; m. Liliane Mann-Khasky, Sept. 8, 1988; children: Toufik, Elie, May. Grad., Cairo U., 1956, Tel Aviv U., 1964; postgrad., Touro Coll., 1991-92. CPA. Chief acct. David Ades & Son, Cairo, 1950-57; acct. Lodzia, Holon, Israel, 1957-61, Bank Leumi, Jaffa, Israel, 1961-64; internal auditor Head Office, Bank Le Melakha, Tel Aviv, 1964-78; auditor, acct. 1st Internat. Bank Israel, Tel Aviv, 1979-84, Greatway Co., N.Y.C., 1985, 88; internal auditor Play Knits Inc., N.Y.C., 1988—. Mem. Rabbinical of Bat-Yam, Israel, 1980-84; judge Bat-Yam City Ct., 1982-84. Officer Israel Army, 1961-84. Avocations: reading poems in English, French, Hebrew and Arabic, helping weak and poor people. Home: 1013 Avenue Y Brooklyn NY 11235-5013 Office: Play Knits Inc 240 W 40th St Fl 3 New York NY 10018-1592

COHILL, MAURICE BLANCHARD, JR., federal judge; b. Pitts., Pa., Nov. 26, 1929; s. Maurice Blanchard and Florence (Clarke) C.; m. Suzanne Miller, June 27, 1952 (dec. May 1986); children: Cynthia Cohill Plattner, Jonathan, Jennifer, Victoria Cohill Rifai. AB, Princeton U., 1951; LLB, U. Pitts., 1956. Bar: Pa. 1957. Judge family div. Common Pleas Ct., Allegheny County, Pitts., 1965-76; judge U.S. Dist. Ct. Pa. (we. dist.), 1976-94, chief judge, 1985-92, sr. judge, 1994—; bd. dirs. Pa. George Jr. Republic, Grove City; bd. visitors Grad. Sch. Social Work, U. Pitts.; chmn. bd. fellows Nat. Center for Juvenile Justice. Served to capt. USMCR, 1951-53. Mem. Am., Pa., Allegheny County bar assns., Nat. Council Juvenile Ct. Judges (v.p.), Pa. Council Juvenile Ct. Judges (past pres.), Pa. Conf. State Trial Judges, Phi Delta Phi. Republican. Presbyterian. Office: US Dist Ct US Courthouse 8th Fl Rm 3 7th and Grant Sts Pittsburgh PA 15219

COHLER, BERTRAM JOSEPH, social sciences educator, clinical psychologist; b. Chgo., Dec. 3, 1938; s. Jonas Robert and Betty (Cahn) C.; m. Anne Meyers, June 11, 1962 (dec. Dec. 1989); children: Jonathan Richard, James Joseph. BA, U. Chgo., 1961; PhD, Harvard U., 1967; cert. in adult analysis, Inst. Psychoanalysis, 1989. Diplomate Am. Bd. Psychoanalysis, Am. Bd. Examiners in Profl. Psychology. Lectr. social relations Harvard U., Cambridge, Mass., 1967-69; assoc. dir. Sonia Shankman Orthogenic Sch., 1969-72, 94-96; dir. Orthogenic Sch. U. Chgo., 1969-72, 94—; asst. prof. U. Chgo., 1969-75, assoc. prof., 1975-81, prof. depts. psychology, edn. and psychiatry, 1981—; co-dir. Univ. Ctr. Health anf Aging Soc., 1987—; sci. and profl. staff dept. psychiatry Michael Reese Hosp., Chgo., 1980-90; cons. The Tresholds, Chgo., 1972-81, Inst. Psychoanalysis, Chgo., 1972—, Ill. State Psychiat. Inst., Chgo., 1977-82; pres. bd. Ctr. Religion and Psychotherapy, Chgo. Author: (with H. Grunebaum et al) Mentally Ill Mothers and Their Children, 1975, 82, Mothers, Grandmothers, and Daughters, 1981, (with others) Parenthood as an Adult Experience, 1983, The Invulnerable Child, 1987, Handbook of Clinical Research on Adolescence, 1993, (with R. Galatzer-Levy) The Essential Other, 1993, (with others) Th ePsychoanalytic Study of Lives Our Time, 1999. Mem. initial rev. group in aging NIMH, Washington, 1982-86, Mental Health Spl. Projects, 1988-96; bd. dirs. Horizons Cmty. Svcs., Chgo. Recipient Quantrell prize U. Chgo., 1975; recipient William Rainey Harper Chair, 1978; fellow Inst. Medicine, 1975. Fellow Gerontol. Soc., Soc. Projective Techniques Am. Orthopsychiat. Assn. (bd. dirs. 1981-84, pres. elect 1991, pres. 1992), Am. Psychol. Assn. (chmn. profl. affairs com. divsn. 39 1981-83, editor Psychoanalytic Psychology 1987-97, pres. sect. II 1992); mem. Am. Sociol. Assn., Am. Anthrop. Assn., Am. Assn. Psychiat. Svcs. to Children (Alexander Gralnick award), Soc. Rsch. in Child Devel., Chgo. Assn. Psychoanalytic Psychology (pres. 1983-84), Am. Psychoanalytic Assn. Home: 5408 S Blackstone Ave Chicago IL 60615-5407 Office: U Chgo 5730 S Woodlawn Ave Chicago IL 60637-1603 *Emphasis on community services has been an important tradition in my family for several generations. This concern includes making knowledge and skills available to others, providing leadership and giving of time where needed. Teaching, writing, and research and clin. svc. are all involved in making the world better for my having been a part of it. My own goal has been to improve the human condition and to inspire my students to carry on this concern for the welfare of others.*

COHN, AARON I., anesthesiologist, educator; b. L.A., Sept. 8, 1959; s. Alan Franklin and Louise Christine (Huff) C.; m. Nicola Ann Bernau, July 1984 (div. Aug. 1986). BS, U. Calif. Riverside, 1980; MA, Rice U., 1984; MD, U. Tex. Galveston, 1987. Diplomate Am. Bd. Anesthesiology. Med. intern Montefiore/Univ. Hosp., Pitts., 1987-88; postdoctoral fellow Ctr. for Med. Informatics, Yale U. Med. Sch., New Haven, 1988-90; resident in anesthesiology Yale-New Haven Hosp., New Haven, 1990-91, St. Elizabeth's Med. Ctr., Boston, 1991-93; asst. prof. dept. anesthesiology U. Tex. Med. Br., Galveston, 1993-96; anesthesiologist North Tex. Anesthesia, Dallas, 1996-97; asst. prof. dept. anesthesiology U. Okla., Oklahoma City, 1997-99, U. Colo., Denver, 1999—; spl. study sect. mem. NIH, Rockville, Md., 1993—; reviewer Jour. Clin. Anesthesia, 1998—. Contbr. articles to profl. jours. Mem. Internat. Anesthesia Rsch. Soc., Am. Soc. Anesthesiologists, N.Y. Acad. Scis. Republican. Jewish. Avocations: bicycling, pistol shooting, computers, SCUBA diving, underwater photography. E-mail: aicohn@ski.uhcolorado.edu. Home: 939 Jersey St Denver CO 80220-4592 Office: U Colo Dept Anes CB B113 4200 E 9th Ave Denver CO 80262

COHN, ANDREW HOWARD, lawyer; b. N.Y.C., Jan. 17, 1945; s. Maurice John and Margaret Ethel (Gordon) C.; m. Marcia Bliss Leavitt, July 10, 1977; children: Marisa Leavitt, David Herman. BA, U. Pa., 1966; AM, Harvard U., 1970, PhD, 1972; JD, Yale U., 1975. Bar: Mass. 1975, U.S. Dist. Ct. Mass. 1976, U.S. Ct. Appeals (1st cir.) 1976. Law clk. to presiding justice U.S. Ct. Appeals (1st cir.), Providence and Boston, 1975-76; assoc. Hill & Barlow, Boston, 1976-80; sr. ptnr. Hale and Dorr, Boston, 1980—; chmn. exec. com. Hale and Dorr, 1990-91, real estate dept., 1991-97, energy group, 1992—; cons. for juvenile justice standards project ABA and Inst. for Judicial Adminstrn., N.Y.C., 1973-74; rsch. fellow MIT-Harvard U. Joint Ctr. for Urban Studies, Cambridge, Mass., 1969-71, Univ. Coll., Nairobi, Kenya, 1968. Contbr. articles to profl. jours.; note and project editor Yale Law Jour., New Haven, 1974-75. Advisor Newton (Mass.) Community SChs. Found., 1987-88. Named Law and Social Sci. fellow Russell Sage Found., 1972-74. Mem. ABA (environ.controls com., bus. law sect.), Am. Coll. Real Estate Lawyers, Boston Bar Assn. (chmn. real estate sect. 95-97), Yale Law Sch. Assn. Mass. (treas. 1985-87). Democrat. Jewish. Office: Hale and Dorr 60 State St Ste 25 Boston MA 02109-1816

COHN, AVERN LEVIN, federal judge; b. Detroit, July 23, 1924; s. Irwin I. and Sadie (Levin) C.; m. Joyce Hochman, Dec. 30, 1954 (dec. Dec. 1989); m. Lois Pincus Cohn, June 1992; children: Sheldon, Leslie Cohn Magy, Thomas. Student, John Tarleton Agrl. Coll., 1943, Stanford U., 1944; J.D., U. Mich., 1949. Bar: Mich. 1949. Practiced in Detroit, 1949-79; mem. firm Honigman Miller Schwartz & Cohn, Detroit, 1961-79; U.S. dist. judge, 1979—. Mem. Mich. Civil Rights Commn., 1972-75, chmn., 1974-75; Mem. Detroit Bd. Police Commrs., 1975-79, chmn., 1979; bd. govs. Jewish Welfare Fedn., Detroit, 1972—. Served with AUS, 1943-46. Mem. ABA, Mich. Bar Assn., Detroit Bar Assn., Am. Judicature Soc. (bd. dirs.), Am. Law Inst.

COHN, BERNARD SAMUEL, anthropologist, historian, educator; b. Bklyn., May 13, 1928; s. Nathan and Blanche (Herc) C.; m. Rella Israly, Mar. 19, 1950; children: Jenny Miriam, Abigail Catherine, Jacob Israly, Naomi Juliet. B.A., U. Wis., 1949; Ph.D. (Social Sci. Research Council fellow), Cornell U., Ithaca, N.Y., 1954. Research assoc., asst. prof. anthropology U. Chgo., 1956-58, vis. asst. prof. history, 1959-60, prof. anthropology and South Asian history, 1964-95, prof. emeritus, 1995—, chmn. dept. anthropology, 1969-72; assoc. prof., chmn. dept. anthropology U. Rochester, 1960-64; vis. prof. history U. Mich., 1967, 79, NYU, 1982, Calif. Inst. Tech., 1987; research fellow Australian Nat. U., 1979, 82; chmn. joint com. on South Asia Social Sci. Research Council-Am. Council Learned Socs., 1983-88; spkr. in field. Assoc. editor: Jour. Asian Studies, 1962-65; editorial bd.: Comparative Studies in Society and History, 1966—, Jour. Peasant Studies; co-author: (with Milton B. Singer) Structure and Change in Indian Society; author: India: The Social Anthropology of a Civilization, 1971, An Anthropologist among the Historians and Other Essays, 1987, Colonialism and Its Forms of Knowledge the British in India, 1996. Served with AUS, 1954-56. Rockefeller Found. fellow, 1957-59; Am. Council Learned Socs. fellow, 1962; Guggenheim fellow, 1964; fellow Center Advanced Study Behavioral Scis., 1967-68; Fellow Am. Inst. Indian Studies, 1975; NEH fellow, 1982-83. Fellow Am. Acad. Arts and Scis.; mem. Assn. Asian Studies (chmn. S. Asia com. 1962-64), Am. Anthrop. Assn., Am. Ethnological Soc. (exec. bd. 1969-72). Home: 5822 S Blackstone Ave Chicago IL 60637-5202 Office: U Chgo Depts Anthropol and History Haskell Hall Rm 324 Chicago IL 60637

COHN, BERTRAM JOSIAH, investment banker; b. Newark, Sept. 12, 1925; s. Julius Henry and Bessie Ruth (Einson) C.; m. Barbara Biard, June 20, 1956; children: Daniel, Susan, Diana. AB cum laude, Harvard, 1949; MBA, NYU, 1957. Vice pres. Decatur Iron & Steel Co., Ala., 1951-67; chmn. bd. Schuylkill Lead Corp., Baton Rouge, 1968-70, DPF, Inc., Hartsdale, N.Y., 1970—, Interstate Bakeries Corp., 1970-82; mem. internat. adv. com. Cohn Inst. for History and Philosophy Sci., Tel Aviv U. Trustee Jewish communal Fund N.Y., Washington Inst. for Near East Policy. With AUS, 1943-46. Home: 125 Woodbine Ave Larchmont NY 10538-3523 Office: First Manhattan Co 437 Madison Ave New York NY 10022-7001

COHN, BOB, public relations executive; b. N.Y.C., Oct. 12, 1934. Grad., U. Ala., 1961. Newspaper reporter, photojournalist, 1961-70; owner Cohn & Wolfe, N.Y.C., 1970-85, CEO, 1985-92, chmn. bd. dirs.; bd. dirs. Burson-Marsteller. Recipient 13 awards AP, UPI; nominee Pulitzer Prize, 1964. Mem. Arthur W. Page Soc. Office: Cohn & Wolfe Ste 2600 303 Peachtree St NE Atlanta GA 30303-1701 Address: Cohn & Wolfe 225 Park Ave S Fl 17 New York NY 10003-1604*

COHN, BRADLEY M., lawyer; b. Chgo., July 5, 1953; s. Charles M. and Marian Cohn C.; m. Janet M. Minow, Mar. 25, 1995; 1 child, Robert M. BA, U. Iowa, 1975; JD, U. Miami, 1978. Assoc. Hanson & Shire, P.C., Chgo., 1978-88; ptnr. Thrun, Tallman & Cohn, Ltd., Mt. Prospect, Ill., 1988—. Dir., officer Ctr. for Enriched Living, Deerfield, Ill., 1989—. Office: Thrun Tallman & Cohn Ltd 111 E Busse Ave Ste 504 Mount Prospect IL 60056-3249

COHN, DAVID HERC, retired foreign service officer; b. Bklyn., July 29, 1923; s. Nathan and Blanche (Herc) C.; m. Verna Elizabeth Peterson, Jan. 29, 1949 (dec. Nov. 1992). A.B., Dickinson Coll., 1948; postgrad., NYU, 1948-49, U. Pa., 1963-64; M.A., U. Miami, 1951. Instr. U. Miami, 1950-51; spl. asst. to div. dir. Dept. Commerce, 1951-56; joined U.S. Fgn. Service, 1956; consul, econ. officer Am. consulate gen., Istanbul, Turkey, 1956-60; 2d sec., economist U.S. Regional Orgn., Paris, 1960-63; economist Office Intelligence Research, Near East and South Asia; economist Bur. Near East and South Asian Affairs Dept. State, 1964-66, economist Pakistan-Afghanistan Country Directorate, 1966-68; dep. prin. officer Am. consulate gen., Karachi, Pakistan, 1968-70; econ. counselor Am. embassy, Kabul, Afghanistan, 1970-73; comml. counselor Am. embassy, Jakarta, Indonesia, 1973-75, econ.-comml. counselor, 1975-76; econ. and social policy adviser Bur. Internat. Orgn. Affairs Dept. State, 1976-77, dir. Internat. Econ. Policy Office, Bur. Internat. Orgn. Affairs, 1977-78, dir. Office Econ. Research and Analysis, Bur. Intelligence and Research, 1978-80, ret., 1980; asst. v.p. U.S.-USSR Trade and Econ. Council, Inc., N.Y.C., 1981-85; program coord. for Chad Internat. Human Assistance Programs, Inc., N.Y.C., 1985-86; UN br. asst. adminstr. Chemical Bank, N.Y.C., 1987-88. Vol. assoc. City of N.Y. Office Bus. Devel. Not-for-Profit sector, 1988-91; vol. tutor N.Y. Pub. Libr. Ctr. for Reading and Writing Harlem Br., 1989-95; vestryman All Saints Episc. Ch., N.Y.C., 1985-90, warden, 1991-99. With AUS, 1943-46. Mem. Nat. League of Nursing, Omicron Delta Kappa. Clubs: Dacor, Dacor House (Washington). Home: 2500 Johnson Ave Apt 16J Bronx NY 10463-4944 Office: All Saints Ch 230 E 60th St New York NY 10022-1402

COHN, DAVID STEPHEN, lawyer; b. Richmond, Va., June 19, 1945; S. Alfred Jerome and Jane Shaffer C.; m. Jane Boyle, Nov. 22, 1970; children: Elizabeth, Sarah. AB, U. Pa., 1967; JD, Harvard U., 1971. Bar: Pa. 1971, Va. 1973, U.S. Dist. Ct. (ea. dist.) Pa. 1971, U.S. Ct. Appeals (3rd cir.) 1971. Assoc. Schnader, Harrison, Segal & Lewis, Phila., 1971-73; asst. prof. law T.C. Williams Sch. Law, U. Richmond, 1973-75; counsel Hunton & Williams, Richmond, 1975-84; mem., chmn., real estate dept. Browder, Russell, Morris & Butcher, P.C., Richmond, 1984-89; ptnr. Mays & Valentine, LLP, Richmond, Va., 1989—; mem. Va. Gov.'s Com. on Efficiency in Govt., Richmond, 1985-87, Va. Gov.'s Regulatory Reform Adv. Bd., 1983-85; chmn. Va. com. Harvard Law Sch. Fund, Cambridge, Mass., 1986-88; lectr. Marshall Wythe Sch. Law, Coll. William and Mary, Williamsburg, Va., 1977-81; arbitrator Am. Arbitration Assn., 1972—. Editor: The Residential Real Estate Transaction, 1975. Assoc. trustee U. Pa., Phila., 1984-94; mem. state ctrl. com. Va. Dem. Party, Richmond, 1985-93; bd. dirs., pres. Sci. Mus. Va. Found., 1987—; mem. Va. Hist. Landmarks Bd., 1988-89; bd. dirs. Richmond Better Housing Coalition, 1988—; chmn., pres. Richmond Goodwill Industries, Inc., 1988—; mem. Va. Vol. Formulary Bd., 1989—; mem. adv. coun. Va. Gov.'s Sch. for Govt. and Internat. Studies for Gifted, 1991-93; mem. regulatory climate subcom. Va. Gov.'s Econ. Recovery Coun., 1991-92. Mem. ABA (chmn. govtl. assistance for real estate programs com. 1989-93), Am. Coll. Real Estate Lawyers (chmn. affordable housing com. 1991-97), Va. Bar Assn. (chmn. real estate com. 1985-87), Va. State Bar (mem. bd. govs. real estate sect. 1984-87). Jewish. Office: Mays & Valentine LLP NationsBank Center PO Box 1122 Richmond VA 23218-1122

COHN, DAVID V(ALOR), oral biology and biochemistry educator; b. N.Y.C., Nov. 8, 1926; s. Ralph and Clara (Schenkman) C.; m. Evelyn Turner, 1947; children: Robert Warren, Emily. BS, CCNY, 1948; PhD, Duke U., 1952; postgrad., Western Res. U., 1953. Faculty U. Kans. Sch. Medicine, Kansas City, 1953-84, prof. biochemistry, assoc. dean rsch., 1974-82; assoc. chief staff for rsch. devel. VA Med. Ctr., Kansas City, Mo., 1953-82; prof. biochemistry U. Mo., Kansas City, 1971-82; v.p. R&D Immuno Nuc. Corp., Stillwater, Minn., 1982; sci. cons. Immuno Nuc. Corp., Stillwater, 1983—; rsch. prof. oral biology and biochemistry U. Louisville Sch. Medicine, Sch. Dentistry, 1984—, chmn. dept. oral health, 1989-91, chmn. dept. biol. and biophys. scis., 1992-97, univ. dir. tech. devel., 1996-99, asst. v.p. econ. devel. and indsl. rels., 1999—; asst. to v.p. rsch. U. Louisville, 1992-95, asst. v.p. econ. devel. and indsl. rels., 1999—; pres. Internat. Conf. on Calcium Regulating Hormones, 1980-86, exec. sec., 1986-89; mem. bd. sci. counselors Nat. Inst. Dental Rsch., Bethesda, Md., 1980-84; chmn. bd. sci. advisors Endotronics, Inc., 1983-85; bd. dirs. Cambridge Med. Tech., Inc., 1985-86. Editor: Hormonal Control of Calcium Metabolism, 1981, Endocrine Control of Bone and Calcium Metabolism, 1984, Calcium Regulation and Bone Metabolism: Basic and Clinical Aspects, 1987, Calcium Regulating Hormones and Bone Metabolism: Basic and Clinical Aspects, vol. II, 1992; editor in chief Bone and Mineral, 1986-94; contbr. articles to profl. jours. With USN, 1945-46. Grantee USPHS, 1957—, Am. Cancer Soc., 1959-60, VA, 1975-82, Ky. Heart Assn., 1991-93. Mem. AAAS, Am. Soc. Molecular Biology and Biochemistry, Am. Chem. Soc., Gordon Rsch. Conf. Chem. and Biol. of Bones and Teeth (chmn. 1974). Achievements include research on calcium metabolism, parathyroid gland parathormone/chromogranin biosynthesis and secretion, bone cell growth, differentiation and hormone responsivity, economic development, entrepreneurship. Home: 5709 Apache Rd Louisville KY 40207-1715 Office: U Louisville Health Scis Ctr Dept Bioland Biophys Scis Louisville KY 40292

COHN, GARY DENNIS, journalist; b. Bklyn., Mar. 9, 1952; s. Morton J. and Claire Cohn; m. Sally Denton, 1980 (div. 1983). BA in Psychology and Polit. Sci., SUNY, Buffalo, 1974; postgrad., U. Calif., Berkeley, 1974-75. Reporter Jack Anderson Column, Washington, 1975-80, Lexington (Ky.) Herald-Leader, 1980-84, Miami bur. Wall St. Jour., N.Y.C., 1984-86, Phila. Inquirer, 1986-93, Balt. Sun, 1993—. Recipient Edward W. Scripps 1st Amendment award, 1980, Inter-Am. Press Assn. award, 1996, Overseas Press Club of Am. award, 1995, 97, Selden Ring award, 1996, 98, 1st Amendment award Soc. Profl. Journalists, 1997, 1st prize for investigative reporting Sigma Delta Chi, 1997, Investigative Reporters and Editors award, 1997, George Polk award, 1997, Pulitzer Prize for Investigative Reporting, 1998. Office: Balt Sun 501 N Calvert St Baltimore MD 21202-3604

COHN, GERALD B., federal judge; b. 1939. BA, Ill. Coll., 1961; JD, U. Chgo., 1964. Magistrate judge Ill. So. Dist., East St. Louis, 1981—. Served with U.S. Army, 1965-67, Res., 1967-71. Office: US Courthouse 750 Missouri Ave East Saint Louis IL 62201-2954

COHN, HARVEY, mathematician; b. N.Y.C., Dec. 27, 1923; s. Morris and Leah (Spielmann) C.; m. Bernice Blaufarb, Mar. 8, 1951; children: Anthony, Susan. BS, CCNY, 1942; MS, NYU, 1943; PhD, Harvard U., 1948. Teaching fellow Harvard U., 1947-48; asst. prof. Wayne U. (now Wayne State U.), 1948-54, assoc. prof., 1955-56; vis. assoc. prof. Stanford U., 1954-55; assoc. prof., then prof., head computer center Washington U., St. Louis, 1956-58; prof. math. U. Ariz., 1958-71; summer lectr. math UCLA, 1960, U. Wis., 1963; Emil Post prof. math. CUNY, 1971-73, distinguished prof., 1973-96; cons. IDA Ctr. for Computing Scis., 1996—; cons. Gen. Motors Corp., AEC computing facility at N.Y.U., Nat. Bur. Standards, Argonne Nat. Labs.; adv. bd. autonomous U. Guadalajara, Mex., 1963—; mem. Inst. for Advanced Study, 1970-71; lectr. U. Copenhagen, 1976-77. Author: Second Course in Number Theory, 1962, Conformal Mapping on Riemann Surfaces, 1967, Classical Invitation to Algebraic Numbers and Class Fields, 1978, Introduction to the Construction of Class Fields, 1985. Served with USNR, 1944-46. Recipient William Lowell Putnam prize Harvard, 1946. Mem. Am. Math. Soc., Math. Assn., Am., Assn. Computing Machinery, Phi Beta Kappa, Sigma Xi. Home: 600 Mckinsey Park Dr Apt 506 Severna Park MD 21146-4550 Office: Ctr for Computing Scis 17100 Science Dr Bowie MD 20715-4300

COHN, HERBERT B., lawyer; b. N.Y.C., Oct. 2, 1912; s. Joseph J. and Lillian (Rosing) C.; m. Kathryn E. Coe, May 24, 1941; 1 child, Elizabeth (Kark) Singer. A.B., Yale U., 1933; LL.B. magna cum laude, Harvard U., 1936. Bar: N.Y. 1936, U.S. Supreme Ct. 1940, D.C. 1978. Mem. legal staff SEC, 1936-48, dir. op. writ. office, 1942-48; mem. legal staff Am. Electric Power Svc. Corp., N.Y.C., 1948-67, v.p., dir., chief counsel, 1954-67; exec. v.p. adminstrv. and corp. svcs. N.Y.C., 1967-72; vice chmn. bd., chief adminstrv. officer Am. Electric Power Service Corp., N.Y.C., 1972-77; dir., mem. exec. com. Am. Electric Power Co., 1966-86, vice chmn. bd., 1972-77, chmn. fin. com., 1976-86; v.p., dir. Appalachian Power Co., Ohio Power Co., other subsidiaries, to 1977; of counsel Morgan, Lewis & Bockius, Washington, 1977-83, Newman & Holtzinger, Washington and successor, Newman, Bouknight & Edgar, 1984-94; sr. advisor Morgan, Lewis & Bockius, Washington, 1995-96; chmn. task force on U.S. energy policy study 20th Century Fund, 1976. Editor: Harvard Law Rev, 1934-36. Chmn. Com. for Capital Formation through Dividend Reinvestment, 1978-87. Served from lt. (j.g.) to lt. comdr. USNR, 1942-46. Mem. ABA (chmn. pub. utility law sect. 1968-69), Am. Arbitration Assn. (mem. arbitration and mediation panels 1982—, mem. secs. arbitration and mediation panels), N.Y. Stock Exch., Nat. Assn. Security Dealers, Am. Stock Exch., Harvard Law Sch. Assn., Edison Electric Inst. (dir. 1964-67, 70-73, chmn. legal com. 1962-64), Nat. Assn. Electric Cos. (chmn. 1977-78, dir., exec. com. 1975-79), Metro Club. Home: Regency at McLean #1712 1800 Old Meadow Rd Mc Lean VA 22102-1819

COHN, HERBERT EDWARD, surgeon, educator; b. Phila., June 4, 1930; s. Robert and Lee (Freed) C.;m. Natalie Mona Brait, Dec. 27, 1953; children: Jeffrey, Richard, David. BS, Rutgers U., 1951; MD, Jefferson Med. Coll., 1955. Diplomate Am. Bd. Surgery, Am. Bd. Cardiothoracic Surgery. Prof. surgery, vice chmn. dept. surgery, program dir. Jefferson Med. Coll., Phila., 1980—; pres. med. staff Thomas Jefferson Univ. Hosp., Phila., 1984-86. Capt. USAF, 1957-59. Recipient Christian and Mary Lindback award for disting. tchg., 1981; named physician of yr. Jewish Nat. Fund, Phila., 1988. Fellow ACS; mem. Am. Assn. Endocrine Surgeons, Soc. Thoracic Surgery, Phi Beta Kappa, Alpha Omega Alpha. Avocations: golf, fishing, travel. E-mail: herbert.cohn@mail.tju.edu. Office: Thomas Jefferson U 1025 Walnut St Philadelphia PA 19107-5001

COHN, HOWARD, retired magazine editor; b. N.Y.C., Nov. 1, 1922; s. Morris and Vivian (Siegel) C.; m. Regina Levy, Apr. 2, 1949; children—Steven B., Robert D. B.A., Am. U., 1947. Assoc. editor Sportfolio mag., 1947-48; assoc. editor, then mng. editor Am. Lawn Tennis mag., 1948-50; assoc. editor Quick mag., 1950-51, Collier's mag., 1951-56; freelance writer, 1957-59; articles editor Pageant mag., 1959, exec. editor, 1959-63; mng. editor True mag., 1964-68; mng. editor Med. World News mag., 1968, exec. editor, 1968-75, editor, 1975-77; exec. editor McGraw-Hill Newsletter Center, 1977-79; sr. staff editor McGraw-Hill Pub. Co., N.Y.C., 1979-81; editor-in-chief Graduating Engr. mag., 1981-88. Served with AUS, 1943-46. Home: 750A Heritage Hls Somers NY 10589-4009

COHN, ISIDORE, JR., surgeon, educator; b. New Orleans, Sept. 25, 1921; s. Isidore and Elsie (Waldhorn) C.; m. Jacqueline Heymann, July 4, 1944 (div. Aug. 1971); children: Ian Jeffrey, Lauren Kerry; m. Marianne Winter Miller, Jan. 3, 1976. MD, U. Pa., 1945; M.Med. Sci. in Surgery, 1952, DMS in Surgery, 1955; LHD (hon.), U. S.C., 1995. Diplomate Am. Bd. Surgery (bd. dirs. 1969-75). Intern Grad. Hosp. U. Pa., 1945-46, resident in surgery, 1949-52; fellow dept. surg. rsch. U. Pa., 1947-48; vis. surgeon Charity Hosp., New Orleans, 1952-62, sr. vis. surgeon, 1962—; surgeon in chief La. State U. Svc., Charity Hosp., New Orleans, 1962-89; prof. surgery La. State U. Sch. Medicine, New Orleans, 1959—; cons. surgeon VA Hosp., New Orleans, Touro Infirmary, New Orleans; instr. surgery La. State U. Sch. Medicine, New Orleans, 1952-53, asst. prof., 1953-56, assoc. prof., 1956-59, prof., 1959—, chmn. dept. surgery, 1962-89; mem. surg. rsch. rev. com. VA, Washington, 1967-68; dir. Nat. Pancreatic Cancer Project, 1975-84; mem. Soc. Surg. Chairmen, 1962-89. Mem. editl. bd. Am. Surgeon, 1963-87, Current Surgery, 1964-90, Am. Jour. Surgery, 1968-96, emeritus, 1997—, Digestive Diseases and Scis., 1978-82, Surg. Gastroenterology, 1982—, Cancer, 1992—, Digestive Surgery, 1995—. Bd. dirs. New Orleans Met. Conv. and Visitors Bur., 1998—. Served to capt. M.C., AUS, 1946-47. Isidore Cohn, Jr. Professorship named in his honor at La. State U., 1987. Fellow ACS (exec. com., bd. govs. 1987-91, vice-chmn. 1989-90, chmn. 1990-91, 1st v.p. 1993-94); mem. AMA, Am. Surg. Assn., So. Surg. Assn. (1st v.p. 1979-80, treas.-recorder 1981-82, pres. 1982-83), La. Surg. Assn. (pres. 1968), So. Med. Assn., La., Orleans Parish med. socs., Soc. Univ. Surgeons, Southeastern Surg. Congress (chmn. forum on progress in surgery 1967-69, councillor for La. 1967-73, pres. 1972), Surg. Biology Club II, Assn. Acad. Surgery, James D. Rives Surg. Soc., Internat. Surg. Soc., Am. Gastroenterol. Assn., Bockus Soc. Gastroenterology, Soc. Surgery Alimentary Tract (trustee 1969-80, recorder 1973-76, pres. 1976-77, chmn. bd. 1977-78), Am. Soc. Microbiologists, Soc. Surg. Oncology, N.Y. Acad. Scis., Am. Assn. Cancer Research, Southeastern Cancer Research Assn. (pres. 1975), Collegium Internationale Chirurgiae Digestivae, Am. Cancer Soc. (vice chmn. clin. investigation adv. com. 1969, chmn. clin. investigation adv. com. 1969-73), Tex. Surg. Soc. (hon.), Sigma Xi, Phi Beta Kappa, Alpha Omega Alpha, Omicron Delta Kappa. Office: La State U Med Sch New Orleans LA 70112

COHN, JANE SHAPIRO, public relations executive; b. N.Y.C., May 19, 1935; d. Harry I. and Ann (Safanie) Shapiro; m. Albert M. Cohn, June 30, 1957 (div. 1972); children: Theodore David, William Alan. BA, Brandeis U., 1956; postgrad., Coll. of New Rochelle, 1974-76; student, Harvard U., 1985. Dir. pub. rels. Hudson River Mus., Yonkers, N.Y., 1976-79; account exec. Dudley-Anderson Yutzy Pub. Rels. Agy. subs. Ogilvy Mather, N.Y.C., 1979-81; dir. communications Haines Lundberg Waehler, N.Y.C., 1981-91; prin. Jane Cohn Pub. Rels., Sherman, Conn., 1991—; cons. to various firms in architecture, engring., and constrn. industry, 1983; spkr., mktg. promotion strategies conf., 1989, AIA N.Y. Chpt., panelist So. New England Chpt.; organizer, co-spkr.Interplan Conv.; organizer and moderator Soc. Mktg. Profl. Svcs. N.Y. Chpt., 1996; spkr. Soc. Mktg. Profl. Svcs. Nat. Conf., 1997; panelist AIA Nat. Conv., 1998. Contbr. articles to profl. jours., chpts. to books. Fellow Soc. Mktg. Profl. Svcs. (cert.; bd. dirs. N.Y. chpt. 1988-89, 92-95, spkr. ann. convs., Gold Medal award 1994); mem. AIA (assoc. 1988, 98, panelist nat. conv. 1998, spkr. ann. conv.), Am. Mktg. Assn. (panelist ann. conv. 1987, moderator profl. services sect. ann. conv. 1988, exec. mem.), Practice Mgmt. Assn. (spkr. promotion strategies conf. 1989). Democrat. Jewish. Avocations: art, sculpture, gardening. Office: Jane Cohn Pub Rels 31 Spring Lake Rd Sherman CT 06784-1201

COHN, JESS VICTOR, psychiatrist; b. Cin., Jan. 1, 1908; s. Samuel L. and Hannah (Pritz) C.; m. Norma J. Hana, Sept. 7, 1947; children: Jess Victor Jr., William S., James D. M.D., U. Cin., 1933. Diplomate Am. Bd. Psychiatry and Neurology. Rotating intern Cin. Gen. Hosp., 1933, resident psychiatry, 1934; resident neurology Bellevue Hosp., N.Y.C., 1935; pres.

neuro-psychiat. dept. Broward Gen. Hosp., Ft. Lauderdale, Fla., 1961, mem. active staff, 1955-63; cons. psychiatry Meml. Hosp., Hollywood, Fla., 1957-63, Mt. Sinai Hosp., Miami Beach, Fla., 1956-63; mem. active staff North Broward Provident Hosp., Ft. Lauderdale, 1956-63, Holy Cross Hosp., Ft. Lauderdale, 1957-63, Ft. Lauderdale Beach Hosp., 1957-63; mem. active staff Boca Raton (Fla.) Community Hosp., 1969-88, emeritus chief div. psychiatry; cons. psychiatry Social Security Adminstrn., 1963-69, 69—, Sinai Hosp., Balt., 1964-69, Carroll County Gen. Hosp., 1965-69, Jerusalem Mental Health Ctr., 1973; asst. supt. Central State Hosp., Indpls., 1948-50; instr. neuro-psychiatry Ind. U. Med. Sch., 1948-50; dir. clerkship in applied practical psychology Butler U., 1949-50; supt. Embreevill (Pa.) State Hosp., 1950-55; assoc. psychiatry U. Pa. Med. Sch., 1952-55, U. Pa. Med. Sch. (Grad. Sch. Medicine), 1952-55; asst. prof. psychiatry U. Miami, 1957; supt. Springfield State Hosp., Sykesville, Md., 1963-69; asst. prof. psychiatry Johns Hopkins Med. Sch., 1963-69; psychiatrist Johns Hopkins Hosp., 1963-69; mem. faculty U. Md. Med Sch., 1963-69; clin. prof. psychiatry U. Miami (Fla.) Sch. Medicine, 1979—; psychiatrist Univ. Hosp., 1963-69; regional dir. mental health for Western Md. Founding mem., chmn. med. adv. com. Mental Health Assn. S.E. Fla., 1944-48; chmn. Fla. commn. Internat. Congress Mental Health, 1948. Author: Sane, Insane, or Maybe: From the Notebook of the Psychiatrist, 1993; contbr. articles to sci. jours., books and bulls. Fellow ACP, AMA, Am. Psychiat. Assn. (life, examining bd. adminstrv. psychiatry); mem. Assn. Med. Supts. Mental Hosps., Am. Assn. Psychiat. Adminstrs. (editor emeritus newsletter, jour.), So. Psychiat. Assn., Pa. Psychiat. Soc., Phila. Psychiat. Soc. (chmn. program com.), Med. Chirurgical Faculty Md., Broward County Med. Assn. (chmn. med. adv. com. to mental health clinic), Broward County Neuropsychiat. Assn. (founding mem., 1st pres.), Fla. Psychiat. Soc., Delaware Valley Group Psychotherapy Soc. 9founding mem., chmn. program com., mem. exec. com.), Am. Acad. Psychotherapists, Eastern Psychoanalytic Assn., Am. Coll. Psychiatrists, Am. Coll. Physicians. Address: 23371 Blue Water Cir Apt C323 Boca Raton FL 33433-7089

COHN, JOSEPH DAVID, surgeon; b. N.Y.C., Jan. 26, 1937; s. Samuel Theodor and Gertrude (Emsheimer) C.; m. Barbara Ester Forst, July 27, 1966; children: Michael, Russell. SB, MIT, 1957; MD, NYU, 1961; MBA, Rutgers U., 1993. Diplomate Am. Bd. Surgery, Am. Bd. Thoracic Surgery, Am. Bd. Critical Care Surgery. Intern Duke Hosp., Durham, N.C., 1961-62; surg. resident Bronx Mcpl. Hosp. Ctr., N.Y., 1962-67; thoracic surgery resident U. Calif., San Diego, 1969-71; from asst. dir. surgery to dir. St. Barnabas Med. Ctr., Livingston, N.J., 1971-83; thoracic surgeon Northfield Surg. Assn., Livingston, 1978—; clin. asst. prof. surgery UMDNJ, Newark, 1972-79, assoc. prof., 1979-90, prof., 1990—; bd. dirs. Daltex Corp., N.Y.C. Editor sci. jours.; author software programs, 1988; contbr. articles to profl. jours. Capt. USAF, 1967-69. Fellow Am. Heart Assn. 1966-67, NIH 1964-66. Fellow ACS, Am. Coll. Critical Care Medicine; mem. Sigma Xi, Phi Lambda Upsilon, Alpha Omega Alpha. Avocations: skiing, scuba, flying. Office: Northfield Surg Assocs 299 E Northfield Rd Livingston NJ 07039-4811

COHN, LAWRENCE STEVEN, physician, educator; b. Chgo., Dec. 21, 1945; s. Jerome M. and Francis C.; BS, U. Ill., 1967, MD, 1971; m. Harriett G. Rubin, Sept. 1, 1968; children: Allyson and Jennifer (twins). Intern, Mt. Zion Hosp., San Francisco, 1971-72, resident, 1972-73; resident U. Chgo., 1973-74; practice medicine specializing in internal medicine, Paramount, Calif.; pres. med. staff Charter Suburban Hosp., 1981-83; mem. staff Long Beach Meml. Hosp., Harbor Gen. Hosp; clin. prof. medicine UCLA. Maj. USAF, 1974-76. Recipient Disting. Teaching award Harbor-UCLA Med. Ctr., 1980, 90; diplomate Am. Bd. Internal Medicine. Fellow Am. Coll. Physicians; mem. A.C.P., AMA, Calif. Med. Assn., L.A. County Med. Assn., Am. Heart Assn., Soc. Air Force Physicians, Phi Beta Kappa, Phi Kappa Phi, Phi Lambda Upsilon, Phi Eta Sigma, Alpha Omega Alpha. Home: 6608 Via La Paloma Palos Verdes Peninsula CA 90275-6449 Office: 16415 Colorado Ave Ste 202 Paramount CA 90723-5054

COHN, LEONARD ALLAN, retired chemical company executive; b. Oskaloosa, Iowa, May 8, 1929; s. Eli A. and Edna C.; m. Rivalie Sideman, Sept. 2, 1951; children: Sheldon, Sylvia, Elliot. B.S. in Ch.E, Iowa State U., 1951; M.B.A., Washington U., St. Louis, 1955. Registered profl. engr., Iowa. Gen. mgr. Carpet Fiber div. Monsanto Co., Atlanta, 1970-72; gen. mgr. Apparel Fiber div. Monsanto Co., St. Louis, 1973-75; gen. mgr. Plastics div. Monsanto Co., 1976-78, v.p. energy and material mgmt., 1979-85, v.p. info. systems, 1986-93; ret., 1993. Mem. AIChe, Am. Chem. soc., Nat. Petroleum Refiners Assn. (bd. dirs. 1980-93, exec. com. 1983-86).

COHN, LUCILE, psychotherapist, nurse; b. Kokomo, Ind., Apr. 17, 1924; d. Jacob and Anna (Kaplan) Kohn; m. Norman Cohn; children: Richard Alan, Robert Irving. PhD, Marquette U. Cert., registered clin. med. hypnotherapist; registered clin. hynotherapist, hosp. hospice grief counsel; diplomate Am. Psychotherapy Assn. Employee counselor Mt. Sinai Med. Ctr., Milw., 1965-70; adminstr. of patient care svcs. Milw., 1970-72; chmn. psychiat. nursing Milw. Region Med. Complex, 1972-82; cons. psychotherapist Cardinal Stritch Coll., Milw., 1982—; pvt. practice psychotherapy Milw., 1980—; prof. nursing Columbia Coll. Nursing, Milw., 1976—, Carroll Coll. Nursing, Waukesha, Wis., 1976—; profl. vol. dying patients and grieving families, nursing homes and hosps.; vol. counselor Alzheimer's victims and their families, 1990—. Contbr. chpts. in textbooks. Bereavement counselor St. Mary's Hosp. Hospice, Milw., 1996—; mem. Women's Am. Orgn. Rehan. Through Tng., URban League, Mt. Sinai Med. Ctr. Aux., Temple Shalom, Pub. Libr. Lit. Soc., Milw. Heart Assn. 1st lt. U.S. Army Nurse Corps. Named 1 of 2000 women of Achievement, London, 1972, Nurse of Yr., Wis. Nurses Assn., 1977. Mem. ANA, Am. Med. Psychotherapists Assn. (diplomate and fellow), Women's Assn. Orgn. Rehab. Through Tng. (pres. Beal chpt., regional v.p.), Am. Assn. Grief Counselors, Nat. Bd. for Hypnotherapy and Hypnotic Anesthesiology, Hadassah, U. Wis. Union. Democrat. Jewish. Avocations: swimming, painting, gardening, world travel, volunteering. Home: 929 N Astor St Unit 2406 Milwaukee WI 53202-3438

COHN, MARJORIE BENEDICT, curator, art historian, educator; b. N.Y.C., Jan. 10, 1939; d. Manson and Marjorie (Allen) Benedict; m. Martin Cohn, Dec. 19, 1960. BA, Mt. Holyoke Coll., 1960; AM, Radcliffe Coll., 1961; DFA, Mt. Holyoke Coll., 1996. Conservator works of art on paper Art Mus. Harvard U., Cambridge, Mass., 1963-89, lectr. fine arts, 1974-77, sr. lectr., 1977—, print curator, 1989—, acting dir., 1990-91; vis. lectr. Boston U., 1972, 73, Wellesley (Mass.) Coll., 1973; vis. asst. prof. Brown U., Providence, 1975. Author: Wash & Gouache, 1977, A Noble Collection: The Spencer Albums of Old Master Prints, 1992, (with S.L. Siegfried) Works by J.A.D. Ingres in Collection of the Fogg Art Museum, 1980, Francis Calley Gray and Art Collecting for America, 1986. Sec. Arlington (Mass.) Hist. Commn., 1972-85. Mem. Am. Acad. Arts and Scis., Print Coun. Am. Democrat. Office: Harvard U Fogg Art Mus 32 Quincy St Cambridge MA 02138-3845*

COHN, MARTIN, advertising executive, consultant; b. N.Y.C, Apr. 9, 1945; s. Adolph J. and Anna (Schiff) C.; m. Kathleen Mandry, Dec. 29, 1973; 1 child, Aaron David. Student, Syracuse U., 1962-67. Copy supr. Ogilvy & Mather, N.Y.C., 1975-80; creative dir. Ogilvy & Mather, San Francisco, 1980-82; cons. San Francisco, 1982-84; ptnr. Cohn & Wells, San Francisco, 1984-95; cons. San Francisco, 1995—; cons., San Francisco, 1995—. Trustee, bd. dirs., French Am. Internat. Sch., San Francisco, 1991—; bd. dirs. Philharm. Baroque Orch., San Francisco, 1998—; pres. Nat. Ctr. Internat. Schs., San Francisco, 1998—. •

COHN, MILDRED, biochemist, educator; b. N.Y.C., July 12, 1913; d. Isidore M. and Bertha (Klein) Cohn; m. Henry Primakoff, May 31, 1938; children: Nina, Paul, Laura. BA, Hunter Coll., 1931, ScD (hon.), 1984; MA, Columbia U., 1932, PhD, 1938; ScD (hon.), Women's Med. Coll., 1966, Radcliffe Coll., 1978, Washington U., St. Louis, 1981, Brandeis U., 1984; Hunter Coll., 1984; ScD (hon.), U. Pa., Phila., 1984, U. N.C., 1985; PhD (hon.), Weizmann Inst. Sci., Israel, 1988; ScD (hon.), U. Miami, 1990. Rsch. asst. biochemistry George Washington U. Sch. Medicine, 1937-38; rsch. assoc. Cornell Med. Coll., 1938-46, Washington U. Sch. Medicine, 1946-58; assoc. prof. biol. chemistry Washington U., 1958-60; assoc. prof. biophysics and phys. biochemistry U. Pa. Med. Sch., 1960-61, prof., 1961-71, prof. biochemistry and biophysics, 1971-82; emerita, 1982—; Benjamin Rush prof. physiol. chemistry U. Pa. Med. Sch., 1978-82; sr. mem. Inst. Cancer Research, Phila., 1982-85; chancellor's vis. prof. biophysics Berkeley U., 1982; vis. prof. biol. chemistry Johns Hopkins U. Med. Sch., 1985-91; research assoc. Harvard U. Med. Sch., 1950-51; established investigator Am. Heart Assn., 1953-59, career investigator, 1964-78. Editorial bd. jour. Biol. Chemistry, 1958-63, 67-72. Recipient Hall of Fame award Hunter Coll., 1973, Disting. Alumni award, 1975, Cresson medal Franklin Inst., 1975, award Internat. Assn. Women Biochemists, 1979, Nat. Medal Sci., 1982, Chandler medal Columbia U., 1986, Disting. Svc. award Coll. Physicians, 1987, Women in Sci. award N.Y. Acad. Sci., 1992, Gov.'s award for excellence in sci., Pa., 1993, Founders medal Magnetic Resonance in Biology, 1994, Stein-Moore award Protein Soc., 1997, Oesper award U. Cin., 1999; Humboldt award, Germany, 1980. Mem. NAS, Am. Philos. Soc. (v.p. 1994—), Am. Chem. Soc. (Garvan medal 1963, Remsen award Md. sect. 1988, chmn. divsn. biol. chemistry 1975-76), Harvey Soc., Am. Soc. Biol. Chemists (pres. 1978-79), Am. Biophys. Soc., Am. Acad. Arts and Scis., Inst. de Biologie Physico-Chemique (fgn.), Phi Beta Kappa, Sigma Xi, Iota Sigma Pi (hon. nat. mem. 1988). Office: U Pa Med Sch Dept Biochemistry & Biophys Philadelphia PA 19104-6089

COHN, MURRAY STEVEN, information technology administrator; b. Phila., Nov. 14, 1948; s. Louis and Norma (Dichter) C.; m. Marcia Lisa Feinberg, June 3, 1979 (div. 1995); m. Ilene Rae Brand, Oct. 20, 1996; children: Tobin, Corbin. BS, U. Del., 1970; MS, Pa. State U., 1972, PhD, 1975. Fellow in biochemistry NIH, Bethesda, Md., 1975-79; from toxicologist to supervisor U.S. Consumer Product Safety Commn., Bethesda, 1979—, info. tech mgr., 1995, Webmaster, 1996—; co-chair formaldehyde subgroup Interagy. Com. Indoor Air Quality, Washington, 1983-84. Referee McLean (Va.) Youth Soccer, 1996—. Avocations: soccer, bridge, boating. Office: US Consumer Product Safety Commn 4330 E West Hwy Bethesda MD 20814-4408

COHN, NATHAN, lawyer; b. Charleston, S.C., Jan. 20, 1918; s. Samuel and Rose (Baron) C.; 1 son, Norman; m. Carolyn Venturini, May 18, 1970. J.D., San Francisco Law Sch., 1947. Bar: Calif. 1947, U.S. Supreme Ct. 1957. Pvt. practice law, San Francisco, 1947—; judge pro tem Mcpl. Ct., Superior Ct. Mem. Calif. State Recreation Commn., 1965-68; former mem. Democratic State Central Com. Served to 1st lt. USAF, 1950-55. Fellow Am. Bd. Criminal Lawyers (past pres. and founder), Am. Bd. Trial Advs. (diplomate, chpt. pres. 1984), Internat. Acad. of Law and Sci., San Francisco Trial Lawyers Assn. (past pres.), Criminal Trial Lawyers Assn. No. Calif., Irish-Israeli-Italian Soc. (co-pres., co-founder), Internat. Footprinters Assn. (chpt. 1 San Francisco), Regular Vets. Assn., Roundtable, Calamari Club, Godfather Club, Press Club (life), Lawyers Club of San Francisco, Masons (32 degree), Shriners, South of Market Boys, Ancient Order Hibernians Am. (hon. life). Jewish. Columnist San Francisco Progress, 1982-86; condr. and author seminars in field. Office: 2107 Van Ness Ave Ste 200 San Francisco CA 94109

COHN, SCOTT, television news correspondent; b. Chgo., Feb. 8, 1960; s. Daniel Harris and Lillian Liselotte (Klopstock) C.; m. Jessica Elizabeth Simonson, Nov. 23, 1985; children: Nathan George, Justin Reid. BA, U. Wis., 1981. Reporter WYEN Radio, Des Plaines, Ill., 1978; reporter, news anchor Wis. Pub. Radio, Madison, 1978-81; reporter, anchor WEAU-TV, WAXX Radio, Eau Claire, Wis., 1981-82, WZZM-TV, Grand Rapids, Mich., 1982-89; corr. CNBC, N.Y.C., 1989-90; chief Medwest corr. CNBC, Chgo., 1990-95, nat. corr., 1995-99; corr. anchor, analyst CNBC, N.Y.C., 1999—. Recipient Citation of Merit, Deadline Club of N.Y., 1994, numerous reporting awards. Mem. Radio-TV News Dirs. Assn. Office: CNBC 2200 Fletcher Ave Fort Lee NJ 07024

COHN, SHERMAN LOUIS, lawyer, educator; b. Erie, Pa., July 21, 1932; s. Jacob and Bella (Kaufman) C.; m. Lucy Diaz, July 5, 1998; children by previous marriage: Ronald Bruce, Jerald Seth, Joshua Biber, Steven David, Leah Sura Guihen. BS in Fgn. Svc. summa cum laude, Georgetown U., 1954, JD, 1957, LLM, 1960, M of Acupuncture (hon.), 1993. Bar: Va. 1957, D.C. 1957, Md. 1978. Law clk. to Judge Burton R. Laub Erie County Ct., Pa., 1955, Walton H. Hamilton, 1957, Judge Charles Fahy, U.S. Ct. of Appeals for D.C. Circuit, 1957-58; staff atty. Appellate sect. Civil div. Dept. Justice, Washington, 1958-62, asst. chief, 1962-65; prof. law Georgetown U. Law Center, Washington, 1965—, dir. continuing legal edn., 1977-84; lectr. Cath. U. Law Sch., 1963-65; vis. prof. Am. U. Law Sch., 1969-78, 92-93, 94-95; adminstr. Preview of U.S. Supreme Ct. Cases, 1975-79; cons., litigation counsel Select Com. on Presdl. Campaign Activities U.S. Senate, 1973-74; mem. Jud. Conf. D.C. Circuit, 1965-70, 71-73, 75, 77-78, 86, Jud. Conf. D.C. Ct. Appeals, 1979-81; reporter Nat. Conf. on Appellate Justice, San Diego, 1976. Contbr. articles to profl. jours. Trustee Am. Inns of Ct. Found., pres., 1985-96; pres. Charles Fahy Am. Inn of Ct., 1985-86, Traditional Acupuncture Found., 1984-88; chmn. Nat. Accredited Commn. Schs. and Colls. Acupuncture and Oriental Medicine, 1983-93; chmn. bd. dirs. Tai Hsuan Found., 1998T, Traditional Acupuncture Inst., 1998—; bd. dirs. Acupuncture and Oriental Medicine Alliance, 1998—. Recipient A. Sherman Christensen award Am. Inns of Ct., 1990, Younger Fed. Lawyer award for outstanding service to U.S., 1964, Civil Justice award Am. Bd. Trial Advocates, 1993. Mem. ABA, Fed. Bar Assn. (pres. D.C. chpt.), D.C. Bar Assn., Va. State Bar, Am. Law Inst., Internat. Assn. Jewish Lawyers and Jurists (pres. Am. sect. 1983-87, dep. pres. internat. 1985-91), Soc. Am. Law Tchrs., Georgetown U. Alumni Assn. (chmn. alumni fund 1985-87, Presdl. citation 1978, 87, John Carroll award 1980). Lodge: B'nai B'rith. Office: Georgetown U Law Ctr 600 New Jersey Ave NW Washington DC 20001-2075

COHN, STEVEN FREDERICK, sociology educator, consultant; b. Chgo., Sept. 5, 1939; s. William Wolf and Sylvia Ann (Wechsler) C.; m. Kathleen Marie Cusick, May 8, 1968 (div. Jan. 1974); 1 child, Iain Cusick-Cohn. BA, Dartmouth Coll., 1961; PhD, Columbia U., 1975. Lectr. U. Strathclyde, Glasgow, Scotland, 1968-69, U. Glasgow, 1969-71; asst. prof. U. Maine, Orono, 1971-77; policy analyst NSF, Washington, 1978-79; assoc. prof. U. Maine, Orono, 1980-85, prof., 1986—; cons. ACTION, Washington, 1970-72, The Royal Soc., London, 1984. Contbr. articles to profl. jours. Fulbright fellow Coun. for Internat. Exch. Scholars, 1984. Mem. Am. Sociol. Assn. (sect. program com. 1995-96), Ea. Soc. Assn. (publs. com. mem. 1990), Phi Beta Kappa. Jewish. Home: 99 N Main St Orono ME 04473-1733 Office: U Maine 201 Fernald Orono ME 04469

COHN, STEVEN LAWRENCE, internist, medical educator; b. Jersey City, N.J., May 23, 1952. AB, Rutgers U., 1973, MS in Physiology, 1974; MD, U. Monterrey, Mex., 1978. Diplomate Am. Bd. Internal Medicine. Intern then resident Downstate Med. Ctr., 1979-82, Kings County Hosp., 1979-82, Bklyn. VA Hosp., 1979-82; dir. med. consultation svc. Kings County Hosp., Bklyn., 1986—; acting chief divsn. internal medicine SUNY Health Sci. Ctr. Univ. Hosp., Bklyn., 1991—, assoc. med. dir. quality assurance, 1993—, clin. assoc. prof. medicine, 1996—. Contbr.: Surgery '89, 1989; contbr. articles to profl. jours. Fellow ACP; mem. Soc. Gen. Internal Medicine, N.Y. Heart Assn. Office: SUNY Health Sci Ctr Box 68 470 Clarkson Ave Brooklyn NY 11203-2012

COHN, THEODORE ELLIOT, optometry educator, vision scientist; b. Highland Park, Ill., Sept. 5, 1941; s. Nathan and Marjorie (Kurtzon) C.; m. Barbara Adler, Nov. 29, 1975; children: Avery Simon, Adrienne Leah, Harris Samuel. SB in Elec. Engring., MIT, 1963; MS in Bioengring., U. Mich., 1965, MA in Math., 1966, PhD in Bioengring., 1969. Asst. prof. U. Calif., Berkeley, 1970-76, assoc. prof., 1976-84, prof., 1985—; vis. fellow John Curtin Med. Sch., Australian Nat. U., Canberra, 1977; vis. scholar U. Calif., San Diego, 1981-90. Author, editor: Visual Detection, 1993. Bd. dirs. Berkeley-Richmond Jewish Cmty. Ctr., 1995—. Fellow Optical Soc. Am. (chairvision tech. group 1984-86); mem. IEEE (sr. mem.), Soc. Neurosci., Sigma Xi. Office: U Calif Sch Optometry 360 Minor Hall Berkeley CA 94720-2020

COHN, VICTOR EDWARD, journalist; b. Mpls., Aug. 4, 1919; s. Louis and Lillian (Bessler) C.; m. Marcella Rigler, Aug. 30, 1941 (dec. Sept. 1980); children: Jeffrey, Deborah, Phyllis. AB, U. Minn., 1941; DS (hon.), Georgetown U., 1986. Editor Minn. Daily, U. Minn., 1940-41; desk man Mpls. Star, 1941-42; copyreader Mpls. Tribune, 1946, reporter, 1946-47, sci. reporter, 1947-67; sci. editor Washington Post, 1968-72, sci.-med. reporter, 1972-84, sr. writer, columnist, 1984-93; incorporator and dir. Coun. Advancement Sci. Writing, 1960-96, fellow, 1996—; vis. lectr. U. Minn. Sch. Journalism, 1966-67; vis. fellow Harvard U. Sch. Pub. Health, 1978, 84, 96—; vis. scholar Johns Hopkins U., 1990-91; rsch. fellow Georgetown U., 1993-94; fellow Am. Statistical Assn., 1994-96. Author: 1999 Our Hopeful Future, 1956, Sister Kenny: The Woman Who Challenged the Doctors, 1976, News & Numbers, 1989, Reporting on Risk, 1990. With USNR, 1942-46. Recipient Disting. Reporting award Sigma Delta Chi Found. of Soc. Profl. Journalists, 1952, 56, 59; citations for service to health Minn. Med. Assn., 1955, Minn. Pub. Health Assn., 1966, Mid-Atlantic chpt. Am. Med. Writers Assn., 1976, 80, March of Dimes Birth Defects Found., 1984, 96, Group Health Assn. of Washington, 1990, D.C. Med. Soc., 1995; Albert Lasker med. journalism award, 1958; Howard W. Blakeslee award Am. Heart Assn., 1963; James T. Grady award Am. Chem. Soc., 1971; Nat. Press Club Consumer Reporting award, 1974; Disting. Achievement award U. Minn., 1978; citation for sci. reporting Exploratorium of San Francisco, 1978; Journalism award Am. Acad. Family Physicians, 1982; Nat. Media award Am. Psychol. Assn., 1983, Consumer Journalism award Penney/U. Mo., 1986, 92; Med. Media award Friends of Nat. Libr. of Medicine, 1995. Fellow AAAS (George Westinghouse award 1951, 59); mem. Nat. Assn. Sci. Writers (pres. 1961-62, Sci.-in-Soc. reporting award 1973, 91), Phi Beta Kappa (Disting. Citizen award 1966). Jewish. Office: 500 23rd St NW Ste B301 Washington DC 20037-2828

COHODES, ELI AARON, publisher; b. Iron Mountain, Mich., Sept. 12, 1927; s. Joseph Harry and Esther Ida (Albert) C.; m. Phyllis Hersh, Jan. 4, 1953; children: Stephen Eliot, David Bruce, Mitchell Joseph, Paul Andrew (dec.). BA, Harvard U., 1950. Assoc. editor Hosp. Mgmt. mag., 1953-54; mng. editor Trustee mag., 1957-59, Modern Hosp. mag., 1959-63; editor Nation's Schs. mag., Chgo., 1963-68; chmn. editorial adv. bd., columnist Nation's Schs. mag., 1968-75; v.p. Instructional Dynamics, Inc., Chgo., 1968-70; chmn. Teach'em, Chgo, 1970—; pres. Bonus Books, Inc., Chgo., 1985—; lectr. profl. writing U. Chgo., 1959-63. Co-author: Planning Flexible Learning Places, 1977; mem. editorial bd. Coll. and Univ. Bus. mag, 1973-75. With AUS, 1945-46. Home: 37 Turnbull Woods Ct Highland Park IL 60035-5135 Office: 160 E Illinois St Chicago IL 60611-3880

COHON, JARED L., university administrator. Pres. Carnegie Mellon U., Pitts. Office: Carnegie Mellon Univ 5000 Forbes Ave Pittsburgh PA 15213-3890 Office: Nuclear Waste Technical Review Board 2300 Clarendon Blvd Ste 1300 Arlington VA 22201-3351*

COIA, ARTHUR A., labor union executive; m. Joanne Coia; 2 children. Student, Providence Coll., Boston U. Bar: U.S. Supreme Ct. Various positions as mem. and laborer Laborer's Internat. Union N.Am., Washington, mgr. New Eng. & Ea. Can. region, bus. mgr. R.I. dist. coun., gen. sec.-treas., 1989-93, gen. pres., 1993—; labor lawyer; v.p. exec. coun. AFL-CIO, mem. blue ribbon com. on health care reform, governing bd. of pres. bldg. and constrn. trades dept., mem. exec. coun. fedn.'s metal trade dept. and pub. employees dept., chmn. organizing com.; trustee AFL-CIO Housing Investment Trust, Union Labor Life Ins. Co., Asian-Am. Free Labor Inst.; co-chmn. Laborers-AGC Edn. and Tng. Trust Fund, Laborer's Nat. Pension Fund, Laborer's Polit. League; bd. dirs. Internat. Labor Rights Edn. Rsch. Fund. Fin. bd. dirs. Dem. Nat. Com.; bd. trustees Providence Performing Arts Ctr., Providence Coll. Adv. Coun.; bd. dirs. Italian Am. Dem. Leadership Coun. Named Samaritan of Yr., Samaritans of Washington, 1994; recipient Labor Social Responsibility award Martin Luther King Ctr., Atlanta, 1996, Human Rights award Nat. Conf. Black Mayors/World Conf. Mayors, 1996. Office: Laborers Internat Union N Am 905 16th St NW Washington DC 20006-1703

COIL, CAROLYN CHANDLER, educational consultant; b. Washington, Aug. 22, 1943; d. William Chandler and Charlotte Eleanor (Lanhardt) Hendrix; m. Paul Douglas Coil; children: Paul William, Johnston Allan. BA, U. Md., 1965; MA, U. South Fla., 1985, MEd, 1990. Cert. gifted tchr., secondary tchr., ednl. leadership tchr., Ga. Tchr. Prince Georges County Sch., Upper Marlboro, Md., 1965-71, Ledyard (Conn.) Pub. Schs., 1971-73; insvc. coord. Ednl. TV for S.E. Ohio, Athens, 1977-81; learning resources specialist Fla. Diagnostic and Learning Rsch., Bartow, 1981-92; ednl. cons. Creative Cons. and Tng., Lilburn, Ga., 1992—. Author: Motivating Underachievers, 1992, Becoming An Achiever, 1994, Eye on Japan, 1995, Eye on Australia, 1995, Teaching Tools for the 21st Century, 1997, Celebrations, 1998, Encouraging Achievement, 1999. Mem. exec. bd. New Beginnings for Youth, Orlando, Fla.; mem. cons. commn. Episcopal Diocese of Atlanta. Avocations: travel, reading. Home: 4141 Wash Lee Ct SW Lilburn GA 30047-7440 Office: Pieces of Learning PO Box 340667 Dayton OH 45434-0667

COIL, CHARLES RAY, printing executive, managed healthcare executive; b. Dallas, June 23, 1940; s. John Charles Jr. and Dixie W. (Riggs) C.; m. Sue Gail Lewis, Jan. 20, 1968; children: Christopher Ryan, Kimberly Ann. BBA, So. Meth. U., 1962. With Provident Life & Accident Ins. Co., Chattanooga, 1962-88; pres., chief exec. officer North Tex. Healthcare Network, Irving, Tex., 1988-98; chmn. bd., pres. Preferred Network Strategies, Allen, Tex., 1996—; pres., CEO, chmn. bd. dirs. Advance Labal & Tag, Inc., McKinney, Tex., 1998—. Republican. Methodist. Avocation: family.

COIN, SHEILA REGAN, organization and management development consultant; b. Columbus, Ohio, Feb. 17, 1942; d. James Daniel Regan and Jean (Hodgson) Cook; m. Tasso H. Coin, Sept. 17, 1967 (div.); children: Tasso, Alison Regan. BS, U. Iowa, 1964. RN Staff nurse VA Hosp., Boston, 1964-66; field rep. ARC, Chgo., 1966-67, chief nurse, 1967; asst. div. dir. Am. Hosp. Assn., sec. Am. Soc. Hosp. Dirs. Nursing, Chgo., 1967-69; owner Coin & Assocs., Chgo., 1975-77; ptnr., orgn. devel. and performance mgmt. sr. cons. Coin, Newell & Assocs., Chgo., 1976-96, Buck Cons., Inc., Washington, 1996—; instr. dept. continuing edn. Loyola U., Chgo., 1975-77, Rock Valley Coll. Mgmt. Inst., Rockford, Ill., 1978-80, Ill. Central Coll. Inst. Personal and Profl. Devel., Peoria, 1979-85, Triton Coll. Continuing Edn., River Grove, Ill., 1983-86, No. Ill. U. Continuing Edn., DeKalb, 1983-86; mem. editorial bd. Tng. Today mag., 1992-94, assoc. editor, 1994-96. Vol. Art Inst., Chgo., 1968-69; mem. Chgo. Beautiful Com., 1968-73; chmn. Mayor Daley's Chgo. Beautiful Awards Project, 1972; mem. jr. bd. Girl Scouts Assn., Chgo., 1975-76; mem. jr. governing bd. Chgo. Symphony Orch., 1971-81, pres., 1977-78; governing mem. Orchestral Assn., Chgo., 1977-81; bd. dirs. Mid-Am. chpt. ARC, Chgo., 1979-81, 91-94, vice chmn. 1986-89, mem. planning & evaluation subcom., 1991-96, chmn. quality mgmt. steering com., 1992-94, bd. dirs. Chgo. dist., 1981-89, chmn. fin. devel. com., 1982-85, vice chmn. dist. bd., 1986-89; bd. dirs. Ill. chpt. Lupus Found. Am., 1991-93; bd. dirs., mem. Survive Alive House Found., 1989-96; dir. Com. for Thalossemia Chgo. Bd., 1981-82; mem. Women's bd. Nat. Com. Prevention Child Abuse, Chgo., 1981-82; mem. State of Ill. Disabled Persons Adv. Coun., 1988-97; academic specialist in mgmt. devel. U.S. Info. Agy., 1994. Mem. ASTD (exec. com. of mgmt. devel. profl. practice area 1992-95), Christ Child Soc., Ill. State Soc., Washington Human Resources Forum. Office: Buck Consultants Inc 1801 K St NW Ste 205L Washington DC 20006-1301

COIR, MARK ALLEN, archivist; b. Detroit, Dec. 15, 1951; s. Donald W. and Alma B.M. (Gnosa) C.; m. Marlene Wolfe, June 17, 1978; children: Alexis, Elizabeth. BA, Wayne State U., Detroit, 1975, MLS, 1977. Libr. Detroit Pub. Libr., 1977-82; prin., v.p. Info. Unltd., Detroit, 1982-86; archivist Cranbrook Edn. Cmty., Bloomfield Hills, Mich., 1986—; cons. archivist Burroughs Corp., Detroit, 1982-86. Author: History of the Detroit Racquet Club, 1984; editor: Saarinen/Swanson Reunion, 1997; contbr. articles to profl. jours. Mem. Detroit Tercentenary Com., 1996—. Recipient Josehans scholarship Detroit Pub. Libr., 1976. Mem. Mich. Archival Assn. (pres. 1996-98), Midwest Archives Conf., Soc. Am. Archivists, Mich. Alliance Cultural Conservation (dir., v.p. 1996-97), Phi Beta Kappa. Democrat. Avocations: violin playing, swimming, nordic skiing, travel. Home: 1221 N Woodward Ave Unit 716 Bloomfield Hills MI 48304-2836 Office: Cranbrook Archives PO Box 801 Bloomfield Hills MI 48303-0801

COIT, R. KEN, financial planner; b. L.A., Aug. 26, 1943; s. Roger L. and Thelma D.C.; BS, U. Ariz., 1967; MBA, Pepperdine U., 1981; m. Donna M. Schemanske, Oct. 8, 1977; children: Kristin M., Shannon, Darren, Lauryn. Prin. Coit Fin. Group, 1981; mem. adj. faculty Coll. Fin. Planning,

Denver, 1978-79; pres. Walnut Creek adv. bd. Summit Bank, 1987-95, Sequoia Equities Securities Corp., Walnut Creek, Calif.; bd. dirs. R.H. Phillips Winery; mem. adv. bd. Mt. Diablo Nat. Bank, 1996—. Mem. dean's adv. bd. Pepperdine U., 1988-91; nat. bd. advisor Coll. Pharmacy U. Ariz.; bd. dirs., chmn. investment com. East Cmty. Found., 1994—. Recipient Outstanding Alumnus award Pepperdine U. Sch. Bus. and Mgmt., 1986. Mem. Internat. Assn. Fin. Planners (chpt. pres. 1978-79), Inst. Cert. Fin. Planners, East Bay Gourmet Club, Blackhawk Country Club. Office: 1655 N Main St Ste 270 Walnut Creek CA 94596-4642

COKE, C(HAUNCEY) EUGENE, consulting company executive, scientist, educator, author; b. Toronto, Ont., Can; s. Chauncey Eugene and Edith May (Redman) C.; m. Sally B. Tolmie, June 12, 1941. BSc with honors, U. Man., MSc magna cum laude; MA, U. Toronto; postgrad., Yale U.; PhD, U. Leeds, Eng., 1938. Dir. rsch. Courtaulds (Can.) Ltd., 1939-42; dir. R & D Guaranty Dyeing & Finishing Co., 1946-48; various exec. R & D positions Courtaulds (Can.) Ltd., Montreal, 1948-59, dir. R & D; mem. exec. com. Hart-Fibres Co., 1959-62; tech. dir. textile chem. Drew Chem. Corp., 1962-63; dir. new products fibers div. Am. Cynamid Co., 1963-68, dir. applications devel., 1968-70; pres. Coke & Assoc., Cons., Ormond Beach, Fla., 1970-78, chmn., 1978—; pres. Aqua Vista Corp. Inc., 1971-74; vis. rsch. prof. Stetson U., 1979—; internat. authority on man-made fibers; guest lectr. Sir George Williams Coll., Montreal, 1949-59; chmn. Can. adv. com. on Internat. Standards Orgn. Tech. Com. 38, 1951-58; mem. Can. Standards Assn., 1958-59; del. Textile Tech. Fedn. Can., 1948-57, bd. dirs., 1957-59. Contbr. articles to Can., U.S., Brit., Australian profl. jours. with translations into Japanese. Vice chmn. North Peninsula adv. bd. Volusia County Coun., 1975-78; mem. Halifax Area Study Commn., 1972-74, Volusia County Elections Bd., 1974-94; bd. dirs. Coun. Assns. North Peninsula, 1972-74, 76-77; pres. Greater Daytona Beach Rep. Mens Club, 1972-75; pres. Rep. Mens Club, 1972-75; pres. Rep. President's Forum, 1976-78, v.p., 1978-81. Recipient Bronze medal Can. Assn. Textile Colourists and Chemists, 1963. Fellow AAAS, Royal Soc. Chemistry (Gt. Britain, life), Soc. Dyers and Colourists (Gt. Britain), Inst. Textile Sci. (co-founder, 3d pres.), Chem. Inst. Can. (life, coun. 1958-61), Am. Inst. Chemists, N.J. Acad. Sci.; mem. Am. Assn. Textile Tech. (life, past pres., bronze medal), Can. Assn. Textile Colourists and Chemists (hon. life, past pres., bronz medal), N.Y. Acad. Scis. (life), U.S. Metric Assn. (life), Chemists Club. Home: 26 Aqua Vista Dr Ormond Beach FL 32176-3109 Office: Coke & Assoc Cons Ormond By The Sea Ormond Beach FL 32176

COKE, FRANK VAN DEREN, museum director, photographer; b. Lexington, Ky., July 4, 1921; s. Sterling Dent and Elisabeth (Van Deren) C.; m. Eleanor Barton, 1943 (div. 1980); children: Sterling Van Deren, Eleanor Browning; m. Joan Gillberry Morgan, 1983. BA, U. Ky., 1956; MFA, Ind. U., 1958; postgrad., Harvard U.; LHD (hon.), San Francisco Acad. of Art, 1986. With Van Deren Hardware Co., Lexington, 1946-56; pres. Van Deren Hardware Co., 1953-56; asst. prof. art U. Fla., 1958-61; assoc. prof. art Ariz. State U., 1961-62; prof., dir. art mus. U. N.Mex., 1962-66, chmn. dept., 1963-70, dir. art mus., 1973-79; dep. dir., then dir. Internat. Mus. Photography, Rochester, N.Y., 1970-72; dir. dept. photography San Francisco Mus. Modern Art, 1979-87; bd. dirs. Internat. Folk Art Found., U. N.Mex. Art Mus., Georgia O'Keeffe Mus., Santa Fe, Mus. Fine Arts, Santa Fe; chmn. Albuquerque Fine Arts Adv. Com.; cons. in field; Disting. vis. prof. art Ariz. State U., 1988-91. Author: books and catalogues, including Taos and Santa Fe; The Artist's Environment, 1882-1942, 1963, The Painter and the Photograph, 1972, One Hundred Years of Photographic History, 1975, Avant-Garde Photography in Germany, 1919-1939, 1981, Faces Photographed, 1984, Joel-Peter Witkin, 1985, Photography: A Facet of Modernism, 1986, Secular and Sacred: Photographs of Mexico by Van Deren Coke, 1992, Forecast: Shifts in Direction, 1994. Served as officer USNR, 1942-45. Recipient Photography Internat. award, 1955, 56 (2), Modern Photography Internat. award, 1956, U.S. Camera Internat. award, 1957, 58, 60, New Talent USA Art in Am. award, 1960, Gov.'s award State of N.Mex., 1986, Educator of Yr. Leica Medal of Excellence, 1987, Joseph Sudek medal Ministry of Culture of the Czech Socialist Republic, 1989, Disting. Internat. Career in Photography award, 1992, Internat. Photomeeting, Rep. San Marino, Peer award The Friends of Photography, San Francisco, 1992, Distinction in Art Adminstrn. award Nat. Coun. Art Adminstrs., 1997; Guggenheim fellow, 1975; Fulbright teaching fellow U. Auckland, N.Z., 1989. Mem. Coll. Art Assn. (bd. dirs. 1973-77, 88-92), Soc. Photog. Edn. (bd. dirs. 1965-70).

COKELET, GILES ROY, biomedical engineering educator; b. N.Y.C., Jan. 7, 1932; s. Roy S. and Anna M. (Trippel) C.; m. Sarah Drew, June 15, 1963; children—Becky, Bradford. B.S., Calif. Inst. Tech., 1957, M.S., 1958; Sc.D., MIT, 1963. Research engr. Dow Chem. Co., Williamsburg, Va., 1958-60; asst. prof. Calif. Inst. Tech., Pasadena, 1964-68; assoc. prof. Mont. State U., Bozeman, 1969-76, prof., 1976-78; prof. U. Rochester, N.Y., 1978-98; rsch. prof. Mont. State U., Bozeman, 1998—. Contbr. articles to profl. jours. Served with U.S. Army, 1954-55, Japan. Recipient Sr. U.S. Scientist award Humboldt-Stiftung, Bonn, Fed. Republic Germany, 1981-82, 88. Fellow AAAS; mem. Biomed. Engring. Soc., Microcirculatory Soc., Am. Inst. Med. and Biol. Engring., Soc. Rheology, No. Am. Soc. Biorheology, Internat. Soc. Biorheology (pres., Poiseville medal 1999), European Microcirculation Soc. Avocations: stamp collecting; hiking. Office: Mont State U Dept Chem Engring Bozeman MT 59717

COKER, CHARLES WESTFIELD, diversified manufacturing company executive; b. Florence, S.C., 1933; m. Joan F. Sasser; 6 children. BA, Princeton U., 1955; MBA, Harvard U., 1957. With Sonoco Products Co., Hartsville, S.C., 1958—, v.p. adminstrn., 1961-67, v.p. gen. mgmt., corp. planning and fin., from 1967, exec. v.p., 1966-70, pres., chief exec. officer, dir., 1970-90, chmn. bd., chief exec. officer, 1990-99, now bd. dirs.; bd. dirs. Carolina Power and Light Co., NCNB Corp., Springs Industries Inc., Sara Lee Corp. Past pres. Pee Dee Area Coun. Boy Scouts Am.; bd. dirs. Hollings Cancer Ctr. 2d lt. USAR, 1957-63. Recipient Silver Beaver award Boy Scouts Am. Mem. Palmetto Bus. Forum, Rotary (past pres. Hartsville). Office: Sonoco Products Co N 2nd St Hartsville SC 29550-3722*

COKER, CHARLOTTE NOEL, political activist; b. New Orleans, Dec. 28, 1930; d. Cecil Eugene and Esta Reed (Williams) Mahaffey; m. Rainey Morris Coker, Nov. 17, 1950; children: Patricia A. Coker Bracey, Carol J. Coker Johnson, Teresa J., Robert M. Student X-ray technician tng., St. Mary's Hosp., Port Arthur, Tex., 1947-48; X-ray therapy, Emory U., 1949. Precinct committeewoman Spokane County Dem. Party, Spokane, Wash., 1970—; 6th legis. dist. leader Spokane County Dem. Party, 1973-74, 77-78; state committeewoman Spokane County Dem. Central Com., 1975-76, 79-80, 81-82; vice chmn. Wash. State Dem. Com., Seattle, 1981; region 6 dir. Wash. State Fedn. Dem. Women's Clubs, 1979-80, state dir., 1981-85; mem. Dem. Nat. Com., 1992—, mem. exec. com., 1995—; tour guide Wash. Ho. of Reps., Olympia, 1975; aide Office of Gov. Dixy Lee Ray, Spokane, 1978-80. Mem. Spokane Quality of Life Coun., 1975-77; mem. Spokane Task Force for Cmty. Devel. Funds, 1978. Mem. Spokane Fedn. Women's Orgns. (pres. 1985—), Nat. Assn. Parliamentarians, Nat. Fedn. Dem. Women, Jane Jefferson Dem. Club (v.p. 1979). Avocations: plate collecting, bridge, public affairs. Home: 2215 E 45th Ave Spokane WA 99223-6466*

COKER, DONALD WILLIAM, economic, management, banking, evaluation & healthcare consultant; b. Mobile, Ala., Nov. 26, 1945; s. William Mack and Gloria Antoinette (Croker) C.; m. Linda Carol Sandlin, July 12, 1969; children: Caroline Tiffany, Brittany Blaire. BA, U. Ala., 1968, postgrad., 1968; postgrad, U. Houston, 1973, Spring Hill Coll., 1996. Approved comml. arbitrator Am. Arbitration Assn. Trust mortgage officer AmSouth Bank, Mobile, 1968-72; sr. loan officer Gibraltar Savs., Houston, 1972-73; mortgage officer, asst. treas. Citicorp Real Estate, Houston, 1973-74; comml. loan officer M Bank-Houston, 1974-77; regional mgr. Comml. Credit Co., 1977-83, Ford Motor Credit, Houston, 1983-84; sr. v.p., mgr. lending and mortgage banking First Fed. Savs., San Antonio, 1984-85; exec. v.p. Home Savs., Houston, 1985-86; also bd. dirs. Home Savs.; supr. banking Tex. Savs. & Loan Dept., Houston, 1986-88; mng. dir. Coker Consulting, Mobile, 1986—, Corp. Intelligence and Analysis, Mobile, 1994—; mng. dir. Present Value Econs., 1989—, Capstone Computer, 1990—, Capstone Ednl. Consulting, 1990—; cons. Prentice-Hall Pub., IRS, FDIC, Resolution Trust Corp.; cons. to fin. instns., attys., corps. and govt. agys.; legis. and govtl. cons.; nat. healthcare and profl. practice valuation cons.; expert witness on valuation, econ., fin., real estate and banking. Author: Complete Guide to Income Property Financing, 1984, Self-Management, 1985; editor: Complete Real Estate Computer Workbook, 1986, The Complete Loan Officers' Handbook, 1999; contbr. numerous articles to profl. jours. and Internet sites. Trustee Katy Ind. Sch. Dist., Houston, 1987; treas. Nottingham Country Civic Club, Houston; precinct leader, del. and dep. voters registrar Rep. party. Mem. Nat. Assn. of State Savs. and Loan Suprs., Tex. Mortgage Bankers' Assn., Am. Bankers Assn., U.S. Savs. & Loan League, Houston C. of C. (bus. devel. com.). Republican. Episcopalian. Clubs: Sweetwater Country. Home and Office: PO Box 91182 Mobile AL 36691-1182

COKER, GEORGINA HARRIS, elementary education educator; b. Chgo., May 6, 1947; d. George Jones and Berta Manning (Hill) Harris; m. Billy Howard Coker, Aug. 13, 1985; 1 child, Christine Elizabeth. BS, U. Memphis, 1970, MEd, 1975. Profl. lic. master career level II tchr. cert. Tenn. Dept. Edn. Tchr. Memphis City Schs., 1970—; kindergarten tchr. Hamilton Accelerated Sch., Memphis, 1986—; Earth day coord. The Childrens Mus. Memphis, 1994—; kindergarten facilitator Family Life Edn. Pub. Hearings, Memphis City Schs., 1994—, elem. sch. sci. fair judge, 1996—; team leader, supervising tchr. early childhood edn. U. Memphis, 1996—. Adult mem. Tenn.-Ark.-Miss. Girl Scout Coun., Memphis, 1994—, Memphis Zool. Soc., Calvery Episcopal Ch., Memphis, 1996—. Recipient Simply the Best award Memphis Assn. for Edn. Young Children, 1993, Amb. award The Edn. Ctr., 1994; Gov.'s Acad. for Tchrs. of Writing grantee Tenn. State Dept. Edn., Knoxville, 1996. Mem. NEA, Nat. Assn. for the Edn. Young Children, So. Early Childhood Assn., Tenn. Edn. Assn., Memphis Edn. Assn., Memphis Early Childhood Assn., Alpha Delta Kappa (Psi chpt. pres. 1975—). Democrat. Avocations: piano, Girl Scouting, gardening. Fax: 901-775-7827. Home: 1887 Manila Ave Memphis TN 38114-1744 Office: Hamilton Elem Sch 1378 Ethlyn Ave Memphis TN 38106-6099

COKER, MARY SHANNON, surgical nurse; b. Pasadena, Tex., May 30, 1947; d. James Edward and Ruby Dee (Langford) Shannon; m. Sherman Leigh Coker, Jan. 25, 1987; children: John Lynn Brinkley, Jamie Leigh Brinkley Kelley, Amanda Renee Coker, Roy Leigh Coker. AAS, Lee Coll., Baytown, Tex., 1990; BSN, U. Tex., Galveston, 1998. Insulator Daniel Constrn., Greenville, S.C., 1985-87; patient care attendant Humana Hosp., Baytown, 1988; staff perioperative nurse Meth. Hosp., Houston, 1989-91, Bay Coast Med. Ctr., Baytown, Tex., 1991-98; staff labor and delivery nurse Lyndon Baines Johnson Hosp., 1999—. Mem. Assn. Operating Room Nurses, Phi Theta Kappa, Sigma Theta Tau. Home: 2111 Utah St Baytown TX 77520-6153

COKER, SALLY JO, sociology educator; b. Springfield, Ill., Aug. 24, 1956; d. Charles D. and Barbara J. (Bailey) Bozeman; m. Joel Dwain Coker, Nov. 7, 1974; 1 child, Corey Alan. BS, U. Houston, 1992, MA, 1995. Rsch. asst. to prof. psychology U. Houston, 1991; student asst. to dean adminstrn. Lee Coll., Baytown, Tex., 1992; instr. sociology, Am. minorities, social problems, marriage and family, San Jacinto C.C., Pasadena, Tex., 1995—; instr. sociology, Am. minorities, social problems, marriage and family Alvin (Tex.) C.C., 1995-97; instr. sociology, Am. minorities, social problems, orgnl. behavior Lee Coll., 1992—; instr. social inequality, prins. of sociology U. Houston, 1999—; human resource mgmt. spkr. H.B. Zachry, Houston, 1995. Mem. AAUP, Am. Sociol. Assn., Tex. C.C. Tchr.'s Assn., Phi Kappa Phi. Democrat. Home: 3607 Trailwood Dr Baytown TX 77521-4835 Office: Lee Coll PO Box 818 Baytown TX 77522-0818

COKER, WILLIAM B., electrical engineer; b. Dumas, Tex., Dec. 2, 1956; s. Oley D. and Betty (Yearwood) C. BSEE, U. Nebr., 1981. Profl. engr. Control engr. Black & Veatch, Overland Park, Ks., 1982-88; electronics engr. Orthman Mfrs., Lexington, Nebr., 1988-92; elec. engr. City of Beatrice, Nebr., 1992—. Patentee in field. Mem. Mayor's Task Force, City of Beatrice. Mem. IEEE, Masons, (master 1996-97, Cryptic Masons master 1996-97, Royal Archmasons high priest 1996-97, Knights Templar comdr. 1996-97), Shriners, Kiwanis, Knight York Cross of Honor (hon.). Achievements include assisting in control panel retrofit at Cooper Nuclear Plant - the first in the U.S. in compliancy with NRC mandates. Office: Beatrice BPW 500 N Commerce St Beatrice NE 68310-1139

COKER, WILLIAM SIDNEY, historian, educator; b. Des Moines, July 18, 1924; s. William McKinnon and Myrtle (Spurgeon) C.; m. Hazel Pauline Gaskin, May 27, 1944 (dec. 1990); children: Judy, Nancy, Elizabeth, Terri; m. Frances Camferdam, April 9, 1992 (dec. 1997). BA with distinction, U. Okla., 1959, PhD, 1965; MA, U. So. Miss., 1962. From asst. to assoc. prof. to U. So. Miss., Hattiesburg, 1966-69; from assoc. prof. to prof. U. West Fla., Pensacola, 1969-87, chmn. dept. history, 1987-91, prof. emeritus, 1992; dir. Papers of Panton, Leslie & Co. U. West Fla., 1973-87. Author: Spanish Censuses of Pensacola, 1981, (with others) Indian Traders of the Southeastern Spanish Borderlands, 1986 (Patrick award 1986, Phi Alpha Theta award 1986), Florida from Beginning to 1992. Recipient Rsch. award Nat. Historic Publs. and Records Commn., 1973-87. Mem. Fla. Hist. Soc. (pres. 1997—). Home: 615 Bayshore Dr Apt 401 Pensacola FL 32507-3565

COKGOR, ILKCAN, neuro-oncologist, neurologist; b. Izmir, Turkey, Mar. 27, 1966; came to U.S., 1993; d. Omer and Tumay Cokgor; m. Haluk Ulubay, Jan. 7, 1998. MD, Hacettepe U., Ankara, Turkey, 1989; postgrad., U. B.C., Vancouver, 1991-93. Diplomate Am. Bd. Psychiatry and Neurology. Rsch. fellow dept. neurosurgery Hacettepe U., Ankara, 1989; gen. practitioner, emergency physician S.S.K. Hosp., Eskisehir, Turkey, 1989-90; resident in neurosurgery Uludag U., Bursa, Turkey, 1990; intern in internal medicine Meridia Huron Hosp., East Cleveland, Ohio, 1993-94; resident in neurology Duke U. Med. Ctr., Durham, N.C., 1994-97; fellow in neuro-oncology, neurology Duke U. Med. Ctr., Durham, 1997-98, vis. assoc. in neuro-oncology, medicine, 1998—. Contbr. articles to profl. jours. Neural Regeneration and Functional Recovery rsch. scholar The Network of Ctrs. of Excellence, 1993. Mem. AMA, Am. Acad. Neurology (scholar ann meeting 1996), Soc. for Neurosci. Home: 113 Rushingwater Dr Cary NC 27513 Office: Duke U Med Ctr Erwin Rd Durham NC 27710

COLACO, JOSEPH P., civil engineer. BS, U. Bombay, 1960; MS, U. Ill., 1962, PhD, 1965. Mem. staff Shalimar Tar Prodn. LTD, 1960-61; sr. structural engr. Skidmore, Owings & Merrill, 1965-69; dir. design computor ops. Ellisor Engrs. Inc., 1969-75; pres. CBM Engrs. Inc., Houston, 1975—; Lectr. Ill. Inst. Tech., Chgo., 1968-69, Rice U., Houston, 1976—, U. Houston, 1978—. Contbr. articles to profl. jours. Mem. Nat. Acad. Engrs., Nat. Soc. Profl. Engrs., Am. Soc. Civil Engrs. (com. chmn. 1991-94), Am. Inst. Steel Construction (special citation award 1973, Archtl. award Excellence 1990), Am. Inst. Architects; fellow Inst. Structural Engrs. (UK chpt.), Am. Concrete Inst. (Maurice Van Buren award 1983). Fax: (713) 629-7772. Office: CBM Engineers Inc 1700 West Loop S Ste 830 Houston TX 77027-3007*

COLAGIOVANNI, JOSEPH ALFRED, JR., lawyer; b. Providence, Dec. 26, 1956; s. Joseph Alfred Sr. and Rosemarie (Giordano) C.; m. Mary Jo Gagliardo, Aug. 9, 1980. AB in Polit. Sci. and Philosophy, Brown U., 1979; JD, Boston U., 1982. Bar: Mo. 1982, U.S. Dist. Ct. (ea. and we. dists.) Mo. 1982, U.S. Ct. Appeals (7th cir.) 1992. Asst. atty. gen. State of Mo., Jefferson City, 1982-84; ptnr., co-leader constrn. group Bryan, Cave, St. Louis, 1984—; adj. prof. of law Wash. U. Sch. of Law, 1997—; hon. vice consul to Italy, 1997—. Mem. ABA, Mo. Bar Assn., Noonday Club. Avocations: tennis, music, collecting matchbooks. Office: Bryan Cave 211 N Broadway Ste 3600 Saint Louis MO 63102-2733

COLAGRECO, JAMES PATRICK, school superintendent; b. Cliffside Park, N.J., Sept. 12, 1929; s. Anthony Edward and Angelina (Giannantonio) C.; B.A., Muhlenberg Coll., 1953; M.A., Seton Hall U., 1959; postgrad. Montclair Coll., 1960-61, Seton Hall U., 1961-64, Columbia U., 1963-64; m. Gloria Padula, June 8, 1952; children—Janice, Jamie, Anthony, June. Tchr., Cliffside Park Public Schs., 1953—, coach football, basketball, baseball, high sch., 1953-60, prin. elem. and high schs., 1960-72, supt. schs., 1972—; cons. Dept. Edn. on evaluation, 1971; hearing officer N.J. State Interscholastic Athletic Assn., 1981-82. Bd. dirs. E. Bergen Tchrs. Fed. Credit Union, 1981—; mem. Cliffside Pk. Library Bd., 1972—; mem. Middle State Evaluation Com., 1974; chmn. Region VI Spl. Edn. Council for Spl. Edn., 1976; participant N.J. Commr. of Edn. Supts. Acad., 1979; mem. Com. on League Re-Alignment, 1981-82. Drug Edn. grantee, 1974; selected to St. Benedict's Prep. Sch. Hall of Fame, 1986, Man of Yr. Bergen County Leonardo de Vinci Soc., 1991. Mem. N.J. Council of Edn., N.J. Sch. Masters, Bergen County Supts. Assn. (pres. 1985-86), N.J. Assn. Sch. Adminstrs., Am. Assn. Sch. Adminstrs., N.J. Sch. Bds. Assn., Assn. for Supervision and Curriculum Devel. Roman Catholic. Clubs: Cliffside Men's (sec.-treas. 1981-82), Cliffside Park Rotary (pres. 1967), Cliffside Park Lions. Home: 2 Fox Ter Cliffside Park NJ 07010-2906 Office: 525 Palisade Ave Cliffside Park NJ 07010-2914

COLAIANNI, JOSEPH VINCENT, judge; b. Detroit, Mar. 19, 1935; s. P. and Marie D. (Mastrantonio) C.; m. Rita Milena Roll, Oct. 13, 1962; children: Marie Elena, Joseph Vincent, Michael Philip, Vincent Gerard. BEE, U. Detroit, 1956; postgrad., Wayne State U., 1956-58; JD with honors, George Washington U., 1961. Bar: Mich. 1962, Ohio 1963, Wash. 1964. Assoc. firm Fay and Fay, Cleve., until 1965; trial atty. civil div. Dept. Justice, Washington, 1965-70; commr. U.S. Ct. Claims, Washington, 1970-73; trial judge U.S. Ct. Claims, 1973-82; judge U.S. Ct. Claims D.C., 1982-84; mng. ptnr. Pennie & Edmonds, Washington, 1984-98; chair intellectual property Patton Boggs LLP, Washington, 1998—; sci. liaison com. Sci. Ct., 1976-84; prof. grad. sch. Patent Resources Inst.; adj. prof. Am. U., 1984-87, Cath. U. Sch. Law, 1997—; adv. com. patents and trademarks U.S. Dept. Commerce, 1987-89; sr. adviser U.S. Claims Ct. Adv. Coun., 1984—; adv. com. U.S. Patent and Trademark Office. Adv. bd. Patent, Trademark and Copyright Jour., 1984-91. District Heights (Md.) Recreation Coun., 1969-70; bd. dirs. Henson Valley Montessori Sch.; pres. Tilden PTA, 1979-81, Lido Civic Club, 1981; trustee Western Coll. Medicine, 1982-85; co-pres. U. Md. at College Park Parents Assn., 1991-97; mem. pres. cabinet U. Detroit Mercy, 1982—, commn. on future Coll. Engring., 1995-96. Mem. Am., Fed. bar assns., Patent Office Soc., Mich., Ohio, Washington bars, Phi Delta Phi, Eta Kappa Nu., Omicron Delta Kappa, Phi Delta Kappa, George Washington U. Law Rev. (1960-61).

COLAIZZI, JOHN LOUIS, college dean; b. Pitts., May 10, 1938; s. Peter Richard and Lena M. (Sebastian) C.; m. Maria Rose Santoro, Aug. 12, 1967; children—James J., Patricia R., John Louis. BS, U. Pitts., 1960; MS, Purdue U., 1962, PhD, 1965. Asst. prof. Sch. Pharmacy, W.Va. U., Morgantown, 1964-65; asst. prof., asso. prof. Sch. Pharmacy, U. Pitts., 1965-76, prof., chmn., asso. dean, 1976-78; prof., dean Coll. Pharmacy, Rutgers U., Piscataway, N.J., 1978—; chmn. Robert Wood Johnson Univ. Hosp., New Brunswick, N.J., 1997—, also bd. dirs.; mem. Medicaid Drug Utilization Rev. Bd. N.J., 1996-97; bioavailability cons. Drug Utilization Rev. Coun. N.J., 1997—. Mem. Am. Pharm. Assn., Am. Assn. Pharm. Scis., Am. Soc. Health-system Pharmacists, Am. Assn. Coll. Pharmacy, Pharm. Care Mgmt. Assn. (deans adv. coun. 1998—), Am. Inst. History of Pharmacy, Rho Chi, Alpha Zeta Omega, Sigma Xi. Democrat. Roman Catholic. Home: 21 Jason Dr East Brunswick NJ 08816-3342 Office: Rutgers U Coll Pharmacy 160 Frelinghuysen Rd Piscataway NJ 08854-8020

COLANDER, PATRICIA MARIE, newspaper publisher; b. Chgo., Oct. 25, 1952; d. Charles L. Colander and Mary Elizabeth Connors; m. Paul Michael Ansell, Aug. 18, 1980 (div. Jan. 1993); children: Charles Thomas, Ida Kay Ansell. BJ, U. Ill., 1973. Staff writer Chgo. Tribune, 1973-77, Chgo. Reader, 1977-81; adj. prof. Medill Sch. Journalism Northwestern U., 1982-87; editor Copley Newspapers, Chgo. suburbs, No. Ill., 1987-92; asst. mng. editor The Times, 1992-93, pub. Ill. edits., 1993—; mng. editor The Times, Munster, Ind.; exec. devel. program Am. Press Inst., Reston, Va., 1994. Author: Thin Air: The Life and Mysterious Disappearance of Helen Brach, 1982, Hugh Hefner's First Funeral and Other True Tales of Love and Death in Chicago, 1985. Recipient awards AP, 1987, 88, 89, Suburban Newspapers Am., 1988, Inland Press Assn., 1991. Mem. So. Suburban Coll. Found. Bd., Soc. Midland Authors, Ill. Press Assn., Soc. Newspaper Design. Office: The Times 601 W 45th Ave Munster IN 46321*

COLANGELO, BRYAN, professional sports team executive. BS in Bus. Mgmt. and Applied Econ., Cornell U., 1987. Scout Phoenix Suns, 1990-92, asst. dir. player personnel, 1992-95, v.p. adminstrn., gen. mgr., 1995-97; alt. gov. bd. govs. NBA; tournament dir. NIKE Desert Classic; pres. Phoenix Arena Sports; bd. dirs. Ariz. Sports Coun., Phoenix Suns Charities, Home Base Youth Svcs. Bd. dirs. Phoenix C. of C., vice chmn. econ. devel., mem. exec com. Named one of top 25 Valley Bus. Leaders, Ariz. Bus. Jour., 1995. Office: Phoenix Suns 201 E Jefferson St Phoenix AZ 85004-2412*

COLANGELO, JAMES JOSEPH, psychotherapist; b. Jamaica, N.Y., Jan. 8, 1950; s. Joseph and Amalia (Bove) C.; m. Kathy DeGuardi, Nov. 12, 1983; children: Nicole, Steven, Christina. BA, Manhattan Coll., 1971; MSEd, St. John's U., 1974; PD, L.I. U., 1987, cert. in marriage, family therapy, 1987; PhD candidate, Calif. Coast U. Diplomate Am. Bd. Sexology; cert. clin. mental health counselor; nat. cert. counselor; registered profl. hypnotherapist; bd. cert. sex therapist; cert. sex counselor. Ind. community mental health counselor Queens, N.Y.; caseworker N.Y.C. Dept. Social Svcs., Queens; clin. cons. Ea. Met. Counseling and Consulting Svcs., Queens; supr. Dept. Health & Human Svcs., Adminstrn. Children & Families, N.Y.C.; specialist Children and Families Program (DHHS/ACF); adj. faculty C.W. Post Ctr., L.I. U.; EEO counselor; mem. Region II AIDS com., DHHS. Recipient C. Eugene Morris award in mental health counseling L.I. U., 1992; named to Nat. Disting. Svc. Registry in Counseling, 1990. Mem. ACA, Am. Assn. Marriage and Family Therapists (clin., approved supr.), Am. Assn. Profl. Hypnotherapists, Am. Assn. Sex Educators, Counselors and Therapists (cert.), Am. Psychotherapy Assn. (diplomate), Internat. Assn. Marriage and Family Counselors, N.Y. Assn. Marriage and Family Counselors, N.Y. Mental Health Counselors Assn. (v.p. N.Y.C. area).

COLANGELO, JERRY JOHN, professional basketball team executive; b. Chicago Heights, Ill., Nov. 20, 1939; s. Larry and Sue (Drancek) C.; m. Joan E. Helmich, Jan. 20, 1961; children: Kathy, Kristen, Bryan. B.A., U. Ill., 1962. Partner House of Charles, Inc., 1962-63; assoc. D.O. Klein & Assocs., 1964-65; dir. merchandising Chgo. Bulls basketball club, 1966-68; gen. mgr. Phoenix Suns basketball club, 1968-87, now also exec. v.p., until 1987, pres., chief exec. officer, 1987—; mng. gen. ptnr. Arizona Diamondbacks, Phoenix, AZ, 1998—. Mem. Basketball Congress Am. (exec. v.p., dir.), Phi Kappa Psi. Republican. Baptist. Clubs: University, Phoenix Execs. Office: Phoenix Suns 201 E Jefferson St Phoenix AZ 85004-2412*

COLANTUONO, THOMAS PAUL, state legislator; b. Newton, Mass., Oct. 4, 1951; m. Pamela E. Chaloge. BA, Duke U., 1973; JD, Boston Coll., 1976. Bar: N.H. 1976. Assoc. Hamblett & Kerrigan, Nashua, N.H., 1976-78; asst. atty gen. N.H. Atty. Gen.'s Office, 1978-81; pvt. practice Derry, N.H., 1981—; state sen. State of New Hampshire, 1990-96; vice chmn. exec. dept., adminstrn. coms.; exec. councilor State of N.H., 1999—; chmn ways and means com., N.H. Senate, mem. capitol budget, fin., judiciary, ins. coms., vice chmn. exec. dept., adminstrn. coms. Mem. ABA, N.H. Bar Assn., Derry Rotary, Londonderry and Hudson C. of C. Office: 23 Birch St Derry NH 03038-2119*

COLASURD, RICHARD MICHAEL, lawyer; b. Navarre, Ohio, Apr. 1, 1928; s. Michael and Adeline (Manack) C.; m. Jane Cooley, Dec. 20, 1986; children: Steven Michael, David Gerard, Cathie Marie. A.B., U. Notre Dame, 1950; J.D., Harvard U., 1953. Bar: Ohio 1953. Practice in Toledo, 1960—; spl. agt. FBI, 1953-56; asst. U.S. atty. charge Northwestern Ohio, 1956-60; mem. firm Shumaker, Loop & Kendrick, 1960-64; asst. city law dir. Toledo, 1964; mem. firm Mulholland, Hickey & Lyman, 1964-73; U.S. commr., 1963-67. Mem. AMA, Ohio Bar Assn., Toledo Bar Assn., Soc. Former Spl. Agts. FBI, Lexington C.C., Rotary. Roman Catholic. Home: 16133 Edgemont Dr Fort Myers FL 33908-3651 Office: 16133 Edgemont Dr Fort Myers FL 33908-3651

COLBATH, BRIAN (BRIAN COLBATH WATSON), actor, script and live performance writer; b. Port Washington, N.Y., July 14; s. H. Desmond Watson and Mary (Colbath) Watson Haynes. BS in Speech and Drama, Ithaca Coll., 1965. Cert. tchr., N.Y. Tchr. speech Canandaigua (N.Y.) Acad., 1965-67; speech pathologist West Seneca (N.Y.) Ctrl. Schs., 1967-70; rsch. mgr. Projects Plus, Inc., N.Y.C., 1994—; mem. Blue Ribbon panel Daytime Emmy Awards, N.Y.C., 1985-91. Appearances include daytime TV programs, Tony Awards show, N.Y.C., 1989-98, various prodns. Studio Arena Theatre, Buffalo; scripwriter indsl. films; writer night club acts. Named one of Outstanding Young Men of Am., 1970. Mem. AFTRA, SAG, Actors' Equity. Home: 15 W 67th St Apt 2RW New York NY 10023-

6226 Office: Projects Plus Inc 145 W 45th St Ste 300 New York NY 10036-4008

COLBAUGH, RICHARD DONALD, mechanical engineer, educator, researcher; b. Pitts., Oct. 31, 1958; s. Richard Donald and Anne Marie (McCue); m. Kristin Lea Glass, July 18, 1987; 1 child, Allison Collette. BS in Mechanical Engring., Pa. State U., 1980, PhD in Mechanical Engring., 1986. Mechanical engr. McDonnell Douglas Corp., Long Beach, Calif., 1980-81; instr. mechanical engring. Pa. State U., State College, 1981-86; asst. prof. mechanical engring. N.Mex. State U., Las Cruces, 1986-90, assoc. prof. mech. engring., 1990-96, prof. mech. engring., 1996—; cons. Dept. Energy, Albuquerque, 1987-- Jet Propulsion Lab., Pasadena, Calif., 1988--. Assoc. editor Internat. Jour. of Robotics and Auto., 1991-93, editor-in-chief, 1993—; assoc. editor Internat. Jour. Environ. Conscious Mfg., 1992—, Intelligent Automation and Soft Computing, 1994—; co-author: Robotics and Remote Systems in Hazardous Environ., 1992; contbr. articles to profl. jours.; guest editor numerous jours. Recipient NASA Space Act Tech. Brief award, 1990, 91, 92, 93, 95, 96, Best Paper award Am. Automatic Control Coun., 1990, 93, Best Presentation award Soc. Indsl. and Applied Math., 1995; NASA/ASEE Summer Faculty fellow, 1991, 92. Mem. IEEE, Am. Soc. Mechanical Engrs., Sigma Xi. Achievements include patent for Obstacle Avoidance Redundant Robots Using Configuration Control; development of first real time control algorithm for robots possessing any combination of kinematic of actuator redundancy, one of first adaptive output stabilizing, tracking and compliance controllers for robots, one of first adaptive stabilizers for underactuated mechanical systems. Office: NMex State U Dept Mechanical Engring PO Box 30001 # 3450 Las Cruces NM 88003-8001

COLBENSON, MARY ELIZABETH DREISBACH, materials engineer; b. New Haven, Nov. 27, 1966; d. Raymond Allen and Dorothy Louise (Seal) Dreisbach; m. Paul Carroll Colbenson, Sept. 7, 1991. BSME and Materials Sci., U. Conn., 1989; MS in Materials Engring., Rensselaer Poly. Inst., 1998; AS in Plastics Engring., Quinebaug Valley Cmty. Tech., 1999. Registered profl. engr., Conn. Mfg. engr. United Technologies Corp., Pratt & Whitney, East Hartford, Conn., 1988-93; sr. mfg. engr. Haydon Switch and Instrument Inc., Waterbury, Conn., 1993-97, sr. project engr., 1997-98, mfg. engring. mgr., 1998—. Bd. dirs. Airpax Fed. Credit Union, 1996-98, supervisory com., 1993-96, chmn., 1996-98, pres., 1998—. Mem. Am. Soc. Materials, Materials Rsch. Soc., Soc. Mfg. Engrs. (cert. mfg. engr.). Home: 492 Prospect St Willimantic CT 06226-2028 Office: Haydon Switch & Instrument 1500 Meriden Rd Waterbury CT 06705-3910

COLBERT, EDWIN HARRIS, paleontologist, museum curator; b. Clarinda, Iowa, Sept. 28, 1905; s. George Harris and Mary (Adamson) C.; m. Margaret Mary Matthew, July 8, 1933; children: George Matthew, David William, Philip Valentine, Daniel Lee, Charles Diller. Student, N.W. Mo. State Tchrs. Coll., 1923-26; BA, U. Nebr., 1928, ScD, 1973; AM, Columbia U., 1930, PhD, 1935; ScD, U. Ariz., 1976, Wilmington Coll., 1984. Student asst. Univ. Mus. U. Nebr., 1926-29; univ. fellow Columbia U., 1929-30, lectr. dept. zoology, 1938-39, prof. vertebrate paleontology, 1945-69, prof. emeritus, 1969—; research asst. Am. Museum Natural History, 1930-32, asst. curator, 1933-42, acting curator, 1942, curator, 1943, chmn. dept. amphibians and reptiles, 1943-44, curator of fossil reptiles and amphibians, 1945-70, chmn. dept. geology and paleontology, 1958-60, chmn. dept. vertebrate paleontology, 1960-66, curator emeritus, 1970—; hon. curator vertebrate paleontology Mus. No. Ariz., Flagstaff, 1970—. Author: Evolution of Vertebrates, 1955, 60, 80, 91, (with M. Morales) Millions of Years Ago, 1958, Dinosaurs, 1961, (with M. Kay) Stratigraphy and Life History, 1965, The Age of Reptiles, 1965, 97, Men and Dinosaurs, 1968, Wandering Lands and Animals, 1973, The Year of the Dinosaur, 1977, A Fossil Hunter's Notebook, 1980, Dinosaurs: An Illustrated History, 1983, Digging into the Past, 1989, William Diller Matthew, Paleontologist, 1992, The Little Dinosaurs of Ghost Ranch, 1995; also sci. papers and monographs. Recipient John Strong Newberry prize Columbia U., 1931, Am. Mus. Natural History medal, 1970, Nat. Ghost Ranch Found. Spl. award, 1986, Disting. Alumni award Dept. Geology, U. Nebr., 1986, George W. Clinton award The Buffalo Soc. Natural Scis., 1987, Hayden medal Geol. award Acad. Nat. Scis. Phila., 1996. Fellow AAAS, Geol. Soc. Am., Paleontol. Soc. (v.p. 1963), N.Y. Zool. Soc.; mem. Soc. Vertebrate Paleontology (sec.-treas. 1944-46, pres. 1946-47, Romer-Simpson medal 1989), Soc. Mammalogy, Soc. Ichthyology and Herpetology, Soc. for Study Evolution (editor 1950-52, v.p. 1957, pres. 1958), Nat. Acad. Sci. (Daniel Giraud Elliot medal 1935), Sigma Xi. Office: Mus of No Ariz 3101 N Fort Valley Rd Flagstaff AZ 86001-8348 *The paramount factor in the development of my scientific career has been a love of original research. Research is creative, and there is true satisfaction in doing creative things.*

COLBERT, ELBERT LYNN, dentist, recording artist; b. Stillwater, Okla., July 11, 1952; s. Oscar James and Hazel Elizabeth (Summit) C.; m. Denise Annette Wilson (div. July 1980); m. Gayla Janyce Burpo, Feb. 27, 1982 (div. Aug. 1995); 1 child, Shane Michael Cheatham. BS in Pre-Medicine, Okla. State U., 1976; DMD cum laude, Washington U., 1977. Pvt. practice dentistry Woodward, Okla., 1977-82, Bear Creek Dental Group, Boulder, Colo., 1982-92, Boulder, 1992—; prin., ind. prodr. Twin Pools Recording Studio. Composer, prodr., musician: Zuriel the Rock of God, 1987, Crown of Thorns, 1986; composer, prodr., singer: First Born, 1985, Delorean's Ride/Lead the Way, 1984, Flyers, 1978-82; composer, singer: Save the Earth, 1989; composer, prodr.: Dark Saying, 1994. Regional coordinator Am. Student Dental Assn., midwestern states, 1976-77. Mem. Nat. Assn. Dental Practitioners, Omicron Kappa Upsilon, Alpha Epsilon Delta. Home: 1727 Eisenhower Dr Louisville CO 80027-1181 Office: 4800 Baseline Rd Boulder CO 80303-6536

COLBERT, GEORGE CLIFFORD, college official; b. Cedar Rapids, Iowa, Mar. 22, 1949; s. Louis Charles and Betty Mae Colbert; m. Marion Patricia Clark, Aug. 4, 1973; children: Bridget, Dontá. AA, Kirkwood C.C., Cedar Rapids, 1972; BA in Criminal Justice and Social Work, Mt. Mercy Coll., Cedar Rapids, 1974; MEd in Leadership Edn., No. Ariz. U., 1993. Coord. continuing edn. Kirkwood C.C., Cedar Rapids, 1978-89; dir. student svcs., dir. continuing edn. Ctrl. Ariz. Coll., Apache Junction, 1989-95; student svc. assoc. Ctrl. Ariz. Coll., Coolidge, 1995—; part-time instr. Ctrl. Ariz. Coll., various locations, 1990—, chmn. enhancement of program offerings, Apache Junction, 1993—; notary public, Ariz., 1993—. Rsch. participant: (book) Profile/Status (Blk) Males in Arizona, 1992, Impace and Challenges of (Blk) Policy Makers in Arizona, 1991. Mem. commn. on excellence in edn. Mesa (Ariz.) C.C., 1993—; mem. nat. coun. instl. adminstrs. All State Cmty. Colls., Ariz., 1990—; v.p. Cedar Rapids br. NAACP, 1978-80; continuing edn. chmn. Kirkwood C.C., 1986-87; founder, chmn. higher ednl. minority scholarship, Cedar Rapids, 1978; vol. probation officer Juvenile Ct., Cedar Rapids, 1974; vol. dept. pub. safety Apache Junction Police Dept., Ariz., 1990. With USMC, 1967-69. Recipient Outstanding Cmty. Svc. award Apache Junction Unified Sch. Dist., 1989, 90, Vol. award Iowa Gov. terry Branstad, 1987. Mem. Am. Vets. Assn. (life mem. Phoenix chpt. Post 15). Avocations: tournament racquetball, youth baseball coaching, car restoration. Home: 6228 E Covina St Mesa AZ 85205-7515

COLBERT, JAMES E., writer, educator; b. New Orleans, Nov. 2, 1951; s. Charles Colbert and Rosemary Schrafft. BA, La. State U., 1980; MFA, U. Ark., 1997. vis. writer U. N.Mex., Albuquerque, 1997-98; short story judge The Faulkner Festival, New Orleans, 1996. Author: (novels) Profit and Sheen, 1986, 96, No Special Hurry, 1988, 92, Skinny Man, 1991, 95, All I Have Is Blue, 1992, 95, (nonfiction) God Bless the Child, 1993 (screenplay with Andrew Vachss) Cross: Genesis, 1996, also graphic novels; contbr. short fiction and poetry to anthologies, articles and revs. to profl. and scholarly publs. With USMC, 1970-71. Recipient Robert Hacke Scholar-Tchr. award Coll. English Assn., 1998. Mem. MLA, Writers Guild, Authors Guild. E-mail: colbert@unm.edu. Home: 4517 Inspiration Dr SE Albuquerque NM 87108 Office: U N Mex Dept English Lang and Lit Humanities Bldg 217 Albuquerque NM 87131-1106

COLBERT, MARVIN JAY, retired internist, educator; b. Spokane, Wash., Nov. 6, 1923; s. John B. and Elizabeth (Peters) C.; m. Eleanor Ruth Rott, June 2, 1951; children: Janet Lynn, James Lee, Lawrence Jay. Student, U. Utah, 1940-43; BS, Yale U., 1946; MD, Boston U., 1949. Diplomate: Am. Bd. Internal Medicine. Intern, resident in internal medicine Presbyn. Hosp., Chgo., 1949-50, VA Hosp., Boston, 1953-54, U. Ill. Rsch. and Ednl. Hosp., 1954-55; pvt. practice internal medicine Belmond, Iowa, 1955-56; mem. faculty U. Ill., Chgo., 1956-58; dir. health svc. Med. Ctr., 1959-78, prof. medicine, 1969-78; dir. employee health svcs. Evang. Hosp. Assn., Oak Brook, Ill., 1978-86; cons. internal medicine radiol. and environ. rsch. div. Argonne (Ill.) Nat. Lab., 1978-79. Pres. Hillcrest PTA, Downers Grove, Ill., 1960-62; Parent-Tchrs. Group Chiengmai Co-Ednl. Ctr., Thailand, 1965-66. Capt. M.C. AUS, 1943-46, 50-52. Fellow ACP; mem. Assn. for Advancement Automotive Medicine (dir. 1969-76). Home: 5600 Plymouth St Downers Grove IL 60516-1231 *While on leave from The University of Illinois, Marvin Jay Colbert was a Visiting Professor of Internal Medicine. Between the years of 1965-66 he taught at The Chiengmai Medical School and Hospital in Chiengmai, Thailand.*

COLBERT, ROBERT B., JR., apparel company executive; b. Columbus, Ga., Sept. 24, 1921; s. Robert B. and Mae (Hindsman) C.; m. Margaret Moore, Mar. 22, 1942; children—Margaret, Bert, John. Student, Emory U., U. Ga. Ret. chmn. bd., dir. Signal Apparel Co. Inc., Chattanooga. With USNR, World War II. Address: 8845 Doveland Dr Cordova TN 38018-6907

COLBERT, ROBERT IVAN, education association administrator; b. Lake Charles, La., Sept. 25, 1950; s. Robert Ivan Sr. and Lou Anna (Duplechin) C.; m. Annick Marie Saint Hubert, July 2, 1977; children: Benjamin David, Catherine Annick, Martin Charles, Sarah Jessica. BA Psychology, U. Dallas, 1972; BA Theology, U. Cath. de Louvain, Belgium, 1973, STB Theology, 1975, MA Theology, 1975. Asst. dean student personnel U. Southwestern La., Lafayette, 1976-78; dir. religious edn. Sts. Peter and Paul Ch., Scott, 1978-81; asst. supt. schs. Diocese of Lafayette, La., 1981-86, diocesan dir. religious edn., 1986-88; asst. prof./coord. field edn. dept. theology St. Mary's U., San Antonio, Tex., 1988-89; dir. pastoral instr., asst. prof. Incarnate Word Coll., San Antonio, 1989-92; assoc. exec. dir. dept. religious edn. Nat. Cath. Edn. Assn., Washington, 1992-94, exec. dir., 1994—; adv. subcom. on catechesis United States Cath. Conf., Washington, 1994—; adv. bd. The Living Light, 1994—. Mem. Assn. Grad. Programs in Ministry, Religious Edn. Assn. Roman Catholic. Office: Nat Cath Ednl Assn 1077 30th St NW Ste 100 Washington DC 20007-3829*

COLBERT, VIRGIS WILLIAM, brewery company executive; b. Jackson, Miss., Oct. 13, 1939; s. Quillie and Eddi C.; grad. Exec. Inst., Earlham Coll.; BS, Ctrl. Mich. U. With Toledo Machining Plant, Chrysler Corp., 1966-79, foreman, 1968-70, gen. foreman, 1970-73, mfg. supt., 1973-77, gen. mfg. supt., 1977-79; asst. to plant mgr. Miller Brewing Co., Reidsville, N.C., 1979-80, prodn. mgr., Ft. Worth, Tex., 1980-81, plant mgr. Milw. Container Plant, 1981-87, asst. dir. can mfg., 1987-88, dir. container and support mfg., 1988-90, v.p. materials mfg. and plant ops., 1990-91, v.p. plant ops., 1991-93, sr. v.p. ops., 1993-95, sr. v.p. worldwide ops., 1995-97, exec. v.p., 1997—; bd. dirs. Delphi Automotive Sys., Inc., AeroQuip-Vickers, Miller Brewing Co., Milw., Columbia Health Svcs., Inc. Fisk Univ., Greater Milw. Open, Thurgood Marshall Scholarship Fund, Milw. Sch. Engring. Mem. exec. com. Boy Scouts Greater Milw.; active NAACP, Nat. Urban League's Black Exec. Exchange Program. Mem. Frontiers Internat. Club, Masons, Shriners, Omega Psi Phi, Sigma Pi Phi. Office: Miller Brewing Co 3939 W Highland Blvd Milwaukee WI 53208-2866

COLBORN, HARRY WALTER, electrical engineering consultant; b. Pitts., May 27, 1921; s. David Lafayette and Leora Blanche (Lane) C.; m. Mary Ellen Meluch, May 31, 1952; children: David, Kurt. Student, Bliss Elec. Sch., Takoma Park, Md., 1940; BS in Elec. Engring., Carnegie Inst. Tech., 1951; postgrad., Oak Ridge Sch. Reactor Tech., 1958. Registered profl. engr., Pa., Md., W.Va. Engr. West Penn Power Co., Pitts. and Greensburg, Pa., 1951-67; system planning mgr. West Penn Power Co., Greensburg, 1967-70; dir. transmission planning Allegheny Power Service Corp., Greensburg, 1970-80; mgr. spl. studies N.Am. Electric Reliability Council, Princeton, N.J., 1980-84; dir. engring. N.Am. Electric Reliability Council, 1984-86; pvt. cons., 1986—; mgr. tech. assessment Electric Power Research Inst., Palo Alto, Calif., 1978-79. Contbr. articles to profl. jours. Served with AUS, 1943-46, ETO. Fellow IEEE (chmn. system planning 1976-82, centennial medal 1984). Republican. Presbyterian. Office: 606 Concord Ln Export PA 15632-1581 *The phrase, "Not in my job description," was never in my job description.*

COLBOURN, TREVOR, retired university president, historian; b. Armidale, New South Wales, Australia, Feb. 24, 1927; came to U.S., 1948; s. Harold Arthur and Ella Mary (Henderson) C.; m. Beryl Richards Evans, Jan. 10, 1949; children—Katherine Elizabeth, Lisa Sian Elinor. B.A. with honors, U. London, 1948; M.A., Coll. William and Mary, 1949, Johns Hopkins, 1951; Ph.D., Johns Hopkins, 1953. From instr. to asst. prof. Pa. State U., 1952-59; from asst. prof. to prof. Am. history Ind. U., 1959-67; dean Grad. Sch., prof. history U. N.H., 1967-73; v.p. for acad. affairs San Diego State U., 1973-77, acting pres., 1977-78; pres. U. Central Fla., Orlando, 1978-89. Author: The Lamp of Experience, 1998, The Colonial Experience, 1966, (with others) The Americans: A Brief History, 1972, 4th edit., 1985; co-editor: (with others) The American Past in Perspective, 1970; editor: (with others) Fame and the Founding Fathers, 1998. Mem. Orgn. Am. Historians, Am. Assn. State Colls. and Univs. Office: U Cen Fla Office Pres Emeritus Orlando FL 32816

COLBURN, DONALD D., lawyer; b. Seward, Nebr., May 20, 1948. BA, U. Nebr., Lincoln, 1970, JD with distinction, 1974. Bar: Ariz. 1974, Tex. 1994. Law clk. for Chief Justice Nebr. Supreme Ct., 1973-74; sr. ptnr. Snell & Wilmer, Phoenix, 1974-99; ptnr. Colburn Law Offices, Phoenix, 1999—. Office: Colburn Law Offices 394 N Third Ave Phoenix AZ 85003*

COLBURN, GENE LEWIS, insurance and industrial consultant; b. Bismarck, N.D., July 12, 1932; s. Lewis William and Olga Alma (Feland) C.; PhD, City U. L.A., 1983. Pres., gen. mgr. Multiple Lines Ins. Agy., Auburn, Wash., 1953-79; ins. and risk mgmt. cons., Auburn, Wash., 1980—; pres. Feland Safe Deposit Corp.; bd. dirs. Century Svc. Corp. subs. Capital Savs. Bank, Olympia, Wash.; mem. exec. com. Great Repub. Life Ins. Co., Portland, Oreg., 1971-75; mem. Wash. State Ins. Commrs. Test Devel. Com., 1986-87. cons. indsl. risk mgmt. Councilperson Auburn City, 1982-85; mayor-pro tem, City of Auburn, 1984; co-incorporator, chmn. bd. SE Community Alcohol Ctr., 1971-75; mem. Wash. State Disaster Assistance Coun., 1981-82, founding mem.; pres. Valley Cities Mental Health Ctr., 1980; mem. instn. rev. com. Auburn Gen. Hosp., 1978—; prin. trustee Dr. R. B. Bramble Med. Rsch. Found., 1980-90; bd. dirs. Wash. Assn. Chs. (Luth. Ch. in Am.), Asian Refugee Resettlement Mgmt. div., 1981-83, Columbia Luth. Home, Seattle, 1985-87, Wash. Law Enforcement Officers and Fire Fighter's Pension Disability Bd., Auburn, 1980-84. Cert. ins. counselor, 1978. Recipient Disting. Alumni award Green River Community Coll., 1982. Fellow Acad. Producer Ins. Studies (charter); mem. Internat. Platform Assn. Lodge: Auburn Lions (past pres.). Office: 720 L St SE Auburn WA 98002-6219

COLBURN, HAROLD LEWIS, dermatologist, state legislator; m. Jane Harrison, 1949; children: Robert, Suzanne. AB, Princeton U., 1947; MD, Albany Med. Coll., 1949. Diplomate Am. Bd. Dermatology. Intern Hosp. Ctr., Orange, N.J., 1949-50; resident in dermatology U. Pa., 1952-55; dermatologist Moorestown and Mt. Holly, N.J., 1955-95; sec. chief emeritus of dermatology Meml. Hosp. Burlington County, Mt. Holly, 1955-92; sect. chief dermatology Zurbrugg Meml. Hosp., Riverside, N.J., 1955-92; asst. clin. prof. dermatology Thomas Jefferson U., 1971; rep. N.J. Assembly, 1984-95, chmn. health and human svcs. com., 1986-89, 91-95, fin. instns. com., 1993-95, drug and alcohol abuse com., 1987-89; ret., 1997; med. dir. N.J. State Bd. Med. Examiners, 1995-97, ret., 1997. Freeholder Burlington County, 1971-84, freeholder dir., 1976, 80, 84. Mem. Burlington County Med. Soc. (past pres.), Med. Soc. N.J. (past trustee), Nat. Assn. Counties (chmn. subcom. for health resources 1977-80).

COLBURN, JULIA KATHERINE LEE, volunteer, educator; b. Columbus, Ohio, Feb. 8, 1927; d. Fred Merritt and Lillian May (Getrost) Lee; m. Joseph Linn Jr., David Laird, Andrew Lee, Julia LeeAnne. BS in Edn., Ohio State U., 1948. Substitute tchr. Columbus Pub. Schs., 1965-69, 79-81, vol. resource person, 1979—. Author: The Six Who Signed Christmas at Valley Forge; editor, compiler (state pub.) Ohio Daughters of 1812, Star and Anchor, 1983-85 (nat. first award 1984, 85). Presiding judge Franklin County Bd. Elections, Columbus, 1959—; pres. Linden Jr. Civic Club, Columbus, 1953, Rhapsody Unit, Columbus Symphony, 1975-77, Arlington Park PTA, Columbus, 1963-64, Linden-McKinley Jr.-Sr. High PTA, Columbus, 1964-66, Northland High PTA, Columbus, 1972-73; organizing pres. Lazarus Cancer Ray, Columbus, 1953; leader Northland coun. Girl Scouts U.S., 1968-70; vol. Vision Ctr., Columbus, 1969-72; v.p. Linden United Meth. Women, Columbus, 1965-66, pres., 1966-68, 96—, various coms., 1963—; pres. Meth. Youth Fellowship, Columbus, 1944-45; adminstrv. bd. Linden United Meth. Ch., Columbus, 1944-45, 52—, spl. membership awards, 1971, 77; dist. chmn. Christian Global Concerns Columbus North Dist. United Meth. Women, 1973-77. Recipient Silver Good Citizenship medal Ohio Soc. SAR, 1978, Medal of Appreciation, Benjamin Franklin chpt. SAR, 1978, Martha Washington medal Ohio SAR, 1989. Mem. Ohio Geneal. Soc. (spkrs. staff 1978—), First Families of Ohio, DAR (Good Citizenship cert. 1945, state rec. sec. 1983-86, state vice regent 1986-89, state regent 1989-92, v.p. gen. 1992-95, nat. vice chmn. Valley Forge belltower restoration 1995-98, various offices and coms. 1976—), NSDAR (spkrs. staff 1983—, chaplain v.p. gen. club 1993-94, parlimentarian nat. vice chmn. club 1994—, v.p. gen. club, historian gen. 1998—), Children of Am. Revolution (sr. pres. state 1976-78, sr. nat. rec. sec. 1982-84, various coms. 1974—, Ohio Svc. award 1979, maj. benefactor 1986, nat. vice chmn. 1980-83), U.S. Daus. of 1812 (parliamentarian, chmn. nat. membership 1985-88, state pres. 1983-85, treas. Nat. Hdqrs. Endowment Trust Fund 1988-91, pres. Assn. of State Pres. 1991-93), Colonial Dames of Am., Dames of the Ct. of Honor, Colonial Dames XVII Century (state first v.p. 1985-87, 95-97, state pres. 1997-99), Daus. Colonial Wars (state historian 1984-86, nat. vice chmn. 1989-92, state custodian 1992-95, state 2nd v.p. 1995-97, state 1st v.p. 1997), Women Desc. Ancient and Honorable Arty. Co. (state rec. sec. 1983-86, state pres. 1986-89, nat. parliamentarian 1989-92, chaplain nat. 1992-95, nat. organizing sec. 1995-98), Daus. Am. Colonists (Old Trails chpt. treas. 1981-85, vice regent 1985-87, regent 1987-89), New Eng. Women (pres. Columbus colony 1984-87, nat. chmn. 1987-95), Colonial Daus. Seventeenth Century, Daus. Union Vets., Ohio Fedn. Women's Club (trustee, chmn. 1974-83), Noreast Women's (v.p. 1994-96), Order of Ea. Star (star point 1961-62), Linden Lawanis, Zeta Phi Eta. Republican. Avocations: genealogy, music, writing. Home: 1887 Northcliff Dr Columbus OH 43229-5332

COLBURN, KEITH W., electronics executive. Chmn. bd., CEO Consolidated Electrical Distrs, Thousand Oaks, Calif. Office: Consolidated Electrical Distrs 31356 Via Colinas Ste 107 Westlake Village CA 91362-3915*

COLBURN, KENNETH HERSEY, financial executive; b. Melrose, Mass., Jan. 8, 1952; s. Warren Edward and Mabelle (Hersey) C.; married. AB, Brown U., 1975; MPPM, Yale U., 1978. Assoc. Credit Suisse 1st Boston Corp./(formerly First Boston Corp.), N.Y.C., 1978-83, v.p., 1983-88, mng. dir., 1988-95; v.p. project and internat. fin. Raytheon Co., Lexington, Mass., 1995-98; chief operating officer Highfields Capital Mgmt. L.P., Boston, 1998—. Trustee Huntington Theatre Co., Boston, Bentley Coll., Waltham, Mass. Mem. Yale Club, Watch Hill Yacht Club, Boothbay Harbor Yacht Club, Dedham Polo and Country Club. Office: Highfields Capital Mgmt 200 Clarendon St Boston MA 02116-5021

COLBURN, RICHARD DUNTON, business executive; b. Carpentersville, Ill., June 24, 1911; s. Cary R. and Daisy (Dunton) C.; children: Richard Whiting, Carol Dunton, Keith Whiting, Christine Isabel, David Dunton, McKee Dunton, Daisy Dunton. Student, Antioch Coll., 1929-33. Pres. Consol. Foundries Mfg. Corp. (and predecessors), 1944-64; chmn. U.S. Rentals Inc., Decco Ltd., U.K. Engring., London, Marlowe Holdings, Edmundson Elec. Ltd., London; dir. Consol. Elec. Distbrs., Inc., Hajoca Corp., Rolled Alloys, Inc.; underwriting mem. Lloyds of London. Home and Office: 1120 La Collina Dr Beverly Hills CA 90210-2616 also: 30 Chester Sq, London SW1W 9HT, England

COLBY, FRANK GERHARDT, scientific consultant; b. Mulhausen, Germany, Apr. 10, 1915; came to U.S., 1946; s. Fritz and Paula (Oppenheimer) Cohn; m. Renee Hiller, Oct. 15, 1952 (dec. Mar. 1995); children: Audrey B., Leonard F. ChemE, U. Geneva, 1939, DSc, 1941. Pvt. practice various cos., Havana, Cuba, 1941-46; rsch. chemist Indsl. Tape Corp., New Brunswick, N.J., 1946-47; chem. lit. specialist Comml. Solvents Corp., Terre Haute, Ind., 1947-51; from dir. rsch. info. to assoc. dir. sci. issues R.J. Reynolds Tobacco, Winston-Salem, N.C., 1951-83; sci. cons. rsch. analysis and product liability N.Y.C., 1983—. Fellow AAAS; mem. Am. Chem. Soc. Home: 186 Riverside Dr Apt 6A New York NY 10024-1007

COLBY, JOY HAKANSON, art critic; b. Detroit; d. Alva Hilliard and Eleanor (Radtke) Hakanson; m. Raymond L. Colby, Apr. 11, 1953; children: Sarah, Katherine, Lisa. Student, Detroit Soc. Arts and Crafts, 1945; BFA, Wayne State U., 1946; DFA (hon.), Coll. Art & Design, 1998, Ctr. for Creative Studies, 1998. Art critic Detroit News, 1947—; originator exhibit Arts and Crafts in Detroit, 1906-1976; at Detroit Inst. Arts, 1976; Mem. visual arts adv. panel Mich. Council for Arts, 1974-79; mayor's appointment Detroit Council for Arts, 1974; mem. Bloomfield Hills Arts Council, 1974. Author: Art and A City, 1956, lead essay in Arts and Crafts in Detroit catalog, 1976; Contbr. articles to art periodicals. Recipient Alumni award Wayne State U., 1967, Art Achievement award, 1983, Headliner award, 1984, award for arts reporting Detroit Press Club, 1984, Art Leadership award Ctr. for Creative Studies, 1989. Office: 615 W Lafayette Blvd Detroit MI 48226-3124

COLBY, MARVELLE SEITMAN, business management educator, administrator; b. N.Y.C., Oct. 31, 1932; d. Charles Edward and Lily (Zimmerman) Seitman; m. Robert S. Colby, Apr. 11, 1954 (div. Apr. 1979); children: Lisa, Eric; m. Selig J. Alkon, Dec. 6, 1986. BA, Hunter Coll., 1954; MA, U. N.Colo., 1973; PhD in Pub. Adminstrn., Nova U., 1977; cert., Harvard Grad. Sch. Bus., 1979. V.p. SE Region URC Mgmt. Services Corp., Washington, 1972-77; dir. devel. Hunter Coll. Woman's Ctr. Community Leadership, N.Y.C., 1977-78; dir. tng. and career devel. Girl Scouts U.S., N.Y.C., 1978-79; dir. Overseas Tour Ops. Am. Jewish Congress, N.Y.C., 1979-81; chief exec. officer Girl Scout Council Greater N.Y.C., 1981-82; prof. bus. mgmt. Marymount Manhattan Coll., N.Y.C., 1982—, chmn. bus. mgmt. and acctg. div., 1982-89, 93-99; adj. prof. NYU, 1986-92; mem. exec. com. Assn. Recreation Mgmt., N.Y.C., 1982; cons. Rockport Mgmt., Washington, 1974-78. Author: Test Your Management IQ, 1984; co-author: Lovejoy's Four Year College Guide for the Learning Disabled, 1985, Introduction to Business, 1991; contbr. articles to profl. jours. Chmn. Met. Dade County Commn. Status Women, Miami, 1975-77; chief planner Met. Dade County U.S. SBA 1st annual conf. Future Women Bus., 1977. Named to Hunter Coll. Hall of Fame, 1986. Mem. Acad. Mgmt., Hunter Coll. Alumni Assn. (bd. dirs. 1978-79), Phi Delta Kappa. Club: Lotos (mem. literary com. 1983-89). Home: 242 E 72nd St New York NY 10021-4574 Office: Marymount Manhattan Coll 221 E 71st St New York NY 10021-4501

COLBY, ROBERT ALAN, retired library science educator; b. Chgo., Apr. 15, 1920; s. Meyer and Ida (Lewis) C.; m. Vineta Blumoff, May 8, 1947. B.A., U. Chgo., 1941, M.A., 1942, Ph.D., 1949; M.S. in L.S, Columbia U., 1953. Instr. English DePaul U., Chgo., 1946-47; asst. prof. English Lake Forest (Ill.) Coll., 1949-51; lectr. English Hunter Coll., N.Y.C., 1951-53; lang., lit. and arts librarian Queens Coll., Flushing, N.Y., 1953-64; assoc. prof. libr. sci. So. Conn. State Coll., 1964-66; assoc. prof. library sci. Queens Coll., 1967-69, prof., 1969-86, prof. emeritus, 1986—; docent N.Y. Pub. Libr., 1986—; asst. editor Wellesley Index to Victorian Periodicals, 1978-89. Author: (with Vineta Colby) The Equivocal Virtue: Mrs. Oliphant and the Victorian Literary Marketplace, 1966, Fiction With a Purpose: Major and Minor Nineteenth-Century Novels, 1967, Thackeray's Canvass of Humanity: An Author and His Public, 1979; editor: spl. issue William Makepeace Thackeray, Studies in the Novel, 1981; contbr. introductions to novels including Introduction to Vanity Fair, 1989; contbr. Victorian Periodicals and Victorian Society, 1994, Storia Della Civilta Letteraria Inglese, 1996; mem. editl. bd. Dickens Studies Ann., Victorian Periodicals Rev. Served with AUS, 1943-46. Penfield fellow N.Y. U., 1942-43; Guggenheim fellow, 1978-79; Newberry Library fellow, summer 1982. Mem. MLA, Typophiles Soc., Victorian Soc. Am., Rsch. Soc. for Victorian Periodicals (bd.

dirs. 1969-95, sr. adv. coun. 1995—), Midwest Victorian Studies Assn. Home: 320 Central Park W Apt 9N New York NY 10025-7659

COLBY-HALL, ALICE MARY, Romance studies educator; b. Portland, Maine, Feb. 25, 1932; d. Frederick Eugene and Angie Fraser (Drown) C.; m. Robert A. Hall, Jr., May 8, 1976 (dec. 1997); stepchildren: Philip, Diana Hall Goodall, Carol Hall Erickson. BA, Colby Coll., 1953; MA, Middlebury Coll., 1954; PhD, Columbia U., 1962. Tchr. French, Latin Orono (Maine) H.S., 1954-55; tchr. French Gould Acad., Bethel, Maine, 1955-57; lectr. French Columbia U., 1959-60; instr. Romance lit. Cornell U., Ithaca, N.Y., 1962-63, asst. prof., 1963-66, assoc. prof., 1966-75, prof. Romance studies, 1975-97, prof. emerita, 1997—, chmn. Romance studies, 1990-96. Author: The Portrait in Twelfth Century French Literature: An Example of the Stylistic Originality of Chrétien de Troyes, 1965; mem. editl. bd. Speculum, 1976-79, Olifant, 1974—. Fulbright grantee, 1953-54; NEH fellow, 1984-85; recipient Médaille des Amis d'Orange, 1985; decorated chevalier de l'Ordre des Arts et Lettres, 1997. Mem. Modern Lang. Assn., Medieval Acad. Am. (councillor 1983-86), Internat. Arthurian Soc., Société Rencesvals, Académie de Vaucluse, Phi Beta Kappa. Republican. Congregationalist. Home: 308 Cayuga Heights Rd Ithaca NY 14850-2107 Office: Cornell U Dept Romance Studies Ithaca NY 14853

COLCORD, HERBERT NATHANIEL, III, food company executive; b. Quincy, Mass., Mar. 21, 1951; s. Herbert Nathaniel Jr. and Audrey Louise (Gunn) C.; m. Deborah Sue O'Brien, Nov. 8, 1975; children: Heather Michele, Jared Scott, Devon Elizabeth. BA in Journalism cum laude, Northeastern U., 1973; MA in Journalism, U. Mo., 1975. Accredited bus. communicator. Staff reporter The Patriot Ledger, Quincy, Mass., 1970-73, Columbia (Mo.) Daily Tribune, 1974-75; pub. affairs asst. Nat. Fire Protection Assn., Boston, 1975-77, mgr. editorial programs, 1977-79; mgr. pub. affairs Ocean Spray Cranberries, Inc., Plymouth, Mass., 1979-82, mgr. consumer affairs, 1982-89; mgr. mktg. comms. Ocean Spray Cranberries, Inc., Lakeville, Mass., 1990-97, mgr. corp. comm. and pub. affairs, 1998—; bd. dirs. Plymouth County Devel. Coun., Pembroke, Mass., 1989-92; bd. dirs. Nat. Guest Rels. Assn., 1984-86, pres., 1984-85. Contbr. articles to profl. jours. Recipient Gold Quill award for Excellence Internat. Assn. Bus. Communicators, 1983, Writing Excellence award Coop. Communicators Assn., 1980-81, Writing Excellence award Nat. Coun. Farmer Coop., 1981-82; named Pub. Rels. Allstar, Food and Beverage Mag., 1995, one of Top 10 Food Industry Pub. Rels. Profls., Food Bus. Mag., 1992. Mem. Internat. Assn. Bus. Communicators, Coop. Communicators Assn. (1st place spl. project awards 1992), Advt. Club Greater Boston, Kappa Tau Alpha. Avocations: basketball, golf, genealogy. Home: 322 Nichols Dr Taunton MA 02780-4373 Office: Ocean Spray Cranberries Inc One Ocean Spray Dr Lakeville MA 02349

COLDEWEY, JOHN CHRISTOPHER, English literature educator; b. Beloit, Wis., June 13, 1944; s. George Henry and Frances Mary (McLoughlin) C.; m. Carolyn Culver (div.); children: Christopher, Devin; m. Christine May Rose, Sept. 9, 1989. BA, Lewis U., 1966; student, U. London, Eng., 1966; MA, No. Ill. U., 1967; PhD, U. Colo., 1972. Acting asst. prof. English U. Wash., Seattle, 1972-73, asst. prof. English, 1973-79, assoc. prof. English, 1979-91, prof. English, 1991—, dir. grad. studies, 1995-99; postdoctoral rsch. fellow Nottingham (Eng.) U., 1979-80; Fulbright exchange prof. U. East Anglia, Norwich, Eng., 1986-87; lectr., speaker and reader in field. Author: Pseudomagia: A 17th Century Neo-Latin Tragicomedy by William Mewe, 1979, Renaissance Latin Drama in England, Vol. IV, 1987, Vol. 14, 1991, Contexts for Early English Drama, 1989, Early English Drama: An Anthology, 1993, Drama: Classical Through Contemporary, 1998; editor: Modern Lang. Quar., 1983-93; contbr. chpts. to books, articles to profl. jours. Bd. dirs. Friends U. Wash. Libr., 1991— (pres. 1995-97); hon. advisor Brit. Univs. Summers Schs. Program, 1977-94. Fellow Medieval Acad. Am., 1974-75; grantee Am. Coun. Learned Socs., 1974-75, 1976-77, 86-87, 89-90, grantee NEH, 1979-80, 82-83, 92-93, fellow, 1999—. Mem. Coun. Editors Learned Jours. (pres. 1992-94, v.p. 1990-92, sec.-treas. 1989-90), Medieval and Renaissance Drama Soc. (exec. coun. 1997-98, v.p. 1998—), Medieval European Drama Coun. (Am. rep. 1997—). Avocations: mountaineering, travel, running. Home: 333 35th Ave E Seattle WA 98112-4923 Office: U Wash Dept English Seattle WA 98195

COLDREN, LARRY ALLEN, engineering educator, consultant; b. Lewistown, Pa., Jan. 1, 1946; s. Roscoe Calvin and Mary (Hutchinson) C.; m. Donna Kauffman, Sept. 4, 1966; children: Christopher William, Bret Allen. BS and AB, Bucknell U., 1968; MS, Stanford U., 1969, PhD, 1972. Registered profl. engr., N.J. Mem. tech. staff Bell Labs., N.J., 1968-84, supr., 1984; prof. U. Calif., Santa Barbara, 1984—. Contbr. 300 papers to tech. jours.; patentee in field. Fellow IEEE (mem. ad com. 1988—), Optical Soc. Am.; mem. Phi Beta Kappa, Tau Beta Pi, Pi Mu Epsilon, Sigma Pi Sigma. Presbyterian. Avocation: flying. Home: 4665 Via Vistosa Santa Barbara CA 93110-2333*

COLDWELL, PHILIP EDWARD, financial consultant; b. Champaign, Ill., July 20, 1922; s. Montgomery Ian and Donna Clare (Rose) C.; m. Norma Elaine Abels, June 1, 1947; children: Douglas Michael, Cameron Iliff. BA, U. Ill., 1946, MS, 1947; PhD, U. Wis., 1952. Teaching asst. U. Ill., at Urbana, 1947; instr. Southwestern La. Inst., Lafayette, 1947-48; asst. prof. Southwestern La. Inst., 1950-51; instr. Mont. State U., 1949-50; research economist Fed. Res. Bank, Kansas City, 1951-52; economist, officer Fed. Res. Bank, Dallas, 1952-62; 1st v.p. Fed. Res. Bank, 1962-68, pres., 1968-74; mem. bd. govs. Fed. Res. System, Washington, 1974-80; fin. cons., 1980—; lectr. Southwestern Sch. Banking, Dallas, 1962-74; dir. Maxus Energy Corp., 1987-93. Trustee Austin Coll., 1977-89; dir. Temp Fund, Fed Fund, Muni Fund, 1980-99. Pilot USNR, 1942-46. Mem. Am. Econ. Assn., So. Finance Assn., Phi Delta Theta. Presbyn. (elder). Club: Economists (Dallas) (founder, 1st pres.). Home: 3330 Southwestern Blvd Dallas TX 75225-7653

COLE, ANN HARRIET, psychologist, communications consultant; b. Phila., Feb. 27, 1949; d. Albert and Deborah (Mann) Brawerman; m. Stephen Cole, June 4, 1969 (div. June 18, 1987); children: Richard David, Robert Walter. BA, SUNY, Stony Brook, 1971, MA, 1975. Dir. field rsch. Opinion Rsch. Assocs., 1974-76; v.p. Social Data Analysts, Inc., 1976-86; rsch. assoc. Jay Schulman, Inc., N.Y.C., 1986-87; cons. Litigation Scis., Inc., N.Y.C., 1988-90, Stanley S. Arkin, P.C., N.Y.C., 1990; cons., Chadbourne & Parke, N.Y.C., 1990-91; pres. Ann Cole Opinion Rsch. and Analysis, N.Y.C., 1991—; CBS news cons., 1994-95. Mem. Am. Soc. Trial Cons. (bd. dirs. 1994-2001, v.p. 1996-97, pres. 1997-99), Internat. Platform Assn., Nat. Coalition to Abolish the Death Penalty, N.Y. Assn. Pub. Opinion Rsch. Office: Ann Cole Opinion Rsch and Analysis 1560 Broadway Ste 813 New York NY 10036-1518

COLE, AUBREY LOUIS, management consultant, forest products company executive; b. Wichita Falls, Tex., Dec. 29, 1923; s. Aubrey Mizell and Lila Ellen (Burge) C.; m. Dorothy Jeanne Willson, Dec. 27, 1944; children—Melissa Ann, Gordon Louis. B.B.A., U. Tex., 1949. Asst. controller Tex. div. Champion Papers Co., Pasadena, 1950-59; corporate controller Champion Papers Co., Hamilton, Ohio, 1959-65; v.p. mgmt. info. systems Champion Papers Co., 1966-69; v.p. planning and control U.S. Plywood-Champion Papers, N.Y.C., 1969-73; v.p. mgmt. info. Champion Internat., Stamford, Conn., 1973-74; sr. v.p. control Champion Internat., 1974-85; vice chmn., dir. Champion Internat. Corp., 1985-89; chmn., dir. Champion Realty Corp., Houston, 1989-97; dir. U.S. Timberlands; pres. Aubrey Cole Assocs. 1985—; mem. adv. council Coll. of Bus. Adminstrn. at U. Tex. Served with USNR, 1942-45. Mem. Fin. Execs. Inst., Nat. Assn. Accountants, Nat. Assn. Corp. Dirs., Alpha Kappa Psi. Office: PO Box 391 Elgin TX 78621*

COLE, BENJAMIN RICHASON, newspaper executive; b. Indpls., July 10, 1916; s. Almon Theodore and Maude (Richason) C.; m. Alice Louise Porteous, Sept. 11, 1937 (dec. 1982); children: Alan Andrew, Amy Alice (Mrs. George E. Martin, Jr.), Benjamin Richason.; m. Kathleen Gibbs Martin, Feb. 12, 1983. Student, Butler U., 1934-35, Ind. State Tchrs. Coll., 1938, Am. Press Inst. of Columbia, 1948. Reporter Terre Haute Tribune-Star Pub. Co., 1938-40, Terre Haute Star, 1940-44; with Indpls. Star, 1944-86, statehouse reporter, 1945-48, asst. city editor, 1948, city editor, 1948-49, Washington Corr., 1949-86; corr. Arizona Republic, Phoenix, 1955-86. Mem. Cosmos Club, Gridiron Club, Nat. Press Club, Press Club Indpls., Masons, Soc. Profl. Journalists. Presbyterian. Home: 4101 N Randolph St Arlington VA 22207-4813

COLE, BETTY LOU MCDONEL SHELTON (MRS. DEWEY G. COLE, JR.), judge; b. Elwood, Ind., June 5, 1926; d. Bernard Miller and Vee Marie (Robertson) McDonel; m. Elbert Shelton, Dec. 13, 1944; children: Steven Elbert, Jeanette Louise; m. 2d, Dewey G. Cole, Jr., Dec. 24, 1975. Student, Ind. U., 1947-50, LLB, 1969; student, Ball State U., 1964-65. Bar: Ind. 1969, Fed. Cts., 1969; cert. sr. judge. Pvt. practice, Muncie, Ind., 1969—, Betty L. Shelton Law Office, 1970-78; sr. ptnr. firm Dunnuck, Cole, Rankin and Wyrick, Muncie, 1978-80; judge Delaware County Superior Ct., 1980-95, ret., 1995. Mem. ABA, Ind. Bar Assn., Muncie Bar Assn., Ind. Judges Assn., Am. Trial Lawyers, Ind. U. Law Alumni Assn., Nat. Assn. Women Judges, LWV (league pres. 1963-64), Riley-Jones Club, Columbia Club; recipient State of Ind. Sagamore of the Wabash award, 1998.

COLE, BRADY MARSHALL, retired naval officer; b. Houston, Sept. 3, 1936; s. Brady Nixon and Ann (Marshall) C.; m. Carol Lorrane Hurst, June 10, 1958; children: Cheryl, Christine, Alan. BBA, U. Tex., 1958; postgrad. in acctg., George Washington U., 1966; MBA, Harvard U., 1969; grad., Indsl. Coll. of Armed Forces, Washington, 1978, Nat. Def. U., 1986. Commd. ensign USN, 1958, advanced through grades to rear adm., 1989; with Ships Parts Control Ctr. USN, Mechanicsburg, Pa., 1969-71; gen. supply officer LPH 10 Tripoli USN, San Diego, 1971-73; adminstrv. contr., Supr. Shipbuilding USN, Newport News, Va., 1973-77; procurement contr. Office Sec. Def. Office Sec. Def., Washington, 1978-80; procurement contr. Naval Regional Contracting Office Washington, 1980-81; procurement mgr. Naval Supply Systems Command Arlington, Va., 1981-84; comdg. officer Naval Supply Ctr. San Diego, 1984-86; fleet supply officer Navy Logistics Command and U.S. Pacific Fleet Pearl Harbor, Hawaii, 1986-89; dep. dir. Def. Logistics Agy. Alexandria, Va., 1989-92; prin. The Cole Cluster, Arlington, Va., 1993-96; exec. v.p. Atlantic Divsn. accts. payable recoveries Bottom Line Enhancement Svcs. Internat., Inc.; gen. mgr. Edn. Svcs. Inst., 1994-96; sr. v.p. planning Navy Fed. Credit Union, 1996-99.; CFO Navy Fed. Credit Union, 1999—. Decorated D.S.M., Legion of Merit with two gold stars, Def. Meritorious Svc. medal, Navy Meritorious Svc. medal with gold star, Navy Commendation medal with Combat V, Def. Disting. Svc. medal; Capstone fellow Nat. Def. U., 1986. Mem. Nat. Contract Mgmt. Assn., Assn. Govt. Accts., Army-Navy Country Club, N.Y. Yacht Club.

COLE, BRUCE MILAN, art historian; b. Cleve., Aug. 2, 1938; s. Jerome I. and Selma (Kaufman) C.; m. Doreen Luff, July 15, 1962; children: Stephaine Wren, Ryan Lawrence. BA, Western Res. U., 1962; MA, Oberlin Coll., 1964; PhD, Bryn Mawr Coll., 1969. Asst. prof. U. Rochester, 1969-73; assoc. prof. Ind. U., Bloomington, 1973-77, prof., 1973-88, disting. prof. fine arts, 1988—. Author: Giott and Florentine Painting 1280-1575, 1976, paperback edit., 1977, Agnolo Gaddi, 1977, Italian Majolica from Midwestern Collections, 1977, Masaccio and the Art of Early Renaissance Florence, 1980, Sienese Painting from Its Origins to the Fifteenth Century, 1969, The Renaissance Artist at Work, 1983, London, John Murray, 1983, Sienese Painting in the Age of Renaissance, 1985, Italian Art 1250-1550: The Relation of Renaissance Art to Life and Soc., 1987, Art of the Western World, Piero della Francesca, 1991, Giotto: The Scrovegni Chapel, Padua, 1993, Studies in Italian Art 1250-1550, 1996, Titian and Venetian Painting, 1450-1590, 1998. Recipient Pres.' award Am. Assn. Italian Studies, 1987; NEH fellow, 1972, Guggenheim Found. fellow, 1975, Am. Coun. Learned Socs. fellow, 1981. Fellow Accademia Senese degli Intronati; mem. Nat. Coun. on the Humanities. Avocation: walking. Office: Ind U Fine Arts # 124 Bloomington IN 47405

COLE, CAROLYN JO, brokerage company executive; b. Carmel, Calif., Apr. 22, 1943; d. Joseph Michael Jr. and Dorothea Wagner (James) C. AB, Vassar Coll., 1965. Mgr. tech. svcs. Aims Group, N.Y.C., 1965-67; editor Standard & Poor's Corp., N.Y.C., 1968-74; sr. v.p. Painewebber, Inc., N.Y.C., 1975-95; exec. v.p. Tucker Anthony, Inc., Boston, 1995-97; chmn. Inst. Econ. & Fin., Inc., N.Y.C., 1997-98; mng. dir. Citibank the Pvt. Bank, N.Y.C., 1998—; guest lectr. Harvard U. Bus. Sch.; lectr. Securities Industry Inst., Wharton Sch. U. Pa.; past chmn. bd. dirs. N.Y. Women's Bldg. Named to YWCA Acad. Women Achievers. Mem. NOW, DAR, N.Y. Soc. Security Analysts (past bd. dirs.), Assn. Investment Mgmt. and Rsch., Soc. Fgn. Analysts, Aspen Inst. Humanistic Studies, Fin. Women's Assn., Women's Econ. Roundtable, Econ. Club N.Y., Women in Need (past bd. dirs.), Vassar Club. Democrat. Office: Citibank The Pvt Bank 153 E 53rd St New York NY 10022-4611

COLE, CHARLES DEWEY, JR., lawyer; b. Lower Merion Twp., Pa., Aug. 12, 1952; s. Charles Dewey and Margaret Ann (Leach) C. AB, Columbia U., 1974; JD, St. John's U., Jamaica, N.Y., 1979; ML Info. Sci., U. Tex., 1982; LLM, NYU, 1988; LLM in Environ. Law, Pace U., 1993; LLM in Trial Advocacy, Temple U., 1999. Bar: N.Y. 1980, Tex. 1980, N.J. 1986, D.C. 1988, U.S. Dist. Ct. (we. and ea. dists.) Tex. 1980, U.S. Dist. Ct. (so. and ea. dists.) N.Y. 1980, U.S. Dist. Ct. (no. dist.) Tex. 1982, U.S. Dist. Ct. (no. dist.) N.Y. 1983, U.S. Dist. Ct. (we. dist.) N.Y. 1984, U.S. Dist. Ct. N.J. 1986, U.S. Dist. Ct. D.C. 1994, U.S. Ct. Internat. Trade 1980, U.S. Tax Ct. 1984, U.S. Ct. Appeals (5th and 11th cirs.) 1981, U.S. Ct. Appeals (Fed. cir.) 1982, U.S. Ct. Appeals (2d cir.) 1984, U.S. Ct. Appeals (D.C. cir.) 1987, U.S. Ct. Appeals (3d cir.) 1993, U.S. Supreme Ct. 1984; solicitor, Eng. and Wales, 1995. Law clk. to chief judge U.S. Dist. Ct. (ea. dist.), Beaumont, Tex., 1979-80, U.S. Ct. Appeals (5th cir.), Austin, Tex., 1981-82; assoc. Moore, Berson, Lifflander & Mewhinney, Garden City and N.Y.C., N.Y., 1982-85; assoc. and ptnr. Newman Schlau Fitch & Burns P.C., N.Y.C. and Mineola, N.Y., 1985-88; assoc. Meyer, Suozzi, English & Klein, P.C., Mineola and N.Y.C., 1988-95; of counsel Newman Fitch Altheim Myers, P.C., N.Y.C. and Newark, 1995—. Author: Law Books as a Charitable Contribution, 1975, The EPA Lender Liability Regulations: EPA's Questionable Authority to Promulgate the Regulations as Part of the National Contingency Plan, 1993; contbr. book revs. to profl. pubs. Mem. The Law Soc., N.Y. State Bar Assn., N.J. State Bar Assn., D.C. Bar, N.Y. County Lawyers Assn. (com. on fed. cts.), Maritime Law Assn. U.S. (proctor), Bar Assn. 5th Fed. Cir., Am. Assn. Law Librs., Law Libr. Assn. Greater N.Y., Brit. and Irish Assn. Law Librs., Osgoode Soc., Am. Soc. for Legal History, Soc. Advanced Legal Studies, Supreme Ct. Hist. Soc., Selden Soc., Federalist Soc. for Law and Pub. Policy, Scribes, Clarity. Republican. Home: 16 94th St Apt 3B Brooklyn NY 11209-6643 Office: Newman Fitch Altheim Myers PC 14 Wall St New York NY 10005-2101

COLE, CHARLES DUBOSE, II, law educator; b. Monroeville, Ala., May 14, 1938. BSBA, Auburn U., 1960; JD cum laude, Samford U., 1966; LLM, NYU, 1971; D (hon.), Faculdade Marcelo Tupinamba, Sao Paulo, Brazil, 1991. Bar: Ala. 1966, U.S. Supreme Ct., 1971, U.S. Ct. Appeals (fed. cir.) 1997, U.S. Ct. Internat. Trade, 1997. Law clk., assoc. atty. Porterfield & Sch., Birmingham, Ala., 1965-66; prof. law Cumberland Sch. Law Samford U., Birmingham, 1966-75, 81—; Lucille S. Beeson prof. law and dir. internat. programs, master comparative law degree program Cumberland Sch. Law, Birmingham, Ala., 1993—; dir. permanent study commn. Ala. Jud. System, 1972-74; dir. Ala. Jud. Conf. Criminal Justice Survey, 1973; dir. adv. com. Ala. jud. article implementation Ala. Dept. Ct. Mgmt., 1974-75; dir. so. regional office Nat. Ctr. for State Cts., Atlanta, 1975-79; adminstrv. dir. cts. Commonwealth of Ky., Frankfort, 1979-81; lectr. Cumberland Inst. for Continuing Legal Edn., Ala. Continuing Legal Edn., Josephson/Kluwer Bar Rev. Ctr. Am., Inc., 1967-87; law and social sci. adv. com. Coll. Liberal Arts/Auburn U., 1991—, chmn. 1992-94, dean's coun., 1996—; chmn. profl. adv. com. Office Advancement Auburn U., 1992-93; reporter civil justice adv. group Middle Dist. Ala., 1991-93; del. Moscow Conf. on Law and Econ. Coop., The Kremlin Palace, 1990; legal specialist (pro bono) Parliament of Ukraine, 1993; v.p. faculty Samford U., 1989-90; policy com. mem. Cumberland Sch. Law, 1989-92; mem. faculty exec. com. Samford U., 1988-89; del. U.S./Japan Bilateral Session, 1988; presenter U.S. Info Agy., Internat. Meeting Brazil/U.S., 1988; participant seminar Claremont McKenna Coll./NEH, 1986. Author: (with Brewer) Alabama Constitutional Law, 1992, 2d edit., 1997; contbr. articles to profl. jours. Bd. dirs. Auburn U. Bar Assn., 1991—. Named Outstanding Prof. Student Bar Assn./Cumberland Sch. Law, 1972-73, 83-84, Outstanding Alumnus, Phi Alpha Delta, 1973, Samford U. Cumberland Sch. Law, 1998. Mem. ABA (lectr. appellate judges seminar 1977-78), Am. Judicature Soc., Supreme Ct. Hist. Soc., Am. Trial Lawyers Assn. (faculty mem.), Ala. Bar Assn. (action group mem. 1984-85, chmn. 1985-88, reporter task force on jud. selection 1988-89, com. on the future of the profession 1990-91, task force on legal edn. 1992—, com. on judicial and legal reform 1994-95, chmn. 1995-96), Ukrainian Legal Found. (bd. fgn. advisors 1993-98), Birmingham Bar Assn. (mem. civil ct. rules com. 1998—), Auburn U. Bar Assn. (adv. bd. 1992—), Phi Alpha Delta. Home: 2337 Star Lake Dr Hoover AL 35226

COLE, CHARLES EDWARD, lawyer, former state attorney general; b. Yakima, Wash., Oct. 10, 1927; married; 3 children. BA, Stanford U., 1950, LLB, 1953. Law clk. Vets. Affairs Commn. Territory of Alaska, Juneau, 1954, Territorial Atty. Gen.'s Office, Fairbanks, Alaska, 1955-56, U.S. Dist. Ct. Alaska, Fairbanks, 1955-56; city magistrate City of Fairbanks, 1957-58; pvt. practice law, 1957-90; atty. gen. State of Alaska, 1990-94; pvt. law comml. litigation, 1995—; profl. baseball player, Stockton, Calif. and Twin Falls, Idaho, summers of 1950, 51, 53. With U.S. Army, 1946-47. Mem. Calif. State Bar, Washington State Bar Assn., Alaska Bar Assn. Office: Law Dept State of AK Office of Atty Gen PO Box 110300 Juneau AK 99811-0300 also: Law Offices of Charles E Cole 406 Cushman St Fairbanks AK 99701-4632

COLE, CHARLES GLASTON, lawyer; b. Washington, Jan. 17, 1952; s. Alan Y. and Gloria G. (Glaston) C.; m. Linda Martin, June 6, 1976; children: Elizabeth, Laura, Alan. BA, Yale U., 1973; JD, Harvard U., 1976. Bar: D.C. 1976, U.S. Dist. Ct. D.C. 1977, U.S. Ct. Appeals (D.C. cir.) 1977, U.S. Supreme Ct. 1982. Law clk. U.S. Ct. Appeals, Washington, 1976-77, U.S. Supreme Ct., Washington, 1977-78; assoc. Steptoe & Johnson, Washington, 1978-83, ptnr., 1983—. Mem. ABA (coun. mem. criminal justice sect. 1986-91, chair ad hoc com. on drug crisis 1990-92), Nat. Assn. R.R. Trial Counsel, Am. Bankruptcy Inst. Office: 1330 Connecticut Ave NW Washington DC 20036-1704*

COLE, CHRISTOPHER ROBERT, cardiologist; b. Berea, Ohio, May 12, 1966; s. George William and Gertrude (Patterson) Colflesh; m. Chee-Hwa Tan, Dec. 18, 1993. BS in Biomed. Engring., Oral Roberts U., 1988; MD, W.Va. U., 1992. Diplomate Am. Bd. Internal Medicine. Intern in internal medicine, then resident Presbyn. Hosp., Dallas, 1993-96; rsch. fellow U. Tex. Southwestern, Dallas, 1996-97; cardiology fellow Cleve. Clinic Found., 1997—. Office: Cleve Clinic Found 9500 Euclid Ave Cleveland OH 44195-0001

COLE, CLARENCE RUSSELL, college dean; b. Crestline, Ohio, Nov. 20, 1918; s. Arthur Leroy and Anita Emma (Stephan) C.; m. Mary Piper, Mar. 15, 1945; children: Carole Ann, Larry Lee, Pamela Sue. Student pre-med., Otterbein Coll., Westerville, Ohio, 1937-39; DVM, Ohio State U., 1943, MS, 1944, PhD, 1947. Instr. dept. vet. pathology Coll. Vet. Medicine Ohio State U., asst. prof., 1947-49, chmn. dept., 1947-67, assoc. prof., 1949-54, prof., 1954-67, asst. dean Coll. Vet. Medicine, 1960-67, dean Coll. Vet. Medicine, 1967—, prof. pathology Coll. Medicine, 1952—, prof. comparative pathology Grad. Sch., 1954—; Regents prof. Ohio Bd. Regents, 1966—; chmn. Merson Ctr. Nat. Security, Ohio State U., 1965-67; mem. U. Coun. Rsch., 1960-67; adminstr. cons. Vet. Rsch., Archtl. Engring. Planning, Animal Med. Ctr., N.Y.C.; cons. nat. adv. rsch. resources coun. NIH, 1972—, NIH Health Manpower Grants Br; mem. nat. adv. com. Nat. Ctr. for Primate Biology, 1967-70; mem. com. on comparative pathology NRC, NAS, 1971—; mem. fellowship com. NATO. Recipient Herzfeld lectr. award Auburn U.; 1st award sci. exhibit Ohio State Med. Assn., 1956; 2nd award AMA. Mem. Men and Women of Sci., Internat. Acad. Pathology (mem. exec. coun.), Internat. Toxoplasmosis Com. (vice-chmn. 1959—), AVMA (Gold award, chmn. adv. bd. vet. med. spltys. 1960-75), Am. Coll. Vet. Pathologists (Disting. citation 1967, pres. 1957, Disting. Mem. 1989), Assn. Am. Vet. Med. Colls. (sec.-treas. 1969—), Sigma Xi, Phi Zeta, Omega Tau Sigma. Club: Torch Internat. Address: 1925 Coffey Rd Columbus OH 43210-1005

COLE, CLIFFORD ADAIR, clergyman; b. Lamoni, Iowa, Nov. 16, 1915; s. Fayette V. and Mable F. (Adair) C.; m. Harriet Lucile Hartshorn, June 28, 1936; children: Alethea Rae (Mrs. Justus S. Allen), Beverly Sue (Mrs. Lloyd G. Hilburn, Jr.), Lawrence Dean. Student, Graceland Coll., Lamoni, 1934-35, 41-42, U. Wyo., 1938; B.S. in Edn, Central Mo. State Coll., 1943; postgrad., U. Iowa, 1946, U. Chgo., 1952; M.A. in Edn, U. Mo. at Kansas City, 1957. Ordained to ministry Reorganized Ch. of Jesus Christ of Latter Day Saints, 1939. High sch. tchr. Lamoni, 1943-46, Bellevue, Ia., 1946-47; min. Iowa, 1947-51; dean students Graceland Coll., 1951-53; dir. dept. religious edn. Reorganized Ch. of Jesus Christ of Latter Day Saints, 1955-58, apostle in council twelve, 1958-80, pres. council, 1964-80, cons. to 1st presidency, 1980-82; ret., 1982. Author: The Prophets Speak, 1954, Working Together in our Families, 1955, Celebrating Together in our Families, 1955, Faith for New Frontier, 1956, The Revelation in Christ, 1963, Modern Women in a Modern World, 1965, The Mighty Act of God, 1984. Mem. Phi Sigma Pi, Zeta Kappa Epsilon, Kappa Delta Pi. *Everyone who thinks deeply must answer the question: "What is the Ultimate Reality undergirding our universe?" The answer is not found in proof but rather in faith. The struggle has led me to a profound and abiding faith in God.*

COLE, CRYSTAL LYNN, artist; b. Toronto, Ont., Can., May 28, 1960; came to U.S., 1971; d. John F. Clark and Lynne Chapple; children: William J., Branden J., Elizabeth A. AA, BFA, Shepherd Coll., 1997. Substitute art tchr. Warren County (Va.) Schs., 1998—; intern Shepherd Coll., London, Italy, and Greece, 1996, 97. Exhibited in group shows at Md. Fedn. Art Emerging Artists Exhibit, 1997 (hon. mention), Blue Ridge Arts Coun., others. Cub scout leader Boy Scouts Am., Herndon, Va., 1988-92; parent advisor Warren County Gifted and Talented Adv. Bd., Front Royal, 1996. Grantee Marion Parks-Lewis Found. for the Arts, Winchester, Va., 1994—; recipient award Liquitex Student Paint Exch./Gallery of Winners-Art on the Internet, 1996, Best in Show award Artstravaganza Shenandoah Arts Coun., 1996. Mem. Coll. Art Assn., Shenandoah Arts Coun., Blue Ridge Arts Coun. (vol. coord. 1992—, gallery intern 1995, student bd. mem. search com. 1997). Roman Catholic. Office: Artique PO Box 282 Linden VA 22642-0282

COLE, DANA T., adult educator, researcher; b. L.A., Sept. 21, 1963; d. Robert Jack and Marlene Cole. BA, Ind. U., 1986; MA, Loyola U., Chgo., 1995. Rsch. asst. Inst. for Urban Life, Chgo., 1992-94; prof. Loyola U., Chgo., 1995-98; adult educator Travelers and Immigrants Aid, Chgo., 1998-99, Morton Coll., Cicero, Ill., 1996—; adult educator in ESL, Kennedy King Coll., Chgo., 1991—; mem. adv. bd. Hands on English, Chgo., 1998—. Author reports and presentations. Avocations: Spanish, Latin music, health, exercise. Email: dcole@megsinet.net. Home: 2825 N Francisco Chicago IL 60618

COLE, DAVID EDWARD, university administrator; b. Detroit, July 20, 1937; s. Edward Nicholas and Esther Helen (Engman) C.; m. Carol Hutchins, July 9, 1965; children: Scott David, Christopher Carl. BS in Mech. Engring. and Math., U. Mich., 1960, MS in Mech. Engring., 1961, PhD, 1966. Engr. GM, Detroit, 1960-65; prof. U. Mich., Ann Arbor, 1967—, dir. Office for Study of Automotive Transp., 1978—; entrepreneur 6 cos., 1975-95; pres. Applied Theory, Ann Arbor, 1980-95; chmn. Automotive Cons. Group, Ann Arbor, 1986-95; bd. dirs. JPE, Ann Arbor, MSX Engring., Detroit, Mech. Dynamics, Ann Arbor, Thyssen U.S., Detroit, Saturn Electronics, Detroit; mem. energy engring. bd. NRC, 1989-94; mem. select panel U.S.-Can. Free trade Pact, 1988-91. Author: Elementary Vehicle Dynamics, 1972; contbr. articles to profl. jours. Bd. trustees Hope Coll., 1994-98. Fellow Soc. Automotive Engrs. (dir. 1980-83, 85-88, Teetor award 1969), Engring. Soc. Detroit; mem. Soc. Mktg. Execs. (Mktg. Educator of Yr. 1998, Rene Dubos Environ. award 1998), Nat. Auto Dealers Assn. Found. (Freedom of Mobility award 1993), Swedens Royal Order of the Polar Star. Republican. Presbyterian. Avocations: hunting, fishing, boating, running, tennis. Office: Office Study Automotive Transp U Mich 2901 Baxter Rd Ann Arbor MI 48109-2150

COLE, DAVID WINSLOW, personal care industry executive; b. Toledo, Sept. 20, 1947; s. Robert Winslow and Marjorie Lucile (Rottman) C.; m. Nancy Carol Gerathy, July 3, 1971; 1 child, Kevin. BS, Miami U., Oxford, Ohio, 1969. From field sales rep. to unit mgr. Procter and Gamble Co., Chgo. and St. Louis, 1970-76; dist. mgr. frozen foods Quaker Oats Co., Detroit, 1976-78; ea. regional mgr. frozen foods Quaker Oats Co., Severna Park, Md., 1978-82; nat. sales mgr. confectionery products Quaker Oats Co.,

Chgo., 1982-85; mgmt. cons. Northeastern Orgn., Inc., Trumbull, Conn., 1985-86; dir. field sales Cadbury U.S.A. subs. Cadbury Schweppes PLC, Stamford, Conn., 1986-88, dir. sales, 1988-89; v.p. sales Personal Care Products divsn. Weyerhauser Co., Federal Way, Wash., 1989, exec. v.p. sales, 1989, v.p., gen. mgr., 1990-93; pres. Paragon Trade Brands, Norcross, Ga., 1993—. Mem. Capital City Club. Avocation: golf. Office: Paragon Trade Brands 180 Technology Pkwy Norcross GA 30092-2907

COLE, DEBORAH S., psychologist; b. Balt.; d. Ray Chenowith Cole and Rena Dale. BS, Towson State U., 1970; MS, Loyola Coll., 1972; PsyD, Pepperdine U., 1992. Lic. psychologist, Md. Sch. psychologist Balt. City Schs., 1980-86; psychology assoc. Patuxent Instn., Jessup, Md., 1992-94; pvt. practice Ellicott City, Md., 1994—. Bd. dirs. Howard County Coalition of Geriatrics, Columbia, Md., 1998. Recipient plaque for svc. to mentally retarded Nat. Assn. for Retarded, 1978. Mem. APA, Md. Psychol. Assn., Howard County C. of C. Avocation: crafts. Office: Ste 100 9380 Baltimore National Pike Ellicott City MD 21042-2806

COLE, DOUGLAS, retired English literature educator; b. N.Y.C., July 25, 1934; s. Ronald and Helen Elizabeth (Bladykas) C.; m. Virginia Ann Ford, Nov. 28, 1957; children: David, Stephen, Karen, Kristin. BA, U. Notre Dame, Ind., 1957; MA, U. Chgo., 1957; PhD, Princeton U., 1961. Instr. English, Yale U., New Haven, 1960-64, asst. prof., 1964-67, assoc. prof., 1967-69; prof. Northwestern U., Evanston, Ill., 1969-98, prof. emeritus, 1998—, chmn. dept. English, 1974-77, acting chmn., 1993, master Humanities Residential Coll., 1981-84, dir. major program in drama, 1980-93, 95-97. Author: Suffering and Evil in the Plays of Christopher Marlowe, 1962, Christopher Marlowe and the Renaissance of Tragedy, 1995; editor: 20th Century Views of Romeo and Juliet, 1970, Renaissance Drama XI: Tragedy, 1980; contbr. numerous articles to profl. jours. Morse fellow, 1966-67; Woodrow Wilson fellow, Danforth fellow Princeton U., 1957-61. Office: Northwestern U English Dept Evanston IL 60208-5638

COLE, ELMA PHILLIPSON (MRS. JOHN STRICKLER COLE), social welfare executive; b. Piqua, Ohio, Aug. 9, 1909; d. Brice Leroy and Mabel (Gale) Phillipson; m. John Strickler Cole, Oct. 3, 1959. AB, Berea Coll., 1930; MA, U. Chgo., 1938. Social work staff, 1930-42; dir. dept. social svc. Children's Hosp. D.C., Washington, 1942-49; cons. pub. coop. Midcentury White House Conf. on Children and Youth, Washington, 1949-51; exec. sec. Nat. Midcentury Com. on Children and Youth, N.Y.C., 1951-53; cons. recruitment Am. Assn. Med. Social Workers, 1953; assoc. dir. Nat. Legal Aid and Defender Assn., 1953-56; exec. sec. Marshall Field Awards, Inc., 1956-57; dir. assoc. orgns. Nat. Assembly Social Policy and Devel., 1957-73; assoc. exec. dir. Nat. Assembly Nat. Vol. Health and Social Welfare Orgns., 1974; dir. edn. parenthood project Salvation Army, 1974-76, asst. sec. dept. women's and children's social svcs., 1976-78, dir. rsch. project devel. bur., 1978-92, ind. cons., 1993—; mem. Manhattan adv. bd., 1975—, sec., 1984—; cons. nat. orgns. Golden Anniversary White House Conf. on Children and Youth, 1959-60; mem. adv. coun. pub. svc. Nat. Assn. Life Underwriters and Inst. Life Ins.; judges com. Louis I. Dublin Pub. Svc. awards, 1961-74; v.p. Blue Ridge Inst. So. Cmty. Svc. Execs., 1977-79, exec. com., 1979-81; mem. awards jury Girls Clubs Am., 1981-93; adv. bd. Nat. Family Life Edn. Network, 1982-97. Com. pub. rels. and fundraising Am. Found. for Blind Commn. on Accreditation, 1964-67; task force on vol. accreditation Coun. Nat. Orgns. for Adult Edn., 1974-78; adv. bd. sexuality edn. project Ctr. for Population Options, 1977-86; bd. dirs., sec. James Lenox House, 1985-89, pres., 1989-94, treas., 1994-98; bd. dirs., sec. James Lenox House Assn., 1985-89, pres., 1989-94, sec., 1994-98; bd. dirs. Values and Human Sexuality Inst., 1980-85, Presbyterian Sr. Svcs., N.Y., 1998, Sexuality Info. and Edn. Coun. of U.S., 1993, exec. com. Mem. Pub. Rels. Soc. Am. (cert.), Nat. Assn. Social Workers (cert.), Nat. Conf. Social Welfare (mem. pub. rels. com. 1961-66, 69-82, chair adminstrn. sect. 1966-67), Soc. Sci. Study Sexuality, Jr. League N.Y., Women's Club of N.Y., Pi Gamma Mu, Phi Kappa Phi. Home: 19 Washington Sq N New York NY 10011-9170

COLE, ELSA KIRCHER, lawyer; b. Dec. 5, 1949; d. Paul and Hester Marie (Pellegrom) Kircher; m. Roland J. Cole, Aug. 16, 1975; children: Isabel Ashley, Madeline Aldis. AB in History with distinction, Stanford U., 1971; JD, Boston U., 1974. Bar: Wash. 1974, Mich. 1989, Kans. 1997, U.S. Supreme Ct. 1980. Asst. atty gen., rep. dept. motor vehicles State of Wash., Seattle, 1974-75, asst. atty. gen., rep. dept. social and health svcs., 1975-76, asst. atty. gen., rep. U. Wash., 1976-89; gen. counsel U. Mich., Ann Arbor, 1989-97, NCAA, Overland Park, Kans., 1997—; presenter ednl. issues various confs. and workshops. Contbr. articles to profl. jours. Mem. Nat. Assn. Coll. and Univ. Attys. (chair profl. devel. com. 1990-91, mem. nominations and site selection coms. 1987-88, 95-96, program 1988-89, 89-90, 91-92, 92-93, 95-96, board ops. 92-93, 95-96, fin., articles and by-laws coms. 1988-89, CLE com. 1995-96, 96-97, co-chair student affairs sect. 1987-88, 88-89, honors and awards ethics com. 1991-92, continuing legal edn. com. 1995-97, pub. com. 1996-97, bd. dirs. 1988-91), Wash. State Bar Assn. (chair law sch. liaison com. 1988-89), Wash. Women Lawyers (pres. Seattle-King County chpt. 1986, v.p. membership, state bd. 1987, 88, state chair candidate endorsement com. 1987, 88), Seattle-King County Bar Assn. Office: NCAA 6201 College Blvd Overland Park KS 66211-2422

COLE, GEORGE THOMAS, lawyer; b. Orlando, Fla., Mar. 14, 1946; s. Robert Bates and Frances (Arnold) C.; m. Peggy Ellen Stimson, May 23, 1981; children—Leslie Elizabeth, Ashley Ellen, Robert Warren. A.B., Yale U., 1968; J.D., U. Mich., 1975. Bar: Ariz. 1975, U.S. Dist Ct. Ariz. 1975, U.S. Ct. Appeals (9th cir.) 1978; cert. real estate specialist Ariz. Bar. Assoc., Fennemore, Craig, von Ammon, Udall & Powers, Phoenix, 1975-81; ptnr., Fennemore Craig, Phoenix, 1981—. Served to lt. (j.g.) USN, 1968-71. Fellow Ariz. Bar Found. (founding); mem. Nat. and Ariz. Assns. Home Builders, Urban Land Inst. (cmty. devel. coun.), Community Assns. Inst., Am. Resort Devel. Assn., Ariz. Bar Assn. (council Real Property sect. 1985—, chmn., 1987-88), Maricopa Bar Assn. Republican. Methodist. Clubs: Yale (pres. 1984), Paradise Valley Country (Phoenix), White Mountain Country (Pinetop, Ariz.). Home: 5102 E Desert Park Ln Paradise Vly AZ 85253-3054 Office: Fennemore Craig 3003 N Central Ave Ste 2600 Phoenix AZ 85012-2913

COLE, GLEN DAVID, minister; b. Tacoma, Dec. 21, 1933; s. Ray Milton and Ruth Evelyn (Ranton) C.; m. Mary Ann Von Moos, June 6, 1953; children: Randall Ray, Ricky Jay. BA in Theology, Cen. Bible Coll., 1956; DD, Pacific Coast Bible Coll., 1983. Pastor Assembly of God, Marion, Ohio, 1957-60, Maple Valley, Wash., 1960-65; assoc. pastor Calvary Temple, Seattle, 1965-67; sr. pastor Evergreen Christian Ctr., Olympia, Wash., 1967-78; sr. pastor Capital Christian Ctr., Sacramento, 1978-95, pastor emeritus, 1995—; dist. supr. Assemblies of God, Sacramento, 1997—; exec. presbyter Assemblies of God, Springfield, 1985—; trustee Bethany Bible Coll., Santa Cruz, Calif., 1979—; bd. dirs. Cen. Bible Coll., Springfield, Mo., 1988—; bd. dirs. Calif. Theol. Sem., Fresno, 1985-90. Mem. Rotary (pres. Olympia chpt. 1977-78). Republican. Office: Assemblies of God 6051 S Watt Ave Sacramento CA 95829 Address: 525 Washoe Ct Roseville CA 95747-8259 *It seems that the people God uses most are not those with greater ability, or more education, or superior talent but those who become totally dependent on him.*

COLE, HEATHER ELLEN, librarian; b. Rochester, N.Y., Nov. 7, 1942; d. Donald M. and Muriel Agnes (Kimball) C.; m. Stratis Haviaras; 1 child, Elektra Maria Muriel. BA, Cornell U., 1964; MS, Simmons Coll., 1973. Mgr. Brentano's, Boston, 1968-70; intern Harvard Coll. Libr., Cambridge, Mass., 1970-73, reference libr., 1973-77, libr., 1977—; libr. Hilles and Lamont Librs., 1977—. Mem. AAUW, ALA, Am. Soc. Info. Sci. (New England chpt.), Assn. Coll. Rsch. Librs. Democrat. Episcopalian. Avocation: gardening. Home: 19 Clinton St Cambridge MA 02139-2303 Office: Harvard Coll Lamont Library Cambridge MA 02138

COLE, HENRY PHILIP, educational psychology educator; b. Buffalo, Jan. 5, 1937; s. Raymond James and Hannah Christina (Shapleigh) C.; m. Marion Margaret Montgomery, Aug. 19, 1961; children: Mark Douglas, David Arthur, Debra Lynn. BS in Chemistry, Nasson Coll., 1958; MEd, SUNY, Buffalo, 1966, EdD, 1968. Chemistry technician WASCO Chem. Co., Sanford, Maine, 1957-58; tchr. physics and sci. Holland (N.Y.) Ctrl. Sch., 1958-59; med. rsch. technician Buffalo Gen. Hosp., 1959-61; tchr. sci. Griffith Inst. and Ctrl. Sch., Springville, N.Y., 1961-65; instr. ednl. psychology SUNY, Buffalo, 1966-68; ednl. psychologist Ea. Regional Inst. for Edn., Syracuse, N.Y., 1968-71; prof. ednl. psychology U. Ky., Lexington, 1971—, prof. preventive medicine, 1990—, head behavioral rsch. aspects safety-health group (BRASH), 1984-97; vis. prof. Syracuse U., 1968-70; rsch. psychologist U.S. Bur. Mines, Pitts., 1988-89; U.S. del. MINESAFE Internat. Conf., Western Australia, 1993; behavioral safety expert ILO, China, 1993. Author: Measuring Learning in Continuing Education for Engineers and Scientists, 1984; contbr. more than 150 tech. reports, articles to profl. jours., chpts. to books. Scoutmaster Boy Scouts Am., Lexington, 1975-77, round table commr., 1976-78; v.p., team. rep. Little League Baseball, Lexington, 1975-78. With U.S. Army, 1959-61. Recipient Disting. Author award Jour. Allied Health, 1981, Best Paper award Am. Soc. Engring. Edn., 1985, Pub. of Yr. award Bur. of Mines-Pitts. Rsch. Ctr., 1987, Tech. Transfer award, 1989, Unsung Hero's award for outstanding rsch. contbns. U. Ky. Mem. AAAS, APA, Am. Ednl. Rsch. Assn., Ky. Safety and Health Network. Republican. Presbyterian. Avocations: jogging, bicycling, reading natural science, farming. Office: University Kentucky Dept Preventive Medicine 1141 Red Mile Rd Ste 102 Lexington KY 40504-2656*

COLE, JACK ELI, physician; b. Matamoras, Pa., Jan. 7, 1915; s. Eli Martin and Louise (Henneberg) C. m. Evelyn Gaston Darragh, Apr. 26, 1941; children: Jack Eli, Thomas, Beverly, Martin, Robert, Leslie, Christopher, Candace, Champa. BS, Pa. State U., 1937; MD, U. Pa., 1941. Diplomate Am. Bd. Family Practice. Intern Wilkes-Barre (Pa.) Gen. Hosp., 1941-42; practice medicine, specializing in family practice Matamoras, Pa., 1946-47; staff St. Luke's Hosp., Bethlehem, Pa., 1948—; practice medicine, specializing in family practice Bethlehem, 1952-68, 1973-89; sec. dept. family practice St. Luke's Hosp., Bethlehem, 1973-88; incorporator, mem. med. staff Muhlenberg Hosp., Bethlehem, 1960—, pres. med. staff, 1961-62; student health physician Lehigh U., Bethlehem, 1948-52; physician Peace Corps, Afghanistan, Swaziland, India, 1968-73; leader mission med. team United Ch. Christ, Honduras, 1987; preceptor Temple U. Med. Sch., Phila., 1978-86. Contbr. poetry to anthologies, children's stories and articles to profl. pubs. Charter mem. mission partnership com. N.E. Pa. conf. United Ch. of Christ, 1984. With U.S. Army, 1942-45. Decorated Purple Heart, Combat Medic badge; recipient Recognition award Temple U. Med. Sch., 1979; Boss of Yr. award Allentown Bus. Womens Assn., 1975. Fellow Am. Acad. Family Physicians; mem. AMA, Northampton County Med. Soc., Pa. Med. Soc., Lehigh Valley Acad. Family Physicians (v.p. 1979-81, pres. 1981-83), Pa. Acad. Family Physicians, Am. Acad. Family Physicians. Republican. Avocation: opera. Home: 782 Barrymore Ln Bethlehem PA 18017-2522

COLE, JANET See **HUNTER, KIM**

COLE, JANICE MCKENZIE, prosecutor; b. Feb. 16, 1947; m. James Carlton Cole. BA summa cum laude, John Jay Coll Criminal Justice, 1975, MPA, 1978; JD, Fordham U., 1979. Bar: N.Y. 1980, N.C. 1983. Asst. U.S. atty. Eastern Dist. N.Y., 1979-83; sole practitioner, 1983-89; with firm Cole & Cole, 1989-90; dist. ct. judge First Jud. Dist. N.C., 1990-94; U.S. atty. N.C. Eastern Dist., 1994—. Office: US Attys Office 310 New Bern Ave Ste 800 Raleigh NC 27601-1461

COLE, JEROME FOSTER, research company executive; b. Cin., Aug. 8, 1940; s. George F. and Arlene M. (McCoy) C.; m. Virginia E. Vaughn, July 6, 1963; children—Cheryl, Robert. B.S. in Pharmacy, U. Cin., 1962, M.S., 1965, Sc.D. in Environ. Health, 1968. Registered pharmacist, Ohio. Indsl. hygienist Procter and Gamble Co., Cin., 1968-69; mgr. environ. health Internat. Lead Zinc Research Orgn., N.Y.C., (moved N.C. 1987—) 1969-73, dep. dir., 1973-75, v.p., 1975-83, pres., 1983—. Served to sgt. USAFR, 1967-68. Mem. Soc. Toxicology, Am. Indsl. Hygiene Assn., N.Y. Acad. Scis., Air Pollution Control Assn., Governors Club. Avocations: sailing, tennis, golf.

COLE, JOANNE W., women's health nurse, researcher; b. Indpls., Dec. 13, 1958; d. James Jamison Jr. and Jean Helen (Cramton) Waygood; m. Dwight Anthony Cole, July 12, 1985. BSN, U. Evansville, 1980; MSN, Indiana U., 1987; postgrad., Ind. U., 1992. Cert. adult nurse practitioner; cert. clinical rsch. coord. Staff nurse James Whitcomb Riley Hosp., Indpls., coord. patient care; nursing mgr. Meth. Hosp. of Indiana Inc., Indpls.; clin. rsch. nurse, study coord., nurse practitioner Metro Health Care of Ind., Indpls.; dept. head advanced practice nurse dept. MetroHealth Care of Ind.; nurse practitioner Meth. Rsch. Inst., Inc.; with Eli Lilly & Co., Indpls. Contbr. articles to profl. jours. Mem. Am. Fertility Soc., Assn. for Care of Children's Health, Ind. Perintology Assn., Sigma Theta Tau. Home: 5662 S County Road 300 W Greencastle IN 46135-8606

COLE, JOHN ADAM, insurance executive; b. Odessa, Tex., May 6, 1951; s. Alling and Millicent (McWilliam) C.; m. Karen Elisabeth Jones, June 28, 1974; children: J. Adam Jr., Robert H., Kathryn E. A in Occupational Studies in Acctg., Bus.i, Utica (N.Y.) Sch. Commerce, 1973; postgrad., New Sch. Social Rsch., 1984, Am. Coll., Bryn Mawr, Pa. ChFC, CLU. Sales mgr. Mohawk Frozen Foods, Marcy, N.Y., 1973-77; sole propr. From the C's, Inc., Rome, N.Y., 1975-77; agt., dist. asst. Equitable Fin. Svcs., Rome, 1978-83; advanced mktg. specialist Farm Family Ins. Cos., Albany, N.Y., 1984, dir. agt. and mgr. devel., 1985-87, dir. devel. and advanced life sales, 1987-96, dir. advanced markets, 1996-97, dir. life sales, 1997—; mem. mktg. com. Farm Bur. Bank, 1998—; adj. instr. various profl. tng. orgns., Rome, Utica & Albany, 1981—. Pres. Rome Cmty. Concerts Assn., 1978-80, Voorheesville (N.Y.) Ctrl. Sch. Bd., 1990—; cubmaster Boy Scouts Am.; mem. Holland Patent (N.Y.) Ctrl. Sch. Bd., 1982-85; mem. parents adv. bd. Pine Bush Little League, New Scotland Pop Warner, Guilderland Babe Ruth League; coach Ea. N.Y. State Champions team Babe Ruth Allstars, 1995; found. dir. Voorheesville Cmty. Schs. Found., 1999—. Mem. Ea. N.Y. Soc. CLUs & ChFCs (bd. dirs. 1986-91), Albany Assn. Life Underwriters (bd. dirs. 1987-92), Mohawk Valley Life Underwriters (pres., chmn. 1980-84), Internat. Platform Assn., Kiwanis, N.Y. State Newsletter award 1992), Masons. Republican. Methodist. Home: 102 Woodview Ct Voorheesville NY 12186-9573 Office: Farm Family Ins Co PO Box 656 Albany NY 12201-0656

COLE, JOHN POPE, JR., lawyer; b. Washington, Jan. 12, 1930; s. John Pope and Helen (Gorman) C.; m. Patsy Nan Moss, Mar. 20, 1960; children—John Moss, Nina Gorman. B.S., Auburn U., 1953; LL.B., George Washington U., 1956. Bar: D.C. 1956, Md. 1956, Ga. 1961. Atty. FCC, Washington, 1956-57; ptnr. Smith & Pepper, Washington, 1957-66, Cole, Raywid & Braverman, Washington, 1966—; staff U.S. Ho. Reps., Washington, 1961-62. Served with USAF, 1948-49. Home: 5309 Portsmouth Rd Bethesda MD 20816-2930 Office: Cole Raywid & Braverman 1919 Pennsylvania Ave NW Washington DC 20006-3458

COLE, JOHNNETTA BETSCH, university president emeritus, educator; b. Jacksonville, Fla., Oct. 19, 1936; d. John Thomas and Mary Frances (Lewis) Betsch; m. Robert Eugene Cole (div. 1982); children: David, Aaron, Ethan; m. Arthur J. Robinson, Jr., 1988. Student, Fisk U., 1953; BA in Sociology, Oberlin Coll., 1957; MA in Anthropology, Northwestern U., Evanston, Ill., 1959, PhD, 1967. Instr. U. Calif., Los Angeles, 1964; dir. black studies Wash. State U., Pullman, 1969-70; prof. anthropology U. Mass., Amherst, 1970-83, assoc. provost undergrad. edn., 1981-83; vis. prof. Hunter Coll., N.Y.C., 1983-84, prof. anthropology, 1983-87, dir. Inter-Am. Affairs Program, 1984-87; pres. Spelman Coll., Atlanta, 1987-97; pres. emeritus, 1997—; corp. bd. dirs. Coca Cola Enterprises, Mgmt. Tng. Corp., Merck & Co., Inc., Home Depot; trustee Rockefeller Found.; presdl. disting. prof. of anthropology women's studies and Afro-Am. studies Emory U., 1998—. Author, editor: Anthropology for the Eighties, 1982, All American Women, 1986, Anthropology for the Nineties, 1988, Conversations: Straight Talk with America's Sister President, 1993, Dream the Boldest Dreams, 1998; mem. editorial bd. The Black Scholar. Recipient numerous hon. degrees. Fellow Am. Anthrop. Assn.; mem. Assn. Black Anthropologists (past pres.). Baptist. Office: Emory U Dept Anthro Geo Scis Rm 214 1557 Pierce Dr Atlanta GA 30322*

COLE, JONATHAN RICHARD, sociologist, academic administrator; b. N.Y.C., Aug. 27, 1942; s. Richard and Sylvia (Dym) C.; m. Joanna Miller Lewis, June 5, 1968; children: Daniel Lewis, Susanna Dora. BA, Columbia U., 1964, PhD, 1969. Asst. prof. sociology Columbia U., N.Y.C., 1969-73, assoc. prof., 1973-76, prof., 1976—, Quetelet prof. social sci., 1989—, dir. Ctr. for Social Scis., 1979-87, v.p. Arts and Scis., 1987-89, provost, 1989-94, profost dean of faculties, 1994—; adj. prof. Rockefeller U., 1983-85; pres. Reid Hall Inc.; cons. Ford Found., NSF, Nat. Acad. Scis., Russell Sage Found., AT&T. Author: Social Stratification in Science, 1973, Fair Science: Women in the Scientific Community, 1979, Peer Review in the National Science foundation, Vol. 1, 1978, Vol. 2, 1981, The Wages of Writing: Per Word, Per Price, or Perhaps, 1986, The Outer Circle, 1990, The Research Library in a Time of Discontent, 1994; editor Am. Jour. Sociology; contbr. articles to profl. jours. Guggenheim fellow, 1975-76, Ctr. for Advanced Study in Behavioral Scis. fellow, 1975-76. Fellow AAAS, Am. Acad. Arts and Scis.; mem. Am. Sociol. Assn., Internat. Sociol. Assn., Eastern Sociol. Assn., Soc. Rsch. Assn. (hon.). Home: 404 Riverside Dr New York NY 10025-1861 Office: Columbia U 205 Low Libr 116th & Broadway New York NY 10027*

COLE, JUNE ANN, safety, health and emergency manager; b. L.A., July 1, 1942; m. Lawrence Dale Cole, Dec. 30, 1960; children: Cathy, Jeff, Caren, Amy. ADN, Mt. Hood Community Coll., 1981; BSN, U. Portland, 1989; MS, Oreg. Health Scis. U., 1994. Cert. audiometric technician, ACLS, CPR instr., respiratory therapy technician, phys. fitness specialist. Staff nurse ICU Mt. Hood Med. Ctr., Gresham, Oreg., 1981-86, occupl. health coord., 1986-88; clin. coord., mgr. Occupational Med. Ctr., Portland, Oreg.; safety, health and emergency mgr. Fujitsu Microelectronics Inc., Gresham, 1989—. Home: 17123 SE Royer Rd Clackamas OR 97015-8746

COLE, KATHLEEN ANN, advertising agency executive; retired social worker b. Cin., Nov. 22, 1946; d. James Scott and Kathryn Gertrude (Borisch) Cole; BA, Miami U., 1968; MSW, U. Mich., 1972; MM, Northwestern U., 1978; m. Brian Brandt, Mar. 21, 1970. Social worker Hamilton County Welfare Dept., Cin., 1969-70, Lucas County Children Svcs. Bd., Toledo, 1970-74, East Maine Sch. Dist., Niles, Ill., 1974-77; account supr. Leo Burnett Advt. Agy., Chgo., 1978-93; primary therapist, Lifeline, Chgo., 1994-95; acct. dir. GreenHouse Comm., 1995—; field instr. Loyola U., Chgo., 1976-77. Mem. Acad. Cert. Social Workers (chair pub. rels. task force), Nat. Assn. Social Workers, Miami U. Alumni Assn. (dir. 1976—), Northwestern U. Prof. Women's Assn., Kellogg Alumni Assn., North Shore United Meth. Congregation. Home: 414 Kelling Ln Glencoe IL 60022-1113

COLE, KENNETH DUANE, architect; b. Ft. Wayne, Ind., Jan. 23, 1932; s. Wolford J. and Helen Francis (McDowell) C.; m. Carolyn Lou Meyer, Apr. 25, 1953; children: David Brent, Denelle Hope, Diana Faith, Dawn Love. Student, Ft. Wayne Art Inst., 1950-51; BS in Architecture, U. Cin., 1957. Draftsman/intern Humbrecht Assocs., Ft. Wayne, 1957-58; ptnr./arch. Cole-Matott, Archs./Planners, Ft. Wayne, 1959-94, Cole & Cole Archs., 1995—; mem. adv. bd. Gen. Services Adminstrn., Region 5, 1976, 78. Archtl. works include: Weisser Pk. Jr. H.S., 1963, Brandt Hall, 1965, Bonsib Bldg., 1967, Lindley Elem. Sch., 1969, Young Elem. Sch., 1972, Study Elem. Sch., 1975, Old City Hall Renovation, 1978, Peoples Trust Bank Adminstrv. Svcs. Ctr., 1979, Cole Residence (Design award 1988), Ossian Office Old 1st Nat. Bank, 1988, Perimeter Security Wall, Ind. State Prison. Bd. dirs. Ft. Wayne Art Inst., 1969-74, Arch, Inc., Ft. Wayne, 1975-77, Downtown Ft. Wayne Assn., 1977-82, Hist. Soc. Ft. Wayne and Allen County, 1982-88, Izaak Walton League Am., Ft. Wayne, 1970-76. Recipient citation Ind. Soc. Archs. for remodeling of Bonsib Bldg., 1978. Mem. Ft. Wayne C. of C., AIA (bd. dirs. No. Ind. 1971-74, pres. 1974), Ind. Soc. Archs. (bd. dirs. 1973-76, sec. 1976), Ft. Wayne Soc. Archs. (pres. 1970-71), Am. Arbitration Assn. (panel of arbitrators 1980-96). Lutheran. Home: 11602 Stellhorn Rd New Haven IN 46774 Office: Cole & Cole Architects 927 S Harrison St Fort Wayne IN 46802-3672

COLE, LEONARD AARON, political scientist, dentist; b. Paterson, N.J., Sept. 1, 1933; s. Morris and Rebecca (Harelick) Cohen; m. Ruth L. Gerber, July 7, 1957; children: Wendy Marcia, Philip Arthur, William Edward. Student, Ind. U., 1951-53; DDS, U. Pa., 1957; BA with highest honors in Polit. Sci., U. Calif., Berkeley, 1961; MA, Columbia U., 1965, PhD, 1970. Dental extern Children's Hosp. East Bay, Oakland, Calif., 1960; pvt. dental practice Hawthorne, N.J., 1961—; lectr. polit. sci. William Paterson Coll., Wayne, N.J., 1970-85; lectr. community dentistry Fairleigh Dickinson U., Teaneck, N.J., 1981-87; adj. prof. New Sch. Social Rsch., N.Y.C., 1986-88; adj. prof. pol. sci., faculty assoc. Program Sci., Tech. and Soc., Rutgers U., Newark, 1987—; vis. rsch. scholar U. Helsinki, summer 1991. Author: Blacks in Power, 1976, Politics and the Restraint of Science, 1983, Clouds of Secrecy, 1988, Element of Risk: The Politics of Radon, 1993, The Eleventh Plague: The Politics of Biological and Chemical Warfare 1996; contbr. articles to profl. jours.; item writer in polit. sci. Ednl. Testing Service. Pres. Glen Rock Human Rels. Coun., 1969-70; chmn. Jewish Community Rels. Coun. No N.J., 1986-89; bd. dirs. Jewish Coun. for Pub. Affairs, 1987—, vice chair, 1991—; bd. dirs. Columbia U. Grad. Sch. of Arts and Scis. Alumni, 1999—. Capt. Dental Corps, USAF, 1957-59. Recipient Ben-Gurion award State of Israel Bonds, 1981, citation for acad. and community leadership N.J. Senate, 1988; fellow NEH, 1981; Rockefeller Found. Scholar-in-Residence, Bellagio, Italy, 1996. Mem. ADA, AAAS, N.Y. Acad. Scis., Am. Polit. Sci. Assn., Phi Beta Kappa. Home: 381 Crest Rd Ridgewood NJ 07450-2436 Office: 723 Lafayette Ave Hawthorne NJ 07506-2348

COLE, LEWIS GEORGE, lawyer; b. N.Y.C., Mar. 9, 1931; s. Ralph David and Emma (Balterman) C.; m. Sara Livingston, June 22, 1952; children: Elizabeth, Peter. BS in Econ., U. Pa., 1951; LLB, Yale U., 1954. Bar: N.Y. 1954. Ptnr. Stroock & Stroock & Lavan, LLP, N.Y.C., 1958—; bd. dirs. Ametek, Inc. Served as 1st lt. U.S. Army, 1954-57. Mem. ABA, Assn. Bar City N.Y., N.Y. State Bar Assn. Office: Stroock & Stroock & Lavan LLP 180 Maiden Ln New York NY 10038-4925

COLE, LINDA SUE, grants planner, computer software professional; b. Orange Park, Fla., Jan. 14, 1951; d. Harold Earl and Alma (Griffis) Cole; m. Stuart Curtis Madsen, June 22, 1974 (div. July 1978). AA, St. John's River C.C., 1971; BS in Journalism, U. Fla., 1973. Cert. tchr. Fla. Public info. specialist Alachua County Bd. of County Commrs., Gainesville, Fla., 1974-76; comms. specialist Jacksonville C. of C., 1976-77; juvenile ct. liason, sr. counselor City of Jacksonville, 1977-78; news reporter Palm Beach (Fla.) Daily News, 1978-80; mgr. Terminus Media, Atlanta, 1980-83; cons. Jr. Achievement of Jacksonville, 1982-83; profl. cons. City of Jacksonville, 1983-84; planning and devel. specialist N.E. Fla. Cmty. Action Agy., Jacksonville, 1984-86, dept. head, 1986-87; grant adminstr. Putnam County Bd. of County Commrs., Palatka, Fla., 1988-91; grant adminstrn. cons. Sims Design Cons., Inc., Jacksonville, 1992-95; tech. support rep. AT&T Solutions/Customer Care, Jacksonville, 1996-98; grants planner/human svcs. program Sterling TQM Bd., Cmty. Svcs. Dept., City of Jacksonville, 1998—. Author: A Smile Goes Wild, 1994; contbr. articles to profl. publs. Cons., spkrs. bur. Jr. Achievement of Jacksonville, 1983-84; annual jail and bail vol. Am. Cancer Soc. of Jacksonville, 1984, 89; mem. Fla. beautification recycling com., Putnam, Fla., 1990-91; bd. dirs. Putnam County Friends of the Libr., Putnam County, 1989-93; staff dir. Citizen's Adv. Task Force for Cmty. Devel., 1989-91. Mem. Am. Assn. Planners, U. Fla. Alumni Assn., Woodmen of World. Democrat. Lutheran. Avocations: reading, writing, sports, computers, sewing. Home: 3145 Belden St Apt 1 Jacksonville FL 32207-3751

COLE, LOIS LORRAINE, retired elementary school educator; b. Rock Lick, Ky., Oct. 18, 1932; d. Charles Lorraine and Gwendolyn Pearl (Johnson) Blanchard; m. John Hamilton Cole, Jr., July 10, 1953; children: Stephen Wesley, Pamela Cole Winningham, Paula Cole Bruner. BS in Elem. Edn. cum laude, Ind. Wesleyan U., Marion, 1954; postgrad., Miami U., Oxford, Ohio, 1974, 82. Cert. kindergarten and elem. tchr., Ohio. Tutor of handicapped Marengo (Ohio) Elem. Sch., 1955-56; tchr. 6th and 7th grade lang. arts Harmony Elem. Sch., Mingo Junction, Ohio, 1957-59; instr. English God's Bible Sch., Cin., 1963-64; tchr. Parents Coop. Kindergarten, Cin., 1964-68; tchr. Mt. Healthy City Schs., Cin., 1968-94, ret., 1994; tutor PALS, Mt. Healthy, Ohio, 1991, Easley (S.C.) Pub. Schs., 1995-96. Tchr., primary supt. Galbraith Rd. Ch. of God Sunday Sch., Cin., 1970-72, Fairfield Ch. of Nazarene Sunday Sch., Fairfield, Ohio, 1973-77; local ch. dir. Wesleyan Women Internat., Easley, 1996-99; former 1st v.p. Newcomers' Club, Easley, 1997. Mem. Mt. Health Edn. Assn. (bldg. rep. 1986-87), Ohio Congress Parents and Tchrs. (life). Republican. Wesleyan. Avocations: reading, photography, travel, flower gardening, music. Home: 245 Andover Turn Easley SC 29642-8803

COLE, LUTHER FRANCIS, former state supreme court associate justice; b. Alexandria, La., Oct. 25, 1925; s. Clem and Catherine (Wiley) C.; m. Juanita Barton, Mar. 9, 1945; children: Frances Jeannette, Jeffrey Martin, Christopher Warren. Student, La. Tech. U., 1943-44; JD, La. State U., 1950. Ptnr. Cole, Mengis & Durant, Baton Rouge, 1950-66; judge 19th Jud. Dist., Baton Rouge, 1966-75, chief judge, 1975-79; judge Ct. Appeals, Baton Rouge, 1979-86; assoc. justice Supreme Ct. La., New Orleans, 1986-92; chmn. Jud. Budgetary Control Bd., 1990-92; mem. La. Bd. Ethics for Elected Ofcls., 1994-95, La. Commn. on Law Enforcement and Adminstrn. of Criminal Justice, 1996—. Rep. La. Legis., Baton Rouge, 1964-66; v.p. Merchants Assn., Baton Rouge, 1954; chmn. awards Boy Scouts Am., Baton Rouge, 1956; mem. Civic Ctr. com., Baton Rouge, 1971-74; bd. dirs. Blundon Home, Baton Rouge, 1984-86. Served to lt. (j.g.) USN, 1943-46. Mem. ABA (ann. meeting 1991, Jury Standards award 1991), La. Bar Assn., Baton Rouge Bar Assn. (pres. 1966), La. Dist. Judges Assn. (pres. 1972-73). Democrat. Baptist. Club: Exchange (Baton Rouge) (pres. 1954). Avocations: hunting, cooking. Home: 9213 Hilltrace Ave Baton Rouge LA 70809-2614

COLE, MAX, artist; b. Hodgeman County, Kans., Feb. 14, 1937; d. Jack Delmont C. and Bertha (Law) Fakes; m. Richard Cole, Sept. 4, 1955 (dec. April 1958); children: Douglas, Janet, Cindy. BA, Fort Hays State U., 1961; MFA, U. Ariz., 1964. Asst. prof. Pasadena (Calif.) City Coll., 1967-78; guest lectr. Claremont (Calif.) Grad. Sch., 1978, Coll. Creative Studies, U. Calif., Santa Barbara, 1977, 79, Contemporary Arts Council, Los Angeles County Mus. Art, 1979, Miami Dade Coll., 1982. One-man shows include Louver Gallery, L.A., 1978, 80, Sidney Janis Gallery, N.Y.C., 1977, 80, Oscarsson Siegeltuch Gallery, N.Y.C., 1986, Zabriskie Gallery, N.Y., 1987, Haines Gallery, San Francisco, 1988, 93, 96, 98, Galerie Schlegl, Zurich, 1990, 96, 99, Mus. Folkwang, Essen, Germany, 1993, Kunstraum Kassel (Germany), 1992, Kyo Higashi Gallery, L.A., 1991, 93, 94, Roswell (N.Mex.) Mus. and Art Ctr., Galerie Conrads, Düsseldorf, Germany, 1996, Stark Gallery, N.Y., Galerie Michael Strum, Stuttgart, 1997, Galerie Appel und Fertsch, Frankfurt, 1997, Mus. Modern Art, Otterndorf, Germany, 1998, Eberhard Ludke Gallery, Cologne, Germany, 1998, Gallerie Spielvogel, Munich, 1999; exhibited in group shows including L.A. County Mus. Art, 1976, Corcoran Gallery Art, Washington, 1977, La Jolla Mus., 1980, Santa Barbara Mus., 1980, Mus. Fine Arts of N.Mex., 1984, Neuberger Mus., Purchase, N.Y., 1984, Marilyn Pearl Gallery, N.Y.C., 1985, Pratt Manhattan Ctr. Gallery, 1985, UCLA, 1988, Nat. Gallery Modern Art, New Delhi, 1988, Panza Found., Verese, Italy, 1995, Aagauer Kunsthaus, Aarau, Switzerland, 1995, Trento (Italy) Mus., 1996, Galerie Conrads, Düsseldorf, 1996, Stark Gallery, N.Y., 1996, Galerie Schlegl, Zurich, 1996, Manif, 1997, Internat. Art Forum, Seoul, 1997, Eberhard Ludke Gallery, Cologne, Germany, 1997, Mus. Modern Art, Otterndorf, Germany, 1998, Haines Gallery, San Francisco, 1998; represented in permanent collections L.A. County Mus. Art, Newport Harbor Mus. Art, La Jolla Mus. Contemporary Art, Mus. N.Mex., Dallas Mus. Art, Santa Barbara Mus., Everson Mus., Tel Aviv Mus., La. Mus., Van Der Heyt Mus., Wuppertal, Germany, Denmark, Panza Collection, Italy, Diozesan Mus., Cologne, Chiat Found., N.Y., Panza Collection, Italy. Address: 195 E 3rd St New York NY 10009-7424

COLE, MONROE, neurologist, educator; b. N.Y.C., Mar. 21, 1933; s. Harry and Sylvia (Firman) C.; m. Merritt Ellen Frindel, June 15, 1958; children: Elizabeth Anne, Victoria, Scott Frindel, Pamela Catherine. A.B. cum laude, Amherst Coll., 1953; M.D. magna cum laude, Georgetown U., 1957. Diplomate Am. Bd. Psychiatry and Neurology. Intern in medicine Seton Hall Coll. Medicine, Jersey City, 1957-58, asst. resident in medicine, 1958-59; asst. resident in neurology Mass. Gen. Hosp., Boston, 1959-60, rsch. fellow in neuropathology, 1960-61, rsch. fellow in neurology, 1961-62; teaching fellow in neurology Harvard U., Cambridge, Mass., 1959-60, 61-62, teaching fellow in neuropathology, 1960-61; clin. instr. in neurology Georgetown U., Washington, 1962-65; asst. prof. neurology, assoc. in anatomy Bowman Gray Sch. Medicine, Wake Forest U., Winston-Salem, N.C., 1965-69; assoc. prof., assoc. in anatomy Bowman Gray Sch. Medicine, Wake Forest U., Winston-Salem, 1969-70; assoc. prof. neurology Case Western Res. U., Cleve., 1970, clin. assoc. prof., 1972—, assoc. prof., 1989-93, prof., 1993—; chief neurology Highland View Hosp., Cleve., 1970-72; neurologist U. Hosps. Cleve. Contbr. chpts. and articles to med. publs. Served to capt. U.S. Army, 1962-65. Fellow ACP, Am. Acad. Neurology, AHA Stroke Coun.; mem. N.Y. Acad. Scis., Acad. of Aphasia, Assn. for Rsch. in Nervous and Mental Disease, Am. Assn. Neuropathologists (assoc.), Am. Neurol. Assn., Alpha Omega Alpha. Office: Univ Hosps Cleve Dept Neurology 11100 Euclid Ave Cleveland OH 44106-1736

COLE, NANCY STOOKSBERRY, educational research executive; b. Brenham, Tex., Nov. 29, 1942; d. Joe Brady and Grace Darling (Pyburn) S.; m. James W.L. Cole, June 4, 1966; 1 child, David Leverett. BA, Rice U., 1964; MA, U. N.C., 1967, PhD, 1968. Rsch. psychologist Am. Coll. Testing Program, Iowa City, 1968-71, dir. test devel., 1971-73, asst. v.p., 1973-74; from assoc. prof. to prof. U. Pitts., 1975-85; prof., dean edn. U. Ill., Champaign, 1985-89; exec. v.p. Ednl. Testing Svc., Princeton, N.J., 1989-93; pres., 1994—. Contbr. articles on ednl. testing to profl. jours. Fellow Am. Psychol. Assn.; mem. Nat. Acad. Edn., Nat. Coun. on Measurement in Edn. (pres. 1983-84), Am. Ednl. Rsch. Assn. (pres. 1988-89). Office: Educational Testing Svc Princeton NJ 08541

COLE, NATALIE MARIA, singer; b. L.A., Feb. 6, 1950; d. Nathaniel Adam and Maria (Hawkins) C.; m. Marvin J. Yancy, July 30, 1976 (div.); m. Andre Fisher (div.). B.A. in Psychology, U. Mass., 1972. Rec. singles and albums, 1975—; albums include Dangerous, 1985, Everlasting, 1987, Inseparable, Thankful, Good To Be Back, 1989, Unforgettable, 1991 (4 grammys, 3 grammys 1992), Too Much Weekend, 1992, I'm Ready, 1992, Take A Look, 1993 (Grammy award nominee best jazz vocal 1994), Holly and Ivy, 1994, Stardust (2 Grammy awards); television appearances include Lily in Winter, USA, 1994. Recipient Grammy award for best new artist, best Rhythm and Blues female vocalist 1975, 76; recipient 1 gold single, 3 gold albums; recipient 2 Image awards NAACP 1976, 77; Am. Music award 1978, other awards. Mem. AFTRA, Nat. Assn. Rec. Arts and Scis., Delta Sigma Delta. Baptist. Office: PMK care Jennifer Allen 955 Carrillo Dr Ste 200 Los Angeles CA 90048-5400*

COLE, PAULA, pop singer, songwriter; b. Rockport, Mass.. Student, Berklee Sch. Music, Boston. Back-up singer Melissa Etheride, Sarah McLachlan, Peter Gabriel; rec. artist Imago Records, 1992; rec. artist Harbinger, 1992, This Fire, 1996. Office: Warner Bros Records Inc 3300 Warner Blvd Burbank CA 91505*

COLE, PETER, linguistics educator; m. Gabriella Hermon. AB in Psychology, Bard Coll., 1962; MA in Linguistics, So. Ill. U., 1971; PhD in Linguistics, U. Ill., 1973. Tchr. English as second lang. N.Y.C. Sch. Sys., 1962-66; instr. English as fgn. lang. Haifa U., Israel, 1967-69; instr. ctr. English as second lang. So. Ill. U., Carbondale, 1969-73; prof. dept. linguistics U. Ill., 1973-90; exchange prof. Tamkang U., Tamsui, Taiwan, 1984-85; prof. linguistics U. Del., Newark, 1988—; vis. prof. dept. English lang. and lit. Nat. U. Singapore, 1992-93; conf. organizer, long distance reflexives Linguistic Soc. Am. Linguistics Inst., Cornell U., Ithaca, N.Y., 1997; workshop organizer Syntax E. Asian Langs., U. Del., 1988-92, U. Ill. , 1978; conf. organizer Northeastern Conf. on Linguistics, 1991. Author: Imbabura Quechua, 1982; mem. editl. bd. Studies in Linguistic Scis., 1974-88, Internat. Jour. Am. Linguistics, 1981—; editor Andean Linguistics Newsletter, 1977-79, 86-88, Syntax and Sementics: Long Distance Reflexives, 1999; mem. internat. adv. bd. Topics in Lang. and Lit., 1995—; squib and discussion editor Linguistic Inquiry, 1996—. Grantee NSF, 1979-83, 92—; grantee Hebrew Cultural Found., 1974-88; recipient Study/Rsch. in Logic and Syntax award Nat. Inst. Mental Health, 1975-76. Mem. Phi Kappa Phi. E-mail: pcole@udel.edu. Office: Dept Linguistics 46 E Delaware Ave Newark DE 19716

COLE, PETER WILLIAM, financial executive; b. Berkeley, Calif., Oct. 8, 1939; s. William Robertson and Bernadette Marie Jordan (Sobernanes) C.; m. Sharleen Martin, June 7, 1969; children: Peter Martin, Megan McKenzie, Christian Granger (dec.), Meredith Elizabeth. BS in Engring., U. Calif., Berkeley, 1962; MBA, U. So. Calif., 1965. Mng. ptnr. Peter Cole & Co., Oakland, 1978—; pres. Bouthillier Capital, 1995—, asst. to v.p. Bechtel Corp., San Francisco, 1965-70; investment officer Am. Express Investmant Mgmt. Co., San Francisco, 1970-76; investment officer Bank Am. Capital Corp., San Francisco, 1976-78, Hambricht & Quist, 1974-76. Served with U.S. Army, 1962. Mem. various hispanic and hist. socs. Home: 1070 Winsor Ave Piedmont CA 94610-1167

COLE, RANSEY GUY, JR., judge; b. Birmingham, Ala., May 23, 1951; s. Ransey Guy and Sarah Nell (Coker) C.; m. Kathleine Kelley, Nov. 26, 1983; children: Justin Robert Jefferson, Jordan Paul, Alexandra Sarah. BA, Tufts U., 1972; JD, Yale U., 1975. Bar: Ohio 1975, D.C. 1982. Assoc. Vorys, Sater, Seymour and Pease, Columbus, Ohio, 1975-78, ptnr., 1980-87, 93—; trial atty. U.S. Dept. Justice, Washington, 1978-80; judge U.S. Bankruptcy Ct., Columbus, 1987-93; circuit judge U.S. Ct. Appeals (6th cir.) Ohio, Cinn., 1996—. Mem. ABA, Nat. Bar Assn., Columbus Bar Assn. Office: US Courthouse 85 Marconi Blvd Columbus OH 43215-2823

COLE, RICHARD A., lawyer; b. Syracuse, N.Y., Feb. 21, 1951; s. Victor and Marie (Pogacar) C.; m. Lois Hallonquist, Sept. 27, 1975. AB, Brown U., 1973; JD, Cornell U., 1976. Bar: Ill. 1976, U.S. Dist. Ct. (no. dist.) Ill. 1976. Assoc. Mayer, Brown & Platt, Chgo., 1976-82, ptnr., 1983—. Trustee U. Notre Dame, London, 1981—. Avocation: travel. Home: 29 Beverley Rd, London SW 13, England Office: Mayer Brown & Platt, 3 Queen Victoria St, London EC4, England

COLE, RICHARD CARGILL, English language educator; b. Kansas City, Kans., Apr. 16, 1926; s. Horace Richard and Iris Verner (Cargill) C.; m. Florence Adaline Mason, June 27, 1956; children: Celia Elizabeth Cole Shaw, Paul Richard. BA, Hamilton Coll., 1950; MA, Yale U., 1951, PhD in English, 1955. English tchr. Manlius (N.Y.) Sch., 1951-52; asst. to dean of freshmen Yale U., New Haven, 1953-54; instr. English U. Tex., Austin, 1954-57; assoc. prof. Radford Va. Coll. (now Univ.), 1957-59, prof. English, 1959-61; prof. English Davidson (N.C.) Coll., 1961-93, prof. emeritus, 1993—. Author: Irish Booksellers and English Writers, 1740-1800, 1986; author, editor: Robert Colvill's Atalanta and Savannah, 1987, John Singleton's Grand Tour, 1815-1817, 1988, The General Correspondence of James Boswell, 1766-1767, 1993, Thomas Mante, Writer, Soldier, Adventurer, 1993, The General Correspondence of James Boswell, 1768-1769, 1997; contbr. articles to profl. jours. Sgt. USAAF, 1944-46, ETO. Robert Warnock rsch. fellow Yale U., 1975-76, rsch. fellow Yale U. Div. Sch., 1978; rsch. grantee Bd. Higher Edn., Presbyn. Ch., 1968, Piedmont U. Ctr. N.C., 1968; grantee Am. Coun. Learned Socs., 1976, Nat. Endowment for the Humanities grantee, 1985, 89. Mem. Phi Beta Kappa. Republican. Presbyterian. Home: 400 Avinger Ln Apt 101 Davidson NC 28036-8894 Office: Davidson Coll PO Box 1719 Davidson NC 28036-1719

COLE, RICHARD GEORGE, public administrator; b. Irvington, N.J., Mar. 11, 1948; s. Warner W. and Laurel M. (Wilson) C. AS in Computer Sci., Control Data Inst., Anaheim, Calif., 1972; BA in Sociology with high honor, Calif. State U., Los Angeles, 1974; MA in Social Ecology, U. Calif., Irvine, 1976; postgrad., So. Oreg. State Coll., 1979. Computer operator Zee Internat., Gardena, Calif., 1971; teaching asst. U. Calif., Irvine, 1974-75; planner Herman Kimmel & Assocs., Newport Beach, Calif., 1976-78; program analyst The Job Council, Medford, Oreg., 1980-81, compliance officer, 1981-82, bus. mgr., 1982—; instr. credential Calif. C.C.; chmn. bd. trustees Job Coun. Pension Trust, Medford, 1982-97; mem. curriculum adv. com. Rogue C.C., Grants Pass, Oreg., 1986; mgr. computer project State of Oreg., Salem, 1983-84; mem. Oreg. Occupational Info. Coordinating Com., Salem, 1982-84. Pres. bd. trustees Vector Control Dist., Jackson County, Oreg., 1985, treas., 1986, bd. dirs., 1984-87, mem. budget com., 1988—, sec., 1988-89; cand. bd. dirs. Area Edn. Dist., Jackson County, 1981; treas. Job Svc. Employer Com., Jackson County, 1987— (Spl. Svc. award 1991); dir. fin. joint pub. venture System Devel. Project, Salem, Oreg., 1986-89; mem. adv. bd. New Jobs Planning, Medford, Oreg., 1987-88, Fin. Audit and Risk Mgmt. Task Force, 1987-91, chm., 1989-90. Fellow LaVerne Noyes, U. Calif., Irvine, 1974; Dr. Paul Doehring Found. scholar, Glendale, Calif., 1973; Computer Demonstration grantee State of Oreg., Salem, 1983; recipient Award of Fin. Reporting Achievement Govt. Fin. Officers Assn. of U.S. and Can., 1989-90, Fin. Ops. recognition Vector Control Dist., Jackson County, Oreg., 1990, Nat. 2d Pl. Chpt. award Jackson County Job Svc. Employer Com., 1989, Oreg. Job Svc. Employer Com. Stat award, 1991, Oreg. Individual Citation award Internat. Assn. Profls. in Employment Security, 1993. Mem. Soc. for Human Resources Mgmt., Assn. So. Oreg. Pub. Adminstrs., Oreg. Employment and Tng. Assn., Pacific N.W. Personnel Mgmt. Assn. (chpt. treas. 1985-87, orgnl. liaison dir. 1988-89, Appreciation award 1985), Govt. Fin. Officers Assn., Oreg. Mcpl. Fin. Officers assn., The Nature Conservancy. Home: 575 Morey Rd Talent OR 97540-9725 Office: The Job Council 673 Market St Medford OR 97504-6125

COLE, RICHARD JOHN, marketing executive; b. N.Y.C., Oct. 18, 1926; s. Arthur and Anna C.; m. Birgitta Ofling, Aug. 26, 1961; children—Catherine Ann, Richard Arthur, John Eric, Christopher Arne. B.A., Yale U., 1946. Pres. Richard J. Cole, Inc., N.Y.C., 1954-61; gen. mgr. Dynasty of Hong Kong, N.Y.C., 1961-67; CEO, M.I. Group div. Manhattan Industries, Inc., 1967-83; mng. dir. B. Barclay Internat., Inc., 1983-87; prin. Richard J. Cole Enterprises, Easton, Conn., 1987-91, Sources Unltd., 1991—, China Connections Internat., Inc., 1993-95, R.&R. Internat., Inc., N.Y.C., 1995—, D&I, Inc., 1997—. Served with USNR, 1943-46, 52-53. Congregationalist. Home: 675 Easton Rd Fairfield CT 06430-1640

COLE, RICHARD LOUIS, political scientist, educator; b. Dallas, Jan. 25, 1946; s. Louis Ray and Mary (Steely) C.; m. Pamela June Jacobs, Nov. 22, 1968; children: Jonathan, Ashley. B.A., North Tex. State U., Denton, 1967, M.A., 1968; Ph.D., Purdue U., 1973. Asst. prof. George Washington U., 1973-78, assoc. prof., 1978-79; research scholar Yale U., New Haven, Conn., 1979-80; prof. polit. sci., dean Sch. Urban and Pub. Affairs U. Tex., Arlington, 1980—; cons. Office Revenue Sharing Rand Corp. Author: Citizen Participation, 1974, Revenue Sharing, 1976, Introduction to Political Inquiry, 1980, Urban Life in Texas, 1986, Texas Politics and Public Policy, 1987, The Politics of American Government, 1994, Introduction to Political and Policy Research, 1996; mem. editl. bd. Am. Politics Quar., 1977-88, Jour. Cmty. Action, 1981—, Pub. Adminstrn. Rev., 1986-89, Jour. Urban Affairs, 1988—; contbr. articles to profl. jours. Mem. Leadership Arlington. Mem. Am. Soc. Pub. Adminstrn. (pres. N. Tex. chpt. 1989-90), S.W. Polit. Sci. Assn. (v.p. 1983-84, pres.-elect 1990, pres. 1991-92), Am. Polit. Sci. Assn. Democrat. Methodist. Home: 614 Portofino Dr Arlington TX 76012-2759 Office: Inst Urban Studies U Tex PO Box 19588 Arlington TX 76019

COLE, RICHARD RAY, university dean; b. Forney, Tex., Apr. 20, 1942; s. Richard W. and G. Gladys C.; m. Lynda F. Painter, May 31, 1968. BJ, U. Tex., 1964, MA, 1966; PhD, U. Minn., 1971. Asst. city editor The News, Mexico City, 1966-67; freelance writer, 1966-67; reporter Harrow Observer, Harrow-on-the-Hill, Eng., 1968; asst. prof. W.Va. U., 1967-68; instr. U. Minn., 1968-71; mem. faculty U. N.C., Chapel Hill, 1971—; prof. journalism U. N.C., 1979—; dean U. N.C. (Sch. Journalism and Mass Communication), 1979—; mem. nat. scholarship com. Freedom Forum, 1980-86, chmn., 1987-93; chief judge H.L. Mencken Nat. Writing Award Competition, 1983-90; mem. journalism awards program steering com. William Randolph Hearst Found., 1981—, chmn., 1991—; chmn. accrediting teams U.S. journalism schs.; mem. faculty adv. com. World Press Inst.; mem. Nat. Accrediting Coun. on Edn. in Journalism and Mass Comm., 1987-96, v.p., 1989-95; cons. to numerous univs., U.S., Chile, Mex., Hong Kong, U.A.E., etc. Co-author: Gathering and Writing The News: Selected Readings, 1975; editor: Communication in Latin America: Journalism , Mass Communication, and Society, 1996; asst. editor Journalism Quar., 1973-85; contbr. articles to profl. jours. Chmn. U. N.C. Bicentennial Observance Planning Com., 1986-87; mem. Bicentennial Policy Com., 1988-94. Recipient Excellence award in undergrad. tchg. Amoco Found., 1978, Freedom Forum medal for lifetime accomplishments in journalism-mass comm. adminstrn., 1992; grantee U. Minn., U. N.C. Dept. State, Internat. Comm. Agy., Internat. Media Fund, U.S. AID, numerous founds. Mem. Assn. Edn. Journalism and Mass Communication (exec. com. 1977-79, 81-84, chmn. coms. 1974-75, 77-79, pres. 1982-83, nat. task force on future mass communication of edn. 1983-84), Internat. Assn. Mass Communication Rsch. (coun. 1980-88, v.p. 1984-88), Assn. Schs. Journalism and Mass Communication (exec. com. 1983-88, 1992-93, pres. 1986-87, mem. nat. steering com. to select 1st journalist in space NASA 1985-86), Inter Am. Press Assn., Sigma Delta Chi, Kappa Tau Alpha. Office: U NC PO Box 3365 Sch of Journalism & Mass Communication Chapel Hill NC 27599-3365

COLE, ROBERT CARLTON, English and journalism educator; b. Beaver, W.Va., June 2, 1937; s. Carlton Enfield and Naomi Ruth (Bowman) C.; children: Cathryn Alisa, Alan Robert; m. Nancy Elaine Knight, Mar. 14, 1973; children: Robin Matthew, Timothy Carlton. AB, Marshall U., 1959; MA, Wake Forest U., 1964; PhD, Lehigh U., 1971. Reporter Herald-Dispatch, Huntington, W.Va., 1957-59; reporter, columnist Jour. and Sentinel, Winston-Salem, N.C., 1959-64; from asst. to assoc. dir. of pubs. Lehigh U., Bethlehem, Pa., 1964-72; asst. prof. English Lehigh U., 1972-73; asst. prof. English Coll. of N.J. (formerly Trenton State Coll.), 1973-83, assoc. prof. English and journalism, 1983-91, prof. English, 1991—; cons. Edison State Coll., Trenton, 1985; dir. Dow Jones Newspaper fund N.J. Copyediting Intern Prog., Trenton, 1989; spkr. N.J. Press Assn., AP Mng. Editors, Am. Soc. Newspaper Editors, 1980—. Contbr. articles to profl. jours. Mem. Planning Commn., Yardley, Pa., 1974-76; dir. social concerns Wesley United Meth. Ch., Bethlehem, Pa., 1969-71. Recipient nat. tchg. award in journalism Am. Soc. Newspaper Editors and Poynter Inst. for Media Studies, 1984, 86; John Ben Snow fellow Am. Press Inst., 1983, 90; named N.J. Prof. of Yr., Coun. for Advancement and Support Edn., 1992. Mem. Am. Fedn. Tchrs., N.J. Press Assn. (Career Achievement award 1994), Sigma Delta Chi. Democrat. Home: 198 S Canal St Morrisville PA 19067-1702 Office: Coll of NJ Dept English Trenton NJ 08650

COLE, ROBERT S., hotel executive. Hotel adminstrn. degree magna cum laude, U. N.H., 1984. Pres. Impac, 1990—; pres., CEO Lodgian (merger Servico and Impac Hotel Group), Atlanta, 1998—. Office: Lodgian Inc # 700 3445 Peachtree Rd Atlanta GA 30326

COLE, ROLAND JAY, lawyer; b. Seattle, Dec. 15, 1948; s. Robert J. and Josephine F. C.; m. Elsa Kircher, Aug. 16, 1975; children: Isabel Ashley, Madeline Aldis. AB in Econs. magna cum laude, Harvard U., 1970, M in Pub. Policy, 1972, PhD in Pub. Policy, JD, 1975. Bar: Wash. 1975, U.S. Supreme Ct. 1980, U.S. Dist. Ct. (we. dist.) Wash. 1984, Mich. 1989. Rsch. scientist Battelle Human Affairs Rsch. Ctrs., Seattle, 1975-83; assoc. Appel and Glueck, P.C., Seattle, 1984-89; gen. counsel Indsl. Tech. Inst., Ann Arbor, Mich., 1990-94; founder, exec. dir. Software Patent Inst., Overland Park, Kans., 1994—; of counsel Shughart Thomson & Kilroy PC, Overland Park, 1997—; founder, dir. MIS; bd. dirs. Cobro Pub., Inc., Lynnwood, Wash., 1984-90. Co-author: Government Requirements of Small Business, 1980, The Containment of Organized Crime, 1984; co-programmer Quadrant I software program, 1983. HUD fellow, 1970-71. Mem. Assn. Personal Computer User Groups (dir., founding pres. 1986), Wash. Athletic Club. Congregationalist. Avocations: squash, racquetball, volleyball, music. Office: 9225 Indian Creek Pkwy Overland Park KS 66210-2009

COLE, RONALD CLARK, lawyer; b. Balt., June 6, 1951; s. Alfred Joseph and Roselda (Katz) C.; m. Sharon Love, June 8, 1974; children: Ryan Scott, Heather Love. BA, Am. U., Washington, 1972; JD, U. Balt., 1975. Bar: Md. 1976. Law clk., atty. Pub. Defender's Office, Glen Burnie, Md., 1976-97; ptnr., founder Scherr Cole & Murphy, Glen Burnie, 1976—; instr. divorce course Anne Arundel C.C., Arnold, Md., 1982-87; panelist weekly radio show Sta-WCBM, Balt., 1997—. Mgr. Little League baseball team, Pikesville (Md.) Recreation, 1984-86, head coach basketball team, 1985-87. Mem. U.S. Tennis Assn. (vol. 1996), Booster Club (vol. 1997). Home: 1 Woodholme Village Ct Pikesville MD 21208-1409 Office: Scherr Cole & Murphy 791 Aquahart Rd Ste 120 Glen Burnie MD 21061-3981

COLE, SALLY ANN, critical care nurse; b. Phila., Jan. 9, 1940; d. William Joseph and Sara Erma (Jones) C.; m. Daniel Cesarini, Feb. 18, 1955 (div. Dec. 1966); children: Daniel Lee, Robert Harold, Richard Dale. Grad., North Montgomery County Area Vocational Tech. Sch., Lansdale, Pa., 1969; ASN, Univ. State N.Y., Albany, 1989. RN, Fla. Nurse North Penn Hosp., Lansdale, 1969-73; LPN St. Petersburg (Fla.) Gen. Hosp., 1974-89, ICU nurse, 1974-95, RN, 1989-95; RN, Fla.; cert. ACLS, Am. Heart Assn. Recipient Best Bedside Nursing Care award North Montgomery County Nursing Assn., 1969. Fellow AACN. Republican. Avocations: camping, canoeing, biking, travel, cooking. Home: 4231 44th Ave N Saint Petersburg FL 33714-3548

COLE, STEPHEN ADAMS, psychiatrist; b. Washington, Dec. 18, 1940; s. Gordon Henry and Malvine Stuart (Gescheidt) C.; m. Dalen Lucia Sciarra; 1 child, Julietta Lorraine. BA with honors, Cornell U., 1961; AM, Harvard U., 1964; MD, Columbia U., 1970. Diplomate Am. Bd. Psychiatry and Neurology. Vol. U.S. Peace Corps, Kathmandu, Nepal, 1964-66; intern Roosevelt Hosp., N.Y.C., 1970-71; resident in psychiatry Albert Einstein Coll. Medicine, Bronx, N.Y., 1971-74, fellow in social and cmty. psychiatry, 1974-75; Robert Wood Johnson Found clin. scholar Columbia U. Coll. Phsycians and Surgeons, N.Y.C., 1975-77; dir. family treatment program N.Y. VA Med. Ctr., 1977-87; chief partial hospitalization program St. Vincent's Hosp. Med. Ctr., N.Y.C., 1988-92, chief continuing day treatment program, 1992-95; med. dir. Healthcare and Rehab. Svc. Southeastern Vt., Bellows Falls, 1995-97; med. dir. outpatient svc. Brattleboro (Vt.) Retreat, 1997—; lectr. in chemistry Amrit Sci. Coll., Kathmandu, 1964-66; instr. in psychiatry Columbia U. Coll. of Physicians and Surgeons, 1976-78; asst. prof. psychiatry, NYU, 1977-84; clin. assoc. prof. psychiatry, 1984-96; assoc. attending physician St. Vincent Hosp. and Med. Ctr., N.Y., 1983-96; asst. attending physician U. Hosp., N.Y.C., 1977-96; attending physician Brattleboro Retreat; examiner Am. Bd. Psychiatry and Neurology, 1980, 83-84, 86; adj. asst. prof. psychiatry Dartmouth Hitchcock Med. Ctr., 1997—; courtesy privileges S.W. Vt. Med. Ctr., Springfield Hosp., Brattleboro Meml. Hosp. Author: (with others) Treatments of Psychiatric Disorders, 1989, 95, Families of the Mentally Ill, 1987, Comprehensive Group Psychotherapy II, 1983, Less Time to Do More, 1993; contbr. articles to profl. jours. Dir. Patient-Family Support Project, N.Y.C., 1981-95; mem. curriculum and tng. com. N.Y. State Alliance for the Mentally Ill, N.Y.C., 1988-95; bd. advisors Friends and Advocates of Mentally Ill, N.Y.C., 1989-95. Lt. comdr. USPHS, 1971-75. Recipient Deans prize for rsch. Columbia Coll. Physicians and Surgeons, 1969, Exemplary Psychiatrist award Nat. Alliance for Mentally Ill, 1993, 96; grad. fellow NSF, 1961-64; internat. fellow Columbia U., 1967-68. Fellow Assn. for Clin. Psychosocial Rsch., N.Y. Acad. of Medicine, Am. Orthopsychiat. Assn., Am. Psychiat. Assn.; mem. Am. Family Therapy Acad., Am. Assn. for Marriage and Family Therapy, Assn. for Adv. Behavior Therapy, Vt. Assn. Hosp. and Cmty. Psychiatrists (co-chmn. 1997—). Democrat. Avocations: gardening, tennis, softball, photography, guitar. Office: Med Dir Outpatient Svcs Brattleboro Retreat Anna Marsh Ln Brattleboro VT 05301-0173

COLE, STEPHEN E., federal judge; b. 1947. BA, U. Wyo., 1969, JD, 1974. Pvt. law practice Worland, Wyo.; judge Worland Mcpl. Ct., 1975-81, Ten Sleep Mcpl. Ct., 1977-81; justice of the peace Washakie County Justice Ct., 1977-81; magistrate judge U.S. Dist. Ct. Wyo., 1975—. Office: PO Box 387 Yellowstone National Park WY 82190-0387

COLE, STEPHEN SALISBURY, bank executive; b. Northampton, Mass., Apr. 11, 1950; s. William Graham Cole and Doris Elinor Williams Yankee; m. Christine Eleanor Garea; children: Taylor Salisbury, Andrew Graham. BA, Lake Forest (Ill.) Coll., 1976. Mgmt. trainee First Nat. Bank of Chgo., 1976-77, personal banking officer, 1977-80, asst. v.p., 1980-82, v.p., 1982-87; pres., chief exec. officer Cash Sta., Inc., Chgo., 1987—; chmn. bd. Electronic Funds Transfer Assn., Washington, 1990-92; mem. Visa, U.S.A. ATM Adv. Coun., San Mateo, Calif., 1985-86; bd. dirs. Primary Payment Sys. Inc. Vice chair, bd. dirs. Anixter Ctr.; bd. dirs. Travellers and Immigrants Aid, Chgo., 1991-96; mem. Ill. EFT Adv. Coun., Chgo., 1991-95; chmn. City of Chgo. ATM Security Adv. Com., 1989; bd. dirs. Met. YMCA, 1995—; trustee Lake Forest Coll., 1999—. Mem. Interlink Network, Inc. (bd. dirs. 1993-96). Avocations: golf, tennis. Home: 1607 Forest Ave Wilmette IL 60091-1529 Office: Cash Station Inc 200 S Wacker Dr Chicago IL 60606-5829

COLE, SUSIE CLEORA, retired government employee relations official; b. Bloomsburg, Pa.; d. Harry E. and Chloe Ann (McKinstry) Cole; m. Richard Edward Miller, July 31, 1959 (div. Aug. 1977); 1 child, Terri Lee Miller; m. Gerald Edward Nelson, Feb. 18, 1978 (div. June 1982). *Mother Chloe Cole was a Marquis Who's Who biographee in the late 1960s and recognized for* *many achievements, primarily for her expertise and compassion in teaching handicapped elementary school children, and her political efforts with the Republican Party in Bloomsburg, Pa. and Eastern Pa. Father Harry E. Cole was a civil engineer. His proudest accomplishment was his genealogy work on "The Coles of Columbia County, Pa.- A Family History Dating from the 1600s in Holland". He researched, wrote, and printed the report from the 1930s until his death in 1963. He worked on the Manhattan Project during World War II, and was commended by President Truman for his accomplishments.* Student in history, No. Va. C.C., 1982; also govt. courses. With Dept. of Navy, Washington, 1957-74; clk., technician U.S. Dept. Navy, Washington, 1957-62, navy mil. pay regulations specialist, 1962-71, mgr. error detection/reduction program mil. pay, 1967-71, fiscal acct., 1971-74; fiscal clk. Dept. State, Washington, 1975-77, sr. retirement claims examiner, 1977-83, employee rels. officer, 1983-94, also mgr. fed. health benefits program, 1983-94, mgr. fed. life ins. program, 1983-94, ret., 1994. *Susie Cole helped the Navy Department develop and implement the pay system for the NASA/NOAA Navy/Marine Corps Astronaut Program. She assisted in formulating guidelines, policy, and implementation of Congressional and Presidential Laws concerning new and old military benefits for all Navy personnel from the 1960s to 1974. She also assisted the State Department in writing policy procedures. She counselled most of the U.S. Iranian Hostages upon their release. She designed and implemented the policy and procedures for the Department's Federal Health Benefits Temporary Continuation of Coverage Program for former spouses, dependents, and children of employees no longer eligible under regular program benefits.* Active Citizen's Band Radio Club, Fairfax, Va., 1974-82, Retarded Children's Ctr., Fairfax, 1981-82. Recipient various govt. awards, including Sustained Exceptional Achievement award Dept. State, 1983-93. Democrat. Avocations: reading, travel, history, music, art. Home: 4910 N Arnold Dr Apt 3 Prescott Valley AZ 86314

COLE, SYLVAN, JR., art dealer; b. N.Y.C., Jan. 10, 1918; s. Sylvan and Dorothy (Stein) C.; m. Vivian Vanderpool, May 1944 (div. 1952); children: Nancy, Robert, James; m. Lillyan Wood, Aug. 20, 1953 (dec. Oct. 1987), m. Mary Rowena Myers Dec. 12, 1998. BA, Cornell U., 1939. Exec. trainee Sears, Roebuck & Co., 1939-41; with Asso. Am. Artists, Inc., N.Y.C., 1946-83; pres., dir. Asso. Am. Artists, Inc., 1958-83, Sylvan Cole Gallery, 1983—. Editor: Raphael Soyer: Fifty Years of Printmaking, 1967, Graphic Work of Joseph Hirsch, 1969, Will Barnet Graphics, 1932-1972, 1972, The Lithographs of John Steuart Curry, 1976; co-editor: Stuart Davis a Catalogue Raisonne of the Prints, 1986. Former pres. N.Y. chpt. Friends of Herbert F. Johnson Mus.; mem. exec. com. Cornell U.; bd. dirs. Manhattan Graphic Art Ctr. Maj. AUS, 1941-46. Recipient Gari Melchers Meml. medal Artists Fellowship, 1989. Mem. Art Dealers Assn. Am. (former dir.), Internat. Fine Print Dealers Assn. (past pres., past v.p.), Appraisers Assn. Am., Nat. Arts Club. Home: 25 Sutton Pl S New York NY 10022-2441 Office: 101 W 57th St New York NY 10019-2215

COLE, TERRI LYNN, organization administrator; b. Tucson, Dec. 28, 1951; m. James R. Cole II. Student, U. N.Mex., 1975-80; cert., Inst. Orgn. Mgmt., 1985. Cert. chamber exec. With SunWest Bank, Albuquerque, 1971-74, employment adminstr., 1974-76, communications dir., 1976-78; pub. info. dir. Albuquerque C. of C., 1978-81, gen. mgr., 1981-83, pres., 1983—; pres. N.Mex. C. of C. Execs. Assn., 1986-87, bd. dirs., 1980—; bd. regents Inst. for Orgn. Mgmt., Stanford U., 1988—, vice chmn., 1990-91, chmn., 1991; bd. dirs. Hosp. Home Health, Inc. Recipient Bus. Devel. award Expn. Mgmt. Inc., 1985, Women on Move award YWCA, 1986; named one of Outstanding Women of Am., 1984. Mem. Am. C. of C. Execs. Assn. (chmn. elect bd. 1992—). Republican. Avocations: skiing, cycling, gardening. Office: Greater Albuquerque C of C PO Box 25100 Albuquerque NM 87125-0100*

COLE, THERON METCALF, engineer; b. Carver, Mass., Sept. 3, 1913; s. Frank Harrison and Florence Jeanette (Shaw) C.; m. Mary Elizabeth Reese, Nov. 26, 1940; children: Theron Jr., Douglas Reese, Gregory Lawrence, Jonathan Reese. BSME, Worcester Polytechnic Inst., 1935. Registered profl. engr., Mass. Mgr. indsl. engring. dept. Atlas Tack Corp., Fairhaven, Mass., 1935-39; gen. mgr. F.H. Cole, N. Carver, Mass., 1939-41; product devel. engr. Norton Co., Worcester, Mass., 1941-65, Bauer Bros. Co., Springfield, Ohio, 1965-69; v.p., engring. rsch. and devel. Parker Metal Corp., Worcester, 1969-90. Patentee in field. Mem. Town Sch. Com., Holden, Mass., 1955-61, chmn., 1957, 61; mem. Town Sch. Union '24, Mass., 1955-61; mem. Mass. Gov. King's Adv. Com. on Edn., 1980s; pres. bd. dirs. Worcester Better Bus. Bur., 1950s. Lt. USNR, 1944-46. Mem. United Ch. of Christ/Congregationalist. Avocations: golf, gardening, travel, music, civic activities. Home: 30 Anderson Ave Holden MA 01520-2121

COLE, THOMAS WINSTON, JR., chancellor, college president, chemist; b. Vernon, Tex., Jan. 11, 1941; s. Thomas Winston and Eva Mae (Sharp) C.; m. Brenda S. Hill, June 14, 1964; children: Kelley S., Thomas Winston. B.S., Wiley Coll., Marshall, Tex., 1961; Ph.D., U. Chgo., 1966. Mem. faculty Atlanta U., 1966-82, prof. chemistry, chmn. dept., 1971-82, Fuller E. Callaway prof., 1969-80, project dir. Resource Ctr. Sci. and Engring., 1978-82, univ. provost, v.p. acad. affairs, 1979-82; pres. Clark Atlanta U., 1988—, W.Va. State Coll., Institute, 1982-86; chancellor W.Va. Bd. of Regents, 1986-88; vis. prof. U. Ill., summer 1972, MIT, 1973-74; summer chemist Miami Valley Lab. Procter and Gamble co., 1967; Celanese Corp., Charlotte, N.C., 1974, UNCF lectr., 1975-84; bd. dirs. C&P Telephone Co., Nat. Pub. TV Stas., United Nat. Bank, Thomas Meml. Hosp.;. Mem. Leadership Atlanta. So. Regional fellow, summer 1961; Woodrow Wilson fellow, 1961-62; Allied Chem. fellow, 1963; Danforth scholar, 1971-82. Mem. Am. Chem. Soc., AAAS, Nat. Inst. Sci., Nat. Orgn. Profl. Advancement Black Chemists and Chem. Engrs., Sigma Xi, Sigma Pi Phi, Alpha Phi Alpha. Lodge: Rotary. Home: 691 Beckwith St SW Atlanta GA 30314-4112 Office: Clark Atlanta U 223 James P Brawley Dr SW Atlanta GA 30314-4385 also: Sta WCLK-FM 111 James P Brawley Dr SW Atlanta GA 30314-4207*

COLE, TODD GODWIN, management consultant transportation; b. Coushatta, La., Mar. 5, 1921; s. Ira and Lucie (Triche) C.; m. Inez Hamilton, Feb. 9, 1953 (div. 1974); children: Michael H., Diane Cole Janusz (dec. 1994); m. Josephine Giovanetti, Oct. 1974 (dec. 1985); m. Pamela Wilds, Mar., 1987. Student, La. State U., 1935-37; LLB, Woodrow Wilson Coll., 1947. CPA, Ga. With Delta Airlines, 1940-63, dir., exec. v.p. adminstrn., 1959-63; sr. v.p. finance and adminstrn., dir. Ea. Airlines, 1963-67, vice chmn., chmn. finance com., dir., 1967-69; v.p., asst. to pres., dir. C.I.T. Fin. Corp., N.Y.C., 1969; v.p. fin. C.I.T. Fin. Corp., 1969-71, mem. exec. com., 1970-86, exec. v.p., 1971-73, pres., chief adminstrv. officer, 1973-80, pres., COO, 1980-83, pres., CEO, 1984-86; CEO, bd. dirs. Frontier Air Lines D.I.P., 1987-89; vice chmn., dir. Ea. Air Lines D.I.P., 1989-91; mng. dir. Simat, Hellesen & Eichner, Inc., 1992-96; pres. Cole & Wilds Assocs., Miami, 1996—; chmn. Arrow Air, Inc., 1997-98, bd. dirs.; bd. dirs. Nacre Corp., Kaiser Steel Corp., Hawaiian Airlines, Inc., Avborne Aviation Support, Inc., Internat. Bus. Network. Mem. Ga. Bar Assn. E-mail: cole@netside.net. Home: 1400 Coral Way Coral Gables FL 33134-4714 Office: 1221 Brickell Ave Ste 1780 Miami FL 33133

COLE, TOM, state official; b. Shreveport, La., Apr. 28, 1949; s. John D. and Helen Gale Cole; m. Ellen Decker; 1 child, Mason. BA, Grinnell Coll., 1971; MA, Yale U., 1974; PhD, U. Okla., 1984. Fellow Yale U., 1974; instr. U. Okla., 1975-78, Okla. Bapt. U., 1981; exec. dir. Okla. Rep. Com., 1980-81; dir. dist. svcs. congressman Mickey Edwards U.S. Congress, 1982-84; exec. dir. Reagan-Bush Campaign, Okla., 1984; chmn. Okla. State Rep. Party, 1985-89; pres. Cole, Hargrave, Snodgrass & Assocs., 1989—; sec. of state State of Okla., 1995-99; chief of staff Republican Nat. Com., Wash., 1999—; lectr. Grinnell Coll., 1977, 79; mem. Cleve. County Rep. Exec. Com., 1979-85, Okla. County Rep. Exec. Com., 1983-85; campaign mgr. Helen Cole for State Rep., 1978, 80, 82, Helen Cole for State Senate, 1984, Ken Wilson for County Commr., 1981, Evelyn Orth for County Commr., 1981; dep. campaign mgr. Daxon for Gov., 1981-82. Fullbright fellow U. London; Watson fellow Inst. Hist. Rsch., London; recipient Robert A. Taft award Okla. Rep. Party, Guardian Small Bus. award Nat. Fedn. Ind. Bus. Mem. Am. Hist. Assn., Inst. Hist. Rsch., Soc. Study Labor History, Ea. London Hist. Soc., Okla. C. of C., Phi Alpha Theta. Methodist. Office: Rep Nat Com 310 1st St SE Washington DC 20003*

COLE, VINSON, tenor; b. Kansas City. Student, U. Mo., Kansas City, Phila. Music Acad., Curtis Inst.; studied under Margaret Harshaw, U. Ind. Opera debut in L'Amico Fritz, San Francisco, 1976; Met. Opera debut, 1987, La Scala debut, 1992; roles have included Rinuccio in Gianni Schicchi, the Duke in Rigoletto, Oedipus Rex, Riccardo in I Puritani, Rodolfo in La Boheme, Don Carmen and Don Jose in Carmen; recordings include (with Patrick Stephens) Works by Bellini and Others. Office: care Columbia Artists Mgmt 165 W 57th St New York NY 10019-2201*

COLE, WAYNE STANLEY, historian, educator; b. Manning, Iowa, Nov. 11, 1922; s. Roy Eldon and Gladys Evelyn (Granseth) C.; m. Virginia Rae Miller, Dec. 24, 1950; 1 child, Thomas Roy. BA with high honors, Iowa State Tchrs. Coll., 1946; MS, U. Wis., 1948, PhD, 1951. Instr. to asst. prof. history U. Ark., 1950-54; asst. prof. to prof. history Iowa State U., 1954-65; prof. history U. Md., College Park, 1965-92, Disting. Scholar tchr., 1989-90, prof. history emeritus, 1992—; Fulbright lectr. U. Keele, Eng., 1962-63. Author: America First, 1953; Senator Gerald P. Nye and American Foreign Relations, 1962; An Interpretive History of American Foreign Relations, 1968, 2d edit., 1974; Charles A. Lindbergh and the Battle Against American Intervention in World War II, 1974; Roosevelt and the Isolationists, 1932-45, 1983; Norway and the United States, 1905-55, 1989; Determinism and American Foreign Relations During the Franklin D. Roosevelt Era, 1995. Served to 1st lt. USAAF, 1943-45. Woodrow Wilson Internat. Center for Scholars fellow 1973, Nat. Endowment for Humanities fellow, 1978-79. Mem. Soc. for Historians of Am. Fgn. Relations (pres. 1973, Graebner award 1994), Norwegian-Am. Hist. Assn. Lutheran. Home: 10203 Mcgovern Dr Silver Spring MD 20903-1612 *Work hard. Give your best. Never give up. Have compassion for those who are different. Remember you stand on shoulders of those who came before. Leave the world a better place than it was. Never forget that you could be wrong.*

COLE, WILLIAM EDWARD, economics educator, consultant; b. Mineola, Tex., Feb. 5, 1931; s. Isaac Harry and Anna Belle (Davis) C.; m. Evelyn Mallory Taylor, June 9, 1967 (div. 1977); 1 child, Mary Kathleen; m. Mary Elizabeth Riddle, Nov. 21, 1978. BA, U. Tex., 1952, PhD, 1965. Auditor Procter and Gamble, Cin., 1955-61; from asst. to assoc. prof. econs. U. Tenn., Knoxville, 1965-70, prof., 1972—; gen. ptnr. Tenn.-Tex. Assocs.; head dept. U. Tenn., Knoxville, 1983-86; indsl. devel. specialist UN Indsl. Devel. Orgn., Vienna, 1970-72; cons. World Bank, Internat. Labor Orgn., TVA, People's Republic of China, 1989, Fgn. Ministry of Japan, 1990; adminstr. UN Productivity Quality Project in Brazil, 1990. Author: Steel and Economic Growth in Mexico, 1967, The Economics of Total Quality Management, 1995; editor: Economic Policy in Mexico, 1987; contbr. articles to profl. jours. Served to 1st lt. U.S. Army, 1952-55, Korea. NDEA fellow Dept. HEW, Washington, 1962-65, Fulbright fellow Dept. HEW, Washington, 1964; grantee Tinker Found., N.Y.C., 1987. Mem. Am. Econ. Assn., N.Am. Econs. and Fin. Assn. (bd. dirs. 1984—), Assn. Evolutionary Econs., Latin Am. Studies Assn. Democrat. Avocation: travel. Home: 9912 Mccormick Pl Knoxville TN 37923-1959 Office: Univ of Tenn Dept Of Economics Knoxville TN 37916

COLE, WILLIAM KAUFMAN, lawyer; b. Hartford, Conn., Oct. 5, 1914; s. Francis Watkinson and Grace (Kaufman) C.; m. Julia Emily Kistler, May 29, 1942 (div. 1955); children: David Brockway, Frank Kistler; m. Marion Beach, June 22, 1957 (dec. July 1990); m. Ula Tenney Duncan, May 9, 1992. BA, Yale U., 1936, LLB, 1939. Bar: Conn. 1939, U.S. Supreme Ct. 1954. Tchr. Laguna Blanca Sch., Santa Barbara, Calif., 1940-42; assoc. firm Robinson, Robinson & Cole, Hartford, 1942-48; partner Robinson, Robinson & Cole, 1949-79, ret. ptnr., 1980—. Pres. Legal Aid Soc., Hartford County, 1955-62, YMCA Greater Hartford, 1964-66; trustee McLean Fund, Simsbury, Conn., 1967-89, chmn., 1980-89, trustee emeritus, 1989—; adv. dir. Hartford Hosp., bd. dirs., 1958-85, vice chmn., chmn., 1961-76; chmn. bd. trustees Conn. Hosp. Assn., 1977-78; bd. dirs. Westchester and So. Conn. Cmty. Health Plans, 1980-82, chmn., 1980-81; mem. Southbury Bd. Selectmen, 1987-94. bd. dirs. Regional Hospice Western Conn., Inc., 1990-93. With S.C. AUS, 1942-45. Fellow Am. Bar Found. (state chmn. 1978-82); mem. ABA, Conn. Bar Found. (bd. dirs. 1973-92, pres. 1975-76), Am. Law Inst., Conn. Bar Assn. (pres. 1974-75), Hartford County Bar Assn. (pres. 1963-64), Hartford Club, Yale Club (N.Y.C.). Republican. Congregationalist. Office: 1 Commercial Plz Hartford CT 06103-3509

COLE, WILLIE, artist; b. Somerville, N.J., 1955. Student, Boston U., 1974-75; BFA, Sch. Visual Arts, N.Y., 1976; student, Art Students League, N.Y., 1976-79. artist-in-residence Studio Mus. Harlem, N.Y., 1989, The Contemporary, Balt., 1994, Pilchuck Glass Sch., Seattle, 1994, Capp St. Project, San Francisco, 1995. One-man shows include Ednl. Testing Svc. Corp., Princeton, N.J., 1986, Inst. Contemporary Arts, L.I., 1990, Peter Miller Gallery, Chgo., 1991, 93, Newark Mus., 1992, St. Louis Art Mus., 1992, Brooke Alexander, N.Y., 1992, 94, Balt. Mus. Industry, 1994, Capp ST. Project, San Francisco, 1995, U. Arts, Phila., 1995, Fabric Workshop Mus., Phila., 1995, Galerie Almine Rech, Paris, 1997, Alexander and Bonin, N.Y., 1997, John Berggruen Gallery, San Francisco, 1998, Mus. Modern Art, N.Y.C., 1998, Brimingham (Ala.) Mus. Art, 1998, Morris Mus., Morristown, N.J., 1999; group shows include Littlejohn-Smith Gallery, N.Y., 1986, Robeson Ctr. Gallery, Rutgers U., 1987, Palais Exposition, Nice, France, 1988, Artworks, Princeton, 1989, Art in General, N.Y., 1990, Brooke Alexander, N.Y., 1991, 93, Weatherspoon Art Gallery, Greensboro, N.C., 1992, Tokushima Modern Art Mus., Japan, 1992-94, Newark Mus., 1993, 97, N.J. Ctr. Visual Arts, Summit, 1994, 96, Josh Baer Gallery, N.Y., 1994, Neuberger Mus. Art, Purchase, N.Y., 1994, 97, Mus. Modern Art, N.Y.C., 1995, 96, K&E Gallery, N.Y., 1995, Whitney Mus. Am. Art, Champion, 1995, City Gallery Chastain, Atlanta, 1996, Rhona Hoffman Gallery, Chgo., Castle Gallery, Coll. New Rochelle, N.Y., 1998, PaineWebber Art Gallery, N.Y., 1998, Alexander and Bonin, N.Y., 1998-99; represented in permanent collections Bronx Mus. Art, Mus. Contemporary Art, Chgo., Dallas Mus. Art, Milw. Art Mus., Newark Mus. Art, N.J., Mus. Modern Art, N.Y.C. Whitney Mus. Am. Art, N.Y., St. Louis Art Mus., State Mus., Trenton, N.J., Nat. Gallery Art, Washington, FRAC Lorraine, Metz. Recipient Joan Mitchell Found. award, 1996; Rutgers Ctr. Innovative Printmaking fellow Rutgers U., 1991; Penny McCall Found. grantee, 1991, Wheeler Found. grantee, 1994, Louis Comfort Tiffany Found. grantee, 1995. Office: c/o Alexander & Bonin 132 Tenth Ave New York NY 10011

COLEMAN, ARLENE FLORENCE, nurse practitioner; b. Braham, Minn., Apr. 8, 1926; d. William and Christine (Judin) C.; m. John Dunkerken, May 30, 1987. Diploma in nursing, U. Minn., 1947, BS, 1953; MPH, Loma Linda U., 1974. RN, Calif. Operating room scrub nurse Calif. Luth. Hosp., L.A., 1947-48; indsl. staff nurse Good Samaritan Hosp., L.A., 1948-49; staff nurse Passavant Hosp., Chgo., 1950-51; student health nurse Moody Bible Inst., Chgo., 1950-51; staff nurse St. Andrews Hosp., Mpls., 1951-53; pub. health nurse Bapt. Gen. Conf. Bd. of World Missions, Ethiopia, Africa, 1954-66; staff pub. health nurse County of San Bernadino, Calif., 1966-68, sr. pub. health nurse, 1968-73, pediatric nurse practitioner, 1973—. Contbr. articles to profl. jours. Mem. bd. dist. missions Bapt. Gen. Conf., Calif., 1978-84; mem. adv. coun. Kaiser Hosp., Fontana, Calif., 1969-85, Bethel Sem. West, San Diego, 1987—; bd. dirs. Casa Verdugo Retirement Home, Hemet, Calif., 1985—; active Calvary Bapt. Ch., Redlands, Calif., 1974—; mem. S.W. Bapt. Conf. Social Ministries, 1993—. With Cadet Nurse Corps USPHS, 1944-47. Calif. State Dept. Health grantee, 1973. Fellow Nat. Assn. Pediatric Nurse Assocs. and Practitioners; mem. Calif. Nurses Assn. (state nursing coun. 1974-76). Democrat. Avocations: gardening, travel, reading. Home: 622 Esther Way Redlands CA 92373-5822

COLEMAN, ARTHUR ROBERT, retired accountant; b. East Brady, Pa., July 16, 1916; s. William Robert and Bertha Etta (Erbe) C.; m. Avanell B. Crawford, Apr. 1, 1938 (dec.); 1 child, Arthur Clyde; m. Catherine Elizabeth Tiedt, Nov. 16, 1985. Student, Internal Corres. Sch., 1932-38, Franklin Comml. Coll., 1938-39, Pa. State U., 1952. Salesman Colonial Life Ins. Co., Butler, Pa., 1939-40; salesman, unit mgr. Comml. Credit Corp., Butler, 1940-42, 45-49; magnetic insp. Curtiss Wright Corp., Beaver, Pa., 1942-45; sales rep. Associates Discount Corp., Butler, 1949-52, 53-59; regional mgr., auditor Borg-Warner Acceptance Corp., Chgo., 1959-61; regional mgr. Westinghouse Credit Corp., Pitts., 1961-62; contr. McGowan Lumber Co., Slippery Rock, Pa., 1962-64, 65-75; sec. and treas. Morgans Restaurants, Butler, 1964-65; Owner A. R. Coleman Ins. Agy., Butler, Pa., 1949-52; co-founder Slippery Rock (Pa.) Plaza, Diamond Investments, Plaza Estates, 1966-75. Founder, chmn. bd. dirs. Tanglewood Sr. Ctr., Lyndora, Pa., 1979-91. Mem. Masons, Am. Assn. Ret. Persons (v.p. local chpt. 1982-85), Acaccia Club (pres. 1966-67), YWCA Mr. & Mrs. Club (pres. 1966-68). Republican. Avocations: wood working, camping, reading. Home: 129 Jarrett Ave Butler PA 16001-1979

COLEMAN, BARBARA MCREYNOLDS, artist; b. Omaha, May 5, 1956; d. Zachariah Aycock and Mary Barbara (McCulloh) McR.; m. Stephen Dale Dent, Mar. 12, 1983 (div. Dec. 20, 1992); children: Madeleine Barbara, Matthew Stephen; m. Ross Coleman, Oct. 16, 1993; 1 child, Marie Jeanne Coleman. Student, U. N.Mex., 1979, MA in Community and Regional Planning, 1984. Artist, 1986-92; lectr. U. N.Mex. Sch. of Architecture, Albuquerque, 1979-82, 91—; assoc. planner, urban designer City of Albuquerque Planning Div., 1982-84; city planner, urban designer City of Albuquerque, N.Mex. Redevel. Div., 1984-88; cons. City of Albuquerque Redevel. Dept., 1987-88; urban design cons. Southwest Land Rsch., Albuquerque, 1991. Columnist for "Kids and Art", 1990-92; author: Coors Corridor Plan (The Albuquerque Conservation Assn. urban design award 1984), Electric Facilities Plan, Downtown Core Revitalization Strategy and Sector Development Plan; contbg. author: Anasazi Architecture and American Design, 1994; contbr. articles to profl. publs.; exhibited in shows at Dartmouth St. Gallery, Albuquerque, Chimayo (N.Mex.) Trade and Mercantile, JoAnne Chappel Gallery, San Francisco, Southwest Arts Festival, Albuquerque, Act I Gallery, Taos, N.Mex. Vol. art tchr. Chaparral Elem. Sch., Roosevelt Mid. Sch., Albuquerque, 1989-97. Recipient First Pl. for Pastels, 20th Ann. Nat. Small Painting Exhibition, N.Mex. Art League, 1991, Best of Show awards Pastel Soc. of N.Mex., 1990, Award of Merit, Pastel Soc. of S.W., 1989, TACA award for Urban Design, 1984. Mem. Pastel Soc. of Am., Pastel Soc. N.Mex. (pres. 1991-92). Democrat. Episcopalian. Avocations: hiking, skiing, running. Works featured in books. Office: U NMex Sch Architecture Albuquerque NM 87131

COLEMAN, BERNELL, physiologist, educator; b. Jefferson County, Miss., Apr. 26, 1929; s. Percy and Julia (Nailor) C.; m. Annie C. Richardson, Jan. 30, 1962; children—Rochelle, Ronald. BS, Alcorn A&M Coll., 1952; Ph.D. (Univ. fellow), Loyola U. Stritch Sch. Medicine, Chgo., 1964. Research asst. in biochemistry U. Chgo., 1956-57; research in cancer Hines (Ill.) VA Hosp., 1957-59; instr. St. Louis U. Sch. Medicine, 1963-65, asst. prof. physiology, 1965-67; asst. prof. Chgo. Med. Sch., 1967-69, asso. prof., 1969-76, prof., 1976; prof. Howard U. Coll. Medicine, Washington, 1976—; chmn. dept. physiology and biophysics Howard U. Coll. Medicine, 1979—; lectr. Cook County Grad. Sch. Medicine, U. Ill. Med. Sch.; vis. prof. Rush Med. Coll.; external examiner Godfrey Huggins Sch. Medicine, U. Zimbabwe, Salisbury, 1981; mem. cardiovascular and pulmonary study sect. Nat. Heart, Lung and Blood Inst./NIH, 1982-83, rsch. tng. rev. com., 1990-94. Peer rev. com. Am. Heart Assn., 1988-93, 95—, rsch. com., 1993—. With U.S. Army, 1953-56, Korea. Recipient research award Chgo. Med. Sch. Bd. Trustees, 1975; NIH research fellow, 1960-61; NIH grantee, 1966-68, 69-74, 74-76, 79—; USPHS fellow, 1961-63; Dept. Def. grantee, 1965-67. Mem. AAUP, Am. Physiol. Soc. (cardiovascular fellow 1985), Am. Heart Assn. (basic sci. coun.), AAAS, Fedn. Am. Socs. Exptl. Biology (vis. scientist for minority instns. programs 1982-83, 1989-90), N.Y. Acad. Scis., Am. Soc. Hypertension (charter), Sigma Xi, Phi Rho Sigma. Democrat. Research, numerous publs. in cardiovascular physiology. Home: 14200 Myer Ter Rockville MD 20853-2350 Office: 520 W St NW Washington DC 20001-2337

COLEMAN, BETH ANN See GLEBA, BETH ANN

COLEMAN, BRITTIN TURNER, lawyer; b. Tuscaloosa, Ala., Dec. 12, 1942; s. Jefferson Jackson and Rose Wallace (Turner) C.; m. Johanna M. Nicol, June 1963 (div. 1967); 1 child, Anna M. Shields; m. Jane M. Kirkman, June 27, 1970; children: Mary Elizabeth, Emily Jane. BA in Am. Studies, U. Ala., 1964, LLB, 1967. Bar: Ala. 1967, U.S. Dist. Ct. (no. dist.) Ala. 1972, U.S. Ct. Appeals (5th cir.) 1975, U.S. Ct. Appeals (11th cir.) 1981, U.S. Dist. Ct. (mid. and so. dists.) Ala. 1986. With Bradley, Arant, Rose & White, Birmingham, Ala., 1971—; ptnr. Bradley, Arant, Rose & White, Birmingham, 1976—; adj. prof. law, coach Nat. Mock Trial teams Cumberland Sch. Law, 1979-84 (2 Nat. Championships); former mem. faculty Ala. Def. Lawyers Assn. Trial Acad., 1992; former mem. Ala. Pattern Jury Instructions Com.; mem. ct.'s adv. group No. Dist. Ala., 1997. Bd. dirs. Downtown YMCA; active Canterbury United Meth. Ch. Capt. JAGC, U.S. Army, 1967-71. Decorated Bronze Star with first oak leaf cluster, Army Commendation medal with first oak leaf cluster, Vietnam Svc. medal. Mem. ABA, Am. Judicature Soc., Birmingham Bar Assn. (past chmn. civil cts. com., mem. exec. com. 1992-94, chmn. grievance com. 1989, past chmn. CLE com., past chmn. ins. com., past Liberty Bell award com., past chmn. election com., past exec. com. young lawyers sect., past chmn. long range planning com., pres. elect 1998, pres. 1999), Am. Inns of Ct., Ala. Law Inst., Am. Bd. Trial Advocates, Ala. Def. Lawyers Assn., Def. Rsch. Inst., Farrah Law Soc., Ala. Law Sch. Found. (pres. 1994-96), Ala. Alumni of Order of Coif (pres. 1992-94), The Club, Inverness Country Club, The Summit Club, Birmingham Inns of Ct. Office: Bradley Arant Rose & White 1400 Park Place Tower 2001 Park Pl Ste 1400 Birmingham AL 35203-2736

COLEMAN, BRYAN DOUGLAS, lawyer, educator, arbitrator, mediator; b. Texarkana, Tex., Aug. 16, 1948; s. William Bryan and Nona Armeda (Crawford) C.; children: Douglas Patrick, Sarah Elizabeth. AS, Texarkana Coll., 1968; BSBA, Stephen F. Austin U., 1970; postgrad. Rice U., 1971-73; JD, South Tex. Coll. Law, 1973; grad. JAG Sch., U.S. Army, 1978, Atty. Mediators Inst., 1991, Am. Arbitration Assn. Mediation Sch., 1991, A.A. White Dispute Resolution Ctr., 1992, SMU Meditation Sch., 1992. Am. Acad. Atty. Mediators, 1993. Bar: Tex. 1973, U.S. Dist. Ct. (ea., no., so. and we. dists.) Tex. 1974, U.S. Tax Ct., 1987, U.S. Ct. Appeals (11th cir.) 1982, U.S. Ct. Appeals (5th cir.) 1975, U.S. Supreme Ct., 1992; cert. Fellow Life Mgmt. Inst. Quality control insp. Lone Star Ammunition Plant, Texarkana, 1966-68; law clk. Fulbright & Jaworski, Houston, 1970-71, Boswell, O'Toole, Davis & Pickering, Houston, 1971-72, Helm, Pletcher & Hogan, Houston, 1972-73; assoc. Law Office Gus Zgourides, Houston, 1973-76, Ray & Coleman, P.C., Houston, 1976-97; gen. counsel Great Southwest Life Ins. Co., 1982-90, United Internat. Life Ins. Co., 1987-90; pres., dir. Conflict Analysis and Resolution, Inc., 1997—; v.p., bd. dirs. Med. Assurance Group, Houston; of counsel Alliance Tex. Life and Health Agts.; instr. U. Houston, 1979-81; v.p. U.S.A. Svc. Corp.; reg. head Neutral Resolute Sys., Inc., 1997—, Jud. Arbitration and Mediation Svc. Endispute, Inc., 1996-97. Served to comdr. Army ROTC, 1972-73, to 1st lt. U.S. Army, 1973-79. Recipient E.E. Townes award, Am. Jurisprudence award South Tex. Coll. Law, 1973. Fellow Houston Bar Found. (life), Assn. Atty.-Mediators, Tex. Bar Found.; mem. ABA, State Bar Tex. (founder law student div. 1973, chmn. grievance com. 1979-81), Am. Arbitration Assn. (panel of arbitrators 1991, meditation instr. 1992), Am. Judicature Soc., Am. Legion, Am. Soc. Law and Medicine, Tex. Assn. Mediators, Houston Trial Lawyers Assn., Soc. Profls. in Dispute Resolution, Rep. Lawyers of Tex. (pres. elect), Rep. Nat. Lawyers Assn., Rep. Presdl. Task Force, Hearthstone Country Club, Alpha Kappa Psi (sec. 1969-70), Alpha Phi Omega (pledge trainer 1970), Delta Theta Phi. Home: 18223 Harrow Hill Dr Houston TX 77084-3228 Office: Conflict Analysis & Resolution Inc 550 Westcott St Ste 300 Houston TX 77007-5043

COLEMAN, CHARLES CLYDE, physicist, educator; b. York, Eng., July 31, 1937; came to U.S., 1941; s. Jesse C. and Geraldine (Doherty) C.; m. Sharon R. Slutsky, Aug. 12, 1976; children: Jeffrey Andrew, Matthew Casey. BA, UCLA, 1959, MA, 1961, PhD, 1968. Asst. prof. physics Calif. State U., Los Angeles, 1968-71; assoc. prof Calif. State U., 1971-76, prof., 1976—; cons. Gen. Dynamics Corp., 1975-77, China Lake Naval Rsch. Labs., 1981; dir. Csula Accelerator Facility; exec. dir. Csula Applied Physics Inst., 1978-83; sr. rsch. fellow Darwin Coll., Cambridge (Eng.) U., 1975-76; project specialist Chinese Provincial Univs. Devel. Project of World Bank, 1987-90; vis. prof. physics U. Istanbul, Turkey, 1969, 72, U. Sydney, Australia, 1977, Arya Mar U., Iran, 1976, U. Natal, South Africa, 1977, UCLA, 1990-91, U. Leicester, U.K., 1995—; mem. NASA review panel, 1992. Contbr. articles to sci. publs.; referee Solid State Electronics, Phys. Rev., Phys. Rev. Letters, Jour. Phys. Chem. Solids. Trustee Calif. State U. L.A. Found., 1981-85. Grantee NSF, 1976—, Rsch. Corp., 1987-91; NATO Collaborative Rsch. grantee, 1991—; NATO Sr. Rsch. fellow Cavendish Lab. (U.K.), 1983-84, Am. Chem. Soc. Rsch. Faculty fellow, 1990. Fellow

Brit. Interplanetary Soc., Royal Philatelic Soc. (London); mem. Am. Phys. Soc., Am. Radio Relay League, Sigma Xi, Phi Kappa Phi, Phi Beta Delta, Sigma Pi Sigma. Office: Calif State U Dept Physics Los Angeles CA 90032

COLEMAN, CLAIRE KOHN, public relations executive; b. New Castle, Pa., Nov. 19, 1924; d. Louis and Florence (Frank) K.; BA, Pa. State U., 1945; m. Frederick H. Coleman, Mar. 10, 1957; children: Franklin, Elliot. Market editor Fairchild Publs., N.Y.C., 1945-48; asst. home editor N.Y. Times, 1949-50; public relations dir. United Wallpaper, Chgo., 1950-53; pub. rels. dir. Assoc.. Am. Artists, N.Y.C., 1953-54; dir. Wallpaper Info. Bur., N.Y.C., 1954; dept. head Roy Bernard, Inc., N.Y.C., 1955-58; pub. rels. dir. The Siesel Co., N.Y.C., 1972—, sr. v.p., 1981-88; pres. Tisch Trask Comm. Resources Pub. Rels. Group, 1988-89; sr. v.p. Anthony M. Franco, N.Y.C., 1989-90; pres. Coleman Comm., N.Y., 1990—. Mem. ctrl. steering com., Sch. Dist. Critical Assessments, New Rochelle, N.Y., 1969-71; bd. dirs., v.p. Beechmont Assn., 1960-74; mem. Mayor's Adv. Coun. on Aging, 1966; mem. Mayor's Adv. Com. on Bd. Edn. Appointments, 1969; v.p. Coun. of PTAs, 1969-70; chmn. women's divsn. United Jewish Appeal, New Rochelle, 1971. Fellow Internat. Furnishings and Design Assn. (formerly Nat. Home Fashions League: founder 1947, nat. treas. 1977-78, nat. pres. 1980-81, N.Y. chpt. v.p. 1994, v.p. mktg. 1998, 99, Cir. of Execellence award 1994, Internat. Hon. Recognition award 1998); mem. Women Execs. Pub. Rels. (bd. dirs. 1983-84, sec. 86-87, pres.-elect 1994-95, pres. 1996-97), Woman Execs. Pub. Rels. Found. (v.p. 1992-93, pres. 1993-94, bd. dirs. 1998, 99).

COLEMAN, COURTNEY STAFFORD, mathematician, educator; b. Ventura, Calif., July 19, 1930; s. Courtney Clemon and Una (Stafford) C.; m. Julia Wellnitz, June 26, 1954; children: David, Margaret, Diane. BA, U. Calif., Berkeley, 1951; PhD, Princeton U., 1955. Asst. prof. Wesleyan U., Middletown, Conn., 1955-58; from asst. prof. to full prof. Harvey Mudd Coll., Claremont, Calif., 1959-98; lectr. Princeton (N.J.) U., 1954-55; rsch. in field. Author, editor: Differential Equations Models, 1983; editor, translator: Local Methods in Nonlinear Differential Equations, 1988; author: (with others) Differential Equations, 1987, Differential Equations Laboratory Workbook, 1992, Ordinary Differential Equations: A Modeling Perspective, 1998, ODE Architect, 1999; mem. editl. bd. Jour. of Differential Equations, 1964—, UMAP Jour., 1980—. Mem. Am. Math. Soc., Math. Assn. Am., Soc. Indsl. Applied Math. Office: Harvey Mudd Coll Math Dept 1250 N Dartmouth Ave Claremont CA 91711

COLEMAN, CURTIS H., financial executive; b. Aug. 19, 1949. BBA, W. Tex. State U., 1976. CPA, Tex. Sr. Arthur Young & Co., Houston, 1976-80; corporate controller Cruthcher Resources, Houston, 1980-87; divns. controller ENSCO, Houston, 1987-90; CFO Metro Networks, Houston, 1990-98; prin. Coleman & Co., Houston, 1998—. E-mail: ccoleman@pdq.net. Home and Office: 1214 Crossfield Dr Katy TX 77450-4302

COLEMAN, CY, pianist, composer, producer; b. N.Y.C.; s. Max and Ida (Prizent) Kaufman. Began playing piano at age four, classically trained pianist; grad., High Sch. of Music and Art; diploma, N.Y. Coll. Music, 1948; pupil, Rudolph Gruen, Adele Marcus, Bernard Wagenaar, Hall Overton.; MusD (hon.), L.I. U., 1994. Pres. Notable Music Co., Notable Records Co. Began performing publicly at age six in N.Y.C.; pianist night clubs throughout U.S., 1948—; TV appearances on Dumont, 1947-48, Date in Manhattan, 1948-51, Kate Smith Show, 1951-52, Art Ford Greenwich Village Party, 1957-58; contbr. John Murray Anderson's Almanac, 1953; provided background music to Compulsion, 1957; appearances with Milw. Symphony Orch., Syracuse (N.Y.) Symphony Pops Orch., Detroit Symphony Orch., Indpls. Symphony Orch., San Antonio Symphony Orch., Ft. Worth, Edmonton (Can.), New Orleans, Toledo, Tulsa, Hartford Pops, Grand Rapids, Honolulu, Middletown and Spokane symphony orchs.; composer music for Broadway shows Wildcat, 1960, Little Me, 1962, Sweet Charity, 1963, also revival, 1986, See-Saw, 1973, I Love My Wife, 1977, On the Twentieth Century, 1978 (Tony award Best Original Score 1978), Barnum, 1980, City of Angels, 1989 (Tony award for Best Original Musical Score, 1990), Welcome to the Club 1989, The Will Rogers Follies, 1991 (Tony award for Best Score, 1991, Grammy award for Best Mus. Show Album, 1992, Grammy award for Record Producer and Composer, 1992), The Life (Best Musical), 1997; also music for motion pictures Heartbreak Kid, Sweet Charity, 1969, Power, 1986, Garbo Talks, Family Business; rec. artist for Westminster, Capitol, Columbia, M.G.M., London records, (recipient Interborough awards Music Edn. League 1934, 35, 36, LaGuardia Meml. award 1961, 2 Emmy awards for TV spl. If They Could See Me Now 1974, Emmy award for Gypsy in My Soul 1975, Drama Desk award for best score I Love My Wife 1977, Cue mag. Golden Apple award for best score I Love My Wife 1977, Tony award Best Score for On the Twentieth Century 1977-78, for City of Angels, 1990); composer popular songs Why Try to Change Me Now, 1952, I'm Gonna Laugh You Out of My Life, 1955, Witchcraft, 1957, Firefly, 1958, It Amazes Me, 1958, You Fascinate Me So, 1958, The Best is Yet to Come, 1959, The Riviera, 1959, Play Boy Theme, 1960, Rules of the Road, 1961, Pass Me By, Pussy Cat, Hey Look Me Over, Big Spender, If My Friends Could See Me Now, Nobody Does It Like Me, I Love My Wife, Hey There Good Times. Recipient Johnny Mercer Songwriters Hall of Fame award, 1995, Elaine Kaufman Cultural Ctr. Honors Creative Arts award, 1999, Lifetime Achievement award Nat. Operatic Dramatic Assn. Eng., 1999; inducted into Songwriters Hall of Fame, Theatre Hall of Fame. Mem. ASCAP (v.p.), Acad. Motion Picture Arts and Scis. Office: 441 E 57th St New York NY 10022-3003

COLEMAN, D. JACKSON, ophthalmologist, educator; b. Waverly, N.Y., Dec. 1, 1934; s. Max Elliot and Frances Agnes (Henton) C.; m. Jane Marie Holmes, July 6, 1963; children: Jeffrey, Jonathan, Jeremy. B.S., Union Coll., 1956; M.D., U. Buffalo, 1960. Intern Columbia Med. Div., Bellevue Hosp., N.Y.C., 1960-61; lt. comdr. USPHS Bur. State Services Heart Disease Control Program, Washington, 1961-64; resident in ophthalmology Edward S. Harkness Eye Inst., Columbia Presbyn. Med. Center, N.Y.C., 1964-67, mem. faculty, staff, 1967-79; John Milton McLean prof. Cornell U. Med. Coll., N.Y.C., 1979—; chmn. dept. ophthalmology N.Y. Hosp.-Cornell Med. Ctr., 1979—, ophthalmologist-in-chief, 1979—. Sr. author: Ultrasonography of Eye and Orbit, 1977; contbr. articles to med. jours. Recipient Wacker award of Club Jules Gonin Internat. Retina Soc., 1976, Lucien Howe medal, 1988; NIH grantee. Fellow ACS, Am. Acad. Ophthalmology; mem. Am. Inst. Ultrasound Medicine (bd. govs. 1970-73), Am. Ophthamolgy Soc., Am. Retina Soc. (v.p. 1989-91, pres. 1991-93), Assn. Rsch. Ophthamology (Weisenfeld award 1996), Societas Interationalis de Diagnostic Ultrasonica in Ophthalmology (exec. bd. 1971-81), World Fedn. Ultrasound Medicine and Biology (exec. bd. 1973-82, sec.treas. 1973-77, treas. 1977-82), Am. Intraocular Lens Soc. (sci. advisor 1976-79), Am. Soc. Ophthalmic Ultrasound (bd. govs. 1976—), AMA, N.Y. County Med. Soc., Am. Eye Study Club, Jules Gonin Club (exec. com. 1992—, v.p. 1993-98, pres. 1998—). Republican. Methodist. Office: NY Presbyterian Hosp-Cornell Med Ctr 525 E 68th St New York NY 10021-4873

COLEMAN, DABNEY W., actor; b. Austin, Tex., Jan. 3, 1932; s. Melvin Randolph and Mary (Johns) C.; m. Ann Courney Harrell, Dec. 21, 1957 (div. June 1959); children: Kelly Johns, Randolph, Mary; m. 2d Carol Jean Hale, Dec. 11, 1961 (div.). Student, Va. Mil. Inst., 1949-51, U. Tex., 1951-57, Neighborhood Playhouse Sch. Theatre, 1958-60. Actor N.Y., Los Angeles, 1960—. Films include: The Slender Thread, The Scalp Hunters, The Other Side of the Mountain, Rolling Thunder, North Dallas Forty, Nothing Personal, How to Beat the High Cost of Living, Melvin and Howard, Nine to Five, Tootsie, War Games, Cloak and Dagger, On Golden Pond, The Man with One Red Shoe, Dragnet, Hot to Trot, Where the Heart Is, 1990, Short Time, 1990, Meet the Applegates, 1991, There Goes the Neighborhood, 1992, Amos and Andrew, 1993, The Beverly Hillbillies, 1993, Clifford, 1994, Devil's Food, 1996, Casanova Falling, 1998, You've Got Mail, 1998, Casanova Falling, 1999, Inspector Gadget, 1999, Stuart Little, 1999; TV includes: Mary Hartman, Forever Fernwood, Apple Pie, Buffalo Bill, The Slap Maxwell Story, Drexell's Class, Madman of the People, Madman of the People, 1996, Recess (voice), 1997, Target Earth, 1998, My Date with the President's Daughter, 1998, Exiled, 1998; TV movie: Maybe Baby, 1988, Never Forget, 1991, Columbo and the Murder of a Rock Star, 1991, In the Line of Duty: Kidnapped, 1995; author: two scripts Bright Promise, NBC, 1972; TV guest appearances include The Fugitive, 1963, I Dream of Jeannie, 1965, The Invaders, 1967, McMillan and Wife, 1971, The Streets of San Francisco, 1972, Love Boat, 1977, others. Served with U.S. Army, 1953-55. Recipient Emmy nomination for Buffalo Bill, 1983, 84, Golden Globe nominee. Mem. Phi Delta Theta. Episcopalian. *

COLEMAN, DALE LYNN, health facility administrator, educator; b. Topeka, June 17, 1958; s. Dale R. Coleman and Linda C. (Parks) Meiergerd; m. Patricia Bermudez, Nov. 20, 1982; 1 child, Athena C. AS in Electronic Engring. Tech. with honors, Cleve. Inst. Electronics, 1987, BS in Electronic Engring. Tech. summa cum laude, 1993, MS in Engring. and Tech. Mgmt. summa cum laude, 1998. Cert. quality engr., regulatory affairs cert. Electronic engring. technician Litton G & CS, L.A., 1979-82; sr. electronics technician Cedars-Sinai Med. Ctr., L.A., 1982-85; svc. engr. Litton AMS, San Diego, 1985-86; elect. engr. tech. IMED Corp. R & D, San Diego, 1987-93, regulatory affairs engr., 1993-98; mgr. regulatory affairs Laborie Med. Technologies, Williston, Vt., 1998-99, dir. RA/QA, 1999—; participant Space Life Scis. mission Space Sta. Freedom, NASA; project mgr. Internat. Space Sta. Infusion Pump Project, 1995-98; adj. prof. engring. and tech. mgmt. So. Calif. U. for Profl. Studies, 1999—. Co-author: The Art of Hsin Hsing Yee Ti Kenpo Kung Fu, 1991; contbr. articles to profl. jours. Active UN Assn., 1979—, bd. dirs., 1994-98; sr. officer USCG Aux., 1980—, aviator, flotilla comdr., 1994-95; USCG liaison U.S. Naval Sea Cadet Corps., NAS Miramar, 1985-98. With USN, 1976-79. Recipient Outstanding Achievement Gold medal U.S. Dept. Transp; named Outstanding Citizen Exch. Club, 1989, Outstanding Grad. Cleve. Inst. Electronics, 1990. Mem. IEEE, Am. Soc. for Quality, Regulatory Affairs Profl. Soc., Alpha Beta Kappa. Achievements include contributions to patents for improved switching power supply and medical device interunit interface connector system; research in H2 generation of reversed biased capacitors, and in lead-acid battery life prolongation. Office: Laborie Medical Techs 310 Hurricane Ln Williston VT 05495-2070

COLEMAN, DANIEL EUGENE, physician; b. Boston, Sept. 12, 1951; s. Bernard John and Lorraine Marie (Walsh) C.; m. Marguerite Marie Horrigan, Aug. 24, 1974; children: Patrick Michael, Daniel Christopher, Erin Kathleen. BA, Boston U., 1973; MD, Georgetown U., 1977. Diplomate Am. Bd. Internal Medicine, cert. pulmonary diseases, crit. care medicine. Resident St. Elizabeth's Hosp., Boston, 1977-80, intern, resident, 1977-80; fellowship Georgetown U. Hosp., Washington, 1980-82; med. dir. ICU Andrews AFB Hosp., Washington, 1983-86; flight surgeon Otis AFB, Cape Cod, Mass., 1986-90; asst. prof. medicine Uniformed Svcs. Hosp., Bethesda, Md., 1983-86; staff pulmonologist Holy Family Hosp., Methuen, Mass., 1986-94, chief of medicine, 1989-93, pres. med. staff, 1996—; asst. clin. prof. medicine Tufts U., Boston, 1990—; med. dir. respiratory tng. No. Essex C.C., Haverhill, Mass., 1984-94; instr. in trauma care Mass. Gen. Hosp., Boston, 1989-94; Col. Mass. Air NG, 1993—, Mass. State Air Surgeon, 1993—; dir. pulmonary rehab. Whittier Rehab. Hosp., Haverhill, 1987-94; dir. cardiac life support tng. Merrimack Valley, Mass., 1987-94. Mem. St. Luke's Guild, Boston, 1989—. Maj. USAF, 1982-86. Fellow Am. Coll. Chest Physicians; mem. AMA, Mass. Med. Soc., Mass. Thoracic Soc. (councillor 1993-96), Aerospace Med. Assn., Soc. State Air Surgeons (pres. 1998—). Roman Catholic. Avocations: skiing, birding, nature, family. Office: 565 Turnpike St North Andover MA 01845-5922

COLEMAN, DAVID CECIL, financial executive; b. Topeka, Sept. 7, 1937; s. Merrill Orda and Cecil Jennie (Warders) C. BS in Fin., Kans. U., 1959; PhD in Bus. Adminstrn., Calif. Western U., 1979. Registered investment advisor. Cost acct. Am. Electronics, Inc., Orange, Calif., 1963-65; fin. mgr. Univ. Calif. San Diego, La Jolla, 1965-67; v.p. fin. Aero Titanium Products, San Diego, 1967-69; contr. Gen. Tire, Tustin, Calif., 1969-70; fin. mgr., satellite telecom. analyst Hughes Aircraft, El Segundo, Calif., 1970-76; proprietor Concept Pub., York, N.Y., 1976—; realtor assoc. Mitchell Pierson Jr., Realtor, Mendon, N.Y., 1980—; instr. MBA prog. Rochester (N.Y.) Inst., 1982-86. Author: Management of the Firm, 1977, For the Long Term Investor, 1979, Consistency in Market Forecasting, 1982, How to Collect Bad Checks, 1989, Tax Tricks for the Proprietor, 1990, Starting a Business for Proprietor, 1992, How to Avoid Audit for the Proprietor, 1992, Asset Protection for the Small Firm, 1995. Fin. mgr. York (N.Y.) Hist. Soc., 1988. 1st Lt. USMC, 1959-63. Home: 2682 Main St Box 500 York NY 14592 Office: Concept Pub 2702 York Rd E York NY 14592

COLEMAN, DAVID DENNIS, II, theater educator; b. Boston, Nov. 18, 1957; s. George Washington Smith and Sallie Lee Coleman; m. Marie Edith Elder, Oct. 11, 1986; children: David Dennis III, Brandon Nathaniel, Christopher Cameron. BA, Boston Coll., 1979; MEd, Boston U., 1982; C.A.G.S., Harvard U., 1984; postgrad., U. Mass., 1993; MFA, Boston U., 1993; postgrad., Lesley Coll. Cert. secondary tchr., speech tchr., spl. edn. tchr., Mass. Teaching intern Mass. Hosp. Sch. for Handicapped Children; studio technician Sta. WGBH-TV, Boston, 1982; assoc. prof. communications Bunker Hill Community Coll., Boston, 1985-87; chmn. dept. arts and humanities, prof. arts and humanities Roxbury Community Coll., Boston, 1987—, artistic dir. artist-in-residency program, 1988—, mng. dir. media arts, 1992-93; instr. photography Digital Equipment Corp., Andover, Mass., 1985; asst. prof. English and lit., Roxbury C.C., 1982-85; tech. dir. Black Folks Theater Co., Boston, 1988-90; adviser Roxbury Outreach Shakespeare Experience, Boston, 1988-90; researcher sta. WGBH-FM, 1981; camera man TV show 10 O'Clock News, 1982; stage mgr. TV show Front Line, 1982, Masterpiece Theatre Mystery, 1982; founding bd. mem. ACT (Artists, Culture and Trade) Roxbury Consortium. Appeared in plays including Lookin' for an Echo, 1987, Macbeth, 1989; tech. dir. play Zooman and the Sign, 1988; writer, dir. play Words of Resistance, 1988, Words of Revolt, 1992, The Mighty Jah Jah, 1992, The Deadly Gift, 1992, Season's Greeting: First Night Boston'96, 1995. Instr. photography Hawthorne Youth Ctr., Boston; cinematographer Ops. Crossroads Africa; group leader, constrn. worker Assn. of Ghana; coord. bike ride Mass. chpt. Arthritis Found. Mem. Performers Ensemble, Mass. Tchrs. Assn., Internat. Brotherhood Elec. Workers, Greater Boston Pan-Hellenic Coun. (v.p.), Phi Beta Sigma (state dir. 1982, area dir. 1983). Avocations: cycling, long-distance running, visual arts, graphic arts, music. Home: 11 Oak Ter Malden MA 02148-1109 Office: Roxbury Community Coll 1234 Columbus Ave Roxbury MA 02120-3423

COLEMAN, DAVID MICHAEL, religious organization executive; b. Cedar Hill, Tenn., Oct. 24, 1942; s. Julian Turner and Dorothy (Cobb) C.; m. Linda Ruth Gholdston, Dec. 21, 1963; children: Melissa Jeanette, Michael Carl. BS, Belmont U., 1965; postgrad., Midwestern Bapt. Theol. Sem., 1965-67, So. Bapt. Theol. Sem., 1979. Cert. fund raising exec. Pastor Maple Grove Bapt. Ch., Dickson, Tenn., 1963-65, Kingsville (Mo.) Bapt. Ch., 1965-67; office mgr. Bapt. Sunday Sch. Bd., Nashville, 1967-69; missionary Zimbabwe So. Bapt. Fgn. Mission Bd., Richmond, Va., 1968-86, assoc. dir. vols. in missions dept, 1986-87, assoc. to v.p. for devel., 1987-89, dir. for devel., 1989-97; exec. dir./CEO Atlanta Union Mission, Atlanta, Ga., 1997—; chmn. Bapt. Internat. Mission Services Bd., Johannesburg, South Africa, 1982-83, 84-85. Co-author: (book) Baptist Beliefs, 1972. Pres. Frank Johnson Sch. PTA, Harare, Zimbabwe, 1975-77; chmn. Planning and Devel. Coun., Harare, 1983-85; chmn. bd. trustees Bapt. Theol. Sem., Gweru, Zimbabwe; mem. Ga. Planned Giving Study Group; mem. com. on gift annuities Am. Assn. Fund Raising Counsel. Mem. Nat. Soc. Fund Raising Execs., Kiwanis (pres. 1963-64, treas. 1965). Republican. Avocations: golf, tennis. Fax:404-588-4016. Home: 4029 Kenway Pl SE Smyrna GA 30082-6410 Office: Atlanta Union Mission PO Box 1807 Atlanta GA 30301-1807

COLEMAN, DERRICK D., professional basketball player; b. Mobile, Ala., June 21, 1967. Student, Syracuse U. Basketball player N.J. Nets, 1990-95, Phila. 76ers, 1995-98; center Charlotte Hornets, 1998—. Named NBA Rookie of the Yr., 1991; named to NBA All-Rookie First Team, 1991, Dream Team II, 1994. Office: Charlotte Hornets Charlotte Coliseum 100 Paul Buck Blvd Charlotte NC 19148*

COLEMAN, DONALD GENE, education educator; b. Ft. Wayne, Ind., June 20, 1934; s. Clarence R. and Ruth F. (Wise) C.; m. Eileen E. Hoffman, Apr. 25, 1959; children: Suzanne Eileen, Jessica Ruth. BS, Ind. U., 1965; MA, St. Francis Coll., 1967; EdD, Ball State U., 1973. Tchr. Ft. Wayne (Ind.) Schs., 1965-67; asst. prof. Ind. U., Ft. Wayne, 1967-74; prof. N.E. Mo. State U., Kirksville, 1974-86, San Diego State U., 1986-88, Calif. State U., Fresno, 1988—; cons. in field. Author: Slams, 1985. With U.S. Army, 1954-56. Danforth Found. grantee, St. Louis, 1990, 91, 92. Mem. Am. Assn. Sch. Adminstrs., Nat. Coun. Profl. Edn. Adminstrs., Nat. Assn. Elem. Sch. Prins., Calif. Profl. Edn. Adminstrn., Assn. Calif. Sch. Adminstrs., Phi Delta Kappa. Office: Calif State U Sch Edn Fresno CA 93740

COLEMAN, DOROTHY ZIPPER, retired educational administrator; b. Louisville, Apr. 18, 1937; d. William Buckner and Florence Marie (Gardner) Zipper; m. Elton B. Coleman, Aug. 16, 1958; children: Sanda Marie Staples, David William Coleman. BABA, Centre Coll. Ky., 1958; MAT, The Citadel, 1974; EdD in Vocat. Edn., U. Ga., 1985. Tchr. Charleston (S.C.) County Pub. Schs., 1968-82; grad. asst. U. Ga., Athens, 1982-85; program coord. So. Ill. U., Carbondale, 1986-97, asst. prof. emeritus, 1997—; adj. prof. Webster U., 1997—. Mem. AAUW, ASTD (bd. dirs., instnl. tech. excellence in leadership award 1994), Carolina Soc. for Tng. and Devel. (bd. dirs. 1990-92), Alpha Delta Kappa (past pres.), Phi Delta Kappa. Avocations: travel, grandchildren. E-mail: dorothyc@awod.com. Home: 677 Highwood Cir Charleston SC 29412-9032

COLEMAN, E. THOMAS, congressman; b. Kansas City, Mo., May 29, 1943; s. Earl T. and Marie (Carlson) C.; m. Marilyn Anderson, June 8, 1968; children: Julie Anne, Emily Catherine, Megan Marie. A.B. in Econs., William Jewell Coll., 1965; M.P.A., NYU, 1969; J.D., Washington U., 1969. Bar: Mo. 1969. Practiced in Gladstone, 1973-76; asst. atty. gen. Mo., 1969-73; mem. Mo. Ho. of Reps., 1973-76; mem. 95th-102nd Congresses from 6th Mo. Dist., 1977—, ranking mem. agr., edn. and labor coms., 1977—; mem. Republican Task Force on Fgn. Policy; chmn. U.S. Congl. Study Group. Office: US Ho of Reps 2468 Rayburn House Bldg Washington DC 20515

COLEMAN, EARL MAXWELL, publishing company executive; b. N.Y.C., Jan. 9, 1916; s. Samuel Sidney and Rose (Ensleman) C.; m. Frances Louise Allan, Mar. 23, 1942 (div. Mar. 15, 1965); children: Allan Douglass, Dennis Scott; m. Ellen Schneid, Aug. 19, 1973. Student, NYU, 1933-34, CCNY, 134-35, Columbia U., 1946. Founder, pres. Plenum Pub. Corp. (and predecessors), N.Y.C., 1946-77; chmn. bd. dirs. Plenum Pub. Corp. (and predecessors), 1960-77, cons., 1977—; founder Earl M. Coleman Enterprises, Inc. (Pubs.), 1977—; pres. Nat. Pubs. The Black Hills Inc., 1984-89; cons. Prentice Hall Coll. div., 1989-90. Contbr. poems, short stories to mags. Served with USAAF, 1941-45. Mem. Info. Industry Assn. (dir. 1971—), Assn. Am. Publishers (exec. com. tech.-sci.-med. div. 1970—), Sci. Tech. Med. Publishers (Holland). Home: 131 Ridge Dr Montville NJ 07045-9473 *Do whatever you do passionately. Never be astonished at the fact that literally all the worldly affairs with which humans busy themselves and into which they pour so much energy, are games, sometimes bloody games, but games. Not only does the passionate player have a greater chance to get ahead in the game, he also enjoys it more than the passive player. Only the person who is willing to be stark naked before his own eyes, which can be the cruelest of mirrors, gets to savor his life to the fullest. Here too, passion serves, for ruthless honesty with self is key to an honest appraisal of anything else.*

COLEMAN, ELIZABETH, college president; b. N.Y.C., Nov. 23, 1937; d. Lewis and Sophie (Brantman) Ginsburg; m. Aaron Coleman, June 14, 1959; children: Daniel, David. B.A., U. Chgo., 1958; M.A., Cornell U., 1959; Ph.D., Columbia U., 1965. Instr. humanities SUNY, N.Y.C., 1960-65; assoc. dean faculty New Sch. Social Research, N.Y.C., 1966-76, dean Coll. Arts and Scis., 1977-84; prof. literature and humanities New Sch. Social Research, 1984-87; pres. Bennington (Vt.) Coll., 1987—; vis. lectr. Hebrew U., 1972, SUNY-Stony Brook, 1975; curriculum cons. Howard U., 1973; chmn. outside evaluating com. CUNY, 1976. Contbr. articles to profl. pubs. Mem. nat. adv. coun. Woodrow Wilson Found., 1990; bd. dirs. Ctrl. Vt. Pub. Svc. Corp., 1990-96; bd. trustees Inst. Ecosystem Studies, 1994. Fellow Ford Found., 1954-58; Woodrow Wilson fellow, 1958-59; F.J.E. Woodbridge fellow Columbia U., 1963-64; Pres.'s fellow Columbia U., 1964-65. Mem. MLA, Am. Assn. Colls. Home and Office: Bennington Coll Office of Pres Off Rte 67A Bennington VT 05201*

COLEMAN, EMMETT See REED, ISHMAEL SCOTT

COLEMAN, ERNEST ALBERT, plastics and materials consultant; b. N.Y.C., Nov. 21, 1929; s. Del Rey and Rozelle (Weed) C.; m. Sonia Dimon, Aug. 22, 1953 (div. 1967); children: Donna Leslie, David Winslow; m. Ann G. Royer, Jan. 20, 1968. BS in Chemistry, Rensselaer Poly. Inst., 1951; MS in Phys. Organic Chemistry, U. Pa., 1955, PhD in Phys. Organic Chemistry, 1959. Sr. rsch. chemist DuPont, Wilmington, Del., 1957-71; phys. sci. Libr. of Congress, Washington, 1971-73; mgr. tech. svc. GAF, Wayne, N.J., 1973-79; mgr. thermoplastics R&D Dart & Kraft Corp., Paramus, N.J., 1979-82; rsch. mgr. Union Carbide, Tarrytown, N.Y., 1982-86, rsch. mgr. Norton Performance Plastics, Wayne, N.J., 1986-88, key technologist Norton Co., Worcester, Mass., 1986-88, cons., 1986—; adj. prof. U. Conn., Stamford, 1982-86, Naugatuck State Tech. Coll., 1992—; CEO CP Tech., Inc. Inventor over 50 patents (U.S. and fgn.) engring. thermoplastics composites, fast crystallizing PET, improvement of mech., chem. andthermal properties of thermoplastic resins and abrasives; assoc. editor Jour. Vinyl & Additive Tech., 1995-96. V.p. consistory Reformed Ch., Kinnelon, N.J., 1982. Ensign USNR, 1951-53. Fellow IBM, 1955-56, Du Pont, 1956. Fellow Soc. Plastics Engrs. (edn. chmn. 1985-86, 91-92, chmn. tech. program 1987-89, 93-95, seminar chmn. 1990-92, nat. publs. com. 1991-96, nat. edn. com. 1991-96, polymer modifiers and additives div.); mem. AAAS, Am. Chem. Soc., Material Rsch. Soc., Assn. Cons. Chemists & Chem. Engrs. (pres 1996-98), Sigma Xi, Phi Lambda Upsilon. Avocations: rehabilitation of injured/orphaned animals, numismatics, woodworking. Home and Office: 293 Janes Ln Stamford CT 06903-4822

COLEMAN, ESTHER MAE GLOVER, educator; b. Cleve., Mar. 22, 1932; d. George Emanuel and Ethel Lee (Greggs) Glover; m. Isaiah Francis Coleman, Jan. 16, 1954; children: Aaron Isaiah, Cynthia Denise. BS in Med. Tech., Youngstown State U., 1975, BS in Comprehensive Sci., 1980. Cert. tchr., Ohio; cert. med. tech. Med. tech. Trumbull Meml. Hosp., Warren, Ohio, 1960-62, St. Elizabeth Hosp., Youngstown, 1962-72; tchr. chemistry, physics and earth sci. Beaver Locale High Sch., Lisbon, Ohio, 1980-82; tchr. chemistry, biology, earth sci. and gen. sci. Mt. Calvary Christian Acad., Youngstown, 1983-84; comprehensive sci. tchr. Youngstown Pub. Schs., 1984-95; tax preparer H & R Block, 1995—. Past pres. Velma Mason Nursery Guild. Mem. Ohio Edn. Assn., Youngstown Edn. Assn., Evergreen Garden Club (past pres., treas., historian, libr.), Fellows Riverside Graden, Ohio Ret. Tchrs. Assn., Mahoning Ret. Tchrs. Assn. Baptist. Avocations: gardening, travel. Home: 577 Bennington Ave Youngstown OH 44505-3401

COLEMAN, GAREY E., state legislative administrator; b. New Haven; s. Julius Jr. and Rebecca A. Coleman. BA in Polit. Sci., Hampton U.; MSW in Cmty. Orgn., U. Conn. Dir. Adult Ctr. of Edn., Urban League of Greater Hartford, Conn., 1980-86; Affirmative Action cons. The Travelers Cos., Hartford, 1986-88; dir. Career Beginnings, Trinity Coll., Hartford, 1990-91; clk. of the House Conn. Gen. assembly, 1989—, chief clk., 1999—; exec. dir. Conn. chpt. Sickle Cell Disease Assn. Am., 1993—. Mem. Leadership Greater Hartford; pres. bd. dirs. new Dawn pre-Sch. and Edn. Ctr., 1986; bd. dirs. Big Bros./Big Sisters, 1984; mem. allocations com. United Way of the Capitol Area, 1986; cons. Jr. Achievemetn Project Bus., 1987; treas., bd. dirs. Nat. Vol. Health Assns., 1997. Combined Health honoree, 1996; named to Outstanding Young Men of Am. Office: State of Conn Gen Assembly State Capitol Rm 109 Hartford CT 06106-1591

COLEMAN, GARY WILLIAM, elementary school educator; b. Davenport, Iowa, Dec. 16, 1945; s. Robert Earl and Mildred Margaret (Mast) C.; m. Janice Marie Coleman, Dec. 29, 1973; children: Heidi Marie, Sean Robert. BS in Elem. Edn., U. S.D., 1987; BSBA, Ariz. State U., 1969. Cert. elem. tchr., EMT, S.D. Tchr. Marty (S.D.) Indian Sch., 1987-91, Parkston (S.D.) Elem. Sch., 1991—; acct./bookkeeper Ulland Bros Constrn., Austin, Minn.; realtor assoc. Myre-Sorenson Real Estate, Albert Lea, Minn.; bldg. constrn. contractor, landscaper, Alcester, S.D. Sgt. USAF, 1969-73. Mem. NEA, Parkston Edn. Assn. (v.p. 1995-96, pres. 1996-97, founder scholarship fund 1997). Office: Parkston Schs Box D Parkston SD 57366

COLEMAN, GEORGE EDWARD, tenor, alto and soprano saxophonist; b. Memphis, Mar. 8, 1935; s. George Edward and Indiana (Lyle) C.; m. Gloria Bell, Aug. 3, 1959; children: George, Gloria; m. Carol Ann Hollister, Sept. 7, 1985. Grad. high sch., Memphis. Ind. saxophonist with numerous jazz combos, 1952-74; leader George Coleman Quartet/Quintet/Octet, 1974—; cons. Lenox (Mass.) Jazz Sch. Music, 1958, L.I. U., 1984—, NYU, 1987—, New Sch. Social Rsch., 1987—, Thelonious Monk Inst., 1996, New Eng. Conservatory, 1998; pvt. instr. Saxophonist B.B. King Band, 1952-53, 55, Max Roach Quintet, 1958-59, MIles Davis quintet, 1963-64, Lionel Hampton Orch., 1965-66, Lee Morgan quintet, 1969, Elvin Jones Quartet, 1970; composer, arranger mus. shows, films: Sweet Love Bitter, 1970, Comedie (French), 1985, Freejack, 1991, The Preacher's Wife, 1996. Grantee NEA, 1975, 81, 85; recipient award for contbns. to music Beale St. Assn., 1977, Tip of the Derby awards, 1978, 79, N.Y. Jazz Audience award, 1979, Gold Note Jazz award, 1985, Key to the City of Memphis, 1991, Lifetime Achievement award Jazz Found. Am., 1997; selected by Internat. Jazz Critics Poll, 1958; named Artist of Yr., Record World mag., 1969. Address: 63 E 9th St New York NY 10003-6302

COLEMAN, GEORGE MICHAEL, chemical company executive; b. Cleve., Mar. 5, 1953; s. George M. and Patricia A. (Harrold) C.; m. Deborah M. Zalar, Feb. 19, 1977 (div. 1989); children: Sean, Kate. BS in Biology, John Carroll U., 1975. Prodn. supr. Republic Steel Copr., Cleve., 1975-79; acct. rep. Calgon Corp. div. Merck and Co., Cleve., 1979-81; mktg. mgr. Calgon Corp. div. Merck and Co., Pitts., 1981-82, regional sales mgr., 1982-83, mgr. mktg., comml. devel., 1983-84; mgr. new bus. devel. biotechnology Standard Oil Chem Co Specialties div. (now BP Chems. Internat.), Cleve., 1984-87; gen. mgr. Adhesive Products div. and Electronic Materials Group BP Chems. Am., Cleve., 1987-90; owner, pres. Innobond Adhesive Corp., Cleve., 1990—. Patentee in field. Republican. Roman Catholic. Clubs: Cleve. Yachting, Holden Arboretum. Avocations: sailboat racing, skiing, scuba, travel. Home: 1235 W 6th St Apt 5D Cleveland OH 44113-1324 Office: Innobond Adhesive Corp 1235 W 6th St Apt 5D Cleveland OH 44113-1324

COLEMAN, GLORIA JEAN, chemical manufacturing company professional; b. Hannibal, Mo., May 9, 1952; d. Gene Hughes and Joan (Wiley) Carroll; m. Larry Dean Coleman, Nov. 25, 1971. BBA, Culver-Stockton Coll., Canton, Mo., 1992. Cert. profl. sec. Sec., bookkeeper, cashier Western-So. Life Ins., Hannibal, Mo., 1970-77; exec. sec. Marion County Mut. Savs. and Loan, Hannibal, 1977; acctg./info. svcs. dept. sec. Am. Cyanamid, Hannibal, 1977-85, users svcs. coordinator, 1985-88, analyst office systems, 1988-90, analyst computer edn. and tng., 1990-94; supr. computer edn. and tng., 1995—; mem. adv. bd. Hannibal area Vocat. Tech. Sch. Bus. Edn. Com., 1985-91; pub. speaker area schs. and svc. orgns., Quincy, Ill., Hannibal, Springfield, Mo., 1986—. Bd. dirs. ARC, Hannibal; mentor Bus. and Profl. Women's Club, Hannibal, 1985-86,also coord. individual devel. program for pub. speaking; fundraiser Convocom Pub. Broadcasting Sta., Quincy, 1986, Hannibal, 1988. Mem. Cert. Profl. Sec. Acad., Profl. Secs. Internat. (sec. Quinsippi chpt. 1984-85, v.p. Heartland chpt. 1988-89, pres. 1989-91, parliamentarian 1991-93, pres. Mo. div. 1993-94, Sec. of Yr. 1985), Kiwanis (Early Bird 1990-94). Mem. Assembly of God Ch. Avocations: walking, traveling, golf, music, sports. Home: 106 Butternut St Hannibal MO 63401-6517 Office: Am Cyanamid 106 Butternut St Hannibal MO 63401-6517

COLEMAN, GREGORY G., magazine publisher. Pub. Reader's Digest mag., Pleasantville, N.Y.; sr. v.p., worldwide pub. Reader's Digest mag., 1997—. Office: Readers Digest Assn 260 Madison Ave New York NY 10016*

COLEMAN, HENRY EDWIN, art educator, artist; b. Charlottesville, Va., Oct. 26, 1938; s. Albin Clayton and Mary Louise (Nay) C.; m. Charlotte Heyne, Dec. 29, 1962 (dec. 1984); children: Edwin Randolph, Mary Clayton; m. Leslie W. Rose, Jan. 4, 1993. AB in Fine Arts, Coll. William and Mary, 1961; MA, U. Iowa, 1963. Instr. art Lawrence Coll., Appleton, Wis., 1963-64; mem. faculty Coll. William & Mary, Williamsburg, Va., 1964-89, prof. fine arts, 1989—, chair dept. fine arts, 1987-90; cons. for purchasing CSX Corp., Richmond, Va., 1985. Illustrator: Oscar Wilde's Remarkable Rocket, 1974; one man shows include Radford Coll., Va., 1975, Gallery II West, St. George, Utah, 1984, U. Maine, Presque Isle, 1989, Andrew & Laura McLain Mus., Florenceville, New Brunswick, Can., 1989, Muscarelle Museum of Art, William & Mary Coll., Williamsburg, Va., 1999; exhibited in group shows at Patio Show, Iowa City, 1962, 63, Des Moines Art Ctr., 1963, Lawrence Coll., Appleton, 1964, 20th Century Gallery, Williamsburg, 1964, 65, 66; Chrysler Mus., Norfolk, Va., 1972, So. Ill. U. at Carbondale, 1975, Peninsula Art Ctr., Newport News, Va., 1980, Nat. Small Image Exhbn., Spokane, Wash., 1984, Am. Drawing Biennial Muscarelle Mus. of Art, Coll. William and Mary, Williamsburg, 1988, 90 (Honorable Mention award), 92, Internat. Culture Exch. Art Exhibit, Neyagawa, Japan, 1988, Bowery Gallery, N.Y.C., 1988, Invitational D'Art Ctr., Norfolk, 1991, Peninsula Fine Arts Mus., Newports News, Va., 1995, 96. Commr. Williamsburg Arts Commn., 1985-91; bd. dirs. Yorktown (Va.) Arts Found., 1989-93; juror Occasion for the Arts, Williamsburg, 1988, 27th Regional Art Exhbn., W.C. Rawls Libr. & Mus., Courtland, Va., 1990. Summer Rsch. grantee Coll. William & Mary, 1976, Semester Faculty grantee, 1985, Faculty Rsch. grantee, 1991-92. Office: Coll William and Mary Andrews Hall Williamsburg VA 23185

COLEMAN, HENRY JAMES, JR., management educator, consultant; b. Cleve., Nov. 28, 1947; s. Henry James and Kathryn Adele (Ketchum) C.; m. Sharon Ann Boothe, Sept. 12, 1971 (div. Jan. 1975). AB, Dartmouth Coll., 1969, MBA, 1970; PhD, U. Calif., Berkeley, 1978. Employment mgr. Lima (Ohio) Meml. Hosp., 1977-78; strategic planner NCR Corp., Dayton, Ohio, 1980-81; vis. asst. prof. Calif. Poly. State U., San Luis Obispo, 1983-85; dean Sch. Mgmt., Columbia Pacific U., San Rafael, Calif., 1985-92; assoc. prof. mgmt. St. Mary's Coll. Calif., Moraga, 1992—; adj. prof. Holy Names Coll., Oakland, Calif., 1987, 90-92; mgmt. cons. Orgn. Dynamics, Berkeley, 1970, Comm. Workers Am., San Francisco, 1971, Exide Corp., Reading, Pa., 1988-89, Retirement Fin. Ctrs. Am., Las Vegas, Nev., 1996. Contbr. articles to profl. jours. Nat. Def. Grad. fellow, 1971. Mem. Western Acad. Mgmt., Phi Beta Kappa. Episcopalian. Avocations: color photography, music appreciation. Office: Saint Marys Coll Calif 1928 Saint Marys Rd Moraga CA 94556-2715

COLEMAN, HOWARD S., engineer, physicist; b. Everett, Pa., Jan. 10, 1917; s. Howard Solomon and Amy (Ritchey) C.; children: Michael Howard, Madeline Frances, Thomas Robert, Carl William, Stephen Mitchell Rosenberg; m. Jeannette Eve Dresher, Dec. 27, 1969. BS, Pa. State U., 1938, MS in Physics, 1939, PhD, 1942. Registered profl. engr., Va., Ariz., Tex. Mem. faculty Pa. State U., 1934-47, dir. optical inspection lab., 1941-47; dir. optical rsch. lab., assoc. prof. physics U. Tex., 1947-51; with Bausch & Lomb, Inc., 1951-62, mgr., v.p. rsch. and engring., 1962-64; head physics rsch. dept., tech. asst. to v.p. charge rsch. Melpar, Inc., Falls Church, Va., 1962-64; dean U. Ariz. Coll. Engring., prof. elec. engring., 1964-68; dir. Spl. Projects Ctr., Schellenger Rsch. Labs., U. Tex., El Paso, 1968-75, Howard S. Coleman and Assos., El Paso, 1975—; dep. dir. solar energy div. ERDA, 1976-77; dep. dir. div. solar energy tech. U.S. Dept. Energy, 1977-78, dir. central solar tech. div., 1978-80, dir. tech. and utilization alcohol fuels, 1980-81, prin. dep. asst. sec. for conservation and renewable energy, 1981-84, dir. Div. Solar Thermal Tech., 1984-90, dir. Office Grants Mgmt., 1990-95, invention coord., 1995—; cons. to industry, govt., 1941—; spl. rsch. optical inspection devices; mem. Ariz. Bd. Tech. Registration.; Mem. adv. vis. com. electronics U. Rochester, 1952; chmn. vis. com. math. Clarkson Coll. Tech., 1953-63. Recipient Joint Svc. award, 1942. Fellow Optical Soc. Am.; mem. Am. Phys. Soc., Meteorol. Soc., Inst. Aero. Scis., Am. Assn. Physics Tchrs., Am. Soc. Metals, Internat. Commn. Optics, Am. Geophys. Union, Am. Inst. Physics, Am. Soc. Engring. Edn., Nat. Soc. Profl. Engrs., N.Y. Acad. Scis., Illuminating Engring. Soc., Soc. Photo-Optical Instrumentation Engrs. Patentee in field. Home: Apt 304N 2111 Jefferson Davis Hwy Arlington VA 22202-3127

COLEMAN, JAMES H., JR., state supreme court justice; b. Lawrenceville, N.J., May 4, 1933; s. James H. Sr. and Neda (Rivers) C.; m. Sophia Coleman, May 12, 1962; 2 children. BA cum laude, Va. State U., 1956; JD, Howard U., 1959. Bar: N.J. 1960, U.S. Dist. Ct. N.J. 1960, U.S. Supreme Ct. 1963. Asst. and/or cons. various N.J. commns. and divs., 1960-64; pvt. practice law Elizabeth and Roselle, N.J., 1960-70; judge N.J. Workers' Compensation Ct., 1964-73, Union County Ct., 1973-78, Law div. N.J. Superior Ct., 1978-81; mem. spl. three-judge resentencing panel N.J. Superior Ct., 1979-81; judge Appellate div. N.J. Superior Ct., 1981-87, presiding judge, 1987-94; assoc. justice Supreme Ct. of N.J., Springfield, 1994—; Mem. various Supreme Ct. coms.; lectr. in field. Chmn. Elizabeth Good Neighbor Coun.; mem. Elizabeth Adv. Bd. on Urban Renewal; incorporator, bd. dirs. Union County Legal Svcs., Elizabeth Anti-Poverty Program; v.p., bd. dirs., counsel to Urban League of Union County; counsel to Elizabeth NAACP; v.p. Scotch Plains-Fanwood Human Rights Coun.; Mem. N.J. Com. on Hiring the Handicapped; mem. Union County Coordinating and Adv. Com. on Higher Edn.;mem. Essex County Coll. Equal Edn. Opportunity Fund Bd., others. Fellow ABA; mem. Nat. Bar Assn. (judicial coun.), N.J. Bar Assn., Union County Bar Assn., Am. Law Inst., Am. Judicature Soc., Garden State Bar Assn., Omega Psi Phi. Baptist. Avocations: tennis, gardening. Office: Supreme Ct of NJ 99 Mt Bethel Rd Warren NJ 07059

COLEMAN, JAMES JULIAN, lawyer; b. New Orleans, May 5, 1915; s. William Ballin and Millie (Davis) C.; m. Dorothy Louise Jurisich, July 30, 1940; children: James Julian, Thomas Blaise, Peter Dee, Dian Judith. *Mrs. Dorothy Coleman, artist, attended Newcomb Art School, runs New Orleans Academy of Fine Arts, a Coleman Family Foundation. James J. Coleman, Jr., Honorary British Consul, graduate of Princeton, attended Oxford and Tulane Law School. In the family law firm, Chairman of family enterprise. Built and developed Windsor Court Hotel, number one hotel in the world by Conde' Nast Traveler. Thomas B. Coleman, Honorary Bangladesh Consul, graduated from Stanford University, now serves as Managing Partner and CEO of International Matex Tank Terminals. Peter D. Coleman, Honorary Barbados Consul, attended Principia College and Tulane Law School. Member of the family law firm. Dian Coleman Winingder, graduate of University of Colorado, with husband, developed Jazzland Theme Park. President and CEO of the family's Holiday Inn Downtown Superdome.* B.A., Tulane U., 1934, J.D., 1937; LL.D. (hon.), Hampden-Sydney Coll., 1982. Bar: La. 1937. Sr. ptnr. Coleman, Johnson & Artigues, New Orleans; past pres. Internat. Trade Mart, New Orleans Philharmonic Symphony; hon. consul gen. Republic of Korea; vice-chmn. La. Jud. Compensation Commn. Past pres. New Orleans C. of C., Jr. Achievement New Orleans, Adult Edn. Ctr.; past bd. dirs. U.S. C. of C., Internat. House, Fed. Rels. Assn.; past chmn. New Orleans coordinating com. NASA; founder Peoples League; trustee emeritus Principia Coll.; past chmn. Tulane U. Bus. Sch. Coun.; chmn. bd. trustees Crimestoppers. Decorated Order of Oranje-Nassau Diplomatic Service Merit Republic Korea; recipient Nat. Achievement award Jr. Achievement, Loving Cup award New Orleans Times-Picayune, 1980, Joseph W. Simon, Jr. award, 1981, Disting. Alumnus award Tulane U., 1982, New Orleans Activist award, 1984, C. Alvin Bertel award, 1985; named to Bus. Hall of Fame, 1984; named Pres. Emeritus, World Trade Ctr., N.Y.C., Chmn. Emeritus, The City Energy Club; recipient Benemerenti Papal Honor, 1989. Mem. ABA, Internat. Bar Assn., La. Bar Assn., New Orleans Bar Assn., Am. Judicature Soc. (past dir.), Beta Gamma Sigma (hon.). Christian Scientist (1st reader 1953-56). Home: 10 Audubon Pl New Orleans LA 70118-5526 Office: 321 Saint Charles Ave New Orleans LA 70130-3145 *Success in Family Enterprises depends on an inbred family loyalty supported by love, compassion and understanding for and between family members and their spouses from generation to generation.*

COLEMAN, JAMES JULIAN, JR., lawyer, industrialist, real estate executive; b. New Orleans, May 7, 1941; s. James Julian Sr. and Dorothy Louise (Jurisich) C.; m. Carol Campbell Owen, Dec. 19, 1970 (dec. Sept. 1979); 1 child, James Owen; m. Mary Olivia Cochrane Cushing, Oct. 12, 1985. BA, Princeton U., 1963; postgrad. in law, Oxford (Eng.) U., 1963-65; JD, Tulane U., 1968. Bar: La. 1969, U.S. Supreme Ct. 1969. Chmn. Internat.-Matex Tank Terminals, New Orleans, 1969—; pres. Coleman Devel. Co., New Orleans, 1969—, IMTT, Quebec, 1993—, Nfld. Transhipment Terminal Inc.; ptnr. Coleman, Johnson & Artigues, New Orleans, 1972—; chmn. DownTown Parking Service, New Orleans, 1978—; pres. City Ctr. Properties, New Orleans, 1980—; chmn. East Jersey R.R. and Terminal Co., 1993; trustee Loving Found., New Orleans, R.L. Blaffer Found., Houston; dir. U.S. Coast Guard Found. Author: Gilbert Antoine de St. Maxent: The Spanish Frenchman of New Orleans, 1975. Mem. Princeton U. History Coun., 1982—; mem. N.J. Commn. on Sci. and Tech., 1992—; bd. dirs. N.J. Mfg. Extension Program, 1998—. Named H.M. Hon. Brit. Consul for La., Brit. Consulate, New Orleans, 1975—, to Order of Brit. Empire, Queen Elizabeth II, London, 1986. Mem. ABA, La. Bar Assn., N.Y. Yacht Club, N.Y. Racquet Club, Newport Reading Room, So. Yacht Club, New Orleans Lawn Tennis Club, USN League (bd. dirs. New Orleans). Republican. Mem. Ch. of Christ Scientists. Office: Coleman Johnson & Artigues 321 St Charles Ave 10th Fl New Orleans LA 70130-3145

COLEMAN, JAMES MALCOLM, marine geology educator; b. Vinton, La., Nov. 19, 1935; s. Leo George and Clara (Gaudet) C.; m. Travis Lucille Alexander, July 28, 1958; children: Thomas M., Sarah E. BS, La. State U., 1958, PhD, 1966. Asst. prof. marine geology Coastal Studies Inst., La. State U., Baton Rouge, 1966-69, assoc. prof., 1969-74, asst. dir., 1971-73, prof., acting dir., 1974-75, prof., dir., 1975-80, Boyd prof., 1980—, dir., 1980-85, chmn. geology and geophysics, 1985-87, head sch. geosci., 1985-89, acting dean Coll. Basic Scis., 1989; exec. vice chancellor La. State U., Baton Rouge, 1989-97; interim vice chancellor Office of Rsch. La. State U., 1997-98; lectr. Am. Assn. Petroleum Geologists, Tulsa, 1976-78, Shell Oil Co., New Orleans, Houston, 1979; mem. devel. coun. Gulf Univ. Rsch. Coun., Baton Rouge, La., 1980; mem. Marine Bd., 1993—; chmn. Marine Bd., NRC, 1997—; mem. Minerals Mgmt. Svc. policy and sci. coms. Outer Continental Shelf Adv. Bd., Washington; cons. numerous oil cos.; chair Gov.'s Higher Edn. Transition Com., 1996. Cons. editor, Royal Soc. Edinburgh, 1984; contbr. articles to profl. jours. Mem. adminstrv. bd. 1st United Methodist Ch., Baton Rouge, 1981. Named Disting. Rsch. Master La. State U., 1976; named Disting. Lectr. La. State U. Found., 1976. Fellow Geol. Soc. Am. (mem. com. on short courses); mem. NAE, Am. Assn. Petroleum Geologists (Leversen medal 1973), Am. Soc. Econ. Paleontologists and Mineralogists (Shepard medal 1980, hon. mem. Gulf Coast sect. 1992), Gulf Coast Assn. Geol. Socs. (Outstanding Educator award 1991), Nat. Sr. Sports Classic IV (bd. dirs. 1992-93), La. Capital Area ARC (bd. dirs. 1991—, chair 1996—), Rotary, Golden Key, Phi Kappa Phi. Republican. Home: 8263 George Brett Dr Cordova TN 38018-8118 Office: La State Univ Coastal Studies Inst 331 Howe Russell Geo Sci Baton Rouge LA 70803*

COLEMAN, JEAN BLACK, nurse, physician assistant; b. Sharon, Pa., Jan. 11, 1925; d. Charles B. and Sue E. (Dougherty) Black; m. Donald A. Coleman, July 3, 1946; children: Sue Ann Lopez, Donald Ashley. Grad., Spencer Hosp. Sch. Nursing, Meadville, Pa., 1945; student, Vanderbilt U., 1952-54. RN, Ga. Nurse, dir. nursing Bulloch Meml. Hosp., Statesboro, Ga, 1948-51, nurse supr. surgery, 1954-67; dir. nursing Bulloch Meml. Hosp., Statesboro, 1967-71; physician's asst., nurse anesthetist Office Dr. Robert H. Swint, Statesboro, 1971-96; physician asst. Office Dr. Earl L. Alderman, Statesboro, 1996-98, Dr. Swaroop Reddy, Statesboro, 1998—; mem. physician's asst. adv. com. Ga. Med. Bd., 1989-97; mem. physician assts. adv. com. Ga. Bd. Med. Examiners, 1987-97, ex-officio mem., 1994-95. Recipient Dean Day Smith Svc. to Mankind award, 1995; named Woman of Yr. in med. field Bus. and Profl. Women, 1980; Paul Harris fellow Rotary Club. Mem. ANA, Am. Acad. Physician Assts., Ga. Nurses Assn., Ga. Assn. Physician Assts. (bd. dirs. 1975-79, v.p. 1979-80, pres. 1980-81). Democrat. Roman Catholic.

COLEMAN, JOEL CLIFFORD, lawyer; b. Reading, Pa., Nov. 6, 1930; s. Thomas and Lee (Jason) Iscovitz; m. Lois M. Schulman, Feb. 4, 1960; children: Teri, Thomas. BS in Econs., U. Pa., 1952, LLB cum laude, 1955. Bar: N.Y. 1956. Assoc. Kaye, Scholer, Fierman, Hays & Handler, N.Y.C., 1955-67; atty. Twentieth-Century Fox Film Corp., N.Y.C., 1967-69; gen. counsel Internat. Playtex, Inc., N.Y.C. and Stamford, Conn., 1969-86; sec. Internat. Playtex, Inc., 1975-86, v.p., 1980-86, also dir.; v.p., gen. counsel, sec. Playtex Inc., 1986-88, Playtex Family Products Corp., 1989-94; v.p., gen. counsel, sec. Playtex Products, Inc., 1994, assoc. gen. counsel, asst. sec., 1994-95. Editor U. Pa. Law Rev., 1953-55, case editor, 1954-55. Trustee Larchmont (N.Y.) Temple, 1973-75; bd. dirs. Jewish Home for the Elderly of Fairfield County, 1996—; bd. dirs. Bruce Mus., Greenwich, Conn., 1997—. Mem. Order of Coif. Home & Office: 61 Ridgeview Ave Greenwich CT 06830-4755

COLEMAN, JOHN MICHAEL, lawyer, consumer products executive; b. Boston, Dec. 28, 1949; s. John Royston Coleman and Mary Norrington Irwin; m. Susan Lee Lavine, Oct. 29, 1978; children: William L., Anne H. L. BA, Haverford (Pa.) Coll., 1975; JD, U. Chgo., 1978. Bar: N.Y. 1978, Pa. 1979, U.S. Ct. Appeals (3rd and 4th cirs.) 1979, U.S. Dist. Ct. (ea. dist.) Pa. 1979, U.S. Dist. Ct. (so. dist.) N.Y. 1981, U.S. Supreme Ct., 1982, N.J. 1988. Law clk. to judge U.S. Ct. Appeals, Richmond, Va., 1978-79; law clk. to chief justice Warren Burger U.S. Supreme Ct., Washington, 1980-81; assoc. Dechert Price & Rhoads, Phila., 1981-86, ptnr., 1986-89; v.p., gen. counsel Campbell Soup Co., Camden, N.J., 1989-90, sr. v.p. law and pub. affairs, 1990-97; sr. v.p., gen. counsel The Gillette Co., Boston, 1998-99; adj. prof. law U. Pa., Phila., 1985-88; bd. dirs. CDI Corp. Contbr. articles to profl. jours. Chmn. bd. trustees Campbell Soup Found., 1990-97; trustee N.J. State Aquarium, 1991-94, Food and Drug Law Inst., 1991-98, Inst. for Law and Econs., 1993-97, Am. Judicature Soc., 1995—; mem. vis. com. U. Chgo. Law Sch., 1993-95; mem. corp. Haverford Coll., 1994—. Mem. Am. Law Inst., Order of the Coif, Phi Beta Kappa. Mem. Religious Soc. of Friends.

COLEMAN, JOHN MORLEY, transportation engineering executive; b. Ottawa, Ont., Can., Dec. 24, 1948; s. Morley Hillis and Marion Sloan (McKelvie) C.; m. Rebecca J. Truxal, June 1, 1974; 1 child, Adam J. BEng, Carleton U., Ottawa, 1971; MBA, U. Western Ont., London, 1973. Registered profl. engr., Ont. Micrographics cons. tech. divsn. Pub. Archives of Can., 1973-77; policy analyst industry br. Ministry State for Sci. and Tech., 1977-81; contracts coord. contract svcs. office Nat. Rsch. Coun. Can., 1981, spl. projects program svcs. secretariat, 1982-85, exec. asst. to pres., 1986-87, coord. transp. program, 1987-88, head indsl. liaison office Inst. Mech. Engring., 1985-89, head ground transp. tech. program Inst. Mech. Engring., 1989-93, gen. mgr. Ctr. for Surface Transp. Tech., 1993—; mem. Can. Railway Rsch. adv. bd., 1993—, Transp. Can. Railway safety consultative com., 1999—. Mem. Transp. Assn. Can. (R & D coun. 1988-99, chmn. heavy vehicle rsch. coordination com. 1989-95, conf. session planning coms., R & D coun. 1992, 93, lectr.), Assn. Profl. Engrs. of Ont., Railway Assn. Can. (chmn. wheel shelling com. 1993—, seminar planning com. 1994, 97, Pub. Svc. Merit award 1985). Home: 20 Shannondoe Cres, Kanata, ON Canada K2M 2H1 Office: Nat Rsch Coun Canada, U-89 Lester Rd, Ottawa, ON Canada K1A 0R6

COLEMAN, JOHN ROYSTON, newspaper publisher; b. Copper Cliff, Ont., Can., June 24, 1921; came to U.S., 1946, naturalized, 1954; s. Richard Mowbray and Mary Irene (Lawson) C.; m. Mary N. Irwin, Oct. 1, 1943 (div. 1966); children: John M., Nancy J., Patty A., Stephen W. BA, U. Toronto, 1943; MA, U. Chgo., 1949, PhD, 1950; LLD (hon.), Beaver Coll., 1963, U. Pa., 1968, Gannon Coll., 1975; L.H.D. (hon.), Manhattanville Coll., 1975, Emory and Henry Coll., 1977, Green Mountain Coll., 1984; DLitt (hon.), Haverford Coll., 1980, Elizabethtown Coll., 1987; D.Litt. (hon.), Marlboro Coll., 1991; DSL (hon.), U. Toronto Victoria Coll., 1994. Rsch. assoc. U. Chgo., 1947-49; instr. econs. Mass. Inst. Tech., 1949-51, asst. prof., 1951-55; asso. prof., asst. head dept. econs. Carnegie Inst. Tech., 1955-60, prof., head dept. econs., 1960-63, dean div. humanities and social sci., 1963-65; assoc. dir. econ. devel. and adminstrn. Ford Found., 1965-66, program officer in charge social devel., 1966-67; pres. Haverford Coll., Pa., 1967-77, Edna McConnell Clark Found., N.Y.C., 1977-86; chmn. Coleman Assocs. Inc., 1985-97; pres. Home Town Press, Inc., 1995—; chmn. bd. dirs. Fed. Res. Bank Phila., 1973-76; labor arbitrator, cons., 1953-85; cons. indsl. rels. rsch. Ford Found. in India, 1960-61; tchr. Am. Economy CBS-TV, 1962-63. Author: Goals and Strategy in Collective Bargaining, 1951, Readings in Economics, 1952, 55, 58, 64, 67, Labor Problems, 1953, 59, Working Harmony, 1955, The Changing American Economy, 1967, Comparative Economic Systems, 1968, Blue Collar Journal, 1974, The Ballad of Clarence Adams, 1992, Pieces from the Quilt, 1993, The Play of the Three Kings, 1995; contbr. numerous articles to mags. Justice of peace, chmn. bd. civil authority Town of Chester, Va., 1991—; prodr., dir. Chester Players Guild, 1991—; dir. Green Mountain Union H.S. Bd., 1998—; v.p. So. Windsor United Way, 1998—. Mem. Religious Soc. of Friends. Home: PO Box 995 Chester VT 05143-0995

COLEMAN, JOHN V., government official; m. Carmela Coleman; 4 children. BS, Pa. State U., 1961. Aviation analyst Civil Aeronautics Bd., Washington, 1963-76, mgr., 1976-82, dir. Bur. Domestic Aviation, 1982-84; dir. Office Aviation Analysis Dept. Transp., Washington, 1985—. Office: USDOT Office Aviation Analysis 400 7th St SW Washington DC 20590*

COLEMAN, JOHN WILLIAM, urologist; b. Jersey City, Jan. 26, 1939; s. John William and Marion Cecille (McAuliffe) C.; m. Rosemary Elizabeth Romano, July 13, 1963 (div. 1984). AB, Georgetown U., 1960, MD, 1964. Diplomate Am. Bd. Urology. Intern, resident, chief resident surgery NY Hosp., 1964-72, asst. attending surgeon urology, 1972-75; assoc. attending urologist NY Hosp./Cornell Med. Ctr., 1975—; assoc. prof. urology Cornell Med. Coll., 1975—; cons. Rockefeller U. Hosp., N.Y.C., 1985—; Vets. Gen. Hosp., Taipei, Taiwan, 1987; bd. dirs. Am. Bur. for Med. Advancement in China. Recipient John K. Lattimer award, 1997, N.Y., N.J. sect. Nat. Kidney Found. award, 1997. Fellow ACS, Am. Acad. Pediatrics; mem. Asian Surg. Soc., Chinese Am. Med. Soc., Soc. Pediat. Urology, Soc. Urologie Internat. Roman Catholic. Avocations: golf, study of southeast Asia. Office: 53 E 70th St New York NY 10021-4941 also: 254 Canal St Rm 3001 New York NY 10013-3501

COLEMAN, JOSEPH EMORY, biophysics and biochemistry educator; b. Iowa City, Iowa, Oct. 11, 1930; s. George Hopkins and Leah Estelle (Rose) C.; m. Phoebe Newman, Apr. 29, 1961; children—Michael Newman, Samuel Hopkins, Julia Heath. B.A., U. Va., 1953, M.D., 1957; Ph.D., MIT, 1964. Intern Peter Bent Brigham Hosp., Boston, 1957-58, resident in medicine, 1963-64; asst. prof. molecular biophysics and biochemistry Yale U., New Haven, 1964-66, assoc. prof., 1966-75, prof., 1975—, chmn. dept. molecular biophysics and biochemistry, 1976-82. Mem. Am. Soc. for Biochemistry and Molecular Biology, Am. Chem. Soc., Biophys. Soc. Home: 855 Ridge Rd Hamden CT 06517-2138 Office: Yale U 309 J W Gibbs Lab PO Box 208114 New Haven CT 06520-8114*

COLEMAN, JOYCE KIT, English literature educator, literary historian; b. Bklyn., Nov. 12, 1949; d. Alexander and Harriet (Yanover) C. BA, Barnard Coll., 1971; MA, U. Tex., 1979; PhD, U. Edinburgh, Scotland, 1993. Proofreader Svc. Typesetters, Austin, Tex., 1976-77; proofreader, prodn. asst. U. Tex. Press, Austin, 1977-79; freelance copy editor, Austin and Berkeley, Calif., 1979-83; copy editor Boston Mag., 1983-84; staff editor Boston Bus. Jour., 1984-85; mng. editor Am. Soc. Law and Medicine, Boston, 1985-88; asst. prof. English lit. U. N.D., Grand Forks, 1994—. Author: Public Reading and the Reading Public in Late Medieval England and France, 1996. Mem. MLA, Early Book Soc., Internat. Courtly Lit. Soc., Medieval Acad. Am., New Chaucer Soc. Avocation: photography. E-mail: jcoleman@badlands.nodak.edu. Office: Univ ND PO Box 7209 Grand Forks ND 58202-7209

COLEMAN, K. VIRGINIA, diaconal minister; b. Hamilton, Ontario, Canada, Oct. 10, 1949; d. LLoyd James and Evelyn Ann (Blackmore) C. Student, McMaster U., 1968-71; diploma, Centre for Christian Studies, 1973-75; student, U. Waterloo, 1976—. Diaconal minister The United Ch. of Canada. Registrar Five Oaks Ctr., Paris, Ontario, Canada, 1971-73; dir. Christian edn. St. Paul's United Ch., Orillia, Ontario, 1975-80; assoc. min. St. Paul's United Ch., Midland, 1981-84; exec. staff ministry personnel svcs Gen. Coun. Divsn. Ministry Personnel and Edn., 1984-92; regional dir. Hamilton Conf. United Ch. of Can., 1992-94; gen. sec., CEO United Ch. Can., 1994—. Vol. leadership devel. programs with Am. Youth Found., Camp Miniwanca, 1969-94. Office: The United Ch of Can, 3250 Bloor St W Ste 300, Etobicoke, ON Canada M8X 2Y4

COLEMAN, KIMBERLEE MICHELE, critical care nurse; b. North Tonawanda, N.Y., July 11, 1962; d. Samuel and Joan (Newhart) C.; married; children: Joshua, Kaylee; m. Ronald L. Coleman, May 23, 1997. AS, Niagara County Community Coll., Sanborn, N.Y., 1982; student, U. Buffalo, 1984. Staff and relief charge nurse, preceptor Erie County Med. Ctr., Buffalo; staff and relief charge nurse Lawnwood Regional Hosp., Ft. Pierce, Fla., Sebastian Humana Hosp., Roseland, Fla.; staff nurse surg. ICU Buffalo Gen. Hosp.; staff nurse Sisters of Charity, Buffalo; spl. care nurse DeGraff Meml. Hosp., North Tonawanda; with Staffbuilders Home Care, Niagara Falls, N.Y. Mem. AACN. Home: 2714 Stenzil Ave North Tonawanda NY 14120-1008

COLEMAN, LEON HORN, real estate investor; b. L.A., Jan. 29, 1931; s. Jack L. and Esther P. Coleman. BS, UCLA, 1953, JD, 1961. Writer, editor Commerce Clearing House, San Francisco, 1966-73; writer, editor Matthew Bender, Inc., San Francisco, 1973-90, author, 1990-93; pres. Leeco Investments, Beaverton, Oreg., 1975—. Author: (chpts.) California Legal Forms, 1982-90, New Jersey Tax Service, 1982-85, Texas Tax Service, 1985-93. Founder, Log Cabin Reps. Oreg., Portland area, 1990; mem. Rep. Party Ctrl. Com., Washington County, 1990—; del. GOP ctrl. com., Oreg., 1999; co-founder Oreg. Rep. Mainstream Com., Portland area, 1995, exec. dir.; mem. Bull Bridge Acad., 1993, dir., 1998; participant Basic Rights Oreg., 1994—. Staff sgt. USAF, 1953-58. Lutheran. Avocation: political communications.

COLEMAN, LESTER L., corporate lawyer. Gen. counsel, exec. v.p. Halliburton Co., Dallas. Office: Halliburton Co 3600 Lincoln Plz 500 N Akard St Ste 3600 Dallas TX 75201-3391

COLEMAN, LESTER LAUDY, otolaryngologist; b. N.Y.C., Mar. 17, 1911; s. Avron and Ann (Blum) C.; m. Felicia Slatkin, Sept. 30, 1945 (dec. 1981); 1 child, Lisa; m. Elizabeth Smith Pantano, Mar. 9, 1986; 1 child, Lynn Ann Dale. BS, Johns Hopkins U.; MD, L.I. Coll. Medicine, 1932. Diplomate: Am. Bd. Otolaryngology. Asst. resident in otolaryngology Johns Hopkins Hosp., 1936-38; pvt. practice medicine specializing in otolaryngology N.Y.C., 1940-99; med. dir. Morton Prince Ctr. Psychotherapy, N.Y.C.; attending surgeon Manhattan Eye, Ear and Throat Hosp., N.Y. Hosp. Cornell Med. Center; asst. clin. prof. Albert Einstein Sch. Medicine; co-founder Internat. Grad. U. Med. columnist: Speaking of Your Health, King Features, Inc.; prodr. show, NBC-TV, 1953-56. Maj. M.C., AUS, 1942. Fellow Am. Trilogical Soc.; mem. Am. Acad. Psychosomatic Medicine (past v.p.). Home: 1000 Park Ave New York NY 10028-0934 Office: 114 E 72nd St New York NY 10021-4245

COLEMAN, LEWIS WALDO, bank executive; b. San Francisco, Jan. 2, 1942; s. Lewis V. and Virginia Coleman; m. Susan G.; children: Michelle, Gregory, Nancy, Peter. BA, Stanford U., 1965. With Bank Calif., San Francisco, 1965-73; With Wells Fargo Bank, San Francisco, 1973-86, exec. v.p., chmn. credit policy com., until 1986; vice chmn., CFO, treas. Bank Am., San Francisco, 1986-95; sr. mng. dir. Montgomery Securities, San Francisco, 1995-98; CEO Nations Bank Mongomery Securities, San Francisco, 1998—.

COLEMAN, LINDA LEE DEVOE, museum educator; b. Pittsfield, Mass., Aug. 15, 1951; d. J. Roland and Loraine A. (Anderson) Devoe; m. Donald W. Coleman, Nov. 27, 1970 (div. Apr. 1997); children: Tiffani Lin, Scott J. BA in Polit. Sci., U. Mass., 1973. Cert. social studies tchr. Mass., N.Mex., N.H. Paralegal Poole, Tinnin & Martin, P.A., Albuquerque, 1980; rsch. and writing cons. for hist. preservation clients N.H., 1983—; paralegal Nixon, Hall & Hess, P.A., Manchester, N.H., 1986-89; substitute tchr. Manchester (N.H.) and Candia (N.H.) Sch. Dist.s, 1990-97; mus. educator Manchester Hist. Assn., 1997—; youth educator U. N.H. Youth Opportunities Unltd., Manchester and Durham, N.H., 1991-92; mus. tchr. Mus. N.H. History, Concord, 1995-97; mus. docent Albuquerque Mus. Art, History and Sci., 1977-80. Zoning com. chair, planning bd. mem. Town of Candia, 1981-83; founder, pres. Candia Chem. People Task Force, 1983-89; bd. dirs. Parent Assn. for Individual Self-Esteem, Manchester, 1983-85, Fitts Mus. Found., Candia, 1990-95; trustee Fitts Mus./Town, Candia, 1992-97. Named Outstanding Young Women of Am., 1988. Mem. Am. Can. Geneal. Soc., N.H. Hist. Soc., Manchester Hist. Assn., Fitts Mus. Found., Phi Beta Kappa. Home: PO Box 221 Candia NH 03034-0221 Office: Manchester Hist Assn 129 Amherst St Manchester NH 03101-1809

COLEMAN, MALCOLM JAMES, JR., band director, music educator, flute educator; b. Mexia, Tex., Feb. 4, 1947; s. Malcolm James and Wilma (Freeman) C. AAS, Navarro Coll., 1967; MusB, U. North Tex., 1970, M in Music Edn., 1975, PhD, 1987; MusD (hon.), London Inst. Applied Rsch., 1991, Inst. Coordinated Rsch., Australia, 1991, Acad. of Scis. Humanities U., Paris, 1991; DSc (hon.), Collegium Sancti Spiritus, Calif., 1991, The Internat. U., Bombay, 1991; Prof. (hon.), European Sci. & Ednl. Instn., Brussels, 1991; Full Accreditation (hon.), Internat. Cultural Correspondence Inst., Madras, India, 1991; MD (hon.), U. Guadalajara, Mexico, 1993. Lic. profl. counselor, Tex., lic. profl. counselor supr.; cert. sch. counselor, TRT counselor. Flute player NORAD Band, Colo., 1970-73; flute player on temporary duty USAF Acad. Band, 1972; band dir. Hubbard High Sch., Tex., 1974-75, Bremond High Sch., Tex., 1977-79; counselor Pecos-Barstow-Toyah Ind. Sch. Dist., Tex., 1979-84; band dir., flute tchr. Pharr-San Juan-Alamo I.S.D., Tex., 1985—; lectr. flute U. Tex., Pan Am, 1995—; flute player USAF Acad. Band, 1972. Flute and piccolo player, McAllen Town Band, Tex., 1985—, First Baptist Ch., Pecos, 1979-84; flute, piccolo player Rio Grande Valley Wind Symphony, 1994-95; prin. flutist Rio Grande Valley Symphony Orch., 1994-95; flute player Brownsville Cmty. Band, 1990-93. Served with U.S. Army, 1970-73. Recipient Commemorative Lifelong Achievemnt medal of Honor, 1987. Mem. NEA, Tex. Tchrs. Assn. (state del. 1981-82), Pecos-Barstow-Toyah Edn. Assn. (v.p. 1981-82, sec. 1983-84), Tex. Music Edn. Assn., Nat. Flute Assn., Tex. Bandmasters Assn., Internat. Parliament for Safety and Peace, Order KT's Jerusalem, Royal Order of Bohemian Crown (knight and baron), Assn. St. George the Martyr (knight), Holy Cross of Jerusalem (knight), Lofsenic Ursinius Order (knight and comdr.), Legion Aigle de Mer (capt.), Order of San Ciriaco (knight) (Italy), Circulo Nobiliario de los Caballeros (knight) (Spain), Ordre Souverain du Saint Sepulcre (Chevalier grand croix).

COLEMAN, MARTIN STONE, retired office furniture company executive; b. N.Y.C., Oct. 22, 1913; s. Adolph H. and Hannah (Stone) C.; m. Janet Mosler, June 30, 1940; children—Ann, John, Nancy. B.S., N.Y. U., 1937. C.P.A., N.Y. Vice pres., treas., dir. Mosler Safe Co., N.Y.C., 1952-61; exec. v.p., treas. Mosler Safe Co., 1961-66, pres., dir., 1966-67, chmn. bd., 1968-72; chmn. bd. Harbor Universal Inc., 1972-94; personal investor, 1995—. Trustee Coleman Found.; Cost insp. Bur. Supplies and Accounts, Navy Dept., 1942-45. Mem. Am. Inst. C.P.A.'s, N.Y. State Soc. C.P.A.'s. Clubs: Sunningdale Country, Harmonie. Home: 740 Park Ave New York NY 10021-4251 Office: 375 Park Ave New York NY 10152-0002

COLEMAN, MARY STALLINGS, retired chief justice; b. Forney, Tex.; d. Leslie C. and Agnes B. (Huther) Stallings; m. Creighton R. Coleman, June 24, 1939 (dec.); children: Leslie Coleman Hagan, Carol Coleman-Sheenson. B.A., U. Md., 1935; J.D., George Washington U., 1939; LL.D., Eastern Mich. U., 1974, Western Mich. U., 1974; L.H.D., Nazareth Coll., 1973; LL.D., Alma Coll., 1973, Olivet Coll., 1973, Detroit Coll. Law, 1975, Adrian Coll., 1976, U. Md., 1978, Saginaw Valley State Coll., 1979, Ferris State U., 1981, Hope Coll., 1981, N.Y. Law Sch., 1982; D.P.A., Albion Coll., 1982, U. Detroit, 1983, Grand Valley State Coll., 1984. Bar: D.C. 1940, Mich. 1950. Practiced in Washington, 1940-46; ptnr. Wunsch & Coleman, Battle Creek, Mich., 1950-61; probate and juvenile ct. judge Calhoun County, Mich., 1961-73; justice Mich. Supreme Ct., 1973-83; dir. K Mart Internat., Nat. Bank Detroit and NBD Bancorp, Biggs/Gilmore; adv. mem. Nat. Bank Detroit, NBD Bancorp. Contbr. articles to profl. publs. Trustee emeritus Albion Coll.; mem. Nat. Commn. for Observance of Internat. Women's Year, 1975-76. Recipient Disting. Alumna award Law Sch., George Washington U., 1973, Alumni Disting. Career Achievement award, 1983, Disting. Alumni award U. Md., 1973, Disting. Mem. award Phi Kappa Phi, 1973, award Calhoun County Bd. Edn., 1964, award NAACP Young Adults, 1969, George award Enquirer & News, 1969, Internat. Wyman award Alpha Omicron Pi, 1975, Disting. Woman award Mich. Bus. and Profl. Women's Club, 1973, Religious Heritage of Am. award, 1974, Disting. Citizen award Mich. State U., 1977, joint resolution of commendation Mich. Legis., 1977, 82, DAR medal of honor, 1978, Disting. Svc. award Mich. Juvenile Detention Assn., 1980, Disting. Alumna award George Washington U., 1980, Award of Merit Am. Judges Assn., 1980, Disting. Vol. Leadership award March of Dimes, 1981, Disting. Jurist award Miss. State U. Pre-Law Soc., 1988; named Woman of Yr. Mich. Assn. Professions, 1976, U. Md. Hall of Fame, 1995, 1 of 10 Top Michigians of Yr., 1980, Disting. Woman Northwood U., 1981, Mich. Women's Hall of Fame, 1983. Fellow Mich. Bar Found. (founder); mem. PEO, Mich. Bar Assn. (Champion of Justice award 1993), Mich. Assn. Woman Lawyers, Bus. and Profl. Women's Club, Am. Legion Aux., Jr. League (hon.), Big Sisters-Big Bros. (hon.), Altrusa Internat. (hon.), Gainesville Golf and Country Club, Beta Sigma Phi, Delta Kappa Gamma, Alpha Delta Kappa, Alpha Omicron Pi. Address: 2805-D214 NW 83rd St Gainesville FL 32606 *My one overriding thought concerning the achievements and honors listed above is that none are truly mine. They are but reflections of the work and good will of many people —importantly, of an extraordinarily helpful and supportive husband and of our admirable children.*

COLEMAN, MARY SUE, academic administrator; b. Richmond, Ky, Oct. 2, 1943. BA, Grinnell Coll., 1965; PhD, U. N.C., 1969. NIH postdoctoral fellow U. N.C., Chapel Hill, 1969-70; NIH postdoctoral fellow U. Ky., 1971-72, instr., rsch. assoc. depts. biochemistry and medicine, 1972-75, asst. prof. dept. biochemistry, 1975-80, assoc. prof. dept. biochemistry, 1980-85, prof. dept. biochemistry, 1985-90; prof. dept. biochemistry and biophysics U. N.C., Chapel Hill, 1990-93; provost, v.p. for academic affairs, prof. biochemistry U. N.Mex., 1993-95; pres., prof. biochemistry, prof. biol. scis. U. Iowa, Iowa City, 1995—; pres. Iowa Health Sys., 1995—; vice chancellor for grad. studies and rsch. U. N.C., 1992-93; assoc. provost, dean rsch. U. N.C., 1990-92; trustee U. Ky. (elected by faculty), 1987-90; assoc. dir. rsch. L.P. Markey Cancer Ctr., U. Ky., 1983-90; dir. grad. studies in biochemistry U. Ky., 1984-87; acting dir. basic rsch. U. Ky. Cancer Ctr., 1980-83; NSF summer trainee Grinnell Coll., 1962; scientific cons. Abbott Labs., 1981-85, Collaborative Rsch., 1983-88, Life Techs., Inc., 1992; bd. dirs. Cardinal Assocs., Inc., 1994-95; editl. bd. Jour. Biol. Chemistry, 1989-93; bd. dirs. Norwest Bank Iowa N.A., 1996—, Gaylord Container Corp., 1996—, Meredith Corp., 1997—; mem. Big Ten Coun. Pres.'s, 1995—. Contbr. numerous articles to profl. jours.; presenter in field. Trustee Grinnell Coll., 1996—; mem. bd. govs. Warren G. Magnuson Clin. Ctr., NIH, 1996—, State of Iowa Gov.'s ACCESS Edn. Commn., 1997—, Inst. Medicine, 1997; bd. dirs. Albuquerque United Way, 1995. Recipient Clayton Found. Biochem. Inst. postdoctoral fellowship U. Tex., 1970-71. Mem. AAAS, Am. Assn. for Cancer Rsch., Am. Soc. Biochemistry and Molecular Biology, NASULGC Coun. Chief Acad. Officers (exec. com. 1993-95). Office: Office of the President 101 Jessup Hall U Iowa Iowa City IA 52242-1316*

COLEMAN, MICHAEL DORTCH, nephrologist; b. Jackson, Tenn., June 19, 1944; s. Ivery R. and Kathleen (Campbell) C.; children by previous marriage: Michael Dortch, Christopher Mathew; m. Stephanie Sherean Summers; 1 child, Cassandra Sherean. BA in Chemistry, U. Ark., 1966; MD, Duke U., 1970. Diplomate Am. Bd. Internal Medicine. Intern, Duke U. Med. Sch., Durham, N.C., 1970-71, resident internal medicine, 1971-72, nephrology fellow, 1972-74; practice medicine specializing in nephrology, Durham, 1972-74, Kannapolis, N.C., 1973-74, Ft. Smith, Ark., 1974—; nephrology cons. Cabarras County Hosp., Kannapolis, 1973; chief dept. nephrology Holt Krock Clinic, Ft. Smith, 1974—, dir. dialysis Holt Krock Dialysis Ctr., 1974—, Sparks Regional Med. Center, Ft. Smith, 1974—, chief medicine, 1994-96; dir. dialysis St. Edward's Mercy Med. Ctr., Ft. Smith, 1980—; assoc. prof. medicine U. Ark., Ft. Smith, 1976—; mem. med. rev. bd. Ark. Kidney Disease Commn., 1974—; nephrology cons., 1974—; mem. exec. com. and med. rev. bd. Ark.-Okla. Endstage Renal Disease Coun., 1977—. Bd. dirs. Ark. Tennis Assn., Jr. Tennis Coun., Holt Krock Clinic, Ft. Smith, Ark.; bd. dirs., mem. fin. com. Holt Krock Clinic. Mem. Internat. Soc. Nephrology, Renal Physician Assn., Am. Soc. Nephrology, Am. Heart Assn., AMA, Ark. Med. Assn., Sebastian County Med. Assn., Ft. Smith Racquet Club (bd. dirs., pres.), Town Club of Ft. Smith, Hardscrabble Country Club, Alpha Omega Alpha. Contbr. articles to med. jours. Office: 1500 Dodson Ave Fort Smith AR 72901-5128

COLEMAN, MICHAEL MURRAY, polymer science educator; b. Herne Bay, Eng., Jan. 24, 1938; s. Ronald and Winifred L. (Legg) C.; m. Mary Jane Ogorek, June 25, 1977; 1 child, David Spencer. BSc in Polymer Sci., Borough Poly., London, 1968; MS in Macromolecular Sci., Case Western Res. U., 1971, PhD in Macromolecular Sci., 1973. Analytical chemist Rhokana Corp. Ltd., Nkana, Zambia, 1955-61, Johnson-Mathey Ltd., Wembley, Eng., 1963-64; rsch. chemist Revertex Ltd., Harlow, Eng., 1968-69, E.I. du Pont de Nemours & Co., Wilmington, Del., 1973-75; asst. prof. polymer sci. Pa. State U., 1975-78, program chmn. polymer sci., 1976-84, assoc. prof., 1978-82, prof., 1982—, head, dept. materials sci. and engring., 1983-91. Author: (with others) The Theory of Vibrational Spectroscopy and its Application to Polymeric Materials, 1982, Specific Interactions and the Miscibility of Polymer Blends, 1991, Fundamentals of Polymer Science, 1994, 2d edit., 1997; contbr. over 190 tech. articles to profl. jours. Mem. Am. Chem. Soc. (polymer and polymeric materials sci. and engring. divsns.), Am. Phys. Soc. (high polymer physics divsn.), Soc. Plastics Engrs. Republican. Fax: (814) 865-2917. E-mail: MMC4@psu.edu. Office: Pa State Univ 330 Steidle Bldg University Park PA 16802-5007

COLEMAN, MORTON, oncologist, hematologist; b. Norfolk, Va., Sept. 15, 1939; s. Isadore and Bessie (Levin) C.; m. Joyce Goodman, May 26, 1968; children: Ingrid Alexandra, Benjamin Lee, Abigail Rachael. AA, Coll. William and Mary, 1958; BA, Johns Hopkins U., 1959; MD, Med. Coll. Va., 1963. Diplomate Nat. Bd. Med. Examiners, Am. Bd. Internal Medicine, Am. Bd. Hematology, Am. Bd. Clin. Oncology. Intern Grady Meml. Hosp.-Emory U. Med. Ctr., Atlanta, 1963-64, resident, 1964-65; resident N.Y. Hosp.-Cornell U. Med. Ctr., N.Y.C., 1967-68, NIH fellow in hematology Cornell U. Med. Coll., 1968-70, asst. prof. medicine, 1970-74, assoc. prof., 1974-86, clin. prof., 1986—; asst. attending N.Y. Hosp., N.Y.C., 1970-74, assoc. attending, 1974-86, attending, 1986—, assoc. dir. oncology svc., 1974-86, assoc. program dir. Nat. Cancer Inst. Clin. Chemotherapy Program in Cancer Control, 1974-80, dir. Ctr. for Lymphoma and Myeloma divsn., hematology-oncology, 1997—; attending staff: Manhattan Eye and Ear Hosp., 1972-82, Doctors Hosp., 1973-90, Beth Israel NorthMed. Ctr., 1990-94, New Rochelle Med. Ctr., 1980-91, Chmn. new agts. com. Cancer and Leukemia Group B, 1975-82; chmn. bd. dirs. Fund for Blood and Cancer Rsch., 1975—; sci. advisor United Leukemia Fund, 1976-82; assoc. editor Cancer Investigation, 1987—; program chmn. N.Y. Cancer Soc., 1993-94, sec., 1994-95, treas., 1995-96, v.p., 1996-97, bd. dirs Cure for Lymphoma Found., 1997; chmn. lymphoma/Hodgkins's diseases symposium com. Internat. Union Against Cancer Congress, 1993-94; internat. adv. bd. Indian Jour. Med. and Pediatric Oncology, 1994—; co-chairman clin. rsch. rev. com. Israel Cancer Rsch. Fund., 1988-93, Chmn. bd. dir., Affiliated Physicians Network, Inc., 1996—, Internat. Adv., Cancer Care Trust and Rsch. Found. India, 1994— V.p. alumni coun. Cornell U. Med. Ctr., 1992-94, pres., 1994-96. Lt. comdr. USN, 1965-67. Disting. Alumni award Old Dominion U., 1994. Fellow ACP; mem. AAAS, AMA, Am. Assn. Cancer Rsch., Am. Fedn. Clin. Rsch., Am. Radium Soc., Am. Soc. Clin. Oncology (mem. com. clin. practice 1997—), Am. Soc. Hematology, Am. Heart Assn., Cornell U. Med. Ctr. Alumni Assn., Harvey Soc., Internat. Soc. Hematology, Internat. Soc. Thrombosis and Hemostasis, N.Y. Acad. Sci., N.Y. State Soc. Med. Oncology and Hematology (mem. exec. com., 1991—), Soc. Study of Blood, N.Y. State Med. Soc., N.Y. County Med. Soc., Alpha Omega Alpha, Sigma Zeta. Research publs. on blood, cancer. Office: 407 E 70th St New York NY 10021-5302 also: NY Hosp-Cornell U Med Ctr Div Hematology-Oncology 525 E 68th St New York NY 10021-4873

COLEMAN, NORM, mayor. BA, Hofstra U.; JD, U. Iowa. Bar: Minn. Asst. atty. gen., solicitor gen., dir. crim. justice policy Minn. Atty. Gen.'s Office, 17 yrs.; mayor City of St. Paul, 1994—; active in creation of Minn. Drug Abuse Resistance Edn. program, also The Partnership for a Drug Free Minn. Humphrey fellow U. Minn. Office: Office of the Mayor 15 W Kellogg Blvd 390 City Hall Saint Paul MN 55102*

COLEMAN, PATRICK J., urban planner; b. Mpls., Oct. 17, 1953; s. Paul Edward and Irene Bernice (Gerald) C.; m. Debra Jane Pederson, May 24, 1974 (div. Apr. 1993); children: Mollie L., Daniel P.; m. Jo Anna Lorichon, Dec. 23, 1995. BS in Urban and Reg. Studies, Mankato (Minn.) State U., 1977, MA in Urban and Reg. Studies, 1978. Planner Mankato Twp., 1976-78, Western UP Planning Reg., Houghton, Mich., 1978-79; cmty. devel. dir. City of Ironwood, Mich., 1979-84; planning divsn. mgr. UP Engrs. & Architects, Marquette, Mich., 1984—. Vice pres. Winter Cities Assn., Can., 1992-97. Mem. Am. Inst. Cert. Planners, Winter Cities Assn. (pres. 1998—), Lions (pres. 1992). Avocations: fishing, skiing, music. Home: 516 Rock St Marquette MI 49855-4530 Office: UP Engrs & Architects 102 W Washington St Ste 217 Marquette MI 49855-4350

COLEMAN, PAUL DARE, electrical engineering educator; b. Stoystown, Pa., June 4, 1918; s. Clyde R. and Catharine (Livengood) C.; m. Betty L. Carter, June 20, 1942; children—Susan Dare, Peter Carter. A.B., Susquehanna U., 1940; M.S., Pa. State U., 1942; Ph.D., Mass. Inst. Tech., 1951, D.Sc. (hon.), 1978. Asst. physics Susquehanna U., 1938-40, Pa. State U., 1940-42; physicist USAF-WADC, Wright Field, Ohio, 1942-46, Cambridge Air Research Center, also; grad. research assoc. Mass. Inst. Tech., 1946-51; prof. elec. engring., dir. electro-physics lab. U. Ill. at Urbana, 1951—. Recipient meritorious civilian award USAAF, 1946. Fellow IEEE-MTT (Disting. Educator award 1994, Centennial medal 1984), Optical Soc. Am., Am. Phys. Soc.; mem. Sigma Xi, Pi Mu Delta, Pi Mu Epsilon, Eta Kappa Nu. Research on millimeter waves, submillimeter waves, relativistic electronics, far infrared molecular lasers, beam wave guides and detectors, chem. lasers, nonlinear optics, solid state electronics. Home: 710 Park Lane Dr Champaign IL 61820-7633 Office: Univ Ill 133 Everitt Lab 1406 W Green St Urbana IL 61801-2918

COLEMAN, PAUL DAVID, neurobiology researcher, educator; b. N.Y.C., Dec. 2, 1927; s. A. Barnett and Martha L. (Michaels) C.; m. Zinia J. Cereska, Mar. 13, 1955 (div. Sept. 1978); children: Laura A., Paul David; m. 2d Dorothy G. Flood, Feb. 26, 1983. AB, Tufts U., 1948; PhD, U. Rochester, 1953. Asst. prof., research assoc. Tufts U., Medford, Mass., 1956-59; assoc. Computer Ctr. MIT, Cambridge, 1957-59; spl. fellow Johns Hopkins Sch. Medicine, Balt., 1959-62; assoc. prof. Sch. Medicine U. Md., Balt., 1962-67; prof. neurobiology and anatomy Sch. Medicine, U. Rochester, N.Y., 1967—. Editor in chief Neurobiology of Aging, 1988—; contbr. articles to profl. jours. 1st lt. U.S. Army, 1953-56. Recipient award for leadership and excellence in Alzheimer's disease Nat. Inst. Aging, NIH, 1990; rsch. grantee NSF, 1958-67, NIH, 1963—; NIH spl. fellow Johns Hopkins U. Sch. Medicine, 1959-62. Mem. Soc. for Neurosci., Am. Assn. Anatomists, AAAS, Gerontol. Soc., Am. Psychol. Assn., Sigma Xi. Club: Yacht (Rochester, N.Y.) (bd. dirs. 1971-72). Home: 35 Atkinson St Rochester NY 14608-2247

COLEMAN, PAUL JEROME, JR., physicist, educator; b. Evanston, Ill., Mar. 7, 1932; s. Paul Jerome and Eunice Cecile (Weissenberg) C.; m. Doris Ann Fields, Oct. 3, 1964; children: Derrick, Craig. BS in Engring. Math., U. Mich., 1954, BS in Engring. Physics, 1954, MS in Physics, 1958; PhD in Space Physics, UCLA, 1966. Rsch. scientist Ramo-Wooldridge Corp. (name now TRW Systems), El Segundo, Calif., 1958-61; instr. math. U. So. Calif., L.A., 1958-61; mgr. interplanetary scis. program NASA, Washington, 1961-62; rsch. scientist UCLA, 1962-66, prof. geophysics, space physics, 1966—; asst. lab. dir., mgr. Earth and Space Scis. divsn., chmn. Inst. Geophysics and Planetary Physics Nat. Lab., Los Alamos, N.Mex., 1981-86; dir. Inst. Geophysics and Planetary Physics UCLA, 1989-92; dir. Nat. Inst. for Global Environ. Change, 1994-96; pres. Univs. Space Rsch. Assn., Columbia, Md., 1981—; bd. dirs. Lasertechnics Inc., Albuquerque, Southeast Interactive Tech., Durham, N.C., Sandia Imaging Sys., Dallas, others; mem. adv. bd. San Diego Supercomputer Ctr., 1986—, chmn., 1987-88, others; trustee Univs. Space Rsch. Assn., Columbia, Md., 1981—, Am. Tech. Initiative, 1990—, Internat. Small Satellite Orgn., 1992-96; vis. scholar U. Paris, 1975-76; vis. scientist Lab. for Aeronomy Ctr. Nat. Rsch. Sci., Verrieres le Buisson, France, 1975-76; com. mem. numerous sci. and ednl. orgns., cons. numerous fin. and indsl. cos. Co-editor: Solar Wind, 1972; co-author: Pioneering the Space Frontier, 1986; mem. editorial bd. Geophysics and Astrophysics Monographs, 1970—; assoc. editor Cosmic Electrodynamics, 1968-72; contbr. revs. to numerous profl. jours. Apptd. to Nat. Commn. on Space, Pres. of U.S., 1985, apptd. to Space Policy Adv. Bd., Nat. Space Coun., v.p. of U.S., 1991; bd. dirs. St. Matthew's Sch., Pacific Palisades, Calif., 1979-82, v.p., 1981-82. 1st lt. USAF, 1954-56, Korea. Recipient Exceptional Sci. Achievement Medal NASA, 1970, 1972, spl. recognition for contributions to the Apollo Program, 1979; Guggenheim fellow 1975-76, Fulbright scholar, 1975-76, Rsch. grantee NASA, NSF, Office Naval Research, Calif. Space Inst., Air Force Office Sci. Research, U.S. Geol. Survey. Mem. AAAS, AIAA, Am. Geophys. Union, Am. Phys. Soc., Internat. Acad. Astronautics, Bel Air Bay Club (L.A.), Birnam Wood Golf Club (Monteceito, Calif.), Cosmos Club (Washington), Explorers Club (N.Y.C.), Eldorado Country Club (Indian Wells, Calif.), Tau Beta Pi, Phi Eta Sigma. Avocations: flying, skiing, racquetball, tennis, golf. Home: 1323 Monaco Dr Pacific Palisades CA 90272-4007 Office: UCLA Inst Geophysics & Planetary Physics 405 Hilgard Ave Los Angeles CA 90095-9000

COLEMAN, RALPH EDWARD, nuclear medicine physician; b. Otwell, Ind., Jan. 2, 1943; s. Ralph H. and Roxie Ellen (Arnold) C.; children: Kathryn Kinsley, Emily Elizabeth, Matthew Edward. BA, U. Evansville, 1965; MD, Washington U., 1968. Diplomate Am. Bd. Nuclear Medicine, Am. Bd. Internal Medicine. Intern Barnes Hosp., St. Louis, 1968-69; med. resident Royal Victoria Hosp., Montreal, Que., Can., 1969-70; resident Mallinckrodt Inst. Radiology, St. Louis, 1972-74, asst. prof., 1974-76; assoc. prof. U. Utah Med. Ctr., Salt Lake City, 1976-78; prof. Duke U. Med. Ctr., Durham, 1978—. Author: ACR Nuclear Radiology Syllabus, 1983, 2d edit., 1990, Diagnostic Nuclear Medicine, 3d edit., 1995; assoc. editor Jour. Nuclear Medicine, 1989—; sr. editor Jour. Positron Imaging, 1997—. Capt. U.S. Army, 1970-72. Fellow Am. Coll. Radiology, Am. Coll. Chest Physicians; mem. Soc. Nuclear Medicine (trustee 1985-88, 89-93, pres. Southeastern chpt. 1987-88), Am. Coll. Nuclear Physicians, Radiol. Soc. N.Am., Inst. for Clin. Positron Emission Tomography (pres. 1990). Office: Duke U Med Ctr PO Box 3949 Rm 1419 Durham NC 27710

COLEMAN, REXFORD LEE, lawyer, educator; b. Hollywood, Calif., June 2, 1930; s. Henry Eugene and Antoinette Christine (Dobry) C.; m. Aiko Takahashi, Aug. 28, 1953 (dec.); children: Christine Eugenie, Douglass Craig; m. Sucha Park, June 15, 1978. Student, Claremont McKenna Coll., 1947-49; A.B., Stanford U., 1951, J.D., 1955; M. in Jurisprudence, Tokyo U., 1960. Bar: Calif. 1955, Mass. 1969. Mem. faculty Harvard U., 1959-69; mem. firm Baker & McKenzie, 1969-83, income ptnr., 1971-73, capital ptnr., 1973-83, mng. ptnr. Tokyo office, 1971-78; sr. ptnr. The Pacific Law Group, L.A., 1983—; adj. prof. McGeorge Sch. Law, U. Pacific, 1989—; lectr. Gray's Inn, The Inns of Ct. Sch. Law, London, 1989; cons. U.S. Treasury Dept., 1961-70; counselor Japanese-Am. Soc. for Legal Studies, 1964—; guest lectr. Ford Seminar on Comparative History, MIT, 1968; lectr. Legal Tng. and Research Inst., Supreme Ct., Japan, 1970-73; guest lectr. Colloguium Scholars, Calif. Luth. U., 1989; chmn. fgn. bus. customs consultative com. Bur. Customs, Ministry of Fin., Govt. of Japan, 1971-72; chmn. fgn. bus. consulatative commn. Japanese Ministry of Internat. Trade and Industry, 1973-76; mem. U.S. Del., U.S.-Japan Income Tax Treaty Negotiations, 1961, internat. bd. advisors, McGeorge Sch. Law, U. Pacific, 1989—. Author: Am. Index to Japanese Law, 1961, Standard Citation of Japanese Legal Materials, 1963, The Legal Aspects Under Japanese Law of an Accident Involving a Nuclear Installation in Japan, 1963, An Index to Japanese Law, 1975; editor: Taxation in Japan, World Tax Series, 1959-70; founding chmn. bd. editors: Law in Japan: An Ann., 1964-67; mem. bd. editors Stanford Law Rev., 1954-55, Japan Ann. Internat. Law, 1970-92; mem. Internat. Adv. Bd., The Transnational Lawyer, 1988—; contbr. articles to profl. jours. Participant in Japanese-Am. Program for Cooperation in Legal Studies, 1956-60; co-chmn. Conf. on Internat. Legal Protection Computer Software, Stanford Law Sch., 1986, Tokyo, Japan, 1987. Served to 1st lt., Inf. AUS, 1951-53; lt. col. Ret. Ford Found. grantee, 1956-60. Mem. ABA, State Bar Calif., Mass. Bar Assn., Japanese-Am. Soc. for Legal Studies, Internat. Fiscal Assn. Japan, Res. Officers Assn. (v.p. army dept. Far East 1974-75), Ret. Officers Assn., Internat. House Japan (Tokyo), Stanford U. Alumni Assn., Gakushi Kai (grads. of former Japanese Imperial Univs. Assn.), Internat. Law Assn. Japan, Japan-Western Assn., Pacific Basin Econ. Council, (U.S. exec. com. 1985-87), Nihon Shihō Gakkai, Nihon Kokusai Hō Gakkai, Nihon Kokusai Shihō Gakkai, Sozei Hō Gakkai, Phi Alpha Delta. Episcopalian (vestryman 1966-69, del. Conv. Episcopal Diocese Mass. 1968, Conv. Episcopal Diocese L.A., 1989-91, Bishop's com. 1983-87, 91-93). Clubs: Tokyo Am; Harvard (N.Y.C.), North Ranch Country. Home: 32314 Blue Rock Rdg Westlake Village CA 91361-3912 Office: The Pacific Law Group 12121 Wilshire Blvd Ste 205 Los Angeles CA 90025-1164

COLEMAN, RICHARD A., JR., career officer. BS in Criminal Justice, U. Nebr., Omaha, 1972; student, Squadron Officer Sch., 1975; M in Criminal Justice, Webster Coll., 1982; student, Air Command and Staff Coll., 1984, Army War Coll., 1990. Commd. 2d lt. USAF, 1972, advanced through grades to brig. gen., 1997; ops. officer 308th Security Police Squadron, Little Rock, 1972-73; Philippine liaison officer, officer in charge Dept. Def. Civilian Guard Force, 3rd Security Police Group, Clark Air Base, The Philippines, 1975; stationed at Lackland AFB, Tex., 1978-83; comdr. and chief 10th

Security Police Squadron, RAF Alconbury, Eng., 1983-86; chief base div. Air Force Office Security Police, Kirtland AFB, N.Mex., 1986-87, chief base def. contingency div., 1988-89; comdr. and chief security police then comdr. 24th Support Group, Howard AFB, Panama, 1990-94; dir. security police Hdqs. Air Combat Command, Langley AFB, Va., 1994-96; chief security police Hdqs. USAF, Pentagon, Washington, 1996-97, dir. security forces, 1997—; comdr. USAF Security Forces Ctr., Lackland AFB, 1997—. Decorated Legion of Merit, Bronze Star, Rep. of Vietnam Gallantry Cross, Rep. of Vietnam Campaign medal. Office: HQ USAF/XOF 1340 Air Force Pentagon Washington DC 20330-1340

COLEMAN, RICHARD WILLIAM, lawyer; b. Brookline, Mass., Dec. 9, 1935; s. Michael John and Mary Ellen (Motherway) C.; m. Mary M. Kilcommins, June 3, 1961; children: Lauren, Christopher. BS, Boston Coll., Newton, Mass., 1957; JD, Boston Coll., Brighton, Mass., 1960. Bar: Mass. 1960, U.S. Dist. Ct. Mass. 1961, U.S. Ct. Appeals (1st cir.) 1981. Field atty. NLRB, Newark, 1960-61; assoc. Segal & Flamm, Boston, 1961-69; labor rels. advisor Scott Paper Co., Phila., 1969-70; labor rels. mgr. Harvard U., Cambridge, Mass., 1970-72; ptnr. Segal, Roitman & Coleman, Boston, 1972-93; pres. Richard W. Coleman, P.C., Needham, 1994—. Contbg. editor Development of Law Under National Labor Relations Act, 1988. Recipient Cushing award Cath. Labor Guild Boston, 1976. Mem. ABA, Am. Prepaid Legal Svcs. Inst. (bd. dirs. 1997—), Indsl. Rels. Rsch. Assn., Mass. Bar Assn., Boston Bar Assn., AFL-CIO Lawyers Coord. Com. Democrat. Roman Catholic. Avocations: golf, reading, choir singing. Office: 214 Garden St Needham MA 02492-2330

COLEMAN, ROBERT ELLIOTT, retired secondary education educator; b. Waterbury, Conn., June 25, 1935; s. William V. and Ethel M. (Brennan) C.; m. Maryan R. Cannon, June 19, 1965; children: Kathryn, William, Becky (dec.), Amy. BA, St. Mary's Sem. & U., Balt., 1957; MA, Fairfield U., 1961, Cert. of Advanced Grad. Study, 1962. Cert. English tchr., grades 9-12. Tchr. Crosby High Sch., Waterbury, 1960-62, Watertown (Conn.) High Sch., 1962-64; dept. chair, guidance counselor Sacred Heart High Sch., Waterbury, 1962-65; dept. chair, tchr. Pomperaug High Sch., Southbury, Conn., 1965-96; ret., 1996; instr. Mattatuck C.C., Waterbury, 1968-72; pres. Ctr. Learning, Watertown, 1975—. Pres. Friends of Huizachera, Cuernavaca, Mex., 1993; sec. Watertown Housing Authority; mem. Dem. Town Com., Watertown; internat. bd. dirs. Vamos!; pres. Human Rights Mex., 1994—. Recipient Am. Tchr. award Walt Disney Co., 1993, Nat. Educator award Milken Family Founds., 1994; inductee Nat. Tchrs. Hall of Fame, 1994; honoree Burger King Excellence in Edn., 1993; named Tchr. of Yr., Conn. State Dept. Edn., 1992, Spl. Edn. Tchr. of Yr., Apple Computer, 1990; NEH fellow, 1993-94; Korea Found. fellow, 1993; Inst. Ednl. Leadership fellow, 1993-94; Fulbright scholar, Beijing, 1996. Mem. ASCD, NEA, Conn. Edn. Assn., Phi Delta Kappa. Roman Catholic. Avocation: computer technology.

COLEMAN, ROBERT GRIFFIN, geology educator; b. Twin Falls, Idaho, Jan. 5, 1923; s. Lloyd Wilbur and Frances (Brown) C.; m. Cathryn J. Hirschberger, Aug. 7, 1948; children: Robert Griffin Jr., Derrick Job, Mark Dana. BS, Oreg. State U., 1948, MS, 1950; PhD, Stanford U., 1957. Mineralogist AEC, N.Y.C., 1952-54; geologist U.S. Geol. Survey, Washington, 1954-57, Menlo Park, Calif., 1958-80; prof. geology Stanford U., Calif., 1981-93, prof. emeritus, 1993—; vis. petrographer New Zealand Geol. Survey, 1962-63; br. chief isotope geology U.S. Geol. Survey, Menlo Park, 1964-68, regional geologist, Saudi Arabia, 1970-71, br. chief field geochemistry and petrology, Menlo Park, 1977-79; vis. scholar Woods Hole Oceanographic Inst., Mass., 1975; vis. prof. geology Sultan Qaboos U., Oman, 1987, 89; cons. geologist, 1993—; instr. geobotany field sch. Siskiyou Inst., Oreg., 1998-99. Author: Ophiolites, 1977, Geologic Evolution of the Red Sea, 1993, Ultrahigh Pressure Metamorphism, 1995; contbr. articles to profl. jours. Named Outstanding Scientist, Oreg. Acad. Sci., 1977; Fairchild scholar Calif. Inst. Tech., Pasadena, 1980; recipient Meritorious award U.S. Dept. Interior, 1981. Fellow AAAS, Geol. Soc. Am. (coun.), Am. Mineral Soc. (coun., editor), Am. Geophys. Union; mem. Nat. Acad. Scis., Russian Acad. Sci. (fgn. assoc.). Republican. Avocations: wood carving, art. Home: 2025 Camino Al Lago Menlo Park CA 94027-5938 Office: Geol & Environ Scis Dept Stanford Univ Stanford CA 94305

COLEMAN, ROBERT J., lawyer; b. Phila., Dec. 24, 1936; s. Francis Eugene and Mary Veronica (McCullough) C.; m. Mary Patricia Coleman, June 26, 1955; children: Debra, Robert P., Linda, Martin S. AB, Villanova U., 1959; JD, Temple U., 1964. Bar: Pa., U.S. Dist. Ct. (ea. dist.) Pa., U.S. Ct. Appeals (3d cir.), U.S. Supreme Ct. With First Pa. Bank, Phila., 1955-57; underwriter Employer's Mut. Co., Phila., 1957-59; claim adjuster Safeco Ins. Co., Phila., 1959-62; claim supr. Gen. Accident Ins., Phila., 1962-64; assoc. Rappaport & Lagakos, Phila., 1964; trial atty. Allstate Ins. Co., Phila., 1964-67; chmn., CEO Marshall, Dennehey, Warner, Coleman & Goggin, Phila., 1967—; bd. dirs. Jeff Banks Inc., Phila., ; hearing com. chmn. Pa. Disciplinary Bd., Phila., 1986-94. Assoc. editor Phila. County Reporter, 1984-96; contbr. articles to legal publs. Bd. dirs. Ins. Soc. Phila.; dir. HERO Scholarship Fund Delaware County; bd. visitors Temple U. Law Sch.; mem. State Bd. Law Examiners. With USAR, 1954-62. Mem. ABA, Pa. Bar Assn., Phila. Bar Assn., Phila. Bar Found. (trustee), Pa. Def. Inst., Internat. Assn. Def. Lawyers, Def. Rsch. Inst. Republican. Roman Catholic. Avocations: tennis, boating, travel. Home: 908 Penn Valley Rd Media PA 19063-1652 Office: Marshall Dennehey Warner Coleman & Goggin 1845 Walnut St Philadelphia PA 19103-4797

COLEMAN, ROBERT LEE, retired lawyer; b. Kansas City, June 14, 1929; s. William Houston and Edna Fay (Smith) C. BMus in Edn., Drake U., 1951; LLB, U. Mo., 1959. Bar: Mo. 1959, Fla. 1973. Law clk. to judge U.S. Dist. Ct. (we. dist.) Mo., Kansas City, 1959-60; assoc. Watson, Ess, Marshall & Engas, Kansas City, 1960-66; asst. gen. counsel Gas Svc. Co., Kansas City, 1966-74; v.p., corp. counsel H & R Block, Inc., Kansas City, 1974-94; retired, 1994. With U.S. Army, 1955-57. Mem. ABA.

COLEMAN, ROBERT MARSHALL, biology educator; b. Bridgton, Maine, Sept. 27, 1925; s. Louis Elmer and Helen (Marr) C.; m. Patricia Ann Stocum, Dec. 29, 1947; children: Mary Deborah, Kevin Robert. B.S., Bates Coll., 1950; M.S., U. N.H., 1951; Ph.D., U. Notre Dame, 1954. Faculty Russell Sage Coll., Troy, N.Y., 1954-62; asst. prof. biology Russell Sage Coll., 1956-58, asso. prof., 1958-62; asso. prof. Boston Coll., 1962-68; prof. biol. scis. U. Mass., Lowell, 1968-97, prof. emeritus, 1997—; cons. AID NSF, India, 1965, 68, Lowell Tech. Inst., 1964-67, Smithsonian Instn., 1976, WHO, Egypt, 1977, NSF Internat. Programs, 1980—, Biotech at Tufts U., 1984, Cath. U., 1985, 86, 87, Harvard U., 1986, Marine Biol. Lab, Woods Hole, Mass., 1988, NSF Young Scholars Program, 1991; ednl. dir. Mass. Bioprocess Ctr., Lowell, 1993; dir. Ctr. for Tropical Diseases, U. Mass., Lowell, 1997. Author: (with others) Fundamental Immunology, 1989, 2d edit., 1992; contbr. articles profl. jours. Served with AUS, 1943-46. Mem. AAAS, Assn. Med. Lab. Immunology, Am. Soc. Parasitology, Am. Soc. Tropical Medicine and Hygiene, Am. Soc. Microbiology, N.Y. Acad. Scis., Sigma Xi, Phi Sigma. Home: 48 Blanchard St PO Box 640 Moody ME 04054-0640 Office: U Mass Lowell Biol Scis Dept Lowell MA 01854

COLEMAN, ROBERT TRENT, social worker, rehabilitation consultant; b. Gary, Ind., Feb. 4, 1936; s. Robert Clinton and Lucille Verna C.; m. Dorothy Agnes, Aug. 1957; children: Sean, Bryce, Daniel; m. 2d, Patricia Lou, June 13, 1976; m. 3d Polly Anderson, Sept. 15, 1984. BA in Speech Therapy, U. Wash., Seattle, 1962; postgrad. in speech U. Redlands, 1963-64; MS in Rehab. Counseling, U. Oreg., 1971. Cert. rehab. counselor, cert. ins. rehab. specialist. Social worker, San Bernardino City Welfare Dept., 1963-64; correctional counselor Calif. Rehab. Center, Norco, 1964-67; sr. counselor Job Corps, Clearfield, Utah, 1967; assoc. dir. Ednl. Systems Corp., Washington, 1968-69; ptnr. Black Fir Jade Mines, Big Sur, Calif., 1971-76; vocat. specialist Internat. Rehab. Assn., San Diego, 1976-77; vocat. rehab. counselor Sharp Hosp., San Diego, 1977-80; clin. coord. San Diego Pain Inst., 1981; cons. in rehab. counseling, career guidance, human rels., Carlsbad, Calif., 1981—; propr. R.T.C. Cons. Svcs., Escondido, 1983—; vocat. rehab. expert Civil Ct., 1983—; sr. social work counselor San Diego Regional Ctr., 1997—. Commr., Handicapped Appeals Commn., San Marcos, Calif., 1981-83. Served with U.S. Army, 1955-58. Mem. ACA, San Diego Career Guidance Assn. (pres. 1984), Assn. Indsl. Rehab. Reps. (pres. 1983), Am. Rehab. Counseling Assn., Nat. Assn. Rehab. Profls. in Pvt. Sector (standards and ethics com. 1986—, chmn. 1988-90). Republican. Home: 538 Glenheather Dr San Marcos CA 92069-2005

COLEMAN, ROBERT WAYNE, airline company executive; b. July 12, 1956. Grad., U. Alaska, 1980. Sales mgr. Van Dusen Aircraft, Mpls., 1981-86; mgr. regional sales Standard Aero, Winnipeg, MB, Can., 1986-96; mgr. engine sales Nat. Airmotive, Oakland, Calif., 1996; mgr. airline sales Airwork Corp., Millville, N.J., 1997—.

COLEMAN, ROBERT WINSTON, lawyer; b. Oklahoma City, Mar. 1, 1942; s. Clint Sheridan and Genevieve (Ross) C.; m. Judith Moore, Sept. 7, 1963; children: Robert Winston, Jr., Claire Elizabeth. BA, Abilene Christian Coll., 1964; JD with hons., U. Tex., 1968. Bar: Tex. 1968, Ga. 1970. Law clk. to presiding justice U.S. Ct. Appeals (5th cir.), Montgomery, Ala., 1968-69; assoc. Kilpatrick, Cody, Rogers, McClatchey & Regenstein, Atlanta, 1969-75, Stalcup, Johnson, Meyers & Miller, Dallas, 1975-77; ptnr. Meyers, Miller, Middleton, Weiner & Warren, Dallas, 1977-80, Jones, Day, Reavis & Pogue, Dallas, 1981-85; dir. Geary, Glast and Middleton, P.C., Dallas, 1985-92; ptnr. Vial, Hamilton, Koch & Knox, LLP, Dallas, 1992—. Mem. exec. com. Dallas County Dem. Com., 1980-87. Mem. ABA, Dallas Bar Found., Dallas Bar Assn., Tex. Bar Assn., Ga. Bar Assn., Am. Judicature Soc. Office: Vial Hamilton Koch & Knox 4400 Bank One Ctr 1717 Main St Ste 4400 Dallas TX 75201-7388

COLEMAN, RODNEY ALBERT, government affairs consultant; b. Newburgh, N.Y., Oct. 12, 1938; s. Samuel C. and Rebecca (Belden) C.; children: Terri Lynn, Stephen Anthony. BArch, Howard U., 1963; grad. exec. devel. program, U. Mich., 1988. Commd. 2nd lt. USAF, 1963, advanced through grades to capt., separated, 1973; White House fellow Washington, 1970-71; exec. asst. to chmn. D.C. City Coun., Washington, 1973-78; archtl. design cons. Pennsylvania Ave. Devel. Corp., Washington, 1978-80; dir. govt. rels. Gen. Motors, Detroit, 1980-85, dir. mcpl. govt. affairs, 1985-90, exec. dir. urban and mcpl. affairs, 1990-94; asst. sec. of Air Force for manpower, Res. affairs, installations, and environ. Dept. of Air Force, Washington, 1994-98; exec. v.p. ICF Kaiser Internat., 1998-99; ptnr. Alcalde & Fay, 1999—. Decorated Bronze Star medal, Air Force Commendation medal Republic of Vietnam, Air Force Meritorious Svc. medal; Honor medal 1st class, 1996; recipient Disting. Alumni award for postgrad. achievement in corp. and govt. svc. Howard U., 1996, Disting. Alumnus award Newburgh Free Acad., 1994, Black Engr. of Yr. dean's award, 1996, Lt. Gen. Benjamin O. Davis Jr. Disting. Achievement award of The Tuskagee Airmen, 1996, decoration for exceptional civilian svc. Dept. of Air Force, 1997, Eagle award Nat. Guard Bur., 1998. Mem. White House Fellows Assn., Exec. Leadership Coun, Air Force Assn., Tuskagee Airmen, Air Force Aid Soc. (trustee 1998—). Methodist. Avocation: golf. Home: 1200 Crystal Dr Arlington VA 22202-4320

COLEMAN, ROGER DIXON, bacteriologist; b. Rockwell, Iowa, Jan. 18, 1915; s. Major C. and Hazel Ruth Coleman; m. Lee Aden Skov, Jan. 1, 1978. AB, UCLA, 1937; postgrad., Balliol Coll., Oxford, Eng., 1944; MS, U. So. Calif., 1952, PhD, 1957. Diplomate Am. Bd. Bioanalysts. Sr. laboratorian Napa (Calif.) State Hosp., 1937-42; dir. Long Beach (Calif) Clin. Lab., 1946-86, pres., 1980-86; mem. Calif. State Clin. Lab. Commn., 1953-57. Author papers to profl. publs. Officer AUS, 1942-46. Mem. Am. Assn. Bioanalysts, Am. Assn. Clin. Chemists, Am. Soc. Microbiologists, Am. Chem. Soc., Am. Venereal Disease Assn., Calif. Assn. Bioanalysts (past officer), Med. Rsch. Assn. Calif., Bacteriology Club So. Calif., Sigma Xi, Phi Sigma (past chpt. pres.). Home: 31086 Montesa Laguna Niguel CA 92677-2721 Office: PO Box 7073 Laguna Niguel CA 92607-7073

COLEMAN, RONALD D. (RON COLEMAN), former congressman; b. El Paso, Tex., Nov. 29, 1941; children: Kimberly Michelle, Michael Robert, Travis Brett. BA, U. Tex., El Paso, 1963; JD, U. Tex., Austin, 1969; postgrad. in law, Kent U., Canterbury, Eng., 1981. Bar: Tex. 1969. Tchr. El Paso Pub. Schs., 1967; practice law El Paso, 1969; asst. county atty. Tex., 1969-71; 1st asst. county atty., from 1971; mem. Tex. Ho of Reps., 1973-82, 98th-104th Congresses from 16th Tex. dist., Washington, 1983-96, House Select Com. on Intelligence, 1993-96; lawyer, sr. v.p. Advantage Assoc. Inc., 1999—; majority whip-at-large, mem. com. on appropriations, subcoms. on mil. constrn., transp. and interior. Author: Pub. Sch. Fin. Act. Tex. Del. Tex. Constl. Conv., 1974. Named One of 10 Best Legislators Tex. Monthly mag., 1977,79, 81; recipient Adminstrn. Justice award State Bar Tex., 1973, Legis. award State Bar Tex., 1979, Environ. award, 1977, award for edn. Tex. Assn. Sch. Adminstrs. and Sch. Bds., 1977, cert. Tex. Compensatory Edn. Assn., 1979. *

COLEMAN, RONALD LEE, insurance claims executive; b. Danville, Va., June 10, 1941; s. Raymond Lee and Mildred Sue (Floyd) C.; m. Stephanie Walther Barton Ewalt; children: Ronald Lee, Christopher Brent. BSBA summa cum laude, Va. Poly. Inst. and State U., 1964; BS in Pub. Adminstrn. summa cum laude, U. Richmond, 1964, postgrad., 1971; postgrad. law sch., U. Va., 1980. Pres. Johnson & Coleman, Ltd., Richmond, 1974-79, Ron Coleman & Assocs., Ltd., Richmond, 1981—; v.p. Schnell, Johnson & Coleman, Ltd., Richmond, Va., 1979-81; adj. prof. U. Tex., Austin, Pa. State U., State College; adv. coun. Pamplin Bus. Sch., Va. Tech. Author: Investigation and Handling of Aviation Claims, 1981, Presentation of Evidence in Accident Reconstruction Cases, 1989, others; editor-in-chief Claimsman mag., 1971-76; contbr. articles to profl. jours. Mem. U.S. Senatorial Bus. Adv. Bd., 1988; mem. adv. coun. Paplin Coll. Bus., Va. Tech.; mem. Rep. Presdl. Task Force, 1988; mem. Va. Rep. Com., Chesterfield County, 1984; mem. The Pres.'s Coun., 1990, Pres. Club Rep. Party; bd. dirs. Va. Tech. Found. Mem. ABA, Richmond Claims Assn. (pres. 1971-72, Man of Yr. award 1971), Torts and Insurance Practice Commn., Va. Claims Assn. (Bob Anderson Humanitarian award), Def. Law Inst., Atlanta Claims Assn., Profl. Claims Assn. Richmond, Truck Ins. Def. Assn., 1872 Soc. at Va. Poly. Inst. and State U., Assn. Lloyds Mems. (London), Ut Prosim Soc. at Va. Poly. Inst. and State U., Va. Tech. Found., 1789 Soc. at Hampdon-Sydney Coll., Soc. of Founders Hampden-Sydney Coll., Reform Club (London), St. James Club (London), Salisbury Country Club, Hurlingham Club (London), Sloane Club (London), Quinnipiack Club (New Haven), Yale Club N.Y.C., Rotunda Soc. U. Va. Methodist. Avocations: jazz, golf. Office: 13408 Village Mill Dr Midlothian VA 23113

COLEMAN, ROY EVERETT, secondary education educator, computer programmer; b. Chgo., Oct. 16, 1942; s. William Everett and Evelyn (Johnson) C.; m. Dianna Joy Uchida, Nov. 12, 1988. BS in Physics, Ill. Inst. of Tech., 1964; MS in Physics, DePaul U., 1974; Sci. Edn., Ill. Inst. of Tech., Chgo., 1990; Computer Sci., Chgo. State U., Chgo., 1984. Physics tchr. Morgan Park H.S., Chgo., 1965—, St. Xavier Coll., Chgo., 1977-80; S.M.I.L.E. staff specialist Ill. Inst. of Tech., Chgo., 1982—, computer edn. staff, 1988—; dir. comp. lit. Chgo. Pub. Sch., 1983-84; treas., pres. Am. Assn. of Physics Tchrs. Chgo. Author: Equipment Evaluation, 1982; coauthor: Physics Text Evaluations, 1984. Mem. Pursuit of Excellence Com., Chgo., 1982-88, Scholarship Com., 1985-89. Recipient Phoebe Aperton Hurst award Nat. PTA, Washington, 1985, Tchr. of Yr. award Chgo. PTA, 1978-80, Presdl. award of Excellence, U.S. Dept. Edn., 1987, Supt. award Chgo. Pub. Schs., 1979, 80, H.S. Tchr. of Astronaut Dr. Mae C. Jemison award, Kohl Internat. Tchg. award, 1994, First pl. Chgo. Rd. Rally Series, 1997; Tandy Tech. scholar, 1995; finalist Golden Apple awards, 1995. Mem. Am. Assn. Physics Tchrs., Sports Car Club Am. (Ind. N.W. region). Avocations: road rallies (rallyemaster, driver SCCA Road Rallye), computer games, auto mechanics. Home: 5436 S Kimbark Ave Chicago IL 60615-5284

COLEMAN, SALLYE TERRELL, retired social studies educator; b. Roanoke, Va.; d. Glen Watson and Addie (Winstead) Terrell; m. William Daniel Coleman, Apr. 14, 1949. BA, Va. State U., 1941; postgrad., NYU, 1951, U. Va., 1962, 63, Interamerican U., Saltillo, Mex., 1966. Cert. tchr., Va. Tchr. Roanoke Pub. Schs., 1941-70, dir. fed. program, 1970-74; presenter clinics at profl. meetings. Mem. Roanoke City Sch. Bd., 1984-92, vice-chmn., 1987-90; bd. dirs. United Way, Roanoke, 1984-87, Coun. Community Svcs., Roanoke, 1983-84, Family Svc., Roanoke, 1981-84; mem. Community Hosp. Vol. Aux., Roanoke, 1975—; bd. govs. Found. of Roanoke Valley, 1993—. Recipient Meritorious Teaching award Nat. Coun. Geographic Edn., Atlanta, George Washington Honor medal Freedom Found., Valley Forge, Pa., Edn. award Roanoke NAACP, Brotherhood citation NCCJ, Roanoke, Disting. Svc. award Va. Congress Parents and Tchrs.; named Gov. Emeritus Found. for Roanoke Valley. Mem. NAACP (life), Va. Sch. Bds. Assn. (bd. dirs. 1990-92, Excellence in Edn. award 1991), Roanoke City Ret. Tchrs., Zeta Phi Beta (Woman Achiever award 1986). Baptist. Avocations: reading, gourmet cooking, travel, volunteer activities. Home: 4700 Grandin Rd SW Roanoke VA 24018-1928

COLEMAN, SIDNEY RICHARD, physicist, educator; b. Chgo., Mar. 7, 1937; s. Harold Albert and Sadie (Shanas) C. B.S., Ill. Inst. Tech., 1957; Ph.D., Calif. Inst. Tech., 1962. Research fellow dept. physics Harvard U., 1961-63, asst. prof., 1963-66, assoc. prof., 1966-69, prof., 1969—; vis. prof. U. Rome, Italy, 1968, Princeton U., 1973, Stanford U., 1979-80, U. Calif., Berkeley, 1989, 95; ptnr. Advent Publs. Author: Aspects of Symmetry, 1985. Trustee Aspen Ctr. Physics. Recipient prize for physics lectures Ettore Majorana Centre Sci. Culture, Boris Pregel award N.Y. Acad. Sci., Disting. Alumnus award Calif. Inst. Tech., Dirac medal Internat. Centre for Theoretical Physics 1990. Fellow NAS (J. Murray Lack award for sci. revs.), Am. Acad. Arts and Sci., Am. Phys. Soc.; mem. Lilapa. Home: 1 Richdale Ave Unit 12 Cambridge MA 02140-2610 Office: Harvard U Physics Dept Cambridge MA 02138

COLEMAN, STEPHEN WILLIAM, community development executive, consultant; b. New Delhi, Oct. 12, 1960; s. John Royston Coleman and Mary Norrington Irwin. Student, Westtown Sch., 1977-79, Haverford Coll., 1979-81, NYU, 1981-82. Intern reporter The MacNeil/Lehrer Report, N.Y.C., 1980-81; program assoc. Am. Friends Svc. Com., N.Y.C., 1982-83; dir. rsch., v.p. for devel. Bus. Execs. for Nat. Security, Washington, 1983-84; cons. Freeze Voter, Washington, 1984-85; prin. S.W. Coleman Cons., Washington, 1984—; dir. program devel. Better World Soc., Washington, 1985-87; founder, pres. Friends of Meridian Hill, Washington, 1990—; exec. dir. Washington Parks and People, Washington, 1996—; pres. FV Tng. Inst., Washington, 1984-86; asst. to pres. Internat. Ctr. Journalists, 1987-89; cons. Natural Resources Coun. Maine, Augusta, 1990-91. Prodr. outdoor music and theater Sunset Series on Meridian Hill, 1990-98, documentary TV series Ending the Arms Race, WTBS/CNN, 1986-87. Pres., founder Save Our Future, Washington, 1983-84; trustee, fin. sec. Washington Innercity Self Help (WISH), 1989-91; sec., pres. Reed-Cooke Neighborhood Assn., Washington, 1989-93, 95-98; founder, coord. Residential Adams Morgan Patrol, Washington, 1990-92, elected Neighborhood Commn., Washington, 1993-95; co-chmn. D.C. Self-Determination Com., 1993-94; sec. Friends of Shenandoah Nat. Park, 1996-98; coord. Potomac Basin Parks Network, 1995-96. Recipient commendation from Pres. of U.S., 1994, from Nat. Park Svc., 1991, 92, 94, U.S. Park Police, 1991, 93, 94, Partnership Leadership award Nat. Park Found., 1994. Mem. Nat. Soc. Fund Raising Execs. (cert.), Com. of 100 on Fed. City (trustee 1994-98, membership chair 1995-98, parks cochair 1996-99). Avocations: hiking, travel, writing. Office: Washington Parks & People 2437 15th St NW Washington DC 20009-6506

COLEMAN, THOMAS YOUNG, lawyer; b. Richmond, Va., Jan. 6, 1949; s. Emmet Macadium and Mary Katherine (Gay) C.; m. Janet Clare Norris, Aug. 30, 1980; children: Dana Alicia, Amanda Gay, Blair Norris. BA, U. Va., 1971, JD, 1975. Bar: Va. 1975, U.S. Dist. Ct. (we. dist.) Va. 1975, U.S. Ct. Appeals (4th cir.) 1976, Calif. 1977, U.S. Dist Ct. (no. dist.) Calif. 1977. Law clk. chief judge U.S. Dist. Ct. (we. dist.) Va., Charlottesville, 1975-76; assoc. Morrison & Foerster, San Francisco, 1976-79; v.p., counsel Calif. 1st Bank (now Union Bank of Calif.), San Francisco, 1979-85; of counsel Orrick, Herrington & Sutcliffe, San Francisco, 1985-86, ptnr., 1987—; speaker in field; vis. atty. Clifford-Turner Solicitors (now Clifford Chance), London, 1984. Mem. bus. gifts com. San Francisco Symphony. Mem. Internat. Bankers Assn. in Calif. (co-counsel). Office: Orrick Herrington & Sutcliffe 400 Sansome St San Francisco CA 94111-3143

COLEMAN, TOMMY LEE, soil science educator, researcher, laboratory director; b. Baxley, Ga., Nov. 8, 1952; s. E.C. and Lucille (Fussell) C.; m. Mildred Cross, Dec. 22, 1974 (div. 1977); m. Edna Thompson, Mar. 6, 1982; children: Sherri, Thomas, Brian. BS in Agronomy, Fort Valley State Coll., 1974; MS, U. Ga., 1977; PhD, Iowa State U., 1980. Soil scientist USDA/Soil Conservation Svc., Statesboro, Ga., 1974-77; rsch. assoc. Iowa State U., Ames, 1977-80; postdoctoral fellow in rsch. Ala. A&M U., Normal, 1981-83, asst. prof., 1983-89, assoc. prof., 1989-93, prof. soil sci. and remote sensing, 1993—, dir. remote sensing lab, 1990-95, dir. Ctr. for Hydrology, Soil Climatology and Remote Sensing, 1995—; rsch. phys. scientist USGS, Reston, Va., 1992-93; dir. Ctr. Hydrology, Soil Climatology, and Remote Sensing, 1995—; cons. Abiola Farms Ltd., Lagos, Nigeria, 1988, U.S. AID-Botswana, Gaborone, 1989-91, 1993—, INRAN-DRE and U.S. AID-Niger, Niamey, 1990. Contbr. articles to profl. jours. Mem. Am. Soc. Agronomy, Soil Sci. Soc. Am., Am. Soc. Photogrammetry and Remote Sensing, NAACP, Profl. Soil Classifiers of Ala., Minorities in Agrl., Natural Resources and Related Scis., North Ala. Golf Club (pres. Huntsville chpt. 1987-92), Omega Psi Phi (Xi Omicron chpt., chair scholarship com. Huntsville chpt. 1986-90). Democrat. Baptist. Office: Ala A&M U Dept Plant & Soil Sci PO Box 1208 Normal AL 35762-1208

COLEMAN, VERONICA FREEMAN, prosecutor. U.S. atty. We. Dist. Tenn., U.S. Dept. Justice, Memphis, 1993—. Office: US Attys Office 800 Federal Office Bldg 167 N Main St Memphis TN 38103-1816

COLEMAN, WADE HAMPTON, III, management consultant, mechanical engineer, former banker; b. Tuscaloosa, Ala., June 24, 1932; s. Wade Hampton, Jr. and Margaret Pauline (James) C.; m. Kate Shannon Stabler, June 2, 1958 (div. 1966); children—Shannon Hunter, Wade Hampton IV; m. Eileen Marie Lincoln, Dec. 23, 1967; 1 child, Lydie Elizabeth. B.A., U. N.C., 1954; B.S. and B.S.M.E., U. Ala., 1960; M.S.I.E., Lehigh U., 1965. Registered profl. engr., Pa. Rsch. engr. Western Electric Co., Princeton, N.J., 1960-65; tech. staff mem. MITRE Corp., Arlington, Va., 1965-66; mgmt. cons. Booz, Allen & Hamilton, Washington, 1967-70; prin. Auerback Corp., Phila., 1970-72; spl. asst. to sec. HEW, Washington, 1972-73; sr. v.p. Citibank, NA, N.Y.C., 1973-85; chmn., chief exec. officer Asbestos Claims Facility Inc, Princeton, N.J., 1985-87; pres. ELW Devel. Group, Lawrenceville, N.J., 1987-89, Coleman & Evans Inc., Princeton, 1989—. Mem. Civic Assn., Lawrenceville, N.J., 1973—, bd. dirs. Lower Eastside Services Ctr., N.Y.C., 1978—, pres. 1986-90; bd. dirs. Capstone Found., Tuscaloosa, 1980—. Served with USN, 1954-57, lt. comdr. res. ret. Mem. Nat. Soc. Profl. Engrs., Am. Bankers Assn., Sigma Pi Sigma, Tau Beta Pi, Delta Kappa Epsilon. Republican. Episcopalian. Home: 4 Monroe Ave Lawrenceville NJ 08648-1606

COLEMAN, WANDA, poet, writer; b. L.A., Nov. 13, 1946; d. George and Lewana Evans; m. Austin Straus, May 1, 1981; children: Anthony, Luanda, Ian Wayne Grant. Author: (books) African Sleeping Sickness, 1990, Hand Dance, 1993, Native in a Strange Land: Trials and Tremors, 1996, Bathwater Wine, 1998. NEA fellow in poetry, 1981, Guggenheim fellow in poetry, 1984. Mem. PEN Ctr. West, Writers Guild Am. Fax: (310) 641-6806. Office: Black Sparrow Press 24 10th St Santa Rosa CA 95401-4714

COLEMAN, WENDELL LAWRENCE, former state legislator; b. Brattleboro, Vt., Oct. 2, 1946; s. Loren Walter and Elizabeth Adele (Ameden) C.; m. Choe Chong Hwa, Feb. 1, 1974; children: Edward, Gretchen. BS in Edn., U. Vt., 1971. Farmer South Londonderry, Vt., 1974—; mem. Vt. Ho. of Reps., Montpelier, 1989—, mem. natural resources com., 1991-94, vice-chair natural resources com., 1995-96, mem. fish wildlife and water resources, 1995, 97-98, mem. natural resources com., 1997-98. Mem. Londonderry Planning Com., 1976-80, chmn., 1980; mem. Flood Brook Union Sch. Bd., Londonderry, 1980-98. With U.S. Army, 1972-73, Korea. E-mail: Wendellcoleman@compuserve.com. Home: RR Box 117 South Londonderry VT 05155-0117

COLEMAN, WILLIAM THADDEUS, JR., lawyer; b. Germantown, Pa., July 7, 1920; s. William Thaddeus and Laura Beatrice (Mason) C.; m. Lovida Hardin, Feb. 10, 1945; children: William Thaddeus III, Lovida Hardin Jr., Hardin L. A.B. summa cum laude, U. Pa., 1941; LL.B. magna cum laude, Harvard U., 1946. Bar: Pa. 1947, D.C. 1977. Law sec. Judge Herbert F. Goodrich, U.S. Ct. of Appeals, 3d Circuit, 1947-48, Justice Felix Frankfurter (asso. justice Supreme Ct. U.S.), 1948-49; assoc. Paul, Weiss, Rifkind, Wharton & Garrison, N.Y.C., 1949-52, Dilworth, Paxson, Kalish, Levy & Green, Phila., 1952-56; ptnr. Dilworth, Paxson, Kalish, Levy & Coleman,

1956-75; sec. Dept. Transp., Washington, 1975-77; sr. counsellor, sr. ptnr. O'Melveny & Myers, Washington, L.A., San Francisco, N.Y.C., Tokyo, London, Hong Kong, Shanghai, China, 1977—; spl. counsel for transit matters City of Phila., 1952-63; rep. atty. gen. Pa. and Commonwealth of Pa. in litigation to remove racial restrictions at Girard Coll., 1965; mem. Pres.'s Com. on Govt. Employment Policy, 1959-61; cons. ACDA, 1963-74; sr. cons., asst. counsel Pres.'s Commn. on Assassination of Pres. Kennedy, 1964; co-chmn. planning sessions White House Conf. to Fulfill These Rights, 1965-66; mem. U.S. del. 24th Session UN Gen. Assembly, 1969; mem. legal adv. com. Council on Environ. Quality, 1970; pub. mem. Pres.'s Nat. Commn. on Productivity, 1970; commr. Price Commn., 1971-72, Phila Fairmount Park Commn., 1967-75, White Ho. Commn. Aviations Safety adn Security, 1996-97; mem. Gov.'s Commn. on Constl. Revision, 1963-65. Contbr. articles to prof. jours. Chmn. bd. NAACP Legal Def. and Ednl. Fund; v.p., trustee, mem. exec. com. Phila. Mus. Art; trustee Brookings Instn., Nat. Gallery Art, 1999; mem. Trilateral Commn.; mem. exec. com. Lawyers Com. for Civil Rights Under Law; bd. overseers Harvard U., 1975-81; bd. dirs., adv. dir. N.Y. City Ballet. Recipient Joseph E. Beale prize, 1946, Presdl. Freedom medal Pres. Clinton, 1995, NAACP Legal Def. Fund Thurgood Marshall Lifetime Achievement award, 1997; Langdell fellow, 1946-47. Fellow Am. Coll. Trial Lawyers; mem. Am. Acad. Appellate Lawyers, Am. Law Inst. (coun.), Phila. Bar Assn. (past chmn. jud. com.), Am. Arbitration Assn. (gov.), Coun. Fgn. Rels., French Legion Honor (officer), Order of Coif, Phi Beta Kappa, Pi Gamma Nu (Wickersham award 1997), Harvard Law Sch. Club, Cosmos Club, Alfalfa Club, Jr. Legal Club (Phila.), Met. Club (Washington). Office: O'Melveny & Myers 555 13th St NW Ste 500W Washington DC 20004-1159

COLEMAN, WILLIAM THADDEUS, III, federal official. BA cum laude, Williams Coll., 1970; JD, Yale U., 1973. Civil rights atty. Hill, Jones & Farrington, Savannah, Ga.; law clk. Hon. Edward T. Gignoux, U.S. Dist. Ct. Maine; assoc. Pepper, Hamilton & Sheetz, Phila., 1975; assoc. Pepper, Hamilton & Sheetz, Detroit, ptnr.; gen. counsel U.S. Army, Washington, 1994—; founder's group mem. Wayne County Devel. Bank; author, lectr. and panelist on employment, affirmative action, defense, ethical and litigation issues; del. 6th Cir. Jud. Conf. Bd. dirs. Wayne County Neighborhood Legal Svcs. Mem. ABA (conf. on minority ptnrs. in majority law firms), U.S. Ct. Fed. Claims, Am. Law Inst., Detroit Bar Assn. (chmn. pub. adv. com. for evaluation of qualifications of Mich. Supreme Ct. jud. candidates, mem. com. on minority and female involvement), Fed. Bar Assn. (exec. bd. for ea. dist. Mich.). Office: Dept of the Army General Counsel 104 Army Pentagon 2E722 Washington DC 20310-0104*

COLEMAN, WINIFRED ELLEN, administrator; b. Syracuse, N.Y., Oct. 3, 1932; d. Peter Andrew and Josephine (Fahey) C. BA, Lemoyne Coll., Syracuse, N.Y., 1954; MA, Marquette U., 1956. Dean of students Cazenovia (N.Y.) Coll., 1957-71; dean of students Trinity Coll., Washington, 1971-81; exec. dir. Nat. Coun. Catholic Women, Washington, 1981-85; pres. St. Joseph Coll., West Hartford, Conn., 1991—; bd. trustees, Lemoyne Coll., Syracuse, 1996—; mem. Nat. Assn. Women Deans, Washington, 1957-81; mem. bd. dirs. Nat. Conf. ITT Hartford Mutual Funds Bd. Vice chmn. Syracuse Commn. for Women, 1986—; commr. Metro Commn. for Aging, Syracuse, 1987—; bd. dirs. Cen City Girl Scout Coun. Hon. Trinity Coll. Alumnae, Washington, 1978, Cazenovia (N.Y.) Coll. Alumnae, 1968, Naming of Winifred E. Coleman Student Union, Cazenovia Coll., 1961; recipient Chantal Award, Catholic Daughters of the Am. 1963. Mem. Alpha Sigma Nu (nat. bd. dirs. 1980-82). Roman Catholic. Avocations: reading, golf, composing lyrics. Home: 27 Buckingham Ln Hartford CT 06117-2758 Office: St Joseph Coll 1678 Asylum Ave Hartford CT 06117-2764

COLEMAN-PORTELL, BI BI, women's health and high risk perinatal nurse; b. Columbus, Ohio, Jan. 23, 1951; d. Frederick Douglas and Rubie Anne (Jackson) Coleman; m. Joseph Philip Portell, Nov. 3, 1978; 1 child, Leslie. RN, St. Anthony Sch. Nursing, Oklahoma City, 1982; student, Ohio State U., 1973-76. RN, Okla., Fla., Tex.; cert. high risk perinatal nurse; cert. inpatient obstetric nurse; cert. gen. nursing practice. Dir. patient care coord. perinatal home care prog. Curaflex Health Svcs., Dallas, 1985; staff nurse Nursefinders, Oklahoma City, 1987-88; charge nurse-perinatal St. Anthony Hosp., Oklahoma City, 1986-87; profl. traveling nurse Nursing Projects Corp., Denver, 1989; prof. traveling nurse Univ. Hosp. Consortium, Oakbrook Terrace, Ill., 1990; asst. head nurse U. Tex. Med. Br., Galveston, 1991-92, nurse clinician IV maternal-fetal medicine, 1993-94; community health nurse Healthy Families-HRS, Tampa, 1994-95; urgent care nurse coord. Cigna Health Care, Tampa, 1994-96; therapeutic apheresis specialist Fla. Blood Svcs., Tampa, 1996-97; travel nurse NET Healthcare, Ft. Lauderdale, 1997-98, Ohio State U. Med. Ctr., Columbus, 1999—. Mem. ARC. Capt. USAR, 1985-96. Recipient Vincent B. Snyder award, 1981. Mem. Am. Assn. Med. Pers. (Nat. Merit award 1983), Internat. Coll. Med. Technologists (v.p. 1984-85, Disting. Citation award 1985). Home: 3124 NW 31st St Oklahoma City OK 73112-6709

COLEMAN-TRIANA, KAREN L., media specialist; b. Miami, Fla., Jan. 29, 1968; d. Ralph Leslie and Leona (Small) Coleman; m. Christopher Charles Triana, Aug. 5, 1995. BS in Secondary Edn., Troy (Ala.) State U., 1992; MS in Edn. Media, Nova Southeastern U., Ft. Lauderdale, Fla., 1998. Cert. educator, Fla. Tchr. English South Dade H.S., Homestead, Fla., 1992-93, Redland Mid. Sch., Miami, 1993-94; tchr. debate, debate coach Southridge H.S., Miami, 1994-98; media specialist North Port Glennallen Elem., Sarasota, Fla., 1998—. Mem. NEA. Avocations: computers, reading, lifelong learning. Office: North Port Glennallen Elem 7050 Glenallen Blvd North Port FL 34287-4158

COLEN, FREDERICK HAAS, lawyer; b. Pitts., May 16, 1947; married, 1972. BSChemE, Tufts U., 1969; JD, Emory U., 1975. Bar: Pa. 1975, Ga. 1975, U.S. Patent Office 1976, U.S. Dist. Ct. (we. dist.) Pa. 1975, U.S. Dist. Ct. (no. dist.) Ga. 1975, U.S. Ct. Appeals (fed. and 3d cirs.) 1975, U.S. Supreme Ct. 1980. Chem. engr. Shell Oil Co., New Orleans, 1969-71; san. engr. USPHS, Morgantown, W.Va., 1971-73; patent atty. Mobay Chem. Corp., Pitts., 1975-79; assoc. Reed Smith Shaw & McClay, Pitts., 1979-86, ptnr., 1986—. Contbr. articles to profl. jours. Mem. ABA, Allegheny County Bar Assn., Pa. Bar Assn., Ga. Bar Assn., Am. Intellectual Property Law Assn. Home: 4940 Ellsworth Ave Pittsburgh PA 15213-2807 Office: Reed Smith Shaw & McClay 435 6th Ave Ste 2 Pittsburgh PA 15219-1886

COLEN, HELEN SASS, plastic surgeon; b. Bytom, Poland, Jan. 9, 1947; came to U.S., 1963; d. Karl Julius and Sabina (Orgel) Sass; m. Stephen Robert Colen, Mar. 25, 1972; children—Kari, Michael. B.A., NYU, 1968, M.D., 1972. Diplomate Am. Bd. Surgery, Am. Bd. Plastic Surgery. Intern, Jefferson U. Hosp., 1972-74; gen. surgeon U. Colo., Denver, 1974-79; plastic surgeon U. Columbia St. Lukes, N.Y.C., 1979-81; microsurgeon Bellevue Hosp., N.Y.C., 1981-82; practice medicine specializing in plastic surgery, N.Y.C., 1982—. Mem. Phi Beta Kappa. Office: 127 Neds Mountain Rd Ridgefield CT 06877-1313

COLER, MYRON A(BRAHAM), chemical engineer, educator; b. N.Y.C., Mar. 30, 1913; s. Marcus and Bertha (Bebarfald) C.; m. Viola Ethel Buchbinder, Nov. 15, 1942 (dec. Jan. 1993); children: Mark D., Sandra Coler Carson; m. Lena Amark, Feb. 16, 1996 (div. Mar. 1998). AB, Columbia U., 1933, BS, 1934, ChE, 1935, PhD, 1937; postgrad., NYU, Bklyn. Poly. Inst. With NYU, N.Y.C., 1941-75, prof., dir. surface tech. program dir. creative sci. program; supr., rsch. scientist Manhattan Project, 1943-45; founder, pres., dir. chmn. bd. Markite Co., Markite Corp., Markite Engring. Co., 1948-67, Coler Engring. Co., 1967—, The Vulcan Press Divsn., Valmath, 1988—; sponsor-in-residence Franklin Inst. Rsch. Labs., 1975-81; cons. numerous cos. and govt. agys. Author: Aircraft Engine Finishes, 1941; editor, contbg. author: Essays on Creativity in the Sciences, 1963, Essays on Invention and Education, 1977; numerous articles to profl. jours.; patentee in field. Bd. dirs. Woodward Envicon, Marcus and Bertha Coler Found.; mem. adv. com. dept. phys. and engring. metallurgy Polytechnic Inst. N.Y.; mem. pres.'s com. for Sch. Continuing Edn., NYU; appointee Nat. Inventors Coun., 1966-74; mem. state tech. svc. com. Dept. Commerce; with divsn. cultural studies UNESCO-Dept. State, 1982. Named hon. prof. Polytechnic Inst. N.Y.; Weston fellow Electrochem. Mem. AAAS, Am. Math. Soc., Materials Rsch. Soc., Am. Nuclear Soc., N.Y. Acad. Sci., Electrochem. Soc., Am. Ceramic Soc., Am. Chem. Soc., Am. Soc. for Metals, Am. Def. Preparedness Assn., Internat. Precious Metals Inst., Sigma Xi, Phi Beta Kappa, Phi Lambda Upsilon, Tau Beta Pi, Epsilon Chi, Kona Kai Club. Address: Empress Hotel 7766 Fay Ave La Jolla CA 92037-4309

COLES, ANNA LOUISE BAILEY, retired university official, nurse; b. Kansas City, Kans., Jan. 16, 1925; d. Gordon Alonzo and Lillie Mai (Buchanan) Bailey; children: Margot, Michelle, Gina. Diploma, Freedmen's Hosp. Sch. Nursing, 1948; B.S. in Nursing, Avila Coll., Kansas City, Mo., 1958; M.S. in Nursing, Cath. U. Am., 1960, Ph.D. in Higher Edn., 1967. Instr. VA Hosp., Topeka, 1950-52; supr. VA Hosp., Kansas City, Mo., 1952-58; asst. dir. in-service edn. Freedmen's Hosp., Washington, 1960-61; adminstrv. asst. to dir. nursing Freedmen's Hosp., 1961-66, assoc. dir. nursing services, 1966-67, dir. nursing, 1967-69; dean Howard U. Coll. Nursing, Washington, 1968-86, dean emeritus, 1986—; cons. pvt. practice, Kansas City, Kans.; dir. minority devel. U. Kans., 1991-95; cons. Gen. Research Support Program, NIH, 1972-76, VA Central Office continuing edn. com., 1976—; pres. Nurses Examining Bd., 1967-68; mem. Inst. Medicine, Nat. Acad. Scis., 1974—; Mem. D.C. Health Planning Adv. Com., 1968-71, Tri-State Regional Planning Com. for Nursing Edn., 1969, Health Adv. Council, Nat. Urban Coalition, 1971-73. Contbr. articles to profl. jours. Bd. dirs. Iona Whipper Home for Unwed Mothers, 1970-72; bd. dirs. Nursing Edn. Opportunities, 1970-72; trustee Community Group Health Found., 1976-77, cons., 1977—; bd. regents State Univ. System Fla., 1977; adv. bd. Am. Assn. Med. Vols., 1970-72. Recipient sustained superior performance award HEW, 1962, Meritorious Pub. Svc. award Govt. of D.C., 1968, medal of honor Avila Coll., 1969, Disting. Alumni award Howard U. Nat. Assn. for Equal Opportunity in Higher Edn., 1990, cmty. svc. award Black Profl. Nurses Kansas City, 1991, lifetime achievement award Assn. Black Nursing Faculty in Higher Edn., 1993, svc. award Midwest Regional Conf. on Black Families and Children, 1994. Mem. ANA, Nat. League Nursing, Freedmen's Hosp. Nursing Alumni Assn., Am. Congress Rehab. Medicine, Am. Assn. Colls. Nursing (sec. 1975-76), Societas Docta (charter, pres. 1996—), Sigma Theta Tau, Alpha Kappa Alpha. Home: 15107 Interlachen Dr Apt 205 Silver Spring MD 20906-5627

COLES, BERTHA SHARON GILES, visual information specialist; b. Paris, Tenn., Aug. 13, 1949; d. Charles Ray and Etter Bell (Lightfoot) Giles. Student, Profl. Edn. Divsn. Dallas, 1979, Dynamic Graphics Ednl. Found., 1980, No. Va. C.C., 1981. Typesetter, illustrator Def. Printing, Washington, 1979-83; editl. asst. Exec. Office of Pres., Washington, 1983; visual info. specialist Naval Media Support Ctr., Washington, 1983—. Design, layout, paste-up specialist for various publs., including USN Medicine, 1981, 83, Bull., 1983, Playbook, 1995; cover design July 1996 issue All Hands Mag.; design, layout Posture Statement Mag., 1997; cover design USN-(Joint Civilian Orientation Conf.)-Dept. Def.; cover design and layout of Dept. Navy Posture Statement, 1998. Bd. dirs. London Woods Cmty. Assn., Capitol Heights, Md., 1995. Democrat. Avocations: painting, gardening, interior decorating, collector. Home: 5634 Onslow Way Capitol Heights MD 20743-3059 Office: Navy Media Support Ctr 2511 Jefferson Davis Hwy Arlington VA 22202-3926

COLES, DONALD EARL, retired aeronautics educator; b. St. Paul, Feb. 8, 1924; s. Courtney J. and Lorna (Addison) C.; m. Ellen Searight, Sept. 11, 1947; children: Christopher Lee, Elizabeth Anne, Kenneth Spencer, Janet Jacqueline. B.Aero. Engring., U. Minn., 1947; M.S., Calif. Inst. Tech., 1948, Ph.D., 1953. Research engr. Jet Propulsion Lab., Pasadena, Calif., 1950-53; research fellow Calif. Inst. Tech., Pasadena, 1953-56; mem. faculty Calif. Inst. Tech., 1953-96, prof. aeros., 1964-96; ret., 1996; cons. to industry, 1954—; mem. Nat. Com. Fluid Mechs. Films, 1960. Producer ednl. film Channel Flow of a Compressible Fluid, 1966. Served with AUS, 1943-46. Fellow AIAA (Lawrence Sperry award 1953, Dryden medal 1985), Am. Phys. Soc. (Otto Laporte award 1996); mem. Nat. Acad. Engring., Sigma Xi. Home: 1033 Alta Pine Dr Altadena CA 91001-1409

COLES, GRAHAM, conductor, composer; b. London, May 7, 1948; arrived in Canada, 1951; s. Walter Harold and Phyllis Irene Gwendoline (Conn) C. MusB, U. Toronto, 1972, MusM, 1974, EdB, 1991. Music dir. Kitchener-Waterloo (Ont.) Chamber Orch., 1985—. Composer numerous instrumental and vocal compositions. Mem. Can. League Composers, Can. Music Ctr. (assoc. composer), Assn. Can. Orchs. Home: 1803 - 81 Church St, Kitchener, ON Canada N2G 4M1 Office: Kitchener Waterloo Chamber Orch, PO Box 34015, Kitchener, ON Canada N2N 3G2

COLES, ROBERT, child psychiatrist, educator, author; b. Boston, Mass., Oct. 12, 1929; s. Philip and Sandra (Young) C.; m. Jane Hallowell; children—Robert, Daniel, Michael. A.B., Harvard U., 1950; M.D., Columbia U., 1954; M.D. (hon.), Temple U., Notre Dame U., Bates Coll., 1972, Wayne State U., 1973, Western Mich. U., Holy Cross Coll., 1974, Hofstra U., 1975, Coll. William and Mary, Bard Coll., U. Lowell, U. Cin., 1976, Stonehill Coll., Lesley Coll., Rutgers U., 1977, Wesleyan U., Columbia Coll., Knox Coll., Cleve. State U., Wooster Coll., 1978, U. N.C., Manhattan Coll., St. Peter's Coll., Coll. New Rochelle, Pratt Inst. and Sch. Design, 1979, Berea Coll., Bklyn. Coll., Emmanuel Coll., 1980, Colby Coll., 1981, Sienna Heights Coll., Salem State Coll., Williams Coll., 1983, Beloit Coll., 1984, Emory U., Fairfield U., Macalaster Coll., Colgate U., 1986, Dartmouth Coll., 1987. Intern U. Chgo. Clinics, 1954-55; resident in psychiatry Mass. Gen. Hosp., Boston, 1955-56, McLean Hosp., Belmont, Mass., 1956-57, Judge Baker Guidance Center-Children's Hosp., 1957-58; mem. staff children's Unit Met. State Hosp., Waltham, Mass., 1957-58; mem. staff alcoholic clinic Mass. Gen. Hosp.; teaching fellow in psychiatry, mem. psychiat. staff and clin. asst. in psychiatry Harvard Med. Sch., 1955-58; research psychiatrist Harvard U. Health Services, 1963—; lectr. gen. edn. Harvard U., 1966—, prof. psychiatry and med. humanities, 1977—; child psychiat. fellow Judge Baker Guidance Center, Children's Hosp., Boston, 1960-61; mem. Nat. Adv. Com. on Farm Labor, 1965—; cons. Appalachian Vols., 1965—, Rockefeller Found., 1969—, Ford Found., 1969—; mem. Inst. of Medicine, Nat. Acad. Scis., 1973-78; vis. prof. public policy Duke U., 1973—; cons. supr. dept. psychiatry Cambridge (Mass.) Hosp., 1976—; cons. Center for Study of So. Culture, U. Miss., 1979—; bd. dirs. Ctr. for Documentary Studies, Duke U.; vis. prof. psychiatry, Dartmouth Coll., 1989. Author: Children of Crisis: A Study of Courage and Fear, 1967, Dead End School, 1968, Still Hungry in America, 1969, The Grass Pipe, 1969, The Image is Yours, 1969; Wages of Neglect, 1969, Uprooted Children: The Early Lives of Migrant Farmers, 1970, Teachers and the Children of Poverty, 1970, Erik H. Erikson: The Growth of His Work, 1970, The Middle Americans, 1970, Migrants, Sharecroppers and Mountaineers, 1972, The South Goes North, 1972, Saving Face, 1972, Farewell to the South, 1972, A Spectacle Unto the World, 1973, Riding Free, 1973, The Darkness and the Light, 1974, The Buses Roll, 1974, Irony in the Mind's Life: Essays on Novels by James Agee, Elizabeth Bowen and George Eliot, 1974, Headsparks, 1975, The Mind's Fate, 1975, Eskimos, Chicanos and Indians, 1978, Privileged Ones, Vol. V of Children in Crisis book series, 1978, (with Jane Hallowell Coles) Women of Crisis Lives of Struggle and Hope, 1978, Walker Percy: An American Search, 1978, Flannery O'Connor's South, 1980, Women of Crisis; Lives of Work and Dreams, 1980, Dorothea Lange: Photographs of a Lifetime, 1982, (with Ross Spears) Agee, 1985, The Political Life of Children, 1986, Dorothy Day: A Radical Devotion, 1987, Simone Weil: A Modern Pilgrimage, 1987, Times of Surrender: Selected Essays, 1988, Harvard Diary, 1988, That Red Wheelbarrow, 1988, The Call of Stories: Teaching and the Moral Imagination, 1989, Rumors of Separate Worlds, 1989, The Spiritual Life of Children, 1990; contbg. editor: The New Republic, 1966—, Am. Poetry Rev, 1972—, Aperture, 1974—, Lit. and Medicine, 1981—, New Oxford Rev, 1981—; mem. editorial bd.: Integrated Edn., 1967—, Child Psychiatry and Human Devel., 1969—, Rev. of Books and Religion, 1976—, Internat. Jour. Family Therapy, 1977—, Grants mag., 1977—, Learning mag., 1978—, Jour. Am. Culture, 1977—, Jour. Edn., 1979—; bd. editors: Parents' Choice, 1978—; editor: Children and Youth Services Rev., 1978—. Bd. dirs. Field Found., 1968—; trustee Robert F. Kennedy Meml., 1968—, Robert F. Kennedy Action Corps, State of Mass., 1968—, Miss. Inst. Early Childhood Edn., 1968—, Twentieth Century Fund, 1971—; bd. dirs. Reading is Fundamental, Smithsonian Inst., 1968—, Am. Freedom from Hunger Found., 1968—, Am. Parents Com., 1971—; mem. corp. Boston Children's Service, 1970; mem. adv. council Inst. for Nonviolent Social Change of Martin Luther King, Jr. Meml. Center, 1971—, Ams. for Children's Relief, 1972—; mem. nat. com. for Edn. of Young Children, 1972—; mem. nat. adv. council Rural Am., 1976—; trustee Austen Riggs Found., Stockbridge, Mass., 1976—; mem. nat. adv. com. Ala. Citizens for Responsive Public Television, 1976—; mem. adv. com. Nat. Indian Edn. Assn., 1976—; visitor's com. mem. Boston Mus. Fine Arts, 1977; bd. dirs. Boys Club Boston, 1977; vis. com. Boston Coll. Law Sch., 1977; adv. Center for So. Folklore, 1978—; mem. children's com. Edna McConnell Clark Found., 1978—; bd. dirs. Lyndhurst Found., 1978—; mem. nat. adv. bd. Foxfire Fund, Inc., 1979—. Recipient Ralph Waldo Emerson prize Phi Beta Kappa, 1967; Anisfield-Wolf award in race relations Saturday Rev., 1968; Hofheimer award Am. Psychiat. Assn., 1968; Sidney Hillman prize, 1971; Weatherford prize Berea Coll. and Council So. Mountains, 1973; Lilliam Smith Award So. Regional Council, 1973; McAlpin medal Nat. Assn. Mental Health, 1972; Pulitzer prize, 1973 (all received for Children of Crisis, Vols. II, III); disting. scholar medal Hofstra U., 1974; William A. Shonfeld award Am. Soc. Adolescent Psychiatry, 1977; MacArthur Found. award, 1981; Josepha Hale award, 1986; fellow Davenport Coll., Yale U., 1976—. Fellow Am. Acad. Arts and Scis., Inst. Soc., Ethics and the Life Scis.; mem. Am. Psychiat. Assn., Am. Orthopsychiat. Assn. (past dir.), Acad. Psychoanalysis, Nat. Orgn. Migrant Children. Office: Harvard U Univ Health Svcs 75 Mount Auburn St Cambridge MA 02138-4960

COLES, ROBERT NELSON, SR., religious organization administrator; b. Aug. 1, 1929; married; 6 children. Grad., Salvation Army Officers Coll., 1956; postgrad., DePaul U., 1968. Field officer Salvation Army, 1960-68; with Vols. Am., 1946-55, 60-80; editor-in-chief Rescue Herald Orgn. Am. Rescue Workers, Phila., 1981-92; ordination com. chmn., dir. spl. svcs. Orgn. Am. Rescue Workers, 1988-96; nat. comm. sec. Am. Rescue Workers, 1980—, also nat. bd. mgrs., 1956—; Ordained; chmn. ordination com., aid-de-camp to gen. Am. Rescue Workers, 1985-96. Editor Rescue Herald. Active Comty. Svc. Coun.; organizer numerous youth baseball and basketball teams, and semi-profl. football team Vols. Am., Elmira, N.Y.; established 3 group homes for children from broken homes, Hagerstown, Md., 1969-81; dir. food program Am. Rescue Workers, Phila., 1981-92. Named to Elmira Sports Hall of Fame, 1990. Mem. Am. Correctional Chaplains Assn., Am. Correction Assn., Md. State Sheriff's Assn., Washington County Ministerial (treas. 1993-94), Scottish Rite Bodies, Masons (32 degree), Hagerstown Exch. Club. Office: Am Rescue Workers Nat Field Office 1209 Hamilton Blvd Hagerstown MD 21742-3340

COLES, ROBERT TRAYNHAM, architect; b. Buffalo, Aug. 24, 1929; s. George Edward and Helena Vesta (Traynham) C.; m. Sylvia Rose Meyn, Mar. 28, 1953; children: Marion Brigette, Darcy Eliot. Student, Hampton Inst., 1947-49; B.A., U. Minn., 1951, B. Arch., 1953; M.Arch., M.I.T., 1955; Litt.D. (hon.), Medaille Coll., 1977. Designer, Perry, Shaw, Hepburn and Dean (Architects), Boston, 1956-57, Shepley, Bulfinch, Richardson and Abbott (Architects), Boston, 1957-58, Carl Koch and Asso., Cambridge, Mass., 1958-59; architect, custom design mgr. Techbuilt, Inc. (housing prefabricators), Cambridge, 1959-60; coordinating architect Deleuw, Cather and Brill, Engrs., Buffalo, 1960-63; prin. Robert Traynham Coles, Architect, P.C., Buffalo, 1963—; Langston Hughes Disting. prof. architecture and urban design U. Kans., 1989; v.p. Buffalo Archtl. Guidebook Corp., 1979-82; cons. housing rsch. Union Carbide Corp., 1963; vis. prof. SUNY, Buffalo, summer 1967, U. Kans., 1969; v.p. Eastside Cmty. Orgn. Inc., 1965-68, pres., 1968-77; chmn. Com. for an Urban U., 1966-67, Goals for Met. Buffalo, 1967-68; pres. Cmty. Planning Assistance Ctr. Western N.Y., Inc., 1972-74, Archtl. Mus. and Resource Ctr., 1980-84; mem. N.Y. State Bd. for Architecture, 1984-94, vice chmn., 1990, chmn., 1991; assoc. prof. architecture Carnegie Mellon U., Pitts., 1990-95. Treas., v.p., editor newsletter Nat. Orgn. Minority Architects, 1972-80; contbr. to: newsletter The Urban Ecosystem: A Holistic Approach, 1974. Mem. coun. Burchfield Art Ctr., Buffalo, 1989-92, nat. adv. com. Arts in Am., 1989, Erie County Horizons Waterfront Commn., 1988-91; bd. dirs. Build a New City, Inc., 1973-75; trustee Preservation League N.Y. State, sec., 1978; trustee Western N.Y. PBS, 1981-87, hon. trustee, 1987—. Recipient Centennial award Medaille Coll., 1975, Alumni Achievement award U. Minn. Coll. Architecture and Landscape Architecture, 1997; Edward H. Moeller scholar, 1949-53, Rotch Travelling Scholar Boston Soc. Architects, 1955; named Citizen of Distinction Mayor of Buffalo, N.Y., 1997. Fellow AIA (mem. nat. housing com. 1969-71, nat. urban design and planning com. 1971-73, chmn. social responsibility com. Buffalo-Western N.Y. chpt. 1970-71, dir. 1978-81, nat. dep. v.p. minority affairs 1974-75, Whitney E. Young award 1981, sec. Coll. of Fellows 1991-93, vice-chancellor 1993-94, chancellor 1995); mem. Nat. Orgn. Minority Architects (treas. 1976-78, dir. 1978, v.p. 1978), Alpha Kappa Mu. Home: 321 Humboldt Pky Buffalo NY 14208-1023 Office: 730 Ellicott St Buffalo NY 14203-1102 *Because they have the ability to see things as they can be, today's architects have a special task which goes beyond simply designing the physical environment. They must be activists involved in the social and political life of the community. They must address their efforts to change in these areas as well, so that people can make the needed adjustments to an increasingly challenging and rich urban world. They must, in their works, build the demonstrative alternative to the way we live today. They must be initiators as well as implementors—leaders more than followers. They must truly be revolutionaries who see their architecture as a broad movement to enchance the quality of life of urban people.*

COLES, WILLIAM HENRY, ophthalmologist, educator; b. Rochester, N.Y.. BA, Ohio Wesleyan U., 1958; MD, Emory U., 1962; MS, La. State U., 1970. Diplomate Am. Bd. Ophthalmology. Intern Grady Hosp., Atlanta, 1962-63; resident Charity-La. State U., New Orleans, 1966-70; prof. ophthalmology Emory U., Atlanta, 1980-86, dir. postgrad. edn., 1981-86; prof. ophthalmology SUNY, Buffalo, 1986—, chmn. dept., 1986—; clin. assoc. prof. Med. Univ. S.C., Charleston, 1980-86; chief of svc. Grady Meml. Hosp., Atlanta, 1981-84; chief ophthalmology svc. VA Hosp., Atlanta, 1984-86; chmn. adv. coun. Opthalmic Surgery, 1998. Author: Ophthalmology: A Diagnostic Text, 1989; sect. editor: Medicine for the Practicing Physician, 1984 (Med. Textbook of Yr. award). Dir. Inst. Health Assessment, 1997—. Nat. Eue Inst. grantee, 1975-78. Mem. AMA, ACS (chair adv. coun. 1997—, regent 1998), AAUP, Am. Acad. Ophthalmology (Disting. Svc. award 1989, sr. honor award 1998), Med. Soc. State of N.Y., Assn. Rsch. and Vision in Ophthalmology, Assn. Univ. Profs. in Ophthalmology (trustee, pres. 1996-97). Home: RR 96 Box 503 E Booth Bay ME 04544 Office: U Buffalo Sch Medicine Cary 211 Buffalo NY 14214

COLESCOTT, WARRINGTON WICKHAM, artist, printmaker, educator; b. Oakland, Calif., Mar. 7, 1921; s. Warrington W. and Lydia (Hutton) C.; m. Frances Myers, Mar. 15, 1971; children by previous marriage: Louis Moore, Julian Hutton, Lydia Alice. A.B., U. Calif. at Berkeley, 1942, M.A., 1947; postgrad., Acad. de la Grand Chaumiere, Paris, France, 1950, 53, Slade Sch. Art, U. London (Eng.), 1957. Mem. faculty U. Wis., Madison, 1949-86; prof. art U. Wis., 1957-86, Leo Steppat chair, prof., 1979-85, emeritus prof., 1986—; printmaker emeritus So. Graphics Coun., 1991; academician Nat. Acad. Design. One-man shows include Perimeter Gallery, Chgo., 1985, 87, 88, 91, 93, 95, 99, Milw. Mus. Art, 1996, Rockford (Ill.) Art Mus., Bradley U., Peoria, Ill.; print retrospective Elvehjem Mus., Madison, Wis., 1989, Nelson-Atkins Mus., Kansas City, 1990, U. Oreg. Art Mus., Eugene, 1992, SUNY, Albany, N.Y., 1995; represented in permanent collections Mus. Modern Art, Victoria and Albert Mus., London, Bibliotechque Nat., Paris, Met. Mus., Chgo. Art Inst., Bklyn. Mus., Phila. Mus. Art, Milw. ARt Mus., Elvehjem Art Mus.; co-author (with Arthur Hove) Progressive Printmakers, 1999. Recipient Print award NAD, 1991, 92, 95, 97, NSAL Award of Excellence, 1993, 99; named Koopman disting. chair in visual arts Hartford Sch. Art, 1995, award Internat. Triennial of Print, Cracow, Poland, 1997; Fulbright fellow, 1957, Guggenheim fellow, 1965, Nat. Endowment Arts Printmaking fellow, 1975, Artist fellow, 1979, 83-84, 93-94. Fellow Wis. Acad. Sci. Arts and Letters. Office: Rt 1 Hollandale WI 53544

COLESON, SARRAH LYNN, women's health nurse, critical care nurse; b. Quonset Point, R.I., June 11, 1954; d. William Peter and Glenda Sue (Young) C. BA, U. Albuquerque, 1978, ADN, 1986. Staff nurse labor and delivery Presbyn. Hosp., Albuquerque, 1980-88; staff nurse ICU, house coord. St. Joseph's Heights Hosp., Albuquerque, 1988-96; house coord. St. Joseph's Health Care Corp., Albuquerque, 1996—.

COLESSIDES, NICK JOHN, lawyer; b. Kavala, Greece, Jan. 14, 1938; came to U.S., 1958; s. John T. and Maroula (Karakas) C.; m. Sophia Simons Symeonidis, Oct. 5, 1970. BS in Polit. Sci., U. Utah, 1963, MS Polit. Sci., 1967, JD, 1970. Bar: Utah 1970, U.S. Dist. Ct. Utah 1970, U.S. Ct. Appeals (10th cir.) 1970, U.S. Dist. Ct. (so. dist.) Ohio 1975, U.S. Ct. Appeals (9th cir.) 1976. Chief deputy county atty. Salt Lake County (Utah) Atty.'s Office, 1970-74; city atty. West Jordan (Utah) City Atty.'s Office, 1971-78, Park City (Utah) Atty.'s Office, 1976-80; atty. pvt. practice, Salt Lake City, 1970—; bd. dirs. Merrill Lynch Bank, U.S.A., Salt Lake City City. Bd. trustees Greek Orthodox Ch., SaltLake City, 1976, 77, 87, 88, 98, 99. Mem. Assn. Trial Lawyers Am., Utah Trial Lawyers Assn., U. Utah Coll. of Law Alumni Assn. (trustee 1995-98), Utah State Bar Assn., Salt Lake County Bar Assn., Am. Inn of Ct. VII (master of the bench, pres. 1997, 98). Greek Orthodox. Avocations: gardening, cooking, reading. Home: 32 Haxton Pl Salt Lake City UT 84102-1410 Office: 466 S 400 E Ste 100 Salt Lake City UT 84111-3325

COLETTA, RALPH JOHN, lawyer; b. Chillicothe, Ill., Dec. 13, 1921; s. Joseph and Assunta Maria (Aromatario) C.; m. Ethel Mary Meyers, Nov. 19, 1949; children: Jean, Marianne, Suzanne, Joseph, Robert, Michele, Renee. BS, Bradley U., 1943; JD, U. Chgo., 1949. Bar: Ill. 1949. Practice law Peoria, Ill., 1949—; pres. White Star Corp., Mark Tidd, Inc.; asst. state's atty. Peoria County. Chmn. United Fund. Served to 1st lt. AUS, 1943-46. Mem. ABA, Peoria County Bar Assn., Chgo. Bar Assn., Ill. State Bar Assn., Creve Coeur Club, Mt. Hawley Country Club, K.C., Union League Club. Republican. Roman Catholic. Home: 301 W Crestwood Dr Peoria IL 61614-7328 Office: 1st Financial Plaza Ste 1714 Peoria IL 61602

COLE WARDELL, KIRSTIN, television news anchor; b. Meriden, Conn., Sept. 11, 1968; d. Chester Albert and Judith Louise Cole; m. John Bennett, Oct. 13, 1990 (div. Apr. 1994); m. Charles B. Wardell, Oct. 5, 1996. BA, Loyola U., Chgo., 1995. Devel. assoc. Conn. Pub. TV, Hartford, 1986-90; prodn. asst. A Current Affair, N.Y.C., 1995; TV news anchor WLNY-TV, Melville, N.Y., 1995-97, WSYX-TV/WTTE-TV, Columbus, Ohio, 1997—. Hon. host Columbus Mus. Art, 1998. Recipient Best in Show award L.I. Press Club, 1996. Mem. Soc. Profl. Journalists. Avocations: skiing, boxing, riding, tennis. Office: WSYX-TV/WTTE-TV 1261 Dublin Rd Columbus OH 43000

COLEY, ELLIOT EDWARD, delivery service executive; b. Dallas, Mar. 1, 1961; s. Daniel Fonviele and Shirley Anne Coley; m. Suzanne Marie Bonoy, Mar. 10, 1985; children: Casey, AJ, Hailey. BA, Norwich U., 1983; MS, Troy State U., 1985. Package car driver UPS, Saddlebrook, N.J., 1987-88; investigator UPS, Secaucus, N.J., 1988-92; loss prevention UPS, Paramus, N.J., 1992-95; project mgr. UPS, Mahwah, N.J., 1995-97, security rep., 1997-98, total quality rep., 1998—. 1st lt. mil. intelligence U.S. Army, 1984-87; major USAR, 1987—. Mem. Project Mgmt. Inst., Am. Soc. Indsl. Security, Toastmasters (pres. 1994-95). E-mail: secoley@bellatlantic.net. Home: 119 Oweno Rd Mahwah NJ 02430

COLEY, LINDA MARIE, secondary school educator; b. Albany, Ga., Apr. 19, 1945; d. Leonard Earl and Hazel (Brady) C. BS in Math., Piedmont Coll., 1966; MS in Math., U. Ga., 1972, postgrad. Cert. tchr., Ga. Tchr. Toccoa (Ga.) Pub. Schs., 1966-67, Hall County Sch. Dist., Gainesville, Ga., 1967-68, Clarke County Sch. Dist., Athens, Ga., 1968—. Sec., 1st v.p. Clarke County Dem. Com., Athens, 1981—, Gov.'s Club. Mem. NEA, Ga. Edn. Assn., Clarke County Assn. Educators (treas., sec.), Alpha Delta Kappa (treas., sec., pres., dist. treas.), Phi Delta Kappa. Democrat. Baptist. Home: 135 Ravenwood Pl Athens GA 30605-3344

COLFACK, ANDREA HECKELMAN, elementary education educator; b. Yreka, Calif., July 17, 1945; d. Robert A. Davis and June (Reynolds) Butler; m. David Lee Heckelman, Sept. 5, 1965 (div. Nov. 1982); children: Barbara, Julie; m. Neal Cleve, Jan. 1, 1984; 1 stepchild, Karl. AB, Calif. State U., L.A., 1966; MA, Calif. State U., Fresno, 1969. Life std. elem. credential, Calif. cert. competence: Spanish, Calif.; ordained to ministry Faith Christian Fellowship Internat., 1987; Calif. preliminary administrv. credential, 1995. Tchr. Tulare (Calif.) City Schs., 1966-67, Palo Verde Union Sch. Dist., 1967-70, Cutler-Orosi (Calif.) Union Sch. Dist., 1979-82, Hornbrook (Calif.) Union Sch. Dist., 1982-84; sales mgr. Tupperware, Fresno, Calif., 1973-79; bilingual tchr. West Contra Costa (Calif.) Unified Sch. Dist., 1984-95; prin. Bayview Elem. Sch. West Contra Costa (Calif.) Unified Sch. Dist., San Pablo, Calif., 1995—; site mentor Bayview Elem. Sch., Richmond, 1990-92; ELD mentor, Richmond, 1992-94, mentor selection com., 1994-95; summer sch. prin. Grant Elem. Sch., Richmond, 1995. Co-author: Project Mind Expansion, 1974. Recipient Calif. Dist. Sch. award, 1998; East Bay C.U.E. Tech. grantee, 1995. Mem. Calif. Assn. Bilingual Educators (sec. Richmond 1990-91), AAUW (pres. Tulare br. 1967-68), Calif. Assn. Sch. Adminstrs., Richmond Assn. Sch. Adminstrs. Democrat. Pentecostal. Avocations: leading music and home bible studies. Home: 5461 Hackney Ln Richmond CA 94803-3830 Office: Bayview Elem Sch 3001 16th St San Pablo CA 94806-2352

COLFAX, RICHARD SCHUYLER, business management and human resources educator; b. N.Y.C., Nov. 2, 1949; arrived in Guam and Federated States of Micronesia, 1994; s. Richard Schoonmaker and Joyce Alta (Bodain) C.; m. Toyoko Suzuki, Dec. 14, 1974; children: Richard Shigemichi, Michael Tyro, Christine Aya. BS in Econs. and Comp. Lit., Sophia U., Tokyo, 1976; MA in Human Resource Leadership, Azusa (Calif.) Pacific U., 1986; MA in Human Devel., Fielding Inst., 1992, PhD in Human & Org. Systems, 1993. Cert. tchr., N.J.; cert. Myers-Briggs Type Indicator trainer, systematic tng. effective parenting trainer, profl. assn. diving instrs. divemaster. Trainer, lang. cons. F.J. Kurdyla & Assocs., K.K., Tokyo, 1974-80; analyst, cons. Sanyo Securities, K.K., Tokyo, 1979-80; head English dept., coord. secondary sch. St. Maur Internat. Sch., Yokohama, Japan, 1980-87; subs. tchr. Hawaii Dept. Edn., Pahoa, 1987-88; adult devel. trainer Hachioji (Japan) Women's Ctr., 1989—; trainer, lectr. Hachioji Nursing Coll., 1989—; program devel. cons., lectr. Nippon Engring. Coll. Hachioji, Hachioji, 1988—; lectr. Tokyo Engring. U., 1994—; cons. human and orgnl. devel. Human Potentials Unltd., Hachioji, 1987—; asst. prof. mgmt. U. Guam, 1994-98, assoc. prof. mgmt. and human resource mgmt., 1998—, chmn. mgmt. and mktg. dept., 1998-99; cons. project devel. Musketeer Info. Rsch., K.K., Yokohama, 1989—; project cons. printing divsn. Japan Treas. Dept., Tokyo, 1990, Geographical Survey Inst. Japan, Tsukuba, Chiba, 1992—; cons. to bd. dirs. Cmty. Environ. Coun. Santa Barbara, 1990; advisor to bd. dirs. Sacred Heart Cath. Ch., Pahoa, 1987-88; staff cons. Liberty Town Devel. Project, Hachioji, 1994—; devel. cons., outreach program mgmt. retreat session facilitator Instnl. Retreat, 1994; club advisor coll. bus. and pub. adminstrn. U. Guam, 1994-96, pub. info. officer, 1995-96, mem. acad. master plan com., 1995-96, mem. univ. cmty. svcs. com., 1995-96, chair 1996-97, chmn. program-conf.-svcs. subcom., 1995, mem. com. human rsch. subjects, 1995—, acting chair 1996-97, univ. acad. affairs com., 1997-99, mem. student affairs adv. coordinating com., 1999—, promotion and tenure com., 1999—; mem. human resources com. Guam Gov.'s Task Force for Vision 2000, 1996—. Author: Stress and the Stress Process Among Japanese Office Workers, 1993; co-author: (with Thomas K. Pinhey) Overweight and Happiness: A Test of the Reflected Self-Appraisal Hypothesis, 1995, Conducting a Successful Business, 1997; co-editor Pacific Rim Jour. Small Bus., 1995, 96, 97, Pacific Rim Jour. Econ. Issues, Bus. Success Monthly Bus. Newspaper, 1999—; assoc. editor Pacific Milestones Monthly Bus. Newspaper, 1997, 99; co-coord. Pacific Rim Jour. Econ. Conf., 1995, 96. Supporting family The Hunger Project, Tokyo, 1987-92; participant 25th Friend's Westtown (Pa.) Seminar on Edn., 1988; supporting mem. WorldWatch Orgn., Boulder, Colo., 1991—; mem. Global Svcs. Corps, San Francisco, 1993—. With USN, 1970-72. Fellow Am. Inst. Stress; mem. Orgnl. Devel. Network, Am. Assn. Higher Edn., Nat. Soc. Internships and Exptl. Edn., Coun. Adult & Exptl. Learning, Forum Corp. Commn. (newsletter editor 1989-90), Visions of New Realities Network (publs. com. 1986-87), Svc. Corps of Ret. Execs. Assn. (counsellor Guam chpt. 1994-97, coord. and facilitator small bus. devel. workshops 1995-97), Guam Inst. Vol. Execs (dir. 1997—), Soc. for Human Resources Mgmt. (Guam conf. presenter 1995, 96, opening spkr. 1996, v.p. student chpts. 1996-98, bd. dirs., faculty advisor, liaison 1997—, pres.-elect 1999-2000), Am. Psychol. Soc., Fielding Alumni Assn., Soc. for Human Resource Mgmt. (v.p. student chpt. 1997—), Chi Omicron Gamma (U. Guam chpt. 1995—), Phi Delta Kappa (membership com. 1986-87, historian 1990-91). Avocations: watercolor painting, writing poetry, scuba diving, whale-watching, Japanese festival drumming. Address: UOG Sta PO Box 5267 Mangilao GU 96923-5267

COLFIN, BRUCE ELLIOTT, lawyer, video producer; b. Bklyn., June 9, 1951; s. Abraham and Sylvia (Laykin) C.; m. Virginia Mary Faszczewski, Sept. 27, 1981. BA, CUNY, 1977; JD, N.Y. Law Sch., 1980. Bar: N.Y. 1982, U.S. Dist. Ct. (so., ea. dists.) N.Y., 1987, U.S. Ct. Internat. Trade, 1990. Audio engr. Snowball Sound Systems, N. Bergen, N.J., 1974-77; producer, dir. cable TV program What's On, N.Y.C., 1976-84; stage mgr. Peter Tosh U.S. tour Rolling Stones Records, 1978; v.p., producer Upswing Artists Mgmt., N.Y.C., 1979-86; pres., producer, dir. LegalVision, Inc., N.Y.C., 1982-87; ptnr. Jacobson & Colfin, N.Y.C. and Washington, 1985-90; mem. Jacobson & Colfin, P.C., N.Y.C. and Washington, 1990—; pres. Fifth Ave. Media, Ltd., N.Y.C., 1996—; spkr. Discovery Ctr., N.Y., 1st Ann. Musicians Seminar, L.I., N.Y. Law Sch. Media Law Soc., 1986; vis. lectr. SUNY, Oneonta, 1988—; panelist New Eng. Music Orgn. Conf., 1998, Emerging Artists and Talent in Music, 1999. Assoc. producer music video Blues Alive, 1982; exec. producer, dir. video series Entertainment Law Video Primer, 1984; monthly columnist Ind. Music Producers Soc. Jour., NARAS N.Y. chpt. newsletter; contbr. articles to profl. jours.; columnist: Replication News, 1998. Mem. ABA (com. on entertainment sports law, subcom. chmn. patent, trademark and copyright com. 1989, subcom. chmn. internat. law and practice, internat. intellectual property rights com., spl. subcom. on multimedia 1994—, editl. advisor pubs. com. internat. law sect. 1990-92, exec. com. entertainment law cir. 1989-91), NATAS (N.Y. chpt.), N.Y. State Bar Assn. (entertainment, arts and sports law sect., com. on talent agys. and talent mgmt., com. on rights of publicity 1994—), Nassau County Bar Assn., Speaker's Bureau (entertainment and sports law comm.), Copyright Soc. U.S.A. (editl. bd. 1986-88), Nat. Acad. of Recording Arts and Scis. (N.Y. chpt.). Jewish. Avocations: traveling, writing, stamp collecting, hockey. E-mail: BRUCE@Thefirm.com. Office: Jacobson & Colfin PC 156 5th Ave Ste 434 New York NY 10010-7002

COLFLESH, GERTRUDE PATTERSON (TRUDY COLFLESH), psychotherapist, author; b. Steubenville, Ohio, June 6, 1939; d. Robert Meade and Gertrude (Lippencott) Patterson; m. George William Colflesh, Aug. 5, 1961; children: Michael, Christopher, Karen (dec.). BA in Religious Studies, Coll. Wooster, 1961; postgrad., Oberlin Sch. Theology, 1962; MA in Counseling and Human Devel., Montclair State U., 1990. Nat. cert. counselor; lic. profl. counselor. Dir. Christian Edn. Calvary Presbyn. Ch., Canton, Ohio, 1961-63; counselor Christian Counseling Ctr., Clifton, N.J., 1990—; founder women's support groups St. Andrew's Presbyn. Ch., Berea, Ohio, 1966-72, elder, 1972; founding v.p. Women's Aglow Fellowship Internat., Miami, Fla., 1973-75, area v.p. Outreach and Retreats, No. N.J., 1980-86. Author: Too Precious to Die, 1984. Mem. Am. Assn. Christian Counselors, N.J. Counseling Assn., Nat. Assn. for Christian Recovery, Phi Kappa Phi. Home: 33 Northwood Dr West Milford NJ 07480-3724 Office: Christian Counseling Ctr 352 Clifton Ave Clifton NJ 07011-2619 *While the accomplishments of my years of service and achievements are presented in this book with pride and delight, my greatest joy is in the accomplishment of Jesus Christ who saved and redeemed me and entered my name in His Book of Life.*

COLFORD, FRANCIS XAVIER, gas industry executive; b. Jersey City, Mar. 18, 1952; s. Joseph Edward and Catherine (Lipsett) C.; m. Trina Claire Peduto, Apr. 12, 1975; children: Courtney, Ryan, Lindsay, Rory. BS in Acctg., St. Peter's Coll., Jersey City, N.J., 1973. CPA, N.J. Sr. acct. Price Waterhouse, Morristown, N.J., 1973-78; acctg. mgr. N.J. Natural Gas, Wall, 1978-80, controller, 1980-82, v.p., treas., 1983-85, sr. v.p., chief fin. officer, treas., 1985-94, sr. v.p. acctg. and fin. control, 1994-96; v.p., contr., 1996—. Mem. Am. Inst. CPA's, N.J. Soc. CPA's, Fin. Execs. Inst., Am. Gas Assn. Home: 13 Barbizon Ct West Long Branch NJ 07764-1273 Office: NJ Natural Gas Co 1415 Wyckoff Rd PO Box 1464 Wall NJ 07719-1464

COLGAN, ANN K., educator; b. Jan. 26, 1950. MS, Iowa State U., 1977; JD, Washburn U., 1984. Pres. Topeka Tech. Coll., 7 yrs.; spl. asst. to sec. of state State of Kans., Topeka, 3 yrs.

COLGAN, GEORGE PHILLIPS, real estate developer, real estate analyst; b. Tokyo, June 3, 1947; s. Jack Phillips and Kimiko (Furukawa) C.; m. Ann Elizabeth Dickerson, Sept. 1, 1968; 1 child, Matthew Seth. Student, Ga. Tech. U., 1965-66; BS in Biology, Ga. State U., 1970. Credit mgr. C&S Nat. Bank, Atlanta, 1969-74; statewide credit mgr. GE Credit Corp., Atlanta, 1974-76; regional v.p. A.L. Williams & Assocs., Atlanta and Houston, 1977-81; dir. sales and mktg. Hooker Barnes Homes, Inc., Atlanta, 1982-84, Brayson/Am. Homes, Atlanta, 1984-87; real estate markets analyst, pres. Whitehall Homes, Inc., Atlanta, 1987-95, residential developer, cons., 1995—. Contbr. articles to profl. jours. Asst. scoutmaster, unit commr. Troop 525 Boy Scouts Am., Norcross, Ga., 1989-94; del. So. Bapt. Conv., Atlanta, 1985; precinct del. Rep. Nat. Party, 1986, 88; pres. Norcross H.S. Wrestling Boosters Club, 1994-96. Mem. Nat. Assn. Home Builders (Cert. of Appreciation 1986). Republican. Presbyterian. Avocations: angling, paleontology, motorcycling. Home: 1590 Keylake Dr Suwanee GA 30024-4263 Office: 3245 Peachtree Pkwy Ste D214 Suwanee GA 30024-1036

COLGAN, SUMNER, manufacturing engineer, chemical engineer; b. Framingham, Mass., Sept. 11, 1934; s. Joseph and Leora C.; student Boston Coll., 1957-61, Boston U., 1961, Banff Climbing Sch.; married; 1 son, Scott Paul. Chem. engr. Beam Tube Corp., Western, Mass., 1962-63; reliability engr. Gen. Motors Corp., Framingham, 1963-86, mfg. engr., 1986-91; chemist Envirotech Operating Systems, North Haven, Conn., 1991-92; lab. mgr. New England Fertilizer, 1992—. Served in USAF, 1953-57. Mem. Hunting Ravine Avalanche Patrol, 1970-78. Mem. Matterhorn Climbers Assn. Zermatt, Pvt. Pilot Assn., Mt. Rainier Summit Climbers Assn. Clubs: Appalachian Mountain, Sea Urchins. Home: PO Box 138 Framingham MA 01704-0138 Office: 97 E Howard St Quincy MA 02169-8711

COLGATE, DORIS ELEANOR, retailer, sailing school owner and adminstrator; b. Washington, May 12, 1941; d. Bernard Leonard and Frances Lillian (Goldstein) Horecker; m. Richard G. Buchanan, Sept. 6, 1959 (div. Aug. 1967); m. Stephen Colgate, Dec. 17, 1969. Student, Antioch Coll., 1958-60, NYU, 1960-62. Rsch. supr. Geyer Moyer Ballard, N.Y.C., 1962-64; administrv. asst. Yachting Mag., N.Y.C., 1964-68; v.p. Offshore Sailing Sch. ltd., Inc., N.Y.C., 1968-78; pres. Offshore Sailing Sch. ltd., Inc., Ft. Myers, Fla., 1978—; pres., CEO On and Off Shore, Inc., Ft. Myers, 1984—; v.p. Offshore Travel, Inc., City Island, 1978-88; chmn. bd. dirs. Women's Sailing Found., 1990—. Author: The Bareboat Gourmet, 1983, Sailing: A Woman's Guide, 1999; contbr. articles to profl. jours. Recipient Betty Cook Meml. Lifetime Achievement award, 1994, Sail Industry Leadership award, 1996. Mem. Royal Ocean Racing Club (London chpt.), Women's Sailing Found (pres. 1998—), Nat. Women's Sailing Assn. (chair nat. women's adv. bd. 1990-94, chair, 1991-94, pres. 1994—), Am. Women's Econ. Devel. Corp. (adv. bd. 1980-86), Internat. Women Boating (bd. dirs.). Avocations: piano, sailing, photography, writing, cooking. Home: 1555 San Carlos Bay Dr Sanibel FL 33957-3423 Office: Offshore Inc 16731 Mcgregor Blvd Fort Myers FL 33908-3843

COLGATE, STEPHEN, small business owner; b. N.Y.C., June 25, 1935; s. Gilbert Colgate and Nina (King) Heiner; m. Doris Eleanor Horecker, Dec. 17, 1969. BA, Yale U., 1957. Chief exec. officer, owner Offshore Sailing Sch., Ltd., Ft. Myers, Fla., 1964—, Offshore Travel, Inc., N.Y.C., 1978-88, On and Offshore, Inc., Captiva Island, Fla., 1975—, Cafe Offshore, Inc., City Island, 1981-84. Author: Colgate's Basic Sailing Theory, 1973, Fundamentals of Sailing, Cruising and Racing, 1978, The Yachtsman's Guide to Racing Tactics, 1981, Steve Colgate on Sailing, 1991, Steve Colgate on Cruising, 1991, Steve Colgate on Sailing Rules, 1991. Served to capt. USAF, 1958-60. Mem. U.S. Sailing Assn., Internat. Sailing Fedn. (vice chair tng. and devel. com.), U.S. Olympians (Fla. chpt.), Nat. Marine Mfrs. Assn., Sail Am. Bd. Republican. Episcopalian. Clubs: N.Y. Yacht (N.Y.C.); Royal Ocean Racing (London); Royal Bermuda Yacht, Cruising of Am. Avocations: bicycling, sailing.

COLGATE, STIRLING AUCHINCLOSS, physicist; b. N.Y.C., Nov. 14, 1925; s. Henry A. and Jeannette (Pruyn) C.; m. Rosemary B. Williamson, July 12, 1947; children: Henry A., Sarah, Arthur S. BA, Cornell U., 1948, PhD in Physics, 1952. Physicist Radiation Lab., Univ. Calif., Berkeley, 1951-52, Lawrence Livermore (Calif.) Lab., 1952-64; pres. N.Mex. Inst. Mining and Tech., Socorro, 1964-74; physicist Los Alamos (N.Mex.) Nat. Lab., 1976—. Contbr. over 200 articles to profl. jours. Served with Merchant Marines, 1943-46. Recipient Rossi prize, 1990, Wetherill prize, 1994. Fellow Am. Phys. Soc.; mem. NAS, Am. Astron. Soc. Home: 422 Estante Way Los Alamos NM 87544-3812 Office: MS B288 Los Alamos Nat Lab Los Alamos NM 87545

COLGATE-LINDBERG, CATHARINE PAMELLA, educator; b. Cedar Rapids, Iowa, Dec. 17, 1939; d. Fred Joseph and Catharine Leona (Hunt) Petrick; m. Gary N. Lindberg; children: Shannon Colgate, Stephen Colgate, Stewart Colgate, Stanley Colgate, Travis Lindberg, Heidi Lindberg Roberts. BS, Ariz. State U., 1973, MA, 1977. Cert. tchr., jr. coll. educator, Ariz. Tchr. English Mesa (Ariz.) Community Coll., Mesa Pub. Schs.; writing specialist Associacao Escola Graduada, Sao Paulo, Brazil; vis. prof. edn. U. Sao Paulo. Patentee sch. lecterns. Mem. NEA, AAUP, Nat. Sch. Bds. Assn., Nat. Coun. Tchrs. English, Mesa Edn. Assn., Ariz. Sch. Bd. Assn., U.S. Air Force Acad. Alumni Parents' Orgn. and Assn., U.S. Mil. Acad. Alumni Parents Orgn., Phi Delta Kappa, Phi Lambda Theta.

COLGLAZIER, E. WILLIAM, science academy administrator, physicist. BS in Theoretical Physics, Calif. Inst. Tech., 1966, PhD in Theoretical Physics, 1971. Rschr. theoretical physics various instns.; congl. sci. fellow U.S. Rep. George Brown, 1976-77; rsch. fellow Ctr. Sci. and Internat. Affairs, Kennedy Sch. Govt. Harvard U.; prof. physics U. Tenn., Knoxville, 1983-91, dir. numerous sci. and tech. policy ctrs.; internat. affairs exec. dir. NRC, 1991-94, exec. dir. Office of Internat. Affairs, 1994; acting exec. officer NAS, NRC, 1994, exec. officer, 1994—; bd. dirs. Fermilab High-Energy Physics Accelerator. Author numerous publs. in field. Bd. dirs. Oak Ridge Associated Univs. Recipient Lifetime Contbn. award sect. environ. and nat. resources adminstrn. ASPA, Commendation, State Planning Coun. on Radioactive Waste Mgmt. Office: NAS & NRC 2101 Constitution Ave NW Washington DC 20418-0007*

COLGRASS, MICHAEL CHARLES, composer; b. Chgo., Apr. 22, 1932; s. Michael Clement and Ann (H) C.; m. Ulla Damgaard, Nov. 25, 1966; 1 child, Neal. MusB, U. Ill., 1956; studied with Paul Price, studied with Eugene Weigle, studied with Darius Milhand, studied with Lukas Foss, studied with Wallingford Riegger, studied with Ben Weber. Author: Tuning the Human Instrument, 1993-94; freelance solo percussionist maj. N.Y. mus. orgns., 1956—, Narrator, Boston Symphony, 1969, Phila. Orch, 1970; dir. : Virgil's Dream, Brighton Festival; Soloist, Danish Radio Orch., 1965; dir. opera Nightingale Inc, U. Ill. Contemporary Music Festival, 1975; author, poet own theatre works, 1966—; composer: Divertimento, 1961, Fantasy Variations, 1961, Wind Quintet, 1962, Light Spirit, 1963, Rhapsody, 1963, Rhapsodic Fantasy, 1965, Sea Shadow, 1966, As Quiet As, 1966, Virgil's Dream, 1967, Three Brothers, 1951, Percussion Music, 1953, Chamber Music for Four Drums and String Quintet, 1954, Chamber Music for Percussion Quintet, 1955, Variations for Four Drums and Viola, 1957, The Earth's a Baked Apple, 1968-69, New People for mezzosoprano, viola, piano, 1969, Nightingale, Inc, Auras for Harp and Orch, 1973, Image of Man, 1974, Concertmasters for 3 violins and orch, 1975, Best Wishes U.S.A. for black and white choruses, folk instruments, jazz band and orch, 1976, Theatre of the Universe for soloists, chorus and orch, 1976, Wolf for solo cello, 1976, Letter from Mozart for orch, 1976, Déjà Vu, 1977 (Pulitzer prize 1978), Mystery Flowers of Spring for soprano and piano, 1978, Something's Gonna Happen, children's musical theatre, 1978; Flashbacks, musical play for 5 brass, 1979; Night of the Raccoon, 5 songs for soprano and 4 players, 1979; Delta, for violin, clarinet, percussion and orch, 1979; Tales of Power, a mus. drama for solo piano on the writings of Carlos Castaneda 1980; Metamusic for solo piano, 1981; Memento for 2 pianos and orch., 1982; Demon for amplified piano, tape, radios and orch., 1983; Chaconne for viola and orch., 1984, Winds of Nagual, for wind ensemble, 1985; Strangers: Irreconcilable Variations for clarinet, viola and piano, 1986, (Jules Leger Chamber Music Prize 1988), Déjà Vu for percusssion quartet and wind ensemble, 1987; Folklines: A Counterpoint of Musics for string quartet and wind ensemble, 1988, The Schubert Birds, 1989, Snow Walker for organ and orch., 1990, arctic Dreams for symphonic band, 1991, Wild Riot of the Shaman's Dreams for solo flute, 1991, Arias for clarinet and orchestra, 1992, Te Tuma Te Papa for solo percussionist, 1994, a Flute in the Kingdom of Drums and Bells, 1994, Urban Requiem for four saxophones and wind ensemble, 1995, "Hammer & Bow" for violin and marimba, 1997, 98, Dream State for solo piano, 1998, Baroque Blues for solo piano, 1998, Drummers for solo piano, 1998; works commd. N.Y. Philharm., CBC, U. Ill. Symphonic and Concert Bands, Boston Symphony, Toronto Symphony Orch., Lincoln Center Chamber Mus. Soc., New Eng. Conservatory Wind Ensemble, Fromm Found., Corp. for Pub. Broadcasting, Ford Found., Spokane, Detroit, Springfield, Minn. symphony orchs., Musica Aeterna Orch. N.Y., Young Concert Artists N.Y., Nat. Arts Centsre Orch. of Can., Calgary Internat. Organ Festival, New World Festival Arts, Delos, Manhattan and Muir string quartets, U. Miami, Nexus percussion ensemble: works recorded various cos.: contbr. articles to publs.; columnist Music Mag. With AUS, 1954-56. Scholar Tanglewood, Mass., 1952, 54, Aspen, Colo., 1953; Guggenheim fellow, 1964-65, 68-69; recipient Fromm award, 1966, Chem. Bank award, 1971, Emmy award for Sta. WGBH-TV film Soundings: The Music of Michael Colgrass for best documentary Nat. Acad. TV Arts and Scis., 1982; Rockefeller grantee, 1967-69; Ford Found. grantee, 1972; recipient Pulitzer prize, 1978; Winds of Nagual winner Louis B. Sudler Internat. Wind Band Composition Competition, 1985, De Moulin prize Nat. Band Assn., 1985, Barlow Internat. prize, 1986. Office: 583 Palmerston Ave, Toronto, ON Canada M6G 2P6 *I see the composer as a person not separate from life and community but indigenous to it. How to bridge the gap that has developed between the artist and people is the biggest challenge I know, but I find the more I reach out to people the less indifferent they are to the artistic experience.*

COLGROVE, THOMAS MICHAEL, landscape architect; b. Painesville, Ohio, Dec. 16, 1930; s. Melvin Samuel and Agnus Mary (Oswald) C.; m. Lois Martha Roffman, June 1, 1957; children: Nancy M., Ruth A., Thomas M., Tracy S. BS, Ohio State U., 1954, B.Landscape Arch., 1955. Reg. landscape architect, Kans. Landscape architect Stuart M. Mertz Assocs., Clayton, Mo., 1955-60, Abbey & Dickens, Inc., Rochester, N.Y., 1960-63; v.p. Hare & Hare, Inc., Kansas City, Mo., 1963-74; dir. landscape arch. G. Butler Assocs., Inc., Kansas City, 1974-89; pres. Thomas Colgrove Assoc., Prairie Village, Kans., 1989—; mem. Coun. Landscape Archtl. Registration Bd., 1989-96. Chmn. City Bd. Parks and Recreation, Prairie Village, Kans., 1972-82; chmn. Kans. Bd. Tech. Professions, Topeka, 1988-96. Recipient Trustee award, Nelson Gallery of Art, 1972, Plant Am. award, Am. Assn. Nurserymen, 1966, 62, 61. Mem. Am. Soc. Landscape Architects (trustee 1965-70), Mo. Parks and Recreation Assn., Nat. Parks and Conservation Assn., Mo. Assn. landscape Architects (pres. 1964-67), Kans. Assn. Landscape Architects (pres. 1967-70), Profl. Grounds Assn. Republican. Episcopalian. Avocations: gardening, golf, fishing. Home: 9024 Rosewood Dr Shawnee Mission KS 66207-2229

COLI, GUIDO JOHN, chemical company executive; b. Richmond, Va., Sept. 12, 1921; s. Guido and Rena (Pacini) C.; m. Vonda L. Coli; children: Pamela, Patricia, Deborah, Rebecca Smith. B.S., Va. Poly. Inst., 1941, M.S., 1942, Ph.D., 1949. Registered profl. engr., N.Y., Va. Asst. engr. Va. Health Dept. bur. indsl. hygiene, 1941; assoc. chemist Naval Research Lab., 1942-43; instr. chem. engring. Va. Poly. Inst., 1947-48; chem. engr. Mobil Oil Co., Paulsboro, N.J., 1949-50; with Allied Chem. Corp., N.Y.C., 1950-72, group v.p. corp., 1968-72, dir., 1970-72; pres. Am. Enka Co., Enka, N.C., 1979-82; dir. Akzo Am. Inc., 1979-86, pres., chief exec. officer, 1982-86; chmn., chief exec. officer Armira, Inc., Asheville, N.C., 1986—; pres., chief operating officer St. Joseph's Health Svcs. Corp., Asheville, 1990—. Mem. Gov. Va. Commn. to Establish Urban Univ. in Richmond Area, 1966-67; mem. adv. council Coll. of Engring., Va. Poly. Inst.; bd. dirs. St. Joseph's Hosp., Asheville, N.C. Lt. USN, 1943-46. Fellow Am. Inst. Chemists; mem. Am. Chem. Soc. (chmn. Va. 1957), Am. Inst. Chem. Engrs., Sigma Xi, Phi Lambda Upsilon, Tau Beta Pi, Phi Kappa Phi, Alpha Kappa Psi. Clubs: University (N.Y.C.); Country of Asheville. Home: 314 Town Mountain Rd Asheville NC 28804-3821 Office: St Joseph's Health Svcs Corp 345 Biltmore Ave Asheville NC 28801-4119

COLIJN, GEERT JAN, academic administrator, political scientist; b. Naarden, The Netherlands, Sept. 23, 1946; came to U.S., 1969; s. Izak and Aaltje Cornelia (Rozeboom) C.; m. Sarah Ellen Griffith, Jan. 4, 1986; 1 child, Cornelia Alice. Kandidaat, U. van Amsterdam, 1969; MA, Temple U., 1971, PhD, 1977. From asst. prof. to assoc. prof. polit. sci. Richard Stockton Coll. N.J., Pomona, N.J., 1978-91, prof., 1991—, chmn. social and behavioral scis., 1982-85, dean of gen. studies, 1988—; trustee Internat. House, Phila., 1990—; mem. steering com. Visions of Higher Edn. Conf., Zurich, Switzerland, 1988-94; vis. fellow U. Warwick, 1987-88; mem. conf. com. Ann. Scholars Conf. on Holocaust and the Chs., 1991—. Co-editor: Confronting the Holocaust, 1997, From Prejudice to Destruction, 1995; contbr. articles to profl. jours. Mem. exec. com. Holocaust Resource Ctr., Pomona, 1988—; trustee Community Justice Inst., Atlantic City, N.J., 1982-85; mem. nat. adv. coun. Anne Frank Ctr., 1992-94; chair Am. com. Internat. Conf. Remembering for Future II. Avocations: classical music, biking, hiking, travel. Home: 135 Old New York Rd Port Republic NJ 08241-9702 Office: Richard Stockton Coll NJ Jimmie Leeds Rd Pomona NJ 08240

COLISH, MARCIA LILLIAN, history educator; b. Bklyn., July 27, 1937; d. Samuel and Daisy (Kartch) C. BA magna cum laude, Smith Coll., 1958; MA, Yale U., 1959, PhD, 1965; DHL (hon.), Grinnell Coll., 1999. Instr. history Skidmore Coll., Saratoga Springs, N.Y., 1962-63; instr. Oberlin Coll., Ohio, 1963-65, asst. prof., 1965-69; assoc. prof. Oberlin Coll, Ohio, 1969-75; prof. history Oberlin Coll., Ohio, 1975—; Frederick B. Artz prof. history Oberlin Coll., 1985—, chmn. dept. history, 1973-74, 78-81, 85-86; vis. scholar Am. Acad. Rome, 1968-69; lectr. history Case Western Res. U., Cleve., 1966-67; editl. cons. W.W. Norton & Co., 1973, John Wiley & Sons, Inc., 1981, SUNY Press, 1983, 85, U. Chgo. Press, 1988, U. Calif. Press, 1988, Princeton U. Press, 1988, 96, 98, U. Notre Dame Press, 1991, 92, 94, U. Ill. Press, 1995, U. Pa. Press, 1995, 97, 97, Yale U. Press, 1997, 98, Oxford U. Press, 1998, Blackwell's, 1998; cons. dept. history Grinnell Coll., 1974, Knox Coll., 1981, St. John's U., 1981, Whitman Coll., 1982, Hope Coll., 1995, Kenyon Coll., 1996; mem. exec. bd. Ohio Program Humanities, 1976-81, exec. bd., 1978-81, vice chmn., 1979-81; writing residency, Villa Serbelloni, Bellagio, 1995; mem. Sch. Hist. Studies, Inst. for Advanced Study, Princeton U., 1986-87. Author: The Mirror of Language: A Study in the Medieval Theory of Knowledge, 2d rev. edit., 1983, The Stoic Tradition from Antiquity to the Early Middle Ages, 1985, enlarged paperback edit., 1990, Peter Lombard, 1994, Medieval Foundations of the Western Intellectual Tradition, 400-1400, 1997, 2d printing, 1998, paperback edit., 1999. Mem. exec. bd. Oberlin ACLU, 1970-74, chmn., 1972-74, rec. sec., 1976-77, vice chmn., 1979-80; mem. exec. bd. Oberlin YWCA, 1966-70. Recipient Wilbur Cross medal Yale Grad. Sch. Alumni Assn., 1993; Samuel S. Fels fellow Yale U., 1961-62, Younger Scholar fellow Inst. for Rsch. in Humanities, U. Wis., 1974-75, Nat. Humanities Ctr. fellow, 1981-82, Guggenheim fellow, 1989-90, Woodrow Wilson Ctr. fellow, 1994-95, NEH fellow, 1968-69, 81-82; NEH summer grantee U. Calif., 1993. Fellow Medieval Acad. Am. (coun. 1987-89, 2d v.p. 1989-90, 1st v.p. 1990-91, pres. 1991-92, Haskins medal 1998); mem. Am. Hist. Assn., Medieval Assn. Midwest (coun. 1978-81), Midwest Medieval Conf. (pres. 1978-79), Renaissance Soc. Am., Cen. Renaissance Conf., Soc. Internat. pour Etude Philosophie Medievale, Internat. Soc. for Classical Tradition, Phi Beta Kappa. Home: 143 E College St Apt 310 Oberlin OH 44074-1759 Office: Oberlin Coll Dept History Oberlin OH 44074

COLKER, EDWARD, artist, educator; b. Phila., Jan. 5, 1927. Grad., Phila. Coll. Art, 1949; B.S., NYU, 1965, M.A., 1985. Instr., critic Phila. Coll. Art, Cooper Union, N.Y.C., 1949-66; assoc. prof. Grad. Sch. Fine Arts, U. Pa., 1968-70; dir. Sch. Art and Design, U. Ill., Chgo., 1972-78; research prof. art Sch. Art and Design, U. Ill., 1977-80; dean of visual arts SUNY, Purchase, 1980-85; chmn. dept. art Cornell U., 1985-86; provost Univ. of the Arts, 1986-91, Cooper Union for the Advancement of Sci. and Art, N.Y.C., 1991-95, Pratt Inst., Bklyn., 1995-98; cons. Nat. Endowment Arts, USIA; cons. in field. One-person shows, Print Club, Phila., 1961, 89, Amel Gallery, N.Y.C., 1965, East Hampton Gallery, N.Y.C., 1969, Douglas Kenyon Gallery, Chgo., 1975, Ctr. Book Arts, N.Y.C., Neuberger Mus., Purchase, U. Ill., Chgo., 1985, 86, SUNY, Albany, 1990, Cooper Union, 1993, U. of Ariz. Mus. of Art, Bates Coll. Mus. of Art, 1998, Neuberger Mus. of Art, 1999, others; represented in permanent collections, Mus. Art, Phila., Library of Congress, Washington, Mus. Modern Art, N.Y.C., Nat. Mus., Stockholm, Rosenwald Collection, NYU, U. Ariz., others. Guggenheim Found. fellow, 1961-62; Ill. Arts Council grantee, 1973, 80; Graham Found. grantee, 1977, R. Florsheim Art Fund grantee, 1997. Mem. Coll. Art Assn. Am., Caxton Club, Grolier Club.

COLL, EDWARD GIRARD, JR., university president; b. Pitts., Aug. 9, 1934; s. Edward G. and Alive V. (Ebeling) C.; m. Carole Hulse, Feb. 3, 1958; children—Thomas, Jean Coll Mendenhall, Peter, Karen, Kelly. BA Duquesne U., 1960, LHD (hon.), 1983. Div. dir. United Fund Allegheny County, Pitts., 1959-61; asst. to exec. v.p. United Fund Dade County, 1961-63; asst. to v.p. for devel. affairs U. Miami, Fla., 1963-66, dir. corp. and found. relations, 1966-67, dir. devel., 1967-72, sec. univ. corp., 1972-73, v.p. for devel. affairs, 1973-82; pres. Alfred U., N.Y., 1982—; lectr. acad. adminstrn.; bd. dirs. Steuben Trust Co. Contbr. articles to profl. jours. Chmn. zoning bd. appeals Dade County, 1973-82; bd. dirs. Nat. Ctr. Child Abuse and Neglect, 1985-90; mem. Pres.'s Com. NCAA, 1988-92, vice chair of div. III, 1990, trustee Coun. for Support and Advancement Edn., Washington, 1981-82, 87-89, chair, 1991-92, divsn. III v.p., 1994—; mem. NCAA Coun., 1993—. With U.S. Army, 1953-56. Univ. Administr. Fulbright fellow U. Warwick, Coventry, Eng., 1985. Mem. Ind. Colls. and Univs. N.Y. (bd. dirs. 1982-86), Duquesne Univ. Alumni Assn., Am. Mktg. Assn. (hon.), Delta Mu Delta, Phi Kappa Phi, Beta Gamma Sigma. Roman Catholic. Clubs: Miami, University, Genesee Valley, Wellsville Country. Office: Office of Pres Alfred U Saxon Dr Alfred NY 14802*

COLL, JIM, gallery director; b. Barcelona, Spain, June 21, 1954; s. Pedro Coll and Rosa Valls. Facultad de Bellas Artes de San Jorge, Barcelona Univ., Barcelona, Spain, 1973-78; Eng. Lang., ILS Coll., Staten Isl., NY, 1981; hist. of U.S., Hunter Coll., New York, NY, 1984. Pres., tech. dir. Montserrat Gallery Inc., N.Y.C., 1989—. The Fine Art Index, New York, 1992, North Amer. Edition, 1992, Art Speak, NY, 1990, Encyclopedia of Living Amer. Artists, (Dirs. Guild), Calif., 1990, Manhattan Arts, NY, 1990. First awd., Mus. Castelldefels, Castelldefels (Barcelona), 1973, Sala Pares awd., Barcelona, 1972, First awd., "Pesebre de Nadal", Town of Sant Llorenc Savall, Barcelona, 1969. Office: Montserrat Gallery 584 Broadway New York NY 10012-3229

COLL, JOHN PETER, JR., lawyer; b. Pitts., Oct. 5, 1943; s. John Peter and Lelia (Nicolussi) C.; m. Nancy Kaye Swan; children: John Peter, Alexis S. AB in Polit. Sci., Duke U., 1965; JD, Georgetown U., 1968. Bar: N.Y. 1969, U.S. Dist. Ct. (so. dist.) N.Y. 1970, U.S. Dist. Ct. (ea. dist.) N.Y. 1974, U.S. Ct. Appeals (2d cir.) 1972, U.S. Supreme Ct. 1974, U.S. Ct. Appeals (5th cir.) 1981, U.S. Ct. Appeals (11th cir.) 1981, U.S. Ct. Appeals (8th cir.) 1980, U.S. Ct. Appeals (6th cir.) 1991, U.S. Ct. Appeals (1st cir.) 1993, U.S. Ct. Appeals (3d cir.) 1994, U.S. Ct. Appeals (9th cir.) 1994, U.S. Dist. Ct. (no. dist.) Calif. 1983, U.S. Dist. Ct. (no. dist.) N.Y. 1984, U.S. Dist. Ct. (we. dist.) N.Y. 1988, U.S. Tax Ct. 1990, U.S. Ct. Appeals (fed. cir.) 1999. Assoc. Donovan Leisure Newton & Irvine LLP, N.Y.C., 1968-76, ptnr., 1976-98, chmn. exec. com., 1989-98; ptnr. Orrick, Herington & Sutcliffe LLP, N.Y.C., 1998—; bd. advisors product safety and liability rep. BNA, 1991—; mem. litigation steering com. Def. Rsch. Inst., 1991—. Contbg. author: Preparing for and Trying the Civil Law Suit, 1987, Supplement, 1997, Commercial Litigation in New York State Courts, 1995, Products Liability in New York, Strategy and Practice, 1997. Mem. ABA (litigation sect. 1983—), Fed. Bar Coun., N.Y. State Bar Assn., Assn. of Bar of City of N.Y., N.Y. Coun. Law Assocs. (mem. steering com. 1971-72), Lawrence Beach Club (bd. govs.), Cherry Valley Club, Univ. Club. Democrat. Roman Catholic. Home: 385 Stewart Ave Garden City NY 11530-4615 Office: Orrick Herrington and Sutcliffe LLP 666 Fifth Ave New York NY 10103

COLL, KATHLEEN M., home care manager; b. Orange, N.J., Jan. 23, 1959; d. Edward Thomas and Rosalie Mary (Tranberg) C. BSN, Coll. Misericordia, Dallas, Pa., 1981; MPH, U. Medicine and Dentistry N.J., Piscataway. RN, N.J. Staff nurse CCU, med., surg. unit Morristown (N.J.) Meml. Hosp.; nurse AT&T, Berkely Heights, N.J.; staff nurse Bell Communications Rsch., Piscataway, N.J.; nurse educator Med. Ctr. Health Care Svcs.; mgr. Overlook Home Care and Hospice. Mem. N.J. State Assn. Occupational Health Nurses (bd. dirs. membership sec. 1990-94), Sigma Theta Tau, Theta Phi.

COLL, STEPHEN WILSON, journalist; b. Washington, Oct. 8, 1958; s. Robert Wilson and Shirley Lee (Baldwin) C.; m. Susan Keselenko, May 17, 1984; children: Alexandra, Emma, Maxwell. BA cum laude, Occidental Coll., 1980. Contbg. editor Calif. mag., L.A., 1983-85; staff writer The Washington Post, 1985-87; Wall St. corr. The Washington Post, N.Y.C., 1987-89; New Delhi bur. chief The Washington Post, 1989-93, investigative journalist, London bur., 1993-95; editor and pub. The Washington Post Mag., 1995-98; mng. editor Washington Post Newspaper, 1998—. Author: The Deal of the Century, 1986, The Taking of Getty Oil, 1987, (with David A. Vise) Eagle on the Street, 1990, On the Grand Trunk Road, 1994. Recipient Pulitzer Prize for explanatory journalism, 1990, Gerald Loeb award UCLA, 1990, Livingston award Molly Parnell Livingston Found., 1992. Mem. Phi Beta Kappa. Office: Washington Post 1150 15th St NW Washington DC 20071-0002

COLLADAY, ROBERT S., trust company executive, consultant; b. Flint, Mich., Sept. 24, 1940; s. Robert Harold and Mary Elizabeth (Strong) C.; m. Joan M. Hartsock; children: David, Jill, James, Christopher. B.A., Alma Coll., 1962; postgrad., Nat. Trust Sch., Northwestern U., 1967. Asst. trust officer Comerica Bank-Detroit, 1968-71, trust officer, 1971-74, v.p., 1974-80, 1st v.p., 1980-83, sr. v.p., 1983-91; sr. v.p. Comerica Inc., 1984-91; pres., prin. cons. Trust Consulting Svcs., Inc., Bloomfield Hills, Mich., 1991—; cons. to bd. dirs. Found. Southeast Mich. Trustee, chmn. investment com. Alma Coll., Mich. Republican. Presbyterian. Avocations: photography; fishing. Home: 22241 Village Pines Dr Franklin MI 48025-3568 Office: Trust Consulting Svcs Inc PO Box 1131 Bloomfield Hills MI 48303-1131

COLLAMORE, THOMAS JONES, corporate executive; b. Hartford, Conn., Jan. 29, 1959; s. H. Bacon Jr. and Elizabeth Caldwell (Jones) C.; m. Jacqueline Ann Kelly, Nov. 21, 1992; children: Thomas Jones Jr., Pauline Elizabeth, Sallie Ann. BA magna cum laude, Drew U., 1981. Personal aide Rome for Gov., Bloomfield, Conn., 1978, dep. dir., 1982; staff asst. George Bush for Pres., Hartford, 1979-80; confidential asst. to sec. commerce Malcolm Baldrige Washington, 1981-82, spl. asst. to sec. commerce, 1982-85; dep. asst. to V.p. of U.S. The White House, Washington, 1985-87, asst. to V.p. of U.S., 1987-89; dir. secretariat Office of Pres.-elect of U.S., Washington, 1988-89; asst. sec. for adminstrn. U.S. Dept. Commerce, Washington, 1989-91, chief of staff, asst. sec. commerce, 1991-92; v.p. corp. affairs policy and adminstrn. Philip Morris Cos. Inc., N.Y.C., 1992-95, v.p. corp. pub. affairs, 1995—; chmn. govt. ops. com. Pres.'s Coun. on Mgmt. Improvement, Washington, 1989-91; mem. bd. advisors George Bush Presdl. Libr., 1996—. Bd. dirs. Malcolm Baldrige Scholarship Fund, Hartford, 1988—; trustee Kingswood-Oxford Sch., West Hartford, 1991—, Drew U., Madison, N.J., 1992—; alt. del. Rep. Nat. Conv., Detroit, 1980, del., Houston, 1992. Mem. Pi Sigma Alpha. Episcopalian. Home: 5206 Norway Dr Chevy Chase MD 20815-6672 Office: Philip Morris Cos Inc 120 Park Ave New York NY 10017-5592

COLLARD, THOMAS ALBERT, transportation executive; b. Paterson, N.J., Nov. 9, 1942; s. Albert Garrison and Katherine Barbara (Adams) C.; BS in Bus. Adminstrn., U. Buffalo, 1964; m. Cynthia Louise Davis, Nov. 6, 1965; children: Elizabeth, Katherine. Various positions Pa. R.R., Cleve. and Buffalo, 1964-69; svc. analyst mktg. dept. Penn Central, Phila., 1969-70, supr. svc. quality control, 1971; mgr. svc. planning Cen. R.R. of N.J., Newark, 1972-74, dir. transp. planning, 1974-75, dir. stas. and intermodal operation, 1975; with Conrail Activation Task Force, 1975-76, dir. svc. planning and performance, 1976-80, dir. svc. devel., 1980-83, mgr. transp. svc. planning and costing, 1983-89; mgr. ea. ops. Nat. Salvage and Svc., 1989-90; mgr. Solid Waste Bus. Group, 1991-92; prin. Cameron Mgmt. Svcs. Co., 1992—; v.p. So. R.R. Co. N.J., 1992—; chmn., chief exec. officer The Elise Corp./N.J. So. Coachways, 1983-90; mem. Transp. Rsch. Forum, 1981—; adv. S. Jersey Transp. Adv. Com., 1982-85. Author children's book: Diesels First, 1977; contbr. articles to tech. publs. Active Big Brother Orgn., Willingboro, N.J., 1972-81; v.p. Big Bros./Big Sisters of Burlington County (N.J.), 1975-76, pres., 1977-78; vol. juvenile probation counselor, 1978; adv. Concerned Citizens North Camden, 1981-85. Mem. Am. Soc. Traffic and Transp. (cert.), ICC Practitioners Assn. Roman Catholic. Home and Office: 30 Topeka Ln Willingboro NJ 08046-4120

COLLAS, JUAN GARDUÑO, JR., lawyer; b. Manila, Apr. 25, 1932; s. Juan D. and Soledad (Garduño) C.; m. Maria L. Moreira, Aug. 1, 1959; children: Juan Jose, Elias Lopes, Cristina Maria, Daniel Benjamin. LLB, U. of Philippines, Quezon City, 1955; LLM, Yale U., 1958, JSD, 1959. Bar: Philippines 1956, Ill. 1960, Calif. 1971, U.S. Supreme Ct. 1967. Assoc., Sy Cip, Salazar & Assocs., Manila, 1956-57; atty. N.Y., N.H. & H. R.R., New Haven, 1959-60; assoc. Baker & McKenzie, Chgo., 1960-63, ptnr., Manila, 1963-70, San Francisco, 1970-95, Manila, 1995—. Contbr. articles to profl. jours. Trustee, sec. Friends of U. of Philippines Found. in Am., San Francisco, 1982—; co-chmn. San Francisco Lawyers for Better Govt., 1982—; chmn. San Francisco-Manila Sister City Com., 1986-92. Recipient Outstanding Filipino Overseas in Law award, Philippine Ministry Tourism Philippines Jaycees, 1979. Mem. ABA, Am. Arbitration Assn. (panelist), Ill. State Bar Assn., State Bar Calif., Integrated Bar of Philippines, Filipino-Am. C. of C. (bd. dirs. 1974-91, 94-96, pres. 1985-87, chmn. bd. dirs. 1987-89, 95-96). Republican. Roman Catholic. Clubs: World Trade, Villa Taverna (San Francisco). Office: Baker & McKenzie 2 Embarcadero Ctr Ste 2400 San Francisco CA 94111-3909

COLLEN, MORRIS FRANK, physician; b. St. Paul, Nov. 12, 1913; s. Frank Morris and Rose (Finkelstein) C.; m. Frances B. Diner, Sept. 24, 1937; children: Arnold Roy, Barry Joel, Roberta Joy, Randal Harry. BEE, U. Minn., 1934, MB with distinction, 1938, MD, 1939. Diplomate Am. Bd. Internal Medicine. Intern Michael Reese Hosp., Chgo., 1939-40; resident Los Angeles County Hosp., 1940-42; chief med. service Kaiser Found. Hosp., Oakland, Calif., 1942-52; chief of staff Kaiser Found. Hosp., Oakland, 1952-53; med. dir. Permanente Med. Group, West Bay Div., 1953-79, dir. med. methods research, 1962-79, dir. tech. assessment, 1979-83, cons. div. research, 1983—; chmn. exec. com. Permanente Med. Group, Oakland, 1953-73; dir. Permanente Services, Inc., Oakland, 1958-73; lectr. Sch. Pub. Health, U. Calif., Berkeley, 1966-78; lectr. info. sci. U. Calif., San Francisco, 1970-85; lectr. U. London, 1972, Stanford U. Med. Ctr., 1973, 75, 84-86, Harvard U., 1974, Johns Hopkins U., 1976, also others; cons. Bur. Health Services, USPHS, 1965-68, chmn. health care systems study sect., 1968-72, mem. adv. com. demonstration grants, 1967; advisor VA, 1968; cons. European region WHO, 1968-72; cons. med. fitness program U.S. Air Force, 1968; cons. Pres.'s Biomed. Research Panel, 1975; mem. adv. com. automated Multiphasic Health Testing, 1971; discussant Nat. Conf. Preventive Medicine, Bethesda, Md., 1975; mem. com. on tech. in health care NAS, 1976; mem. adv. group Nat. Commn. on Digestive Diseases, U.S. Congress, 1978; mem. adv. panel to U.S. Congress Office of Tech. Assessment, 1980-85; mem. peer rev. adv. group TRIMIS program Dept. Def., 1978-90; program chmn. 3d Internat. Conf. Med. Informatics, Tokyo, 1980; chmn. bd. sci. counselors Nat. Library Medicine, 1985-87; mem. lit. selection tech. rev. com. Nat. Libr. of Medicine, 1997-01; cons. Nat. Libr. Med., 1985-88. Author: Treatment of Pneumococcic Pneumonia, 1948, Hospital Computer Systems, 1974, Multiphasic Health Testing Services, 1978, Medical Informatics: A Historical Review, 1995; editor: Permanente Med. Bull., 1943-53; mem. editl. bd. Preventive Medicine, 1970-80, Jour. Med. Sys., Methods Info. Medicine, 1980-97, Diagnostic Medicine, 1980-84, Computers in Biomed. Rsch., 1987-94; contbr. articles to med. jours., chpts. to books. Recipient Computers in Health Care Pioneer award, 1992; Johns Hopkins Centennial scholar, 1976; fellow Ctr. Advanced Studies in Behavioral Scis., Stanford U., 1985-86; scholar-in-residence Nat. Libr. Medicine, 1987—. Fellow ACP, Am. Coll. Cardiology, Am. Coll. Chest Physicians, Am. Inst. Med. and Biol. Engring.; mem. AMA, Inst. Medicine of NAS (chmn. tech. subcom. for improving patient records 1990, chmn. workshop on informatics in clin. preventive medicine 1991), Am. Fedn. Clin. Rsch., Am. Coll. Med. Informatics (pres. 1987-88, Morris F. Collen medal named in his honor 1993), Salutis Unitas (v.p. 1972), Soc. Adv. Med. Sys. (pres. 1973), Nat. Acad. Practice in Medicine (chmn. 1982-88, co-chmn. 1989-91), Am. Med. Informatics Assn. (bd. dirs. 1985-96), Internat. Health Evaluation Assn. (pres. 1995-96, Lifetime Achievement award 1992, David E. Morgan award for achievement in health care info. 1998), Internat. Med. Informatics Assn. Sr. Officers Club, Alpha Omega Alpha, Tau Beta Pi. Home: 4155 Walnut Blvd Walnut Creek CA 94596-5834 Office: 3505 Broadway Oakland CA 94611-5714

COLLEN, SHELDON ORRIN, lawyer; b. Chicago, Ill., Feb. 7, 1922; s. Jacob Allen and Ann (Andalman) C.; m. Ann Blager, Apr. 8, 1946; 1 child, John O. B.A. magna cum laude, Carleton Coll., 1944; J.D., U. Chgo., 1948. Bar: Ill. 1949, Minn. 1976, U.S. Dist. Ct. (no. dist.) Ill. 1949, U.S. Supreme Ct. 1965. Assoc. Adcock, Fink & Day, Chgo., 1948-51; mem. Simon & Collen, Chgo., 1951-59, Friedman & Koven, Chgo., 1959-86, Epton, Mullin & Druth, Ltd., Chgo., 1986-89; of counsel Lawrence Walner and Assocs., Ltd., 1989-90; prin. Sheldon O. Collen P.C., 1990—; specialist fed. antitrust litigation; sec. Jupiter Industries, Inc. and subs., Chgo., 1961-86. Mem. adv. bd. Antitrust Bull. and Jour. Reprints for Antitrust Law and Econs. Curator Prince Art Gallery, Chgo.; mem. bd. edn. U. Chgo. Law Rev., 1948-49; bd. dirs. J.G. Inds. Inc., Lower Northcenter, Chgo. Youth Ctrs., Union League Found. for Boys and Girls, Contemporary Art Workshop, Edward P. Martin Soc., Ctr. for Study of Multiple Births; sec., bd. dirs. 3750 Lake Shore Dr., Inc., 1982-87; pres. Union League Civic and Arts Found., 1984-86, life trustee. With AUS, 1943-46. Fellow Norwegian Am. Mus., Decorah, Iowa. Mem. ABA, Am. Judicature Soc., Chgo. Bar Assn. (coun. corp. and securities law coms., chmn. antitrust 1976-77), Bar Assn. 7th Cir., Am. Arbitration Assn. (arbitrator), Art Inst. Chgo., Mus. Contemporary Art, Lawyers for Creative Arts, Chgo. Hist. Soc. Home: 3750 N Lake Shore Dr Apt 16C Chicago IL 60613-4234

COLLEN, TOM, coach. B in Health and Phys. Edn., Bowling Green U., 1977; M in Health Edn., Miami U. of Ohio, 1982, M in Recreational Programming, 1983. Asst. coach Miami of Ohio, 1982-84, U. Utah, 1984-86, Purdue U., 1987-93; asst. coach, asst. head coach U. Ark., 1994-97; head coach women's basketball Colo. State U., Ft. Collins, 1997—. Office: Colo State U Dept Athletics 215 D Moby Arena Fort Collins CO 80523-0120*

COLLENETTE, DAVID M., Canadian government official; b. London, 1946; m. Penny Hossack, Oct. 11, 1975; 1 child, Christopher. BA, York U., 1969; postgrad., Carleton U. Exec. v.p. Mandrake Mgmt. Cons., Toronto and Ottawa, Can.; adminstrv. officer Int. Life Ins. Co., London, 1970-72; coord. 41st Ann. Couchiching Conf., 1972; exec. dir. Liberal Party of Ont., 1972-74; M.P. from Don Valley East dist. Ho. of Commons, Ottawa, Ont., Can., 1974-79, 80-84; min. state multiculturalism, 1983-84; sec. gen. Liberal Party Canada, 1985-87; min. nat. def., min. vets. affairs Govt. of Can., Ottawa, 1993-97; min. transport Govt. of Can., 1997—; del. NATO, Brussels, UN, N.Y.C., EEC, Strasbourg, S.Am.; party sec. to Postmaster Gen., Dep. Govt. House Leader; chmn. Standing Com. Energy Legis.; vice chmn. External Affairs and Nat. Def., Subcom. on Van. Rels. with L.Am. and Caribbean, 1982-83. Vol. overseas dem. devel. work; monitor elections in Haiti, Chile, Romania, Czech Republic. Mem. Univ. Club (Toronto), Nat. Liberal Club (London). Anglican. Avocations: squash, swimming, classical music, theatre. Office: Transport Can, 330 Sparks St, Ottawa, ON Canada K1A ON5*

COLLENS, LEWIS MORTON, university president, legal educator; b. Chgo., Feb. 10, 1938. BS, U. Ill., Urbana, 1960, MA, 1963; JD, U. Chgo., 1966. Bar: Ill. 1966. Assoc. Ross, Hardies, Chgo., 1966-67; spl. asst. to gen. counsel EEOC, Washington, 1967-68; asst. prof. Ill. Inst. Tech., Chgo. Kent Coll. Law, 1970-72, assoc. prof., 1972-74, prof., 1975—; dean Coll. Law, Ill. Inst. Tech., 1974-90, pres., 1990—; bd. dirs. Amsted Industries, Inc., Dean Foods Co., Inc. Bd. dirs. Met. Plan Coun., pres. Coun. of Pres. of the Tchrs. Acad. for math. and Sci., dir. Ill. Coalition; pres. Leadership Greater Chgo. Mem. ABA, Ill. Bar Assn., Chgo. Bar Assn., Am. Law Inst., Econ. Club of Chgo. (dir.), Order of Coif. Office: Ill Inst Tech 10 W 33rd St Rm 223 Chicago IL 60616-3730*

COLLERAN, KEVIN, lawyer; b. Spalding, Nebr., July 16, 1941; s. James Edward and Helen Marcella (Vybiral) C.; m. Karen Ann Rooney, Aug. 1, 1964; children: Mary Jane, Patrick. BS, U. Nebr., 1964, JD with distinction, 1968. Bar: Nebr. 1968, U.S. Dist. Ct. Nebr. 1968, U.S. Dist. Ct. (we. dist.) La. 1975, U.S. Dist. Ct. (no. dist.) Tex. 1978, U.S. Supreme Ct. 1980, U.S. Ct. Appeals (8th cir.) 1981. Law clk. U.S. Dist. Ct. Nebr., 1968-69; assoc. Cline, Williams, Wright, Johnson & Oldfather, Lincoln, Nebr., 1969-74; ptnr., 1975—, mng. ptnr., 1985-89, 96—. Bd. dirs. Lancaster County unit Am. Cancer Soc., 1972-83, pres., 1979. Fellow Am. Coll. Trial Lawyers; mem. ABA, Am. Bd. Trial Advocates, Nebr. Bar Assn. (chmn. worker's compensation com. 1980-82), Internat. Assn. Def. Counsel, Nat. Assn. Trial Attys., Order of Coif. Democrat. Office: Cline Williams Wright Johnson & Oldfather Firs Tier Bank Bldg Lincoln NE 68508

COLLETT, JENNIE, principal. Prin. OB Whaley Sch, San Jose, Calif., 1995—. Recipient Elem. Sch. Recognition award U.S. Dept. Edn., 1989-90. Office: O B Whaley Sch 2655 Alvin Ave San Jose CA 95121-1609*

COLLETT, MERRILL JUDSON, management consultant; b. Winona Lake, Ind., Feb. 20, 1914; s. Charles Alfred and Dora (Jenkins) C. BA, Stanford (Calif.) U., 1934; MPA, Syracuse (N.Y.) U., 1938. With Pub. Adminstrn. Svs., Chgo., 1940-43; U.S. Bur. of Budget, 1945-46; pers. dir. Bonneville Power Adminstrn., Portland, Oreg., 1946-50; dir. pers. and mgmt. prodn., mktg. adminstrn. USDA, Washington, 1950-52; dir. wartime organizational planning Office Def. Mobilization, Washington, 1954-58; co-owner Collett and Clapp, P.R., 1958-65; founder, pres. Exec. Mgmt. Svc., Arlington, Va., 1967-82; editor-at-large The Bureaucrat, Washingt, 1981—. Contbr. articles to profl. jours. Moderator Calvary Bapt. Ch., Washington, 1981-83; bd. dirs. Efforts from Ex-Convicts, Washington, 1967-83, Bacone Coll., Muskogee, Okla., 1980-86, 91-94, Tucson Met. Ministry, 1989-91. Lt. USNR, 1943-46. Mem. Internat. Pers. Mgmt. Assn. (hon. life, Stockberger award), Ariz. Pers. Mgmt. Assn. (hon. life).

COLLETT, ROBERT LEE, financial company executive; b. Ardmore, Okla., July 1, 1940; s. Pat (Dowell) Conway; m. Sue Walker Healy; 1 child, Catherine April. BA in Math., Rice U., 1962; MA in Econs., Duke U., 1963. Chief actuarial asst. Am. Nat. Ins. Co., Galveston, Tex., 1963-66; actuary Milliman & Robertson, Inc., Phila., 1966-70; prin. Milliman & Robertson, Inc., Houston, 1970-89, pres., 1990; pres., CEO Milliman & Robertson, Inc., Houston and Seattle, 1991-92, Seattle, 1992—. Bd. dirs. Seattle Symphony, 1992—. Fellow Soc. Actuaries (chmn. internat. sect. 1992—); mem. Rainier Club. Episcopalian. Avocations: tennis, traveling, music, reading. Office: Milliman & Robertson Inc 1301 5th Ave Ste 3800 Seattle WA 98101-2646

COLLETTE, FRANCES MADELYN, retired tax consultant, lawyer; b. Yonkers, N.Y., Aug. 5, 1947; d. Morris Aaron and Esther (Gang) Volbert; m. Roger Warren Collette, Dec. 25, 1971; children: Darren Roger, Bonnie Frances. BEd summa cum laude, SUNY, Buffalo, 1969; JD cum laude, U. Miami, 1980. Bar: Fla. 1980. Employment counselor Fla. Bur. Employment Security, Miami, Fla., 1969-73; unemployment claims adjudicator Fla. Bur. Unemployment, Miami, 1973-77; owner Unemployment Svcs. Fla., Inc., Miami, 1977-93; cons. Fla. unemployment tax and personnel; lectr. in field. Ad hoc comm. students with Asperger's Syndrome Dade County Pub. Schs., 1998—; vol. child advocate Exceptional Student Edn., 1996—. Mem. BBB S. Fla. (1st v.p. 1980-81, bd. govs., 2d vice chmn. 1990-91). Jewish.

COLLETTI, TERESA ANN, polymer chemist; b. Balt., Aug. 26, 1967; d. John Bruce and Elizabeth Grace (Schmidt) Schott; m. Ronald Francis Colletti, Sept. 23, 1989; 1 child, Christopher Robert. BS, U. So. Miss., 1989. Chemist, microscopist Monsanto, Pensacola, Fla., 1990-92, process engr., 1992-93, new product engr., 1993-94; process tech. team leader Monsanto, Greenwood, S.C., 1994-96; sr. mktg. tech. svc. specialist Solutia, St. Louis, 1996-99, sr. credit analyst, 1999—; presenter in field. Contbr. articles to sci. jours. Mem. Am. Chem. Soc. (mem. women chemist com. 1993-94, 95-01, treas. Pensacola sect. 1991-93), Soc. of Plastics Engrs. Home: 257 Harbour Pointe Dr Wildwood MO 63040-1956

COLLEY, JANET SCRITSMIER, investment consultant; b. Pomona, Calif., May 21, 1960; d. Jerome Lorenzo and Mildred Joan (Lloyd) Scritsmier; children: Justin Michael, Corey Gray, Cody James; m. Glenn Turner Colley, Dec. 27, 1996. Student Calif. State Poly. U., 1978-79. Vice pres. sales E.L.A. Co., Industry, Calif., 1979-84; investment cons. Cameron Properties Inc., Covina, Calif., 1980—. Asst. instr. Dale Carnegie Sales Course, 1981-82, Human Relations, 1983. Republican. Mormon. Home: 1440 E Puente St Covina CA 91724-3214

COLLEY, JOHN SCOTT, college president, English literature educator; b. Charlottesville, Va., June 29, 1942; s. Alred Gordon and Lottie Tupper (Pugh) C.; m. Christine H. Colley, Apr. 3, 1981; 1 child, Gwen Hilary. BA, Randolph-Macon Coll., 1964, LHD (hon.), 1991; MA, U. Chgo., 1965, PhD, 1969. Prof. English, Vanderbilt U., Nashville, 1968-88; provost Hampden-Sydney (Va.) Coll., 1988-98; pres. Berry Coll., Mount Berry, Ga., 1998—; chair governing coun. Wye Faculty Seminar, Wye Woods, Md., 1998—; mem. commn. on women in higher edn. Am. Coun. on Edn., Washington, 1999&; commr. So. Assn. Colls. and Schs., Atlanta, 1998—; bd. dirs. Ga. Coun. for Econ. Edn., Atlanta, 1998—. Author: Richard's Himself Again, 1994. Mem. Phi Beta Kappa. Home: 2148 Martha Berry Blvd Rowe GA 30165 Office: Berry Coll Mount Berry GA 30149

COLLEY, KAREN J., medical educator, medical researcher; b. Nov. 3, 1958. BS in Chemistry, Duke U., 1981; PhD in Molecular Biology, Washington U., St. Louis, 1987. Postdoctoral fellow dept. biol. chemistry UCLA, 1987-91; asst. prof. dept. biochemistry U. Ill., Chgo., 1991-97, assoc. prof., 1997—; mem. med. adv. bd. Leukemia Rsch. Found., reviewer study sect., 1994—; outside reviewer NSF Grants, 1995—, VA Rsch. Grants, 1995—; reviewer Jour. Biol. Chemistry, Jour. Cell Biology, Molecular and Chem. Neuropathology, Jour. Cell Sci., Devel. Biology. Contbr. articles to profl. jours.; patentee in field. Postdoctoral fellow NIH, 1990, grantee, 1992; Sr. fellow Am. Cancer Soc., 1991, grantee, 1992; U. Ill. grantee, 1992, 96, Leukemia Rsch. Found., Inc., 1993; recipient Established Investigator award Am. Heart Assn., 1996. Mem. AAAS, Am. Soc. Cell Biology, Am. Soc. Biochemistry and Molecular Biology, Soc. Glycobiology, Sigma Xi. Office: U Ill Dept Biochemistry and Molecular Biology 1819 W Polk St Chicago IL 60612-7331

COLLI, BART JOSEPH, lawyer; b. Englewood, N.J., Feb. 13, 1948; s. Bart Joseph and Marie (Burns) C.; m. Mary Ellen Diemer, May 20, 1972; 1 son, Michael John. BA summa cum laude, Fordham Coll., 1968; JD cum laude, Harvard U., 1971. Bar: N.Y. 1972, Tex. 1975, N.J., 1988. Assoc. White & Case, N.Y.C., 1971-75; ptnr. Hughes & Luce, Dallas, 1976-85, McCarter & English, L.L.P., Newark, 1985—; adj. prof. law Seton Hall U.; judge Entrepreneur of the Yr. awards program, 1993, 95, 96, North Jersey Venture Fairs, 1993, 94, N.J. Family Bus. of Yr. awards program, 1997; lectr. in field; mem. resources com. Edison Partnership Tech. Contbr. numerous articles to legal publs. Trustee Tri-County Scholarship Fund, No. N.J. chpt. Leukemia Soc. Am., Inc., Morris County unit Am. Cancer Soc.; coun. Lincoln Ctr. Bus. Coun. of the Consol. Fund. Capt. M.I., USAR, 1968-76. Mem. ABA (fed. regulation of securities com., sect. on corp.k), N.Y. State Bar Assn. (securities law com., chmn. bus. orgn. com. of the corp. and bus. law sect.), Phi Beta Kappa. E-mail: bcolli@mccarter.com. Office: McCarter & English LLP 4 Gateway Ctr 100 Mulberry St Newark NJ 07102-4096

COLLIAS, NICHOLAS ELIAS, zoology educator, ornithologist; b. Chicago Heights, Ill., July 19, 1914; s. Elias and Marina (Giatras) C.; m. Elsie Cole, Dec. 21, 1948; 1 child, Karen. BS, U. Chgo., 1937, PhD, 1942. Instr. biology Amherst (Mass.) Coll., 1946-47; instr. zoology U. Wis., Madison, 1947-51; postdoctoral fellow Cornell U., Ithaca, N.Y., 1953-54; prof. zoology Ill. Coll., Jacksonville, 1954-58; from asst. prof. to prof. zoology UCLA, 1958—. Author: Evolution of Nest-building in the Weaverbirds, 1964, Nest Building and Bird Behavior, 1984; editor: External Construction by Animals, 1976. 1st lt. USAAC, 1943-46. Guggenheim fellow, 1962-63; NSF grantee, 1960-80. Fellow AAAS, Am. Ornithologists Union (Elliott Coues award 1980), Animal Behavior Soc.; mem. Cooper Ornithol. Soc. (hon.), Wilson Ornithol. Soc. (Margaret Morse Nice medal 1997). Avocations: natural history, birding. Office: U Calif Dept Biology/Ecology U Calif Los Angeles CA 90095-1606

COLLIE, H. CRIS, III, trade association executive; b. Cape Girardeau, Mo., Jan. 30, 1945; s. H.C. and Amelia (Richardson) C.; m. Susan Bishop, Apr. 24, 1971; children: Megan, Chad. BSBA, S.E. Mo. State U., 1966. Employment mgr. Motorola, Inc., Chgo., 1966-72; exec. v.p. Employee Relocation Coun., Washington, 1972—; bd. dirs. Greater Washington Bd. Trade, 1986-87, 93—; pres. Washington Assn. Rsch. Found., 1985. Contbg. author: Meetings and Administration: A Textbook and Reference Book for Non-Profit Assns.; contbr. articles to profl. jours. Leader adult com. N.W. Fairfax (Va.) Young Life; active YMCA Ptnr. with Youth; mem. Leadership Washington. With U.S. Army, 1966-72. Mem. Am. League Lobbysits, Am. Soc. Assn. Execs. (frequent program and panel presenter), Greater Washington Soc. Assn. Execs. (chmn. bd. 1986-87), Profl. Conv. Mgmt. Assn. (bd. dirs. 1995—, chmn. govt. rels. com., spkr. ann. conv.), U.S. C. of C. (assn. com. of 100, 1993—), Coun. of Human Resource Mgmt. Assns. (coun.), Nat. Eagle Scout Assn. (life), The SKEE (pres., chmn. bd. 1991-92), Capitol Hill Club, Sigma Chi (life). Episcopalian. Avocations: golf, skiing, running. Office: Employee Relocation Council 1720 N St NW Washington DC 20036-2900*

COLLIE, JOHN, JR., insurance agent; b. Gary, Ind., Apr. 23, 1934; s. John and Christina Dempster (Wardrop) C.; m. Jessie Fearn Shaw, Aug. 1, 1964; children: Cynthia Elizabeth Lunsford, Douglas A.H., Jennifer Fearn. Student, Purdue U., 1953; AB in Econs., U. Ind., 1957; assoc. risk mgmt. (A.R.M.). Operator Collie Optical Lab., Gary, 1957-62; owner, operator Collie Ins. Agy., Gary, 1962—; pres. Collie Realty and Investment, Ins. and Fin. Advisory, Lake Mich. Global Industries; lectr. High Frontier; dist. chmn. 1st dist. Ind. for com. to secure High Frontier; mem. employer support Guard & Res., Dept. Def.; registered rep. WMA Securities, Inc.; affiliated broker Pickart Ins. Agy. Inc., Merrillville. Lt. col. U.S. Army Res., 1957-86; instr. Command and Gen. Staff Coll., 1973-77. Mem. Ind. Ins. Agts. Assn., Mil. Order World Wars, Res. Officers Assn. (sec., pres. N.W. Ind. chpt., v.p. Ind. chpt.), Leadership Coun. Am., Nat. Fedn. Ind. Bus. (guardian), Merrillville C. of C. (legis. com.), Masons (32 degree), Shriners, Phi Kappa Psi. Republican. Methodist. Home: 871 Camelot Mnr Portage IN 46368-6632 Office: PO Box 10148 5600 Broadway Merrillville IN 46411-0148

COLLIE, KELSEY EUGENE, producer, educator, director, playwright; b. Miami, Fla., Feb. 21, 1935; s. James George and Elizabeth Malinda (Moxey) C.; m. Doris Jean Sims, June 13, 1959 (div. 1985); children: Kim Denyse, Vaughn Hayse; m. Joyce Jenkins Brown, Dec. 28, 1995. BA, Hampton U., 1957; MFA, George Washington U., 1967; PhD, Howard U., 1979. Asst. to pub. rels. dir. Hampton (Va.) Inst., 1958; documents libr. Libr. Congress, Washington, 1960-70; prof. theatre Howard U., Washington, 1970-95, dir. Children's Theatre, 1973-91; artistic dir. KEC Playmakers Repertory Co., Washington, 1976—, Color Me Human Players, Inc., Washington, 1987—, Friends of the Children, mem. adv. bd., 1996—; talent agt., mgr. KEC Talent Assocs., Washington, 1988—; exec. dir. KEC Children's Theatre Experience, 1991—. Dir. plays including The Fantasticks, 1986, Tales, Tales and More Tales, 1989; musical revue Night of The Divas, 1987; playwright plays including Black Image/Black Reflection, 1974, Brother, Brother, Brother Mine, 1979, Mimes and Yarns, 1982, In and Out of Africa, 1993, Urban Voices: Cries and Whispers, 1995, The Wonderful Wizard of Utama, 1996; appeared in play Ceremonies in Dark Old Men, 1990. With AUS, 1958-60. Mem. AFTRA, Black Theatre Network, African-Am. Children's Theatre League (exec. dir.). Democrat. Episcopalian. Avocations: piano playing, cooking. Home: 1924 Shepherd St NE Washington DC 20018-3230

COLLIER, ALBERT M., pediatric educator, child development center director; b. Elba, Ala., May 3, 1937; s. Milford William and Ida Ruth C.; m. Mary Gaynell Wehler, July 17, 1960; children: Albert Mark, Dennis Murray, Jonathan Lee. BS, U. Miami, 1959, MD, 1963. Pediatric resident U. Miami, Coral Gables, Fla., 1963-66; infectious diseases fellow U. N.C., Chapel Hill, 1968-70, from asst. prof. to assoc. prof., 1971-80, prof., 1980—, divsn. chief infectious disease, 1980—, assoc. dir. ctr. environ. med. lung bio, 1980—, acting dir. Frank Porter Graham Child Devel. Ctr., 1990-92; assoc. chmn. of pediatrics for rsch. U. N.C., 1997—. Contbr. over 100 articles to profl. jours. Recipient Louis Dienes award Internat. Orgn. Mycoplasmology, Vienna, Austria, 1988. Mem. Gideons (zone leader 1990-93). Baptist. Office: U NC Chapel Hill Dept Pediatrics 535 Burnett-Womack CB 7220 Chapel Hill NC 27599

COLLIER, ALICE ELIZABETH, retired community organization executive; b. Akron, Ohio, June 9, 1927; d. Christian and Virginia (Schulmeister) Becker; m. John Robert Fenwick, Aug. 28, 1954 (div. Apr. 1968); 1 child, Beth Alice; m. Thomas Collier, Mar. 8, 1980. BA in Edn., Heidelberg Coll., Tiffin, Ohio, 1949; MA in Ednl. Adminstrn., U. Akron, 1968. Cert. tchr., ednl. adminstr., Ohio. Tchr. Air Force Dependent Schs., Fed. Republic Germany and Eng., 1960-64; tchr. Akron Pub. Schs., 1964-80, adminstr., 1968-80; dep. mayor City of Akron, 1980-84; pres. Collier Pub. Rels./Mktg., Akron, 1984-86; gen. mgr. Coldwell Banker Real Estate, Akron, 1986-90; dir. comm. and devel., asst. exec. dir. Area Agy. on Aging, Akron, 1990-94; v.p. Mktg. and Creative Solutions, 1994-97; ret., 1997. Author, editor: (Manual) Visual-Motor Training for the Developmentally Disabled Child, 1972, Different Strokes for Little Folks, 1974. Chmn. adv. coun. U. Akron, 1977-88; active Akron Health Comm., 1978-80, Akron Sr. Citizens Commn., 1980—, Nat. Adv. Coun. on Aging, Bethesda, Md., 1982-84; pres. Tri-County Employee Assistance Program, Summit, Medina and Portage, 1985—; charter rev. commn. Summit County, 1991; mem. women's adv. coun. Summa Health Sys., 1994—; v.p. Women's Network, Akron, 1987-88; trustee Comty. Health Rsch. Group, Inc., 1980—, Cuyahoga Falls Gen. Hosp. Found., 1992—; pub. rels. chmn. Atty. Gen. Health Info. Com.; bd. trustees NEC Invitational Firestone Country Club World Series of Golf, 1999—. Recipient Svc. to Elderly award Am. Gerontol. Soc., 1982, Excellence in Comm. award Nat. Assn. Area Agys. on Aging, 1991. Mem. Am. Mktg. Assn. (pres. Akron-Canton chpt. 1988-89, Spl Merit award 1990), Ohio Assn. Realtors (trustee 1988-90), Akron Bd. Realtors (Salesperson of Yr. award 1988, Hall of Fame award 1988), Heidelberg Coll. Alumni Assn., Akron Woman'c City Club, Medina Country Club, Mission Valley Country Club, Venice, Fla., Pi Lambda Theta. Republican. Avocations: church organist, golf, tennis, collecting Hummel figurines. Home summer: Beechwood # 11 333 N Portage Path Akron OH 44303-1218 Home winter: 255 The Esplanade N Apt 204 Venice FL 34285-1518

COLLIER, BEVERLY JOANNE, elementary education educator; b. Grand Haven, Mich., Oct. 28, 1936; d. Joseph Frank and Anne (Mary) Snyder; divorced; children: Ann, Cindy. Student, U. Mich., 1955-57; BA, Western Mich. U., 1965. Cert. elem. tchr., Mich. 1st grade tchr. Fruitport (Mich.) Community Schs., 1965-93; retired, 1993. Contbr. articles to local newspapers. Active Grand Haven (Mich.) Presbyn. Ch., 1955—. Mem. ASCD, NEA, Muskegon Edn. Assn., Mich. Edn. Assn. (past regional rep.), West Mich. Edn. Assn., Mich. Assn. Ret. Sch. Personnel (Muskegon County chpt.). Avocations: reading, writing, biking, theater, hiking. Home: 1235 Washington Ave Grand Haven MI 49417-1627 Office: Fruitport Cmty Sch 305 Pontaluna Rd Fruitport MI 49415-9652

COLLIER, CHARLES ARTHUR, JR., lawyer; b. Columbus, Ohio, Apr. 18, 1930; s. Charles Arthur and Gertrude Clara (Roe) C.; m. Linda Louise Biggs, Aug. 5, 1961; children: Sheila Collier Rogers, Laura Collier Prescott. AB magna cum laude, Harvard U., 1952, LLB, 1955. Law clk. U.S. Dist. Ct. (cen. dist.) Calif., L.A., 1959-60; assoc. Freston & Files, L.A., 1960-66; assoc., ptnr. Mitchell, Silberberg & Knupp, L.A., 1967-82; ptnr. Irell & Manella, L.A., 1982-95, of counsel, 1995—; lectr. Calif. Continuing Edn. of Bar, 1976-89; advisor Restatement of Property, Donative Transfers, 1990—; speaker numerous local bar assns. Contbr. articles to profl. jours. Recipient Arthur K. Marshall award Probate and Trust sect. L.A. County Bar Assn. Fellow Am. Coll. Trust and Estate Counsel (chmn. state laws com. 1986-89, regent 1989-98, joint editl. bd. uniform probate code com. 1988—, chmn. expanded practice com. 1989-92, chmn. nominating com. 1998-99, spkr. 1988, exec. com. 1989-98, treas. 1992-93, sec. 1993-94, v.p. 1994-95, pres.-elect 1995-96, pres. 1996-97, immediate past pres. 1997-98), ABA Found.; mem. ABA (mem. real property, trust and probate law sect. spkr. 1985, 89, moderator teleconf. 1998, coun. 1989-93, chmn. com. trust adminstrn. 1982-85, chmn. task force on fiduciary litigation 1986-89, sr. lawyers divsn., mem. wills, probate and trusts com., others), Estate Planning, Trust and Probate Law Sect. of State Bar Calif. (chmn. 1980-81,vice chmn. 1979-80, mem. exec. com. 1977-82, advisor 1982-85, chmn. probate com. 1977-78, mem. legislation com. 1977-80, sect. liaison to Calif. Law Revision Commn. 1982-88), Internat. Acad. Estate and Trust Law, Harvard Alumni Assn. (dir. 1975-77, v.p. 1979-82), Harvard Club So. Calif. (pres. 1970-72). Republican. Methodist. Office: Irell & Manella LLP 1800 Ave Of Stars Ste 900 Los Angeles CA 90067-4276

COLLIER, CURTIS LYNN, lawyer; b. Marianna, Ark., Oct. 4, 1949; s. Lenzora and Lucille (Edwards) C.; m. Cheryl Elaine Hollingshed, July 17, 1975; children: Galen, Cayanna, Christian. BS, Tenn. State U., 1971; JD, Duke U., 1974. Bar: Ark., Tenn., U.S. Dist. Ct. (ea. dist.) Tenn. 1995. Asst. U.S. atty. for ea. dist. La., Dept. Justice, New Orleans, 1979-87; supervisory asst. U.S. atty. for ea. dist. Tenn. Dept. Justice, Chattanooga, 1987-95; U.S. dist. judge U.S. Dist. Ct., Chattanooga, 1995—; dir. A.I.M. Ctr., Chattanooga, 1988-93. Bd. dirs. Girl Scouts U.S.A., Chattanooga, 1990—. Capt. JAGC, USAF, 1974-79. Mem. Chattanooga Bar Assn. (com. mem. 1988—), Tenn. State U. Alumni Assn. (treas. 1990—), Omega Psi Phi (parliamentarian 1988-90). Baptist. Avocations: reading, jogging, kiting, stereo. Office: US District Court PO Box 831 Chattanooga TN 37401-0831

COLLIER, DIANA GORDON, publishing executive; b. Ottawa, Ont., Can., June 15, 1945; came to U.S., 1984; d. Edward Cecil and Vera (Lowrie) C.; m. Y. Naim, Apr. 17, 1982; 1 child, Sundiata. BA, U. B.C., 1963; MA, U. Montreal, 1975. Writer, 1972-83; editor Black Rose Books, Montreal, Que., Can., 1973-75; bus. mgr. Studies Polit. Economy, Ottawa, Ont., Can., 1980-82; pub. Clarity Press, Inc., Atlanta, 1984—; dir. communications, editor newsletter Internat. Human Rights Assn. of Am. Minorities, Chgo., 1988—. Author: Invisible Women of Washington, 1989 (Best of U.S. Small Press 1989), Minnesota Review, 1988; editor: Restructuring of America, 1991, Israeli Peace-Palestinean Justice, 1994, A Popular Guide to Minority Rights, 1995, American Indians: Stereotypes and Realities, 1996, Societal Development and Minority Rights, 1997, A Land to Die For, 1998, The Legacy of Ibo Landing: Gullah Roots of African American Culture, 1999, The Piracy of America: Profiteering in the Public Domain, 1999, Discovering America As It Is, 1999. Pub. grantee European Human Rights Found., Brussels, 1992; Can. Coun. grantee, Ottawa, 1975, 77; Bell Can. fellow, Montreal, 1973, 74. Mem. NAACP, ACLU, Soc. Scholarly Pub., Pub. Mktg. Assn. Office: Clarity Press Inc 3277 Roswell Rd NE Ste 469 Atlanta GA 30305-1854

COLLIER, DUAINE ALDEN, manufacturing and distribution company executive; b. Chambersburg, Pa., Aug. 19, 1950; s. Clyde Alden and Etta Jean (Browell) C.; m. Trudy Jean Shoap, Aug. 22, 1970; children: Patrick, Crystal. BS in Math., Shippensburg U., 1972. Product specialist ITT Domestic Pump, Shippensburg, 1972-77; pres., CEO College Town, Inc., Shippensburg, 1971—; gen. mgr. Shippensburg Pump Co., Inc., 1985—; bd. dirs., sec.-treas. Beidel Printing House, Inc., Shippensburg, 1975—, White Mane Pub. Co., Inc., Shippensburg, 1987—. Committeeman Franklin County Rep. Party, 1989-92; pres. Shippensburg Area Devel. Corp., 1983-84, bd. dirs., 1982-84; bd. dirs. Shippensburg Midget Football Assn., Inc., coach, 1984-94, head coach, 1991-94; pres. Maroon & Grey Football Club, 1991-94; bd. dirs. Shippensburg U. Found., 1995—; bd. dirs., pres. Shippen Place, Inc., 1996-99; mem. adv. bd. Orrstown Bank, 1998—; v.p. Main St. Non-profit Redevel. Corp. Mem. The Wednesday Club, Masons (master Orrstown lodge 1979), Shippensburg Lions Club (pres. 1989-90), Sons of the Am. Legion. Methodist. Avocations: hunting, fishing, skiing, photography, painting. Office: College Town Inc PO Box 337 17 W Burd St Shippensburg PA 17257-1223

COLLIER, EVELYN MYRTLE, elementary school educator; b. Newton, Ala., Dec. 11, 1942; d. Palmer Lee and Jessie Beryl (Williams) C. BA, Samford U., 1965; M Religious Edn., Southwestern Sem., 1967; MS, Troy State U., 1977. Youth dir. Calvary Bapt. Temple, Savannah, Ga., 1967-69; tchr. Newton Elem. Sch., 1969-77, prin., 1977-94; asst. prof. elem. edn. Fla. Bapt. Theol. Coll., Graceville, Fla., 1994—. Mem. ASCD, Ala. Assn. Elem. Sch. Prins. (exec. bd. 1984-94, sec. 1985, dist. IX pres. 1983, dist. IX Disting. Prin. award 1986, 89, 92), Ala. Coun. Sch. Adminstrs. and Suprs. (bd. dirs. 1991-94), Nat. Assn. Elem. Sch. Prins., Delta Kappa Gamma (Alpha Kappa chpt., Beta state exec. bd. 1987-96, pres. Ala. chpt. 1991-93, 1st v.p. 1989-91, 2d v.p. 1987-89, Golden Gift Fund award 1983, Internat. scholar 1996), Phi Delta Kappa, Kappa Delta Pi. Baptist. Avocations: singing, reading, swimming. Office: Fla Bapt Theol Coll 5400 College Dr Graceville FL 32440-1831

COLLIER, HERMAN EDWARD, JR., retired college president; b. St. Louis, Aug. 8, 1927; s. Herman E. and Evelyn (Savill) C.; m. Jerline L. Weston, Mar. 25, 1948; children: Herman Edward III, Michael F., Thomas W. B.S., Randolph-Macon Coll., 1950, Sc.D., 1977; M.S., Lehigh U., 1952, Ph.D., 1955, LL.D., 1971; Litt.D., Coll. of Charleston, 1976; LHD, Muhlenberg Coll., 1986, Moravian Coll., 1987. Chmn. dept. chemistry Moravian Coll., 1955-57; research chemist E. I. duPont de Nemours Co., Wilmington, Del., 1957-63; prof. chemistry, chmn. div. natural scis. Moravian Coll., 1963-69, pres., 1969-86; pres., dir. I&I Planning Assocs., 1987—; interim pres. Salem Acad. and Coll., 1991, N.C., Wesleyan Coll., 1994-95, Chowan Coll., 1995-96, Lees-McRae Coll., 1997-98; sr. cons. Acad. Search Consultation Svc., 1998—; bd. dirs. Horizon Health Sys. Inc.; cons. sci. adv. bd. EPA, 1979-85; chmn. Commn. Ind. Colls. and Univs. Pa.; bd. dirs. Bethlehem Steel Corp., 1987-95. Mem. Com. to Employ the Handicapped, 1970-75; mem. Northampton County Citizens for Regional Progress; bd. dirs. United Fund Bethlehem, Hist. Bethlhem, Inc., Moravian Music Found., 1992-94, Roanoke Island Hist. Assn., Inc., 1996—; trustee St. Luke's Hosp., R.K. Laros Found., Moravian Acad., Salem Acad. & Coll., 1995—. With USN, 1945-46. Mem. Lehigh Valley Assn. Ind. Colls. (dir.), Am. Chem. Soc., AAUP, Lehigh Valley Automobile Assn. (dir. 1981-86), Bethlehem C. of C. (dir.), Phi Beta Kappa, Sigma Xi, Omicron Delta Kappa, Kappa Alpha. Club: Saucon Valley Country (dir.), Duckwoods Country Club. Patentee mfg. tech. and product quality organo-lead compounds; sodium tetraphenyl boron for potassium detection; periodic table for lecture room, 1953; flame spectra Metallic ions from the H-F Flame, 1957.

COLLIER, JAMES WARREN, lawyer; b. Dallas, July 31, 1940; s. J.W. and Mary Gertrude (Roberts) C.; m. Judith Lane, Dec. 27, 1964; children: Anne Elizabeth, Jennifer Susan. BA, U. Mich., 1962, JD, 1965. Bar: N.Y. 1966, Mich. 1968. Assoc. Simpson Thacher & Bartlett, N.Y.C., 1965-66; tax atty. office gen. counsel Ford Motor Co., 1966-67; assoc. Dykema Gossett, Detroit, 1967-73, ptnr., 1973—; mem. Dykema Gossett. Contbr. articles to profl. jours. Mem. ABA, Mich. Bar Assn., Detroit Bar Assn., Econ. Club Detroit, Lochmoor Club. Office: Dykema Gossett 400 Renaissance Ctr Ste 3800 Detroit MI 48243-1603

COLLIER, KEN O., editor; b. Mpls., Oct. 7, 1952. BA, Carleton Coll., 1976; MSc, UCLA, Santa Barbara, 1978. Instr. geology Carleton Coll., Northfield, Minn., 1980; owner Custom Furniture, Mpls., 1980-87; assoc. editor The Family Handyman Mag., Mpls., 1987-91; exec. editor Custom Furniture, Mpls., 1995—; sr. editor New Bus. Devel., Mpls., 1991-95; chief editor Am. Woodworker Mag./Home Svc. Publ., Eagan, Minn., 1999—. Office: Home Svcs Publ 2915 Commers Dr Ste 700 Eagan MN 55121-2398

COLLIER, LACEY ALEXANDER, federal judge; b. Demopolis, Ala., June 23, 1935; s. James Porter and Virginia Slade (Lacey) C.; m. Beverly Anne Brady, Sept. 1, 1956; children: Lorrie Collier Berry, Teri Collier Siebert, Frank. Student. U. Ala., 1953-55; BA in Govt. and Internat. Rels., U.S. Naval Postgrad. Sch., 1970; MA in Polit. Sci., U. West Fla., 1972, BA in Acctg., 1975; JD with honors, Fla. State Sch. Law, 1977. Bar: Fla. 1978, U.S. Dist. Ct. (no. dist.) Fla. 1978, U.S. CT. Appeals (5th cir.) 1978, U.S. Ct. Appeals (11th cir.) 1981. Commd. USN, 1955, advanced through grades to lt. comdr., ret., 1975; asst. state atty. Office of State Atty. 1st. Jud. Cir. of Fla., 1977-84; cir. judge 1st Jud. Cir., 1984-91; U.S. dist. judge U.S. Dist. Ct. (no. dist.) Fla., 1991—; adj. prof. polit. sci. U. West Fla., 1973; adv. grand juries 1st Jud. Cir., 1978-84; lectr. La. Judges Conf., 1986, Robert A. Taft Inst. Govt., 1989—; faculty Fla. New Judges' Coll., 1989-92. Pres. St. Paul's Cath. Ch. Men's Club, 1972; chmn. leadership in action program Pensacola Jaycees, 1971-72; divsn. leader CFC/United Way, 1973; mem. public safety task force Action '76, 1974; vice chmn. Escambia County charter com., 1978-79; bd. dirs. Fla. State Law Sch. Alumni Assn., 1980-81; pres. city-county Drug Abuse Commn., 1982-83; chmn. City Pensacola Revenue Study Com., 1985-86; official adv. Escambia Govtl. Study Commn., 1986-87; mem. Presdl. Search Com. U. W. Fla., 1987; chmn. Edn. Conf. subcom. Fla. Conf. Crct. Judges, 1987-89; trustee, pres.U. W. Fla. Found., 1988—; mem. adv. bd. students in free enterprise U. W. Fla., 1989—; trustee Pensacola Little Theater/Cultural Ctr., 1989—; lectr., mem. adv. bd., chmn. Nativity Cath. Ch., 1990—; chmn. Pensacola com. Nat. Mus. Naval Aviation Found., 1990—; bd. dirs. Big Brother/Big Sister of NW Fla., sec., 1990-92; mem. adv. bd. African-Am. Heritage Soc., 1990—; mem. adv. bd. Sacred Heart Hosp., 1991—. Recipient 11 air medals; named Disting. Alumni U. W. Fla., 1988, Pensacola BIP Profl. Leader of Yr., 1989. Mem. ABA, Fla. Bar (standard jury instrns. com. civil 1989—), Okalossa-Walton Bar Assn., Escambia-Santa Rosa Bar Assn., Am. Inns of Court (exec. bd. Pensacola chpt., founding mem.), Assn. Naval Aviation, Gulf Coast Econs. Club (v.p. 1990-92, pres. 1993—), Fla. State Law Sch. Alumni Assn. (bd. dirs. 1981-81), Fla. Conf. Cir. Judges, C. of C. (chmn. Com. 100 1987-89, task force on port/airport devel., chmn. bldg. and sites task force 1989—). Office: US Courthouse 100 N Palafox St Pensacola FL 32501-4839*

COLLIER, RICHARD BANGS, philosopher, foundation executive; b. Hastings, Nebr., Aug. 12, 1918; s. Nelson Martin and Stella (Butler) C. BA, U. Wash., 1951. Fgn. aid officer GS14, air traffic control supr. gen. & airway comms. engr., civil aviation Am. embassy, Bangkok, Thailand, 1958-63; founder, dir. Pleneurethics Society, Tacoma, 1985—; founder Inst. Ethics & Sci., Tacoma, 1988—, Pleneurethics Inst., 1995—. Carnegie fellow Inst. Pub. Affairs, Grad. Sch., U. Wash., 1950-51. Nat. adv. bd. Am. Security Council. Capt. USAF, 1965-66. Recipient Rep. Presdl. Legion of merit, Medal of Freedom, Rep. Senatorial, 1964. Mem. Assn. Supervision & Curriculum Devel., Soc. Health & Human Values, Senatorial Trust (U.S. Senatorial Medal of Freedom), Royal Inst. Philosophy (Eng.), Nat. Rep. Senatorial Inner Circle (Presdl. commn.), Rep. Nat. Com. (life, Eisenhower commn., charter mem. chmn.'s. adv. bd.). Author: Pleneurethic, 20 vols., 1964-93, Pleneurethics: A Philosophical System Uniting Body, Brain and Mind, 2d edit. 1990, contrb. to Journal of Pleneurethics. Home: 319 Tacoma Ave N Apt 1607 Tacoma WA 98403-2722

COLLIER, R(OBERT) JOHN, biomedical researcher, academic dean; b. Wichita Falls, Tex., Aug. 6, 1938; s. Eric Knox and Julia (Spearman) C.; m. Joan McCarthy, June 23, 1962; children: Andree, Erin, Brittany. BA in Biology, Rice U., 1959; PhD in Biology, Harvard U., 1964. Postdoctoral fellow Molecular Biology Inst., Geneva, 1964-66; asst. prof. bacteriology UCLA, 1966-70, assoc. prof. bacteriology, 1970-74, prof. microbiology, 1974-84; prof. microbiology and molecular genetics Harvard Med. Sch., Boston, 1984-88, faculty dean for grad. edn., 1988-94, Maude and Lillian Presley prof. microbiology and molecular genetics, 1989—; DuPont lectr. Harvard U., 1981; chmn. Gordon Conf., Microbial Toxins and Pathogenicity, 1982; cons. Cetus Corp., Berkeley, 1989-93, Virus Rsch. Inst., 1992—. Mem. editl. bd. Infection and Immunity, Molecular Microbiology, Microbiol. Revs.; assoc. editor Protein Sci., 1995—. Guggenheim fellow, 1973-74; recipient Eli Lilly award, 1972, co-recipient Pierce Immunotoxin award, 1988, Paul Ehrlich prize, 1990. Mem. NAS, Am. Acad. Arts and Scis., Am. Field Svcs. (treas. local chpt. 1986-90), Norwegian Acad. Scis. and Letters, Phi Beta Kappa. Office: Harvard Med Sch Dept Microbiol/Molec Genet 200 Longwood Ave Boston MA 02115-5701

COLLIER, ROBERT STEVEN, broadcast technician; b. Louisville, Nov. 13, 1952; s. James Wesley and Mildred Louise C.; m. Sharon Lee Smith, Nov. 1, 1989; children: David, Stephanie. B Music Edn., Pikeville Coll., 1980. Disc jockey Stas. WPKE-AM/WDHR-FM, Pikeville, Ky., 1976-80; news dir. Sta. WPRT-AM-FM, Prestonsburg, Ky., 1980-82; police beat reporter Sta. WLEX-TV, Lexington, Ky., 1982-90; videographer, field prodr. WLEX-TV Ky. Sunrise Lives, Lexington, 1990—; stage mgr. Peach Orchard Players, Pikeville, 1976-81; videographer, cons. Rudibaguh Pix, Lexington, 1983—; pub. affairs chief, master sgt. 133d Mobile Pub. Affairs Detachment, Ky. ARNG, Frankfort, 1984—; command in formation non-commn. officer-in-charge Task Force Eagle, Operation Joint Forge, 1999; broadcast supr. VII Corps Pub. Affairs Office Operation Desert Shield/Storm, 1990-91; producer, videographer Ky. Ptnrs. Am., Quito Ecuador, 1987. Writer, producer radio commentary: Victims in the News, 1981 (Best Entry award 1982); producer, videographer TV shows: La Iquala MEDRETE, 1986, Ambassadors in Camo, 1989 (1st place award U.S. Army), Thought for Food, 1989 (2d place Keith L. Ware award Dept. Army 1990); writer, producer, videographer TV short: Coal Mining: What's It Like, 1982 (1st pl. Cochran award); writer, videographer TV short: Coal Mining Weather, 1983; writer, producer, videographer, editor TV shorts Operation Desert Heart:

VII Corps Civil Affairs, 1991 (1st place award U.S. Army 1991), Neijmegen March (1st place award U.S. Army 1994), N.G. Spl. Forces in Haiti (2d place Keith L. Ware award Dept. Army 1995); producer, mixer, contbr. radio news program Desert Dispatches (1st place Keith L. Ware award Dept. Army 1991), Three TV Stories: Nat. Guard in Panama, 1996, Memorial Day: A Photo Essay Videography (2d pl. Keith L. Ware award Dept. Army 1995). Master sgt. Ky. Army NG. Recipient spl. svc. award U.S. Weather Svc., 1982, Meritorious Svc. medal for contbns. to U.S. Army Pub. Affairs, 1995; named Ky. Col., Commonwealth of Ky., 1982, 88, N.G. Broadcaster of Yr., 1994. Mem. VFW, NRA (instrs. award 1980), Am. Legion. Avocations: reading, running, travel, family.

COLLIER, ROGER MALCOLM, minister; b. Richmond, Va., Nov. 10, 1950; s. Edward Malcolm and Vallie Pauline (Cuthbertson) C.; m. Sarah Catherine Carter, Apr. 5, 1980; children: Leigh Anne, Paula Kay, Edward Malcolm II. BA, U. Richmond, 1972; postgrad., Yale U. Div. Sch., 1972-73; MDiv, Southeastern Bapt. Theol. Sem., 1976; D of Ministry, Union Theol. Sem., Richmond, 1984; postgrad., Waldensian Sem., Rome, 1995. Ordained to ministry So. Bapt. Conv., 1975. Min. Hunton Bapt. Ch., Glen Allen, Va., 1975-85, West End Bapt. Ch., Suffolk, Va., 1985-86, Glen Allen Bapt. Ch., 1986—. Trustee Cmty. Rels. Referral Bd. Henrico County, Richmond, 1989-95; pres. Glen Allen Elem. Sch. PTA, 1990-91; bd. dirs. Virginians for Integrity in Govt., 1991—; citizen mem. Va. Bd. Funeral Dirs. Named Outstanding Young Religious Leader, Glen Allen Jaycees. 1981. Mem. Bapt. Gen. Assn. Va. (chmn. Christian Life Com. 1982-85), Laurel Glen Allen Mins.' Conf. (pres. 1976, 84), Kiwanis of North Richmond (bd. dirs. 1994—), PhiBeta Kappa. Home: 2909 Susan Sheppard Ct Glen Allen VA 23060-2035 Office: Glen Allen Bapt Ch PO Box 1245 Glen Allen VA 23060-1245

COLLIER, SAMUEL MELVIN, aerospace engineer; b. Atlanta, Aug. 19, 1941; d. Samuel Roland Collier and Dixie Pauline (Sorrells) Terry; m. Gail Lee Grenfel Simmons, Sept. 22, 1962 (div. 1982); children: Phyliss, Sheri, Suzan, Samuel, Donica, Michele; m. Betty Lou Morris, Feb. 22, 1985. Grad., Officer's Candidate Sch., 1964; BS, U. Tex., 1973; MBA, U. No. Colo., 1977. Enlisted U.S. Army, 1959, advanced through grades to maj., ret., 1979; staff engr. LTV Missiles & Electronics, Grand Prairie, Tex., 1979-85; engrng. project mgr. LTV Aircraft, Dallas, 1985-93, ret., 1993; technology transfer mgr. La. State U., Shreveport, 1996-97; sr. staff engr. Lockheed-Martin, Dallas, 1999—; grants cons. Town of Vivian, 1993-95. Pres. Hist. Soc. North Caddo, Vivian, 1995-99; grants review panelist Shreveport Regional Arts Coun., 1996, 97; mem. Vivian Preservation Commn., 1995-96. Mem. Ret. Officers Assn., Inst. Ops. Rsch. and Mgmt. Sci. Avocations: bass fishing, archery, genealogy; achievements include leading the operations research engineering team in the highly competitive joint tactical missile system production program won by the company; managing research and development programs that defined future military aircraft designs based upon the application of stealth technologies; authoring winning grant applications for small, local non-profit corporations. Home: 1701 N Pine St Vivian LA 71082-9515

COLLIER, SIMON, history educator; b. Harpenden, Eng., June 6, 1938; came to U.S., 1991; s. Daniel Henry and Margery Kate (Winter) C. BA, Cambridge (Eng.) U., 1961, PhD, 1965. Prof. history U. Essex, Colchester, Eng., 1965-91, Vanderbilt U., Nashville, 1991—. Author: Ideas and Politics of Chilean Independence, 1967, From Cortes to Castro, 1974, The Life, Music and Times of Carlos Gardel, 1985; co-editor: Cambridge Encyclopedia of Latin America, 1985, Mining in Chile's Norte Chico, 1998; co-author: Tango, 1995, A History of Chile, 1808-1994, 1996. Mem. Chilean Acad. History (corr. academician), Buenos Aires Lunfardo Acad. (corr. academician), Nat. Acad. of Tango (corr. academician), Chilean Soc. for History and Geography (corr.). Avocations: music, literature. Office: Vanderbilt U PO Box 2 Nashville TN 37202-0002

COLLIER, TOM WARD, musician, educator; b. Puyallup, Wash., June 30, 1948; s. Ward L. and Ethel M. (Turner) C.; m. Cheryl Anne Zilbert, May 31, 1970; children: Cara, Nina. BA, MusB, U. Wash., 1971. Freelance musician Seattle Symphony/Northwest Chamber Orch., 1967-74; drummer, vibraphonist Northwest Jazz Quintet, Seattle, 1972-80; studio musician various artists and shows including Barbra Streisand, Ry Cooder, American Music Awards, Harry O., Los Angeles, 1975-78; timpanist L.A. Repertoire Orch., 1976-77; jazz drummer Howard Roberts Quartet/Bill Smith Trio, Los Angeles, Seattle, 1975-82; freelance percussionist various artists including Johnny Mathis, Paul Williams, Jermaine Jackson, Sammy Davis Jr., Bob Hope, Barbra Streisand, Ry Cooder, Olivia Newton-John, The Beach Boys, Bud Shank, Earl "Fatha" Hines, Diane Schurr, Los Angeles, Seattle, 1976-91; jazz vibraphonist Collier/Dean Duo, Seattle, 1977—; rec. artist, leader band Tom Collier, Seattle, 1987—; faculty, dir. percussion studies U. Wash., Seattle, 1980—, sound prodn. evening degree adv. bd. dirs., 1994—; leader Tom Collier Duo/Trio, Wash. State Arts Commn. Cultural Enrichment Program, 1980-95, Arts in Edn. Program, 1996—; owner Mallet Head Music, 1979—, T.C. Records, 1987—; dir. N.W. Percussion Inst., Seattle, U. Wash. Jazz Inst., 1989—; bd. dirs. South Ctr. Sch. Dist., Seattle, 1987-91. Rec. artist: (records) Whistling Midgest, 1981, Illusion, 1987, Pacific Aire, 1991; author: History of Jazz, Lecture Notes, Overheads and Listening Examples, 1997, (book/records) Jazz Improvisation and Ear Training, 1983, Studio Call simulated Recording Sessions, 1984; composer: Quintet for Percussion Ensemble, 1972, Xenolith for String Quartet, 1973, Piece for Electric Bass, Vibraphone and Orch., 1979, Nina's Joy, Busy Body, Tightwad, Subito Sox, 1991. Mem. arts adv. bd. Fed. Way Sch. Dist., 1992-94. Grantee Rockefeller Research, U. Wash., 1967-71. Mem. ASCAP (Spl. award 1981—), Percussive Arts Soc., Nat. Assn. Jazz Educators (Outstanding Service award 1980), Music Educators Nat. Conf. (faculty advisor, 1986-88), Musicians Union. Office: U Wash Sch Music 353450 Seattle WA 98195

COLLIER, ZENA, author; b. London, Jan. 21, 1926; came to U.S., 1946; d. Benjamin and Rebecca Feldman; m. Louis Shumsky, May 3, 1945 (div. 1967); children—Jeffrey A. (dec.), Paul E.; m. Thomas M. Hampson, Dec. 30, 1969. Tchr. Writers Workshop, Adult Edn., Rochester, N.Y., 1968-78, Writers Workshop, Nazareth Coll., Rochester, N.Y., 1984-94; guest lectr. Chautauqua Inst., 1991. Author: (novels) A Cooler Climate, 1990, Ghost Note, 1992; (children's books) The Year of the Dream (as Jane Collier), 1962; (as Zena Shumsky with Lou Shumsky) First Flight, 1962, Shutterbug, 1963; A Tangled Web (as Jane Collier), 1967; Next Time I'll Know, 1981; Seven for the People, 1979; contbr. short stories in Prairie Schooner, Southwest Rev., Lit. Rev., So. Humanities Rev., McCalls, others; contbr. articles in Pubs. Weekly, Money, Family Circle, L.A. Times Book Rev., others. Bd. dirs. Friends of Rochester Pub. Library, 1967-70, 79-85; mem. community adv. bd. WXXI Pub. TV-AM-FM, 1983-95. Resident fellow MacDowell, Yaddo, Va. Ctr. Creative Arts; writer-in-residence Just Buffalo lit. ctr., 1984, Niagara-Erie Writers, 1986, N.Y. State, So. Tier Libr. System, 1985. Recipient Hoepfner prize, Citation on Honour Roll of Best Am. Short Stories; nomination for Pushcart prize. Mem. Authors Guild, Writers & Books, Poets and Writers Inc. Democrat. Jewish. Address: c/o Harvey Klinger 301 W 53rd St New York NY 10019-5766

COLLIGAN, JOHN C. (BUD COLLIGAN), multimedia company executive; married; 3 children. BS in Internat. Econs., Georgetown U., 1976; MBA, Stanford U., 1983. With Macintosh divsn. Apple Computer Corp., 1983-85, head higher edn. mktg. and sales, 1985-89; pres., CEO Authorware, Inc., 1989-92; chmn. Macromedia, Inc., San Francisco, 1992-98; ptnr. Accel Ptnrs., Palo Alto, Calif., 1998—; bd. dirs. S3 Corp., c/net Inc. Mem. Interactive Multimedia Assn. (bd. dirs.). Office: Accel Ptnrs 428 University Ave Palo Alto CA 94301*

COLLIN, THOMAS JAMES, lawyer; b. Windom, Minn., Jan. 6, 1949; s. Everett Earl and Genevieve May (Wilson) C.; m. Victoria Gatov, Oct. 11, 1985; children: Arielle, Elise, Sarah. BA, U. Minn., 1970; AM, Harvard U., 1972; JD, Georgetown U., 1974. Bar: Ohio 1975, U.S. Dist. Ct. (no. dist.) Ohio 1975, U.S. Ct. Appeals (10th cir.) 1977, U.S. Supreme Ct. 1980, U.S. Ct. Appeals (6th cir.) 1981, U.S. Ct. Appeals (8th cir.) 1982, U.S. Ct. Appeals (7th cir.) 1997. Law clk. to Judge Myron Bright U.S. Ct. Appeals, 8th Cir., St. Louis, Mo., 1974-75; assoc. Thompson, Hine & Flory, LLP, Cleve., 1975-82, ptnr., 1982—. Author: Ohio Business Competition Law, 1994, (with others) Criminal Antitrust Litigation Manual, 1983; editor: Punitive Damages and Business Torts: A Practitioner's Handbook, 1998; contbr. articles to profl. jours. Active Citizens League, Cleve., 1987—, bd. trustees, 1994—, v.p., 1995-97, pres. 1997—. Mem. ABA (chair bus. torts and unfair competition com., antitrust sect. 1995-98), Ohio State Bar Assn. (bd. govs. antitrust sect. 1988-98). Republican. Avocations: book collecting, music. Home: 7879 Oakhurst Dr Cleveland OH 44141-1123 Office: Thompson Hine & Flory LLP 127 Public Sq Cleveland OH 44114-1216

COLLINA, KATHLEEN ALICE, corrugated box company executive; b. N.Y.C., Oct. 24, 1938; d. Louis Orville and Evelyn Dorothy (Cosgrove) Seawood; m. Nido Edward Collina, Sept. 14, 1957; children: Susan B. Collina Schulte, Gary E., Jill A. Collina Labar, Douglas J., Steven J. Grad. high sch., Easton, Pa. Svc. rep. Bell Telephone Co. of Pa., Easton, 1956-59, Stanley Home Products, Westfield, Mass., 1962-78; exec. asst. MA 500, Inc., Nazareth, Pa., 1973-86, Century Packaging Inc., Whitehall, Pa., 1987—. Capt. leadership team capital campaign Notre Dame High Sch., Easton, 1991-92. Mem. Ladies Ancient Order of Hibernians (pres. 1993-96, treas. 97—, Anna Malia Ruddy award 1997). Home: 3825 Church Rd Easton PA 18045-2909 Office: Century Packaging Inc 5217 Kemmerer St Whitehall PA 18052-1848

COLLING, KENNETH FRANK, hospital administrator; b. Watertown, N.Y., Apr. 17, 1945. BA, Cornell U., 1967, M Hosp. Adminstrn., 1969. Adminstrv. res. New Britain (Conn.) Gen. Hosp., 1968; asst. prof. Baylor Army program Healthcare Adminstrn., San Antonio, 1971-73; asst. adminstr. Kaiser Found. Hosp., Fontana, Calif., 1973-75, assoc. adminstr., 1979-81; asst. adminstr. Kaiser Found. Hosp., Panorama City, Calif., 1975-79; adminstr. Kaiser Found. Hosp., San Diego, 1981—, sr. v.p., area mgr. Contbr. articles to profl. jours. Mem. Calif. Hosp. Assn. (exec. com., trustee). Home: 3024 Cadencia St Carlsbad CA 92009-8307 Office: Kaiser Found Hosp 4647 Zion Ave San Diego CA 92120-2507*

COLLINGE, WILLIAM JOSEPH, humanities educator; b. Erie, Pa., July 14, 1947; s. William Klumb and Rita Anne (Magner) C.; m. Susan Ruth Harris, June 16, 1972; children: William O., Matthew J., Daniel P. AB, Georgetown U., 1969; MPhil, Yale U., 1971, PhD, 1974. Asst. prof. philosophy Loyola Marymount U., L.A., 1974-80; assoc. prof. theology Mt. St. Mary's Coll., Emmitsburg, Md., 1980-89; prof. theology and philosophy Mt. St. Mary's Coll., Emmitsburg, 1989—, Forker prof. of Cath. soc. tchg., 1997—. Author: Historical Dictionary of Catholicism, 1997; co-author: St. Augustine: Four Anti-Pelagian Writings, 1992; contbr. articles to profl. jours. Bd. dirs. Interfaith Ctr. Peace & Justice, Gettysburg, Pa., 1989—, pres. 1993-95. Mem. Am. Acad. Religion, Am. Philos. Assn., Coll. Theology Soc. (bd. dirs. 1989-92), Cath. Theol. Soc. Am., Theta Alpha Kappa (sec. 1991—). Democrat. Roman Catholic. Office: Mt St Mary's Coll 16300 Old Emmitsburg Rd Emmitsburg MD 21727-7700

COLLINGS, MICHAEL ROBERT, poet, educator; b. Rupert, Idaho, Oct. 29, 1947. Grad. with highest honors, Bakersfield Coll., 1967, Whittier Coll., 1969; PhD in English, U. Calif., Riverside, 1977. Instr. English UCLA, 1978-79; prof. English Pepperdine U., 1979—; mem. awards selection com. Internat. Assn. for Fantastic in Arts, 1986; judge Dialogue poetry contest, 1986; participant, panelist L.A. Sci.-Fantasy Soc., Pasadena, 1989; panelist, workshop dir., poetry guest Life, the Universe, and Everything: Brigham Young U. Symposium on Sci. Fiction and Fantasy, Provo, 1987-97; poetry workshop instr. Borders Books and Music, Thousand Oaks, Calif., 1996—; judge Calif. State Poetry Soc., 1983-98; lit. judge Artasia '97, '98, '99, Thousand Oaks, 1997-99; poet guest of honor Brigham Young U., 1992-95; scholar guest of honor Mythopoeic Soc., Clark Kerr campus U. Calif., Berkeley, 1995; poet-in-residence Seaver Coll., Pepperdine U., 1997—; lectr. in field. Editor: The Lamp Post, 1981-83, Thaumaturge newsletter, 1982-85; poetry editor: Dialogue: A Jour. of Modern Thought, 1984-88; co-editor: Retooling for the Renaissance in the 3d Millenium: Earthwords III, 1995; guest editor: Ygdrasil jour., 1996, consulting editor, 1999—; assoc. editor: Catharsis...: The Healing Effect of Therapeutic Poetry, 1997—; reviewer numerous publs. including Owlflight, 1981-83, Sci. Fiction and Fantasy Book Rev., 1981-83, Mystery Scene, 1987-91, N.Y. Rev. Sci. Fiction, 1995—; contbr. to numerous scholarly studies and vols. of poetry, also poetry and fiction chapbooks. Chorus accompanist Glenwood Elem. Sch., 1988; merit badge councilor Boy Scouts Am., 1985-95; organist, choir dir., music dir., tchr. Ch. of Jesus Christ of Latter-day Saints, others, 1960—. Recipient numerous poetry awards including Bay Area Poets Coalition, 1981, Mid-south Poetry Festival, 1983, Triton Coll. Salute to Arts Competition, 1991, 92, 93, 95, 1st pl. award Poet Mag. Ima Willism Inspirational Poetry Competition, 1992, 1st pl. award Phantom Press Poetry Contest, 1995; NDEA fellow U. Calif.-Riverside, 1971-73. E-mail: mcollings@pepperdine.edu. Office: Pepperdine U Humanities/Tchr Edn Divsn Malibu CA 90263

COLLINGS, ROBERT BIDDLECOMBE, judge; b. Aug. 31, 1942; s. Harry Biddlecombe and Juanita Beatrice (Huber) C.; m. Mary Clare Flintoft, Sept. 14, 1968; children: John Richard Biddlecombe, Christopher James More, Clare Yung Hee. AB, Hamilton Coll., 1964; JD, Harvard U., 1967. Bar: Mass. 1968, N.H. 1970, U.S. Ct. Mil. Appeals 1970, U.S. Dist. Ct. Mass. 1971, U.S. Ct. Appeals (1st cir.) 1971, U.S. Ct. Appeals (5th cir.) 1979, Temporary Emergency Ct. Appeals 1980. Asst. U.S. atty. Dept. Justice, Boston, 1971-82, chief criminal divsn., 1976-82, 1st asst. U.S. atty., 1978-81; U.S. magistrate judge U.S. Dist. Ct., Boston, 1982-99, chief magistrate judge, 1999—; lectr. law Harvard Law Sch., 1988-92, Northeastern U. Sch. Law, 1989-90; mem. Magistrate Judge Ednl. Com. of Fed. Judicial Ctr., 1990-96, Def. Svcs. Com. Judicial Conf. U.S., 1991-97; mem. joint adv. group Adminstrv. Office of U.S. Cts., 1998—. Co-editor: Federal Court Civil Litigation in the First Circuit, 1994. Lt. USNR, 1967-71. Mem. ABA (chair magistrate judges' com. nat. conf. fed. trial judges 1999—), Nat. Coun. U.S. Magistrates (treas. 1990-91), Fed. Magistrate Judges Assn. (2d v.p. 1991-92, 1st v.p. 1992-93, pres.-elect 1993-94, pres. 1994-95, past pres. 1995-96, legis. chmn. 1995—, Founders award 1998), N.H. Bar Assn., Mass. Bar Assn., Boston Bar Assn. Home: 155 Haverhill St North Reading MA 01864-2426 Office: US Courthouse 1 Courthouse Way Boston MA 02210

COLLINGS, ROBERT L., lawyer; b. May 22, 1950. AB, Harvard U., 1972; JD, Boston Coll., 1977. Bar: Pa. 1977, U.S. Ct. Appeals (3d and D.C. cirs.), U.S. Dist. Ct. (ea. and mid. dists.) Pa. Atty. U.S. EPA, 1977-84, sect. chief, 1979-81, br. chief, 1981-84; ptnr., co-chair environ. practice group Schnader, Harrison, Segal & Lewis LLP, Phila. Editor: Environmental Spill Reporting Handbook; contbr. Municipal Solicitors Handbook, 1994, Brownfields: A Comprehensive Guide, 1997. Mem. Phila. Bar Assn. (chair environ. law com. 1986), Pa. Bar Assn. (nominating com. environ. mineral and natural resources law sect. 1992), Water Resources Assn. (sec. exec. com. 1990—), Am. Soc. Testing and Materials. Office: Schnader Harrison Segal & Lewis LLP 1600 Market St Ste 3600 Philadelphia PA 19103

COLLINGWOOD, TRACY LYNN, academic advisor, career counselor; b. Jamestown, N.Y., Aug. 9, 1964; d. Edward William and Kay Collingwood. AA Social Scis., Jamestown C.C., 1992; BA in Psychology, SUNY, Fredonia, 1994; EdM in Coll. Student Svcs. and Devel., SUNY, Buffalo, 1997. Motor rte. mgr. Post Jour., Inc., Jamestown, 1987-92; cmty. living skills instr. The Resource Ctr., Jamestown, 1994—; commuter svcs. coord. SUNY, Buffalo, 1995-96, peer edn. supr., 1996-97; acad. affairs advisor SUNY, Fredonia, 1997; mem. faculty, counselor Jamestown (N.Y.) C.C., 1997—; career counselor SUNY, Fredonia, 1998—; Internet steering com. SUNY, Buffalo, 1995-96, career counselor, 1996; tchg. asst. SUNY, Fredonia, 1994; mem. SUNY Career Devel. Orgn. Vol. Rosa Parks Scholarship Program, Fredonia, 1997, The Resource Ctr., 1994—. Seager Presdl. scholar SUNY, Fredonia, 1992-94, Crecraft Olsen scholar, 1993-94. Mem. Nat. Assn. Student Pers. Adminstrs., Am. Coll. Pers. Assn., Coll. Student Pers. Assn., Nat. Acad. Advising Assn., Psi Chi, Phi Theta Kappa. Avocations: singing, songwriting, guitar. Office: SUNY at Fredonia Central Ave Fredonia NY 14063 also Office: Jamestown CC Counseling & Career Devel 10807 Bennett Rd Dunkirk NY 14048-3507

COLLINS, ALLAN MEAKIN, cognitive scientist, psychologist, educator; b. Orange, N.J., Aug. 7, 1937; s. Clinton and Sarah Amy (Meakin) C.; m. Anne Marjorie Linstead, Aug. 24, 1963; children: Antony, Elizabeth. MA in Communication Scis., U. Michigan, 1962, PhD in Psychology, 1970. Sr. scientist Bolt, Beranek & Newman Inc., Cambridge, 1967-82, prin. scientist, 1982—; prof edn. and social policy Northwestern U., Evanston, Ill., 1989-98; co-dir. Ctr. for Tech. in Edn., Bank St. Coll. of Edn., N.Y.C., 1991-94; rsch. prof. of edn. Boston Coll., 1998—; lectr. various colls. and univs. Editor: Representation and Understanding, 1975, Cognitive Science, 1976-80, Readings in Cognitive Science, 1988; author: The Cognitive Structure of Emotions, 1988. Guggenheim fellow, 1974, Sloan fellow, 1980. Mem. AAAS, Nat. Acad. Edn., Cognitive Sci. Soc. (chmn. 1979-80, goving. bd. 1979-87), Am. Assn. for Artificial Intelligence (fellow 1990), Am. Ednl. Rsch. Assn. Achievements include launched research on human semantic memory (with R. Quillian); development of first intelligent tutoring system (with J.R. Carbonell); development of cognitive apprenticeship (with J.S. Brown). Home: 135 Cedar St Lexington MA 02421-6516 Office: School of Education Boston College Chestnut Hill MA 02467

COLLINS, ALLEN HOWARD, psychiatrist; b. Washington, Sept. 6, 1942; s. Murray and Bertha (Baccalman) C.; m. Stephanie Evelyn Awn, May 22, 1976; children: Sasha Marie, Matthew Allen, Alyssa Beth. AB, Columbia Coll., 1964; MD, Tufts U., 1968; MPH, Columbia U., 1974. Diplomate Am. Bd. of Psychiatry and Neurology; Nat. Bd. of Med. Examiners; cert. psychoanalysis. Mental health career develop. fellow NIMH, Rockville, Md., 1968-74; staff psychiatrist Region II NIMH, N.Y.C., 1972-74, psychiat. cons., 1974-90; chief psychiat. consultation liaison svcs. Lenox Hill Hosp., N.Y.C., 1974-76, chief psychiat. inpatient svc., 1976-78, chief of psychiatry svc., 1978-86, dir. dept. of psychiatry, 1986—; examiner in psychiatry Am. Bd. of Psychiatry and Neurology, Evanston, Ill., 1979—, chief proctor, 1991—; clin. prof. of psychiatry N.Y. Med. Coll., Valhalla, 1988-90; tng. and supervisory psychoanalyst divsn. of psychoanalytic tng., 1986-90; assoc. clin. prof. psychiatry Cornell U. Med. Coll., 1990-93; clin. prof. psychiatry NYU Med. Ctr., 1993—. Author: (with others) Provider's Guide To Hospital-Based Services, 1986; contbr. articles to profl. jours. Pres. med. bd. Lenox Hill Hosp., 1994-96. With USPHS, 1968-74. Fellow Am. Psychiatr. Assn., Am. Acad. of Psychoanalysis, N.Y. Acad. Medicine. Avocations: tennis, golf, reading biographies, history.

COLLINS, ALMA JONES, English educator, writer; b. New London, Conn., June 14, 1921; d. Walter Melville Jones and Anne Teresa Harrington; m. Daniel Francis Collins, Apr. 9, 1994. BA, Conn. Coll., 1943; MA, Trinity Coll., 1952, U. Conn., 1962. Tchr., counselor W. Hartford (Conn.) Bd. Edn., 1947-72; pres. Arts Universal Rsch. Assocs., Inc., 1978—. Contbr. articles to profl. jours. Mem. Phi Beta Kappa, Delta Kappa Gamma. Avocations: writing poetry and fiction, working with artists and galleries. Home: 275 Steele Rd A318 West Hartford CT 06117

COLLINS, AMY AMANDA, research assistant; b. Trenton, N.J., July 2, 1964; d. Lawrence Edward and Janet Swan (Tom) C. AB magna cum laude with honors in psych., Hamilton Coll., 1986. Rsch. asst. 1 psychology dept. Princeton (N.J.) U., 1987-89, rsch. asst. 2 psychology dept., 1989-92, sr. rsch. asst. psychology dept., 1992—; cons. Sensor Electronics, Mt. Laurel, N.J., 1988-90; co-organizer conf. Tactile Rsch. Group, Washington, 1993, Phila., 1997. Author: (book chpt.) Psychology of Touch, 1991; contbr. articles to profl. jours. Mem. pastor nominating com. Lawrence Rd. Presbyn. Ch., Lawrenceville, N.J., 1988, elder, 1991—, advisor youth program, 1987—. Mem. Acoustical Soc. Am. (mem. tech. organizing com. 1991), Sigma Xi (assoc., Cert. of Recognition 1986), Psi Chi. Office: Princeton U Psychology Dept Green Hall Princeton NJ 08544

COLLINS, ANITA MARGUERITE, research geneticist; b. Allentown, Pa., Nov. 8, 1947; d. Edmund III and Virginia (Hunsicker) C. BSc in Zoology, Pa. State U., 1969; MSc in Genetics, Ohio State U., 1972, PhD in Genetics, 1976. Instr. biology Mercyhurst Coll., Erie, Pa., 1975-76; rsch. geneticist Honey Bee Breeding Lab. Agrl. Rsch. Svc., USDA, Baton Rouge, 1976-88; rsch. leader Honey Bee Rsch. Lab. Agrl. Rsch. Svc., USDA, Weslaco, Tex., 1988-95; rsch. geneticist Bee Rsch. Lab. Agrl. Rsch. Svc., USDA, Beltsville, Md., 1995—. Co-author: Bee Genetics & Breeding, 1986; contbr. articles to profl. jours. Mem. Entomol. Soc. Am. (chair sect. C, 1997), Assn. for Women in Sci. (pres. Baton Rouge chpt. 1982), Am. Beekeeping Fedn. (rsch. com. 1990, 92-94), Am. Genetics Assn., Animal Behavior Soc., Internat. Union for Study of Social Insects, Sigma Xi, Soc. for Cryobiology. Office: USDA ARS Bee Rsch Bldg 476 BARC-East Beltsville MD 20705

COLLINS, ANN N., secondary school educator; b. Bronx, Nov. 11, 1967; d. Sean J. and Mary (Conneely) C. BA, CUNY, N.Y.C., 1989; MA, CUNY, Bronx, 1994. Tchr. 7th grade St. Jude's Sch., N.Y.C.; tchr. English N.Y.C. Pub. Schs., Bronx, Yonkers (N.Y.) Pub. Schs.; adj. prof. Lehman Coll., CUNY, Bronx. Home: 344 Central Park Ave B20 Scarsdale NY 10583

COLLINS, AUDREY B., judge; b. 1945. BA, Howard U., 1967; MA, Am. U., 1969; JD, UCLA, 1977. Asst. atty. Legal Aid Found. L.A., 1977-78; with Office L.A. County Dist. Atty., 1978-94, dep. dist. atty., 1978-94, head dep. Torrance br. office, 1987-88, asst. dir. burs. ctrl. ops. and spl. ops., 1988-92, asst. dir. atty., 1992-94; judge. U.S. Dist. Ct. (Ctrl. Dist.) Calif., 1994—; dep. gen. counsel Office Spl. Acad. scholar Howard U.; named Lawyer of Yr., Langston Bar Assn., 1988; honoree Howard U. Alumni Club So. Calif., 1989; recipient Profl. Achievement award UCLA Alumni Assn., 1997. Mem. FBA, Nat. Assn. Women Judges, Nat. Bar Assn. (life), State Bar Calif. (com. bar examiners, chmn. subcom. on moral character 1992-93, co-chmn. 1993-94), Los Angeles County Bar Assn. (exec. com. litigation sect.), Assn. Los Angeles County Dist. Attys. (pres. 1983), Black Women Lawyers Los Angeles County, Women Lawyers L.A. (life), Los Angeles County Bar Assn. Inn of Ct., Order of Coif, Phi Beta Kappa. Office: US Dist Ct Edward R Roybal Fed Bldg 255 E Temple St Ste 680 Los Angeles CA 90012-3334

COLLINS, BARBARA-ROSE, former congresswoman; b. Detroit, Apr. 13, 1939; d. Lamar N. Sr. and Versa (Jones) R.; widowed; children: Cynthia Lynn, Christopher Loren. Student, Wayne State U. Commr. Human Rights Commn., Detroit, 1974-75; Mich. state rep., 1975-81; councilwoman City of Detroit, from 1982; mem. 102nd-103rd Congresses from 13th (now 15th) Mich. dist., 1991-96, ranking minority mem. govt. reform & oversight subcom. on postal svc., mem. transp. & infrastructure com.; regional coord. Nat. Black Caucus of Local Elected Officials, 1984. Chmn. Detroit City Coun. Task Force on Teenage Violence, 1985. Recipient Disting. Cmty. Svc. award Shrines of Black Madonna Pan African Orthodox Christian Ch., 1981, Devoted Svc. award Metro Boy Scouts Am., 1984, Invaluable Svc. award Pershing H.S., Detroit, 1985. *

COLLINS, BERT, insurance executive; b. Austin, Tex., Nov. 9, 1934; s. James Kirk and Marie (Edmondson) C.; m. Carolyn Porter; children: Suane, Carolyn E., Bert E. BS, Huston-Tillotson Coll., 1955; MBA, U. Detroit, 1959; JD, N.C. Cen. U., 1970. Bar: N.C. 1970; CPA, Mich. Chief acct. Sidney A. Sumby Meml. Hosp., Detroit, 1956-61; sr. staff acct. Austin, Washington & Davenport, CPA's, Detroit, 1962-67; adminstrv. asst. N.C. Mut. Life Ins. Co., Durham, 1967-70, asst. v.p., 1970-74, v.p., contr., 1974-82, sr. v.p. adminstrn., 1983-87, exec. v.p., chief oper. officer, 1987-90, pres., chief exec. officer, 1990—; vice chmn., bd. dirs. Mut. Cmty. Savs. Bank, Durham, The Am. Coll. Life Ins. Conf., Wachovia Bank, Pub. Svc. Co. of N.C. Bd. govs. U. N.C.; bd. dirs. Nat. Boys Club Am., 1989—. Mem. ABA, AICPA, Nat. Bar Assn., Nat. Ins. Assn., N.C. Bar Assn., Mich. Assn. CPAs, Rotary, Sigma Pi Phi. Democrat. Mem. Ch. of Christ Scientist. Office: NC Mut Life Ins Co 411 W Chapel Hill St Durham NC 27701-3642

COLLINS, BEVERLY ANN, obstetrical, gynecological nurse practitioner; b. Indpls., Sept. 13, 1942; d. Spaulding and Mary Louise (Roberts) Mills.; m. Clarence Scott, May 7, 1967 (div. 1973); children: Carron M. Scott, Clarence J. Scott, Jr.; m. Albert Burrell, Jan. 1975 (div. 1979); m. Allen Collins, May 2, 1993; stepchildren: Cetra Collins, Angela Collins. RN diploma, Glendale Sch. of Nursing, 1964. RN, Calif.; cert. ob/gyn. nurse. Asst. head nurse U. So. Calif. Med. Ctr., L.A., 1964-68; pvt. duty nurse Saratoga Nurses Residency, Westwood, Calif., 1968; asst. head nurse St. Luke's Hosp., Pasadena, Calif., 1969-70; staff nurse Calif. State U., L.A., 1970-73, asst. head nurse, 1973-84, ob-gyn. nurse practitioner, 1984-90; ob-gyn. nurse practitioner Kaiser South San Francisco, 1990-93, East Valley Community Health Ctr., West Covina, Calif., 1993—; clin. preceptor ob-gyn. Edn. Programs Assocs., Campbell, Calif., 1985; staff commr. Commn. of Status of Women, 1989-90. Family planning lectr. Summer Program Economically Disadvantaged Youth, City of L.A., 1970-73; rep. calif. State U. Divsn., Svc. Employee Internat. Union, 1985-90; speaker in several legis. coms., Sacramento. Recipient Cert. of Appreciation Planned Parenthood, 1989, Appreciation award Calif. State U. Divsn. SEIU, 1990. Mem. Calif. Coll. Health Nurse Assn., Pacific Coast Coll. Health Assn., Calif. State U. L.A. Com. of Quality Assurance, Nat. Assn. of Nurse Practitioner in Reproductive Health. Democrat. Avocations: stained glass, music, traveling. Home: 10470 N Lynn Cir Apt H Mira Loma CA 91752-1352 Office: East Valley Community Health Ctr 420 S Glendora Ave West Covina CA 91790-3001

COLLINS, CARDISS, former congresswoman; b. St. Louis, Sept. 24, 1931; m. George W. Collins (dec.); 1 child, Kevin. Ed., Northwestern U.; hon. degree, Winston-Salem State U., Spelman Coll., John Marshall Law Sch., Rosary Coll., Forest Inst. Profl. Psychology. Barber Scotia Coll.; mem. 93d-104th Congresses from 7th Ill. Dist., 1973-97; ret., 1997; ranking minority mem. govt. reform & oversight com.; former chair. govt. activity and transp. subcom.; former chair commerce, consumer protection and competition subcom.; former majority whip-at-large; former asst. regional whip; former chair Congl. Black Caucus, sec.; former chair Congl. Black Caucus Found.; former chair Mems. Congress for Peace through Law. Recipient award Roosevelt U., Loyola U. Mem. NAACP, Nat. Coun. Negro Women (v.p.), Chgo. Urban League, Black Women's Agenda, The Chgo. Network, The Links, Dem. Nat. Com., Alpha Kappa Alpha. Democrat. Baptist. Home: 1110 Roundhouse Ln Alexandria VA 22314-5934

COLLINS, CARL RUSSELL, JR., corporate services; b. Williamsport, Pa., Dec. 29, 1926; s. Carl Russell, Sr. and Annis (Kilmer) C.; m. Rita Thomas, Oct. 3, 1959; children—James, Michael, Nancy. Student, Drexel Inst. Tech., 1947-49; B.S. in Indsl. Engring., Pa. State U., 1953. Div. sales mgr. Fla. Power Corp., St. Petersburg, 1961-64, asst. div. mgr., 1964-65, dist. mgr., 1965-67, div. mgr., 1967-79, v.p., 1979-85; v.p. George F. Young Inc., architects and engrs., St. Petersburg, 1986-91. Bd. dirs. United Way, St. Petersburg, 1978, Com. of 100, 1981; v.p. Suncoasters, Inc., St. Petersburg, 1982; mem. adv. bd. Salvation Army, 1964—; active Meth. Ch., pres. Meth. Men, chmn. adminstrv. bd., lay leader, chmn. fin. com. With USN, 1944-46, as lt., 1953-56. Mem. Pa. State U. Alumni Club (life), Tau Beta Pi. Republican. Lodge: Kiwanis (pres. 1984). Avocations: photography; fishing; boating. Home: 5937 Tangerine Ave S Saint Petersburg FL 33707-4059 Office: George F Young Inc 299 9th St N Saint Petersburg FL 33701-3126

COLLINS, CAROLYN HERMAN, school media specialist, legislative aide; b. Lenoir, N.C., May 25, 1944; d. William Richard and Madeline Edith (Harris) Herman; m. Walter William Collins, Dec. 30, 1989. BA in English, Old Dominion U., 1968, cert. advanced study in ednl. adminstrn., 1992; MS in LS, Fla. State U., 1977. Cert. secondary prin. and libr., tchr. English, French, profl. librarian. Librarian Southampton County (Va.) Schs., 1973-79, TRADOC Army Library, Fort Monroe, Va., 1980-81; media specialist Portsmouth (Va.) Pub. Schs., 1981—; legis. aide Va. House of Dels., Richmond, 1984-97.; moderator White House Conf. on Libraries, Washington, 1991; state del. Gov's. Conf. on Libraries, Richmond, Va., 1990; York regional dir. Va. Ednl. Media Assn. (VEMA), 1992-94. Del. Virginia Beach City Rep. Conv., 1985-87; mem. Red, White and Blue Club, Virginia Beach, 1987-88; elected rep. Rep. City Com., Virginia Beach, 1987-89; category 1 rehabilitator Va. Wildlife Response. Mem. Va. Ednl. Media Assn. (regional dir. 1992-94), Va. Reading Assn., Va. Assn. Tchrs. of English, Va. Square Dancing Assn., Libr. of Congress Assocs., Nat. Hist. Soc., Old Dominion Alumni Assn. (v.p. English chpt. 1987-89, House Dels. 1993-97), Fla. State U. Alumni Assn., Virginia Beach Shag Club, Alpha Delta Kappa (chpt. pres. 1978-80, dist. sec. 1980-82), Beta Phi Mu, Phi Kappa Phi. Republican. United Methodist. Avocations: square, ballroom and shag dancing, oil painting, traveling, reading, skiing. Home: 4026 B Tanglewood Trl Chesapeake VA 23325-2252

COLLINS, CATHERINE, health administrator, educator; b. Buffalo, N.Y.; d. Herman and Catherine (Lynch) Fisher; m. Clyde Collins, Dec. 31, 1973 (dec. 1995); children: Laura Collins Harris, Clyde, Tim. BS, Buffalo State Coll., 1975; MS in Allied Health Edn., U. Buffalo, 1979, EdD in Ednl. Adminstrn., 1990. RN, N.Y.; cert. pediatric nurse practitioner. Nurse Sisters Hosp., Buffalo, 1963-70; sch. nurse Buffalo Bd. Edn., 1970-71; with Model City, Buffalo, 1971-73; agy. adminstr. Health Systems Agy., Buffalo, 1973-86, Erie County Med. Ctr., Buffalo, 1986-88; mem. faculty Erie C.C., Buffalo, 1988-92; assoc. prof. Empire State Coll., Buffalo, 1992—; cons. health edn., Buffalo, 1980; cons. Ednl. Opportunity Ctr., Buffalo, 1989, Head Start of Buffalo, 1997. Contbr. articles to profl. jours. Mem. HopeVale, Orchard Park, N.Y.,1994-97; mem. N.Y. State Commn. on Correction, Albany, 1975-80; chmn. Jess Nash Health Ctr., 1970-72. Recipient Black Achievers award 1490 Enterprises, 1991, various Cmty. Svc. awards. Mem. Western N.Y. Diabetes Assn., Links of Buffalo (treas. 1991), Jack and Jill of Am. (regional dir. 1993-95). Methodist. Avocations: golf, painting. Office: SUNY Empire State Coll 617 Main St Buffalo NY 14203-1400

COLLINS, CURTIS ALLAN, oceanographer; b. Des Moines, Sept. 16, 1940; s. Ralph Charlie and Noma Lovella (Buckley) C.; m. Judith Ann Petersen, Dec. 22, 1962; children: Nathaniel Christopher and Hillary Victoria. BS, U.S. Mcht. Marine Acad., 1962; MS, Oreg. State U., 1964, PhD, 1967. Instr. Chapman Coll. (Calif.) in Barcelona, Spain, 1964; 3d mate on ship Reynolds Metals, Corpus Christi, Tex., 1967-68; research scientist Govt. of Can., Nanaimo, B.C., 1968-70; ocean engr. Cities Svc. Oil, Tulsa, 1970-72; program dir. NSF, Washington, 1972-87, prof., dept. oceanography, Naval Postgrad. Sch., Monterey, 1987—, chmn. 87-94; guest investigator Woods Hole Oceanographic Instn. (Mass.), 1983; commr. Moss Landing Harbor Dist., 1993-94, pres. 1994. vis. prof. U. Calif., Santa Cruz, 1998. Oceanography editor Geophys. Rsch. Letters, 1996-98. Served to capt. USNR. Decorated Nat. Def. medal; recipient Admiral E.S. Land award Dept. Commerce, 1962, Meritorious Service award NSF, 1987, grad. fellow NSF, 1995, Fulbright fellow Instituto Investigaciones Oceanológicas U. Autonomia de Baja, Calif., 1994-95. Mem. Am. Geophys. Union (Oceans Scis. award 1985, pres. ocean scis. sect., 1993-94), Ocean Soc. Japan, Am. Meteorol. Soc. Home: 24010 Ranchito Del Rio Ct Salinas CA 93908-9652 Office: Naval Postgrad Sch Code Occo-833 Dyer Rd Rm 331 Monterey CA 93943

COLLINS, DANA JON, financial executive; b. Grand Rapids, Mich., July 15, 1956; s. Daniel Hiltz and JoAnne M. (Smee) C. BBA with honors, U. Mich., 1978. CPA, Mich. Staff acct. Ernst & Whinney, Jackson, Mich., 1978-82; mgr. Ernst & Whinney, Jackson, 1982-86; CFO, treas. Fetzer Broadcasting Svc., Inc., Kalamazoo, 1986—, also bd. dirs.; asst. sec., asst. treas. Jacobson Stores Inc., Jackson, Mich., 1997—; exec. v.p., treas., bd. dirs. W.C.A. Holdings, Inc. Mem. AICPA, Mich. Assn. CPAs, Inst. Mgmt. Accts. (treas. 1984-86, exec. v.p. 1989, pres. 1990-91, bd. dirs. local chpt. 1984-92, nat. bd. dirs. 1992—). Republican. Avocations: golf, tennis, sports, square dancing. Home: 7094 Jamaica Ln Portage MI 49002-9400 Office: Jacobson Stores Inc 3333 Sargent Rd Jackson MI 49201-8800

COLLINS, DANIEL FRANCIS, lawyer; b. N.Y.C., Mar. 5, 1942; s. Daniel Joseph and Madeline Elizabeth (Berger) C.; m. Margaret Mary Heyden, Jan. 15, 1966; children: Matthew C., Elizabeth C. BA in History and Polit. Sci., Hofstra U., 1964; JD, Am. U., 1967. Bar: D.C. 1968. Law clk. to E. Barrett Prettyman, U.S. Ct. Appeals, Washington, 1967-68; assoc. Ross, Marsh & Foster, Washington, 1970-74, mem., 1974-78; ptnr. Brackett & Collins, P.C., Washington, 1978-87; v.p. regulatory law, The Coastal Corp., 1987—. Office: Coastal Corp 2000 M St NW Washington DC 20036-3307

COLLINS, DANIEL W., accountant, educator; b. Marshalltown, Iowa, Sept. 1, 1946; s. Donald E. and Lorine R. (Metge) C.; m. Mary L. Packer, June 27, 1970; children—Melissa, Theresa. BBA with honors, U. Iowa, 1968, PhD, 1973. Asst. prof. acctg. Mich. State U., East Lansing, 1973-76, assoc. prof., 1976-77; vis. assoc. prof. U. Iowa, Iowa City, 1977-78, assoc. prof., 1978-81, prof., 1981-83, Murray chaired prof. acctg., 1983-88; Henry B. Tippie prof. of acctg. U. Iowa, 1989—; vis. IBM prof. bus. Fuqua Sch. Bus., Duke U., 1988-89, chmn. dept. acctg., 1995—; mem. Fin. Acctg. Stds. Adv. Coun., acad. adv. bd. Deloitte & Touche; mem. Arthur Andersen doctoral dissertation awards com., 1996—; bd. dirs. Ira B. McGladrey Inst., Mercantile Bank, Iowa City, Christian Ret. Svcs., Iowa City. Assoc. editor Acctg. Rev., 1980-86; mem. editl. bd. Jour. Acctg. and Econs., 1978—, Jour. Acctg., Auditing and Fin., 1986—; contbr. articles to profl. jours. 2d lt. U.S. Army, 1972. Recipient All Univ. Tchr. scholar award Mich. State U., 1976, Gilbert Maynard Excellence in Tchg. award U. Iowa, 1985, Collegiate Tchg. award, 1998; Univ. Faculty scholar U. Iowa, 1980-82. Mem. Am. Acctg. Assn. (disting. vis. faculty mem. Doctoral Consortium 1980, 89, dir. Doctoral Consortium 1987, program dir. ann. conv. 1988, dir. publs. 1989-91, exec. com. 1989-91), Acctg. Rschrs. Internat. Avocations: jogging; gardening. Home: 11 Wildberry Ct NE Iowa City IA 52240-9173 Office: U Iowa Coll Bus W252 PBAB Iowa City IA 52242-1000

COLLINS, DAVID BROWNING, religious institution administrator; b. Hot Springs, Ark., Dec. 18, 1922; s. Charles Frederick and Agnes Elizabeth (George) C.; m. Maryon Virginia Moise, Oct. 14, 1945; children: Melissa, Christopher, Matthew, Geoffrey. BA, U. of the South, 1943, BD, 1948, STM, 1962, DD, 1974. Ordained to ministry Episcopal Ch. as deacon, 1948, as priest, 1949. Rector St. Andrew's Episc. Ch., Marianna, Ark., 1948-53; priest-in-charge Holy Cross Episc. Ch., West Memphis, Ark., 1949-53; chaplain and assoc. prof. of religion U. of the South, Sewanee, Tenn., 1953-66; dean Cathedral of St. Philip, Atlanta, 1966-84; exec. dir. Windsong Ministries, Inc., 1984—; pres. House of Deps. Episcopal Ch., 1985-91; trustee Ch. Pension Fund, N.Y.C., 1976-88; mem. Bd. of Clergy Deployment, N.Y.C., 1971-76. Contbr. articles to profl. jours. Pres. Christian Council of Met. Atlanta, 1977-78; chaplain Atlanta Braves Booster Club, 1966-84. Served to lt. (j.g.) USNR, 1943-46. Avocation: baseball. Home and Office: 132 Hearthstone Dr Woodstock GA 30189-5298

COLLINS, DENNIS ARTHUR, foundation executive; b. Yakima, Wash., June 9, 1940; s. Martin Douglas and Louise Constance (Caccia) C.; m. Mary Veronica Paul, June 11, 1966; children: Jenifer Ann, Lindsey Kathleen. BA, Stanford U., 1962, MA, 1963; LHD, Mills Coll., 1994. Assoc. dean admissions Occidental Coll., Los Angeles, 1964-66, dean admissions, 1966-68, dean of students, 1968-70; headmaster Emma Willard Sch., Troy, N.Y., 1970-74; founding headmaster San Francisco U. High Sch., 1974-86; pres. James Irvine Found., San Francisco, 1986—; trustee Coll. Bd., N.Y.C., 1981-85, Ind. Ednl. Svcs., Princeton, N.J., 1981-85, Calif. Assn. Ind. Schs., L.A., 1982-86, Branson Sch., 1987-89, Aspen Inst. Nonprofit Sector rsch. Fund, 1992—; chmn. bd. So. Calif. Assn. Philanthropy, L.A., 1989-91, No. Calif. Grantmakers, 1987-90; dir. Rebuild L.A., 1992-93. Trustee Cathedral Sch. for Boys, San Francisco, 1976-82, Marin Country Day Sch., Corte Madera, Calif., 1978-84, San Francisco Exploratorium, 1984-86, Ind. Sector, Washington, 1987-95, Am. Farmland Trust, Washington, 1992—; bd. dirs., vice chmn. Children's Hosp. Found., San Francisco, 1984-86; chmn. bd. dirs. Coun. for Cmty. Based Devel., Washington, 1989-92. Mem. Council on Founds. Democrat. Episcopalian. Clubs: World Trade, University; California (L.A.). Home: 432 Golden Gate Ave Belvedere Tiburon CA 94920-2447 Office: The James Irvine Found Steurt Tower 1 Market St Ste 2500 San Francisco CA 94105

COLLINS, DENNIS GLENN, mathematics educator; b. Gary, Ind., June 26, 1944; s. Glenn and Irene Martha (Richman) C.; m. Barbara Jean Hamilton, July 14, 1979; 1 child, Glenn H. BA, Valparaiso U., 1966; MS, Ill. Inst. Tech., 1970, PhD, 1975. Temp. instr. Mich. State U., East Lansing, 1975-76; instr. U. New Orleans, 1976-79; asst. prof. Valparaiso (Ind.) U., 1979-82; from asst. prof. to prof. math. U. P.R., Mayaguez, 1982—, chmn. math. dept. pers. com., 1994-95; vis. assoc. prof. dept. math. Mich. State U., 1988-89; judge computer sci. 38th Internat. Sci. and Engring. Fair, San Juan, P.R., 1987; presenter econ. modelling World Bank, 1994; presenter optical echo theory of quasars Seminario Interuniversitaio de Investigación Matematica, Rio Piedras, P.R., 1995 and Am. Math. Soc., Orlando, Fla., 1996; presenter Eighth Quadrennial Internat. Conf. on Graph Theory, Kalamazoo, Mich., 1996, 10th Internat. Math. Conf., Chgo., 1998, Atlanta, 1998. Created copyrighted set postcards of mathematicians and physicists, 1983; composed short Columbus Cantata and short Spaceship Cantata. NSF fellow, 1966-67; vis. scholar Mich. State U., 1988-89, 96-97. Mem. Internat. Soc. for Sys. Sci. (presenter 42nd meeting Atlanta 1998), Soc. Photo-optical Instrumentation Engrs., Internat. Soc. for Optical Engring., Am. Math. Soc. (presenter ann. meetings 1985-87, invited address 5th Internat. Conf. on info. rsch., informatics and cybernetics 1990, presenter Internat. Symposium on Econ. Modelling, World Bank 1994, Detroit meeting 1997, dialog com. to rector 1997—, poster session 10th internat. math. conf. Chgo. 1998), Soc. Indsl. and Applied Mathematicians, N.Y. Acad. Scis., Sigma Xi. Lutheran. Home: 7108 Grand Blvd Hobart IN 46342-6628 Office: U PR Dept Math Mayaguez PR 00681

COLLINS, DIANA JOSEPHINE, psychologist; b. Potsdam, N.Y., Apr. 27, 1944; d. Philip Joseph and Janet Dorothy (Lynke) C.; grad. with high honors, SUNY; Psy.D., Mass. Sch. Profl. Psychology, 1981. Psychologist, N.H. Hosp., Concord, 1974-79; asst. dir. forensic unit, 1979-80; founder, dir. Victim/Witness Service County of Hillsborough, Manchester, N.H., 1980-84; pvt. practice, Bedford, N.H.; adj. assoc. prof. U. N.H., 1974; adj. assoc. prof. Antioch Coll. of New Eng. Mem. APA, Assn. Applied Psychophysiology and Biofeedback, Biofeedback Soc. Am. (cert.), N.H. Psychol. Assn. (bd. dirs.), Mass. Psychol. Assn., Eastern Psychol. Assn., Internat. Assn. Psychotherapists and Counselors, Am. Assn. Female Execs., Roman Catholic. Home: 17 Pine Ln Warner NH 03278-4630 Office: 40 S River Rd Unit 63 Bedford NH 03110-6724

COLLINS, DOROTHY CRAIG, retired educational administrator; b. Evansville, Ind., Oct. 11, 1912; d. Edmund Lawrence and Mable Irene (Ross) Craig; m. Ralph Leonard Collins, June 13, 1940; 1 child, David Harrington. BA cum laude, Western Coll. for Women, 1934; MA, U. Chgo., 1937. Rsch. asst. Kinsey Inst., Ind. U., Bloomington, 1951-56; asst. dir. Instnl. Rsch., Ind. U., Bloomington, 1963-64; rsch. asst. Office of Pres., Ind. U., Bloomington, 1965-69; rsch. and editl. assoc. Office of Univ. Chancellor, Ind. U., Bloomington, 1969-92; ret., 1992. Co-author: Pictorial History of Indiana University, 1992. V.p. United Way of Monroe County, Bloomington, 1974; pres. bd. dirs. Bloomington Hosp., 1963; pres. Monroe County Comprehensive Health Planning, Bloomington, 1971-73. Mem. Univ. Women's Club (pres.), Consumers Health Task Force, Theatre Circle (pres.), Friends of Lilly Libr. (bd.), Office of Women's Affairs (adv. bd.), Collins Living-Learning Ctr. (adv. bd.). Democrat. Avocations: reading, travel, theatre attendance, art appreciation. Home: 919 Juniper Pl Bloomington IN 47408-1285

COLLINS, DUANE E., manufacturing executive. BSME, U. Wis.; postgrad., Harvard U. Sales engr. Parker Hannifin Corp., Cleve., 1961, gen. sales mgr., ops. mgr. hose products divsn., gen. mgr., 1973-76, v.p. ops. fluid connectors group, 1976-80, pres. fluid connectors group, 1980-83, corp. v.p., 1983-87, pres. internat., 1987-88, corp. exec. v.p., pres. internat., 1988-92, vice chmn., 1992-93, pres., CEO, 1993—; bd. dis. Nat. City Bank, Sherwin-Williams Co. Bd. dirs. Greater Cleve. Growth Assn.; bd. trustees Cleve. YMCA. Office: Parker Hannifin Corp 6035 Parkland Blvd Cleveland OH 44124-4141*

COLLINS, EARLINE BROWN, medical and surgical and nephrology nurse; b. Canton, Miss., Apr. 30, 1955; d. Oresa and Thelma Holbert (Nichols) Brown; m. James Byron Collins, Jan. 23, 1982 (div. Dec. 1995). Cert., Holmes Jr. Coll., Goodman, Miss., 1975; AAS, Shelby State C.C., Memphis, 1989. Nurse Canton Nursing Home; charge nurse Canton Manor; nurse St. Dominic, Jackson, Miss.; staff nurse nephrology med./surg. unit, 1979-90; nurse hemodialysis unit Meth. Hosp., Memphis, 1990-91, patient educator peritoneal dialysis, 1991—, acting renal coord., 1996, nurse mgr. acute hemodianlysis unit, 1996—; clin. instr. nursing asst. program Rice Coll., 1989-90. Mem. Am. Nephrology Nurses Assn., Phi Theta Kappa. Home: 4132 Arrowhead Rd Memphis TN 38118-2116

COLLINS, EDWARD J., JR., city financial officer. BSBA in Fin., Boston Coll., JD in Corp. and Tax Law. Bar: Mass. Tax atty. Deloitte & Touche Consulting Group; tax mgr., tax counsel various nat. corps., Boston; dep. commr. dept. revenue, divsn. local svcs. Commonwealth of Mass., 1978-91; town mgr., CEO Town of Saugus, Mass., 1991-96; CFO, collector-treas. City of Boston, 1996—. Elected mem. Town Meeting, 1976-91; chmn. Zoning Bd. Appeals; former mem. bd. selectmen, pers. com., water and sewer rate study com.; chmn. sign bylaw com., chmn. site plan rev. com. Recipient Disting. Svc. award Mass. Mcpl. Ass.n, 1991, Lyman H. Ziergler Outstanding Svc. award Mass. Taxpayers Found., 1987, Mass. Assn. Assessing Officers award, 1989, Mass. Sheriff's Assn. award, 1990. Mem. Nat. League Cities and Towns, Nat. Assn. Tax Adminstrs., Internat. Assn. Assessing Officers (conf. spkr. 1987), Govt. Fin. Officers Assn. (spkr. 81st Ann. Conf., 1987), Mass. Govt. Fin. Officers Assn., Mass. Treasurers and Collectors Assn. Office: City of Boston Finance Cabinet One City Hall Plz Rm 603 Boston MA 02201*

COLLINS, EILEEN MARIE, astronaut; b. Elmira, N.Y., Nov. 19, 1956; d. James Edward and Rose Marie (O'Hara) C.; m. James Patrick Youngs, Aug. 1, 1987. AS in Math., Sci., Corning C.C., 1976; BA in Math., Econs., Syracuse U., 1978; grad., USAF Undergrad. Pilot Tng., Vance AFB, Okla., 1979, USAF Test Pilot Sch., Edwards AFB, Calif., 1990; MS in Ops. Rsch., Stanford U., 1986; student, USAF Inst. Tech., 1986; MA in Space Systems Mgmt., Webster U., 1989. Commd. 2d lt. USAF, 1978, advanced through grades to lt. col., 1993; instr. pilot 71st flight tng. wing USAF, Vance AFB, 1979-82; aircraft comdr. 86th mil. airlift squadron USAF, Travis AFB, Calif., 1983-85; asst. prof. math. USAF Acad., Colorado Springs, Colo., 1986-89; astronaut Johnson Space Ctr. NASA, Houston, 1990—; second in command, space shuttle Discovery, 1995, space shuttle Atlantis, 1997. Decorated Air Force Commendation medal with one oak leaf cluster, Meritorious svc. medal with one oak leaf cluster, Air Force Expeditionary medal, Def. Meritorious Svc. medal; 1st woman pilot of the Space Shuttle. Mem. U.S. Space Found., Am. Inst. Aeronautics and Astronautics, Air Force Assn., Women Mil. Aviators, Order Daedalians.

COLLINS, EUGENE BOYD, medical chemist, molecular pathologist, consultant; b. L.A., May 28, 1917; s. Harold Porter and Mina Rosannah (Eversoll) C.; m. Frances Louise File, Aug. 4, 1946 (div. May 1962); children: Dana, Diane, Eric; m. Helen Lucille Schultz, Oct. 16, 1966; 1 child, Dane. BS in Chemistry, UCLA, 1951, diploma in edn., 1962; BSChE, De Landas U., 1940, DSc (hon.), 1952; cert. advanced med. tech., Calif. State U., Dominguez Hills, 1977; MD, U. Cen. del Este, San Pedro, Dominican Republic, 1982. Lic. clin. lab. scientist, Calif.; cert. tchr., Calif. Assoc. dir. spectroscopy Union Oil Co. (Unocal), Wilmington, Calif., 1951-57; prof. chemistry Los Angeles Harbor Coll., Wilmington, 1957-74; cons. chemist Collins and Assocs., Carson, Calif., 1974-79, 83-92, Selma, Ala., 1992—; pres. Boyd Collins Co., South Gate, Calif., 1960-70; cons. Holley Carburetor Co. Research Lab., San Pedro, Calif., 1957-60; lectr. biology and clin. science Calif. State U., Dominquez Hills, 1988-92. Contbr. articles to profl. jours. Commr. Boy Scouts Am., Long Beach, Calif., 1958-59. Staff sgt. U.S. Army, 1944-46, ETO. Fellow Am. Inst. Chemists, Royal Soc. Arts; mem. AAAS, Am. Chem. Soc., Internat. Union of Pure and Applied Chemistry (affiliate), Am. Pharm. Assn., Acad. Pharm. Scis., N.Y. Acad. Scis., Am. Assn. Clin. Chemistry (molecular pathology divsn.). Avocations: history, chess, internat. affairs. Office: Collins and Assoc 470 Deepwoods Dr Selma AL 36701-0467

COLLINS, FRANCIS S., medical research scientist. PhD in Phys. Chemistry, Yale U., 1974; MD, U. N.C., 1977. Former staff mem. Howard Hughes Med. Inst., U. Mich. Med. Ctr., Ann Arbor; now dir. Nat. Human Genome Rsch. Inst. NIH, Bethesda, Md. Co-recipient Gairdner Found. Internat. award for work on cystic fibrosis, 1990. Mem. NAS. Office: Nat Human Genome Rsch Inst Bldg 31 Rm 4B09 31 Center Dr MSC2152 Bethesda MD 20892-2152

COLLINS, FRANCIS WINFIELD, chemical company executive; b. N.Y.C., Jan. 5, 1927; s. Francis W. and Lillian A. (Schaeffler) C.; m. Rhoda Henry Collins, May 30, 1952; children: Sharon, Russell, Margaret, Cynthia, Wayne. BA cum laude, Amherst Coll., 1948; MA, Columbia U., 1949. From control chemist to asst. dept. head Merck and Co., Rahway, N.J., 1949-60; tech. rep. E.I. DuPont de Nemours, Wilmington, Del., 1960-65; from supt. to sr. market rschr. E.I. DuPont de Nemours, Gibbstown, N.J., 1965-85; ret., 1985; pres. Brandywine Cons., Inc., Wilmington, Del., 1985—; tchg. and tutoring, 1985—. Chair Hanby Civic Assn., Wilmington, 1978-80, West Milford (N.J.) Adv. Commn., 1969; chpt. chair Svc. Corps Ret. Execs., 1991-93, regional mktg. coord., 1994-95, regional computer coord., 1994-96 (spl. award 1996, Platinum award 1997); counselor Internat. Exec. Svc. Corps, 1993—; asst. chmn. bd. trustees Minikin Opera, Wilmington, 1985-94. Recipient Platinum award for outstanding svc. Svc. Corp. Ret. Execs., 1998. Avocations: world travel, sailing, camping, gardening. Home and Office: 2401 Dorval Rd Wilmington DE 19810-3528

COLLINS, FRANK CHARLES, JR., industrial and service quality specialist; b. El Paso, Tex., Oct. 29, 1927; s. Frank Charles Sr. and Lucile Ellen (Reynolds) C.; m. Esther Frances Shiell, Aug. 16, 1948; children: Lucile Frances Collins Silveira, Sue Ellen Collins Hekman, Francene C. Collins Newman, Virginia Ann Collins Friesen, Melissa Esther Collins Fry, Laura Beth Collins Leach, Frank Charles III. BA in Sociology, La. State U., 1949; grad., Naval War Coll., 1966; postgrad., UCLA, 1976-77; PhD, Kennedy Western U., 1995. Enlisted USNR, 1945-46; commd. ensign USN, 1951, advanced through grades to rear adm. (upper half), 1951; comdr. U.S.S. LSS(L) 65, 1953-54, U.S.S. Saline CTY LST 1101, San Diego, 1957-59, U.S.S. John A. Bole DD 755, 1967-69; ops. officer Naval Support Activity, Danang, Vietnam, 1966-67; comdr. COMDESRON Nine, San Diego, 1974-76, Devel. and Tng. Center/Fleet Maintenance Assistance Group, Pacific, San Diego, 1976-78; chief Navy Sect., Army Mission, Mil. Assistance Adv. Group, Iran, 1978-79; dir. logistics plans Office Chief of Naval Ops., Washington, 1979-81; exec. dir. quality assurance Def. Logistics Agy., 1981-83, ret., 1983; v.p. quality ops. Avco Corp. and Textron, Inc., Providence, 1983-86; pres. Frank Collins Assocs. Survival Twenty-One, Alexandria, Va., 1987—; chmn. bd. dirs. The Collins Group Internat., Inc., Washington. Author: Sixteen Steps in Establishing a Quality Improvement Process, 1986, Quality—The Ball in Your Court, 1987, Twenty Steps in Establishing a Quality Culture, 1991, Chiko and the Guv, 1992; contbg. author: Energy and Sea Power, 1981, Vietnam: The Naval Story, 1986; contbr. articles to profl. jours. Mem. exec. bd. Iran Am. Friendship Found., Washington, 1985—; bd. dirs. Malcolm Baldridge Nat. Quality Award Consortium, Milw., 1988-92, Nat. Found. Inc., Washington, 1988-93; mem. pastor's cabinet, lay preacher Alexandria Free Meth. Ch., 1990-93. Decorated Legion of Merit (2), Bronze Star, Navy Commendation medal (all with Combat V), Def. Superior Service medal, Def. Meritorious Service medal., Def. Disting. Service medal. Mem. Am. Soc. for Quality Control (chmn. aerospace and def. div. 1987-88, vice chmn. energy div. 1989-91), Assn. for Quality and Participation, Ret. Officers Assn., U.S. Naval Inst., Navy League, Nat. Security Indsl. Assn., Navy Surface Warfare Assn. Republican. Avocations: writing poetry, quality management doctrine, history of Iranian revolution and the overthrow of the Shah. *In an era now characterized by humanism and relativism, I thank God for having grown up in a period which recognized absolutes—absolutes of morality, self-discipline, individual effort, and national leadership and purpose. I pray we can set an example of concern for others, and as a nation set goals which can bring about a revival of justice, peace, morality and belief in a sovereign God and risen Christ.*

COLLINS, FUJI, mental health professional; b. Tokyo, Nov. 3, 1954; s. Boyd Leslie and Kimiko (Terayama) C.; 1 child, Lacey Nichole. BS, Ariz. State U., 1977; MS, Ea. Wash. U., 1989; MA, The Fielding Inst., 1993, PhD, 1994. Registered clin. therapist. Commd. 2d lt. U.S. Army, 1978, advanced through grades to maj., 1989, lt. platoon leader, adminstrv. officer, 1978-79; lt. bat. adjutant 509th Airborne Bat. Combat Team, 1977-80; capt., air def. fire coordination officer U.S. Army, 1981-83, capt. battery comdr., 1983-85, capt., 1985-86; clin. therapist Wash. State Patrol, 1985-95; dir. of adminstrn., Japanese Counseling Program Richmond Area Multi-Svcs., Inc., San Francisco, 1995-97, dir. children and youth svcs., 1995-97; prof. psychology Ctrl. Wash. U., Ellensburg, 1997—; adj. prof. John F. Kennedy U.; coord. Wash. State Patrol Critical Incident/Peer Support Team, Wash. State Hostage Negotiator; mem. Thurston/Mason County Critical Incident Stress Debriefing Team; dir. Richmond Counseling Ctr., 1995—; vis. lectr. Georgetown U., 1996—; faculty Nat. Asian Am. Psychology Tng. Ctr., San Francisco, 1996—. Vol. Thurston/Mason County Crisis Clinic; mem. steering com. Thurston/Mason County Critical Incident Team. Mem. ACA, APA, Wash. State Psychol. Assn., Asian Am. Psychol. Assn., Soc. for Psychol. Study of Ethnic Minority Issues, Am. Critical Incident Stress Found., Wash. State Hostage Negotiation Assn., Assn. Police Planning and Rsch. Officers. Home: 400 S Walnut St Ellensburg WA 98926-3823 Office: Dept Psychology Ctrl Washington U Ellensburg WA 98926-7575

COLLINS, GEORGE EDWIN, computer scientist, mathematician, educator; b. Stuart, Iowa, Jan. 10, 1928; s. Martin Wentworth and Linnie (Fry) C.; m. Dorothy Day Guise, Sept. 4, 1954 (dec. Aug. 1986); children: Cynthia Day, Nancy Helen Rusch, Rebecca Lynne. BA in Math., State U. Iowa,

1951, MS in Math., 1952; PhD in Math., Cornell U., 1955; DrRerNat honoris causa, Tübingen U., 1996. Mathematician IBM Corp., Yorktown Heights, N.Y., 1955-59, rsch. staff, 1959-66; from assoc. prof. to prof. U. Wis., Madison, 1966-86; prof. Ohio State U., Columbus, 1986-91; vis. prof. Johannes Kepler U., Linz, Austria, 1991-96; rsch. prof. U. Del., 1996—; chmn. dept. U. Wis., Madison, 1970-72; vis. prof. Stanford (Calif.) U., 1972-73, U. Kaiserslautern, West Germany, 1974-75, U. Karlsruhe, West Germany, 1978. Editor, author: Computer Algebra, 1982; editor: Jour. of Symbolic Computation; contbr. articles to profl. jours. With USN, 1946-47. Rsch. grantee NSF, 1968-91, 97—, Austrian Sci. Found., 1992-96. Mem. Math. Assn. Am., Assn. for Computing Machinery. Achievements include pioneering work in computer algebra; invention of method for cylindrical algebraic decomposition and quantifier elimination. Office: Dept Computer & Info Scis University of Delaware Newark DE 19716

COLLINS, GEORGE J., JR., surgeon; b. Nov. 19, 1939. BS, Tex. A&M U., 1961, MS, 1963; MD, U. Tex. Med. Br., 1966. Chief vascular surgery svc. Brooke Army Med. Ctr., 1982-83; chief vascular surgery svc. Walter Reed Army Med. Ctr., 1983-86, chief dept. of surgery, 1984-86; chief cardiovascular/thoracic surgery Madigan Army Med. Ctr., 1997—. E-mail: collins@seanet.com. Home: C-303 3008 North Narrows Dr Tacoma WA 98407

COLLINS, GEORGE TIMOTHY, computer software consultant; b. Connersville, Ind., Aug. 21, 1943; s. Robert Emerson and Oma (Richie) C.; m. Martha Elizabeth Holt, Apr. 30, 1966; children: Kirsten Stephanie, Eowyn Erika. BA in Math., Ind. U., 1966; MS in Computer Sci., Rensselaer Poly. Inst., 1971. Engr. program analyst Sikorsky Aircraft, Stratford, Conn., 1966-70; research mathematician Peter Eckrich, Ft. Wayne, Ind., 1970-75; sr. systems analyst Pyrotek Data Service, Ft. Walton Beach, Fla., 1975-77; sr. aerosystems engr. Gen. Dynamics, Ft. Worth, 1977-79; sr. specialist Electronic Data Systems, Las Vegas, Nev., 1979-81; sr. assoc. CACI Fed., San Diego, 1981-82; prin., gen. mgr. Structured Software Systems, Escondido, Calif., 1982-88; sr. software engr. Sci. Applications Internat. Corp., San Diego, 1988-94; pvt. practice cons. Escondido, 1994-96; prin. engr. Orbital Scis. Corp., 1996—; cons. Hi-Shear Corp., Los Angeles, 1973-75. Developer (computer model and data base) Aircraft Stores Interface, 1975, (computer model) TAC Daystripe, 1981; co-developer (computer model) Tactical Air Def., Battle Model, 1978, Tactical Air and Land Ops., 1980; prime contbr. (computer data collection and analysis sys.) Mobile Sea Range, 1988-90; contbr. (computer comm. sys.) Lightweight Deployable Comm., 1990, Joint Advanced Spl. Ops. Radio Sys., 1992, Orbital Scis. Corp.'s Maj. Constituent Analyzer Environ. Control/Life Scis. Sys. for Internat. Space Station (team received NASA Manned Flight Awareness award 1994), Orbital Scis. Corp. Software Lead Meterology Sensor Module, 1996, Point of Contact Support MCA Integration in Internat. Space Station, 1998, Software Engr. MCA EDP bd. self-test debug, 1998. Bd. dirs. Family and Children's Service, Ft. Wayne, 1974. Mem. N.Y. Acad. Scis., North County Chess Club. Unitarian. Avocations: chess, tennis, astronomy. Home: 121 W 8th Ave Escondido CA 92025-5001 also: Orbital Scis Corp 2771 N Garey Ave Pomona CA 91767-1809

COLLINS, HARKER, economist, manufacturing executive, publisher, marketing, financial, business and legal consultant; b. Denver, Nov. 24, 1924; s. Clem Wetzel and Marie (Harker) C.; m. Emily Harvey, Aug. 23, 1957; children: Catherine Emily, Cynthia Lee, Constance Marie. B.S., U.S. Naval Acad., 1945. Asst. buyer Montgomery Ward & Co., N.Y.C., 1947-51; prodn. mgr. Diamond Hosiery Mills, High Point, N.C., 1953-55; v.p. Vanette Hosiery Mills, Dallas, 1955-59; v.p., dir. Grote Mfg. Co., Madison, Ind., 1959-71; group v.p., gen. mgr. Bendix Corp., South Bend, Ind., 1971-73; pres., dir. Bandag, Inc., Muscatine, Iowa, 1973-78; chief exec. officer Bandag, Inc., 1974-78; pres., chief exec. officer, bd. dirs. Harker Collins & Co., Lubbock, Tex., 1978-98; pub. newsletters The Economy and You, Update, 1978—; econ. counsel Automotive Svc. Industry Assn., 1978-91; exec. v.p., bd. dirs. Indsl. Molding Corp., Lubbock, 1993-97; pres., bd. dirs. Indl. Molding Corp., Lubbock, 1997; instr. U. Denver, 1948; Bd. dirs. Hwy. Users Fedn., 1970-86; chmn. automotive industry liaison com. with Dept. Transp., 1968-86, automotive industry excise tax com., 1964-70, automotive industry tariff com., 1964-70, joint operating com. for automotive trade shows, 1969-77. Mem. Pres.'s Com. Hwy. Safety, 1966-68; Bd. dirs. Iowa Ind. Coll. Found., 1976-86; bd. fellows Northwood Inst., 1974—; alderman City of Rancho Viejo, Tex., 1980-87. Served to ensign USN, 1945-47; to lt. USNR, 1951-53. Recipient Automotive Industry Leadership award, 1965, 74; Fin. World award as chief exec. of yr., 1975, 77. Mem. Automotive Svc. Industry Assn. (vice chmn. 1966-67, chmn. 1968-69, chmn. heavy duty exec. com. 1969-71, chmn. safety and environ. protection com. 1962-67, 70-78), Automotive Sales Coun. (bd. dirs. 1966-67, sec. 1971-72, v.p. 1972-73, pres. 1973-74), Am. Nat. Standards Inst. (chmn. task force on used vehicle standards 1966-74), Home Products Safety Coun. (pres. 1960-63), Medicine Cabinet Mfg. Coun. (pres. 1960-63, bd. dirs. 1960-68), Truck Safety Equipment Inst. (pres. 1960-63, dir. 1960-68).

COLLINS, HARRY DAVID, construction consultant, forensic engineering specialist, mechanical and nuclear engineer, retired army officer; b. Brownsville, Pa., Nov. 18, 1931; s. Harry Alonzo and Cecelia Victoria (Morris) C.; BS in Mech. Engring., Carnegie Mellon U., 1954; MS in Physics, U.S. Naval Postgrad. Sch., 1961; postgrad., U.S. Army Command and Gen. Staff Coll., 1970; postgrad. in exptl. physics, George Washington U., 1971-72; m. Suzanne Dylong, May 11, 1956; children: Cynthia L. Mabel, Gerard P. Commd. 2d lt. C.E., U.S. Army, 1954, advanced through grades to lt. col. 1969; comdr. 802d Heavy Engr. Constrn. Bn., Korea, 1972-73; dep. dist. engr. and acting dist. engr. Army Engr. Dist., New Orleans, 1973-75; v.p. deLaureal Engrs., Inc., New Orleans, 1975-78; v.p. Near East mktg. and project mgmt. Kidde Cons., Inc., 1978-82; dir. new bus. devel. and project mgmt. for North Africa, Middle East, Am. Middle East Co., Inc., 1982-84; sr. cons. Wagner, Hohns, Inglis, Inc., 1984-91; chief engr. bd. commrs. Orleans Levee Dist. State of La., 1991-92; pres. Harry D. Collins and Assocs., 1992—; pres. La. Security Products & QuTech, 1994-97. Contbr. articles to profl. jours. Decorated Legion of Merit, Bronze Star with oak leaf cluster, Meritorious Service medal with oak leaf cluster, Joint Svc. Commendation medal, Armed Forces Expeditionary medal, Vietnam Svc. medal, Vietnam Nat. Commendation medal, Vietnam Tng. Svc. medal; registered profl. engr., Miss., La. Mem. ASME, Am. Soc. Mil. Engrs. (past pres. La Post), La. Engring. Soc., NSPE, Am. Nuclear Soc., Am. Arbitration Assn. (panel of arbitrators and mediators), Nat. Acad. Forensic Engrs. (diplomate, cert.), Sigma Xi. Home: 2024 Audubon St New Orleans LA 70118-5518

COLLINS, HARVEY TALIAFERRO, chemist; b. Thomaston, Ga., July 12, 1929; s. Walter Clinton and Elnora (Harvey) C.; m. Rosalind Wyatt, Feb. 12, 1948; 1 child, Rasheedah Najii Abdur-Rahman. BS in Chemistry, Ft. Valley State U., 1945, BS in Pre-Med., 1945; postgrad., Atlanta U., 1947-49. Head Toxicity Studies of Animals Goldblatt Cancer Rsch. U. Chgo., 1949-52; chief coord. std. solutions Lever Bros., Hammond, Ind., 1952-88; founder, chmn., CEO Collins Pharm., Inc., Chgo., 1984—. Patentee in method and sys. for treatment of AIDS, others, 2 patents for Herpes medication. Avocations: bridge, chess, table tennis, volleyball, travel. Home: 1486 E 56th St Chicago IL 60637-1866

COLLINS, HENRY JAMES, III, insurance company executive; b. Washington, July 9, 1927; s. Henry James and Genevieve (Downey) C.; m. Josephine Ann McDonald, July 13, 1946; children: Jonathan Alexander, Thomas James, Patricia Ann. B.C.S., Strayers Coll., 1951. With Govt. Employees Ins. Co., Washington, 1945, 46-80; treas. Govt. Employees Ins. Co., 1965-77, comptroller, 1972-80, v.p., 1977-80; v.p. Govt. Employees Life Ins. Co., 1980-83; with Collins Contracting, 1983—; treas. Govt. Employees Corp., Washington, 1966-74, Govt. Employees Fin. Corp., Washington, 1966-74; asst. treas. Criterion Ins. Co., 1961-70, treas., 1970-72; dir. Md. Ins. Guaranty Fund.; Mem. auditors and comptrollers adv. com. Nat. Assn. Ins. Commrs. Treas. Oakview Citizens Assn., 1952-53. Served with AUS, 1945-46. Mem. Soc. Ins. Accountants, Ins. Accounting and Statis. Assn., Nat. Assn. Ind. Insurers (com. blanks and uniform accounting 1964—, fed. taxes com. 1969-74), Fin. Execs. Inst. (pres. D.C. chpt. 1979-80), Izaak Walton League Am., Am. Legion. Club: Bassmasters. Home: 13878 Foggy Bottom Ct Mount Airy MD 21771-4608 Office: 13812 Penn Shop Rd Mount Airy MD 21771-4626

COLLINS, H(ERSCHEL) DOUGLAS, retired physician; b. Caribou, Maine, Jan. 19, 1928; married, 1950, 87; 3 children.; BA, U. Maine, 1949; MD, Harvard U., 1952. Diplomate Am. Bd. Internal Medicine. Intern Mass. Gen. Hosp., 1952-53, asst. resident in medicine, 1953-54, 72-73, resident, 1954-55; sr. asst. surgeon USPHS, 1955-57; pvt. practice Caribou, 1957-72, 73-75, 1980-84, group practice, 1984-87; dir. Ctrl. Maine Family Practice Residency, 1975-79, Maine-Dartmouth Family Practice Residency, 1979-80; gov. Am. Bd. Internal Medicine, 1988-91. Mem. Inst. Med.-Nat. Acad. Sci., AMA, ACP (master). Home: RFD Box 2179 Kingfield ME 04947

COLLINS, J. BARCLAY, II, lawyer, oil company executive; b. Gettysburg, Pa., Oct. 21, 1944; s. Jennings Barclay and Golda Olevia (Hook) C.; m. Janna Claire Fall, June 25, 1966; children: J. Barclay III, L. Christian. AB magna cum laude, Harvard U., 1966; JD magna cum laude, Columbia U., 1969. Bar: N.Y. 1969. Law clk. to presiding judge U.S. Ct. Appeals (2d cir.), N.Y.C., 1969-70; assoc. Cravath, Swaine and Moore, N.Y.C., 1970-78; v.p., asst. gen. counsel City Investing Co., N.Y.C., 1978-84; exec. v.p., gen. counsel Amerada Hess Corp., N.Y.C., 1984—, also bd. dirs.; bd. dirs. Dime Bancorp Inc. Trustee Bklyn. Hosp.-Caledonian Hosp., Plymouth Ch. of the Pilgrims, Bklyn.; bd. dirs. United Hosp. Fund N.Y., John Milton Soc. for Blind; past gov. Bklyn. Heights Assn. Mem. ABA, N.Y. Bar Assn., N.Y.C. Yacht Club. Clubs: Heights Casino (Bklyn.); Harvard N.Y.C. Office: Amerada Hess Corp Ste 810 1185 Avenue Of The Americas Fl 800 New York NY 10036-2601

COLLINS, J. MICHAEL, public broadcasting executive; b. Buffalo, Feb. 17, 1935; s. John Lloyd and Celestine (Buhrle) C.; m. Marilyn Anne Mercer, Aug. 5, 1961; children: Kevin Michael, Timothy David, Sheila Anne, Jeanne Mary, Julie Lynn. BS in Social Scis., Canisius Coll., 1957, LHD (hon.), 1978; postgrad., Mich. State U., 1957-58. Promotion mgr. Western N.Y. Pub. Broadcasting Assn. (Stas. WNED-TV-AM-FM, WNEQ-TV, WNJA-FM), Buffalo, 1959-60, dir. devel., 1961-62, asst. sta. mgr., 1963-65, gen. mgr., 1966-69, pres., 1970-98; sr. cons., 1998-99. Co-author: ETV: The Farther Vision, 1967. Mem. ho. of dels. United Way of Buffalo and Erie County, 1967-98; trustee Ea. Ednl. Network, 1965-95, treas., 1967-70, exec. com., 1967-74, 78-81, 84-85, 88-90, 92-94, chmn. budget and fin. com., 1967-70, pres., 1971-72, chmn., 1973-74, v.p., 1980-81, 88-90, 92-93, adv. bd. interregional progam svc., 1984-90; trustee Am. Program Svc., 1993-96, exec. com., 1993-96, fin. com., 1994-96; mem. CATV com., devel. adv. com. NAEB; exec. bd. Niagara Frontier coun. Boy Scouts Am., 1971-76; exec. com. Cantalician Ctr., 1978-85; trustee St. Joseph's Collegiate Inst., 1978-85; chmn. PBS Border Sta. Consortium, 1986-88; bd. dirs. PBS, 1972-78, 80-86, vice-chmn., 1975, nat. program policy com., 1990-95; mem. Governance Task Force, 1996; bd. dirs. PBS Enterprises, 1985-90, Nat. Data Cast, Inc., 1989-90; trustee Assn. Am. Pub. TV Stas., 1987-93, exec. com., 1989-93, chmn. nominating com., 1989; mem. Kenmore-Tonawanda Pub. Schs. Bd. Edn., 1974-81, v.p., 1977, pres., 1978; trustee Chautauqua Instn., 1988-96, devel. com., 1989, program com., 1988-95, exec. com., 1989-95, personnel com., 1990-95, mktg. com., 1994-95, fin. com., 1995-96, bldg. and grounds com., 1995-96, edn./youth/recreation com., 1989-93, 96-97, chmn., 1989-93, mission policy com., 1997—; bd. dirs. Buffalo Coun. World Affairs, 1994-95, Blue Shield West N.Y., 1990-92; fin. coun. St. Amelia Ch., 1990—, chmn. stewardship com., 1993—. Recipient Focus award Buffalo Courier Express, 1978, Signum Fidei award St. Joseph's Collegiate Inst., 1984, Man of Yr. award Nat. Columbus Day Com., 1985, 92, Matrix award Women in Comm., 1985; named one of 100 Most Influential People in Western N.Y., Bus. First, 1996; inducted into Burralo Broadcast Pioneers Hall of Fame, 1999. Mem. N.Y. State Ednl. Radio and TV Assn. (trustee, pres. 1964-65, treas. 1963, editor newsletter 1962), Pub. Rels. Assn. Western N.Y. (pres. 1966), Nat. Assn. Ednl. Broadcasters, Canisius Coll. Alumni Assn. (bd. govs. 1960-62, 70-73, named Outstanding Alumnus 1977). Avocations: reading, collecting and tasting wine, photography. Office: Sta WNED-TV PO Box 1263 Buffalo NY 14240-1263

COLLINS, JAMES DUFFIELD, marine engineer, editor; b. Logansport, Ind., Dec. 20, 1919; s. Louis Duffield and Gaynelle May (Mobley) C.; m. Barbara Cook, Mar. 12, 1949; children: Barbara Cook Jr., James Duffield II. BS in Marine Engring., U.S. Mcht. Marine Acad., 1946. Process engr. Gen. Motors Corp., Indpls., 1940-44; marine engr. Moore McCormack Lines, N.Y.C., 1946; sr. project engr. rsch. and devel. Gen. Motors Corp., Indpls., 1946-82; editor-at-large Marcel Dekker, Inc., N.Y.C., 1986—. Contbr. author: Materials and Processes, 1985; author: Bowline Knot, 1972; contbr. articles to profl. jours; patentee in field. Lt. (j.g.) USNR, 1946-57, ret. Mem. Soc. Naval Architects and Marine Engrs., Masons. Avocations: music, concert master, orchestra and symphony member. Home and Office: 5228 Bevedere Dr Indianapolis IN 46228-2137

COLLINS, JAMES FRANCIS, lawyer, financial consultant; b. Evanston, Ill., July 31, 1943; s. James Francis Jr. and Jeanne (Moss) C.; m. Ann Peake Rogers, Apr. 5, 1983. BSc in Mktg., U. Louisville, 1969, JD, 1977; JD, Xavier U., 1971; MEd in Bus. Adminstrn. Bar: Ky. 1977, Ill. 1977, Fla. 1978, U.S. Dist. Ct. (we. dist.) Ky. 1978, U.S. Mil. Ct. Appeals 1978, U.S. Tax Ct. 1978, U.S. Customs Ct. 1978, U.S. Ct. Appeals (6th cir.) 1980, U.S. Supreme Ct. 1980, U.S. Dist. Ct. (so. dist.) Ind. 1981, U.S. Dist. Ct. (mid. dist.) Fla. 1982, Wis. 1989 (inactive status), Ind. 1989; cert. secondary tchr., Ill., Ky. Br. mgr., mcht. rep. Household Fin. Corp., Chgo., 1962-66; tchr. bus. Jefferson County Bd. Edn., Louisville, 1968-77; pvt. practice Louisville, 1977-82; criminal def. trial lawyer Pub. Defender, Sanford, Fla., 1982-83; pvt. practice Schaumburg, Ill., 1984-96, Louisville, 1997—; arbitrator, chairperson Cir. Ct. Cook. County, Mandatory Ct. Annexed Arbitration, 1990—; part-time instr. in comml. and internat. law Watterson Coll., Louisville, 1974-75. Dist. ct. judge candidate Jefferson County, Ky., 1981; cir. ct. judge candidate Dem. Primary, Chgo., 1986, 88, 92, 96; appellate ct. judge candidate, Chgo., 1990, Dem. Primary, Chgo., 1994; Dem. cir. ct. judge candidate, 1996; mem. S.E. Side Community Orgn.; legal counsel election day Dem. Party of Proviso Twp., 1985-90, 37th Ward of Chgo., 1991-94, 27th Ward of Chgo., 1991-94, election day legal counsel to Sen. Rickey Hendon, 1989—; mem. Berkeley (Ill.) Citizens Party, 1987; life mem. United Helenic Voters Asn., 1996—; life mem. Gary Marinaros Reg. Dem. Orgn., Proviso Twp., Ill., Sen. Rickey Hendon's 27th Ward of Chgo. Progressive Dem. Orgn.; mem. Maine Twp. (Ill.) Dem. Com., 1996—; mem. peoples assembly of Congressman Danny K. Davis of 7th Congl. Dist. Chgo.; mem. Alderman Percy Giles 37th Ward Dem. Orgn., Chgo., Alderman Madeline Haithcock 2d Ward Regular Dem. Orgn.; mem. or polit. cons. Polit. Action Com. Jean Kohn and Rev. Melvin Dlep, Chgo.; mem. Jean Soliz for Congress, Dem. Orgn. Chgo.; mem. Donald and Karen Marie Smith S.W. Side Chgo. 12th Ward and 23d Ward Polit. Cons. Orgn. for Regular Dems.; mem. Robert Bachs Dep. Committeeman of West Provciso Dem. Orgn., Melrose Prk, Ill.; assoc. Alderman Richard Mell 33d Ward Dem. Orgn., Chgo.; mem. Ill. State Senator Robert Mulano Regular Dem. Orgn., Committeeman Andy Prysbo Maine Twp. of Cook County Regular Dem. Orgn.; mem. Rep. Nat. Com., chmn. cons. nonpartisan com. Recipient ICLE 32 Hour Bankruptcy Course award, 1985, Recognition award Berkeley (Ill.) Citizens party, 1986, Continuing Legal Edn. Recognition award Ky. Bar Assn., 1987, 91, 92, 93, 94, 95, 96, 97, 98, Recognition awards Westside Chgo. Black Polit. Leaders Assn., 1990, 92, Recognition award Cook County Dem. Party Fair Coalition, 1992, Continuing Legal Edn. Recognition award Ky. Bar Assn., 1996; named Disting. Citizen of Louisville, Ky. by Mayor Harvey Stone, 1976, Hon. Cpt. Belle Louisville by County Judge Exec. Todd Hollenbach, 1974, Hon. Ky. Col. by Gov. Wenden Ford, Lt. Gov. Thelma Stoval, 1974. Mem. Ky. Bar Assn. (Clie award 1998), Louisville Bar Assn., Internat. Platform Assn., Chgo. Bar Assn. (Ill. indsl. comm. workers's compensation com., adminstrv. law com.), U. Louisville Bus. Sch. Alumni Assn., Xavier U. Alumni Assn., U. Louisville Law Sch. Alumni Assn., United Hellenic Voters of Am. (life), Sigma Delta Kappa. Avocation: politics.

COLLINS, JAMES FRANCIS, toxicologist; b. Balt., Jan. 26, 1942; s. James Murphy and Mary M. (Dolan) C.; m. Barbara Joan Betka, June 21, 1969; children: Chris, Cavan. BS, Loyola Coll., Balt., 1963; PhD, U.N.C., 1968. Diplomate Am. Bd. Toxicology. Fellow NIH, Bethesda, Md., 1968-75; faculty mem., rsch. chemist U. Tex. Health Sci. Ctr. and VA Med. Ctr., San Antonio, 1975-86; staff toxicologist Calif. EPA and Dept. Health Svcs., Berkeley, Calif., 1986—; instr. U. Calif. Berkeley/Extension, 1987-95; instr. U. San Francisco, 1995—. Contbr. numerous articles to profl. jours., publs. Mem. Am. Soc. Biochemistry and Molecular Biology. Democrat. Roman Catholic. Avocations: youth soccer, hiking. Home: 822 Rogers Way Pinole CA 94564-2409 Office: Calif EPA 1515 Clay St Fl 16 Oakland CA 94612-1499*

COLLINS, JAMES FRANCIS, wildlife artist; b. Haverhill, Mass., Aug. 9, 1952; s. Francis Stanley and Elinor Marie (Clohecy) C.; m. Susan Elaine Woodburn, Sept. 24, 1977. Plumber Stark & Cronk, Groveland, Mass., 1975-84; truck driver various cos., Mass., 1984-89; wildlife artist self employed, Plaistow, N.H., 1989—. Recipient award for N.J. Trout Stamp Design, 1995, Ind. Trout Stamp Design, Dept. Fish and Wildlife, 1997, Vt. Waterfowl Stamp Design, 1997, N.H. Migratory Waterfowl Stamp Design, 1998, N.J. Pheasant Stamp Design, 1999. Mem. N.H. Artist Assn. (Miriam Sawyer award 1995), Haverhill Artist Assn., Ducks Unltd., NRA (life). Republican. Roman Catholic. Avocations: hunting, fishing, woodworking, hiking, photography. Home: 37 Harriman Rd Plaistow NH 03865-2520

COLLINS, JAMES FRANKLIN, ambassador. Dir. for intelligence policy Nat. Security Coun., Washington; dep. exec. sec. for Europe and L.Am. U.S. Dept. of State, Washington; vice counsel U.S. Dept. of State, Izmir, Turkey; polit. counselor U.S. Dept. of State, Amman, Jordan; dep. chief of mission Am. Embassy U.S. Dept. of State, Moscow, 1990-93; coord. for regional affairs for New Ind. States U.S. Dept. of State, 1993-94; sr. coord. Office of Ambassador-at-Large for New Ind. State U.S. Dept. of State, Washington, 1994-97; amb. to Russia Moscow, 1997—. Office: Am Embassy Moscow Russia Dept State Washington DC 20521-5430*

COLLINS, JAMES MICHAEL, principal; b. Sept. 12, 1947. MS, Hunter Coll., 1972; Cert. Adv. Study, Hofstra U., 1976. Math/sci. coord. Selden (N.Y.) Mid. Sch., 1982-86, asst. prin., 1986-88; prin. Islip (N.Y.) Mid. Sch., 1988-92, Harry B. Thompson Mid. Sch., Syosset, N.Y., 1992—. E-mail: jcollins@syosset.k12.ny.us. Office: 98 Ann Dr Syosset NY 11791-5900

COLLINS, JEAN KATHERINE, English educator; b. Norfolk, Va., June 14, 1928; d. Elwood Brantley and Katherine Belle (Lambertson) C. BA in Liberal Arts, James Madison U., Harrisonburg, Va., 1945-49; MA in English, U. Richmond, 1950-51; edn. credits, U. Va., Eastern Shore of Va., 1950, 60; art edn. credits, Millersville State Tchrs. Coll, summer 1970. Continuity writer Radio Station WLEE, Richmond, Va., 1949; English, critic tchr. Farmville H.S., Longwood Coll., Va., 1951-53; English tchr., art tchr. Hermitage H.S., Richmond, Va., 1953-55; prin., art tchr. Cape Charles (Va.) H.S., 1957-59; head English dept., tchr. Northampton H.S., Eastville, Va., 1960-63; art tchr. Pvt. Studio, Cape Charles, Va., 1964-90; pres. Lambda chpt. Delta Kappa Gamma Soc., Eastern Shore of Va., 1966-68; recording sec. Iota State Delta Kappa Gamma Soc., Headqtrs., Richmond, Va., 1967-69; adv. bd. Eastern Shore Pub. Libr., Accomac, Va., 1981-89; bd. dirs. Eastern Shore of Va. Hist. Soc., Onancock, Va., 1957-60. Author: (poetry) Madison Quarterly, 1948, 49; author, illustrator: An Eastern Shore Sampler, 1975; author: History of Trinity United Methodist Church, 1993. Named Woman of Yr. Young WOmen's Club of Cape Charles, Va., 1958. Mem. Eastern Shore of Va. Hist. Soc., Cape Charles Hist. Soc., Trinity United Meth. Ch., Delta Kappa Gamma Soc.. Republican. Methodist. Avocations: painting, needlework, history, theater, dance, writing.

COLLINS, JEFFREY HAMILTON, research facility administrator, electrical engineering educator; b. Luton, Bedfordshire, Eng., Apr. 22, 1930; came to U.S., 1966; s. Ernest Frederick and Dora Gladys (Bromley) C.; m. Sally Parfitt, Mar. 31, 1956; children: Adrian Vincent, Kevin Allan. BS, London U., 1950, 51, MS, 1954, DSc, 1987; D of Engring. (hon.), Napier, 1997. Chartered engr., chartered physicist, Eng. Sci. staff mem. GEC Hirst Rsch. Ctr., London, 1951-56; sr. staff mem. Ferranti Ltd., Edinburgh, Scotland, 1956-57; sr. lectr. U. Glasgow, Scotland, 1947-66; rsch. engr. Stanford (Calif.) U., 1966-68; dir. phys. sci. Rockwell Internat., Anaheim, Calif., 1968-70; prof. elec. engring., then head dept. U. Edinburgh, 1977-84, emeritus prof., 1984; dir. Automation and Robotics Rsch. Inst., Ft. Worth, 1987-90; sr. tech. specialist L0thian Regional Coun., Edinburgh, Scotland, 1990-93; specialist adviser to prin. Napier U., Edinburgh, 1994-97, prof., 1995-97; prof. elec. engring. U. Tex., Arlington, 1987-90; bd. dirs. advent tech., Edinburgh, 1981-86, chmn. tech. adv. com., 1985-88; mem. Computer Bd. Univs. and Rsch. Couns., Eng., 1985-86, Info. Sys. com. U.K. Univs. Coun., 1992-94; chmn. Edinburgh Parallel Computing Centre, 1990-94; chmn. Scottish Electronics Mfg. Ctr., 1994-96. Editor: Computer-Aided Design of SAW Devices, 1976; editor Conf. Proc. Tech. and Edn., 1988-89; contbr. numerous articles to profl. jours. Recipient Hewlett Packard Europhysics prize European Phys. Soc., Paris, 1979, Bulgin Premiums, Marconi Premium Inst. Electronics and Radio Engr., London, 1974, 77, 78. Fellow Instn. Elec. Engrs. (Eng., chmn. electronics div. 1985-86, counc. mem. 1984-87), IEEE, Royal Soc. Edinburgh, Royal Acad. Engring. (Eng., coun. mem. 1984-87), Inst. Physics (Eng.). Address: 28 Muirfield Park, Gullane EH31 2DY, Scotland

COLLINS, JENNY GALLOWAY, poet, disc jockey, radio talk show host; b. Cumberland, Ky., Sept. 5, 1950; d. Estill Galloway and Lena Carruba; m. Bobby Joe Collins, May 6, 1967 (div. Feb., 1998); children: Norman, Robbie, Jason. AA in Arts, Humanities, U. Ky., 1991. Editor Mt. Rev. Appalshop, Inc., Whitesburg, Ky., 1987-90; writer-in-residence S.E. C.C., Cumberland, Ky., 1991-93, 96-99; editor Pine Mt. Sand and Gravel, Whitesburg, Ky, 1993-96; resource person Letcher and Harlan County (Ky.) Schs., 1991—; panel mem. Ky. Arts Coun., Frankfort, 1991—; adv. bd. Appalshop, Inc., 1996—. Author: (poetry prose) Blackberry Tea, 1988, A Cave and a Cracker, 1997; lyricist (record album) Stonega Run, 1997; playwright Stonega Run, 1999. Mem. So. Appalachin Writers. Avocations: dancing, reading, gardening, herbology. E-mail: jgcoll@pop.uky.edu. Home: Wolfpen Dr Thornton KY 41855 Office: SE C.C. 700 School St Cumberland KY 40823

COLLINS, JERRY CLAYTON, biomedical engineering educator; b. Nashville, Mar. 19, 1941; s. Seldon Clayton and Hilda (Copeland) C.; m. Sandra Lynn Johnson, Aug. 22, 1964; children: Leslie, Reid, Erin. B of Engring., Vanderbilt U., 1962; MSEE, Purdue U., 1965; PhD, Duke U., 1970. Registered profl. engr., Tenn. Asst. prof. U. Ky., Lexington, 1968-74, cons. dept. surgery, 1974, sr. rsch. assoc., 1975-77; rsch. instr. Vanderbilt U., Nashville, 1977-81, rsch. asst. prof., 1981-87, rsch. assoc. prof., 1987—; cons. Clin. Rsch. Ctr. Meharry Med. Coll., Nashville, 1987-90, dir. computers and biostats., 1990-93; cons. Aids Clin. Trials Unit, Meharry Med. Coll., 1993-96. Author 85 articles and 95 abstracts. Deacon Southside Ch. of Christ, Lexington, 1974-77, Otter Creek Ch. of Christ, Nashville, 1980-93; mem. exec. bd. Youth Hobby Shop, Nashville, 1982, 84, pres. exec. bd., 1983; bd. dirs. Christian Campus Ministries, Inc., Nashville, 1989-90, pres. bd. dirs., 1991-97; adv. bd. Internat. Christian U., Vienna, Austria, 1995—, bd. dirs., Zoe Music Group, Nashville, 1997—. Fellow AAAS, Am. Inst Med. Biol. Engrs.; mem. Am. Physiol. Soc., Biomed. Engring. Soc. (sr. mem., bull. editor 1991—, bd. dirs. 1996—, chair interface with industry com. 1997—), Tau Beta Pi, Eta Kappa Nu, Sigma Xi. Democrat. Office: Vanderbilt Univ AA-3228 Med Ctr N Nashville TN 37232

COLLINS, JOAN HENRIETTA, actress; b. London, May 23, 1933; came to U.S., 1938; d. Joseph William and Elsa (Bessant) C.; m. Anthony Newley (div.); children: Tara, Sacha; m. Ronald S. Kass, Mar., 1972 (div.); 1 child, Katy; m. Peter Holm (div.); m. Maxwell Reed. Ed., Francis Holland Sch., London; student, Royal Acad. of Dramatic Art. Films include: Cosh Boy, Our Girl Friday, I Believe in You, Girl in the Red Velvet Swing, Sea Wife, Rally Round the Flag Boys, Island in the Sun, Seven Thieves, Road to Hong Kong, Sunburn, The Stud, Game for Vultures, The Bitch, The Big Sleep, The Good Die Young, Land of the Pharoahs, The Bravados, Esther and the King, Warning Shot, The Executioner, Subterfuge, Revenge, Quest for Love, Tales From the Crypt, The Bawdy Adventures of Tom Jones, The Opposite Sex, The Virgin Queen, Quest for Love, Decadence, 1994, In the Bleak Mid-Winter, 1995, The Clandestine Marriage, 1998, The Flintstones-Viva Rock Vegas, 1999; theater appearances include: Jassey, Claudia, The Skin of Our Teeth, The Praying Mantis, The Last of Mrs. Cheyney, The 7th Veil, A Doll's House, Private Lives (London, Broadway, also tour); TV films include: Drive Hard, Drive Fast, 1973, The Man Who Came to Dinner, Paper Dolls, 1982, The Wild Women of Chastity Gulch, 1982, The Cartier Affair, The Making of a Male Model, 1983, Her Life as a Man, 1984; miniseries: The Moneychangers, 1976, Sins, 1986, Monte Carlo, 1986, Tonight at 8:30, 1991, Dynasty: The Reunion, 1992; appeared in Faerie Tale Theater (Showtime TV), 1982; star TV series: Dynasty, 1981-89; other TV appearances: Roseanne (ABC), 1993, Mama's Back spl., 1993, Annie: A Royal Adventure (TV Movie), 1995, Hart to Hart spl., (TV movie), 1995, Pacific Palisades, (TV Series), 1997, Sweet Deception (TV Movie), 1998; video spl. Secrets of Fitness and Beauty, 1994; author: Past Imperfect (autobiography), 1978, Katy, A Fight for Life, Joan Collins Beauty Book, (novels) Prime Time, 1988, Love and Desire and Hate, 1991, My Secrets, 1994, Too Damn Famous, 1995, Second Act (autobiography), 1996, My Friends Secrets, 1999. Recipient Emmy nomination, Golden Globe award, Ace award, People's Choice award; named to Order Brit. Empire. Avocations: travel, 18th Century art.

COLLINS, JOHN ALFRED, obstetrician-gynecologist, educator; b. Kitchener, Ont., Can., Oct. 2, 1936; s. John Bandel and Vera (Hannahson) C.; m. Carole Joanne Sedwick West; children: John Bruce, Blayne Linda, Anne Catherine. MD, U. West Ont., 1960. Intern Victoria Hosp., London; resident ob-gyn. U. West Ont., 1961-65; McLaughlin Found. fellow Univ. Coll. Hosp., London; with clin. endocrinology rsch. unit U. Edinburgh, U.K., Middlesex Hosp., London, 1965-67; clin. rsch. fellow Ont. Cancer Found. London Clinic, 1967-76; with dept. ob-gyn. U. West Ont., 1967-77, asst. dean undergrad. edn. faculty medicine, 1975-77; prof., head dept. ob-gyn. Dalhousie U., 1977-83; prof., chmn. dept. ob-gyn. McMaster U., Hamilton, Ont., 1983-93. Mem. editl. bd. New Eng. Jour. Medicine, 1991-96, Fertility and Sterility, 1991-96; contbr. articles to profl. jours. Mem. Royal Coll. Physicians and Surgeons Can., Am. Coll. Obstetricians and Gynecologists, Am. Soc. Reproductive Medicine, Can. Fertility Soc., Soc. Obstetricians and Gynecologists Can., Can. Med. Assn. Home: RR#1 Mahone Bay, Nova Scotia, ON Canada B0J 2E0 Office: McMaster U Faculty, Health Scis 1200 Main St W, Hamilton, Canada L8N 3Z5

COLLINS, JOHN FRANCIS, landscape architect, educator; b. Norristown, Pa., July 12, 1936; s. William Finn and Florence Roscoe (Manning) C.; m. Sandra Elizabeth Snowdon, Sept. 12, 1959; children: Kathleen M., John R., Christopher S., Matthew M. BS in Landscape Architecture, Pa. State U., 1959; MLA, Harvard U., 1961. Lic. landscape architect, Pa., Md., Conn., Mass. With Sasaki Walker Assocs., Boston, 1961-63; prin. own firm, Phila., 1963-71, Delta Group, 1971—; prof., chmn. dept. landscape architecture & horticulture Temple U., Phila., 1988—; vis. lectr./critic Harvard U., Washington U., La. State U., Ohio State U., Pa. State U., Temple U., U. Mich., Queens U. Belfast, Iowa State U., Rutgers U., U. Toronto, Auburn U., U. Colo., Morgan State U., Cornell U., U. Va.; vis. prof. Sch. Architecture & Planning, New Delhi, India, 1977; adj. assoc. prof. U. Pa.; also instr. in Drexel U. and Cornell U. Depts. Architecture. Work pub. in various mags. & books; projects include renewal of downtown Salem, Mass., new towns of Reston, Va. and Coldspring, Md.; restoration of Trans-Alaska Pipeline right-of-way; Schuylkill Park, Phila., Environ. Planning Program South Fork of Long Island. Mem. archtl. adv. bd., Camden, N.J.; past mem. Balt. Design Adv. Panel, also design rev. bds. of Salem, Mass., Reading, Pa., and Atlantic City, N.J.; past mem. Coun. of Pa. Horticultural Soc.; founder Phila. Landscape and Nursery Tng. (PLANT) program Phila. Prison, PLANT Ctr. City Landscape Maintenance program, Collins Nursery. Alumni fellow Pa. State U., 1995; recipient Disting. Achievement award Pa. Hort. Soc., 1995. Fellow Am. Soc. Landscape Archs.; mem. Am. Planning Assn. Roman Catholic. Avocations: camping, gardening, tree nursery.

COLLINS, JOHN JOSEPH, communications consultant; b. Boston, Dec. 22, 1945; m. Denise M. Denon, Apr. 18, 1970; children: Christopher, Brendan, Mark. BA, Boston Coll., 1967, MEd, 1970; EdD, U. Mass., 1980. Tchr. various sch. systems, 1967-75; project dir. Network Inc., Andover, Mass., 1975-95; owner Ctr. for Effective Comms., West Newbury, Mass., 1995—. Author: Developing Writing and Thinking Skills, 1992, Survivor's Guide to the Research Paper, 1994, Implementing the Cumulative Writing Folder, 1988, The Effective Writing Teacher, 1987. Office: Ctr for Effective Comms 320 Main St PO Box 957 West Newbury MA 01985-0957

COLLINS, JOHN ROGER, transportation company executive; b. Tulsa, Jan. 13, 1941; s. John Leland and Velma (Jones) C.; m. Mary Susan Lanphier, Aug. 29, 1964; children: John Burkett, Stephanie Lanphier, Elizabeth Arnold. AB, Princeton U., 1963; MBA, U. Chgo., 1967. Officer program Continental Ill. Nat. Bank, Chgo., 1963-65; economist Skelly Oil Co., Tulsa, 1967-70, asst. treas., 1970-72; exec. v.p. Vanply, Inc., Tulsa, 1972-76; v.p. adminstrn. Parker Drilling Co., Tulsa, 1976-79, sr. v.p., 1979-86; dir. econ. devel. NORDAM, Tulsa, 1987-91; gen. mgr. aircraft modification divsn. NORDAM, Tulsa, Okla., 1992-94, gen. mgr. mfg. divsn., 1994-96; v.p. adminstrn. Arrow Trucking Co., Tulsa, 1996—; chmn. bd. dirs. Am. Nursery Products, Tulsa, 1995—; bd. dirs. Bank of Lakes, Owasso, Okla.; pres. bd. dirs. Relvue Royalty Corp., Collins Energy Corp., Tulsa; trustee Jones Found., Bristow, Okla., 1981—; founder, dir. Custer County Bank, Colo., 1979-86; dir. Comty. Bank, Bristow, 1974-86. Author: The Vision of a Creature, 1963. Vice chmn. Tulsa Area United Way, 1975; trustee Hillcrest Med. Ctr. and its Found., Tulsa, 1978-86, 87-92; mem. alumni coun. Princeton (N.J.) U., 1979-85; bd. dirs. Tulsa Opera, Inc., 1980-82, Tulsa Internat. Visitors Coun., 1981-83, Tulsa area Campfire Girls, 1978-80. Mem. So. Hills Country Club, Summit, Tulsa Tennis (past pres., bd. dirs.), Tulsa Ozark Club (past pres. bd. dirs.). Presbyterian. Avocations: fishing, hunting, literary collecting. Office: 4230 S Elwood Ave Tulsa OK 74107-5823

COLLINS, JOHN W., nurse practitioner, lecturer; b. Chgo., Jan. 13, 1950; s. Joseph Theodore and Christine Pebble (Sisco) C.; m. Julia Marie Watson, July 20, 1984. BS in Civil Engring., U. Tex., 1973; ADN, San Antonio Coll., 1978; MSN, Vanderbilt U., 1983. RN; cert. diabetic educator; cert. adult and family nurse practitioner. Family nurse practitioner Cmty. Health Ctr., Alberta, Ala., 1984-86, Project Concern Internat., San Diego, 1986-87; nurse practitioner Prime Health Med. Group, Inc., Kansas City, Mo., 1987—; clin. instr. in family nurse practitioner program U. Kans. Sch. Nursing, Kansas City, 1994—; lectr. in grad. nurse practitioner program U. Mo. Sch. Nursing, Kansas City, 1994-99. Contbr. articles to The Nurse Practitioner. Mem. ANA (nurses in advanced practice com.), Am. Acad. Nurse Practitioners, Am. Diabetes Assn. Avocations: running, golf, tennis, guitar. Office: Stadium Care Ctr 9150 E 41st Ter Kansas City MO 64133-1448

COLLINS, JOHN WILLIAM, III, librarian; b. North Adams, Mass., June 1, 1948; s. John William and Josephine Theresa (O'Connell) C.; m. Linda Elizabeth Dawson, Sept. 25, 1971; children: Hannah, Dylan. BA in English Lit., U. Mass., 1974; MLS, U. Ky., 1975; EdD in Ednl. Leadership, Boston U., 1985. Student supr. stack maintenance U. Mass., 1972-74; grad. asst. instrnl. svcs. U. Ky., 1974-75; asst. libr., inst. libr. sci. Glenville (W.Va.) State Coll., 1975-79, project dir. Coun. on Libr. Resources, Robert F. Kidd Libr., 1977-78; asst. head bibliographic svcs., Mugar Meml. Libr. Boston U., 1979-82, head Ednl. Resources Libr., 1982-85; libr. Grad. Sch. Edn., mem. faculty Harvard U., Cambridge, Mass., 1985—; mem. ERIC redesign study panel, Dept. Edn., 1986. Author: The Taming of the Dinosaur, 1975, (with Leslie DiBona) Harvard Graduate School of Education: A Bibliography of Doctoral Dissertations, 1918-1987, 1989, (with others) A National Information Clearinghouse for Citizens in Education: A Feasibility Study Report to the John D. and Catherine T. MacArthur Foundation, 1985; contbr. articles to profl. jours. Trustee Boyden Libr., Foxboro, Mass., 1983—, chmn., 1986-90; councilman City of Glenville, 1978-79. With USN, 1968-70. Mem. ALA, Assn. Coll. and Rsch. Librs. (bibliographic instrn. conf. planning com. 1986, chmn. 1984, bibliographic instrn. sect. com. 1984-86, chmn. 1986, bibliographic instrn. exec. com. 1984-86, univ. libr. sect. steering com. 1988, pres.'s program planning com. 1991, chpts. coun.), Am. Ednl. Rsch. Assn., New Eng. Assn. Coll. and Rsch. Librs. (v.p.-1993, pres. 1994, bd. dirs. 1993-95), New Eng. On-Line Users Group, W.Va. Libr. Assn. (exec. com. 1979, chair JMRT sect. 1979), S.E. Libr. Assn. (bibliographic instrn. com. 1979), Tri-State Assn. Coll. and Rsch. Librs., Beta Phi Mu. Home: 118 East St Foxboro MA 02035-2257 Office: Harvard U Monroe C Gutman Libr 6 Appian Way Cambridge MA 02138-3704*

COLLINS, JOSEPH JAMESON, communications executive; b. Troy, N.Y., July 27, 1944; s. Mark Francis and Olive Elizabeth (Jameson) C.; m. Maura McManmon, June 3, 1972; children: Maura Farley, Elizabeth Dempsey, Joseph Jameson Jr., Kathryn M. AB, Brown U., 1966; MBA, Harvard U., 1972. Dir. mktg. Am. TV Communication Corp., Orlando, Fla., 1972-73, gen. mgr. Orlando cable system, 1973-74; div. mgr. Am. TV Communication Corp., Denver, 1974-76; v.p. ops. Am. TV Communication Corp., 1976-78, sr. v.p., 1978-80, exec. v.p., 1980-82, pres., 1982-84; chmn., chief exec. officer Am. TV Communication Corp., Stamford, 1988-90; pres. Home Box Office, Time Inc., 1984-88; chmn., CEO Time Warner Cable, 1990—; bd. dirs. TBS Inc., Ga., Tristar Pictures, N.Y.C. Lt. USNR, 1967-72. Mem. Nat. Cable TV Assn. (vice chmn. 1991). Roman Catholic. Office: Time Warner Cable 290 Harbor Dr Stamford CT 06902-7475*

COLLINS, KATHLEEN ANNE, artistic director; b. Elmira, N.Y., Dec. 20, 1951; d. James G. and Joyce (Balmer) C.; m. Andrew Stephon Elston, May 28, 1977; children: Megan, Kate. BA, SUNY, Albany, 1974; MA in Theatre, U. Wash., 1976, MFA in Theatre, 1979. Dir. edn. Seattle Children's Theatre, 1975-78; instr. drama Lakeside Sch., Seattle, 1978-79; artistic dir. Honolulu Theatre for Youth, 1979-83, Fulton Opera House, Lancaster, Pa., 1983-98; guest lectr. U. Wash., Seattle, 1979, U. Hawaii, Honolulu, 1981. Contbg. author: Drama With Children, 1979. Bd. dirs. PTO, Lancaster, 1990-98. Mem. Am. Assn. Theatre Educators, Assn. and Soc. for Theatre and Children. Democrat. Roman Catholic.

COLLINS, KEITH, federal executive. BS in Math., Villanova U., 1969; MS in Econs., U. Conn., 1973; PhD in Econs. and Stats., N.C. State U., N.C. State U., 1977. With USDA, Washington, 1978—, dir., econ. analysis staff, 1986-92, acting asst. sec. econs., 1993-95, chief economist, 1996—; mem. Sr. Exec. Svc. Recipient Presdl. Rank award, 1990, 92, 96. Office: USDA Office Chief Economist Rm 112-A Whitten Bldg Washington DC 20250-3810

COLLINS, LARRY, author, journalist; b. Hartford, Conn., Sept. 14, 1929; s. John Laurence and Helen (Cannon) C.; m. Nadia Hoda Sultan, Sept. 17, 1966; children—John Lawrence III, Michael Kevin. Grad., Loomis Inst., Windsor, Conn., 1947; B.A., Yale U., 1951. With advt. dept. Proctor & Gamble, Cin., 1951-52; With U.P.I., 1956-59; corr. U.P.I., Middle East, 1957-59; Middle East editor Newsweek mag., 1959-61; chief Newsweek mag. (Paris bur.), 1961-64. Author: (with Dominique La Pierre) Is Paris Burning, 1965, Or I'll Dress You in Mourning, 1967, O, Jerusalem!, 1972, Freedom at Midnight, 1975, The Fifth Horseman, 1980, Mountbatten and the Partition of India, 1982, Fall from Grace, 1985, Maze, 1989, Black Eagles, 1993, Le Jour du Miracle: D Day Paris, 1994, Tomorrow Belongs to Us, 1998. With AUS, 1953-55, ETO. Recipient Lit. prize Deauville Film Festival, 1985, Mannesmann-Talley Lit. prize, 1989. Address: La Biche Niche, 83350 Ramatuelle France

COLLINS, LARRY WAYNE, small business owner, information systems specialist; b. Plainville, Ind., Mar. 23, 1941; s. Virgil Raymond and Eva Pauline (Hedden) C.; m. Donna Kay Miller, July 25, 1961 (div. Apr. 1983); children: Rex Aaron, Jill Renee; m. Mary Ellen McConn, Dec. 15, 1983; 1 child, Ann Marie. AS, Vincennes U., 1961; BS, U. Indpls., 1968, MBA, 1981. Computer programmer State of Ind., Indpls., 1963-64, systems analyst, 1964-65, asst. ops. mgr., 1965-66; mgr. systems and programming Community Hosp. of Indpls., 1966-67, dir. data processing, 1967-77, v.p. hosp. systems, 1977-84; v.p., mgr. Bethesda N. Hosp., Cin., 1984-85, group v.p., 1985-86; sr. v.p. Bethesda Oak Hosp., Cin., 1986-91; sr. v.p., chief info. officer Bethesda Hosp., Inc., Cin., 1991-95; ptnr. RHI, Inc., Maineville, Ohio, 1995-98; prin. Collins Cons., Maineville, 1998—. Bd. dirs. Tri-State Community Cancer Orgn., 1986-92, chmn., 1989-92; chmn. bd. dirs. Hospice of Cin., Inc., 1987-91. Mem. Ind. Cen. U. Alumni Assn. (bd. dirs. 1984-88), Am. Coll. Healthcare Execs., Tri-State Health Adminstrs. Forum, Am. Mgmt. Assn., Am. Acad. Med. Adminstrs. (bd. dirs. 1993-98, chmn. elect 1996, chmn. 1997), Kiwanis (bd. dirs. Montgomery chpt. 1984-87). Methodist. Avocations: golf, photography. Home: 7667 Hopkins Rd Maineville OH 45039-8682 Office: Collins Cons 7667 Hopkins Rd # 101 Maineville OH 45039-8682

COLLINS, LINDA LOU POWELL, manager of contracts; b. Michigan City, Ind., May 6, 1957; d. Ronald Edward Powell and Betty Louise (Gruenberg) Will; m. Aug. 15, 1981 (div. May 18, 1983); m. Edward T. Collins, oct. 14, 1989; 1 child, Elizabeth Louise. BA in English, Purdue U., 1980; MBA, St. Francis Coll., Fort Wayne, Ind., 1988. Cert. purchasing mgr.; cert. profl. contracts mgr. Head expeditor Graham Electronics, Ft. Wayne, Ind., 1981-82; expeditor solid state Raytheon Sys. Co. (formerly Magnavox Electronic Sys. Co.), Ft. Wayne, 1982-83, assoc. buyer, 1983-85, buyer, 1985-87, subcontract adminstr., 1987-88, sr. contract adminstr., 1988-93, contract mgr., 1993-96, mgr. contracts, 1996—; bus. writing instr. Ind.-Purdue U., Ft. Wayne, 1990-91; seminar instr. Nat. Contract Mgmt. Assn., 1991-92. Mem. Civic Theater Dirs.' Cir., Ft. Wayne, 1989—; property trustee St. Joseph United Meth. Ch., Ft. Wayne, 1992, choir mem., 1993-95; vol. tutor Study Connection, 1995-97. Recipient Woman of Achievement award YWCA, 1996. Fellow Nat. Contract Mgmt. Assn. (program chair 1990-91, v.p. 1991-92, mem. chair 1992-93, v.p. programs/facilities 1993-94, v.p./sec. 1994-95, regional mem. chair 1994-96, nat. functional dir. mem. retention 1994-95, v.p. membership 1995-96, nat. dir. 1996-97, pres.-elect 1997-98, pres. 1998-99, N. Ctrl. region nat. v.p.-elect 1999—, regional fellows chair 1996, James E. Cravens Mem. award 1993, 96, Blanch Witte Hon. Mention award 1996); mem. Philips Electronics Credit Union (bd. dirs. 1997—), Purdue U. Alumni Assn. (life), Magna Health Club (v.p. 1990-91, mem. chair 1991-95, sec. 1995-96), Magnavox Mgmt. Club Ind. (facilities chair 1990-91, bd. dirs. 1993-96), Alpha Gamma Delta (altruism chair 1977-78). Republican. Avocations: reading, writing, fitness. Office: Raytheon Systems Co 1010 Production Rd Fort Wayne IN 46808-4106

COLLINS, LYNN M., oncology clinical nurse specialist; b. St. Paul, Oct. 10, 1960; d. Bruce W. and Marianne (Palla) Baumann; m. Robert H. Collins Jr., Sept. 14, 1985. BSN, Winona State U., 1982; M in Nursing, UCLA, 1990. Cert. advanced oncology nurse. Staff clin. nurse II Baylor U. Med. Ctr., Dallas, supr., 1984-87; acting nurse mgr. Children's Hosp. of L.A., 1987-89; rsch. asst. UCLA Sch. Nursing; oncology clin. nurse specialist Sammons Cancer Ctr. Baylor U. Med. Ctr., Dallas, 1990-97; oncology nurse cons. Dallas, 1997—. Asst. editor for Clin. Practice, ONS, On-line. Mem. Oncology Nursing Soc. (nat. Congress com. 1989, 90, nat. Fall inst. com. 1991, 92, chair nat. Fall inst. com. 1993), Leukemia Soc. Am. (N. Tex. chpt., bd. trustees 1995—, chair patient svcs. com. 1997), Sigma Theta Tau. Home: 6439 Westlake Ave Dallas TX 75214-3438

COLLINS, MARIBETH WILSON, foundation president; b. Portland, Oreg., Oct. 27, 1918; d. Clarence True and Maude (Akin) Wilson; m. Truman Wesley Collins, Mar. 12, 1943; children: Timothy Wilson and Terry Stanton (twins), Cherida Smith, Truman Wesley Jr. BA, U. Oreg., 1940. Pres. Collins Found., Portland, Oreg., 1964—; dir. Collins Pine Co., Collins Holding Co., Ostrander Resource Co. Mem. exec. com., sec. bd. trustees Willamette U., Salem, Oreg., also mem. coms. on orgn. and campus religious life. Mem. Univ. Club, Gamma Phi Beta. Republican. Methodist. Home: 2275 SW Mayfield Ave Portland OR 97225-4400 Office: Collins Found Ste 305 1618 SW 1st Ave Portland OR 97201-5708

COLLINS, MARK, professional football player; b. San Bernardino, Calif., Jan. 16, 1964. Student, California State U., Fullerton. With N.Y. Giants, 1986-94; cornerback Kansas City Chiefs, 1994-97; with Green Bay Packers, 1997, Seattle Seahawks, 1998—. Recipient All-America team defensive back, The Sporting News, 1985. Played in Super Bowls XXI (1986), XXV (1990); Dr. Z's All-Pro Team, 1994. Office: Seattle Seahawks Kingdome 11220 NE 53d St Kirkland WA 98033*

COLLINS, MARTHA, English language educator, writer; b. Omaha, Nov. 25, 1940; d. William E. and Katheryn (Essick) C.; m. Theodore M. Space, Apr. 1991. AB, Stanford U., 1962; MA, U. Iowa, 1965, PhD, 1971. Asst. prof. N.E. Mo. U., Kirksville, Kirksville, 1965-66; instr. U. Mass., Boston, 1966-71, asst. prof. English, 1971-75, assoc. prof., 1975-85, prof. English, 1985—, co-dir. creative writing, 1979—, chair dept. English, 1994-96; prof., co-dir. creative writing Oberlin (Ohio) Coll., Boston, 1997—. Author (poetry): The Catastrophe of Rainbows, 1985, The Arrangement of Space, 1991, A History of Small Life on a Windy Planet, 1993, Some Things Words Can Do, 1998. Fellow Bunting Inst., 1982-83, Ingram Merrill Found., 1988, NEA, 1990; recipient Pushcart prize, 1985, 96, 98, Di Castagnola award, 1990. Mem. Poetry Soc. Am., Assoc. Writing Programs. Democrat. Office: Oberlin Coll Rice Hall Oberlin OH 44074

COLLINS, MARY, management consultant, former Canadian legislator; b. Vancouver, B.C., Can., Sept. 26, 1940; d. Fredrick Claude and Isabel Margaret (Copp) Wilkins; children: David, Robert, Sarah. Student, U. B.C., Queen's U., Kingston, Ont., Can.; LLD (hon.), Royal Rds. Mil. Coll., 1994. Mem. Can. Ho. of Commons, 1984-93; pres., CEO B.C. Health Assn., 1994-97; pres. Amarok Holdings, Ltd.; mem. fed. cabinet Can., assoc. min. nat. def., 1989-92, min. Western econ. diversification, 1993, min. state environ., 1993, min. responsible for status of women, 1990-93, min. of health, 1993; dir. Can. Blood Svcs.; sec., treas. Vancouver Bd. Trade. Trustee Queen's U.; bd. dirs. Vancouver Libr., Vancouver C.C.; dir. Can. Blood Svcs. Mem. Internat. Womens Fedn. Mem. Progressive Conservative Party. Home: 201-1315 W 7th Ave, Vancouver, BC Canada V6H 1B8 Office: Amarok Holdings Ltd, 1315 W 7th Ave Ste 201, Vancouver, BC Canada V6H 1B8

COLLINS, MARY ELLEN, human resources executive; b. Indpls., Jan. 24, 1949; d. Carl William and Hester (Dawson) McConn; m. Thomas N. Wininger, June 19, 1971 (div. 1981); m. Larry Wayne Collins, Dec. 15, 1983; 1 child, Ann Marie. Diploma in nursing, Holy Cross Coll., 1969; BS, Coll. of St. Francis, 1981; MS, Ind. U., 1984; PhD in Orgnl. Behavior, Union Inst., Cin., 1993. Edn. coord. Cmty. Hosp., Indpls., 1969-84; dir. tng. Middletown (Ohio) Regional Hosp., 1984-87; pres. People Power Cons. Svc., Cin., 1987—; adj. prof. Coll. Mt. St. Joseph, Ohio, 1988-93; faculty MBA program Xavier U., Cin., 1996—. Editl. bd. Strategic Governance for Non Profit Orgns., (newsletters) Teamwork, Quality One. Adminstrv. chair Deerfield Ch., Maineville, 1987-89. Mem. ASTD (bd. dirs. Cin. chpt. 1988-89), Assn. for Psychol. Type (pres., founder Greater Cin. chpt. 1992—, bd. dirs. Gt. Lakes region, Internat. New Leader award 1993, internat. conf. chair 1997, dir. membership com. 1997—), Assn. Quality Participation (healthcare adv. bd., Disting. Faculty mem.), Internat. Visitors Ctr., Women Entrepreneurs, Inc. Methodist. Avocation: gourmet cooking.

COLLINS, MAX ALLAN, writer; b. Muscatine, Iowa, Mar. 3, 1948; s. Max Allan, Sr. and Patricia Jane Mull, June 1, 1968; 1 child, Nathan Allan. AA, Ea. Iowa C.C., Muscatine, 1968; BA, U. Iowa, 1970, MFA, 1972. Writer Dick Tracy Comic Strip Tribune Media Svcs., Chgo., 1977-93; writer Batman and other features DC Comics, N.Y.C., 1988—; writer, co-creator feature Mike Danger Big Entertainment, 1993-97; screenwriter Axis Films, Hollywood, Calif., 1993-95; instr. fiction writing Miss. Valley Writers Conf., Rock Island, Ill., 1973—; pres. The Mommy Co., L.C., Muscatine, Iowa, 1994—. Author: (books) True Detective, 1983 (Best Novel award Pvt. Eye Writers of Am./Shamus award 1983), Stolen Away, 1991 (Best Novel award Pvt. Eye Writers of Am./Shamus 1991), numerous others 1973—; screenwriter, dir.: (films) Mommy, 1995, Mommy's Day, 1996 (Best Screenplay Iowa Motion Picture awards 1996). Recipient Inkpot award for outstanding achievement in comic arts San Diego Comic Conv., Calif., 1982, Edgar Allan Poe Spl. award Mystery Writers of Am., N.Y.C., 1984, Disting. Alumnus award Muscatine C.C., 1984, Susan Glaspell award for Fiction, Quad-City Times, Davenport, Iowa, 1990. Mem. Pvt. Eye Writers of Am. (bd. dirs. 1991—), Mystery Writers of Am. (bd. dirs. 1980—), Iowa Motion Picture Assn. (bd. dirs. 1994—, pres. 1998-99), Iowa Screenwriters Alliance (bd. dirs. 1997—). Avocations: keyboardist/singer with rock groups, collector of original comics, pin-up and paperback-cover art. Home: 301 Fairview Ave Muscatine IA 52761-4929

COLLINS, MELISSA ANN, oncological nurse; b. Wichita Falls, Tex., June 6, 1951; d. Foley D. Jr. and Pathea Jo (Thornton) C. BS, U. Tex., Austin, 1973. Cert. oncology nurse, med. radiologic technologist. Nurse technologist U. Tex. System Cancer Ctr. at M.D. Anderson Hosp., Houston; staff nurse, technologist Hermann Hosp., Houston; nurse/radiation therapist Park Plaza Hosp., Houston. Mem. Oncology Nursing Soc.

COLLINS, MERLE, English educator; b. Oranjestaad, Aruba, Sept. 29, 1950; d. John and Dorothy Helena Collins. BA, U. West Indies, 1972; MA, Georgetown U., 1981; PhD, U. London, 1990. Cert. in translation. Sr. lectr. Caribbean Studies U. North London, Eng., 1990-94; prof. English and Comparative Lit. U. Md., College Park, 1995—; dir. U. Md. Study in Mexico City, 1997; vis. prof. St. George's U., Grenada, 1998; cons. editor Jour. of Caribbean Women Writers, Miami, 1998—. Author: Angel, 1987, Rain Darling, 1990, Rotten Pomerack, 1992; co-editor: Watchers and Seekers, 1987;. Grantee U. Md., 1996. Mem. Assn. of Caribbean Women Writers and Scholars, Caribbean Studies Assn. E-mail: mc188@umail.umd.edu. Office: U Md Dept English 3101 Susquehanna Hall College Park MD 20742

COLLINS, MICHAEL A. (MAC COLLINS), congressman; b. Ga., Oct. 15, 1944; m. Julie Watkins; 4 children. Owner Collins Trucking Co.; former chmn. Butts County Commn.; mem. 2 terms Ga. State Senate; mem. Congress from 3d Ga. dist., 1992—; mem. House com. ways and means, mem. House com. on the budget, dep. majority whip; mem. House Com. on Ways and Means; dep. majority whip. Republican. Office: US House Representatives 1131 Longworth Bldg Washington DC 20515-1003

COLLINS, MICHAEL EDWARD, religious newspaper editor; b. Columbus, Ohio, Nov. 17, 1938; s. Martin Patrick and Monica Louise (Metzger) C. Student, MIT, 1956-57, Ohio State U., 1957-61. Staff writer Cath. Times, Columbus, 1962-66, news editor, 1966-70, editor, 1970-95, cons. editor, 1995—; pres. Cath. Men's Luncheon Club, 1972-73, Holy Name Parish Coun., 1972-73; chmn. comm. Diocesan Coun. Cath. Men, 1964-67; chmn. comm. sect. Cath. Conf. Ohio, 1978-80; instr. Gabriel Richard Inst., 1963-69. Contbr. articles to religious jours. Mem. Cath. Press Assn. (mem. various coms.), Soc. Profl. Journalists (pres. Ctrl. Ohio chpt. 1980-82), Mensa, Press Club Ohio, KC. Home: 82 Georgian Dr Columbus OH 43214-1671 Office: The Cath Times 197 W Gay St Columbus OH 43215-2830 *I think it is impossible to be a Christian by yourself. If a person is to follow Matthew 25, he or she has to be involved in a real church—one with old people, young people, poor people, sick people, people who need each other.*

COLLINS, MICHAEL JAMES, investment company executive; b. Orange, N.J., July 30, 1944; s. James Mitchel and Dorothy (Dann) C.; m. Wynnell Madison Roach, Nov. 14, 1982; children: Malcolm James, Catherine Elise, Miles Benjamin. B.A., Stanford U., 1967; M.B.A., Harvard U., 1970; spl. degree program, Am. Inst. Fgn. Trade, 1968. Chmn. bd., pres., chief exec. officer, chief operating officer Fidelity Union Life Ins. Co., Dallas, 1972-82; pres. Allianz Investment Corp., Dallas, 1980-82; pres., chief exec. officer Collins Capital, Dallas, 1982—; mng. gen. ptnr. Collins Capital Diversified Fund, Collins Capital, Ltd., Gold Mining & Minerals Ltd., Fgn. Capital Ltd.; ptnr. and chmn. investment commn. Taylor & Turner Assocs. Venture Capital. Trustee KERA-TV Pub. Boradcasting Sta., Dallas Mus. Art, Baylor Hosp., Colo. Outward Bound Sch.; bd. dirs., v.p. Carr P. Collins Found., Dallas; bd. dirs. Dallas County C.C. Dist. Found.; internat. edn. chmn. Young Pres.'s Orgn... Named One of 10 Outstanding Young Men of Am. U.S. Jaycees, 1978, Outstanding Young Texans of Decade by Nations Bus. Mem. Young Pres. Orgn. Clubs: Petroleum, Preston Trail Golf. Office: Collins Capital 3131 Turtle Creek Blvd Ste 888 Dallas TX 75219-5437

COLLINS, MICHAEL SEAN, obstetrician and gynecologist, educator; b. Yankton, S.D., Sept. 8, 1951; s. Edward Daniel and Joyce (Slatky) C.; m. Judy Furman, Sept. 20, 1975; children: Lauren, Sean, Carolyn. BS, Davidson Coll., 1973; MD, Med. U. S.C., 1977. Diplomate Am. Bd. Ob-Gyn. Chief resident in ob-gyn Med. U. S.C., Charleston, 1980-81; instr. ob-gyn U. Oreg. Health Scis. Ctr., Portland, 1981—; chmn. dept. ob-gyn Good Samaritan Hosp., Portland, 1983-85; cons. Prepared Childbirth Assn., Portland, 1981—, Triplet Connection, L.A., 1985—. Fellow ACOG (adv. coun. 1991—, chmn. Oreg. sect.); mem. AMA, Oreg. Med. Assn., Oreg. Ob-Gyn. Soc., Pacific Coast Ob-Gyn. Soc., Pacific N.W. Ob-Gyn. Soc., Am. Fertility Soc., Porsche Club Am., Oreg. Ob-Gyn. Soc. (vice-chmn. 1991-94, chmn. 1995—), Am. Assn. Gynecologic Laparoscopists, Internat. Soc. Advancement Humanistic Studies Medicine, Alpha Omega Alpha. Republican. Roman Catholic. Avocations: photography, jogging, travel, skiing, hiking. Home: 716 NW Rapidan Ter Portland OR 97210-3129 Office: Portland Ob-Gyn Assocs 1130 NW 22nd Ave Ste 120 Portland OR 97210-2934

COLLINS, MONICA ANN, journalist; b. Rockville Center, N.Y.; d. Louis Andrew and Eileen Ann Collins. B.A., Vassar Coll., 1973. Writer, editor

The Real Paper, Cambridge, Mass., 1975-79; TV critic Boston Herald Am., 1979-83, USA Today, Arlington, Va., 1983-89; columnist Boston Mag., 1983-85, TV Guide, 1989-93; TV critic, editl. page columnist Boston Herald, 1989—. Roman Catholic. Office: The Boston Herald 1 Herald St Boston MA 02118-2200

COLLINS, ORAL EDMOND, theology educator, archaeologist; b. Alton, N.Y., May 9, 1928; s. Johnston Homer and Thelma Inez (Davis) C.; m. Joyce Irene Towle, June 7, 1952; children: Sandra, Rodney, Roger, Judith, Paula. BA in Theology, New England Sch. Theology, Brookline, Mass., 1950; B of Divinity, Gordon Divinity Sch., South Hamilton, Mass., 1953; MA, Brandeis U., 1966, PhD, 1977. Instr. New Testament and Greek Berkshire Christian Coll., Lenox, Mass., 1950-54, assoc. prof. bible, dir. libr., 1954-68, prof. New Testament studies, dir. libr., 1968-76, prof. bibl. studies, 1976-88; prof. Bible The Berkshire Inst. for Christian Studies, Lenox, Mass., 1988—; sq. supr. archaeology, Kh. el-Maqatir, West Bank, Israel, Assocs. for Bibl. Rsch., Walkersville, Md., 1995—; mem. task force on history Advent Christian Gen. Conf., Charlotte, N.C., 1979—; exec. bd. dirs. The Berkshire Inst. Christian Studies, 1996—. Co-author: Manual of Ministerial Practice and Procedure, 1982; contbr. articles to profl. jours. and ency.; editor adult Sunday sch. quarterly Advent Christian Gen. Conf., 1989—. First elder Hope Ch., Lenox, 1991—. Mem. Assocs. Bibl. Rsch., Evang. Theol. Soc., Soc. Bibl. Lit., Near East Archaeol. Soc. Republican. Advent Christian. Avocations: photography, genealogy. Home: 152 Old Stockbridge Rd Lenox MA 01240-2811 Office: Berkshire Inst Christian Studies 175 Kemble St Lenox MA 01240-2817

COLLINS, PATRICIA A., lawyer, judge; b. Camp Lejeune, N.C., Mar. 12, 1954; d. Thomas and Margaret (Parrish) C. BA, U. Va., 1976; JD, Gonzaga U., 1982. Bar: Alaska 1982, U.S. Dist. Ct. Alaska, U.S. Ct. Appeals (9th cir.) 1982. Assoc. Guess & Rudd, Anchorage and Juneau, 1982-84, 85-87; asst. pub. defender Alaska Pub. Defender's Office, Ketchikan, 1984-85; prin. Collins Law Office, Juneau, 1987-95; judge Alaska Dist. Ct., Ketchikan, 1995-1999, Juno Superior Ct., Alaska, 1999—; part time fed. magistrate judge U.S. Cts., Juneau, 1988-95, Kitchikan, 1996—; adj. prof. U. Alaska, Juneau, 1991-95. Mem. Alaska Bar Assn., Ketchikan Sailing Club. Office: Alaska Superior Ct 114100 Juneau AK 99811-4100*

COLLINS, PAUL DANIEL, principal. Prin. Amherst (N.H.) Mid. Sch. Recipient Blue Ribbon Sch. award Dept. Edn., 1986-87, 90-91, 94-96. Mem. Nat. Assn. Elem. Prin. (pres. 1979-80), Nat. Assn. Secondary Sch. Prin., N.H. Assn. Sch. Prin. (pres. 1998-99). Office: Amherst Mid Sch Cross Rd PO Box 966 Amherst NH 03031-0966

COLLINS, PAUL JOHN, banker; b. West Bend, Wis., Oct. 26, 1936; s. Curtis Alvin and Adele (Stopenbach) C.; m. Carol Lee Hoffmann, May 8, 1965; children: Ronald Alvin, Julia Downing. BBA, U. Wis., 1958; MBA, Harvard U., 1961. With Citibank, N.Y.C., 1961—; investment analyst, portfolio mgmt. Citibank, 1961-70, sr. v.p., chmn. investment policy com., 1970-75, sr. v.p., head corp. planning, 1976-77, sr. v.p., head fin. div., 1977-79, exec. v.p. acctg. and control, 1980-81, group exec. investment br., 1982-85, sr. corp. officer N.Am., 1985-88, vice chmn., 1988-98, also bd. dirs., Citigroup vice chmn., 1998—; bd. dirs. Citicorp, Kimberly Clark Corp., Nokia Corp. Carnegie Hall, Ctrl. Park Conservancy, Glyndebourne Arts Trust. Republican. Congregationalist. Home: 29 Wilton Crescent, London SW1 X8SA, England Office: Citibank House, 33 Cavendish Sq, London W1A 2SY, England

COLLINS, PAUL STEVEN, vascular surgeon; b. Portsmouth, Ohio, July 24, 1954; s. Paul Whitney and Geralda Pearl (Hoskins) C.; m. Cathy Ann McWicker, Jan. 17, 1981; children: Lauren Elizabeth, Paul McWicker, Andrew Steven. BS, Davidson Coll., 1976; MD, U. South Fla., 1979. Diplomate Am. Bd. Surgery, spl. qualifications in gen. vascular surgery and surg. critical care; diplomate Nat. Bd. Med. Examiners; lic. surgeon, Fla., Va. Commd. 2d lt. U.S. Army, 1979, advanced through grades to lt. col., 1990; resident in gen. surgery Walter Reed Army Med. Ctr. U.S. Army, Washington, 1979-84; chief gen. surg. U.S. Army, Würzburg, West Germany, 1984-86; fellow peripheral vasc. surgery Walter Reed Army Med. Ctr. U.S. Army, Washington, 1986-87; chief vascular surgery Letterman Army Med. Ctr. U.S. Army, San Francisco; resigned U.S. Army, 1992; pvt. practice St. Petersburg, Fla., 1990—; asst. clin. prof. surgery U. S. Fla., Tampa, 1995—; asst. clin. prof. surgery Uniformed Svcs. U. of Health Scis., Bethesda, Md., 1984—; chief of surgery St. Anthony's, 1998—; profl. mem. Keystone, Tampa, Fla., 1993-97; pres. Bay Blaza Outpatient Surgry; dir. vascular lab. St. Anthony's Hosp., St. Petersburg, 1994-97, chmn. dept. surgery, 1998—; bd. dirs, trustee St. Anthony's Found; team surgeon Tampa Bay Devil Rays Baseball Team, 1996—. Contbr. chpts. to books, articles to med. jours. Bd. dirs. St. Anthony's Found. Recipient Physicians Recognition award AMA, 1992, Sigvaris award Camp Internat., 1987. Fellow ACS (Regional Trauma award 1984), Internat. Soc. for Cardiovascular Surgeons; mem. So. Assn. for Vascular Surgery (Pres.'s award 1992), Fla. Vascular Soc., Fla. Med. Assn., Pinellas County Med. Soc. (bd. govs.). Avocations: golf, tennis, snow and water skiing, gardening. Office: 1201 5th Ave N Ste 200 Saint Petersburg FL 33705-1410

COLLINS, PHILIP REILLY, lawyer, educator; b. New Orleans, July 26, 1921; s. James Mark and Katherine (Gallaher) C.; m. Mary Catherine O'Leary, Feb. 9, 1946. BA, Loyola U., New Orleans, 1939, JD, 1942; MA in Govt. and Internat. Law and Rels., Georgetown U., 1948, PhD, 1950; LLM, George Washington U., 1952. Bar: La. 1942, Mass. 1948, D.C. 1953, Md. 1963, Va. 1986. Atty. Bur. Land Mgmt., Dept. Interior, Washington, 1946-47; asst. legis. counsel Office of Solicitor, P.O. Dept., 1947-48; pvt. practice Washington, 1954-77, 79—; ptnr. MacCracken, Collins & Hawes, 1960-69; chief counsel, staff dir. com. on rules U.S. Ho. of Reps., 1977-78; spl. counsel Fed. Home Loan Bank Bd., 1961-69, Ky. Savs. and Loan League, 1967-68, State of Alaska, 1967-68; vis. prof., spl. asst. to pres. for labor rels. Queens Coll., 1969-70; lectr. pub. adminstrn. Sch. Social Scis. Cath. U. Am., 1954-56, lectr. Sch. Law, 1954-60. Mem. adv. com. on wills, trusts and other bequests Loyola U., New Orleans, 1966-69, charter mem. bd. visitors Law Sch., 1968-85, mem. pres.'s coun., 1976-85. Capt USAAF, 1942-46, PTO; maj. USAF, Korea; col. Res., ret. Mem. ABA, La. Bar Assn., Mass. Bar Assn., D.C. Bar Assn., Assn. of Bar of City of N.Y., Md. Bar Assn., Va. State Bar, KC, Mil. Order of Carabao, Univ. Club (Washington), Delta Theta Phi, Phi Alpha Theta. Democrat. Roman Catholic. Home: 1300 Crystal Dr Apt 209 Arlington VA 22202-3234

COLLINS, RICHARD FRANCIS, microbiologist, educator; b. St. Paul, Minn., Jan. 22, 1938; s. Francis Bernard and Maude Roegene (Night) C.; m. Deanne Margaret Scafati, Dec. 28, 1960 (div. 1970); children: Lisa, Mark, Michael; m. Judy A. Wright, Feb. 15, 1978; children: Kristyn, Todd. AB, Shepherd Coll., 1962; MA, Wake Forest U., 1968; PhD, U. Okla., 1973. Tchr. Alexandria (Va.) Schs., 1962-66; instr. U. Okla., Oklahoma City, 1972-73; lab. dir. Infectious Disease Svc. U. Ill./Rockford Sch. of Medicine, 1974-80; asst. prof. U. Ill., Rockford, 1973-80; assoc. prof. U. Osteo. Medicine and Health Scis., Des Moines, 1980-85, faculty pres., 1990-91, pres.-elect, 1997-98, prof., dept. head, 1985-95; prof., divsn. head Ariz. Coll. Osteo. Medicine, Glendale, 1997—; cons. U.S. EPA, Washington, 1975-81; mem. Nat. Bd. Podiatry Examiners, Princeton, N.J., 1983-96, Nat. Bd. Osteo. Med. Examiners, Des Plaines, Ill., 1994-97; participant mission project Christian Med. Soc., Dominican Republic, 1977. Mem. editorial bd. African Jour. Clin. Exptl. Immunology, 1979-83; contbr. articles to profl. jours. Vol. Blank Guild, Iowa Meth. Hosp., Des Moines, 1988-91. Recipient awards NSF, 1962-67, fellowship NIH, 1969-70, Gov.'s Vol. awards State of Iowa, 1988, 89. Mem. Am. Soc. for Microbiology, Am. Soc. Tropical Medicine and Hygiene, Iowa Acad. of Sci., Sigma Xi (pres. 1987-90, 96-97, treas. 1990-91). Avocations: photography, auto restoration. Home: 4131 W Tierra Buena Ln Phoenix AZ 85053-3717 Office: Midwestern U Ariz Coll Osteo Medicine 19555 N 59th Ave Glendale AZ 85308-6813

COLLINS, RICHARD LAWRENCE, magazine editor, publisher, author; b. Little Rock, Nov. 28, 1933; s. Leighton Holden Collins and Sarah Aloysia (Banks) Polk; m. Ann Terry Slocomb, Feb. 14, 1958; children—Charlotte, Sarah, Richard Jr. Chief pilot Ben M. Hogan Co., Little Rock, 1957-58; mng. editor Air Facts mag., Princeton, N.J., 1958-68; sr. editor Flying mag., N.Y.C., 1968-77, editor in chief, 1977-88; editor in chief, pub. Pilot, sr. v.p. Aircraft Owners and Pilots Assn., Frederick, Md., 1988-89; aviation cons., 1989—. Author numerous aviation books including: Flying Safely, 1977, Tips to Fly By, 1980, Thunderstorms and Airplanes, 1982, Flight Level Flying, 1985, Air Crashes, 1986, The Perfect Flight, 1988, Pilot Upgrade, 1989, Mastering the Systems, 1991; contbr. articles to mags. Chmn. Ark. Aero. Commn., Little Rock, 1976. Served with U.S. Army, 1955-57. Recipient Earl D. Osborn award Aviation Writers, 1978, Sherman Fairchild award Flight Safety Found., 1965; named to Ark. Aviation Hall of Fame, 1988. Mem. Flying Physicians Assn. (hon.), Lawyer Pilots Bar Assn. (hon.), Civil Aeromed. Assn. (hon.). Clubs: Quiet Birdmen. Avocation: sailing. Office: 500 W Putnam Ave Greenwich CT 06830-6086

COLLINS, RICHARD WAYNE, English literature educator; b. Eugene, Oreg., Sept. 4, 1952; s. Alva Corder and Reba Voneta (Tannehill) C.; m. Leigh Frances Guillory, June 6, 1992; 1 child, Cyleste. BA in English, U. Oreg., 1977; MA in English, U. Calif., Irvine, 1979, PhD in English, 1984. Asst. prof. La. State U., Baton Rouge, 1982-92; assoc. prof. Am. U. of Bulgaria, Blagoevgrad, 1995-97, Xavier U., New Orleans, La., 1997—. Author: (books) Foolscape, 1983, John Fante: A Literary Portrait, 1999. Recipient Fulbright Rsch. Grant, London, 1980-81, Leverhulme Commonwealth-USA fellowship, Wales, 1984-85; named Fulbright Sr. Lectr., U.S. Info. Agy., Bucharest Romania, 1992-93, Timisoara, Romania, 1993-94. Avocation: fencing. E-mail: rnlcoll@bellsouth.net. Home: 2480 Dauphine St New Orleans LA 70117 Office: Xavier U La 7325 Palmetto St New Orleans LA 70125

COLLINS, ROBERT ARNOLD, English language educator; b. Miami, Fla., Apr. 25, 1929; s. John William and Edna (Arnold) C.; m. Laura Virginia Roberts, June 3, 1960; 1 child, Judith. BA in English, U. Miami, Coral Gables, Fla., 1951; MA in English, U. Ky., 1960, PhD in English, 1968. Chair English Midway (Ky.) Jr. Coll., 1960-64; assoc. prof. English No. Ill. U., DeKalb, 1964-68, Morehead (Ky.) State U., 1968-69; from assoc. prof. to prof. English Fla. Atlantic U., Boca Raton, 1970—; founder, dir. Internat. Conf. on the Fantastic in the Arts, Ft. Lauderdale, Fla., 1980—. Author: Thomas Burnett Swann: A Critical Biography, 1980, Science Fiction and Fantasy Book Review Annual, 1987-91; editor: Scope of the Fantastic, 1985, Modes of the Fantastic, 1995; editor Fantasy Rev., 1981-87; mng. editor Jour. of the Fantastic in the Arts, 1995—; contbr. articles to profl. jours. Recipient World Fantasy award World Fantasy Conv., New Haven, 1982, Balrog award Sword and Shield, 1982, 83. Home: 1320 SW 5th St Boca Raton FL 33486-4404 Office: Fla Atlantic U English Dept 777 Glades Rd Boca Raton FL 33431-6424

COLLINS, ROBERT CRAIG, business educator; b. El Paso, Tex., Apr. 9, 1958; s. Robert Claude and E. Howellyn (Smith) C.; m. Grace Susann Sawyer, Aug. 5, 1989; children: Grace, Diane. BBA in Computer Info. Sys., U. Tex., El Paso, 1995; postgrad., U. North Tex., 1996—. Asst. mgr. Furr's Cafeterias, Inc., El Paso, 1986-88; night mgr. Farm Fresh Produce, Inc., El Paso, 1988-95; tech. writer Creative Edn. Inst., Waco, Tex., 1996; instr., asst. program chair Tex. State Tech. Coll., Waco, 1996—, dept. chair, 1999—. Author: Mastering Today's Software: Paradox, 1993, Mastering Today's Software: Access, 1994, Mastering Today's Software: I.M., 1995, Productivity Software: Paradox, 1995. Mem. St. Alban's Sch. Bd., Waco, 1997—, v.p., 1999—. Mem. Data Processing Mgmt. Assn., Alpha Chi (pres. 1993-95). Office: Texas State Tech Coll 3801 Campus Dr Waco TX 76705-1607

COLLINS, ROBERT ELLWOOD, surgeon; b. Cottage City, Md., Aug. 4, 1932; s. Edward Clarence and Edith (Blough) C.; m. Barbara Kauffmann Murray, June 28, 1964; children: Garret, Randy, Robin, Bill, Bruce, Brad, Beth. BS, Ea. Mennonite Coll., 1954; MD, Med. Coll. Va., 1958. Diplomate Am. Bd. Orthopaedic Surgeons. Intern Washington Hosp. Ctr., 1958-59, orthopaedic resident, 1961-64; pvt. practice medicine Broadway, Va., 1959-60; resident in gen. surgery Med. Coll. Va., Richmond, 1960-61; pvt. practice medicine specializing in orthopaedic surgery Washington, 1964—; acting orthopaedic chief Children's Hosp., 1970-72; chief orthopaedics Washington Hosp. Ctr., 1973-75, vice-chmn. dept. orthopaedics, 1975-80, bd. dirs., pres. med. and dental staff, 1981, 83-85; assoc. prof. Georgetown U. Hosp., 1975—; courtesy staff Sibley Meml. Hosp.; pres. med. staff Nat. Rehab. Hosp., Washington, 1988; bd. dirs. Medlantic Health Corp., Washington. Bd. dirs. Easter Seal Soc. of Washington and Md., 1986—, chmn. bd. dirs., 1990-92; bd. dirs. Nat. Orthopedic Hosp., Washington, 1990; bd. dirs. Nat. Easter Seals Soc., 1995—. Recipient Teaching award Georgetown U., Washington, 1985; Children's Orthopaedic's fellow Children's Hosp., 1963, Cerebral Palsy fellow Children's Rehab. Inst. Johns Hopkins U., 1965. Fellow ACS (chmn. D.C. trauma com.), Am. Acad. Cerebral Palsy, Am. Acad. Orthopaedic Surgeons, Am. Acad. Orthopaedic Foot Surgeons; mem. Med. Soc. D.C. (pres. 1985-86), Washington Clin. Club (past pres.), Georgetown Club, Congl. Country Club (Bethesda, Md.). Presbyterian. Office: Drs Collins Gordon Johnson PC 106 Irving St NW Ste 318 Washington DC 20010-2993

COLLINS, ROBERT G(EORGE), literature educator, writer; b. Danbury, Conn., June 6, 1926; s. Thomas Arthur and Sara M. (Lowe) C.; m. May, July 17, 1981. B.A. with honors, Miami U., Oxford, Ohio, 1950, M.A., 1952; Ph.D. in Comparative Lit., U. Denver, 1959. Asst. prof. Colo. State U., Fort Collins, 1956-57, 58-59, Pa. State U., University Park, 1957-58; assoc. prof. San Jose State U., Calif., 1963-65; vis. prof. Colgate U., Hamilton, N.Y., 1975-76; prof. lit. U. Manitoba, Winnipeg, Can., 1968-76, U. Ottawa, Ont., Can., 1976—; chmn. grad. English studies U. Manitoba, 1970-74; cons.-assessor Canadian Fedn. Humanities, 1983, Publs. MLA, N.Y.C., 1983. Author/editor The Colo. Review, Mosaic, Thalia. Served in USN, 1943-47, ETO, PTO. Named finalist First Novel award Books in Can., 1983;/grantee Can. Council, Social Scis. Humanities Research Council. Mem. MLA of Am. (pres. Conf. Editors of Learned Jours. 1975-77), The Bronte Soc., Canadian Assn. Univ. Tchrs., Canadian Assn. Am. Studies. Home: PO Box 6 Falls Village CT 06031

COLLINS, ROBERT OAKLEY, history educator; b. Waukegan, Ill., Apr. 1, 1933; s. William George and Louise Van Horsen (Jack) C.; m. Janyce Hutchins Monroe, Oct. 6, 1974; children by previous marriage: Catharine Louise, Randolph Ware, Robert William. BA, Dartmouth Coll., 1954; AB (Marshall scholar 1954-55), Balliol Coll., Oxford U., 1956, MA, 1960; MA (Ford fellow), Yale U., 1958, PhD, 1959. Instr. history Williams Coll., Williamstown, Mass., 1959-61; lectr. U. Mass. Extension, Pittsfield, 1960-61; vis. asst. prof. history Columbia U., N.Y.C., 1962-63; asst. prof. history Williams Coll., 1963-65; mem. faculty U. Calif., Santa Barbara, 1965—, prof. history, 1969-94, dir. Ctr. for Study Developing Nations, 1967-69, acting vice chancellor for research and grad. affairs, 1970-71, dean grad. div., 1971-80; prof. emeritus, 1994—; vis. sr. assoc. fellow St. Antony's Coll., Oxford U., Eng., 1980-81; Trevelyan fellow Durham U., 1986—; dir. Washington Ctr. U. Calif., Santa Barbara, 1992-94; mem. Internat. Adv. Group for the Nile Basin, World Bank, 1997. Author: The Southern Sudan, 1883-1898, 1962, King Leopold, England and the Upper Nile, 1968, Problems in African History, 1968, The Partition of Africa, 1979, Land Beyond the Rivers: The Southern Sudan, 1898-1918, 1971, Europeans in Africa, 1971, An Arabian Diary, 1969, The Southern Sudan in Historical Perspective, 1975, Shadows in the Grass: Britain in the Southern Sudan, 1983, The British in the Sudan, 1898-56, 84, The Waters of the Nile: Hydropolitics and the Jonglei Canal, 1900-1988, 1990, Western African History, Eastern African History, Central and Southern African History, 1990, The Nile Waters: An Annotated Bibliography, 1991, Problems In African History, The Pre-Colonial Centuries, 1993, Requiem for the Sudan, 1994, Historical Problems of Imperial Africa, 1994, Problems in the History of Modern Africa, 1996. Recipient Gold class award Order Scis. and Arts Dem. Republic of Sudan, 1980; John Ben Snow Found. prize, 1984; NDEA lang. fellow, 1960-61, Social Sci. Rsch. Coun. fellow, 1962-63; Rockefeller Found. scholar-in-residence Bellagio, Italy, 1979, 87; Ford Found. fellow, 1979-81; Fulbright sr. rsch. fellow, 1982, 90; Woodrow Wilson fellow, 1983; vis. fellow Trevelyan Coll. mem. Soc. Fellows Durham U., 1986, fellow Balliol Coll., Oxford U., 1986-87; fellow Am. Coun. Learned Soc. 1990. Fellow Am. Philos. Soc.; mem. Am. Hist. Assn., African Studies Assn., Western River Guides Assn., Sudan Studies Assn., Explorers Club, Phi Beta Kappa. Home: PO Box 1378 Santa Barbara CA 93102-1378 Office: U Calif Dept History Santa Barbara CA 93106

COLLINS, ROBERT T., publisher. Pres., pub. Asbury Park Press, Neptune, N.J. Office: Asbury Park Press/The Gannett Co PO Box 1550 3601 Hwy 66 Neptune NJ 07754-1551*

COLLINS, RONALD WILLIAM, psychologist, educator; b. N.Y.C., Jan. 6, 1947; s. Edward H. Collins Jr. and Estelle Lott. BA, Rutgers U., 1969; MS, Nova U., 1987; EdD, Fla. Internat. U., 1990; PhD, Saybrook Inst., 1996. Lic. profl. counselor, Mont., mental health counselor, Fla., psychologist, Colo. Spl. agt., ret. U.S. Secret Svc., Miami, Fla., 1971-91; asst. prof. Ea. Mont. Coll., Billings, 1991-94, Mont. State U., Billings, 1994-95; psychol. intern Inst. for Psychol. Growth, Ft. Lauderdale, Fla., 1994-95; adj. prof. instrnl. analysis/design Fla. Internat. U., Ft. Lauderdale, 1995-96; psychologist Dept. Corrections, Canon City, Colo., 1998-99, in pvt. practice, Miami, 1999—; adj. prof. St. Thomas U., Miami, 1990-91. Author: The Kabiroff Papers, 1988, Transfer of Learning, 1990; contbr. articles to profl. jours. Mem. Billings Family Violence Task Force, 1992. Mem. APA, Am. Ednl. Rsch. Assn., Mental Health Assn. Broward County. Episcopalian. Avocations: skiing, horseback riding, flying, fiction writing, jogging. Home: PO Box 2053 Fort Lauderdale FL 33303-2053 Office: PO Box 2053 Fort Lauderdale FL 33310

COLLINS, ROSE ANN, minister; b. Pitts., July 5, 1935; d. Joseph and Rochelle (McCrary) Covington; m. Frank Collins, June 30, 1960 (div. 1978); children: Gar Andre, Guy Tracy. BA, Ctrl. Bible Coll., Springfield, Mo., 1987; MDiv, Assemblies of God Theol. Sem., Springfield, Mo., 1989. Ordained to ministry, 1990. Assoc. minister Deliverance Temple World Outreach Ministries, Springfield, 1988-90; evangelist Deliverance Temple World Outreach Ministries, Springfield and Pitts., 1991-93; chaplain Western Ctr., Canonsburg, Pa., 1993-96; trustee Northside Ch. of God in Christ, Pitts., 1982-87, bd. dirs., 1983-87. Vol. Ctr. Victims Violent Crime. Mem. Soc. Chaplains (Western chpt.), Pa. Coun. Chs., Ret. Enlished Assn. (hon., Steel City chpt. 72 chaplain 1994-96). Avocations: reading, walking. Home: 6290 Auburn St Apt 622 Pittsburgh PA 15206-3136

COLLINS, RUSSELL AMBROSE, advertising executive, creative director. BA, U. Calif., Berkeley, 1976; postgrad., U. Calif., Irvine, 1978-80. Project dir. Douglas Boyd Design & Mktg., L.A., 1980-82; pres., exec. creative dir. Fattal & Collins, Santa Monica, Calif., 1982-87; pres., exec. creative dir., vice chmn. GEM/Fattal & Collins, Santa Monica, 1987—. Recipient Clio award Art Dirs. Club N.Y.; Belding award Art Dirs. Club L.A., Lulu award, Key Art award. Office: Grey Entertainment & Media Fattal & Collins 4640 Admiralty Way Ste 900 Marina Del Rey CA 90292*

COLLINS, SAMUEL W., JR., judge; b. Caribou, Maine, Sept. 17, 1923; s. Samuel Wilson Collins & Elizabeth Black C; m. Dorothy Small, 1952; children: Edward, Elizabeth, Diane. BA, U. Maine; JD, Harvard U. Lawyer Rockland, Maine, 1947—; justice Supreme Jud. Ct., Portland, Maine. Trustee Rockland Sch. Dist, 1949-61; Maine State Senate Dist. 21, 1975-84, Majority Leader, 1981-82, Minority Leader, 1983-84. Recipient Disting. Svc. award Jaycees, 1978. Mem. Maine Bar Assn., Rotary, Phi Beta Kappa, Phi Kappa Phi, Delta Tau Delta. Unitarian Universalist. Republican. Office: Knox County Courthouse 62 Union St Rockland ME 04841-2836

COLLINS, S(ARAH) RUTH KNIGHT, education educator; b. Northumberland, Pa., May 13, 1939; d. Walter Brown and Alice Marie (Neighbour) Knight; m. Frank Gibson Collins, June 13, 1960; children: James, Pamela Collins Williams. BA, Wheaton Coll., 1960; MA, U. Tex., Austin, 1974; PhD, Vanderbilt U., 1980. Tchr. various levels Evanston, Ill., 1960-61, Berkeley, Calif., 1961-71; demonatration tchr. for head start and kindergarten U. Tex., Austin, Tex., 1969-74; tchr. in early childhood U. Tex., Austin, 1972-74; tchr. reading Motlow State C.C., Tullahoma, Tenn., 1977-91, coord. of English, 1979-81, prof. edn., 1982-93, coord. social scis., 1986-93; mem. state-wide adv. coun. for tchr. edn. and cert., 1987-90, state-wide adv. coun. for minorities in tchr. edn., 1990-91; pres. faculty coun. Motlow C.C., 1979-80, tchr. 1978; adj. prof. edn. Mid. Tenn. State U., 1979-89; presenter at profl. confs. Writer and proofreader for religious sci. tech. editor, Tullahoma Telesis, 1980—, columnist, 1996—; writer for HealthWise, 1998—. Actress Cmty. Playhouse, Tullahoma, 1973-87; storyteller various librs. and pub. schs., 1974—; violinist Mid. Tenn. Symphony Orch., Murfreesboro, 1987-89; presenter programs on grief and loss at various profl. confs. and cmty. orgns., 1973—; bd. mem., yearly speaker Compassionate Friends, 1985—; active Unitarian Universalist Ch., Tullahoma, 1993—; home vol. Hospice Highland Rim.; tchr. competitve swimming, diving, water ballet, program dir., 1949-68; panelist (TV series) How to Combat Juvenile Delinquency, Chgo., 1956; vol. Harton Regional Med. Ctr., 1997—. Recipient Gov. Ned McWherter's cert. of recognition Tenn. Collaborative Leadership Acad., 1991. Mem. NEA, ASCD, AAUP (v.p. 1986-87, sec. 1990-91), Assn. Tchr. Educators, Bus. and Profl. Women's Club, Tenn. Edn. Assn., Internat. Reading Assn., Nat. Assn. for Edn. of Young Children (pres.-elect local chpt. 1972-73), Phi Delta Kappa, Kappa Delta Pi. Avocations: reading, sewing, playing and teaching violin, public speaking. Home and Office: 1703 Country Club Dr Tullahoma TN 37388-4831

COLLINS, STEPHEN BARKSDALE, retired health care executive; b. Houston, Mar. 14, 1932; s. Ray George and Ruth Ella (Davis) C.; m. Katherine Jane Justice, June 6, 1955; children: Nancy Catherine, Rebecca Jane, Ruth Anne, Stephen Barksdale, Cynthia Marye. B.A., Baylor U., 1954; M.H.A., Washington U., 1956. Asst. adminstr., adminstr. Good Samaritan Hosp., Vincennes, Ind., 1959-65; adminstr. Rosewood Gen. Hosp., Houston, 1965-72; chief exec. officer Lake Charles Meml. Hosp., La., 1972-85; v.p. shareholder rels. and membership VHA, Inc., Irving, Tex., 1985-97; ret., 1997. Bd. dirs. Better Bus. Bur. Served with USAF, 1956-59. Decorated Meritorious Service medal, Commendation medal. Fellow Am. Coll. Hosp. Adminstrs.; mem. C. of C. (dir.), Southeastern Hosp. Conf. (bd. dirs. 1981-82, exec. com. 1983, chmn.-elect 1984), La. Hosp. Assn. (chmn.-elect 1981, chmn. 1982), Am. Hosp. Assn. Baptist. Club: Rotary. Home: 3541 Meadowside Dr Bedford TX 76021-3546

COLLINS, STEVEN M., lawyer; b. Atlanta, Oct. 22, 1952; s. E.B. and Judith (Morse) C.; divorced; 1 child, Erin M.; m. Anne Frances Garland, Oct. 31, 1987; 1 child, Timothy G. AB, Harvard U., 1974, JD, 1977. Bar: Ga. 1977, U.S. Dist. Ct. (no. dist.) Ga. 1977, U.S. Ct. Appeals (5th cir.) 1977, U.S. Ct. Appeals (11th cir.) 1981, U.S. Dist. Ct. (mid. dist.) Ga. 1982, U.S. Tax Ct. 1984, U.S. Ct. Appeals (4th cir.) 1986, U.S. Supreme Ct. 1994. Assoc. Alston & Bird, Atlanta, 1977-83, ptnr., 1983—; editor-in-chief Ga. State Bar Journal, Atlanta, 1982-84. Mem. ABA, State Bar Ga., Atlanta Bar Assn. Office: Alston & Bird One Atlantic Ctr 1201 W Peachtree St NW Atlanta GA 30309-3424

COLLINS, SUSAN FORD, leadership consultant; b. N.Y.C., Dec. 8, 1939; d. Eugene Elwood and Mary Elizabeth Crighton Ford; m. Donald J. Collins, Sept. 9, 1962 (div. 1973); children: Catherine Lyn Rosenberg, Margaret Ann Chaneles. Student, Smith Coll., 1958-60; BA, U. Richmond, 1961. Rsch. psychologist NIMH, Bethesda, Md., 1962-64; rschr. success and leadership strategies Miami, Fla., 1964—; creator The Technology of Success, The Leadership Relay; ptnr. Success Internat., Miami, 1985-86, co-dir., 1988-93; v.p. Winterstreet Corp. USA, Miami, 1986-88; pres. Our Children Are Watching, Inc., Miami, 1993—; cons. Arthur Andersen, CNN, Am. Express, Digital Equipment, Kimberley-Clar, Ryder Sys., Fla. Power and Light, IBM, Levitz Furniture, Coopers and Lybrand, City of Miami, City of Seaside, Fla., Palm Beach County, Fla.; spkr. in field. Author: The Me Book: A Manual for Being Human, 1983, Our Children Are Watching: Ten Skills for Leading the Next Generation to Success, 1995, Intuition At Work, 1996; author foreword Women and Leadership, 1996; guest TV and radio shows. Fellow The Leadership Trust; mem. Nat. Spkrs. Assn., Nat. Writers Assn., Phi Beta Kappa, Psi Chi, Pi Kappa Delta, Phi Kappa Phi. E-mail: scollins33@aol.com. Address: Tech of Success Inc 12040 NE 5th Ave Miami FL 33161-6260

COLLINS, SUSAN M., senator; b. Caribou, Maine, Dec. 7, 1952. BA in Govt. magna cum laude, St. Lawrence U., 1975. Prin. advisor bus. affairs U.S. Senator Bill Cohen; commr. Maine Dept. Profl. and Fin. Regulation; dir. New England ops. U.S. Small Bus. Adminstrn.; exec. dir. Ctr. Family Bus., Husson Coll., Bangor, Maine; U.S. senator from Maine, 1997—; staff dir. Senate Subcom. on Oversight Govt. Mgmt., 1981-87; chair Cabinet Coun. on Health Care Policy, State of Maine; mem. U.S. Senate com. health, edn., labor and pensions, 1997—, subcom. on children and families, 1997—, subcom. on pub. health and safety, 1997—, com. on govtl. affairs, 1997—; chmn. permanent subcom. on investigations, 1997—; mem. spl. com. on aging. Rep. candidate for Gov., State of Maine, 1994. Recipient Outstanding Alumni award St. Lawrence U., 1992. Mem. Bangor Rotary Club, Phi Beta Kappa. Roman Catholic. Office: 172 Russell Sen Office Bldg Washington DC 20510

COLLINS, TERRY, professional baseball manager; b. Midland, Mich., May 27, 1949. Mgr. Houston Astros, 1994-96, Anaheim Angels, 1996—. Office: Anaheim Angels 2000 Gene Autry Way Anaheim CA 92806-6100*

COLLINS, THEODORE JOHN, lawyer; b. Walla Walla, Wash., Oct. 2, 1936; s. Robert Bonfield and Catherine Roselle (Snyder) C.; m. Patricia Spengler Pasieka, May 11, 1968; children: Jonathan, Caitlin, Matthew, Patrick, Flannary. BA, U. Notre Dame, 1958; postgrad., U. Bonn, Fed. Republic Germany, 1959; LLB, Harvard U., 1962. Bar: Wash. 1962, U.S. Supreme Ct. 1982, U.S. Ct. Appeals (fed. cir.) 1982, U.S. Dist. Ct. (ea. dist.) Wash. 1965, U.S. Dist. Ct. (we. dist.) Wash. 1962. Ptnr. Perkins Coie Law Firm, Seattle, 1962-86; v.p., gen. counsel The Boeing Co., Seattle, 1986-98, sr. v.p., gen. counsel, 1998—. Mem. ABA, Boeing Mgmt. Assn., Wash. State Bar Assn., King County Bar Assn., Wash. Athletic Club. Office: Boeing Co PO Box 3707 MS 13-08 Seattle WA 98124-2207*

COLLINS, THOMAS JOSEPH, English language educator, university official; b. London, Ont., Can., Aug. 23, 1936; s. Joseph Benedict and Margaret Jean (Collins) C.; div.; children: Mark, Kristen, Brendan; m. 1985. BA, U. Western Ont., 1959, MA, 1961; PhD, Ind. U., 1965. Prof. English, U. Western Ont., London, 1965—, chmn. dept., 1974-82, dean faculty arts, 1982-86, acad. v.p., provost, 1986-95. Author: Robert Browning's Moral-Aesthetic Theory: 1833-55, 1967. Editor: Letters from the Brownings to the Tennysons, 1971, Letters of Robert Browning to the Rev. J.D. Williams, 1976, (with J. Pettigrew) Robert Browning: The Poems, 1981, (with R.J. Shroyer) Robert Browning: The Plays, 1988, Robert Browning: Centennial Issue of Victorian Poetry, 1989, (with R.J. Shroyer) Robert Browning Concordance, 7 vols., 1996; mem. editorial bd. Victorian Poetry, 1974—, Victorian Studies, 1979—. Can. Council research grantee, 1974; grantee U. Western Ont. Acad. Devel. Fund., 1982, Social Sci. and Humanities Research Council, 1983. Mem. Can. Assn. U. Tchrs., MLA (exec. com. Victorian group 1972-75), Internat. Browning Soc. (bd. dirs. 1976), Com. Chairmen English Ont. (pres. 1979-81), Can. Assn. Chairmen English (pres. 1979-80), Council Deans Arts and Scis. Ont. (chmn. 1983-85), Ontario Assn. Triathletes. Office: Univ of Western Ont, Dept English, London, ON Canada N6A 3K7

COLLINS, THOMAS WILLIAM, caterer, consultant; b. Lewiston, Idaho, Nov. 4, 1926; s. William James and Mary (Egan) C.; m. Mary Charlene Tracy, Aug. 1, 1947 (dec. Apr. 1984); children: Kathleen, William, Charles. Grad. high sch., Staples, Minn., 1944. Owner Collins Cafe, Park Rapids, Minn., 1947-63, Tom Collins Restaurant, Walker, Minn., 1963-83, Tom Collins Catering, Walker, 1983—. Author: Collins Cooking Secrets, 1981. Fundraiser DFL, 1976-83; adv. bd. Lake Country Food Bank, Mpls., 1981-86. Served with USN, 1945-46, 51-52. Recipient Recognition award Mont. Gov., 1978, cert. of Spl. Congl. Recognition, 1995; Tom Collins Day proclaimed by Minn. Gov., 1977. Mem. Assn. Great Lakes Outdoor Writers, Am. Legion. Lodge: Masons (sr. warden 1958), Shriners. Avocations: hunting, fishing, photography. Home and Office: PO Box 33 Walker MN 56484-0033

COLLINS, TIMOTHY CLARK, holding company executive; b. Frankfort, Ky., Oct. 8, 1956; s. Frank Dane and Betty (Cunningham) C.; m. Andrea Shaffer, Jan. 15, 1983; children: Dane Andrew, Matthew Ramsey. BA in Philosophy, DePauw U., 1978; M in Pub. and Pvt. Mgmt., Yale U., 1982. Assoc. Booz Allen & Hamilton, Chgo., 1982-84; v.p. Lazard Freres & Co., N.Y.C., 1984-90; sr. mgr. dir. Onex Corp., N.Y.C., 1990-95; CEO Ripplewood Holdings LLC, N.Y.C., 1996—; bd. dirs. Dayton Superior Corp., Danielson Holding Corp. Bd. dirs. Lenox Hill Neighborhood House; trustee DePauw U. Mem. Siwanoy Country Club, Knickerbocker Club, Hollenbeck Club (Conn.), Racquet and Tennis Club (N.Y.C.), Bronxville Field Club. Presbyterian. Office: Ripplewood Holdings LLC 712 5th Ave Fl 49 New York NY 10019-4108

COLLINS, TUCKER, pathologist, molecular biologist; b. Lorain, Ohio, Nov. 3, 1952; s. Robert James and Catherine (Meisner) C.; m. Mary Judith Whitley, June 15, 1985. BA, Amherst Coll., 1975, DSc (hon.), 1998; MD, PhD, U. Rochester, 1981. Diplomate Am. Bd. Pathology. Clin., rsch. fellow Brigham and Women's Hosp., Boston, 1981-85; from instr. to prof. pathology Harvard Med. Sch., Boston, 1985-98, prof. pathology, 1998—; staff pathologist Brigham and Women's Hosp., 1992—; charter mem., chmn. pathology study sect. NIH. Author: Pathologic Basis of Disease, 1999, assoc. editor Am. Jour. Pathology; contbr. articles to profl. jours. Scholar Pew Scholars Program, 1987-91; grantee NIH, 1985, 90, 93, 96, 97, Am. Heart Assn. Established Investigator, 1991-96; recipient Warner-Lambert/Parke-Davis award Am. Society for Investigative Pathology, 1994. Master Francis Weld Peabody Soc. (assoc.); mem. Am. Assn. Pathologists (v.p.), Am. Assn. Univ. Pathologists, N.Am. Vascular Biology Orgn. Achievements include research in the structure and regulation of platelet-derived growth factor, structure and regulation of genes for leukocyte-endothelial adhesion molecules. Home: 160 Fairoaks Ln Cohasset MA 02025-1314 Office: Brigham and Women's Hosp Boston MA 02115

COLLINS, VICKI TICHENÉ, critical care and emergency room nurse; b. Germany, Dec. 1, 1944; children: David, Michael, Amy. Diploma, St. Anthony Sch. Nursing, Columbus, Ohio, 1968. Night nurse Fairfax Hosp., Falls Church, Va., 1977—. Mem. No. Va. Emergency Nurses Assn. Home: 11 Edgecliff Ln Stafford VA 22554-5118

COLLINS, VINCENT PATRICK, radiologist, physician, educator; b. Toronto, Ont., Can., Nov. 11, 1912; came to U.S., 1940, naturalized, 1945; s. John and Laura (Doyle) C.; m. Lois Cowan, Dec. 26, 1942; children: Cowan, Ross, Christopher. M.D., U. Toronto, 1937; J.D., U. Houston, 1964. Diplomate: Am. Bd. Radiology. Intern Toronto Gen. Hosp., 1937-38; demonstrator anatomy, fellow physiology U. Toronto, 1938-39; research fellow Banting Inst., 1939-40; sr. resident pathology N.E. Deaconess Hosp., Boston, 1940-42; resident surg. pathology, instr. surgery Presbyn. Hosp., Columbia, 1942-43, resident radiology, 1945-47, attending radiologist, 1950-52; instr. radiology Columbia U., 1947-49; cons. radiology USPHS Marine Hosp., S.I., 1948-52; asst. prof. Columbia U., 1949-50, assoc. prof. radiology, 1950-52; chief radiotherapy Francis Delafield Hosp., 1950-52; prof. radiology, chmn. dept. Baylor U., 1952-68; radiologist-in-chief Jefferson Davis Hosp., Houston, 1952-68, Ben Taub Gen. Hosp., Houston, 1963-68; chief cons. radiology VA Hosp., Houston, 1952-68; attending radiologist Meth. Hosp., Houston, 1955-68; cons. radiology Tex. Children's Hosp., Houston, 1956-68; dir. radiotherapy Rosewood Gen. Hosp., 1969-82, cons., 1982—; cons. radiotherapy Ochsner Clinic, New Orleans, 1968-82, U. Tex. Med. Br., Galveston, 1969-84; prin. cons. radiology Nat. Inst. Gen. Med. Scis., Bethesda, Md., 1966, Lawrence Labs. U. Calif. at Berkeley, 1972-77; med. dir. Houston Inst. for Cancer Research, Detection and Treatment, 1974—; mem. med. adv. com. U.S. Nuclear Regulatory Commn., clin. prof. radiology therapy dept., U. Tex. Med. Br., 1984—. Served from 1st lt. to capt., M.C. AUS, 1943-45. Decorated Silver Star. Fellow Am. Coll. Radiology, Am. Coll. Legal Medicine; mem. Am. Roentgen Ray Soc., Radiol. Soc. N.Am., Tex. Radiol. Soc., Soc. Surg. Oncology, Am. Radium Soc., N.Y. Acad. Scis., Arthur Purdy Stout Soc., Am. Soc. Therapeutic Radiologists, A.A.A.S., Internat. Acad. Pathology, Sigma Xi. Home: 105 Shasta Dr Houston TX 77024-6914 Office: 8811 Gaylord St Ste 100 Houston TX 77024-2923

COLLINS, WALTER LLOYD GEORGE, editor; b. Broken Arrow, Okla., Dec. 6, 1917; s. Dow Otho and Myrtle Hester (Campbell) C.; m. Ruth Leona Hamilton, Sept. 3, 1935; children: Mary, Walter, Alvin, Shirley. *George and wife, Ruth, are both descendants of generations of pioneers. One of his great grandmother's sisters was Daniel Boone's wife. His great grandfather was a cousin of Lt. General Nathan Bedford Forrest. His grandfather built one of the early stone houses in Indian Territory. His father worked for Frank Phillips as he built his oil empire in the 1920s. Ruth's family, the Hamiltons, moved from Maryland to Missouri about 1780. He and Ruth have four children: Mary Ellen Moore, Walter Lewis, Alvin Lloyd and Shirley Marie Wilks. They have eighteen grandchildren, thirty-nine great grandchildren, and two great, great grandchildren.* BA, Pan Am. U., 1966; MA, U. Tulsa, 1975. Aviation cadet USAAF, 1942; advanced through grades to maj. USAF, 1962; exec. in charge C-E Installation Project NATO, Europe, North Africa, Mid. East, 1956-57; sr. editor radar and missiles project USAF, 1957-58; ops. officer C-E divsn. Def. Atomic Support Agy., Alburquerque, 1959-63; dir. comm.-elec., spacetrack NORAD, Colorado Springs, 1963-64; ret., 1964; gen. mgr. Desert Lodge, Moab, Utah, 1967-68; design engr., planner Beech Aircraft Corp., Wichita, Kans., 1968-72; dir. internat. student affairs Spartan Sch. Aeronautics, Tulsa, 1979-83; pres. R&W Internat., Tulsa, 1984-88, Alpha-Omega Press, Tulsa, Ponca City, Okla., 1990—; adv. bd. Higher Edn. Com. Okla. Acad. State Goals, 1977-95. Author: On the Razor's Edge, 1990. Mem. Kay County (Okla.) Rep. Com., 1993—; commr. Ponca City Traffic Comm., 1997—. Mem. Acad. Am. Poets, Nat. Author's Registry, Nat. Order Battlefield Commns., Am. Air Mus. in Great Britain, Air Force Assn., Ret. Officers Assn. Avocations: writing, editing, photography. Office: Alpha-Omega Press PO Box 2163 Ponca City OK 74602-2163

COLLINS, WAYNE WINFORD, protective services official; b. Balt., July 19, 1943; s. James Winford and Clyde Kellys (Braddock) C.; m. Barbara Anne Beabout, June 22, 1962 (div. Jan. 1990); m. Diane Christopher, June 23, 1990; children: Dane Allen, Dawn Rene. Student, Houston C.C., 1971-74, U. State N.Y., 1987-88; grad., Ga. Police Acad./Ga. Fire Acad., Internat. City Mgmt. Assn. Tng. Inst.; BS in Fire Scis., Western States U., MS in Fire Svc. Adminstrn. Cert. fire officer VI, police officer; expert witness fire and arson investigation; pvt. investigator; cons. security and fire loss control. Firefighter City of Galveston, Tex., 1964-66; firefighter/emergency fire apparatus operator City of Houston Fire Dept., 1966-73, capt.-fire co. comdr./sta. officer, 1973-77, sr. capt. ctrl. command divsn., 1977-81, tng. officer comm. divsn., 1978-79, mem. fire chiefs staff/divsn. chief, 1981-85, chief officer fire and emergency med. svc. comm. divsn., 1985-87; fire chief City of Thomaston, Ga., 1987-91, City of Columbus, Ga., 1991—; faculty pub. svc. divsn. Houston C.C., 1979-80; appointed chmn. Ga. Firefighters Stds. and Tng. Coun., 1995; mem. Fire Safe Ga. State Commn. Fire Protection, 1991; specialist cons. weapons of mass destruction; dir. arson task force Muscogee County. Chmn. mid. Ga. chpt. Nat. Kidney Found., 1989; chmn. Upson County Coun. Child Abuse, Ga., 1990; advisor fire explorer program Boy Scouts Am. With USN, 1960-64. Recipient Svc. award Ga. Ins. Commr., 1993, Svc. award Office of Mayor of Columbus, 1994, Arron Cohn award Juvenile Cts. System, 1994. Mem. Nat. Fire Protection Assn., Ga. Firefighters Assn., Ga. Assn. Fire Chiefs, Southeastern Assn. Fire Chiefs, Internat. Assn. Fire Chiefs, Internat. Assn. Firefighters (mem. exec. bd. Houston chpt. 1973-77, editor Houston Firefighter 1976-77, mem. City Hall com., chmn. speakers bur., Internat. Labor Press Assn. Nat. award), Metro Fire Chiefs Assn., Fellowship Christian Firefighters Internat., Assn. County Commrs. Ga. (mem. pub. safety com. 1994), Am. Legion (Vietnam era mem.), Exch. Club Columbus. Avocations: hunting, fishing, traveling, civil war history. Office: Columbus Fire Dept Pub Safety Complex 510 10th St Columbus GA 31901-2827

COLLINS, WHITFIELD JAMES, lawyer; b. Dallas, Aug. 26, 1918; s. Jasper and Gertrude (James) C.; m. Beth Cooper, June 5, 1951 (dec. Aug. 1980); children: Whitfield James Jr., Kay, Cooper R. AA, Kemper Mil. Sch., 1936; BA, U. Tex., 1938, JD, 1940; LLM, Harvard U., 1941. Bar: Tex. 1940, U.S. Dist. Ct. (no. dist.) Tex. 1950, U.S. Ct. Claims 1978, U.S. Tax Ct. 1949, U.S. Ct. Appeals (5th cir.) 1981. Atty. Office Gen. Counsel Treasury Dept., Washington, 1941-42, Office Chief Counsel, IRS, Washington and N.Y.C., 1946-48; assoc. Cantey, Hanger, Johnson, Scarborough & Gooch, Ft. Worth, 1949-54; ptnr. Cantey & Hanger and predecessor firms, Ft. Worth, 1954-96, of counsel, 1996—; sec., bd. dirs. Vol. Purchasing Groups, Inc., Bonham, Tex., 1968-95; pres. Fifth Ave. Found. and C.J. Wrightsman Ednl. Fund, 1980—; bd. dirs., sec.-treas. T.J. Brown and C.A. Lupton Found., Ft. Worth; former chmn. bd. Intercultura, Inc., Ft. Worth. Contbr. articles in field to profl. jours. Bd. dirs., past pres. Moncrief Radiation Ctr., Ft. Worth, Ft. Worth Art Assn., Arts Council Ft. Worth and Tarrant County, Ft. Worth Art Commn.; bd. dirs. Van Cliburn Found., Ft. Worth Opera Assn. Served to lt. commdr. USNR, 1942-46. Fellow ABA (life), State Bar Tex. (chmn. taxation sect. 1964-65); mem. Tarrant County Bar Assn. (Blackstone award 1995). Episcopalian. Home: 6732 Brants Ln Fort Worth TX 76116-7202 Office: Cantey & Hanger 801 Cherry St Ste 2100 Fort Worth TX 76102-6898

COLLINS, WILLIAM EDWARD, aeromedical administrator, researcher; b. Bklyn., May 16, 1932; s. William Edward and Loretta Agnes (Brasier) C.; m. Corliss Jean Barnes, June 20, 1970; 1 child, Corliss Adora. B.S., St. Peter's Coll., 1954; M.A., Fordham U., 1956, Ph.D., 1959. Lic. psychologist, Okla. Psychol. rsch. asst. Fordham U., 1954-56, teaching fellow, 1958, grad. instr., 1958-59, rsch. asst., 1958-59; rsch. psychologist U.S. Army Med. Rsch. Lab., Ft. Knox, Ky., 1959-61; research psychologist Aviation Psychology Lab. FAA Civil Aeromed. Inst., Oklahoma City, 1961-63, chief sensory integration sect., 1963-65, lab. supr., 1965-86, human resources rsch. br. mgr., 1986-88, dep. dir., 1988-89, dir., 1989—; adj. assoc. prof. psychology U. Okla., Norman, 1963-70, adj. prof., 1970-89; adj. assoc. prof. research psychology dept. psychiatry and behavioral scis. U. Okla. Health Scis. Ctr., Oklahoma City, 1965-71, adj. prof., 1971—; mem. Nat. Acad. Sci.-NRC Com. on Vision, 1963-82, mem. exec. council, 1973-81; mem. Nat. Acad. Sci.-NRC Com. on Hearing, Bioacoustics and Biomechanics, 1963-87; appearances before House Sub-Com. on Pub. Health and Environ., 1971, House Sub-Com. on Investigations and Oversight, 1983, House Sub-Com. on Transp., Aviation and Materials, 1987, 88; judge Okla. State Sci. and Engring. Fair, Ada, 1980, 81, 82; mem. Okla. Bd. Examiners Psychologists, 1981-84, chmn., 1982-84; evaluator proposals NSF, 1968-82, HEW, 1971-80; lectr. in field. Contbr. chpts., numerous articles to profl. publs.; numerous research presentations in field. Served to capt. Med. Services Corps, U.S. Army, 1959-61. Recipient Silver Medal award South African Soc. Aerospace and Environ. Medicine, 1998. Fellow AAAS, APA (abstractor Psychol. Abstracts 1962—, citation 1973), N.Y. Acad. Scis., Aerospace Med. Assn. (Raymond F. Longacre award 1971, presdl. exec. com. 1982-84, exec. coun. 1982-85, editorial bd. Aviation, Space and Environ. Medicine 1974—, assoc. editor 1980—, Pres.'s Citation 1993, Harry G. Moseley award 1998), Am. Psychol. Soc. (charter), Aerospace Human Factors Assn. (charter, Paul T. Hansen award 1998); mem. Assn. Aviation Psychologists (pres. 1974-75), Okla. Psychol. Assn. (Disting. Psychologist award 1984), South African Soc. Aerospace and Environ. Medicine (Silver award 1998). Home: 8900 Sheringham Dr Oklahoma City OK 73132-4764 Office: FAA Civil Aeromed Inst AAM-3 PO Box 25082 Oklahoma City OK 73125-0082

COLLINS, WILLIAM F., JR., neurosurgery educator; b. New Haven, Conn., Jan. 20, 1924. MD, Yale U., 1947. Diplomate Am. Bd. Neurol. Surgery. Intern Barnes Hosp., St. Louis, 1947-49, asst. resident in neurosurgery, 1951-52, resident, 1952-53; fellow neurophysiology Washington U., 1953-54; instr. neurosurgery Western Res. U., Cleve., 1954-55, sr. instr., 1955-57, asst. prof., 1957-60, assoc. prof., 1960-63; prof., chmn. div. neurosurgery Med. Coll. Va., 1963-67; prof. Yale U., New Haven, 1967—, chmn. sect. neurosurgery, 1967-86, chmn. dept. surgery, 1986-93, prof. neurosurgery, 1993-94, prof. neurosurgery emeritus, 1994—. With M.C., U.S. Army, 1949-51. Office: Yale Sch Medicine Dept Neurosurgery PO Box 20882 New Haven CT 06520-8082

COLLINS, WILLIAM LEROY, telecommunications engineer; b. Laurel, Miss., June 17, 1942; s. Henry L. and Christene E. (Finnegan) C. Student, La Salle U., 1969; BS in Computer Sci., U. Beverly Hills, 1984. Sr. computer operator Dept. Pub. Safety, Phoenix, 1975-78, data communications specialist, 1978-79, supr. computer ops., 1981-82; mgr. network control Valley Nat. Bank, Phoenix, 1979-81; mgr. data communications Ariz. Lottery, Phoenix, 1982-85; mgr. telecommunications Calif. Lottery, Sacramento, 1985—; Mem. Telecomm. Study Mission to Russia, Oct. 1991. Contbr. to profl. publs. Served as sgt. USAF, 1964-68. Mem. IEEE, Nat. Sys. Programmers Assn., Centrex Users Group, DMS Centrex User Group, Accunet Digital Svcs. User Group, Telecomms. Assn. (v.p. edn. Sacramento Valley chpt. 1990-94, pres. 1995, chpt. assn. dir. 1996-97, chpt. past pres. 1996, Prestigious Svc. award 1997), Telecom. Assn. (chmn. corp. edn. com. 1994-95, conf. com. 1994-95, co-chair conf. program com. 1996, program dir. edn. 1996, corp. dir. edn. 1996-97, pres.-elect 1998, pres. and ceo, 1999), SynOptics User Group, Timeplex User Group, Assn. Data Comm. Users, Soc. Mfg. Engrs., Data Processing Mgmt. Assn., Am. Mgmt. Assn., Assn. Computing Machinery, Am. Soc. for Quality Control, Bldg. Industry Cons. Svc. Internat., Assn. for Quality and Participation, KC, Calif. Integrated Svcs. Digital Network User Group, Computer Security Inst., Assn. Pub. Comms. Officials, Armed Forces Comms. and Electronics Assn., Assn. Info. Tech. Profls., H.P. Open View Forum. Roman Catholic. Home: 116 Valley Oak Dr Roseville CA 95678-4378 Office: Calif State Lottery 600 N 10th St Sacramento CA 95814-0393

COLLINS, WILLIAM THOMAS, retired pathologist; b. Omaha, Feb. 21, 1922; s. John Maurice and Bess (Ewing) C.; m. Ann E. Adams, May 30, 1942; children: William Thomas, Carol Ann, John Mark, Donald Brian. B.S., U. Ky., 1942; M.D., U. Mich., 1944. Diplomate Am. Bd. Pathology. Intern Good Samaritan Hosp., Cin., 1944-45; resident in pathology Cin. Gen. Hosp., 1945-46, asst. attending pathologist, 1948-51; pathologist, dir. labs Good Samaritan Hosp., Cin., 1952-56; fellow in exfoliative cytology Free Hosp. for Women, Brookline, Mass., 1949; assoc. pathologist Blodgett Meml. Hosp., Grand Rapids, Mich., 1956-57; assoc. pathologist Lima Meml. Hosp., Ohio, 1957-58, pathologist, dir. lab., 1958-87; instr. in pathology Coll. Medicine, U. Cin., 1948-51, asst. prof. pathology, 1951-56; assoc. clin. prof. pathology Med. Coll. Ohio, Toledo, 1972—; pres. med. staff Lima Meml. Hosp., 1968-70; chmn. adv. group Northwestern Ohio Regional Med. Program, 1970-71; mem. exec. com. bd. dirs., sec.-treas. Gt. Lakes Regional Quality Assurance Assn.; mem. cert. lab. assts. com. Nat. Accrediting Agy. for Clin. Lab. Scis., 1974-76; chmn. bd. dirs. Ohio Region III PSRO, 1977-80; mem. Ohio Statewide Profl. Standards Rev. Council, 1980-81. Bd. dirs. Allen County chpt. ARC, pres., 1972-73; bd. dirs. Allen County unit Am. Cancer Soc., pres., 1973-75, mem. exec. com. Ohio divsn., sec., 1979-80, v.p., 1980-81, pres., 1981-82, nat. del., 1985-92; nat. bd. dirs. Am. Cancer Soc., 1992-95; bd. dirs., exec. com. Cancer Control Consortium Ohio, 1980-86; bd. dirs. Lima Symphony Orch., 1963-69, United Fund Greater Lima, 1970-72. Lt. (j.G.) M.C. USNR, 1946-48. Mem. Lima and Allen County Acad. Medicine (sec.-treas. 1972-79), Ohio Med. Assn., AMA, Ohio Soc. Pathologists (pres. 1970-71), Am. Soc. Investigative Pathology, Am. Soc. Clin. Pathologists, Coll. Am. Pathologists, Internat. Acad. Pathology, Sigma Xi. Republican. Presbyterian. Lodges: Rotary (pres. 1964-65). Home: 4030 S Wapak Rd Lima OH 45806-9409 *Always complete an objective or task, no matter how small before undertaking a new one.*

COLLINS BLOCK, CATHY, education educator, writer, educational consultant; b. Madison, Wis., Dec. 11, 1948; d. Charles Douglas and Jo Ann (Jiru) Zinke; m. Stanley Byron Block, June 31, 1991; 1 child, Michael Donegan. BS in Elem. Edn., Lamar U., 1970; M in Elem. Edn., U. North Tex., 1974; PhD in Curriculum and Instrn., U. Wis., 1976. Cert. tchr. Tex., Okla. Tchr. elem. sch. Beaumont (Tex.) Ind. Sch. Dist., 1970-71, Oklahoma City Ind. Sch. Dist., 1971-72, Azle (Tex.) Ind. Sch. Dist., 1972-74; grad. rsch. asst. U. Wis., Madison, 1974-76; asst. prof. edn. So. Ill. U., Carbondale, 1976-77; prof. edn. Tex. Christian U., Ft. Worth, 1977—; ednl. cons. 300 sch. dists., U.S., Can., Poland, Russia, Hungary, 1976—, Walt Disney Corp., Burbank, Calif., 1995—, Scholastic Inc., N.Y.C., 1997—. Author: Teaching Language Arts, 1993, 3d edit., 1999, Power Thinking for Success, 1997; contbr. 50 articles to profl. jours. including Scholastic, Inc., Walt Disney. Bd. dirs. Nobel Edn. Dynamics, Media, Pa., 1996—. Mem. APA (mem. editl. adv. bd. Jour. Ednl. Psychology 1996—), Internat. Reading Assn. (pres. spl. interest group for gifted and creative readers 1991—). Jewish. Avocations: running, piano. Office: Tex Christian U 2800 S University Dr PO Box 297900 Fort Worth TX 76129

COLLINS BURNS, LISA DIANE, art educator; b. Long Beach, Calif., Sept. 20, 1967; d. Jimmy Royce and Cloa Mae (Westbrook) C. BS Art Edn., BA Comml. Art, Kennesaw State Coll., Marietta, Ga., 1991; student, U. Ga. Studies Abroad, Cortona, Italy, 1988, Kennesaw State Coll. Studies, San Miguel, Mex., 1989; postgrad., State U. West Ga., Carrollton. Instr. studio art for children Kennesaw State U., 1988—; art educator Josh Powell Camp, Kennesaw, 1990-92; art tchr. Floyd Middle Sch., Mableton, Ga., 1991—; freelance artist; prodn. asst. Share Mag., Kennesaw State Coll., 1990-91, coop. tchr. to upcoming art tchrs., 1993—; dir. Floyd Celebrates Arts at Mable House Gallery, 1991—; judge Paulding County Fine Arts Assn. Exhibit, 1993. Bd. dirs. South Cobb Arts Alliance, 1996—. Named Tchr. of Yr., Floyd Mid. Sch., 1996. Mem. ASCD, Profl.. Assn. Ga. Educators., Nat. Art Edn. Assn., Pi Lambda Theta. Home: 3800 Parks Dr Powder Springs GA 30127-2720

COLLINSON, DALE STANLEY, lawyer; b. Tulsa, Okla., Sept. 1, 1938; s. Harold Everett and Charlotte Elizabeth (Bonds) C.; m. Susan Waring Smith, June 7, 1969; children—Stuart, Eleanor. A.B. summa cum laude in Politics and Econs., Yale U., 1960; LL.B., Columbia U., 1963. Bar: N.Y. 1963, U.S. Tax Ct. 1977. Law clk. U.S. Ct. Appeals (2d cir.), N.Y.C., 1963-64; law clk. to Justice Byron R. White, U.S. Supreme Ct., Washington, 1964-66; asst. prof. Stanford (Calif.) Law Sch., 1966-68, assoc. prof., 1968-72; atty.-advisor Office of Tax Policy, U.S. Dept. Treasury, Washington, 1972-73, assoc. tax legis. counsel, 1973-74, dep. tax legis. counsel, 1974-75, tax legis. counsel, 1975-76; now tax ptnr. Willkie Farr & Gallagher, N.Y.C.; panel mem. Practising Law Inst. programs, 1981, 82, 84, 86, 88, Am. Law Inst.-ABA program, 1984, Investment Co. Inst. programs, 1992, 94. Fellow Am. Coll. of Tax Counsel; Mem. ABA, N.Y. State Bar (chmn. tax sect. 1985), Assn. of Bar of City of N.Y. (tax coun. 1990-93, vice chmn. taxation of corps. com. 1990-93), Nat. Assn. Bond Lawyers. Republican. Contbr. articles to legal jours. Home: 320 King St Chappaqua NY 10514-2729 Office: Willkie Farr & Gallagher 787 7th Ave New York NY 10019-6099 *Our country is becoming dangerously dependent on computers. Not that using a computer is bad, but that we are more and more lacking the human resources (in computer hardware and software technicians) to keep them working. To be self reliant in the future, one must be able to keep his own computer working.*

COLLINSON, VIVIENNE RUTH, education educator, researcher, consultant; b. Kitchener, Ont., Can., July 30, 1949; d. Earl Stanley and Mary Magdalena (Sauder) Feick; m. Charles L. Collinson, May 21, 1983. BA, Wilfrid Laurier U., Waterloo, Ont., 1974; MEd, U. Windsor, Ont., 1989; PhD, Ohio State U., 1993. Cert. adminstr., Md. Tchr. Waterloo County Bd. Edn., 1969-84, Windsor Bd. Edn., 1984-89; vis. asst. prof. U.Windsor, 1989-90; vis. asst. prof. U. Md., College Park, 1993-94, asst. prof. edn., 1994-98; adj. prof. Mich. State U., 1998—. Author: Teachers As Learners, 1994, Reaching Students, 1996. Charter mem. Eleanor Roosevelt Found., 1989—; benefactor Stratford (Ont.) Shakespearean Festival Found. Recipient Ont. Silver medal for piano U. We. Ont. Conservatory of Music, 1965, McGraw-Hill awrd, 1969; Ont. scholar, 1968; Wilfrid Laurier U. grad. scholar. Mem. AAUW, Am. Ednl. Rsch. Assn., Fedn. Women Tchrs. Assn. Ont. (provincial resource leader 1988-94), Nat. Soc. for Study of Edn., Delta Kappa Gamma (Doctoral Dissertation award 1994), Phi Kappa Phi. Avocations: music, theatre, travel. Office: 736 Bedford Rd Grosse Pointe MI 48230-1803

COLLIPP, BRUCE GARFIELD, ocean engineer, consultant; b. Niagara Falls, N.Y., Nov. 7, 1929; s. Planton G. and Audrey O. Collipp; m. Priscilla Jane Milbury, Dec. 25, 1954; children: Gary, Richard. BS, MIT, 1952, MS, 1954. Registered profl. engr., Tex.; lic. marine engr. Engring. offficer Lykes Bros., New Orleans, 1951, 53; teaching asst. MIT, Cambridge, Mass., 1954; designer, contractor Shell Oil, 1954-56, mgr. design constrn. and operation semisubmersible rig, 1956-61, prin. lectr. floating drilling and subsea completions, 1961; divsn. engr. Shell Oil, L.A., 1962-65, Lafayette, La., 1965-70; sr. staff rschr. Shell Oil, 1970-74, offshore designer Gulf of Mex., 1974-78, constrn. engr., 1978-80, project mgr., 1980-83, cheif naval architect, 1984, designer, contractor, 1985-87; cons. Shell Offshor Inc., Shell Oil Co., Exxon, World Bank, Reading and Bates Drilling C., U. of Texas, Austin, Noble Denton, PMB Systems Engring., British Petroleum, Elf Acquitaine Petroleum, Homestake Mining Inc., CBS Engring., Shell Pecten Internat., ARCO Internat., Lemle and Kelleher, 1987—; vis. prof. U. Tex., Austin, 1976—. Author: Buoyancy and Stability, 1976; contbr. over 50 tech. papers to profl. jours. Mem. marine bd. Nat. Rsch. Coun., Washington, 1993—. Lt. USNR. Recipient Holley medal Am. Soc. Mech. Engrs., 1979, Gibbs Bros. medal Nat. Acad. Scis., 1991; Fulbright scholar. Mem. Nat. Acad. Engring., Soc. Naval Arch. and Marine Engring. (Blakley Smith medal 1993, Offshore Energy Ctr. Hall of Fame 1998), Sigma Xi. Republican. Presbyterian. Achievements include patents for drill barge anchor system, floating drilling platform, pitch period reduction apparatus for tension leg platforms, curved conductor well template, tension leg platform anchoring method and apparatus; invention of semisubmersible drilling rig. Home: 511 Kickerillo Dr Houston TX 77079-7428

COLLIS, CHARLES, aircraft company executive; b. Bklyn., Aug. 6, 1920; s. Charles and Marie (Barnaby) C.; m. Margaret Howell, July 11, 1942; children: Jane, Joy. BSMechE, Brown U., 1942. V.p. Stratos div. Fairchild Hiller Corp., 1946-65, sr. v.p. Republic Aviation div., 1965-67, exec. v.p. corp., 1967-81; pres. Fairchild Hiller-F.R.G. Corp., 1966-69; pres. Fairchild Republic Co., 1973-75, ret., 1981; mgmt. cons. Babylon, N.Y., 1982—; mem. grad. mgmt. engrng. adv. council C.W. Post Coll., L.I., 1965-66. Served as lt. USNR, 1942-45. Mem. AIAA, L.I. Assn. Commerce and Industry (bd. dirs. 1964-66). Clubs: Babylon Yacht, Southward Ho Country; SEA Island (Ga.). Home and Office: 116 Peninsula Dr Babylon NY 11702-3336

COLLIS, JOHN STANLEY, neurosurgeon; b. Lexington, Ky., Apr. 6, 1931; s. John Stanley and Elizabeth (Stefanis) C.; m. Helen Levas; children: Maribeth, John. BS, U. Ky., 1950; MD, U. Louisville, 1955. Program dir. Good Samaritan Hosp., Lexington, 1956; resident in gen. surgery Cleve. Clinic, 1957, resident in neurol. surgery, 1958-61, head spinal surgery, 1968-74, neuro anatomy instr., 1964-69, mem. neurosurgery dept., 1963-74; assoc. prof. neurosurgery Case Western Res. U., Cleve., 1976-82; neurosurg. adv. coun. Alcon Surg., 1983; dir. neurosurgery St. Luke's Hosp., Cleve., 1974-83, St. Vincent Charity Hosp., Cleve., 1984—, Luth. Med. Ctr., Cleve., 1988—; founder Cleve. Spine and Arthritis Ctr., 1988, co-dir.; lectr. in field. Inventor surg. hood, surg. instruments for total disc replacement, laminectomy retractor, surg. see-0thru-barrier drape; contbr. articles to profl. jours.; editl. bd. Principle and Technic of Spinal Surgery, 1989. Chmn. sect. ch. and soc. Archdiocese Coun., Orthodox Ch., N.Y., 1983-84, co-chmn. fin. com. for Pitts.-Cleve. Diocese, mem. coun., 1984—; chmn. expansion com. St. Constantine & Helen, Cleve., 1985-87, co-chmn. expansion fund, tchr. adult edn., 1988-96; pres. Hawken Sch. Swimming Booster Club, 1979-80; mem. Hellenic Univ. Club, 1984; me., trustee Leadership 100, N.Y.C., 1986-97; exec. com. bd. trustees Hellenic Coll., Boston, 1997-98. Recipient St. Paul award Orthodox Ch., 1992. Mem. AMA, AAAS, Am. Assn. Neurol. Surgeons, Ohio State Neurosurg. Soc., Congress of Neurol. Surgeons, N.E. Ohio Neurosurg. Soc., Fellowship of Acad. Neurosurgeons, Cleve. Surg. Soc., Ohio State Med. Assn., N.Am. Lumbar Spine Assn., Order of St. Paul, Order of St. Andrew. Republican. Greek Orthodox. Avocations: Bible study, philosophy. Office: Cleveland Spine and Arthritis Ctr 2709 Franklin Blvd Cleveland OH 44113-2912

COLLIS, KAY LYNN, professional beauty consultant; b. Dallas, July 15, 1958; d. Martin Edward and Norma June C. AA, Tyler Jr. Coll., 1978; BBA, Sam Houston State U., 1982. Mgr. World Fin. Corp., Bryan, Tex., 1977-81; ops. analyst Republic Bank Dallas, 1983-85; asst. v.p. MBank, Dallas, 1985-87; v.p., Murray Fed. Savs., 1987-90; owner KC Enterprises, 1990—; team leader Mary Kay, 1994—; advisor Collis Cons. Co., Sulphur Springs, Tex., 1983—. Columnist Contemporary Singles Lifestyles, 1993-96; contbr. articles to mags. Vol. Speaker Bur. Mem. NAFE, Fin. Women Internat. (group pres. 1989-90, Tex. mktg./pub. rels. 1990-91), Las Vegas C. of C. (Mentor Com.1997—), Toastmasters Internat. (divsn. gov. 1996-97). Republican. Episcopalian. Home and Office: 7844 Desert Candle Way Las Vegas NV 89128-7368

COLLIS, SIDNEY ROBERT, retired telephone company executive; b. Oak Park, Ill., Mar. 24, 1924; s. Sidney John and Celia (Steele) C.; m. Lois E. Harding, Feb. 23, 1946 (dec.); children—Robert H., Elizabeth A., Gail M., April L. Student, Ill. Inst. Tech., 1941-43, U. Santa Clara, 1943-44; B.S. in Elec. Engring, Northwestern U., 1947. Registered profl. engr., Ill. With Ill. Bell Telephone Co., 1947-54, 60-61; with Am. Tel. & Tel. Co., 1954-60, 61-62, asst. v.p., 1968-83; v.p. Am. Tel. & Tel. Communications, 1984; asst. v.p. N.Y. Telephone Co., 1962-63, v.p., 1963-68. Home: 70 Fieldstone Dr Basking Ridge NJ 07920-1607

COLLISON, JIM, business executive; b. Blue Earth, Minn., May 24, 1933; s. Elliott Eugene and Rosa Theresa (Whitcomb) C.; m. Valerie Ann Thul, Oct. 28, 1954; children: Judith, Michelle, Daniel, Michael, Rebecca, David. BA, St. John's Univ., 1955. Sports editor Blue Earth Post and Faribault County Register, 1953; staff writer St. Cloud (Minn.) Daily Times, 1953-55, Waterloo (Iowa) Courier, 1955-57, Mason City (Iowa) Globe Gazette, 1958-63; bus. and edn. cons. Jim Collison Assocs., Mason City, 1963-77; exec. dir. Employers of Am., Mason City, 1978-81, pres., 1981—; pres., pub. Sunburst Publ., Mason City, 1990—; co-founder Employers of Am., 1978; chmn. bd. ISBE Ins. Alliance, Mason City, 1986—, Select Advantage, Inc., ISBE Bus. Ins. Assn., ISBE Employer Benefits Assn.; pres. Am. Corp. Advisors, Inc.; workshop presenter. Author: Skill Building in Advanced Raeding, 1968, Mental Power in Reading, 1970; sr. editor: Complete Employee Handbook Made Easy, 1994, 97, The Employer Protection Workshop, 1996, (newsletter) Smart Workplace Practices. Asst. min. Orchard (Iowa) Congreg. Ch., 1985—; designer Adult Literacy and Employment Reading Training Program. Democrat. Avocations: flower gardening, hiking. Home: 310 Meadow Ln Mason City IA 50401-1717 Office: Employers of Am 520 S Pierce Ave Ste 224 Mason City IA 50401-2751

COLLMAN, JAMES PADDOCK, chemistry educator; b. Beatrice, Nebr., Oct. 31, 1932; married. B.Sc., U. Nebr., 1954, M.S., 1956; Ph.D. (NSF fellow), U. Ill., 1958; Ph.D. (hon.), U. Nebr., 1988; Docteur Honoris Causa, U. Dijon, France, 1988, U. Borgogne, France, 1988; D (hon.), U. Nebr., 1988. Instr. chemistry U. N.C., Chapel Hill, 1958-59; asst. prof. U. N.C., 1959-62, asso. prof., 1962-67; prof. chemistry Stanford U., 1967—; George A. and Hilda M. Daubert prof. chemistry Stanford U., 1980—; Frontiers in Chemistry lectr., 1964, Nebr. lectureship, 1968; Venable lectr. U. N.C., 1971; Edward Clark Lee lectr. U. Chgo., 1972; vis. Erskine fellow U. Canterbury, 1972; Plenary lectr. French Chem. Soc., 1974; Dreyfus lectr. U. Kans., 1974; Disting. inorganic lectr. U. Rochester, 1974; Reilley lectr. U. Notre Dame, 1975; William Pyle Philips lectr. Haverford Coll., 1975; Merck lectr. Rutgers U., 1976; FMC lectr. Princeton, 1977; Julius Steiglitz lectr. Chgo. sect. Am. Chem. Soc., 1977; Pres.'s Seminar Series lectr. U. Ariz., 1980; Frank C. Whitmore lectr. Pa. State U., 1980; Plenary lectr. 3d IUPAC Symposium on Organic Synthesis, 1980, 2d Internat. Kyoto Conf. on New Aspects Inorganic Chemistry, 1982, Internat. Symposium on Models of Enzyme Action, Brighton, Eng., 1983, Internat. Symposium, Italy, 1984; Brockman lectr. U. Ga., 1981; Samuel C. Lind lectr. U. Tenn., 1981, Syntex Disting. lectr. Colo. State U., 1983; Disting. vis. lectr. U. Fla., 1983; vis. prof. U. Auckland, New Zealand, 1985; Nelson J. Leonard lectr. U. Ill., 1987; plenary lectr. Internat. Symposium on Activation of Dioxygen and Homogeneous Catalytic Oxygenations, Tsukuba, Japan, 1987; plenary lectr. 12th Internat. Symposium on Macrocyclic Chem., Hiroshima, Japan, 1987; lectr. Texas A&M, 1988; J. Clarence Karcher lectr. U. Okla., 1989; Musselman lectr. Gettysburg Coll., 1990; Davis lectr. U. New Orleans, 1991; PLU lectr. Okla. State U., 1991; lectr. 5th Internat. Fischer Symposium, Karlsruhe, Ger., 1991; lectr. Euchem Conf., 1991; Pratt lectr. U. Va., 1992, others; lectr. series Harvard/MIT, 1992, Yale U., 1993; invited speaker symposia, univs., confs. Recipient Disting. Teaching award Stanford U., 1981, Calif. Scientist of Year award, 1983, Allan V. Cox medal for excellence in fostering undergrad. rsch., 1988, LAS Alumni Achievement award Coll. Liberal Arts and Scis. U. Ill., 1994, John C. Bailar Jr. medal, 1995, Joseph Chatt medal Royal Soc., 1998; named George A. and Hilda M. Daubert Prof. Chemistry (endowed chair, Stanford U.), 1980; Guggenheim fellow, 1977-78, 85-86, Churchill fellow, Cambridge, 1977—, Bing fellow, 1996. Fellow Calif. Acad. Scis. (hon.); mem. Am. Chem. Soc. (Calif. sect. award 1972, sec. award in inorganic chemistry 1975, Arthur C. Cope scholar 1986, Pauling award Puget Sound and Oreg. sect. 1990, Disting. Svc. award in inorganic chemistry 1991, Alfred Bader award in bioinorganic or bioorganic chemistry 1997, Joseph Chatt lectr. 1998, Basolo lectr. and medallist 1999), N.Y. Acad. Sci., Chem. Soc. (London), Nat. Acad. Sci., Am. Acad. Arts and Scis., Phi Beta Kappa, Sigma Xi, Phi Lambda Upsilon, Alpha Chi Epsilon. Office: Stanford U Dept Chemistry Stanford CA 94305

COLLMER, ROBERT GEORGE, English language educator; b. Guatemala, Central Am., Nov. 28, 1926 (parents Am. citizens); s. G. Russell and Constance Ethel (Cravener) C.; m. Linnie Maffett Burney, Jan. 5, 1948 (dec. 1979); children: Carol Linda Collmer McLaren, Mark Wesley; m. Alys Edney, July 4, 1981. BA, Baylor U., 1948, MA, 1949; PhD, U. Pa., 1953. Asst. instr. U. Pa., Phila., 1949-52; instr. Phila. Coll. of Bible, Phila., 1952-54; from assoc. prof. to prof., chmn. dept. English, Hardin-Simmons U., Abilene, Tex., 1954-58, 61; Smith-Mundt vis. prof. Inst. Tecnologico, Monterrey, Mex., 1958-60; independent researcher U. Leiden, Netherlands, 1960; academic dean, prof. Wayland Baptist U., Plainview, Tex., 1961-66; Fulbright vis. prof. Universidad Nacional, Asuncion, Paraguay, 1966-67; prof. English, Tex. Tech U., Lubbock, 1967-73; prof., chmn. dept. English, Baylor U., Waco, 1973-80, dean grad. studies and rsch., 1979-92, disting. English prof., 1992-97,emeritus disting. English prof., 1997—, visiting English prof. U. of Jordan, fall 1997. Editor: (with others) American Bypaths, 1980, The English Journals of Lodewijck Huygens, 1982, Bunyan in Our Time, 1989. Contbr. articles to profl. jours. Served to cpl. U.S. Army, 1945-46. Fellow Rockefeller Found. 1958, Smith-Mundt, 1958-60, Fulbright-Hays, 1966-76, Hon. Rsch. fellow U. Glasgow, 1994; grantee Dutch Ministry Edn. Scis., 1981, Fulbright-Hays sr. research grantee 1982, Am. Philosophical Soc. grantee, 1976. Mem. Deans Conf. So. Assn. Bapt. Schs. (pres. 1963-64), S. Central Renaissance Conf. (pres. 1970-71), Assn. Tex. Grad. Schs. (pres. 1982-83), Conf. Christianity and Lit. (pres. 1982-85), Conf. Coll. Tchrs. of English (pres. 1983-84). Democrat. Avocations: traveling to Latin Am. and Europe, book collecting. E-mail: RCoL1017eaol.com. Home: 2801 Wooded Acres Dr Waco TX 76710-1252

COLLMER, RUSSELL CRAVENER, data processing executive, educator; b. Guatemala, Jan. 2, 1924; s. G. Russell and Constance (Cravener) C.; m. Ruth Hannah Adams, Mar. 4, 1950; 1 child, Reed Alan. MS in Meteorology, Calif. Inst. Tech., 1944; BS in Math., U. N.Mex., 1951; MS in Math., State U. Iowa, 1955. Staff mem. Lincoln Lab., MIT, Lexington, 1955-57; mgr. systems modeling, computer dept. GE, Phoenix, 1957-59; mgr. ARCAS Thompson Ramo Wooldridge, Inc., Canoga Park, Calif., 1959-62; assoc. mgr., tech. dir. CCIS-70 Bunker-Ramo Corp., L.A., 1962-64; sr. assoc. Planning Rsch. Corp., L.A., 1964-65; pres. R. Collmer Assocs., Benson, Ariz., 1965—; pres. Benson Econ. Enterprises Corp., 1968-69; lectr. computer scis. Pima C.C., Tucson, 1970—. With USAAC, 1942-46, capt. USAF, 1951-53. Mem. IEEE, Am. Meteorol. Soc., Assn. for Computing Machinery, Assn. Instnl. Rsch., Phi Delta Theta. Office: R Collmer Assocs PO Box 864 Benson AZ 85602-0864

COLLOMB, BERTRAND PIERRE, cement company executive; b. Lyon, France, Aug. 14, 1942; came to U.S., 1985; s. Charles and Helene (Traon) C.; m. Marie Caroline Wirth, July 1, 1967; children: Cedric, Alex, Stephanie. Engring. student, Ecole Poly., Paris, 1960-62; engring. degree, Ecole des Mines, Paris, 1963-66; law degree, U. Nancy, France, 1968; PhD in Mgmt., U. Tex., 1972. Mining engr. Ministry of Industry, France, 1967-74; spl. asst. to Minister of Edn. Paris, 1974-75; with Lafarge, 1975—; regional v.p. Ciments Lafarge, Paris, 1976-77, pres., 1978-82; pres., CEO Orsan, Paris, 1982-85; CEO Gen. Portland, Inc., Dallas, 1985-87, Lafarge Corp., Paris, 1987-88; chmn. bd. Lafarge Corp., Reston, Va., 1989—; sr. v.p. Lafarge, Paris, 1988-89, chmn., CEO, 1989—; bd. dirs. Crèdit Commercial de France, Elf; adv. dir. Unilever; chmn. French Inst. de l'Entreprise; supervisory bd. Allianz. Home: 4 rue de Lota, 75116 Paris France Office: Lafarge, 61 rue des Belles Feuilles, 75116 Paris France also: Lafarge Corp 11130 Sunrise Valley Dr Ste 300 Reston VA 20191-4329

COLLONS, RODGER DUANE, decision sciences educator; b. Glenn, Neb., Jan. 8, 1935; s. Rodger Bernard and Ethel Bernice (Littrel) C.; m. Cynthia Carolyn Dyer, May 6, 1961; children: Kevin Rodger, Theresa Rene. BCE, U. Tex., El Paso, 1957; JD, George Washington U., 1961; MBA, Ga. State U., 1965, DBA, 1967. Bar: Va. 1961, Ga. 1963; registered U.S. patent atty.; CLU. Patent examiner U.S. Patent Office, Washington, 1957-60; assoc. counsel Strauch, Nolan & Neale, Washington, 1960-61; asso. patent counsel Lockheed Ga. Co., Atlanta, 1961-64; teaching fellow Ga. State U., 1964-65; asst. prof. mgmt. Ga. So. Coll., 1965-66; asst. prof. quantitative analysis Ga. State U., 1966-68; dir. div. adminstrv. scis. Grad. Coll. W.Va., 1969-71; dean Coll. Bus. and Adminstrn., Drexel U., 1971-76, prof. decision scis., 1976—; James S. Bingay vis. prof. creative leadership Am. Coll., 1979-81. Author: (with Donald Del Mar) Classics in Scientific Management, 1976; editor: Decision Line, 1969-72; contbg. editor: Creative Leadership Rev., 1980-82; bi-monthly series Best's rev., 1980-83. Bd. dirs. Phila. Civic Ballet, 1974-86, pres. 1979-82; bd. dirs. Rosemont-Villanova (Pa.) Civic Assn., 1976—, pres., 1980-86. Recipient cert. of appreciation Allied Social Scis. Assns., 1976. Fellow Decision Scis. Inst. (Disting. Service award 1971, pres. 1972-73, dir. 1969-76, chmn. fellows 1979-81); mem. Middle Atlantic Assn. Colls. Bus. Adminstrn. (pres. 1975-76), Alpha Iota Delta (pres. 1971-72, 73-74, Disting. Svc. award 1976, dir. 1972—). Kiwanis (dir. Phila. club 1973-76). Patentee container closure, sealing method. Home: 1909 Firethorn Ln Villanova PA 19085-1809 Office: Coll Bus and Adminstrn Drexel U Philadelphia PA 19102

COLLOTON, JOHN WILLIAM, university health care executive; b. Mason City, Iowa, Feb. 20, 1931; s. Harold and Miriam (Kelly) C.; m. Mary Ann Hagglund, Oct. 8, 1960; children—Steven, Laura, Ann. B.A. with high honors, Loras Coll., 1953; M.A., U. Iowa, 1957. Hosp. relations rep. Hosp. Service Inc. of Iowa, Des Moines, 1957-58; with U. Iowa, Iowa City, 1958—; assoc. dir. U. Iowa Hosps. and Clinics, 1969-71, dir., asst. to univ. pres. for statewide health svcs., 1971-93; v.p. statewide health svcs. U. Iowa, 1993—; bd. dirs. Baxter Internat., Inc., Nat. Med. Waste Inc., Iowa State Bank & Trust Co., MidAm. Energy Co., Premier Anesthesia, Atlanta, 1992, Assn. Health Svcs. Rsch., 1992; cons. HIH; pres. adminstrv. bd. Assn. Am. med. Colls. Coun. of Teaching Hosps., 1979-80; mem. presdl. search com. Assn. Am. Med. Colls., 1984; mem. adv. bd. Duke U. Hosp., 1985; mem. task force on acad. health ctrs. Commonwealth Fund, chmn. selection com. exec. nurse leadership program, 1983; mem. prospective payment commn. Congl. Office Technology Assessment, 1983; chmn. bd. dirs. Iowa-S.D. Health Svcs. Corp. (now Blue Cross and Blue Shield Iowa, Blue Cross S.D.), 1993—. Contbr. articles to profl. publs. Served with Finance Corps U.S. Army, 1953-55. Fellow Am. Coll. Hosp. Adminstrs.; mem. Inst. Medicine NAS, Am. Hosp. Assn. (coun. on financing 1977, med. edn. com. 1984-87), Iowa Hosp. Assn. (chmn. bd. trustees 1977-78, trustee 1978—), Am. Assn. Hosp. Planning, Assn. Am. Med. Colls. (chmn. 1987-88, disting. svc. mem. 1991), Johnson County (Iowa) Med. Soc., U. Iowa Alumni Assn., Rotary. Roman Catholic. Office: U Iowa Hosps & Clinics 200 Hawkins Dr Iowa City IA 52242-1009*

COLLUMB, PETER JOHN, communications company executive; b. Newark, July 29, 1942; s. Peter A. and Rose M. (Coffey) C.; 1 child, Alexandra Christine. Student, Tex. A&M, Commerce, 1967; postgrad in Bus. Adminstrn., U. Dallas, 1988. Registered lobbyist. Dir. pers./labor rels. Roper Corp., Chattanooga, Tenn., 1969-71; v.p. human resources Nat. Sharedata Corp., Dallas, 1971-74; dir. pers./labor Dallas Times Herald, 1975-78; dir. econ. devel. divsn. Tex. Dept. Community Affairs, Austin, 1978-80; dep. dir. Tex. Dept. Cmty. Affairs, 1978-81; legis./adminstrv. dir. U.S. Senator John G. Tower, Washington and Dallas, 1980-83; member U.S. Senate Armed Services Com., U.S. Senate Banking, Finance and Labor Com.; v.p. fin., sec.-treas. Diversified Packaging Co., Inc., Dallas, 1983-85; pres. N.Am. Systems, Inc., Dallas, 1981—; chmn. of bd., pres. Collumb, Hess, Navarro Pub. Rels., Dallas, Austin, Washington, Sacramento, 1991—; chmn., pres. Collumb Communications Co., Dallas, 1983—; chmn. Komatsu, Ashcraft and Collumb Inc.; personal envoy Ronald W. Reagan, Pres. of U.S., Washington, 1981-82; cons. Market Solutions, Inc., 1997—; adj. prof. Bishop Coll., Dallas; bd. dirs. Tex. Housing Agy., Govs. Coms. on Aging and Migrant Affairs; guest lectr. So. Meth. U., Dallas, 1988—; chmn. bd. D.S.P. Corp., Dallas, 1985—, C.H.N. Internat., Washington, Geneva, London and Tokyo; advisor to U.S. Sec. of Labor, Houston Econ. Summit, 1990; labor cons. Kullman, Lange, Inman & Bee, New Orleans; dir. Drug Prevention and Treatment Divsn., Tex. Dept. Cmty. Affairs; cons. City of Westminster, Tex. Author: Political Process, 1982; contbr. articles to profl. publs. bd. dirs. Plano Child Guidance Ctr., Collin County Mental Health-Mental Retardation Coun., Edna Gladney Ctr., Ft. Worth, 1979—, Free Shakespeare Festival, Dallas, 1978-85, v.p. finance; pres. Family Coun. Heritage Park; bd. dirs. Outstanding Young Men Am., Atlanta, 1982—, Nat. Com. Adoption, 1986—, Bus. Continuation/Disaster Recovery Inst., 1987—, Ark. State Vocat./Tech. Schs., Ft. Worth State Sch. for the Retarded, Beautify Tex. Coun., 1980-85, Westminster Ind. Sch. Dist. Bd.; lobbyist, City of Fairview, Tex.; mem. advance staff Reagan/Bush Presdl. Campaign, Washington, 1978-85, Sam Johnson for Congress Campaign, 1991, Edwin Edward for Gov. Campaign, Bush-Quayle 1992 Presdl. Campaign; vice-chmn., dir. fin. Fair Housing Coun., 1988—; mem. community adv. coun. Coord. Bd. Tex. Colls. and Univs.; mem. Rep. Presdl. Task Force, 1984—; co-chair, parents counc., Mary Baldwin Coll., chmn. Fourth Border Conf. on Drug Abuse; candidate U.S. Ho. Reps., Dallas, 1982-84; del. White House Confs. on Aging, Small Bus. and the Family, Tex. Rep. Party Convs., 1984, 88, 92; pvt. advisor to Pres. U.S.: Ronald Reagan and George Bush; exec. dir., receiver Dallas County Community Action Com.; cons. U.S. Can. Free Trade Commn., Washington, 1986-87, Plano Sister Cities, Inc., Big Brothers & Sisters, others; chmn., v.p. fin., v.p. devel. Tex. World of Children; chmn. Pres.'s Adv. Coun., HUD Tech. Adv. Coun., Plano Ballet Theatre, N.E. Tex. Coun. of Svcs., Hillcrest Acad. Found., 1986-91, George W. Bush Re-Election Campaign, 1994, Hutchinson for U.S. Senate, 1994, Ralph Hall for Congress Re-Election Campaign; Welfare to Work Pilot Project, State of Tex., office at Gov. George W. Bush. Named to Outstanding Young Men Am., Jaycees, 1981, Amigo Extradonaire, Govt. of Mexico, 1984. Mem. Centros de Juv Mexico (chmn. 1980-84), North Dallas C. of C. (bus. resource, internat. affairs, govt. affairs com.), Lions (v.p. Mena, Ark. chpt. 1976-77), Rotary, Lambda Chi Alpha (pres. 1967-69, chmn. Alumni control bd., pres. Alumni Assn.), Stallion Club (pres.), Tex. Sheriffs Assn. (charter), East Tex. State U. Alumni Assn. Republican. Presbyterian. Avocations: tennis, golf, reading, politics. Office: Collumb Communication Co 3404 Mission Ridge Rd Ste 100 Plano TX 75023-8115

COLLYER, GEORGE STANLEY, JR., magazine editor; b. Beech Grove, Ind., Feb. 1, 1932; s. George Stanley and Esther (Ritz) C. BA, Duke U., 1954; PhD in Russian History, Free U., Berlin, 1973. Lectr. Schiller Coll., Berlin, 1969-73; journalist Bus. Internat./ McGraw Hill, Vienna, Austria, 1974-75; lectr. Ind.-Purdue U., Ft. Wayne, Ind., 1975; owner, pres. The Glassworks, Louisville, Ind., 1977-84; exec. dir. The Competition Project, Inc., Louisville, 1986—; adv. bd. Parsons Sch. Design, N.Y.C., 1998-99; adv. com. Gateway Park Competition, Covington, Ky., 1993-94; mem. competition task force AIA, Washington, 1996-97, bldg./site com. Pub. Radio Partnership, Louisville, 1997-98. Author: (dissertation) Riazan, an Ancient Russian Principality, 1974; editor (jour.) Competitions, 1991—. With U.S. Army, 1954-57, Germany. Office: The Competition Project Inc PO Box 20445 Louisville KY 40250-0445

COLLYER, MICHAEL, lawyer; b. N.Y.C., Feb. 5, 1942; s. Clayton Johnson and Heloise (Green) C.; m. Karen Machon, Nov. 4, 1963 (div. July 1979); m. Sandra Karen Schaum, July 28 1979; children: Sophie Marie; stepdaughter Shelley Malia. BA, Williams Coll., 1963; LLB, Columbia U., 1966. Bar: N.Y. 1966, Assoc., Becker & London, N.Y.C., 1966-70; ptnr. Kay Collyer & Boose and predecessors, N.Y.C., 1970—; legal adviser NATAS, N.Y.C., 1978—, trustee, 1982—, nat. officer, 1982—, chmn., 1990—; instr. bus. law Columbia U., N.Y.C., 1966-69; speaker conv. Practicing Law Inst., 1977, mem. chpt. motion pictures and TV under new copyright statute, 1978. Trustee George Heller Meml. Scholarship Fund; active N.Y.C. Mayor's Adv. Coun. Film and Broadcasting, 1993. With U.S. Army, 1966-71. Mem. Assn. of Bar of City of N.Y. (com. Entertainment Law 1992—), N.Y. Bar Assn. (author TV sect. entertainment law 1995), Internat. Radio and TV Soc., Internat. Coun. Nat. Acad. Arts and Scis. (bd. dirs.), N.Y. Yacht Club. Home: 25 Chester Ct Cortlandt Mnr NY 10567-6361 Office: Kay Collyer & Boose LLP One Dag Hammarskjold Pla New York NY 10017-2299

COLLYER, ROBERT B., trade association administrator; b. Decatur, Ill., Oct. 16, 1932; s. Murray Gordon and Frances Mary (Evans) C.; m. Margaret Mary Hebel, Feb. 27, 1960; 1 son, Bryan. BA, Humboldt Coll., 1956. Cons. DeLeuw Cather & Co., 1957-59; claims and mgr. govt. relations Indsl. Indemnity Co. Calif., San Francisco, San Jose, Sacramento, 1960-73; exec. asst. UBA Inc., Washington, 1974-81; dep. under sec. Employment Standards Adminstrn. U.S. Dept. Labor, Washington, 1981-84; pres. The Collyer Co., 1984—; exec. dir. Internat. Assn. Indsl. Accident Bds. and Commns., 1990-96; exec. dir., sec.-treas. Internat. Workers' Compensation Found., 1990—; dean Internat. Workers' Compensation Coll., 1990-96; co-founder, dir. Nat. Symposium Workers Compensation U. Maine, 1976-80; dir. Western States Self-Ins. Colloquim, Inc., Nat. Employers' Adv. Council on Workers Compensation; cons. Nat. Indsl. Council; mem. Nat. Adv. Commn. on State Workers Compensation Law Compliance U.S. Dept. Labor; mem. Nat. Adv. Commn. on Indsl. Rehab. Research and Tng. Program U. N.C.; mem. steering com. Nat. Workers Compensation Info. Exchange Group; mem. steering com. Permanent Disability Study Adv. Commn. NSF; mem. steering com. U.S. Longshoremen and Harbor Workers' Reform Group. Pres. Marin county Republican Council, (Calif.), 1973; mem. Calif. Rep. Central Com., 1970-73; asst. county chmn. Com. to Re-elect Pres., 1972. Named Republican of Yr. Marin County, 1972.

COLMAN, JOHN P., publishing executive. Pres., chief exec. officer Spy. Office: Spy Sussex Pubs Inc 49 E 21st St Fl 11 New York NY 10010-6213

COLMAN, RICHARD THOMAS, lawyer; b. Boston, Sept. 22, 1935; s. Albert Vincent and Marie Catherine (Henehan) C.; m. Marilyn Flavin, Dec. 1, 1962; children: Elizabeth B., Catherine B., Richard T. Jr., Patrick B. AB magna cum laude, U. Notre Dame, 1957; LLB cum laude, Boston Coll., 1962. Bar: Mass. 1962, D.C. 1966. Trial atty. Antitrust Div. U.S. Dept. Justice, Washington, 1962-66; ptnr. Howrey & Simon, Washington, 1970—. Trustee Indian Mountain Sch., Lakeville, Conn., 1992-98; regional del. Boston Coll. Law Sch. Alumni Assn., 1992—. Mem. ABA, Internat. Bar Assn., Fed. Bar Assn., D.C. Bar Assn., Wianno Club, Beach Club. Democrat. Roman Catholic. Office: Howrey & Simon 1299 Pennsylvania Ave NW Washington DC 20004-2420

COLMAN, ROBERT WOLF, physician, medical educator, researcher; b. N.Y.C., June 7, 1935; s. Jack K. and Miriam (Greenblatt) C.; m. Roberta Fishman, June 16, 1957; children: Sharon, David. AB summa cum laude, Harvard U., 1956, MD cum laude, 1960. Intern Boston City Hosp., 1960-61; resident Beth Israel, Brookline, Mass., 1961-62; clin. assoc. USPHS, NIH, 1962-64; resident Barnes Hosp., St. Louis, 1964-65, fellow in hematology, 1965-67; assoc. in medicine Harvard Med. Sch., Cambridge, Mass., 1967-69, asst. prof., 1969-73, assoc. prof., 1973; assoc. prof. U. Pa., Phila., 1973-77, prof. medicine, 1977-78; prof. medicine Temple U. Sch. Medicine, Phila., 1978—, prof. thrombosis rsch., 1981—, prof. physiology, 1992—, dir. Sol Sherry Thrombosis Rsch. Ctr., 1979—, Sol Sherry prof. of medicine, 1989—; mem. hematology study sect. NIH, Bethesda, Md., 1977-81; mem. parent com. to review SCORs in Ischemic Heart Disease; mem. chemistry spl. emphasis panel to review SBIR, STTR grants, NIH; invited lectr. Gordon confs., Internat. Congress Hemostasis and Thrombosis, Fedn. Am. Socs. Exptl. Biology meetings; plenary lectr. and chair Gordon Conf. Internat. Soc. Kallikreins and Kinins, others. Editor: Hemostasis and Thrombosis, 3d edit., 1994; editor Platelet Jour.; mem. editorial bd. Jour. Clin. Investigation, Blood, Procs. Soc. Exptl. Biology, Thrombosis Rsch. Platelets, Thrombosis Hemostasis; contbr. numerous articles to profl. jours. Surgeon USPHS, 1962-64. Recipient Leon Resnick prize Harvard U., Career Devel. award NIH, Sr. Investigator award S.E. Pa. chpt. Am. Heart Assn., Disting. Career award Internat. Soc. Thrombosis and Hemostasis. Fellow ACP; mem. Assn. Am. Physicians. Am. Soc. Clin. Investigation, Am. Soc. Biochemistry and Molecular Biology, Internat. Soc. Hemostasis and Thrombosis (councillor 1989-95), Peripatetic Club, Interurban Clin. Club, Phi Beta Kappa, Sigma Xi, Alpha Omega Alpha. Office: Temple U Sch Medicine Sol Sherry Thrombosis Rsch Ctr 3400 N Broad St Philadelphia PA 19140-5104

COLMAN, SAMUEL, assemblyman; b. Wadowice, Poland, Jan. 14, 1933; came to the U.S., 1954; s. Jacob and Sara R. (Cizner) Zollman; m. Clara Shifra Schwed, Sept. 11, 1957; children: Miriam, Jacob, Abraham. BEE, CCNY, 1963. Legislator County of Rockland, N.Y., 1974-85, chmn., 1978-80, majority leader, 1980-82, vice chair, 1982-84; assemblyman N.Y. State Legislature, Albany, 1985—. Del. Dem. Nat. Conv., N.Y.C., 1976, 92; pres. Young Dems., Rockland County, 1968-70. Recipient Humanitarian award Venture of Rockland, ARC, Pub. Svc. award Yeshiva of Spring Valley, N.Y., Hebrew Inst. Rockland County, Svc. award Rockland County Irish Arts Forum, 1994. Avocations: reading, biographies, history. Office: NY State Assembly PO Box 1549 1 Blue Hill Plz Ste 1116 Pearl River NY 10965-3100

COLMANT, ANDREW ROBERT, lawyer; b. Bklyn., Oct. 10, 1931; s. Edward J. and Mary Elizabeth (Byrne) C.; children: Stephen, Robert, Elizabeth, Carolyn. BBA, St. Johns U., Jamaica, N.Y., 1957, LLB, 1959. Bar: N.Y. 1959, U.S. Dist. Ct. (so. and ea. dists.) N.Y. 1961, U.S. Ct. Appeals (2nd cir.) 1969, U.S. Ct. Appeals (4th cir.) 1977, U.S. Supreme Ct. 1991. Assoc. Hill, Rivkins, Carey, Loesberg, O'Brien & Mulroy and predecessor firms, 1959-73, ptnr., 1973-87; of counsel Jerrold E. Hyams, 1988-91, Peter F. Broderick, 1992; proctor in admiralty; active USMC amphibious reconnaissance Army Gen. Intelligence Sch. Author: Outline of General Average. Cpl. USMC, 1952-54. Mem. ABA, Assn. Trial Lawyers of Am., N.Y. State Bar Assn., N.Y. County Lawyers Assn., Maritime Law Assn. (life), Asia Pacific Law Assn., Pacific Rim Maritime Law Assn., Assn. Internat. de Droit des Assurances. Home: Bethany Manor 500 Broad St Apt 11Y Keyport NJ 07735-1640

COLMENARES, NARSES JOSE, electrical engineer; b. Caracas, Venezuela; came to U.S., 1977, naturalized, 1992; s. Jose and Isabel (Guevara) C.; m. Linda Burns, July 23, 1988; 1 child, Leah R. Communications Engr., Escoelfa, Caracas, 1974; Elec. Engr., Metropolitana U., Caracas, 1976; MS in Engring, Princeton U., 1980; M in Project Mgmt., George Washington U., 1996. Asst. prof. Simon Bolivar U., Caracas, 1975-77; systems engr. CSEE, Paris and Caracas, 1981-82; telecom. engr. CE Caracas Telecom. Group, Bloomfield, N.J., 1982-83; systems engr. Ram Broadcasting Corp., Avenel, N.J., 1983-85, Metromedia Telecommunications, Englewood City, N.J., 1985-86; communications engr. N.Y. Power Authority, White Plains, N.Y., 1986-87; tech. staff AT&T Bell Labs., Holmdel, N.J., 1987-93; project mgmt. cons. AT&T Svcs. Co. Inc., Whippany, N.J., 1993-94; project mgr. AT&T Network Wireless Systems, Whippany, 1994-95, Motorola Inc., Glen Rock, N.J., 1995-96; program mgr. Next Wave Telecom, Inc., Hawthorne, N.Y., 1996—; asst. researcher Princeton U., N.J., 1978-79; cons. Thevenin S.A., Caracas, 1974-77. Contbr. articles to profl. jours. and books. Lt. Venezuelan Navy, 1965-75. Recipient scholarship Venezuela Sec. of Defense, 1972, GMA Found., 1977. Mem. IEEE, Venezuela Assn. Elec. and Mech. Engrs. (former exec. dir.), Project Mgmt. Inst., N.Y. Acad. Scis. Avocation: daughter's education. Office: Next Wave Telecom, Inc 3 Skyline Dr Ste 3 Hawthorne NY 10532-2163

COLMERY, BENJAMIN HERRING, III, veterinarian; b. Battle Creek, Mich., Oct. 14, 1945; s. Benjamin Herring Jr. and Anne Renkes (Brainard) C.; m. Barbara Lemlein, Apr. 25, 1970 (div. Sept. 1986); m. Charlie L. Adams, Sept. 26, 1992; 1 child, Benjamin Herring IV. BS, Mich. State U., 1967, DVM, 1968. Diplomate Am. Vet. Dental Coll. Assoc. vet. Patterson Animal Hosp., Ann Arbor, Mich., 1968-72; hosp. dir. Westarbor Animal Hosp., Ann Arbor, 1972-93; chief dentistry Animal Med. Ctr., N.Y.C., 1993-95; staff dentist, oral surgeon Mich. Vet. Specialists, Southfield, 1995—; asst. prof. Mich. State U., East Lansing, 1975-92; past pres. Washtenaw Acad. Vet. Medicine, 1976-78, 84-85; pres. bd. dirs. Animal Emergency Clinic, Ann Arbor, 1997; spkr. in field. Contbr. articles to profl. jours. Named U.S. Jaycee Outstanding Young Men of Am., 1977. Fellow Acad. Vet. Dentistry (charter, pres. 1992); mem. Am. Vet. Med. Assn., Am. Vet. Dental Coll. (bd. dirs. 1989, treas. 1989-95, Peter Emily award 1996), Am. Animal Hosp. Assn., Am. Vet. Dental Soc. (co-founder, acting sec./treas. 1975-84, treas. 1984-92, pres. 1987-88), Southeastern Mich. Vet. Med. Assn., Mich. Vet. Med. Assn. (bd. dirs. 1974, pres. 1993), Ann Arbor Western Kiwanis Club (pres. 1972-73), Jackson Rd. Bus. Assn. (bd. dirs. 1975), Mt. Brighton Ski Patrol (asst. patrol dir. 1974-75), Phi Zeta. Avocations: scuba diving, golfing, skiing. Office: Mich Vet Specialists 21600 W 11 Mile Rd Southfield MI 48076-3709

COLN, WILLIAM ALEXANDER, III, pilot; b. Los Angeles, Mar. 20, 1942; s. William Alexander and Aileen Henrietta (Shimfessel) C.; m. Lora Louise Getchel, Nov. 15, 1969 (div. July 1979); 1 child, Caryn Louise. BA in Geography, UCLA, 1966. Cert. airline transport pilot, flight engr. Commd. USN, Pensacola, Fla., 1966; pilot, officer USN, Fighter Squadron 102, 1969-71, Port Mugu, Calif., 1975-77; pilot, officer USNR, Port Mugu, Calif., 1971-75, advanced through grades to lt. comdr., 1978; ret. USNR, 1984; capt. Delta Airlines, Inc. (formerly Western Airlines Inc.), Los Angeles, 1972—. Recipient Nat. Def. medal USN, 1966. Mem. Nat. Aero. Assn., Airline Pilots Assn., Aircraft Owners and Pilots Assn., UCLA Alumni Assn., Am. Bonanza Soc., Internat. Platform Assn., Santa Barbara Yacht Club. Democrat. Club: Santa Barbara (Calif.) Athletic, Santa Barbara Yacht. Avocations: sailing, scuba diving, flying, computers, electronics. Home: 486 Cota Ln Montecito CA 93108 Office: Delta Air Lines Inc LA Internat Airport Los Angeles CA 90009

COLODNY, EDWIN IRVING, lawyer, retired airline executive; b. Burlington, Vt., June 7, 1926; s. Myer and Lena (Yett) C.; m. Nancy Dessoff, Dec. 11, 1965; children: Elizabeth, Mark, David. AB with distinction, U. Rochester, 1948; LLB, Harvard U., 1951; D in Comml. Sci. (hon.), Robert Morris Coll., 1985; LLD (hon.), Middlebury Coll., 1986; HHD (hon.), Kings Coll., 1988. Bar: N.Y. 1951, D.C. 1958. With Office Gen. Counsel, GSA, 1951-52, CAB, 1954-57, USAirways Inc. (formerly Allegheny Airlines Inc.), 1957-91; exec. v.p. mktg. and legal affairs USAirways, Inc. (formerly Allegheny Airlines Inc.), 1969-75, pres., 1975-90, chief exec. officer, 1975-91, chmn. bd. dirs., 1978-92, ret., 1992; also chmn. USAirways Group, Inc., 1978-92; of counsel Paul, Hastings, Janofsky and Walker, Washington, 1991—; chmn. bd. dirs. COMSAT Corp. Lt. AUS, 1952-54. Recipient James D. McGill Meml. award U. Rochester, Wright Bros. Meml. award, 1990, Tony Jannus award, 1990. Mem. ABA, U. Rochester (bd. trustees).

COLOGNE, GORDON BENNETT, lawyer; b. Long Beach, Calif., Aug. 24, 1924; s. Knox M. Cologne; m. Patricia Cologne; children: Steven J., Ann Maureen Meyer. BS, U. So. Calif., 1948; LLB cum laude, Southwestern U. Sch. of Law, L.A., 1951. Bar: Calif. 1951, U.S. Supreme Ct. 1961. Trial atty. U.S. Dept. of Justice, Jacksonville, Fla., 1951-52; pvt. practice Indio, Calif., 1952-61; mayor Indio City Coun., 1954; mem. state assembly Calif. Legis., Sacramento, 1961-65; mem. senate Calif. State Senate, Sacramento, 1965-72; justice Ct. of Appeal, San Diego, 1972-84; govt. rels. atty. Sacramento, 1984-99. With USN, 1944-46. Named one of Outstanding Young Men of Calif., Calif. Jr. C. of C., 1961; recipient Freedom Found. award, 1965.

COLOM, VILMA, alderman; b. San Juan, P.R., June 7, 1954; d. Andres and Niza (Miranda) C.; divorced; 1 child, Omar Otero. BA, Northeastern U., 1978; MA, U. Ill., 1980. Mem. U.S. Sen. Task Force, Washington, 1983-90; chmn. Nat. Puerto Rican Forum, N.Y.C., 1986-89; pres. Colom Internat. & Assocs., 1986-88; bilingual educator Richard Yate Pub. Sch., 1993-95; alderman, committeeman 35th ward City of Chgo., 1995—; with nat. Hispanic affairs Allstate Ins., 1983-90. Asst. dir. U. Ill., Chgo., 1990-93; mem. adv. bd. LeadershipAm., 1994—; bd. dirs. Nat. Network Latino Women, 1995—; chmn. Chgo. office Nat. Puerto Rican Forum, N.Y.C., 1986-89, mem. adv. bd. nat. hqrs.; mem. aux. bd. Golden Apple Found., fundraising chmn., 1995—; mem. corp. nat. bd. Nat. Svc. Jobs for Progress. Recipient Signature award Leadership Am., 1994, Hispanic State Law Enforcement award, 1996, Law Enforcement award Hispanic Inst., 1996, Internat. award Logan Sq. Lions Club, 1996; named Hispanic of Yr., 1996. Mem. Nat. Women's C. of C., Omega Sigma Alpha. Democrat. Office: 2535 N Kedzie Blvd Chicago IL 60647-2655*

COLOMBATTO, MARTIN J., technology company executive. BSET, Calif. Polytech. U., Pomona. Various sales positions LSI Logic Corp.; dir. mktg. for networking and broadband access bus. units Broadcom Corp., Irvine, Calif., v.p., gen. mgr. networking bus. unit. Office: Broadcom Corp 16215 Alton Pkwy Irvine CA 92618

COLOMBO, JOHN ROBERT, poet, editor, writer; b. Kitchener, Ont., Can., Mar. 24, 1936; s. John Anthony and Irene (Nicholson) C.; m. Ruth Florence Brown, May 11, 1959. BA, U. Toronto, 1959, postgrad., 1959-60, DLitt (hon.), 1998. Editorial asst. U. Toronto Press, 1957-59; asst. editor Ryerson Press, Toronto, 1960-63; sr. adv. editor McClelland & Stewart, Toronto, 1964-70; publ. cons. Toronto, 1971—; editor Tamarack Rev., Toronto, 1960-82; Spl. instr. Atkinson Coll., York U., Toronto, 1965-68; mem. adv. arts panel Can. Council, 1968-70; advisor Ont. Council Arts, 1965-68. Author over 110 books, including Colombo's Canadian Quotations, 1974, (with Nikola Roussanoff) The Balkan Range: A Bulgarian Reader, 1976, Colombo's Canadian References, 1976, anthology The Poets of canada, 1978, Other Canadas: An Anthology of Science Fiction and Fantasy, 1979, Colombo's Hollywood, 1979, 222 Canadian Jokes, 1981, Friendly Aliens, 1981, Selected Poems, 1982, Selected Translations, 1982, Songs of the Indians, 1983, (with George Faludy) Learn This Poem of Mine by Heart, 1983, Canadian Literary Landmarks, 1984, 1001 Questions about Canada, 1986, Colombo's New Canadian Quotations, 1987, poetry Off Earth, 1987, Mysterious Canada, 1988, Extraordinary Experiences, 1989, 999 Questions About Canada, 1989, Songs of the Great Land, 1989, Mysterious Encounters, 1990, Mackenzie King's Ghost, 1991, UFOs Over Canada, 1991, The Dictionary of Canadian Quotations, 1991, Worlds in Small, 1992, Dark Visions, 1992, The Little Blue Book of UFOs, 1992, Walt Whitman's Canada, 1992, The Mystery of the Shaking Tent, 1993, Colombo's All-Time Great Canadian Quotations, 1994, Ghost Stories of Ontario, 1995, Voices of Rama, 1995, Strange Stories, 1995, Shapely Places, 1996, Haunted Toronto, 1996, All about Us, 1998, Marvellous Stories, 1998, More Iron Curtains, 1998, Closer than You Think, 1998, Quatable Canada, 1998, Interspaces, 1999, Self-Schrift, 1999; gen. editor The Canadian Global Almanac, 1992—, Ether, 1997, What is What, 1998. Recipient Can. Centennial medal, 1967, Order Cyril and Methodius 1st class, Esteemed Knight of Mark Twain, lit. prize Philips Info. Systems, 1985. Mem. P.E.N., League Can. Poets (provisional coordinator 1966-67), Assn. Can. TV and Radio Artists. Fax: 1 (416) 782-0285. E-mail: jrc@inforamp@nat. Home and Office: 42 Dell Park Ave, Toronto, ON Canada M6B 2T6

COLÓN, CARLOS WILDO, librarian; b. Shreveport, La., Apr. 23, 1953; s. Wildo Domingo and Mercedes (Alejandro) C.; m. Alma Maria Mutzi, June 17, 1979; 1 child, Gina Marie. BA in English, La. State U., Shreveport, 1975; MLS, La. State U., 1977. Ref. libr. Memphis-Shelby County Pub. Libr. and Info. Ctr., 1978-81; ref./reader's adv. supr. Shreve Meml. Libr., Shreveport, 1981—; libr. practicum instr. La. State U., Shreveport, 1982—. Author: The Worst of Almira Gulch, 1984, Almira Gulch: Confessions of a Social Wallflower, 1987, Jiminy Limericks, 1991, 94, Blue Jay on a Bowling Pin, 1991, Mountain Climbing, 1993, Clocking Out, 1996; (with Alexis K. Rotella) Nothing Inside, 1996, Sassy, 1998; editor: Shreve Memorial Library Public Service Statistics 1922-89, 1990; sr. editor A Selective Index to the Shreveport Journal, 1985-91, A Selective Index to the Shreveport Times, 1985-96; co-editor: Area Agencies and Organizations Directory, 1985—; contbr. articles to profl. jours. Vol. disk jockey Sta. WEVL, Memphis, 1981; lit. panel chmn. Shreveport Regional Arts Coun., 1990—, bd. dirs., 1991—. Named Outstanding Young Man of Am., Outstanding Young Men of Am., 1986; recipient Pushcart Prize nomination, 1994. Mem. ALA, La. Libr. Assn., Am. Contract Bridge League, Shreveport Bridge Assn., Poets & Writers, Haiku Soc. Am., Shreveport Writers Club, Yellow Bus Tour, LogJam. Roman Catholic. Home: 185 Lynn Ave Shreveport LA 71105-3523 Office: Shreve Meml Libr 424 Texas St Shreveport LA 71101-5452

COLÓN, PHYLLIS JANET, city official; b. Taylor, Tex., Sept. 1, 1938; d. Jack and Lydia Windmeyer; m. Henry J. Colón, Feb. 12, 1977; children: Walter N. Barnes III, Bradley H. Barnes, Mark A. Barnes. AA in Pub. Adminstrn., Del Mar Coll.; postgrad. in Acctg., Durham Jr. Coll.; BAAS in Pub. Adminstrn., Tex. A&I U., 1987; postgrad., Art Inst. Dayton. Registered profl. appraiser, Tex., assessor, Tex.; cert. tax adminstr., Tex.; lic. real estate borker, Tex. Mgr. info. Med. Arts Lab., Dayton, Ohio, 1970-73; appraiser Nueces County Appraisal Dist., Corpus Christi, 1973-82; tax assessor, collector Flour Bluff Ind. Sch. Dist., Corpus Christi, 1982, dir. spl. svcs., 1992-93; tax assessor, collector City of Laredo, Tex., 1993—; mem. Profl. Stds. Com. Bd. Tax Profl. Examiners, 1991, vice chmn., 1992, chmn. 1994—. Mem. advance planning bd. Corpus Christi Libr.; chmn. ad hoc planning com. Del Mar Coll., 1989—. Recipient achievement award State of Tex., Hero award City of Corpus Christi. Mem. NAFE, AAUW (bd. dirs. Corpus Christi br.), Tex. Assn. Assessing Officers, Tex. Sch. Assessors Assn., Inst. Cert. Tax Adminstrs., Am. Soc. Notaries, Corpus Christi C. of C., Art Mus. South Tex., Kiwanis (treas. Corpus Christi 1989-90, pres. 1990—; 2d v.p. Laredo United Way, 1995—, pres. Laredo chpt. 1997). Republican. Lutheran. Avocations: art, photography, reading. Home: 323 Manor Rd Laredo TX 78041-2752 Office: City of Laredo PO Box 329 1110 Houston St Laredo TX 78040-8019

COLONEY, WAYNE HERNDON, civil engineer; b. Bradenton, Fla., Mar. 15, 1925; s. Herndon Percival and Mary Adore (Cramer) C.; m. Anne Elizabeth Benedict, June 21, 1950; 1 child, Mary Adore. B.C.E. summa cum laude, Ga. Inst. Tech., 1950. Registered profl. engr. and surveyor, Fla., Ga., Ala., N.C. Project engr. Constructora Gen. S.A., Venezuela, 1948-49, Fla. Rd. Dept., 1950-55; hwy. engr. Gibbs & Hill, Inc., Guatemala, 1955-57; project mgr. Gibbs & Hill, Inc., Tampa, Fla., 1957-59; project engr., then assoc. J.E. Greiner Co., Tampa, 1959-63; ptnr. Barrett, Daffin & Coloney, Tallahassee, 1963-70; pres. Wayne H. Coloney Co., Inc., Tallahassee, 1970-78, chmn., bd. chief exec. officer, 1978-85; pres., sec. Tesseract Corp., 1975-85; dep. chmn. Howden Airdynamics Am., Tallahassee, 1985-90; pres. Coloney Co. Cons. Engrs., Inc., 1978—; v.p., dir. Howden Coloney Inc., Tallahassee, 1985-90; prin. Coloney-Von Soosten & Assocs. Inc., Tallahassee, 1990—; chmn. adv. com. Area Vocat. Tech. Sch., 1965-78; pres. Retro Tech. Corp., 1983-93, Profl. Mgmt. Con. Group, 1983-87; pres., bd. dirs. Internat. Enterprises Inc., 1967-73; bd. dirs., exec. com. GTO, Inc., 1990—. Patentee roof framing system, dense packing external aircraft fuel tank, tile mounting structure, curler rotating device, bracket system for roof framing; contbr. articles to profl. jours. Pres. United Fund Leon County, 1971-72; bd. dirs. Springtime Tallahassee, 1970-72, pres., 1981-82; bd. dirs. Heritage Found., 1965-71, pres., 1967; mem. Pres.'s Adv. Council on Indsl. Innovation, 1978-79; bd. dirs. LeMoyne Art Found., 1973, v.p., 1974-75; bd. dirs. Goodwill Industries, 1972-73, Tallahassee-Popoyan Friendship Commn., 1968-73; mem. Adv. Com. for Hist. and Cultural Preservation, 1969-71; vice chmn. Govs. Commn. for Purchase from the Blind, 1980—. Served with AUS, 1943-46. Fellow ASCE, Nat. Acad. Forensic Engrs.; mem. NSPE, Am. Def. Industries Assn., Fla. Engring. Soc. (sr.), Fla. Inst. Cons. Engrs., Fla. Surveying and Mapping Soc., Anak, Koseme Soc., Am. Arbitration Assn., Fla. Small Bus. Assn. (pres. 1981), Gov.'s Club, Phi Kappa Phi, Omicron Delta Kappa, Sigma Alpha Epsilon, Tau Beta Pi. Episcopalian. Home: 503 McDaniel St Tallahassee FL 32303-6254 Office: Coloney Co Cons Engrs 1014 N Adams St Tallahassee FL 32303-6133

COLONNA, WILLIAM MARK, accountant; b. Joliet, Ill., Jan. 18, 1956; s. William and Lorraine (Govednik) C. BA in Acctg., Lewis U., 1974-78. Cost acct., asst. acctg. mgr. Insta-Foam Products, Joliet, Ill., 1978-86; cost acct. Durkee Foods, Joliet, 1986-88; chief acct. mgr. Lennon Wallpaper Co., Shorewood, Ill., 1988-90; pres., owner William M. Colonna Acctg. and Tax Svc., Crest Hill, Ill., 1990—; contr. Whiteford Warehouse & Distbn., Joliet, 1992—, Midwest Motor Svc. Co. of Ill., Inc., Joliet, 1992—; sec., Joliet St. Anne Credit Union, Crest Hill, Ill., 1980-99, also bd. dirs. Home: 1718 Dearborn St Joliet IL 60435-2550

COLONNIER, MARC LEOPOLD, neuroanatomist, educator; b. Quebec, Que., Can., May 12, 1930; s. Jean and Enilda (Bourguignon) C.; m. Lise De Gagne, Oct. 24, 1959; 1 son, Jean. B.A., B.Ph., U. Ottawa, 1951, M.D., 1959, M.S., 1960; Ph.D., U. Coll. London, 1963. Asst. prof. anatomy U. Ottawa, 1963-65; asst. prof. dept. physiology U. Montreal, Que., Can., 1965-67; assoc. prof., assoc. fellow neurol. scis. group Med. Research Council Can., 1967-69; prof., head dept. anatomy U. Ottawa, 1969-76; prof. dept. anatomy Laval U., Quebec City, Que., 1976-91; ret., 1991. Recipient Lederle Med. Faculty award, 1966, Charles Judson Herrick award Am. Assn. Anatomists, 1967. Fellow Royal Soc. Can.; mem. Am. Assn. Anatomists; Mem. Soc. Neurosci.; mem. Can. Assn. Anatomists (pres. 1973-75). Club: Cajal.

COLOSI, THOMAS R., educator; b. May 25, 1934. BS, Cornell U., 1958. Internat. rep. dist. SO United Mine Workers Am., N.Y., 1958-61; commr. U.S. Fed. Mediation and Conciliation Svc., Buffalo, 1961-68; corp. dir. employee rels. Monogram Industries, L.A., 1968-71; v.p. alt. dispute resolution Am. Arbitration Assn., Washington, 1971-99; cons. alternate dispute resolution. E-mail: TCOLOSI@aol.com. Home: 1348 Hunter Mill Rd Vienna VA 22182

COLOSIMO, STEVEN FRANCIS, counselor; b. Greensburg, Pa., July 22, 1974; s. Lewis David and Joan Charlotte (Frye) C. BA in History, Washington and Jefferson Coll., Washington, Pa., 1996. Cash rep. Owens & Minor, Greensburg, 1996-97; counselor Adelphoi Village, Latrobe, Pa., 1997—; tchr. Trinity Area Sch. Dist., Washington, Pa., 1999—. Mem. Phi Beta Kappa, Alpha Tau Omega, Phi Alpha Theta. Republican. Roman Catholic. Avocations: Special Olympics volunteering, bike riding, reading, running. Home: 1220-11 Green Valley Dr Pittsburgh PA 15220

COLP, NORMAN BARRY, photographic artist, curator; b. Bronx, N.Y., Sept. 3, 1944; s. Joseph Johnny Colp and Martha (Berman) Colp Levine; m. Marsha Stern, July 18, 1981. BA in Art, CUNY, 1967; postgrad., Pratt Inst., 1967, Parsons Sch. Design, 1971. Archtl. modelmaker Milton Glaser Inc., N.Y.C., 1978-80; assoc. curator Alternative Mus., N.Y.C., 1979-80; curator exhibits Ctr. for Book Arts, N.Y.C., 1980-83, exhbn. coord., 1983; instr. Pratt Graphics Ctr., N.Y.C., 1983-84; instr. Sch. Visual Arts, N.Y.C., 1982-86, acad. advisor, 1984-87; photog. artist, curator N.Y.C., 1978—; cons. curator Anchorage Mus. History and Art, 1990, Golden & Dresnin Design, Phila., 1990, Islip Art Mus., East Islip, N.Y., 1990, Boca Raton (Fla.) Mus. Art, 1991; cons. on book Exploring Color Photography, 1991, 97; artist-in-residence Pub. Sch. 1, Long Island City, N.Y., 1977-78, Cabin Creek Ctr. for Work and Environ. Studies, N.Y.C., 1979; workshop presenter-in-residence Mus. Holography, N.Y.C., 1985; cons. Artists Found., Inc., Boston, 1986, juror, 1989; lectr. in field. Author: Freud's Recipe, Crazy Hair, A Primer on Art Criticism, 1983; one-man shows include Victoria and Albert Mus., London, 1991, Islip Art Mus., 1993, UCLA, 1994, Coll. of Charleston, 1997, Hugo de Pagano Gallery, N.Y.C., 1998; numerous group shows, 1970—, including Mus. Modern Art Libr., Mus. Fine Arts, St. Petersburg, Fla., Boca Raton Mus., Corcoran Galley of Art, Washington, U. Art Mus., U. Calif., Berkeley, Wadsworth Atheneum, Hartford, Conn., The Ralls Collection, Washington; represented in permanent collections Nat. Libr., Paris, Victoria and Albert Mus., Corcoran Gallery, Libr. Congress, Mus. Modern Art Libr., N.Y.C., N.Y. Pub. Libr., Queens Mus. of Art, Flushing, N.Y., Islip Art Mus., East Islip, N.Y., Bklyn. Mus. of Art, Archives of Am. Art, Smithsonian Instn., Washington. Grantee Com. for Visual Arts, 1980, Met. Transit Authority, 1991, Fieldcrest Cannon Inc., 1991. Avocations: collecting American art and Japanese redware pottery and gutta-purcha frames. Home and Studio: 180 W End Ave Apt 3R New York NY 10023-4913

COLSEY, ALAN BLAIR, public safety executive; b. Nyack, N.Y., Mar. 12, 1952; s. Lloyd Corwin and Joan (Claypoole) C.; m. Margaret W. Cromwell, Aug. 28, 1976 (div. Oct. 1986); 1 child, Blair Cromwell; m. Virginia Mary Sansone, Oct. 10, 1987; children: Benjamin Alan, Allison Blair. BA, Haverford Coll., 1974; MS, Iona Coll., 1994; postgrad., St. Thomas Aquinas Coll., 1998—. Police officer South Nyack (N.Y.) Police Dept., 1973-77, cpl., 1977-80; police chief South Nyack-Grand View Police Dept., 1980—; pres. Avstar Corp., Nyack, 1998—; adj. faculty mem. Nyack Coll., 1990—. Bd. mgrs. YMCA of Rockland County, Nyack, 1986-91; pres. O'Grady-Brown Meml. Scholarship Fund, Nyack, 1988—. Mem. N.Y. State Assn. of Chiefs of Police, Internat. Assn. of Chiefs of Police, Police Chiefs Assn. of Rockland County (pres. 1987-89), Mid-Hudson Assn. of Chiefs of Police (pres. 1992-93), Police Chiefs Found. of Rockland County (exec. dir. 1991-94), Nyack C. of C. (award 1982), Haverford Coll. Alumni Assn. (rep. 1975—, co-chmn. 1993—), Rotary (pres. 1989-90, award 1981), Elks (Valor award 1982). Episcopal. Avocations: reading, gourmet cooking, classical and jazz music, photography, travel. E-mail: ABC@aol.com. Home: 341 Deer Track Ln Valley Cottage NY 10989 Office: South Nyack-Grand View 282 Broadway South Nyack NY 10960

COLSKY, ANDREW EVAN, lawyer, mediator, arbitrator; b. Miami, Fla., Nov. 20, 1964; s. Jacob and Irene Vivian (Belen) C. BA, U. Fla., 1986, JD, 1989; LLM in Litigation, Emory U., 1990. Bar: Fla. 1989, Ga. 1990, D.C. 1990, U.S. Dist. Ct. (no. dist.) Ga. 1990, U.S. Dist. Ct. (so. dist.) Fla. 1990, U.S. Ct. Appeals (D.C. cir.) 1990, U.S. Ct. Appeals (11th cir.); cert. mediator Fla. Supreme Ct. Pvt. practice Miami, Fla., 1992—; pres. The Am. Mediation Inst., Miami, Fla., 1995—; CEO Am. Conflict Mgmt. Inst., 1998—; mem. trial team U. Fla., Gainesville, 1988-89, co-founder U. Miami Collaboration in Advanced Dispute Resolution Edn. program. Mem. Golden Key Honor Soc., Phi Delta Phi, Omicron Delta Kappa, Phi Kappa Phi, Alpha Lambda Chi (pres. 1985-86). Office: 6619 S Dixie Hwy # 220 Miami FL 33143-7919

COLSON, ANNY-ODILE, chemist; b. Montcy, France, Sept. 9, 1966; came to U.S., 1988; d. Yvon Colson and Gabrielle (Marteau) C. BSc in Biochemistry magna cum laude, Oakland U., 1990, PhD in Chemistry, 1995. Rsch. asst. Oakland U., Rochester, 1990-95; rsch. assoc. Mt. Sinai Med. Sch., N.Y.C., 1995-98; scientist Procter & Gamble Pharms., Mason, Ohio, 1998—. Contbr. articles to profl. jours. including Jour. of Phys. Chemistry, Internat. Jour. of Rad. Biol. Biophys. Jour., Jour. Biol. Chemistry, Biochemistry Jour. Grantee NIDDK/NIH, 1997-98. Mem. AAAS, N.Y. Acad. Scis., Biophys. Soc., Radiation Rsch. Soc., Sigma Xi. Office: Procter & Gamble Pharms 8700 S Mason Montgomery Rd Mason OH 45040-9462 Address: 9286 Carriage Run Circle Lovland OH 45140

COLSON, BARBARA, publishing executive. Dir. Cambridge Univ. Press, N.Y.C., 1993-98, spl. projects dir., 1998—. Office: Cambridge Univ Press 40 W 20th St New York NY 10011-4211*

COLSON, EARL MORTON, lawyer; b. Bklyn., Mar. 8, 1930; s. Abraham and Rebecca (Hecker) C.; m. Helen Thereša Austern, Apr. 24, 1960; children: Adam Thomas, Amy Esther, Deborah Austern. BS magna cum laude, Syracuse U., 1950; LLB magna cum laude, Harvard U., 1957. Bar: N.Y. 1958, D.C. 1960. Assoc. Chadbourne, Parke, Whiteside & Wolff, N.Y.C., 1957-60, Arent, Fox, Kintner, Plotkin & Kahn, Washington, 1960-68; partner Arent, Fox, Kintner, Plotkin & Kahn, 1968—; adj. prof. law Georgetown U., 1970—; lectr on tax subjects. Author: Capital Gains and Losses, 1975; co-author: Federal Taxation of Estates, Gifts and Trusts, 1975. Bd. dirs. Washington Hebrew Congregation, 1979—, v.p., 1984-90, pres., 1990-92; trustee Kingsbury Ctr., 1978-81; mem. N.Y. bd. overseers Hebrew Union Coll., 1995-97; bd. dirs. D.C. chpt. Am. Jewish Com., 1995-98. Mem. ABA (chmn. estate and gift tax com. sect. taxation 1972-73), D.C. Bar Assn. (chmn. tax com. 1971-72, treas., bd. govs. 1974-76), Am. Law Inst., Assn. of Bar of City of N.Y., Cosmos Club Washington. Office: 1050 Connecticut Ave NW Washington DC 20036-5303

COLSON, ELIZABETH FLORENCE, anthropologist; b. Hewitt, Minn., June 15, 1917; d. Louis H. and Metta (Damon) C. BA, U. Minn., 1938, MA, 1940; MA, Radcliffe Coll., 1941, PhD, 1945; PhD (hon.), Brown U., 1978, D of Sociology, 1979; D.Sc., U. Rochester, 1985, U. Zambia, 1992. Asst. social sci. analyst War Relocation Authority, 1942-43; research asst. Harvard, 1944-45; research officer Rhodes-Livingstone Inst., 1946-47, dir., 1948-51; sr. lectr. Manchester U., 1951-53; assoc. prof. Goucher Coll., 1954-55; research assoc., assoc. prof. African Research Program, Boston U., 1955-59, part-time, 1959-63; prof. anthropology Brandeis U., 1959-63; prof. anthropology U. Calif.-Berkeley, 1964-84, prof. emeritus, 1984—; vis. prof. U. Zambia, 1987; Lewis Henry Morgan lectr. U. Rochester, 1973; vis. rsch. assoc. Refugee Studies Program Queen Elizabeth House, Oxford, 1988-89. Author: The Makah, 1953, Marriage and the Family Among The Plateau Tonga, 1958, Social Organization of the Gwembe Tonga, 1960, The Plateau Tonga, 1962, The Social Consequences of Resettlement, 1971, Tradition and Contract, 1974, A History of Nyempeo, 1992; jr. author Secondary Education and the Formation of an Elite, 1980, Voluntary Efforts in Decentralized Management, 1983, sr. author For Prayer and Profit, 1988; sr. editor: Seven Tribes of British Central Africa, 1951; jr. editor People in Upheaval, 1987. AAUW travelling fellow, 1941-42, fellow Ctr. Advanced Study Behavioral Scis., 1967-68, Fairchild fellow Calif. Inst. Tech., 1975-76. Fellow Am. Anthrop. Assn., Brit. Assn. Social Anthropologists, Royal Anthrop. Inst. (hon.); mem. Nat. Acad. Sci., Am. Acad. Arts and Scis., Am. Assn. African Studies (Disting. Africanist award 1988), Soc. Applied Anthropology, Soc. Woman Geographers, Phi Beta Kappa. Avocations: walking, opera, reading. Office: U Calif Dept Anthropology Berkeley CA 94720

COLSON, STEVEN DOUGLAS, research director, chemistry educator; b. Idaho Falls, Idaho, Aug. 16, 1941; s. Robert William and Ellen Laurine (Pederson) C.; m. Donna Marie Lovell, Sept. 14, 1962; children: Maria, Susan, Douglas, David, Spencer, Steven, Brent. B.S., Utah State U., 1963; Ph.D., Calif. Inst. Tech., 1968. Postdoctoral fellow NRC, Ottawa, Ont., Can., 1967-68; asst. prof. chemistry Yale U., New Haven, 1968-73, assoc. prof., 1973-80, prof. chemistry, 1980-89; assoc. dir. chem. structure and dynamics environ. molecular sci. lab. Battelle Pacific Northwest Nat. Lab., Richland, Wash., 1990—; adj. prof. Wash. State U., 1990—; affiliate prof. U. Wash. Home: 2626 Appaloosa Way Richland WA 99352-7727 Office: Battelle Pacific Northwest National Lab Environ Molecular Scis Lab PO Box 999 Richland WA 99352-0999

COLTEN, HARVEY RADIN, pediatrician, educator; b. Houston, Jan. 11, 1939; s. Oscar Aaron and Zina Mae (Radin) C.; m. Susan J. Kaplowitz, July

29, 1959; children: Jennifer J., Lora, Charles Thomas. BA, Cornell U., 1959; MD, Western Res. U., 1963; MA (hon.), Harvard U., 1978. Diplomate Am. Bd. Allergy and Clin. Immunology, Am. Bd. Pediats. Intern Univ. Hosps., Cleve., 1963-64, resident in pediat., 1964-65; resident in pediat. Children's Hosp. of D.C., Washington, 1968-69; rsch. assoc. Nat. Inst. Child and Human Devel., NIH, Bethesda, Md., 1965-67; asst. prof. pediat. George Washington U., 1969-70; asst. prof. pediat. Harvard U., 1970-73, assoc. prof., 1973-79, prof., 1979-86; chief divsn. cell biology, dir. cystic fibrosis program Children's Hosp. Med. Ctr., Boston, 1976-86; Harriet B. Spoehrer prof. pediat. Washington U. Med. Sch., St. Louis, 1986-97, chmn. dept. pediat., 1986-95, prof. molecular microbiology, 1986-97; pediatrician-in-chief Children's and Barnes Hosps., 1986-95, Jewish Hosp., 1986-90; pediatrician Children's Barnes Jewish Christian Hosp. Sys., 1995-97; dean, v.p. med. affairs Northwestern U. Sch. Medicine, 1997—; past chmn. pediat. allergy Nat. Inst. Allergy and Infectious Disease Task Force on Asthma and Allergy; past mem. Nat. Inst. Child and Human Devel. Task Force on Cystic Fibrosis; past bd. dirs. rsch. rev. com. Nat. Cystic Fibrosis Found.; past mem. pulmonary diseases adv. com. NIH. Assoc. editor Jour. Immunology, 1971-74, Immuno-chemistry, 1972-75, Jour. Allergy and Clin. Immunology, 1977-80, New Eng. Jour. Medicine, 1978-81, Jour. Clin. Investigation, 1982-85, Am. Jour. Respiratory Cell and Molecular Biology, 1988-91, New Insights into CF, 1993; mem. editl. bd. Molecular and Cellular Biochemistry, 1983-87, Jour. Pediat., 1981-88, Jour. Clin. Immunology, 1985-89, Ann. Rev. Immunology, 1986-90, Clin. Immunology and Immunopathology, 1987-91, Blood, 1987-92, New Eng. Jour. Medicine, 1990-97, Jour. Biomed. Sci., 1992—, Proc. Assn. Am. Physicians, 1995—; contbr. Encyclopedia of Life Scis., 1997—; contbr. articles to profl. jours. Vice chmn. bd. dirs. Parents As Tchrs. Nat. Ctr.; bd. mem. The Oasis Inst.; past mem. pediat. scientist program selection com. AMSPDC; mem. sci. adv. coun. March of Dimes; mem. Nat. Heart, Lung, Blood Adv. Coun., NIH; past bd. mgrs. Ctrl. Inst. for Deaf. Recipient Spl. Faculty Rsch. award Western Res. U., 1963, E. Mead Johnson award, 1979. Fellow AAAS, Am. Acad. Allergy and Immunology, Am. Acad. Pediat.; mem. Fedn. Am. Socs. for Exptl. Biology, Inst. Medicine NAS (vice chmn. coun.), E. Mead Johnson Award Program Com. (past chmn.), Am. Assn. Immunologists (past sec.-treas., Disting. Svc. award), Am. Soc. Clin. Investigation, Assn. Am. Physicians, Soc. Pediat. Rsch., Am. Pediat. Soc., Am. Thoracic Soc., Am. Soc. Biochem. & Molecular Biol., St. Louis Pediat. Soc., Hungarian Soc. Immunology (hon.). Office: Northwestern U Sch Medicine Morton Bldg 303 E Chicago Ave Rm 4-656 Chicago IL 60611-3093

COLTMAN, JOHN WESLEY, physicist; b. Cleve., July 19, 1915; s. Robert White and Louise (Tyroler) C.; m. Charlotte Waters Beard, June 10, 1941; children—Sally Louise, Nancy Jean. B.S. in Physics, Case Inst. Tech., 1937; M.S., U. Ill., 1939, Ph.D. in Physics, 1941. Research scientist Research Labs. Westinghouse Electric Corp., Pitts., 1941-49; mgr. electronics and nuclear physics dept. Westinghouse Electric Corp., 1949-60, asso. dir. research labs., 1960-64, dir. research math. and radiation, 1964-69, dir. research industry, def. and pub. systems, 1969-74, dir. research and devel. planning, 1974-80; mem. adv. group on electron devices Dept. Def., 1958-62; mem. Naval Intelligence Sci. Adv. Com., 1971-73, NRC Commn. on Human Resources, 1977-80; privately sponsored rschs. on acoustics of the flute. Contbr. articles to profl. jours. Recipient Longstreth medal Franklin Inst., 1960; Roentgen medal Remscheid, W. Ger., 1970; Gold medal Radiol. Soc. N.Am., 1982. Fellow Am. Phys. Soc., IEEE; mem. Nat. Acad. Engring., Am. Musical Instrument Soc. Republican. Presbyterian. Inventor x-ray image amplifier, scintillation counter. E-mail: coltmanjw@worldnet.att.net. Home: 3319 Scathelocke Dr Pittsburgh PA 15235-5122

COLTON, CLARK KENNETH, chemical engineering educator; b. N.Y.C., July 20, 1941; s. Sidney and Goldie (Chases) C.; m. Ellen Ruth Brandner, June 20, 1965; children: Jill Erin, Jason Adam, Michael Ross, Brian Scott. B of Chem. Engring., Cornell U., 1964; PhD, MIT, 1969. Asst. prof. chem. engring. MIT, Cambridge, 1969-73, assoc. prof., 1973-76, prof., 1976—, Bayer prof. chem. engring., 1980-85, dep. head dept. chem. engring., 1977-78, chmn. centennial chem. engring. edn., 1988; cons. to NIH, FDA, various indsl. orgns.; mem. adv. bd. mil. personnel supplies NRC, 1971-75. Mem. editl. bd. Jour. Membrane Sci., 1975-81, 97, Jour. Bioengring., 1976-79, Preparative Chromatography, 1988-94, Isolation and Purification, 1994—, ASAIO Jour., 1985-94; mem. editl. bd. Cell Transplantation, 1991-94, 97, assoc. editor, 1997—; contbr. articles to sci. jours. Ford found. fellow, 1969-70; recipient Tchr./Scholar award Camille and Henry Dreyfus Found., 1972, Lifetime Contbn. award in bioartificial organs Engring. Found., 1998. Fellow AAAS; mem. N.Y. Acad. Scis., Am. Inst. Chem. Engrs. (dir. food, pharm. and bioengring. div. 1978-81, Allan P. Colburn award 1977), Am. Soc. Artificial Internal Organs (editorial bd. 1978-84), Am. Diabetes Assn., Am. Soc. for Apheresis, Am. Soc. for Engring. Edn. (Curtis W. McGraw rsch. award 1980), North Am. Membrane Soc., Am. Heart Assn., Cell Transplantation Soc. (sec. 1994—), Internat. Soc. on Oxygen Transport to Tissue, Am. Chem. Soc., Am. Inst. Med. and Biological Engring., Internat. Soc. Articificial Organs, Internat. Soc. Blood Purification (Gambro award 1986), Biomed. Engring. Soc., Cornell Club, Sigma Xi, Tau Beta Pi, Phi Lambda Upsilon. Home: 279 Commonwealth Ave Chestnut Hill MA 02467-1012 Office: MIT Dept Chem Engring Cambridge MA 02139

COLTON, DAVID LEM, mathematician, educator; b. San Francisco, Mar. 14, 1943; s. Ellis and Myrl (Crowder) C.; m. Renate, Dec. 20, 1968; children—Claire, Natasha. BS, Calif. Inst. Tech., 1964; MS, U. Wis., 1965; PhD, U. Edinburgh, Scotland, 1967, DSc, 1977. Asst. prof. math. Ind. U., 1967-71, assoc. prof., 1972-74; prof. U. Strathclyde, Glasgow, Scotland, 1975-78; prof. U. Del., Newark, 1978—, Unidel prof., 1996—; vis. prof. McGill U., 1968-69, U. Glasgow, 1971-72, U. Konstanz, 1974-75. Author various rsch. monographs; rschr. numerous publs. in field. Mem. Soc. Indsl. and Applied Math. (assoc. editor jour.). Office: U Del Dept Math Newark DE 19716

COLTON, FRANK BENJAMIN, retired chemist; b. Bialystok, Poland, Mar. 3, 1923; came to U.S., 1934, naturalized, 1934; s. Rubin and Fanny (Rosenblat) C.; m. Adele Heller, Mar. 24, 1950; children—Francine, Sharon, Laura, Sandra. B.S., Northwestern U., 1945, M.A., 1946; Ph.D., U. Chgo., 1949. Research fellow Mayo Clinic, Rochester, Minn., 1949-51; with G.D. Searle & Co., Chgo., 1951-86, asst. dir. chem. research, 1961-70, research advisor, 1970-86. Contbr. articles to profl. jours. Pioneer in organic and steroid chemistries. Patentee first oral contraceptive. Recipient Discovery medal for first oral contraceptive Nat. Assn. Mfrs., 1965, Profl. Achievement award U. Chgo., 1978, Achievement award Indsl. Research Inst., 1978; inducted in Nat. Inventors Hall of Fame, 1988. Mem. Am. Chem. Soc., Chgo. Chemists Club. Home: 1419 Lorete Ln Northbrook IL 60062-5142

COLTON, JOEL, historian, educator; b. N.Y.C., Aug. 23, 1918; s. Philip and Theresa (Cotler) C.; m. Shirley Baron, May 8, 1942; children—Valerie Beth, Kenneth Richard. BA magna cum laude, CCNY, 1937, MS, 1938; MA, Columbia U., 1940; PhD, 1950. Lectr. history Columbia U., 1946-47; successively instr., asst. prof., assoc. prof., prof. history Duke U., 1947-89, prof. emeritus, 1989—, chmn. dept. history, 1967-74, chmn. acad. council, 1971-73; dir. for humanities Rockefeller Found., 1974-81; U.S. mem. Internat. Commn. on History of Social Movements and Social Structures, 1975—, v.p., 1980-85, co-pres., 1985-90, hon. pres., 1990—; vis. prof. U. Wis., Makerere U., Uganda; lectr. Cadi-Ayyad U., Morocco. Author: Compulsory Labor Arbitration in France, 1936-39, 1951, Léon Blum: Humanist in Politics, 1966, (French transl. 1968), rev. edit., 1987, Twentieth Century: Time-Life Great Ages of Man Series, 1968, rev. edit., 1980; co-author: (with R.R. Palmer) A History of the Modern World, 8th edit., 1995 (transl. into Arabic, Persian, Swedish, Finnish, Spanish, Italian and Chinese), A Study Guide for a History of the Modern World, 8th edit., 1995; editor: The Humanities in an International Context, 1976, The Search for a Value Consensus, 1978, Toward the Restoration of the Liberal Arts Curriculum, 1979; co-editor: Technology, The Economy and Society, 1987; bd. editors: Jour. Modern History, 1967-70, Third Republic/Troisième République, 1975-85, Hist. Abstracts, 1981—, French Hist. Studies, 1985-88; contbr. articles to profl. jours., encys., internat. conf. procs. and yearbooks. Mem. adv. bd. Duke U. Press, 1982-88; trustee Triangle Univs. Ctr. for Advanced Studies, N.C., 1982-85. 1st lt., U.S. Army, 1942-46, M.I., 1944-46, ETO. Recipient book award Mayflower Soc., 1967, Townsend Harris medal CCNY Alumni Assn., 1980, Disting. Tchg. award Duke U., 1986, award for contbns. to study and tchg. French history Western Soc. for French History, 1994; Guggenheim fellow, 1957-58, fellow Rockefeller Found., 1961-62, sr. fellow NEH, 1970-71. Fellow Am. Acad. Arts and Scis.; mem. Am. Hist. Assn. (mem. com. on internat. hist. activities 1980-85), So. Hist. Assn. (chmn. European sect. 1975-76), Soc. French Hist. Studies (v.p. 1972-73), PEN Am. Ctr., Century Assn., Phi Beta Kappa (vis. scholar 1983-84, assocs. 1985—). Home: 6 Stoneridge Cir Durham NC 27705-5510 Office: Duke U Dept History Durham NC 27708-0719

COLTON, STERLING DON, lawyer, business executive, missionary; b. Vernal, Utah, Apr. 28, 1929; s. Hugh Wilkins and Marguerite (Maughan) C.; m. Eleanor Ricks, Aug. 6, 1954; children: Sterling David, Carolyn, Bradley Hugh, Steven Ricks. BS in Banking and Fin., U. Utah, 1951; JD, Stanford U., 1954. Bar: Calif. 1954, Utah 1954, D.C. 1967. Ptnr. Van Cott, Bagley, Cornwall & McCarthy, Salt Lake City, 1957-66; former vice chair, sr. v.p., gen. counsel, bd. dirs. Marriott Internat., 1993-95; former pres. Can. Vancouver Mission Ch. of Jesus Christ of Latter Day Saints, 1995-98, also bd. dirs.; v.p. Colton Ranch Corp., Vernal, 1987—; former bd. dirs. Megaherz Corp. and Dyncorp; former chmn. bd. dirs. Nat. Chamber Litigation Ctr. Former bd. dirs. Polynesian Cultural Ctr.; former chmn. nat. adv. coun. U. Utah, Ballet West, nat. adv. counsel; mem. adv. coun. The Nat. Conservancy. Maj. JAG, U.S. Army, 1954-57. Mem. ABA, Calif. Bar Assn., Utah Bar Assn., D.C. Bar Assn., Washington Met. Corp. Counsel Assn. (former pres., dir.), Sigma Chi. Republican. Mem. LDS Ch.

COLTON, SUSAN ADAMS, educational administrator; b. Jamestown, N.Y., Sept. 26, 1950; d. Emmett Robert and Jeanne Ellen (Moynihan) Franklin; m. Charles Ira, June 30, 1990. BA in edn., Fla. Atlantic U., 1977, MEd, 1984. Tchr. grade 1 Tamarac (Fla.) Elem., 1977-79; tchr. Cresthaven Elem, Pompano Beach, Fla., 1979-84; ednl. cons. Macmillan Pub. Co., N.Y.C., 1984-86; tchr. grade 1 Maplewood Elem., Coral Springs, Fla., 1986-87; asst. prin. Coral Springs (Fla.) Elem., 1987-92; prin. Forest Hills Elem. Sch., Coral Springs, 1992; cons. Broward County Schs., Ft. Lauderdale, Fla., 1986—; mem. adv. bd. dirs. Broward County Reading Coun., Broward City, Fla., 1990—; sec. adv. bd. Coalition Essential Schs. Active Coral Springs Edn. Task Force, 1990—; vol. Child Care Connection, Ft. Lauderdale, 1987—. Grantee Broward County Schs., 1990; Fla. Commrs. prin. Achievement award for Outstanding Leadership Fla. Commr., 1999. Mem. NAESP, ASCD, Internat. Reading Assn., Fla. Reading Assn. (Honor Coun. 1989), Broward County Reading Assn. (pres. 1988-89, honor coun. 1989), Fla. Assn. Elem. Sch. Prins., Broward Assn. Elem. Sch. Prins. (pres.), Phi Delta Kappa, Delta Kappa Gamma. Republican. Episcopalian. Avocations: photography, reading, teddy-bear collecting, crafts. Office: Forest Hills Elem Sch 3100 NW 85th Ave Coral Springs FL 33065-4699

COLTRIN, STEPHEN HUGH, public relations, advertising and marketing executive; b. Rupert, Idaho, June 7, 1945; s. Ira Hugh and Beverly (Luke) C.; m. Gwen Moore; children: Stephanie Ann, Jennifer Lynn, Susan Michelle, Wilson Stephen, Joel, Bryce, Gretel Cundick. B.S. in Psychology, Brigham Young U., 1970. Sales and mktg. rep. Burroughs Wellcome, Tucson, 1970-73; spl. rep. to med. ctrs. Burroughs Wellcome, Salt Lake City, 1973-76; product mgr., spokesman Pharm. Mfrs. Assn., Washington and Raleigh, N.C., 1976-78; dir. eastern pub. relations Ch. of Jesus Christ of Latter-day Saints, N.Y.C., 1978-82; chmn. Coltrin & Assocs., N.Y.C., 1982—; dir. Internat. Radio and TV Found., N.Y.C; v.p. Internat. Radio and TV Soc.; pvt. sect. broadcast adv. com. Voice of Am. Named Pharm. Industry Spokesman of Yr., Pharm. Mfrs. Assn., 1974, Outstanding Young Man, Jaycees, 1982. Republican. Mormon. Avocations: skiing, tennis. Office: Coltrin & Assocs 1212 Avenue Of The Americas New York NY 10036-1602

COLUCCI, JOSEPH MICHAEL, mechanical engineering consultant; b. Bklyn., Aug. 12, 1937; s. Michael Louis and Frances (Papaleo) C.; m. Suzanne Holden, Aug. 31, 1957; children: Michael, Cathryn, Christopher. BSME, Mich. State U., 1958; MSME, Calif. Inst. Tech., 1959. Asst. dept. head fuels & lubricants GM Rsch. Labs, Warren, Mich., 1970-72, dept. head fuels & lubricants, 1972-92; exec. dir. materials rsch. GM R&D Ctr., Warren, Mich., 1992-95; pres. Automotive Fuel Consulting, Inc., Clarkston, Mich., 1995—; bd. dirs. Mich. State U. Coll. of Engring. Rsch. Adv. Com., Lansing, 1978-82, Coordinating Rsch. Coun., Atlanta, 1992-97. Editor: (book) Future Automotive Fuels, 1977. Named Exec. of Yr., Harti-IRI Publs., 1991, 95. Fellow Soc. Automotive Engrs. (bd. dirs. 1990-93, bd. trustees 1996—), Sigma Xi. Avocations: photography, skiing, travel, sail boarding. Home: 7155 Hillside Dr Clarkston MI 48346-1432 Office: Automotive Fuels Consulting Inc 7155 Hillside Dr Clarkston MI 48346-1432

COLUCCIO, JOSEPHINE CATHERINE, primary and elementary school educator; b. Bklyn., Oct. 21, 1952; d. Dominic Anthony and Catherine (Pomponio) Ferone; m. Frank Anthony Coluccio, June 26, 1976; 1 child, Nancy Marie. BA in Edn. cum laude, Bklyn. Coll., 1974. Cert. nursery, kindergarten, and elem. tchr., N.Y., nursery and elem. tchr., N.J. Elem. math. and sci. tchr.-coord. Our Lady of Perpetual Help Sch., Bklyn., 1974-77; pub. rels. coord. McDonald's Corp., S.I., N.Y., 1977-78; day care group tchr. Congress of Italian Am. Orgns., Bklyn., 1979-80; elem. math. and sci. tchr.-coord. Resurrection Elem. Sch., Bklyn., 1980-83; owner, dir. Little Yellow House, Toms River, N.J., 1984-90, Little Explorers-An Ed U Care Program, Toms River, 1990—. Active Rep. Nat. Com., Washington, 1991—. Mem. ASCD, Nat. Assn. for Edn. Young Children, Nat. Safety Coun., Soc. Children's Book Writers and Illustrators (assoc.). Republican. Roman Catholic. Avocations: piano playing, bowling, arts and crafts, cooking.

COLUMBUS, CHRIS JOSEPH, film director, screenwriter; b. Spangler, Pa., Sept. 10, 1958; s. Alex Michael and Mary Irene (Puskar) C.; m. Monica Devereux, Aug. 6, 1983; children: Eleanor, Patricia. BFA, NYU, 1980. Writer: (films) Reckless, 1983, Gremlins, 1984, Goonies, 1985, Young Sherlock Holmes, 1985, Little Nemo, 1992; dir.: (films) Adventures in Babysitting, 1987, Home Alone, 1990, Home Alone 2: Lost in New York, 1992, Mrs. Doubtfire, 1993, (television series-episodic) Amazing Stories, Twilight Zone, Alfred Hitchcock Presents, Bicentennial Man, 1999; dir., writer: (films) Heartbreak Hotel, 1988, Only the Lonely, 1991; dir., writer, prodr.: Nine Months, 1995; dir., prodr.: Stepmom, 1998; prodr.: Jingle All the Way, 1996, Monkey Bone, 1999. Democrat. Roman Catholic. Office: CAA c/o Beth Swofford 9830 Wilshire Blvd Beverly Hills CA 90212-1804*

COLUMBUS, R. TIMOTHY, lawyer; b. West Bend, Wis., Mar. 17, 1949; s. Robert M. and Dena (Eggabean) C.; m. Penny G. Baker, June 16, 1979; children: Alexandra Baker, Robert Benjamin. BA, Harvard U., 1971; JD, U. Va., 1974. Bar: Va. 1974, D.C. 1975. Assoc. Collier, Shannon, Rill & Scott, PLLC, Washington, 1974-80, ptnr., 1980—. Home: 6011 Nevada Ave NW Washington DC 20015-2527 Office: Collier Shannon Rill & Scott PLLC 3050 K St NW Washington DC 20007-5108

COLUSSY, DAN ALFRED, aviation executive; b. Pitts., June 3, 1931; s. Dan and Viola E. (Andreis) C.; m. Helene Graham, June 6, 1953; children: Deborah, Jennifer. B.S. U.S. Coast Guard Acad., 1953; M.B.A., Harvard U., 1965. Applications engr. Jet Propulsion div. Gen. Electric Co., 1956-63; dir. ops. Am. Airlines, N.Y.C., 1965-66; v.p. mktg. N.E. Airlines, Boston, 1966-69; v.p. Wells, Rich, Green Advt. Agy., N.Y.C., 1969-70; v.p. mktg. devel. Pan Am. World Airways, N.Y.C., 1970-72, v.p. passenger mktg., 1972-74, sr. v.p. passenger mktg., 1974, sr. v.p. field ops., 1974-75, sr. v.p. mktg. and services, 1975-76, exec. v.p. mktg. and services, dir., 1976-78, pres., chief operating officer, mem. exec. com., 1978-80; chmn., chief exec. officer Columbia Air, Balt., 1981-82; pres., CEO Can. Airlines Internat., Vancouver, B.C., 1982-84, chmn., 1985-86; bd. dirs., mem. exec. com. Can. Pacific Hotels, 1983-84; pres., chief exec. officer UNC Inc., Annapolis, Md., 1985-97, chmn. bd., chmn. exec. com., 1989-97; chmn. Gemini Capital, Palm Beach Gardens, Fla., 1997—. Mem. bd. visitors Coll. Bus. and Mgmt. U. Md.; pres. adv. bd. St. John's Coll.; mem. Johns Hopkins Medicine Bd. Visitors.; bd. dirs. Balt. Gas and Electric o., Hist. Annapolis Found.; chmn. Care First Inc. Mem. Campaign Cabinet, U.S. Naval Inst., Chesapeake Bay Found. (pres.' coun.), Larchmont Yacht, Annapolis Yacht, Harvard (N.Y.C.) Club, Old South Country Club, Wings Club (N.Y.C.), Econ. Club Washington, Met. Club Washington, Order of St. John (Can.), Chartwell Country Club, Ballen Isles Country Club. Office: 20 St Thomas Dr Palm Beach Gardens FL 33418

COLVAN, CAROLYN W., federal agency administrator. BS in Bus. Adminstrn., Morgan State U., MBA; postgrad., Harvard U. Sec. Md. Dept. Human Resources; dep. commr. for policy and external affairs Social Security Adminstrn., Balt., 1994; dep. commr. for programs and policy Social Security Adminstrn., dep. commr. for ops. Grad. Greater Balt. Leadership Program. Mem. Nat. Coalition 100 Black Women, Nat. Forum Black Pub. Adminstrs. (Md. chpt.), Women Execs. in State Govt. Office: Social Security Adminstrn Rm 1204 W High Rise Bldg 6401 Security Blvd Baltimore MD 21235

COLVARD, DEAN WALLACE, emeritus university chancellor; b. Ashe County, N.C., July 10, 1913; s. W. P. and Mary (Shepherd) C.; m. Martha Lampkin, July 7, 1939; children: Carol Lampkin, Mary Lynda, Dean Wallace. B.S., Berea Coll., 1935; M.A., U. Mo., 1938; Ph.D., Purdue U., 1950, D.Agr., 1961; L.H.D. (hon.), Belmont Abbey Coll., 1978; D. Public Service, U. N.C., Charlotte, 1979. Instr. agr., farm mgr. Brevard Coll., 1935-37; supt. N.C. Mountain Expt. Sta., 1938-46; prof. animal sci. N.C. State Coll., 1947-48, head dept. animal sci., 1948-53; dean agr., 1953-60; pres. Miss. State U., 1960-66; chancellor U. N.C., Charlotte, 1966-78, chancellor emeritus, 1978—; mng. cons. Sci. Mus. of Charlotte, 1980-81; dir. Fed. Res. Bank of Richmond, 1955-60, dep. chmn., 1959-60; dir. Mut. Savs. & Loan, 1975-91; Spl. cons. ICA, Bangkok, Thailand, 1960; mem. Gov.'s Rsch. Triangle Devel. Coun., 1957-59; co-ordinator Agr. Rsch. Mission in Peru, S. Am., 1954-60; mem. agr. adv. com. W. K. Kellogg Found., 1954-60; chmn. Miss. Gov.'s Com. on Latin Am. Edn., 1961. Author: Mixed Emotions: As Racial Barriers Fell-A University President Remembers, 1985; co-author: (with W.L. Carpenter) Knowledge is Power, 1987, (with Orr and Bailey) University Research Park: The First Twenty Years, 1988; contbr. to publs. in animal sci., agrl. econs., ednl. adminstrn. Chmn. Miss. Rhodes Scholar Com., 1965-66; chmn. N.C. Rhodes Scholar Com., 1967, 78; mem. Miss. Jr. Coll. Commn., 1960-66; vice chmn. Dimensions for Charlotte-Mecklenburg, 1973-76; mem. N.C. Council on State Goals and Policy, 1972-76, So. Growth Policies Bd., 1977-85, Mecklenburg and Union Counties Health and Hosp. Council, 1967-76; chmn., 1974-76; bd. dirs., exec. com. U. Research Park, Charlotte, 1967-87, vice chmn., 1974-79; trustee Berea Coll., 1956-76, St. Andrews Coll., 1969-76, Cordell Hull Found. for Internat. Edn., 1961-67; chmn. bd. trustees N.C. Sch. Sci. and Math., 1978-83. Recipient Disting. Svc. award N.C. Farm Bur., 1956, Disting. Svc. award Miss. Farm Bur., 1965, Disting. Svc. award N.C. Grange, 1958, Outstanding Civilian award U.S. Dept. Army, 1966, Charlotte News Man of Yr. award, 1977, Disting. Alumnus award Berea Coll., 1980, U. N.C. Disting. Svc. award, 1989, N.C. Disting. Pub. Svc. award, 1990, Lifetime Achievement award Nat. 4H CLub Found., 1998; named Man of Yr. in Agr. in N.C., 1954. Mem. Nat. Assn. State Univs. and Land Grant Colls. (co-chmn. joint com. edn. for govt. svc. 1961-65, chmn. president's coun. 1966), Am. Coun. Edn. (commn. internt. edn. 1966-68, chmn. com. higher adult edn. 1966-68), Am. Assn. State Colls. and Univs. (bd. dirs. 1978), Charlotte C. of C. (bd. dirs. 1968-70), Charlotte Country Club, Blue Key, Sigma Xi, Omicron Delta Kappa, Phi Kappa Phi, Gamma Alpha, Alpha Gamma Rho, Gamma Sigma Delta, Alpha Zeta. Clubs: Charlotte Country, Charlotte Rotary (pres. 1978, hon. 1984—). Home: U NC 1530 Queens Rd Charlotte NC 28207-2574

COLVILLE, DAVID ALEXANDER, artist; b. Toronto, Aug. 24, 1920; s. David Harrower and Florence (Gault) C.; m. Rhoda Wright, Aug. 5, 1942; children: Graham, John, Charles, Ann. B.F.A., Mt. Allison U., 1942. One-man shows include Kestner Gesellschaft, Hanover, Germany, 1969, Marlborough Mus. Fine Art, London, 1970, Gemeentmuseum, Arnhem, Netherlands, 1977, Städtische Kuntsthalle, Düsseldorf, Germany, 1977, Fischer Fine Art, London, 1977, Mira Godard Gallery, Toronto and Montreal, 1978, Art Gallery Ont., Toronto, 1983, Staatliche Kunsthalle, Berlin, 1983, Mus. Ludwig, Cologne, Germany, 1983, Beijing Exhbn. Hall, China, 1984, Mus. U. Hong Kong, 1985, Telen Art Mus., Tokyo, Canada House, London, 1985, Drabinsky Gallery, Toronto, 1991, Montreal Mus. Fine Art, 1994, Mira Godard Gallery, Toronto, 1999; represented in permanent collections, Nat. Gallery Can., Mus. Modern Art, N.Y.C., Mussee National d'Art Moderne, Paris, Sammlung Ludwig, Aachen, Germany, Boymans-Van Beuningen Mus., Netherlands, Rotterdam, Montreal Mus. Fine Arts, Mus. Ludwig, Cologne, Germany, Art Gallery Ont.; vis. artist, U. Calif.-Santa Cruz, 1967, Berliner Kunstler Programm, 1971. Served with Canadian Army, 1942-46. Decorated companion Order of Can. Home and Office: Box 550, Wolfville, NS Canada B0P 1X0

COLVIN, BURTON HOUSTON, mathematician, government official; b. West Warwick, R.I., July 12, 1916; s. Asa Burton and Sara Elsie (Houston) C.; children: Daniel Burton, David Walter, Thomas Alan. AB, Brown U., 1938, AM in Math., 1939; PhD in Math., U. Wis., 1943. Instr. math. and mechanics, dept. math. U. Wis., Madison, 1943, instr. math., asst. prof. math., 1946-51; tech. aide nat. def. rsch. com. Office Sci. Rsch. and Devel., 1944-45; cons., applied mathematician phys. rsch. staff Boeing Co., Seattle, 1951-55; supr. math. analysis group Boeing Co., 1955-58; with Boeing Sci. Rsch. Labs., Seattle, 1958-72; head math. rsch. lab. Boeing Sci. Rsch. Labs., 1958-70, acting head info. scis. lab., 1966-70, head math. and info. scis. lab., 1970-72; chief div. applied math. Nat. Bur. Standards, Dept. Commerce, Washington, 1972-78, dir. Ctr. for Applied Math., 1978-86; dir. acad. affairs Nat. Inst. Standards and Tech., Gaithersburg, Md., 1986-91, dep. dir. acad. affairs, 1991-94; ret., 1994; NSF lectr., 1957; mem. council Conf. Bd. Math. Scis., 1964, 70-77, chmn., 1975-77; adv. bd. Sch. Math. Study Group, 1963-71, chmn., 1965-66; chmn. computer sci. adv. com. Stanford U., 1970-71. Recipient Silver medal U.S. Dept. Commerce, 1978, Gold medal, 1981, Presdl. Meritorious Rank award, 1980, Equal Employment Opportunity award Nat. Inst. Standards and Tech., 1988. Fellow AAAS (coun. 1965-67, chmn. task force on tech., edn. 1968-69); mem. NEA, Soc. Indsl. and Applied Math. (vis. scientist lectr. 1962-63, trustee 1962-65, 67-70, 78-80, pres. 1971-72), Math. Assn. Am. (vis. lectr. 1963-65), nat. Phys. Sci. Consortium (bd. dris. 1988-93, v.p. 1992-93), Am. Math. Soc., Inst. Math. Stats., Assn. Women in Math., Nat. Coun. Tchrs. Math., Phi Beta Kappa, Sigma Xi.

COLVIN, CONNIE LOU, administrative specialist, author; b. Peoria, Ill., Feb. 4, 1951; d. Edward Franklin Sr. and Emily Annette (Anderson) Smith; m. Ivan C. Colvin, Jr., Mar. 15, 1969; children: Christopher Alan, Catrina Annette. Grad. h.s., Peoria, Ill. Catering sec. Peoria Hilton Hotel, 1976-80; adminstrv. specialist IV City of Peoria, Ill., 1980—. Author/writer news articles Co-Operwriter, 1996-98; news stories, Observer, Peoria Journal Star. Leader Girl Scouts of U.S., Peoria, 1983-86; sec. City of Peoria Mcpl. Employees Assn./ Am. Fedn. State, City, Mcpl. Employees, 1986—; mem. allocation com. United Way of Peoria, 1990—, co-chair fund distbn. com., 1997—. Mem. Writers Coop. (steering com. 1996-98). Democrat. Avocations: writing, reading, crafts. Home: 2925 W Malone Ave Peoria IL 61605-1324 Office: City of Peoria 419 Fulton St Rm 106 Peoria IL 61602-1276

COLVIN, DANIEL L., English educator; b. Amarillo, Tex., Mar. 10, 1947; s. Orville L. and Doris Ann Colvin; m. Nancy Esther Clark, Apr. 12, 1969; 1 child, Christina Beth. BA, Wheaton Coll., 1969; MA, Northwestern U., 1970, PhD, 1975. Prof. English Western Ill. U., Macomb, 1972—; mem. the Bible as Literature sem. NEH, Ann Arbor, Mich., 1992; mem. interactive Shakespeare project Coll. of Holy Cross, 1998-99. Author: (monograph) Shakespeare--A Study Guide, 1997; editor: Measure for Measure, 1998. Chair bd. trustees Western Ill. Youth for Christ, Macomb, 1990-96; chair coun. Ill. Youth for Christ, Peoria, Ill., 1998-99; bd. dirs. Wesley Village, Macomb, 1998—. Recipient Examining Shakespeare Through Performance award NEH, 1996-97. Mem. Shakespeare Assn. Am., Macomb Philosophy Club (pres. 1995-96). Presbyterian. Fax: (309) 298-2974. E-mail: DL-Colvin@wiu.edu. Home: 320 S Lafayette Macomb IL 61455 Office: Western Ill U Dept English 1 University Cir Macomb IL 61455

COLVIN, HARRY WALTER, JR., physiology educator; b. Schellsburg, Pa., Dec. 5, 1921; s. Harry Walter and Maude Elizabeth (Girven) C.; m. Marie Catherine McNinch, Apr. 8, 1950; children: Sarah Lee, William McNinch. BS, Pa. State U., 1950; PhD, U. Calif., Davis, 1957. Instr. Okla. State U., Stillwater, 1955-57; assoc. prof. physiology U. Ark., Fayetteville, 1957-65; prof. U. Calif., Davis, 1965—; cons. Pel-Freez Biologicals, Inc., Rogers, Ark., 1960-65. Assoc. editor Hilgardia, 1981-92; contbr. articles to profl. jours. Served with U.S. Army, 1942-45, ETO. Recipient Fulbright award CIES, Washington, 1972, 86. Mem. Am. Dairy Sci. Assn., Am. Soc. Animal Sci., Sigma Xi, Phi Kappa Phi, Alpha Zeta, Gamma Sigma Delta, Phi Sigma , Phi Eta Sigma. Republican. Club: El Macero (Calif.) Country.

Avocations: golf, flying. Home: 3340 Biscayne Bay Pl Davis CA 95616-2602 Office: U Calif Davis Dept Neurobiol & Physiol Behavior Davis CA 95616

COLVIN, (OTIS) HERBERT, JR., musician, educator; b. El Dorado, Ark., Mar. 18, 1923; s. Otis Herbert and Irene (Hammons) C.; m. Mary Ila Ullom, June 18, 1948; children: Carol Kay Colvin Smith, Mary Edith Colvin Reitmeier, Susan Elizabeth Colvin White. B.A., Baylor U., 1944, B.Mus., 1948; M.Mus., U. Colo., 1950; Ph.D., U. Rochester, 1958. Grad. asst. U. Colo., 1948-50; instr. music Tex. Tech. Coll., 1950-55; grad. asst. Eastman Sch. Music, 1955-57; asst. prof. piano Baylor U., 1957-62, chmn. dept., 1958-62, assoc. prof. theory, 1962-64, prof., 1964-93; prof. emeritus Baylor U. Sch. Music, 1993—; chmn. dept. Baylor U., 1962-76, coordinator theory div., 1976-85, dir. acad. studies, 1985-88, univ. carillonneur, 1988—. Concert accompanist, organist, 7th and James Bapt. Ch., 1969-99; editor choral compositions.; Composer: Organ Voluntaries Based on Early American Hymn Tunes, 1964, Short Pieces for Organ, 1971, For Sunday; six organ pieces based on modal melodies, 1972, Gloria; anthem for mixed voices and organ, 1974, Nine Hymn Settings for Organ, 1975, For Sunday Volume II; six organ pieces based on modal melodies, 1976, Sheep May Safely Graze; six organ-piano duets on compositions by Bach and Billings, 1977, Surely the Lord Is in This Place; anthem for mixed voices, accompanied, 1977, Four Madrigals; mixed-voice choral settings of A.E. Housman poems, 1978, They That Wait Upon the Lord, 1980, anthem for mixed voices, accompanied, Once in Royal David's City (anthem for mixed voices, children's choir, oboe and organ); editor choral compositions; contbr. articles to profl. jours. Served with USNR, 1944-46, CBI. Mem. Am. Guild Organists (dean Waco chpt. 1958-60, 68-69, 79-80, treas. 1990-92), Music Tchrs. Nat. Assn., Guild of Carillonneurs N.Am. (bd. dirs. 1996—), Tex. Soc. Music Theory, Phi Mu Alpha Sinfonia, Pi Kappa Lambda, Masons (32 degree). Baptist. Office: Sch Music Baylor U Waco TX 76798

COLVIN, JOHN ALEXANDER, campus minister; b. N.Y.C., Sept. 14, 1950; s. Donald Roy Colvin and Alice Justine (Berry) Stone; m. Linda Lorraine Duxbury, July 1, 1982; children: Hana Lyn, Dena Bari. BA, U. Balt., 1983; MDiv., Unification Theol. Sem., 1986; MA, U. Balt., 1990. Ordained to ministry Unification Ch., 1986. Lay missionary Unification Ch., Balt., 1976-83; dir. outreach Unification Theol. Sem., Barrytown, N.Y., 1984-86; state dir. Unification Ch., Ohio, 1986; dir. campus ministry Unification Campus Mins. Assn., Balt., 1989—; state dir. Am. Constitution Com., Md., 1987—; staff Orgn. Interfaith Activity in N.Y.C., Assembly of World Religions, McAttra, N.J., 1985; participant Youth Seminar on World Religions, various countries, 1985; dir. United Christian Citizens, Md., 1987—; exec. dir. Family Fedn. world Peace, 1996-99. Contbr. articles to jours. bd. dirs. Am. Freedom Coalition of Md., 1987—, sec.-treas. 1990-93; co-founder, dir. pub. rels. Univ. Balt., Fgn. Affairs Coun., 1989—; co-founder, sec. Coalition for Harmony, Balt., 1990-93; treas. Ann Arundel Sch. Bd. Nominating Conv., Anne Arundel County, Md., 1990—. Named Outstanding Young Men of Am., 1987. Mem. Internat. Religious Fedn., Federalist Soc., Anne Arundel County Elephant Club. Home: 205 Marie Ave Glen Burnie MD 21060-6514 Office: Am Constitution Com 205 Marie Ave Glen Burnie MD 21060-6514 *The challenge of life is to be a good person. When I succeed in maintaining my own personal integrity and directing my actions in the service of God and mankind, problems are transformed into exciting growth experiences and the blessings of love, success, and joy are assured.*

COLVIN, JOHN O., federal judge; b. 1946. AB, U. Mo., 1968; JD, Georgetown U., 1971, LLM in Taxation, 1978. Tax counsel Office of Sen. Bob Packwood, 1975-84; senate fin. com. chief counsel, 1985-87; chief minority counsel U.S. Senate, 1987-88; judge U.S. Tax Ct., Washington, 1988—; adj. prof. law Georgetown U. Law Ctr., 1987—. Served with USCG, 1971-75. Mem. Fed. Bar Assn. Office: US Tax Ct 400 2nd St NW Washington DC 20217*

COLVIN, O. MICHAEL, medical director, medical educator; b. Princeton, Ind., June 15, 1936; s. Jack Gene and and Evelyn Mae (Satkamp) C.; m. Arline Mae Lockerbie, Aug. 23, 1959; children: Michael Eric, Jennifer Susan, Kimberly Anne, Christopher Andrew. BA in Chemistry, Ind. U., 1957; MD, Wash. U., St. Louis, 1961. Intern, resident Johns Hopkins Hosp., Balt., 1961-64; clin. assoc. Nat. Cancer Inst., Bethesda, Md., 1964-66; fellow in pharmacology Johns Hopkins U., Balt., 1966-68, physician, 1968-95, from asst. prof. to prof. medicine, 1968-95; dir. Duke Comprehensive Cancer Ctr. Duke U. Med. Ctr., Durham, N.C., 1995—; grant rev. study sect. Nat. Cancer Inst., Bethesda, 1968—. Recipient Career Devel. award Nat. Cancer Inst., 1975-80. Mem. AAAS, Am. Soc. Clin. Oncology, Am. Soc. Bone Marrow Transplantation, Am. Assn. Cancer Rsch. Home: 208 Arcadia Ln Chapel Hill NC 27514-1472 Office: Duke Comprehensive Cancer Ctr Duke U Med Ctr PO Box 3843 Durham NC 27702-3843

COLVIN, SHAWN, recording artist, songwriter; b. Vermillion, S.D., Jan. 10, 1956. Past mem., founder Shawn Colvin Band, Carbondale, Ill.; past mem. Dixie Diesels, Austin, Tex. Albums include Live Tape, 1988, Steady On, 1989, Fat City, 1992, Cover Girl, 1994, Round of Blues, 1995, Live '88, 1995, Few Small Repairs, 1996, (single Grammy award Record of the Year for Sonny Came Home, 1998), (single) I Don't Know Why, 1992, (extended play single) Every Little Thing, 1994; background vocals, arranger I Know, 1987; background vocals Solitude Standing, 1987, Ghosts Upon the Road, 1989, Ben & Jerry's Newport Folk, 1989, Festival, 1989, State of the Heart, 1989, Long Road, 1990, Days of Open Hand, 1990, Stages, 1991, Come on Come on, 1992, Life is Messy, 1992, Stones in the Road, 1994, House on Fire, 1995, Strangers World, 1995, Down in There, 1996, Last Tango, 1996; vocals, guitar Samp, 1988, Bob Dylan's 30th Anniversary, 1993, Concert, 1993, Columbia Records Radio Hour (vol. 1), 1994, Best of Columbia Records Radio Hour, 1996; vocals Standing Eight, 1989, Time Was, 1995; harmony vocals Land of the Bottom Line, 1992, Road to Ensenada, 1996; vocals, prodr., Tin Cup, 1996; prodr. Tide, 1994; vocals, background vocals Shooting Straight in the Dark, 1990, others; appearances include (off-broadway) Pump Boys and Dinettes, Diamond Studs, Lie of the Mind, (film) It Could Happen to You, Grace of My Heart. Recipient Grammy award Song of the Year, 1998. Office: care Sony Music 550 Madison Ave New York NY 10022-3211*

COLVIN, THOMAS STUART, agricultural engineer, farmer; b. Columbia, Mo., July 17, 1947; s. Charles Darwin and Miriam Elizabeth (Kimball) C.; m. Sonya Marie Peterson, Sept. 11, 1982; children: Christopher, Kristel. BS, Iowa State U., 1970, MS, 1974, PhD, 1977. Registered profl. engr., Iowa. Farmer Hawkeye and Cambridge, Iowa, 1970—; rsch. assoc. Iowa State U., Ames, 1972-77; agrl. engr. USDA/Agrl. Rsch. Svc., Ames, 1977—; cons. WillowCreek Cons., Manning, Iowa, 1978-85. Sgt. USAF, 1970-72, Vietnam. Recipient Air Force Commendation medal USAF, 1971. Mem. Am. Soc. Agrl. Engrs. (power machinery stds. com. St. Joseph, Mich. 1989—, Iowa sec., Young Engr. of Yr. 1986), Am. Soc. Agronomy, Soil and Water Conservation Soc., Iowa Acad. Sci. (chair agrl. scis. sect. 1991-92), Sigma Xi, Alpha Epsilon (pres. 1978), Gamma Sigma Delta, Phi Mu Alpha. Achievements include design and development of first computer program to help farmers manage tillage and residue cover for erosion control. Office: Nat Soil Tilth Lab USDA ARS 2150 Pammel Dr Ames IA 50011-4420

COLVIN-HERRON, GAYLE ANN, mental health consultant, psychotherapist, health facility administrator, columnist writer; b. L.A., Sept. 21, 1953; d. Robert Owen Sr. and Rachel Rebecca (Lemley) Colvin; m. Curtis William Herron Sr., Feb. 14, 1997; children: Fred Phillips II, Brian Scott Phillips, Curtis (Ian) II. AA in Psychology, Okla. City Community Coll., Oklahoma City, 1986; BS in Sociology, Okla. State U., 1990, BS in Psychology, 1991, MS in Counseling, 1992; MSW, U. Nev., Las Vegas, 1996. Adminstr., fin. cons. Security Fin. Cons., Oklahoma City, 1980-88; case worker Big Bros./Big Sisters, Stillwater, Okla., 1988-89; counselor Payne County Family Practices, Stillwater, 1989; social worker Dept. Human Svcs. Child Welfare, Stillwater, 1990; instr. Langston (Okla.) U., 1992; counselor Payne County Dept. Guidance Clinics and Health, Stillwater and Cushing, Okla., 1992-93, Christian Counseling Assocs., Stillwater, 1993-95; clin. dir., clin. psychotherapist New Beginnings Clin. Svcs. Corp., Las Vegas, 1996—; clin. dir., CEO, New Beginnings Diagnostic and Clin. Svcs., Brunswick City, N.C., 1997—. Columnist Brunswick County News, 1997-98. Disaster vol. ARC, Oklahoma City, 1987-88; vol. disaster inquiry team, Oklahoma City, Las Vegas, 1995; vita site coord. IRS, Oklahoma City, 1982-84; emergency room EMT Hillcrest Hosp., Oklahoma City, 1994; EMT/intermediate paramedic Amcare Ambulance Svcs., 1994. mem. ACA, APA, NASW, Am. Assn. for Christian Counselors, Nat. Assn. Social Workers, Okla. Psychol. Assn., Okla. Assn. Counseling and Devel., Assn. for Humanist Psychology, Phi Theta Kappa, Psi Chi. Democrat. Mem. LDS Ch., Roman Catholic. Avocations: traveling, drafting, hiking, flying, sports. Home: PO Box 4121 Calabash NC 28467-9820 Address: PO Box 1241 Pawleys Island SC 29585-1241

COLVIS, JOHN PARIS, aerospace engineer, mathematician, scientist; b. St. Louis, June 30, 1946; s. Louis Jack and Jacqueline Betty (Beers) C.; m. Nancy Ellen Fritz, Mar. 15, 1969 (div. Sept. 16, 1974); 1 child, Michael Scott; m. Barbara Carol Davis, Sept. 3, 1976; 1 child, Rebecca Jo; stepchildren: Bruce William John Zimmerly, Belinda Jo Zimmerly Little. Student, Meramec Community Coll., St. Louis, 1964-65, U. Mo., 1966, 72-75, Palomar Coll., San Marcos, Calif., 1968, U. Mo., Rolla, 1968-69; BS in Math., Washington U., 1977. Assoc. system safety engr. McDonnell Douglas Astronautics Co., St. Louis, 1978-81; sr. system safety engr. Martin Marietta Astronautics Group-Strategic Systems Co., Denver, 1981-87; sr. engr. Martin Marietta Astronautics Group-Space Launch Systems Co., Denver, 1987-95, Lockheed Martin Astronautics Co.-Space Launch Sys., Denver, 1995—; researcher in field. Precinct del., precinct committeeman, congl. dist. del., state del. Rep. Party. Lance cpl. USMC, 1966-68, Vietnam. Mem. VFW (post 4171), Colo. Home Educators' Assn. (pres. 1989), Khe Sanh Vet Incorp. Evangelical. Achievements include the quantum postulate and the quantum philosophy of science and mathematics; identification and correction of empirical flaw in foundations of science and mathematics; resolution of several ancient and contemporary conjectures in science and mathematics through application of revolutionary new, complete and verifiable logic-quantum synthesis; correction of fundamental misconception concerning integral and differential limits of calculus; identification of principles and dynamics of nature responsible for such things as relativity, consistency, wave/particle duality, quantum events, black holes, chaos, and irreversibility; clarification and expansion of the Second Law of Thermodynamics allowing for more comprehensive, diverse, and pervasive applications; development of mathematical algorithm which greatly enhanced accuracy and efficiency in which engineering component failure analysis of large complex systems is performed. Avocations: camping, hiking, swimming. Home: 4978 S Hoyt St Littleton CO 80123-1988 Office: Lockheed Martin Astronautics Group-SLS PO Box 179 Denver CO 80201-0179

COLWELL, CHRISTOPHER SCOTT, telecommunications industry executive; b. Toledo, June 6, 1959; s. Ronald Edward and Frances Anne (Kirkham) C.; m. Debra Ann Runyon, July 12, 1986; children: Christopher Scott, Jr., Veronica Anne. BA, Xavier U., 1998. Fin. dir. Citizens for Kasich, Columbus, Ohio, 1984-85, Franklin County Rep., Columbus, 1985-86; v.p. Mamais and Assocs., Columbus, 1986-89; fin. dir. Voinovich for Gov., Columbus, 1989-91; govt. affairs dir. Cin. Bell Tel., 1991-95, v.p. govt. affairs, 1995-97, v.p. govt. rels./pub. affairs, 1997—. Mem. Big Bros., Big Sisters, Columbus, 1985-91, cmty. chest govt. affairs United Way, Cin., 1992—; mem. bd. dirs. Ohio Host Com. Inc., Nat. Conf. State Legis., 1991-92, Good Samaritan Hosp. Found., Cin., 1996—; mem. telecomm. task force Am. Legis. Exch. Coun., Washington, 1995—. Mem. U.S. Tel. Assn., Ind. Tel. Telecomm. Alliance, Ohio Tel. Assn. Avocations: golf, running, football, baseball, landscaping. Office: Cin Bell Tel 201 E 4th St # 102 900 Cincinnati OH 45202-4122

COLWELL, DAVID RUSSELL, software engineer; b. Madison, Wis., Mar. 7, 1972; s. Gerald Lynn and Barbara Kay Colwell. BS in Computer Sci., U. Wis., 1995. Software engr. Quad/Graphics, Inc., Pewaukee, Wis., 1995—. Avocations: bicycling, skiing, camping, gaming. E-mail: clavelvis@sprynet.com.

COLWELL, DENIS, music director. Grad., Carnegie Mellon, postgrad. Condr., founder Carnegie Mellon Youth Brass Band; condr., founder River City Brass Band, cornetist to asst. prin. solo cornetist, 1982, assoc. condr., 1994—, music dir., 1994—; assoc. prof. music Carnegie Mellon U., Pitts., asst. head dept. of music, 1988-95; music dir. Carnegie Mellon Wind Ensemble. Former mem. Carnegie Brass Quintet. Office: River City Brass Band PO Box 6346 Pittsburgh PA 15212

COLWELL, GENE THOMAS, engineering educator; b. Chattanooga, Aug. 3, 1937; s. William Clarence and Mary Virginia (Smith) C.; m. Peggy Ann Fletcher, June 1, 1973. BSME, U. Tenn., 1959, MSME, 1962, PhD, 1966. Rsch. engr. Oak Ridge (Tenn.) Nat. Lab., 1959-62; instr. U. Tenn., Knoxville, 1962-65; rsch. engr. Oak Ridge Nat. Lab., 1965-66; asst. prof. Ga. Inst. Tech., Atlanta, 1966-71, assoc. prof., 1971-77, prof., 1977-95; prof. emeritus, 1995—; assoc. dir. Ga. Inst. Tech., Atlanta, 1984-87; vis. prof. U. Carabobo, Venezuela, 1971; cons. in field. Patentee in field; contbr. articles to profl. jours. Recipient numerous Rsch. grants. Fellow ASME (life); mem. Sigma Xi, Pi Tau Sigma. Avocations: tennis, golf, hiking. Home: 9145 Prestwick Club Dr Duluth GA 30097-2442

COLWELL, HOWARD OTIS, advertising executive; b. New Rochelle, N.Y., Sept. 16, 1929; s. Robert Talcott and Louise (Otis) C.; m. Barbara Elaine Hrosenchik, Aug. 14, 1954; children: John Robert, Christian, Mary Louise. A.B., Colgate U., 1953. Copy group head Batten, Barton, Durstine & Osborn, N.Y.C., 1953-59; v.p., creative dir. Tatham-Laird & Kudner, N.Y.C., 1959-68; sr. v.p., creative dir. William Esty Advt., N.Y.C., 1968-87; v.p., corp. creative dir. Combe, Inc., White Plains, N.Y., 1987-98; guest lectr. NYU, 1979-81, Pace U., 1980-84, adj. prof., 1982-83. Chmn. YMCA Indian Guides Norwalk-Wilton, 1966; chmn. Wilton Voice on Edn., 1972-75, Wilton Arts Council, 1980-83; v.p. bd. dirs. Wilton Orch., 1985—, pres., 1986-87. Mem. Phi Beta Kappa. Congregationalist. Office: 1101 Westchester Ave White Plains NY 10604-3503

COLWELL, JOHN EDWIN, retired aerospace scientist; b. Bellaire, Kans., Sept. 2, 1930; s. Clyde Theodore and Ida Mae (Swank) C. BS in Chemistry, Kans. State U., 1952; postgrad., Harvard U., 1952-53; PhD in Phys. Chemistry, U. Pa., 1958. Rsch. chemist Shell Oil Co., Wood River, Ill., 1952; staff scientist Rocketdyne divsn. N.Am. Aviation, Canoga Park, Calif., 1958-61; mem. tech. staff The Aerospace Corp., El Segundo, Calif., 1961-72, cons., 1972-73; cons. NASA, 1970-72. Bd. dirs. Ctrl. Kans. Libr. System, Great Bend, 1977-81, 89-93; vice chmn. Smith County Rep. Ctrl. Com., 1986-90, chmn., 1990-94, 96—; trustee Blaine Twp., Lebanon, 1981-98; treas. Smith County Hist. Soc., 1990-93. 1st lt. USAF, 1953-55. Fellowships Harvard fellow Harvard U., 1952-53, NSF fellow U. Pa., 1957-58. Mem. Am. Legion (post comdr. 1991-93), Sigma Xi, Phi Kappa Phi, Theta Xi. Republican. Avocations: music, gardening, fishing. Home: RR 2 Box 54 Lebanon KS 66952-9500

COLWELL, KENT LEIGH, venture capitalist; b. Pasadena, Calif., Feb. 21, 1931; s. Max F. and Ruth (Chamberlain) C.; m. Margaret Hayes, Nov. 9, 1963; children: David, Hilary, Stacy. BA, Stanford U., 1951; MBA, Harvard U., 1957. Asst. to pres. Transam. Corp., San Francisco, 1962-64, v.p. real estate svcs., 1977-96; fin. v.p. Bankers Mortgage Co., San Francisco, 1965-68, pres., 1968-84; trustee, sec. Mortgage Trust Am. (name later Transam Realty Investors), San Francisco, 1969-72, trustee, pres., 1973-86; pres. Transam Realty Svcs., San Francisco, 1972-96, Ventana Inn, Inc., Big Sur, Calif., 1980-97; ltd. ptnr. Montreux Equity Ptnrs., 1997-98; prin. Parthenon Assocs., San Francisco, 1998—; trustee Mortgage & Realty Trust, Elkins Park, Pa.; bd. dirs. Bridge Housing Corp., San Francisco. Lt. USN, 1952-55. Baker scholar Harvard U. Bus. Sch., 1957. Mem. Am. Soc. Real Estate Counselors (cert.), Urban Land Inst., Nat. Assn. Real Estate Investment Trusts (nat. pres.), Bankers Club, Lagunitas Club (Ross, Calif.), Phi Beta Kappa, Lambda Alpha. Office: Parthenon Assocs Penthouse 10 220 Montgomery St San Francisco CA 94104-3402*

COLWELL, RITA ROSSI, microbiologist, molecular biologist, educator, federal agency administrator; b. Nov. 23, 1934; m. Jack H. Colwell, May 31, 1956; children: Alison E.L., Stacie A. BS in Bacteriology with distinction, Purdue U., 1956, MS in Genetics, 1958; PhD, U. Wash., 1961; DSc, Heriot-Watt U., Edinburgh, Scotland, 1987; DSc (hon.), Hood Coll., 1991; DSc, Purdue U., 1993; LLD, Notre Dame Coll., 1994; DSc (hon.), U. Surrey, Eng., 1995, U. Bergen, Norway, 1999. Rsch. asst. genetics lab. Purdue U., West Lafayette, Ind., 1956-57; rsch. asst. U. Wash., Seattle, 1957-58, predoctoral assoc., 1959-60, asst. rsch. prof., 1961-64; asst. prof. biology Georgetown U., Washington, 1964-66, assoc. prof. biology, 1966-72; prof. microbiology U. Md., 1972—, v.p. for acad. affairs, 1983-87; dir. Ctr. Marine Biotech., 1987-91; pres. Md. Biotech. Inst. U. Md., 1991-98; dir. NSF, 1998—; hon. prof. U. Queensland, Brisbane, Australia, 1988, Quindao U., China, 1995; cons., advisor Washington area comms. media, congressman, legislators, 1978—; external examiner various univs. abroad, 1964—; mem. coastal resources adv. com. dept. natural resources State of Md., 1979; NAS ocean scis. bd., 1977-80, vice-chair polar rsch. bd., 1990-94; mem. Nat. Sci. Bd., 1984-90, sci. adv. bd. Oak Ridge Nat. Labs., 1988-90, 93-96, adv. com. FDA, 1991-92, food adv. com., 1993-96, sci. bd., 1996—. Author 18 books including (manual numerical taxonomy) Collecting the Data, 1970, (with M. Zambruski) Rodina-Methods in Aquatic Microbiology, 1972, (with L. H. Stevenson) Estuarine Microbial Ecology, 1973, (with R. Y. Morita) Effect of the Ocean Environment on Microbial Activities, 1974, (with A. Sinsky and N. Pariser) Marine Biotechnology, 1983, Vibrios in the Environment, 1985, Nucleic Acid Sequence Data, 1988, (with others) Marine Biotechnology, 1995, Microbial Diversity, 1996; mem. editorial bd. Microbial Ecology, 1972-91, Applied and Environ. Microbiology, 1969-81, Oil and Petrochemical Pollution, 1980-91, Jour. Washington Acad. Scis., 1981-87, Johns Hopkins U. Oceanographic Series, 1981-84, Revue de la Fondation Oceanographique Ricard, 1981—, Estuaries, 1983-89, Zentralblatt fur Bacteriologie, 1985—, Jour. Aquatic Living Resources, 1987—, System. Applied Microbiology, 1985—, World Jour. Microbiology and Biotechnology, 1988-95; contbr. more than 500 articles and revs. to profl. jours. including Can. Jour. Fisheries and Aquatic Scis., Soc. Gen. Microbiology, Jour. Bacteriology, Applied & Environ. Microbiology, others. Recipient Gold medal Internat. Biotech. Inst., 1990, Purkinje Gold medal Achievement in Scis. Czechoslavakian Acad. Scis., 1991, Civic award Gov. Md., 1990, Woman of the Yr. award Women Legislators of Md., 1996, Cert. Recognition NASA, 1984, Alice Evans award Am. Soc. Microbiol., 1988, Andrew White medal Loyola Coll., 1994, medal of distiction Barnard Coll./Columbia U., 1996; named Prof. Extraordinairo, U. Catolica Valparaiso, Chile, 1976, one of Outstanding Women on Campus, U. Md., 1979, Scholar of Yr., Phi Kappa Phi, 1992. Fellow AAAS (chmn. sect. biol. scis. 1993-94, pres. 1995, chmn. bd. 1996), Grad. Women Sci., Can. Coll. Microbiologists, Am. Acad. Microbiology (chmn. bd. govs. 1989-99), Washington Acad. Scis. (bd. mgrs. 1976-79, pres. 1996-98), Marine Tech. Soc. (exec. com. 1982-88), Sigma Delta Epsilon; mem. Am. Soc. Microbiology (various sci. coms. 1961—, pres. 1985, chmn. program com. REGEM-1 1988, Fisher award 1985), World Fedn. Culture Collections, Internat. Union Microbiol. Soc. (v.p. 1986-90, pres. 1990-94), Am. Inst. Biol. Scis. (bd. govs. 1976-82), Am. Soc. Limnology and Oceanography, Internat. Coun. Sci. Unions (gen. com., exec. bd. 1993-96), U.S. Fedn. Culture Collections (governing bd. 1978-88), Soc. Indsl. Microbiology (bd. govs. 1976-79, Charles Thom award 1997), Classification Rsch. Group Eng. (charter), Soc. Gen. Microbiology, French Soc. Microbiology, (hon.), Israeli Soc. Microbiology (hon.), Soc. Applied Microbiology (hon.), Bangladesh Soc. Microbiology (hon., fgn.), Phi Beta Kappa, Sigma Xi (Ann. Achievement award 1981, Rsch. award 1984, nat. pres. 1991), Omicron Delta Kappa, Delta Gamma (Delta Gamma Rose award, 1989). Achievements include research in marine biotechnology, marine and estuarine microbial ecology, survival of pathogens in aquatic environment, ecology of Vibrio cholerae and related organisms, microbial systematics, marine microbiology, antibiotic resistance, indexing of E. coli to identify sources of fecal contamination in water, environmental aspects of Vibrio cholerae in transmission of cholera, global climate and cholera transmission. Office: NSF Office of the Dir 4201 Wilson Blvd Ste 1205 Arlington VA 22230-0001

COLWELL, SUE ELLEN, English educator; b. Danville, Ill., Dec. 3, 1952; d. Cary Allen and Mary Elizabeth (Smith) Thurman; m. William Vincent Colwell, May 28, 1977. BA in English with honors, Ea. Ill. U., 1975; MEd, Nat. Louis U., Evanston, Ill., 1984. Cert. tchr., Ill. Tchr. English Danville (Ill.) Sch. Dist. #118, 1977—. Named Outstanding Tchr. of the Yr., Danville Pub. Schs., 1994. Mem. Nat. Coun. Tchrs. English, Ill. Coun. Tchrs. English. Avocations: golf, travel. Office: Danville Sch Dist 118 516 N Jackson St Danville IL 61832-4677

COLWILL, JACK MARSHALL, physician, educator; b. Cleve., June 15, 1932; s. Clifford V. and Olive A. (Marshall) C.; m. Winifred Stedman, 1954; children: James F., Elizabeth Ann, Carolyn. BA, Oberlin Coll., 1953; MD (George Whipple scholar), U. Rochester, 1957. Diplomate Am. Bd. Med. Examiners, Am. Bd. Internal Medicine, Am. Bd. Family Practice. Intern Barnes Hosp., Washington U. Sch. Medicine, St. Louis, 1957-58; resident in medicine U. Washington Affiliated Hosps., Seattle, 1958-60; chief resident U. Hosp., 1960-61; instr. medicine, dir. med. outpatient dept. U. Rochester (N.Y.) Sch. Medicine and Dentistry, 1961-62, sr. instr. medicine, dir. med. outpatient dept., 1962-64; asst. dean, asst. prof. medicine, asst. prof. community health and med. practice U. Mo. Sch. Medicine, Columbia, 1964-67; assoc. dean, asst. prof. U. Mo. Sch. Medicine, 1967-69, assoc. dean for acad. affairs, asst. prof., 1969-70, assoc. dean, assoc. prof., 1970-76, interim chmn. dept. family and community medicine, 1976-77, prof., 1976-97; prof. emeritus, 1999—; chmn. dept. U. Mo. Sch. Medicine, 1977-97; cons. Office Div. Dir., USPHS, 1977—, Bur. Health Manpower, NIH, 1969-75; mem. Coun. on Grad. Med. Edn. Health Resources and Svcs. Adminstrn., 1990-96; mem. Am. Bd. Family Practice, 1998—. Contbr. articles to profl. jours. Dir. Robert Wood Johnson Found. Generalist Physician Initiative, 1991—. Mem. AMA, Assn. Med. Am. Colls. (chmn. Midwest-Gt. Plains Group on Student Affairs 1971-73, nat. vice chmn. Group 1973-74, chmn. working group on non-cognitive assessment-adv. to com. on admissions assessment 1974-77), Soc. Tchrs. Family Medicine (bd. dirs. 1978-82, 83-87, pres.-elect 1987-88, pres. 1988-89), Am. Acad. Family Physicians (commn. on govtl. legis. affairs 1984-87,), Inst. Medicine NAS, Alpha Omega Alpha. Office: U Mo-Columbia Sch Medicine Dept Family and Medicine Columbia MO 65212

COLWIN, ARTHUR LENTZ, biologist, educator; b. Sydney, Australia, Jan. 26, 1911; came to U.S., 1936, naturalized, 1942; m. Laura North Hunter, June 15, 1940. B.Sc., McGill U., 1933, M.Sc., 1934, Ph.D. (NRC Can. fellow), 1935-36; Moyse Travelling fellow, Cambridge (Eng.) U., 1934-35; Seessel fellow, Yale, 1936-37, Royal Soc. Can. fellow, 1937-38. Mem. faculty Queens Coll., 1940-73, prof., 1957-73, emeritus, 1973; adj. prof. Rosensteil Sch. Marine and Atmospheric Sci., U. Miami, Fla., 1973—; Fulbright research fellow Tokyo U., 1953-54; vis. scientist Nat. Inst. Med. Research, London, Eng., 1960. Mem. editorial bd. Jour. Exptl. Zoology, 1964-68, Jour. Morphology, 1964-68, Biol. Bull, 1969-73, Am. Zoologist, 1970-75; contbr. articles to profl. jours. Trustee Marine Biol. Lab., Woods Hole, Mass., 1962-72. Served to capt. USAAF, 1943-46. Fellow N.Y. Acad. Scis., AAAS; mem. Internat. Inst. Developmental Biology, Internat. Soc. Cell Biology, Am. Soc. Zoologists, Soc. Study Devel. and Growth, Soc. for Study of Reprodn., Electron Microscope Soc. Am. Asso. Spl. research fertilization, devel. biology, cell contacts and assn., membrane structure and behavior. Home: 320 Woodcrest Rd Miami FL 33149-1322 Office: U Miami Rosenstiel Sch Marine & Atmospheric Sci 4600 Rickenbacker Cswy Miami FL 33149-1031

COLY, LISETTE, foundation executive; b. N.Y.C., Apr. 6, 1950; d. Robert Raymond and Eileen (Lyttle-Garrett) C.; children: George Robert Damalas, Anastasia Eileen Damalas. BA cum laude, Hunter Coll., 1973. Sec. Parapsychology Found., Inc., N.Y.C., 1972-75, assoc. editor, 1975—, v.p., 1978—, exec. dir., 1999—. Assoc. editor Parapsychology Rev. and Procs. Ann. Internat. Parapsychology Found. Confs., 1978—; editor, conf. coord. Procs. Ann. Internat. Confs., 1989—. Office: Parapsychology Found Inc 228 E 71st St New York NY 10021-5136

COLYER, KIRK KLEIN, insurance executive, real estate investment executive; b. Fayetteville, N.C., Jan. 30, 1956; s. Joe Bill and Charlotte (Klein) C. Assoc. in Bus., SUNY, Albany, 1977; BBA in Polit. Sci., Incarnate Word Coll., 1980; student, Leonard's Tng. Sch., 1985, Tex. Crime Prevention Inst., 1985. Lic. recording agt. Councilman City of Balcones Heights, San Antonio, Tex., 1977-82, mayor, 1982-86, mayor emeritus, 1986; pres. Colyer Real Estate Investments, San Antonio, 1980—; pres., founder Colyer Ins. Agy., San Antonio, 1982—; pres. Colyer Oil Co., San Antonio, 1982—; campaign dir. Congl. Rep. nominee Carl Bill Colyer, San Antonio; campaign treas. Gerry Richkoff County Clk., Bexar County, 1994; mem. dinner com. U.S. Congress Dist. 20 Candidate Charlie Gonzalez, 1998—. Vice pres. Balcones C. of C., San Antonio, 1978, San Antonio Young Reps., 1991; bd. mem. Beautify San Antonio, 1982, South Tex. Charities, 1998; pres. Tex. Mcpl. League Region 7, San Antonio, 1985; founder Bexar County Young

Reps., 1995; bd. dirs. San Antonio March of Dimes, 1985; grad. Leadership San Antonio, 1985; pres. Lulac Coun. 602, 1998-99; host. Com. for Nat. Rep. Conv. 2000 Bid for San Antonio, Tex. Named one of Outstanding Mems. of Am., U.S. Jaycees, 1977-91; Rey Feo XLIX, 1996-97. Mem. IHIO Corridor (founder, pres. 1984-86), San Antonio Ind. Car Dealers Assn. (founder, pres. 1993—), Tex. Auto Dealers Assn. (bd. dirs. 1994—), San Antonio City Club, San Antonio Plaza Club (life), Rey Feo '97, Distributive Edn. Clubs of Am. (life), Lions (bd. dirs. Balcones chpt. 1976-78), Tex. Jaycees (dist. bd. dirs. 1978, pres. Balcones Hts. chpt. 1977, Top Recruiter 1980), San Antonio Crime Stoppers (bd. dirs. 1984—), San Antonio Martini Found. (bd. dirs. 1988—), San Antonio P.A.R.T.I. Found. (bd. dirs. 1998—), South Tex. Charities. Avocations: fishing, hunting, hiking, jogging, roller blading. Home: 13290 Hunters View St San Antonio TX 78230-2032 Office: Colyer Ins Agy 4311 IHIOW San Antonio TX 78201

COMANDINI, MICHELE LOUISE, newspaper reporter; b. Somerville, N.J., Oct. 11, 1973; d. Alexander William and Beth Adele (Sutton) C. BA in Polit. Sci., BS in Journalism, Boston U., 1995; MS in Journalism, Columbia U., 1998. Reporter, rewrite editor City News Bur., Chgo., 1995-96; reporter Bergen Record, Hackensack, N.J., 1996—; mem. adv. and alumni bd. Daily Free Press, Boston, 1995—. Coord. youth ministry retreat St. Helen's Ch., Westfield, N.J., 1989-91, 97-98. Scholar N.J. Press Assn., 1993, Nathan Miller journalism scholar Boston U., 1993. Mem. Soc. Profl. Journalists. Avocations: travel, reading, watching college basketball. Office: Bergen Record 150 River Rd Hackensack NJ 07601

COMANOR, WILLIAM S., economist, educator; b. Phila., May 11, 1937; s. Leroy and Sylvia (Bershad) C.; m. Joan Thall; children: Christine, Katherine, Lauren, Gregory. Student, Williams Coll., 1955-57; BA, Haverford Coll., 1959; MA, PhD, Harvard U., 1963; postgrad., London Sch. Econs., 1963-64. Spl. econ. asst. to asst. atty. gen. Antitrust div. U.S. Dept. Justice, Washington, 1965-66; asst. prof. econs. Harvard U., Cambridge, Mass., 1966-68; assoc. prof. Stanford (Calif.) U., 1968-73; dir. bur. econs. FTC, Washington, 1978-80; prof. econs. U. Calif., Santa Barbara, 1975—, dept. chmn., 1984-87; prof. Sch. Pub. Health U. Calif., L.A., 1990—. Author: National Health Insurance in Ontario, 1980, Advertising and Market Power, 1974, Competition Policy in Europe and North America, 1990, Competition Policy in the Global Economy, 1997; contbr. articles to profl. jours. Mem. Am. Econ. Assn. Home: 519 S Arden Blvd Los Angeles CA 90020-4737 Office: U of Calif Santa Barbara Dept Econs Santa Barbara CA 93106

COMBE, IVAN DEBLOIS, drug company executive; b. Fremont, Iowa, Apr. 21, 1911; s. Louis Abel and Elsie (Mange) C.; m. Mary Elizabeth Deming, Dec. 10, 1938; children—Diana M. Combe Bickford, Juliette M. Combe Larson, Christopher Bryan. BS, Northwestern U., 1933, postgrad. Law Sch., 1933-35. Salesman, sales promotion exec. Nat. Dairy Products, Chgo., 1935-36; div. sales mgr. Wilbert Products Co., N.Y.C., 1936-40; merchandising account exec. Young & Rubicam, Inc., N.Y.C., 1940-43; v.p. sales and advt. Pharmacraft Corp. (subs. Seagram Distillers), N.Y.C., 1944-49; pres., founder Combe Inc., White Plains, N.Y., 1949-70; chmn. , 1970—. Chmn. Council on Family Health, N.Y.C., 1972-79; bd. dirs. White Plains Hosp. Ctr., 1962—; trustee Northwestern U., 1968—, life trustee, 1979—, life regent. Recipient Alumni Service award Northwestern U., 1962, Merit award, 1971. Mem. U.S. Nonprescription Drug Mfrs. Assn. (bd. dirs., exec. com. 1958—, chmn. 1964-66), World Fedn. Proprietary Medicine Mfrs. (bd. dirs., exec. com. 1977—, chmn. 1977-79), Met. Club (N.Y.C.), Blind Brook Club (Purchase, N.Y.), Country Club of Fla. (Delray), Ekwanok Country Club, (Manchester, Vt.), Svc. Club, Rotary, Alpha Delta Phi. Home: 25 Wilshire Rd Greenwich CT 06831-2723*

COMBE, JOHN CLIFFORD, JR., lawyer; b. New Orleans, Jan. 5, 1939; s. John Clifford and Gladys Ann (Reine) C.; m. Lynne Wendel Watson, July 11, 1964; children: John, Wendy, Holly. BBA, Tulane U., 1960, LLB, 1965. Bar: La. 1965, U.S. Dist. Ct. (ea. and mid. dists.) La. 1965, U.S. Ct. Appeals (5th cir.) 1965, U.S. Supreme Ct. 1971, U.S. Ct. Appeals (11th cir.) 1981, U.S. Dist. Ct. (we. dist.) La. 1986. Assoc. Jones, Walker, Waechter, Poitevent, Carrere & Denegre, New Orleans, 1965—, ptnr., 1970—, sr. ptnr., 1989—. Editor: La. Bar Jour., 1975-77; contbr. articles to legal jours. Organizer, mem. Crestmont Pk. Improvement Assn.; organizer Greater New Orleans Law Explorer program Boy Scouts Am., 1974; mem. St. Catherine of Siena Parish Sch. Bd., 1976-89; trustee Acad. of Sacred Heart, 1993-96. Lt. (j.g.) USN, 1960-62. Fellow ABA (mem. ho. of dels. 1982-88), Am. Coll. Trial Lawyers, Am. Bar Found., La. State Bar Found.; mem. Internat. Assn. Def. Counsel (speaker 1989, mem. faculty trial acad. 1991), La. Assn. Def. Counsel (bd. dirs. 1969-75), Am. Judicature Soc. (mem. bd. govs. 1982-86), Def. Rsch. Inst., Nat. Conf. Bar Pres., So. Regional Conf. Bar Pres., La. Bar Assn. (pres. 1979-80, mem. bd. govs. 1973-74, 75-76, 77-78, 78-80, sec.-treas. 1975), Metairie Country Club, Bienville Club, Boston Club, Cactus Club, Crescent Club, Neptune Club, Stratford Club (pres. 1993-95). Republican. Roman Catholic. Office: Jones Walker Waechter Poitevent Carrere & Denegre 201 Saint Charles Ave Ste 50 New Orleans LA 70170-1000

COMBEST, LARRY ED, congressman; b. Memphis, Tex., Mar. 20, 1945; s. Lawrence Nelson and Callie (Gunter) C.; m. Sharon McCurry, Sept. 10, 1981; children—Tonya Lee, Haydn Cudd. BBA, W. Tex. State U., 1969. Farmer, stockman Memphis, 1965-71; county trainee Dept. Agr., Graham, Tex., 1971; spl. asst. Senator John Tower, Washington, 1971-78; owner Combest Distbg., Lubbock, Tex., 1978-85; mem. 99th-106th Congresses from 19th Tex. dist., Washington, 1985—; chmn. agriculture com., vice-chmn. small bus. com. Recipient Santa Fe award Future Farmers Am., 1962, Gerald W. Thomas Outstanding Agriculturalists award for pub. svc., 1989. Republican. Methodist. Lodges: Rotary, Lions. Office: US Ho of Reps 1026 Longworth Bldg Washington DC 20515-4319

COMBOPIANO, CHARLES ANGELO, opera company executive; b. Rome, N.Y., Aug. 8, 1935; s. Joseph and Felicia (Bravo) C.; m. Claire Ermina Rebecchi, Aug. 13, 1967; children: Michael, Kevin, Nina. B. Music magna cum laude, Syracuse U., 1957; PhD in Musicology, NYU, 1970. Instr. music dept. SUNY, Stonybrook, 1969-70; asst. prof. music Earlham Coll., Richmond, Ind., 1970-76; artistic dir., gen. mgr., founder Sorg Opera Co., Inc., Middletown, Ohio, 1990—; gen. mgr., founder Whitewater Opera Co., Inc., Richmond, 1972-97, artistic dir., 1972—; conductor Whitewater Opera, Richmond, 1972—, Sorg Opera, Middletown, 1972—; guest conductor Orch. Sinfonico De San Remo, San Remo, Italy, 1985, many Midwest arts orgns., Ind., Ohio, 1976—; music dir., conductor Peterloon Opera Festival, Cin., 1982-84; spl. lectr. Ind. U. East, Richmond, 1978-79; arts cons. many orgns. throughout U.S., 1977—. Subtitle author 12 operas. Mem. City Plan Commn., Richmond, 1989. Named Ky. Col., 1982. Mem. Ind. Presenters Network (charter bd. dirs., treas. 1985—), Consortium of Ind. Advocates of Opera (founding mem., pres. 1979-85, treas. 1985-89), Ind. Assembly of Arts Couns. (charter bd. dirs. 1978-85), Nat. Opera Assn. (Ind. gov. 1983-89), Ind. Arts Commn. Music Panel (chmn. 1981-86), Wayne County Arts Consortium (bd. dirs., pres. 1976-77), Rotary (pres. 1980). Home: 861 Hidden Valley Ln Richmond IN 47374-5163 Office: Sorg Opera Co 63 S Main St Middletown OH 45044-4055*

COMBS, JANET LOUISE, sales and advertising company executive; b. Houston, Jan. 13, 1959; d. James Lee and Mary Lynn (Woolley) Combs. BSBA, U. Ark., 1981. With Exxon Chem. Co., Houston, 1981-82; account exec. Promotional Products Co., Houston, from 1982, asst. v.p., 1982-86, v.p., 1986—. Adminstrv. bd. mem., leisure ministries core team mem. Chapelwood Meth. Ch. Mem. Houston Downtown Rotary, Houston Young Profl. Reps., Girls' Cotillion, Mortar Bd., Blue Key, Houston C. of C., Kappa Alpha Theta (Founder's Meml. scholar 1980-81), Beta Gamma Sigma, Alpha Mu Alpha, Omicron Delta Kappa, Arkansas Alumni Assn. (Houston chpt. bd. mem.). Republican. Methodist. Home: 12611 Trail Hollow Dr Houston TX 77024-4010 Office: Promotional Products Co Inc 1700 W Sam Houston Pkwy N Houston TX 77043-2797

COMBS, ROBERT KIMBAL, museum director; b. Oklahoma City, Mar. 5, 1955; s. Harold Lee and Joanna Jane (Barton) Combs; m. Lynn Marie Robison, June 9, 1979 (div. 1984); 1 child, Caitlyn. BA in History, San Francisco State U., 1978; cert. in museology, U. Calif., Berkeley, 1979; MA in Museology, John F. Kennedy U., 1980. Curator San Mateo (Calif.) County Mus., 1978-79; intern Smithsonian Instn., Washington, 1979; San Francisco Fine Arts Mus., 1979-81; curator Presidio Army Mus., San Francisco, 1981-83; dir. U.S. Army Engr. Mus., Ft. Leonard Wood, Mo., 1983—; prof. history Columbia Coll., Ft. Leonard Wood, 1984—; cons. Nat. Park Svc., San Francisco, 1978; dir. mus. educators forum, 1983-85; historian 2d Inf. Divsn., 1994-95; guest lectr. Kookmin U., Seoul, 1995. Editor: Fort Leonard Wood, 1941, 1991; contbr. articles and monographs to mags. and newspapers; appeared in numerous TV documentaries and programs. Pres. Parents Without Ptnrs., Rolla, Mo., 1985-86; bd. dirs. South Ctrl. Mo. Arts Coun., Rolla, 1991. Mem. Am. Assn. Mus., Am. Assn. State and Local History, Internat. Commn. on Mus., Commn. on Mil. Mus. in Am., Rolls Royce Owners Club. Avocations: travel, archaeology. Office: US Army Engr Mus ATTN: AZTZ-PTM-OM Fort Leonard Wood MO 65473-5165

COMBS, RONALD T., music educator; b. War Creek, Ky., July 2, 1936; s. Joseph Lester and Bessie B. (Miller) C. BS in Music Edn., U. Cin., 1958; MMus, Cin. Conservatory of Music, 1960; DMA, Northwestern U., 1969. Prof. music U. Wis., Stevens Point, 1969-75, Northeastern Ill. U., Chgo., 1975—. Composer: (choral music) Chicrister's Guild, 1973, (operas) The Patriots, A Christmas Carol; author: Learning to Sing Non-Classical Music, 1996. Avocations: reading, walking. Home: 917 W Castlewood Ter Chicago IL 60640-4218 Office: Northeastern Ill Univ 5500 N Saint Louis Ave Chicago IL 60625-4679

COMBS, ROY JAMES, JR., analyst, researcher; b. Marion, Va., Dec. 11, 1954; s. Roy James and Mary Cathleen Mitchem C.; m. Eva Sue Smith, March 17, 1973 (div. Aug. 1991); children: Crystal Michelle, Mark Nicholas; m. Kathryn Michelle Howard, June 25, 1994. Student, U. Va., 1992-93; MPA, Harvard U., 1995; postgrad., U. So. Calif., Washington, 1995—. Analyst CIA, Washington, 1977-98; program mgr. Nat. Imagery and Mapping Agy., Bethesda, Md., 1998—. Asst. coach Fairfax (Va.) Police Youth Club, 1993-94; fund raiser Harvard Graduate Sch., Washington, 1998; vol. Christmas in April, Arlington, Va., 1995; sec., treas., Purple Sage Homeowners Assn., Reston, Va., 1995—. Mem. Am. Soc. Pub. Adminstrs. Avocations: sailing, rollerblading, biking, reading.

COMBS, SANDRA LYNN, state parole board official; b. Lancaster, Pa., Aug. 31, 1946; d. Clyde Robert and Violet (Sensenig) Boose; m. Allen Evans Combs, Aug. 30, 1969; children: Evan McKenzie, Leslie Ann. AAS in Nursing, Thomas Nelson C.C., Hampton, Va., 1980; BS in Psychology, Juniata Coll., 1968. RN, Va. Dir. vols. in probation Yorktown (Va.) Juvenile Ct., 1973-74; emergency nurse assoc. to pvt. practice physician Hampton, Va., 1980-82; chmn. bd. dirs., CEO Hampton Roads Gulls Profl. Hockey Team, Hampton, 1981-82; mem. sch. bd. York County Pub. Schs., Yorktown, 1985-94; vice chmn. Va. Parole Bd., Richmond, 1994—; mem. supt.'s adv. coun. York County Pub. Schs., 1984-94, mem. long range strategic planning com., 1989-94; trustee New Horizons Tech. Ctr., Gov.'s Sch., Hampton, 1991-94; mem. Va. edn. tech. adv. com. Va. Dept. Edn., 1992-95; mem. Va. Bd. Correctional Edn., 1994—, Va. Adult Basic Edn. and Literacy Adv. Coun., 1994—. Pres. Hampton Med. Soc. Aux, 1977-78, Dare Elem. PTA, York County, 1979-81, York County Coun. PTA, 1983-84; chmn. York County Rep. Com., 1984-90, 1st Dist. Rep. Congl. Com., Va., 1990-94; adviser edn. policy George Allen for Gov., Richmond, 1992-93. Capt. USAF, 1968-73, Vietnam. Decorated Bronze Star medal, Cross of Gallantry (Vietnam), Air Force Commendation medal. Mem. ASCD, VFW, Va. Sch. Bds. Assn. (bd. dirs. 1990-94, award of Excellence 1990, 91, 92), Mil. Order World Wars. Methodist. Avocations: reading, travel, ice hockey. Home: 103 Jernigan Ln Yorktown VA 23692-3127 Office: Va Parole Bd 6900 Atmore Dr Richmond VA 23225-5644

COMBS, SEAN, record company executive, producer; b. N.Y.C., 1971; 1 child. Promoter hip-hop events Howard U., Washington, 1980s; intern Uptown Records, 1991, head A&R dept., 1991; pres., CEO Bad Boy Entertainment, 1994—. Prodr.: Forever My Lady (Jodeci), 1991, Diary of a Mad Band (Jodeci), 1993, What's the 411? (Mary J. Blige), 1993, My Life (Mary J. Blige), 1994, Project: Funk Da World (Craig Mack), 1994, Ready to Die (The Notorious B.I.G.), 1994, Think of You (Raymond Usher), 1994, Faith (Faith Evans), 1995; also prodr. records by Supercat, 7669, Keith Sweat, Caron Wheeler, Mix Tape Volume 2, 1997, Money Talks, 1997, In Tha Beginning...There Was Rap, 1997, Diana, Princess of Wales: Tribute, 1997, Chef Aid: The South Park Album, 1998; artist: No Way Out, 1997. Office: Bad Boy Entertainment 1540 Broadway 30th Fl New York NY 10036*

COMBS, STEPHEN PAUL, pediatrician, health facility administrator; b. Bristol, Tenn., Feb. 11, 1966; s. Paul Willis and Janis Rose C. BS, East Tenn. State U., 1988, MD, 1992. Diplomate Nat. Bd. Med. Examiners, Am. Bd. Pediat., Am. Bd. Forensic Examiners, Am. Bd. Forensic Medicine. Resident in pediat. Duke U., Durham, N.C., 1992-95; asst. chief pediat. residents Duke Children's Hosp. Duke U., 1994-95; ptnr. Mountain Region Pediats., Kingsport, Tenn., 1995-98, sec., 1999—; pediatrician Gray (Tenn.) Sta. Pediat., 1996—; dir. pediat. intensive care, chmn. pediat. critical care Wellmont Health Sys., Holston Valley Med. Ctr., Kingsport, Tenn., 1996—; chmn. dept. pediat. Indian Path Med. Ctr.; mem. med. adv. bd. Am. Homepatient, Nashville, 1995—; regional faculty PALS Tenn. chpt. AHA, 1995—; mem. child fatality rev. bd. jud. dist. II State of Tenn., 1995—; asst. prof. family medicine, asst. prof. internal medicine E. Tenn. State U., James H. Quillen Coll. of Med.; chmn. Quality Improvement, Wllmont. Contbr. articles to profl. jours. Recipient Forty Under 40 award Bus. Jour. Fellow AAP (resident rep. 1993-95); mem. AMA, Tenn. Med. Assn., N.C. Med. Assn., Duke Med. Alumni Assn., East Tenn. State U. Med. Alumni Assn. (rep. 1992—), History of Appalachia Soc. Republican. Baptist. Avocations: Civil War, Revolutionary War, gardening, snow skiing, golf. Home: 405 Westfield Dr Kingsport TN 37664-5410 Office: Gray Sta Pediat 2103 Forest Dr Ste 5 Gray TN 37615-8423

COMBS, STEVEN PAUL, orthopedic surgeon; b. Ft. Dodge, Iowa, Apr. 9, 1944; s. Eugene Charles and Marie Wilhelmina (Mack) C.; m. Penelope Ann Calvey, July 6, 1974; children: Patrick, Mary Katherine, Meaghan, Bridget. BS, U. Iowa, 1966, MD, 1970; MBA, Lake Erie Coll., 1991. Diplomate Am. Bd. Orthopedic Surgery. Intern Robert Packer Hosp., Sayre, Pa., 1970-71; resident in orthopedics Cleve. Clinic, 1971-75; orthopedic surgeon Drs. DeMarco & Irwin, Willoughby, Ohio, 1979—; pres. med. staff Lake Hosp. Sys., 1998—. Served to maj. USAF, 1975-79. Fellow ACS; mem. AMA, Am. Acad. Orthopedic Surgeons, Orthopedic Rsch. Soc., Coll. Physician Execs., Lake County Med. Soc. (pres. 1991), Lake Hosp. Found. (chmn. 1993-96), Ohio State Med. Assn. (alt. del. AMA 1997—, chmn. legis. com. 1997—). Republican. Roman Catholic. Home: 8685 King Memorial Rd Mentor OH 44060-7960 Office: Drs DeMarco & Irwin Inc 36100 Euclid Ave Ste 170 Willoughby OH 44094-4497

COMBS, SUSAN, commissioner of agriculture; married; 3 children. Grad., Vassar Coll.; JD, U. Tex. Formerly asst. dist. atty. Dallas; mem. Tex. Legislature, 1993-96; owner, operator ranch in West Tex.; commr. of agr. State of Tex., 1999—. Named Outstanding Legis. Crimefighter, Greater Dallas Crime Commn., 1993. Mem. Tex. Wildlife Assn. (bd. dirs.), Tex. and Southwestern Cattle Raisers Assn. (bd. dirs.). Office: Tex Dept Agr PO Box 12847 Austin TX 78711

COMBS, W. WILLIAM, college administrator; b. Thayer, Mo., Sept. 12, 1946; s. Willie Cleve and Martha Larona (Farrow) C.; children: Brenda, Betsy, Billy, Beverly. AA, Williams Bapt. Coll., Walnut Ridge, Ark., 1966; BA, S.W. Bapt. U., Bolivar, Mo., 1968; MDiv, Midwestern Bapt. Sem., Kansas City, Mo., 1993; PhD, LAEL, St. Louis, 1993. Ordained to ministry Baptist Ch. Min. of pastoral care First Bapt. Ch., Broken Arrow, Okla., 1979-81; sr. pastor First Bapt. Ch., Troy, Mo., 1982-93; exec. dir. extension Mo. Bapt. Coll., St. Louis, 1993—; chaplain USAF Res., 1981-93; pres. La. Mission Bd., Troy, 1991-92. Contbr. articles to profl. jours. Mem. hosp. chaplaincy Lincoln County Hosp., 1982-92; bd. dirs. Four County Mental Health, Troy, 1990-91. Office: Mo Bapt Coll One College Park Dr Saint Louis MO 63141

COMBS, W(ILLIAM) HENRY, III, lawyer; b. Casper, Wyo., Mar. 18, 1949; s. William Henry and Ruth M. (Wooster) C.; divorced; 1 child, J. Bradley. Student, Northwestern U., 1967-70; BS, U. Wyo., 1972, JD, 1975. Bar: Wyo. 1975, U.S. Dist. Ct. Wyo. 1975, U.S. Ct. Appeals (10th cir.) 1990, U.S. Supreme Ct. 1990. Assoc. Murane & Bostwick, Casper, 1975-77, ptnr., 1978—. Mem. com. on resolution of fee disputes, 1988-92. Mem. ABA (tort and ins. practice, law office mgmt. sects.), NRA, Natrona County Bar Assn., Def. Rsch. Inst., Am. Judicature Soc., Wyo. Assn. Trial Def. Counsel, Assn. Ski Def. Attys., Nat. Bd. Trial Advocacy (cert.), U.S. Handball Assn., Waterski USA, Casper Boat Club, Casper Petroleum Club, Porsche Club Am., BMW Club Am. Republican. Episcopalian. Avocations: handball, waterskiing, snow skiing, climbing, driving. Office: Murane & Bostwick 201 N Wolcott St Casper WY 82601-1922

COMEAU, KATHY DARR, publishing executive; b. Miami, Fla., Dec. 26, 1956; d. William Holmes and Susan Marie (Standish) Darr; m. Mark Lesin Comeau, Dec. 30, 1978 (div. July 1985); children: Ryan William, Chase Lesin. Student, No. Va. C.C. Asst. mgr., trainer Times Cmty. Newspapers, Leesburg, Va.; asst. mgr. Connection Newspapers, McLean, Va.; regional mgr. PT Bull., Alexandria, Va. Office: PT Bulletin 333 N Fairfax St Ste 400 Alexandria VA 22314-2632

COMEAU, LORENE ANITA EMERSON, real estate developer; b. Haverhill, Mass., Sept. 6, 1952; d. Russell Paul and Jeannette (La Course) Emerson; m. Peter Robert Comeau, May 6, 1950; children: Stephen David, Michelle Patricia. BA with honors, Northeastern U., 1975. Lic. real estate broker. Housing rep., pub. liaison U.S. Dept. HUD, Boston, 1975-78; devel. mgr. John M. Corcoran & Co., Milton, Mass., 1978-84, v.p., 1984-94; ptnr. Corcoran Realty Assocs., Milton, 1994—; co-owner, treas. Refrigeration Engring. & Contracting Co., Inc., 1995—; bd. dirs. Stoneham Coop. Bank, 1992—, mem. bd. affairs com., 1992-93, mem. security com., 1993—, chmn. bldg. com., 1997—; v.p. Merrimack Valley Housing Partnership, Lowell, Mass., 1986-89. Treas. Andover (Mass.) bd. Merrimack Valley YMCA, 1986-88, vice chair, 1988-90, chair, 1990-92; mem. Andover Fair Housing Com., 1982-87, Andover Housing Partnership Com., 1990—, Andover Planning Bd., 1993-96; mem. Andover Master Plan Com., 1982-84, chmn. com. housing component and master plan, 1989-90; assoc. mem. Andover Zoning Bd. Appeals, 1984-87; mem. fin. com., cor. bd. Merrimack Valley YMCA, Lawrence, Mass., 1984-86, 91-94, treas. corp. fin. com., 1992-94; mem. low income housing subcom. corp. bd. 1992—; mem. and vice chmn. adv. bd. Caritas Cmtys., 1994-97, chmn. adv. bd., 1998—; mem. Fessenden Sch. Parent's Orgn., 1995-97; mem. Shady Hill Sch. Parents Coun., 1998-99. Mem. LWV (fin. chmn. Andover chpt. 1981-83, budget chmn. 1983-84, 86-87), New England Women in Real Estate (seminars com. 1992, cmty. rels. com. 1992-97, program com. 1996—, chmn. 1998—, mem. steering com. 1997—, spl. events com. 1999, v.p. 1999—), Nat. Assn. Indsl. and Office Properties (pub. affairs com. 1992—, vice chair land use com. 1999—), Nat. Pvt. Developers Coun., Svc. Club of Andover, Sanborn Sch. PTO (curriculum enrichment com. 1988-95) West Mid. Sch. PAC (curriculum enrichment com., women's history month 1993-95). Republican. Episcopalian. Home: PO Box 4108 Andover MA 01810-0812 Office: John M Corcoran & Co 500 Granite Ave Milton MA 02186-5610

COMEAU, MICHAEL GERARD, lawyer; b. Balt., July 13, 1956; s. Joseph Gerard and Irma (Cullison) C.; m. Penny Lee Derrickson, Apr. 14, 1984; children: Joseph Gerard, Nicole Lee. BA, Randolph-Macon Coll., 1978; JD, U. Balt., 1981; postgrad., George Washington U., 1982-83, U.S. Army Judge Advocate Gen.'s Basic Course, 1992; Advanced Course, 1994. Bar: Md. 1981, U.S. Dist Ct. Md. 1982, U.S. Ct. Mil. Appeals 1982, U.S. Ct. Appeals (4th and D.C. cirs.) 1982, D.C. 1984, U.S. Dist Ct. D.C. 1984, U.S. Supreme Ct. 1985. Law clk. Balt. County Solicitor's Office, Towson, Md., 1980-81; assoc. county atty. Prince George's County, Upper Marlboro, Md., 1981-84, 86-89; assoc. Knight, Manzi, Brennan & Ostrom, Upper Marlboro, 1984-86; chief dep. clk. Ct. Spl. Appeals, Annapolis, Md., 1986; asst. atty. gen. State of Md., Towson, 1989-94; chief of litigation, asst. county atty. Balt. County Atty.'s Office, Towson, Md., 1994—; mem. adv. com. Loyola Coll. Bar Rev., Balt., 1982; mem. gen. assembly's task force on gaming laws in Prince George's County, 1987. Mem. ch. coun. All Saints Luth. Ch., Bowie, Md., 1986-88, pres., 1987-88; mem. Dem. State Ctrl. Com. for Harford County, 1995-98; mem. procurement adv. coun. State of Md., 1995-98, Gubernatorial Transition Team, 1994-95; mem. judiciary com. Md. Ho. of Dels., Harford County, 1997-99. Maj. Md. Army N.G., 1991—. Recipient Exceptional Svc. award, Md. Atty. Gens.'s Office, 1991. Mem. Md. Bar Assn., Harford County Bar Assn., Baltimore County Bar Assn., Prince George's County Bar Assn. (bd. dirs. 1988-90), Kappa Alpha. Democrat. Avocations: baseball card collecting, softball. Home: 3509 Glen Oak Dr Jarrettsville MD 21084-1837 Office: Old Court House 400 Washington Ave Fl 2 Towson MD 21204-4606

COMEAU, SUSAN, bank executive. Exec. v.p. State St. Corp., Boston. Office: State St Corp 225 Franklin St Boston MA 02110-2804

COMEAUX, KATHARINE JEANNE, realtor; b. Richland, Wash., Jan. 18, 1949; d. Warren William and Ruth Irma (Remington) Gonder; m. Jack Goldwasser, May 25, 1992; 1 child, Thelma Morrow. AA, West Valley Coll., 1970; student, San Jose State U., 1970-71. Cert. realtor. Realtor Value Realty, Cupertino, Calif., 1975-79, Valley of Calif., Cupertino, 1979-81, Coldwell Banker, Cupertino, 1981-82, Fox & Carskadon, Saratoga, Calif., 1984-90. With Los Gatos-Saratoga Bd. Realtors Polit. Action, 1984-89; v.p. Hospice of Valley Svc. League, Saratoga, 1984-89; Big Sister Big Bros./Big Sisters, San Jose, Calif., 1976-90; bd. dirs. Mountain Energy Inc., Energia Natural, Honduras, Boys and Girls Club, 1996-98, United Way of Josephine Co., 1995-98. Avocations: reading, drawing, writing, needlepoint, photography. Home: 4330 Fish Hatchery Rd Grants Pass OR 97527-9547

COMEFORO, JEAN ELIZABETH, hearing-impaired educator; b. Urbana, Ill., June 2, 1947; d. Jay E. and Jean Carolyn (Raff) Comeforo. BS in Biology, Coll. St. Elizabeth, 1969; MEd of Deaf, Smith Coll., 1972; MEd, Cheyney State Coll., 1982. Cert. tchr. of deaf, N.J., Pa., tchr. biol. and comprehensive scis., oral interpreter for deaf. Houseparent Katazenbach Sch. for Deaf, West Trenton, N.J., 1969-70; math. and sci. tchr. Western Pa. Sch. for Deaf, Edgewood, 1971-76; tchr. of deaf Delaware County Intermediate Unit, Media, Pa., 1976-98, itinerant hearing therapist; presenter in field. Leader Girl Scouts U.S.; chaperone Miss Deaf Pa., 1987-89. Recipient citation for inspirational teaching of sci. subjects Buhl Planetarium, Annie Sullivan award; named Best Producer Community Svc. TV Program, Am. Cablevision Pa. Mem. Alexander Graham Bell Assn. (bd. dirs. Marion Quick chpt. 1983-91, pres. 1989-91), Internat. Orgn. Of Hearing Impaired (Tchr. of Yr. award 1990-91), Delaware Valley Assn. Oral Hearing Impaired, Quota Clubs (gov. dist. II 1985-87), Optimists Internat. (sec. 1995-96, pres. 1996-98, chair Pa. Upper Delaware dist. Comm. Contest for the Deaf and Hard-of-Hearing 1995-98, lt. gov. zone 2 1998-99), Beta Beta Beta Nat. Biology Honor Soc. Home: 315 Catch Penny Ln Media PA 19063-5420

COMER, BRAXTON BRAGG, II, entrepreneur; b. Eufaula, Ala., Aug. 5, 1951; s. Richard Johnson and Anne Laurie C.; m. Mary Anna Fay, July 22, 1972; children: Margaret Laurie, Braxton Bragg Jr. BBA, U. Tex., Austin, 1974; MBA, Vanderbilt U., 1982. Projects mgr. acctg. Avondale Mills, Sylacauga, Ala., 1978, asst. v.p., asst. contr., 1979-81, corp. contr., asst. v.p., 1981-82, v.p., contr., 1982-85; mdse. mgr. Yarn Dyes & Indigo Avondale Fabrics, 1985-89; owner, pres. CX Enterprises Inc., Sylacauga, 1989—; bd. dirs. City Nat. Bank of Sylacauga. Bd. dirs. Sylacauga Libr., Ala. Pub. Libr. Svc., chmn., trustee; bd. advisors McCallic Sch. Mem. Sylacauga C. of C. (past bd. dirs.), Rotary (past dir., pres.). Home: 8 Mountain Ridge Rd Sylacauga AL 35150-4641 Office: CX Enterprises PO Box 418 Sylacauga AL 35150-0418

COMER, DEBRA RUTH, management educator; b. Phila., Apr. 11, 1960; d. Nathan Lawrence and Rita (Ellis) C.; m. James Michael Maloney; children: Rudy Gabriel Malcom and Jacob Eli Malcom (twins). BA, Swarthmore Coll., 1982; MA, Yale U., 1984, MPhil, 1985, PhD, 1986. Instr. Yale U., New Haven, 1983-84; orgnl. devel. cons. Port Authority of N.Y. & N.J., N.Y.C., 1984-87; asst. prof. mgmt. Hofstra U., Hempstead, N.Y., 1987-93; assoc. prof. mgmt. Hofstra U., Hempstead, 1993—, chairperson dept. mgmt. and GB, 1995-97, assoc. dean faculty devel. Sch. of Bus., 1997-98. Contbr. articles to profl. jours. Yale U. fellow, 1982-86, Joshua B. Lippincott fellow Swarthmore Coll., 1982; Hofstra U. grantee, 1988-99. Mem. APA, Acad. Mgmt., Ea. Acad. Mgmt., Orgnl. Behavior Teaching Soc. Jewish. Avocations: music, fitness, cooking, reading. Office: Hofstra U Dept Mgmt and Gen Bus 228 Weller Hall Hempstead NY 11549

COMER, DONALD, III, investment company executive; b. N.Y.C., June 23, 1938; s. Donald and Isabel (Anderson) C.; m. Jane Stephens, May 4, 1962; children: Jason Legare, Luke McDonald, Carrie St. George. B.S., U. Ala., 1962. With Cowikee Mills, Eufaula, Ala., 1962-82; plant mgr. Cowikee Mills, 1965-66, v.p., 1966-68, pres., treas., dir., 1968-82; pres., dir. Aurizon Inc., 1982—; past pres., treas., dir. Avondale Mills., Sylacauga, Ala. Past chmn. Ala. Ethics Commn. Served with USAF, 1961-64. Club: Mountain Brook Country (Birmingham). Home: 3905 Hillock Dr Birmingham AL 35213-3223

COMER, EVAN PHILIP, manufacturing company executive; b. Cumberland Gap, Tenn., May 29, 1927; s. Evan Mitchell and Margaret Nola (Estep) C.; m. Mary Blanc, Aug. 28, 1948; children: Vivian, Jane. BA, Carson-Newman Coll., Jefferson City, Tenn., 1948; MA, Columbia U., 1949. Asst. prof. psychology, dir. student personnel and placement Furman U., Greensville, S.C., 1949-52; self-employed writer, 1952-53; supervisory conf. leader Union Carbide Nuclear Co., Oak Ridge, 1953-55; instr. in-plant tng. U. Tenn., Knoxville, 1955-56; with Foote Mineral Co., 1956-67, 69—, v.p., gen. mgr. chems. and minerals div., 1970-80; pres., chief exec. officer Foote Mineral Co., Exton, Pa., 1980-84, also bd. dirs.; pres., chief exec. officer, chmn. bd. Ashram Farm, Inc., Rutledge, Tenn., 1984-98; mem. Pa. adv. bd. Liberty Mut. Ins. Co.; exec. com. , dir. Phila. Mfrs. Mut. Ins. Co. Pres. Southeastern Community Coll., Whiteville, N.C., 1964-69; mem. adv. bd. Carson-Newman Coll.; bd. dirs. Pa. Sci. and Engring. Found.; mem. Pa. Gov's Sci. Adv. Com.; mem. adv. coun. Pa. Tech. Assistance Program, Pa. State U.; chmn. bd. Chester County Pvt. Industry Coun., 1983-84. With USNR, 1945-46. Mem. AIME, Ferroalloys Assn. (chmn. bd. dirs. 1983—), Am. Mining Congress, Mining Club (N.Y.C.). Republican. Baptist. Home: 1548 Smoky View Dr Dandridge TN 37725-6328

COMER, JAMES PIERPONT, psychiatrist, educator; b. East Chicago, Ind., Sept. 25, 1934; s. Hugh and Maggie (Nichols) C.; m. Shirley Ann Arnold, June 20, 1959 (dec. Apr. 1994); children: Brian Jay, Dawn Renee. AB, Ind. U., 1956; MD, Howard U., 1960; MPH, U. Mich., 1964; DSc (hon.), U. New Haven, 1977; LittD (hon.), Calumet Coll., 1978; LHD (hon.), Bank St. Coll., N.Y.C., 1987, Albertus Magnus Coll., 1989, Quinnipiac Coll., 1990, DePauw U., 1990; DSc (hon.), Ind U., 1991, Wabash Coll., 1991; EdD (hon.), Wheelock Coll., 1991; LLD (hon.), U. Conn., 1991; LHD (hon.), SUNY Buffalo, 1991, New Sch. for Social Rsch., 1991; D Pedagogy (hon.), R.I. Coll., 1991; DSc (hon.), Amherst Coll., 1991; LHD (hon.), John Jay Coll. Criminal Justice, 1991, Wesleyan U., 1991; DH (hon.), Princeton U., 1991; DSc (hon.), Northwestern U., 1991, Worcester Poly. Inst., 1991; LHD (hon.), U. Pa., 1992; DPD (hon.), Niagara U., 1992; LHD (hon.), Hamilton Coll., 1992; DSc (hon.), Brown U., 1992; LHD (hon.), U. Mass. at Lowell, 1992; DSc (hon.), Med. Coll. Ohio, 1992, Howard U., 1993, W.Va. U., 1993; LLD (hon.), Lawrence U., 1993; DSc (hon.), Morehouse Sch. Medicine, 1993; LLD (hon.), Columbia U., 1994, Boston Coll., 1994; LHD (hon.), Briarwood Coll., 1994, Cleve. State U., 1996; DSc (hon.), St. Mary's Coll., Md., 1996. Served with USPHS, Washington and Chevy Chase, Md., 1961-68; intern St. Catherine's Hosp., East Chicago, 1960-61; resident Yale Sch. Medicine, 1964-67; asst. prof. psychiatry Yale Child Study Center and dept. psychiatry, 1968-70, assoc. prof., 1970-75, prof., 1975-76, Maurice Falk prof. psychiatry, 1976—; assoc. dean Yale Med. Sch., New Haven, 1969—; dir. pupil svcs. Baldwin-King Sch. Project, New Haven, 1968-73; dir. sch. devel. program Yale Child Study Ctr., 1973—; dir. Conn. Energy Corp., 1976—, Nat. Acad. Found. N.Y., N.Y.C., 1993—; co-dir. Black Family Roundtable Greater New Haven, 1986—; cons. Joint Commn. on Mental Health of Children, Nat. Commn. on Causes and Prevention of Violence, NIMH; mem. nat. adv. mental health coun. HEW; Henry J. Kaiser Sr. fellow Center for Advanced Study in the Behavioral Scis., Stanford, 1976-77. Author: Beyond Black and White, 1972, Black Child Care, 1975, 2d edit., 1992, School Power, 1980, 2d. edit., 1993, Maggie's American Dream, 1988, Rallying the Whole Village: The Comer Process for Reforming Education, 1996, Waiting For a Miracle: Why Schools Can't Solve Our Problems-And How We Can, 1997; mem. editl. bd. Am. Jour. Orthopsychiatry, 1969-76, Youth and Adolescence, 1971-87, Jour. Negro Edn., 1973-83; guest editor Jour. Am. Acad. Child Psychiatry, 1985; columnist Parents mag.; contbr. articles to profl. jours. Bd. dirs. Field Found., 1981-88, Dixwell Soul Sta. and Yale Afro-Am. House; trustee Hazen Found., 1974-78, Wesleyan U., 1978-84, Nat. Coun. for Effective Schs., 1985—, Albertus Magnus Coll., 1989—, Carnegie Corp., 1990, Milton S. Eisenhower Found., Washington, 1991—, Conn. State U., 1991-94; bd. dirs., mem. profl. adv. bd. Children's TV Workshop, 1972-88; mem. profl. adv. coun. Nat. Assn. Mental Health; mem. ad. hoc adv. com. Conn. Rsch. Commn.; mem. adv. coun. Nat. Com. for Citizens in Edn.; mem. nat. adv. coun. Hogg Found. for Mental Health, 1983-86; mem. adv. com. adolescent pregnancy prevention Children's Def. Fund, 1985—; mem. adv. coun. Nat. Com. for Citizens in Edn., 1983—; mem. nat. adv. coun. Hogg Found for Mental Health, 1983-86; mem. edn. adv. bd., bd. dirs. (hon.) Kids Voting USA, 1997—; mem. nat. evaluation adv. coun. Kellogg Youth Initiative Partnerships W.K. Kellogg Found., 1997—. Recipient Child Study Assn.-Wel-Met Family Life book award, 1975, Howard U. Disting. Alumni award, 1976, Rockefeller Public Service award, 1980, Media award NCCJ, 1981, Cmty. Leadership award Greater New Haven C. of C., 1983, Disting. Fellow award Conn. chpt. Phi Delta Kappa, 1984, Elm and Ivy award New Haven Found., 1985, Disting. Svc. award Conn. Assn. Psychologists, 1985, Disting. Educator award Conn. Coalition of 100 Black Women, 1985, Outstanding Leadership award Children's Def. Fund, 1987, Whitney M. Young Jr. Svc. award Boy Scouts Am., 1989, Prudential Leadership award Prudential Found., 1990, Harold W. McGraw Jr. prize in Edn., 1990, James Bryant Conant award Edn. Commn. States, 1991, Charles A. Dana prize in Edn., 1991, Disting. Svc. award Coun. Chief State Sch. Officers, 1991, Family Focus Nat. award, 1991, Charles A. Dana award for pioneering achievement in edn., 1991, Ind. U. Disting. Alumni Svc. award, 1992, Burger King Disting. Svc. to Edn. award, 1992, Conn. Assn. for Human Svcs. Pres. award, 1992, Golden Acorn award Bronx C.C., 1994, Presdl. citation Am. Ednl. Rsch. Assn., 1995, Health Trac Found. prize, 1996, Heinz Family award, 1996, Lehigh U. Outstanding Svc. to Coll. Edn. award, 1996, Ann Vanderbilt Achievement award for ednl. leadership, 1997, Great Friend to Kids award Assn. Youth Mus., 1997, Disting. Svc. medal Tchrs. Coll., 1997; John and Mary Markle Found. scholar, 1969—; James Comer NIMH Minority Fellowship established in his honor, 1991. Mem. APA (Disting. Svc. award 1993), Am. Acad. Child Adolescent Psychiatry, Nat. Med. Assn., Nat. Mental Health Assn. (Lela Rowland Prevention award 1989), Am. Psychiat. Assn. (Agnes Purcell McGavin award 1990, Solomon Carter Fuller award 1990, Spl. Presdl. Commendation 1990, Disting. Svc. award 1993), Am. Orthopsychiat. Assn. (Vera S. Paster award 1990), Am. Acad. Child Psychiatry, Black Psychiatrists of Am., NAACP, Black Coalition of New Haven, Greater New Haven Black Family Roundtable (co-dir. 1986—), Alpha Omega Alpha, Alpha Phi Alpha. Avocations: photography, travel, sports fan. Office: Yale U Child Study Ctr PO Box 207900 New Haven CT 06520-7900 *As a black child, I sometimes had doubts about my future opportunities for success in our predominantly white country. My parents counselled me never to let the issue of race stand in my way; that the time of greater opportunity for blacks would come. They advised me to work hard, prepare myself, to strive to be the best or among the best in every undertaking, and at the same time be respectful of all people, regardless of their abilities, race, beliefs, or station in life. I have lived by this advice and it has served me well. I have learned not to strive for top position but to let my work take me where it will in line with my interests.**

COMER, NATHAN LAWRENCE, psychiatrist, educator; b. Phila., Nov. 10, 1923; s. Rubin L. and Fannie (Cassover) C.; m. Rita Ellis, June 19, 1949 (dec. Mar. 1978); children: Robert, Susan Comer Kitei, Debra R., Marc J. BA, U. Pa., 1944; MD, Hahnemann Med. Coll., 1949; postgrad., U. Pa. Diplomate Am. Bd. Psychiatry and Neurology, Am. Bd. Profl. Disabiligy Cons., Sr. Disability Analyst of Am. Bd. Disability Analysts, Am. Bd. Forensic Examiners, Am. Bd. Forensic Medicine. Intern Hahnemann Med. Coll., Phila., 1949-50; resident, NIMH fellow Inst. of Pa. Hosp., Phila., 1951-53, sr. attending psychiatrist, 1968—, resident in psychiatry, 1951-53; chief of psychiatry Ford Rd. campus Thomas Jefferson U. Hosp., Phila., 1978-94; clin. assoc. prof. psychiatry and human behavior Jefferson Med. Coll., Thomas Jefferson U., Phila., 1994—; clin. assoc. prof. psychiatry Med. Coll. Pa. and Hahnemann U., 1978—; pres. med. staff Belmont Ctr. Comprehensive Treatment, 1975-77, emeritus sr. attending physician, 1988—; pres. med. staff Inst. of Pa. Hosp., 1983-85. Contbr. articles to profl. jours. Bd. dirs. Temple Adath Israel of Main Line, Merion, Pa., 1958-78. Fellow Coll. Physicians Phila., Am. Psychiat. Assn. (life); mem. AMA, Am. Soc. for Adolescent Psychiatry, Hahnemann Med. Coll. Alumni Assn. (pres. 1973-74), B'nai B'rith. Republican. Jewish. Home: 1100 Hillcrest Rd Narberth PA 19072-1224 Office: Inst Pa Hosp 111 N 49th St Philadelphia PA 19139-2718 *Do things to the best of your ability and be willing to go that extra mile. Alsobe willing to express your opinion if you think you're right even if you seem to be in the minority. Being respected is more important than being liked.*

COMEROTA, ANTHONY JAMES, vascular surgeon, biomedical researcher; b. Newark, Aug. 4, 1948; s.Louis Anthony and Eleanor Dorothy (Dombroski) C.; m. Elsa Benavides, Aug. 18, 1973; children: Anthony James, Maya Christine, Mark Anthony. BA, Millikin U., 1970; MD, Temple U., 1974. Diplomate Am. Bd. Surgery. Surg. resident Temple U. Hosp., Phila., 1974-78; vascular surgery fellow Good Samaritan Hosp., Cin., 1979-81; from asst. prof. to prof. surgery Temple U. Hosp, Temple U. Sch. Medicine, Phila., 1981-88, prof. surgery, chief vascular surgery, 1988—; dir. Ctr. for Vascular Diseases Temple U. Hosp., Temple U. Sch. Medicine, Phila., 1995—; dir. ctr. vascular diseases Temple U. Sch. Medicine, Phila., 1995—. Editor: Thrombolytic Therapy for Peripheral Vascular Disease, 1995; co-editor: Prevention of Venous Thromboembolism, 1994. Fellow ACS, Royal Australian Coll. Surgeons; mem. Am. Surg. Assn., Soc. Vascular Surgery, Internat. Soc. Cardiovascular Surgery, Phila. Acad. Surgery (pres. 1996-97), Temple U. Sch. Medicine Alumni Assn. (pres. 1993-95), Alpha Omega Alpha. Office: Temple Univ Dept of Surgery Broad & Ontario St Philadelphia PA 19140

COMES, ROBERT GEORGE, research scientist; b. Bangor, Pa., July 7, 1931; s. Victor Francis and Mabel Elizabeth (Mack) C.; student U. Detroit, 1957-58, Oreg. State Coll., 1959-60, U. Nev., 1960, Regis Coll., 1961-62; m. Carol Lee Turinetti, Nov. 28, 1952; children: Pamela Jo, Robert G. II, Shawni Lee, Sheryl Lynn, Michelle Ann. Tech. liaison engr. Burroughs Corp., Detroit, 1955-60, mgr. reliability and maintainability engring., Paoli, Pa., 1962-63, Colorado Springs, Colo., 1963-67; sr. engr. Martin Marietta Corp., Denver, 1960-62; program mgr., rsch. scientist Kaman Scis. Corp., Colorado Springs, 1967-75; dir. engring. Sci. Applications, Inc., Colorado Springs, 1975-80; mgr. space def. programs Burroughs Corp., Colorado Springs, 1980-82; tech. staff Mitre Corp., Colorado Springs, 1982-85; dir. Colorado Springs opn. Beers Assoc., Inc., 1985; dir. space programs Electro Magnetic Applications, Inc., Colorado Springs, 1985-87; dir. Space Systems, Profl. Mgmt. Assocs., Inc., 1987-88; mgr. Computer Svcs., Inc., Colorado Springs, 1989—; dir. mktg. Proactive Techs., Inc., Colorado Springs, 1990—; chmn. Reliability and Maintainability Data Bank Improvement Program, Govt.-Industry Data Exch. Program, 1978-80—; cons. in field. Youth dir. Indian Guides program YMCA, 1963-64; scoutmaster Boy Scouts Am., 1972-73; chmn. bd. dirs. Pikes Peak Regional Sci. Fair, 1972-84. Served with USAF, 1951-55. Mem. AAAS, IEEE, Inst. Environ. Scis., Soc. Logistics Engrs., Am. Soc. Quality Control. Lutheran. Club: Colorado Springs Racquet. Author: Maintainability Engineering Principles and Standards, 1962. Inventor Phase Shifting aircraft power supply, 1957. Home and Office: Proactive Tech Inc 4309 Tipton Ct Colorado Springs CO 80915-1034

COMEY, RACHEL MICKYLA, gallery curator and director, sculptor; b. Manchester, Conn., Oct. 7, 1972; d. Dale Raymond and Marilyn Ann (Phillips) C. BA in Studio Art, U. Vt., 1994. Curator, dir. Exquisite Corpse Artsite, Burlington, Vt., 1995—; designer MME, Burlington, 1996—; panel spkr. Fleming Mus., Burlington, 1997; juror Vt. Caucus for Arts, Burlington, 1997. Work reviewed by various publs., including Art New Eng., Yankee mag. Cons. Burlington City Arts, Arts Alive. Mem. Met. Mus. Art, Fleming Mus. Office: Equisite Corpse Artsite 47 Maple St Burlington VT 05401-4784

COMFORT, ALEXANDER, physician, author; b. London, Feb. 10, 1920; s. Alexander Charles and Daisy Elizabeth (Fenner) C.; m. Ruth Muriel Harris, 1943 (div. 1973); 1 child, Nicholas Alfred Fenner; m. Jane Tristram Henderson, June 8, 1973 (dec. 1991). BA, Cambridge (Eng.) U., 1943, MB, BCh, 1944, MA, 1945; PhD, London U., 1949, DSc, 1962, DCH, 1946. Licentiate Royal Coll. Physicians. House physician London Hosp., 1944; resident Royal Waterloo Hosp., London, 1945-46; lectr. physiology London Hosp., 1948-51; Nuffield rsch. fellow Univ. Coll. London, 1951-65; head Med. Rsch. Coun. Group on Aging, 1965-72, dir. rsch., 1972-74; lectr. dept. psychiatry Stanford, 1974-83; prof. dept. pathology U. Calif. Med. Sch., Irvine, 1976-78; adj. prof. Neuropsychiat. Inst., UCLA, 1979-85; cons. geriatric psychiatry Brentwood VA Hosp., Los Angeles, 1978-91. Author: (poetry) A Wreath for the Living, 1973, The Songs of Lazarus, 1945, The Signal to Engage, 1947, And All But He Departed, 1951, Haste to the Wedding, 1961, Poems, 1979, Mikrokosmos, 1994; (essays) Art and Social Responsibility, 1947, Barbarism and Sexual Freedom, 1948, Darwin and the Naked Lady, 1961, What Is a Doctor?, 1980, Writings Against Power and Death, 1993; (novels) No Such Liberty, 1941, The Almond Tree, 1943, The Power House, 1944, On This Side Nothing, 1948, A Giant's Strength, 1952, Come Out to Play, 1961, The Patient, 1987, Walsingham's Drum, 1989, The Philosophers, 1989; (counseling books) The Joy of Sex, 1973, More Joy, 1974, A Good Age, 1976, New Joy of Sex: The Gormet Guide to Lovemaking in the 90s, 1991; (with Jane T. Comfort) The Facts of Love, 1979; also author numerous other works; editor: Experimental Gerontology, from 1965; contbr. articles to profl. jours. Recipient Karger Meml. prize in gerontology, 1969. Mem. Royal Coll. Surgeons, Coll. Physicians and Surgeons (Sask.), Royal Soc. Medicine (London), Brit. Soc. Rsch. on Aging (pres. 1969), Am. Psychiat. Assn. Address: Chacombe House, Chacombe Nr Banbury, Oxon OX17 2SL, England

COMFORT, CLIFTON C., management consultant, fraud examiner; b. Dallas, June 19, 1943; s. Clifton C. and Nola B. (Harris) C.; m. Jacquelynn S. Henderson, June 27, 1964 (div. Nov. 1981); 1 child, Amy Elizabeth (Mrs. James Pratt). BBA in Acctg. with honors, U. Tex., Arlington, 1964; MBA, U. Phoenix, 1989. CPA, cert. internal auditor, cost analyst, fraud examiner, Tex. Auditor U.S. Govt., Dallas, 1964-75, fin. mgr., 1975-78, audit mgr., 1978-83; mgmt. cons. C.C. Comfort Cons., Dallas, 1983-86, Scottsdale, Ariz., 1992—; dir. compliance Litton Industries, Tempe, Ariz., 1986-92; fraud examiner Maricopa County Attorney's Office, Phoenix, Ariz., 1999—; mem. Fed. Exec. Bd., Dallas, 1979-82, Intergovtl. Audit Forum, Dallas, 1979-82; co. rep. to Electronic Industries Assn., Washington, 1986-92, Machinery and Alied Products Inst., Washington, 1986-92; presenter seminars in field. Contbr. articles to profl. jours. Bd. dirs. Assn. Govt. Accts., 1983-84; res. dep. sheriff Sheriff's Dept. Dallas, 1976-83; pres. U. Tex.-Arlington Alumni Assn., 1984-85. Recipient Cert. of Merit Sheriff's Dept. Dallas, 1980, Best Tech. Article award Assn. Govt. Accts., 1979. Mem. ABA, AICPA, Am. Health Lawyers Assn., Soc. for Advancement of Mgmt. (bd. dirs. 1984-85), Nat. Contract Mgmt. Assn. (v.p. 1994-95), Assn. Cert. Fraud Examiners (bd. dirs. 1994-95), Inst. Mgmt. Cons. Avocations: travel, hiking, reading, teaching. E-mail: CCComfortCFE@MartindaleMail.com. Office: CC Comfort Cons 3370 N Hayden Rd Ste 123 Scottsdale AZ 85251-6632

COMFORT, IRIS TRACY, writer; b. Racine, Wis.; d. Arnold Thomas and Iva Dorothea Tracy; widowed; 1 child, Alain James. Student, U. Wis., U. Minn. Reporter St. Paul Dispatch, 1937-38; mem. pub. rels. staff Allis-Chalmers, Milw., 1942-45; editor-in-chief Where Mag., Chgo., 1946-47; owner, operator pub. rels. agy. Milw., 1948-49; freelance writer Milw. and Orlando, Fla., 1948—; lectr. Dept. Def. Schs., Germany, 1991-92; lectr., presenter workshops in field. Author: Earth Treasures, 1970, Joey Tigertail, 1973, Lets Grow Things, 1974, Let's Read About Rocks, 1975, Echoes of Evil, 1981 (Book Club choice), Shadow Masque, 1982 (Book Club choice), Florida's Geological Treasures, 1998, also others. Mem. Mystery Writers Am., Authors' Guild, Nat. Speleological Soc., Ctrl. Fla. Mineral and Gem Soc., Fla. Mineral Friends, Romance Writers Am. Avocations: caving, photography, exotic and tropical gardening, rock and mineral collecting, psychic investigation. Home and Office: 2902 Oxford St Orlando FL 32803-6821

COMFORT, JANE, choreographer, director. BA in Painting, U. N.C. Artistic dir. Jane Comfort and Co., N.Y.C.; produced by Lincoln Ctr.'s Serious Fun! Festival, Off-Broadway at Classic Stage Co., The Joyce Theater, Performance Space 122 and Dance Theater Workshop in N.Y., The Am. Ctr./Paris, Antwerp's Dance/USA Festival, Jacob's Pillow Dance Festival, The Walker Art Ctr., The Balt. Art Mus., Actors Theatre of Louisville. Choreographer (Broadway musical): Passion (recipient four Tony awards, including Best Musical), (theater dance musicals) Faith Healing, 1993, S/he, 1995, (film) Franchesca Page, 1997; (off broadway) TellTale Underground River, 1998, Macbeth at Dance Theater Workshop, 1999, Sondheim on Sondheim, 1999. Grantee Nat. Endowment for the Arts, N.Y. Found. for Arts, N.Y. State Coun. on the Arts, Joyce Mertz-Gilmore Found., Dance Mag. Found., Harkness Founds. for Dance, Found. for Contemporary Performance Art. E-mail: jjcomfort@earthlink.net. Office: Jane Comfort and Co 55 N Moore St New York NY 10013-2349

COMFORT, PRISCILLA MARIA, college official, human resources professional; b. Ft. Dix, N.J., Feb. 20, 1947; d. Jennie Rita (Manes) McGuire; children: James, Aimee. BS, Montclair State Coll., 1969; MEd, Trenton State Coll., 1980. Cert. tchr., guidance counselor, pub. mgr., N.J. Tchr. Burlington (N.J.) Twp. and City Schs., 1969-72; employment svc. interviewer N.J. Dept. Labor and Industry, Trenton, 1972-74; prin. career devel. specialist N.J. Dept. Civil Svc., Trenton, 1974-76, prin. pers. technician, 1976-79; dir. pers. svcs. Stockton State Coll., Pomona, N.J., 1979-89; asst. v.p. human resources Stockton Coll., Pomona, 1990-95, assoc. v.p. human resources, 1995—; with N.J. Gov.'s task force on sexual harassment, 1993. Bd. dirs. Betty Bacharach Rehab. Hosp. Found., 1993—; tchr. CCD Assumption Ch., Pomona, 1981-84, mem. CCD adv. bd., 1983-84; active Little League, PTO, 1977-84; mem. pers. com. Big Bros./Big Sisters Adv. Com., 1988; mem. cmty. adv. bd. Jewish Family Svcs., 1991—; mem. adv. bd. pers. com. Atlantic City C. of C., 1985. Recipient Tribute to Women in Industry award YWCA (twin), 1987, Mgmt. Merit award, 1986, 88, SUN Mag. award, 1988, Community Recognition award Chapel of the Four Chaplains, 1988. Mem. ASPA, Cert. Pub. Mgrs. Assn., N.J. Atlantic County Pers. Assn., Assn. Affirmative Action in Higher Edn. (panelist), N.J. Pers. Adv. Bd., N.J. Coll. and Univ. Pers. Assn. (chmn., sec.-treas., chmn. mem. sect.), Coll. and Univ. Pers. Assn. (nat. bd. dirs. 1993, nat. legis. com. 1989-93, bd. dirs. ea. region 1990-96, sec. 1990-93, bd. dirs., mem. exec. com. nat. found. 1996-99, active other coms., Disting. Svc. award 1997, Ea. Region Svc. award 1996), Coll. and Univ. Pers. Assn. Ea. Acad. for Human Resource Excellence (chair 1994-95, found. bd. 1996). Roman Catholic. Avocations: reading, travel, collecting bells, books, candles. Office: Richard Stockton Coll NJ Jim Leeds Rd Pomona NJ 08240

COMFORT, ROBERT DENNIS, lawyer; b. Camden, N.J., Nov. 22, 1950; s. Joseph Albert Sr. and Elizabeth (Rogers) C.; m. Loretta Masullo, Aug. 24, 1974; 1 child, Adam. AB summa cum laude, Princeton U., 1973; JD magna cum laude, Harvard U., 1976. Bar: Pa. 1976, N.J. 1977, U.S. Dist. Ct. N.J. 1977, U.S. Dist. Ct. (ea. dist.) Pa. 1977, U.S. Ct. Appeals (3d cir.) 1977, U.S. Tax Ct. 1978, U.S. Claims Ct. 1983. Law clk. to Hon. James Hunter III U.S. Ct. Appeals 3d Cir., Phila., 1976-77; law clk. to Lewis F. Powell Jr. U.S. Supreme Ct., Washington, 1977-78; assoc. Morgan, Lewis & Bockius, Phila., 1978-82; ptnr. Morgan, Lewis & Bockius, 1982—; adj. prof. U. Pa. Law Sch., Rutgers-Camden Law Sch. Mem. ABA, Phila. Bar Assn. (vice chair tax sect. 1990-92, chair 1993-94). Avocations: golf, camping, music, history, fishing. Office: Morgan Lewis & Bockius 1701 Market St Philadelphia PA 19103-2903*

COMFORT, WILLIAM TWYMAN, JR., banker; b. Ellsworth, Kans., Aug. 3, 1937; s. William Twyman and Leoti Dora (Shackleford) C.; m. Nathalie Pierrepont, June 6, 1964; children: Nathalie Pierrepont, William Twyman III, James Theodore, Stuyvesant Pierrepont. BA, Okla. U., 1959, LLB, 1961; LLM, NYU, 1964. With W.E. Hutton & Co., N.Y.C., 1962-73, ptnr., 1969-73, sr. v.p., 1973-74; sr. v.p. Citibank, N.Y.C., 1974—; exec. dir. Citicorp Internat. Bank Ltd., London, 1976-78; chmn. bd. dirs. 399 Venture Ptnrs. Inc., Citicorp Venture Capital, Ltd.; chmn. bd. dirs. CourtSquare Capital Ltd.; adj. prof. Columbia Bus. Sch., N.Y.C.; bd. dirs. Citicorp Info. Tech. Industries Ltd. Trustee NYU Law Ctr. Found.; former trustee Pine Mano Coll., Chestnut Hill, Mass.; advisor to bd. dirs. Old Westbury (L.I.) Gardens. With U.s. Army, 1961. Mem. N.Y. Bar Assn., Okla. Bar Assn., Piping Rock Club (Locust Valley, N.Y.), Jupiter Island Club (Hobe Sound, Fla.). Home: Duck Pond Rd Locust Valley NY 11560 Office: 399 Park Ave Unit 14 New York NY 10022-4600

COMFORT, WILLIAM WISTAR, mathematics educator; b. Bryn Mawr, Pa., Apr. 19, 1933; s. Howard and Elizabeth (Webb) C.; m. Mary Constance Lyon, Mar. 30, 1957; children: Martha Wistar, Howard III. BA, Haverford Coll., 1954; MS, U. Wash., 1957, PhD, 1958; MA ad eundem gradum, Wesleyan U., Middletown, Conn., 1969. Tchg. asst., rsch. asst. U. Wash., Seattle, 1954-58; B. Peirce instr. Harvard U., Cambridge, Mass., 1958-61; asst. prof. U. Rochester, N.Y., 1961-65; assoc. prof. U. Mass., Amherst, 1965-67; prof. math. Wesleyan U., 1967—, Edward Burr Van Vleck prof. math., 1982—, chmn. dept., 1969-70, 80-82, 96-97; vis. prof. U. Ark., 1965, McGill U., Montreal, 1970-71, U. Heidelberg, 1974, Istituto Matematico Leonida Tonelli, Pisa, Italy, 1974, Athens U., Greece, 1978, Univ. Nacional Autonoma de Mex., 1983, Univ. São Paolo, 1983, Vrije Univ. Amsterdam, 1984, 95, Technische Hochschule Darmstadt, Germany, 1991, Univ. Jaume I. Castellon, Spain, 1995. Author: (with S. Negrepontis) The Theory of Ultrafilters, 1974, Continuous Pseudometrics, 1975, Chain Conditions in Topology, 1982; mem. editorial bd. Procs. Am. Math. Soc., 1972-75, mng. editor, 1974-75; mem. editorial bd. Topology Procs., 1976—, Am. Math. Monthly, 1983-86, Karachi Jour. Math., 1984—, Mathematica Japonica, 1992—, Topology and Its Applications, 1993—; contbr. articles to profl. jours. Bd. mgrs. Haverford Coll., 1971-74; trustee Ind. Day Sch., Middlefield, Conn., 1972-75. Recipient Excellence-in-teaching award U. Rochester, 1966. Mem. AAUP, Math. Assn. Am., Am. Math. Soc. (coun. 1972-75, 82-93, assoc. sec. Ea. region 1982-93), N.Y. Acad. Scis., Conn. Acad. Sci. and Engring., Assn. Concerned Scientists, Phi Beta Kappa. Mem. Religious Soc. of Friends. Home: 26 Pine St Middletown CT 06457-3113 Office: Wesleyan U Math Dept Middletown CT 06459

COMINGS, DAVID EDWARD, physician, medical genetics scientist; b. Beacon, N.Y., Mar. 8, 1935; s. Edward Walter and Jean (Rice) C.; m. Shirley Nelson, Aug. 9, 1958; children: Mark David, Scott Edward, Karen Jean.; m. Brenda Gursey, Mar. 20, 1982. Student, U. Ill., 1951-54; BS, Northwestern U., 1955, MD, 1958. Intern Cook County Hosp., Chgo., 1958-59; resident in internal medicine Cook County Hosp., 1959-62; fellow in med. genetics U. Wash., Seattle, 1964-66; dir. dept. med. genetics City of Hope Med. Ctr., Duarte, Calif., 1966—; mem. genetics study sect. NIH, 1974-78; mem. sci. adv. bd. Hereditary Disease Found., 1975—, Nat. Found. March of Dimes, 1978-92. Author: Tourette Syndrome and Human Behavior, 1990, Search for the Tourette Syndrome and Human Behavior Genes, 1996, The Gene Bomb, 1996; editor: (with others) Molecular Human Cytogenetics, 1977; mem. editorial bd.: (with others) Cytogenetics and Cell genetics, 1979—; editor in chief Am. Jour. Human Genetics, 1978-86. Served with U.S. Army, 1962-64. NIH grantee, 1967—. Mem. Assn. Am. Physicians, Am. Soc. Clin. Investigation, AAAS, Am. Soc. Human Genetics (dir. 1974-78, pres. 1988), Am. Soc. Cell Biology, Am. Fedn. Clin. Research, Western Soc. Clin. Research, Council Biology Editors. Office: City of Hope Med Ctr 1500 Duarte Rd Duarte CA 91010-3000

COMINGS, WILLIAM DANIEL, JR., mortgage banker, housing development executive; b. Orange, N.J., June 5, 1938; s. William Daniel and Margaret E. Comings; m. Margaret Bunting, Dec. 22, 1962; children: Scott B., Douglas N. BA, Dartmouth Coll., 1960. Dir. land disposition and devel. D.C. Redevel. Land Agy., 1962-69; with Nat. Corp. for Housing Ptnrships., Washington, 1969-87, exec. v.p. multifamily devel., 1978-87; exec. v.p. The Patrician Mortgage Co., 1987—, The Patrician Fin. Co., 1990-97, pres., 1997—. Served to lt. (j.g.) USNR, 1960-62. Office: The Patrician Fin Co 4550 Montgomery Ave # 1150 Bethesda MD 20814-3304*

COMINI, ALESSANDRA, art historian, educator; b. Winona, Minn., Nov. 24, 1934; d. Raiberto and Megan (Laird) C. BA, Barnard Coll., 1956; MA, U. Calif., Berkeley, 1964; PhD with distinction, Columbia U., 1969. Teaching asst. U. Calif., Berkeley, 1964; vis. instr. U. Calif., 1967; preceptor Columbia U., 1965-66, 67-68, instr., 1968-69, asst. prof., 1969-74; vis. asst. prof. So. Methodist U., summers 1970, 72, assoc. prof. art history, 1974-75, prof., 1975—, Univ. disting. prof., 1983—; Alfred Hodder resident humanist Princeton U., 1972-73; disting. vis. lectr. Oxford U., 1996; vis. asst. prof. Yale U., 1973; vis. humanist various univs.; lectr. in English, German and Italian; keynote spkr. Gewandhaus Symposia, Leipzig, Germany, 1983, 85,

87, 89, Mahler Internat Congress, Amsterdam, 1988, 95, Hamburg, 1989, Oxford, 1996, Montpellier, 1996, Internat. Mahler Fest, Boulder, Colo., 1998; featured spkr. Purchase, N.Y., 1989, Leningrad, 1990, Stockholm, 1991, Berlin, 1993, Bethoven Extravaganza, Milw., 1994, Schiele Symposium, Indpls., 1994, Helsinki, 1996, Schubertiads at Curtis Inst., Phila., Reed Coll., Oreg. and So. Meth. U., 1997, Santa Fe Opera, 1997, 98, 99, Mozart Internat. Symposium, Dublin, Ireland, 1999; panelist NEH Mus. and Pub. Programs, 1978—; lectr. for the Santa Fe Opera, 1997, 98, 99. Author: Schiele in Prison, 1973, Egon Schiele's Portraits, 1974 (Nat. Book award nominee 1975, reissued 1990, Charles Rufus Morey Book award 1975), Gustav Klimt, 1975, reissued 1986, 90, 93, also German, French and Dutch edit., Egon Schiele, 1976, reissued 1986, 94, also German, French and Dutch edits., The Fantastic Art of Vienna, 1978, The Changing Image of Beethoven, 1987, Egon Schiele: Nudes, 1995; contbg. author: World Impressionism, 1990, Käthe Kollwitz, 1992, Egon Schiele, 1994, Violetta and her Sisters, 1994, Salome, 1996, By a Finnish Fireside: An Evening with Akseli Gallen-Kallela and Gustav Mahler, 1997, Irony and Gustav Mahler, 1997, The Visual Wagner, 1997; contbr. numerous articles to Stagebill, Arts Mag., English Nat. Opera, Chgo. Lyric Opera; also author various catalogue and book introductions, also book revs. for N.Y. Times, Women's Art Jour. Awarded Grand Decoration of Honor for svcs. to Republic of Austria, 1990; recipient Charles Rufus Morey Book award Coll. Art Assn. Am., 1976, Laural award AAUW, 1979; named Outstanding Prof., 1977, 79, 83, 85, 86, 87, 88, 90, 98; AAUW travel fellow, 1966-87; NEH grantee, 1975; named Meadows Disting. Teaching Prof., 1986-87, Tchr./Scholar of Yr., United Meth. Ch., 1996. Mem. MSCAP, Nat. Mus. for Women in the Arts (nat. bd. 1997—), Coll. Art Assn. Am. (bd. dirs. 1980-84), Women's Caucus for Art (bd. dirs. 1974-78, Life Achievement award 1995), Tex. Inst. Letters. Democrat. Home: 2900 McFarlin Blvd Dallas TX 75205-1920 Office: So Meth U Art History Divsn Dallas TX 75275

COMISKEY, MICHAEL PETER, lawyer; b. Oak Park, Ill., Oct. 13, 1948; s. John B. and Jeanne M. (Platt) C.; m. Barbara A. Twardowski, Apr. 24, 1981; children: Julianne, Bridget, Eleanor, Michael Patrick. BA, U. Notre Dame, 1970; JD, Harvard U., 1975. Bar: Ill. 1975, U.S. Dist. Ct. (no. dist.) Ill. 1975. Ptnr. Lord, Bissell & Brook, Chgo., 1983—. Office: Lord Bissell & Brook 115 S La Salle St Ste 3200 Chicago IL 60603-3972*

COMISKEY, NANCY, newspaper editor. Mng. editor features The Indpls. News; dep. mng. editor features and readership The Star & The News, Indpls., 1998—. Office: The Indpls News PO Box 145 Indianapolis IN 46206-0145

COMISKY, HOPE A., lawyer; b. Phila., Apr. 23, 1953; married; three children. BA with distinction, Cornell U., 1974; JD, U. Pa., 1977. Bar: Pa. 1977, U.S. Dist. Ct. (ea. dist.) Pa. 1978, D.C. 1979, U.S. Ct. Appeals (3d cir.) 1979, U.S. Supreme Ct. 1987, U.S. Dist. Ct. (mid. dist.) Pa. 1991, N.Y. 1993. Law clerk ea dist. U.S. Dist. Ct., Pa., 1977-78; assoc. Dilworth, Paxson, Kalish & Kauffman, Phila., 1978-84, ptnr., 1985-91; ptnr. Anderson Kill & Olick, P.C., Phila., 1992-98; mng. ptnr. Phila. office Anderson Kill & Olick, P.C., 1995-98; ptnr. labor & employment dept. Office of Pepper Hamilton, 1998—; spkr. in field. Contbr. articles to profl. jours. Bd. dirs. Phila. Sch., 1989—; hon. bd. dirs. Fedn. Day Care Svcs., 1991-97, mem. exec. com., chmn. pers. practices com., 1985-91; bd. dirs. Ctr. for Literacy, 1996—, Women's Law Project, 1998—; mem. Phila. Regional Employment Adv. Com. Am. Arbitration Assn., 1996. Mem. Am. Arbitration Assn. (comml. and employment arbitrator), Phi Beta Kappa, Mortar Bd. Office: Pepper Hamilton LLP 3000 Two Logan Sq 18th & Arch Sts Philadelphia PA 19103-2799

COMISKY, IAN MICHAEL, lawyer; b. Phila., Feb. 5, 1950; s. Marvin and Goldye (Elving) C. BS magna cum laude, U. Pa., 1971, JD, 1974; LLM in Taxation, U. Miami, 1984. Bar: Pa. 1974, Fla. 1976, D.C. 1976, U.S. Ct. Appeals (3rd and 11th cirs.), U.S. Ct. Claims, U.S. Tax Ct., U.S. Supreme Ct., U.S. Dist. Ct. (ea. dist.) Pa., U.S. Dist. Ct. (so. dist.) Fla., U.S. Dist. Ct. (mid. dist.) Fla. Law clk. to Hon. Alfred Luongo Jr. U.S. Dist. Ct. Pa., Phila., 1974-75; asst. dist. atty. Office of Dist. Atty., Philadelphia County, Phila., 1975-78; asst. U.S. atty. So. Dist. Fla., 1978-80; spl. asst. Office of Dist. Atty., So. Dist. Fla., 1980; ptnr. tax dept. Blank Rome Comisky & McCauley, Phila., 1980—; presenter various profl. confs. seminars, 1981—; guest TV and radio programs, 1990. Co-author: Tax Fraud and Evasion (2 vols.); contbr. articles to profl. publs. Sec. Mann Music Ctr.; participant Fedn. Jewish Agys. Mem. ABA (past chmn. civil and criminal tax penalties com. tax sect., mem. CLE com. tax sect., cogs spl. projects, mem. various coms. criminal justice and litig. sect.), ATLA, Am. Law Inst., Am. Coll. Tax Counsel, Fed. Bar Assn., Pa. Bar Assn., Fla. Bar Assn. (bd. govs. 1998), D.C. Bar Assn., Phila. Bar Assn., Assn. Fellows and Legal Scholars or Ctr. for Internat. Legal Studies (hon.). Avocations: sailing, gardening, karate, jogging. Office: Blank Rome Comisky & McCauley 1200 N Fed Hwy Ste 309 Boca Raton FL 33432 also: 1200 N Federal Hwy Ste 309 Boca Raton FL 33432-2846

COMISKY, MARVIN, retired lawyer; b. Phila., June 5, 1918; m. Goldie Elving; children: Ian M., Hope A., Matthew J. B.S.C. summa cum laude, Temple U., 1938; LL.B., U. Pa., 1941; LL.D., Dickinson Sch. Law, 1970. Bar: Pa. 1942. Law clk. Pa. Superior Ct., 1941-42; law clk. to presiding justice Pa. Supreme Ct., 1946; assoc. Lemuel B. Schofield, Phila., 1946-54; ptnr. Brumbelow & Comisky, 1954-59; ptnr. Blank, Rome, Comisky & McCauley LLP, Phila., 1959-68, mng. ptnr., 1968-88; chmn. Blank, Rome, Comisky & McCauley, Phila., 1988-90, chmn. emeritus, 1991-99, ret., 1993; mem. Pa. Bd. Law Examiners, 1974-75; former dir. Midlantic Bank. Co-author: Judicial Selection, Compensation, Ethics and Discipline, 1986. Gen. counsel Pa. Constl. Conv., 1967. Fellow Am. Bar Found., Am. Coll. Trial Lawyers, Internat. Acad. Trial Lawyers; mem. ABA (del. 1965, 70), Phila. Bar Assn. (chancellor 1965), Pa. Bar Assn. (past pres.), Order of Coif, Beta Gamma Sigma. Office: Blank Rome Comisky & McCauley LLP One Logan Square Philadelphia PA 19103

COMISSIONA, SERGIU, conductor; b. Bucharest, Romania, June 16, 1928; came to U.S., 1969; naturalized, 1976; s. Isaac and Jean L. (Haufrecht) C.; m. Robinne Florin, July 16, 1949. Studied with Constantin Silvestri and Eduoard Lindenberg, 1928; ed. music conservatoire, Bucharest; Mus.D. (hon.), Peabody Conservatory Music, 1972; LHD (hon.), Loyola Coll., Balt., 1973, Towson State U., 1980; D.F.A. (hon.), Washington Coll., Chestertown, Md., 1980, Western Md. Coll., 1977, U. Md., 1981, Johns Hopkins U., 1982. Operatic conducting debut in Faust at Sibiu, 1945, conducting debut Bucharest Opera Orch., 1946; violinist Bucharest Radio Quartet, 1946, Rumanian State Ensemble Orch., 1947, asst. condr., 1948, music dir., 1950-55; prin. condr. Rumanian State Opera, 1955-59, Asian Youth Orch., 1995; founder, condr. Ramat Gan (Israel) Chamber Orch., 1960-67; music dir. Haifa (Israel) Symphony, 1960-66, Israel Chamber Orch., 1960-67, Goteburg (Sweden) Symphony Orch., 1966-67, Balt. Symphony Orch., 1969-84, condr. laureate, 1995—; music dir. Houston Symphony Orch., 1983-88, N.Y.C. Opera, 1987-89, Helsinki Philharm. Orch. (also chief condr.), 1990-93, Vancouver Symphony, 1990—, Orquesta Sinfonica de RTVE, Madrid, 1990-97, Asian Youth Orch., 1995—, Vancouver Symphony Orch., 1990—; Am. debut with Phil. Orch., 1965; mus. adviser, condr. No. Ireland Orch., 1967-68; artistic dir. Temple U. Music Festival, 1976-80, music advisor, prin. condr., 1977-80; music dir., prin. condr. Chautauqua Symphony Orch. Summer Festival, 1976-80; music adviser Am. Symphony Orch., 1978-82; artistic advisor Houston Symphony Orch., 1980-83; permanent guest condr. Radio Philharm. Orch. of Netherlands, 1982-83, chief condr., 1983-89; with London Symphony, Stockholm Philharm., Swedish Radio Orch.; founder Joseph Meyerhoff Hall, Balt. Decorated Order Merit 2d Class Rumania; winner internat. competition for young condrs. Besancon, France, 1954; recipient Gold medal award City of Goteborg, 1973, Ditson Condr.'s award Columbia U., 1979. Mem. Royal Swedish Acad. Music (hon.); Knight Order Arts Letters (France). Home: ICM Artists Classical Divsn 10 W 66th St Apt 20F New York NY 10023 Office: c/o Vancouver Symphony Orch, 601 Smithe St, Vancouver, BC Canada V6B 5G1*

COMITAS, LAMBROS, anthropologist; b. N.Y.C., Sept. 29, 1927; s. Dennis and Magdaline (Livanis) C.; m. Irene Mousouris. AB, Columbia U., 1948, PhD in Anthropology, 1962. Instr. anthropology Columbia U., N.Y.C., 1958-61, asst. prof., 1962-64, assoc. prof. anthropology and edn. Tchrs. Coll., 1965-67, prof., 1967-87, Gardner Cowles prof. anthropology and edn., 1988—, dir. div. philosophy, social scis. and edn., 1979-96, dir. Inst. Latin Am. and Iberian Studies, 1977-84; dir. Rsch. Inst. for Study of Man, 1985—; mem. drug abuse, clin., behavioral and psychosocial rsch. rev. com. Nat. Inst. Drug Abuse, 1977-81. Author books and articles in field. With U.S. Army, 1946-47. Office Edn. fellow, 1968-69, Guggenheim fellow, 1971-72; Fulbright grantee, 1957-58, Nat. Inst. Drug Abuse grantee, 1975-79. Mem. Soc. Applied Anthropology (pres. 1970-71), Am. Anthrop. Assn., Am. Ethnol. Soc., Nat. Acad. Edn. (chmn. com. anthropology and edn.), N.Y. Acad. Scis. Home: 1107 5th Ave New York NY 10128-0145 Office: Teachers Coll Columbia U New York NY 10027

COMIZIO-ASSANTE, DELVA MARIA, nurse, clinical nurse specialist; b. Yonkers, N.Y., Nov. 8, 1964; d. Vito Joseph and Delva Maria (Ciucci) Comizio; m. William J. Assante, Nov. 5, 1988. BSN, Coll. Mt. St. Vincent, Bronx, N.Y., 1986; postgrad., Pace U. RN, N.Y., Va. Staff nurse St. Joseph's Med. Ctr., Yonkers, N.Y., 1986-87, sr. nurse, 1987-89, nurse clinician, 1989-90; med.-surg., ambulatory surgery-recovery rm. nurse Community Hosp at Dobbs Ferry, N.Y., 1991—; mem. quality assurance coun. St. Joseph's Med. Ctr., Yonkers, 1989, chmn. nurse practice coun., 1987-90, mem. leadership coun., 1987-90, mem. exec. coun., 1987-90, mem. documentation com., 1989, mem. com. for the system of nursing care delivery, 1989. Mem. All County Head Nurse Assn., Am. Soc. Post-Anesthesia Nurses, N.Y. State Post-Anesthesia Nurses Assn., Sigma Theta Tau (chpt. treas. 1987-92, chpt. v.p. 1992-93). Republican. Roman Catholic. Avocations: Christian ministries, pro-life advocacy. Home: 137 Hosner Mt Rd Hopewell Junction NY 12533 Office: Community Hosp Dobbs Ferry 128 Ashford Ave Dobbs Ferry NY 10522-1924

COMMANDAY, PETER MARTIN, educator; b. N.Y.C., Oct. 4, 1932; s. Joseph and Dorothy (Kaplan) C.; m. Susan Nancy Shair, Apr. 28, 1962; children: Lisa, Clifford. BS in Graphic Arts, Rochester Inst. Tech., 1959; MS in Adminstrv./Supr. Edn., Manhattan Coll., Riverdale, N.Y., 1967. Cert. peacemaking instr.; cert. crisis intervenor; cert. peace officer. Dean, tchr. N.Y.C. Bd. Edn., South Bronx, N.Y., 1964-79; coord. profl. tng. divsn. sch. safety N.Y.C. Bd. Edn., 1979-91; peacemaker, educator, dir. Commanday Peacemaking Inst. Corp., Congers, N.Y., 1991—; cons. crisis intervention, resolution, prevention. Author: Peacemaking: The Management of Confrontation, 1979, Crisis Without Violence, 1980; appeared on Today Show, Geraldo Rivera Show, Phil Donahue Show, 20-20 Show, UN Radio. Trustee Solomon Schechter Sch., Rockland County, N.Y., 1972-84. With USAF, 1952-56. Recipient PONY award Fed. Govt., 1967. Home and Office: Commanday Peacemaking Inst 7 Greenfield Ter Congers NY 10920-2606

COMMANDAY, SUE NANCY SHAIR, English language educator; b. N.Y.C., Oct. 9, 1938; d. Leonard Allan and Sally (Bernstein) Shair; m. Peter Martin Commanday, Apr. 28, 1962; children: Lisa Robin Commanday Durow, Clifford Martin Commanday. BA cum laude, Syracuse U., 1959; MA with honors, Columbia U., N.Y.C., 1960; PhD with honors, NYU, N.Y.C., 1973. Adj. instr. English Rockland C.C., Suffern, N.Y., 1968-75, asst. coord., then coord. Israel and Judaic studies, 1975-93, coord. telecourses and distance learning, 1978-94, prof. English, 1994—; sec., mem. exec. com. faculty coun. SUNY, 1993-94; mem. bd. trustees Consortium Distance Learning, N.Y.-N.J., 1990-94; cons. development of distance learning programs for various ednl. instns., 1980s—; mem. planning and evaluation coms. Annenberg-funded telecourses; presenter profl. confs. Contbr. articles on Henry James, English composition, internat. edn., telecourse and distance learning to profl. jours. Founding mem., sec. Solomon Schechter PTA, 1970-75; mem. exec. com. Jewish Family Svc., 1993-95; trustee Jewish Fedn. Rockland County, 1985-95, mem. exec. com., chairperson long-term planning, 1994-95; mem. women's commn. Rockland County Legislature, 1987—, editor newsletter, editor com. reports, 1988—; mem. area Dem. com., N.Y.C., 1994—; coord. (with others) Gov. Mario Cuomo campaign in Rockland County, 1994; campaign writer N.Y. State Assemblyman Sam Colman, 1994, local legislator Harriet Cornell, Clarkstown, 1991-94; pub. rels. dir., writer for campaign of Bob Axelrod, Rockland County Legislature, 1997. Recipient SUNY Chancellor's award for Profl. Svc., 1991, Svc. to Students with Disabilities award, 1997; award for tchg. Nat. Inst. Staff and Orgnl. Devel., 1999. Mem. Delta Tau Kappa, Kappa Delta Pi, Pi Lambda Theta, Rho Delta Pi, Phi Kappa Phi, Eta Pi Upsilon. Avocations: knitting, crocheting, bead work, gardening. Office: Rockland Cmty Coll 145 College Rd Suffern NY 10901-3611

COMMANDER, CHARLES EDWARD, lawyer, real estate consultant; b. Jacksonville, Fla., Aug. 17, 1940; s. Charles Edward Jr. and Eleanor (Wood) C.; m. Victoria Coxe, Aug. 10, 1963; children: Eleanor, Charles IV, Christopher. BS in Commerce, Washington & Lee U., 1962; JD, U. Fla., 1965. Bar: Fla. 1966. Atty., assoc. ptnr. Mahoney, Hadlow, Chambers and Adams, Jacksonville, 1966-73; pres. Barnett Winston Properties, Jacksonville, 1973-74; founding ptnr. Commander, Legler, Werber, Dawes, Sadler & Howell, Jacksonville, 1974-91; ptnr., mgmt. com. Foley & Lardner, Jacksonville, 1991—; cons. First Union Nat. Bank Fla., Jacksonville, 1990-95; chmn. bd. dirs. First Nat. Bank, Jacksonville, 1979-84; chmn. Property Investment Svcs., Inc., Jacksonville, 1974—; bd. advisors Alliance Mortgage Co.; trustee Builders Investment Group, King of Prussia, Pa. and Fullerton, Calif., 1977-80; dir. Koger Equity Inc., 1993-95, Computer Power, 1974-79, 86-92, First Alliance Bank, 1998—. Editor Law Review U. Fla., 1964-65; reporter Fla. Law Revision Coun., 1975-76. Trustee The Bolles Sch., Jacksonville, 1980-90; pres. U. No. Fla. Found., 1994-97, Cummer Gallery of Art, 1993—; bd. dirs. Jacksonville Housing Authority, 1995—; vice chmn. Mus. Sci. and History, Jacksonville, 1968-73, Jacksonville Zool. Soc., 1972-76; bd. dirs. The River Club, Jacksonville, 1977-84, also pres. Episcopalian. Avocations: fishing, hunting, boating, farming. Office: Foley & Lardner The Greenleaf Bldg PO Box 240 Jacksonville FL 32201-0240

COMMANDER, EUGENE R., lawyer; b. Sioux City, Iowa, Jan. 10, 1953. BA in Architecture, Iowa State U., 1975; JD with distinction, U. Iowa, 1977. Bar: Iowa 1977, Colo. 1981. Mem. Hall & Evans, LLC, Denver, 1981—. Mem. ABA (forum com. on constrn. industry, subcoms. on bonds, liens, ins. and contract documents, tort and ins. practice sect. coms. on fidelity, surety law, property ins.), AIA (profl. affiliate, Colo. chpt.), Am. Arbitration Assn. (panel constrn. industry arbitrators 1983—), Am. Law Firm Assn. (constrn. industry practice group), Def. Rsch. Inst. (constrn. law and fidelity and surety law coms.), Profl. Liability Underwriting Soc. Office: Hall & Evans LLC 1200 17th St Ste 1700 Denver CO 80202-5817

COMMINS, ERNEST ALTMAN (ERNIE COMMINS), certified financial planner; b. Charleston, S.C., Feb. 13, 1946; s. John Commins and Marie Edna (Crosby) Jenkins; m. Nancy Palmer Redd, May 11, 1968; children: Scott Palmer, Ashley Redd. BS in Indsl. Mgmt., Clemson U., 1968; MBA, Wichita State U., 1972. Cert. fin. planner, Colo.; registered stock broker. Broker Mick, Stack & Smartt Investors, Wichita, Kans., 1971-72; div. mgr. Ortho Pharm. Corp., Raritan, N.J., 1972-82; dist. mgr., fin. planner IDS/Am. Express, Mpls., 1982-87; fin. planner Ctr. for Fin. Planning, Inc., Pensacola, Fla., 1987-88; registered investment advisor Money Profls. Group, Inc., Pensacola, 1988—; instr. Pensacola Jr. Coll., 1988, Okaloosa-Walton Jr. Coll., 1989, Clemson U., 1992; bd. dirs. Cordova Sq. Owners Assn., Pensacola. Coach YMCA, Pensacola, 1984-87, Youth Basketball League, Pensacola, 1987—, Men's Softball League, Pensacola, 1983—; vice chmn. sch. adv. coun. Washington H.S., Escambia County Sch. Dist., 1992-93; bd. dirs. Child Discovery Ctr., 1992—; elder and trustee First Presbyn. Ch., 1992. Capt. USAF, 1968-72. Mem. Nat. Soc. Fund Raising Execs., Internat. Bd. Cert. Fin. Planners, Registry Cert. Fin. Planning Lic. Practitioners, N.W. Fla. Planned Giving Coun. (charter), Gulf Coast Econ. Club. Republican. Presbyterian. Avocations: water sports, basketball, softball. Office: 4400 Bayou Blvd Ste 54C Pensacola FL 32503-1909

COMMIRE, ANNE, playwright, writer, editor; b. Wyandotte, Mich.; d. Robert and Shirley (Moore) C. BS, Eastern Mich. U., 1961; postgrad., Wayne State U., NYU. Author: (plays) Shay, 1973, Put Them All Together, 1978, Transatlantic Bridge, 1977, Sunday's Red, 1982, Melody Sisters, 1983, Starting Monday, 1988, (book) (with Mariette Hartley) Breaking the Silence, 1990; editor: Something About the Author, 1970-90, Yesterday's Authors of Books for Children, 1977-78, Historic World Leaders, 1994, Women in World History: An Encyclopedia, 1999. Recipient Eugene O'Neill Theatre award, 1973, 78, 83, 88; Creative Artists Program grantee, 1975; Rockefeller grantee for playwriting, 1979. Mem. PEN, Authors Guild, Dramatists Guild, Writers Guild Am. Home: 11 Stanton St Waterford CT 06385-1400

COMMONER, BARRY, biologist, educator; b. Bklyn., May 28, 1917; s. Isidore and Goldie (Yarmolinsky) C.; m. Lisa Feiner, 1980; children by previous marriage: Lucy Alison, Frederic Gordon. AB with honors, Columbia U., 1937; MA, Harvard U., 1938, PhD, 1941; DSc (hon.), Hahnemann Med. Coll., 1963; D.Sc. (hon.), Clark U., 1967, Grinnell Coll., 1968, Lehigh U., 1969, Williams Coll., 1970, Ripon Coll., 1971, Colgate U., 1972, Cleve. State U., 1980; LL.D. (hon.), U. Calif., 1974, Grinnell Coll., 1981; D.Sc. (hon.), St. Lawrence U., 1988; D.H.L. (hon.), Lowell U., 1990; DSc (hon.), Conn. Coll., 1992. Asst. biology Harvard, 1938-40; instr. biology Queens Coll., 1940-42; asso. editor Sci. Illus., 1946-47; asso. prof. plant physiology Washington U., St. Louis, 1947-53; prof. Washington U., 1953-76, chmn. dept. botany, 1965-69; dir. Washington U. (Center for the Biology of Natural Systems), 1965-81, Univ. prof. environ. sci., 1976-81; prof. dept. geology Queens Coll., Flushing, N.Y., 1981-87, prof. emeritus, 1987—, dir. Center for the Biology of Natural Systems, 1981—; vis. prof. cmty. health Albert Einstein Coll. of Medicine, N.Y.C., 1981-87; disting. univ. prof. indsl. policy U. Mass., Lowell, 1992-95; pres. St. Louis Com. for Nuclear Info., 1965-66, bd. dirs., 1966; mem. Nat. Tb Commn. on Air Conservation, 1966-68; bd. dirs. Scientists Inst. Pub. Info., 1963—, co-chmn., 1967-69, chmn., 1969-78, chmn. exec. com., 1978—; chmn. spl. cons. group sonic boom Dept. Interior, 1967-68; mem. adv. coun. on environ. edn. Office Edn., HEW, 1971; mem. internat. sponsoring com. Chaim Weizmann Centenary Celebration, 1974-75; mem. adv. com. Coalition Health Communities, 1975; mem. sec.'s adv. coun. Dept. Commerce, 1976; mem. sci. adv. coun. on dioxin Vietnam Vets. Am. Found., 1985—; mem. sci. adv. N.Y. State Com. on Sci. and Tech., 1981—; mem. adv. bd. Com. for Responsible Genetics, 1983—. Author: Science and Survival, 1966, The Closing Circle, 1971 (Phi Beta Kappa award), (Internat. prize City of Cervia, Italy), La Technologia del Profitto, 1973, The Poverty of Power, 1976 (Premio Iglesias award, Sardinia, Italy 1978), Ecologia e Lotte Sociali, 1976, l'energia alternativa, 1978, The Politics of Energy, 1979 (Premio Iglesias award 1982), Se Scoppia La Bomba, 1984, Il Cerchio Da Chiudere, 1986, Making Peace With the Planet, 1990; editorial bd. World Book Ency., 1968-73, Environment mag., 1977; mem. adv. bd. Science Year, 1967-72; editorial adv. bd. Hon. Chemosphere, from 1972; bd. sponsors In These Times, 1976—. Bd. cons. experts Rachel Carson Trust for Living Environment, 1967—; adv. com. Center for Devel. Policy, 1978; mem. bd. Univs. Nat. Anti-War Fund; adv. bd. Fund for Peace, 1978, Citizens Party candidate for pres. of U.S., 1980. Served to lt. USNR, 1942-46. Recipient Newcomb Cleveland prize AAAS, 1953; 1st Humanist award Internat. Humanist and Ethical Union, 1970; medal AIA, 1979; decorated comdr. Order of Merit Italy, 1977. Fellow AAAS (chmn. com. sci. in promotion of human welfare 1958-65, dir. 1967-74, chmn. com. on environ. alterations 1969-72), Am. Sch. Health Assn. (hon.); mem. Soc. Biol. Chemists, Soc. Gen. Physiologists, Am. Soc. Plant Physiologists, Sierra Club, Nat. Parks Assn. (trustee 1968-70), Soil Assn. Eng. (hon. life v.p.), Am. Chem. Soc., Am. Soc. Biol. Chemists, Fedn. Am. Scientists, Ecol. Soc. Am., Inst. Environmental Edn. (trustee), Phi Beta Kappa, Sigma Xi. Office: Queens Coll Ctr for Biol Natural Systems Flushing NY 11367

COMOSS, PATRICIA B., cardiac rehabilitation nurse, consultant; b. Shamokin, Pa., Apr. 20, 1947; d. William J. and Lucille M. (Shipulski) McCall; m. Eugene J. Comoss, Nov. 25, 1970. Diploma, St. Joseph's Hosp., Reading, Pa., 1968; BS in Health Care Mgmt., Pa. State U., Harrisburg, 1982. CCU staff nurse Polyclinic Med. Ctr., Harrisburg; head nurse, cardiac rehab. Rehab. Hosp., Mechanicsburg, Pa.; dir. edn. AMSCO/Rehab., Mechanicsburg; founder, pres. Nursing Enrichment Consultants, Harrisburg. Co-author: Cardiac Rehabilitation: A Comprehensive Nursing Approach, 1979; co-editor: Cardiac Rehabilitation: A Guide to Practice in the 21st Century, 1999; contbr. articles to profl. jours. Fellow Am. Assn. Cardiovascular and Pulmonary Rehab. (bd. dirs. 1986-88, v.p. 1988-90, pres.-elect 1990-91, pres. 1992, chair fed. project on clin. practice guidelines on cardiac rehab. 1992-95); mem. ANA, AACCN, Am. Coll. Sports Medicine, Am. Heart Assn. Home: 4100 Elmerton Ave Harrisburg PA 17109-1327

COMP, PHILIP CINNAMON, medical researcher; b. Kewanee, Ill., Feb. 28, 1945; s. Franklin Howard and Alberta (Cinnamon) C.; m. Carol Lee Winter, May 11, 1974; children: Vanessa Cinnamon, Justin Philip, Aubrie Elizabeth. BA, Reed Coll., 1967; MD, U. Wash., 1971; PhD, U. Okla., 1978. Intern, then resident U. Pa. Hosp., Phila., 1971-74; fellow allergy sect. U. Okla. Health Sci. Ctr., Oklahoma City, 1974-76, asst. prof. medicine, 1976-82, assoc. prof. medicine, 1982-88, prof. medicine, 1988—, dir. thrombosis/coagulant lab., 1979—, dir. Okla. Ctr. for Molecular Medicine, 1990—; attending physician Allergy Clinic State of Okla. Teaching Hosps., Oklahoma City, 1976-89; attending physician med. svc. VA Med. Ctr., Oklahoma City, 1976—, assoc. chief of staff rsch., 1992—; dir. Adult sect. Okla. Comprehensive Hemophilia Treatment Ctr., Oklahoma City, 1980—; mem. cardiovasc. biology rsch. program Okla. Med. Resident Found., Oklahoma City, 1988—. Avocations: amateur mycology, breadmaking. Office: Okla Univ Hosp EB 400 Oklahoma City OK 73126

COMPAGNON, ANTOINE MARCEL, French language educator; b. Brussels, July 20, 1950; came to U.S., 1985; s. Jean and Jacqueline (Terlinden) C. Ecole, Nat. des Ponts et Chaussees, Paris, 1975; D es Lettres, U. Paris VII, 1985. Rsch. attache Centre Nat. de la Recherche Scientifique, Paris, 1975-78; lectr. Ecole Poly., Paris, 1978-85, French Inst., London, 1980-81, U. Rouen, France, 1981-85; prof. Columbia U., N.Y.C., 1985—, Blanche W. Knopf prof., 1991—; vis. prof. U. Pa., Phila., 1986, 90; prof. U. Le Mans, France, 1989-90, U. Paris, Sorbonne, 1994—. Author: La Seconde Main, 1979, Ferragosto, 1985, Proust entre deux Siecles, 1989; editor: Marcel Proust, Sodome et Gomorrhe, 1988. Fellowship Found. Thiers, 1975-78, Guggenheim Found., 1988, All Souls Coll., Oxford U., 1994. Mem. Am. Acad. Arts and Scis. Office: Columbia U 517 Philosophy Hall New York NY 10027

COMPANS, RICHARD W., microbiology educator; b. Syracuse, N.Y., Sept. 15, 1940; m. Marian Merly Compans. BA magna cum laude, Kalamazoo Coll., 1963; PhD, Rockefeller U., 1968. Asst. prof. The Rockefeller U., 1969-73, assoc. prof., 1973-75; prof. dept. microbiology The U. Ala., Birmingham, 1975-92, prof. dept. biochemistry, 1985-92; prof., chmn. dept. microbiology and immunology Emory U., 1992—; guest investigator Inst. Cancer Rsch., Villejuif, France, 1968; hon. fellow John Curtin Sch. Med. Rsch., Canberra, Australia, 1968-69; vis. investigator Scripps Clinic and Rsch. Found., 1982; vis. prof. U. Geneva, 1988-89, U. Marburg, Germany, 1999; numerous univ. appointments including sr. scientist Cancer Ctr., U. Ala., 1975-92; dir. Electron Microscope Core Facility, 1975-92dir. Molecular Cell Biology Grad. Program, 1982-92, others; vis. scientist Nat. Inst. Med. Rsch., Mill Hill, U.K., 1998-99; mem. various virology task forces. Editor: Virus Research, 1983—; editorial bd.: Jour. Gen. Virology, 1972-77, Jour. Virology, 1974-82, 91-94, Intervirology, 1974-90, Virology, 1974-76, CRC Handbook Series in Clin. Lab. Sci., Archives of Virology, 1980-83, Jour. Biol. Chemistry, 1983-88, Current Topics Microbiology and Immunology, 1985—, Virology, 1992—; contbr. numerous articles to profl. jours. Recipient Wright A. Gardner award Ala. Acad. Scis., 1988, Alexander von Humboldt Rsch. award, 1999; grantee NIH, 1972—, others. Mem. Am. Acad. Microbiology, Am. Soc. Virology, Am. Soc. Biol. Chemists, Am. Soc. Cell Biology, Am. Assn. Immunologists, Soc. Gen. Microbiology, Am. Soc. Microbiology, Soc. Mucosal Immunology, Phi Beta Kappa. Office: Emory U Sch Med Dept Micro & Immunology Rm 3001 1510 Clifton Rd NE Atlanta GA 30322-4218

COMPO, LAWRENCE JUDD, sales and marketing executive; b. Freeport, N.Y., June 18, 1955; s. Lawrence Charles and Marilyn Anne (Volz) C.; m. Lorraine Mary Schwarz, Sept. 13, 1980; children: Caitlin Laura, Dylan Lawrence. BS, Ithaca (N.Y.) Coll., 1977; MBA, St. John's U., N.Y.C., 1980. Sales and mktg. analyst Merrill Lynch, Pierce Fenner & Smith, N.Y.C., 1977-81; sr. mktg. dir. Transamerica Relocation Svc., Greenwich, Conn., 1981-85; dir. bus. devel. Coldwell Banker Relocation Mgmt., Norwalk, Conn., 1985-87; v.p., regional mgr. Assocs. Relocation Mgmt. Co., Stamford, Conn., 1987-89; sr. v.p. Assocs. Relocation Mgmt. Co., Dallas, 1989-92; v.p. Coop. Resource Svcs., Ltd., Dallas, 1992—; sr. v.p. ProSource Properties, Ltd. subsidiary of CRS, Ltd., Dallas, 1995—. Mem. Am. Mgmt. Assn., Assn. for MBA Execs., Employee Relocation Coun. (cert. relocation profl., Meritorious Svc. award), Omicron Delta Epsilon. Home: 2904 Cottonwood

Ln Colleyville TX 76034-5124 Office: Coop Resource Svcs Inc PO Box 503 Colleyville TX 76034-0503

COMPONATION, PAUL JOSEPH, industrial and systems engineer, educator; b. Glendale, W.Va., June 9, 1959; s. Paul Joseph and Jean C.; m. Kimberly Marie LaPlante, Dec. 26, 1981; children: Justin, Seth, Ian. BS in industrial engr., W. Va. Univ., Morgantown, 1982; MS in mgmt., Troy State Univ., 1987; PhD in industrial engr., W. Va. Univ., 1995. Engring. officer U.S. Air Force, 1983-89; engr. Sonoco Products Co., Orlando, Fla., 1991-92; instr. W.Va. Univ., Morgantown, 1992-95; resident assoc. Ctr. for Entrepreneurial Studies & Devel., Morgantown, W.Va., 1995-96; asst. prof. indsl. engr. Univ. Ala., Huntsville, 1996—; dir. Internat. Coun. Systems Engrs. Contbr. articles to profl. jours. Capt. U.S. Air Force, 1983-89. Decorated Air Force Commendation Medal, 1985; named Outstanding Young Men of Am., 1987, 88. Mem. Inst. of Indsl. Engrs. (sr.), Internat. Coun. of Systems Engrs. Office: Univ Ala ISEEM Dept Th N134 Huntsville AL 35899

COMPTON, ALLEN T., state supreme court justice; b. Kansas City, Mo., Feb. 25, 1938; m. Sue Ellen Tatter; 3 children. B.A., U. Kans., 1960; LL.B., U. Colo., 1963. Pvt. practice Colorado Springs, 1963-68; staff atty. Legal Svcs. Office, Colorado Springs, 1968-69, dir., 1969-71; supervising atty. Alaska Legal Svcs., Juneau, Alaska, 1971-73; pvt. practice Juneau, 1973-76; judge Superior Ct., Alaska, 1976-80; justice Alaska Supreme Ct., Anchorage, 1980-98, chief justice, 1995-97, ret., 1998. Mem. 4 bar assns. including Juneau Bar Assn. (past pres.). Office: Alaska Supreme Ct 303 K St Anchorage AK 99501-2013

COMPTON, ANN WOODRUFF, news correspondent; b. Chgo., Jan. 19, 1947; d. Charles Edward and Barbara (Ortlund) C.; m. William Stevenson Hughes, Nov. 25, 1978; children: William Compton, Edward Opie, Ann Woodruff, Michael Stevenson. BA, Hollins (Va.) Coll., 1969. Reporter, anchorwoman WDBJ-TV (CBS), Roanoke, Va., 1969-70; polit. reporter, state capitol bur. chief WDBJ-TV (CBS), Richmond, Va., 1971-73; fellow Washington Journalism Center, 1970, trustee, 1978-93; corr. ABC News, N.Y.C., 1973-74; White House corr. ABC News, Washington, 1974-79, 81-84, 89—, congl. corr., 1979-81, 84-86, chief Ho. of Reps. corr., 1987-88. Trustee Hollins Coll., 1987-93; bd. dirs. Freedom Forum Ctr. for Media Studies, N.Y., 1984—. Named Mother of Yr., Nat. Mother's Day Com., 1987. Mem. White House Corrs. Assn. (dir. 1977-79), Radio-TV Corrs. Bd. (chmn. 1987). Office: ABC News Washington Bur 1717 DeSales St NW Washington DC 20036-4407*

COMPTON, ASBURY CHRISTIAN, state supreme court justice; b. Portsmouth, Va., Oct. 24, 1929. BA, Washington and Lee U., 1950, LLB, 1953, LLD, 1975. Bar: Va. 1957. Mem. firm May, Garrett, Miller, Newman & Compton, Richmond, 1957-66; judge Law and Equity Ct., City of Richmond, 1966-74; justice Supreme Ct. Va., Richmond, 1974—. Trustee Collegiate Schs., Richmond, 1972-89, chmn. bd., 1978-80; former chmn. adminstrv. bd. Ginter Park United Meth. Ch., Richmond; former mem. adminstrv. bd. Trinity United Meth. Ch., Richmond; trustee Washington and Lee U., 1978-90. With USN, 1953-56, USNR, 1956-62. Decorated Letter of Commendation. Mem. Va. Bar Assn., Va. State Bar, Bar Assn. City Richmond, Washington and Lee U. Alumni Assn. (past pres., dir.), Omicron Delta Kappa, Phi Kappa Sigma, Phi Alpha Delta. Club: Country of Va. Office: Va Supreme Ct 100 N 9th St Richmond VA 23219-2335

COMPTON, CHARLES DANIEL, chemistry educator; b. Elizabeth, N.J., Jan. 8, 1915; s. Charles Daniel and Janie (Little) C.; m. Ida Lightman, Dec. 19, 1953. AB cum laude, Princeton U., 1940; PhD in Chemistry, Yale U., 1943. Rsch. chemist Calco Chem. Co., 1943; instr. Princeton, 1944-46; rsch. assoc. Manhattan Dist. Project, Princeton, 1943-45; faculty Williams Coll., 1946—, prof., 1957—, chmn. chemistry dept., 1964-74, Halford R. Clark prof. natural sci., 1966-72, Ebenezer Fitch prof. chemistry, 1972-77, Ebenezer Fitch prof. chemistry emeritus, 1977—; lectr. chemistry New Coll., U. South Fla., 1979-81. Author: Introduction to Chemistry, Inside Chemistry; contbr. articles to profl. jours. Allied Chem. and Dye Co. fellow, Yale U., 1942-43. Fellow AAAS; mem. Am. Chem. Soc., Phi Beta Kappa, Sigma Xi. Home: 1050 Riverside Dr Apt A304 Palmetto FL 34221-5056

COMPTON, DALE LEONARD, retired space agency executive, consultant; b. Pasadena, Calif., June 18, 1935; s. John Leonard and Gladys Imnachuck (Foster) C.; m. Marilyn Doris Garland, June 21, 1959 (dec. Mar. 1997); children: David, Debora. BSME, Stanford U., 1957, MS in Aero. Engring., 1958, PhD, 1969; MMS in Mgmt. Sci., MIT, 1975. Rsch. scientist NASA-Ames Rsch. Ctr., Moffett Field, Calif., 1957-72, Tech. asst. to dir., 1972-73, dep. dir. astronautics, 1973-74, chief space sci. div., 1974-80, mgr. IRAS Project, 1980-81, dep. dir. astronautics, 1981-82, dir. engring. & computer systems, 1982-85, dep. dir., 1985-88, dir., 1988-94; Sloan fellow MIT, Cambridge, Mass., 1974-75. Recipient NASA's Outstanding Leadership and Disting. Svc. medals, SES Presdl. Ranks of Meritorious and Disting. Exec. Fellow AIAA (named Outstanding Engr./Astro. 1983-84), AAAS; mem. Internat. Acad. Astronautics, Tau Beta Pi, Sigma Xi. Avocations: woodworking, reading, sailing, bird watching. Home: 10131 Phar Lap Dr Cupertino CA 95014-1113

COMPTON, DAVID BRUCE, international management consultant; b. Dayton, Ohio, Sept. 27, 1952; s. Hall W. and Joan E. (Reinheimer) C.; m. Danielle M. Dufour, Apr. 19, 1986; children: Kyle Hall, Benjamin David, Zachary James. BS, No. Ariz. U., 1976; M in Internat. Mgmt., Am. Grad. Sch. Internat. Mgmt., 1977. Microsoft cert. profl.; Microsoft cert. solutions provider. Cons. Harris Graham and Ptnrs., London, 1978-81, Wyatt Co., Stamford, Conn., 1981-84; mgr. internat. benefits dept. Motorola, Inc., Chgo., 1984-86; dir. internat. benefits dept. Dart & Kraft, Chgo., 1986; dir. employee benefits dept. Premark Internat. subs. Dart & Kraft, Chgo., 1986-89, dir. internat. compensation and benefits dept., 1989—; pres., dir. HR Solutions, Inc., 1991—. Mem. Soc. Human Resource Mgmt., Assn. Human Resource Systems Profls. Avocations: guitars, cooking, Tai Chi, Aikido, computers. Home: 550 Carpenter Dr Palatine IL 60067-3706 Office: HR Solutions 616 N North Ct Ste 100 Palatine IL 60067-8199 *Personal philosophy: Always strive for improvement and maintain honesty and integrity in everything you do.*

COMPTON, HAZEL LOUISE, office administrator; b. Sept. 16, 1950. Grad., Ft. Gay (W.Va.) H.S., 1968. Accts. payable Family Urgent Care Ctr., Huntington, W.Va., 1986-88; fin. and ins. mgr. Ron Perry Auto Mall, Louisa, Ky., 1988-90; asst. to comptr. Coggin Motor Mall, Ft. Pierce, Fla., 1990-98; office mgr. Ron Perry Auto Mall, 1998—. Home: Rte 6 Box 905 Louisa KY 41230-0684

COMPTON, JOHN JOSEPH, philosophy educator; b. Chgo., May 17, 1928; s. Arthur Holly and Betty Charity (McCloskey) C.; m. Marjorie Ann Yaple, July 8, 1950; children: Elizabeth Holly, Catherine Marchus, John Arthur. BA, Coll. of Wooster, 1949; MA, Yale U., 1951, PhD, 1953. Asst. prof. philosophy Vanderbilt U., Nashville, 1952-55, assoc. prof., 1955-68, prof., 1968-98, prof. emeritus, 1998—, chmn. or acting chmn. dept., 1966-73, 84-85, 88-89, 93-95; vis. prof. Colo. Coll., Colorado Springs, 1977, Wesleyan U., Middletown, Conn., 1984. Contbr. articles to profl. jours. and chpts. in books. Mem. bd. advisers Matchette Found., 1968—; trustee Coll. of Wooster, Ohio, 1975—. Recipient Harbison award for disting. teaching Danforth Found., 1966; fellow Belgian-Am. Edn. Found., 1956-57, sr. fellow NEH, 1974-75, fellow Ctr. for Humanities, Wesleyan U., 1974-75. Mem. AAAS, AAUP, Am. Philos. Assn. (sec. ea. div. 1970-73, v.p. 1974), Metaphys. Soc. Am. (pres. 1979), Soc. for Phenomenology and Existential Philosophy, So. Soc. for Philosophy and Psychology, Philosophy of Sci. Assn., Soc. for Values in Higher Edn. (Kent fellow 1951), Phi Beta Kappa. Democrat. Avocations: hiking, camping, gardening, choral singing, cooking. Home: 3708 Whitland Ave Nashville TN 37205-2430 Office: Vanderbilt U Dept Philosophy Nashville TN 37235

COMPTON, JOHN ROBINSON, rake company executive; b. Elmira, N.Y., Feb. 24, 1923; s. William Randall and Ada (Viele) C.; m. Jean Elinor York, Apr. 17, 1943; children—John York, Jan Elizabeth (Mrs. Harriss M. Ganey), Julie Ann Compton Cook. B.S. cum laude, Syracuse U., 1950. Acct., factory mgr. York Modern Corp., Unadilla, N.Y., 1947-51, pres., 1969-95; CEO, treas. bd. dirs., acct. Brewer-Titchener Corp., Binghamton, N.Y., 1951-52, chmn., 1996—; divsn. contr. Riegel Paper Corp., Riegelwood, N.C., 1953-65, corp. contr., 1966-69; pres. Mail-Print, Inc., 1970—; CEO York Modern Corp., Unadilla, N.Y., 1995—. Served to 2d lt. USAAF, World War II. Methodist. Home: 1681 County Road 39 Bainbridge NY 13733-4211 Office: York Modern Corp PO Box 488 Unadilla NY 13849

COMPTON, NORMA HAYNES, retired university dean, artist; b. Washington, Nov. 16, 1924; d. Thomas N. and Lillian (Laffin) Haynes; m. William Randall Compton, Mar. 27, 1946; children: William Randall, Anne Elizabeth. AB, George Washington U., 1950; MS, U. Md., 1957, PhD, 1962; D of Letters, Purdue U., 1996. Rschr. Julius Garfinckel & Co., Washington, 1955; tchr. Montgomery Blair High Sch., Silver Spring, Md., 1955-57; instr. U. Md., 1957-60, teaching and rsch. fellow Inst. Child Study, 1960-61, assoc. prof., 1962-63; psychology extern St. Elizabeths Hosp., Washington, 1962-63; assoc. prof. Utah State U., 1963-64, prof., 1964-68, head dept. clothing and textiles, 1963-68, dir. Inst. for Rsch. on Man and His Personal Environment, 1967-68; dean Sch. Home Econs. Auburn (Ala.) U., 1968-73; dean Sch. Consumer and Family Scis. Purdue U., 1973-87, prof. family studies, 1987-90; faculty The Edn. Ctr., Longboat Key, Fla., 1991—, mem. edn. adv. bd., 1995-98; cons. Burgess Pub. Co., Mpls., 1975-81, Nat. Advt. Rev. Bd., N.Y.C., 1978-82; bd. dirs. Armour & Co., Phoenix, 1976-82, Home Hosp., Lafayette, Ind., 1983-89; adv. com. Women's Resource Ctr. of Sarasota, Fla., 1992-96; chair Adv. Commn. Status Women, Sarasota, 1993-96; mem. advocates coun. Family Law Network Sarasota, 1994—; exec. bd. Sarasota-Manatee Phi Beta Kappa Assn., 1996—. Author: (with Olive Hall) Foundations of Home Economics Research, 1972, (with John Touliatos) Approaches to Child Study, 1983, Research Methods in Human Ecology/ Home Economics, 1988; contbr. articles to profl. jours. Recipient Woman of Impact Lifetime Achievement award, 1997. Mem. APA, AAUW, PEO, Am. Assn. Family and Consumer Sci., Nat. League Am. Pen women, Fine Arts Soc. of Sarasota, Phi Beta Kappa, Sigma Xi, Phi Kappa Phi, Omicron Nu, Psi Chi. Episcopalian.

COMPTON, OLIN RANDALL, consulting electrical engineer, researcher; b. Parsons, W.Va., Apr. 12, 1925; s. Troy William and Strauda Belle (Robinson) C.; m. Patricia Ruth Osborne, June 3, 1947; children: Patricia Randall, Olin Bryan, Lisa Adrienne, Barry Christopher. BSEE, W.Va. U., 1949; Cert., Advanced Sch. Electric Utility Engring., Pitts., 1961. Registered profl. engr., Va. Jr. engr. Va. Electric & Power Co., Richmond, 1949-56, asst. supt elec. equipment, 1956-59, supt. elect. equipment, 1959-64, asst. substa. engr., 1965-79, elec. systems coord., 1979-83, corp. engring. advisor, 1983-85, prin. engr., 1985-91; pvt. practice cons., elec. rsch. Richmond, 1991—; chmn. C76 Am. Nat. Standards Inst., Washington, 1968-72, C29, 1983-86; U.S. expert on transformers Internat. Electrochem. Commn., Geneva, Switzerland, 1982-86, on insulators, 1986-89. Contbr. 60 articles to profl. jours. Dir. Ctrl. Va. Ednl. TV Group, Richmond, 1972-79; commr. Tuckahoe Little League, Richmond, 1972-80; dir. United Meth. Lay Tng. Sch., Richmond, 1973-79; Native Am. Ministries coord., Va. Conf. United Meth. Ch., 1995—; chmn. State Spl. Edn. Adv. Com., Richmond, 1976-79; constrn. chmn., 1995-97, bd. mem. Richmond Metro Mabitat for Humanity, Inc., 1995—. 2d lt. USAAF, 1943-47. Fellow IEEE (chmn. substa. com. 1976-78, chmn. transformer com. 1985-88, Disting Svc. awards, best paper prizes 1948, 89). Republican. Avocation: Bible study. Home and Office: 8423 Kalb Rd Richmond VA 23229-4133*

COMPTON, RALPH THEODORE, JR., electrical engineering educator; b. St. Louis, July 26, 1935; s. Ralph Theodore and Ethel (Evans) C.; m. Lorraine Fielding, Nov. 9, 1957; children: Diane Marie, Ralph Theodore III, Richard Thomas. S.B., MIT, 1958; M.Sc., Ohio State U., 1961, Ph.D., 1964. Jr. engr. DECO Electronics, Leesburg, Va., 1958-59; sr. engr. Battelle Meml. Inst., Columbus, Ohio, 1959-62; asst. supr. Antenna Lab., Columbus, 1962-65; asst. prof. Case Inst. Tech., Cleve., 1965-67; fellow, guest prof. Tech. Hochschule, Munich, W. Ger., 1967-68; assoc. prof. Ohio State U., Columbus, 1968-78, prof. elec. engring., 1978-91; pres. Compton Rsch., Inc., Columbus, 1992—; cons. to various orgns., U.S., Europe, Israel, 1969—. Author: Adaptive Antennas-Concepts and Performance, 1988; contbr. chpts. to books, articles to profl. jours. Fellow Battelle Meml. Inst., 1961; NSF fellow, 1967; recipient Outstanding Paper awards Ohio State Electro-Sci. Lab., 1978, 80, 82, M. Barry Carlton award IEEE Aerospace and Electric Systems Soc., 1983, Sr. Research award Ohio State U. Engring. Coll., 1983. Fellow IEEE (assoc. editor Jour. Trans. on Antennas Propagation 1970); mem. Antenna and Propagation Soc. (chmn. Columbus chpt. 1971-72), Sigma Xi (sec.-treas. Case Inst. Tech. chpt. 1965-67), Pi Mu Epsilon. Home and Office: 477 Poe Ave Worthington OH 43085-3036

COMPTON, ROBERT H., lawyer. Adminstrv. v.p., gen. counsel Ashland (Ky.) Petroleum Co., until 1988; adminstrv. v.p. Ashland Oil, Inc., Russell, Ky., 1988-92; bus. cons., atty pvt. practice, Ashland, 1992—; chmn. West Penn/W.Va. AAA, 1999—; magistrate Juvenile Ct., Lawrence County, Ohio. Office: HO-7th Fl 1401 Winchester Ave Ashland KY 41101-7555

COMPTON, W. DALE, physicist; b. Chrisman, Ill., Jan. 7, 1929; s. Roy L. and Marcia (Wood) D.; m. Jeanne C. Parker, Oct. 14, 1951; children: Gayle Corinne, Donald Leonard, Duane Arthur. B.A., Wabash Coll., 1949; M.S., U. Okla., 1951; Ph.D., U. Ill., 1955; D.Eng. (hon.), Mich. Technol. U., 1976. Physicist U.S. Naval Ordnance Test Sta., China Lake, Calif., 1951-52, U.S. Naval Research Lab., Washington, 1955-61; prof. physics U. Ill. at Urbana, 1961-70, dir. coordinated sci. lab., 1965-70; dir. chem. and phys. scis., exec. dir. sci. research staff, v.p. research Ford Motor Co., Dearborn, Mich., 1970-86; sr. fellow Nat. Acad. Engring., 1986-88; disting. prof. indsl. engring. Purdue U., West Lafayette, Ind., 1988—, interim head sch. indsl. engring., 1998—; mem. Presdl. Commn. for Award of Medal of Sci., 1978-80; mem. vis. com. Nat. Bur. Stds., 1975-79, chmn. vis. com., 1979; mem. coun. Nat. Acad. Engrs., 1990-96; bd. govs. NRC, 1991-95, mem. com. engring. and tech. sys., 1996-97, chmn., 1997—; bd. dirs. Advanced Refractory Techs., Inc. Author: (with J.H. Schulman) Color Centers in Solids, 1962; editor: Interaction of Science and Technology, 1969, Design and Analysis of Integrated Manufacturing Systems, 1988; co-editor (with J. Heim): Manufacturing Systems, Foundations of World Class Practice, 1992, Engineering Management: Creating and Managing World Class Operations, 1997. Bd. dirs. Mich. Cancer Found., 1975-86, Coordinating Rsch. Coun., 1983-85; adv. com. Combustion Rsch. Facility, Sandia Nat. Lab., 1983-86; mem. energy rsch. adv. bd. Dept. Energy, 1979-80; bd. govs. Argonne Nat. Lab., 1983-86. Fellow AAAS, Am. Phys. Soc., Soc. Automotive Engrs., Engring. Soc. Detroit, IC2 Inst. U. Tex.; mem. Rsch. Soc. Am.

COMRIE, KEITH BRIAN, city administrative officer; b. Schenectady, N.Y., Oct. 3, 1939; s. Arthur James and Therese (Johnson) C.; married; children: Shannon, Colleen. BBA, U. So. Calif., 1963, M of Pub. Adminstrn. in Local Govt., 1966. Adminstrv. analyst city adminstrv. office City of Los Angeles, 1963-69, city adminstrv. officer, 1979—; prin. adminstrv. analyst chief adminstrv. office County of Los Angeles, 1969-71, bur. dir. dept. pub. social services, 1971-73, asst. dir. dept. pub. social services, 1973-76, dir. dept. pub. social services, 1976-79; now city adminstrv. officer City of L.A. Mem. Los Angeles 2000 Com., 1986-89; mem. bd. councillors U. So. Calif. Sch. Pub. Adminstrn., Los Angeles, 1984—; bd. dirs. United Way, Los Angeles, 1985—. Fellow Nat. Acad. Pub. Adminstrn., 1986; recipient Bowron award U. So. Calif., 1986, All Pro Mgmt. Team award City and State mag., 1987, Alumni award of merit U. So. Calif., 1989. Mem. Internat. City Mgmt. Assn., Am. Mgmt. Assn., Am. Soc. Pub. Adminstrn. (Dykstra award 1986), Los Angeles C. of C. (centennial com. 1986-87), Govt. Fin. Officers Assn. Avocations: automobiles, architecture. Office: City of Los Angeles Room 300 City Hall E 200 N Main St Los Angeles CA 90012-4110

COMRIE, SANDRA MELTON, human resource executive; b. Plant City, Fla., Sept. 15, 1940; d. Finis and Estelle (Black) Melton; m. Allan Crecelius; children: Shannon Melissa, Colleen Megan. BA, UCLA, 1962, grad. exec. program, 1984. Div. mgr. City of L.A., 1973-77, asst. pers. dir., 1977-84; v.p. Transam. Life Cos., L.A., 1984-89; chief operating officer Treacy & Rhodes Consultants, Solana Beach, Calif., 1989-92; exec. dir. Reward Strategy Group, Inc., Del Mar, Calif., 1992—; bd. dirs. Found. for Employment and Disability, Sacramento, Clif.; mem. Asian Pacific Employment Task Force, Los Angeles, 1986-89. Bd. dirs. L.A. Urban League, 1985-92, Vols. of Am.-L.A., 1985-89; active United Way Downtown Bus. Consortium, Child Care Task Force, L.A., 1985-86; mem. adv. bd. L.A. City Child Care, 1987-89. Recipient Young Woman of Achievement award Soroptimists of Los Angeles, 1979. Mem. Internat. Pers. Mgmt. Assn. (mem. assessment coun., co-chair program com. for 1982 nat. conf., chair human rights com. 1983, pres. 1985), So. Calif. Pers. Mgmt. Assn., Planning Forum, Human Resource Planning Soc., Soc. for Human Resource Mgmt., Am. Compensation Assn., Am. Mgmt. Assn., L.A. C. of C. (human resources com. 1986-89). Democrat. Avocation: travel. Office: Reward Strategy Group Inc 2775 Via De La Valle Ste 200 Del Mar CA 92014-1920

COMSTOCK, DALE ROBERT, mathematics educator; b. Frederic, Wis., Jan. 18, 1934; s. Walter and Frances (Lindroth) C.; m. Mary Jo Lien, Aug. 18, 1956; children—Mitchell Scott, Bryan Paul. BA, Ctrl. Wash. State Coll., 1955; MS, Oreg. State U., 1962, PhD, 1966. Tchr. math. Kennewick (Wash.) High Sch., 1955-57, 59-60; instr. Columbia Basin Coll., Pasco, Wash., 1956-57, 59-60; programmer analyst Gen. Electric Co., Hanford Atomic Works, Richland, Wash., 1963; prof. math. Cen. Wash. U., Ellensburg, 1964—, dean Grad. Sch. and Research,, 1970-90; on leave as sr. program mgr. U.S. ERDA, also Presdl. interchange exec., 1976-77; mem. Pres.'s Commn. on Exec. Devel., 1976-77; bd. dirs. Council Grad. Schs. in U.S., 1981-84, dean in residence, 1984-85; cons. Indian program NSF, 1968, 69, USIA, India, 1985, NSF, Saudi Arabia, 1986; mem. grant proposal rev. panels NSF, 1970, 71, 76, 77, 89, 90; pres. Western Assn. Grad. Schs., 1979-80, sec.-treas. 1984-90; pres. N.W. Assn. Colls. and Univs. for Sci., 1988-89; Russian exch. prof., St. Petersburg, 1993; vis. prof. U. Wash., 1990-91. With U.S. Army, 1957-59. NSF fellow, 1960-61; grantee, summer 1964. Mem. Am. Math Soc., Math. Assn. Am., Assn. Computing Machinery (exec. com.), Soc. Indsl. and Applied Math., Northwest Coll. and Univ. Assn. for Sci. (pres. 1980-83). Methodist. Office: Cen Wash U Dept Math Ellensburg WA 98926

COMSTOCK, REBECCA ANN, lawyer; b. Mpls., Mar. 13, 1950; d. Clark Franklin and Ruth Carolyn (Sundt) C. Student, Conn. Coll., 1968-70; BA summa cum laude, U. Minn., 1973; JD Order of St. Ives, U. Denver, 1977. Bar: Minn. 1978, U.S. Dist. Ct. Minn. 1978, U.S. Ct. Appeals (8th cir.). Ptnr. Dorsey & Whitney, Mpls., 1982—. Bd. dirs. St. Paul Chamber Orch., 1996—. Mem. ABA, Minn. Bar Assn. (chmn. adminstrv. law sect. 1989-90, exec. coun. environ. and natural resources law sect. 1992-94), Hennepin County Bar Assn. (co-chmn. environ. com. 1998—), Legal Aid Soc. of Mpls. (bd. dirs. 1988-93), Minn. Women Lawyers (bd. dirs. 1979-81). Avocations: skiing, sailing, golf, music, theatre. Office: Dorsey & Whitney LLP 220 S 6th St Ste 2200 Minneapolis MN 55402-1498

COMSTOCK, ROBERT DONALD, JR., real estate executive; b. Miami, Fla., Sept. 28, 1921; s. Robert Donald Sr. and Gertrude (Quigg) C.; m. Mary Evans, Oct. 12, 1949; children: Carol Frances, Robert Donald III (dec.). BS in Commerce, U. Miss., 1943. Lic. real estate broker. Acct. New Orleans Pub. Service Co., 1946-47; salesman, br. mgr. Capitol Records, Inc., New Orleans and Charlotte, N.C., 1948-51; regional v.p. Atlanta, 1952-57; owner, pres. Comstock Distbg. Co., Atlanta, 1957-74, Comstock and Assocs., Atlanta, 1968-74, Cartridge Control Corp., Atlanta, 1968-80, Comstock Properties, Atlanta, 1980—; pres. Ctr. for Rehab. Tech., Ga. Tech. U., Atlanta, 1987-91, chmn. bd., 1991—. Mem. Atlanta Arts Alliance, 1970—, Atlanta Symphony, 1970—; bd. dirs. Christian Council Met. Atlanta, 1975-77; trustee So. Ctr. for Internat. Studies; mem. Atlanta Hist. Soc. Served as lt. USN, 1943-46, PTO. Named #1 Distbr. CBS Records, Columbia Broadcasting, N.Y.C., 1965, 69, Outstanding Distbr. Columbia Phonographs, Columbia Broadcasting, 1968, 70-72. Mem. Atlanta Bd. Realtors, Capital City Club, Commerce Club, Breakfast Club (pres. 1970-71), Trinity Presbyn. Ch. Men's Club (pres. 1977, Rotary (pres. Atlanta Midtown 1978-79), Omicron Delta Kappa. Avocations: golf, swimming, foreign affairs. Home: 3400 Ridgewood Rd NW Atlanta GA 30327-2418 Office: 1447 Peachtree St NE Ste 804 Atlanta GA 30309-3029

COMSTOCK, ROBERT RAY, journalism educator, newspaper editor; b. N.Y.C., Sept. 17, 1927; s. Kenneth Franklin and Phyllis Abigail (Taylor) C.; m. Barbara Sylvia Corner, June 30, 1956; children: Eric Taylor, Katherine Sylvia. Litt.B. in Journalism, Rutgers U., 1952. Reporter Ridgewood (N.J.) News, 1953; successively reporter, polit. writer, public affairs editor, asst. editor Hackensack (N.J.) Record, 1954-75, v.p., exec. editor, 1977-88; talk show moderator sta. WNET-13, Newark, 1970-71; instr. Seton Hall U., S. Orange, N.J., 1974-75; dir. public info. State of N.J., Trenton, 1975-77; mem. N.J. Public Broadcasting Authority, 1978-86, chmn., 1979-80; lectr. journalism, asst. dir. Journalism Resources Inst., Rutgers U., New Brunswick, N.J., 1988—; sr. cons. The Marcus Group, Secaucus, N.J., 1988—. Mem. N.J. Com. for Humanities, 1982-89, adv. com. on jud. conduct N.J. Supreme Ct., 1990-97; trustee Bergen Mus. Art and Sci., Paramus, N.J., 1990-94. With USNR, 1945-48. Mem. Am. Soc. Newspaper Editors, N.J. Legis. Corr. Club (pres. 1965-67), Soc. Profl. Journalists (pres. N.J. chpt. 1969-71). Home: 67 Park Gate Dr Edison NJ 08820-4032

COMSTOCK, WALTER, biologist, educator; b. Chgo., Sept. 29, 1946; s. George and Una (Feldman) C.; m. Mary Beth Lederer, Dec. 28, 1968; two children. BS, Coll. Emporia, 1970. Tchr. Kenton County Schs., Erlanger, Ky., 1970-71; tchr. biology Forest Hills Schs., Cin., 1971—. Co-editor: Biology: A Molecular Approach, 1989. Coach Acad. Quiz team, 1989—. Avocations: wood turning, wood sculpting. Home: 1144 Round Bottom Rd Milford OH 45150-9559

CONABOY, RICHARD PAUL, federal judge; b. Scranton, Pa., June 12, 1925; m. Marion Hartnett; children: Mary Ann, Richard, Judith, Conan, Michele, Kathryn, Patrick, William, Margaret, Janet, John, Nancy. BA, U. Scranton, 1945; LLB, Cath. U. Am., 1950. Bar: Pa. 1951. Ptnr. firm Powell & Conaboy, Scranton, 1951-54; dep. atty. gen., 1953-62; assoc. firm Kennedy O'Brien & O'Brien, 1954-62; judge Pa. Ct. Common Pleas, 1962-79, pres. judge, 1978-79; judge U.S. Dist. Ct. (mid. dist.) Pa., Scranton, 1980—, chief judge, 1989-93, now sr. judge; pres. Pa. Joint Council on Criminal Justice System, 1971-79; mem. Nat. Conf. Juvenile Justice, Nat. Conf. Corrections. Contbr. articles to legal jours. Bd. dirs. Marywood Coll., U. Scranton; apptd. chmn. U.S. States Sentencing Commn., 1994. Mem. Pa. Conf. State Trial Judges (pres. 1976-77, v.p. 1973-76, sec. 1968-73), ABA, Pa. Bar Assn., Am. Judicature Soc. Office: US Dist Courthouse & Post Office Bldg PO Box 189 Scranton PA 18501*

CONAN, ROBERT JAMES, JR., chemistry educator, consultant; b. Syracuse, N.Y., Oct. 30, 1924; s. Robert James and Helen M. (O'Brien) C. B.S., Syracuse U., 1945, M.S., 1947; Ph.D., Fordham U., 1950. Instr. Fordham U., N.Y.C., 1947-49; asst. prof. Le Moyne Coll., Syracuse, 1949-54, assoc. prof., 1954-58, prof. chemistry, 1958-89, prof. emeritus, 1990—; cons. Carrier Corp., Syracuse, 1949-63, Owl Wire and Cable Co., Oneida, N.Y., 1952-62, Edison Audio Archives, Syracuse, 1972-86; researcher U. Stockholm, Sweden, 1953, Swiss Fed. Inst. Tech., 1967, U. South Fla., 1988—; mem. com. Onondaga Lake Sci. Coun., Syracuse, 1964-65; vis. prof. U. South Fla., 1988—. Contbr. over 50 articles to profl. jours. Recipient Plaque award Le Moyne Coll., 1989. Mem. Am. Chem. Soc. (chmn. Syracuse sect. 1958, 72, nat. councillor 1982-85, Unique Plaque Svc. award 1989, Spl. 50 Yr. Pin, life mem.), Tech. Club Syracuse (pres. 1981-82, plaque award). Republican. Roman Catholic. Avocations: music, Irish genealogy. Home: 263 Robineau Rd Syracuse NY 13207-1643 also: 5406 Seminole Ave Tampa FL 33604-7048

CONANT, ALLAH B., JR., lawyer; b. Waco, Tex., July 24, 1939; s. Allah B. and Frances Louise (James) C.; m. Sheila Conant; children: Heather Lee Arsham, Lisa Lynn, Leslie Marie; stepchild, Thomas R. Bone II. B.A., N. Tex. State Coll., Denton, 1961; J.D. cum laude, Baylor U., 1963. Bar: Tex. 1963, U.S. Ct. Dist. (no. dist.) Tex. 1964, U.S. Dist. Ct. (so. dist.) Tex. 1969, U.S. Dist. Ct. (ea. dist.) Tex. 1986, U.S. Dist. Ct. (we. dist.) Tex. 1986, U.S. Ct. Appeals (5th cir.) 1970, U.S. Ct. Appeals (8th cir.) 1975, U.S. Ct. Appeals (4th and 7th cirs.)1978, U.S. Ct. Appeals (3d and 11th cirs.) 1981, U.S. Ct. Appeals (10th cir.) 1987, U.S. Tax Ct. 1963, U.S. Supreme Ct. 1971. Since practiced in Dallas; ptnr. Shank, Irwin, Conant, Lipshy & Casterline, 1964-90; of counsel Whittenburg Whittenburg and Schachter, 1990; mem. Conant Whittenburg French & Schachter, Dallas, 1991—; owner ABC Ranch, 1981-89. Contbr. to legal jours. Trustee St. John's Episcopal Sch., 1987-90. Fellow Am. Bar Found. (life), Tex. Bar Found. (life), Dallas Bar Found. (life); mem. ABA (coun. gen. practice sect. 1977-80, chmn. 1982-83, del. 1983-86), Dallas Bar Assn., State Bar Tex., Trial Attys. Am., Baylor

Law Sch. Counsellors, Baylor Law Alumni Assn. (dir. 1979-82), Baylor Law Rev. Ex-Editors Assn., N.Tex. State U. Alumni Assn. (dir., v.p.), Sigma Phi Epsilon, Omicron Delta Kappa, Phi Delta Phi (historian 1962). Clubs: Petroleum (Dallas). Avocations: swimming, reading, travel, boating. Home: 8247 Forest Hills Blvd Dallas TX 75218-4410

CONANT, HOWARD ROSSET, steel company executive; b. Chgo., Sept. 30, 1924; s. Louis J. and Fredericka (Rosset) Cohn; m. Doris S. Kaplan, Dec. 14, 1947; children: Alison Sue, Howard R., Meredith Ann. B.S., U. Pa., 1947. Pres., dir. Interstate Steel Co., Des Plaines, Ill., 1947-71; chmn. bd. Interstate Steel Co., 1971-90; pres., dir. Elliott Paint & Varnish Co., Chgo., 1961-76; bd. dirs. Interstate Steel Supply Co., Phila., Artra Group, Inc.; chmn. bd. dirs. White Products Corp., 1965-67. Discussion leader Center Study of Continuing Edn., 1955-62; dir. Com. for Sane Nuclear Policy, 1964-69; mem. Bus. Execs. Move for Vietnam Peace, 1965-73. Served with AUS, 1943-46, PTO. Mem. World Pres.' Orgn., Chgo. Pres.' Orgn. (dir.), Ridge and Valley Tennis Club, Carlton Club, East Bank Club. Home: 736 Greenacres Ln Glenview IL 60025-3204 Office: 445 N Wells St Ste 403 Chicago IL 60610-4534

CONANT, HOWARD SOMERS, artist, educator; b. Beloit, Wis., May 5, 1921; s. Rufus P. and Edith B. (Somers) C.; m. Florence C. Craft, June 18, 1943; children: Judith Lynne Steinbach, Jeffrey Scott. Student, Art Students League of N.Y., 1944-45; B.S., U. Wis.-Milw., 1946; M.S., U. Wis.-Madison, 1947; Ed.D., U. Buffalo, 1950. Instr. art, asst. head housefellow U. Wis., 1946-47; asst. prof. art SUNY, Buffalo, 1947-50, prof. art, 1950-55; chmn. dept. art and art edn. also chmn. art collection NYU, 1955-76; head dept. art U. Ariz., Tucson, 1976-86, prof. art, 1986-87; profl. artist, 1987—; art edn. cons. NBC-TV, also Girl Scouts Am. TV series, 1958-60; field reader, also Title III program cons. U.S. Office of Edn.; adviser N.Y. State Council on Arts, 1962-63, Conn. Commn. on Arts, 1967-68; cons. Ford Found., 1973, Children's Theatre Assn., 1973, Getty Trust, 1985; examiner Internat. Baccalaureate Orgn., 1998. Moderator: weekly TV program Fun to Learn About Art, WBEN-TV, Buffalo, 1951-55; numerous one man shows; represented maj. group exhbns. pub. art mus. and coll. art collections; represented by Sol Del Rio Gallery, San Antonio, Art Source Inc., Tulsa; executed mural Sperry High Sch., Henrietta, N.Y., 1971, Good Samaritan Med. Ctr., Phoenix, 1982, Valley Nat. Bank, Tucson, 1983; one-man retrospectives, Amarillo (Tex.) Art Mus., 1989, Sun City (Ariz.) Art Mus., 1996; author: (with Arne Randall) Art in Education, 1959, 63; author, editor: Art Workshop Leaders Planning Guide, 1958, Masterpieces of the Arts, New Wonder World Cultural Library, Vol. 4, 1963, Art Education, 1964, Seminar on Elementary and Secondary School Education in the Visual Arts, 1965, Lincoln Library of the Arts (2 vols.), 1973; art editor: Intellect, 1975-78, USA Today, 1978-85; assoc. editor Arts mag., 1973-75; contbr. articles profl. publs. Dept. State lectr., India, 1964; Dir. Waukesha County (Wis.) YMCA Art Program, 1946-48; pres., dir. Children's Creative Art Found., 1959-60; mem. adv. com. Coll. of Potomac, 1966; mem. cultural exchange mission to Mex., Ptnrs. of the Ams., 1988, 90; Lt. USAAF, 1943-46. Recipient 25th Ann. medal Nat. Gallery Art, 1966, Disting. Alumnus award U. Wis.-Milw., 1968, Purchase award Richard Florsheim Art Fund, 1992; Disting. fellow Nat. Art Edn. Assn., 1985, Nat. Endowment Arts sr. fellow in painting, 1985. Mem. Coll. Art Assn., Nat. Art Edn. Assn., Internat. Art Critics Assn., Alliance for Arts in Edn., Nat. Assn. Schs. Art and Design, AAUP, Nat. Com. Art Edn. (council, chmn. 1962-63), Inst. Study of Art in Edn. (bd. govs. 1965-72, pres. 1965-68). Club: Torch (N.Y.C.) (pres. 1965-66). Studio: 6954 E Cicada Ct Tucson AZ 85750 *I have learned to freely follow my interests from one area of concern or involvement to another without feeling guilty about "putting off until tomorrow what one can do today." I have learned to be an innovator and an enjoyer, rather than a solemn plodder. I have learned how to do three, four, even five things more or less at once, much like an organist handling contrapuntal melodies. As a result, I am a happy artist, author, lecturer and private human being whose multiple interests seem highly compatible and, indeed, essential to one another.*

CONANT, ROBERT SCOTT, harpsichordist, music educator; b. Passaic, N.J., Jan. 6, 1928; s. Frederick Banks and Bessie Trimble (Scott) C.; m. Nancy Lydia Jackson, Oct. 10, 1959; children: Elizabeth Scott, Andrew Frederick. BA, Yale U., 1949, MusM, 1956. Recorded with various labels including: RCA Victor, CBS, Decca, Musurgia, Kapp, Ex Libris, FBM, 1958—; asst. prof. music Yale U., New Haven, 1961-66; fellow Silliman Coll., 1961-66, assoc. fellow, 1967-71; assoc. prof. music history and harpsichord Roosevelt U., Chgo., 1967-71, prof. music history and harpsichord, 1971-86, prof. emeritus, 1986—; vis. artist Aspen Inst. Humanistic Studies, 1988-89, N.C. Sch. Arts, 1990. Concert harpsichordist N.Y. Town Hall recital debut, 1953, ann. tours as recitalist, chamber music player, U.S., Europe, Can., 1953—; appeared with Pitts., Chgo., and Denver Symphonies, soloist, Casals Festival, 1963, lectr. performer numerous colls., univs., mem. Viola da Gamba Trio of Basel, 1968-94, Robert Conant Baroque Trio, 1987—, Nova/Antiqua (new music trio) 1987—; author: (with others) Twentieth Century Harpsichord Music: A Classified Catalog, 1974; contbr. articles to profl. jours. Founder, pres. Found. for Baroque Music, Inc., Greenfield Center, N.Y., 1959—. Served with AUS, 1951-53. Recipient Lifetime Achievement award Saratoga County Arts Coun., 1992. Mem. Coll. Music Soc. (treas. 1971-74), Am. Musicol. Soc., Am. Mus. Instrument Soc. Democrat. Club: The Cliffdwellers (Chgo.). Avocations: photography, mountain climbing. Home and Office: Found for Baroque Music Inc 165 Wilton Rd Greenfield Center NY 12833-1704

CONANT, STEVEN GEORGE, psychiatrist; b. Elkhart, Ind., July 8, 1949; s. Hubert Eugene and Ruth (Weaver) C. BA in Zoology with distinction, DePauw U., 1971; MD, Ind. U., 1975. Diplomate Am. Bd. Psychiatry and Neurology. Intern Ind. U. Med. Ctr., Indpls., 1975-76, resident in psychiatry, 1976-78, asst. prof. psychiatry, 1978-80, asst. clin. prof. psychiatry, 1988-93; cons. psychiatry Gallahue Mental Health Ctr., Indpls., 1979-85; staff psychiatrist Metro Health, Indpls., 1983-97; staff privileges at Meth. Hosp., Indpls., 1979—; cons. psychiatrist Ind. Prison Sys., 1986, Ctrl. State Hosp., 1992-94, Hamilton Ctr., 1994—. Mem. Conductor's Cir. Indpls. Symphony, 1984-96, Indpls. Symphonic Choir Orch., 1976-83; life trustee Indpls. Mus. Art, 1988—. Mem. AMA, Am. Acad. Clin. Psychiatrists, Mensa, The Hoosier Group, Wash. DePauw Soc. Republican. Presbyterian. Avocations: European and American literature, classical piano, American modernist and contemporary art, early Chinese ceramics.

CONARD, FREDERICK UNDERWOOD, JR., lawyer; b. Bklyn., July 11, 1918; s. Frederick U. and Julia Ellmaker (Hand) C.; m. Annette Hall, June 19, 1943; children: Frederick U., Virginia H. BA with distinction in English, Wesleyan U., 1940; JD, Yale U., 1943. Bar: Conn. 1943, U.S. Dist. Ct. Conn. 1948, U.S. Dist. Ct. (no. dist.) N.Y. 1967, U.S. Dist. Ct. Vt. 1973, U.S. Ct. Appeals (2d cir.) 1960, U.S. Tax Ct. 1950, U.S. Supreme Ct. 1959. Assoc., Shipman & Goodwin, Hartford, Conn., 1943-49, ptnr., 1950-90, of counsel, 1990-93; justice of peace, West Hartford, Conn., 1973-74, 77—; mem. adv. com. to Waller Tenn. Trust, 1953-70, trustee, 1970—; pres. Sunset Farm Corp., 1987-91; panel mem. Am. Arbitration Assn., 1992—, Stafed, Inc., 1993-95. Bd. dirs. YMCA of Met. Hartford, sec., 1944-50, bd. dirs., 1967-78, 79-85, pres., 1970-74, trustee, 1978-79, 85—, chmn. numerous coms., del. Nat. Coun. YMCA, 1981-83, bd. dirs. YMCA of USA, 1981-83; bd. dirs. Am. Sch. for the Deaf, Hartford, 1956-93, sec., 1956-68, 2d v.p., 1968-75, exec. com., 1968-93; corporator Conn. Inst. for Blind, Inst. for Living, 1959-94; trustee Hartford Coll. for Women, 1954-84, 86-93, hon. trustee, 1993—; corporator Hartford Public Library, 1963—; bd. dirs. Almada Lodge-Times Farm Corp., 1964-93; active Asylum Hill Congl. Ch., 1937—, elder, 1968—, mem. pastoral search com., 1974, deacon, 1962-68, 1980-83; mem. Con. Gen. Assembly, 1955-57, com. on judiciary, com. on rules, mem. interim rules com., 1955-57; mem. 10th Dist. Rep. Com., 1961-95; mem., vice chmn. charter revision commn. Town of West Hartford, 1963-64, chmn., 1964-65; del. Constl. Conv. of Conn., 1965; mem. jud. performance evaluation com. Conn. State Jud. Dept., 1983-84; mem. jud. adv. panel Judicial Performance Evaluation Program Comm. State Jud. Dept., 1984-90; state trial referee Jud. Dept., 1984—; spl. masters U.S. Dist. Ct. Conn., parajudicial U.S. Dist. Ct., 1992—. Recipient Greater Hartford Jr. C. of C. Disting. Svc. award, 1946; Robert C. Knox, Jr. YMCA Disting. Leadership award, 1980; Am. Sch. for the Deaf award of Merit for Disting. Svc., 1982. Mem. ABA (ho. of dels. 1976-80, com. on prepaid legal svcs. 1980-81, com. on constn. and bylaws 1981-87, chmn. com. sr. lawyers divsn., mem. coun. 1995-97, numerous other coms.), Conn. Bar Assn. (chmn. and mem. numerous coms., v.p. 1976-77, pres. 1978-79, bd. govs. 1976-80, ho. of dels. 1976-80, com. on jud. evaluation 1982-83, chmn. task force on jud. eval. 1979-81, gen. practice 1982-85, rep. to conf. on state bar gen. practice leaders 1981), Hartford County Bar Assn. (com. on unauthorized practice of law 1961-80, chmn. 1969-80, chmn. com. on lawyer referral 1980-97), New Eng. Bar Assn. (bd. dirs. 1977-78, 80-82, v.p. 1984-85, pres. 1985-86), Am. Bar Found. (fellow, Conn. State chmn. 1990-95), Am. Law Inst., Marine Hist. Assn. of Mystic, Conn. River Watershed Council, Inc., Wadsworth Atheneum, Inc., Supreme Ct. Hist. Soc., Yale Law Sch. Assn. (exec. com. 1990—), Greater Hartford C. of C. (local govt. com. 1966-92), Yale Alumni Club of Harford, Wesleyan Univ. Alumni Club (pres. 1948, 70, v.p. 1965-69), 20th Century Club, Hartford Club, Beta Theta Pi. Mem. United Ch. of Christ. Home and Office: B519 The McAuley 275 Steele Rd West Hartford CT 06117-2716

CONARD, JOHN JOSEPH, financial official; b. Coolidge, Kans., June 30, 1921; s. Joseph Harvey and Jessie May (Shanstrom) C.; m. Virginia Louise Powell, Sept. 13, 1947; children—Joseph Harvey II (dec.), James Powell, Spencer Dean, John Joseph. B.A., U. Kans., 1943, M.A., 1947; D. Internat. Law, U. Paris, 1951. Instr. polit. sci. U. Kans., 1946-49, asst. to chancellor, 1970-75; spl. asst. U.S. Mut. Security Agy., Paris, France, 1951-54; editor, pub. Kiowa County Signal, Greensburg, Kans., 1955-70; exec. officer bd. regents State of Kans., Topeka, 1976-82; pres. Higher Edn. Loan Program of Kans., Inc., Overland Park, Kans., 1982-86; v.p. Higher Edn. Assistance Found., 1982-86; legis. liaison Gov. of Kansas, 1987-88; dir. Haviland (Kans.) State Bank. Mem. Kans. Ho. of Reps., 1959-69; mem. State Fin. Council, 1961-69; speaker of House, 1967-69; exec. asst. to Gov. Kans., 1975-76; trustee William Allen White Found., 1959—. Served to ensign USNR, 1943-45. Summerfield scholar, 1939-42; Rotary Found. fellow, 1949-50. Mem. VFW, Rotary, Phi Beta Kappa, Sigma Delta Chi, Pi Sigma Alpha, Tau Kappa Epsilon. Republican. Methodist. Home: 421 Woodring Rd Lecompton KS 66050-9501

CONARD, NORMAN DALE, secondary education educator. Tchr. social studies Uniontown (Kans.) High Sch., 1987—. Recipient State Tchr. of Yr. Social Studies award, Kans., 1992. Office: Uniontown High Sch 601 E 5th St Uniontown KS 66779-0070*

CONARROE, JOEL OSBORNE, foundation administrator, educator, editor; b. West Orange, N.J., Oct. 23, 1934; s. Elvin Hamn and Elizabeth (Lofland) C. BS, Davidson Coll., 1956, LHD (hon.), 1987; MA, Cornell U., 1957; PhD, NYU, 1966; LHD (hon.), Rhodes Coll., 1983; PhD (hon.), U. Md., 1989, Tulane U., 1996. Asst. prof. English U. Pa., 1966-71, assoc. prof., 1971-77, prof., 1977—, univ. ombudsman, 1971-73, chmn. dept. English, 1973-77, master Van Pelt Coll. House, 1974-77, dean faculty arts and scis., 1983-85; pres. John Simon Guggenheim Meml. Found., 1985—; exec. dir. MLA, N.Y.C., 1978-83; mem. selection com. Commonwealth Award in Lit., 1980-83; v.p. Nat. Book Critics Circle, 1981-85; chmn. Nat. Book Award Fiction Jury, 1988, Pulitzer Prize Fiction Jury, 1989, 94, 97, Nat. Book Found., 1991-94; bd. dirs. PEN, Am. Acad. Poets, Yaddo. Author: William Carlos Williams' Paterson: Language and Landscape, 1970, John Berryman: An Introduction to the Poetry, 1977, Six American Poets, 1992, Eight American Poets, 1994, essays and revs.; editor PMLA, 1978-83. With U.S. Army, 1957-58. Recipient Founders Day award NYU, 1966, Lindback Teaching award U. Pa., 1970, Disting. Alumni award NYU, 1995; Yaddo fellow, 1973, 76, Guggenheim fellow, 1977-78. Mem. MLA, Century Assn., Phi Beta Kappa. Office: John Simon Guggenheim Meml Found 90 Park Ave New York NY 10016-1301

CONARY, DAVID ARLAN, investment company executive; b. South Paris, Maine, Mar. 3, 1937; s. Wilfred Grindle and Arline (Whitney) C.; m. Frances Jane Harrison, June 8, 1957; children: Lee Harrison, Neil Whitney. AB, Bowdoin Coll., 1959; postgrad. Northeastern U., 1965-66, Mass. Inst. Tech., 1966-67; Boston U., 1967. Securities trader H.C. Wainwright & Co., Boston, 1959-60; securities trader May & Gannon, Boston, 1960-65, v.p., dir. rsch., 1968-71; securities analyst, adminstr. The Boston Co., Boston, 1965-68; mgr. instl. trading Fahnestock & Co., Boston, 1971-72; resident mgr. G.A. Saxton & Co., Boston, 1972-75; instl. trader Baker, Weeks & Co., N.Y.C., 1975; equities trader State St. Research & Mgmt. Co., Boston, 1976-87; v.p. Howard, Weil, Inc., 1987-88; sr. v.p. Boettcher & Co., Inc., Denver, 1989-90; dir. Astra Corp., Security 1 Specialists, Inc.; pres., chmn. Granite Solid State, Inc., Conifer Holding Corp., Inc.; ptnr. Mustang Capital, L.L.C.; lectr. in field. Dist. dir. Mass. Bay United Fund, 1966. Recipient Editors Choice award Nat. Libr. of Poetry, 1993; named to Internat. Poetry Hall of Fame, 1996. Mem. Nat. Security Traders Assn., Boston Securities Traders Assn. (gov. 1972-73, 81-82), Boston Investment Club (pres. 1985-94), Bowdoin Club of Boston (dir. 1965-66, dir. 175th anniversary campaign 1973-74), Mensa, Theta Delta Chi. Club: Weymouth Sportsmen's (sec. 1965-66, 71-72). Republican. Home: PO Box 69 Bryant Pond ME 04219-0069

CONATON, MICHAEL JOSEPH, financial service executive; b. Detroit, Aug. 3, 1933; s. John Martin and Margaret Alice (Cleary) C.; m. Nancy D. Kelley, June 13; children: Catherine, Macaira (dec.), Michael, Margaret, Elizabeth. B.S., Xavier U., 1955. Public accountant Stanley A. Hitter, C.P.A., Cin., 1956-58; controller The Moloney Co., Albia, Iowa, 1958-61; v.p. fin. The Midland Co., Cin., 1961-80, sr. v.p., chief fin. officer, 1980-83, exec. v.p., chief fin. officer, 1983-88, pres., chief operating officer, 1988—, also dir., vice-chmn., 1998—; bd. dirs. Key Corp Bank, BBI Mktg. Svcs., Inc.; interim pres. Xavier U., 1990-91. City councilman, Albia, 1959-61; trustee, chmn. bd. Xavier U., 1983—. Served to lt. USMC, 1955-56. Mem. Fin. Execs. Inst., New Ohio Inst. (chmn.), Cin. Soc. Fin. Analysts, Athenaeum of Ohio (trustee), Met. Club (chmn. bd.). Home: 736 Elsinboro Dr Cincinnati OH 45226-1706 Office: The Midland Company PO Box 1256 Cincinnati OH 45201-1256

CONAWAY, MARY ANN, behavioral studies educator; b. Pulaski, Ill., Nov. 3, 1940; d. Harry Sr. and Anna Mary (Walsh) Tolar, m. Larry Kay Conaway, June 25, 1960; children: Mary Kay, Larissa Jean, Stephen Patrick. BS, So. Ill. U., 1962; MEd, U. Mo., 1980; PhD, St. Louis U., 1991. Cert. secondary tchr., Mo.; lic. profl. counselor, Mo. Secondary tchr. Equality (Ill.) High Sch., 1962-63; data processor Blue Bell Meat Packing Plant, DuQuoin, Ill., 1963-64; secondary tchr. Dixon (Mo.) High Sch., 1964-66; ednl. cons. St. Louis, 1980-83; marriage, family therapist Christian Psychol. and Family Svcs., St. Louis, 1983-87, Psychologists & Educators, St. Louis, 1987-88; min. single adults and family Fee Fee Bapt. Ch., Bridgeton, Mo., 1988-89; min. edn. Concord Bapt. Ch., St. Louis, 1989-91; assoc. prof. psychology Mo. Bapt. Coll, St. Louis, 1992-93, dean of students, 1993-96. Mem. ACA, Am. Assn. Marriage and Family Therapists, So. Bapt. Assn., Family Mins., Pi Lambda Theta, Chi Sigma Iota. Democrat. Avocations: reading, cooking.

CONBOY, KENNETH, lawyer, former federal judge; b. 1938. AB, Fordham Coll., 1961; JD, U. Va., 1964; MA in History, Columbia U. 1980. Asst. dist. atty., exec. asst. dist. atty. Manhattan Dist. Atty.'s Office, 1966-77; dep. commr., gen. counsel N.Y. Police, 1978-83; criminal justice dir. N.Y.C., 1984-86; N.Y.C. commr. of investigation, 1986-87; judge U.S. Dist. Ct. (so. dist.) N.Y, 1987-93; sr. litigation ptnr. Mudge, Rose, Guthrie, Alexander & Ferdon, N.Y.C., 1994-95; ptnr. Latham & Watkins, N.Y.C., 1995—; summer faculty Cornell Law Sch.; adj. prof. of law Fordham Law Sch. Author: Grand Jury Examination of the Recalcitrant Witness, 1977; contbr. articles to profl. jours. Mem. N.Y. State Crime Control Planning Bd., N.Y. Sovern Commn. Capt. U.S. Army, 1964-66. Mem. Am. Soc. Legal History, N.Y. State Bar Assn., Assn. of Bar of City of N.Y., Fed. Bar Coun. Office: Latham & Watkins 885 3rd Ave Ste 1000 New York NY 10022-4834

CONBOY, MARTIN DANIEL, insurance broker, historian; b. Chgo., Nov. 27, 1954; s. Martin Daniel and Margaret Ann (Hartnett) C.; m. Jeanne Elizabeth Jones, Oct. 2, 1982 (div. Mar. 1987); m. Karen Ann Bolton, Feb. 18, 1989; 1 child, Natalie Ann. BA, Western Ill. U., Macomb, 1977. Chartered property and casualty underwriter Am. Inst., Malvern, Pa., 1990—; instr. Ins. Libr., Boston, 1997; mentor, tutor Boston Ptnrs. in Edn., Boston, 1993-97. Bd. dirs. Home Health and Child Care, Boston, 1993-97; candidate U.S. Congress, Rep. party, Boston, 1992. Recipient Outstanding Svc. award Boston Ptnrs. in Edn., 1997. Lutheran. Avocations: cross training, justice of the peace. Office: Lynch & Conboy Ins 31 Plain St Brockton MA 02301-7102

CONCANNON, JAMES M., law educator, university dean; b. Columbus, Ga., Oct. 2, 1947; s. James M. Jr. and Mary Jane (Crow) C.; m. Melissa P. Masoner, June 9, 1988. BS, U. Kans., 1968, JD, 1971. Law clk. Kans. Ins. Commn., Topeka, 1971; rsch. atty. Kans. Supreme Ct., Topeka, 1971-73; asst. prof. law Washburn U., Topeka, 1973-75, assoc. prof. law, 1976-81, prof., 1981—, dean, 1988—; vis. prof. law Washington U., St. Louis, 1979; active Kans. Commn. on Pub. Understanding of Law, 1983-89, Task Force on Law Enforcement Consolidation, Topeka, 1991-92; mem. Nat. Conf. Commrs. on Uniform State Laws, 1998—. Co-author: Kans. Appellate Practice Manual, 1978, Kansas Statutes of Limitations, 1988; sr. contbn. editor: Evidence in America-Federal Rules in the States, 1987. Coord. Citizens to Keep Politics Out of Our Courts, Topeka, 1984; co-reporter Citizens Justice Initiative, 1997—. chmn. legal com. Concerned Citizens Topeka, 1995—; bd. dirs. United Funds, Inc., 1997—. Master Topeka Am. Inn of Ct.; fellow Am. Bar Found., Kans. Bar Found.; mem. Kans. Bar Assn. (CLE com. 1976—, Outstanding Svc. award 1982), Assn. Am. Law Schs. (com. on bar admission, lawyer performance 1994-97), Washburn Law Sch. Alumni Assn. (life), Order of Coif. Office: Washburn U Law Sch 1700 SW College Ave Topeka KS 66621-0001

CONCANNON, MATTHEW JEROME, plastic surgeon; b. Feb. 9, 1962. BA, St. Louis U., 1983; MD, U. Mo., 1987. Clin. instr. surgery Harvard Med. Sch., Boston, 1994-95; dir. hand and microsurgery U. Mo., Columbia, 1996—. E-mail: mjc@surgery.missouri.edu.

CONCEPCIÓN, DAVID ALDEN, arbitrator, educator; b. Carmel, Calif., Aug. 6, 1935; s. Don Dominador Cuales Concepción and Elma Elizabeth Davis; m. Ann Martin Worster, Dec. 3, 1960; children: Leslie Martin Concepción Mayns, David Worster. BA, U. Calif., Santa Barbara, 1959. Adminstrv. exec. Lawrence Berkeley Lab. U. Calif., Berkeley, 1962-70, dir. mgmt. analysis, 1970-75; assoc. dean adminstrn. Hastings Coll. Law U. Calif., San Francisco, 1975-80; pvt. practice Berkeley, 1980—; mem. adv. bd. Calif. Pub. Employee Rels. at U. Calif., Berkeley, 1978—. Contbr. articles to profl. jours. Capt. USMC, 1959-62. Mem. Nat. Acad. Arbitrators (mem. com. 1995—), Am. Arbitration Assn. (mem. No. Calif. Adv. Coun. 1980—, mem. nat. bd. dirs. 1980-86, Disting. Svc. award 1990), Soc. Profls. in Dispute Resolution, Indsl. Rels. Rsch. Assn., Soc. Fed. Labor Rel. Profls. Democrat. Mem. United Ch. Christ. Office: 92 Park St Portland ME 04101-3825

CONCHA, MAURICIO, epidemiologist, educator, neurologist; b. Apr. 20, 1963; came to U.S., 1990; MD, Inst. of Sci. and Health, Medellin, Columbia, 1986; MHS, Johns Hopkins U, 1992. Co-investigator and field epedemiologist U. Valle, Cali, Colombia, 1987-89; asst. prof. neurology U. Miami, Fla., 1997—. Office: 1150 NW 14th St Ste 304 Miami FL 33136-2114

CONCILIO, CHARLES BENNETT, retired chemist, educator; b. Waco, Tex., June 11, 1935; s. Paul Ground and Mary Margaret (Fant) C.; m. Norma Jerice Murdock, July 17, 1954; children: Michael Paul, Rebecca Lynn, David Earle. BS in Chemistry, U. Houston, 1959, MEd in Sci. Edn., 1988. Cert. tchr., Tex. Technician Baroid Divsn., Houston, 1954-59, technologist, 1959, from technologist to sr. scientist, 1963-85; tchr. sci. St. Pius X H.S., Houston, 1986-98; ret. Contbr. articles to profl. jours. Deacon Cy-Fair Assembly of God Ch., Cypress, Tex., tchr. Sunday sch. Lt. comdr. USN, 1959-63. Recipient Tex. Excellence award for outstanding high sch. tchrs. U. Tex. Ex-Students Assn., 1991. Mem. Am. Rifle assn., Tex. rifle Assn., Mensa. Republican. Avocations: computing, hunting, shooting. Home: 12303 Oralia Dr Houston TX 77065-1514

CONCORDIA, CHARLES, consulting engineer; b. Schenectady, N.Y., June 20, 1908; s. Francis G. and Susie Elizabeth (Decker) C.; m. Frances Butler, Dec. 18, 1948. ScD, Union Coll., 1971; ScD (hon.), Iowa State U., 1993. Reg. profl. engr., N.Y., Fla. With GE, Schenectady, 1926-73, in lab., 1926-31, participant, tchr. advanced engring. program, 1932-35, in power system engring. dept., 1936-73, applications engr., 1936-49, in aircraft devel., 1941-45, cons. engr., 1949-73; cons. electric power systems engring. Venice, Fla., 1973—; lectr. various univs. Author: Synchronous Machines, 1951; contbr. over 130 articles to profl. jours.; patentee in field. Recipient Coffin award Gen. Electric Co., 1942, Steinmetz award, 1973. Fellow IEEE (Lamme medal 1961, Centennial award 1984, Power life award 1992, First chmn. of First Com. on Computing Devices, 1946, medal of hon. 1999), ASME, AAAS; mem. NAE, NSPE (Engr. of Yr. award 1963), Assn. Computing Machinery (founding mem.), Conf. Internationale des Grands Reseaux Electriques a Haute Tension (Philip Sporn award 1989), Sigma Xi, Tau Beta Pi. Republican. Presbyterian. Clubs: Venice Yacht, Mohawk Golf. Patentee in field (6). Home and Office: 900 Tamiami Trl S Apt 316 Venice FL 34285-3625

CONDAX, KATE DELANO (KATE DELANO CONDAX DECKER), marketing and public relations executive; b. Phila., Mar. 23, 1945; d. John and Laura Foster (Delano) C. Student, Sweet Briar Coll., 1964-67, U. St. Andrews, Scotland, 1966-67, U. Pa., 1975-76. Legis. aide to Sen. Samuel J. Ervin, Jr. Subcom. Separation of Powers, Com. on Judiciary U.S. Senate, Washington, 1970-73; ptnr. U.S. Trade Trip to People's Republic China, 1973; assoc. producer, asst. dir. KYW-TV, Phila., 1973-74; account exec. Aitkin, Kynett Pub. Rels., Phila., 1975-77, ICPR Pub. Rels., N.Y.C., 1977-79; dir. pub. rels. Am. Heritage Pub. Co., Inc., N.Y.C., 1979-81; account exec. Howard J. Rubenstein Pub. Rels., Inc., N.Y.C., 1981-82; rsch. assoc. Nordeman Grimm Exec. Search Firm, N.Y.C., 1982-84; prin. Kate Delano Condax & Assocs. Mktg., N.Y.C., 1984-89; nat. dir. mktg. and pub. rels. Allmilmo Corp., Fairfield, N.J., 1989-92; mktg. and media cons.; exec. dir. Philadelphia 100. Author: Horse Sense: Cause and Correction of Problems, 1979, 2d edit., 1990, Riding: A Guide for New Riders, 1995, 101 Training Tips for Your Dog, 1994, 6th edit., 1997. Probono housing counselor to elderly, N.Y.C., 1980—; exec. dir. Phila. 100, 1991-94; bd. dirs., mktg. dir. Interfaith Caregivers, 1993—; dir. pub. affairs Recording for the Blind & Dyslexic, Princeton, N.J., 1995-97. Mem. Brit. Horse Soc. (instr.), Am. Horse Shows Assn. (ex-officio, judge), Soc. Mayflower Descendants, Nat. Soc. Colonial Dames Am., Acorn Club. Office: 314 E Central Ave Moorestown NJ 08057-3637

CONDAYAN, JOHN, retired foreign service officer, consultant; b. Addis Ababa, Ethiopia, Sept. 1, 1933; s. Vahram Hagop and Sirvart (Parthog) C.; m. Eileen Mary Ferguson, Nov. 6, 1965; children: Christopher Charles, Alicia Elizabeth. BS, Bucknell U., 1955; MPA, Syracuse U., 1974; postgrad., Nat. Def. U., 1978. Mng. dir. V.H. Condayan & Co., N.Y.C., 1955-63; joined Fgn. Service, Dept. State, 1965; adminstrv. officer Am. embassy, Niamey, Niger, 1965-67; gen. services officer Am. embassy, Manila, 1967-69; spl. asst. to dep. asst. sec. Dept. State, Washington, 1969-71; adminstrv. officer Am. embassy, Copenhagen, 1971-73, exec. dir. Office Fgn. Bldgs., 1974-75, spl. exec. dir. to asst. sec. of state for adminstrn., 1975-77; counselor of embassy Am. embassy, Moscow, 1978-80, Bangkok, Thailand, 1980-82; exec. dir. Bur. E. Asian and Pacific Affairs, 1982-83; dep. asst. sec. for ops. bur. adminstrn. U.S. Dept. State, Washington, 1983-87, dir. office fgn. missions, 1987-89; minister-counsellor Am. Embassy, London, 1989-91; assoc. dir. for mgmt. USIA, Washington, 1991-94; pvt. cons., 1994—. Bd. dirs. Internat. Sch., Copenhagen, 1970-71, Anglo-Am. Sch., Moscow, 1978-80, Am. Employee Assn., Moscow, 1978-80, Am. Employee Support Orgn., Bangkok, 1980-82; mem. assets and liability com. State Dept. Fed. Credit Union, 1985, 92-93, bd. dirs., 1993-98, treas., 1994-95. Recipient Presdl. Humanitarian award (The Philippines), 1968, Meritorious Honor award Dept. State, 1975, Superior Honor award, 1985, 92, Presdl. Meritorious award, 1987, Dir.'s award for Superior Achievement, 1993. Mem. Armenian Orthodox Ch. Avocations: photography; reading; sports.

CONDE, CARLOS DANACHE, journalist; b. San Benito, Tex.; m. Dorothy Macksyne; children: Carlos V., Carla C., Carmela M. BA in Journalism, U. Tex., 1960; student, U. Mayor San Marcos, Lima, Peru, 1965-66, Am. U., 1976. With AP, Austin, Tex., Dallas Morning News, 1961-64; Washington corr. Copley News Svc., 1966; fgn. corr. Copley News Svc., Caracas, Venezuala, 1967; with Houston Chronicle, 1968-69; dir. info. Pres.'s Cabinet Com. Hispanic Affairs, 1970, U.S. Commn. Civil Rights, 1971; staff asst. Hispanic affairs Office Comm., The White House, 1972-73; chief info. InterAm. Devel. Bank, Washington, 1973-78; chief regional info. activities InterAm. Devel. Bank, Lima, 1978-88; dep. rep. InterAm. Devel. Bank, Nassau, Bahamas, 1989-95; freelance journalist, 1998—. Inter-Am. Press

Assn. scholar, 1965; nominee Pulitzer prize, 1968. Roman Catholic. Home: 2416 Chestnut St Falls Church VA 22043-3052

CONDE, MIGUEL A., hematologist, oncologist; b. 1958. MD, Columbia U., 1986. Diplomate Am. Bd. Internal Medicine, Am. Bd. Hematology, Am. Bd. Oncology. Resident medicine George Washington U. Hosp., Washington, 1986-89, fellow hematology and oncology, 1989-91; fellow rsch. FDA/Nat. Cancer Inst., 1991-93; mem. staff St. Barnabas Med. Ctr., Livingston, N.J., 1993—. Mem. ACP, AMA, Assn. Medicine N.J., Am. Soc. Clin. Oncology, N.J. Med. Soc., Am. Soc. Blood and Marrow Transplantation, Am. Soc. Hematology, Soc. for Neuro-Oncology. E-mail: MConde@SBHCS.com. Office: St Barnabas Cancer Ctr East Wing 2nd Fl Livingston NJ 07039

CONDE, YVONNE MENÉNDEZ, freelance journalist; b. Havana, Cuba, Oct. 28, 1950; came to the U.S., 1961; d. Pedro M. and Maria L. (de Quesada) C.; m. B. Loret de Mola, Apr. 10, 1989. BA in Communication, SUNY, N.Y.C., 1989; MA in Journalism, NYU, 1991. Freelance journalist various publs., N.Y.C., 1991—. Author: Operation Pedro Pan, 1999; contbg. editor: Hispanic Bus. Mag. Recipient award for best news and pub. affairs work Nat. Assn. Coll. Broadcasters, 1991. Mem. Nat. Assn. Hispanic Journalists, Internat. Women's Writing Guild. Roman Catholic. Avocation: sporting clays. Home: 340 E 64 St Apt 23B New York NY 10021-7510

CONDELLONE, TRENT PETER, real estate developer; b. Belleville, Ill., Sept. 28, 1969; s. Peter Charles and Carroll Helen (Malano) C.; m. Angela Marie Trader, June 21, 1991 (div. Oct. 1995). Student, Mo. So. State U., 1990, Evangel Coll., Springfield, Mo., 1991. Pres. Edgewater software Corp., Matthews, N.C., 1985-87; owner Sta. KØ8AT-TB, Cabool-Houston, Mo., 1988-89; chief res. officer City of Willard, Mo., 1991-93; pres. Condellone Properties, Springfield, Mo., 1990-98; chief of police City of Battlefield, Mo., 1993-94; pres. Mo. Property Investments, L.L.C., Springfield, 1994—; owner Flying Armadillo Restaurants, Inc., Springfield, 1996-97; sec. bd. advisors Meml. Hosp., Houston, 1988-91; project dir. Old St. Frances Hosp. renovation, 1994—; pres. Creative Bail Bond Agy., 1998—. Author: Iron Wondea-Clipless Stand Machine, 1998. State chmn. Teen Age Reps., 1987-90 (Mo. Teen Age Rep. of Yr. 1990); state bd. dirs. Young Reps., 1987-90, Coll. Reps., 1989-90; pres. Evangel Coll. Reps., 1989-90; elected to 5th ward Rep. Com., 1996-98. Mem. Internat. Callulator Collectors, Pacyderms. Republican. Avocations: collecting adding machines, calculators, clipless stand devices and teletypes. Office: Condellone Properties PO Box 2741 Springfield MO 65801-2741

CONDEMI, JOHN J., physician; b. Nov. 15, 1931. BA, Columbia U., 1953; MD, Albany Med. Sch., 1957. Pres. Allergy Asthma Imm. of Rochester, N.Y., 1985—; dir. clin. rsch. AAIR Rsch., 1990—. Office: 919 Westfall Rd Rochester NY 14618

CONDIE, VICKI COOK, nurse, educator; m. Michael J. Condie; children: Jennifer, Jamie, Stephen. Diploma, Deaconess Hosp. Sch. Nursing, 1969; BSN summa cum laude, SUNY, 1983; MS, Syracuse U., 1986; cert. advanced study in nursing edn., Widener U., 1991. RN, N.Y. Dir. nursing edn. Cayuga C.C., N.Y., 1987—, prof. nursing; SIDS educator Western N.Y. SIDS Ctr., 1987—; chmn. utilization rev. com. Cayuga County Dept. Health, 1985—, profl. adv. com. for Cert. Home Health Agy., 1987—; adj. prof. SUNY Health Sci. Ctr., Syracuse.; active N.Y. State Coun. ADN Programs. Active Florence Nightingale Mus. Assn., London. Recipient Chancellors' award for excellence in profl. svc. SUNY, 1998. Mem. ANA, N.Y. State Nurses Assn. (mem. coun. nursing edn.), Omicron Alpha, Sigma Theta Tau.

CONDIT, GARY ADRIAN, congressman; b. Salina, Okla., Apr. 21, 1948. AA, Modesto Jr. Coll., 1970; BA, Calif. State Coll., 1972. Councilman City of Ceres, Calif., 1972-74, mayor, 1974-76; supr. Stanislaus County, Calif., 1976-82; assemblyman State of Calif., 1982-89; mem. 101st-105th Congresses (now 106th Congress) from 15th (now 18th) Calif. Dist., 1989—; ranking minority mem. Ag. subcom. on nutrition & fgn. ag., mem. govt. reform & oversight, agriculture coms. Democrat. Office: US Ho of Reps 2245 Rayburn Washington DC 20515-0518

CONDIT, LINDA FAULKNER, economist; b. Denver, May 30, 1947; d. Claude Winston and Nancy Isobel (McCallum) Faulkner; BA, U. Ark., 1969; MA, U. Wis., 1970; postgrad. U. Minn., 1974-77; m. John Michael Condit, Dec. 20, 1970; 1 child, David Devin. Economist, St. Louis Fed. Res. Bank, 1971-73; ops. analyst No. States Power Co., Mpls., 1973-76; energy economist, 1976-78; economist Pennzoil Co., Houston, 1978-79, sr. economist, 1979-81, mgr. econ. research dept., 1981-84, dir. corp. planning and econs. dept., 1984-86; dir. treasury ops., 1986-90, corp. sec., 1990—, v.p., corp. sec., 1995-98; v.p., corp. sec. Pennzoil-Quaker State Co., Houston, 1998—; research asst. U. Wis., 1969-70; econ. cons. Jr. Achievement, 1983. Recipient Alumni award U. Ark., 1969. Mem. Internat. Assn. Energy Economists (pres., v.p., treas.), Nat. Assn. Bus. Economists, Internat. Bus. Council (v.p.), Am. Econ. Assn., N. Am. Soc. Corp. Planners, Am. Soc. Corp. Sec. (membership chmn.), Hits Theatre (bd. dirs.), Corp. Alliance to Eliminate Ptnr. Violence (bd. dirs.), Harvard Discussion Group Indsl. Economists, Phi Beta Kappa, Mortar Bd., Kappa Alpha Theta. Unitarian. Clubs: Forest, River Oaks Women's Breakfast (v.p., pres.). Home: 11822 Village Park Cir Houston TX 77024-4418 Office: Pennzoil-Quaker State Co PO Box 2967 Houston TX 77252-2967

CONDIT, PHILIP MURRAY, aerospace executive, engineer; b. Berkeley, Calif., Aug. 2, 1941; s. Daniel Harrison and Bernice (Kemp) C.; m. Madeleine K. Bryant, Jan. 25, 1963 (div. June 1982); children: Nicole Lynn, Megan Anne; m. Janice Condit, Apr. 6, 1991. BS MechE, U. Calif., Berkeley, 1963; MS in Aero. Engring., Princeton U., 1965; MS in Mgmt., MIT, 1975. Engr. The Boeing Co., Seattle, 1965-72, mgr. engring., 1973-83, v.p., gen. mgr., 1983-84, v.p. sales and mktg., 1984-86, exec. v.p., 1986-89, exec. v.p., gen. mgr. 777 div., 1989-92, pres., 1992-96, chmn., CEO, 1996—; mem. adv. coun. Dept. Mech. and Aerospace Engring., Princeton (N.J.) U., 1984—; chmn. aero. adv. com. NASA Adv. Coun., 1988-92; bd. dirs. The Fluke Corp., 1987—, Nordstom, Inc., 1993—. Co-inventor Design of a Flexible Wing, 1965. Mem. Mercer Island (Wash.) Utilities Bd., 1975-78; bd. dirs. Camp Fire, Inc., 1987-92; mem. exec bd. chief Seattle coun. Boy Scouts Am., 1988-90; trustee Mus. of Flight, Seattle, 1990—. Co-recipient Laurels award Aviation Week & Space Tech. magazine, 1990; Sloan fellow MIT, Boston, 1974. Fellow AIAA (aircraft design award 1984, Edward C. Wells tech. mgmt. award 1982, Wright Brothers Lectureship Aeronautics 1996), Royal Aero. Soc.; mem. NAE, Soc. Sloan Fellows (bd. govs. 1985-89), Soc. Automotive Engrs. Clubs: Rainier, Columbia Tower (Seattle). Office: The Boeing Co 7755 E Marginal Way S Seattle WA 98108-4000*

CONDITT, MARGARET KAREN, scientist, policy analyst; b. Mobile, Ala., Aug. 7, 1953; m. David Joseph Bruno, Feb. 13, 1988; 2 stepchildren: Josh, Holly. BS in Chemistry, U. Ala., Tuscaloosa, 1975; PhD in Chemistry, U. Colo., 1984. Field hydrologist U.S. Geol. Survey, Tuscaloosa, 1975; sci. aide II Geol. Survey Ala., Tuscaloosa, 1975-77; tchg. asst. U. Ala., Tuscaloosa, 1977-79; rsch. asst. U. Colo., Boulder, 1979-84; sr. scientist Procter & Gamble, Cin., 1984—; reviewer sci. edn. grant proposals NSF, Washington, 1988; mem. water sci. and tech. bd. com. Nat. Acad. Scis., Washington, 1989-91. Author: (chpt.) Advanced Techniques in Synthetic Fuels Analysis, 1983; contbr. articles to profl. jours. Inter Colo. Gov.'s Sci. and Tech. Adv. Coun., 1981-83; appointee Liberty Twp. Bd. Zoning Appeal, 1994-97, elected trustee Liberty Township, 1998—; trustee, sec. Woodmoor Ter. Homeowner's Assn. Bd., 1993-97, pres. 1996-97. Recipient fellowship Mining and Mineral Resources and Rsch. Inst., 1980, Rsch. fellowship U. Colo. Grad. Sch., 1981, Browns-Rickett grant AAUW, 1982. Mem. Am. Chem. Soc. Roman Catholic. Avocations: Internet Webmaster, collecting antiques, Boy Scouts. Home: 6959 Rock Springs Dr Liberty Township OH 45011-9376

CONDO, JAMES ROBERT, lawyer; b. Somerville, N.J., Mar. 2, 1952; s. Ralph Vincent and Betty Louise (MacQuaide) C.; m. Rhonda H. King, June 7, 1997. BS in Bus. and Econs., Lehigh U., 1974; JD, Boston Coll., 1979. Bar: Ariz. 1979, U.S. Dist. Ct. Ariz. 1979, U.S. Ct. Appeals (9th cir.) 1982, U.S. Ct. Appeals (D.C. cir.) 1989, U.S. Ct. Appeals (10th cir.) 1989, U.S. Supreme Ct. 1983, U.S. Ct. Appeals (6th cir.) 1991, U.S. Ct. Appeals (4th cir.) 1994. Assoc. Snell & Wilmer, Phoenix, 1979-84, ptnr., 1985—; judge pro tem Ariz. Ct. Appeals. Bd. dirs. Ariz. Town Hall. Fellow Ariz. Bar Found.; mem. ABA, State Bar Ariz., Maricopa County Bar Found. E-mail: jcondo@swlaw.com. Office: Snell & Wilmer One Arizona Ctr Phoenix AZ 85004

CONDON, CHARLES MOLONY, state attorney general; b. Charleston, S.C., May 2, 1953; s. James Joseph and Harriet (Molony) C.; m. Emily Yarbrough, June 21, 1980; children: Charles Molony Jr., Patrick Monaghan, Doreen Yarbrough, Emily Elliot. Student, Saltzburg (Austria) Summer Sch., 1972, U. Innsbruck, Austria, 1972-73; BA, U. Notre Dame, 1975; JD, Duke U., 1978. Bar: S.C. 1978, U.S. Dist. Ct. S.C. 1978, U.S. Ct. Appeals (4th cir.) 1987, U.S. Supreme Ct. 1988. Assoc. Nexsen, Pruet, Jacobs & Pollard, Columbus, S.C., 1978-79; asst. solicitor S.C. 9th Jud. Cir., Charleston, 1979-80, solicitor, 1980-92; atty. gen. State of S.C., Columbia, 1992—; lectr. Med. U. S.C., 1982, U. S.C., 1983, Coll. Charleston, 1986, various confs.; bd. visitors com., Charleston, 1992—; panel mem. Nat. Inst. for Drug Abuse, Washington; prosecuter City of Isle Palms, S.C., 1993—; cons. Nat. Consortium for Justice Info. and Stats. profl. rep. So. Environ. Network, 1990-91. profl. rep. So. Envion. Network., 1990-91. Mem. com. Charleston County Criminal Justice Task Force; sect. chmn. govtl. divsn. United Way; bd. dirs. com. for drug free soc. Charleston County Sch. Dist., 1989, Children's Ctr., Charleston, S.C., 1990-91, S.C. Commn. on Presecution Coord., 1991-92; ex-officio mem. Friends of Charleston County Courthouse. Mem. ABA, S.C. Bar Assn., Richland County Bar Assn., Charleston Lawyers Club, S.C. Cir. Solicitors Assn. (v.p. 1987-88, pres. 1988-89), S.C. Law Enforcement Assn., Notre Dame Club, Silver Elephant Club. Republican. Home: 835 Middle St Sullivans Island SC 29482-8728 Office: Office of Attorney General PO Box 11549 Columbia SC 29211-1549*

CONDON, FRANCIS EDWARD, retired chemistry educator; b. Abington, Mass., Oct. 12, 1919; s. Maurice Francis and Eva Isabel (Cole) C.; m. Mary Anna Medvetz, Jan. 9, 1943; children: Francis E., Mary Ellen (Mrs. George Laessig III), John M., Arthur T., Dorothy A. (Mrs. Ronald G. Waldt), James M., Rita C. A.B., Harvard, 1941, Ph.D., 1944. Research chemist Phillips Petroleum Co., Bartlesville, Okla., 1944-52; asst. prof. chemistry CCNY, 1952-61, assoc. prof., 1962-66, prof., 1967-82, ret., 1982, Louis J. Curtman prof., 1976-78; founder, chmn. Seven Siblings Found., Ltd., 1977-94; vis. prof. Purdue U., 1960. Author: (with H. Meislich) Introduction to Organic Chemistry, 1960, Study Projects in Physical Chemistry, 1963, Chess monographs, 1992—, also articles; contbr. chpt. to Catalysis, 1958. Mem. planning bd. Borough of Bogota, N.J., 1963; Trustee, pres. Bogota Swim Club, Inc., 1967-71. Petroleum Research Fund grantee, 1967-70; NSF Sci. Faculty fellow U. So. Calif., 1964-65. Mem. Am. Chem. Soc. (dir. N.Y. sect. 1967-68), U.S. Chess Fedn. (life), Glen Rock (N.J.) Chess Club (pres. 1975-79, Washington Twp. (N.J.) Chess Club (pres. 1990-92), Dumont (N.J.) Chess Mates (sec. 1992—), St. Joseph's Holy Name Soc. (pres. 1974-75, sec. 1992—), Alpha Chi Sigma, Sigma Xi. Home: 471 Larch Ave Bogota NJ 07603-1058

CONDON, GEORGE EDWARD, journalist; b. Fall River, Mass., Nov. 6, 1916; s. John Joseph and Mary Agnes (O'Malley) C.; m. Marjorie Philona Smith, May 9, 1942; children—Theresa, John, George, Katherine, Mary, Susan. BSc in Journalism, Ohio State U., 1940. Publicity dir. Mt. Union Coll., Alliance, Ohio, 1941; info. dir. Agrl. Adjustment Adminstrn. for Ohio, 1941-42; mem. staff Cleve. Plain Dealer, 1943-84, gen. columnist, 1962-84; pres. George Condon & Assocs., Inc., 1985—. Author: Cleveland-The Best-Kept Secret, 1967, Laughter from the Rafters, 1968, Stars in the Water, 1972, Yesterday's Cleveland, 1976, Yesterday's Columbus, 1977, Cleveland: Prodigy of the Western Reserve, 1979, History of Ohio Farmers Insurance Company, 1985, Gaels of Laughter and Tears, 1995, The Man in the Arena, 1995. Recipient Ohioana Library Assn. Lit. award, 1975, Cleve. Women's City Club Lit. award, 1975, Emily Gray Burke Meml. award lit., 1979; award Cleve. Newspaper Guild; awards for public service, copy editing and column writing Press Club Cleve.; Disting. Service award Nat. Soc. Profl. Journalists, 1980; named to Cleve. Journalism Hall of Fame, Press Club Cleve., 1990. Mem. Sigma Delta Chi, Pi Sigma Alpha. Home: 19235 S Sagamore Rd Fairview Park OH 44126-1619

CONDON, ROBERT EDWARD, surgeon, educator, consultant; b. Albany, N.Y., Aug. 13, 1929; s. Edward A. and Catherine (Kilmartin) C.; m. Marcia Jane Pagano, June 16, 1951; children: Sean Edward, Brian Robert. AB, U. Rochester, 1951, MD, 1957; MS, U. Wash., 1965. Diplomate Am. Bd. Surgery, Nat. Bd. Med. Examiners. N.Y. Bd. Regents scholar U. Rochester, 1957; intern King County Hosp., Seattle, 1957-58; resident dept. surgery U. Wash. Sch. Medicine (and affiliated hosps.), 1958-65; postdoctoral rsch. fellow Nat. Heart Inst., 1961-63; asst. prof. surgery Baylor Coll. Medicine, Houston, 1965-67; assoc. prof. surgery U. Ill. Coll. Medicine, Chgo., 1967-69, prof., 1969-70; prof., head dept. surgery U. Iowa Coll. Medicine, Iowa City, 1971-72; prof. surgery Med. Coll. Wis., Milw., 1972—, chmn. dept. surgery, 1979-95; chief surg. svcs. Wood VA Hosp., Milw., 1972-81; attending surgeon Froedtert Meml. Luth. Hosp., 1982-98; cons. Columbia Hosp., Milw., St. Joseph Hosp., Milw. Author: (with others) Abdominal Pain: A Guide to Rapid Diagnosis, 2d edit., 1995, Manual of Surgical Therapuetics, 9th edit., 1996, Hernia, 4th edit., 1995, Surgical Care, 1980. Recipient sr. class award as Outstanding Faculty Member Baylor U. Coll. Medicine, 1966, Excellence in Teaching award Phi Chi, 1967, Cert. Appreciation U. Iowa Coll. Medicine, 1971, Tchr. of Yr. award 1972, Med. Coll. Wis., 1983; rsch. fellow Guggenheim Found., 1963-64. Mem. ACS, Am. Surg. Assn. (v.p.) , Surg. Infection Soc. (pres.), Am. Assn. Surgery of Trauma, Internat. Soc. Surgery, Collegium Internationale Chirurgiae Digestivae (pres.), Assn. for Acad. Surgery, Cen. Surg. Assn. (pres.), So. Surg. Assn., Western Surg. Assn., Wis. Surg. Soc. (pres.), Milw. Surg. Soc. (pres.), Chgo. Surg. Soc., Soc. U. Surgeons, Soc. Clin. Surgery, Milw. Acad. Medicine, Soc. Surgery Alimentary Tract (v.p.), Milw. Acad. Surgery (pres.). Home and Office: 2722 86th Ave NE Clyde Hill WA 98004-1653

CONDON, THOMAS BRIAN, hospital executive; b. Beverly, Mass., June 1, 1942; s. Thomas William and Marguerite Mary (Welch) C.; m. Carol Therese Sicilliano, Apr. 29, 1969; children: Therese Beth, Tara Bridget, Colleen Margarite, Caroline Susan. BA in English, Boston Coll., 1964; MPA, U. New Haven, 1973, MA in Community Psychology, 1975, MA in Indsl. and Organizational Psychology, 1977. Dir. unit mgmt. Yale New Haven Hosp., 1971—, asst. adminstr., 1975, v.p., 1980-94, v.p. clin. adminstrn., 1994—; assoc. prof. Quinnipiac Coll., Hamden, 1982—; bd. dirs. Nat. Inst. Cmty. Health Edn., Hamden, Conn., Spectronics, Phila.; bd. dirs. New Eng. Organ Bank, 1996—; chmn. bd. dirs. Gateway Tech. and C.C. Found., New Haven, 1988-96. Elected mem. Cheshire (Conn.) Planning and Zoning Commn., 1976-87; chmn., dir. Conn. Student Loan Found., Rocky Hill, 1976—; mem. Gov.'s Task Force on Student Aid, Hartford, Conn., 1986-87; bd. dirs. So. Conn. Jr. Achievement, 1994—; bd. advisors Clelian Ctr. Adult Day Care Ctr., Hamden, 1990. Capt. U.S. Army, 1964-70. Recipient Community Svc. award Bd. Trustees Conn. State Coll., 1991, Disting. Alumni award U. New Haven, 1997. Mem. Grad. Club Assn. New Haven (bd. dirs. 1993—), Lyman Orchards Golf Club. Roman Catholic. Avocations: golf, antiques, netsuke, film collector, golf. Home: 150 Hotchkiss Rdg Cheshire CT 06410-3041 Office: Yale New Haven Hosp 20 York St New Haven CT 06510-3220

CONDON, THOMAS JOSEPH, university historian; b. New Haven, July 27, 1930; m. Ann Kathleen Gorman, 1962; children: Katherine, Caroline, Gregory. B.A., Yale U., 1952; M.A., Boston Coll., 1953; Ph.D., Harvard U., 1962. Teaching fellow history Harvard U., 1959-62; asst. prof. history U. N.B. (Can.), Fredericton, 1962-66; exec. asso. Am. Council Learned Socs., N.Y.C., 1966-70; vis. asso. prof. history Ind. U., 1967-68, City U. N.Y., 1968-69; prof. history, dean of Arts U. N.B., 1970-77; prof. history, dean and v.p. U. N.B. (St. John Campus), 1977-79, acting pres., 1979-80, v.p., 1980-87, prof. history, 1977-96, v.p. emeritus, gov. emeritus, 1996—; hon. rsch. fellow Inst. U.S. Studies, U. London, 1975-76; mem. Humanities Rsch. Coun. Can., 1972-73, Commn. on Fgn. Students Policy, Can. Bur. Internat. Edn., Ottawa, 1980-83, Maritime Provinces Higher Edn. Commn., 1982-85; chmn. adv. com. on arts in N.B. Min. of Youth, 1973-75; bd. govs. Rothesay Collegiate Sch., 1977-88, U. N.B., 1977-87, 90-96; chmn. engring. task force Maritime Provinces Higher Edn. Commn., 1977-78; chmn., pres. Bi-Capitol Project, Inc., 1982-91; chmn. Festival by the Sea, Sur Mer, 1985, Bi-Capitol Found., 1984—; bd. govs., exec. com. Can. Conf. Arts, 1988-94; bd. dirs. Writers Devel. Trust; bd. govs. Internat. Scholarship Found., 1996—. Author: New York Beginnings: The Commercial Origins of New Netherland, 1968; Mem. editorial bd.: Computers and the Humanities, 1969-70, Acadiensis, 1970—; contbr. articles to profl. jours. V.p. St. John Can. Games, 1977-87. Served with USNR, 1953-57. Recipient Lescarbot award Can. govt., 1991, Commemorative medal for 125th anniversary of Confedn. of Can., 1992; Can. Coun. grantee, 1964, 65. Mem. Am. Hist. Assn., Can. Assn. Am. Studies, Can. Hist. Assn. Home: 268 Princess St, Saint John, NB Canada E2L 1L3 Office: Box 5050, Saint John, NB Canada E2L 4L5

CONDON, THOMAS JOSEPH, editor, writer; b. N.Y.C., Sept. 10, 1934; s. Thomas Joseph and Mary Josephine (Tully) C.; m. Teresa Elvira Garcia, Feb. 14, 1982. BS in Social Studies, Fordham U., 1962; MS in English Edn., Long Island U., 1977. Journalist Long Island Daily Press, Jamaica, N.Y., 1964-77; equal opportunity specialist U.S. EEOC, Washington, 1979-83; writer-editor office of the asst. sec., pub. affairs Dept. of Def., Rosslyn, Va., 1983-84; supr. writer-editor office of sec., Pentagon Dept. of Def., Washington, 1984-98; freelance writer-editor, 1999—. Author, editor: (manual) DoD Directives System Procedures, 1994. With USN, 1952-54. Mem. Nat. Press Club (affil.), Dramatists Guild (assoc.), KC (3d deg.). Democrat. Roman Catholic. Avocations: play writing, physical fitness, traveling, reading. Home: 512 Vivienne Dr Watsonville CA 95076-3563

CONDON, WILLIAM (BILL), director, writer, producer; b. Nov. 22, 1955. Degree in philosophy, Columbia Coll. T.V. and motion picture dir., writer, prodr. Writer, dir. Gods and Monsters, 1998 (Best Writing Oscar award 1999, Flanders Internat. Film Festival award 1998, Golden Satellite award 1999, Ind. Spirit award 1999, others); dir. films Sister, Sister, 1987, Candyman: Farewell to the Flesh, 1995; T.V. films include Murder 101, 1991, White Lie, 1991, Dead in the Water, 1991, Deadly Rels., 1993, The Man Who Wouldn't Die, 1995. Office: c/o DGA 7920 Sunset Blvd Los Angeles CA 90046*

CONDON, WILSON LESLIE, commissioner; b. Livingston, Mont., Sept. 28, 1939; m. M. Susan Stuardi. AB in Polit. Sci., Stanford U., 1963, JD, 1971. Asst. dir. fin. aid Stanford U., 1965-68; asst. atty. gen. State of Alaska, 1971-75, dep. atty. gen., 1975-80, atty. gen., 1980-82; ptnr. Hellen, Partnow & Condon, 1983-91, Condon, Partnow & Sharrock, 1991-95; commr. Dept. Revenue, Juneau, Alaska, 1995—. Mem. ABA (adminstrv. law, pub. utilities and natural resources and environ. law sects.), Alaska Bar Assn., Stanford Environ. Law Soc. (founding mem.). Office: Dept of Revenue PO Box 110400 Juneau AK 99811-0400

CONDRAN, CYNTHIA MARIE, gospel musician; b. Avon Park, Fla., Apr. 29, 1953; d. Kenneth Dale and Ruth Mae (Garber) Grubb; m. Lee Light Condran, July 3, 1971. Student, Lebanon Valley Coll., 1970-72. Piano tchr. Sebring, Fla., 1968-70, Annville, Pa., 1971—; gospel musician, writer, arranger Condran Music Co., Annville, Pa., 1972—, also recording engr.; writer comml. jingles. Sang by spl. invitation at Elipse of The White House, 1982; composer The Only Thing Holding You Back, 1977, Just A Few More Rivers, 1975, The Patchwork Quilt, 1978, Freedom, 1976, The Little Things, 1980, We're America, Heavens Fiesta, He's the Lord of Everyday, 1989, I've Never Known Such Love, 1990, I Just Want To Talk To You, 1990, Sweep Our Sins, 1990, Eternal Friends, 1991, The Precious Jewels At Christmas Time, 1992, Lost On My Way Back Home, 1993, I Believe in the Power of Love, 1993, To Speak Your Name, 1994, Forever, 1994, We Praise You Lord, 1994, R.D. #11, Heaven, 1996, Surprise, 1997, Patience, 1998, His Healing Blood, 1999, Just A Few More Rivers, 1999. Recipient Contemporary Country Artists of Yr. award Internat. Country Gospel Music Assn., Internat. Star Music award, 1997. Mem. Gospel Music Assn., Broadcast Music Inc., Christian Bus. and Prof. Women (music chmn.), So. Gospel Music Guild. Republican. Avocations: skiing, golf, swimming, tennis, racquetball. Home: 935 N Route 934 Annville PA 17003-9803

CONDRON, BARBARA O'GUINN, metaphysics educator, school administrator, publisher; b. New Orleans, May 1, 1953; d. Bill Gene O'Guinn and Marie Gladys (Newbill) Jackson; m. Daniel Ralph Condron, Feb. 29, 1992; 1 child, Hezekiah Daniel. BJ, U. Mo., 1973; MA, Coll. Metaphysics, Springfield, Mo., 1977, DD, D in Metaphysics, 1979. Cert. counselor; ordained min. Interfaith Ch. Metaphysics. Field rep. Sch. Metaphysics, New Orleans, 1978-80; dir. Interfaith Ch. Metaphysics, 1884-89; pres. Nat. Hdqs., Sch. Metaphysics, Windyville, Mo., 1980-84, prof., 1989—, chmn. bd. dirs., 1991-98, mem. coun. elders, bd. govs. internat. edn., 1998—; CEO SOM Pub., Windyville, 1989-98; guest lectr., instr. Wichita State U., 1977, U. New Orleans, 1979, La. State U., 1981, Am. Bus. Womens Assn., 1982, U. Mo., Kansas City, 1984, Unity Village, 1985, Kans. Dept. Social Svcs. Conf., Topeka, 1986, U. Mo., Columbia and St. Louis, 1986, Mo. Tchrs. Conf., St. Louis, 1991, U. Okla., Norman, 1988-89, Parliament of World's Religions, Chgo., 1993, many others; creator Sch. Metaphysics Assocs., 1992; initiator Universal Hour Peace, 1995; initiator, internat. coord. Nat. Dream Hotline, 1988—; radio and TV guest, 1977—. Author: What will I do Tomorrow?, Probing Depression, 1977, Search for a Satisfying Relationship, 1980, Strangers in My Dreams, 1987, Total Recall: An Introduction to Past Life & Health Readings, 1991, Kundalini Rising, 1992, Dreamers Dictionary, 1994, The Work of the Soul: Past Life Recall & Spiritual Enlightenment, 1996, Uncommon Knowledge, 1996, First Opinion: 21st Century Wholistic Health Care, 1997, Spiritual Renaissance Elevating Your Conciousness for the Common Good, 1999; author series When All Else Fails; editor-in-chief Thresholds Jour., 1990—; editor Wholistic Health and Healing Guide, 1992—; also numerous poems. Mem. Internat. Platform Assn., Am. Bus. Women's Assn., Interfaith Ministries, Kundalini Rsch. Network, Planetary Soc., Heritage Found., Sigma Delta Chi. Office: Sch Metaphysics World Hdqs Nat Hdqs Windyville MO 65783

CONDRON, CHRISTOPHER M. KIP, investment company executive; b. Scranton, Pa.. B Bus., U. Scranton. Sr. v.p. C.S. McKee & Co., Pitts.; founder, pres. Ayco, 1985-88; head pvt. client group The Boston Co. (now Mellon Pvt. Asset Mgmt.), 1989-93, exec. v.p., 1993-95; pres., COO Boston Co. Asset Mgmt., 1995; pres., CEO Dreyfus Corp., N.Y.C., 1995—; vice chmn. Mellon Bank Corp., pres., COO, 1998—. Trustee U. Scranton, St. Sebastian's Country Day Sch., Needham, Mass.; former bd. dirs. Mass. Bankers Assn.; vice chmn. bd. trustees Wang Ctr. for Performing Arts; mem. Jobs for mass. Inc.; mem. Coord. Com., Boston. Office: Dreyfus Corp 200 Park Ave Fl 7W New York NY 10166-0039

CONDRON, DANIEL RALPH, academic administrator, metaphysics educator; b. Chillicothe, Mo., Jan. 30, 1953; s. Ralph Wesley and Rosa Irene (Garber) C.; m. Barbara Gail O'Guinn, Feb. 29, 1992; 1 child, Hezekiah Daniel. BS, U. Mo., 1975, MS, 1978; DDiv, Coll. Metaphysics, Springfield, Mo., 1982, D in Metaphysics, 1985. Cert. counselor; ordained to ministry Interfaith Ch. of Metaphysics. Dir. Sch. Metaphysics, Des Moines, 1980, Kansas City, Mo., 1981; regional dir. Sch. Metaphysics, Colo., 1982-85, Chgo. and Detroit, 1985-90; pres. bd. nat. hdqs. Sch. Metaphysics, Windyville, Mo., 1988—; chancellor, prof. Coll. Metaphysics, Windyville, Mo., 1990—; tchg. asst. U. Mo., Columbia, 1977; sales and mgmt. cons. Am. Media, Des Moines, 1980-83; speaker in field including Parliament of the World's Religions, Chgo., 1993. Author: Dreams of the Soul, 1991, Permanent Healing, 1992, Universal Language of Mind, 1994, Understanding Your Dreams, 1994, Uncommon Knowledge, Seven Secret Keys to Prosperity and Abundance, 1996, Superconscious Meditation, 1997; pub. jour. Thresholds Quar., 1988—; internat. radio and TV guest including BBC, Radio Hong Kong, Voice of Am., 1979—. Mem. Sch. Metaphysics Assocs. (pres.), Nat. Space Soc., Planetary Soc., Alpha Gamma Rho, Alpha Zeta. Republican. Achievements include implementer and designer of organic and bio-dynamic farming and agriculture at the 1500 acre College of Metaphysics campus, landscape designer and artist for 1500 acre college of metaphysics campus, discoverer and developer of many aspects of the Universal language of mind as it applies to dreams, to the Bible and other holy works; discoverer of specific attitudes that cause specific disease and disorders in the body. Avocations: photography, horticulture, landscaping, designing and inventing, space research. Home: Box 15 Windyville MO 65783-9703 Office: Sch Metaphysics Nat Headquarters Windyville MO 65783

CONDRY, ROBERT STEWART, retired hospital administrator; b. Charleston, W.Va., Aug. 16, 1941; s. John Charles and Mary Louise (Jester) C.; m. Mary Purcell Heinzer, May 21, 1966; children: Mary-Lynch, John

Stewart. BA, U. Charleston, 1963; MBA, George Washington U., 1970. Asst. hosp. dir. Med. Coll. of Va., Richmond, 1970-73, assoc. adminstr., 1973-75; assoc. hosp. dir. McGaw Hosp., Loyola U., Maywood, Ill., 1975-84, hosp. dir., 1984-93, ret., 1993; pres. Inter-Hosp. Planning Assn. of Western Suburbs, Maywood, 1983-93; bd. dirs. PentaMed, Inc., San Antonio. Bd. dirs. Met. Chgo. Healthcare Coun., 1985-93, mem. exec. com., 1989-93; bd. dirs. Cath. Hosp. Alliance, 1992, chmn. bd. dirs., 1992, mem. exec. com. 1988-94; mem. Ill. Gov.'s Adv. Bd. on Infant Mortality Reduction, 1988-93, Rev. Bd. on Emergency Medicine Svcs., 1989-93. With U.S. Army, 1964-66. Recipient preceptorship George Washington U., 1985, U. Chgo., 1984, St. Louis U., 1984, Tulane U., 1984, Yale U., 1991. Fellow Am. Coll. Healthcare Execs., Am. Acad. Med. Adminstrs.; mem. Am. Hosp. Assn., Cath. Hosp. Assn., Am. Mgmt. Assn. Republican. Roman Catholic. Avocations: golf, tennis, camping, travel.

CONE, CAROL LYNN, public relations executive; b. N.Y.C., June 7, 1950; d. William Addison Cone and Harriet (Gurney) Brown. BA, Brandeis U., 1972; MS, Boston U., 1978. Account exec. Newsome and Co., Boston, 1977-80; pres., CEO Cone Communications, Boston, 1980—. Mem. Gov.'s Entrepreneurial Adv. Council, Boston, 1982, Dukakis for Pres. campaign nat. fin. com., Boston, 1987. Named Outstanding Female Entrepreneur La Salle Jr. Coll., Newton, Mass., 1986, YWCA Achievement Entrepreneur, Boston, 1986, Entrepreneur of Yr. Arthur Young/Venture Mag., 1988; recipient Golden Quill award Internat. Assn. Bus. Communicators, 1987. Mem. Counselor's Acad. of Pub. Relations Soc. Am., Pub. Relations Soc. Am. (Silver anvil 1987), Am. Mktg. Assn. Avocations: skiing, windsurfing, walking. Office: Cone Comm Inc 90 Canal St Boston MA 02114-2018*

CONE, DAVID BRIAN, professional baseball player; b. Kansas City, Mo., Jan. 2, 1963. Baseball player Kansas City Royals, 1986-87, N.Y. Mets, 1987-92, Toronto Blue Jays, 1992, 94-95, Kansas City Royals, 1992-94, New York Yankees, 1995—. Mem. Nat. League All-Star team, 1988, Am. League All-Star team, 1992, 94, Sporting News A.L. All-Star team, 1994; recipient Cy Young award Am. League, 1994; shares Nat. League single-game rec. most strikeouts. Player in World Series, 1992; Pitched a no-hit game (perfect) on July 18, 1999. Office: NY Yankees Yankee Stadium E 161st St and River Ave Bronx NY 10451*

CONE, EDWARD CHRISTOPHER, newspaper publisher; b. Montclair, N.J., Mar. 29, 1937; s. Edward della Torre and Patricia Clapp (Laurence) C.; divorced; children: David Christopher, Jennifer Lynn. BA, Princeton U., 1958. Lic. lay preacher, eucharistic minister Diocese Newark, 1992. Missionary Holy Cross Mission, Bolahun, Liberia, 1958-83, commissary, 1984—; asst. to editor West Essex Tribune, Livingston, N.J., 1963-68, mng. editor, 1968-80, pub., pres., 1980—; cons. Vols. in Tech. Assistance, Washington, 1964—, Assn. Episc. Colls., 1985—. Author: Automotive Operation and Maintenance, 1973. Trustee North Essex United Way, Montclair, N.J., 1982-98, Livingston Symphony Orch., 1978—, Livingston Coun. for Arts, 1991—, Salisbury Scholarship Fund, 1982—; sole sponsor Korea-Vietnam Veterans Meml., Livingston, 1987; sponsor Occupational Ctr. Sheltered Workshop, Livingston, 1981; tech. mgr. Studio Players Theater, Montclair, 1963-68; vestryman Grace Episc. Ch., Madison, N.J., 1991-96, verger, 1996—; lay assoc. Coll. Preachers, Washington Cathedral, 1989—; bishops' soc. Gen. Theol. Sem., N.Y.C., 1989—; mem. Verger's Guild Episc. Ch., 1994—; mem. Scholarly Engagement with Anglican Doctrine, 1994—; regional dir. Washington Nat. Cathedral Assn., 1993—; St. John's soc. Episc. Div. Sch., Cambridge, Mass., 1993—. Mem. N.J. Press Assn. (editl. com. 1968—, bd. dirs. 1988—, v.p. 1993-96, pres. 1997, chmn. 1998, trustee N.J. Press Found. 1993—), Nat. Newspaper Assn., Livingston Coun. Arts, Livingston C. of C. (bd. dirs. 1981-92). Republican. Episcopalian. Avocations: vegetable gardening, musicology. Office: West Essex Tribune 495 S Livingston Ave PO Box 65 Livingston NJ 07039-0065

CONE, EDWARD TONER, composer, emeritus music educator; b. Greensboro, N.C., May 4, 1917; s. Julius Washington and Laura Barbara (Weill) C. A.B., Princeton U., 1939, M.F.A., 1942; D.Mus. (hon.), U. Rochester, 1973, New Eng. Conservatory Music, 1984; D.F.A. (hon.), U. N.C.-Greensboro, 1983. Asst. prof. dept. music Princeton U., 1947-52, assoc. prof., 1952-60, prof., 1960-85, prof. emeritus, 1985—; Andrew D. White prof.-at-large Cornell U., 1979-85; Treas. Am. sect. Internat. Soc. Contemporary Music, 1950-52. Composer numerous compositions, 1 symphony, other works for piano, voice, chorus, orch., chamber combinations, 1939—. Author: Musical Form and Musical Performance, 1968, The Composer's Voice, 1974, Music: A View from Delft, 1989; co-editor: Perspectives of New Music, 1965-69, adv. editor, 1969-72. Guggenheim fellow in composition, 1947-48. Mem. AAUP, Am. Philos. Soc., Am. Acad. Arts and Scis. Club: Century.

CONE, FRANCES MCFADDEN, data processing consultant; b. Columbia, S.C., Oct. 20, 1938; d. Joseph Means and Francis (Graham) McFadden; m. Charles Cone Jr., May 1962 (div. Sept. 1964); 1 child, Deborah Ann Cone Craytor. BS, U. S.C., 1960, MEd, 1973, M Math., 1977. Systems svc. rep. IBM, 1960-62; programmer/analyst Ga. Power Co., Atlanta, 1964-68, S.C. Fin. and Data Processing, Columbia, 1968-69; instr., head dept. Midlands Tech. Coll., Columbia, 1969-75; tng. coord. S.C. Nat. Bank, Columbia, 1975-79; systems analyst S.C. Dept. Health and Environ. Control, Columbia, 1979-80; project analyst So. Co. Svcs., Atlanta, 1980-89; cons. George Martin Assocs., Atlanta, 1989-93; sr. sys. developer Emory U., Atlanta, 1993-97; sys. analyst Southland Life Ins. Co., Atlanta, 1997-99, team leader, 1999—; adj. prof. Golden Gate U., Sumter, S.C., 1976-80. Vol. Ga. Wildlife Found., Save the Manatee Club, Names Project. Mem. Nat. Mgmt. Assn. (sec., treas., awards comn. 1981-89). Episcopalian. Avocations: reading, embroidery, grandchildren. Office: Southland Life Ins Co 5780 Powers Ferry Rd NW Atlanta GA 30327-4349

CONE, JAMES HAL, theologian, educator, author; b. Fordyce, Ark., Aug. 5, 1938; s. Charlie M. and Lucy (Frost) C. BA, Philander Smith Coll., 1958; BD, Garrett Theol. Sem., 1961; MA, Northwestern U., 1963, PhD, 1965. Asst. prof. religion and philosophy Philander Smith Coll., Little Rock, 1964-66; asst. prof. religion Adrian (Mich.) Coll., 1966-69; asst. prof. theology Union Theol. Sem., N.Y.C., 1969-70; asso. prof. Union Theol. Sem., 1970-73, prof., 1973-77, Charles A. Briggs prof. systematic theology, 1977-87, Briggs disting. prof., 1987—; vis. prof. Afro-Am. history U. of Pacific, Stockton, Calif., summer, 1969; vis. asso. prof. religion Barnard Coll., N.Y.C., 1969-71, 74; vis. prof. theology Drew U., Madison, N.J., 1973; lectr. systematic theology Woodstock Coll., N.Y.C., 1971-73; vis. prof. theology Princeton (N.J.) Theol. Sem., 1976, Notre Dame Sch. Theology, New Orleans, summer, 1977, Howard U. Sch. Religion, Washington, 1980. Author: Black Theology and Black Power, 1969 (transl. into Dutch, 1970, German, 1971, Japanese, 1971, Korean, 1979), A Black Theology of Liberation, 1970 (transl. into Spanish, 1973, Italian, 1973, Japanese, 1974), The Spirituals and the Blues: An Interpretation, 1972 (transl. into German, 1973, Japanese, 1975, Korean, 1987), God of the Oppressed, 1975 (transl. into Japanese, 1976, Italian, 1978, Korean, 1978, German, 1982, French, 1989), My Soul Looks Back, 1982 (transl. into Japanese, 1987), For My People, 1984 (transl. into German, 1987), Speaking the Truth, 1986, Martin and Malcom and America: A Dream or a Nightmare, 1991; contbr. articles to profl. publs.; mem. editorial bd.: Jour. Religious Thought, 1975—, Jour. Interdenominational Theological Ctr.; co-editor: Black Theology: A Documentary History, 1966-79, 1979. Rockefeller Found. grantee, 1973-74. Mem. Black Theology Project Theology in Ams., Am. Acad. Religion, Soc. Study Black Religion, Ecumenical Assn. Third World Theologians. Mem. African Methodist Episcopal Ch. Office: Union Theol Sem 3041 Broadway New York NY 10027-5710

CONE, MICHAEL MCKAY, venture capitalist; b. Washington, Oct. 14, 1947; s. Montie Fowler and Eleanor Newcomb (Faulk) C.; m. Constance Ann Hennessy, July 21, 1971. AB, Princeton U., 1969; MPhil, Yale U., 1973, PhD, 1976. Chemist E.I. DuPont de Nemours, Wilmington, Del., 1977-81; area supt. E.I. DuPont de Nemours, LaPlace, La., 1981-84; bus. analyst E.I. DuPont de Nemours, Wilmington, 1984-85, tech. svc. specialist, 1985-86; devel. mgr. E.I. DuPont de Nemours, Parlin, N.J., 1986-89; cons. E.I. DuPont de Nemours, Wilmington, 1989-94; mgr. new bus. devel. E.I. DuPont de Nemours, Deepwater, N.J., 1994-98; ptnr. Crossway Ventures, Toms River, N.J., 1998—; bd. dirs. Wayn-Tex Inc., Waynesboro, Va., F.T. Industries, LLC, Franklinville, N.J. Patentee in field. Mem. AAAS, Am. Chem. Soc., Product Devel. & Mgmt. Assn. (dir. sponsor devel. 1994-97), Sigma Xi, Princeton Club N.Y. Avocations: sailing, skiing, music. Home: 1910 Spruce St Philadelphia PA 19103-6613 Office: Crossway Ventures 864 Rt 37 W Ste 16 Toms River NJ 08755

CONE, THOMAS CONRAD, communications executive; b. Bryan, Tex., Nov. 4, 1948; s. Conrad Bryan and Monica Bonnell (Sappington) C.; m. Linda Arnold, Nov. 2, 1968 (div. 1978); m. Miriam Stose, July 26, 1997. BA in Journalism, Tex. A&M U., 1973; postgrad., U. Houston, 1973-75. Print, radio, TV asst. Tex. Agrl. Extension Svc., College Station, 1970-73; field rep. Rice Coun. Am., Houston, 1973-75, dir. Africa ops., 1975-80, dir. comm., 1975-81; pres. Cone Comm., Houston, 1981—; host, prodr. city-wide radio pub. svc. program, Houston, 1978-81. Sgt. USMC, 1966-69, Vietnam. Mem. Houston Jaycees (bd. dirs., advisor 1978-83, nominee one of 5 Outstanding Young Texans 1981,82), Houston Advt. Fedn. (bd. dirs. 1978-85), Houston C. of C. (named one of 5 Outstanding Young Houstonians 1981), Soc. Profl. Journalists, Rotary (bd. dirs. 1983-86). Methodist. Avocations: guitar playing, singing, photography. Home and Office: 2805 Creasey Dr Temple TX 76501-1413

CONERLY, ALBERT WALLACE, academic administrator, dean; b. Tylertown, Miss., Dec. 14, 1935; m. Francis Marie Bryan; children: Albert Wallace Jr., Charles Franklin. BS, Millsaps Coll., 1957; MD, Tulane U., 1960. Diplomate Am. Bd. Internal Medicine, Am. Bd. Pulmonary Disease. Intern The McLeod Infirmary, S.C., 1960-61; fellow in medicine sect. on cardiology Ochsner Found. Hosp., New Orleans, 1971; resident in medicine Sch. Medicine U. Miss., Jackson, 1971-72, fellow in pulmonary disease, 1972-74, asst. instr. medicine, 1971-73, asst.prof. medicine divsn. pulmonary diseases, 1974-79, prof. respiratory care Sch. Health-Related Professions, 1978-93, assoc. prof. medicine, 1990-94, prof., vice chancellor health affairs, dean Sch. Medicine, 1994—; attending physician Univ. Hosp., U. Miss. Med. Ctr. - Univ. Hosps. and Clinics, Jackson, 1973—; med. dir. adult ICU Univ. Hosp., U. Miss. Med. Ctr., Jackson, 1977-79, med. dir. acute care lab., 1978-82, dir. divsn. continuing health profl. edn., 1979-93, asst. vice chancellor, 1981-94, vice chancellor health affairs and deans, 1994—; dean Sch. Medicine U. Miss., Jackson; vis. prof. U. Ky. Sch. of Medicine Dept. of Anesthesiology, 1981; mem. attending staff Miss. Bapt. Hosp., St. Dominic Hosp. and Hinds Gen. Hosp., Jackson, Miss., 1966-70; med. dir. dept. respiratory therapy U. Hosps. and Clinics, U. of Miss., 1973-94, med. dir. dept. of respiratory care Sch. of Health-Related Professions, 1975-93; med. advisor Tri-State Respiratory Therapy Conf., Ala., La., Miss., 1975-85, 90—; med. cons. Respiratory Care Svcs., Inc., Jackson, 1976-84; mem. health and human svcs. coun. So. Regional Ednl. Bd., 1992-95; med. cons. Tb Control Unit, Miss. State Bd. of Health, 1976-82; oral examiner Nat. Bd. for Respiratory Care, 1977-79, others. Mem. editl. rev. bd. Jour. Respiratory Diseases, 1981-82; contbr. articles to profl. jours. Bd. dirs. Capital Area United Way; mem. cmty. adv. coun. Jr. League Jackson, 1994—. With USAF, 1960-66. Grantee Am. Lung Assn., 1975-78, VA grant U. Miss. Med. Ctr., 1975-83. Mem. AMA, ACP (commr. commn. on accreditation of allied health edn. programs 1994—), Aerospace Med. Assn., Am. Acad. of Gen. Practice, Am. Soc. Internal Medicine, Miss. Acad. Scis., Miss. State Med. Assn., Ctrl. Med. Soc. of Miss., Am. Coll. Chest Physicians (mem. Am. Coll. Chest Physicians-AMA joint rev. com. for respiratory therapy edn., com. on allied health edn. accreditation 1992-94), Am. Thoracic Soc., So. Assn. Colls. and Schs. (accreditation site visitor 1984—), Miss. Thoracic Soc., Assn. of Am. Med. Colls., Miss. Soc. of the Am. Assn. for Respiratory Care (med. advisor 1974-85, 91—), Univ. Club Jackson (bd. dirs.), Rotary (bd. dirs. Downtown Jackson chpt.). Office: U Miss Med Ctr 2500 N State St Jackson MS 39216-4500*

CONERLY, EVELYN NETTLES, educational consultant; b. Baton Rouge, Aug. 25, 1940; d. Noel Douglas and Evelyn Elsie (Pratt) Nettles; children from previous marriage: Douglas Wayne, Kelee Lynne. BS, La. State U., 1962, MEd, 1965, PhD, 1973. Tchr., East Baton Rouge Parish Pub. Schs., La., 1962-67, elem. librarian, 1967-73, prin., 1973-81, elem. library supr., 1981-83, prin., 1983-84; edn. cons., Baton Rouge, 1984—, co-owner, Acad. Learning Ctr., 1986-92; dir. Libr. Power Project, East Baton Rouge Parish, DeWitt Wallace-Reader's Digest Fund, 1992-96; vol. pub. sch.; with Nat. Libr. Power Program Network of Conss., 1996—; program evaluator La. State Bd. Elem. and Secondary Edn., 1996-98; supr. office field experiences Southeastern La. U. Coll Edn., 1997-98; program adminstr. La. State Bd. Elem. and Secondary Edn. Co-author: Principals' Pointers for Parents, 1985. Mem. ALA, AASL, Assn. Tchr. Educators (pres. La. 1981-82), Internat. Reading Assn., La. Reading Assn., La. Ret. Tchrs. Assn., La. Libr. Assn., Inst. Reality Therapy (cert.), Phi Kappa Phi, Phi Delta Kappa, Delta Kappa Gamma. Presbyterian. Home: 3727 Woodland Ridge Blvd Baton Rouge LA 70816-2772

CONERLY, RICHARD PUGH, retired corporation executive; b. Jackson, Ala., May 6, 1924; s. William L. and Eunice (Pugh) C.; m. Iva Jean Brightwell, Aug. 12, 1956; children: William Edward, Robert Andrew, Christopher Brightwell, Elizabeth Anne. Student, Howard Coll., Birmingham, Ala., 1942; B.J., U. Mo., 1948; LL.B., Harvard U., 1952. Bar: Mo. 1952. Practice in St. Louis, 1952-65; assoc., partner Thompson & Mitchell, 1952-65; v.p., gen. counsel, exec. v.p. Peabody Coal Co., St. Louis, 1965-69; pres. Pott Industries Inc., St. Louis, 1969-87; vice-chmn. Houston Natural Gas Corp., 1979-85; chmn. Orion Capital Inc., St. Louis, 1988-94. Served with USAAF, 1942- 46. Home: 339 Hawthorne Ave Saint Louis MO 63119-2511

CONERLY-PERKS, ERLENE BRINSON, retired chemist; b. Jackson, Miss., Nov. 16, 1938; d. Alvin Bryan and Erlene (Brinson) Conerly; m. Paul Allen Perks, May 4, 1991. BS, Millsaps Coll., 1959; MS in Tech. Mgmt., Am. U., 1978. Chemist NIH, Bethesda, Md., 1962-78; research biologist Dynamac, Rockville, Md., 1979-80; chemist EPA, Washington, 1980-94; ret., 1994. Democrat. Episcopalian. Avocations: madrigal singing, wildlife.

CONETTA, TAMI FOLEY, lawyer; b. Akron, Ohio, Aug. 29, 1965; d. Charles David and Roxanne (Onyett) Foley; m. Anthony Joseph Conetta, July 29, 1989; 1 child, Emory Elizabeth Conetta. BA in Polit. Sci., Furman U., 1987; JD with honors, U. Fla., 1990. Bar: Fla. 1991; bd. cert. estates, trusts and wills Fla. Bar Bd. Legal Specialization. Ptnr. Gassman & Conetta, PA, Clearwater, Fla., 1990-98, Ruden, McClosky, Smith, Schuster & Russell, PA, Sarasota, Fla., 1998—. Contbr. articles to profl. jours. Recipient Am. Jurisprudence awards in Estate Planning and Taxation of Gratuitous Transfers, 1990. Mem. Am. Bus. Womens Assn., Sarasota County Bar Assn., Clearwater Bar Assn. (chair law week 1994, Pres.'s award 1994), Clearwater Bar Probate Com. (chair 1996-98), Southwest Fla. Estate Planning Coun. Avocations: golf, reading. Office: Ruden McClosky Smith Schuster & Russell PA 1549 Ringling Blvd Ste 600 Sarasota FL 34236-6772 also: PO Box 49017 Sarasota FL 34230-6017

CONEY, AIMS C., JR., lawyer, labor-management negotiator; b. Cleve., Sept. 22, 1929; s. Aims Chamberlain and Elizabeth (Lee) C.; m. Rita Newbold Platt, Feb. 20, 1954; children: Aims C. III, Sylvia L., Anne F. B.A., Yale U., 1951; J.D., U. Pa., 1954. Bar: Pa. Assoc. Kirkpatrick, Lockhart, Johnson & Hutchison, Pitts., 1956-69; ptnr. Kirkpatrick & Lockhart, Pitts., 1969-89, of counsel, 1990—. Contbr. articles in field of union-management relations to profl. jours. Bd. dirs. Arthritis Found., Pitts., 1967—, pres., 1972-75; bd. dirs. Ellis Sch., Pitts., 1974-91, Freedom House Amb. Svc., 1968-75, Indian Lake (N.Y.) Zoning Commn., 1993-95, Transitional Svcs. Inc., 1992-98; bd. dirs. Pace Sch., Pitts., 1980-94, pres., 1990-91. With U.S. Army, 1954-56. Mem. Pa. Bar Assn. (chmn. client security fund com. 1991-93), Allegheny County Bar Assn. Republican. Home: 516 Glen Arden Dr Pittsburgh PA 15208-2809 Office: Kirkpatrick & Lockhart 1500 Oliver Building Pittsburgh PA 15222-2312

CONEY, CAROLE ANNE, accountant; b. Berkeley, Calif., Aug. 11, 1944; d. Martin James and Ida Constance (Ditora) Skuce; m. David Michael Coney, June 20, 1964; children: Kristine Marie, Kenneth Michael. BS cum laude, Calif. State Poly. U., 1985, MBA, 1988. Tax cons., instr. H&R Block, Portland, Oreg., 1969-71; acct., asst. sec.-treas. Surety Ins. Co., La Habra, Calif., 1973-76; bookkeeper Homemakers Furniture, Downers Grove, Ill., 1976-79; office mgr., acct. Helen's Pl. Printing, Upland, 1979-80; bookkeeper Vanguard Cos., Upland, 1980-82; dir. acctg. Coll. Osteopathic Medicine of Pacific, Pomona, Calif., 1982-89; fiscal svcs. mgr. City of Ontario, Calif., 1989—. Pres. Brea/La Habra Newcomers, 1975; treas. Alta Loma (Calif.) Com. to Elect Robert Neufeld, 1981. Mem. NAFE, Nat. Assn. Coll. and Univ. Bus. Officers, Calif. Soc. Mcpl. Fin. Officers, Govt. Fin. Officers Assn., Assn. Coll. and Univ. Auditors, Coun. Fiscal Officers, Soroptimists, Ontario Kiwanis, Delta Mu Delta, Alpha Iota. Democrat. Roman Catholic. Avocations: fishing, crafts, sewing, golf. Home: PO Box 4910 24581 San Moritz Dr Crestline CA 92325-4910 Office: City of Ontario 303 E B St Ontario CA 91764-4196

CONEY, ELAINE MARIE, English and foreign languages educator; b. Magnolia, Miss., Aug. 9, 1952; d. Allen Leroy and Katie Jane (McLeod) C. BA in Spanish, Millsaps Coll., 1974; MA in Spanish, U. Interam. Saltillo Coahuila, Mex., 1975, PhD, 1977; MEd, U. So. Miss., 1979, EdS in Higher Edn. Adminstrn., 1997. Tchr. fgn. langs. South Pike High Sch., Magnolia, Miss., 1977-91; tchr. English Amite County Schs., Liberty, Miss.; instr. Jackson (Miss.) State U.; GED instr. South Pike Schs., Magnolia, Miss.; instr. Spanish, French and English composition S.W. Miss. Community Coll., Summit, 1989—. Mem. NEA (del. conv. 1986, 88), MLA, Am. Coun. Tchrs. Fgn. Langs., Am. Assn. Tchrs. French, Am. Assn. Tchrs. Spanish and Portuguese, Miss. Assn. Educators (instructional profl. devel. com.), Nat. Coun. Tchrs. English, Miss. Fgn. Lang. Assn. (pres. 1991-93, Disting. Svc. award 1998), SPAE (treas.). Home: PO Box 208 Magnolia MS 39652-0208

CONFER, ANTHONY WAYNE, veterinary pathologist, educator; b. Hot Springs, Ark., July 29, 1947; s. Edwin M. and Gloria V. (Parker) C.; m. Carolyn Gay Pope, Aug. 15, 1970; children: Andrew W., Aaron J., Michael E., Christina A. DVM, Okla. State U., 1972; MS, Ohio State U., 1974; PhD, U. Mo., 1978. Diplomate Am. Coll. Vet. Pathologists. Assoc. prof. La. State U., Baton Rouge, 1978-81; assoc. prof. Okla. State U., Stillwater, 1981-85, prof., 1985—, dept. head, 1986-99, assoc. dean for rsch. Coll. Vet. Medicine, 1999—, endowed chair food animal rsch., 1995—; vis. prof. U. B.C., Vancouver, 1990-91; cons. Ft. Dodge (Iowa) Lab., 1987-92, Baxter Healthcare Corp., Round Lake, Ill., 1988-89, Vet. Reference Lab., Dallas, 1988-89, Smith Kline Beechan Ltd., Lincoln, Nebr., 1990; mem. Conf. Rsch. Workers-Animal Diseases, 1981—; cons. Diamond Animal Health, Des Moines, 1994-98. Mem. editl. bd. Am. Jour. Vet. Rsch., 1993—, Vet. Pathology, 1995-97. V.p. Stillwater Soccer Assn., 1987-91, pres., 1992-93; pub. rels. specialist Stillwater H.S. Soccer Club, 1990-96; cub master Cub Scout pack 22, Stillwater, 1987-89. Capt. USAF, 1974-76. Recipient Beecham award for Rsch., Smith Kline Beecham Lab., 1985, Norden Disting. Tchr. award Norden Labs., 1987. Mem. AVMA (Vet. Rsch. award 1992), Am. Coll. Vet. Pathologists (chair standing edn. com. 1994-96, program chair 1995), Morris Animal Found. (sci. advisor 1991-95), Sigma Xi (chpt. lectr. 1993). Mormon. Avocations: physical fitness, youth sports, guitar, cooking. Home: 2817 W 28th Ave Stillwater OK 74074-2212 Office: Dept Anatomy Pathology and Pharmacology Okla State Univ Stillwater OK 74078

CONFORTI, MICHAEL PETER, museum director, art historian; b. Bradford, Mass., Apr. 3, 1945; s. Sven and Cecile Conforti; m. Licia Peterson; children: Peter, Julia. BA, Trinity Coll., Hartford, Conn., 1968; MA, Harvard U., 1973, PhD, 1977. Cataloguer Sotheby & Co., London, 1968-69; dir. tng. program Sotheby & Co., N.Y.C., 1969-71; curator sculpture and decorative arts Fine Arts Mus., San Francisco, 1977-80; chief curator, Bell curator decorative arts and sculpture Mpls. Inst. Arts, 1980-94; dir. Sterling and Francine Clark Art Inst., Wiliamstown, Mass., 1994—. Exhbns. include: Sweden: A Royal Treasury, 1988, The American Craftsman and the European Tradition, 1620-1820, 1989, Art and Life on the Upper Mississippi, 1890-1915, 1994, A Grand Design--The History of London's Victoria and Albert Museum, 1997; author jour. articles on sculpture, decorative arts, collecting and mus. history. Decorated Order of Polar Star (Sweden); recipient Robert Smith award, 1987, Charles Montgomery award, 1990; Bush fellow, 1985, Nat. Endowment Arts Mus. fellow, 1974, Am. Acad. in Rome fellow, 1975-77; Getty Guest scholar, 1988; Andrew Mellon fellow Ctr. for Advanced Study in the Visual Arts, Nat. Gallery of Art, 1993. Mem. Harvard Club, Psi Upsilon. Office: Sterling and Francine Clark Art Inst Williamstown MA 01267

CONGALTON, CHRISTOPHER WILLIAM, lawyer; b. N.Y.C., Apr. 8, 1946; s. William Alexander and Jacqueline Rose (Ryan) C.; m. Susan Tichenor, May 29, 1971. AB, Fairfield (Conn.) U., 1968; JD, Georgetown U., 1971. Bar: N.Y. 1972, U.S. Dist. Ct. (so. dist.) N.Y. 1974, U.S. Ct. Appeals (2d cir.) 1974, U.S. Supreme Ct. 1976, Ill. 1988, Colo. 1990. Assoc. Dunnington, Bartholow & Miller, N.Y.C., 1971-78; asst. gen. counsel Diamond Internat. Corp., N.Y.C., 1978-82; gen. counsel, v.p. Children's TV Workshop, N.Y.C., 1987-88; chmn. and ceo Moffitt Co., Schiller Park, Ill., 1988—. Mem. ABA, (corp. banking & bus. sect.), Am. Corp. Counsel Assn., N.Y. State Bar Assn., Assn. of Bar of City of N.Y., Chgo. Bar Assn., Eagle Springs Golf Club. Home: 1500 N Lake Shore Dr Chicago IL 60610-1607 Office: Moffitt Co 9347 Seymour Ave Schiller Park IL 60176-2206

CONGALTON, SUSAN TICHENOR, lawyer; b. Mt. Vernon, N.Y., July 12, 1946; d. Arthur George and M. Marjorie (McDermott) Tichenor; m. Christopher William Congalton, May 29, 1971. BA summa cum laude, Loretto Heights Coll., 1968; JD, Georgetown U., 1971. Bar: N.Y. 1972, Ill. 1986, Colo. 1990. Assoc. Reavis & McGrath (now Fulbright & Jaworski), N.Y.C., 1971-78, ptnr., 1978-85; v.p., gen. counsel, sec. Carson Pirie Scott & Co., Chgo., 1985-87, sr. v.p. fin. and law, 1987-89; mng. dir. Lupine LLC (formerly known as Lupine Ptnrs.), Chgo., 1989—; bd. dirs. Harris Trust & Savs. Bank, Harris Bankcorp, Inc., Harris Bankmont, Inc., Bankmont Fin. Corp.; chmn. Community Reinvestment Act Com., 1990-97, chmn. audit and examining com., 1997—. Mem. editorial staff Georgetown U. Law Jour., 1969-70, editor, 1970-71. Mem. bd. overseers Ill. Inst. Tech., Chgo., Chgo. Kent Coll. Law, 1985-89; mem. bus. adv. coun. Bus. Sch., U. Ill., Chgo., 1987-90; mem. planning com. Ann. Corp. Counsel Inst., 1986-89; bd. dirs. Ill. Inst. Continuing Legal Edn., 1992-95; mem. Chgo. Workforce Bd., 1995-98; chmn. Strategic Planning Task force, 1995-96, chmn. Performance Rev. Com., 1996-98. Mem. ABA, Econ. Club Chgo., Chgo. Club (bd. dirs. 1996—). Office: Lupine LLC 1520 Kensington Rd Ste 112 Oak Brook IL 60523

CONGDON, JOHN RHODES, transportation executive; b. Balt., Feb. 17, 1933; s. Earl Everett and Lillian Francis (Herbert) C.; m. Barbara Natalie Neblett, June 17, 1952; children: Susan Lee, John Rhodes, Jeffrey Whitefield. Student, U. Richmond, 1952-53. Driver Old Dominion Freight Line, 1951, vice chmn.; founder, chmn. Old Dominion Truck Leasing, 1963—; vice chmn. Old Dominion Freight Line. Deacon River Rd. Ch., 1971-81; pres. Dorset Woods Civic Assn., 1973-74. With U.S. Army, 1953-55. Mem. Va. Hwy. Users Assn. (pres. 1976-78), River Rd. Citizens, Country Club of Va., Masons, Shriners. Home: 109 Walsing Dr Richmond VA 23229-7640 Office: 7511 White Pine Rd Chesterfield VA 23832

CONGDON, ROGER DOUGLASS, theology educator, minister; b. Ft. Collins, Colo., Apr. 6, 1918; s. John Solon and Ellen Avery (Kellogg) C.; m. Rhoda Gwendolyn Britt, Jan. 2, 1948; children: Rachel Congdon Lidbeck, James R., R. Steven, Jon B., Philip F., Robert N., Bradford B., Ruth A. Mahner, Rebecca York Skones, Rhoda J. Miller, Marianne C. Potter, Mark Alexander. BA, Wheaton Coll., 1940; postgrad, Eastern Bapt. Sem., 1940-41; ThM, Dallas Theol. Sem., 1945; ThD, Dallas Theology Sem., 1949. Ordained to ministry Bapt. Ch., 1945. Exec. sec., dean Altanta Bible Inst., 1945-49; prof. theology Carver Bible Inst., Atlanta, 1945-49; prof. Multnomah Bible Coll., Portland, Oreg., 1950-87; pastor Emmanuel Bapt. Ch., Vancouver, Wash., 1985—; past dean of faculty, dean of edn., v.p., chmn. libr. com., chmn. achievement-award com., chmn. lectureship com., advisor grad. div. and mem. pres.'s cabinet Multnomah Bible Co.; chmn. Chil Evang. Fellowship of Greater Portland, 1978—; founder, pres. Preaching Print Inc., Portland, 1953—. Founder, speaker semi-weekly radio broadcast Bible Truth Forum, KPDQ, Portland, Oreg., 1989-98, KPAM 1999—, DZAM, Manila, Philippines, 1996—, Radio Africa 2, 1998—; author: The Doctrine of Conscience, 1945. Chmn. Citizen's Com. Info. on Communism, Portland, 1968-75. Recipient Outstanding Educators of Am. award, 1972, Loraine Chafer award in Systematic Theology, Dallas Theol. Sem. Mem. Am. Assn. Bible Colls. (chmn. testing com. 1953-78), N.Am. Assn. Bible Colls. (N.W. rep. 1960-63), Near East Archaeol. Soc., Evang. Theol. Soc. Republican. Home: 16539 NE Halsey St Portland OR 97230-5607 Office: Emmanuel Bapt Ch 14810 NE 28th St Vancouver WA 98682-

8357 *A base person's problems usually consist in selecting between overt evils. The average person chooses between the shady and the good. But the truly noble person, who follows Jesus Christ, never bothers with evils or shady acts; he ever seeks to discern the transcendent, to choose the best of all good choices.*

CONGEL, FRANK JOSEPH, federal agency administrator, physicist; b. Syracuse, N.Y., Mar. 6, 1943; s. Frank Richard and Emily (Crimi) C.; m. Mary Ellen Taylor, July 10, 1965; children: Karin, Suzanne, Frank A. BS, LeMoyne Coll., 1964; MS, Clarkson U., 1967, PhD, 1969. Postdoctoral fellow Argonne (Ill.) Nat. Lab., 1968-69; asst. prof. physics Macalester Coll., St. Paul, 1969-72; radiation physicist AEC, Washington, 1972-74; radiation physicist, tech. mgr. U.S. Nuclear Regulatory Commn., Washington, 1974-81, sr. tech. mgr., nuclear power reactors, 1981—; cons. U.S. Govt. Response Commn. for Nuclear Emergencies. Washington, 1984—. Contbr. articles to profl. jours. Mem. U.S. Del. to Vienna to discuss the Chernobl nuclear accident, 1986. Mem. Health Physics Soc., Izaak Walton League (Damascus, Md.). Republican. Roman Catholic. Avocation: photography. Home: 7400 Cutty Sark Way Gaithersburg MD 20882-4301 Office: US Nuclear Regulatory Commn TWFN 4-D-27 Washington DC 20555

CONGER, BOB VERNON, plant and soil science educator; b. Greeley, Colo., July 2, 1938; s. Vernon Fred and Florence Violet (Pierce) C.; m. Donna Dee Russell, June 5, 1960; children: Gregory, Rhonda, Stephen, Michael. BS, Colo. State U., 1963; PhD, Wash. State U., 1967. Asst. prof. Wash. State U., Pullman, 1967-68; asst. prof. U. Tenn., Knoxville, Oak Ridge, 1968-73, assoc. prof., 1973-78; prof. dept. plant and soil sci. U. Tenn., Knoxville, 1978-86, Austin disting. prof., 1986—, dir. grad. program in plant physiology and genetics, 1990-92; cons. Joint Food and Agrl. Orgn./IAEA Divsn., Vienna, Austria, 1986-87. Author, editor: Cloning Agricultural Plants in Vitro Techniques, 1981; editor Critical Revs. in Plant Scis., 1981—; assoc. editor In Vitro Cellular and Devel. Biology-Plant, 1991-98; editorial bd. mem. Environ. Exptl. Botany, 1976-98; contbr. articles to profl. jours. Predoctoral trainee NASA, 1964-67; Chancellor's rsch. scholar U. Tenn., 1985, Profl. Leave award, 1986-87. Fellow AAAS, Am. Soc. Agronomy, Crop Sci. Soc. Am.; mem. Am. Soc. Gravitational and Space Biology, Soc. In Vitro Biology, Internat. Soc. Plant Molecular Biology, Internat. Assn. Plant Tissue Culture, Sigma Xi, Phi Kappa Phi, Alpha Zeta, Beta Beta Beta, Gamma Sigma Delta. Methodist. Home: 723 Robertsville Rd Oak Ridge TN 37830-8260 Office: U Tenn Dept Plant and Soil Sci PO Box 1071 Knoxville TN 37901-1071

CONGER, CYNTHIA LYNNE, financial planner; b. Omaha, Dec. 8, 1948; d. Bob Bruce Ashton and Cleo (Artz) Ashton Taplin; m. Terry H. Conger, Dec. 21, 1969 (div. June 1989); children: Cynthia T., Scott A. BA in Acctg., U. Ark., Little Rock, 1980, MBA in Fin. and Econ., 1983. CPA, Ark.; cert. fin. planner. Staff acct. Leaseway Ark., Inc., Little Rock, 1981-83; rsch. asst. Indls. Rsch. and Econ. Com., Little Rock, 1983; agt. Conn. Mutual Life, Little Rock, 1983-84; v.p., fin. planner Ark. Fin. Group, Inc., Little Rock, 1984-94, pres., 1995—; pres. Cynthia L. Conger, CPA, PA, Little Rock, 1989—. Mem. Civitan, Little Rock, 1985-89. Mem. LWV (adv. bd. 1997—), Internat. Assn. Fin. Planning (Ark. chpt., v.p. 1986-87, pres. 1987-89, nat. bd. dirs. 1994-98, Delphi rsch. task force 1991), Ret. and Sr. Vols. (adv. bd. 1995—), Registry Fin. Planning Practitioners. Methodist. Avocations: reading, crewel embroidery, cooking. Office: Ark Fin Group Inc 225 E Markham St Ste 275 Little Rock AR 72201-1636

CONGER, HARRY MILTON, mining company executive; b. Seattle, July 22, 1930; s. Harry Milton Jr. and Caroline (Gunnell) C.; m. Phyllis Nadine Shepherd, Aug. 14, 1949 (dec.); children: Harry Milton IV, Preston George; m. Rosemary L. Scholz, Feb. 22, 1991. D in Bus. Adminstrn. (hon.), S.D. Sch. Mines and Tech., 1983; D. in Engring. (hon.), Colo. Sch. Mines, 1988, hon. degrees. Registered profl. engr., Ariz., Colo. Shift foreman Asarco, Inc., Silver Bell, Ariz., 1955-64; mgr. Kaiser Steel Corp. Eagle Mountain Mine, 1964-70; v.p., gen. mgr. Kaiser Resources, Ltd., Fernie, B.C., Can., 1970-73, Consolidation Coal Co. (Midwestern div.), Carbondale, Ill., 1973-75; v.p. Homestake Mining Co., San Francisco, 1975-77, pres., 1977-78, pres., chief exec. officer, 1978-82, chmn., pres., chief exec. officer, 1982-86, chmn., chief exec. officer, 1986-96, chmn., 1996-98, chmn., CEO emeritus, also bd. dirs., 1998—; bd. dirs. ASA Ltd., Pacific Gas & Electric Co., Apex Silver Mines; chmn. Am. Mining Congress, 1986-89, World Gold Coun., 1995-97. Chmn. World Gold Coun.; trustee Calif. Inst. Tech. With C.E., U.S. Army, 1956. Recipient Disting. Achievement medal Colo. Sch. Mines, 1978, Am. Mining Hall of Fame, 1990, Disting. Svc. award Am. Mining Congress, 1995. Mem. NAE, Am. Inst. Mining Engrs. (disting., Charles F. Rand gold medal 1990), Mining and Metallurgy Soc. Am., Mining Club, Bohemian Club, Commonwealth Club, Pacific Union Club, World Trade Club. Republican. Episcopalian. Office: Homestake Mining Co 500 Ygnacio Valley Rd Ste 250 Walnut Creek CA 94596-8209

CONGER, JOHN JANEWAY, psychologist, educator; b. New Brunswick, N.J., Feb. 27, 1921; s. John C. and Katharine (Janeway) C.; m. Mayo Trist Kline, Jan. 1, 1944; children: Steven Janeway, David Trist. BA magna cum laude, Amherst Coll., 1943; MS, Yale U., 1947, PhD, 1949; DSc (hon.), Ohio U., 1981, Amherst Coll., 1983, U. Colo., 1989. Asst. prof. psychology Ind. U., 1949-53; chief staff psychologist U.S. Naval Acad., 1951-52; mem. faculty U. Colo. Sch. Medicine, prof. psychology, 1957-88, assoc. dean, 1961-63, v.p. for med. affairs, 1963-70, dean, 1963-68, acting chmn. dept. psychiatry, 1983-84, acting chancellor, 1985-86, prof. emeritus, 1988—; fellow Ctr. for Advanced Study in Behavioral Scis., Stanford, Cal., 1970-71; vis. scholar Inst. Human Devel., U. Calif., Berkeley, 1978; v.p., dir. health program John D. and Catherine T. MacArthur Found., 1980-83, cons., 1983-85; cons. to NIH, VA, USPHS; vice chmn. Colo. Bd. Psychology Examiners, 1961-64; mem. Gov. Colo. Com. Mental Health, 1957; chmn. mental health adv. council Colo. Dept. Pub. Health, 1957-61; mem. tng. com. Nat. Inst. Mental Health, 1959-62; mem. Western council mental health research and tng. Western Interstate Commn. Higher Edn., 1959-66; chmn. research com. President's Com. Traffic Safety, 1960-63; vice chmn. nat. motor vehicle safety adv. council Dept. Transp., 1967-70; mem. inter-council com. constrn. univ.-affiliated facilities for mentally retarded Dept. Health, Edn. and Welfare, 1967-70, mem. sec.'s adv. com. traffic safety, 1966-69; council research and planning Am. Hosp. Assn., 1965-68; nat. adv. mental health council USPHS, 1965-69; nat. adv. com. John F. Kennedy Center for Research on Edn. and Human Devel., 1965-76, chmn., 1970-74; mem. adv. com. on undergrad med. edn. AMA, 1969-70; adv. com. on casualty ins. Dept. Transp., 1970; mem. Pres.'s Task Force on Hwy. Safety, 1970, President's Commn. on Mental Health, 1977-78; mem. com. study nat. needs for biomed. and behavioral sci. research personnel Nat. Acad. Scis., 1976-80; mem. Inst. Medicine/Nat. Acad. Scis., 1983—, bd. mental health and behavioral medicine, 1986-92. Author: Child Development and Personality, 7th edit., 1990, Readings in Child Development, 1964, 3d edit., 1984, Personality, Social Class and Delinquency, 1965, Adolescence and Youth: Psychological Development in a Changing World, 5th edit., 1997, The Shape of the Tree: Selected Poems, 1993, Basic and Contemporary Issues in Developmental Psychology, 1975, Contemporary Issues in Adolescent Development, 1975, Psychological Development: A Life-Span Approach, 1979, Essentials of Child Development and Personality, 1980, also articles; mem. editl. coun. Applied and Preventive Psychology, 1991—. Served to lt. USNR, 1944-46, 51-52. Recipient Stearns Alumni medal for extraordinary service U Colo., 1970, U. Colo. medal, 1986, disting. profl. achievement award Am. Bd. Profl. Psychology, 1979. Fellow APA (mem. policy and planning bd. 1967-70, rec. sec., dir. 1974-79, pres. 1980-82, award for outstanding contbns. health psychology 1983, award for disting. contbns. psychology in pub. interest 1986), AAAS, Soc. Rsch. in Child Devel. (program chmn. 1975, fin. com. 1989-93, Disting. Contbns. to Pub. Policy for Children award 1995); mem. Am. Psychol. Found. (bd. dirs. 1982-86, pres. 1985-86), Denver Med. Soc. (hon. mem.), Colo. Psychol. Assn. (pres. 1959, Disting. Svc. award 1963, 84), Colo. Med. Soc. (Disting. Svc. award 1970), Phi Beta Kappa, Sigma Xi, Alpha Omega Alpha (hon.). Home: 130 S Birch St Denver CO 80246-1017

CONGER, SUE ANN, computer information systems educator; b. Akron, Ohio, Nov. 6, 1947; d. Scott Stanley and Norma Marie (Bauknecht) Summerville; m. David Boyd Conger, July 3, 1971 (dec. June 1997); 1 child, Kathryn Summerville. BS, Ohio State U., 1970; MBA, Rutgers U., 1977; PhD, NYU, 1988. Programmer, analyst USDA, Washington, 1970-72; project leader Ednl. Testing Svc., Princeton, N.J., 1972-73; 2d v.p. Chase Manhattan Bank, N.Y.C., 1973-77; tech. dir. Lambda Technology, Inc., N.Y.C., 1977-80; sr. cons. Mobil Corp., N.Y.C., 1980-83; asst. prof. computer info. systems Ga. State U., Atlanta, 1988-90; asst. prof. Baruch Coll. CUNY, 1990-94; assoc. prof. So. Meth. U., Dallas, 1994—; freelance cons., educator, 1970—. Author: The New Software Engineering, 1994, Planning and Designing Effective Web Sites, 1998; contbr. articles to profl. jours. Grantee, U.S. Army Info. Systems Engring. Command, 1989. Mem. IEEE, Assn. for Computing Machinery, Acad. of Mgmt. Avocations: reading, sports, cooking. Office: So Meth U MIS Dept Edwin L Cox Sch Bus Dallas TX 75275

CONGER, WILLIAM FRAME, artist, educator; b. Dixon, Ill., May 29, 1937; s. Robert Allen and Catherine Florence (Kelly) C.; m. Kathleen Marie Onderak, May 23, 1964; children: Sarah Elizabeth, Clarisa Lynn. Student, Art Inst. Chgo., 1954, 56-57, 60, 62; BFA, U. N.Mex., 1960; MFA, U. Chgo., 1966. asst. prof. Rock Valley Coll., Rockford, 1966-71; vis. lectr. Beloit Coll., 1969; prof., chmn. dept. art DePaul U., Chgo., 1971-85; vis. artist U. Chgo., 1976, 83, Cornell U., 1980; Sch. Art Inst. Chgo., 1985, Univ. Iowa; adj. prof. So. Ill. U., 1984; prof., chmn. dept. art theory and practice Northwestern U., Evanston, Ill., 1985—; numerous lectures; cons. Puresol, Inc. One man shows Burpee Mus., Rockford, Ill., 1971, Douglas Kenyon Gallery, Chgo., 1974, 75, Krannert Ctr. for Arts, Urbana, Ill., 1976, Zaks Gallery, Chgo., 1978, 80, 83, Roy Boyd Gallery, Chgo., 1985, 87, 90, 92, 94, 96, 97, 98, 99 Janus Gallery, Santa Fe, 1992, Tarbel Mus., Ill., 1993, Univ. Club Chgo., 1998, Jonson Mus., Albuquerque, 1998; group shows include Art Inst. Chgo., 1963, 71, 73, 78, 80, 84-85, Mus. Contemporary Art, Chgo., 1976, 96-97, Krannert Mus., Urbana, 1976, Ill. State Mus., 1978, 88-89, E.B. Crocker Gallery, Sacramento, 1977, Phoenix Mus., 1977, Mitchell Mus., 1980, Notre Dame U., 1981, Sonoma State U., 1983, Cowles Mus., 1983, Arts Club Chgo., 1983-97, Sheldon Meml. Gallery, U. Nebr., 1984, Anchorage Fine Arts Mus., 1985, Ark Art Ctr., 1985, Block Gallery, Northwestern U., 1986, 90, 96-97, Smart Mus., 1996; represented in permanent collections Art Inst. Chgo., Mus. Contemporary Art, Chgo., Smart Mus., U. Chgo., Ill. State Mus., Chgo., No. Ill. U., DePaul U., Jonson Mus., U. N.Mex., Block Gallery, others; also pvt. collections U.S. and worldwide; numerous catalogs, revs. and commentary in Arts mag., Art Forum, Art in Am., Ciamese, Art News, Art Criticism, Art & Antiques; others; author essays in Whitewalls, Chicago/Art/Write, Psychoanalytic Perspectives on Art, Psychoanalytic Studies of Biography, Critical Inquiry, other jours. Bd. dirs. Ox Bow Art Sch., 1982-86; adv. bd. Renaissance Soc., 1988—; bd. trustees St. Benedict H.S., Chgo., 1994—; referee NEH, 1989; interviewee TV and radio programs including Am. Art Forum. Recipient Bartels award Art Inst. Chgo., 1971; Clusmann award, 1973; Friedman awards U. Chgo., 1965, 66, Ill. Acad. of Fine Arts Nominee award, 1992. Mem. Coll. Art Assn. Am., Phi Sigma Tau. Office: Northwestern U Dept Art Theory & Practice Rm 244 Kresge Hall Evanston IL 60201 Home: 3500 N Lake Shore Dr Chicago IL 60657-1823

CONGER-WHITE, CHRISTINE KATHLEEN, utilization management coordinator; b. Chgo.; m. Donald A. White, Sept. 4, 1992; 1 child, Jason S. AS, RN, Morton Coll., 1977; BA, George Williams Coll., 1971; post-grad., 1991—. RN, Ariz.; cert. psychiat. and mental health nurse; cert. profl. in utilization rev. Psychiat. and mental health nurse St. Mary Nazareth Hosp., Chgo., 1978-85; crisis ctr. intake assessment nurse Maricopa Med. Ctr., Phoenix, 1997—; psychiat. charge nurse E. Valley St. Luke's Hosp., Chandler, Ariz.; profl. svcs. rev. coord. Behavioral Med. Resources, Tempe, Ariz.; reimbursement specialist Charter Hosp. E. Valley, Chandler; quality analyst Maricopa Med. Ctr.-Psychiat. Annex, Chandler, 1989—; quality analyst dept. quality mgmt. Maricopa Med. Ctr., Phoenix, utilization mgmt. coord., 1998—. Mem. ANA, Nat. Assn. Quality Assurance Profls., Ariz. Assn. Quality Assurance Profls. Home: 1691 W Harvard Ave Gilbert AZ 85233-2908

CONIDI, DANIEL JOSEPH, private investigation agency executive; b. Chgo., Mar. 11, 1957; s. Joseph Frank and Gloria (Zimmerman) C. BS, SUNY, Albany, 1983; MA, Chgo. State U., 1987. Lic. pvt. detective, Ill., Wis., Ind. Owner, mgr. Conidi Enterprises, Chgo., 1979-81; pres. Daniel J. Conidi-Assocs., Chgo., 1981—; cons. Office Cook County Sheriff, Chgo., 1983-90; freelance lectr., 1983—. Author: Professional Investigative Methods, 1984, Private Investigators Training Manual, 1986. Del. Cook County Rep. Conv., 1987. Recipient cert. of appreciation Boys Town, 1982; named Ky. col. State of Ky., 1987. Mem. World Assn. Detectives, Internat. Police Congress, Coun. Internat. Investigators, Nat. Assn. Investigations and Security, Fraternal Order Police, NRA (life), Navy League (life), Univ. Club, Masons, Shriners. Presbyterian. Avocations: flying, writing. Home: 500 Ashland Ave River Forest IL 60305-1825 Office: 734 N La Salle Dr Ste 1082 Chicago IL 60610-3530

CONIGILARO, PHYLLIS ANN, retired elementary education educator; b. Ilion, N.Y., Nov. 27, 1932; d. Gus Carl and Jennie Margaret (Marine) Denapole; m. Paul Anthony Conigilaro, July 16, 1983. BS cum laude, SUNY, Cortland, 1955; MA in Edn., Psychology, Cornell U., 1961. Cert. tchr., N.Y. Elem. classroom tchr. Mohawk (N.Y.) Central Sch., 1955-88. Contbr. articles to profl. jours. Bd. dirs. United Fund of Ilion, Herkimer, Mohawk and Frankfort, 1984-86, pres., 1986; pres. bd. edn. St. Mary's Parochial Sch., 1978; mem. Herkimer County Hist. Soc., 1988—, trustee, 1994-97; bd. dirs. local Federal Emergency Mgmt. Agy., 1987-96. Mem. N.Y. State United Tchrs., Mohawk Tchrs. Assn. (past pres.), AAUW (pres. Herkimer chpt. 1981-82), N.Y. State Ret. Tchrs. Assn. (past legis. chmn. Herkimer County chpt.), Rep. Women's Club, Kappa Delta Pi. Republican. Roman Catholic. Avocations: golf, travel, reading, music. Home: 137 7th Ave Frankfort NY 13340-3612

CONINE, ERNEST, newspaper commentator, writer; b. Dallas, Dec. 31, 1925; s. Ernest and Myrtle Eva (Elkins) C.; m. Phyllis Joan Hoyland, Nov. 28, 1953 (dec.); m. Ulla Fisher, Jan. 10, 1981. B.S., So. Methodist U., 1948. Staff writer UPI, Dallas, 1948-51; Washington corr. Dallas Times Herald, 1952-55; successively Washington corr., Moscow corr., New Eng. mgr. Bus. Week mag., 1955-63; fgn. corr. L.A. Times, Vienna, 1963-64; public affairs columnist, mem. editorial bd. L.A. Times, 1964-87, contbr., 1988-92; mem. Ctr. Internat. and Strategic Affairs, UCLA, 1975-90, Internat. Inst. for Strategic Studies, 1984-98; mem. Calif. Seminar Internat. Security and Fgn. Affairs, 1970-93, L.A. Com. Fgn. Affairs, 1973-93. Contbr. articles to nat. magazines. Served with AUS, 1944-46, 51-52. Mem. Soc. Profl. Journalists. Home and Office: 205 Dasher Dr Austin TX 78734-5040

CONINE, JEFFREY GUY, professional baseball player; b. Tacoma, Wash., June 27, 1966. Student, UCLA. With Kansas City Royals, 1992; outfielder Fla. Marlins, 1993-97, Kansas City Royals, 1997-98, Balt. Orioles, 1999—. Named So. League Most Valuable Player, 1990, Nat. League All-Star Team, 1994-95, Most Valuable Player All-Star Game, 1995. Office: Balt Orioles Camden Yards 333 W Camden St Baltimore MD 21201*

CONINO, JOSEPH ALOYSIUS, lawyer; b. Hammond, La., Aug. 17, 1920; s. Dominic and Catherine (Tamborella) C.; m. Mae Evelyn Moragas, Feb. 27, 1943; children: Joseph Aloysius Jr., Robert Carl. BBA, Tulane U., 1950; JD, Loyola U., 1961; MBA, U. Pa., 1951. Bar: La. 1961, U.S. Dist. Ct. (ea. dist.) La. 1961, U.S. Ct. Appeals (5th cir.) 1972, U.S. Supreme Ct. 1989. Pvt. practice Jefferson, La., 1961—; county judge State of La. Parish, Jefferson, 1970; del. State of La. Constnl. Conv., Baton Rouge, 1973-74; asst. atty. Parish of Jefferson, 1977—. With USN, 1942-45. Mem. La. Bar Assn. (ho. of dels. 1963-92, bd. dirs. 1981-83, 96—), Jefferson Bar Assn. (pres.), New Orleans C. of C. (bd. dirs. 1974-77), Kiwanis (pres. Metairie, La. chpt.). Avocations: golf, swimming, tennis. Office: 1920 Jefferson Hwy Jefferson LA 70121-3816

CONISON, JAY, lawyer; b. Cin., Oct. 21, 1953; s. Allan Abraham and Theresa (Yudofsky) C.; m. Nancy Jo Kelber, Sept. 7, 1980; children: Alexander, David. BA, Yale U., 1975; MA, U. Minn., 1978, JD, 1981. Bar: Ill. 1981, U.S. Dist. Ct. (no. dist.) Ill. 1980, U.S. Dist. Ct. (ea. dist.) Wis. 1984, U.S. Dist. Ct. (no. dist. trial) Ill. 1985, U.S. Ct. Appeals (7th cir.) 1986, U.S. Dist. Ct. (we. dist.) Okla. 1990, U.S. Supreme Ct. 1990. Atty. Sonnenschein, Carlin, Nath & Rosenthal, Chgo., 1981-90; asst. prof. Oklahoma City U. Sch. Law, 1990-92, assoc. prof., 1992-94, prof., assoc. dean, 1994-97, interim dean, 1997—. Author: Employee Benefit Plans in a Nutshell, 1993. Mem. ABA (Forum com. franchising). Home: 2103 Chandana Trl # E Valparaiso IN 46383-2295 Office: Okla City U Sch Law 2501 N Blackwelder Ave Oklahoma City OK 73106-1402

CONKEL, ROBERT DALE, lawyer, pension consultant; b. Martins Ferry, Ohio, Oct. 13, 1936; s. Chester William and Marian Matilda (Ashton) C.; m. Elizabeth A. Cargill, June 15, 1958; children: Debra Lynn Conkel McGlone, Dale William, Douglas Alan; m. Brenda Jo Myers, Aug. 2, 1980; 1 child, Chelsea Ashton. BA, Mt. Union Coll., 1958; JD cum laude, Cleve. Marshall Law Sch., 1965; LLM, Case Western Res. U., 1972. Bar: Ohio 1965, U.S. Tax Ct. 1974, U.S. Supreme Ct. 1974, Tex. 1978, U.S. Ct. Appeals (5th cir.) 1979. Supr., Social Security Adminstrn., Cleve., 1958-65; trust officer Harter Bank & Trust Co., Canton, Ohio, 1965-70; exec. v.p. Am. Actuaries, Inc., Grand Rapids, Mich., 1970-73, pension cons., southwest regional dir., Dallas, 1974-88; mgr. plans and rsch. A.S. Hansen, Inc., Dallas, 1973-74; pvt. practice, Dallas, 1973—; sr. cons., Coopers & Lybrand, Dallas, 1989; pres. Robert D. Conkel, Inc., 1989—; mem. devel. bd. Met. Nat. Bank, Richardson, Tex.; instr. Am. Mgmt. Assn., 1975, Am. Coll. Advanced Pension Planning, 1975-76. Sustaining mem. Rep. Nat. Com., 1980-88. Enrolled actuary, Joint Bd. Enrollment U.S. Depts. Labor and Treasury. Mem. ABA (employee benefit com. sect. taxation), Ohio State Bar Assn., Tex. Bar Assn., Dallas Bar Assn., Am. Soc. Pension Actuaries (dir. 1973-81), Am. Acad. Actuaries. Contbr. articles to legal publs.; mem. editl. adv. bd. Jour. Pension Planning and Compliance, 1974-83. Office: 100 N Central Expy # 519 Richardson TX 75080-5332

CONKIN, PAUL KEITH, history educator; b. Chuckey, Tenn., Oct. 25, 1929; s. Harry Thomas and Dorothy (Staten) C.; m. Dorothy L. Tharp, 1954; 3 children. BA, Milligan Coll., 1951; MA, Vanderbilt U., 1953, PhD, 1957. Asst. prof. history U. Southwestern La., 1957-59; asst. prof., assoc. prof., prof. U. Md., 1959-67; prof. U. Wis., Madison, 1967-76, Merle Curti prof., 1976-79; disting. prof. history Vanderbilt U., Nashville, 1979—, chmn. dept. history, 1984-87. Author: The New Deal, 1967, F.D.R. and the Origins of the Welfare State, 1967, Puritans and Pragmatists, 1968, Self-Evident Truths, 1974, Prophets of Prosperity, 1980, Gone with the Ivy: A Biography of Vanderbilt U., 1985, Big Daddy from the Pedernales: Lyndon Baines Johnson, 1986, The Southern Agrarians, 1988, Cane Ridge: America's Pentecost, 1991, Four Foundations of American Government, 1994, The Uneasy Center: Reformed Christianity in Antebellum America, 1995, American Originals: Homemade Varieties of Christianity, 1997, When All the Gods Trembled: Darwinism, Scopes, and American Intellectuals, 1998; co-author: The Heritage and Challenge of History, 1971; author: (with others) A History of Recent America, 1974; co-editor: New Directions in American Intellectual History, 1979. Guggenheim fellow, 1965-66; sr. fellow Nat. Endowment for Humanities, 1972-73, 90. Mem. Am. Hist. Assn. (Beveridge award 1958), Orgn. Am. Historians, So. Hist. Assn. (pres. 1996-97). Home: 1003 Tyne Blvd Nashville TN 37220-1026

CONKLIN, DONALD RANSFORD, retired pharmaceutical company executive; b. Bound Brook, N.J., Sept. 10, 1936; s. Walter Ransford and Dorothy Ann (Haase) C.; m. Louise Sealey, July 13, 1960; children: Elizabeth, Edward. BA, Williams Coll., 1958; MBA, Rutgers U., 1961; grad. program for mgmt. devel., Harvard U., 1970. Dir. mktg. Schering Corp. U.S.A. (name changed to Schering-Plough 1971), Kenilworth, N.J., 1970-74; dir. mktg. Europe div. Schering-Plough, Lucerne, Switzerland, 1975-76; v.p. internat. mktg. Schering-Plough, Kenilworth, 1977-79; regional dir., sr. v.p. Latin Am. div. Schering-Plough, Miami, Fla., 1980-83; sr. v.p. internat. hdqrs. Schering-Plough, Kenilworth, 1984—, pres., 1985, group v.p. pharm. ops., 1986, exec. v.p. pharm. ops., 1987-89, pres. pharm. ops., 1989-94, pres. healthcare products, 1994-96; ret., 1996; bd. dirs. Vertex Pharms., Biotransplant, Inc. Home: 120A Youngs Rd Basking Ridge NJ 07920

CONKLIN, GEORGE MELVILLE, retired food company executive; b. Roselle Park, N.J., Dec. 29, 1921; s. Melville Guy and Anna Elizabeth (McMahon) C.; m. Jean Austin Wiley, Feb. 19, 1944; children: Andrea, Blair. B.S., Clarkson Coll. Tech., 1947; M.S., Newark Coll. Engring., 1951; D.Sc. (hon.), Clarkson U., 1987. Draftsman Babcock & Wilcox, N.Y.C., 1939-42; indsl. engr. Johns-Manville Co., Manville, N.J., 1947-48, Western Electric Co., Kearny, N.J., 1948-50, Gen. Ceramics, Keasby, N.J., 1950-51; indsl. engring. supr. Gen Electric Co., Bloomfield, N.J., 1951-52; with M & M/Mars, Hackettstown, N.J., 1952—; pres. M & M/Mars, 1968-78, chmn., 1980-82; group pres. Mars, Inc., 1979-80. Trustee Clarkson U., 1976-86. Served with inf. AUS, 1943-45. Decorated Combat Inf. badge; named Hon. Commodore, Lake Waco, Tex; recipient Key to City of Cleveland, Tenn. Mem. Tex. Rangers (hon.), Tau Beta Pi, Somerset Hill Golf Club (Bernardsville, N.J.), Willoughby Golf Club (Stuart, Fla.). Home: 1305 SE Brewster Pl Stuart FL 34997-5611 *Be a leader that most people do not notice so that when a job is done well, the people believe that they did it themselves.*

CONKLIN, HAROLD COLYER, anthropologist, educator; b. Easton, Pa., Apr. 27, 1926; s. Howard S. and May W. (Colyer) C.; m. Jean M. Morisuye, June 11, 1954; children: Bruce Robert, Mark William. A.B., U. Calif.-Berkeley, 1950; Ph.D., Yale U., 1955. From instr. to assoc. prof. anthropology Columbia U., 1954-62; lectr. anthropology Rockefeller Inst., 1961-62; prof. anthropology Yale U., 1962-96, chmn. dept., 1964-68, Crosby prof. anthropology, 199096; curator of anthropology Yale Peabody Mus. Natural History, 1974-96, dir. divsn. anthropology, 1994-96, prof. emeritus, curator emeritus, 1996—; mem. Inst. for Advanced Study, Princeton, N.J., 1972; fellow Ctr. for Advanced Study in Behavioral Scis., Stanford, Calif., 1978-79; field rsch. in Philippines, 1945-47, 52-54, 55, 57-58, 61, 62-65, 68-69, 70, 73, 80-81, 82-85, 90-91, 95, Malaya and Indonesia, 1948, 57, 83, Melanesia, 1987, N.Y., 1943, 49, 51, Calif., 49, 51, Guatemala, 1959, Peru, 1987; dir., com. problems and policy Social Sci. Rsch. Coun., 1963-70; bd. dirs. Survival Intnerat. USA; spl. cons. Internat. Rice Rsch. Inst., Los Baños, Philippines, 1962—; book rev. editor Am. Anthropologist, 1960-62; mem. Pacific sci. bd. Nat. Acad. Scis.-NRC, 1962-66. Author: Hanunóo Agriculture, 1957, Folk Classification, 1972, Ethnographic Atlas of Ifugao, 1980; other publs. on ethnol., linguistic and ecol. topics. Served with AUS, 1944-46. Guggenheim fellow, 1973; recipient Internat. Sci. prize Fyssen Foundation, 1983. Mem. NAS; Fellow Am. Acad. Arts and Scis., Am. Anthrop. Assn. (exec. bd. 1965-68), Royal Anthrop. Inst., N.Y. Acad. Scis. (sec. sect. anthropology 1956); mem. Am. Ethnol. Soc. (councilor 1960-62, pres. 1978-79), Koninklijk Inst. voor Taal- Land- en Volkenkunde, Conn. Acad. Arts and Scis., Linguistic Soc. Am., Kroeber Anthrop. Soc., Phila. Anthrop. Soc., Am. Geog. Soc., Am. Oriental Soc., Assn. Asian Studies, Classification Soc., Linguistic Soc. Philippines, Indo-Pacific Prehistory Assn., Soc. Econ. Botany, Internat. Assn. Plant Taxonomy, AAAS, Phi Beta Kappa, Sigma Xi. Home: 106 York Sq New Haven CT 06511-3625 Address: TYale Univ DEPT of Anthopogy PO Box 208277 New Haven CT 06520-8277

CONKLIN, JACK LARIVIERE, education educator; b. Pt. Jefferson, N.Y., Dec. 9, 1942; s. John Agustus and Jeanne (Lariviere) C.; m. Susan J. Kuceluk, July 25, 1981; children: Susanne, Danielle, Genevieve, Michelle. BA, Dowling Coll., 1967; MA, Adelphi U., 1970; PhD, U. So. Calif., L.A., 1972. Tchr. Comsewogue Sch. Dist., Pt. Jefferson Sta., N.Y., 1967-70; asst. principal intern Toll Jr. High Sch., Glendale, Calif., 1971-72; prof. edn. Mass. Coll. Liberal Arts, 1972—; chmn. edn. dept. North Adams (Mass.) State Coll., 1982-92, cert. officer, 1988-93; chmn. Commonwealth Tchr. Edn. Consortium, 1981-83; cons. U.S. Dept. Edn. Drug Free Schs. and Communities, 1989—; field reader safe and drug-free schs. program U.S. Dept. Edn., 1990—. Bd. dirs. Berkshire Ctr. for Families and Children, Pittsfield, Mass., 1977, South Forty Alternatives, North Adams, 1978, Old Castle Theatre Co., Bennington, Vt., 1994-98; vestry mem. St. John's Episcopal Ch., Williamstown, Mass., 1983-84, St. John's Episcopal Ch., N. Adams, Mass., 1996-98; cons. N.E. Regional Ctr. for Drug Free Schs., 1988-94; mem. sch. coun. Mt. Greylock Regional Sch. Dist., Williamstown, 1996—. Mem. Am. Assn. Colls. for Tchr. Edn. (adv. coun. state reps.), Mass. Assn. Colls. for Tchr. Edn. (pres. 1988-89), North Adams State Faculty Assn. (pres. 1980-83), Cmty. Edn. Legis. Task Force, Mass. State Senate, 1998—Joint Task force on Tchr. Preparation, Phi Delta Kappa, Pi Lambda Theta (nat. officers nominating com.). Democrat. Avocations: jazz-cocktail piano, sailing. Home: 85 Hawthorne Rd Williamstown MA 01267-2700 Office: Mass Coll Liberal Arts Hopkins Hall Church St North Adams MA 01247-4100

CONKLIN, JOHN EVAN, sociology educator; b. Oswego, N.Y., Oct. 2, 1943; s. Evan Nelson and Susan Estelle (Brenner) C.; m. Ruth Tiffany Edmonds, July 10, 1965 (div. Oct. 1974); children: Christopher Perry, Anne

Tiffany; m. Sarah Hubbard Belcher, Jan .2, 1982; children: Lydia Catherine, Gillian Jane. AB, Cornell U., 1965; PhD, Harvard U., 1969. Research assoc. Harvard U. Law Sch., Cambridge, Mass., 1969-70; asst. prof. sociology Tufts U., Medford, Mass., 1970-76, assoc. prof. sociology, 1976-81, prof. sociology, 1981—, chmn. dept. sociology, 1981-86, 90-91. Author: Robbery and the Criminal Justice System, 1972, The Impact of Crime, 1975, Illegal But Not Criminal, 1977, Criminology, 1981, 6th edit., 1998, Sociology: An Introduction, 1984, 2d edit., 1987, Art Crime, 1994; editor: The Crime Establishment, 1973, New Perspectives in Criminology, 1996. Mem. Am. Sociol. Assn., Am. Soc. Criminology. Avocations: collecting books, movie memorabilia, marbles. Office: Tufts U Dept of Sociology Eaton Hall Medford MA 02155

CONKLIN, JOHN ROGER, retired electronics company executive; b. Poughkeepsie, N.Y., Dec. 20, 1933; s. Leland Thomas and Eleanor (Warren) C.; m. Catharine Becker, Dec. 28, 1956 (div. Apr. 1976); children: Thomas Stephen, Todd Roger; m. Nancy Plank, July 16, 1983. BS in Mil. Sci., U.S. Mil. Acad., 1956; postgrad., Xavier U., Cin., 1961-62, Northeastern U., 1974. Engr. Procter & Gamble Co., Cin., 1960-64; sales engr. Orville Simpson Co., Cin., 1964-67; various sales positions DeLaval Separator Co., Poughkeepsie, 1967-74, pres., 1974-78; pres. Standard Gage Co., Poughkeepsie, 1979-86; pres., owner Discount Data Products, Inc., Poughkeepsie, 1988-97; adv. bd. Dutchess divsn. Bank of N.Y., Poughkeepsie, 1974-98. Contbr. articles to profl. jours.; patentee basket centrifuge. Bd. dirs. Area Fund-Dutchess County, Poughkeepsie, 1975, Poughkeepsie C. of C., 1981-86, YMCA, Poughkeepsie, 1982; campaign chair United Way, Dutchess County, N.Y., 1986. 1st lt. U.S. Army, 1956-60. Mem. D.C. Mycological Soc., D.C. Hist. Soc. Avocations: skiing, trout fishing, gardening, mycology. Home: 4 Dutchess Ter Rhinecliff NY 12574

CONKLIN, KENNETH EDWARD, lawyer, industry executive; b. Keota, Iowa, Aug. 21, 1939; s. Cleo W. and Viola C.; children: David S., Steven J. Student, St. Ambrose Coll., 1957-59, Ariz. State U., 1960-61; B.S., N.E. Mo. State U., 1966; J.D., Washington Coll. Law Am. U., 1969. Bar: Md., D.C., U.S. Supreme Ct., U.S. Ct. Appeals, U.S. Ct. Claims. Atty. Pub. Defender Office, 1969-70; partner firm Conklin & Noble, Chevy Chase, Md., 1970-76, Leighton, Conklin, Lemov, Jacobs and Buckley, Washington, 1977-83; pres. CEO. Noramco Internat., Inc., Noramex Trading Corp.; bd. dirs. Ea. Pines Devel. Corp., Personal Protection Internat. Inc., Korume Internat., Inc., Falls Church Profl. Ctr. Adviser, atty. Legal Aid, 1969-75; mem. Montgomery County (Md.) Rep. Club, v.p., 1972-73. Served with spl. forces AUS, 1962-65, Vietnam. Mem. Am., Montgomery County, Md. State, D.C. bar assns., Assn. Trial Lawyers Am. Home: 1510 12th St N Apt 603 Arlington VA 22209-3634 Office: Noramco Intenat Inc 200 Little Falls St Ste 508 Falls Church VA 22046-4302

CONKLIN, MARA LORAINE, public relations executive; b. Vallejo, Calif., July 28, 1962; d. Kenneth J. and Laura T. (Siegrist) Cichosz; m. Rex D. Conklin, Sept. 6, 1986; children: Elisabeth, Emily, Margaret. BA, Marquette U., 1984. Nat. news editl. staff Nat. Safety Coun., Chgo., 1984-85; corp. comm. specialist Household Internat., Prospect Hgts., Ill., 1985-86; acct. supr. Posner McGrath Ltd., Lincolnshire, Ill., 1986-90, v.p., 1990-92, sr. v.p., 1992-94, exec. v.p., 1994-97, pres., 1997-98; pres. Clarus Comms. Ltd., Libertyville, Ill., 1998—. Recipient Spectra award Internat. Assn. Bus. Communicators, 1992, 94, Silver Trumpet award Publicity Club Chgo., 1993. Mem. Marquette Club Chgo. (chair alumni com. 1986-94, pres. 1994-96). Office: Clarus Comms Ltd 620 Mullady Pkwy Libertyville IL 60048-3729

CONKLIN, ROBERT EUGENE, electronics engineer; b. Loveland, Ohio, Apr. 21, 1925; s. Charles and Alberta (Reynolds) C.; m. Virginia E. McCann, June 14, 1952; children—Carl Lynn, Jill Elaine Conklin Bradford. B.S. in Edn., Wilmington Coll., 1949, B.S. in Sci., 1949. Electronic scientist Electronic Technol. Lab., Wright-Patterson AFB, Ohio, 1951-55; electronic engr. AF Avionics Lab., Wright-Patterson AFB, 1956-60 supervisory elec. engr., 1960-72, cons. electronic engr., 1972-78, supervisory electronic engr., 1978-82, electronic engr. (VHSIC), 1982-84; cons. engr. REC Electronics, Fairborn, Ohio, 1984—; mem. Inst. Nav., 1968-72. Mgr. Babe Ruth Boys' Baseball, 1969-74; mgr. and pres. Little League, Fairborn, 1965-68. Served with USAAC, 1943-46. Mem. IEEE. Republican. Quaker. Lodge: Lions (Fairborn) Home: 114 Wayne Dr Fairborn OH 45324-5228 Office: 47 N Broad St Fairborn OH 45324-4863

CONKLIN, SARAH C., health education educator; b. Aug. 15, 1944. MA, United Theol. Sem. Twin Cities, New Brighton, Minn., 1994; PhD, U. Pa., 1996. Curriculum specialist Minn. Instnl. Materials Ctr., White Bear Lake, 1976-77, Coop. Edn. Svc. Agy. 11, Turtle Lake, Wis., 1989-91; asst. prof. health and secuality edn. U. Wyo., Laramie, 1996—. E-mail: conklins@uwyo.edu.

CONKLIN, THOMAS WILLIAM, lawyer; b. Chgo., Mar. 1, 1938; s. Clarence Robert and Ellen Pauline (Gleason) C.; children: Thomas William, Sarah Adrienne. BA, Yale U., 1960; JD, U. Chgo., 1963. Bar: Ill. 1964, Mich. 1997. Ptnr. Upton, Conklin & Leahy, Chgo., 1969-72, Conklin, Leahy & Eisenberg, Chgo., 1972-79, Conklin & Adler, Ltd., Chgo., 1979-87, Conklin & Roadhouse, Chgo., 1988-95; Rivkin, Radler & Kremer, Chgo., 1995-97; ptnr. Conklin Murphy & Conklin, Chgo., 1997—; of counsel Luyendyk & Assocs., Muskegon, Mich. Contbr. numerous articles to legal jours. With USAF, 1963-64. Mem. ABA, Fed. Bar Assn., Am. Arbitration Assn., Internat. Assn. Ins. Counsel, Chgo. Bar Assn., Maritime Law Assn., Mich. Bar Assn., Union League Club Chgo. Home: PO Box 189 43 148 CR 681 Bangor MI 49013 Office: Conklin Murphy & Conklin 53 W Jackson Blvd Ste 1750 Chicago IL 60604-3790

CONKLING, ROGER LINTON, consultant, business administration educator, retired utility executive; b. Bloomington, Ill., July 12, 1917; s. Robert Edwin and Helen (Ricketts) C.; m. Meta Baskerville, Apr. 4, 1941; children—Mary Beth, Jane Linton, Roger Marc. B.B.A., Northwestern U., 1941; M.A., U. Oreg., 1948; LL.D., U. Portland, 1972. With Pub. Service Co. of No. Ill., Chgo. and Joliet, 1936-42; economist Bonneville Power Adminstrn., Portland, Oreg., 1945-47, asst. to power mgr., 1948-51, chief system devel., 1952-53, chief customer service, 1954, dir. budget and mgmt., 1955-56, asst. to adminstr., 1957; v.p., assoc. H. Zinder & Assocs., Inc., Washington, 1958-61; pres., cons. Conkling, Inc., Portland, 1962-67; v.p. N.W. Natural Gas Co., Portland, 1967-76, sr. v.p., 1976-82, ret., 1982; cons., 1982—; adj. prof. bus. adminstrn. U. Portland, 1988—; former pres., dir. Pacific Western Pipeline Corp., Portland; mem. grad. faculty Oreg. System Higher Edn., Portland, 1946-56. Past pres., chmn. Oreg. United Appeal; pres. Delauney Inst. Mental Health, 1964; mem. Gov.'s Com. Child Care, 1964; bd. dirs. Cath. Charities, Inc., Portland, 1957-58, 61-64; pres. Oreg. State Soc., Washington, 1960; chmn. exec. com. Nat. Found., 1958-60; chmn. March of Dimes campaign, Portland, 1957; bd. dirs. Mental Health Assn., 1957-58, Cath. Services for Children, 1954-57, Oreg. Symphony Assn., NCCJ, 1980-82, Found. Oreg. Research and Edn., 1967-80; chmn. bd. regents U. Portland; trustee Providence Children's Center; chmn. ann. fund dr. Oreg. Symphony, 1981; mem. fin. council Archdiocese of Portland, 1988-98. Served with USNR, 1942-45. Recipient Distinguished Service award Dept. Interior, Arthur S. Fleming award Jr. C. of C., Papal honor, Benemerenti medal. Mem. Am. Econ. Assn., Western Econ. Assn., Fed. Govt. Accts. Assn., Am. Gas Assn., Pacific Coast Gas Assn., Assn. Wash. Gas Utilities (trustee, past pres.), Beta Gamma Sigma, Delta Mu Delta. Club: Multnomah Athletic (Portland). Home and Office: 2539 SW Hill Crest Dr Portland OR 97201-1749

CONLAND, STEPHEN, publishing company executive; b. Hartford, Conn., Apr. 22, 1916; s. Henry Holton and Caroline Mathilde (Henschel) C.; m. Gladys Bett Burton, Mar. 10, 1944; 1 son, Robert Stephen. A.B., Yale U., 1939; M.B.A., Harvard U., 1941. Adminstrv. mgr. Burlington Industries, N.Y.C., 1948-55; with Berkley Pub. Corp., N.Y.C., 1956-77; pres. Berkley Pub. Corp., 1959-77; assoc. Moseley Assos., Inc. (pub. cons.), N.Y.C., 1979. Served to lt. col. Q.M.C., AUS, World War II; Res. ret. Decorated Bronze Star. Clubs: Yale (N.Y.C.); Harvard Business School of No. Conn; Hempstead Hill (West Granby, Conn.); Hartford (Conn.); Yale (Hartford); Army and Navy (Washington). Home: PO Box 291 West Granby CT 06090-0291

CONLEY, CARROLL LOCKARD, physician, emeritus educator; b. Balt., May 14, 1915; s. Harry Lewis and Harriet (Coulbourne) C.; m. Edith DeYoung, Feb. 27, 1943; children: Anne Marie (Mrs. R.J. Weaver), Jean Alice. AB, Johns Hopkins U., 1935; MD, Columbia U., 1940. Intern Presbyn. Hosp., N.Y.C., 1940-42; fellow medicine Johns Hopkins, 1946, instr. to assoc. prof. medicine, 1947-56; prof. medicine Johns Hopkins U., 1956—, Disting. Service prof., 1976-80, emeritus, 1980—; dir. hematology div. Johns Hopkins Hosp., 1947-80, dir. labs., 1956-66; hon. assoc. prof. medicine Guy's Hosp. Med. Sch., London, Eng.; cons. USPHS, FDA, Army, VA, WHO, NASA; mem. com. on blood NRC, 1954-63, chmn. subcom. on thrombosis and hemorrage, 1962-64; chmn. hematology study sect. NIH, 1962-65; sickle cell disease adv. com. Dept. HEW, 1971-73; disting. sr. clinician USPHS, 1980-81. Editorial bd.: Archives of Internal Medicine, 1959-65, Blood, the Jour. of Hematology, 1954-67, Bull. of Johns Hopkins Hosp, 1963-70; Contbr. med. textbooks and profl. jours. Served from lt. to maj. M.C. AUS, 1942-45. Recipient Bicentennial medal Coll. Physicians and Surgeons, 1967. Fellow AAAS, ACP (master 1983, Disting. Tchr. award 1983), Royal Coll. Physicians (London); mem. AMA, Soc. for Exptl. Biology and Medicine, Assn. Am. Physicians, Am. Soc. Clin. Investigation, Am. Soc. Hematology (exec. com. v.p. 1973-74, pres. 1975-76), European Soc. Hematology (corr. mem.), Interurban Clin. Club, Phi Beta Kappa, Alpha Omega Alpha (Leader in Medicine 1988). Home: 717 Maiden Choice Ln Apt 520 Baltimore MD 21228-6173 Office: Johns Hopkins Hosp Baltimore MD 21205

CONLEY, DARLENE ANN, actress; b. Chgo.; d. Raymond and Melba (Manthey) C.; m. William Woodson, Oct. 1959 (div. 1966); 1 child, Raymond. Actress Broadway prodns. including: The Baker's Wife, The Night of the Iguana;. actress feature films including: Tough Guys, Faces, Minnie and Moscowitz, Play it As it Lays, Lady Sings the Blues, Valley of the Dolls, The Birds; TV movies include: I Want to Live, The Fighter, The Choice, Return Engagement, The President's Plane is Missing; TV episodes include: Get Christie Love, Scarecrow and Mrs. King, Highway to Heaven, Murder She Wrote, Bill Cosby Show, Little House on the Prairie; continuing role on The Young and The Restless, 1980-88, The Bold and The Beautiful, 1989—. Emmy nominee for Outstanding Supporting Actress, 1991, 92; statue made for Madame Tussaud's Wax Mus., 1998. Office: Bell-Phillip TV Prodns Inc 7800 Beverly Blvd # 3371 Los Angeles CA 90036-2112

CONLEY, EUGENE ALLEN, retired insurance company executive; b. Nebraska City, Nebr., Oct. 3, 1925; s. Melville Evans and Margaret (Allen) C.; m. Erma Grace Fuller, June 27, 1948; children: Tom, Roger, John, Carol Sue. B.S., U. Nebr., 1949; D.Sc. (hon.), U. Nebr. Med. Ctr.; LL.D. (hon.), Nebr. Wesleyan U. C.L.U. Agt. Am. Mut. Life Ins. Co., Omaha, 1948-54; supr., supt. agts., v.p., dir. agts., dir. Am. Mut. Life Ins. Co., Des Moines, 1954-72; exec. v.p., dir. Guarantee Mut. Life Co., Omaha, 1972-76; pres. Guarantee Mut. Life Co., 1976-89, chmn. bd., 1989-90; retired, 1990. Bd. dirs. Omaha Zool. Soc.; trustee, past chmn. Nebr. Ind. Coll. Found.; bd. trustees U. Nebr. Found., Lincoln; civilian aide to sec. Army; mem. pres.'s adv. coun. Creighton U.; past chmn. bd. govs. Nebr. Wesleyan U.; co-chmn. fund drive United Way Midlands, 1976-77, pres., 1979-80; past crusade chmn. Am. Cancer Soc.; co-chmn. NCCJ; chmn. bd. Bishop Clarkson Coll., 1990; chmn. Omaha Community Found., 1991.. Served with USNR, 1943-46. Recipient Americanism citation B'Nai B'rith, 1982, Builder award U. Nebr.; named Citizen of Yr. United Way, 1983. Mem. Nat. Assn. Life Underwriters, Coll. Life Underwriters, Omaha C. of C. (chmn. dir.), Phi Kappa Psi. Clubs: Omaha, Omaha Country, Plaza, Masons, Shriners. Home: 9715 Brentwood Rd Omaha NE 68114-4970 Office: Guarantee Centre 8801 Indian Hills Dr Omaha NE 68114-4059

CONLEY, JEFF, company executive. BA, Drew U., 1975. Prin. Strat@Comm, 1995—. Office: 2d Fl 818 Connecticut Ave NW Washington DC 20006

CONLEY, JOHN JOSEPH, philosophy educator, priest; b. Phila., Nov. 25, 1951; s. Peter Thomas and Mary Broderick Conley. BA, U. Pa., 1973; LTh, Ctr Sevres, Paris, 1983; PhD, Cath. U. Louvain, Belgium, 1988. Ordained priest Roman Cath. Ch., 1983. Instr. Wheeling (W.Va.) Coll., 1977-79; assoc. pastor Holy Trinity Ch., Washington, 1984-85; prof. philosophy Fordham U., Bronx, N.Y., 1988—, chmn. philosophy dept., 1996—; mem. exec. com. John Paul II Symposium, Rome, 1990—. Editor: Prophecy and Diplomacy, 1999; assoc. editor Internat. Philos. Quar., 1994—; contbr. articles to profl. jours. Mem. Bronx Arts Com., 1990—. Recipient Essay award Pax Christi, 1991; Folger inst. grantee, 1998. Mem. Am. Philos. Assn., Am. Cath. Philos. Assn., Soc. for Study of Women Philosophers, United Faculty for Life, Phi Beta Kappa. E-Mail: jconley@murray.fordham.edu. Home: Spellman Hall Bronx NY 10458 Office: Fordham U Dept Philosophy Bronx NY 10458

CONLEY, KATHARINE, language educator; b. Washington, Aug. 10, 1956; d. James Daniel and Jane (Harris) C.; m. Richard Stamelman, Sept., 1997. BA, Harvard U., 1979; MA, U. Colo., 1988; PhD, U. Pa., 1992. Asst. editor Old-House Jour., Brooklyn, N.Y., 1980-81; assoc. editor Victorian Homes mag., Brooklyn, N.Y., 1981-83; asst. prodn. mgr. Shambhala Publs., Boulder, Colo., 1983-85, Westview Press, Boulder, Colo., 1985-86; assoc. prof. French, Italian Dartmouth U., Hanover, N.H., 1992—. Author: Automatic Women, 1996; co-editor: La Femme sèntête, 1998. Mem. Am. Assn. Tchrs. French, Am. Coun. Québec Studies, Women in French, MLA. Democrat. Avocations: singing, hiking. Office: Dartmouth Coll French & Italian 6087 Dartmouth Hall Hanover NH 03755-3511

CONLEY, KATHERINE LOGAN, religious studies educator; b. Rutherford, N.C., Sept. 3, 1911; d. Claude Joseph and Mary (Beam) Logan; m. Jesse William Conley, Dec. 26, 1942. BS in Edn., Asheville (N.C.) Coll., 1936; postgrad., Presbyn. Ch. Christian Edn., Richmond, Va., 1939-40. Dir Christian edn. Presbyn. Ch., Spartanburg, S.C., 1940-41, Knoxville, 1941—; chmn. bldg. com. Seventh-Day Adventist Ch., Rutherford, N.C., 1963; lay speaker United Meth. Ch., Rutherfordton, 1973-91. Mem. Genealogical Soc., DAR (regent 1976-78), Amnesty Internat., Am. Bible Soc. (silver). Democrat. Avocations: gardening, arts and crafts, hiking. Home: 4429 Us 64 Hwy Rutherfordton NC 28139-8198

CONLEY, MICHAEL ALEXANDER, track and field athlete; b. Chicago, Oct. 5, 1962. Grad., U. Ark., 1985. Olympic triple jumper Barcelona, Spain, 1992. Recipient Triple Jump Gold medal Olympics, Barcelona, 1992. Office: care US Track and Field 1 Rca Dome Ste 140 Indianapolis IN 46225-1023*

CONLEY, PATRICK, clinic administrator; b. Roby, Tex., Oct. 10, 1921; s. Boerne Lurl and Mary Esther (Barlow) C.; m. Lucy Ann Webster, Sept. 26, 1942; children: Christopher Redifer, Peter Lurl, Molly Catherine. BSEE, Rice U., 1942; MS in Comm. Engring., Harvard U., 1946, PhD in Applied Physics, 1948, MBA, 1955. V.p. Boston Consulting Group; vis. prof. Carnegie Mellon U., Pitts.; v.p. Westinghouse Elec., Pitts.; gen. mgr. Westinghouse Aerospace, Balt.; dir. devel. Westinghouse Def. Prodn., Balt.; mgr. electronics and nuc. physics Westinghouse Rsch. Labs.; dir., acting CEO Am. Overseas Clinics Corp. Contbr. articles to profl. jours.; patentee in field. Pres. Friends of Manchester (Mass.) Trees, 1992, Manchester Hist. Soc., 1994. Lt. comdr. USN, 1942-46. Named Outstanding Engring. Alumnus, Rice U., Houston, 1988. Mem. Am. Orchid Soc. (accredited judge), Harvard Club Boston, Singing Beach Club, Manchester Yacht Club (bd. dirs. 1981-83). Avocations: gardening, orchid growing. Home: PO Box 32 Manchester MA 01944-0032

CONLEY, PHILIP JAMES, JR., retired air force officer; b. Providence, May 22, 1927; s. Philip James and Lillian Loretta (Burns) C.; m. Shirley Jean Andrews, Jan. 26, 1956; children: Sharon, Kathleen, Anne, James. BS, U.S. Naval Acad., 1950; MS, U. Mich., 1956, Rensselaer Poly. Inst., 1963. Commd. 2d lt. USAF, 1950, advanced through grades to maj. gen., 1979; dep. chief staff, ops. Air Force Systems Command, Andrews AFB, Washington, 1974-75; chief staff Air Force Systems Command, 1975-78; comdr. Air Force Flight Test Center, Edwards AFB, Calif., 1978-82; vice-comdr. Electronic Systems Divn. Hanscom AFB, Mass., 1983; ret., 1983. Decorated Disting. Svc. medal (2), Legion of Merit (2), Disting. Flying Cross, Bronze Star, Air medal (3). Mem. Air Force Assn., Order of Daedalians, U.S. Naval Acad. Alumni Assn., Am. Legion, Vikings Club (L.A.), Santa Barbara Yacht Club, Monticeto Country Club. Roman Catholic. Home: 930 Camino Viejo Santa Barbara CA 93108-1920

CONLEY, RAYMOND LESLIE, English language educator; b. Manhattan, Kans., Feb. 25, 1923; s. Orville Ray and Goldie Gladys (Wallack) C. AB with honors, Park Coll., 1947; postgrad., Nebr. U., 1948-50; MA, Northwestern U., Evanston, Ill., 1958; postgrad., Ol Dominion U., 1968. Cert. tchr. speech, English, social scis. Dep. county clk. Nemaha County, Auburn, Nebr., 1942-45; tchr., English, speech St. Edward (Nebr.) High Sch., 1948-50, Oakland (Nebr.) High Sch., 1950-52, Nebraska City (Nebr.) High Sch., 1952-56, Galesburg (Ill.) High Sch., 1956-58, Maine Twp. High Sch. East, Park Ridge, Ill., 1958-65; asst. prof. English, speech Meth. Coll., Fayetteville, N.C., 1966-77; English prof. Campbell U., Buies Creek, N.C., 1980-83; aux. faculty Campbell U., Fort Bragg, N.C., 1978—; coach Nebr. State Debate Champs, 1951, 52; judge Iowa State Speech Contest, 1952, 53; mem. Coun. Status of Women, Fayetteville, 1965-68; aux. faculty Campbell U., Pope AFB, N.C., 1985—; speech coach, judge local and sectional contests Toastmistress Club. Actor Fort Bragg Vietnam War Tng. Films. Precinct officer Dem. party, Fayetteville, 1964-68; coord. Congrl. Dist. Common Cause, 1978, mem. state program action com., state and gov. bd. 1976-78, 95—; dir. state governance bd. Common Cause, N.C., 1995—; mem. Congress Watch/Pub. Citizen, People for the Am. Way, ACLU, N.C. ACLU; conservation coord. Sierra Club, 1978; mem. Amnesty Internat.; vol. Fayetteville Mus. Art. Recipient Am. Legion Citizenship award, 1938. Mem. NOW, AAUP, Internat. Platform Assn., Fayetteville Fgn. Film Soc. (co-founder 1967), Inst. for So. Studies, World Future Soc., Found. For Nat. Progress, N.C. Alliance For Democracy, Amnesty Internat., Ams. United for Separation Ch. and State, Lambda Chi Alpha. Presbyterian. Home: 1076 Stamper Rd Fayetteville NC 28303-4191 Office: Campbell U Bldg 284 Rm 218 Pope AFB NC 28308-2373

CONLEY, ROBERT T., educational administrator. Pres. Union Inst., Cin. Office: Union Inst 440 E Mcmillan St Cincinnati OH 45206-1925*

CONLEY, SARAH ANN, health facility administrator; b. Richmond, Ind., Sept. 14, 1942; d. Harry Herbert and Mary Janet Kercheval; m. Philip Howard Conley, Apr. 5, 1963 (dec.); children: Christine L., Philip Douglas. BS, Purdue U., 1964; postgrad., U. Cin., 1965. Elem. tchr. Southwest Local Schs., Harrison, Ohio, 1964-66; svc. office mgr. Renault of Dayton (Ohio), 1970-73; mgr. Office of Charlotte Ames, Xenia, Ohio, 1974-77; bus. mgr. Radiol. Physicians, Inc., Dayton, 1977-79, Nat. Tractor Pullers Assn., Columbus, Ohio, 1979-85; HMO adminstr. Cen. Benefits Mutual Ins. Co., Columbus, 1985-90; adminstr. Orthopedic and Neurol. Cons., Columbus, 1990-97, Peripheral Vascular Surgery, Columbus, 1997—. Mem. Am. Coll. Med. Practice Execs. (cert.), Ohio Med. Group Mgmt. Assn. (pres. 1993-94), MidOhio Med. Mgmt. Assn., Med. Group Mgmt. Assn., Licking County Bus. and Profl. Women (pres. 1989-91). Democrat. Methodist. Avocations: piano, organ, church choir, teaching sunday school. Office: Peripheral Vascular Surgery 300 E Town St Ste 613 Columbus OH 43215-4632

CONLEY, TOM CLARK, literature educator; b. New Haven, Dec. 7, 1943; s. Walter Frederick and Hazel Mason (Hatch) C.; m. Verena Andermatt; children: David, Francine. BA, Lawrence U., 1965; MA, Columbia U., 1966; PhD, U. Wis., 1971. Prof. U. Minn., Mpls., 1971-95; prof. renaissance lit., cinema Harvard U., Cambridge, Mass., 1995—, dir. grad. studies in French; vis. prof. U. Calif., Berkeley, 1978-79, CUNY Grad. Ctr., 1985-87, Miami U., Ohio, 1989, UCLA, 1995; instr. Folger Inst., 1998; summer seminar leader NEH, 1998. Author: Lectura de Bunuel, 1988, Film Hieroglyphs, 1991, Graphic Unconscious, 1992, Self-Made Map, 1995; translator, 5 books; editor jour. Lendemains, 1985—; corr. jour. Litterature, 1988—; contbr. articles to profl. jours. Woodrow Wilson fellow, 1965-66, Fulbright fellow, 1968-69, study fellow Am. Coun. Learned Socs., 1975-76, summer fellow NEH, 174, 89, Inst. for Rsch. in Humanities fellow, 1990, Newberry Libr. Fellow, 1992, Soc. Humanities fellow, 1998. Mem. MLA, Renaissance Soc. Am., Assn. Study Dada/Surrealism, Midwest MLA (mem. exec. com. 1977-80), Sixteenth Century Studies Soc. (exec. com. 1994—), Alpha Omega Alpha. Avocations: handball, fishing, mycology. Office: Harvard U Romance Langs 201 Boylston Hall Cambridge MA 02138

CONLIN, ROXANNE BARTON, lawyer; b. Huron, S.D., June 30, 1944; d. Marion William and Alyce Muraine (Madden) Barton; m. James Clyde Conlin, Mar. 21, 1964; children: Jacalyn Rae, James Barton, Deborah Ann, Douglas Benton. BA, Drake U., 1964, JD, 1966, MPA, 1979; LLD (hon.), U. Dubuque, 1975. Bar: Iowa 1966. Assoc. Davis, Huebner, Johnson & Burt, Des Moines, 1966-67; dep. indsl. commr. State of Iowa, 1967-68, asst. atty. gen., 1969-76; U.S. atty. So. Dist. Iowa, 1977-81; ptnr. Conlin, P.C., Des Moines, 1983—; adj. prof. law U. Iowa, 1977-79; chmn. Iowa Women's Polit. Caucus, 1973-75, del. nat. steering com., 1973-77; cons. U.S. Commn. on Internat. Women's Year, 1976-77; gen. counsel NOW Legal Def. and Edn. Fund, 1985-88, pres., 1986-88; lectr. in field. Contbr. articles to profl. jours. Nat. committeewoman Iowa Young Dems.; pres. Polk County Young Dems., 1965-66; del. Iowa Presdl. Conv., 1972; Dem. candidate for gov. of Iowa, 1982; bd. dirs. Riverhills Day Care Ctr., YWCA; chmn. Drake U. Law Sch. Endowment Trust, 1985-86; bd. counselors Drake U., 1982-86; pres. Civil Justice Found., 1986-88, Roscoe Pound Found., 1994-97; chair Iowa Dem. Party, 1998—. Recipient award Iowa ACLU, 1974, Iowa Citizen's Action Network, 1987, Alumnus of Yr. award Drake U. Law Sch., 1989, ann. award Young Women's Resource Ctr., 1989, Verne Lawyer award as Outstanding Mem. Iowa Trial Lawyers Assn., 1994, Rosalie Wahl award Minn. Women Lawyers, 1998; named one of Top Ten Litigators Nat. Law Jour., 1989, 100 Most Influential Attys., 1991, 50 Most Powerful Women Attys. Nat. Law Jour., 1998; scholar Reader's Digest, 1963-64, Fishcher Found., 1965-66. Mem. NOW (bd. dirs. 1986-88), ABA, ATLA (chmn. consumer and victims coalition com. 1985-87, chmn. edn. dept. 1987-88, parliamentarian 1988-89, sec. 1989-90, v.p. 1990-91, pres.-elect 1991-92, pres. 1992-93), Iowa Bar Assn., Assn. Trial Lawyers Iowa (bd. dirs.), Internat. Acad. Trial Lawyers, Iowa Acad. Trial Lawyers, Higher Edn. Commn. Iowa (co-chmn. 1988-90), Inner Circle of Advocates, Phi Beta Kappa, Alpha Lambda Delta, Chi Omega (Social Svc. award). Office: 300 Walnut St Ste 5 Des Moines IA 50309-2239

CONLIN, THOMAS (BYRD), conductor; b. Arlington, Va., Jan. 29, 1944. BMus, Peabody Conservatory Music, 1966, MMus, 1967; studied with Leonard Bernstein, Erich Leinsdorf, Sir Adrian Boult. Artistic dir. Chamber Opera Soc., Balt., 1966-72; assoc. condr. N.C. Symphony Orch., 1972-74; music dir. Queens (N.Y.) Orchestral Soc., 1974-76; condr. Amarillo (Tex.) Symphony Orch., 1976-84, W.Va. Symphony Orch., 1983—; asst. prof. mus. CUNY, 1974-76. Mem. Am. Symphony Orch. League, Nat. Opera Assn., Condrs. Guild, Opera America. Office: West Va Symphony Orch 1210 Virginia St E Charleston WV 25301-2913

CONLON, BRIAN THOMAS, promotion executive; b. Oceanside, NY, Mar. 19, 1958; s. Thomas James and Joan Anna (Erickson) C.; m. Mary Jane Lewis, Nov. 12, 1988; children: Brendan Lewis, Ryan Bradshaw Erickson, Emily Rose Mary. BA in English, Hofstra U., 1979. Asst. account exec. DR Group, N.Y.C., 1981-82, account exec., 1982-83; account exec. D.L. Blair, Inc., Garden City, N.Y., 1983-85, v.p./account supr., 1985-90, sr. v.p., 1990-91, exec. v.p., 1991—. Roman Catholic. Office: DL Blair Inc 1051 Franklin Ave Garden City NY 11530-2931

CONLON, EUGENE, artist, administrator; b. Boston, Dec. 17, 1925; s. James Edward and Mary Honor (Dalton) C.; m. Marie Elizabeth Hommel, Sept. 1, 1952; children: Michelle, Meridith, Sally, Eugenia. BFA, Mass. Coll. Art, 1950. Designer-illustrator Rust Craft Pubs., Boston, 1953-61, MIT, Cambridge, 1961-66; instr. painting Mass. Coll. Art, Boston, 1966-67; artist-designer Avco Research Inc., Everett, Mass., 1967-70; art dir. Donnelly Advt., Boston, 1970-78, Ackerley Communications, Stoneham, Mass., 1978-91; commd. 22 paintings Bd. Room Internat. Silver Co., Meriden, Conn., 1976. One-man exhbns. include Springfield, Mo. Mus. of Fine Arts exhibit in Republic of China, 1985, Aisling Gallery of Irish Art, Hingham, Mass., Munson Gallery, Chatham, Mass., Santa Fe. Served with USN, 1943-46. Recipient Purchase prize S.W. Mo. Mus., 1966, Wichita Centennial, 1970; Gold medal Acad. Artists Assn., 1978, 1st prize Cape Cod Art Assn., 1982, Gold Medal of Honor award, 1990, 1st prize New Eng. Juried Show, 1992. Mem. Am. Watercolor Soc., New Eng. Watercolor Soc. (sec.-treas.), Watercolor U.S.A. Honor Soc., Guild Boston Artists, Nat. Acad. Design, Boston Art Dirs. Club. Home: 74 Proctor Rd Braintree MA 02184-7638*

CONLON, JAMES JOSEPH, conductor; b. N.Y.C., Mar. 18, 1950; s. Joseph Michael and Angeline (Leibinger) C; m. Jennifer Ringo; 2 daughters. Mus.B., Juilliard Sch., 1972. Condr. opera prodn. Juilliard Sch., 1972; mem. orchestral conducting faculty, 1972-75; condr. N.Y. Philharmonic, 1974—, Met. Opera, N.Y.C., 1976—, major symphony orchs. in U.S. and Can., including, N.Y.C., Phila., Cleve., Chgo., Boston, Pitts., Washington, also orchs. and opera cos. in Gt. Britain, Germany, Italy, France and The Netherlands, Berlin Philharm., 1979—, London Philharm., 1978—, Covent Garden, 1979—, Paris Opera, 1982—, l'orchestra di Santa Cecilia, Rome, Maggio Musical Fiorentino, 1985—, London Symphony Orch., 1977—, Orchestre de Paris, 1980—, Orchestre Nationale, 1983, Dresdner Staatskapelle, 1993—, La Scala, 1993—, Kirov Opera, 1994—; music dir., Cin. May Festival, 1979—; music dir. Rotterdam Philharm. Orch., 1983-91; chief condr. Cologne Opera, 1989; gen. music dir. City of Cologne, 1990—; prin. condr Opéra Nat. de Paris, 1996—. Decorated Officier de l'ordre des Arts et des Lettres, French Ministry of Culture, 1996; recipient Samuel Chotzinoff awards Aspen Music Festival, 1968, 69, Nat. Orchestral Assn. award, 1972, Grand Prix du Disque, Cannes Classical award, ECHO award for recording of Zemlinsky's The Dwarf, 1997. Mem. Am. Fedn. Musicians. Office: Shuman Assocs 120 W 58th St New York NY 10019-2141

CONLON, KATHRYN ANN, county official; b. Mankato, Minn., July 30, 1958; d. Ralph Raymond and Joan Margaret (Meyer) Walter; m. James Alan Conlon, Oct. 1, 1977; children: Jessica Marie, Brian Michael. Student, Mankato Vocat. Sch., 1976-77. Teller Minn. Valley Fed. Credit Union, 1977; clk. Nicollet County Credit Bur., 1977-78; abstracter Lorna Holmquist, St. Peter, Minn., 1978-82; dep. recorder, abstracter Nicollet County, 1982-84, county recorder, abstracter, 1984—, sec. to dept. heads, 1985, chmn. dept. heads, 1986. Mem. Spina Bifida Assn. Minn., 1981—, Spina Bifida Assn. S.W. Minn., 1983—; bd. dirs. Children's Cen. Child Care, 1985-87, United Way, 1990-91. Mem. Minn. Assn. County Recorders (2nd v.p. 1994, pres. 1995), VFW Aux., Am. Legion Aux., St. Peter Lions. Avocations: handcrafting, camping, gardening. Home: RR 3 Box 116 Saint Peter MN 56082-9542 Office: Nicollet County Recorder PO Box 493 Saint Peter MN 56082-0493

CONLON, MICHAEL WILLIAM, lawyer; b. Wilkes Barre, Pa., Nov. 9, 1946; s. William Peter and Dorothy (Stone) C.; m. Alice Cario, June 14, 1969; children: Michele, Stacia. A.B., Cath. U., 1968; J.D., Duke U., 1971. Bar: Tex. 1971, D.C. 1993. Ptnr. Fulbright & Jaworski, Houston, 1978-93, 98—; ptnr. in charge Fulbright & Jaworski, Washington, 1993-98. Office: Fulbright & Jaworski 1301 McKinney Houston TX 72020

CONLON, PATRICK C., family nurse practitioner; b. Sioux City, Iowa, July 24, 1962; s. James Ambrose and Mary Lee Emily (Donahue) Conlon. Diploma in Nursing, St. Joseph Mercy Hosp., Sioux City, 1986; BSN, Briar Cliff Coll., Sioux City, 1988, BA in Psychology; MSN, U. N.Mex., 1998. Cert. FNP, gen. nursing practice; cert. diabetes educator; cert. BCLS; cert. case mgr. Staff nurse, charge nurse Marian Health Ctr., Sioux City, 1979-89; staff nurse Western Med. Svcs., Sioux City, 1987-89; asst. nurse mgr., orthopaedic nurse adminstr. Michael Reese Hosp. and Med. Ctr., Chgo., 1989-91; edn. dir. ADA Iowa Diabetes Childrens Camp, 1989-93; health team coord., nurse educator, teaching faculty Triangle D Childrens Diabetes Camp, No. Ill., 1990-93; dir., clin. coord. diabetes edn. Mt. Sinai Hosp., 1991-96; grad. tching. asst. U. N.Mex., Albuquerque, 1996-97; diabetes specialist St. Josephs Hosp/S.W. Endocrinology Assocs., Albuquerque, 1997; N.P.-C Sinai Family Health Ctr., Chgo., 1998—. Manuscript reviewer Jour. of Care Mgmt., Jour. of Woman's Health in Primary Care; contbr. articles to profl. jours. Mem. ANA (chmn. 1992-94), Am. Nurses Credentialing Ctr., Am. Diabetes Assn. (bd. dirs., camp com. No. Ill. affiliate, peer reviewer of recognition program 1994-97), Iowa Nurses Assn. (nursing adminstrn. commn. 1993-97), Am. Psychol. Soc. (charter), Nat. Nurses in Bus. Assn. (charter), St. Joseph Mercy Sch. Nursing Alumni Assn., Endocrine Soc., Am. Assembly for Men in Nursing, Am. Assn. Diabetes Educators (manuscript reviewer jour.), Diabetes Educators Chgo. Area (v.p. 1991-92, pres.-elect 1992-93, pres. 1993-94, past pres./symposium chair 1994-95), Am. Acad. Nurse Practicioners, Sigma Theta Tau, Alpha Tau Delta, Psi Chi. Home: 2059 Roundtable Rd Sergeant Bluff IA 51054-9743 Office: Sinai Family Health Ctrs Westside Family Health Ctr 3606 W 16th Chicago IL 60623

CONLON, SUZANNE B., federal judge; b. 1939. AB, Mundelein Coll., 1963; JD, Loyola U., Chgo., 1968; postgrad., U. London, 1971. Law clk. to judge U.S. Dist. Ct. (no. dist.) Ill., 1968-71; assoc. Pattishall, McAuliffe & Hostetter, 1972-73, Schiff Hardin & Waite, 1973-75; asst. U.S. atty. U.S. Dist. Ct. (no. dist.) Ill., 1976-77, 82-86, U.S. Dist. Ct. (cen. dist.) Calif., 1978-82; exec. dir. U.S. Sentencing Commn., 1986-88; spl. counsel to assoc. atty. gen., 1988; judge U.S. Dist. Ct. (no. dist.) Ill., 1988—; asst. prof. law De Paul U., Chgo., 1972-73, lectr., 1973-75; adj. prof. Northwestern U. Sch. Law, 1991-95; vice chmn. Chgo. Bar Assn. Internat. Inst., 1993—; vis. com. U. Chgo. Harris Grad. Sch. Pub. Policy, 1997—. Mem. ABA, FBA, Fed. Judges Assn., Nat. Assn. Women Judges, Am. Judicature Soc., Internat. Bar Assn. Judges Forum, Chgo. Bar Assn., Law Club Chgo., Legal Club Chgo. (pres. 1996-97). Office: US Dist Ct No Dist Everett McKinley Dirksen Bldg 219 S Dearborn St Ste 2356 Chicago IL 60604-1802

CONLON, THOMAS JAMES, marketing executive; b. N.Y.C., July 30, 1935; s. Kenneth Charles and Catherine (Gavaghan) C.; m. Joan Anna Erickson, Jan. 19, 1957; children: Brian T., Michael K., Keith J.K. Ed., Art Students' League, N.Y.C., 1951-53, St. Peter's Coll., Jersey City, 1953-56. Staff artist N.Y. News, N.Y.C., 1953-57; spl. features writer-reporter N.Y. News, 1957-59; mktg. mgr. Tricolator Inc., Wantagh, N.Y., 1959-64; assoc. dir. promotion Benton & Bowles, N.Y.C., 1964-68; COO D.L. Blair Inc., Garden City, N.Y., 1968—; chmn. PMI, Inc., Atlanta, 1986—, DLB/W, Beverly Hills, Calif., 1987—; mng. dir./gerant Blair Europe, Paris, 1991-98. Illustrator for various mags., 1952-53. Home: Wolver Hollow Rd Upper Brookville NY 11771-4301 Office: DL Blair Inc 1051 Franklin Ave Garden City NY 11530-2931

CONLY, JOHN FRANKLIN, engineering educator, researcher; b. Ridley Park, Pa., Sept. 11, 1933; s. Harlan and Mary Jane (Roberts) C.; m. Jeannine Therese McDonough, Apr. 14, 1967; children: J. Paul, Mary Ann. B.S., U. Pa., 1956, M.S., 1958; Ph.D., Columbia U., 1962. Instr. U. Pa., Phila., 1956-58; research asst. Columbia U., N.Y.C., 1959-62; asst. prof. engring. San Diego State U., 1962-65, assoc. prof., 1965-69, prof., 1969—, chmn. dept., 1971-74, 77-85, wind tunnel dir., 1978—. D. and F. Guggenheim fellow, 1958. Assoc. fellow AIAA (sect. chmn. 1970 best U.S. sect.). Republican. Episcopalian. Office: San Diego State U Dept Aerospace Engring San Diego CA 92182

CONMY, PATRICK A., federal judge; b. 1934. BA, Harvard U., 1955; JD, Georgetown U., 1959. Bar: Va. 1959, N.D. 1959. Ptnr. Lundberg, Conmy et al, Bismarck, N.D., 1959-85; mem. Bismarck City Commn., 1968-76; state rep. N.D. House Reps., Bismarck, 1976-85; judge U.S. Dist. Ct. N.D., Bismarck, 1985—. Office: US Dist Ct Fed Bldg 220 E Rosser Ave Rm 411 PO Box 1578 Bismarck ND 58502-1578

CONN, ERIC EDWARD, plant biochemist; b. Berthoud, Colo., Jan. 6, 1923; s. William Elmer and Mary Anna (Smith) C.; m. Louise Carolyn Kachel, Oct. 17, 1959; children: Michael E., Kevin E. BA in Chemistry, U. Colo., 1944; PhD in Biochemistry, U. Chgo., 1950. Instr. biochemistry U. Chgo., 1950-52; instr. U. Calif., Berkeley, 1952-53, asst. prof., 1953-58; assoc. prof. U. Calif., Davis, 1958-63, prof., 1964—. Author: (with P.K. Stumpf) Outlines of Biochemistry, 1963, 5th edit., 1987; editor: (with P.K. Stumpf) (book series) Biochemistry of Plants, 1980-90. With U.S. Army, 1944-46. Fellow USPHS, 1960; Fulbright Rsch. grantee, 1965; recipient Pergamon Phytochemistry prize and cert., 1994. Mem. NAS, Phytochem. Soc. N.Am. (hon. life mem., pres. 1971-72, editor in chief 1984-89), Am. Soc. Plant Physiologists (pres. 1986-87, Charles Reid Barnes life mem.), Am. Soc. Biol. Chemistry, Phytochemistry Soc. Europe, Am. Soc. Pharmacognosy. Democrat. Avocations: gardening, philately. Office: U of Calif Sect Molecular & Cellular Biol Davis CA 95616

CONN, GORDON BRAINARD, JR., lawyer; b. St. Louis, Dec. 20, 1944. BA, Macalester Coll., 1967; JD, U. Mich., 1970. Bar: Minn. 1970, U.S. Supreme Ct. 1986; cert. in bus. bankruptcy law Am. Bd. Certficiation. Law clk. to Chief Justice Minn. Supreme Ct., St. Paul, 1970-71; with Faegre & Benson, Mpls., 1971—. Mem. ABA, Am. Bankruptcy Inst., Minn. State Bar Assn., Comml. Law League Am., Nat. Assn. Bankruptcy Trustees. Office: Faegre & Benson 2200 Norwest Ctr 90 S 7th St Ste 2200 Minneapolis MN 55402-3901

CONN, HADLEY LEWIS, JR., physician, educator; b. Danville, Ind., May 6, 1921; s. Hadley L. and Fyrne (Holtsclaw) C.; m. Betty Jean Aubertin, Sept. 18, 1946; children: Eric Hadley, Jeffrey Wood, Thomas Brian, Andrew Randall, Lisabeth Ann. B.A., U. Ind., 1942, M.D., 1944; M.S. (hon.), U. Pa., 1972. Assoc. scientist Brookhaven Nat. Lab., N.Y., 1953-55; asst. prof. U. Pa. Sch. Medicine, Phila., 1956-59; assoc. prof. U. Pa. Sch. Medicine, 1959-64, prof. medicine, 1964-72; dir. Clin. Research Center Hosp. of U. Pa. Sch. Medicine, 1970-72; chmn. dept. medicine Presbyn.-U. Pa. Med. Center, Phila., 1964-69; vis. prof. medicine Am. U. Beirut, 1969-70; chmn. dept. medicine Univ. Medicine and Dentistry N.J.-Rutgers Med. Sch., Piscataway, 1972-83, dir. Cardiovascular Inst., 1982-91, prof. medicine, chmn. emeritus, 1992. Author: Myocardial Cell, 1966, Cardiac and Vascular Disease, 1971, Platelets, Prostaglandins and Lipids, 1980, Health and Obesity, 1983. Sec. Nat. Bd. Med. Examiners, 1962-65; bd. govs. Am. Heart Assn., 1969-72; pres. Heart Assn. S.E. Pa., 1967, Detweiler Found., 1973-85. Served to capt. M.C., AUS, 1946-48. Mem. ACP, Am. Coll. Cardiology (trustee 1963-69), AMA, Am. Soc. Clin. Investigation, Am. Clin. and Climatological Soc., Assn. Univ. Cardiologists, Am. Phys. Soc., Assn. Profs. Medicine, Phi Beta Kappa, Alpha Omega Alpha. Republican. Clubs: Rittenhouse; Merion Cricket (Phila.). Home: 253 Wendover Dr Princeton NJ 08540-2434

CONN, HAROLD O., physician, educator; b. Newark, Nov. 16, 1925; s. Joseph H. and Dora (Kobrin) C.; m. Marilyn Barr, May 2, 1951; children: Chrysanne, Steven A., Dorianne. BS, U. Mich., 1946, MD, 1950; MS, Yale U., 1972. Diplomate: Am. Bd. Internal Medicine. Intern Johns Hopkins Hosp., 1950-51; asst. resident Grace New Haven Community Hosp., 1951-52, chief resident, 1955-56; James Hudson Browne research fellow, 1952-53; dir. med. edn. Middlesex Meml. Hosp., 1956-57; clin. investigator VA, 1957-61; chief med. svc. VA Hosp., West Haven, Conn., 1959-60; chief hepatic rsch. lab. VA Hosp., 1961-89; instr. Yale Sch. Medicine, 1955-58, asst. prof., 1958-66, assoc. prof., 1966-71, prof., 1971-91, prof. emeritus, 1991—, dir. continuing med. edn. program, 1988-91; clin. prof. surgery divsn. liver/intestinal transplantation U. Miami, 1986—; dir. continuing med. edn. program Yale Univ., 1988-91; vis. assoc. prof. Washington U. Sch. Medicine, 1982-83; CEO, Med., Med.-Legal and Consultations; dir. Continuing Med. Edn. dept. medicine Yale U. Sch. Medicine, 1990-92. Author: (with M.M. Lieberthal) The Hepatic Coma Syndromes and Lactulose, 1979, (with J. Rodes, M. Navasa) Spontaneous Bacterial Peritonitis, 1999; co-author: (with G. Klatskin) Histopathology of the Liver, 1990; editor: Cyanidanol in Diseases of the Liver, 1981; (with J. Palmaz, J. Rösch, and M. Rössle) Transjugular Intrahepatic Partal-Systemic Stent-shunts: TIPS, 1995; mem. editl. bd. Gastroenterology, 1970-80, Italian Jour. Gastroenterology, 1977—, Jour. Internal Medicine, 1988-99; assoc. editor Hepatology, 1980-90; book editor: Hepatology, 1985-88; editor Hepatology, 1985-91; editor: (with J. Bircher) Hepatic Encephalopathology: Management with Lactulose and Related Carbohydrates, 1988, (with J. Bircher) Hepatic Encephalopathy: Syndromes and Therapies, 1994. Bd. dirs. Am. Liver Found., 1977-80. Ensign USNR, 1943-44; 1st lt. USAR, 1953-54, USAFR, 1954-55. Recipient Rorer award, 1973, William Beaumont award clin. rsch., 1974. Fellow ACP; mem. Assn. Am. Physicians, Am. Soc. Clin. Investigation, Internat. Assn. Study Liver, Sydenham Soc. (sec. 1968-88, mem. med. adv. bd. Seminars and Symposia 1974-80), Am. Assn. Study Liver Disease (v.p. 1971, pres. 1972), Am. Fedn. Clin. Rsch., Am. Gastroenterol. Assn. (councillor 1974-77, Hugh Butt-Miles and Shirley Fiterman award for clinical rsch. in hepatology 1990), Nat. Assn. Va. Physicians (bd. dirs. 1986-88, chmn. continuing med. edn. com. 1987-89); hon. mem. Australian Soc. Gastroenterology, Brazilian Assn. for Study of Liver, China Med. Assn. (Shanghai br.; Taiwan), Hungarian Gastroent. Soc. (hon.), Nominated for Distinguished Educator Awd., Amer. Gastro Assn., 1998. Home and Office: 160 Morgan Ave East Haven CT 06512-4519 Home (summer): 1800 S Ocean Blvd Apt Phb Pompano Beach FL 33062-7922 *It is among my professional goals to apply the principles of the laboratory to the bedside, to enhance and enliven medical writing and to introduce a modicum of humor into the somber realm of the medical literature.*

CONN, REX BOLAND, JR., physician, educator; b. Marengo, Iowa, Aug. 3, 1927; s. Rex Boland and Helena Dorothea (Schoenfelder) C.; m. Victoria Grace Sellens, Dec. 28, 1950; children: Elizabeth Marian, Victoria Anne, Mary Catherine. BS, Iowa State U., 1949; MD, Yale U., 1953; BSc, U. Oxford, Eng., 1955; MS, U. Minn., 1960. Prof. pathology, dir. clin. labs. W.Va. Med. Center, Morgantown, 1960-68; prof. lab. medicine, dir. dept. Johns Hopkins Med. Instns., Balt., 1968-77; prof. pathology and lab. medicine, dir. clin labs. Emory U., Atlanta, 1977-87; prof. and vice chmn. dept. pathology and cell biology, dir. clin. labs. Thomas Jefferson U., Phila., 1987-97; prof. emeritus Jefferson Med. Coll., Phila., 1997—; mem. pathology tng. com. NIH, 1972-73, mem. pathology A study sect., 1968-72; cons. Walter Reed Army Med. Center, 1972-77; cons. Armed Forces Inst. of Pathology, 1984-88. Editor: Current Diagnosis, 1997, Yearbook of Pathology and Clinical Pathology, 1980, Applied Laboratory Medicine, 1992. Served with USNR, 1945-46. Mem. Coll. Am. Pathologists, Am. Soc. Clin. Pathologists (dir. 1975-81, pres. 1993-94), Acad. Clin. Lab. Physicians and Scientists (pres. 1972). Office: Thomas Jefferson Univ Jefferson Alumni Hall 212 Philadelphia PA 19107

CONN, ROBERT WILLIAM, engineering science educator; b. N.Y.C., Dec. 1, 1942; s. William Conrad and Rose Marie (Albanese) C.; children: Carole, William. BChemE, Pratt Inst., 1964; MS in Mech. Engring., Calif. Inst. Tech., 1965, Ph.D. in Engring. Sci., 1968. NSF postdoctoral fellow Euratom Cmty. Rsch. Center, Ispra, Italy, 1968-69; rsch. assoc. Brookhaven Nat. Lab., Upton, N.Y., 1969-70; vis. assoc. prof. U. Wis., Madison, 1970-72, assoc. prof., 1972-75, prof., 1975-80, dir. fusion tech. program, 1974-79, Romnes faculty prof., 1977-80; prof. engring. and applied sci. UCLA, 1980-93, dir. Inst. Plasma and Fusion Rsch., 1987-93; dean Sch. Engring. U. Calif., San Diego, 1994—; founder, chmn. bd. Trikon Techs., Inc. (now Trikon Techs., Inc.), L.A., 1986-93; chair, sec. Energy's Fusion Energy Adv. Com., 1991-96; cons. to govt. and industry. Author papers, chpts. in books. Recipient Curtis McGraw Rsch. award Am. Assn. Engring. Edn., 1982, Outstanding Svc. cert. U.S. Dept. Energy, E.O. Lawrence Meml. award, 1984, Fusion Power Assocs. Leadership award, 1992, Disting. Assoc.'s award Sec. of Energy, Dept. of Energy, 1996, Calif. U. Tech. Disting. Alumni Yr. award, 1998; named San Diego Outstanding Educator of Yr., 1997. Fellow Am. Nuclear Soc. (Outstanding Achievement award for excellence in research fusion div. 1979), Am. Phys. Soc.; mem. NAE. Office: U Calif San Diego Jacobs Sch ENgring 9500 Gilman Dr La Jolla CA 92093-0403*

CONNABLE, ALFRED BARNES, retired business executive; b. Kalamazoo, Feb. 20, 1904; s. Alfred B. and Frances (Peck) C.; m. Dorothy Jean Malcomson, Apr. 15, 1927 (div. 1972); children: Nancy M., Alfred B. III, John Lee (dec.); m. Tenho S. Hindert, Nov. 11, 1972. Student, Culver Mil. Acad., 1921; A.B., U. of Mich., 1925; M.B.A., Harvard, 1929; H.H.D., Western Mich. U., 1962. Sales asst. Kalamazoo Vegetable Parchment Co., 1925-28; asst. sec. Selected Securities Corp. of Detroit, 1928-30; successively asst. sec., asst. v.p. and dir. of investment analysis dept. Detroit Trust Co., 1930-43; state price adminstr. for Mich. OPA, 1942-43; state mgr. Wendell L. Willkie presdl. campaign, 1943-44; instr. investments and econs. Detroit Inst. Tech., 1929-30; chmn., dir. Monroe Calculating Co., 1944-58; chmn. Lafourche Realty Co., Inc., Kalamazoo; dir. Hayes-Albion Co., 1967-74, Albion Malleable Iron Co., 1945-67, Am. Nat. Bank & Trust Co. of Mich., 1946-76, Kalamazoo Sled & Toys Co., Inc., 1944-68, Kalamazoo Ice and Fuel Co., 1945-72, Hayes Industries, Inc., Jackson, Mich., 1947-67, KVP Sutherland Paper Co., 1946-66, Litton Industries, 1958-61; Regent U. Mich., 1942-58, emeritus, 1960. Trustee Douglas Community Assn.; trustee emeritus Western Mich. U.; mem. exec. com. Community Chest; dir., past pres. Kalamazoo Symphony Orch. Soc.; mem. adv. council Assn. Governing Bds. Univs., Colls.; past pres. Assn. of Governing Bds. of State Univs. and Colls., Am. Symphony Orchestra League (dir.); mem. exec. com. Mich. Artrain, Inc.; former mem. Mich. State Council for the Arts. Recipient Man of Achievement award Arts Coun. Greater Kalamazoo, award Boy Scouts Am. Mem. Pi Delta Epsilon, Alpha Kappa Psi, Delta Kappa Epsilon. Republican. Presbyn. Clubs: Rotarian. (Detroit and Kalamazoo), U. of Mich. (Detroit and Kalamazoo); Harvard (N.Y.). Home: 1400 N Drake Kalamazoo MI 49007-5281 Office: Old Kent Bank Bldg 136 E Michigan Ave Ste 1201 Kalamazoo MI 49007-3918*

CONNAIR, STEPHEN MICHAEL, financial analyst; b. Fredericksburg, Va., Sept. 10, 1950; s. Thomas Joseph Jr. and Wilma Melvina (McCarty) C.; m. Karen Lee Matusoff, Feb. 15, 1986. BA in Philosophy, Duns Scotus Coll., 1973; MA in Religious Studies, U. Dayton, 1976; PhL in Philosophy, Cath. U. Am., 1983; MPA, Va. Tech., 1992; grad., Air Command & Staff Coll., 1990, Naval War Coll., 1995, Nat. Def. U., 1996. Tchr. Cath. Sch. Sys., Cin., 1973-83; fin. analyst USAF The Pentagon, Washington, 1985—. Mem. Smithsonian resident assoc. program, Washington, 1987—; sec., bd. dirs. Arlington Run Homeowners Assn., 1990-92; v.p. Sleepy Hollow Woods Civic Assn., 1996-97, pres., 1997-98. Mem. Am. Soc. Mil. Comptrs. (Profl. award 1990, Outstanding Analysis and Evaluation award 1992), Soc. Cost Estimating and Analysis, Am. Cath. Philos. Assn., Air Force History Found., Air Force Assn., Naval War Coll. Found., Nat. Air and Space Soc., Wilson Ctr. Assn., Nat. Trust for Hist. Preservation, Am. Acad. Polit. Sci., Am. Soc. Pub. Adminstrn., Am. Econ. Assn., George C. Marshall Found., James Madison Inst., Nat. Hist. Soc., Va. Hist. Soc., Arlington County Hist. Soc., Fairfax County Hist. Soc., Soc. for Mil. History, Nat. Assn. Scholars, Libr. of Congress Assn., Hon. Order of Ky. Cols., Pi Alpha Alpha. Roman Catholic. Avocations: civil war buff, American history, movies, reading. Home: 3808 Moss Dr Annandale VA 22003-1917

CONNALLY, ANDREW DAVID, historian, educator; b. Atlanta, Jan. 22, 1956; s. Charles Price Jr. and Florence Shropshire (Daley Meros) C. BA in History magna cum laude, Fla. State U., 1977, JD with honors, 1982; MS in Edn. summa cum laude, St. Joseph's Univ., Phila., 1989. Cert. social studies tchr. Pa. Staff atty., legal editor Mcpl. Code Corp., Tallahassee, 1983-85, 87, The Fla. Bar, Tallahassee, 1985-86; tchr. The Episcopal Acad., Merion, Pa., 1987-88, The Agnes Irwin Sch., Rosemont, Pa., 1988—; park ranger Independence Nat. Hist. Park, Phila., 1989-92, 95-96, 98—. Editor: Codes of Ordinances For: 20 Cities in Missouri, Fla., Ga., & Mass., 1983-87. Tenor soloist, chorister St. John's Episcopal Ch., Norristown, Pa. 1992-98, Ch. of the Good Shepherd, Rosemont, Pa., 1998—. Mem. Phi Beta Kappa, Pi Gamma Mu, Phi Alpha Theta. Democrat. Avocations: travel, film, gothic fiction, cooking, theater. Home: 5 E Athens Ave Apt C Ardmore PA 19003-2201 Office: The Agnes Irwin Sch Ithan Ave & Conestoga Rd Rosemont PA 19010

CONNALLY, ERNEST ALLEN, retired federal agency administrator; b. Groesbeck, Tex., Nov. 15, 1921; s. Ernest Lackey and Pauline (Allen) C.; m. Janice Muriel Wegner, Aug. 28, 1951; children: Mary Allen, John Arnold. Student, Rice U., 1939-40, U. Tex., 1940-42, U. Florence, Italy, 1947; BArch, U. Tex., 1950; MA, Harvard U., 1952, PhD, 1955. Asst. prof. architecture Miami U., Oxford, Ohio, 1952-55; assoc. prof. Washington U., St. Louis, 1955-57; vis. prof. Washington U., 1962; assoc. prof. U. Ill., Urbana, 1957-61; prof. U. Ill., 1961-67; assoc. Ctr. for Advanced Study, 1966-67; asst. dir. Nat. Park Svc., U.S. Dept. Interior, Washington, 1967-72, assoc. dir., 1972-78; chief appeals officer cultural resources Nat. Park Service, Dept. Interior, Washington, 1982-92; assoc. dir. Heritage Conservation and Recreation Service, 1978-79; cons. restoration hist. bldgs., 1952—; cons. UNESCO, Nepal, 1968, mem. working group for Sukhotai Hist. Park, Thailand, 1982-88; sec.-treas, U.S. com. Internat. Coun. on Monuments and Sites, 1969-73, chmn., 1973-75, sec.-gen., ICOMOS, Paris, 1975-81; Fulbright prof. U. Melbourne, Australia, 1963; U.S. del. UNESCO Conf. on Cultural Property, 1968; U.S. rep. Internat. Conf. on Rec. Hist. Monuments, Prague, Czechoslovakia, 1969; U.S. del., v.p. Gen. Assembly, Internat. Centre for Study of Preservation and Restoration of Cultural Property, Rome, 1971, 77, mem. exec. bd., 1971-75; mem. U.S.-USSR Joint Working Group on Urban Environ., 1973-81; bd. dirs. Pa. Ave. Devel. Corp., Washington, 1974-78; charter mem. Sr. Exec. Svc. of U.S.A., 1979. Author: Printed Books on Architecture, 1485-1805, 1960; also articles in jours., encys.; important works include restoration of Louis Bolduc house, 1956-57, Bolduc-LeMeilleur house, St. Genevieve, Mo., 1967. Maj. USAAF, 1942-46, lt. col. Res., 1956-58. Decorated Officier Ordre des Arts et des Lettres, France, 1986; recipient Research award Am. Philos. Soc., 1957, Disting. Service award Dept. Interior, 1978, Crowninshield award Nat. Trust Hist. Preservation, 1980, AIA Presdl. citation, 1990; named Membre d'Honneur ICOMOS, 1981, Trustee of Am., 1986, recipient Prix Gazzola, 1996. Mem. AIA (hon.), SAR, Soc. Archtl. Historians (past bd. dirs.), Nat. Trust for Hist. Preservation (past trustee), Fulbright Assn., Nat. Pks. and Conservation Assn., Assn. for Preservation Va. Antiquities, Gargoyle, Cosmos Club, Harvard Club (Washington), Alpha Rho Chi, Tau Sigma Delta, Phi Kappa Phi. Episcopalian. Home: 1601 Ruffner Rd Alexandria VA 22302-4121

CONNAUGHTON, DAVID MICHAEL, management consultant; b. Youngstown, Ohio, Feb. 19, 1943; s. James M. and Dorothy Edith Roberts C.; m. Marilyn Jane Goscewski, Dec. 31, 1966; children; Erin, James. BS in Math., USAF Acad., 1965; MBA, Harvard U., 1973. Asst. to COO Burton Duenke Constrn. Co., St. Louis, 1973-74; sr. cons. Cambridge (Mass.) Comm. Group, 1975-77; fin. mgr. IBM, Armonk, N.Y., 1980-91; prin. Gemini Cons., Morristown, N.J., 1991-96; ptnr. Organizational Dynamics, Burlington, Mass., 1997-98; dir. Benchmarking Ptnrs., Cambridge, 1998—; cons. in field. Mem. Sabre Soc. Avocations: pilot, artist, triathlete. Home: 2 Laurel St LExington MA 02421 Office: Benchmarking Ptnrs 1 Main St Cambridge MA 02124

CONNEEN, MARI M., artist; b. Allentown, Pa., Dec. 21, 1946; d. Edward Charles and Margaret Florence (Reiter) Leidig; m. Joseph Lawrence Conneen Jr., Aug. 3, 1965; children: Christopher Joseph, Matthew Ward, Michael Walker. One-woman shows include 1st Fed. Savs. of Mid Fla., Deland, 1983, Brevard Art Ctr. and Mus., Melbourne, Fla., 1983, Fla. Frame House Gallery, Winter Pk., 1983, Cielo Gallery, Westfield, Mass., 1984, Galleries Internat., Winter Pk., 1986, Ctr. for the Arts, Vero Beach, Fla., 1986, Ormond Beach (Fla.) Meml. Art Gallery, 1986, Deland Art Mus., 1985, Naples (Fla.) Art Gallery, 1987, Seminole C.C., Sanford, Fla., 1988, The Hartley Gallery, Winter Pk., 1989, Herr-Chambliss Gallery, Hot Springs, Ark., 1990, Hobe Sound (Fla.) Gallery, 1990, J. Lawrence Gallery, Melbourne, 1991-96, Brevard Mus. Art and Sci., Melbourne, 1997, Brevard Art Ctr. and Mus., 1997; exhibited in group shows at Adirondacks Nat. Exhibit of Am. Watercolors, Old Forge, N.Y., 1984-96 (numerous awards), Nat. Arts Club, N.Y.C., 1984, La. Watercolor Soc. Annn. Internat. Exhbns., 1985, 95 (awards), 1985, Orlando (Fla.) Mus. of Art, 1985, 90-91, Tampa Mus. of Art, 1986, Ky. Watercolor Soc., 1986, 92, 93, 95 (Grumbacher Gold medallion and award 1986, award 1992), San Diego Watercolor Soc., 1987, 93, Miss. Watercolor Soc., 1995 (Gold medallion), Fla. Watercolor Soc., 1979-97 (awards), Okla. Arts Ctr., 1987-95 (awards), Mus. Arts and Scis., Daytona Beach, Fla., 1988, Boca Raton (Fla.) Mus. Art, 1990, 91, 92, So. Watercolor Soc. Ann. Juried Exhbn., 1984-97 (awards), Springfield (Mo.) Art Mus., 1993 (honor soc.), Samford U., Birmingham, Ala., 1996 (award), Lafayette (La.) Art Gallery (award), numerous others; represented in numerous pub. and pvt. collections; contbr. art work to numerous publs., books in field. Recipient 2d pl. award Invitational Wildlife Exhbn., Atlanta, 1978, Best of Show award Artists Showcase, Miami, Fla., 1981, 1st pl. award Fla. Watercolor Soc. Ann. Juried Exhbn., 1982, Best of Show award, 1983, 2d pl. Festival of the Masters, Lake Buena Vista, Fla., 1982-83, 1st pl., 1987, Best of Show award Brevard Art Ctr. Ann. Juried Exhbn., Melbourne, 1983-84, Best of Show and 1st pl. awards Winter Pk. Art Festival, 1983, Best of Show award St. Stephens Arts Festival, Coconut Grove, Fla., 1983, Beaux Arts Festival of the Arts, Lowe Art Mus., Miami, 1983, Miami Beach Festival of the Arts, 1983, Coconut Grove Arts Festival, 1983, 1st pl., 1988, Artists Three award Orlando Mus. Art, 1985, Best of Show award La. Watercolor Soc. Ann. Juried Exhbn., New Orleans, 1985, Natural Resources award Adirondacks Nat. Exhibit of Am. Watercolors, 1985, award, 1988, Experts Choice award Artists Soc. Internat., San Francisco, 1987, Jurors award San Diego Watercolor Soc., 1987, 2d pl., Purchase award Nat. Watercolor Soc. Ann. Exhbn., 1993, 1st pl. award Fla. Artists Group, Mus. Arts and Scis., Daytona Beach, 1994, Purchase award Bank of Newport, Brea, Calif., 1994. Mem. Am. Watercolor Soc., Guild of Natural Sci. Illustrators, Am. Artist Profl. League, Nat. Watercolor Soc. (signature), Nat. Mus. Women in the Arts, Watercolor USA (honor soc.), Fla. Watercolor Soc. (signature), So. Watercolor Soc. (signature), Ky. Watercolor Soc. (signature), Ala. Watercolor Soc. (signature), Fla. Artists Group Inc., Miss. Watercolor Soc. (signature), Okla. Watercolor Soc., Brevard Mus. Art and

Sci., Brevard Cultural Alliance. Democrat. Roman Catholic. Home: Apt C-14 441 N Harbor City Blvd Melbourne FL 32935-6844

CONNELL, ALASTAIR MCCRAE, physician; b. Glasgow, Scotland, Dec. 21, 1929; came to U.S., 1970; s. Alex McCrae and Maud (Crawford) C.; m. Joyce Dethlefs, 1983; children: Stewart, Fiona, Alison, Iain, Andrew. BS, U. Glasgow, 1951, MB, ChB, 1954, MD, 1969. Intern Western Infirmary, Glasgow, 1954-55; resident in gastroenterology Cen. Middlesex and St. Mark's Hosp., London, 1957-60; practice medicine specializing in gastroenterology, 1960—; mem. med. staff Med. Rsch. Coun., 1960-64; sr. lectr. clin. sci. Queen's U., Belfast, No. Ireland, 1964-70; Mark Brown prof. medicine Med. Ctr., U. Cin., 1970-79, dir. div. digestive diseases, 1970-79, prof. physiology, 1972-79, assoc. dean, 1975-77; dir. Office Clin. Affairs, 1975-77; dean Coll. Medicine, U. Nebr. Med. Ctr., 1979-84, prof. internal medicine, 1979-84; v.p. health scis. Va. Commonwealth U., Richmond, 1984-88; scholar-in-residence Inst. Medicine, 1988-89; vice chancellor health scis. Ea. Carolina U., 1989-90; dir. Office Healthcare Inspections, Dept. Vets. Affairs, Washington, 1991-96; adj. prof. med. George Washington U., 1992—; vis. prof. dept. moral philosophy U. St. Andrews, Scotland, 1984-86; mem. sci. adv. bd. Nat. Found. for Ileitis and Colitis, 1974-80, chmn. rsch. devel. com., 1974-78; mem. Personal Health Com. Ohio, 1974-76; trustee Medco Peer Rev., 1974-79; adj. prof. health adminstrn. Va. Commonwealth U., 1996—; med. dir. Williamsburg Landing. Author: Clinical Tests of Gastric Function, 1973; Assoc. editor: Am. Jour. Digestive Diseases; Contbr. articles to profl. jours. Served with M.C. Royal Army, 1955-57. Fellow Royal Coll. Physicians (Edinburgh), ACP; mem. Am. Gastroent. Assn., Brit. Soc. Gastroenterology, Internat. Group for Study Intestinal Motility (past pres.). Address: 208 Jones Mill Ln Williamsburg VA 23185

CONNELL, CHARLES W., provost; m. Lynn Gardner. Grad., U. Cin., postgrad.; doctoral degree, Rutgers U., 1969. Interim vice provost, dean of faculty Ariz. State U. West Campus, dir. faculty of arts and scis., dir. 21st century project; sr. v.p. for acad. affairs U. South Ala., 1991-95; provost Northern Ariz. U., 1995—. Bd. dirs. United Way, Mus. Northern Ariz. Fellowship Am. Coun. of Edn. Nat. Endowment for the Humanities, Rutgers U. Office: Northern Ariz U Box 4120 Flagstaff AZ 86011

CONNELL, EVAN SHELBY, JR., author; b. Kansas City, Mo., Aug. 17, 1924; s. Evan Shelby and Elton (Williamson) C. Student, Dartmouth, 1941-43; AB, U. Kans., 1946-47; grad. study, Stanford U., 1947-48, Columbia U., 1948-49. Editor Contact mag., Sausalito, Calif., 1960-65. Author: The Anatomy Lesson and Other Stories, 1957, Mrs. Bridge, 1959, The Patriot, 1960, Notes From a Bottle Found on the Beach at Carmel, 1963, At the Crossroads: Stories, 1965, The Diary of a Rapist, 1966, Mr. Bridge, 1969, Points for a Compass Rose, 1973, The Connoisseur, 1974 (Calif. Literature Silver medal 1974), Double Honeymoon, 1976, A Long Desire, 1979, The White Lantern, 1980, St. Augustine's Pigeon, 1980, Son of the Morning Star: Custer and the Little Bighorn, 1984 (Nat. Book Critics Circle award nomination 1984, L.A. Times Book award 1985), The Alchymist's Journal, 1991, Mesa Verde, 1992, Collected Stories, 1996; editor: Jerry Stoll's I Am A Lover, 1961, Women by Three, 1969. Served as naval aviator 1943-45. Eugene Saxton fellow, 1953, Guggenheim fellow, 1963; Rockefeller Found. grantee, 1967; recipient Am. Acad. Inst. Arts and Letters award, 1987. Mem. AAAL. Address: care Don Congdon 156 5th Ave New York NY 10010-7002*

CONNELL, GEORGE EDWARD, former university president, scientist; b. Saskatoon, Sask., Can., June 20, 1930; s. James Lorne and Mabel Gertrude (Killins) C.; m. Sheila Harriet Horan, Dec. 27, 1955; children: James, Caroline, Thomas, Margaret. BA, U. Toronto, Ont., Can., 1951, PhD in Biochemistry, 1955; DSc, U. Toronto, 1993; LLD (hon.), McGill U., 1987. NSF postdoctoral fellow, 1956-57; asst. prof. biochemistry U. Toronto, 1957-62, assoc. prof., 1962-65, prof., chmn. dept. biochemistry, 1965-70, assoc. dean faculty of medicine, 1972-74, v.p. rsch. and planning, 1974-77, pres., 1984-90; pres. U. Western Ont., London, 1977-84; chair Nat. Round Table on Economy and Environ., 1990-95; vice chair Environ. Assessment Bd., Ont., 1990-93; chmn. TC207, Internat. Stds. Orgn., 1993-96; prin. adviser Commn. Inquiry on Blood Sys. Can., 1993-95; chmn. bd. protein engring. Nat. Ctr. Excellence, 1995-97; chmn. Task Force on Funding and Delivery Med. Care in Ont., 1995-96; sr. policy advisor Can. Found. for Innovation, 1997; bd. dirs. Allelix Biopharms., Inc.; mem. Ont. Press Coun., 1996—; trustee McLaughlin Found., 1996—. Recipient Order of Can., 1987. Fellow Chem. Inst. Can., Royal Soc. Can.; mem. Am. Soc. Biol. Chemists, Can. Biochem. Soc. (pres. 1973-74), Queen's Club (Toronto).

CONNELL, GROVER, food company executive; b. N.Y.C., Apr. 12, 1918; s. Grover Clevel and Violet Regina (Connell) C.; m. Patricia Day, July 31, 1940; children—Ted, Terry, Toni. B.S. in Bus. Adminstrn, Columbia, 1939. With The Connell Co. (formerly Connell Rice & Sugar Co., Inc.), Westfield, N.J., 1939—, pres., chmn. bd., 1950—. Lt. USNR, 1942-46. Democrat. Presbyterian. Home: 207 Watchung Fork Westfield NJ 07090-3813 Office: Connell Co 45 Cardinal Dr Westfield NJ 07090-1019

CONNELL, HUGH P., foundation executive; b. Bethlehem, Pa., May 7, 1931; s. Joseph B. and Mary A. (McFadden) C.; m. Susan Hobbs, July 2, 1965; children: Hugh Richardson, Andrew Warfield, Edward William. AB, Moravian Coll., 1953; JD, U. Pa., 1956; student, Hague (The Netherlands) Acad. Internat. Law, 1959; LLM, U. London, 1960. Bar: Pa. 1956, N.Y. 1963. Intelligence analyst AUS Counter Intelligence Corp., Berlin, 1956-58; lectr. internat. law Univ. London, 1960-62; with Coudert Bros. Law Firm, N.Y.C., 1962-65; gen. counsel J. Walter Thompson Co., N.Y.C., 1966, v.p., 1967, sec., 1972, sr. v.p., 1973, exec. v.p., dir., 1974; exec. v.p., dir. JWT Group Inc., N.Y.C., 1980-86; founder, owner Crosswoods Vineyards Inc., N. Stonington, Conn., 1981-90; pres., CEO, trustee Sea Rsch. Found. Inc., Mystic, Conn., 1991—; trustee, past chmn. bd., chmn. exec. com. Jackson Lab., Bar Harbor, Maine, 1978—. Mem. Pilgrims of U.S., Union Club, N.Y.C., Wadawanuck Club, Stonington, Conn. Office: Sea Rsch Found 55 Coogan Blvd Mystic CT 06355-1927

CONNELL, JOHN GIBBS, JR., former government official; b. Atlanta, Sept. 26, 1914; s. John Gibbs and Vena Estelle (Turner) C.; m. Bernice E. Siewerdsen, Oct. 2, 1941; children: Sharon Elaine, Candace Anne. AA, George Washington U., 1948, AB, 1952. With U.S. Civil Service Commn., 1935-38, U.S. Housing Authority, 1938-40; with War Dept. and Army Dept., 1940-79; personnel mgr. Office of Sec. Army, 1942-54, asst. for security and personnel, 1954-62, dep. adminstrv. asst. to sec. army, 1962-66, adminstv. asst. to sec. army, 1966-79; Chmn. Army Security Screening Bd., 1953-66; prin. adminstrv. officer Army Loyalty-Security Program, 1950-79; mem. Army Bd. Correction Mil. Records, 1947-62; Army Dept. rep. interdepartmental com. to study govt. employee security programs for Pres. Truman, 1951-52; Army rep. Exec. Officers Group, 1968-79; mem. Dept. Def. Concessions Com., 1966-79; Army rep. Fed. Exec. Bd., 1969-79; mem. adv. com. Nat. Archives and Records Service, 1973. Bd. dirs. Army-Air Force Civilian Welfare Fund, Youth Devel. Inst. Served to 2d lt. USAAF, 1943-45; 1st lt. OSS, 1945-46; maj. M.I. Army Res. Recipient Army Exceptional Civilian Svc. medal, 1973, 75, 79, 40-Yr. cert. of svc. award, 1975, Meritorious Civilian Svc. award, 1977, sculpture award Faculty-Student Show, Art League, Alexandria, Va., 1982, 89; hon. mention for sculpture Young at Art Exhbn., 1991, hon. mention, 1992, 93. Mem. Fed. Sr. Exec. Svc. (charter), Nat. Assn. Ret. Fed. Employees, Art League of Alexandria, Coun. Former Fed. Execs., Sculptor, Sigma Nu. Presbyterian (elder). Home: 302 Cloverway Dr Alexandria VA 22314-4818 *I try to govern my life so as to serve others as I would have them serve me. I believe in the inherent dignity of man as an individual.*

CONNELL, MARION FITCH, government official; b. New London, Conn., May 4, 1940; d. Avery Williams and Marion Booth (Gammons) Fitch; m. Lawrence Connell, 1965 (div. 1988); children: Elizabeth Cunningham, Rachel Avery. AB, Mt. Holyoke Coll., 1962; MPA, U. Hartford, 1974. Program officer Peace Corps, Washington, 1962-65; social sci. advisor U.S. Dept. Labor, Women's Bur., Boston, 1974-76; exec. dir. Internat. Women's Yr. Coord. Com., Hartford, Conn., 1977; program analyst HUD, Washington, 1978-80, program officer Office Field Ops., 1980-86, dir. urban homesteading Office Urban Rehab., 1986-89, dir. programs div. Office Fair Housing Enforcement, 1989-90, program advisor Office Insured Single Family Housing, 1990-96; dir. Manufactured Housing & Standards Divsn., Washington, 1996-98; mgr. Real Estate Assessment Ctr. Manufactured Housing & Standards Divsn., 1998—; adminstr. Expt. in Internat. Living, 1966-76. Commr. Town Planning and Zoning Commn., Glastonbury, Conn., 1973-77; rep. Regional Planning Commn., Hartford, 1974, Neighborhood Sch. Coun., Washington, 1979-80. Recipient Vice-President's Hammer award, 1998. Mem. Nat. Assn. Housing and Redevel. Ofcls., Am. Soc. Pub. Adminstrn. (pres. Conn. chpt. 1976-77, bd. dirs. Nat. Capital Area chpt., 1993-95). Democrat. Unitarian. Avocations: tennis, music, travel. Office: HUD 451 7th St SW Washington DC 20410-0001

CONNELL, PHILIP FRANCIS, food industry executive; b. Hamilton, Ont., Can., Jan. 20, 1924; s. Maurice W. and Kathleen (Richardson) C. BA, McMaster U., Can., 1946. Chartered acct. With Clarkson Gordon & Co. (Ernst & Young), Hamilton and Toronto, 1946-57; comptroller Canadian Westinghouse Co. Ltd., Hamilton, 1957-67; controller Domtar Ltd., Montreal, 1967-68; v.p. fin. George Weston Ltd., Toronto, Ont., 1968-75, Loblaw Cos., Ltd., Toronto, Ont., 1972-75; exec. v.p. Oshawa Group Ltd., Toronto, Ont., 1976-92, dir., 1976-97. Fellow Inst. Chartered Accts.; mem. Fin. Execs. Inst. (pres. Hamilton chpt. 1966-67), Ont. Inst. Chartered Accts., Hamilton Club, Nat. Club. Home: 400 Walmer Rd Apt 2510, Toronto, ON Canada M5P 2X7

CONNELL, SHIRLEY HUDGINS, public relations professional; b. Washington, Oct. 5, 1946; d. Orville Thomas and Mary (Beran) H.; m. David Day Connell, Dec. 13, 1980 (div. 1985). BA, U. R.I., 1968, MA, 1970. Lic. property, casualty broker, N.Y. Clk., editor MGM Studios, Culver City, Calif., 1970-72; scriptor, talent Monarch Records, Studio City, 1972-73; communications specialist U. So. Calif., L.A., 1973-81; dir. pub. rels. Six Flags Movieland, Buena Park, Calif., 1981-82; dir. pub. rels. Donald J. Fager & Assocs., N.Y.C., 1982-93, dir. policy holder/pub. rels., 1993—; cons. Children's TV Workshop, N.Y.C., 1978; ind. beauty cons. Mary Kay Cosmetics, 1991—; instr. Princeton Rev., 1990-91. Editor: Coastal Ocean Space Utilization III, 1995; contbr. articles to profl. jours.; contbg. editor Greater N.Y. Doctor's Shopper mag., 1987—. Pres. bd. trustees Oaks at North Brunswick Condominium Assn., 1987—; founding mem. Mcpl. Svcs. Com., North Brunswick; mgr. Animal Rescue Force, 1988—; chair environ. com. Twp. of North Brunswick, 1990—; snuggler pediat. and neonatal units St. Peter's Hosp.; Blue Belt Tiger Schulmann's Karate, 1997. Mem. NAFE, Marine Tech. Soc. (vice chmn. 1980-81), Mensa (pub. rels. adv. com. 1989—, pub. rels. coord. Ctrl. N.J. chpt. 1992—, bd. dirs. 1992—), Oceanic Soc. (bd. dirs. 1979-81), Stony Brook Millstone Watershed Assn. (water qualification monitor 1994—), Lawrence Brook Watershed Assn. (bd. dirs. 1997—). Avocations: photography, reading, swimming, wood finishing, writing.

CONNELL, WILLIAM FRANCIS, diversified company executive; b. Lynn, Mass., May 12, 1938; s. William J. and Theresa (Keaney) C.; m. Margot C. Gensler, May 29, 1965; children: Monica Cameron, Lisa Terese, Courtenay Erin, William Christopher, Terence Alexander, Timothy Patrick. BS magna cum laude, Boston Coll., 1959; MBA, Harvard U., 1963. Contr. Olga Co., Inc., Van Nuys, Calif., 1963-65; asst. treas. Litton Industries, Inc., 1965-68; pres. div. Marine Tech., Inc., 1965-68; treas. Ogden Corp., N.Y.C., 1968-69; v.p., treas. Ogden Corp., 1969-71, sr. v.p., 1971-72, exec. v.p., 1980-85; chief exec. officer, chmn. bd. Ogden Leisure, Inc.; chmn. bd., chief exec. officer Ogden Food Service, Inc., Ogden Recreation, Inc., Ogden Security, Inc., Ogden Svcs. Inc.; bd. dir. Ogden Corp., various Ogden subs., 1969-85; chmn., chief exec. officer, pres. Avondale Industries, Inc. 1985-87; chmn., chief exec. officer Connell Ltd. Partnership, 1987—. Active fund raising Boston Coll., trustee, 1974-86, 88—, chmn. bd. trustees, 1981-84; trustee St. Elizabeth Hosp., Boston, Boston 200 Corp. 1st lt. AUS, 1959-61. Mem. Greater Boston C. of C. (chmn. bd. dirs. 1988-90), Algonquin Club, Univ. Club (Boston), Tedesco Country Club, Knights of Malta Club, Beta Gamma Sigma, Alpha Sigma Nu, Alpha Kappa Psi. Roman Catholic. Home: 111 Ocean Ave Swampscott MA 01907-2413 Office: Connell Ltd Partnership One International Pl Boston MA 02110-2600

CONNELLAN, WILLIAM WESLEY, higher education administrator; b. Detroit, Apr. 25, 1945; s. Thomas Kennedy and Florence Irene Connellan; m. Mary Emma Solonika Simms, Aug. 17, 1969 (div. Jan. 1979); 1 child, Brian Patrick; m. Catherine Joanne Marine, Oct. 12, 1985. BA, Oakland U., Rochester, Mich., 1967; MA, U. Mich., 1971, PhD, 1981. Reporter Detroit News, 1965-70; acting v.p., assoc. provost, dir. pub. rels. Oakland U., 1970-97, vice provost, 1997—; vis. scholar U. Mich., Ann Arbor, 1987; participant Inst. for Edn. Mgmt., Harvard U., Cambridge, Mass., 1993. Mem. exec. com. Met. Detroit Conv. and Visitors Bur., 1979—, chair, 1999; mem. Rochester Hills (Mich.) Bldg. Authority, 1981-97; mem. Avon Twp. Charter Commn., Rochester Hills, 1982-84; active Habitat for Humanity. Mem. Am. Assn. Higher Edn., Earthwatch Inst., Detroit Econ. Club, Sigma Xi. Democrat. Presbyterian. Avocations: international research projects, recreational sports. Home: 804 Augusta Ct Rochester MI 48309 Office: Oakland U 205 Wilson Hall Rochester MI 48309

CONNELLY, ALBERT R., lawyer; b. N.Y.C., Mar. 24, 1908; s. John E. and Julia (Broughey) C.; m. Eleanor Milburn, June 17, 1930 (dec. 1997); children: Mary, Jean. BA, Yale, 1929, LLB, 1932. Bar: N.Y. 1933. Since practiced in N.Y.C.; partner Cravath Swaine & Moore (and predecessors), from 1941, now ret. ptnr. Trustee emeritus Berkshire Sch. Fellow Am. Bar Found., Am. Coll. Trial Lawyers, N.Y. Bar Found.; mem. ABA, N.Y. State Bar Assn., N.Y. County Bar Assn., Assn. Bar City of N.Y., Union Club, Yale Club of N.Y.C., Met. Club (Washington). Office: Worldwide Pla 825 8th Ave New York NY 10019-7416

CONNELLY, COLIN CHARLES, lawyer; b. Hopewell, Va., Nov. 1, 1956; s. Charles Bernell and Doris Louise (Beasley) C.; m. Stephanie Paige Lowder, May 9, 1981. AA, Richard Bland Coll., 1977; BA, Va. Commonwealth U., 1979; JD, U. Richmond, 1983. Bar: Va. 1983, U.S. Ct. Appeals (4th cir.) 1983. Assoc. Tuck, Freasier, & Herbig, Richmond, Va., 1984-87; ptnr. Tuck & Connelly Profl. Assocs., Inc., Richmond, Va., 1988-95, Connelly & Associs., P.C., Chester, Va., 1996—; bd. dirs., v.p. Cen. Title Ins. Agy., Richmond, 1988—; agt. Chgo. Title Ins. Corp., Richmond, 1988—. Mem., assoc./counsel Home Builders Assn. South Side Va. Mem. ABA, Va. Bar Assn., Richmond Bar Assn., Southside Bd. Realtors (affiliate), Chester Jaycees, Omicron Delta Kappa, Phi Kappa Phi, Phi Alpha Delta (justice 1983-86). Baptist. Avocations: biking, racquetball, basketball. Home: 14206 Masada Ct Chesterfield VA 23838-8725 Office: Connelly & Assocs 4830 W Hundred Rd Chester VA 23831-1746

CONNELLY, DAVID O'BRIEN, museum administrator, journalist; b. Canton, Ohio, Apr. 25, 1952; s. Harold O'Brien and Mary Louise (Wells) C. BA in English summa cum laude, Mt. Union Coll., 1974; MA, Bowling Green State U., 1975; MA in Latin Am. Studies, U. Tex., Austin, 1995, postgrad., 1977-78. Dir. men's housing Southwestern U., Georgetown, Tex., 1975-76; cmty. educator, publicist Planned Parenthood Assn. Summit County, Akron, Ohio, 1976-77; arts/entertainment editor Shreveport (La.) Jour., 1978-90; asst. grants dir. Mus. Fine Arts, Houston, 1991-93; pub. rels. dir., grants writer Mus. Fine Arts, St. Petersburg, Fla., 1996—; staff writer The Archer M. Huntington Art Gallery, U. Tex., Austin, 1993-95; staff rep. long-range plan com. bd. trustees Mus. Fine Arts, St. Petersburg. Editor: Mosaic; contbr. articles to profl. jours. Organizing com. Inner City Soup Kitchen, Shreveport, 1986-87; organizing com., first sec. exec. com., grants writer N.W. La. AIDS Task Force, Shreveport, 1988-91. Harmon O. DeGraff Meml. scholar Akron YMCA, 1977; Emmett Walter fellow U. Tex., 1977-78, Music Critics Inst. fellow, 1980; named one of Outstanding Young Men of Am., 1989; grantee Tinker Found., 1994. Mem. Am. Assn. Mus., Fla. Assn. Mus., St. Petersburg Mus. Consortium, Blue Key, Phi Kappa Phi, Psi Kappa Omega. Democrat. Jewish. Avocations: reading, travel, swimming, film, the arts. Home: 5190 Salmon Dr SE Apt B Saint Petersburg FL 33705-6351 Office: Mus Fine Arts 255 Beach Dr NE Saint Petersburg FL 33701-3498

CONNELLY, DIANE CECILE, communications executive; b. Mpls., Sept. 27, 1945; d. Howard R. Bloomquist and Ingrid (Brostrom) Bloomquist Pope; m. William Mowry Connelly, Aug. 19, 1967; children: Karin Ingrid, Susan Anne, Heather Mowry. BA in English, Smith Coll., 1967. Assoc. rsch. editor Readers Digest, N.Y.C., 1967-70; freelance writer, editor, rschr. Readers Digest, Time, Bus. Week, Nation, others, 1970-86; mgr. strategic comm. Rockwell Automation, Cleve., 1986-95, Eaton Corp., Cleve., 1996—. V.p. bd. trustees Ruffing Montessori Sch., Cleveland Heights, 1980-84; pub. rels. rep. parent bd. Shaker Heights (Ohio) H.S., 1986. Mem. Internat. Assn. Bus. Communicators (v.p. 1994, pres. 1995, sr. del. 1996). Mem. United Ch. of Christ. Home: 2742 Rocklyn Rd Shaker Hts OH 44122-2115 Office: Eaton Corp Eaton Ctr Cleveland OH 44114

CONNELLY, DONALD PRESTON, electric and gas utility company executive; b. Newark, Del., Nov. 27, 1939; s. Walton Theodore and Edna Rocelia (Lee) C.; m. Margaret Burnetta Boylan, Oct. 29, 1940; children: Donald Preston Jr., Pamela Margaret. AS, U. Del., 1970, BS, 1980. Clk. Delmarva Power, Wilmington, Del., 1961-66, supr., 1966-67, spl. acct., 1967-72, sr. acct., 1972-73, gen. supr., 1973-76, coordinator customer info. system, 1976-79, mgr., 1979-85, mgr., asst. sec., 1985, corp. sec., 1985-88; corp. sec., ethics officer Delmarva Power Subs. Cos., Wilmington, Del., 1988-98, ret., 1998. 1st v.p. Civic League for New Castle County, Wilmington, 1985-86, treas., 1987-91; mem. Metroform Coun. Civic Assns., 1993-96, Churchman's Crossing Civic Assn., 1996—. With USN, 1957-60. Mem. Am. Soc. Corp. Secs. (nat. bd. dirs. 1994-97, exec. steering com. 1995-97, v.p. Mid Atlantic chpt. 1989-91, pres. 1991-92, adv. com. 1988-97), Ethics Officer Assn. Methodist. Avocations: hiking, coin collecting, photography. Home: 7 Greenridge Rd Newark DE 19711-6704 Office: Delmarva Power & Light Co 800 N King St Wilmington DE 19801-3518

CONNELLY, ELIZABETH ANN, state legislator; b. N.Y.C.; d. John Walter and Alice Marie (Mallon) Keresey; m. Robert Vincent Connelly; children: Alice, Robert, Margaret, Therese. Grad. H.S., Bronx; LLD (hon.), Wagner Coll., 1996. Telephone sales Pan Am. World Airways, N.Y.C., 1946-54; mem. N.Y. State Assembly, Albany, 1973—, chair com. on mental health, retardation/devel. disabilities, 1977-92, chair com. on standing coms., 1993-95, speaker pro tem, 1995—, chair intern com., 1995—; chair Legis. Women's Caucus, N.Y. State, 1993-95. Recipient over 250 awards and honors including S.I. Hosp. Vol. of Yr. award, 1972-73, Cert. Appreciation Willowbrook chpt. Benevolent Soc. Retarded Children, 1978, Legislator of Yr. award N.Y. State Coun. on Alcoholism, 1983, Woman of Yr. award Epilepsy Ctr., 1984, Disting. Humanitarian of Yr. award S.I. Ctr. Ind. Living, 1987, Alliance for Mentally Ill of N.Y. State award, 1988, Thomas G. Gilbert Meml. award N.Y. State Mental Health Soc., 1989, Nat. Barrier Awareness Found., 1990, Irish Am. Heritage Mus., 1991, N.Y. State Head Injury Assn. Pub. Policy award, 1994, N.Y. State Cath. Conf. Pub. Policy award 1996, St. John's U. Pres.' medal, 1998. Democrat. Office: NY State Assembly 1150 Forest Hill Rd Staten Island NY 10314-6316

CONNELLY, JAMES P., prosecutor; b. Hartford, Conn., Apr. 15, 1947. BA, Marquette U., 1969; JD, Georgetown U., 1972. Bar: Wis. 1972. Spl. asst. to Sec. of Treasury, 1975-76; ptnr. Foley & Lardner, Milw.; U.S. atty. U.S. Dist. Ct. (ea. dist.) Wash., Spokane, 1994—. Editor-in-chief Georgetown Law Jour., 1971-72. Mem. State Bar Wis., Phi Alpha Delta. Office: U S Atty Office U S Courthouse PO Box 1494 920 W Riverside Ave Spokane WA 99210-1494*

CONNELLY, JOAN BRETON, art educator. BA, Princeton U., 1976, MA, 1979; PhD, Bryn Mawr Coll., 1984. Assoc. prof. classical art, arch. NYU. Office: NYU Dept Fine Arts 303 Main Bldg 100 Washington Sq E New York NY 10003

CONNELLY, JOHN DOOLEY, social service organization executive; b. Sept. 8, 1946; s. John Joseph and Mary (Dooley) C. BS, Xavier U., 1968; MA, Northeastern Ill. U., 1973; PhD, Cornell U., 1976. Spl. edn. tchr. Spl. Edn. Dist., Lake County, Gurnee, Ill., 1969-73; asst. prof. spl. edn. Ea. Ky. U., Richmond, Ky., 1973-76; divsn. dir., acting exec. dir. City of Chgo. Health Sys., 1977-80; exec. dir. Jobs for Youth Chgo., 1980—. Bd. dirs. Emergency Loan Fund, Chgo., 1982-88, Health and Medicine Policy Rsch. Group, Chgo., 1983-84, 92-98, Chgo. Literacy Coordinating Coun., 1988-90, Clarence Darrow Comty. Ctr., Chgo., 1983-88, Gov.'s Task Force on Youth, 1986-87, AIDS Care, 1992-94; founding mem. Health and Medicine Jour., 1984; chmn. Pegasus Players Theatre, Chgo., 1982-87; mem. steering com. Chgo. Initiative, 1992-96; co-chair Chgo. Lab. for Change; active Soc. Svcs. Adv. Coun., Ill. Dept. Pub. Aid, 1989-91; mem. Chgo. Com. Urban Opportunity, 1993-95, Mayor's Task Force on Youth, 1994-95, adv. com. City Chgo. Comty. Devel, 1994-96. Roman Catholic. E-mail: jackconly@aol.com. Office: Jobs for Youth Chgo 50 E Washington St Chicago IL 60602-2100

CONNELLY, JOHN F., communications executive. Chmn., CEO GE Am. Comms., Princeton, N.J. Office: GE Am Comm Inc 4 Research Way Princeton NJ 08540-6618*

CONNELLY, JOHN J., federal judge. JD, U. Notre Dame, 1952. Bar: N.Y. Ptnr. Lindquist & Vennum; asst. U.S. atty. U.S. Dept. Justice; bankruptcy judge for so. and ea. dists. N.Y., U.S. Bankruptcy Ct., White Plains, 1995—; adj. prof. U. Minn. Sch. Law. With USN, 1944-46. Office: US Bankruptcy Ct US Courthouse 300 Quarropas St White Plains NY 10601-4140

CONNELLY, JOHN JAMES, retired oil company technical specialist; b. Lima, Ohio, Aug. 14, 1935; s. Robert Vincent and Helen Josephine (Hay) C.; m. Aug. 22, 1959 (dec. Aug. 1991); children: Thomas, Kathleen, Joseph, Patrick; m. Virginia Connelly, July, 1993. BSChemE, Ohio State U., 1958; MBA with honors, Baldwin Wallace U., 1975. Registered profl. engr., Ohio. Engr. Std. Oil of Ohio, Lima, 1958-63; rsch. assoc. Battelle Meml. Inst., Columbus, Ohio, 1963-65; tech. specialist Owens Corning Fiberglas, Granville, Ohio, 1965-67; sr. engr. Std. Oil of Ohio, Lima, 1967-71; tech. program analyst Std. Oil of Ohio, Cleve., 1971-74, linear program specialist, 1974-78, fed. affairs analyst, 1978-81; project leader Std. of Ohio/Brit. Petroleum Am., Cleve., 1981-92; tech. specialist BP Am., Cleve., 1992-95; retired, 1995; part time technical specialist Paramount Tech. Svcs., 1995—; instr. Ohio State U., Lima, 1961-63. Advisor Jr. Achievement, Lima, 1960-62; treas. Harding Middle Sch. PTA, Lakewood, Ohio, 1975-77, Music Parents Assn., Lakewood, 1978-80, Sch. Bd. Candidate Treas., Lakewood, 1981; mem. Vols. for Internat. Tech. Assistance, 1988—. Mem. Soc. of Friends. Avocations: reading, biking, needlework. Home: 23749 Wonneta Pkwy Westlake OH 44145-2733

CONNELLY, LEWIS BRANCH SUTTON, lawyer; b. St. Louis, Sept. 17, 1950; s. Lewis Branch and Mary Ellen (Henneberger) C.; m. Anna Kristina Cook, Oct. 15, 1977; children: Christopher Sutton, Jeffrey Scott, Sarah Elizabeth. B.A., Vanderbilt U., 1972; J.D., U. Tenn., 1977. Mem. Smith, Cohen, Ringel, Kohler & Martin, Atlanta, 1977-79, Cook & Connelly, Summerville, Ga., 1979—; city atty. Summerville, 1989—. Staff mem. Tenn. Law Rev., 1975-77; apptd. to the magistrate selection com. U.S. Dist. Ct. (no. dist.) Ga., 1990. Mem. ABA (complex crime com. litigation sect. 1982—); atty. sch. bd. Chattooga County Schs., 1989-96, consumer affairs com. corp. banking sect. 1982—), Assn. Trial Lawyers Am., Ga. Assn. Trial Lawyers, Nat. Assn. Criminal Def. Lawyers, Ga. Assn. Criminal Def. Lawyers. Democrat. Presbyterian. Office: Cook & Connelly 128 S Commerce St Summerville GA 30747-1339

CONNELLY, MARGERY ANNETTE, research pathologist, educator; b. Patchogue, N.Y., Nov. 19, 1962; d. Joseph and Faithmarie Martha (Gehrke) Perino; m. Martin Edward Connelly, Aug. 9, 1986; children: Christopher Martin, Kelly Ann. BS in Biochemistry, SUNY, Stony Brook, 1984, PhD in Immunology and Pathology, 1992. Alexander Hollaender Post-doctoral fellow Brookhaven Nat. Lab., Upton, N.Y., 1993-96; adj. faculty C.W. Post Campus, Long Island U., Brookville, N.Y., 1995-96; mem. faculty Southampton (N.Y.) campus L.I. U., Southampton, N.Y., 1996-97; mem. faculty SUNY, Stony Brook, 1997—. Contbr. articles to profl. jours. Mem. AAAS, AAUW, Am. Heart Assn. Republican. Roman Catholic.

CONNELLY, MARK, writer, educator; b. Phila., July 8, 1951; s. Edward James and Hilda Virginia (Pfleger) C. BA in English and History, Carroll Coll., 1973; MA in Creative Writing, U. Wis., Milw., 1974, PhD in English, 1984. Instr. English Milw. Area Tech. Coll., 1986—; cons. Great Lakes Precision Products. Author: The Diminished Self: Orwell and the Loss of Freedom, 1987, The Sundance Reader, 1997, Orwell and Gissing, 1997. Sec. Irish Cultural and Heritage Ctr. of Wis., 1993—. Recipient Ann. Fiction award Milw. Mag., 1982, 1st Place Fiction award Ind. Mag., 1982. Presbyterian. Avocations: reading, travel, Irish studies. Office: Milw Area Tech Coll 700 W State St Milwaukee WI 53233-1419

CONNELLY, MARY CREEDON, insurance company executive; b. Niagara Falls, N.Y., Apr. 1, 1950; d. Daniel Francis and Anne Walle (Moynihan) C. BA, Coll. New Rochelle, 1972. Dir. divsn. ins. Fed. Savs. and Loan Ins. Corp., Washington, 1984-86, dep. exec. dir., 1987-88, exec. dir., 1989; assoc. dir. FDIC, Washington, 1989-91; COO Farm Credit Sys. Ins. Co., McLean, Va., 1991—. Mem. Women in Housing and Fin. Avocation: watercolors. Home: 4315 31st St N Arlington VA 22207-4115 Office: Farm Credit Sys Ins Corp 1501 Farm Credit Dr Mc Lean VA 22102-5004*

CONNELLY, MARY JO, lawyer; b. Chgo., May 19, 1949; d. Joseph Anthony and Veronica Colette (Casey) C. BSN, Coll. St. Teresa, 1971; JD, DePaul U., 1980. Bar: Ill. 1980, U.S. Dist. Ct. (no. dist.) Ill. 1980, U.S. Dist. Ct. (ctrl. dist., no. dist.) Ill. 1990. Head nurse neurosurgery St. Mary's Hosp., Rochester, Minn., 1971-73; head nurse ambulatory care U. Calif., San Francisco, 1973-77; ptnr. Sweeney & Riman Ltd., Chgo., 1980-98. Mem. ABA, Women's Bar Assn. Ill., Ill. Bar Assn., Chgo. Bar Assn. (investigator hearing, bd. dirs. jud. evaluation com. 1984-89). Home: 340 W Diversey Pky Apt 618 Chicago IL 60657-6242

CONNELLY, PATRICIA LORRAINE, travel executive; b. Phila., Mar. 29, 1944. BA, Western State U., 1987; postgrad., Holy Family Coll., 1988. Mgr. Transeair Travel Inc., Phila.; assn. tax acct. Gen. Refractories Co., Phila.; travel mgr. Morgan, Lewis & Bockius, LLP, Phila.; adv. bd. Four Seasons Hotel. Mem. Nat. Passenger Traffic Assn., Delaware Valley Corp. Travel Mgrs. Assn. (asst. v.p.), Am. Soc. Travel Agts. (cert.), Meeting Planners Internat., Internat. Soc. Meeting Planners (cert. meeting planner). Avocations: antiquing, golfing, sailing, traveling.

CONNELLY, SHARON RUDOLPH, lawyer, federal official; b. Kingwood, W.Va.; d. John E. and Lorene E. Rudolph; 1 child, John. BS, W.Va. State U., 1966; MBA, Ind. U., 1968; JD, Cath. Univ., 1976; LLM in Taxation, Georgetown U., 1995. Bar: Va. 1977. Mgr. IRS, Washington, 1969-76; asst. contr. Mfrs. Hanover, N.Y.C., 1976-77; compliance chief D.C. Dept. Labor, Washington, 1977-79; dir. compliance U.S. Dept. Commerce, Washington, 1979-82; asst. insp. gen. NASA, Washington, 1982-84; dir. insp. office Nuclear Regulatory Commn., Washington, 1984-89; spl. asst. internal controls Nuclear Regulatory Commn., 1989-98. Contbr. articles to profl. jours.

CONNELLY, TERRENCE JOHN, SR., television station executive; b. Chgo., Aug. 23, 1947; s. Charles Bernard, Jr. and Margaret Agnes (Gilmore) C.; m. Andrea Susan Hahn, Feb. 12, 1972; children: Terrence John, Jr., Bridget Colleen. BS in Comms., U. Ill., 1970. Reporter WITI-TV, Milw., 1970-73, WRGB-TV, Schenectady, N.Y., 1973-74; news dir. WNYT-TV, Albany, N.Y., 1974-76, WDAF-TV, Kansas City, Mo., 1976-78; exec. news producer WMAQ-TV, Chgo., 1978-80; v.p. TV news Taft Broadcasting, Cin., 1980-86; v.p., gen. mgr. WCPO-TV, Cin., 1986-88, WKRC-TV, Cin., 1988-92, WSYX-TV, Columbus, Ohio, 1992-95; pres., gen. mgr. WJLA-TV, Washington, 1995-98; sr. v.p. programming and prodn. The Weather Channel, Atlanta, 1999—; dir. teletext, Taft Broadcasting, Cin., 1981-86; mem. broadcast adv. bd. UPI, N.Y.C., 1983-85. Editor/gen. mgr.: WCPO TV news, 1987 (Peabody award for investigative report 1987). Bd. dirs. United Way, Washington, 1995—, Easter Seals Bd., Washington, 1995—, Muscular Distrophy Assn., Columbus, 1992-95; chmn. Neediest Kids, Inc., Washington, 1995—. With U.S. Army, 1970-76. Mem. Soc. Profl. Journalists, Radio-TV News Dirs. Assn., Nat. Assn. TV Program Execs., Rotary. Roman Catholic. Office: The Weather Channel 300 Interstate North Pkwy Atlanta GA 30339*

CONNER, FRED L., lawyer; b. Hutchinson, Kans., Nov. 30, 1909; s. Hugh and Ida (Guldner) C.; m. Helen Opie, Sept. 15, 1940; 1 child, Brian. JD, U. Kans., 1934. Bar: Kans. 1934. Assoc. Andrew F. Schoeppel, Ness City, Kans., 1934-37; sole practice Gt. Bend, Kans., 1937-38; ptnr. Conner & Opie and predecessor firms, Gt. Bend, 1938—; dir. Insured Titles, Inc.; mem. faculty Philmont Scout Ranch, 1956; mem. Kans. Jud. Council Com. to Redistrict Dist. Cts. of Kans., 1968. Served to lt. comdr. USN, 1942-45. Fellow Am. Coll. Trust and Estate Counsel (chmn. Kans. sect. 1974-78), Probate Attys. Assn. (rsch. and editl. bd. 1959-62); mem. ABA (admissions com. 1951-58), Kans. Bar Assn. (program com. chmn. 1955-56, profl. ethics chmn. 1962-69, nominating com. chmn. 1969-70, Outstanding Svc. award 1970-71, 78-79, pres. 1980-81), S.W. Kans. Bar Assn., Kans. Bar Found. (trustee 1958-61), Barton County Bar Assn. (pres. 1946), Rotary (pres. Gt. Bend 1948), Masons, Am. Legion, Phi Delta Phi. Republican. Methodist. Home and Office: PO Box 763 Salina KS 67402-0763

CONNER, JAMES LEON, II, lawyer, mediator; b. Roanoke, Va., June 29, 1956; s. James Leon and Avis Christine (Craig) C.; m. Lorraine Joyce McNamara, Aug. 11, 1979 (div. 1987); children: Patrick James, Daniel Silas; m. Kathy Lynelle Watson, July 28, 1996; children: Benjamin Micah, Caleb Thomas. AB, Duke U., 1978; JD, U. N.C. Bar: N.C. 1983, U.S. Dist. Ct. (mid. dist.) N.C. 1984; U.S. Ct. Appeals (4th cir.). Vis. law instr. U. Ill. Coll. Law, Champaign, 1983-84; assoc. editor Environ. Law Inst., Washington, 1984-85; ptnr. Abernathy, Roberson & Conner, Graham, N.C., 1985-88; recycling dir. Alamance County, Burlington, N.C., 1988-89; assoc. atty. Brooks Pierce Mclendon Humphrey & Leonard, Greensboro, N.C., 1989-93; lead environ. atty. Kennedy Covington Lobdell & Hickman, Charlotte, N.C., 1993-95; prin. atty. J. Conner & Assocs., Durham, N.C., 1995—; mem. coun. environ. and natural resources law sect. N.C. Bar Assn., 1987-91. Contbr. articles to profl. jours. Mem. Durham (N.C.) City and County Environ. Affairs Bd., 1995—, vice chair 1997-98, chmn. 1998—; bd. dirs. Piedmont Land Conservancy, Greensboro, 1992-93; elder Presbyn. Ch.; founder U. N.C. chpt. Equal Justice Found., 1982; bd. dirs. North State Legal Svcs., 1986-89. Recipient Chpt. Svc. award N.C. Sierra Club, 1990, Am. Jurisprudence award. Avocations: hiking, canoeing, golf. Office: J Conner & Assocs 311 E Main St Durham NC 27701-3717

CONNER, KATHRYN GAMBLE, nurse; b. Orlando, Fla., Apr. 11, 1959; d. Thomas Edward and Gertrude (Whitty) Gamble; m. Keith Devaughn Conner, May 1, 1982; children: Andrew Devaughn, Kevin Devaughn. AA, Seminole Community Coll., 1978; BSN, U. Fla., 1980; M in Nursing, Emory U., 1988. LPN Ga., ARNP, Fla. Pediatric nurse Henrietta Egleston Hosp. for Children, Atlanta, 1985-86; specialist in hematology/oncology U. Fla., Gainesville, 1988-91; pediatric nurse Shands Tchg. Hosp., Gainesville, Fla., 1981-85, 87-88, clin. nurse specialist pediatric oncology, 1991-93; nursing supr./educator Shands Tchg. Hosp., Gainesville, 1993-95, coordinated care mgr., 1995—; mem. adj. faculty Coll. Nursing, U. Fla., 1989—. Mem. Assn. Pediatric Oncology Nurses, Pediatric Oncology Group, Oncology Nursing Soc.,Sigma Theta Tau. Democrat. Methodist. Office: Shands Teaching Hosp Dept Nursing Box 100335 1600 SW Archer Rd Dept Nursing Gainesville FL 32610-3001

CONNER, LABAN CALVIN, retired librarian; b. Ocala, Fla., Feb. 18, 1936; s. Laban Calvin and Dorothy Helen (Todd) C. B.Gen.Edn., U. Nebr., 1959; M.S. in Library Edn., Emporia State U., 1964; Ed.S., Nova U., 1979; Ph.D., Pacific Western U., 1980. Tchr., Liberty City Elem. Sch., Dade County, Fla., 1959-63; library/media specialist Dade County Pub. Schs., 1963-68, coordinator library services, 1968-70; asst. prof. library Miami-Dade Community Coll., 1970-73; library/media specialist Dade County Pub. Schs., 1973-81; dir. libraries Fla. Meml. Coll., Miami, 1981-98, ret., 1998. Mem. Dade County Media/Specialists Assn., ALA, Fla. Library Assn., Kappa Delta Phi (Phi Eta chpt.). Served with USAF, 1956-59. Democrat. African Methodist Episcopal. Home: 18601 NW 39th Ave Opa Locka FL 33055-2820

CONNER, LELAND LAVON, Indian lorist; b. Logan, Ohio, May 9, 1930; s. Foster Everett and Ida May (Cullison) C.; m. Doris Ann Keller, 1953; children: Lavonna Sue, Gregory Lee, Kay Annette, Melinda Lou. Indian lore speaker Conner Indian Show, Logan, 1960—. Author: The Vengeance of Lewis Wetzel, 1980; contbr. articles to profl. publs. Pres. Hocking County Hist. Soc., Logan, 1977-78, v.p., 1975-76; chmn. ARC Blood Program, Logan, 1976-77. With U.S. Army, 1951-53. Recipient Schiele award for Excellence in Indian Lore Schiele Mus., Gastonia, N.C., 1987, Proclamation of Recognition Ohio Ho. Reps., 1988. Mem. Am. Indian Lore Assn. (nat. dir. 1988—, Catlin Peace Pipe award 1979), Continental Confederation of Adopted Indians (Continental chief 1988—), Pipestone Indian Shrine Assn. Avocations: camping, nature hiking, teaching wilderness survival, fossil hunting. Home and Office: Am Indian Lore Assn 960 Walhonding Ave Logan OH 43138-1868

CONNER, LEONARD WAYNE, banker, association administrator, layworker; b. Kansas City, Mo., Aug. 5, 1944; s. Clyde Page and Daisy Marie (Clevenger) C.; m. Joanne Marie Di Bianca, Jan. 6, 1968; 1 child, Brett Page. BA, U. Mo., 1968; MBA, Widener U., 1975. V.p. Continental Bank, Norristown, Pa., 1971-85; adminstrv. v.p. First Pa. Bank, Phila., 1985-86; AVP Centerre Bank, Kansas City, Mo., 1986-88; v.p., cashier Bank of Lee's Summit, Mo., 1988-92; bus. adminstr. Internat. Union Gospel Missions, North Kansas City, Mo., 1992—; bd. dirs. Englewood Assembly of God, Independence, Mo., 1993-94. Squadron commdr. Kingsway Power Squadron, Cherry Hill, N.J., 1986. Capt. U.S. Army, 1968-70, Vietnam. Recipient Golden Telephone award Greater Phila. C. of C., 1972. Mem. Christian Mgmt. Assn. Avocations: fishing, weight lifting, power walking, re-modeling. Office: Internat Union Gospel Miss 1045 Swift Ave North Kansas City MO 64116

CONNER, LEWIS HOMER, JR., lawyer; b. Chattanooga, Mar. 21, 1938; s. Lewis H. Sr. and Cleo (Johnson) C.; m. Ashley Whitsitt, June 1, 1960; children: Holland Ashley, Lewis Forrest. BA, Vanderbilt U., 1960, JD, 1963. Bar: Tenn. 1963, U.S. Dist. Ct. (all dists.) Tenn. 1963, U.S. Ct. Appeals (6th cir.) 1963, U.S. Ct. Mil. Appeals 1964, U.S. Supreme Ct. 1990; cert. mediator, Tenn. Founding ptnr., atty. Dearborn & Ewing, Nashville, 1972-80; judge Ct. Appeals Middle Dist., Nashville, 1980-84; sr. ptnr., atty. Waller Lansden Dortch & Davis, Nashville, 1985-89, Boult, Cummings, Conners & Berry, Nashville, 1989-96; of counsel Stokes & Bartholomew, Nashville, 1997—; chmn. Willis Coroon, Tenn., 1996—; spl. chief justice Supreme Ct. Tenn., 1980-81; lectr. law Vanderbilt U. Sch. Law, Nashville, 1984-93; life del. Sixth Cir. Ct. Appeals Jud. Conf. Mng. editor Vanderbilt Law Rev. Elder Westminster Presbyn. Ch.; bd. dirs. Tenn. Golf Assn., Nashville, 1965—, pres., 1985, chmn. 1994-95, 98—; fin. co-chmn. Alexander for Gov., 1974-78; chmn. Tenn. Rep. Fin. Com., 1975, Tenn. Corrections Overcrowding Commn., 1985-86; bd. dirs. Boys & Girls Club Middle Tenn., 1980—, pres., 1991-92; bd. govs. Tenn. State Mus., 1987—, vice chmn. bd., 1988-89, chmn. bd., 1990-91; mem. nat. fin. com. Bush for Pres., 1988, 92; bd. dirs., exec. com. Nashville Sports Coun., 1994—; bd. dirs. BellSouth Sr. Classic, Nashville, 1994—; nat. fin. co-chmn. Lamar Alexander for Pres., Inc., Nashville, 1995-96, 1999-2000. Fellow Am. Acad. Matrimonial Lawyers, Am. Bar Found., Tenn. Bar Found., Nashville Bar Found.; mem. ABA, Am. Arbitration Assn. (bd. dirs. 1990—, chmn. Tenn. large complex case panel 1992—, panel of arbitrators 1995, panel of mediators 1995—), Tenn. Bar Assn., Tenn. Jud. Conf., Nashville Bar Assn. (pres. 1986-87, bd. dirs., 1984-87), Commn. on the Future of the Cts. in Tenn., Order of the Coif, PGA of Am. (hon. Tenn. sect.), The Golf Club Tenn. (founder, exec. com. 1991-97), Richland Country Club (bd. dirs. 1976-79, pres. 1978-79), Belle Meade Country Club, The Honors Course, Quail West Golf Club, Nashville City Club, Nashville Cumberland Club, Nashville Stadium Club, Tenn. Golf Assn. (amateur player of yr., 1973). Republican. Avocations: golf, basketball, softball, politics. Home: 163 Charleston Park Nashville TN 37205-4703 Office: Stokes & Bartholomew 424 Church St Ste 2800 Nashville TN 37219-2386

CONNER, RUTH MARTHA EDONE, nonprofit executive; b. N.Y.C., May 13, 1950; d. Anthony Charles and Ruth Natalie (Weireter) Edone; m. Michael E. Conner, 1985 (div. Feb. 1992). BA, NYU, 1972; MDiv, Union Theol. Sem., N.Y.C., 1976; student, U. Tuebingen, Germany, 1977. Tchr. various schs., N.Y.C., 1977-79; editor Book of the Month Club, N.Y.C., 1979-85; tech. writer AT&T, Freehold, N.J., 1985-87; editor for grad. mktg. comm. Rutgers U., New Brunswick, N.J., 1987-89, dir. alumni comm., 1989-97; v.p. individual support Nat. Med. Fellowships, N.Y.C., 1997-99; dir. devel. Nat. Charities Info. Bur., N.Y.C., 1999—. Author: Getting Organized, 1981; contbr. articles to profl. jours. and trade mags. Bd. dirs. Union Sem. Libr. Friends, N.Y.C., 1992-94; v.p. Duncan Hill Block Assn., Jersey City, 1994—. Recipient Woman of Action award Mayor of Jersey City, 1997. Mem. AAUW, Nat. Soc. Fundraising Execs., Coun. for Advancement and Support of Edn. Episcopalian. Avocation: oil painting. Office: Nat Charities Info Bur 19 Union Square W New York NY 10003

CONNER, STEWART EDMUND, lawyer; b. Louisville, Oct. 7, 1941; s. James Pleasant and Lucille (Winter) C.; m. Joan E. Fish, May 20, 1989; children: Shannon Lynn, Erin Eileen, Margaret Eisele; stepchildren: Hunt Rounsavall, Gibbs Rounsavall, Christine Rounsavall. BS, U. Louisville, 1963, JD cum laude, 1966. Bar: Ky. 1966, U.S. Dist. Ct. (ea. and we. dists.) Ky. 1966, U.S. Tax Ct. 1967. Assoc. Wyatt, Tarrant & Combs, Louisville, 1966-72, ptnr., 1972—, chmn. gen. corp. sect., 1980-90, mng. ptnr., 1988—. Author, editor: Kentucky Business Practice Handbook, 1988; editor Kentucky Legal Forms, 1988; contbr. to U. Ky. Law Rev. Bd. dirs. Coun. on Higher Edn., 1992-95, Louisville Water Co., 1990—, Lincoln Heritage coun. Boy Scouts Am., 1989—, dePaul Sch., 1996—. With U.S. Army, 1968-69, Vietnam. Fellow Am. Bar Found., Ky. Bar Found.; mem. ABA (banking com. 1983), Ky. Bar Assn., Louisville Bar Assn. (chmn. ethics com. 1980), Ky. C. of C. (bd. dirs. 1992-96), Louisville C. of C. (bd. dirs. 1996—), Law Club, Harmony Landing Country Club, Louisville Boat Club. Republican. Office: Wyatt Tarrant & Combs 2800 Citizens Plz Louisville KY 40202

CONNER, SUSAN GORDON, nurse, organization official, consultant; b. Long Branch, N.J., Sept. 2, 1948; d. Louis Samuel and Elizabeth Isabel (Van Brunt) Scalpati; children: Ainsley Price, Alison Beth. BS, Old Dominion U., 1974; MS, U. Md., Balt., 1989; advanced cert. in policy sci., U. Md., Balt. County, 1989. Cert. BLS, ACLS. Commd. 1st lt. U.S. Army, 1974, advanced through grades to lt. col.; head nurse US Army Health Clinic, Ft. Monroe, Va., 1976-77; head nurse ICU U.S. Army Hosp., Ft. Eustis, 1977-78; instr. William Beaumont Army Med. Ctr., El Paso, Tex., 1978-79; supr. Williamsburg (Va.) Community Hosp., 1980; head nurse surg. U.S. Army Hosp., Ft. Eustis, 1980-82; head nurse ICU U.S. Army Hosp., Ft. Campbell, Ky., 1983-85; br. chief Acad. Health Scis., Ft. Sam Houston, Tex., 1985-87; chief quality improvement Walter Reed Army Med. Ctr., Washington, 1989-93; ret., 1993; dir. nursing Lorien Nursing and Rehab. Ctr., Columbia, Md., 1993-95; dir. subacute Meridian-Spa Creek, Annapolis, Md., 1995-96; cons. Ctr. for Health Policy Studies, 1996-98; mng. cons., rsch. dir. The Gallup Orgn., Rockville, Md., 1998—; cons. in quality improvement Walter Reed Army Med. Ctr. Region, 1992-93; cons. Office Pers. Mgmt., Washington, 1990-93; med. legal cons., internat. cons. quality assurance; preceptor grad. and undergrad. U. Md., Cath. U., George Washington U., 1989-93. Awarded Legion of Merit; U.S. Senate fellow, 1989; decorated Meritorious Svc. award, Army Commendation medal, Army Achievement medal. Mem. ANA (nurses strategic action team), Md. Nurses Assn. (legis. com., task force on health care reform, conv. planning com. 1991, 92), U.S. Naval Acad. Sailing Assn., Eastport Yacht Club, Seaford Yacht Club, Optimists (bd. dirs. Annapolis chpt.), Sigma Theta Tau, Delta Phi Omega. Avocations: sailing, politics, cooking. Home: 140 Spring Place Way Annapolis MD 21401-7295 Office: The Gallup Orgn One Church St Ste 900 Rockville MD 20850

CONNER, TROY BLAINE, JR., retired lawyer, writer; b. Moundsville, W.Va., Jan. 23, 1926; s. Troy Blaine and Ethel (Barbour) C.; m. Betty Lenore Luzier, Dec. 29, 1953; children: Troy Blaine III, Kimberly Ann Motteler, Robert James, David Jefferson. AB, W.Va. U., 1946, JD, 1948. Bar: W.Va. 1948, D.C. 1969, U.S. Ct. Appeals (3d cir.) 1975, U.S. Ct. Appeals (4th cir.) 1979, U.S. Ct. Appeals (5th cir.) 1978, U.S. Ct. Appeals (6th cir.) 1988, U.S. Supreme Ct. 1957. Pvt. practice Morgantown, W.Va., 1948-53; trial atty. criminal and internal security divs. Dept. Justice, 1953-58; the trial counsel AEC, 1958-70; exec. dir. CAB, 1970-71; ptnr. Reid & Priest, N.Y.C. and Washington, 1971-73; sr. ptnr. Conner, Hadlock & Knotts (and successor firms), Washington, 1973-90; chmn. KMC, Inc., 1976-90; mem. adv. council environ. edn. HEW, 1976-77. Trustee Salem Coll., 1975-80; bd. dirs. W.Va. U. Found., 1974-95, campaign exec. com., 1987-94, W.Va. U., Order of Vandalia, 1996; mem. W.Va. Coll. Law Nat. Coun., 1985-94; mem. Lit. Vol. Am., 1990-91. Fellow Internat. Acad. Law and Sci.; mem. ABA, Am. Nuclear Soc., W.Va. Bar Assn., D.C. Bar Assn., Fed. Bar Assn., U.S. Coun. for Energy Awareness, W.Va. U. Alumni Assn., Md. Rep. Eagles (chmn. 1988-91), Montgomery Rep. Club (pres. 1994-95), Nat. Aero. Assn., U.S. Naval Inst., Emerald Shillelaghs Chowder and Marching Soc., NRA, Aero Club, Circus Saints and Sinners Club, Nat. Lawyers Club, Capitol Hill Club, Phi Sigma Kappa. Republican. Methodist. Home: 9416 Firethorn Ct Potomac MD 20854-1561

CONNER, WILLIAM CURTIS, judge; b. Wichita Falls, Tex., Mar. 27, 1920; s. D.H. and Mae (Weeks) C.; m. Janice Files, Mar. 22, 1944; children: William Curtis, Stephen, Christopher, Molly. B.B.A., U. Tex., 1941, LL.B., 1942; postgrad., Harvard, 1942-43, Mass. Inst. Tech., 1943. Bar: Tex. bar 1942, N.Y. State bar 1949. Asso., mem. firm Curtis, Morris & Safford (and predecessor firm), N.Y.C., 1946-73; judge U.S. Dist. Ct. (so. dist.) N.Y., White Plains, 1973—, now sr. judge. Editor Tex. Law Rev. Served to lt. USNR, 1942-45, PTO. Recipient Jefferson medal N.J. Patent Law Assn. Mem. Am. Judicature Soc., N.Y. Patent Law Assn. (pres. 1972-73). Presbyterian (elder). Club: St. Andrews Golf. Office: US Dist Ct US Courthouse 300 Quarropas St White Plains NY 10601-4150

CONNERS, JOHN BRENDAN, insurance company executive; b. Boston, Oct. 6, 1945; s. Stephen Edward and Josephine (McMahon) C.; m. Jean Marie McLean, June 15, 1968; children: James, Michael, Colleen. AB, Boston Coll., 1967. Cert. casualty actuary. Actuarial asst. Liberty Mut. Ins. Co., Boston, 1969-70, actuarial analyst, 1970-73, asst. actuary, 1973-75, assoc. actuary, 1975-79, asst. v.p., assoc. actuary, 1979-80, v.p., assoc. actuary, 1980, v.p., actuary, 1980-82, v.p., mgr. personal risks, 1982-83, sr. v.p., mgr. personal market, 1983-87, exec. v.p. personal market, 1987—. Mem. Ins. Rsch. Coun.; bd. dirs. Hwy. Loss Data Inst., Washington, Advocates for Hwy. and Auto Safety, Washington, ARC, Mass. Bay, SADD. Mem. Casualty Actuarial Soc. (bd. dirs. 1983-85), Casualty Actuaries New Eng. (pres. 1980). Roman Catholic. Avocations: golf, gardening. also: Liberty Mutual 175 Berkeley St Boston MA 02116*

CONNERY, SEAN (THOMAS CONNERY), actor; b. Edinburgh, Scotland, Aug. 25, 1930; s. Joseph and Euphamia C.; m. Diane Cilento, 1962 (div.); 1 son, Jason; m. Micheline Roquebrune, 1975; 1 stepdaughter. D.Litt. (hon.), Heriot-Watt U., 1981. Dir. Tantallon Films Ltd., 1972—; first theater appearance in road show co. of South Pacific, Eng., 1953, also in Macbeth, Judith; films include: Let's Make Up, 1955, No Road Back, 1956, The Hill, 1965, Action of the Tiger, 1957, Another Time, Another Place, 1957, Hell Drivers, 1958, Tarzan's Greatest Adventure, 1959, Darby O'Gill and the Little People, 1959, On the Fiddle, 1961, The Longest Day, 1962, The Frightened City, 1962, Woman of Straw, 1964, Marnie, 1964, A Fine Madness, 1966, Shalako, 1968, The Molly Maguires, 1968, The Red Tent, 1969, The Anderson Tapes, 1970, The Offence, 1973, Zardoz, 1973, Ransom, 1974, Murder on the Orient Express, 1974, The Wind and the Lion, 1975, The Man Who Would be King, 1975, Robin and Marian, 1976, A Bridge Too Far, 1977, The Great Train Robbery, 1979, Cuba, 1979, Meteor, 1979, The Outland, 1981, Time Bandits, 1981, Sword of the Valiant, 1982, Wrong is Right, 1982, Five Days One Summer, 1982, The Name of the Rose, 1986, The Untouchables, 1987 (Acad. award for best supporting actor), The Presidio, 1988, Indiana Jones and the Last Crusade, 1989, Family Business, 1989, The Hunt for Red October, 1990, The Russia House, 1990, Highlander 2: The Quickening, 1991, Robin Hood: Prince of Thieves, 1991, (also exec. prodr.) Medicine Man, 1992, Rising Sun, 1993, A Good Man in Africa, 1994, Just Cause, 1995, First Knight, 1995, The Rock, 1996, (voice) Dragon Heart, 1996; actor, co-exec. prodr.: Medicine Man, 1992; James Bond films include: Dr No, 1963, From Russia with Love, 1964, Goldfinger, 1965, Thunderball, 1965, You Only Live Twice, 1967, Diamonds are Forever, 1971, Never Say Never Again, 1983; TV appearances include Requiem For a Heavyweight, 1957, Anna Karenina, The Crucible; prodr., dir.: The Bowler and the Bonnet (film documentary), I've Seen You Cut Lemons (London stage); prodr.: Something Like the Truth, Playing by Heart, 1998, (narrator) Macbeth, 1999; exec. prodr. Finding Forrester, 1999; exec. prodr., actor The Avengers, 1998, Entrapment, 1999. Served with Brit. Royal Navy. Named Star of the Yr., Nat. Assn. Theater Owners, 1987, Commander of Arts, France; recipient Tribute award Brit. Acad. Film and Television Arts, 1990, Cecil B. DeMille Golden Globe award Hollywood Fgn. Press Assn., 1996; recipient Lifetime Achievement award ShoWest Conv., 1999, Career Achievement award Nat. Bd. Rev., 1993. Office: CAA 9830 Wilshire Blvd Beverly Hills CA 90212-1804*

CONNES, ALAIN, education educator. Prof. Inst. des Hautes Etudes Sci, Coll. de France. 1982 FIELDS MEDAL WINNER.

CONNEY, ALLAN HOWARD, pharmacologist; b. Chgo., Mar. 23, 1930; s. Leo Younkers and Celia (Gasway) C.; m. Diana, Sept. 5, 1954; children—Michael Raymond, Steven Herbert. BS, U. Wis., 1952, MS, 1954, PhD, 1956. Research asst. McArdle Lab., Madison, Wis., 1952-56; guest investigator Nat. Heart Inst., Bethesda, Md., 1957-58, pharmacologist, 1958-60; head dept. biochem. pharmacology Burroughs Wellcome & Co., Tuckahoe, N.Y., 1960-70; dir. dept. biochemistry Hoffmann-La Roche Inc., Nutley, N.J., 1970-71, dir. dept. biochemistry and drug metabolism, 1971-83, assoc. dir. exptl. therapeutics, 1979-83, dir. lab. exptl. carcinogenesis and metabolism, 1983-85; head Lab. of Exptl. Carcinogenesis and Metabolism Roche Inst. Molecular Biology, Nutley, N.J., 1985-87; chmn. dept. chem. biology Rutgers U. Coll. Pharmacy, Piscataway, N.J., 1987—. Mem. NAS, AAAS, Am. Soc. Biol. Chemists, Am. Soc. Pharmacology and Exptl. Therapeutics (ASPET award), Am. Assn. Cancer Rsch. (G.H.A. Clowes award), Soc. Toxicology, Inc. (Arnold J. Lehman award). Office: Rutgers U Coll Pharmacy/Lab Canc Rsch 164 Frelinghuysen Rd Piscataway NJ 08854-8020

CONNICK, CHARLES MILO, retired religion educator, clergyman; b. Conneaut Lake Park, Pa., Mar. 23, 1917; s. Walter and Iola Belle (Wintermute) C.; m. Genevieve Shaul, June 7, 1941 (dec. June 1992); children: Joy (Mrs. J. Bruce Parker), Christopher Milo, Nancy (Mrs. David F. Jankowski); m. Sonja J. Banisch, July 24, 1994. Student, Edinboro State U., 1935-36; AB, Allegheny Coll., 1939, DD, 1960; DMin, Boston U., 1942, PhD, 1944; Roswell R. Robinson fellow, Harvard U., 1942-43; postgrad., Episcopal Div. Sch., 1942-44. Ordained deacon United Meth. Ch., 1941, elder, 1942; assoc. minister St. Paul's Methodist Ch., Lowell, Mass., 1940-41, Copley Meth. Ch., Boston, 1941-42; dir. Wesley Found., Harvard U.; also minister to students Harvard Epworth Meth. Ch., Cambridge, Mass., summers 1943-44; sr. instr. pub. speaking Curry Coll., Boston, 1942-44; head Bible dept. Northfield Sch., East Northfield, Mass., 1944-46; prof. religion, chmn. dept. philosophy, religion Whittier (Calif.) Coll., 1946-82, prof. religion emeritus, 1982—; chmn. social sci. div., 1950, 60, pres. faculty senate, 1970-71, dir. coll. study tour to Europe, Middle East, around the world, summers 1955-69; pres. I-TAC, 1976-87; Danforth assoc., 1959—, Danforth sr. assoc., 1964-82; spl. lectr. Bibl. lit. Sch. Religion, First Congl. Ch., Los Angeles, 1948-61; mem. Western Pa. Conf., United Meth. Ch., 1942—; exec. sec. Presdl. Selection Com., 1969-70; cons. for colls. and univs. seeking new presidents, 1971-82; adv. council Calif. Christian Com. for Israel, 1974-82. Author: Build on The Rock, You and the Sermon on the Mount, 1960, Jesus, the Man, the Mission, and the Message, 1963, 2d edit., 1974, The Message and Meaning of the Bible, 1965, The New Testament: An Introduction to its History, Literature and Thought, 1972, 2d edit., 1978; editorial adviser to maj. pubs., 1964-88; contbr. articles to religious jours. and mags. Trustee Whittier Coll., 1982—. Recipient Distinguished Alumnus award Boston U., 1971, Gold award Allegheny Coll., 1989; C. Milo Connick chair in religion established Whittier Coll., 1982. Mem. Consumers Coop. Whittier Inc. (pres. 1949-53), AAUP (Whittier pres. 1970-72), Pacific Coast Assn. for Religious Studies (exec. com. 1947-60), Am. Acad. Religion (pres. Western Region 1953-54), Soc. Bibl. Lit., Am. Oriental Soc., Am. Christian Assn. for Israel (mem. nat. adv. com. 1964-69), Phi Sigma Tau, Kappa Phi Kappa, Chi Delta Sigma, Omicron Delta Kappa. Home: 6249 Roundhill Dr Whittier CA 90601-3836 Office: Whittier Coll 13421 Philadelphia St Whittier CA 90601 *Perhaps the greatest misunderstanding about courtship and marriage is the nature of love. A person does not "fall in love." Love is not an accident; it is an achievement. One falls into passion and climbs into love.*

CONNICK, ROBERT ELWELL, retired chemistry educator; b. Eureka, Calif., July 29, 1917; s. Arthur Elwell and Florence (Robertson) C.; m. Frances Spieth, Dec. 19, 1952; children—Mary Catherine, Elizabeth, Arthur, Megan, Sarah, William Beach. B.S., U. Calif. at Berkeley, 1939, Ph.D., 1942. Mem. faculty U. Calif., Berkeley, 1942-88, researcher Manhattan project, 1943-46, asst. prof. then assoc. prof. chemistry, 1945-52, prof., 1952-88, chmn. dept. chemistry, 1958-60, dean Coll. Chemistry, 1960-65, vice chancellor acad. affairs, 1965-67, vice chancellor, 1969-71, acting dean Coll. Chemistry, 1987-88. Contbr. articles profl. jours. Guggenheim fellow, 1949, 59. Mem. Am. Chem. Soc., Nat. Acad. Scis., Phi Beta Kappa, Sigma Xi, Pi Mu Epsilon. Home: 50 Marguerita Rd Kensington CA 94707-1020

CONNIFF, RICHARD, writer; b. Jersey City, N.J., Mar. 2, 1951; s. James C.G. and Dorothy E. (Donnelly) C.; m. Karen Ward Braeder, May 23, 1981; children: James F., Benjamin B., Clare E. BA, Yale U., 1973. Reporter The Star Ledger, Newark, 1973-75; freelance writer N.J., 1975-79; sr. writer Next Mag., N.Y.C., 1979-81; freelance writer Conn., 1981-83, 85—; mng. editor Geo Mag., N.Y.C., 1983-85. Author: The Devil's Book of Verse, 1983, Irish Walls, 1986, Spineless Wonders, 1996; Every Creeping Thing, 1998, screenwriter documentaries for Discovery Channel, Nat. Geographic, WNET, PBS, BBC; contbr. articles to Smithsonian, Nat. Geographic, others. Recipient Nat. Mag. award Mag. Publs. Assn., 1997. Mem. Authors Guild, Writers Guild Am. Democrat. Roman Catholic. Office: The Spieler Agy 154 W 57th St New York NY 10019-3321

CONNINGTON, MARY ELLEN, health facility administrator; b. N.Y.C., July 6, 1954; d. John A. and Alice C. (Neville) Walsh; m. Kevin W. Connington, June 17, 1978; children: Kevin, Tara, Sean. Diploma, Misericordia Sch. Nursing, N.Y.C., 1974; BSN, Coll. Mt. St. Vincent, 1981; student, Columbia U. Supr. Misericordia Hosp. and Med. Ctr., Bronx, N.Y., 1974-81; dir. nursing qualtiy assurance St. Joseph's Med. Ctr., Yonkers, N.Y., 1985-89, dir. nursing quality assurance and staff devel., 1989-90; corp. dir. quality assurance Cath. Med. Ctr., Jamaica, N.Y., 1990-98; v.p. Fidelis Care, Rego Park, N.Y., 1998—; mem. faculty Borough Manhattan C.C., CCNY, 1981-87; cons. in field. Author: Nursing Qualtiy Assurance Unit Based and Patient Centered. Mem. ANA, AACN, Am. Assn. Quality Assurance Profls., No. Westchester Assn. Quality Assurance, Sigma Theta Tau (v.p. 1989-90). Office: Fiedlis Care 95-25 Queens Blvd Rego Park NY 11374

CONNOLA, DONALD PASCAL, JR., management consultant, educator; b. New Brunswick, N.J., Sept. 25, 1948; s. Donald Pascal and Josephine (Montalbano) C. AB, Rutgers U., 1970, MBA, 1973; JD, Bklyn. Law Sch., 1977. Mktg. control analyst Gen. Foods Corp., White Plains, N.Y., 1973-74, product analyst, 1974, sr. fin. analyst, 1974-75, fin. assoc., 1975-79, fin. specialist, 1979, internal mgmt. cons., 1979-82, mgmt. cons., 1983—; prof. mgmt. Fairleigh Dickinson U., Rutherford, N.J., 1983-86, dir. MBA program, dir. undergrad. student svcs., 1986-94; prof. bus. adminstrn. Concordia Coll., Bronxville, N.Y., 1995—. Mem. N.J. State Bar Assn., Am. Soc. Tng. and Devel., Assn. MBA Execs., Soc. for Human Resource Mgmt. Home: 1220 Cellar Ave Apt 12 Clark NJ 07066-2044 Office: 171 White Plains Rd Bronxville NY 10708-1923

CONNOLLY, EDWARD S., neurological surgeon; b. Omaha, 1934. MD, Creighton U., 1960. Diplomate Am. Bd. Neurological Surgery (pres. 1994). Intern U. Calif. Med. Ctr., 1960-61, resident in gen. surgery, 1961-62, resident in neurosurgery, 1962-67; neurol. surgeon Ochsner Clinic, New Orleans; prof. neurol. surgery La. State U. and Tulane U.; clin. prof.; pvt. practice New Orleans. Fellow ACS; mem. AMA, Am. Assn. Neurol. Surgeons, Neurol. Soc. Am., Am. Acad. Neurol. Surgeons, Soc. Neurol. Surgeons, Congress Neurol. Surgeons. Office: 1514 Jefferson Hwy New Orleans LA 70121-2429

CONNOLLY, ELMA TROUTMAN, artist, contractor, designer; b. Middleburg, Pa., May 10, 1931; d. Benjamin F. and Eva Ellen (DeLong) Hollenback; m. Kenneth R. Troutman, Aug. 15, 1950; children: Kenneth, Linda, Robert; m. Jerome P. Connolly, Apr. 15, 1973. Student, Lock Haven State Tchrs. Coll., 1949. Instr. Sunbury, Pa.; cons. for exceptions unit Pa. Tax Bur., Harrisburg; owner, founder, pres. Arts ETC Co., Sunbury, Pa.; bus. cons. Cohen, Danville, 1970-72. Murals (with Jerome Connolly): Nature Ctr., Winston Salem, N.C., 1974, South Am. Hall-Smithsonian Nat. History Mus., Washington, 1975, George Page Mus. of La Brea Discoveries, L.A., 1976, Makah Mus., Neah Bay, Wash., 1978, Woolly Mammoth Background Provincial Mus. B.C., Can., 1979, The African Hall Springfield (Mass.) Sci. Mus., 1980, Big Cypress Nature Ctr., Naples, Fla., 1982, Indian Hall Ill. State Mus., 1984, Edn. Ctr. Taipei, Taiwan, 1987, African Water Hole, American Kudu, Carnagie Mus. Nat. History, Pa., 1992, Alaskan Brown Bear, Carnagie Mus. Natural History, Pitts., 1994; sculpture, murals George Page Mus., Provincial Mus., Springfield Sci. Mus., Big Cypress Nature Ctr. Fla. Pres. Susquehanna Art League, 1999. Named Woman of Yr., ABI, 1991; recipient Am. Women's award. Mem. NAFE, Sunbury Mchts. Coun. (pres.), C. of C. (govt. affairs com.), Susquehanna Art Soc. (pres.), Internat. Platform Assn. Republican. Avocations: sculpture, writing, civic affairs, art, bldg. contractor. E-mail: connolly@postoffice.ptd.net. Home: RR 2 Box 176n3 Selinsgrove PA 17870-9657

CONNOLLY, GERALD EDWARD, lawyer; b. Boston, Oct. 13, 1943; s. Thomas E. and Grace J. (Fitzgerald) C.; m. Elizabeth Heidi Eckert, Jan. 6, 1968; children: Matthew F., Dennis F., David D., Edward F. BS, Coll. of Holy Cross, 1965; JD, U. Va., 1972. Bar: Wis. 1972, U.S. Tax Ct. 1973. From assoc. to ptnr. Whyte & Hirschboeck S.C., Milw., 1972-78; ptnr. Minahan & Peterson S.C., Milw., 1978-91; Quarles & Brady, 1991—; v.p., bd. dirs., sec. Reinhart FoodService, Inc.; bd. dirs., sec. Reinhart Real Estate Group, Inc., Reinhart Retail Group; sec. Hometown Inc.; bd. dirs. Viterbo Coll., LaCrosse, Wis., Hatco Corp., Milw., Adaptive Engring. Lab., Inc., Diversatek, Inc., Medovations, Sunlite Plastics, Inc., Milw.; sec. The Medalcraft Mint, Inc., Radisson LaCrosse Hotel, Water Blasting. Trustee Emory T. Clark Family Charitable Found., D.B. Reinhart Family Found.; chmn. Pres. Coun. Children's Hosp. Wis. Lt. USN, 1966-69. Mem. ABA, Order of Coif, Milw. Club, Milw. Yacht Club, North Shore Country Club. Home: 860 E Ravine Ln Milwaukee WI 53217-1469 Office: Quarles & Brady 411 E Wisconsin Ave Ste 2550 Milwaukee WI 53202-4497

CONNOLLY, JANET ELIZABETH, retired sociologist and criminal justice educator; b. New Rochelle, N.Y., June 28, 1929; d. Michael A. and Vincentia (Bonitatibus) Dandry; m. Edward C. Connolly, June 7, 1952; children: Michael, Matthew, Christopher, Benedict, Andrew. BA, Chestnut Hill Coll., Phila., 1951; MA, Temple U., Phila., 1970, PHD, 1975; hon. degree, Rilski Neofit U., Blagoevgrad, Bulgaria, 1992. Intelligence clk. CIA, Washington, 1951-52; tchr. Prince George's County Bd. Edn., Hyattsville, Md., 1952-53; rsch. assoc. Pa. Prison Soc., Phila., 1974-76; field dir. rsch. Georgetown U. Law Sch., Washington, 1976-77; rsch. dir. Phila. Commn. for Effective Criminal Justice, 1977-78; mem. faculty dept. criminal justice Temple U., Phila., 1980-91; mem. faculty dept. sociology Am. U. in Bulgaria, Blagoevgrad, 1991-96; guest lectr. Sch. Law Kiril E Metodi Univerzitet, Skopje, Macedonia, 1993; cons. Bucks County Correctional Facility, Doylestown, Pa., 1987-91; evaluator Phila. Prison System, 1973. Campaign chairperson, Doylestown, Pa., 1980, 82, 84, 86, 90; pres. Bucks County Assn. for Corrections and Rehab., Doylestown, 1988-91; trustee Bucks County Community Coll., Newtown, Pa., 1989-91; bd. dirs. ARC, Bucks County chpt., Doylestown, 1980-82; mem. New Hope (Pa.) Civil Svc. Commn., 1986-91; bd. dirs. Planned Parenthood, 1986-88. U.S. Justice Dept. dissertation grantee, Washington, 1972. Mem. ACLU, LWV, Law and Soc. Assn., Am. Correctional Assn., Balkan Ednl. and Sci. Assn. (mem. sci. senate). Democrat. Avocations: gardening, embroidery, oil painting. Home: 130 N Main St New Hope PA 18938-1317

CONNOLLY, JOHN EARLE, surgeon, educator; b. Omaha, May 21, 1923; s. Earl A. and Gertrude (Eckerman) C.; m. Virginia Hartman, Aug. 12, 1967; children: Peter Hart, John Earle, Sarah. AB, Harvard U., 1945, MD, 1948. Diplomate: Am. Bd. Surgery (bd. dirs. 1976-82), Am. Bd. Thoracic and Cardiovascular Surgery, Am. Bd. Vascular Surgery. Intern. in surgery Stanford U. Hosps., San Francisco, 1948-49, surg. research fellow, 1949-50, asst. resident surgeon, 1950-52, chief resident surgeon, 1953-54, surg. pathology fellow, 1954-55, 1957-60, John and Mary Markle Scholar in med. scis., 1957-62; surg. registrar professional unit St. Bartholomew's Hosp., London, 1952-53; resident in thoracic surgery Bellevue Hosp., N.Y.C., 1955; resident in thoracic and cardiovascular surgery Columbia-Presbyn. Med. Ctr., N.Y.C., 1956; from instr. to assoc. prof. surgery Stanford U., 1957-65; prof. U. Calif., Irvine, 1965—, chmn. dept. surgery, 1965-78; attending surgeon Stanford Med. Ctr., Palo Alto, Calif., 1959-65; chmn. cardiovascular and thoracic surgery Irvine Med. Ctr. U. Calif., 1968—; attending surgeon Children's Hosp., Orange, Calif., 1968—, Anaheim (Calif.) Meml. Hosp., 1970—; vis. prof. Beijing Heart, Lung, Blood Vessel Inst., 1990, A.H. Duncan vis. prof. U. Edinburgh, 1984; Hunterian prof. Royal Coll. Surgeons Eng., 1985-86; Kinmonth lectr. Royal Coll. Surgeons, Eng., 1987, Hume Lectr. Soc. for Clin. Vascular Surgery, 1998, Dist. Prof. Lectr. Unified Svcs. Med. Ctr., 1998; mem. adv. coun. Nat. Heart, Lung, and Blood Inst.-NIH, 1981-85; cons. Long Beach VA Hosp., Calif., 1965—. Contbr. articles to profl. jours.; editorial bd.: Jour. Cardiovascular Surgery, 1974—, chief editor, 1985—; editorial bd. Western Jour. Medicine, 1975—, Jour. Stroke, 1979—, Jour. Vascular Surgery, 1983—. Bd. dirs. Audio-Digest Found., 1974—; bd. dirs. Franklin Martin Found., 1975-80; regent Uniformed Svcs. U. of Health Scis., Bethesda, 1992—. Served with AUS, 1943-44. Recipient Cert. of Merit, Japanese Surg. Soc., 1979, 90. Fellow ACS (gov. 1964-70, regent 1973-82, vice chmn. bd. regents 1980-82, v.p. 1984-85), Royal Coll. Surgeons Eng. (hon.), Royal Coll. Surgeons Ireland (hon.), Royal Coll. Surgeons Edinburgh (hon.); mem. Am. Surg. Assn., Soc. U. Surgeons, Am. Assn. Thoracic Surgery (coun. 1974-78), Pacific Coast Surg. Assn. (pres. 1985-86), San Francisco Surg. Soc., L.A. Surg. Soc., Soc. Vascular Surgery, Western Surg. Assn., Internat. Cardiovascular Soc. (pres. 1977), Soc. Internat. Chirurgie, Soc. Thoracic Surgeons, Western Thoracic Surg. Soc. (pres. 1978), Orange County Surg. Soc. (pres. 1984-85), James IV Assn. Surgeons (councillor 1983—), San Francisco Golf Club, Pacific Union Club, Bohemian Club (San Francisco), Harvard Club (N.Y.C.), Big Canyon Club (Newport Beach, Calif.), Cypress Point Club (Pebble Beach). Home: 7 Deerwood Ln Newport Beach CA 92660-5108 Office: U Calif Dept Surgery Irvine CA 92717

CONNOLLY, JOHN JOSEPH, health care company executive; b. Worcester, Mass., Feb. 4, 1940; s. Nicholas John and Margaret Anne (Flynn) C.; m. Ingrid Schlemminger, Apr. 11, 1964; children: Sean Timothy, Cheryl Lea. BS, Worcester State Coll., 1962; MA., U. Conn., 1963; EdD, Columbia U., 1972; LLD, Mercy Coll., 1980. Pres. Dutchess C.C., Poughkeepsie, N.Y., 1972-81; pres., CEO N.Y. Med. Coll., Valhalla, N.Y., 1981-92, Castle Connolly Med. Ltd., N.Y.C., 1992—; bd. dirs. Mortons Restaurant Group, Charlie Browns Restaurant, Inc.; chmn. Alpha Gene Inc. Bd. dirs. United Way of Dutchess County, pres., 1978; chmn. bd. trustees St. Francis Hosp., Poughkeepsie, 1976-80; chmn. Dutchess County Indsl. Devel. Agy., 1978-81; trustee N.Y. Med. Coll., chmn. acad. affairs com.; trustee Culinary Inst. Am., 1976-99, chair, 1996-98; trustee Poughkeepsie Area Fund, 1973-78, St. Agnes Hosp., White Plains, 1988-91; bd. dirs. Econ. Devel. Corp. Dutchess County, Westchester County Mental Health Assn., S.L.E. (Lupus) Found., 1995-97, Am. Lyme Disease Found., 1993—; hon. chmn. Dutchess/Columbia br. Am. Lung Assn., 1979; pres. Westchester Hist. Soc., 1985-88; mem. Pres. Adv. Coun. United Hosp. Fund; mem. bd. advisors White Inst. for Biomed. Rsch.; mem. exec. com. Funding First, Inc. Recipient Disting. Svc. award Poughkeepsie Jaycees, 1974, Marie Y. Martin award Assn. Community Coll. Trustees, 1978; named Man of Yr. Dutchess County Legislature, 1980, One of 100 Outstanding Young Leaders in Higher Edn. Change Mag., 1979. Fellow N.Y. Acad. Medicine; mem. N.Y. Acad. Sci., Assn. Colls. Mid-Hudson Area (pres. 1976-79), Friends of the Nat. Libr. Medicine (dir.), Friends of Hudson Valley (chmn. 1990), Westchester County Assn. (bd. dirs. 1991—), Phi Delta Kappa. Roman Catholic.

CONNOLLY, JOSEPH FRANCIS, II, educational executive, government consultant; b. Quincy, Mass., Feb. 15, 1944; s. Joseph Francis and Flora Frances C.; m. Donna M. Cameron, May 4, 1968; children: Jennifer S., Joseph F. III. BA magna cum laude, Park Coll., Parkville, Mo., 1971; LLB, Blackstone Sch. Law, Chgo., 1972, JD, 1977; postgrad., U. South Fla., 1977-79, Fla. Inst. Tech., Melbourne, Liberty U., Lynchburg, Va., Am. Mil. U., Manassas, Va.; grad., Inst. Tng. in Mcpl. Adminstrn. of Internat. City Mgmt. Assn., USAF Air Command and Staff Coll., Indsl. Coll. of the Armed Forces. Cert. EMT, firefighter and law enforcement officer, Fla. Former coord. emergency med. svcs. City of Quincy, 1971-73; former EMT Boston Ambulance Squad, 1973-74; former coord. 14-community emergency med. svcs. program, 1974; formerly safety tng. coord., lead instr. Fire Tng. Acad. Orange County Pub. Schs., Fla., 1979-82; former dir. pub. safety Poinciana, Fla., 1985-86; sr. cons. Resource, Studies, and Devel. Internat., Inc., 1988-91; CEO Connolly, Hudson, Taylor & Assocs., Orlando, Fla., 1988-91; pres. Joseph F. Connolly II, P.A., Fla., 1982-95; adj. faculty mem. Pikes Peak Community Coll., Valencia Community Coll., Fla. Inst. Tech., Nat. Fire Acad., So. Coll.; tng. counselor emeritus NRA; med. cons. State of Bahrain Def. Force; former mem. Health Planning Coun. Greater Boston; dir. Royal Nat. Lifeboat Instn., Ireland, U.K.; dir. U.S. Jujitsu Fedn. Mem. Orange County subcom. Health Systems Agy. of East Ctrl. Fla.; fire commr. Conway Fire control Dist. of Orange County, 1980-84; former combat lt., staff capt. reserve program Orange County Fire Dept.; com. chmn. Orange County Rep. Exec. Com., 1985-93; former Safety Tng. Coord. Orange County Pub. Schs., Fla., pres. Coun. of Vol. Coords., Orange County, 1987; mem. Rep. Presdl. Task Force, Natl. Rep. Senatorial Commn.; active Boy Scouts Am., 1954—; life mem. Nat. Eagle Scout Assn., ret. lt. col. CAP, 1989; operational auxiliarist USCG Aux. Master sgt. Army Spl. Forces, 1961-96. Decorated Purple Heart with two oak leaf clusters, 24 other U.S. and fgn. mil. decorations or citations, Knight Sovereign Mil. Order St. John of Jerusalem (Austria); recipient Gill Robb Wilson award CAP, Aerospace Edn. Achievement award, 1987, Resolution of Tribute award Orange County Sch. Bd., 1989, Presdl. Sports award for martial arts, 1996; named Vietnam Vet. of the Yr., Vietnam Vets. Ctrl. Fla., Inc., 1988; named to Order Knights Templar, 1985, Grandmaster of Yr., Internat. Martial Arts Hall of Fame, 1998; inducted into Hall of Fame, Fla. Martial Arts, 1997. Mem. Aircraft Owners and Pilots Assn., Boat/US, Sons of the Union Vets. of the Civil War, Ducks Unltd., VFW (life), DAV (life), Nat. Fire Acad. Alumni Assn. (pres. 1984-92), U.S. Martial Arts Assn. (nat. dir.), Nat. Assn. of Vet. Police Officers, Internat. Assn. Counselors and Therapists, Am. Counseling Assn., Intertel, Nat. Eagle Scout Assn. (life), Legion of Frontiersmen of the British Commonwealth, Third Order St. Francis, Mil. Order of Purple Heart, Mensa, Masons, U.S. Judo Assn. (life, black belt in karate, 8th degree black belt in jujitsu, 9th degree black belt in judo, inducted into World Martial Arts Hall of Fame, 1996), Asahi Internat. Dojo (pres.), Midori Yama Budokai, U.S. Yudo Assn. (founder 1998). Anglican Catholic. Office: PO Box 620533 Orlando FL 32862-0533

CONNOLLY, K. THOMAS, lawyer; b. Spokane, Wash., Jan. 23, 1940; s. Lawrence Francis and Kathleen Dorothea (Hallahan) C.; m. Laurie Samuel, June 24, 1967; children: Kevin, Megan, Amy, Matthew. BBA, Gonzaga U., Spokane, Wash., 1962; JD, Gonzaga U., 1966; LLM in Taxation, NYU, 1972. Bar: Wash. 1966, U.S. Ct. Mil. Appeals 1967, U.S. Tax Ct. 1983. Assoc. Witherspoon, Kelley, Davenport & Toole, Spokane, 1972-77; ptnr./prin. Witherspoon, Kelley, Davenport & Toole, 1977—; assoc. prof. law Gonzaga Sch. Law, 1973-77. Bd. overseers Gonzaga Prep. Sch., Spokane, 1988-89; bd. trustees Spokane Guild Sch. for the Handicapped, 1975-78, Wash. State U. Found. Bd., 1992-97, Whitman Coll. Planned Giving Coun., 1994—. Capt. U.S. Army, 1966-70. Recipient Wall St. Jur. award, 1962; decorated Bronze Star medal. Mem. Wash. State Bar Assn. (founder, chmn. health law sect. 1989-92, health law coun. 1989-94, pres. tax sect. 1987-88, mem. tax coun. 1984—), ABA (chmn. health care subcom. 1990-94). Republican. Avocations: tennis, astronomy. Office: Witherspoon Kelley Davenport & Toole 1100 Old National Bldg Spokane WA 99201

CONNOLLY, KEVIN JUDE, lawyer; b. N.Y.C., May 25, 1954; s. John William and Beatrice Joan (Fallon) C.; m. Audrey Mason, May 25, 1995; children: Shea Alexander, Ciaran Jude. BA cum laude, Fordham Coll., 1976; JD, Fordham U., 1985. Bar: N.Y. 1990. Assoc. Stroock & Stroock & Lavan, N.Y.C., 1985-89, Shapiro & Byrne, P.C., Mineola, N.Y., 1989-92; counsel Schreiber, Simmons, MacKnight & Tweedy, N.Y.C., 1992-94, Eaton & Van Winkle, N.Y.C., 1994-97; assoc. Robinson, Silverman, Pearce, Aronsohn & Berman LLP, N.Y.C., 1998—; vis. lectr. Sch. Visual Arts, N.Y.C., 1996—; dir. Internet Soc., N.Y.C. chpt., 1997—; outside counsel Internet Policy Adv. Body, Geneva, Switzerland, 1997—, Internet Coun. Registrars, Geneva, 1997-98, Hatewatch, Inc., 1998—. Tactical field trainer U.S. Mil. Acad., West Point, 1989—. Avocations: antiques, paintball. E-mail: jawz@cybersharque.com. Home: 522 Lincoln Blvd Long Beach NY 11561-2312 Office: Robinson Silverman Pearce Aronsohn & Berman 1290 Ave of Amers New York NY 10104

CONNOLLY, MATTHEW B., JR., conservationist; b. Norwood, Mass., July 28, 1941; s. Carolyn (Masciarelli) C.; m. Stephanie Leach, 1969; children: Allison, Caroline. AS Stockbridge Sch. Agr., Amherst, Mass., 1964; BS, U. Mass., 1968. State ornithologist Mass. divsn. Fish and Game, Boston, 1968-73; dir. Coastal Zone Mgmt. Commonwealth Mass., Boston, 1973-76, Fisheries and Wildlife, Boston, 1976-79; exec. v.p. N.Am. Wildlife Found., 1985-87; exec. v.p. Ducks Unltd., Inc., Memphis, 1987—; COO Wetlands Am. Trust, 1987—; pres. N.E. Assn. Fisheries and Wildlife agys., 1978; chmn. N.Am. Waterfowl Mgmt. Plan Implementation Bd., Washington, 1988-90; apptd. chmn. by Bush and Clinton Adminstrns. to N.Am. Wetlands Conservation Coun., Washington, 1990—; mem. European Waterfowl Habitat Fund, Brussels, 1987—, Wildlife Habitat Coun. Bd., Washington, 1989—, chancellors exec. com. U. Mass., Amherst, 1989-93; bd. govs. Ams. Clean Water Found., Washington, 1990—; chmn. mgmt. com. Inst. for Internat. Waterfowl and Wetlands Rsch., 1991—; mem. adv. bd. Non-Point Source Fedn., Kansas City, Mo. Named Conservationist of Yr., Times Mirror-Chevron, 1995. Avocations: fishing, hunting, reading. Office: Ducks Unltd Inc 1 Waterfowl Way Memphis TN 38120-2351*

CONNOLLY, RUTH CAROL, urological nurse practitioner; b. Pitts., Oct. 2, 1944; d. Chester John and Mary Elizabeth (Sansbury) Williams; divorced; children: Patrick L., Sean M. Diploma in nursing, Allegheny Gen. Hosp., Pitts., 1965; cert. nurse practitioner, Allegheny Gen. Hosp., 1983, La Roche Coll., Pitts., 1983. RN, Pa. Staff nurse critical care Divine Providence Hosp., Pitts.; asst. clin. supr. Allegheny Gen. Hosp., clin. supr. neuroscis. unit; nurse practitioner Triangle Urol. Group, Pitts. Contbr. articles to nursing jours. Mem. AACN, Am. Urol. Assn. Allied (founding mem. and pres.-elect Pitts. chpt.), Am. Assn. Office Nurses, Soc. Urol. Nurses and Assocs. Home: 5549 Pocusset St Pittsburgh PA 15217-1912

CONNOLLY, THOMAS EDMUND, educator. BS, Fordham U., 1939; MA, U. Chgo., 1947, PhD, 1951. Lectr. English Loyola U., Chgo., 1947-50; instr. English U. Idaho, Moscow, 1950-51; asst. prof. English Creighton U., Omaha, 1951-53; asst. prof. English U. Buffalo (N.Y.), 1953-59, assoc. prof., 1959-64; prof. English SUNY, Buffalo, 1964-87, dir. MA in humanities program, 1978-81, prof. emeritus, 1987—; vis. prof. English and Am. Lit. U. Coll., Dublin. Ireland, 1966-67; acting provost faculty arts and letters SUNY, 1970-71; mem. adv. bd. The Irish Tradition, Global Village, N.Y.C., 1988-90; bd. overseers Mellen U. Turks & Caicos Islands, 1998—; presenter in field. Author: The Personal Library of James Joyce, 1955, James Joyce's Scribbledehobble, 1961, (with Selig Adler) From Ararat to Suburbia, 1960, Swinburne's Theory of Poetry, 1964, James Joyce Exhibition: A Catalogue, 1978, Faulkner's World, 1988, A Neo-Aristotelian and Joycean Theory of Poetic Forms, 1995, James Joyce's Books, Portraits, Manuscripts, Notebooks, Typescripts, Page Proofs, Together with Critical Essays about Some of His Works, 1997, Essays on Fiction: Dickens, Melville, Hawthorne and Faulkner, 1999; editor: Joyce's Portrait, 1962, Nathaniel Hawthorne: Young Goodman Brown, 1968, Hawthorne's Scarlet Letter, 1970. Summer Rsch. fellow, 1963. Mem. AAUP, MLA, James Joyce Found. Avocations: golf, gardening. E-mail: tecconnolly@earthlink.net. Home: 426 Vista Dorado Ln Oak Park CA 91377-3721

CONNOLLY, THOMAS EDWARD, judge; b. Boston, Nov. 7, 1942; s. Thomas Francis and Catherine Elizabeth (Skehill) C. AB, St. John's Sem., Brighton, Mass., 1964; JD, Boston Coll., 1969. Bar: Mass., 1969. Assoc. Schneider & Reilly, Boston, 1969-73; ptnr. Schneider, Reilly, Zabin, Connolly & Costello, P.C., Boston, 1973-85, Connolly Leavis & Rest, Boston, 1986-90; judge Mass. Superior Ct., Boston, 1990—; instr. law Northeastern Law Sch., Boston, 1975-76. Mem. governing coun. Boston Coll. Law Sch. Alumni Coun., 1980—. Mem. ABA (vice chmn. products liability sect. 1978—), Trial Lawyers Assn. Am. (nat. gov. 1977-80), Mass. Acad. Trial Lawyers (gov. 1976—), Am. Coll. Trial Lawyers, Univ. Club (Boston), Algonquin Club (Boston). Democrat. Roman Catholic. Home: 253 Marlborough St # 4 Boston MA 02116-1731 Office: The Superior Ct Boston MA 02108

CONNOLLY, THOMAS JOSEPH, bishop; b. Tonopah, Nev., July 18, 1922; s. John and Katherine (Hammel) C. Student, St. Joseph Coll. and St. Patrick Sem., Menlo Park, Calif., 1936-47, Catholic U. Am., 1949-51; JCD, Lateran Pontifical U., Rome, 1952; DHL (hon.), U. Portland, 1972. Ordained priest Roman Cath. Ch., 1947. Asst. St. Thomas Cathedral, Reno, 1947, asst., rector, 1953-55; asst. Little Flower Parish, Reno, 1947-48; sec. to bishop, 1949; asst. St. Albert the Gt., Reno, 1952-53; pastor St. Albert the Gt., 1960-68, St. Joseph Ch., Elko, 1955-60, St. Theresa's Ch., Carson City, Nev., 1968-71; bishop Baker, Oreg., 1971—; Tchr. Manogue High Sch., Reno, 1948-49; chaplain Serra Club, 1948-49; officialis Diocese of Reno; chmn. bldg. com., dir. Cursillo Movement; moderator Italian Cath. Fedn.; dean, mem. personnel bd. Senate of Priests; mem. Nat. Bishops Liturgy Com., 1973-76; region XII rep. to adminstrv. bd. Nat. Conf. Cath. Bishops, 1973-76, 86-89, mem. adv. com., 1974-76; bd. dirs. Cath. Communications Northwest, 1977-82. Club: K.C. (state chaplain Nev. 1970-71). Office: Bishop of Baker PO Box 5999 911 SE Armour Dr Bend OR 97702-1489*

CONNOLLY, WILLIAM M., state supreme court justice. Former judge Nebr. Ct. of Appeals, Lincoln; assoc. justice Nebr. Supreme Ct., Lincoln. Office: Nebr Supreme Ct PO Box 98910 2413 State Capitol Bldg Lincoln NE 68509*

CONNOLLY-WEINERT, FRANCIS DAVID, theology educator; b. Phila., Sept. 27, 1941; s. Philip Walter and Mary (McGuigan) W.; m. Kathleen Grusky Connolly, May 23, 1987 (dec. May 20, 1990); 1 child, James Bernard. BS, St. Joseph's U., 1963; MA, Maryknoll Sch. Theology, 1967; PhD, Fordham U., 1979. Lectr. theology St. John's U., Jamaica, N.Y., 1967-75, assoc. prof. theology, 1980—; from asst. to assoc. prof. theology Coll. St. Elizabeth, Convent Station, N.J., 1975-80, chair dept. religious studies, 1976-80; regional sec., treas. Mid-Atlantic Am. Acad. Religion, N.Y.C., 1988—. Contbr. Eerdman's Dictionary of the Bible, Liturgical Press Introductory Dictionary of Theology and Religious Studies, articles to theological jours. Recipient 2nd prize Nat. Libr. Poetry, 1997; named Outstanding Chpt. Moderator Nat. Hon. Soc. Religious Studies, 1996. Mem. AAUP, Am. Acad. Religion, Nat. Physics Hon. Soc., Soc. Biblical Literature, Cath. Biblical Assn., Coll. Theology Soc. Democrat. Roman Catholic. Office: St John's U Dept Theology Grand Central And Utopia Pkwy Jamaica NY 11439-0002

CONNOR, CAROL J., library director. BA in History, Molloy Coll., 1964; MA in History, Georgetown U., 1970; MS in Libr. Sci., Drexel U., 1972. Various adminstrv. positions in ednl. fields various U.S. Cities, 1964-72; spl. asst. tech. processes divsn. Lincoln (Nebr.) City Librs., 1972-73, coord. tech. processes divsn., 1973-76, asst. dir., 1976-78, dir., 1978—. Mem. Mayor's Com. for Internat. Friendship, Lincoln, 1973—; adv. com. U. Nebr., search for dean of librs., 1984-85; del. to cmty. retreat, Star Venture, 1986, edn. task force, 1987-88, vocat. edn. task force, 1988-89, downtown child care task force, 1988-89; mem. cmty. adv. com. Lincoln Pub. Schs. Search for English Cons., 1991, Search for Media Dir., 1992; mem. Nebr. Ctr. for Book Bd., 1990-95, Nebr. Libr. Commn. state adv. coun. 1985-86, Nebr. Lit. Festival Com., 1990-92; bd. dirs. Postsecondary Ednl. Librs. and Resource Ctrs. of Nebr. 1981-84, chair 1982; mem. edn. com. Am. Cancer Soc., Lancaster County, Nebr., 1989-91, Family Svcs. Bd., 1991—, vice chair chair elect 1992, chair, 1994; leadership Lincoln VI 1990-91; mem. Lincoln Cancer Ctr. adv. bd., 1988-94, vice chair 1991-94. Mem. ALA, (bylaws com., membership com., LITA/LAMA conf. com. 1996-97), Mountain Plains Libr. Assn. (chair continuing edn. com. 1984-85; membership devel. com. 1986-87, vice chair and chair of pub. libr. sect. 1975-77, v.p./ pres. elect 1996-97, pres. 1997-98), Nebr. Libr. Assn. (chair intellectual freedom com. 1975-76, state rep. to Mountain Plains Libr. Assn., 1984-86, vice chair and chair of pub. libr. sect. 1987-89), Urban Librs. Coun. (leadership programs 1994-95), Capitol Bus. and Profl. Women (v.p. 1983), Downtown Lincoln Assn. (mktg. com. 1988-89). Office: Lincoln City Librs 136 S 14th St Lincoln NE 68508-1899

CONNOR, CATHERINE BROOKS, educational media specialist; b. Dothan, Ala., Oct. 29, 1955; d. James Bolling and Margaret Elizabeth (Jones) Brooks; m. Joseph Yauger Whealdon, Jr., June 12, 1983 (div. Aug. 1990); 1 child, Joseph Yauger III; m. William Christopher Connor, Dec. 28, 1991. BS, Fla. State U., 1980, MS in Libr. Sci., 1990. Cert. profl. media specialist, Fla. Asst. br. mgr. City Fed. Savs. and Loan, Birmingham, Ala., 1976-77; elem. tchr. Louise S. McGehee Sch., New Orleans, 1981-85; kindergarten tchr. Lafayette Elem. Sch., New Orleans, 1986; grad. asst. Fla.

State U. Sch. Libr. Sci., Tallahassee, 1990; media specialist Lely H.S., Naples, Fla., 1990-91; media specialist Frank M. Golson Elem. Sch., Marianna, Fla., 1991—, chmn. sch. adv. coun., 1995-98, leadership team, 1994—. Bd. dirs. Jackson County Pub. Libr.-Friends of Libr., Marianna, 1992-94, mem. adv. bd. 1998—, sec. 1998—; bd. dirs. Jackson County unit Am. Cancer Soc., 1998—, novinatina com. chair, 1998—; charter mem. Libr. of Congress, Washington, 1994—; mem. Panhandle Pub. Libr. Coop. Sys. Bd., 1998—. Mem. Daus. of Am. Revolution, Colonial Dames, Descendants of the Knights of the Garter. Democrat. Episcopalian. Avocations: genealogy, travel. Home: PO Box 507 Marianna FL 32447-0507 Office: Frank M Golson Elem Sch 4258 2d Ave Marianna FL 32446-1905

CONNOR, CHARLES WILLIAM, airline pilot; b. Miami, Fla., Aug. 2, 1935; s. Robert Hugh and Mary (Cauthen) C.; m. Retha Moeller, Mar. 12, 1988; children: Charles W. Jr., Christine Wendy, Elizabeth Tammy. MAS with distinction, Embry Riddle Aero. U., 1970, MBA with distinction, 1970; PhD in Behavioral Psychology/Aero. Sci., Columbia Pacific U., 1982. Exptl. test pilot Boeing Vertol Co., 1962-65; C-5A program contract adminstr. Lockheed Ga. Aircraft Corp., 1965-66, Delta Air Lines, Inc., Atlanta, 1966—; v.p. Aviation Systems Concepts, Inc., 1983—; recovery pilot Project Mercuty (participated in the tng. and recovery of astronauts Glenn, Carpenter, Schirra & Cooper); capt. L-1011 aircraft; adj. prof., grad. curriculum advisor Emory Riddle Aero. U., 1979-82; pres. aerospace Behavioral Engrng. Tech., 1982—, chmn. SAE HBT, G-10 Internat. Aviation Human Factor Stds., chmn. industry subcom. outdoor laser tech. hazards navigable airspace; planning chmn. over 100 tech. sessions on aerospace behavioral engrng. tech.; designer APD L-1011; check airmen B-727, L-1011; U.S. rep. on laser hazards to flight crews Internat. Civil Aviation Orgn., 1998, Internat. Fedn. Airline Pilots Assn. tech. rep. on flight deck laser hazards, 1998; Flight Safety Found. mem. of CFIT approach and landing accidents, 1999. Contbr. articles, reports to profl. publs., confs. Selected by Internat. Fedn. Airline Pilots Assn. as U.S. tech. rep. to Internat. Civil Aviation Orgn. which represents 184 nations attempting to establish internat. operational stds. for flight crews and ground-based laser activities. With USMC, 1957-62. Recipient Chinese Air Force Wings, Chinese Govt., 1959, Presdl. award Outstanding Contbns. to Air Safety, 1995. Fellow Soc. Exptl. Test Pilots (assoc.); mem. AIAA, Soc. Automotive Engrs. (mem. gen. com. aerospace div. 1985—, div. chmn. engrng. and activity bd. 1989—, proc. editor for confs., Forest R. McFarland award 1986, 93, Tech. Bd. award 1988), Inst. Navigation, Human Factors Soc., Air Line Pilots Assn. (bd. dirs. 1968-74, nat. spokesman 1980—, Presdl. Citation Outstanding Svc. 1995), Soc. Exptl. Test Pilots, Nat. Aviation Club. Achievements include development of line oriented flight training scenarios for air carrier crew members, progressive cognitive branching concept for advanced adaptive air crew training; developing operational cognitive model for information management through integrated systems architecture and adaptive protocol. Home: 206 Elm Ave Melbourne Bch FL 32951-2420 Office: Delta Airlines Inc Flight Ops Atlanta Hartsfield Int Atlanta GA 30320

CONNOR, FRANCES PARTRIDGE, retired education educator; b. Bklyn., May 4, 1919; d. Horace K. and Sybil V. (Rafters) P.; m. Leo E. Connor, June 7, 1952. BA, St. Joseph's Coll., 1940; MA, Columbia U., 1948, EdD, 1953; LLD (hon.), Coll. New Rochelle, 1976. Cert. history, social studies tchr., spl. edn. tchr., N.Y. Tchr. history/econs. Haverstraw (N.Y.) Schs., 1940-42; tchr. N.Y. State Rehab. Hosp., West Haverstraw, 1942-49; lectr. Hunter Coll., CCNY, N.Y.C., 1946-54; tchr. spl. edn. Ramapo Ctrl. Schs., Suffern, N.Y., 1949-53; coord. spl. edn. U. Ga., Athens, summers 1952-53; rsch. assoc. U.S. Office of Edn., Washington, 1954-58; survey assoc. Tchrs. Coll., Columbia U., N.Y.C., 1953-54, prof., dir. Rsch. and Demonstration Ctr./Inst. for LD, 1955-87, dept. chair, 1962-85, Richard March Hoe prof. emeritus, 1987—; mem. profl. adv. bd. Willowbrook Consent Decree, N.Y. State Dept. of Mental Retardation/Devel. Disabilities, Albany, 1977—; mem. bd. dirs. Family Resource Assocs., Shrewsbury, N.J. Author: Education of Homebound and Hospitalized Children, 1964, Experimental Curriculum for Young Mentally Retard Children, 1964; editor: Critical Issues for Low Incidence Populations, 1987. Mem. bd. trustees Mt. Saint Mary Coll., Newburgh, N.Y., 1970—, Human Resources Schs., Albertson, N.Y., 1984—; mem. Pres.'s Com. on Employment of Handicapped, Washington, 1972-89; del., mem. steering com. White House Conf. on the Handicapped, Washington, 1975-78; mem. Coalition of Disabled Women and Their Advocates, Ocean County, N.J., 1990—. Recipient Behavioral Sci. award Nat. Hemophilia Found., 1968, Pioneer in Spl. Edn. award Hofstra U., 1986. Fellow Am. Assn. on Mental Retardation; mem. Coun. for Exceptional Children (pres. 1964-65, Wallin award 1982, Outstanding Contbr. award 1992, R.P. MacKie award 1998), Com. Rehab. Internat. Roman Catholic. Avocations: choral/choir singing, swimming. Home: 23343 Blue Water Cir (B113) Boca Raton FL 33433

CONNOR, GEOFFREY MICHAEL, lawyer; b. Washington, Oct. 2, 1946; s. John Thomas and Mary (O'Boyle) C.; m. Maud Holly Pyne, July 24, 1976; children: Taylor Pyne, Michael Buck, Grafton Wright. BA, Williams Coll., 1968; JD, Harvard U., 1973. Bar: N.Y. 1974, N.J. 1975. Clk. to presiding judge U.S. Ct. Appeals (2d cir.), N.Y.C., 1973; assoc. Cleary, Gottlieb, Steen & Hamilton, N.Y.C. and London, 1974-79, Shanley & Fisher, N.J., 1979-83; v.p. Carteret Savs. Bank, FA, N.J., 1984-86; sr. v.p. Carteret Savs. Bank, FA, Morristown, N.J., 1987-90; commr. N.J. Dept. Banking, Trenton, 1990-94; pntr. Reed, Smith, Shaw & McClay, Princeton, N.J., 1994—. Lt. (j.g.) USN, 1968-70. Mem. ABA, N.J. State Bar Assn. Democrat. Roman Catholic. Home: 52 Potterstown Rd PO Box 355 Oldwick NJ 08858-0355 Office: 136 Main St Princeton Forrestal Village Princeton NJ 08540-5799

CONNOR, JAMES EDWARD, JR., retired chemical company executive; b. New Haven, Feb. 14, 1924; s. James Edward and Rose Marie (McGovern) C.; m. Margery Hawe, Apr. 7, 1951; children: James, Anne, William, Joan, Margery, Peter. B.A., Harvard U., 1944, M.A., 1948, Ph.D., 1950. Research chemist Atlantic Refining Co., 1949-60, asst. mgr. research, 1960-61, mgr. research, 1961-66; mgr. research Arco Chem. Co., Glenolden, Pa., 1966-78; mgr. R & D Arco Chem. Co., 1978-79, v.p. chems. R & D, 1979-81; v.p. research Arco Chem. Co. div. Atlantic Richfield Co., Newtown Square, Pa., 1981-86; v.p. R & D ARC Chem. Co. div. Atlantic Richfield Co., Newtown Square, 1985-86; ret. Atlantic Richfield Co., Newtown Square, 1986. Served with USN, 1944-46. Mem. Am. Chem. Soc. Democrat. Roman Catholic. Patentee in field. Home: 1421 Hillside Rd Wynnewood PA 19096-2406

CONNOR, JAMES RICHARD, foundation administrator; b. Indpls., Oct. 31, 1928; s. Frank Elliott and Edna (Felt) C.; m. Zoe Ezopov, July 7, 1954; children: Janet K., Paul A. BA with highest distinction, U. Iowa, 1951; M.S., U. Wis., 1954, Ph.D., 1961. Asst. prof. history Washington and Lee U., 1956-57, Va. Mil. Inst., 1958-61; asst. dir. Salzburg Seminar in Am. Studies, 1961-62; joint staff mem. Wis. Coordinating Com. Higher Edn., 1962-63; dir. Inst. Analysis; asst. prof. history U. Va., 1963-66; assoc. prof. history, assoc. provost No. Ill. U., 1966-69; provost, acad. v.p., prof. history Western Ill. U., 1969-74; chancellor, prof. history U. Wis., Whitewater, 1974-91, chancellor, prof. emeritus, 1991; exec. dir. James S. Kemper Found., Long Grove, Ill., 1991—; assoc. dir. Va. Higher Edn. Study Com., 1964-65; intern acad. adminstrn. Am. Coun. Edn., Stanford U., 1965-66; staff dir. Study of Governance of Acad. Med. Ctr., Josiah Macy Jr. Found., 1968-70; mem. commn. on higher edn. North Ctrl. Assn. 1970-75, 79-84, cons.-examiner, 1972-91; chair adv. com. on alcohol and drug use U. Wis. System, 1984-85; mem. nat. adv. com. Woodrow Wilson Nat. Fellowship Found., 1990-96, trustee, 1996—; dir. Fairhaven Retirement Corp., 1994—. Author: Studies in Higher Education, 1965; contbr., Ency. Brit. Served with AUS, 1946-47, 51-53. Woodrow Wilson fellow, 1953-54; So. fellow, 1957-58. Mem. AAUP, Orgn. Am. Historians, Blue Key, Golden Key, Order of Omega, Phi Beta Kappa, Phi Eta Sigma, Phi Kappa Phi, Phi Delta Kappa, Beta Gamma Sigma, Phi Alpha Theta, Delta Sigma Pi. Home: N7447 Linden Dr Whitewater WI 53190-4357 Office: James S Kemper Found 1 Kemper Dr Long Grove IL 60049-0001

CONNOR, JOHN MURRAY, agricultural economics educator; b. Attleboro, Mass., July 7, 1943; s. John Murray Sr. and Victoria Rose (Moro) C.; m. Ulla Maija Niemelä, Apr. 3, 1972; 1 child, Timo. BA cum laude, Boston Coll., 1965; MA, U. Fla., 1974; MS, U. Wis., 1974, PhD, 1976. Vol. U.S. Peace Corps, Nigeria, Uganda, 1966-68; agrl. economist Econ. Rsch. Svc. USDA, Madison, 1976-79; head food mfg. rsch. Econ. Rsch. Svc. USDA, Washington, 1979-83; assoc. prof. agrl. econs. Purdue U., West Lafayette, Ind., 1983-89; prof. Purdue U., West Lafayette, 1989—, asst. dept. head, 1985-88; ajd. prof. Catholic U. Sacred Heart, Piacenza, Italy, 1991—; vis. prof. Åbo (Finland) Akademi U., 1994; cons. subcom. on multinats. U.S. Senate, Washington, 1974-76, select com. on nutrition, 1977-78; cons. UN Ctr. on Transnats. and Dept. Justice, N.Y.C., 1981-82; chair Orgn. and Performance World Food Systems, 1988-93. Author: Market Power of Multinationals, 1977, Food Processing: An Industrial Powerhouse in Transition, 1988, 2d edit., 1997, (with others) Food Manufacturing Industries, 1985; contbr. articles to profl. jours., chpts. to books. Grantee U.S. Office Tech. Assessment, 1984-85, Inst. Food Technologists, 1986-88, 94-95, Ind. Dept. Commerce, 1987-91, Econ. Rsch. Svc., USDA, 1988-89, Coop. State Rsch. Svc., USDA, 1989—. Mem. AAUP (pres. Purdue U. chpt. 1988-90, exec. bd. ind. conf. 1990-94, nat. coun. 1991-92), Am. Agrl. Econs. Assn. (policy award 1980, comm. award 1985, Disting. Extension Program award 1993), Indsl. Orgn. Soc., Am. Econs. Assn., ACLU. Home: 180 Sumac Dr West Lafayette IN 47906-2157 Office: Purdue U Dept Agrl Econs West Lafayette IN 47907-1445

CONNOR, JOHN THOMAS, retired bank and corporate executive, lawyer; b. Syracuse, N.Y., Nov. 3, 1914; s. Michael J. and Mary (Sullivan) C.; m. Mary O'Boyle, June 22, 1940; children: John Thomas, Geoffrey, Lisa Forrestal. AB magna cum laude, Syracuse U., 1936; JD, Harvard U., 1939; DSc, Phila. Coll. Pharmacy, 1959, Hahnemann Med. Coll., 1964; LLD, Rutgers U., 1964; DHL, Ohio No. U., 1965; LLD, St. Louis U., 1965, Boston Coll., 1965, Syracuse U., 1965, Manhattan Coll., 1967, Mt. Mary Coll., 1967, N.J. Coll. Medicine and Dentistry, 1967, St. Peters Coll., 1968, Pratt Inst., 1969, Fairleigh Dickinson U., 1973; DE, Stevens Inst., 1976. Bar: N.Y. 1939. Assoc. Cravath, deGersdorff, Swaine & Wood, 1939-42; gen. counsel OSRD, 1942-44; counsel Office Naval Rsch., also spl. asst. to sec. navy, 1945-47; gen. atty. Merck & Co., Inc., Rahway, N.J., 1947, sec., 1947-51, counsel, 1947-53, v.p., 1950-55, pres., chief exec. officer, 1955-65; U.S. sec. commerce, 1965-67; pres. Allied Chem. Corp., 1967-68, chief exec. officer, 1968-79, chmn., 1969-79; ret. chmn. Schroders, Inc., N.Y.C.; mem. bus. coun. Coun. Fgn. Rels. Trustee Syracuse U. Served to capt. USMCR, 1944-45. Recipient Presdl. certificate of merit, 1948; N.J. Brotherhood award NCCJ, 1959; Jefferson medal N.J. Patent Law Assn., 1962; Harvard Bus. Club award, 1965; named N.J. Bus. Statesman of Year, 1964; recipient Pub. Services award Advt. Council, 1967. Mem. Phi Beta Kappa. Home: 11854 Turtle Beach Rd No Palm Beach FL 33408-3351

CONNOR, JOHN THOMAS, JR., lawyer; b. N.Y.C., June 16, 1941; s. John Thomas and Mary (O'Boyle) C.; m. Susan Scholle, Dec. 18, 1965; children: Seanna, Marin, John. BA cum laude, Williams Coll., 1963; JD, Harvard U., 1967. Bar: N.Y. 1968, D.C. 1980. Assoc. Cravath, Swaine & Moore, N.Y.C., 1967-71; dep. dir. Office Econ. Policy and Case Analysis, Pay Bd., Washington, 1971-72, Bur. East-West Trade, U.S. Dept. Commerce, Washington, 1972-73; sr. v.p. U.S.-USSR Trade and Econ. Coun., Moscow, 1973-76; assoc. Milbank, Tweed, Hadley & McCloy, N.Y.C., 1976-79; ptnr. Curtis, Mallet-Prevost, Colt and Mosle, Washington, 1980-82; v.p., gen. counsel, sec. PHH Corp., 1982-88; v.p., asst. gen. counsel Prudential Ins. Co. Am., Newark, 1988-90; ptnr. Sills Cummis, Newark, 1990-94; counsel Chadbourne & Parke, N.Y.C., 1994-96, Patterson, Belknap, Webb & Tyler, LLP, 1996-98; chmn. Great Am. Life Corp., 1993—, ROSGAL Group Fin Cos., Moscow, 1993—; portfolio mgr., chmn. Third Millennium Funds, 1998—. Exec. dir. Dem. Party N.J., 1969-70; pres., trustee Newark Boys Chorus Sch.; Fulbright tutor Ferguson Coll., Poona, India, 1963-64; chmn. Coun. on Econ. Priorities. Mem. ABA, N.Y. State Bar Assn., D.D. Bar Assn., Coun. Fgn. Rels., Am. Law Inst., Baltusrol Cub N.J., Met. Club (Washington), Union Club (N.Y.C.), Chevy Chase Club (Md.), Wianno Club (Cape Cod), Mountain Lake Club (Fla.), Phi Beta Kappa. Home: 40 Royal Oak Dr Far Hills NJ 07931-2569 Office: Third Millennium Funds 32d Fl 1185 Ave of the Americas New York NY 10022

CONNOR, JOSEPH E., accountant; b. N.Y.C., Aug. 23, 1931; s. Joseph E. Connor; m. Cornelia B. Camarata, Apr. 17, 1958 (dec. Oct. 11, 1983); children: Anthony, Cornelia, David; m. Sally Howard Johnson, Dec. 27, 1992. AB summa cum laude, U. Pitts.; MS in Bus., Columbia U.; DHL (honoris causa), Georgetown U., 1989. Joined Price Waterhouse & Co., N.Y.C., 1956; ptnr. Price Waterhouse & Co., 1967-92, ptnr. in charge So. Calif., 1973-76; mng. ptnr. Western region Price Waterhouse & Co., Los Angeles, 1976-78; chmn. policy bd. U.S. Price Waterhouse & Co., 1978-88, chmn. World Firm, 1988-92, ret., 1992; Disting. prof. bus. Georgetown U., 1992-94; under-sec. gen. UN, N.Y.C., 1994—; cons. fgn. direct investment program U.S. Dept. Commerce; project adv. rsch. study AICPA; lectr. in field.; mem. adv. coun. Columbia U. Grad. Sch. Bus.; bd. visitors U. Pitts. Grad. Sch. Bus., Georgetown U. Sch. Bus.; chmn. U.S. Coun. for Internat. Bus., 1987—; mem. Pres.'s Mgmt. Adv. Coun., Pres.'s Pvt. Sector Survey on Cost Control. Contbr. articles to profl. lit. Trustee YMCA Greater N.Y.; bd. overseers Meml. Sloan Kettering Cancer Inst.; bd. dirs. Georgetown U., 1982-92; mem. coun. Brookings Instn. Served to 1st lt. U.S. Army, 1954-56. Mem. N.Y. State Soc. CPAs (chmn. internat. ops. com., mem. acctg. and auditing com., real estate acctg. com.), Calif. Soc. CPAs (legis. com.), Internat. C. of C. (exec. bd. 1989-94, pres. 1990-92), Met. Club (Washington), Links Club, Univ. Club. Office: UN UN Plz New York NY 10021

CONNOR, JOSEPH PATRICK, III, lawyer; b. Phila., Apr. 15, 1953; s. Joseph Patrick Jr. and Wanda Delores (Filipkowski) C.; m. Mary Margaret Kazanicka, Aug. 13, 1977; children: Cathleen Marie, Christopher Joseph, Christine Anne. BA in Polit. Sci., Villanova U., 1974; JD, St. Mary's U., San Antonio, 1974. Bar: Pa. 1977, U.S. Dist. Ct. (ea. dist.) Pa. 1977, U.S. Dist. Ct. (mid. dist.) Pa. 1997, U.S. Ct. Appeals (3d cir.) 1977, U.S Supreme Ct. 1982. Assoc. ptnr. Gibbons, Buckley, Smith, Palmer & Proud, Media, Pa., 1977-82; pres. Connor & Weber, P.C., Phila., Paoli, 1982—. Mem. ABA (tort & litigation sects.), Pa. Bar Assn., Pa. Def. Inst., Def. Research Inst., Pa. Trial Lawyers Assn., Chester County Bar Assn. Republican. Roman Catholic. Club: Overbrook County (Bryn Mawr). Avocations: flying, golf, swimming, traveling. Office: Connor & Weber PC 2401 Pennsylvania Ave Philadelphia PA 19130-3061

CONNOR, JOSEPH ROBERT, editor; b. N.Y.C., Jan. 31, 1927; s. Joseph M. and Ethel May (Ball) C.; m. Marie Louise Zolezzi, Sept. 6, 1952; children: Jeanne Marie, Robert Brian, Ellen Louise. B.A., Hunter Coll., 1951. Copy editor sports desk N.Y. Mirror, N.Y.C., 1950-52; mng. editor Mechanix Illustrated Mag. div. Fawcett Publs., N.Y.C., 1953-70; editor in chief CBS Publs., N.Y.C., spl. interest publs., 1970-72; editor in chief Motor Mag. div. Hearst Corp., N.Y.C., 1972-77; editor Construction Contracting, 1978-79; editor in chief Graduating Engr. McGraw-Hill, Inc., 1979-81, 88-90; editor Bus. Week New Product Devel., 1981—, Bus. Week Almanac, 1981—; editor in chief Bus. Week Careers, 1982-87; editor-in-chief Graduating Engr., 1988-90; exec. editor Graduating Engr. Peterson's-Cog Publs., 1990-91; freelance writer, editorial cons., 1991—; editor MOTORScoop Mag., GRG Publs. Inc., 1995-96. Author: A Job With A Future in Automotive Mechanics, 1969, (with Heinz Ulrich) The National Job-Finding Guide, 1981; Cracking the Over-50 Job Market, 1992; contbr. numerous articles to popular mags. Served with AUS, 1945-46. Mem. Internat. Motor Press Assn. (pres. 1966-67), Am. Soc. Mag. Editors. Home: 8 Woodvale Ln Huntington NY 11743-2324

CONNOR, LAURENCE DAVIS, lawyer; b. Columbus, Ohio, May 14, 1938; s. Laurence R. and Gladys C. (Davis) C.; m. Clare Elizabeth Hartwick, Aug. 8, 1964; children: Jeffrey H., Lynne D. BA, Miami U., Oxford, Ohio, 1960; JD, U. Mich., 1965. Bar: Mich. 1966, U.S. Dist. Ct. (ea. dist.) Mich. 1966, U.S. Ct. Appeals (6th cir.) 1973, U.S. Supreme Ct. 1979. Assoc. Dykema Gossett, Detroit, 1965-73, ptnr., 1973—, mem. exec. com., 1984-90, dir. litigation sect., 1987-91; mem. coun. sect. on alternative dispute resolution State Bar of Mich., 1992—, chairperson, 1996-97; pres. Vis. Nurse Assn. Met. Detroit, 1980-81, Vist. Nurse Corp., Detroit, 1986-88; adj. prof. U. Mich. Law Sch. Mem. ABA, Am. Judicature Soc., Mich. Def. Trial Counsel, Country Club Detroit, Detroit Athletic Club, Yondotega Club. Office: Dykema Gossett 400 Renaissance Ctr Ste 3800 Detroit MI 48243-1603

CONNOR, LEO EDWARD, special education administrator; b. Phila., Sept. 5, 1922; s. Leo A. and Margaret (McMahon) C.; m. Frances Partridge, June 7, 1952. BA, LaSalle U., 1945; MA, U. Pitts., 1949; EdD, Columbia U., 1955. Cert. tchr. spl. edn., adminstr., audiologist. Tchr. Pitts. and Phila. schs., 1945-49; elem. prin., dir. elem. edn. Clarkstown Cen. Sch. Dist., New City, N.Y., 1950-57; ednl. dir. Lexington Sch. for the Deaf, N.Y.C., 1957-68, exec. dir., 1968-85; exec. dir. Lexington Ctr. for Hearing Impaired, N.Y.C., 1985-88; chmn. N.Y. Schs. for Deaf and Blind, Albany, N.Y., 1968-83, Coun. on Edn. of Deaf, Washington, 1976-78, Nat. Adv. Com. on Media for Handicapped, Washington, 1978-80; adj. prof. edn. Columbia U., N.Y.C.; instr. NYU, N.Y.C. Author: Administration of Special Education, 1960, History of Research, 1978, History of the Lexington School for the Deaf, 1988, Review of Oral Education, 1980; editor: Speech for the Deaf Child, 1971, Lexington Education Series, 1965-80; contbr. articles to profl. jours. Chmn. Bd. Zoning Adjustment, Borough of Spring Lake, N.J., 1989-96, chmn. lake com., 1990-95; trustee New Rochelle (N.Y.) Coll. Recipient annual award N.Y. Coun. Exceptional Children, Albany, 1988. Fellow Am. Speech/Hearing/Lang. Assn. (clin. cert. competency); mem. Alexander Graham Bell Assn. (Honors of the Assn. award 1986, pres. 1970-72), Coun. for Exceptional Children (pres. 1968-69). Roman Catholic. E-mail: franleo@worldnet.att.net. Home: 23343 Blue Water Cir Boca Raton FL 33433

CONNOR, MARY RODDIS, foundation administrator; b. Marshfield, Wis., May 14, 1909; d. Hamilton and Catherine S. (Prindle) Roddis; m. Gordon R. Connor, July 20, 1929 (dec. 1986); children: Mary I. Pierce, Gordon P., Catherine Dellin, David (dec.), Sara W. Connor. Student, Wellesley Coll., 1927-28; student, U. Wis., 1929. Corp. sec. Connor Lumber and Land Co., Connor Forest Industries, Wausau, Wis., 1954-78; co-founder, exec. dir. Camp Five Mus. Found., Inc., Laona, 1968—; bd. dirs., v.p. Hamilton Roddis Found.; pres. Connor Found., Forest History Assn. Wis., 1975-87; v.p. Gordon R. Connor Charitable Found.; mem. Nat. Women's Adv. Coun., Am. Forest Products Inst., 1960-78; active Mary Roddis Connor U. Wis. Endowment Fund, 1992. Author: A Century with Connor Timber, 1972, Forestry Futures and Conservation Misconcepts, 1946, 2d rev. edition, 1947; contbr. articles to various publs. Legis. chmn. 7th Dist. Wis. Fedn. Rep. Women, 1963-65, bd. dirs., 1955-65, vice chmn. 1955-59; del. Rep. county, state, nat. conventions, 1962; vice chmn. Marathon County; Rep. vice chmn. Recipient Gov.'s Wis. Heritage Tourism award, 1993, State Hist. Soc. Wis. award of merit, 1970, 90, U.S. EPA, 1987, Forest History Assn. Wis. Mus. award, 1978, Nat. Award in Edn. Arbor Day Found., 1975. Mem. Wis. Mayflower Soc., Colonial Dames (Wis. Soc.), The Hugenot Soc. of Wis., Bascom Hill Soc. (U. Wis.), Lake States Resource Alliance, Inc., Lake States Women in Timber, Inc., Forest History Assn. of Wis., State Hist. Soc. of Wis., Nat. Trust for Hist. Preservation, Wausau chpt. DAR (nat. vice chmn. resolutions 1965-68, Wis. state chmn. nat. def., 1962-65, nat. conservation chmn. 1974-77, recipient many awards). Home: 1220 Easthill Dr Wausau WI 54403-9223

CONNOR, PAUL EUGENE, social worker; b. Atchison, Kans., Aug. 11, 1921; s. Samuel Walters and Juanita Marie (Fry) C.; m. Louise Dorothy Schiddel, June 28, 1959 (div. 1964). BS in History with honors, Columbia U., 1962, MA, 1963; grad. cert. in social work, Fordham U., 1973; postgrad. summer history program, Cambridge U., 1990-96. Lectr. Am. History Rutgers State U., 1966-67; lectr. S.E. Asian history New Sch. Social Rsch., 1967-68; caseworker Bergen Ctr., South Bronx, N.Y., 1970-73; caseworker Protective Svcs. Bur. of Child Welfare, Bronx, N.Y., 1973-76; caseworker preventive svcs. Spl. Svcs. for Children, N.Y.C., 1976-83; supr. I family program Crisis Intervention Svcs., N.Y.C., 1983-87; tchr. The Internat. Ctr., N.Y.C., 1977-86. Rec. sec. Bronx Coun. for Environ. Quality, 1981-83, bd. dirs., 1983—; docent Mus. of City of N.Y., 1988-91, Abigail Adams Smith Mus., 1993-95, South St. Seaport Mus., 1993-96. Mem. Internat. Coun. Social Welfare, Asia Soc., Am. Hist. Assn., S.C. Hist. Soc., N.C. Lit. and Hist. Assn., Soc. of Boonesborough, Clan Buchanan Soc. in Am., English Speaking Union, Benjamin Franklin Reform Dem. Club. Democrat. Home: 2755 Reservoir Ave Apt 5A Bronx NY 10468-2730

CONNOR, ROBERT W., JR., federal judge; b. 1942. Magistrate judge U.S. Dist. Ct. Wyo., Sheridan, 1977—. Office: PO Box 607 Sheridan WY 82801-0607

CONNOR, SEYMOUR VAUGHAN, historian, educator, writer; b. Paris, Tex., Mar. 4, 1923; s. Aikin Beard and Gladys (Vaughan) C.; 1 son, Charles Seymour. B.A., U. Tex., 1948, M.A., 1949, Ph.D., 1952. Archivist W.Tex. State U., 1952-53, Tex. State Library, 1953-55; prof. history, dir. S.W. collection Tex. Tech. U., Lubbock, 1955-64; prof. history Tex. Tech. U., 1965-79, prof. emeritus, 1979—; vis. prof. Angelo State Coll., 1964-65. Author: Preliminary Guide to Texas Archives, 1956, Peters Colony of Texas, 1959, A Biggers Chronicle, 1961, Adventure in Glory, 1965, Texas: A History, 1971, (with others) The Battles of Texas, 1967, The Capitols of Texas, 1970, (with Odie Faulk) North America Divided: The Mexican War, 1846-1848, 1971, La Guerra de Intervencion, 1948-1848, 1975, Texas in 1776, 1975, (with W.C. Pool) Texas, the 28th State, 1971, (with J.M. Skaggs) Broadcloth and Britches: The Santa Fe Trade, 1976, Orange Connor and His Descendents 1792-1992; editor: Texas Treasury Papers (3 vols.), 1955, The West Is for Us, 1957, Builders of the Southwest, 1959, Saga of Texas (6 vols.), 1965, Dear America, 1971, Panhandle-Plaines Hist. Rev., 1953-57, Tex. Tech. Mus. Jour., 1970-72, Catalogs and Ofcl. Bulletins, 1965-70; contbr. articles to profl. jours. With AUS, 1943-45, ETO; with USAR, 1946-53. Fellow Tex. State Hist. Assn. (exec. council 1957-70, pres. 1967-68); mem. Phi Kappa Tau, Phi Kappa Psi, Phi Alpha Theta. Home: 3503 45th St Lubbock TX 79413-3416

CONNOR, WALTER ROBERT, classics educator, humanities center administrator; b. Worcester, Mass., Aug. 30, 1934; m. Carolyn Loessel; children: Christopher, Stephan. BA, Hamilton Coll., 1956, LHD, 1991; PhD in Classics, Princeton U., 1961; LHD, Knox Coll., 1993. Instr. U. Michigan, Ann Arbor, 1960-63; jr. fellow Ctr. Hellenic Studies, 1963-64; asst. prof. Princeton U., Princeton, N.J., 1964-70, assoc. prof., 1970-72, prof., 1972-89, Andrew Fleming West prof. classics, 1978-89, chmn. dept. classics, 1972-77, chmn. com. Hellenic studies, 1979-85, chmn. coun. humanities, 1982-89; pres., dir. Nat. Humanities Ctr., Rsch. Triangle Pk., N.C., 1989—; prof. classics Duke U., Durham, N.C., 1989—; vis. prof. U. Mich., U. Colo., Breadloaf Sch. of English, Inst. Advanced Study, 1985-86; mem. overseers' com. to visit the classics Harvard U., 1976-84, com. to visit the Meml. Ch., 1995—; mem. univ. coun. com. on lit. Yale U., 1979-83; mem. mng. com. Am. Sch. Classical Studies in Athens, 1973-89, exec. com., 1976-80, 85-89; trustee William Alexander Procter Found., 1980-89, Princeton U. Press, 1989, The Glaxo Wellcome Found., 1995—; mem. adv. bd. U. N.C., Asheville, 1990-94, Athens (Greece) Coll., 1996—. Author: Greek Orations, 1966, Theopompus and Fifth Century Athens, 1968, The New Politicians of Fifth Century Athens, 1971, Thucydides, 1984; (with C.L. Connor) Life of St. Luke of Steiris, 1994. Alumni trustee Princeton U., 1993-97. Fulbright fellow U. Coll., Oxford, 1956-57, U. Melbourne; Woodrow Wilson fellow, Danforth Fellow, Am. Coun. Learned Socs. fellow, NEH fellow; recipient Howard Behrman award, 1986. Fellow Am. Acad. of Arts and Scis.; mem. Am. Philos. Soc., Princeton Club, Century Assn., Am. Philol. Assn. (pres. 1987-88), Phi Beta Kappa. Office: Nat Humanities Ctr PO Box 12256 Research Triangle Park NC 27709

CONNOR, WILDA, government health agency administrator; b. Pleasantville, N.J., Apr. 9, 1947; d. Herman Smith and Rubina (Miraglilo) Cooney; m. James J. Connor Jr., Nov. 5, 1966; 1 child, James J. III. BSBA cum laude, Rowan U., 1985; MS, U. Pa., 1995. Employee services coord. Turning Point Drug Outpatient Program, Collingswood, N.J., 1976-78; mgmt. specialist Camden County Ctr. Addictive Diseases, Lakeland, N.J., 1978-87; adminstr. Family Practice Ctrs. Camden (N.J.) County Health Dept., 1988—; fiscal analyst Camden County Dept. Health & Human Svcs., Lakeland, N.J., 1995—. Com. fund raiser Camden County Dem. Congl. Campaign, Stratford, N.J., 1986; mem. Solid Waste Adv. Coun., Camden County; mem. Coastal Resources Adv. Commn. Dept. Environ. Protection. Mem. N.J. Assn. Alcoholism Counselors, N.J. Substance Abuse Cert. Bd. (cert. 1987, 89 MSA), LWV, Solid Waste Adv. Council. Roman Catholic. Avocations: jogging, aerobics, skiing, traveling. Home: 228 Vasey Ave Lindenwold NJ 08021-2249 Office: Camden County Dept Health & Human Svcs Jefferson House 6th Fl Lakeland NJ 08012-0009

CONNOR, WILLIAM ELLIOTT, physician, educator; b. Pitts., Sept. 14, 1921; s. Frank E. and Edna S. (Felt) C.; m. Sonja Lee Newcomer, Sept. 19, 1969; children: Rodney William, Catherine Susan, James Elliott, Christopher French, Peter Malcolm. B.A., U. Iowa, 1942, M.D., 1950. Diplomate Am.

Bd. Internal Medicine, Am. Bd. Nutrition. Intern USPHS Hosp., San Francisco, 1950-51; resident in internal medicine San Joaquin Gen. Hosp., Stockton, Calif., 1951-52; practice medicine specializing in internal medicine Chico, Calif., 1952-54; resident in internal medicine VA Hosp., Iowa City, 1954-56; cons., 1967-75; mem. faculty U. Iowa Coll. Medicine, 1956-75, prof. internal medicine, 1967-75; acting dir., then dir. Clin. Research Center, 1967-75, dir. lipid-atherosclerosis sect., cardiovascular div., 1974-75; vis. prof. Basic Sci. Med. Inst., Karachi, Pakistan, Ind. U., 1961-62, Baker Med. Rsch. Inst., Melbourne, Australia, 1982; vis. fellow clin. sci. Australian Nat. U., Canberra, 1970; prof. cardiology and metabolism-nutrition, dept. medicine, 1975-79, head sect. clin. nutrition, 1979-90, acting head, head div. endocrinology, metabolism and nutrition, 1984-90, prof. sect. clin. nutrition, 1990—, dir. lipid-atherosclerosis lab., assoc. dir. Clin. Rsch. Ctr., Oreg. Health Scis. U. Portland, 1975-94; chmn. heart and lung program project com. Contbr. numerous articles to med. jours.; editor Jour. Lab. and Clin. Medicine, 1970-73; mem. editorial bds., reviewer profl. jours. Mem. Johnson County (Iowa) Cen. Dem. Com., 1965-69; mem. nat. council Fellowship Reconciliation; nat., North Central and Pacific Northwest bds. Am. Friends Service Com. Served with AUS, 1943-46. Research fellow Am. Heart Assn., 1956-58; ACP traveling fellow Sir William Dunn Sch. Pathology, Oxford, Eng., 1960; recipient Career Devel. Research award Nat. Heart Inst., 1962-73, Discovery award Med. Research Found. Oreg. Mem. AAAS, ACP, AMA, AAUP (pres. U. Iowa chpt. 1968-69, pres. Oreg. Health Sci. U. chpt. 1978-79), Am. Diabetes Assn. (vice chmn. food and nutrition com. 1972-74), Am. Dietitic Assn. (hon.), Am. Fedn. Clin. Rsch., Am. Heart Assn. (chmn. coun. arteriosclerosis 1975-78, exec. com. coun. epidemiology 1967-70, exec. com. coun. cerebral vascular disease 1966-68, C. Lyman Duff meml. lectrue 1989), Am. Soc. Clin. Nutrition (pres. 1978), Nat. Acad. Sci. (food and nutrition bd. 1986-89), Am. Inst. Nutrition, Am. Oil Chemists Soc., Am. Physiol. Soc., Am. Soc. Clin. Investigation, Am. Soc. Study Arteriosclerosis, Assn. Am. Physicians, Ctrl. Soc. Clin. Rsch., Nutrition Soc., Soc. Exptl. Biology and Medicine (coun. 1971-72, pres. Iowa sect. 1971-72), Western Assn. Physicians, Western Soc. Clin. Rsch., Phi Beta Kappa, Sigma Xi, Alpha Omega Alpha. Research in nutrition, lipid metabolism, blood vessel diseases. Home: 2600 SW Sherwood Pl Portland OR 97201-2285 Office: Oreg Health Scis U L465 Portland OR 97201*

CONNORS, CHRISTOPHER, geology educator; b. Erie, Pa., Feb. 12, 1962; s. Robert E. and Elousie Connors; m. Lisa M. Kohn, May 12, 1990; children: Maureen, Kevin. BS, Pa. State U., 1984; MS, U. Pitts., 1990; PhD, Princeton U., 1999. Tchr. Millcreek Sch. Dist., Erie, Pa., 1986-87; geologist Texaco, Bellaire, Tex., 1995-99; prof. geology Washington and Lee U., Lexington, Va., 1999—. Contbr. articles to sci. jours., including Jour. Geophys. Rsch. Mem. Geol. Soc. Am., Am. Assn. Petroleum Geologists, Am. Geophys. Union, Soc. Exploration Geophysicists. Avocations: rock climbing, canoeing, hiking, gardening. Fax: 540-463-8142. E-mail: connorsc@wlu.edu.

CONNORS, DORSEY, television and radio commentator, newspaper columnist; b. Chgo.; d. William J. and Sarah (MacLain) C.; m. John E. Forbes; 1 dau., Stephanie. BA cum laude, U. Ill. Fl. reporter WGN-TV Rep. Nat. Conv., Chgo., Dem. Nat. Conv., L.A., 1960. Conducted: Personality Profiles, WGN-TV, Chgo., 1948-49, Dorsey Connors Show, WMAQ-TV, Chgo., 1949-58, 61-63, Armchair Travels, WMAQ-TV, 1952-55, Homeshow, NBC,1954-57, NBC Today Show, Dorsey Connors program, WGN, 1958-61, Tempo Nine, WGN-TV, 1961, Society in Chgo, WMAQ-TV, 1964; writer: column Hi! I'm Dorsey Connors, Chgo. Sun Times, 1965—; Author: Gadgets Galore, 1953, Save Time, Save Money, Save Yourself, 1972, Helpful Hints for Hurried Homemakers, 1988. Founder Ill. Epilepsy League; mem. woman's bd. Children's Home and Aid Soc., mem. women's bd. USO. Named one of Am.'s Outstanding Irish Am. Women, World of Hibernia mag., 1995. Mem. AFTRA, NATAS (Silver Cir. award 1995), SAG, Mus. Broadcast Comm. (founding mem.), Soc. Midland Authors, Chgo. Hist. Soc. (guild com., costume com.), Chi Omega. Roman Catholic. Office: Chgo Sun Times 401 N Wabash Ave Chicago IL 60611-5642

CONNORS, EUGENE KENNETH, lawyer, educator; b. Dobbs Ferry, N.Y., Oct. 3, 1946; s. Edward Micheal and Eileen (Burke) C.; children: Kevin Patrick, Kathryn Margaret. BA in English, Holy Cross Coll., Worcester, Mass., 1968; JD, Columbia U., 1971. Bar: Pa. 1971. Assoc. Reed Smith Shaw & McClay, Pitts., 1971-76, ptnr., 1977—; adj. prof. St. Francis Coll. Grad. Sch., Loretto, Pa., 1975—; ski instr. Holiday Valley Ski Area, Ellicottville, N.Y., 1987—; bd. dirs. Green Garden Inc., 1985—. Contbr. articles to profl. jours. Bd. dirs. Sch. Vol. Assn. Pitts., 1973-78, TEC/Pa. Small Bus. United, 1993-94, Pitts. Pub. Theater, 1998—. Persuaded U.S. Supreme Ct. to overturn 9-0 employment discrimination decision adverse to employers 442 U.S. 366 (1979). Mem. ABA, Pa. Bar Assn., Allegheny County Bar Assn., Pitts. Human Resources Assn. (bd. dirs. 1988-95, treas. 1987-95), Tri-State Employers Assn. (bd. dirs. 1992-93), Profl. Ski Instrs. Am. Avocations: alpine (downhill) skiing, scuba diving, golf. Office: Reed Smith Shaw & McClay PO Box 2009 435 6th Ave Ste 2 Pittsburgh PA 15219-1886

CONNORS, FRANK JOSEPH, lawyer; b. N.Y.C., Oct. 8, 1944; s. Frank Joseph and Nina Florence (Kirk) C.; m. Evelyn Noreen Mills, Oct. 14, 1983. BA, UCLA, 1965; MA, Columbia U., 1966; JD, Harvard U., 1969. Bar: N.Y. 1970, Fla. 1982, Mass. 1986, U.S. Supreme Ct. 1973. Assoc. Dewey, Ballantine, Bushby, Palmer & Wood, N.Y.C., 1969-75; asst. atty. gen. N.Y. State Spl. Prosecutor, N.Y.C., 1975-77; gen. atty. Am. Broadcasting Cos., Inc., N.Y.C., 1977-85; atty. Harvard U., Cambridge, Mass., 1985—; acting gen. counsel, 1992; arbitrator N.Y.C. Civil Ct., 1980-85; comml. arbitrator Am. Arbitration Assn., N.Y.C., 1984-85. Bd. dirs. World Teach, Inc., 1992—. Mem. Am. Judicature Soc., N.Y. State Bar Assn. (copyright com. 1981-85), Assn. of Bar of City of N.Y. (profl. discipline com. 1983-85). Republican. Methodist. Office: Harvard U 1350 Massachusetts Ave Cambridge MA 02138-3846

CONNORS, JAMES PATRICK, lawyer; b. N.Y.C., May 28, 1952; s. Joseph Patrick Connors and Edna Theresa Fitzgerald; m. Gloria Ann Ciccarelli, Jan. 12, 1974; children: Nicholas, Patrick, Jamie Cathleen. BA, Herbert H. Lehman Coll., 1974; JD, N.Y. Law Sch., 1977; LLM, NYU, 1985. Bar: N.Y. 1978, U.S. Dist. Ct. (so. and ea. dists.) N.Y. 1978. Assoc. Bower & Gardner, N.Y.C., 1978-80, Joseph W. Conklin, N.Y.C., 1980-82; ptnr. Jones, Hirsch, Connors & Bull, N.Y.C., 1982—; lectr. NYU Sch. Medicine, 1983, N.Y. Law Jour., 1984, Bellevue Hosp., 1984, Hillcrest Gen. Hosp., 1984, Mt. Sinai Hosp., 1985, Am. Coll. Ophthalmologists, 1986-88. Contbr. articles to profl. jours. Recipient Am. Jurisprudence award Lawyers Pub. Coop., 1977. Mem. ABA, N.Y. State Bar Assn., N.Y. County Bar Assn., Def. Assn. of N.Y. Home: 85 Mayflower Dr Yonkers NY 10710-3801

CONNORS, JIMMY (JAMES SCOTT CONNORS), professional tennis player; b. East St. Louis, Ill., Sept. 2, 1952; s. James and Gloria (Thompson) C.; m. Patti McGuire; children: Brett David, Aubree Leigh. Student, UCLA. Joined World Championship Tennis, Inc., 1972; now in Men's Seniors' Circuit. Recipient Player of Year award, 1974; named All-Am., 1971; ranked number 1 male tennis player in U.S. and World, 1976; ranked number 1 in world, 1978; elected to Tennis Hall of Fame, 1998. Winner Australian Men's Singles, 1974, Wimbledon Men's Singles, 1974, 82, Wimbledon Men's Doubles (with Ilie Nastase), 1973, U.S. Pro Championship Men's Singles, 1973, Cologne Cup, 1976, U.S. Clay Ct. Championship-Men's Singles, 1974, 76, 78, 79, U.S. Open Men's Singles, 1974, 76, 78,82, 83, U.S. Indoor Open Men's Singles, 1973, 74, 75, 78, 79, 83, 84, Pro Indoor Men's Singles, 1976, 78, 79, 80, U.S. Open Men's Doubles (with Ilie Nastase), 1975, U.S. Indoor Men's Doubles (with Frew McMillan), 1974, (with Ilie Nastase), 1975, U.S. Clay Ct. Men's Doubles (with Ilie Nastase), 1974, S.African Men's Singles, 1973, 74, World Championship Tennis Singles, 1977, Grand Prix Masters Championship, 1978, U.S. Nat. Indoor Men's Singles, 1978, Australian Indoor Men's Singles, 1978, Suntory Cup, 1986, D.C. Tennis Classic, 1987, Olympia Open, Toulouse, France, 1987, Toulouse Grand Prix, 1989; mem. Davis Cup Team, 1976, 81, World Cup Team, 1976, 85(winning team). Office: Tennis Mgmt Inc 109 Red Fox Rd Belleville IL 62223-2242 also: RHB Ventures 1320 18th St NW Ste 100 Washington DC 20036*

CONNORS, JOHN MICHAEL, JR., advertising agency executive; b. Boston, June 9, 1942; s. John Michael and Mary (Horrigan) C.; m. Eileen Marie Ahearn; children: John, Timothy, Susanne, Kevin. Grad., Boston Coll., 1963. Mktg. rep. Campbell Soup Co., Boston, 1963-65; account exec. Batten, Barton, Durstine & Osborne, New York and Boston, 1965-68; chmn., CEO Hill, Holliday, Connors, Cosmopulos, Inc., Boston, 1968—; bd. dirs. Am. Ireland Fund, John Hancock Mut. Life Ins. Trustee Boston Coll., 1979—; chmn. bd. trustees Brigham and Women's Hosp., Boston; bd. dirs. Boys and Girls Club Boston. Mem. Advt. Club Greater Boston (past pres.), New Eng. Broadcasting Assn. (past pres.), Sportsmen's Tennis Club (bd. dirs.), Braeburn Country Club, Oyster Harbors Country Club, Eastward Ho! Country Club. Roman Catholic. Office: Hill Holliday Connors Cosmopulos Inc John Hancock Tower 200 Clarendon St Boston MA 02116-5021*

CONNORS, JOSEPH CONLIN, lawyer; b. Mineola, N.Y., Sept. 9, 1948; s. Gerard Edward and Mary Helen (Conlin) C.; m. Mary Napolitano, May 29, 1971; children: J.C., Ryan. BA, SUNY-Oneonta, 1970; JD, Fordham U., 1973. Bar: N.Y. 1974, Tenn. 1985. Confidential law sec. to judge N.Y. Supreme Ct., Cortland, 1973-75; atty. Chevron Corp., Perth Amboy, N.J., 1975-76, Schering-Plough Corp., Kenilworth, N.J., 1976-82; assoc. gen. counsel Schering-Plough Corp., Memphis, 1982-87; staff v.p., planning and bus. devel. Schering-Plough Corp., Madison, N.J., 1987, dep. gen. counsel, 1987-91, v.p., gen. counsel, 1991-92, sr. v.p., gen. counsel, 1992-96, exec. v.p. and gen. counsel, 1996—; mem. adv. com. Met. Corp. Counsel; sr. advisor N.J. Corp. Counsel Assn. Mem. ABA (com. of corp. gen. counsel), N.Y. Bar Assn., Tenn. Bar Assn. (former chmn. corp. sect.), Assn. Nat. Advertisers (bd. dirs. 1987-90), N.J. Legal Aid andDefender Assn. (corp. adv. com.), N.J. Corp. Counsel Assn. (sr. advisor), N.J. Panel of the CPR Inst. for Dispute Resolution (bd. dirs.), Food and Drug Inst. (trustee, editl. adv. bd.), Pharm. Rsch. and Mfrs. Am. (exec. com. law sect. 1998). Roman Catholic. Avocations: travel, golf. Office: Schering Plough Corp 1 Giralda Farms Madison NJ 07940-1010*

CONNORS, KENNETH ANTONIO, retired chemistry educator; b. Torrington, Conn., Feb. 19, 1932; s. Peter Francis and Adeline (Gioia) C.; m. Patricia R. Smart, Dec. 30, 1972. B.S., U. Conn., 1954; M.S., U. Wis., 1957, Ph.D., 1959. Rsch. assoc. dept. chemistry Ill. Inst. Tech., Chgo., 1959-60, Northwestern U., Evanston, Ill., 1960-61; asst. prof. U. Wis. Sch. Pharmacy, Madison, 1962-65, assoc. prof., 1965-72, prof., 1972-97, prof. emeritus, 1997—, acting dean, 1991-93. Author: A Textbook of Pharmaceutical Analysis, 3d edit., 1982, Reaction Mechanisms in Organic Analytical Chemistry, 1973, Chemical Stability of Pharmaceuticals, 2d edit., 1986, Binding Constants, 1987, Chemical Kinetics, 1990. Served with U.S. Army, 1961. Fellow AAAS, Acad. Pharm. Scis., Am. Assn. Pharm. Scis.; mem. Am. Chem. Soc., N.Y. Acad. Scis. Office: U Wis Sch Pharmacy 425 N Charter St Madison WI 53706-1508

CONNORS, MICHELE PERROTT, wholesale beverage company executive; b. Ft. Lauderdale, Fla., June 28, 1952; d. Samuel R. and Mariette (Larouche) Perrott; m. Robert Gary Connors, Apr. 14, 1973; children: Eva Marie, Colleen Elizabeth. AA, Daytona Beach Community Coll., Fla., 1972. Legal sec. Richard Krause, Ormond Beach, Fla., 1972-74; sec. S.R. Perrott, Inc., Ormond Beach, 1974-79, v.p., ops. mgr., 1979-83, pres., chief exec. officer, 1983—; prin., pres. Michele & Group Modeling Talent Agy., 1989—. Bd. dirs. Daytona Beach Easter Seals Soc., 1985—, chmn. fundraising, 1983-86; bd. dirs. Am. Cancer Soc., 1989—. Mem. Beer Industry Fla., Nat. Beer Wholesalers, Ormond Beach C. of C. (pres. 1984), Oceanside Country Club, Trails Racquet Club. Republican. Roman Catholic. Office: S R Perrott Inc PO Box 836 Ormond Beach FL 32175-0836

CONNORS, ROBERT LEO, city official; b. Kings County, N.Y., June 11, 1940; s. John Leo and Emma Mae (Bayers) C.; children from former marriage: Anne, Laura, Kathleen; m. Sharon M. Skeels, Jan. 20, 1996; 1 child, Sarah. B. Profl. Studies, Pace U., 1974, MS in Indsl. Labor Relations, 1976. Police officer, trustee, fin. sec. exec., 1st v.p. Patrolmen's Benevolent Assn., N.Y.C. Police Dept., 1965-77; dep. commr., dir. labor relations Dept. Gen. Services City of N.Y., 1977-83; dir. personnel adminstrn. City of Fall River, Mass., 1984-85, city adminstr., 1985—; lectr. in field. Co-author: Comprehensive Reorganization of Municipal Government, 1986. Mem. Fall River Regional Task Force, 1984—. Served with USAF, 1957-61. Recipient Community Relations Service award, U.S. Justice Dept., Boston, 1985. Mem. Am. Mgmt. Assn., Nat. League of Cities, Internat. City Mgmt. Assn., Greater Fall River Personnel Council, Internat. Personnel Mgmt. Assn., Soc. of Profls. in Dispute Resolution. Democrat. Lodge: Masons. Avocations: golf, carpentry. Home: 26 Primrose Dr Seekonk MA 02771-5916 Office: City of Fall River One Government Ctr Fall River MA 02722

CONNORS, WILLIAM EDWARD, lawyer; b. Madison, Wis., Dec. 7, 1962; s. William James and Carol Mae (Nachtwey) C.; m. Joan Camille Sorteberg, Aug. 24, 1991; 1 child, Cara Brigid Sorteberg. BA in History, U. Wis., 1985, MA in Pub. Policy and Adminstrn., JD, 1989. Bar: Minn. 1989, Wis. 1989. Judicial law clk. U.S. Bankruptcy Ct., Mpls., 1989-91; assoc. lawyer Fredrikson & Byron, Mpls., 1991-95; legis. fiscal analyst Minn. Ho. of Reps., St. Paul, 1995-97; dir. tax increment fin. divsn. Office of the State Auditor, Minn., 1997—. Pres. Macalester-Groveland Cmty. Coun., St. Paul, 1997. Mem. Minn. State Bar Assn., State Bar Wis. Roman Catholic. Avocation: lacrosse. Home: 1900 Jefferson Ave Saint Paul MN 55105-1662 Office: Ste 505 1600 University Ave W Saint Paul MN 55104-3825

CONNORS, WILLIAM FRANCIS, JR., psychology educator; b. Bklyn., Mar. 31, 1945; s. William Francis and Ethel Lucille (Sester) C.; AB, St. Anselm Coll., 1966; MEd, Springfield Coll., 1967; MPA, Long Island Univ., 1980; m. Susan Edwards, Nov. 20, 1971; children: Terence Michael, Corinne Elizabeth, Kristin Michelle, Jessica Marie. Counselor, Suffolk Community Coll., Selden, N.Y., 1967-72, asst. prof. psychology, 1972-73, assoc. prof., 1974-79, prof., 1979—, asst. dean instrn., 1973-87, assoc. dean instrn., 1987-97, dean of faculty, 1997—, acting dean students, 1987, acting dean instrn., 1993-94. Trustee, v.p. Emma S. Clark Meml. Library, 1984-92; mem., pres. sch. bd. Sts. Philip and James Sch., St. James, N.Y., 1984-93; mem., pres. Three Village Bd. Edn., 1994—. Roman Catholic. Home: 39 Cinderella Ln East Setauket NY 11733-1708 Office: Suffolk County CC Brentwood NY 11717-1092

CONOBY, JOSEPH FRANCIS, chemist; b. Albany, June 12, 1930; s. Joseph Francis and Helen Emma (Brucker) C.; m. Mary Joan A. Ryan, June 21, 1958; children: James Francis, Mark Joseph. BS, Union Coll., 1952. Sr. tech. svc. engr. Allied Chem. Corp., Syracuse, N.Y., 1956-66; rsch. chemist Conversion Chem. Corp., Rockville, Conn., 1966-69; environ. engr., indsl. hygienist Honeywell Bull, Billerica, Mass., 1969-97, mgr. environ. and health engring., 1969-97; mgr. environ. engring. Bull HN Worldwide Info. Sys., 1987-95; sr. scientist Concorp, Inc., Acton, Mass., 1996—; adv. bd. Mass. Water Resources Authority Sewer Use (rules and regulations, policy and procedures, and facilities planning task forces); cons. exptl. project course Mass. Inst. Tech., 1977-78. Contbr. articles to profl. jours.; patentee in field. Lt. USN, 1952-56. Mem. Am. Indsl. Hygiene Assn., Nat. Assn. Environ. Mgmt. Home: 5 Samuel Parlin Dr Acton MA 01720-3206 Office: Concorp Inc PO Box 2766 Acton MA 01720-6766

CONOLE, CLEMENT VINCENT, business administrator; b. Binghamton, N.Y., Sept. 29, 1908; s. P.J. and Briget (Halleran) C.; m. Marjorie Anable, Sept. 26, 1931; children: Barbara McElroy, Marjorie A. Hargrave, Richard C., Jacalyn Harman. BSCE, Clarkson Coll. Tech., Potsdam, N.Y., 1931; postgrad., Cornell U., NYU, Yale U.; MBA, Fla. Atlantic U. Licensed profl. engr. and land surveyor, N.Y., Pa. Engr. City of Binghamton, also N.Y. State, 1930-32; ptnr. Richmeyer, Harding and Conole, 1932-33; engr. Dept. of Interior, 1933-35; dist. dir. Fed. Works Adminstrn.; dist. supt. N.Y. Unemployment Ins. Div., 1936-37; asst. state indsl. commr. Binghamton and Rochester, N.Y., 1937-39; dep. indsl. commr. State of N.Y., 1939-43; dir. indsl. bur. C. of C. Bd. of Trade of Phila., 1943-44, operating mgr., 1945-46, exec. v.p., 1946-52; also editor, pub. Greater Phila. mag., 1945-50; v.p. Bankers Securities Corp., 1952-55; pres. Mcpl. Publs., Inc., 1947-50; pub. relations cons. Phila.-Balt. Stock Exchange, 1947-52; chmn. bd., pres., dir. Hearn Dept. Stores, Inc., N.Y.C., 1952-54; dir., chmn. bd. James McCutcheon & Co., 1956-57; ptnr. Franklin D. Roosevelt Jr., 1954-59; chmn. bd., dir. Bus. Supplies Corp. Am., Skytop, Pa., 1962-65; chmn. bd. dir., pres. Tabulating Card Co., Inc., Princeton, N.J., 1955-62; chmn. bd. dir. Am. Bus. Mgmt. Co., 1955-62, Whiting Paper Co., Inc., 1959-62, Sky Meadow Farms, Inc., 1965-68; prof. adminstrn. Fla. Atlantic U., 1972-74; chmn. bd. trustees, pres. Am. Coll. Adminstrs. Execs. Mgrs., Laguna Hills, Calif.; dean Grad. Sch. Adminstrn. Coll. of Boca Raton, Fla.; exec. head mgmt. engring. divsn. S.D. Leidesdorf & Co., 1954-55; dir. City Stores Corp., City Stores Mer. Co., Inc., City Splty. Stores Co., Inc., Oppenheim Collins & Co., Franklin Simon Co., N.Y.C., R.H. White Co., Boston, Wise Smith & Co., Hartford, Conn. Mem. Broome County Planning Commn., 1936-38, Pa. War Manpower Commn.; chmn. War. Emergency Bd. N.Y. State, 1941; industry mem. appeals com. Nat. War Labor Bd., 1943-45; cons. HOLC and FHA, 1936-39; chmn. Armed Forces Regional Council, Pa. and Del., 1950-52; mem. adv. com. 2d Army, 4th Naval Dist.; pres. 175th Anniversary of the Signing of the Declaration of Independence, 1951; pres. Phila. Conv. and Visitors Bur., 1953; chmn. United Com. Fund, Princeton; apptd. mem. State Commn. to reorgn. Govt. City N.Y., 1953; apptd. mem. Mayor's Adv. Council, chmn. com. on city mgmt. and adminstrn., 1954; Citizens Com. to Keep N.Y. Clean, 1955, Citizens Com. on Cts., 1955; pres. Quiet City Campaign, 1956; vice chmn., sec. Phila. Parking Authority.; trustee William Shelton Harrison Found., Hun School, Princeton, N.J., Clarkson Coll. of Tech. Named Adm., Flagship Fleet, Am. Airlines, 1942, to Honorable Order of Ky. Colonels, 1950, Amb., TWA, 1957. Mem. Am. Mgmt. Assn., Am. Inst. Mgmt. (pres. coun., charter mem. adv. bd.), Nat. Retail Rsch. Inst. (bd. dirs.), Bronx Bd. Trade (bd. dirs. 1954-64), Ave. of Americas Assn. (bd. dirs. 1952-55), Soc. for Advancement Mgmt., Nat. Assn. Cost Accts., Commerce and industry Assn. N.Y. (treas., bd. dirs., exec. com. 1954-58), Lambda Iota (pres.), Delta Upsilon (trustee), Midday Club (Phila.), Phila. Country Club, Lake Placid Club, Skytop Club, Merion Cricket Club, Racquet Club, Poor Richard Club, Pen and Pencil Club, Economic Club, Union League, Nat. Golf Links Am., Uptown Club, Springdale Golf Club, Rotary, Nassau Club, Laguna Hills Golf Club, Pinehurst Country Club, Royal Palm Yacht and Country Club (gov.), Mission Viejo Country Club, El Niguel Country Club, P.G.A. Nat. Golf Club, Calif. Club, Phi Beta Lambda. *

CONOMIKES, MELANIE REMINGTON, marketing executive; b. Chgo., Sept. 3, 1966; arrived in Australia, 1995; d. George Spero Conomikes and Cynthia Stoll Chandler. BFA, NYU, 1988; postgrad., UCLA, 1993-94. Publs. dir. Conomikes Assns., Inc., L.A., 1987-92; comm. mgr. Frank O. Gehry & Assoc., Santa Monica, Calif., 1992-95; pres. Melanie Conomikes Consulting, L.A., Melbourne, Australia, 1995—; mktg. dir. Eye Media Pty Ltd, Melbourne, 1996—. Active L.A. planning com. Share Our Strength's "Taste of The Nation", 1995, Women are Info. Tech., Melbourne, 1997—. Office: Eye Media Proprietary Ltd, Level 1 10 Cremorne St, Richmond VIC 3121, Australia

CONOUR, WILLIAM FREDERICK, lawyer; b. Indpls., June 21, 1947; s. William E. and Marian L. (Smith) C.; m. Jennifer Hentges; children: Tonja, Andrea, Erin, Rachel, Tyler. AB in History, Ind. U., 1970, JD cum laude, 1974. Bar: Ind. 1974, U.S. Dist. Ct. (so. dist.) Ind. 1974, U.S. Dist. Ct. (no. dist.) Ind. 1996, U.S. Ct. Appeals (7th cir.) 1975, U.S. Supreme Ct., 1982; cert. mediator Ind. Supreme Ct., 1992—. Dir. training Ind. Pros. Attys. Council, Indpls., 1974-82; ptnr. Conour & Davis, Indpls., 1974-86; pvt. practice Indpls., 1986-88; ptnr. Conour Doehrman, 1988—; assoc. prof., adjunct faculty Ind. U. Purdue U. Indpls., 1974—; lectr. Ind. Law Enforcement Acad.; rsch. analyst Ind. Criminal Law Study Commn., 1973-74. Contbg. author Indiana Criminal Procedure Sourcebook, 1974, Indiana Prosecuting Attorney's Deskbook; editor profl. bulletins; contbr. articles to profl. jours. Guarantor Butler U. Clowes Hall; patron Ind. Repertory Theatre, Indpls. Symphony Orch.; mem. Gov.'s club Ind. Dems., Conner Prairie Pioneer Settlement, Nat. Safety Coun., Hoosier Safety Coun. Recipient commendation Drug Enforcement Adminstrn. U.S. Dept. Justice, 1977, Commendation award Hoosier Safety Coun., 1989, Commendation award Ind. State Bar Assn. Criminal Justice Sect., 1990. Fellow Roscoe Pound Found. (life), Found. Am. Bd. Trial Advocates (sr. life), Indpls. Bar Found. (life); mem. ABA (litigation sect.), Am. Bd. Trial Advocates (pres. Ind. chpt.), Am. Soc. Safety, Ind. Bar Assn. (sec. litigation 1981-82, ad hoc com. on legal cert., mem. litigation sect., criminal justice sect., sec. 1977-78, treas. 1981-82), Indpls. Bar Assn. (grievance com. 1983-91, litigation sect.), Assn. Trial Lawyers Am. (cert. Nat. Coll. Advocacy 1979, Advanced Coll. Advocacy 1981, cons. site litigation group, M Club, lectr.), Coll. of Legal Medicine, Am. Coll. of Legal Medicine, Ind. Trial Lawyers Assn. (sustaining mem., bd. dirs., lectr., amicus curie com., rule of evidence com.), Ind. Lawyers Commn. (ad hoc com. on criminal justice standards and goals 1976-80), Am. Bd. Trial Advs., Trial Lawyers for Pub. Justice (sustaining founder), Woodburn Guild (life), Ind. U. Alumni Assn. (life), Aquatic Injury Safety Assn., Indpls. Law Club, Indpls. Athletic Club, US Equestrian Team (contbg. mem.), US Dressage Fedn. Ind. Dressage Soc. (dir.), Indpls. Mus. Art, Phi Delta Phi (hon.). Democrat. Clubs: Inpls. Athletic; Ind. Soc. Chgo., Atla "M". Home: 10858 Sedgemoor Cir Carmel IN 46032-9189 Office: 10333 N Meridian St Ste 100 Indianapolis IN 46240

CONOVER, DOROTHY NANCY LEVER, medical practice administrator, nurse; b. Abington, Pa., Jan. 11, 1941; d. Charles Ambler and Dorothy Nancy (Greenway) Lever; m. Albert Paul Conover, Dec. 23, 1960 (div. Aug. 1981); 1 child, Hollie Marie. Degree in nursing, Phila. Gen. Hosp. Sch. Nursing, 1960. Staff and pvt. duty nurse Morton Plant Hosp., Clearwater, Fla., 1963; med. asst., sec. Office of E.E. Wilkison, MD, Tallahassee, 1966-69; med. sec. Urology Clinic Assocs., Houston, 1977-78; adminstr. glenn A. Helwig, M.D.-Coastal Women's Ctr., Clearwater, 1979-98, Digestive Disease Assn. Clearwater, 1998—. Editor (newsletter) People with AIDS, 1995. V.p. Meadows Swim Team Booster Club, Stafford, Tex., 1974, Meadows Cmty. Improvement Assn., Stafford, 1975; bd. dirs. Bay House Condo Assn., Clearwater, 1987-96; ruling elder Presbyn. Ch., Sugarland, Tex., 1976. Mem. Assn. Healthcare Mgrs., Profl. Assn. Healthcare Office Mgrs., Am. Acad. Procedural Coders (adv. bd. 1994-95), Med. Group Mgmt. Assn. Ob-gyn. Assembly (sec.-treas. 1996, pres.-elect 1997, pres. 1998, newsletter editor ob-gyn. assembly 1995-96, adv. bd. Ob Prac Mgmt Newsletter 1997-98, gastroenterology adminstrn. assembly 1998—), Clearwater Bus. and Profl. Womens Club (treas. 1985-86). Republican. Presbyterian. Avocations: gardening, needlepoint, depression era glassware. Home: 246 Temple Ln Largo FL 33770-1966 Office: Digestive Disease Assn Clearwater Drs Weston Berner & Aviles 1330 S Ft Harrison A4 Clearwater FL 33756-5326

CONOVER, HARVEY, retired publisher; b. New Rochelle, N.Y., Oct. 23, 1925; s. Harvey and Dorothy (Jobson) C.; m. Isabel McIver Toner, Dec. 27, 1980; children: Harvey III, Stephen, Jeffrey, Cynthia. B.S., U.S. Naval Acad., 1949. With Mill & Factory mag., 1953-54, Purchasing mag., 1954-56; dist. mgr. Volume Feeding mag., 1956-57; sales mgr. Volume Feeding mag., 1958-59; pub. Boating Industry mag., 1959-62; exec. v.p. Conover-Mast Publs., Inc., 1962-64, pres., 1964-68; pres. Conover-Mast div. Cahners Pub. Co., Inc., N.Y.C., 1968-73; v.p. branch ops. Cahners Pub. Co., divsn. Reed Internat., 1973-91. Served to lt. (j.g.) USN, 1949-53. Mem. N.Y. Yacht Club. Home: 7 Half Moon Way Dolphin Cove Stamford CT 06902

CONOVER, JILL M., freelance writer; b. Maine, 1967; m. Michael E. Conover; 1 child, Brian. Dir. publs. Nat. Assn. Real Estate Investment Trusts, Inc., Washington, 1993-94; sr. prodn. editor Aspen Pubs., Inc., Gaithersburg, Md., 1994-95; writer Exec. Office of Pres., White Ho., Washington, 1995-96; freelance writer, editor and reporter, Frederick, Md., 1996—; Tutor in English and lang. arts, Frederick, 1998—. Editor bus. newsletters, including Best Practices in Customer Svc., 1998. Clinton assoc. Dem. Nat. Conv., N.Y.C., 1992; campaign asst. Bill Clinton for Pres. Campaign, Westchester County, N.Y., 1992; mem. Dem. Nat. Com., 1992—, Dem. Leadership Coun., 1992—. Brodbeck scholar Hood Coll. Mem. NEA, Soc. Profl. Journalists.

CONOVER, MONA LEE, retired adult education educator; b. Lincoln, Nebr., Nov. 9, 1929; d. William Cyril and Susan Ferne (Floyd) C.; m. Elmer Kenneth Johnson, June 14, 1953 (div. 1975); children: Michael David, Susan Amy, Sharon Ann, Jennifer Lynne. AB, Nebr. Wesleyan U., 1952; student, Ariz. State U., 1973-75; MA in Edn., No. Ariz. U., 1985. Cert. tchr., Colo., Ariz. Tchr. Jefferson County R-1 Sch., Wheat Ridge, Colo., 1952-56, Glendale (Ariz.) Elem. Sch. 40, 1972-92; dir. Glendale Adult Edn., 1987-92; ret., 1992. Author: ABC's of Naturalization, 1989. Mem. AAUW, Phoenix Bot. Gardens, Heard Mus., Phoenix Zoo, Order of Ea. Star. Republican. Methodist. Avocations: music, travel, photography, history.

CONOVER, NELLIE COBURN, retail furniture company executive; b. Lebanon, Ohio, Dec. 21, 1921; d. Frank C. and Isabel (Murphy) Coburn; student public schs.; m. Lawrence E. Conover, Jan. 11, 1941; children—Lawrence R., Carol, David C., Constance, Christina. Co-founder, 1949, since exec. sec.-treas. Larry Conover Furniture & Appliance, Inc., and predecessor, Milford, Ohio, also trustee co. pension fund. Mem. Milford C. of C., Cin. Hist. Soc., Milford Hist. Soc., DAR. Democrat. Roman Catholic. Address: 438 Main St Milford OH 45150-1128

CONOVER, RICHARD CORRILL, lawyer; b. Bridgeport, Nebr., Jan. 12, 1942; s. John Cedric and Mildred (Dunn) C.; m. Cathy Harlan, Dec. 19, 1970; children—William Cedric, Theodore Cyril. B.S., U. Nebr., Lincoln, 1965, M.S., 1966; J.D., Cornell U., 1969. Bar: N.Y. 1970, Mont. 1982, U.S. Dist. Ct. (so. and ea. dists.) N.Y. 1971, U.S. Supreme Ct. 1977, U.S. Ct. Customs and Patent Appeals 1979, U.S. Ct. Claims 1980, U.S. Dist. Ct. Mont. 1984, U.S. Tax Ct. 1986. Assoc. Brumbaugh, Graves, Donohue & Raymond, N.Y.C., 1969-73; assoc. Townley, Updike, Carter & Rodgers, N.Y.C., 1974-75; assoc. gen. csl. legal office Automatic Data Processing, Inc., Clifton, N.J., 1975-77; assoc. Nims, Howes, Collison & Isner, N.Y.C., 1977-81; sole practice, Mont., 1981—; lectr. indsl. and mech. engrng. dept. Mont. State U., 1981-97. Mem. Mont. Gov.'s Bd. Sci. and Tech., 1985-87. Mem. ABA, Assn. Bar City N.Y., Mont. Bar Assn., Am. Pat. Law Assn. Home: PO Box 1329 Bozeman MT 59771-1329 Office: 104 E Main St Ste 404 Bozeman MT 59715-4732

CONOVER, ROBERT WARREN, retired librarian; b. Manhattan, Kans., Oct. 6, 1937; s. Robert Warren and Grace Darline (Grinstead) C.; BA, Kans. State U., 1959; MA, U. Denver, 1961. Librarian, supervising librarian County of Fresno, Calif., 1961-66; county librarian County of Yolo, Woodland, Calif., 1967-68; dir. City of Fullerton (Calif.) Pub. Library, 1968-73, City of Pasadena (Calif.) Pub. Library, 1973-80, Palos Verdes Library Dist., Palos Verdes Peninsula, Calif., 1980-85, City of Commerce (Calif.) Pub. Library, 1985-97, ret. Pres. Kapalua Bay (Hawaii) Villas, Inc. Recipient Pres.'s award Fresno Jaycees, 1963. Mem. ALA, Orange County Libr. Assn. (pres. 1971), Spl. Librs. Assn., Calif. Libr. Assn. (pres. Yosemite chpt. 1965, mem. coun. 1981), Santiago Libr. System Coun. (pres. 1972), Met. Coop. Libr. System (exec. com. mem., 1994, vice chair 1995, chair 1996), Univ. Club, Pi Kappa Alpha. Episcopalian. Home: Kapalua Bay Villas 500 Bay Dr # 17g-5 Lahaina HI 96761-9034

CONOVER, WILLIAM JAY, statistics educator; b. Hays, Kans., Dec. 6, 1936; s. William Joseph Conover and Viola Marie (Herman) Beishline; m. Patricia Louise Solomon, June 11, 1960 (div. Apr. 1994); children: Christopher Michael, Robert Andrew, Judith Ann, Therese Marie, William Joseph; m. Susan Theresa Mole, Dec. 27, 1996. BS, Iowa State U., 1958; MA, Cath. U., 1962, PhD, 1964. Asst. prof. stats. Kans. State U., Manhattan, 1964-67, assoc. prof. stats., 1967-73; vis. prof. stats. U. Zürich, Switzerland, 1970-71; prof. stats. Tex. Tech U., Lubbock, 1973-81, Horn prof., 1981—, area coord. of info. systems/quantitative scis., assoc. dean, 1978-88; vis. prof. U. Calif., Davis, 1976-77; vis. staff mem. Los Alamos (N.Mex.) Sci. Labs., 1976—; cons. Sandia Labs., Albuquerque, 1979—. Author: Practical Nonparametric Statistics, 1971, 2d edit., 1980, Modern Business Statistics, 1983, 2d edit., 1989; co-author 9 textbooks on statistics; contbr. numerous articles to profl. jours. Served to lt (j.g.) USN, 1958-61. Recipient Rushing Faculty Research award Tex. Tech Dad's Assn., 1983. Fellow Am. Statis. Assn. (Don Owen award San Antonio chpt. 1986); mem. Inst. Math. Stats., Biometric Soc., Inst. Decision Scis. Roman Catholic. Avocations: chess, basketball. Office: Tex Tech U Coll Bus Adminstrn Lubbock TX 79409

CONQUEST, (GEORGE) ROBERT (ACWORTH), writer, historian, poet, critic, journalist; b. Malvern, Worcestershire, Eng., July 15, 1917; s. Robert Folger Westcott and Rosamund Alys (Acworth) C.; m. Joan Watkins, 1942 (div. 1948); children: John, Richard; m. Elizabeth Neece, Dec. 1, 1979. Student, Winchester Coll., Eng., 1931-35, U. Grenoble, France, 1935-36, U. Oxford, 1936-39; MA, U. Oxford, Eng., 1972; DLitt, U. Oxford, 1975. First sec. H.M. Fgn. Svc., Sofia, Bulgaria, U.N., London, 1946-56; rsch. fellow London Sch. Econs., 1956-58; vis. poet U. Buffalo, N.Y., 1959-60; lit. editor The Spectator, London, 1962-63; sr. fellow Russian Inst. Columbia U., N.Y.C., 1964-65; fellow Woodrow Wilson Internat. Ctr., Washington, 1976-77; sr. rsch. fellow Hoover Inst., Stanford (Calif.) U., 1977-79, 81—; disting. vis. scholar Heritage Found., Washington, 1980-81; adv. bd. Freedom House, N.Y.C., 1980—; rsch. assoc. Ukrainian Rsch. Inst. Harvard U., Cambridge, Mass., 1983—; adj. fellow Washington Ctr. Strategic Studies., 1984—. Author: Poems, 1955, A World of Difference, 1955, Common Sense About Russia, 1960, Power and Policy in the USSR, 1961, The Pasternak Affair, 1962, Between Mars and Venus, 1962, (with Kingsley Amis) The Egyptologists, 1965, Russia after Khrushchev, 1965, The Great Terror, 1968, Arias from a Love Opera, 1969, The Nation Killers, 1970, Where Marx Went Wrong, 1970, V I Lenin, 1972, Kolyma: The Arctic Death Camps, 1978, Coming Across, 1978, The Abomination of Moab, 1979, Forays, 1979, Present Danger: Towards a Foreign Policy, 1979, We and They: Civic and Despotic Cultures, 1980, (with Jon M. White) What to do When the Russians Come, 1984, Inside Stalin's Secret Police: NKVD Politics 1936-39, 1985, The Harvest of Sorrow: Soviet Collectivization and the Terror-Famine, 1986, New and Collected Poems, 1988, Stalin and the Kirov Murder, 1988, Tyrants and Typewriters, 1989, The Great Terror: A Reassessment, 1990, Stalin: Breaker of Nations, 1991, Demons Don't, 1999, Reflections on a Ravaged Century, 1999. Capt. inf. Brit. Army, 1939-46, ETO. Decorated Officer Order of the Brit. Empire, London, 1955, Companion Order St. Michael and St. George, London, 1996; recipient Alexis de Tocqueville award, 1992Light Verse award Acad. Arts and Letters, 1997; Jefferson lectr. in the humanities, Washington, 1993; Royal Soc. Lit. fellow, 1972. Fellow Brit. Acad., Brit. Interplanetary Soc.; mem. Soc. for Promotion of Roman Studies. Club: Travellers (London). Home: 52 Peter Coutts Cir Stanford CA 94305-2506 Office: Stanford U Hoover Inst Stanford CA 94305-6010

CONRAD, ANDREW WILLIAM, dean, writer; b. Johnson City, N.Y., Dec. 23, 1941; s. George Emery Conrad and Cora Belle Barnes; m. Mary Ann Blaskowsky, June 27, 1970 (div. Apr. 1981); children: Heather K. Conrad Bradley, Emery David Conrad. AB, Barrington Coll., 1963; MDiv, Gordon-Conwell Theol. Sem., 1967; ThM, Princeton Theol. Sem., 1971; MA, Princeton U., 1975, PhD, 1977. Dean R.I. Sch. Deaf, Providence, 1967-71; instr., dir. writing Princeton (N.J.) U., 1977-80; freelance cons., writer Princeton, 1980-87; assoc. prof. English, dir. learning, dean Mercer County C.C., Trenton, N.J., 1987—. Author, editor: The Spread of English, 1977, Post-Imperial English, 1996; contbr. articles to profl. jours. pres., bd. dirs. Friends Trenton Pub. Libr., 1995—; chair bd. dirs. Rick Redner AIDS Libr., Trenton, 1995—. Mem. Assn. Princeton Grad. Alumni (bd. dirs, mem. chair 1993—). E-mail: conrada@mccc.edu. Home: 6 Servis Rd Skillman NJ 08558 Office: Mercer County C C 1200 Old Trenton Rd Trenton NJ 08690

CONRAD, CRAIG EDWARD, electronic distribution executive; b. Oak Park, Ill., Nov. 3, 1951; s. George Conrad and Mary Jane Graber Larsen; m. Ann Kathleen Frankowiak, Aug. 30, 1975; children: Terry, Allison. AA, Coll. of DuPage, Glen Ellyn, Ill.; BS in Mktg., No. Ill. U., 1975. Product mgr. Semi Specs, Elmhurst, Ill., 1976; ops. mgr. Kierulff Electronics, Elk Grove, Ill., 1976-78, product dir., 1978-79; gen. mgr. Schweber/Lex, Atlanta, 1979-83; regional v.p. Lex Electronics, Elk Grove, 1983-86; sr. v.p. mktg. Lex Electronics, Westbury, N.Y., 1986-90; v.p. mktg. Avnet, Culver City, Calif., 1990-93; v.p. sales/mktg. TTI, Ft. Worth, Tex., 1993—. Mem. Nat. Electronics Distbn. Assn. (bd. dirs. 1994, treas. 1996—, treas. edn. found. 1996—). Avocations: boating, golf, fishing, basketball. Office: TTI 2441 Northeast Pky Fort Worth TX 76106-1816

CONRAD, DAVID PAUL, business broker, retired restaurant chain executive; b. Greensboro, N.C., Jan. 11, 1946; s. Lucas Lee and Elizabeth Gertrude (Kincaid) C.; 1 child, Lucas Wilfong. BSBA, East Carolina U., 1970; cert. in real estate, Forsyth Tech. Coll., 1979. From cashier to cook Libby Hill Seafood, Greensboro, N.C., 1962-64; plant mgr. Libby Hill Seafood Restaurants, Inc., Greensboro, N.C., 1970-76; mgr. Libby Hill Seafood Restaurants, Inc., Winston-Salem, N.C., 1976-85; v.p., dir. ops. Libby Hill Seafood Restaurants, Inc., Greensboro, N.C., 1985-93, also bd. dirs., 1985-93; comml. real estate broker Allied Comml. Real Estate, Kernersville, N.C., 1993—; franchise owner Swisher Maids of West Greensboro, N.C., 1994—, regional dir., 1996-98; broker-in-charge VR Bus. Brokers; pres. Jonathan's Proprietorships, L.L.C.; broker VR Bus. Brokers. Mem. Greensboro Jaycees, 1973-81; vol. St. Jude's Children's Rsch. Hosp. Staff sgt. N.C. N.G., 1968-74. Mem. Masons. Republican. Methodist. Avocation: family. Fax: (336) 854-2202. Office: VR Business Brokers Four Seasons Exec Ctr 9A Terrace Wayrden St Greensboro NC 27403

CONRAD, DONALD GLOVER, insurance executive; b. St. Louis, Apr. 23, 1930; s. Harold Armin and Velma Glover (Morris) C.; m. Stephania Shimkus, Feb. 8, 1980; 1 child, Christina; 1 stepchild, Alexa Sanzone; children by previous marriage: Marcy Conrad Tramont, Suzanne Jones, Mark. Student, Wesleyan U., 1948-49; BS, Northwestern U., 1952; MBA, U. Mich., 1957. With Exxon Co., 1957-70; fin. adv. Exxon Co. (Esso Natural Gas), The Hague, Netherlands, 1965-66; treas. Exxon Co. (Esso Europe), London, 1966-70; sr. v.p. Aetna Life & Casualty Co., Hartford, Conn., 1970-72; exec. v.p., dir. Aetna Life & Casualty Co., 1972-88, ret., 1988; prin. owner, chmn. Hartford Whalers Hockey Club, 1988-92; chmn. Lang Capital Assocs.; sr. advisor to the pres. World Bank, Washington, 1995—; bd. dirs. Chevy Chase (Md.) F.S.B. Chmn. emeritus Am. Coun. for Arts N.Y., Greater Hartford Arts Coun. Lt. USNR, 1952-55. Mem. Watch Hill Yacht Club, The Club at Windermere, Bath and Tennis Club (Palm Beach), Teton Pines Country Club (Jackson Hole). Office: The World Bank 1818 H St NW Washington DC 20433-0002

CONRAD, FLAVIUS LESLIE, JR., minister; b. Hickory, N.C., May 5, 1920; s. Flavius Leslie and Mary Wilhelmina (Huffman) C.; m. Mary Elizabeth Isenhour, Nov. 4, 1944; children: Ann Meisner (dec.), Susan Amis. AB, Lenoir Rhyne Coll., 1941; MDiv, Luth. Theol. So. Sem., 1944; MST, Temple U., 1955, STD, 1959. Ordained to ministry Evang. Luth. Ch. Am., 1944. Pastor St. Timothy Luth. Ch., Hickory, 1944-49, Holy Comforter Luth. Ch., Belmont, N.C., 1949-50; youth dir. United Luth. Ch. Am., Phila., 1950-60; pastor St. Luke's Luth. Ch., Richardson, Tex., 1960-86, pastor emeritus, 1986—; dean Dallas and East Tex. dist. Luth. Ch. Am., 1973-77, mem. publ. bd., 1974-82; del. convs. Luth. Ch. Am., 1968, 74, 76; exec. sec. Luther League Am., 1950-60; mem. exec. bd. and gen. assembly Nat. Coun. Chs. of Christ in U.S.A., 1954-60. Author: A Study of Four Non-Denominational Youth Movements, 1955, Poetic Potshots at People and Preachers, 1977; pub. sermons for The Clergy Jour., worship materials for The Minister's Annual Manual, 1996-97; contbg. editor Ch. Mgmt. mag., 1966-74; corr. The Lutheran from S.W., 1962-76; contbr. sermons, articles and poems to various mags. V.p. Piedmont (N.C.) coun. Boy Scouts Am., 1948-49. Winner Nat. Poetry Contest, 1960. Home: 1108 Pueblo Dr Richardson TX 75080-2913

CONRAD, FRANCIS G., federal judge; b. 1946. BA, Manhattan Coll., 1967; MBA, Iona Coll., 1972; JD, Fordham U., 1977. Bar: N.Y. Acct. Peat, Marwick, Mitchell & Co., 1973; pvt. practice., 1978-85; vis. bankruptcy judge for ea. dist. N.Y. and Vt., U.S. Bankruptcy Ct., Westbury, 1985—. With U.S. Army, 1968-70. Office: US Bankruptcy Ct 1635 Privado Rd Westbury NY 11590-5298

CONRAD, GEOFFREY WENTWORTH, archaeologist, educator; b. Boston, Dec. 24, 1947; s. Albert Austin and Ruth Wentworth (Cadieux) C.; m. Karen Ann Hildebrant, June 12, 1971; children: Matthew, Peter, Marc. AB, Harvard U., 1969, PhD, 1974. Curatorial asst. Smithsonian Inst., Washington, 1974-75; asst. prof. and asst. curator Harvard U., Cambridge, Mass., 1976-81, assoc. prof. and assoc. curator, 1981-83; dir. William Hammond Mathers Mus. Ind. U., Bloomington, 1983—, assoc. prof. anthropology, 1983-91, prof., 1991—, chair, 1991-95; cons. Nat. Geog. Soc., Washington, 1982-83. Co-author (books): Religion and Empire, 1984, The Andean Heritage, 1982; co-editor (book) Ideology and Precolombian Civilizations, 1992; contbr. articles to profl. jours.; mem. editl. bd. Jour. of Field Archaeology, 1986-96. Bd. dirs. Monroe County Hist. Soc., Bloomington, 1989-92. NSF grantee, 1978, 85; Ind. Humanities Coun. grantee, 1983, 86, 88; Wenner-Gren Found. grantee, 1987. Fellow AAAS; mem. Archaeol. Inst. Am. (pres. Cen. Ind. chpt. 1989-91, acad. trustee 1994-97), Soc. Am. Archaeology, Assn. for Field Archaeology, Am. Assn. Mus., Midwest Mus. Conf., Assn. Coll. and Univ. Mus. and Galleries (Midwest rep. 1990-91). Home: 3130 Saint James Ct Bloomington IN 47401-7105 Office: Mathers Mus Ind U 601 E 8th St Bloomington IN 47408-3812 also: Ind U Dept Anthropology Student Bldg Bloomington IN 47405

CONRAD, GEORGE JOHN, retired design engineer, planner; b. N.Y.C., Apr. 24, 1943; s. George John and Bridget Anne (Kelly) C.; m. Marita Margaret Teuber, Apr. 24, 1971; children: Tracey Lynn, Kimberly Ann, Christopher George. BEE, Manhattan Coll., 1965. With Phila. Naval Shipyard, 1965-95, supr. field design, 1973-79, gen. engr., 1979-84, design br. head, 1984-85, asst. chief design engrng., 1985-87, advance planning supr., 1987-90, waterfront supr., 1987-95, ret., 1995; transp. coord. Lakewood Pathology, 1998—; CEO Conrad Properties, Atco, N.J., 1973—; transp. coord. Lakewood Pathology Assocs., 1998—. Coach Waterford Twp. Athletic Assn., 1987-94; chief YMCA Indian Guides, Echelon, N.J., 1987-93; founder Winslow Crossing Civic Assn., 1972. Mem. Fed. Mgrs. Assn. (v.p. chpt. 4 1984-90). Roman Catholic. Avocations: financial planning, hiking, canoeing. Home: 635 Raritan Ave Atco NJ 08004-1830

CONRAD, GLEN E., federal judge; b. 1949. Magistrate judge U.S. Dist. Ct. (we. dist.) Va., Roanoke, 1976—. Fax: (540) 857-2497. Office: US Dist Ct (we dist) Va 201 Franklin Rd SW Roanoke VA 24011

CONRAD, HANS, materials engineering educator; b. Konradstahl, Germany, Apr. 19, 1922; came to U.S., 1926, naturalized, 1944; s. Henry K. and Martha Ann (Bader) C.; m. Emma Ann Bort, June 10, 1944; children—Sandra Joy, Roberta Lee, Gary Richard. Student, Washington and Jefferson Coll., 1940-42; B.S. in Metall. Engrng, Carnegie Inst. Tech., 1943; M.Eng., Yale, 1951, D.Eng., 1956. Research metallurgist Chase Copper & Brass Co., Waterbury, Conn., 1953-55; supervisory engr. Westinghouse Research Labs., Churchill Boro, Pa., 1955-59; sr. research specialist Atomics Internat., Canoga Park, Calif., 1959-61; head dept. physics Aerospace Corp., El Segundo, Calif., 1961-64; tech. dir. Franklin Inst. Research Labs., Phila., 1964-67; prof., chmn. dept. metall. engrng. and materials sci., assoc. dir. Inst. Mining and Minerals Research, U. Ky., Lexington, 1967-80; prof., head dept. materials engrng., dir. minerals and materials research programs N.C. State U., 1981-85, prof., 1985—; Japan Soc. Promotion Sci. vis. prof. 1976; Disting. vis. prof. Am. U., Cairo, 1983, Soviet Acad. Scis, 1984; Ministry Metall. Industry, PRC, 1986. Contbr. articles to profl. jours. and books. Recipient Rsch. award U. Ky., 1971, U.S. Sr. Scientist award Alexander von Humboldt-Stiftung, 1974; Alcoa Rsch. award N.C. State U., 1985, Alumni Rsch. award, 1991. Fellow Am. Soc. Materials; mem. AIME, Rheol. Soc., ASME, Sigma Xi, Tau Beta Pi. Home: 205 Glasgow Dr Cary NC 27511-6517

CONRAD, HAROLD AUGUST, retired religious pension board executive; b. Cleve., Dec. 18, 1928; s. August and Olga (Heise) C.; m. Anne (Chernosky) Conrad, July 10, 1948 (widowed Mar. 1956); children: Deborah Anne Hamer, Loren Harold Conrad, Rebecca Faith Towle; m. Naomi Ruth (Sweeny) Conrad, Dec. 31, 1960; 1 child, Paul Alan Conrad, MD. BA, Anderson U., Ind., 1952; MDiv, Christian Theo. Sem., Indpls., 1970; DD, Mid-Am. Bible Coll., Oklahoma City, 1975. Pastor Akron Ch. of God, Akron, Ind., 1952-63, First Ch. of God, Winchester, Ky., 1963-66, Glendale Ch. of God, Indpls., 1966-74; exec. sec. treas. Bd. of Pensions of Ch. of God, Anderson, Ind., 1974-93; ret., 1993; state chmn. Ind. Ministerial Assembly, Indpls., 1961-62; vice chmn. Ky. Ministerial Assembly, Winchester, Ky., 1965-66; bd. mem. Bd. of Pensions of Ch. of God, Anderson, Ind., 1964-74; bd. dirs. Exec. Coun. of Ch. of God, Anderson, Ind., 1976-84, 87-90. Mem. Nat. Ch. Pensions Conv. (pres. 1985). Republican. Mem. Ch. of God. Avocations: stamp collecting, gardening, walking, reading, traveling. Home: 810 Northwood Dr Anderson IN 46011-1072

CONRAD, HAROLD THEODORE, psychiatrist; b. Milw., Jan. 25, 1934; s. Theodore Herman and Alyce Barbara C.; m. Elaine Marie Blaine, Sept. 1, 1962; children: Blaine, Carl, David, Erich, Rachel. *Wife Elaine is an accomplished musician. She studied piano in Rome and at Newcomb College. Son Blaine is a graduate in Economics and is currently studying computer applications for health data management. Son Carl is an attorney in private practice. Son David is an expert in environmental preservation and safety. He has a graduate degree in the field and works for the Council of Energy Resource Tribes, a Native American group. Daughter Rachel is a physician and an officer in the U.S. Air Force. Son Erich is a student at the LSU Medical School in New Orleans.* AB, U. Chgo., 1954, BS, 1955, MD, 1958. Diplomate Am. Bd. Psychiatry. Intern USPHS Hosp., San Francisco, 1958-59, commd. sr. asst. surgeon, 1958, advanced through grades to med. dir., 1967; resident psychiatry USPHS Hosp., Lexington, Ky., 1959-61, Charity Hosp., New Orleans, 1961-62; chief of psychiatry USPHS Hosp., New Orleans, 1962-67, clin. dir., 1967; dep. dir. div. field investigation NIMH, Chevy Chase, Md., 1968; chief NIMH Clin. Rsch. Ctr., Lexington, 1969-73; cons. psychiatry region IX USPHS, HEW, San Francisco, 1973-79; dir. adolescent unit Alaska Psychiat. Inst., Anchorage, 1979-81, supt., 1981-85; clin. assoc. prof. psychiatry U. Wash. Med. Sch., 1981-85; med. dir. Bayou Oaks Hosp., Houma, La., 1985—. Contbr. to publs. in field. Recipient Decorated Commendation Medal, various community awards for contbns. in field of drug abuse and equal employment opportunity for minorities. Fellow Royal Soc. Health, Royal Soc. Medicine, Am. Psychiat. Assn.; mem. AMA, Alpha Omega Alpha, Alpha Delta Phi. Office: 855 Belanger St Houma LA 70360-4452

CONRAD, JOHN R., corporate executive; b. Chgo., Dec. 3, 1915; s. Nicholas John and Irene Edna (Billups) C.; m. Ruth Osborne Good, June 14, 1940 (div. 1957); children: Lynn, Joanne, Catherine; m. Arlys Mafra Streitmatter, Apr. 11, 1958. Student, Yale U., 1934-36; BS in Econs., U. Chgo., 1937; postgrad., Boeing Sch. Aeros., 1938; LHD (hon.), Ill. Inst. Tech., 1991. Mem. staff engrng. and mfg. Douglas Aircraft, Santa Monica, Calif., 1938-44; mgr. properties Douglas Aircraft, Long Beach, Calif., 1944-45; v.p. S&C Electric Co., Chgo., 1945-52, pres., 1952-88, chmn., CEO, chmn. bd. dirs., 1988—; bd. dirs. S&C Electric Can. Ltd., Toronto, Ont. Patentee terminal constrn. 1957. Mem. Mid-Am. Com., Chgo., 1983—, Chgo. Com. Chgo. Coun. on Fgn. Rels., 1980—; mem. Ill. Coalition; mem. Northwestern U. J.L. Kellogg Grad. Sch. Mgmt. Adv. Bd.; mem. Pres. Coun. U. Ill.; mem. adv. bd. Exec. Club Chgo.; gov. mem. John G. Shedd Aquarium Soc.; mem. St. Francis Hosp. of Evanston Founders Soc. (Founders' Day award 1983). Recipient Progress award Soc. Mfg. Engrs., 1972, Bus. in the Arts award Esquire/Bus. Com. for Arts, 1975, Spl. award for support and contbns. to switchgear industry IEEE Power Engrng. Soc. Switchgear Com., 1990, Citizen's Coun. Cmty. Svc. award Gateway Found., 1991, 25th Anniversary Cmty. Svc. award Gateway Found., 1992, Civic award Loyola U., 1993, award for excellence in power distbn. engrng. IEEE, Inc. Power Engrng. Soc., 1994. Mem. IEEE (life), Conf. Internat. Grandes Reseaux Electriques (U.S. nat. com., U.S. v.p. 1971-72), Ill. Bus. Roundtable, Mid-Am. Club. Avocations: reading, off-shore dayboating. Office: S&C Electric Co 6601 N Ridge Blvd Chicago IL 60626-3925*

CONRAD, JOHN REGIS, lawyer, engineering executive; b. Bloomington, Ind., Feb. 23, 1955; s. John Francis and Patricia Ann (English) C.; m. Paula Jane Vessels, July 4, 1980; children: William Celestine Vessels, John Paul Vessels, M. Alexander Vessels, David Thomas Kelamalamalamanokeakua Vessels, Rachel Elizabeth Ho'ouluolaikealoha Vessels. AB cum laude, Harvard U., 1977; MBA, JD, Ind. U., 1981. Bar: Hawaii 1981, Fla. 1994, Tex. 1994, N.C. 1995, U.S. Dist. Ct. Hawaii 1981, U.S. Ct. Appeals (9th cir.) 1981, U.S. Ct. Claims 1981, U.S. Tax Ct. 1981. Assoc. Cades, Schutte, Fleming & Wright, Honolulu, 1981-85, 89-90, Thompson & Chan, Honolulu, 1985-89; ptnr. Cades Schutte Fleming & Wright, Honolulu, 1991-94; regional bus. mgr. Kimley-Horn and Assocs., Inc., West Palm Beach, Fla., 1994-96, regional prodn. mgr., 1996-98; regional bus. mgr. Kimley-Horn and Assocs., Inc., Phoenix, 1999—; lectr. law Kapiolani C.C., Honolulu, 1984-86; adj. prof. Richardson Sch. Law, U. Hawaii, 1989-90. Author: A Conrad Genealogy, 1979, Hawaii Probate Sourcebook, 1985, rev. 1986, rev. 1992; co-author: Beyond the Basics: Hawaii Estate Planning & Probate, 1985, Hawaii Wills & Trusts Sourcebook, 1986, Hawaii Guardianship Sourcebook, 1988; editor HICLE Fin. and Estate Planning Manual, vol. II, 1989, vol. I, 1990. Planned giving com. Hawaii Heart Assn., Honolulu, 1983-86; arbitrator Hawaii Ct. Annexec Arbitration Program, 1989-94; sch. bd. Star of the Sea Sch., Honolulu, 1992-94, pres., 1993-94, chair Carnival, 1992; chair Cub Scout Pack Aloha Coun. Boy Scouts Am., den leader Cub Scout Pack, Gulf Stream Coun.; lector Good Shephert of the Hills Ch., Cave Creek, Ariz. Fellow Am. Coll. Trust and Estate Coun.; mem. ABA, Am. Arbitration Assn., Hawaii Bar Assn. (chmn. estate and gift tax com. 1984-85, CFO probate and estate planning sect. 1989-90), Hawaii Bar Found. (bd. dirs. 1985-92, v.p. 1989, pres. 1989-91), Hawaii Estate Planning Coun. (bd. dirs. 1991-94, sec. 1993). Roman Catholic. Avocations: running, genealogy, coin collecting, scouting. Home: 33214 N 61st St Cave Creek AZ 85331 Office: Kimley-Horn and Assocs Inc 7600 N 15th St # 250 Phoenix AZ 85020

CONRAD, JOSEPH HENRY, animal nutrition educator; b. Cass County, Ind., Dec. 7, 1926; s. Ferdinand M. and Marie E. (Hubenthal) C.; m. Frances Ash, June 18, 1950; children: Kenneth A., Leonard J., Carol Ann, Joseph C. B.S., Purdue U., 1950, M.S., 1954, Ph.D., 1958; prof. honoris causa, Fed. U. Viçosa, Brazil, 1965. Asst. prof. Purdue U., West Lafayette, Ind., 1958-63, assoc. prof., 1963-68, prof., 1968-71; animal scientist Fed. U. Viçosa, 1961-65; prof. and coordinator tropical animal sci. programs, U. Fla., Gainesville, 1971-95. Co-author: Swine Production, 1982; contbr. monographs and numerous articles on animal nutrition and tropical animal prodn. to profl. jours. Served with USN, 1944-46. Recipient Disting. Nutritional award Distillers Feed Research Council, 1964; Moorman fellow, 1989. Mem. Am. Soc. Animal Sci. (Internat. Animal Agrl. award 1985, Bohstedt award 1987, Internat. Mktg. award 1989, Fellow award 1993), Sociedade Brasileira de Zootecnia, Latin Am. Soc. Animal Prodn., World Assn. Animal Prodn. (v.p.), Sigma Xi, Gamma Sigma Delta, Purdue U. Alumni Assn. (life; pres.'s council). Republican. Lutheran. Home: 1824 NW 10th Ave Gainesville FL 32605-5312 Office: PO Box 110910 Gainesville FL 32611-0910

CONRAD, JUDY L., insurance company executive; b. Reading, Pa., May 22, 1952; d. Willard Martin and Mary Eleanor (Strecker) Conrad; m. Mark A. Stead, Feb. 14, 1988 (dec. 1990); stepchildren: Matthew, Mark Jr., Adrian, Angela. BS in Edn., West Chester (Pa.) U., 1974. CFP, CLU. Tchr. Auscilla Christian Acad., Monticello, Fla., 1980-82; sales agt. Alden Levin Assocs., Phila., 1977-80, John Hunt Assocs., Tallahassee, Fla., 1982-84; life and employee benefits mgr. Corp. Risk Assocs., Tallahassee, Fla., 1982-84; acct. exec. Cigna/INA Cos., Phila., 1985-86; fin. svcs. rep. The Travelers Ins. Cos., Orlando, Fla., 1986-90; fin. svcs. mgr. The Travelers Ins. Cos., Orlando and Tampa, 1990-95; estate planning and ins. specialist, v.p. Salomnon Smith Barney, Orlando, 1995—; pub. speaker, lectr. in field. With Free Fin. Clinics, Orlando Sentinel sponsored hotline 1992, local TV & radio shows St. Petersburg, Jacksonville, Orlando. Recipient Life Citation award INA/CIGNA, 1984. Mem. Am. Soc. CLU, Ctrl. Fla. Soc. ICFP (edn. dir. 1991—, v.p. 1992—, pres.-elect 1993, pres. 1994, chmn. 1995, state rep. 1996), Am. Coll. CLU & ChFC, Nat. Assn. Life Underwriters, Gen. Agts. and Mgrs. Assn., Internat. Assn. Fin. Planners. Republican. Avocations: swimming, scuba diving, ballroom dancing, golf, racquetball. Office: Smith Barney Inc Ste 100 338 W Morse Blvd Winter Park FL 32789-4241

CONRAD, KELLEY ALLEN, industrial and organizational psychologist; b. N.Y.C., June 29, 1941; s. Allen and Dorothy Etta (McAtee) C.; m. Barbara Rae Bedessem, July 8, 1976. BS in Behavioral Science, Mont. State U., 1963; MA in Psychology, SUNY, Geneseo, 1970; PhD in Psychology, Iowa State U., 1973. Lic. psychologist, Wis. Cons. indsl. psychologist Humber, Mundie & McClary, Milw., 1988-96; v.p. Human Resources Devel. Ctr., 1988-95, pres., 1995-96; mgr. Human Resources Devel. Ctr., Naples, Fla., 1996-98, Conrad Cons. Internat., Inc., 1998—; pvt. practice indsl. and orgnl. psychology Naples, 1996—. Contbg. author Learning by Experience—What, Why, How, 1978; co-editor: A Handbook of Psychological Assessment in Business, 1991; co-author: Current Perspectives in Industrial Organizational Psychology, 1998; contbr. articles to profl. jours. Mem. Naples Free Net, co-chmn. help desk, 1997-99, chmn. intership com., 1997—, mem. strategic planning com., 1997-98, bd. dirs., sec. 1998-98, pres., 1999—; mem. Bus. Solutions Network, Inc.; mem. Home Organ Festival, newsletter editor, 1992—, co-dir., 1999—. Lt. USN, 1964-68, Vietnam. Recipient Eli Tash award Wis. Assn. for Children with Learning Disabilities, 1983, 93. Fellow Am. Psychol. Soc., Wis. Psychol. Assn. (sec. 1984-86, pres. indsl./organizational divsn. 1984-85); mem. APA, ASTD (bd. dirs. 1980), Nat. Psychol. Cons. to Mgmt. (pres. 1988-89, sec.-treas. 1990—), Midwest Psychol. Assn., Fla. Psychol. Assn. (assoc.), Midwest Human Resources Planning Assn., Milw. Area Psychol. Assn. (pres. 1985-86), Coun. Police Psychol. Svcs., Acad. Mgmt., Kiwanis (bd. dirs. Milw. 1978-80, com. chmn. 1980, 91),

Sigma Xi, Psi Chi. Congregationalist. Republican. Avocations: computer programming, music, jogging, sking, photography. Home and Office: 7657 San Sebastian Way Naples FL 34109-7168

CONRAD, KENT, senator; b. Bismarck, N.D., Mar. 12, 1948; m. Lucy Calautti, Feb. 1987; 1 child, Jessamyn Abigail. Student, U. Mo., 1967; BA, Stanford U., 1972; MBA, George Washington U., 1975. Asst. to tax commr. State of N.D. Tax Dept., Bismarck, 1974-80, tax commr., 1981-87; U.S. senator from N.D. Washington, 1987—; mem. agr. nutrition and forestry com., mem. budget com. and fin. coms., ethics com., Indian affairs com., senate Dem. steering and coord. com., forestry com. Democrat. Office: US Senate 530 Hart Senate Office Bldg Washington DC 20510

CONRAD, LORETTA JANE, educational administrator; b. Wooster, Ohio, Aug. 9, 1934; d. Donald William and Celia Irene (Smith) C.; B.Mus. Edn. cum laude, Coll. of Wooster, 1956; M.Mus. Edn., U. Colo., 1969; postgrad. cert. supervision/adminstrn. (Univ. scholar), John Carroll U., 1978. Tchr., Avon Lake (Ohio) public schs., 1956-61, Dept. Def., Europe and Far East, 1961-64, Bay Village (Ohio) Bd. Edn., 1964-73, Elyria (Ohio) public schs., 1973-78; asst. prin. Bay Village Bd. Edn., Bay High Sch., 1978-84, Bay Middle Sch., 1984-89; edn. dir. Riverside Acad.; music clinician, adjudicator; pvt. tchr. piano; accompanist, dir. ch. choir, Luth. Ch., 1966-80, children's choir Lakewood United Meth. Ch., 1989-92. Area rep. for recruitment Coll. of Wooster, mem. music com., women adv. bd. Presser scholar, 1955-56; Annie Webb Blanton scholar, Delta Kappa Gamma, 1968. Mem. Ohio Assn. Secondary Sch. Prins., Nat. Assn. Secondary Sch. Prins., Assn. Secondary Curriculum Devel., Ohio Middle Schs. Assn., Cuyahoga Fairview Ret. Tchrs. Assn. (pres. 1998—), Phi Delta Kappa, Delta Kappa Gamma, Alpha Delta (state music rep.), Coll. Club West (bd. dirs., historian), Three Arts Club Lakewood (chmn. scholarship grant fund, v.p. 1997-99, pres. 1999—). Democrat. Lutheran. Club: Quota (pres. 1985-87). Home: 1650 Cedarwood Dr Cleveland OH 44145-1862

CONRAD, MARCEL EDWARD, hematologist, educator; b. N.Y.C., Aug. 15, 1928; s. Marcel Edward and Lulu Marie (Geraghty) C.; m. Marcia Louise Grove; children: Marcel Edward, III, Mark E., Carol J., Erin E., Julia P. BS, Georgetown U., 1949, MD, 1953. Diplomate Am. Bd. Internal Medicine, Am. Bd. Hematology. Intern Walter Reed Gen. Hosp., Washington, 1953-54; resident, then chief resident in internal medicine Walter Reed Gen. Hosp., 1955-60; mem. staff Walter Reed Army Inst. Rsch., 1961-74, chief dept. hematology, 1965-74; chief clin. investigation svc. Walter Reed Army Med. Ctr., 1971-74; clin. asst. prof., then clin. assoc. prof. medicine Georgetown U. Med. Sch., 1964-74; prof. medicine U. Ala. Med. Sch., Birmingham, 1974-83, also dir. div. hematology and oncology, 1974-83; prof. medicine, pathology, dir. divsn. hematology, oncology U. South Ala., Mobile, 1983—, dir. USA Cancer Ctr., 1985—. Contbr. numerous articles to med. publs. Commd. 1st lt. M.C. U.S. Army, 1953; advanced through grades to col. 1968. Decorated Legion of Merit with oak leaf cluster; recipient Skinner medal U.S. Army, 1955, Hoff medal, 1962, John Shaw Billings award, 1967, William Beaumont award, 1972, Walter Reed award, 1974. Fellow Internat. Soc. Hematology, ACP (Laureate award 1989); mem. AAAS, Assn. Am. Physicians, Internat. Soc. Hematology, Am. Soc. Clin. Investigation, Am. Physiol. Soc., Internat. Soc. Blood Transfusion, Am. Soc. Hematology, Am. Soc. Clin. Oncology, Am. Chem. Soc., Soc. Exptl. Biology and Medicine, So. Soc. Clin. Investigation, Am. Fedn. Clin. Rsch. Roman Catholic. E-mail: mconrad@usamail.usouthal.edu. Home: 28451 Perdido Pass Dr Orange Beach AL 36561-3602 Office: U South Ala USA Cancer Ctr Mobile AL 36688

CONRAD, MARIAN SUE (SUSAN CONRAD), special education educator; b. Columbus, Ohio, May 3, 1946; d. Harold Marion Griffith and Susie Belle (House) Goheen; m. Richard Lee Conrad, Jan. 23 1971. BS, Ohio State U., 1967. Tchr. spl. edn. West High Sch., Columbus, Ohio, 1967-70; spl. edn. work study coord. North High Sch., Columbus, 1974-79, Whetstone High Sch., Columbus, 1979-80, Briggs High Sch., Columbus, 1980-97, West High Sch., Columbus, 1970-97; ret., 1997. Bd. dirs. Jr. Div., The Columbus Symphony Club, 1972-79; vice chmn. Zoofari, Columbus, 1978-97; bd. dirs., life mem. Wazoo, Columbus, 1974-87; bd. dirs., chair coms. Jr. League, Columbus, 1982—; vice chmn. devel. com. Dublin (Ohio) Counseling Ctr., 1987-97; trustee Columbus Zoo, 1991—. Recipient Mayors Award for Vol. Svc., Columbus, 1988. Mem. Am. Bus. Women's Assn. (v.p. 1979-80, bd. dirs., Woman of Yr. 1980), Coun. Exceptional Children (pres. 1988-89, Educator of Yr. 1989), Ohio Assn. Suprs. and Work Study Coords., Dublin Women in Bus. and Professions, Country Club at Muirfield, Dublin Women's Club, Iota Lambda Sigma. Republican. Methodist. Avocations: golf, gardening, travel, family, cooking. Home: 8039 Crossgate Ct S Dublin OH 43017-8432

CONRAD, MELVIN LOUIS, biology educator; b. Kiowa, Kans., Mar. 10, 1927; s. Marvin Bearl and Elsie Louise (Murphy) C.; m. Eula Montes Vieira, Apr. 3, 1954; children: Albert Vieira Conrad, Celia Conrad Theiler, Daniel Vieira Conrad. BA in Biology, Southwestern Coll., 1950; MA, George Peabody Coll. Tchrs., 1956; PhD, U. Mo., 1980. Ednl. missionary Meth. Ch., Brazil, 1950-54; tchr. biology and gen. sci. McLeansboro (Ill.) Twp. High Sch., 1956-58; asst. prof. biology Oxford (Ga.) Coll. Emory U., 1958-67; from asst. prof. to prof. plant taxonomy N.E. Mo. State U. (name changed to Truman State U.), Kirksville, 1967-91, prof. emeritus, 1991—; vis. instr. botany U. Ga., Athens, 1967; mem. teaching staff Reis Biol. Sta., St. Louis U., nr. Steelville, Mo., 1988—; reviewer Army C.E., 1985. Bd. dirs. ARC, Kirksville, 1984-93, chmn. Adair County chpt. 1985, dir. blood svcs., 1993; bd. dirs. The Border Line Theatre, Inc., v.p., 1997—; chmn. Kiowa City Tree Bd., 1996—; bd. dirs. Kiowa Alumni Assn., chmn., 1997—; lay leader Kiowa United Meth. Ch., 1996, 97. Mem. Mo. Native Plant Soc. (pres. 1983-85), Am. Soc. Plant Taxonomists, Kans. Wildflower Soc., Am. Legion (post comdr. 1997—), Lions Internat. (dist. gov. 1983-84, other offices), Beta Beta Beta, Phi Sigma. Republican. Avocations: gardening, carpentry, photography, family genealogy. Home: 1014 Dickinson St Kiowa KS 67070-1726

CONRAD, PAUL ERNEST, transportation consultant; b. Hartford, Conn., June 11, 1927; s. Ernest and Agnes Anita (Eis) c.; m. Audrey Grace Lindner, June 17, 1947; children: Cynthia Dale, Robin Sue, Kristen Diane. BS, U. Conn., 1949. Hwy. engr. Fed. Hwy. Adminstrn., Southeast U.S., Conn. and N.Y., 1949-55; prin. assoc. Wilbur Smith & Assocs., Columbia, S.C., 1955-69, sr. v.p., 1969-72, exec. v.p., 1972-91, also bd. dirs. Bd. dirs. Spring Valley Homeowners Assn., 1976-77, 97-98. With USN, 1945-46. Mem. NSPE, ASCE, Inst. Transp. Engrs., Am. Cons. Engrs. Coun., Spring Valley Country Club (bd. govs. 1993-96, v.p. house). Lutheran. Home: 103 Enclave Loop Columbia SC 29223-3260

CONRAD, PAUL FRANCIS, editorial cartoonist; b. Cedar Rapids, Iowa, June 27, 1924; s. Robert H. and Florence G. (Lawler) C.; m. Barbara Kay King, Feb. 27, 1954; children: James, David, Carol, Elizabeth. B.A., U. Iowa, 1950. Editorial cartoonist Denver Post, 1950-64, L.A. Times, 1964-93; cartoonist L.A. Times Syndicate, 1973—; Richard M. Nixon chair Whittier Coll., 1977-78. Exhibited sculpture and cartoons, Los Angeles County Mus. Art, 1979; author: The King and Us, 1974, Pro and Conrad, 1979, Drawn and Quartered, 1985, CONArtist: Thirty Years With The Los Angeles Times, 1993, Drawing The Line, 1999. Served with C.E. AUS, 1942-46, PTO. Recipient Editorial Cartoon award Sigma Delta Chi, 1963, 69, 71, 81-82, 88, 97, Pulitzer prize editorial cartooning, 1964, 71, 84, Overseas Press Club award, 1970, 81, Journalism award U. So. Calif., 1972, Robert F. Kennedy Journalism award, 1st Prize, 1985, 90, 92, 93, Hugh M. Hefner 1st Amendment award, 1990, Lifetime Achievement award Am. Assn. Editl. Cartoonists, 1998. Fellow Soc. Profl. Journalists; mem. Phi Delta Theta. Democrat. Roman Catholic. Office: LA Times Syndicate 2121 Rosecrans Ave Ste 2370 El Segundo CA 90245-4745

CONRAD, PETER, sociology educator; b. N.Y.C., Apr. 12, 1945; s. George and Gertrude (Rosenthal) C.; m. Ylisabeth Bradshaw, Apr. 12, 1975; children: Rya, Jared. BA, SUNY, Buffalo, 1967; MA, Northeastern U., 1970; PhD, Boston U., 1976. From instr. to asst. prof. sociology Suffolk U., Boston, 1971-75; asst. prof. sociology Drake U., Des Moines, Iowa, 1975-78; from asst. prof. to prof. Brandeis U., Waltham, Mass., 1979—, Harry Coplan prof. social scis., 1993—; vis. asst. prof. NYU, N.Y.C., 1978. Co-author: Deviance and Medicalization, 1980, Having Epilepsy, 1983; editor: Sociology of Health and Illness, 1997; co-editor: Health and Health Care Developing Countries, 1992, Qualitative Sociology, 1982-87. Bd. dirs. Codman Cmty. Farm, Lincoln, Mass., 1987-92; commr. Conservation Commn., Lincoln, 1992—. Shannon grantee NIH, 1994-96; vis. scholar Harvard Med. Sch., Boston, 1986, Godjah Mada U., Yogyakata, Indonesia, 1989-90, Disting. Fulbright scholar Queen's U., Belfast, Ireland, 1997; recipient Charles Horton Cooley award, 1981. Mem. Am. Sociol. Assn. (chair med. sociology 1987-89), Soc. for Study of Social Problems (pres. 1995-96), Eastern Sociol. Soc. Avocations: biking, hiking, films, cooking Greek food, travel. Office: Brandeis U Dept Sociology Waltham MA 02254-9110

CONRAD, RICHARD A., opera singer, educator; b. N.Y.C., Aug. 12, 1935; s. Lester Alexander and Mildred Lillian (Murley) C. AAS, N.Y. State U., 1955; BFA, Boston U., 1957. artistic dir. Boston Acad. of Music, 1980—. Opera debut Am. premiere of Mozart's La Finta Semplice, Boston, 1961; recital debut Philips Collection, Washington, 1961; opera appearances with cos., orchs. on radio, TV in U.S., Can., Europe, Gt. Britain, Africa, 1961—; opera recordings on Decca/London, Pearl, CRI, Teldec, Westminster, Video of Bel Canto, among others.

CONRAD, ROAN, federal agency administrator; b. Bismarck, N.D., June 2, 1940. BA, Stanford U.; AM, Harvard U. Dir. Sustainable Devel. and Intergovernmental Affairs, Washington, 1998—. Office: Nat Oceanic/Atmospheric Adminstrn Dept of Commerce 14th Constitution Ave NW Washington DC 20230

CONRAD, ROBERT (CONRAD ROBERT FALK), actor, singer, producer, director; b. Chgo., Mar. 1, 1935. Ed., Northwestern U. Chief exec. officer Black Sheep Prodns., 1966—. Starred in TV series Hawaiian Eye, 1959-63, Wild Wild West, 1965-69, The D.A, 1971-72, miniseries Centennial, 1978, High Mountain Rangers, 1987; starred and directed TV series Baa Baa Black Sheep, 1976-78, The Duke, 1979, A Man Called Sloane, 1979, (film pilot) High Mountain Rangers, 1987, Jesse Hawkes, 1989, Search and Rescue, 1995—; appeared in films Thundering Jets, 1958, Palm Springs Weekend, 1963, Young Dillinger, 1965, Murph the Surf, 1975, Sudden Death, 1975, Wrong is Right, 1980, The Woman in Red, 1984, Moving Violations, 1985, Uncommon Courage, 1985, Anything to Survive, 1990, Wild Wild West, 1999; produced, starred in films Coach of the Year, 1980, TV films Will: G. Gordon Liddy, 1981, Hard Knox, 1983, Two Fathers' Justice, 1984, Charley Hannah, 1986; appeared in TV films Wild, Wild West Revisited, 1979, More Wild, Wild West, 1980, Breaking Up Is Hard To Do, 1980, Sullivan, 1985, Assassin, 1986, Glory Days, 1988, Anything To Survive, 1990, Mario and the Mob, 1991, (TV) Sworn to Vengeance, 1993, Search and Rescue, 1993, Two Fathers: Justice for the Innocent, 1993, (feature film) Jingle All The Way, 1996, New Jersey Turnpike's, 1998, Wild Wild West, 1999; actor (TV) Search and Rescue, 1994; dir. Crossfire, 1967, The Bandits, 1967, A Man Called Sloan, 1979, High Mountain Rangers, 1988, Glory Days, 1988; TV guest appearances include Maverick, Temple Houston, Mission: Impossible, Mannix. Office: care David Shapira & Assocs Inc 15301 Ventura Blvd Ste 345 Sherman Oaks CA 91403-3129*

CONRAD, ROBERT DAVID, broadcast executive, educator; b. Kankakee, Ill., July 17, 1933; s. Clarence P. and Geneva (Beatty) C.; m. Jean Smith, July 11, 1959; children: Caroline, Allison, Christopher, Susan, Andrea. BS, Northwestern U., 1955; DFA (hon.), Baldwin Wallce Coll., 1983; MusD (hon.), Cleve. Inst. Music, 1998. Announcer KULA, KAIM, Honolulu, 1956-57, WKAN, Kankakee, 1947-51; announcer, program dir. WEAW AM/FM, Evanston, Ill., 1951-54; announcer WFMT, Chgo., 1954-55, announcer, ops. mgr., 1957-60; program dir. WDTM, Detroit, 1960-62; v.p., program mgr. WCLV, Cleve., 1962-92, pres., broadcast mgr., 1992—; prodr., commentator Cleve. Orch., 1965—; broadcasting instr. Cuyahoga C.C., Cleve., 1984-91; adj. prof. broadcasting Case Western Res. U./Cleve. Inst. Music, 1991—. Bd. dirs., trustee Cleve. Music Sch. Settlement, 1995—, Friends of Cleveland Sch. of the Arts, 1998—. Named Program Dir. of Yr., Billboard Mag., N.Y., 1982. Mem. Concert Music Broadcasters Assn. (bd. dirs., pres. 1980-83), City Club Cleve. (past bd. mem., v.p. 1975-78). Office: WCLV 26501 Renaissance Pkwy Cleveland OH 44128-5798

CONRAD, STEVEN ALLEN, physician, biomedical engineer, educator, researcher; b. St. Martinville, La., Aug. 23, 1953; s. Karl Donovan and Dolores Beatrice (Bienvenu) C.; m. Mona Theresa Hollier, Aug. 9, 1974; children: David, Lesley, Taylor. BS, U. S.W. La., 1974; MD, La. State U., Shreveport, 1978; MS, Case Western Reserve, Cleve., 1980, PhD, 1985; MS in Engring., La. Tech. U., 1981. Diplomate Am. Bd. Internal Medicine, Critical Care Medicine, Am. Bd. Emergency Medicine; cert. nutritional support physician. Postdoctoral trainee in biomed. computing Case Western Res., 1979-80; resident internal medicine La. State U., Shreveport, 1981-84; fellow in critical care medicine Mayo Grad. Sch. Medicine, Rochester, 1984-86; asst. prof. medicine La. State U. Med. Ctr., Shreveport, 1986-91, assoc. prof. medicine, 1991—, dir. crit. care medicine tng. program, 1987—, dir. med. ICU, 1986—, assoc. prof. emergency medicine, 1996-97, chmn. dept. emergency medicine, 1996—; instr. in computer sci. Winona State U., 1985-86, asst. prof. physiology, 1988-91; adj. assoc. prof. biomed. engring. La. Tech. U., Ruston, 1989—, adj. prof. human ecology, 1996—, prof. emergency medicine and internal medicine, 1997—; adj. assoc. prof. mech. engring. Inst. for Micromanufacturing, 1994—; cons. physician critical care VA Med. Ctr., 1986—, dir. extracorporeal life support program, 1993—, co-dir. nutritional support svc., 1994—, transplant intensivist Willis Knighton Regional Heart Transplant Program, 1994—, attending physician in pediat. ICU, 1994—; mem. emergency med. svcs. task force Shreveport Fire Dept., 1992—; prin. investigator in multiple device and drug trials. Editor: Pulmonary Function Testing: Principles and Practice, 1984; manuscript reviewer ASAIO Jour., Artificial Organs; abstract reviewer Critical Care Medicine; contbr. chpts. to books and articles to profl. jours. Grantee Am. Heart Assn. Fellow ACP, Am. Coll. Crit. Care Med., Am. Coll. Chest Physicians, Am. Coll. Emergency Physicians; mem. IEEE, Biomed. Engring. Soc., Shock Soc., Am. Soc. Artificial Internal Organs, Internat. Soc. for Artificial Organs, Soc. for Acad. Emergency Medicine, Am. Soc. for Parenteral and Enteral Nutrition, Alpha Omega Alpha, Sigma Xi, Phi Kappa Phi. Office: La State U Med Ctr 1501 Kings Hwy Shreveport LA 71103-4228

CONRAD, THOMAS, basketball coach; b. McSherrytown, Pa.; m. Cheryl Conrad; children: Kyle, Liza. BS, Old Dominion U. Asst. basketball coach Old Dominion U., 1979-80, U. N.C., Asheville, 1988-91; asst. varsity coach, head coach jr. varsity Ky. Wesleyan U., 1981-83; head coach St. Michael's Coll., Vt., 1983-88, Charleston (S.C.) So. U., 1992—. Office: Charleston So U PO Box 118087 Charleston SC 29423-8087*

CONRAD, WILLIAM MERRILL, architect; b. Sapulpa, Okla., Sept. 5, 1926; s. William Samuel and Lillian Lorraine (Strain) C.; m. Esther Marian Lenz, Nov. 8, 1952. BS in Architecture, U. Kans., 1950, BSBA, 1951. Lic. architect. Prin., architect William M. Conrad, F.A.I.A., Kansas City, Mo., 1956—; asst. prof., Sch. of Architecture and Urban Design U. Kans., Lawrence, 1956-59; mem. adv. com. U. Kans. Sch. of Architecture and Urban Design, 1974-86; vis. Fulbright prof., U. Helsinki, 1958-59. Mem. Kans. City-St. Joseph Bldg. Commn., 1970-82. With USN, 1944-46. Recipient Patriotic Svc. award Dept. Army, 1974, 84, Nat. Friend of Park and Recreation award Nat. Assn. Park and Recreation Ofcls., 1982, Urban Design award Mcpl. Art Com., Kansas City, 1976, Disting. Alumnus award U. Kans. Sch. Arch. and Urban Design, 1993. Fellow AIA (treas. nat. conv. 1979, Kansas City chpt. pres. 1968, past sec., other offices, mem. numerous coms., Cmty. Svc. award 1990, numerous other awards); mem. SAR (Good Citizenship award 1997), Mo. Coun. Architects (past dir. and treas.), People to People Internat. (pres. Greater Kansas City chpt. 1972-74, chmn. Gt. Plains regional coun. 1974-77, chmn. bd. dirs., trustee 1985-89, internat. pres. 1988-91, Disting. Mem. award 1986, Eisenhower Lifetime Achievement award 1996), Optimists (past pres. Honor Club), Masons, Scottish Rite, Shriners (pres. 1990), Sertoma Kans. dist. gov. 1984-86, pres. Honor Club 1982-84, Sertoman of Yr. 1987, Outstanding Regional Sec. award 1995), Tau Beta Pi (life), Tau Sigma Delta. Presbyterian. Home: 6120 W 69th St Overland Park KS 66204-1411 Office: Plaza Ctr Bldg 800 W 47th St Kansas City MO 64112-1251

CONRAD, WINTHROP BROWN, JR., lawyer; b. Detroit, May 26, 1945; s. Winthrop Brown and Dolores (Millard) C.; m. Ellen Rouse, May 12, 1973; children: Parker Rouse, Louisa Katherine, Frances Winthrop. AB, Yale U., 1967; JD, Harvard U., 1971. Bar: N.Y. 1972, U.S. Dist. Ct. (so. dist.) N.Y. 1975, U.S. Ct. Appeals (2d cir.) 1975. Ptnr. Davis, Polk & Wardwell, N.Y.C., 1979—, Paris Office, 1985-88. Bd. dirs. Found. for Joffrey Ballet, N.Y.C., 1985-86, British-Am. Ednl. Found.; trustee Episcopal Diocese of N.Y.; trustee Estate and Property of the Conv. of the Diocese of N.Y., Ch. Pension Fund; dir., BAR Vermont Inc. Mem. ABA, Assn. of Bar of City of N.Y. Home: 1120 5th Ave New York NY 10128-0144 Office: Davis Polk & Wardwell 450 Lexington Ave New York NY 10017-3911 also: 856 Old Post Rd Bedford NY 10506-1215

CONRAD-ENGLAND, ROBERTA LEE, pathologist; b. Meriden, Conn., Aug. 25, 1950; d. Hans and Emma Ann (Bort) Conrad; m. Gary Thomas England, June 6, 1976; children: Eric Bryan, Christopher Ryan. BS in Microbiology, U. Ky., 1972, MD, 1976. Diplomate Nat. Bd. Med. Examiners, Bd. Am. Pathologists. Resident anatomic and clin. pathology Emory U. Affiliated Hosps., Atlanta, 1976-80; pathologist Western Bapt. Hosp., Paducah, Ky., 1980—; cons. Marshall County Hosp., Benton, Ky., 1985—, chair infection control com., 1985—. Mem., com. chairperson PTA, Paducah, Ky., 1993-94; mother's asst. Boy Scouts Am., Paducah, 1991-94. Fellow Coll. Am. Pathologists, Am. Soc. Clin. Pathologists; mem. Ky. Med. Assn., Ky. Soc. Pathologists, Ky. Women Mentors in Sci., Alpha Omega Alpha, Phi Beta Kappa. Avocations: swimming, snorkeling, interior decorating.

CONRADER, CONSTANCE RUTH, artist, writer, librarian; b. Vandalia, Mo., Apr. 13, 1919; d. Gilbert Fordyce and Elizabeth Florence (Cleghorn) Stone; m. Jay Merten Conrader, Nov. 29, 1941 (dec. 1996). Student, Carroll Coll., 1938-40, North Park Coll., 1940-41. Cert. pub. libr. Artist, author Oconomowoc, Wis., 1940—; libr. Oconomowoc Pub. Libr., 1947-82, vol. 1982—; illustrator Turtox classroom charts Gen. Biol. Supply House, Chgo., 1940-60; manuscript critique Baha'i Pub. Trust, Wilmette, Ill., 1970-89, editor, 1988. Author, illustrator: Blue Wampum, 1958; co-editor: Tokens From the Writings of Baha'u'llah, 1973, Baha'i newsletter, 1997—; illustrator: Northwoods Wildlife Region, 1983; co-author, illustrator articles to profl. jours.; co-editor regional Baha'i Newsletter, 1997—. Chair UN Day, Oconomowoc, 1976-86. Avocations: gardening, music, reading.

CONRADES, GEORGE HENRY, information systems company executive; b. St. Louis, Feb. 26, 1939; s. Ralph Andrew and Elizabeth (Quermann) C.; m. Patricia Ruth Belt, Feb. 9, 1963; children: Elizabeth, Laura, George, Mary Emma, Anna. BA in Physics and Math., Ohio Wesleyan U., 1961; MBA, U. Chgo., 1971. With IBM Corp., 1961-93; pres. data processing div. IBM Corp., White Plains, N.Y., 1980-82; corp. v.p. IBM Corp., Armonk, 1981-82, pres. nat. accounts div., 1982-83; corp. v.p., asst. group exec. Info. Systems and Tech. Group IBM Corp., Harrison, N.Y., 1983-84; corp. v.p., group exec. Asia/Pacific Group IBM Corp., Tokyo, 1984-86, sr. v.p., group exec. Info. Systems and Products Group, 1986-87; corp. sr. v.p. IBM Corp., Armonk, 1986—; gen. mgr. Personal Systems IBM Corp., White Plains, N.Y., 1988, U.S. Mktg. & Svcs., IBM Corp., White Plains, 1988-90; sr. v.p., gen. mgr. IBM U.S. IBM Corp., White Plains, 1990-91; dir. BBN Corp., Cambridge, Mass., 1993-94; chmn., CEO GTE Internetworking, Cambridge, Mass., 1994—; mem. bd dirs. Westinghouse. Chmn. bd. trustees Ohio Wesleyan U., Delaware, Ohio, Coun. Grad. Sch. Bus. U. Chgo. Mem. Electrical Mfrs. Club. Office: GTE Internetworking 150 Cambridgepark Dr Cambridge MA 02140-2322

CONRAN, JOSEPH PALMER, lawyer; b. St. Louis, Oct. 4, 1945; s. Palmer and Theresa (Bussmann) C.; m. Daria D. Conran, June 8, 1968; children: Andrew, Lisabeth, Theresa. BA, St. Louis U., 1967, JD with honors, 1970. Bar: Mo. 1970, U.S. Ct. Mil. Appeals 1971, U.S. Ct. Appeals (8th cir.) 1974. Assoc. Husch and Eppenberger, St. Louis, 1974-78, ptnr., 1978—, chmn. litigation dept., 1980-95, chmn. mgmt. com. 1995—; mem. faculty Trial Practice Inst. Capt., JAGC, USAF, 1970-74. Mem. Bar Assn. Met. St. Louis (Merit award 1976,77), Mo. Bar Assn. (bd. govs. 1987-92), Mo. Athletic (pres. 1986-87), Norwood Hills Country Club. Roman Catholic. Home: 53 Hawthorne Est Saint Louis MO 63131-3035 Office: Husch & Eppenberger 100 N Broadway Ste 1300 Saint Louis MO 63102-2789

CONROY, CATHERINE MARTIN, public relations executive; b. Bklyn., Dec. 29, 1948; m. Robert Ellsworth Conroy, 1972; 1 child, Amy Elizabeth. BA, Bklyn. Coll., 1970. Adminstrv. dir. Met. Golf Assn., N.Y.C., 1970-74; v.p. Blyth, Eastman Dillon & Co., Inc., N.Y.C., 1975-78; asst. v.p. Merrill Lynch, N.Y.C., 1978-83; sr. v.p. Donaldson, Lufkin & Jenrette, Inc., N.Y.C., 1983—. Mem. Pub. Rels. Soc. Am., Fin. Comm. Soc. Office: Donaldson Lufkin & Jenrette Inc 277 Park Ave New York NY 10017-2016*

CONROY, PAT (DONALD PATRICK CONROY), writer; b. Atlanta, Oct. 26, 1945; s. Donald and Frances Dorothy (Peek) C.; m. Barbara Bolling, 1969 (div. 1977); children: Jessica, Melissa, Megan; m. Lenore Gurewitz, 1981 (div. 1995); children: Gregory, Emily, Susannah. BA in English, The Citadel, 1967. Author: The Boo, 1970, The Water Is Wide, 1972 (Anisfield-Wolf award Cleve. Found. 1972), The Great Santini, 1976, The Lords of Discipline, 1980 (Lillian Smith award for fiction So. Regional Council 1981), The Prince of Tides, 1986, Beach Music, 1995; screenwriter: (TV movie) Invictus, 1988, (with Becky Johnson) The Prince of Tides, 1991 (Academy Award nomination best adapted screenplay 1991), Beach Music, 1997. Ford Found. Leadership Devel. grantee, 1971; recipient NEA award for achievement in education, 1974, Ga. Gov.'s award for Arts, 1978, Golden Plate award Am. Acad. Achievement, 1992, Thomas Cooper Libr. Soc. Literary award U. S.C., 1995, S.C. Gov.'s award in the Humanities for disting. achievement, 1996, Humanitarian award Ga. Commn. on the Holocaust, 1996, Lotos medal of Merit for outstanding literary achievement, 1996. Mem. Authors Guild Am., Writers Guild, PEN. Democrat. Office: care Doubleday 1540 Broadway New York NY 10036-4039*

CONROY, ROBERT JOHN, lawyer; b. Newark, Feb. 17, 1953; s. Michael John and Frances (Goncalves) C.; m. Mary Catherine McGuire, June 7, 1975; children: Caitlin Michaela, Michael Colin. BS, St. Peter's Coll., 1977; M in Pub. Adminstrn., CUNY, 1981; JD, N.Y. Law Sch., 1981; MPH, Harvard U., 1985. Bar: N.Y. 1981, N.J. 1981, U.S. Dist. N.J. 1981, Calif. 1982, U.S. Dist. Ct. (so. and ea. dists.) N.Y. 1982, U.S. Dist. Ct. (we. dist.) Calif. 1990, U.S. Ct. Appeals (2d, 3d and 11th cirs.) 1982, Fla. 1984, D.C. 1984, U.S. Supreme Ct. 1984. Asst. corp. counsel City of N.Y., 1981-83, dep. chief med. malpractice unit, 1983, chief med. malpractice unit, 1984; assoc. Jones, Hirsch, Connors & Bull, N.Y.C., 1985-88; counsel Kern & Augustine, P.A., Morristown, N.J., 1988-90; prin. Kern Augustine Conroy & Schoppmann, P.C., Bridgewater, N.J. and Lake Success, N.Y., 1990—; spl. counsel pro bono med. malpractice rsch. project, N.Y.C., 1985-88. Solomon scholar, N.Y. Law Sch., 1979. Fellow Coll. Law Practice Mgmt.; mem. ABA (chmn. govt. mgmt. com. 1984-86, mgr. products media bd. 1985-92, chmn. document retrieval com. 1985-86, vice chmn. ins. and malpractice com. 1986-88, co-chmn. glass ceiling task force 1992-95, vice chmn. law practice mgmt. phb. bd. 1992-95, coun. mem. 1989-95, co-chmn. law practice mgmt. pub. bd. 1995-98), N.J. Bar Assn. (dir., chmn. health hosp. sect. 1993-95, mem. com. health law litigation, mem. subcom. profl. licensing 1997—, del. gen. coun. adminstrn. sect. 1995-97), Soc. Health Care Risk Mgmt. N.J. (chmn. legis. com. 1987-96), Westfield Sr. Citizens Housing Corp., Inc. (trustee 1994—, v.p. 1996-98, pres. 1998—), Cmty. Health Law Project N.J., Inc. (trustee 1988-91), Assn. of Bar of City of N.Y., N.Y. Bar Assn. (mem. health law sect. 1996—), Harvard Club, Phi Alpha Alpha. Home: 905 Pennsylvania Ave Westfield NJ 07090-3433 Office: Kern Augustine Conroy & Schoppmann PC 1120 Rt 22 Bridgewater NJ 08807

CONROY, SARAH BOOTH, columnist, novelist, speaker; b. Valdosta, Ga., Feb. 16, 1927; d. Weston Anthony and Ruth (Proctor) Booth; m. Richard Timothy Conroy, Dec. 31, 1949; children: Camille Booth, Sarah Claire. B.S., U. Tenn., 1950. Continuity writer Sta. WNOX, 1945-48; commentator, writer Sta. WATO, 1948-49; reporter, architecture columnist Knoxville News Sentinel, 1949-56; assoc. editor The Diplomat mag., 1956-58; columnist Washington Post, 1957-58, design editor, columnist, 1970-82, feature writer, columnist, 1982-94, Chronicles columnist, 1986—; reporter, art critic Washington Daily News, 1968-70; regular contbr. N.Y. Times, 1968-70; mem. adv. bd. Horizon mag., 1978-85. Author: Refinements of

Love A Novel about Clover and Henry Adams, 1993. Recipient Raven award Mystery Writers Am., 1990, U. Tenn. Disting. Alumni award, 1995, Mortar Bd. award, 1997. Mem. AIA (hon.). Home: 5016 16th St NW Washington DC 20011-3842 Office: The Washington Post 1150 15th St NW Washington DC 20071-0002

CONROY, TAMARA BOKS, artist, special education educator, former nurse; b. Most, Bohemia, Czechoslovakia; came to U.S., 1947; d. Alois and Tatiana (Shapilova) Boks; m. John P. Conroy, Aug. 19, 1950 (dec. Oct. 1973); 1 child, Michael Thomas (dec.). Student, U. Graz, Austria, 1945-47; RN, New Rochelle (N.Y.) Med. Ctr., 1950; student, Coll. of William & Mary, 1958, 59, Cath. U. Am., 1960; BS in Nursing Edn., Columbia U., 1963, MA in Spl. Edn., 1965. RN, N.Y.; cert. spl. edn. tchr., N.Y. Nurse accident rm. New Rochelle Hosp./Med. Ctr., 1950-51; pub. health nurse Va. Dept. of Health, Richmond, 1958-59; tchr. spl. edn. Southern Westchester Bd. Coop. Edn. Svcs., Portchester, N.Y., 1965-83; freelance artist and painter N.Y.C. and Pelham, N.Y., 1969—; asst. to chmn. math. dept. Columbia U., N.Y.C., 1975-76. Author math. program Learning Numbers-Step by Step, 1977. Pres., founder Classical Music Lovers' Exch., Pelham, N.Y., 1980-98. Mem. Am. Fedn. Tchrs., N.Y. State United Tchrs., BOCES Tchrs. Assn. (profl.), Women's Mus. Group, Mamaroneck Artists Guild, Silvermine Artists Guild, Westchester Musicians Guild (assoc.), Kappa Delta Pi. Avocations: flying, reading, music, fashion designing.

CONROY, THOMAS FRANCIS, insurance company executive; b. Chgo., Sept. 26, 1938; s. Thomas Francis and Eleanor Althea (Heatherly) C.; m. Mary Elizabeth Schaeffer, June 19, 1965; children: Alexandra B., Margaret E. BSc, De Paul U., 1959; MBA, U. Chgo., 1969. CPA, CDP. Mgr. Ernst & Whinney, Chgo., 1959-74; exec. v.p. fin., treas., contr. Security Life of Denver, 1974-93; prin. Ea. Hemisphere Trading Corp., Denver, 1990—; pres. Security Life Reins., 1993—, ING Reins., 1993-98; bd. dirs. Buffalo Mountain Met. Dist. Bd. trustees Denver Chamber Orch., 1988-93. Capt. U.S. Army, 1960-62. Fellow Life Mgmt. Inst. Roman Catholic. Office: 1290 Broadway Denver CO 80203-2122

CONROY, WILLIAM B., university administrator; b. Malone, N.Y.; m. Patricia Conroy; children: Kathryn, William Michael, David, Carol, Kevin. B in History magna cum laude, U. Notre Dame, 1953; MEd, Syracuse U., 1959, D in Social Sci., 1963. Tchr. U. Tex., U. Wash., Tex. Tech. U.; exec. v.p. N.Mex. State U., Las Cruces, 1985-97, interim pres., 1994-95, pres., 1997—. Mem. Nat. Coun. Geog. Edn., Assn. Am. Geographers, Southwestern Social Sci. Assn. (past pres.), N.Mex. Coun. Univ. Presidents, Las Cruces C. of C. (bd. trustees town-gown com.). Fax: (505) 646-6344. E-mail: wconroy@nmsu.edu. Office: Box 30001 Las Cruces NM 88003-8001

CONROY-LACIVITA, DIANE CATHERINE, city administrator; b. Niskayuna, N.Y., Aug. 22, 1965; d. William John and Bernice Mary (Paluch) Conroy; m. Joseph James LaCivita, Nov. 5, 1988; children: Frances Catherine LaCivita, Catherine Elizabeth LaCivita, Louis Philip LaCivita. BA, SUNY, Oswego, 1986; Master's degree, SUNY, Albany, 1991. Exec. dir. Shaker Heritage Soc., Albany, N.Y., 1988-92; asst. dir. tng. N.Y. State Martin Luther King Jr. Commn. & Inst., Albany, 1992-96; asst. exec. dir. Latham (N.Y.) Area C. of C., 1996-97; dep. town clk. Town of Colonie, N.Y., 1997—; cons. N.Y. State Dept. Corrections, Albany, 1996-97. V.p., mem. Friends of the Pruyn House, 1997—; mem. Latham Ridge PTA, 1996—; mem. Colonie Women's Rep. Com., 1997—, Colonie Youth Ctr. Ann. Dinner Com., 1998, 99. Mem. Capital Region Aviation Assn. (bd. dirs., publicity chair), Shaker Heritage Soc. (bd. dirs.), Albany Airport Rotary Club (newsletter editor 1997—). Avocations: private pilot training, gardening, speed skating. Office: Town of Colonie Memorial Town Hall 534 Loudon Rd Newtonville NY 12110-5316

CONRY, THOMAS FRANCIS, mechanical engineering educator, consultant; b. West Hempstead, N.Y., Mar. 7, 1942; s. Thomas and Bridget Anne (Walsh) C.; m. Sharon Ann Silverwood, June 10, 1967; children: Christine Elizabeth, Carolyn Danielle, Anne Marie. BS, Pa. State U., 1963; MS, U. Wis.-Madison, 1967, PhD, 1970. Registered profl. engr., Wis., Ill. Engr. Gen. Motors Corp., Milw., 1963-66; sr. research engr. Gen. Motors Corp., Indpls., 1969-71; asst. prof. gen. engring. U. Ill., Urbana, 1971-75, assoc. prof. gen. and mech. engring., 1975-81, prof. gen. and mech. engring., 1981—; co-dir. mng. engring. program Coll. Engring., Urbana, 1986-89, head dept. gen. engring., 1987-98, coord. program in tech. and bus., 1995-98; sr. visitor U. Cambridge (Eng.), 1978; cons. Zurn Industries, 1974-83; staff cons. Sargent & Lundy, Engrs., 1977, 79; cons.-evaluator commn. on instns. of higher edn. North Ctl. Assn., 1983—; cons. indsl. firm on machine dynamics, optimization and tribology. NSF trainee, 1968-69; NASA/ASEE summer faculty fellow, 1974-75. Contbr. articles to profl. jours. Mem. Bd. Edn. St. Matthews Parish Roman Catholic Ch., Champaign, 1981-84. Fellow ASME (chmn. design engring. divsn. 1979-80, tech. editor Jour. Vibration, Acoustics, Stress and Reliability in Design, 1984-89, mem. bd. on communications 1989-93, 96—, mem. com. on fin. and investment 1999—); mem. Am. Soc. Engring. Edn., Rotary, Sigma Xi, Lambda Chi Alpha, Phi Kappa Phi. Home: 3301 Lakeshore Dr Champaign IL 61822-5205 Office: 104 S Mathews Ave Urbana IL 61801-2925

CONSAGRA, SOPHIE CHANDLER, academy administrator; b. Radnor, Pa., Apr. 28, 1927; d. Alfred D. and Carol (Ramsay) Chandler; children: Maria, Pierluigi, Francesca, George. B.A., Smith Coll., 1949; M.A., Cambridge (Eng.) U., 1952. Exec. dir. Del. Arts Council, 1972-78; dir. visual arts and architecture N.Y. State Council Arts, 1978-80; dir. Am. Acad. in Rome, 1980-84, pres., 1984-88, pres. emerita, vice chmn./spl. projects, 1988-90; cons. Nat. Endowment Arts. Recipient Smith Coll. award, 1986, Centennial medal Am. Acad. in Rome, 1995. Address: 955 Lexington Ave New York NY 10021-5107

CONSER, WALTER HURLEY, JR., religion and philosophy educator; b. Riverside, Calif., Apr. 4, 1949; s. Walter Hurley and Barbara Healy C.; m. Janet Gunter, June 7, 1986; 1 child, Emily. BA, U. Calif., Irvine, 1971; MA, Brown U., 1974, PhD, 1981. From vis. asst. prof. to prof. U. N.C., Wilmington, 1985—. Author: Church and Confession, 1984, God and the Natural World, 1993; editor: Experiences of the Sacred, 1992, Sacred Spaces, 1999; mem. adv. bd. Jour. So. Religion, 1997—. Mem. Am. Hist. Assn. Mem. Am. Acad. Religion. Office: Dept Philosophy and Religion U NC 601 S College Rd Wilmington NC 28403-3297

CONSEY, KEVIN EDWARD, museum administrator; b. N.Y.C., Jan. 15, 1952; s. Edward and Dorothy (Kemmann) C.; m. Susan Mary Kirsch, Aug. 26, 1972. BA, Hofstra U., 1974; M in Mus. Practice, MA, U. Mich., 1977. Dir. Emily Lowe Gallery, Hofstra U., Hempstead, N.Y., 1977-80, San Antonio Mus. Art., 1980-83; dir., chief exec. officer Newport Harbor Art Mus., Newport Beach, Calif., 1983-89, Mus. Contemporary Art, Chgo., 1989—; panelist profl. devel. Nat. Endowment for Arts, Washington, 1987-88, panelist challenge grant, 1988, panelist mus. program, 1989-90, panelist F.A.C.I.E., 1991-94. Hofstra U. scholar, 1970-74, Guggenheim Mus. intern, 1976; grantee Nat. Mus. Act, 1976-77. Mem. Assn. Art Mus. Dirs., Coll. Art Assn. Office: Mus Contemporary Art 220 E Chicago Ave Chicago IL 60611-2604*

CONSIDINE, JOHN JOSEPH, advertising executive; b. Jersey City, N.J., Sept. 6, 1941; s. Joseph Patrick and Helen (Hrezak) C.; m. Catherine Christine Noone, Nov. 26, 1966; children: Elizabeth, Laura, Adam, Kate. BA, St. Peter's Coll., Jersey City, 1963. Rsch. analyst Prudential Ins. Co., Newark, 1964-66; asst. rsch. mgr. The Mennen Co., Morristown, N.J., 1966-68; rsch. mgr. The Gillette Co., Boston, 1968-69; rsch. dir. W. B. Doner & Co., Detroit, 1969-74, sr. v.p., corp. rsch. dir., 1974-82, exec. v.p., corp. dir. strategic planning, 1982-94, vice chmn., 1994—. Mem. Pine Lake Country Club (West Bloomfield, Mich.). Home: 3652 Erie Dr West Bloomfield MI 48324-1524 Office: W B Doner & Co 25900 Northwestern Hwy West Bloomfield MI 48075-1067*

CONSIGLIO, HELEN, nursing educator and consultant; b. Wyandotte, Mich., June 21, 1962; d. Francis and Helen (Grabowski) Zgoda; m. Anthony Consiglio, Nov. 10, 1989. BSN, Madonna Coll., 1984; postgrad., U. Mich., Dearborn, 1984-85, Madonna Coll., 1987. RN, Mich. Student tutor Ctr. for Personalized Instrn., Madonna Coll., Livonia, Mich., 1981-84; nursing asst. Wyandotte (Mich.) Hosp. and Med. Ctr., 1983-90, staff nurse, critical care instr.; nurse surg.-ICU Henry Ford Hosp., Detroit, 1990-91; staff nurse, consultant Nurses Plus, Inc., Wyandotte, Mich., 1991-96; staff nurse pre-op/post anesthesia care unit Oakwood Hosp. and Med. Ctr., Dearborn, Mich., 1996—; speaker, researcher in field; adj. clin. faculty Oakland Community Coll., Union Lake, Mich., 1992-94. Producer ednl. videotape. Mem. Am. Assn. Critical Care Nurses, Sigma Theta Tau. Office: Nurses Plus Inc 140 Elm St Wyandotte MI 48192-5921

CONSILIO, BARBARA ANN, legal administrator, management consultant; b. Cleve., June 22, 1938; d. Joseph B. and Anna E. (Ford) C. BS, Kent State U., 1962; MA, U. Detroit, 1973. Cert. social worker, Mich. Tchr. Chagrin Falls (Ohio) High Sch., 1962-64; probation officer Macomb County Juvenile Ct., Mt. Clemens, Mich., 1965-68, casework supr., 1968-74; dir. children's svcs. Macomb County Juvenile Ct., Mt. Clemens, 1974-79; mgr. foster care and instns. Oakland County Juvenile Ct., Pontiac, Mich., 1979-83; ct. adminstr. Oakland County Probate Ct., Pontiac, 1983-93, ret., 1993. Bd. dirs. Children's Charter Cts. of Mich., Lansing, Statewide Adv. Bd. on Sexual Abuse, Lansing, Havenwyck Hosp., Auburn Hills, Orchards Children's Svcs., Southfield, Oakland County Coun. Children at Risk, Pontiac; mem. Nat. Women's Polit. Caucus, N.Y.C.; bd. dirs. Care House, Pontiac. Mem. Nat. Coun. Juvenile and Family Ct. Adminstrs. Group, Mich. Probate and Juvenile Register's Assn., Mich. Juvenile Ct. Adminstrs. Assn., Nat. Assn. Ct. Mgrs., Supreme Ct. Task Force on Racial and Ethnic Bias, Office of Children and Youth Svcs. (state foster care system rev. com.), Nat. Coun. Juvenile and Family Ct. Judges (Outstanding Ct. Adminstr. award, 1993). Avocations: music, sports, sports cars. Home: 958 Canyon View Rd Sagamore Hls OH 44067-2279

CONSOLI, MARC-ANTONIO, composer; b. Catania, Italy, May 19, 1941; came to U.S., 1956, naturalized, 1967; s. Francesco Gabriele Settimio and Rosa (Puglisi) C.; m. Elizabeth Jean Szlek, June 19, 1971. B.Mus., N.Y. Coll. Music, 1966; M.Mus., Peabody Conservatory, 1967; M.Mus. Arts, Yale U., 1971, D.Mus. Arts, 1977. lectr. Bridgeport U.; vis. prof. U. Western Ont., 1975. Composer, works performed by Balt. Symphony Orch., N.Y. Philharm., Los Angeles Philharm., Louisville Orch.,, Ensemble Kontrapunkte, Vienna, Austria, Monday Evening Concerts, Los Angeles, Berkshire Music Center, Yale Players for New Music, Gaudeamus Festival, Netherlands, Royan Festival, France; commns. for Graz (Austria) radio sta., Royan Festival, others; performer, dir.-mem., Yale Players for New Music, 1969-71, The Experiment, 1974, Equinox I, 1967, Equinox II, 1968, Isonic, 1970, Interactions I-V, 1970-71, Profiles, 1972-73, Music for Chambers, 1974, Canti Trinacriani, 1975, Sciuri Novi I, 1974, Sciuri Novi II, 1975, Tre Canzoni, 1976, Odefonia, 1976, Vuci Siculani, 1979, Tre Fiori Musicali, 1979, Naked Masks, 1980, The Last Unicorn, 1981, Orpheus' Meditation, 1981, Saxlodie, 1981, Afterimages, 1982; String Quartet, 1983, Fantasia Celeste, 1983, Ancient Greek Lyrics, 1984, 88, Musiculi II (summer), 1985, Reflections, 1986, Eyes of the Peacock, 1987, Sans Parole I and II, 1988, Cello Concerto, 1988, String Quartet II, 1989, Arie Mutate, 1990, Musiculi IV (winter), 1990/92, Musiculi III (autumn), 1992/94, Games for 2 and 3, 1994/95, Cinque Canti, 1995, Varie Azioni, Di-ver-ti-mento, (Games for 4), 1995—, Sciuri Novi III, 1997, Pensieri Sospesi, 1997, Rounds & Relays, 1997. Recipient award Nat. Inst.-Am. Acad. Arts and Letters, 1975; Guggenheim Found. fellow, 1971-72, 79-80; Fulbright fellow Poland, 1972-74; Creative Artists Pub. Service grantee, 1975; Nat. Endowment for Arts grantee, 1979, 81, 85. Mem. Broadcast Music Inc., Am. Composers Alliance, Am. Music Center.

CONSTABLE, BURT WILSON, newspaper columnist; b. Lafayette, Ind., Dec. 3, 1957; s. Wilson Wayne and Lois Yvonne (Schembs) C.; m. Cheryl Ann Terhorst, Mar. 26, 1988; children; Ross Terhorst, Benjamin Wilson. BS in Journalism, Northwestern U., Evanston, Ill., 1980. Reporter Washington (Iowa) Evening Jour., 1980-81; reporter, copy editor Daily Herald, Arlington Heights, Ill., 1981-88, columnist, 1988—. Big brother Cmty. Response, Oak Park, Ill., 1992—. Recipient Lisajor award Chgo. Headline Club, 1989, 91, 93, 1st pl. columnist UPI, 1989. Avocation: travel.

CONSTABLE, JOHN, advertising executive; b. 1943. Pvt. practice London, 1964-76; with Cramer Krasselt Co., Milw., 1976-78; ptnr. Laughlin/Constable Inc., Milw., 1978—, now v.p., sec., ptnr., creative dir., art dir., 1978—. Office: Laughlin/Constable Inc 207 E Michigan St Stop 1 Milwaukee WI 53202-4996*

CONSTABLE, WILLIAM GORDON, real estate development executive, lawyer; b. Manchester, N.H., May 5, 1950; s. William McMillan and Barbara (Fischer) C.; m. Katharine Preston (div. 1985); 1 child, W. Malcoln. BA, Williams Coll., 1972; M in Forestry and Environ. Studies, Yale U., 1974; JD, Boston U., 1979. Bar: Mass., 1979. Of counsel Warner & Stackpole, Boston, 1979—; sr. v.p. A.W. Perry, Inc., Boston, 1985—; chmn. Lincoln (Mass.) Land Conservation Trust, 1988—; adj. faculty Lincoln Inst. Land Policy, Cambridge, 1992—; bd. dirs. Old South Meeting House, Boston, Move Mass. 2000, Boston, Environ. League Mass., Boston. Editor: Guide to Lincoln Conservation, 1991. Chmn. Lincoln Planning Bd., 1979-89; mem. Lincoln Housing Commn., 1989-94; pres. Met. Area Planning Coun., Boston, 1995-97. Recipient Profl. Leadership award N.E. Am. Planning Assn., 1989; Loeb fellow Harvard Grad. Sch. Design, Cambridge, Mass., 1993-94. Mem. Greater Boston Real Estate Bd. Avocations: kayaking, fly fishing, community building. Office: AW Perry Inc 5th Fl 20 Winthrop Sq Fl 5 Boston MA 02110-1229

CONSTANCE, BARBARA ANN, financial planner, small business owner, consultant; b. Springfield, Mass., Dec. 24, 1945; d. Edward F. and Margaret E. (Price) Corcoran; m. Thomas F. Tiedgen, Apr. 27, 1968 (div. 1975); m. G. Lawrence Gadsby Jr., May 5, 1978 (div. 1991); m. F. David Constance, Dec. 6, 1991. AA, Vt. Coll., Montpelier, 1965. CLU; chartered fin. cons. Adminstrv. asst. Mass. Mut. Life Co., Springfield and Hartford, Conn., 1965-75; office mgr. Am. Nat. Life Ins. Co., Springfield, 1976; traveling trainee Conn. Gen. Life Ins. Co., Bloomfield, 1976; sales rep. Conn. Gen. Life Ins. Co., Springfield, 1976-77; dir. mktg. NN Life Ins. Services, Johnston, R.I., 1978-80; sales rep. New Eng. Mut. Life Co., Providence, 1980-82; pvt. practice fin. planner Tiverton, R.I., 1982-97; pres., founder Heritage Prodns., Ltd., Tiverton, R.I., 1988-91; cons. Northwestern Mutual Life Ins. Co., Providence, 1986-87; co-founder, bd. dirs. Career Connections, Inc.; co-capt. SV/Nootka, 1997—. Bd. dirs. YWCA of Greater R.I., Big Sister Assn. of R.I. Mem. Am. Soc. CLUs and ChFC (past pres. R.I. chpt.), Nat. Assn. Life Underwriters, R.I. Life Underwriters, Assn. Health Ins. Agts., Newport County Women's Network (co-founder), R.I. Woman's Career Network, R.I. Bus. Esch., R.I. Estate Planning Coun. Republican. Episcopalian. Home: 434 Bliss Rd Longmeadow MA 01106-1548

CONSTANDY, JOHN PETER, lawyer; b. N.Y.C., June 11, 1924; s. Peter Kosta and Cecelia (Grammas) C.; m. Ruth Corrine Mitchel, Nov. 10, 1951 (dec. Nov. 1984); m. Arlette Nicole Schmitt, Jan. 26, 1985. Student, Okla. A&M U., 1943, U. Bridgeport, 1946-47, U. Miami, 1947-49; LL.B., Northeastern U., 1951. Bar: N.Y. 1954, D.C. 1975. Asst. dist. atty. New York County, N.Y.C., 1955-58; asst. counsel U.S. Senate Select Com. on Improper Practices in the Labor and Mgmt. Field, Washington, 1958-59; asst. chief counsel U.S. Ho. of Reps. Spl. Subcom. on Fed. Aid Hwy. Program, Washington, 1959-69, U.S. Ho. of Reps. Subcom. on Investigations and Oversight, Washington, 1969-71; chief counsel U.S. Senate Permanent Subcom. on Investigations, Com. on Govt. Ops., 1971-73; fgn. service officer U.S. Dept. State, Washington, 1973-74; asst. sec., dep. insp. gen. of fgn. assistance U.S. Dept. State, 1974-76; sole practice law Washington, 1977—. Author: Military Law, 1951. Served to 2d lt. USAAC, 1943-45; PTO; to 1st lt. USSAF, 1951-52. Decorated Bronze Star, Air medal; Meritorius Civilian Svc. medal Sec. Def. Mem. D.C. Bar Assn., N.Y. State Bar Assn., Frank S. Hogan Assn., Diplomatic and Consular Officers Ret. Greek Orthodox. Avocation: photography. Home: The Colonnade 2801 New Mexico Ave NW Washington DC 20007-3921

CONSTANT, ANITA AURELIA, publisher; b. Youngstown, Ohio, Jan. 5, 1945; d. Sandu Nicholas and Erie Marie (Tecau) C. BA, Ind. U., 1967; postgrad., Northwestern U., Evanston, Ill., 1991. Sales rep. Economy Fin. Inc., St. Louis, 1967-69; recruiter Case Western U. Hosp., Cleve., 1969-70; sales rep. Internat. Playtex Inc., Chgo., 1970-71, John Wiley & Sons, Inc., Chgo., 1971-77; sr. product mgr. CBS Pub. Inc., The Dryden Press, Chog., 1977-80; exec. editor Dearborn Fin. Pub., Inc., Chgo., 1980-81, v.p., 1981-89, sr. v.p., prin., 1989-97; cons. to pub. industry, 1997-98; prin. Ea. European investment venture EUROTEC, 1998—; sr. v.p., editor-in-chief Southwestern Coll. Pub. divsn. ITP Inc., 1988-94. Bd. dirs. Romanian Heritage Ctr., Detroit, 1988—, Orthodox Brotherhood of Am., Detroit, 1985—. Mem. Chgo. Women in Pub. (keynote speaker 1988), Real Estate Educators Assn. (conv. coord. 1989), Internat. Assn. of Fin. Planners, Chgo. Book Clinic (bd. dirs. 1987-88, v.p. 1988-90), pres. 1990-91, past pres. 1991-92, Mary Alexander award 1995), Nat. Assn. Women Bus. Owners. Eastern Orthodox. Avocations: property development and renovation, hiking, bicycling. Office: 5101 Madison Rd Cincinnati OH 45227-1427

CONSTANT, WILLIAM DAVID, chemical engineer, educator; b. Bunkie, La., May 15, 1954; s. Warren LeRoy and Montez Henning (Haas) C.; m. Donna Gail Hall, Nov. 14, 1987; 1 child, Justin Glen Germany. BSChemE, La. State U., 1977, MSChemE, 1980, PhD, 1984. Registered chem. and environ. engr., La. Lab. tech. U.S. Forest Svc., Pineville, La., 1973, 74; chem. engr. Ethyl Corp., Baton Rouge, La., 1977-78; Exxon fellow dept. chem. engring. La. State U., Baton Rouge, 1978-84, asst. prof. petroleum engring., 1984-88, asst. dir. hazardous waste rsch. ctr., 1988-91, dir. hazardous waste rsch. ctr., 1991-99, asst. dir. hazardous substance rsch. ctr. south and S.W., 1991—, assoc. prof. dept. civil & environ. engring., 1994-97, dir. La. water resources rsch. inst., 1989-99, prof. dept. civil and environ. engring., 1997—; dir. Civil & Environ. Infrastructure Rsch. Ctr./La. State U., 1998—; cons. in field. Contbr. articles to profl. jours. Recipient numerous Rsch. grants, 1985—. Mem. Am. Inst. Chem. Engrs., U. Coun. on Water Resources, Am. Water Resources Assn., Gamma Beta Phi, Tau Beta Pi, Pi Epsilon Tau, Phi Lambda Epsilon (chpt. pres. 1980-81). Republican. Methodist. Avocations: golf. Office: CEIRC La State U 3221 CEBA Baton Rouge LA 70803

CONSTANTINE, JAN FRIEDMAN, lawyer; b. N.Y.C., Jan. 22, 1948; d. Howard J. and Elayne (Sercus) Friedman; m. Lawrence Levien, Oct. 11, 1970 (div. Sept. 1974); m. Lloyd E. Constantine, June 22, 1975; children: Isaac, Sarah, Elizabeth. BA, Smith Coll., Northampton, Mass., 1970; JD, George Washington U., 1973. Bar: N.Y. 1974, U.S. Dist. Ct. (so. and ea. dists.) N.Y. 1975, U.S. Ct. Appeals (2d cir.) 1975. Staff atty. div. spl. projects FTC, Washington, 1973-75; staff atty. N.Y. office FTC, N.Y.C., 1975-77; asst. atty. U.S. Dist. Ct. (ea. dist.) N.Y., Bklyn., 1977-82; litigation counsel Macmillan, Inc., N.Y.C., 1982-84, assoc. gen. counsel, 1985-90, dep. gen. counsel, 1990-91; sr. v.p. and dep. gen. counsel News Am. Inc., N.Y.C., 1992—; sr. v.p. and gen. counsel News Am. Mktg. and Pub. Groups, N.Y.C.; sr. v.p. The News Corp. Ltd., N.Y.C., 1996—; vis. asst. prof. George Washington U. Law Sch., Washington, 1974. Mem. Assn. of Bar of City of N.Y. (mem. consumer protection com. 1981-84, corp. law com. 1987-90, media law com. 1991-94, women in the law com. 1994-96, comm. and media law com. 1996—, chair 1999-2001). Avocation: tap dancing, tennis. Home: 10 W 66th St New York NY 10023-6206 Office: The News Corp Ltd 1211 Ave Of The Americas New York NY 10036-8701

CONSTANTINE, MICHAEL, actor; b. Reading, Pa., May 22, 1927; s. Theoharis and Andromache (Foteadou) Efstration; m. Juliana McCarthy, Oct. 5, 1953 (div. 1969); children: Thea Eileen, Brendan Neil. Actor (TV programs) Room 222, 1969-74 (Emmy award), Sirotas Court, Hey Landlord, 1965, Murder She Wrote, 1988, 89, The Love Boat, 1983, Homicide, 1993, Law and Order, 1993, 94, (films) The Hustler, 1959, If It's Tuesday This Must Be Belgium, Deadfall, 1993, My Life, 1993, The Juror, 1995, Steven King's 'Thinner,' 1995, (plays) Inherit the Wind, 1955, The Egg, 1965, Compulsion, 1967, The Miracle Worker, 1969, Arturo VI, 1972, A Walk in the Woods, 1986 (San Diego Drama Critics award), Three Sisters, 1991, Meshugah or Lost Souls, 1998. Recipient Emmy award, 1970, San Diego Drama Critics award, 1986, Dramalogue, Hollywood Fgn. Press, also numerous nominations.

CONSTANTINEAU, CONSTANCE JULIETTE, retired banker; b. Lowell, Mass., Feb. 18, 1937; d. Henry Goulet and Germaine (Turner) Goulet-Lamarre; m. Edward Joseph Constantineau; children: Glen Edward, Alan Henry. Student, Bank Adminstrn. Inst. and Am. Inst. Banking, 1975-87. Mortgage sec. The Cen. Savs. Bank, Lowell, 1955-57; head teller First Fed. Savs. & Loan, Lowell, 1957-59, Lowell Bank & Trust Co., Lowell, 1973-74; br. mgr. Century Bank & Trust Co., Malden, Mass., 1975-78; v.p. purchasing, mgr. support svcs. First Security Bank of N.Mex. (formerly First Nat. Bank Albuquerque), 1983-96; ret., 1996; mem. planning purchasing mgr.'s conf. Bank Adminstrn. Inst., San Antonio, Orlando, Fla., New Orleans; treas. polit. action com. First Nat. Bank, 1986. Bd. dirs., historian Indian Pueblo Cultural Ctr., Albuquerque, 1986-89. Home: 13015 Deer Dancer Trl NE Albuquerque NM 87112-4831

CONSTANTINESCU, GHEORGHE M., veterinarian; b. Bucharest, Ilfov, Romania, Jan. 20, 1932; came to U.S., 1984; U.S. citizen 1989; s. Mircea and Elisabeta (Mateescu-Capetineanu) C.; m. Ileana Anghelina, Mar. 1, 1979; children: Alexandru Razvan, Adina Elizabeth. Student, Liceul Gh. Lazar, Bucharest, 1950; DVM, Faculty Vet. Medicine, Bucharest, 1955, PhD, 1964; PhD (hon.), U. Agrl. Scis. Banat-Timisoara, Romania, 1992, U. Agrl. Scis., Bucharest, 1995. Bd. cert. in vet. diagnostic lab. pathology. Lab. chief Faculty of Vet. Medicine, Bucharest, 1955; scientific researcher Zootech. Rsch. Inst., Bucharest, 1958-59; doctor-medic vet. Zool. Garden, Bucharest, 1959-62; circuit doctor-medic vet. Agrl. Coun., Panciu-Galati, Romania, 1962-63; head breeding sect. Agrl. Coun., Panciu-Galati, Romania, 1963-65; head and assoc. prof. vet. anatomy Faculty of Vet. Medicine, Timisoara, Romania, 1965-82; assoc. prof. vet. anatomy U. Mo. Coll. Vet. Medicine, Columbia, 1984-92, prof., 1992—; v.p. Agrl. Coun., Panciu-Galati, 1963-65; sci. sec. Agronomic Inst. Timisoara, Romania, 1974-76; assoc. dean Faculty of Vet. Medicine, Timisoara, 1976-77; mem. internat. com. on vet. gross anatomical nomenclature, 1988—. Author: Comparative Anatomy, 4 vols., 1971-74, Comparative and Topographic Anatomy of Domestic Animals, 1978, Topographic Anatomy Domestic Mammals, 1982, Clinical Dissection Guide for Large Animals, 1991, Illustrated Veterinary Anatomical Nomenclature, 1992. Mem. European Assn. Vet. Anatomists, Union Soc. Med. Scis. Romania, Romanian Vet. Med. Assn., Am. Assn. Vet. Anatomists, Am. Assn. Anatomists, World Assn. Vet. Anatomists, Fedn. Am. Socs. for Exptl. Biology, Nat. Computer Graphics Assn. E-mail: constantinescuG@missouri.edu. Home: 5800 Spiva Crossing Rd Hallsville MO 65255-9717 Office: U Mo Coll Vet Medicine 1600 W Rollins Rd Columbia MO 65203-5120

CONSTANTINI, JOANN M., information management consultant; b. Danbury, Conn., July 30, 1948; d. William J. and Mathilda J. (Ressler) C. BA, Coll. White Plains, N.Y., 1970; postgrad., Ctrl. Conn. State Coll., 1977-78, U. Hartford, 1985-88, U. Jacksonville, 1991; MS, Nova Southeastern U., 1996. cert. records mgr., 1987; lic. realtor, N.C. Psychiat. social worker N.Y. State Dept. Mental Hygiene, Wassaic, 1970-73; with N.E. Utilities, Hartford, Conn., 1973-88; methods analyst N.E. Utilities, Hartford, 1979-82, records and procedures mgmt. adminstr., 1982-88; document contr., mgr. Ralph M. Parsons Co., Fairfield, Ohio, 1990-91, St. Johns River Power Park, Jacksonville, 1991—; mem. faculty Ctrl. Piedmont C.C., 1989-90, Fla. C.C., Jacksonville, 1993-95. Bd. dirs. Meriden YWCA, Conn., 1978-79; vol. Queen City Friends, Charlotte, 1988-89, Cath. Charities AIDS Ministries, Jacksonville, 1996—; mem. Greater Charlotte Bd. Realtors, 1989-91; mem. adv. coun. Greater Hartford C.C., 1986, Clermont Coll., Cin., 1990-91, Jacksonville C.C., 1991-94; mem. St. Augustine Diocesan Task Force Alternative Ministries, 1997—. Mem. AAUW, NACDLGM, Assn. Record Mgmt. and Adminstrs. (sec. 1984-85, bd. dirs. 1984-86, internat. chair industry action program 1989-93, chair industry action com. for pub. utilities 1986-89, profl. issues com. 1997—), Assn. Image and Info. Mgmt. (dir. 1984-86), Women Bus. Owners, Assn. Configurement Data Mgmt., Electric Coun. New Eng. (chair records mgmt. com. 1985-87), Coll. White Plains Alumnae Assn., Nat. Trust for Hist. Preservation, Inst. Cert. Records Mgrs., Am. Platform Assn., N.E. Utilities Women's Forum Club (treas. 1983-88), Beta Sigma Phi. Democrat. Roman Catholic. Avocations: antiques, fund raising, traveling, investing. Home: 11538 Jonathan Rd Jacksonville FL 32225-1314

CONSTANTINI, LOUIS ORLANDO, financial consultant, stockbroker; b. Columbus, Ga., Jan. 12, 1948; s. Louis T. and Edna G. (Spears) C.; m. Mary Ann Jennings, Feb. 9, 1974; children: Rachel J., Emily J. BA, U. Fla., 1972.

Cert. fin. mgr., N.Y. Intelligence officer CIA, Washington, 1972-76; v.p., fin. cons. Merrill Lynch & Co., El Paso, Tex., 1976-84; fin. cons. Merrill Lynch & Co., Las Cruces, N.Mex., 1984—, v.p., 1988—. Chmn. El Paso Estate Planning Coun., 1982. Decorated Bronze Star, Combat Infantryman Badge, Cross of Gallantry with Gold Star (Republic of Vietnam). Mem. Sigma Phi Epsilon. Avocation: Arctic exploration. E-mail: Newmex@IBM.net. Home: 5155 Hunters Chase Rd Las Cruces NM 88011 Office: Merrill Lynch & Co 425 S Telshor Blvd Ste 101C Las Cruces NM 88011-8211

CONSTANTINIDES, DINOS DEMETRIOS (CONSTANTINE CONSTANTINIDES), music educator, composer, conductor; b. Ioannina, Greece, May 10, 1929; came to U.S., 1957, naturalized, 1966; s. Demetrios Constantine and Magdalini (Papastergiou) C.; m. Judith Rose Hursh, July 1, 1962; children: Lenna, John. Diploma, Greek Conservatory, Athens, 1950, 57, Juilliard Sch., 1960; MM, Ind. U., 1965; PhD, Mich. State U., 1968. 1st violinist State Orch. Athens, Radio Symphony Athens, 1952-63; concertmaster Little Orch. Athens, 1961-62; 1st violinist Indpls. Symphony, 1963-65; concertmaster Indpls. Sinfonietta, 1963-65; prin. 2d violin Lansing (Mich.) Symphony, 1965-66; guest concertmaster Kalamazoo Symphony, 1966; Boyd prof. La. State U., Baton Rouge, 1966—, chmn. Festival Contemporary Music, 1974—, dir. New Music Ensemble, 1983—; concertmaster Baton Rouge Symphony, 1966-88, Beaumont (Tex.) Civic Opera, 1966-72, Baton Rouge Gilbert and Sullivan, 1978-89, Baton Rouge Opera, 1984-87; condr., music coord. Baton Rouge Symphony Chamber Orch., 1982-90; guest composer, condr., educator People's Republic China, 1990; music dir., condr. La. Sinfonietta, 1990—. Composer: (opera) Intimations, 1975 (awards 1981, 85), (opera in 3 acts) Antigone, 1993, (works for orch.) Symphony No. 2, 1983, Hymn to the Human Spirit, 1983, China I-Shanghai for soprano, bassoon and strings, 1991; guest composer, performer U.S. Poland, Eng., France, Greece, 1966—. Mem., performer Contemporary Arts Ctr., New Orleans, 1985—. Cpl. Greek Army, 1947-51. Recipient Disting. Svc. award Am. New Music Consortium, 1985, Glen award L'Ensemble composition contest, Lifetime Achievement award Gov. La.; Greek Govt. Found. grantee, 1957-60; named disting. tchr. White House Commn. on Presdl. Scholars, 1994. Mem. ASCAP (21 Standard awards 1975-96), Music Tchrs. Nat. Assn. (exec. bd. 1982-86, awards 1970, 79, 82, 88), Soc. Composers, Inc. (nat. coun. 1983-84, 88-89), Coll. Music Soc., Nat. Composers Assn. USA (nat. bd. dirs. 1991—). Democrat. Greek Orthodox. Avocations: art films, chess, travel. Home: 947 Daventry Dr Baton Rouge LA 70808-5830 Office: Sch Music La State U Baton Rouge LA 70803

CONSTANTINOU, CLAY, lawyer, ambassador; b. N.Y.C., Sept. 4, 1951; s. Dan and Eleni (Maouris) C.; m. Eileen Calamari, Mar. 6, 1976; children: Jennifer, Dan. BA, Jersey City State Coll., 1973; JD, Seton Hall U., 1981; LLM, NYU, 1986; program cert., Harvard U., 1996. Ptnr. Constantinou & Carroll Law Offices, West Orange, N.J., 1981-86; pvt. practice Clay Constantinou Law Offices, West Orange, 1986-95. Commr. N.J. Turnpike Authority, New Brunswick, 1990—; supreme pres. Cyprus Fedn. Am., N.Y.C., 1986-90; mem. Jersey City State Coll. Devel. Fund, 1991—; trustee Dem. Nat. Com., Washington, 1988-91; N.J. state fin. chair Dem. Primary and Gen. Election, 1988-89. Recipient Ellis Island Medal Honor, 1995, Disting. Grad. Yr. award Seton Hall U. Sch. Law, 1997; named Disting. Almnus Jersey City State Coll., 1991. Mem. N.J. State Bar Assn. Office: PO Box 10 Woodbridge NJ 07095-0958 Address: Psc 9 Box 9500 APO AE 09123-9998*

CONSTON, HENRY SIEGISMUND, lawyer; b. Dresden, Germany, Dec. 18, 1928; came to U.S., 1947, naturalized, 1952; BSBA, NYU, 1955, JD, 1958, LLM, 1961. Bar: N.Y. 1959. With Calif. Tex. Oil Corp., N.Y.C., 1947-61; sr. counsel Walter, Conston, Alexander & Green, N.Y.C., 1961—. Contbr. articles to profl. jours. Bd. dirs. Margaret Tietz Center for Nursing Care, N.Y. Found. Nursing Homes, Inc. Mem. Internat. Fiscal Assn., Internat. Bar Assn. Office: 90 Park Ave New York NY 10016-1301

CONTA, RICHARD VINCENT, actuary; b. N.Y.C., Sept. 4, 1946; s. Antonion and Eugenia Theresa (Cavalli) C.; m. Joanne Shultis, July 14, 1979 (div. 1990); children: Kerry, Gregory; m. Maureen Fitzgerald, June 8, 1991; 1 child, Tracy. BA, Fordham U., 1968; actuarial student, U.S. Life Ins. Co., N.Y.C., 1969-74. Pension clk. Tchrs. Retirement Sys., City of N.Y., 1968-69; pension actuary Laiken, Siegel & Co., N.Y.C., 1974-75; enrolled actuary Guardian Life Ins. Co., N.Y.C., 1975-99; ptnr. Fitzgerald & Conta Pension Svcs., Bloomfield, N.J., 1990—. Mem. Am. Acad. Actuaries, Am. Soc. Pension Actuaries. Roman Catholic. Fax: (973) 338-7834. Office: Fitzgerald & Conta Pension Svcs 104 Davis Ave Bloomfield NJ 07003-4140

CONTE, ANDREA, retail executive, health care consultant, community activist; b. Great Barrington, Mass., Feb. 13, 1941; d. Louis William and Rosalie (Salvini) C.; m. Philip Norman Bredesen, Nov. 22, 1974; 1 child, Benjamin Conte. BS in Nursing, U. Wash., 1968; MBA, Tenn. State U., 1983. RN. Nurse various hosps. and med. ctrs., Mass. and Calif., 1961-68, Vis. Nurse Service, Boston, 1968-70; clin. coordinator Reg. Med. Program, Boston City Hosp., 1970-72; trainer computer systems Searle Medidata, Lexington, Mass., 1973-75; dir. nursing mgmt. services Hosp. Corp. Am., Nashville, 1975-78; cons. various health care cos., Nashville, 1978-81; mgr. Ernst and Whinney, Nashville, 1981-83; pres. Conte Philips, Nashville, 1983—; founder, pres. You Have The Power, Inc., 1993—. Bd. dirs. Family and Children's Svc., 1988-91, Cumberland Sci. Mus., 1988-93, Shepherd's Ctr. of West End, 1989-91, Tenn. Performing Arts Ctr., 1989-97, NCCJ, 1991-94, St. Thomas Hosp., Fisk U., 1995—, First Ctr. Visual Arts, 1998—; mem. Commn. on Future of Tenn. Jud. Sys., Juvenile Justice Reform Commn., 1998; chmn. You Have The Power Com. Roman Catholic. Avocations: cooking, gardening, skiing, herbs, hiking.

CONTE, JULIE VILLA, nurse, administrator; b. Manila, July 4, 1951; came to U.S., 1970; d. Gregorio Cortes and Lourdes (Villa) Dirige; m. Michael Don Conte, Jan. 22, 1983. BSN, Calif. State U., L.A., 1974; MBA, U. Phoeniz, San Diego, 1993. RN, Calif. Staff nurse Santa Monica (Calif.) Hosp., 1976-78; pub. health nurse Kaiser Found. Hosp., Panorama City, Calif., 1978-85; nursing supr. Nat. Med. Homecare, L.A., 1985-86; dir. home health Holy Cross Hosp., Mission Hills, 1986-88; dir. profl. svcs. Care Home Health, San Diego, 1988—; dir. nursing Health Prime Home Health Svcs. of San Diego, Inc., 1988-92; dir. home health svcs. Alvardado Home Health Agy., San Diego, 1993-94; expert consulting Home Health and Bus. Cons., San Diego, 1994—; dir. patient care svcs. Unlimited Care, Inc., 1995—; pub. health nurse cons. Able Home Health Care, Wilmington, Calif., 1984; bd. dirs. nursing Health Prime, Inc.; CEO, adminstr. We Care Home Health Svcs., Inc., 1996—. Pres. Bapt. Nursing Fellowship, Calif., 1997. Mem. NAFE, Nat. Assn. Home Care, Associational Woman's Missionary Union (dir.), San Diego So. Bapt. Assn., Bapt. Nursing Fellowship (pres. Calif. chpt. 1996—), Alpha Delta Chi. Republican. Baptist. Avocations: travel, foreign language, collecting, piano, organ. Home: 5851 Despejo Pl San Diego CA 92124-1003

CONTE, LOU, artistic director, choreographer; b. DuQuoin, Ill., Apr. 17, 1942; s. John and Floy Mae (Saunders) C. Student Ellis DuBoulay Sch. Ballet, Chgo., 1961-68, So. Ill. U., 1960-62, Am. Ballet Theatre Sch., N.Y.C., 1964-66. Choreographer musicals Mame, 1972, Boss, 1973; choreographer Milw. Melody Top, 1966; dir. Lou Conte Dance Studio, Chgo., 1974—; artistic dir. Hubbard St. Dance Co., Chgo., 1977—; lectr. Mem. Actors Equity Assn., AFTRA. Office: Hubbard St Dance Co 218 S Wabash Ave Chicago IL 60604-2306*

CONTI, CAROLYN ANN, elementary school educator; b. Ellwood City, Pa., Jan. 23, 1950; d. Leonard Louis and Leona Wanda (Sutkowski) Wolfe; m. Stanley James Conti, July 19, 1969; children: Raechel, Stanley Jason, Anthony, Nicholas. BS in Elem. Edn., Edinboro U., 1971; MS in Elem Edn., Slippery Rock U., 1993. Cert. elem. tchr. and tchr. emotionally disturbed,reading specialist, Pa., instrnl. II. Elem. educator Neason Hill Sch., Meadville, Pa., 1971-72, Seneca Valley Sch. Dist., Harmony, Pa., 1989—; mem. Whole Lang. Network, 1990—; mem. math. curriculum com., progress report com., strategic planning com., 1992-93; mem. children's learning workshops devel. com. Seneca Valley Sch. Dist., 1993, portfolio com. Mem. NEA, Nat. Coun. Tchrs. of English, Pa. State Edn. Assn., Primary English Tchrs. Assn., Internat. Reading Assn. Democrat. Roman Catholic. Avocation: reading. Home: 204 Whispering Oaks Dr Cranberry Township PA 16066-3172 Office: Haine Middle Sch Haine Sch Rd Cranberry Township PA 16066

CONTI, JAMES JOSEPH, chemical engineer, educator; b. Coraopolis, Pa., Nov. 2, 1930; s. James Joseph and Mary (Smrekar) C.; m. Concetta Razziano, May 13, 1961; children—Lori Ann, James Robert. B.Chem. Engring., Poly. Inst. Bklyn., 1954, M.Chem. Engring., 1956, D. Chem. Engring., 1959. Sr. engr. Bettis atomic power div. Westinghouse Electric Corp., 1958-59; mem. faculty Polytech. U. N.Y., 1959-90, prof. chem. engring., 1965-90, chmn. dept., 1964-70, provost, 1970-78, v.p. edn1. devel., 1978-90; pres. Webb Inst. Naval Architecture, Glen Cove, N.Y., 1990—; cons. to industry and govt., 1960—. Author articles. Trustee Webb Inst. Naval Architecture. Fellow Am. Inst. Chemists, AAAS; mem. Am. Inst. Chem. Engrs., Am. Soc. Engring. Edn., Soc. Naval Architects and Marine Engrs., Am. Soc. Naval Engrs., Sigma Xi, Tau Beta Pi, Phi Lambda Upsilon, Omega Chi Epsilon. Patentee in field. Home: 26 Miami Rd Bethpage NY 11714-2229 Office: Webb Inst Crescent Beach Rd Glen Cove NY 11542-1398

CONTI, JOY FLOWERS, lawyer; b. Kane, Pa., Dec. 7, 1948; d. Bernard A. Flowers and Elizabeth (Tingley) Rodgers; m. Anthony T. Conti, Jan. 16, 1971; children: Andrew, Michael, Gregory. BA, Duquesne U., 1970, JD summa cum laude, 1973. Bar: Pa. 1973, U.S. Dist. Ct. (we. dist.) Pa. 1973, U.S. Ct. Appeals (3rd cir.) 1976, U.S. Supreme Ct. 1993. Law clk. Supreme Ct. Pa., Monessen, 1973-74; assoc. Kirkpatrick & Lockhart, Pitts., 1974-76, 82-83, ptnr., 1983-96; shareholder Buchanan, Ingersoll, P.C., Pitts., 1996—; prof. law Duquesne U., Pitts., 1976-82; hearing examiner Pa. Dept. State, Bur. Profl. Occupation and Affairs, 1978-82; chairperson search com. for judge U.S. Bankruptcy Ct. (we. dist.) Pa., 1987, 95; active Pa. Futures Commn. on Justice in 21st Century, 1995-97. Contbr. articles to profl. jours. Mem. disciplinary hearing com. Supreme Ct. Pa., 1982-88; v.p. Com. for Justice Edn., Pitts., 1983-84; mem. Leadership Pitts., 1987-88. Named One of Ten Outstanding Young Women in Am., 1981. Fellow Am. Bar Found. (Pa. state chair 1991-97); mem. ABA (ho. of dels. 1980-86, 91-97), Am. Law Inst., Am. Coll. Bankruptcy, Pa. Bar Assn. (gov. 1993-95, ho. of dels. 1978—, corp. banking and bus. law sect. coun. 1983-89, treas. 1991-93, v.p. 1993-95, chair-elect 1995-97, chmn. 1997-99, chmn. commn. comml. law 1990-93, co-chair 1995—, chairperson civil rights and responsibilities com. 1986-89, Achievement award 1982, 87, 99, Anne X. Alpern award 1995), Nat. Conf. Bar Pres. (exec. coun. 1993-96), Allegheny County Bar Assn. (adminstrv. v.p. 1984-86, 90, chairperson corp. banking and bus. law sect. 1987-89, treas. 1988-90, gov. 1991, pres.-elect 1992, pres. 1993), Internat. Women's Insolvency and Restructuring Confedn. (chair Tri-State Network 1996), Pa. Bar Inst. (dir. 1991-97), Duquesne Club, Treesdale Country Club. Roman Catholic. Home: 3469 Palomino Dr Gibsonia PA 15044-8965 Office: Buchanan Ingersoll PC 301 Grant St Fl 20 Pittsburgh PA 15219-1410

CONTI, LEE ANN, lawyer; b. Astoria, Oreg.. BA with honors, So. Ill. U., 1970; JD summa cum laude, De Paul U., 1976. Bar: Ill. 1976, U.S. Dist. Ct. (no. dist.) Ill. 1976. Ptnr. Mayer, Brown & Platt, Chgo., 1983-94; assoc. gen. counsel Citizens Utilities Co, Stamford, 1994—. Contbr. articles to profl. jours. Mem. Bd. Edn. Cmty. Consol. Sch. Dist. 89, Du Page County, 1987-93. Recipient Am. Jurisprudence awards in Torts, Remedies. Mem. ABA, Am. Corp. Counsel Assn., Ill. State Bar Assn., Du Page County Bar Assn., Chgo. Bar Assn., Phi Kappa Phi, Pi Sigma Alpha, Phi Lambda Pi. Office: Citizens Utilities Co 1000 Internationale Pkwy Woodridge IL 60517-4924

CONTI, LISA ANN, epidemiologist, veterinarian; b. Amityville, N.Y., July 10, 1963; d. Daniel Desiderio and Lorraine Conti; m. Thomas Lee Seal, Oct. 21, 1989. BS, U. Miami, Coral Gables, Fla., 1984; DVM, U. Fla., 1988; MPH, U. South Fla., 1993. Diplomate Am. Coll. Vet. Preventive Medicine. Relief vet. various clinics, Tallahassee, 1988—; vet. epidemiologist Fla. Dept. Health, Tallahassee, 1988-89, epidemiologist, 1989-94, med. health care program analyst, 1994-97, program adminstr., 1997-98, state pub. health vet., 1998—; mem. rabies control adv. com. Fla. Dept. of Health, 1997—. Assoc. editor Fla. Jour. Pub. Health. Vol. Lit. Vols. Am., Tallahassee, 1995—. Mem. AVMA (pub. health rep. coun. pub. rels. 1997—), Nat. Assn. State Pub. Health Vets. (Psittacosis compendium com. 1996-98, Rabies compendium com. 1999—), Fla. Vet. Med. Assn. (pub. health chmn. 1994—), Big Bend Vet. Med. Assn. (pres. 1991-92). Avocations: stained glass, folk dancing, hiking. Office: Fla Dept Health Bin A-12 2020 Capital Cir SE Tallahassee FL 32399-1734

CONTI, LOUIS THOMAS MOORE, lawyer; b. Phila., Aug. 31, 1949; s. Alexander and Yolanda (DiLorenzo) C.; m. Christina M.S. Moore, May 1, 1982; children: Charles Alexander, Whitney Caroline. BS, LaSalle Coll., 1971; MBA, Drexel U., 1972; JD, Creighton U., 1975; LLM, Temple U., 1981. Bar: U.S. Claims Ct. 1975, U.S. Tax Ct. 1975, Pa. 1975, U.S. Dist. Ct. (ea. dist.) Pa. 1978, U.S. Ct. Appeals (3d cir.) 1979, U.S. Supreme Ct. 1981, Fla. 1982, U.S. Dist. Ct. (mid. dist.) Fla. 1988. Tax atty. Office Chief Counsel IRS, Washington and Phila., 1975-81; tax mgr. Touche Ross & Co., Phila., 1981-84; assoc. Saul, Ewing, Remick & Saul, Phila., 1984-87; shareholder Swann & Haddock, P.A., Orlando, Fla., 1987-89; ptnr., chmn. corp. tax and securities dept. Holland & Knight, Orlando, 1989—. Mem. fin. com. S.E. Pa. chpt. ARC, Phila., 1984-87; advisor Vol. Lawyers for Arts, Phila., 1984-87; bd. dirs. Fla. Hosp. Found., 1989—, Ctrl. Fla. Planned Giving Coun., 1989-97, Cmty. Found. Ctrl. Fla. Inc., 1993—, World Trade Ctr., Orlando, 1992-95; mem. internat. bus. adv. bd. Metro Orlando; grad. Leadership Orlando, 1994, Leadership Fla., 1996; chair recruiting com. East Ctrl. Region of Leadership Fla., 1997, bd. dirs. Orlando Performing Arts & Edn. Ctr., Inc., 1998—. Mem. ABA (tax and bus. law sect., chmn. task force on drafting prototype ltd. liability co. operating agreements 1998—, chmn. Fla. Bar drafting com. 1999), Fla. Bar Assn. (tax and bus. law sect., chmn. drafting com. ltd. liability co. act 1998—, vice chair corps. and securities com., bus. law sect. 1997-99, chair long-range planning com. tax sect. 1999—), Orange County Bar Assn. (chmn. tax sect. 1990-91), Seminole County C. of C. (bd. dirs. 1994-97), Racquet Club, Alaqua Country Club, Citrus Club. Republican. Avocations: traveling, skiing, golfing, tennis, theatre. Home: 3003 Timpana Pt Longwood FL 32779-3108 Office: Holland & Knight PO Box 1526 Orlando FL 32802-1526

CONTI, PETER SELBY, astronomy educator; b. N.Y.C., Sept. 5, 1934; s. Attilio Carlo and Marie (Selby) C.; m. Carolyn Safford, Aug. 26, 1961; children—Michael, Karen, Kathe. BS, Rensselaer Poly. Inst., 1956; PhD, U. Calif-Berkeley, 1963; Honoris Causa degree, U. Utrecht, 1993. Research fellow Calif. Inst. Tech., Pasadena, 1963-66; asst. prof. astronomy U. Calif./Santa Cruz, 1966-71; astronomer Lick Obs., Santa Cruz, 1966-71; prof., fellow Joint Inst. Lab. Astrophysics U. Colo., Boulder, 1971—, chmn., 1989-90, chmn. dept. astrophys., planetary and atmospheric scis., 1980-86; Chmn. bd. dirs. Assoc. Univs. for Research in Astronomy Inc., Tuscon, 1983-86; vis. prof. U. Utrecht, The Netherlands, 1969-70, minnaert prof. U. Utrecht, 1995. Editor: Mass Loss and Evolution of O-type Stars, 1979, O Stars and Wolf Rayet Stars, 1988; contbr. articles to profl. jours. Served to lt. (j.g.) USNR, 1956-59. Recipient Gold medal U. Liege, Belgium, 1975; Fulbright fellow, 1969-70. Fellow AAAS (chmn. sect. D in astronomy 1980); mem. Am. Astron. Soc. (councillor 1983-86), Astron. Soc. of Pacific, Internat. Astron. Union (organizing com. 1983-85, v.p. 1985-88, pres. 1988-91, commn. 29 stellar spectra). Democrat. Home: 817 Racquet Ln Boulder CO 80303-2972 Office: U Colo-Boulder Joint Inst Lab Astrophysics Campus Box 440 Boulder CO 80309-0440

CONTI, RONALD SAMUEL, electronics engineer, fire prevention engineer; b. PIitts., June 23, 1948; s. Eugene H. and Helen V. (Pietrzak) C.; m. Mary Ann Pagano, May 6, 1972; children: Ronald S. Jr., Ryan A., Renai L. BS in Electronics Engring., Point Park Coll., 1979. Fire prevention engr., supr. gen. engr. response group Pitts. Rsch. Lab of NIOSH, 1970—; mem. nat. mine rescue assn. Pa. Dept. Environ. Protection; PADEP adv. bd. of mine rescue subcom. coord. open industry briefings on mine fire preparedness and mine rescue team tng. simulations. Author: Combustion Science and Technology, 1991, also abstracts; patentee inflatable partition for fighting fires (spl. achievement award 1996), trigger device for explosion barriers (spl. achievement award 1980). Pres. Brookline Youth Soccer Assn., Pitts., 1985-86; coach Little League, Pitts., 1980-89, BYSA Soccer, City League Soccer, Pitts., 1982-90, Brookline Boxing, Pitts., 1981-82. Sgt. USMC, 1968-70, Vietnam. Recipient PE 5 Star award Pollution Engring., Washington, 1982; named Tech. Transfer Person of Yr., Pitts. Rsch. Ctrs., 1992. Mem. Combustion Inst., Nat. Mine Rescue Assn., Pleasant Hill Hall Assn. (bd. dirs. 1984-90), Vietnam Vets Inc., Am. Legion, Pleasant Hills Guthrie Lodge (past master). Roman Catholic. Office: Pitts Rsch Lab NIOSH PO Box 18070 Pittsburgh PA 15236-0070

CONTI, SAMUEL, federal judge; b. L.A., July 16, 1922; s. Fred and Katie C.; m. Dolores Crosby, July 12, 1952; children: Richard, Robert, Cynthia. BS, U. Santa Clara, 1945; LLB, Stanford U., 1948, JD. Bar: Calif. 1948. Pvt. practice, San Francisco and Contra Costa County, 1948-60; city atty. City of Concord, Calif., 1960-69; judge Superior Ct. Contra Costa County, 1968-70; judge U.S. Dist. Ct. (no. dist.) Calif., San Francisco, 1970-88, sr. judge, 1988—. Mem. Central Contra Costa Bar Assn. (pres.), Concord C. of C. (pres.), Alpha Sigma Nu. Office: US Dist Ct PO Box 36060 San Francisco CA 94102

CONTI, TOM, actor, writer, director; b. Paisley, Scotland, Nov. 22, 1941; s. Alfonso and Mary (McGoldrick) C.; m. Kara Drummond Wilson, July 2, 1967; 1 child, Nina. Appeared in plays on London's West End, Jesus My Son, 1998, Chapter Two, The Ride Down Mount Morgan, Savages, Other People, The Black and White Minstrels, Don Juan, The Devil's Disciple, Romantic Comedy, Chapter Two, Jesus My Boy: Broadway debut in Whose Life Is It Anyway, 1979 (Tony award), Jeffrey Bernard is Unwell, 1990; appeared in They're Playing Our Song, 1980; dir. Before the Party, 1980; dir., star Present Laughter, 1993; film appearances include Galileo, Eclipse, Merry Christmas Mr. Lawrence, Reuben, Reuben, 1983, American Dreamer, 1984, Saving Grace, Miracles, Heavenly Pursuits, Beyond Therapy, The Dumb Waiter, White Roses, Shirley Valentine, Someone Else's America, 1995, Sub Down, Something To Believe In, 1996, Don't Go Breaking My Heart, 1998, Out of Control, 1997; appeared in TV plays including the Beaux Strategem; appeared in American TV prodns. Princess and the Pea, Faerie Tale Theatre, the Beate Klarsfeld Story, The Quick and the Dead, Fatal Dosage, When Rabbit Howls, Wright Verdicts, The Inheritance, Friends; appeared in Brit. TV prodns. The Glittering Prizes, Norman Conquests, Madame Bovary. Club: Garrick (London). Address: Chatto & Linnit, 123 A Kings Rd, London NW3 4PL, England

CONTIE, LEROY JOHN, JR., federal judge; b. Canton, Ohio, Apr. 2, 1920; s. Leroy John and Mary M. (DeSantis) C.; m. Janice M. Zollars, Nov. 28, 1953; children: Ann L., Leroy John III. BA, U. Mich., 1941, JD, 1948; JD (hon.), U. Akron, 1993. Bar: Ohio 1948, U.S. Dist. Ct. (no. dist.) Ohio, 1953, U.S Supreme Ct. 1959. Law dir. City of Canton, 1952-60; chmn. Canton City Charter Commn., 1963; mem. Stark County Bd. Elections, Canton, 1964-69; judge Common Pleas Ct., Stark County, 1969-71, U.S. Dist. Ct., No. Dist. Ohio, Cleve., 1971-82, U.S. Ct. Appeals (6th cir.), Cin., 1982—; now senior judge U.S. Ct. Appeals (6th cir.). Trustee Stark County Legal Aid Soc., Canton chpt. ARC; mem. adv. bd. Walsh U., Canton, U. Akron Law Coll. With AUS, 1942-46. Mem. Am., Ohio, Stark County, Summit County, Cuyahoga County, Akron bar assns., Am. Judicature Soc., U.S. Jr. C. of C. (internat. senator), Canton Jr. C. of C. (trustee), Stark County Hist. Soc., Stark County Wilderness Soc., Am. Legion, Sigma Phi Epsilon (Nat. citation award), Phi Alpha Delta., Omicron Delta Kappa, K.C. Club (4 deg.), Elks Club. Republican. Office: US Ct Appeals 365 US Courthouse 2 S Main St Akron OH 44308-1813

CONTILLO, LAWRENCE JOSEPH, financial and computer company executive; b. Washington, Mar. 3, 1960; s. Lawrence and Kathleen Grace (O'Neill) C. BS in Acctg. and Fin., U. Md., 1981; MBA, George Washington U., 1982. CPA, Md. Financial analyst Fed. Home Loan Mortgage Corp., Washington, 1982-83; budget analyst Am. Security Bank, 1983-84; mgr. MCI, Arlington, Va., 1984-86; cons. Laventhol & Horwath, Washington, 1986-87; mgr. Watkins, Meegan, Drury & Co., Bethesda, Md., 1987-91; pres., founder, CEO Rennaissance Computing Ltd., Greenbelt, Md., 1991—. Mem. Md. Assn. CPAs (com. mem.).

CONTINETTI, ROBERT E., chemistry educator. Assoc. prof. dept. chemistry U. Calif. San Diego, La Jolla, Calif., 1990—. Recipient Packard Found. fellow, 1994. Office: U Calif San Diego 9500 Gilman Dr Dept 332 La Jolla CA 92093-0332

CONTINO, ROSALIE HELENE, drama educator, costume designer and historian, playwright; b. Bklyn., Apr. 1, 1938; d. Nicholas and Domenica Helen (Nostro) C. EdB, Fordham U., 1959; MA in Ednl. Theater, NYU, 1980, PhD in Ednl. Theater, 1997. Teaching fellow NYU Ednl. Theater Dept., N.Y.C., 1980-83; resident costume designer TRG Prodn., N.Y.C., 1979-89, B.F.R. Prodn., N.Y.C., 1980-82, Studio Theatre, 1985-88; co-host Internat. Arts Festival, NYU. Author: (poem) Trees (Editor's Choice award Nat. Book of Poetry); assoc. prod. Art for All, Art for the Disabled, Channel 25/58 Cablevision, Riverhead, N.Y., The Telegram, My Grandmother's Garden; playwright: Ricky, Transitions, Kids, Kids, Kids, Twixt 'n' Tween. Former mem. Ladies' Aux. Victory Meml. Hosp., Bklyn., 1964-74. Mem. Am. Alliance for Theatre and Edn., United Fedn. Tchrs., U.S. Inst. Theater Tech., Dramatists Guild, NYU Grad. Student Orgn. (treas. 1984-92), Costume Soc. Am., Theatre Libr. Assn., Pi Lambda Theta (Rho chpt., exec. bd. 1987—, region I editor). Roman Catholic. Avocations: tennis, bike riding, reading. Home: 74 Bay 10th St Brooklyn NY 11228-3412

CONTI-O'BRIEN, YVONNE, elementary education educator; b. Oceanside, Calif., May 21, 1967; d. Thomas Joseph and Rose Marie (Corsino) Conti; m. Dennis Richard O'Brien, Dec. 29, 1990; children: Shane Patrick, Alec Richard. BA in Spanish, BA in Journalism, Salve Regina U., 1989; tchg. cert., Sacred Heart U., 1995-96, postgrad., 1996—. Asst. prodr. juvenile audio-home video Random House, Inc., N.Y.C., 1989-91; mgr. for audio/filmstrip Weston (Conn.) Woods, 1991; tchr. 6th grade lang. arts, tchr. 6th, 7th, 8th grade Spanish All Saints Cath. Sch., Norwalk, Conn., 1993-96; tchr. 8th grade Spanish and French Flood Middle Sch., Stratford, Conn., 1996—; team leader Flood Middle Sch., Stratford, 1998—; ednl. cons. Good Friends Prodns., Bridgeport, Conn., 1996. Asst. coach Stratford Pony Baseball, 1997. em. ASCD, Sigma Phi Sigma, Sigma Delta Pi. Democrat. Roman Catholic. Avocations: bicycling, arts and crafts, reading, family activities. Home: 1188 Nichols Ave Stratford CT 06614-2624 Office: Flood Mid Sch 490 Chapel St Stratford CT 06614-1690

CONTIS, GEORGE, medical services company executive. MD, MPH. Pres. Med. Svc. Corp. Internat. E-mail: msci@iamidgex.net. Fax: 703-276-3017. Address: 1716 Wilson Blvd Arlington VA 22209-2504

CONTNEY, JOHN JOSEPH, trade association administrator; b. Milw., Oct. 15, 1932; s. Francis Anthony and Rose (Nowicki) C.; m. Dawn Georgette Wintz, Sept. 7, 1963; children: Wade Anthony, Ross Joseph. B.S., Marquette U., 1954, M.B.A., 1965; M.S., Barry U., 1975. Asst. to v.p. Boston Store, Milw., 1950-56; exec. v.p., sales mgr. Records Unlimited, Inc., Milw., 1956-59; exec. v.p. Columbia S.E., Miami, Fla., 1959-63; sales controller Color Corp., Tampa, Fla., 1964-65; mgr. mktg. Textile Rental Svcs. Assn., Miami, 1965-72, asst. exec. dir., 1973, gen. mgr., 1974-75, exec. dir., 1975-98; cons., 1998—; lectr. various groups.; chmn. Clean '93 Edn. com., sponsor, World Ednl. Congress for Laundering & Dry Cleaning; chmn. organizing com. World Textile Rental Congress, 1998. Contbr. articles to profl. jours. Served with AUS, 1954-56. Mem. Am. Soc. Assn. Execs., Fla. Soc. Assn. Execs. (past pres., Exec. of Yr. 1982), Alliance Textile Care Assn. (past pres.), South Fla. Soc. Assn. Execs. (bd. dirs.), Found. for Internat. Meetings (chmn). Home: 601 Grand Concourse Miami FL 33138-2473 Office: Textile Rental Svcs Assn Am Ste B 1130 E Hallandale Beach Blvd Hallandale FL 33009-4432

CONTO, ARISTIDES, advertising agency executive; b. N.Y.C., Feb. 10, 1931; s. Gus Dimitrios and Osee (Kenney) C.; BA, Champlain Coll., 1953; MS in Journalism, UCLA, 1958, certificate in indsl. rels., 1965; m. Phyllis Helen Wiley, June 22, 1957; 1 son, Jason Wiley. Reporter, City News Svc., L.A., 1958; dir. pub. rels. Galaxy Advt. Co., Los Angeles, 1959-60; news media chief Los Angeles County Heart Assn., 1960-61; pub. rels. assoc. Prudential Ins. Co., L.A., 1961-64; advt. mgr. Aerospace Controls Co., L.A., 1964-65; comml. sales promotion coord. Lockheed-Calif. Co., Burbank, 1965-73; pres. Jason Wiley Advt. Agy., L.A., 1973-92; dir. Tower Master, Inc., L.A. With U.S. Army, 1955-56. Recipient advt. awards. Mem. Nat. Soc. Published Poets, L.A. Press Club, Bus.-Profl. Advt. Assn. L.A.s, Pub. Rels. Soc. Author: The Spy Who Loved Me, 1962; The Diamond Twins,

1963, Edit Me Dead, 1992, I Marcus, 1994, A Short Life, 1995, (screenplays) Lannigan, 1973, Haunted Host, 1976, Captain Noah, 1977, Government Surplus, 1983.

CONTOS, PAUL ANTHONY, engineer, investment consultant; b. Chgo., Mar. 18, 1926; s. Anthony Dimitrios and Panagiota (Kostopoulos) C.; m. Lilian Katie Kalkines, June 19, 1955 (dec. Apr. 1985); children: Leslie, Claudia, Paula, Anthony. Student, Am. TV Inst., Chgo., 1946-48, U. Ill., 1949-52, 53-56, Ill. Inst. Tech., 1952-53, U. So. Calif., 1956-57. Engr. J.C. Deagan Co., Inc., Chgo., 1951-53, Lockheed Missile and Space Co., Inc., Sunnyvale, Calif., 1956-62; engrng. supr. Lockheed Missile and Space Co., Inc., Sunnyvale, 1962-65, staff engr., 1965-88; pres. PAC Investments, Saratoga, Calif., 1984-88; pres. PAC Investments, San Jose, Calif., 1988—, also advisor, 1984—. Mem. Pres. Coun. U. Ill., 1994—. With U.S. Army, 1944-46, ETO. Decorated Purple Heart. Mem. DAV (life, commdr. Chgo. unit 1948-51), VFW (life), Pi Sigma Phi (pres. 1951-53). Republican. Greek Orthodox. Home and Office: 1009 Blossom River Way Apt 105 San Jose CA 95123-6305

CONTRACTOR, FAROK, business and management educator; b. Bombay, Dec. 24, 1946; came to U.S., 1967; s. Jamshed Phirozshaw and Hilla C.; m. Joan Forbes, June 6, 1970; children: Cyrus, Sahm, Eric. BSME, U. Bombay, 1967; MS in Indsl. Engring., U. Mich., 1968; MBA, U. Pa., 1977, PhD in Managerial Sci. and Applied Econs., 1980. Staff indsl. engr. Max Factor, Inc., L.A., 1969; rsch. fellow U. Mich., Ann Arbor, 1969-70; exec. officer, asst. to mng. dir. TATA Group subs. TATA Adminstrv. Svcs., India, 1970-74; asst. instr. bus. and mgmt. Wharton Sch. Bus., U. Pa., Phila., 1975-77, instr., 1977-80; assoc. prof. Grad. Sch. Mgmt., Rutgers U., Newark and Piscataway, N.J., 1980-90, prof. internat. bus., 1991—, chmn. internat. bus. dept., 1986-88, 90-93; lectr. Wharton Sch. Bus., U. Pa., 1985-86; vis. scholar UN Ctr. on Transnat. Corps., N.Y., fall 1988; mem. Internat. Bus. Inst., Rutgers U., 1986—, rsch. dir. CIBER, 1997-99, com. mem., 1980-90; NSF reviewer, 1980, 84, 94; organizer, co-chmn. joint conf. on coop. ventures in internat. bus. Rutgers U. and Wharton Sch. Bus., U. Pa., 1986; licensing and tech. transfer agreements cons.; Unilever Group vis. fellow, vis. prof. Indian Inst. Fgn. Trade, New Delhi, spring 1994; vis. prof. Copenhagen Bus. Sch., 1995, Lubin sch. Pace U., 1997; presenter in field. Author: (books) International Technology Licensing: Compensation, Costs and Negotitation, 1981, Licensing In International Strategy: A Guide for Planning and Negotiation, 1985, Government Policies And Foreign Direct Investment, 1991, Economic Transformation In Emerging Countries: The Role of Investment, Trade and Finance, 1998, (with Peter Lorange) Cooperative Strategies in International Business, 1990, Economic Transformation in Emerging Countries: The Role of Investment, Trade and Finance, 1998, others; Co-Author: Introduction to International Business, 1986. Esmee Fairbairn fellow U. Reading, Eng., 1982, Fulbright fellow, 1991-92; grantee The German Marshall Fund of U.S., 1986, Carnegie Bosch Found., 1996-98. Fellow Acad. Internat. Bus. (bd. dirs., sec.-treas. 1992-94); mem. Licensing Execs. Soc., Acad. Mgmt. (exec. bd. 1997—, pre-conf. workshop chair San Diego meeting 1998, prgm. chair Chicago meeting 1999), European Internat. Bus. Assn., Zoroastrian Assn. Greater N.Y., Internat. Trade and Fin. Assn. (bd. dirs. 1995-97). Avocations: antique restoration, skiing, trekking, canoeing, interior design. Home: 52 Old Denville Rd Boonton NJ 07005-8835 Office: Rutgers Univ Grad Sch Mgmt 81 New St Newark NJ 07102-1820

CONTRENI, JOHN JOSEPH, JR., humanities educator; b. Savannah, Ga., Aug. 31, 1944; s. John Joseph Sr. and Elfriede Johanna (Hille) C.; m. Margarita Lee Partridge, July 3, 1986; children: Judith, Rachel, Daniel, Maureen, Jennifer Rogers, Paul Rogers. BA, St. Vincent Coll., 1966, HHD (hon.), 1996; PhD, Mich. State U., 1971. From asst. prof. to prof. history Purdue U., West Lafayette, Ind., 1971—, head dept. history, 1985-97, asst. dean Sch. Humanities, Social Sci. and Edn., 1981-85, interim head dept. fgn. langs. and lits., 1983-85; pres. Midwest Medieval Conf., 1980-81. Author: The Cathedral School of Laon from 850 to 930: Its Manuscripts and Masters, 1978, (John Nicholas Brown prize 1982), Codex Laudunensis 468: A Ninth-Century Guide to Virgil, Sedulius, and the Liberal Arts, 1984; co-author: Glossae Divinae Historiae: The Biblical Glosses of John Scottus Eriugena, 1997: translator: Education and Culture in the Barbarian West, Sixth Through Eighth Centuries (Pierre Riché), 1976, Carolingian Learning, Masters, and Manuscripts, 1992; co-editor: Religion, Culture, and Society in the Early Middle Ages: Studies in Honor of Richard E. Sullivan, 1987, French Historical Studies, 1991—; contbr. articles to profl. jours. and chpts. to books. Pres., bd. trustees Brookston-Prairie Twp. Pub. Libr. Grantee Am. Philos. Soc., 1973, 76, 82, 86, NEH, 1973, 86, Am. Council Learned Socs., 1975, 77-79, 83, 89, Purdue U., 1973, 75-76, 81, 83, 89. Mem. Am. Hist. Assn., Soc. for Promotion Eriugenian Studies, Medieval Acad. Am. (councillor 1987-90, grantee 1973), Phi Beta Kappa. Home: 504 W 5th St Brookston IN 47923-8100 Office: Purdue Univ Dept of History Univ Hall West Lafayette IN 47907-1358

CONTRERAS, DEE (DORTHEA CONTRERAS), municipal official, educator; b. Kansas City, Mo., Nov. 13, 1945; d. Robert MacGregor Hubsch and Dorothea Ann (Bauer) Wilson; m. Michael Raul Contreras, May 1969 (div. Nov. 1979); 1 child, Jason Michael Raul. BA in Anthropology, UCLA, 1967; JD with honors, Western State U., 1979. Bar: Calif. 1979. Sr. social worker San Diego County, 1968-80; sr. field rep. Svc. Employees Internat. Union Local 535, San Diego, 1980-88; bus. rep. Stationary Engrs. Local 39, Sacramento, 1988-90; sr. employee rels. rep. City of Sacramento, 1990-95, dir. labor rels., 1995—; mem. exec. bd. San Diego Imperial County Labor Coun., 1985-88; tchr. labor history U. Calif. Davis Ext., Sacramento, 1989—. Recipient Bread and Roses award Coalition of Labor Union Women, San Diego, 1981. Mem. Indsl. Rels. Assn. No. Calif. (mem. exec. bd. 1988-94, pres. exec. bd. 1994-96). Democrat. Avocations: reading, writing. Office: City of Sacramento Ste 601 921 10th St Sacramento CA 95814-2711

CONTRERAS, THOMAS J., JR., naval officer; b. Morenci, Ariz.; m. Gloria Rachel Gutierrez, Sept. 4, 1965; children: Naomi, Thomas. BS in Chemistry and Secondary Edn., No. Ariz. U., 1967; MS in Phys. Organic Chemistry, U. Utah, 1969; PhD in Physiology, Uniformed Svcs. U. Health Sci., 1983. Commd. lt. (j.g.) M.C., USN, 1971, advanced through grades to capt.; prin. investigator Naval Blood Rsch. Lab., Boston, 1972-76, Armed Forces Radiobiology Rsch. Inst., Bethesda, Md., 1976-79, Naval Med. Rsch. Inst., Bethesda, 1982-85; rsch. area mgr. combat casualty care Naval Med. R&D Command, Bethesda, 1985-87; tech. area mgr. biomed. and chem./ biol. warfare def. program Office of Naval Tech., Office of Chief of Naval Rsch., Arlington, Va., 1987-91, dep. dir. support technologies directorate, 1987-91; exec. officer Naval Health Rsch. Ctr., San Diego, 1991-95; comdg. officer Naval Med. Rsch. Inst., Bethesda, 1995-98, Naval Med. Rsch. Ctr., Forest Glen, Md., 1998—. Contbr. articles to profl. jours. Decorated Joint Svc. Commendation medal, Meritorious Svc. medal with 2 gold stars, 1984, 91, 95; recipient Hispanic Engring. Nat. Achievement award for profl. achievement in govt., 1991, Hispanic Mag. Role Model of the Yr. award, 1992, Nat. Image Inc. Meritorious Svc. award, 1993, No. Ariz. U. Disting. Citizen award, 1995, Outstanding Alumnus award of Dept. Chemistry, 1995. Mem. Soc. Armed Forces Med. Lab. Scientists, Soc. for Advancement of Chicanos and Native Americans in Sci., Assn. Naval Svc. Officers (Mil. Outstanding Vol. Svc. medal). Office: Naval Medical Research Ctr 8901 Wisconsin Ave Bethesda MD 20889-5607

CONVERSE, ELIZABETH SHEETS, artist, writer; b. Springfield, Ill., Jan. 17, 1946; d. Frank Thomas and Frances Converse (Deal) Sheets; m. Daniel B. A. Richter, Apr. 12, 1979 (div. Dec. 1994); children: William, Joan Clair. BA in Anthropology, Lake Forest Coll., 1964-67; student Writing Ctr., Sarah Lawrence Coll., N.Y.C., 1991; M in Pub. Arts of Literacy, Pacific Oaks Coll., 1999. anthropol. field worker, interviewer NIMH, Chgo., 1967-70; v.p., creative dir. Prodn. Sys., Inc., N.Y.C., 1984-89; intern grad. tchr. program Pacific Oaks Coll., 1997. Performer Absolute Reality Theatre, N.Y.C., The Bridge Collective, N.Y.C., The Performance Group, N.Y.C., 1971-78; dir., performer Whitney Counterweight, N.Y.C., 1971-78; writer, dir. Uto Theatrical Experiment, N.Y.C., 1971-78; writer, dir., actor: (short film) Mercy, 1971-78; prodr., writer, actor: (ind. film) Alexyx, 1978-83; works included in publs. Artweek, Visions, Pasadena Weekly, L.A. Reader, mus. and galleries; author: (fiction) The Pursuit of Happiness, The Clearing, Imbroglio, Wild Thing, Dust and Gold, The Citadel, Stories for Our Times, Our Dream; exhibited in group shows Pierce Coll., Sierra Madre Libr., SouthBay Contemporary Mus., Restaurant Lozano, The Armory, Pasadena; commns. include Susan Chen, Above the Rest, Jim Grancich, Carol Tannenbaum, Judy Webb-Martin, Little Stuga, Eddie Truman, City of Sierra Madre, Dopkins Chapel, Lozano Restaurant. Chair Gooden Sch. Silent Auction, Sierra Madre, Calif., 1992, Harvest Ball Silent Auction, Greenwich, Conn., 1987. Avocations: bicycling, gardening, horse racing, traveling. Home: 823 Canyon Crest Dr Sierra Madre CA 91024-1313

CONVERSE, JAMES CLARENCE, agricultural engineering educator; b. Brainerd, Minn., Apr. 2, 1942; s. James L. and Doris E. (Beck) C.; m. Marjorie A. Swanson, Aug. 6, 1965; children—James, Julie, Mark, Katherine. A.A., Brainerd Jr. Coll, 1962; B.S. in Agrl. Engring., N.D. State U., 1964, M.S. in Agrl. Engring., 1966; Ph.D. in Agrl. Engring., U. Ill., 1970. Asst. prof. agrl. engring. U. Wis., Madison, 1970-75, assoc. prof., 1975-80, prof., 1980—, chmn. dept., 1988-96. Fellow Am. Soc. Agrl. Engring. (Gunlogson countryside engrng. award 1984). Roman Catholic. Avocations: scouts, soccer. Office: U Wis Dept Agrl Engring 460 Henry Mall Madison WI 53706-1533

CONVERSE, JOSEPH THOMAS, archivist, records manager; b. Glasgow, Ky., July 22, 1950; s. Henry Thomas and Betty Rue (Lee) C.; m. Myra Massey, June 24, 1974; 1 child, Emma Victoria. BA, U. Ky., 1972, MLS, 1978; postgrad. studies, U. Ga., 1972-74, U. Va., 1974-76. Br. chief Ky. State Archives, Frankfort, 1979-85; vice consul U.S. Embassy U.S. Dept. State, Guatemala City, Guatemala, 1986-88, U.S. Consulate Gen., Barcelona, Spain, 1989-90; consul U.S. Embassy, Managua, Nicaragua, 1990-91; chief libr. Nat. Archives, Washington, 1991-93; chief records mgmt. Inter Am. Devel. Bank, Washington, 1993—. Mem. Soc. Am. Archivists, Assn. Records Mgrs. and Adminstrs., Ky. Coun. on Archives, Archaeol. Inst. Am., Acad. Cert. Archivists. Democrat. Unitarian. Avocations: reading, cooking, travel. Home: 10461 Red Granite Ter Oakton VA 22124-2714 Office: Inter Am Devel Bank 1300 New York Ave NW Washington DC 20577-4710

CONVERSE, PHILIP ERNEST, social science educator; b. Concord, N.H., Nov. 17, 1928; s. Ernest Luther and Evelyn (Eaton) C.; m. Jean Gilmore McDonnell, Aug. 25, 1951; children: Peter Everett, Timothy McDonnell. B.A., Denison U., 1949, D.H.L. (hon.), 1974; M.A., State U. Iowa, 1950; cert., U. Paris, 1954; M.A., U. Mich., 1956, Ph.D., 1958; D.H.L. (hon.), U. Chgo., 1979. Asst. prof. sociology U. Mich., 1960-65, prof. sociology and polit. sci., 1965-89, Robert C. Angell Disting. prof., 1975-89; asst. study dir. Inst. Social Rsch. U. Mich., 1956-58, study dir., 1958-65, program dir., 1965-82, dir. Ctr. for Polit. Studies, 1982-86, dir. Inst. Social Rsch., 1986-89; dir. Ctr. Advanced Study in Behavioral Scis., 1989-94; trustee Ctr. Advanced Study in Behavioral Scis., 1980-86, 94—, Russell Sage Found., 1982-92. Co-author: The American Voter, 1960, Elections and the Political Order, 1966, The Human Meaning of Social Change, 1972, The Quality of American Life, 1976, Political Representation in France, 1986; contbr. articles to profl. jours. Served with U.S. Army, 1950-52. Recipient Disting. Faculty Achievement award U. Mich., 1973; Fulbright fellow, 1959-60; NSF fellow, 1967-68; Guggenheim fellow, 1975-76; Ctr. Advanced Study in Behavioral Scis. fellow, 1979-80. Mem. AAAS, Am. Sociol. Assn., Am. Polit. Sci. Assn. (pres. 1983-84), Internat. Soc. Polit. Psychology (pres. 1980-81), Nat. Acad. Scis., Am. Acad. Arts and Scis., Am. Philos. Soc. Home: 9 Haverhill Ct Ann Arbor MI 48105-1406

CONVERSE, WILLIAM RAWSON MACKENZIE, retired librarian; b. Sherbrooke, Que., Can., Nov. 25, 1937; s. Augustus Mackenzie and Violet Naomi (Ward) C.; m. Valerie Noel Williams, Jan. 12, 1965 (div., 1989); children: David, Benjamin. BA, Bishop's U., Lennoxville, Que., 1959, MA, 1962; PhD, U. Adelaide, South Australia, 1968; MLS, U. Western Ont., London, Can., 1970. Collections librarian Meml. U. of Nfld., St. John's, 1970-73; humanities librarian U. Calgary, Alta., Can., 1973-74, dep. chief librarian, 1974-78, acting chief librarian, 1978, area librarian, 1979-82; univ. libr. U. Winnipeg, Man., Can., 1982-98. Bd. dirs. Man. Assn. for Rights and Liberties, Winnipeg, 1985-87, West Broadway Cmty. Ministries, 1996-97. Research grantee The Can. Council, Ottawa, Ont., 1968-69. Mem. Can. Libr. Assn. (pres. 1985-86), Can. Civil Liberties Assn., WIN (Winnipeg in the Nineties) (steering com. 1991-94). Avocations: film, music, reading, travel. Office: U Winnipeg Libr, 515 Portage Ave, Winnipeg, MB Canada R3B 2E9*

CONVERY, FREDRICK RICHARD, retired surgeon, orthopedist; b. Olympia, Wash., June 12, 1932; m. Martha Ann Minteer; children: Kristine Helen, Linda Lea, Mark Richard. BA, U. Wash., 1954, MD, 1958. Diplomate Am. Bd. Orthopaedic Surgery (examiner 1980-91). Intern Mpls. Gen. Hosp., 1958-59; resident U. Wash., Seattle, 1961-66; fellow in arthritis Rancho Las Amigos, Downey, Calif., 1966-67; instr. orthopedics U. Wash., Seattle, 1967-68, asst. prof., 1968-71, assoc. prof., 1971-72; assoc. prof. U. Calif., San Diego, 1972-77, surgeon in residence, prof. surgery, 1977-97. Inventor prosthetic fixation technique. Mem. med. and sci. com. Western Wash. chpt. The Arthritis Found., 1968-72, San Diego chpt., 1973, chmn., 1977-78; mem. Calif. State Arthritis Coun., 1974-76. With USNR. Grantee Johnson & Johnson, 1994. Fellow Am. Acad. Orthopaedic Surgeons (exam. and evaluation com. 1974-82, Kappa Delta award 1972); mem. Am. Rheumatism Assn. (sect. arthritis, program com. 1973-75), Western Orthopaedic Assn. (Vernon P. Thompson award for Resident Rsch. 1964), Acad. Orthopaedic Soc., Am. Orthopaedic Assn. (resident guest 1966), Orthopaedic Rsch. Soc., Internat. Soc. of the Knee, Assn. for Arthritic Hip and Knee Soc., Wilson-Bost Interurban Club.

CONVERY, PATRICK GEORGE, orthopedic surgeon; b. Paterson, N.J., July 4, 1953; s. Patrick Hugh and Constance (Donato) C.; m. Marilyn Jean Glaser, Aug. 3, 1975; children: Kristen, Ellen, Matthew, Steven. BA in Chemistry, Montclair State Coll., 1975; MD, Bowman Gray Sch. Medicine, 1979. Diplomate Am. Bd. Orthopedic Surgery. Resident Pa. State U., Hershey, 1979-84; practice medicine specializing in orthopedic surgery Budd Lake, N.J., 1984-85; orthopedic surgeon Univ. Mednet, 1985—, chief dept. surgery, 1994—; active staff Lake County Hosp., Willougby, 1986—, Euclid Gen. Hosp., 1986-94, Univ. Hosps. Cleve., 1994—; chief dept. surgery Univ. Mednet, 1994—; mem. adv. bd. Kerr Brumbaugh Rehab. Ctr., Mentor, Ohio, 1987-91; med. dir. Lake Hosps. Rehab. and Wellness Ctr., 1992-97. Fellow Am. Acad. Orthopaedic Surgeons; mem. Ohio State Med. Assn., Lake County Med. Soc. (pres. 1992—), Cleve. Orthopaedic Soc. Democrat. Roman Catholic. Avocation: sports. Home: 8280 Eagleridge Ln Concord OH 44077-9797 Office: Mednet Euclid Clinic 18599 Lake Shore Blvd Euclid OH 44119-1054

CONVISER, RICHARD JAMES, law educator, lawyer, publications company executive; b. Chgo., Apr. 4, 1938; s. Jack and Florence Conviser; 1 child, Ryan Elizabeth. B.A., U. Calif.-Berkeley, 1959, J.D., 1962; Dr. Jur, U. Cologne, Fed. Republic Germany, 1964. Bar: Calif. 1962, Ill. 1965. Assoc. Baker & McKenzie, Chgo., 1965-67; dep. European dir. European Office of Ill., Brussels, Belgium, 1968-69; prof. law DePaul U., Chgo., 1969-73, Chgo.-Kent Coll. Law, Ill. Inst. Tech., 1973—; sr. v.p. Harcourt Brace Pubs., N.Y.C., from 1980; chmn., chief exec. officer Harcourt Profl. Edn. Group, Chgo., 1967—; founder, dir. BAR/BRI Bar Rev., Chgo.; founder, dir. Conviser & Duffy CPA Rev., Chgo.; bd. dirs. Harcourt Profl. Edn., Exchange Nat. Bank, Chgo., Conviser-Duffy CPA Rev. Author: The Modern Philanthrophic Foundation: A Comparative Legal Analysis, 1965, The Law of Agency and Partnership, 1993; mng. editorial dir. Gilbert Law Summaries, L.A., 1978—. Mem. North Dearborn Pk. Assn.; trustee Emory U. Sch. Law, Atlanta, Libr. Internat. Rels., Inst. Internat. Edn. Fellow Col. W. Dinkelspiel Found., 1960-62, Newhouse Found., 1960-62; Ford Found. internat. law fellow, 1962-64. Mem. ABA, Calif. Bar Assn., Ill. Bar Assn., Chgo. Bar Assn. Clubs: Racquet of Chgo., Saddle and Cycle (Chgo.). Home: 1518 N Dearborn Pky Chicago IL 60610-1402 Office: Harcourt Profl Edn Group 111 W Jackson Blvd Fl 7 Chicago IL 60604-3502*

CONWAY, ANNE CALLAGHAN, federal judge; b. Cleve., July 30, 1950. AB, John Carroll U., 1972; JD, U. Fla., 1975. Bar: Fla. 1975, U.S. Supreme Ct. 1981, U.S. Ct. Appeals (5th and 11th cirs.), U.S. Dist. Ct. (mid., no. and so. dists.) Fla. Law clk. to justice U.S. Dist. Ct., Orlando, Fla., 1975-77; from assoc. to ptnr. Wells, Gattis & Hallowes, Orlando, 1978-81; assoc. Carlton, Fields, Ward, Emmanuel, Smith & Cutler, P.A., Orlando, 1982-85, ptnr., 1985-91; judge U.S. Dist. (Mid. Dist.) Fla., Orlando, 1991—; mem. adv. com. on local rules U.S. Dist. Ct., Orlando, 1990-91, grievance com. Orlando div., mid. dist., 1986-91. Bd. dirs. So. Ballet Theatre, Winter Park, Fla., 1985-89, adv. bd., 1985-89; bd. dirs. Greater Orlando Area Legal Svcs., 1978-85. Mem. ABA, Orange County Bar Assn. (chairperson state and fed. trial practice com. 1989-90). Office: US Courthouse 80 N Hughey Ave Rm 646 Orlando FL 32801-2231*

CONWAY, BRIAN PETER, ophthalmologist, educator; b. N.Y.C., Dec. 20, 1942; s. Francis Xavier and Marie Theresa (Bohan) C.; m. Dora Linda Rubin, July 23, 1971 (div. Dec. 1995); children: Jennifer, Matthew, Michael. AB in Econs., Georgetown U., 1964, MD, 1968. Intern Peter Bent Brigham Hosp., Boston, 1968-69, asst. resident in internal medicine, 1969-70; resident in ophthalmology Johns Hopkins Hosp., Balt., 1972-75, asst. chief of svc., 1976-77; asst. prof. Johns Hopkins U., Balt., 1977-78; prof. ophthalmic surgery, chmn. dept. U. Va. Med. Sch., Charlottesville, 1978—; mem. data monitoring com. Nat. Eye Inst., Bethesda, Md., 1982—. Lt. cmdr. USPHS, 1970-72. Retinal disease fellow Bascom Palmer Eye Inst., Miami, Fla., 1975-76. Presbyterian. Office: Univ of Va Sch Medicine Dept of Ophthalmology PO Box 10009 Charlottesville VA 22906-0009*

CONWAY, CONNIE ANNE See **HELLYER, CONSTANCE ANNE**

CONWAY, DAVID ANTONY, communications executive, marketing professional; b. N.Y.C., Dec. 31, 1941; s. David A. and Elizabeth (Reidy) C.; m. Rosanne Kearney, July 30, 1966; children: Jennifer Stanton, Caroline Sloane. BS in Econs., Fordham Coll., 1963, MS in Econs., 1965. With Allied Chem. Corp., N.Y.C., 1967-68, CBS Inc., N.Y.C., 1968-75, Goldman Sachs & Co., N.Y.C., 1975-76; v.p. adminstrn. Keene Corp., N.Y.C., 1976-86, KDI Corp., Cin., 1986-93, also bd. dirs.; pres. Modern Edn. Svcs., N.Y.C., 1994-97, also bd. dirs.; pres., CEO Waterchef Inc., Glen Head, N.Y., Phoenix, 1997—, also bd. dirs. Served to 1st lt. U.S. Army, 1965-67. Republican. Roman Catholic. Club: Manhasset Bay Yacht (Port Washington, N.Y.). Office: Waterchef Inc 13026 N Cave Creek Rd Ste 206 Phoenix AZ 85022-5199

CONWAY, DENNIS, geography educator; b. Whitehaven, Eng., Mar. 26, 1941; came to U.S., 1969; s. Ernest and Constance May (Pratt) C.; m. Ruth Janet Hope, Jan. 6, 1966; children: Rebecca, Michael. BA with honors, Cambridge (Eng.) U., 1962; MA in Geography, U. Tex., 1974, PhD, 1976. Asst. prof. geography Ind. U., Bloomington, 1976-82, assoc. prof., 1982-92, prof., 1992—, chair dept. geography, 1993-97; Co-author: Caribbean: Endless Diversity, 1992, Caribbean Self Help Housing, 1997; contbr. chpts. to books, numerous articles to profl. jours. Office: Ind U Bloomington IN 47405

CONWAY, DOROTHY JEAN WILLIAMS, economist; b. Elizaville, Ky., Apr. 13, 1927; d. John Downing and Maud (Knight) Williams; m. Gene Farris Conway, Sept. 1, 1950; children: Lisa Ann Conway Allen, Janet Lee Conway Fleenor, Linda Knight Conway Hensley. Student, Ky. Wesleyan Coll., Winchester, 1945-46; BS, U. Ky., Lexington, 1949; student, Drexel Inst. Tech., Phila., 1952. Extension svc. agt. U. Ky., Maysville, 1949-52; tchr. home econ. Dayton (Ky.) H.S., 1952; therapeutic dietitian Doctor's Hosp., Phila., 1952-53; rsch. and devel. lab. asst. Pillsbury Ballard, Louisville, Ky., 1953-54; home svc. adv. Indpls. Power and Light, 1954, The Gas Svc. Co., Topeka, Kans., 1954-56; lectr. home mgmt. U. Cin., 1963. Bd. mem. Mary P. Shelton Pub. Libr., Georgetown, Ohio, 1979-93; bd. United Way. Allocations Com. Cin., 1985-94; bd. mem., chmn. Georgetown United Meth. Ch., 1981-87; mem., pres., sec. U. Cin. Women's Club, 1958-98. Mem. DAR, Am. Home Econ. Assn., Brown County Gen. Hosp. Aux., Cin. Women's Club, Phi Epsilon Omicron. Methodist. Home: 315 E State St Georgetown OH 45121-1416

CONWAY, DWIGHT COLBUR, chemistry educator; b. Long Beach, Calif., Nov. 14, 1930; s. Dee A. and Ruth (Mills) C.; m. Diane Faye Coulter, Aug. 25, 1962; children—Kathleen Coulter Jurell, Karyn Mills, Michael Dwight, Patrick Hugh. B.S., U. Calif. at Berkeley, 1952; M.S., U. Chgo., 1953, Ph.D., 1956. Postdoctoral student Purdue U., West Lafayette, Ind., 1956-57; asst. prof. Purdue U., 1957-63; assoc. prof. chemistry Tex. A.&M. U., College Station, 1963-67; prof. Tex. A.&M. U., 1967—. U.S. Rubber Co. fellow, 1953-54; DuPont teaching fellow, 1954-55; recipient Excellence in Teaching award Standard Oil Co. of Ind., 1969. Mem. Am. Chem. Soc. (chmn.), Am. Phys. Soc., Am. Soc. Mass Spectrometry, Phi Beta Kappa, Sigma Xi (pres. local chpt.), Alpha Chi Sigma. Home: 1909 Bee Creek Dr College Station TX 77840-4871 Office: Tex A&M U Dept Chemistry College Station TX 77843

CONWAY, GENE FARRIS, cardiologist; b. Cynthiana, Ky., 1928; s. Farris Lee and Cora Jane (Hall) C.; m. Dorothy Jean Williams, Sept. 1, 1950; children: Lisa Ann, Janet Lee, Linda Knight. BS, U. Ky., 1949; MD, U. Cin., 1952. Cert. in internal medicine, specialty in cardiovasc. disease. Intern Phila. Gen. Hosp., 1952-53; resident in medicine Louisville Gen. Hosp., 1953-54; resident in rsch. medicine Indpls. Gen. Hosp.; resident in medicine Cin. Gen. Hosp., 1957, 58-59, fellow in cardiology, 1959-61; with U. Hosp. Cin.; prof. med., assoc. dir. internal medicine U. Cin. Coll. Medicine, 1988—; mem. adv. com. Area Health Edn. Ctrs., Ohio Bd. Regents, Columbus, 1977-85; mem. adv. com. Regional Med. Planning, Cin., 1978-82; chair Adv. Group to VA on Cardiac Catheterization, Washington, 1973-75. Contbr. sci. papers to profl. jours. Vice chair Ohio Legis. Com. on Health Care, Columbus, 1994; mem. adv. com. geriatrics Ohio Bd. Regents, Columbus, 1978-80. Fellow Am. Coll. Cardiology, Coun. on Clin. Cardiology; mem. Am. Coll. Physician Execs., Am. Heart Assn., Cen. Soc. for Clin. Rsch., Cin. Soc. Internatl Medicine (pres. 1988-89), Soc. Sigma Xi. Republican. Methodist.

CONWAY, HOBART MCKINLEY, JR., geo-economist; b. Hackleburg, Ala., Nov. 1, 1920; s. Hobart McKinley and Eva (Kelly) C.; m. Rebecca Warner Kellam, Sept. 17, 1942; children—Linda, Laura. B.S., Ga. Inst. Tech., 1940, B.A. in Engring., 1941. Research engr. NASA, 1941-44, 46-47; dir. So. Assn. Sci. and Industry, Atlanta, 1948-53; pres. Conway Research, Inc., Atlanta, 1954—; dir. Sitenet, 1983—; mem. U.S. Devel. Mission to S.E. Asia, 1962; cons. AID, 1963-68; chmn. Ga. Sci. and Tech. Commn., 1965-66, Caracas Interam. Devel. Seminar; indsl. devel. cons., 15 countries. Editor: Industrial Development mag, 1954-64, Site Selection Handbook, 1954-64, Weather Handbook, 1974, Industrial Facility Planning, 1976, Industrial Park Growth, 1979, Site Net World Guide, 1988—; editor Site World, 1990, 92; author: The Airport City, 1977, 93, Pitfalls in Development, 1978, Marketing Industrial Buildings and Sites, 1980, Disaster Survival, 1981, The Good Life Index, 1981, Facility Planning Technology, 1987, A Glimpse of the Future, 1992, Geo-Economics, The New Science, 1994, The Telcom Coup, 1994, Development Highlights of the Twentieth Century, 1997; also rsch. reports on facilities planning. Mem. Ga. Senate from 41st Dist., 1963-64, 67-68; sponsor The Safe Skies award, 1989—. With USNR, 1944-46. Recipient medal Time mag., 1953. Fellow AAAS; mem. World Devel. Fedn. (chmn.), Internat. Devel. Rsch. Coun. (founder, dir., recipient award 1979), Aircraft Owners and Pilots Assn. Presbyterian. Home: 4292 Ridgegate Dr Duluth GA 30097-2318 Office: Site Selection Ste 150 35 Technology Park Norcross GA 30092-2900*

CONWAY, HOLLIS, track and field athletie, Olympic athlete; b. Chgo., Jan. 8, 1967. Student, Southwestern La. U., 1989—. high jumper Reebok Racing Club. Ranked No. 4 in the world, 1988, No. 3, 1989, No. 1, 1990, 92; winner NCAA Am. Record, 1989, Olympic Festival, 1989; winner World Indoor Championship, Seville, Spain, 1991, USA/Mobil crown, 1991, World Univ. Games, 1991, many other awards. Office: care USA Track & Field 1 Rca Dome Ste 140 Indianapolis IN 46225-1023*

CONWAY, JAMES DONALD, internist, educator; b. Newark, May 2, 1946; s. James M. and Dorothy (Kelly) C. Home and Office: 4300 Houma Blvd Ste 205 Metairie LA 70006-2924

CONWAY, JAMES JOSEPH, physician; b. Chgo., July 1, 1933; s. Frank and Mary (Tuohy) C.; m. Dolores Mazer, June 30, 1956; children: Laurie, John, Cheryl. BS, DePaul U., 1959; MD, Northwestern U., 1963. Asst. instr. U. Pa., 1964-68; assoc. in radiology McGaw Med. Ctr. Northwestern U., Chgo., 1968-71, asst. prof. to assoc. prof. radiology, 1974-80; attendant radiology, chief nuclear medicine div. Children's Meml. Hosp., Chgo., 1968-

98, prof. radiology, 1980—. Contbr. over 110 articles to profl. jours. Served with U.S. Army, 1953-55. Recipient Gold medal Chgo. Radiol. Soc., 1993. Fellow Am. Coll. Nuclear Physicians, Am. Coll. Radiology; mem. P.R. Soc. Nuclear Medicine (hon.), Radiol. Soc. N.Am. (Scroll of Appreciation award 1983), Soc. Nuclear Medicine (pres. 1994-95). Avocation: collector of Chgo. memorabilia. Office: Children's Meml Hosp 2300 N Childrens Plz Chicago IL 60614-3394

CONWAY, JAMES VALENTINE PATRICK, forensic document examiner, former postal service executive; b. Scottdale, Pa., July 16, 1917; s. James Aloysius and Mary Margaret (Yahner) C.; m. Mildred E. Garypie, Aug. 6, 1936; children: James W., Ruth A. Conway Masonek, Colleen L. Conway Weyland, Judith Conway Henderson. Student, St. Vincent Coll., Latrobe, Pa., 1931-34, Cambria-Rowe Bus. Coll., Greensburg, Pa., 1935-36. Diplomate Am. Bd. Forensic Document Examiners. With U.S. Postal Svc., 1939-80; regional chief insp. U.S. Postal Svc., San Francisco, 1971-73; exec. asst. to Postmaster Gen., Washington, 1973-75; sr. asst. postmaster gen. for employee and labor rels., 1975-78; dep. Postmaster Gen., 1978-80, bd. govs., 1978-80; forensic document examiner Alameda, Calif., 1980—. Author: Evidential Documents, 1959; contbr. articles to profl. jours. Bd. dirs. Regional Civil Def. Bd., Santa Rosa, Calif., 1964-69. Recipient Benjamin Franklin award Postmaster Gen.'s, 1980; named Staff Man of Yr. Fed. Bus. Assn., San Francisco, 1957. Fellow Am. Acad. Forensic Scis. (chmn. document sect. 1960-61, chmn. adv. council 1960-61); mem. Internat. Assn. Chiefs Police (life), Internat. Assn. Identification (chmn. subcom. questioned document 1953-56), Am. Soc. Questioned Document Examiners (pres. 1988-90). Democrat. Roman Catholic. Lodge: Elks. Avocations: cantoring, tennis. *Professional competence is a must but necessarily subordinate to absolute personal integrity. Call things the way they are, not the way others, e.g., clients might wish them to be.*

CONWAY, JOHN E., federal judge; b. 1934. BS, U.S. Naval Acad., 1956; LLB magna cum laude, Washburn U., 1963. Assoc. Matias A Zamora, Santa Fe, 1963-64; ptnr. Wilkinson, Durrett & Conway, Alamogordo, N.Mex., 1964-67, Durrett, Conway & Jordon, Alamogordo, 1967-80, Montgomery & Andrews, P.A., Albuquerque, 1980-86; city atty. Alamogordo, 1966-72; mem. N.Mex. State Senate, 1970-80, minority leader, 1972-80; chief fed. judge U.S. Dist. Ct. N.Mex., Albuquerque, 1986—. 1st lt. USAF, 1956-60. Mem. Nat. Commrs. on Uniform State Laws, Fed. Judges' Assn. (bd. dirs.), 10th Cir. Dist. Judges' Assn. (pres.), N.Mex. Bar Assn., N.Mex. Jud. Coun. (vice chmn. 1973, chmn. 1973-75, disciplinary bd. of Supreme Ct. of N.Mex. vice chmn. 1980, chmn. 1981-84), Albuquerque Lawyers Club. Office: US Dist Ct 333 Lomas Blvd NW #770 Albuquerque NM 87102

CONWAY, JOHN K., lawyer. Gen. counsel Kemper Ins. Co., Long Grove, Ill. Office: Lumbermens Mutual Casualty Co 1 Kemper Dr Long Grove IL 60049-0001

CONWAY, JOHN PAUL, retired steel executive; b. Summit, N.J., May 20, 1924; s. Thomas Francis and Mary Magdalene (Spencer) C.: m. Helen Elizabeth Hermes, Sept. 4, 1948; children: Agnes, John Paul, Edward, Mary M., Raymond F., Anne, Joseph, Hugh G., Margaret, Frances. BA, Loras Coll., 1949; postgrad., No. Ill. U. Acct. Northwestern Steel & Wire Co., Sterling, Ill., 1950-65, mgr. acctg., 1965-70, asst. contr., 1970-75, contr., 1975-80, v.p. fin., sec., treas., dir., 1980-86; adv. dir. Allendale Midwest Adv. Bd., Chgo., 1982-86; bd. dirs. Dillon Found., Sterling, 1980—, Cath. Found. of the Rockford (Ill.) Diocese, 1991—. Vol. bus. mgr. St. Mary's Ch., Sterling; bd. dirs. United Way, Sterling, 1975-80. Served with USN, 1943-46, ETO, PTO. Home: 1408 1st Ave Sterling IL 61081-2317

CONWAY, JOHN S., history educator; b. London, Dec. 31, 1929; s. Geoffrey S. and Elsie (Philips) C.; m. Ann P. Jefferies, Aug. 10, 1957; children—David, Jane, Alison. B.A., Cambridge U., Eng., 1952; M.A., Cambridge U., 1955, Ph.D., 1956. Asst. prof. U. Man., Can., 1955-57; asst. prof., assoc. prof., then prof. history U. B.C., Vancouver, 1957-94, prof. emeritus, 1995—; mem. editorial bd. dirs. Holocaust and Genocide Studies, Kirchliche Zeitgeschichte; Smallman Disting. vis. prof. history U. Western On., 1998. Author: The Nazi Persecution of the Churches, 1968, 2d edit., 1997. Contbr. numerous articles on churches and the holocaust to topical publs. Pres. Tibetan Refugee Aid Soc., Can., 1971-81; chmn. Vancouver Coalition with World Refugees, 1982-84. Recipient Queen's Silver Jubilee medal, 1977. Mem. Can. Inst. Internat. Affairs, German Studies Assn., Can. Hist. Assn. Anglican. Home: 4345 Locarno Crescent, Vancouver, BC Canada V6R 1G2 Office: U BC, Dept History, Wesbrook Mall, Vancouver, BC Canada V6T 1Z1

CONWAY, JOHN THOMAS, government official, lawyer, engineer; b. N.Y.C., May 10, 1924; s. John Joseph and Johannah (Stanley) C.; m. Priscilla Harris, Sept. 13, 1947 (div. 1978); children: John, Daniel, Sean, Thomas, Christopher, Johannah; m. Virginia McLaughlin, Mar. 17, 1989. B.N.S., Tufts U., 1945, B.S. in Engring., 1947; J.D., Columbia U., 1949. Bar: N.Y. 1949, U.S. Supreme Ct. 1952. Spl. agt. FBI, Washington, 1950-56; asst. dir. U.S. Congress Joint Com. on Atomic Energy, Washington, 1956-62, exec. dir., 1962-68; exec. asst. to chmn. Consol. Edison, N.Y.C., 1968-78, exec. v.p., 1982-89; chmn. Def. Nuclear Facilities Safety Bd., Washington, 1989—; pres. Am. Nuclear Energy Council, Washington, 1978-82, chmn. bd., 1983-89; bd. dirs. Empire State Energy Research Com., N.Y., 1970-76, Atomic Indsl. Forum, 1976-78; mem. oversight com. U.S. Com. Energy Awareness, Washington, 1982-89. Bd. dirs. Americans for Energy Independence, Washington, 1982-89, Youth for Energy Independence, Washington, 1982-89, Assn. For A Better N.Y., 1982-89, N.Y. Fire Safety Found., 1984-89; mem. N.Y.C. Mayor's Com. for Sci., 1969-76. Lt. (j.g.) USN, 1943-46. Mem. Am. Legion (life), U.S. Army Ft. Myers Officer Club, Democratic Club (Washington). Democrat. Roman Catholic. Office: Defense Nuclear 625 Indiana Ave NW Ste 700 Washington DC 20004-2909

CONWAY, KEVIN, actor, director; b. N.Y.C., May 29, 1942; s. James John C. and Margaret O'Brien; m. Mila Quiros, Apr. 5, 1966. Broadway and Off-Broadway appearances include: Elephant Man, Of Mice and Men, Moonchildren, Red Ryder, One Flew Over the Cuckoo's Nest, Life Class, Other Places, King John, Other People's Money, 1988 (Outer Critics Circle award for best actor, 1989), On the Waterfront; films include: Slaughterhouse Five, Portnoy's Complaint, FIST, Paradise Alley, The Funhouse, Flashpoint, Homeboy, Jesse, One Good Cop, Ramblin Rose, Jennifer 8, Gettysburg, Lawnmower Man II, Whipping Boy, The Quick and the Dead, Rage of Angels, The Scarlet Letter, The Deadliest Season, The Lathe of Heaven, Elephant Man, Something About Amelia, When Will I Be Loved, Breaking the Silence, (miniseries) Gettysburg, Streets of Laredo, Calm at Sunset, (films) Looking for Richard, Mercury Rising, The Confession, (TV) Miami Vice, Law and Order, Jag, Equalizer; dir.: (plays) Off-Broadway and Lincoln Ctr. Mecca, Old Flames, Milk Train Doesn't Stop Here, Chgo. and L.A. prodn. Other Peoples Money, 1990; star, dir.: (feature film) The Sun and the Moon, 1985. Bd. dirs. Second Stage Co. Served with USN, 1960-62. Recipient Village Voice Obie award, 1973; recipient Drama Desk award, 1973-74. Mem. Screen Actors Guild (bd. dirs. 1979-81), Nat. Acad. TV Arts and Scis. Home and Office: 25 Central Park W New York NY 10023-7253

CONWAY, LOWAVA DENISE, data processing administrator; b. Galesburg, Ill., Mar. 27, 1958; d. Richard Eugene and Lowava Jeanine (Squire) Corbin; m. James Dean Rutledge, June 17, 1977 (div. May 1981); 1 child, Tiffany Michelle; m. Dennis Lane Conway, May 26, 1995. Computer operator cert., Carl Sandburg Coll., 1977, student, 1976-86; student, IBM Edn., Chgo., 1979-87. Keypunch operator Fin. Industry Systems, Galesburg, Ill., 1977-79; computer operator Solution Assocs., Peoria, Ill., 1979-80; programmer, data processing mgr. May Co., Galesburg, 1980-81; programmer Kirkendall Gen. Offices, Galesburg, 1981-82; programmer, data processing mgr. Munson Transp., Monmouth, Ill., 1982-85, programmer/analyst, dir. data processing, 1985-87, dir. mgmt. info. systems, 1987-89; ind. contract programmer analyst Oklahoma City, Okla., 1989-92; product line mgr. Innovative Computing Corp., 1992-94; sr. programmer analyst, dir. info. resources Freymiller Trucking, Inc., Oklahoma City, 1994-96; ptnr. D&D Computers, Inc., 1996—. Mem. Ch. of God. Address: 1061 W Losey St Galesburg IL 61401-3441

CONWAY, LYNN, computer scientist, electrical engineer, educator; b. Mt. Vernon, N.Y., Jan. 2, 1938. BS, Columbia U., 1962, MSEE, 1963; D (hon.), Trinity Coll., 1997. Rsch. staff IBM Corp., Yorktown Heights, N.Y., 1964-68; sr. staff engr. Memorex Corp., Santa Clara, Calif., 1969-73; rsch. staff Xerox Corp., Palo Alto, Calif., 1973-78, rsch. fellow, mgr. VLSI systems area, 1978-82, rsch. fellow, mgr. knowledge systems area, 1982-83; asst. dir. for strategic computing Def. Advanced Research Projects Agy., Arlington, Va., 1983-85; prof. elec. engring. and computer sci., assoc. dean U. Mich. Coll. Engring., Ann Arbor, Mich., 1985—; vis. assoc. prof. elec. engring. and computer sci. MIT, Cambridge, Mass., 1978-79; sci. adv. bd. USAF, 1987-90. Co-author: textbook Introduction to VLSI Systems, 1980; contbr. articles to profl. jours.; patentee in field. Mem. coun. Govt.-Univ.-Industry Rsch. Roundtable, 1993—; mem. corp. Charles Stark Draper Lab., 1993—; mem. bd. visitors USAF Acad., 1996—, presdl. appt. Recipient Ann. Achievement award Electronics mag., 1981, Harold Pender award U. Pa., 1984, Wetherill Medal Franklin Inst., 1985, Sec. of Def. Meritorious Civilian Svc. award, 1985. Fellow IEEE; mem. NAE, Am. Assn. for Artificial Intelligence, Soc. Women Engrs. (Ann. Achievement award 1990), Assn. Computing Machinery. Avocations: motocross racing, whitewater canoeing, natural landscaping. E-mail: conway@engin.umich.edu. Office: U Mich 146 ATL Bldg Ann Arbor MI 48109-2110

CONWAY, MARK ALLYN, lawyer; b. Dayton, Ohio, Dec. 13, 1957; s. Allyn Walter and Doris Jean (Wright) C.; m. Dawn Elizabeth Manning, July 31, 1982; children: Ashley Wright, Alexandra Mills. BA, Denison U., 1980; JD, Calif. Western Sch. of Law, 1983; LLM in Taxation, Georgetown U., 1984. Bar: D.C. 1983, U.S. Tax Ct. 1983, Calif. 1988, Ohio 1991. Ptnr. Thompson, Hine & Flory LLD, Dayton, 1990—. Mem. ABA (real property, probate and trust law sect.), D.C. Bar Assn. (taxation sect. Washington chpt.), Calif. Bar Assn. (real property, probate and trust law sect. 1988—), Dayton Racquet Club. Republican. Presbyterian. Avocations: tennis, skiing, sailing. Home: 5712 Price Hill Pl Dayton OH 45459-1428 Office: Thompson Hine & Flory LLD 2000 Courthouse Plz NE Dayton OH 45402

CONWAY, MICHAEL MAURICE, lawyer; b. St. Joseph, Mo., Mar. 11, 1946; s. Michael Maurice and Genevieve (Hepburn) C.; m. Kathleen Stevens; children: Michael, Cara, Mary. BS in Journalism, Northwestern U., 1968; JD, Yale U., 1973. Bar: Ill. 1973, U.S. Dist. Ct. (no. dist.) Ill. 1973, U.S. Tax Ct. 1975, U.S. Ct. Claims 1976, U.S. Ct. Appeals (7th cir.) 1976, U.S. Ct. Appeals (1st cir.) 1979, U.S. Supreme Ct. 1980, U.S. Ct. Appeals (5th and 11th cirs.) 1981, U.S. Ct. Appeals (fed. cir. 1982),. Ptnr. Hopkins & Sutter, Chgo., 1979—; counsel U.S. Ho. Reps. com. on judiciary impeachement inquiry Richard M. Nixon, 1974. Chmn. Ill. Lawyers Com. Clinton/Gore, Chgo., 1992; alt. del. Dem. Nat. Conv., 1992, del., 1996. Mem. Am. Coll. Trial Lawyers, Union League Club. Roman Catholic. Avocations: baseball coaching. Office: Hopkins & Sutter 3 1st Nat Plz Chicago IL 60602

CONWAY, NANCY ANN, editor; b. Foxboro, Mass., Oct. 15, 1941; d. Leo T. and Alma (Goodwin) C.; children: Ana Lucia DaSilva, Kara Ann Martin. Cert. in med. tech., Carnegie Inst., 1962; BA in English, U. Mass., 1976, cert. in secondary edn., 1978. Tchr. Brazil-Am. Inst., Rio de Janeiro, 1963-68; freelance writer, editor Amherst, Mass., 1972-76; staff writer Daily Hampshire Gazette, North Hampton, Mass., 1976-77; editor Amherst Bull., 1977-80, Amherst Record, 1980-83; features editor Holyoke (Mass.) Transcript/Telegram, 1983-84; gen. mgr. Monday-Thursday Newspapers, Boca Raton, Fla., 1984-87; dir. editorial South Fla. Newspaper Network, Deerfield Beach, 1987-90; pub., editor York (Pa.) Newspapers, Inc., 1990-95; exec. editor, v.p. Alameda Newspaper Group, Pleasanton, Calif., 1996—. Bd. dirs. Math.: Opportunities in Engring., Sci. and Tech.-Pa. State, York, 1991-95. Recipient writing awards, state newspaper assns. Mem. Am. Soc. Newspaper Editors, Soc. Profl. Journalists. Avocations: literature, photography, communication gardening. Office: 66 Jack London Sq Oakland CA 94607-3726

CONWAY, NEIL JAMES, III, title company executive, lawyer, writer; b. Cleve., Feb. 15, 1950; s. Neil J. and Jeanne Louise (Gensert) C.; m. Maureen Dolan; children: Seanna, Neil James IV, Declan, Liam. BSBA, John Carroll U., 1972; MBA, Suffolk U., 1974; JD, Antioch Sch. Law (named change to The U. of D.C.), 1983. Bar: Ohio, 1983, U.S. Dist. Ct. (no. dist.) Ohio, 1983, U.S. Supreme Ct., 1987, D.C., 1988. Auditor U.S. Dept. Interior, Arlington, 1974-77; systems acct. Mil. Dist. Washington, 1978-79; legal intern Govt. Accountability Project, Washington, 1980-81; jud. intern presiding judge U.S. Dist. (no. dist.) Ct. Ohio, 1982; legal asst. Spiegel & McDiarmid, Washington, 1982-83; pvt. practice Painesville, Ohio, 1983—; from title examiner to pres. Conway Land Title Co., Painesville, 1983—; adj. prof. legal studies Lake Erie Coll., Painesville, Ohio. Author: American Protestants for Truth About Ireland; editor in chief Antioch Law Jour., 1982-83, Am. Soc. for Internat. Law Human Rights Newsletter, 1995; pub. The Ohio Irish Times, 1993—; contbr. articles to profl. jours. Mem. Lake County Econ. Devel. Coun.; mem. Lawyers Com. for Human Rights, N.Y.C. Capt. USAR, 1972-81. Mem. ABA, Am. Soc. Internat. Law (Dean Rusk award 1980), Ohio Bar Assn., Lake County Bar Assn. (co-author real estate symposium 1989), Brehon Law Soc. N.Y., Ohio Land Title Assn., Lake County Bd. Realtors (Affiliate of Yr. 1986), Painesville Title Assn. (pres. 1985-86), Irish Am. Cultural Inst. (Editl. citation Ohio Irish Bull. 1990), Amnesty Internat. Democrat. Roman Catholic. Avocations: racquetball, youth hockey. Home: 10930 Bradley Ct Concord OH 44077-2443

CONWAY, PAUL GARY, neuropharmacologist; b. Monson, Mass., July 31, 1952; s. Andrew Paul and Joan Sarah (Haley) C.; m. Malana Frances Seniuk, Aug. 21, 1976. BS in Pharmacy, Ohio No. U., 1975; MS in Pharmacology, U. Toledo, 1978; PhD in Pharmacology, Ohio State U., 1982. Postdoctoral fellow U. Pa., Phila., 1982-84; sr. rsch. pharmacologist Hoechst Roussel Pharm. Inc., Somerville, N.J., 1984-86, rsch. assoc., 1986-88, group leader, 1988-92, project mgr., 1992-95, sr. project mgr., 1995-96; dir. project planning Janssen Rsch. Found., Titusville, N.J., 1996-98; dir. project planning & contract adminstrn. Clin. Studies Ltd., Providence, R.I., 1998—; adj. asst. prof. Fairleigh-Dickinson U., Madison, N.J., 1986; pharmacology instr. Ohio No. U., Ada, 1975-76. Editor Clin. Neuropharmacology, 1991; contbr. more than 40 articles to profl. jours.; patentee in field. Mem. Am. Soc. Pharmacology and Exptl. Therapeutics, Soc. for Neurosci., Internat. Brain Rsch. Orgn., Drug Info. Assn., Sigma Xi. Avocations: sailing, golf. Office: CLin Studies Ltd 10 Dorrance St Ste 400 Providence RI 02903-2018*

CONWAY, REBECCA ANN KOPPES, lawyer; b. Colorado Springs, Colo., May 18, 1952; d. Virgil Lee and Betty J. Koppes; children: Kelley, Kathrine; m. Sean P. Conway, Nov. 26, 1994. BA, U. Colo., 1975, JD, 1978. Bar: Colo. 1978, U.S. Dist. Ct. Colo. 1978. Atty. EEOC, Denver, 1978-79, Dist. Atty.'s Office, Adams County, Brighton, Colo., 1979-80; ptnr. Gutierrez & Koppes, Greeley, Colo., 1980-92; pvt. practice Law Office of Rebecca Koppes Conway, Greeley, 1992—; mem. Colo. Pub. Defenders Commn., 1985-95, chair, 1990-95. Chmn. Placement Alternatives Commn., Weld County, Colo., 1987-89; mem. Our Saviors Luth. Ch., Greeley, 1985—, exec. dir., 1987-89; chmn. bd. dirs. Colo. Rural Legal Svcs., Denver, 1983-86, 93-96; vice-chair Weld Child Care Network, 1988. Fellow ABA Found., Colo. Bar Found. (dir. 1998—, bd. dirs. 1999—); mem. ABA (house of dels. 1994-97), Colo. Bar Assn. (com. mem., exec. coun. 1986-90, bd. govs. 1983-90, 94—, pres.-elect. 1996-97, pres. 1997-98, chair young lawyers divsn. 1988-89, Outstanding Young Lawyer 1988, v.p. 1989-90), Weld County Bar Assn. (pres. 1992-93, dem. state exec. com. 1998-99, state ctrl. com. 1993—, Weld County exec. com. 1993—). Avocation: reading. Home: 2595 56th Ave Greeley CO 80634-4503 Office: 912 8th Ave Greeley CO 80631-1112

CONWAY, RICHARD ASHLEY, environmental engineer; b. Weymouth, Mass., Nov. 10, 1931; s. George and Helen Mildred (Baker) C.; m. Anne; children: Dianne Marie Conway Clay, David Ashley. BS, U. Mass., 1953; MS, MIT, 1957. Registered profl engr., W.Va.; Diplomate Am. Acad. Environ. Engrs. (trustee 1996-98, Kappa award 1999). Sr. corp. fellow Union Carbide Corp., South Charleston, W.Va., 1957-97; pvt. cons., 1997—; mem. NRC; cons. sci. adv. bd. EPA, DOD Strategic Environ. R&D Program, 1992-98; mem. NRC Bd. Army Sci. and Tech., Comm. Geoscis., Environ. and Resources. Author: Industrial Waste Disposal, 1980; editor: Hazardous Solid Waste Testing, 5 vols., 1981-87, Environmental Risk Analysis, 1982; patentee in field. Served to 1st lt. U.S. Army, 1954-56. Recipient Personal Achievement award in Chem. Engring., Chem. Engring. mag., N.Y.C., 1986, Kappa award, Am. Acad. Environ. Engrs., 1999. Fellow ASCE (chmn. environ. engring. divsn. 1975, Hering medal 1974); mem. NAE, ASTM (Dudley medal 1984), Internat. Water Quality Assn. (governing bd. 1978-88), Soc. Environ. Chemistry and Toxicology (bd. dirs. 1983-86, Rachel Carson award 1997), Assn. Environ. Engring. Profs. (affiliate), Water Environ. Fedn. (Gascoigne medal 1967, Rudolfs medal 1974, 83). Avocations: running, tennis. E-mail: conwayenv@aol.com.

CONWAY, RICHARD FRANCIS, investment company executive; b. Greenwich, Conn., Jan. 4, 1954; s. Francis Xavier and Marie (Bohan) C.; m. Greta Weil, Oct. 29, 1988; children: Signe Charlotte Weil, Anna Augusta Weil. BA, Harvard Coll., 1976; MBA, Yale U., 1981. Mgmt. trainee Citibank, N.Y.C., 1976-79; assoc. L.F. Rothschild, Unterberg, Towbin Inc., N.Y.C., 1981-83, v.p., 1983-86, prin., 1986-88; v.p. Salomon Bros. Inc., N.Y.C., 1988-90, Security Pacific Mcht. Bank, N.Y.C., 1990-91; sr. v.p. Needham and Co. Inc., N.Y.C., 1992-94; v.p. Smith Mgmt. Co., N.Y.C., 1994-97, Lone Star Securities Mgmt., Inc., N.Y.C., 1998-99; ptnr. Lampe, Conway & Co., LLC, N.Y.C., 1999—. Trustee Choate Rosemary Hall Sch., Wallingford, Conn., 1974-78; class com. Harvard Coll. Fund, Cambridge, Mass., 1991. Mem. Harvard Club (N.Y.C.), Knickerbocker Club (N.Y.C.), Georgica Assn. (Wainscott, N.Y.). Roman Catholic. Home: 1361 Madison Ave New York NY 10128-0713 Office: Lampe Conway & Co LLC 32nd Fl 730 Fifth Ave 21st Fl New York NY 10019

CONWAY, RICHARD WALTER, computer scientist, educator; b. Milw., Dec. 12, 1931; s. Ralph Walter and Tennie May (Mitchell) C.; m. Edythe Davies, Aug. 29, 1953; children—Kathryn Dimiduk, Ralph, Evan. B.M.E., Cornell U., 1954, Ph.D, 1958. From instr. to prof. computer sci. Cornell U., Ithaca, N.Y., 1956-84, Emerson prof. mfg. Johnson Grad. Sch. Mgmt., 1984—; sr. scientist DataWorks Corp. Author numerous books including: Theory of Scheduling, 1967; Introduction to Programming, 3d edit., 1979; Programming for Poets, 1979; XCELL Simulation System, 1986. Mem. Nat. Acad. Engring., Tau Beta Phi. Office: Cornell U Sage Hall Ithaca NY 14853-4201

CONWAY, ROBERT GEORGE, JR., lawyer; b. Albany, N.Y., Apr. 26, 1951; s. Robert George Sr. and Kathryn Ann (Kelly) C.; m. Lynda Rae Christenson, Dec. 15, 1979; 1 child, Phillip Christopher. AB, Dartmouth Coll., 1973; JD, Union U., 1976; diploma, U.S. Army JAGC Sch., 1986. Bar: Pa. 1978, U.S. Ct. Mil. Appeals 1978, N.C. 1983, U.S. Dist. Ct. (ea. dist.) N.C. 1983, U.S. Dist. Ct. (no. dist.) N.Y. 1998, U.S. Army Ct. Mil. Rev. 1986, U.S. Supreme Ct. 1986, U.S. Ct. Appeals (4th and fed. cirs.) 1987, N.Y. 1998; cert. USMC judge advocate. Commd. 2d lt. USMC, 1975, advanced through grades to maj., 1983; gen. staff sec. USMC, Camp Lejeune, N.C., 1982-83, chief rev. officer, 1983-84, spl. asst. U.S. atty., 1984-85; dir. joint law ctr. air sta. USMC, Cherry Point, N.C., 1986-88, chief rsch. officer air sta., 1988; dep. asst. staff judge adv. to comdt. USMC, Washington, 1989; mil. justice officer Marine Corps Base, Quantico, Va., 1990-91; assoc. counsel for land use law Ea. Area Counsel Office USMC Dept. of Navy Office of Gen. Counsel, Camp Lejeune, N.C., 1991-96; ret. USMC, 1996; counsel N.Y. State Divsn. Mil. and Naval Affairs, Latham, 1996—; adj. faculty mem. Ga. Inst. Tech., 1993, Webster U., 1994-96; spkr. in field. Trustee Cath. student ctr. Aquinas House, Dartmouth Coll., Hanover, N.H., 1973-89, sec. Dartmouth class of 1973, 1994—. Recipient Legion of Merit, 1996. Mem. ABA, Pa. Bar Assn., N.C. Bar Assn., N.Y. Bar Assn., Fed. Bar Assn. (contbg. author assn. news and jour. 1990), Dartmouth Lawyers Assn., Am. Legion, U.S. Naval Inst., Marine Corps Assn., KC (adv. 1984-85), Rotary, Dartmouth Club Ea. N.Y. (v.p. 1998—). Roman Catholic. Home: 27 Manor Dr Glenmont NY 12077-3326 Office: NY State Divsn Mil and Naval Affairs Attn MNLA 330 Old Niskayuna Rd Latham NY 12110-3514

CONWAY, SEAN, press secretary; b. Denver, Sept. 16, 1959. BA, Ft. Lewis Coll., 1982. Staff dir. Office of U.S. Senator Williams Armstrong, Colo., 1982-90; south Colo. dir. Office of U.S. Senator Williams Armstrong, 1982-95, north Colo. dir., 1986-89, state dir., 1989-90; area dir. Office of Congressman Mike Strange, Colo., 1985; dist. area dir., press sec. Office of U.S. Rep. Wayne Allard, Colo., 1991-96; co. press sec. Office of Senator Wayne Allard, Colo., 1997-98; press sec. Office of Senator Wayne Allard, 1998—. Office: 513 Senate Hart Office Bldg Washington DC 20510-0604 also: Ste 3Q 3400 16th St Greeley CO 80631

CONWAY, WILLIAM GAYLORD, zoologist, zoo director, conservationist; b. St. Louis, Nov. 20, 1929; s. Frederick Eldridge and Alice Harriet (Gaylord) C. AB, Washington U., 1951; ScD (hon.), St. Lawrence U., 1979, Fordham U., 1981, Trinity Coll., 1984. Curator birds St. Louis Zoo, 1951-56; curator birds N.Y. Zool. Soc. (now The Wildlife Conservation Soc.), N.Y.C., 1956-72, assoc. dir., 1960-61, zoo dir., 1962—, gen. dir., 1966—, pres., 1992—; mem. expdns. to Trinidad, Argentina, Boliva, China; dir. Asa Wright Nature Ctr., Trinidad; advisor Fundación Patagonia Natural, Argentina. Contbr. articles to profl. jours. Decorated comdr. Order of the Golden Ark (The Netherlands); recipient Mayor's award of honor for arts and culture, 1979, Marlin Perkins award AAZPA, 1986, Disting. Achievement award Soc. for Conservation Biology, Disting. Svc. medal Am. Assn. Mus., 1998. Fellow N.Y. Zool. Soc.; mem. Am. Ornithologists Union, Cooper Ornithol. Soc., Brit. Avicultural Soc. Wilson Ornithol. Club, Internat. Survival Svc. Commn., Cultural Instns. Group (past pres.), Am. Conservation Assn. (bd. dirs.), Am. Assn. Zool. Pks. and Aquariums (past pres., bd. dirs.), Am. Zoo and Aquarium Assn. (chmn.). Office: Wildlife Conservation Soc 2300 St Southern Blvd Bronx NY 10460*

CONWAY-GERVAIS, KATHLEEN MARIE, reading specialist, educational consultant; b. Bklyn., Apr. 18, 1942; d. John Joseph and Mary Josephine Conway; m. Stephen Paul Gervais, July 10, 1976; 1 child, John Joseph. BA, Coll. Mt. St. Vincent, 1970; MS, Hunter Coll. of N.Y.C., 1973, Reading Specialization, 1974. Cert. reading and social studies tchr., nursery and elem. ecuator, N.Y., N.J. Elem. tchr. Archdiocese of N.Y., N.Y.C., 1963-74; reading specialist Malverne (N.Y.) Union Free Sch. Dist., 1974-86, dist. reading, testing coord., 1986-91, reading specialist, 1992-95; reading specialist East Meadow (N.Y.) Union Free Sch. Dist., 1995-96; reading cons., tchr. trainer Uniondale (N.Y.) Union Free Sch. Dist., 1996—; adv. bd. mem. Newsday in Edn., Melville, 1982—; adj. prof. Nassau C.C., Garden City, N.Y., 1995—. Active Getting Out the vote presdl. election, N.Y., 1992. Recipient Ambassador in Edn. award Newsday, Melville, 1982, Congruence Model Project award N.Y. State Dept. Edn., Albany, 1988, Elizabeth Ann Seton award Office of Cathechesis and Worship, Long Island, 1991. Mem. ASCD, Internat. Reading Assn., N.Y. State Reading Assn., Orton Dyslexia Soc., Nassau Reading Coun. (bd. dirs.). Democrat. Roman Catholic. Avocations: travel, reading, theater, swimming, computer. Home: 174 Nassau Blvd West Hempstead NY 11552-2218 Office: Uniondale Union Free Sch Dist 50 Lawrence Rd Hempstead NY 11550-7535

CONWAY-WELCH, COLLEEN, dean, nurse midwife; b. Monticello, Iowa, Apr. 26, 1944; d. John Andrew and Lorraine (Digman) Conway; m. Ted Houston Welch, Mar. 31, 1985. BSN, Georgetown U., 1965; CNM, Catholic Maternity Inst., 1969; MSN, Catholic U., Washington, 1969; PhD, NYU, 1973. Staff nurse Georgetown U. Hosp., Washington, 1965; staff nurse labor & delivery Queens Med. Ctr., Honolulu, 1966; nurse cons. U. So. Calif. Med. Ctr., L.A., 1967; staff assoc. Nat. League Nursing, N.Y.C., 1969-70; asst. prof. Downstate Med. Ctr., Bklyn., 1970-74; asst. prof. Georgetown U., 1974-76, assoc. dean, 1975-76; assoc. prof. George Mason U., Fairfax, Va., 1976-78, Calif. State U., Long Beach, 1978-80; prof. nursing U. Colo., Denver, 1980-84; dean Vanderbilt Sch. Nursing, Nashville, 1984—; mem. Presdl. Commn. on HIV Epidemic, Washington, 1988, adv. coun. NIH Nat. Ctr. Nursing Rsch., Washington, 1989-93, bd. trust Healthcare Leadership Coun., Washington, 1990; chair nursing leadership coun. Inst. Healthcare Improvement, 1992; bd. dirs. Diversicare, Franklin, Tenn., Nat. League Nursing Community Health Accreditation, N.Y.C., Commonwealth Fund Nurse Exch. Fellowship Program, N.Y.C. Contbr. articles to profl. jours. Bd. govs. United Way, Middle, Tenn., 1989; active Mayor's Task Force for Substance Abuse, 1990, JFK Adv. Com. on Arts, Washington, 1991, Jr. League, 1973—. Recipient Dempsey Humanitarism award St. Clare's Hosp. AIDS Ctr., 1989; commencement speaker, Columbia Sch. Nursing, 1991. Fellow Am. Acad. Nursing; mem. Soc. Advancement Women's Health Rsch. (bd. dirs. 1991—), Rotary Club, Cosmos Club, Sigma Theta Tau (bd. dirs. 1968—). Avocations: snow skiing, scuba diving, hiking, reading. Home: 109

Lynnwood Ter Nashville TN 37205-2911 Office: Vanderbilt U Sch Nursing 111 Godchaux 461 21st Ave S Nashville TN 37240-0008*

CONWELL, ESTHER MARLY, physicist; b. N.Y.C., May 23, 1922; d. Charles and Ida (Korn) C.; m. Abraham A. Rothberg, Sept. 30, 1945; 1 son, Lewis J. BA, Bklyn. Coll., 1942; MS, U. Rochester, N.Y., 1945; PhD, U. Chgo., 1948; DSc, Bklyn. Coll., 1992. Lectr. Bklyn. Coll., 1946-51; mem. tech. staff Bell Telephone Labs., 1951-52; physicist GTE Labs., Bayside, N.Y., 1952-61; mgr. physics dept. GTE Labs., 1961-72; vis. prof. U. Paris, 1962-63; Abby Rockefeller Mauze prof. M.I.T., 1972; prin. scientist Xerox Corp., Webster, N.Y., 1972-80; rsch. fellow Xerox Corp., 1981-98; adj. prof. U. Rochester, 1990—; cons., mem. adv. com. engrng. NSF, 1978-81. Author: High Field Transport in Semiconductors, 1967, also research papers; mem. editorial bd. Jour. Applied Physics; Proc. of IEEE; patentee in field. Fellow IEEE (Edison medal 1997), Am. Phys. Soc. (sec.-treas. divsn. condensed matter physics 1977-82); mem. AAAS, NAS, NAE, Soc. Women Engrs. (Achievement award 1960). Office: 800 Phillips Rd 0114/22D Webster NY 14580-9720

CONWELL, HALFORD ROGER, physician; b. Cin., Jan. 28, 1924; s. Halford Fredrick and Erma Pearl (Cornelius) C.; BA, U. Wooster, 1948; MA, U. Louisville, 1950; MD, U. Cin., 1955, ATP; diplomate crew coordination tng. Continental Airlines; m. Margaret Ann King, Dec. 15, 1965; children: Mark A., Sherri L., John H. Aviation medicine, Huntsville, Tex., 1959—; mem. staff Huntsville (Tex.) Meml. Hosp., chief of staff, 1974-75, chief medicine, 1976-80, bd. trustees, 1991—; sr. U.S. med. officer Brit. Caledonian Airways, 1977-89; cons. Aeromexico; chief flight surgeon Continental Airlines, 1996—; mem. Walker County Hosp. Dist., 1975-79, chmn., 1976-79; asst. dean of men, instr. psychology Heidelberg U., Tiffin, Ohio, 1950-51; instr. psychology Cin. Coll.; sr. med. examiner FAA; sr. examiner C.A.A. (U.K.), C.A.A. (Australia); newspaper columnist, 1992—. Trustee Biol. Analysis and Research Found.; capt. (hon.) Tex. Internat. Airline; founder Bomber Command Mus. (R.A.F.). Served to lt. USNR, 1942-46. Recipient safe pilot award Nat. Pilots Assn., Pilot Proficiency award FAA, Profl. Svc. Citation. mem. Brit. Assn. Aerospace Medicine, Latin Am. Aviation Med. Assn., Scottish Assn. Aviation Med. Examiners; mem. Airline Med. Dirs. Assn., Civil Aviation Med. Assn. (v.p. 1968-80, dir. 1968—, pres. 1980-81, award of merit 1994, 97), Mitchell Pediatric Soc., Academie Internationale de Medicine Aeronatque et Spatiale, Aircraft Owners and Pilots Assn. (med. adv. panel), Confederate Air Force (founding mem.), Airline Transp. Assn. (med. com.), Order Ky. Cols., Quiet Birdmen, Masons, Psi Chi, Alpha Psi Omega (hon.). Office: 2800 Lake Rd Huntsville TX 77340-5632

CONWELL, THERESA GALLO, financial services representative; b. Utica, N.Y., Mar. 6, 1947; d. Ernest and Anna (Caiazzo) Gallo; m. Charles Ray Conwell, Aug. 19, 1978. BS in Edn., SUNY-Potsdam, 1968; MA in Edn., SUNY-Cortland, 1978; Cert. tchr., N.Y.; CLU; chartered fin. cons., registered rep.; ChFc. Tchr. pub. schs., Clinton, N.Y., 1969-78, Portland, Conn., 1978-80; supr. mktg. services Phoenix Home Life Ins. Co. (now Phoenix Home Life Ins. Co.), Hartford, Conn., 1980-82, assoc. mgr. agt. tng., 1982-84, mgr. agt. tng., 1984-85, dir. agt./mgmt. devel., 1985-88, fin. svcs. rep., 1988—; speaker to small bus. orgns., women's groups, N.Y., New Eng., 1986—. Mem. NAFE, NOW, Am. Soc. CLU, Nat. Assn. Life Underwriters, Internat. Assn. Fin. Planners, Hartford Assn. Life Underwriters, Conn. Assn. Life Underwriters, Nat. Assn. Profl. Saleswomen, Bus. and Profl. Women of Glastonbury (pres. 1995), Pres. Club (assoc. 1991). Democrat. Avocations: tennis, golf, swimming, aerobics, reading. Home: 191 Knollwood Dr Glastonbury CT 06033 Office: Phoenix Home Life Ins Co Commerce Ctr One 333 E River Dr Ste 504 East Hartford CT 06108-4219

CONYERS, CLAUDE BRUNSON, retired publishing executive; b. Cartersville, Ga., June 19, 1934; s. Claude Brunson and Rachel Keith (Stephens) C. BA, Vanderbilt U., 1956; MA, Columbia U., 1962; dance tng., New Dance Group, N.Y.C., 1959, Sch. of Am. Ballet, N.Y.C., 1960, Ballet Russe Sch., N.Y.C., 1961-64. Sr. editor Prentice-Hall, Inc., Englewood Cliffs, N.J., 1960-64; dancer PACT Ballet, Johannesburg, South Africa, 1965-66, Les Grands Ballets Canadiens, Montreal, 1967; editl. dir. Greystone Press, N.Y.c., 1968-70; editl. cons. N.Y.C., 1970-74; spl. projects editor Praeger Pubs., N.Y.c., 1975; sr. projects editor Macmillan Pub. Co., N.Y.c., 1975-87; editl. dir., scholarly and profl. reference Oxford U. Press, N.Y.C., 1988-98; mem. publs. com. N.Y. Acad. Scis., 1990-95. Bd. dirs. The George Balachine Found., 1999—. Lt. (j.g.) USNR, 1956-58. Recipient R.R. Hawkins award Profl. and Scholarly Pub./Assn. Am. Pubs., 1991, 93, 96, 98, Dartmouth medal ALA, 1987, 99. Mem. Am. Acad. Religion, Soc. Archtl. Historians, Soc. Dance History Scholars (advisor, editl. bd. 1988—), Columbia Club, World Dance Alliance, Soc. for Scholarly Pub. Democrat. Episcopalian.

CONYERS, JOHN, JR., congressman; b. Detroit, May 16, 1929; s. John and Lucille (Simpson) C.; m. Monia Estes; children: John Jr., Carl Edward. B.A., Wayne State U., 1957, J.D., 1958; LL.D., Wilberforce U., 1969. Bar: Mich. 1959. Legis. asst. to Congressman John Dingell, 1959-61; sr. ptnr. firm Conyers, Bell & Townsend, 1959-61; referee Mich. Workmen's Compensation Dept., 1961-64; mem. 89th-105th Congresses from 1st (now 14th) Mich. dist., 1964—; former chmn. Govt. Ops. Com., former chmn. subcom. on legis. and nat. security; ranking mem. Judiciary Com.; Past dir. edn. Local 900, United Auto Workers; mem. adv. council Mich. Liberties Union; gen. counsel Detroit Trade Union Leadership Council; vice chmn. nat. bd. Ams. for Democratic Action; vice chmn. adv. council ACLU; an organizer Mems. Congress for Peace through Law; bd. dirs. numerous other orgns. including African-Am. Inst., Commn. Racial Justice, Detroit Inst. Arts, Nat. Alliance Against Racist and Polit. Repression, Nat. League Cities. Sponsor, contbg. author: Am. Militarism, 1970, War Crimes and the American Conscience, 1970, Anatomy of an Undeclared War, 1972; contbr. articles to profl. jours. Trustee Martin Luther King Jr. Ctr. for Non-Violent Social Change. Served to 2d lt. U.S. Army, 1950-54, Korea. Recipient Rosa Parks award SCLC. Mem. NAACP (exec. bd. Detroit), Kappa Alpha Psi. Democrat. Baptist. Office: 2426 Rayburn Bldg Washington DC 20515-2214*

COODY, CHARLES S., federal judge; b. 1946. BS, Spring Hill U., 1968; JD, U. Ala., 1975. Law clk. hon. T. Embry Ala. Supreme Ct., 1975; assoc. Smith, Bowman, Thaggard, Crook & Culpepper, 1976-78; gen. counsel Ala. State Bd. Edn., 1978-87; magistrate judge State of Ala., Montgomery, 1987—. With U.S. Army, 1968-72. Mem. Ala. State Bar Assn., Montgomery Inns Ct. Fax: 334-223-7114. Office: US Courthouse 15 Lee St Montgomery AL 36104

COOEY, WILLIAM RANDOLPH, economics educator; b. Wheeling, W.Va., Feb. 23, 1942; s. William Earl and Marguerite Ruth (Potts) C.; m. Linda Faye Whiteman, Aug. 11, 1973; children: William Justin, Crissa Kaye. BA, Bethany Coll., 1964; MS, W.Va. U., 1966; postgrad., Miss. State U., 1973-74. Prof. Bethany (W.Va.) Coll., 1966—; v.p., bd. dirs. Cooey-Bentz Co., Wheeling, 1986-90; part-time assoc. prof. Ohio U., St. Clairsville, 1967-86, W.Va. U., West Liberty, 1976-84; pvt. practice legal cons., Bethany, 1975—. Contbr. articles to profl. publs. Advisor Boy Scouts Am., Bethany, 1986-90; asst. coach Little League Baseball, Bethany, 1986-90. Mem. Midwestern Econs. Assn., Beta Beta Beta, Omicron Delta Epsilon, Gamma Sigma Kappa. Avocations: woodworking, making videos, computers. Home: 102 Pt Breeze Dr Bethany WV 26032 Office: Bethany Coll Cochran Hall Bethany WV 26032

COOGAN, FRANK NEIL, health and social services administrator; b. Watertown, Wis., June 14, 1929; s. Neil Christopher and Lilian (Nelson) C.; m. Mary Louise Block, Apr. 14, 1951; children: Michael, Thomas, Karen. BS, U. Wis., 1951, MSW, 1955. Psychiatric social worker VA, 1955-62; dist. mental health cons. Wis. State Div. Mental Hygiene, 1962-65; dir. Bur. Alcohol and Other Drug Abuse, Wis. Dept. Health, 1965-77; v.p. DePaul Health Corp., 1977-90; behavioral health cons. Corphealth, West Allis, Wis., 1990-94; psychotherapist Midwest Clin Svcs., 1994—. With U.S. Army, 1951-53. Fellow Am. Coll. Addiction Treatment Adminstrs.; mem. Alcohol and Drug Problems Assn. N. Am. (chmn. membership com.), Wis. Alcohol and Drug Treatment Providers Assn. (bd. dirs.), Wis. Assn. Alcohol and Other Drug Abuse (bd. dirs., Outstanding Profl. award 1990), Am. Legion. Lutheran. Avocations: hiking, golf, fishing, cycling, cross country skiing. Home: 2127 S 99th St Milwaukee WI 53227-1452

COOGAN, MELINDA ANN STRANK, chemistry educator; b. Davenport, Iowa, Mar. 29, 1955; d. Gale Benjamin and Margie Delene (Admire) Strank; m. James Daniel Coogan, July 10, 1976; children: James Benjamin, Jessica Ann. AA, Stephens Coll., Columbia, Mo., 1975; BS, E. Carolina U., Greenville, N.C., 1978. Biology, physical science educator York (Pa.) Catholic H.S., 1989-90; science adv. Bettendorf (Iowa) Children's Mus., 1993; gifted, chemistry and physics educator St. Katherine' Coll. Prep. Sch., Bettendorf, 1994; biology educator Lewisville (Tex.) H.S., 1995, chemistry educator, 1996—; ALS rsch. asst. U. Tex. Southwestern Med. Ctr., Dallas, 1998; violinist Augustana Symphony Orchestra, Rock Island, Ill., 1993-94; pres. bd. dirs. Flower Mound (Tex.) Cmty. Orchestra, 1994-95; founder, instr. Northlakes Violin Acad., Flower Mound, 1994—; violinist Waterforde Women's String Ensemble, Lewisville, 1995-98. Mem. Roanoke Art Mus. (docent 1983-86), Jr. Bd. of Quad City Symphony (chair promotion 1987-88), Jr. Svc. League Moline (Ill.) (chair Riverfest 1987-88), Jr. League of York (Pa.) (chair thrift shop spl. sales 1989-92), Jr. League of Quad Cities (nom./placement 1993-94), Jr. League of Dallas (sustaining 1995-96), Gamma Beta Phi, Chi Beta Phi, Phi Kappa Phi. Republican. Roman Catholic. Home: 2629 Bierstadt Dr Highland Village TX 75077-6700

COOGAN, PHILIP SHIELDS, pathologist; b. Peoria, Ill., Feb. 13, 1938; s. Paul Mathew and Elizabeth Ann (Shields) C.; m. Carol Jean Gerlach, June 18, 1960 (div. 1985); children: Mary Brighid, Philip Gerlach, Joseph Baker, Clare Ann; m. Joan C. Storozynski, Dec. 24, 1987. Student, U. Notre Dame, 1955-58; M.D., St. Louis U., 1962. Diplomate: Am. Bd. Pathology. USPHS summer research trainee pathology St. Louis U. Med. Sch., 1959-61; intern Presbyn.-St. Luke's Hosp., Chgo., 1962-63; resident Presbyn.-St. Luke's Hosp., 1963-67; research pathologist, chief histopathology U.S. Air Force Sch. Aerospace Medicine, 1967-69; asst. prof. pathology Rush Med. Coll., Chgo., 1971-73; assoc. prof. Rush Med. Coll., 1972-75; assoc. prof. pathology Northwestern U., Chgo., 1974-78; dir. anatomic pathology Northwestern Meml. Hosp., Chgo., 1974-78; prof., chmn. dept. pathology James H. Quillen Coll. Medicine, East Tenn. State U., Johnson City, 1978—; cons. FDA, 1972-81, USPHS, 1962-67. Assoc. editor: Year Book Pathology and Clinical Pathology, 1978-80. Served with USAF, 1967-69. Recipient Hektoen award Chgo. Path. Soc., 1969; named Outstanding Tchr. East Tenn. State U. Coll. Medicine, 1980, 81, 83, 84, 85. Mem. AMA, AAAS, U.S. and Can. Acad. Pathology, Am. Soc. Exptl. Pathology, Am. Soc. Clin. Pathology, Coll. Am. Pathology, Am. Soc. Investigative Pathology, Alpha Omega Alpha. Roman Catholic. Home: 3409 Stoneridge Dr Johnson City TN 37604-2182 Office: East Tenn State U Dept Pathology Johnson City TN 37614 *"Don't shoot the wounded." As a teacher of medical students and residents, it is advisable to treat those struggling under adversity with special care. They often become the most empathetic physicians.*

COOK, ALBERT SPAULDING, comparative literature and classics educator, writer; b. Exeter, N.H., Oct. 28, 1925; s. Albert Spaulding and Adele (Farrington) Cook Ventura; m. Carol Rubin, June 19, 1948; children: David, Daniel, Jonathan. AB, Harvard U., 1946, MA, 1947, postgrad., 1947-48. Asst. prof. U. Calif., Berkeley, 1953-56; assoc. prof., then prof. Western Res. U., Cleve., 1957-63; prof., chmn. SUNY, Buffalo, 1963-66, prof., dir. comparative lit., 1964-71, prof. English and comparative lit., 1971-78; prof. comparative lit. Brown U., Providence, 1978—, prof. comparative lit. and classics and English, 1983—, Ford Found. prof., 1986-88, prof. emeritus, 1988—; Fulbright prof. U. Munich, W. Ger., 1956-57, U. Vienna, Austria, 1960-61; sr. fellow Center for Advanced Study Behavioral Scis., 1966-67; vis. prof. U. Bologna, 1997. Author: (criticism) The Dark Voyage and the Golden Mean, 1949, 66, The Meaning of Fiction, 1960, The Classic Line, 1966, Prisms, 1967, The Root of the Thing: Job and the Song of Songs, 1968, Enactment: Greek Tragedy, 1971, Shakespeare's Enactment, 1976, Myth and Language, 1980, French Tragedy: The Power of Enactment, 1981, Changing the Signs: The Fifteenth Century Breakthrough, 1985, Figural Choice, 1985, Thresholds, 1985, History/Writing, 1988, Dimensions of the Sign in Art, 1988, Soundings, 1991, The Burden of Sufferance: Women Poets of Russia, 1993, Temporalizing Space/Piero Della Francesca, 1992, Canons and Wisdoms, 1993, The Reach of Poetry, 1995, The Stance of Plato, 1996, The Burden of Prophecy, 1996, (poetry) Progressions, 1963, The Charges, 1970, 72, Adapt the Living, 1981, Midway, 1991, Modulars, 1992, Delayed Answers, 1992, Modes, 1994, Affability Blues, 1993, Reasons for Waking, 1996, The Future Invests, 1997, Haiku, 1997, The Sometime Master, 1998; author, prodr.: (plays) Double Exposure, 1958, Night Guard, 1962, Big Blow, 1964, Check, 1966, The Death of Trotsky, 1971; translator: Oedipus Rex, 1957, 60, The Odyssey of Homer, 1967, 93; author: Oedipus Rex: A Mirror for Greek Drama, 1963, 82, Plays for the Greek Theatre, 1972, 83, 97, The Odyssey: A Critical Edition, 1972, 93; contbr. articles in field to profl. jours., poems to various periodicals. Harvard U. jr. fellow, 1948-51; Fulbright fellow U. Paris, 1952-53; Guggenheim fellow Paris, 1969-70; fellow classical studies Found. Hardt, Geneva, 1968, 75, 87; sr. fellow Soviet Ministry Edn., Internat. Research and Exchange Bd., 1972; Camargo Found. fellow, 1977; fellow Clare Hall, Cambridge U., 1982, Bellagio, 1989, Am. Acad. in Rome, 1991. Mem. MLA, Internat. Assn. Univ. Profs. English, Am. Soc. Aesthetics, Am. Comparative Lit. Assn., Internat. Assn. Philosophy and Lit. Episcopalian. Home: 92 Elmgrove Ave Providence RI 02906-4136 Office: Brown U Box E Providence RI 02912-9105

COOK, ALBERT THOMAS THORNTON, JR., financial advisor; b. Cleve., Apr. 24, 1940; s. Albert Thomas Thornton and Tyra Esther (Morehouse) C.; m. Mary Jane Blackburn, June 1, 1963; children: Lara Keller, Thomas, Timothy. BA, Dartmouth Coll., 1962; MA, U. Chgo., 1966. Asst. sec. Dartmouth Coll., Hanover, N.H., 1972-77; exec. dir. Big Brothers, Inc., N.Y.C., 1977-78; underwriter Boettcher & Co., Denver, 1978-81; asst. v.p. Dain Bosworth Inc., Denver, 1981-82, Colo. Nat. Bank, Denver, 1982-84; pres. The Albert T.T. Cook Co., Denver, 1984—; arbitrator Nat. Assn. Securities Dealers, N.Y.C., 1985—, Mcpl. Securities Rulemaking Bd., Washington, 1987-98. Pres. Etna-Hanover Ctr. Community Assn., Hanover, N.H., 1974-76; mem. Mayor's Task Force, Denver, 1984; bd. dirs. Rude Park Community Nursery, Denver, 1985-87, Willows Water Dist., Colo., 1990—, pres., 1998—; trustee The Iliff Sch. Theol., Denver, 1986-92; mem. Dartmouth Coll. Com. on Trustees, 1990-93. Mem. Dartmouth Alumni Coun. (exec. com., chmn. nominating and trustee search coms. 1987-89), University Club (chmn. admissions com. 1997-98), Cactus Club (Denver), Dartmouth Club of N.Y.C., Yale Club, Lions (bd. dirs. Denver chpt. 1983-85, treas. 1986-87, pres. Denver Found. 1987-88), Delta Upsilon. Congregationalist. Avocations: fly fishing, furniture making, running, skiing, backpacking. Home: 7099 E Hinsdale Pl Englewood CO 80112-1610 Office: One Tabor Ctr 1200 17th St Ste 960 Denver CO 80202-5835

COOK, ALEXANDER BURNS, museum curator, artist, educator; b. Grand Rapids, Mich., Apr. 16, 1924; s. Gorell Alexander and Harriette Florence (Hinze) C.; m. Marilyn Bierschwal Coffey, Aug. 11, 1992; B.A., Ohio Wesleyan U., 1949; M.S., Case Western Res. U., 1967. Editorial cartoonist, artist Cleve. Plain Dealer, 1949-55; account exec. Edward Howard & Co., Cleve., 1955-61; spl. art tchr. Cleve. Pub. Schs., 1964-88; curator exhibits Inland Seas Maritime Mus. (formerly Gt. Lakes Mus.), Vermilion, Ohio, 1970-78, curator, 1978—, chmn. mus. operating com., 1977—. Trustee, Berkshire Condominium Owners Assn., 1981-83, pres., 1982-83; trustee Shaker Hist. Soc., 1999—. Served with AUS, 1943-45. Recipient award of honor Ohio Wesleyan U., 1955; Distinguished Achievement award Gt. Lakes Hist. Soc., 1973; 1st pl. award for editorial cartoons Union Tchr. Communications Assn., 1980, 81, 82, 87. Mem. Gt. Lakes Hist. Soc. (exec. v.p. 1959-64, v.p. 1964—, trustee, mem. exec. com. 1959—), Ohioana Library Assn., Art Inst. Chgo., Akron Art Mus., Cleve. Mus. Art, Am. Soc. Marine Artists (artist mem.), Assn. for Great Lakes Maritime History, Chgo. Maritime Soc., Ohio Acad. History, Northeastern Ohio Inter-Mus. Coun., Delta Tau Delta, Pi Delta Epsilon, Pi Sigma Alpha. Republican. Episcopalian. Contbr. editorial cartoons to Reid Cartoon Collection, U. Kans. Jour. Hist. Center, The Critique, 1975-88; editorial adviser, columnist Inland Seas Quar. Jour., 1957—, The Chadburn, 1976—; cover illustrations for Ohioana Quar., 1979—; book cover illustrations Dodd, Mead & Co., 1984. Paintings represented in pvt. collections, 1960—; executed mural depicting Gt. Lakes shipping Gt. Lakes Mus., 1969. Mem. The English Speaking Union. Avocations: gardening, sailing, model railroading. Home: 2449 Saybrook Rd University Heights OH 44118-4440

COOK, ANDREA JENELLE, newspaper editor, rancher; b. Huron, S.D., Nov. 22, 1949; d. Charles Alfred and Iris Adelade (Privett) Brown; m. Jerald Leon Cook, Feb. 19, 1972; children: Wendy Cara, Jeremy Wade. BS in Agrl. Journalism, S.D. State U., 1973. Staff writer S.D. State U. News Bur., Brookings, 1973-74; editor The Pioneer Rev./Ravelette Pub., Philip, S.D., 1975-81, 89—. Author feature stories and editls. Pres. Haakon Cmty. Libr. Bd., Philip, 1995-97; mem. Philip Cmty. Betterment, 1995-97; dir. edn. United Ch., Philip, 1986-90. Recipient Celebrity Literacy award Pierre Area Reading Coun., 1994. Mem. S.D. Newspaper Assn., Order Eastern Star (Worthy Matron). Home: HC 84 Box 13 Quinn SD 57775-9510 Office: The Pioneer Rev/Ravelette PO Box 788 Philip SD 57567-0788

COOK, ANN JENNALIE, English language educator; b. Wewoka, Okla., Oct. 19, 1934; d. Arthur Holly and Bertha Mable (Stafford) C.; children: Lee Ann Merrick, Amy Ceil Leonard; m. Gerald George Calhoun, Apr. 1994. BA, U. Okla., 1956, MA, 1959; PhD, Vanderbilt U., 1972. Instr. English, U. Okla., 1956-57; tchr. English, N.C. and Conn., 1958-61; instr. So. Conn. State Coll., 1962-64; asst. prof. U. S.C., 1972-74; adj. asst. prof. Vanderbilt U., Nashville, 1977-82, assoc. prof., 1982-89, prof., 1990-98, prof. emeritus, 1998—; exec. sec. Shakespeare Assn. Am., 1975-87; chmn. Internat. Shakespeare Assn., 1988-96, v.p. 1996—. Author: Privileged Playgoers of Shakespeare's London, 1981, Making a Match: Courtship in Shakespeare and His Society, 1991; assoc. editor Shakespeare Studies, 1973-80; mem. editorial bd. Medieval and Renaissance Drama in Eng., Shakespeare Quar., Shakespeare Studies, Internat. Studies in Shakespeare and His Contemporaries; contbr. articles to profl. jours. Trustee Folger Shakespeare Libr., 1985-90, Shakespeare Birthplace Trust (life); patron Friends of the Shakespeare Birthplace Trust. Recipient Letseizer award, 1956, Nat. Leadership award Delta Delta Delta, 1956; Danforth fellow, 1968-72, Folger summer fellow, 1973, Donelson fellow, 1974-75, fellow Rockefeller Found., 1984, Guggenheim Found., 1984-85; grantee Folger seminar NEH, 1992-93. Mem. Shakespeare Assn. Am., MLA, AAUP, Shakespeare Inst., Deutsche Shakespeare Gesellschaft, Soc. Values in Higher Edn., Renaissance Soc. Am. (bd. dirs.), Southeastern Renaissance Soc., Phi Beta Kappa. Episcopalian. Home: 114 Prospect Hill Nashville TN 37205-4721 Office: Vanderbilt U Dept English Nashville TN 37235

COOK, ARTHUR JOHN DAVID, labor arbitrator; b. Quillota, Chile, Dec. 15, 1915; came to U.S., 1924; s. Arthur Thompson and Sara Anne (Franz) C.; m. Frances Jean Francisco, June 2, 1951; children: Elizabeth Jean Cook Cayce, Arthur J. Franz. PhD in Econs., U. Kans., 1957. Tchg. asst. in econs. U. Kans., Lawrence, 1947-48; indsl. rels. specialist Raymond-Hegeman, San Tome, Venezuela, 1948-49; insdl. rels. specialist W.R. Grace & Co., N.Y.C., 1957-60; instr. mgmt. tng. Ohio U., Athens, 1953-55; assoc. prof. bus. adminstrn. Fairleigh Dickenson U., Rutherford, N.J., 1960-62, Temple U., Phila., 1962-68; prof. bus. adminstrn. U. Tenn., Chattanooga, 1968-84; labor arbitrator Fed. Mediation and Concilation Svc., Washington, 1978—; bus. cons. to univs., Kans., Ohio, N.J., Pa., Tenn., 1955-84; mem. AID edn. program Syracuse U., Medellin, Colombia, 1965-67. Staff sgt. Signal Intelligence, U.S. Army, 1943-46. Avocations: golf, reading. history. Home: Browview 18 100 James Blvd Signal Mountain TN 37377-1860

COOK, AUGUST JOSEPH, lawyer, accountant; b. Devine, Tex., Sept. 25, 1926; s. August E. and Mary H. (Schmidt) C.; m. Matie M. Brangan, July 12, 1952; children: Lisa Ann, Mary Beth, John J. BS, Trinity U., 1949; BBA, U. Tex., 1954; JD, St. Mary's U., 1960. Bar: Tex. 1960, Tenn. 1975. Bus. mgr., corp. sec. Life Enterprises, Inc. and affiliated cos., San Antonio, 1950-58, also dir.; mgr. Ernst and Whinney, San Antonio, 1960-69, ptnr. Memphis, 1970-84; ptnr. McDonnel Boyd, Memphis, 1984-91; counsel Harris, Shelton, Dunlap and Cobb, Memphis, 1991-97; counsel Pietrangelo Cook, Memphis, 1997—. Author newspaper column A.J.'s T ax Fables, 1983—. Author: A.J. $ Tax Court, 1987; contbr. articles to profl. jours. Alderman City of Castle Hills, Tex., 1961-63, mayor, 1963-69; chmn. Bexar County Coun. Mayors, 1967-69; v.p. Tex Mcpl. League, 1968-69; bd. dirs. San Antonio Met. YMCA. With U.S. Army, 1945-46, PTO. Mem. AICPA, Tex. Soc. CPAs, Tex. Bar Assn., Estate Planning Coun. San Antonio (pres. 1967), Tenn. Soc. CPAs, Tenn. Bar Assn. (chmn. tax, probate and trust sect., 1993-95), Estate Planning Coun. Memphis (pres. 1983-84), Toastmasters (pres. 1963), Delta Theta Phi, Kappa Pi Sigma. Roman Catholic. Clubs: University (Memphis); Canyon Creek Country (San Antonio) (bd. dirs.); Chickasaw Country. Lodges: Optimists (bd. dirs.), Rotary (treas. 1978, bd. dirs. 1986-87, 1997-98). Home: 6785 Slash Pine Cv Memphis TN 38119-5617 Office: Pietrangelo Cook PLC 6410 Poplar Ave Ste 190 Memphis TN 38119-4841

COOK, B. THOMAS, lawyer; b. Dallas, July 15, 1946; s. Bryan Jennings and Winifred Texana (Tipps) C.; m. Nancy Illback, Nov. 8, 1969; children: Rachel Lynn, David Thomas, Hayden Paul. AB, Wheaton Coll., 1968; JD, U. Tex., 1974. Bar: Tex. 1974, U.S. Ct. Appeals (5th cir.) 1975, U.S. Dist. Ct. (so. dist.) Tex. 1975, U.S. Dist. Ct. (ea. dist.) Tex. 1981, U.S. Dist. Ct. (no. dist.) Tex. 1985, U.S. Dist. Ct. (we. dist.) 1990. Atty., ptnr. Bracewell & Patterson L.L.P., Houston, 1974—. Capt. U.S. Army, 1968-71. Named Disting. Military Grad. U.S. Army, 1968. Fellow Houston Bar Found.; mem. Houston Bar Assn., Houston Club, Forest Club. Avocation: skiing. Office: Bracewell & Patterson LLP 711 Louisiana St Ste 2900 Houston TX 77002-2781*

COOK, BERNADINE FERN, book publisher, writer; b. Saginaw, Mich., Sept. 6, 1924; d. Luke C. and Evelyn Estella (Rands) Smith; m. George Cook, Jr., Oct. 25, 1942 (dec. Mar. 1964); children: George Daniel, Joan Louise, Marcie Ann, Lisë Dawn, Brian Lee. Corr., reporter Owosso (Mich.) Argus Press, 1960-62; freelance writer Durand, Mich., 1962-64; sec. Congl. Ch., Durand, 1964-68, 70-71; receptionist, copywriter WNEM-TV Sales Office, Flint, Mich., 1968-69; bookkeeper, copywriter Rossano Assoc. Ad Agy., Flint, 1969-70, Comm. Ctr. Ad Agy., Flint, 1972; vol. coord., pub. info. officer Saginaw County Mental Health, 1973-78; office mgr. WNBY Radio, Newberry, Mich., 1980; pres., pub. Little Peoples' Press, Durand, 1994—. Author: Little Fish That Got Away, 1956, The Curious Little Kitten, 1956, Looking For Susie, 1959, Little Puppy That Lost It's Tail, 1995, Shorty and That Cat, 1999. Mem. Shiawassee Scribblers (pres. 1995-96). Avocations: genealogy, knitting, reading, gardening, travel. Home and Office: 10625 Garrison Rd Durand MI 48429-1814

COOK, BLANCHE WIESEN, history educator, journalist; b. N.Y.C., Apr. 20, 1941; d. David Theodore and Sadonia (Ecker) Wiesen. B.A., Hunter Coll., 1962; M.A., Johns Hopkins U., 1964, Ph.D., 1970. Instr. Hampton Inst., Va., 1963; instr. Stern Coll. for Women, Yeshiva U., N.Y.C., 1964-67; prof. history John Jay Coll., Grad. Faculty CUNY, 1968—; disting. prof., 1995—; producer, broadcaster program stas. WBAI and WPFK, N.Y.C. and L.A., 1978—; vis. prof. UCLA, 1982-83; syndicated journalist; bd. dirs. Women's Fgn. Policy Adv. Coun., v.p., co-chair Fund for Open Info. and Accountability; mem. freedom to write com. PEN. Author: Crystal Eastman on Women and Revolution, 1978, Declassified Eisenhower, 1981, Biography of Eleanor Roosevelt, vol. 1, 1992 (L.A. Times Book award), vol. 2, 1999; sr. editor: The Garland Library of War and Peace, 360 vols., 1970-80, Jewish Women's Encyclopedia, 1997; contbr. articles to various publs. Appointed to com. on documents for fgn. rels. U.S. Dept. State, 1986-90. Named Scholar of the Yr. N.Y. Coun. Humanities, 1996, Alumna of Yr. Hunter Coll. Hall of Fame, 1999; recipient Breakthrough award Women, Men and Media, 1992, Feminist of Yr. award Feminist Majority Found., 1992, Lambda Lit. Prize, 1992; faculty fellow CUNY, 1978, 84, 91. Mem. Orgn. Am. Historians (co-chair freedom of info. com.), Am. Hist. Assn. (v.p. for rsch. 1991-94), Coordinating Com., Women in Hist. Profession (pres. N.Y.C. chpt. 1969-71), Berkshire Women Historians, Soc. Historians Am. Fgn. Rels., Conf. on Peace Rsch. in History (bd. dirs., v.p.), Women's Internat. League for Peace and Freedom, Pi Sigma Alpha, Phi Alpha Theta. Office: CUNY John Jay Coll Dept History 445 W 59th St New York NY 10019-1104

COOK, BRUCE LAWRENCE, research analyst, educator; b. Chgo., Dec. 12, 1942; s. David Charles III and Anna Mae (Lawrence) C.; m. Carolyn Winslow Smith Hammock (div. Dec. 1972); 1 child, Steven Winslow; m. Eileen Clare McPeak, Jan. 3, 1973; children: Christopher David, Helen Clare, Bruce Michael. BA in Radio-TV, Ohio Wesleyan U., 1965; MA in Speech Arts, San Diego State U., 1967; PhD in Comm., Temple U., 1979. Trustee comm. rsch. David C. Cook Found., Elgin, Ill., 1972-83; dir. Ill.

Mcpl. Inst., Dundee, 1983-88; mng. editor Sr. Am. Newspapers, Dundee, 1988-90; dir. Cook Comm., Dundee, 1990-95; rsch. analyst Fox Valley Press/Copley Newspapers, Plainfield, Ill., 1995—; instr. Columbia Coll., Chgo., 1989—, Keller Grad. Sch. Mgmt., Oakbrook, Ill., 1991—. Author: (monograph) Understanding Pictures in Papua, 1981, (booklet) Serving Mentally Impaired People, 1983. Trustee Village of Sleepy Hollow, Ill., 1983-87; campaign advisor DeLoris Doederlein, Algonquin, Ill., 1986; alt. bd. rev. Kane County, Batavia, Ill., 1993-95; v.p. gen. edn. adv. bd. De Vry Inst. Tech., 1997—. Capt. USAF, 1967-72. Mem. Newspaper Assn. Am., Rsch. Fedn., Am. Legion. Republican. Home: 1211 Carol Crest Dr Sleepy Hollow IL 60118-2643 Office: Copley Chgo Newspapers 3101 N Us Highway 30 Plainfield IL 60544-9604

COOK, BRYSON LEITCH, lawyer; b. Balt., Apr. 17, 1948; s. A. Samuel C. B.A. magna cum laude, Princeton U., 1970; J.D. cum laude, U. Pa., 1973, M.B.A., 1973. Bar: Md. 1974, U.S. Dist. Ct. Md. 1976, U.S. Tax Ct. 1977. Assoc. Alex Brown & Sons, Balt., 1973-75, Venable, Baetjer & Howard, Balt., 1975-81, ptnr., 1981; adj. prof. U. Md. Law Sch., Balt., 1981, Loyola U. Bus. Sch., Balt., 1980-82. Contbr. articles to legal jours.; author tax mgmt. portfolios. Trustee, Balt. Ballet, 1980-83, Keswick Home for the Incurables, Balt., 1983—; bd. dirs. Balt. City Jail, 1980-82; counsel Md. Hist. Soc., Balt., 1981—. Recipient Gordon A. Block award U. Pa. Law Sch., 1973. Mem. Bar Assn. Balt. City, Md. State Bar Assn., ABA, Internat. Fiscal Assn., Order of Coif. Republican. Methodist. Club: Elkridge (Balt.). Home: 201 Woodbrook Ln Baltimore MD 21212-1037 Office: Venable Baetjer & Howard LLP 1800 Mercantile Bank & Trust Bldg 2 Hopkins Plz Ste 2100 Baltimore MD 21201-2982

COOK, CAMILLE WRIGHT, law educator; b. Tuscaloosa, Ala.; d. Reuben Hall and Camille Tunstall (Searcy) Wright; children: Sydney, Reuben, Cade, Camille. AB, U. Ala., 1945, JD, 1948. Bar: Ala. 1948. Asst. prof. law, Law Sch. Auburn (Ala.) U., 1968; mem. faculty Sch. Law U. Ala., 1968-93, assoc. dean, dir. continuing legal edn., prof. law, Law Sch., 1975-93, asst. acad. v.p., 1984-85; ret., 1993; bd. dirs. U. Ala. Law Sch. Found., Am/South. Mem. Smithsonian Coun., Washington, 1972-78, Ala. Air Pollution Commn., 1971-81; vestry Christ Episcopal Ch. Recipient outstanding commitment to tchg. award U. Ala., 1990, disting. alumni award, 1996. Fellow Am. Bar Found., Ala. Bar Assn. (award merit 1973); mem. ABA (Rawles Spl. Merit award 1983), Farrah Law Soc. (trustee 1972—, disting. alumnae award 1992), Am. law Inst. (coun., Rawles Spl. Merit award 1983). Episcopalian. Home: 32 Ridgeland Tuscaloosa AL 35406-1607 Office: PO Box 870382 Tuscaloosa AL 35487-0382

COOK, CATHY WELLES, state senator; b. New London, Conn.. BA, Conn. Coll.; postgrad., U. Conn., U. R.I. Mem. Eastern Conn. Long Island Sound Commn., 1990-92, Conn. State Senate, Hartford, 1993—; adminstr. Bartink & Gianocoplos, P.C., Groton, Conn.; chmn. environ. com., tourism subcom.; vice-chmn. edn. com.; mem. commerce and exportation com.; ranking mem. appropriations com., subcoms. on govt., transp. and conservation and devel. Republican. Office: Conn State Senate State Capitol Hartford CT 06106 Address: PO Box 3528 Groton CT 06340-8206*

COOK, CHARLES DAVENPORT, pediatrician, educator; b. Mpls., Nov. 30, 1919; s. Henry W. and Ellen (Davenport) C.; m. Carolyn Crowther, June 12, 1976; 1 child, Deborah; children by previous marriage: Andrew D., Sheila D., Peter G., Charles Davenport II; stepchildren: Peter C. Brinzey, Christopher F. Brinzey. A.B., Princeton U., 1941; M.D., Harvard U., 1944; M.A. (hon.), Yale U., 1964. Intern U. Minn. Hosp., 1944-45; fellow Mayo Clinic, 1945-46; resident Mass. Gen. Hosp., 1948-49; chief resident Children's Hosp., Boston, 1949-51; assoc. clin. prof. pediatrics Harvard Med. Sch., 1963-64; prof., chmn. dept. pediatrics Yale Sch. Medicine, 1964-74; vis. prof. U. Conn. Health Center, 1974-75; prof. pediatrics Downstate Med. Center, State U. N.Y., Bklyn., 1975-81; chmn. dept. Downstate Med. Center, State U. N.Y., 1975-81; Edward H. Townsend, Jr. emeritus prof. pediatrics U. Rochester, N.Y., 1990—; chief pediatrics Rochester (N.Y.) Gen. Hosp., 1982-90, Anthony Jordan Health Ctr., Rochester, N.Y., 1990-92; lectr. dept. pediatrics Yale Sch. Medicine, New Haven, 1992—, Yale Sch. Nursing, New Haven, 1995—; pediatrician Hill Health Ctr., New Haven, 1993-94; vis. scholar Japan Soc. Promotion Sci., Nagoya, 1974; vis. prof. Ben Gurion U. Negev, Beersheva, Israel, 1976, U. Hong Kong, 1989; pres. Monroe County Bd. Health, 1989-91; health dir. Town of Old Lyme, Conn., 1994-96. Served with M.C. AUS, 1945-47. Mem. Am. Pediatric Soc. (sec., treas. 1964-75). Researcher med. care, med. edn. and quality assurance. Home: 3-1 Meetinghouse Ln Old Lyme CT 06371-1623 *On the basis of training as an academic pediatrician, my work for the past several decades has been and continues to be directed to the development of techniques for the evaluation of physicians and for the assurance of quality care for children. While quality care for all is still a distant goal, third party payors and consumers are beginning to demand accountability and computers are beginning to facilitate the quality assurance programs we have developed.*

COOK, CHARLES DAVID, international lawyer, arbitrator, consultant; b. Saginaw, Mich., Apr. 5, 1924; s. Charles Christian and Grace (Robins) C.; m. Bobette Ringland, Oct. 30, 1947 (dec. 1984); children: Ian Ainsworth, Kendra. AB, U. Mich., 1947; LLB, Columbia U., 1950, MA in Internat. Affairs, 1950. Bar: N.Y. 1951, D.C. 1965, Fed. Dist. Ct. So. N.Y 1965, Supreme Ct. U.S 1967. Assoc. dir. Inst. World Affairs seminar, Twin Lakes, Conn., summer 1950; mem. U.S. Mission to UN, 1950-62, dep. counselor, chief polit. sect., 1956-60, counselor, 1960-62; ptnr. Barco, Cook, Patton & Blow, 1962-67; sr. counsel Gen. Tel. & Electronics Internat., 1967-72; v.p., gen. counsel, sec., dir. GTE Internat., 1972-78; gen. counsel, cons. Copadco Ltd., 1978-81, 85-95; of counsel Patton, Boggs & Blow, Washington, 1981-87; resident Law Office of Ismail S. Nazer, 1981-85; adj. prof. internat. bus. transactions Bklyn. law Sch., 1980; mem. panel arbitrators Ministry Fgn. trade, Govt. of Poland, 1987—; arbitrator Internat. Ct. Arbitration, Internat. C. of C., Paris, 1989, World Intellectual Property Orgn., Geneva, 1993—; lectr. in field; counselor U.S. dels. UN Gen. Assemblies, 1958-61; accompanied Amb. Adlai Stevenson on Presdl. mission to S.Am., 1961; mem. U.S. del. disarmament com., Geneva, Switzerland, 1962; adviser U.S. del. WHO, Geneva, 1962; spl. cons. Pres. Nixon's Commn. for Observance of 25th Anniversary of UN; biographee Oral History Project on Eisenhower Yrs., Columbia U.; assoc. Inst. of World Affairs, Twin Lakes, Conn., 1993—. Chmn. bd. dirs. Maxwell Inst., Inc., Bronxville, N.Y., 1989-96; chmn. Bronxville Little Forum, 1987-89; trustee Bronxville Adult Sch., 1990-93, treas., 1992-93; mem. adv. bd. Maxwell Inst. of St. Vincent's Hosp. Westchester, Harrison, N.Y., 1996—. With USNR, 1943-46. Univ. seminar assoc. Columbia U., N.Y.C., 1961-73, 86—. Mem. Assn. Bar City N.Y. (past com. on lawyers role in search for peace), Am. Arbitration Assn. (internat. arbitrator, panel arbitrators 1964—), Bronxville Field Club, Faculty House of Columbia U., Columbia Club N.Y. Home: PO Box 53 181 Interlaken Rd Lakeville CT 06039-0506 Office: PO Box 188 Bronxville NY 10708-0188

COOK, CHARLES FRANCIS, insurance executive; b. Hackensack, N.J., Mar. 23, 1941; s. John Cooper and Emily (Morse) C.; m. Barbara Ann Dotter, Sept. 8, 1962; children: Melanie, Tammy, Cynthia. AB, Princeton U., 1963; MBA, St. Mary's of Tex., 1974. Asst. actuary Continental Ins. Cos., N.Y.C., 1965-68; actuary Gen. Accident, Phila., 1968-70; v.p., actuary USAA, San Antonio, 1970-75; sr. v.p. Am. Internat. Underwriters, N.Y.C., 1975-80, N.H. Ins. Co., Manchester, 1980-83; pres. Am. Universal Group, Providence, 1983-88; pvt. cons. practice in actuarial and ins. mgmt. Barrington, R.I., 1988-89; Bristol, R.I., 1989-90; pres. The HuroCook Group, Inc., 1989-95, Ins. for Animals, Inc., 1989-95, MBA, Inc., 1991—, Cook Cons., Inc., 1990—, PetHealth, Inc., 1995—. Contbr. articles to profl. jours. Pres. St. John and St. Matthew Emanuel Luth. Ch., Bklyn., 1978-80; bd. dirs. United Way S.E. New Eng., 1985-89; bd. dirs., stewardship chmn. St. James Evang. Luth. Ch., 1988-89. Fellow Casualty Actuarial Soc. (bd. dirs. 1971-74, 85-88, gen. chmn. exam com., recipient Woodward Fondiller Prize 1968), Conf. Cons. Actuaries (bd. dirs. 1998—, v.p. casualty 1999—); mem. Am. Acad. Actuaries, Soc. CPCU's (cert.), Internat. Assn. Actuaries. Home: 9 Lakeview Ter Montville NJ 07045-9158 Office: 36 Midvale Rd Mountain Lakes NJ 07046-1330

COOK, CHARLES WILKERSON, JR., banker, former county official; b. Nashville, Sept. 10, 1934; s. Charles Wilkerson and Virginia (Jones) C.; m. Sally Randolph Frierson, June 24, 1961; children: Charles Wilkerson III, John Stephenson Frierson. B.S., Yale U., 1956; postgrad., Stonier Grad. Sch. Banking, Rutgers U., 1964-66. With Third Nat. Bank, Nashville, 1959-85, pres., 1979-83, chmn., 1983-85, also dir.; with Third Nat. Corp., Nashville, 1985-89, pres., chief exec. officer, 1985-87, chmn. bd. dirs., chief exec. officer, 1987-89, dir., 1983-90; exec. v.p. Sun Trust Banks, Inc., 1989-90; dir. fin. Met. Govt. of Nashville-Davidson County (Tenn.), Nashville, 1991-93; pres., CEO, dir. Union Planters Bank of Mid. Tenn., N.A., Nashville, 1993—; bd. dirs. Nashville Electric Power, chmn. bd. dirs., 1998—; bd. dirs. Quality Industries, Inc., Centennial Med. Ctr, Richland Place, Inc. Author: History of a Bank Merger, 1969. Mem. Nashville-Davidson County Govt. Social Svcs. Commn., 1970-85; sr. warden Christ Episcopal Ch., Nashville, 1970-71; pres. Episc. Churchmen of Tenn., 1974; mem. bishop and coun. Episc. Diocese of Tenn., 1979-81; chmn., bd. dirs. United Way Nashville, 1984-85, 1993-97; chmn. Project PENCIL, 1988-89, Jr. Achievement of Nashville, Bill Wilkerson Hearing and Speech Ctr., Nashville, 1970-80, Ensworth Sch., 1978-81, Better Bus. Bur. Nashville, 1980-83, Nashville Meml. Hosp., 1974-89, Tenn. Performing Arts Mgmt. Corp., 1985-89, vice-chmn., 1987-89, Tenn. State Mus. Found., 1986-89; mem. adv. bd. Salvation Army, Nashville, 1976-79; bd. dirs. Episcopal Ch. Found., 1991-92, St. Luke's Cmty. House, 1999—; campaign chmn. United Way Mid. Tenn., 1994. With USN, 1956-59; capt. Res., 1977-84. Mem. Nashville C. of C. (bd. govs. 1982-84, 95—), Belle Meade Country Club (bd. dirs. 1996—, pres. 1999—), Army-Navy Club (Washington), Yale Club of N.Y.C., Cumberland Club (Nashville). Office: 401 Union St Nashville TN 37219-1708

COOK, CHARLES WILLIAM, aerospace consultant, educator; b. Yankton, S.D., Sept. 27, 1927; s. William O. and Kathryn S. (Eymer) C.; m. Virginia M. Fosness, May 30, 1950; children: Jennifer Cook Clark, William O. II, Amy Cook Lewandowski. AB summa cum laude, U. S.D., Dean Akeley fellow, 1951; MS, Calif. Inst. Tech., 1954, PhD, 1957. Head nuclear physics Convair Corp., San Diego, 1957-60; chief Ballistic Missile Def. br. Advanced Rsch. Project Agy., Washington, 1961; corp. dir. elec. rsch. and devel. No. Am. Aviation Inc., El Segundo, Calif., 1961-67; dep. div. chief. CIA, Washington, 1961-71; asst. dir. def. rsch. and engring. Dept. Def., Washington, 1971-74; dep. under sec. for space systems, acting dir. NRO Air Force, 1974-79, dep. asst. sec. for space plans and policy, 1979-88; adj. prof. George Mason U., Fairfax, Va., 1988-90; cons. aerospace engring., plans and policy Inst. Def. Analyses, Alexandria, Va., Sys. Planning Corp., Arlington, Def. Sci. Bd., Pentagon, Global Outpost Inc., Alexandria, ANSER, Arlington, George Washington U., VEDA, Alexandria, Kistler Aerospace, Kirkland, Wash., McGraw-Hill Inc., 1988—. Contbr. articles to profl. jours., chpts. to books. With A.C. AUS, 1944-47. Decorated Air Force Exceptional Civilian Svc. award with three oak leaf clusters; recipient Meritorious Civil Svc. award Sec. Def., 1974, Disting. Svc. award Sec. Def., 1976, Disting. Alumni award U. S.D., 1982, Cert. of Appreciation Intelligence R & D Coun., 1987, Disting. Svc. medal NASA, 1988, Nat. Intelligence medal of achievement, 1988, Disting. Svc., Mission Nat. Reconnaissance Office, 1998; named to Coyote Hall of Fame, U. S.D., 1976; U. S.D. Dean Akeley fellow, 1951, Calif. Inst. Tech. Dobbins fellow, 1953, Calif. Inst. Tech. fellow, 1954-56. Fellow AIAA; mem. IEEE (sr.), Am. Phys. Soc., Am. Inst. Physics, Sigma Xi, Phi Beta Kappa, Sigma Pi Sigma. Achievements include determination of astrophysical significance of B12 with respect to element synthesis in stellar interiors. Home: 1180 Daleview Dr Mc Lean VA 22102-1540 Office: Inst for Def Analyses 1801 N Beauregard St Alexandria VA 22311-1733

COOK, CHARLES WILLIAM, JR., manufacturing executive; b. St. Louis, July 13, 1944; s. Charles William and Mildred (Bush) C.; m. Renee Marie Marre, May 10, 1969; children: Cynthia, Christina. BA in Economics, Denison U., 1966; MBA, Washington U., 1968. Various sales and mktg. positions Monsanto Co., St. Louis, 1968-82; dir. mktg. Avery Internat., Painesville, Ohio, 1983-84; v.p. Monsanto Electronic Materials, Tokyo, 1985-89; corp. v.p. MEMC Electronic Materials, St. Peters, Mo., 1990-96; chmn., CEO MEMC Pasadena, Inc., St. Peters, Mo., 1997-98; v.p., gen. mgr. electronic chems. divsn. Ashland Chem. Co., Dublin, Ohio, 1998—; bd. dirs. MEMC S.W., Sherman, Tex. Exec. in residence U. Ill., Champaign, 1997. Mem. Washington U.-Olin Sch. Alumni Assn. (exec. com. 1997), Japan Am. Soc. St. Louis (bd. dirs. 1990—, pres. 1994, 96), Bellerive Country Club, Hawk's Nest Golf Club, Country Club at Muirfield Village.. Avocations: golf, jogging, photography.

COOK, CHAUNCEY WILLIAM WALLACE, retired food products company executive; b. Hugo, Okla., June 22, 1909; s. Chauncey William and Minnie Malona (Cherry) C.; m. Ethel Frances Crain, Dec. 27, 1934; children: David William, Frances Ann (Mrs. Ann C. Cole). B.S., U. Tex., 1930; postgrad., Columbia U., 1930-31; LL.D., C.W. Post Coll., L.I. U., 1967, Babson Inst. Bus. Adminstrn., 1967, Iona Coll., 1968; L.H.D., Pace Coll., 1969; D.Eng., Mich. Tech. U., 1969. Prodn. engr. Procter & Gamble Co., 1931-37, plant engr., 1937-42; chief engr. Gen. Foods Corp., 1942-44; mgr. mfg. and engring. Maxwell House div. Gen. Foods Corp., Hoboken, N.J., 1944-46, prodn. mgr., 1946-51, product mgr., 1951-52, mgr. sales and advt., 1952-53, asst. gen. mgr., 1953-55, gen. mgr., 1955-59; v.p. Gen. Foods Corp., 1955-59, exec. v.p., 1959-62, pres., 1962-65, pres., chief exec. officer, 1965-66, chmn., chief exec. officer, 1966-73, chmn., pres., chief exec. officer, 1972, chmn., 1973-74, chmn. exec. com., 1974-80; mem. Bus. Coun., 1966—; chmn. food sub-coun. Nat. Indsl. Pollution Control Coun., 1970-73. Trustee Com. for Econ. Devel., 1965-74, Coun. of Americas, 1965-74, The Conf. Bd., 1964-76, chmn., 1972-73; bd. dirs. Coun. Better Bus. Burs., 1970-73; mem. devel. bd. U. Tex. System, 1969-74, chmn. devel. bd., 1981-83, mem. exec. com. Chancellor's Coun. Recipient Distinguished Engring. grad. award U. Tex., 1963; Distinguished Achievement award U. Tex. Ex-Students Assn. N.Y., 1963; Distinguished Alumnus award Ex-Students Assn. U. Tex., 1965; Alumni medal Columbia U. Alumni Assn., 1969; C. Walter Nichols award N.Y. U. Grad. Sch. Bus. Adminstrn., 1972; Herbert Hoover award Am. Wholesale Grocers Assn., 1979. Mem. Tex. Philos. Soc., Pi Sigma Epsilon (hon.), Tau Beta Pi, Beta Gamma Sigma, Eta Kappa Nu, Delta Chi. Clubs: Austin, Headliners (Austin, Tex.). Home and Office: 1801 Lavaca St Apt 11J Austin TX 78701-1331

COOK, CHRISTOPHER DIXON, communications company executive; b. Santa Monica, Calif., Sept. 14, 1942; s. Albert and Virginia (Dixon) C.; m. Elizabeth Burkman, June 18, 1966 (div. 1983); two children. BA, N.C. State U., 1964; MA, U. Va., 1966. English instr. U. N.C., Charlotte, 1966-69; acct. exec. K. Drake Assocs., Detroit, 1969-72; pub. rels. acct. supervisor, advt. acct. exec. Cochrane Chase & Co., Newport Beach, Calif., 1972-76; pres. Cook Comms. Svcs., Inc., Irvine, Calif., 1976-91, Atlanta, 1992—. Office: Cook Comms Svcs Inc 6065 Roswell Rd NE Ste 2258 Atlanta GA 30328-4011

COOK, CLARENCE EDGAR, research facility scientist; b. Jefferson City, Tenn., Apr. 27, 1936; s. Edgar Marion and Lillie Grey (Hodge) C.; m. Gail O'Connor McKee, June 1, 1957; children—David Grey, Lisa O'Connor Priebe, Kevin McKee. BS, Carson-Newman Coll., 1957; PhD, U. N.C., 1961; postdoctoral, U. Cambridge, Eng., 1961. Chemist, sr. chemist Rsch. Triangle Inst., Research Triangle Park, N.C., 1962-68, group leader, 1968-71, asst. dir. chem. life sci., 1971-75, dir. life sci. bioorganic chemistry, 1975-80, dir. bioorganic chemistry, 1980-85, research v.p., 1983-96; chief scientist Rsch. Triangle Inst., Research Triangle Park, 1996—; adj. prof. Sch. Pharmacy, U. N.C., Chapel Hill, 1985-96. Mem. editorial adv. bd. Drug Metabolism and Disposition, 1977-93; contbr. articles to profl. jours., chpts. to books; patentee in field. Fellow N.Y. Acad. Scis.; mem. AAAS, Am. Chem. Soc., Am. Soc. Pharmacology and Exptl. Therapeutics, Coll. on Problems of Drug Dependence, Nat. Inst. on Drug Abuse (biomed. rsch. rev. com. 1985-89). Avocation: gardening. Office: Research Triangle Inst PO Box 12194 Durham NC 27709-2194

COOK, CLARENCE SHARP, physics educator; b. St. Louis Crossing, Ind., Aug. 18, 1918; s. Clarence C. and Musa Gladys (Sharp) C.; m. Marian Norma Waring, June 19, 1943; children: Sherma Louise, Wayne William. *Great great great grandfather, William Ludlow, was one of two men who decided in 1803 to locate Miami University at Oxford, Ohio. He was president of Miami University Trustees, 1810-1813. His father, Cornelius Ludlow, was lieutenant colonel whose troops were detailed to cover Washington's retreat across New Jersey after evacuation of New York in 1776.* A.B., DePauw U., 1940; M.A. in Physics, Ind. U., 1942, Ph.D. in Physics, 1948. Asst. prof. physics Washington U., St. Louis, 1948-53; head nuclear radiation br. U.S. Naval Radiol. Def. Lab., San Francisco, 1953-60, head nucleonics div., 1960-62, physics cons. to sci. dir., 1962-65, head radiation physics div., 1965-69; lectr. U. Santa Clara, Calif., 1969-70; prof. physics U. Tex., El Paso, 1970-85, prof. emeritus, 1985—, chmn. dept., 1970-72, 80-83; Mem. com. on dose assignment and reconstrn. for service personnel at nuclear weapons tests NRC, 1984-86. Author: Modern Atomic and Nuclear Physics, 1961, Structure of Atomic Nuclei, 1964; Contbg. author: (Reinhold) Ency. of Physics; Contbr. articles to profl. jours. Mem. bd. Civil Service Examiners for Scientists and Engrs., Pasadena, Calif., 1955-58, chmn., 1957-58; bd. dirs., exec. bd. El Paso Radiation Center Found., 1971-80; bd. dirs. El Paso Public TV Found., 1972-81; mem. univ. coordinating com. Tex. Energy Adv. Council, 1975-79. Served to capt. AUS, 1942-46. Fulbright research scholar Aarhus (Denmark) U., 1961-62. Fellow Am. Phys. Soc., Calif. Acad. Scis., AAAS; mem. Am. Assn. Physics Tchrs., Health Physics Soc., Phi Beta Kappa, Sigma Xi. Club: Explorers (fellow). Achievements include experimental verification of the Fermi theory of beta decay; understanding the radiations from an explosion of a nuclear weapon; understanding the possibilities and problems related to the use of alternate energy resources. Home: 285 Maricopa Dr El Paso TX 79912-4401 Office: U Tex at El Paso Physics Dept 500 W University Dr El Paso TX 79968-0515

COOK, CLAYTON HENRY, rancher; b. Moundridge, Kans., Apr. 21, 1912; s. Herbert and Bertha (Wilkening) C.; m. Margery Maxine Manning, Apr. 13, 1941; children: Larry Clayton, Ronald Leigh, Michael Craig, Melanie Beth. Student, public schs., Moundridge. Rancher Vega, Tex.; profl. actor. Mem. Tex. Econ. Commn., 1950-57-59, 62—; mem. Gov.'s Com. on Aging, Tex. Constn. Revision Com.; play critic, judge Tex. U. Interscholastic League; past mem. governing bd. Amarillo Little Theatre; mem. governing bd. High Plains Center Performing Arts; bd. dirs. Friends of Fine Arts West Tex. State U., Amarillo Symphony; chmn. Oldham County Democratic Exec. Com. Mem. Internat. Platform Assn. (chmn.), Masons, Kiwanis (lt. gov. Tex.-Okla. dist. 1959, chmn. new club bldg. 1960, chmn. past lt. govs. 1967), Amarillo Knife and Fork Club (dir.). Methodist. Home: PO Box 57 Vega TX 79092-0057

COOK, COLIN BURFORD, psychiatrist; b. London, Jan. 20, 1927; came to U.S., 1952, naturalized, 1975; s. Bertram William and Anna Marie (Forster-Jones) C.; M.D., London U., 1951. Diplomate Am. Bd. Psychiatry and Neurology, 1979. Rotating intern Bridgeport (Conn.) Hosp., 1952-53; resident Goodmayes Hosp., Warlingham Park Hosp., London, 1955-57; gen. med. practitioner, London, 1960-66; resident in psychiatry Marquette Sch. Medicine, Wis., 1968-69; resident in psychiatry Cornell U., White Plains, N.Y., 1969-71; fellowship Nat. Hosp. Neurol. Disease U. London, 1973; practice medicine, specializing in psychiatry, Stamford, Conn., 1975—; prof. psychiatry, Columbia U., N.Y.C., 1992-95; attending physician, psychiatrist Regional Network Programs, Inc., Conn., 1995-96. Author (as Alan Phillips) Jazz Improvisation and Harmony, 1965, 4th edit., 1998. Served with Brit. Navy, 1953-55, 57-59. Mem. AMA, Authors League. Club: Masons (32 degree). Address: 373 Strawberry Hill Ave Stamford CT 06902-2512

COOK, DAVID, editor; b. Boston, Dec. 28, 1946; s. Theodore N. and Charlotte M. (Stachelhaus) C.; m. Linda Markarian, Dec. 19, 1981; children: Matthew D., Christopher E., Timothy T. BA, Principia Coll., 1969; postgrad., Columbia U., 1977, Mich. State U., 1979-81. Staff writer Christian Sci. Monitor, Boston and Washington, 1971-77; bus. corr. Christian Sci. Monitor, Boston, 1981-82; Washington corr. Christian Sci. Monitor, 1982-88; chief bur. McGraw Hill World News, Detroit, 1977-79; dep. chief McGraw Hill World News, Chgo., 1980-81; corr. Bus. Week Mag., Detroit, 1979-80; mng. editor Monitor TV, Boston, 1988-92; editor Monitor Radio, Boston, 1992-94, The Christian Sci. Monitor, Boston, 1994—. With U.S. Army, 1969-71. Christian Scientist. Avocation: reading. Office: Christian Sci Monitor One Norway St Boston MA 02115-3122

COOK, DAVID ALASTAIR, pharmacology educator; b. Haslemere, Surrey, Eng., May 19, 1942; emigrated to Can., 1967; s. James W. and Monica (Reekes) C. M.A., Oriel Coll., Oxford U., D.Phil. Postdoctoral fellow U. Alta., Edmonton, 1967-70, asst. prof., 1970-74, assoc. prof., 1974-79, prof., 1979—, chmn. dept. pharmacology, 1981-91, dir. div. study med. edn., 1990—. Contbr. articles to profl jours. Named Tchr. of Yr., Med. Students Assn., 1974, 79, 81, 83, 94, Hon. Graduating Class Pres., 1987; recipient Pharm. Soc. Jour. award, 1977; 3M Tchg. fellow, 1996. Mem. Pharm. Soc. Can., Can. Soc. Clin. Pharmacology, Can. Assn. Med. Edn., Western Pharm. Soc., Soc. Toxicology of Can., Brit. Pharm. Soc., Soc. Dirs. Rsch. in Med. Edn. (sec.). Office: Divsn Studies Med Edn U Alta, Edmonton, AB Canada T6G 2R7

COOK, DIERDRE RUTH GOORMAN, school administrator, secondary education educator; b. Denver, Nov. 4, 1956; d. George Edward and Avis M. (Wilson) Goorman; m. Donald Robert Cook, Apr. 4, 1981; 1 child, Christen. BA in Theatre Arts, Colo. State U., 1980, MA in Adminstrn., MEd, 1995. Cert. secondary tchr. Tchr. Centennial High Sch., Ft. Collins, Colo., 1983-87; tchr., also dir. student activities Poudre H.S., Ft. Collins, 1987-95; asst. prin. Lesher Jr. H.S., Ft. Collins, 1995—; mem. curriculum devel. com. Poudre R-1 Sch. Dist., Ft. Collins, 1984, mem. instrnl. improvement com., 1985-94, trainer positive power leadership, 1986-87, mem. profl. devel. com. 1992-94; comm. cons. Woodward Gov. Com., Ft. Collins, 1991, 92, 95; mem. evaluation visitation team North Ctrl. Evaluation, Greeley, Colo., 1991. Campaign worker Rep. Party, Littleton, Colo., 1980, Ft. Collins, 1984, 88; mem. Colo. Juvenile Coun., Ft. Collins United Way, 1986, 88, loaned exec., 1987; bd. dirs. Youth Unltd., 1994-95; mem. Leadership Ft. Collins, 1992-93; troop leader Girl Scouts U.S., 1991-94. NEH scholar, 1992; named Disting. Tchr. 1993 Colo. Awards Coun.; recipient Tchr. Excellence award Poudre High Sch., 1992. Mem. NEA, ASCD, Colo. Edn. Assn., Poudre Edn. Assn. (rep. 1989-91), Nat. Speech Comm. Assn., Nat. Forensics League (degree for outstanding distinction 1992), Nat. Platform Soc., Kappa Kappa Gamma (pres. Epsilon Beta chpt. 1985-90, mem. corp. house bd., alumni pres. Ft. Collins 1996-97), Evangelica Free Ch. Avocations: water skiing, snow skiing, gardening, golf. Home: 2809 Lake Dr Loveland CO 80538-3130 Office: Poudre R-1 Sch Dist 1400 Stover St Fort Collins CO 80524-4249

COOK, DORIS MARIE, accountant, educator; b. Fayetteville, Ark., June 11, 1924; d. Ira and Mettie Jewel (Dorman) C. BSBA, U. Ark., 1946, MS, 1949; PhD, U. Tex., 1968. CPA, Okla., Ark. Jr. acct. Haskins & Sells, Tulsa, 1946-47; instr. acctg. U. Ark., Fayetteville, 1947-52, asst. prof., 1952-62, assoc. prof., 1962-69, prof., 1969-88, Univ. prof. and Nolan E. Williams lectr. in acctg., 1988-97, emeritus disting. prof., 1997—; mem. Ark. State Bd. Pub. Accountancy, 1987-92, treas., 1989-91, vice chmn. 1991-92; mem. Nat. Assn. State Bds. of Accountancy, 1987-92; appointed Nolan E. Williams lectureship in acctg., 1988-97. Mem. rev. bd. Ark. Bus. Rev., Jour. Managerial Issues; contbr. articles to profl. jours. Recipient Bus. Faculty of Month award Alpha Kappa Psi, 1997, acct. of yr. in edn. award U. Ark., 1996, outstanding faculty award Ark. Tchg. Acad., 1997. Mem. AICPA, Ark. Bus. Assn. (editor newsletter 1982-85), Am. Acctg. Assn. (chmn. nat. membership 1982-83, Arthur Carter scholarship com. 1984-85, membership Ark. 1985-87), Am. Women's Soc. CPAs., Ark. Soc. CPA's (life, v.p. 1975-76, pres. N.W. Ark. chpt. 1980-81, sec. Student Loan Found., 1981-84, treas. 1984-92, pres. 1992-97, chmn. pub. rels. 1984-88, 93-95, Outstanding Acctg. Educator award 1991), Acad. Acctg. Historians (life, trustee 1985-87, rev. bd. of Working Papers Series 1984-92, sec. 1992-95, pres.-elect 1995, pres. 1996), Ark. Fedn. Bus. and Profl. Women's Clubs (treas. 1979-80), Fayetteville Bus. and Profl. Women's Clubs (pres. 1973-74, 75-76, Woman of Yr. award 1977) Mortar Bd., Beta Gamma Sigma, Beta Alpha Psi (editor nat. newsletter 1973-77, nat. pres. 1977-78), Phi Gamma Nu, Alpha Lambda Delta, Delta Kappa Gamma (sec. 1976-78, pres. 1978-80, treas. 1989—), Phi Kappa Phi. Home: 1115 N Leverett Ave Fayetteville AR 72703-1622 Office: U Ark Dept Acctg Fayetteville AR 72701

COOK, EDWARD JOSEPH, college president; b. N.Y.C., July 8, 1925; s. Clinton J. and Catherine A. (Cullen) C.; m. Dorothy A. Collins, July 21, 1951; children: Barbara A., Thomas E., Patricia M. B.S. summa cum laude, Fordham U., 1949, Ph.D., 1958; M.A., Columbia U., 1950. Assoc. prof., chmn. dept. econs. Sch. Bus., Fordham U., N.Y.C., 1950-62; asst. dean Sch. Bus., chmn. econs. dept. St. John's U., N.Y.C., 1962-64; prof. econs., dir. div. bus. C.W. Post Coll., Greenvale, N.Y., 1964-69; exec. dean Sch. Bus. Adminstrn. C.W. Post Coll., 1969-73; pres. C. W. Post Center, L.I. U.,

Greenvale, 1973-86; mgmt. cons. to U.S. Navy and pvt. industry, 1969-73. Author: Causes of Commercial Bank Failures in New York State, 1958, (with R. Vizza) The Marketing Concept, 1968, (with A.F. Chapman) Peter Drucker, Contributions to Business Enterprises, 1970, (with J.N. Macri) Maternal Serum Alpha-Fetoprotein Patient-Specific Risk Reporting: Its Use and Misuse, 1990, (with J.N. Macri) Maternal Serum Down Syndrome Screening: Free Beta Protein, 1990. Chmn., L.I. Regional Planning Bd. Served with U.S. Army, 1942-45. Decorated Purple Heart. Mem. Am. Econ. Assn. Roman Catholic. Office: Long Island U Ctr C W Post Greenvale NY 11548

COOK, EDWARD WILLINGHAM, diversified industry executive; b. Memphis, June 19, 1922; s. Everett Richard and Phoebe (Willingham) C.; m. Patricia Long, Mar. 17, 1973; children: Patricia Kendall, Mark W.; children by previous marriage: Edward Willingham, Jr., Everett Richard II, Barbera Moore Cook Brooks. A.B., Yale U., 1944. Dir. First Tenn. Corp., Memphis, 1969-88; chmn. 1st Presdl. Bank, U.K., 1986-94, Innovations Group Plc, U.K., 1987-94; mng. gen. ptnr. Palm Beach Capital, 1987-95, Cook Forest Products, 1998—; chmn. Mid-South Internat. Agricenter, Memphis, 1979-82 (chmn.); mem. President's Export Council, 1973-79; dir. Chgo. Bd. Trade, 1974-76. Chmn. Memphis-Shelby County Airport Authority, 1968-81; Squire, Shelby County Ct., 1948-66; bd. dirs. Palm Beach Civic Assn., 1984—; vice chmn. Hospice Found. of Palm Beach. Maj. USAAF, 1943-45, MTO. Decorated D.F.C., Bronze Star, Air medal with 4 oak leaf clusters. Mem. So. Cotton Assn. (past pres.), Cotton Council Am. (bd. dirs. 1962-65), Cotton Council Internat. (bd. dirs. 1964-65), Am. Cotton Shippers Assn. (past pres.). Episcopalian. Clubs: Memphis Country, Memphis Hunt and Polo; Links (N.Y.C.); Everglades, Bath and Tennis (Palm Beach, Fla.); Boodles (London). Address: 340 Royal Palm Way Palm Beach FL 33480-4307

COOK, EUGENE AUGUSTUS, lawyer; b. Houston, May 2, 1938; s. Eugene A. and Estelle Mary (Stiner) C.; m. Sondra Attaway, Aug. 27, 1968; children: Laurie Ann, Eugene A. BBA, U. Houston, 1961, JD, 1966; LLM, U. Va., 1992. Bar: Tex. 1966, U.S. Dist. Ct. (so. dist.) Tex. 1967, U.S. Ct. Appeals (5th cir.) 1969, U.S. Supreme Ct. 1971, U.S. Ct. Claims 1972, U.S. Tax Ct. 1974, U.S. Ct. Appeals (11th cir.) 1982, U.S. Dist. Ct. (no., we. and ea. dists.) Tex. 1983. Ptnr. Butler & Binion, Houston, 1966-85; founding ptnr. Cook, Davis & McFall, 1985-88; justice Tex. Supreme Ct., Austin, 1988-93, chmn. jud. edn. exec. com., chmn. professionalism com., 1988-92; sr. ptnr. Bracewell & Patterson, Houston, 1993—; adj. asst. prof. law U. Houston, 1971-72, 74. Editor in chief, contbg. author: Creditors Rights in Texas, 2d edit., 1981; bd. dirs. U. Houston Law Rev., 1978-79; contbr. articles to profl. jours. Vice-chmn. bd. YMCA, 1977; bd. dirs. Spl. Olympics, Tex., 1989-95, chmn. bd. dirs., 1994. Recipient Disting. Alumnus award U. Houston Law Ctr., 1990, Am. Inns of Ct.-Lewis F. Powell Jr. award, 1992. Fellow Am. Coll. Trial Lawyers, Am. Acad. Matrimonial Lawyers, Internat. Acad. Matrimonial Lawyers, Am. Bar Found., Tex. Bar Found. (Outstanding Pub. Svc. award 1990); mem. ABA, Am. Inns of Ct. (pres. Austin Inn 1990-91), Tex. Bar Assn. (chmn. grievance com. 1971-72, vice chmn. consumer law sect. 1976-77, chmn. consumer law sect. 1979-80, Presdl. Citation 1979, dir. family law sect. 1984-88, Presdl. Cert. Merit, 1983, 84, 86, Pres.'s award as most outstanding lawyer in Tex., 1989, chmn. pubs. com. 1981-82, Achievement award 1982, chmn. litigation sect. 1982-84, chmn. CLE, 1988-89), Houston Bar Assn. (seminar com. 1976-77, Chmn. of Yr. award, 1976-77, chmn. insts. com. 1977-78, Outstanding Svc. award 1977-78, chmn. CLE com. 1978-79, Pres.'s award, 1978-79, 96-97; chmn. consumer law sect. 1978-79, vice-chmn. family law sect. 1981-82, chmn. family law sect. 1982-83, Officers award 1983, chmn. staff and staffing com. 1985-86, chmn. Spl. Oympics Com. 1987-88, chmn. long range planning and devel. com. 1988-89, dir. 1984-86, 2d v.p. 1986-87, 1st v.p. 1987-88, pres. elect 1988-89, pres. 1989-90, chmn. profl. com. 1996-97), Texas Bd. Legal Specialization (cert.), Civil Trial and Family Law, Nat. Bd. Trial Advocacy (bd. cert. civil trial law), Tex. Assn. Cert. Civil Trial Lawyers, Gulf Coast Family Law Specialists Assn., Tex. Acad. Family Law Specialists, ABA, State Bar Tex., Phi Kappa Phi, Phi Theta Kappa (chmn. bd. dirs. 1966-71, 87-88, Most Disting. Alumnus in Nat. award, 1988), Omicron Chi Epsilon, Omicron Delta Kappa, Phi Rho Pi, U. Houston Alumni Assn. (bd. dirs. 1996—). Office: Bracewell & Patterson LLP S Tower Pennzoil Pl 711 Louisiana St Ste 2900 Houston TX 77002-2781

COOK, FERRIS, writer, illustrator; b. N.Y.C., Dec. 28, 1950; d. Norman and Nancy (Burge) C.; m. Kenneth L. Krabbenhoft Jr., Feb. 26, 1979; 1 child, Isaac. Student, Skowhegan (Maine) Sch. Painting and Sculpture, 1971; BA, Bennington Coll., 1972; MA, NYU, 1993. Author, illustrator: The Garden Trellis, 1996; illustrator, editor: Garden Dreams, 1991 (Quill & Trowel awards for illustration and book design 1991), Remembered Gardens, 1993, Odes to Common Things by Pablo Neruda, 1994, Odes to Opposites by Pablo Neruda, 1995 (Excellence in Graphics award New England Bookshow 1996), The Rose Window by R.M. Rilke, 1997, A Murmur in the Trees by Emily Dickinson, 1998, The Sonnets, 1999, The Poems of St. John of the Cross, 1999; editor: Invitation to the Garden, 1992 (Quill & Trowel award for garden communication 1993), The Sonnets by William Shakespeare, 1999, The Poetry of St. John of the Cross, 1999. Avocations: painting, gardening, cello playing. Home: 2 Washington Square Vlg Apt 4B New York NY 10012-1703

COOK, FIELDER, producer, director; s. George Lindsey and Marion (Fielder) C.; children: Rebecca Eden, Lindsey Fielder. BA cum laude in English Lit., Washington and Lee U.; postgrad. Elizabethan drama, U. Birmingham, Eng.; DFA, Washington and Lee U. Exec. J. Walter Thompson (advt.); ptnr. Unit Four. Dir. Lux Video Theatre; prodr., dir. Kraft TV Theatre, Kaiser Aluminum Hour; TV prodr., dir. Am. Jewish Com; freelance dir. Studio One, Philco-Goodyear Playhouse, U.S. Steel-Goodyear Playhouse, Playhouse 90, pres. Eden Prodns., Inc.; prodr., dir. Du Pont Show of Week; TV pilot films for series Ben Casey, The 11th Hour, The Waltons, Beacon Hill; dir. motion pictures Patterns, Home is the Hero, A Big Hand for the Little Lady, How to Save a Marriage and Ruin Your Life, Prudence and the Pill, London, Eagle in a Cage, Yugoslavia, The Hideaways, Too Far to Go, Seize the Day; theatrical Broadway prodns. A Cook for Mr. General, off-Broadway prodn. Manuvers; author: original TV plays Zone Four, The Moment of the Rose, Throw Me a Rope; Recipient TV awards for: Snapfinger Creek, A Profile in Courage, Throw me a Rope, Project Immortality, A Big Deal in Lorado, Brigadoon, Teacher, Teacher, The Price, Sam Hill: Who Killed the Mysterious Mr. Foster, Goodbye Raggedy Ann, The Homecoming, The Hands of Cormac Joyce, Miracle on 34th Street, This Is the West that Was, Miles to Go Before I Sleep, Beacon Hill, The Pilot, Judge Horton and the Scottsboro Boys, Beauty and the Beast, A Love Affair: The Eleanor and Lou Gehrig Story, Too Far to Go, I Know Why the Caged Bird Sings, Gangin the Savage, Family Reunion, The Francis Farmer Story, Why Me?, (mini series) Evergreen, A Special Friendship, Sweet Talk, A Member of The Wedding. Mem. Acad. Motion Picture Arts and Scis. (bd. govs.), Dirs. Guild Am. (v.p., mem. nat. bd.). Clubs: Players (N.Y.C.), N.Y. Athletic (N.Y.C.); Riviera Country (Los Angeles).

COOK, FRANCES D., diplomat; b. Charleston, W.Va., Sept. 7, 1945; d. Nash and Vivian Cook. BA, Mary Washington Coll. of U. Va., 1967; MPA, Harvard U., 1978; LLD, Shenandoah U., 1998. Certificats d'Etudes, Université d'Aix-Marseille (France), 1966. Commd. fgn. svc. officer Dept. State, 1967; spl. asst. to R.S. Shriver amb. to France, Paris, 1968-69; mem. U.S. Del. Paris Peace Talks on Viet-Nam, 1970-71; cultural affairs officer, consul Am. Consul Gen., Sydney, Australia, 1971-73; cultural affairs officer, first sec. Am. Embassy, Dakar, Senegal, 1973-75; personnel officer for Africa USIA, Washington, 1975-77; dir. office public affairs African Bur. Dept. State, Washington, 1978-80; amb. to Republic of Burundi Dept. State, Bujumbura, 1980-83; consul gen. Dept. State, Alexandria, Egypt, 1983-86; dep. asst. sec. of state for refugees Dept. State, Washington, 1986-87, dir. Office of West African Affairs, 1987-89; amb. to Cameroon Dept. State, Yaoundé, 1989-93; U.S. coord. for Sudan Dept. State, 1993; dep. asst. sec. of state for political-military affairs Dept. of State, Washington, 1993-95; amb. to Oman Dept. of State, Muscat, 1996. Recipient various honor awards Dept. State. Mem. AAUW, Am. Fgn. Svc. Assn., Coun. of Fgn. Rels., Harvard Club of N.Y.C., Army-Navy Club/Washington, Phi Beta Kappa (alumni). Office: Am Embassy Muscat Unit 73000 Box 1 APO AE 09890-3000

COOK, GARY L., management professional; b. Salem, Ohio, Mar. 4, 1953; s. Steve and Ada Mae (Williams) C.; m. Brenda Joyce Rankin, Apr. 8, 1989; children: Garrett & Emily (twins). BA, Thiel Coll., 1975; MA in Pub. Adminstrn., U. Akron, 1978; MBA, Kent State U., 1983. Exec. dir. Info. Line, Inc., Akron, Ohio, 1979-84; mng. fin. analysis Loral Aircraft Braking Sys. Corp., Akron, 1984-92; dep. dir. Area Agy. on Aging, Akron, 1992—; regional adv. coun. Ameritech, 1994—. Cmty. team leader Boy Scouts Am., Green, Ohio, 1993—; social svcs. adv. bd. Summit County, Akron, 1989-92. Mem. Masons.

COOK, GARY RAYMOND, university president, clergyman; b. Little Rock, Ark., Sept. 27, 1950; s. Raymond C. and Vada (James) C.; m. Sheila Gayle Raymer, Dec. 28, 1974; children: David Daniel, Mark Andrew. BA, Baylor U., 1972; MDiv, So. Sem., Louisville, 1975; MA, U. North Tex., 1977; D in Ministry, Southwestern Sem., 1977. Pastor 1st Bapt. Ch., McGregor, Tex., 1976-78; dir. denomination and community rels. Baylor U., Waco, Tex., 1978-88; pres. Dallas Bapt. U., 1988—. Author: Retirees in Mission, 1977; co-editor: Abner McCall: One Man's Journey, 1981. Mayor pro tem City of Waco, 1983-84, mem. city coun., 1981-84; past bd. dirs. Tex. Dept. on Aging; past internat. bd. dirs. Habitat for Humanity. Recipient Humanitarian award Waco Conf. Christians and Jews, 1986. Mem. Rotary (sustaining). Home and Office: 3000 Mountain Creek Pky Dallas TX 75211-9209

COOK, GEORGE, songwriter. Songwriter Song Machine, Mississauga, Ont., Can. Songwriter 166,050 songs, Can., 5 casettes; record albums include Anthology of Early Country Songs. Home: 2820 E North St Inverness FL 34453-9551

COOK, GEORGE EDWARD, electrical engineering educator, consultant; b. Memphis, Apr. 4, 1938; s. John Walter and Kizzie Mae (Burkett) C.; m. Mary Elizabeth Spell, June 26, 1965. BEngring, Vanderbilt U., 1960, PhD, 1965; MS, U. Tenn., 1961. V.p., dir. R & D Merrick Engring. Inc., Nashville, 1964-69; tech. dir. Indsl. Electronics Lab., Nashville, 1969-72; v.p., dir. R & D Advanced Control Engring., Nashville, 1972-74, The Merrick Corp., Nashville, 1974-81; mgr. R & D CRC Welding Systems, Inc., Nashville, 1981-83; asst. prof. elec. engring. Vanderbilt U. Engring. Sch., Nashville, 1964-67, assoc. prof. elec. engring., 1967-73, prof. elec. engring., 1973—, assoc. dean, 1987-95; bd. dirs. Arnet Corp., Nashville. Contbr. over 175 articles and book chpts. to profl. publs.; holder 14 U.S. patents, over 50 fgn. patents. Recipient Gold award James F. Lincoln Arc Welding Found., 1981, Franklin-Jefferson award Small Bus. High Tech. Inst., 1984, NASA Space Act award, 1987, cert. recognition Space Act Tech Brief award, 1987. Fellow IEEE, Am. Welding Soc. (Comfort A. Adams lecture award 1987); mem. ASME, Am. Soc. for Materials, Am. Soc. for Mfg. Engrs., Am. Soc. for Engring. Edn. Presbyterian. Avocation: amateur radio. Home: RR 6 1203 Hood Dr Brentwood TN 37027-6512 Office: Vanderbilt U Dept Elec Engring Box 1824 Station B Nashville TN 37235

COOK, GEORGE VALENTINE, lawyer; b. Glendale, N.Y., Feb. 14, 1927; s. Walter Preston and Ida Ruth (Smith) C.; m. Edith Wengler, Sept. 4, 1948; children: George V., James, Robert, Laura, Barbara, Mary, Walter, Elizabeth. B.A., Columbia U., 1949, LL.B., 1952. Bar: N.Y. 1953, U.S. Dist. Ct. (so. dist.) N.Y. 1955, U.S. Dist. Ct. (ea. dist.) N.Y. 1955, U.S. Ct. Appeals (2d cir.) 1955, U.S. Ct. Appeals (3d cir.) 1982, US. Dist. Ct. (no. dist.) N.Y. 1987. Assoc. Dewey, Ballantine, Bushby, Palmer & Wood, N.Y.C., 1952-56; mem. legal staff N.Y. Telephone Co., N.Y.C., 1956-59, 60-61; atty. AT&T, N.Y.C., 1959-60, 61-65, v.p., 1973-76; v.p. regulatory matters Western Electric Co., Inc., N.Y.C., 1966-72, v.p. gen. counsel, 1976-83, also dir.; exec. v.p., gen. counsel AT&T Technologies, Inc., N.Y.C., 1984-85; counsel Hunton & Williams, 1985-90; cons., 1990—. Contbr. articles to profl. jours. Active alumni activities Columbia U. Served to 2d lt. U.S. Army, 1945-47. Fellow Am. Bar Found.; mem. ABA, N.Y. State Bar Assn., Assn. Gen. Counsel, Assn. of Bar of City of N.Y. Home: 127 Somerset Ave Garden City NY 11530-1348

COOK, GERALD, electrical engineering educator; b. Hazard, Ky., Oct. 31, 1937; s. Rudolph H. and Rose I. (Boyer) C.; m. Nancy Anne Gillispie, June 9, 1962; children: Gerald Boyer, Allan Binford. B.S., Va. Poly. Inst., 1961; M.S., MIT, 1962, Sc.D., 1965. Registered profl. engr., Va. Lectr. U. Colo., Colorado Springs, 1966-68; asst. prof. U.S. Air Force Acad., Colorado Springs, 1966-68; assoc. prof. U. Va., Charlottesville, 1968-73, prof., 1973-81; prof., dept. chmn., Vanderbilt U., Nashville, 1981-85; Earle C. Williams prof. elec. engring. George Mason U., Fairfax, Va., 1985—; chmn. Dept. Elec. and Computer Engring., 1990-98; vis. prof., Tech. U. Denmark, 1979-80; vis. rschr. Night Vision Lab., Ft. Belvoix, 1998-99. Editor-in-chief IEEE Trans. on Indsl. Electronics, 1984-91. Recipient Outstanding Rsch. award USAF Office Aerospace Rsch., 1968, Cert. of Achievement, U.S. Army, 1981; NSF fellow, 1961-64. Fellow IEEE (pres. Indsl. Electronics Soc. 1982-84, Centennial medal 1984, Eugene Mittelmann Achievement award 1989), Am. Soc. Engring. Edn. (Outstanding Research award, Southeast sect. 1971), Sigma Xi, Eta Kappa Nu, Phi Kappa Phi, Tau Beta Phi. Home: 4821 Fox Chapel Rd Fairfax VA 22030-4508 Office: George Mason U Dept Elec Engring Fairfax VA 22030

COOK, GLORIA JEAN, writer; b. Scott City, Kans., June 1, 1948; d. John Alfred and Norma Jean (Russell) C.; m. Billy Chris Batman, June 28, 1975 (div. Apr. 1993); 1 child, Stephanie Jo Geraghty. Student, U. Colo., 1966-68; BA, U. No. Colo., 1971, MA, 1978. Tech. writer M.D.C. Holdings, Inc., Denver, 1987-88; mgr. documentation J.D. Edwards & Co., Denver, 1988-93, sr. editor, 1993-95; freelance writer Evergreen, Colo., 1995—; elected mem. State Pers. Employees Exec. Coun., Greeley, Colo., 1983-84. Author: The Shaman's Spell, 1995, numerous software manuals, 1985-96; contbr. articles to profl. jours. Regents' scholar U. Colo., 1966-68. Mem. Rocky Mtn. Fiction Writers. Avocations: neo-shamanism, skiing, hiking, biking.

COOK, HAROLD DALE, federal judge; b. Guthrie, Okla., Apr. 14, 1924; s. Harold Payton and Mildred Arvesta (Swanson) C.; children: Harold Dale II, Caren Irene, Randall Swanson; m. Kristen Elizabeth Ward; stepchildren: Kimberley Ward, Stephanie Ward, Erica Ward. BS in Bus., U. Okla., 1950, LLB, 1950, JD, 1970. Bar: Okla. 1950. Pvt. practice law Guthrie, Okla., 1950; county atty. Logan County, Okla., 1951-54; asst. U.S. atty. Oklahoma City, 1954-58; assoc. Butler, Rinehart and Morrison, Oklahoma City, 1958-61; ptnr. Rinehart, Morrison and Cook, 1961-63; legal counsel and adviser to Gov. State of Okla., 1963-65; ptnr. Cook & Ming, Oklahoma City, 1965, Cook, O'Toole, Ming & Tourtellotte, Oklahoma City, 1966-68, Cook, O'Toole & Tourtellotte, 1969-70, Cook & O'Toole, 1971; gen. counsel Shepherd Mall State Bank, Oklahoma City, 1967-71; pres. Shepherd Mall State Bank, 1969-71, chmn. bd., 1969-71; dir. Bur. of Hearings and Appeals, Social Security Adminstrn., HEW, 1971-74; judge U.S. Dist. Ct., Tulsa, 1974-79; chief judge U.S. Dist. Ct. (no. dist.) Okla., Tulsa, 1979-91, sr. judge, 1992; mem. legal adv. coun. Okla. Hwy. Patrol, 1969-70; mem. magistrates com. Jud. Conf. U.S., 1980-88; mem. indsl. adv. coun. Bur. Bus. and Econ.Rsch., U. Okla., 1970-71. First v.p. PTA, Sunset Elementary Sch., 1959-60; v.p. Parent-Tchrs. & Students Assn., John Marshall High Sch., Oklahoma City, 1970-71, pres., 1971; mem. Econ. Opportunity Com., Okla., 1963-65; tchr. Sunday sch. classes for coll., high sch. and adult ages Village Methodist Ch., Oklahoma City, 1959-65; mem. bd. of stewards First Meth. Ch., Guthrie, Okla., 1951-54. Served with USAAF, 1943-45. Recipient Secretary's Spl. Citation HEW, 1973. Fellow Am. Bar Found.; mem. ABA, Fed. Bar Assn., Okla. Bar Assn. (del. to state bar convs.), Oklahoma City C. of C. Republican. Clubs: So. Hills Country, Shriners, Masons, Tulsa, Order Eastern Star (past worthy patron Okla.). Office: Tulsa Fed Bldg Ste 241 224 S Boulder Ave Tulsa OK 74103-3026*

COOK, HAROLD RODNEY, military officer, medical facility administrator; b. Sterling, Colo., Feb. 13, 1944; s. Harold E. Cook and Adelaide Cook; 1 child, Dawn. BS in Bus. and Psychology, Kearney State Coll., 1973; MA in Human Rels., Webster U., 1983; MHA, Baylor U., 1985. Commd. 2d lt. U.S. Army, 1974, advanced through grades to maj., 1986; med. adminstr. U.S. Gen. Hosp., Nürnberg, Germany, 1975-78; comdr. 560th Ambulance Co., Korea; chief ops. med./surg. div. Acad. of Health Sci., Ft. Sam Houston, Tex., 1980-83; with health care adminstrn. Baylor U., Waco, Tex., 1983-85; surgery adminstr. Fitzsimons Army Med. Ctr., Aurora, Colo., 1985—; dep. comdr. USAHC, St. Louis, 1988-90; with adminstr. directorate ancillary svcs. Brook Army Med. Ctr., Ft. Sam Houston, 1991-92; with Team Am. Consulting, San Antonio, 1992—; exec. dir., pres. Colo. Petrolon Inc., 1986-88, regional v.p., 1988—; pres. Team Am. Cons.; pres. Mars Cons.; co-pub., investigative editor MLM Insider. Mem. Am. Coll. Hosp. Adminstrs., Am. Soc. Mgmt., Nat. Assn. Collegiate Vets. (exec. bd.), Fitz Alpine Club (pres. 1985-87), Colo. Pantera Club. Office: Team Am Consulting 7704 Painted Ridge Dr San Antonio TX 78239-4074

COOK, HARRY CLAYTON, JR., lawyer; b. Washington, Mar. 25, 1935; s. Harry Clayton and Lillian June (A'harrah) C.;m. Jane Clare Melius, 1963 (div. 1974); children: Christianne Pier, Nicole, Harry Clayton III; m. Judith Ann Tabler, 1994; children: Rebecca Lyeth Kelsey, Parker Burr Kelsey. B-SChemE, Princeton U., 1956; LLB, U. Va., 1960. Bar: Colo. 1960, N.Y. 1961, Pa. 1966, D.C. 1973. Assoc. Sullivan & Cromwell, N.Y.C., 1960-63, Holme Roberts & Owen, Denver, 1964, Pepper Hamilton & Scheetz, Phila., 1965-69; ptnr. Pepper Hamilton & Scheetz, 1969-70, 73; on assignment as sr. tax counsel Sun Oil Co., Phila., 1970; ptnr. Cadwalader Wickersham & Taft, Washington, 1974-87, Bishop, Cook, Purcell & Reynolds, Washington, 1988-90; pvt. practice Langley, Va., 1991—; of counsel Bastianelli, Brown and Kelley, Washington, 1992—; page to U.S. Sen. E.D. Millikin, Colo., 1950-52; gen. counsel Maritime Adminstrn.; mem. Maritime Subs. Bd., U.S. Dept. Commerce, Washington, 1970-73; U.S. del. to Soviet Union for Maritime Agreement between U.S. and USSR, 1971-73; mem. Adminstrv. Conf. U.S., 1980-90, chmn. com. on jud. rev., 1982-88, sr. fellow, 1988-90; mem. Nat. Def. Exec. Res., U.S. Mil. Sealift Command, 1983-91, mem. emeritus, 1991—, U.S. Office of Tech. Assessment; mem. citizens adv. panel on U.S. Maritime Ind., 1982-85, cargo policy workshop participant, 1984-85. Mem. editorial bd. Va. Law Rev., 1958-59, exec. editor, 1959-60; contbr. articles to profl. jours. Dir. Com. on the Present Danger; bd. dirs. Inst. for Fgn. Policy Analysis; bd. govs. United Svcs. Orgn., 1997—; maritime adv. bd. Rep. Liberia. Mem. ABA (tax sect. 1965—, adminstrv. practice sect. 1974—), D.C. Bar Assn., Fed. Bar Assn. (com. gen. counsels 1970—), Am. Law Inst. (life), Maritime Law Assn. U.S. (marine fin. com., proctor in admiralty), Chevy Chase (Md.) Club, Cosmos Club (Washington), Fishers Island Club (N.Y.), Hay Harbor Club (N.Y.), Racquet Club Phila., Univ. Club (N.Y.C.) (San Francisco), Order of Coif, The Raven Soc. Phi Delta Phi. Home: 1011 Langley Hill Dr McLean VA 22101-1709 Office: Two Lafayette Centre 1133 21st St NW Ste 500 Washington DC 20036-3390

COOK, HARRY EDGAR, engineering educator; b. Americus, Ga., Feb. 14, 1939; m. 1961; 2 children. BS, Case Inst. Tech., 1960; MS, Northwestern U., 1962, PhD in Materials Sci., 1966. Sr. rsch. scientist Ford Motor Co., Detroit, 1967-69, sr. engr., 1969-70, prin. engr. chassis, engine, 1970-71, supr., 1971-72, sr. rsch. scientist metallurgy, 1977-78, mgr. materials engring., 1978-79, body component engr., 1979-81, mgr. body component engring. and metallurgy dept., 1981-85; from assoc. prof. to prof. metallurgy and mech. engring. U. Ill., Champaign-Urbana, 1972-77; dir. auto rsch. Chrysler Motors, Detroit, 1985-90; J. Gauthier prof. dept. mech. and indsl. engring. U. Ill., Champaign-Urbana, 1990-98, head dept. gen. engring., 1998—. Recipient Robert Lansing Hardy medal Am. Inst. Mining and Metall. Engrs. Fellow Am. Soc. Metals, Am. Soc. Automotive Engrs. (Teetor award 1977); mem. Nat. Acad. Engring. Achievements include research contributing to knowledge of phase transformation and friction materials; studies in competitiveness and leadtime. Home: 4004 Pinecrest Dr Champaign IL 61822-9216 Office: U Ill Dept Gen Engring Urbana IL 61801

COOK, HARVEY CARLISLE, law enforcement official; b. Cambridge, Md., June 19, 1936; s. John Morrison and Lula Arbelia (Warfield) C.; m. Shirley Marie Cox, Aug. 4, 1973; children: Brenda, Claudine, John, Anne. AA in Police Sci., Charles Ct. Community Coll., LaPlata, Md., 1973; BBA, U. Md., 1979, cert. in paralegal, 1980; cert. in criminal justice, FBI Nat. Acad., Quantico, Va., 1983. USCG Masters lic., 1988. Inspector Tidewater Fisheries Dept., Hughesville, Md., 1958-61, dist. inspector, 1962-64; lt. Md. State Marine Police, Hughesville, 1965-69; capt. Md. State Marine Police, LaPlata, 1970-72, Md. Natural Resources Police, LaPlata, 1973-75; maj. Md. Natural Resources Police, Annapolis, 1976-86, dep. supt., 1986-88; dir. Hovercraft tng. and ops. Hover Systems, Inc., 1988-93; dir. health & indsl. safety Mech. Constrn. Inc., 1994—; dir. marine & indsl. safety & security Cook & Assocs., 1995—; liaison officer Emergency Mgmt. Agy., Pikesville, Md., 1974-86, USCG Aux., Balt., 1982-86. Bd. dirs. Charles County Fair, LaPlata, 1985. Recipient Ann. Safe Boating award USCG Aux., 1975, Disting. Svc. award Gov. of Md., 1987; named Best Engring. Soldier Md. N.G. 121st Engr. Battalion, 1967, Disting. Citizen, Mass. Gov.'s Office, 1983; commd. Ky. Col., Gov. Ky., 1983. Mem. FOP, NRA (life), Nat. Police Officers Assn. Am. (charter), Hoverclub Am., U.S. Hovercraft Soc. Inc. (bd. dirs. 1987, v.p. 1990-92, pres. 1993), USCG Auxiliary (vice flotilla comdr. 1996, comdr. 1997-98, flotilla staff officer 1999), Dr. Samuel A. Mudd Soc. Inc. (treas. 1987), So. Md. Bd. Realtors, Md. Chiefs Police Assn., Charles County Cmty. Coll. Alumni Assn. (pres. 1984). Republican. Methodist. Avocations: hunting, fishing, power boating, antiques. Home: 408 Briarwood Rd Wallingford PA 19086-6503 Office: Cook & Assocs 408 Briarwood Rd Wallingford PA 19086-6503

COOK, J. ROWLAND, lawyer; b. Dallas, July 20, 1942; s. John Hubbard and Nancy Eva (Watson) C.; m. April Beall, Dec. 24, 1966 (div. 1984); children: Matthew Rowland, Samantha, Joshua Malcolm, Abigail; m. Diane E. Ireson, Aug. 10, 1990; stepchildren: Eric Perlmutter, Lindsay Perlmutter. Student, Tex. A&M U., 1960, So. Meth. U., 1961; BBA, U. Tex., 1964, LLB, 1965. Tax law specialist IRS, Washington, 1965-66; adminstrv./legis. asst. U.S. congressman J. J. Pickle, Washington, 1966-69; spl. counsel, staff atty. div. corp. fin. SEC, Washington, 1969-76, chief, asst. dir. Office of Disclosure Policy and Proceedings div. corp. fin., 1976-79; asst. atty. gen. ins., banking and securities dept. State of Tex., Austin, 1979-80; from assoc. to ptnr. Salmanson, Smith & Mouer, Austin, 1980-81; ptnr., mem. Johnson & Wortley, P.C., Austin, 1981-95; ptnr. Jenkens & Gilchrist, P.C., Austin, 1995—; bd. dirs., pres. Travis County Dispute Resolution Ctr., 1990-95. Contbr. articles to profl. jours. Mem. Met. Club. Office: Jenkens & Gilchrist PC 2200 One American Center 600 Congress Ave Austin TX 78701-3238

COOK, JAMES, magazine editor; b. Schenectady, N.Y., Nov. 9, 1926; s. Harold James and Ruth May (Turner) C.; m. Claire Rose Kehrwald, Sept. 12, 1953; children—Karen Louise, Cassandra Claire. A.B., Bowdoin Coll., 1947; A.M., Columbia U., 1948. Instr. English Yankton (S.D.) Coll., 1948-49, Ohio U., 1949-52; editor Popular Publs., N.Y.C., 1952-53; mng. editor Railroad mag., 1953-55; assoc., sr. editor Forbes mag., N.Y.C., 1955-76; exec. editor Forbes mag., 1976-92; reviewer Forbes Restaurant Guide, 1970-71; editor Forbes in Arabic, 1975-76; free lance writer, 1992—. Author: Fellow Travelers, 1999. Home and Office: 200 W 16th St New York NY 10011-6165

COOK, JAMES ANTHONY, artist, educator; b. Mar. 28, 1950. BFA, U. Calif., Berkeley, 1982; MFA, Calif. Coll. Arts and Crafts, Oakland, 1988. Artist, sculptor self employed, Berkeley, also Ithaca, N.Y., 1985—; lectr. art Calif. Coll. Arts and Crafts, 1992-94; asst. prof. art Elmira (N.Y.) Coll., 1994—. Email: jetcook@clarityconnect.com.

COOK, JAMES IVAN, clergyman, religion educator; b. Grand Rapids, Mich., Mar. 8, 1925; s. Cornelius Peter and Cornelia (Dornbos) C.; m. Jean Rivenburgh, July 8, 1950; children: Mark James, Carol Jean, Timothy Scott, Paul Brian (dec.). BA, Hope Coll., 1948; MA, Mich. State U., 1949; BD, Western Theol. Sem., 1952; ThD, Princeton Theol. Sem., 1964. Ordained to ministry Reformed Ch. America, 1953. Pastor Blawenburg Reformed Ch., N.J., 1953-63; from instr. to asst. prof. bibl. langs. Western Theol. Sem., Holland, Mich., 1963-67, prof. bibl. langs. and lit., 1967-77, Anton Biemont prof. New Testament, 1977-95, prof. emeritus, 1995—; chmn. Theol. Commn., Reformed Ch. Am. N.Y.C., 1980-85; pres. Gen. Synod-Reformed Ch. Am., N.Y.C., 1982-83. Author: Edgar Johnson Goodspeed, 1981, Shared Pain and Sorrow: Reflections of a Secondary Sufferer, 1991, One Lord/One Body, 1991; editor Reformed Rev.; contbg. editor: Grace Upon Grace, 1975, Saved by Hope, 1978, The Church Speaks, 1985; contbg. editor Perspectives: A Jour. of Reformed Thought, 1986-90. Served with U.S. Army, 1943-45, ETO. Mem. Soc. Bibl. Lit. Home: 1004 S Shore Dr Holland MI 49423-4539 Office: Western Theol Sem 101 E 13th St Holland MI 49423-3622

COOK, JANICE ELEANOR NOLAN, retired elementary school educator; b. Middletown, Ohio, Nov. 22, 1936; d. Lloyd and Eleanor Lee (Caudill) Nolan; m. Kenneth J. Cook, May 16, 1980; children: Gerald W. Fultz Jr., Jana Linn Perkins, Jennylee Haines. BSEd, Miami U., 1971; MEd, reading specialist cert., Xavier U., 1982, rank 1 cert., 1987, spl. edn. cert., 1988. Tchr. pre-sch. and elem. Middletown (Ohio) Pub. Schs., 1957-58, 71-80; tchr. Boone County Schs., Florence, Ky., 1980-99; ret., 1999; resource tchr. Ky. Internship Program, 1985-95. Fellow ABI Rsch. Assn. (life); mem. NEA, Nat. Assn. Edn. Young Children, Internat. Reading Assn., Nat. Coun. Tchrs. English, Ky. Edn. Assn., Boone County Edn. Assn., Assn. Childhood Edn. Internat., Nat. Coun. Tchrs. Math. Home: 926 Pine Needle Ct Mainesville OH 45039 Office: New Haven Elem Sch 10854 Us Highway 42 Union KY 41091-9596

COOK, JAY MICHAEL, accounting company executive; b. N.Y.C., Sept. 16, 1942; s. Gerald Cook and Mary Elizabeth (McGill) Totten; m. Mary Anne Griffith, July 11, 1964; children—Jennifer Lynn, Angela Marie, Jeffrey Thomas. B.S. in Bus. Adminstrn. cum laude, U. Fla., 1964. C.P.A., N.Y., Fla., Conn. Staff acct. Deloitte, Haskins & Sells, Fort Lauderdale, Fla., 1964-70; mgr. Deloitte, Haskins & Sells, Miami, Fla., 1970-74; ptnr. Deloitte, Haskins & Sells, N.Y.C., 1974-81; ptnr.-in-charge Deloitte, Haskins & Sells, Miami, 1981-83; mng. ptnr. Deloitte, Haskins & Sells, N.Y.C., 1983-86, chmn., 1986-89; chmn., CEO Deloitte & Touche, 1989—; exec. com. Securities Regulation Inst.; chmn. World Congress Accts., 1992; adv. coun. Internat. Acctg. Standards Com. Mem. N.Y.C. Partnership, U.S. Coun. for Internat. Bus.; chmn. United Ways of Tri-State, 1990-92; bd. govs., past chmn. United Way Am.; past chmn. bd. dirs. Catalyst; mem. dean's adv. coun. Columbia Bus. Sch.; adv. com. Sch. Bus., U. Fla., Gainesville; mem. Rep. Eagles; past chmn. bd. trustees Acctg. Found.; vice chmn. Drugs Don't Work Leadership Coun. Recipient Disting. Alumnus award U. Fla. Mem. AICPA (chmn. SEC regulations 1980-83, mem. coun. 1983—, vice chmn. 1985-86, chmn. 1986-87), Conf. Bd., U.S. C. of C. (commerce svcs. industries coun.), Advt. Coun. (industries adv. coun.), U.S. Japan Coun., Econ. Club N.Y. (trustee), Greenwich (Conn.) Country Club, Blind Brook Club. Republican. Methodist. Avocations: tennis; golf; skiing. Home: 980 Lake Ave Greenwich CT 06831-3032 Office: Deloitte & Touche LLP 10 Westport Rd Wilton CT 06897-4522

COOK, JEANNE GARN, historian, genealogist; b. Wadsworth, Ohio; d. Ralph D. and Rose M. Garn; m. William A. Cook; children: William Jeffrey, Julie L. Cook Boatwright, James A. BA, Hiram Coll., 1947. Woman's supr. City Recreation Dept., Wadsworth, 1947-51; libr. Cleve. City Schs., 1953-55; physician's office receptionist Cleve., 1978-81; self-employed genealogist, historian various orgns., Parma Heights, Ohio, 1982—; lectr. in field. Editor Cleve. Colony Mayflower Newsletter, 1991-95, 97—; author: (poetry) The Blue of Autumn, 1990 (Golden Poet award), also numerous genealogies and slide programs. Vol. craft instr. City of Parma Heights, 1968-75. Mem. Western Res. Hist. Soc. (vol. libr. 1980—, mem. geneal. com. 1981—), Parma-Cuyahoga Genealogy Soc. (pres. 1986-97, editor newsletter 1997—, v.p. 1999), Daus. Am. Colonists (state sec. 1993—, regent local chpt. 1979-81, 91-95, state 1st vice regent 1999—), 1st Families of Ohio (lectr. 1982—), Cleve. Colony Mayflower Descendants (bd. assts., pub. rels. com. 1987—), Hiram Coll. Club of Women, Parma Heights Book Discussion Club, Flagon and Trencher. Avocations: composing music, displays, crafts, sewing, travel. Home: 6428 Nelwood Rd Parma Heights OH 44130-3211

COOK, JEANNINE SALVO, library consultant; b. N.Y.C., Apr. 11, 1929; d. Ernest August and Edith Agatha (Lombardo) S.; m. Donald Carter Cook, June 9, 1962; 1 child, Carter Steven. BA, Hunter Coll., 1951; MLS, Columbia U., 1958, postgrad., 1973. Chemist Charles Pfizer and Co., Inc., Bklyn., 1951-56, lit. chemist, 1956-58; cen. med. librarian Am. Cyanamid, N.Y.C., 1958-60; sr. profl. adminstr. Engrng. and phys. scis. library Columbia U., N.Y.C., 1960-62; assoc. librarian SUNY, Stony Brook, 1962-63; dir. Emma S. Clark Meml. Library, Setauket, N.Y., 1966-93; cons. Bro Dart, Williamsport, Pa., 1990—; editorial adv. bd. Gale, Rsch. Pub., Detroit, 1989, adv. bd., 1986-88; design com. Gaylord Bros., Syracuse, N.Y., 1987. Pres. bd. dirs. 3 Village Community Youth Coun., Stony Brook, 1978-88; bd. dirs. Ministries Coun., Setauket, 1978-85, 3 V Schs.-Community Youth at Risk, Stony Brook, 1989—; co-chmn. edn. com. Assn. Community Univ. Cooperative, Stony Brook, 1973-80; v.p. Health House, 1991-93; bd. dirs. 3 Village Civic Assn., 1991-95; aux. mem. Mather Meml. Hosp., 1991—. Recognized for voluntarism Brookhaven Youth Bur., Setauket, 1984, for Outstanding Service Community Youth Services, Stony Brook, 1988; recipient Pub. Relations award Library Pub. Relations Coun., 1978. Mem. ALA (pub. relations award 1987), Brookhaven Library Dirs. (pres. 1976-80), Pub. Library Dirs. Assn. (exec. bd. 1976—), Spl. Library Assn., Med. Library Assn. Home and Office: 40 Seabrook Ln Stony Brook NY 11790-3328

COOK, JOHN, professional golfer; b. Toledo, Oct. 2, 1957. Winner Bing Crosby Nat. Pro-Am., 1981, Canadian Open, 1983, The Internat., 1987; ranked 5th on PGA Tour CVS Clarity Classic, 1992; winner of Bob Hope Classic, 1992; winner United Airlines Hawaiian Open, 1992, Las Vegas Invitational, 1992, FedEx St. Jude Classic, 1996, CVS Clarity Classic, 1996, Bob Hope Chrysler Classic, 1997, GTE Byron Nelson Golf Classic, 1998; mem. Ryder Cup Team, 1993. Office: PGA Tour 112 Tpc Blvd Sawgrass Ponte Vedra Beach FL 32082-3077 also Office: PGA of Am PO Box 109601 100 Avenue of the Americas Palm Beach Gardens FL 33410*

COOK, JOHN C., lawyer; b. Detroit, July 9, 1941. BA, Carleton Coll., 1963; JD, U. Mich., 1966; MS in Internat. Law, U. London, 1967. Bar: Calif. 1967. Ptnr. Cook & Roos, San Francisco. Mem. ABA, Bar Assn. San Francisco, The State Bar of Calif. Office: Cook & Roos 333 Bush St Fl 26 San Francisco CA 94104-2806

COOK, JOHN ROSCOE, JR., insurance executive; b. Houston, Apr. 17, 1943; s. John Roscoe and Ruth Mildred (Spargo) C.; m. Loxi June Gumienny, Aug. 28, 1964 (dec.); children: John T., Andrew J., Wesley A. BA, U. Houston, 1968. With Allstate Ins., Houston, 1968-72, Northbrook, Ill., 1972-74, pub. affairs mgr., Roanoke, Va., 1974-78, Valley Forge, Pa., 1978-80, Northbrook, 1980; v.p. pub. affairs Am. Ins. Assn., Washington, 1980-85; sr. v.p. Ins. Inst. for Hwy. Safety, Washington, 1985-87, exec. v.p., 1987-89; sr. v.p., chief comm. officer USAA, San Antonio, Tex., 1989-97; sr v.p., chief comm. officer Nationwide Ins. Enterprise, Columbus, Ohio, 1997—. Chmn. walkamerica March of Dimes, Franklin County, Ins. Edn. Found., Columbus Jazz Arts, Riverwalk, Live at the Landing, Buckeye Ranch Found., Coll. Fellows, Pub. Rels. Soc. Am. Mem. Nat. Press Club, Capitol Hill Club, The Lakes Country Club, The Capitol Club, Club Giraud. Home: 2433 Edington Rd Columbus OH 43221-3047

COOK, JOHN WESLEY, foundation administrator; b. Mar. 1, 1933; m. Phyllis Carol Depp, Apr. 14, 1962; children: Stephanie, Clayton. BA, Baylor U., 1954; MDiv, Yale U., 1957, MPhil, 1973, PhD, 1975; LLD (hon.), Valparaiso U., 1995. Ordained minister United Ch. of Christ, 1963. Prof. religion and arts Yale U., New Haven, 1971-92, prof. emeritus, 1992—; pres. The Henry Luce Found., N.Y.C., 1992—; lectr. in field; lectr. twentieth century art Lady Margaret Hall, Oxford, England, 1996; dir. Yale Inst. Sacred Music, New Haven, 1984-92, dir. religion and the arts program, 1978-84; minister 1st Congregational Ch., Derby, Conn., 1965-68, River Oaks Ch., Houston, 1963-65; cons. NEH, 1976, 77; vis. prof. Kalamazoo (Mich.) Coll., 1974, 76. Co-author: Conversations with Architects, 1973; contbr. articles to profl. jours. Fulbright fellow, 1970-71, NDEA fellow, 1968-70; recipient disting. alumnus award Baylor U., Waco, Tex., 1993; grantee The Henry Luce Found., 1977-80, Lilly Endowment, 1987-93, Menil Found., 1991; Rayzor scholar fellow, 1960-62. Office: The Henry Luce Found 111 W 50th St New York NY 10020-1202

COOK, JULIAN ABELE, JR., federal judge; b. Washington, June 22, 1930; s. Julian Abele and Ruth Elizabeth (McNeill) C.; m. Carol Annette Dibble, Dec. 22, 1957; children: Julian Abele III, Peter Dibble, Susan Annette. BA, Pa. State U., 1952; JD, Georgetown U., 1957, LLD (hon.), 1992; LLM, U. Va., 1988; LLD (hon.), U. Detroit, 1996, Wayne State U., 1997. Bar: Mich. 1957. Law clk. to judge Pontiac, Mich., 1957-58; pvt. practice Detroit, 1958-78; judge U.S. Dist. Ct. (ea. dist.) Mich., Detroit, 1978, chief judge, 1989-96, sr. judge, 1996—; spl. asst. atty. gen. State of Mich., 1968-78; adj. prof. U. Detroit Sch. Law, 1971-74; gen. counsel pub. TV Sta. WTVS, 1973-78; labor arbitrator Am. Arbitration Assn. and Mich. Employment Rels. Commn., 1975-78; mem. Mich. State Bd. Ethics, 1977-78; instr. trial advocacy workshop Harvard U., 1988—, trial advocacy program U.S. Dept. Justice, 1989-90; com. on fin. disclosure Jud. Conf. U.S., 1988-93, chmn., 1990-93; screening panel NYU Root-Tilden-Snow Scholarship Program, 1991, 96—; mem. U.S. Sentencing Commn. Judicial Adv. Group, 1996—; mem. nat. bd. trustees Am. Inn Ct., 1996—; mem. adv. com. Nat. Publs., 1994-96, chmn. nat. nominations and election com., 1994-95; pres. chpt. XI, Master of Bench, 1984-95. Contbr. articles to profl. jours. Exec. bd. dirs., past pres. Child and Family Svcs. Mich.; bd. dirs. Am. Heart Assn. Mich., 1984-89, Hutzel Hosp., 1984-95; chmn. Mich. Civil Rights Commn., 1968-71; co-chair exec. com. Walter P. Reuther Libr. Labor and Urban Affairs, Wayne State U.; mem. bd. visitors Georgetown U. Law Ctr., 1992—. With Signal Corps, U.S. Army, 1952-54. Recipient Merit citation Pontiac Area Urban League, 1971, Pathfinders award Oakland U., 1977, Svc. award Todd-Phillips Home, Inc., 1978, Disting. Alumnus award Pa. State U., 1987, Georgetown U., 1989, Focus and Impact award Oakland U., 1985; Named Disting. Citizen of the Year, NAACP, Oakland County, MI, 1970; resolution Mich. Ho. of Reps., 1971, Outstanding Community Svc. award Va. Park Community Investment Assocs., 1992, 1st Ann. Trailblazers award D. Augustus Straker Bar Assn., 1993, Renowned Jurist award Friends of African Art, 1993, Brotherhood award Jewish War Vets. U.S., 1994, Paul R. Dean award Georgetown U. Law Sch., 1997; named Boss of Yr., Oakland County Legal Secs. Assn., 1974, one of Mich. Most Respected Judges, Mich. Law Weekly, 1990-91; named one of the Best Judges, Detroit Monthly, 1991. Fellow Am. Bar Found., Mich. Bar Found. (vice-chmn. 1992-93, chmn. 1993—); mem. NAACP (mem. state constl. revision and legal redress com. 1963, Disting. Citizen of Yr. 1970, Presdl. award North Oakland County, Mich. chpt. 1987), ABA, Fed. Bar Assn. (fed.-state ct. seminar lectr. Detroit chpt. 1981—), Am. Law Inst., Mich. Bar Assn. (chmn. constl. law com. 1969, vice-chmn. civil liberties com. 1970, co-chmn. profl. devel. task force 1984-87, U.S. cts. com. 1988-95, com. on professionalism 1991—, Champion of Justice 1994), Mich. Tribunal Assn. (bd. dirs. 3rd cir. 1992—), Detroit Bar Assn. (Bench-Bar award 1987), Oakland County Bar Assn. (chmn. continuing legal edn. com. 1968-69, jud. liaison Dist. Ct. com. 1977, unauthorized practice law com. 1977), Wolverine Bar Assn. (Bench-Bar award 1987, D. Augustus Straker award 1988), Mich. Assn. Black Judges, Am. Inn of Ct. (founder Met. Detroit chpt., pres., master of bench, chmn. 6th cir. com. on standard jury instructions 1986—), Am. Law Inst., Union Black Episcopalians (Detroit chpt., Absalom Jones award 1988), Justice Frank Murphy Honor Soc.

COOK, KARLA JOAN, elementary education educator; b. L.A., June 24, 1939; d. Charles Paul and Helen Barbara (Hamel) Belanger; m. John Rencoret, Aug. 1962 (div. 1964); 1 child, Renee; m. John Cook, Mar. 15, 1973 (div. 1983); children: Michael Donovan, Melody Marie. AB, Compton Jr. Coll., 1963; BA, Calif. State U., L.A., 1970. Cert. life tchr., Calif. Bookkeeper, asst. 1st Nat. Bank, N.Y.C., 1957-58; bookkeeper, vault teller 1st Western Bank, L.A., 1958-61; Blue-line operator County Sanitation, L.A., 1963-66; tchr. Long Beach (Calif.) Unified Sch. Dist., 1971-72, L.A. Unified Sch. Dist., Calif., 1974-94, 96—, Anaheim (Calif.) Sch. Dist., 1994-96; film background artist many casting cos., 1994—. Founder, dir. Crisis Intervention Resource and Referral Agy., South Gate/Paramount, Calif., 1991; dir. Sunday sch. program Lynwood Ch. of God, 1995. Mem. Christian Blue Collar Workers (pres. 1990-91), United Tchrs. L.A. (chpt. chair 1990-91). Democrat. Avocations: painting, dancing, acting, poetry writing, sculpture. Home: 16106 1/2 Eucalyptus Ave Bellflower CA 90706-4708

COOK, LARRY NORMAN, pediatrician, neonatologist, educator; b. Erie, Pa., Dec. 8, 1943; s. Charles Fremonst and Virginia June (Weinheimer) C.; m. Christine Louise DuBois, June 17, 1973; children: Brian, Amelia. BS with honors, U. Louisville, 1964, MD with highest honors, 1968. Diplomate Am. Bd. Pediat., Am. Bd. Neonatal-Perinatal Medicine; cert. in neonatal advanced life support; cert. in controlled substances Drug Enforcement Adminstrn.; cert. in aspects of AIDS, Ky. Straight pediatric intern U. Colo. Med. Ctr., Denver, 1968, resident in pediat., 1969; fellow in neonatology U. Louisville Sch. Medicine, 1970-72, asst. clin. prof. pediat., 1972-74, asst. clin. prof. ob.-gyn., 1972-79, assoc. prof. pediat. and ob-gyn., 1979-84, prof. pediat., 1984—, billy F. Andrews prof., chmn. dept., 1994—, co-dir. divsn. neonatology, 1974-94; pvt. practice, Louisville, 1984—; cons. on neonatology Ireland Army Hosp., Ft. Knox, Ky., 1974—, St. Joseph's Informary, Louisville, 1974-76; chief staff Kosair Children's Hosp., Louisville, 1994—; pres. Med. Sch. Fund, Louisville, 1994—; numerous presentations in field. Contbg. author: Fetal and Maternal Medicine, 1980, Management of High Risk Pregnancy, 1980, 85; contbr. over 200 articles and abstracts to med. jours., including Pediat., Am. Jour. Ob-Gyn., Am. Jour. Diseases of Children, Jour. Ky. Med. Assn., Archives Perinatal Medicine. Mem. med. adv. ad hoc com. Louisville area region ARC Blood Svcs., 1982-84; bd. dirs., mem. exec. com. Univ. Pediat. Found., Inc., Louisville, 1983—, acting pres., 1992-94, pres., 1995—; trustee Children's Hosp. Found., Alliant Health Sys., Louisville, 1991—; pres. Louisville Pediatric Found., Inc., 1993—. Maj. M.C., U.S. Army, 1972-74. Named Outstanding Young Man of Ky., Ky. Jaycees, 1977; recipient Lawrence Grever award Nat. Assn. Residents and Interns, 1993, Order of Merit award U. Louisville Alumni Assn., 1996, Roger J. Fox award Kosair Charities, 1998; alumni scholar U. Ky., 1964, summer rsch. scholar, 1965-67, Pfizer med. scholar, 1966, John Walker Moore scholar, 1967; Norman Joliffe med. student fellow, 1967; numerous grants, 1974—, including Burroughs Wellcome Co., WHAS Crusade for Children, Humana Inc., Univ. Health Care, Inc. Mem. AMA, Am. Acad. Pediat. (manuscript reviewer Pediat. 1991—), Assn. Am. Med. Colls., Assn. Med. Sch. Pediatric Dept. Chairmen (exec. com. 1993—), Extracorporeal Lif Support Orgn. (treas. 1989—), Am. Pediatric Soc., So. Perinatal Assn., So. Soc. for Pediatric Rsch., Ky. Pediatric Soc. (exec. com. 1993—), Ky. Med. Assn. (maternal and child health adv. bd. 1974—), Calif. Perinatal Assn., Jefferson County Med. Soc., Louisville Pediatric Soc., Med. Sch. Practice Assn. (pres. 1993—), Alpha Omega Alpha. Avocations: fly fishing, hiking, interior design. Office: U Louisville Dept Pediat 571 S Floyd St Ste 300 Louisville KY 40202-3829

COOK, LINDA KAY, critical care nurse; b. Olean, N.Y., Jan. 14, 1955; d. William Reese and Helen Cora (Torrey) Miller; m. B. Bruce Cook, May 23, 1981. Diploma in Nursing, Genesee Hosp. Sch. Nursing, Rochester, N.Y., 1976; AS, Monroe Community Coll., 1976; BS in Nursing, Alfred U., 1979; MS, U. Md., 1997. Cert. CCRN; cert. ACLS instr. Staff nurse Doctor's Cmty. Hosp., Lanham, Md., 1979-86, 86-94; cardiac rehab. coord. Doctor's Cmty. Hosp., Lanham, 1994—; asst. clin. dir., patient care coord. Doctor's Community Hosp. PG County, Lanham, 1986-94; coord. cardiac rehab. Drs. Cmty. Hsop., Lanham, 1994-98, clin. edn. specialist, 1998—. Mem. Am. Assn. Critical Care Nurses, Heart Failure Soc. Am. Home: 7128 Cipriano Springs Dr Lanham Seabrook MD 20706-3835

COOK, LISLE, farmer; b. Marshalltown, Iowa, Sept. 27, 1936; s. Maurice J. and Fern (Frazer) C.; m. Margaret A. Cook, Nov. 23, 1958; children: Jeff, Scott, Daniel, Paul. BS, Iowa State U., 1960. Farmer Hubbard, Iowa. Mem. Ho. of Reps, State of Iowa, 1981-83; mem. Iowa Farm Bur. Bd., 1976-80; sec. U.S. Feed Grains Coun., Washington, 1997-98, treas., 1998-99. Mem. Pork All Amer., Corn Growers (state pres.). Home: Deere Rd Hubbard IA 50122

COOK, LYLE EDWARDS, retired fund raising executive, consultant; b. Astoria, Oreg., Aug. 19, 1918; s. Courtney Carson and Fanchon (Edwards) C.; m. Olive Freeman, Dec. 28, 1940; children: James Michael (dec.), Ellen Anita Cook Otto, Mary Lucinda Cook Vaage, Jane Victoria. A.B. in History, Stanford U., 1940, postgrad., 1940-41. Instr. history Yuba Jr. Coll., Marysville, Calif., 1941-42; methods analyst Lockheed Aircraft Corp., 1942-45; investment broker Quincy Cass Assocs., Los Angeles, 1945-49; mem. staff Stanford U., 1949-66, asso. dean Sch. Medicine, 1958-65; sr. staff mem. Lester Gorsline Assocs., Belvedere, Calif., 1966-72, v.p., 1967-70, exec. v.p., 1970-72; v.p. univ. relations U. San Francisco, 1973-75; fund-raising and planning cons., 1975; dir. fund devel. Children's Home Soc. Calif., 1976-78; exec. dir. That Man May See, Inc., San Francisco, 1978-87; co-founder, trustee, chmn. bd. The Fund Raising Sch., 1977-86; spl. cons. NIH, 1960-62. Mem. Marin County Grand Jury, 1987-88. Mem. Nat. Soc. Fund Raising Execs. (bd. dirs. 1976-88, chmn. certification bd. 1988-90, recipient first Nat. Chmn.'s award 1981, named Outstanding Fund Raising Exec. 1987), Stanford Assocs., Stanford Founding Grant Soc. (dir. 1994—), Belvedere Tennis Club, Theta Delta Chi. Democrat. Episcopalian. Home: 25 Greenwood Bay Dr Tiburon CA 94920-2252*

COOK, LYNN J., nursing educator; b. Newark, Aug. 18, 1950; d. George Roy Cook and Jean Aileen (Wegner) Cook Ainsley; m. Troy Wagner Ray, Mar. 11, 1995. Diploma, Mass. Gen. Hosp. Sch. Nursing, 1971; BSN, U. Va., 1975; MPH, Boston U. Sch. Pub. Health, 1986. RN, Pa.; cert. neonatal nurse practitioner. From staff nurse newborn ICU to nursing dir. for neonatal transport and perinatal outreach edn. U. Va., Charlottesville, 1973-83, nat. coord. for the perinatal continuing edn. program, 1983—; coord. perinatal edn. for Poland/Project HOPE, Millwood, Va., Krakow, Poland, 1986-89; lectr., gen. faculty U. Va. Sch. Medicine, 1992—; staff NICU Hosp. U. Pa., Phila., 1991-93; mem. Va. Perinatal Svcs. Adv. Coun. to Va. Dept. Health, 1979-83; fellow Project HOPE, Hangzhou, China, 1985. Author: Perinatal Continuing Education Program, 1978—; contbr. articles to profl. jours. Recipient outstanding instrnl. devel. award Nat. Soc. Performance & Instrn., 1979. Mem. AWHONN, Nat. Assn. Neonatal Nurses, Nat. Perinatal Assn., Phila. Perinatal Soc., Pa. Perinatal Assn., Del. Valley Assn. Neonatal Nurses. Office: U Va Health Sci Ctr Dept Pediatrics Box 386 Perinatal Cont Edn Program Charlottesville VA 22908

COOK, MARCELLA KAY, drama educator; b. Albuquerque, Dec. 22, 1949; d. Joseph Raymond and Vivian Francis (Mullinax) Murdick; m. James Rogers Cook, Mar. 25, 1975 (dec. Aug. 1991); 1 child, Amanda Kay. BA, U. Albuquerque, 1971; MA, Eastern N.Mex. U., 1973. Prof. theatre, speech Vernon (Tex.) Regional Jr. Coll., 1973-97; fine arts chair Vernon Regional Jr. Coll., 1982-87, 97—; actress, dir. Bill Fegan Attractions, Raton, N.Mex., 1974; costume designer Eastern N.Mex. Univ., Portales, 1972-73; head wardrobe mistress Cinegai Films, Rome, 1971. Wrote and dir. 3 plays for Waggoner Ranch's Entry in Tex. Ranch Roundup, 1987, 88, 89. Recipient humanitarian svc. award Tex. Army Nat. Guard, 1979, Outstanding Young Women in Am., 1978, Am. Coll. Theatre Festival awards of Excellence in Directing, 1987, 97; grantee The Stokes Found., Ft. Worth. Mem. Tex. Ednl. Theatre Assn., Southwest Theatre Assn., Drama League of N.Y., Alpha Psi Omega, Delta Psi Omega. Avocations: sculpting, traveling, horseback riding, trout fishing. Home: 4608 Leonard St Vernon TX 76384-4931 Office: Vernon Regional Jr Coll 4400 College Dr Vernon TX 76384-4005

COOK, MARCY LYNN, mathematics educator, consultant; b. Culver City, Calif., Mar. 5, 1943; d. Lloyd Everett and Theresa J. (Matusek) Rude; m. Robert Lee Cook, Aug. 26, 1968; children: Bob, Jim. BA, U. Calif., Santa Barbara, 1964; MA, Stanford U., 1968. Tchr. 5th and 6th grades Sunnyvale (Calif.) Sch. Dist., 1964-67; tchr. Thessaloniki (Greece) Internat. H.S., 1968-70; tchr. primary grades Carmel (Calif.) Unified Sch. Dist., 1970-72; faculty of edn. Calif. State U., Fullerton, 1973-80; tchr. gifted and talented Newport Mesa Unified Sch. Dist., Calif., 1980-85; math. cons. Newport Beach, Calif., 1985—; lectr. in field nationally and internationally. Author over 100 books including Act It Out, Assessing Math Understanding, Basic Games, Book A, Book B, Clues and Cues, Communicating with Tiles, Contrasting Facts, Coop Thinking, Crack The Code Book A, Book B, Do Math, Do Talk It Over, Duo Do Dominoes, Follow the Clues, I Have, Justify Your Thinking, Numbers Please! Questions Please!, Positive Math at Home and School, I, II, Primary Today is the Day, Reason Together, Show Me and Stump Me, Talk It Over, Think in Color, Tile Awhile, many others. Stanford U. fellow, 1968. Mem. Calif. Assn. Gifted, Calif. Math. Coun., Nat. Coun. Tchrs. Math., Assn. for Advancement of Internat. Edn., Nat. Coun. Suprs. of Math. Avocation: travel. Home and Office: PO Box 5840 Newport Beach CA 92662-5840

COOK, MARY MARGARET, steamfitter; b. Royal Oak, Mich., Apr. 28, 1944; d. John Patrick and Agnes Hannah (Anderson) McMahon; m. Barney Albert Cahill, Aug. 19, 1967 (div. Apr. 1971); m. Frank Melvin Cook, Jan. 26, 1974. BA in Elem. Edn., Ariz. State U., 1971; cert. United Assn. instr., Mich. State U., 1990; Cert., Ariz. Community Coll. Cert. elem. tchr., Ohio, Ariz.; lic. mech. journeyman. Tchr. St. Agnes Elem. Sch., Phoenix, 1967-71, Bevis Elem. Sch., Cin., 1971-73; GED instr. Scottsdale, Ariz., 1975-78; steamfitter United Assn. Local 469, Phoenix, 1978—; instr. apprentices Rio Salado C.C., Phoenix, 1984-90; math. cons. Ariz. Dept. Edn., 1988-90; state dir. AFL-CIO Apprenticeship Awareness Program, 1990-92. Chair State Con. Emerging Careers for Women, 1992-98; mem. Apprenticeship Adv. Coun., 1990-97, chair, 1995-97; staff dept. of commerce Workforce Devel. Coun., 1997—; mem. Gov.'s Commn. on Nontraditional Employment for Women; Ariz. dir. Project Nontraditional Assistance and Info. Link, 1992—; extended staff Gov.'s Workforce Devel. Policy, 1997—. Mem. Ariz. State U. Alumni Assn. (life), Toastmasters Internat. Avocations: swimming, weightlifting, computers, reading, writing. Home: 15827 N 23rd Dr Phoenix AZ 85023-4136

COOK, MAURICE GAYLE, soil science educator, consultant; b. Frankfort, Ky., Dec. 26, 1931; s. Price Cash and Evelyn (Moore) C.; m. Eva Nancy Blalock, Aug. 27, 1966; 1 child, Stephen Price. BS, U. Ky., 1957, MS, 1959; PhD, Va. Poly. Inst., 1961. From asst. prof. to prof. N.C. State U., Raleigh, 1961-92, Alumni Disting. prof., 1975; ret., 1992; spl. advisor Gov. N.C., 1999—. Author: Concepts in Soil Science, 1973; contbr. numerous articles to profl. jours. With U.S. Army, 1957; col. USAR, 1962-90. Fellow Soil Sci. Soc. Am., Am. Soc. Agronomy, Soil and Water Conservation Soc. (bd. dirs. 1979-88, pres. 1986-87), Nat. Assn. Colls. and Tchrs. Agr.; mem. Soil Sci. Soc. N.C. (Achievement award 1991), N.C. Divsn. Soil and Water Conservation (exec. dir. 1982-84), Am. Water Resources Assn., Internat. Erosion Control Assn., Gamma Sigma Delta (Merit award 1986), Epsilon Sigma Phi, Alpha Zeta (pres. 1976-85). Democrat. Baptist. Home: 3458 Leonard St Raleigh NC 27607-6827 Office: NC State U Dept Soil Science Raleigh NC 27695-7619

COOK, MELANIE, lawyer. Ptnr. Bloom Hergott Cook Diemer & Klein, Beverly Hills, Calif. Office: Bloom Hergott Cook Diemer & Klein 150 S Rodeo Dr Flr 3 Beverly Hills CA 90212-2410*

COOK, M(ELVIN) GARFIELD, chemical company executive; b. Woodbury, N.J., June 17, 1940; s. Melvin Alonzo and Wanda (Garfield) C.; m. Margo Dawn Taylor, Aug. 24, 1965; children: Dawn Ann, Melvin, Katherine, JoAnn, Carol, Mary, Taylor, Stephen, Michael. BS in Physics, U. Utah, 1966. Rsch. assoc. IRECO Chems., Salt Lake City, 1966-67; gen. mgr. Mesabi Blasting, Inc., Biwabik, Minn., 1967-69; v.p. ops. IRECO Chems., 1969-71; from v.p. ops. to pres., CEO IRECO Chems., Salt Lake City, 1971-89; chmn. Non-Invasive Med. Tech. Corp., 1989—; dir. Def. Systems, Inc., Salt Lake City, Nobel Ins. Ltd.; advisor on explosives and propellants Dept. Def., Washington, 1979-81—; chmn. bd. govs. Inst. of Makers of Explosives, Washington, 1972-89. Author: Everlasting Burnings, 1981, Ency. Modern Explosives, 1972—; (with M.A. Cook) Science and Mormonism, 1967, Cornerstones of the Restoration, 1999. V.p. N.E. Bench Region Coun., Salt Lake City, 1974; vice chmn. Utah Symphony, 1988-90; chmn. voting dist. Rep. Party, 1973. With USAR, 1958-66. Mem. Mayflower Soc., Rotary. Mem. LDS Ch.

COOK, MERRILL A., congressman, explosives industry executive; b. Phila., May 6, 1946; s. Melvin A. and Wanda (Garfield) C.; m. Camille Sanders, Oct. 24, 1969; children: Brian, Alison, Barbara Ann, David, Michelle. BA magna cum laude, U. Utah, 1969; MBA, Harvard U., 1971. Profl. staff cons. Arthur D. Little, Inc., Cambridge, Mass., 1971-73; mng. dir. Cook Assocs., Inc., Salt Lake City, 1973-78; pres. Cook Slurry Co., Salt Lake City, 1978-97; mem. com. on banking and fin., sci. and transp. and infrastructure 105th Congress (now 106th Congress) from 2d Utah dist., 1997—. Patentee in field. Del. Rep. Nat. Conv., Kansas City, Mo., 1976, San Diego, 1996. Mem. Salt Lake City C. of C., Phi Kappa Phi. Mormon. Home: 631 16th Ave Salt Lake City UT 84103-3704 Office: US House of Reps 1431 Longworth HOB Washington DC 20515-4402 also: 125 S State St Ste 2311 Salt Lake City UT 84138-1131

COOK, MICHAEL ALLAN, social sciences educator; b. Newark, Eng., Dec. 24, 1940; s. John Manuel and Enid May (Robertson) C. BA, Cambridge (Eng.) U., 1963. Lectr. Sch. Oriental and African Studies U. London, 1966-84, reader, 1984-86; Cleveland E. Dodge prof. Near Ea. studies Princeton (N.J.) U., 1986—. Author: Early Muslim Dogma, 1981, Muhammad, 1983, others; contbr. articles to profl. jours. Fellow Royal

Asiatic Soc.; mem. Am. Oriental Soc. Office: Princeton Univ Dept Near Eastern Studies Princeton NJ 08544

COOK, MICHAEL ANTHONY, financial services executive; b. Kingston, Jamaica, Jan. 10, 1956; came to U.S., 1979; s. Noel Keith and Edna Elaine (Walsh) C.; m. Maida E. Rivera, June 7, 1985; 1 child, Yvette. Diploma, Coll. Arts, Scis. and Tech., Kingston, 1976; BS, CUNY, 1982; MBA, Baruch Coll., 1984. Registered profl. engr., N.J., Jamaica; cert. fin. planner. Transmitter engr. Radio Jamaica Ltd., Kingston, 1976-79; acct. South Bklyn. Health Ctr., 1981-83; fin. cons. Tri-Star Fin. Svcs., Queens, 1983-85; fin. planner John Hancock, Queens, 1985-87; chief exec. officer M.A.C. Assocs., Queens, 1987—; cons. Tri-Star Fin. Svcs., 1985—; bd. dirs. Scudder's Trucking, Inc., Bronx, Expressways, Inc., Bklyn. Inventor high voltage, high frequency isolating transformer. Recipient Econs. award Am. Econs. Assn., 1982. Mem. Internat. Assn. for Fin. Planners, Inst. Cert. Fin. Planners, Nat. Soc. Pub. Accts., N.Y. Soc. Ind. Accts., IEEE, Masons, Rosicrucian. Home: 85-12 169th St Jamaica NY 11432-2630 Office: MAC Assocs 89-32 210th St Queens Village NY 11427-2227

COOK, MICHAEL BLANCHARD, government executive; b. Buffalo, May 8, 1942; s. Gerhard Albert and Lura (Lincoln) C.; m. Le Thi Kim Oanh, Feb. 10, 1942; children: Arthur, Benjamin. BA, Swarthmore Coll., 1963; postgrad., Princeton U.; B in Philosophy, Oxford U., 1966. Field advisor Agy. for Internat. Devel., Saigon, Vietnam, 1966-68; model cities rep. HUD, Phila., 1968-70; consular officer Dept. of State, Udorn, Thailand, 1971-73; exec., Water Programs EPA, Washington, 1973-80, superfund dir., 1980-81, dep. dir. hazardous waste, 1981-85, dir. drinking water, 1985-91, dir. waste-water enforcement and compliance, 1991-94, dir. wastewater mgmt., 1994—. Author numerous articles on sewage treatment, hazardous waste and drinking water. Rhodes scholar Rhodes Trust, Oxford U., Eng., 1964; recipient Meritorious Honor awards U.S. Dept. of State, 1967, 72, Gold, Silver, Bronze medals EPA, 1975-87, Disting. Exec. award, Pres. Ronald Reagan, 1987. Avocations: coaching wrestling, running marathons, tri-athlete. Home: 3406 Rose Ln Falls Church VA 22042-4015 Office: EPA Wastwater Mgmt 401 M St SW # 4201 Washington DC 20460-0002

COOK, MICHAEL LEWIS, lawyer; b. Rochester, N.H., Mar. 5, 1944; s. Israel J. and Molly L. Cook; m. Roberta Tross, Feb. 25, 1995; children: Jonathan, Alexander. AB, Columbia U., 1965; JD, NYU, 1968. Bar: N.Y. 1968. Assoc. Weil, Gotshal & Manges, N.Y.C., 1970-75, ptnr., 1975-80; ptnr. Skadden, Arps, Slate, Meagher & Flom, LLP, N.Y.C., 1980—; adj. prof. law NYU Sch. Law, 1975—. Co-author: A Practical Guide to the Bankruptcy Reform Act, 1979, Creditors' Rights, Debtors' Protection and Bankruptcy, 1985, rev. edit., 1997; contbr.: Collier on Bankruptcy, 1979, rev. edit., 1998, Collier Bankruptcy Practice Guide, 1996; editor and contbg. author: Bankruptcy Litigation Manual, rev. edit., 1998. Bd. dirs. Goddard Riverside Cmty. Ctr.; bd. dirs., vice-chair Lawyers Alliance for N.Y. Fellow Am. Coll. Bankruptcy; mem. ABA, Assn. of Bar of City of N.Y., Practicing Law Inst. (mem. bankruptcy law adv. com.), Columbia Coll. Alumni Assn. (bd. dirs., v.p.), Soc. of Columbia Grads. (bd. dirs.). Home: 45 E 89th St New York NY 10128-1251 Office: Skadden Arps Slate Meagher & Flom LLP 919 3rd Ave New York NY 10022-3902

COOK, MICHELLE JO, marketing professional; b. Manitowoc, Wis., Jan. 17, 1965; d. Howard Bert and Patricia Ann (Goodman) Zimmerman. BBA, U. Tex., 1987. Mktg. coord. Brown & Root, Houston, 1989-92, mgr. proposal devel., 1996—; coord., proposal mktg. S:B Infrastructure, Houston, 1993-95; mktg. rep. Info. Bldrs., Houston, 1995-96. Vol. coord. Tex. Children's Hosp., Houston, 1990-92; mem. jr. bd. Am. Cancer Soc., Houston, 1993-96, mem. bd. starlight gala, 1996—; bd. dirs. Texas Exes, Houston, 1995—.

COOK, NANCY W., state legislator; b. May 11, 1936. Ed. U. Del. Mem. Del. Senate from 15th Dist.; mem. Kent County Dem. Com. Democrat. Home: PO Box 127 Kenton DE 19955-0127 Office: Del State Senate Legislative Hall PO Box 1401 Dover DE 19903-1401*

COOK, NOEL ROBERT, manufacturing company executive; b. Houston, Mar. 19, 1937; s. Horace Berwick and Leda Estelle (Houghton) C.; children: Laurel Jane, David Robert. Student, Iowa State U., 1955-57; BS in Indsl. Engring., U. Mich., 1960. Registered profl. engr., Mich.; cert. Fluid Power Engr. Engr. in tng. Eaton Mfg., Saginaw, Mich., 1960-61; mgr. mfg. and contracting J.N. Fauver Co., Madison Heights, Mich., 1961-65; pres. Newton Mfg., Royal Oak, Mich., 1965—; sec. Indsl. Piping Contractors, Birmingham, Mich., 1969-75; pres. RNR Metal Fabricators, Inc., Royal Oak, 1974-78; chmn. bd. dirs. Kim Internat. Sales Co., 1978-88; pres. Newton Sales Co., Royal Oak, 1978-90, Power Package Windsor Ltd., Windsor, Ont., Can., 1981—. Patentee in field. With U.S. Army, arty. officer, 1960-61. Mem. ASME, Fluid Power Soc., Nat. Fluid Power Assn., Birmingham Jr. C. of C. (past bd. dirs.), Delta Tau Delta. Home: 4481 Cherry Hill Dr Orchard Lake MI 48323-1615 Office: Newton Mfg Co 4249 Delemere Blvd Royal Oak MI 48073-1897

COOK, NORMA BAKER, consulting company executive; b. North Wilkesboro, N.C.; d. Charles Chauncey and Mildred Baker. BA in Bus. and Econs., Meredith Coll.; postgrad., Alliance Francaise, N.Y.C., 1980-83, N.Y. Sch. Interior Design, 1983-84. Cert. tchr., N.C. Pres., owner John Robert Powers Sch. Fashion Careers, Raleigh, N.C., 1971-87, NBC of Raleigh, Inc., 1979—; mem. adv. commn. N.C. Pvt. Bus., Trade and Corr. Schs., 1986; exec. distbr. NuSkin Internat., 1989—; bus. broker, 1991-93; instr. continuing edn. Meredith Coll., Raleigh, 1994—; pres. Fast Forward Concepts tm, 1996—. Author articles on fashion and success motivation and personal devel. Established Norma Baker Cook Art Scholarship at Meredith Coll., 1989; vice chmn. Meredith Coll. Bd. Assocs., 1991-92; charter mem. Meredith Coll. Heritage Soc., Raleigh. Recipient Svc. award Am. Cancer Soc., 1978. Mem. AFTRA, The Fashion Group, Inc., Greater Raleigh C. of C., North Raleigh Civitans, Am. Assn. of Univ. Women. Avocations: art, writing, cooking, music. Office: 3528 Wade Ave Ste 123 Raleigh NC 27607-4048

COOK, PAMELA MARGARET, French educator; b. Gateshead, Eng., Apr. 11, 1955; came to U.S., 1983; d. John Andrew and Doreen Cook; m. Philip Edward Mirowski, June 14, 1986; 1 child, Alexander John Daniel Mirowski. BA with honors, U. Nottingham, Eng., 1977; MA, Tufts U, 1985, Yale U., 1991; MPhil, Yale U., 1991, PhD, 1991. Tchr. Sawston Coll., Cambridge, Eng., 1978-83; asst. head dept. Hitchin Sch., Herts, Eng., 1983-85; part-time asst. prof. French St. Mary's Coll., Notre Dame, ind., 1990—. Mem. Hoosier Environ. Coun., Indpls., 1997—; mem. Ind. Opera North. Christine Jankowski fellow, 1984. Mem. MLA. Avocations: singing, flute, piano, theater.

COOK, PAUL CHRISTOPHER, engineering psychologist; b. Corpus Christi, Tex., Mar. 24, 1953; s. William Eckford and Nelle (Gladney)C. AA, Ocean City Coll., Md., 1973; BA, U. Ariz., Tucson, 1978; MA, U. Ariz., 1981, PhD, 1987. Oceanographer Dept. Natural Resources, State of Md., Annapolis, 1973-75; researcher Child Psychology Lab., Tucson, 1977-78; behavioral and video cons. Intermt. Ctrs. for Human Devel., Tucson, 1978-79; rsch. assoc. Family & Community Medicine Ariz. Health Sci. Ctr., Tucson, 1982-84, rsch. cons., 1989—; rsch. and analysis assoc. U. Ariz., Tucson, 1980-87, rsch. cons. Coll. Medicine, 1989—; sr. human factors engr. U.S. Army Electronic Proving Ground, Ft. Huachuca, Ariz., 1986-87; engring. psychologist U.S. Army Yuma Proving Ground, Ariz., 1988; cons. engr. Cook Enterprises, Tucson, 1989-91; pres. World Trade Assocs. Ltd. Sterling (Va.), Inc., Tucson, Lake Havasu, Ariz., 1991—; pres., ptnr. Unicus Imports, Inc., 1997—; rsch. cons. Coll. Medicine Ariz. Health Scis. Ctr., U. Ariz., Tucson, 1989—; pres. World Trade Assocs. Ltd. of Sterling, Inc., Tucson, Sterling, Va. and Lake Havasu, Ariz., 1990—. *Over 20 years experience in medical research and in the field of research and development, feasibility, developmental and operational field and lab testing at the senior levels of Engineering Psychologist and senior levels of Human Factors Engineering. Contracted deliverables to the Electronic, Desert and Jungle Proving Grounds of the United States Military: Global Positioning System, Navigation System Timing and Ranging, Mobile Subscriber Equipment, Position Location Information and Distribution System, Position Location Reporting System, XM21 Remote Sensing Chemical Agent Alarm, Tactical Explosive System, Remotely Piloted Vehicle, Plaster Works Radio, Securable Remote Control Unit, Electronic Information Delivery System and others.* Scuba diver Pima County Sheriff's Dept., 1985-90; plank owner USN Meml., Washington. Mem. Navy League, U.S. Naval Inst., Human Factors Soc., Internat. Platform Assn., Profl. Assn. Diving Instrs., U.S. C. of C. Republican. Methodist. E-mail: uexport@cwix.com. Home: 6537 E Santa Elena Tucson AZ 85715-3132 Office: Trail Dust Town #10 PO Box 10 6541 E Tanque Verde Rd Tucson AZ 85715-3813

COOK, PAUL MAXWELL, technology company executive; b. Ridgewood, N.J.. BSChemE, MIT, 1947. With Stanford Rsch. Inst., Menlo Park, Calif., 1948-53, Sequoia Process Corp., 1953-56; with Raychem Corp., Menlo Park, Calif., 1957-95, founder, former pres., CEO, until 1990, chmn., bd. dirs., until 1995; chmn., CEO CellNet Data Sys., San Carlos, Calif., 1990-94, also bd. dirs.; chmn., bd. dirs. SRI Internat., 1993-98; chmn. DIVA Sys. Corp., Menlo Park, Calif., 1995—. Mem. exec. com. San Francisco Bay Area Coun., 1988-94, chmn., 1990-91. Recipient Nat. Medal Tech., 1988. Mem. NAE, Am. Acad. Sci., Environ. Careers Orgn. (past chmn., bd. trustees), MIT Corp. (life). Office: Diva Sys Corp Bldg 205 333 Ravenswood Ave Menlo Park CA 94025-3453

COOK, PEGGY JO, psychotherapist, consultant; b. Greenville, Miss., Jan. 2, 1931; d. Bertram R. Coffing and Mary Josephine (Rodgers) McCarthy; m. Jack Storey Cook, July 15, 1951 (div. 1969); children: Bill S., Paul K., Monte C., Carol Rose Doss. BS in Psychology, SUNY, Albany, 1979; MEd in Counseling, U. North Tex., 1980, PhD in Counseling and Student Svcs., 1987. Co-founder, dir. Family Counseling Ctr., Ctr. for Creative Living, Ft. Worth, 1968-97; pvt. practice. Home: 6516 Parkway Ave North Richland Hills TX 76180-4309

COOK, PHILIP CARTER, lawyer; b. Atlanta, Nov. 4, 1946. BS, Ga. Inst. Tech., 1968; JD cum laude, Harvard U., 1971. Bar: Ga. 1972. Law clk. to Hon. Lewis R. Morgan U.S. Ct. Appeals (5th cir.), 1971-72; mem. Alston & Bird, Atlanta. Pres. Harvard Journal of Legislation 1970-71. Fellow Am. Coll. Tax Counsel; mem. ABA (chmn. sect. taxation, com. on banking and savs. instns. 1995), D.C. Bar, State Bar Ga. (chmn. taxation sect.), Am. Law Inst., Atlanta Tax Forum (trustee 1986-91, pres. 1991), Phi Kappa Phi, Omicron Delta Kappa. Office: Alston & Bird 1 Atlantic Ctr 1201 W Peachtree St NW Ste 4200 Atlanta GA 30309-3424*

COOK, QUENTIN LAMAR, lawyer, healthcare executive, church leader; b. Sept. 8, 1940; s. J. Vernon and Bernice (Kimball) C.; m. Mary Gaddie, Nov. 30, 1962; children: Kathryn Cook Knight, Quentin Laurance, Joseph Vernon III. BS, Utah State U., 1963; JD, Stanford U., 1966. Bar: Calif. 1966. Assoc. Carr, McClellan, Ingersoll, Thompson & Horn, Burlingame, Calif., 1966-69, ptnr., 1969-93; interim pres., CEO Calif. Healthcare Sys., San Francisco, 1993-94, pres., CEO, 1994-95; vice chmn. Sutter Health/Calif. Healthcare Sys., San Francisco, 1996; gen. authority LDS Ch., 1996—. City atty. Town of Hillsborough, Calif., 1982-93; mem. adv. bd. Utah State U., Logan, 1985-95; mem. bd. visitors Brigham Young U. Law Sch., Provo, 1994-96.

COOK, RALPH D., state supreme court justice. Former judge Ala. Cir. Ct. (10th jud. dist.), Ala. Dist. Ct.; assoc. justice Ala. Supreme Ct., Montgomery. Office: 300 Dexter Ave Montgomery AL 36104-3741*

COOK, REBECCA MCDOWELL, state official; m. John Larkin Cook; children: Hunter, Morgan. BA in Polit. Sci., U. Mo., 1972, JD, 1975; DEd (hon.), Mo. We. State Coll., 1997. Former clerk, assoc., partner Limbaugh, Limbaugh & Russell Law Firm, Cape Girardeau, Mo.; v.p. Oliver, Oliver, Waltz & Cook Law Firm, 1979-92; delegate to Mo. State Dem. Convention, 1980, mem. Mo. State Bd. Elem. & Sec. Edn., 1990-94; sec. of state State of Mo., 1994—. Mem. Future of South Commn., Dem. Nat. com., 1995—. Recipient Order of Barristers Awd, 1992, Woman of Achievement Awd, Cape Girardeau Zonta Club, 1994, James C. Kirkpatrick Excellence in Governance award; Henry Toll fellow. Mem. Southeast Mo. State U. Found., Southeast Mo. Hosp. Found., Nat. Assn. Secretaries of State (dir., exec. com.), Coun. Econ. Edn., Mo. K-16 Coalition, Lift Mo., Inc. Presbyterian. Office: PO Box 778 Jefferson City MO 65102-0778

COOK, RICHARD BORRESON, architect; b. Harvard, Ill., May 23, 1937; s. Ernest Keller and Clara Matilda (Borreson) C.; m. Shirley Jean Antrup,; children: Alan Blair, Elizabeth Ann, Rebecca Alica. BArch, U. Ill., 1962. Registered architect, Calif., Fla., Ill., Ind., Mich., Mo., N.D., N.Y., Ohio, Wis. Intern architect Skidmore, Owings & Merrill, Chgo., 1962-64, Ulrich Franzen & Assocs., N.Y.C., 1964-65; assoc. I.W. Colburn & Assocs., Chgo., 1965-70, Metz, Train, Olson & Youngren, Chgo., 1970-78; pres. Orput Associs., Wilmette, Ill., 1978-81, Stowell Cook Frolichstein, Chgo., 1981—, Green Cook Ltd., Chgo., 1981; bd. dirs., pres. Chgo. Archtl. Assistance Ctr., 1983; chmn. handicapped subcom. Mayor's Commn. Bldg. Code Amendments, Chgo., chmn. constrn. industry affairs com.; speaker, presenter papers in field. Prin. projects with Stowell Cook Frolichstein and Cook, Hiltscher Assoc. include Countryside Mall, Fla., Orange Park Mall, Fla., Trinity Evangel. Div. Sch., Rolfing Libr. addition and renovation, Deerfield, Ill, renovation main br. U.S. Postal Svc., Chgo., City Colls. of Chgo., Main St. Sq. Shopping Ctr., Downers Grove, Ill., Chgo. Bd. Edn.; with Orput Assocs. Kenosha (Wis.) County Pub. Safety Bldg., Burnham Terr. Apts. for Elderly, Rockford, Ill., addition and renovation Garrett-Evangel. Sem. Libr., addition Elmhurst (Ill.) Pub. Libr., addition Lake Forest (Ill.) Sch. Mgmt., apt. bldg. renovation Gt. Lakes (Ill.) Naval Sta., Hickory Hills (Ill.) Mcpl. Bldg.; with Metz Train, Olson & Youngren, Inc. office and computer ctr. Lumbermen's Mut. Casualty Co., Long Grove, Ill., Safeguards Analytical Lab. Bldg. Argonne (Ill.) Nat. Lab., Cancer Virus Rsch. Lab. U. Chgo., pub. bldg. commn. John Hope Middle Sch., Chgo.; with I.W. Colburn & Assocs. Geophys. Sci. Bldg. U. Chgo, Cathedral Christ the King, Kalamazoo, dormitory complex and dining facilities Bryn Mawr Coll, Pa., lab. and office bldg. Standard "T" Chem. Co., Lisle, Ill., Temple Jeremiah, Northbrook, Ill. Mem. plann commn. Evanston, 1997. Fellow AIA (dir. Ill. region 1988-89, chmn. T6B documents com., chmn. 1987 nat. conv., chmn. membership svcs. task force, mem. goals and grassroots '82 com.); mem. Ill. Council AIA (bd. dirs., pres., co-chmn. Midwest Regional Conf., mem. fin. and nominating coms.), Chgo. chpt. AIA (sec., v.p., 1st v.p., pres., mem. 1992 World's Fair Rev. Com., chmn. nominating com., mem. Logan Sq. Design Ctr.), Am. Arbitration Assn., Chgo. chpt. AIA Found. (pres.). Democrat. Congregationalist. Avocations: sculpture, photography. Home: 1330 Wesley Ave Evanston IL 60201-4141 Office: Stowell Cook & Frolichstein 33 W Grand Ave Chicago IL 60610-4306*

COOK, RICHARD KELSEY, aerospace industry executive; b. White Plains, N.Y., Nov. 14, 1931; s. Albert James and Frances Elizabeth (Butler) C.; m. Marjorie S. Schellabarger, Sept. 10, 1959 (div.); children: Geoffrey, Patrick, Sarah, Catherine; m. Fleur Wales-Baillie, Oct. 14, 1987. Postgrad., Stanford U., 1979; BA, George Washington U., 1958. Legis staff Am. Trucking Assn., 1959-61; adminstrv. asst. Rep. Edwin B. Dooley, 1961; legis. asst. Rep. Oliver P. Bolton, 1963-65; profl. staff mem. Banking and Currency Com., U.S. Ho. of Reps., Washington, 1965-69; spl. asst. to Pres. of U.S., Washington, 1969-71, dep. asst., 1971-73; v.p. Lockheed Corp., Washington, 1973-94, sr. v.p., 1994-95; pres. RKC Ltd., 1995—; spl. adv. O'Connor & Hannan, Washington; cons. to major U.S. and South African Companies, with offices in Johannesburg and Washington; cons. to PanAmSat Cpr., 1999—. Served with USAF, 1949-53. Mem. Tau Kappa Epsilon. Clubs: Aero. (pres. 1979), Met; Burning Tree (Washington), Captiva Yacht Club, Fla.; Nnanda Metropolitan (D.C.), Johannesburg. Office: O'Connor & Hannon 1919 Pennsylvania Ave NW Washington DC 20006-3404

COOK, RICHARD W., motion picture company executive; b. Bakersfield, Calif., Aug. 20, 1950. Ed., U. So. Calif. Saels rep. Disneyland, 1971-74, sales mgr., 1974-77; mgr. pay TV and non-theatrical releases Disney Studios, 1977-80; asst. domestic sales mgr. Buena Vista, 1980-81, v.p., asst. gen. sales mgr., 1981-84, v.p., gen. sales mgr., 1985-88, sr. v.p. domestic distbn., 1988-94; pres. Buena Vista Pictures Distbn., 1994; pres. worldwide mktg. Buena Vista Pictures Mktg., 1994-97; chmn. Walt Disney Motion Pictures Group, Burbank, Calif., 1997—. Office: Walt Disney Studios 500 S Buena Vista St Burbank CA 91521-0004*

COOK, ROBERT CROSSLAND, research chemist; b. New Haven, June 5, 1947; s. Russell C. and Tensia (Veazey) C. BS in Chemistry, Lafayette Coll., 1969; MPh in Phys. Chemistry, Yale U., 1971, PhD in Theoretical Chemistry, 1973. Mem. faculty Lafayette Coll., Easton, Pa., 1973-81; staff scientist Lawrence Livermore (Calif.) Nat. Lab., 1981—; instr. Calif. State U., Hayward, 1985-86, 94, Chabot Coll., 1986-90, Las Positas Coll., 1990-92; mem. vis. faculty Dartmouth Coll., Hanover, N.H., 1977, 78, 79, Colo. State U., Ft. Collins, 1980. Contbr. articles to profl. jours. Grantee in field. Mem. Am. Chem. Soc., Am. Phys. Soc., Sigma Xi. Office: Lawrence Livermore Nat Lab L-481 PO Box 808 Livermore CA 94551

COOK, ROBERT DONALD, financial service executive; b. Chicago Heights, Ill., Nov. 1, 1929; s. Webster Warren and Gladys (Miner) C.; m. Maxine Jensen, Nov. 11, 1950; children: Carolyn Jean, Robert Donald II. BS in Bus., U. Md., 1956; grad. advanced mgmt. program, Harvard U., 1973. CPA, Md. Audit mgr. Arthur Andersen & Co. (CPAs), Washington, 1956-63; comptroller Peoples Drug Stores, Washington, 1963-68; v.p., controller Booz, Allen & Hamilton, Inc., Chgo., 1968-72; pres. Cookemper Rentals, Inc., Barrington, Ill., 1971-73; controller Esmark, Inc., Chgo., 1973-77; pres., chief operating officer Castle & Cooke, Inc., San Francisco, 1977-86; chmn. R.D. Cook Mgmt. Corp., 1986—; chmn. bd., dir. Yorkshire Foods Inc., 1997—; chmn. bd. dirs. Am. Nursery Products, Inc.; bd. dirs. Redwood Empire Bancorp, PAFCO, Inc. Served with USNR, 1948-52. Mem. Inst. CPAs, Fin. Execs. Inst., Beta Alpha Psi. Clubs: Masons (32 deg.), Shriners. Home and Office: RD Cook Mgmt Corp 75 Rolling Hills Rd Belvedere Tiburon CA 94920-1501

COOK, ROBERT EDWARD, plant ecology educator, research director; b. Providence, R.I., Sept. 26, 1946; s. John Edward and Suzanne Marie (Boisvert) C. A.B., Harvard U., 1968; Ph.D., Yale U., 1973. Instr. Yale U., New Haven, 1973-74; postdoctoral fellow Harvard U., Cambridge, Mass., 1974-75; asst. prof. Harvard U., Cambridge, 1975-80, assoc. prof., 1980-83, Arnold prof., 1989—; assoc. dir. Harvard U. Herbaria, Cambridge, Mass., 1998—; program dir. NSF, Washington, 1982-83; assoc. prof. Cornell U., Ithaca, N.Y., 1983-88, dir. Cornell Plantations, 1983-88; dir. Arnold Arboretum, Boston, 1989—; vis. prof. Cornell U., Ithaca, 1981-82. Contbr. articles to profl. jours. Capt. U.S. Army, 1968-74. NSF grantee. Office: Harvard U Arnold Arboretum 125 Arborway Jamaica Plain MA 02130-3500

COOK, ROBERT S., JR., lawyer; b. Syracuse, N.Y., Apr. 5, 1940; m. Sally Williams. BA, Amherst Coll., 1962; LLB, Yale U., 1965. Bar: N.Y. 1966. Assoc., Hancock, Ryan, Shove & Hust, Syracuse, N.Y., 1965-68; urban renewal rep. HUD, N.Y.C., 1968-71; exec. dir. The Parks Council, Inc., N.Y.C., 1972-73; v.p., co-founder Project for Pub. Spaces, Inc., N.Y.C., 1974-77; cons., N.Y.C., 1978-80; assoc. Tufo & Zuccotti, N.Y.C., 1981-86; assoc., then ptnr., Brown and Wood, N.Y.C., 1986-94, ptnr. DeForest & Duer, N.Y.C., 1995—; v.p., bd. dirs. Citizens Housing and Planning Council, 1985; cons. The Denver Partnership, 1981; mem. N.Y. State Freshwater Wetlands Appeals Bd., 1991-94. Author: Zoning for Downtown Urban Design, 1980. Design project fellow Nat. Endowment for Arts, Washington, 1978-79; Graham Found. for Advanced Studies in the Fine Arts fellow, Chgo., 1979. Mem. N.Y. State Bar Assn., Assn. Bar City N.Y. (com. environ. law 1979-82, com. land use planning and zoning, 1994—, chmn., 1997—). Office: DeForest & Duer 90 Broad St Fl 18 New York NY 10004-2276

COOK, ROBERTA LYNN, agricultural economist, educator; b. Oceanside, Calif., Feb. 27, 1954; d. Robert Merold and Wanda Eugenia (Wright) C.; m. José Canela-Cacho, May 12, 1999. BA, Mich. State U., 1976, MS, 1981, PhD, 1985. Grad. rsch. asst. Mich. State U., East Lansing, 1978-81, 84; cons. Banco de Mexico, Mexico City, 1981-84; ext. economist, prof. U. Calif., Davis, 1985—; appointed to the Agricult. trade adv. Com. (ATAC) for Fruits and Vegs. by the US Trade Rep., 1997-98, bd. dirs. Calif. Kiwifruit Commn., Sacramento, chair, 1997-98; bd. dirs. Calif. Tomato Commn., Market Devel. Com. Chair, 1997—, Fresno; mem. Internat. adv. coun. Produce Mktg. Assn., Newark, Del., 1994-97, Ag Bennet Round Table, 1997—; mem. USDA Adv. Panel on Food Losses, 1998—; cons. OECD, Colombian Govt., Trade Bur., U.S. AID, World Bank, UN, others; chair S-222 Regional Rsch. Group on Fruits and Vegetables, 1991-93; appointee USTR and U.S. Sec. Agr. to Agrl. Trade Adv. Com. for fruits and vegetables. Contbr. articles to profl. jours. Bd. dirs. Katalysis Found., Stockton, Calif., 1987-91; chair U. Calif./Legis. Task Force on Cooperatives, Davis, 1987-88. Recipient Grad. Inst./Coop. Leadership award U.S. Dept. Agr., U. Mo., Columbia, 1986, Affirmative Action award U. Calif., 1991. Mem. Food Dist. Rsch. Soc. (bd. mem. 1995—, v.p. for programs 1997-98), Am. Agrl. Econs. Assn. (various coms. 1984—), Produce Mktg. Assn. (various coms. 1987—), United Fresh Fruit and Vegetable Assn. (various coms. 1987—), Internat. Soc. Hort. Sci. (v.p. econ. divsn. 1992-96). Avocations: travel, tango, cooking/wine, history. Office: U Calif Davis Dept Agr and Resource Econs Davis CA 95616

COOK, ROBIN, author; b. N.Y.C., May 4, 1940; s. Edgar Lee and Audrey (Koons) C.; m. Barbara Ellen Mougin, July 18, 1979. BA, Weslyan U., 1962; MD, Columbia U., 1966. Resident in gen. surgery Queen's Hosp., Honolulu, 1966-68; resident in ophthalmology Mass. Eye and Ear Infirmary, Boston, 1971-75, mem. staff, from 1975; clin. instr. Harvard U. Med. Sch., 1972. Author: The Year of the Intern, 1972, Coma, 1977, Sphinx, 1979, Brain, 1981, Fever, 1982, Godplayer, 1983, Mindbend, 1986, Outbreak, 1987, Mortal Fear, 1988, Mutation, 1989, Harmful Intent, 1990, Vital Signs, 1990, Blindsight, 1991, Terminal, 1992, Fatal Cure, 1994, Acceptable Risk, 1995, Invasion, 1997, Chromosome 6, 1997, Toxin, 1998. Lt. comdr. USN, 1969-71. Avocations: skiing, surfing, painting, cooking. Home: 4601 Gulf Shore Blvd N # P4 Naples FL 34103-2221 Office: care Putnam Pub 200 Madison Ave New York NY 10016-3903*

COOK, RON A., management company executive. Pres. Boykin Mgmt. Co. LLC, Clev. Office: Boykin Mgmt Co LLC 50 Public Sq # 1500 Cleveland OH 44113

COOK, SHARLA J., military officer. BS in Edn. with honors, Brigham Young U., 1971; disting. grad., Officer Tng. Sch., 1972; aircraft maintenance officer course, Chanute AFB, Ill., 1973; M in Logistics Mgmt., Air Force Inst. of Tech., 1977; grad., Air Command and Staff Coll., 1985; disting. grad., Indsl. Coll. of Armed Forces, 1993. Commd. 2d lt. USAF, 1972, advanced through grades to brigadier gen., 1998; wing job control officer U-Tapao Air Base, Thailand, 1975-76; aide-de-camp air logistics ctr. comdr. Sacramento Air Logistics Ctr., McClellan AFB, Calif., 1981-82, dep. br. chief inventory and scheduling br., 1982-84; comdr. 374th Orgnl. Maintenance Squadron, Clark Air Base, The Philippines, 1985-87; maintenance ops. officer 58th Tactical Tng. Wing, Luke AFB, Ariz., 1988-90; asst. dep. comdr. for maintenance 58th Tactical Tng. Wing, Luke AFB, 1990-91; dep. comdr. 58th Support Group, Luke AFB, 1991-92; comdr. 8th Logistics Group, Kunsan Air Base, South Korea, 1993-94; chief maintenance engring. Hdqs. Pacific Air Forces, Hickam AFB, Hawaii, 1994-95, asst. dir. logistics, 1995-96; dir. aircraft directorate Ogden Air Logistics Ctr., Hill AFB, Utah, 1996-97; dir. logistics Hdqs. Air Edn. and Tng. Command, Randolph AFB, Tex., 1997—. Decorated Legion of Merit, Meritorious Svc. medal with 4 oak leaf clusters. Office: HQ AETC/LG 555 E St E Randolph AFB TX 78150-4440

COOK, STANTON R., media company executive; b. Chgo., July 3, 1925; s. Rufus Merrill and Thelma Marie (Borgerson) C.; m. Barbara Wilson, Sept. 23, 1950 (dec. Nov. 1994). BS in Mech. Engring., Northwestern U., 1949. With Shell Oil Co., 1949-51; with Chgo. Tribune Co., 1951-81, v.p., 1967-70, exec. v.p. and gen. mgr., 1970-72, pres., 1972-74, pub., 1973-90, CEO, 1974-76, chmn., 1974-81; dir. Tribune Co., 1972-96, v.p., 1972-74, pres., 1974-88, chmn., 1989-92, CEO, 1974-90; chmn. Chgo. Nat. League Ball Club, Inc., 1990-94; bd. dirs. AP, 1975-84, 2d vice chmn., 1979-84; bd. dirs. Newspaper Adv. Bur., 1973-92, Am. Newspaper Pubs. Assn., 1974-82; dep. chmn., bd. dirs. Fed. Res. Bank Chgo., 1980-83, chmn., 1984-85; bd. dirs. Robert R. McCormick Tribune Found., 1990—. Trustee Robert R. McCormick Trust, 1972-90, Savs. and Profit Sharing Fund of Sears Employees, 1991-94, U. Chgo., 1973-87, Mus. Sci. and Industry, Chgo., 1973—, Field Mus. Natural History, Chgo., 1973—, Gen. Douglas MacArthur Found., 1979—, Northwestern U., 1987—, Shedd Aquarium Soc., 1987—, Am. Newspaper Pubs. Assn. Found., 1973-82. Mem. Newspaper Assn. Am. (bd. govs. 1992),

Chgo. Coun. Fgn. Rels. (bd. dirs. 1973-93), Comml. Club (past pres.), Econ. Club (past pres., life mem.). Home: 224 Raleigh Rd Kenilworth IL 60043-1209

COOK, STEPHEN ARTHUR, mathematics and computer science educator; b. Buffalo, Dec. 14, 1939; s. Gerhard Albert and Lura (Lincoln) C.; m. Linda Marie Craddock, May 4, 1968; children—Gordon, James. B.S. in math., U. Mich., 1961; S.M. in math., Harvard U., 1962, Ph.D. in math., 1966. Asst. prof. U. Calif.-Berkeley, 1966-70; assoc. prof. U. Toronto, 1970-75, prof., 1975—, univ. prof., 1985—. Contbr. articles to profl. jours. E.W.R. Staecie Meml. fellow, 1977-78; Killam research fellow Can. Council, 1982-83; recipient ACM Turing award Assn. Computing Machinery, 1982, Killam prize Can. Coun., 1997. Fellow Royal Soc. Can., Royal Soc. London; mem. Nat. Acad. Scis., Am. Acad. Arts and Scis. Home: 6 Indian Valley Crescent, Toronto, ON Canada M6R 1Y6 Office: Dept Computer Sci U Toronto, Toronto, ON Canada M5S 3G4

COOK, STEPHEN BERNARD, homebuilding company executive; b. Balt., June 26, 1947; s. Allen Bernard and Evelyn Naomi (Thomas) C.; m. Marlena Marie Sapia, Dec. 27, 1969; children—Geoffrey Matthew, Katherine Marie. B.S. in Acctg., Loyola Coll., Balt., 1969. C.P.A., Md. Audit mgr. Ernst & Whinney, Balt., 1977-81; v.p., treas. U.S. Fidelity and Guaranty Co., Balt., 1982-85, v.p., controller, 1985-91; v.p. corp. controller The Ryland Group Inc., Balt., 1992—. Fellow Life Mgmt. Inst.; mem. Fin. Execs. Inst. (bd. dirs. Balt. chpt. 1989-92), Md. Assn. CPAs (chmn. ins. com. 1980-85, outstanding com. chmn. award 1984-85), Hillendale Country Club (bd. govs. 1985-94, pres. 1990-91). Roman Catholic. Avocations: golf, tennis, bridge, theater. Home: 1 Norwick Lutherville Cir Timonium MD 21093-2930 Office: The Ryland Group Inc 11000 Broken Land Pkwy Columbia MD 21044-3562*

COOK, STEPHEN CHAMPLIN, retired shipping company executive; b. Portland, Oreg., Sept. 20, 1915; s. Frederick Stephen and Mary Louise (Boardman) C.; m. Dorothy White, Oct. 27, 1945 (dec. Sept. 1998); children: Mary H. Cook Goodson, John B., Samuel D., Robert B. (dec.). Student, U. Oreg., 1935-36. Surveyor U.S. Engrs. Corp., Portland, Oreg., 1934-35; dispatcher Pacific Motor Trucking Co., Oakland, Calif., 1937-38; manifest clk. Pacific Truck Express, Portland, 1939; exec. asst. Coastwise Line, San Francisco, 1940-41, mgr. K-Line svc., 1945-56; chartering mgr. Ocean Svc. Inc. subs. Marcona Corp., San Francisco, 1956-75, ret., 1975; cons., San Francisco, 1976-78. Author 1 charter party, 1957. Mem. steering com. Dogwood Festival, Lewiston, Idaho, 1985-92; sec. Asotin County Reps., Clarkston, Wash., 1986-88; adv. bd. Clarkston Pt. Commrs., 1989-92. Lt. USN, 1941-45, PTO. Recipient Pres.'s award Marin (Calif.) coun. Boy Scouts Am., 1977, Order of Merit, 1971, 84, Skillern award Lewis Clark coun., 1982, Silver Beaver award 1987; Lewis-Clark Valley Vol. award, 1987, Youth Corps award Nat. Assn. Svc. and Conservation Corps, 1990, Pres.'s Spl. award Clarkston C. of C., 1983. Mem. VFW, Asotin County Hist. Soc. (hon. life pres. 1982-83, bd. dirs.), Asotin C. of C. (v.p. 1994-95). Republican. Mem. Stand for United Ch. of Christ. Avocations: hiking, camping, stamp collecting.

COOK, STUART DONALD, physician, educator; b. Boston, Oct. 23, 1936; s. Martius and Nina (Schwartzman) C.; m. Josepha Emdin, June 26, 1960; children—Andrew, Peter, Jonathan. AB, Brandeis U., 1957; MS, U. Vt., 1959, MD, 1962. Diplomate: Am. Bd. Psychiatry and Neurology. Intern Upstate Med. Center, Syracuse, N.Y., 1962-63; resident in neurology Albert Einstein Coll. Medicine, Bronx, N.Y., 1965-67; chief resident Albert Einstein Coll. Medicine, Bronx, 1967-68, instr. dept. neurology, 1968-69; asst. prof. neurology Coll. Physician and Surgeons, Columbia U., N.Y.C., 1969-71; prof. medicine N.J. Med. Sch., Newark, 1971—, chmn. dept. neuroscis., 1972-98, acting dean, 1987-89; chief neurology svc. VA Med. Ctr., East Orange, N.J., 1971-86; pres. U. Medicine and Dentistry N.J., 1998—; vis. scientist div. virology Nat. Inst. Med. Research, London, 1977-78; vis. scientist Swiss Inst. for Cancer Research, 1985. Contbr. articles to profl. jours. Served with USN, 1963-65. Mem. Am. Acad. Neurology (S. Weir Mitchell award 1968), Am. Assn. Neuropathologists, AAUP, Am. Fedn. Clin. Research, Assn. Univ. Profs. Neurology, Harvey Soc., Am. Neurol. Assn., Sigma Xi, Alpha Omega Alpha. Home: 26 Dogwood Dr Morristown NJ 07960-3310 Office: U Medicine and Dentistry NJ MS Dept Neuroscis 185 S Orange Ave Newark NJ 07103-2757

COOK, SUSAN FARWELL, alumni relations director; b. Boston, Apr. 28, 1953; d. Benjamin and Beverly (Brooks) Conant; m. James Samuel Cook Jr., Aug. 17, 1985; children: Emily Farwell, David McKendree. AB, Colby Coll., 1975. Bank teller Boston 5 Cent Savs. Bank, 1975-76; asst. technician plan cost John Hancock Mut. Life Ins. Co., Boston, 1976-77, technician plan cost, 1977-78, sr. technician plan cost, 1978-79, asst. mgr. group pension plan cost, 1979-81; assoc. dir. alumni rels. Colby Coll., Waterville, Maine, 1981-86; dir. alumni rels. Colby Coll., Waterville, 1986-97, assoc. dir. planned giving, 1997—; co-dir. adv. bd. women's studies Colby Coll., 1987-89, adv. women's group, 1987-89. Bd. dirs., newsletter sec. Literacy Vols. Am., Waterville, 1986-89, 91-92, v.p., 1995-97, pres., 1997-99; bd. dirs. Congress Lake Assns., Yarmouth, Maine, 1988-92; treas. Pitcher Pond Improvement Assn., 1988-95; treas. Gagnon/100 Campaign, 1996, 98. Mem. AAUW (sec. Waterville br. 1989-91, pres. 1991-93, co-pres. 1993-95), Coun. Advancement and Support of Edn., CASE Dist. I (exec. bd. dirs. 1994-97, sec. 1996-97, nominating com. 1997-99). Avocations: skiing, sewing, golf. Home: 6 Pray Ave Waterville ME 04901-5339 Office: Colby Coll 4373 Mayflower Hl Waterville ME 04901-8843

COOK, TONY MICHAEL, legislative staff member; m. Joy Cook; children: Michael, Libby. BA, Wash. State U., 1970; JD, Stanford U., 1973. With Senate Rsch. Ctr., 1973, U. Wash.; mem. staff Utilities and Transp. Commn., 1977; counsel Wash. State Senate, 1991, sec., 1999—; counsel Legis. Ethics Bd. Fax: 360-786-7520. E-mail: cookúto@leg.wa.gov. Office: Wash State Senate PO Box 40482 306 Legislative Bldg Olympia WA 98504-0482

COOK, VICTOR JOSEPH, JR., marketing educator, consultant; b. Durant, Okla., June 25, 1938; s. Victor Joseph and Athelene Ann (Arduser) C.; m. Linda Lee Potter, June 6, 1960 (div. 1971); children: Victor Joseph III, William Randall, Christopher Phelps; m. Barbara Brainard, Dec. 29, 1989 (div. 1997). BA, Fla. State U., 1960; MS, La. State U., 1962; PhD, U. Mich., 1965. Rsch. assoc. Mktg. Sci. Inst., Phila., 1965-68, assoc. rsch. dir., Boston, 1968-69; asst. prof. U. Chgo., 1969-75; pres., dir. Mgmt. & Design, New Orleans, 1975-78; prof. Freeman Sch. Bus. Tulane U., 1978—; pres. The Styjl Furniture, 1998—; cons. Ford Motor Co., Dearborn, Mich., 1964-67, IBM, N.Y.C., 1968-72, Sears, Roebuck & Co., Chgo., 1975-77, Internat. Computers Ltd., ICL, London, 1982-91, The DuPont Co., Wilmington, 1986—, The Bases Group, Cin., 1986-89. Author: Brand Policy Determination, 1967, Readings in Marketing Strategy, 1989; designer, patentee furniture, frameworks, 1976. Mem. Am. Mktg. Assn., Am. Econ. Assn., Inst. for Ops. Rsch. and the Mgmt. Scis., Beta Gamma Sigma, Phi Beta Kappa. Republican. Methodist. Avocations: furniture making, cooking, art collecting, furniture design. Office: Tulane U AB Freeman Sch Bus New Orleans LA 70118

COOK, WILLIAM HOWARD, architect; b. Evanston, Ill., Dec. 19, 1924; s. Clare Cyril and Matilda Hermine (Schuldt) C.; m. Nancy Ann Dean, Feb. 1, 1949; children: Robert, Cynthia, James. BA, UCLA, 1947; BArch, U. Mich., 1952. Chief designer Fabrica de Muebles Camacho-Roldan, Bogota, Colombia, S.Am., 1949-52; assoc. architect Orus Eash, Traverse City, Mich., Ft. Wayne, Ind., 1952-60; ptnr. Cook & Swaim (architects), Tucson, 1961-68; project specialist in urban devel. Banco Interamericano de Desarrollo, Buenos Aires, Argentina, 1968-69; pres. Cain, Nelson, Wares, Cook and Assocs., architects, Tucson, 1969-82; vis. lectr. architecture U. Ariz., 1980-89; coord. archtl. exch. with U. LaSalle, Mexico City, 1983, 85, 87, 89, 93. Lt. (j.g.) USNR, 1943-46. Served to lt. (j.g.) USNR, 1943-46. Fellow AIA (pres. So. Ariz. 1967); mem. Ariz. Soc. Architects (pres. 1970), Ariz. Soc. of AIA (Architect's medal 1981). Presbyterian. Home and Office: PO Box 347 Sonoita AZ 85637-0347

COOK, WILLIAM LESLIE, JR., lawyer; b. July 1, 1949; s. William Leslie and Mary Elizabeth (Roberts) C.; m. Mary Jo Dorr, July 17, 1976; children: Leslie Patton, William Roberts, Maribeth Dorr. BA, U. Miss., 1971, JD, 1974. Bar: Miss. 1974, U.S. Dist. Ct. (no. dist.) Miss. 1974, U.S. Dist. Ct. (we. dist.) Tenn. 1986. Assoc. Bailey & Trusty, Batesville, Miss., 1974-79; ptnr. Bailey, Trusty & Cook, Batesville, Miss., 1980-90, Bailey & Cook, Batesville, Miss., 1990-92, Bailey, Cook & Womble, Batesville, Miss., 1992—; Chmn., Miss. Coll. Rep. Clubs, 1973, Panola County March of Dimes, Batesville, 1976-78; Miss. chmn. Nat. Orgn. Social Security Claimants Reps., 1981-82; rep. Honor Coun., U. Miss. Sch. Law, 1974. Paul Harris fellow 1998—. Mem. ABA (torts and ins. practice sect. 1979—, vice chmn. com. on delivery of legal svcs. tothe disabled young lawyers divsn. 1983-85, gen. practice sect. 1985-86), ATLA, Miss. State Bar (state bd. bar admissions 1978-79, mem. ethics com. 1980-83, bd. dirs. Young Lawyers sect. 1980-83, chmn. com. on unauthorized practice of law 1983-86, workers compensation sect., mem. com. on Kid's Second Chance 1992), Panola County Bar Assn. (pres. 1979-80), Miss. Trial Lawyers Assn. (membership com. 1983-84), Ct. Practice Inst. (diplomate), Lawyer-Pilots Bar Assn., Lamar Soc. Internat. Law, Batesville Jaycees (legal counsel 1975-77), Masons, Shriners, Rotary (pres. 1991-92, 96-97, asst. dist. gov. 1997—, dist. gov. nominee 1999—, Paul Harris fellow), Omicron Delta Kappa, Pi Sigma Alpha, Delta Theta Pi. Methodist. Home: 110 Shagbark Dr Batesville MS 38606-8470 Office: Panola Plz 118 Highway 6 W Batesville MS 38606-2507

COOK, WILLIAM WILBERT, English language educator; b. Trenton, N.J., Aug. 4, 1933; s. Cleve and Frances (Carter) C. BA, Coll. of N.J., 1954; MA, U. Chgo., 1976; PhD, Rivier Coll., Manchester, N.H., 1994. Tchr. William G. Cook Sch., Trenton, 1954-56, Jr. H.S. 1, Trenton, 1956-61; tchr., chmn. English dept. Princeton (N.J.) H.W., 1961-73; prof. English, Dartmouth Coll., Hanover, N.H., 1973—, chmn. dept., 1994—, Israel Evans prof. oratory and belles lettres, 1993; workshop leader, cons., in-svc. tchr. trainer various sch. sys., 1973—, Nat. Faculty Arts and Scis., Atlanta, 1976—. Author: Hudson Hornet and Other Poems, 1989, Spiritual and Other Poems, 1999, (play) Flight to Canada, 1982; editor: Tapping Potential, 1985; contbr. essays and poems to various jours. Selection panel mem., workshop leader Nat. Endowment for the Humanities Nat. Endowment for the Arts; founder, v.p. African Grove Inst. for Arts, 1996—. With U.S. Army, 1957-59. Recipient Disting. Alumni citation Coll. of N.J., 1977; named N.H. Prof. of Yr., Coun. for Advancement and Support Edn., 1993. Mem. MLA, Nat. Coun. Tchrs. English (exec. com. 1971-73), Conf. on Coll. Composition and Comm. (asst., assoc. chmn. 1990-92). Democrat. Baptist. Avocations: acting, painting, reading. Office: Dartmouth Coll Box 6032 Hanover NH 03755

COOK, WILLIE CHUNN, retired elementary school educator; b. Uriah, Ala., Feb. 3, 1935; d. Thompson Ann and Minnie Lee (Jay) Chunn; m. Clifford Thomas Cook, Feb. 3, 1974; children: Wendelin Marin Boothe, Melanie Martin. BS, Livingston U., 1956, MEd, 1972. Elem. tchr. Jefferson County Pub. Sch. System, Birmingham, Ala., 1956-58, Mobile County Pub. Sch. System, Mobile, Ala., 1958-60, Norfolk (Va.) City Pub. Sch. System, 1960-61, Mobile County Pub. Sch. System, 1961-66, Pinellas County Pub. Sch. System, Clearwater, Fla., 1966-73; mid. sch. sci. tchr. St. Bernard Pub. Sch. System, Chalmette, La., 1973-76; elem. tchr. Jefferson Parish Pub. Sch. System, Gretna, La., 1976-98, ret., 1998; mem. system textbook adoption com. Pinellas County pub. Sch. System, Clearwater, 1970, Jefferson Parish Pub. Sch. System, Gretna, 1978-79; coordinating tchr. Yearly Sch. Sci. Fairs, Pinellas County, Fla., 1969-72, Jefferson Parish, La., 1981-92, yearly extended class field trips, Jefferson Parish, 1984-92; sponsor Jefferson Parish Nat. Acad. Games teams, 1981-85; workshop presenter. Treas. Caddo Presbytery Cumberland Presbyn. Women, Marshall, Tex., 1982-83; chmn. Faith Ch. Cumberland Presbyn. Women, Kenner, La., 1980; mem. Christian edn. com. Faith Cumberland Presbyn. Ch., Metairie, La., 1988—; com. on polit. effectiveness Jefferson Fedn. Tchrs., coun. mem. 1987-89, chmn. Ednl. Issues Com. 1987-89, mem. Govs. Edn. Adv. Com. 1987-88, lobbyist in state legis., Jefferosn Parish, and Baton Rouge, 1985-88. Mem. Am. Fedn. Tchrs., La. Fedn. Tchrs., Jefferson Fedn. Tchrs., Nat. Sci. Tchrs. Assn., La. Sci. Tchrs. Assn. Democrat. Avocations: travel, sewing, cooking, camping, reading. Home: 25 Trinidad Dr Kenner LA 70065-3112

COOKE, ALEX "TY", JR., mayor; b. Wichita, Kans., July 26, 1944; m. Judy Kay Cornelison; children: Alex K. III, Kimperly Cooke Powell. BBA, Tex. Tech. U., 1968. Commd. salesman, then officer, dir., co-owner Fields & Co., Lubbock, Tex., 1962-84; former dir., chmn. loan rev. com. and bus. devel. com. Tex. Commerce Bank, Lubbock, 1985-93; gen. ptnr. Coppercreek Land and Cattle, Lubbock; mng. ptnr. Cooke Cattle Co., Lubbock; mayor City of Lubbock; city councilman, 1996—; bd. dirs. State Nat. Bank; del. South Plains Assn. Govts.; pres. West Tex. Mcpl. Power Agy.; dir., pres. Tex. Pub. Power Assn.; mem. wastewater improvement com., temporary transp. adv. com. City of Lubbock; mem. pres.'s coun. Jenn-Air Corp.; mem. adv. panel GE Distbrs. Past mem. Friends of Libr. Health Scis. Bd., Tex. Tech U. Health Scis. Ctr.; past mem. found. bd. Meth. Hosp.; past dir. and pres. South Plains Childrens' Shelter; past bd. dirs. Lubbock Symphony Orch. Mem. West Tex. Home Builders Assn. (bd. dirs.), Wholesale Distbrs. Assn. (adv. com.), West Tex. Mus. Assn. (bd. dirs.), Lubbock Area Found. (founder), Lubbock Country Club (past pres.). Office: Office of Mayor PO Box 2000 Lubbock TX 79457-0001*

COOKE, CARLTON LEE, JR., mayor; b. Marion, Ala., July 12, 1944; s. Carlton Lee and Willie (Rinehart) C.; divorced; 1 child, Kimberly Ann. Student, U. Hawaii, 1962-65; BA, La. Tech. U., 1966; postgrad., U. Tex., 1970-72. Mfg. engr. Tex. Instruments, Austin, 1972-75, site personnel mgr., 1975-81, mktg. mgr., 1981-83; pres., CEO Greater Austin C. of C., 1983-87; mayor City of Austin, Austin, 1988—; chmn., CEO Habitek Internat., Inc., 1991—; pres., CEO, U.S. Med. Systems, Inc., 1992—; bd. dirs. Bill Concepts Corp., U.S. Long Distance Corp., Tanisys Tech. Corp., Sharps Compliance, Corp., Med. Polymers Tech., Inc.; participant U.S. Conf. Mayors, Washington, 1991; mem. Anthony Commn., U.S. Congress. Contbr. editor to mags. Mem. Austin City Coun., 1977-81, mayor pro tem, 1979; co-chmn. Jerry Lewis Telethon, Austin, 1986-87; chmn. United Negro Telethon, 1991, Tex. Housing Fin. Corp., 1992, Austin Charter Com., 1993-94, Tex. Walk of Stars, 1991—. Capt. USAF, 1966-72. Decorated Bronze Star (Vietnam); recipient Carl Burnett Cmty. award, 1981, Disting. Austin Citizen's award, 1992, Excellence award Real Estate Coun. of Austin, 1992; named Jaycee of Yr. Austin Jaycees, 1976, one of Five Outstanding Young Texans Tex. Jaycees, 1979. Mem. Nat. League Cities (chair fin. steering com.), Tex. Mcpl. League (pres. 1991), Austin-San Antonio Corridor Coun. (pres. 1988, 91), VFW. Baptist. Avocations: travel, reading, civic work, movie history, art. E-mail: usmedsys@onr.com. Home: PO Box 50442 Austin TX 78763-0442 Office: Office of Mayor 515 Congress Ave Ste 2520 Austin TX 78701-3503

COOKE, CHANTELLE ANNE, writer; b. Denver, Apr. 9, 1971; d. Frederick Blaize and Claire Gail (Jones) C. Student, Collin County C.C., Plano, Tex., 1989-93. Author: (poetry chapbook) Songs From Stars, 1995, (poetry cassette tape) Visions, 1997; contbg. editor tech. articles for computer industry, 1994-96; freelance writer articles and poems. Recipient Star of Loyalty, Paralyzed Vets. Am., 1996. Mem. Internat. Soc. Poets, Acad. Am. Poets, Poetry Connection, Magic Cir. Democrat. Roman Catholic. Avocations: mosaic art, home interior decorating, pistol target shooting, needlepoint. Home: 5003 Birdie Ln Doylestown PA 18901-2872

COOKE, CONSTANCE BLANDY, librarian; b. Woodbury, N.J., Mar. 7, 1935; d. John Chase and Josephine Spond (Black) Blandy; m. Len B. Cooke Jr., Jan. 7, 1978 (div. 1987). BA, U. Pa., 1956; MA, U. Denver, 1957. Adult cons. Onondaga Library System, Syracuse, N.Y., 1965-66; asst. dir. Mt. Vernon (N.Y.) Public Library, 1966-75; dep. dir. Queens Borough Public Library, Jamaica, N.Y., 1975-79; dir. Queens Borough Public Library, 1980-94; founder pres. Literacy Vols. Mt. Vernon, 1972-74. Trustee METRO, 1980-81, v.p., 1985-88, pres., 1988-91; mem. N.Y. State Libr. Svcs. and Constrn. Act Adv. Coun., 1982-88, chmn., 1986-87; bd. dirs. Queens Coun. on the Arts, 1988-94, v.p., 1989-93; bd. dirs. Queens Mus. of Art, 1988-98, v.p., 1994-96, pres. 1996-98; bd. dirs. Queens Libr. Found., 1996—. Mem. ALA, Queens C. of C. (dir. 1982-98), Circumnavigators Club. Democrat. Episcopalian. Home: 16625 Powells Cove Blvd Apt 2F Beechhurst NY 11357-1505

COOKE, DAVID OHLMER, government official; b. Buffalo, Aug. 31, 1920; s. Lot Howell and Thekla Thusnelda (Ohlmer) C.; m. Marion Louise McDonald, Nov. 21, 1947; children: Michele C., Lot H., David O. B.S., SUNY, Buffalo, 1941; M.S., SUNY, Albany, 1942; LL.B., George Washington U., 1950. Bar: D.C. 1950. Mem. faculty U.S. Sch. Naval Justice, 1951-54; mem. staff JAG, Office of Navy, 1957-61; mem. Reorgn. Task Force, Dept. Def., 1958; mem. staff Office of Organizational and Mgmt. Planning, OSD, 1961-64, dir., 1964-69; dep. asst. sec. for adminstrn. Dept. Def., Washington, 1969-88, dir. adminstrn. and mgmt., 1988—; dir. Washington Hdqrs. Services, 1977—. Mem. Interagency Coun. on Adminstrv. Mgmt.; chair local Fed. coord. com. Combined Fed. Campaign of Nat. Capital Area. Recipient Disting. Svc. medal Dept. Navy, 1967, Disting. Civilian Svc. medal Dept. Def., 1971, medal with bronze palm, 1973, medal with silver palm, 1975, with gold palm, 87, 93, 97, Sec. Def. medal for outstanding pub. svc., 1977, medal for disting. pub. svc., 1981, with bronze palm, 1989, Meritorious Exec. award, 1980, Roger W. Jones award for Exec. Leadership, Am. U., 1983, Jack Niles medal of honor Pub. Employees Roundtable, 1990, Benjamin L. Hooks Disting. Svc. award NAACP, 1994, Govt. Exec. Leadership award, 1995, Presdl. Disting. Rank award, 1995, Nat. Pub. Svc. award, 1997, Presdl. Disting. Fed. Civilian Svc. award, 1998. Mem. ABA, Fed. Bar Assn., Maritime Law Assn. (bd. grad. sch., dept. agr. 1973-80, 84-88), Am. Soc. Pub. Adminstrn. (pres. Nat. Capital Area chpt. 1989-90), Nat. Acad. Pub. Adminstrn. (nat. coun. 1993-95), Am. Consortium for Internat. Pub. Adminstrn. Home: 1412 23rd Rd S Arlington VA 22202-1560 Office: Dir Adminstn and Mgmt Office Sec Def The Pentagon Rm 3D972 Washington DC 20301-1950

COOKE, EILEEN DELORES, retired librarian; b. Mpls., Dec. 7, 1928; d. Walter William and Mary Frances C. BSLS, Coll. St. Catherine, 1952; extension courses, U. Minn. Bookmobile libr. Mpls. Pub. Libr., 1952-57; br. asst. Queensborough Pub. Libr., 1957-58; br. asst., hosp. libr., pub. rels. specialist Mpls. Pub. Libr., 1958-63; asst. dir. Washington office ALA, 1964-68, asso. dir., 1968-69, dep. dir., 1969-72, dir., 1972-94, ret., 1994; lectr. U. Mich., Ann Arbor; mem. steering com. White Conf. on Libr. and Info. Svcs. Task Force. Contbr. articles to profl. jours. Mem. bd. visitors Sch. Libr. and Info. Sci., Cath. U.; mem. Pres. Forum, Coll. St. Catherine, 1992—. Mem. ALA (life, hon.), Minn. Libr. Assn. (life), D.C. Libr. Assn., Joint Coun. Ednl. Telecom. (past pres.), Higher Edn. Group Washington, World Future Soc., Women's Nat. Book Assn., Home and Sch. Inst., Nat. Adv. Coun., Minn. Ctr. for the Book (bd. dirs. 1995—). *Success in working for the common good requires patience, persistence, and giving credit to others.*

COOKE, FRED CHARLES, real estate broker; b. Winchester, Tenn., Dec. 3, 1915; s. Warner Cleveland and Emma (Lancaster) C.; m. Pamela Burr, Dec. 27, 1942; children: Gary Donald, David Charles, Pamela Ann, Alexander Campbell. AB, Lincoln Meml. U., 1939; grad., Realtor's Inst., 1988. Commd. USAF, 1942, advanced through ranks to lt. col.; project officer, R & D engr. specialist USAF, Eglin AFB, Fla., 1951-53; resigned USAF, 1953; realtor Ft. Walton Beach, Fla., 1956—. With USAF Res. Decorated DFC, Air medal with oak leaf cluster; inducted into Alumni Athletic Hall of Fame, 1987. Mem. Ft. Walton Beach Bd. Realtors (pres. 1959-60, 65), Fla. Assn. Realtors (dist. v.p. 1965, pres. Diamond Pin Club 1988), Nat. Assn. Realtors (bd. dirs. 1983-86, realtor emeritus 1993), Fla. Real Estate Exchangors (founder 1972), Greater Ft. Walton Beach C. of C. (chmn. waterways and reefs com. 1983-87, Award of Excellence), Fla. Waterways Adv. Bd., Ft. Walton Yacht Club (vice commodore 1984, commodore 1989, dir. 1990-95), Ft. Walton Power Squadron (commdr. 1972-73), Civitan (pres. 1961-62, dist. v.p. Birmingham 1963), Emerald Coast Sailing Assn. (founder 1992). Republican. Episcopalian. Home: 354 Sudduth Cir NE Fort Walton Beach FL 32548-5125 Office: 79 Beal Pky NE Fort Walton Beach FL 32548-4822

COOKE, GORDON RICHARD, retail executive; b. Winnipeg, Man., Can., May 18, 1945; came to U.S., 1959; s. Walter Gordon and Ethel Cecilia (Long) C.; m. Jennifer Lee Osborn, Sept. 4, 1975; children: Lauren Ashley, Erica Lee. BA in U.S. History, U. Puget Sound, 1967; MBA in Mktg., U. Oreg., 1968. Dir. mktg. The Bon Marche, Seattle, 1968-73; v.p. sales promotion Burdines, Miami, Fla., 1973-75; sr. v.p. sales promotion Macy's, N.Y.C., 1975-77; exec. v.p. sales promotion Bloomingdale's, N.Y.C., 1977-91; chief exec. officer Bloomingdale's By Mail, N.Y.C., 1991—; pres. Time Warner Interactive Merchandising, 1993; pres., CEO DM Mgmt., Hingham, Mass., 1996—. Recipient Man of Yr. award United Jewish Appeal, 1976, Retailing Man of Yr. award Retailing Advt. Conf., 1985. Mem. Retail Advt. and Mktg. Assn. (vice chmn. 1985—), Direct Mktg. Assn. Avocations: golf, tennis. Home: 400 E 57th St Apt 14K New York NY 10022-3030 Office: DM Mgmt 25 Recreation Park Dr Ste 200 Hingham MA 02043-4214*

COOKE, JAMES BARRY, civil engineer, consultant; b. London, Apr. 28, 1915; became U.S. citizen; BS, U. Calif., 1939. Engr. Pacific Gas and Electric Co., 1939-52, assoc. cons., 1952-61; cons. Tiburon, Calif., 1961—. Contbr. articles to profl. jours. Mem. ASCE (Rickey medal 1960, James Laurie prize 1961, Thomas A. Middlebrooks award 1961, Terzaghi lectr. 1982), Nat. Acad. Engrs., Sigma Xi. Home and Office: 1661 Mar West St Belvedere Tiburon CA 94920-1829*

COOKE, JOHN F., entertainment company executive. Exec. v.p. corp. affairs Walt Disney Co., Burbank, Calif. Office: Walt Disney Co 500 S Buena Vista St Burbank CA 91521-0004*

COOKE, JOHN KENT, professional sports management executive; b. Toronto, Sept. 27, 1941; s. Jack Kent Cooke and Barbara Jean (Carnegie) Berwald; m. Rebecca Ann Gilliam, Mar. 12, 1966 (div. 1988); children: John Kent Jr., Thomas Kent; m. Rita Bernadette Donoghue, Sept. 27, 1991. Student, Waterloo U., Can., 1958-59. Trainee, dir., prodr. Associated TV, London, 1958-60; with QM Prodns., L.A., 1961-63; asst. gen. mgr. Am. Cablevision, L.A., 1964-70; v.p. California Sports, Inc., Inglewood, Calif., 1965-78; dir. Jack Kent Cooke, Inc., Middleburg, Va., 1979—; exec. v.p. Pro-Football, Inc., Washington, 1981-97, pres., 1997—; commr. search com. Nat. Football League, N.Y.C., 1989, mem. mgmt. coun. exec. com., 1991-95. Mem. N.Y. Yacht Club. Avocations: sailing, fly fishing, collecting Am. antiques. Office: Pro-Football Inc 21300 Redskin Park Dr Ashburn VA 20147-6100 also: Washington Redskins Dulles Airport PO Box 17247 Washington DC 20041-7247

COOKE, JOHN P., cardiologist, medical educator, medical researcher. BA in Biology, Cornell U., 1976; MD, Wayne State U., 1980; PhD in Physiology, Mayo Grad. Sch. of Medicine, 1985. Diplomate Am. Bd. Internal Medicine, Am. Bd. Cardiovascular Disease; cert. instr. advanced cardiac life support Am. Heart Assn. Assoc. physician Brigham and Women's Hosp., Boston, 1987-90; asst. prof. medicine Harvard Med. Sch., Boston, 1987-90; asst. prof. medicine Stanford (Calif.) U. Sch. of Medicine, 1990-95, dir. sect. vascular medicine, 1991—, assoc. prof. medicine, 1995—, dir. sect. cardiovascular medicine, 1995—. Mem. editl. bd. Jour. Vascular Medicine and Biology, 1990—; contbr. articles to profl. jours. Rsch. fellow Mayo Grad. Sch. of Medicine, 1980-87; Merck fellow Am. Coll. Cardiology, 1985-86; recipient Henry Christian award Am. Fedn. Clin. Rsch., 1990, Vascular Acad. award NIH, 1991. Mem. Soc. Vascular Medicine and Biology (founder). Office: Stanford U Divsn Cardiovascular Medicine 300 Pasteur Dr Palo Alto CA 94304-2203*

COOKE, KENNETH LLOYD, mathematician, educator; b. Kansas City, Mo., Aug. 13, 1925; s. Sidney Kenneth and Mildred Blanche (Brown) C.; m. Margaret Sarah Burgess, Aug. 18, 1950; children: Catherine Sarah, Robert K., Susan E. BA, Pomona Coll., 1947; MS, Stanford, 1949, PhD, 1952. Instr., then asst. prof. math. State Coll. Wash., Pullman, 1950-57; mem. faculty Pomona Coll., 1957-93, Joseph N. Fiske prof. math., 1963—, chmn. dept., 1961-71, W.B. Keck disting. service prof., 1985-93; cons. RAND Corp., 1956-65; mathematician Rsch. Inst. Advanced Studies, Balt., 1963-64; NSF sci. faculty fellow Stanford, 1966-67; Fulbright rsch. scholar U. Florence, Italy, 1971-72; vis. prof. Brown U., 1978-79, Inst. Math. Applications, U. Minn., 1983, Cornell U., 1987; Fulbright lectr. U. São Paulo, Sao Carlos, Brazil, 1987. Author: (with Richard Bellman) Differential-Difference Equations, 1963, Modern Elementary Differential Equations, 2d edit., 1971, (with Richard Bellman and J.A. Lockett) Algorithms, Graphs and Computers, 1970, (with Donald Bentley) Linear Algebra with Differential Equations, 1973, (with Colin Renfrew) Transformations: Mathematical Approaches to Culture Change, 1979, (with Stavros Busenberg) Vertically Transmitted Diseases, 1993; co-editor: Differential Equations and Applications in Ecology, Epidemics, and Population Problems, 1981, Differential Equations and Applications to Biology and to Industry, 1995. Served with USNR, 1944-46. Mem. Am. Math. Soc., Math. Assn. Am., Soc. Indsl. and

Applied Math., Soc. Math. Biology, Phi Beta Kappa, Sigma Xi. Mem. United Ch. Christ. Home: 654 N Northwestern Dr Claremont CA 91711-4149*

COOKE, LAWRENCE HENRY, lawyer, former state chief judge; b. Monticello, N.Y., Oct. 15, 1914; s. George L. and Mary (Pond) C.; m. Alice McCormack, Nov. 25, 1939; children—Edward M., George L., II, Mary L. Cooke Opie. BS cum laude, Georgetown U., 1935; LLB, Union U., 1938, LLD (hon.), 1975; LLD (hon.), Siena Coll., 1964, N.Y. Law Sch., 1979, Bklyn. Law Sch., 1980, Pace U., 1980, N.Y. Law Sch., 1981, Syracuse U., 1985. Bar: N.Y. 1939. Pvt. practice Monticello, 1939-53, Sullivan County judge, 1954-61; Supreme Ct. justice 3d Jud. Dist., 1962-68; assoc. justice Appellate div. 3d Dept., Albany, 1969-74; assoc. judge N.Y. State Ct. Appeals, Albany, 1975-78; chief judge N.Y. State Ct. Appeals, 1979-84; sr. counsel Hall, Dickler, Lawler, Kent & Friedman, N.Y.C., 1985-87, Couch, White, Brenner, Howard & Feigenbaum, Albany, N.Y., 1987—; Dist. scholar in residence Pace U. Sch. Law, N.Y., 1989-92; arbitrator internat. law cases, 1986—; chmn. Conf. Chief Justice, 1982-83; pres. Nat. Ctr. for State Cts., 1982-83, adv. com., 1989—; chmn. N.Y. Fair Trial, Free Press Conf., 1979-84; chmn. adv. coun. Nat. Symposium on Civil Justice Issues, 1986; chmn. assocs. com. Nat. Ctr. for State Cts., 1985-86; lectr. Brookings Inst., 1984, 86; John F. Sonnett Meml. lectr. Fordham U. Law Sch., 1981; Charles Evans Hughes Meml. lectr. N.Y. County Lawyers Assn., 1981; keynote spkr. Internat. Jewish Jurists and Lawyers Conv., Jerusalem, 1981, Gender Task Force Anniversary, 1996; mem. Sen. Daniel P. Moynihan Jud. Screening Com., 1985-93; chair Gov. Pataki Jud. Screening Com., 1995-97; hon. chair State Instl. Commentary, 1996. Supr. Town of Thompson, N.Y., 1946-49; chmn. Sullivan County Bd. Suprs., 1947-48; bd. visitors Sch. Law Fordham U., 1987—; bd. dirs. State Justice Inst., 1986-88; formerly chair local dist. Boy Scouts Am., Monticello dist. ARC, Monticello March of Dimes, Sullivan County United Fund Drive, Monticello Cath. Charities Drive; hon. chair Sullivan County Assn. Retarded Citizens; former trustee Ethelbert Crawford Meml. Libr.; bd. dirs. St. Joseph's Sanatorium, Sullivan County Hist. Soc., Sullivan County Cerebral Palsy Assn. Recipient Torch of Liberty award B'nai B'rith, 1967, Friend of Press award N.Y. State Soc. Newspaper Editors, 1985, 1st Amendment award Deadline Club, 1985, Seymour medal Am. Arbitration Assn., 1985, Toney Rivers Watson award Jud. Friends of Nat. Bar Assn., 1984, award of merit Am. Judges Assn., 1983, Law Day award N.Y. State Trial Lawyers' Assn., 1983, John Carroll award Georgetown U. Alumni Assn., 1982, Golda Meir Meml. award Jewish Lawyers Guild, 1983, Grange 50 yr. mem. award, 1989, Disting. Founders award N.Y. State Assn. Cmty. Dispute Resolution Ctrs., Inc., 1991, Sullivan County Cath. of Yr. award, 1993, Shields award Sullivan County, 1991, Gold medal Albany Law Sch., 1995, Nat. Ctr. for State Cts. Recognition dinner, 1995, Monticello Masons De Witt Clinton award, 1995, Gender Fairness award N.Y. State Assn. Women Judges, 1996, keynote spkr. anniversary of Gender Bias Task Force Report, 1996, Judiciary award Sullivan co-chpt. NAACP, 1996, Rosen award Orange-Sullivan Women's Bar Assn., 1996, Golden Trumpet award Firefighters Assn. State N.Y., 1997; Sullivan County courthouse renamed Lawrence H. Cooke Sullivan County Courthouse, 1997; named Grand Marshal, Sullivan County Firefighter's Ann. Parade, 1998. Fellow Am. Bar Assn. Found.; mem. ABA, N.Y. State Bar Assn. (past chmn. young lawyers sect., Gold medal 1985), Assn. of Bar of City of N.Y., Albany County Bar Assn., N.Y. State Women's Bar Assn. (hon.), Sullivan County Bar Assn. (pres.), Am. Law Inst., Am. Judicature Soc. (bd. dirs. 1987-90), Nat. Ctr. for State Cts. (Disting. Svc. award 1987), Rockland County Magistrates' Assn. (Disting. Svc. award 1987); pres. Hudson Valley Vol. Fireman's Assn., 1965-66, Sullivan County Vol. Fireman's Assn., Monticello Fire Dept. Democrat. Roman Catholic. Office: Couch White Brenner Howard & Feigenbaum PO Box 22222 540 Broadway Ste 1 Albany NY 12201*

COOKE, LLOYD MILLER, former organization executive; b. LaSalle, Ill., June 7, 1916; s. William Wilson and Anna (Miller) C.; m. Vera E. Schlegel, June 29, 1957; children: Barbara Anne Williams, William E. B.S., U. Wis., 1937; Ph.D., McGill U., 1941; LL.D. (hon.), Coll. of Ganado. Lectr. McGill U., 1941-42; sect. leader Corn Products Refining Co., Argo, Ill., 1942-46; group leader Films Packaging div. Union Carbide Corp., Chgo., 1946-49; dept. mgr. Films Packaging div. Union Carbide Corp., 1950-54, asst. to mgr. tech. div., 1954-57, asst. dir. research, 1957-65, mgr. market research, 1965-67, mgr. planning, 1967-70; dir. urban affairs Union Carbide Corp., N.Y.C., 1970-78, corp. dir. univ. relations, 1973-76; corp. dir. community affairs Union Carbide Corp., 1976-77, sr. cons., 1978-81; mem. Nat. Sci. Bd., 1970-82; cons. Office of Tech. Assessment, U.S. Congress, 1972-79, NSF, 1991—; vice chmn. Econ. Devel. Coun. of N.Y., 1978-81; pres. Nat. Action Coun. on Minorities in Engring., 1981-83, pres. emeritus, 1983-90; cons. Internat. Found. on Edn. and Self-Help, 1984-87, K-12 math and sci. curricula, 1986—; pres. LMC Assocs., 1988-98. Contbr. articles to profl. jours. Mem. Cmty. Conf. Bd., Downers Grove, Ill., 1968-70; trustee McCormick Theol. Sem., 1976-80, N.Y. Found. for Sci. and Tech., 1985-95, N.Y. Hall of Sci., 1985-90, N.Y.C. Commn. Sci. and Tech., 1985-90. Recipient Proctor prize sci. Sci. Research Soc. Am., 1970. Fellow Am. Inst. Chemists (honor scroll Chgo.), N.Y. Acad. Scis.; mem. Am. Chem. Soc., AAAS, Chgo. Chemists Club, N.Y.C. Chemists Club, Sigma Xi, Phi Kappa Phi, Beta Kappa Chi. Home: 71 Kendal Dr Oberlin OH 44074-1903

COOKE, MARGUERITE K., nurse, mayor; m. Steven John Cooke. AA in Journalism and French, Grand Rapids Jr. Coll., 1968; BA in Social Scis., Western Mich. U., 1970; MA in Counseling, Mich. State U., 1975; BSN, Northwestern U., Chgo., 1980; cert. critical care nurse, Loyola U., Maywood, Ill. RN, Ga. Substitute tchr. Kent Intermediate Sch. Dist., Kent County, Mich., 1971-72; tchr. French and history Rogers Sr. H.S., Wyoming, Mich., 1972-73; tchr. adult edn. Wyoming, Godwin and South Kent Pub. Schs., Wyoming and Kentwood, Mich., 1973-77; rehab. counselor Christian Outreach to Handicapped, Chgo., 1977-79; staff nurse rehab., orthopedic and gynecology unit U. Ill. Hosp., Chgo., 1981-82; part-time staff nurse adolescent psychiat. unit Hinsdale (Ill.) Hosp., 1982-88; part-time staff nurse adult affective disorders unit Good Samaritan Hosp.-Ctr. for Mental Health, Downers Grove, Ill., 1987-92; Christian counselor Minirth-Meier New Life Clinic (now New Life), Smyrna, Ga., 1996-97; mem. city coun. City of Berkeley Lake, Ga., 1996-98, mayor, 1998—; staff nurse behavioral medicine unit Northside Hosp., Atlanta, 1997—; off-campus counselor Coll. of DuPage, Glen Ellyn, Ill., 1991-94; psychotherapist Minirth-Meier Clinic, P.C., Wheaton, Ill., 1992-94; interim instr. med. asst. dept. Gwinnett Tech. Inst., Lawrenceville, Ga., 1997. Mem. Kappa Delta Pi. Fax: 770-368-8810. E-mail: margcooke@aol.com. Home: 4055 Berkeley View Dr Duluth GA 30136-3070 Office: City of Berkeley Lake 4040 Berkeley Lake Rd Berkeley Lake GA 30096-3016

COOKE, MARVIN LEE, sociologist, consultant, urban planner; b. Tulsa, Dec. 9, 1947; s. Marvin Joel and Mary Lee (Sleeper) C.; m. Sandra Pauline Creason, Dec. 23, 1967 (div. Mar. 1979); 1 child, Francis Wesley; m. Mary Lou Albitz, Nov. 25, 1981. BA summa cum laude, Cen. State U., Edmond, Okla., 1970; PhD, Okla. State U., 1993; M in Divinity summa cum laude, Phillips U., Enid, Okla., 1975. Ordained to ministry United Meth. Ch., 1972, withdrew, 1985. Pastor Carmen (Okla.) United Meth. Ch., 1973-75, Turley United Meth. Ch., Tulsa, 1975-78; assoc. dir. Tulsa Met. Ministry, 1978-82, exec. dir., 1982-88; planner urban devel. City of Tulsa, 1992-98; divsn. chair Tulsa Cmty. Coll., 1998—. Recipient O.D. Duncan award, Rsch. Excellence award Okla. State U., 1993. Mem. Am. Planning Assn., Am. Sociol. Assn. Democrat. Episcopalian. Avocations: running, biking, hiking. Home: 302 N Santa Fe Ave Tulsa OK 74127-6923

COOKE, M(ERRITT) TODD, banker; b. Phila., Mar. 20, 1920; s. Merritt Todd and Beatrice (Crawford) C.; m. Mary T. Cooke, Sept. 24, 1949 (dec.); children—Mary Marshall, Merritt Todd; m. Margaret S. Groome, Dec. 4, 1965. B.A., Princeton, 1942; M.C.P., Mass. Inst. Tech., 1947. Exec. dir. Del. County Planning Commn., Media, Pa., 1951-55; v.p. W.A. Clarke Mortgage Co., Phila., 1956-60; asst. v.p. First Pa. Bank, Phila., 1961-65; with The Phila. Saving Fund Soc., 1966-87, pres., 1971-78, chmn., chief exec. officer, 1979-86, vice chmn., 1986-87; former trustee Mut. Assurance Co., Phila.; dir. Provident Mut. Ins. Co. Pres. United Fund Phila., 1974-76; bd. dirs. Pa. Hosp., Phila., chmn., 1969-75; v.p. United Way Phila., 1976-85; bd. dirs. Phila. Urban Coalition, Ctr. Phila. Devel. Corp., Curtis Inst. Music; treas. Marlboro Sch. Music, 1986—; former pres. Phila. Orch. Assn., chmn., 1988-92; trustee Phila. Mus. Art. Served with AUS, 1942-46. Mem. Phi Beta Kappa, Lambda Alpha. Home: Greenlands 620 Newtown Street Rd Media PA 19063-1047

COOKE, PAUL LEWIS, state fire marshall; b. Rochester, N.Y., Oct. 4, 1957; s. Percy Charles and June Mary (Oswold) Cooke; m. Linda Gail Hinds, July 6, 1978 (div. Oct. 1986); 1 child, Jennifer; m. Sherry Elaine Webster, Oct. 14, 1986; children: Stephanie, Paul Jr., Jessica. AAS in Fire Suppression, Red Rocks C.C., 1985, AAS in Fire Prevention, 1985; BS in Fire Svcs. Adminstrn., Met. State Coll., 1989. Fire protection specialist Buckley ANG Base Fire Dept., Aurora, Colo., 1981-82; fire chief Cunningham Fire Protection Dist., Denver, 1982-91; dep. dir. Colo. Divsn. of Fire Safety, Denver, 1991-93, dir., state fire marhsall, 1993—; v.p. Nat. Fire Info. Coun., dir. v.p. 1991-99. Adult leader Boy Scouts Am., Aurora, Colo., 1994—. With U.S. Army, 1975-81. Mem. Colo. State Fire Chiefs Assn. (legis. liaison 1989-91), Nat. Assn. of State Fire Marshals (com. chair 1992—), Nat. Fire Protection Assn., Internat. Assn. of Fire Chiefs. Protestant. Avocations: hiking, camping. Fax: 303-239-4405. E-mail: plcooke@worldnet.att.net. Office: Colo Divsn Fire Safety 700 Kipling St Ste 1000 Denver CO 80215

COOKE, PHILIP HOWARD, television director, producer; b. Charlotte, N.C., Aug. 31, 1954; s. Bill Howard and Thelma (Blackwelder) C.; m. Kathleen Rene Paille, Mar. 22, 1977; children: Kelsey Taylor, Bailey Christine. BA, Oral Roberts U., 1976; MA in Journalism, U. Okla., 1986. Dir. Oral Roberts TV, Tulsa, 1978-90; exec. prodr. Phil Cooke Pictures, Inc., Burbank, Calif., 1990—; cons. various TV prodn. facilities, 1983—. Producer, dir. numerous TV programs. Recipient Addy award Am. Advt. Fedn., 1981, 82, 83, Angel awards Religion in the Media, Los Angeles, 1985, 86, 96, 3 awards Okla. Film Festival award 1982, Videography award, 1998, Covenant award, 1998. Mem. Acad. TV Arts and Scis., Am. Film Inst., Nat. Religious Broadcasters (bd. dirs.). Republican. Office: Phil Cooke Pictures Inc PO Box 1515 Burbank CA 91507

COOKE, R(ICHARD) CASWELL, JR., architect; b. Richmond, Va., Dec. 19, 1935; s. Richard Caswell and Caroline (Kellock) C.; m. Mary Gibson, June 6, 1962; children: Richard, Frederick, Gordon, Molly. BArch, U. Va., 1962; MArch, Yale U., 1967. Registered architect, Mass., Conn., Va., N.C., S.C., Ill., N.J., Pa., N.S., Colo., R.I. Project mgr. Clinch Crimp Brown & Fischer, Boston, 1962-64, Paul Rudolph Architect, New Haven, 1964-65; prin., dir. Geotactics, Inc., New Haven, 1965-82; gen. mgr. Gulf Consult Architects, Al Khobar, Saudi Arabia, 1982-86; prin. Fellows, Read, Leoncavallo & Cooke, Princeton, N.J., 1986-89; v.p., dir. arch. Raytheon Engrs. & Constructors, Inc., Phila. and London, 1989—; pres. Raytheon Architects, Phila. and London; lectr. Quinnipiac Coll., New Haven, St. Paul's Ch., Kiwanis Club; juried design Yale U. Prin. works include design of Petromin Corp. Bldg., Riyadh, Saudi Arabia, Baxter Health Care Facility, Calif., Roche Carolina Campus, S.C., Can. Red Cross Facility, N.S., Derby (Conn.) Elderly Housing. Chmn. New Haven Harbor Commn., 1976, Conn. Regional Planning Com., 1976; bd. dirs. Am. Businessmen's assn., Saudi Arabia, 1986; pres. Yale Alumni Assn. Sch. Architecture, 1978; past bd. dirs. Conn. Soc. Architects. Recipient Christchurch Sch. Alumni award, 1975, first design award Milford Yacht Club, 1977, Alpha Rho Chi award U. Va., 1962. Mem. AIA, N.J. Soc. Archs., Nat. Coun. Archtl. Registration Bds., Assn. of Yale Alumni, Yale Club of Princeton (past pres.), Constrn. Specification Inst., Illuminating Engrs. Soc., Am. Soc. Landscape Archs., Sons of the Revolution (N.J. bd. dirs.), Henry Found. for Bot. Rsch. Episcopalian. Office: Raytheon Archs LLC 510 Carnegie Ctr Princeton NJ 08540-6241

COOKE, ROBERT EDMOND, physician, educator, former college president; b. Attleboro, Mass., Nov. 13, 1920; s. Ronald Melbourne and Renee Jeanne (Wuillumier) C.; m. Sharon Riley, Nov. 20, 1978; children: Susan R., Anne R.; children from previous marriage: Robyn (dec.), Christopher, Wendy, W. Robert, Kim. BS, Yale U., 1941, MD, 1944, postgrad., 1948-50; DSc (hon.), U. Miami, 1970; D in Med. Sci. (hon.), Yale U., 1994. Intern, then asst. resident dept. pediat. New Haven Hosp., 1944-46; instr. pediat. Yale U., New Haven, 1950-51, asst. prof. pediat. and physiology, 1951-54, assoc. prof., 1954-56; from resident to assoc. pediatrician Grace-New Haven Cmty. Hosp., 1951-56; pediatrician-in-chief Johns Hopkins Hosp., 1956-73; chmn. dept. Johns Hopkins Sch. Medicine, 1956-73; Grover Powers prof. pediat. Nat. Assn. Retarded Children, 1957-59, Given Found. prof., 1962-73; vis. prof. Harvard U., 1972-73; vice chancellor health scis., prof. pediat. U. Wis., 1973-77; pres. Med. Coll. Pa., 1977-80; A. Conger Goodyear prof., med. dir. SUNY, Buffalo, 1982-88, prof. emeritus, 1988—, chmn. dept. pediat., 1985-88; pediatrician-in-chief Children's Hosp. of Buffalo, 1985-88; chief med. officer Spl. Olympics Internat.; with Mass. Dept. Mental Health, 1980-82; chmn. med. adv. bd. Kennedy Found.; mem. adv. bd. Nat. Ctr. Rehab. Rsch., Nat. Inst. Child Health and Human Devel., 1991—. Editor, contbr. to pediat. textbooks, profl. jours. Trustee Children's Rehab. Inst. Capt. M.C., AUS, 1946-48. NIH postdoctoral fellow Sch. Medicine Yale U., 1948-50, John and Mary Markle scholar, 1951-55; recipient Mead Johnson award in pediat., 1954, Kennedy Internat. award for disting. svc. in field of mental retardation, 1968, Howland medal, 1992, medallion of the Surgeon Gen., 1993. Fellow Am. Acad. Pediat., Am. Psychiat. Assn. (disting.); mem. APHA, Am. Pediat. Soc. (John Howland award 1991), Soc. for Pediat. Rsch. (pres. 1965-66), Am. Soc. for Clin. Investigation, Md. Med. Soc., Am. Fedn. Clin. Rsch., Inst. of Medicine, Aurelian Hon. Soc., Phi Beta Kappa, Sigma Xi, Alpha Omega Alpha. Home: 865 Painted Bunting Ln Vero Beach FL 32963-2026 *My goal has been the enjoyment of socially useful achievement. To achieve that has required periods of self renewal to adapt to a rapidly changing world.*

COOKE, ROGER ANTHONY, lawyer; b. Bklyn., June 11, 1948; s. John J. and Virginia (Humphreys) C.; m. Joan J. Cirillo, June 19, 1976; children: Julia Cirillo, Elizabeth Cirillo. AB, Georgetown U., 1970, JD, 1973. Bar: N.Y. 1974. Assoc. Simpson, Thacher and Bartlett, 1973-80; dep. gen. counsel, sec. Pan Am. World Airways, N.Y.C., 1981-90; sr. v.p., gen. counsel Fred Meyer Inc., 1990—. Mem. Assn. of Bar of City of N.Y. (aeros. com.). Office: Fred Meyer Incorporated 3800 SE 22nd Ave PO Box 42121 Portland OR 97242-2999*

COOKE, STEVEN JOHN, chemical engineer, consultant, scientist; b. Grand Rapids, Mich., Oct. 1, 1954; s. Edward G. and Annette M. (Minnema) C.; m. Marguerite K. Oldenburger, June 18, 1977; children: Allison, Jonathan. BS in Chemistry, Calvin Coll., 1977; M in Chem. Engring., Ill. Inst. Tech., 1987; postgrad. in Engring., Calif. Coast U. Registered profl. engr., Ill.; cert. profl. chemist, quality engr., quality auditor. Chemist, lab. supr. Matheson Gas Products, Joliet, Ill., 1977-80; chief chemist Cardox, Countryside, Ill., 1980-85; scientist Am. Air Liquide, Countryside, 1985-92; asst. quality mgr. Alphagaz Divsn. of Liquid Air, Countryside, 1992-93; quality assurance/quality control mgr. Am. Air Liquide, Countryside, 1993-95; quality mgr. Carbonic Industries Corp., 1995-98, Airgas Carbonic, Duluth, Ga., 1998—. Contbr. articles on quality systems to profl. jours. Group leader Hazardous Materials Emergency Response Team; treas. Christian Reformed Ch. Mission, Western Springs, Ill., 1982-93, Chicagoland Diaconal Task Force Bd., Palos Heights, Ill., 1989-92. Fellow Am. Inst. Chemists; mem. Am. Soc. Quality Control, Am. Chem. Soc. (publicity chair I&E divsn. 1989-95, chair I&E divsn. 1999), Compressed Gas Assn. (CO2 task force, gas specifications com.). Achievements include patent for portable gas analyzer. Office: Airgas Carbonic 3700 Crestwood Pkwy NW Ste 200 Duluth GA 30096-5599

COOKE, THOMAS PAUL, education educator; b. Panama Canal, Oct. 12, 1948; s. Thomas Paul and Sarah Anne (Downing) C.; m. Sharon Anne Raver, Dec. 18, 1968 (div. June 1975); 1 child, James Mitchell; m. Marrianne McKinley, Apr. 14, 1990. BA, U. South Fla., 1970, MA, 1971; PhD, Vanderbilt U., 1974. Coord. spl. edn. Sonoma State U., Rohnert Park, Calif., 1982-88; prof. edn. Sonoma State U., Rohnert Park, 1983—, chmn. dept. edn., 1988-92. Author: Exceptional Children: Assessing and Modifying Social Behavior, 1976, Towards Excellence: Achievements in Residential Arrangements, 1980, Early Independence: A Curriculum System, 1981, Self Instructional Curriculum Development, 1981, A New Look at Guardianship, 1984; contbr. articles to profl. jours. Chmn. bd. Found. for Ednl. Devel., Napa, Calif., 1993-96. Avocations: sea kayaking, river kayaking, skiing.

COOKE, WALTA PIPPEN, automobile dealership owner; b. Shreveport, La., Oct. 18, 1940; d. Billy Burt and Eula (Heaton) Pippen; m. John William Cooke II, Dec. 20, 1958; children: Cheryl Cooke Williams, John William III. BA, Baylor U., 1963. Co-owner, sec.-treas. Pippen Motor Co., Carthage, 1972-80, owner, sec.-treas., 1980—; dir. Sabine River Authority Tex., 1993—, v.p., sec. bd. dirs., 1996, pres., 1996-97, also chmn. lower basin project com., chmn. 50th anniversary celebration, 1999, mem. by-laws com. Bd. dirs. Toledo Bend Joint Project Opeartion, L.A., Tex.; pianist for sanctuary choir Ctrl. Bapt. Ch., Carthage, 1986—; adv. dir. Panola County Found. Mem. Carthage 32 Club, Carthage Book Club (rec. sec. 1995-97). Avocations: reading, gardening, travel, music. Home: 200 Timberlane Dr Carthage TX 75633-2231 Office: Pippen Motor Co 1300 W Panola St Carthage TX 75633-2346

COOK-SATHER, SCOTT DOUGLAS, pediatric anesthesiology educator; b. Golden Valley, Minn., July 23, 1963; s. Douglas Ray and Carol Ann (Henrikson) Sather; m. Alison Mary Cook, May 22, 1993. BS with distinction and honors, Stanford U., 1985, MD, 1990. Diplomate Am. Bd. Anesthesiology. Intern U. Calif., San Francisco, 1990-91; resident in anesthesia Hosp. of U. Penn., Phila., 1991-94; fellow in pediatric anesthesia Children's Hosp. Phila.-U. Pa., 1994, fellow in pediat. cardiac anesthesiology, 1995, instr., 1995-97, asst. prof., 1997—. Contbg. author: Balliere's Clinical Anaesthesiology, 1996, Complications in Anesthesiology, 1999, Atlas of Anesthesia, 1999; contbr. articles to profl. jours. All Coll. scholar Aid Assn. for Luths., 1981-85. Mem. Soc. for Pediatric Anesthesia, Am. Soc. for Anesthesiologists, Sierra Club, Phi Beta Kappa. Avocations: travel, hiking, biking, swimming, piano. Office: Children's Hosp Phila Dept Anes and Crit Care Med 34th St and Civic Ctr Blvd Philadelphia PA 19104-4399

COOKSEY, JOHN CHARLES, congressman, ophthalmic surgeon; b. Alexandria, La., Aug. 20, 1941; s. Henry Oscar and Ruth (Lee) C.; m. Dorothy Ann Grabill, Dec. 30, 1969; children: Karen, Carol Ann, Catherine. MD, La. State U., New Orleans, 1966. Practice medicine specializing in ophthalmology, Monroe, La., 1972-96; mem. Congress from 5th La. Dist., 1996—; mem. teaching staff E.A. Conway Hosp., Monroe , 1972—; vis. lectr. Alton Ochsner Med. Found., New Orleans, 1978—; asst. clin. prof. La. State U. Med. Sch., New Orleans, 1979—. Contbg. author: Cataract and Intraocular Lens Surgery, 1984. Lay leader St. Paul's United Meth. Ch., Monroe, 1978-80; mem. La. Rep. Cen. Com., 1974-82; del. Rep. Nat. Conv., Kansas City, Mo., 1976. Served to capt. USAF, 1967-69. Mem. AMA, La. Med. Soc., Ouachita Parish Med. Soc. Avocation: breeding quarter horses. Address: 1310 N 19th St Monroe LA 71201-5044

COOKSON, ALAN HOWARD, electrical engineer, researcher; b. London, July 3, 1939; came to U.S., 1968; s. Joseph and Rachel (Wiseman) C.; m. Elizabeth Rosamond Ritblat, Oct. 24, 1965; children: Richard Jonathan, Simon Charles. B.Sc. in Engring. with 1st class honors, Queen Mary Coll., London U., 1961, Ph.D. in Elec. Engring., 1965. Chartered engr., Gt. Brit. Rsch. fellow Queen Mary Coll., London, 1964-65; rsch. officer Cen. Elec. Rsch. Labs., Leatherhead, Eng., 1965-68; sr. engr. Westinghouse R & D Ctr., Pitts., 1968-75; mgr. gas cable rsch. Westinghouse Power Circuit Breaker, Westborough, Mass., 1975-80; mgr. polymers, dielectrics and advanced batteries Westinghouse Sci. & Tech. Ctr., Pitts., 1980-92; assoc. dir. Electronics and Elec. Engring. Lab. divsn. Nat. Inst. Stds. and Tech., Gaithersburg, Md., 1992—; U.S. rep. advanced materials for electro tech. com. Internat. Conf. Large Elec. Systems, 1996—; convener Working Group on Gas Insulated Cables, Internat. Conf. Large Elec. Systems, 1980-90. Editor: Digest of Literature on Dielectrics, 1970; contbr. articles to profl. jours.; patentee in field. Mem. adv. com. Miss. State U., 1983. Fellow IEEE (pres. Dielectrics and Elec. Insulation Soc. 1993-94), Inst. Elec. Engrs. London; mem. Phys. Soc., Inst. Physics London. Home: 15717 Bondy Ln Darnestown MD 20878-2114 Office: Nat Inst Standards/Tech Bldg 220 Rm B358 Gaithersburg MD 20899

COOKSON, ALBERT ERNEST, telephone and telegraph company executive; b. Needham, Mass., Oct. 30, 1921; s. Willard B. and Sarah Jane (Jack) C.; m. Constance J. Buckley, Sept. 10, 1949 (dec. July 1987); children: Constance J., William B.; m. Lorraine B. Hirsch, Dec. 29, 1987. BEE, Northeastern U., 1943; MEE, MIT, 1951; ScD, Gordon Coll., 1974. Group leader Research Lab. Electronics, Mass. Inst. Tech., 1947-51; lab. dir. ITT Fed. Labs., Nutley, N.J., 1951-59; v.p., dir. operations ITT Fed. Labs. (Internat. Elec. Corp. div.), Paramus, N.J., 1959-62; pres. ITT Intelcom, Falls Church, Va., 1962-65; dep. gen. tech. dir. Internat. Tel. & Tel. Corp., N.Y.C., 1965-66, v.p., tech. dir., 1966-68, sr. v.p., gen. tech. dir., 1968-84, ret., 1984; pres., chief exec. officer Richmond Properties, 1982—; chmn. bd. ITT Interplan; pres., chmn. Comtexco Industries, 1980—; chmn. tech. adv. bd. U.S. Postal Svc., 1983-91; bd. dirs. Internat. Standard Electric, ITT Industries; mem. Def. Communications Satellite Panel; adviser research and engring. on def. communications satellite systems Dept. Def.; mem. indsl. panel sci. and tech. NSF; mem. Fairfax County Econ. and Indsl. Devel. Com., 1962-65; mem. nat. coun. Northeastern U.; mem. pride com. U. Hartford, 1973-76; elec. engring./computer adv. bd. MIT, 1977-82. Bd. dirs. Fundacion Chile, 1983-89. Served with USNR, 1943-46. Fellow IEEE; mem. Armed Forces Communications and Electronics Assn., Am. Mgmt. Assn., Am. Inst. Aeros. and Astronautics, Electronic Industries Assn., Sigma Xi, Tau Beta Pi. Patentee frequency search and track system.

COOKSON, PETER WILLIS, JR., sociologist, writer; b. N.Y.C., Nov. 17, 1942; s. Peter Willis and Maureen (Grey) C.; m. Susan Stern, Sept. 16, 1968; children: Alexandra Genvieve, Aram Nathaniel. BA, NYU, 1966, MA, 1968, PhD, 1981; cert. advanced study, Harvard U., 1991. Prof., dir. ctr. ednl. outreach innovation Columbia U.; pres. Cookson and Assocs. Author: School Choice and the Struggle for the Soul of American Education, 1994, Preparing for Power: America's Elite Boarding Schools, 1985, The International Handbook for Educational Reform, 1992, Making Sense of Society, 1993, Exploring Education, 1994, Choosing Schools, 1996, Autonomy and Choice in Context, 1997, A Parent's Guide to Standardized Tests in School, 1998; contbr. articles to profl. jours. With USAR, 1963-69. Rsch. grantee found., govt. and pvt. sector. Mem. N.Y. Acad. Scis., Am. Sociol. Assn. (Congrl. fellow 1993), Am. Ednl. Rsch. Assn. Democrat. Roman Catholic. Home: 116 Valleyview Rd Irvington NY 10533 Office: Tchrs Coll Columbia U 525 W 120th St New York NY 10027

COOLEDGE, RICHARD CALVIN, lawyer; b. Charleston, S.C., Apr. 20, 1943; s. Russell Clarence and Lorena Ann (Weymuth) C.; m. Nancy Jean Western, June 15, 1965 (div. Dec. 1986); children: Dean Richard, Mark Alan, Jocelyn Joy; m. Jeanine Diana Smith, Apr. 12, 1989 (div. Nov. 1993). BA in Econs. with honors, U. Mo., Columbia, 1965; JD, U. Mich., 1968. Bar: Ariz. 1969, U.S. Dist. Ct. Ariz. 1969, U.S. Ct. Appeals (9th cir.) 1973, U.S. Supreme Ct. 1973. Mem. Brown & Bain P.A., Phoenix, 1968—. Contbg. editor: Banking and Lending Institutions Forms, Business Workouts Manual; contbr. articles to profl. jours. Mem. Phoenix Rolls Royce Owners (pres. 1970-72), Harley Owners Group, Ariz. Arms Assn., Motorcycle Safety Found. (instr.). Avocations: motorcycling, golf, music. Office: Brown & Bain PA 2901 N Central Ave Fl 20 Phoenix AZ 85012-2700

COOLEN, PHYLLIS ROSE, community health nurse; b. Monterey, Calif., Oct. 13, 1950. BSN, U. Wash., 1973, MSN, 1981. Hospice clinician Providence Med. Ctr., Seattle, 1980-86; nursing cons. home health Dept. Social and Health Svc. Med. Asst. Adminstrn., Olympia, 1986, nursing care cons., 1987-87, nursing cons. advisor, 1987-93; nursing cons. adv., quality care coord. Dept. Social and Health Svc. Med. Asst. Adminstrn., Olympia, Wash., 1993-95, acting dir. divsn. utilization svcs., 1995-97; dir. divsn. health svcs. quality support Dept. Social and Health Svc. Med. Asst. Adminstrn., Olympia, 1997—; theory, clin. instr. fundamentals and advanced med.-surg. Kauai C.C., Lihue, Hawaii, 1983-85; clin. instr. advanced med.-surg. Seattle C.C., 1985-86; nursing cons. advisor. Home Health Phys. Medicine and Rehab., Medically Intensive Home Care Program, Dept. Social and Health Svcs., Med. Assistance Adminstrn., Olympia. Lt. comdr. USNR, 1989-96. Mem. SEARCHIN Cmty. Health Nurse Rsch., Wash. State Assn. for Health Care Quality. Home: 14040 Prairie Pky SW Olympia WA 98512-9267 Office: Med Assistance Adminstrn Divsn Svcs Quality Support PO Box 45506 Olympia WA 98504-5506

COOLEY, ANDREW LYMAN, corporation executive, former army officer; b. St. Louis, Oct. 14, 1934; s. Andrew L. and Algretta R. (Carr) C.; m. Joan Lynn Wheatley, Jan. 9, 1958; children: Cathleen Wheatley, Caroline Carr. BA, George Washington U., 1964, MA, 1967; MS, U.S. Army Command and Gen. Staff Coll., 1966; postgrad., U.S. Army War Coll., 1972-73. Commd. 2d lt. U.S. Army, 1955; advanced through grades to maj. gen. U.S. Army, Continental U.S. and Hawaii, 1955-64; bn. adv. Vietnam, 1964-65; aide to chief of staff SHAPE, Belgium, 1967-69; tank bn. comdr. Germany, 1969-70; mem. staff Dept. of Army Pentagon, 1970-72; brigade comdr. and div. chief of staff Korea, 1975-77; exec. to comdr. in chief Pacific Hawaii, 1978-79; asst. div. comdr. 101st Airborne Div., 1979-81; asst. dep. dir. for politico-mil. affairs, plans and policy directorate Joint Chiefs of Staff, Washington, 1981-83; mil. adviser Habib-Draper Mission, Lebanon, 1982-83; dir. strategy, plans and policy Dept. Army, Washington, 1983-85; comdg. gen. 24th Inf. Div. (Mech.) and Fort Stewart, Hunter Army Air Field, Fort Stewart, Ga., 1985-87; chief Office Military Cooperation, Cairo, 1987-89; ret., 1989; program mgr. Vinnell Brown Root, Turkey Base Maintenance Agreement, 1989-91; project mgr. ops. and maintenance Brown and Root Svcs. Corp., Houston, 1991-94; program mgr. Project Restore Hope Somalia, 1993; ind. cons. with expertise in Africa, Croatia, Bosnia and Haiti, 1994-97; dir. ops. Dyncorp Internat. Tech. Svcs., 1988—. Author: Diplomatic Significances of the Great White Fleet, 1966, Realistic Deterrence in NATO, 1973. Decorated Def. D.S.M. with oak leaf cluster, Legion of Merit with oak leaf cluster, Bronze Star, Air medal, others; Fed. Exec. fellow Brookings Instn., 1977-78; named to Officer Candidate Sch. Hall of Fame, 1979. Mem. Assn. U.S. Army, Armor Assn. Episcopalian. Home: 17202 De Chirico Cir Spring TX 77379-6269

COOLEY, DENTON ARTHUR, surgeon, educator; b. Houston, Aug. 22, 1920; s. Ralph C. and Mary (Fraley) C.; m. Louise Goldsborough Thomas, Jan. 15, 1949; children: Mary, Susan, Louise, Florence, Helen. B.A., U. Tex., 1941; M.D., Johns Hopkins U., 1944; Doctorem Medicinae (hon.), U. Turin, Italy, 1969; H.H.D. (hon.), Hellenic Coll., 1984, Holy Cross Greek Orthodox Sch. of Theology, 1984; DSc honoris causa, Coll. of William and Mary, 1987. Diplomate: Am. Bd. Surgery, Am. Bd. Thoracic Surgery. Intern Johns Hopkins Sch. Medicine, Balt., 1944-45; resident surgery Johns Hopkins Sch. Medicine, 1945-50; sr. surg. registrar thoracic surgery Brompton Hosp. for Chest Diseases, London, Eng., 1950-51; assoc. prof. surgery Baylor U. Coll. Medicine, Houston, 1954-62; prof. surgery Baylor U. Coll. Medicine, 1962-69; clin. prof. surgery U. Tex. Med. Sch., Houston, 1975—; founder, surgeon-in-chief Tex. Heart Inst., 1962—. Served as capt., M.C., 1946-48. Named one of ten Outstanding Young Men in U.S., U.S. C. of C., 1955, Man of the Yr. award Kappa Sigma, 1964; recipient Rene Leriche prize Internat. Surg. Soc., 1967, Billings Gold medal Am. Surg. Soc., 1967, Vishnevsky medal Vishnevsky Inst., USSR, 1971, Theodore Roosevelt Award, 1980, Presdl. Medal of Freedom, presented by Pres. Reagan, 1984, Gifted Tchr. award Am. Coll. Cardiology, 1987, Disting. Svc. award AMA, 1997, Nat. Medal of Tech., U.S. Dept Commerce, 1998. Hon. fellow Royal Coll. Physicians and Surgeons of Glasgow, Royal Coll. Surgeons of Ireland, Royal Australasian Coll. Surgeons, Royal Coll. Surgeons of Eng.; mem. ACS, Am. Surg. Assn., Internat. Cardiovascular Soc., Am. Assn. Thoracic Surgery, Soc. Thoracic Surgery, Soc. Univ. Surgeons, Am. Coll. Cardiology, Am. Coll. Chest Physicians, Soc. Clin. Surgery, Soc. Vascular Surgery, Western Surg. Assn., Tex. Surg. Soc., Halsted Soc. Performed numerous heart transplants; implanted 1st artificial heart, 1969. Office: Tex Heart Inst PO Box 20345 Houston TX 77225-0345 *As a person progresses along the path of life, he may achieve certain goals he set for himself as a youth. But to be more completely fulfilled, he must forever extend his goals to utilize his talents and accomplishments more fully. Too often, a man receives recognition for his deeds early in life and contents himself prematurely with living in peace and self-satisfaction.*

COOLEY, HILARY ELIZABETH, county official; b. Leesburg, Va., May 8, 1953; d. Thomas McIntyre and Helen Strong (Stringham) C. BA in Econs., U. Pitts., 1976; postgrad. in bus. adminstrn., Hood Coll., Frederick, Md., 1985-90. Mgr. Montgomery Ward, Frederick, 1976-80, merchandiser, 1980-82; asst. bus. mgr. Arundel Comm., Leesburg, 1982-84; bus. mgr. Loudoun Country Day Sch., Leesburg, 1984-85, bd. trustees, 1989-93, sec. bd. trustees, 1989-90, v.p., 1990-92; contr. Foxcroft Sch., Middleburg, Va., 1984-86, 91-92; corr. Loudoun Times Mirror, Leesburg, 1985-87; estate mgr. Delta Farm Inc., Middleburg, Va., 1988-98; cmty. ctr. mgr. County of Loudoun, 1998—. Area chmn. Keep Loudoun Beautiful, Middleburg, 1983-90, pres., bd. dirs. 1993-96; pres. Waterford (Va.) Citizens' Assn., 1985-86, Waterford Players, 1986-88; bd. dirs. Waterford Found., Inc., 1992-95, pres. 1995-98; bd. dirs. Loudoun Hist. Soc., Leesburg, 1987, Mt. Zion Ch. Preservation Assn., 1996—; treas. Amendment 1 Inc., 1997—. Mem. Penn Hall Alumnae Ann. (pres. 1987-92). Democrat. Episcopalian. Avocations: photography, music, drama, tennis. Home and Office: 171 Blue Ridge Acres Harpers Ferry WV 25425

COOLEY, JACOB ALAN, painter; b. Sydney, Australia, Feb. 9, 1968; came to U.S., 1969; s. Phillip Chester and Gretchen (Slick) C. Student, Antioch Coll., 1986-88; BFA, U. Ga., 1990; MFA, U. N.C., 1993. Editl. intern Inst. for So. Studies, Durham, N.C., 1988; asst. preparator Ga. Mus. Art, Athens, 1988-91; tchg. asst. in drawing U. N.C., Chapel Hill, 1991-93, instr. painting, 1993; instr. drawing Duke U. Crafts Ctr., Durham, N.C., 1996-97; instr. painting Durham Arts Coun., 1996-99, Duke U. Continuing Edn., Durham, 1997. Exhibited in group shows, 1995—, including Tyndall Gallery, Durham, Trinity Gallery, Atlanta, Ctr. of Earth Gallery, Charlotte, N.C., Raleigh (N.C.) Contemporary, Craven Allen Gallery, Durham; exhibited in solo shows including Lowe Gallery, Atlanta, Duke U. Mus. Art, Durham, Ackland Art Mus., Chapel Hill, Durham Art Guild, Durham Arts Coun., Gallerie 454, Grosse Pointe Park, Mich., Greenhill Ctr. for N.C. Art, Greensboro. Emerging Artists grantee Durham Arts Coun., 1994. Office: 2101 Chapel Hill Rd Durham NC 27707-1405

COOLEY, JAMES WILLIAM, retired executive researcher; b. N.Y.C., Sept. 18, 1926; s. William F. and Anna (Fanning) C.; m. Ingrid Uddholm, May 1, 1957; children: William, Anna-Carin, Lars. B.A., Manhattan Coll., Riverdale, N.Y., 1949; M.A., Columbia U., 1951, Ph.D., 1961. Programmer Inst. Advanced Study, Princeton, N.J., 1953-56; research staff Courant Inst., NYU, 1956-62; research staff mem. IBM Watson Research Ctr., Yorktown Heights, N.Y., 1962-91; with dept. elec. engring. U. R.I., Kingston, 1991-93; ret., 1993. Inventor fast fourier transform. Served with USAAF, 1945-46. Fellow IEEE.

COOLEY, WES, former congressman; b. L.A., Calif., Mar. 28, 1932; married; 4 children. AA, El Camino C. C.; BS in Bus., U. So. Calif., 1958. Asst. to pres. Hyland Labs. divsn. Baxter Labs. Allergan Pharmaceuticals; asst. to chmn. bd. ICN, divsn. mgr., dir. drug regulatory affairs; v.p. Virateck divsn.; founder, co-owner Rose Labs., Inc., 1981—; mem. Oregon State Senate, 1992-94; congressman 104 Congress from 2nd Oreg. dist., 1994-96; mem. House Com. Agriculture, House Com. Resources, House Com. Veteran Affairs, Subcommittee Gen. Farm Commodities, Subcommittee on Livestock, Dairy and Poultry, Subcommittee on Nat. Pks., Forests and Lands, Subcom. Water and Power Resources. With U.S. Army Spl. Forces, 1952-54. Address: 25550 Walker Rd Bend OR 97701-9323

COOLEY, WILLIAM EDWARD, regulatory affairs manager; b. St. Louis, Mar. 7, 1930; s. Charles Frederic and Lillian Marie (Williams) C.; m. Marion Grace Sherman, June 5, 1952; children: Charles, Marilyn, Harold, Noele. AB, Cen. Coll., 1951; PhD, U. Ill., 1954. Rsch. chemist Procter & Gamble Co., Cin., 1954-61, product devel. chemist, 1961-65, product devel. group leader, 1965-75, product devel. regulatory sect. mgr., 1975-90, regulatory affairs sect. mgr., 1990-91; worldwide regulatory coordination sect. mgr., 1991-94; pres. Cooley Cons., Inc., 1994—; bd. dirs. Nonprescription Drug Mfrs. Assn., Washington, 1987-91. Contbr. articles to profl. jours.; inventor, patentee in field. Mem. Am. Assn. Dental Rsch., Internat. Assn. Dental Rsch., Drug Info. Assn., Assn. Food Drug Ofcls., Regulatory Affairs Profl. Soc. (bd. editors 1990). Republican. Avocations: music, motorcycling, railroading, flying, astronomy. Home: 531 Chisholm Trl Cincinnati OH 45215-2517 Office: Cooley Cons Inc 531 Chisholm Trl Wyoming OH 45215

COOLEY, WILLIAM EMORY, JR., radiologist; b. Charlottesville, Va., Jan. 28, 1941; s. William Emory Sr. and Madelle Elizabeth (Fullen) C.; m. Janella Mahoney Haney, Dec. 26, 1966; children: Angela Janette, William Emory, James Haney. BA, Emory U., 1963; MD, U. Va., 1967. Diplomate Am. Bd. Radiology. Rotating intern. U.S. Naval Hosp., Phila., 1967-68; resident radiology U.S. Naval Regional Med. Ctr., Phila., 1972-75; radiologist U.S. Naval Regional Med. Ctr., Portsmouth, Va., 1975-76, asst. chief radiology, 1976-77; radiologist Bloomington (Ill.) Radiology S.C., 1977-79, pres., 1979—; chief radiologist Brokaw Hosp., Normal, Ill., 1979-85, St. Joseph Hosp., Bloomington, Ill., pres. med. staff, 1981; med. dir. radiology Bromen Health Care System, Bloomington, 1985—, pres. med. staff, 1990. Mem. citizens adv. coun. Sch. Dist. 87, Bloomington, 1981-84; v.p. McLean County unit Am. Cancer Soc., 1989-90, pres., 1990-94. Comdr. USN, 1966-77. Fellow Am. Coll. Radiology (alt. councillor 1987-92, councillor 1993-99, mem. commn. on small and rural practices 1999); mem. AMA, Radiol. Soc. N.Am., Am. Roentgen Ray Soc., Am. Inst. Ultrasound Medicine, Ill. Radiol. Soc. (exec. com. 1986-99, pres. 1994-95), Ctrl. Ill. Radiol. Soc. (pres. 1990-91), Clin. Magnetic Resonance Soc., Bloomington Country Club, Masons. Republican. Presbyterian. Avocations: book collecting, tennis, personal computers. Office: Bloomington Radiology SC 200 S Towanda Ave Normal IL 61761-2155

COOLEY-PARKER, SHEILA LEANNE, psychologist, consultant; b. Oakland, Calif., July 25, 1956; d. Philips Theadore and Helen Ellene (Newbill) C.; Kenneth Louis Parker. BA, St. Leo Coll., 1979; MS, U. So. Miss., 1986; PhD, Miss. State U., 1990. Lic. psychologist, Ky. Counselor Charter Counseling Ctr., Jackson, Miss., 1988-89; staff psychologist Rivendell Psychiat. Ctr., Bowling Green, Ky., 1989-90; program dir. Mid-South Hosp., Memphis, 1990-91; resource ctr. dir. MidSouth Resource Ctr., Ridgeland, Miss., 1991-92; partial hosp. dir. Pathways Partial Hospitalization, Ridgeland, 1991-92; edn. specialist, sr. position Miss. Dept. of Edn., Bur. Spl. Svcs., Jackson, 1993-94; psychologist Western State Hosp., Hopkinsville, Ky., 1994—, Caring Connections, Hopkinsville, Ky., 1995; pvt. practice Hopkinsville, Ky., 1996—. Campaign organizer for Dem. mayor, Jackson, 1992. Mem. APA, Ky. Psychol. Assn., Phi Delta Kappa, Psi Chi, Theta Pi Sigma. Baptist. Home: 4081 Singletree Dr Hopkinsville KY 42240-9191 Office: PO Box 2200 Hopkinsville KY 42241-2200

COOLIDGE, ANNE R., investment company executive. AB cum laude, Harvard U., 1991; MBA in Fin., Columbia U., 1997. Exec. asst. dept. estates and appraisals, asst. dept. 19th century paintings, asst. legal dept. Christie Manson Woods Internat., Inc., N.Y.C., 1991-93; asst. to chmn. W.P. Carey & Co., Inc., N.Y.C., 1993-97, 2d v.p., 1997-98, v.p., 1998-99, 1st v.p., 1999—; exec. v.p., portfolio mgr. Corp. Property Assocs. 10 Inc., N.Y.C., 1999—; v.p. W.P. Carey Found., N.Y.C., 1999—. Avocations: travel, volunteer work, leisure sports.

COOLIDGE, ARCHIBALD CARY, JR., English language educator, literature researcher; b. Oxford, Eng., June 9, 1928; s. Archibald Cary and Susan Thistle (Jennings) C.; m. Lillian Dobbel Merrill, June 29, 1951; children: Lillian, Emily, Sarah, Archibald, Anne, John, Alexander. BA, Harvard U., 1951; MA, Brown U., 1954, PhD, 1956. Instr. English, U. Iowa, Iowa City, 1956-59, asst. prof., 1959-65, assoc. prof., 1965-74, prof., 1974—. Author: Charles Dickens as Serial Novelist, 1967, Beyond the Fatal Flaw: A Study of the Neglected Forms of Greek Drama, 1980, A Theory of Story, 1989, English Law and American Problems, 1995. With USMC, 1945-46, CBI. Mem. U. Iowa Rsch. Club, Phi Beta Kappa. Avocations: fishing, movies. Home: 304 Brown St Iowa City IA 52245-5802 Office: U Iowa Dept English Iowa City IA 52242

COOLIDGE, CHARLES H., JR., career officer. BS in Basic Sci., USAF Acad., 1968; student undergrad. pilot tng., Moody AFB, Ga., 1968-69; M in Physics, Air Force Inst. Tech., 1974; student, Air Command and Staff Coll., 1979, Nat. War Coll., 1988. Commd. 2d lt. USAF, 1968, advanced through grades to maj. gen., 1996, various pilot/instr. pilot assignments, 1969-72; instr. and assoc. prof. dept. physics USAF Acad., Colorado Springs, Colo., 1974-77, br. chief cadet parachute program airmanship div., 1977-78; KC-135 pilot 4017th Combat Crew Tng. Squadron, Castle AFB, Calif., 1979; stationed at 911th Air Refueling Squadron, Seymour Johnson AFB, N.C., 1979-83; various assignments USAF, 1983-87; vice comdr. then comdr. 301st Air Refueling Wing, Malmstrom AFB, Mont., 1988-91; asst. dep. chief staff requirements and test Hdqs. Strategic Air Command, Offutt AFB, Nebr., 1991-92; vice comdr. Tanker Airlift Control Ctr. Hdqs. Air Mobility Command, Scott AFB, Ill., 1992-93; various comdr. positions USAF, 1993-96; dir. plans and ops. then dir. ops. Hdqs. Air Edn. and Tng. Command, Randolph AFB, Tex., 1996-97; dir. ops. and logistics U.S. Transp. Command, Scott AFB, 1997—. Decorated Legion of Merit with oak leaf cluster, D.F.C., Air medal with four oak leaf clusters, Rep. Vietnam Gallantry Cross with Palm. Office: USTranscom 508 Scott Dr Ste 200 Scott Air Force Base IL 62225

COOLIDGE, MARTHA, film director; b. New Haven, Aug. 17, 1946; Ed. RISD, Columbia U. Dir. films: Valley Girl, 1983, The City Girl, 1983, Joy of Sex, 1984, Real Genius, 1985, Plain Clothes, 1988, Rambling Rose, 1991, Crazy in Love, 1991, Lost in Yonkers, 1993, Angie, 1994, Three Wishes, 1995, Out to Sea, 1997; dir. TV shows and TV films Sledge Hammer pilot episode, 3 episodes The Twilight Zone, CBS miniseries The Winners, Roughhouse pilot episode, 1988, Trenchcoat in Paradise, 1989, Bare Essentials, 1991, Crazy in Love, 1992, Boston Grace pilot episode, Introducing Dorothy Dandridge, 1999; dir. documentaries David: On and Off, 1972, More Than A School, 1973, Old Fashioned Woman, 1974, Not A Pretty Picture, 1976 (all winners Am. Film Festival awards). Office: care Beverly Magid Guttman Assoc 118 S Beverly Dr Ste 201 Beverly Hills CA 90212-3016

COOLIO, popular musician. Albums include It Takes a Thief, 1994, Gangsta's Paradise, 1995. Recipient World Wide Music award, Favorite Rap Artist Am. Music award, Billboard Music award, 1995, Best Rap Solo Performance Grammy award, 1996. Office: Tommy Boy Records 902 Broadway Fl 13 New York NY 10010-6098*

COOMBE, GEORGE WILLIAM, JR., lawyer, retired banker; b. Kearny, N.J., Oct. 1, 1925; s. George William and Laura (Montgomery) C.; A.B., Rutgers U., 1946; LL.B., Harvard, 1949; m. Marilyn V. Ross, June 4, 1949; children—Susan, Donald William, Nancy. Bar: N.Y. 1950, Mich. 1953, Calif. 1976, U.S. Supr. Ct. Practice in N.Y.C., 1949-53, Detroit, 1953-69; atty., mem. legal-staff Gen. Motors Corp., Detroit, 1953-69, asst. gen. counsel, sec., 1969-75; exec. v.p., gen. counsel Bank of Am., San Francisco, 1975-90; ptnr. Graham and James, San Francisco, 1991-95; sr. fellow Stanford Law Sch., 1995—. Served to lt. USNR, 1942-46. Mem. Am., Mich., Calif., San Francisco, Los Angeles, N.Y.C. bar assns., Phi Beta Kappa, Phi Gamma Delta. Presbyterian. Home: 2190 Broadway St Apt 2E San Francisco CA 94115-1311 Office: Am Arbitration Assn Asia Pacific Ctr 225 Bush St San Francisco CA 94104

COOMBE, V. ANDERSON, valve manufacturing company executive; b. Cin., Mar. 5, 1926; s. Harry Elijah and Mary (Anderson) C.; m. Eva Jane Romaine, Sept. 26, 1957; children—James, Michael, Peter. B.E., Yale, 1948. Asst. to pres. Wm. Powell Co., Cin., 1953-57, v.p., 1957-63, exec. v.p., 1963-69, pres., treas., 1969-91, chmn. bd., 1991—, also bd. dirs.; bd. dirs. Firstar Bank Cin. Clubs: Camargo (Cin.), Queen City (Cin.), Cincinnati Country (Cin.). Home: 6 Corbin Dr Cincinnati OH 45208-3302 Office: 2503 Spring Grove Ave Cincinnati OH 45214-1729

COOMBS, JANET, advertising executive. Pres. Wunderman-Cato-Johnson, N.Y.C. Office: Wunderman Cato Johnson 675 Ave of Americas New York NY 10010

COOMBS, KERRY LELAND, veterinarian, educator; b. Mesa, Ariz., Sept. 19, 1957; s. Roy Leland and Illa Mae (Rogers) C.; m. Robin G. Miller, June 23, 1982; children: Nolan, Kaitlyn. AS, Ricks Coll., 1980; BS, Brigham Young U., 1982; DVM, Colo. State U., 1986. Assoc. veterinarian Ken Caryl Animal and Bird Hosp., Littleton, Colo., 1986-87, Woodlawn Vet. Clinic, Littleton, 1987-89, Columbine Animal Hosp., Littleton, 1989-90; program dir. vet. tech. Omaha Coll. Health Careers, 1990-94, Midland (Tex.) Coll., 1994—. Contbr. to book: Questions for Veterinary Technicians, 1996. Troop instnl. rep. Boy Scouts Am., Midland, 1994, 96. Mem. AVMA, Assn. vet. Technician Educators, Tex. Vet. Med. Assn. (mem. vet. technician testing com. 1996-97). Avocations: sports, scouts, ranching. Office: Midland Coll 3600 N Garfield St Midland TX 79705-6329

COOMBS, ROBERT HOLMAN, behavioral scientist, medical educator, therapist, author; b. Salt Lake City, Sept. 16, 1934; s. Morgan Scott and Vivian (Holman) C.; m. Carol Jean Cook, May 29, 1958; children: Robert Scott, Kathryn, Lorraine, Karen Youn Jung, Holly Ann, Krista Ho Jung, David Jeremy. BS, U. Utah, 1958, MS, 1959; PhD, Wash. State U., 1964. Asst. prof. sociology Iowa State U., 1963-66; fellow Behavioral Sci. Ctr.-Bowman Gray Sch. Medicine/Wake Forest U, 1966, asst. prof., 1966-68; assoc. prof. Behavioral Sci. Center, Bowman Gray Sch. Medicine, Wake Forest U., 1968-70; career rsch. specialist Calif. Dept. Mental Hygiene, Camarillo, 1970-73; assoc. rsch. sociologist UCLA, 1970-77, assoc. prof. biobehavioral scis. Sch. Medicine, 1977-78, prof., 1978—; chief Camarillo Neuropsychiat. Inst., 1970-78; asst. dir. rsch. UCLA Neuropsychiat. Inst., Center for Health Scis., 1978-81; dir. Office Edn. of Neuropsychiat. Inst., 1980-90, UCLA Family Learning Center, Oxnard, Calif., 1977-84; cons. World Fedn. for Med. Edn., 1990-92; dir. grief and bereavement program UCLA, 1993-99. Author: Psychosocial Aspects of Medical Training, 1971, Junkies and Straights: The Camarillo Experience, 1975, Socialization in Drug Abuse, 1976, Mastering Medicine: Professional Socialization in Medical School, 1978, Making It in Medical School, 1979, Inside Doctoring: Stages and Outcomes in the Professional Socialization of Physicians, 1986, The Family Context of Adolescent Drug Use, 1988, Drug Testing: Issues and Options, 1991, Handbook on Drug Abuse Prevention, 1995, Drug-Impaired Professionals, 1997, Surviving Medical School, 1998, Cool Parents/Drug Free Kids, 1999, Addiction Recovery Tools: A Practitioner's Handbook, 2000; assoc. editor Family Rels.: Jour. Applied Family and Child Studies, 1970-80, Clin. Sociology Rev., Jour. Clin. Sociology, Jour. Marriage and the Family, 1982-96, Qualitative Health Rsch., 1990-94, Family Dynamics and Addiction Quar., 1990-94; corr. editor Med. Edn. (U.K.); contbg. editor Jour. Drug Issues, 1977; series editor Sage Book Series on Medical Student Survival, 1998—; contbr. articles to profl. jours., chpts. to books. Bishop Winston-Salem (N.C.) Ward, Ch. Jesus Christ of Latter-day Saints, 1969-70, Camarillo (Calif.) Ward, 1972-77; mem. Calif. Atty.-Gen.'s Commn. on Prevention of Drug and Alcohol Abuse, 1985-86; high risk youth prevention grant rev. com. USPHS, 1990—; com. to combat drug abuse World Fedn. Mental Health, 1989—. With U.S. Army, 1958. Grantee NIMH, 1968-73, Nat. Fund Med. Edn., 1969-71, Law Enforcement Assistance Adminstrn., 1971-76, Nat. Inst. Drug Abuse, 1977-80, Calif. Dept. Alcohol and Drug Programs, 1977-78, Father Flanagan's Boys Home, 1977-79, CETA, Ventura County, Calif., 1978. Fellow AAAS, APS, Am. Assn. Applied and Preventive Psychology; mem. Internat. Sociol. Assn., Internat. Family Therapy Assn., World Fedn. Menal Health (mem. com. to combat drug abuse), Assn. Am. Med. Colls., Am. Psychotherapy Assn. (cert.), Sigma Xi, Phi Kappa Phi. Democrat. Office: UCLA Sch Medicine Dept Psychiatry Biobehavioral Scis 760 Westwood Plz Los Angeles CA 90095-8353 *I have surrounded myself with superior people, those whose specialized talents have enriched my thinking and productivity. I actively pursue the association and assistance of those whose skills exceed or compliment my own.*

COOMES, SALLY PAYNE, secondary educator; b. Chgo., Apr. 2, 1937; d. William Barrie and Marjorie (Thomas) Payne; m. Roger Kellogg Coomes, Aug. 1, 1959; children: Brian, Barbara, Bradley. BA in English and Biology, No. Ill. U., 1959; MS in Reading, Mankato State U., 1974; postgrad., U. Ariz., 1989-90. Math. tchr. Tilden Tech. H.S., Chgo., 1959; English tchr. Beloit (Wis.) Meml. H.S., 1959-60; reading instr., student tchr. supr. Mankato (Minn.) State U., 1974-79, Gustavus Adolphus Coll., St. Peter, Minn., 1977-79; reading, English tchr. Mankato Pub. Schs., 1979-89, assurance of mastery lead tchr., reading cons., 1990—; regional reading cons. Minn. Reading Best Practice Network, 1995—; curriculum adv. com. Mankato Pub. Schs., 1993-96, chair profl. growth com. staff devel. assn., 1996—. Fundraiser Habitat for Humanity, Mankato, 1989—; pres. Ch. Women United, Mankato, 1970-71; bd. dirs. Minn. Reading Assn., 1979-81; pres. S.W. Minn. Reading Coun., 1979-81. Mem. ASCD, Internat. Reading Assn. Presbyterian. Avocations: reading, sewing. Home: RR 5 Box 54 Mankato MN 56001-9306 Office: Dakota Meadows Middle Sch 1900 Howard Dr North Mankato MN 56003

COON, PENNY K., religious organization official; b. Penn Yan, N.Y., May 21, 1959; d. Wilfred Orval and Marilyn Estelle (Wells) Knapp; m. Thomas Allen Gray, Aug. 30, 1980 (div. July 1990); m. David Charles Coon, May 23, 1992; 1 child, Rachel Mariah. BSW, Keuka Coll., 1980. Residence counselor Cath. Charities Residential Program, Penn Yan, 1981-82, residence mgr., 1982-92, residential supr., 1992—; bd. dirs. Yates County (N.Y.) ARC, Penn Yan, 1993-98, mem. incident rev., 1989—; co-chmn. Keuka Lake Conf. Com., Rochester, N.Y., 1986—; mem. Yates County Rep. Com.; mem. parent adv. coun. and bldg. level team Dundee (N.Y.) Ctrl. Sch., 1998—. Election inspector, Yaks County Bd. Elections, 1996—; mem. Yaks County Rep. Com., Yaks County Women's Rep. Club. Recipient Direct Care award, N.Y. State Assn. Community Residence Adminstrs. Mem. DAR, Daughters Am. Colonists. Republican. Avocations: reading, pets, camping. Home: 2599 Knapp Rd Dundee NY 14837-9730 Office: Cath Charities Residential Program 607 W Washington St Geneva NY 14456-2119

COON, SHARON ANN, writer, public relations executive, educator; b. Euclid, Ohio, July 7, 1968; d. Earl L. and Jean Ann C. BA, Hiram Coll., 1990; MBA, Lake Erie Coll., 1995. Cert. tchr., Ohio. Freelance writer, 1990—; pub. rels. dir. Lake Erie Coll., Painesville, Ohio, 1991-96, resident dir., 1994-98, alumni dir., 1996-97; founds. chair Learning About Bus., Painesville, 1997—; publ. supr. Cuyahoga C. C., 1998—; rep. Painesville Image Enhancement Com., 1995-96; pub. rels. chair provisional bd. Key Bank Hunter Jumper Classic, Chagrin Falls, 1996-97. Contbr. articles to profl. jours. Mem. Cleve. Com. Higher Edn., 1991-96. Recipient Bronze award North Coast Print Prodn., Cleve., 1995, Cert. of Merit award Women in Comm., 1996. Mem. Pub. Rels. Soc. Am., Omicron Delta Kappa, Alpha Lambda Delta. Roman Cath. Avocations: photography, writing, horseback riding. Home: 9032 Sherman Rd Chesterland OH 44026-2214 Office: Cuyahoga C C 700 Carnegie Ave Cleveland OH 44115

COON COME, MATTHEW, Native American tribal chief; b. Bush-Mistissini, Que., Can., Apr. 13, 1956; s. Alfred and Harriet (Etapp) C.; m. Mary Ann Matoush; children: Justus, Marilyn, Ryan, Sarah, Emma. LLD (hon.), Trent U., 1998. Dep. chief Mistissini, Quebec, 1978-81, chief, 1980-81, 85-86; grand chief Grand Coun. of the Crees (of Quebec), 1987—; chmn. Cree Regional Authority, 1987—, James Bay Eeyou Co., 1987—, SODAB, 1991—; dir. Cree Regional Econ. Enterprises Co., 1987-94, Cree Constrn. Co., First Nations Bank Can.; bd. dirs. Air Creebec. Dir. James Bay Cree Cultural Edn. Ctr., Cree Health Bd., Cree Ednl. Authority, James Bay Native Devel. Corp., Ctr. Indigenous Environ. Resources; hon. patron Waseskun House; mem. dean's adv. bd. U. Toronto Faculty of Forestry; hon. chmn. Aanishchaaukamikw Fund Raising Campaign. Recipient Equinox Environ. award Eqinox Canadian Mag., 1993, Goldman Global Environ. prize Goldman Found., 1994, Conde Naste award Environ. Condé Nast Traveler, 1994, Environ. award Nat. Aboriginal Achievement award, 1995, Achievement award James Bay Cree Comm. Soc., 1995. Avocations: hunting, fishing, trapping. Office: Grand Coun Crees Eeyou, Estchee 2 Lakeshore Rd, Nemaska, PQ Canada J0Y 3B0

COONELLY, FRANCIS X., lawyer. Gen. counsel maj. league baseball Office Commr. Baseball, N.Y.C. Office: Maj League Baseball Office Commr Baseball 245 Park Ave New York NY 10167

COONEY, DAVID FRANCIS, lawyer; b. Chgo., Sept. 21, 1954; s. John Thomas and Margaret (Bonner) C.; m. René Marie Struzzieri, June 20, 1987; children: Lauren René, Cailin Anne, David Brenden. BBA in Fin. magna cum laude, U. Notre Dame, 1975, JD, 1978. Bar: Fla., U.S. Dist. Ct. (so. dist.) Fla., U.S. Ct. Appeal (5th, 8th and 11th cirs.). Assoc. Grimmett, Scherer & James, Ft. Lauderdale, Fla., 1978-82; ptnr. Conrad, Scherer & James, Ft. Lauderdale, 1982-92, Cooney, Mattson, Lance, Blackburn, Richards & O'Connor, Ft. Lauderdale, 1992—. Mem. Am. Bd. Trial Advs. (assoc.). Roman Catholic. Home: 2839 NE 24th Pl Fort Lauderdale FL 33305-2821 Office: Cooney Mattson 2312 Wilton Dr Fort Lauderdale FL 33305-1249

COONEY, DAVID MARTIN, organization administrator, retired naval officer; b. Los Angeles, Aug. 5, 1930; s. Arthur B. and Margaret M. (Metcalf) C.; m. Beverly Satchwell, Feb. 22, 1952; children—Kathleen Cooney Lambert, David Martin, Karen L. Newman, Kacy Lypka. B.A., U. So.

Calif., 1951; M.S., George Washington U., 1965; grad., Naval War Coll., 1965. Commd. ensign U.S. Navy, 1951, advanced through grades to rear adm., 1976; pub. affairs officer 6th Fleet, cre; pub. affairs officer comdr. in chief U.S. Atlantic Command, 1967-71; asst. chief of info. Dept. Navy, Washington, 1971-73; dep. chief of info. Dept. Navy, 1973-75, chief of info., 1975-80, asst. to sec. of Navy for mgmt., 1980-81; ret., 1981; pres. Goodwill Industries Internat. Inc., Washington, 1981-95; CEO Partnership Umbrella Inc., Alexandria, Va., 1996-99; exec. dir. human resource devel. Lifecare Mgmt. Inc., 1999—; chmn. com. on spl. wages U.S. Dept. Labor, 1987-93; mem. quadrennial rev. bd. Social Security Adminstrn.; cons. Argentine Ms. World Bank, 1998—. Mem. nat. coun. Boy Scouts Am., 1978-90; treas. Rehab. Internat., 1988-95; bd. trustees Naval Inst. Found., 1993. Decorated Legion of Merit with gold star; recipient Disting. Svc. medal, Alumni Merit award U. So. Calif., 1979, Excellence in Nat. Leadership award, 1993, Presdl. Disting. Pub. Svc. award, 1993, others. Office: Lifecare Ste 300 6601 Little River Turnpike Alexandria VA 22312

COONEY, JOAN GANZ, broadcasting executive; b. Phoenix, Nov. 30, 1929; d. Sylvan C. and Pauline (Reardan) Ganz; m. Timothy J. Cooney, 1964 (div. 1975); m. Peter G. Peterson, 1980. BA, U. Ariz., 1951; hon. degrees, Boston Coll., 1970, Hofstra U., Oberlin Coll., Ohio Wesleyan U., 1971, Princeton U., 1973, Russell Sage Coll., 1974, U. Ariz., Harvard U., 1975, Allegheny Coll., 1976, Georgetown U., 1978, U. Notre Dame, 1982, Smith Coll., 1986, Brown U., 1987, Columbia U., 1991, NYU, 1991. Reporter Ariz. Republic, Phoenix, 1953-54; publicist NBC, 1954-55, U.S. Steel Hour, 1955-62; producer Sta. WNET, Channel 13; pub. affairs documentaries Sta. WNET, Channel 13, N.Y.C., 1962-67; TV cons. Carnegie Corp. N.Y., N.Y.C., 1967-68; exec. dir. Children's TV Workshop (producers Sesame Street, Electric Company, others), N.Y.C., 1968-70, pres., trustee, 1970-88, chmn., chief exec. officer, 1988-90, chmn. exec. com., 1990—; trustee Channel 13/Ednl. Broadcasting Corp., Columbia Presbyn. Med. Ctr., Mus. of TV and Radio; dir. Johnson & Johnson, Met. Life Ins. Co. Mem. Pres.'s Commn. on Marijuana and Drug Abuse, 1971-73, Nat. News Council, 1973-81, Council Fgn. Relations, 1974—, Pres.'s Commn. for Agenda for 80's, 1980-81, Adv. Com. for Trade Negotiations, 1978-80; mem. Gov.'s Commn. on Internat. Yr. of the Child, 1979, Carnegie Found. Nat. Panel on High Sch., 1980-82. Recipient numerous awards for Sesame Street and other TV programs including Nat. Sch. Pub. Relations Assn. Gold Key 1971; Disting. Service medal Columbia Tchrs. Coll., 1971; Soc. Family Man award, 1971; Nat. Inst. Social Scis. Gold medal, 1971; Frederick Douglass award N.Y. Urban League, 1972; Silver Satellite award Am. Women in Radio and TV; Woman of Yr. in Edn. award Ladies Home Jour., 1975; Women of Decade award, 1979; NEA Friends of Edn. award; Kiwanis Decency award; NAEB Disting. Service award; 5th Women's Achiever award Girl Scouts U.S.A.; Stephen S. Wise award, 1981; Harris Found. award, 1982; Ednl. Achievement award AAUW, 1984; Disting. Service to Children award Nat. Assn. Elem. Sch. Prins., 1985; DeWitt Carter Reddick award Coll. Communications, U. Tex.-Austin, 1986; Emmy Lifetime Achievement award Acad. TV Arts and Scis., 1989, Presdl. medal of Freedom, 1995; named to Hall of Fame Acad. TV Arts and Scis., 1990. Mem. Nat. Acad. TV Arts and Scis., Nat. Inst. Social Scis., Internat. Radio and TV Soc., Am. Women in Radio and TV. Office: Children's TV Workshop 1 Lincoln Plz New York NY 10023-7129*

COONEY, JOHN GORDON, lawyer; b. Bklyn., Jan. 21, 1930; s. John Philip and Josephine (Gordon) C.; m. Patricia Ruth McEwen, June 8, 1957; 1 child, J. Gordon Jr. AB, St. John's U., 1951, JD, 1953. Bar: N.Y. 1953, Pa. 1962, D.C. 1970. Asso. Patterson, Belknap & Webb, N.Y.C., 1953-55; staff counsel U.S. Industries, N.Y., 1956-57; atty. SEC, Washington, 1957-59, FTC, 1959-61; ptnr. Schnader, Harrison, Segal & Lewis, Phila., 1962-97; bd. dirs. PH II, Inc.; arbitrator Am. Arbitration Assn., 1964—; public mem. nat. com. on arbitration Nat. Assn. Securities Dealers, 1977-83; dir. Attys. Liability Assurance Soc., 1979-85. Dir., pres. Strafford Village Assn., 1969-70; bd. govs. N.Y.C. Young Republican Club, 1957. Recipient Superior Service award FTC, 1961. Fellow Am. Bar Found.; mem. ABA (coun. sect. corp. banking and bus. law 1980-84, 93-97), Am. Law Inst. (life mem., adviser project on corp. governance: analysis and recommendations 1980-92), D.C. Bar Assn., N.Y. State Bar Assn., Pa. State Bar Assn., Phila. Bar Assn., Union League Club, Overbrook Golf Club, Merion Cricket Club. Roman Catholic. Home: 320 Gatcombe Ln Bryn Mawr PA 19010-3628 Office: Schnader Harrison Segal & Lewis 1600 Market St Ste 3600 Philadelphia PA 19103-7240 *Deceased.*

COONEY, J(OHN) GORDON, JR., lawyer; b. Alexandria, Va., Mar. 22, 1959; s. John Gordon Sr. and Patricia Ruth (McEwen) C. BA, Wesleyan U., 1981; JD magna cum laude, Villanova U., 1984. Bar: Pa. 1984, U.S. Dist. Ct. (ea. dist.) Pa. 1986, U.S. Ct. Appeals (3d cir.) 1988. Law clk. to hon. judge J. William Ditter Jr. U.S. Dist. Ct. (ea. dist.) Pa., Phila., 1984-86; assoc. Morgan, Lewis & Bockius, LLP, Phila., 1986-92, ptnr., 1992—; adj. lectr. Villanova U. Sch. of Law, 1993—; barrister U. Pa. Law Sch. Inn of Ct., 1994-96. Editor-in-chief Villanova U. Law Rev., 1983-84; mem. lawyer's editl. bd. The Legal Intelligencer, 1997—. Trustee Rosemont Sch. of the Holy Child, 1997—; alumni bd. mgrs. Episcopal Acad., 1996—. Mem. ABA (com. on class actions and derivative suits), Pa. Bar Assn., Phila. Bar Assn. (profl. guidance com., fed. cts. com.), Union League Phila., Merion Cricket Club, Wesleyan U. Alumni Assn. (pres. Phila. area 1993-96), Arthritis Found. (bd. dirs Ea. Pa. chpt. 1993-96), Order of Coif. Republican. Roman Catholic. Office: Morgan Lewis & Bockius LLP 1701 Market St Philadelphia PA 19103-2903

COONEY, JOHN PATRICK, JR., lawyer; b. Chgo., Oct. 18, 1944; s. John Patrick and Katherine (Rafferty) C.; m. Joan Oberbeck, Dec. 7, 1968 (div. 1990); children: John, Brian, Anne; m. Jane Elizabeth Hewett, Oct. 3, 1992; children: Luke, Nathaniel. BS, Ind. U., 1966; JD, Duke U., 1969. Bar: N.Y. 1970, U.S. Ct. Appeals (2nd, 5th cir.) 1972, U.S. Dist. Ct. (so. dist.) N.Y. 1972, U.S. Dist. Ct. (ea. dist.) N.Y. 1977. Assoc. Davis Polk & Wardwell, N.Y.C., 1969-72, 77-80, mem. firm, 1980—; asst. U.S. atty. U.S. Atty.'s Office for So. Dist. N.Y., N.Y.C., 1972-77, chief narcotics unit, 1976-77; instr. trial advocacy program Harvard Law Sch., 1976-90, Fordham U. Law Sch., 1978, Cardoza Law Sch., 1995. Note editor Duke Law Jour., 1968-69. Fellow Am. Coll. of Trial Lawyers; mem. Fed. Bar Coun., Com. for Modern Cts., Criminal Justice Act Panel, Assn. Bar City of N.Y., N.Y. Coun. of Def. Lawyers, Supreme Ct. Hist. Soc. (chmn. N.Y. chpt.), Wong Sung Soc. San Francisco, Am. Alpine Club, Knickerbocker Club. Roman Catholic. Avocation: mountain climbing. Home: 50 Hillside Rd Rye NY 10580-2013 Office: Davis Polk & Wardwell 450 Lexington Ave New York NY 10017-3911

COONEY, JOHN THOMAS, retired banker; b. Warren, Pa., Jan. 20, 1927; s. Willis Edward and Elaine (Blanden) C.; m. Clara Jean Ellberg, Dec. 22, 1950; children: John B., Michael T., Lisa J. BS in Bus., Gannon U., 1951. Asst. personnel mgr. Nat. Biscuit Co., Houston, 1951-52; v.p. Bank of Southwest, Houston, 1956-80, exec. v.p., and sr. trust officer, 1980-85; vice chmn. M Trust Corp., 1985-90, Ameritrust Tex. N.A., Houston, 1990-92; adv. dir. Legacy Trust Co., 1993—; bd. dirs. Marine Safety Systems, Inc., 1996—; mem. SEI II Bd. of Trustees, 1994—. Pres. Mental Health Assn., Houston; bd. dirs. Am. Heart Assn., state treas., Tex.; established TBA Tex. Sch. of Trust Banking (chmn. 1978). Served as cpl. U.S. Army, 1945-46. Recipient Medal of Honor Gannon U., 1951. Mem. Tex. Bankers Assn. (trust divsn. chmn. 1982-83), Lakeside Country Club, The Houstonian Club. Republican. Roman Catholic.

COONEY, LEO MATHIAS, JR., geriatrician, educator; b. Providence, Nov. 30, 1943. MD, Yale U. Diplomate Am. Bd. Internal Medicine, Am. Bd. Geriatric Medicine, Am. Bd. Rheumatology. Intern Boston City Hosp., 1969-70, resident, 1970-71, resident in internal medicine, 1973-74, fellow in arthritis, 1974; prof. medicine Yale U. Sch. Medicine, New Haven, 1975—; mem. staff Yale-New Haven Hosp. Recipient Nascher/Manning award Am. Geriatrics Soc., 1994. Office: Humana Prof Geriatric Medicine Yale School of Med Yale N Haven Hospital/20 York St TMP Rm 17B New Haven CT 06504

COONEY, MIKE, state official; b. Washington, Sept. 3, 1954; s. Gage Rodman and Ruth (Brodie) C.; m. Dee Ann Marie Gribble; children: Ryan Patrick, Adan Cecelia, Colin Thomas. BA in Polit. Sci., U. Mont., 1979. State rep. Mont. Legislature, Helena, 1976-80; exec. asst. U.S. Sen. Max Baucus, Butte, Mont., 1979-82, Washington, 1982-85, Helena, Mont., 1985-89; sec. of state State of Mont., Helena, 1988—. Bd. dirs. YMCA; mem. adv. panel Fed. Clearinghouse. Mem. Nat. Secs. of State (pres.), Nat. Assns. Secs. of State (pres. 1997). Home: PO Box 754 Helena MT 59624-0754 Office: Office Sec of State PO Box 20281 225 E 6th Ave Helena MT 59620-4026

COONEY, M(URIEL) SHARON TAYLOR, medical/surgical nurse, educator; b. Edenton, N.C., Oct. 12, 1947; d. Howard Russell and Evelyn Louise (Phelps) Taylor; children: Michael James, Patrick Russell. BSN, East Carolina U., 1969; MS in Nursing, St. Louis U., 1972. Cert. orthopaedic nurse. Staff nurse Johns Hopkins Hosp., Balt., 1969-71, Barnes Hosp., St. Louis, 1971-72, Person County Meml. Hosp., 1989—; cardiovascular clin. nurse specialist Jackson Meml. Hosp., Miami, 1973-74; instr. Shepherd Coll., Shepherdstown, W.Va., 1983-84, Piedmont Community Coll., Roxboro, N.C., 1989-90, Watts Sch. Nursing, Durham, N.C., 1990—; clin. instr., lectr. Shepherd Coll.; home health care supr., mgr. Coord. Coun. for Sr. Citizens, 1985. Mem. ANA, Nat. Assn. Orthopaedic Nurses, Nat. League for Nursing, Acad. Med.-Surg. Nursing, N.C. Alliance Hosp.-Based Schs. Nursing, N.C. Nurses Assn. (coun. of clin. specialists, med.-surg. coun., chmn. coun. nurse educators). Home: 4812 Bahama Rd Rougemont NC 27572

COONEY, PATRICIA RUTH, civic worker; b. Englewood, N.J.; d. Charles Aloysius and Ruth Jeannette (Foster) McEwen; m. J. Gordon Cooney, June 8, 1957; 1 child, J. Gordon, Jr. Student, Fordham U., 1950-51; DHL honoris causa, Phila. Theol. Sem. St. Charles Boromeo, 1991. Blood bank chmn. Strafford Village Civic Assn., 1968-69, sec., 1970-71; vice chmn. Spl. Gifts Com. Cath. Charities Appeal of Archdiocese of Phila., 1980—, chmn., 1985. Mem. Coun. of Mgrs. Archdiocese of Phila., 1982-88, sec., exec. com., 1983-88; bd. dirs. Cath. Charities of Archdiocese of Phila., 1984—, sec., exec. com., 1988-90, v.p., exec. com., 1991—; bd. dirs. Village of Divine Providence, Phila., 1982—, sec., 1983-85, v.p. exec. com., 1990—; bd. dirs. St. Edmond's Home for Crippled Children, Phila., 1984—, v.p. exec. com., 1990—; bd. dirs. Don Guanella Village of Archdiocese of Phila., 1984—, v.p. exec. com., 1990— ; mem. Archdiocesan Adv. Com. on Renewal, 1991—; mem. Women's Com. Wills Eye Hosp., 1973—, mem.-at-large, 1st v.p.; mem. Women's Aux. St. Francis Country House, Darby, Pa., 1976—, treas., 1978-82; exec. com. United Way of Southeastern Pa., 1984-90, sec., 1986-88; bd. dirs. Chapel of Four Chaplains, 1984-89, Phila. Criminal Justice Task Force, 1989-90. Decorated Cross Pro Ecclesia et Pontifice, 1982, Lady Order St. Gregory the Gt., 1998. Republican. Avocations: reading, tennis, sailing. Home: 320 Gatcombe Ln Bryn Mawr PA 19010-3628

COONEY, PATRICK LOUIS, writer; b. Bellflower, Calif., Apr. 7, 1947; s. Jack William and Lauretta (Jenkins) C.; m. Rosemary Santana Cooney, Sept. 10, 1967; 1 child, Carl. BA in Sociology, Fla. State U., 1969; MA, PhD, U. Tex., 1976; MBA, Fordham U., 1979; cert. in Field Botany, N.Y. Bot. Garden, Bronx, 1993. Asst. prof. sociology Coll. Mount St. Vincent, Bronx, 1975-77; mktg. exec. pub. firms, 1980-89; Cert. in Field Botany; spkr. Martin Luther King Jr. Inst. for Non-Violence, Westchester County, N.Y., 1994; presenter in field. Author: Discovering the Mid-Atlantic: Historical Tours, 1991, Seeing the United States as the South and the World Community of the North: Using the Approach of Martin Luther King Jr. to Invigorate the Next Civil Rights Movement, 1994, The Role of Multiculturalism in Establishing A New Period of Separate but Equal Segregation in the United States: A Comparison of the Periods After and First and Second Civil Wars, 1997. Civil rights activist. With Army Nat. Guard, 1966-73. Dissertation fellow Sweden-Am. Inst., N.Y.C., 1973-74. Mem. Torrey Bot. Club (chairperson field com.). Democrat. Mem. Soc. of Friends. Home: 221 Mount Hope Blvd Hastings On Hudson NY 10706

COONEY, PATRICK RONALD, bishop; b. Detroit, Mar. 10, 1934; s. Michael and Elizabeth (Dowdall) C. B.A., Sacred Heart Sem., 1956; S.T.B., Gregorian U., Rome, 1958, S.T.L., 1960; M.A., Notre Dame U., 1973. Ordained priest Roman Cath. Ch., 1959 ordained bishop, 1983. Assoc. pastor St. Catherine Ch., Detroit, 1960-62; asst. chancellor Archdiocese of Detroit, 1962-69, dir. dept. worship, 1969-83; rector Blessed Sacrament Cathedral, 1977-83; regional bishop Roman Cath. Ch., Detroit, 1983-89; apptd. bishop Diocese of Gaylord, Mich., 1989—. Office: Diocese of Gaylord Pastoral Ctr 1665 W M 32 Gaylord MI 49735*

COONEY, WILLIAM J., lawyer; b. Augusta, Ga., July 31, 1929; s. John F. and Ellen (Joy) C.; m. Martha L. Whaley, May 1, 1971; children: William J. IV, Sarah C. BS, U. Notre Dame, 1951; JD, Georgetown U., 1954, LLM, 1955. Bar: Ga. 1963, Calif. 1961, D.C. 1954. Law clk. U.S. Ct. Appeals, Washington, 1954, U.S. Claims Ct., Washington, 1955; asst. U.S. atty. Washington, 1958-60, San Francisco, 1960-63; sole practice Augusta, 1963—. Capt. JAGC, U.S. Army, 1955-58. Mem. State Bar Ga., Spl. Master State Bar Ga., Augusta Bar Assn. (mem. exec. com., arbitrator), Am. Arbitration Assn. (arbitrator). Roman Catholic. Office: 1 Habersham Sq 3602 Wheeler Rd Augusta GA 30909-1826

COONROD, DELBERTA HOLLAWAY (DEBBIE COONROD), elementary education educator, consultant, freelance writer; b. Eldon, Mo., Oct. 21, 1937; d. Delbert Leland and Zealoth (Stevens) Hollaway; m. Charles Ralph Coonrod, Aug. 26, 1961; children: Charles Leland, Marcia Renee. BS in Edn., U. Kans., 1961; MS in Edn., Ind. U., 1972, EdD in Edn., 1977; postgrad., U. Tex., Tex. Women's U. Cert. elem. tchr., Kans. Classroom tchr. Hood Sch. & Heizer Elem., Barton County, Kans., 1957-60, Emporia (Kans.) Pub. Schs., 1961-62, Lincoln (Nebr.) Pub. Schs., 1964-66, South Bend (Ind.) Sch. Corp., 1967-72; assoc. instr., vis. asst. prof. Ind. U., Bloomington, 1972-79; asst. prof. Ind. State U., Terre Haute, 1975-76; pres. Debcon, Inc., Bloomington, 1979-81; pvt. practice cons. Bloomington, 1981-85; classroom tchr. Ft. Worth Ind. Sch. Dist., 1985—; cons. Ft. Hays State U., Kans., 1990, Edison Cmty. Coll., Piqua, Ohio, 1994; instr. Tarrant County (Tex.) Jr. Coll., 1992-94; adj. asst. prof. Tex. Woman's U., Denton, 1987—; adj. prof. Tex. Christian U., Ft. Worth, 1991-92; adminstrv. project dir. Monroe County Sch. Corp., Bloomington, 1983-85; instr. Weatherford Coll., 1996-97; kindergarten cons. Penn-Harris-Madison Sch. Corp., Mishawaka, Ind., 1970-71; head adminstr. Hoosier Cts. Nursery Sch., Ind. U., 1978-79; nat. approved trainer Head Start, 1982-85; chair emeritus Who's Who in Am. Edn. adv. bd.; mem. FWISD Dist. adv. com., 1996—. Contbr. articles to profl. jours. Bd. dirs. 4C's of Monroe County, 1979-85; mem. Greater Ft. Worth Lit. Coun., 1990—; pres. IRA-Ft. Worth Coun., 1993 (Celebrate Literacy honoree); mem. Hist. Commn., City of Bedford, Tex., 1993—; chmn. early literacy com. Tex. State Reading Assn., 1993-96; com. co-chair Campaign for Children, 1st Tex. coun. Camp Fire, 1992-94; educator Ft. Worth Sister Cities, 1991—; Harashin Educator scholar Nagaoka, Japan, 1992; bd. dirs. Ft. Worth Assn. Edn. Young Children, 1986-87; chmn. speakers bur. Ind. Gov.'s Com. for Internat. Yr. of the Child, 1979-80, others. Recipient Excellence in English Edn. award Tex. Joint Coun. Tchrs. English, 1990, Ethel M. Leach award Tex. Woman's U., 1990; named Woman of Yr., Monroe County (Ind.) Girls Club, 1985, Yellow Rose of Tex., 1989, Dillard Tchr. of Week, 1992-93; named to Hon. Order Ky. Cols., 1987; Joe E. Mitchell Disting. Educator honoree Tex. Wesleyan U., 1991; honored Tex. Edn. Agy. Early Childhood Promising Practices (inclusion model), 1993-94, NYL Care Health Plans Chair for Tchg. Excellence in Early Childhood Edn., 1997-98. Mem. NEA, Internat. Reading Assn., Ind. Assn. Edn. Young Children (bd. dirs. 1974-80, pres. 1979-80), Pi Lambda Theta (nat. v.p. 1985-89, pres. 1982-84, pres. Great Lakes Region II 1993-97, Greater Ft. Worth area chpt. Internat. Recognition award region VI Outstanding Pi Lambda Thetan 1992, pub. adv. bd. 1995-97, Edn. Endowment bd. 1996—), Delta Theta Tau, Delta Kappa Gamma. Republican. Baptist. Avocations: poetry, piano, photography, public speaking. Home: 701 Hurst Dr Bedford TX 76022-7425 Office: Ft Worth Ind Sch Dist 100 N University Dr Fort Worth TX 76107-1360

COONROD, ROBERT T., federal agency administrator. Grad., Fordham U., 1966; postgrad., Union U., George Washington U., 1976. Fgn. svc. officer U.S. Info. Agy., Italy, Yugoslavia, 1967; sr. positions Bur. Ednl. and Cultural Affairs U.S. Info. Agy., dir. Am. studies; dep. dir. Voice of Am.; exec. v.p., COO Corp. for Pub. Broadcasting, Washington, 1992-97, pres., CEO, 1997—. U.S. Info. Agy. Jefferson fellow George Washington U., 1976. Office: Corp for Pub Broadcasting 901 E St NW Washington DC 20004-2037

COONS, BARBARA LYNN, public relations executive, librarian; b. Peoria, Ill., June 1, 1948; d. Harold Leroy and Norma (Brauer) C. BA, Stephens Coll., Columbia, Mo., 1970; MA, U. N.C., 1972; MLS, Cath. U., 1982. Research asst. Am. Revolution Bicentennical Office Library of Congress, Washington, 1974-76, editorial asst., office of the Asst. Librarian, 1976-78; ednl. liaison specialist Library of Congress, Washington, 1978-82; dir. rsch. svc. Gray and Co., Washington, 1982-85, v.p., 1985-86; v.p., dir. rsch. svcs. Hill and Knowlton Pub. Affairs Worldwide, Washington, 1986-92, sr. v.p., 1992-95, sr. mng. dir., 1996—; dir. rsch. svcs. Hill and Knowlton USA, 1997—; pres. Library of Congress Profl. Assn., 1982. Mem. Spl. Libraries Assn., Stephens Coll. Alumnae Club of Greater Washington (pres. 1987). Lutheran. Home: 532 N West St Alexandria VA 22314-2159 Office: Hill & Knowlton Pub Affairs Worldwide 600 New Hampshire Ave NW Washington DC 20037-2403

COONS, LARRY R., public parks administrator; b. Drain, Oreg., Mar. 22, 1933; s. Lloyd L. and Frederica B. C.; m. Patricia J. Peterson, Sept. 10, 1955; children: R. Gregory, C. Geoffrey. BS in Polit. Sci., U. Oreg., 1961. Asst. dir. Eugene (Oreg.) Renewal Agy., 1959-60, Portland (Oreg.) Devel. Commn., 1960-65; dir. comty. devel. Town of Salem, Oreg., 1965-68; asst. to city mgr. City of Inglewood, Calif., 1968-72; city mgr. City of Richland, Wash., 1972-77; dir. environ. mgmt. Fairfax (Va.) County, Va., 1978-83; asst. planning and devel. then dir. parks and recreation County of Santa Clara, San Jose, Calif., 1984-94; gen. mgr. open space authority County of Santa Clara, San Jose, 1994—. With U.S. Army Signal Corps, 1953-56. Mem. Internat. City and County Mgmt. Assn. (pres. Wash. 1970), Nat. Assn. of Housing and Redevel. Officials, Am. Soc. for Pub. Adminstrn. E-mail: lcoons@openspaceauthority.org. Office: Santa Clar County Open Space Authority 6146 Carmino Verde Dr Ste D San Jose CA 95119-1460

COONS, RONALD EDWARD, historian, educator; b. Elmhurst, Ill., July 24, 1936; s. William A. and Madeline Louise (Theisen) C. B.A., DePauw U., Greencastle, Ind., 1958; A.M., Harvard U., 1959, Ph.D., 1966. Teaching fellow history Harvard U., 1961-62, 63-66; research fellow Inst. Europäische Geschichte, Mainz, Germany, 1962-63; mem. faculty U. Conn., Storrs, 1966—, prof. history, 1979—, dir. grad. studies, dept. history, 1983-87, 90-98, assoc. chmn., 1993-94, interim chmn., summer 1994. Author: Steamships, Statesmen and Bureaucrats: Austrian Policy Towards the Steam Navigation Company of the Austrian Lloyd, 1836-1848, 1975, I primi anni del Lloyd Austriaco, 1983; editor: Over Land and Sea. Memoir of an Austrian Rear Admiral's Life in Europe and Africa, 1857-1909 (Ludwig Ritter von Höhnel), 1999; mem. editl. bd. Austrian History Yearbook, 1992-94, 96-97, mem. adv. bd., 1994-96, also articles and revs. Mem. exec. com. St. Mark's Episcopal Ch., Storrs, 1976-82, 83-85, asst. organist, 1980-87; mem. exec. com. U. Conn. Friends of Soccer, 1989-98, v.p., 1993-95, pres. 1995-97; mem. exec. com. New Eng. Hosta Soc., 1989-92; co-chair interim com. St. Paul's Episcopal Ch., Willimantic, 1998—. Nat. Endowment Humanities summer fellow, 1969; Am. Council Learned Socs. grantee, 1974, Am. Philos. Soc. grantee, 1974; NIH grantee, 1979; Gladys K. Delmas Found. grantee, 1983-84; Am. Council Learned Socs. grantee, 1985. Mem. AAUP, Am. Hist. Assn., Conf. Group Cen. European History, German Studies Assn., Soc. for Austrian and Habsburg History (exec. com. 1992-97, exec. sec. 1994-96), New Eng. Hist. Assn., Vienna Hist. Soc., Conn. Acad. Arts and Scis., Conn. Hort. Soc., Am. Hosta Soc., New Eng. Hosta Soc., Phi Beta Kappa (chpt. sec. 1976-86, v.p. 1987-88, 99—, pres. 1988-89), Phi Alpha Theta, Phi Mu Alpha. Democrat. Home: 476 Prospect St Willimantic CT 06226-2028 Office: U Conn Dept History 241 Glenbrook Rd Storrs Mansfield CT 06269-2103

COONTS, STEPHEN PAUL, novelist; b. Morgantown, W.Va., July 19, 1946; s. Gilbert Gray and Violet (Gadd) C.; m. Nancy Quereau, Feb. 19, 1971 (div. 1985); children: Rachael Diane Quereau, Lara Danielle Quereau, David Paul; m. Deborah Buell, Apr. 12, 1995. AB in Polit. Sci., W.Va. U., 1968; JD, U. Colo., 1979. Commd. ensign USN, 1968; with attack squadron 196 USN, Whidbey Island, Wash.; flight instr. USN, asst. catapult-arresting gear officer USS Nimitz; pvt. practice Hymes & Coonts Attys., Buckhannon, W.Va., 1980-81; in-house counsel Petro-Lewis Corp., Denver, 1981-86; freelance novelist, 1986—. Author: Flight of the Intruder, 1986 (Author of Yr. award U.S. Naval Inst. 1986), Final Flight, 1988, The Minotaur, 1989, Under Siege, 1990, The Cannibal Queen: An Aerial Odyssey Across America, 1992, The Red Horseman, 1993, The Intruders, 1994, War In the Air, 1996, Fortunes of War, 1998, Cuba, 1999. Trustee W.Va. Wesleyan Coll., 1990-98. Inductee Acad. of Dist. Alumni W.Va. U., 1992.

COOP, FREDERICK ROBERT, retired city manager; b. San Diego, Mar. 1, 1914; s. Ernest Frederick and Hazel (Angier) C.; m. Jean Haven, Feb. 11, 1939; children—Susan, Robert, Thomas, Elizabeth. A.B., U. Calif. at Berkeley, 1935; M.S. in Pub. Adminstrn, U. So. Calif., 1937. Pers. technician Calif. Personnel Bd., 1937-41; pers. dir. Pasadena, Calif., 1941-49; pers. cons. UN, 1947; city mgr. Inglewood, Calif., 1949-56, Fremont, Calif., 1956-58; chief pub. svcs. div. U.S. Ops. Mission to Yugoslavia, 1958-61; city mgr. Newport Beach, Calif., 1961-64, Phoenix, 1964-69; regional dir. HEW, San Francisco, 1969-71; dir. pub. adminstrn. svcs. Arthur D. Little, Inc., San Francisco, 1972-78; pres. Robert Coop Assocs., Moraga, Calif., 1978-81, Coop Mgmt. Svcs. Inc., 1981-91; pres., bd. dirs. Pub. Svc. Skills Inc. Served to lt. comdr. USNR, World War II. Named Young Man of Year, 1947, Young Man of Year Pasadena Jr. C. of C. Mem. Internat. City Mgmt. Assn. (pres. Calif. 1956, regional v.p.), Am. Soc. Pub. Adminstrn. (bd. dirs.), Nat. Acad. Pub. Adminstrn., League Calif. Cities (hon. life. city mgrs. dept.).

COOPER, ALAN MICHAEL, psychiatrist; b. Balt., Mar. 14, 1950; s. William I. and Barbara (Stein) C.; m. Elizabeth Ann Mumper, May 31, 1980; children: William, Leigh. SB, MIT, 1972; MD, Med. Coll. of Va., 1976. Diplomate Am. Bd. Psychiatry and Neurology. Intern neurology Med. Coll. Va., 1976-77, resident psychiatry, 1977-78; resident psychiatry U. Va. Hosps., 1978-79, fellow pain clinic, 1979-80, fellow child and adolescent psychiatry, 1981; instr. psychiatry Harvard Med. Sch., Boston, 1980-81; assoc. in anesthesia (psychiatry) Brigham & Women's Hosp., Boston, 1980-81; dir. diagnostic and evaluation unit David C. Wilson Hosp., Charlottesville, Va., 1982-84; clin. adminstr. psychiatry Va. Bapt. Hosp., Lynchburg, 1984-85; chief psychiatrist Ctrl. Va. Cmty. Svcs., Lynchburg, 1985-92; cons. psychiatrist Ctrl. Va. Tng. Ctr., Lynchburg, 1992—; asst. prof. clin. family medicine U. Va. Sch. Medicine, Charlottesville, 1997—; mem. faculty Lynchburg Family Practice Residency Program, 1997—. Bd. dirs. First Unitarian Universalist Ch. of Lynchburg. MIT Nat. scholar, 1968. Mem. Am. Psychiat. Assn., Am. Soc. Clin. Hypnosis, Psychiat. Soc. of Va., Lynchburg Acad. Medicine, Nat. Assn. for the Dually Diagnosed. Office: Central Virginia Tng Ctr PO Box 1098 Lynchburg VA 24505-1098

COOPER, ALAN SAMUEL, lawyer, educator; b. June 13, 1942; s. Rudey and Rosalie (Schwartz) C.; m. Maxine Jacobs, Aug. 13, 1966 (dec.); children: Lauren K., Jennifer D.; m. Linda Morguelan Klein, April 18, 1999. BA, Vanderbilt U., 1964, JD, 1968. Bar: Tenn. 1968, D.C. 1969, U.S. Dist. Ct. D.C. 1969, U.S. Supreme Ct. Appeals (Fed. cir.) 1975, U.S. Supremem Ct. 1980. Law clk. U.S. Dist. Ct. (mid. dist.), Tenn., 1967-68; assoc. Browne, Schuyler & Beveridge and Browne, Beveridge & DeGrand, Washington, 1968-72, Schyler, Birch, Swindler, McKie & Beckett, Washington, 1972-74; ptnr. Schyler, Banner, Birch, McKie & Beckett, Washington, 1974-94; mem. bd. dirs., shareholder Banner & Witcoff, Ltd., Washington, Chgo., Boston, 1995-97; ptnr. Shaw Pittman Potts & Trowbridge, Washington, N.Y.C., Londo, 1997—; adj. prof. Georgetown U. Law Ctr., 1985—; adviser on trademark law to U.S. del. to Diplomatic Conf. on Revision of Paris Conv. for Protection of Indsl. Property, Nairobi, Kenya, 1981. Mem. ABA (faculty Nat. Insts. on Trademark Litigation 1978-79), Internat. Trademark Assn., D.C. Bar, Bar Assn. D.C., Tenn. Bar Assn., Bethesda Country Club. Jewish. Office: 2300 N St NW Washington DC 20037-1122

COOPER, ALCIE LEE, JR., insurance executive; b. Gadsden, Ala., Aug. 3, 1939; s. Alcie Lee and Jettie Merle (Farabee) C.; m. Audrey May MacAuslan, Sept. 3, 1976. AB, Asbury Coll., 1961; MDiv, St. Paul Sch. Theology, 1966; student, Workers Compensation Coll., 1979. CPCU, Am. Inst. Property and Liability Underwriters, 1991. Claims adjuster Sentry Ins. A Mut. Co., St. Louis, 1967-69; claim supr. Sentry Ins. A Mut. Co., Kansas City, Kans., 1969-72; regional claims supr. Sentry Ins. A Mut. Co., Dallas, 1972-77; home office workers compensation cons. Houston Gen. Ins. Co., Ft. Worth, 1977-79, asst. claims mgr., 1979-82, worker's compensation claims mgr., 1982-85, dir. Field Claim Ctr., asst. v.p. claims, 1986-93; ptnr. Al Cooper & Assocs., distbrs. Amway products, Ft. Worth, 1977—; br. mgr. Hammerman & Gainer, Inc., 1993—; instr. Workers Compensation Sch., 1977-85. Mem. Rep. Presdl. Task Force; bd. dirs. Am. Heart Assn., Tarrant County, Tex., 1983-89. Mem. CPCU Soc. (sec. Ft. Worth chpt. 1994-95, v.p. 1995-96, pres.-elect 1996-97, pres. 1997-98, bd. dirs. 1998-99), Amway Distbrs. Assn. Office: 4425 W Airport Fwy Ste 210 Irving TX 75062-5833

COOPER, APRIL HELEN, nurse; b. Evergreen Park, Ill., Dec. 24, 1951; d. Frank and Anne (Mirocha) Stevens; m. Michael Dennis, June 20, 1970; children: Christine Michelle, Brian Michael, Jeannette Michelle. AAS, Ohio U., 1981, BSN, 1996. RN Ohio; cert. med./surg. nurse, ANCC. Supr. home health care Med. Pers. Pool, Cambridge, Ohio, 1989-91; primary nurse pediat. home care Primary Care Nursing Svcs., Dublin, Ohio, 1989-91; case mgr. Buckeye Home Health Svc., Zanesville, Ohio, 1990-91; with home health svcs. Genesis Home Care, Zanesville, 1981-98. Mem. ANA, Golden Key, Phi Kappa Phi, Sigma Theta Tau, Gamma Pi Delta. Republican. Methodist. Avocations: reading professional journals, interior decorating. Home: 2750 Red Fox Duncan Falls OH 43734-9740

COOPER, ARNOLD COOK, management educator, researcher; b. Chgo., Mar. 9, 1933; s. Millard and Sarah Ellen C.; m. Jean Phillips Lord, Sept. 12, 1959; children: Katherine Lord, David Andrew. BS in Chem. Engring., Purdue U., 1955, MS in Mgmt., 1957; D in Bus. Adminstrn., Harvard U., 1962. Engr. Proctor & Gamble, Cin., 1957-58; asst. prof. Harvard U., Cambridge, Mass., 1961-63; assoc. prof. Purdue U., West Lafayette, Ind., 1963-70; prof. Purdue U., West Lafayette, 1970-84, Weil prof. mgmt., 1984—; vis. assoc. prof. Stanford Univ., Palo Alto, Calif., 1967-68; vis. prof. Manchester (Eng.) Bus. Sch., 1972, IMEDE Mgmt. Devel. Inst., Lausanne, Switzerland, 1977-78; past dir. Grad. Profl. Programs, chmn. Mgmt. Policy Com., Purdue U., West Lafayette; mem. Ind. Employment Devel. Commn., 1982-89, Fed. Adv. Com. on Indsl. Innovation, 1978-79. Author: The Founding of Technologically Based Firms, 1971; co-author: Small Business Management, 1966, Technical Entrepreneurship: A Symposium, 1972, The Entrepreneurial Function, 1977, New Business in America, 1990; contbr. numerous articles to profl. jours. and bus. publs.; mem. editorial bd. Stategic Mgmt. Jour., 1979—, Jour. of Bus. Venturing, 1985—, Acad. of Mgmt. Jour., 1978-84, Jour. High Tech. Mktg., 1986-87. 2d lt. U.S. Army, 1956. Named Sagamore of the Wabash, Gov. of Ind., 1988; recipient Honeywell Master Tchr. award, 1990, Disting. Scholar award Internat. Coun. on Small Bus., 1987, Ten Year Author award, Babson Entrepreneurship Conf., 1990. Mem. Acad. Mgmt. (chmn. bus. policy and strategy divsn. 1978-79, Outstanding Paper award Entrepreneurship Divsn. 1991, 92, Coleman Entrepreneurship Mentor award, 1993, Soc. Fellows/Internat. award for entrepreneurship and small bus. rsch. 1997), Internat. Coun. Small Bus., Strategic Mgmt. Soc. (bd. govs. 1984-86). Home: 616 Ridgewood Dr West Lafayette IN 47906-2367 Office: Purdue Univ Krannert Sch of Mgmt 1310 Krannert West Lafayette IN 47907-1310

COOPER, ARTHUR MARTIN, magazine editor; b. N.Y.C., Oct. 15, 1937; s. Benjamin Albert and Elizabeth (Sadock) C.; m. Amy Levin, June 9, 1979. B.A., Pa. State U., 1959. Writer, reporter Harrisburg Patriot (Pa.), 1964-66; corr. Time mag., N.Y.C., 1966-67; assoc. editor Newsweek, N.Y.C., 1967-76; editor Penthouse mag., N.Y.C., 1976-77, CBS Family Weekly, N.Y.C., 1978-83; editor-in-chief Gentlemen's Quar., Conde-Nast Publs., N.Y.C., 1983—. Served to lt. (j.g.) USN, 1960-63. Profl. journalism fellow Stanford U., 1970-71, Alumni fellow Pa. State U., 1990. Mem. Am. Soc. Mag. Editors (Editor of Yr. 1985). Home: 60 Sutton Pl S Apt 16C New York NY 10022-4168 Office: Conde Nast Publs Gentlemen's Quar 350 Madison Ave New York NY 10017-3704*

COOPER, ARTHUR WELLS, ecologist, educator; b. Washington, Aug. 15, 1931; s. Gustav Arthur and Josephine (Wells) C.; m. Jean Farnsworth, Aug. 30, 1953; children: Paul Arthur, Roy Alan. BA, Colgate U., 1953, MA, 1955; PhD, U. Mich., 1958. Asst. prof. botany N.C. State U., Raleigh, 1958-63, assoc. prof., 1963-68, prof., 1968-71, prof. forestry, 1976-80, 94—, head dept. forestry, 1980-94, faculty athletics rep., 1990—; asst. sec. N.C. Dept. Natural and Econ. Resources, Raleigh, 1971-76; mem. N.C. Coastal Resources Commn., Raleigh, 1976-89, N.C. Environ. Mgmt. Commn., Raleigh, 1989-91; chmn. Com. Scientists for Nat. Forest Mgmt. Act, Washington, 1977-79, 82, Govs. Task Force on Forest Sustainability, 1995-96; bd. dirs. N.C. Environ. Def. Fund, 1987-90, So. Environ. Law Ctr., 1987-90. Trustee N.C. Nature Conservancy, Chapel Hill, N.C., 1977-87; mem. coun. NCAA, 1995-96, mem. Divsn. I mgmt. coun., 1996—. Recipient Am. Motors Conservation award, 1972; Sol Feinstone award SUNY Coll. Environ. Sci. and Forestry, Syracuse, 1982; named Conservationist of Yr., N.C. Wildlife Fedn., 1982. Fellow AAAS, Soc. Am. Foresters (chmn. N.C. chpt. 1984, Appalachian Soc. 1990); mem. Ecol. Soc. Am. (cert. sr. ecologist 1982-97, v.p. 1974, pres. 1981, Disting. Svc. award 1984), N.C. Acad. Sci. (pres. 1979), Assn. Southeastern Biologists. Democrat. Home: 719 Runnymede Rd Raleigh NC 27607-3103 Office: NC State U Dept Forestry Raleigh NC 27695-8008

COOPER, AUSTIN MORRIS, chemist, chemical engineer, consultant, researcher; b. Long Beach, Calif., Feb. 1, 1959; s. Merril Morris and Charlotte Madeline (Wittmer) C. BS in Chemistry with honors, Baylor U., 1981; BSChemE with honors, Tex. Tech U., 1983, MSChemE with honors, 1985. Solar energy researcher U.S. Dept. Energy, Lubbock, Tex., 1983-85; advanced mfg. and process engring. mgr. McDonnell Douglas Space Systems Co., Huntington Beach, Calif., 1986-87, chem.-process line mgr., 1987-89, sr. material and process engr., 1989—. Contbr. articles to profl. jours. Mem. Am. Inst. Chem. Engrs., Am. Chem. Soc., Soc. Advancement of Materials and Process Engrs., Sigma Xi, Omega Chi Epsilon, Kappa Mu Epsilon, Beta Beta Beta. *

COOPER, B. JAY, public relations executive; b. Waterbury, Conn., June 9, 1950; s. Harold and Phyllis Ruth Lillian (Fidler) C.; divorced; children: Sarah Chisamore, Jenny Fidler, Kathryn Jeanne. B.A. in Journalism, Northeastern U., 1973. Reporter Waterbury (Conn.) Rep., 1973-79, editor, 1979-81; press sec., dir. pub. affairs U.S. Dept. Commerce, Washington, 1981-87; dep. White House press sec., dep. asst. to the Pres. Washington, 1987-88, 88-89; dir. comm. Rep. Nat. Com., Washington, 1989-93; sr. v.p. APCO Assocs. Inc., Washington, 1994-97, sr. v.p. stragetic command, 1998—; dir. pub. affairs Yale U., New Haven. Co-author: (series) Regeneration of a City, 1978 (UPI award 1978). Dir. rsch. Sarasin Gov. com., Hartford, Conn., 1978; dir. communications Reagan-Bush Com., Hartford, 1980. Jewish. Home: 760 Elba Rd Alexandria VA 22306

COOPER, BARBARA, federal agency administrator. Dir. spl. projects Office Health Affairs Dept. Def., Washington; with Health Care Fin. Adminstrn., Washington, dir. Office Rsch. and Demonstrations, dir. Office Legislation, acting dep. Office Legislation and Policy, dir. strategic planning. Recipient Presdl. Meritorious Exec. Rank award, 1998. Office: Health Care Financing Adminstrn Rm 323-H Humphrey Bldg 200 Independence Ave SW Washington DC 20201

COOPER, BOBBIE (MINNA LOUISE MORGAN COOPER), volunteer; b. Pierce County, Wash., Nov. 21, 1913; d. William Clarence and Eda (Krause) Morgan; m. Vincent Leon Cooper, Feb. 14, 1936 (div. Oct. 1979); children: Marjorie Suzanne, Nancy Jane, O. Leon. Student, Ariz. State U., Tempe, 1954-57, Grand Canyon U., 1962-63, Phoenix Coll., 1984-87. Supr. Hallmark Cards, Kansas City, Mo., 1930-41; with Iron Lung-Polio Meml. Hosp., Phoenix, 1951-52; ch. and civic vol. Telephone Rsch. & Svcs. Vol., Phoenix, 1952-60, 60-94; music rschr. KOY, 1970-80. Officer Oasis Women's Club, Gen. Fedn. Women's Clubs, Phoenix, 1943-88; chmn. bd. dirs. 21st Century Charter Schs. of Ariz., 1995—. Mem. Valley Innkeepers Assn. Republican. Baptist. Avocations: travel, meditating, cross word puzzles, family.

COOPER, CARDELL, housing and urban development administrator. B in Polit. Sci., Montclair State U., 1974; MPA, Rutgers U. Mayor East Orange, N.J.; with Solid Waste and Emergency Response Program, EPA, Washington; asst. sec. Office of Cmty. Planning and Devel., Dept. Housing and Urban Devel., Washington; mem. U.S. Conf. of Mayors Delegation to Poland, 1990; N.J. chmn. Bill Clinton-Al Gore 1996 Coordinated Victory Campaign, 1996; mem. adv. bd. U.S. Conf. of Mayors, chair health and human svcs. com., task force on immigration; mem. Nat. League Cities Transp. and Comm. Com. Office: Office of Cmty Planning and Devel 451 7th St SW Washington DC 20410-0001

COOPER, CAROL DIANE, publishing company executive; b. Williamsport, Pa., Aug. 14, 1953; d. Ray Calvin and Norma Jane (Stiger) C. BA, Colgate U., 1975; cert. in pub., Radcliffe Coll., 1975; MA, Syracuse (N.Y.) U., 1977. Editorial and promotion asst. St. Martin's Press, N.Y.C., 1977-78; sales rep., 1978-79; dir. sales, v.p. Clearwater Pub. Co., Inc., N.Y.C., 1979-80, dir. mktg., 1980-81, v.p., 1980-83; exec. v.p. K.G. Saur Inc., N.Y.C., 1983-87; v.p., pub. R.R. Bowker Co., N.Y.C., 1987-90; v.p. internat. pub. ops. Bowker, Martindale Hubbell, N.Y.C., 1990-92; v.p. internat. pub. ops. Reed Reference Pub., New Providence, N.J., 1992-96, also bd. dirs., 1996; v.p., assoc. pub. Martindale-Hubbell, New Providence, 1996—. Mem. ALA (com. microform standards rsch. and tech. standards div. 1986). Office: Martindale Hubbell 121 Chanlon Rd New Providence NJ 07974-1544

COOPER, CAROLINE ANN, hospitality faculty dean; b. Gardner, Mass., Oct. 16, 1943; d. Frank D. and Florence M. (O'Neil) Toohey; m. Paul Geoffrey Cooper, Apr. 16, 1972; children: Geoffrey Paul, Heather Ann. BS, Russell Sage Coll., 1966; MBA, Bryant Coll., 1983; postgrad., U. Mass., Boston. Adminstrv. dietitian Mass. Gen. Hosp., Boston, 1967-68; with rsch., devel., mktg. Mkt. Forge Co., Everett, Mass., 1968-71; food svc. administr. Jane Brown R.I. Hosp., Providence, 1971-74; self-employed pres., cons. pvt. practice, Attleboro, Mass.; from instr. to assoc. prof. Johnson & Wales U., Providence, 1978-86, acad. coord., 1984-86, dept. chair HRI, Hospitality, Food Svc. mgmt. and tourism, 1986-91; asst. dean Hospitality Coll., 1991-94, dean, 1995—; del. White House Conf. on Travel and Tourism, 1995, mem. implementation team, 1995-96; mem. adv. bd. Ednl. Found. of the nat. Restaurant Assn., 1998—; mem. bd. advisors Acad. Travel and Tourism, 1997—. Vol. Parent Orgn. for Sch., 1978-91, Pub. Sch. System, 1981-84, Cmty. Sports Program, 1989-95. Recipient Hon. Doctorate medallion N.Am. Foodsvc. Assn. Mfrs.; named Pacesetter Nat. Roundtable for Women, 1989. Mem. Am. Dietetic Assn., Am. Hotel Motel Assn. (trustee Ednl. Inst. 1990—, nominating com. 1996-99, chmn. 1999—, exec. com. 1998—, chmn. certification commn., 1998—, Outstanding Educator 1990), Am. Hotel and Motel Industry, Computer Application Food Svc. Edn. (pres. 1987-89), Internat. Coun. on Hotel Restaurant Inst. Edn. (bd. dirs., pres. N.E. chpt. 1992-93, pres. 1994-95, chmn. bd. 1995-96). Office: Johnson and Wales U Abbott Park Pl Providence RI 02903

COOPER, CHARLEEN FRANCES, special and elementary education educator; b. Jamaica, N.Y., Oct. 23, 1948; d. Charles and Dolly (Oakes) Fells; m. Chris M. Cooper, June 23, 1969 (div.); children: Chris A., Scott F. BS in Spl. Edn. cum laude, Coll. of St. Joseph, Rutland, Vt., 1985; postgrad., The Provider; MA in Edn., Castleton State Coll., 1994. Cert. spl. and elem. edn. tchr., Vt.; cert. learning specialist/consulting tchr. spl. edn. Spl. edn. and resource rm. tchr. Rutland City Pub. Sch., 1985-88; tchr. spl. edn., multi-handicapped Rutland Cen. Supervisory Union, 1988-91; spl. edn. and resource rm. tchr. Addison-Rutland Supervisory Union, 1991-92; mktg. instr. Stafford Tech. Ctr., Rutland City Pub. Schs., 1992-93; vocat. rehab. employment facilitator State of Vt., 1995-96; chpt. 1 title 1 head instr. Bennington Sch., Inc., 1996-97; title 1 head instr. Catamount Elem., Bennington, Vt., 1997—; resource rm. tchr. Catamount Elem., Bennington, 1998; coord. program, instr. Integration of Proctor High Sch. Students with Spl. Needs, 1989-91. Coll. of St. Joseph scholar. Avocations: gardening, motorcycling, flying. Home: PO Box 40 North Clarendon VT 05759-0040 Office: Catamount Elem Sch School St Bennington VT 05201

COOPER, CHARLES DONALD, association executive, editor, retired career officer; b. Exeter, N.H., Dec. 19, 1932; s. Herbert Almon and Mildred (Pitcher) C.; m. Beverly Lorraine Hummel, May 18, 1957; children: Liane, Dale, Kristin. BS, Northwestern U., 1954; grad., Indsl. Coll. Armed Forces, Washington. Commd. 2d lt. USAF, 1954, advanced through grades to col., 1977; mem. ops. staff USAF, various AF bases, 1955-76; dep. chief pub. affairs USAF Fifth AF, Yokota Air Base, Japan, 1975-77; dep. chief community rels. USAF, Washington, 1977-78, dep. chief media rels., 1978-80, chief media rels., 1980-82, dir. internal info., 1982-83; vol. community svc. Springfield, Va., 1984-86; exec. editor The Ret. Officer Assn., Alexandria, Va., 1986-88, dir. publs., 1988-96. Contbr. articles to mags. and newspapers in field. Trustee Messiah United Meth. Ch., Springfield, 1985-96, mem. adminstrv. bd., 1998—, asst. treas., 1999—. Decorated Meritorious Svc. Medal, D.F.C., Air medal with five oak leaf clusters, Legion of Merit. Mem. Pub. Rel. Soc. Am., Daedalian Club, Masons, Shriners. Avocations: gardening, snow skiing.

COOPER, CHARLES GILBERT, toiletries and cosmetics company executive; b. Chgo., Apr. 4, 1928; s. Benjamin and Gertrude Cooper; m. Miriam Meyer, Feb. 11, 1951 (dec. Oct. 17, 1984); children: Debra, Ruth, Janet, Benjamin; m. Nancy Cooper. BS in Journalism, U. Ill., 1949. With sales promotion dept. Maidenform Co., N.Y.C., 1949-51; with circulation promotion dept. Esquire mag., Chgo., 1951-52; with Helene Curtis Industries Inc., Chgo., 1953-96, pres. salon div., 1971-75, pres. consumer products div., 1975-82, corp. exec. v.p., 1982-85, exec. v.p., COO, 1985-93, sr. v.p., 1993-96; sr. ptnr. GCG Ptnrs.; bd. dirs. Devon Bank. Bd. dirs. Coun. for Jewish Elderly. With AUS, 1952-53. Office: 225 W Wacker Dr Ste 1800 Chicago IL 60606-1229

COOPER, CHARLES GORDON, insurance consultant, former executive; b. Providence, May 31, 1927; s. Irving and Helen Christina (Skog) C.; m. Barbara Caroline Termohlen, June 17, 1950; 1 dau., Marie Suzanne. B.A., Ohio Wesleyan U., 1949. C.L.U. Group rep. Washington Nat. Ins. Co., 1949-53, asst. mgr., 1953-58, mgr., 1958-63, dir. assn. field services, 1963-65, asst. sec., 1965-67, 3d v.p., 1967-72, 2d v.p., 1972-77, v.p., 1977-79, sr. v.p., 1979-83; exec. v.p. Washington Nat. Ins. Co., Evanston, Ill., 1983-85; dir., mem. exec. com. Washington Nat. Ins. Co., 1979-85; sr. v.p.-mktg. Washington Nat. Corp., parent co. Washington Nat. Ins. Co., Evanston, 1983-85; cons. Washington Nat. Corp., parent co. Washington Nat. Ins. Co., 1985—; dir. Washington Nat. Trust Co., 1974-85, chmn. exec. com., 1979-85; chmn., dir. Washington Nat. Fin. Services, Inc., 1979-85; pres., dir. Washington Nat. Equity Co., 1973-85, chmn. bd., 1983-85. Bd. dirs. North Shore Assn. for Retarded, Evanston, 1983—. Served with USNR, 1945-46, PTO. Mem. Am. Coll. Life Underwriters, Chartered Life Underwriters, Nat. Assn. Life Underwriters, Chgo. Life Underwriters Assn., Nat. Assn. Health Underwriters, Chgo. Health Underwriters. Republican. Club: Ivanhoe (Ill.). Lodges: Masons, Shriners.

COOPER, CHARLES HOWARD, photojournalist, newspaper publishing company executive; b. Clinton, N.C., July 17, 1923; s. John Howard and Ella Jane (Bass) C.; m. Nell Elizabeth Slaughter, Jan. 2, 1943; children: Charles Howard, John Phillip. Grad., U.S. Air Force Sch. Photography, 1943. Chief photographer, mgr. photo dept. Durham Herald Co. (N.C.), 1945-85; pub. Durham Morning Herald, 1945, Durham Sun, 1945-85; chmn. Miss Nat. Press Photographer Pageant, 1952, 53, 55. Mem. Citizens Safety Com., Durham, 1961-71. Served with USAAF, 1942-45, ETO. Mem. Nat. Press Photographers Assn. (life, exec. dir. 1963—Fellowship award, Joseph A. Sprague award 1961, Pres.'s medal 1964, 67, Merit award 1965, Joseph Costa award 1977, exec. dir. emeritus 1998), Carolinas Press Photographers Assn. (life, pres. 1952-54). Democrat. Baptist. Office: Nat Press Photographers 6 Lucerne Ln Durham NC 27707-3839

COOPER, CHESTER LAWRENCE, research administrator; b. Boston, Jan. 13, 1917; s. Israel and Hannah (Levenson) C.; m. Orah Pomerance, July 23; children: Joan Laurence Gould, Susan Louise Cooper. BS, NYU, 1939, MBA, 1941; PhD, Am. U., Washington, 1960. Asst. dep. dir. CIA, Washington, 1947-62; sr. staff White House/NSC, Washington, 1962-66, U.S. Dept. State, Washington, 1966-70; dir. internat. div. Inst. Def. Analysis, Arlington, Va., 1970-72; fellow Woodrow Wilson Internat. Ctr. Scholars, Washington, 1972-75; dep. dir. Inst. Energy Analysis, Oak Ridge, Tenn., 1975-83; dep. dir., acting dir. Internat. Inst. Applied Systems Analysis, Laxenburg, Austria, 1983-85; coord. internat programs Resources for the Future, Washington, 1985-92; dep. dir. Battelle Pacific N.W. Labs., Washington, 1992—; cons. Aspen Inst., Sci. Policy Assocs., Washington, Screenscope Films, Washington. Author: The Lost Crusade, 1971 (award 1971), The Lion's Last Roar, 1977; editor: Growth in America, 1976, Science for Public Policy, 1987. Nat. War Coll. scholar, Washington, 1952-53, Internat. Inst. Applied Systems Analyses hon. scholar, Laxemburg, Austria, 1986. Mem. Coun. Fgn. Rels., Poets, Essayists, Novelists, Cosmos Club. Avocations: fishing, gardening, sculpting, 18th Century Furniture and Silver. Home: 7514 Vale St Chevy Chase MD 20815-4004 Office: Battelle Pacific NW Labs 901 D St SW Washington DC 20024-2169

COOPER, CLARENCE, federal judge; b. 1942. BA, Clark Coll., 1964; JD, Emory U., 1967; MA, Harvard U., 1978. Atty. Atlanta Legal Aid Soc., 1967; asst. dist. atty. Fulton County, 1968-75; judge City of Atlanta Mcpl. Ct., 1975-80, Fulton County Superior Ct., 1980-90, Ga. Ct. Appeals, 1990-93; dist. judge U.S. Dist. Ct. (no. dist.) Ga., Atlanta, 1994—; co-chair Supreme Ct. Commn. Racial & Ethnic Bias in Ct. Sys. Mem. adv. com. Internat. Friendship Force; active Butler St. YMCA, Atlanta Conv. and Visitors Bur., 100 Black Men of Atlanta, Ga. Health Decisions. With U.S. Army, 1968-70. Decorated Bronze Star; recipient Al Thompson Award for Cmty. Svc., Thurgood Marshall award, Outstanding Jurist, 1974. Mem. ABA, NAACP, Nat. Bar Assn., State Bar Ga., Atlanta Bar Assn., Fed. Bar Assn., Gate City Bar Assn., Omega Phi Psi (Omega Man of Yr. award 1991), Kappa Boule, Lawyers Club Atlanta, Old Warhorse Lawyer's Club. Office: Richard B Russell Fed Bldg 1721 US Courthouse 75 Spring St SW Atlanta GA 30303-3309*

COOPER, CLEMENT THEODORE, lawyer; b. Miami, Fla., Oct. 26, 1930; s. Benjamin Leon and Louise (Bethel) C.; m. Nan Coles Cooper; children: Patricia, Karen, Stephanie, Bridgette, Jessica (dec.), Stacy. AB, Lincoln U., 1952; postgrad., Boston U., 1954-55; JD, Howard U., 1958; PhD in Bus. Adminstrn. honoris causa, Colo. Christian Coll. Bar: D.C. 1960, Mich. 1960, U.S. Supreme Ct. 1963. Sole practice Washington, 1960—; adj. prof. Strayer U., Washington; legal cons. No. Calif. Mining Assn. Author: Sealed Verdict, 1964; contbr. articles to legal jours. Mem. adv. coun. D.C. Dept. Welfare, 1964-66; mem. adv. bd. Com. on Irish Ethnicity, N.Y.C. Mem. ABA, ATLA, D.C. Bar Assn., Nat. Bar Assn., ACLU, Am. Judicature Soc., Rocky Mountain Mining Law Found., Internat. Platform Assn., Nat. Assn. Securities Dealers (arbitrator), Alpha Phi Alpha. Home: 728 Dahlia St NW Washington DC 20012-1844 Office: PO Box 76135 Washington DC 20013-6135

COOPER, CYNTHIA, professional basketball player; b. Apr. 14, 1963. Degree in phys. edn., U. So. Calif., 1986. Basketball player Segovia, Spain, 1986-87, Parma, Italy, 1987-94, 96-97, Alcamo, Italy, 1994-96; basketball player Houston Comets Women's NBA, 1997—; mem. U.S. Goodwill Games, 1986, 90, World Championships, 1986, 90, Pan Am Games, 1987. Recipient Gold medal Pan Am Games, 1987, Gold medal U.S. Olympic basketball, 1988, Bronze medal, 1992; named MVP Women's NBA Championship, 1997, 98. Office: Houston Comets Two Greenway Plz Ste 400 Houston TX 77046-3865*

COOPER, DAVID E.K., foundation executive; b. Honolulu, Aug. 12, 1941; s. Robert Lewis and Lucy Kapuakela (Kamakaú C.; m. Katherine S. Arakaki, June 16, 1962; children: Troy A.K., Bradley H.K., Ethan Scott K.K. BA in English, U. Hawaii Manoa, Honolulu, 1963; MA in English Lit., U. Mo., Kansas City, 1974; MS in Counseling Psychology, L.I. U., 1976; postgrad., Harvard U., 1992. Cert. fin. planner. Commd. 2d lt. U.S. Army, 1963, advanced through grades to brig. gen., 1993, ret., 1993; pres. Pacific Am. Found., Washington, 1993—; CEO Hana Engring., Inc., Honolulu, 1994—, Pacific Nations Internat., Washington, 1997—. Contbr. articles to army mags. Chmn. Fed. Adv. Com. on Minority Vets., Washington, 1995—; bd. govs. Japanese Am. Nat. Mus., L.A., 1996—. Decorated Silver Star with oak leaf cluster, Combat Inf. badge; Coun. on Fgn. Rrels. fellow, 1985. Mem. U. Hawaii Alumni Assn. (pres. Nat. Capital Region chpt. 1997—), Kamehameha Alumni Assn. (dir. East Coast chpt. 1994—), Inst. for Cert. Fin. Planners, 173rd Soc., 25th Inf. Divsn. Soc., Phi Kappa Phi. Avocations: tennis, running, biking. Home: 1106 W Abingdon Dr Alexandria VA 22314-1201

COOPER, DENNIS LAWRENCE, oncologist, educator; b. Chgo., Apr. 15, 1954; s. Marvin and Gwendolyn (Janowicz) C.; m. Jean Bolognia, Aug. 25, 1984. BS, Loyola, Chgo., 1975; MD, Rush Med. Coll., 1979. Diplomate Am. Bd. Internal Medicine, Am. Bd. Oncology. Intern internal medicine Yale-New Haven Hosp., 1979-80, resident internal medicine, 1980-82; chief resident internal medicine U. Pitts., 1982-83; fellow oncology Yale U., New Haven, 1983-86, asst. prof. internal medicine, 1986-93, assoc. prof., 1993—, dir. stem cell transplant program, 1994-97, clin. dir. bone marrow and stem cell transplant program, 1997—; clinic chief Oncology Outpatient Svc., New Haven, 1995-98; dir. Oncology Fellowship Program, New Haven, 1993-97, Inpatient Svc. Oncology, New Haven, 1994—. Editl. bd. Cancer Investigation, 1993—, Cancer Therapeutics, 1998—; contbr. articles to profl. jours. Basketball coach Orange (Conn.) Recreation League, 1991-92. Mem. Internat. Soc. Hematotherapy and Graft Engring., Am. Soc. Clin. Oncology, Conn. Oncology Assn. Avocations: softball, baseball. Home: 140 Patten Rd North Haven CT 06473-2830 Office: Yale U Sch Medicine 333 Cedar St New Haven CT 06510-3289

COOPER, DIANN CARYN, critical care nurse, staff development specialist; b. Meadville, Pa., May 13, 1965; d. James Dennis and Mary Ann (Graves) Ainsworth; m. Bard Eugene Cooper, Sept. 16, 1989. BSN, Villa Maria Coll., Erie, Pa., 1987; MSN, Edinboro U. of Pa., 1995. Cert. CPR instr. Clin. nurse Hamot Med. Ctr., Erie, 1987-92, staff devel. coord., 1992—. Mem. AACN, Nat. Nurses Staff Devel. Orgn., Sigma Theta Tau.

COOPER, DONALD LEE, physician; b. Columbus, Kans., Aug. 11, 1928; s. Calvin M. and J. Pearl (Mullen) C.; m. Dona Faye Maddux, June 4, 1950; children—Donald Lee, Catherine Susan, Cheryl Lyn, Tad Houston. A.B., Kans. State Coll., 1949; M.D., U. Kans., 1953. Intern St. Mary's and Childrens Mercy hosps., Kansas City, Mo., 1953-54; pvt. practice medicine Manhattan, Kans., 1956-57; team physician, asst. dir. Health Center Kans. State U., 1957-60; dir. health service, team physician Okla. State U. Hosp. and Clinic, Stillwater, 1960-90, dir. athletic medicine, 1990—; vis. lectr. div. sportsmedicine, dept. orthopedic surgery Coll. Medicine U. Okla. Health Scis. Center, 1974—; liaison officer Am. Coll. Health Assn. to Nat. Athletic Trainers Assn., 1963—; Am. chmn. 1st Am.-Soviet Conf. on Student Health, Moscow, Russia, 1967; team physician U.S. Olympic Team, 1967-68; mem. Pres.'s Coun. Phys. Fitness and Sports, 1981-92, del. to Moscow to rev. phys. culture and olympic tng. sites in Russia, 1989; team physician U.S. Deaf Olympic Team, Los Angeles, 1985; elected chmn. Joint Commn. on Competitive Safegaurds and Med. Aspects of Sports, 1986. Author: (with others) Standard Nomenclature of Athletic Injuries, 1966; Contbr. (with others) articles med. jours. Served to capt. USAF, 1954-56. Recipient Pres.'s Challenge Sportsmedicine award Nat. Athletic Trainers Assn., 1974, Bill Coltrin Meml. award Western Athletic Conf. Sports Writers Assn., 1974, Edward Hitchcock award Am. Coll. Health Assn., 1975; named among 10 healthy American fitness leaders Nat. Jaycees, Pres.'s Coun. on Physical Fitness and Sports, Allstate Ins. Co., 1995; inductee Okla. Hall of Fame, 1998. Mem. AMA (chmn. com. med. aspects sports 1971-76, chmn. 1976-77, mem. coun. sci. affairs 1976-79), Nat. Collegiate Athletic Assn. (med. cons. to football rules com. 1969-75), Am. Coll. Health Assn. (past pres., exec. com.), Southwestern Coll. Health Assn. (past pres.), Nat. Athletic Trainers Assn., Alpha Omega Alpha, Nu Sigma Nu. Presbyterian (elder 1971—). Club: Lion. Home: 1001 W Liberty Ln Stillwater OK 74075-2113 Office: OK State U Hosp and Clinic Stillwater OK 74074 *We must realize and accept that life is neither fair nor unfair; one must accept it as a unique journey composed of all types of experiences. It is not so much what happens to us as we go along in life, it is how we react to what happens that is so very important.*

COOPER, DORIS JEAN, market research executive; b. N.Y.C., Dec. 17, 1934; d. James N. and Georgina N. (Cassidy) Breslin; student Sch. of Commerce, N.Y. U., 1953-55, Hunter Coll., 1956-57; m. S. James Cooper, June 17, 1956; 1 son, David Austin. *Considers herself the embodiment of the American Dream. First generation of Scottish parents who immigrated during the Great Depression. Well educated in NYC Public School system. Married many years to same man. Have one son who is currently on leave from The Department of Defense returning to the Pentagon in January, 2000 having earned a Doctorate in non-proliferation. Doris Cooper established and continues to successfully run a business in the field of Market Research. She has earned the affection of good friends and feels her life to be full and* *rich and is grateful for all of these blessings.* Asst. coding supr. Crossley S-D Surveys, N.Y.C., 1955-57; asst. field supr. Trendex, Inc., N.Y.C., 1957-59; coding dir. J. Walter Thompson Co., N.Y.C., 1960-63, Audits & Surveys, N.Y.C., 1964-65; pvt. practice cons., N.Y.C., 1965-73; pres. Cooper Svcs., Hastings-on-Hudson, N.Y., 1973—; pres., CEO computer tabulation and lang. manipulation Doris J. Cooper Assocs., Hastings-on-Hudson, N.Y., 1989—; cons. market rsch. Mem. Am. Mktg. Assn. (N.Y. chpt.), Nat. Bus. Women Owners Assn., Am. Assn. Pub. Opinion Researchers (N.Y. chpt.), Acad. Health Svcs. Mktg., Hastings C. of C. Republican. Episcopalian. Office: Doris J Cooper Assocs Ltd 1 North St Hastings On Hudson NY 10706-1542

COOPER, EDWARD HAYES, lawyer, educator; b. Highland Park, Mich., Oct. 13, 1941; s. Frank Edward and Margaret Ellen (Hayes) C.; m. Nancy Carol Wybo, June 29, 1963; children: Lisa, Chandra. A.B., Dartmouth Coll., 1961; LL.B., Harvard U., 1964. Bar: Mich. 1965. Law clk. Hon. Clifford O'Sullivan, U.S. Ct. of Appeals, 1964-65; practice law, Detroit, 1965-67; adj. prof. Wayne State U. Law Sch., 1965-67; assoc. prof. U. Minn. Law Sch., 1967-72; prof. law U. Mich. Law Sch., Ann Arbor, 1972-88, assoc. dean for acad. affairs, 1981-94; Thomas M. Cooley prof. of law, 1988—; advisor Restatement of the Law, 2d Judgments, 1976-80, Complex Litigation Project, Restatement of the Law, 3d Torts-Apportionment, Transnational Procedure Project; reporter fed. state juridstiction com. Jud. Conf. U.S., 1985-91; mem. civil rules adv. com., 1991-92, reporter, 1992—; reporter Uniform Transfer of Litigation Act, 1989-91. Author: (with C.A. Wright and A.R. Miller) Federal Practice and Procedure: Jurisdiction, Vols. 13-19, 1975-81, 3d edit., 1999—; contbr. articles to law revs. Mem. ABA, Mich. Bar Assn., Am. Law Inst. (council). Office: U Mich 408 Hutchins Law Sch Ann Arbor MI 48109

COOPER, EDWARD SAWYER, cardiovascular internist, educator; b. Columbia, S.C., Dec. 11, 1926; s. Henry Howard and Ada Crosland (Sawyer) C.; m. Jean Marie Wilder, Dec. 2, 1951; children—Lisa Marie Cooper Hudgins, Edward Sawyer Jr. (dec.), Jan Ada, Charles Wilder. A.B., Lincoln U., Pa., 1946; M.D., Meharry Med. Coll., Nashville, 1949; M.S., U. Pa., 1972. Diplomate Nat. Bd. Med. Examiners, Am. Bd. Internal Medicine. Intern Phila. Gen. Hosp., 1949-51, resident in medicine, 1951-54, NIH fellow in cardiology, 1956-57, pres. med. staff, 1969-71, co-dir. Stroke Research Ctr., 1968-74, chief med. service, 1973-76; prof. emeritus medicine U. Pa., Phila., 1973—; dir. Independence Blue Cross; mem. adv. bd. Hypertension Detection and Followup Program, Phila., 1974—. Trustee Am. Found. Negro Affairs, 1969—, Rockerfeller U., 1992—. Served to capt. USAF, 1954-56. Fellow Phila. Coll. Physicians (council), Am. Coll. Chest Physicians; mem. ACP (master), Am. Heart Assn. (chmn., dir., past nat. pres.), Alpha Omega Alpha. Democrat. Methodist. Research on stroke and hypertension. Home: 6710 Lincoln Dr Philadelphia PA 19119-3155 Office: University of Pa Hosp 3400 Spruce St Philadelphia PA 19104-4204

COOPER, EDWIN LOWELL, anatomy educator; b. Oakland, Tex., Dec. 23, 1936; s. Edwin Ellis and Ruthesther (Porché) C.; m. Helene Marie Antoinette Tournaire, Sept. 13, 1969; children—Astrid Madeleine, Amaury Tournaire. B.S., Tex. So. U., 1957; M.S., Atlanta, 1959; Ph.D., Brown U., 1963. UHPHS postdoctoral fellow UCLA, 1962-64, asst. prof. anatomy, 1964-69; assoc. prof., 1969-73, prof., 1973—; vis. prof. Instituto Politecnico Nacional, Mexico City, 1966; Mem. adv. com. Office Sci. Personnel, NRC, 1972-73; mem. bd. sci. counselors Nat. Inst. Dental Research, 1973—. Author: Comparative Immunology; Editor: Phylogeny of Transplantation Reactions, 1970, Invertebrate Immunology, 1974; founding editor: Internat. Jour. Developmental and Comparative Immunology, 1977—. Guggenheim fellow, 1970; Fulbright scholar, 1970; Eleanor Roosevelt fellow Internat. Union Against Cancer, 1977-78. Fellow AAAS (council 1971, chmn. sect. 1976); mem. Soc. Invertebrate Pathology (founding), Pan Am. Congress Anatomy (founding), Am. Assn. Anatomy, Transplantation Soc., Am. Assn. Immunologists, Am. Soc. Zoologists (program officer 1974—, founder div. comparative immunology 1975, pres.), Brit. Soc. Immunology, Societe d'Immunologie Francaise, Sigma Xi. Office: UCLA Sch Medicine Dept Neurobiology 10833 Le Conte Ave Los Angeles CA 90095-3075 *Aims must always be high, so that when fate is cruel, there is somewhere to fall. Aiming for the bottom leaves nowhere to fall.*

COOPER, ELAINE JANICE, physical therapist; b. Detroit, Apr. 26, 1937; d. Morris and Sally (Mack) Braverman; divorced; children: Jeffrey, Michael, Jonathan. BS, U. Mich., 1959; cert. in massage therapy. Supr. Rehab. Inst., Detroit, 1959-61; cons. Redford (Mich.) Community Hosp., 1963-73; cons. in field Detroit, 1970-78; asst. dir. William Beaumont Hosp., Royal Oak, Mich., 1979-81; pres., cons. Cooper Ctr. for Phys. and Massage Therapies, Inc., Farmington Hills, Mich., 1981—; cons. Drs. Sobel & Castle, Detroit, 1965-66; peer reviewer ins. co. Mem. Am. Phys. Therapy Assn. (edn. com. 1969), Mich. Phys. Therapy Assn., Biofeedback Soc. Mich., Am. Massage Therapy Assn., Mich. Dance Assn., Mich. State C. of C. (health care com.), Brookfield Highlands Club (chmn. land devel., restrictions coms. 1979-85). Avocations: dance, running, aerobics, skiing, karate (Black Belt Isshinryu Karate). Office: Cooper Ctr for Phy and Massage Therapies Inc 31800 Northwestern Hwy Ste 110 Farmington Hills MI 48334-1663 *Personal philosopy: The greatest thing in the world is not so much where we stand, as in what direction we are moving. (Oliver Wendell Holmes).*

COOPER, ELVA JUNE, artist, writer; b. Wilmore, Ky., Mar. 18, 1933; d. Scott Combs and Rhoda Mae (Hundley) Bishop; m. Lowell Howard Cooper, Nov. 29, 1952; children: Lowell Scott, Linda Janet, Candace Lea, Connie Lynn, June Roxanne. Student, Georgetown Coll., 1952-53, Southwestern Jr. Coll., 1961, U. West Fla., 1994, Pensacola Jr. Coll., 1998. Owner June Bug Art and Gifts, Pensacola, Fla., 1973-94, The Studio, Pensacola, Fla., 1986-94. Cons. editor Church Recreation, 1993-95; contbr. articles to mags. Drama writer, dir. Myrtle Grove Bapt. Ch., Pensacola, Fla., 1977-96, artist in residence, 1973-96, discipleship tng. dir., 1973-79, 88-97; sec. Lillian (Ala.) First Bapt. Ch., 1984-95; writer Bapt. Sunday Sch. Bd., Nashville, Tenn., 1987-98; state recreation leader Fla. Bapt. Conv., Jacksonville, 1994-98; discipleship tng. dir. Pensacola Bay Bapt. Assn., 1994-96. Three time winner of Peggy award Popular Ceramics Mag., 1970; numerous other awards in art shows. Mem. Quayside Art Gallery (asst. publicity, 1984), Foley Art Assn., Art Study Club. Baptist. Avocations: porcelain doll making, sewing, flower arranging, stained glass artist. Office: The Studio 710 N 69th Ave Pensacola FL 32506-4548

COOPER, ERIC, multimedia executive. BA in Math., Harvard U.; PhD in Computer Sci., U. Calif., Berkeley. Chmn., co-founder, CEO FORE Syss., Warrendale, Pa., 1990—; past prof. computer sci. Carnegie Mellon U. Office: FORE Syss 1000 Fore Dr Warrendale PA 15086-7502*

COOPER, EUGENE BRUCE, speech, language pathologist, educator; b. Utica, N.Y., Dec. 20, 1933; s. Clements Everett and Beulah (Wetzel) C.; m. Crystal Silverman, Sept. 12, 1965; children: Philip Adam, Ivan Bruce. BS, SUNY, Geneseo, 1955; MEd, Pa. State U., 1957, DEd, 1962. Pathologist speech and lang. Franklin County Schs., Chambersburg, Pa., 1957-59; asst. prof. Ohio U., 1962-64, Pa. State U., 1964-66; program specialist U.S. Office Edn., 1966; exec. sec. sensory study sect., rsch. and demonstrations Rehab. Services Adminstrn., HEW, Washington, 1966-67; faculty U. Ala., Tuscaloosa, 1967-96, prof. speech-lang. pathology, 1969-96, chmn. dept. communicative disorders, dir. Speech and Hearing Ctr., 1967-96, prof., chair emeritus, 1996—; Disting. prof. comm. scis. and disorders Nova Southeastern U., 1997—; chmn. Ala. Bd. Examiners Speech Pathology and Audiology, 1979; cons.-at-large Nat. Student Speech-Lang.-Hearing Assn., 1983-88. Author: Personalized Fluency Control Therapy, 1976, Understanding Stuttering: Information for Parents, 1979, revised edit., 1990; (with Crystal Cooper) The Cooper Personalized Fluency Control Therapy Program, 1985, Cooper Assessment for Stuttering Syndromes, 1995; contbr. articles to profl. jours. Fellow Am. Speech, Lang. and Hearing Assn. (legis. coun. 1971-72, 85-97), Divsn. Fluency and Fluency Disorders (steering com. 1993-99, divsn. coord. 1994-99), Am. Speech, Lang. and Hearing Found. (chmn. adv. and devel. bd. 1988-89, trustee 1989-94); mem. Coun. Exceptional Children (pres. divsn. children comm. disorders 1975-76), Nat. Coun. Grad. Programs in Speech, Lang. Pathology and Audiology (pres. 1978-80), Nat. Coun. State Bds. Examiners Speech-Lang. Pathology and Audiology (pres. 1980, 91, mem. exec. bd. 1988-91), Nat. Coun. Comm. Disorders (chmn. 1982), Nat. Alliance Prevention and Treatment on Stuttering (pres. 1985-86), Internat. Fluency Assn. (bd. dirs. 1991-96, pres. 2d world congress on fluency disorders 1997, chmn. specialty commn. on fluency disorders 1997-99).

COOPER, FRANCIS LOREN, advertising executive; b. Dodge Center, Minn., Nov. 30, 1919; s. Harold U. and Grace (Miller) C.; m. Shirley Edith Garniss, Jan. 27, 1945; children: Donald R., Lynne A. Cooper Lichtermann. B.A., U. Minn., 1941. Newspaper reporter Mpls., Rochester, Minn., Waseca, Minn., 1932-41; with N.Y. Life Ins. Co., N.Y.C., 1946-80; pub. rels. counsel N.Y. State Commn. on Organizational Structure of Govt. of City of N.Y., 1952-54; asst. v.p. N.Y. Life Ins. Co., 1961-65, 2d v.p., 1965-67, v.p., 1967-79; mktg. cons. Media Networks, Inc., Dunedin, Fla., 1980—. Chmn. Wilton (Conn.) Charter Revision Com., 1972-73; chmn. Wilton Rep. Com., 1962-70; ofcl. Little League Baseball, 1954-79; chmn. pub. rels. adv. com. City of Dunedin (Fla.), 1983-91; trustee Mease Manor, Inc., Dunedin, 1982—, chmn. bd., 1993—. With USMC, 1941-45, 50-52; lt. col. res., ret. Recipient Meritorious Service award Life Ins. Advertisers Assn., 1980; The Gus Cooper Award named in his honor Life Communicators Assn., 1997. Mem. Pub. Relations Soc. Am. (accredited), Life Ins. Advertisers Assn. (pres. 1971-72), Am. Legion. Presbyterian. Clubs: Masons, Dunedin Country.

COOPER, FREDERICK EANSOR, lawyer; b. Thomasville, Ga., Jan. 18, 1942; s. Martin Milner and Margeret (Philips) C.; m. Helen Dykes, Dec. 20, 1966; children: Frederick Eansor Jr., Johnson Joseph. B.A., Washington and Lee U., 1964; J.D., U. Ga., 1967. Bar: Ga. 1967. Ptnr. firm Herndon & Cooper, Thomasville, 1972-73; gen. counsel Flowers Industries, Inc., Thomasville, 1973-74; gen. counsel, sec. Flowers Industries, Inc., 1974-83, corp. v.p., 1978-83, exec. v.p., 1983-84, pres., 1984-86, vice chmn., 1986-89; of counsel Jones, Day, Reavis & Pogue, Atlanta, 1989-98; chmn. bd., CEO Cooper Smith, Inc. Chmn. Ga. Rep. Com., 1981-83, Am. Bakers Assn., 1994-95; mem. exec. com. U. Ga. Found.; state chmn. George Bush for Pres. campaign. Presbyterian. Club: Rotary. Home: 170 W Paces Ferry Rd NW Atlanta GA 30305-1352*

COOPER, GARY ALLAN, lawyer; b. Bristol, Va., Feb. 3, 1947; s. Earl Clarence and Reba Evelyn (Jenkins) C.; m. Lynn Ellen Weir, Feb. 17, 1973; chidlren: Drew Kelsey, Gavin Morgan. BS in Journalism, U. Tenn., 1969, JD, 1972. Bar: Tenn. 1972, U.S. Dist. Ct. (ea. dist.) Tenn. 1972, U.S. Supreme Ct. 1979, Fla. 1981. Assoc. Luther, Anderson & Ruth, Chattanooga, 1972-76; ptnr. Luther, Anderson, Cleary, Luhowiak & Cooper, Chattanooga, 1976-79, Luther, Anderson, Cleary & Cooper, Chattanooga, 1979-80, Anderson, Cleary & Cooper, Chattanooga, 1981, Fleissner & Cooper, Chattanooga, 1982, Fleissner, Cooper & Marcus, Chattanooga, 1983-88, Fleissner Cooper Marcus & Steger, Chattanooga, 1988-89, Fleissner Cooper Marcus & Quinn, Chattanooga, 1990-97, Franklin, Cooper & Marcus, PLLC, Chattanooga, 1998—. Author: Tennessee Forms for Trial Practice, 1977, 4th edit., 1994, Tennessee Law Office Adminstration, 1977, Tenesee Forms for Trial Practice-Damages, 1997. With USAR, 1972-79. Recipient Herman Hickman Postgrad. scholarship for Athletes U. Tenn., 1969. Mem. ABA, Chattanooga Bar Assn. (bd. dirs. 1984-86), Fla. Bar Assn. (mem. out-of-state practitioners com. 1983-86), Tenn. Bar Assn., Tenn. Def. Lawyers Assn. (chmn. amicus curiae com. 1987-89), Phi Delta Phi, Signal Mt. Golf and Country Club. Republican. Methodist. Avocations: golf, reading. Home: 55 Carriage Hl Signal Mountain TN 37377-2331 Office: Franklin Cooper & Marcus PLLC 837 Fortwood St Chattanooga TN 37403-2317

COOPER, GEORGE, superintendent animal welfare Oklahoma City. DVM, Tukegee Inst., 1966. Supt. animal welfare Okla. City, Okla., 1992—. Mem. Okla. Vet. Med. Assn., Ctrl. Okla. Vet. Med. Assn., Soc. Animal Welfare Adminstrs. Office: Animal Welfare 2811 SE 29th St Oklahoma City OK 73129-8305*

COOPER, GEORGE KILE, business educator; b. Bushnell, Ill., Apr. 5, 1920; s. George Kile and Lula Belle (Robison) C.; m. June Anna Cardell, June 12, 1948; children: Kyle, Ernest, Ruth Anne, William, Jean, Andrew. BEd, Western Ill. State U., 1942; MBA, Ind. U., 1951; PhD, U. Mich., 1962. Cert. secondary sch. tchr., Ill. Bus. tchr. Reynolds (Ill.) Community High Sch., 1946-47; student teaching coordinator Western Mich. U., Kalamazoo, 1948-55, head bus. edn. dept., 1955-62; head bus. edn. and adminstrv. office mgmt. dept. Eastern Ill. U., Charleston, 1962-73, prof. bus. edn. and adminstrv. office mgmt., 1962-82, prof. emeritus, 1982—; vis. research and devel. specialist Ctr. for Vocat. and Tech. Edn., Ohio State U., Columbus, 1973-74. Treas. Wesley United Meth. Ch., Charleston, 1983-93, trustee, 1994-97; chmn. Ill. Curriculum Coun., 1980-81. With AUS, 1942-46. Recipient Alumni Achievement award Western Il.. U., 1994; Cooper Hall named in honor, Ea. Ill., U., 1991. Mem. Ill. Bus. Edn. Assn. (pres. 1971-72, disting. svc. award 1975), Ill. Vocat. Asns. (treas. 1965-69), Ill. State U. Annuitants Assn. (pres.-elect 1986-87), Eastern Ill. U. Annuitants Assn. (pres. 1984-86), Pi Omega Pi (nat. pres. 1966-68), Delta Pi Epsilon (pres. chpt. 1960-61), Phi Delta Kappa (pres. chpt. 1980-81, alt. del. 1986-87). Home: 708 Taft Ave Charleston IL 61920-4135

COOPER, GERALD RICE, clinical pathologist; b. Scranton, S.C., Nov. 19, 1914; s. Robert McFadden and Viola Lavender Cooper; m. Lois Corrina Painter, Mar. 9, 1946; children: Annetta, Gerald Jr., Rodney. AB, Duke U., 1936, MA, 1938, PhD, 1939, MD, 1950. Cert. Am. Bd. Clin. Chemistry. Intern Atlanta VA Hosp., 1950-51, resident, 1951-52; rsch. assoc. Duke U. Sch. Medicine, Durham, N.C., 1939-46; chief chemistry, hematology and pathology Ctrs. for Disease Control, Atlanta, 1952-72; rsch. med. officer Ctrs. for Disease Control, Nat. Ctr. Environ. Health, Atlanta, 1973—. Author (with others) books; contbr. articles to profl. jours. Col. USPHS. Decorated commendation medal, Superior Svc. award, Disting. Svc. medal, Asst. Sec. for Health award for exceptional achievement; recipient Hektoen Silver medal AMA, 1954, Fulton County Med. Achievement award, 1954, Billings Silver medal, 1956, Sigma Xi rsch. award, 1997. Mem. Am. Assn. for Clin. Chemistry (pres. 1984, bd. dirs. 1975-77, chmn. bd. editors of selected methods 1967-80, bd. editors Clin. Chemistry jour. 1970-76, Fischer award 1975, Dade Internat. award 1975, N.J. Gerulat award 1979, SE Sect. Meritorious Svc. award 1989, Outstanding Contbn. Clin. Chemistry award 1992), Internat. Fedn. Clin. Chemistry (apolipoprotein expert panel 1985), Am. Soc. Clin. Pathologists (chmn. clin. chemistry coun. 1974, Continuing Edn. award 1967, 77). Methodist. Home: 2165 Bonnevit Ct NE Atlanta GA 30345-4126 Office: Ctrs for Disease Control Chamblee 102/2319 F20 4770 Buford Hwy NE Atlanta GA 30341-3724

COOPER, GINNIE, library director; b. Worthington, Minn., 1945; d. Lawrence D. and Ione C.; m. Richard Bauman, Dec. 1995; 1 child, Daniel Jay. Student, Coll. St. Thomas, U. Wis., Parkside; BA, S.D. State U.; MA in Libr. Sci., U. Minn. Tchr. Flandreau (S.D.) Indian Sch., 1967-68, St. Paul Pub. Schs., 1968-69; br. libr. Wash. County Libr., Lake Elmo, Minn., 1970-71, asst. dir., 1971-75; assoc. adminstr., libr. U. Minn. Med. Sch., Mpls., 1975-77; dir. Kenosha (Wis.) Pub. Libr., 1977-81; county libr. Alameda County (Calif.) Libr., 1981-90; dir. librs. Multnomah County Libr., Portland, Oreg., 1990—. Chair County Mgr. Assn.; county adminstr. Mayor's Exec. Roundtable. Mem. ALA (mem. LAMA, PLA and RASD coms., elected to coun. 1987, 91, mem. legislation com. 1986-90, mem. orgn. com. 1990—), Calif. Libr. Assn. (pres. CIL, 1985, elected to coun. 1986, pres. Calif. County Librs. 1986), Oreg. Libr. Assn., Pub. Libr. Assn. (pres. 1997-98). Office: Multnomah County Libr 205 NE Russell St Portland OR 97212-3708

COOPER, GLORIA, editor, press critic; b. Oak Park, Ill., Jan. 8, 1931; c. Sam and Madelyn (Brandt) Glaser; m. Wallace J. Cooper, June 3, 1950; children—Alison, Julie. B.A. summa cum laude, Briarcliff Coll., 1970; M.A., Columbia U., 1974. From asst. editor to mng. editor Columbia Journalism Rev., N.Y.C., 1974—. Editor: Squad Helps Dog Bite Victim, 1980, Red Tape Holds Up New Bridge, 1987; contbr. articles, revs., editorials to Columbia Journalism Rev., 1974—. Mem. Soc. Prof. Journalists, Princeton Club (N.Y.C.). Home: 91 Long Hill Rd E Briarcliff Manor NY 10510-2611 Office: Columbia U Columbia Journalism Rev 707 Journalism Bldg New York NY 10027*

COOPER, HAL, television director; b. N.Y.C., Feb. 23, 1923; s. Benjamin and Adeline (Raichman) C.; m. Mary Patricia Meikle, Dec. 21, 1944 (div. 1971); children: Bethami, Pamela; m. Marta Lucille Salcido, June 26, 1971; 1 child, James Benjamin. BA, U. Mich., 1946. Ind. TV dir., writer, producer various prodn. cos., 1948—. Performer Big Bro.'s Rainbow House, Mut. Network, 1936-41, asst. dir. Dock Street Theatre, Charleston, S.C., 1946-48; writer, producer TV Babysitter, DuMont TV Network, 1948-52, The Magic Cottage, 1950-56; dir., producer various daytime TV shows including Search For Tomorrow, others, 1950-57; producer stage play The Troublemakers, London, 1952; dir. numerous TV shows (various episodes) including Death Valley Days, 1965-67, Dick Van Dyke Show, 1962, Gilligan's Island, 1966, I Dream of Jeannie, 1965-69, I Spy, 1966, That Girl, 1967-69, Courtship of Eddie's Father, 1968-71, The Odd Couple, 1970-72, Mary Tyler Moore, 1972, All in the Family, 1972, (pilots) Hot L Baltimore, 1974, One Day At a Time, 1975, All's Fair, 1976, Nancy Walker Show, 1976, The Time of Their Lives, 1987; dir., exec. producer: TV shows including Maude, 1972-78, Phyl and Mikky, 1980, Love, Sydney, 1982-83, Gimme a Break, 1983-87, Empty Nest, 1988-89, Dear John, 1989-92, The Powers That Be, 1992-93. Served to lt. (j.g.) USNR, 1943-46, PTO. Mem. Writers Guild Am., ASCAP, Screen Actors Guild, AFTRA, Actors Equity Assn., Dirs. Guild Am. (mem. dirs. council, nat. bd. dirs.).

COOPER, HAL DEAN, lawyer; b. Marshall County, Iowa, Dec. 8, 1934; s. Truman Braton and Golda Frances (Chadwick) C.; m. Constance Bellinger Simms, Dec. 31, 1960; children: Shannon, Charles, Ellen. Student, Neb. U., 1952-54; B.S. in Mech. Engring., Iowa State U., 1957; JD with honors, George Washington U., 1963. Bar: Iowa 1963, Ohio 1963, U.S. Supreme Ct. 1971. Assoc., ptnr. Fay & Fay, Cleve., 1962-67; ptnr. Meyer, Tilberry & Body, Cleve., 1967-69, Yount, Tarolli, Weinshenker & Cooper, Cleve, 1969-72; trial judge U.S. Ct. Claims, Washington, 1972-75; ptnr. Jones, Day, Reavis & Pogue, Cleve., 1975-95; owner Halco Enterprises, Ltd., Austinburg, Ohio, 1995—. Served with AUS, 1957-59. Mem. Cleve. Intellectual Property Law Assn., Rowfant Club, Clifton Club, Union Club, Rotary. Episcopalian.

COOPER, HARRY EDWIN, historian; b. Oak Park, Ill., Sept. 2, 1939; s. William Cortland Jr. and Adelaide Elizabeth (Beggs) C.; m. Kathleen Mary Lewandowski, Oct. 30, 1985; children: Sean Patrick, Meaghan Mary Kathleen. BS in Bus. Adminstrn., U. Wis., 1965. Cert. scuba diver. Customer svc. mgr. Motorola, Elk Grove Village, Ill., 1965-69; inventory control mgr. No. Petrochem., Des Plaines, Ill., 1969-76; dir. pers. Consumer Periodical, Schaumburg, Ill., 1983-85; v.p. NPC Co., Marion, Iowa, 1985-87; pres. Sharkhunters, Hernando, Fla., 1983—; organizer, leader various hist. trips, 1987—; leading expert on history, activities and pers. of German U-Boats during World War II; founder, exec. dir. Eaglehunters. guest Today in Chgo., 1969; sportscaster Motorsports Internat, 1969; substitute news anchor U.S. Cable 6:00 News, 1980; asst. hist. data for documentaries; contbr. articles to profl. jours.; author: Sponsorship, 1978, 1001 Things to do in Florida for Free, 1984. Sgt. USAF, 1957-61. Class Champion major drag racing event, 1964, set 2 nat. records, 1964, nat. class champion, 1965. Avocation: drag racing. Home: 6885 N Beechnut Loop Hernando FL 34442-3806 Office: Sharkhunters PO Box 1539 Hernando FL 34442-1539

COOPER, ILENE LINDA, magazine editor, author; b. Chgo., Mar. 10, 1948; d. Morris and Lillian (Friedman) C.; m. Robert Seid, May 28, 1972 (div. 1995). BJ, U. Mo., 1969; MLS, Rosary Coll., 1973. Head of children's svcs. Winnetka (Ill.) Libr. Dist., 1974-80; editor children's books Booklist Mag., ALA, Chgo., 1981—. Author: Susan B. Anthony, 1983, Choosing Sides, 1990 (Internat. Reading Assn.-Children's Book Coun. choice 1990), Mean Streak, 1991, (series) Frances in the Fourth Grade, 1991, The Dead Sea Scrolls, 1997, numerous others. Mem. Soc. Midland Authors, Soc. Children's Book Writers, Children's Reading Roundtable. Jewish. Office: Booklist Mag 50 E Huron St Chicago IL 60611-5295

COOPER, IRBY, real estate development company executive; b. Memphis, June 20, 1929; s. Louis and Sade (Kantor) C.; m. Bernice Schramm, June 11, 1950; children: Laurie, Debra, Cynthia, Pace, David. BA, Washington U., St. Louis, 1951. Sports writer Comml. Appeal, Memphis, 1948-54; developer, organizer Cooper Cos., Memphis, 1954—. Pres. NCCJ, Memphis; bd. mem. Jewish Community Ctr., Memphis, Commn. for Improvement for Shelby County, Memphis; pres. Yeshiva of South, Memphis, Hebrew Acad., Memphis; active Better Bus. Bur., also bd. dirs. Recipient Pres.'s award Union Orthodox Jewish Congress Am., 1978. Mem. Home Builder's Assn. (pres.), Memphis C. of C. (bd. dirs.). Club: Memphis State Rebounders (pres.). Office: Cooper Cos 1407 Union Ave Ste 400 Memphis TN 38104-3616

COOPER, J. MICHAEL, advertising executive; b. 1949. Grad., Southwest Mo. State U., 1971. CPA. With Associated Wholesale Grocers, 1971-72, Gen. Grocer Co., 1972-73, McLean Enterprises, 1973-74, Paul Mueller Co., 1974-78; pvt. practice as acct., 1978-81; with Lawrence Photo-Graphic, 1981-84; with Noble & Assocs., Springfield, Mo., 1984—, now sec., CFO. Office: Noble & Assocs 2155 W Chesterfield Blvd Springfield MO 65807*

COOPER, JACK ROSS, pharmacology educator, researcher; b. Ottawa, Ont., Can., July 26, 1924; came to U.S., 1948; s. Harry and Jean (Levine) C.; m. Helen Achbar, Aug. 14, 1951; children: Marilyn, Sheila, Nancy. B.A., Queen's U. Kingston, Ont., 1948; M.A., George Washington U., 1952, Ph.D., 1954; M.A. hon., Yale U., 1971. Asst. prof. pharmacology Yale U., New Haven, 1953-63, assoc. prof., 1963-71, prof., 1971—. Author: The Biochemical Basis of Neuropharmacology, 7th edit., 1996. Served with RCAF, 1944. Smith, Kline and French research fellow, 1950-52; USPHS predoctoral fellow, 1952-54; postdoctoral fellow USPHS, 1954-56; spl. fellow USPHS, London, 1965-66. Mem. Am. Soc. Neurochemistry, Internat. Soc. Neurochemistry, Am. Soc. Pharmacology and Exptl. Therapeutics, Soc. Neurosci. Democrat. Jewish. Home: 11 Jenick Ln Woodbridge CT 06525-1935 Office: Yale U Sch Medicine 333 Cedar St New Haven CT 06510-3289

COOPER, JACKIE, actor, director, producer; b. Los Angeles, Sept. 15, 1922; m. Barbara Kraus, 1954; children: John, Russell, Julie, Cristina. V.p. in charge West Coast Screen Gems, Inc., 1963-69. Began performing at age three; appeared in Our Gang short features; motion pictures include Skippy, 1931, The Champ, 1931, The Bowery, 1933, Treasure Island, 1934, The Love Machine, 1970, The Chosen Survivors, 1973, Superman, 1978, Superman II, 1981, Superman III, 1983, Superman IV, 1987, Surrender, 1987; Broadway plays include King of Hearts; star TV series People's Choice, NBC-TV, 1955-58, Hennessey, CBS-TV, 1959-62, Mobile One, ABC-TV, 1975; numerous TV appearances include Ironside, The Rockford Files, TV films Mobile Two, 1975, Operation Petticoat, 1977; dir. films Stand Up and Be Counted, 1972, Go For the Gold, 1984; dir. and producer numerous TV spls. including Zenith Salutes 25 Years of Television, 1973; dir. numerous TV movies including Perfect Gentlemen, 1978, Rainbow, 1978, Sex and the Single Parent, 1979, Marathon, 1980, White Mama, 1980, Rodeo Girl, 1980, Leave 'Em Laughing, 1981, Rosie: The Rosemary Clooney Story, 1982, Glitter, 1984, The Night They Saved Christmas, 1984, Izzy and Moe, 1985; author: autobiography (with Dick Kliener) Please Don't Shoot My Dog, 1981. Served with USNR, World War II; capt. Res. ret. Decorated Legion of Merit, Navy Commendation medal; recipient Emmy award for best comedy dir. for program M, also best dramatic dir. NATAS, 1974. Office: Contemporary Artists 1317 5th St Ste 200 Santa Monica CA 90401-2358*

COOPER, JAMES ALBERT, JR., electrical engineering educator; b. Columbus, Miss., Feb. 5, 1946; s. James Albert and Juanita (Perkins) C.; m. Barbara Crowder, Aug. 3, 1968; children: David Alan, Katherine Liann. BSEE, Miss. State U., 1968; MSEE, Stanford U., 1969; PhD, Purdue U., 1973. Mem. tech. staff Sandia Labs., Albuquerque, N.Mex., 1968-69; grad. rsch. asst. Sch. Elec. Engring. Purdue U., West Lafayette, Ind., 1970-72, prof., 1983—, dir. Purdue Optoelectronics Rsch. Ctr., 1986-89; mem. tech. staff Bell Labs., Murray Hill, N.J., 1973-83. Contbr. numerous articles to jours., chpts. to books; patentee in field. Fellow IEEE (assoc. editor Trans. on Electron Devices 1983-86). Republican. Mem. United Methodist Ch. Achievements include 10 patents in field; co-origination of the Time-of-Flight measurement technique for the study of high-field transport of electrons along semiconductor/insulator interfaces; design of Bell System's first microprocessor chip; co-development of first silicon carbide nonvolatile memory chips, first silicon carbide monolithic integrated circuits and first SiC DMOS power transistors. Office: Purdue U Sch Elec & Computer Engring 1285 EE Bldg West Lafayette IN 47907-1285

COOPER, JAMES CLINTON, social services administrator, consultant; b. Brinson, Ga., Feb. 3, 1929; s. James and Hattie Lue (Speights) C.; m. Anne

Elizabeth Brown, July 14, 1959. BA, Savannah State U., 1956; MSW, Atlanta U., 1958. Lic. ind. social worker, Ohio. Clin. social worker VA Hosp., Tuskegee, Ala., 1958-61; social work supr. State Hosp., Fulton, Mo., 1961-64; dir. resident ctr. Community Action for Youth, Cleve., 1964-67; exec. dir. Goodrich-Bell Social Settlement, Cleve., 1967-69; dir. social svc. Cleve. State Hosp., 1969-74, Fairhill Mental Health Ctr., Cleve., 1974-84; dir. social svc. Cleve. Psychiat. Inst., 1984-85, cons. on quality assurance, 1985-95; owner Northcoast Vending Co., Cleve., 1992—; pres., chief exec. officer Wayne Morrie, Inc., cons., Cleve., 1983—. Bd. dirs. Hough Area Devel. Corp., Cleve., 1967-77, 1st vice-chmn., 1976-77. Sgt. U.S. Army, 1951-53. Recipient Editors' Choice award Nat. Libr. Poetry, 1993, 96; NASW fellow U. Pitts., 1977-79. Mem. NASW, Acad. Cert. Social Workers, Nat. Assn. Quality Assurance Profls., Internat. Platform Assn. Avocations: reading, writing, bowling, jazz. Home: 14420 Onaway Rd Cleveland OH 44120-2841

COOPER, JAMES HAYES SHOFNER (JIM COOPER), investment company executive, former congressman, lawyer; b. Nashville, Tenn., June 19, 1954; s. William Prentice Jr. and Hortense (Powell) C.; m. Martha Hays; children: Mary Argentine Adams, John James Audubon, Hayes Hightower. BA, U. N.C., 1975, Oxford U., 1977; JD, Harvard U., 1980. Atty. Waller, Lansden, Dortch & Davis, Nashville, 1980-82; mem. 98th-103rd Congresses from 4th Tenn. dist., Washington, 1983-94; mem. budget com. 98th-103rd Congresses from 4th Tenn. dist., mem. energy and commerce com.; mng. dir. Equitable Securities, 1995-99; chmn. bd. Brentwood Capital Adv., 1999—. Bd. dirs. Resources for the Future, 1997—. Rhodes scholar, 1975, Morehead scholar, 1972. Mem. Am. Acad. Ophthalmology (trustee 1996—), Phi Beta Kappa. Democrat. Episcopalian. *

COOPER, JAMES MELVIN, healthcare executive, consultant; b. Prescott, Ariz., Oct. 29, 1940; s. Audrey Louise Cooper; m. Marlene Kitay, Oct. 29, 1960; children: Jamie Lynn Hill, David Paul. BS in Adminstrn., George Washington U., 1976, MBA, 1979. Cert. healthcare exec. Enlisted USN, 1959, advanced through grades to capt.; officer-in-charge pers. support detachment Naval Hosp., San Diego, 1979-81; dir. for ambulatory care Naval Hosp., Camp Pendleton, Calif., 1981-83; manpower analyst The Pentagon, Washington, 1983-85; dir. for adminstrn. Naval Med. Clinics, San Diego, 1985-88; exec. officer Naval Hosp., Long Beach, Calif., 1988-91; comdg. officer U.S. Naval Hosp., Naples, Italy, 1991-93; ret. USN, 1993; v.p. Capital Health Svcs., San Diego, 1994-97; treas. Ramona/Julian Health Care Adv. Coun., 1996—. Bd. dirs., chmn. Ramona (Calif.) Food and Clothes Closet, 1995—. Decorated Legion of Merit, Meritorious Svc. medal (3). Fellow Am. Acad. Med. Adminstrs.; mem. Am. Coll. Healthcare Execs. (diplomate), Am. Coll. Managed Care Execs., San Diego Women in Health Adminstrn., Fed. Health Care Execs. Inst. (life), DAV (life), Assn. Med. Svc. Corps Officers (chmn. mentoring com. 1996—), Kiwanis of Ramona (pres. 1996-97), VFW (life). Avocations: jogging, horseback riding, leather tooling. Home: 2148 Cook Pl Ramona CA 92065-3214 Office: Ambulatory Care Cons PO Box 1912 Ramona CA 92065-0925

COOPER, JAMES MICHAEL, education educator; b. Steubenville, Ohio, July 29, 1939; s. James Stanley and Regina Marie (Coen) C.; m. Susan Callaway, Sept. 1, 1962 (div. June 1978); children: Jeffrey, Craig, Cynthia; m. Shamim Sisson, June 13, 1987. AB in History with distinction, Stanford U., 1961, AM in Edn., 1962, AM in History, 1966, PhD in Edn., 1967. Tchr. Jordan Jr. High Sch. of Palo Alto (Calif.) Unified Sch. System, 1961-63, Palo Alto High Sch., 1963-65; lectr. Stanford U. Sch. Edn., 1967; asst. prof. edn. U. Mass., Amherst, 1968-71; assoc. prof. U. Houston, 1971-74, prof., 1974-84; Commonwealth prof. U. Va. Curry Sch. Edn., Charlottesville, 1984—, dean, 1984-94; chmn. U. Houston faculty senate, 1982; mem. exec. bd. dirs. Holmes Group, East Lansing, Mich., 1985-94; mem. unit accreditation bd. Nat. Coun. Accreditation of Tchr. Edn., Washington, 1986-90. Co-author: Those Who Can, Teach, 8th edit., 1998; editor: Developing Skills for Instructional Supervision, 1984, Classroom Teaching Skills, 6th rev. edit., 1999; co-editor: Kaleidoscope: Readings in Education, 8th edit., 1998. Recipient Florence B. Stratemeyer award Assn. for Student Teaching, Washington, 1967, Fulbright-Hays award Portugal Coun. Internat. Exch. Scholars, Washington, 1980, Outstanding Leader in Tchr. Edn. award Assn. Tchr. Educators, 1990. Mem. ASCD, Am. Ednl. Rsch. Assn., Am. Assn. Colls. for Tchr. Edn. (bd. dirs. 1990-93), Raven Soc., Phi Delta Kappa, Omicron Delta Kappa. Democrat. Roman Catholic. Avocations: golf, traveling. Office: U Va Curry Sch Edn 405 Emmet St Charlottesville VA 22903

COOPER, JAMES RALPH, engineering executive; b. Muskegon, Mich., May 23, 1943; s. Earl Ralph and Henrietta Kathryn (Sebolt) C.; m. Mary Lu Geiger Marony, Jan. 13, 1962 (div. 1964); 1 child, Kenneth James; m. Kathleen Starr Walsh, Oct. 22, 1964; children: Peter, Kevin Shawn, Rhonda Reneé. BS in applied biology, Ferris State Coll., 1974, BS in vocat. edn., 1987; MPA, Golden Gate U., 1983; DEd in higher edn. admin., U. Fla., 1997; grad., C.C. Bus. Officers Acad., 1996. Draftsman Dresser Industries, Muskegon, Mich., 1966-70; sr. engineer, public Dresser Industries, 1974-76; reliability engineer NWL Controls, Kalamazoo, 1976-78; sr. publs. mgr. Teledyne Camera Sys., Arcadia, Calif., 1978-79; sr. rsch. engineer General Dynamics Corp., San Diego, 1979-81; sr. staff engineer, admin. staff asst. Martin Marietta Corp., Denver, 1981-98; assoc. exec. dir. Cmty. Coll. Bus. Officers, Gainesville, Fla., 1995-98; dept. head, tchr. Antelope Valley Christian Schs., Lancaster, Calif., 1998—; cons. engineer U.S. Govt. Kalamazoo, 1975-76, Rancho Cucamonga, Calif., 1984. Author: Engineering Operations Manual, 1982, An Analysis of the Attitudes, Perceptions, and Beliefs of Community College Chief Business Officers and Chief Academic Officers, 1998. Vol. probation officer Probate Ct., Traverse City, Mich. 1989-95. With U.S. Army, 1960-61, 71. Mem. Cmty. Coll. Bus. Officers, Am. Assn. Cmty. Colls. (coun. of chairs). Republican. Lutheran. Avocations: auto restoration, private pilot. Home: 44150 35th St W Apt 3 Lancaster CA 93536-1005 also: 1732 Sunburst Grawn MI 49637-9702 Office: Antelope Valley Christian Sch Lancaster CA 93536-1004

COOPER, JAMES ROBERT, III, computer software company executive, mobile communications consultant; b. Mobile, Ala., Nov. 21, 1938; s. James Robert Jr. and Mary Nell (McMichael) C.; m. Marion Griser (div.); m. Nina Jessica Dotterer; children: Jessie Cameron, Charles Dotterer. BS in Sociology and Psychology, Spring Hill Coll., 1965. With sales and mktg. Proctor & Gamble, 1963-69; cons. to marine industry, 1969-79; pres., founder BCI Utilities Constn., Clearwater, Fla., 1979-84; v.p. aviation and navigation, cofounder ComGrafix, Inc., Clearwater, 1984-94; pres. Satellite Data, LLC; CEO Cooper Rsch., SP; former mem. com. Radio Tech Commn., Washington, Cooper Rsch.; mem. mgmt. systems coun. ATA, interstate truckload corriers conf. Patentee in field. Bd. dirs. Mus. Yachting, Ida Lewis Yacht Club. With USAR, 1958-63. Fellow Royal Inst. Navigation; mem. Nat. Marine Election Assn., Wild Goose Assn., U.S. Yacht Racing Assn. (contbg. mem.). Republican.

COOPER, JAMES RUSSELL, retired law educator; b. New Kensinston, Pa., July 21, 1928; s. John Edward and Isabella Bird (Bowen) C.; m. Carolyn Hocker, Sept. 21, 1953 (div. Dec. 1975); children: L. Rachel, Julia Anderoni, Evan Lloyd, Jennifer Meyer; m. Leigh Ann Brian, Feb. 25, 1995. BS in Econs., U. Pa., 1952, JD, 1955. Bar: D.C., 1955, U.S. Supreme Ct., 1964. Pres., chmn. Radio WKPA-AM, WYDD-FM, New Kensington, 1959-64; urban renewal dir. Redevelopment Authority, New Kensington, 1964-68; assoc. prof. U. Ill., Champaign-Urbana, 1968-74; prof. legal studies Ga. State U., Atlanta, 1974-94, emeritus prof., 1994—. Author: Twilights Last Gleaming, 1992, Real Estate Investments, 3d edit. 1982. Sgt. U.S. Army, 1946-48. Mem. Fed. Bar Assn., D.C. Bar Assn., Am. Real Estate Soc. (founder, dir.). Home: Two West Wesley Rd #4NW Atlanta GA 30305-3500

COOPER, JANE TODD (J. C. TODD), poet, writer, educator; b. Bklyn., Dec. 24, 1943; d. John Curtis and Margaret E. (Johnston) C.; m. William Hudson Shoff; children: Donald Charles Taylor, Eamon Robert Shoff, Savannah Elizabeth Cooper-Ramsey. BA in Lit., Duquesne U., 1965; MFA in Creative Writing, Warren Wilson Coll., 1990. Instr. high sch., Pitts., 1967-73; ednl. dir. drug and alcohol treatment facility Pa. Dept. Corrections, Camp Hill, 1974-78; project mgr. domiciliary care, boarding home provider tng. Pa. State Coll. Medicine, Hershey, 1979-80, 82; dir. primary health care projct Elizabethtown Hosp., Pa., 1980-81; cons. Pa. Council on Arts, 1979-91; creative writing instr. Coll. N.J., 1992-94; bd. dirs. Poetry Ctr., Phila., 1990-97, dir., 1994-97. Author: (poetry) Entering Pisces, 1985, 2nd edit., 1993, Nightshade, 1995. Artist in residence N.J. State Arts Council, Pa. Council on the Arts, 1982—, Lit. fellow, 1998, Geraldine R. Dodge Found., 1987—, Carroll scholar, 1964-65; Warner Lambert/Nat. Merit scholar, 1961-65; fellow poetry Hambidge Ctr., 1991-93, Va. Ctr. Creative Arts, 1997, Pa. Coun. on Arts Fellowship in Poetry award 1998, Disting. Tchg. Artist award N.J. State Arts Coun., 1999-2001. Mem. Poets and Writers, Poetry Soc. Am., Friends of Writers. Fax: 215-629-3656. E-mail JCTODD66@aol.com. Studio: 119 Herr St # A Harrisburg PA 17102-3303 also: 339 S 4th St Philadelphia PA 19106-4219

COOPER, JANELLE LUNETTE, neurologist, educator; b. Ann Arbor, Mich., Dec. 11, 1955; d. Robert Marion and Madelyn (Leonard) C.; children: Lena Christine, Nicholas Dominic. BA in Chemistry, Reed Coll., 1978; MD, Vanderbilt U., 1986. Diplomate Nat. Bd. Med. Examiners; diplomate in neurology Am. Bd. Psychiatry and Neurology; registered med. technologist Am. Soc. Clin. Pathologists. Med. technologist Swedish Hosp. Med. Ctr., Seattle, 1978-80, U. Wash. Clin. Chemistry, Seattle, 1980-82, Vanderbilt U. Hosp., Nashville, 1983-84; intern medicine Vanderbilt U. Med. Ctr., Nashville, 1986-87, resident neurology, 1987-90; instr. neurology Med. Coll. Pa., Phila., 1990-91, asst. prof., clerkship dir., 1991—, mem. curriculum com., 1990-91, vis. asst. prof., 1991-95; neurologist Greater Ann Arbor Neurology Assocs., 1991-93; dir. neurol. svcs., med. dir. Indsl. Rehab. Program St. Francis Hosp., Escanaba, Mich., 1993-98; founder, dir. No. Neuroscis., Escanaba, 1993-98; pres. HolderLady, Ltd., 1996—; chmn. dept. medicine St. Francis Hosp., Escanaba, Mich., 1998—; dir. LaSalle Clinic Memory Ctr., Oshkosh, Wis., 1998—; med. dir. Memory Clinic of the Upper Peninsula, Escanaba, Mich., 1998—; neurologist LaSalle Clinic, Oshkosh, Wis., 1998—; physician MCP Neurology Assocs., Phila., 1990-91; emergency rm. physician Tenn. Christian Med. Ctr., 1989-90. Contbr. articles to Annals of Ophthalmology, Ophthalmic Surgery. Vol. Rape and Sexual Abuse Ctr., Nashville, 1988-90; mem. adminstrv. bd. Edgehill United Meth. Ch., Nashville, 1989-90; mem. editorial bd. Nashville Women's Alliance, 1989-90; bd. dirs. Upper Peninsula Physicians Network, 1995-98; mem. adv. bd. Perspective Adult Daycare Ctr., 1996-99; founding dir. Memory Clinic of Upper Peninsula, 1998—. Recipient Svc. award for outstanding contbns. Rape and Sexual Abuse Ctr., 1990; epilepsy minifellow Bowman Gray U., 1995. Mem. AMA (physician's Recognition award 1989—), NOW, AAAS, NAFE, Am. Med. Women's Assn., Am. Acad. Neurology, Am. Psychol. Soc., Mich. State Med. Soc., N.Y. Acad. Scis., Upper Peninsula Neuro Assn. (v.p. 1998—, trustee 1998—), Upper Peninsula Physician Network (bd. dirs. 1995-98), Aircraft Owners and Pilots Assn., Women in Aviation Internat. (charter), Air Force Assn. (life patron). Democrat (mem. nat. com.). Methodist. Achievements include first synthesis of Difluoromethanedisulfonic Acid; research on neurobehavioral disorders; on neuroendocrinology of sexual development, identity and orientation; on the history of women in medicine; clinical investigation trials for new medications for dementias and epilepsy. Home: 108 Country Club Ln Oshkosh WI 54901-7459 Office: LaSalle Clinic Dept Neurology 2725 Jackson St Oshkosh WI 54901-1513

COOPER, JANIS CAMPBELL, public relations executive; b. Laurel, Miss., July 26, 1947; d. Clifton B. and Hilna Mae (Welch) Campbell; m. William R. Cooper, Sept. 18, 1971; 1 child, Emily Susanne. BS, U. So. Miss., 1969. Certified home economist. Staff home economist Maytag Co., Newton, Iowa, 1969-73, supr. home econs., 1973-81, mgr. consumer edn., 1981-86; mgr. corp. pub. affairs Maytag Corp., Newton, 1986-87, asst. dir. corp. pub. affairs, 1987-88, corp. dir. pub. affairs, 1988-89, corp. v.p. pub. affairs, 1989-96, dir. found. programs, 1996—. žhmn. bd. trustees Newton Cmty. Edn. Found., 1992-95; campaign vice chmn. United Way, Newton, 1996, campaign chmn., 1997, bd. dirs., 1997-98, pres., 1998, mem. exec. com., 1999—; bd. dirs. YMCA, 1997—. Mem. Assn. Family and Consumer Scis., Pub. Rels. Soc. Am., Home Economists in Bus. (nat. chmn. 1981-82, Disting. Svc. award 1986, Nat. Bus. Home Economist of Yr. 1991), Iowa Assn. Bus. and Industry (bd. dirs., mem. exec. com. 1990-96), Assn. Home Appliance Mfrs. (treas. 1988-89, 1st vice chmn. 1989-90, chmn. 1990-92, chmn. Major Appliance Divsn. Bd. 1993-95), Maytag Mgmt. Club (Cmty. Svc. award 1997), Kiwanis Internat. Avocations: golfing, reading, travel. Office: Maytag Corp PO Box 39 403 W 4th St N Newton IA 50208-3034

COOPER, JEAN SARALEE, judge; b. Huntington, N.Y., Mar. 7, 1946; d. Ralph and Henrietta (Halbreich) C.; stepchildren: Mitzi Concklin Prochnow, John Todd Concklin. B.A., Sophie Newcomb Coll. of Tulane U., 1968; J.D., Emory U., 1970. Bar: La. 1970, Ga. 1970, U.S. Dist. Ct. (ea. dist.) La. 1970, U.S. Ct. Appeals (5th cir.) 1972, U.S. Ct. Appeals (2d cir.) 1976, U.S. Ct. Appeals (4th cir.) 1979, U.S. Ct. Appeals (fed. cir.) 1982, U.S. Supreme Ct. 1974. Trial atty. Office of Solicitor, U.S. Dept. Labor, Washington, 1970-73, spl. projects asst., 1973, sr. trial atty., 1973-77; adminstrv. judge Bd. Contract Appeals, HUD, Washington, 1977—, acting chmn. and chief judge, 1980-81, vice chmn., 1983—; cons., lectr. Contbr. articles to profl. jours. Recipient Moot Court award Tulane Law Sch., 1968. Fellow ABA (standing com. on jud. selection, tenure and compensation 1992-95, jud. divsn. 1979—, sec. Nat. Conf. Adminstrv. Law Judges 1996-97, vice chmn. 1997-98, chair-elect 1998-99, chair 1999—, vice chmn. debarment and suspension com. pub. contracts sect. 1992-97, adminstrn. law sect.); mem. La. Bar Assn., Am. Law Inst., Am. Inns of Ct. Found. (trustee 1992-98, leadership coun. 1998—), Prettyman-Leventhal Am. Inn of Ct. (past pres., master of bench), Am. Judicature Soc., BCA Bar Assn., Nat. Assn. Women Judges (founding mem.), Contract Appeals Judges Assn. (bd. dirs.). Republican. Home: 2800 Flagmaker Dr Falls Church VA 22042-2200 Address: HUD Bd Contract Appeals 1707 H St NW 11th Fl Washington DC 20006 *My approach to life has been "anything is possible." That removed the boundaries in my mind, so that I could move past the boundaries that might hold me back. I take real joy in both work and play, family and friends. I firmly believe in mentoring young people so that they, too, will see past boundaries real and imagined.*

COOPER, JEROME A., lawyer; b. Brookwood, Ala., Jan. 15, 1913; s. Marks Benjamin and Etta (Temerson) C.; m. Lois Harriet McMillen, Aug. 16, 1938; children: Ellen (Mrs. Benjamin L. Erdreich), Carol. A.B. Cum laude, Harvard, 1933, LL.B., 1936. Bar: Ala. bar 1936. Practice in Birmingham, 1946—; law clk. U.S. Dist. Judge Davis, 1936-37, U.S. Supreme Ct. Justice Hugo L. Black, 1937-40; regional atty. Solicitors Office, Dept. Labor, 1940-41; partner firm Cooper, Mitch & Crawford, 1950-98; of counsel Gardner, Middlebrooks, Fleming & Gibbons, PC, Birmingham, 1999—; mem. Pres. Kennedy's Lawyers' Com. for Civil Rights Under Law, 1963—; pres. adv. coun. Pub. Radio Sta. WBHM, 1980—. Mem. editorial adv. bd. The Ala. Lawyer. Mem. Birmingham area Manpower Resource Devel. Planning Bd., 1969; chmn. cmty. devel. com. Operation New Birmingham; mem. Jefferson County Drug Abuse Coordinating Com., 1970-76; pres. Jefferson County Assn. Mental Health, Birmingham Jewish Cmty. Ctr., United Jewish Fund; mem. Southeastern regional adv. bd. Anti Defamation League, 1981; exec. bd. Birmingham Concentrated Employment Program; pres. Positive Maturity; sec., exec. bd. Jefferson County Com. Econ Opportunity; pres. Crisis Ctr., 1976; mem. Gov.'s Task Force on Unemployment, 1983; Democratic candidate for Ala. Senate, 1966; bd. dirs. Birmingham Symphony Assn., 1979-80, Ruffner Mountain Nature Ctr., 1985—, v.p., 1990, pres. 1991-93; bd. dirs. Friends of U. Ala. in Birmingham Psychiatry, 1987, Birmingham Civil Rights Inst., 1992—, adv. com. (HAER) Birmingham Hist. Soc., 1992—. Served to lt. comdr. USNR, 1942-45. Fellow Internat. Soc. Barristers, Coll. Labor and Employment Lawyers (emeritus); mem. Ala. Law Inst., Adminstrv. Conf. U.S., Birmingham Audubon Soc. (v.p. exec. com. 1989—), Disting. Fellow Birmingham-So. Coll., 1995. Jewish (trustee temple). Home: 42 Fairway Dr Birmingham AL 35213-4211 Office: Ste 450 McAdory Bldg 2013 1st Ave N Birmingham AL 35203

COOPER, JEROME MAURICE, architect; b. Memphis, Jan. 24, 1930; s. Samuel and Bessie (Phillips) C.; m. Jean Kanter, Dec. 29, 1957; children: David Franklin, Samuel Randolph, Beth Lauren. B.S., Ga. Inst. Tech., 1952, B.Arch., 1955; postgrad., U. Rome, Italy, 1956-57. Fulbright fellow Rome, 1956-57; pres. Cooper, Carry & Assos., Inc., Atlanta, 1960—; vis. artist Am. Acad. Rome. Prin. works include Coll. of Architecture bldg. Ga. Inst. Tech., Siemens Corp. Hdqrs., Nat. Svc. Industries Corp. Hdqrs., Adtraw Corp. Hdqrs., Huntsville, Ala., Scientific Atlanta Corp. Hdqrs, Lazarus Dept. Store, Pitts., Clin. Info. Mgmt. Ctr., Drake U. Med. Ctr., Sch. of Theology, Mercer U., Green Hill Mall (AIA design award), Heritage Village at Sea Pines, Underground Atlanta, C&P Hdqrs., No. Va., Rich's Dept. Store, Northpoint Mall, Atlanta, Jordan Marsh Dept. Store, Natick Mall, Boston. Trustee Nat. Bldg. Mus. Served to lt. (j.g.) USN, 1952-54. Recipient Rothschild medal, 1985, Silver medal Atlanta chpt. AIA, 1987. Fellow AIA (pres. chpt., nat. dir., task force on ethics, task force on certification, task force on long span buildings, Silver medal firm award Atlanta chpt. 1987), Nat. Jud. Council. Home: 1070 Judith Way NE Atlanta GA 30324-2905 Office: Cooper Carry & Assocs Inc 3520 Piedmont Rd NE Ste 200 Atlanta GA 30305-1595

COOPER, JERROLD STEPHEN, historian, educator; b. Chgo., Nov. 24, 1942; s. Emanuel Cooper and Adele (Faberson) Smith; m. Elaine Abrams, Dec. 22, 1962 (div. 1969); children: Nina Lynn, Sari Jean; m. Carol Manson Bier, Nov. 18, 1982; 1 child, Jenny Alexandra. AB, U. Calif., Berkeley, 1963, MA, 1964; PhD, U. Chgo., 1969. Asst. prof. Johns Hopkins U., Balt., 1968-74, assoc. prof., 1974-79, prof., 1979—, chmn. dept. Near Eastern Studies, 1983-91; acting chmn. Near Eastern Studies, 1992-93; acting chmn. classics Johns Hopkins U., Balt., 1988-91; vis. prof. UCLA, 1975, U. Calif., Berkeley, 1981, U. Padua, Italy, 1992, U. Rome, 1998. Author: The Return of Ninurta, 1979, The Curse of Agade, 1983, Sumerian and Akkadian Royal Inscriptions, 1985; assoc. editor Jour. of Cuneiform Studies, 1972-89. NEH grantee, 1980-86. Mem. Am. Oriental Soc. (dir. 1982-85), Am. Schs. of Oriental Rsch. (trustee 1987-97). Avocations: early music. Office: Johns Hopkins U Dept Near East Studies Baltimore MD 21218

COOPER, JOEL, psychology educator; b. N.Y.C., Dec. 3, 1943; s. Samuel Cooper and Sarah Tobias; m. Barbara Orenstein, Dec. 17, 1966; children: Jason, Aaron, Grant. BS, CCNY, 1965; PhD in Social Psychology, Duke U., 1969. Asst. prof. psychology Princeton (N.J.) U., 1969-73, assoc. prof., 1973-78, prof., 1978—, chmn. psychology dept., 1985-92, dir. grad. studies dept. psychology, 1976-83; chmn. Inst. Rev. Bd. Princeton U., 1974-81, 84-87, 96—, com. appointments and advancements, com. on grad. sch.; sr. fellow East-West Population Inst., 1975. Author: Understanding Social Psychology, 1976, 5th edit. 1991; editorial bd. Jour. Personality, Jour. Exptl. Social Psychology, Social Psychology Quar.; contbr. chpts. to books in field, articles to profl. jours. Office: Princeton U Dept Psychology Green Hall Princeton NJ 08544

COOPER, JOHN, university football coach; b. Powell, Tenn., July 2, 1937; m. Helen Cooper; children: John Jr., Cindy. BS, Iowa State U., 1962. Freshman football coach Iowa State U., 1962-63; asst. football coach Oreg. State U., 1963-67; defensive coord. U. Kans., 1967-72; asst. coach U. Ky., 1972-77; coach U. Tulsa, 1977-84, Ariz. State U., 1985-87; head football coach Ohio State U., Columbus, 1987—; coach East-West Shrine Bowl Game, Hula Bowl, Japan All-State games. Active civic orgns., Columbus, including Big Bros./Big Sisters, Alzheimer's Found., Arthur James Cancer Hosp., Children's Hosp. With U.S. Army. Named Nat. Coach of Yr., 1986; winner Rose Ball games with Pac-10 and Big Ten conf. teams. Mem. Am. Football Coaches Assn. (past pres.). Office: Ohio State U Athletic Dept St John Arena 401 Woody Hayes Dr Columbus OH 43210*

COOPER, JOHN ALFRED, JR., community development company executive; b. Memphis, Sept. 13, 1938; s. John Alfred and Mildred (Borum) C.; m. Pat McInnis, Oct. 23, 1965; children: Mary Virginia, John Alfred III, Borum. Student, U. Ark., 1961. With Cherokee Village Devel. Co., Inc., 1962—, exec. v.p., 1967—; pres. John A. Cooper Co., 1968-90; pres. Cooper Communities Inc., 1972-90, vice chmn., 1990-91; chmn. Cooper Communities, Inc., 1991-97, pres., CEO, 1997—; bd. dirs. Wal-Mart Stores, Inc., Entergy Corp., 1st Nat. Bank of Sharp County, J.B. Hunt Transport Svcs., Inc. Clubs: Memphis Country, Little Rock Country. Office: Cooper Communities Inc 1801 Forest Hills Blvd Bella Vista AR 72715-2395*

COOPER, JOHN ALLEN DICKS, medical educator; b. El Paso, Tex., Dec. 22, 1918; s. John Allen Dicks and Cora (Walker) C.; m. Mary Jane Stratton, June 17, 1944; children: Margaret Ann, John Allen Dicks, Patricia Alison, Randolph Arend Stratton. B.S. in Chemistry, N.Mex.State U., 1939, LL.D. (hon.), 1971; Ph.D. in Biochemistry, Northwestern U., 1943, M.D., 1951, D.Sc. (hon.), 1972; D.Honoris Causa, U. Brasil, 1958; D.Sc. (hon.), Duke U., 1973, Med. Coll. Ohio, Toledo, 1974, Med. Coll. Wis., 1978, N.Y. Med. Coll., 1981, Wake Forest U., 1985, Georgetown U., 1986; D.Med. Sci (hon.), Med. Coll. Pa., 1973; DHL (hon.), Thomas Jefferson U., 1984. Intern Passavant Meml. Hosp., Chgo., 1951; mem. attending staff Passavant Meml. Hosp., 1955-69; mem. faculty Northwestern U., 1943-69, prof. biochemistry, 1957-69; asso. dean Northwestern U. (Med. Sch.), 1959-63, dean scis., 1963-69; mem. faculty Georgetown U., Washington, 1970-90; prof. practice of health policy Duke U., Durham, N.C., 1973-78; faculty Baylor Coll. Medicine, Houston, 1987-96; Disting. physician VA, 1987-92; vis. prof. U. Brasil, 1956, U. Buenos Aires, 1958, Harvard Med. Sch., 1985; mem. policy adv. bd. Argonne Nat. Lab., 1957-63, mem. review com. divs. biol. and med. research and radiol. physics, 1958-63, chmn. review com., 1958-62; mem. com. on licensure AEC, 1956-69, cons. div. edn. and tng., 1963; mem. adv. council on health research facilities NIH, 1965-69; organizing com. Pan Am. Fedn. of Assn. Med. Colls., 1962-64, treas., 1963-76; adv. com. personnel for research Am. Cancer Soc., 1962-66; cons. commr. food and drugs FDA, 1965-70; spl. cons. to dir. NIH, 1968-70; cons. to div. physician and health professions edn. Bur. Health Manpower Edn. NIH, 1970-73; mem. Inst. Medicine, Nat. Acad. Scis., 1972—; mem. bd. higher edn., Ill., 1964-69; chmn. Gov.'s Sci. Adv. Council, State Ill., 1967-69; mem. council Asso. Midwest Univs., 1963-68, v.p., bd. dirs., 1964-65, pres., bd. dirs., 1965-66; v.p., bd. trustees Argonne Univs. Assn., 1965-68; bd. dirs. Nat. Fund Med. Edn., 1970-79. Editor: Jour. Med. Edn, 1962-71. Trustee Georgetown U., 1986-89. Served to 1st lt., San. Corps AUS, 1945-47. Recipient Outstanding Alumnus award N.Mex. State U., 1960; Alumni medal Northwestern U., 1976; Abraham Flexner award Assn. Am. Med. Colls., 1985; John and Mary R. Markle scholar in acad. medicine, 1951-56. Mem. AMA, Am. Hosp. Assn. (hon.), Inst. Medicine of NAS, Am. Soc. Biol. Chemists, Assn. Am. Med. Colls. (del. numerous confs., mem. various coms., pres. 1969-86, pres. emeritus 1986), Asociación Venezolana Para el Avance de la Ciencia (hon.), Sigma Xi, Alpha Omega Alpha. Home: 800 Caledonian Way Birmingham AL 35242-0501

COOPER, JOHN CHARLES, writer, educator; b. Charleston, S.C., Apr. 3, 1933; s. Chauncey Miller and Marguerite Anna (Gerard) C.; m. Celia Ann Johnston, June 6, 1954 (div. 1986); children: Martin Christopher, Catherine Marie, Cythia Ann, Paul Conrad; m. Victoria Davis, May 19, 1988; 1 child, Sean Christopher. AB cum laude, U. S.C., 1955; MDiv, Luth. Sem., Columbia, S.C., 1958; ThM, Chgo. Luth. Sem., Maywood, Ill., 1960; MA, U. Chgo., 1964, PhD, 1966. Instr. religion and philosophy Thiel Coll., Greenville, Pa., 1959-60; pastor Faith Luth. Ch., Tampa, Fla., 1960-61; asst. prof. to prof. Newberry (S.C.) Coll., 1961-68; prof., chmn. dept. Eastern Ky. U., Richmond, 1968-71; prof., academic dean Winebrenner Sem., Findlay, Ohio, 1971-82; prof., chmn. dept. Susquehanna U., Selinsgrove, Pa., 1982-89; dir. seminars and rsch. The Zoe Corp., Burgin, Ky., 1989-90, Transylvania U., 1990-91, Eastern Ky. U., 1990-96, Asbury Coll., Wilmore, Ky., 1990-97; pastor Lord of the Seas Luth. Ch., Big Pine Key, Fla., 1997—. Author: (novel) Cast A Single Shadow, 1996, 3 vols. of poetry, also 40 books on religion, sociology, politics, and intellectual history; contbr. articles to profl. jours. Served as sgt. USMC, 1950-52, Korea. Democrat. Home: 70 E Cahill Ct Big Pine Key FL 33043-3304

COOPER, JOHN JOSEPH, lawyer; b. Vincennes, Ind., Oct. 20, 1924; s. Homer O. and Ruth (House) C.; m. Nathalie Brooke, 1945. A.B., Stanford, 1950, LL.B., 1951; LL.M., U. So. Calif., 1964. Bar: Calif. 1952. Pvt. practice San Francisco, 1951-54, Los Angeles, 1954-61, Palo Alto, 1961-90; gen. counsel, v.p. Varian Assocs., Palo Alto, 1970-90, sr. v.p., 1990, also bd. dirs.; speaker, lectr. Am. Law Inst., ABA, other legal orgns. Contbr. articles to law revs. and profl. jours. Aviator USNR, 1942-45. Mem. ABA, Calif. Bar Assn. Home: 191 Ramoso Rd Portola Valley CA 94028

COOPER, JOHN MADISON, philosophy educator; b. Memphis, Nov. 29, 1939; s. Marion Armon and Bernardine (Sheehan) C.; m. Marcia Louise Coleman, Aug. 21, 1965; children: Stephanie Coleman, Katherine Alexander. AB magna cum laude, Harvard U., 1961; BPhil, Corpus Christi Coll., Oxford, England, 1963; PhD, Harvard U., 1967. Asst. prof. philosophy and the classics Harvard U., Cambridge, Mass., 1966-71; assoc. prof. U. Pitts., 1971-76, prof., 1976-81, chmn. philosophy dept., 1977-81; prof. Princeton U., N.J., 1981—, chmn. philosophy dept., 1984-92, Stuart prof., 1998—. Author: Reason and Human Good in Aristotle, Seneca: Moral and Political Essays, Plato: Complete Works, Reason and Emotion; mem. editl. bd. Am. Philos. Quar., 1977-80, History of Philosophy Quar., 1983-86, The Monist, 1987—, Ratio, 1988, Archiv für Ges. d. Phil., 1994—; contbr. articles to profl. jours. Recipient Ctr. for Advanced Studies fellow U. Ill., 1969-70, NEH fellow, 1982-83, John Simon Guggenheim fellow, 1987-88, Ctr. for Advanced Study in the Behavioral Scis. fellow, 1992-93. Mem. Am. Philos. Assn. (ea. divsn. exec. com. 1984-87, chmn. com. def. profl. rights 1983-88, ea. divsn. nominating com. 1991-94, chmn. ea. divsn. program com. 1980, v.p. 1998-99). Home: 182 Western Way Princeton NJ 08540-7208 Office: Princeton Univ Dept of Philosophy 1879 Hall Princeton NJ 08544

COOPER, JOHN MILTON, JR., history educator, author; b. Washington, Mar. 16, 1940; s. John Milton and Mary Louise (Porter) C.; m. Judith Karin Widerkrantz, June 9, 1962; children: John Milton III, Elizabeth Karin Doyle. AB summa cum laude, Princeton U., 1961; MA, Columbia U., 1962, PhD, 1968. Instr. history Wellesley (Mass.) Coll., 1965-67, asst. prof., 1967-70; asst. prof. history U. Wis., Madison, 1970-71, assoc. prof., 1971-76, prof., 1976-87, William Francis Allen prof. history, 1987—, chmn. dept., 1988-91; Fulbright prof. Coun. Internat. Exch. Scholars, Moscow, 1987. Author: Vanity of Power, 1969, Walter Hines Page, 1977, Warrior and Priest, 1983, Pivotal Decades, 1990; editor: Causes and Consequences of World War I, 1971, The Wilson Era, 1991. Woodrow Wilson Found. fellow, 1961, NEH fellow, 1969, 91, Guggenheim Found. fellow, 1979. Mem. Am. Hist. Assn., Orgn. Am. Historians, So. Hist. Assn., Coun. Fgn. Rels., Rotary, State Hist. Soc. Wis. (bd. curators), Ctr. for Nat. Policy, Phi Beta Kappa. Democrat. Congregationalist. *

COOPER, JON CHARLES, environmental science educator, lawyer; b. N.Y.C., Sept. 28, 1948; s. Joseph Irving and Fay Phylis (Rubin) C.; m. Nancy Louise Hoffman, July 17, 1986; 1 child, Emily Maxwell. BA cum laude, Lawrence U., 1969; MS, U. Wis., 1971, PhD, 1974; JD, Pace U., 1993. Bar: N.Y. 1993, N.J. 1994, Conn. 1994, U.S. Supreme Ct. 1997. Tech. dir. Tex. Instruments, Buchanan, N.Y., 1976-79; staff biologist U.S. EPA, Washington, N.Y., 1979-83; sci. dir. Hudson River Found., N.Y.C., 1983-87; pres. Internat. Sch. Environ. Studies Found., New Haven, 1986—; prin. scientist TAMS, N.Y.C., 1987-90; sci. policy dir. Louis Berger & Assocs. Inc., East Orange, N.J., 1990-99; assoc. prof. environ. sci. SUNY, Purchase, 1990—; v.p. natural resources and environment Marasco Newton Group Ltd, Arlington, Va., 1999—. Contbr. numerous articles to profl. jours. Mem. tree subcom. Town of Greenwich (Conn.), 1990-93. Mem. Am. Chem. Soc., N.Y. Bar Assn., Am. Soc. Limnology, Sigma Xi. Avocations: horseback riding, tennis. Office: Marasco Newton Group Ltd 2801 Clarendon Blvd Ste 100 Arlington VA Office: Louis Berger & Assocs Inc 1819 H St NW Washington DC 20006-3603

COOPER, JOSEPH, political scientist, educator; b. Boston, Sept. 10, 1933; s. Charles and Esther (Balder) C.; m. Frances Lorna Wollin, Aug. 24, 1965; children: Samuel Wollin, Meryl Charlotte. AB summa cum laude, Harvard U., 1955, AM, 1959, PhD, 1961. Asst. prof. govt. Harvard U., 1963-67; mem. faculty Rice U., Houston, 1967-91; prof. polit. sci. Rice U., 1970-91, chmn. dept., 1967-72, Lena Gohlman Fox prof., 1978-89; dean Rice U. (Sch. Social Scis.), 1979-88; Herbert S. Autrey prof. social scis. Rice U., 1989-91; pres. Rice Inst. for Policy Analysis Rice U. (Sch. Social Scis.), 1989-91; provost, v.p. for acad. affairs Johns Hopkins U., 1991-96, prof. dept. polit. sci., 1991—; vis. Olin prof. polit. sci. Stanford U., 1988-89; staff dir. commn. adminstrv. rev. U.S. Ho. Reps., 1976-78; vis. prof. govt. Harvard U., 1984-85; bd. dirs. Dirksen Congl. Ctr., 1994—, Consortium of Social Sci. Orgns., 1994-97, regional bd. dirs., 1994-97; bd. dirs. Public Campaign, 1997—. Author: The Origins of the Standing Committees and the Development of the Modern House, 1970, Congress and Its Committees, 1988; also articles; co-editor Sage Yearbook on Electoral Studies, 1975-82; mem. bd. editors Congress and the Presidency, Ency. of U.S. Congress, Legis. Studies Quar., 1987-90; assoc. editor Ency. of Am. Legis. Sys., Congress of U.S., 1789-1989. Mem. Adv. Com. on Records of Congress U.S. Congress and Nat. Archives, 1995—; bd. editors Legis. Studies Quar., 1987-90; bd. dirs. Balt. Hebrew Univ. Brookings rsch. fellow Harvard U., 1959-60; NEH sr. fellow, 1973; recipient Press award Congl. Quar., 1989. Mem. Am. Polit. Sci. Assn. (sec. 1979, program chmn. 1985, nominations chmn. 1992), Southwestern Polit. Sci. Assn. (pres. 1977), So. Polit. Sci. Assn., Midwest Polit. Sci. Assn., D.C. Area Polit. Sci. Assn. (mem. coun. 1993-94, v.p. 1994, pres. 1996), Jefferson Davis Assn. (dir. 1980-91), Asia Soc. (bd. dirs. 1990-92), Phi Betta Kappa, Sigma Xi. Office: Dept Polit Sci Johns Hopkins Univ Baltimore MD 21218-2685

COOPER, JOYCE BEATRICE, medical/surgical nurse; b. Marston, Mo., Sept. 29, 1941; d. Lester Hendrex and Fannie Beatrice (McCool) McGruder; m. Joe Taylor Cooper, Oct. 4, 1957; children: Terry Joe, Tracy James, Timothy John. Creative writing degree, Chgo. Writers Inst., 1973; diploma, Kokomo Sch. Practical Nursing, 1977; ADN, Marian Coll., 1987; BSBA, Ind. Wesleyan U., 1996. Cert. ob-gyn. nurse, trauma nurse, cardiac and respiratory nurse, life support care nurse. Nurse Vis. Nurse Assn. North Cen. Ind., Elwood; dir. nursing Tipton (Ind.) Nursing Ctr., 1991-97, Windsor Estates, Kokomo, Ind., 1997-98; intake coord. SCCI-Kokomo-Long-Term Acute Care Hosp., 1998—. Mem. NAACOG, ANA, Vis. Nurse Assn., Soc. Nursing Profls. Home: Box 205 309 McClellan Windfall IN 46076

COOPER, KAREN RENÉ, health facility administration nurse; b. Pleasanton, Calif., Oct. 15, 1957; d. Homer L. and Rosa B. (Upton) C.; m. Tommy Joe McCarty, Nov. 1, 1981. BSN, U. Ala., Birmingham, 1980. Cert. in profl. healthcare quality; healthcare cert. Bd. Nat. Commn. Certifying Agencies; cert. in profl. utilization rev.; cert. Interqual Nat. Registry; cert. chemotherapy, rehab. nurse, tissue therapy. Internship in SICU/MICU Cedars of Lebanon Hosp., Miami, Fla., 1980; mem. head injury/CVA and chronic pain team Spain Rehab. Ctr. U. Ala. Hosps., Birmingham, 1980-82, rheumatology charge nurse Spain Rehab. Ctr., 1982-88, staff nurse, 1988-90, coord. utilization rev./quality assurance med. care rev., 1990-91, coord. quality improvement med. care rev., 1991-93, sr. nurse coord. med. care rev., 1993, interim dir. med. care rev., 1993-94, sr. coord. dept. quality resources, 1994—; Mem. Com. for Quality Improvement U. Ala. Birmingham Hosps., mem. Discharge Planning Com., Emergency Svcs. Quality Improvement, 1991-93, Key 100 Com., Med./Dental Staff Task Force, Mobile Med. ICU Quality Com. APACHE Study, 1990-92, Neurology Quality Com., 1990-92, Nursing Stds. Com., 1982-85, Nursing Task Force Com., 1984-88, Resuscitation Com., 1990-94, Skin Care/Tissue Therapy Com., 1986-89, Surg. Quality Improvement Com., 1991-93; mem. Arthritis Newsletter Com. U. Ala. Birmingham Multi-Purpose Arthritis Ctr., 1983-89; active Value Improvement Project of Birmingham Hosp. Network; participant, presenter numerous confs. and workshops in field. Contbr. articles to Arthritis Today and Arthritis Newsletter of U. Ala. Birmingham Multi-Purpose Arthritis Ctr., 1983-90. Pres. Coalnugget Ala. Mining Mus., 1987-89, chair literacy daycamp, 1990-92; participant Ala. State Fair Family Craft Divsn., 1975-94; co-chair AHPA Nat. Nursing Coun., 1986-88; vol. Children's Hosp., Dixie Wheelchair Assn. Regional Wheelchair Games, Goodwill Industries Doll Sale, Caring and Sharing Drive; troop leader Cahaba Coun. Girl Scouts Am., 1982—, POGO advisor, 1985-93, advisor outdoor interest group, 1995-98, mem. program operating unit, 1984-93, coun. trainer, 1984—, cons. svc. area events/programs, 1984-92, bd. dirs., 1992-94, svc. area mgr. Upper 78 West, 1995-98, assn. chair, 1991-92, camp nurse, 1992-97, mem. nominating com., 1993-95, facilities com., 1992-94, chair long-range property planning com., 1993, del. to nat. conv., 1993, del. to nat. coun., 1993-99, life mem., 1993, mem. World of People Interest Group, 1997-98; mem. Ala. Assn. Healthcare Quality, Am. Juvenile Arthritis Orgn., 1982-88, Arthritis Found., 1982-90, liaison ACT Club support group, 1984-86; mem. UHC: Quality and Risk Mgmt. Coun., United Way/Benevolent Fund com. U. Ala. Birmingham Hosps., 1990. Recipient Thanks award Girl Scouts Am. Cahaba Coun., 1989; fellow Girl Scouts U.S.A., 1976. Mem. NAFE, Nat. Assn. Healthcare Quality, U. Ala. Birmingham Alumni Assn. Avocations: painting, poetry, crafts, dolls, dogs. Home: 30 Scurlock Rd Dora AL 35062-4221 Office: Dept Quality Resources U Ala Birmingham Hosp Birmingham AL 35223-6507

COOPER, KATHLEEN BELL, economist; b. Dallas, Feb. 3, 1945; d. Patrick Joseph and Ferne Elizabeth (McDougle) Bell; m. Ronald James Cooper, Feb. 6, 1965; children—Michael, Christopher. B.A. in Math. with honors, U. Tex., Arlington, 1970, M.A. in Econs, 1971; Ph.D. in Econs, U. Colo., 1980. Research asst. econs. dept. U. Tex., Arlington, 1970-71; corp. economist United Banks of Colo., Denver, 1971-79, chief economist, 1980-81; v.p., sr. fin. economist Security Pacific Nat. Bank, Los Angeles, 1981-83, 1st v.p., sr. economist, 1983-85, sr. v.p., economist, 1985-86, sr. v.p., chief economist, 1986-87, exec. v.p., chief economist, 1988-90; chief economist Exxon Corp., Irving, Tex., 1990—. Trustee Scripps Coll., Com. for Econ. Devel.; mem. Dallas Com. on Fgn. Rels., Internat. Women's Forum. Mem. Nat. Assn. Bus. Economists (past pres. Denver and L.A. chpts.; bd. dirs. 1975-78, pres. 1985-86), Nat. Bur. Econ. Rsch. (bd. dirs., exec. com.), Am. Bankers Assn. (econ. adv. com. 1979-81, 86-90, chmn. 1989-90), U.S. Assn. Energy Econs. (pres. 1996), Am. Econ. Assn., Conf. Bus. Economists (tech. cons. to bus. coun. 1993-94). Office: Exxon Corp 5959 Las Colinas Blvd Irving TX 75039-2298*

COOPER, KEN ERROL, management educator; b. Bryan, Ohio, Mar. 10, 1939; s. George Wayne and Agnes Anibel (Fisher) C.; m. Karen Cremean, June 17, 1961; children: Kristin, Andrew. B.S., Bowling Green State U., 1961; M.B.A., Miami U., Oxford, Ohio, 1962; Ph.D., U. Minn., 1984. Instr. Miami U., 1962-63; lectr. U. Minn., 1965-67, 84-86; group v.p. Land O'Lakes, Inc., Mpls., 1967-82; v.p. fin. and adminstrn. Hamline U., 1982-84; dean Coll. Bus., Ohio No. U., Ada, 1986-90, prof., 1990—; prof., post chair for ethics and professions Am. Coll., Bryn Mawr, Pa., 1994-95; vis. prof. (on leave) Coll. of St. Thomas, St. Paul, 1981-82. Trustee Westmar Coll., 1980-86; bd. dirs., sec.-treas. Acad. Mgmt., 1989-95; mem. Iowa Supreme Ct. Adv. Council, 1972-75, North Central Devel. Found. Republican. Methodist. Office: Ohio No U Coll Bus Adminstrn Ada OH 45810

COOPER, KENNETH BANKS, business executive, former army officer; b. Ft. Leavenworth, Kans., Nov. 12, 1923; s. Avery John and Ona Carey (Gibson) C.; m. Virginia Leah Adkins, Dec. 29, 1979; children by previous marriage: Kenneth, Robert. BS, U.S. Mil. Acad., 1944; MS, MIT, 1951. Commd. 2nd lt. U.S. Army, 1944; advanced through grades to lt. gen., 1975; World War II svc. in S. Pacific Philippines, Japan, 1944-46; assigned to Manhattan Project-Armed Forces Spl. Weapon Project, N.Mex., Eniwetok, and Washington, 1946-48; mem. nuclear weapons staff AEC, Washington, 1951-55; nuclear weapons planning officer SHAPE, Paris, 1955-58; project mgr., ballistic missile def. rsch. Advanced Rsch. Projects Agy., Washington, 1959-63; bn. comdr. Korea, 1963-64; dir. Army Nuclear Power Program, 1965-66; with Def. Com. Planning Group, 1966-68; exec. to Sec. of Army, 1968-70; brigade comdr. Vietnam, 1970-71; dep. dir. civil works Office Chief of Engrs., Washington, 1971-72, asst. chief engrs., 1972-75; dep. comdr.-in-chief U.S. Army, Europe, Heidelberg, Germany, 1975-77; dep. adviser to Sec. of Def., 1977-78, ret., 1978; gen. mgr. Svc. and Constrn. Group ITT, Nutley, N.J., 1978-79; dep. asst. sec. def. for plans and resources Office Asst. Sec. Def. C3I, Washington, 1980-81; pres. SPC Internat., Arlington, Va., 1981-84; cons. BMD (Ballistic Missile Def., formerly SDI), Alexandria, Va., 1985-88, Inst. Def. Analysis, 1988—. Decorated Legion of Merit (2), D.S.M. (2), D.D.S.M. Mem. Soc. Mil. Engrs, Army Navy Country Club. Office: IDA 1801 Beauregard St Alexandria VA 22311-1772

COOPER, KENNETH STANLEY, educational administrator; b. Oxford, N.C., May 17, 1948; s. Stephen and Helen (Norman) C.; m. Nancy Robinson, June 26, 1971; children: Danielle Jamilla, Janine Kandyce. AS, Miami Dade Community Coll., 1971; BS in Criminal Justice, Fla. Internat. U., 1973, MS in Adult Edn., 1974; postgrad., Fla. Atlantic U., 1976, Ind. U., 1978. Police officer City of Miami (Fla.) Police Dept., 1971-72; tchr. Dade County Pub. Schs., Miami, 1974-76, 80-83, adminstr., asst. prin., 1983-89, prin. intern exec. tng. program, 1987-88, asst. prin., 1983-90; grad. asst. Dept. Social Studies U. Ind., Bloomington, Ind., 1976-78; pres. Cooper Williamson Auto Brokerage, Miami, 1978-80; prin. Jan Mann Opportunity Sch., Miami, Fla., 1990-92, Robert Renick Ednl. Ctr., Opa Locka, Fla., 1992-96, Pine Villa Elem. Sch., Goulds, Fla., 1996-97, Mays Mid. Cmty. Sch., Goulds, 1997—. Guest columnist Miami Times, 1988; contbr. articles to profl. jours. Organizer, activist Young Democrats of South Fla., 1967-68; mem. United Tchrs. of Dade County, Miami, 1974-76, 80-83; sec. bd. dirs. Cmty. Crusade Against Drugs, Miami, 1995-96. Served with U.S. Army, 1969-70. Named Adminstr. of Yr., Dade County Assn. for Counseling and Devel., 1993. Mem. NAACP. Home: 12840 SW 187th St Miami FL 33177-3000 Office: Mays Mid Cmty Sch 11700 SW 216th St Goulds FL 33170-2935

COOPER, LARRY S., carpet industry consultant; b. Bklyn., June 14, 1957; s. Jack and Evelyn (Weinfeld) C.; m. Tryna Lee Giordano, Dec. 31, 1975; children: Jonathan, Jennifer, Jillian. Student, U. Colo., 1975-78. Cert. master cleaner, sr. level carpet insp. Inst. of Inspection, Cleaning and Restoration. Owner Cooper's Carpet Cleaners, Boulder, Colo., 1975-79; pres. Profl. Cleaning Network, Denver, 1979-97; owner Textiles Cons., Denver, 1986—. Chmn. Broomfield (Colo.) Connection, 1988-90; mayor pro-tem City of Broomfield, 1995-96, mem. city coun., 1996—. Named Cleanfax Man of Yr., Clean Fax Mag., 1990. Mem. Profl. Carpet and Upholstery Cleaners Assn. (pres. 1980-81, 84-86), Internat. Inst. of Carpet and Upholstery Cert. (v.p. 1984-85, pres. 1985-87, chmn. bd. dirs. 1988, chmn. cert. bd. 1990—, hon. dir.). Avocations: snow mobiling, fishing. Office: Textile Cons Inc PO Box 21373 Denver CO 80221-0373

COOPER, LEON MELVIN, lawyer; b. L.A., July 24, 1924; s. Harry and Edith (Goldman) C.; m. Shirley Abbey, July 9, 1978; children: Katharine Lee, Victoria Lee, Wendy Elizabeth, Christopher. AB with honors, UCLA, 1944; JD, Harvard U., 1949; LLM, U. S.C., 1965. Bar: Mass. 1949, Calif. 1950. Ptnr. Knight, Gitelson & Ashton, L.A., 1953-58, Cooper, Wyatt, Tepper & Plant (and predecessor firms), L.A., 1958-79; sr. ptnr. Pacht, Ross, Warne, Bernhard & Sears, L.A., 1979-86, Shea & Gould, L.A., 1986-89, Cooper & Dempsey, L.A., 1989-94; ptnr. Lewis, D'Amato, Brisbois & Bisgaard, L.A., 1994—. *Mr. Cooper's legal career includes the representation of corporations and individuals involved in public offerings, private placements, mergers, acquisitions, and filings and negotiations with the United States Securities and Exchange Commission and securities commissioners or divisions of various states. He has also represented corporations in connection with restructuring and reorganization involving Chapter 11 situations. His practice includes consultation in real estate matters, as well as trusts, estates and employment and labor matters. He organized the health care legal group at the firm of Lewis, D'Amato, Brisbois & Bisgaard, where he is a partner and the group leader of the Business and Transaction Group.* Bd. dirs. Santa Catalina Island Conservancy, 1983—, chmn. bd. dirs., 1986—; mem. Alcoholic Beverage Control Appeals Bd., Calif., 1965-67; chmn. Alcoholic Beverage Control Bd., L.A., 1966-67; So. chmn. Calif. Dem. Ctrl. Com., 1968-71. Lt. comdr. USNR, WWII, Korea. Decorated medal of Commendation with battle clasp. Mem. ABA, Calif. Bar Assn., L.A. Bar Assn., State Bar Mass., L.A. Yacht Club, Transpacific Yacht Club, St. Francis Yacht Club, Harvard Club (N.Y.C.), Royal Hawaiian Ocean Racing Club, The Calif. Club, Phi Beta Kappa. Office: Lewis D'Amato Brisbois & Bisgaard 221 N Figueroa St Ste 1200 Los Angeles CA 90012-2646*

COOPER, LEON N., physicist, educator; b. N.Y.C., Feb. 28, 1930; s. Irving and Anna (Zola) C.; m. Kay Anne Allard, May 18, 1969; children: Kathleen Ann, Coralie Lauren. AB, Columbia U., 1951, AM, 1953, PhD, 1954, DSc, 1973; DSc hon. degrees; DSc, U. Sussex, Eng., 1973, U. Ill., 1974, Brown U., 1974, Gustavus Adolphus Coll., 1975, Ohio State U., 1976, U. Pierre et Marie Curie, Paris, 1977. NSF postdoctoral fellow, mem. Inst. for Advanced Study, 1954-55; rsch. assoc. U. Ill., 1955-57; asst. prof. Ohio State U., 1957-58; assoc. prof. Brown U., Providence, 1958-62, prof., 1962-66, Henry Ledyard Goddard U. prof., 1966-74, Thomas J. Watson Sr. prof. sci., 1974—; dir. Ctr. for Neural Sci., Providence, 1978-91; dir. Inst. for Brain and Neural Systems Brown U., Providence, 1991—; lectr. pub. lectures, internat. conf. and symposia; vis. prof. various univs. and summer schs.; cons. indsl., ednl. orgns.; sponsor Fedn. Am. Scientists; mem. Def. Sci. Bd., 1989-93; co-chair Nester Inc., assoc. Neurosci. Rsch. Program. Author: Introduction to The Meaning and Structure of Physics, 1968, Structure and Meaning, 1992, How We Learn, How We Remember: Toward an Understanding of Brain and Neural Systems, 1995; Contbr. articles to profl. jours. Recipient Nobel prize (with J. Bardeen and J.R. Schrieffer), 1972, award of Excellence, Grad. Faculties Alumni of Columbia U., 1974, Descartes medal Acad. de Paris, U. Rene Descartes, 1977, John Jay award Columbia Coll., 1985, award for Disting. Achievement Columbia U., 1990, Alexander Hamilton award Columbia Coll., 1995; Alfred P. Sloan Found. rsch. fellow, 1959-66, John Simon Guggenheim Meml. Found. fellow, 1965-66. Fellow AAAS, Am. Phys. Soc., Am. Acad. Arts and Scis.; mem. Am. Philos. Soc., Nat. Acad. Scis. (Comstock prize with J.R. Schrieffer 1968), Soc. Neurosci., Internat. Neural Network Soc., Phi Beta Kappa, Sigma Xi. Office: Brown U Box 1843 Physics Dept Providence RI 02912-1843*

COOPER, LYNN DALE, retired minister, retired navy chaplain; b. Aberdeen, Wash., Aug. 11, 1932; s. Lindsey Monroe and Mattie Ann (Cattron) C.; m. Doris Marlene Aydelott, June 2, 1956; children: Kevin Dale, Kathy Cooper O'Briant, Karen Doris Cooper Henthorn. Student, Gray's Harbor Coll., 1950-51; BTh, Northwest Christian Coll., 1955; MDiv, Phillips U., 1961, D Ministry, 1977. Ordained to ministry Christian Ch., 1954. Commd lt. (j.g.) USN, 1965, advanced through grades to comdr., 1988, ret., 1988; assoc. pastor First Christian Ch., Olympia, Wash., 1955-57; minister First Christian Ch., Aline, Okla., 1957-61, Sumner, Wash., 1961-66; chaplain U.S. Navy, 1966-88; minister Cen. Christian Ch., Prosser, Wash., 1988-97; bd. dirs. Jubilee Ministries, Prosser, Wash., 1988-96. Recipient many Navy and Marine Corps awards and medals; decorated Bronze Star medal. Mem. Mil. Chaplains Assn. U.S.A. (life), Disciples of Christ Hist. Soc. (life), Navy League of U.S., Ret. Officers Assn. (life), Kiwanis (past pres. Prosser, Wash. chpt.), De Molay (past master councillor 1950—). Avocations: hiking, snowshoeing, backpacking. Home: 1818 Benson Ave Prosser WA 99350-1547

COOPER, MARK FREDRICK, artist, sculptor, art educator; b. Evansville, Ind., Oct. 5, 1950; s. I. Phillip and J. Janice (Crystal) C.; m. Danette English, Aug. 22, 1987; children: Alexandra Carrey, Jack English. BS, Ind. U., 1972; MFA, Tufts U., 1980. Asst. prof. art Boston Coll., Chestnut Hill, Mass., 1978—; mem. permanent faculty Sch. Mus. Fine Arts, Boston, 1978—. One man exhbns. include Sun Valley (Idaho) Gallery, 1975, 79, Helen Shlien Gallery, Boston, 1980, 81, 82, 85, Allan Stone Gallery, N.Y.C., 1987, Hartje Gallery, Frankfurt, Germany, 1988, Howard Yezerski Gallery, Boston, 1989, 90, 95, New England Bio-Tech Gallery, 1990, 91, Ctr. St. Studio Gallery, Boston, 1995, Models Inc., Boston, 1997, others; group exhbns. include Almeditteranea, Spain, 1993, Polaroid Gallery, Tokyo, 1994, Polaroid Gallery, Cambridge, Mass., 1995, G.W. Einstein Gallery, N.Y.C., 1995, DNA Gallery, Provincetown, Mass., 1995, John Wayne Airport, Costa Mesa, Calif., 1996, Northwest Mo. State U., Maryville, Mo., 1996, Bernard Toale Gallery, Boston, 1996, U. Hawaii, Honolulu, 1996, Cambridge Multicultural Arts Ctr., 1996, 99, Baum Fine Arts Galleries, U. Ctrl. Ark., Conway, 1997, numerous others; mus. exhbns. include Danforth (Mass.) Mus., 1988, 89, 90, Whitney Mus. Philip Morris, 1999, Inst. Contemporary Art, Boston, 1994, Fuller Mus., Brockton, Mass., 1994, Kuntsmuseum, Cologne, Germany, 1992, 96; Boston Coll. Mus., 1994, Capital Children's Mus., Washington, 1995, 96, Corcoran Mus. Art, Washington, 1995, N.D. Mus. Art, Grand Forks, 1996, Revolving Mus., Boston, 1997, numerous others; commns. include First Night Boston, 1992, 93, 94, House of Blues Corp., 1994, Lyons Group, 1995, numerous others; works and Project Against Violence subject numerous publs. and TV features, 1976—. Dir. Project Against Violence, Boston, Washington, N.Y.C., 1991—; bd. dirs. Creativity in the 21st Century. Grantee Ruth Mott Fund, 1995-96, Cafritz Found., 1994, NEA, 1993; recipient pub. svc. award Mayor of Boston, 1995; fellowship Open Soc. Inst., 1998-00, Mass Cultural Coun. sculpture award, 1999. Home and Studio: 52 Saint James Ave Somerville MA 02144-2930

COOPER, MARSH ALEXANDER, mining company executive; b. Toronto, Ont., Can., Oct. 8, 1912; s. Frederick W. and Gertrude (Marsh) C.; m. Doris Elsie Roos, Sept. 13, 1941. BASc, MASc, U. Toronto, 1935; postgrad., Harvard U., 1938-39; D.Sc. (hon.), St. Francis Xavier U., 1974; LL.D. (hon.), Laurentian U., 1984. Ptnr. James, Buffam & Cooper, 1937-67; pres., CEO McIntyre Mines, Ltd., 1967-69, Falconbridge Ltd., Toronto, 1969-80, M.A. Cooper Cons. Inc., 1980—. Bd. dirs. W.M. Keck Found. Mem. Soc. Econ. Geologists, Assn. Profl. Engrs. Province of Ont., Am. Inst. Mining, Metall. and Petroleum Engrs., Can. Inst. Mining and Metallurgy. Office: Ste 1004, 95 Wellington St, Toronto, ON Canada M5J 2V4

COOPER, MARSHALL, information company executive; b. N.Y.C., Nov. 20, 1967; s. Norman and Marilyn Cooper; m. Kristine Ann Cooper, Sept. 1, 1996. BA, U. Mich., 1989; MBA, Dartmouth Coll., 1993. Aide-comms. The White House, Washington, 1989-91; dir. K-III Info., N.Y.C., 1993-95; mgr. The N.Y. Times Co., N.Y.C., 1995-96; exec. v.p. Kennedy Info., LLC, Fitzwilliam, N.H., 1996—; ptnr. Internat. Info. Investors, L.A., 1997—. Office: Kennedy Info LLC 1 Kennedy Pl Rte 12 S Fitzwilliam NH 03447

COOPER, MARTIN, electronics company executive; b. Chgo., Dec. 26, 1928; s. Arthur and Mary C.; children from previous marriage: Scott David, Lisa Ellen; m. Arlene Harris, Jan. 26, 1991. BSEE, Ill. Inst. Tech., 1950, MSEE, 1957. Research engr. Teletype Corp., Chgo., 1953-54; with Motorola, Inc., Schaumburg, Ill., 1954-83, ops. dir., 1967-76, div. mgr., 1977-78, v.p., corp. dir. research and devel., 1978-83; chmn., chief exec. officer Cellular Bus. Systems, Inc., 1983-86, Cellular Pay Phone Inc., Chgo. and Del Mar, Calif., 1986-92, Arraycomm, Inc., San Jose, Calif., 1992—; mem. computer-telecommunications bd. NRC, 1979-83; mem. indsl. adv. bd. U. Ill.-Chgo., 1980-90. Served with USNR, 1950-54. Fellow IEEE (pres. vehicular tech. soc. 1973-74, telecommunications policy bd. 1976—, award for contbns. to radiotelephony, Centennial medal awardee), Internat. Electronics Consortium (disting. lectr., adv. bd.), Radio Club of Am. (Fred Link award); mem. Ill. Inst. Tech. Alumni Assn. (v.p.). Patentee in field. Home and Office: Arraycomm Inc 100 Via De La Valle Del Mar CA 92014-2031 *It is essential that we conduct ourselves as though each of our fellow humans is honest, values his or her word, is ethical and moral. They will rise to our honorable expectations just as they can sink to our base suspicions.*

COOPER, MARY CAMPBELL, information services executive; b. Meadville, Pa., Aug. 14, 1940; d. Paul F. and Margaret (Webb) Campbell; m. James Nicoll Cooper, June 8, 1963; children: Alix, Jenny. BA, Mt. Holyoke Coll., 1961; MLS, Simmons Coll., 1963; MEd, Harvard U., 1965. Cert. museum adminstrn. With Harvard U. Libr., Cambridge, Mass., 1961-63, Carleton U. Libr., Ottawa, Can., 1965-85; archive cons. U.S., Can., 1985-86; info. mgr. Haley & Aldrich Inc., Cambridge, 1986-88, Tsoi/Kobus & Assocs., Cambridge, 1988-90; pres., founder Cooper Info., Cambridge, 1990—; bd. dirs. Mass. Com. for Preservation of Archtl. Records, Boston. Author: Records in Architectural Offices, 1992, Records and Information Management: Meeting the Challenge, 1994, Records and Information Management: Order Out of Chaos, 1996. Bd. dirs. Berkshire Hist. Soc., Pitts., Mass. Travel grantee Nat. Hist. Pub. Records Commn., 1991. Mem. Spl. Librs. Assn., Am. Mus. Assn., Assn. Ind. Info. Profls., Assn. Moving Image Archivists, Assn. Records Mgrs. and Adminstrs. (nat. com. 1991—). Avocations: travel, tennis, swimming. Home and Office: 5 Ellery Pl Cambridge MA 02138-4200

COOPER, MARY LITTLE, federal judge, former banking commissioner; b. Fond du Lac, Wis., Aug. 13, 1946; d. Ashley Jewell and Gertrude (McCoy) Little; m. John Francis Parell, May 28, 1972 (div. 1990); children: Christie, Morgan, Shawn, John Brady; m. John F. Cooper, Dec. 26, 1997. AB in Polit. Sci. cum laude, Bryn Mawr Coll., 1968; JD, Villanova U., 1972; LLD (hon.), Georgian Ct. Coll., 1987. Bar: N.J. 1972. Assoc. McCarter & English, Newark, 1972-80, ptnr., 1980-84; commr. N.J. Dept. Banking, Trenton, 1984-90; assoc. gen. counsel Prudential Property & Casualty Ins. Co., Holmdel, N.J., 1991-92; judge U.S. Dist. Ct. N.J., 1992—; chmn. bd. Pinelands Devel. Credt Bank. Bd. trustees Exec. Commn. Ethical Standards, Trenton, 1984-90, Corp. Bus. Assistance, Trenton, 1984-91, N.J. Housing & Mortgage Fin. Agy., Trenton, 1984-90, N.J. Cemetery Bd. Assn., 1984-90, N.J. Hist. Soc., 1976-79, YMCA of Greater Newark, 1973-76, Diocesan Investment; mem. Supreme Ct. N.J. Civil Practice Com., 1982-84, Supreme Ct. N.J. Dist. Ethics Com., 1982-84; lay assesor Ecclesiastical Ct. Episc. Diocese Newark, 1980-84. Fellow Am. Bar Found.; mem. ABA, N.J. Bar Assn., Princeton Bar Assn., John J. Gibbons Am. Inn of Ct. Office: US Courthouse 402 E State St Ste 5000 Trenton NJ 08608-1507

COOPER, MATTHEW MARC, cardiothoracic surgeon; b. Yonkers, N.Y., Jan. 6, 1957; s. Leon M. and Ida C.; m. Nina Irene Germaniuk, Aug. 25,

1985. BA in Math. and Biology magna cum laude, Franklin and Marshall Coll., 1979; MD with honors, NYU, 1983; student, Harvard U., 1997. Diplomate Am. Bd. Thoracic Surgery, Am. Bd. Surgery; cert. Nat. Bd. Med. Examiners. Surg. house officer numerous N.Y.C. Hosps., 1983-85; med. staff fellow surgery br. Nat. Heart, Lung, Blood Inst. NIH, Bethesda, Md., 1985-87; chief and sr. resident U. Iowa Hosps. and Clinics Iowa City (Iowa) VA Med. Ctr., 1987-89; chief resident and resident cardiothoracic surgery Columbia-Presbyn. Med. Ctr., Babies Hosp., N.Y.C., 1989-91; sr. registrar cardiothoracic surgery Hosp. for Sick Children, London, 1991-92; cardiothoracic surgeon Meml. Hosp., Colorado Springs, Colo., 1992-93, Boulder City (Nev.) Hosp., 1998—, Vencor Hosp., Las Vegas, 1996—, St. Rose Dominican Hosp., Henderson, Nev., 1994—, various hosps., Las Vegas, 1994—, Cardiovasc. Surgery Assocs., Las Vegas, 1994—; clin. asst. prof. dept. surgery U. Nev. Sch. Medicine, 1995—; chief cardiovasc. and thoracic surgery Mountain View Hosp., 1996-97, 99—, chmn. dept. surgery, 1997—; chief pediat. cardiac surgery Meml. Hosp., 1992-93, cardiac svcs. monitoring and evaluation com., 1992-93; mem. data com. Rocky Mountain Heart Consortium, 1993; vice chmn. dept. surgery Sunrise Hosp. and Med. Ctr., 1997-98, chief cardiovasc. and thoracic surgery, 1997-98, chmn. dept. surgery, 1999—; chmn. Las Vegas Cardiovasc. IPA, 1997; quality improvement reviewer Desert Springs Hosp., 1994—; mem. med. adv. com., bd. dirs. Nev. Donor Network. Guest reviewer Annals Thoracic Surgery, 1992—; contbr. articles to profl. jours.; presenter in field. Mem. coun. on cardiothoracic and vascular surgery Am. Heart Assn., 1997—. Fellow ACS; mem. AMA, Internat. Soc. Cardiac Biol. Implants, Internat. Soc. Heart and Lung Transplantation, Andrew G. Morrow Soc. Cardiovasc. Surgeons (Traveling fellowship award 1988), The John Jones Surg. Soc., Soc. Thoracic Surgeons, Nev. State Med. Soc. (med. legal screening panel 1997—), Clark County Med. Assn., Las Vegas Pediat. Soc., Wilderness Med. Soc., United Network Organ Sharing, Phi Beta Kappa, Mu Upsilon Sigma. Republican. Jewish. Avocations: parrots, music-clarinet and saxophone, skiing, biking, scuba diving. Fax: 702-367-3884. E-mail: cophud@aol.com. Office: Cardiovascular Surgery Assocs 1090 E Desert Inn # 202 Las Vegas NV 89109

COOPER, MAX DALE, physician, medical educator, researcher; b. Hazlehurst, Miss., Aug. 31, 1933; s. Ottis Noah and Lily (Carpenter) C.; m. Rosalie Lazzara, Feb. 6, 1960; children: Owen Bernard, Melinda Lee Cooper Holladay, Michael Kane, Christopher Byron. Student, Holmes Jr. Coll., 1951-52, U. Miss., 1952-54; postgrad., U. Miss. Med. Sch., 1954-55; MD, Tulane U., 1957. Diplomate Am. Bd. Pediatrics. Intern Saginaw (Mich.) Gen. Hosp., 1957-58; resident dept. pediatrics Tulane Med. Sch., New Orleans, 1958-60; house officer Hosp. for Sick Children, London, 1960, rsch. asst. dept. neurophysiology, 1961; allergy fellow dept. pediatrics U. Calif. Med. Ctr., San Francisco, 1961-62; instr. Tulane Med. Sch., New Orleans, 1962-63; med. fellow specialist U. Minn., Mpls., 1963-64, instr., 1964-66; asst. prof. dept. pediats. U. Ala., Birmingham, 1967-71, assoc. prof. dept. microbiology, 1967-71, dir. rsch. Rehab. Rsch. and Tng. Ctr., 1968-70, prof. dept. microbiology, 1971—, dir. Cell. Identification Lab., 1987-90, dir. Ctr. Interdisciplinary Rsch. in Immunological Diseases, 1987-95, dir. Div. Devel./Clin. Immunology, 1987—, prof. dept. medicine, 1987—, investigator Howard Hughes Med. Inst., 1988—; sr. scientist Comprehensive Cancer Ctr. U. Ala., Birmingham, 1971—, Multipurpose Arthritis Ctr., 1979—, Cystic Fibrosis Rsch. Ctr., 1981—; dir. Cellular Immunobiology Unit of Tumor Inst. U. Ala., Birmingham, 1976-87; vis. scientist tumor immunology unit dept. zoology, U. Coll. London, 1973-74, Inst. D'Embryologie, Nogent-Sur-Marne and Inst. Pasteur, Paris, 1984-85. Co-author: Acute Hemiplegia in Childhood, 1962, Ontogeny of Immunity, 1967, Immunologic Incompetence, 1971, Immunodeficiency in Man and Animals, 1975, numerous others; mem. editl. bds. Immunology Today, 1986, Immunodeficiency Revs., 1987-94, Clin. Immunology and Immunopathology, 1987-90, Internat. Immunology, 1988—; assoc. editor Jour. Immunology, 1972-76, 77-79, Arthritis and Rheumatism, 1985-90, Jour. Clin. Immunology, 1979-83; co-editor Seminars in Immunopathology, 1988-91; editor Current Topics in Microbiology and Immunology, 1981—; contbr. numerous 450 articles to profl. jours. Faculty rsch. assoc. Am. Cancer Soc., 1966-71; mem. bd. sci. advisors St. Jude Hosp., Memphis, 1981-84, 91—, Becton-Dickinson Monoclonal Antibody Ctr., 1980-90; mem. med. adv. com. Immune Deficiency Found., 1981-99; mem. bd. sci. counselors Nat. Cancer Inst., Bethesda, Md., 1982-86, Nat. Inst. Allergy and Infectious Diseases, 1978-82, 90-95, Inst. Merieux, Lyons, France, 1985-90, Med. Biology Inst., La Jolla, Calif., 1986; mem. internat. sci. adv. bd. Basel (Switzerland) Inst. Immunology, 1987-91; NIH Immunobiology Study Sect., 1974-78; trustee Leukemia Soc. Am., 1983-88. Special Postdoctoral Rsch. fellow USPHS, 1964-66; recipient Teaching Traineeship award Nat. TB Assn., 1962-63, Samuel J. Meltzer Founder's award Soc Exptl. Biology and Medicine, 1966, Life Scis. award 3M, 1990, Sandoz Prize for Immunology, 1990. Mem. NAS, AAAS, AAUP, Am. Assn. Immunologists (pres. 1988-89, councilor 1983-86, chmn. mem. com. 1974-77), Am. Soc. Exptl. Pathology, Am. Soc. Clin. Investigation, Am. Assn. Cancer Rsch., Am. Acad. Pediatrics, Am. Pediatric Soc., Fedn. Am. Scientists, Med. Assn. State Ala., Internat. Soc. Devel. and Comparative Immunology, Soc. Francaise d'Immunologie (life Membre d'Honneur), Soc. Pediatric Rsch. (v.p. 1978), So. Soc. Pediatric Rsch. (pres. 1975), Cen. Soc. Clin. Rsch., Jefferson County Med. Assn., Clin. Immunology Soc., Am. Acad. Scis., Inst. Medicine, Am. Acad. Arts and Scis., Soc. Mucosal Immunology, Alpha Omega Alpha, Sigma Xi. Achievements include research in developmental immunobiology with emphasis on B cell and T cell differentiation, in clinical immunology with emphasis on immunodeficiency diseases and lyhmphoid malignancies. Office: Howard Hughes Med Inst U Ala Birmingham Wallace Tumor Inst Rm 378 Birmingham AL 35294

COOPER, MICHAEL ANTHONY, lawyer; b. Passaic, N.J., Mar. 29, 1936. B.A., Harvard U., 1957, LL.B., 1960. Bar: N.Y. State 1961, U.S. Supreme Ct. 1969. With firm Sullivan & Cromwell, N.Y.C., 1960—; ptnr. Sullivan & Cromwell, 1968—; pres. Legal Aid Soc., 1981-83; bd. fellows Inst. Jud. Adminstrn. Co-chair Lawyers Com. for Civil Rights Under Law, 1993-95; bd. dirs. Fund for Modern Cts., Vols. of Legal Svcs. Fellow Am. Coll. Trial Lawyers; mem. ABA, N.Y. State Bar Assn., Assn. Bar City N.Y. (chmn. exec. com. 1996-97, v.p. 1997-98, pres. 1998—), Fed. Bar Coun. (trustee), Am. Law Inst., Am. Judicature Soc. Office: Sullivan & Cromwell 125 Broad St Fl 28 New York NY 10004-2489

COOPER, MILTON, real estate investment trust executive; b. N.Y.C., Mar. 15, 1929; s. Aaron and Fannie (Liebowitz) Cooper; m. Shirley Mandelker, Sept. 9, 1950; children: Clifford, David, Matthew, Todd. BBA, CCNY, 1949; LLB, Bklyn. Law Sch., 1952. Bar: N.Y. 1952. Ptnr. Jaffin, Schneider, Kimmel & Galpeer, N.Y.C., 1952-66, Galpeer & Cooper, N.Y.C., 1966-70; chmn. Kimco Realty Corp., New Hyde Park, N.Y., 1966—; bd. dirs. Getty Realty Corp., Blue Ridge Real Estate Cos. Trustee Mass. Mut. Corp. Investors, Mass. Mut. Participation Investors, Springfield. Mem. Nat. Assn. Real Estate Investment Trusts (chmn. bd. govs.). Office: Kimco Corp 3333 New Hyde Park Rd New Hyde Park NY 11042-1205*

COOPER, N. LEE, lawyer; m. Joy Clark; children: Clark, Catherine. BS, U. Ala., 1963, LLB, 1964. Pvt. practice Birmingham, Ala., 1966—; founder Maynard, Cooper & Gale, P.C., Birmingham. Articles and Notes editor Ala. Law Rev., 1962-64. Nat. bd. dirs. U. Ala.; trustee Ala. Law Sch. Found. 1st lt. U.S. Army, 1964-66, capt. USAR. Fellow Am. Bar Found.; mem. ABA (chair, litig. sect. 1985-86, sec. litig. sect. 1976-78, Birmingham bar del. to ho. of deps. 1979-80, Ala. del. to ho. of dels. 1980-89, chair ho. of dels. drafting com. on model rules of profl. conduct 1982-84, mem. commn. on professionalism 1985-87, chair select com. on ho. of dels. 1989-90, chair ho. of dels. 1990-92, pres.-elect 1995-96, pres. 1996-97), Am. Judicature Soc. (dir.), Am. Bar Endowment (dir.), Am. Law Inst. (council, advisor project on restatement of law governing lawyers), Ala. Bar Assn. (pres. young lawyers sect. 1974-75, Merit award 1976), Birmingham Bar Assn. (sec.-treas. 1972, vice chair congl. commn. on structural alts. for the fed. cts. of appeals, dir. lawyers com. for civil rights). Office: AmSouth Harbert Plz 1901 6th Ave N Ste 2400 Birmingham AL 35203-4604

COOPER, NORMAN STREICH, pathologist, medical educator; b. N.Y.C., Dec. 23, 1920; s. Samuel and Edith (Streich) C.; m. Evelyn Fickler, Apr. 13, 1945; 1 child, Jonathan Samuel. BA, Columbia Coll., 1940; MD, U. Rochester, 1943. Diplomate Am. Bd. Pathology. Intern, resident pathology N.Y. Hosp., N.Y.C., 1944-46, intern in medicine, 1948-49; scientist Oak Ridge Nat. Lab., Tenn., 1947-48; instr. microbiology NYU Sch. Medicine, N.Y.C., 1949-51, instr. pathology, 1951-54, asst. prof., 1954-56; assoc. prof. NYU Sch. Medicine, 1956-67, prof. pathology, 1967—; chief pathology and lab. medicine svc. DVA Med. Ctr., N.Y.C., 1967-97; cons., 1997—; founding pres. Assn. VA Lab. Service Chiefs, 1974-76. Mem. editorial bd. Clin. Immunology and Immunopathology, 1979-82. Vice pres., treas. Arthritis Found., N.Y. chpt., 1978-84. Served to capt. U.S. Army, 1946-48. Mem. Am. Assn. Immunologists, Am. Soc. for Investigative Pathology, U.S. and Can. Acad. Pathology, Transplantation Soc., Assn. VA Pathologists (pres. 1987-89), Soc. for In Vitro Biology, Am. Soc. for Cell Biology, Army and Navy Club (Washington), Dunes Racquet Club. Home: PO Box 1887 228 Cove Hollow Rd East Hampton NY 11937-0902 Office: NYU/DVA Med Ctrs 423 E 23rd St New York NY 10010-5050

COOPER, NORTON J. (SKY COOPER), liquor, wine and food company executive; b. Phila., Aug. 16, 1931; s. Maurice J. and Elsie (Goldstein) C.; divorced; children: John Amos, Rob. B.A., Cornell U., 1953. With Charles Jacquin et Cie Inc., Phila., 1955—, pres., chief exec. officer, prin. owner, 1979—; pres., chief exec. officer, prin. owner Chambord et Cie, France, Doumen Canton Liquer Co. Ltd., Guandong, People's Republic of China, St Dalfour et Cie, Marmande, France; pres. Lost Horizons Wines Pty, Capetown, South Africa. Author: off-Broadway prodn. Ballad of Jazz Street, 1959. Served to 1st lt. AUS, 1953-55. Decorated Ordre de Chevalier de Provence. Mem. Confrerie des Chevalier, du Tastevin.

COOPER, PAUL, mechanical engineer, research director; b. Mt. Holly, N.J., May 21, 1934; s. Frederick and Katherine Lena (Sixt) C.; m. Therese Adams, Apr. 11, 1959; children: Margaret Mary, Gregory, Timothy Richard, Peter Dunstan. BSME, Drexel U., 1957; MSME, MIT, 1959; PhD in Engring., Case Western Res. U., 1972. Registered profl engr., Ohio. Rsch. asst. MIT, Cambridge, 1957-59; instr. Case Western Res. U., Cleve., 1968, 72; fluids engring. specialist TRW Inc., Cleve., 1959-77; researcher, sr. staff Ingersoll-Rand Rsch., Inc., Princeton, N.J., 1977-85; dir. hydraulic tech. Ingersoll-Rand Co., Phillipsburg, N.J., 1986-87, dir. R&D Pump Group, 1987-92; dir. advanced tech. Ingersoll-Dresser Pump Co., Phillipsburg, N.J., 1992-99; mem. adv. bd. Internat. Pump Symposium, Tex. A&M U., 1983—; bd. dirs. R&D Coun. N.J., 1987-92. Contbr. articles to profl. jours. Recipient George Stephenson Rsch. prize Instn. of Mech. Engrs., London, 1984. Fellow ASME (exec. com. fluids engring. divsn. 1982-87, fluid machinery design award 1992, Henry R. Worthington medal 1993, Robert Henry Thurston lectr. 1995); mem. Sigma Xi (assoc.), Pi Tau Sigma, Tau Beta Pi. Episcopalian. Achievements include patents relating to aircraft fuel pumps and commerical industrial pumps; avocation: private pilot. Home: 415 Pennington Titusville Rd Titusville NJ 08560-2012 Office: Ingersoll-Dresser Pump Co 942 Memorial Pkwy Phillipsburg NJ 08865-2741

COOPER, PAUL DOUGLAS, lawyer; b. Kansas City, Mo., July 22, 1941; s. W.W. and Emma Marie (Ringo) C.; m. Elsa B. Shaw, June 15, 1963 (div. 1991); children: Richard, Dean; m. Kay J. Rice, Aug. 30, 1992; 1 child, Natanya. BA in English, U. Mich., 1963; LLB, U. Calif., Hastings Coll. Law, 1966. Bar: Colo. 1966, U.S. Dist. Colo. 1966, U.S. Ct. Appeals (10th cir.) 1967, U.S. Supreme Ct. 1979. Dep. dist. atty. Denver, 1969-71; asst. U.S. atty. Dist. of Colo., 1971-73; ptnr. Yegge, Hall & Evans, Denver, 1973-80; pres., dir. Cooper & Kelley, P.C., Denver, 1980-94, Cooper & Clough, P.C., Denver, 1994—; mem. faculty trial practice seminar Denver U. Law Sch., 1982; spl. asst. U.S. atty. Dist. of Colo., 1973-75; spl. prosecutor Mar. 1977 term, Garfield County Grand Jury; pres. Bow Mar Owners, Inc., 1976-77; bd. dirs. Colo. Physicians Health Program 1986-88, Def. Counsel Trial Acad. Boulder, Colo., 1991. Recipient Spl. Commendation for Outstanding Service, 1972. Mem. ABA, Am. Bd. Trial Advs., Colo. Bar Assn. (interprofl. com., bd. govs.), Denver Bar Assn. (trustee, 1st v.p. 1982-83), Colo. Med. Soc. (chmn. interprofl. com., Denver bar liaison com.), Internat. Assn. Def. Counsel (mem. exec. com. 1989-92). Republican. Club: Denver Athletic. Office: 1512 Larimer St Ste 600 Denver CO 80202-1610 Home: 1890 Bellaire St Denver CO 80220-1051

COOPER, PAULA, art dealer; b. Mass., Mar. 14, 1938. Student, Pierce Coll., Athens, Greece, Sorbonne, Paris, Goucher Coll.; DFA (hon.), R.I. Sch. Design, 1995. Asst. World House Galleries, N.Y.C., 1959-61; pvt. dealer, 1962-63; with Paula Johnson Gallery, N.Y.C., 1964-65; dir. Park Place Gallery, N.Y.C., 1965-67, Paula Cooper Gallery, N.Y.C., 1968—; chmn. bd. dirs. Kitchen Ctr., N.Y.C., 1985-95. Mem. Art Dealers Assn. Am. (chmn. bd. dirs. 1982-86, 88-90, 97—). Office: Paula Cooper Gallery 534 W 21st St New York NY 10011-2812

COOPER, PAULETTE MARCIA, writer; b. Antwerp, Belgium, July 26, 1942; came to U.S., 1948; naturalized, 1951; d. Ted S. and Stella R. (Toepfer) C.; m. Paul Noble. B.A. with honors, Brandeis U., 1964; M.A., CUNY, 1968. Free-lance writer, 1968—. Recipient Edgar Allan Poe spl. award Mystery Writers Am., 1975. Mem. Am. Soc. Journalists and Authors (Spl. award 1988, Conscience-in-Media award 1992), Travel Journalists Guild, Nat. Acad. of TV Arts & Sci. Author 9 books including: The Scandal of Scientology, The Medical Detectives; also 1000 articles. Address: 401 E 74th St New York NY 10021-3919

COOPER, R. JOHN, III, lawyer; b. East Orange, N.J., Mar. 2, 1942; s. Russell John and Cynthia Rhe (Runser) C.; m. Unni Irene Langaanes, June 20, 1964; children—Kirsten Elizabeth, R. John IV. A.B., Amherst Coll., 1964; postgrad., U. Oslo, 1965; J.D., Harvard U., 1968. Chief law clk. Supreme Jud. Ct. Mass., Boston, 1968-69; assoc. Cravath, Swaine & Moore, N.Y.C., 1969-77; ptnr. Casey Lane & Mittendorf, N.Y.C., 1977-82; gen. counsel video group Time Inc., N.Y.C., 1982-84; exec. v.p., gen. counsel, sec. Young & Rubicam, Inc., N.Y.C., 1984-94, also bd. dirs.; of counsel Davis, Weber & Edwards, N.Y.C., 1995—; bd. dirs. Dentsu Young & Rubicam Partnerships, N.Y.C., Tokyo, DWD, Tokyo, Y&R Sovero, Moscow. Editor: Cablespeech, 1983. Clk. of vestry Christ Ch., Short Hills, N.J., 1978-82, lay min., 1980—; trustee N.J. Shakespeare Fest, 1986; chmn. Millburn-Short Hills Cable TV Com., 1986-94; prof. Salzburg Seminars, Austria, 1986; pres. Juniper Point Village Improvement Soc., Boothbay Harbor, Maine, 1997—. Amherst Coll. fellow, Oslo, Norway, 1964-65. Mem. ABA (governing com., forum com. on sports and entertainment industries 1983-86), Assn. Bar City N.Y. (mem. antitrust and trade regulation com. 1982-84, corp. law depts. com. 1986-92), Am. Assn. Advt. Agys. (govt. rels. com. 1986-94). Republican. Episcopalian. Clubs: Short Hills (N.J.); Boothbay Harbor Yacht (Maine). Home: 9 East Ln Short Hills NJ 07078-3202 Office: Davis Weber & Edwards PC 100 Park Ave New York NY 10017-5516

COOPER, RACHEL BREMER, accountant; b. Oak Park, Ill., Dec. 21, 1950; d. James Louis and Betty Charlene (Barfield) B.; m. Terry Linn Cooper, Aug. 14, 1981. BS in Acctg., Murray State U., 1982. CPA, Tenn. Gen. bookkeeper The Paducah (Ky.) Sun, 1975-80; staff acct. Kraft Bros., Esstman, Patton, & Harrell, CPAs, Nashville, 1983; acquisition analyst Freeman Cos., Nashville, 1984; asst. controller Surg. Care Affiliates, Nashville, 1984-86; sr. staff acct. O'Neill & Co. CPAs, Nashville, 1986, EQUICOR, Nashville, 1987; acctg. mgr. Times Pub. Co., DBA The St. Petersburg (Fla.) Times, 1987-93; pres. Eco Solutions, Inc., St. Petersburg Beach, 1993—; pres., owner The Cover Story, Inc., Clearwater, Fla., 1996—; pres., owner Lady Rachael Imports, Nashville, 1986-87. Officer Don Cesar Property Owners Corp., St. Petersburg Beach, 1988-90. Named to Dean's List Paducah Community Coll., 1978, 79, Murray State U., 1980-82. Mem. Tenn. Soc. CPAs, Fla. Inst. CPAs, AICPA. Republican. Avocations: chess, painting, writing, photography, kayaking. Home: 178 Oswego St Lake Oswego OR 97035-1079

COOPER, REBECCA, art dealer; b. Phila., July 11, 1957; d. Frank N. Cooper and Bernice Silverstein; m. Michael J. Waldman, June 27, 1982. *Grandfather, Louis Silverstein, entrepreneur and philanthropist of Philadelphia, Pennsylvania, University of Pennsylvania Hospital Silverstein Pavillion and I.S. Ravdin Wing, owner Eagle's Football Team 1960's and Spectrum, yellow cabs of Philadelphia, waterfront real estate and Camden Fibre Mills in his lifetime. With grandmother, Hilda Lieberman Silverstein, Rosehilde Breeding Farm Bucks County, Pennsylvania, winning trotters include Cardigan Bay Worth Seein, Albatross.* BA NYU, MA, postgrad. Cert. appraiser. Owner Gallery Rebecca Cooper, Washington; pres. Rebecca Cooper Fine Art, N.Y.C., 1980s-90s; hon. chairperson N.Y. Women Bus. Owners Art Roundtable, 1981; lectr. Resources Coun., 1983, N.Y. Mayor's com. on interior design and furnishings, 1983; sec. bd. assocs. Am. Craft Mus., lectr. Collectors Circle; nat. patron Am. Fed. Art., Ind. Curators Inc. Patron, Mus. Modern Art; benefactor New Mus. Dirs. Forum; exhbn. assoc., mem. edn. com. Whitney Mus. Mem. Am. Appraisers Assn. (assoc.), Nat. Women's Rep. Club, Women's Investment Club, Women's 008 Investment Club, Pvt. Art Dealers Assn., Nat. Arts Club, Lotos Club, Guggenheim Mus. (internat. cir.).

COOPER, REGINALD RUDYARD, orthopedic surgeon, educator; b. Elkins, W.Va., Jan. 6, 1932; s. Eston H. and Kathryn (Wyatt) C.; m. Jacqueline Smith, Aug. 22, 1954; children—Pamela Ann, Douglas Mark, Christopher Scott, Jeffrey Michael. B.A. with honors, W.Va. U., 1952, B.S., 1953; M.D., Med. Coll. Va., 1955; M.S., U. Iowa, 1960. Diplomate Am. Bd. Orthopedic Surgeons (examiner 1968-70). Orthopedic surgeon U.S. Naval Hosp., Pensacola, Fla., 1960-62; assoc. in orthopedics U. Iowa Coll. Medicine, Iowa City, 1962-65; asst. prof. orthopaedics U. Iowa Coll. Medicine, 1965-68, assoc. prof. orthopedics, 1968-71, prof. orthopedics, 1971—, chmn. orthopedics, 1973-99; research fellow orthopedic surgery Johns Hopkins Hosp., Balt., 1964-65; exchange fellow to Britain for Am. Orthopedic Assn., 1969. Trustee Jour. Bone and Joint Surgeons, 1989-94, chmn. 1993-94. Trustee Nat. Easter Seals Research Found., 1977-81, chmn., 1979-81. Served to lt. comdr. USNR, 1960-62. Mem. Iowa, Johnson County Med. Socs., Orthopedic Rsch. Soc. (sec.-treas. 1970-73, pres. 1974-75), Am. Acad. Orthopedic Surgeons (Kappa Delta award for outstanding rsch. in orthopedics 1971), Canadian, Am. Orthopedic Assns., N.Y. Acad. Sci., Assn. Bone and Joint Surgeons, AMA, Am. Rheumatism Assn., Am. Acad. Cerebral Palsy, Am. Acad. Orthopedic Surgeons (chmn. exams. com. 1978-82, sec. 1982, 2d v.p. 1985-86, 1st v.p. 1986-87, pres. 1987-88, ortho residency rev. com. 1989-95, chmn. 1993-95). Home: 201 Ridgeview Ave Iowa City IA 52246-1625 Office: U Iowa Hosps & Clinics 450 Newton Rd Iowa City IA 52242

COOPER, RICHARD ALAN, hematologist, college dean, health policy analyst; b. Milw., Sept. 23, 1936; s. Peter and Annabelle (Schlomovitz) C.; m. Jaclyn Koppel, June 22, 1958 (dec.); children: Stephanie, Jonathan; m. Andrea Pastor, Aug. 20, 1988. BS, U. Wis., 1958; MD, Washington U., St. Louis, 1961. Intern Harvard U. med. services Boston City Hosp., 1961-63, resident in medicine, 1965-66, fellow in hematology Thorndike Meml. Lab., 1966-69; asst. prof. medicine Harvard U. Med. Sch., 1969-71; chief hematology div. Thorndike Meml. Lab. and Harvard Med. Services, Boston City Hosp., 1969-71; prof. medicine, dir. Cancer Center, chief hematology-oncology sect. U. Pa., Phila., 1971-85; prof. medicine, exec. v.p., dean Med. Coll. Wis., Milw., 1985-94, dir. health policy inst., 1992—. Mem. editorial bd. Blood, 1979-84, Lipid Research, 1983-84. Served with USPHS, 1963-65. NIH grantee. Mem. Am. Soc. Hematology, Am. Fedn. Clin. Rsch., Am. Soc. Clin. Investigation, Assn. Am. Physicians, Am. Clin. Climatol. Assn., Phi Beta Kappa., Alpha Omega Alpha. Office: 8701 W Watertown Plank Rd Milwaukee WI 53226-3548

COOPER, RICHARD CASEY, lawyer; b. Tulsa, Jan. 20, 1942; s. Winston Churchill and Frances Margaret (Coppinger) C.; m. Ireen Lysbeth Evans, Nov. 24, 1965; children: Christopher Casey, Kimberly Ireen. BSBA, U. Tulsa, 1965, JD, 1967. Bar: Okla. 1967, U.S. Dist. Ct. (no., ea. and we. dists.) Okla. 1967, U.S. Ct. Mil. Appeals 1967, U.S. Ct. Appeals (10th cir.) 1972. Assoc. Boesche, McDermott & Eskridge, Tulsa, 1972-76, ptnr., 1977-92, mng. ptnr., 1990—. Editor in chief: Tulsa Law Jour., 1967. Counsel Tulsa Philharm. Orch., 1990-92; trustee Mervin Bovaird Found., Tulsa, 1991—, pres., 1995—; trustee The Philbrook Mus. Art, 1997—. Lt. USNR, 1967-71, mil. judge JAGC, 1970-71. Villard Martin scholar U. Tulsa, 1967, recipient Order of the Curule Chair, 1967. Mem. ABA, Okla. Bar Assn., Tulsa County Bar Assn., So. Hills Country Club. Republican. Avocations: family activities, fly fishing, travel. Home: 2923 E 58th St Tulsa OK 74105-7453 Office: Boesche McDermott Eskridge 100 W 5th St Ste 800 Tulsa OK 74103-4291

COOPER, RICHARD FRANCIS, computer company executive; b. Rouses Point, N.Y., May 27, 1946; s. Richard Charles and Bernice (Traynor) C.; m. Cheryl Jones, Aug. 9, 1975. Student, Albany Bus. Coll., 1965, Plattsburgh State U., 1966-67. Coding clk., asst. data processing F.W Myers, Inc., Rouses Point, N.Y., 1965-67; operator, programmer No. Data Processing, Plattsburgh, N.Y., 1967; data processing supr. Au Sable Valley Telephone Co., Keeseville, N.Y., 1967-69; data processing mgr. John H. McGaulley CPA, Plattsburgh, 1969-71; owner Computer Bus. Systems, Plattsburgh, 1971—; mgr. Roctest, Inc., Plattsburgh, 1977-85; sales assoc. Met. Life Ins., Plattsburgh, 1976; chief exec. officer Four-Star Heritage Group, Plattsburgh, 1985—; pres. Am. RR Transpn. Co., Plattsburgh, 1980—; v.p. No. Sports & Recreation, Plattsburgh, 1982—; chief exec. officer Computer Bus. Systems, Plattsburgh, 1985—; v.p. Ardcom Satellite Comm. Svcs., Plattsburgh, 1992—. Episcopalian. Avocations: model RR, hiking, camping. Office: 21 Track Side Plattsburgh NY 12901-3089

COOPER, RICHARD LEE, newspaper editor, journalist; b. Grand Rapids, Mich., Dec. 8, 1946; s. Harold Ralph and Elizabeth (DeSchipper) C.; m. Carol Jean Bonjernoor, Sept. 5, 1968; children—Jason Adam, Jessica Lynne. Student, Grand Rapids Jr. Coll., 1965-67; BA, Mich. State U., 1969. Reporter Rochester (N.Y.) Times-Union, 1969-77; reporter Phila. Inquirer, 1977—, Neighbors editor, 1983—, asst. city editor, 1988-91, Main Line editor, 1991—; editor Main Line & Del. County Neighbors, 1993—; editor Main Line, Del. County and Chester County Neighbors, 1995—, asst. regional editor, 1997—; instr. journalism Temple U., 1980—. Recipient N.Y. State Asso. Press Spot News First Place award, 1972, 76; Pulitzer prize for gen. local reporting, 1972; Distinguished Alumni award Grand Rapids Jr. Coll., 1974; Outstanding Contbn. in Pub. Info. award N.Y. State Bar Assn., 1977; 1st prize for investigative reporting Gannett News, 1977; Mich. Journalism fellow, 1990—. Mem. Pen and Pencil Club, Swan Creek Sailing Assn., Chesapeake Bay Triton Fleet, Rock Hall Sailing Club, Sigma Delta Chi. Presbyterian. Office: Phila Inquirer 400 N Broad St Philadelphia PA 19130-4099

COOPER, RICHARD NEWELL, economist, educator; b. Seattle, June 14, 1934; s. Richard Warren and Lucile (Newell) C.; m. Carolyn Jane Cahalan, June 5, 1956 (div. 1980); children: Laura Katherine, Mark Daniel; m. Ann Lorraine Hollick, Jan. 1, 1982 (div. 1994). AB, Oberlin Coll., 1956, LLD (hon.), 1978; MSc, London Sch. Econs., 1958; PhD, Harvard U., 1962; MA (hon.), Yale U., 1966. Sr. staff economist Council Econ. Advisers, 1961-63; asst. prof. econs. Yale U., 1963-65, prof., 1966-77, provost, 1972-74; dep. asst. sec. state internat. monetary affairs Dept. State, 1965-66, undersec. for econ. affairs, 1977-81; prof. econs. Harvard U., Cambridge, Mass., 1981—; chmn. Fed. Res. Bank Boston, 1990-92; chmn. Nat. Intelligence Coun., 1995-97; bd. dirs. Phoenix Home Mut. Life Ins. Co., Circuit City, Inst. Internat. Econs., Warburg-Pincus Funds, Ctr. Naval Analysis; trustee Oberlin Coll., 1993-98. Author: Economics of Interdependence, 1968, Currency Devaluation in Developing Countries, 1971, Economic Policy in an Interdependent World, 1986, The International Monetary System, 1987, Economic Stabilization and Debt in Developing Countries, 1992, (with others) Boom, Crisis and Adjustment, 1993, Environ. and Resource Policies for the World Economy, 1994; editor, contbr. A Reordered World, 1973, The International Monetary System under Flexible Exchange Rates, 1982, Can Nations Agree?, 1989, Trade Growth in Transition Economies, 1997; contbr. articles to profl. jours. Fellow Am. Acad. Arts and Scis.; mem. Am. Econ. Assn., Coun. Fgn. Rels., German-Am. Academic Coun. (mem. trilateral commn.). Office: Harvard U Ctr for Internat Affairs 1737 Cambridge St Cambridge MA 02138-3016

COOPER, ROBERT CARL, JR., veterinary medicine educator; b. Macon, Miss., Aug. 11, 1950; s. Robert Carl and Kathryn Emma (Woodcock) C.; m. Deborah Anne Roach, Aug. 26, 1972; children: Benjamin Andrew, Samuel Adam, Elizabeth Anne. Student, Miss. State U., 1971; DVM, Auburn U., 1975, MS, 1979. Diplomate Am. Coll. Vet. Surgeons. Assoc. veterinarian W. Broward Animal Hosp., Ft. Lauderdale, Fla., 1975-76; instr. anatomy and histology Auburn (Ala.) U., 1976-79; coord. surg. svcs. Miss. State U., Starkville, 1984-89, chmn. dept. clin. scis., 1989-91, prof. vet. medicine, 1995—. Contbr. articles to Am. Jour. Vet. Rsch., Vet. Medicine, Vet. Surgery. Asst. Scout Master Boy Scouts Am., Starkville, 1993—. Recipient Carl J. Norden Disting. Tchr. award Smith Kline Beecham, 1994, 99. Mem. AVMA, Phi Kappa Phi, Phi Zeta, Sigma Xi (chair univ. faculty senate 1999). Presbyn. Home: 110 Kirkside Dr Starkville MS 39759-4114 Office: Miss State Univ Coll Vet Med PO Box 9825 Mississippi State MS 39762-9825

COOPER, ROBERT ELBERT, state supreme court justice; b. Chattanooga, Oct. 14, 1920; s. John Thurman and Susie Inez (Hollingsworth) C.; m. Catherine Pauline Kelly, Nov. 24, 1949; children: Susan Florence Cooper Hodges, Bobbie Cooper Martin, Kelly Ann Smith, Robert Elbert Jr. B.A., U. N.C., 1946; J.D., Vanderbilt U., 1949. Bar: Tenn. 1948. Asso. Kolwyck and Clark, 1949-51; partner Cooper and Barger, 1951-53; asst. atty. gen. 6th Jud. Ct. Tenn., 1951-53; judge 6th Jud. Circuit Tenn., 1953-60; judge Tenn. Ct. Appeals, 1960-70, presiding judge Eastern div., 1970-74; justice Tenn. Supreme Ct., 1974-90, chief justice, 1976-77, 84-85; chmn. Tenn. Jud. Coun., 1967-90; chmn. Tenn. Code Commn., 1976-77, 84-85; mem. Tenn. Jud. Standards Commn., 1971-77. Mem. exec. bd. Cherokee council Boy Scouts Am., 1960-64; bd. dirs. Met. YMCA, 1956-65, St. Barnabas Nursing Home and Apts. for Aged, 1966-69. With USNR, 1941-46. Recipient Nat. Heritage award Downtown Sertoma Club, Chattanooga, 1989. Mem. Am., Tenn., Chattanooga bar assns., Conf. Chief Justices, Phi Beta Kappa, Order of Coif, Kappa Sigma, Phi Alpha Delta. Democrat. Presbyterian. Clubs: Signal Mountain Golf and Country, Masons (33 deg.), Shriners. Home and Office: 196 Woodcliff Cir Signal Mountain TN 37377-3147

COOPER, ROBERT JAMES, purchasing consultant; b. St. Louis, Dec. 27, 1929; s. William McKinley and Lucille Evelyn (Floyd) C.; m. Joan Kathleen Gray, Nov. 20, 1932; children: Bruce John, Anne Muriel. Student, Ruskin Coll., Oxford, Eng., 1954-55. Asst. purchasing agt. Absorbant Cotton Co., St. Louis, 1960-65; purchasing agt. Christian Hosp., St. Louis, 1965-67; dir. purchasing St. John's Mercy Med. Ctr., St. Louis, 1967-86; purchasing cons. St. Louis, 1986—; lectr. in field; condr. seminars/workshops in field. Contbr. articles to profl. jours. With USAF, 1950-54. Mem. Nat. Assn. Purchasing Mgmt., Nat. Assn. Hosp. Purchasing Mgmt. (pres. 1974-76, fellow), Assn. Hosp. Purchasing Agts. of Greater St. Louis (pres. 1968). Democrat. Episcopalian. Avocations: oil painting, stained glass, sculpture. Home: 7955 Big Bend Blvd Saint Louis MO 63119-2703 *Personal philosophy: Work hard, be honest and love people.*

COOPER, ROBERT SHANKLIN, engineering executive, former government official; b. Kansas City, Mo., Feb. 8, 1932; s. Robert S. and Edna A. (Pobanz) C.; m. Benita A. Sidwell, Oct. 5, 1985; children—Jonathan A., James G. BS in Elec. Engring, U. Iowa, 1954; MS, Ohio State U., 1958; ScD, MIT, 1963, Sc.D. (Ford Found. postdoctoral fellow), 1965. Mem. staff elec. engring. dept. Mass. Inst. Tech., 1958-65; mem. staff Lincoln Lab., 1965-72; asst. dir. def. research and engring. Dept. Def., 1972-75; dep. dir. Goddard Space Flight Center, Greenbelt, Md., 1975-76; dir. Goddard Space Flight Center, 1976-79; v.p. engring. Satellite Bus. Systems, McLean, Va., 1979-81; asst. Sec. Def. Washington, 1983-85; dir. Def. Adv. Research Projects Agy., Arlington, 1981-85; pres., chief exec. officer, chmn. bd. Atlantic Aerospace Electronics Corp., Greenbelt, Md., 1985—; bd. dirs. Lear Astonics Corp., Santa Monica, Calif., Trimble Navigation Ltd., Sunnyvale, Calif., GEC-Marconi N.Am., Inc., Wayne, N.J., 1998—; chmn. bd. dirs. Talarian Corp., Mountainview, Calif., 1989—; mem. def. sci. bd. Office Sec. Def., 1996—; mem. strategic adv. group U.S. Strategic Command, 1982—. Served with USAF, 1954-56. Westinghouse fellow, 1958; recipient Sec. Def. Meritorious Civilian Service award, 1975. Fellow AAAS, AIAA, IEEE; mem. Sigma Xi, Tau Beta Pi, Eta Kappa Nu. Office: Atlantic Aerospace Elec Co 6404 Ivy Ln Ste 300 Greenbelt MD 20770-1407*

COOPER, ROGER MERLIN, information technology executive,federal government official, school administrator; b. Scottsbluff, Nebr., Feb. 25, 1943; s. Dean P. and Bette Jane (Ward) C.; m. Erica Feuer: children: Gregory Joseph, Lis Jane. BS, U. Utah, 1964; MSA, George Washington U., 1970; MBA, U. So. Calif.; grad., Fed. Execs. Inst. U. Utah, 1980, Harvard U. Kennedy Sch. Govt., 1984. Master's lic. USCG. Mgr. sys. programming Larwin Group, Beverly Hills, Calif., 1973-74; chief teleprocessing sect. U.S. CSC, Washington, 1974-76, chief info. tech. divsn., 1976-77; dir. Office Automated Sys. Devel., Macon, Ga., 1977-78; asst. dir. U.S. Office Pers. Mgmt., Washington, 1979-82; dir. med. info. resources mgmt. office VA, Washington, 1982-85; dep. asst. sec. for info. sys. U.S. Dept. Treasury, Washington, 1985-88; dep. adminstr. Farmers Home Adminstrn., Washington, 1988-91; dep. asst. atty. gen. info. mgmt. U.S. Dept. Justice, Washington, 1991-95; v.p. I-NET Inc., Bethesda, Md., 1995-96; dir. info. tech. Fairfax County Pub. Sch. Sys., 1996—; CEO The Cooper Group, Ltd.; mem. Coun. of Prins., Nat. Communications Systems, Coun. Sch. Networks; mem. adv. bd. FTS2000; chmn. Nat. Computer Security and Privacy Bd.; exec. bd. Inter-agy. Coun. on Info. Resources Mgmt., Fed. Micro Adv. Bd.; active Fed. Info. Ctr. Adv. Coun., Fed. Info. Rsch. Policy Coun., Fed. Data Ctrs. Dirs. Conf.; bd. dirs. Armed Forces Electronics, Naval Liaison Office. Lt. USN, 1964-69; capt. USNR. Recipient Dept. Def. Joint Svc. achievment medal, 1988. Mem. ASPA. Home: 2002 Windmill Ln Alexandria VA 22307-1951

COOPER, SARAH JEAN, nursing educator; b. Wallace, Idaho, Oct. 3, 1940; d. Kenneth Albert and Jean Saxsonia (Horton) Merryweather; m. George Harlan Cooper, Aug. 5, 1961; children: John, Matthew, Thomas. Diploma, Sacred Heart Sch. Nursing, 1961; BSN, Pacific Luth. U., 1974; MN, U. Wash., Seattle, 1979. Assoc. dir. nursing St. Alphonsus Hosp., Boise, Idaho; asst. dir. nursing and staffing St. Luke's Regional Med. Ctr., Boise, mgr. patient care support svcs.; instr. nursing Walla Walla C.C. Kellogg Found. fellow; Pew grantee. Mem. Am. Soc. Quality, Sigma Theta Tau.

COOPER, SAUL, producer, public relations executive; b. N.Y.C., July 31, 1934; s. Joseph Matthew and Libby (Benson) C.; m. Karin Granath, June 23, 1957; children: Louis, Andrew, Michael, David, Elisabeth. BA, NYU, 1955; MS, Columbia U., 1957. Account exec. Lynn Farnol Group, N.Y.C., 1952-58; nat. publicity coordinator Paramount Pictures, N.Y.C., 1958-63; dir. mktg. Robert Rossen Prodns., N.Y.C., 1963-64; unit publicist 20th-Century Fox/MGM/Columbia Pictures, Rome, London, 1964-67; dir. prodn. publicity United Artists, London, Paris, 1967-70; dir. European film prodn. United Artists, Paris, 1970-72; prodr. 6 films including Les Films de la Seine, Les Gaspards, L'Agression, Paris, 1972-76; mktg. supr. Eon Prodns., London, N.Y.C., 1976-77; v.p. internat. advt. and publicity United Artists, N.Y.C., 1978-80; v.p. worldwide publicity and promotion 20th Century-Fox, L.A., 1980-82; prodr., Contact French CBS-Fox Video, L.A., 1982-83; pub. rels. cons. Saul Cooper Consultancy, L.A., 1983-88; dir. internat. mktg. ITC Entertainment Group, Studio City, Calif., 1988; v.p. Warfield (James Bond) Prodns., Inc., Culver City, Calif., 1988-92. Author 10 books including Dillinger, Sex on Celluloid, Hatari!, The Jayhawkers, Paris When It Sizzles; editor: Rodgers & Hammerstein Fact Book, 2d edit.; exec. prodr. Madeline (nominee 4 Emmy awards, 6 Humanitas awards), 39 animated shows from 1988-96; prodr. film Madeline, 1998. Mem. Acad. Motion Picture Arts and Scis. Home: 2439 Santa Barbara St Santa Barbara CA 93105-3549

COOPER, SHARON MARSHA, marketing, advertising executive; m. Steven Jon Cooper; children: Robin Eve, Erik Scott. BA, Northeastern Ill. U., Chgo., 1974; MEd, Loyola U., Chgo., 1977. Adj. asst. prof. Chgo. Med. Sch., North Chicago, Ill., 1974-79; edn./media coordinator Humana Hosp., Aurora, Colo., 1980-82; v.p. Healthcare Mktg. Corp., Denver, 1982-84; pres. Sharon Cooper Assocs., Ltd., Englewood, Colo., 1984—; cons./speaker Jason Pharms., Balt., 1988—; cons. Am. Soc. Bariatric Physicians; lectr. in field; guest lectr. U. Denver, 1988—. Illustrator: A Manual of Radiographic Positioning, 1973; contbr. articles to profl. jours. Bd. dirs., v.p. The Barre Assn./Colo. Ballet, Denver, 1989—; bd. dirs. Am. Diabetes Assn., Denver, 1983—, Am. Cancer Soc., Denver, 1988—, Hospice of St. John, Denver, 1986-90; mem. adv. bd. U. Colo. Denver Sch. of the Arts, 1997—. Named Co-Woman of the Yr., Lerner Newspapers, Chgo., 1973, Silver Microphone award, 1988, Golden Leaflet award, Colo. Hosp. Assn., 1981, 84. Mem. Am. Hosp. Assn., Assn. Healthcare Pub. Rels. and Mktg. (reg. rep. 1987—), Colo. Soc. Health Care Pub. Rels., Pub. Rels. Soc. Am., Zonta, Toastmasters (sec. 1972-84). Avocations: writing, art, aerobics. Office: Sharon Cooper Assocs Ltd 10 Inverness Dr E Ste 210 Englewood CO 80112-5612

COOPER, SHELDON MARK, medical educator, immunology researcher, rheumatologist; b. N.Y.C., Dec. 5, 1942; s. Alex and Sylvia (Silverman) C.; m. Amy Diane Freedman, Nov. 23, 1966; 1 child, Jonas Eric. BS cum laude, Hobart Coll., 1963; MD, NYU, 1967. Diplomate Am. Bd. Internal Medicine, Am. Bd. Rheumatology. Intern, asst. resident in internal medicine King's County Hosp. Ctr., Bklyn., 1967-69; fellow rheumatic disease study unit NYU Med. Ctr., N.Y.C., 1970-72; asst. prof. medicine U. So. Calif. Sch. Medicine, L.A., 1974-80; assoc. prof., rsch. coord., 1980-82; assoc. prof. medicine, dir. rheumatology and clin. immunology unit U. Vt., Coll. Medicine, Burlington, 1982-86, prof. medicine, dir. rheumatology and clin. immunology unit 1986—; mem. staff L.A. County U. So. Calif. Med. Ctr., 1974-82, Med. Ctr. Hosp. of Vt., Burlington, 1982—. Contbr. articles to profl. jours. Mem. exec. com., Vt. chpt. Arthritis Found., Burlington, 1982—, chmn., trustee, 1990—; mem. panel gen. and plastic surgery devices FDA. Served to maj. USAF, 1972-73. NIH fellow, 1971; Nat. Cancer Inst. grantee, 1976, NIAMS grantee, 1984—, NIH grantee, 1984—. Mem. Am. Coll. Rheumatology, Am. Fedn. Clin. Research, Am. Assn. Immunologists, Reticuloendothelial Soc., Physicians for Social Responsibility, Union Concerned Scientists. Democrat. Jewish. Avocations: jogging, swimming, travel, cinema. Home: Barstow Rd Shelburne VT 05482 Office: U Vt Given Bldg D301 Burlington VT 05405

COOPER, SHEROD MONROE, JR., retired English language educator; b. Norristown, Pa., Jan. 28, 1927; s Sherod Monroe and Louise (Morley) C.; m. Janet Williams, June 27, 1953; children: Sherod M. III, Stephen O., David L., Elizabeth C. Judy. BS with honors, Temple U., 1951, MA, 1953; PhD, U. Pa., 1963. English tchr. Woodstown (N.J.) H.S., 1952-54; instr. English Westminster Coll., New Wilmington, Pa., 1954-56; instr. English U. Md., College Park, 1957-63, asst. prof. English, 1963-67, assoc. prof. English, 1967-89, assoc. prof. emeritus, 1995—. Author: The Sonnets of Astrophel and Stella, 1968, S.S. John W. Brown: Baltimore's Living Liberty, 1991, Liberty Ship: The Voyages of the John W. Brown, 1942-46, 1997. With U.S. Merchant Marine, 1945-46, U.S. Army, 1946-47. Mem. Project Liberty Ship (historian 1988—, bd. dirs. 1990—), Nat. Maritime Hist. Soc., Steamship Hist. Soc. of Am., Naval Inst., Civitan Internat. Home: 922 Mastline Dr Annapolis MD 21401-6857

COOPER, SIMON F., hotel executive. Pres. Delta Hotels & Resorts, Toronto, Ont., Can., 1998, Mariott Lodging Can., Etobicoke, Can., 1998—. Office: Marriott Lodging Can, 10 Carlson Ct Ste 640, Etobicoke, ON Canada M9W 6L2

COOPER, STEPHEN HERBERT, lawyer; b. N.Y.C., Mar. 29, 1939; s. Walter S. and Selma (Herbert) C.; m. Linda Cohen, Aug. 29, 1965 (dec.); m. Karen Gross, Sept. 6, 1981; 1 child, Zachary Noel. A.B., Columbia U., 1960, J.D. cum laude, 1965. Bar: N.Y. 1965. Assoc. Breed, Abbott & Morgan, N.Y.C., 1965-66; assoc. Weil, Gotshal & Manges, N.Y.C., 1966-73, ptnr., 1973—; lectr. Nat. Inst. Securities Regulation U. Colo., Boulder, 1985, Practicing Law Inst. 25th Annual Nat. Inst. Securities Regulation, N.Y.C., 1993, Law Jours. Seminars, 1997, 98. Served to lt. USNR, 1960-62. Fellow Am. Bar Found.; mem. ABA (com. fed. regulation securities, subcom. internat. securities matters, co-chmn. 1990—). Home: 1125 Park Ave New York NY 10128-1243 Office: Weil Gotshal & Manges LLP 767 5th Ave Fl Concl New York NY 10153-0119

COOPER, STEVE NEIL, art gallery owner, photographer; b. N.Y.C., July 19, 1944; s. Felix Cooper and Sybil Koff. AAS, Rochester (N.Y.) Inst. Tech., 1964, BFA, 1966; cert. in film, NYU, 1992. Owner Steve Cooper Studio, N.Y.C., 1972—, Sybille Art Gallery, N.Y.C., 1985—. Recipient NE Pocket Billiards Champion NCAA, 1966, award Soc. Publ. Designers, 1975, N.Y.C. Art Dirs. Club award, 1978, Award of Excellence Decor Mag., 1987; N.Y. State Regents Coll. scholar, 1962. Mem. Am. Soc. Mag. Photographers, Assn. Ind. Video and Filmmakers. Jewish. Avocation: chess. Office: Sybille Gallery 5 W 31st St New York NY 10001-4414

COOPER, STEVEN JON, healthcare management consultant, educator; b. Oct. 19, 1941; m. Sharon M.; children: Robin E., Erik S. BA, U. Calif., L.A., 1966; MEd, Loyola U., 1973; PhD, Union Sch., 1979. Ednl. coord. dept. radiology Mt. Sinai Hosp. Med. Ctr., Chgo., 1969-72; chmn. dept. radiol. scis. U. Health Scis., Chgo. Med. Sch., VA Hosp., North Chicago, 1972-79; v.p. C&S, Inc., Denver, 1980-81; pres. Healthcare Mktg. Corp., Denver, 1981-84; corp. officer, exec. v.p. Sharon Cooper Assocs. Ltd., Englewood, Colo., 1984—; cons. HEW; lectr. in field. Contbr. articles to profl. publs. Pres. bd. dirs. Hospice of St. John. With USAF, 1960-64, USAFR, 1964-66. W.K. Kellogg Found. grantee. Mem. AMA (com. on allied health edn. and accreditation), Am. Soc. Radiol. Tech. (mem. edn., curriculum rev. coms., task force), Ill. Soc. Radiol. Tech. (chmn. annual meeting 1976, program Midwest conf. 1977), Coll. Radiol. Scis., Am. Hosp. Radiology Adminstrs. (mem. edn. com., treas. Midwest region, nat. v.p.), Kiwanis Club Inverness (charter, pres., lt. govt. divsn. 15 1997-98), Sovereign Order of St. John of Jerusalem, Knights of Malta, Inverness Club (bd. dirs.), Sigma Xi. Office: 10 Inverness Dr E Ste 210 Englewood CO 80112-5612

COOPER, STUART LEONARD, chemical engineering educator, researcher, consultant; b. N.Y.C., Aug. 28, 1941; s. Jacob and Anne (Bloom) C.; m. Marilyn Portnoy, Aug. 29, 1966; children: Gary, Stacey. B.S., MIT, 1963; Ph.D., Princeton U., 1967. Asst. prof. chem. engring. U. Wis., Madison, 1967-71, assoc. prof., 1971-74, prof., 1974, chmn. dept., 1983-89, 92, Paul A. Elfers prof., 1989-93; dean, H. Rodney Sharp prof. Coll of Engring. U. Del., Newark, 1993-98; v.p., chief acad. officer, P. Danforth prof. engring. Ill. Inst. Tech., 1998—; vis. assoc. prof. U. Calif.-Berkeley, 1974; vis. prof. Technion, Haifa, Israel, 1977; cons. in field; trustee Argonne Univs. Assn., Argonne Nat. Lab., 1975-81. Editor: Multiphase Polymers, 1979, Biomaterials: Interfacial Phenomena and Applications, 1982, The Vroman Effect, 1992, Polymer Biomaterials: In Solution as Interfaces and as Solids, 1995; author: Polyurethanes in Medicine, 1986, Polyurethanes in Biomedical Applications, 1997; contbr. numerous articles in field to profl. jours. Lady Davis fellow, 1977. Fellow AIChE (Charles M.A. Stine award 1987), AAAS, Am. Phys. Soc., Am. Inst. Med. and Biol. Engrs. (founding), Soc. for Biomaterials (pres. 1996-97, Clemson award for basic rsch. 1987); mem. Am. Chem. Soc. (best paper award 1976), Am. Soc. Artificial Internal Organs, Soc. Rheology, Soc. Plastics Engrs. Office: Ill Inst Tech 10 W 32d St Rm 117-E-1 Chicago IL 60616

COOPER, THOMAS ASTLEY, banking executive; b. Phila., July 19, 1936; s. Thomas Astley and Elmira (Betts) C.; m. Anita June Danenberger, Sept. 7, 1957; children: Aleta Cooper Bossert, Anita Cooper Barbato, Alane Cooper Inacker, Allison, Anne Cooper Fleming, Thomas Astley III. BA, Haverford Coll., 1957; BD, Drew U., 1960; postgrad., Pa. U., 1972; Program for Mgmt. Devel., Harvard U., 1976. Pres. Girard Bank, Phila., 1978; vice chmn. Mellon Bank, Mellon Nat. Corp., Pitts., 1982; pres. Bank of Am., Bank Am. Corp., San Francisco, 1984; chmn. Investment Svcs. for America, Tampa, Fla., 1986-90; pres., CEO Goldome, Buffalo, 1986-90; prin. TAC Assocs., Buffalo, 1992—; CEO Chase Fed. Bank, Miami, Fla., 1993-96; chmn. Flatiron Credit, Denver, 1997; dir. Dela. No. Cos., Buffalo, Rennaisance Reins, Bermuda; CEO TAC Assocs. Inc., Triton Systems, Gulfport, Miss., BISYS, Little Fall, N.J. Mem. Island Country Club, Brant Beach Yacht Club (N.J.). Office: 1291 Laurel Ct Marco Island FL 34145-2351

COOPER, THOMAS LOUIS, lawyer; b. Pitts., Mar. 16, 1938; s. Louis D. and Gertrude V. (Edmonds) C.; m. Leah Mary Meyers, Aug. 5, 1961; children—Marcia, Jeffrey, Daniel. B.A., Dartmouth Coll., 1959; LL.B., U. Pitts., 1962. Bar: Pa. 1962, U.S. Dist. Ct. (we. dist.) Pa. 1962, U.S. Ct. Appeals (3d cir.) 1962, U.S. Supreme Ct. 1962. Assoc. McArdle & McLaughlin, Pitts., 1962-69; ptnr. Gilardi & Cooper, Pitts., 1969—; mem. civil procedural rules com. Pa. Supreme Ct., 1985-92, continuing legal edn. bd., 1992—, common pleas automation implementation team, 1990-92; adj. prof. U. Pitts. Sch. Law, 1986—. Fellow Am. Coll. Trial Lawyers; mem. Pa. Bar Assn. (v.p. 1989, pres. elect 1990-91, pres. 1991-92, bd. govs., ho. of dels.), Allegheny County Bar Assn. (pres. 1984), Allegheny County Acad. Trial Lawyers (pres. 1982), Pa. Trial Lawyers Assn. (bd. govs.), Western Pa. Trial Lawyers Assn. (bd. govs.). Contbr. articles to profl. jours. Office: Gilardi & Cooper 808 Grant Building Pittsburgh PA 15219-2200

COOPER, THOMAS LUTHER, retired printing company executive; b. Statham, Ga., Sept. 30, 1917; s. William Henry and Ovelia Jane (Arnold) C.; m. Helen Brown, Aug. 30, 1941; 1 son, Thomas Luther. Student, Ga. State U., 1938-39, High Mus. Art, Atlanta, 1946. With Constn. Pub. Co., Atlanta, 1936-50, head photoengraving and art dept., 1947-50; pres. So. Engraving Co., Atlanta, 1950-75, Photo Process Engraving Co., Atlanta, 1954-75; pres., gen. mgr. So. Photo Process Engraving Co., Atlanta, 1955-75; v.p., dir. Perry Communications, 1976-90, Beck Engraving Co., Inc., Phila., 1968-75; bd. dirs. J.M. Tull Metals Co., Inc. *Thomas Cooper served as Captain in the USAF. He served as photo-intelligence officer in the 8th Air Force in England 1943-45. He was awarded 6 battle stars. At wars end, he served as target intelligence briefing officer on the staff of a Commanding General.* Exec. bd. Atlanta Area council Boy Scouts Am., Silver Beaver award, 1972; trustee Shorter Coll., Rome, Ga.; mem. adv. council Ga. State U.; chmn. bd. Ga. State U. Found. Recipient Craftsman of Year award Inland Printer and Am. Lithographer mag., 1961. Mem. Internat. Assn. Printing House Craftsmen (pres. 1959-60), Am. Photoengravers Assn. (exec. com. 1952-54), Southeastern Photoengravers Assn. (pres. 1951-52), Nat. Soc. Art Dirs., Printing Industry Assn. Ga., Advt. Club Atlanta, Mil. Order World Wars, Am. Legion, Capital City Club, Masons, Shriners, Rotary (pres. Atlanta 1975, dist. gov. Ga. dist. 6900 1981-82). Baptist. Home: 1002 Dunwoody Chace NE Atlanta GA 30328-6012

COOPER, TIMOTHY ROBERT, neonatologist, pediatrician, educator, consultant; b. Panama City, Fla., Apr. 15, 1954; s. James Robert and June Koch Cooper; m. Deborah Sue Hulsey, Mar. 12, 1985; children: Peter Michael, Christopher Robert, Benjamin James. BA in Biochemistry, Rice U., 1976; MD, Baylor Coll. Medicine, 1979. Diplomate Am. Acad. Pediat., Am. Bd. Neonatology. Intern Baylor Coll. Medicine, Houston, 1980, resident, 1981-82, fellow in neonatology, 1983-84, instr. pediat., 1985-89, asst. prof., 1989—, asst. prof. ethics, 1994—; mem. adv. bd. Snyder Comm., Bethesda, Md., 1993—. Author, editor: Contemporary Diagnosis and Management of Neonatal Respiratory Disease, 1995, 2d edit., 1998; editor: Guidelines for the Acute Care of the Neonate, 1993, 6th edit., 1998; contbr. articles to med. jours., including Pediat., Jour. Clin. Ethics. Webelos den leader pack 1040, bd. dirs. pack 1040, Boy Scouts Am., Houston, 1998—. Fellow Am. Acad. Pediat.; mem. Tex. Med. Assn. (del.), Tex. Pediatric Soc. (chmn. subcom. 1992—). Avocations: photography, piano, scouting. E-mail: timothyc@bcm.tmc.edu. Home: 10711 Valley Forge Houston TX 77042 Office: Baylor Coll Medicine Dept Pediat 1 Baylor Plz Houston TX 77030

COOPER, WARREN F., retail executive; b. Evanston, Ill., Nov. 27, 1944; s. Warren F. and Beatrice (Monahan) C.; m. Sharon A. Bell, Aug. 20, 1966; children: Blake, Justin. BS, Ball State U., 1967, MA, 1968. Employment mgr. United Air Lines, Elk Grove Village, Ill., 1969-71; corp. v.p. Sears, Roebuck & Co., Chgo., 1972-95; sr.v.p. Gen. Cable Corp., Highland, Ky., 1995-96; exec. v.p. K-Mart Corp., Troy, Mich., 1996—; mem. adv. bd. Oakland U. Bus. Sch., Rochester, Mich., 1996—. Mem. Conf. Bd. (adv. bd. 1995—). Avocations: reading, gardening, horses. Office: K-Mart Corp 3100 W Big Beaver Rd Troy MI 48084-3163

COOPER, WENDY FEIN, lawyer; b. Irvington, N.J., May 10, 1946; d. Jacob and Rose (Rothman) Fein; m. James C. Faltot, Apr. 4, 1971 (div. 1982); m. Leonard J. Cooper, June 19, 1983; children: Jennifer Regan, Ian Joshua. AB cum laude, Bryn Mawr Coll., 1968; JD, Temple U., 1973, LLM in Taxation, 1983. Assoc. Beitch & Block, Phila., 1973-76, ptnr., 1976-80; assoc. Narin & Chait, Phila., 1980-83, ptnr., 1983-85; assoc. Griffith & Burr P.C., Phila., 1985-87; shareholder Dolchin, Slotkin & Todd, P.C., Phila., 1987—. Bd. dirs., sec. Phila. Festival Theatre for New Plays, 1981-97. Mem. ABA, N.J. Bar Assn., Phila. Bar Assn. Home: 1603 Harris Rd Laverock PA 19038-7206 Office: Dolchin Slotkin & Todd PC 2005 Market St 24th Fl Philadelphia PA 19103-7035

COOPER, WILLIAM ALLEN, banking executive; b. Detroit, July 3, 1943. BS in Acctg., Wayne State U., 1967. CPA, Mich. With Touche, Ross & Co., Detroit, 1967-71; chm. Minn. Rep Party; sr. v.p. Mich. Nat. Bank of Detroit, 1971-72; sr. v.p. Mich. Nat. Corp., 1971-78; exec. v.p. Huntington Nat. Bank, Columbus, Ohio, 1978-83, pres., 1983-84; pres., Am. Savs. & Loan Assn. of Fla., Miami, 1984-85 , also dir.; chmn. bd., chief exec. officer TCF Bank, FSB, Mpls., 1985—; chmn., TCF Fin. Corp., Mpls., from 1987, now chmn. bd., past chief exec. officer, bd. dirs. Mem. AICPA. Office: TCF Bank Office of Chmn Bd 801 Marquette Ave Minneapolis MN 55402-3475 Office: Minn Rep Party 480 Ceder Street Ste 560 Castle Rock MN 55010*

COOPER, WILLIAM CLARK, physician; b. Manila, P.I., June 22, 1912 (father Am. citizen); s. Wibb Earl and Pearl (Herron) C.; MD, U. Va., 1934; MPH magna cum laude, Harvard U., 1958; m. Ethel Katherine Sicha, May 1, 1937; children: Jane Willoughby, William Clark, David Jeremy, Robert Lawrence. Intern, asst. resident U. Hosps., Cleve., 1934-37; commd. asst. surgeon USPHS, 1940, advanced through grades to med. dir., 1952; chief occupational health Field Hqrs., Cin., 1952-57; mem. staff div. occupational health USPHS, Washington, 1957-62, chief div. occupational health, 1962-63; ret., 1963; rsch. physician, prof. occupational health in residence Sch. Pub. Health, U. Calif.-Berkeley, 1963-72; med. cons. AEC, 1964-73; sec.-treas. Tabershaw-Cooper Asso., Inc., 1972-73, v.p., sci. dir., 1973-74; v.p. Equitable Environ. Health Inc., 1974-77; cons. occupational medicine, 1977-94. Served to 1st lt. M.C., U.S. Army, 1937-40. Diplomate Am. Bd. Internal Medicine, Am. Bd. Preventive Medicine, Am. Bd. Indsl. Hygiene. Fellow AAAS, Am. Pub. Health Assn., Am. Coll. Chest Physicians, Am. Coll. Occupational Medicine, Royal Soc. Medicine (London); mem. Internat. Commn. on Occupational Health, Western Occupational Med. Assn., Am. Indsl. Hygiene Assn., Cosmos Club. Contbr. articles to profl. jours. Home: 8315 Terrace Dr El Cerrito CA 94530-3060

COOPER, WILLIAM COPELAND, public library director; b. Laurens, S.C., Aug. 3, 1946; s. James Lafayette Jr. and Dorothy (Copeland) C. Ba in History, Presbyn. Coll., 1968; MA in History, Wake Forest U., 1969; MS in Libr. Sci., U. N.C., 1971. Tchr. Wade Hampton H.S., Greenville, S.C., 1969-70; reference asst. U. N.C. Libr., Chapel Hill, 1970-71, reference libr., 1971-72; head reference dept. Greenville County Libr., 1972-74; dir. Laurens County Libr., 1974—. Contbr. articles to profl. jours. Treas. Laurens Hist. Soc., 1990-99, Laurens County Arts Coun., 1994-97; preas. Cmty. Concert Assn., Clinton, 1980-82. Mem. ALA, Southeastern Libr. Assn., S.C. Libr. Assn., Piedmont Libr. Assn. (pres. 1998-99), Pub. Libr. Adminstrs. (pres. 1982, treas. 1997-99), Laurens County C. of C., Kiwanis (preas. 1998). Avocations: piano and organ, running, swimming, historical houses. E-mail: cooplib@infoAve.net. Home: PO Box 42 Laurens SC 29360 Office: Laurens County Libr 1017 W Main St Laurens SC 29360

COOPER, WILLIAM EDGAR, animal behaviorist, educator; b. Richmond, Va., Apr. 23, 1945; s. William Edgar Sr. and Elizabeth Mae Cooper; m. Carolyn Taylor Fitchett; 1 child, Charles Austin; m. Donetta Lynn Hornsby, Jan. 27, 1982; children: Anna Lynn Jones, Elizabeth Alexandra. BA in Psychology, U. Richmond, 1966; MS in Physiol. Psychology, Kans. State U., 1970, PhD in Environ. Biology, 1972. Postdoctoral fellow in biomath. N.C. State U., Raleigh, 1972-74; population ecologist Tex. Instruments, Verplanck, N.Y., 1974-75; from asst. prof. to prof. Auburn U., Montgomery, Ala., 1976-91; prof. biology Ind. U.-Purdue U., Ft. Wayne, 1991—, chair dept. biology, 1991-93. Assoc. editor Herpetologica, 1989-91, Herpetol. Natural History, 1996—; contbr. some 150 articles to profl. jours. John ellerman scholar, 1993. Mem. Am. Soc. Ichthyologists and Herpetologists (bd. govs. 1998—), Soc. for Study of Amphibians and Reptiles, Societas Europeae Herpetologica, Animal Behavior Soc., Herpetologists League, Phi Beta Kappa, Sigma Xi. Avocations: guitar, camping, gym rat, swimming, Spanish. E-mail: cooperw@ipfw.edu. Home: 8336 Sagimore Ct Fort Wayne IN 46835 Office: Ind U-Purdue U Dept Biology 2101 E Coliseum Blvd Fort Wayne IN 46805

COOPER, WILLIAM EDWIN, university president, educator; b. Balt., Mar. 20, 1951; s. William Daniel and Mildred (Hively) C.; m. Clarissa Holmes, July 5, 1984; children: Ashley, Courtney. AB magna cum laude, Brown U., 1973, AM, 1973; PhD, MIT, 1976. NIH postdoctoral fellow speech comm. group MIT Rsch. Lab. Electronics, Cambridge, 1976-78, rsch. affiliate, 1978-83; asst. prof. psychology Harvard U., Cambridge, 1978-81, assoc. prof. psychology, 1981-83; prof. psychology U. Iowa, Iowa City, 1983-89, assoc. dean for R&D Coll. Liberal Arts, 1987-89; prof. psychology Tulane U., New Orleans, 1989-96, dean Coll. Arts and Scis., 1989-91, dean faculty liberal arts and scis., 1991-96; prof. linguistics and psychology Georgetown U., Washington, 1996—, exec. v.p. main campus, 1996-98; pres. U. Richmond, Va., 1998—; fellow Newcomb Coll., 1989-96. Author: Speech Perception and Production: Studies in Selective Adaptation, 1979; co-author: Syntax and Speech, 1980, Fundamental Frequency in Sentence Production, 1981; editor: Cognitive Aspects of Skilled Typewriting, 1983; co-editor:

Sentence Processing: Psycholinguistic Studies Presented to Merrill Garrett, 1979; contbr. articles to profl. jours. Recipient Harold Schlosberg Meml. award in psychology, 1973, Acoustical Soc. Am. Biennial award, 1986; NSF grad. fellow, 1973, John Simon Guggenheim fellow, 1983; Fulbright Sr. scholar U. Fed. de Minas Gerais, Belo Horizonte, Brazil, 1984. Mem. Phi Beta Kappa, Sigma Xi. Office: U Richmond Office of Pres Richmond VA 23173

COOPER, WILLIAM EUGENE, consulting engineer; b. Erie, Pa., Jan. 11, 1924; s. William Hall and Ruth E. (Dunn) C.; m. Louise I. Ferguson, June 23, 1946; children: Margaret, Glenn, Keith, Joyce, Carol. Student, Stevens Inst. Tech., 1941-43; BS, Oreg. State Coll., 1947, MS, 1948; PhD, Purdue U., 1951. Instr. Purdue U., 1948-52; cons. engr. Knolls Atomic Power Lab., GE, 1952-63; engring. mgr. Lessells and Assos., Waltham, Mass., 1963-68; sr. v.p., tech. dir. Teledyne Materials Rsch., Waltham, Mass., 1968-76; cons. engr. Teledyne Engring. Svcs., Woburn, 1976-94; staff cons. Teledyne Brown Engring., Marion, Mass., 1994-95. Contbr. articles to tech. jours. Served with AUS, 1943-46. Named Distinguished Engring. Alumnus Purdue U., 1974. Mem. ASME (hon., B.F. Langer Nuclear Codes and Standards award 1978, hon. mem. boiler and pressure vessel com. 1980, v.p. codes and standards and mem. exec. com. of council 1980-81, sr. v.p. codes and standards 1981-84, Pressure Vessel and Piping medal 1983, codes and standards medal 1986), NAE, Soc. Exptl. Mechanics (Murray lectr. 1977), Am. Nat. Standards Inst. (dir. 1981-84), Sigma Xi, Pi Tau Sigma, Sigma Pi Sigma. Achievements include development of comprehensive design criteria for pressure vessels and piping in critical services. Home: 1010 Waltham St Apt 352C Lexington MA 02421-8064

COOPER, WILLIAM EWING, JR., retired army officer; b. Birmingham, Ala., June 19, 1929; s. William Ewing and Margaret (Tate) C.; m. Mary Jane Beers, Feb. 16, 1952; children—William Ewing III, Leslie Beers. B.A. in History, Citadel, 1951; M.A. in History, U. Miami, 1961; postgrad., Georgetown U., 1970-72, U.S. Army Command and Gen. Staff Coll., 1961-62, Armed Forces Staff Coll., 1966-67, Army War Coll., 1970-71. Commd. 2d lt. U.S. Army, 1951, advanced through grades to maj. gen., 1979; comdr. arty. group U.S. Army, Darmstadt, Germany, 1972-73; sr. liaison officer to Brit. Army U.S. Army, Germany, 1973-75; comdg. gen. arty. brigade U.S. Army, Homestead AFB, Fla., 1976-79; chief of staff NORAD U.S. Army, Peterson AFB, Colo., 1979-81; comdg. gen. 32d Army Air Def. Command U.S. Army, Darmstadt, Fed. Republic Germany, 1981-83; dep. dir. Def. Intelligence Agy. U.S. Army, Washington, 1983-85; ret., 1985; assoc. Burdeshaw Assocs. Ltd., Bethesda, Md., 1986-93; ret., 1993. Decorated D.S.M., Def. Superior Service medal with oak cluster, Legion of Merit, Bronze Star with V and 2 oak leaf clusters, Air medal with 3 oak leaf clusters, Army Meritorious Service medal; knights cross (Germany), Honor medal (Vietnam). Mem. Phi Alpha Theta, Phi Sigma Alpha. Democrat. Presbyterian. Clubs: Fla. Citadel (v.p. 1976-78); Colo. Citadel (pres. 1980-81). Avocations: golf; skiing; hunting. Home: 4925 Old Creek Dr Sarasota FL 34233

COOPER, WILLIAM JAMES, JR., history educator; b. Kingstree, S.C., Oct. 22, 1940; s. William James and Mamie (Mayes) C.; m. Patricia Holmes, Sept. 1, 1962; children: William James III, Michael Holmes. A.B., Princeton U., 1962; Ph.D., Johns Hopkins U., 1966. Asst. prof. history La. State U., Baton Rouge, 1968-70, assoc. prof., 1970-78, prof., 1978—, dean Grad. Sch., 1982-89; Boyd prof., 1989—. Author: The Conservative Regime: South Carolina 1877-1890, 1968, The South and the Politics of Slavery 1828-1856, 1978, Liberty and Slavery: Southern Politics to 1860, 1983; co-author: The American South: A History, 1990, 2d edit., 1995; co-editor: A Master's Due: Essays in Honor of David Herbert Donald, 1985, Writing the Civil War: The Quest to Understand, 1998; editor: Social Relations in Our Southern States (Daniel Hundley), 1979, So. Biography Series, 1979-93; also articles. Served to capt. U.S. Army, 1966-68. Sr. fellow Inst. So. History, Johns Hopkins U., 1971-72; rsch. fellow Charles Warren Ctr. Studies in Am. History, Harvard U., 1975-76; Guggenheim fellow, 1980-81, NEH fellow, 1988-89; named Disting. Rsch. Master La. State U., 1980. Mem. Am. Hist. Assn., Orgn. Am. Historians, So. Hist. Assn. Presbyterian. Home: 250 Amherst Ave Baton Rouge LA 70808-4603 Office: La State U Dept History Baton Rouge LA 70803

COOPER, WILLIAM MARION, physician; b. Pitts., Jan. 12, 1919; s. Lardin Monroe and Sophia Antoinette (Swartz) C.; m. Sara Georgia Thomas, Jan. 19, 1942; children—Mikell Lee Cooper Schenck, William Marion, Thomas L., George Robert. B.S., Pa. State U., 1939; M.D., Hahnemann Med. Coll., 1943; JD, U. Pitts., 1987. Diplomate: Am. Bd. Internal Medicine, Am. Bd. Hematology; cert. in Geriatrics. Intern Shadyside Hosp., Pitts., 1943; resident U. Pitts. Sch. Medicine, 1946-48, Cleve. Clin. Found., 1948; practice medicine specializing in internal medicine and hematology Pitts., 1948—; mem. staff Presbyn.-Univ., Shadyside; chief dept. medicine Shadyside Hosp., 1980-91; mem. med. faculty U. Pitts., 1948—, clin. prof. medicine, 1958—, dir. div. continuing edn., 1970-80, assoc. dean continuing edn., 1974-80; dir. continuing edn. Univ. Health Center, Pitts., 1975-80; sr. asst. vice-chancellor Univ. Health Ctr. Pitts., 1979-80; Med. dir. Central Blood Bank, Pitts., 1951-60, Pitts. Skin and Cancer Found., 1958-65. Contbr. articles to med. jours. Served with M.C. U.S. Army, 1944-45. Mem. AMA, AAAS, ACP (bd. govs. 1965-71), Pa., Allegheny County med. socs., Am., Internat. Socs. Hematology, Am. Soc. Internal Medicine, Am. Coll. Legal Medicine. Clubs: Oakmont (Pa.) Country. Home: The Mews 302 Fox Chapel Rd Pittsburgh PA 15238-2335 Office: Shadyside Hosp Dept Medicine 5230 Centre Ave Dept Medicine Pittsburgh PA 15232-1381

COOPER, WILLIAM SECORD, information science educator; b. Winnipeg, Man., Can., Nov. 7, 1935; m. Helen Clare Dunlap, July 22, 1964. BA, Principia Coll., 1956; M.Sc., MIT, 1959; Ph.D., U. Calif.-Berkeley, 1964. Alexander von Humboldt scholar U. Erlangen, Germany, 1964-65; asst. prof. info. sci. U. Chgo., 1966-70; assoc. prof. info. sci. U. Calif., Berkeley, 1971-76, prof., 1976-94, prof. grad. sch., 1994-96, prof. emeritus, 1996—; Miller prof. Miller Inst., Berkeley, 1975-76. Hon. research fellow Univ. Coll., London, 1977-78; ACM/SIGIR Triennial Rsch. award, 1994. Mem. AAAS, Am. Soc. Info. Sci., ACM. Office: Univ Calif Sch Info Mgmt and Sys Berkeley CA 94720

COOPER, WYLOLA, retired special education educator; b. Cleve., Feb. 12, 1926; d. William Wilkins and Leola Anderson; m. Henry J. Cooper, Apr. 4, 1948 (dec. May 1992); children: Henry J. Jr., Wylola Jr., Antigone, Yolanda Lee. BE, Chgo. State U., 1967; MA, Roosevelt U., 1974. Itinerant tchr. Dist. 117 Elem. Level, Hickory Hills, Ill., 1968-71; tchr. learning disabled, emotionally and behaviorally handicapped Conrady Jr. High Sch. Dist. 117, Hickory Hills, 1971-86, behavior disorders tchr., 1986-91, dept. chairperson spl. edn. dept., 1988-94, tchr. emotionally disturbed, 1991-94; ret., 1994; staff S.W. Coop. of Cook County for Spl. Edn., Oak Forest; mem. organizing com. Ill. Spl. Edn. Program, Springfield, 1971-72. Mem. Coun. Exceptional Children, Am. Fedn. Tchrs. Union, S.W. Coop. for Spl. Edn. Democrat. Roman Catholic. Avocations: swimming, counseling. Home: 1451 E 55th St Chicago IL 60615-5429

COOPER-AVRICK, ANITA BEVERLY, television stage manager; b. Ottawa, Ont., Can.; d. Albert and Edith (Sobie) Cooper; m. Andrew Jay Avrick, Apr. 15, 1984; 1 child, Ashley Nicole. AA, L.A. Valley Coll., 1968; BS in Bus. Adminstrn., Calif. State U., Northridge, 1974; LLM, Southwestern Sch. Law, 1984. Field rep., contract adminstr. AFTRA, Hollywood, Calif., 1975-80; stage mgr. Dirs. Guild Am., L.A., 1980—; segment producer Nat. Leukemia Telethon Nat. Leukemia Broadcasting Coun., L.A., 1989, 90, 91; adminstr. Doctor's Urology Group, 1997-98; trustee Dirs. Guild of am. and Prodrs. Pension and Health Fund. Stage mgr. (TV series) Soap, 1980-81, Lewis & Clark, 1981-82, The People's Court, 1982-83, Filthy Rich, 1982-83, Reggie, 1983, Nine to Five, 1983-84, This Is Your Life, 1983-84, Mr. Belvedere, 1985-90, Kids Incorporated, 1986, Jay Leno Special, 1987, Davis Rules, 1990-91, Fresh Prince of Bel Air, 1991, Dudley, 1993, Herman's Head, 1993-94, Daddy's Girls, 1994, Blame It On Ernie, 1995, Mr. Willoughby's Christmas Tree, 1995, Minor Adjustments, 1995-96, Social Studies, 1996, America's Funniest Home Videos, 1997; (TV pilots) Weekends, 1982, Sam, 1985 Charlie & Co., 1985, Real Life, 1988, Homeroom, 1989, The Johnsons Are Home, 1989, Babes, 1990, The Brave New World of Charlie Hoover, 1991, The Office, 1994, Minor Adjustments, 1995, Just One of the Girls, 1997, America's Funniest Home Videos, 1997-98; assoc. dir. (TV shows) Mr. Belvedere, 1990. Trustee pension and health bd. Dirs. Guild. Mem. AFTRA, Dirs. Guild Am. (nat. bd. mem., chairperson Assoc. Dir.-Stage Mgr.-Prodn. Assoc. Coun., various other coms.). Avocations: needle point, knitting, swimming, skiing, movies.

COOPERMAN, ALVIN, television and theatrical producer; b. Bklyn.; s. Nathan and Marietta (Steinmann) C.; m. Marilyn Frances Fisher; Children: Karen Lynn, Audrey Joan, Margot Jane. Exec. dir. booking Shubert Theatre Enterprises, N.Y.C., 1963-68; v.p. spl. programs NBC, N.Y.C., 1967-68; exec. v.p. Madison Sq. Garden Ctr., Inc., N.Y.C., 1968-72; pres. Madison Sq. Garden Prodns., N.Y.C., 1968-72; chief exec. officer Athena Communications Corp., N.Y.C., 1972—. Developed and produced spl. program Wide Wide World, 1955; exec. prodr. Producer's Showcase, 1955-56, Big Event, 1976-77, Screen Gems, 1957-58; prodns. include Dodsworth, Rosalinda, Jack and the Beanstalk, Shirley Temple Storybook, 1956-57, The Untouchables, 1962-63, Bolshoi Ballet Romeo and Juliet (Emmy award nomination 1976), Pele's Last Game, Amahl and the Night Visitors, A Tribute to Toscanini (Emmy award 1980), An Evening with Jerome Robbins (Emmy award 1981), The Life of Pope John Paul II, Ain't Misbehavin, 1985 (Emmy award, Best Musical of the Year award NAACP), My Two Loves, 1986, Safe Passage, 1987, Family Album, 1987, Witness to Survival, 1988-90; prodr./writer animated spl. NBC-TV Fourth King, 1984; prodr./dir./writer TV spl. Mobs and Mobster, 1993; prodr. cable TV show The Higgins Boys and Gruber Show, 1993 (Ace award nominee), ABC movie: Follow the River, 1994; writer: (stage musical) Honky Tonk Heaven, 1995, (ABC spl.) Susan B. Anthony Slept Here, 1995 (Am. Women in Radio and TV Best Documentary award), (feature film) Charity Royall, 1997-98; creator, writer: (websites) The Stork Club, Platinum, 1996; writer, lyricist (musical) The Life and Adventures of Santa Claus, 1998, weathertainment.com, 1999. Creative cons. Rep. Nat. Conv., 1972; mem., trustee Judy Holliday Meml. Com. for Am. Med. Ctr., Denver; chmn. N.Y. chpt. Arthritis Found. Recipient Peabody award, 1957, Christopher award, 1957, Judy Holliday Humanitarian award, 1972. Mem. Newcomen Soc. N.Am., Am. Theatre Planning Bd., Players Club. Home: 146 Central Park W New York NY 10023-2005

COOPERMAN, BARRY S., educational administrator, educator, scientist; b. N.Y.C., Dec. 11, 1941; married, 1963; 2 children. B.A., Columbia U., 1962; Ph.D. in Chemistry, Harvard U., 1968. NATO fellow biochemistry Pasteur Inst., 1967-68; from asst. prof. to assoc. prof. dept. chemitry U. Pa., 1968-72, prof. bioorganic chemistry, 1977—, vice provost for rsch., 1982-95; dir. French Inst., 1993—. Trustee Assoc. Univs., Inc., 1983—, chmn. bd., 1989-91; mem. policy governing bd. Advanced Tech. Ctr. S.E. Pa., 1984-88; bd. mgrs. Morris Arboretum, 1985-91; bd. dirs. Wistar Inst., 1987. Mem. Am. Soc. Biol. Chemists, Am. Chem. Soc. Research in mechanism of phosphoryl transfer enzymes; ribosomes; serum serine protease inhibitors; ribonucleotide reductase. Office: Univ Pa Dept Chemistry 358 Chemistry Philadelphia PA 19104

COOPERMAN, SAUL, foundation administrator; b. Newark, Dec. 18, 1934; s. Louis Frank and Lucille (Swarthberg) C.; m. Paulette Beth Koch, Aug. 17, 1958; children: Suzanne, Deborah, David. B.S., Lafayette Coll., 1956; M.Ed., Rutgers U., 1964, Ed.D., 1969; D.H.L. (hon.), Drew U., 1984. Tchr. North Plainfield High Sch., N.J., 1960-64; prin. Belvidere High Sch., N.J., 1964-68; research asst. Rutgers U., New Brunswick, N.J., 1968-69; supt. schs. Montgomery Twp., N.J., 1969-74, City of Madison, N.J., 1974-82; commr. N.J. State Dept. Edn., Trenton, 1982-90; pres. Educate Am., 1990—; chmn. edn. adv. panel New Am. Sch. Devel. Corp., 1990-97. Author: How Schools Really Work: Practical Advice to Parents from an Insider; contbr. articles to profl. jours.; columnist: Star Ledger. Pres. 10,000 Mentors, Newark, 1996—. Served with USNR, 1956-82. Avocations: reading; athletics; travel. Address: 181 Round Top Rd Bernardsville NJ 07924-2106

COOPERRIDER, TOM S., botanist; b. Newark, Ohio, Apr. 15, 1927; s. Oscar Harold and Ruth Evelyn Cooperrider; m. Miwako Kunimura, June 13, 1953; children: Julie Ann, John Andrew. BA, Denison U., 1950; MS, U. Iowa, 1955; PhD, 1958. Instr. biol. scis. Kent (Ohio) State U., 1958-61, asst. prof., 1961-65, assoc. prof., 1965-69, prof., 1969-93, emeritus prof., 1993—, curator herbarium, 1968-93, dir. bot. gardens, 1972-93; mem. editorial bd. Univ. Press, 1976-79; on leave as asst. prof. dept. botany U. Hawaii, 1962-63; NSF rschr. Mountain Lake Biol. Sta., U. Va., summer 1958; faculty mem. Iowa Lakeside Lab., U. Iowa, summer 1965; cons. endangered and threatened species U.S. Fish and Wildlife Svc. Dept. Interior, 1976-83; cons. Davey Tree Expert Co., 1979-85, Ohio Natural Areas Coun., 1983, regional reviewer Flora of North Am., 1993—. Author: Ferns and Other Pteridophytes of Iowa, 1959, Vascular Plants of Clinton, Jackson and Jones Counties, Iowa, 1962, The Dicotyledoneae of Ohio, Part 2, 1995; editor, co-author: Endangered and Threatened Plants of Ohio, 1983. Active YMCA-YWCA Students in Govt., Washington, 1950; personnel placement U.S. Census Bur., Washington, 1950-51; Quaker Internat. Vol., Fed. Republic Germany, 1951. Served with U.S. Army, 1945-46. Recipient Osborn award Ohio Biol. Survey, 1994; dedicatee Kent Bog State Nature Preserve, Ohio Dept. Natural Resources, 1995; NSF predoctoral fellow, 1957-58. Fellow AAAS, Ohio Acad. Scis. (chair Ohio flora com. 1969-97), Explorers Club; mem. Am. Soc. Plant Taxonomists, Internat. Assn. Plant Taxonomists, Bot. Soc. Am., Nature Conservancy, Wilderness Soc., So. Appalachian Bot. Soc., Blue Key, Sigma Xi. Home: 548 Bowman Dr Kent OH 44240-4512

COOPERSTEIN, PAUL ANDREW, lawyer, business consultant; b. New Bedford, Mass., Dec. 16, 1953; s. Leon I. and Dorothea (Silverman) C.; m. Beverly S. Schultz, July 16, 1983. BS summa cum laude, Ithaca Coll., 1974; JD, Western New Eng. Coll., 1978; cert. in dispute resolution, Cornell U., 1996. Bar: Mass. 1978, U.S. Ct. Appeals (1st cir.) 1979. Assoc. Law Office Irving Sheff, Boston, 1976-77; ptnr. Prince & Cooperstein, Boston and Cambridge, Mass., 1977-79, Cooperstein & Cooperstein, Cambridge, 1979-83; gen. counsel Carlyle-Omni Realty Investors, Inc., Lexington, Mass., 1986-88; pvt. practice Cambridge, 1983-85, 89-92; pres. Strategic Intervention Assocs., Inc., Cambridge, 1992—; dir. bus. devel. New Eng. Stereo, Inc., Boston, 1997-98. Mem. Milton (Mass.) Conservation Commn., 1988-92; co-chmn. The Partnership Fund., 1997—; bd. dirs. Temple Shalom, Milton, 1997—. Mem. ASTD, Am. Mgmt. Assn., Soc. for Intercultural Tng. and Rsch. Home: 118 Cary Ave Milton MA 02186-4223

COOPERSTEIN, SHERWIN JEROME, medical educator; b. N.Y.C., Sept. 14, 1923; s. Joseph and Bessie (Berger) C.; m. Alice Ruth Peskin, June 1, 1947; children—Rhoda Ann, Lawrence Alan. B.S., Coll. City N.Y., 1943; D.D.S., N.Y. U., 1948; Ph.D. in Anatomy, Western Res. U., 1951. Instr. biology Coll. City N.Y., 1943, 46-48; research asso. physiology N.Y. U., 1946-48; instr. anatomy Western Res. U., 1948-49, fellow anatomy, 1949-51, sr. instr., 1951-52, asst. prof. anatomy, 1952-55, asso. prof., 1955-64, asst. dean, 1957-64; prof., head dept. anatomy U. Conn. Schs. Medicine and Dental Medicine, Farmington, 1964-92, prof. emeritus, acting head dept. 1992-94; prof. emeritus, 1994—; Mem. adv. panel on med. student research NSF, 1960-61; mem. anatomical scis. tng. com. Nat. Inst. Gen. Med. Scis., 1966-70; mem. spl. study sect. on diabetes centers NIH, 1973-75, mem. ad hoc study sect. on research tng. grants in systems and integrative biology, 1977; mem. adv. panel on research personnel needs in basic biomed. sci. Nat. Acad. Scis./NRC, 1976-83. Contbr. articles profl. jours.; editorial adviser: Diabetes Lit. Index, 1966-79. Served with AUS, 1943-44. Mem. AAAS, Am. Chem. Soc., Marine Biol. Lab., Am. Assn. Anatomists, Am. Soc. Biol. Chemists, Am. Diabetes Assn., Sigma Xi. Home: 10 Hillsboro Dr West Hartford CT 06107-1011 Office: U Conn Health Ctr Farmington Ave Farmington CT 06030

COOR, LATTIE FINCH, university president; b. Phoenix, Sept. 26, 1936; s. Lattie F. and Elnora (Witten) C.; m. Ina Fitzhenry, Jan. 18, 1964 (div. 1988); children: William Kendall, Colin Fitzhenry, Farryl MacKenna Witten; m. Elva Wingfield, Dec. 27, 1994. AB with high honors (Phelps Dodge scholar), No. Ariz. U., 1958; MA with honors (Univ. scholar, Universal Match Found. fellow, Carnegie Corp. fellow), Washington U., St. Louis, 1960, PhD, 1964; LLD (hon.), Marlboro Coll., 1977, Am. Coll. Greece, 1982, U. Vt., 1991. Adminstrv. asst. to Gov. Mich., 1961-62; asst. to chancellor Washington U., St. Louis, 1963-67, asst. dean Grad. Sch. Arts and Scis., 1967-69, dir. internat. studies, 1967-69, asst. prof. polit. sci., 1967-76, vice chancellor, 1969-74, univ. vice chancellor, 1974-76; pres. U. Vt., Burlington, 1976-89; prof. public affairs, and pres. Ariz. State U., Tempe, 1990—; cons. HEW; spl. cons. to commr. U.S. Commn. on Edn., 1971-74; chmn. Commn. on Govtl. Rels., Am. Coun. on Edn., 1976-80; dir. New Eng. Bd. Higher Edn., 1976-89; co-chmn. joint com. on health policy Assn. Am. Univs. and Nat. Assn. State Univs. and Land Grant Colls., 1976-89; mem. pres. commn. NCAA, 1984-90, chmn. div. I, 1989; mem. Ariz. State Bd. Edn., 1993-98. Trustee emeritus Am. Coll. Greece. Mem. Nat. Assn. Stae Univs. and Land Grant Colls. (chmn. bd. dirs. 1991-92), New Eng. Assn. Schs. and Colls. (pres. 1981-82), Am. Coun. on Edn. (bd. dirs. 1991-93, chmn. Pacific 10 Conf. 1995-96), Kellogg Commn. on Future of State and Land-Grant Univs. Office: Ariz State U Office of Pres Tempe AZ 85287

COORDSEN, KAREN GAIL, medical/surgical nurse; b. Orlando, Fla., May 27, 1946; d. Russell P. Jr. and Joyce Gwendolyn (Davis) Sullivan; m. Robert Lee Coordsen, June 27, 1984; children: Wesley Aaron Aho, Candace Yvette Aho, Michelle Lynn Coordsen, Shawn Marie Coordsen. ADN, Brevard Community Coll., Cocoa, Fla., 1973; BSN with high honors, U. Fla., 1981. Staff nurse Holmes Regional Med. Ctr., Melbourne, Fla.; staff and charge nurse Shands Teaching Hosp., Gainesville, Fla. Recipient 2-yr. scholar award U. Fla. Mem. Fla. Nurses Assn. (chmn. coms. arrangements and scholastics, conf. com.), Sigma Theta Tau (Alpha Theta chpt.), Phi Kappa Phi, Phi Theta Kappa, Golden Key. Home: 3904 SW 102nd Way Gainesville FL 32607-4658

COORS, WILLIAM K., brewery executive; b. Golden, Colo., Aug. 11, 1916. BSChemE, Princeton U., 1938, grad. degree in chem. engring., 1939. Pres. Adolph Coors Co., Golden, Colo., from 1956, Chmn. bd., 1970—, also corp. pres. Office: Adolph Coors Co 16000 Table Mountain Pkwy Golden CO 80403-1640*

COOTS, LAURIE, advertising executive. Chief mktg. officer TBWA Chiat/Day L.A., Venice, Calif.; now COO TBWA Chiat/ Day L.A., Playa Del Rey, Calif. Office: TBWA Chiat/Day LA 5353 Grosvenor Blvd Playa Del Rey CA 90296

COOVER, DORIS DIMOCK, artist; b. Beaverdam, Wis., Aug. 8, 1917; d. Almon Crowe and Alma Josephine (Johnson) Dimock; m. Francis Merle Coover, Apr. 11, 1945; children: Cheryl, Danelle. Student in Fashion and Design, Woodbury U., 1937. One-woman shows include Chappqua (N.Y.) Pub. Libr., 1964-79, Katonah (N.Y.) Gallery, 1967-72, Briarcliff (N.Y.) Coll., 1969, Silvermine (Conn.) Guild of Artists, 1965-81, Am. Can Corp., Greenwich, Conn., 1971—, Village Gallery at Gallmofry, Croton, N.Y., 1974-81, Manhattan Savs. Bank N.Y.C.-White Plains, 1963-68; gallery artist Virginia Barrett, Chappqua, 1964-98; exhibited in groups shows at Okla. Art Ctr., Oklahoma City, 1959, Tex. Oil Industry, Dallas, 1958, Delgado Mus., New Orleans, 1958, Dallas Mus. art, 1958-59, Westchester Art Soc., White Plaine, N.Y., 1962-74, Silvermine Guild Artists, 1970-81, Crocker Art Mus. Art Auction, 1981-98, Neuberger Mus., Purchase, N.Y., 1985, Sacramento Fine Arts, 1985 and many others; cover artist Sci. and Tech. Mag., 1966; work included in Am. Refs., 1978, Who's Who in Am. Art, 1996-97, Rockport Pubs.-Painting Color, 1997, 98, Sketching and Drawing, 1998. Mem., historian Officers Club, L.A., 1940-45; artist judge No. Westchester chpt. Cancreare, Bedford Village, N.J., 1958. Recipient numerous awards for art, including Helbein award Western Colo. Watercolor Soc. Mem. Nat. Watercolor Soc. (assoc.), Am. Watercolor Soc. (assoc.), Nat. Mus. Woman in Arts (charter), Crocker Art Mem. Republican. Avocations: visiting galleries with friends, reading mysteries, experimenting with art.

COOVER, HARRY WESLEY, manufacturing company executive; b. Newark, Del., Mar. 6, 1919; s. Harry Wesley and Anna (Rohm) C.; m. Muriel Zumbach, Sept. 17, 1941; children—Harry Wesley, Stephen R., Melinda Coover Paul. BS in Chemistry (Southerland prize), Hobart Coll., Geneva, N.Y., 1941; MS, Cornell U., 1942, PhD, 1944. Rsch. chemist Eastman Kodak Co., Rochester, N.Y., 1944-49; sr. rsch. chemist Tenn. Eastman Co., Kingsport, 1949-54; rsch. assoc. Tenn. Eastman Co., 1954-63, head polymers div., 1963-65, dir. rsch., 1965-73, v.p., 1970-73, exec. v.p., 1973-81; v.p. Eastman Kodak Co., Kingsport, 1981-84; internat. mgmt. cons. Kingsport, 1984-85; pres. New Bus. Devel. Loctite Corp., Newington, Conn., 1985-88, Mgmt. Cons., Kingsport, Tenn., 1988—. Author, patentee in field. Mem. NAE, N.Y. Acad. Scis., Internat. Union Pure and Applied Chemistry, Am. Chem. Soc. (So. Chemist award 1960, Speaker of Yr. award N.E. Tenn. sect. 1962, Earle B. Barnes award 1985, Chem. Pioneers award 1986), AAAS, Am. Inst. Chemists, Assn. Rsch. Dirs., Dirs. Indsl. Rsch., Indsl. Rsch. Inst. (pres. 1981-82, medal award 1984), Soc. Chem. Industry, Masons. Presbyterian. Office: 1201 Eastman Rd PO Box 3866 Kingsport TN 37664-0866

COOVER, JAMES BURRELL, music educator; b. Jacksonville, Ill., June 3, 1925; s. James Verans and Flod Elizabeth (Burrell) C.; m. Georgena A. Walker; children: Christopher, Mauri, Regan. AB, U. No. Colo., 1949, MA, 1950; MA, U. Denver, 1953. Asst. dir. Bibliog. Ctr. for Research, Denver, 1950-53; head Dickinson Music Library Vassar Coll., Poughkeepsie, N.Y., 1953-67; Ziegele prof. music, dir. music library SUNY, Buffalo, 1967—, Disting. Svc. Prof., 1992—; cons. Middle States Assn. Colls. and Secondary Schs., Newark, 1961—. Author: Music Lexicography, 1952, 58, 71, Musical Instrument Collections, 1981, Music Publishing, Copyright and Piracy, 1985; co-editor: Richard S. Hill: Tributes from Friends, 1987, Music at Auction: Puttick & Simpson of London (1794-1971), 1988, Antiquarian Catalogues of Musical Interest, 1988; contbr. articles and revs. to profl. jours., 1953—. Reader NEH, 1981—, Australian Rsch. Coun., 1989—. Served with U.S. Army, 1943-45, ETO. Grantee Am. Council Learned Soc., 1982, SUNY, Research Found., 1980, 82. Mem. Internat. Assn. Music Libraries, Music Library Assn. (pres. 1959-60), Papers and Lectures. Home: 111 Marjann Ter Buffalo NY 14223-1471 Office: SUNY Dept Music Baird Hall Amherst NY 14260

COOVER, ROBERT, writer, scriptwriter, educator; b. Charles City, Iowa, 1932. BA, Ind. U., 1953; MA, U. Chgo., 1965. Disting. prof. Brown U., Providence, 1979-81. Author: The Origin of the Brunists, 1966, The Universal Baseball Association, Inc., J. Henry Waugh, Prop., 1968, Pricksongs and Descants (short stories), 1969, On a Confrontation in Iowa City (film), 1969, A Theological Position (plays), 1972, The Public Burning, 1977, Hair o' the Chine, 1979, Charlie in the House of Rue, 1980, A Political Fable, 1980, Spanking the Maid, 1982, In Bed One Night and Other Brief Encounters, 1983, Gerald's Party, 1986, A Night at the Movies (short stories), 1987, Whatever Happened to Gloomy Gus of the Chicago Bears?, 1987, Pinocchio in Venice, 1991, John's Wife, 1996, Briar Rose, 1997, Ghost Town, 1998. Mem. Am. Acad. Arts and Letters (dept. lit.). Office: Brown U Dept English Providence RI 02912-1152

COOVER, RODERICK LUIS, anthropologist; b. Poughkeepsie, N.Y.; s. Robert Lowell and Pilar Sans C. BA, Cornell U., 1989; MA in English, Brown U., 1993; PhD in History of Culture, U. Chgo., 1999. Digital media producer/dir. Fire Escape Films, Chgo., 1994-98; lectr./instr. Japenese Edn. Bd., Tochigi, Japan, 1990-92; lectr./prof. Art Inst. Chgo., 1997-99. Author: (cd-rom) Rhetorics of Montage, 1998; dir. video documentary, Performances in Ghenua, Penelope Project; editor: Iphegenian Cycle. Recipient Fulbright Scholar, USIS, Ghana, 1993; numerous film and rsch. grants including U. Chgo., Art Inst. Chgo., others. Mem. Fire Escape Films (chmn.), Am. Anthropol. Assn., Soc. Cinema Studies.

COOX, ALVIN DAVID, history educator; b. Rochester, N.Y., Mar. 8, 1924; s. Irving and Ruth (Werner) C.; m. Hisako Suzuki, Apr. 7, 1954; 1 child, Roy Alan. BA, NYU, 1945; MA, Harvard U., 1946, PhD, 1951. Teaching fellow Harvard U., Cambridge, Mass., 1948-49; sr. historian Johns Hopkins U., Washington, 1949-54; lectr. U. Calif. Far East Div., Tokyo, 1954-56, U. Md. Far East Div., Tokyo, 1956-64; prof. history San Diego State U., 1964—, dir. Japanese Studies, 1985-97, dir. Asian Studies, 1966-79; scholar-diplomat in residence Dept. State, 1981; rsch. assoc. Japanese Nat. Inst. for Def. Studies, Tokyo, 1984—; vis. prof. Shiga Nat. U., Hikone-Otsu, Japan, 1954-55; historian Japanese Rsch. Div., Tokyo, 1955-57; adj. prof. U.S. Naval War Coll., San Diego, 1985—; dir. AASCU/JSI nat. summer inst. for Japan Studies, San Diego and Tokyo, 1987—. Author: Year of the Tiger, 1964, Japan: The Final Agony, 1970, Tojo, 1975, Anatomy of a Small War, 1977, Nomonhan 1939, 1985, The Unfought War, Japan 1941-42, 1992; co-editor: China and Japan, 1978, The Japanese Image, 1965-66; editor

Orient/West Mag., 1958-65. Decorated Order of Rising Sun with gold rays (Japan); named outstanding prof., Calif. State Univ. System, 1973; recipient Samuel Eliot Morison award Am. Mil. Inst., 1987, Yokohama Culture Prize (Japan), 1993, nat. faculty award Phi Beta Delta, 1994; fellow Rockefeller Found., 1961-64, Japan Found., 1983-84, 90-91, NEH, 1985, Fulbright Rsch. Fellow, 1989. Mem. Assn. Calif. State Univ. Profs., Assn. Asian Studies, Internat. House Japan, Calif. Pacific Rim Commn., Am. Mil. Inst., Phi Beta Kappa (pres. Nu chpt. 1973). Avocation: writing. Office: 5025 College Gardens Ct San Diego CA 92115-1103

COPANS, KENNETH GARY, accountant; b. Stamford, Conn., Dec. 6, 1946; s. Lawrence W. and Rosaline (Davidoff) C.; m. Jo Ellen Silbert, Apr. 25, 1972; children: Richard Harris, Mark Adam. BS in Acctg., Bucknell U., 1968. CPA, N.Y. With Arthur Andersen & Co., N.Y.C., 1968; with Copans, Copans & Piccone, N.Y.C., 1971-74, ptnr., 1974-84, mng. ptnr., 1984—; instr. Long Island U., Found. for Acctg. Edn. Bd. dirs. Congregation Aqudas Israel, Newburgh, N.Y., 1980—. Served with U.S. Army, 1968-70. Mem. AICPAs, N.Y. State Soc. CPAs, S.C. Soc. CPAs, N.J. Soc. CPAs, Am. Assn. Personal Fin. Planners. Republican. Lodge: Rotary (local bd. dirs. 1980-84). Avocations: fishing, golf, tennis. Home: 43 Parkhill Dr New Windsor NY 12553-6437 Office: Copans & Co 540 Gidney Ave Newburgh NY 12550-3129

COPE, DANIEL, package good industry executive; b. Cin., Dec. 15, 1945; s. Paul Eugene and Virginia Brug C.; m. Mary Ladd Dixon, Apr. 19, 1975; children: Jennifer Dixon, Mary Abigail, Alexander David. BA, De Pauw U., 1968. Sales rep. Procter & Gamble, Cin., 1968-70, dist. field rep., 1970-71; unit mgr. Procter & Gamble, St. Louis, 1971-77; assoc. sales mdse. mgr. Procter & Gamble, Cin., 1977-81, project mgr., 1981-83, sr. project mgr., 1983-85, assoc. dir. sales, 1985-89, v.p. bus. devel., 1989-93; v.p. sales Advanced Promotion Tech., Boca Raton, Fla., 1993-96; sr. v.p. mktg. Info. Resources, Inc., Chgo., 1996-98; pres. Cope & Assocs., Inc., Boca Raton, 1999—; spkr. in field. 1st v.p. United Home Care, Cin., 1980-83; dir. Sch. Adv. Coun., Palm Beach County, Fla., 1997-99. Staff sgt. USAFR, 1968-94. Avocations: travel, computers, fitness, reading, tennis. E-mail: Dan@Cope.net. Home and office: 1980 NW 25th St Boca Raton FL 33431

COPE, DERRIKE, professional race car driver; b. Spanaway, Wash., Nov. 3, 1958; m. Renee Cope. winner NASCAR Late Model Sportsman series, 1980, Winston West 500, Riverside, 1982, Winston Cup Daytona 500, 1990, Dover, 1990; 6 top-20s Winston Cup series, 1994. Named NASCAR Late Model Sportsman Rookie of Yr., 1980, NASCAR Winston West Series Rookie of Yr., 1984. Avocations: golf, horses. Office: c/o Bahari Racing 208 Rolling Hill Rd Mooresville NC 28117*

COPE, HAROLD CARY, former university president, higher education association executive; b. Westown, Pa., Aug. 9, 1918; s. Joshua A. and Edith (Cary) C.; m. Ann Elizabeth Reeves, Apr. 17, 1943; children: David Harold, Sarah Ann, Elizabeth R., Hannah Sue. BS, Cornell U., 1941; postgrad., U. Omaha, 1953-54, U. Mich., 1959. Supr. student union cafeteria Cornell U., 1941-42; dietician Earlham Coll., 1946-49, mgr. resident halls, 1949-52, mgr. resident halls, accountant, 1952-55, asst. comptroller, 1955-58, bus. mgr., 1958-67, v.p. bus. affairs, 1967-72; pres. Friends U., Wichita, Kans., 1972-79, pres. emeritus, 1979—, cons., staff worker deferred giving, 1979-82, chmn. fin. com., 1980-82; exec. dir. Friends Assn. Higher Edn., 1985-87; mem. Kans. State adv. bd. Title I Funds, 1974-79. Active Cub Scouts Am., 1947-51; chmn. stewardship and fin. bd. 5 Years Meeting, Soc. of Friends, 1960-66, mem. exec. coun., 1960-70, nat. bd. com., 1966-72; pres. Friends Extension Corp., 1963-72; bd. dirs., treas. Friends Fellowship Retirement Home, 1964-70; clk. White Water Monthly Meeting of Friends, 1963-66, Ind. Yearly Meeting, 1965-71, Univ. Friends Ch., 1970-82; mem. nat. bd. dirs. Am. Friends Svc. Com., 1968-74, 79-84, mem. exec. com., 1970-74; chmn. Richmond (Ind.) Housing Authority, 1968-72; mem. Sedgwick County Zoo Adv. Bd., 1973-79, Wichita Alcoholism Task Force, 1972-74; sec. Kans. Found. Pvt. Coll.-Secondary Schs., 1973-75; Bd. dirs., sec. Quaker Hill Found., 1969-72; treas., bd. dirs. Partnership for Productivity Found., 1969-72, 84-87, sec. bd. dirs., 1984-88; bd. dirs., mem. exec. com. Richmond YMCA, 1969-72; bd. dirs. Sunflowers Ednl. TV Corp., 1972-74, Salvation Army, 1976-82; bd. dirs. Wichita United Way, 1977-82, chmn. planning div., 1979-82; trustee Friends United Meeting, 1971-83, chmn., 1975-83; chmn. fin. com. Friends World Com. for Consultation, 1980-85; mem. Friends Com. on Legis., 1989-92, exec. com., 1990, fin. com., 1990-93; chmn. bd. advs. Earlham Sch. Religion Sem., 1979-84; v.p., bd. dirs. Wellspring Retirement Cmty., 1987-90; trustee, chmn. fin. com. Friends Elem. Sch., 1988-90; bd. dirs. Friends Ctr., 1983-88, v.p., 1985-88; bd. dirs. Pendle Hill, 1987-93, exec. com., 1990-94; bd. dirs. Peace Tax Fund Inc., 1986-91, chmn. fin. com. 1987-91; trustee Sandy Spring Meeting, 1992-95, trustee Sandy Springs Friends Sch., 1990-95. Mem. Ind. Assn. Bus. Officers (pres. 1960-61), Central Assn. Bus. Officers (mem. exec. com. 1970-71), Am. Assn. Pres.'s Ind. Colls. and Univs. (sec. 1974-76), Wichita C. of C., Y's Mens Club (pres. 1959-60, dist. gov. 1960-61), Kiwanis (bd. dirs. 1967-72), Rotary. Home: 1014 Quaker Knoll Rd Sandy Spring MD 20860-1270

COPE, JAMES DUDLEY, trade association executive; b. Nelsonville, Ohio, Apr. 22, 1932; s. James Wesley Cope; m. Katherine Clark Bealle, July 9, 1994. BA, Denison U., 1954; student, Inst. Orgn. Mgmt., Yale U., 1959. Exec. dir. Ohio State Pharm. Assn., Columbus, 1957-61; corp. sec. Nonprescription Drug Mfrs. Assn., Washington, 1961-66, v.p., sec., 1966-67, exec. v.p., 1967-73, pres., 1973-99; pres. name changed to Consumer Healthcare Products Assn., Washington, 1999—; pres. Nat. Conf. Pharma. Orgns., Washington, 1975, 83, 88, 98; bd. overseers U. Calif. Sch. Pharmacy, San Francisco, 1997—; exec. v.p. adv. com. Am. Assn. Colls. Pharmacy. Contbr. articles to profl. jours. Pres. Glen Mar Pk. Civic Assn., Bethesda, Md., 1963; pres. bd. trustees Faith United Meth. Ch., Rockville, Md., 1978; bd. dirs. Coun. on Family Health, N.Y.C., 1967—, Children's Hosp., 1968-76. Cpl. U.S. Army, 1954-56. Recipient Achievement medal Alpha Zeta Omega, 1960, Alumni citation Denison U., 1979, FDA Commrs.'s spl. citation, 1987, 99; named Man of Yr., Am. Druggist, 1959. Mem. Am. Soc. Assn. Execs. (bd. dirs. 1979-82), Greater Washington Soc. Assn. Execs., Denison U. Alumni Assn., World Self-Medication Industry (vice chmn. 1979-86, 89—), Nat. Assn. Execs. (pres. 1984), Met. Club (Washington), Congl. Country Club (Potomac, Md.). Republican. Home: 5916 Halpine Rd Rockville MD 20851-2409 Office: Consumer Healthcare Products Assn 1150 Connecticut Ave NW Washington DC 20036-4104

COPE, JEANNETTE NAYLOR, executive search consultant; b. Corpus Christi, Tex., Feb. 9, 1956; d. Glen R. and Jeannine (Withington) N.; m. John R. Cope, May 22, 1993. BA in Psychology and Sociology, Trinity U., 1978. Asst. fin. dir. Jim Baker for Atty. Gen. Campaign, Houston, 1978; fin. dir. Rep. Party of Tex., Austin, 1979-81; regional Eagle rep. Rep. Nat. Com., Washington, 1981-83; devel. officer Nat. Endowment for the Arts, Washington, 1983-87; sr. project mgr. Internat. Skye Assocs., Washington, 1988; spl. asst. to Pres. of U.S. The White House, 1989-90, dep. asst. to Pres. of U.S., dep. dir. of presdl. pers., 1990-93; pres. J. Naylor Cope Co., Washington, 1994—; NEA liaison Pres.' Com. on Arts and Humanites, Washington, 1985-87; dir. Internat. Skye Advisor, Washington, 1988; bd. dirs. Bush/Quayle Alumni Assn., 1991—; mem. Officer Pers. Mgmt.'s Task Force on Exec. and Mgmt. Devel., Washington, 1990. Chmn. alumni admissions coun. Trinity U., Washington, 1986-87; bd. dirs. Coop. Urban Ministry Ctr., Washington, 1987-89, Pennsylvania Ave. Devel. Corp., 1993-96, Decatur House, Washington, 1998—; vestrywoman St. John's Episcopal Ch., Washington, 1990-94, co-chmn. outreach com., 1991-94, chmn. search com. for 14th rector, jr. warden, 1994-97, sr. warden, 1998—. Tex. Coun. of Ch. Related Colls. scholar, 1974. Mem. Am. Soc. Assn. Execs. (exec. recruiter), Tex. State Soc. (chmn. membership com. 1981), Nat. Trust for Hist. Preservation, Smithsonian Instn., Am. Film Inst., Mcpl. Art Soc. (N.Y.C.), 1925 F Street Club (chmn. mems. com.), President's Club, Columbia Country Club (Chevy Chase, Md.), Tex. Breakfast Club, Blue Key (sec. 1976-78), City Tavern Club, Chi Beta Epsilon (v.p. San Antonio coun. 1976). Republican. Episcopalian. Office: J Naylor Cope Co PO Box 40069 Washington DC 20016-0069

COPE, JOHN R(OBERT), lawyer; b. San Angelo, Tex., May 30, 1942; s. Robert Lloyd and Meta (Young) C.; m. Jeannette L. Naylor; 1 child, Lloyd Chapman. BBA, U. Tex., 1964, JD, 1966. Bar: Tex. 1966, D.C. 1976. Ptnr. Bracewell & Patterson, Attys., Houston, 1966-76; ptnr. Bracewell & Patterson, Attys., Washington, 1976—, mem. adv. mgmt. com., 1987-90; sr. ptnr., 1994—; vice chmn. bd. dirs., gen. counsel Century Nat. Bank, Washington, 1982—; bd. dirs., gen. counsel Columbia Nat. Bank, Washington, 1987-90; bd. dirs., v.p., gen. counsel Century Bancshares, Washington, 1985—; mem. fed. savs. and loan adv. coun. Fed. Home Loan Bank Bd., Washington, 1980-81; chmn., lectr. Practicing Law Inst. Seminars on Energy Litigation, Washington, 1980, 81; chief judge Wake Island Ct., Wake Island, North Pacific Ocean, 1989. Bd. govs. Wesley Theol. Sem., Washington, 1997—; mem. devel. bd. Lon Morris Coll., Lake Jackson, Tex., 1974-76; mem. Southwest U. Spl. Edn. Found., San Marcos, Tex., 1973-76; v.p., dir. Harris County Easter Seal Soc., Houston, 1972-76; bd. dirs., sec. Nemours Wildlife Found., Yemassee, S.C., 1993—; treas. Dem. Party Harris County, Houston, 1976-77; mem. nat. fin. coun. Dem. Nat. Com., Washington, 1976-80; cert. lay spkr. United Meth. Ch., dist. dir. lay speaking dist. Washington-Columbia. Mem. ABA (mem. litigation sect.), D.C. Bar Assn. (mem. litigation and govt. contracts sect.), Tex. Bar Assn. (mem. litigation sect.), Houston Bar Assn. (mem. gen. litigation sect.), Orton Soc. Republican. Office: Bracewell & Patterson 2000 K St NW Ste 500 Washington DC 20006-1872

COPE, KENNETH WAYNE, chain store executive; b. Rifle, Colo., May 31, 1924; s. William Grant and Mary (Park) C.; m. Patricia Miller, Feb. 1, 1946; children: Kimberly Ann, Bradley Mark. B.A., La Sierra Coll., Arlington, Calif., 1948; postgrad., U. Wash., 1948-50. C.P.A., Calif. From staff accountant to mgr. Price Waterhouse & Co., C.P.A.s, Los Angeles, 1950-58; resident mgr. Price Waterhouse & Co., C.P.A.s, Phoenix, 1959-63; regional controller Lucky Stores, Inc., San Leandro, Calif., 1963-68; v.p., corp. controller Lucky Stores, Inc., 1968-83, sr. v.p. adminstrn., 1984-86, v.p. corp. affairs, 1986-87, ret., 1987. Served with AUS, 1943-46. Mem. Am. Inst. CPA's, Calif. Soc. CPA's, Fin. Execs. Inst. Republican. Episcopalian. Office: Lucky Stores Inc 6300 Clark Ave Dublin CA 94568-3098

COPE, LAURENCE BRIAN, utilities company executive, economic consultant; b. White Plains, N.Y., May 28, 1951; s. Lawrence Lyndon and Dorothea Anne (Herrick) C.; m. Ana Virginia Ambrosini, June 7, 1986 (div.). BS, Fla. So. Coll., 1974; MS in Govt. and Pub. Adminstrn., So. Ill. U., Edwardsville, 1980; postgrad. in Econs., George Washington U., 1982. Mgr. cost estimating Potomac Electric Power Co., Washington, 1974-77, systems and tng. specialist, 1977-82, project mgr., 1982-84, mem. spkrs. bur., 1978-84; project mgr., cons. Nat. Rural Utilities Coop. Fin. Corp., Herndon, Va., 1984—; econ. cons. Cope Assocs., Washington, 1978-84; trustee Cope Family Trusts; chmn. budget com. Oakton Condominium Assn., 1986-88. Author articles in field. Co-chmn. Christian Young Adults Group, Washington, 1983. Mem. ASTD (reporter chpt. organ The Torch 1977, 78), Am. Soc. Pub. Adminstrn. (budget and fin. divsn.), Nat. Economists Club (rapporteur 1985—), CFC Investment Club (pres. 1995). Roman Catholic. Home: 5407 Newington Rd Bethesda MD 20816-3317 Office: Nat Rural Utilities Coop Fin Corp Woodland Pk 2201 Cooperative Way Herndon VA 20171-3081

COPE, LEWIS, journalist; b. Sweetwater, Tex., June 24, 1934; s. Millard L. and Margaret Wallace (Kilgore) C.; m. Betty Joan Ball, June 28, 1958; children—Margaret, Elizabeth, Mary Amelia. BA, Washington and Lee U., 1955. Reporter Greenville (Tex.) Herald-Banner, 1957-60; copy editor Richmond (Va.) Times Dispatch, 1960-62; copy editor, news editor San Antonio Express, 1962-66; sci. reporter Mpls. Star and Tribune, 1966-95; freelance science writer, newspaper cons., 1995—; bd. dirs. Coun. Advancement of Sci. Writing, 1996—; writer-in-residence Nat. Cancer Inst., 1976. Author: Save Your Life, 1979. Served as officer AUS, 1955-57. Recipient Merit award Am. Assn. Blood Banks, 1974, Journalism award Am. Acad. Family Physicians, 1976, 79, Penney award lifestyle reporting U. Mo., 1977, Nat. Media award Am. Cancer Soc., 1977, Blakeslee award Am. Heart Assn., 1979, Cecil award Arthritis Found., 1982, Harvey award Am. Med. Writers Assn., 1993; Sci. Writing fellow Columbia U. Grad. Sch. Journalism, 1963-64. Mem. Nat. Assn. Sci. Writers (exec. com. 1982-93, treas. 1985-88, v.p. 1989-90, pres. 1991-92), Sigma Delta Chi (pres. Minn. chpt. 1973-74, dep. regional dir. 1974-86). Episcopalian. Home: 5217 W 91st St Minneapolis MN 55437-1819

COPE, MAURICE ERWIN, art history educator; b. Detroit, Feb. 4, 1926; s. Henry Erwin and Myragene (Mead) C.; m. Beatrice L. Everson, June 18, 1949 (div. Jan. 1975); children: Thomas M., Cynthia E.; m. C. Penelope Bass, Dec. 23, 1977 (div. Feb. 1981); 1 child, Nicholas M. MA in English, U. Chgo., 1949, PhD in Art History, 1965; postgrad., U. Florence, Italy, 1954-56. Instr. English, Valparaiso (Ind.) U., 1949-51; instr., asst. prof. humanities U. Chgo., 1954, 56-60; asst. prof. art history Pomona Coll., Claremont, Calif., 1960-65; assoc. prof., prof. Ohio State U., Columbus, 1965-72; prof. U. Del., Newark, 1972-97, prof. emeritus, 1997—; dir. fund raising in ctrl. and south Ohio, Com. To Rescue Italian Art after Floods of 1966, 1966-67, rep. in Italy, 1967-68, rep. to UNESCO meeting on Venice, 1968; reader in art history Ednl. Testing Svc., Princeton, N.J., 1972-77. Contbg. author: The Friedrick W. Schumacher Collection, 1976, Atti del Convegno Tintoretto, 1995; author: The Venetian Chapel of the Sacrament in the 16th Century, 1979, (catalogues) James Turrell: Jida, 1984, Philipp Fehl: Birds of a Feather, 1991; editor The Arts, Ohio State U., 1969-72. With USN, 1944-46. Fulbright fellow, Florence, 1954-56; rsch. fellow NEH, Florence and Venice, 1967-68, Delmas Found., Venice, 1986. Mem. Coll. Art Assn. (com. for 1964 meeting, session chmn. 1979), Renaissance Soc. Am., Italian Art Soc. Avocations: music, art and political collecting. Home: 602 Delaware St New Castle DE 19720-5058

COPE, RANDOLPH HOWARD, JR., electronic research and development executive, educator; b. Cleve., Nov. 19, 1927; s. Randolph Howard and Helen Eunice (Smith) C.; m. Elizabeth Louise Barton, July 1, 1950; children: David, Margaret. BS in Physics, Case Inst. Tech., 1949; MEE, Poly. Inst. Bklyn., 1958. Electronic engr. Hazeltine Corp., Little Neck, N.Y., 1949-54, sr. engr., 1957-71; assoc. dir. rsch. Hazeltine Corp., Greenlawn, N.Y., 1971-75, dir. rsch. labs., 1975-79, v.p. rsch., 1979-88; dir. grad. program in indsl. mgmt., dept. tech. and society SUNY, Stony Brook, 1989-93, lectr., grad advisor in indsl. mgmt., 1993-98. Lt. (j.g.) USNR, 1954-57. Office: SUNY at Stony Brook Coll Engring and Applied Scis Stony Brook NY 11794-2250

COPE, ROBERT GARY, management educator, author, consultant; b. Chgo., June 13, 1936; s. Henry Jasper and Alicia (Vecellio) C.; m. Claudette Holm, June 16, 1961 (div. Mar. 1985); children: Kathryn, Robin, Peter, Michael, Linda; m. Nancy Louise Junak, Aug. 1, 1987 (div. Aug. 1997). BBA, U. Mich., 1959, AM, 1961, PhD, 1967. Dir. instl. research and planning U. Mass., Amherst, 1966-69; prof. U. Wash., Seattle, 1969-92; founder, dir. Northwoods (Mich.) Ctr. and Inst., 1992—; founder Eagle Harbor Inst., Mich., 1994-97; lectr. Snowmass (Colo.) Inst., 1979—; cons. in field, 1972—. Author: Revolving College Doors, 1974, European Camping and Caravaning, 1974, Strategic Policy Planning, 1978, Strategic Planning Management and Decision-Making, 1981, High Involvement Strategic Planning, 1989, El Plan Estrategico, 1991, Opportunity From Strength, 1987, Total Management for Organisations, 1991, Total Management (in Russian) 1993, High Involvement Strategic Planning (in Russian), 1993, El Totalmente Plan Estrategico, 1995, Profits for Small Business Operations (in Russian) 1996. Vis. fellow U. Melbourne (Australia), 1977, Australian Nat. U., Canberra, 1976, Nat. Ctr. for Mgmt. Systems, Boulder, Colo., 1981. Mem. Acad. Mgmt., Am. Assn. for Higher Edn., Internat. Assn. Astacologists, Assn. for Instl. Research. Avocation: nature conservation. Home: 2439 US Hwy 41 Ishpeming MI 49849-9451 Address: PO Box 534 Friday Harbor WA 98250 Office: Northwoods Ctr RR 1 Ishpeming MI 49849-9801

COPE, THOM K., lawyer; b. Bremen, Fed. Republic Germany, Feb. 26, 1948; came to U.S., 1960; s. Ray and Gabriele E. (Meyer) C.; m. Melba D. Van Hemert, Nov. 8, 1980. BA with honors, Syracuse U., 1969; JD, U. Nebr., 1972. Bar: Nebr. 1972, U.S. Dist. Ct. Nebr. 1972, U.S. Ct. Appeals (8th cir.) 1972, Calif. 1976, U.S. Dist. Ct. (no. dist.) Calif. 1976, U.S. Ct. Appeals (9th cir.) 1976, U.S. Supreme Ct. 1987, U.S. Claims Ct. 1988, U.S. Ct. Appeals (D.C. cir.) 1990. Agy. legal counsel Nebr. Workers' Compensation Ct., Lincoln, 1972-73; assoc. counsel Fireman's Fund Ins. Co., San Francisco, 1973-76; asst. gen. counsel Argonaut Ins. Co., Menlo Park, Calif., 1976-78; assoc. counsel Ins. Svcs. Office, N.Y.C., 1978-82; assoc. atty. Tate & Assocs., Nebr., 1982-83, Bailey, Polsky, Cada & Todd, Nebr., 1983-84; ptnr. Bailey, Polsky, Cope & Knapp, Lincoln, 1984-97, Polsky Cope Shiffermiller & Coe, Lincoln, 1997—; judge Nebr. Commn. of Indsl. Rels., 1986-91; mem. Nebr. Supreme Ct. Gender Bias Task Force; mem. Nebr. Motor Vehicle Industry Licensing Bd.; mem. Fed. Practice Adv. Com.; lectr. in field; bd. dirs. Nat. Org. Women. Author: Executive Guide to Employment Practices, 1985, 3d edit., 1999. Bd. dirs. Friends of Elderly Found., Lincoln, 1986-90, Capital Humane Soc., Planned Parenthood Lincoln, 1997—, v.p., 1998, pres. 1999-00; bd. dirs. Child Advocacy Ctr., 1995-97; bd. trustees Lincoln Bar Assn. Fellow Coll. Employment and Labor Law; mem. Nat. Employ & Lawyers Assn., Nebr. Bar Assn. (labor and employment sect., exec. com., sec.), Nebr. Trial Lawyers Assn. Avocation: golf. Fax: (402) 484-7714. Home: 2244 Heritage Pines Ct Lincoln NE 68506-2874 Office: Polsky Cope Shiffermiller and Coe 3901 Normal Blvd Ste 102 Lincoln NE 68506-5200

COPE, THOMAS FIELD, lawyer; b. Oak Park, Ill., Feb. 29, 1948; s. Benjamin Thomas and Myra Norma (Lees) C.; m. Ann Wattis, Mar. 21, 1970; children: Elizabeth Ann, Philip Thomas. BA, U. Denver, 1970, MA, 1976, JD, 1974; postgrad., U. Chgo., 1978-81. Bar: Colo. 1974, Ill. 1978, Wyo. 1996, U.S. Dist. Ct. Colo. 1974, U.S. Ct. Appeals (10th cir.) 1989. Assoc. Holme Roberts & Owen, Denver, 1974-78, 81-83, ptnr., 1984—; instr. IIT/Chgo.-Kent Coll. Law, 1980, Loyola U. Sch. Law, Chgo., 1980-81. Co-editor: Colorado Environmental Law Handbook, 1989, 4th rev. edit., 1996, Colorado Environmental Compliance Update, 1993-96; contbg. editor Oil & Gas Law and Taxation Rev., Oxford, Eng., 1987-93; mng. editor Shepard's Environ. Liability in Comml. Transactions Reporter, 1990-92; mem. bd. editors Denver Law Jour., 1972-74; contbr. articles to profl. jours. Bd. dirs. Colo. Fourteeners Initiative, 1996—. Mem. Am. Law Inst., Am. Soc. Legal History, Irish Legal History Soc., Selden Soc. (state corr. Colo. 1997—), Rocky Mountain Mineral Law Found. (mem. grants com. 1983-95, chmn. 1995—), Order St. Ives, Am. Alpine Club, Colo. Mountain Club. Democrat. Mem. Orthodox Ch. in Am. Avocations: mountaineering, history. Home: 2800 S University Blvd Unit 108 Denver CO 80210-6072 Office: Holme Roberts & Owen LLP 1700 Lincoln St Ste 4100 Denver CO 80203-4541

COPE, WENDY, poet; b. 1945. Tchr. Portway Jr. Sch., London, 1967-69, Keyworth Jr. Sch., London, 1969-73, Cobourg Primary Sch., 1973-81, Brindishe Primary Sch., 1984-86; writer, TV columnist The Spectator, London, 1986-90; arts educator ILEA Contact Tchrs. Newspaper, 1982-84. Author: Across the City, 1980, Hope and the 42, 1984, Making Cocoa for Kingsley Amis, 1986, Poem from a Colour Chart of Housepaints, 1986, Men and Their Boring Arguments, 1988, Does She Like Word-Games?, 1988, Twiddling Your Thumbs, 1988, The River Girl, 1991, Serious Concerns, 1992; editor: Is That the New Moon?, Poems By Women Poets, 1989, The Orchard Book of Funny Poems, 1993, The Funny Side, 1998. Recipient Cholmondeley award for poetry, 1987, Michael Braude award AAAL, 1995. Fellow Royal Soc. Lit. Office: Faber & Faber, 3 Queen Sq, London WC1N 3AU, England

COPELAND, BENNY JAMES, transportation agent; b. Alton, Ill., Apr. 9, 1948; s. Jesse J. and Suda M. (Counts) C.; m. Linda Kay, Apr. 26, 1969; children: Davin, Shaun. Student, So. Ill. U., 1966-68, Lewis & Clark Coll., Godfrey, Ill., 1971-73. Ticket agt. Gulf Mobile & Ohio R.R., Alton, 1968-72; operator Ill. Ctrl. Gulf R.R., Wood River, 1972-79; chief clk. Ill. Ctrl. Gulf R.R., Venice, 1979-87; transp. agt. So. Pacific R.R., Wood River, 1987-97; with spl. svcs. Union Pacific R.R., 1997-99. Office: Union Pacific RR 301 Rueter Rd Wood River IL 62095-1444

COPELAND, CAROLYN ABIGAIL, retired university dean; b. White Plains, N.Y., May 5, 1931; d. Robert Erford and Mary Terwilliger; B.A. (CEW scholar), U. Mich., 1973, M.A. (Rackham Grad. Student scholar), 1979, postgrad. 1992—; m. William E. Copeland, Aug. 16, 1964; children—Rob Cameron, Diana Elizabeth Bosworth. With dean's office Coll. Lit., Sci. and Arts, U. Mich., Ann Arbor, 1967-91, asst. dean, 1980-84, assoc. dean, 1984-91. Mem. Mortar Bd., Phi Beta Kappa (v.p. Alpha chpt. 1984-86, pres. Alpha chpt. 1986-88). Author: Tankas from the Koelz Collection, 1980; Walter Norman Koelz, A Biography, in progress. Research in Buddhist art history. Home: 520 Darwin Rd Pinckney MI 48169-8113 Office: U Mich Ann Arbor MI 48109

COPELAND, CHARLENE CAROLE, lawyer; b. Gloversville, N.Y., July 22; d. Joseph Frank and Marion (Dye) Born; m. E. Allen Copeland, June 18; children: Christopher, Todd, Tiffani. BS in Polit Sci., Lamar U.; JD, John Marshall U. Bar: Ill. 1991, U.S. Dist. Ct. (no. dist.) Ill. 1991, U.S. Ct. Appeals (7th cir.) 1993, Fed. Trial Bar, 1993. Assoc. Brenner, Mavrias & Alm, New Lenox, Ill., 1992-96; assoc. civil divsn. Will County State's Attys. Office, Joliet, Ill., 1997—. Mem. Will County Pro Bono Project; pres. Jaycettes, Port Authur, Tex., 1970-71; fin. chmn. League of Women Voters, 1971, pres. Joliet Region, 1979-81; area capt. March of Dimes Mothers' March, 1971; day chmn. George Bush for Senate Campaign, 1970; mem. Village of Shorewood Ad Hoc Com. on Ordinances, 1975, Fin. Com., 1976-78; pres. United Meth. Women of Grace Meth. Ch., 1980-81; crusade chmn. Shorewood Residential Cancer Crusade, 1982. Named Outstanding Pro Bono Vol., 1995. Mem. ATLA, Ill. State Bar Assn., Will County Bar Assn., Will County Arbitration Panel, Will County Women's Bar Assn. Home: 516 Ca Crest Dr Shorewood IL 60431-9729 Office: Will County States Atty 54 N Ottawa St Joliet IL 60432-4345

COPELAND, CHRISTINE SUSAN, therapist; b. Milw., Jan. 8, 1949; d. Walter Horace and Doris Esther (Becker) C. BA in Psychology, Valparaiso (Ind.) U., 1971; MS in Psychology, U. Wis., 1974. Psychologist Curative Workshop, Green Bay, Wis., 1974-77, No. Wis. Ctr. for Developmentally Disabled, Chippewa Falls, Wis., 1977-86; behavior therapist Midelfort Clinic, Eau Claire, Wis., 1986-93, Systems Counseling and Cons., Inc., Eau Claire, 1994-95; pvt. practice, Chippewa Falls, Wis., 1995—; ind. computer cons. Mem. APA (assoc.), Am. Assn. Mental Retardation, Assn. for Advancement of Behavior Therapy, Wis. Psychol. Assn., C.H.A.D.D., Beta Sigma Phi (officer Wis. chpt. 1977—, Woman of Yr. 1979). Home and Office: 17884 54th Ave Chippewa Falls WI 54729-8754

COPELAND, DONALD EUGENE, research marine biologist; b. Mendon, Ohio, Feb. 6, 1912; s. Arland Murlin and Chloe (Severns) C.; m. Marjorie Groves, June 20, 1941; children: Sandra Kay, Jane Hance, Diana Sue. A.B., Rochester U., 1935; M.A., Amherst Coll., 1937; Ph.D., Harvard U., 1941. Instr. zoology U. N.C., 1941-42; asst. then assoc. prof. zoology Brown U., 1946-51; chief aviation physiologist Office Surgeon Gen., USAF, 1951-53; profl. assoc. Nat. Acad. Scis.-NRC, 1953-56; exec. sec. NIH, 1956-59; prof. zoology Tulane U., 1959-77, prof. emeritus, 1977—, chmn. dept., 1959-65; mem. (Marine Biol. Lab.), Woods Hole, Mass., 1948—; ind. investigator (Marine Biol. Lab.), 1977—; Mem. morphology and genetics study sect., physiology study sect. NIH, 1952-53. Served to capt. USAAF, 1942-46. Mem. Am. Assn. Anatomists, Am. Soc. Zoologists, Soc. Study Devel. and Growth, Am. Soc. Cell Biologists, Am. Physiol. Soc. Research histophysiology and ultra structure salt secreting mechanisms, gas secretion in swim bladders, oxygen elevation in fish eye, secretion of aqueous humor in fish eye, cytology of luminescent organs in deepsea fish. Home: 41 Fern Ln Woods Hole MA 02543-1111 Office: Marine Biol Lab 41 Water St Woods Hole MA 02543-1023

COPELAND, EDWARD JEROME, lawyer; b. Chgo., Oct. 29, 1933; s. Harvey and Lilyan (Rubin) C.; m. Ruth Caminer, Sept. 2, 1962; children: Ellyn, Bradley. BA, Carleton Coll., 1955; JD, Northwestern U., 1958. Bar: Ill. 1959, N.Y. 1981. Mem. Ill. Legislature, Springfield, 1967-71; ptnr. Foss, Schuman, Drake & Barnard, Chgo., 1971-86, Wood,Lucksinger & Epstein, Chgo., 1986-88, Shefsky & Froelich, Ltd., Chgo., 1988-89, Schuyler, Roche & Zwirner, Chgo., 1989—; chmn. Bank of the North Shore, Northbrook, Ill., 1976-81. Mem. Ill. Bd. Edn., 1975-83, chmn., 1981-83. Mem. ABA, Ill. Bar Assn., Chgo. Bar Assn. Republican. Office: Schuyler Roche & Zwirner 130 E Randolph St Ste 3800 Chicago IL 60601-6317

COPELAND, EDWARD MEADORS, III, surgery educator; b. Augusta, Ga., Oct. 6, 1937; s. Edward Meadors Jr. and Louise (Leggitt) C.; m. Martha Patterson, Ar. 24, 1964; children: Edward Meadors IV, Catherine Leggit. BA, Duke U., 1959; MD, Cornell U., 1963. Diplomate Am. Bd. Surgery (bd. dirs. 1983-91, chmn. 1990-91). Intern in surgery U. Pa. Hosp., Phila., 1963-64, resident in gen. surgery, 1964-69; resident surg. oncology Anderson Hosp., Houston, 1971-72; asst. prof. to prof. U. Tex. Med. Sch.,

Houston, 1972-82, U. Tex. M.D. Anderson Hosp. and Tumor Inst., Houston, 1972-82; prof., chmn. dept. U. Fla. Coll. Medicine, Gainesville, 1982—; project dir. Nat. Large Bowel Cancer Project, Nat. Cancer Inst., Houston, 1981-82. Bd. dirs. Sun Bank, Gainesville, 1987—. Maj. U.S. Army, 1969-71, Vietnam. Decorated Bronze Star Rep. Vietnam; recipient Seale Harris award So. Med. Assn., 1984, Disting. Alumnus award M.D. Anderson Hosp. and Tumor Inst., 1987. Fellow Am. Surg. Assn., So. Surg. Assn. (pres. 1998-99); mem. ACS (chmn. bd. govs. 1995-96, bd. regents 1997—), Assn. for Acad. Surgery (pres. 1978-79), Soc. Surg. Oncology (pres. 1998-99), Soc. Surg. Chmn. (pres. 1996-98), Southeastern Surg. Congress (v.p. 1999—), Soc. Univ. Surgeons, Gainesville Golf and Country Club. Avocations: fishing, golf, tennis. Home: 2605 NW 7th Rd Gainesville FL 32607-2600 Office: Univ Fla Coll Medicine Dept of Surgery PO Box 100286 Gainesville FL 32610-0286

COPELAND, FLOYD DEAN, lawyer; b. Jackson, Miss., Apr. 11, 1939; s. Clyde Xenephon and Dorothy Russell (Dean) C.; m. Linda Gail Langston, Dec. 22, 1965; children: Albion Ehlers, Russell Braden. BA, U. Miss., 1961, U. Oxford, Eng., 1963; LLB, Yale U., 1965. Bar: Ga. 1967, Tenn. 1998. Assoc. Alston, Miller & Gaines, Atlanta, 1967-71; ptnr. Alston & Bird, Atlanta, 1972-97; exec. v.p., gen. coun. Provident Cos., Inc., Chattanooga, 1997—. Bd. dirs. Atlanta Metro Boys and Girls Clubs, 1986-97; sec. State and Dist. Rhodes Scholarship Selection Coms., Atlanta, 1976-97. Capt. U.S. Army, 1965-67. Rhodes scholar, 1961, Carrier scholar, 1957. Mem. Am. Law Inst. Presbyterian. Avocations: recreational basketball, reading, travel. Home: 214 Camden Rd NE Atlanta GA 30309-1512 Office: Provident Cos Inc One Fountain Sq Chattanooga TN 37402*

COPELAND, HENRY JEFFERSON, JR., former college president; b. Griffin, Ga., June 13, 1936; s. Henry Jefferson and Emory (Drake) C.; m. Laura Harper, Dec. 21, 1958; children—Henry Drake, Eleanor Harper. B.A., Baylor U., 1958; Ph.D, Cornell U., 1966. Instr. Cornell U., Ithaca, N.Y., 1965-66; asst. prof. history Coll. Wooster, Ohio, 1966-69; assoc. dean Coll. Wooster, 1969-74, dean, 1974-77, pres., 1977-95, prof. history, 1995-98. Woodrow Wilson fellow, 1960. Democrat. Presbyterian.

COPELAND, HUNTER ARMSTRONG, real estate executive; b. Birmingham, Ala., Oct. 22, 1918; s. Miles Axe and Leonora (Armstrong) C.; m. Suzanne Curl, 1942 (div. 1954); children: Susan Diane, Hunter Armstrong; m. Patricia Ann McGregor, 1956 (div. 1976); children: John McGregor, Miles, Ann; m. Courteney Bass, May 27, 1978. Student, U. Ala., 1936-37; grad. advanced mgmt. course, Harvard U., 1952. Mortgage appraiser Prudential Ins. Co. Am., Birmingham, 1946-54; mortgage broker Huntoon-Paige, N.Y.C., 1954-57; pres. Huntoon Copeland & Hedin, N.Y.C., 1958-70; exec. dir. Hunter Copeland and Assocs., N.Y.C., 1970-75; v.p. Colwell Co., N.Y.C., 1970-75; pres. Copeland-Tresnan & Hornblower Inc., N.Y.C., 1975-78, Hunter Copeland and Assocs., Birmingham, Ala., 1978—; trustee Md. Realty Trust, Balt.; organizer, dir. New Canaan Bank & Trust Co., Conn.; mem. Ala. Cert. Bd. Alcoholism and Drug Counselors. Mem. Am. Coun. on Alcoholism; exec. dir. Alcohol and Drug Abuse Coun. With inf. AUS, 1941-45; maj. USAF, 1952-54. Decorated Legion of Merit, Silver Star, Bronze Star with 4 oak leaf clusters, Purple Heart with oak leaf cluster., Legion of Merit, Croix du Combattant Voluntaire (France), War Cross Royal Yugoslav Army Peter II King of Yugoslavia, Medaille Commemorative Francaise, Medaille de France Liberee; named to Inf. Officers Hall of Fame, Ft. Benning, Ga., 1982. Mem. Mortgage Bankers Assn. Am., Mortgage Bankers Assn. N.Y. (gov.), Am. Pub. Health Assn., Nat. Assn. Alcoholism and Drug Abuse Counselors, ASCD, Internat. Coun. Alcohol & Addictions, Vets. of Battle of the Bulge, Newcomen Soc., Commerce Exec. Soc. U. Ala., Chi Phi. Clubs: Kiwanis; Union League (N.Y.C.), Met. (N.Y.C.); Country of Birmingham. Office: Alcohol and Drug Abuse Coun 1923 14th Ave S Birmingham AL 35205-4905

COPELAND, JACQUELINE TURNER, music educator; b. Birmingham, Ala., Mar. 22, 1939; d. Charles Smith and Julia (Northrop) Turner; m. William Edward Copeland, Apr. 20, 1962; children: Denise Arlene, Dawn Alane. B in Music Edn., Birmingham-So. Coll., 1960; M in Music Edn., Wichita State U., 1977. Cert. music tchr. grades K-12, Ala., Ga., Kans., La., Va. Music tchr. Jefferson County Bd. Edn., Birmingham, 1960-62, 63-64, DeKalb County Bd. Edn., Decatur, Ga., 1965-68; choral music tchr. Fairfax (Va.) County Bd. Edn., 1968-69, Derby (Kans.) Unified Sch. Dist. #260, 1977-80, Maize (Kans.) Unified Sch. Dist. #266, 1980-84; music tchr. Montgomery (Ala.) County Pub. Schs., 1984-85; instr. voice and piano Acad. Performing Arts, Montgomery, 1985-95, Studio of Jacqueline T. Copeland, Montgomery, 1995—; accompanist County-Wide Music Festivals, Birmingham, 1960-65; sect. leader Dekalb Cmty. Chorus, Decatur, Ga., 1965-68; sect. leader, exec. bd. New Orleans Concert Choir, 1970-74; asst. dir., dir. chorale Wichita Choral Soc., 1974-84; dir. opening ceremony Bicentennial Fair, Wichita, 1976; mem. Montgomery (Ala.) Civic Chorale, 1984-87; musical dir. for theatre depts. Performing Arts Jr. High, Performing Arts H.S., Faulkner U., 1986—. Author: Music Teacher Handbook, 1967; editor, contbg. author: Teacher Advisement Handbook, 1980. Secret svc. wife White House Wives, Washington, 1968-70; leader, trainer, area chmn. Camp Fire Girls, New Orleans, 1970-74; leader, membership com., exec. bd. Camp Fire Girls, Wichita, 1974-82; elected ofcl. Citizens Participation Orgn., Wichita, 1984; area chmn. Am. Heart Assn., Montgomery, 1988-94; vol. DA Election, Montgomery, 1994. Recipient Groovey Tchr. award WQXI Radio, Atlanta, 1967, Gov.'s commendation Revolutionary Bicentennial Com., Wichita, 1976; named Outstanding Young Women of Am., New Orleans, 1971. Mem. NOW, AAUW, Music Tchrs. Nat. Assn., Ala. Music Tchrs. Assn., Montgomery Music Tchrs. Forum, Alpha Chi Omega (Montgomery chpt. treas. 1995-99, pres. 1999—), Alpha Chi Omega Alumnae (del. to 4 nat. convs., pres., v.p.). Democrat. Baptist. Avocations: searching for collectibles for country decor. Home: 6121 Bell Road Mnr Montgomery AL 36117-4362

COPELAND, JAMES E., JR., financial service executive. Mng. ptnr. Deloitte & Touche LCP, Wilton, Conn., 1994-99, CEO, 1999—. Office: Deloitte & Touche LLP PO Box 820 10 Westport Rd Wilton CT 06897-0820*

COPELAND, JOHN ALEXANDER, III, physicist; b. Atlanta, Feb. 6, 1941; s. John Alexander and Gay Elise (Stafford) C.; m. Sandra Jeanne Chandler, June 18, 1960; children: Brian Christopher, Trudi Kathleen. BS, Ga. Inst. Tech., 1962, MS, 1963, PhD, 1965. Mem. tech. staff Bell Tel. Labs., 1965-82, supr., 1967-76; head repeater research dept. Bell Tel. Labs., Holmdel, N.J., 1976-82; v.p. engring. tech. Sangamo Weston/Schlumberger, Atlanta, 1982-85; v.p. systems engr. Hayes Microcomputer Products, Atlanta, 1985-93; rsch. physicist Ga. Inst. Tech., Atlanta, 1965; CEO Ga. Ctr. Advanced Telecomm. Tech., 1993-96; also bd. dirs. Ga. Ctr. Advanced Telecom. Tech., Ga. Inst. Tech., Atlanta; prof. Ga. Inst. Tech., Atlanta, 1993-96; Wetnauer chair School of Elec. and comp. engnr. GA Inst. Tech., Atlanta, GA, 1993—. Recipient Disting. Svc. award Atlanta Civil Def., 1965, Best Paper award Internat. Solid States Cirs. Conf., 1967. Fellow IEEE (editor trans. electron devices 1971-73, Morris N. Liebmann award 1970); mem. Am. Phys. Soc., Sea Bright Lawn Club. Patentee gallium arsenide microwave devices, magnetic-bubble computer memories, silicon integrated circuits. Home: 1070 Greenway Atlanta GA 30350-1707 Office: Ga Inst Tech ECE 0250 Atlanta GA 30332

COPELAND, JOHN DEWAYNE, law educator; b. Wichita Falls, Tex., Apr. 9, 1950; s. Howard R. and Lorene (Sharp) C.; m. Vannette Sue Thomas, July 2, 1970; children: Aaron, Seth, Sarah. BA, U. Tex., Arlington, 1971; JD, So. Meth. U., 1974; LLM, U. Ark., 1986, EdD, 1997. Bar: Tex. 1974, Ark. 1986, U.S. Dist. Ct. (no. dist.) Tex. 1974, U.S. Dist. Ct. (ea. and we. dists.) Ark. 1986, U.S. Ct. Appeals (5th cir.) 1975, U.S. Ct. Appeals (8th cir.) 1987, U.S. Supreme Ct. 1979. Ptnr. Short & Copeland, Wichita Falls, 1974-76, Helton, Copeland & Southard, Wichita Falls, 1976-78, Oldham, Copeland & Barnard, Wichita Falls, 1978-81; mem. Russell, Tate & Gowan, Wichita Falls, 1981-84; assoc. Roy & Lambert, Springdale, Ark., 1985-88; vis. asst. prof. U. Ark. Sch. Law, Fayetteville, Ark., 1988-89; dir. and rsch. prof. law Nat. Ctr. for Agrl. Law Rsch. and Info., Fayetteville, Ark., 1989-98; exec. v.p. for ethics, food safety and environ. compliance Tyson Foods, Springdale, Ark., 1998—; cons. environ. com. Nat. Pork Producers Coun., Des Moines, 1991-98, Am. Meat Inst., Washington, 1994-98, mem. environ. compliance com. Dairy Quality Assurance Bd. Author: Understanding the Farmers Comprehensive Personal Liability Policy, 1992, Recreational Access to Private Land: Liability Issues and Solutions, 1995; author book chpts.; contbr. articles to profl. jours. Legal advisor City Charter Revision Commn., Wichita Falls, 1976-77; bd. dirs. Wichita County Bar Assn., Wichita Falls, 1976-78, treas., 1978-79, dir. lawyer referral, 1982-84. Recipient grad. fellowship U. Ark. Sch. Law, 1984. Mem. ABA (vice chair agrl. law com. 1990-91), Am. Agrl. Law Assn. (bd. dirs. 1997—, Excellence in Profl. Scholarship award 1996). Baptist. Home: 5059 Tall Pine Cir Springdale AR 72762-2577 Office: Univ Ark Leflar Law Ctr Fayetteville AR 72701

COPELAND, LEWIS, principal. Prin. W.P. Davidson High Sch., Mobile, Ala., 1982—. Recipient Blue Ribbon Sch. award U.S. Dept. Edn., 1990-91, 95-96; named Secondary Prin. of Yr., Ala. State PTA, 1993-94, Outstanding Sch. Adminstr., Ala. Music Educators Assn., 1997. Office: WP Davidson HS 3900 Pleasant Valley Rd Mobile AL 36609-2022

COPELAND, LOIS JACQUELINE (MRS. RICHARD A. SPERLING), physician; b. Malden, Mass., Sept. 16, 1943; d. Arnold Alan and Ann (Goldfarb) C.; m. Richard A. Sperling, June 7, 1970; children: Mark Edward, Larissa Lynn, Lauren Anne, Lorraine Elizabeth. BA magna cum laude with distinction, Cornell U., 1964, MD, 1968. Intern N.Y. Hosp., N.Y.C., 1968-69, resident, 1969-70; resident Bellevue Hosp., NYU Med. Ctr., 1970-72; tchg. asst. internal medicine NYU Med. Ctr., 1971—; attending physician Pascack Valley Hosp., Westwood, N.J., 1974—; mem. courtesy staff Valley Hosp., Ridgewood, N.J., 1980—. Mem. secondary schs. com. Cornell U., 1978—; bd. dirs. Found. for Free Enterprise; steering com. physicians coun. Heritage Found., 1993—; pres. Coun. Cornell Women, 1993-95. Mem. Bd. Assn. Am. Physicians and Surgeons, Assn. Am. Physicians and Surgeons (bd. dirs. 1991—; pres. 1995, N.J. chpt. 1998), Assn. Liberty Choice and Individual Responsibility (pres. 1998), Phi Beta Kappa, Phi Kappa Phi, Alpha Lambda Delta. Achievements include being originator and physician-plaintiff in landmark constitutional lawsuit Stewart v. Sullivan, which reaffirmed the right to senior citizens to contract privately with physicians, and Amicus in United Seniors v. Shalala for the right to pay privately for medical services. Home: 25 Sparrowbush Rd Upper Saddle River NJ 07458-1411 Office: 47 Central Ave Hillsdale NJ 07642-2118

COPELAND, PHILLIPS JEROME, former academic administrator, former air force officer; b. Oxnard, Calif., Mar. 22, 1921; s. John Charles and Marion Moffatt) C.; student U. So. Calif., 1947-49; BA, U. Denver, 1956, MA, 1958; grad. Air Command and Staff Coll., 1959, Indsl. Coll. Armed Forces, 1964; m. Alice Janette Lusby, Apr. 26, 1942; children: Janette Ann Copeland Bosserman, Nancy Jo Copeland Briner. Commd. 2d lt. USAAF, 1943, advanced through grades to col. USAF, 1964, pilot 8th Air Force, Eng., 1944-45; various flying and staff assignments, 1945-51; chief joint tng. sect. Hdqrs. Airsouth (NATO), Italy, 1952-54; asst. dir. plans and programs USAF Acad., 1955-58; assigned to joint intelligence, Washington, 1959-61; plans officer Cincpac Joint Staff, Hawaii, 1961-63; staff officer, ops. directorate, then team chief Nat. Mil. Command Center, Joint Chiefs Staff, Washington, 1964-67; dir. plans and programs USAF Adv. Group, also adviser to Vietnamese Air Force, Vietnam, 1967-68; prof. aerospace studies U. So. Calif., L.A., 1968-72, exec. asst. to pres., 1972-73, assoc. dir. office internat. programs, 1973-75, dir. adminstrv. services Coll. Continuing Edn., 1975-82, dir. employee relations, 1982-84. Decorated D.F.C., Bronze Star, Air medal with 3 clusters; Medal of Honor (Vietnam). Mem. Air Force Assn., Order of Daedalians. Home: 81 Cypress Way Palos Verdes Peninsula CA 90274-3416

COPELAND, POPPY CARLSON, psychotherapist; b. Evanson, Ill., Dec. 18, 1939; d. Frederick Winsor and Polly (Packard) C.; m. Marshall S. Johnson (div. 1979), children: Erica Winsor, Lara Siree; m. Lawrence E. Carlson, June 15, 1985. BA, U. Calif., Berkeley, 1962; MA, U. Denver, 1975; ABD (hon.) in Internat. Studies, U. Colo., 1980; M in Psychology, Counseling Inst. Transpersonal, Palo Alto, Calif., 1992. Lic. profl. counselor, Colo.; lifetime tchg. credential, Calif. Tchr. Temple City (Calif.) Sch. Dist., 1965-67; chmn. sch. assistance Mitrapah Found., Bangkok, Thailand, 1969-73; rsch. assoc. edn. Commn. of States, Denver, 1976-78; rsch. assoc. Boulder County Bd. Developmental Disabilities, Boulder, Colo., 1978-79; social policy writer Boulder Camera, Denver Post, 1981-84; sr. trainer Tucker Internat., Boulder, 1984—; psychotherapist in pvt. practice Boulder, 1990—; dir. Internat. Women's Week, U. Colo., 1981-83, Internat. Pedestrian Conf., City of Boulder, 1981-83; cons. Colo. Civil Rights Commn., 1987-89; bd. dirs. Rocky Mountain Survivors Ctr. Dir. Boulder Peace Consortium, 1983-86, Friendship City Nicaragua, Boulder, 1984-86; series chair Conf. on World Affairs, U. Colo., 1999. Mem. ACA. Avocations: skiing, bicycling, hiking, gardening. Home: 2541 Bluff St Boulder CO 80304-3721 Office: 711 Walnut St Ste 200 Boulder CO 80304

COPELAND, ROBERT BODINE, internist, cardiologist; b. Arab, Ala., Jan. 24, 1938; s. Haden Paul and Jimmie Alice (Bodine) C.; m. Jenny Trammell, June 26, 1960; children: Robert Theodore, Haden McTieyre. BS, Auburn U., 1960; MD, U. Ala., Birmingham, 1963. Diplomate Am. Bd. Internal Medicine; cert. internal medicine, cardiovascular diseases and geriatrics. Intern then resident, clin. rsch. fellow in cardiology Mass. Gen. Hosp., Harvard Med. Sch., Boston, 1963-67; physician Clark Holder Clinic, LaGrange, Ga., 1967-77; founder, dir. Ga. Heart Clinic, LaGrange, 1972—; founder, pres. So. Cardiopulmonary Assocs., LaGrange, 1977—; clin. prof. med. U. Ala., Birmingham, 1980—, Emory U., Atlanta, 1980—; bd. govs. Am. Bd. Internal Med., Phila., 1980-86, Joint Commn. on Accreditation of Healthcare Orgns., Chgo., 1991-97. Contbr. articles to profl. jours. Recipient Disting. Alumni award U. Ala., Birmingham, 1985. Fellow ACP (gov. Ga. chpt. 1987-91, Master 1993, regent 1993, chair bd. regents 1998—), Am. Coll. Cardiology; mem. Am. Heart Assn. (pres. Ga. affiliate 1985-86), Nat. Acad. Sci., Inst. of Medicine. Office: 1551 Doctors Dr Lagrange GA 30240-4139

COPELAND, ROBERT GLENN, lawyer; b. San Diego, Mar. 15, 1941; s. Glenn Howard and Luella Louise (Schmid) C.; m. Harriet S. Smith, June 27, 1964 (div. Jan. 1977); children: Katherine Louise, Matthew Robert; m. Marcia Diane Cummings, Jan. 8, 1977 (div. June 1990); m. Lynne Newman, Oct. 10, 1993; 1 child, Zachary Newman. AB, Occidental Coll., 1963; JD, U. So. Calif., 1966. Bar: Calif. 1966, U.S. Dist. Ct. Calif. (so. dist.), 1967. Ptnr. Gray, Cary, Ware & Freidenrich, San Diego, 1966-95, Luce, Forward Hamilton & Scripps LLP, 1995—. Mem. ABA, Calif. Bar Assn. Republican. Avocations: shooting, fishing, hiking, racquetball. Office: Luce Forward et al 600 W Broadway Ste 2600 San Diego CA 92101-3311

COPELAND, ROBERT MARSHALL, music educator; b. Douglas, Wyo., Jan. 30, 1945; s. Wilbur Clyde and Arvilla Estella (Walkinshaw) C.; m. Louise Margaret Edgar, June 10, 1966; children: Thomas Edgar, Anne Louise, Kathryn Elizabeth. BS, Geneva Coll., 1966; MM, U. Cin., 1970, PhD, 1974; postgrad., Westminster Choir Coll., 1981-82, Emory U., 1988. Asst. prof. to prof. music Mid-Am. Nazarene Coll., Olathe, Kans., 1971-81; prof. music, chmn. dept. music, dir. choral activities Geneva Coll., Beaver Falls, Pa., 1981—; vis. lectr. U. Kans., Lawrence, 1977; trustee, sec. Ref. Presbyn. Theol. Sem., Pitts., 1981-93, vis. lectr., 1983-84. Author: Spare No Exertions, 1986, Isaac Baker Woodbury: The Life and Works of an American Musical Populist, 1995; co-editor: The Book of Psalms for Singing, 1973; contbr. articles to profl. jours. Dir. music Internat. Covenanter Conf., Northfield, Minn., 1970, 76, 80, 84; ruling elder Ref. Presbyn. Ch., 1973—; moderator, Synod of the Ref. Presbyn. Ch. of N.Am., 1995-97; mem. Rep. County Com., 1992—. With AUS, 1966-68. NDEA fellow, 1968-71. Mem. AAUP (v.p. Kans. Conf. 1980-81), Am. Musicological Soc. (v.p. Allegheny chpt. 1987-89, 97-99, pres. 1989-91, 99—, coun. mem. 1992-95), Sonneck Soc. for Am. Music (founding mem., program com. 1982), Am. Choral Dirs. Assn. (co-editor Pa. Newsletter 1983-85, editor 1985-90), Soc. for Ethnomusicology, Huguenot Fellowship (bd. dirs. 1987—), Presbyn. and Ref. Joint Commn. on Chaplains and Mil. Personnel (sec. 1995—). Republican. Home: 3111 5th Ave Beaver Falls PA 15010-3616 Office: Geneva Coll 3200 College Ave Beaver Falls PA 15010-3557

COPELAND, STEWART, composer, musician; b. Maclean, Va., July 16, 1952. Mem. Curved Air; founder, drummer The Police, 1976-83; founder The Rhythmatists, 1994. Scores include (films) Rumblefish, 1983, Out of Bounds, 1986, Wallstreet, 1987, Talk Radio, 1988, She's Having A Baby, 1988, See No Evil, Hear No Evil, 1989, Hidden Agenda, 1990, The First Power, 1990, Taking Care of Business, 1990, Men at Work, 1990, Riff Raff, 1991, Highlander 2: The Quickening, 1991, Wide Sargasso Sea, 1993, Airborne, 1993, Raining Stones, 1993, Bank Robber, 1993, Decadence, 1993, Fresh, 1994, Surviving the Game, 1994, Rapa Nui, 1994, Silent Fall, 1994, The Saddness of Sex, 1994, Boys, 1996, The Pallbearer, 1996, The Leopard Son, 1996, Gridlock'd, 1997, Little Boy Blue, 1997, The Big Red, 1997, Good Burger, 1997, Very Bad Things, West Beyrouth, Pecker, 1998, She's All That, 1999, (TV) The Ewoks and Droids, 1985, The Equalizer, 1986, After Midnight, 1989, TV 101, 1990, Fugitive Among Us, 1992, Afterburn, 1992, Babylon 5, 1993, Lear, 1985, Tyson, 1995, White Dwarf, 1995, The Insiders, 1997, Legalese, 1998, (opera) Holy Blood and Crescent Moon, 1989, Horse Opera, 1993, Cask of Amontillado, 1994, (ballet) Lear, Prey, 1994, The Stars That Played with Lucky Joes Cards, 1994 (LDS) Klark Kent, Rumble Fish, Rhythmatist, Equalizer and other Cliffhangers, Rapa Nui, Silent Fall, (symphonies) Noah's Ark, Salcheeka; albums include (with the Police) Outlandos d'Amour, 1979, Regatta de Blanc, 1979, Zenyatta Mondatta, 1980, Ghost in the Machine, 1982, Synchronicity, 1983, Every Breath You Take: The Singles, 1986 (solo) The Rhythmatist, 1985. Recipient Music in Film Visionary Award, Hollywood Film Festival, 1998. Office: Kinetic Kollections 9729 Culver Blvd Culver City CA 90232-2739 Office: Columbia Artists Management Inc 165 W 57th St New York NY 10019-2201*

COPELAND, WILLIAM EDGAR, SR., physician; b. Huntington, W.Va., Nov. 22, 1920; s. Orville Edgar and Clara Gertrude (Naylon) C.; m. Carolyn Ann Varin, Jan. 31, 1948; children—William Edgar, Christopher Marsh, Stephen Jeffrey. M.D., Med. Coll. Va., 1945. Intern Stuart Circle Hosp., Richmond, Va., 1945-46; resident in obstetrics gynecology Hosp. U. Pa., Phila., 1948-51; practice medicine specializing in obstetrics and gynecology Phila., 1951-53, Columbus, Ohio, 1953—; mem. staff Ohio State U. Hosp., Columbus; chief of staff Ohio State U. Hosp., 1985-87; med. dir. Univ. Health Plan, 1985; mem. staff Childrens Hosp., Riverside Meth. Hos., Columbus; mem. faculty Ohio State U., 1953-90, prof. ob-gyn, 1970-87, dir. clin. div., dept., 1971-73, emeritus prof. ob-gyn, 1987—. contbr. articles to profl. jours. Mem. adv. com. Planned Parenthood, YMCA. Served with USN, 1943-47. Fellow Am. Coll. Obstetricians and Gynecologists, ACS, Am. Soc. Study Fertility; mem. Central Assn. Obstetricians and Gynecologists, AMA, N.Am. Obstet. and Gynecol. Soc., Ohio Med. Soc., Ohio State U. Health Ctr. Med. Soc., Assn. Am. Med. Colls. Clubs: Scioto Country, Faculty, Zanesfield Rod and Gun, Grand Hotel Hunt, Ohio State U. Pres., League Ohio Sportsmen. Home: 2495 Sherwin Rd Columbus OH 43221-3621 Office: Kingsdal Gynecol Assocs 1800 Zollinger Rd Columbus OH 43221-2849*

COPELAND, W(ILLIAM) JOEL, JR., clergyman; b. Pitts., June 1, 1946. BS, United Wesleyan Coll., 1967; MDiv, Asbury Sem., 1970; STM, Luth. Theol. Semin., 1976; D of Ministry, Asbury Sem., 1980. Ordained to ministry Wesleyan Ch., 1968. Student pastor Red Lion United Meth. Ch., Franklin, Ohio, 1967-70; pastor Parkway Wesleyan Ch., Wilmington, Del., 1970-83, First Wesleyan Ch., Batavia, N.Y., 1983-88, Zion Evang. Congl. Ch., Myerstown, Pa., 1988-95, Rexmont (Pa.) Evang. Congl. Ch., 1995-98; chaplain Coatesville (Pa.) VA Med. Ctr., Lebanon, Pa., 1993—, Batavia, 1996—; advisor Salvation Army, Wilmington, 1979-83, City Youth Bur., Batavia, 1984-88,Children's Chapel, Wilmington, 1973-83, Youth for Christ, Batavia, 1985-88; dist. sec. West N.Y. dist. The Wesleyan Ch., 1984-88. Co-editor E.C. Doors and Windows, 1991-95. Mem. Wesleyan Theol. Soc. Republican. Avocations: collecting stamps, coins, sports cards, reading. Home: PO Box 113 Myerstown PA 17067-0113 Office: VA Med Ctr 1400 Blackhorse Hill Rd Coatesville PA 19320-2040

COPEN, MELVYN ROBERT, management educator, university administrator; b. N.Y.C., Jan. 23, 1938; s. Samuel L. Copen and Frieda (Kroun) Zucker; m. Linda B. Kopans, Feb. 17, 1960 (div. 1991); children: Erika Beth Ellingsen, Susan Andrea Holtey; m. Beverly Joyce Stein, Sept. 7, 1991. BS in Bus., Engring Adminstrn., MIT, 1958, MS in Indsl. Mgmt., 1959; DBA in Prodn., Internat. Mgmt., Harvard U., 1967. Various positions Gen. Elec. Co., various locations, 1959-61; program assoc., rsch. fellow Harvard Bus. Sch., Boston, Ahmedabad, India, 1961-67; assoc. dean, prof., dir. grad. studies U. Houston, 1967-71; dir. office mgmt. improvement automated decision sys. U.S. Dept. Agr., Washington, 1971-74; dir. strategic planning Westinghouse Corp., Pitts., 1974-75; dir. internat. planning Gould, Inc., Rolling Meadows, Ill., 1975-77; assoc. dean, dean grad. studies coll. bus. adminstrn. Ga. State Univ., Atlanta, 1977-80; v.p. acad. affairs Babson Coll., Wellesley, Mass., 1980-87; rector Ctrl. Am. Inst. Bus. Adminstrn., Alajuela, Costa Rica, 1987-91; dean sch. internat. mgmt. Internat. Univ. Japan, Urasa, Tokyo, 1991-94; chmn., CEO Global Enterprises, Atlanta, 1991—; sr. v.p. acad. affairs, prof. internat. mgmt. Am. Grad. Sch. Internat. Mgmt., Glendale, Ariz., 1995-98; exec. v.p. global ops. Am. InterContinental U., Atlanta, 1998—; membership chmn. audit com. Nat. Bank Ga.-1st Am., Atlanta, 1980-87. Co-author: International Manangement and Economic Development, 1971, Production Management, 1972; contbr. articles to profl. jours. Bd. dirs. White House Fellows Found., Washington, 1973-74, Epilepsy Found. Ga., Atlanta, 1979-80, Hemophilia Ga., Atlanta, 1978-80, Nat. Bank Ga., Atlanta, 1979088; chmn. Arts in Progress, Roxbury, Mass., 1985-87, Am. Coll., Atlanta, 1996—; mem. Greater Phoenix Econ. Coun., 1997—. With USAR, 1960. Recipient Command Gen. Citation, U.S. Transp. Corps., 1960; White House fellow, 1970-71. Mem. Beta Gamma Sigma, Omicron Delta Epsilon. Avocations: tennis, travel, outdoor activities, flying. Home: 3870 Adams Rd Cumming GA 30041 Office: Am InterContinental Univ 500 Embassy Row 6600 Peachtree-Dunwood Rd Atlanta GA 30328

COPENBARGER, LLOYD GAYLORD, lawyer; b. Geary, Okla., Feb. 25, 1941; s. Lloyd G. and Audrey G. C.; m. Laura M. Drinnon, Mar. 6, 1943; children: Gwendolyn Ann, Larry G. BS, U. Okla., 1968, JD, 1971, LLM, 1988. Bar: Okla. 1971, Ohio 1976, Calif. 1979. Ptnr. Copenbarger & Welch, Norman, Okla., 1971-76; gen. counsel Rex Humbard Found., Akron, Ohio, 1976-79; prin. Lloyd, Copenbarger & Assoc. (formerly Copenbarger & Copenbarger), Irvine, Calif., 1979—. Office: 4675 Macarthur Ct Ste 700 Newport Beach CA 92660-1842

COPENHAVER, JOHN THOMAS, JR., federal judge; b. Charleston, W.Va., Sept. 29, 1925; s. John Thomas and Ruth Cherrington (Roberts) C.; m. Camille Ruth Smith, Oct. 7, 1950; children: John Thomas III, James Smith, Brent Paul. A.B., W.Va. U., 1947, LL.B., 1950. Bar: W.Va., 1950. Law clerk to presiding judge U.S. Dist. Ct. (so. dist.) W.Va., 1950-51; mem. firm Copenhaver & Copenhaver, Charleston, 1951-58; U.S. bankruptcy judge So. Dist. W.Va. Charleston, 1958-76; U.S. dist. judge, 1976—; adj. prof. law W.Va. U. Coll. Law, 1970-76; mem. faculty Fed. Jud. Center, 1972-76; Pres. Legal Aid. Soc. Charleston, 1954; Chmn. Mcpl. Planning Commn. City of Charleston, 1964; chmn., pres. W.Va. Housing Devel. Fund, 1969-72; chmn. vis. com. W.Va. U. Coll. Law, 1980-83; mem. adv. com. on bankruptcy rules Jud. Conf. U.S., 1978-84. Contbr.: articles in fields of bankruptcy and comml. law to Bus. Lawyer, Am. Bankruptcy Law Jour., Personal Fin. Law Quar., W. Va. Law Rev., others. Served with U.S. Army, 1944-46. Recipient Gavel award W.Va. U. Coll. Law, 1971, Outstanding Judge award W. Va. Trial Lawyers Assn., 1983. Fellow Am. Bar Found.; mem. ABA, W.Va. Bar Assn., Kanawha County Bar Assn., Nat. Bankruptcy Conf., Nat. Conf. Bankruptcy Judges (past pres.), Phi Delta Phi, Beta Theta Pi. Republican. Presbyterian. Office: US Courthouse PO Box 2546 Charleston WV 25329-2546*

COPENHAVER, MARION LAMSON, state legislator; b. Andover, Vt., Sept. 26, 1925; d. Joseph Fenwick and Christine (Forbes) Lamson; m. John H. Copenhaver, June 30, 1946; children: John III, Margaret, Christine, Eric, Lisa. Student, U. Vt., 1945-46. Mem. N.H. Ho. of Reps., Concord, ranking Dem. health and human svcs. com., 1973—, mem. adminstrv. rules com., 1982—, mem. health and human svcs. oversight, 1990—. Chair Grafton County Dems., 1986-91; assoc. supr. Grafton County Soil Conservation Dist., 1980—; mem. Hanover (N.H.) Dem. Town Com., 1992; mem.-at-large Dem. State Com., Concord, 1992; bd. dirs. Dartmouth Hitchcock Found., Hanover, 1991—; bd. incorporators Dartmouth Hitchcock Med. Ctr., Lebanon, N.H., 1984—; bd. dirs. Grafton County Sr. Citizens Coun., Inc., 1995-96. Named N.H. Legislator of Yr. N.H. Nurses Assn., 1989; recipient Meritorious award N.H. Women's Lobby, 1996, James A. Hamilton award

N.H. Hosp. Assn., 1997. Mem. NOW, Bus. and Profl. Women's Club (Outstanding mem. 1990). Democrat. Unitarian. Avocations: golf, skiing. Home: 14 Woodcock Ln Etna NH 03750-4402

COPENHAVER, W. ANDREW, lawyer; b. Roanoke, Va., Nov. 10, 1946; s. William Pierce and Jane Foote (Farrier) C.; m. Anne Phillips, July 7, 1973; children: William, Catherine, Andrew. BA, Duke U., 1969; cert. in internat. law, U. London, 1971; JD, U. N.C., 1972. Bar: N.C. 1972, U.S. Supreme Ct. 1981. Rsch. and teaching asst. Inst. Govt., 1970-72; assoc. Womble Carlyle Sandridge & Rice, Winston-Salem, N.C., 1972-77; ptnr. Womble, Carlyle, Sandridge & Rice, Winston-Salem, N.C., 1978—; head anti-trust and trade regulations sect. Womble Carlyle Sandridge & Rice, Winston-Salem, N.C., 1992—; mem. Fed. Bar Adv. Coun., N.C., 1992-99, chmn., 1994-95. Bd. dirs. Winston-Salem Arts Coun., 1992-97, vice chmn., 1995-97; bd. dirs. U. N.C. Law Alumni Assn./Law Found., Inc., 1994—, The Summit Sch., 1984-91, chmn., 1988-90; trustee Centenary United Meth. Ch., 1992-94. Mem. Winston-Salem Rotary Club (bd. dirs. 1993-96), Old Town Club, Piedmont Club. Home: 2540 Warwick Rd Winston Salem NC 27104-1944 Office: Womble Carlyle Sandridge & Rice PO Box 84 Winston Salem NC 27102-0084

COPES, PARZIVAL, economist, researcher; b. Nakusp, B.C., Can., Jan. 22, 1924; s. Jan Coops and Elisabeth Catharina Coops-van Olst; m. Dina Gussekloo, May 1, 1946; children: Raymond Alden, Michael Ian, Terence Franklin. BA, U. B.C., 1949, MA, 1950; PhD, London Sch. Econs., 1956; D of Mil. Sci. (hon.), Royal Roads Mil. Coll., Victoria, B.C., Can., 1991; Dr. Philos. (hon.), U. Tromsö, Norway, 1993. Economist, statistician Dominion Bur. of Stats., Ottawa, Can., 1953-57; from assoc. prof. to prof. Meml. U. Nfld., St. John's, Can., 1957-64; founding dir. econ. rsch. Inst. Social and Econ. Rsch. Meml. U. Nfld., St. John's, 1961-64; prof. Simon Fraser U., Burnaby, B.C., Can., 1964-91, head dept. econs. and commerce, 1964-69, chmn. dept. econs. and commerce, 1972-75, dir. Ctr. for Can. Studies, 1978-85, founding dir. Inst. of Fisheries Analysis, 1980-94, prof. emeritus, 1991—; governor Inst. Can. Bankers, Montreal, Que., 1967-71; dir. "Can.-Fgn. Arrangements Project," Can. Govt. Dept. Environment, 1976; pres., chmn. Pacific Regional Sci. Conf. Orgn., 1977-85; spl. advisor to Minister of Fisheries, B.C., 1998. Author: St. John's and Newfoundland: An Economic Survey, 1961, The Resettlement of Fishing Communities in Newfoundland, 1972. Lt. Can. Army, 1945-46, 50-51. Fgn. fellow Acad. Natural Scis. of Russia, Moscow, 1992. Mem. Internat. Inst. Fisheries Econs. and Trade (exec. com. 1982-86, Disting. Svc. award 1996), Internat. Assn. for Study of Common Property, Can. Regional Sci. Assn. (pres. 1983-85), Can. Econs. Assn. (v.p. 1972-73), Assn. for Can. Studies, Western Regional Sci. Assn. (pres. 1977-78), Social Sci. Fedn. Can. (dir., v.p. 1979-83), Can. Assn. Univ. Tchrs., Internat. Arctic Sci. Com. Achievements include some of earliest research contributions to establish sub-discipline of fisheries economics; research and international consulting in fisheries resource management. Home: 2341 Lawson Ave, West Vancouver, BC Canada V7V 2E5 Office: Simon Fraser U, Dept Economics, Burnaby, BC Canada V5A 1S6

COPITHORNE, DAVID A., public relations executive. BS, Harvard U., 1975. CEO, co-founder Copithorne & Bellows, Boston, 1988—. Office: Copithorne & Bellows 855 Boylston St 8th Fl Boston MA 02116*

COPLANS, JOHN RIVERS, artist; b. London, June 24, 1920; came to U.S., 1960; s. Joseph Moses and Celia (Taneborne) C.; divorced; children: Barbara Ann, Joseph John. Student, L'academie de la grande chaumiere Paris, 1947-49. sr. lectr. Maidstone Coll. Art, Eng., 1956-60; vis. prof. U. Calif., Berkeley, 1960-61; Disting. vis. prof. Am. U., Cairo, 1983; Koopman Disting. chair U. Hartford, Conn., 1991; dir. art gallery U. Calif. at Irvine, 1965-70; sr. curator Pasadena (Calif.) Mus. Modern Art, 1967-71; founding editor ARTFORUM Mag., San Francisco, 1962, editor in chief, N.Y.C., 1971-76; dir. Akron (Ohio) Art Inst., 1978-80; pub., editor Dialogue mag., Ohio, 1978-80. Exhibited paintings and photographs in one-man mus. shows Chgo. Art Inst., 1961, 81, 89, M.H. de Young Mus., San Francisco, 1963, Musée du Nouveau Monde, La Rochelle, 1986, San Francisco Mus. Modern Art, 1988, Mus. Modern Art, N.Y., 1988, Musée de la Vieille Charité, Marseille, 1989, Frankfurter Kunstverein, 1990, Mus. Boymans-van Beunigen, Rotterdam, 1990, Gulbenkian Found., Lisbon, Portugal, 1992, Centre Georges Pompidou, Paris, 1994, Ludwig Forum, Aachen, 1995, PS1 Contemporary Art Ctr., N.Y., 1997, Paco Das Artes, Sao Paulo, 1998, Scottish Nat. Gallery of Modern Art, Edinburgh, 1999; represented in collections, Met. Mus., N.Y.C., Mus. Modern Art, N.Y.C., Cleve. Mus., Art Inst. Chgo., High Mus., Atlanta, Wadsworth Atheneum, Conn., Israel Mus., Fogg Art Mus., Cambridge, Mass., Jerusalem, Mcpl. Mus., Amsterdam, Netherlands, Bibliotheque Nationale, Paris, Centre Georges Pompidou, Paris, Mus. des Beaux-Arts, Strasbourg, Victoria and Albert Mus., Musee De Art Contempaino, Que., Winnipeg Art Mus., Manitoba, Tate Gallery, London, Arts Coun. Gt. Britain, Nat. Gallery Can., Ottawa, Bklyn. Mus., Internat. Mus. Photography, Rochester, L.A. County Mus., San Francisco Mus. Modern Art, Mpls. Inst. Art, Mus. of Contemporary Art, Chgo., Whitney Mus. Am. Art, Honolulu Contemporary Mus. and Acad. of Arts, Hawaii, Mus. of Fine Art, Houston, Milw. Art Mus., Yale U. Art Gallery, New Haven, Conn., Wis., Mus. Contemporary Art, Helsinki, Boston Mus. of Fine Arts, Mus. Folkwang, Essen, Ludwed Forum, Aachen, Musée Art Modern, St. Etienne, Staatsgalerie, Stuttgart, Fed. Republic Germany, Swedish State Collection; author: Cezanne Watercolors, 1967, Serial Imagery, 1968, Andy Warhol, 1970, Roy Lichtenstein, 1972, Ellsworth Kelly, 1973, Decisions, Decisions, 1976, Weegee The Famous, 1968, A Body of Work, 1987, Provocations, 1996, A Self-Portrait, 1997; organized numerous mus. exhbns. and, articles for art mags. Served with RAF, 1938-40; served to capt. King's African Rifles, 1940-46. Recipient Frank Jewitt Mather award, 1974, Best Photography Exhbn. award Internat. Assn. Art Critics, 1998; Guggenheim fellow, 1969, 85; NEA fellow, 1975, 80, 86, 92.

COPLEY, CYNTHIA SUE LOVE, insurance adjuster; b. Defiance, Ohio, Oct. 26, 1957; d. Thomas Lee and Pauline Ann (Brandt) Love, Jr.; m. James Earl Copley, Jr., Oct. 19, 1985. B.Criminal Justice, Ohio U., 1981, A. in Law Enforcement, 1979, A in Fire and Safety Tech., 1982. Cert. profl. ins. woman. With Spangler Candy Co., Bryan, Ohio, 1976-77; guard Juvenile Detention Ctr., Chillicothe, Ohio, 1978; security officer J.C. Penney Corp., Inc., Chillicothe, Ohio, 1979, Rink's Bargain City, Chillicothe, Ohio, 1979; with Rubbermaid Sales Corp., Chillicothe, Ohio, 1980; asst. dept. sec. and computer lab asst. Ohio U., Chillicothe, 1977-81; supr. collections and investigation Bur. of Support, Ross County, Chillicothe, 1981-82; asst. mgr. Tecumseh Claims Svc., Chillicothe, 1982—; owner Copley Adjusting, Chillicothe, 1982—; part-time employe Ross County Bd. Elections, 1998—. Poll worker Rep. Party, Chillicothe, 1983-98. Mem. So. Ohio Claims Assn., Ohio Assn. Ind. Ins. Adjusters (sec.-treas. 1994, v.p. 1995, pres. 1996), Ohio Assn. Mut. Ins. Cos., Nat. Soc. Profl. Ins. Investigators. Lutheran. Avocations: golf, cooking, weekend trips. Home and Office: Tecumseh Claims Svc PO Box 15 Chillicothe OH 45601-0015

COPLEY, DAVID C., newspaper publishing company executive; s. Mrs. James S. Copley. BSBA, Menlo Coll. Formerly pres. Copley Press, Inc., La Jolla, Calif., pres., CEO, 1988—, also mem. exec. com., chmn. sr. mgmt. bd. and bd. dirs.; chair, CEO Fox Valley Press, Inc.; pres. Copley N.W., Inc., Puller Paper Co.; pres. Copley News Svc.; pub. Borrego Sun. Mem. editl. bd. San Diego Union-Tribune. Pres., trustee James S. Copley Found.; trustee Canterbury Sch., San Diego Crew Classic Found.; trustee emeritus La Jolla Playhouse, Am. Craft Coun., Mus. Photog. Arts; bd. dirs. San Diego Mus. Art, St. Vincent de Paul Soc.; pres. assocs., pres. adv. com., exhibits com. Zool. Soc. San Diego; adv. bd. San Diego Automotive Mus.; pres. coun. Scripps Clinic and Rsch. Found., San Diego Kind Corp.; active Pres. Club U. San Diego, San Diego Aerospace Mus., San Diego Hall Sci., San Diego Hist. Soc. Mem. Nat. Newspaper Assn., U.S. Humane Soc., F.O.C.A.S., Bachelor Club San Diego. Office: Copley Press PO Box 1530 La Jolla CA 92038-1530

COPLEY, EDWARD ALVIN, lawyer; b. Memphis, Jan. 17, 1936; s. Edward Alvin and Ethel Marie (Fooshee) C.; m. Connie James Patterson, Nov. 17, 1990; children: Julie, Ward, Drew, Kelly, Zeke. BA, So. Meth. U., 1957, JD, 1960. Bar: U.S. Dist. Ct. (no. dist.) Tex., U.S. Ct. Claims 1962, U.S. Supreme Ct. 1963, U.S. Tax Ct. 1966, U.S. Ct. Appeals (5th cir.) 1968. Atty. U.S. Dept. Justice, Washington, 1960-64, Ft. Worth, 1964-66; assoc. Akin, Gump, Strauss, Hauer & Feld, Dallas, 1966-67, ptnr., 1968—. Mem. ushering com., benevolence com. Highland Park Presbyn. Ch., Dallas, 1982. Fellow Am. Coll. Probate Counsel; mem. Internat. Acad. Estate Trust Law, Dallas Bar Assn. (tax sect.), Dallas Estate Coun. (pres. 1975-76), So. Meth. U. Law Sch. Alumni Assn. (pres. 1978-79), Salesmanship Club (legal counsel 1984), Order of Woolsac, Barristers, Dallas Petroleum Club, Dallas Country Club, Phi Alpha Delta. Avocations: racquetball, photography, hunting, fishing, reading. Home: 3711 Shenandoah St Dallas TX 75205-2120 Office: Akin Gump Strauss Hauer & Feld Ste 4100 1700 Pacific Ave Dallas TX 75201-4675

COPLEY, HELEN KINNEY, newspaper publisher; b. Cedar Rapids, Iowa, Nov. 28, 1922; d. Fred Everett and Margaret (Casey) Kinney; m. James S. Copley, Aug. 16, 1965 (dec.); 1 child, David Casey. Attended, Hunter Coll., N.Y.C., 1945. Assoc. The Copley Press, Inc., 1952—, chmn. exec. com., chmn. corp., dir., 1973—, chief exec. officer, sr. mgmt. bd., 1974—; chmn. bd. Copley News Svc., San Diego, 1973—; chmn. editorial bd. Union-Tribune Pub. Co., 1976—; pub. The San Diego Union-Tribune, 1973—; bd. dirs. Fox Valley Press, Inc. Chmn. bd., trustee James S. Copley Found., 1973—; life mem. Friends of Internat. Ctr., La Jolla, Mus. Contemporary Art, San Diego, San Diego Hall of Sci., Scripps Meml. Hosp. Aux., San Diego Opera Assn., Star of India Aux., Zool. Soc. San Diego; mem. La Jolla Town Coun. Inc., San Diego Soc. Natural History, YWCA, San Diego Symphony Assn.; life patroness Makua Aux.; hon. chmn., bd. dirs. Washington Crossing Found.; hon. chmn. San Diego Coun. Literacy. Mem. Inter-Am. Press Assn., Newspaper Assn. Am., Calif. Press Assn., Am. Press Inst., Calif. Newspaper Pubs. Assn., Calif. Press Inst., San Francisco Press Club, L.A. Press Club. Republican. Roman Catholic. Clubs: Aurora (Ill.) Country, Army and Navy (D.C.), Univ. Club San Diego, La Jolla Beach and Tennis, La Jolla Country. Office: Copley Press Inc 7776 Ivanhoe Ave La Jolla CA 92037-4574

COPLEY, STEPHEN JEAN, minister; b. Lawton, Okla., Oct. 13, 1961; s. Albert Jean and Mary Lou (Carnes) C.; m. Judith Ann Wallace, May 18, 1966. BA, U. Ctrl. Ark., 1984; MDiv, So. Meth. U., 1999. Minister Lamar Circuit United Meth. Ch., Barnesville, Ga., 1985-86; youth dir. Nashville (Ark) U. Meth. Ch., 1986; minister Prestwich (Eng.) Whitefield Circuit, 1986-87; youth minister Woodstock (Ga.) United Meth. Ch., 1987-88; minister Lamar/Mount Olive United Meth. Ch., 1988-89; asst. dir. Luton Indsl. Coll., Luton, Eng., 1989-92; minister Horatio (Ark.)/Winthrop United Meth. Ch., 1992-95; dir., founder Ouachita Regional Enterprise Fund, 1995-96; min. Hampton Circuit United Meth. Ch., 1996—; bd. dirs. Atlanta Clerty and Laity Concerned, 1985-86, Inst. Indsl. and Comml. Ministries, 1988-89, Meth. Fedn. for Social Action, 1993; mem. Little Rock Conf.-United Meth. Ch. Bd. Global Ministries, 1993—; founder, bd. dirs. Ouachita Regional Enterprise Fund, 1995—; cons. United Meth. Ch. Concern for Worker's Task Force, 1997-98; polit. dir. SEIO, 1998-99. Senator Ga. Jaycees Legislature, 1985; chair Ga. Jaycees-Multiple Sclerosis, 1985-86, Dem. Party. Com. Abroad, U.K., 1992; commr. Sevier County Housing Authority, 1993—; chaplain Little River Hist. Soc., 1992—, Sevier County Literacy Coun., 1992—, Horatio City Coun., 1995, Leadership Ark., 1995—, Ark. State Jaycees, 1993—; pres. Horatio Recreation Assn., 1993-95; bd. dirs. Little River C. of C., 1994, Ark. South Tourism Bd., 1996; chmn. Horatio Parks Commn.; dep. chair Dem. Party, Ark., 1994—; mem. social affairs com. Ark. Interfaith Conf., 1996, Ouachita River United Way; bd. dirs. Hogskin Holidays, Ark. South Tourism Assn.; leader Leadership Ark., 1995-97; chair Ark. JWJ Religion-Labor Com., 1997—. Recipient Jaycees Young Outstanding Arkansas award, 1994; named Town and Country Pastor of Yr., United Meth. Rural Fellowship Hope Dist., 1993, 94. Mem. Am. Acad. Religion, Horatio Mchts. Assn., Sevier County C. of C., Little River C. of C., Horatio Lions Club (pres. 1994-95, zone chair 1995-97), DeQueen Rotary Club, Little Rock Civitan Club, Young Dems. of Ark. (v.p. fin.), Hampton/Calhoun County C. of C. (pres.). Avocations: tennis, golf. Home: PO Box 477 Hampton AR 71744-0477

COPLEY, STEPHEN MICHAEL, materials science and technology engineer, consultant; b. Urbana, Ill., Apr. 29, 1936; s. Michael Joseph and Marion Elizabeth (Partlow) C.; m. Marcia Elizabeth Thornton, Nov. 28, 1957 (div. Nov. 1983); children: Michael Thornton, Sara Marie, Philip Stephen, Paul Ellis, Peter Leland, Susan Elizabeth, Stephen Joseph; m. Judith Ann Todd, Aug. 3, 1984; 1 child, Amy Elizabeth. B.A., U. Calif. at Berkeley, 1959, M.S., 1961, Ph.D., 1964. Research assoc., sr. research assoc., group leader, sect. supr. Advanced Materials Research and Devel. Lab., Pratt & Whitney Aircraft Co., Middletown, Conn., 1964-70; assoc. prof. materials sci. and mech. engring. U. So. Calif., Los Angeles, 1970-76; Kenneth T. Norris prof. U. So. Calif., 1972-90, chmn. dept. materials sci. and engring., 1975-81, 83-88, founder, dir. mfg. engring. program, 1976, prof. materials sci. and mech. engring., 1976-90; prof. metall. and materials engring. dept. Armour Coll., Ill. Inst. Tech., Chgo., 1990-95; chmn. metall. and materials engring. dept. Ill. Inst. Tech., Chgo., 1990-91, vice provost for acad. planning and budgeting, 1991-92, dean Armour Coll. Engring. and Scis., 1992-95; dir. Mfg. Inst., prof. mech., materials and aerospace engring dept., 1995-96; pres., CEO STE, Inc., Naperville, Ill., 1996; CEO Parker Engring. Inc., 1997-98; pres., CEO The Packer Group, Inc., Naperville, Ill., 1997—; bd. dirs. STE, Inc., 1993-96, The Packer Group, Inc., 1997—, Packer Engring., Inc., 1997—, K&P Agile, Inc., 1997—, Smart Signal Corp., 1997—. Subject editor Ency. of Materials Sci.; contbr. articles to profl. jours.; patentee in field. Recipient Edn. Achievement award Soc. Mfg. Engrs., 1978, Vanadium award Inst. of Metals, Eng., 1990. Fellow Am. Soc. Metals (mem.); mem. ASM Internat. (truse 1986-92, pres. 1990-91), ASME, SME, Am. Foundrymen's Soc., Sigma Xi. Home: 307 Briargate Ter Hinsdale IL 60521-2819

COPLIEN, JAMES O., engineering researcher; b. Monroe, Wis., Jan. 7, 1954; s. Dwight Clayton and Joyce Elaine (Grinnell) C.; m. Sandra Kay Trader, Jan. 7, 1977; children: Christopher James, Lorelei Marie, Andrew Michael. BSCE, U. Wis., 1977, MS, 1979. Head systems programmer Engring. Computer Lab., Madison, Wis., 1977-79; MTS Bell Labs., Naperville, Ill., 1979-97, Disting. MTS, 1997—; mem. emeritus The Hillside Group, Champaign/Urbana, Ill. Author: (book) Advanced C , 1991, Multi-Daradign Desigh for C , 1998, Multi-Paradigm Design in C , 1999; editor: (book) Plopd Series, 1995-96; co-inventor in field. Recipient Jolt Productivity award Software Devel. Mag., 1991, Top Ten Books award Jour. of Object-Oriented Programming, 1994-96. Mem. Wis. Ct. Chevaliers. Lutheran. Office: Bell Labs ILL650 1G341 1000 E Warrenville Rd Naperville IL 60563-1444

COPLIN, MARK DAVID, lawyer; b. Balt., Dec. 1, 1928; m. Judith Charlotte Levinson, Jan. 27, 1991. BA, U. Md., 1949, LLB, 1952. Bar: Md. 1952. Law clk. presiding justice U.S. Ct. Appeals (4th cir.), 1952-53; assoc. Weinberg and Green, LLC, Balt., 1953-60, mem., 1960-98; spl. counsel Saul Ewing Weinberg & Green, Balt., 1998—. Pres. Md. chpt., Am. Jewish Congress, 1971-74, Balt. Jewish Coun., 1976-78; pres. HIAS of Balt., Inc., 1972-74; mem. adv. com. Md. Blue Sky, 1968-92; bd. dirs. Jewish Family Svc., 1992-98; chmn. bd. trustees Balt. Hebrew U., 1987-89; mem. bd. visitors Balt. City Coll., 1990-97, sec., 1992-97. Mem. ABA, Md. Bar Assn., Balt. City Bar Assn., Balt. Bar Found. (pres. 1991-93), Order of Coif, Omicron Delta Kappa, Jewish.

COPP, JAMES HARRIS, sociologist, educator; b. Thief River Falls, Minn., Apr. 28, 1925; s. Vivian Emery and Irene (Sorenson) C.; m. Veronica Fliegel, Sept. 12, 1953; children—Christine, John, Karen, Sarah, Martha. B.A., U. Minn., 1949, M.A., 1951; Ph.D., U. Wis.-Madison, 1954. Research dir. 4-H Club Wis., Madison, 1953-54; asst. prof. rural sociology Kans. State U., 1954-55, U. Wis.-Madison, 1955-56; asst. prof. Pa. State U., 1956-62, assoc. prof., 1962-66, prof., 1966-67; chief br. human resources Econ. Research Service U.S. Dept. Agr., Washington, 1967-72; prof., head dept. sociology and anthropology Tex. A&M U., 1972-81, prof., head dept. rural sociology, 1972-80, prof. dept. sociology and rural sociology, 1981—; vis. prof. Mich. State U., 1960, U. Wis.-Madison, 1966; cons. Office Tech. Assessment U.S. Congress, Nat. Inst. on Aging, HEW, Bd. Agrl. and Renewable Resources NRC. Editor: Our Changing Rural Society, 1964, Rural Sociology, 1976-79, Southern Rural Sociology, 1984-87; co-editor: (with John M. Wardwell) Population Change in the Rural West, 1997; assoc. editor Rural Sociology, 1992-94. Recipient State 4-H Alumni award Minn. 4-H, 1964. Mem. Am. Sociol. Assn., Rural Sociol. Soc. (pres. 1972, Disting. Rural Sociologist award 1991), Southwestern Sociol. Assn., So. Sociol. Soc. (Outstanding Teaching award 1991), Internat. Rural Sociol. Assn. (coun. 1985-88), So. Assn. Agrl. Scientists, Phi Beta Kappa. Home: 1101 Pershing Dr College Station TX 77840-3082 Office: Tex A&M U Dept Sociology College Station TX 77843

COPPELMAN, PETER DAVID, lawyer, government official; b. Boston, Aug. 1, 1942; s. Leonard and Lillian (Hoffman) C.; m. Victoria Joan DeGoff, May 2, 1971 (div. 1978); m. Carolyn Marie Beckett, Dec. 28, 1979; children: Alexander Beckett, Elizabeth Beckett. AB magna cum laude, Harvard U., 64; JD, Cornell U., 1968. Bar: Calif. Directing atty. Calif. Rural Legal Assistance, San Francisco, 1970-74; prin., mng. ptnr. Coppelman & Hiestand, Oakland, Calif., 1974-78; trial atty. gen. litigation sect., land and natural resources divsn. Dept. Justice, Washington, 1978-81; gen. counsel The Wilderness Soc., Washington, 1981-90, dir. forest wilderness programs, 1981-84, sr. counsel resource planning and econs. dept., 1984-87, v.p., 1987-90; counsel fed. legal affairs Greenfield Environ., Washington, 1990-94; prin. dep. asst. atty. gen. environ. and natural resources Dept. Justice, Washington, 1994—; former chmn. Ashoka Environ. Group. Vice chmn., bd. dirs. Cathedral Coll. of Laity, Washington Nat. Cathedral; bd. dirs. Ams. for the Environ., Mt. Vernon Unitarian Ch.; vice-chmn., bd. dirs. Nat. Consumer Law Ctr. Reginald Heber Smith Cmty. Law fellow, 1968-70; Fulbright scholar, 1964-65. Mem. Harvard U. Alumni Assn. (mem. career adv. svc.). Home: 405 High St Alexandria VA 22302-4109 Office: Dept Justice Environ & Nat Resource Divsn 10th & Constitution Ave NW Washington DC 20530

COPPENS, PHILIP, chemist; b. Amersfoort, Holland, Oct. 24, 1930; s. Alexander and Sophie (Berkeley) C.; m. Marguerite Louise Anholt, Aug. 6, 1957; children—Alon, Eldad, Daniel David. PhD, U. Amsterdam, Netherlands, 1960; Dr. honoris causa, U. Nancy, France, 1989. Chemist Weizmann Inst. Sci., Rehoboth, Israel, 1957-60, 62-65, Brookhaven Nat. Lab., Upton, L.I., N.Y., 1960-62, 65-68; prof. chemistry SUNY, Buffalo, 1968—; adj. prof. applied physics and engring. sci. Cornell U., 1982-87; disting. prof. SUNY, Buffalo, 1992—, H. M. Woodburn chair chemistry, 1999—; vis. prof. Fordham U., 1966-67, Aarhus U., Denmark, 1973, U. Grenoble, France, 1974-75, 87, U. Calif., Santa Barbara, 1992; gov. consortium of advanced radiation sources U. Chgo., 1994—; materials rsch. adv. com. NSF, 1980-82; exec. com. Nat. Synchotron Light Source User, 1983-85, adv. com. High Flux Beam Reactor Program, Brookhaven Nat. Lab., 1985-90; steering com. Advanced Photon Source Argonne Nat. Lab, 1991-94. Recipient Harker award Hauptman-Woodward Med. Inst., 1995, George Aminoff award Swedish Acad. Scis., 1996. Fellow AAAS; mem. Internat. Coun. of Scientific Unions (gen. com. 1996—), Am. Crystallographic Assn. (v.p. 1977, pres. 1978, Buerger award 1994), Internat. Union Crystallography (exec. com. 1987—, pres. 1993-96), Internat. Coun. Sci. Unions (gen. com. 1996—), Am. Chem. Soc. (Schoelkopf award Western N.Y. sect. 1996), Materials Rsch. Soc., Royal Dutch Acad. Scis. (corr.). Office: SUNY Dept Chemistry Buffalo NY 14260

COPPER, JOHN FRANKLIN, Asian studies educator, consultant; b. Omaha, Oct. 30, 1940; s. Russell B. and Ina Belle (Townsend) C.; m. Lei Wang, Mar. 1, 1996; 1 child, Royce Wellington. BA, U. Nebr., 1961; MA, U. Hawaii, 1965; postgrad., U. Calif., Berkeley, 1966-68; PhD with Distinction, U. S.C., 1975. Lectr. U. Md., Tokyo, 1971-76; rsch. fellow Hoover Instn., Stanford, Calif., 1976-77; assoc. prof. Southwestern Coll., Memphis, 1977-83; exec. dir. Asian Studies Ctr., Washington, 1983-84; grad. prof. J.F.K. Ctr., Ft. Bragg, N.C., 1984-85; Stanley J. Buckman disting. prof. internat. studies Rhodes Coll., Memphis, 1985—. Author: A Matter of Two Chinas, 1979, China's Global Role, 1980 (Clarence Day Found. award 1981), Taiwan's Elections, 1984, Human Rights in Post-Mao China, 1985, A Quiet Revolution, 1988, Taiwan: Nation-State or Province?, 1990, 2d edit., 1996, China Diplomacy, 1992, Historical Dictionary of Taiwan, 1993, Taiwan's 1991 and 1992 Non-Supplemental Elections, 1994, The Bamboo Gulag: Human Rights in the People's Republic of China, 1991-92, 94, Words Across the Taiwan Strait, 1995, The Taiwan Political Miracle, 1997, Coping with a Bad Global Image, 1997, Taiwan's Mid-1990s Elections, 1998; contbr. articles to profl. jours. Bd. govs. East-West Ctr., 1983-89. Winner Internat. Comms. award, 1997. Mem. Am. Assn. Chinese Studies (bd. dirs.), Internat. Studies Assn., Assn. Asian Studies, Am. Mensa Ltd. Republican. Presbyterian. Office: Rhodes Coll Dept Internat Studies 2000 N Parkway Dept Internat Memphis TN 38112-1690

COPPER, WILLIAM P., composer, computer consultant; b. Augusta County, Va., Aug. 29, 1953; s. John M. and Frances E. (Mausteller) C.; m. Mary E. Urann, Mar. 27, 1993; children: Mary H., Ellen R. Student, MIT, 1971-72; BMus, Eastman Sch., Rochester, N.Y., 1979; postgrad., Akademia Muzyczne, Krakow, Poland, 1979-80. Pres. Hartenshield Group Inc., Wilmington, Del., 1987—; grant rev. panel Md. State Arts Coun., Balt., 1996; mem. panel Mid Atlantic Arts Found., Balt., 1994; edn. grant panel Del. State Arts Coun., Wilmington, 1995. Composer (chamber music) Piano Trio, 1994, (opera) The Other Half, 1993, (Symphony) From the Old World, 1995, (concerto) Whistler for Violin and Orch., 1996. Bd. dirs. Newark Symphony Orch., pres., 1997—. Recipient 1st prize S.E. Composers League, 1982; Fulbright scholar, 1979; Del. Individual Arttist fellow, 1991, 94. Mem. Mid-Atlantic Chamber Music Soc. (pres. 1994-98), Arts Am. (founder), Am. Music Ctr., Soc. for Composers Inc., Am. Composers Forum. Achievements include development of database video system for home video on demand. Avocations: walking, fencing, history, child development. Home: 2314 Ridgeway Rd Wilmington DE 19805-2629

COPPERFIELD, DAVID (DAVID KOTKIN), illusionist, director, producer, writer; b. Metuchen, N.J., 1956. Student, Fordham U. prof. magic NYU, 1974; creator, founder Project Magic, 1982. Levitated across Grand Canyon, 1984; walked through Great Wall of China, 1986; escaped from Alcatraz prison, 1987, vanished Statue of Liberty, 1989, survived bldg. implosion challenge, 1989; went over Niagara Falls, 1990; vanished Orient Express, 1991, introduced flying illusion, 1992; escaped from burning ropes 13 stories above ground before 15,000 people, Caesar's Palace, 1993; performer, dir., producer, writer (TV spls.) The Magic of David Copperfield annually since 1978; presdl. command performance, 1981, 82, 85, 87, 92; performer (musical) Magic Man, 1974; appeared in film Terror Train, 1980. Nat. spokesperson at Olympics U.S. Orgn. Disabled Athletes, Seoul, Republic of Korea, 1988. Recipient Emmy awards and/or nominations, 1979, 80, 81, 83, 84, 85, 86, 88, 89, 90, 91, 92, Golden Rose award Montreux Film Festival, 1987, Bambi award-European equivalent of Oscars, 1993; named Magician of Yr. Acad. Magical Arts, 1980, 87; named Entertainer of Yr. Am. Guild Variety Artists, 1981, City of Atlantic City, 1986, Nat. Assn. Campus Activities, 1987; named one of Ten Outstanding Young Men in Am. U.S. Jaycees, 1985; named one of Top Ten Entrepreneurs (age 30 or under) Young Entrepreneur Orgn., 1987; named America's Fastest Rising Star by Forbes Mag., 1993. Am. producer to premiere Am. TV spl. in Peoples Republic of China, 1986; Broke box office attendance records Miami Knight Ctr., 1984, Warner Theater, Washington, 1985, Caesars Palace, Las Vegas, Nev., 1985, Taipei Sports and Cultural Stadium, 1987, Premier Theater, Mexico City, 1987, Coliseum, Hong Kong, 1988, World Trade Ctr., Singapore, 1988, Putra World Trade Ctr., Kuala Lumpur, 1988, Giganto Arena, Porto Allegre, Brazil, 1988, Fox Theatre, Detroit, 1989, 92; broke European attendance record Dortmond, Germany, 1993.

COPPERMAN, STUART MORTON, pediatrician; b. Bklyn., June 5, 1935; s. Irving and Anne (Reisfield) C.; m. Renee Stein, Aug. 17, 1958; children: Beth, Alan, Cara. B.A. cum laude, Bklyn. Coll., 1956; M.D., SUNY-Bklyn., 1960. Diplomate Am. Bd. Pediat. Rotating intern. L.I. Jewish Hosp., New Hyde Park, N.Y., 1960-61, resident in pediat., 1961-63; practice medicine specializing in pediat. Merrick, N.Y., 1965—; mem. staff L.I. Jewish Hillside Med. Ctr., Schneider Children's Hosp., New Hyde Park, Nassau County Med. Ctr., East Meadow, Winthrop U. Hosp., Mineola, North Shore Univ. Hosp., Manhasset; clin. assoc. prof. pediat. SUNY Med. Sch., Stony Brook, 1972—; asst. prof. clin. health studies SUNY Sch. Allied Health, Stony Brook, 1977—; clin. instr. physicians asst. program Stony Brook Med. Ctr., 1972—; prof. pediat. St. George's Med. Coll., St. Vincent, W.I., acting chmn. pediat., 1979-80; med. advisor Assn. Children with Downs Syndrome, 1971—; mem. com. for handicapped Bellmore Sch. Dist., 1976-86; mem. ad hoc com. on cmty. as sch. Merrick-Bellmore Schs., 1976-90; bd. dirs. North Shore-L.I. Jewish I.P.O., L.I. Sch. Health Edn. Coalition, North Shore Physicians Orgn., North Shore - L.I. Jewish PHO; mem. Nassau County Sch. Health Edn. Commn., 1990-93; mem. ad hoc com. on prevention of birth defects March of Dimes; preceptor in pediat. Physicians Asst. Program; mem. doctor's adv. com. Shaare Zedek Hosp., Jerusalem, 1974—; med. cons. Matchbox Toys, 1985-88, Proctor & Gamble, 1988, Carnation Co., 1989-90, Disney Ednl. Svcs., 1990-95, vaccine divsn. Merck Corp., 1997—; cons., mem. spkrs. bur. N.Y. State Senate Com. Mental Hygiene, 1988—; mem. spkrs. bur. Lederle Labs., 1989-95, Merck Labs., 1996—, Wallace Labs., 1996—, ucb Pharma, 1999—; author, co-founder, pres., bd. dirs. Child Health Imagery Prodns., 1997. Appearance TV shows on Downs Syndrome, learning disabilities, CPR, first aid, infant exercise programs, TV's effects on children, infectious disease, parent-infant bonding, enuresis, toilet training, prevention of cigarette smoking among children, 1972—, also on HealthLinks (Life Time TV), 1990-93; mem. editl. adv. bd. Jour. Assn. for Physician Assts., 1987—; editl. cons. Jour. Pediat. Mgmt., 1991—; contbr. articles to profl. jours.; contbr. chpt. to Textbook Pediat. Sports Medicine; developer Babycise (infant parent interactive program in video tape and book form), 1985; rschr. on hetacillin, 1966, pyridoxine effect on serotonin level and performance in children with Down's Syndrome, 1970-75, Alice in Wonderland syndrome as presenting sympton of infectious mononucleosis, 1966-77, on transmission of group A Beta hemolytic strep infection from pet reservoirs to children, 1963-81; med. editor Air Fair Mag., 1991-93, L.I. Parent Mag., 1985-93, L.I. Family Mag., 1994-95. Mem. sch. bd. Temple Beth Am., Merrick, 1972-78, mem. exec. com., 1973-74, chmn. com. Israel and World Affairs, 1976-78, mem. sch. com., 1976-78, mem. ritual com., 1976-93; mem. N.Y. State Senate com. on mental hygiene, 1990—; mem. profl. adv. bd. So. Shore divsn. YM-YWHA; benefactor Merrick Libr., 1992—. With U.S. Army, 1963-65. Recipient Physician Recognition award AMA, 1966—, testimonial dinner and plaque Assn. Children with Down Syndrome, 1972, Best Clin. Tchrs. of Pediat. award Nassau County Med. Ctr., 1981-82; named Merrick Profl. of Yr., 1994. Fellow Am. Acad. Pediat. (chmn. com. TV effects on children 1976—, mem. nat. com. comm. and pub. info. 1984-85, mem. nat. com. on substance abuse 1998-2001, media spokesperson 1988—, tobacco, alcohol and drug-free generation coord. 1988—, chmn. substance abuse com. 1992—, N.Y. state chmn. substance abuse com. 1992-94, managed care com. chpt. 2 1993-95), Internat. Coll. Pediat.; mem. AMA, N.Y. State Med. Soc., Nassau County Med. Soc. (com. on mental health 1980—, project assist 1992—, Nassau Acad. Medicine Pub. Health com. 1991—, libr. com. 1993—, chmn. pediat. sect. 1995—), Nassau Pediat. Soc. (mem. exec. bd. 1972—, chmn. com. on mental health 1972-88, v.p. 1994-95, pres. 1996-97). A Non-Smoking Generation Internat. (organizer, med. dir. Am. divsn.), Am. Lung Assn., Nassau-Suffolk Lung Assn. (life mem., dir. 1982-84), Am. Physicians Fellowship for Israel Med. Assn., Assn. Children with Learning Disabilities (mem. profl. adv. bd.), La Leche League, Latin Am. Parents Assn., L.I. Sch. Health Edn. Coun. (bd. dirs. 1989-92), Alpha Epsilon Pi (chancellor Phi Theta chpt. 1955-56), Phi Delta Epsilon (consul Zeta chpt. 1960), B'nai Brith. Office: 3137 Hewlett Ave S Merrick NY 11566-5328 *No one person can do everything - but every person can do something. If you want something done, give it to a busy person. We must live for today with an eye toward tomorrow. I'd like my epitaph to read "While alive, he lived."*

COPPERSMITH, SAM, lawyer; b. Johnstown, Pa., May 22, 1955; m. Beth Schermer, Aug. 28, 1983; children: Sarah, Benjamin, Louis. AB in Econs. magna cum laude, Harvard U., 1976; JD, Yale Law Sch., 1982. Fgn. svc. officer U.S. Dept. State, Port of Spain, Trinidad, 1977-79; law clk. to Judge William C. Canby Jr. U.S. Ct. Appeals (9th cir.), Phoenix, 1982-83; atty. Sacks, Tierney & Kasen, P.A., Phoenix, 1983-86; asst. to Mayor Terry Goddard City of Phoenix, 1984; atty. Jones, Jury, Short & Mast P.C., Phoenix, 1986-88, Bonnett, Fairbourn & Friedman P.C., Phoenix, 1988-92; mem. 103d Congress from 1st Ariz. Dist., 1993-95; atty. Coppersmith Gordon Schermer Owens & Nelson PLC, 1995—. Former dir., pres. Planned Parenthood Ctrl. and No. Ariz.; former chair City of Phoenix Bd. of Adjustment; former dir. Ariz. Cmty. Svc. Legal Assistance Found., 1986-89; chair Ariz. Dem. Party, 1995-97; trustee Devereux Found., 1997—. Mem. ABA, State Bar of Ariz., State Bar of Calif., Maricopa County Bar Assn. Democrat. Office: Coppersmith Gordon Schermer Owens & Nelson PLC Ste 300 2633 E Indian School Rd Phoenix AZ 85016-6759

COPPERSMITH, SUSAN NAN, physicist; b. Johnstown, Pa., Mar. 18, 1957; d. Wallace Louis and Bernice Barbara (Evans) C.; m. Robert Daniel Blank, Dec. 20, 1981. BS in Physics, MIT, 1978; postgrad., Cambridge U., 1979; MS in Physics, Cornell U., 1981, PhD in Physics, 1983. Rsch. assoc. Brookhaven Nat. Labs., 1983-85; postdoctoral mem. tech. staff AT&T Bell Labs., Murray Hill, N.J., 1985-86, mem. tech. staff, 1987-90, disting. mem. tech. staff, 1990-95; prof. physics U. Chgo., 1995—; vis. lectr. Princeton U., 1986-87; vis. professorship for women NSF, 1986-87; gen. mem. Aspen Ctr. for Physics, 1991—; chancellor's disting. lectr. U. Calif., Irvine, 1991. Trustee Aspen Ctr. for Physics, 1993-96. Winston Churchill scholar, 1978-79, Bell Labs. GRPW fellow, 1979-83. Fellow Am. Phys. Soc. Home: 5807 S Dorchester Ave Apt 5E Chicago IL 60637-1775

COPPIE, COMER SWIFT, state official; b. Washington, Oct. 19, 1932; s. John Lee and Marion (Peck) C.; m. Judith Ann Wright, Apr. 29, 1961; children: Cynthia, Sean, Scott. AB, Hamilton Coll., 1955; M in Pub. Adminstrn., Syracuse U., 1959. Budget analyst Bur. of Budget, State of Md., Balt., 1958-62; exec. dir., trustee Md. State Colls., Balt., 1963-68; dep. budget dir. Govt. of D.C., Washington, 1968-69; dir. Office of Budget and Mgmt. Systems, Washington, 1969-78; exec. dir. N.Y. State Fin. Control Bd., N.Y.C., 1978-86; CFO U.S. Postal Svc., Washington, 1986-92; 1st dep. compt. Office of State Compt., Albany, N.Y., 1993-99; ret., 1999. Dir., 1st v.p. Homeless and Travelers Aid Agy., Albany; dir. Grand Ctrl. Social Svcs. Corp., N.Y.C. Served with USN, 1955-57. Recipient Gold medal Fin. Officers Assn. of U.S. and Can., 1978. Mem. Cosmos Club (Washington), Univ. Club (Washington). Episcopalian. Avocation: swimming.

COPPINGER, RAYMOND PARKE, biologist, educator; b. Boston, Feb. 7, 1937; s. John Raymond and Frances (Sheppard) C.; m. Lorna L. Baxter, Dec. 27, 1958; children: Karyn D., Timothy L. A.B., Boston U., 1959; M.A., U. Mass., 1965; four-coll. Ph.D., U. Mass., Amherst Coll., Smith Coll., Mt. Holyoke Coll., 1968. Postdoctoral research assoc. Amherst Coll., Mass., 1968-70; prof. biology Hampshire Coll., Amherst, 1970—; lectr. on animal behavior, human and canine behavior; cons. UN Devel. Program, Chad, Africa, Caribbean Area. Co-author 13 week TV series on human adaptation; contbr. articles to publs. Mem. adv. bds. various local instns. Recipient various pvt. and fed. grants for predator control research. Mem. Explorers Club, Am. Soc. Mammalogists, Sigma Xi. Home: 111 E Chestnut Hill Rd Montague MA 01351-9558 Office: Hampshire Coll Box FC Amherst MA 01002

COPPLE, WILLIAM PERRY, federal judge; b. Holtville, Calif., Oct. 3, 1916; s. Perry and Euphie (Williams) C.; m. Nancy Matson, May 30, 1981; children by previous marriage—Virginia (Mrs. Richard Schilke), Leonard W., Steven D. A.B., U. Calif. at Berkeley, 1949, LL.B., 1951. Bar: Ariz. 1952. Various positions with U.S. Govt., also pvt. employers, 1936-48; practice in Yuma, Ariz., 1952-65; U.S. dist. atty. Dist. Ariz., Phoenix, 1965-66; judge U.S. Dist. Ct. Dist. Ariz., 1966—, now sr. judge; Mem. Ariz. Hwy. Commn., 1955-58, Gov. Ariz. Com Fourteen for Colo. River, 1963-65; chmn. Yuma County Democratic Central Com., 1953-54, 59-60. Mem. Am. Bar Assn. Office: US Dist Ct US Courthouse & Fed Bldg 230 N 1st Ave Ste 3007 Phoenix AZ 85025-0230*

COPPOCK, ADA GREGORY, theatre executive; b. Midland, Tex., Aug. 22, 1960; d. Richard Raymond and Ruth Irene (Jones) Gregory; m. Lawrence H. Coppock Jr., May 26, 1984. BFA in Theatre Arts and Acting, Baylor U., 1982; MS in Arts Adminstrn., Drexel U., 1989. Bookkeeper Murray Fin., Vorhees, N.J., 1984-86; adminstrv. asst. Drexel U., Phila., 1986-89; gen. mgr. Phila. Theatre Co., 1989—. Mem. Theatre Assn. Greater Phila. Avocation: travel. Home: 114 Station Rd PO Box 177 Cheyney PA 19319-0177 Office: The Phila Theatre Co 1811 Chestnut St Ste 300 Philadelphia PA 19103-3703

COPPOCK, JANET ELAINE, mental health nurse; b. Tipton, Ind., June 2, 1954; d. Jack Donavon and Bonnie Ruth (Luse) Weismiller; divorced; children: Jonathan Andrew, Daniel Jason. Student, Ball State U., 1972-73; ASN, Ind. U., Kokomo, 1977. RN, Ind., Mich. RN charge staff and med.-surg. Tipton County Meml. Hosp., Ind., 1977-79; RN psychiatric staff Howard Cmty. Hosp., Kokomo, 1987-89; pvt. nurse Kokomo, 1989-95; RN psychiatric and addiction treatment, instr. Koala Hosp. & Counseling Ctr. Behavioral Healthcare Corp., Kokomo, 1995-98; RN psychiatric and addiction treatment Lafayette (Ind.) Behavioral Health System, 1998—; instr. parenting edn. Kinsey Youth Ctr., Kokomo, 1995-96; co-developer Koala Halfway House, Behavioral Healthcare Corp., Kokomo, 1996, house mgr., 1996-98. Author: Poetic Reflections, Expressions and Inspirations, 1986, Faithful Resolutions, 1993, Coming to Terms, 1998. Recipient Golden Poet award World Poetry Orgn., 1987, 88. Mem. Ind. State Nurses Assn., Internat. Platform Assn., Nurses Svc. Orgn., Writers' Ctr. Indpls., Ind. U. Alumni Assn. (life), Kokomo H.S. Band Boosters, Rose-Hulman Parent's Assn. Republican. Avocations: musical instruments, art, movies, basketball. Home: 2711 President Ln Kokomo IN 46902-3066

COPPOCK, RICHARD MILES, nonprofit association administrator; b. Salem, Ohio, Mar. 17, 1938; s. Guy Lamar and Helen Angeline (Johnston) C.; m. Rita Mae McArtor, June 20, 1961 (div. 1973); 1 child, Carole; m. Trelma Anne Kubacak Hafer, Nov. 21, 1973; children: James, Lori. BS, USAF Acad., 1961; MSME, U. Colo., 1969. Commd. 2d lt. USAF, 1961, advanced through grades to lt. col., 1983, ret., 1983; pres., CEO, Assn. Grads. USAF Acad., Colo., 1983-99, also bd. dirs.; bd. dirs. Air Acad. Nat. Bank, Colo.; v.p. Nat. Assns. in Colorado Springs. Decorated DFC (4), Air medal (29); named Outstanding Alumnus Salem H.S., 1980. Mem. Colorado Springs C. of C. (mil. affairs coun. 1985-90), VFW (life), Am. Legion, Air Force Assn., Ret. Officers Assn., Elks. Republican. Methodist. Avocations: music, history. Home: 2513 Mirror Lake Ct Colorado Springs CO 80919-3515 Office: USAF Acad Assn Grads 3116 Academy Dr U S A F Academy CO 80840

COPPOLA, ANTHONY, electrical engineer; b. Bklyn., July 14, 1935; s. Frank and Barbara (Tambasco) C.; children: Stephen, Paul, Dominic, Jane. BA in Physics, Syracuse U., 1956; MS in Engring. Adminstrn., 1966; cert. of completion, Air War Coll., Griffiss AFB, N.Y., 1981. Lic. pvt. pilot. Electronic engr. Rome Air Devel. Ctr., USAF, Griffiss AFB, N.Y., 1956-60, group leader, 1960-72, sect. chief, 1972-89, comdr.'s spl. asst. for total quality mgmt., 1989-92; sr. engr. IIT Rsch. Inst., 1992—; guest instr. Air Force Inst. Tech., 1964-78, George Washington U., 1969-70, Air Force Acad., 1973. Editor RAC Jour. (formerly RAC Quar.), 1992—; contbr. articles to profl. jours. Advisor Mohawk Valley Engrs. Exec. Council, Utica, N.Y., 1978-82. N.Y. state scholar, 1952; recipient Superior Performance award USAF, 1965, 81, 86, Cert. of Merit USAF Systems Command, 1979, Meritorious Civilian Svc. award Dept. Air Force, 1986, Outstanding Civilian Career award USAF, 1992. Fellow IEEE (editor Reliability Soc. newsletter 1981, recipient svc. medal 1993, sect. chmn. 1975, gen. chmn. ann. reliability and maintainability symposium 1990, Centennial medal 1984); mem. Armed Forces Mgmt. Assn., Pi Delta Epsilon. Office: IIT Rsch Inst 201 Mill St Rome NY 13440-6916

COPPOLA, ELAINE MARIE, librarian; b. Dunkirk, N.Y., Aug. 5, 1947; d. Henry Stanley and Althea May Hruby; m. Joseph Arthur McCoy III, Sept. 27, 1969 (div. 1972); 1 child, Richard Henry; m. Joseph Angelo Coppola, Aug. 15, 1981. BA, St. Bonaventure U., 1969; MLS, Syracuse U., 1979, MS Sc, 1989. Asst. mgr. manpower planning and devel. Oneida (N.Y.) Ltd., 1972-74, asst. mgr. pub. rels., 1974-78; libr. SUNY Inst. Tech., Utica, 1979; catalog libr. E.S. Bird Libr., Syracuse U., 1979-89, social scis. ref. bibliographer, 1989-99, head ref. dept., 1999—. Author: Political Science Annotations within the Supplement to the Guide to Reference Books, 1992, Political Science Annotations in Guide to Reference Books, 11th edit., 1996. Mem. Dem. com. Town of Manlius, town councilor, 1998—. Mem. ALA, N.Y. Libr. Assn., Assn. of Coll. and Rsch. Librs. (ea. N.Y. chpt. pres. 1992-93, v.p. 1991-92, sec. 1989-91, Libr. of the Yr. 1996), Beta Phi Mu. Home: 103 Kenny St Fayetteville NY 13066-1230 Office: ES Bird Libr Syracuse Univ Syracuse NY 13244-2010

COPPOLA, FRANCIS FORD, film director, producer, writer; b. Detroit, Apr. 7, 1939; s. Carmine C.; m. Eleanor Neil; children: Gian-Carlo (dec.), Roman, Sofia. B.A., Hofstra U., 1958; Master of Cinema, UCLA, 1968. Pub. mag. San Francisco, 1975-76. Artistic dir., Zoetrope Studios.; dir. films including Dementia 13, 1964, You're a Big Boy Now, 1967, Finian's Rainbow, 1968, The Rain People, 1969, One from the Heart, 1981, Peggy Sue Got Married, 1986, Gardens of Stone, 1987, Tucker: The Man and His Dream, 1988, Bram Stoker's Dracula, 1992, The Rainmaker, 1997; writer films This Property Is Condemned, 1966, Reflections In a Golden Eye, 1967, The Rain People, 1969, Is Paris Burning, 1966, Patton, 1970, The Great Gatsby, 1974; co-writer, dir. The Cotton Club, 1984, Life Without Zoe (segment in New York Film Stories), 1990; writer, prodr. and dir. films The Godfather (Acad. awards for Best Screenplay and Best Picture, nominee for Best Dir., Film Dir.'s award Dirs. Guild Am. 1972), The Godfather, Part II, 1974 (Acad. awards for Best Screenplay, Best Dir. and Best Picture), The Conversation, 1974 (Golden Palm award Cannes Film Festival 1974), Apocalypse Now, 1979 (Golden Palm award Cannes Film Festival 1979), Rumble Fish, 1983; writer, dir. The Godfather: Part III, 1990, The Rainmaker, 1997; prodr., dir. films The Outsiders, 1983, Jack, 1996, The Rainmaker, 1997; prodr. films THX 1138, 1971, The Escape Artist, 1982, The Black Stallion Returns, 1983; exec. prodr. films Black Stallion, 1979, Hammett, 1983, Lionhart, 1987, The Secret Garden, 1993, Mary Shelley's Frankenstein, 1994, My Family/Mi Familia, 1995, Don Juan DeMarco, 1995, Buddy, 1997; co-exec. prodr. Mishima, 1985; dir. TV Movie The People; prodr. TV series White Dwarf, 1995; exec. prodr. TV movie Dark Angel, 1996; exec. prodr. TV mini-series The Odyssey, 1997; dir. play Private Lives, opera The Visit; appeared in TV movie Marlon Brando: The Wild One, 1996. Mem. Dirs. Guild Am. Inc. *

COPPOLA, JOHN FRANCIS, exhibits director; b. Hackensack, N.J., July 26, 1947. BA, Thiel Coll., 1969; MS, Northwestern U., 1970. Program mgr. Arts Am. U.S. Info. Agy., Washington, 1982-86, chief Bur. Internat. Expositions, 1986-91; dir. Office Exhibits Ctrl. Smithsonian Inst., Washington, 1991-95; curator, exhbn. developer Washington, 1995—; cons. Mus. Latin Am. Art, Long Beach, Calif., Nat. Bonsai Mus., Washington, Panama Canal Mus., Ethnographic Mus. U. Buenos Aires, Nat. Mus., San Jose, Costa Rica; lectr. U. Victoria, B.C., Can. Numerous one man and group shows. Mem. Am. Assn. Mus., Internat. Coun. Mus., Nat. Assn. for Mus. Exhbn., Nat. Artist's Equity Assn. and Fund. Home and Office: 229 13th St SE Washington DC 20003-1432

COPPOLA, NICOLAS See CAGE, NICOLAS

COPPOLA, SARAH JANE, special education educator; b. Alton, Ill., Apr. 20, 1957; d. Howard Earl and Dorothy Elizabeth (Eads) Cox; m. Daniel Joseph Coppola Jr., June 26, 1977; children: Daniel Joseph III, Shawn Marie. BS, Trenton State Coll., 1979; M Counseling Edn., Kean Coll. of N.J., 1995. Cert. guidance counselor, substance abuse counselor, N.J., early childhood cert., CIE coop. coord. cert. 1998, WECEP cert. Substitute tchr. Dunellen (N.J.) Bd. Edn., 1979-87, Greenbrook (N.J.) Bd. Edn., 1979-87, Middlesex (N.J.) Bd. Edn., 1979-87, Bound Brook (N.J.) Bd. Edn., 1983-84; tchr. of handicapped Piscataway (N.J.) Bd. Edn., 1987—, prin. adv. bd., 1990-91, editl. yearbook advisor, 1998—. Youth group advisor Trinity Reformed Ch., North Plainfield, N.J., 1983-91, deacon, 1985-87, elder, 1997—, head Christian Edn., 1997—. Mem. NEA, N.J. Edn. Assn., Piscataway Edn. Assn., Kean Coll. Alumni Assn. (vol. Fish Hospitality program). Avocations: reading, needlework, church choir. Home: 334 Runyon Ave Middlesex NJ 08846-2225 Office: Piscataway Bd Edn 100 Behmer Rd Piscataway NJ 08854-4161

COPPOLECCHIA, ROSA, internist; b. Hoboken, N.J., Mar. 28, 1964; d. Sergio and Maria Corrada (Annese) C. BS in Biology, St. Peter's Coll., 1986; DO, U. Medicine & Dentistry N.J., 1992. Diplomate Nat. Bd. Osteo. Med. Examiners, Am. Bd. Internal Medicine. Intern Union Hosp., U. Medicine and Dentistry of N.J., 1992-93; resident in internal medicine Overlook Hosp., Summit, N.J., 1993-96; post-doctoral fellow environ. and occupl. medicine UMDNJ-Robert Wood Johnson Med. Sch., Piscataway, N.J., 1996-98; asst. dir. employee health svcs. Schering Plough Corp., Kenilworth, N.J. Mem. AMA, ACP (assoc.), ACPM, AWMA, Am. Coll. Occupl. and Environ. Medicine, Am. Osteo. Assn., N.J. Med. Soc.

COPPS, MICHAEL JOSEPH, commerce administrator; b. Milw., Apr. 23, 1940; s. Edmund J. and Ruth E. (Klemm) C.; m. Elizabeth Miller, Sept. 5, 1970; children: Robert, Mary, Michael, William, Claire. BA, Wofford Coll., 1963; PhD, U. N.C., 1967. Asst. prof. history Loyola U., New Orleans, 1967-70; adminstrv. asst. to U.S. Sen. Ernest F. Hollings U.S. Senate, Washington, 1970-85; dir. govt. affairs Collins & Aikman Corp., Washington, 1985-89; sr. v.p. Am. Meat Inst., Washington, 1989-93; dep. asst. sec. Dept. Commerce, Washington, 1993-98, asst. sec. for trade devel., 1998—. Mem. Phi Beta Kappa, Pi Gamma Mu. Democrat. Avocations: reading, automobiles. Home: 6916 Baylor Dr Alexandria VA 22307-1703 Office: US Dept Commerce Basic Industries Rm 3832 Washington DC 20230

COPPS, MICHAEL WILLIAM, retail and wholesale company executive; b. Stevens Point, Wis., Aug. 29, 1939; s. Donald William and Mary Jane (Krembs) C.; B.S., U. Wis., 1963, LL.B., 1967; m. Priscilla Lynn Reichardt, July 10, 1971; children—Clinton, Carolyn. Legis. analyst Wis. Taypayers Alliance, Madison, 1967-68; intern Supermarket Inst., Chgo., 1968-70; with Copps Corp., Stevens Point, Wis., 1970—, successively warehouse supt., exec. v.p., vice chmn. bd., now chmn. bd. Bd. dirs. YMCA, Stevens Point, 1978—. Republican. Lutheran. Office: Copps Corp 2828 Wayne St Stevens Point WI 54481-4100*

COPPS, SHEILA, Canadian government official; b. Hamilton, Ont., Can., Nov. 27, 1952; d. Victor Kennedy and Geraldine (Guthro) C.; 1 child, Danelle Lauran Copps. BA in French, English with hons., U. Western Ont., London; postgrad., U. Rouen, France, McMaster U., Hamilton. Reporter Ottawa Citizen, 1974-76, Hamilton Spectator, 1977; asst. to Ont. Liberal leader Stuart Smith, Hamilton, 1977-81; mem. Legis. Assembly Ont., Toronto, 1981-84, House of Commons, Ottawa, 1984-97; apptd. dep. leader Liberal Party Can., Ottawa, Ont., 1990—; dep. prime min. Govt. of Can., Ottawa, 1993-97, min. environ., 1993-96, min. of Can. heritage, 1996—. Author: Nobody's Baby, 1986. Mem. Liberal Party. Office: House of Commons Rm 511S, Ottawa, ON Canada K1A 0A6

COPSETTA, NORMAN GEORGE, real estate executive; b. Pennsauken, N.J., Mar. 11, 1932; s. Joseph J. and Mary P. (DeMello) C.; m. Patricia Fitzpatrick, Mar. 5, 1971; children: Gregory, Margaret, Andrew, Norman G. Jr.; stepchildren: Samuel Sassano, James Sassano. Cert. real estate, Rutgers U. Extension, Camden, N.J., 1952; AA, Internat. Accts. Soc. Schl. Acctg., Chgo., 1968. Lic. title insurance agent, N.J. Settlement clk. Market Street Title Abstract Co., Camden, 1949-53; settlement administrator West Jersey Title & Guaranty Co., Camden, 1953; title examiner, abstract adminstr. Realty Abstract Co., Cherry Hill, N.J., 1954-64; mcpl. treas., tax collector Borough of Somerdale, N.J., 1961-65; title examiner, legal adminstr. Davis, Reberkenny & Abramowitz, Cherry Hill, 1974-97; pres., title officer Cooper Abstract Co., Cherry Hill, 1974—; N.J. fgn. commr. of deeds in and for Pa., 1959—; mem. faculty Title Acad. N.J. Custodian of funds Somerdale Bd. Edn., 1960-64. Mem. ABA (assoc.), N.J. Title Ins. Agts. Assn., Haddonfield (N.J.) Hist. Soc., Camden County Hist. Soc. Avocation: local history. Office: Cooper Abstract Co 401 Cooper Landing Rd Ste C6 Cherry Hill NJ 08002-2598

COQUILLETTE, DANIEL ROBERT, lawyer, educator; b. Boston, May 23, 1944; s. Robert McTavish and Dagmar Alvida (Bistrup) C.; m. Judith Courtney Rogers, July 5, 1969; children: Anna, Sophia, Julia. A.B., Williams Coll., 1966; M.A. Juris., Univ. Coll., Oxford U., Eng., 1969; J.D., Harvard U., 1971. Bar: Mass. 1974, U.S. Dist. Ct. Mass. 1974, U.S. Ct. Appeals (1st cir.) 1974. Law clk. Mass. Supreme Ct., 1971-72; to Warren E. Burger, chief justice U.S. Supreme Ct., 1972-73; assoc. Palmer & Dodge, Boston, 1973-75, ptnr., 1980-85; assoc. prof. law Boston U., 1975-78; dean, prof. Boston Coll. Law, 1985-93, prof., 1993-96, J. Donald Monan univ. prof. law, 1996—; vis. assoc. prof. law Cornell U., Ithaca, N.Y., 1977-78, 84; vis. prof. law Harvard U., 1978-79, 84-85, 94-95, 95-96, 96-97, 97-98, mem. overseers com.; reporter com. rules and procedures Jud. Conf. U.S.; mem. task force on rules of atty. conduct Supreme Jud. Ct. of Mass., 1996-97. Author: The Civilian Writers of Doctors Commons, London, 1988, Francis Bacon, 1993, Lawyers and Fundamental Moral Responsibility, 1995, Working Papers on Rules Governing Attorney Conduct, 1997, (with Basile, Beston, Donahue) Lex Mercatoria and Legal Pluralism, 1999, The Anglo-American Legal Heritage, 1999; editor: Law in Colonial Massachusetts, 1985, Moore's Federal Practice, 3d edit., 1997; bd. dirs. New Eng. Quar., 1986—; contbr. articles to legal jours. Trustee, sec.-treas. Ames Found; bd. overseers vis. com. Harvard Law Sch.; treas. Byron Meml. Fund; propr., trustee Boston Athenaeum. Recipient Kaufman prize in English Williams Coll., 1966; recipient Sentinel of the Republic prize in polit. sci. Williams Coll., 1965; Hutchins scholar, 1966-67; Fulbright scholar, 1966-68. Mem. ABA (com. on profl. ethics 1990-93), Am. Law Inst., Mass. Bar Assn. (task force on model rules of profl. conduct), Boston Bar Assn., Am. Soc. Legal History (bd. dirs. 1985-89), Mass. Soc. Continuing Legal Edn. (bd. dirs. 1985-89), Selden Soc. (state corr.), Colonial Soc. Mass. (v.p., mem. coun.), Anglo-Am. Cathedral Soc. (bd. dirs.), Mass. Hist. Soc., Am. Antiquarian Soc., Phi Beta Kappa. Democrat. Quaker. Home: 12 Rutland St Cambridge MA 02138-2503 Office: Boston Coll Sch Law 885 Centre St Newton MA 02459-1154

COQUILLETTE, WILLIAM HOLLIS, lawyer; b. Boston, Oct. 7, 1949; s. Robert McTavish and Dagmar (Bistrup) C.; m. Mary Katherine Templeton, June 19, 1971 (div. Oct. 1984); 1 child, Carolyn Patricia; m. Janet Marie Weiland, Dec. 8, 1984; children: Benjamin, Weiland, Madeline Marie, Elizabeth Charlotte. BA, Yale U., 1971, Oxford U., 1973; JD, Harvard U., 1975. Bar: Ohio 1976, Mass. 1976. Law clk. to presiding justice Mass. Supreme Ct., Boston, 1975-76; assoc. Jones, Day, Reavis & Pogue, Cleve., 1976-83, ptnr., 1984—. Trustee Greater Cleve. Cmty. Foodbank, Playhouse Sq. Found., Greater Cleve. Com. on Hunger. Mem. Kirtland Club, Yale Club (N.Y.C.), Union Club (Cleve.), Cleve. Skating Club, Rowfant Club, N.Y. Yacht Club. Office: Jones Day Reavis & Pogue 901 Lakeside Ave E Cleveland OH 44114-1116

CORACE, JOSEPH RUSSELL, automotive parts company executive; b. Mt. Clemens, Mich., July 22, 1953; s. Joseph Anthony and Josephine (Coniglario) C.; m. Judith Agnes Cynowa, June 24, 1977; children: Christina Marie, Joseph R., Anthony Casmier. AA, Macomb Coll., 1973; BSME, Wayne State U., 1976; MBA, Mich. State U., 1980. Staff engr. GM Corp., Warren, Mich., 1976-81; mgr. Volvo Cars N. Am., Rockleigh, N.J., 1981-85; dir. Volvo Automated Systems, Sterling Heights, Mich., 1985-88; pres., chief exec. officer Inalfa Roof System, Auburn Hills, Mich., 1988-98; pres., CEO, owner Forum Motors Group, 1999—. Mem. Rockleigh Sch. Bd., 1986, Holy Name Ch., 1987; lector St. Fabian Ch. Recipient Disting. Engring. Alumnus award Wayne State U.; named to Wayne State U. Hall of Fame; Sloan fellow Volvo Cars N.Am., 1981. Mem. Soc. Automotive Engrs. (jour. contbr.), Soc. Mfg. Engrs., Young Pres. Orgn. (pres. East Mich. chpt. 1997, bd. dirs., officer), Legatus (bd. dirs., pres. Detroit chpt. 1998—), Oakland Hills Country Club, Engring. Soc. Detroit, Detroit Econ. Club, Am. Mgmt. Assn. (pres.'s coun.), Walnut Creek Country Club (bd. dirs., pres.), Rochester Racquet Club, Detroit Athletic Club, KC (officer Detroit 1979). Roman Catholic. Avocations: racquetball, golf. Home: 5658 Springbrook Dr Troy MI 48098-5351

CORAM, DAVID JAMES, marketing professional; b. San Diego, Oct. 17, 1962; s. Thomas Harry and Joan Catherine (Reuter) C.; m. Irma Elizabeth Aquino, Jan. 14, 1989 (dec. July 1991); children: Catherine May, Corinna Briann, Carston James, Caitlin Kay; m. Corinna Kay Ward, May 6, 1995. AS with honors, Miramar Coll., 1989; honor grad. sheriff acad. basic trng., Southwestern Coll., 1986. Computer oper. Cubic Data Systems, San Diego, 1981-83, Electronic Data Systems, San Diego, 1983-84; ct. svc. officer San Diego County Marshal, 1985-86, dep. marshal, 1986—; pres. Coram Cons. Group, 1994—; owner franchise Fantastic Sams Hair Salon, 1998. Mediator San Diego Community Mediation Ctr., 1990—; soccer coach Temecula Valley Soccer Assn., dir. referees; mem. nominating com. Outstanding Young Women Am. Awarded Gold medal soccer Ariz. Police Olympics, 1990, 91, Silver medal, 1993, Marksmanship award San Diego Marshal, Outstanding Young Men Am. award, 1989; 2d pl. Mid. Weight San Diego Gold's Gym Classic, 1993, Bronze medal Bodybuilding Calif. Police Olympics, 1994. Mem. Calif. State Marshal's Assn. (dir. on state bd. 1994), San Diego County Marshal's Assn. (parliamentarian 1988, dir. 1989-91, 93-94), San Diego County Marshal's Athletic Fedn. (dir. 1993-95), Nat. Physique Com. (contest judge). Republican. Avocations: golf, baseball, camping, computers, weight lifting. Office: Coram Cons Group 45620 Corte Montril Temecula CA 92592-1206

CORAN, ARNOLD GERALD, pediatric surgeon; b. Boston, Apr. 16, 1938; s. Charles and Ann (Cohen) C.; m. Susan Myra Williams, Nov. 17, 1960; children: Michael, David, Randi Beth. AB, Harvard U., 1959, MD, 1963. Diplomate Am. Bd. Surgery, Am. Bd. Thoracic Surgery, Am. Bd. Pediat. Surgery. Intern in surgery Peter Bent Brigham Hosp., Boston, 1963-64, resident in general and thoracic surgery, 1964-69; resident in pediatric surgery Children's Hosp., Boston, 1966-68; chief pediat. surgery, assoc. prof. surgery U. South Calif. Med. Sch., L.A., 1972-74; chief pediat. surgery, prof. surgery U. Mich., Ann Arbor, 1974—; surgeon in chief C.S. Mott Childrens Hosp., Ann Arbor, 1981—. Contbr. articles to profl. jours. Lt. comdr. USN, 1970-72. Avocations: skiing, golf, running. Home: 505 E Huron St Apt 802 Ann Arbor MI 48104-1541 Office: CS Mott Childrens Hosp Rm F3970 Ann Arbor MI 48109-0245

CORASH, RICHARD, lawyer; b. N.Y.C., Mar. 31, 1938; s. Paul and Mildred (Spanier) C.; m. Carol A. McKevitt, Dec. 11, 1966; children: Richard Jr., Sharon, Peter, Amy. BA, Harpur Coll., SUNY, Binghampton, 1959; MA, Bklyn. Law Sch., 1966; JD, Rutgers U., 1963. Bar: N.Y. 1964, U.S. Dist. Ct. D.C. 1964, U.S. Sup. Ct. 1972. Pvt. practice, N.Y.C., 1964-77; pres. Corash & Hollender, P.C., N.Y.C., 1977—; pres. Kobe Trading Co., N.Y.C.; chmn. North Eastern Fiscal Mgmt. Co., N.Y.C.; pres. North Eastern Abstract Assn.; counsel Caywood Homeowners Assn. Mem. N.Y. State Bar Assn. (real estate sect., guest panelist grievance procedures 1989), N.Y. Bankruptcy Bar Assn. (chmn. grievance com.), Richmond County Bar Assn. Democrat. Address: 81 Roxiticus Rd Far Hills NJ 07931-2225

CORAY, JEFFREY WARREN, assistant principal, instructor; b. Chgo., July 16, 1958; s. Warren George and Rose (Paul) C. Student, U. Calif., Berkeley, 1976-77; BA, Occidental Coll., 1980; MA, Calif. State U., San Bernardino, 1996. Instr. Damien High Sch., La Verne, Calif., 1982-98, dir. student activities, 1983-87, chair social sci. dept., 1986-88, asst. prin. student activities, 1987-88, asst. prin. acad. affairs, instr. social sci., 1988-98; mgr. tech. support and tng., project mgr. Netel Ednl. Systems, Inc., Claremont, Calif., 1998-99; project mgr., tng. supr. SICORP, Inc., Rockville, Md., 1999—; cons. advanced placement program N.J. Coll. Bd., 1987-98, exam reader, 1988-98. Mem. Omicron Delta Epsilon, Phi Kappa Phi. Republican. Roman Catholic. Avocations: music, theatre, opera. Home: PO Box 116 La Verne CA 91750-0116

CORBALLY, JOHN EDWARD, foundation director; b. South Bend, Wash., Oct. 14, 1924; s. John Edward and Grace (Williams) C.; m. Marguerite B. Walker, Mar. 12, 1946; children: Jan Elizabeth, David William. BS, U. Wash., 1947, MA, 1950; PhD, U. Calif., Berkeley, 1955; LLD, U. Md., 1971; LL.D., Blackburn Coll., 1972, Ill. State U., 1977, Ohio State U., 1980; Litt.D., U. Akron, 1979. Tchr. Clover Park High Sch., Tacoma, 1947-50; prin. Twin City High Sch., Stanwood, Wash., 1950-53; asst. prof., then assoc. prof. edn. Ohio State U., Columbus, 1955-60, prof., 1960-69, dir. pers. budget, exec. asst. to pres., 1960-64, v.p. adminstrn., 1964-66, provost, v.p. acad. affairs, 1966-69; chancellor, pres. Syracuse (N.Y.) U., 1969-71; pres. U. Ill., Chgo. and Urbana-Champaign, 1971-79; pres. emeritus U. Ill., 1979—; disting. prof. higher edn. U. Ill., Urbana-Champaign, 1979-82, disting. prof. emeritus, 1982—; pres. John D. and Catherine T. MacArthur Found., 1979-89, dir., 1979—, chmn., 1995—; cons. Heidrick & Struggles, 1989-90; bd. dirs. Global Partnerships, Seattle; mem. Gov's Task Force on Med. Malpractice, 1985; chmn. Nat. Coun. Ednl. Rsch., Nat. Inst. Edn., 1973-79; trustee Mus. Sci. and Industry, Chgo., 1971-79; chmn. Commn. Curricular Outcome, Ill. Bd. Edn., 1985-88; chmn. Chgo. Sch. Reform Authority, 1988-89. Author: Introduction to Educational Adminstration, 6th edit, 1983, Educational Administration: The Secondary School, 2d edit, 1965, School Finance, 1962. Bd. dirs. U. Wash. Found., 1989-93, Ill. Ednl. Consortium, 1973-79, Found. for Tchg. Econs., 1978-85, Rural Devel. Inst., Seattle, Exec. Svc. Corps of Wash., 1990-96, 98—, Snonet, Everett, Wash., 1994—; mem. commn. on govt. rels. Am. Coun. on Edn., 1972-76. Lt. (j.g.) USNR, 1943-46. Recipient Centennial medal U. Calif. Alumni Assn. and Sch. Edn. Alumni Soc., 1976, Disting. Eagle award Boy Scouts Am., 1978, Van Miller award Ill. Assn. Sch. Adminstrs. and Ednl. Adminstrn. Alumni Assn. U. Ill., 1986, Humanitarian award No. Ill. U., 1986, Disting. Alumnus award U. Wash. Coll. Edn., 1987, Disting. Achievement award U. Wash. Coll. Arts and Sci., 1995; named Alumnus Summa Laude Dignatus, U. Wash., 1988, Laureate, Lincoln Acad. Ill., 1989. Mem. U. Ill. Alumni Assn. (life, Disting. Svc. award 1986), U. Wash. Alumni Assn. (life), Tavern Club, Wayfarers Club, Phi Beta Kappa, Phi Kappa Sigma. Home: 1507 151st Pl SE Mill Creek WA 98012-1591

CORBAT, PATRICIA LESLIE, special education educator; b. Washington, Feb. 28; d. Kenneth Lee and Stella Mary (Brey) C.; m. Noah Hughes Palmer IV, Aug. 16, 1975 (div.). BA, Coll. William and Mary, Williamsburg, Va., 1975, MEd, 1981. cert. learning disabilities/diagnostic prescriptive tchr. Learning disabilities resource/spl. edn. educator Virginia Beach (Va.) City Pub. Schs., 1981—, drama coach, 1997-98, 99—; sec. spl. edn. eligibility com. Virginia Beach City Schs., 1981-87, chmn. gifted and talented selection com., 1985-86. Del. Va. State Dem. Conv., Norfolk, 1984, Roanoke, 1992; lobbyist Va. Gen. Assembly, Richmond, 1985; mem. Virginia Beach City Dem. Com., 1985-86; bd. dirs. Art and Company Contemporary Art Ctr. of Virginia, 1993-98, Contemporary Art Ctr. Va., 1993—, sec., 1994, treas. 1995. Mem. Virginia Beach Soc. for the Prevention of Cruelty to Animals Auxillary Com., Contemporary Art Ctr. of Virginia. Avocations: drawing, painting, fashion designing, weight-lifting/exercising, reading. Office: Virginia Beach City Schs Mcpl Ctr 2512 George Mason Dr Virginia Beach VA 23456-9105

CORBATO, CHARLES EDWARD, geology educator; b. Los Angeles, July 12, 1932; s. Hermenegildo and Charlotte Carella (Jensen) C.; m. Patricia Jeanne Ferg, May 18, 1957; children: Steven, Barbara, Susan. B.A., UCLA, 1954, Ph.D., 1960. Instr. geology U. Calif., Riverside, 1959; Instr. geology U. Calif., Los Angeles, 1959-60, asst. prof., 1960-66; assoc. prof. Ohio State U., Columbus, 1966-69; prof. Ohio State U., 1969-92, chmn. dept. geology and mineralogy, 1972-80, assoc. provost office of acad. affairs, 1987-92, prof., assoc. provost emeritus, 1992—; geophysicist U.S. Geol. Survey, 1966-74; dir. State Postsecondary Rev. Entity, Ohio Bd. Regents, 1994-95, dir. info. svcs., 1995—. Fellow Geol. Soc. Am.; mem. Am. Geophys. Union, Am. Inst. Profl. Geologists, Internat. Assn. Mathematical Geology, Delta Tau Delta. Home: 2400 Buckley Rd Columbus OH 43220-4616 Office: Ohio State U 125 S Oval Mall Columbus OH 43210-1308

CORBATO, FERNANDO JOSE, electrical engineer and computer science educator; b. Oakland, Calif., July 1, 1926; s. Hermenegildo and Charlotte (Jensen) C.; m. Isabel Blandford, Nov. 24, 1962 (dec. July 1973); children: Carolyn Suzanne, Nancy Patricia; m. Emily Susan Fish, Dec. 6, 1975; stepchildren: David Lawrence Gish, Jason Charles Gish. Student, UCLA, 1943-44; BS, Calif. Inst. Tech., 1950; PhD, MIT, 1956. With Computation Ctr. MIT, Cambridge, Mass., 1955-66; dep. dir. MIT, Cambridge, 1963-66, head computer sys. rsch. group of project MAC, 1963-72, co-head sys. rsch. divsn., 1972-74, co-head automatic programming divsn., 1972-74, faculty mem., 1962—, prof. elec. engring. and computer sci., 1965-96, prof. emeritus, 1996—, assoc. dept. head computer sci. and engring., 1974-78, 8393, Cecil H. Green prof. computer sci. and engring., 1978-80, dir. computing and telecomm. resources, 1980-83, Ford prof. engring., 1993-96. Co-author: The Compatible Time Sharing System, 1963, Advanced Computer Programming, 1963. With USNR, 1944-46. Recipient Harry Goode Meml. award Am. Fedn. Info. Processing Socs., 1980, Computer & Comms. prize Found. for Computer & Comms. Promotion, Japan, 1998. Fellow IEEE (W.W. McDowell award 1966, Computer Pioneer award IEEE Computer Soc. 1982), AAAS; mem. NAE, Am. Acad. Arts and Scis., Assn. Computing Machinery (coun. 1964-66, A.M. Turing award 1990), Am. Phys. Soc., Sierra Club, Sigma Xi. Home: 88 Temple St Newton MA 02465-2307 Office: Rm 613 545 Technology Sq Cambridge MA 02139-3539

CORBEN, HERBERT CHARLES, physicist, educator; b. Portland, Dorset, Eng., Apr. 18, 1914; came to U.S., 1946, naturalized, 1950; s. Harold Frederick and Margaret (Hart) C.; m. Mulaika Barclay, June 7, 1941 (div. 1955); m. Beverly Balkum, Oct. 25, 1957; children: Deirdre McGowan, Sharon Schafer, Gregory. B.A., U. Melbourne, 1933, B.Sc., 1934, M.A., 1936, M.Sc., 1936; Ph.D., Cambridge U., 1939. Lectr. math. and physics New Eng. U. Coll., Armidale, Australia, 1941; lectr. math., physics U. Melbourne, Australia, 1942-46; acting dean Trinity Coll., Melbourne, 1942-46; asso. prof. Carnegie Inst. Tech., 1946-51, prof., 1951-56; part-time lectr. physics U. Pitts., 1947; Fulbright vis. prof. U. Genoa, Milan, and Bologna, 1951-53; part-time lectr. physics U. So. Calif., 1957-58; asso. dir. Research Lab. Ramo-Wooldridge Corp. and Space Tech. Labs, Inc., Los Angeles, 1956-60; dir. Quantum Physics Lab., 1961-68; chief scientist Phys. Research Center, 1966-68; distinguished vis. prof. physics Queens Coll., 1968; acting dean faculties Cleve. State U., 1968-69, dean faculties, 1969-70, v.p. acad. affairs, 1970-72, dean Coll. Grad. Studies, prof. physics, 1968-72; prof. physics Scarborough Coll., U. Toronto, 1972-78, vis. prof., 1980-82, chmn. phys. scis. group, 1972-76; faculty Harvey Mudd Coll., Claremont, Calif., 1978-80, scholar-in-residence, 1982-85, sr. prof., 1985-88; Commonwealth Fund fellow U. Calif. and; Princeton U., 1939-41. Author: Classical and Quantum Theories of Spinning Particles, 1968, The Struggle to Understand, A History of Human Wonder and Discovery, 1992, A Scientist's Spring and Other Poems, 1995; co-author: Classical Mechanics, 1950, 2d edit., 1960, internat. edit., 1974, Dover reprint, 1994; contbr. International Dictionary of Physics and Electronics, 1956; contbr. tech. papers to profl. pubs. Fellow Am. Phys. Soc.; mem. Am. Soc. Physics Tchrs. Home: 4304 O'Leary Ave Pascagoula MS 39581-2352 *Faith in the order of nature is a source of both certainty and wonder. This certainty is my foundation; the wonder is my religion. Together, they form the quest for truth that influences every area of my life. I am fascinated by the unsolved problems both of science and mankind, and I am dedicated to finding accurate solutions. In sharing knowledge through research and teaching, I believe that the certainty is reinforced, the wonder multiplied, and truth interpreted and carried forward.*

CORBET, RICHARD HUGH, trade policy specialist, educator, writer; b. Perth, Australia, Nov. 18, 1936; came to U.S., 1990; s. John Arthur and Freda Marian (Sherwood) C.; m. Rosalind Mary Willett Bevan, June 10, 1961 (div. Oct. 1978); children: Zoe Mary Louisa, John Llewelyn Guy Sherwood. BA, U. Adelaide, Australia, 1960; postgrad., U. Keele, Eng., 1990-93. Cert. journalist Brit. Inst. Journalists. Rsch. asst. Cazenove & Co., stockbrokers, London, 1961-62; rsch. asst. conservative backbench com. on European cmty. Brit. Ho. of Commons, London, 1962-63; econs. corr. Thomson Newspapers, London, 1963-65; specialist writer The Times, London, 1965-68; dir. Trade Policy Rsch. Ctr., London, 1968-89; mng. editor The World Economy, Boston and Oxford, Eng., 1977-89; guest scholar Woodrow Wilson Internat. Ctr. for Scholars and the Brookings Inst., Washington, 1990-92; sr. fellow Manhattan Inst., N.Y. and Washington, 1992-93; dir. trade policy program Sigur Ctr. for Asian Studies George Washington U., Washington, 1993-97; pres. Cordell Hull Inst., Washington, 1998—; spl. advisor Opposition Spokesmen on Trade, Brit. Ho. of Commons, London, 1978-79; cons. on trade policy Internat. C. of C., Paris, 1979-83; mem. adv. com. on studies in internat. trade policy U. Mich. Press, Ann Arbor, 1989—; mem. adv. bd. The World Economy, Oxford and Boston, 1990—; cons. European Inst. Japanese Studies, Stockholm, 1994-97; cons. Swiss-Asia Found., Lausanne, 1996—. *At the Trade Policy Research Centre, in the 1970's, Hugh Corbet initiated the debate on extending the multilateral trading system to trade in services. From 1982-86, as part of the international effort to launch the Uruguay Round negotiations, he convened seven "informal meetings" of trade ministers, senior officials, business leaders and independent experts. Four were held in the Asia-Pacific region, hosted by the Australian, Korean, Japanese and Indonesian governments, respectively. For the first meeting, the Centre's report yielded the Australian proposal in 1983 for regular consultations among Western Pacific trade officials, which led in 1989 to the Asia-Pacific Economic Cooperation (APEC) initiative.* Co-author: Trade Strategy for the Asia-Pacific Region, 1970; co-editor: Europe's Free Trade Area Experiment, 1970, Commonwealth Policy in a Global Context, 1971, In Search of a New World Economic Order, 1974; rapporteur various profl. reports, including Economic Policy for the European Community, 1974, Trade Routes to Sustained Economic Growth, 1987, Public Scrutiniy of Protection, 1987; contbr. articles to profl. jours. Served with Australian Army, 1955-56; with Citizen Mil. Forces Australian Army, 1957-61; with Royal Ulster Rifles Brit. Territorial Army, 1961-62. Fax: 202-338-0327. Home: 2400 Pennsylvania Ave NW Washington DC 20037-1729

CORBETT, FRANK JOSEPH, advertising executive; b. N.Y.C., July 5, 1917; s. Daniel and Frances (Manson) C.; m. Dolores Pierce, May 23, 1959; children: Kenneth, Beverly. Ph.G., Columbia U., 1938; postgrad., U. So. Calif., 1947, UCLA, 1947, NYU, 1945-46. Pharmacy mgr. N.Y.C., 1938-41; sales rep. Upjohn, Inc., N.Y.C., 1941-43; dist. sales mgr., mgr. market research dept. William R. Warner Co., N.Y.C., 1944-46; dir. product devel. and market research, advt. mgr., also asst. to dir. sales Harrower Lab., Inc., Glendale, Calif., 1946-51, Jersey City, 1946-51; account exec. Jordan-Sieber Advt. Agy., Chgo., 1951-55; ptnr., v.p. Jordan, Sieber & Corbett (advt.), 1955-60; cons. pharm. field, 1960-61; founder, pres. Frank J. Corbett, Inc. (advt.), 1961-78, chmn. bd., 1978-93, vice chmn., 1993—. Inductee Med. Advt. Hall of Fame, 1998. Mem. Nat. Wholesalers Drug Assn., Midwest Pharm. Advt. Club, Pharm. Mfrs. Assn. Home: 1320 N State Pky Chicago IL 60610-2118 Office: Frank J Corbett Inc 211 E Chicago Ave Ste 1600 Chicago IL 60611-2660*

CORBETT, GERARD FRANCIS, electronics executive; b. Phila., Apr. 6, 1950; s. Eugene Charles and Dolores Marie (Hoffmann) C.; 1 child, Daniel Gerard. AA, C.C. Phila., 1974; BA in Pub. Rels., San Jose State U., 1977. Sci. programmer Sverdrup Inc., NASA Ames Rsch. Ctr., Moffett Field, Calif., 1970-77; sr. writer Four-Phase Sys., Inc., Cupertino, Calif., 1977-78; with Nat. Semicondr. Corp., Santa Clara, Calif., 1978-79; sr. acct. exec. Creamer Dickson Basford, Providence, 1979-81; mgr. tech. and exec. comm. Internat. Harvester Co., Chgo., 1981-82; mgr. corp. tech. comm. Gould Inc., Rolling Meadows, Ill., 1982-83; dir. corp. pub. rels. Gould Inc., 1983-86, bd. dirs. corp. comm., 1986-89; sr. corp. comm. exec. ASARCO Inc., N.Y.C., 1989-94; v.p. corp. comms. Loral Corp., N.Y.C., 1994-95; dir. corp. comm. Hitachi Am. Ltd., Brisbane, Calif., 1995—; pub. rels. and comm. cons. on high tech.; chmn. profl. adv. bd. pub. rels. degree program San Jose State U. Recipient Vice Presdl. award of honor Calif. Jaycees, 1977; named 1993 All Star Inside PR mag. Mem. AIAA (sr.), Nat. Investor Rels. Inst., Pub. Rels. Soc. Am. (accredited, nat. honors and awards com. 1996—, coll. fellows 1998—, Pres.'s citation 1981), N.Y. Pub. Rels. Soc., Nat. Assn. Sci. Writers Consortium, Sales and Mktg. Execs. Internat., Capital Hill Club, Commonwealth Club Calif., Meadow Club (Rolling Meadows, Ill.), Kappa Tau Alpha. Republican. Roman Catholic. Fax: 650-244-7920. E-mail: gerard.corbett@hal.hitachi.com. Home: 3350 Geoffrey Dr San Bruno CA 94066-1627

CORBETT, JAMES JOSEPH, retired computer programmer; b. Glens Falls, N.Y., Feb. 29, 1944; s. John Howard and Margaret Claire (Tupper) C.; m. Elaine Cecile Smith, Nov. 16, 1974. BA, Siena Coll., 1965; MA in Am. Studies, U. Md., 1967. Logistics intern U.S. Army Logistics Intern Tng. Ctr., Texarkana, Tex., 1967-68; supply specialist U.S. Army Electronics Command, Phila., 1968-70; computer programmer, analyst U.S. Army Logistics Systems Support Ctr., St. Louis, 1970-99. Contbr. articles to jours. Mem. Blueliners, Inc., St. Louis, 1970—, pres. 1983-85; mem. Bridge Line Hist. Soc., Albany, N.Y., 1990—; mem. choir Assumption Parish, 1994—; mem. Year 2000 Task Group, LSSC, 1996-99. Recipient Comdr.'s award for Civilian Svc., U.S. Army, 1987. Mem. Nat. Railway Hist. Soc. Roman Catholic. Avocations: railroad history, ice hockey, basketball, flags. Office: US Army Cecom LSSC 1222 Spruce St Saint Louis MO 63103-2818

CORBETT, JOHN DUDLEY, chemistry educator; b. Yakima, Wash., Mar. 23, 1926; s. Alexander Hazen and Elizabeth (Dudley) C.; m. Irene Lienkaemper, Aug. 7, 1948(wid. Nov. 1996); children: John Scott, Julia Barton, James Dudley. B.S. cum laude, U. Wash., 1948, Ph.D. (duPont research fellow), 1952. Asst. prof., asso. chemist Iowa State U. dept. chemistry and Ames Lab. AEC (now Dept. of Energy), 1952-58; asso. prof., chemist Iowa State U. and Ames Lab. AEC, 1958-63, prof., sr. chemist, 1963—, disting. prof. scis. and humanities, 1983—, chmn., div. chief, 1968-73, program dir., materials chemistry, 1974-78; chmn. molten salts Gordon Research Confs., 1963, mem. council, 1964-67; cons. E.I. duPont de Nemours & Co., 1956-63, 73-79, Oak Ridge Nat. Lab., 1969-72, Monsanto, 1977-78. Contbr. articles to profl. jours. Served with USNR, 1944-46. Recipient A. von Humboldt Sr. U.S. scientist award, 1985, Outstanding Sci. Accomplishments award U.S. Dept. Energy, 1987, Sustained Outstanding Rsch. in Materials Chemistry award, 1995, J.C. Bailar Jr. medal U. Ill., 1988. Mem. Nat. Acad. Scis., Am. Chem. Soc. (councilor, past chmn. Ames sect., Iowa award 1984, Midwest award 1985, award in inorganic Chemistry 1986), AAUP, Sigma Xi, Phi Lambda Upsilon, Phi Kappa Phi, Pi Mu Epsilon, Delta Tau Delta. Episcopalian. Home: 2337 Woodview Dr Ames IA 50014-8259

CORBETT, JOSEPH EDWARD, neurosurgeon; b. Burlington, Vt., May 24, 1954; s. Joseph Edward and Mae Nina (Johnson) C.; m. Jean Marie Murphy, Nov. 3, 1984; children: Joseph, John, Jim, Jeff. AB, Middlebury Coll., 1976; MD, U. Vt., 1982. Diplomate Am. Bd. Neurosurgery. Physician Vt. Neurosurg. Assocs., Rutland, Vt., 1993—. Office: Vt Neurosurg Assocs 231 Mussey St Rutland VT 05701-4843

CORBETT, LENORA MEADE, community college educator; b. Reidsville, N.C., Aug. 1, 1950; children: Kenneth Russell Johnson, Ralph Nathaniel Brown. AAS in Electromechanics, Tech. Coll. of Alamance, 1985, AAS in Electronics, 1986; BS in Indsl. Tech., Electronics, N.C. A&T State U., 1996. Cloth inspector Burlington (N.C.) Industries, 1971-74; electrician's helper Williams Electric, Greensboro, N.C., 1978, Nobility Mobile Homes, Reidsville, N.C., 1979; instr. math. and physics Alamance C.C., Graham, N.C., 1985—, chmn. learning resources, 1993. Contbr. poems to profl. publs. (Golden Poet award 1991, Merit award 1990, 92). Mem. sr. choir Jones Cross Rd. Ch., Reidsville, 1988-94, pastor's aide mem., 1988-90, jr. Sunday sch. tchr., 1989-91, asst. choir sec., 1988-94. Mem. AAUP, AAUW, Alamance C.C. Alumni Assn., Golden Key, N.C. A&T State U. Alumni Assn. Baptist. Avocations: cooking, reading, writing poetry, drawing, singing. Office: Alamance CC 1247 Jimmie Kerr Rd Graham NC 27253

CORBETT, SIOBHAN AIDEN, surgeon; b. Aug. 11, 1959. Diplomate Am. Bd. Surgery. Postdoctoral fellow Princeton (N.J.) U.; asst. prof. surg. scis. Robert Wood Johnson Med. Sch., New Brunswick, N.J., 1997—. Recipient Clin. Sci. award Am. Heart Assn., 1995-96. Office: Robert Wood Johnson Med Sch Dept Surg Med Edn Bldg One Robt Wood Johnson Pl New Brunswick NJ 08903-0019*

CORBETT, SUZANNE ELAINE, food writer, marketing executive, food historian; b. St. Louis, Jan. 23, 1953; d. George Edward and Opal Laverne (Duncan) Traxel; m. James Joseph Corbett, Jr., July 17, 1970; 1 child, James J. III. BA, Webster U., 1994, MA in Media Comm., 1995. Cert. culinary profl. Tchr. Inst. Continuing Edn. St. Louis C.C., 1976—; tchr. cmty. edn. Lindbergh Sch. Dist. Pub. Schs., St. Louis, 1983-89; confectioner/caterer Suzanne Corbett Seasonal Confections, St. Louis, 1977-84; test baker Fleishman's Yeast, St. Louis, 1983; food stylist St. Louis, 1980—, rsch. cons./food mktg. and rsch. food/product history, 1994; rsch. cons. PanCor Prodns., 1994—; food historian/folklorist St. Louis County Parks and Recreation, Mo. Hist. Soc., St. Louis Art Mus., Colonial Dames Am.; food media trainer Internat. Assn. Culinary Profls., 1990; ALHFAM lectr. in field. Author: Cowpuncher's Provision, 1988, River Fare, 1990, Pharoh's Pheast-Food from the Nile, 1991, Tips from Missouri Win Country, 1993, Pushcarts & Stalls: The Soul and Market History Cookbook, 1999; food writer, cookbook editor St. Louis Bugle food editor, 1991-96, columnist, 1991-96; columnist Sr. Circuit Newspaper; food writer, columnist News Weekly. Bd. dirs. St. Louis South sect. Am. Heart Assn., Historyonics Theatre Co.; mem. Mo. Grape and Wine Adv. Bd. Recipient Folklife Greentree grant award Ralston Purina, 1989, grant award Commerce Bank, 1990, grant award Wetterau Foods, 1991. Mem. Women in Communications (pres. St. Louis chpt. 1996, Communication awards 1989, 90, 91, 92, 93, 94, 95, 96, 97, 98), Nat. Fedn. Press Women (v.p. Mo. chpt.), Mo. Press Women (past pres., Communication award 1989, 96, 97, Communicator of Yr. 1993), Victorian Soc. Am. (past pres. St. Louis chpt.), James Beard Found. (charter), Am. Inst. Wine and Food, Internat. Assn. Culinary Profls. (cert., culinary historian Boston and Ann Arbor, internat. conf. com. 1990), Assn. Ind. Video and Filmmakers, St. Louis Press Club (former co-editor Courier, interim dir., Pres.' award, Press Club Charitable Fund pres. 1993-94), Nat. Fedn. Press Women (Communication and Writing awards), Nat. Trust for Hist. Preservation, St. Louis Culinary Soc. (sec., bd. dirs.), Order Eastern Star. Roman Catholic. Avocations: herb gardening, travel, civil war reenacting hist. preservation, folklife crafts. Home and Office: 5850 Pebble Oak Dr Saint Louis MO 63128-1412

CORBETT, THOMAS WINGETT, JR., lawyer; b. Phila., June 17, 1949; s. Thomas Wingett and Mary Bernadine (Diskin) C.; m. Susan Jean Manbeck, Dec. 16, 1972; children: Thomas Wingett III, Katherine. BA, Lebanon Valley Coll., 1971; JD, St. Mary's U., 1975. Bar: Pa. 1976, U.S. Dist. Ct. (we. dist.) Pa. 1976, U.S. Ct. Mil. Appeals 1979, U.S. Supreme Ct. 1984. Asst. dist. atty. Allegheny County, Pitts., 1976-80; asst. U.S. atty. Office U.S. Atty. for Western Dist. Pa., Pitts., 1980-83; assoc. Rose, Schmidt, Hasley & DiSalle, Pitts., 1983-86, former ptnr., from 1986; U.S. atty. We. Dist. Pa., Pitts., mem. U.S. atty. gen.'s adv. com., 1991—, chmn., 1993; Atty. Gen. State of Pa., Harrisburg, 1995-97; ptnr. Thorp, Reed & Armstrong, Pitts., 1993-95, 97-98; ast. gen. counsel for govt. affairs Waste Mgmt. Inc., Pitts., 1998—. Pres. St. Mary's Parent-Tchr. Guild, Glenshaw, Pa., 1983-85; mem. Allegheny County Republican Com., 1985-89; mem. Shaler Twp. Bd. Commrs., 1988-89. Mem. ABA, Pa. Bar Assn., Allegheny County Bar Assn. (judiciary com.). Roman Catholic. Avocations: skiing, golf, reading. Office: Waste Mgmt Inc Park West Two Ste 420 2000 Cliff Mine Rd Pittsburgh PA 15225

CORBETT, VIOLET JANE, farmer, contracter; b. Ft Worth, Tex., Apr. 18, 1949; d. Ellsworth Bryan and Hannah Hsu Sams; m. Ronnie R. Corbett, Feb. 14, 1968; children: Jeffrey, Joseph, John Deere. Grad. h.s., Knob Noster, Mo. Area clk. Amoco Oil Co., Inc., Warrensburg, Mo., 1967-72; agrl. profl. Ronnie Corbett & Sons, Knob Noster, 1968—; v.p. Ronnie Corbett Dozer Work, Inc., Knob Noster, 1996—. Charter mem., treas. Heartland Parliamentary, Warrensburg, Mo., 1999; regent Nat. Fedn. Rep. Women, Alexandria, Va., 1999; pres. Johnson County Farm Bur., Warrensburg, 1993, 94, 95, Johnson County Ext. Coun., Warrensburg, 1990; mem. 4th Congl. Dist. MFRW, pres., 1999—, Johnson County Cen. Com., committeewoman, v.p. Recipient Mo. Farm Bur. Pres.'s award Mo. Farm Bur., 1995; named Outstanding Johnson County Rep., Cen. Com., 1997. Mem. Mo. Fedn. Rep. Women (2d v.p. 1998-99), Mo. State Assn. Parliamentarians, Parliamentary Club. Home: 1127 NE 175 Knob Noster MO 65336

CORBETT, WILLIAM JOHN, government and public relations consultant, lawyer; b. Bklyn., Mar. 15, 1937; s. John Joseph and Mildred (Bauer) C.; m. Ann Virginia Teplitz, June 25, 1966; children: William John, Spencer Thomas, Sally Ann. BA, Hobart Coll., 1959; JD, Fordham U., 1965. Bar: N.Y. 1966, U.S. Dist. Ct. (fed. dist.) 1968, Customs Ct. 1968, U.S. Supreme Ct. 1990. Info. officer USAF, Greenville, S.C., 1959-62; trial lawyer Nassau County Legal Aid Soc., Mineola, N.Y., 1965-67; asst. dist. atty. County of Nassau, 1967-68; corp. dir. pub. rels. Avon Products, Inc., N.Y.C., 1968-84; v.p. comm. AICPA, N.Y.C., 1984-90; chmn. Corbett Assocs., Inc., 1990—; pub. rels. advisor USIA, Washington, 1981-93; cons. status UN Office Info. and ECOSOC, N.Y.C., 1979-84, 90-93; pros. atty. Inc. Village of Floral Park, N.Y., 1975-84, acting village justice, 1984-98, adj. asst. prof. Iona Coll. Grad. Sch. Comm. Mem. adv. bd. Pub. Rels. News (Leadership award 1984); mem. Commn. on Pub. Rels. Edn. Participant White House Conf. on Indsl. World Ahead, 1972, White House Mini Conf. on Consumer Elderly, 1979, White House Conf. on Small Bus., 1986, 95, White House Conf. on Librs. and Info. Svcs., 1991; staff mem. N.Y. State Senate, Albany, 1962-63. Capt. USAF, 1959-62. Decorated Air Force Commendation medal; recipient Legion of Honor Internat. Coun. Order DeMolay, 1982, Hobart Coll. Alumni award, 1984, N.Y. State Conspicuous Svc. medal, 1970, Pinnacle award, 1990; named to Hall of Fame, U.S. Dept. Def. Info. Sch., 1990. Mem. Internat. Pub. Rels. Assn. (bd. dirs. 1984-90, pres. 1990), Pub. Rels. Soc. Am. (accredited, Fellow Pres. award 1985, 88), Pub. Rels. Soc. N.Y. (past pres.), Corp. Forum N.Y., Ctr. for Study Presidency (adv. bd.), Pub. Affairs Coun. (bd. dirs. 1976-78), Nat. Assn. Corp. Dirs. N.Y. (v.p. 1993-94). Home: 102 Chestnut Ave Floral Park NY 11001-2421 Office: 111 S Tyson Ave Floral Park NY 11001-1822

CORBIN, BARRY, actor, writer; b. Lamesa, Tex., Oct. 16, 1940; s. Kilmer Blaine and Alma LaMerle (Scott) C.; m. Elyse Corbin, 1968 (div. 1971); m. Susan James Berger, May 29, 1976 (div. 1992); children: James Barry, Christopher Clayton, Shannon Katy, Bernard Weiss. Student, Tex. Tech. U.,

1959-64, U. Colo., summer 1964. Freelance actor, 1965—; faculty N.C. State U., Raleigh, 1966-67. Playwright: Suckerrod Smith and the Cisco Kid, 1974 (Theater U.S.A. award 1974), Throckmorton, Tx., 76083, 1983; screenwriter The Wildcatters, 1986; films include Any Which Way You Can, 1980, Urban Cowboy, 1980, Dead and Buried, 1981, The Night the Lights Went Out in Georgia, 1981, Six Pack, 1982, The Best Little Whorehouse in Texas, 1982, Honkytonk Man, 1982, The Ballad of Gregorio Cortez, 1983, WarGames, 1983, The Man Who Loved Women, 1983, Hard Travelling, 1985, My Science Project, 1985, Nothing in Common, 1986, What Comes Around, 1986, Under Cover, 1987, Off the Mark, 1987, Permanent Records, 1988, Critters 2: The Main Course, 1988, It Takes Two, 1988, Who is Harry Crumb?, 1989, Short Time, 1990, Ghost Dad, 1990, The Hot Spot, 1990, Career Opportunities, 1991, Curdled, 1996, Solo, 1996, Kiss & Tell, 1997, Inconvenienced, 1999; TV series: Boone, 1983-84, Spies, 1987, Northern Exposure, 1990-95 (Emmy nomination, Supporting Actor - Drama, 1993, 94) The Big Easy, 1996; mini-series: The Thorn Birds, 1983, Lonesome Dove, 1989, Moon Shot, 1994 (host); TV movies Rage, 1980, This House Possessed, 1981, The Killing of Randy Webster, 1981, Murder in Texas, 1981, Bitter Harvest, 1981, A Few Days in Weasel Creek, 1981, Fantasies, 1982, Prime Suspect, 1982, Travis McGee, 1982, Flight #90: Disaster on the Potomac, 1984, The Jesse Owens Story, 1984, Fatal Vision, 1984, Ratings Game, 1984, Death in California, 1985, The Defiant Ones, 1986, Firefighter, 1986, C.A.T. Squad, 1986, Warm Hearts, Cold Feet, 1987, LBJ: The Early Years, 1987, Secret Witness, 1988, Man Against the Mob, 1988, The People Across the Lake, 1988, Stranger on My Land, 1988, Red King, White Night, 1989, I Know My First Name Is Steven, 1989, Spooner, 1989, Last Flight Out, 1990, The Chase, 1991, Conagher, 1991, Siringo, 1994, Virus, 1995, Deadly Family Secretes, 1995, The Pandora Directive, 1996, My Son Is Innocent, 1996, Columbo: A Trace of Murder, 1997, The Hired Heart, 1997, Judgement Day: The Ellie Nesler Story, 1998, A Face to Kill For, 1999. Pvt. USMCR, 1962-64. Recipient Western Image award Dallas Apparel Mart, Buffalo Bill Cody award Nebraskaland Days, Wrangler award Nat. Cowboy Hall of Fame. Mem. Screen Actors Guild (bd. dirs. 1985, 87-90), Actors Equity Assn., AFTRA, Dramatists Guild, Acad. Motion Picture Arts and Scis. Avocations: cutting, cow penning, trail riding. Office: care Elkins Entertainment 8306 Wilshire Blvd # 438 Beverly Hills CA 90211-2382*

CORBIN, DONALD L., state supreme court justice; b. Hot Springs, Ark., Mar. 29, 1938. BA, U. Ark., 1964, JD, 1966. Bar: Ark. 1966, U.S. Dist. Ct. (we. dist.) Ark. 1966. Lawyer Lewisville and Stamps, 1967-80; judge Ark. Ct. Appeals, 1981-87, chief judge, 1987-90; assoc. justice Ark. Supreme Ct., Little Rock, 1991—; state rep. Ark. Gen. Assembly, 1971-80. Served with USMC, 1955-59. Mem. ABA, Ark. Bar Assn., SW Ark. Bar Assn., Sigma Alpha Epsilon. Democrat. Avocation: duck hunting. Office: Supreme Ct Justice Bldg 625 Marshall St Little Rock AR 72201-1054*

CORBIN, HERBERT LEONARD, public relations executive; b. Bklyn., Mar. 30, 1940; s. H. Dan and Lillian Corbin; m. Carol Heller, June 2, 1963; children: Jeffrey, Leslie Faith. BA, Rutgers U., 1961. Staff corr. Newark News, 1961-63; asst. dir. pub. relations Rutgers U. News Service, New Brunswick, N.J., 1963-65; account exec. A.A. Schechter Assocs., N.Y.C., 1965-66, Barkis & Shalit, Inc., N.Y.C., 1965-66; sr. account exec. Daniel J. Edelman, Inc., N.Y.C., 1967-69; founder, pres., mng. ptnr. KCSA Pub. Rels. Worldwide, N.Y.C., 1969—. Mem. nat. coun. Am. Jewish Com., White Plains Pub. Access Cable TV Commn.; mem. mktg. adv. com. United Jewish Appeal-Fedn. N.Y., Met. Jewish Health. Sys. Mem. Pub. Rels. Soc. Am. (counsellors Acad.), Soc. Profl. Journalists, Old Oaks Country Club (bd. dirs.), City Athletic Club. Home: 31 Hathaway Ln White Plains NY 10605-3610 Office: KCSA Pub Rels Worldwide 800 2nd Ave New York NY 10017-4709

CORBIN, JAMES H., executive engineer, meteorologist, oceanographer. BS in Elec. Engring., U. Nebr., 1971; MS in Oceanography and Meteorology, Naval Postgrad. Sch., Monterey, Calif., 1977. Commd. U.S. Navy, 1962, advanced through grades to, various sea and shore commands, 1962-77; spl. projects officer Naval Oceanography Command Ctr., Guam, 1977-80; meteorol. and oceanographic officer Aircraft Carrier John F. Kennedy, 1980-82; officer in charge Naval Oceanography Command Detachment, Monterey, Calif., 1982-86; dir. operational oceanography ctr. U.S. Naval Oceanographic Office, 1986-90; mgr. exptl. ctr. for mesoscale ocean prediction Inst. for Naval Oceanography, 1990-92; dir. Ctr. for Air Sea Tech. Miss. State U., Stennis Space Ctr., Miss., 1992—. Office: Miss State U Ctr Air Sea Tech Bldg 1103 Stennis Space Center MS 39529*

CORBIN, KENDALL BROOKS, physician, scientist; b. Oak Park, Ill., Dec. 31, 1907; s. William Sherman and Emma (Heacock) C.; m. Eryl Portia Wallace, Jan. 2, 1932; children: Kendall Wallace, Edwin Malcolm. Student, UCLA, 1926-30; AB cum laude, Stanford, 1931, MD, 1935. Diplomate: Am. Bd. Psychiatry and Neurology. Instr. anatomy Stanford, 1934-38; NRC fellow in medicine Neurology Inst., Northwestern U., 1937-38; assoc. prof. anatomy Tenn. U., then prof. and chief div. anatomy, 1938-46, in charge neurology, 1943-45; prof. neurology Mayo Found., Minn. U., and; cons. in neurology Mayo Clinic, 1946-72, head sect. neurology, 1956-63, sr. cons. neurology, 1963-72, pres. staff, 1968; asso. dir. Mayo Found. for Med. Edn. and Research, Grad. Sch. of U. Minn., 1950-54; chmn. bd. devel. Mayo Found., 1969-73, emeritus, 1973—; mem. residency rev. com., neurology and psychiatry, 1952-56. Contbr. articles on nervous system to med. jours., chpts. to med. books. Bd. dirs. United Fund Rochester, 1962-68. Mem. AMA, Am. Neurol. Assn., Am. Acad. Neurology, Minn. Med. Assn., Phi Beta Kappa, Sigma Xi, Alpha Omega Alpha. Home: 211 2nd St NW Apt 1817 Rochester MN 55901-2899 Office: Mayo Clinic Rochester MN 55901 *Avoid succumbing to the Peter Principle: 1. Obtain the best, most complete training in your field of specialization. Do not use short-cuts. 2. Avoid tempting promotions or job offers, especially involving administrative duties, which will interfere with progression in your chosen field. 3. Similarly, avoid offers which appear to enhance your power, prestige or financial status, if such interfere with growth and experience in your field of knowledge.*

CORBIN, KRESTINE MARGARET, manufacturing company executive, fashion designer, columnist; b. Reno, Apr. 24, 1937; d. Lawrence Albert and Judie Ellen (Johnston) Dickinson; m. Lee D. Corbin, May 16, 1959 (div. 1982); children: Michelle Marie, Sheri Karin. BS, U. Calif., Davis, 1958. Asst. prof. Bauder Coll., Sacramento, 1974—; columnist Sacramento Bee, 1976-81; owner Creative Sewing Co., Sacramento, 1976—; pres., chief exec. officer Sierra Machinery Inc., Sparks, Nev., 1984, also bd. dirs.; nat. sales and promotion mgr. Westwood Retail Fabrics, N.Y.C., 1985—; bd. dirs. Sierra Pacific Resources, Sierra Pacific Power Co., NEWTRAC; cons. in field. Author: Suede Fabric Sewing Guide, 1973, Creative Sewing Book, 1978, (audio-visual) Fashions in the Making, 1974; producer: (nat. buyers show) Cream of the Cream Collections, 1978—, Style is What You Make It!, 1978-83. Named Exporter of Yr. State of Nev., 1989. Mem. Crocker Art Gallery Assn., 1960-78, Rep. Election Com., Sacramento, 1964, 68; apptd. by Gov. of Nev. to Internat. Program Adv. Com.; elected head Bd. Federal Reserve Bank 12th Dist., 1995—. Mem. Home Economists in Bus., Am. Home Econs. Assn., Internat. Fashion Group, Women's Fashion Fabrics Assn., Nat. Machine Tool Builders Assn. (mem. internat. export com.), Nat. Fluid Power Assn., Nev. World Trade Coun. (bd. dir.), Omicron Nu. Office: Sierra Machinery Inc 1651 Glendale Ave Sparks NV 89431-5912 also: PO Box 435 Reno NV 89504-0435

CORBIN, SOL NEIL, lawyer; b. N.Y.C., Apr. 16, 1927; s. Nathan I. and Sarah (Kaiser) C.; m. Tanya Jacobs, Aug. 7, 1963; 1 son, David J. BS, Columbia U., 1948; JD cum laude, Harvard U., 1951. Bar: N.Y. 1952. Practiced N.Y.C., 1952—; law clk. Judge Charles D. Breitel, 1954-56; counsel Gov. of N.Y., 1962-65; ptnr. Corbin, Silverman & Sanseverino LLP, N.Y.C., 1970-96, sr. counsel, 1997—; mem. N.Y. State Banking Bd., 1969-76; Chmn. N.Y. State Commn. Constl. Conv., 1966-67; mem. N.Y. State Commn. Local Govt. Powers, 1971-73; chmn. N.Y. State Crime Control Planning Bd., 1974-75; mem. Chief Judge's Com. to Recruit State Ct. Adminstr., 1973; trustee in bankruptcy Franklin N.Y. Corp., 1974-90; spl. counsel v.p. U.S., 1975. Trustee N.Y. Pub. Libr., 1977—; mem. Chief Judge's com. on Availability of Legal Svcs., 1988-90. With USNR, 1945-46. Mem. ABA, N.Y. State Bar Assn., Assn. Br. City N.Y., New York County Bar Assn., Am. Law Inst., Lotos Club. Home: 1100 Park Ave New York NY 10128-1202 Office: 805 3rd Ave New York NY 10022-7513

CORBIN, TRACY DIANNE, researcher; b. Dec. 18, 1964. BA in Social Work, So. Ill. U., 1987, BA in Anthropology, 1997, MA in Pub. Adminstrn., 1999. Rehab. counselor So. Ill. Comty. Correctional Ctr., Carbondale, 1986-87; legal advocate Women's Ctr., Carbondale, 1987-95; rschr. So. Ill. U., Carbondale, 1995-99; owner, operator The Book Rack, 1999—. E-mail: tcorbin@midwest.net.

CORBITT, DORIS ORENE, real estate agent, dietitian; b. Warrior, Ala., Oct. 25, 1929; d. Olen J. and Begie Pernie (Motte) Florence; m. Wallace R. Cornett, Nov. 29, 1952 (div. 1980); children: Wallace R. Jr., Kris J., Brett T.; m. Weldon Plant Corbitt, Jr., Apr. 21, 1984. BS in Dietetics, Maryville Coll., 1950; postgrad., Duke U., 1950-51. Registered dietitian; lic. real estate agt., Fla. Asst. dir. dietary St. Mary's Hosp., Knoxville, 1952-53; dir. dietary Soldier and Sailor Sch. for Children, Bloomington, Ill., 1966-68; tchr. Nashville Area Vocat. Sch., 1971-73; dir. dietary Westside Hosp., Nashville, 1973-79, Meml. Hosp., Tampa, Fla., 1980-85; realtor assoc. Coldwell Banker, Tampa, 1986—; Spkr. in field. Devel. original curriculum for Food Svc. Workers and Suprs., Tenn.; co-author first diet manual for Nashville Dietetic Assn. Sec. Galleria Homeowners Assn., Tampa, 1986-87; Sunday sch. tchr. Recipient Internat. Citizenship award, 1995; named The Honourable, Prince Kevin of Australia, 1996. Mem. Am. Dietetic Assn., Tampa Dietetic Assn., Tampa Bd. Realtors, Million Dollar Club. Republican. Mem. Ch. of Christ. Avocations: music, movies, reading, church work, walking. Home: 11515 Galleria Dr Tampa FL 33624-4752 Office: Coldwell Banker Residential Real Estate Inc 14502 N Dale Mabry Hwy Ste 100 Tampa FL 33618-2076

CORBOY, JAMES MCNALLY, investment banker; b. Erie, Pa., Nov. 3, 1940; s. James Thomas and Dorothy Jane (Schluraff) C. ; m. Suzanne Shaver, July 23, 1965; children: Shannon, James McNally. BA, Allegheny Coll., 1962; MBA, U. Colo., 1986. Sales staff Boettcher & Co., Denver, 1964-70; sales staff Blyth Eastman Dillon, Denver and Chgo., 1970-74, William Blair & Co., Chgo., 1974-77; mgr. corp. bond dept. Boettcher & Co., Denver, 1977-79; ptnr. in charge William Blair & Co., Denver, 1979-86; first v.p. Stifel, Nicolaus & Co., Denver, 1986-88; pres., CEO SKB Corboy Inc., Denver, 1988-97, Century Capital Group Inc., 1997-98; ptnr. Corboy and Jerde, LLC, Englewood, Colo., 1999—. With USMC, 1962-67. Mem. Nat. Assn. Securities Dealers, Country Club at Castle Pines, Met. Club. Republican. Presbyterian. Home: Castle Pines Village 870 Homestake Ct Castle Rock CO 80104-9081 Office: 400 Inverness Dr S # 200 Englewood CO 80112

CORBRIDGE, JAMES NOEL, JR., law educator; b. Mineola, N.Y., May 27, 1934; s. James Noel Sr. and Edna (Springer) C.; children: Loren, Stuart. AB, Brown U., 1955; LLB, Yale U., 1963. Assoc. Lord, Day & Lord, N.Y.C., 1963-65; asst. prof. law U. Colo., Boulder, 1965-67, assoc. prof., 1967-73, prof., 1973—, v.p. student affairs, 1970-72, v.p. student and minority affairs, 1972-74, vice chancellor acad. affairs, 1974-77, interim vice chancellor acad. services, 1979-81, acting vice chancellor acad. affairs, 1986, chancellor, 1986-94; vis. scholar Inst. for Advanced Legal Studies U. London, 1977, 85, Univ. Linkoping, Sweden, 1985, 1997. Contbr. articles to profl. jours. Served to lt. (j.g.) USNR, 1957-60. Mem. Colo. Bar Assn., Boulder County Bar Assn., Internat. Assn. Water Lawyers, Internat. Water Resources Assn. Episcopalian. Club: Boulder Country. Avocations: golf, bird carving, birding. Home: 7229 Four Rivers Rd Boulder CO 80301-3737 Office: U Colo PO Box 401 Boulder CO 80309-0401

CORBY, FRANCIS MICHAEL, JR., manufacturing company executive; b. Chgo., Feb. 2, 1944; s. Francis M. and Jean (Wolf) C.; m. Diane S. Orselli, Aug. 5, 1972; children: Francis Michael III, Brian A., Christopher S. B.A., St. Mary of the Lake, 1966; M.B.A., Columbia U., 1969. With Chrysler Corp., 1969-80; treasury mgr. Chrysler Peru S.A., Lima, 1973-74; fin. dir. Chrysler Wholesale Ltd., London, 1974-76; mng. dir. Chrysler Comml. S.A. de C.V., Mexico City, 1976-77; v.p., treas. Chrysler Fin. Corp., Troy, Mich., 1977-80; treas. Joy Mfg. Co., Pitts., 1980-83; controller Joy Mfg. Co., 1983-86, v.p., 1984-86; sr. v.p. fin., CFO Harnischfeger Industries, Inc., Milw., 1986-94, exec. v.p. fin. and adminstrn., 1994—; bd. dirs. Harnischfeger Industries, Inc., Harnischfeger Corp., Industries Ins. Corp., Dobson Park, PLC, Harnischfeger Found., Inc., Joy Techs., Inc. Mem. Fin. Execs. Inst. Club: Westmoor Country. Office: Harnischfeger Industries Inc PO Box 554 Milwaukee WI 53201-0554

CORCORAN, ANDREW PATRICK, JR., lawyer; b. Fredrick, Md., Nov. 20, 1948; s. Andrew Patrick and Beatrice Josephine (Poletti) C.; m. Margaret Cecila Boyle, July 3, 1971; children: Maureen Meredith, Andrew Patrick III. BA, Villanova U., 1970; JD, Seton Hall U., 1973. Bar: Pa. 1973, U.S Dist. Ct. (ea. dist.) Pa. 1974, U.S. Ct. Appeals (7th cir.) 1976, U.S. Ct. Appeals (3d cir.) 1977, U.S. Supreme Ct. 1982. Atty. Pa. Cen. Transp. Co., Phila., 1973-75, sr. atty., 1975-79; asst. gen. atty. Consol. Rail Corp., Phila., 1979-82, gen. atty., 1982-85, sr. gen. atty., 1985-92, assoc. gen. counsel, 1992-99; gen. atty. Norfolk (Va.) So. Corp., 1999—. Mem. Conf. of Rwy. and Airline Labor Lawyers, Assn. of Am. R.R.'s (legal affairs com.). Republican. Roman Catholic. Home: 3132 Hunters Chase Dr Virginia Beach VA 23452 Office: Norfolk So Corp Three Commercial Pl Norfolk VA 23510-9241

CORCORAN, C. TIMOTHY, III, bankruptcy judge; b. Kansas City, Mo., Dec. 18, 1945; s. Clement T. and Bette Lou (Hohl) C. BA, U. N.C., 1967; JD, U. Va., 1973. Bar: Fla. 1973, U.S. Dist. Ct. (mid. dist.) Fla. 1973, D.C. 1974, U.S. Dist. Ct. (no. and so. dists.) Fla. 1975, U.S. Supreme Ct. 1979, U.S. Ct. Appeals (11th cir.) 1981. Law clk. U.S. Dist. Ct., Tampa, Fla., 1973-75; assoc. Carlton, Fields, Ward, Emmanuel, Smith & Cutler, P.A., Tampa, 1975-78, ptnr., 1978-89; judge Bankruptcy Ct. (mid. dist.) Fla., Orlando, 1989-93, Tampa, 1993—; dir. Bay Area Legal Svcs., Inc., Tampa, 1993—; dir. Bay Area Legal Svcs., Inc., Tampa, 1983-89, v.p., 1987, pres., 1988; bd. dirs. Fla. Coun. Bar Pres., 1982-88, pres., 1986-87; arbitrator Ct. Annexed Arbitration Program, U.S. Dist. Ct. (mid. dist.) Fla., 1984-89; counselor U. Tampa, 1981-86, fellow, 1986-89. Co-author: Conflicts of Interest, 1984; contbr. articles to legal jours. Lt. USNR, 1967-70. Mem. ABA (litigation sect., co-chair comm. com. 1990-92, chair book pub. bd. 1992-98, assoc. editor Litigation News 1982-87, mng. editor 1987, editor-in-chief 1988-90, Nat. Conf. of Lawyers and Reps. of Media 1992-95, mem. adv. com. on nominations 1994-95, chair media-law roundtable 1994, chair sect. officers conf. com. on non-dues revenue 1995-96, mem. working group on ABA bus. plan for pub. 1995-96, standing com. on pub. oversight 1996—), Fla. Bar (chmn. voluntary bar liaison com. 1985-86, chmn. grievance com. 13-D 1986-88, chmn. legal edn. com. 1981-82, Most Productive Young Lawyer award 1981), Am. Judicature Soc., Hillsborough County Bar Assn. (Red McEwen award 1980, pres. 1982-83), Am. Inns of Ct. (Master of the Bench 1990-93, 96—). Roman Catholic. Office: Sam M Gibbons US Courthouse 801 N Florida Ave Tampa FL 33602-3899

CORCORAN, COLLEEN MARIE, grant and contract administrator; b. Sept. 20, 1968. BA, Wells Coll., 1990; MPA, U. Mass., Amherst, 1994. Grant adminstr. Health Rsch., Inc., Rensselaer, N.Y., 1994-98; clin. rsch. adminstr. Rsch. Found. for Mental Hygiene, Inc., Albany, N.Y., 1998—. E-mail: cmckae@juno.com. Home: 61 South Pine Ave Albany NY 12208

CORCORAN, DAVID, newspaper editor; b. N.Y.C., July 22, 1947; s. William and Ruth (Brody) Diebold; m. Karrie Olick; children: Thomas, Daniel, Katie. BA, Amherst Coll., 1969; fellow journalism, Stanford U., 1976-77. Tchr. Rockland Country Day Sch., Congers, N.Y., 1969-70; reporter Hackensack (N.J.) Record, 1969-73, from editorial writer to asst. editor, 1973-77, editor editorial page, 1977-87, chief news editor, 1987-88; copy editor N.Y. Times, 1988-92, asst. to nat. editor, 1992-93, dep. op-ed editor, 1993-95, dep. N.J. editor, 1995-96, dep. graphics dir., 1996-98, edn. editor., 1999—; instr. journalism Seton Hall U., S. Orange, N.J., 1977-78. Trustee Ctr. Analysis of Pub. Issues, 1983-91. Mem. Am. Soc. Newspaper Editors, Nat. Conf. Editorial Writers, Soc. Profl. Journalists (dir. N.J. chpt. 1980—, pres. N.J. chpt. 1983-84). Home: 437 Wildwood Rd Northvale NJ 07647-1221 Office: NY Times 229 W 43rd St New York NY 10036-3959

CORCORAN, JAMES JOSEPH, JR., health plan administrator, physician; b. Ithaca, N.Y., May 8, 1956. AB, Harvard U., 1978; MD, Pa. State U., 1982; MPH, Johns Hopkins U., 1995. Diplomate Am. Bd. Internal Medicine, Am. Bd. Preventive Medicine. Intern Brockton (Mass.) Hosp., 1982-83; resident in internal medicine Med. Coll. Ga., Augusta, 1983-85; pvt. practice Greenville, S.C., 1985-93; resident in preventive medicine Johns Hopkins Sch. Pub. Health, Balt., 1994-96; med. dir. Blue Cross Blue Shield Fla., Jacksonville, 1996—. Mem. ACP, AMA, Am. Coll. Preventive Medicine. Office: 4800 Deerwood Campus Pky Jacksonville FL 32246-6498

CORCORAN, JAMES MARTIN, JR., lawyer, writer, lecturer; b. Evanston, Ill., Nov. 12, 1932; s. James M. and Ethel M. (Fitzgerald) C.; m. Catherine F. Howland, Aug. 6, 1955; children: Mary Carol, John Kevin, Lawrence T., Rosemary C., Pauline M., Moira E., Daniel P. AB, U. Notre Dame, 1955, JD, 1956. Bar: Ill. 1956, U.S. Dist. Ct. (no. dist.) Ill. 1956, U.S. Tax Ct. 1957, U.S. Supreme Ct. 1987. Practiced in Evanston, 1956-78; partner Corcoran & Corcoran (attys.), Evanston, 1957-63; sr. partner Corcoran & Corcoran (attys.), 1964-72; pres. Corcoran & Corcoran, Profl. Corp., Evanston, 1973-78, Chgo. and Evanston, 1983—; ptnr. D'Ancona & Pflaum, 1979-83; assoc. reporter ALI-ABA study project, Buying, Selling and Merging Businesses, 1970-74. Author: Alternatives to Probate, 1972, Suggested Will and Trust Forms for Lawyers, 1974, In the Office-A Form Book for Lawyers, 1973, 74, Probate Forms for Estates of Minors, Incompetents and Decedents, 1976, Estate and Gift Taxation for The General Practitioner, 1975-80 (6 edits.); (with others) Drafting Wills and Trust Agreements, 10 edits., 1967-90, sr. author 1987-95, chmn. com. authors, 1989-95; (with others) Buying and Selling Businesses, 5 edits., 1967-83, Contested Estates, 1984-96; contbr. chpts. to continuing legal edn. books, articles to profl. jours.; estate planning, pobate and trust law editor Ill. Bar Jour., 1955-87; mng. editor Notre Dame Lawyer, 1955-56. Mem. sch. bd. St. Mary's Sch., 1969-72. Recipient Harrison Tweed award Assn. Continuing Legal Edn. Adminstrs., 1975; Distinguished Service award Chgo. Estate Planning Council, 1975; Francis Rawle spl. award of merit ABA-Am. Law Inst. Com. on Continuing Profl. Edn., 1985. Fellow Am. Coll. Trust and Estate Counsel (editorial bd. Probate Notes 1975-78); mem. ABA (gen. practice sect., probate and estate planning com. 1983—, vice chmn. 1989-92, sole practitioners & small firms com., vice chmn. 1983-84, 85), Ill. S tate Bar Assn. (bd. govs. 1972-75, chmn. pub. rels. com. 1962-64, estate planning, probate & trust law coun. 1971-72, fed. tax course, chmn. 1974, co-chmn. 1977, Virgil Tipton Jr. Pubs. award 1986), Chgo. Bar Assn. (com. on adoption laws 1957-61, probate practice com. 1977—, fed. tax com. 1979—, Chgo. estate planning coun. 1973-). Roman Catholic. Home: 929 Sheridan Rd Evanston IL 60202-1426 Office: Corcoran & Corcoran Profl Corp 221 N La Salle St Ste 2230 Chicago IL 60601-1502*

CORCORAN, KEVIN JAMES, town planner; b. Plattsburgh, N.Y., July 10, 1962; s. Francis William and Mary Theresa (Maxwell) C.; m. Patricia Ann McNamara, Sept. 19, 1987; children: Conor James, Shannon Kathleen. BA in Environ. Sci., SUNY, Plattsburgh, 1984; M Regional Planning, SUNY, Albany, 1987. Sr. planner, planner Oneida County, Utica, N.Y., 1986-89; town planner Town of Glenville, N.Y., 1989—; mem. planning com. Capital Dist. Transp. Com., Albany, 1993—; mem. Traffic Safety Com., Glenville, 1991—, Econ. Devel. Zone Adminstrn. Bd., Schenectady, 1994-97. Contbr. articles to profl. jours. Mem. Am. Planning Assn., N.Y. Planning Fedn. Avocations: hiking, softball, guitar playing, skiing, reading. Home: 10 Vernon Blvd Scotia NY 12302-2606 Office: Town of Glenville Planning Dept 18 Glenridge Rd Schenectady NY 12302-4518

CORCORAN, MARY ALICE, retired medical surgical nurse, educator; b. West Point Twp., Wis., Sept. 19, 1934; d. Roman P. and Agnes M. (Ryan) Boehmer; m. Edward J. Corcoran, Aug. 16, 1958; children: Patrick, Bridget (dec.). Diploma, St. Mary's Sch. Nursing, Milw., 1955; cert. pub. health nurse, Marquette U., 1957. RN, Wis.; cert. diabetes educator. Nurse clinician IV U. Wis. Univ. Health Svc., Madison, 1967-98; ret., 1998. Mem. hypertension faculty Am. Heart Assn., 1978-94. Mem. Am. Diabetes Assn. (Wis. bd. dirs. 1985-91, Vol. of Yr. award 1988, Program Vol. of Yr. award 1994, Outstanding Svc. award), Am. Assn. Diabetes Educators. Office: U Wis Health Svc 1552 University Ave Madison WI 53705-4084

CORCORAN, MAUREEN ELIZABETH, lawyer; b. Iowa City, Feb. 4, 1944; d. Joseph and Velma (Tobin) C. BA in English with honors, U. Iowa, 1966, MA in English, 1967; JD, Hastings Coll. of Law, San Francisco, 1979. Bar: Calif. 1979, D.C. 1988, U.S. Ct. Appeals (9th cir.), 1979, U.S. Dist. Ct. (no. dist.) Calif., 1979, U.S. Dist. Ct. (cen. dist.) Calif., 1979, U.S. Ct. Appeals (D.C. cir.) 1983. Assoc. Hassard Bonnington Rogers & Huber, San Francisco, 1979-81; spl. asst. to gen. counsel HHS, Washington, 1981-83; assoc. Weissburg & Aronson, San Francisco, 1983-84; gen. counsel U.S. Dept. Edn., Washington, 1984-86; of counsel Pillsbury, Madison & Sutro, San Francisco, 1987-; chmn. bd. Hastings Coll. Law U. Calif., San Francisco, 1993—; chmn. Managed Health Care Conf., 1989; mem. AIDS adv. com. Ctrs. for Disease Control, 1989-91; speaker health law mtgs. Author: (book) Managed Care Contracting: Advising the Managed Care Organization, 1996; contbr. articles on health law to profl. jours. Mem. U.S. delegation to 1985 World Conf. to Review and Appraise Achievements of UN Decade for Women, Nairobi, Kenya, 1985; mem. Adminstrv. Conf. U.S., Washington, 1985. Mem. ABA (sect. health law), Calif. State Bar Assn., Am. Health Lawyers Assn. Office: Pillsbury Madison & Sutro LLP 235 Montgomery St Fl 16 San Francisco CA 94104-3074

CORCORAN, PAUL JOHN, physician; b. Washburn, Wis., June 8, 1934; s. Thomas F. and Mary Rose (McCauley) C., m. Patricia Ann Bounds, Nov. 10, 1956; children: Mary Colbourne, Ann Campbell, Clare Bounds, Thomas Bounds, Peter Campbell, David Pusey. BS, Georgetown U., 1955, MD, 1959; MS in Phys. Medicine and Rehab., U. Wash., 1968. Diplomate Am. Bd. Phys. Medicine and Rehab. Intern U. Oreg. Hosps., 1959-60; resident in rehab. medicine NYU, 1963-66; postdoctoral fellow dept. rehab. medicine HEW-Social and Rehab. Services; Acad. Career trainee dept. rehab. medicine U. Wash. Med. Center, 1966-68; asst. attending physiatrist Presbyn. Hosp. City N.Y.; asst. prof. rehab. medicine Columbia U., 1968-72; dir. residency tng. in rehab. medicine Columbia-Presbyn. Med. Center, N.Y.C., 1969-72; assoc. prof. rehab. medicine Boston U., 1972-76; chief rehab. medicine Boston City Hosp., 1975-77; from assoc. prof. to prof. Tufts U., 1976-85, clin. prof., 1985—, acting chmn. dept. rehab. medicine, 1976-77, 89-90, chmn. dept., 1977-81; physiatrist-in-chief Rehab. Inst., New England Med. Ctr. Hosp., Boston, 1976-81, 89-90; chief rehab. medicine service Boston VA Med. Center, 1980-85; med. dir. Easter Seal Soc./N.H., Manchester, 1985-91; chief phys. medicine and rehab. New England Sinai Hosp. and Rehab. Ctr., Stoughton, Mass., 1989-90, Newton-Wellesley (Mass.) Hosp., 1991-93; dir. rehab. medicine Spaulding Rehab. Hosp., Boston, 1992-96; interim dir. divsn. phys. medicine and rehab. Harvard Med. Sch., Boston, 1993-96; assoc. in neurology Mass. Gen. Hosp., Boston, 1993-96; lectr. phys. medicine and rehab. Harvard Med. Sch., 1997—; instr. NYU Grad. Sch. Prosthetics and Orthotics, 1970-77; vis. physician rehab. medicine U. Hosp., Boston, 1972-76; project dir. New England Regional Rehab. Rsch. and Tng. Ctr., 1977-81; chief med. cons. Mass. Rehab. Commn., 1991-96; vis. prof. Harvard Med. Sch., Boston, 1993-96. Contbr. chpts. to books, articles to profl. pubs.; editorial bd. Archives Phys. Med. and Rehab., 1971-77. Trustee Easter Seal Rsch. Found., 1975-78, 88-90, Carroll Rehab. Ctr. for Blind, 1975-78; mem. rehab. svcs. nat. adv. com. HEW, 1976-77; chmn. Mass. Interagy. Coun. on Ind. Living, 1977-79. Lt. M.C., USN, 1960-63. Recipient Licht award Am. Congress Rehab. Medicine, 1985, Physician of Yr. award Pres.'s Com. on Employment of Handicapped, 1986, Disting. Clinician award Am. Acad. Phys. Medicine and Rehab., 1995. Mem. Am. Assn. Acad. Physiatrists (pres. 1981-83, Outstanding Svc. award 1996). Home: 37 Main St Hancock NH 03449-5321 Office: New England Sinai Hosp and Rehab Ctr 150 York St Stoughton MA 02072

CORCORAN, PHILIP E., wholesale distribution executive. CEO Comark, Bloomingdale, Ill. *

CORCORAN, ROBERT JOSEPH, fund raising executive; b. Boston, Dec. 1, 1929; s. John William and Mary Magdelen (Ryan) C.; m. Edith Therese Fidler, Nov. 3, 1956 (dec. Feb. 1989); children: Robert J. Jr., Gerard J., Michael I.; m. Marie Murphy Clausen, May 31, 1991; children: Mark V., Jeanmarie Whittaker, Annmarie Bremser. AB in Econs. with honors, Boston Coll., Chestnut Hill, 1951; MA, Georgetown U., 1956. Cryptographer Nat. Security Agy., Washington, 1951-52; with bus. tng. program GE, Ashland, Mass., 1955-58; area dir. Mass. div. Am. Cancer Soc., Boston, 1958-63; v.p. The Lavin Co., Boston, 1963-70; sr. v.p. Instl. Fundraising Inc., Boston, 1970-71; pres. Robert J. Corcoran Co., Boston,

1971—. Lt. USN, 1952-55. Mem. Nat. Soc. Fund Raising Execs. (cert.), Boston Coll. Alumni Soc., Boston Latin Sch. Alumni Soc. Democrat. Roman Catholic. Avocations: reading, travel, golf, tennis, swimming. Home and Office: 5 Loew Cir Ste 150 Milton MA 02186-1043

CORCORAN, THOMAS JOSEPH, hotel executive; b. Clay Center, Kansas, Jan. 22, 1949. BA, Washburn U., 1976, JD, 1978. Operator, franchisor ShowBiz Pizza Time, Inc.; with Integra-A Hotel and Restaurant Co., 1979-90, pres., CEO, 1986-90; chmn., pres., CEO Fiesta Foods, Inc., 1990-91; co-founder, pres., CEO FelCor Inc., 1991-94; pres., CEO FelCor Lodging Trust, Irving, Tex., 1994—. Office: FelCor Lodging Trust #1300 545 E John Carpenter Frwy Irving TX 75062

CORDARO, MATTHEW CHARLES, utility executive, energy developer, engineer; b. N.Y.C., July 25, 1943; s. Matteo C. and Josephine (Picone) C.; m. Janet Chick, June 24, 1967; children: Anne-Marie, Allison; m. Martha Warnock, July 18, 1987; 1 child, Marie Elena. B.S., C.W. Post Coll., 1965; M.S. in Nuclear Engring., NYU, 1967; Ph.D. in Engring.and Physics, Cooper Union, 1970. Asst. engr. L.I. Lighting Co., Hicksville, N.Y., from 1966, successively assoc. engr., nuclear physicist, sr. environ. engr., mgr. environ. engring., v.p. engring., 1978-84, v.p. engring. and adminstrn., 1984-85, sr. v.p. ops. and engring., 1985-88; pres. Long Lake Cogeneration Corp., Melville, N.Y., 1988-93; sr. v.p. Long Lake Energy Corp., N.Y.C., 1988-93; pres. and CEO Nashville Electric Svc., 1993—; cons. Bechtel, CMS, GE, Panhandle, Shoreham Project, 1992-93; guest rsch. assoc. Brookhaven Nat. Lab., 1968-71; adj. assoc. prof. nuclear engring. Poly. Inst. N.Y., 1979-80; adj. asst. prof. engring. C.W. Post Coll., 1968-72; former bd. dirs. ctr. for energy studies Adelphi U. Contbr. articles to profl. jours. Mem. Coun. overseers C.W. Post Coll., 1968-72; former mem. campaign coun. L.I. U.; former mem. cmty. adv. bd. Sta. WLIW Pub. TV, Garden City, N.Y.; bd. dirs. Nashville C. of C., Nashville Urban League, Nashville BBB, Nashville Jr. Achievement, Nashville Heart Assn., Tenn. Mcpl. Elec. Power Assn., Tenn. Valley Pub. Power Assn., Nature Conservancy of Tenn.; chmn. Mid. Tenn. U.S. Savs. Bond Campaign, 1995-97; mem. corp. bd. Nashville Bapt. Hosp.; mem. adv. com. Nashville Girl Scouts; trustee Elec. Power Rsch. Inst. AEC fellow, 1965-66. Mem. Am. Pub. Power Assn. (bd. dirs.). Office: Nashville Electric Svc 1214 Church St Nashville TN 37246-0002 *One must try with all their heart to achieve anything of value on this earth. The tragedy of life is not giving your full effort for fear of failure. Never give up, never give in.*

CORDASCO, FRANCESCO, sociologist, educator, author; b. N.Y.C., Nov. 2, 1920; s. Giovanni and Carmela (Madorma) C.; m. Edna Vaughn, Oct. 22, 1946; children—Michael, Carmela. B.A., Columbia, 1942; M.A., N.Y. U., 1945, Ph.D., 1959; student, U. London, U. Salamanca. Prof. English L.I.U., 1946-53; prof. edn. Fairleigh Dickinson U., then; Seton Hall U., 1953-63; prof. edn. Montclair (N.J.) State U., 1963—; vis. prof. N.Y. U., City U. N.Y., U. London, U. P.R.; cons. migration div. Commonwealth P.R., U.S. Office Edn., also municipal, county, state and fed. anti-poverty programs; cons. com. edn. and labor com. U.S. Ho. of Reps., labor and welfare com. U.S. Senate; mem. N.J. adv. council Elementary and Secondary Edn. Act Title III Programs; mem. N.J. Adv. Council Vocat. Edn.; mem. com. on racism and social justice Nat. Council for Social Studies. Author: Research, 1948, 15th edit., 1974, Junius Bibliography, 1949, rev. edit., 1974, 18th Century Bibliographies, 1950, Adam Smith: A Bibliographical Checklist, 1950, Bohn Libraries, 1951, Daniel Coit Gilman and the Protean Ph.D.: The Shaping of American Graduate Education, 1960, A Brief History of Education, 1963, 5th edit., 1981, Educational Sociology, 1965, Education in the Urban Community, 1969, School in the Social Order, 1970, Puerto Rican Community and its Children, 1968, 3d edit., 1982, Jacob Riis Revisited: Poverty and the Slum in Another Era, 1968, Minorities in the American City, 1970, Teacher Education in the United States: A Guide for Foreign Students, 1971, Puerto Ricans on the U.S. Mainland, 1972, Italians in the United States, 1972, Puerto Rican Experience, 1973, Italian American Experience, 1974, Equality of Educational Opportunity, 1973, The Puerto Ricans, 1973, The Italians: Social Backgrounds of an American Group, 1974, Studies in Italian American Social History, 1975, Bibliography of American Educational History, 1975, Bilingual Schooling in the United States, 1976, Immigrant Children in American Schools, 1976, Spanish for Hospital and Medical Personnel, 1977, Tobias G. Smollett, M.D, 1978, Sociology of Education, 1978, Bilingual Education in American Schools, 1979, Medical Education in the U.S, 1979, American Ethnic Groups, 1980, The White Slave Trade and the Immigrants, 1981, American Medical Imprints, 1820-1910: A Bibliography, 1985, Crime in America, 1985, Immigrant Woman in North America, 1985, Junius and His Works, 1986, The New American Immigration, 1987, Italian Emigration to the United States, 1992, Theodore Besterman: Editor and Bibliographer, 1992, Medical Publishing in 19th Century America, 1991, The Archives of American Educational History, 1997, Bilingual Education: An Overview & Inventory, 1998, America & The Quest for Equal Educational Opportunity, 1999, also numerous articles.; Editor: Social History of Poverty, 15 vols, 1968-70, Puerto Rican Experience, 33 vols, 1975, Italian American Experience, 39 vols, 1975, Bilingual Education in the U.S., 40 vols, 1978, American Ethnic Groups: The European Heritage, 47 vols, 1981, Dictionary of American Immigration History, 1990, Homeopathy in the United States, 1991. Mem. bd. edn. Newark Archdiocese; mem. exec. bd. Mt. Carmel Guild; trustee Christ Hosp., Jersey City. Served with AUS, World War II. Recipient Brotherhood award NCCJ, Order Merit Republic Italy. Fellow Am., Brit. sociol. assns.; mem. Soc. Advancement Edn. (trustee). Home: 6606 Jackson St West New York NJ 07093-1705 Office: Montclair State Univ Dept Edn Upper Montclair NJ 07043

CORDASCO, MARTHA ANN, therapist, social worker, consultant; b. Detroit, May 5, 1953; d. Edward Michael and Martha Ann (Bickel) C.; m. Jerome Herb Reaper, Nov. 14, 1986; children: Laura, Valerie, Christopher. BSW, U. Dayton, 1974; MSW Adminstrn., Case Western Res. U., 1984. Lic. ind. social worker, Ohio. Residential counselor DeVeaux Sch., Niagara Falls, N.Y., 1975; social worker Grandview Hosp., Dayton, Ohio, 1981-82; therapist, social worker Assoc. Counselors, Shaker Heights, Ohio, 1984, Dunn Ctr., Richmond, Ind., 1984; therapist, social worker Preble County Counseling Ctr., Eaton, Ohio, 1984-85, clin. coord., 1985-87, acting exec. dir., 1987; pvt. practice Dayton, 1990—. Contbr. articles to profl. jours. Facilitator Mothers At Home, Dayton, 1990. Mem. NASW, Acad. Cert. Social Workers, Network Group. Avocations: equestrian activities, ballroom dancing, antiques, music. Home: 2620 Loris Dr Dayton OH 45449-3225

CORDELL, A(LFRED) ROBERT, cardiothoracic surgeon, educator; b. Union, S.C., Oct. 16, 1924; s. Carl Eugene and Ann Louise (Elsmore) C.; m. Dewitt Cromer, June 4, 1956 (dec. Feb. 1984); children: Alfred Robert Jr., Carl Dewitt, Mark Bynum. BS, U. N.C., 1945; MD, Johns Hopkins U., 1947. Diplomate Am. Bd. Surgery, Am. Bd. Thoracic Surgery. Surg. intern Johns Hopkins U. Hosp., Balt., 1947-48; asst. resident, surgery Yale VA Surg. Svc., Newington, Conn., 1948-50; med. corps, surgeon, chief surg. svc. USNR, Korea and Va., 1950-52; asst. resident gen. and thoracic surgery N.C. Bapt. Hosp., Winston-Salem, 1952-55, resident gen. and thoracic surgery, 1955-56; asst. prof. surgery, assoc. prof. Wake Forest U.-Bapt. Med. Ctr., Winston-Salem, 1958-61, 61-70, prof. surgery, 1970-79, Howard Holt Bradshaw Prof. Surgery, dept. chmn., 1979-91, emeritus prof., 1995—. Contbr. chpts. to books, articles to profl. jours. Bd. mem. Piedmont Opera Theatre Inc., Winston-Salem, Triad Meth. Home, Winston-Salem, Centenary Meth. Ch., Winston-Salem. Recipient Gold Heart Forsyth-Stokes-Davie County (N.C.) Med. Soc., 1997. Fellow Assn. Physician Assts. in Cardiovasc. Surgery (hon.); mem. ACS (bd. govs. 1983-89, Surgeon of Yr. N.C. chpt. 1997), N.C. Stroke Assn. (bd. dirs.), Soc. Thoracic Surgeons, Thoracic Surgery Found. for Rsch. and Edn., Am. Heart Assn. (chmn. mid-Atlantic region 1970-71, bd. dirs. 1966-67), Am. Assn. Thoracic Surgery, So. Thoracic Surg. Assn. (pres. 1971-72), N.C. Heart Assn. (pres. 1966-67, bd. dirs. 1956-75), So. Assn. Vascular Surgery (pres. 1984), Thoracic Surgery Found. (bd. dirs. 1994—). Methodist. Avocations: bonsai, opera, symphony, United Way of Forsyth County. Home: 349 Arbor Rd Winston Salem NC 27104-1909 Office: Wake Forest U Sch Medicine Bapt Med Ctr Medical Center Blvd Winston Salem NC 27157

CORDELL, BEULAH FAYE, special education educator; b. Clifty, Ark., Mar. 5, 1939; m. Jack Cordell; children: Dennis, Kevin. B in English and Social Studies, U. Ark., 1987, M in Spl. Edn. and Reading, 1994. Cert. tchr. K-12, Ark. Tchr. Benton County Alternative Sch., Rogers, Ark., 1988-90, Job Tng. Partnership Act at Fayetteville, Ark., 1990-91; reading and study skills tchr. N.W. Ark. C.C., Rogers, 1991-94; dir. spl. edn. tutoring The One-Room Sch., Springdale, 1993—; kindergarten tchr. Springdale, 1994-96; tchr. ESL and GED N.W. Tech. Inst., 1996—. Contbg. writer The Mailbox Mag., 1999—. Bd. dirs. Ozark Literacy, Inc., Fayetteville, 1984-90; contbg. mem. Beaver Lake Lit., Inc., Rogers, 1994—. Recipient Tchg. Excellence award Gamma Beta Phi, 1993, Outstanding Achievement cert. Internat. Biog. Inst., Cambridge, Eng., 1998. Mem. Coun. for Exceptional Children, Am. Assn. Mentally Retarded, Poets and Writers Assn. Avocations: oil painting, writing poetry and children's fiction. Home: 1100 N Monitor Rd Springdale AR 72764-9024 Office: 807 C Bailey St Springdale AR 72764-4247

CORDELL, FRANCIS MERRITT, instrument engineer, consultant; b. South Pittsburg, Tenn., Sept. 11, 1932; s. Lucien Hall and Sara Frances (Taliaferro) C.; m. Olivia Elizabeth West, June 17, 1950; 1 child, Francis Merritt Jr. LittB, Hamilton Coll., 1966; PhD in Physics, U. Del., 1973. Low speed code operator Dept. Army, Ft. Devens, Mass., 1949-52; materials tester TVA, Stevenson, Ala., 1952-53; instrument mechanic TVA, Stevenson, 1953-57, sr. instrument mechanic, 1957-80, instrumentation supr., 1980-86; prin. restorer, telescope and observatory project U. of the South, Sewanee, Tenn., 1982—; info. cons. South Pittsburg, 1980—; mem. Tenn. Vis. Scientists Program, Associated Univs. for the Tenn. Acad. Sci., Oak Ridge, 1989—. contbng. writer Barnard Astronomical Soc. Jour., 1973—. Recipient Llewellyn Evans award Barnard Astronomical Soc., Chattanooga, 1983. Mem. AAAS, Barnard Astronomical Soc., Instrument Soc. Am., Tenn. Acad. Sci., Astronomical Soc. Pacific. Achievements include restoration of Alvan Clark & Sons refractor and observatory (renamed Cordell-Lorenz Obs.). Home: Medius Lodge Dogwood Trail South Pittsburg TN 37380 Office: Info Consulting 1018 Holly Ave South Pittsburg TN 37380-1432

CORDELL, STEVEN MARK, small business owner; b. Kansas City, Mo., Aug. 18, 1955; s. Arthur Orville and Eva (Miller) C.; m. Sandra Sue Price, Oct. 24, 1981; 1 child, Elizabeth Ann. AA, Penn Valley Coll., 1975; BA, U. Mo., 1977; MBA, Mid Am. Nazarene U., 1994. Store mgr. Radio Shack, Kansas City, 1977-78; sales rep. Harris-Hansen Co., Grandview, Mo., 1978-80; jr. ptnr. Palatine Engring., Mission, Kans., 1980-82; sales engr. T. L. Dowell and Assoc., Overland Park, Kans., 1983-85; sales mgr. Independent Electric, Kansas City, 1985-89; gen. mgr. North Supply div. United Telecom, North Kansas City, 1989-91; lead quality facilitator network ops. Sprint Corp., Overland Park, Kans., 1991-94; owner Money Mailer of South Johnson County, Olathe, Kans., 1994—. Mem. Kansas City Blues Soc., Rotary of Olathe, Olathe C. of C., Phi Theta Kappa. Avocations: hunting, travel, music, music history. Home: 14405 S Kaw Dr Olathe KS 66062-4864 Office: Money Mailer South Johnson County 14405 S Kaw Dr Olathe KS 66062-4864

CORDER, BILLIE FARMER, clinical psychologist, artist; b. Sept. 12, 1934; d. Lee Kennith and Jimmy Louise (Hawkins) Farmer; m. Robert Floyd Corder, July 11, 1961. BS, Memphis State U., 1957; MA, Vanderbilt U., 1959; postgrad., Memphis Acad. Art, 1959, N.C. State U., 1971-75; EdD, U. Ky., 1966. Intern U. Tenn. Sch. Medicine, Memphis, 1959; staff psychologist Ea. State Hosp., Lexington, Ky., 1960-65, Child Guidance Clinic, Lexington, 1965-67; asst. prof. psychology Inter-Am. U., P.R., 1967-68; dir. psychology adolescent day care Area Cmty. Mental Health Ctr., Washington, 1968-70; dir. psychol. svcs. Alcoholic Rehab. Ctr., Butner, N.C., 1970-71; co-dir. psychol. svcs. in child psychiatry Dix Hosp., Raleigh, N.C., 1971—; mem. adv. bd. Raleigh Developmental Evaluation Clnic, 1976-80; adj. faculty psychology dept. N.C. State U., Raleigh, 1975—, U. N.C. Sch. Medicine, 1975—. Contbr. articles to profl. jours.; dir. editl. bd. N.C. Jour. Mental Health, 1974—; adj. editl. rev. bd. Hosp. and Cmty. Psychiatry, Quar. Jour. Studies on Alcohol, Raleigh Acad. Women, 1993. Mem. Wake County Youth Adv. Bd., 1979-80; mem. adv. com. Raleigh Arts Commn., 1980-82; bd. dirs. Haven House for Children, 1980-85, Nazareth House for Children, 1980-85. Recipient best rsch. award N.C. Dept. Mental Health, 1965, cert. of appreciation Washington Tchrs. Assn., 1969, Outstanding Youth Svcs. award Wake Coun., 1991, Hargrove Rsch. award N.C. Mental Health Rsch. Found., 1995, numerous awards for art, including Purchase award N.C. Mus. Art, 1976, awards N.C. Watercolor Soc., 1978, 79; numerous rsch. grants. Mem. APA, AAUW, Southeastern Psychol. Assn., N.C. Psychol. Assn., Am. Assn. Psychiat. Svcs. for Children (program chmn. 1976-77), Raleigh Artists Guild (pres.), Raleigh Fine Arts Soc., N.C. Art Soc., Women's Equity Action League, N.C. Women's Polit. Caucus, Durham Artists Guild, N.C. Watercolor Soc. (v.p.), Wake Visual Artists Assn. (pres.). Office: Dix Hospital Child Psychiatry Clinic Raleigh NC 27611

CORDERO, WILFREDO NIEVA, professional baseball player; b. Mayaguez, P.R., Oct. 3, 1971. Grad. high sch., P.R. Shortstop Montreal Expos, 1992-95, Boston Red Sox, 1996-97, Chgo. White Sox, 1997-98; outfielder Cleve. Indians, 1999—. Named "The Sproting News" Nat. League Silver Slugger Team, 1994, Nat. League All-Star Team, 1994. Office: Cleve Indians Jacobs Field 2401 Ontario St Cleveland OH 44115*

CORDES, ALEXANDER CHARLES, lawyer; b. Buffalo, Aug. 14, 1925; s. Alexander J. and Margaret (Markens) C.; m. Jane Wells, Feb. 9, 1976; children by previous marriage: John J., Ann T., Susan A. BA, Yale U., 1947; LLB, U. Buffalo, 1950. Bar: N.Y. 1950. Assoc. Kenefick, Bass, Letchworth, Baldy & Phillips, 1950-54; asst. U.S. atty. Western Dist. N.Y., 1954-56; ptnr. Phillips, Lytle, Hitchcock, Blaine & Huber, Buffalo, 1956-90, of counsel, 1990—; Mem. Erie County Bd. Suprs., 1960-61. Trustee The Park Sch. Buffalo, 1993-96. With USNR, 1943-46. Fellow Am. Coll. Trial Lawyers, Am. Bar Found., N.Y. Bar Found.; mem. Tennis and Squash Club Buffalo, Pundit Club Buffalo. Presbyterian. Home: 470 Village Pl Apt 316 Longwood FL 32779-6031

CORDES, EUGENE HAROLD, pharmacy and chemistry educator; b. York, Nebr., Apr. 7, 1936; s. Elmer Henry and Ruby Mae (Hofeldt) C.; m. Shirley Ann Morton, Nov. 9, 1957; children: Jennifer Eve, Matthew Henry James. B.S., Calif. Inst. Tech., 1958; Ph.D., Brandeis U., 1962. Instr. chemistry Ind. U., Bloomington, 1962-64, asst. prof., 1964-66, assoc. prof., 1966-68, prof., 1968-79, chmn., 1972-78; exec. dir. biochemistry Merck Sharp and Dohme Research Labs., Rahway, N.J., 1979-84, v.p. biochemistry, 1984-87; v.p. research and devel. Eastman Pharmaceuticals, Malvern, Pa., 1987-88; pres. Sterling Winthrop Pharms. Rsch. div. Sterling Winthrop Inc., Collegeville, Pa., 1988-94; prof. U. Mich., Ann Arbor, 1995—. Author: (with Henry Mahler) Biological Chemistry, 1966, 2d. edit., 1971, Basic Biological Chemistry, 1969, (with Riley Schaeffer) Chemistry, 1973; also articles. NIH Career Devel. award, 1966; Alfred P. Sloan Found. fellow, 1968. Mem. AAAS, Am. Soc. Biol. Chemists. Home: 220 Barton North Dr Ann Arbor MI 48105-1016

CORDES, JOHN F., JR., federal agency administrator. LLB, Georgetown U., 1974. Acting dir. commn. appellate adjudication Nuclear Regulatory Commn., Washington, 1998—. Office: Nuclear Regulatory Commn MS 15B18 Washington DC 20555

CORDES, LOVERNE CHRISTIAN, interior designer; b. Cleve., Feb. 13, 1927; d. Frank Andrew and Loverne Louise (Brown) Christian; m. William Peter Cordes, Nov. 14, 1959; children: Christian Peter, Carey Pomeroy. BS, Purdue U., 1949. Owner, mgr. Loverne Christian Cordes, Chagrin Falls, Ohio, 1967—; tchr. John Carroll U., Cleve., 1976-77. Interior designer, Fred Epple Co., Cleve., 1949-67. Fellow Am. Soc. Interior Designers, AIA, Nat. Home Fashion League (past pres. Ohio chpt.), Am. Inst. Interior Designers (past pres. Ohio chpt., nat. bd. dirs. 1969-75, nat. v.p. East Central region 1972-75, nat. exec. bd. 1972-75, recipient 1st Presdl. citation 1973, 74, 75); mem. Soc. Collectors Dunham Tavern Mus. (bd. dirs. 1961-62), Dunham Dames (past pres.), Western Reserve Hist. Soc., Cleve. Mus. Art, Cleve. Garden Center, Chagrin Falls Hist. Soc., Nat. Trust for Hist. Preservation, Internat. Platform Assn., Am. Furniture Collectors (bd. dirs. 1998—, decorative arts trust v.p. 1998), Audobon Soc., Confrérie de la Chaine des Rôtisseurs, Wallkill Golf Club, Chagrin Valley Country Club, Dogwood Garden Club, Intown Club, Arcadian, Kappa Kappa Gamma. Republican. Congregationalist. Avocations: golf, cross country skiing, wine maker, calligraphy. Address: 60 S Franklin St Chagrin Falls OH 44022-3235 *We must never stop striving to make this world a more beautiful, healhful, safer place for all people and creature to live and enjoy harmoniously.*

CORDINGLEY, MARY JEANETTE BOWLES (MRS. WILLIAM ANDREW CORDINGLEY), social worker, psychologist, artist, writer; b. Des Moines, Jan. 1, 1918; d. William David and Florence (Spurrier) Bowles; m. William Andrew Cordingley, Mar. 17, 1942 (dec. Dec. 1996); children: William Andrew, Thomas Kent, Constance Louise. Student, Stephens Coll., 1936; BA, Carleton Coll., 1939; postgrad., U. Denver, 1944-45; MA in Psychiat. Social Work, U. Minn., 1948, grad. art student, 1963; MA in Counseling Psychology, Pepperdine U., 1985. Co-pub. Univ. News, 1939-40; with U.S.O. Travelers Aid Svc., 1942-44; clin. psychiat. social worker U. Minn. Hosp., 1947-48; social worker cmty. svc. project neuropediats. U. Minn.ue, Mpl, 1964-65; med. dir. med. sch. svc. Mont. Deaconess Hosp., 1970-74; instigator, pres. Original Pioneer Prints Notepaper Co.; therapist Mental Health Ctr., 1977-82. paintings in variety of galleries and traveling shows; exhibited in numerous one-woman shows including Chas. Russell Gallery, Mont., Student Union U. Minn., Nat. Biennial League Am. Pen Women, 1968, 70, U. Mont., 1974, Mont. Traveling Exhibit, 1966-67, Mus. of the Rockies hist. show, 1976, Bergen Art Guild, 1976, 78, U.S. Traveling Show, 1987-89, Russell Auction, 1977, 91, Kessel Long Gallery, Scottsdale, 1991, Great Falls Pub. Libr. hist. art show oil exhibit, 1995, Ariz. Terrain show, Mayo Clinic, Scottsdale, 1991—; illustrator: The Tobacco Route, Geol. Soc. Guide Book, 1992; Mont. Artist Exhibit-Gov.'s Mansion, 1990; graphic artist in metal etchings; co-author: State Arts Coun. Series on Mont. Instns.; author: Speaking With a Brush; represented in Iowa Archives. Mem. Jr. League, Des Moines, 1943, bd. dirs., sec., Mpls., 1951-56; organizer Hazeltine Nat. Golf Club Women's Assn., 1962-64, I & R Ctr., 1967; pres. adv. bd. Mont. State U.; past mem. bd. dirs. United Way; mem. arts adv. bd. Sierra Nev. Coll.; pres. Dollars & Sense, 1965—; former mem. Youth Guidance Home Bd. Recipient various awards. Mem. NASW, State Arts Coun. (art instr. Ariz.), Scottsdale Jr. League (sustainers 1986—), Nat. Mus. Women in Arts (participating). Home: 428 S Cooke St Helena MT 59601-5146

CORDNER, TOM, advertising executive. Co-chmn. bd., creative dir. Team One Advertising, El Segundo, Calif. Office: Team One Advertising Ste 700 1960 E Grand Ave El Segundo CA 90245*

CORDONI, BARBARA KEENE, special education educator; b. Peoria, Ill., Dec. 21, 1933; d. Edward Leland Keene and Grace (Wolpert) Werner; m. Gregory Walter Kupiec, June 9, 1984; children: Mark, Heather, Lance, Tara. BA, Southwestern U., 1955; MEd, Duke U., 1974, EdD, 1976; D in Ednl. Psychology. Certified Sch. Psychologist Specialization in Learning Disabilities. Tchr. Catskills (N.Y.) Pub. Sch., 1955-56, Oneonta (N.Y.) Pub. Sch., 1956-57; dir. Nursery Sch., Woodstock, N.Y., 1959-62; dir. pvt. sch. Merritt Island, Fla., 1967-72; resource tchr. Brevard County Schs., Merritt Island, 1972-73; clin. instr. Duke U., Durham, N.C., 1973-75; asst. prof. Greensboro (N.C) Coll., 1975-77, So. Ill. U., Carbondale, Ill., 1977-81; assoc. prof. So. Ill. U., Carbondale, 1981-87, prof., 1987—; coordinator So. Ill. U. Clin. Ctr. Achieve Program, Carbondale, 1977—; cons. in field. Author: Living with a Learning Disability, 1987, 2d rev. edit., 1990; contbr. numerous articles to profl. jours. Mem. Ill. Gov.'s Adv. Council, Springfield, Ill., 1982-90; participant Pres.'s Commn. for Employment of the Handicapped, Washington. Named Outstanding Woman of the Year, 1970, Brevard County Tchr. of the Year, 1972, Fla. Dist. Tchr. of the Year, 1973; recipient Disting. Teaching award, 1977, Wallace Phillips Meml. Award for Outstanding Svc. in the Field of Learning Disabilities, 1977. Mem. Coun. for Exceptional Children, Learning Disabilities Assn. Am. (Lifetime Achievement award 1997), N.C. Assn. for Rsch. in Edn., Am. Ednl. Rsch. Assn., Internat. Dyslexia Assn., Internat. Acad. for Rsch. in Learning Disabilities, Golden Key, Kappa Delta Pi, Phi Delta Kappa. Democrat. Methodist. Avocations: bird watching, travel abroad. Home: 2037 W Lake Rd Murphysboro IL 62966-5630 Office: So Ill U Dept Ednl Psych/Spl Edn Carbondale IL 62901

CORDOVA, DENISE A., foreign language educator; b. N.Y.C., Jan. 22, 1947. BA, Bklyn. Coll., 1968; MS in Edn., SUNY, New Paltz, 1978; EdD, Fla. Internat. U., 1997. Tchr. adult basic edn.-high sch. equivalency Occupations, Inc., Goshen, N.Y., 1976-80; tchr. French/Spanish Orange County C.C., Middletown, N.Y., 1979-80, Burke H.S., Goshen, 1980-82, Chester Unified Free Sch. Dist., N.Y., 1982-86, Broward County Sch., Fla., 1986—.

CORDOVA, DONALD E., lawyer; b. Trinidad, Colo., Jan. 26, 1938. AB, Regis Coll., 1961; JD, U. Colo., 1964. Bar: Colo. 1964. Asst. U.S. atty. Colo., 1964-68; ptnr. Zarlengo, Mott & Carlin; mem. Denver County Ct. Judicial Selection Commn., 1968-71; ptnr. Cordova, DeMoulin, Harris & Mellon, P.C., Denver; judge U.S. Bankruptcy Ct., Denver; mem. Judicial Conf. Adv. Com. Bankruptcy Rules, 1994—. Mem. ABA (mem. ho. of dels. 1996-98), Denver Bar Assn. (v.p. 1981-82, pres. 1987-88) Colo. Bar Assn. (v.p. 1978-79, mem. bd. govs 1970-72, 80-82, 86-89, Supreme Ct. com. on pattern jury instructions 1987-90), Nat. Conf. Bankruptcy Judges (bd. govs. 1996-99), Hispanic Bar Assn. (pres. 1984), Denver Law Club (pres. 1977-78). Office: US Bankruptcy Ct US Custom House 721 19th St Denver CO 80202-2500

CORDOVA, JEANNE ROBERT, publisher, journalist, activist; b. Bremerhaven, Germany, July 18, 1948; d. Frederick Benedict Jr. and Joan Frances (McGuinness) C.; life ptnr. Lynn Harris Ballen, Aug. 19, 1995. BA, UCLA, 1970, MSW, 1972. Pub. Lesbian Tide Mag., L.A., 1971-80; advt. exec. Cordova Promotional Svcs., L.A., 1980-82; pub. Cmty. Yellow Pages, So. Calif.'s Gay and Lesbian Phone Book, L.A., 1982—, The Spirit of Todos Santos, 1996—; pres. Internat. Gay and Lesbian Archives, L.A., 1995-97; v.p. Connexxus Women's Ctr., L.A., 1984-88. Author: Sexism; It's A Nasty Affair, 1976, Kicking the Habit, 1990; editor: L.A. Free Press, 1973-76; contbr. articles to mags. and anthologies. Mem. Calif. Dem. Party, sec., 1980; pres. Stonewall Dem. Club, 1979-81; organizer Nat. Lesbian Conf., Calif., 1973. Avocations: conversation, psychology, spirituality, creating new organizations. Office: 1604 Vista Del Mar St Los Angeles CA 90028-6420

CORDOVA, MARTIN KEEVIN (MARTY CORDOVA), baseball player; b. Las Vegas, July 10, 1969. Grad. H.S., Las Vegas; student, Orange Coast Coll., Calif., U. Nev., Las Vegas. Outfielder Minn. Twins, 1995—. Named A.L. Rookie of the Yr. Baseball Writers' Assn. of Am., 1995. Office: Minn Twins 34 Kirby Puckett Pl Minneapolis MN 55415-1596*

CORDOVER, RONALD HARVEY, business executive, venture capitalist; b. N.Y.C., Mar. 4, 1943; s. Jack and Ida Cordover; m. Barbara A. Popkin, June 9, 1963; children: Valerie Jill, Jeffrey A. BS and MS in Elec. Engring. and Econ., MIT, 1964, PhD EE, 1967. Researcher, tchr. MIT, Cambridge, 1964-67; ptnr. Newhouse Investing Co., Wayne, N.J., 1983-98; chmn. bd. dirs. Corber Corp., Wayne, 1986—; chmn. bd. The Berkline Corp., Morristown, Tenn., 1988-95; cons. various fin. cmty. and indsl. corps., N.Y.C., 1967—. Contbr. articles to profl. jours. Mem. MIT Edn. Coun., Cambridge, 1982-92, MIT Coun. for Arts, 1986—; pres. bd. trustees The Children's Ctr., Bergen County, N.J., 1972-73; bd. dirs. Daughters of Miriam Found., Wayne, 1987-89. Mem. Tau Beta Pi, Eta Kappa Nu, Sigma Xi. Avocations: squash, art. Office: 400 Newark Pompton Tpke Wayne NJ 07470-6641*

CORDTS, THOMAS JAMES, elementary education educator; b. Cumberland, Md., June 27, 1963; s. Harold John and Jeanne Estella (Moore) C. BS, Frostburg State U., Md., 1985, MEd, 1986. K-12 Advanced Profl. Teaching Cert., Md. Elem. phys. edn. tchr. Hillsmere Elem. Sch., Annapolis, Md., 1986-89, Windsor Farm Elem. Sch., Annapolis, Md., 1989—; asst. boys' soccer coach Annapolis Sr. H.S., 1986-94, head girls' soccer coach, 1995—; summer camp soccer coach U.S. Naval Acad., Annapolis, Md., 1989—, Frostburg State U., 1985—; mem. drown proffing curriculum rewrite com. Anne Arundel County Pub. Schs., 1990. Recipient Gov.'s citation for tchg. excellence, 1993, Capital A Tchr. Recognition, 1993, Md. Phys. Edn. Demonstration Ctr. award President's Coun. on Phys. Fitness and Sports, 1993—, Anne Arundel County Tchr. of Yr. award, 1995, citation Anne Arundel County Coun., 1995, Md. Dept. Edn., 1995. Mem. NEA, AAH-

PERD, Md. Tchrs. Assn., Tchrs. Assn. Anne Arundel County, Md. Assn. Health, Phys. Edn., Recreation and Dance (conv. planning com. 1990-93, v.p. for phys. edn. 1993-94, McNeely merit award 1992), Phi Epsilon Kappa. Avocations: coaching soccer, golf, camping. Office: Windsor Farm Elem School 591 Broadneck Rd Annapolis MD 21401-5503

CORE, DAVID L., federal judge; b. 1940. AB, W.Va. U., 1962, JD, 1970. Magistrate judge U.S. Dist. Ct. (no. dist.) W.Va., Elkins, 1979—. Fax: (304) 637-6210. Office: US Dist Ct (no dist) WVa Jennings Randolph Fed Ctr 300 3d St Rm 200 Elkins WV 26241

CORE, HARRY MICHAEL, psychiatric social worker, mental health therapist and administrator; b. Core, W.Va., Oct. 7, 1933; s. Earl Lemley and Freda Bess (Garrison) C.; m. Jane Ann Boggs, Oct., 1976; children: Kevin M., Brian D., Jennifer T. BS, W.Va. U., 1955; MSW, U. N.C., 1957. Psychiat. social worker Lake County Mental Health Ctr., Mentor, Ohio, 1960-67, asst. dir., 1967-72, exec. dir., 1972-87; psychiat. social worker Simon & Bertschinger MDs, Inc., Eastlake, Ohio, 1966-92; clin. assoc. Kent A. Young, PhD & Assocs., Mentor, Ohio, 1992—; trustee Tri-Care, Inc., Westlake, Ohio, 1986-87. Trustee Western Res. Counseling, Inc., 1988—, Point One Behavioral Health Svcs., 1997—. 1st lt., U.S. Army, 1957-60. Fellow Am. Orthopsychiat. Assn. (life); mem. Acad. Cert. Social Workers, NASW, Ohio Coun. Cmty. Mental Health Agys. (trustee 1981-84, v.p. 1984). Democrat. Mem. Christian Ch. (Disciples of Christ). Home: 6707 Stratford Rd Painesville OH 44077-1533 Office: Lake Ambulatory Care Ctr 9500 Mentor Ave Ste 320 Mentor OH 44060-8702

COREA, CHICK (ARMANDO COREA), pianist, composer; b. Chelsea, Mass., June 12, 1941; s. Armando John and Anna (Zaccone) C.; m. Gayle Moran; children—Thaddeus, Liana. Student, Columbia, 1960, Juilliard Sch. Music, 1961. Founder Stretch Records, L.A., 1992—. Pianist with Mongo Santamaria, 1962; pianist, composer with Blue Mitchell, 1965, Stan Getz, 1966-68; pianist with Miles Davis, 1969-71, Sarah Vaughan, 1970; founder, leader, pianist with group Return to Forever, 1971—; author: The Jazz Style of Chick Corea, 1972; founder group The Elektric Band, 1986; over 100 recs. including Piano Improvisations 1 & 2, Leprechaun, My Spanish Heart, Mad Hatter, Delphi 1, 2, & 3, Light as a Feather, Romantic Warrior, Hymn of the Seventh Galaxy, Music Magic, (with Steve Kujala) Voyage, 1984; toured, recorded The Chick Corea Elektric Band, 1986, Light Years, 1987, (Grammy award, 1989), Eye of the Beholder, 1988 (Best Keyboard Album 1988), Chick Corea Akoustic Band, 1989; record with Elektric Band Inside Out, 1990, Chick Corea Akoustic Band Alive!, 1991, Elektric Band Beneath the Mask, 1991; album Early Circle, 1992, solo album Expressions, 1994, Paint the World, 1993, Time Warp, 1995, Remembering Bud Powell, 1997, Native Sense, 1997, Origin, 1998, Change, 1999; numerous collaborations and appearances on albums with other groups. Recipient 8 Grammy awards and 33 nominations to include Grammy awards, 1990, 6 Playboy Music Poll awards; 19 Downbeat awards including Best Electric Pianist, 1987, Best Electric Group, 1988, Best Electric Piano, 1988, 17 Keyboard Mag. Readers Poll awards, Best Overall Keyboardist, 1988, 89, Best Jazz Piano, 1989, Best Jazz Keyboards, 1988, 89, other awards; named Jazz Life Musician of World, Jazz Forum Music Poll, Europe, 1974, Jazzman of Yr., Swing Jour., Japan, 1978, Swing Jour. Critics Poll, 1980; named Best Electric Jazz Group Downbeat Readers Poll, 1990, Best Acoustic Pianist Jazz Times Reader Poll, 1990, Best Jazz Piano, 1990, Keyboard Sythesist, 1990, Overall Best Keyboardist Keyboard Mag. Readers Poll, 1990, Top Jazz Keyboardist, 1990, Top Jazz Pianist, 1990, #1 in Field of Jazz, 1990, Best Keyboard Player Swing Jour. Mag., 1990. Mem. Ch. of Scientology. Address: 2635 Griffith Park Blvd Los Angeles CA 90039-2519 *I always knew that music would be my life's work, but learning to live life itself has been a constant search for the right way. I searched through rebellion, drugs, diets, mysticism, religions, intellectualism, and much more only to begin to find, with the help of the incredible teachings of L. Ron Hubbard, that truth is basically simple and feels good, clean, and right. And that learning to know myself and communicate with my surroundings with an honest and unafraid intention to really look and be willing to see what's there is the surest way to success.*

COREIL, RAYMOND CLYDE, English educator; b. Ville Platte, La., Nov. 29, 1939; s. Armand Bernard and Thelma (Perrodin) C.; m. Vivian Jr Yi Tsao, June 5, 1976. BA in English, U. Southwe. La., 1961; MFA in Theatre, Carnegie-Mellon U., 1976; PhD in Linguistics, CUNY, 1992. Writer-journalist Daily Advertiser Newspaper, Lafayette, La., 1961-62, La. State U., Baton Rouge, 1963-67; tchr. English U. Hue, Vietnam, 1967-68, U. Abdulaziz, Jeddah, Saudi Arabia, 1968-69, 77-80, U. Saigon, Vietnam, 1970-74, New Jersey City Univ., 1981—; founder Ctr. for Imagination in Lang. Learning, 1997. Playwright numerous stageplays and screenplays; songwriter Remembering Hue, 1968—; editor-founder Jour. Imagination, 1993—. Recipient Edward Sapir award N.Y. Acad. Scis., 1992; Fulbright grantee U.S. Govt., 1972; grantee Nat. Endowment Arts, 1976. Roman Catholic. Avocations: photography, music, painting, linguistics. Home: 17 Fuller Pl Brooklyn NY 11215-6006 Office: New Jersey City Univ 2039 Kennedy Blvd Jersey City NJ 07305-1527

CORELL, ROBERT WALDEN, science administration educator; b. Detroit, Nov. 4, 1934; s. George W. and Grace (Hagland) C.; m. Billie Jo Proctor, June 16, 1956; children: Robert Walden, David Richard, Beth Anne. BSME, Case Inst. Tech., 1956; MS, MIT, 1959, PhD, 1964. Engr. GE, Cleve., 1955, program engr., Lynn, Mass., 1956-57; instr. U. N.H., 1957-58, asst. prof., 1959-60, assoc. prof., 1964-66, prof., 1966-90, chmn. dept. mech. engring., 1964-72, dir. marine program, 1975-87; asst. dir. geoscis. NSF, Arlington, Va., 1987—; rsch. engr. Huggins Hosp., Wolfeboro, N.H., 1957-60, Highland View Hosp., Cleve., 1960-64; vis. investigator Woods Hole Oceanographic Inst., 1965; rsch. assoc., vis. prof. Scripps Instn. Oceanography, 1971-72; vis. prof. U. Wash., 1985; chair U.S. Global Change Rsch. Com. of U.S. Govt., 1987—; numerous positions as chair of interagy. sci. coms. and internat. bodies. Contbr. articles to profl. jours. Founding chair Internat. Group of Funding Agencies for Global Change Rsch., 1988-90; chair Implementation Com. for Inter-Am. Inst. for Global Change Rsch., 1992—; dir. White House Conf. on Sci. and Econs. to Global Change Rsch., 1990. Mem. AAAS, Sigma Xi, Tau Beta Pi, Sigma Alpha Epsilon. Mem. AAAS, Am. Soc. Engring. Edn., IEEE, Marine Tech. Soc., Sigma Xi, Tau Beta Pi, Sigma Alpha Epsilon. Achievements include research in global change, climate and environmental research, medicine, medical engineering, ocean science and technology. Home: 7008 Channel Village Ct # 2L Annapolis MD 21403-5322 Office: NSF Geosciences 4201 Wilson Blvd Arlington VA 22230-0001*

COREY, DAVID THOMAS, invertebrate zoology specialist; b. Saratoga Springs, N.Y., Apr. 12, 1960; s. Raymond Roy and Eleanor Ann (Ahrens) C. AA, U. Cen. Fla., 1981, BS, 1982, MS, 1987; PhD, So. Ill. U., 1993. Sr. mgr. Davgar Restaurants Inc., Winter Park, Fla., 1981-86; rsch. asst. genetics lab. U. Cen. Fla., Orlando, 1984-86, biol. scientist II, 1986-88; rsch. asst. fisheries So. Ill. U., Carbondale, 1989, teaching asst., 1990-93; adj. instr. John A. Logan Coll., 1993; full-time instr. Midlands Tech. Coll., Columbia, S.C., 1994—, Beltline sci. coord. 1996; presenter, manuscript reviewer, reviewer textbook chpts. in field; reviewer grant proposal for Nat. Geographic Soc. Contbr. articles to profl. jours. Recipient Padgett scholarship So. Ill. U. chpt. Sigma Xi, 1993; grantee Exline-Frizzell Fund for Arachnological Rsch., Calif. Acad. Scis., 1983, 87, Fla. Entomol. Soc., 1990, 93. Mem. Am. Arachnol. Soc., Brit. Arachnol. Soc., Lambda Chi Alpha. Avocations: tropical fish, model ship building, scuba diving, photography. Office: Sci Dept Beltline Midlands Tech Coll PO Box 2408 Columbia SC 29202-2408

COREY, ELIAS JAMES, chemistry educator; b. Methuen, Mass., July 12, 1928; s. Elias and Tina (Hashem) C.; m. Claire Higham, Sept. 14, 1961; children: David, John, Susan. BS, MIT, 1948, PhD, 1951; AM (hon.), Harvard U., 1959; DSc (hon.), U. Chgo., 1968, Hofstra U., 1974, Colby Coll., 1976, Oxford U., 1982, U. Liege, 1985, U. Ill., 1985, Kenyon Coll., 1989, Helsinki Coll., 1990, Ariz. U., 1990, Merrimac Coll., 1990, Hokkaido U., 1991, Boston Coll., 1992. From instr. to asst. prof. U. Ill., Champaign-Urbana, 1951-55, prof., 1955-59; prof. chemistry Harvard U., Cambridge, Mass., 1959—, Sheldon Emory prof., 1968—. Contbr. articles to profl. jours. Bd. dirs. phys. sci. Alfred P. Sloan Found., 1967-72; mem. sci. adv. bd. dirs. Robert A. Welch Found. Recipient Intrasci. Found. award, 1968, Ernest Guenther award in chemistry, 1968, Harrison Howe award, 1971, Ciba Found. medal, 1972, Evans award Ohio State U., 1972, Linus Pauling award, 1973, Dickson prize in sci. Carnegie Mellon U., 1973, George Ledlie prize in sci. Harvard U., 1973, Nichols medal, 1977, Buchman award Calif. Inst. Tech., 1978, Franklin medal in sci. Franklin Inst., 1978, Sci. Achievement award CCNY, 1979, J.G. Kirkwood award, Yale U., 1980, C.S. Hamilton award U. Neb., 1980, Chem. Pioneer award, Am. Inst. Chemists, 1981, V.D. Mattia award Roche Inst. Molecular Biology, 1985, Wolf prize (chem.), Wolf Found., 1986, Silliman award, 1986, Japan prize, 1989, Nat. Med. Sci., 1988, Nobel prize in chemistry, 1990, Gold Medal Award, AIC, 1990, Roger Adams award Am. Chem. Soc. 1993, numerous others; fellow Swiss-Am. Exch., 1957, Guggenheim Found., 1957-58, 68-69, Alfred P. Sloan Found., 1956-59. Mem. Am. Acad. Arts and Scis., AAAS, Am. Chem. Soc. (hon., award in synthetic chemistry 1971, Pure Chemistry award 1960, Fritzche award 1968, Md. sect. Remsen award 1974, Arthur C. Cope award 1976, Roger Adams award organic chemistry 1993, Madison Marshall award 1985), Nat. Acad. Sci., Franklin Inst., Chem. Soc. Japan (hon.), Sigma Xi. Office: Harvard U Dept Chemistry 12 Oxford St Cambridge MA 02138-2902*

COREY, GORDON RICHARD, financial advisor, former utilities executive; b. Osceola, Wis., Sept. 27, 1914; s. Ralph Watson and Bessie Mabel (Simpson) C.; m. Margarete Moeller Grenn, 1967; children by previous marriage: Eleanor Corey Tatge, Margaret Corey Amundson, Gordon Ralph, Martha Elizabeth. B.A., U. Wis., 1936; M.B.A., Northwestern, 1940. CPA, Ill. V.p. Commonwealth Edison Co., 1952-62, exec. v.p., 1962-64, chmn. finance com., 1964-73, vice chmn., from 1973; now ret., now pvt. fin. adv. Clubs: Commercial, Wayfarers. Home: 2511 Park Pl Evanston IL 60201-1315

COREY, JEFF, actor, director, educator; b. N.Y.C., Aug. 10, 1914; s. Nathan and Mary (Peskin) C.; m. Hope Victorson, Feb. 26, 1938; children: Eve Corey Poling, Jane, Emily. Student, Feagin Sch. Drama, 1930-32, UCLA, 1955. Prof. drama Calif. State U.-Northridge, 1966-71, Chapman Coll.'s World Campus Afloat, 1973—; founder creative drama workshop Los Angeles Juvenile Hall, 1968; guest lectr. U. Tex., Austin, Ball State U., Muncie, Ind., U. So. Calif., L.A.; mem. faculty Am. Film Inst.; mem. faculty grad. program dramatic writing Tisch Sch. of Art, NYU; mem. adv. coun. Calif. Edn. Theater Assn.; bd. dirs. Ojai Music Festivals Inc.; guest artist U. Ill., Bloomington. Stage actor, N.Y.C., 1932-40, appeared in Hamlet as Rosencranz with Leslie Howard, God Bless Our Bank with Ann Sothern, King Lear, In the Matter of J. Robert Oppenheimer; dir. TV films, various films, 1970—, profl. actors workshop, Hollywood, 1951—; actor numerous films including True Grit, Butch Cassidy and the Sundance Kid, Little Big Man, The Color of Night, Surviving the Game, (starring roles TV series) Helltown, Morning Star/Evening Star; contbr. articles on film, stage acting to profl., popular publs. Served with USNR, 1943-45. Recipient citation USN, 1945. Mem. Acad. Motion Picture Arts and Scis. (actors com. 1970—), Screen Actors Guild (dir.), Dirs. Guild Am., Actors Equity Assn.

COREY, JO ANN, senior management analyst; b. Methuen, Mass., Jan. 26, 1965; d. Joseph Augustine and Marie Ellen (Dowe) C. BA, Calif. State U., Fullerton, 1987, MPA, 1989. Adminstrv. intern City of Brea, Calif., 1987-90; mgmt. analyst City of Mission Viejo, Calif., 1990-92, sr. mgmt. analyst, 1992—. Mem. Mcpl. Mgmt. Assts. So. Calif. (programming com. 1987—, sec. 1997), Calif. Parks and Recreation Soc., Calif. League of Cities, Phi Alpha Theta. Democrat. Roman Catholic. Avocations: music, concerts, trivia, sports. Office: City of Mission Viejo 25909 Pala Mission Viejo CA 92691-2778

COREY, JUDITH ANN, educator; b. Peoria, Ill., Dec. 1, 1937; d. Lyle William and Eileen A. (Zigrang) Springston; m. Thomas W. Corey, Aug. 12, 1961; children: John William, Jeffrey Michael, Gregory Lyle, Mark Andrew. BA in Bus., English, Marycrest Coll., 1960; MA in Counseling, Bradley U., 1972. Lic. tchr. K-12, Ill.; lic. clin. profl. counselor. Tchr. Riverview Sch., Spring Bay, Ill., 1960-61, Lincoln Sch., East Peoria, Ill., 1963-64; counselor Bradley U., Peoria, 1972-73; clin. psychologist intern Zeller Zone Ctr., Peoria, 1973; dean students Morton (Ill.) High Sch., 1974-85; tchr. Jefferson Sch., Morton, 1985—. Contbr. poem to Worlds Greatest Contemporary Poems, 1981 (Hon. Mention). Campaign work Grace Bunn Lievens Ill. Rep., 89th Dist. Ill., Morton, 1994; mem. exec. bd. Ill. State Deans' Assn., 1980-84, historian, 1980-82, membership com., 1982-84. Named to Outstanding Young Women in Am., 1973. Mem. NEA, Ill. Edn. Assn., Morton Edn. Assn. (newsletter editor 1987-90, mem. exec. com. and maj. negotiator 1987-97, v.p. 1993-95), Assn. Play Therapy, Phi Kappa Phi (life), Kappa Gamma Pi, Pi Lambda Theta. Roman Catholic. Avocations: reading, writing, photography, music, nature. Home: 20432 Tennessee Ave Morton IL 61550-9777 Office: Jefferson Sch 220 E Jefferson St Morton IL 61550-2003

COREY, KAY JANIS, business owner, designer, nurse; b. Detroit, Aug. 22, 1942; d. Alexander Michael Corey and Lillian Emiline (Stanley) Kilborn; divorced; children: Tonya Kay, William James, Jason Ronald. Student, C.S. Mott Community Coll., 1960-62, Mich. State U., 1962-64; AA, AS in Nursing, St. Petersburg Jr. Coll., 1978; student, U. South Fla., 1985-86. RN; cert. perioperative nurse; cert. varitypist. Mgr. display Lerner Shops, Flint, Mich., 1960-62; layout artist Abdulla Advt., Flint, 1966-67; varitypist, artist City Hall Print Shop, Flint, 1967-70; nurse Suncoast Hosp., Largo, Fla., 1976-78; nurse, coord. plastic surgery svc., perioperative staff nurse Largo Med. Ctr. Hosp., 1978-81, 84-90; assoc. dir. nursing Roberts Home Health Svc., Pinellas Park, Fla., 1982-84; co-owner Sand Castle Resort, White Bay, Jost Van Dyke, Brit. Virgin Island, 1990-95; perioperative nurse Columbia Golf Coast Surgery Ctr., 1996—; designer, artist K.J. Originals clothing line, 1990-95, The Magic Needle clothing line, 1998; insvc. edn. instr., dir. video edn., team leader oncology dept. Largo Med. Ctr. Hosp., 1980-81, now part-time nurse. Editor, illustrator: (book) Some Questions and Answers About Chemotherapy, 1981, Thoughts for Today, 1981; illustrator (cookbooks) Spices and Spoons, 1982, Yom Tov Essen n' Fressen, 1983; various brochures and catalogues; art work in permanent collection of C.S. Mott Jr. Coll., Flint, 1962; artist, designer of casual and hand painted clothing for children and adults. Historian Am. Businesswomen's Assn., Flint, 1968-73 (scholarship 1976); outreach chmn. Temple B'nai Israel, Clearwater, Fla., 1981-85; regional outreach coord. Union of Am. Hebrew Congregations, N.Y.C., 1983-85. Mem. Assn. of Oper. Rm. Nurses, Phi Theta Kappa. Republican. Jewish. Avocations: sailing, scuba diving, tennis, original teddy bear making. Office: Columbia Gulf Coast Surgery 411 2nd St E Bradenton FL 34208-1001 also: 1500 53rd Ave W Palmetto FL 34221-5510

COREY, KENNETH EDWARD, geography and urban planning educator, researcher; b. Cin., Nov. 11, 1938; s. Kenneth and Helen Ann (Beckman) C.; m. Marie Joann Fye, Aug. 26, 1961; children: Jeffrey Allen, Jennifer Marie. BA with honors, U. Cin., 1961, MA, 1962, M of Community Planning, 1964, PhD, 1969. Instr. U. Cin., 1962-65, asst. prof. community planning, 1965-69, assoc. prof., 1969-74, prof., 1974-79, head grad. community planning and geography, 1969-78; assoc. prof. community planning and geography U. R.I., 1966-67; prof. geography, planning, chmn. dept. geography, dir. urban studies U. Md., 1979-89; prof. geography and urban and regional planning, dean Coll. Social Sci. Mich. State U., East Lansing, 1989-99, sr. rsch. advisor to v.p. for rsch. and grad. studies, 1999—; vis. prof. geography Univ. Wales, Aberystyth, 1974-75, Peking U., 1986; chmn. Cin. Model Cities Bd., 1974; Fulbright rsch. scholar Inst. S.E. Asian Studies, Singapore, 1986, Fulbright group study abroad, Sri Lanka, 1983; trustee Met. Washington Housing Planning Assn., 1980-82. Author: The Local Community, 1968, Community Internships for Undergraduate Geography Students, 1973, The Planning of Change, 3d edit., 1976. Bd. dirs. Potomac River Basin Consortium, Washington, 1982-85. Recipient Service award Community Chest and Council Cin., 1979; recipient Service award Planning Div., 1979, Service award Coalition of Neighborhoods, Cin., 1979, 83, medal of city Mayor of Seoul, South Korea, 1980. Fellow Royal Geog. Soc.; mem. Am. Inst. Cert. Planners, Am. Planning Assn., Assn. Am. Geographers (award spl. group on planning and regional devel. 1985), Assn. Asian Studies, Asia Soc., Pacific Rim Coun. on Urban Devel., World Future Soc. Democrat.

COREY, MARK, historic site director; b. DeKalb, Ill., Aug. 3, 1950. BA, U. Miss., Oxford, 1972. Supt. Ocmulgee Nat. Park, Macon, Ga., 1988-92, Andrew Johnson Nat. Hist. Site, Greenville, Tenn., 1992—. Office: Andrew Johnson Nat Hist Site College and Depot Sts Greeneville TN 37743 also: PO Box 1088 Greeneville TN 37744-1088

COREY, STEPHEN DALE, magazine editor, poet, educator; b. Buffalo, N.Y., Aug. 30, 1948; s. Dale Burton and Julienne Barbara (Holmes) C.; m. Mary Elizabeth Gibson, Jan. 28, 1970; children: Heather, Miranda, Rebecca, Catherine. BA, SUNY, Binghamton, 1971, MA, 1974; PhD, U. Fla., Gainesville, 1979. Instr. English U. Fla., 1979-80; asst. prof. English U. S.C., Columbia, 1980-83; asst. editor The Ga. Rev. U. Ga., Athens, 1983-86, assoc. editor, 1986—. Author: The Last Magician, 1981, Synchronized Swimming, 1985, All These Lands You Call One Country, 1992; editor: Necessary Fictions, 1986, Keener Sounds, 1987, Mortal Fathers and Daughters, 1999. Ga. Coun. Arts literary grantee, 1985-86, 88-89; lit. fellow S.C. Arts Commn., 1981-82; named Author of Yr. Poetry Ga. Coun. Authors & Journalists, Atlanta, 1992, 93. Mem. South Atlantic Modern Lang. Assn., Assoc. Writing Programs. Home: 357 Parkway Dr Athens GA 30606-4951 Office: The Georgia Rev U Ga Athens GA 30602-9009

COREY, STUART MERTON, minister; b. Tacoma, Wash., Apr. 20, 1933; s. Harold Marvin and Vera Lydia (Wonderly) C.; m. Laraine Kathryn Ober, May 1, 1956; children: Nathan, Rebecca, MaryBeth. BS, U.S. Naval Postgrad. Sch., 1961, MS, 1965. Ordained to ministry, 1984. Commd. USN, 1955, advanced through ranks to capt., 1977; served in Korea, Vietnam, ret., 1978, Bible tchr., conf. speaker, 1961—; pres., founder Island Ministries, Oak Harbor, Wash., 1979—; owner Corey Oil Co., Oak Harbor, Wash., 1978—. Adv. coun. Coupeville (Wash.) Pub. Sch., 1982-83; mem. Econ. Devel. Coun., Island County, Wash., 1984-85. With USNR, 1950-53. Mem. North Whibey Ministerial Assn., Petroleum Marketers Assn., Aircraft Pilots & Owners Assn. Home: 431 S Race Rd Coupeville WA 98239-9536 Office: Island Ministries 3124 300th Ave E Oak Harbor WA 98277-3020

CORIGLIANO, JOHN PAUL, composer; b. N.Y.C., Feb. 16, 1938; s. John and Rose (Buzen) C. B.A. cum laude, Columbia U., 1959. disting. prof. music Lehman Coll., N.Y.C.; mem. faculty Juilliard Sch. of Music. Composer: Violin Sonata, 1963, Tournaments Overture, 1965, The Cloisters for Voice and Orch., 1965, Concerto for Piano and Orch., 1988, A Dylan Thomas Trilogy: A Choral Symphony, 1961-76, Concerto for Oboe and Orch., 1975, Etude Fantasy for Piano, 1976, Concerto for Clarinet and Orch., 1977, Promenade Overture, 1981, Summer Fanfare, 1982, Pied Piper Fantasy: Concerto for Flute and Orch., 1982, Fantasia on an Ostinato for Orch., 1985, The Ghosts of Versailles, 1987, Symphony # 1, 1991 (Grawemeyer award 1991), Troubadours (Variations for Guitar and Chamber Orch.), 1993, Fanfares to Music, 1993, Phantasmagoria for Cello and Piano, 1993, String Quartet, 1996, The Red Violin (chaconne for violin and orch.), 1997 (Genie award Best Original Score 1998); film scores Altered States, 1981, Revolution, 1985, The Red Violin, 1998; commns. from N.Y. Philharm., Boston Symphony Orch., James Galway, Van Cliburn Found., Inc., Met. Opera Assn. Guggenheim fellow, 1968; nominee Acad. award and Grammy award for film score Altered States, 1981; recipient Anthony Asquith award for Best Film Score, Brit. Film Inst., 1985, Acad. Inst. Arts and Letters award, 1989, Grawemeyer award for Symphony Number 1, 1991, 2 Grammy awards for Symphony No. 1, 1992, Internat. Classical Music award Composition of Yr. The Ghosts of Versailles (opera), 1992; named Composer of Yr., Musical America, 1992, 2 Grammy awards for string quartet, 1996, Grammy for Symphony No. 1, 1996 (Classical CD of Yr.). Mem. ASCAP, Assn. Classical Music, Acad. Inst. Arts and Letters, Bohemian. Home: 365 W End Ave New York NY 10024-6511 Office: care G. Schirmer Inc 257 Park Ave S 20th Fl New York NY 10010-7304

CORINTHIOS, MICHAEL JEAN GEORGE, electrical engineering educator; b. Cairo, Jan. 19, 1941; arrived in Can., 1965; s. Jean George and Gisèle Michel (Cabbabe) C.; m. Maria Scigalski, Nov. 18, 1967; children: Angela, Gisèle, John. Student, Leonardo DaVinci Art Sch., Cairo, 1952-56; BSc, Ain Shams U., Cairo, 1962; MASc, U. Toronto, 1968, PhD, 1971. Engr. Radio Transmission, Abu Zaabal, Cairo, Egypt, 1962-65; engr. Bell Can., Toronto, Ont., 1965-66, Litton Systems Canada, Toronto, 1968-69; asst. prof. Ecole Poly., Montreal, Que., Can., 1971-74; prof. Ecole Poly., Can., 1977—; vis. scientist U. Nice, France, 1979-80; engring. cons. Huntec Exploration Corp., Toronto, 1970-71; prin. investigator Def. Research Lab., Victoria, B.C., Canada, 1977-81; acad. visitor Imperial Coll. Sci., Tech. and Medicine, London, Eng., 1992-93; pres. Corinthian Games Ltd., Montreal, 1980—; chmn. 2d Internat. Spectral Workshop, Montreal, 1986. Author: How to Patent Your Invention, 1971; Analyse des Signaux Ecole Polytech., 1982; paintings reproduced in Guide Vallee, 1993, Louis Bruens, 1995; contbr. chpts. to books, numerous papers to sci. and profl. jours. Mary H. Beatty fellow U.Toronto, 1969. Fellow IEEE; mem. N.Y. Acad. Sci., (1st prize art competition Montreal chpt. 1979), Art Group 80 (Montreal). Achievements include patents for processors for high speed vector transformation, 1973, for trademarked symmetric chess game Ministers, 1977. Home: # 1204, 5999 Monkland Ave, Montreal, PQ Canada H4A 1H1 Office: Ecole Poly Montreal, CP 6079 Succ A, Montreal, PQ Canada H3C 3A7

CORIO, MARK ANDREW, electronics executive; b. Buffalo, July 18, 1961; s. Anthony Jack and Gertrude Irene (Nordin) C.; m. Lisa Marie Mitchell, May 18, 1985; 1 child, Joshua Robert. BSEE, SUNY, 1983. Elec. engr. Monarch Machine Tool Co., Cortland, N.Y., 1983-85; electronic des. engr. Landis Tool Co., Waynesboro, Pa., 1985-87; controls engr. The Gleason Works, Rochester, N.Y., 1987-88; sr. lab. engr. U. Rochester, 1988-91; sr. devel. engr. Eastman Kodak Co., Rochester, N.Y., 1991-95; pres. Rochester MicroSystems, Inc., 1994—, chmn. bd., 1994—. Patentee in field. Mem. IEEE, Planetary Soc., Internat. Soc. for Analytical Cytology, Internat. Soc. for Optical Engring. Home: 37 Bucky Dr Rochester NY 14624-5407 Office: Rochester MicroSystems Inc 200 Buell Rd Ste 9 Rochester NY 14624-3183

CORK, DONALD BURL, electrical engineer; b. Terre Haute, Ind., Aug. 10, 1949; s. Clay Jr. and Margaret M. (Ellis) C.; m. Carolyn R. Lewis, Nov. 18, 1978. BSEE, U. Evansville, Ind., 1971. Owner Ellcor Electric, West Union, Ill., 1971-73; test engr. Zenith Radio, Paris, Ill., 1973-78, mfg. engr., 1978-81; design engr. TRW Electronics, Marshall, Ill., 1981-84, electrical engr. coord., 1984-88, program mgr., 1988—. Mem. West Union (Ill.) Fire Dept., 1969—, trustee, 1995—; elder West Union Christian Ch. Mem. Eta Kappa Nu, Ea. Ill. Hamateurs (pres. 1971-73), West Union Firemans Assn. (v.p. 1977-78, treas. 1989), Old Nat. Trail Firefighters'. Republican. Avocation: amateur radio. Home: 321 S Walnut St West Union IL 62477-1045 Office: TRW TED PO Box 279 Marshall IL 62441-0279

CORK, EDWIN KENDALL, business and financial consultant; b. Toronto, Ont., Can.; m. Eve Slater, Dec. 31, 1960; children: Sarah, John, Peter, Mary. B in Commerce, U. Toronto, 1954. With Noranda Inc., Toronto, 1959-88; sr. v.p., treas., mng. dir. Sentinel Assocs. Ltd., Toronto, 1988—; bd. dirs. Bank of N.S., Strongco, McCain Foods, United Corp., Rsch. in Motion, Internetsecure, U. Toronto Press; vice-chmn., bd. dirs., E.-L Fin. Corp., chmn., pres., 1991-97; mem. Can. Inst. Internat. Affairs, 1975—; governing coun. U. toronto, 1979-88. Recipient Disting. Bus. Grad. prize U. Toronto, 1987. Christian Science. Clubs: National, Caledon Ski, Hart House.

CORK, LINDA KATHERINE, veterinary pathologist, educator; b. Texarkana, Tex., Dec. 14, 1936; d. Albert James and Martine Sessions (Buntyn) Collins; m. P.S. Cork Jr., Mar. 1955 (div. 1965); children: Robin E., Jerald W. BS, Tex. A&M U., 1969, DVM, 1970; PhD, Wash. State U., 1974. Diplomate Am. Coll. Vet. Pathologists. Fellow Wash. State U., Pullman, 1970-74; asst. prof. U. Ga., Athens, 1974-76; asst. prof. Johns Hopkins U., Balt., 1976-82, assoc. prof., 1982-88, assoc. dir. rsch. Alzheimer's Disease Rsch. Ctr., 1985-93, prof., 1988-93; prof., chmn. Dept. Comparative Medicine Stanford U., 1994—; coun. mem. NIH div. Rsch. Resources, Bethesda, Md., 1985-89; adv. bd. Registry Comparative Pathology, Bethesda. Grantee Nat. Inst. on Aging, 1985-89, Nat. Inst. Health, 1986-91, 86-93, 87-92. Mem. Inst. Medicine, Am. Assn. Neuropathologists (chmn. June 1988), Am. Assn. Pathology, U.S.-Can. Acad. Pathology. Methodist. Avocation: music. Office: Stanford Univ Dept Comparative Medicine MSOB Bldg Stanford CA 94305-5415*

CORKERY, JAMES CALDWELL, retired Canadian government executive, mechanical engineer; b. East Orange, N.J., June 23, 1925; S. Kirk James and

Helen May (Caldwell) C.; m. Jane Woodruff, Sept. 19, 1953; children—Kirk, Candace. B.A. Sc., U. Toronto, Ont., Can., 1948, M.A. Sc., 1950. Registered profl. engr., Ont. Plant mgr. Can. Gen. Electric, Montreal, Que., 1956-61; plant mgr. Can. Gen. Electric, Oakville, Ont., 1961-68; mng. mfg. Can. Gen. Electric, Toronto, 1968-70; regional gen. mgr. Can. Post, Toronto, 1970-77; dep. postmaster gen. Can. Post, Ottawa, Ont., 1977-82; pres. Royal Can. Mint., Ottawa, 1982-86, chmn. bd., 1986-95; pres. Gold. Inst., 1986-88;. Chmn. bd. Oakville Trafalgar Hosp., 1968-72; chmn. Easter Seal Campaign, Ottawa, 1985; chmn. bd. Ottawa Children Treatment Hosp., 1986-89. With RCAF, 1943-45. Mem. Profl. Engrs. Ont., Mint Dirs. Conf. (sec. 1984-86). Anglican. Lodge: Rotary. Avocations: furniture refinishing; antiques; gardening.

CORKERY, PAUL JEROME, author, editor; b. Everett, Mass., Nov. 5, 1946; s. James Richard and Eileen Elizabeth (Collins) C. BA, Harvard U., 1968; postgrad., Clare Hall, Cambridge, Eng., 1968-69. Reporter Boston Herald, 1969-71; asst. to dean Harvard U., Cambridge, 1970-72; editor Boston Phoenix, 1973-74, Boston Mag., 1974-76; articles editor Nat. Enquirer, Lantana, Fla., 1977-79; editl. staff L.A. Herald-Examiner, 1979-82; columnist TV Guide, 1984-85; editor The PJ Page, San Francisco, 1982—; script and tech. cons. various TV and movie prodns., 1981—; editor various books; host Movers and Shakers TV talk show, 1984; frequent guest various TV and radio talk shows, 1984—. Contbr. numerous articles to pubs. including Slate, Harper's, The New Republic, The New Yorker, People, Rolling Stone, TV Guide, Spy, Vanity Fair; author: Carson, 1987. Mem. Selective Svc. Bd., Everett, Mass., 1970-73; mem. Fourth St. Dem. Club, San Francisco, 1992—. Knox fellow Harvard U., 1968. Mem. Authors Guild, Cold Day Club, Harvard Club (Silicon Valley and San Francisco). Office: # 306 1072 Folsom St San Francisco CA 94103-4023

CORKRAN, VIRGINIA B., realtor; b. N.Y.C., Feb. 13, 1924; d. Stuart H. and Bessie (Moses) Bowman; m. Sewell H. Corkran, Jr., June 15, 1946; children: Sewell H. III, Leslie C. Price. BA, Conn. Coll., 1945. Tchr. Low-Heywood Sch., Stamford, Conn., 1946-47; editor North Shore Calendar, Winnetka, Ill., 1955-59; real estate assoc. Lodge McKee Realty Inc., Naples, Fla., 1969—. Elected Naples City Coun., 1974-78; pres. Old Naples Assn., 1995-97; past bd. dirs. Big Cypress Nature Ctr., Naples, Southwest Heritage, Inc., Naples, The Conservancy, Inc., Collier County LWV. Recipient Guy Bradley award Collier County Audubon, ONA award Old Naples Assn., 1998. Office: Lodge McKee Realty Inc 600 5th Ave S Naples FL 34102

CORLE, FREDERIC WILLIAM, II, government relations executive; b. Phila., June 20, 1945; s. Frederic William and Marjorie (Dudley) C.; m. Pamela Gaus White, Apr. 16, 1983 (div. May 1987); children: Alison Gaus, Louise Armour; m. Morrell T. Taggart, Dec. 9, 1995. BA, Marietta Coll., 1967; MBA, U. Denver, 1973. Supply mgmt. officer Fed. Deposit Ins. Corp., Washington, 1970-72; program analyst Exec. Office of Pres., Washington, 1973-77; dir. Commn. on Budget U.S. Ho. of Reps., Washington, 1977-78; v.p. City Sports Mgmt., Inc., Washington, 1978-82; asst. to adminstr. White House, Washington, 1983-84; dir. mktg. Interand Corp., Washington, 1984-85; spl. asst. Dept. of Interior, Washington, 1985-86; mgr. fed. mktg. Datapoint Corp., Washington, 1987-89; chief exec. officer Mktg. Solutions Internat., Inc., Washington, 1989—; bd. dirs., dir. fed. mktg. Sun Microsystems Fed. Inc., Washington, 1991—; ptnr. Potomac Rsch. Group, Washington, 1996—. Served as lt. (j.g.) USN, 1967-70. Mem. Armed Forces Communications and Electronics Assn., Am. Electronics Assn. (govt. and bus. com.), Nat. Assn. Mfrs., Calif. Policy Steering Com., City Tavern Club, Army Navy Country Club. Republican. Episcopalian.

CORLESS, DOROTHY ALICE, nurse educator; b. Reno, Nev., May 28, 1943; d. John Ludwig and Vera Leach (Wilson) Adams; children: James Lawrence Jr., Dorothy Adele Carroll. RN, St. Luke's Sch. Nursing, 1964. Clinician, cons., educator, grant author, adminstr. Fresno County Mental Health Dept., 1970-94; pvt. practice mental health nurse Fresno, 1991-94; instr. police sci. State Ctr. Tng. Facility, 1991-94; pvt. practice, mental health con., educator Florence, Oreg., 1994—. Res. asst. officer ARC, Disaster Mental Health Svcs., 1993—. Maj. USAFR, 1972-94. Mem. NAFE, Forensic Mental Health Assn. Calif., Calif. Peace Officer's Assn., Critical Incident Stress Found. Office: 2006 Highway 101 Florence OR 97439-9723

CORLETO, RAYMOND ANTHONY, lawyer; b. Bklyn., Nov. 27, 1931; s. Sal A. and Ida (Cianci) C.; m. Annette Grasso, Aug. 30, 1958; children: Anthony, Brian, Suzann, Todd. BA, Bklyn. Coll., 1953; LLB, Bklyn. Law Sch., 1959. Bar: N.Y. 1960, U.S. Ct. Appeals (2d cir.) 1991, U.S. Claims Ct. 1991, U.S. Supreme Ct. 1991. Assoc. Morris, Duffy, Ivone & Jensen, N.Y.C., 1976-82; ptnr. Schiavetti, Begos & Nicholson, N.Y.C., 1982-88, Rossano, Mosé, Hirschhorn & Corleto, Garden City, N.Y., 1988—; mem. med. malpractice panels Supreme Ct. Nassau County, 1982-91. Cpl. U.S. Army, 1953-55, Germany. Mem. Nassau County Bar Assn., Nassau Suffolk Trial Lawyers, Def. Rsch. Inst., Def. Assn. N.Y., Columbian Lawyers Nassau. Republican. Roman Catholic. Avocations: golf, chorus. Office: Rossano Mose Corleto & Andron PC 595 Stewart Ave Ste 700 Garden City NY 11530-4742

CORLETT, CLEVE EDWARD, government administrator; b. Boise, Idaho, July 19, 1940; s. Edward John and Bertha (Wagner) C.; m. Ruth Ann Augspurger, Dec. 26, 1961; children: Christopher Sean, Gregory Cleve. Student, Coll. of Idaho, 1958-60; BA, George Washington U., 1963. Reporter UPI, Washington, 1960-64; Washington corr. Fed. Publs., Washington, 1964-68; press sec. U.S. Senator Frank Church, Washington, 1968-75, 76-81, U.S. Senator Joseph R. Biden, Washington, 1975-76, U.S. Senator John H. Chafee, Washington, 1981-87; dir. pub. affairs U.S. Gen. Acctg. Office, Washington, 1987-95, dir. external affairs, 1996—. Episcopalian. Avocation: photography. Office: Gen Acctg Office Pub Affairs 441 G St NW Washington DC 20548-0002

CORLETT, WILLIAM ALBERT, retired aerospace engineer; b. Talala, Okla., Mar. 5, 1938; s. William Forest and Floy Opal (Gill) C.; m. Patricia Anne Harrison, May 31, 1964; children: William Edward, Cynthia Anne, Mary Anne. BS, U. Okla., 1962. Aerospace engr. NASA, Langley Rsch. Ctr., Hampton, Va., 1962-75, head exptl. methods sect., 1975-79, head unitary wind tunnel ops. office, 1979-95; ret., 1995; exptl. aerodynamics cons. Dept. of Def., prin. investigator aero-space plane project. Contbr. articles to profl. jours. Deacon Hampton Bapt. Ch., 1991—. Recipient Apollo Achievement award, NASA, 1969, Lightweight Fighter Prototype Support Team Achievement award, 1976, Superior Accomplishment award, 1990. Fellow AIAA (assoc.). Baptist. Home: 24 Laurel Wood Rd Newport News VA 23602-6111

CORLEW, JOHN GORDON, lawyer; b. Dyersburg, Tenn., July 13, 1943; s. Emmett Atkins and Margaret Elizabeth (Swann) C.; m. Elizabeth Lee Scott, July 8, 1967; children: John Scott, William Heath, Carey Elizabeth. BA, U. Miss., 1965; JD, Vanderbilt U., 1968. Bar: Miss. 1968. Clk. to judge U.S. Dist. Ct. (so. dist.) Miss., 1968-69; assoc., then ptnr. Megehee, Brown, Williams & Corlew, Pascagoula, Miss., 1969-74; sole practice Pascagoula, 1975-78; ptnr. Corlew, Krebs & Hammond, Pascagoula, 1978-84, Watkins & Eager, Jackson, Miss., 1984. Mem. Miss. State Senate, 1974-80, chmn. appropriations com., 1979, chmn. constn. com., 1975-79, chmn. legis. audit com., 1978; chmn. Miss. State Bd. Pub. Welfare, 1980-84. Mem. ABA, Miss. Bar Assn., Hinds County Bar Assn., Miss. Bar Found., Order of Coit, Phi Delta Phi. Democrat. Methodist. Home: 2124 Eastover Dr Jackson MS 39211-6719 Office: Emporium Bldg 400 E Capitol St Jackson MS 39201-2602

CORLEY, CAROL LEE, school nurse; b. Waco, Tex., Feb. 2, 1943; d. Henry Lee (dec.) and Irma Geraldine (King) Cranfill; m. Thomas Lane Corley, May 22, 1965; 1 child, Christopher Lyn. ADN, McLennan C.C., 1974; BSN, U. Tex.-Arlington, 1983. Staff nurse ICU Providence Health Ctr., Waco, Tex., 1974; sch. nurse Crawford (Tex.) Ind. Sch. Dist., 1975-79; coord. sch. nurse Midway Ind. Sch. Dist., Waco, 1979—. Mem. ANA, Tex. Nurses Assn. (dist. 10 pres. 1992-94, past v.p.), Tex. Assn. Sch. Nurses (dist. 12 pres. 1990), Tex. Sch. Nurses Adminstrs. Assn., Sigma Theta Tau. Home: 8930 Raven Dr Waco TX 76712-3453 Office: Midway ISD 1205 Foundation Dr Waco TX 76712-6899

CORLEY, CHARLES J., middle school educator. Middle sch. tchr. McCall Middle Sch. Recipient Tchr. Excellence award Internat. Tech. Edn. Assn., 1992. *

CORLEY, JEAN ARNETTE LEISTER, infosystems executive; b. Charleston, S.C., June 16, 1944; d. William Audley and Arnette (Mason) Leister; m. Fred G. Wix, Aug. 27, 1995; children: Arnette Elizabeth, Daniel Lee, Heather, Gretchen. BS, Med. Coll. Ga., 1970; MBA, M of Pub. Adminstrn., Georgetown U., 1980. Various positions health care orgns., Augusta, Ga., 1960-70; office mgr., counselor Info. Ctr. for Alcohol and Drug Abuse, Augusta, 1970-71; planner health care systems Nat. Med. Assn. Found., Washington, 1971-72; research assoc., systems analyst GEOMET, Inc., Gaithersburg, Md., 1972-74; dir. med. records Georgetown U. Hosp., Washington, 1974-80; dir. med. info. svcs. Lahey Clinic Med. Ctr., Burlington, Mass., 1980-84; nat. sales mgr. 3M Health Info. Systems, Boston and Atlanta, 1984-91; mktg. mgr. 3M Health Info. Systems, Salt Lake City, 1992—. Contbr. articles to profl. jours. Mem. adv. bd. various colls., 1973-96; grad. proctor U. Ala., U. Utah, Brigham Young U., Ohio State U.; active Habitat for Humanity, Leadership Utah. Mem. Am. Health Info. Mgmt. Assn. (program com. 1977-80, chmn. 1981-82, fed. health program adv. com. 1978-80, computerized health info. task force 1983-87, subcom. on edn. 1990-93, Workgroup on Electronic Data Interchange 1992-94), Computer-based Patient Record Inst., Women in Info. Processing, New Eng. Med. Records Conf. (exec. dir. 1984-88), LWV, Emily's List, Utah Women's Polit. Caucus. Democrat. Presbyterian. Avocations: reading, restoring old houses, boating, cooking. Home: 545 De Soto St Salt Lake City UT 84103-2134

CORLEY, JENNY LYND WERTHEIM, elementary education educator; b. Lincoln, Ill., June 18, 1937; d. Robert Glenn and Nancy Lynd (Hoblit) Wertheim; m. William Gene Corley, Aug. 9, 1959; children: Anne Lynd Corley Baum, Robert William, Scott Elson. BS in Music Edn., U. Ill., 1959, MS in Music Edn., 1961; postgrad., U. Ill., Loyola U., 1985—. Tchr. choral music Mahomet (Ill.)/Seymour K-12, 1959-61; supr. music Fairfax County (Va.), 1961-63; Tchr. music Highland Park (Ill.) 107, 1969, dir. gifted edn., 1969-70; tchr. music Glenview (Ill.) 34, 1981—; v.p. Corley Agroleum Properties, 1993—; water safety instr./trainer ARC; lifeguard instr./trainer Cmty. First Aid & Safety, 1995. Dir. mid-Am. bd. ARC, Chgo., 1980-86; mem. Chgo. Symhony Orch. Chorus, 1965-75. Recipient Heart of Gold United Way, 1992, Community Svc. award Ill. Park & Recreation Assn./Ill. Assn. Park Dists., 1994, Disting. Svc. award Boys and Girls Swimming Official, Ill. High Sch. Assn., 1994. Mem. Music Edn. Nat. Conf., North Shore Music Tchrs. Assn. (treas. 1987-90), Jr. League Chgo. (treas. 1978-81), Sigma Alpha Iota, Phi Delta Kappa (found. chmn. 1994—), U. Ill. Music Alumnae (pres. bd. dirs. 1995-97). Presbyterian. Home: 744 Glenayre Dr Glenview IL 60025-4411 Office: Springman Sch 2701 Central Rd Glenview IL 60025-4134

CORLEY, JOHN D. W., military officer. BS in Engring., USAF Acad., 1973; grad., Squadron Officer's Sch., 1978; MBA, U. of The Philippines, Manila, 1984; grad., Air Command and Staff Coll., 1985, Naval Command and Staff Coll., 1986; M in Nat. Security and Strategic Studies, 1986; grad., Army War Coll., 1992. Commd. 2d lt. USAF, 1973, advanced through grades to col., 1994; instr. pilot, flight examiner 64th Flying Tng. Wing, Reese AFB, Tex., 1974-78, 49th Tactical Fighter Wing, Holloman AFB, N.Mex., 1979-82; flight comdr. 26th Aggressor Squadron, chief Aggressor Ops., Clark Air Base, The Philippines, 1982-85; analyst advanced tactical fighter Air Force Ctr. for Studies and Analyses, Washington, 1986-88; analyst comdr.'s action group Tactical Air Command, Langley AFB, Va., 1988-90; ops. officer 7th Fighter Squadron, comdr. 8th Fighter Squadron, 49th Fighter Wing, Holloman AFB, N.Mex., 1990-92; comdr. 33d Ops. Group, 33d Fighter Wing, Eglin AFB, Fla., 1993-95; chief Western Hemisphere divsn. Directorate of Strategic Plans and Policy, J-5 Joint Staff, 1995-97; comdr. 355th Wing, Davis-Monthan aFB, Ariz., 1997—. Decorated Def. Superior Svc. medal, Def. Meritorious Svc. medal, Meritorious Svc. medal with 4 oak leaf clusters. Office: 355 WG/CC 5275 E Granite St Davis Monthan A F B AZ 85707

CORLEY, ROSE ANN MCAFEE, government official; b. Lawton, Okla., Aug. 21, 1952; d. Claude James and Mary Margaret (Holman) McAfee; m. Gary Michael Griffin, Feb. 14, 1973 (div. Oct. 1984); m. Terry Joe Corley, July 31, 1988; stepson Troy Justin Corley. BS, Cameron U., Lawton, Okla., 1970; diploma, Army Command and Staff Coll., Ft. Leavenworth, Kans., 1989; MCJA, Oklahoma City U., 1990; cert., Army Mgmt. Staff Coll., Ft. Belvoir, Va., 1991. Cert. in Distbn. Mgt. Supply clk. Dept. of Army, Ft. Sill, Okla., 1972-80, supply mgmt. asst., 1980-82; supply systems analyst Dept. of Army, Ft. Lee, Va., 1982; supply tech. Dept. of Army, Ft. Sill, Okla., 1982-83, supr. inventory mgmt. specialist, 1983-86, manprint program mgr., 1986-91; weapon system advisor Def. Logistics Agy., San Antonio, 1991-96; customer svc. rep. Def. Logistics Agy., Robins AFB, Ga., 1996-98; dir. supply mgmt. NIH, Rockville, Md., 1998—; equal employment counselor USA Field Artillery Sch., Ft. Sill, Okla., 1976-82; mentor Fed. Women's Program, Kelly AFB, Tex., 1991-96. Recipient Cert. of Appreciation, Sec. of Def., Washington, 1984, Cert. of Appreciation, Directorate of Engring. and Housing, Ft. Sill, 1986; decorated Order of St. Barbara, U.S. Army Arty. Sch., Ft. Sill, 1991. Mem. Fed. Women's Program, Soc. Logistics Engrs., Fed. Mgrs. Assn., Kelly Mgmt. Assn., World Affairs Coun. of San Antonio, Internat. City Mgmt. Assn., Tex. Corvette Assn. Avocations: autocrossing, reading, golf, crafts. Home: 11706 Balsamwood Ter Laurel MD 20708-3175 Office: NIH Office Logistics Mgmt 6011 Executive Blvd Rockville MD 20852-3804

CORLEY, SARAH TAYLOR, physician; b. Great Lakes, Ill., May 19, 1956; d. Frank Winston and Alice Jean Corley. BS in Chemistry, Va. Commonwealth U., 1982; MD, U. Va., 1986. Intern in internal medicine Stamford Hosp.; resident in internal medicine U. Va.; staff physician Group Health Assocs., Annandale, Va., 1989-94; physician Internal Medicine Assocs., Arlington, Va., 1994—; bd. dirs. Practice Ptnr. Rsch. Network, Charleston, S.C., 1996—. Vol. physician Arlington Free Clinic, 1996—. Fellow ACP (mem. coun. Va. chpt. 1996—), Phi Kappa Phi. Avocations: scuba diving, in-line skating. Office: 4840A 31st St S Arlington VA 22206-1654

CORLEY, WILLIAM GENE, engineering research executive; b. Shelbyville, Ill., Dec. 19, 1935; s. Clarence William and Mary Winifred (Douthit) C.; m. Jenny Lynd Wertheim, Aug. 9, 1959; children: Anne Lynd, Robert William, Scott Elson. BS, U. Ill., 1958, MS, 1960, PhD, 1961. Lic. profl. engr., Ill., Va., Wash., Calif., Miss., Fla., La., Pa., Ala., Hawaii, Tenn., Tex., Utah, Mich., Mo., S.D., Tenn.; lic. structural engr., Ill.; chartered structural engr., U.K. Devel. engr. Portland Cement Assn., Skokie, Ill., 1964-66, mgr. structural devel. sect., 1966-74, dir. engring. devel. div., 1974-86; v.p. Constrn. Tech. Labs., Inc. (formerly Portland Cement Assn.), Skokie, 1986—; mem. adv. panels NSF. Contbr. articles to tech. and profl. jours. Pres. caucus Glenview (Ill.) Sch. Bd., 1971-72; elder United Presbyn. Ch., 1975-79; sec. bd. dirs. Assn. Ho., Chgo., 1976, treas., 1977, pres., 1978-79; chmn. bd. dirs. North Cook dist. ARC, bd. dirs. Mid-Am. chpt., chmn. North Region Coun., 1988-92; mem. Gov.'s (Ill.) Earthquake Preparedness Task Force. Recipient Wason medal for Research, 1970; Martin Korn award Prestressed Concrete Inst., 1978; Reinforced Concrete Rsch. Coun. Authur J. Boase award, 1986. Fellow ASCE (T.Y. Lin award 1979, lifetime achievement award 1994), Inst. Structural Engrs., Am. Concrete Inst. (Bloem award 1978, Reese structural rsch. award 1986, Henry C. Turner award 1988, Ferguson lectr. 1991, bd. dirs. 1994-97, Henry Crown award 1997); mem. NSPE, Reunion Internationale des Laboratoires d'Essais et Recherchas sur Materiaux Construction, Earthquake Engring. Rsch. Inst. (chpt. sec., treas. 1980-82, chmn. 1984-86), Internat. Assn. Bridge and Structural Engring., Structural Engrs. Assn. Ill. (pres. 1986-87, meritorious publ. award 1993, 97, John Parmer award 1997), Nat. Coun. Structural Engrs. Assns. (pres. 1996-97), Post-Tensioning Inst., Chgo. Com. High-Rise Bldgs. (vice chmn. 1978-82, chmn. 1982-84), Bldg. Seismic Safety Coun. (vice-chmn. 1983-85, sec. 1985-87). Presbyterian. Home: 744 Glenayre Dr Glenview IL 60025-4411 Office: Construction Tech Labs Inc 5420 Old Orchard Rd Skokie IL 60077-1053

CORLISS, JOHN OZRO, zoology educator; b. Coats, Kans., Feb. 23, 1922; s. Clark L. and Catharine (Smith) C.; children: Susan Elizabeth, Joan Alison, Kimberley Ann, Jeniffer Sara Corliss; m. Yuemei Geng, June, 1992. BS, U. Chgo., 1944; BA, U. Vt., 1947; PhD, NYU, 1951; DSc (hon.), Universite de Clermont, France, 1973. Postdoctoral fellow AEC, Coll. de France, Paris, 1951-52; instr. zoology Yale, 1952-54; asst. prof. to prof. zoology U. Ill., Urbana, 1954-64; prof., head dept. biol. scis. U. Ill., Chgo. Circle, 1964-69; dir. systematic zoology NSF, 1969-70; prof., chmn. dept. zoology U. Md., College Park, 1970-87, prof., 1987-89, emeritus prof., 1989—; adj. prof. U. N.Mex., Albuquerque, 1988-96; hon. rsch. assoc. zoology Univ. Coll., London, 1960-61; vis. prof. zoology U. Exeter, Eng., 1961-62; vis. prof. protozoology, Shanghai, China, 1980, 86, Geneva, 1980; mem. panel systematic biology NSF, 1966-69; active Nat. Com. Internat. Biol. program, 1966-68; mem. Internat. Commn. on Zool. Nomenclature, 1972-96; mem. corp. Marine Biol. Lab., Woods Hole, Mass. Author: The Ciliate Protozoa, 1961, 2d edit., 1979; joint editor 5 books on protistology, 1984-91; contbr. articles on protozoology/protistology to profl. jours. Served to capt. USAAF, 1943-46. Fellow AAAS, Am. Inst. Biol. Scis., Am. Acad. Microbiology; mem. Soc. Protozoologists (past pres, mem. editl. bd., past editor), Am. Micros. Soc. (past editor, past pres.), Am. Zool. Soc. (hon.), French Zool. Soc. (hon.), Spanish Zool. Soc. (hon.), Mexican Zool. Soc. (hon.), Italian Zool. Soc. (hon.), Coun. Biology Editors (past chmn., CBE Meritorious award 1982), Am. Soc. Zoologists (past pres.), Soc. Systematic Zoology (past pres.), Am. Soc. Parasitologists, Am. Soc. Microbiology (U.S. Fedn. Culture Collections/J. Roger Porter award 1994), Internat. Congress Systematic and Evolutionary Biology (convenor 1970-74, 76-80), Internat. Union Biol. Scis. (chmn. U.S. nat. com. 1971-73), numerous others. Home: 730 Yale Rd Bala Cynwyd PA 19004-2116 Address: PO Box 2729 Bala Cynwyd PA 19004-6729

CORMAN, EUGENE HAROLD, motion picture producer; b. Detroit, Sept. 24, 1927; s. William and Anne (High) C.; m. Nan Chandler Morris, Sept. 4, 1955; children: Todd William, Craig Allan. B.A., Stanford U., 1948. Vice-pres. Music Corp. Am., Beverly Hills, Calif., 1950-57; owner, operator Corman Co., Beverly Hills, 1957—; pres. Penelope Prodn. Inc., Los Angeles, 1965—, Chateau Prodn. Inc., Los Angeles, 1972—; v.p. 20th Century Fox TV, Beverly Hills; exec. v.p. 21st Century Film Corp. of Worldwide Prodn. Producer: The Big Red One, 1978-79, F.I.S.T, 1977-78. Recipient Emmy award for A Woman Called Golda, Cath. Christopher award for A Woman Called Golda. Mem. Acad. Motion Picture Arts and Scis., TV Acad. Arts and Scis., Los Angeles County Mus. Art (patron), Beverly Hills Tennis Club, Theta Delta Chi. Roman Catholic. Office: 20th Century Fox TV PO Box 900 Beverly Hills CA 90213-0900

CORMAN, JACK BERNARD, lawyer, investment manager; b. Hillsboro, Tex., Nov. 16, 1926; s. Maxwell A. and Lillie (Wood) C.; children from previous marriage: Michael, Catherine, Laura; m. Annette Adler, Sept. 1991. BBA, U. Tex., 1948, LLB, 1948. Bar: Tex. 1948. Assoc. Conway & Schaff, Waco, Tex., 1948-50; lawyer Stanolind Oil & Gas Co., Ft. Worth, 1950-52; lawyer The Brit. Am. Oil Co., Dallas, 1952-56, gen. counsel, 1958-65; assoc. Carrington Gowan Law Firm, Dallas, 1956-58; assoc. gen. counsel Tenneco, Houston, 1965-66; pres. Opco Oil & Gas. Co., Dallas, 1966-70; pvt. practice Dallas, 1970—; bd. dirs. Forum Cos., Dallas, 1970—, Forum Oil and Gas. Co., Dallas, 1970—. 1st lt. U.S. Army, 1943-44. Home: 7364 Meadow Oaks Dr Dallas TX 75230-4227 Office: 10830 N Central Expy Ste 160 Dallas TX 75231-1022

CORMAN, JULIE ANN, producer, director; b. Omaha, June 22, 1942; d. Gordon Francis Halloran and Mary Julia (Corcoran) Halloran-Ferrier; m. Roger William Corman, Dec. 26, 1970; children: Catherine, Roger, Brian, Mary. BA, UCLA, 1964. V.p. New World Pictures, L.A., 1971-83; exec. v.p. Concorde-New Horizons Pictures, Inc., L.A., 1984—; pres. Trinity Pictures, Inc., L.A., 1984—; conf. chmn. UCLA Extension, 1991. Producer (films) Boxcar Bertha, 1972, Crazy Mama, 1975, Lady in Red, 1976, The Dirt Bike Kid, 1985, DA, 1988, A Cry in the Wild (Silver medal Houston Internat. Film Festival 1990), (TV movie) Drop Out Mother, 1988, White Wolves series, 1990-95, Max is Missing, 1995, Legend of the Lost Tomb, 1996, The Westing Game, 1997. Mem. Air Resources Bd., Calif., Internat. Women's Forum, 1990. Named Prodr. of Yr. Acad. Family Film, 1996. Mem. Women in Film. Roman Catholic. Office: Trinity Pictures 11600 San Vicente Blvd Los Angeles CA 90049-5102

CORMAN, MARVIN LEONARD, surgeon, educator; b. Phila., Dec. 17, 1939; s. Joseph Mayer and Dorothy Frances (Stern) C.; children: John Mayer, Alexander Stern. BA, U. Pa., 1961, MD, 1965. Diplomate Nat. Bd. Med. Examiners, Am. Bd. Surgery, Am. Bd. Colon and Rectal Surgery; lic. surgeon, Mass., N.J., Fla., Calif. Sr. registrar, vis. lectr. gen. infirmary, prof. surg. unit U. Leeds, Eng., 1968-69; surg. intern Boston City Hosp.-Fifth (Harvard) Surg. Svc., 1965, surg. resident, 1966-68, surg. resident, chief surg. resident, 1969-71; staff surgeon divsn. colon and rectal surgery, dept. surgery Lahey Clinic Med. Ctr., Boston, 1971-81, Sansum Med. Clinic, Santa Barbara, Calif., 1981-95; surgeon divsn. colon and rectal surgery UCLA, 1996-98; prof. surgery U. So. Calif. Sch. Medicine, 1998—; instr. surgery Sch. Medicine Harvard U., Boston, 1972-77, clin. asst. prof. surgery, 1977-82, prof. surgery UCLA, 1996—; co-dir. tng. program colon and rectal surgery Sansum Med. clinic, 1981-95, chmn. divsn. edn., 1983-90; credentials com. Santa Barbara Cottage Hosp., 1984-95, mem. libr. com., 1985-95, mem. com. on grad. med. edn., 1989-94, vice-chmn. dept. surgery, 1994-95; pres. alumni assn. Harvard Surg. Svc., Boston City Hosp., 1983-84; vis. prof. U. Tex. Health Sci. Ctr., San Antonio, 1982, Throckmorton Surg. Soc., Des Moines, 1985, Ogden (Utah) Surg. Soc., 1985, 20th ann. Surg. Congress Orange County Surg. Soc., Newport Beach, Calif., 1988, Royal Australasian Coll. Surgeons, Adelaide, Australia, 1989, Northwest Permanente Dept. Surgery, Portland, Oreg., 1990, Hahnemann U., Phila., 1991, El Colegio de Cirujanos Gererales de Mexicali, Mexico, 1991, Cleve. Clinic Fla., Ft. Lauderdale, Fla., 1992, Univ. Hosp. de Clinicas do Parana, Curitiba, Brazil, 1993; Ralph Coffey vis. prof. Sch. Medicine, U. Mo., Kansas City, 1988; Ralph B. Samson Meml. lectr. Grant Med. Ctr., Columbus, Ohio, 1991; Louis A. Buie vis. lectr. Mayo Med. Sch., Rochester, Minn., 1992; ann. vis. surgeon Queen Elizabeth Hosp. Ctr. of Montreal, Que., 1993; vis. prof. U. So. Calif. Sch. Medicine, L.A., 1995; Neil Swinton vis. prof. Lahey-Hitchcock Med. Ctr., Burlington, Mass., 1997; del. leader Citizen Amb. Program Colon and Rectal Surgery Del. to Russia, Hungary and Czechoslovakia, 1992. Author: (textbook) Colon and Rectal Surgery, 1984, 89, 93; assoc. editor: Diseases of the Colon and Rectum, 1977-92, Lahey Clinic Bull., 1972-81; contbr. numerous articles to profl. jours. Recipient Hoffman-LaRoche award, 1965, Piedmont Proctologic Soc. award, 1973, 1st prize of Med. Book award, 1985. Fellow ACP; mem. ACS (So. Calif. chpt.), AMA (chmn. residency rev. com. for colon and rectal surgery 1985-86), Internat. Soc. Univ. Colon and Rectal Surgeons, Am. Soc. Colon and Rectal Surgeons (v.p. 1995-96), Am. Surg. Assn., Am. Med. Writers Assn. (hon.), Am. Coll. Gastroenterology, Assn. for Program Dirs. in Colon and Rectal Surgery, We. Surg. Assn., Pan Am. Med. Assn. (coun. sect. on colon and rectal surgery 1989—), Royal Australasian Coll. Surgeons (hon., sect. colon and rectal surgery 1989), New Eng. Surg. Soc., Calif. Med. Soc., New Eng. Soc. Colon and Rectal Surgeons (sec.-treas. 1977-81), Boston Surg. Soc., Northeastern Soc. Colon and Rectal Surgeons, Soc. Surgery Alimentary Tract, Santa Barbara County Med. Soc., So. Calif. Soc. Colon and Rectal Surgeons, Piedmont Proctologic Soc. (hon.). Office: Divsn of Colon and Rectal Surgery USC Sch of Medicine 1450 San Pablo St Ste 5400 Los Angeles CA 90033-1042

CORMAN, RANDY, lawyer; b. El Paso, Tex., Sept. 24, 1960; s. Theodore Howard and Joan (Golaszewski) C.; m. Kathleen Glynn, July 27, 1996; 1 child, William Joseph. BA, Rutgers U., 1982; JD, Rutgers U., Newark, 1985. Bar: N.J. 1985. Assoc. counsel State Senate Rep. Staff, Trenton, N.J., 1986-92; state senator N.J. Senate, Trenton, 1992-94; of counsel Donington, Karcher, Salmond, Ronan and Rainone, Edison, N.J., 1994-95, Karcher and Rainone, Sayreville, 1996-97; counsel Perth Amboy City Coun., 1995-96; borough atty. Borough of Spotswood, 1996-97; dir. of law N.J. Tpk. Authority, 1997—; vice chmn. Senate Environment Com., 1992-94. Mem. Bd. of Edn., Sayreville, N.J., 1980-84; councilman Borough of Sayreville, 1985-92; chmn. Sayreville Rep. Com., 1986-87, 94-98; trustee St. Stanislaus Kostka Roman Cath. parish, 1998—. Decorated knight comdr. Order of Merit of St. Angilbert, knight Order of Noble Companions of the Swan, knight Order of Merit of the Bear of Alabama. Mem. Phi Beta Kappa. Republican. Roman Catholic. Office: NJ Tpk Authority PO Box 1121 New Brunswick NJ 08903-1121

CORMAN, ROGER WILLIAM, motion picture producer, director; b. Detroit, Apr. 5, 1926; s. William and Anne C.; m. Julie Ann Halloran, Dec. 26, 1970; children: Catherine Ann, Roger Martin, Brian William, Mary Tessa. AB, Stanford, 1947; postgrad., Oxford (Eng.) U., 1950; D in Fine Arts (hon.), Am. Film Inst., 1998. Founder, pres. New World Pictures, 1970-83, Concorde-New Horizons Corp., 1983—. Prodr.: Carnosaur, The Fantastic Four, I Never Promised You a Rose Garden, St. Jack, Battle Beyond the Stars, Deathrace 2000, Piranha, Avalanche, Munchies, Crime Zone, The Terror Within, Black Scorpion, others; dir.: Five Guns West, 1955; prodr., dir.: The Intruder, Fall of the House of Usher, Masque of the Red Death, Machine Gun Kelly, Little Shop of Horrors, The Trip, Von Richthofen and Brown, Frankenstein Unbound, 1989, others; distbr.: Cries and Whispers, Autumn Sonata, Amarcord, Small Change, The Tin Drum, Cabeza de Vaca, others; films shown at numerous film festivals; prodr., dir., screenwriter: Roger Corman's Frankenstein Unbound; exec. prodr.: Hollywood Boulevard, Rock and Roll High School; chmn. bd. Wometco Theaters; actor The Silence of the Lambs, The Godfather, Part III, Philadelphia, Apollo 13. Recipient Grand prize Venice Film Festival, 1979, Lifetime Achievement award L.A. Film Critics, 1997, 1st Prodrs. of Century award Cannes Film Festival, 1998. Mem. Producers Guild Am., Dirs. Guild Am. Office: Concorde-New Horizons Corp 11600 San Vicente Blvd Los Angeles CA 90049-5102

CORMIA, FRANK HOWARD, industrial engineering administrator; b. Montreal, Que., Can., Nov. 17, 1936; s. Frank Edward Cormia and Elizabeth Kulp (Hall) St. Louis; m. Mary Irene Porter, Aug. 29, 1959; children: John Howard, Carl William, Ross Michael, Judith Anne. BS in Engring., Calif. Inst. Tech., 1960. Indsl. engr. Alcoa, Vernon, Calif., 1960-64; chief indsl. engr. Warrick ops. Alcoa, Evansville, Ind., 1968-76; mgr. indsl. engring. Tenn. ops. Alcoa, 1976-95; chief indsl. engr. Wear-ever Aluminum, Chillicothe, Ohio, 1964-68. Past chmn. bd. dirs. Sch. Indsl. Sys. Engring., Ga. Inst. Tech., Atlanta; bd. dirs., past chmn. dept. indsl. sys. engring. Va. Poly. Inst. and State U., Blacksburg; chmn. long range planning com. Smoky Mountain coun. Boy Scouts Am., 1988-89. 1st lt. USAR, N.G., 1960-66. Episcopalian.

CORMIE, DONALD MERCER, investment company executive; b. Edmonton, Alta., Can., July 24, 1922; s. George Mills and Mildred (Mercer) C.; m. Eivor Elisabeth Ekstrom, June 8, 1946; children: John Mills, Donald Robert, Allison Barbara, James Mercer, Neil Brian, Buce George, Eivor, Robert. BA, U. Alta., 1944, LLB, 1945; LLM, Harvard U., 1946. Bar: Alta. 1947. Queens counsel, 1964; sessional instr. faculty law U. Alta., 1947-53; sr. ptnr. Cormie, Kennedy, Edmonton, Barristers, 1954-87; instr. real estate law Dept. of Extension, U. Alta., 1958-64; pres., bd. dirs. Collective Securities, Ltd., Cormie Ranch, Inc., Sea Investors Corp.; With Can. Mcht. Marine, 1943-44. Recipient Judge Green Silver medal in law. Mem. Dean's Coun. of 100 Ariz. State U., World Pres.'s Orgn., Chief Execs. Orgn. (bd. dirs. 1976-79), Can. Bar Assn. (mem. coun. 1961-76, chmn. adminstrv. law 1963-66, chmn. taxation 1972-82, v.p. Alta. 1968-69), Found. Legal Rsch. Can. (hon. life). Home and Office: 5101 N Casa Blanca Dr Unit 314 Scottsdale AZ 85253-6989

CORMIER, JEAN G., communications company executive; b. Campbellton, N.B., Can., May 3, 1941; s. Simon and Leona (Arsenault) C.; m. Helen Morrison, Sept. 9, 1965; children—Paul, Michel. B.A. in Philosophy, Bathurst Coll., N.B., 1963; postgrad., McMaster U., Hamilton, Ont., Can., 1963-64. Dir. pub. affairs Dofasco, Hamilton, 1970-75; v.p. pub. relations Can. Nat., Montreal, Que., Can., 1975-79; pres. CN Hotels and Tower, Montreal, 1979-81; sr. v.p. corp. affairs B.C. Resources Investment Corp., Vancouver, Can., 1981-86; pres. Cormier Communicators, Inc., Vancouver, 1986—. Contbr. articles to profl. jours. Fellow Internat. Assn. Bus. Communicators (bd. dirs. 1983-89, past chmn. 1987-88); mem. Can. Pub. Rels. Soc. (accredited), Vancouver Club, Marine Dr. Golf Club (pres. 1999—), Roman Catholic. Avocation: photography. Office: Cormier Comm Corp, 1050 W Pender St Ste 910, Vancouver, BC Canada V6E 2N7

CORMIER, ROBERT EDMUND, writer; b. Leominster, Mass., Jan. 17, 1925; s. Lucien Joseph and Irma Margaret (Collins) C.; m. Constance B. Senay, Nov. 6, 1948; children: Roberta Susan, Peter Jude, Christine Judith, Renee Elizabeth. Student, Fitchburg (Mass.) State Coll., 1943-44, Litt.D. (hon.), 1977. Script/comml. writer Radio Sta. WTAG, Worcester, Mass., 1946-48; reporter, columnist Worcester Telegram & Gazette, 1948-55; reporter, columnist, asso. editor Fitchburg Sentinel & Enterprise, 1955-78; writing coach, cons. Worcester Telegram & Gazette. Author: Now And At the Hour, 1960, A Little Raw on Monday Mornings, 1963, Take Me Where the Good Times Are, 1965, The Chocolate War, 1974, I Am the Cheese, 1977, After the First Death, 1979, Eight Plus One, 1980, The Bumblebee Flies Anyway, 1983, Beyond the Chocolate War, 1985, Fade, 1988, Other Bells For Us to Ring, 1990, I Have Words To Spend, 1991, We All Fall Down, 1991, Tunes For Bears To Dance To, 1992, In the Middle of the Night, 1995, Tenderness, 1997, Heroes, 1998; contbr. short stories to, Redbook, McCalls, Saturday Evening Post, Sign, St. Anthony Messenger. Trustee Leominster Pub. Libr., 1977-92. Recipient Best News Story in New Eng. award AP, 1959, 74, K.R. Thomson prize Thomson Newspapers, Inc., 1974, ALAN award Adolescent Lit. Assembly of Nat. Coun. Tchrs. English, 1982, Margaret A. Edwards award ALA Young Adult Svcs. Div./Sch. Libr. Jour., 1991; named Mass. Author of the Yr., Mass. Libr. Assn., 1985; Bread Loaf Writers' Conf. fellow, 1968. Mem. L'Union St. Jean Baptiste d'Amerique Club, PEN Club. Roman Catholic. Home: 1177 Main St Leominster MA 01453-1765 *To write with clarity, the simple telling word or phrase, omitting unnecessary adjectives or adverbs; to write the truth, however it sears or burns or perhaps soars; to select words that move and dance and sing upon the page; to make the reader say: My God, that's how it is.*

CORN, ALFRED DEWITT, poet, fiction writer, critic, educator; b. Bainbridge, Ga., Aug. 14, 1943; s. A.D. and Grace (Lahey) C.; m. Ann Rosalind Jones, July 24, 1967 (div. 1971). BA, Emory U., 1965; MA, Columbia U., 1970. Preceptor Columbia Coll., N.Y.C., 1968-70; free-lance writer N.Y.C., 1971-77; vis. lectr. Yale U., New Haven, 1977-79; assoc. prof. Conn. Coll., New London, 1978-81; lectr. Columbia U., N.Y.C., 1983; vis. lectr. Sch. Arts, writing div. Columbia U., 1985, 87; lectr. CUNY, 1983-84; vis. lectr. Silliman Coll. Yale U., 1986; Elliston prof. poetry U. Cin., 1989; lectr. Columbia U., 1987, Eugene Lang. Coll., 1991; vis. lectr. Parsons New Sch., N.Y.C., 1988, Ezra Stiles Coll. Yale U., 1992; vis. prof. UCLA, 1990, Columbia U., 1992, 93-98, Bell vis. prof. U. Tulsa, 1992. Author: All Roads at Once, 1976, A Call in the Midst of the Crowd, 1978, The Various Light, 1980, Notes from a Child of Paradise, 1984, The Metamorphoses of Metaphor, 1987, The West Door, 1988, Autobiographies, 1992, Part of His Story, 1997, Present, 1997, The Poem's Heartbeat, 1997; editor: Incarnation: Contemporary Writers on the New Testament, 1990. Recipient award Nat. Endowment for Arts, 1979, 90; Levinson prize Poetry mag., 1982; Spl. award Am. Acad. and Inst. Arts and Letters, 1983; fellow Acad. Am. Poets, 1988, Ingram Merrill Found., 1974, N.Y. Found. for the Arts, 1986, Guggenheim Found., 1986-87. Mem. PEN, Nat. Book Critics Circle, Poetry Soc. Am. Home: 720 Fort Washington Ave New York NY 10040

CORN, LOVICK P., retired foundation executive; b. Macon, Ga., Aug. 14, 1922. AB, U. N.C., 1947; hon. degree, LaGrange (Ga.) Coll., 1994. Vice chmn. Bradley-Turner Found., from 1950, now ret.

CORN, MILTON, academic dean, physician; b. Berlin, Jan. 17, 1928; came to U.S., 1934; m. Gilan Akbar Tocco; children: Stephanie, Sarah, Paul, Rhoya Tocco. BS with highest honors, Yale U., 1952, MD with highest honors, 1955. Diplomate Nat. Bd. Med. Examiners, Am. Bd. Internal Medicine, Am. Bd. Hematology. Intern then resident Peter Bent Brigham Hosp., Boston, 1955-58; fellow in hematology Johns Hospkins Sch. Med., Balt., 1958-60; asst. prof. medicine Seton Hall Coll. Medicine, 1960-63; from asst. to assoc. prof. medicine George Washington U., 1963-72, prof. medicine, 1972-73; chief of hematology D.C. Gen. Hosp. div. George Washington U., 1963-73, chief of medicine, 1970-73; dir. blood bank and emergency dept. Geogetown U., Washington, 1973-78; dir. clerkship jr. medicine, dir. med. residency tng. program Georgetown U., Washington, 1978-84, also vice chmn. medicine, 1978-84, assoc. dean hosp. liaison, 1984, med. dir. hosp., 1984-85; dean Sch. Medicine, Georgetown U., Washington, 1985-89; dir. Office of Clin. Informatics Georgetown U. Med. Ctr., Washington, 1989-90; spl. cons. to dir. Nat. Libr. Medicine, 1990—, assoc. dir. extramural programs, 1990—; dir. med. edn., hematologist St. Michael's Hosp., Newark, 1960-63; cons. hematology FDA, 1978—; chief physician Cath. Relief Svcs. Refugee Capt, Thailand, 1981, 83; regional dir. rev. courses CX ACP, 1981-87; mem. UN Relief and Works Agy. Inspection Team for Palestinian Refugee Camps, 1984; guest lectr. U. Southampton, Eng., 1981; keynote speaker India Med. Soc., New Delhi, 1985. Co-editor Hematology Revs., 1984—; contbr. articles to profl. publs. Recipient Golden Apple award Georgetown U. Student Med. Assn., 1971, 83, Teaching award Kaiser Permanente, 1983, Maimonides award Anti Defamation League, 1989. Home: 6404 Goldleaf Dr Bethesda MD 20817-5830 Office: Nat Libr Medicine NIH Biomed Communications Bethesda MD 20894

CORN, MORTON, environmental engineer, educator; b. N.Y.C., Oct. 18, 1933; s. Julius and Sophie (Haber) C.; m. Jacqueline Karnell, Aug. 21, 1955; children: Matthew Irwin, Frederick Eliot. B.S. in Chem. Engring, Cooper Union, 1955; M.S., Harvard U., 1956, Ph.D., 1961. Asst. san. engr. USPHS, Cin., 1956-58; research asso. Harvard, 1960-61; asst. prof. U. Pitts., 1962-65, assoc. prof., 1965-66, prof. Grad. Sch. Pub. Health and Sch. Engring., 1967-79; prof. and div. head environ. health engring. Sch. Hygiene and Public Health, Johns Hopkins U., Balt., 1980-97; prof. emeritus Johns Hopkins U., Balt., 1998—; pres. Morton Corn; Assocs., Cons. Engrs., 1977—; cons. div. biology and medicine AEC, 1965-74; chmn. air pollution rsch. grants com. EPA, 1968-71, mem. sci. adv. bd., 1978-84; mem. com. on biol. effects air pollution NAS, 1971, mem. com. risk assessment, 1982-83; mem. expert panel occupational health WHO, 1973—; asst. sec. labor for occupational safety and health U.S. Dept. Labor, 1975-77; mem. Allegheny County Air Pollution Adv. Com., 1967-72; mem. nat. adv. com. health vital stats. Dept. HHS 1979-81, mine health rsch. adv. com. Nat. Inst. Occupational Safety and Health, 1986-89, GM/UAW joint health and safety adv. com., 1988-92; chmn. OTA Commn. Preventing Injury and Illness in the Workplace, 1982-84; chmn. tech. adv. bd. Clean Sites, Inc., Alexandria, Va., 1984-87; trustee Assoc. Univ., Inc., 1991-93; mem. Hanford tank adv. panel DOE, 1993—, cons. Health, Safety and Environment, 1993. Chmn. Gov. of Md.'s Toxic Coun., 1986-89. NSF postdoctoral fellow U. London, 1961-62; WHO fellow, 1970; Guggenheim fellow, 1972. Fellow Am. Pub. Health Assn.; mem. Am. Soc. Safety Engrs., Am. Indsl. Hygiene Assn., Am. Conf. Govt. Indsl. Hygienists (chmn. 1983-84). Home: 3208 Bennett Point Rd Queenstown MD 21658-1126 Office: Johns Hopkins U 615 N Wolfe St Baltimore MD 21205-2103

CORNABY, KAY STERLING, lawyer, former state senator; b. Spanish Fork, Utah, Jan. 14, 1936; s. Sterling A. and Hilda G. Cornaby; m. Linda Rasmussen, July 23, 1965; children: Alyse, Derek, Tara, Heather, Brandon. AB, Brigham Young U., 1960; postgrad. law, Heidelberg, Germany, 1961-63; JD, Harvard U., 1966. Bar: N.Y. 1967, Utah 1969, U.S. Patent and Trademark Office 1967. Assoc. Brumbaugh, Graves, Donahue & Raymond, N.Y.C., 1966-69; ptnr. Mallinckrodt & Cornaby, Salt Lake City, 1969-72; sole practice Salt Lake City, 1972-85; mem. Utah State Senate, 1977-91, majority leader, 1983-84; shareholder Jones, Waldo, Holbrook & McDonough, Salt Lake City, 1985—. Mem. Nat. Commn. on Uniform State Laws, 1988-93; mem. adv. bd. U. Mich. Ctr. for Study of Youth Policy,1990-93; mem. Utah State Jud. Conduct Commn., 1983-91, chmn., 1984-85; bd. dirs. KUED-KUER Pub. TV and Radio, 1982-88; bd. dirs. Salt Lake Conv. and Visitors Bur., 1985—. Mem. N.Y. Bar Assn., Utah Bar Assn., Utah Harvard Alumni Assn. (pres. 1977-79), Harvard U. Law Sch. Alumni Assn. (pres. 1995—). Office: Jones Waldo Holbrook & McDonough 1500 Wells Fargo Bank Plz 170 S Main St Salt Lake City UT 84101-1605

CORNACCHIO, JOSEPH VINCENT, engineering educator, computer researcher, consultant; b. N.Y.C., Dec. 27, 1934; s. Vincent and Elena (Vuolo) C.; m. Carole Ester Taber, Aug. 27, 1960; children—Karen Marie, Kevin Joseph. B.S.E.E., Pa. State U., 1956; M.E.E., Syracuse U., 1959, Ph.D., 1962. Adv. engr. IBM Corp., Endicott, N.Y., 1962-72; postdoctoral fellow, 1965; assoc. prof. SUNY-Binghamton, 1972-74, prof. engring., 1974—, dept. chmn., 1981-84; cons. ptnr. Usability Services, Binghamton, 1982—; cons. N.Y. Dept. Commerce, Albany, N.Y., 1978-80, N.Y.-Pa. Health Plan, Binghamton, 1975-76. Editor and author System Complexity Jour., 1976; contbr. articles to profl. jours.; patentee in field. Bd. dirs. Am. Arthritis Assn., Binghamton, 1980—; mem. Mark Twain Soc., Elmira, N.Y., 1984—; assoc. mem. Danforth Found., St. Louis, 1974—. Grantee SUNY, 1971, State of N.Y., 1977-78. Mem. IEEE (chpt. pres. 1974-75), Assn. Computing Machinery. Home: 3120 Belmont Ave Vestal NY 13850-2802 Office: SUNY Dept Engring Binghamton NY 13901

CORNATZER, WILLIAM EUGENE, retired biochemistry educator; b. Mocksville, N.C., Sept. 23, 1918; s. William Pinkston and Stella Augusta (Vogler) C.; m. Margaret Virginia Freeman, Mar. 30, 1946; children—Nancy Freeman, William Eugene. Student, Mars Hill Coll., 1935-37; B.S., Wake Forest Coll., 1939; M.S., U. N.C., 1941, Ph.D., 1944; postgrad., Oak Ridge Inst. Nuclear Studies, 1948; M.D., Bowman Gray Sch. Medicine, 1951; DSc (hon.), Univ. N. Dak., 1992. Student asst. zoology Wake Forest Coll., 1937-38, Wake Forest Coll. (phys. chemistry), 1938-39; grad. and student asst. biol. and food chemistry U. N.C., 1939-41, Fels Research fellow, 1941-45; asst. prof. biochemistry Bowman Gray Sch. Medicine, 1946-51; prof., head dept. biochemistry med. sch. U. N.D., Grand Forks, 1951-83; Chester Fritz disting. prof. U. N.D., 1973—, Univ. prof., 1983, prof. emeritus, 1983—; also dir. Ireland Research Lab.; Mem. biochem. test com. Nat. Bd. Med. Examiners; mem. White Ho. Com. for Orgn. Conf. on Food, Nutrition and Health, 1969. Mem. bd. editors: Jour. Clin. Chemistry, 1971-81; mem. editorial bd.: Jour. Nutrition, 1975-79; author: Clinical Significances of Laboratory Tests, 1986, The Role Of Nutrition In Health And Disease, 1989; contbr. articles sci. jours. Recipient Frank Billing award for original investigation; Silver medal AMA, 1951; Nat. Scis. Travel award to Internat. Congress Biochemistry Paris, 1952; Nat. Scis. Travel award to Internat. Congress Biochemistry Tokyo, 1967; travel award Internat. Congress Cancer, London, Eng.; travel award Am. Assn. for Cancer Research, 1958; travel award to 1st Internat. Congress Pharmacology, Stockholm, 1961; travel award to Internat. Union Physiol. Sci.; NSF Travel award to 7th Internat. Congress Biochemistry, Tokyo, 1967; travel award 8th Internat. Congress Nutrition; travel award Am. Inst. Nutrition, Prague, 1969; travel award 9th Congress, Mex., 1972; Distinguished Service award U. N.C., 1970; Outstanding Sci. Research award U. N.D. chpt. Sigma Xi, 1970; Distinguished Alumnus award Bowman Gray Med. Sch., 1976. Fellow A.C.P., N.Y. Acad. Scis., Am. Inst. Chemists, AAAS; mem. Am. Assn. Oil Chemists, Nat. Acad. Clin. Chemistry, Am. Bd. Clin. Chemistry (dir.), Am. Assn. Clin. Chemists (nat. exec. com. 1957), Am. Assn. for Study of Liver Disease, Central Soc. for Clin. Research, Radiation Research Soc., Am. Chem. Soc., Am. Soc. Biol. Chemistry, So. Soc. for Clin. Research, Am. Fedn. for Clin. Research, Soc. Exptl. Biology and Medicine, AAUP, Am. Inst. Nutrition, Elisha Mitchell Sci. Soc., N.D. Acad. Scis. (pres. 1956), N.D. Diabetic Assn., Royal Soc. Medicine. Baptist. Research in properties of proteins, quinine metabolism, anti-malarial testing, phospholipide metabolism, radioactive isotopes, biol. effects of radiation. Home: 1810 Edgemere Ct SE Huntsville AL 35803-3634 *Faith in yourself and your Creator/Positive thinking/High Objectives/Hard work.*

CORNBLATT, ALAN JACK, lawyer; b. Balt., Aug. 31, 1936; s. Harold A. and Sara (Kellar) C.; m. Nancy O'Donell; children: Lawrence Paul, Wendy Ellen. LLB, JD, U. Md., 1962. Bar: N.J. 1962, U.S. Dist. Ct. N.J. 1962, U.S. Supreme Ct. 1968. Assoc. Mirne and Nowels, Asbury Park, N.J., 1962-66; ptnr. Mirne, Nowels, Fundler & Cornblatt, Asbury Park, 1966-70; sole practice Brick, N.J., 1971—; judge Brick (N.J.) Mcpl. Ct., 1971-73; pres. Ethical Mediation Inc., Brick, 1986—; instr. family law Ocean County Coll., N.J., 1974; county penal system study commn. mem. State of N.J., 1974; spkr. World Congress on Family Law, Sydney, Australia, 1993. Contbr. articles to profl. jours.; columnist Family Law 1988. Pres. Temple Beth Or Men's Club, Brick, 1972; bd. dirs. Temple Beth Or, 1971-74. Served with U.S. Army, 1955-57, Korea. Fellow Am. Acad. Matrimonial Lawyers (bd. mgrs. N.J. chpt. 1990—), Internat. Acad. Matrimonial Lawyers; mem. N.J. Bar Assn. (exec. com., family law sect. 1984-86), Ocean County Bar Assn. (family law com., trustee 1999-2000), Ocean County Inns of Ct. (master 1992—), Asbury Park Jaycees (pres. 1965, Disting. Svc. award 1966, internat. senator 1967), B'nai B'rith, Jewish War Vets., Masons, Kiwanis (pres.). Republican. Avocations: travel, sailing. Office: 44 Princeton Ave Brick NJ 08724-3550 *Notable cases include: D'Onofrio vs. O'Onofrio, 200 N.J. super. 361 App. Div., 1985 in which antenuptial agreements made in contemplation of divorce are valid; Moidl vs. Schreiber, 214 N.J. super. 513 App. Div., 1986 in which support payments for child continues after father's death; Kelly v. Kelly, 217 su. 147 Ch., 1986 in which post-divorce overnight visitation permitted with children in presence of paramour; N.N. v. G., 219 su. 334 Ch., 1987, in which child is permitted to assume stepfather's surname.*

CORNELIO, ALBERT CARMEN, insurance executive; b. Winsted, Conn., Feb. 9, 1930; s. Carmine E. and Mary (Petrunti) C.; m. Elizabeth Ann Lach, June 2, 1956; children: Charles C., Catherine M., Michael J., Julia A. Student, Washington-Jefferson Coll., 1947-50; LL.B., Boston U., 1957. Bar: Mass. 1957. Atty. Berkshire Life Ins. Co., Pittsfield, Mass., 1957-60; counsel Berkshire Life Ins. Co., 1960-65, assoc. gen. counsel, 1965-68, v.p. and gen. counsel, 1968-70, sr. v.p., 1970-71, sr. v.p. mktg. and ins. services, 1971-76, exec. v.p.-mktg., 1977-82, pres., chief exec. officer, 1982-95; chmn. bd. dirs. Berkshire Life Ins. Co. Served with USNR, 1950-54. Mem. Am. Soc. CLUs, Life Mgmt. Inst. Home: 84 Spadina Pky Pittsfield MA 01201-8122 Office: 700 South St Pittsfield MA 01201-8212

CORNELISON, FLOYD SHOVINGTON, JR., retired psychiatrist, former educator; b. San Angelo, Tex., Apr. 30, 1918; s. Floyd Shovington and Nannie Lee (Brewer) C.; m. Erwina Ladelle Bode, Aug. 30, 1940 (div. 1966); 1 child, Ann Brewer; m. Ruth Reeder Williams, Sept. 17, 1966. B.A., Baylor U., 1939; postgrad., Northwestern U., 1939-40, Columbia U., 1943-45; M.D., Cornell U., 1950; M.S., Boston U., 1958. Diplomate Am. Bd. Psychiatry and Neurology. Intern Grasslands Hosp., Valhalla, N.Y., 1950-51; resident in psychiatry Mass. Meml. Hosp., Boston U. Sch. Medicine, also Boston State Hosp., 1951-54; from asst. in psychiatry to instr. Boston U. Sch. Medicine, 1951-58; lectr. psychology Tufts Coll., 1954-56; successively asst. prof., assoc. prof., cons. prof. psychiatry U. Okla. Sch. Medicine, 1958-64; prof. psychiatry Jefferson Med. Coll., Thomas Jefferson U., Phila., 1962-83; hon. prof. Jefferson Med. Coll., Thomas Jefferson U., 1983—, chmn. dept., 1962-74; past mem. staff numerous hosps.; med. staff Wilmington Med Center; cons. area hosps., 1962—; med. dir. Freedom From Fear, Inc., 1980-83; dir. Marka T. du Pont Inst. Human Behavior, Wilmington, Del., 1971-75; initiated self-image experience, photog. confrontation technique in psychiat. rsch. Author articles; producer films in field. Fellow psychiat. films Med. Audio-Visual Inst., Assn. Am. Med. Colls., 1951-53; candidate Boston Psychoanalytic Inst., 1954-58. Fellow Am. Coll. Psychiatrists (emeritus), Am. Psychiat. Assn. (life), Royal Australian and New Zealand Coll. Psychiatrists (hon.); mem. AMA, Del. Psychiat. Soc., Del. County Med. Soc., New Castle County Med. Soc., Sigma Xi. Home and Office: 16 Stone Hill Rd Wilmington DE 19803-4411

CORNELIUS, JEFFREY MICHAEL, music educator; b. Chgo., Apr. 26, 1943; s. George Edward and Helen (Benjamin) C.; m. Betty Wallace, June 10, 1967; children: Benjamin Michael, Lisa Louise. BA, King Col., 1965; B in Music magna cum laude, Westminster Choir Col., 1970; M in Music, Temple U., 1972, EdD, 1986. Tchr. Bristol Tenn. Sch. Sys., 1965-68; adj. music instr. Mercer County C.C., Trenton, N.J., 1970-71; music instr. La Salle Col., Phila., 1971-72; music prof. Temple U., Phila., 1972—; dean of Esther Boyer Col. Music Temple U., 1993—; lectr. Phila. Orch., 1982—; conductor, adjudicator Music Educators Assn., Eastern States, 1989—; adv. bd. Phila. Ave. Arts, 1993—, Station WRTI, Pa., 1994-96;. Choral singer with numerous major orchs. including Phila. Orch., N.Y. Philharmonic, L.A. Philharmonic, Am. Symphony Orch., 1968—; contbr. articles to profl. jours. Cons. City of Phila., 1992; panel member City of Phila. Cultural Fund, 1993-96; bd. dir. Singing City, Phila., 1987-90. Recipient Cert. of Merit Temple U. Alumni Assn., 1981. Mem. Am. Choral Dirs. (Pa. chpt., pres. 1984-86), Music Educators Nat. Conf., Musical Fund Soc. Phila., Nat. Assn. Schs. Music (evaluator 1994—), Internat. Coun. Fine Arts Deans, Nat. Soc. Sci. Honor Soc., Pi Kappa Lambda. Avocations: photography, travel, history. Office: Esther Boyer Col Music Temple Univ Philadelphia PA 19122

CORNELIUS, KENNETH CREMER, JR., finance executive; b. Plainwell, Mich., Sept. 7, 1944; s. Kenneth Cremer and Hollie Jane (Tupper) C.; m. Mary Patricia Hagen, Aug. 19, 1967; children: Kari, Jay, Lee Ann. BA, Carleton Coll., 1966; MBA, U. Mich., 1967. Mgr. acctg. divsn. Maremont Corp., Nashville, 1972-74, mgr. regional acctg. divsn., 1974-75, divsn. contr., 1975-79, corp. contr., 1979-89; v.p., CFO Maremont Corp., Chgo., 1980-89, M-C Industries, Ann Arbor, Mich., 1989-92, Prestolite Electric Inc., Ann Arbor, 1992—. Capt. USAF, 1968-72. Mem. Phi Beta Kappa. Home: 3465 Ridgeline Ct Ann Arbor MI 48105-2500 Office: Prestolite 2100 Commonwealth Blvd Ann Arbor MI 48105-1560

CORNELIUS, MARIA G., financial advisor; b. Washington, Apr. 19, 1961; d. James C. and Rose Marie; m. Frederick J. Cornelius, Apr. 13, 1991; children: Patrick Joseph, Michael James. BS, Mt. St. Mary Coll., 1983. CFP. Adminstrv. asst. AFC Adv. Svcs., Silver Spring, Md., 1984-89; fin. planner AFC Adv. Svcs., Silver Spring, 1990-91, Montgomery Advisors, Rockville, Md., 1989-90, Nat. Bank Washington, 1990, Profl. Fin. Planning, Gaithersburg, Md., 1991-93; v.p. Burt Assocs., Inc., Bethesda, Md., 1992—; pres. MGC Fin. Advisors, Rockville, Md., 1993—. Mem. Inst. CFP, Md. Soc. Inst. CFP, Bethesda C. of C. (com. svcs. mem. 1998). Greek Orthodox. Avocations: walking, hiking, spending time with family. Office: Burt Assocs Inc 7910 Woodmont Ave Ste 1055 Bethesda MD 20814-3081

CORNELL, ANNIE AIKO, nurse, administrator, retired army officer; b. L.A., Sept. 23, 1954; d. George and Fumiko (Iwai) Okubo; m. Max A. Cornell, Dec. 10, 1990. BSN, U. Md., 1976. RN, Calif. Enlisted U.S. Army, 1972, advanced through grades to maj.; clin. staff nurse surg. ICU U.S. Army, Presidio of San Francisco; clin. head nurse ICU U.S. Army, Seoul, Korea; clin. head nurse gen. medicine ward U.S. Army, Ft. Ord, Calif., chief nursing adminstrn.; ret. U.S. Army, 1992; nursing supr. Home Health Plus; dir. patient svcs. Hollister Vis. Nurses Assn., Calif.; asst. dir. patient svcs. Monterey Vis. Nurses Assn., Calif.; case mgr. supr. Cmty. Hosp. Home Health Svcs., Monterey, asst. mgr. Recipient Walter Reed Army Inst. nursing scholarship. Mem. Sigma Theta Tau. Home: 199 Linde Cir Marina CA 93933-2206

CORNELL, DAVID ROGER, health care executive; b. Glens Falls, N.Y., Apr. 5, 1944; s. Junius R. and Isabelle (Richardson) C.; m. Alma Files (dec. 1967); children: Kimberley Anne Farley, Kelly Elizabeth. B.A., U. Vt., 1966; cert. phys. therapy Duke U., 1967; M.B.A., U. S.C., 1973; PhD Columbia Pacific U., 1986 . Dir. phys. therapy Univ. Hosp., Augusta, Ga., 1970-72, adminstrv. resident, 1972; adminstrv. asst. Drs. Hosp., Augusta, 1973-74; asst. adminstr. Cypress Community Hosp., Pompano Beach, Fla., 1974; assoc. adminstr. North Ridge Gen. Hosp., Ft. Lauderdale, Fla., 1975-77, adminstr., 1977-79; pres. Mont. Deaconess Med. Center, Great Falls, 1979-88; pres. Western Res. Care System, Youngstown, Ohio, 1988-91; pres., CEO Albany (N.Y.) Med. Ctr., 1991-94; COO New England Med. Ctr., Boston, 1995-97; pres., CEO New Eng. Med. Ctr. Internat., Boston, 1997—. Served with U.S. Army, 1968-69. Fellow Am. Acad. Med. Adminstrs., Am. Coll. Health Care Execs.; mem. Am. Hosp. Assn. (del. 1984-91), Med. Group Mgmt. Assn.

CORNELL, ERIC ALLIN, physics educator; s. Allin and Elizabeth (Greenberg) C.; m. Celeste Landry; 1 child, Eliza. BS in Physics with honors, Stanford U., 1985; PhD in Physics, MIT, 1990. Tchr. English as Fgn. Lang. Taichung YMCA, Taiwan, 1982; rsch. asst. Stanford (Calif.) U., 1982-85; tchg. fellow Harvard Ext. Sch., 1989; postdoctoral Rowland Inst., Cambridge, Mass., summer 1990; postdoctorate Joint Inst. Lab. Astrophysics, Boulder, Colo., 1990-92; asst. prof. adj. dept. physics U. Colo., Boulder, 1992-95; staff scientist Nat. Inst. Stds. and Tech., Boulder, 1992—; fellow JILA U. Colo and Nat. Inst. Stds. and Tech., Boulder, 1994—. Contbr. over 30 articles to profl. jours.; patentee in field. Recipient Grad. fellowship NSF, 1985-88, Undergrad. Rsch. award for excellence Firestone, 1985, Samuel Wesley Stratton award, 1995, Newcomb-Cleveland prize, 1995-96, Carl Zeiss award, 1996, Fritz London prize in low temperature physics, 1996, Gold medal Dept. Commerce, 1996, Presdl. Early Career award in sci. and engring., 1996, I.I. Rabi prize in atomic, molecular and optical physics Am. Phys. Soc., 1997, King Faisal Internat. prize in sci., 1997, Alan T. Waterman award NSF, 1997. Office: Univ Colo JILA Campus Box 440 Boulder CO 80309-0440*

CORNELL, JAMES FRASER, JR., entomologist, educator; b. Charlotte, N.C., Dec. 19, 1940; s. James Fraser and Catherine Odom (Parker) C.; m. Sandra Johnson, June 13, 1965; children: James F. III, Thomas Alexander Duncan. BS in Geology, U. N.C., 1963; MS in Entomology, N.C. State U., 1965; PhD, Oreg. State U., 1971. Asst. prof. biology Appalachian State U., Boone, N.C., 1968-71; prof. N.C. State U., Raleigh, 1971-72; prof. biology Lees McRae U., Banner Elk, N.C., 1972-73; pres. Scientific Equipment Co., Inc., Charlotte, N.C., 1973-85; with internat. studies program Charlotte-Mecklenburg Sch. System, 1986-91, with internat. baccalaureate program, 1991—; cons. forensic entomology Charlotte Mecklenburg Police Dept., 1991—; ad hoc grant reviewer NSF; hon. curator Colcoptera N.C. State U. Entomology Dept., 1995—. Contbr. articles to profl. jours. Fulbright grantee, 1990, 92; Dept. of Energy fellow, 1995; scholar Charlotte World Affairs Coun., 1994. Mem. Pacific Entomol. Soc., Washington Entomol. Soc., Am. Topical Assn. (pres. biology unit 1988-92), N.C. Entomol. Soc., Coleopterists Soc. (charter). Achievements include research in anophthalmic edaphic and nidicolous Coleoptera, and rare and endangered insects, particularly beetles. Home: 1616 Euclid Ave Charlotte NC 28203-4738 Office: Charlotte Mecklenburg Sch 1967 Patriot Dr Charlotte NC 28227-4123 *Entomologists are listed behind only presidential advisors as the longest lived group of professionals. The constant joy of discovery, the opportunity to travel and investigate one's world, these are things that make a long life something to look forward to - and I do.*

CORNELL, JOHN ROBERT, lawyer; b. Boston, Nov. 7, 1943; s. Robert Cole Cornell and Thelma Marjorie (Bassett) Strout; m. Susan Lindsay Jordan, June 11, 1966; children: Jared, Joshua, Alexandra, Margaret. AB, Colby Coll., 1965; JD, Georgetown U., 1968; LLM in Taxation, NYU, 1972. Bar: N.Y. 1969, Maine 1972, U.S. Dist. Ct. Maine 1972, Ohio 1982, U.S. Tax Ct. 1990. Assoc. Dewey, Ballantine, Bushby, Palmer & Wood, N.Y.C., 1968-72; from assoc. to ptnr. Drummond, Woodsum, Plimpton & MacMahon, Portland, Maine, 1972-81; ptnr. Jones, Day, Reavis & Pogue, Cleve., 1981-98, Atlanta, 1998—; former chmn. tax group's employee benefits sect. Jones, Day, Reavis & Pogue; lectr. in field. Overseer Colby Coll., 1992-97, trustee, 1997—; trustee Cleve. San Jose Ballet, 1994-98, treas., 1995-98. Mem. ABA, Maine Bar Assn. (chmn. tax sect. 1980-81), Colby Coll. Alumni Assn. (chmn. 1979-82), Cleve. Yachting Club (Rocky River, Ohio), Anglers Club (N.Y.C.), Megantic Club (Eustis, Maine), DKE Club (N.Y.C.). Republican. Avocations: sailing, bicycling, skiing, fly fishing, water fowl hunting. Office: Jones Day Reavis & Pogue 3500 Sun Trust Plz 303 Peachtree St NE Atlanta GA 30308-3242

CORNELL, KENNETH LEE, lawyer; b. Palo Alto, Calif., Feb. 23, 1945; s. Clinton Burdette and Mildred Lucy (Sheafer) C.; m. Barbara J. Smith, June 26, 1966; children: Melinda Lee, Geoffery Mark. BBA, BA in Social Sci., Pacific Union Coll., 1966; JD, U. Wash., 1971. Bar: Wash. 1971, U.S. Dist. Ct. (we. dist.) Wash. 1971, U.S. Supreme Ct. 1974. Ptnr. Keller & Rohrback, Seattle, 1971-75, Richard, Rossano & Cornell, Seattle, 1975-77, Moren, Lageschulte (now Cornell, Hansen, Bugni & McConnell), Seattle, 1978-87, Cornell, Hansen, Bugni & McConnell PS (firm name change), 1995-98; pvt. practice Seattle, 1998—; cons. atty. Town of Clyde Hill, Wash. 1980-87. Editor Wash. U. Law Rev., 1970-71. Bd. dirs. Kirkland (Wash.) Seventh Day Adventist Sch., 1972-78, Auburn (Wash.) Acad., 1974-80, Western Wash. Corp. Seventh Day Adventists, Bothell, 1974-80. Mem. Assn. Trial Lawyers Am., Wash. State Bar Assn., Wash. State Trial Lawyers Assn., Order of Coif. Democrat. Avocations: skiing, reading, gardening. Office: 11320 Roosevelt Way NE Seattle WA 98125-6228

CORNELL, PETER MCCAUL, economic consultant, former government official; b. Thunder Bay, Ont., Can., Nov. 28, 1926; s. Maurice Leo and Jeanette Ethel (McCoy) C.; m. Kathryn Elizabeth Griffin, Sept. 7, 1949 (dec. May 1984); children—Allison, Ellen, Peter G.; m. Judith May Fagan, Sept. 14, 1991; stepchildren: Andrew Slater, Kathryn Slater. B.A. in Econs., Queen's U., Kingston, Ont., Can., 1951, M.A. in Econs., 1952; Ph.D. in Econs., Harvard U., 1956. Research officer Bank of Can., Ottawa, Ont., Can., 1956-66; economist, project dir. Econ. Council of Can., Ottawa, Ont., Can., 1966-81, dir., 1981-86. Author monographs, also articles in profl. jours. Comdr. Can. Navy, 1943-68. Mem. Ottawa Econs. Assn., Naval Officers Assn. Can. Avocations: skiing, golf, fishing. Home: 20 Cherrywood Dr, Nepean, ON Canada K2H 6G7

CORNELL, RALPH LAWRENCE, JR., publishing executive; b. Albany, N.Y., Nov. 26, 1951; s. Ralph Lawrence and Madeline (Hitchcock) C. Student, Purdue U., 1986-87. Mem. housekeeping staff Vets. Hosp., Albany, 1976-78; food svcs. supr. Univ. Aux. Svcs. SUNY, Albany, 1981-89, 95-99; owner, editor R.C. Publs., Albany, 1988—; fl. mgr. Food Court Sunya, Albany, 1994—. Author: The Moods of Madness, 1985, 3d edit., 1999, Mindless Wanderings, 1986, Tales of the Streets, 1993; editor poetry newsletter Ralph's Rev., Opportunity Digest, RC's Stamp Hotline, Notre Dame Scrapbook, 1993; editor UAS News, 1997-98. With USN, 1971-74. Recipient Golden Poet award World of Poetry, 1993. Mem. Am. Philatelic Soc. Roman Catholic. Avocations: art, bicycling, stamp and coin collecting, old books, oil painting. Home and Office: RC Publs 129A Wellington Ave Albany NY 12203-2637

CORNELL, RICHARD GARTH, biostatistics educator; b. Cleve., Nov. 18, 1930; s. Russell Gervas and Grace (Garlick) C.; m. Valma Yvonne Edwards, June 3, 1961; children: Sharon Cornell Murray, Russell Glenn, Carol Elizabeth Wheelock. B.A., U. Rochester, 1952; M.S., Va. Poly. Inst., 1954, Ph.D., 1956. Statistician, Nat. Communicable Disease Center, Atlanta, 1956-58; chief lab. and field sta. stats. unit Nat. Communicable Disease Center, 1958-60; asso. prof. stats. Fla. State U., 1960-68, prof. stats., 1968-71; prof., biostats. U. Mich., Ann Arbor, 1971-96, prof. emeritus biostats., 1996—; chmn. dept. U. Mich., 1981-84, 90-93, interim dean pub. health, 1993-95; cons. to govt. and industry. Served with USPHS, 1956-58. Mem. Biometric Soc. (program chmn. 1968, 71, pres. Eastern N.Am. region 1975, council 1978—), Am. Statist. Assn. (chmn. biometrics sect. 1973, program chmn. ann. meeting 1981), Phi Beta Kappa, Sigma Xi., Phi Kappa Phi, Pi Mu Epsilon. Baptist (deacon 1962—). Research, publs. in biometrics to sci. jours. Home: 6149 Water Works Rd Saline MI 48176-8811

CORNELL, ROB, hotel executive. Sr. v.p. Preferred Hotels and Resorts Worldwide, Chgo., 1994—. Office: Preferred Hotels & Resorts Worldwide 311 S Wacker Dr Ste 1900 Chicago IL 60606-6620*

CORNELL, ROBERT ARTHUR, retired international government official, consultant; b. Mineola, N.Y., Sept. 8, 1936; s. Herbert and Clara (Lange) C.; m. Nadine E. Dittmer, May 4, 1962 (div. June 1993); children: Robert Arthur Jr., James E., Suzanne N.; m. Catherine Rescoussie, Aug. 29, 1995. AB, Columbia U., 1958, postgrad., 1965-66; postgrad., Pacific Luth. U., 1960-61, Am. U., 1964-65; MBA, NYU, 1963. With Grace Nat. Bank, N.Y.C., 1961-63, U.S. Govt., Washington, 1963-69, IBM World Trade Corp., 1970, S.J. Rundt & Assocs., N.Y.C., 1970-71; dep. dir. Office Econ. Research U.S. Internat. Trade Commn., Washington, 1971-76, dir. Office Trade and Industry, 1976-77, dep. dir. ops., 1977-79; asst. dir. for stockpile trans. GSA, Washington, 1979-80; dep. asst. sec. for internat. trade and investment policy U.S. Treasury Dept., Washington, 1980-88; dep. sec.-gen. OECD, Paris, 1988-95; cons., editor Sannois, France, 1995—; mem. faculty U. Md., 1968; pvt. cons. in econs. and fin. Contbr. articles to profl. jours. With USN, 1958-61. Recipient Arthur S. Flemming award, 1974. Mem. Am. Econ. Assn., Western Econ. Assn., Nat. Economists Club, Nat. Assn. Bus. Economists. Lutheran. Home: 5 Place du General Leclerc, 95110 Sannois France

CORNELL, ROBERT WITHERSPOON, engineering consultant; b. Orange, N.J., Aug. 16, 1925; s. Edward Shelton and Helen Lauretta (Lawrence) C.; m. Patricia Delight Plummer, June 24, 1950; children: Richard W., Delight W. Cornell Dobby, Elizabeth Cornell Wilkin, Roberta Shelton. BSME, Yale U., 1945, MSME, 1947, D in Engring., 1950. Registered profl. engr., Conn., N.Y. Instr. math. New Haven Jr. Coll., 1947-48; analytical engr. Pratt & Whitney Aircraft, East Hartford, Conn., 1947; with Hamilton Standard, Windsor Locks, Conn., 1948-87, chief applied mechanics and aerodynamics, 1961-87; instr. engring. Hillyer Coll., Hartford, 1955; pres. Cornell Cons., 1973—, Cornell Enterprises, West Hartford, 1984—; adj. prof. Yale U., 1985, 90. Contbr. articles to profl. jours. Patentee in field. Bd. dirs., treas. Yale Sci. and Engring. Assn., 1969—; Conn. State Taxpayers Assn., Stratford, 1984-86; past pres., bd. dirs. West Hartford Taxpayers Assn., 1972-97; rep. state senatorial candidate 5th dist. State of Conn., 1988, 94, state rep. candidate 18th dist., 1990; mem. Svc. Corps. Ret. Execs., 1989—, chmn. 1998—; dir. Agawam Coun., 1993—. With USN, 1943-46. Fellow ASME; mem. Yale Club (Hartford, Conn. and N.Y.C.), Hartford Golf Club, Sigma Xi, Tau Beta Pi. Avocations: tennis, squash, jogging, swimming, gardening. Home and Office: 40 Belknap Rd Hartford CT 06117-2819

CORNELL, RYAN SCOTT MICHAEL, communications company executive; b. Newburgh, N.Y., Apr. 18, 1972; s. Richard Harry Cornell and Donna Marie DeCrosta. BBA cum laude, U. Miami, Coral Gables, Fla., 1994. Nat. mgr. sales and mktg. Campuslink Comms., Stamford, Conn., 1994-96; v.p. Donna Cornell Enterprises, Inc., 1996—. Bd. dirs. St. Catherine's Youth Ministry, Riverside, Conn. Mem. Stamford C. of C., Golden Key Nat. Honor Soc., Beta Gamma Sigma, Phi, Kappa Phi. Republican. Roman Catholic. Avocations: boating, traveling, golf, racquetball. Home: 674 River Rd Newburgh NY 12550-1350

CORNELL, THOMAS BROWNE, artist, educator; b. Cleve., Mar. 1, 1937; s. Norman Monrod and Betty (Browne) C.; m. Christa Vaughan Kinkel, May 1, 1976; children: Anna Olivia, Nicolas Browne, Diana Camille. B.A., Amherst Coll., 1959; postgrad. art and architecture, Yale U., 1959-60. Faculty U. Calif., Santa Barbara, 1960-62; prof. art Bowdoin Coll., Brunswick, Maine, 1962—; mem. visual arts program Princeton U., 1969-70. Author: The Monkey with 11 etchings, 1959, The Defense of Gracchus Babeuf with 21 etchings, 1964, Voiceprints with 5 etchings, 1988; one-man shows, Yale U. Art Gallery, Williams Coll. Art Mus., Santa Barbara Mus. Art, 1965, Wesleyan U., Conn., 1967, Bowdoin Coll., Maine, Princeton U., 1971, Muhlenberg Coll., 1976, Barridoff Galleries, Maine, U. Bridgeport, Conn., 1977, U. Redlands, Calif., 1979, A. M. Sachs Gallery, N.Y.C., 1979, 81, Santa Barbara (Calif.) Mus. Art, 1980, Morehead State U., Ky., 1986, G.W. Einstein Co., N.Y.C., 1986, 89, 97, Bowdoin Coll. Mus. Art, Maine, 1990; group shows include, DeCordova Mus., Lincoln, Mass., 1963, Mus. Modern Art, N.Y.C., 1966, Pa. State U., 1974, Maine State Mus., Bklyn. Mus., 1976, Cleve. Mus. Art, 1976, USIA, 1977, U. Va. Art Mus., 1978, Tatistcheff & Co., N.Y.C., 1979, Nat. Portrait Gallery, Washington, Artists Choice Mus., N.Y.C., Weatherspoon Art Gallery, N.C., Pratt Graphic Center, N.Y.C., 1980, Brit. Internat. Print Biennele, West Yorkshire, 1982, Robert Schoelkopf Gallery Ltd., N.Y.C., 1982, 84, 89, Twentieth Century Am., travelling exhbn., 1984-85, G.W. Einstein Co., N.Y.C., 1985, 86, 87, 88, 91, 92, 93, 94, 95, 96, Bayly Art Mus., U. Va., 1987, Bank of Boston, Plein Air-an Exhibition, 1986, So. Alleghenies Mus. Art, 1988, Robert Schoelkopf Gallery, N.Y.C., 1989, Kuznutsky Most Exhbn. Hall, Moscow, 1989, The Baxter Gallery, Portland, Maine, 1989, The Ark. Arts Ctr., Little Rock, 1989; The Mus. of Modern Art, art adv. svc. exhbn. at Am. Express Co., 1987, 88, 94, Md. Inst. Coll. Art, 1989, Douglas F. Cooley Meml. Art Gallery, Portland, Oreg., 1990, Noyes Mus., Oceanville, N.J., 1990, Ark. Arts Ctr., Little Rock, 1990, 94, U. Maine, Augusta, 1990, So. Alleghenies Mus. Art, 1991, Barn Gallery, Ogunquit, Maine, 1991, Nat. Acad. Design, N.Y.C., 1991, 93, 94, 96, 97, Webster U., St. Louis, 1992, The Monmouth Mus., Lincroft, N.J., 1992, Portland Mus. of Art, Portland, Maine, 1993, Ark. Arts Ctr., 1994, Icon Gallery, Brunswick, Maine, 1994, J.S. Ames Fine Art, Belfast, Maine, 1995, Bowdoin Coll. Mus., Brunswick, 1996. Recipient Louis Comfort Tiffany award, 1961, Nat. Inst. Arts and Letters award, 1964; Nat. Found. on Arts and Humanities fellow, 1966-67; Fulbright grantee Inst. for Internat. Edn., 1966; grantee Ford Found., 1969-70, Pollock-Krasner Found., 1993. Mem. Coll. Art Assn., Figurative Alliance N.Y., NAD, Union Maine Visual Artists (pres. 1990-91). *

CORNELL, THOMAS CHARLES, peace activist, writer; b. Bridgeport, Conn., Apr. 11, 1934; s. Thomas Charles Cornell and Ann (Caruso) Cornell Rice; m. Monica Mary Ribar, July 7, 1964; children: Thomas Christopher, Deirdre Ann. AB in English, Fairfield U., 1956; MS in Secondary Edn., U. Bridgeport, 1962; diaconate, St. Thomas Sem., 1988; DLH (hon.), Fairfield U., 1990. Ordained deacon Roman Catholic Ch., 1988. Instr. English and Latin pub. schs., Brookfield, Conn., 1959-62; mng. editor The Catholic Worker, N.Y.C., 1962-64; program dir. Fellowship of Reconciliation, Nyack, N.Y., 1965-79; nat. sec. Cath. Peace Fellowship, N.Y.C., 1965—; freelance writer and lecturer, 1979-81; instr. Enlish and Latin pub. schs., Conway, N.H., 1981-82; soup kitchens dir. Waterbury Area Coun. Churches, Conn., 1982-92; coord. Peter Maurin Cath. Worker Farm, Marlborough, N.Y., 1993—; adj. prof. religion, Mercy Coll., Dobbs Ferry and Peekskill, N.Y., 1979-81, St. Joseph Sem., Yonkers, N.Y., 1997—; contbg. editor, The Catholic Worker, 1994—; del. Third World Congress Laity, 1967, Bishops' Bicentennial Call to Action, 1976. Editor: (with James H. Forest) A Penny a Copy: Readings from The Catholic Worker, 1968, expanded edit. (with R.E. Ellsberg and J.H. Forest), 95; contbr. articles to profl. jours. and newspapers. Mem. exec. com. War Resisters League, 1970-72; co-founder and mem. Pax Christi, USA, organized first pub. demonstration against U.S. participation in Vietnam, 1963, first group act resistance againt Vietnam draft, 1965, imprisoned, Danbury Fed. Corectional Inst., 1968, pardoned by Pres. Jimmy Carter, 1978. Recipient Catholic Peace Fellowship award, 1985, Liberty Bell award Waterbury Bar Assn., 1986. Democrat. Home: Peter Maurin Farm 41 Cemetery Rd Marlborough NY 12542 Office: Catholic Peace Fellowship 55 E 3d St New York NY 10003-9003

CORNELL, WILLIAM DANIEL, mechanical engineer; b. Valley Falls, Kans., Apr. 17, 1919; s. Noah P. and Mabel (Hennessy) C.; m. Barbara L. Ferguson, Aug. 30, 1942; children—Alice Margaret, Randolph William. BS in Mech. Engring., U. Ill., 1942. Registered profl. engr., N.Y. Research engr. Linde Air Products Co., Buffalo, 1942-48, cons. to Manhattan Dist. project, 1944-46; project engr. devel. of automatic bowling machine Am. Machine and Foundry, Buffalo, 1948-55; cons. Gen. Electric Co., Hanford, Wash., 1949-50; project engr. devel. of automatic bowling machine Brunswick Corp., Muskegon, Mich., 1955-59, mgr. advanced engring., 1959-72; mgr. advanced concepts and tech. Sherwood Med. Industries div. Am. Home Products Corp., St. Louis, 1972-85; mem. faculty Coll. Engring., U. Buffalo, 1946-47; cons. Cornell Engring., St. Louis, 1985—; mem. faculty Coll. Engring. Washington U., St. Louis, 1993-94. Patentee numerous inventions, including automatic golf and bowling game apparatus, med. instruments; developer new method of measuring hemoglobin and new method of counting platelets in whole blood. Recipient Navy E award, 1945, Manhattan Project Recognition award, 1945, Merit award Maritime Commn., 1945. Republican. Presbyterian. Home and Office: 907 Camargo Dr Ballwin MO 63011-1506 *My daughter says "He uses the think system".*

CORNELL, WILLIAM HARVEY, clergyman; b. Pitts., May 27, 1934; s. Floyd Anderson and Audrey Fern (Wasson) C.; m. Betty Jean Yates, July 24, 1954; children: Deborah Jean, William Mark, Darla Ruth. AA, Central (S.C.) Wesleyan Coll., 1953; AB in Religion, Ind. Wesleyan U., 1956. Ordained to ministry Wesleyan Meth. Ch., 1958. Clergyman Wilgus Wesleyan Meth. Ch., Gypsy, Pa., 1956-59, Wolf Summit (W.Va.) Wesleyan Meth. Ch., 1959-63, Canal Wesleyan Meth. Ch., Utica, Pa., 1968-73, Greenville (Pa.) Wesleyan Meth. Ch., 1973-76, Salem (Ohio) Wesleyan Meth. Ch., 1976-78, Sagamore (Pa.) Wesleyan Meth. Ch., 1963-68, 78-95, Niles (Ohio) Wesleyan Meth. Ch., 1995—; mem. mission bd. Allegheny Wesleyan Meth. Connection, 1965—, sec., 1973-98, editor ann. jour., 1973-98, mem. adv. bd., 1978-98; sec. N.W. Indian Bible Sch., Alberton, Mont., 1969—. Republican. Avocations: hunting, travel. Home and Office: 960 Lafayette Ave Niles OH 44446-3160

CORNELSON, GEORGE HENRY, IV, retired textile company executive; b. Spartanburg, S.C., July 12, 1931; s. George Henry III and Elizabeth Marshall (Woodward) C.; m. Ann Martin Shaw, Oct. 6, 1956; children: George Henry V, Martin Shaw, Scott Montgomery, Elizabeth Woodward. Student, Davidson Coll., 1949-51; BS in Textiles, N.C. State U., 1953; postgrad., Harvard U., 1953-54, Harvard U. With indsl. engring. dept. Clinton (S.C.) Mills, Inc., 1954-55, 57-58, v.p., 1958-70, exec. v.p., 1970-79, pres., 1979-86, chief exec. officer, 1985-86; v.p. Clinton Mills Sales Corp., 1958-70; pres. Clinton Investment Co., 1985-86; bd. dirs. Elastic Fabrics of Am., N.C. Textile Found. (also exec. com.), Clinton Mills of Geneva (also past pres.); vice chmn. bd. dirs. Bailey Fin. Corp., 1996-99; mem. S.C. Gov.'s Trade Mission to Far East, Hong Kong, Singapore, Kuala Lumpur, Malaysia, Taiwan. *While serving as organzing Chairman of the Greater Clinton Planning Commission, planning was initiated to remove the Columbia, Newberry and Laurens Railroad Tracks in downtown Clinton in order to improve auto traffic. Also planning was initiated with the So. Car. Hwy. Dept. to construct the ring road by-pass for hwy. 72 and hwy. 56. Planning was also commenced for the construction of the Clinton City Hall in 1967-68.* Trustee Presbyn. Coll., Clinton, 1959-68, 94—; trustee Davidson (N.C.) Coll., 1992-95, bd. visitors, 1986-91; trustee Ind. Coll. and Univs. S.C., 1971-92, life trustee, 1993—; trustee Thornwell Home for Children, Clinton, 1968-76, exec. comn., 1973-74, sec. bd. trustees, 1974; organizing chmn. Greater Clinton Planning Commn., 1967; pres. Cmty. Chest and United Fund, 1963-64; chmn. Laurens County dist. Boy Scouts Am., 1973, exec. bd. Blue Ridge Coun., 1974-94; deacon 1st Presbyn. Ch., Clinton, 1959-67, elder, 1967-73, 76-81, 83-87, 88-93; chair adv. com. Bailey Found., 1969-99; bd. regents Leadership Laurens County, 1988-91; dir. S.C. State Mus. Found., 1986-89; expansion com. Carolina's NFL, 1988-92; bd. dirs. Colombia Theol. Sem., Decatur, Ga., 1990-93; trustee Laurens County Health Care Sys., 1996—, chmn. 1997-99. Served in USAF, 1955-57. Recipient Disting. Service award Clinton Jr. C. of C., 1962, Outstanding Young Alumnus award N.C. State U., 1965, Disting. Alumnus award McCallie Sch., 1989, Disting. Alumnus award N.C. State U., 1999. Mem. Am. Textile Mfrs. Inst. (rsch. and tech. svcs. com. 1964-71, vice chmn. crafted with pride in U.S.A. com. 1985-87, vice chmn. edn. com. 1975-76, mem. cotton com. 1981-82, safety and health com. 1981-82), S.C. Textile Mfrs. Assn. (bd. dirs. 1973-82, pres. 1979-80), S.C. C. of C. (bd. dirs., exec. com. 1975-79), Clinton C. of C. (bd. dirs. 1959-61, 66, v.p. 1968, pres. 1969), Lions, Musgrove Mill Golf Club (founding mem., bd. dirs. 1982-99), Phi Psi, Kappa Alpha. Home: Rte 2 Box 354 Merrie Oaks Clinton SC 29325 *1967- While serving as organizing Chairman of the Greater Clinton Planning Commission, planning was initiated to remove the Columbia, Newberry and Laurens Railroad Tracks in downtown Clinton in order to improve auto traffic. Also planning was initiated with the So. Car. Hwy. Dept. to construct the ring road by-pass for hwy. 72 and hwy. 56. Planning was also commenced for the construction of the Clinton City Hall in 1967-68.*

CORNELY, PAUL BERTAU, retired physician, educator; b. Guadeloupe, French W.I., Mar. 9, 1906; came to U.S., 1921, naturalized, 1934; s. Eleodore and Adrienne (Mellon) C.; m. Mae Stewart, June 23, 1934; 1 child, Paul Bertau. A.B., U. Mich., 1928, M.D., 1931, Dr. P.H., 1934, D.Sc. (hon.), 1968; D. Pub. Service (hon.), U. of Pacific, 1972; ScD (hon.), Howard U., 1992. Diplomate: Bd. Preventive Medicine and Pub. Health. Intern Lincoln Hosp., Durham, N.C., 1931-32; mem. faculty Howard U. Coll. Medicine, Washington, 1934—; chief div. phys. medicine and rehab. Howard U. Coll. Medicine, 1959-64, prof., chmn. dept. preventive medicine and pub. health, 1955-73, prof. emeritus, 1973—; pres. Tech. Assos., Inc., 1977-84; med. dir. Freedmen's Hosp., Washington, 1947-58; chmn. bd. dirs. Profl. Exam. Service, 1978-81; cons. AID, 1960-74; asst. to exec. med. officer United Mine Workers Welfare and Retirement Fund, Inc., 1971-74; sr. med. cons. System Scis. Inc., Bethesda, Md., 1973-81; mem. Pres.'s Commn. on Population and Am.'s Future, 1970-72; mem. com. of cons. on cancer Senate Com. on Labor and Pub. Welfare, 1970-72; mem. exec. com. Pres.'s Com. on Employment of Handicapped, 1971-85; bd. dirs. Physicians Forum, 1947-67, pres., 1960-61; pres. Community-Group Health Found., 1968-73. Bd. dirs. Pub. Citizen Found., 1992. Recipient Sesquicentennial award U. Mich., 1967; Nat. Merit award Delta Omega Soc., 1979; Disting. U.S. Immigrant award Citizens Com. Immigration Reform, 1982. Fellow Am. Coll. Preventive Medicine, Am. Coll. Hosp. Adminstrs. (hon.); mem. Med. Soc. D.C. (Community Service award 1964), Am. Cancer Soc. (v.p. 1962- 63), Am. Pub. Health Assn. (exec. com. 1964-71, pres. 1969-70, chmn. exec. bd. 1970-71, Sedgwick Meml. award 1972), D.C. Pub. Health Assn. (pres. 1963-65, Disting. Service award 1971). Home: 1220 E West Hwy Apt 622 Silver Spring MD 20910-3271

CORNETT, DONNA J., counselor, alcohol moderation administrator; b. Calif., Jan. 26, 1949; d. L.D. and Shirley A. Cornett. BA in Psychology, San Jose State U., 1972, MA in Psychology, 1973. Founder dir., Drink/Link Moderation Program, Santa Rosa, Calif., 1987—; founder, dir. The Responsible Drinking Inst. Am., Santa Rosa, 1994—; mem. Responsible Hospitality Project, San Rafael, Calif., 1993-95. Author: 7 Weeks to Safe Social Drinking: How to Effectively Moderate Your Alcohol Intake, 1996; copyrighted moderation program developer, 1987. Mem. Calif. State Psychol. Assn. Avocations: writing, gardening, moderate drinking, psychology. Office: The Drink/Link Moderation Program PO Box 5441 Santa Rosa CA 95402-5441

CORNETT, GREGG, newspaper publisher, newspaper editor, computer company executive; b. Dayton, Ohio, May 12, 1954. PhD in Computer Sci. Pres. Computer Commuter, Batesville, Ark., 1982-87, Gregg Cornett Assocs., Batesville, Bald Knob, Searcy, Ark., 1984—; pub., editor Bald Knob Banner, 1987—; CEO G.C.A. Computer Svcs., 1993—; v.p. Wood Nursery, Inc., 1995-96; systems analyst Arkansas Pub., 1996—; police photographer Bald Knob Police Dept., 1988—; computer cons. Gregg Cornett Assocs., 1984—, freelance journalist, Bald Knob, 1987—. Author (booklet) Neighborhood Crime Prevention, 1989; contbr. articles to newspapers. Area coord. City Crime Prevention, Bald Knob, 1988—; assoc. KARK-TV Community Network, Little Rock, 1990—; acting city clk. City of Bald Knob, 1991; rural community cons. City of Bald Knob, 1988—; founding bd. dirs. Rsch. Internat., Aruba. Recipient Better Newspaper Advt. award Ark. Press Assn., 1988; Gregg Cornett Day proclaimed by City of Bald Knob, 1990. Fellow Rotary; mem. C. of C. (bd. dirs. 1988—). Avocations: writing, photography, electronics.

CORNETT, LLOYD HARVEY, JR., retired historian; b. Seminole, Okla., Aug. 29, 1930; s. Lloyd Harvey and Edna Lee (Walker) C.; children from previous marriage: Lloyd Harvey III, Rosemary Lynne, Carlton Wayne, Curtis Lee; m. Sarah Frances Missildine, Apr. 15, 1992. B.A., U. Okla., 1951, M.A., 1954; postgrad., U. N.Mex., 1965, Auburn U., 1977. Asst. dir. command history 2d Air Force, U.S. Air Force, 1955-57; historian Air Def. Command, 1957-58, asst. dir. command history Continental Air Def. Command, 1958-59, asst. dir. command history N.Am. Air Def. Command, 1959-61, center historian Air Force Missile Devel. Center, 1961-70, historian Air Force Spl. Weapons Center, 1970-72, command historian Aerospace Def. Command, 1972-73, command historian Air Tng. Command, 1973-74; dir. U.S. Air Force Hist. Rsrch. Ctr., Maxwell AFB, Ala., 1974-89; prin. Ind. Hist. Rsch./Adv. Svc., Montgomery, Ala., 1989—; Mem. Gov.'s Com. for Ala. Conf. on Library and Info. Services; bd. advisors Ala. Hist. Commn. Co-editor: Vol. of Am. Astronautical Soc. Hist. and (sch. text) Hist. of Ala., 1998; contbr. to hist. jours. Committeeman Boy Scouts Am., 1963-70, 75-79; mem. at large adminstrv. bd. Meth. Ch., 1978-81. Served with USMCR, 1951-53. Mem. AIAA (chmn. tech. com. on history 1983-96), Am. Astronautical Soc. Hist. Com., Western History Assn., Soc. for History in Fed. Govt. Democrat. Home and Office: 3751 Marie Cook Dr Montgomery AL 36109-1509

CORNETT, RICHARD ORIN, research educator, consultant; b. Driftwood, Okla., Nov. 14, 1913; s. Grover Cleveland and Essie (Richardson) C.; m. Lorene Huston, May 26, 1943; children: Linda, Robert, Stanley. B.S., Okla. Baptist U., 1934; M.S., U. Okla., 1937; postgrad., U. Ill., 1938-39; Ph.D., U. Tex., 1940; D.Sc., Hardin-Simmons U., 1954; Litt.D., Jacksonville U., 1964; LL.D., Belknap Coll., 1967. Instr. physics Okla. Bapt. U., 1935-37, assoc. prof., 1940-41, prof., 1941; asst. supr. physics Pa. State Engring., Sci., Mgmt., Def. Tng. Program, 1941-42; lectr. electronics Harvard U., 1942-45; spl. research asso. OSRD, 1945; asst. to pres. Okla. Baptist U., 1945-46, v.p., 1946-47, exec. v.p., 1947-51; exec. sec. Edn. Commn., So. Bapt. Conv., 1951-58, So. Assn. Bapt. Colls. and Schs., 1951-58; editor So. Bapt. Educator, 1951-58; specialist for coll. and univ. orgn. and adminstrn. U.S. Office Edn., 1959, exec. asst. to dir. div. higher edn., 1959-61, acting asst. commr., dir., 1961-64, dir. div. ednl. orgn. and adminstrn., 1964-65; v.p. Gallaudet Coll., Washington, 1965-75, research prof., dir. cued speech programs, 1976-84; prof. emeritus Gallaudet U. (formerly coll.), 1985—; prin. investigator field test of wearable electronic lipreading aid for deaf, 1988-89; mem. U.S. del. UNESCO Conf. on Devel. Higher Edn. in Africa, 1962; dir. Ann. Inst. on Coll. and Univ. Planning, Soc. for Coll. and Univ. Planning, 1975-77; nat. lectr. Sigma Xi, 1983-85. Author: (with White, Weber, Manning) Practical Physics, 1943, Algebra, A Second Course, 1945, Electron Tubes and Circuits, 1947, Cued Speech lessons in 33 langs., Cued Speech Handbook for Parents, 1971, Cued Speech Resource Book for Parents of Deaf Children, 1992. Recipient Disting. Svc. award Nat. Coun. on Communicative Disorders, 1992. Republican. Baptist. Achievements include originator of Cued Speech communication method for deaf, adapted to 56 languages and major dialects as of May 1994; originator, co-developer electronic lipreading aid for deaf; author of recorded lessons in cued speech in 33 languages and major dialects; patentee in field. Home: 8702 Royal Ridge Ln Laurel MD 20708-2458 Office: Gallaudet U Florida Ave And 7th St Washington DC 20002 *If one is to be included in the company of those who give their very best, he must be able to create within himself a vision of success and have the courage* *to follow that vision. Two kinds of men follow visions: those who are fools and those who do great things. The man who sees a vision and has the impulse to follow it is not permitted to know in advance which he will turn out to be.*

CORNETTE, WILLIAM MAGNUS, scientist, technical advisor; b. San Francisco, Apr. 17, 1945; s. William Magnus and Elisabeth Louise (Stone) C.; m. Patricia Ruth King, Mar. 24, 1968 (div. Oct. 1981); children: Christopher Scott, David Warren; m. Sylvia Annette Martin, Jan. 6, 1982; 1 child, Jennifer Nicole. BS with high honors, U. Fla., 1967; MS, U. Chgo., 1969; PhD, U. Denver, 1973. Mathematician Naval Weapons Ctr., China Lake, Calif., 1973-77; specialist engr. Boeing Co., Seattle, 1977-80; v.p., dir. Photon Research Assocs., La Jolla, Calif., 1980-95, Observables Tech., 1989, Adv. Phenomenologies and Models, 1992; sci. advisor for def. modeling and simulation Nat. Imagery and Mapping Agy., Bethesda, Md., 1995—; cons. Denali Software Systems, San Diego, 1983-91. Contbr. articles to profl. jours. With USAF, 1969-73. Mem. Optical Soc. Am., Wilderness Soc., Sierra Club, Am. Geophys. Union, German Philatelic Soc. (working group chmn. 1985-89), U.S. Figure Skating Assn., Phi Beta Kappa, Sigma Xi. Avocations: backpacking, river running, photography. Home: 9529 Stevebrook Rd Fairfax VA 22032-2033 Office: Nat Imagery and Mapping Agy P-23 12310 Sunrise Valley Dr # P23 Reston VA 20191-3414*

CORNFELD, DAVE LOUIS, lawyer; b. St. Louis, Dec. 24, 1921; s. Abraham and Rebecca (David) C.; m. Martha Herrmann, May 30, 1943; children: Richard Steven, James Allen, Lawrence Joseph. A.B., Washington U., St. Louis, 1942, LL.B. (editor Law Quar. 1943), 1943. Bar: Mo. 1943. Practice law St. Louis; ptnr. Husch & Eppenberger, 1954—; adj. prof. Washington U., 1966-87. Co-author: Missouri Estate Planning, Will Drafting and Estate Administration, 2 vol., 1988, supplement, 1998. Bd. dirs. Jewish Fedn., St. Louis, 1977-80, 83-88, Jewish Ctr. for Aged, 1981-88; mem. adv. com. U. Miami Inst. Estate Planning, 1979—. Served with AUS, 1945-46. Mem. ABA (past chmn. com. taxation income estates and trusts, vice chmn. sect. taxation 1977-80, editor-in-chief Tax Lawyer 1977-80, sr. assoc. editor Probate and Property), St. Louis Bar Assn. (past chmn. taxation com), Am. Law Inst., Am. Coll. Trust and Estate Counsel (regent 1984-90), Am. Coll. Tax Counsel (regent 1980-88), Internat. Acad. Estate and Trust Law, Order of Coif. Jewish (trustee temple 1967-91). Club: Masons. Home: 834 Oakbrook Ln Saint Louis MO 63132-4812 Office: Husch & Eppenberger 100 N Broadway Ste 1300 Saint Louis MO 63102-2789

CORNFIELD, MELVIN, lawyer, university institute director; b. Chgo., June 5, 1927; s. Harry and Annabelle (Maltz) C.; m. Edith Pauline Haas, June 24, 1951; children: Daniel Benjamin, Deborah S. Cornfield Alexander. AB, U. Chgo., 1948, JD, 1951. Bar: D.C. 1951, N.Y. 1958. Atty. durable goods div. Office Price Stblzn., Washington, 1951-53; atty., advisor Chief Counsel's Office IRS, Washington, 1953-58; assoc. Willkie, Farr, Gallagher, Walton & FitzGibbon, N.Y.C., 1958-63; dir. taxes NBC, Inc., 1963-66; staff v.p. tax affairs RCA Corp., N.Y.C., 1966-76, v.p., treas., 1976-82, v.p. tax affairs, 1982-85; dir. NYU Tax Inst., 1985-94. With USAAF, 1946-47. Home: 4703 Iselin Ave Bronx NY 10471-3323

CORNFORTH, SIR JOHN WARCUP, chemist; b. Sydney, Australia, Sept. 7, 1917; s. John William and Hilda (Eipper) C.; m. Rita H. Harradence, Sept. 27, 1941; children: Brenda (Mrs. David Osborne), John, Philippa (Mrs. William Horder). BSc, U. Sydney, 1937, MSc, 1938; DPhil, Oxford U., 1941, DSc (hon.), 1976; DSc (hon.), E.T.H. Zurich, 1975, Trinity Coll., Dublin, Univs. Liverpool, Warwick, Aberdeen, Hull, Sussex, Kent and Sydney. Mem. sci. staff Med. Research Council, London, 1946-62; dir. Milstead Lab. Chem. Enzymology, Shell Research Ltd., Sittingbourne, Kent, Eng., 1962-75; Royal Soc. rsch. prof. Sch. Chemistry and Molecular Scis. U. Sussex, Brighton, Eng., 1975-82. Contbr. articles on chemistry of penicillin, total synthesis of steroids and other biologically active natural products, chemistry of heterocyclic compounds, biosynthesis of steroids, enzyme chemistry to profl. jours. Decorated comdr. Brit. Empire; knighted, 1977; apptd. Companion of the Order of Australia, 1991; recipient Stouffer prize, 1967, Prix Roussel, 1972, Nobel Prize in Chemistry, 1975. Fellow Royal Soc., 1953 (Davy medal 1968, Royal medal 1976, Copley medal 1982), Royal Soc. Chemistry (Corday-Morgan medal 1953, Flintoff medal 1966), Am. Chem. Soc. (Ernest Guenther award 1969); mem. Biochem. Soc. (CIBA medal 1966), Am. Soc. Biol. Chemists (hon.), Am. Acad. (hon. fgn. mem.), Australian Acad. Sci. (corr.), Netherlands Acad. Sci. (fgn.), NAS (fgn. assoc.). Home: Saxon Down, Cuilfail, Lewes BN7 2BE, England Office: U Sussex Sch Chemistry, Physics & Environ Sci, Falmer Brighton BN1 9QJ, England

CORNGOLD, STANLEY ALAN, German and comparative literature educator, writer; b. Bklyn., June 11, 1934; s. Herman and Estelle (Bramson) C.; m. Marie Josephine Brettle, July 29, 1961 (div. May 1969); 1 child, Isabel Anna; m. Regine Schmidt-Üllner, Feb. 18, 1995. AB, Columbia U., 1957; postgrad., Sch. Oriental and African Studies-U. London, 1957-58; M.A., Cornell U., 1963, Ph.D., 1969; postgrad., U. Basel (Switzerland), 1965-66. Instr. English U. Md. European div., 1959-62; teaching asst. English Cornell U., 1963-64; teaching asst. French Cornell U, 1964-65; asst. prof. German Princeton U., 1966-72, assoc. prof., 1972-79, assoc. prof. German and comparative lit., 1979-81, prof., 1981—, dir. grad. studies dept. German, 1979-82, 85, 93-95, 96-97. Author: The Commentators' Despair, 1973, The Fate of the Self, 1986, 2d edit., 1994, Franz Kafka: The Necessity of Form, 1988, Complex Pleasure: Forms of Feeling in German Literature, 1998; co-author: Borrowed Lives, 1991; editor: Ausgewählte Prosa by Max Frisch, 1968, Aspekte der Goethezeit, 1975, Thomas Mann, 1875-1975, Norton Critical Edition of the Metamorphosis (Franz Kafka), 1996; translator, editor: The Metamorphosis (Franz Kafka), 1972; translator: essays Walter Benjamin, Selected Writings, 1996. Served with U.S. Army, 1955-57. Named Am. Coun. Learned Socs. fellow, 1965-66, NEH fellow, 1973-74, Guggenheim Found. fellow, 1977-78, Fulbright fellow, 1986, Hölderlin Residence fellow, 1990, 98, Literarisches Colloquium, Berlin fellow, 1990. Mem. PEN, MLA (exec. com. divsn. on philos. approaches to lit. 1993-97, past chair, pub. com. 1993-95), Acad. Lit. Studies, N.Am. Nietzsche Soc., Kafka Soc. Am. (past pres.), Heidelberg Club Internat. Home: 51 Ridgeview Cir Princeton NJ 08540-7603 Office: Princeton U Dept German 224 E Pyne Bldg Princeton NJ 08544

CORNIES, LARRY ALAN, journalist, educator; b. Leamington, Ont., Can., Apr. 4, 1953; s. William Walter and Helen Louise (Rempel) C.; m. Jacquelyn Ann Brown, Aug. 17, 1974; children: Darryl, Graeme, Andrew, Natalie. BA in Religious Studies, U. Waterloo, 1975; postgrad., Wichita State U., 1981-84; MA in Journalism, U. Western Ontario, 1986. Comm. officer Conrad Grebel Coll., Waterloo, Ont., 1974-75; secondary sch. tchr. United Mennonite Ednl. Inst., Leamington, 1975-80; assoc. editor The Mennonite, Newton, Kans., 1980-84; comm. dir. Mennonite Ch. Hdqs., Newton, 1984-85; mng. editor London (Ont.) Mag., 1986-88; arts and entertainment editor The London Free Press, 1989-93, cluster editor, 1993-97, asst. city editor, 1997-98, Forum editor, 1998—; adj. prof. faculty info. and media studies U. Western Ont., 1987—; corr. World Report, Washington, 1983-85, Ecumedia News, N.Y.C., 1982-85; bd. govs. Conrad Grebel Coll., U. Waterloo, Ont., 1994-97. Author: Essays in Journalism, 1986. Bd. dirs. divsn. gen. svcs. Gen. Conf. Mennonite Ch., Newton, Kans., 1995—. Recipient Derose-Hinkhouse award Religious Pub. Rels. Coun., 1985. Mem. Coun. Ch. and Media (chmn. 1991-93). Avocations: music, baseball. Home: 759 Barclay Rd, London, ON Canada N6K 1K4 Office: London Free Press, 369 York St, London, ON Canada N6A 4G1

CORNING, JOY COLE, former state official; b. Bridgewater, Iowa, Sept. 7, 1932; d. Perry Aaron and Ethel Marie (Sullivan) Cole; m. Burton Eugene Corning, June 19, 1955; children: Carol, Claudia, Ann. BA, U. No. Iowa, 1954; hon. degree, Allen Coll. Nursing. Cert. elem. tchr., Iowa. Tchr. elem. sch. Greenfield (Iowa) Sch. Dist., 1951-53, Waterloo (Iowa) Cmty. Sch. Dist., 1954-55; mem. Iowa Senate, Des Moines, 1984-90, asst. Rep. leader, 1989-90; lt. gov. State of Iowa, Des Moines, 1991-99; past chmn. Nat. Conf. Lt. Govs. Mem. Iowa Legacy 150 Inst.; mem. policy bd. Performing Arts Ctr., U. No. Iowa, also bd. dirs. Found.; bd. dirs. Nat. Conf. Cmty. and Justice, Des Moines Symphony, The Caring Found. Legacy 150, U. No. Iowa, NCCJ. Named Citizen of Yr., Cedar Falls C. of C., 1984; recipient ITAG Disting. Svc. to Iowa's Gifted and Talented Students award, 1991, Pub. Svc. award Iowa Home Econs. Assn., 1994, Friend of Math. award Iowa Coun. Tchrs. of Math., 1995, Iowa State Edn. Assn. Human Rels. award, 1996, Govs. Affirmative Action award, Spl. Recognition award Nat. Foster Parent Assoc., Des Moines Human Rights Commn. award, Pub. Svc. award Coalition for Family and Children's Svcs in Iowa, Friends of Iowa Civil Rights, Inc. award, Martin Luther King Jr. Lifetime Svc. award, 1999; recognized for Extraordinary Advocacy for Children of Iowa chpt. Nat. Com. for Child Abuse, award for leadership Early Care and Edn. Congress. Mem. AAUW, LWV, PEO, Nat. Assn. for Gifted Children (mem. adv. bd. 1991—), Delta Kappa Gamma, Alpha Delta Kappa. Republican. Mem. United Ch. of Christ. Home: 4323 Grand Ave Apt 324 Des Moines IA 50312-2443

CORNING, NICHOLAS F., lawyer; b. Seattle, Nov. 8, 1945; s. Frank C. and Jessie D. (Weeks) C.; m. Patricia A. Tomlinson, Dec. 14, 1968; children: Kristen Marie, Lauren Margaret. BCS cum laude, Seattle U., 1968; JD, U. Wash., 1972. Bar: Wash. 1972, U.S. Ct. Appeals (9th cir.) 1972, U.S. Dist. Ct. (we. dist.) Wash. 1973, U.S. Supreme Ct. 1976, U.S. Ct. Claims 1981. Assoc. Jennings P. Felix, Seattle, 1972-75; ptnr. Lagerquist, McConnell & Corning, Seattle, 1975-77; pres., ptnr. Treece, Richdale, Malone, Corning & Abbott, Inc., P.S., Seattle, 1977-99; atty. Corning Law Firm, Seattle, 1999—; pres. Windermere Corp., Seattle, 1988, also bd. dirs. Recipient Am. Jurisprudence award in Criminal Law U. Wash., 1971. Mem. Assn. Trial Lawyers Am., Nat. Inst. Trial Advocacy, Wash. State Bar Assn., Wash. State Trial Lawyers Assn. (pres. 1994-95, bd. dirs.), King County Bar Assn. (spkrs. bur. 1983-85, chmn. pub. info. com. 1985-87), Ballard C. of C. (bd. dirs., pres. 1989-92), Beta Gamma Sigma (Key award 1968). Home: 5640 NE 55th St Seattle WA 98105-2835 Office: The Corning Law Firm 5301 Ballard Ave NW Seattle WA 98107

CORNISH, EDWARD SEYMOUR, magazine editor; b. N.Y.C., Aug. 31, 1927; s. George Anthony and Elizabeth Furniss (McLeod) C.; m. Sally Woodhull, Oct. 12, 1957 (dec. Mar. 1992); children: George Anthony, Jefferson Richard Woodhull, Blake McLeod. Diplome d'etudes, U. Paris, France, 1948; AB, Harvard U., 1950. Copy boy, cub reporter Evening Star, Washington, 1950-51; staff corr. U.P. Assn., Richmond, Va., 1951-52, Raleigh, N.C., 1952-53, London, 1953-54, Paris, 1954-55, Rome, 1956; staff writer Nat. Geog. Soc., 1957-69; founder, pres. World Future Soc., Washington, 1966—; creator, editor The Futurist Mag., 1966—; editor World Future Soc. Bull., 1968-77; cons. to govt., bus. and ednl. orgns. Author: The Study of the Future, 1977; editor: Resources Directory for America's Third Century, 1977, The Future: A Guide to Information Sources, 1977, 1979; The World of Tomorrow, 1978, Communications Tomorrow, 1982, Global Solutions, 1984, The Computerized Society, 1985, Careers Tomorrow, 1988, The 1990s and Beyond, 1989; editor: Exploring Your Future: Living, Learning and Working in the Information Age, 1996; editl. cons.: Nat. Goals Rsch. Staff, 1970, White House Report Toward Balanced Growth, 1970. Bd. dirs. World Watch Inst., 1974—; adv. bd. Inst. for Alternative Futures. Home: 5501 Lincoln St Bethesda MD 20817-3723 Office: World Future Soc 7910 Woodmont Ave Bethesda MD 20814-3002

CORNISH, ELIZABETH TURVEREY, stockbroker; b. Ionia, N.Y., Dec. 31, 1919; d. Clifford Dwight and Mildred Althea (Spicer) T.; m. Louis Joseph Cornish, June 21, 1941 (div. June 1955); 1 child, Carol Cornish Reeves. BS, Cornell U., 1941. Lic. stockbroker N.Y. Stock Exch., Prin. Reg. Options Prin., Commodity prin., Insur. prin. Teletype operator, sec. to mgr. Carl M. Loeb Rhoades & Co., Ithaca, N.Y., 1955-65; reg. rep. Carl M. Loeb Rhoades & Co., Ithaca, 1962-75; branch mgr. Loeb, Rhoades & Co., Ithaca, 1975-82; registered rep. Shearson Loeb Rhoades, Shearson Am. Express, Ithaca, 1982-86, Hutton, Shearson, Ithaca, 1986-88, First Albany Corp., Ithaca, 1988-91; registered rep., br. office mgr. A.G. Edwards & Sons, Inc., Ithaca, 1991-97, investment broker, 1998—; charter mem. Nuveen Adv. Coun., 1984, 85, 86; instr. stock market and various br. office jobs for coll. interns; bd. dirs. McGraw House. Mem. Planning Com. Downtown Mall, Ithaca, N.Y., 1972-75; chmn. campaign United Way Tompkins County, Ithaca, 1983, dir., 1983-89; bd. dirs. Ithaca Neighborhood Housing, Leadership Tompkins, 1986-88; pres. Friends of Ithaca Coll., 1985-86. Mem. Downtown Bus. Women (pres. 1971-72), Tompkins County C. of C. (bd. dirs. 1974-77, 83-86, v.p. 1980-81, pres.-elect 1989, pres. 1990), Ithaca Yacht Club (bd. dirs. 1988-90). Republican. Episcopalian. Avocations: boating, reading, letter writing, coach of Cornell Women's Rifle Team, 1942-55. Office: A G Edwards & Sons Inc 2 Graham Rd W Ithaca NY 14850-1113

CORNISH, GEOFFREY ST. JOHN, golf course architect; b. Winnipeg, Man., Can., Aug. 6, 1914; came to U.S., 1947, naturalized, 1955; m. Carol Burr Gawthrop, Mar. 31, 1951. B.S.A., U. B.C., Can., 1935; M.S., U. Mass., 1952, Dr. Sci. (hon.), 1987. Golf course architect Thompson-Jones & Co., Toronto, Ont., Can., 1935-47; instr. U. Mass., 1947-52; pvt. practice golf course architecture Amherst, Mass., 1952—; vis. lectr. U. Mass. Coauthor: The Golf Course, 1981, rev. edit., 1987, The Architects of Golf, 1993, Golf Course Design, 1998; subject of Interview mag., Apr. 1987; contbr. numerous articles on golf course design and turfgrass to profl. publs. Served to maj. Can. Army, 1940-45. Recipient Disting. Service award Golf Course Supts. Am., 1981; named Can. Golf Hall of Fame, 1996. Mem. Am. Soc. Golf Course Architects (pres. 1975, Donald Ross award 1982), Brit. Assn. Golf Course Architects (hon.), Soil Sci. Soc. Am., Sigma Xi, Phi Kappa Phi. Epsicopalian. Home and Office: Fiddlers Grn 1030 S East St Amherst MA 01002-3078

CORNISH, KENT M., television executive; b. Topeka, Kans., Nov. 29, 1954. BS in Journalism, U. Kans., 1976. V.p., gen. mgr. KTKA TV, Topeka, 1991—. Office: KTKA TV 2121 SW Chelsea Dr Topeka KS 66614*

CORNISH, RICHARD JOSEPH, international affairs consultant, retired diplomat; b. Omaha, Nov. 7, 1925; s. Lebbeus Morrison and Lydia Christine (Herrmann) C.; m. Beverly Anne Cormier, July 28, 1958; children—Pamela Anne, Allyson Juillette, Carolyn Lydia. B.A., Yale U., 1949; M.A., Am. U., 1965; diploma U.S. Air War Coll., 1976. Commd. fgn. service officer Dept. State, 1959; 2d sec., vice consul U.S. Embassy, Rangoon, Burma, 1959-62; 2d sec., consul U.S. Embassy, Lome, Togo, 1964-66; regional dir. AID, Savannakhet and Vientiane, Laos, 1967-71; polit. adviser Dept. Def., Frankfurt, Germany, 1973-75; dir. mil. assistance Dept. Def., Addis Ababa, Ethiopia, 1975-77; 1st sec. for polit. and econ. affairs U.S. embassy, Yaounde, Cameroon, 1979-81; 1st sec., polit. affairs, U.S. Embassy, London, 1981-85; ret., 1985; cons. London Diplomatic Assn., 1985-87, The Parvus Co., 1985-90, Trefoil Partnership, Ltd., London, 1987-90; chmn. bd. dirs. Cornish Assocs., 1987—. Author: The Development of Nationalism in Burma, 1966, The National Decision Making Process, 1975, Deployment of Military Forces, 1975. With USAAF, 1944-46, Asia Pacific Theater; served to lt. col. USAFR, 1949-77. Mem. Diplomatic and Consular Officers Ret., Am. Fgn. Service Assn., Assn. Diplomatic Studies, Assn. Asian Studies, Royal Commonwealth Soc., Kipling Soc. Clubs: Chevy Chase (Md.); Travellers, RAF (London); University (Washington); Yale (N.Y.C.). Lodges: Rotary (bd. dirs. 1976-77), Masons.

CORNISH, RICHARD POOL, lawyer; b. Evanston, Ill., Sept. 9, 1942; s. William A. and Rita (Pool) C.; children: William Darby, Richard Gordon. B.S., Okla. State U., 1964; LL.B., U. Okla., 1966. Bar: Okla. 1966, U.S. Dist. Ct. (ea. dist.) Okla. 1969, U.S. Supreme Ct. 1979. Ptnr., Baumert & Cornish, McAlester, Okla., 1967-71, Cornish & Cornish, Inc., McAlester, Okla., 1971-77; magistrate U.S. Dist. Ct. Eastern Dist. Okla., 1976—; prin. Richard P. Cornish, Inc., McAlester, Okla., 1977—. Bd. dirs. McAlester Boys Club, 1970-80, pres., 1974. Served to capt. JAGC, USAR, 1966-78. Mem. Okla. Bar Assn. (mem. legal aid to servicemen com., legal specialization com.), Pittsburg County Bar Assn., McAlester C. of C. (dir. 1973-75). Roman Catholic. Home: 611 E Creek Ave Mcalester OK 74501 Office: PO Box 1106 Mcalester OK 74502-1106

CORNWALL, DEBORAH JOYCE, consulting firm executive, management consultant; b. Wilmington, Del., Dec. 9, 1946; d. Samuel and Norma (Bram) Handloff; m. Barry Newland Cornwall, June 22, 1968; 1 child, Deborah Leigh. BA, Mount Holyoke, 1968; MBA, Boston U., 1975. Editor Houghton Mifflin Co., Boston, 1967-69; editor Harbridge House, Inc., Boston, 1969-73, cons., 1973-74, assoc., 1974-75, sr. assoc., 1975-77, prin., 1977-79, v.p., 1979-81, v.p., divsn. mgr., 1981-83, sr. v.p., divsn. mgr., 1983-90; founder and mng. v.p. Korn/Ferry Orgnl. Cons., Boston, 1991-96; founder and mng. dir. The Corlund Group, L.L.C., Boston, 1996—; mem. mid. mgmt. excellence com. City of Boston, 1986. Bd. dirs. Mass. divsn. Am. Cancer Soc., 1994-97. Mem. Phi Beta Kappa, Beta Gamma Sigma. Office: The Corlund Group LLC 75 Federal St Boston MA 02110-1913

CORNWALL, JOHN MICHAEL, physics educator, consultant, researcher; b. Denver, Aug. 19, 1934; s. Paul Bakewell and Dorothy (Zitkowski) C.; m. Ingrid Linderos, Oct. 16, 1965. AB, Harvard U., 1956; MS, U. Denver, 1959; PhD, U. Calif., 1962. NSF postdoctoral fellow Calif. Inst. Tech., Pasadena, 1962-63; mem. Inst. Advanced Study, Princeton, N.J., 1963-65; prof. physics UCLA, 1965—; vis. prof. Niels Bohr Inst., Copenhagen, 1968-69, Inst. de Physique Nucleaire, Paris, 1973-74, MIT, 1974, 87, Rockefeller U., N.Y.C., 1988; faculty RAND Grad. Sch., 1999; cons. Inst. Theoretical Physics, Santa Barbara, Calif., 1979-80, 82, bd. dirs., 1979-83; assoc. Ctr. Internat./Strategic Affairs, UCLA, 1987—; cons. MITRE Corp., Aerospace Corp., Los Alamos Nat. Labs., RAND Corp.; mem. dir.'s adv. com. Lawrence Livermore Labs., 1991—; mem. Def. Sci. Bd., 1992-93, mem. task force, 1996; chmn. External Rev. com. Accelerator Oper. and Technol. Divsn., Los Alamos Nat. Labs., 1995-97; chmn. external rev. com. Ctr. for Internat. Security and Arms Control, Stanford U., 1996; adv. commn. Accelerator Prodn. Tritium Project, 1997—; cons. John D. and Catherine T. MacArthur Found.; prof. RAND Grad Sch., 1998—. Author: (with others) Academic Press Ency. of Science and Technology, other encys. and books; contbr. numerous articles to profl. jours. With U.S. Army, 1956-58. Grantee NSF, NASA; NSF pre/postdoctoral fellow 1960-63, A.P. Sloan fellow, 1967-71. Fellow AAAS; mem. Am. Phys. Soc., Am. Geophys. Union, N.Y. Acad. Sci. Avocations: jogging, bicycling, golf, bridge. Office: UCLA Dept Physics Los Angeles CA 90095

CORNWELL, DAVID GEORGE, biochemist, educator; b. San Rafael, Calif., Oct. 8, 1927; s. John Nevius and Nora (Jonasen) C.; m. Normagene Conn, Mar. 14, 1959; children: Karen Sue, David Andrew. BA with honors, Coll. Wooster, 1950; MA, Ohio State U., 1952; PhD, Stanford U., 1955. NRC fellow Harvard U., 1954-56; faculty Ohio State U., 1956-92, prof. medical biochemistry, 1963-92; part-time prof., 1993—; chmn. dept. medical biochemistry Ohio State U., 1965-80, asso. dean acad. affairs Coll. Medicine, 1979-92, prof. and assoc. dean emeritus, 1992—; mem. nutrition study sect. NIH, 1966-70, nutrition sci. tng. rev. sect., 1970-73; hon. prof. Tongji Med. U., Wuhan, China, 1993—. Mem. editl. bd. Jour. Lipid Rsch., 1962-66, 88-95, Jour. Nutrition, 1969-72; mem. adv. bd. Jour Lipid Rsch., 1974-78, Chem. Abstracts, 1979-84; contbr. articles to profl. jours. Trustee Children's Hosp. Rsch. Found., Columbus, 1982-93. With AUS, 1946-47. Co-recipient hon. mention for research 6th Internat. Congress Hematology, 1956. Mem. Am. Chem. Soc., Biophys. Soc., Am. Soc. Biol. Chemists, Am. Oil Chemists Soc., Am. Inst. Nutrition, Alpha Omega Alpha, Sigma Xi. Presbyterian (elder). Home: 2290 Middlesex Rd Columbus OH 43220-4646

CORNWELL, DAVID JOHN MOORE See LE CARRÉ, JOHN

CORNWELL, GIBBONS GRAY, III, physician, medical educator; b. West Chester, Pa., Jan. 17, 1933; s. Gibbons Gray and Eva Chambers (Parke) C.; m. Mary Helen Fortmiller, Sept. 13, 1958; children: Gibbons Gray IV, Heidi Cornwell Trout, Holly Fortmiller. BS, Yale U., 1954; MD, U. Pa., 1963; MA (hon.), Dartmouth Coll., 1993. Diplomate Am. Bd. Internal Medicine, Am. Bd. Hematology. Resident in medicine Hosp. U. Pa., Phila., 1963-64, 65-66; research fellow Cambridge U., Eng., 1964-65; hematology fellow Hosp. U. Pa., Phila., 1966-68; biochemistry fellow Dartmouth Med. Sch., Hanover, N.H., 1968-70, asst. prof. medicine, 1971-74, assoc. prof., 1974-80, prof., 1980-95, prof. pathology, 1990-95, prof. emeritus medicine and pathology, 1995—, assoc. dean student and acad. affairs, 1973-76, chmn. sect. hematology-oncology, 1977-84; vis. prof. Inst. Immunology, Oslo, 1976-77; dir. clin. rsch. Norris Cotton Cancer Ctr., Hanover, 1978-91; bd. dirs. Cancer and Leukemia Group B, Boston, 1978-91; trustee, chmn. Hitchcock Found., Hanover, 1978-90; staff bd. govs. Mary Hitchcock Meml. Hosp., Hanover, 1981-88; vis. scientist Inst. Pathology/Swedish Med. Rsch. Coun., Uppsala, Sweden, 1987. Contbr. articles to profl. jours. Bd. dirs. Upper Valley Hospice, Lebanon, N.H., 1980; mem. sch. bd. Town of Lyme, N.H., 1973-76, health officer, 1970-74, mem. conservation com., 1970-74, budget com., 1996—; trustee Lyme (N.H.) Found., Lyme, 1998—. Capt. USAF, 1955-59. Clin. research grantee NIH, 1978-91. Fellow ACP; mem. Am. Fedn. Clin. Research (emeritus), Am. Soc. Hematology, N.H. Med. Soc. Republican. Episcopalian. Avocations: cycling, stamp collecting, whale watching, computer animation, scuba. E-mail: gibb@dartmouth.edu. Home: 1 Orfordville Rd Lyme NH 03768-3305 Office: Dartmouth-Hitchcock Med Ctr Lebanon NH 03756-1417

CORNWELL, MARGUERITE KELSEY, college administrator; b. Port Chester, N.Y., Nov. 1, 1957; d. Harvey Marion and Anne (Talcott) Kelsey; m. Grant H. Cornwell Jr., Aug. 30, 1980; children: Tanner, Kelsey, MacIntosh. BA in Econs., St. Lawrence U., 1979, MEd, 1994. Asst. v.p. Chem. Bank, Chgo., 1979-86; asst. dir. career planning St. Lawrence U., Canton, N.Y., 1987-89, 91-95, dir. career planning, 1995—; advisor Women's Resource Ctr., Canton, 1995—. Bd. dirs., pres. Canton Day Care Ctr., 1991-97; referee Nat. Women's Lacrosse Assn., Canton, 1991-94. Mem. Am. Coll. Pers. Assn., Nat. Assn. Student Pers. Adminstrs., Eastern Assn. Coll. Employers, Omicron Delta Kappa. Avocations: skiing, hiking, reading.

CORNWELL, PATRICIA DANIELS, author; b. 1956. Grad., Davidson Coll. Police reporter Charlotte (N.C.) Observer, 1979-81; computer analyst Office Chief Med. Examiner, Richmond, Va., from 1985. Author: (biography) A Time for Remembering, 1983, (novels) Postmortem, 1990, Body of Evidence, 1991, All that Remains, 1993, Cruel and Unusual, 1993, From Potter's Field, 1995 (One of Top 15 Bestsellers for 1995 Pubs. Weekly), Hornet's Nest, 1997, Unnatural Exposure, 1997, Ruth, A Portrait, 1997, Point of Origin, 1998. Vol. police officer. Address: ICM 40 W 57th St New York NY 10019-4001*

CORNWELL, PAUL M., JR., architect; b. Wheeling, W.Va., Jan. 28, 1966; s. Paul M. Sr. and Penny S. (Kain) C. BS, Kent State U., 1988, BArch, 1989. Registered architect, Ohio. Estimator/field rep. Evick Cons., Inc., St. Clairsville, Ohio, summer 1987, summer 1988; intern architect Brubaker/Brandt, Inc., Columbus, Ohio, 1989-92, Maddox-NBD/Brubaker-Brandt, Inc., Dublin, Ohio, 1992-93, NBBJ, Columbus, 1993-95, Fanning/Howey Assocs., Dublin, Ohio, 1995—; ind. contractor Amway Corp., Ada, Mich., 1991—; architect/engr. C.H.K. Degvel., Belmont, Ohio. Scolar Ruritan Internat., Am. Inst. Architects, Honors Coll. Kent State U. Republican. Lutheran. Avocations: 20th century U.S. history, transportation history, photography, model railroading. Home: 624 Foxbury Ct Apt C Columbus OH 43228-2656 Office: Fanning/Howey Assocs Inc 4930 Bradenton Ave Dublin OH 43017-3520

CORNWELL, WILLIAM JOHN, lawyer; b. Wheeling, W.Va., Nov. 9, 1959; s. James Miller Cornwell and Judith (Shock) Clark; m. Leslie Glickstein, May 23, 1987. BBA, Ga. State U., 1982, JD, 1985. Bar: Ga. 1985, U.S. Dist. Ct. (no. and mid. dists.) Ga. 1985, U.S. Ct. Appeals (11th cir.) 1985, Fla. 1988. Gov.'s intern Coun. for Maternal and Infant Health, Atlanta, 1982; adminstrv. asst. Coun. Juvenile Ct. Judges, Atlanta, 1983; law clk. HHS, Atlanta, 1984; legal intern Office Fulton County Dist. Atty., Atlanta, 1984-85; ptnr. Pope, McGlamry, Kilpatrick & Morrison, Atlanta, 1985-97; active Cuban Detainee Assistance Program, 1985-87. Mem. Ga. Bar Assn. (moot ct. com. 1987), Atlanta Bar Assn. (pub. rels. com. 1988), Fla. Bar Assn., Assn. Trial Lawyers Am., Ga. Trial Lawyers Assn., Ga. State U. Law Alumni Assn., Phi Alpha Delta. Democrat. Methodist. Avocations: water skiing, tennis, softball, history. Fax: 561-218-3552. Office: Pope McGlamry Kilpatrick & Morrison 83 Walton St NW Ste 400 Atlanta GA 30303-2123

CORNYN, JOHN, state attorney general; b. Feb. 2, 1952; married; 2 children. BA, Trinity U., 1973; JD, St. Mary's U., 1977; postgrad., U. Va. Cert. personal injury trial law Tex. Bd. Legal Specialization. Assoc., ptnr. Groce, Locke & Hebdon, San Antonio, 1977-84; judge 37th Dist. Ct., Bexer County, 1985-90; presiding judge 4th Adminstrv. Jud. Region, 1989-92; justice Supreme Ct. Tex., Austin, 1991-98; atty. Thompson & Knight; atty. gen. State of Tex., Austin, 1999—; Tex. Supreme Ct. liaison Bd. LAw Examiners, 1991—, Gender Bias Task Force, 1993-95; lectr. CLE programs. Bd. vis. Trinity U., Pepperdine U. Sch. Law. Fellow Tex. Bar Found., San

Antonio Bar Found.; mem. Am. Law Inst., William Sessions Inn of Ct. (master bencher 1988-90, pres. 1989-90), Robert W. Calvent Inn of Ct. (pres. 1994-95). Office: Office of Atty Gen PO Box 12548 Austin TX 78711-3697*

CORO, ALICIA CAMACHO, federal executive; b. Havana, Cuba, Mar. 28, 1937; came to U.S., 1964; d. Daniel and Alicia (Mignagaray) Camacho; m. Carlos J. Coro (dec.); children: Alicia, Carlos, Christina; m. Kenneth M. Hoffman, Mar. 1997. BA in English and Edn., U. Havana, 1961; MEd, U. Md., 1972. Elem. sch. tchr. Havana, 1956-59; tchr., supr. Montgomery County Pub. Schs., Rockville, Md., 1966-71; edn. specialist HEW, Washington, 1971-75, staff asst. to sec., 1975-77, program analyst, br. chief, 1977-80; dir. Horace Mann Learn Ctr. Dept. Edn., Washington, 1981-85, dep. asst. sec. for civil rights, 1985-86, acting asst. sec. for civil rights, 1986—; bd. dirs. Montgomery Community TV, Rockville, 1984—. Council mem. United Way, Rockville, 1985—; mem., vol. activites com. Chevy Chase (Md.) Rep. Women's Club, 1980—, Hispanic Rep. Club Montgomery County, Bethesda, Md., 1981—; mem. Rep. Nat. Hispanic Assmebly, Washington, 1972—; advisor at large Spanish-Speaking Community Md., Inc. Recipient Outstanding Achievement award Nat. Assn. Cuban-Am. Women, Nat. Council Hispanic Women, Cuban Circle of Md., 1986. Mem. Am. Soc. for Tng. and Devel., Am. Assn. for Adult-Continuing Edn., Fed. Exec. Inst. Alumni Assn., Soc. Fed. Linguists, Tchrs. English to Speakers of Other Langs., Nat. Assn. Cuban Women (dir. at large), Nat. Council Hispanic Women (bd. dirs.). Roman Catholic. Club: Who's Who Internat. (Marina del Ray, Calif.). Home: 909 Parsons Dr Madison MD 21648 Office: Dept of Edn 400 Maryland Ave SW Washington DC 20202-0001

CORODEMUS, STEVEN JAMES, state legislator, lawyer; b. Newark, Jan. 14, 1952; m. Michele Russell; 2 children. BA, Rutgers U., 1974; JD, Seton Hall U., 1979. Bar: N.J. 1979, Calif. 1981. Councilman Borough of Atlantic Highlands, 1986-88; vice-chmn. Monmouth County Planning Bd., 1989-92; mem. N.J. Gen. Assembly, 1991—; ptnr. Corodemus & Corodemus, Metuchen, N.J. Republican. Greek Orthodox. Office: PO Box 266 40 1st Ave Atlantic Highlands NJ 07716-1243*

CORONITI, FERDINAND VINCENT, physics educator, consultant; b. Boston, June 14, 1943; s. Samuel Charles and Ethel Marie (Havlik) C.; m. Patricia Ann Smith, Aug. 30, 1969; children: Evelyn Marie, Samuel Thomas. A.B., Harvard U., 1965; Ph.D., U. Calif.-Berkeley, 1969. Research physicist UCLA, 1967-70, asst. prof. physics, 1970-74, assoc. prof., 1974-78, prof. physics and astronomy, 1978—; cons. TRW Systems. Contbr. articles to sci. jours. NASA grantee, 1974, NSF grantee, 1974—. Fellow Am. Geophys. Union, Am. Phys. Soc.; mem. Am. Astron. Soc., Internat. Union Radiol. Sci. Home: 10475 Almayo Ave Los Angeles CA 90064-2301 Office: UCLA Dept Physics & Astronomy 405 Hilgard Ave Los Angeles CA 90095-9000

COROTIS, ROSS BARRY, civil engineering educator, academic administrator; b. Woodbury, N.J., Jan. 15, 1945; s. A. Charles and Hazel Laura (McCloskey) C.; m. Stephanie Michal Fuchs, Mar. 19, 1972; children: Benjamin Randall, Lindsay Sarah. SB, MIT, Cambridge, 1967, SM, 1968, PhD, 1971. Lic. profl. engr., Ill., Md., Colo., structural engr., Ill. Asst. prof. dept. civil engring. Northwestern U., Evanston, Ill., 1971-74, assoc. prof. dept. civil engring., 1975-79, prof. dept. civil engring., 1979-81; prof. dept. civil engring. Johns Hopkins U., Balt., 1981-82, Hackerman prof., 1982-83, Hackerman prof., chmn. dept. civil engring., 1983-90, Hackerman prof., assoc. dean engring., 1990-94; dean Coll. Engring. and Applied Sci. U. Colo., Boulder, 1994—; mem. bldg. research bd. Nat. Research Council, Washington, 1985-88; lectr. profl. confs. Editor in chief Internat. Jour. Structural Safety, 1991—; contbr. articles to profl. jours. Mem. Mayor's task force City of Balt. Constrn. Mgmt., 1985. Recipient Engring. Teaching award Northwestern U., 1977; named Md. Engr. of Yr., Balt. Engrs. Week Coun., 1989; rsch. grantee NSF, Nat. Bur. Standards, U.S. Dept. Energy, 1973-96. Fellow ASCE (chmn. safety bldgs. com. 1985-89, chmn. tech. adminstrv. com. structural safety and reliability 1988-92, chmn. probabilistic methods com. 1996-98, v.p. Md. chpt. 1987-88, pres. 1988-89, Walter L. Huber rsch. prize 1984, Civil Engr. of Yr. award Md. chpt. 1987, Outstanding Educator award Md. chpt. 1992); mem. Internat. Assn. for Structural Safety and Reliability (chair exec. bd. 1998—), Am. Soc. for Engring. Edn. (mem. pub. policy com. 1998—, mem. exec. bd. 1998—), Am. Concrete Inst. (chmn. structural safety com. 1986-88), Am. Nat. Stds. Inst. (chmn. live loads com. 1978-84). Office: U Colo Coll Engring & Applied Sci PO Box 422 Boulder CO 80309-0422

CORPORON, JOHN ROBERT, broadcasting executive; b. Arcadia, Kans., Mar. 1, 1929; s. George William and Portteus (Stephens) C.; m. Harriett Sloan; children: John Robert Jr., David Sloan. BS in Journalism, U. Kans., 1951, MA in Polit. Sci., 1953. Reporter Pitts. Sun, 1950, UP, New Orleans, 1955; bur. chief UP, Baton Rouge, 1956, New Orleans, 1956-58; correspondent Sta. WDSU-TV, New Orleans, Washington, 1958-60, La. and Miss., 1960-62; news dir. Sta. WDSU-TV-AM, New Orleans, 1962-66; v.p., news dir. Sta. WNEW-TV, Metromedia, N.Y.C., 1967; v.p. news Metromedia TV, N.Y.C., Los Angeles, Washington and Kansas City, 1967-68; v.p., gen. mgr. Sta. WTOP-TV, Washington, 1968-71; exec. producer Newsweek Broadcast Service, 1971-72; v.p., news dir. Sta. WPIX, N.Y.C., 1972-83, sr. v.p., 1983-96; founding pres. Ind. TV News Assn., 1980; co-founder Ind. Network News, 1980. spl. reporter London Economist, Washington Post, 1960's. Mem. Park Slope Civic Assn.; trustee William Allen White Found., U. Kans., 1994—. Served with U.S. Army, 1953-55. Recipient Nat. Emmy award Acad. Arts and Scis., 1965. Mem. N.Y. State Associated Press Broadcasters (bd. dirs. 1984-96, pres. 1986-87), Radio TV News Dirs. Assn. (bd. dirs. 1988-91), Nat. AP Broadcasters (bd. dirs. 1989—, pres. 1995-97), N.Y. Press Club, Overseas Press Club (pres. 1996—). Democrat. Avocations: jogging, tennis, swimming. Home: 671 10th St Brooklyn NY 11215-4501 Office: Overseas Press Club 320 E 42nd St New York NY 10017-5900

CORPREW, BARBARA ANNE, lawyer; b. Washington, Sept. 16, 1949; d. Theodore Elias and Daisy (McLeod) C. BA in Polit. Sci. cum laude, Tufts U., 1971; JD, U. Pa., 1974. Bar: Pa. 1974. Staff atty. Pub. Defender Svc. for D.C., Washington, 1974-79; trial atty. fraud sect., criminal divsn. Dept. Justice, Washington, 1979-88, chief def. procurement fraud unit, criminal divsn., 1988-90, dep. chief fraud sect., criminal def. divsn., 1990—. Bd. dirs. Art and Drama Therapy Ctr., Washington, 1996—; chair ministerial rels. com. All Souls Ch. Unitarian, Washington, 1995—. Recipient Mathew Schure award N.Y. Inst. Tech., 1995. Mem. ABA (co-chair white collar crime com. 1998). Unitarian. Avocation: running. Home: 1442 Corcoran St NW Washington DC 20009-3855

CORR, EDWIN GHARST, ambassador; b. Edmond, Okla., Aug. 6, 1934; s. E.L. and Rowena C.; m. Susanne Springer, Nov. 24, 1957; children: Michelle Ruth, Jennifer Jean, Phoebe Rowena. BS, U. Okla., 1957, MA, 1961; MA, U. Tex., 1969. Fgn. service officer Dept. State, Washington, 1961-62; assigned to Mex., 1962-66; Peace Corps dir. Cali, Colombia, 1966-68; Panama desk officer Dept. State, 1969-71; program officer Inter Am. Found., 1971; exec. asst. to ambassador Am. embassy, Bangkok, Thailand, 1972-75; counselor polit. affairs Am. embassy, Quito, Ecuador, 1976, dep. chief of mission, 1977-78; dep. asst. sec. internat. narcotics matters Dept. State, 1978-80; ambassador to Peru Dept. State, Lima, 1980-81; ambassador to Bolivia Dept. State, La Paz, 1981-85; ambassador to El Salvador San Salvador, 1985-88; Dept. State diplomat-in-residence U. Okla., 1988-90, prof. polit. sci., 1990-96; assoc. dir. Internat. Programs Ctr., dir. Energy Inst. Americas, 1996—. Author: The Political Process in Colombia, 1971, Low-Intensity Conflict: Old Threats in a New World, 1992; contbr. to books and profl. jours. Served to capt. USMC, 1957-60. Mem. Am. Fgn. Service Assn. Home: 544 Shawnee St Norman OK 73071-4631

CORR, JAMES VANIS, furniture manufacturing executive, investor, lawyer, accountant; b. Selma, Ala., June 28, 1922; s. Mark Stroud and Julia (Dozier) C.; m. Judith Ann Hackney, Feb. 3, 1971; children by previous marriage: James Jr., William V., Emily S., Julia D. BS, U. Ala., 1948, LLB, 1951. CPA, Ala., Ga. Ptnr. Dent & Corr, CPA's, Birmingham, Ala., 1954-61; exec. v.p. Buck Creek Industries, Inc., Atlanta, 1961-70, pres., 1970-77, also bd. dirs.; v.p. Sperry & Hutchinson Co., N.Y.C., 1976-78; group v.p. furnishings div. Sperry & Hutchinson Co., Atlanta, 1976-78; pres. JVC Enterprises, Inc., Atlanta, 1978—; speaker tax clinic U. Ala., 1954—. Bd. dirs. Met. YMCA, Birmingham. With AC, USMCR, 1944-46. Decorated D.F.C., Air medal with 2 oak leaf clusters. Mem. Ala. Soc. CPA's (past chmn. Birmingham chpt.), Ga. Soc. CPA's, ABA, Ala. Bar Assn., Am. Inst. CPA's, Ala. Textile Assn., Ga. Textile Assn., Exchange Club (Birmingham), Mountain Brook (Ala., past pres.). Home: 545 River Chase Pt NW Atlanta GA 30328-3555

CORR, ROBERT MARK, computer company executive; b. Macon, Ga., Oct. 17, 1948; s. Edward and Nancy (Green) C.; m. Patricia Ann McKibben, Mar. 14, 1970; children: Kevin Matthew, Amy Elizabeth. Bachelor of Indsl. Engring., Ga. Tech. U., 1971; MBA with honors, Mich. State U., 1985. Sr. engr. assembly div. GM, Atlanta, 1968-75; sr. staff asst. assembly div. GM, Warren, Mich., 1975-78; supt. mfg. assembly div. GM, Framingham, Mass., 1978; planning dir. GM, Mexico City, 1978-80; sr. adminstr. fin. staff Gen. Motors, Detroit, 1980-84; dir. internat. Pacific ops. Electronic Data Systems, Warren, 1984-86; dir. tech. planning Electronic Data Systems, Troy, Mich., 1986-87, regional mgr., 1988-91; divsn. mgr. EDS Capital Svcs., Detroit, Mich., 1992-95, EDS VSSM, Troy, Mich., 1995-97; exec. in charge EDS/GM Access, Troy, Mich., 1997—; pres. Advancement of Tech. Through Strategic Cooperation, Warren, 1986-87. Contbg. editor Info World, 1985-88. Mem. Founders Soc., Detroit Inst. Arts, 1987—; commr. Boy Scouts Am., Detroit, 1984-86. Mem. Internat. Platform Assn., Strategic Planning Inst., Am. Productivity and Quality Ctr., Phi Kappa Phi, Beta Gamma Sigma. Avocations: bridge, applied mathematics, atomic clocks, skiing, skeet shooting.

CORRADA DEL RIO, ALVARO, bishop; b. Santurce, P.R., May 13, 1942. ordained priest Roman Cath. Ch., 1974. Pastoral coordinator Northeast Cath. Hispanic Ctr., N.Y., 1982-85; titular bishop of Rusticiana and aux. bishop Washington, 1985—; apostolic adminstr. Diocese of Caguas, P.R. Office: Bishop's House PO Box 8698 Caguas PR 00726*

CORRADA DEL RIO, BALTASAR, supreme court justice; b. Morovis, P.R., Apr. 10, 1935; s. Romulo and Ana Maria (del Rio) Corrada del R.; m. Beatrice Betances, Dec. 24, 1959; children: Ana Isabel, Francisco Javier, Juan Carlos, Jose Baltasar. BA in Social Scis., U. P.R., 1956, JD, 1959. Bar: P.R., 1959. Ptnr. McConnell Valdes Sifre & Ruiz Suria, San Juan, 1959-75; atty., chmn. Civil Right Commn., P.R., 1970-72; mem., resident commr. from P.R. 95th-98th Congress; mayor City of San Juan, P.R., 1985-89; atty. Baltasar Corrada Law Office, 1989-92; sec. of state Govt. of P.R., 1993-95; Puerto Rico assoc. justice Supreme Ct., P.R., 1995—; pres. New Progressive Party, 1986-89. Pres. editorial bd. P.R. Human Rights Rev., 1971-72. Bd. dirs. P.R. Teleradial Inst. Ethics. Recipient Great Cross of Civil Merit of Spain King Juan Carlos I, 1987. Mem. ABA, Fed. Bar Assn., P.R. Bar Assn. Roman Catholic. Club: Exchange, San Juan Rotary. Office: P R Supreme Ct PO Box 9022392 San Juan PR 00902-2392

CORRADINI, DEEDEE, mayor. Student, Drew U., 1961-63; BS, U. Utah, 1965, MS, 1967. Adminstrv. asst. for public info. Utah State Office Rehab. Svcs., 1967-69; cons. Utah State Dept. Community Affairs, 1971-72; media dir., press sec. Wayne Owens for Congress Campaign, 1972; press sec. Rep. Wayne Owens, 1973-74; spl. asst. to N.Y. Congl. Rep. Richard Ottinger, 1975; asst. to pres., dir. community rels. Snowbird Corp., 1975-77; exec. v.p. Bonneville Assocs., Inc., Salt Lake City, 1977-80; pres. Bonneville Assocs., Inc., 1980-89, chmn., CEO, 1989-91; mayor Salt Lake City, 1992—; pres. U.S. Conf. of Mayors, 1998—, mem. unfunded fed. mandates task force, mem. crime and violence task force; chair Mayor's Gang Task Force; mem. interngovtl. policy adv. com. U.S. Trade Rep., 1993-94; mem. transp. and comm. com. Nat. League of Cities, 1993-94. Bd. trustees Intermountain Health Care, 1980-92; bd. dirs., exec. com. Utah Symphony, 1983-92, vice chmn., 1985-88, chmn., 1988-92; dir. Utah chpt. Nat. Conf. Christians and Jews, Inc., 1988; bd. dirs. Salt Lake Olympic Bid Com., 1989—; chmn. image com. Utah Partnership for Edn. and Econ. Devel., 1989-92; co-chair United Way Success by 6 Program; pres. Shelter of the Homeless Com.; active Sundance Inst. Utah Com., 1990-92; disting. bd. fellow So. Utah U., 1991; active numerous other civic orgns. and coms. Mem. Salt Lake Area C. of C. (bd. govs. 1979-81, chmn. City/County/Govt. com. 1976-86). Office: Office of Mayor City Hall 451 S State St Rm 306 Salt Lake City UT 84111-3104

CORRADO, FRED, food company executive; b. Mt. Vernon, N.Y., May 20, 1940; s. Anthony Edward and Rose (Capone) C.; children: David, Paul, Christopher. BBA in Acctg, Manhattan Coll., 1961; grad. Advanced Mgmt. Program, Harvard U., 1983. CPA, N.Y. Sr. auditor Arthur Andersen & Co., N.Y.C., 1961-65; contr. Romney Cosmetics Co. div. Pfizer Co., Stamford, Conn., 1966-68; with ITT Corp., 1968-69, Kenton Corp., 1969-73, Nabisco Brands USA (formerly Standards Brands Inc.), 1973-86; pres. Planters div. Nabisco Brands USA (name formerly Standard Brands Inc.), East Hanover, N.J., 1980-84; exec. v.p., COO, Nabisco Brands Ltd., Toronto, Ont., Can., 1984-85, pres., COO, 1985-86, also bd. dirs.; vice chmn. fin. and adminstrn., CFO, bd. dirs. Great Atlantic and Pacific Tea Co., Inc., Montvale, N.J., 1987—. Bd. dirs. Covenant House. Mem. AICPA, Fin. Execs. Inst., N.Y. State Soc. CPAs. Office: Gt Atlantic & Pacific Tea Co Inc 2 Paragon Dr Montvale NJ 07645-1718

CORRAL, EDWARD ANTHONY, fire marshal; b. Chgo., July 4, 1931; s. Lewis and Carmen (Alvarez) C.; m. Rima Herrera, Dec. 31, 1963; children: Eddie L., Robert J. Cert. in elec. engring., U. Houston, 1955; cert. in fire protection arson investigation, Tex. A&M U., 1968; cert. in mgmt., Houston Community Coll., 1988; student, U.S. Fire Acad., 1984. Firefighter Houston Fire Dept., 1956-69, fire insp., 1969-73, chief insp., 1973-81, fire marshal, 1981—; bd. dirs. Juvenile Firesetters Prevention Program, Houston, 1981—, fire protection advisory com. State Fire Marshal's Office, Austin, 1986—; advisor state fire code com. State of Tex. Legis., Austin, 1982—, Tex. Advisory Coun. on Arson, Austin, 1981—. Author: (program) Fire Prevention-Cease Fire Club; contbr. articles to Fire Service Today & Fire Command, 1982. Adminstrv. aide to mayor, City of Houston, 1969-73; bd. dirs. Boy Scouts Am., Houston, 1983—, U. Tex. Sch. Pub. Health, Houston, 1986—, Escape Ctr.- Child Abuse Prevention, Houston, 1984; chmn. two sects. United Way, Houston, 1984; sponsor Lifesaving Legis.-Houston Fire Codes. Recipient Outstanding Pub. Svc. award V.P. Bush's office, Houston, 1981, Gov. Clements of Tex., Austin, 1981, Gov. Briscoe of Tex., Austin, 1973, Outstanding Citizen award Big Brothers of Houston, 1983. Mem. Fire Marshall's Assn. of N.Am. (exec. bd.), Nat. Fire Protection Assn., Internat. Assn. Fire Chiefs, Internat. Assn. Arson Investigators, Internat. Soc. Fire Svcs. Instrs., Rotary, Cen. Optimist (pres. 1970), Masons, Shriners. Avocations: music, reading, painting, sculpture. Home: 7807 Prestwood Dr Houston TX 77036-2819 Office: Fire Dept 1205 Dart St Houston TX 77007-4223*

CORRALES, FRANK CAMPA, composer, writer, guitarist; b. San Antonio, Dec. 30, 1931; s. Candelario Chavez and Benigna (Campa) C.; m. Yolanda Oyervides, May 30, 1959; children: Frank Jr., Cecilia, Nancy, Jackie, Steven. Student, Tex. Vocat. Coll., Amistad Sch. mem. adv. com. KLRN-PBS TV Prodns., San Antonio, 1996—; toured with Air Force shows, 1954-56, Tejano bands in U.S., 1957-67; clk., salesperson So. Music Co. Book Dept., 1968-76; recording artist for Talking Taco Records, 1979—. Author: Easy Guide to Conjunto, 1987, Mariachi Guitar for Beginners, 1995, Tex-Mex Music for Guitar, 1998. With USAF, 1952-56. Avocations: scrapbook collection, cartooning, composing, recording, old photographs. Home: 801 E Ashby Pl San Antonio TX 78212-4146

CORRALLO, CARL ANTHONY, lawyer; b. Medina, N.Y., Feb. 24, 1944. BA, Syracuse U., 1965; JD, Georgetown U., 1968. Capt., judge advocate USAF/Office JAG, 1969-74; dep. asst. gen. counsel Fed. Energy Adminstrn., Washington, 1974-77; U.S. Dept. of Energy solicitor Spl. Counsel for Compliance, 1977-81; solicitor Econ. Regulatory Adminstrn., 1981-86; dir. of litigation The Coastal Corp., Houston, 1986-90, dir. litigation, dep. gen. counsel, 1986-90, 90-93, gen. counsel, 1993—. Mem. Tex. Bar, N.Y. Bar, D.C. Bar, U.S. Supreme Ct. Bar. Office: The Coastal Corp Nine Greenway Pl Ste 830 Houston TX 77046*

CORREA, ALONSO VELEZ, neurosurgeon; b. Copacabana, Colombia, Feb. 12, 1939; s. Bernardo and Bertha (Valez) C.; children: Sonya, Yvonne, Lara. Degree, Javeriana U., 1963. Intern Maimonides Hosp., Bklyn., 1964-69; resident in surgery N.Y. Med. Coll., Valhalla, 1969; resident in neurosurgery Mt. Sinai Hosp. and Sch. Medicine, N.Y.C., 1969-74; dir. neurosurgery USPHS, 1975-82; asst. prof. clin. neurosurgery Mount Sinai Sch. of Medicine, N.Y.C., 1984-91. Office: St Joseph's Hosp and Med Ctr Suite J243 703 Main St Ste J243 Paterson NJ 07503-2621

CORREDOR, EVA LIVIA, foreign language educator; b. Budaörs, Hungary, Mar. 7, 1936; d. Michael and Eva (Albecker) Sarlos-Schaeffer; m. Juan S. Corredor, 1960 (div. 1968); 1 child, Livia Corredor Duffee. Diploma, The Sorbonne, Paris, 1959; MA, Columbia U., 1968, PhD, 1975. Instr. of French Barnard Coll., N.Y.C., 1968-73, Columbia U., N.Y.C., summers 1968-73; asst. prof. French Douglass Coll., New Brunswick, N.J., 1973-78; vis. asst. prof. French Reed Coll., Portland, Oreg., 1978-79, U. Wash., Seattle, 1979-80; asst. prof. French Mills Coll., Oakland, Calif., 1980-83; prof. French and German U.S. Naval Acad., Annapolis, Md., 1983—; fellow sch. criticism and theory U. Calif., Irvine, summer 1977; exchange lectr. Britannia Royal Naval Coll., Dartmouth, Devon, Eng., 1987-88. Author: György Lukács and the Literary Pretext, 1987, Lukács After Communism, 1997. Mem. Annapolis Rotary Club (Paul Harris fellow 1992, dir. internat. svc. 1996-97, team leader study tour Eastern Europe 1997). Avocations: literature, music, art, history. Office: US Naval Acad 589 Mcnair Rd Annapolis MD 21402-1323

CORREIA, ROBERT, state legislator; b. Fall River, Mass., Jan. 3, 1939; s. Manuel and Mary Perreira (Gomes) C.; m. Patricia Fogarty; children: Robert, Susan, Mark. BSBA, U. Mass., Dartmouth, 1962; MEd, Bridgewater State Coll., 1968; DPA (hon.), U. Mass., Dartmouth, 1989. Founding charter mem., bd. dirs., treas., mgr. Our Lady of Angels Fed. Credit Union, Fall River, 1962-92; tchr. math & sci. Henry Lord Jr. High Sch., Fall River, 1962-77; state rep. Commonwealth of Mass., Boston, 1977—. Mem. Dem. City Com., Fall River, 1979—; legis. liaison Sr. Senate of Mass., Fall River, 1979—; mem. U. Mass.-Dartmouth Labor Edn. Ctr., 1985-93. Served with USMC, 1962. Awarded Order of Prince Henry/rank of Knight Comdr., Portuguese Govt. Democrat. Roman Catholic. Home: 1290 Plymouth Ave Fall River MA 02721-2534

CORRELL, ALSTON DAYTON, JR., forest products company executive; b. Brunswick, Ga., Apr. 28, 1941; s. Alston Dayton and Elizabeth (Flippo) C.; m. Ada Lee Fulford, June 23, 1963; children: Alston Dayton, Elizabeth Lee. B.S.B.A., U. Ga., 1963; M.S. in Pulp and Paper Tech., U. Maine, 1966, M.S. in Chem. Engring., 1967. Pres. paperboard div. Mead Corp., Dayton, Ohio, 1977-80, pres. paperboard group, 1980, group v.p. paperboard, 1980, group v.p. paper, 1980-81, group v.p. forest products, 1981-83, sr. v.p. forest products, 1983-88; sr. v.p. pulp and printing paper Ga.-Pacific Corp., Atlanta, 1988-89, exec. v.p. pulp and paper, 1989-91, pres., COO, 1991-93, pres., CEO, 1993, CEO, chmn. bd. and pres., 1993—; dir. Ga. Kraft Co., Rome, Brunswick Pulp & Paper Co., Ga., Northwood Pulp & Timber Ltd., Prince George, B.C., Can., B.C. Forest Products Ltd., Vancouver; pres., CEO, dir. Gr. Nd. Nekoosa Corp.; pres. Mead Tumber Co. Bd. dirs. Atlanta Symphony Orch., Miami Valley (Ohio) Boy Scouts, Nature Conservancy, Keep Am. Beautiful Inc., Ga. Rsch. Alliance; trustee U. Ga. Found., Robert W. Woodruff Arts Ctr.; chmn. United Negro Coll. Fund, vice chmn. Atlanta Campaign; mem. Atlanta Action Forum; chmn. Ctrl. Atlanta Progress; bd. councilors The Carter Ctr. Recipient Nat. Brotherhood award, 1991, Disting. Alumnus award U. Ga., Terry Coll. Bus., 1994, Inst. Human Rels. award Am. Jewish Com., 1995; named one of 100 Most Influential Georgians, Ga. Trend Mag., 1994. Mem. Ga. C. of C. (bd. dirs.), Atlanta C. of C. (bd. dirs., Forward Atlanta Policy Group), Commerce Club (Atlanta, bd. dirs.). Republican. Presbyterian. Office: Ga-Pacific Corp PO Box 105605 133 Peachtree St NE Atlanta GA 30303-1847*

CORRELL, DAN EUGENE, physical education educator; b. Moline, Il., June 29, 1960; s. Ronald Guy and Ilene Ida (Havens) C.; m. Cara Lisa Lawwill, Aug. 12, 1989; m. Benjamin Louis Correll, Nov. 21, 1994. AA, Black Hawk Coll., 1986; BA, Morehead State U., 1988. Instr. Black Hawk Coll., Moline, Ill., 1989-93; tutor chpt. I United Twp. High Sch., East Moline, Ill., 1993-98; health, driver edn. tchr. Westmer H.S., Joy, Ill., 1998—. Swimming instr. Am. Red Cross, Moline, 1990-91. Mem. Ill. Assn. Health, Phys. Edn. and Recreation, AAHPERD, Am. Assn. Health Edn., Nat. Assn. Sport and Phys. Edn. Republican. Presbyterian. Avocations: golf, softball, basketball, baseball, football. Home: 2411 20th Ave Rock Island IL 61201-4743

CORRENTI, JOHN DAVID, steel company executive; b. Rochester, N.Y., Apr. 1, 1947; s. Nicholas William and Sara Rita (Annalora) C.; m. Dawn Jane Major, Nov. 22, 1980; 1 child, Nicholas John. BCE, Clarkson U., 1969. Supr. of contrn. U.S. Steel, Pitts., 1969-80; v.p., gen. mgr. Nucor Corp., Plymouth, Utah, 1980-87, Nucor/Yamato Steel Co., Blytheville, Ark., 1987-91; pres., vice chmn., CEO Nucor Corp., Charlotte, N.C., 1993—.

CORRERO, ANTHONY JAMES, III, lawyer; b. Monroe, La., Dec. 15, 1941; s. Anthony James Jr. and Robbie Lee (Pace) C.; m. Margaret Aline O'Meara, May 31, 1966; children: Margaret Hollis, Edward Thomas Eliot, Marshall Alan. BA, N.E. La. U., 1962; LLB, La. State U., 1965. Bar: La. 1965, U.S. Supreme Ct. 1968. Spl. asst. atty. gen. State of La., Baton Rouge, 1965-68; assoc. Jones, Walker, Waechter, Poitevent, Carrere & Denegre, New Orleans, 1968-72, ptnr., 1972-94; ptnr. Correro, Fishman & Casteix, LLP, New Orleans, 1994-96, Correro Fishman Haygood Phelps Walmsley & Casteix, LLP, New Orleans, 1996—; adj. prof. law La. State U., Tulane U., Loyola U.; bd. dirs. Avondale Industries, Inc., New Orleans, T.L. James & Co., Inc., Ruston, La., La. Partnership for Tech. 1st lt. USAR, 1965-71. Mem. ABA, La. Bar Assn. (chmn. sect. corp. and bus. law 1978-79), Am. Law Inst. Democrat. Roman Catholic. Office: Correro Fishman et al 201 Saint Charles Ave New Orleans LA 70170-1000

CORRIERE, JOSEPH N., JR., urologist, educator; b. Easton, Pa., Apr. 3, 1937; s. Joseph N. and Rosa Ada (Poinsetta) C.; m. Evelyn Pavia Mossey, June 25, 1960 (div. July 1984); children—Joseph N., Christopher John, Gregory James, Evelyn Anne; m. Eileen Doyle Brewer, Oct. 17, 1987. B.A., U. Pa., 1959; M.D., Seton Hall Coll. Medicine, 1963. Diplomate Am. Bd. Urology (trustee). Intern Pa. Hosp., Phila., 1963-64; asst. instr. surgery, fellow in Harrison Dept. Surg. Research, Hosp. U. Pa., Phila., 1964-65, asst. instr. urology, 1965-68, USPHS urol. research trainee, 1967-68, instr. urology, 1968-69, assoc. in urology, 1969-71, asst. prof. urology, 1971-74; venereal disease trainee Phila. Dept. Pub. Health, 1965; radioisotope trainee William H. Donner Ctr. for Radiology, Phila., 1965-66; prof., dir. div. urology, dept. surgery U. Tex. Med. Sch., Houston, 1974-93, interim chmn. dept. surgery, 1980-82, assoc. chmn. dept. surgery, 1984-86; chief urology service Hermann Hosp., 1974-93, Tex. Med. Ctr., Houston; cons. residency rev. com. in urology Lyndon Baines Johnson Hosp., 1993-99; cons. NASA. Contbr. numerous articles to profl. jours. Trustee Am. Bd. Urology, 1992-98. Served to maj. USAF, 1969-71. Mem. ACS, Am. Urol. Assn. (dir. edn. 1993—), Soc. Univ. Surgeons, Soc. Univ. Urologists (pres. 1987-88, sec.-treas. 1984-86, pres. 1987-88), Am. Assn. Genitourol. Surgery, Am. Assn. for Surgery of Trauma. Roman Catholic. Home: 7511 Morningside Dr Houston TX 77030-3619 Office: U Tex Med Sch Dept Urology 6431 Fannin St Ste 6018 Houston TX 77030-1501

CORRIERE, JULIE ANNE, family therapist; b. Bethlehem, Pa., May 11, 1968; d. Donald Blaise and Carol Ann (Kroenig) C.; m. Patrick Joseph Santoro, Oct. 1, 1994 (div Sept. 1994). BA, Lehigh U., 1990; MA, Fairfield U., 1994; cert. sch. counseling, Kutztown U., 1997; postgrad. in PhD program, Seton Hall U., 1997. Cert. secondary sch. counselor, Pa.; nat. cert. counselor. Pvt. practice family therapy, Bethlehem, 1994—; therapist intermediate unit Florence Child Guidance Ctr., Allentown, Pa., 1994-97; sch.-based therapist partial hospitalization program Intermediate Unit. Mem. ACA, APA (assoc.), Am. Assn. for Marriage and Family Therapists (assoc.). Roman Catholic. Avocations: reading, animals, piano, running, working out. Home: 1560 E Raders Ln Bethlehem PA 18015-5533 Office: 433 E Broad St Bethlehem PA 18018-6312

CORRIGAN, E(DWARD) GERALD, investment banker; b. Waterbury, Conn., 1941. BS, Fairfield U.; MA, PhD, Fordham U. Group v.p. mgmt. and planning Fed. Res. Bank of N.Y., 1976-80; spl. assignment to chmn. bd. govs. Fed. Res. Sys., 1979-80; pres. Fed. Res. Bank of Mpls., 1981-84, Fed. Res. Bank of N.Y., N.Y.C., 1985-93; chmn. internat. advisors Goldman, Sachs & Co., N.Y.C., 1994-96, mng. dir., 1997—; Trustee The Am. Ditchley Found., The Bretton Woods Com., The Chgo. Mercantile Exch., WNET Channel 13, Pub. Broadcasting, Fairfield U., fin. svcs. vol. corps steering com. The Group of Thirty, The Inst. for Fin. Stability, Bank for Internat.

Settlements, The Trilateral Commn.; co-chmn. Aspen Inst. Mem. Aspen Inst. (co-chmn.), Econ. Club of N.Y. Office: Goldman Sachs and Co 85 Broad St New York NY 10004-2456

CORRIGAN, FAITH, journalist, educator; b. Cleve., Oct. 16, 1926; d. William John and Marjorie (Wilson) C.; m. Sigvald Matias Refsnes, Sept. 18, 1957 (dec. Feb. 1994); children: Marjorie Refsnes, Sunniva Collins, Stephen Refsnes. *Faith Corrigan is the granddaughter of Lieutenant Edward Corrigan of the Cleveland Police Dept, who shot it out with the Blinky Morgan Gang in 1886 and Gilbert Daniel Wilson of Brandon, Manitoba, an educator, newspaper editor and mayor. Father, William J. Corrigan, was the leading trial attorney in Ohio. Mother, Marjorie Wilson, a pioneer woman journalist from 1913-1925, covered the Cox-Harding Presidential Campaign.* BA, Ohio State U., 1948; MAT, Kent State U., 1987. Cert. tchr. English, reading, Ohio. Staff writer women's news N.Y. Times, N.Y.C., 1953-57; investigative reporter Cleve. Plain Dealer, 1962-66; dir. pub. info. Cuyahoga County Bd. Commrs., Cleve., 1966-69; dir. news, publs. Huron Rd. Hosp., East Cleveland, Ohio, 1970-73; lectr. II U. Akron, Ohio, 1990-91; adj. prof. Kent State U., North Canton, Ohio, 1996—; lectr. Fordham U., N.Y.C., 1956; expert witness U.S. Senate Medicare Hearings, Cleve., 1965; mgr. Cuyahoga County Welfare Levy Campaign, Cleve., 1966. Contbr. articles to newspapers. TESOL, Lit. Vols. Am.; mem. bd. mgrs. Eleanor B. Rainey Meml. Inst., Cleve., 1966-78; officer, trustee Lake County Cmty. Svcs. Coun., 1984-90; mem. adv. bd. Lake Geauga Legal Aid Soc., Painesville, Lake County, 1984-87; chair Initiative Petition Campaign on Environ. Waste Plant Issue, Willoughby, Ohio, 1991; officer, founder Ohio State U. chpt. Am. Newspaper Guild, 1947-48; del. rep. assembly N.Y. Newspaper Guild, 1954-57; poll judge Lake County Bd. Elections, 1984-98; field rep. U.S. Census Bur., 1989—; recruiter, crew leader U.S. Census 2000. Recipient award of achievement Press Club of Cleve., 1964, Pulitzer nominee Cleve. Plain Dealer, 1964, 1st in state Ohio Newspaper Women's Assn., 1964, 1st in state Pub. Contest of Am. Heart Assn., 1972, 1st pl. publs. award Internat. Assn. Bus. Communicators, 1971-72. Mem. VFW (Ladies Aux.), Willoughby Hist. Soc. (v.p. 1997—), Ohio Bicentennial Hist. Markers Rsch. Democrat. Roman Catholic. Avocations: expert on American china, glass, American labor history. Home: 37550 Euclid Ave Willoughby OH 44094-5622

CORRIGAN, JAMES JOHN, JR., pediatrician, dean; b. Pitts., Aug. 28, 1935; s. James John and Rita Mary (Grimes) C.; m. Carolyn Virginia Long, July 2, 1960; children: Jeffrey James, Nancy Carolyn. B.S., Juniata Coll., Huntingdon, Pa., 1957; M.D. with honors, U. Pitts., 1961. Diplomate: Am. Bd. Pediatrics (hematology-oncology). Intern, then resident in pediatrics U. Colo. Med. Center, 1961-64; trainee in pediatric hematology-oncology U. Ill. Med. Center, 1964-66; asso. in pediatrics Emory U. Med. Sch., 1966-67; asst. prof. Emory U. Med. Sch., Atlanta, 1967-71; mem. faculty U. Ariz. Coll. Medicine, Tucson, 1971-90; prof. pediatrics U. Ariz. Coll. Medicine, 1974-90; chief sect. pediatric hematology-ongology, also dir. Mountain States Regional Hemophilia Center, U. Ariz., Tucson, 1978-90; chief of staff U. Med. Ctr. U. Ariz., Tucson, 1984-86; prof. pediatrics, vice dean for acad. affairs Tulane U. Sch. Medicine, New Orleans, 1990-93, interim dean, 1993-94, dean, 1994—. Assoc. editor Am. Jour. Diseases of Children, 1981-89, 90-93, interim editor, 1993; contbr. numerous papers to med. jours. Grantee NIH, Mountain States Regional Hemophilia Ctr., Ga. Heart Assn., GE, Am. Cancer Soc. Mem. Am. Acad. Pediatrics, Am. Soc. Hematology, Soc. Pediatric Rsch., Western Soc. Pediatric Rsch., Am. Heart Assn. (coun. thrombosis), Internat. Soc. Thrombosis and Haemostasis, Am. Pediatric Soc., World Fedn. Hemophilia, Pima County Med. Assn. (v.p., 1986—, pres. 1988—), Alpha Omega Alpha. Republican. Roman Catholic. Office: Tulane U Sch Medicine Office of Dean 1430 Tulane Ave New Orleans LA 70112-2699

CORRIGAN, JOHN EDWARD, JR., banker, lawyer; b. Chgo., Sept. 26, 1922; s. John Edward and Veronica (Mulvey) C.; m. Eileen Williams, Nov. 4, 1950 (div. 1979); m. Sylvia Dennison McElin, Sept. 24, 1983. B.A., Harvard U., 1943, J.D., 1949. Bar: Ill. 1950. With First Nat. Bank Chgo., 1949-79, asst. v.p., 1960-61, v.p., 1961-72, sr. v.p., 1972-79; prin. Hedberg, Tobin, Flaherty & Whalen P.C., Chgo., 1980-87; of counsel Hedberg, Tobin, Flaherty & Whalen Inc., Chgo., 1988-92. Served with AUS, 1943-46, 51-52. Home: 560 Greenwood Ave Kenilworth IL 60043-1024

CORRIGAN, MAURA DENISE, lawyer, judge; b. Cleve., June 14, 1948; d. Peter James and Mae Ardell (McCrone) C.; m. Joseph Dante Grano, July 11, 1976; children: Megan Elizabeth, Daniel Corrigan. BA with honors, Marygrove Coll., 1969; JD with honors, U. Detroit, 1973; LLD (hon.), No. Mich. U., 1999. Bar: Mich. 1974. Jud. clk. Mich. Ct. Appeals, Detroit, 1973-74; asst. prosecutor Wayne County, Detroit, 1974-79, asst. U.S. atty., 1979-89, chief appellate divsn., 1979-86; chief asst. U.S. Atty. Wayne County, 1986-89; ptnr. Plunkett & Cooney PC, Detroit, 1989-92; judge Mich. Ct. Appeals, 1992-98, chief judge, 1997-98; justice Mich. Supreme Ct., 1999—; vice chmn. Mich. Com. to formulate Rules of Criminal Procedure, Mich. Supreme Ct., 1982-89; mem. Mich. Law Revision Commn., 1991-98; mem. com. on standard jury instrns., State Bar Mich., 1978-82; lectr. Mich. Jud. Inst., Sixth cir. Jud. Workshop, Inst. CLE, ABA-Cin. Bar Litigation Sects., Dept. Justice Advocacy Inst. Contbr. chpt. to book, articles to legal revs. Vice chmn. Project Transition, Detroit, 1976-92; mem. citizens Adv. Coun. Lafayette Clinic, Detroit, 1979-87; bd. dirs. Detroit Wayne County Criminal Advocacy Program, 1983-86; pres. Rep. Women's Bus. and Profl. Forum, 1993—, bd. dirs., 1990-91. Recipient award of merit Detroit Commn. on Human Rels., 1974, Dir.'s award Dept. Justice, 1985, Outstanding Practitioner of Criminal Law award Fed. Bar Assn., 1989, award Mich. Women's Commn., 1998. Mem. Mich. Bar Assn., Detroit Bar Assn., Fed. Bar Assn. (pres. Detroit chpt. 1990-91), Inc. Soc. Irish Am. Lawyers (pres. 1991-92), Federalist Soc. (Mich. chpt.). Office: Mich Supreme Ct 20th Fl 500 Woodward Ave Detroit MI 48226-3435

CORRIGAN, PAULA ANN, military officer, internist; b. Cheyenne, Wyo., Feb. 17, 1961; d. Patrick Joseph and Eleanor Marie (Kasun) C. BS, U. Notre Dame, 1983; MD, U. N.Mex., 1987; degree, Tulane Sch. Diplomate Am. Bd. Internal Medicine. Advanced through ranks to lt. col. USAF; chief internal medicine clinic USAF, Holloman AFB, N.Mex., 1990-93, flight surgeon Hosp. 48 RQS, 1993-94; flight comdr. 18 AMDS/SGPF USAF, Kadena AB, Japan, 1996-98; res., Aerospace Med. Brooks AFB, TX, 1999—. Mem. ACP, Am. Heart Assn. (coun. mem. 1992-93), Am. Soc. of Tropical Medicine and Hygiene. Roman Catholic. Avocation: scuba diving. Home: 19275 Stone Oak Pkwy #711 San Antonio TX 78258 Office: USAF SAM/AF 49th Med Group SGP Brooks AFB TX 78235

CORRIGAN, ROBERT ANTHONY, academic administrator; b. New London, Conn., Apr. 21, 1935; s. Anthony John and Rose Mary (Jengo) C.; m. Joyce D. Mobley, Jan. 12, 1975; children by previous marriage: Kathleen Marie, Anthony John, Robert Anthony; 1 stepdau., Erika Mobley. A.B., Brown U., 1957; M.A., U. Pa., 1959, Ph.D., 1967; LHD (hon.), 1995. Researcher Phila. Hist. Commn., 1957-59; lectr. Am. civilization U. Gothenburg, Sweden, 1959-62, Bryn Mawr Coll., 1962-63, U. Pa., 1963-64; prof. U. Iowa, 1964-73; dean U. Mo., Kansas City, 1973-74; provost U. Md., 1974-79; chancellor U. Mass., Boston, 1979-88; pres. San Francisco State U., 1988—. Author: American Fiction and Verse, 1962, 2d edit., 1970, also articles, revs.; editor: Uncle Tom's Cabin, 1968. Vice chmn. Iowa City Human Rels. Commn., 1970-72, Gov.'s Commn. on Water Quality, 1983-84; mem. Iowa City Charter Commn., 1972-73; chmn. Md. Com. Humanities, 1976-78, Assn. Urban Univs., 1988-92; mem. Howard County Commn. Arts, Md., 1976-79; bd. dirs. John F. Kennedy Libr.; trustee San Francisco Econ. Devel. Corp., 1989-92, Modern Greek Studies Found., Found. of Spain and U.S., Adv. Coun. of Calif. Acad. Scis., Bishop Desmond Tutu South African Refugee Scholarship Fund, Calif. Historical Soc., 1989-92; co-chmn., bd. dirs. Calif. Compact, 1990-93; mem. exec. com. Campus Compact, 1991—, chmn., 1995—; Mayor's Blue Ribbon Commn. on Fiscal Stability, 1994-95; chmn. Pres. Clinton's Steering Com. of Coll. Pres. for Am. Reads and Am. Counts, 1996-97. Smith-Mundt prof., 1959-60; Fulbright lectr., 1960-62; grantee Standard Oil Co. Found., 1968, NEH, 1969-74, Ford Found., 1969, Rockefeller Found., 72-75, Dept. State, 1977; recipient Clarkson Able Collins Jr. Maritime History award, 1956, Pa. Colonial Soc. Essay award, 1958, 59, William Lloyd Garrison award Mass. Ednl. Opportunity Assn., 1987; Disting. Urban Fellow Assn. Urban U., 1992. Mem. San Francisco C. of C. (bd. dirs.), San Francisco World Affairs Coun. (bd. dirs.), Pvt. Industry Coun. (bd. dirs.), Boston World Affairs Coun. (1983-88), Greater Boston C. of C. (v.p. 1987-89), Fulbright Alumni Assn. (bd. dirs. 1978-80), Univ. Club, City Club, World Trade Club, Commonwealth Club (bd. dirs. 1995—), Phi Beta Kappa. Democrat. Office: San Francisco State U 1600 Holloway Ave San Francisco CA 94132-1722

CORRIGAN, ROBERT FOSTER, business consultant, retired diplomat; b. Cleve., Sept. 12, 1914; s. Francis Patrick and Ethel (Foster) C.; m. Jane Carswell, May 15, 1952; children: Kevin, Mary, Martha, Robert Foster, Susan. Student, Washington and Lee U., 1932-34; BA, Stanford U., 1937; postgrad., Central U. Venezuela, 1939-40, Heidelberg U., Fed. Republic Germany, 1950. Dep. collector IRS, Cleve., 1937-39; corr. N.Y. Times, Venezuela, 1939-41; sec. to U.S. ambassador to Venezuela, 1939-41; vice consul, attache Am. Embassy, Rio de Janeiro, 1941-45; prin. officer Am. Consulate, Natal, Brazil, 1945-46; polit. officer Berlin and Frankfort, Fed. Republic Germany, 1947-48; polit. adviser to comdr.-in-chief European Command, Heidelberg, Fed. Republic Germany, 1948-52; Am. consul Dakar, French West Africa, 1952-54; 1st sec. Am. Embassy, Chile, 1954-57; assigned to Nat. War Coll., 1957-58; dep. chief protocol Dept. State, Washington, 1958-59; dep. chief mission, counselor of embassy, consul gen. Am. Embassy, Guatemala, 1960-64; minister, polit. adviser to comdr.-in-chief U.S. So. Command, C.Z., 1965-68; consul gen. Sao Paulo, Brazil, 1968-72; ambassador to Rwanda, 1972-73; dep. asst. sec. def. Internat. Security Affairs, Washington, 1973-75; Washington rep. United Brands Co., 1975-90; cons. Chiquita Brands Internat., 1990—. Ensign USNR, 1939-41. Mem. Am. Fgn. Svc. Assn., SAR, Washington Inst. Fgn. Affairs (dir.), Diplomatic and Consular Officers Ret., Res. Officers Assn., Mil. Order Malta, Cosmos Club, Nat. Press Club, Army and Navy Club (Washington). Roman Catholic. Address: 5304 Saratoga Ave Chevy Chase MD 20815-3723

CORRIGAN, TERENCE MARTIN, tax specialist, accountant; b. Medford, Mass., July 30, 1971; s. John Joseph and Mary Cecelia (Lee) C. B Accountancy, Bentley Coll., 1993, M Taxation, 1994. CPA, Mass. Sr. acct. O'Connor & Drew, Quincy, Mass., 1994-96; with tax dept. Coopers & Lybrand, Boston, 1996; fin. and tax mgr. Astra USA, Inc., Westborough, Mass., 1997-98; tax mgr. Boston Sci. Corp., 1999—. Mem. AICPA, Mass. Soc. CPA's. Roman Catholic. Avocations: basketball, golf, weightlifting, stock market. Home: 130 Wollaston Ave Arlington MA 02476-7165

CORRIGAN, WILFRED J., data processing and computer company executive; b. 1938. Divsn. dir. Motorola, Phoenix, 1962-68; pres. Fairchild Camera & Instrument, Sunnyvale, Calif., 1968-80; chmn. bd., CEO LSI Logic Corp., Milpitas, Calif., 1980—, also dir. Office: LSI Logic Corp 1551 Mccarthy Blvd Milpitas CA 95035-7451

CORRIGAN, WILLIAM THOMAS, retired broadcast news executive; b. Bridgeport, Conn., Sept. 18, 1921; s. Thomas F. and Anna M. (Callan) C.; m. Harriett Bell, Sept. 1, 1951; children: Kevin, Brian. BS, Am. U., 1948. Reporter Bridgeport Herald, sports broadcaster sta. WUST, Washington, 1947; writer, reporter, producer NBC News, 1948-51; producer, editor NBC-TV (newsreel), 1951-52; assignment editor NBC-TV News, 1952-53; Washington mgr. CBS Newsfilm, Washington bur. chief, 1953-59; dir. news and pub. affairs Sta. KNXT-TV, West Coast bur. chief CBS TV News, 1959-61; Am. Networks producer, editor Eichmann Trial, Jerusalem, Israel, 1961; mgr. Washington bur. NBC News, 1962; producer Huntley Brinkley Report, Wash., 1963-65; dir. news ops. NBC, N.Y.C., 1965-68; gen. mgr. operations NBC News, N.Y.C., 1968-73; gen. mgr. NBC News, 1973-79, dir. broadcast service, 1979-81. Sgt. USAAF, World War II. Decorated D.F.C., Air medal. Mem. Radio-TV News Dirs. Assn., White House Photographers Assn., Radio-TV Corrs. Assn., Nat. Press Club, Phi Sigma Kappa, Soc. Profl. Journalists, Venice Yacht Club, Bath Club (Nokomis). Home: 710 Bird Bay Dr W Venice FL 34292-4031

CORRIPIO, ARMANDO BENITO, chemical engineering educator; b. Mantua, Cuba, Mar. 6, 1941; came to U.S., 1961; s. Bernardo Manuel and Maria Teresa (Pedraja) C.; m. Consuelo Lucia Careaga, June 9, 1962; children: Consuelo T., Bernardo M., Mary A., Michael G. BChemE, La. State U., 1963, MChemE, 1967, PhD, 1970. Registered profl. engr., La. Systems engr. Dow Chem. Co., Plaquemine, La., 1963-68; instr. La. State U., Baton Rouge, 1968-70, asst. prof., 1970-74, Disting. Faculty fellow, 1974, assoc. prof., 1974-81, prof. dept. chem. engring., 1981-98, Jay Affolter prof., 1998—; pvt. cons., 1968—; vis. engr. MIT, Cambridge, 1978-79. Author: Tuning of Industrial Control Systems, 1990, Design and Application of Industrial Control System, 1998; co-author: Automatic Process Control, 1985, 2d edit., 1997; contbr. numerous articles to profl. jours. Chmn. St. George Bd. Edn., Baton Rouge, 1975-77; lector St. Aloysius Cath. Ch., Baton Rouge, 1989—. Recipient Excellence in Instrn. award Exxon Co., 1986, Excellence in Teaching award Dow Chem. Co., 1989, Faculty Professionalism award La. Engring. Found., 1997. Fellow Am. Inst. Chem. Engrs. (instr. 1977-87, chmn. Baton Rouge sect. 1990, Charles E. Coates Meml. award with Am. Chem. Soc. 1990); mem. Instrument Soc. Am. (sr. mem.; instr. 1977—), Tau Beta Pi, Phi Lambda Upsilon, Phi Kappa Phi, Sigma Xi. Avocations: sailing, swimming, reading, computer programming. Home: 9344 Bermuda Ave Baton Rouge LA 70810-1121 Office: La State Univ Dept of Chem Engring Baton Rouge LA 70803

CORRIPIO AHUMADA, ERNESTO CARDINAL, retired archbishop; b. Tampico, Mexico, June 29, 1919. Ordained priest Roman Catholic Ch., 1942. Aux. bishop, Zapara, Mex. 1953; named bishop of Tampico, 1956, of Artequera, 1967, of Puebla de los Angeles, 1976; archibishop of Mexico City, primate of Mex., 1977-94, archbishop emeritus, 1994—, created cardinal, 1979; tchr. sem., Tampico, 1945-50.

CORROTHERS, HELEN GLADYS, criminal justice official; b. Montrose, Ark., Mar. 19, 1937; d. Thomas and Christene (Farley) Curl; m. Edward Corrothers, Dec. 17, 1968 (div. Sept. 1983); 1 child, Michael Edward. AA in Liberal Arts magna cum laude, Ark. Bapt. Coll., 1955; BS in Bus. Adminstrn. Mgmt., Roosevelt U., 1965; grad. officer leadership sch., WAC Sch., 1965; grad. Inst. Criminal Justice, Exec. Ctr. Continuing Edn., U. Chgo., 1973; postgrad., Calif. Coast U., 1981—. Enlisted U.S. Army, 1956, advanced through grades to capt., 1969; chief mil. pers. U.S. Army, Ft. Meyer, Va., 1965-67; dir. for housing Giessen Support Ctr., Germany, 1967-69; resigned, 1969; social interviewer Ark. Dept. Corrections, Grady, 1970-71; supt. women's unit Ark. Dept. Corrections, Pine Bluff, 1971-83; commr. U.S. Parole Commn., Burlingame, Calif., 1983-85, U.S. Sentencing Commn., Washington, 1985-91; fellow U.S. Dept. Justice, Washington, 1992-95; criminal justice cons., 1996—; instr. women & crime U. Md., College Park, 1994; instr. corrections U. Ark.-Pine Bluff, 1976-79; mem. bd. visitation Jefferson County Juvenile Ct., Pine Bluff, 1978-81; bd. dirs. Vols. in Cts., 1979-83, Vols. Am., 1985-94; mem. Am./Can. study team Mex. penal system Am. Correctional Assn., Islas Marias, Mex., 1981; mem. Ark. Commn. Crimes and Law Enforcement, 1975-78; mem. U.S. Atty. Gen.'s Correctional Policy Study Team, 1987. Mem. Ark. Commn. on Status of Women, 1976-78; bd. dirs. Com. Against Spouse Abuse, 1982-83; mem. nat. adv. bd. dept. criminal justice Xavier U., Cin., 1993-97; bd. dirs. Bapt. Mission Found. of Md./Del., Columbia, Md., 1993-98. Recipient Ark. Woman of Achievement award Ark. Press Women's Assn., 1980, Human Rels. award Ark. Edn. Assn., 1980, Outstanding Woman of Achievement award Sta. KATV-TV, Little Rock, 1981, Correctional Svc. award Vols. Am., 1984, William H. Hastie award Nat. Assn. Blacks in Criminal Justice, 1986, Outstanding Victim Advocacy award Nat. Victim Ctr., 1991, Appreciation cert. Dept. Justice Office for Victims of Crime, 1994; recipient testimonial for svc. to fed. judiciary Adminstrv. Office of Cts., 1991. Mem. NAFE, Am. Correctional Assn. (treas. 1980-86, v.p. 1986-88, pres.-elect 1988-90, pres. 1990-92, E.R. Cass Correctional Achievement award 1993, mem. Del. Assembly 1993—, chmn. rsch. coun. 1997—), N.Am. Assn. Wardens and Supts., Ark. Law Enforcement Assn., Nat. Coun. on Crime and Delinquency, Am. Soc. Criminology, Ark. Sheriff's Assn. (hon.), Delta Sigma Theta (local sec. 1976-79, local parliamentarian 1983). Baptist. Avocations: reading, music. Office: Am Correctional Assn 4380 Forbes Blvd Lanham Seabrook MD 20706-4863

CORRY, CHARLES ELMO, geophysicist, consultant; b. Salt Lake City, May 15, 1938; s. Elmo Leigh Corry and Sylvia Birch; children: Christopher Charles, Matthew Lee. BS in Geology, Utah State U., 1970; MS in Geophysics, U. Utah, 1972; PhD in Geophysics, Tex. A&M U., 1976. Electronic missile checkout GD Convair-Astronautics, San Diego, 1960-64; rsch. assoc. Scripps Inst. Oceanography, La Jolla, Calif., 1965-68, Woods Hole (Mass.) Oceanographic Inst., 1968; mgr. geophys. rsch. AMAX, Golden, Colo., 1977-82; v.p. Nonlinear Analysis, Inc., Bryan, Tex., 1982-84; vis., adj., assoc. prof. geophysics Tex. A&M U., College Station, 1983-87; assoc. prof. geophysics U. Mo., Rolla, 1984-89; coord. world ocean circulation experiment Woods Hole Oceanographic Inst., 1990-95; cons. Golden, Denver, Colorado Springs, 1995—. Author: Laccoliths, Mechanics of Emplacement and Growth, 1988, Geology of the Solitario, Trans-Pecos Texas, 1990 (award); contbr. articles to profl. jours. and conf. procs., including Trans. Am. Geophys. Union, Jour. Applied Geophysics, others. Cpl., USMC, 1956-59, Calif. Fellow Geol. Soc. Am.; mem. Am. Geophys. Union, Soc. Exploration Geophysicists. Buddhist. Achievements include overturning of paradigm that had existed for over 150 years, regarding galvanic current flow in ore bodies; discovery that ore minerals are commonly ferroelectrics and that ore bodies behave as a polarized dielectric medium, or solid plasma, in electrical surveys; development of the controlled source audiomagnetotelluric method for electrical exploration; field and theoretical studies of magmatic intrusions; terrestrial heat flow studies in the North Pacific; coordination of hydrographic program of World Ocean Circulation Experiment; relational database design and data modeling. E-mail: ccorry@pcisys.net. Home: 455 Bear Creek Rd Colorado Springs CO 80906-5820

CORRY, DALILA BOUDJELLAL, internist; b. El-Arrouch, Algeria, July 7, 1943; came to U.S., 1981; MD, U. Algiers, 1974. Intern Hosp. Mustapha Algiers, 1972-73; resident Hosp. Tenon, Paris, 1975-79; fellow in nephrology UCLA, 1981-83; chief renal divsn. Olive View-UCLA Med. Ctr., Sylmar, Calif., 1983—; assoc. prof. medicine UCLA Sch. Medicine, 1993—; assoc. prof. clin. medicine UCLA. Recipient Clinician-Scientist award Am. Heart Assn., 1995-96. Mem. Am. Hosp. Assn., Am. Soc. Nephrology. Office: Olive View-UCLA Med Ctr 14445 Olive View Dr Sylmar CA 91342-1437

CORRY, EMMETT BROTHER, librarian, educator, researcher, archivist; b. N.Y.C.; s. Patrick Joseph and Bridget Corry. BA, St. Francis Coll., N.Y.C., 1960; MS, Columbia U., 1962; PhD, NYU, 1977. Tchr. Franciscan Bros. Schs., Bklyn., 1960-69; libr. St. Francis Coll., Bklyn., 1970-71, St. Anthony's High Sch., Smithtown, N.Y., 1971-77; prof. divsn. libr. and info. sci. St. John's U., Jamaica, N.Y., 1977-94; archivist Franciscan Bros., 1994—; dir. St. John's U., Jamaica, N.Y., 1988-93; cons. N.Y.C. Bd. Edn., 1984-88, St. Francis Coll., 1996—. Author: Grants for Libraries, 1982, 2d edit., 1986. Pres. N.Y. Irish History Roundtable, 1994-96. Mem. Cath. Libr. Assn. (pres. 1989-91, Libr. of Yr. 1991), N.Y. Irish History Roundtable (pres. 1994-96). Avocations: classical music, history of the Irish in N.Y.C. Home: St Francis Coll Faculty House 185 Joralemon St Brooklyn NY 11201 Office: St Francis Monastery 135 Remsen St Brooklyn NY 11201-4212

CORRY, JAMES MICHAEL, insurance executive, educator; b. N.Y.C., Apr. 27, 1947; s. Patrick Joseph and Bridget (Cosgrave) C.; m. Maureen Patricia Grogan; children: Matthew, Michael. BS, Manhattan Coll., 1968; MS, CUNY, 1971; PhD, U. Oreg., 1975. Health specialist N.Y.C. Bd. Edn., 1968-71; teaching asst. U. Oreg., Eugene, 1971-73; asst. dir. health Oreg. Bd. Edn., Salem, 1973-74; asst. prof. Worcester (Mass.) State Coll., 1974-76, U. North Tex., Denton, 1976-81; dir. health edn. dept. Mt. Sinai Med. Ctr., N.Y.C., 1981-88, asst. dean for continuing edn. Sch. Medicine, 1981-88; dir. health and fitness programs Met. Life Ins. Co., N.Y.C., 1988—; cons. Tex. Dept. Edn., Austin, 1975-76; grant dir., researcher State of Tex. Rsch. Fund, Denton, 1976-80. Author: Consumer Health: Facts, Skills and Decisions, 1983, Drugs: Facts, Alternatives, Decisions, 1984, Implementing Health/Fitness Programs, 1986; contbr. articles to profl. jours. Bd. dirs. Silvermine Community Assn., New Canaan, Conn., 1981-83, Mid Fairfield Hospice, Norwalk, Conn., 1982-84. Diocese of Bklyn. and U. of Oreg. scholar, 1964, 71. Fellow Nat. Ctr. for Health Edn.; mem. APHA, Assn. Adv. Health Edn. Educators, Soc. for Pub. Health Edn., Assn. for Worksite Health Promotion. Democrat. Roman Catholic. Avocations: sailing, skiing, running, tennis. Home: 7 Peter Cooper Rd 2F New York NY 10010 Office: Met Life Ins Co 1 Madison Ave New York NY 10010-3603

CORSARO, FRANK ANDREW, theater, musical and opera director; b. N.Y.C., Dec. 22, 1924; s. Joseph and Marie (Quarino) C.; m. Mary Cross Bonnie Lueders, May 30, 1971; 1 child, Andrew. Grad. in Drama, Yale, 1947. Tchr. pvt. acting class for singers; artistic dir. Julliard Opera Ctr., Julliard Sch.; head music drama div. opera/music theatre Inst. N.J.; trustee Nat. Opera Inst. Dir.: Broadway prodn. A Hatful of Rain, 1955-56, The Night of the Iguana, 1961-62, Treemonisha, 1975, Cold Storage, 1978, Whoopee, 1979, Knockout, 1979, It's So Good to be Civilized, 1987; off-Broadway prodn. Master Class, 1986; dir.: N.Y.C. Opera, 1958—, Washington Opera Soc., 1970-74, St. Paul Opera, 1971, Houston Grand Opera, 1973-77, assoc. artistic dir., 1977—, Glyndebourne Festival, 1982-85, Deutsches Oper, Berlin, 1983, Chgo. Lyric Opera, 1984, 96, Covent Garden, 1984, Met. Opera, 1984, Spitalfields Festival, London, 1985, Den Norske Opera, Oslo, 1985, Australian Opera, 1986. appeared in: Broadway prodn. Mrs. McThing, 1951; film Rachel, Rachel, 1967; author: adaptation L'Histoire du Soldat, 1974, Memoir Maverik, 1978; Love for Three Oranges Glyndebourne Version, 1985, (double bill) Where the Wild Things Are, Higgeldy Piggelby Pop, 1985, Los Angeles Opera, 1986, Amsterdam Netherlanders Opera, 1986, Montreal Opera, 1986; Ravel: L'enfant et les Sortileges, L'heure Espagnol, Glyndebourne Festival, 1987, Hansel and Gretel, Houston Can. Opera Co.; (libretto) Heloise and Abelard. Mem. Dirs. Guild Am., Soc. Stage Dirs., Choreographers, Am. Guild Mus. Artists. Home: 33 Riverside Dr New York NY 10023-8012

CORSE, JOHN DOGGETT, university official, lawyer; b. Jacksonville, Fla., Mar. 16, 1924; s. Herbert Montgomery and Carita Ann (Doggett) C.; m. Margaret Murchison, Aug. 4, 1951; children: Carita Doggett, Cameron Murchison, John Doggett, Margaret Murchison. BS, U.S. Naval Acad., 1946; LLB, U. Va., 1957. Bar: Fla. 1957, Ga. 1974. Commd. ensign U.S. Navy, 1946, advanced through grades; resigned, 1954; ptnr. Ulmer, Murchison, Ashby & Ball, Jacksonville, 1957-75, Powell, Goldstein, Frazer & Murphy, Atlanta, 1975-92; sr. dir. devel. U. Va. Law Sch. Found., Charlottesville, 1992—; pres. Gt. Am. Mgmt. Corp., Atlanta, 1972-75, chmn. bd., 1975; sr. v.p., dir. UniCapital Corp., Atlanta, 1972-75; mng. trustee Gt. Am. Mortgage Investors, 1972-75. Editor-in-chief: Va. Law Rev, 1956-57. Mem. ABA, Fla. Bar Assn., D.C. Bar Assn., Va. Bar Assn., Ga. Bar Assn., Piedmont Driving Club (Atlanta), Farmington Country Club (Charlottesville). Home: 2600 Ridge Rd Charlottesville VA 22901-9423 Office: U Va Law Sch Found 580 Massie Rd Charlottesville VA 22903-1738

CORSER, DAVID HEWSON, pediatrician, retired; b. Mpls., Aug. 4, 1930; s. John and Mary (Griswold) C.; m. Bettyrose Nerlich, June 10, 1954; children—William, Diana, Joan, Carolyn, Bonnie, Jennifer. A.B., Washington U., 1951, M.D., 1954. Diplomate Am. Bd. Pediatrics. Intern Mpls. Gen. Hosp., 1954-55; resident M U. Minn. Hosps., Mpls., 1955-57; practice medicine specializing in pediatrics Skemp Walk In Clinic, LaCrosse, Wis., 1959-95; clin. asst. prof. pediatrics U. Wis., Madison, 1959-95; retired, 1995; mem. staff St. Francis Hosp. Served with U.S. Army, 1957-59. Mem. Am. Acad. Pediatrics, LaCrosse County Med. Assn., Wis. Med. Assn., AMA. Roman Catholic. Club: Optimist. Home: 804 28th St S La Crosse WI 54601-5156

CORSI, PHILIP DONALD, lawyer; b. N.Y.C., Oct. 11, 1928; s. Edward and Emma Catherine (Gillies) C.; m. Marcia Munro, June 3, 1953 (div. 1976); children: Martina Jane O'Donnell, Charles Edward, Philip Munro, Christopher Matthew; m. Lois Joann Cobb, July 20, 1983. A.B., Princeton U., 1950; LL.B., Columbia U., 1953. Bar: N.Y. 1955, U.S. Dist. Ct. N.Y. 1970. Assoc. Willkie Farr & Gallagher, N.Y.C., 1955-69, ptnr., 1969-88, ret., 1988. Bd. dirs., pres. LaGuardia Meml. House, N.Y.C., 1964—. Mem. Garden City Golf Club. Republican. Avocations: golfing, reading, history. Home: 59 Osborne Rd Garden City NY 11530-3126

CORSIGLIA, ROBERT JOSEPH, electrical construction company executive; b. Chgo., Jan. 22, 1935; s. John Robert and Marie Virgina Corsiglia; m. Patricia Ann Ryan, Jan. 26, 1960 (div. Jan. 1984); children: Nancee, Thomas, Karen; m. Emilie Joe Clementz, Sept. 10, 1989. BSEE, Ill. Inst. Tech., Chgo., 1963. Registered profl. engr., Ill., Ind., Calif., Tex., Fla. CEO, pres. Hyre Electric Co. Ind., Highland, 1970-90, JWP/Hyre Electric Co.

Ind., Highland, 1990—; CEO Midwestern region JWP Mech./Elec. Svcs. Inc., Oak Brook, Ill., 1991-93; chmn. C & H Engring. Co., Inc., Highland, 1984-90; sec.-treas. Adventures in Travel, Highland, 1984-95; bd. dirs. Bank One, Highland. Bd. dirs. No. Ind. Arts Assn., Munster, 1989-93, v.p. devel., 1990; bd. dirs. N.W. Ind. United Way, Highland, 1985, Chgo. Engring. Found., 1991-97; bd. dirs. IIT Alumni Bd., Chgo., 1985, v.p. adminstrn., 1986; mem. IIT Pres.' Coun., 1985—; mem. Legacy Found. Inc. Lake County, Griffith, Ind., 1993—; mem. exec. bd. Boy Scouts of Am. Calumet Coun., 1993—; pres. Nat. Elec. Contractors Assn., 1975, 76, 77. Served with U.S. Army, 1964-70. Mem. Internat. Brotherhood of Elec. Workers (hon.), Chgo. Pres. Orgn., Young Pres. Orgn., World Pres. Orgn., Union League Club. Republican. Roman Catholic. Avocations: collecting, golf. Home: 8701 Northcote Ave Munster IN 46321-2726

CORSO, FRANK, JR., architect, educator; b. Elmhurst, Ill., Jan. 12, 1946; s. Frank and Jane (Kennedy) C.; m. Kathleen Angela Largay, June 18, 1971; children: Angela, Anthony, Kristina. Student, St. Ambrose U., Davenport, Iowa, 1964-67; BArch, U. Okla., 1970; postgrad., U. Ill., Springfield, 1997—. Lic. architect, Wis., Ill.; registered interior designer, Ill. Designer, drafter Filmore Designs, Oklahoma City, 1971, Lankton-Ziegele-Terry Assocs., Peoria, Ill., 1971-74; project architect J.L. Heiniger & Assocs., Morton, Ill., 1977-78; prodn. contract doc. Kenyon & Assocs., Peoria, 1977-78; prof. Ill. Ctrl. Coll., East Peoria, Ill., 1974—; pvt. practice archtl. cons. Peoria, 1975—. Com. author: Peoria I, 1976, Peoria II, 1977, Peoria III, 1980, Peoria IV, 1981. Commr. Historic Preservation Commn., Peoria, 1995—, Neighborhood Devel. Commn., Peoria, 1997; pres. East Bluff Neighborhood Housing Svcs., Peoria, 1997. Recipient Cert. of Merit, East Bluff Neighborhood Housing Svc., Peoria, 1997, Good Neighbour award City of Peoria, 1997, Dorothy Richardson award Neighborhood Reinvestment Corp. and NeighborWorks Network, 1997. Mem. AIA (svc. award Peoria sect. 1982), Nat. Trust Historic Preservation. Office: Ill Ctrl Coll 1 College Dr Peoria IL 61635-0001

CORSO, FRANK MITCHELL, lawyer; b. N.Y.C., July 28, 1928; s. Joseph and Jane (DeBenedetto) C.; m. Dorothy G. McVeety, Apr. 7, 1951; children: Frank, Elaine, Patricia, Dorothy. LLB, St. John's U., 1952. Bar: N.Y. 1954, D.C. 1981, U.S. Ct. Mil. Appeals 1954, U.S. Sup. Ct. 1960. Ptnr. Corso & Fertig, 1957-61, Corso & Petito, 1966-69, Corso & Landa, Jericho, N.Y., 1971-73, Corso & Engelberg, 1973-82; sr. ptnr., Mitchell Corso, P.C., Westbury, N.Y., 1982—. Appointed bd. dirs. UN Devel. Corp. by N.Y. Gov., N.Y. Mcpl. Bond Bank Agy.; lectr. St. John's U. Sch. of Law; U.S. congl. candidate, N.Y.; trustee WLIW pub. TV channel. With U.S. Army 1951-53. Named Man of Yr., Am.-Itals of L.I., 1966. Mem. ABA, N.Y. State Bar Assn., Nassau Bar Assn., Assn. Trial Lawyers Am., Internat. Bar Assn., World Assn. Lawyers (founding mem.), Vatican Knight of Holy Sepulchre. Contbr. articles to legal jours.; TV commentator legal topics. Home: 1 Southdown Ct Huntington NY 11743-2548 Office: 350 Jericho Tpke Jericho NY 11753

CORSO, LEE, former football coach, football analyst; b. Jan. 22, 1944. BA in Phys Edn., Fla. State U., 1957, M in Adminstrn. and Supervision, 1958. Coach U. Louisville, 1969-72, India. U., 1973-83, No. Ill. U., 1984-85, Orlando Renegades, 1985; gen. mgr. Orlando Thunder, 1991; analyst Coll. Football Assn. telecasts ESPN, 1987-88, football analyst, studio analyst Coll. GameDay, 1987—. Office: care ESPN 935 Middle St No 2 Bristol CT 06010

CORSO, SUSAN FALK, minister; b. Mineola, N.Y., Oct. 12, 1957; d. Morris Stephen and Linda (Jackson) Falk; m. Antony Corso, Jan. 23, 1987 (div. Mar. 1991); 1 child, Isaac Stephen (dec.). BA, Smith Coll., Northampton, Mass., 1979; DDiv, Coll. of Divine Metaphysics, Pasadena, Calif., 1992. Ordained to ministry, 1991. Profl. theater mgr.; minister Celebration Unity, Richland, Wash., 1992-93; minister, ch. cons. River of Life Met. Cmty. Ch., Richland, 1992-93; cons. U.S. Dept. Energy, Richland, Wash., 1993-95; minister, spkr. Vaud, various locations, 1993—. Author: The Peace Diet, 1996. Mem. Smith Coll. Alumni Assn. Office: 250 W 20th St Apt 1re New York NY 10011-3550

CORSON, J. JAY, IV, lawyer; b. Richmond, Va., May 19, 1935; s. John Jay III and Mary Turner (Tilman) C.; children: John Jay V, Catherine Anne, Clare Tilman, Jennifer Page. BA, U. Va., 1957, LLB, 1960. Bar: Va. 1960. Assoc. Davis, Polk, Wardwell, Sunderland & Kiendl, N.Y.C., 1960, Boothe, Dudley, Koontz & Blankingship, Fairfax, Va., 1963-68; ptnr. McGuire, Woods, Battle & Boothe & predecessor firms, McLean, Va., 1968—. Capt. USAF, 1960-63. Fellow Am. Coll. Trial Lawyers, Am. Bar Found., Va. Law Found.; mem. Va. Assn. Def. Attys. (pres. 1981-82), Va. State Bar (pres. 1988-89, del. ABA 1989-96). Episcopalian. Avocations: golf, skiing, fishing, gardening. Home: 3137 Trenholm Dr Oakton VA 22124-1329 Office: McGuire Woods et al 1750 Tysons Blvd Ste 1800 Mc Lean VA 22102

CORSON, SHAYNE, professional hockey player; b. Barrie, Ont., Can., Aug. 13, 1966. Selected 1st round NHL entry draft Montreal Canadiens, 1984, left wing, 1985-92, 96—; traded Edmonton Oilers, 1992-95; signed to an offer sheet St. Louis Blues, 1995-96; played in NHL All-Star Games, 1990, 94; capt. Edmonton Oilers, 1994-95. Office: Montreal Canadiens, 1260 de La Gauchetiere St W, Montreal, PQ Canada H3B 5E8*

CORSON, THOMAS HAROLD, manufacturing company executive; b. Elkhart, Ind., Oct. 15, 1927; s. Carl W. and Charlotte (Keyser) C.; m. Dorthy Claire Scheide, July 11, 1948; children: Benjamin Thomas, Claire Elaine. Student, Purdue U., 1945-46, Rennsselaer Poly. Inst., 1946-47, So. Meth. U., 1948-49. Chmn. bd. Coachmen Industries, Inc., Elkhart, Ind., 1965-97, chmn. emeritus, dir., 1997—; bd. dirs. First State Bank, Middlebury, R.C.R. Sci. Inc., Goshen, Ind., Micrology Labs., Inc., Goshen, Great Lakes Capital, L.L.C., Morristown, N.J.; chmn., sec. Greenfield Corp., Middlebury. Adv. coun. U. Notre Dame; past trustee Ball State U.; dir., past trustee, past vice chmn. Interlochen (Mich.) Arts Acad. and Nat. Music Camp. Served with U.S. Naval Air Force, 1945-47. Mem. Ind. Mfrs. Assn. (past dir.), Elkhart C. of C. (past dir.), Ind. C. of C. (bd. dirs.), Ind. Hist. Soc. (dir.), Capitol Hill Club, Royal Poinciana Golf Club, Elcona Club (past dir.), Masons, Shriners. Methodist. Home: PO Box 504 Middlebury IN 46540-0504 Office: Coachmen Industries Inc 601 E Beardsley Ave PO Box 3300 Elkhart IN 46515-3300

CORSON, WALTER HARRIS, sociologist; b. Phila., June 16, 1932; s. Bolton Langdon and Carolyn Reeves (Davis) C.; m. Sarah Peabody Lord, Sept. 21, 1964 (div. 1979); children: Trevor C. Corson, Ashley P. Corson; m. Ann Stevens Dusel, Oct. 24, 1981. BSChemE, Princeton (N.J.) U., 1954; PhD in Sociology, Harvard U., 1971. Rsch. engr. G&W.H. Corson, Inc., Plymouth Meeting, Pa., 1956-63; rsch. assoc. U. Mich., Ann Arbor, 1969-71; vis. scholar John Hopkins U., Washington, 1971-73; rsch. assoc. World Population Soc., Washington, 1974-77; ptnr. Corson Investment Co., Plymouth Meeting, 1977—; sr. assoc. Global Tomorrow Coalition, Washington, 1984-95; trustee Janelia Found., Washington, 1991—; bd. dirs. Rachel Carson Coun., Bethesda, 1992—, World Population Soc., Washington, 1992—; trustee Internat. Ctr., Washington, 1982—; adj. prof., dir. environ. politics program George Washington U., Washington, 1994—. Author: Measuring Conflict and Cooperation Intensity, 1971, Global Environmental Issues and Sustainable Resource Management, 1994, Priorities for a Sustainable Future, 1996; editor: The Global Ecology Handbook, 1990; contbr. articles to profl. jours. Mem. steering com. Soc. for Sustainable Future, Washington, 1993—; mem. task force Blueprint for the Environment, Washington, 1987-89; bd. dirs. New Directions, Washington, 1977-81. With U.S. Army, 1954-56. Rsch. grant NSF, 1971; recipient Sustainable Devel. award Global Tomorrow Coalition, 1991. Mem. AAAS, Ecol. Soc. Am., U.S. Assn. for the Club of Rome (bd. dirs. 1992-96). Achievements include development of a ranking of priorities for alleviating major global problems and achieving sustainable econ. and social development: reduced population growth, sustainable agriculture, sustainable energy use, forest protection, poverty reduction, sustainable water use, reduced waste generation. Home: 1399 Orchard St Alexandria VA 22302-4215

CORTA, NANCY RUTH, nurse; b. Galveston, Tex., Feb. 15, 1957; d. Dale Newton and Perelene Ruth (Wright) Johnson; 1 child, Joseph Henry Johnson. BSN, Tex. Woman's U., Denton, 1980. Staff nurse Baylor U. Med. Ctr., Dallas, 1980-81; charge nurse ICU/CCU DeLeon Hosp., Tex., 1981-82; staff nurse MICU/CCU VA Med. Ctr., Phoenix, 1982-83; staff nurse Harris Hosp. Meth., Ft. Worth, 1983-84, Tex. Dept. Health, Stephenville, 1984-95; nurse Dublin Ind. Sch. Dist., 1995—. Mem. Tex. Woman's U. Alumni Assn., Epsilon Sigma Alpha. Lodge: Order Eastern Star. Home: RR 1 Box 192 De Leon TX 76444-9801 Office: 701 Thomas St Dublin TX 76446-1617

CORTAZAR, ALEJANDRO, educator; b. Rio Bravo, Tamaulipas, Mex., Sept. 16, 1963; came to U.S., 1981; s. Gabriel and Maria Guadalupe C. BA, Ariz. State U., 1988, MA, 1992; PhD, U. Iowa., 1997. Grad. teaching asst. Ariz. State U., Tempe, 1989-91; asst. prof. Spanish Phoenix Coll., 1991-92; grad. teaching asst. U. Iowa, Iowa City, 1993-97; asst. prof. Spanish Tex. A&M U., Kingsville, 1997—. Assoc. editor Torre de Papel, 1993-97; corr. Culturadoor, 1995—; contbr. articles to profl. jours. Mem. Modern Lang. Assn. Avocations: guitar, reading, soccer, racquetball. Home: 1100 W Corral Ave #204 Kingsville TX 78363 Office: Tex A&M U Dept Lang & Lit Kingsville TX 78363

CORTES, DENNIS ALFREDO, internist; b. San Juan, P.R., Aug. 20, 1962; s. Alfredo Cortes and Virgenmina Feliciano. Student, U. P.R., Rio Piedras, 1984, Universidad Central del Caribe, Cayey, P.R., 1988. Lic. physician, P.R., Fla. Staff physician VA, San Juan, 1992-95; emergency physician CAC-United Health Care, Miami, Fla., 1995—. Mem. AMA, ACP, Inter-american Coll. Physicians and Surgeons. Avocations: golf, reading, business and finances, online investment and research.

CORTES, IVETTE, elementary education educator. Tchr. Republica de Mex., San Juan, P.R. Recipient State Tchr. of Yr. Home Econs. award P.R., 1992. Office: Republica de Mexico 50 Street SE La Rivera San Juan PR 00921

CORTES, RON, reporter; ž; Reporter Phila. Inquirer. Office: Phil Inquirer 400 N Broad St Philadelphia PA 19101-8263

CORTESE, ALFRED WILLIAM, JR., lawyer, consultant; b. Phila., Apr. 2, 1937; s. Alfred William and Marie Ann (Coccio) C.; m. Rosanna S. Zimmerman, Aug. 18, 1962 (div. Aug. 1981); children: Aline Elizabeth, Alfred William III, Christina Nicole. BA cum laude, Temple U., 1959; JD, U. Pa., 1962. Bar: Pa. 1963, U.S. Supreme Ct. 1972, D.C. 1977. Assoc., ptnr. Pepper, Hamilton & Scheetz, Phila., 1962-71; asst. exec. dir. FTC, Washington, 1972-73; assoc. Dechert, Price & Rhoads, Phila., 1974-76; ptnr. Clifford & Warnke, Washington, 1977-81; chmn., chief exec. officer Cortese & Loughran Inc., Washington, 1982-84; ptnr. Kirkland & Ellis, Washington, 1985-94, Pepper Hamilton, LLP, Washington, 1994-98; mng. mem. Cortese PLCC, Washington, 1999—; cons. Gen. Motors Corp., Detroit, 1985—. Lt. U.S. Army, 1959-60. Mem. ABA, Am. Law Inst., Pa. Bar, D.C. Bar Assn., Def. Rsch. Inst., Lawyers for Civil Justice (mem. exec. com., bd. dirs.), Racquet Club (Phila.), Univ. Club, Capitol Hill Club. Avocations: vintage automobile racing and restoration, art & antique collecting, cooking. Fax: 202-637-9797. Home: 113 3rd St NE Washington DC 20002-7313 Office: Cortest PLLC 600 Hamilton Sq 600 1th St NW Washington DC 20005

CORTESE, ANTHONY JOSEPH, sociologist; b. Dallas, June 15, 1954; s. Joseph and Rachel C.; m. Patricia Jean Nocita, Apr. 7, 1979 (div. Aug. 1989); 1 child, Amber Richelle. BA, Bellevue U., 1975; MA, PhD, Notre Dame U., 1980. Asst. prof. Colo. State U., Ft. Collins, 1980-85; assoc. prof. Ill. State U., Normal, 1985-89, So. Meth. U., Dallas, 1989—. Author: Ethnic Ethics, 1990, Provocateur, 1999. Fulbright grantee, 1990-91. Mem. Am. Sociological Assn. (com. prof. ethics). Roman Catholic. Avocations: matrial arts, percussin, biking, swimming, travel. Home: 15622 Ranchita Rd Dallas TX 75248 Office: So Meth U PO Box 336 Dallas TX 75275

CORTESE, DAN, actor; b. Sewickley, Pa., Sept. 14, 1967. T.V. series include MTV Sports, 1992, Rt. 66, 1993, Traps, 1994, Melrose Place, 1995, The Single Guy, 1995, Veronica's Closet, 1997—; T.V. movies include Weekend in the Country, 1996, The Lottery, 1996, Volcano: Fire on the Mountain, 1997, also T.V. guest appearances. Office: c/o Bright-Kaufmann-Crane Prodns Bldg 140 Rm 130 300 S Lorimar Plz Burbank CA 91522

CORTESE, EDWARD, marketing and public relations executive. Sr. v.p. mktg. and pub. rels. Lefrak Orgn Inc, Rego Park, N.Y. Office: Lefrak Orgn Inc 97-77 Queens Blvd Rego Park NY 11374*

CORTESE, JOSEPH SAMUEL, II, lawyer; b. Des Moines, Aug. 17, 1955; s. Joseph Anthony and Kathryn Mary (Marasco) C.; m. Diane Caniglia, Aug. 5, 1978; children: Joseph III, James David, Kathryn Elizabeth. BA, Ind. U., 1977; JD with honors, Drake U., 1980. Bar: Iowa 1981, U.S. Dist. Ct. (no. and so. dists.) Iowa 1981, U.S. Ct. Appeals (8th cir.) 1984. Assoc. Jones, Hoffman & Huber, Des Moines, 1981-85; ptnr. Huber, Book, Cortese, Happe & Brown, P.L.C., Des Moines, 1985—. Mem. ABA, ATLA, Iowa State Bar Assn., Polk County Bar Assn., Def. Research Inst., Iowa Trial Lawyers Assn. Roman Catholic. E-mail: jcortese@desmoineslaw.com. Fax: 515-243-5481. Home: 2915 Sherry Ln Urbandale IA 50322-6813 Office: Huber Book Cortese Happe & Brown PLC 317 6th Ave Ste 200 Des Moines IA 50309-4127

CORTESE, RICHARD ANTHONY, computer company executive; b. New London, Conn., Dec. 4, 1942; s. Anthony John and Winifred Silvia (Beebe) C.; m. Susan Louise Turner, Feb. 13, 1965 (div. 1973); m. Cindy Sue Folsom, Feb. 9, 1982; children: Cynthia Ann, Jennifer Lynn. BS, U. So. Calif., 1965, MBA, 1967. Fin. dir. Nat. Semiconductor Corp., Santa Clara, Calif., 1973-78; fin. control dir. TRW Corp., Los Angeles, 1978-79; v.p. fin. Northern Telecom Systems Corp., Minn. and Calif., 1979-80; v.p., gen. mgr. Gen. Automation Inc., Anaheim, Calif., 1980-82; pres., chief exec. officer Alpha Microsystems, Santa Ana, Calif., 1982-87, also bd. dirs.; pres., chief exec. officer Hugin Sweda, Pine Brook, N.J., 1987-89; pres., CEO, vice-chmn. BOD, 1990-96; pres., chief exec. officer Racotek, Burnsville, Minn., 1990-96; pres. RMB Assocs., Durango, Colo., 1996—; mem. adv. bd. Bus.-to-Bus., RimTech, Los Angeles, 1985—; bd. dirs. So. Calif. Tech. Network. Active Young Pres.'s Orgn., N.J. Named All-Am. in track and field NCAA, 1964, All-Am. in track and field AAU, 1964. Mem. Computer Communication Industry Assn. (mem. exec. com. 1983—), SoCal 10 (founding mem., bd. dirs. 1983—). Club: Chancellor's. Avocation: reading.

CORTEZ, RICARDO LEE, investment management executive; b. N.Y.C., Mar. 9, 1950; s. Eddie Adam and Marian Ruth (Lee) C.; children: Vanessa, Natalie, Rebecca; m. Harriet Anne Howard, Jan. 16, 1993. BA cum laude, CUNY, 1971; postgrad., Columbia U., 1971-73; cert. investment mgmt. analyst, U. Pa., 1993. Sr. stock market analyst Merrill Lynch, N.Y.C., 1971-76; exec. v.p. Trident Investment-Grace Capital, N.Y.C., 1976-78; pres. Liberty Capital Mgmt., N.Y.C., 1978-84, Cortez Capital Mgmt., N.Y.C., 1984-89; v.p., dir. fixed income Summit (N.J.) Trust Co., 1985-86; 1st v.p., dir. programs and communications Prudential Securities, N.Y.C., 1989-96, nat. sales dir. investment mgmt. svcs., 1996—; No. divsn. dir. Prudential Investments, 1998—, nat. dir. investment mgmt. svcs. divsn.; lectr. stock market analysis N.Y. Inst. Fin., N.Y.C., 1973-75. Author: (with Edson Gould) Industry and Stock Forecast, 1976. Named Speaker of Yr., Mcpl. Treas.'s Assn. Calif., 1981. Avocation: former lead guitar for Mitch Ryder, Jay and the Americans, Coasters, other musical rock groups. Office: Prudential Investments Three Gateway Plaza Newark NJ 07102

CORTINEZ, VERONICA, literature educator; b. Santiago, Chile, Aug. 27, 1958; came to U.S. 1979; d. Carlos Cortinez and Matilde Romo. Licenciatura en Letras, U. Chile, 1979; MA, U. Ill., Champaign, Ill., 1981, Harvard U., 1983; PhD, Harvard U., 1990. Teaching asst. U. Chile, Santiago, 1977-79, U. Ill., Champaign, 1979-80; teaching fellow Harvard U., 1982-86, instr., 1986-89; assoc. prof. colonial and contemporary Latin Am. lit. UCLA, 1989—; fgn. corres. Caras, Santiago, 1987—. Editorial bd. Mester/Dept. Spanish and Portuguese of UCLA, 1989—; editor Plaza mag., 1981-89, Harvard Rev., 1983-89; contbr. articles to profl. jours. Recipient award for Tchg. Excellence Derek Bok Ctr., Harvard U., 1982, 83, 84, 85, 86, Tchg. prize Romance Lang. Dept., Harvard U., 1986, Disting. Tchg. award UCLA, 1998; Whiting fellow. Mem. Cabot House, Phi Beta Phi. Avocations: reading, classical films, writing. Office: UCLA Dept Spanish and Portuguese 5310 Rolfe Hall Los Angeles CA 90095

CORTLUND, JOAN MARIE, educator; b. Ponoka, Alta., Can., Aug. 22, 1947; came to U.S., 1961; d. Chester Doty and Kathleen Mary (Fowler) Cook; children: Kimberly Rae Hall, David James Chesley. AA, Green River C.C., Auburn, Wash., 1981; BA in Edn., Pacific Luth. U., 1988; MEd, U. Wash., Tacoma, 1995, credentials in adminstrn., 1996. Cert. tchr., Wash. Instrnl. asst. White River Sch. Dist., Buckley, Wash., 1981-88; tchr. Sumner (Wash.) Sch. Dist., 1988-97, adminstr., chief tech. officer, 1997—. Recipient Wash. State Excellence in Edn. award State of Wash., 1994.

CORTNER, HANNA JOAN, science administrator, research scientist, educator; b. Tacoma, Wash., May 9, 1945; d. Val and E. Irene Otteson; m. Richard Carroll Cortner, Nov. 14, 1970. BA in Polit. Sci. magna cum laude with distinction, U. Wash., 1967; MA in Govt., U. Ariz., 1969, PhD in Govt., 1973. Grad. tchg. and rsch. asst. dept. govt. U. Ariz., Tucson, 1967-70, rsch. assoc. Inst. Govt. Rsch., 1974-76, rsch. assoc. forest-watershed and landscape resources divsns. Sch. Renewable Natural Resources, 1975-82, adj. assoc. prof. Sch. Renewable Natural Resources, 1983-89; exec. asst. Pima County Bd. Suprs., 1985-86; adj. assoc. prof. renewable natural resources, assoc. rsch. scientist Water Resources Rsch. Ctr. U. Ariz., Tucson, 1988-89, prof., rsch. scientist Water Resources Rsch. Ctr., 1989-90, prof., rsch. scientist, dir. Water Resources Rsch. Ctr., 1990-96, prof., rsch. scientist Sch. Renewable Resources, 1997—; program analyst USDA Forest Svc., Washington, 1979-80; vis. scholar Inst. Water Resources, Corps of Engrs., Ft. Belvoir, Va., 1986-87; com. arid lands AAAS, 1986-89; com. natural disasters NAS/NRC, 1988-91, com. on planning and remediation of irrigation-induced water quality impacts, 1994-95; rev. com. nat. forest planning Conservation Found., Washington, 1987-90; chair adv. com. renewable resources planning techs. for pub. lands Office of Tech. Assessment U.S. Congress, 1989-91; mem. policy coun. Pinchot Inst. Conservation Studies, 1991-93; co-chair working party on evaluation of forest policies Internat. Union Forestry Rsch. Orgns., 1990-95, chair working party on forest instns. and forestry adminstrn., 1996; vice chair Man and the Biosphere Program, Temperate Directorate, U.S. Dept. State, 1991-96; bd. dirs. 7th Am. Forest Congress, 1994-96, mem. comtys. com. steering com. and rsch. com., 1996—; mem. sci. adv. com. Consortium for Environ. Risk Evaluation, 1996-97; cons. Greeley and Hansen, Cons. Engrs., U.S. Army Corps Engrs., Ft. Belvoir, U.S. Forest Svc., Washington, Portland, Oreg., Ogden, Utah. Assoc. editor Society and Natural Resources, 1992-94; book reviewer Western Polit. Sci. Quar., Am. Polit. Quar., Perspectives, Natural Resources Jour., Climatic Change, Society and Natural Resources, Jour. of Forestry Environment; mem. editl. bd. Jour. Forest Planning, 1995—; co-author: The Politics of Ecosystem Management, 1999; pub. papers and monographs; contbr. articles to profl. jours. Bd. dirs. Planned Parenthood So. Ariz., 1992-94, mem. planning com., 1992, mem. bd. devel. and evaluation com., 1994; bd. dirs. N.W. Homeowners Assn., 1982-83, v.p., 1983-84, pres., 1984; vice chmn., chmn. Pima County Bd. Adjustment Dist. 3, 1984; active Tucson Tomorrow, 1984-88; mem. water quality subcom. Pima Assn. Govts., 1983-84, mem. environ. planning adv. com., 1989-90, chmn., 1984, mem. Avra Valley task force, 1988-90; bd. dirs. So. Ariz. Water Resources Assn., 1984-86, 87-95, sec., 1987-89, mem. com. alignment and terminal storage, 1990-94, mem. CAP com., 1988-92, chairperson, 1989-90, mem. basinwide mgmt. com., 1983-86, chairperson, 1992-93; active Ariz. Interagy. Task Force on Fire and the Urban/Wildland Interface, 1990-92; mem. wastewater mgmt. adv. com. Pima County, 1988-92, mem. subcom. on effluent reuse Joint CWAC-WWAC, 1989-91, mem. citizens water adv. com. Water Resources Plan Update Subcom., 1990-91; bd. dirs. Ctrl. Ariz. Water Conservation Dist., 1985-90, mem. fin. com., 1987-88, mem. spl. studies com., 1987-88, mem. nominating com., 1987; mem. Colo. River Salinity Control, 1989-90; chairperson adv. com. Tucson Long Range Master Water Plan, 1988-89; active water adv. com. City of Tucson, 1984. Travel grantee NSF/Soc. Am. Foresters; Rsch. grantee US Geol. Survey, US Army Corps of Engrs., USDA Forest Svc., Soil Conservation Svc., Utah State U., Four Corners Regional Commn., Office of Water Rsch. & Tech.; Sci. & Engring. fellow AAAS, 1986-87; recipient Copper Letter Appreciation cert. City of Tucson, 1985, 89, SAWARA award, 1989. Mem. Am. Water Resources Assn. (mem. nat. award com. 1987-90, mem. statues and bylaws com. 1989-90, tech. co-chairperson ann. meeting 1993), Am. Forests Assn. (mem. forest policy ctr. adv. coun. 1991-95), Soc. Am. Foresters (mem. task force on sustaining long-term forest health and productivity 1991-92, mem. com. on forest policy 1994-96), Am. Polit. Sci. Assn., Western Polit. Sci. Assn. (mem. com. on constrn. and bylaws 1976-80, chairperson 1977-79, mem. exec. coun. 1980-83, mem. com. on profl. devel. 1984-85, mem. com. on status of women 1984-85), Nat. Fire Protection Assn. (mem. tech. com. on forest and rural fire protection 1990-94), Phi Beta Kappa. Democrat. Achievements include research in political and socioeconomic aspects of natural resources policy, administration, and planning, water resources management, ecosystem management, wildland fire policy and management. Home: 1425 W Calle Tiburon Tucson AZ 85704-1023 Office: U Ariz Sch Renewable Nat Resources 325 Bio Sci E Tucson AZ 85721

CORTNER, JEAN ALEXANDER, physician, educator; b. Nashville, Nov. 10, 1930; s. Roy Alexander and Ruth Elizabeth (McGaw) C.; m. Jean Gibson Morgan, Mar. 24, 1956; children: John Alexander, Ruth Morgan, Stephen Lee. BA in Chemistry, Vanderbilt U., 1952, MD, 1955. Diplomate Am. Bd. Pediatrics. Intern Vanderbilt Hosp., Nashville, 1955-56; resident in pediatrics Babies Hosp., Columbia U., N.Y.C., 1956-58; chief resident, instr. Vanderbilt U., Nashville, 1958-59; NIH vis. fellow depts. pediatrics and biochemistry Babies Hosp., Columbia U., N.Y.C., 1961-63; guest investigator, asst. physician dept. human genetics Rockefeller Inst., N.Y.C., 1962-63; chief dept. pediatrics Roswell Pk. Meml. Inst., Buffalo, 1963-67; asst. rsch. prof. pediatrics SUNY, Buffalo, 1963-67, prof., chmn. dept. pediatrics, 1967-74; physician-in-chief Children's Hosp. of Buffalo, 1967-74; prof., chmn. dept. pediatrics U. Pa. Sch. Medicine, Phila., 1974-86; physician-in-chief Children's Hosp. of Pa., Phila., 1974-86; prof. pediatrics in human genetics U. Pa. Sch. Medicine, Phila., 1975-89; dir. lipid-heart rsch. ctr. Children's Hosp. Phila., 1980—, dir. nutrition ctr., 1985—. Contbr. articles to med. and sci. jours. Hon. rsch. fellow dept. human genetics and biometry Galton Lab., U. Coll., London, 1972-73. Fellow Am. Acad. Pediatrics, Coll. Physicians Phila.; mem. Am. Soc. Human Genetics, AAAS, Am. Fedn. for Clin. Rsch., Soc. for Pediatric Rsch., John Morgan Soc., Assn. Med. Sch. Pediatric Dept. Chmn., Am. Pediatric Soc. Home: 422 Penn Valley Rd Narberth PA 19072-1631 Office: Children's Hosp Phila Off of Dir of Nutrition Ctr 34th And Civic Center Blvd Philadelphia PA 19104

CORTO, DIANA MARIA, lyric-coloratura, producer, educator; d. Samuel and Margaret C.; 1 child, Christian Miles Stomsvik. BA, CUNY, 1977, MA, 1978; studied drama, Am. Place Theatre; studied voice with Maria Kurenko, Bolshoi Theatre, Moscow, studied ballet with Maria Nevelska. Founder, dir. Am. Opera Musical Theatre Co., Inc., 1995—; mem. voice faculty Calif. State U., L.A., also stage dir. opera program; founder, dir. Am. Opera/Mus. Theatre Co. Starred as Maria in West Side Story in numerous opera houses in Spain, Germany, Switzerland, Austria, 1984; appeared on Broadway in Her First Roman, Status Quo Vadis, Thirteen Daughters, West Side Story, Stop the World, I Want To Get Off; producer West Side Story for Kennedy Ctr. Opera House, 1985; concert tours in U.S., S.Am., Moscow, 1989-91; lead singer City of Angels Opera, Met. Studio; lyric-coloraturist in operas in U.S. and Europe; road tours include King and I, Man of La Mancha, Kismet; prodr. (N.Y. debut performance) The Jewel Box by Mozart/Griffiths; co-prodr. The Jewel Box with N.J. State Opera, Dmitiri Shostakovich concert with Fedn. of Russia, La Bohème, and others.

CORTOR, ELDZIER, artist, printmaker; b. Richmond, Va., Jan. 10, 1916; s. John and Ophelia (Twisdale) C.; m. Sophia Schmidt, Aug. 20, 1951; children: Michael, Mercedes, Stephen, Miriam. Student, Art Inst. Chgo., 1936-41, Inst. Design, 1942, 43, 47, Columbia U., 1946. Painting instr. Centre D'Art, Port au Prince, Haiti, 1949-51; printmaker Pratt Inst., Bklyn., 1972-74. One man shows include Le Musee de Peuple Haitien, Port-au-Prince, Haiti, 1950, Ctr. d'Art, Port-au-Prince, 1950, Elizabeth Nelson Gallery, Chgo., 1951, James Whyte Gallery, Washington, 1953; exhibited in group shows Met. Mus. Art, N.Y.C., 1950, Studio Mus. Harlem, N.Y.C., 1973, 82, Boston Mus. Fine Arts, 1975, Museo de Arte Moderno La Pertulia, Cali, Colombia, 1976, Columbia Mus. Art, S.C., 1980, Kenkeleba Gallery, N.Y.C., 1988, Taipei Fine Arts Mus., 1988, San Antonio Mus. Art, 1994, Michael Rosenfeld Gallery, N.Y.C., 1995, 96, 97, Mus. Contemporary Art, Chgo., 1996-97, M. Rosenfeld Gallery, 1998-88, Schomburg Ctr., N.Y.C., 1998, Flint (Mich.) Inst. Arts, 1999; represented in permanent collections Smithsonian Inst., Washington, Am. Fedn. Art, N.Y.C., Mus.

Modern Art, N.Y.C., IBM Corp., N.Y.C., Portland, Oreg. Art Mus., Art Inst. Chgo. Recipient Bertha A. Florsheim award Art Inst. Chgo., 1945; recipient William H. Bartels award, 1946, Carnegie Inst. award, 1947; Julius Rosenwald fellow, Chgo., 1945-47; John Simon Guggenheim fellow, N.Y.C., 1949-50. Home: 35 Montgomery St Apt 19E New York NY 10002-6531

CORTRIGHT, BARBARA JEAN, writer; b. Oxford, Miss., Dec. 29, 1927; d. Lewis Stephen and Lucile (Chevalier) Grandy; m. Lem R. Cortright, Aug. 19, 1946; children: Lewis Stephen, Clyde Kenneth, Eric Allen, Barbara Edith. BFA with honors, Ariz. State U., 1949, MA in Humanities, 1977, MA in German Lang., 1979; PhD in Art History, U. N.Mex., Albuquerque, 1993. Instr. in art history Scottsdale (Ariz.) Coll., 1974-78; newsletter editor Heard Mus., Phoenix, 1978-79; lectr. in non-fiction Ariz. State U., Tempe, 1979-80; publicist O.K. Harris West Gallery, Scottsdale, 1981-84. Author: The Reach of Solitude, 1984; contbr. articles to profl. jours. NEA fellow, 1976. Mem. Phi Kappa Phi, Alpha Mu Gamma. Democrat. Episcopalian. Home: 516 E Erie Dr Tempe AZ 85282-3713

CORTS, JOHN RONALD, minister, religious organization executive; b. Hammond, Ind., Jan. 26, 1936; s. Charles Harold and Hazel (Vernon) Corts; m. Jo-Ann Ketchum, 1956; 1 child, Alicia Beth. BA, Trinity Coll., Clearwater, Fla., 1956. Ordained to ministry Gospel Tabernacle Ch., 1957. Pastor Christian Fellowship Ch., Tampa, Fla., 1957-58; registrar Trinity Coll., Clearwater, 1957; pastor First Evang. Bapt. Ch., St. Petersburg, Fla., 1958-62; exec. dir. Youth for Christ, Tampa, 1962-64; crusade assoc. Billy graham Assn., 1964-80; pastor Idlewild Bapt. Ch., Tampa, 1980-83; pres., COO Billy Graham Evangelistic Assn., Mpls., 1983—. Avocations: sports, drama, journalism. Office: Billy Graham Evangelistic Assn 1300 Harmon Pl Minneapolis MN 55403-1925*

CORTS, PAUL RICHARD, college president; b. Terre Haute, Ind., Sept. 15, 1943; s. Charles H. and Hazel Corts; m. Diane Stevens, May 29, 1965; children: Kenneth Stevens, Daniel Paul, Susan Diane. BA, Georgetown Coll., 1965; MA, Ind. U., 1967, PhD, 1971. Assoc. prof. speech communication Western Ky. U., Bowling Green, 1968-78, dir. internat. edn., 1973-76, dir. univ. honors program, 1972-78, asst. dean for instrn., 1973-78, assoc. v.p. for instrn., 1978; exec. v.p., chief adminstrv. officer Okla. Bapt. U., Shawnee, 1978-83; pres. The Corts Co., Shawnee, 1983, Wingate (N.C.) Coll., 1983-91, Palm Beach Atlantic Coll., West Palm Beach, Fla., 1991—; cons. bd. govs. U. N.C., Chapel Hill, 1987-88. Co-author: Fundamentals of Effective Group Communication, 1979, Let's Talk Business, 1983. Pres. coun. pres.' Carolinas Intercollegiate Athletic Conf., 1986-88; mem. edn. com. Bapt. World Alliance, McLean, Va., 1990—; bd. dirs. United Way Cen. Carolinas, Monore and Charlotte, 1984-91. Mem. Am. Assn. Pres. Ind. Colls. and Univs. (bd. dirs.), Charlotte Area Ednl. Consortium (pres. 1987-88), Am. Coun. Edn., Ind. Colls. and Univs. Fla. (sec. 1995—), Williamsburg Pres. Colloquy (chmn. 1990), Palm Beach Lit. Soc. (pres. 1992—), Rotary. Office: Palm Beach Atlantic Coll Office of Pres PO Box 24708 West Palm Beach FL 33416-4708

CORTS, THOMAS EDWARD, university president; b. Terre Haute, Ind., Oct. 7, 1941; s. Charles Harold and Hazel Louise (Vernon) C.; m. Marla Ruth Haas, Feb. 15, 1964; children: Jennifer Ruth Corts Fuller, Rachel Anne Corts Wachter, Christian Haas. BA, Georgetown (Ky.) Coll., 1963; MA, Ind. U., 1968, PhD, 1972; DLitt (hon.), Georgetown Coll., 1991; DHL (hon.), Campbell U., 1995. Asst. to pres. Georgetown Coll., 1963-64, 67-69, asst. prof., 1967-69, exec. dean, 1969-73; exec. v.p. Georgetown Coll., Ky., 1973; coord. Higher Edn. Consortium, Lexington, Ky., 1973-74; pres. Wingate (N.C.) Coll., 1974-83, Samford U., Birmingham, Ala., 1983—; bd. dirs. Samford U. Found., 1990—, Found. Ind. Higher Edn., 1988-92; chmn. Ala. Commn. on Sch. Performance and Accountability. Contbr. articles to profl. jours. Bd. dirs. Birmingham chpt. ARC, 1983-89; mem. adv. bd. Salvation Army, 1987—; mem. exec. coun. Boy Scouts Am., Birmingham, 1984—; bd. dirs. Leadership Birmingham, 1984—, Birmingham Summerfest, 1984—, Ala. Poverty Project, Inc., Brookwood Bapt. Ch., 1984. Recipient Outstanding Alumnus award Georgetown Coll., 1987, Jefferson award Downtown Action Com., Birmingham, 1988, Outstanding Educator award Ala. Assn. Coll. and Univs.-Ala. Assn. Women, Birmingham, 1989, Good Shepherd award Assn. Bapt. for Scouting, 1990, Citizen of Yr., 1990, Most Supportive Pres. award Am. Assn. of Colls. for Tchr. Edn., 1991. Mem. Am. Assn. Pres. of Ind. Colls. and Univs. (v.p. 1990-92, pres. 1992-95, bd. dirs. 1989—), Coun. for Advancement of Pvt. Colls. in Ala. (past pres.), Ala. Assn. Ind. Colls., Nat. Fellowship Bapt. Educators (pres. 1988-89), Assn. So. Bapt. Colls. and Schs. (v.p. 1988-89, pres. 1990-91), So. Assn. Colls. and Schs. (trustee 1991-98, mem. commn. on colls., vice chmn. 1991, chmn. exec. coun. 1992-94, pres. 1996), Coun. Higher Edn. Accreditation (bd. dirs. 1995-97), Assn. Governing Bds. (president's commn., vice-chmn., 1998), Ala. Acad. Honor, Country Club Birmingham, The Club, The Summit Club, Rotary. Democrat. Office: Samford U 800 Lakeshore Dr Birmingham AL 35229-0002

CORTY, ANDREW P., publishing executive; b. Wilmington, Del., June 16, 1952; s. Claude and Susanne Corty; m. Betty L. Wallace, Apr. 30, 1983; children: Robert Wallace, Edward Wallace. AB, Harvard U., 1974; MBA, Stanford U., 1978. Copy editor The Morning News, Wilmington, 1974-75; reporter The Record, Havre de Grace, Md., 1975-76; asst. to pub. The St. Petersburg (Fla.) Times, 1978-80; gen. mgr. Fla. Trend mag., St. Petersburg, 1981-85, pub., 1984-85; gen. mgr. Washington Post mag., 1985-89; mktg. dir. St. Petersburg Times, 1989-91; v.p., bd. dirs. Times Pub. Co., St. Petersburg, 1991—; vice chmn. Congrl. Quar., Inc., Washington, 1991—; pres. Fla. Trend, St. Petersburg, 1991—. Office: St Petersburg Times PO Box 1121 Saint Petersburg FL 33731-1121

CORVA, ANGELO FRANCIS, architect; b. N.Y.C., Apr. 9, 1948; s. Frank John and Angelina (Di Gennaro) C.; m. Susan Aiuto, May 5, 1973; children: Christopher Francis, Katherine Mary. BA in Sci., N.Y. Inst. Tech., 1972. Registered architect, Calif., Conn., Ill., La., Maine, Mass., Mich., Minn. N.J., N.Y., Ohio, Pa., Vt., Va., Wis., Fla., Ga. Project architect Gencorelli & Salo, Mineola, N.Y., 1968-77; prin., founder Angelo Francis Corva Assoc. Architects, Garden City, N.Y., 1977—; Cons. architect N.Y. State Thoroughbred Racing Capital Investment Fund. Contbr. articles on architecture to N.Y. Times, 1984. Committeeman Nassau County Rep. Orgn., Merrick, Garden City, Manhasset, 1978-95; trustee of N.Y. Inst. of Technology; past v.p. Merrick Rep. Com.; mem. Garden City Rep. Com., Rep. Pres. Task Force, Rep. Senatorial Inner Circle; adv. bd. mem. State Bank L.I., 1983—, N.Y. State Transp. Com.; chmn. Town of Hempstead Landmarks Preservation Com.; former vice-chmn. North Hempstead Landmarkers Com.; mem. Heart Fund Ball Com., St. Francis Hosp. Challenge Fund. Recipient Masonry Inst.award. Mem. AIA (L.I. chpt., Bldg. Archtl. Design award 1984), Construction Specifications Inst., N.Y. C. of C. (Bldg. Design award Queens chpt. 1983, 90, 91, Bldg. Design award Riverhead Mfg. Facility chpt. 1985), Merrick Hist. Soc., Roslyn Hist. Soc., Nat. Trust Hist. Preservation, Queens C. of C. Roman Catholic. Lodges: Kiwanis, KC. Avocations: photography, golf. Office: Angelo Francis Corva & Assoc PO Box 4321 1691 Northern Blvd Manhasset NY 11030-3026*

CORVINO, ERNESTA, ballet dancer; b. Bklyn., Feb. 27, 1952; d. Alfredo Alfonso and Marcella (Rubin) C. AA in English with honors, Manhattan C.C., 1972. Soloist Md. Ballet Co., Balt., 1966-68; mem. corps de ballet Met. Opera Ballet, N.Y.C., 1970-71, Radio City Music Hall, N.Y.C., 1972-74; dir., prin. dancer Ernesta Corvino's Dance Cir. Co., N.Y.C., 1981—; co-dir., tchr. Dance Cir., N.Y.C., 1968-93; tchr. ballet Sarah Lawrence Coll., Bronxville, N.Y., 1993-94; artist-in-residence U. Nev., Las Vegas, 1995—; guest artist Randolph-Macon Woman's Coll., Lynchburg, Va., 1987-91, N.Y. Baroque Dance Co., N.Y.C., 1991-95, Danspace, Oakland, Calif., 1990—; pres. Dance Cor Inc., N.Y.C., 1989—. Choreographer (ballets) Charlie & Co., 1981, Holmes Sweet Holmes, 1984, Somnus, 1987, Sujets d'Art, 1997.

CORWELL, ANN ELIZABETH, public relations executive; b. Battle Creek, Mich.; d. James Albert Corwell and Marion Elizabeth (Petersen) Shertzer. BA, Mich. State U., 1971, MBA, 1981; cert. fin., Wharton Sch., 1986. Sr. publicist City of Dearborn, Mich., 1972-76; sr. assoc. Gen. Motors Corp., Detroit, 1976-77; media coord. Gen. Motors Corp., N.Y.C., 1977; mgr. community rels. Gen. Motors Corp., Pontiac, Mich., 1977-81; mgr. internal communications Gen. Motors Corp., Pontiac, 1981-82; dir. pub. rels. Pillsbury Co., Mpls., 1982-85, Avon Products Inc., N.Y.C., 1985-87; exec. v.p. MECA Internat., Flat Rock, Mich., 1987—. Dir. Mich. State U. Nat. Alumni Bd. Mem. Pub. Rels. Soc. Am., Women In Communications, Oakland County C. of C. (dir. 1988-91), Dearborn C. of C. (dir. 1989-91).

CORWIN, ANDREW DAVID, physician; b. N.Y.C., July 25, 1958; s. Leonard J. and Phoebe T. Corwin; m. Mary-Joan Marron, Oct. 1988; children: Matthew T., Timothy J., Katherine T. BA, Grinnell Coll., 1980; MD, Far Ea. U., Manila, 1986. Diplomate Am. Bd. Ob-Gyn. Software engr. Health Products Rsch., Inc., Whitehouse, N.J., 1980-81, Burroughs Corp., Flemington, N.J., 1981-82; intern St. Michaels Med. Ctr.-Holy Name Hosp., Newark/Teaneck, N.J., 1986-87; resident in ob/gyn. N.Y. Infirmary Beekman Downtown Hosp., N.Y.C., 1987-90, chief resident in ob/gyn., 1990-91; assoc. attending physician Overlook Hosp., Summit, N.J., 1991—; mem. exec. com. dept. ob-gyn. Overlook Hosp., Summit, 1998—; assoc. attending physician Morristown (N.J.) Meml. Hosp., 1993—; asst. clin. prof. ob-gyn., asst. attending physician Columbia Presbyn. Med. Ctr., N.Y.C., 1996-98, mem. com. quality assurance for ambulatory care network corp, 1997-98, mem. com. on prenatal care assistance program, 1997-98; dir. obstetrics, attending physician St. Vincents Hosp. and Med. Ctr., N.Y.C., 1999—; com. on continuing quality improvement mgmt. maternal labor Overlook Hosp., Summit, 1993-94; mem. pharmacy and therapeutics com. Empire Blue Cross Blue Shield N.J., 1998—. Fellow Am. Coll. Obstetrics and Gynecology; mem. N.J. Obstet. Soc., Assn. for Computing Machinery, Med. Soc. N.J., Union County Med. Soc. Office: 90 Millburn Ave Millburn NJ 07041-1933

CORWIN, BERT CLARK, optometrist; b. Rapid City, S.D., Oct. 4, 1930; s. Meade and Adeline (Clark) C.; m. Lydia M. Forehand; children: B. Clark II, Kelley Linette Fromm. AS, S.D. State U., 1952; BS, Ill. Coll. Optometry, Chgo., 1956, OD, 1957. Pvt. practice optometry Rapid City, 1957—; projects chmn. S.D. Lions Sight and Svc. Found., 1964; chmn. med. adv. com. to S.D. Dept. Pub. Welfare, 1968-76; mem. S.D. Adv. Coun. for Regional Med. and Health Planning, 1971; cons. S.D. Dept. Human Svcs., 1989—; mem. adv. bd. S.D. Dept. of Svc. to Visual Impaired; bd. dirs. Super 8 Motel Developers; bd. dirs. Rapid City Regional Airport, 1997—; chmn. bd. dirs. Transaction Network, Inc., 1997—. Contbr. articles to profl. jours. Pres. Cleghorn PTA, Rapid City, 1968-70; bd. dirs. Am. Optometric Found., 1989-90, v.p., 1990-94, pres., 1994-96. Fellow Am. Acad. Optometry (diplomate contact lens sect., sec.-treas. 1985-86, pres.-elect 1987-88, pres. 1988-90, chmn. 1st internat. meeting 1992); mem. Am. Optometric Assn. (exec. com. 1974-76, Am. Optometrist of the Yr. 1993), S.D. Optometric Soc. (pres. 1970-71), North Ctrl. State Optometric Conf. (bd. dirs. 1970-71), Black Hills Optometric Soc. (sec.-treas. 1958-69), S.D. State Bd. Examiners (pres. 1982-85), Nat. Acad. Practice Optometry (sec.-treas. 1990-94, Disting. Practitioners award, co-chair 1994-96). Republican. Methodist. Club: Black Hills Water Ski (pres. 1963). Lodges: Masons, Elks, Lions (pres. Rushmore chpt. 1961-62, Robert Tyler award 1998). Avocations: skiing, water skiing, hunting, piloting, public speaking. Home: 5436 Timberline Trl Rapid City SD 57702-1806 Office: 810 Mountain View Rd Rapid City SD 57702-2520

CORWIN, GREGG MARLOWE, lawyer; b. Mpls., May 4, 1947; s. Gerald Sidney Corwin and Shirley Mae (Nathenson) Nadler; m. Frances Gail Shapiro, mar. 21, 1971; children: Mitchell, David. BA summa cum laude, U. Minn., 1969, JD cum laude, 1972. Bar: Minn. 1972, U.S. Dist. Ct. Minn. 1972, U.S. Ct. Appeals (8th cir.) 1976, U.S. Supreme Ct. 1977. Assoc. Fred Burstein Law Firm, Mpls., 1972-77; ptnr. Cortlen Cloutier, Mpls., 1977-78; pvt. practice, Mpls., 1978—. Capt. USAF. Mem. ABA, Minn. Bar Assn., Hennepin County Bar Assn., Phi Beta Kappa. Democrat. Jewish. Avocations: reading, music, sports. Office: 1660 Hwy 100 Ste 508 E Minneapolis MN 55416-1534

CORWIN, JOYCE ELIZABETH STEDMAN, construction company executive; b. Chgo.; d. Cresswell Edward and Elizabeth Josephine (Kimbell) Stedman; m. William Corwin, May 1, 1965; children: Robert Edmund Newman, Jillanne Elizabeth McInnis. Pres. Am. Properties, Inc., Miami, Fla., 1966-72; v.p. Stedman Constrn. Co., Miami, 1971—; owner Joy-Win Horses, Gray lady ARC, 1969-70. Guidance worker Youth Hall, 1969-70; sponsor Para Med. Group of Coral Park High Sch., 1969-70; hostess, Rep. presdl. campaign, 1968; aide Rep. Nat. Conv., 1972. Mem. Dade County Med. Aux. (chmn. directory com. 1970), Marion County Med. Aux., Fla. Psychiat. Soc. Aux., Fla. Morgan Horse Assn., Fla. Thoroughbred Breeders Assn. Clubs: Coral Gables Jr. Women's (chmn. casework com.), Golden Hills Golf and Turf, Heritage, Royal Dames of Ocala. Home: Windrift Farm 8500 NW 120th St Reddick FL 32686-4513

CORWIN, SHERMAN PHILLIP, lawyer; b. Chgo., June 29, 1917; s. Louis C. and Becky (Goodman) Cohen; m. Betty C. Corwin (dec. Jan. 1998); children: Susan M. Rothberg, Laurie L. Grad. valedictorian, Wilson Jr. Coll., 1937; B.A., U. Chgo., 1939, J.D. cum laude, 1941. Bar: Ill. 1941, Mich. 1946, Colo. 1946. Assoc. Lederer, Livingston Kahn & Adsit, Chgo., 1941-43; assoc. Sonnenschein Nath & Rosenthal, Chgo., 1946-60, ptnr., 1960—, head estate planning and probate group, 1970-88. Editor: Estate Planning Handbook for Lawyers, 6th edit., 1976, 7th edit., 1980. Bd. dirs., officer North Suburban Synagogue Beth El, Highland Park, Ill., 1959-80; bd. dirs. Congregation Moriah, Deerfield, Ill., 1980-84; chmn. profl. adv. com. (estate planning) Jewish Fedn. Met. Chgo., 1985-87. Served to 1st lt. U.S. Army, 1944-46. Fellow Am. Coll. Trust and Estate Counsel; mem. Chgo. Bar Assn. (chmn. trust law com. 1970, chmn. Am. citizenship com. 1955), Chgo. Estate Planning Coun. (pres. 1983), Nu Sigma Kappa (past pres. local chpt.), Nu Beta Epsilon (past pres. local chpt.). Home: 400 E Ohio St Apt 2104 Chicago IL 60611-4615 Office: Sonnenschein Nath Et Al 8000 Sears Tower 233 S Wacker Dr Ste 8000 Chicago IL 60606-6342

CORWIN, STANLEY JOEL, book publisher; b. N.Y.C., Nov. 6, 1938; s. Seymour and Faye (Agress) C.; m. Donna Gelgur; children: Alexandra, Donna, Ellen. AB, Syracuse U., 1960. Dir. subsidiary rights, v.p. mktg. Prentice-Hall, Inc., Englewood Cliffs, N.J., 1960-68; v.p. internat. Grosset & Dunlap, Inc., N.Y.C., 1968-75; founder, pres. Corwin Books, N.Y.C., 1975; pres., pub. Pinnacle Books, Inc., L.A., 1976-79; pres. Stan Corwin Prodns. Ltd., 1980—; pres., CEO Tudor Pub. Co., N.Y.C. and L.A., 1987-90; lectr. Conf. World Affairs, U. Colo., 1976, U. Denver, 1978, Calif. State U., Northridge, 1980, The Learning Annex; participant Pubmart Seminar, N.Y.C., 1977, UCLA, 1985, 93; guest lectr. U. So. Calif., 1987—; expert witness nat. media trials. Author: Where Words Were Born, 1977, How to Become a Best Selling Author, 1984, 3d edit., 1999; contbr. articles to L.A. Times, N.Y. Times, short stories to Signature Mag.; prodr. motion picture Remo Williams-The Adventure Begins, 1986, (golf video) How to Golf with Jan Stephenson, 1987; exec. prodr. The Elvis Files TV Show, 1991, The Marilyn Files, 1993; pub. The Movie Script Libr., 1994; columnist Buddhascape Internet Network. Mem. Pres. Carter's U.S. Com. on the UN, 1977. Served with AUS, 1960. Nat. prize winner short story contest Writers' Digest, 1966. Mem. Assn. Am. Pubs., PEN. Home and Office: 1185 Coldwater Canyon Dr Beverly Hills CA 90210-2420

CORWIN, VERA-ANNE VERSFELT, small business owner, consultant; b. Glen Ridge, N.J., Nov. 12, 1932; d. Porter LaRoy and Vera Anna (Price) Versfelt; m. John M. Corwin, Apr. 9, 1955; children: Gail Elizabeth Corwin Bayne, Gregory John, Lynn B. Corwin Byers. BS, Upsala Coll., 1954; MEd, Wayne State U., 1972, PhD, 1977. Instr. Wayne (N.J.) Sch. Dist., 1954-55; engr., spec., analyst Chrysler Corp., Highland Park, Mich., 1955-56, 78-85; instr. Royal Oak (Mich.) Sch. Dist., 1968-78; sr. systems engr. Electronic Data Systems, Troy, Mich., 1985-87; owner, pres. Unique Solutions, Inc., Royal Oak, 1987—; adj. prof. U. Mich., Dearborn, 1989, Wayne State U., 1989; expert cons. Teltech, Inc., Mpls., 1990—. Author: (tng. manuals) Statistical Process Control Philosophies and Tools, 1988, Design of Experiments Philosophies and Tools, 1989. Pres. Arlington Park Homeowners Assn., Royal Oak, 1984-85, road commr., 1984-90; trustee First Presbyn. Ch. of Royal Oak, 1990-93, sec. 1993, Presbys. sec. 1994, choir mem., 1958-72, 97—, ch. children's computer lab. cons., instr., 1997—; sec. bd. dirs. Cmty. Concert Assn. of Troy, 1996—; vol. Oakland County Mobile Meals, 1996—. N.J. scholar, 1950-51. Fellow Am. Soc. for Quality (standing rev. bd. 1996—); mem. Soc. Automotive Engrs. (trainer 1991—), Automotive Industry Action Group (chmn. design expts. subgroup 1988-94), Soc. Mfg. Engrs. (sr., trainer 1987-91), Am. Statis. Assn. Avocations: skiing, piano, travel. Office: Unique Solutions Inc PO Box 1711 Royal Oak MI 48068-1711

CORY, ANGELICA JO, author, spiritual consultant; b. Marshalltown, Iowa, Feb. 28, 1950; d. Douglas Alan and Mary Lou (Brewster) Beckwith; m. Phillip Charles Cory, Feb. 24, 1971 (div. Feb. 1985); children: Shane Douglas, Sean Phillip. BS in BA, U. N.Mex., 1971. Lic. real estate broker, Ariz.; lic. pilot, Ariz. Bookkeeper Goodyear Tires, Inc., Albuquerque, 1968-71; instr., model Barbizon Sch. Modeling, Phoenix, 1972-75; cons., pilot Cory's Gasoline Sta., Inc., Mesa, Ariz., 1975-80; dir., cons. Sunshine Fuels, Mesa, 1980-83; dir. mgmt. and real estate Cimmarron Devel., Phoenix, 1984-86; owner, broker KCB Brokerage, Mesa, 1986-91; owner, dir. Ultimate Practices, Mesa, 1989-91; spiritual cons. Mesa, 1991—. *After her divorce, Angelica raised her two surviving sons while creating a Commercial Real Estate Company, in addition to a Medical Consulting firm both personally owned. In 1991, she withdrew from the corporate world to follow her heart's dream of inspirational writing and consulting those ones whom were choosing to become self-empowered to their hearts' dreams. Angelica, then founded the TARA-ANGELICA FOUNDATION committed to the Enlightenment of Humanity, preserving spiritual integrity through the development of supportive programs for the peace and serenity of mind, body and soul. She continues to write and consult spreading hope and inspiration into the world.* Author: Reflections of Perfections, 1995, Reflections of the Mind, 1995, Reflections of the Heart, 1996, Thoughts to Ponder, A Treasure Chest of Golden Rays of Light, 1998; contbg. composer: (cassette-CD) Light of the World, 1996, (5 cassette-CDs) Sound of Poetry, 1996-98; contbg. author: (poetry) Morning Song, 1996, Best Poems of 1997, 1996-97, Best Poems of 1998, Prisms of Thought, 1997, The Scenic Route, 1997, Sketches of the Soul, 1997; contbr. articles, poetry to profl. jours. Founder Tara-Angelica Found., 1997. Recipient Poet's Choice award, 1997, Nat. Libr. of Poets Internat. Poet of Merit, 1997. Mem. Internat. Soc. Poets (Disting. Mem. 1996—). Avocations: writing, international travel, fixed wing and hot air balloon pilot.

CORY, JEFFREY, television, film, stage, event and creative director; b. Johannesburg, Rep. of South Africa, Oct. 10, 1945; came to U.S., 1990; s. Isaac and Flora (Moshal) Kwitz. BS, Jerusalem U., 1967. Freelance stage and event dir. U.K. and Israel, 1963-68; dir. ITC TV Sta., Israel, 1969-74; CEO, dir. Jeffricory Prodns., Israel, 1974-75; CEO San Hill Prodns., Rep. of South Africa, 1975-78; founder, exec. dir. Performing Arts Workshop Coll., Rep. of South Africa, 1983-87; CEO Screen Machine Prodns., Rep. of South Africa, 1978-90; pres., dir. Scene Internat., N.Y.C., 1990—; exec. dir. Performing Arts Workshop Coll., Rep. of South Africa, 1983-87. Dir.: (TV/film prodn.) Loerie (award 1990), N.Y. Film Festival (Bronze award 1985). Recipient advt. design awards, 1995, 96, 97, 98, 99, Gold Statue award Houston Film Festival, 1989, 99; finalist N.Y. Film Festival, 1984, 85, Israels Citizen's award for TV, 1971. Mem. Mtg. Planners Internat., S.A. Film and TV Technicians Union, Internat. Platform Assn., WIZO (hon. life), Graphic Artists Guild, Am. Inst. of Graphic Artists, Art Dirs. Guild. Jewish. Avocations: music, theatre, art, travel. Office: Scene Internat 300 W 55th St Ste 4J New York NY 10019-5163

CORY, PETER DE CARTERET, retired Canadian supreme court justice; b. Windsor, Ont., Can., Oct. 25, 1925; s. Andrew and Mildred (Beresford Howe) C.; m. Edith Nash, Sept. 13, 1947; children: Christopher, Andrew, Robert. BA, U. Western Ont., 1947; LLL, Osgoode Hall Law Sch., 1950. Bar: Ont. 1950; Queen's counsel 1963. Justice Supreme Ct. of Ont., Ottawa, 1974-89; mem. Ct. of Appeals, Ottawa, 1981-89; puisne judge Supreme Ct. of Can., Ottawa, 1989-99. Pilot RCAF, 1943-45. Mem. Law Soc. Upper Can. (bencher 1971-74), Can. Bar Assn. (former councilman), Advs. Soc. (pres.). *

CORY, WILLIAM EUGENE, retired consulting company executive; b. Dallas, Apr. 5, 1927; s. William Leroy and Maude (Cole) C.; m. Doris Garlington, Jan. 4, 1947; children: William E., II, Madeline K. B.S. in Elec. Engring, Tex. A&M U., 1950; M.S., UCLA, 1959. Registered profl. engr., Tex.; cert. electromagnetic compatibility engr. Elec. engr., supervisory elec. engr. USAF Security Service, San Antonio, 1950-57; electronic systems engr., aircraft devel. engr. specialist Lockheed Aircraft Co., Burbank, Calif., Marietta, Ga., 1957-59; sr. rsch. engr., 1959-61; mgr. comms. Lockheed Aircraft Co., 1961-65; dir. electronic sys. divsn. Southwest Research Inst., 1965-72; v.p. electronic systems rsch. divsn. Southwest Rsch. Inst., San Antonio, 1972-89; pres. Cory Cons., 1989—; ret.; bd. dirs. MIDCON, Dallas and Chgo., 1977-84. Contbr. articles to various publs. Served with USN, 1945-46; maj. USAF, 1951-87, ret. Decorated Air Force Res. medal, Nat. Def. Svc. medal, World War II Victory medal, Am. Campaign medal. Fellow IEEE (bdf. dirs. 1972-73), IEEE Electromagnetic Compatiblity Soc. (pres. 1974-75, dir. 1971-75, 80-85, 90-93, Laurence G. Cumming award 1983, Interant. EMC award 1992, Richard B. Stoddard award 1995). Patentee in field. Home and Office: 4135 High Sierra San Antonio TX 78228-1916

CORYELL, GLYNN HEATH, financial service executive; b. Lexington, Ky., May 8, 1929; s. Glynn Lawrence and Allie May (Heath) C.; m. Diane Garnett Dobyns, Dec. 27, 1955 (div. Aug. 1981); children: Heather Diane, Holly. *Mr. Coryell's wife, now deceased, was a wonderful mother, raising two very fine daughters. Daughter Heather, born 1/22/64, A.B. Cum Laude, Harvard U., 1986, M.B.A. Wharton School of Finance, 1993, is a principal for American Management Systems. Daughter Holly, born 7/12/65, B.A. Cum Laude, Haverford College, 1988, is a teacher in Prague, Czech Republic. Before moving to Prague, Holly was an editor with the Associated Press. Between High School and College, Holly was a singer, pianist, and dancer with Up With People.* Grad., Culver (Ind.) Summer Cavalry Sch., 1947; A.B., Harvard U., 1951; student, Harvard Law Sch., 1951-52, 54-55; M.B.A., Northwestern U., 1957. Supr. cost accounting Procter & Gamble Co., Cin., 1957-60; sr. financial analyst Socony Mobil Oil Corp., N.Y.C., 1961-62; dir. corp. profit planning, corp. economist Libby, McNeill & Libby, Chgo., 1962-67; treas. Lyntex Corp., N.Y.C., 1968-69; asst. treas. Standard Brands, Inc., N.Y.C., 1969-71; v.p. adminstr. and ops. Standard Brands Foods Co., N.Y.C., 1971-73; financial v.p. Grand Union Co., Elmwood Park, N.J., 1973-76; exec. v.p., chief fin. officer, dir. Cramer Electronics, Inc., Newton, Mass., 1976-79; sr. v.p., chief fin. officer, dir. Kuhn's-Big K Stores Corp., Nashville, 1979-81; v.p. fin. and adminstrn., sec. Sunmark, Inc., St. Louis, 1981-83; corp. fin. cons. Lemoyne, Pa., 1984-88; pres. Glynn H. Coryell & Assocs. Inc. doing bus. as Travel Agts. Internat., Falls Church, Va., 1988-94; corp. fin. cons. Alexandria, Va., 1994—. Served with Intelligence U.S. Army, 1953-54. Mem. Alumnus Kellogg Grad. Sch. Mgmt. Northwestern U. (pres. Washington chpt.). Republican. Baptist. Home and Office: 1105 Quaker Hill Ct Alexandria VA 22314-4742

COSBEY, ROGER B., federal judge; b. 1950. BA, Western Mich. U., 1972; JD, U. Toledo, 1975. With Heckner & Assocs., Ligonier, Ind., 1975-81; judge Superior Ct., Noble County, Ind., 1982-90; magistrate judge U.S. Dist. Ct. (no. dist.) Ind., Ft. Wayne, 1990—. Maj. JAGC, USAR. Mem. Ind. State Bar Assn., Allen County Bar Assn., Fed. Magistrate Judges Assn. Office: 1130 Federal Bldg 1300 S Harrison St Fort Wayne IN 46802-3495

COSBY, BILL, actor, entertainer; b. Phila., July 12, 1937; s. William Henry and Anna C.; m. Camille Hanks, Jan. 25, 1964; children: Erika Ranee, Erinn Chalene, Ennis William (dec.), Ensa Camille, Evin Harrah. Student, Temple U.; MA, U. Mass., 1972, EdD, 1977. Pres. Rhythm and Blues Hall of Fame, 1968—. Appeared in numerous night clubs, including The Gaslight, N.Y.C., Hungry I, San Francisco, Shoreham Hotel, Washington, Basin St. East, N.Y.C., Hilton, Las Vegas, Nev., Harrah's Lake Tahoe; guest appearances on numerous TV shows, including The Electric Co. 1972, Capt. Kangaroo; co-star: TV show I Spy, 1965-68; star: TV show The Bill Cosby Show, 1969-71, The New Bill Cosby Show, 1972-73, (host, voices) Fat Albert and the Cosby Kids, 1972-79, Cos, 1976, (host, voices) The New Fat Albert Show, 1979-82, The Cosby Show, 1984-92, The Cosby Mysteries, 1994-95, Cosby, 1996; host, TV game show You Bet Your Life, 1992-93; exec. producer TV show A Different World, 1987-93, Here and Now, 1992-93; TV movies include I Spy Returns, 1994, The Bill Cosby Mystery Movies, 1994; recs. include: Revenge (Grammy award Nat. Acad. Performing Arts and Scis. 1967), To Russell, My Brother, With Whom I Slept, Top Secret, 200 M.P.H, Why Is There Air, Wonderfulness, It's True, It's True, Bill Cosby is a Very Funny Fellow...Right, I Started Out as a Child, 8:15, 12:15, Hungry; Reunion, 1982, Bill Cosby...Himself, 1983, Those of You With or Without Children, You'll Understand, (jazz albums) Where You Lay Your Head, 1990, My Appreciation, 1991; films include Hickey and Boggs, 1972, Man and Boy, 1972, Uptown Saturday Night, 1974, Let's Do It Again, 1975, Mother, Jugs and Speed, 1976, A Piece of the Action, 1977, California Suite, 1978, (voice) Aesop's Fable, 1978, Devil and Max Devlin, 1979, Bill Cosby...Himself, 1985, Leonard: Part VI, 1987, Ghost Dad, 1990, The Meteor Man, 1993, Jack, 1996; recipient 4 Emmy awards 1966, 67, 68, 69, 8 Grammy awards, named number 1 in comedy field Top Artists on Campus Poll (album sales) 1968; author: The Wit and Wisdom of Fat Albert, 1973, Bill Cosby's Personal Guide to Power Tennis, Fatherhood, 1986, Time Flies, 1988, Love and Marriage, 1989, Childhood, 1991. Served with USNR, 1956-60. Set concert attendance record Radio City, 1986. *

COSBY, JOHN CANADA, lay professional church worker, retired; b. Greensboro, N.C., Nov. 24, 1929; s. John Canada and Mildred Bernice (Cooper) C., m. Mary-Stuart Parker, June 5, 1954; children: J. Stuart, Williams C., Ellen Parker, Laura Elizabeth. BS, Furman U., 1951; postgrad., Episcopal Div. Sch., Cambridge, Mass., 1980. Cert. camp dir. Reporter, copy desk staff The Greenville (S.C.) News, 1951-58; dir. Miramar Conf. Ctr., Newport, R.I., 1958-61; exec. sec. spkrs. bureau Episcopal Ch., N.Y.C., 1961-64, dir. diocesan press svc., 1964-67; asst. ecumenical officer Episcopal Ch. Ctr., N.Y.C., 1967-71; dir. Bement Camp & Conf. Ctr., Charlton Depot, Mass., 1972-81; exec. dir. Summit Conf. Ctr., Browns Summit, N.C., 1981-82; ret., 1999; exec. dir. Huston Camp & Conf. Ctr., Gold Bar, Wash., 1983-88; mgr. Wash. Mktg. Group, Inc., Monroe, 1988-93; chmn. religious affiliated camps, 1988-92; asst. to the pres. Coun. on Christian Unity, Indpls. Christian Ch., 1994-98. Recipient Vol. of Year award Wash. State Reformatory, Monroe, 1993. Mem. Am. Camping Assn. (bd. dirs.), Lions. Episcopalian. Avocations: music, theater, art, cooking. travel. Home: PO Box 539 Floyd VA 24091-0539

COSBY, RITA KAREN, newscaster; b. Bklyn., Nov. 18, 1964; d. Richard Roger and Adda Otilia (Arenfeldt) C. Honors degree, Conn. Sch. Broadcasting, 1983; BA in Broadcast Journalism, BA in Spanish, U. S.C., 1989. Nat. sales mgr. Basic Wallpaper, Inc., Stamford, Conn., 1983-86; bus. cons. Lin-Gor, Inc., Clifton, N.J., 1986-89; announcer, control operator Sta. WACH-TV, Columbia, S.C., 1989; intern, asst. CBS Evening News, N.Y.C., 1989; anchor, reporter Sta. KERO-TV, Bakersfield, Calif., 1989-92, Sta. WBTV-CBS, Charlotte, N.C., 1992-95; sr. corr. FOX News, Washington, 1995—; news anchor S.C. Pub. Radio, Columbia, 1988-89; host, interviewer, prodr. Bus. and Fin. Shows, Bakersfield, 1989-92; host, interviewer Community Affairs Show, Bakersfield, 1989-92, Take One Prodns., N.Y.C., 1989—, Spanish Cable TV Show, Charlotte, 1993-95. News editor (newspaper) The Gamecock, 1987-89; writer (newspaper) The State, 1988-89; columnist (Hispanic newspaper) El Progreso Hispano, 1993—. Mem. adv. bd. Youth Involvement Coun., Charlotte, 1992-95; host, fundraiser United Negro Coll. Fund, Charlotte, 1993-95, Children's Miracle Network Telethon, Charlotte, 1993-95, Muscular Dystrophy Assn., Bakersfield, 1990-92; speaker, reader Charlotte-Mecklenburg Schs., Charlotte, 1992-95; vol., speaker Girl Scouts U.S., 1989—; motivational speaker anti-drug program DARE. Recipient Outstanding Sr. award U. S.C., 1989, Best Reporting award Kern County Press Club, 1991. Mem. NATAS (Emmy 1992, 95, listed as Outstanding Young Am. 1989, mem. nominating bd. 1997—), L.Am. Coalition (speaker 1993—), L.Am. Women's Assn. (speaker 1994—), Soc. Profl. Journalists (student pres. 1987—), Alpha Epsilon Rho (pub. info. officer 1987-89), Omicron Delta Kappa. Avocations: foreign languages. Office: Fox Network News 400 N Capitol St NW Ste 550 Washington DC 20001-1502

COSCO, JOHN ANTHONY, health care executive, educator, consultant; b. Cin., July 13, 1947; s. Adolph John and Pasqualina Marie (Saluppo) C.; m. Anne Patricia Ward, Aug. 5, 1978; children: Stephen Ward, Justin Thomas. BS, Xavier U., Cin., 1969, MEd, 1972, MBA, 1975; postgrad. U. Cin., 1972, PhD in Health Svcs. and Mgmt., Columbia-Pacific U., 1986; asst. dir. edn. and staff devel. Jewish Hosp., Cin., 1972-77; exec. dir. Region IX Peer Rev. Systems, Inc., Portsmouth, Ohio, 1977-78; exec. dir. Region II Med. Rev. Corp., Dayton, Ohio, 1978-81; asst. adminstr., sr. v.p. Mercy Hosp., Tiffin, Ohio, 1981-87; adminstr. Grafton (W.Va.) City Hosp., 1987-89; sr. v.p., COO, The St. Francis Acad., Inc., Salina, Kans., 1989—; ptnr. Hos-Con & Assocs., 1974-79; pres. & CEO hale foster & stunning, 1993—; bd. dirs. Sunflower Health Network, Inc., Salina, Kans., WSFA, Phila., N. Ctrl. Kans. PHO, Salina; instr. Kans. State U., Salina, 1996—; adj. asst. prof. Kan. Wesleyan U., 1997—. Lt. AUS, 1969-71. Fellow Am. Coll. Health Care Execs. Roman Catholic. Office: St Francis Academy Inc 509 E Elm St Salina KS 67401-2348

COSE, ELLIS, journalist, author; b. Chgo., Feb. 20, 1951; m. Lee Llambelis. BA in Psychology, U. Ill., Chgo., 1972; MA in Sci. Tech. and Pub. Policy, George Washington, 1978. Columnist, reporter, editor Chgo. Sun-Times, 1970-77; sr. fellow, dir. energy policy studies Joint Ctr. Polit. Studies, Washington, 1977-79; editl. writer, columnist Detroit Free Press, 1979-81; resident fellow NAS, 1981-82; spec writer USA Today, 1982-83; pres. Inst. Journalism Edn., 1983-86; pres. Gannett Ctr. Media Studies Columbia U., N.Y.C., 1987; contbg. editor, essayist Time mag., N.Y.C., 1989-90; chmn. editl. bd. N.Y. Daily News, 1991-93; contbg. editor, essayist Newsweek mag., N.Y.C., 1993—. Author: Energy and Equity, Some Social Concerns, 1978, Energy and the Urban Crises, 1978, Decentralizing Energy Decisions: The Rebirth of Community Power, 1983, The Press, 1988, A Nation of Strangers, 1992, The Rage of a Privileged Class, 1994, A Man's World, 1995, Color Blind, 1997, The Best Defense, 1998. Fellow Ford Found., Andrew Mellon Found.; grantee Rockefeller Found., Aspen Inst. for Humanistic Studies; recipient Ill. UPI award, Lincoln U. award, N.Y. Assn. Black Journalists award, Myers Ctr. Study of Human Rights in N.Am. award, others. Office: Newsweek 251 W 57th St New York NY 10019-1802

COSENTINO, PATRICIA BYRNE, English educator, poet; b. Boston, June 6, 1927; d. Charles E. and Patricia (McDermott) Byrne; m. E. McDonough (div. 1953); 1 child, Peter E. McDonough; m. Kenneth Rosenfield, Aug. 29, 1954 (div. 1968); 1 child, R. Noah Rosenfield; m. David Cosentino, June 28, 1990. AS, Newton (Mass.) Jr. Coll., 1967; BS, Boston U., 1972; MA, Regis Coll., 1984. Dir. learning lab. Newton (Mass.) Jr. Coll., 1965-70; asst. to dir. MAT Sch. Edn. Harvard U., Cambridge, Mass., 1970-72; tchr. Wellesley (Mass.) High Sch., 1972-90; cons. East-West Nexus/Prota, Cambridge, 1987—, writing tchr. Mt Wachusett C.C., Gardner, Mass., 1999, Adv. Bd. Educators Pubs., Cambridge, Mass. Author: Cat in the Mirror, 1970, Whetstone, 1990. Sec., treas. North Ctrl. (Mass.) Assn. Small Bus., 1991—; sec. Gardner-Athol (Mass.) Area Mental Health Assn., 1994—; bd. dirs. Opportunities Unltd., Heywood Hosp. Volunteer/Admitting, Gardner, Mass., 1991-97. Recipient Mary F. Lindsley award N.Y. Poetry Forum, 1972. Mem. Am. Acad. Poets, Poetry Soc. Am., Gardner Cultural Coun. Avocations: golf, music, travel, education, theater. Home: 33 Leo Dr Gardner MA 01440-1211 Office: Reliable Fin & Antiques 177 West St Gardner MA 01440-2121

COSENZA, ARTHUR GEORGE, opera director; b. Phila., Oct. 16, 1924; s. Luigi and Maria (Piccolo) C.; m. Marietta Muhs, Sept. 16, 1950; children: Louis John, Arthur William, Maria. Student, Ornstein Sch. Music, Phila., 1946-48, Berkshire Music Festival, 1947, Am. Theater Wing, N.Y.C., 1948-50. asso. prof. Coll. Music, Loyola U. of South, 1954-84, dir. opera workshop, 1954-84; dir. Opera Program for City of New Orleans, 1955-73. Performed leading baritone roles with opera cos. throughout, U.S., Can., 1947-70; baritone, New Orleans Opera, 1954-70; producer operas, 1960-74; resident stage dir., 1965-70, gen. dir., 1970-96, artistic dir. 1970-98. Served with AUS, 1943-45. Decorated Purple Heart medal; cavaliere Order Star Italian Solidarity; cavaliere Ufficiale dell' Ordine al Merito Italy; officier Ordre des Arts et des Lettres. Mem. Am. Guild Mus. Artists (hon. life), Blue Key. Home: 1720 Soniat St New Orleans LA 70115-4919 Office: New Orleans Opera Assn 305 Baronne St New Orleans LA 70112-1624

COSENZA, VINCENT JOHN, accountant; b. Bklyn., Aug. 12, 1962; s. Vincent James and Rosalie Theresa (Ferraro) C. BS in Acctg., NYU, 1984. CPA, N.Y. Mgr. fin. adminstrn. Jr. Achievemnt N.Y. Inc., N.Y.C., 1984-85; staff acct. Rosenshein, Neiman & Weiss, CPA's, N.Y.C., 1985-87; sr. acct., mgr. Pepper, Gelbord, Roth & Co. LLP, N.Y.C., 1987—; assoc. acct. Sheldon Plotnick, Bklyn., 1986-88. Mem. AICPA, N.Y. State Soc. CPAs. Democrat. Roman Catholic. Avocations: stamp collecting, volleyball, reading, travel. Home: 1393 E 53rd St Brooklyn NY 11234-3226 Office: Pepper Gelbord Roth & Co LLP 60 E 42nd St Ste 1201 New York NY 10165-1299

COSER, LEWIS ALFRED, sociology educator; b. Berlin, Nov. 27, 1913; came to U.S., 1941, naturalized, 1948; s. Martin and Margarete (Fehlow) C.; m. Rose Laub, Aug. 25, 1942; children: Ellen, Steven. Student, Sorbonne, Paris, France, 1935-38; PhD in Sociology, Columbia U., 1954; D (hon.), Humboldt U., Berlin, 1993. Instr. U. Chgo., 1948-50; mem. faculty Brandeis U., 1951-68, prof. sociology, 1960-68; Disting. prof. SUNY, Stony Brook, 1969-87; adj. prof. sociology Boston Coll., 1987-97, Boston Univ., 1997—; fellow Ctr. for Advanced Study Behavorial Scis., Stanford, Calif., 1968-69, 79-80; vis. prof. U. Calif., Berkeley, 1957-58. Author: The Functions of Social Conflict, 1956, (with B. Rosenberg) Sociological Theory, 1957, 5th edit., 1982, (with Irving Howe) The American Communist Party, 1957, 2d edit., 1962, Sociology Through Literature, 1963, rev. edit., 1971, Men of Ideas, 1965, Georg Simmel, 1965, Political Sociology, 1967, Continuities in the Study of Social Conflict, 1967, Masters of Sociological Thought, 1971, enlarged edit., 1977, Greedy Institutions, 1974, (with Kadushin and Powell) The Culture and Commerce of Publishing, 1982, Refugee Scholars in America, 1984, A Handful of Thistles, 1988; editor: Maurice Halbwachs: On Collective Memory, 1992, Everett C. Hughes: On Work Race and the Sociological Imagination, 1994. Named Disting. Prof. Emeritus, 1986. Mem. Am. Acad. Arts and Scis., ACLU, Am. Sociol. Assn. (pres. 1975-76), Eastern Sociol. Soc. (pres. 1964-65). Home: 27 Shepard St Cambridge MA 02138-1504

COSETTI, JOSEPH LOUIS, federal judge; b. Youngstown, Ohio, May 8, 1929; s. Raymond and Mary Cosetti; m. Marilyn Sullivan, Nov. 23, 1973; children: Maura Kelly, John Sullivan. BS, Ohio State U., 1951, MBA, 1953; JD, Duquesne U., 1975. Bar: Pa. 1975, U.S. Dist. Ct. (we. dist.) Pa. 1975. Analyst U.S. Steel Corp., Pitts., 1953-58; mgr. market rsch. Virginia-Carolina Chem. Corp., Richmond, Va., 1958-59; prin. economist Jones & Laughlin Steel Corp., Pitts., 1959-70; city sch. treas. City of Pitts., 1970-77; atty. Titus, Marcus & Shapiro, Pitts., 1978-80; bankruptcy judge U.S. Bankruptcy Ct. we. dist. Pa., Pitts., 1980—, chief bankruptcy judge, 1985-94; ski patrol, Blue Knob (Pa.) Ski Resort. Bd. dirs. Consumer Credit Counseling of Western Pa., Pitts. Col. ret., USAR. Mem. ABA, Allegheny County Bar Assn., Pa. Bar Assn., Am. Bankruptcy Inst., Am. Coll. Bankruptcy. Republican. Baptist. Avocation: skiing. Office: US Bankruptcy Ct 600 Grant St Ste 5436 Pittsburgh PA 15219-2702

COSGRIFF, JAMES ARTHUR, physician; b. Lamberton, Minn., Mar. 18, 1924; s. James Arthur and Elsie Ann (Forster) C. BS summa cum laude, Coll. St. Thomas, 1944; MD, U. Minn., 1946. Diplomate Am. Bd. Family Practice. Intern St. Mary's Hosp., Duluth, Minn.; pvt. practice Olivia, Minn., 1949—. With USN, 1947-49. Fellow Am. Acad. Family Physicians; mem. Minn. Acad. Family Physicians (pres. 1963, Merit award 1964), Alpha Omega Alpha. Roman Catholic. Avocations: travel, photography, reading, music. Home: 802 E Park Ave Olivia MN 56277-1361 Office: Olivia Clinic 619 E Lincoln Ave Olivia MN 56277-1349

COSGRIFF, STUART WORCESTER, internist, consultant, medical educator; b. Pittsfield, Mass., May 8, 1917; s. Thomas F. and Frances Deford (Worcester) C.; m. Mary Shaw, Jan. 23, 1943; children: Mary, Thomas, Stuart, Richard, Robert. B.A. cum laude, Holy Cross Coll., 1938; M.D., Columbia U., 1942, D.Med. Sci., 1948. Diplomate: Am. Bd. Internal Medicine. Intern Presbyterian Hosp., N.Y.C., 1942-43; asst. resident in medicine, 1943, 46-47, chief resident, 1947-48; instr. in medicine Columbia U., N.Y.C., 1948-50, clin. asst. prof. medicine, 1951-63, clin. assoc. prof., 1963-73, clin. prof. medicine, 1973-83, clin. prof. emeritus, 1983—; attending physician Presbyn. Hosp., N.Y.C., 1948-83; cons. emeritus Presbyn. Hosp., 1984—; individual practice medicine, specializing in internal medicine and vascular diseases, 1948—; cons. in medicine to dir. Selective Svc., N.Y.C., 1957-73, N.Y. Giants Baseball Club, 1951-57, San Francisco Baseball Club, 1958-61; dir. thrombo-embolic clinic Vanderbilt Clinic, N.Y.C., 1948-83. Contbr. articles to med. jours. Served to capt. M.C., U.S. Army, 1943-45, ETO. Fellow ACP, Pan Am. Med. Assn.; mem. Am. Heart Assn., N.Y. Heart Assn., Alpha Omega Alpha. Roman Catholic. Club: Knickerbocker Country (Tenafly, N.J.). Home and Office: 11 Park St Tenafly NJ 07670-2217 Office: 161 Ft Washington Ave New York NY 10032-3713

COSGROVE, CAMERON, technology executive; b. Arcadia, Calif., July 25, 1957; s. Joseph Patrick Jr. and Marion (Barrons) C.; (div.); children: Christopher Farley, Steven Patrick. BS in Mgmt., Calif. State U., Long Beach, 1980. V.p. Pacific Life Ins. Co., Newport Beach, 1982—. Co-author city ordnance Regulation of Ozone, Depleting Compounds, 1989-90; contbr. articles to newspaper. Fin. commr. City of Irvine, Calif., 1983-87, planning commr. 1987-88, city councilman, 1988-90; bd. dirs. Irvine Transp. Authority, 1988-90.; founding advisor Irvine Conservancy, advisor, 1986-88, Irvine Infrastructure Authority, 1988-90; founder San Joaquin Marsh Adv. Com., chair 1988-90. Recipient Sea and Sage Audubon Conservation award, 1990. Mem. Life Office Mgmt. Assn. (tech. and mgmt. com. 1990-96). Republican. Avocation: environmentalist. Office: Pacific Life Ins 700 Newport Center Dr Newport Beach CA 92660-6307

COSGROVE, JAMES, artist, industrial designer; b. Phoenix; s. Donald and Evelyn (Dresden) C.; m. Madeline Matranga, Sept. 20, 1969 (div. June 1986); children: Shannon, Kenneth, Marcia, Daniel. AA in Liberal Arts, Mt. San Antonio Coll., 1974; AA in Fine Art, Sacramento City Coll., 1994, AS in Metals Tech., 1995. With Mattel Toys, L.A., 1973-78; prin. Cos Design Group, Sacramento, 1994—. Inventor, designer in field. Recipient Award of Merit, State of Calif. Works Exhibit, 1995, Award of Excellence, 1996. Mem. Artist-Blacksmith Assn. N.Am., Calif. Blacksmith Assn. Studio: 8371 Jackson Rd Sacramento CA 95826-3902

COSGROVE, JOHN FRANCIS, lawyer, state legislator; b. Coral Gables, Fla., July 1, 1949; s. Francis Freheil and Vivian Adair (Rafferty) C.; m. Bernadine Elizabeth Cosgrove, Dec. 19, 1981; children—Michael, Tiffany, Colleen. A.A., U. Fla., 1969, B.S. in Journalism, 1971; J.D., Cumberland Sch. Law, 1975. Bar: Fla., U.S. Dist. Ct. (so. dist.) Fla., U.S. Ct. Appeals (5th cir.), U.S. Supreme Ct. Assoc., Hall & Hedrick, Miami, Fla., 1975-80; sole practice, Miami, 1980—; mem. Fla. Ho. of Reps., 1981-84, 1986—; gen. counsel Biscayne Coll.; columnist Miami Rev.: Juris Conspectus, 1975—; chair Nat. Conf. State Legislatures Com. on Commerce and Comm.; chair property and casualty com., mem. exec. com. Nat. Conf. Ins. Legislatures. Chmn. Coral Gables Code Enforcement Bd.; mem. Coral Gables Econ. Devel. Bd.; mem. Jr. Orange Bowl Com.; chmn. Metro-Dade Econ. Devel. Bd., Miami Budget Rev. Com.; mem. South Miami Hosp. Assocs. Mem. ABA, Fla. Bar Assn. (Jud. Selection, Adminstrn. and Tenure Com., vice chmn. jud. nominating com.), Dade County Bar Assn. (3d v.p.), Am. Judicature Soc., Assn. Trial Lawyers Am., Pvt. Industry Council of Dade County, Emerald Soc. of South Fla., Miami Springs-Hialeah C. of C., Coral Gables C. of C., Greater Miami C. of C., Blue Key, Phi Kappa Tau. Democrat. Roman Catholic (chmn. Cath. Service Bur.-50th anniversary). Clubs: Serra, Viscayans Civic, Le Lega Civic; Greater Miami Leadership Prayer Breakfast. Lodges: K.C. (grand knight Coral Gables; pres. Dade County chpt.), Kiwanis, Knight of Malta. Home: 8230 SW 192nd St Miami FL 33157-8013 Office: 201 W Flagler St Miami FL 33130-1510

COSGROVE, JOHN PATRICK, editor; b. Pittston, Pa., Sept. 25, 1918; s. Raymond Patrick and Alice (Gilroy) C.; m. Patricia Ellen O'Hara, Mar. 26, 1951. Ed. pub. schs., Pa. Reporter, Wilkes-Barre (Pa.) Record, 1936-37, AP, Washington, 1938-40; writer, research Nat. Republican Congl. Com., Washington, 1940; exec. asst. U.S. Senator Hiram W. Johnson, 1941-42; free lance writer, 1946-48; dir. publs. Broadcasting Publs., Inc. (pubs. Broadcasting Businessweekly, Television monthly, Broadcasting Yearbook), Washington, 1948-68. Author: The Gendreau Story: War History of DE 639; editor: SHRDLU-An Affectionate Chronicle of the first fifty years of the Nat. Press Club, 1959. Publicity dir. Honor Am. Day Celebration, 1970; exec. dir. Am. Hist. and Cultural Soc., Inc., 1970-88; sec. Nat. Christmas Pageant of Peace, 1974—, v.p., 1985—, mem. com. to light nat. Christmas tree; Washington rep. Nat. Com. Neurol. Disorders and Stroke, 1972-78, R.R. Task Force for Northeast Region, 1973-75; bd. dirs. Am. Irish Found., 1967-87, pres., 1971-73; bd. dirs. Washington chpt. Nat. Multiple Sclerosis Soc., 1962-70, Am. Ireland Fund, 1987—; mem. bd. dirs. USN Meml. Found., Washington, 1986—, sec. and chmn. dedication com., 1987; bd. dirs. Ellis Island Restoration Commn., N.Y., 1989—, Destroyer-Escort Hist. Found., 1993—; vice chmn. Am. Fedn. Irish Heritage, 1988—; bd. dirs. Internat. Svc. Agys., 1992—. Served with USNR, 1942-46; assigned Office Censorship, Washington 1942; U.S.S. Gendreau 1944-46. Named Gael of Yr., Washington D.C. St. Patrick's Parade, 1999. Mem. VFW (life), White House Corrs. Assn. (hon.), Soc. Profl. Journalists, Destroyer-Escort Sailors Assn. (life, bd. dirs. 1981-96), Am. Legion (life), Nat. Press Club (Post no. 20, comdr. 1999—), Soc. Friendly Sons of St. Patrick (life, bd. dirs. 1976-82), Nat. Headliners Club (Atlantic City), Circus Saints and Sinners Club (exec. v.p., dir. P.T. Barnum tent 1973-89, pres. 1989-91), Nat. Press Club (Washington) (bd. govs. 1956-59, v.p. 1960, pres. 1961, chmn. awards com. 1974, chmn. election com. 1978). Roman Catholic. Home: 7906 Jensen Pl Bethesda MD 20817-4671 Office: 1124 National Press Bldg Washington DC 20045

COSGROVE, WILLIAM E., English literature educator; b. South St. Paul, Minn., Jan. 29, 1939; s. Emmett Edward and Margaret Mary (Sweeney) C.; m. Margaret T. Froehlich, Sept. 3, 1966; children: Courtney Ann, Shannon Margaret, Cristin Marie. BA, U. St. Thomas, St. Paul, 1962; MA, Marquette U., 1966; PhD, U. Iowa, 1972. English tchr. Cretin H.S., St. Paul, 1962-64; grad. tchg. asst. Marquette U., Milw., 1964-66; grad. tchg. asst. U. Iowa, Iowa City, 1966-69, grad. fellow, 1969-70; asst. prof. N.D. State U., Fargo, 1970-76, assoc. prof., 1976-81, prof., 1981—, chair dept. English, 1991-97. Performer An Evening with Mark Twain, the Trouble Begins at Eight, 1983—; contbr. articles to profl. jours. Mem. MLA (Am. Lit. sect.), Nat. Coun. Tchrs. English, N.D. Coun. Tchrs. English (affiliate dir.). Democrat. Roman Catholic. Avocations: tennis, biking. Home: 1001 4th Ave S Fargo ND 58103-1716 Office: ND State U Dept English Minard Hall 322 Fargo ND 58105

COSIER, RICHARD A., business educator, consultant; b. Jackson, Mich., May 18, 1947; s. Roy A. and Wilma M. (Braund) C.; m. Rae L. Pettelle, June 14, 1969 (div. Feb. 1985); children: Jeffrey R., Nathan R.; m. Lynn M. Hays, Aug. 30, 1986; children: Courtney M., Kelsey L. BS, Mich. State U., 1969; MBA, Loyola U., 1972; PhD, U. Iowa, 1976. From asst. to assoc. prof. mgmt. Ind. U., Bloomington, 1976-86, prof. mgmt., 1986-92, chairperson, prof. mgmt., 1983-90, assoc. dean for acads., prof. mgmt., 1990-92; dean, Fred E. Brown chair U. Okla., Norman, 1993-99; dean and leads prof. mgmt. Purdue U., 1999—; cons. in field. Contbr. over 75 articles and book chpts. to profl. jours.; inventor patented packaging technique. Mem. Acad. Mgmt., Decision Scis. Inst. Republican. Home: 4701 Sundance Ct Norman OK 73072-3900 Office: Krannert Sch Mgmt Purdue U West Lafayette IN 47907-1310

COSLET, BRUCE N., professional football coach; b. Oakdale, Calif., Aug. 5, 1946; s. James A. and Mae C. (Coon) C.; m. Kathleen Joseph; children: Jonathan James, Amy Kathleen. BA, U. of Pacific, 1968. Player Edmonton (Alta., Can.) Eskimos, CFL, 1968; player, capt. Cinn. Bengals, NFL, 1969-76, coach spl. teams, 1981-83, coach wide receivers, 1984-85, coach, offense coord., 1986-89, 95-96; coach spl. teams San Francisco 49ers, 1980; head coach N.Y. Jets, 1990-93, Cincinnati Bengals, 1996—; owner Coslet Devel., Stockton, Calif., 1977-80. Author: Youth Passing and Receiving, 1989. Named to Pacific Sports Hall of Fame U. Pacific, 1984, Oakdale (Calif.) Sports Hall of Fame, (charter) 1987. Mem. LDS Ch. Avocations: golf, fishing, reading, music. Office: Cincinnati Bengals One Bengals Dr Cincinnati OH 45204*

COSLIK, STEPHEN, real estate executive; b. Rochester, N.Y., Feb. 10, 1949; s. Stephen and Gertrude (Wagner) C.; m. Marie Alice Hay; 1 child, Erik James. BBA with honors, Calif. State U., San Diego, 1971. Regional asst. mgr. Lincoln Nat. Life, San Francisco, 1973-77; exec. v.p. Comml. Properties and Investments, Hurst, Tex., 1977-81; pres. Woodmont Corp., Ft. Worth, 1981—. Contbr. articles to profl. jours. Bd. dirs. Ft. Worth Ballet, First United Meth. Ch., Ft. Worth; mem. fin. com. Trinity Valley Sch. Bd., Ft. Worth. Mem. Urban Land Inst. (assoc.), Internat. Council Shopping Ctrs. (assoc.), Nat. Assn. Indsl. and Office Parks. Republican. Club: Ft. Worth. Avocations: marathon running, camping, tennis. Office: Woodmont Corp 6500 West Fwy Ste 900 Fort Worth TX 76116-2190

COSMAN, FRANCENE JEN, government official; b. Windsor, Ont., Can., Jan. 14, 1941; d. John Douglas and Dorothy Mae (Machel) McCarthy; m. David Killam Cosman, July 25, 1964; children: Lara Machel, Andrea Leigh. Diploma in Nursing, St. John Gen. Hosp., N.B., 1962; postgrad. diploma, Margaret Hague Hosp., Jersey City, 1963. RN, Can. Various nursing positions, 1963-68; county councillor County of Halifax, N.S., 1976-79; mayor Town of Bedford, N.S., 1979-82; pres. Adv. Coun. on Status of Women, N.S., 1982-86; exec. dir. N.S. Liberal Party, 1989-93; mem. Legis. Assembly, House of Assembly of N.S., Halifax, 1993—, dep. spkr., min. comty. svcs., 1995—; chair Sr. Citizens Secretariat, 1997—; min. responsible adminstrn. Adv. Coun. Status Women Act, 1997—; min. Cmty. Svcs., 1997—; min. responsible Disabled Persons Commn. Act, 1997—. Contbr. numerous reports, brief, documents to provincial and fed. levels of govt.; opinion col. writer Chronicle Herald Newspaper, 1987-88. Liberal Party, United Ch. Avocations: artist, writing poetry, swimming, healing touch practitioner. Office: Legis Assembly Office of Spkr, POB 1617 Sta Central, Halifax, NS Canada B3J 2Y3*

COSMATOS, GEORGE PAN, film director; b. Jan. 4, 1941. Ed., London U. Dir.: (films) The Cassandra Crossing, 1977, Restless, 1978, Escape to Athena, 1979, Rambo: First Blood Part II, 1985, Cobra, 1986; dir., co-screenwriter Massacre in Rome, 1973. Mem. Dirs. Guild Am.

COSNOTTI, RICHARD LOUIS, development director; b. Pitts., Jan. 27, 1952; s. Frank Paul and Mary Louise (Paich) C.; B.S. in Sociology, Brigham Young U., 1973; M.Div., Princeton Theol. Sem., 1976; Advanced Mgmt. Studies, Yale, 1989; m. Margaret Lynn Jackson, June 27, 1981 (div. 1984); 1 son, Andrew Elliott. Ordained to ministry Presbyterian Ch., 1976-85; asst. minister Brick Presbyn. Ch., N.Y.C., 1976-79; minister Appleby Manor Meml. Presbyn. Ch., Ford City, Pa., 1980-83, 1st Presbyn. Ch., Cedar Falls, Iowa, 1983; guest chaplain U.S. Senate, 1983; assoc. dir., then dir. Ketchum, Inc., Pitts., 1984—, then sr. dir., 1989-91; assoc. v.p. Sacred Heart U., Fairfield, Conn, 1991-92; exec. dir., dir. Inner City Found. for Charity and Edn., Bridgeport, Conn., 1992-94; dir. development Gen. Theol. Seminary Episc. Ch., N.Y.C., 1994—; chmn. career panel on religion, counseling and social work Princeton U., 1978. Bd. dirs. Good News Communications, 1978-81; adv. bd. Armstrong County Drug and Alcohol Prevention Unit, 1981-82; mem. planned giving adv. com. Episc. Ch. Found. Recipient Good Turn award Boy Scouts Am., 1979, hon. God and country award, 1979; Freedom Found. George Washington medal of Honor for sermon, 1982, Ark. Traveler award, State of Ark., 1986. Mem. Nat. Soc. Fund-Raising Execs., Nat. Ctr. for Nonprofit Bds., Newcomen Soc. U.S. Republican. Episcopalian. Clubs: Princeton (N.Y.C.); University (Pitts.), Nassau (Princeton, N.J.). Composer music.

COSPER, SAMMIE WAYNE, educational consultant; b. Greggton, Tex., Oct. 8, 1933; s. Sammie Hampton and Mabel Viola (Byrd) C.; m. Shirley Ann Aguillard, May 13, 1954; children: Ann Caprice, Michelle Marie, Renée Elizabeth. BS in Physics, U. Southwestern La., 1960, DSc (hon.), 1991; PhD in Nuclear Physics, Purdue U., 1965. Postdoctoral appointee Lawrence Radiation Lab. U. Calif. Berkeley, 1965-67; head Dept. Physics, dean Coll. Liberal Arts, Acad. v.p. U. Southwestern La., Lafayette, 1967-89; commr. higher edn. La. Bd. Regents, Baton Rouge, 1990-94; cons. higher edn. Lafayette, 1994—; com. mem. State Hi-Ed Exec. Officers, Denver, 1990—; com. mem. La. Assn. Bus., Industry Edn. Coun., Baton Rouge, 1986—; bd. dirs. La. Coun. Econ. Edn., Baton Rouge. Contbr. articles to profl. jours. Named Communicator of Yr. La. Pub. Rels. Assn., 1993; fellow Woodrow Wilson Found., 1960. Mem. Coun. for Better La. (bd. dirs.), Krewe Gabriel Mardi Gras Assn., Krewe Triton Mardi Gras Assn. (bd. dirs.), Krewe Zeus Mardi Gras Assn. (bd. dirs.). Republican. Roman Catholic. Avocations: hunting, fishing, reading. Home: 240 Thibodeaux Dr Lafayette LA 70503-4442

COSPOLICH, JAMES DONALD, electrical engineering executive, consultant; b. New Orleans, Dec. 19, 1944; s. Clarence James and Olga Marie

C.; m. Shirley Patricia Knipper, Feb. 4, 1967; children: Brian James, Jeffery Donald, Stephen William. BEE, La. State U., 1967, MEE, 1972. Registered profl. engr., La., Calif., Tex. Geophysicist Pan Am. Petroleum Corp. subs. AMOCO, New Orleans, La., 1967; elec. engr. Waldemar S. Nelson & Co., New Orleans, 1967-74, asst. v.p., mgr. elec. engring., 1974-83, v.p., mgr. elec. engring., 1983-85, sr. v.p. ops., 1985-91, exec. v.p., 1991—; mem. Nat. Elec. Code Panel 14. Mem. Rep. Nat. Com., Washington, 1988; v.p. Ormond Civic Assn., Destrehan, La., 1985, pres., 1986; mem. representing St. Charles Parish, New Orleans Internat. Airport Noise Abatement Com. With USCGR, 1964-72. Mem. NFPA (nat. elec. code com.), IEEE, NSPE, Instrument Soc. Am. (sr., mem. various coms. 1975—), Am. Petroleum Inst. (com. recommended practice stds.), Gas Processors Assn., La. Engring. Soc., Ormond Country Club, The City Energy Club of New Orleans. Republican. Roman Catholic. Avocations: fishing, tennis, golf, skiing, boating, woodworking. Home: 61 Rosedown Dr Destrehan LA 70047-2529 Office: Waldemar S Nelson & Co Inc 1200 Saint Charles Ave New Orleans LA 70130-4334

COSS, JOHN EDWARD, archivist; b. Spring Valley, Ill., Apr. 2, 1947; s. Edward Francis and Doris (Leonard) C.; m. Sherry Lee Ushman, June 4, 1973 (div. May 1979); 1 child, Stephen John; m. Brenda Lynn Gibson, May 30, 1981; 1 stepchild, Anthony Robert. AA, Ill. Valley Community Coll., 1967; BA, Northwest Mo. State U., 1970. Archivist Ill. State Archives, Springfield, 1971—. Mem. Ill. Fedn. Archivists, Archival Technicians & Photographers, Springfield Trades & Labor Coun. (del.). Methodist. Avocations: music, reading, golf. E-mail: jcoss@ccgate.sos.state.il.us. Home: 10470 E State Route 54 Buffalo IL 62515-7148 Office: Dept Archives and Records Ill Sec State Archives Bldg Springfield IL 62756

COSSA, DOMINIC FRANK, baritone; b. Jessup, Pa., May 13, 1935; s. Domenico and Pasquina (Stella) C.; m. Janet Edgerton, Dec. 26, 1956; children: Francine, Gian-Antonio. BS in Psychology, U. Scranton, Pa., 1959; MA, U. Detroit, 1961; postgrad., Detroit Inst. Mus. Arts, 1960-61, Phila. Acad. Vocal Arts, 1961-63; LHD (hon.), U. Scranton, 1982. Leading baritone N.Y.C. Opera, 1961—, San Francisco Opera, 1970, Met. Opera, N.Y.C., 1970-76; prof. of voice, chair voice/opera dept. U. Md., College Park; former mem. voice faculty Manhattan Sch. Music; hon. life bd. mem. Am. Guild Mus. Artists, trustee Am. Guild Mus. artists pension fund, 1985—. Debut, N.Y.C. Opera, 1961, Met. Opera, N.Y.C., 1970, San Francisco Opera, 1970; rec. artist for, London Records, Elixir of Love, Les Huguenots, RCA Victor, Julius Caesar; appeared in title role in: world premiere of Gian Carlo Menotti's The Hero, 1976. Recipient Liederkrantz award; Met. Nat. Coun. 1st pl. prize; winner Am. Opera Auditions; winner WGN Auditions; inducted into Great Am. Singers Hall of Fame, Phila. Acad. Vocal Arts; Rockefeller grantee. Republican. Roman Catholic. Avocations: antiques, wine collecting, gardening, collecting early American pressed glass. *One must keep a sense of balance and proportion. Whenever thoughts of success and career become foremost in my mind, I try to place it in a larger perspective. There are certainly issues of greater importance in life than my success or failure. In a word, I try to be honest with myself even if it's painful.*

COSSACK, ROGER, newscaster. Bar: Calif. U.S. Dist. Ct. (cen. dist.) Calif., U.S. Supreme Ct., U.S. Ct. Appeals (2d, 9th and 10th cirs.). Anchor CNN, Atlanta; correspondent Burden of Proof (CNN), Atlanta. Office: Cable Network News PO Box 105366 Atlanta GA 30348-5366*

COSSÉ, R. PAUL, realty company executive; b. Nashville, July 11, 1956; s. Xavier B. and Irene E. (Amburgey) C.; 1 child, Michelle Reneé. Student, Belmont Coll., 1974-75, Aquinas Jr. Coll., 1975-76, U. Tenn., Knoxville, 1976—, Middle Tenn. State U., 1980-81. Mktg. dir. First Tenn. Bank, Murfreesboro, Tenn., 1980-83; exec. v.p. First Federal, Columbia, Tenn., 1983-88; exec. v.p., mng. officer Security Trust Fed., Knoxville, 1988-89; pres., CEO Prudential Vol. Realty, 1989-98; pres. Home Mortgage Brokers, Inc., Knoxville, 1990-98; pres., CEO Fin. Investor Svcs. of Tenn., Inc., Knoxville, 1992-98, Ins. and Fin. Svcs. Group, Inc., Knoxville, 1992-98; realtor Prudential Vol. Realty, 1998—; pres./CEO Southeastern Holdings of Tenn., Inc., 1995-98; bd. dirs. YMCA, Knoxville; cons. in field. Pres. Big. Bros. and Big Sisters Maury County, Columbia, Tenn., 1987-88; bd. dirs. YMCA, Columbia, 1988; chmn. Saturn Run, Columbia, 1987-88; chmn. realtor divsn. Am. Heart Assn. and United Way, Knoxville. Mem. Tenn. League Savs. (leadership bd., publicity com.), Exch. Club. Republican. Avocations: golf, tennis. Office: Vol Realty Co PO Box 30808 Knoxville TN 37930-0808

COSSINS, EDWIN ALBERT, biology educator, academic administrator; b. Havering, Eng., Feb. 28, 1937; came to Can., 1962; s. Albert Joseph and Elizabeth H. (Brown) C.; m. Lucille Jeannette Salt, Sept. 1, 1962; children: Diane Elizabeth (dec. 1995), Carolyn Jane. B.Sc., U. London, 1958, Ph.D., 1961, D.Sc., 1981. Research assoc. Purdue U., Lafayette, Ind., 1961-62; from asst. prof. to prof. U. Alta., Edmonton, Can., 1962-96, acting head dept. botany, 1965-66, assoc. dean of sci., 1983-88, prof. biol. scis. emeritus, 1996—; mem. grant selection panel Natural Scis. and Engring. Research Council, Ottawa, Ont., Can., 1974-77, 78-81. Author: (with others) Plant Biochemistry; 1980, 1988, Folates and Pterins, 1984. Assoc. editor Can. Jour. Botany, 1969-78. Contbr. numerous articles to profl. jours. Recipient Centennial medal Govt. of Can., 1967. Fellow Royal Soc. Can. (life); mem. Can. Soc. Plant Physiologists (western dir. 1968-70, pres. 1976-77, gold medal 1998), Japanese Soc. Plant Physiologists, Am. Soc. Plant Physiologists. Clubs: Faculty (U. Alta.), Derrick Golf and Winter. Avocations: gardening; golf; curling; cross-country skiing. Home: 99 Fairway Dr, Edmonton, AB Canada T6J 2C2 Office: U Alta, Dept Biological Sciences, Edmonton, AB Canada T6G 2E9

COST, FRANCIS HOWARD, JR., physician; b. Hagerstown, Md., Sept. 24, 1938; s. Francis Howard and Mary Elizabeth C. AB, Gettysburg Coll., 1962; MD, U. Md., 1966. Diplomate Am. Bd. Internal Medicine, Am. Bd. Cardiovascular Disease, Am. Bd. Pulmonary Disease. Resident in internal medicine USPHS, S.I., 1967-68; resident in internal medicine U. Hosp., Balt., 1969-70, fellow in cardiology, 1970-72; fellow in pulmonary disease Temple U. Hosp., Phila., 1972-73; fellow in nuclear medicine Johns Hopkins Hosp., Balt., 1984-85, fellow in med. ICU, 1986-88. Lt. comdr. USPHS, 1967-69. Fellow Am. Coll. Chest Physicians; mem. Am. Coll. Cardiology, Am. Coll. Physicians, Laennec Soc. Phila. Avocations: sailing, music. Home: 1101 Potomac Ave Hagerstown MD 21742-3439

COST, STEPHEN JAMES, principal; b. N.Y.C., June 16, 1950; s. Stephen Stauros and Elizabeth Jane (Kearing) C.; m. Patricia Coelyn Oradorff; children: Stephen Cobert, Caleigh Coelyn. BS, Southwestern Coll., 1979; MS in Ednl. Adminstrn., Emporia State U. Art tchr. Bluestein H.S., Leoni, Kans., 1974-78; art tchr. Andover (Kans.) H.S., 1982-98, asst. prin., 1998—. Mem. event chair, treas. El Dorado Jaycees, 1983-84; leader Boy Scouts Am., El Dorado, 1994-95. Mem. Kans. Assn. Secondary Prins., Elks. Roman Catholic. Avocations: photography, oil painting. Home: 347 Hillside El Dorado KS 67042 Office: Andover HS 1744 N Andover Rd Andover KS 67002

COSTA, ALBERT BERNARD, retired science history educator; b. Hayward, Calif., Aug. 14, 1929; s. Albert Francis and Cynthia Carolyn (Bernard) C. BS, St. Mary's Coll., 1952; MS, Oreg. State U., 1954; PhD, U. Wis., 1960. Asst. prof. liberal arts St. Mary's Coll., Calif., 1959-62; prof. history Duquesne U., Pitts., 1963-91. Author: Michel Eugene Chevreul, 1962; assoc. editor Jour. Ecumenical Studies, 1966-69; contbr. articles to profl. jours. Grantee NSF, 1960, GTE Found., 1988. Mem. History of Sci. Soc., Sigma Xi (chpt. pres. 67-68). Democrat. Roman Catholic. Avocations: travel, music.

COSTA, DANIEL LAWRENCE, architect; b. Providence, R.I., Feb. 16, 1953; s. Dimas and Laurinda (Diogo) C.; m. Shepley Patterson Metcalf, May 31, 1980 (div. Mar. 1988); 1 child, Hilary Metcalf. AB, Brown U., 1974; MArch, Harvard U., 1980. Architect Archtl. Resources Cambridge (Mass.), Inc., 1980-87, Shepard/Quraeshi Assocs., Watertown, Mass., 1987-88; prin. Costa/Flenniken Assocs., Boston, 1988-90, Dan Costa AIA, Boston, 1990—; mem. Somerville (Mass.) Design Rev. Bd., 1988; bd. dirs. Somerville Hist. Preservation Commn., 1991-96. Recipient Home of Yr. award Met. Home Mag., 1997, Best in Am. Living award Profl. Builder Mag., 1995, Southern Home award So. Living Mag., 1995. Mem. AIA, Boston Soc. Architects. Office: 368 Congress St Fl 4 Boston MA 02210-1864

COSTA, ERMINIO, pharmacologist, cell biology educator; b. Cagliari, Italy, Mar. 9, 1924; s. Oreste and Gigina (Murgia) C.; divorced; children: Max, Robert Henry, Michael John; m. Ingeborg Hanbauer, July 13, 1973. MD, U. Cagliari, 1947, PhD in Pharmacology, 1953; PhD in Biol. Sci. (hon.), U. Cagliari, Italy, 1986; DSc (hon.), Georgetown U., 1992; MD (hon.), U. Tampere, Finland, 1992. Asst. prof., assoc. prof. U. Cagliari, 1948-54, prof. pharmacology, 1954-56; physician II, med. rsch. assn. Thudichum Psychology Rsch., Galesburg, Ill., 1956-60; vis. scientist NIH, Bethesda, Md., 1960-61; dep. chief lab. chem. pharmacology Nat. Heart Inst., Bethesda, 1961-63, head sect. clin. pharmacology, 1963-65; assoc. prof. pharmacology Columbia U., N.Y.C., 1965-68; chief lab. preclin pharmacology St. Elizabeth's Hosp., Washington, 1968-85; dir. Fidia-Georgetown Inst. for the Neuroscis. Georgetown U., Washington, 1985-94; McDonnel vis. prof. neurology Washington U. Sch. Medicine, St. Louis, 1994—; scientific dir., prof. biochemistry in psychiatry U. Ill. at Chgo. Psychiat. Inst., 1996—. Editor Neuropharmacology, 1967, Advance Biochem Psychopharmacology, 1968; contbr. 915 articles to profl. jours. Recipient Bennet award and Gold medal Soc. Biol. Psychiatry, Gold medal Fed. II Univ., Naples, 1990, Premio Fiuggi award Fiuggi Rsch. Found., 1988. Mem. NAS, Academia Nazionale Lincei, Am. Soc. Pharmacology and Exptl. Theareutics., Am. Soc. Physiology., Am. Soc. Biol. Chemistry and Molecular Biology, Cosmos Club, Pepipathetic Club. Office: Psychiatric Ins Univ of Illinois at Chicago 1601 W Taylor St Chicago IL 60612-4310*

COSTA, GEORGE GEORGE (ADEL GEORGE COSTANDY), physician; b. Cairo, Jan. 27, 1951; came to U.S., 1981; s. George Toma Costandy and Elain R. Mosa. MD with honors, Cairo U., 1975. Cert. Ednl. Commn. for Fgn. Med. Grads. Rotating intern Cairo U. Hosp., 1975-76, Army Hosp., 1976-77; lab. technician, phlebotomist N.Y. labs., 1977-79; ear, nose and throat resident Cairo, 1978-79, 82-83, 1984-86; respiratory therapist trainee Mt. Vernon (N.Y.) Hosp., 1989; pediatric clk. Interfaith Med. Ctr., Bklyn., 1990; resident in internal medicine Woodhull Hosp., Bklyn., 1991. Mem. N.Y. Acad. Sci. Address: 5929 Reno Ave Temple City CA 91780-1529

COSTA, GUSTAVO, Italian language educator; b. Rome, Mar. 21, 1930; came to U.S., 1961; s. Paolo and Ida (Antonangelo) C.; m. Natalia Zalessow, June 8, 1963; 1 child, Dora L. Maturità Classica, Liceo Virgilio, Rome, 1948; D Philosophy cum laude, U. Rome, 1954. Asst. Istituto di Filosofia, Rome, 1957-60; instr. Italian Univ. de Lyon, Lyons, France, 1960-61; instr. Italian U. Calif., Berkeley, 1961-63, asst. prof., 1963-68, assoc. prof., 1968-72, prof., 1972-91, prof. emeritus, 1991—, chmn. dept. Italian, 1973-76, 88-91; vis. prof. Scuola di Studi Superiori, Naples, 1984, Inst. Philosophy, U. Rome La Sapienza, 1992; reviewer RAI Corp., Rome, 1982-89. Author: La critica di Thomas Blackwell (1701-1757), 1959, La leggenda dei secoli d'oro nella lett. ital., 1972, Le antichità germaniche nella cultura italiana, 1977, Il sublime e la magia da Dante a Tasso, 1994, Vico e l'Europa: Contro la boria delle nazioni, 1996; mem. editl. bd. Romance Philology, Nouvelles de la Rèpublique des Lettres, New Vico Studies, L'anello che non tiene, Cuadernos Sobre Vico. Istituto Italiano Studi Storici fellow, Naples, Italy, 1954-57, Guggenheim Meml. Found. fellow, N.Y.C., 1977; grantee French Govt., Paris, 1956, Belgian Govt., Brussels, 1956, Targa d'oro Apulia, Italy, 1990. Mem. Am. Assn. Tchrs. Italian, Am. Soc. for Eighteenth-Century Studies, Renaissance Soc. Am., Am. Soc. for Aesthetics, Dante Soc. Am., Faculty Club (Berkeley). Avocations: gardening, stamp collecting. Office: U Calif Dept Italian Studies Berkeley CA 94720

COSTA, GUY, city official. Sutdent, DuKane U. Exec. dir. Pitts. Parking Authority, 1994-98, dir. gen. svcs., 1998—. Office: Pittsburgh Parking Authority 414 Grant St Rm 526 Pittsburgh PA 15219*

COSTA, JOHN ANTHONY, loan assistant; b. San Francisco, Oct. 20, 1946; s. Henry Milton and Martha Florence (Seineke) C. BA, San Francisco State Univ., 1969; student, George Washington Univ., 1969-73, Univ. San Francisco, 1987-88. Cert. legal asst., Pa. Analyst internat. rels. Libr. Congress Congl. Rsch. Svc., Washington, 1969-82; coord. Family Svc. Agy. San Mateo County, Burlingame, Calif., 1984-87, loan asst. Family Loan Program, 1998—. Pres., v.p., sec. Bentana Park Condominium, Reston, Va., 1977-81; bd. dirs. St. Dunstan Sch., Millbrae, Calif., 1991-92, Shelter Creek Condominium, San Bruno, Calif., 1999—. Mem. Internat. Studies Assn. (chpt. sec. 1970-71), Internat. Platform Assn., Worl Affairs Coun. No. Calif., Commonwealth Club San Francisco. Office: Family Svc Agy 1870 El Camino Real Ste 107 Burlingame CA 94010-3190

COSTA, KEVIN, post secondary education educator; b. Fall River, Mass., Oct. 25, 1956; s. Serafin and Angelina (Franco) C.; m. Helena Medeiros. Cert., U. de Lisboa, Portugal, 1977; BA, U. Mass., 1979; Cert., U. dos Acores, Azores, Portugal, 1988; MA, Brown U., 1989. Instr. of English Internat. Orgn. on Migration/UN, Azores, 1980-83, U.S. State Dept., Azores, 1980-83; instr. Portuguese Bristol C.C., Fall River, 1984-88; instr. labor edn. U. Mass., Dartmouth, 1989-91; tchg. assoc. in polit. sci. U. Mass., Amherst, 1991—; adv. bd. Dia de Portugal Celebracoes, New Bedford, Mass., 1997-98. Bd. dirs. Human Rels. Taskforce, Fall River, 1995-98, Portuguese Am. Congress, Providence, 1987-98, Portuguese Am. Organizing Coalition, Fall River, 1996-98. Recipient univ. fellowship U. Mass., Amherst, 1991, Mellon fellowship Mellon Found., 1988, fellowship for fgn. rsch. Inst. Cultural Portuguese, Lisbon, 1977. Mem. Am. Polit. Sci. Assn., Northeastern Polit. Sci. Assn., New Eng. Polit. Sci. Assn., Brazilian Studies Assn., Harvard Orgn. of Portuguese Spkrs., Northeastern Brazilian Studies Assn., Internat. Conf. Group on Portugal, Genocide Studies Assn. Avocations: Western European and Brazilian travel, classical music, theater, visual arts, history. Home: 417 Belmont St Fall River MA 02720-3603 Office: Polit Sci Dept U Mass Amherst Amherst MA 01003

COSTA, MANUEL ANTONE, recreational facility manager; b. Lawrence, Mass., Oct. 26, 1933; s. Manuel Joaquin and Mellie Theresa (Perry) C.; m. Barbara Susan Cournoyer, Dec. 2, 1967; children: David Manuel, Julia Lynn, Jeffrey David. BA in Bus., Mktg., Columbia Pacific U., San Rafael, Calif., 1983. Cert. facility exec. Dir. advt./promotions Volvo Penta of Am., Norfolk, Va., 1974-77; pres. Drummond Yachts, Inc., Dania, Fla., 1977-79; regional rep. Ga. Dept. Industry/Trade, Augusta, Ga., 1979-81; dir. Ga. Mountains Ctr., Gainesville, 1981-85, Myrtle Beach (S.C.) Conv. Ctr., 1985-88; exec. dir. Chattanooga Conv. and Trade Ctr., 1988-90; facility cons. Melbourne Beach, Fla., 1990-91; dir. Florence (S.C.) Civic Ctr., 1991-95; bd. dirs. S.C. Music and Entertainment Commn. Bd. dirs. S.C. Music & Entertainment Commn.; sec. S.C. Music & Entertainment Hall of Fame; sector coord. summer Olympics, Atlanta, 1996. With USMC, 1951-54. Mem. Internat. Assn. Audit Mgrs. (dist. v.p. 1987-89, bd. dirs. 1987-89, facility instr. 1990-91), Mid-Atlantic Bldg. Mgrs. Assn., Country Music Assn., Internat. Country Music Buyers Assn. Republican. Roman Catholic. Avocations: golf, reading. Address: 1468 The Crossing Niceville FL 32578

COSTA, MAX, health facility administrator, pharmacology educator, environmental medicine educator; b. Jan. 10, 1952. BS in Biology, Georgetown U., 1974; PhD in Pharmacology, U. Ariz., 1976. Rsch. asst. NIMH, Bethesda, Md., 1970-72, Lab. Tumor Cell Biology, Nat. Cancer Inst., Bethesda, Md., 1972-74; rsch. assoc., divsn. radiation oncology U. Ariz. Sch. of Medicine, Tucson, 1976; asst. prof. lab. medicine U. Conn. Sch. Medicine, Farmington, Conn., 1977-79; asst. prof. dept pharmacology and toxicology Coll. Medicine, Tex. A & M Univ., Coll. Sta., Tex., 1979-80; asst. prof. dept. pharmacology U. Tex. Medical Sch., Houston, 1980-81, assoc. prof. dept pharmacology, 1981-85, prof. dept. pharmacology, 1985-86; prof. environ. medicine and pharmacology NYU Med. Ctr., N.Y.C., 1986-92; dep. dir. Inst. Environ. Medicine, NYU Med. Ctr., N.Y.C., 1986-92, prof., chmn. dept. environ. medicine, 1993—; dir. The Nelson Inst. Environ. Medicine, Tuxedo, N.Y., 1993—; Burroughs Wellcome prof. U. South Ala. Coll. Medicine, 1996; expert witness testified U.S. Congressional Hearing, 1979, Dept. Labor, OSHA, 1990; cons. Amax, Inc., 1977-80, NiPera, 1981, 82; vis. prof. Kurume U., Japan, 1989; invited lectr., speaker Nat. Cancer Ctr. Rsch. Inst., Tokyo, Kitasato U., Tokyo, Shizuoka Coll., Japan, Kurume U., Japan, Robert Wood Johnson Med. Sch., N.J., Temple U., Pa., U. Milan, Italy, U. Tenn., U. Calif., Rutgers U., Cornell U., Brown U., and numerous others. Author: Metal Carcinogenesis Testing: Principles and In Vitro Methods, 1980; Editor: Environmental Carcinogenesis Chemosphere, 1981-83, Biology of Metals, 1988-90, Journal of Pharmacology and Experimental Therapeutics, 1992—; editorial bd. Cell Biology and Toxicology, 1987—, Biological Trace Element Research, 1988—, BioMetals, 1992—; editor in chief Molecular Toxicology, 1989-91, editl. adv. bd. Toxicology and Applied Pharmacology, 1996—; bd. assoc. editors Environ. Health Perspectives, 1996—; contbr. to numerous profl. jours. including Journal Biological Chemistry, Biochemistry Journal, Science, Cancer Research and numerous others;. Recipient Young Environ. Scientist award NIH, 1978-81, Kenneth Morgareidge award Internat. Life Scis. Inst., 1984; Hoffmann-La Roche Inc. grantee, 1974-76, Conn. Rsch. Found, 1977-78, NIH-NIEHS, 1978-81, 78-79, 79-80, 80-81, 88—, 89—, 90—, 91—,, NIH-NCI CA, 1982-85, 85-90, Amax. Inc., 1978, 79, U.S. EPA, 1980-84, 1985-88, 90-93, U.S. Dept. Energy, 1981-86, Chem. Mfr. Assn., 1987-88, Rutgers U., 1994—. Mem. AAAS, Am. Soc. Cell Biology, Am. Soc. Biochemistry and Molecular Biology, Am. Soc. Pharmacology and Experimental Therapeutics, Soc. Toxicology, Am. Assn. Cancer Rsch., Internat. Assn. Bioinorganic Scientists, Internat. Assn. Environ. Analytical Chemistry. Office: NYU Med Ctr Inst of Environ Medicine 550 1st Ave New York NY 10016-6481*

COSTA, MICHAEL F., multimedia communications executive; b. N.Y.C., May 10, 1968; s. Nicholas and Sandra (McClure) C. BSBA, U. So. Calif., 1991. Account exec. Bear Stearns & Co., L.A., 1991-93; CEO Vision Digital Comms., Irvine, Calif., 1993-98; v.p. Genesis Intermadia, Costa Mesa, Calif., 1999—; mem. adv. bd. Speedway, Newport Beach, Calif., 1997—. Multiple patents in field. Avocations: sports, scuba diving, auto racing.

COSTA, PAT VINCENT, automation sciences executive; b. Cambridge, Mass., Sept. 4, 1943; s. Vincent James and Mary Florence (Mercurio) C.; m. Kathleen Ann Valachovic, Aug. 9, 1975; children: Jessica Kate, Hannah Pat. BSEE, Northeastern U., 1966; SM, MIT, 1969; MBA, Harvard U., 1977. Exec. v.p. GCA Corp., Bedford, Mass., 1977-84; pres., chief exec. officer, chmn. Robotic Vision Systems, Inc., Hauppauge, N.Y., 1984—. Mem. Automated Industries Assn. (chmn. bd.), Machine Vision Assn., Soc. Mech. Engrs., Robotic Industries Assn., Navy League of U.S. Avocations: racquetball. Office: Robotic Vision Systems Inc 5 Shawmut Rd Canton MA 02021-1408

COSTA, TERRY ANN, educational administrator; b. Huntington, W.Va., Jan. 9, 1951; d. Hobart G. and Beatrice (Chaput) Owens; m. Joseph M. Costa, June 5, 1970; children: Carrie Lynn, Anthony Martin. BA, Marshall U., 1972, MA, 1979; EdS, Nova U., 1988. Cert. specific learning disabilities, mentally and emotionally handicapped, varying exceptionalities, ESOL, speech tchr., coach, ednl. leadership, Fla. Tchr. spl. edn. Cabell County Sch. System, Huntington, 1973-77, 80-86, coach, 1980-86; adj. instr. Marshall U., Huntington, 1979-80; tchr. spl. edn., dept. chmn. Palm Beach County Sch. Sys., West Palm Beach, Fla., 1986-94, coord. exceptional student edn., dept. chairperson, coach, 1989-94; chmn. tng. and devel. Palm Beach County Sch. System, West Palm Beach, Fla., 1988-89; asst. prin. Loggers' Run Cmty. Mid. Sch., Boca Raton, Fla., 1994-98; prin. Christa McAuliffe Cmty. Mid. Sch., Boynton Beach, Fla., 1998—; chmn. exceptional student edn. instructional materials coun. for math. and sci. Fla. Dept. Edn., West Palm Beach, 1988, clin. educator, 1986-91. Coord., vol. Spl. Olympics, Cabell County, 1974-76; religious tchr., coord. Diocese of Wheeling-Charleston, W.Va., 1980-86; leader Girl Scouts U.S.A., W.Va., 1984-86; sch. campaign chmn. United Way, Palm Beach County, 1988-89. Mem. ASCD, Nat. Assn. Secondary Sch. Prins., Coun. for Exceptional Children (sec. W.Va. 1973-74, corr. sec. 1992-93, Palm Beach County Tchr. of Yr. award chpt. 200, 1989, grantee, 1988, 89, 90, 92), Fla. Assn. Sch. Adminstrs., Palm Beach County Sch. Adminstrs. Assn. (exec. bd. sec. 1996—), Prins. Assn. (sec.), Phi Delta Kappa (v.p. membership, Kappan of Yr. 1999). Democrat. Roman Catholic. Avocations: tennis, water skiing, running, fishing, needlecrafts. Home: 8381 Mildred Dr W Boynton Beach FL 33437-1031 Office: Christa McAuliffe Cmty Mid Sch 6500 Le Chalet Blvd Boynton Beach FL 33437-2304

COSTA, THOMAS CHARLES, priest; b. Queens, N.Y., Nov. 16, 1950; s. James B. and Catherine M. (Pensa) C. BA in English magna cum laude, Cathedral Coll., Douglaston, N.Y., 1972; MDiv, Immaculate Conception Sem., Huntington, N.Y., 1977; cert. in cross-cultural ministry studies, Cath. Theol. Union., Chgo., 1995. Ordained priest, Roman Catholic Ch., 1978. Customer svc. rep. Wallach's, Garden City, N.Y., 1972-73; assoc. pastor St. Boniface Ch., Elmont, N.Y., 1978-82, St. Rose of Lima Ch., Massapequa, N.Y., 1982-84, St. Ignatius Loyola Ch., Hicksville, N.Y., 1984-88; co-pastor St. John of God Ch., Central Islip, N.Y., 1988-94; assoc. pastor for ethnic ministry St. Brigid Ch., Westbury, N.Y., 1994-98; pastor St. Patrick Ch., Glen Cove, N.Y., 1998—; mem. dea. Founding sch. bd. pres. Our Lady of Providence Regional Sch., Central Islip, 1991-94; chmn. corp., All Saints Regional Sch., Glen Cove, 1998—; mem. deafness adv. bd. Cath. Charities, Rockville Centre, N.Y., 1988-92; nat. deaf vocat. adv. bd. DePaul Project, Yonkers, N.Y., 1992—; adv. bd. Haitian Civic Assn., Central Islip, 1988-94; mem. continuing edn. bd. Diocese of Rockville Centre, 1995-98; dir. spirituale Comitato Italiano Della Comunita, Westbury, N.Y., 1994-98; dir. espiritual Consejo Pastoral, Westbury, 1994-98; assoc. diocesan chaplain for the deaf Diocesan Deaf Apostolate, Rockville Centre, 1978—; procurator-adv. Diocesan Marriage Tribunal, Diocese of Rockville Centre, N.Y., 1981—; pastoral worker Nat. Cath. Office of the Deaf. Capt. USAFR, 1982-88. Mem. Am. Legion, K.C. (trustee 1994-98, past grand knight Sign of Cross Coun. 1993-94), Internat. Cath. Deaf Assn. (life). Republican. Office: Saint Patrick Roman Cath Ch 235 Glen St Glen Cove NY 11542-3059

COSTA, VICTOR CHARLES, fashion designer; b. Houston, Dec. 17, 1935; s. Russell and Mary (Candelari) C.; m. Mary Therese Tschumy, June 28, 1958 (div.); children: Kevin, Adrienne. BA, U. Houston, 1958; cert., Ecole Chambre Syndicale de la Couture Parisienne, 1958. Designer Murray Hamburger, 1959, Pandora, N.Y.C., 1960-64; designer, v.p. Suzy Perette, N.Y.C., 1965-73; pres. designer Victor Costa, Inc., Dallas, 1973-95; designer Victor Costa, Inc., N.Y.C., 1996. Pres. Fashion Industry Found., Dallas. Bd. dirs. Dallas Opera; pres. Fashion Industry Found., Dallas. Recipient Am. Designer award May Co. Calif., Stix, Baer, Fuller Golden Fashion award, Dallas Flying Colors Fashion award, 1980, Tommy award Am. Printed Fabric Coun., 1983, 84, 85, 86, 93, L.S. Ayers Look award, 1987, Cert. of Merit, City of Atlanta, 1983, Dallas Mart Fashion award, 1980, 87, 91, 97; named Outstanding Alumnus U. Houston, 1990, Northwood Inst. Businessman of Yr., 1991, Designer of Yr., Syracuse U., 1997. Mem. Coun. Fashion Designers Am., Am. Fashion Assn., Fashion Industry Found. (founder 1988), Fashion Group Internat. Roman Catholic. Office: 530 7th Ave New York NY 10018-4878

COSTABILE-HEMING, CAROL ANNE, humanities educator; b. Hazleton, Pa., June 5, 1963; d. Fiore and Anne (Boyle) Costabile; m. Ralf Heming, May 19, 1993. BA, U. Pa., 1985, MA, 1989; PhD, Wash. U., 1992. Instr. S.E. Mo. State U., Cape Girardeau, 1991-92; asst. prof. Pa. State U., University Park, 1992-97; asst. prof. S.W. Mo. State U., Springfield, 1997-99, assoc. prof., 1999—. Author: Intertextual Exile, 1997. Mem. Am. Assn. Tchrs. German, Women in German, German Studies Assn. Office: SW Mo State U Dept Modern and Class Langs 901 S National Ave Springfield MO 65804-0088

COSTA-GAVRAS (KONSTANINOS GAVRAS), director, writer; b. Athens, Greece, Feb. 13, 1933; naturalized French citizen; m. Michele Ray, Sept. 12, 1968; children: Alexandre, Helene, Romain. Student, U. Sorbonne, Paris. Diplomate Inst. Higher Cinematic Studies. Ballet dancer Greece; asst. to film dirs. Yves Allegret, Jacques Demy, Rene Clair, Rene Clement, Jean Giorno; pres. Cinematheque francaise, 1982—. Dir., screenwriter films The Sleeping Car Murders, 1964, Z, 1969 (Acad. award for best fgn. lang. film, 1970, Jury Prize, Cannes Film Festival 1969, Raoul-Levy prize 1969, Golden Globe award 1970), Missing, 1982 (Golden Palm award Cannes 1982, Acad. Award for best screenplay 1982); dir. films Un Homme de Trop, 1966 (Moscow Film Festival prize), L'Aveu (The Confession), 1970, State of Siege, 1973 (Louis Delluc prize 1973), Special Section, 1975 (Cannes Film Festival award 1975), Madame Rosa (also actor), 1978, Clair de Femme, 1979, Hanna K, 1983, Conseil de Femme, 1986, Family Business, 1986, Betrayed, 1988, Music Box, 1990 (Golden Bear award Berlin film festival 1990), Little Apocalypse, 1992, Mad City, 1996; dir. opera Il Mondo Dela Luna (Joseph Haydn), 1994, Mad City, 1997; co-dir. A Propos de Nice, 1995, Lumiere and Compagnie, 1995. Named Best Dir., Cannes Film Festival 1975; decorated

Comdr. Arts and Letters, France, Chevalier Legion d'Honneur; recipient Life Achievement award De l'Academie Francaise, 1998.

COSTAGLIOLA, FRANCESCO, former government official, macro operations analyst; b. Cranston, R.I., Aug. 24, 1917; s. Luigi and Rose (Lubrano) C.; m. Agnes Mary Ross, June 14, 1952 (dec.); children: Francesca Gensler, Marisa Costagliola, Antonia Burns, Roseanne Rubin. Student U. R.I., 1935-37; BSEE, U.S. Naval Acad., 1941; postgrad. Naval Postgrad. Sch., 1946-47, MIT, 1947-49, Cath. U. Am., 1967-71; MBA, Am. U., Washington, 1974. Commd. ensign U.S. Navy, 1941, advanced through grades to capt., 1960; served in U.S.S. Phoenix in 24 ops. PTO, 1941-46; comdg. officer U.S.S. Halsey Powell, Korea, 1951-52; various positions naval sea and shore assignments involving atomic energy, 1952-64; mil. asst. to asst. to Sec. Def., 1964-67; ret., 1968; commr. AEC, 1968-69; engr. RCA, 1974-76; staff mem. Joint Congressional Com. on Atomic Energy, Washington, 1967-68, 69-71, 76-77; staff mem. Office of Sec. of Senate, Washington, 1977-86; mem. Md. Radiation Control Adv. Bd., 1973-81. Contbr. articles to profl. jours. Decorated Legion of Merit, Bronze Star with Combat V (2). Mem. AAAS, Inst. Ops. Rsch. & Mgmt. Scis., Am. Nuc. Soc., U.S. Naval Inst., Pearl Harbor Survivors Assn., Naval Acad. Alumni Assn., Mil. Order World Wars, Mil. Order Carabao, Army and Navy Club (Washington). Roman Catholic. Home: 307 Gibbon St Alexandria VA 22314-4129

COSTAMAGNA, GARY, fire chief City of Sacramento; b. Sacramento, Calif.. AS in Fire Tech., Am. River C.C.; BS in Bus. Adminstrn., Calif. State U., Sacramento. Fireman Sacramento Fire Dept., 1968-73, capt., 1973-83, battalion chief, 1983-86, dep. chief, 1986-89, chief, 1989—; chmn. Calif. Fire & Rescue Svcs. Adv. Com, Fire Scope bd. dirs.; mem. state Fire Marshal's Pub. Edn. Adv. Com. Mem. Nat. USAR Steering Com. With USAF 1966-70. m. Sacramento County Fire Chiefs' Assn. (past pres.), Calif. Met. Fire Chiefs'Assn. (chmn.). Office: Fire Dept 1221 1st St Ste 401 Sacramento CA 95814

COSTANDY, ADEL GEORGE See COSTA, GEORGE GEORGE

COSTANTINI, MARY ANN C., writer, editor, retired elementary educator; b. Steubenville, Ohio, June 13, 1955; d. Thomas and Anna M. (Slabdorf) Colsh; m. William J. Costantini; children: Thomas Kyle, Susan Michelle. BS in Elem. Spl. Edn., U. Steubenville, 1977; MS in Sch. Counseling, U. Dayton, Steubenville, 1986; MS in Multihandicapped Edn., Ohio U., St. Clairsville, 1991. Cert. K-8 spl. edn., elem. tchr., Ohio. Substitute tchr. St. John's Elem. Sch., Wellsburgh, W.Va., 1977-78; mid. sch. tchr. All Saints Consol. Elem. Sch., Steubenville, 1979-80; elem. tchr., tchr. spl. edn. Steubenville City Sch. System, 1978-79; pvt. tutor, counselor, 1976-79; elem. tchr., tchr. spl. edn. Edison Local Sch. Dist., Hammondsville, Ohio, 1985-90; freelance writer and editor Steubenville, Ohio, 1995—. Coach Spl. Olympics, 1977, 79; instr. ARC; mem. Girl Scouts USA. With USMC, 1981-82. Mem. Nat. Writers Assn, Internat. Soc. Poetry, Am. Acad. Poetry.

COSTANTINO, FRANK MATHEW, architectural illustrator; b. Boston, May 18, 1946; s. Mathew Peter and Rose Margaret (Caruso) C.; m. Linda Carroll DeRoo, Dec. 7, 1968; children: Matthew Abbott, Noel Lamb, Cory Robert. Degree in architecture, Pratt Inst., 1966, Boston Archtl. Ctr., 1968. Archtl. designer, illustrator Parson, Brinckerhoff, Quade and Douglas, 1967-69, Corp. Design Cons., 1969-72; prin. archtl. illustration firm, 1972-87; pres. F. M. Costantino, Inc., Winthrop, Mass., 1987—; instr. R.I. Sch. Design, Providence, 1974-78, Boston Archtl. Ctr., 1970-75, Harvard Grad. Sch. Design, Cambridge, Mass., 1987-89; lectr. Pa. State U., 1992, U. Man., Winnipeg, Can., 1993, MIT, Cambridge, 1993-94, Balt. Arch. Found., 1994, Headlands Ctr. for Arts, San Francisco, 1994, JARA Conv., Osaka, Japan, 1995, Lawrence Tech. U., Mich., 1995, 96, Boston Ctr. for Arts, 1996, Korean Archtl. Renderers Assocs., Seoul, 1996, Queensland U. of Tech., Brisbane, Australia, 1997—; prof. workshops Boston Ctr. for Arts, Queensland U. of Tech., Brisbane, Ulmo Art Ctr., Sydney, Melbourne Sch. Art, Australia, 1997, The Art Ctr., 1998, Cesar Pelli & Assocs., 1998, The Art Cellar, Conn., 1998, Block Island, R.I., 1998. Contbr. author/artist/editor to profl. publs., including Boston Architecture, 1975-1990, 1992, Watercolor in Architectural Illustration, 1991, The Art of Architectural Illustration, 1994, Architecture of the Imagination, 1994, The Art of Architectural Illustration 2, 1995, Architecture in Perspective Catalogues No. 2 through No. 14, The Illustrated Room: Interior Rendering in the 20th Century, 1997, Cesar Pelli Recent Themes, rev. edit., 1999, Michael Doyle Color Drawing, rev. edit., 1999, The Art of Architectural Illustration 3, 1999; exhbns. include Architecture in Perspective, Boston, 1985, 90, 96, Dallas, 1987, L.A., 1988, Chgo., 1989, 93, N.Y.C., 1991, Toronto, Ont., Can., 1992, San Francisco, 1994, 99, Seattle, 1995, Baltimore, 1996, Memphis, 1997, Atlanta, 1998, Arch. Found., 1996, Balt. Arch. Found., 1997, Kans. State U., 1998, Octagon Mus., 1998, N.Y. Architects, Frankfurt, Germany, 1989, Tokyo, Osaka, Nagoya, Japan, 1989-99, Seoul, Korea, Tokyo, Japan, 1996; Copenhagen, 1996; artist/designer paintings for postcards, 1991-93. Bd. dirs. Winthrop Revitalization Com., 1988-94, Winthrop Improvement and Hist. Assn., 1990-97. Recipient Gov.'s citation Commonwealth of Mass., 1983, citation Mass. State Ho. Reps., 1984, Citation of Am., Winthrop Bicentennial Com., 1990, 36th Ann. Awards Program citation Chgo. Pub. Libr., 1989, Category A award Am. Soc. Archtl. Perspectivists, 1990, Arthur Ross award for Archtl. Rendering, Classical Am., 1991, Beautification award Winthrop C. of C., 1992, Inst. Honors award AIA, 1995; named Elks Citizen of Yr., 1994. Fellow Soc. Archtl. Illustrators Eng.; mem. AIA (assoc.), Am. Soc. Archtl. Perspectivists (co-founder, pres. emeritus, adv. coun., Award of Excellence 1987-99), Japan Archtl. Renderers Assn., Boston Soc. Archs. (affiliate), Marblehead Art Assn. Avocations: gardening, woodworking, karate, philosophy, watercolor painting. Office: 13B Pauline St Winthrop MA 02152-3011

COSTANZA, MARIE, secondary education educator; b. Rochester, N.Y., Nov. 25, 1955; d. Michael S. and Loretta (DiCrisci) Pace; m. John Westerman, Nov. 17, 1979 (div. Mar. 1997); 1 child, Jeffrey; m. Jay Costanza, May 8, 1998; 1 child, Michelle. BA in English, Brockport Coll., 1977; MS in Reading, Nazareth Coll., 1979. Cert. English tchr. grades 7-12, reading cert. grades K-12. English/journalism tchr. Sch. of the Arts, Rochester, 1977—; lead tchr. Rochester City Sch. Dist., 1988—; coll. instr. Brockport (N.Y.) Coll., 1993—; cons. Creative Curriculum Design, Rochester, 1997—. Mem. ASCD, Nat. Coun. Tchrs. English, Phi Delta Kappa. Roman Catholic. Avocations: photography, desktop publishing. Home: 4229 St Paul Blvd Rochester NY 14617 Office: Rochester Sch of the Arts 45 Prince St Rochester NY 14607

COSTANZO, HILDA ALBA, retired banker; b. Newark, Feb. 4; d. Smeraldo Louis and Giovanna Marianna (Mancuso) C. Pub. rels. cert., Princeton U., N.J. Bankers Assn. Sch., 1965; pre-standard cert., Am. Inst. Banking, 1967, standard cert., 1972; BA in English summa cum laude, Caldwell Coll., 1992. Various positions Howard Savs. Bank, Newark, 1943-66, asst. sec., 1966-74, asst. to pres., 1974-76, corp. sec., 1976-80, v.p., corp. sec., 1980-87, ret., 1987. Mem. Nat. Assn. Bank Women, Zonta (v.p. 1973-74), Alpha Sigma Lambda, Kappa Gamma Pi. Republican. Roman Catholic. Avocations: reading, music, travel. Home: 1400 Route 70 Apt 431 Lakewood NJ 08701-5949

COSTAS, BOB (ROBERT QUINLAN COSTAS), sportscaster; b. N.Y.C., Mar. 22, 1952; s. John George and Jayne (Quinlan) C.; m. Carole Randall Krummenacher, June 24, 1983; children: Keith Michael, Taylor. Student, Syracuse U., 1970-74. Sportscaster Sta. KMOX-AM, St. Louis, 1974-81; sportscaster, host sports programs NBC Sports, N.Y.C., 1980—; former host Later with Bob Costas. Recipient 11 Emmy awards, 8 for outstanding sports broadcaster, 2 Emmy awards for writing, 1 Emmy award for interview show, 1996; named Nat. Sportscaster of Yr., Nat. Sportscasters and Sportwriters Assn., 1985, 87, 88, 91, 92, 95, 97.

COSTA-ZALESSOW, NATALIA, foreign language educator; b. Kumanovo, Macedonia, Dec. 5, 1936; came to the U.S., 1951; d. Alexander P. and Katarina (Duric) Z.; m. Gustavo Costa, June 8, 1963; 1 child, Dora. BA in Italian, U. Calif., Berkeley, 1959, MA in Italian, 1961, PhD in Romance Langs. and Lits., 1967. Tchg. asst. U. Calif., Berkeley, 1959-63; instr. Mills Coll., Oakland, Calif., 1963; asst. prof. San Francisco State U., 1968-74, assoc. prof., 1974-79, prof., 1979-98, coord. Italian program, 1992-98, prof. emerita, 1998—. Author: Scrittrici italiane dal XIII al XX secolo, Testi e critica, 1982; editor: Anima, 1997; transl.: Her Soul, 1996; contbr. articles to profl. publs. Sidney M. Ehrman scholar U. Calif., Berkeley, 1957-58, Gamma Phi Beta scholar U. Calif., Berkeley, 1958, Herbert H. Vaughan scholar U. Calif., Berkeley, 1959-60, Advanced Grad. Traveling fellow in romance lang. and lit. U. Calif., Berkeley, 1964-65. Mem. MLA, Am. Assn. Tchrs. Italian, Renaissance Soc. Am., Dante Soc. Am., Croatian Acad. Am. Roman Catholic. Avocations: swimming, hiking, opera, symphony, gastronomy. Office: San Francisco State U Dept Fgn Lang and Lit San Francisco CA 94132

COSTEA, NICOLAS VINCENT, physician, researcher; b. Bucharest, Romania, Nov. 10, 1927; came to U.S., 1957; s. Nicolas and Florica (Ionescu) C.; m. Ileana Paunescu, Apr. 20, 1973. B.A., Nat. Coll. Bucharest, 1946; M.S., U. Paris, 1949, M.D., 1956. Intern St. Francis Hosp., N.Y.C., 1956-57; resident L.I. Jewish Hosp., 1957-59; fellow in hematology Tufts U., 1959-62; dir. clinic Pratt Clinic, Boston, 1962-63; clin. investigator Va. West Side Med. Ctr., Chgo., 1963-68; chief hematology U. Ill., Chgo., 1968-70; prof. medicine U. Ill., 1970-72; chief hematology-oncology UCLA-VA Hosp., Sepulveda, 1972-87; prof. UCLA, 1972-83; vis. prof. Nat. Acad. Scis., 1972. Contbr. numerous chpts., articles to profl. publs. Recipient Lederle award Lederle Industries, 1966. Mem. Am. Soc. Hematology, Am. Soc. Immunology, N.Y. Acad. Scis., Western Soc. Clin. Research. Home: 3651 Terrace View Dr Encino CA 91436-4019

COSTELLO, AMELIA FUSCO, educator; b. Schenectady, Apr. 12, 1946; d. Alfonso and Adele (D'Andrea) Fusco; m. Thomas Michael Costello, July ll, 1981; 1 stepchild, Jason Sean. BA in English, Russell Sage Coll., 1971, MS in Elem. Edn., 1974. Cert. tchr., N.Y. Tchr. English, theater arts Averill Park (N.Y.) Ctrl. Schs., 1971—; assisting in adminstrn. Averill Park H.S., 1996, asst. prin., 1997-98. Contbr. to various profl. publs. Sec. Troy (N.Y.) Charter Revision com., 1978; mem. Rensselaer Dem. Com., Troy, 1978-82; class agt. vol. Russell Sage Coll.; Averill Park Ctrl. Shared Decision Making Dist. Com., 1994-97. Named Labor Person of Yr., Troy Labor Coun., 1982. Mem. AFL-CIO (pres. Troy area labor coun. 1980-82), LWV (pub. rels. chair 1981), Am. Fedn. Tchrs., N.Y. State United Tchrs., Averill Park Tchrs. Assn. (v.p. 1989-94, grievance com. 1990-94), St. Jude's Rosary Soc., Russell Sage Troy Club (v.p. 1977-78), Russell Sage Alumni (admissions vol. 1992—), Capitol Dist. Assn. Women Adminstrs. (co-chair 1997-99, Spl. award 1999), Phi Delta Kappa (exec. bd. dirs.). Roman Catholic. Avocations: reading, writing, antique collecting, church work. Home: 28 Goodman Ave Troy NY 12180-8814 Office: Averill Park High Sch 146 Gettle Rd Ste 2 Averill Park NY 12018-9799

COSTELLO, ANDREW F., newspaper editor; b. Norwood, Mass., Sept. 18, 1947. BEngring, BA, U. Mass., 1969. Exec. editor Boston Herald, 1994—. Office: Boston Herald One Herald Sq Boston MA 02106-2096*

COSTELLO, DANIEL BRIAN, lawyer, consultant; b. Arlington, Va., Apr. 23, 1950; s. James Russell and Hazel Virginia (Caudle) C.; m. Margaret Ruth Dow, June 13, 1970; children: James Brian, Rebecca Ruth, Kathleen Marie. BA, U. Va., 1972; JD, Coll. of William and Mary, 1975. Bar: Va. 1975, U.S. Dist. Ct. (ea. dist.) Va. 1979, U.S. Ct. Appeals (4th cir.) 1979, U.S. Bankruptcy Ct. (ea. dist.) Va. 1979, D.C. 1984. Reporter Globe Newspapers, Vienna, Va., 1965-68; freelance journalist Williamsburg, Va., 1972-73; news dir. Sta. WMBG, WBCI-FM, Williamsburg, 1973-76; spl. asst. atty. gen. Commonwealth of Va., Suffolk, Va., 1976-78; asst. atty. gen. Commonwealth of Va., Richmond, Va., 1978-80; ptnr. Dameron, Costello & Hubacher, Alexandria, Va., 1980-89, Costello & Hubacher, Alexandria, 1989-99; pvt. practice Alexandria, 1999—; corp. sec., gen. counsel Olivares U.S.A., Inc., Fairfax, Va., 1999—; press rels. cons. Va. Bar Assn., No. Va. Dem. Combined Campaign; spl. commr. in chancery Alexandria Cir. Ct. Author: Land Use Planning and Eminent Domain, 1997, Foreclosure in Virginia, 1991; co-editor, co-author The Layman's Guide to Virginia Law, 1977; editor night news Sta. WINA, 1969-72; contbr. articles to profl. jours. Mem. Va. State Bar, Alexandria Bar Assn., D.C. Bar, Soc. Alumni Coll. of William and Mary, U. Va. Alumni Soc., Rolling Hills Club. Presbyterian. Avocations: hunting, fishing, coin collecting. Office: D. Brian Costello 429 N Saint Asaph St Alexandria VA 22314-2317

COSTELLO, DANIEL WALTER, retired bank executive; b. Mich., June 17, 1930; s. Walter William and Rose Angela (Dimond) C.; m. Sylvia Michael; children: Michael Joseph, Colleen Marie. BS in Engring. Sci, Purdue U., 1952. Various sales, mktg. and real estate positions Shell Oil Co., 1955-63; dir. real estate and constrn., planning mgr. Ford Motor Co., U.S. and Can., 1963-71; dir. real estate devel. and constrn. Ford Land Devel. Corp., Dearborn, Mich., 1971-75; chmn. Am. Express Realty Mgmt. Co., N.Y.C., 1975-82; corp. sr. v.p. real estate and gen. svcs. Am. Express Co. and subs., N.Y.C., 1975-82; exec. v.p. corp. real estate div. Bank of Am., San Francisco, 1982-95, ret. 1995. Commdr. U.S. Army, 1952-55; Korea. Mem. Nat. Assn. Rev. Appraisers (bd. dirs.), Internat. Real Estate Inst. (bd. govs.), Urban Land Inst., Nat. Assn. Corp. Real Estate Execs. (cert. master corp. real estate), Bldg. Owners and Mgrs. Assn., Meadow Club, Country Club, San Francisco Bankers Club, Theta Xi.

COSTELLO, ELVIS (DECLAN PATRICK MCMANUS), musician, songwriter; b. London, 1954; s. Ross McManus; m. Cait O'Riordan, 1986; 1 child from previous marriage. Songs composed include Alison, 1977, Watching the Detectives, 1977, (I Don't Want To Go To) Chelsea, 1979, Crawling to the USA, 1978, Radio Radio, 1978, Stranger in the House, 1978, Girls Talk, 1979, Oliver's Army, 1979, Boy With a Problem, 1982, Every Day I Write the Book, 1983, others; albums include My Aim is True, 1977, This Year's Model, 1978, Armed Forces, 1979, Get Happy!!, 1980, Trust, 1980, Almost Blue, 1981, Taking Liberties, Imperial Bedroom, 1982, Goodbye Cruel World, 1984, Punch the Clock, 1984, The Best Of, 1985, Blood and Chocolate, 1986, King of America, 1986, Spike, 1989, Girls, Girls, Girls, 1990, Mighty Like a Rose, 1991, (with Steve Nieve, Pete Thomas, Bruce Thomas and Nick Lowe) Brutal Youth, 1994 (with the Brodsky Quartet) The Juliet Letters, 1993, The Very Best of Elvis Costello and the Attractions, 1994, Kojak Variety, 1995, All This Useless Beauty, 1996, Extreme Honey, 1997, Painted From Memory, 1998 (Grammy, 1999); appears in concert U.S. and Eng., 1978—; appeared in film Americathon, 1979. Address: care Warner Bros Records 3300 Warner Blvd Burbank CA 91505-4632*

COSTELLO, FRANCIS WILLIAM, lawyer; b. Cambridge, Mass., Apr. 16, 1946; s. Frank George and Anna M. (Sinnott) C. B.A., Columbia U., 1968, J.D., 1973. Bar: N.Y. 1974, Calif. 1977. Assoc., Whitman & Ransom, N.Y.C., 1973-74, Los Angeles, 1976-82, ptnr., Los Angeles, 1982-93; ptnr. Whitman, Breed, Abbott & Morgan, 1993—; bd. dirs. Oreg. Ctrl. Corp., Portland, Sunritz Corp., L.A., Japan Travel Bur. Internat., L.A. Served with U.S. Army, 1968-70, Vietnam. Mem. State Bar Calif., Los Angeles County Bar Assn., Pumpkin Ridge Golf Club (Oreg.), Wilshire Country Club (L.A.), Calif. Club (L.A.). Home: 415 Knight Way La Canada Flintridge CA 91011-2725

COSTELLO, GERALD MICHAEL, editor; b. Utica, N.Y., May 17, 1931; s. Michael Francis and Catherine Theresa (O'Malley) C.; m. Jane Hansen Van Saun, Dec. 18, 1954; children: Nancy Rishty, Eileen Marx, Michael, Brian, John, Robert. Student, Fordham U., 1952-53; BA, U. Notre Dame, 1952; LittD (hon.), St. John's U., 1997. Reporter Paterson (N.J.) News, 1953-58; editor Suburban Trends, Riverdale, N.J., 1958-62; news editor The Advocate, Newark, N.J., 1962-64; asst. suburban editor The Herald-News, Passaic, N.J., 1964-66; mng. editor The Beacon, Paterson, 1966-81; editor in chief Catholic N.Y., N.Y.C., 1981-91, ret., cons. editor, 1991-96; bd. dirs. The Christophers, N.Y.C., 1980—, Carroll Pub. Co., Washington. Author: Mission to Latin America, 1979, Without Fear or Favor, 1984 (Cath. Press Assn. award 1985). Served with U.S. Army, 1953-55. Named Knight of St. Gregory, 1981. Roman Catholic. Home: 3 Van Allen Pl Pompton Plains NJ 07444-1510

COSTELLO, JAMES JOSEPH, retired electrical manufacturing company executive; b. Boston, Feb. 15, 1930; s. James Joseph and Jennie Theresa (Boyle) C.; m. Mary Virginia Bird, May 7, 1960; children: James, Susan, Maureen, Thomas, Daniel. BSBA, Northeastern U., 1953. With GE, various locations, 1956-71; fin. mgr. AC Motor divsn. GE, Schenectady, 1971-76; fin. mgr. components and materials group GE, Pittsfield, Mass., 1976-77; staff exec. tech. systems and materials sector GE, Fairfield, Conn., 1977-79, v.p., compt., 1979-92; ret., 1992; dir. Latin Comm. Group, Inc., N.Y.C. Trustee Sacred Heart U., Fairfield, Conn.; dir. nat. coun. Northeastern U., Boston. Officer USN, 1953-56. Mem. Fin. Execs. Inst.

COSTELLO, JERRY F., JR., congressman, former county official; b. Sept. 25, 1949. County bd. chmn. St. Clair County, Ill.; dir. ct. services and probation 20th Jud. Cir. Campaign; chmn. Heart Assn., Belleville, Ill., 1983; vice chmn. Ill. div. United Way, 1984, chmn., 1985; mem. 100th-105th Congresses from 21st (now 12th) Ill. Dist., 1988—; mem. budget com., mem. transp. and infrastructure com. Bd. dirs. Ill. Ctr. for Autism; active St. Clair County Big Bros./Big Sisters, Belleville Women's Crisis Ctr., Children's Ctr. for Behavioral Devel.; helped establish St. Clair County chpt. Vets. Outreach Info. Ctr.; mem. East St. Louis Econ. Opportunity Comm., Ill.; vice chmn. Southwestern Ill. Bus. Devel. Fin. Corp., 1985—; bd. dirs. So. Ill. Leadershp Council; pres. Urban Counties Council of Ill. Recipient cert. of Appreciation, Bus. and Profl. Women's Assn., 1985; honored Citizens League for Adequate Social Services; 1985 AAHMES Court #84, Daus. ISIS Ann. Humanitarian award, Gene Hughes award Ill. Ct. Services and Probation Assn. Office: US Ho of Reps 2454 Rayburn House Off Bldg Washington DC 20515-1312*

COSTELLO, JOHN, military officer; b. Pottsville, Pa., Apr. 24, 1947; s. Samuel J. and Blanche (McAndrew) C.; m. Michele Marie Vonnegut, Jan. 25, 1970; children: Patrick M., Adrienne. BA in Polit. Sci., Citadel, 1969; MA in Fgn. Affairs, U. Va., 1975; M of Mil. Arts and Sci., Command and Gen. Staff Coll., Ft. Leavenworth, Kans., 1982; ed. program for sr. execs., Harvard U., 1996. Commd. 2nd lt. U.S. Army, 1969, advanced through grades to lt. gen., 1998; comdr. 1st bn. 59th Air Def. Arty., Schwabach, Germany, 1984-86; chief materiel and logistics Combat Devels., Ft. Bliss, Tex., 1987-88; comdr. 35th Air Def. Arty. Brig., Ft. Lewis, Wash., 1988-90; chief of staff 32nd Army Air Def. Command, Darmstadt, Germany, 1990-92, comdg. gen., 1992-93; asst. divsn. comdr. 1st Armored Divsn., Germany, 1993; dir. roles and missions Office of Dep. Chief of Staff Ops., Washington, 1994; comdg. gen. U.S. Army Air Def. Ctr., Ft. Bliss, 1995-98; comdr. U.S. Army Space and Missile Def. Command, Arlington, Va., 1998-99, lt. gen., 1998—. Contbr. articles to mil. pubs. Decorated D.S.M., Legion of Merit with 2 bronze oak leaf clusters; recipient Star award El Paso (Tex.) C. of C., 1997. Mem. Citadel Alumni Assn., Rotary (El Paso), El Paso Citadel Club (v.p.). Avocations: reading, tennis. Home: 317 Jackson Ave # A Fort Myer VA 22211-1202

COSTELLO, JOHN H., III, business and marketing executive; b. Akron, Ohio, June 2, 1947; s. John H. Jr. and Lia Costello; children from previous marriage, Michael, Jeffrey, Matthew. BS in Indsl. Mgmt., Akron U., 1968; MBA, Mich. State U., 1970. Mktg. dir. Procter & Gamble Co., Cin., 1971-84; sr. v.p. Pepsi-Cola USA, Purchase, N.Y., 1984-86; exec. v.p. Wells, Rich, Greene, Inc., N.Y.C., 1986-88; pres., chief oper. officer Nielsen Mktg. Rsch. U.S.A., Chgo., 1988-93; sr. exec. v.p. Sears, Roebuck & Co., Hoffman Estates, Ill., 1993-98; pres. Auto Nation, Inc., Ft. Lauderdale, Fla., 1999—; sr. mktg. execs. panel Conf. Bd., N.Y.C., 1985-87; industry speaker on bus. trends and issues, 1985—; bd. dirs. The Quaker Oats Co, Sears Can. Mem. exec. bd. N.E. Ill. coun. Boy Scouts Am., 1993-97; trustee Multiple Sclerosis Soc., Chgo., 1990—, vice chmn., 1995—; bd. dirs. Nat. Multiple Sclerosis Soc., 1989—, chair fundraising, 1990-94, mem. exec. com., 1990—, chair nominating com., 1996—. Mem. Assn. Nat. Advertisers (bd. dirs. 1995—, vice chmn. 1998, chmn. 1999), Direct Ad Coun. (bd. dirs. 1996—, vice chmn. 1998), Direct Retail Advt. and Mktg. Assn. (bd. dirs. 1995—, Retail Mktg. Hall of Fame 1997), Lake Forest Club, Econ. Club Chgo., Conway Farms Golf Club. Episcopalian. Avocations: skiing, golf, travel. Home: 860 Gloucester Xing Lake Forest IL 60045-4902 Office: Republic Industries 110 SE 6th St Fort Lauderdale FL 33301

COSTELLO, JOHN WILLIAM, lawyer; b. Chgo., Apr. 16, 1947; s. William John and June Ester (O'Neill) C.; m. Maureen Grace Matthews, June 13, 1970; children—Colleen, William, Erin, Owen. BA, John Carroll U., 1969; JD, DePaul U., 1972. Bar: U.S. Dist. Ct. (no. dist.) Ill. 1982. Assoc. Arvey, Hodes, Costello & Burman, Chgo., 1972-76; ptnr., 1976-90, ptnr. Wildman, Harrold Allen & Dixon, 1990—. Co-author: (manual) The Bankrupcy Reform Act of 1978, 1981. Served to capt. U.S. Army, 1972-73. Mem. ABA (bus. bankruptcy com., jurisdiction and venue and secured creditors subcoms.), Ill. State Bar Assn. (former vice chmn., chmn. comml. banking and bankrupcy law sect. 1979-81), Am. Bankruptcy Inst., Turnaround Mgmt. Assn. (former bd. dirs. Midwest sect.). Democrat. Roman Catholic. Office: Wildman Harrold Aller & Dixon 225 W Wacker Dr Chicago IL 60606-1224

COSTELLO, JOSEPH ANTHONY, JR., circuit court judge, educator; b. Monroe, Mich., Aug. 27, 1956; s. Joseph A. and Mary A. (Michelin) C.; m. Amy J. Cronenwett, May 22, 1981; children: Monica R., James S. AA, Monroe County C.C., Monroe, 1976; BA, U. Mich., 1978; JD, Detroit Coll. Law, 1982. Bar: Mich. 1982. Gen. laborer Chrysler Corp., Trenton, Mich., 1976, 77; substitute tchr. Monroe County Pub. Schs., Monroe, Dundee, Carleton, 1978-79; assoc. Office Jack Vitale, Monroe, 1982, Czeryba, Dulany & Godfroy, Monroe, 1982-85; probate judge Monroe County Probate Ct., Monroe, 1985-96; presiding judge family divsn. 38th Cir. Ct., Monroe, 1997—; adj. prof. Monroe County C.C., 1994—. Charter mem., mem. alumni bd. Monroe County C.C., 1992—, found. mem., bd. dirs. Named Vol. of Yr., Child Advocacy Network, Monroe, 1989, Alumnus of Yr. award St. Mary Cath. Ctrl. H.S., 1995, Monroe County C.C., 1997; recipient Spes Unica award Boysville of Mich., Monroe, 1994. Mem. Italian-Am. Bd., State Bar Mich., Mich. Judges Assn., Monroe County Bar Assn., NAACP, Kiwanis. Roman Catholic. Avocations: travel, golf, water activities. Office: 38th Jud Circuit 106 E 1st St Monroe MI 48161-2115

COSTELLO, RICHARD NEUMANN, advertising agency executive; b. Phila., Sept. 2, 1943; s. Joseph Neumann and Katherine Cash (Birkhead) C.; m. Ann M. Dodds, Oct. 24, 1970; children—Brian Stuart, Gregory Scott. B.A. in English, U. Pa., 1965, M.B.A. in Mktg. 1967. Account mgr. Ogilvy & Mather, Inc., N.Y.C., 1967-71; v.p. Rosenfeld, Sirowitz & Lawson, Inc., N.Y.C., 1971-73; pres. Baron, Costello & Fine, Inc., N.Y.C., 1973-77, TBWA Advt., Inc., N.Y.C., 1977-95; internat. bd. dirs. TBWA Advt., Inc., 1984-96, chief operating officer, 1987-94; pres., CEO TBWA Chiat/Day-East, 1995-96; pres. universal strategic mktg. group Universal Studios Inc., University City, Calif., 1996-98; pres. New Bus. Initiatives Univ. Studios, Inc., 1998—. mem. Young Pres.'s Orgn. Office: Universal Studios Inc 100 Universal City Plz Universal City CA 91608

COSTELLO, THOMAS JOSEPH, bishop; b. Camden, N.Y., Feb. 23, 1929; s. James G. and Ethel A. (Dupont) C. Lic. in Sacred Theology, Cath. U. Am., 1954, JCB, 1960. Ordained priest Roman Cath. Ch., 1954. Sec. Diocesan Tribunal, Diocese of Syracuse, 1958; supt. schs. Cath. Diocese of Syracuse, 1960-75; pastor Our Lady Lourdes Ch., Syracuse, N.Y., 1975-78; aux. bishop Syracuse, 1978—. Home: 1515 Midland Ave Syracuse NY 13205-1447 Office: PO Box 511 240 E Onondaga St Syracuse NY 13202-2608

COSTENBADER, CHARLES MICHAEL, lawyer; b. Jersey City, Dec. 9, 1935; s. Edward William and Marie Veronica (Danaher) C.; m. Barbara Ann Wilson, Aug. 1, 1959; children: Charles Michael Jr., William E., Mary E. BS in Acctg., Mt. St. Mary's Coll., 1957; JD, Seton Hall U., 1960; LLM in Taxation, NYU, 1968. Bar: NJ 1960; U.S. Tax Ct. 1961, U.S. Ct. Appeals (3d cir.) 1973, U.S. Supreme Ct. 1983. Trial atty. office regional counsel IRS, N.Y.C., 1961-69; tax assoc. Shanley & Fisher, Newark, 1969-76; tax ptnr. Stryker, Tams & Dill, Newark, 1976-98; spl. counsel McCarter & English, Newark, 1998—. Mem. N.J. State and Local Expenditure and Revenue Commn., 1985-88. Mem. ABA, N.J. Bar Assn. (chmn. taxation sect. 1984-85), N.J. State C. of C. (chmn. cost of govt. com. 1988—), Am. Coll. Tax Counsel. Republican. Roman Catholic. Avocations: gardening, reading, sports. Home: 8 Neptune Pl Colonia NJ 07067-2502 Office: McCarter & English Gateway Four Ctr 100 Mulberry St Newark NJ 07101-4096

COSTERTON, JOHN WILLIAM FISHER, microbiologist; b. Vernon, B.C., Can., July 21, 1934; married, 1955; 4 children. BA, U. B.C., 1955, MA, 1956; PhD in Microbiology, U. Western Ont., Can., 1960. Prof.

biology Baring Union Christian Coll., Punjab, India, 1960-62, dean sci., 1963-64; fellow bot. Cambridge (Eng.) U., 1965; prof. assoc. microbiology McGill U., 1966-67, asst. prof., 1968-70; assoc. prof. U. Calgary, Alta., Can., 1970-75, prof. microbiology, 1975-93, indsl. rsch. chair biofilm microbiology, 1985-93; dir. Ctr. Biofilm Engring. Mont. State U., Bozeman, 1993—. Author 2 books on biofilms; contbr. more than 750 articles to profl. jours. Recipient Sir Frederick Haultain prize, 1985, Isaac Walton Killam prize, 1990. Mem. Can. Soc. Microbiology, Am. Soc. Microbiology. Achievements include research in architecture of bacterial cell walls and including extracellular carbohydrate coats; originator of universal biofilm theory in microbiology; thought of as leader in the biofilm concept in engring., medicine, dentistry, and environ. sci. Office: Montana State Univ-Bozeman Ctr Biofilm Engineering 366 ETS Bldg Bozeman MT 59717

COSTES, NICHOLAS CONSTANTINE, aerospace technologist, university educator, retired government official; b. Athens, Greece, Sept. 20, 1926; came to U.S., 1948, naturalized, 1959; s. Constantine Nicholas and Anna (Papadopoulou) C.; m. Polytime Andros, Nov. 22, 1958; children: Constantine Nicholas, Anna Amalia, Christina Smaragtha. Diploma, Sci. Sch., Athens Coll., 1945; student, Athens Nat. Tech. U, 1945-48; A.B., Darthmouth Coll., 1950, M.S.C.E. (George W. Davis scholar), 1951; A.M., Harvard U., 1962, M.E.N., 1962; M.S., N.C. State U., 1955, Ph.D. (Ford Found. fellow), 1965. Registered profl. engr., N.C., Ill. Teaching fellow dept. civil engring. N.C. State U., Raleigh, 1951-53, instr., 1962-63; materials engr. N.C. State Hwy. and Pub. Works Commn., Raleigh, 1953-56; research civil engr. U.S. Army Cold Regions Research and Engring. Lab., Hanover, N.H., 1956-62; sr. research scientist space sci. lab Marshall Space Flight Center, NASA, Huntsville, Ala., 1965-98, team leader Apollo II Soil Mechanics Investigation Sci. Team, co-prin. investigator Apollo 12, 13 Lunar Geology Experiment, Apollo 14-17 Soil Mechanics Expt., 1991—, prin. investigator, co-investigator, project scientist Mechanics of Granular Materials Microgravity Expt., 1991—; cons. geotech. engring., 1965—; adj. prof. U. Colo., Boulder, 1998. Contbr. articles and tech. reports to profl. jours. Recipient Dartmouth Soc. Engrs. prize, 1951; recipient NASA awards including cert. of appreciation, 1970, Group Achievement award Lunar Roving Vehicle Team, 1971, invention award, 1971, Astronauts' Silver Snoopy award, 1972, dirs. commendation achievement, 1973, Group Achievemnt award Flow Process Modeling Space Shuttle Main Engine, 1985, Group Achievement awards Environs Definition of Space Shuttle Solid Rocket Motor Team, Challenger Incident, 1986, Mechanics of Granular Materials (MGM) Microgravity Expt. Fellow ASCE (life, Norman medal 1972, chmn. program com. aerospace council 1973-75, exec. com. aerospace div. 1976-82, chmn. 1980-81, profl. coordination com. 1982—), AIAA (assoc. fellow, dir. Ala./Miss. sect. 1976-79, Outstanding Aerospace Engr. award 1976, Martin Schilling award 1979, Herman Oberth award 1998); mem. NSPE, AAAS, Am. Geophys. Union, Dartmouth Soc. Engrs., Soc. Harvard Engrs. and Scientists, Assn. Civil Engrs. Greece (hon.), N.Y. Acad. Scis., Am. Men and Women of Sci., Sigma Xi, Phi Kappa Phi, Chi Epsilon. Greek Orthodox. Home: 4216 Huntington Rd SE Huntsville AL 35802-1144

COSTIGAN, CONSTANCE FRANCES, artist, educator; b. Hoboken, N.J., July 3, 1935; d. Charles Francis and Joan Aletta (Visser) C.; m. John Francis Christian, June 6, 1959 (div. 1972); m. Michael Krausz, May 14, 1976. B.S., Simmons Coll. and Boston Mus. Sch. Fine Arts, 1957; M.A., Am. U., 1965; postgrad., U. Calif.-Berkeley, 1971, U. Va.-Fairfax, 1968-69, U. D.C., 1972-73. Cert. tchr. Va. Designer Smithsonian Instn., Washington, 1957-59, mus. services staff mem., 1962-68, drawing and design instr., 1971-76; art and crafts instr. Arlington County (Va.) Pub. Schs., 1970-75; prof. fine arts George Washington U., Washington, 1976—; curator Arlington Art Ctr., Va., 1980; disting. vis. prof. Am. U. in Cairo, 1980-81; vis. prof. in drawing Haystack Mt. Sch. Crafts, Deer Isle, Maine, 1990; jurist and judge art show D.C. area, 1975, 76, 90, 82, area show Del. Ctr. for Contemporary Arts, 1985; judge art show Sussex County Arts Coun. Mems. Show, 1991. Author: Leonardo, 1982, Elements of Art: Line, 1980; one-woman shows: Corkran Gallery, Rehoboth Art League, Del., 1998, Soho 20 Gallery, N.Y.C., 1997, Hampshire Coll. Gallery Hampshire Coll., Amherst, Mass., 1996, Dimock Gallery, George Washington U., 1987, Franz Bader Gallery, Washington, 1985, 90, No. Va. Community Coll., Alexandria, 1983, Barbara Fiedler Gallery, Washington, 1979, 82, Phillips Collection, Washington, 1977, Gulbenkian Gallery, U. Kent, Canterbury, Eng., 1975, Talbot Rice Arts Ctr., Edinburgh, Scotland, 1974, Design Ctr. Gallery, Cleve., 1974, Annenburg Arts Ctr., Phila., 1973, numerous group invitational and juried shows; represented pub. collections Hirschborn Mus. and Sculpture Garden, Washington, Phillips Collection, Washington, U. Iowa Mus., Iowa City, Dimock Gallery, George Washington U., Del. Mus. Art, others; included in numerous pvt. collections. Fellow Macdowell Colony, 1977; fellow Ossabaw Island project, 1980; grantee Lester Hereward Cooke Found., 1978-79, G.W.U., grantee GSAS Facilitating Fund 1990. Fellow Royal Soc. Arts; mem. Am. Craft Council, Coll. Art Assn. Home: 2456 20th St NW Washington DC 20009-1574 Office: George Washington U Art Dept 801 22nd St NW Washington DC 20037-2515

COSTIGAN, EDWARD JOHN, investment banker; b. St. Louis, Oct. 31, 1914; s. Edward J. and Elizabeth Keane; m. Sara Louise Guth, Mar. 30, 1940 (dec. Nov. 1988); children: Sally Edward John, James, Betsy, Robert, David, Louise; m. Mildred F. Fabick, Dec. 27, 1995. A.B., St. Louis U., 1935; M.B.A., Stanford U., 1937. Analyst, v.p. Whitaker & Co., St. Louis, 1937-43; ptnr. Edward D. Jones & Co., 1943-72; sr. v.p. Stifel Nicolaus & Co. Inc., St. Louis, 1972-74, pres., 1974-79, vice chmn., 1979-83, emeritus, 1983; gov. Nat. Assn. Securities Dealers, 1967-70, Investment Bankers Assn., 1968-69, Midwest Stock Exchange, Chgo., 1962-64; bd. dirs. 12 cos. Trustee Calvary Cemetery Assn., St. Louis, 1956—. Mem. St. Louis Soc. Fin. Analysts (pres. 1956), Harvard Club St. Louis (pres. 1955), Bellerive Country Club, Mo. Athletic Club, Old Warson Country Club, Noonday Club, University Club. Republican. Roman Catholic. Office: 501 N Broadway 8th Fl Saint Louis MO 63102-2110

COSTIKYAN, EDWARD N., lawyer; b. Weehawken, N.J., Sept. 14, 1924; s. Mihran Nazar and Berthe (Muller) C.; m. Barbara Heine, Mar. 6, 1977; children: Gregory John, Emilie Berthe. AB, Columbia U., 1947, LLB, 1949. Bar: N.Y. 1949, U.S. Dist. Ct. (so. dist.) N.Y. 1950, U.S. Ct. Appeals (2d cir.) 1950, U.S. Supreme Ct. 1964. Law sec. to judge Harold R. Medina U.S. Dist. Ct., N.Y.C., 1949-51; ptnr. Paul, Weiss, Rifkind, Wharton & Garrison, N.Y.C., 1960-93, of counsel, 1994—; spl. advisor to mayor on sch. and borough governance City of N.Y., 1994-96, chairperson mayor's investigative commn. on sch. safety, 1995-96; mem. Commn. on Integrity in Govt., N.Y.C., 1986, mem. joint com. on jud. adminstrn., 1985-92; adj. fellow Ctr. for Edn. Innovation, 1997—. Author: Behind Closed Doors: Politics in the Public Interest, 1966, How to Win Votes: The Politics of 1980, 1980; co-author: Re-Structuring the Government of New York City, 1972, New Strategies for Regional Cooperation, 1973; rsch. editor Columbia Law Rev.; mem. editl. bd. City Jour., 1992—; mem. bd. editors N.Y. Law Jour., 1976—; contbr. articles on legal and polit. subjects to profl. publs. Chmn. N.Y. State Task Force on N.Y.C. Juristiction and Structure, 1971-72; vice chmn. State Charter Revision for N.Y.C., 1972-77; county leader New York County Dem. Com., 1962-64; Dem. presdl. elector, 1964, 88; trustee, mem. exec. com., chmn. alumni adv. bd. Columbia U., 1981-93, trustee emeritus, 1993—; bd. dirs., mem. coun. Mcpl. Art Soc., 1993-98; chmn. bd. dirs. N.Y. Found. for Sr. Citizens, 1993—. 1st lt. inf. U.S. Army, 1943-46. Recipient William J. Brennan Jr. award for Outstanding Cont. to Pub. Discourse, 1997. Fellow Am. Coll. Trial Lawyers; mem. Assn. of Bar of City of N.Y. (mem. exec. com. 1986-90), Century Club. Unitarian. Home: 50 Sutton Pl S New York NY 10022-4167 Office: Paul Weiss Rifkind Wharton & Garrison Ste 3910 1285 Avenue Of The Americas Fl 21 New York NY 10019-6065

COSTIN, JAMES D., performing arts company executive. BA in Theater, U. Calif., L.A., 1959; MA in Theater, U. Mo., Kansas City, 1966. Cert. German linguist, 1956. Mgr. Fox West Coast Theatres, L.A., Calif., 1954-56; German linguist Army Security Agency, U.S. Army, 1956-59; editor Great Lakes News, 1960-61; asst. stage mgr to stage mgr. Am. Ballet Theatre, 1961-62, co. mgr., 1962-63; asst. gen. mgr. Washington D.C. Ballet Guild/Am. Ballet Theatre, 1963-64; co-founder, adminstrv. dir. Mo. Repertory Theatre, U. Mo., Kansas City, 1964-67; playwright in residence U. Mo., Kansas City, 1966-67; adminstrv. dir. of theatre U. Mo., 1968-72, asst. to the provost, dir. office of cultural events, 1972-76, asst provost for performing arts mgmt., 1976-79, vice provost, chief academic fiscal officer, 1979—; exec. dir./playwright in residence Mo. Repertory Theatre, Inc., 1979—; cons. Internat. Theatre Inst., Great Lakes Shakespeare Festival, Kansas City Ballet. Author: (play) Laity, 1964, Lee, 1966, Ageina, 1969, The Curious Adventures of Alice, 1988, Jekyll, 1989; (stage productions) Ageina, The Curious Adventures of Alice, Jekyll; (co-author play with James Lee) The Holy Terror, 1967. Com. mem. Mayor's Com. Save The Starlight Theater, Save the Phiharmonic Orchestra; bd. dirs. State Ballet Mo., Kans. City Arts Coun. Lt. USNR 1968-71. Recipient Best Playwright award UCLA, 1959, Pirouette award, 1987. Office: Mo Repertory Theatre 4949 Cherry St Ste 307 Kansas City MO 64110-2269

COSTIN, JOHN EDWARD, graphic artist; b. Detroit, Oct. 9, 1955; s. Sanford John and Barbara Costin. AA, Polk C.C., Winter Haven, Fla., 1976; BA, U. South Fla., 1982. Solo shows include Edison C.C., Ft. Myers, Fla., 1988, Warehouse teatre, Tampa, Fla., 1993, 94, Mus of Sci. and Industry, Tampa, 1996, Estate of the Arts, Mansfield, Ohio, 1996; exhibited in group shows at Clemson (S.C.) U., 1985, Zanner Gallery, 1986, Somerstown Gallery, Somers, N.Y., 1986, Tampa Mus. Art, 1986, 87, Scarfone Gallery, U. Tampa, 1986, Polk Mus. Art, Lakeland, Fla., 1987, Clayton Gallery, 1988, Arts coun. Hillsborough County, Tampa, 1990, Fla. Ctr. Contemporary Art, Tampe, 1990, Polk C.C., Winter Haven, Fla., 1991, Am. Embassy, Madrid, 1991, Anderson Marsh Gallery, St. Petersburg Beach, 1992, Grand Ctrl. Gallery, Tampa, 1992, Still and Moving Gallery, Tampa, 1993, Tampa Mus. Art, 1995, others; works in permanent collectoins at City of Tampa, Barnett Bank, Tampa, Fla. C. of C., Tallahassee, GM Corp., chgo., Eckerd Coll., St. Petersburg, State Libr. of Fla., Tampa Tribune, Tampa Mus. Art, IBM, Chgo., USAA Ins. Co., City of St. Petersburg, others. Home and Office: 1905 N 36th St Tampa FL 33605-4437

COSTIN, J(OSEPH) LAURENCE, JR., information services executive; b. Chgo., Mar. 14, 1941; s. Joseph Laurence and Maribel (Cummings) C.; m. Joan Gayley, June 20, 1964 (dec. June 1998); children: Jennifer, Michael. BA, U. Chgo., 1966. Divsn. mgr. Marshall Field and Co., Chgo., 1967-81; sr. v.p. Seligman and Latz, Inc., N.Y.C., 1981-83; exec. v.p. CCC Info. Svcs., Inc., Chgo., 1983-93, vice-chmn., 1993—. With Ill. Army N.G., 1963-69. Mem. Am. Ins. Svcs. Group (com. automobile phys. damage), Internat. Assn. Automobile Theft Investigators, I-Car Edn. Found. (past chmn., bd. trustees), Nat. Ins. Crime Bur.-Fed. Anti-Car Theft Act, Inc. (bd. trustees), Westmoreland Country Club, Chgo. Curling Club, East Bank Club, Contemporary Arts Coun. Roman Catholic. Avocations: golf, curling, contemporary art, urban history. Office: World Trade Ctr Chgo 444 Merchandise Mart Plz Chicago IL 60654-1005

COSTLE, ELIZABETH ROWE, commissioner. BA, Harvard U.; MPA, U. Calif., Berkeley; JD, Georgetown U. Bar: Vt., D.C., U.S. Dist. Ct. (fed. dist.), U.S. Ct. Appeals D.C. Assoc. Arnold & Porter, Washington; corp. counsel Satellite Bus. Systems; asst. gen. counsel Fed. Nat. Mortgage Assn.; gen. counsel Vt. Dept. Banking, Ins., Securities and Health Care Adminstrn., Montpelier, 1988, dep. commr. securities divsn., commr., 1992—. FAX: (802) 828-3306. Office: Vt Dept Banking Ins Securities and Health Care Adminstrn 89 Main St # Montpelier VT 05602-2948

COSTNER, KEVIN, actor; b. L.A., Jan. 18, 1955; m. Cindy Silva (div.); children: Annie, Lily, Joe. Degree in mktg., Calif. State U., Fullerton, 1978. Owner prodn. co. TIG Prodns. Film appearances include Sizzle Beach U.S.A., 1974, Shadows Run Black, 1981, Chasing Dreams, 1981, Frances, 1982, Night Shift, 1982, Table for Five, 1983, Stacy's Knights 1983, The Gunrunner, 1983, The Big Chill, 1983, American Flyers, 1985, Fandango, 1985, Silverado, 1985, The Untouchables, 1987, No Way Out, 1987, Bull Durham, 1988, Field of Dreams, 1989, Revenge (also exec. prodr.), 1990, Dances with Wolves (also co-prodr., dir.) 1990 (Acad. award for best dir. 1991, Star of Tomorrow award Nat. Assn. Theatre Owners 1987, Hasty Pudding Man of Yr., Harvard U. 1990, Acad. award for best picture, 1991, Acad. award nominee best actor 1991, Dir's. Guild Am. award Best Dir. Feature Film 1991), Robin Hood: Prince of Thieves, 1991, JFK, 1991, Truth or Dare, 1991, The Bodyguard (also co-prodr.) 1992, A Perfect World, 1993, Wyatt Earp, 1994, The War, 1994, Waterworld (also co-prodr.), 1995, Tin Cup, 1996, The Postman (also dir., prodr.) 1997, Message in a Bottle (also prodr.), 1999, For Love of the Game, 1999; host, exec. prodr. (TV series) 500 Nations; co-prodr. China Moon, 1993; exec. prodr. Rapa Nui, 1994; TV movies include Testament (PBS) 1983. Office: TIG Prodns 4000 Warner Blvd Bldg 5 Burbank CA 91522-0001

COSTON, SUZANNE, television producer; m. Harold Coston; 2 children. Formerly creative asst. to Berry Gordy, Motown Records, Detroit, v.p., later pres. Motown Prodns., from 1982; ptnr. Gordy/de Passe Prodns., to 1992; founder pres., chmn., CEO de Passe Entertainment, L.A., 1992—. Prodr. miniseries including Lonesome Dove, Small Sacrifices, Return to Lonesome Dove, The Jacksons: An American Dream, Buffalo Girls, Streets of Laredo, Dead Man's Walk; exec. prodr. telefilms Callie and Son, Someone Else's Child, others; exec. prodr. comedy series Sister, Sister, also Lonesome Dove: The Outlaw Years. Recipient Emmy awards for Motown 25: Yesterday, Today, Forever, 1983, Motown Returns to the Apollo; Crystal award Women in Film, 1988, Revlon Bus. Woman of Yr. award, 1994, Essence Bus. award, 1989; named to Black Filmmakers Hall of Fame, 1990. Office: care DePasse Entertainment 5750 Wilshire Blvd Ste 640 Los Angeles CA 90036

COSTONIS, JOHN J., law educator, lawyer; b. 1937. A.B., Harvard U., 1959; LL.B., Columbia U. Bar: D.C. 1967, Ill. 1968. Asst. prof. U. Pa., 1965-69; assoc. Ross, Hardies, O'Keefe, Babcock & Parsons, Chgo., 1968-70; vis. assoc. prof. U. Ill.-Chgo., 1970, prof., 1972-77; former prof. NYU, from 1978—; now dean law sch. Vanderbilt U., Nashville; prof. environtl. law Vanderbilt U., 1998; vis. lectr. internat. law U. Chgo., 1968; vis. prof. U. Calif.-Berkeley, 1975-76; advisor to pres. Adv. Council of Hist. Preservation, to Nat. Endowment for Arts, NSF, Sec. Interior, and Nat. Trust for Hist. Preservation; chancellor La. State U. Law Sch., Baton Rouge, 1998—. Past articles editor: Columbia Law Rev. Served to 1st lt. I.C. U.S. Army, 1960-62. Mem. Am. Law Inst., Am. Planning Assn. Office: La State U Sch Law Office of Chancellor 21st Ave S Baton Rouge LA 70803*

COSTRELL, LOUIS, physicist; b. Bangor, Maine, June 26, 1915; s. Solomon Nathan and Annie (Cohen) C.; m. Esther Klaiman, Apr. 11, 1942; children: James A., Daniel N., Robert M. B.S., U. Maine, 1939; postgrad., U. Pitts., 1940-41; M.S., U. Md., 1949. With Elliot Co., Ridgeway, Pa., 1940, Westinghouse Corp., East Pittsburgh, 1940-41, Bur. Ships, Dept. Navy, Washington, 1941-46; with Nat. Bur. Standards, Dept. Commerce, Washington, 1946—; chief radiation instrumentation sect. Nat. Bur. Standards, Dept. Commerce, 1952-81; physicist Ctr. for Radiation Research Nat. Bur. Standards, Dept. Commerce, Gaithersburg, Md., 1981—; Tech. adviser to U.S. Nat. Com. for Internat. Electrotech. Commn., 1962—; chmn. AEC Nuclear Instrument Modules Com. (now Dept. Energy Nat. Instrumentation Methods), 1964—. Recipient Meritorious Service award Dept. Commerce, 1955, Disting. Service award, 1968, Spl. Service award, 1963; Edward Bennett Rosa award, 1979. Fellow IEEE (chmn. profl. group on nuclear sci. 1960-61, H. Diamond meml. award 1975, Nuclear and Plasma Sci. merit award 1975, Disting. Mem. award 1987), Nuclear and Plasma Sci. Soc. (Computer Applications in Nuclear and Plasma award 1993), Washington Acad. Sci.; mem. Am. Phys. Soc., Am. Nat. Stds. Inst. (chmn. com on radiation instruments 1960—), Tau Beta Pi, Phi Kappa Phi. Office: Ctr for Radiation Rsch Dept Commerce Stds Nat Inst Stds & Tech Gaithersburg MD 20899

COSUE, LAMBERTO GUTIERREZ, III, internist; b. Manila, May 8, 1964; came to U.S., 1992; s. Lamberto C. Jr. and Celeste (Gutierrez) C. BS in Med. Tech. cum laude, U. Santo Tomas, Manila, 1985, MD, 1989. Cert. in internal medicine. Intern Luth. Med. Ctr., Bklyn., 1992-93, resident in internal medicine, 1993-95; med. staff North Sunflower County Hosp., Ruleville, Miss., 1995—; dir. emergency rm. dept. North Sunflower County Hosp., Ruleville, 1997—. Mem. ACP, AMA, Miss. State Med. Assn., Med. Soc. State of N.Y. Office: North Sunflower County Hosp PO Box 369 840 N Oak Ave Ruleville MS 38771-3227

COTA, JOHN FRANCIS, utility executive; b. Mason City, Iowa, Oct. 28, 1924; s. Sylvester D. and Ina (McAlpine) C.; m. Margaret Louise Allen, Oct. 22, 1945; children—David J., Julie A., Daniel A., Kim F. Student, Drake U., 1942; B.S., Iowa State U., 1947. Cadet engr. Iowa Power & Light Co., Des Moines, 1948; project mgr. Iowa Power & Light Co., 1949, chief gas engr., 1954-57; v.p., gen. mgr. Winnebago Natural Gas Corp., Kaukauna, Wis., 1957-58; pres., dir. Natural Gas Distbrs., Inc., Madison, Wis., 1958; asst. v.p. Wis. Gas Co., Milw., 1960-64; v.p. ops. Wis. Gas Co., 1964-69, exec. v.p., 1969-75; dir., 1968-75; v.p., asst. to chmn. Am. Natural Resources, Detroit, 1975-78; v.p. engring. and constrn. Mich. Wis. Pipe Line Co., Detroit, 1978-86; cons. ANR Pipe Line Co., 1984; ret., 1986; pres. Marjac Investments, Inc., San Diego, 1993—. Served with USNR, 1942-45. Mem. Am., Midwest gas assns., Mich. Utilities Assn. Clubs: Bernardo Heights Country, Rancho Bernardo Swim and Tennis (San Diego). Home: 13193 Polvera Ave San Diego CA 92128-1147

COTCHETT, JOSEPH WINTERS, lawyer, author; b. Chgo., Jan. 6, 1939; s. Joseph Winters and Jean (Renaud) C.; children—Leslie F., Charles P., Rachael E., Quinn Carlyle, Camilla E. B.S. in Engring., Calif. Poly. Coll., 1960; LL.B., U. Calif. Hastings Coll. Law, 1964. Bar: Calif. 1965, D.C. 1980. Ptnr. Cotchett, Pitre & Simon, Burlingame, Calif., 1965—; mem. Calif. Jud. Coun., 1975-77, Calif. Commn. on Jud. Performance, 1985-89, Commn. 2020 Jud. Coun., 1991-94; select com. on jud. retirement, 1992—. Author: (with R. Cartwright) California Products Liability Actions, 1970, (with F. Haight) California Courtroom Evidence, 1972, (with A. Elkind) Federal Courtroom Evidence, 1976, (with Frank Rothman) Persuasive Opening Statements and Closing Arguments, 1988, (with Stephen Pizzo) The Ethics Gap, 1991, (with Gerald Uelmen) California Courtroom Evidence Foundations, 1993; contbr. articles to profl. jours. Chmn. San Mateo County Heart Assn., 1967; pres. San Mateo Boys and Girls Club, 1971; bd. dirs. U. Calif. Hastings Law Sch., 1981-93. With Intelligence Corps, U.S. Army, 1960-61; col. JAGC, USAR, ret. Fellow Am. Bar Found., Am. Bd. Trial Advs., Am. Coll. Trial Lawyers, Internat. Acad. Trial Lawyers, Internat. Soc. of Barristers, Nat. Bd. Trial Advs. (diplomate civil trial adv.), State Bar Calif. (gov. 1972-75). Clubs: Commonwealth, Press (San Francisco). Office: 840 Malcolm Rd Burlingame CA 94010-1401 also: 12100 Wilshire Blvd Ste 1100 Los Angeles CA 90025-7124

COTE, DAVID EDWARD, state legislator; b. Nashua, N.H., Oct. 28, 1960; s. Edward David and Dorothy Eliza (Soucy) C. Mem. N.H. Ho. of Reps., 1982-88, 89—, asst. Dem. whip, 1991-92, dep. Dem. whip, 1992-96; mem. House Dem. Leadership, 1996—. Del. N.H. Constl. Conv., 1984, N.H. Dem. Convs., 1982—; mem. N.H. Civil Liberties Union, 1982; mem. platform com. N.H. Dem. Com., 1984; chmn. Nashua City Dem. Com., 1985-86; active various Dem. campaigns. Home: 96 W Hollis St Nashua NH 03060-3146 Office: NH Ho of Reps N State St Rm 306 Concord NH 03301-3229

COTE, DENISE LOUISE, federal judge; b. St. Cloud, Minn., Oct. 13, 1946; d. Donald Edward and Dorothy (Garberson) C.; m. Howard F. Maltby, Dec. 24, 1987. BA, St. Mary's Coll., 1968; MA, Columbia U., 1969, JD, 1975. Bar: N.Y. 1976, U.S. Dist. Ct. (so. and ea. dist.) N.Y. 1976, U.S. Ct. Appeals (2d cir.) 1984. Law clk. to Hon. Jack B. Weinstein U.S. Dist. Ct. (ea. dist.) N.Y., 1975-76; assoc. Curtis Mallet-Prevost, N.Y.C., 1976-77; asst. U.S. Attys. Office (so. dist.), N.Y.C., 1977-85; dep. chief criminal divsn. so. dist. U.S. Attys. Office, N.Y.C., 1983-85, chief criminal divsn. so. dist., 1991-94; atty. Kaye Scholer Fierman Hays & Handler, N.Y.C., 1985-88, ptnr., 1988-91; judge U.S. Dist. Ct. (so. dist.) N.Y., 1994—. Mem. Assn. of Bar of City of N.Y. Office: 1040 US District Court 500 Pearl St New York NY 10007-1316*

COTE, MICHAEL RICHARD, bishop; b. Sanford, Maine, June 19, 1949. Student, Our Lady of Lourdes Sem., Cassadaga, N.Y., St. Mary's Sem. Coll., Balt., Gregorian U. Rome, Cath. U. Washington; JCL, Cath. U., 1981. Ordained priest Roman Cath. Ch., 1975. Asst. SS Athanasius & John, Rumford, Maine, 1975-78; assoc. Holy Rosary, Caribou, 1978-79; notary Vice-Officialis Diocesan Tribunal, Portland, 1980-89; sec. Apostolic Nunciature, Washington, 1989-94; pastor Sacred Heart, Auburn, Maine, 1994-95; titular bishop Diocese of Cebarades, 1995—; auxiliary bishop Diocese of Portland, 1995—. Office: PO Box 11559 Portland ME 04104-7559*

COTÉ, RALPH WARREN, JR., mining engineer, nuclear engineer; b. Berkeley, Calif., Oct. 5, 1927; s. Ralph Warren and Clara Maria (Neves) C.; m. Lois Lydia Maddox, Aug. 8, 1950; children: Ralph Warren III, Michele Marie. BSME, N.Mex. Inst. Mining and Tech., 1952. Registered profl. nuclear engr., Calif.; grad. Realtor Inst. Resident engr. Am. Smelting and Refining Co., Page, Idaho, 1952-54; shift boss Bunker Hill Co., Kellogg, Idaho, 1954-57, gen. mine foreman, 1958-60; project engr. Union Carbide Nuclear Co., Grand Junction, Colo., 1957-58; shift supr. GE, Richland, Wash., 1960-63; shift supr. GE, Vallecitos, Calif., 1963-66, maintenance mgr., 1966-67; start-up shift supr. GE, San Jose, Calif., 1967-71; project start-up mgr. Bechtel Power Corp., San Francisco, 1971-89; realtor retirement real estate Prudential Preferred Properties, Sun City West, Ariz. Served to 2d lt. U.S. Army and U.S. N.G., 1946-50. Mem. VFW, Am. Legion. Republican. Home: 14610 W Sky Hawk Dr Sun City West AZ 85375-5925 Office: Prudential Perferred Properties 13576 W Camino Del Sol Ste 20 Sun City West AZ 85375-4428

COTE, RICHARD JAMES, pathologist, researcher; b. L.A., May 10, 1954; s. Richard Patrick and Kathrine (Bisbas) C.; m. Anne Louise Foxen, Feb. 8, 1992; children: Nicholas Foxen, Juliet Anne, Grace Elizabeth. BS in Biology, U. Calif., Irvine, 1976, BA in Chemistry, 1976; MD, U. Chgo., 1980. Diplomate Am. Coll. Pathologists. Intern in surgery U. Mich. Hosp., Ann Arbor, 1980-81; rsch. fellow, immunology Meml. Sloan-Kettering Cancer Ctr., N.Y.C., 1981-83; rsch. assoc., immunology Meml. Sloan-Kettering Hosp., N.Y.C., 1983-85, fellow, pathology, 1987-88, chief fellow, pathology, 1988-90; resident, pathology Cornell U. Med. Ctr., N.Y.C., 1985-87; asst. prof., pathology U. So. Calif., L.A., 1990-95, assoc. prof., 1995-99, prof., 1999—; attending pathologist Kenneth Norris Cancer Ctr., L.A., 1990—; dir. genitourinary program U. So. Calif./Norris Cancer Ctr., 1997—; founder, dir. Impath, Inc., N.Y.C., 1987—; scientific dir. Neoprobe Corp., Columbus, Ohio, 1992-97; sci. dir. ChromaVision Med. Sys., Inc., San Juan Capistrano, Calif., 1997—; sci. dir. John Wayne Cancer and Rsch. Inst., Santa Monica, Calif.; mem. numerous nat. and internat. adv. bds. in field. Author: Immunomicroscopy, 1994; editor Modern Surg. Pathology; assoc. editor Applied Immunohistochemistry; contbr. scientific papers to profl. jours., book chpts. Patentee in field. Am. Cancer Soc. fellow, 1988; recipient rsch. grants, awards NIH, ACS, others, 1981—. Mem. Soc. for Basic Urologic Rsch., Internat. Soc. for Hematotherapy, Phi Beta Kappa. Avocations: golf, photography, skiing, writing. Office: U So Calif 1441 Eastlake Ave Los Angeles CA 90033-1048

COTHERMAN, AUDREY MATHEWS, management and policy consultant, administrator; b. St. Paul, May 20, 1930; d. Anthony Joseph and Nina Grace (Harmon) Mathews; m. Richard Louis Cotherman, Dec. 30, 1950 (div. 1973); children: Steven, Michael, Bruce, Gen Elizabeth. BA, Hamline U., 1952; MA, U. Wyo., 1973, EdD, 1977. Communications coord. Natrona Sch. Dist., Casper, Wyo., 1968-69; hostess TV program KTWO-TV, Casper, 1970-71; exec. dir. United Way, Casper, 1971-73, Wyo. Coun. Humanities, Laramie, 1973-79; dep. state supt. Wyo. Dept. Edn., Cheyenne, 1979-90; devel. officer Coll. Edn. U. Wyo., Laramie, 1990-91; pres. Connections: Mgmt. and Policy Cons., Casper, 1991—; spl. asst. U.S. Dept. Edn. Region VIII, 1996—; exec. sec. Wyo. Bd. Edn., 1979-90; dir. comty. programs HSS, Cheyenne, 1986-90; cons. Wyo. Atty. Gen., Cheyenne, 1990; dealer Profiles, Internat. Dem. precinct chair, Laramie, 1986-90. State exec. policy fellow U.S. Dept. Edn., 1985. Mem. LWV (past pres. local chpts., Wyo. chpt.), Am. Assn. Pub. Adminstrs. (pres. 1987-88), Wyo. Assn. Pub. Adminstrs. (Pub. Adminstr. of Yr. 1982), Phi Delta Kappa. Presbyterian. Avocations: writing, spending time with grandchildren, reading, gardening. Home: 1250 Galapago St Apt 106 Denver CO 80204-3594

COTHERN, BARBARA SHICK, county official; b. Okmulgee, Okla., Mar. 5, 1931; d. Roy and Irene Maude (Baldwin) Shick; m. George Albert Cothern, Mar. 21, 1954; children: Cynthia Lou, Deborah Sue, James Albert. BA in Human Resources, Seattle U., 1980, MBA, 1983. Owner Human Resource Svc., 1980-85; mem. Wash. Ho. of Reps., Olympia, 1992-94; chair Northshore Shoreline Health & Safety Network, 1995—; exec. dir. Northshore Pub. Edn. Found., Wash. State Pub. Disclosure Commn., 1996-97. Crisis counselor, 1979—; pres. Northshore Sch. Bd., Bothell, Wash., 1990-91, bd. dirs., 1987—, legis. rep., 1989-91; mem. resolutions com. Wash. State Sch. Dis. Assn., 1989—; pres. Shoreline Sch. Bd., 1971-74; chair Northshore Legis. Coalition, 1989-91; mem. Snohomish County Com. for Improved Transp., 1992; numerous other civic activities. Mem. AAUW, Nat. Women's Polit. Caucus. Mem. Reorganized Ch. of Jesus Christ of Latter Day Saints. Avocation: music. Home: 20006 4th Ave SE Bothell WA 98012-9659

COTHORN, JOHN ARTHUR, lawyer; b. Des Moines, Dec. 12, 1939; s. John L. and Marguerite (Esters) C.; m. Connie Cason, Aug. 6, 1996; children: Jeffrey, Judith. BS in Math., U. Mich., 1961, BS in Aero. Engring., 1961, JD, 1980. Bar: Mich. 1981, U.S. Dist. Ct. (ea. dist.) Mich. 1981, U.S. Ct. Appeals (6th cir.) 1981, U.S. Dist. Ct. (we. dist.) Mich. 1986, U.S. Supreme Ct. Exec. U.S Govt., 1965-78; asst. prosecutor Washtenaw County, Ann Arbor, Mich., 1981-82; ptnr. Kitch, Saurbier, Drutchas, Wagner & Kenney P.C., Detroit, 1982-94, Meganck & Cothorn P.C., Detroit, 1994-97, Meganck, Cothorn & Stanczyk P.C., Detroit, 1997-98, Cothorn & Stanczyk, P.C., Detroit, 1998—. Served to capt. U.S. Army, 1961-65. Mem. ABA, Nat. Bar Assn. (numerous fed. and state coms.), Soc. Automotive Engrs., Assn. Def. Trial Counsel, Phi Alpha Delta. Republican. Avocations: bridge, golf. Office: 535 Griswold St Ste 1525 Detroit MI 48226-3689

COTRAN, RAMZI S., pathologist, educator; b. Haifa, Palestine, Dec. 7, 1932; came to U.S., 1956; s. Suliman T. and Fadwa (Khoury) C.; m. Kerstin Larson, OCt. 5, 1957; children: Paul, Leila, Suzanne, Nina. BA, Am. U. Beirut, Lebanon, 1952, MD, 1956; MA (hon.), Harvard U., 1972. Diplomate Am. Bd. Pathology. Intern and resident in pathology Boston City Hosp., Mallory Inst. Pathology, Boston, 1956-59; fellow in pathology Meml. Sloan Kettering Cancer Ctr., N.Y.C., 1959-60; from instr. to assoc. prof. pathology Harvard Med. Sch., Boston, 1960-72, F.B. Mallory prof. pathology, 1972—; assoc. dir. Mallory Inst. Pathology, Boston, 1969-74; chmn. dept. pathology Brigham & Women's Hosp., Boston, 1974—; pathologist in chief Children's Hosp. Med. Ctr., Boston, 1990—; chmn. sci. adv. bd. St. Jude Children's Rsch. Hosp., Memphis, 1986-89. Sr. author: Pathologic Basis of Disease, 5th edit., 1994, Renal Pathophysiology, 1976, 3d edit., 1986, Current Topics in Inflammation and Infection, 1982. Recipient Rsch. Career Devel. award NIH, 1966-74. Fellow AAAS, Am. Acad. Arts and Sci.; mem. Inst. Medicine (elected mem. 1986), Inst. of Medicine of NAS, Am. Assn. Pathologists (mem. coun. 1980-86, pres. 1986-87), Am. Soc. Nephrology (pres.-elect), Fed. Am. Soc. Exptl. Biology (mem. exec. bd. 1981-84), Assn. Am. Physicians, Alpha Omega Alpha. Democrat. Home: 57 Chatham St Brookline MA 02446-5451 Office: Brigham & Women's Hosp 75 Francis St Boston MA 02115-6106*

COTRUBAS, ILEANA, opera singer, lyric soprano, retired; b. Galati, Romania; d. Vasile C. and Maria C. m. Manfred Ramin, 1972. Student, Scoala speciala de Musica, Bucharest, Ciprian Porumbescu Conservatory, Bucharest, Musikakademie, Vienna, Austria. tchr. master-classes, interpretation and operatic roles. Debut as Yniold in Pelleas et Melisande, Bucharest Opera, 1964; appeared with Frankfurt (Fed. Republic Germany) Opera, 1968-71, Staatsoper, Vienna, 1970—, Covent Garden, London, 1971—, Staatsoper, Munich, 1973—, Lyric Opera Chgo., 1973-75, 83—, Opera Paris, 1974—, La Scala, Milan, 1975—, Met. Opera, N.Y.C., 1977—, San Francisco Opera, 1978, Ehrenmitglied Vienna Staats oper, 1991; major roles include: Zerlina, Susanna, Pamina, Norina, Gilda, Violetta, Elisabetta (Don Carlos), Mimi, Tatyana, Micaela, Manon, Antonia, Melisande; ret., 1990; author: Opera Truths, Truth in and about Opera, 1998. Recipient 1st prize Internat. Singing Competition, Hertogenbusch, Netherlands, 1965; 1st prize Munich Radio Competition, 1966; Kammersängerin Vienna Staatsoper, 1981; Great Officer of the Order Sant' Iago da Espada, Portugal, 1990.

COTRUVO, JOSEPH ALFRED, federal agency administrator; b. Toledo, Aug. 3, 1942; s. Nicholas and Angela (Campanale) C.; m. Marcia J. Ramm, Dec. 28, 1968 (div. 1970); m. Karen Shrum, June 18, 1983; 1 child, Joseph Alfred Jr. BS in Chemistry, U. Toledo, 1963; PhD, Ohio State U., 1968; postgrad., U. Bologna, Italy, 1969. Mgr. R & D Chem. Samples Co., Columbus, Ohio, 1970-72; programs analyst EPA, Washington, 1973-76, dir. drinking water criteria and stds. divsn., 1976-90, dir. health and environ. rev. divsn., 1990-92; dir. risk assessment divsn., 1992-96; sr. regulatory exec. NSF Internat., Washington, 1996—; v.p. Environ. Health Scis., NSE Internat., 1998—; coun. pub. health cons. Nat. Sanitation Found., Ann Arbor, Mich., 1996-98; dir. NSF Internat./WHO Collaborating Ctr. for Water Safety and Tech.; adj. prof. environ. scis. Am. U., 1997; mem. rsch. adv. bd. Nat. Water Rsch. Inst.; mem. sci. adv. bd. Santa Ana River Water Quality and Health; ind. adv. bd. Tampa Water Resource Reuse Panel, 1997-98. Co-editor: Ozone/Chlorine Dioxide, 1978, Water Chlorination, 1983, Procs. Safe Drinking Water in Small Sys.: Tech., Ops. and Econs., 1999; chmn., editor book series NATO/CCMS Drinking Water Pilot, 1980; contbr. articles to jours. in field. Recipient Environ. Leadership award Nat. Sanitation Found., Ann Arbor, 1988, Donald R. Boyd award Assn. Met. Water Agys., 1990; named Meritorious Exec., Pres. U.S., 1983. Mem. Am. Chem Soc., Am. Water Works Assn. (life, mem. editorial adv. bd. Jour., 1987-90). Roman Catholic. Avocations: woodworking, light construction. Office: NSF Internat 1301 K St NW # 225 Washington DC 20005-3317

COTSAKOS, CHRISTOS MICHAEL, internet financial services company executive; b. Paterson, N.J., July 29, 1948; s. Michael John and Lillian (Scoulikas) C.; m. Hannah Batami Fogel, July 1, 1973; 1 child, Suzanne Renee. BA in Communications and Polit. Sci., William Paterson Coll., 1972; MBA, Pepperdine U., 1984. Tour guide Universal Studios, Burbank, Calif., 1973; courier Fed. Express Corp., Burbank, 1973-74; sales rep. Fed. Express Corp., Long Beach, Calif., 1974; sta. mgr. Fed. Express Corp., San Jose, Calif., 1974; we. dist. mgr. Fed. Express Corp., 1974; region engring. mgr. Fed. Express Corp., Denver, 1975; mng. dir. Fed. Express Corp., Chgo., 1975-80; v.p. Fed. Express Corp., Sacramento, Calif., 1980-92; pres., chief operating officer Nielsen, Europe, Middle East, Africa, 1992-93; pres., chief exec. officer Nielsen Internat., 1993-95; pres., co-chief exec. officer, chief operating officer, dir. A.C. Nielsen, Inc., 1995-96; pres., chief exec. officer E*TRADE Group, Inc., Palo Alto, Calif., 1996—; instr. Consumers River Coll., Placerville, Calif., 1985-86; bd. dirs. Airlifeline, Sacramento, Nat. Processing, Inc., Louisville, Forté Software, Inc., Oakland, 4th Comms. Network, San Jose, Datacard, Mpls. Served as sgt. U.S. Army, 1967-70, Vietnam. Decorated Bronze Star, 1967, Purple Heart, 1967. Mem. World Econ Forum (Davos, Switzerland), Sutter Club, Comstock Club. Office: E*TRADE Group Inc 2400 Geng Rd Palo Alto CA 94030

COTSONAS, NICHOLAS JOHN, JR., physician, medical educator; b. Boston, Jan. 28, 1919; s. Nicholas John and Louise Catherine (Lapham) C.; m. Betty Borge, Nov. 21, 1970; children by previous marriage: Nicholas III, Bruce, Elena. A.B., Harvard, 1940; M.D. cum laude, Georgetown U., 1943. Intern D.C. Gen. Hosp., Washington, 1944; resident in chest diseases D.C. Gen. Hosp., 1946-47, asst. med. resident, 1947-48, chief med. resident, 1948-49; asst. prof. medicine Georgetown U. Sch. Medicine, 1949-53; chief med. officer, med. div. D.C. Gen. Hosp., 1951-53; asst. prof. medicine U. Ill. Coll. Medicine, Chgo., 1953-57; assoc. prof. U. Ill. Coll. Medicine, 1957-62, prof., 1962-70; dean, prof. medicine Peoria Sch. Medicine, U. Ill., 1970-79; prof. medicine U. Ill., Chgo., 1979-90, prof. emeritus, 1989—, assoc. vice chancellor for acad. affairs, 1979-82; mem. Bradley Assocs., 1972-79; bd. dirs. Ill. Heart Assn., 1972-79, pres., 1976-77; bd. dirs. Ill. Central Health Systems Agy., 1976-79, Planned Parenthood Assn. Greater Peoria Area, 1971-79; mem. Statewide Health Coordinating Council, 1978-79; bd. dirs. Chgo. Heart Assn., 1980-82, Inst. Religion and Medicine, 1980; mem. task force on older women Ill. Council on Aging, 1985-86; chmn. Commn. on Health Resources Allocation, Peoria, Ill., 1985-87. Asst. editor: Disease-A-Month, 1960-77; asso. editor, 1977-80, editor, 1980-86, emeritus, 1987. Served to capt. AUS, 1944-46. Recipient Raymond Allen award U. Ill. Coll. Medicine, 1955, Faculty of Yr. award, 1978. Fellow A.C.P., Am. Heart Assn. (council clin. cardiology 1963), Am. Coll. Cardiology, Inst. Medicine Chgo., Am. Geriatrics Soc.; mem. Am. Fedn. Clin. Research, Chgo. Soc. Internal Medicine, Harvard Soc. Chemists, Sigma Xi, Alpha Omega Alpha.

COTTAM, KEITH M., librarian, educator, administrator; b. St. George, Utah, Feb. 13, 1941; s. Von Bunker and Adrene (McArthur) C.; m. Laurel Springer, June 16, 1961; children—Mark Patrick, Lisa Diane, Andrea Jill, Brian Lowell, Heather Dawn. BS, Utah State U., 1963; MLS, Pratt Inst., 1965. Trainee Bklyn. Pub. Library, 1963-65, asst. instr. reading improvement program, 1964-65, adult services librarian, 1965; asst. social scis. librarian, instr. So. Ill. U., Edwardsville, 1965-67; head, social sci. librarian, instr. asst. prof. Social Scis. Library, Brigham Young U., Provo, Utah, 1967-72; supr., inst. Library Technician Program Brigham Young U., Provo, Utah, 1969-72; head undergrad. library, assoc. prof. U. Tenn., Knoxville, 1972-75, asst. dir. libraries, assoc. prof., 1975-77; asst. dir. for pub. services and employee relations Vanderbilt U. Library (formerly Joint Univ. Libraries), Nashville, 1977-80, assoc. dir., 1980-82, acting dir., 1982-83; dir. libraries, prof. U. Wyo., Laramie, 1983—; vis. lectr. U. Tenn., 1972-77; vis. asst. prof. Vanderbilt U., 1979-80; adj. prof. journalism U. Wyo., 1987-89; vis. lectr. comm. and mass media, 1990, 94; cons., adv. to various orgns. in Tenn., Ill., Wyo.; advisor Nat. Inst. Adminstrn., Saigon, Vietnam, 1971; pres. Tenn. Libr. Assn., 1979-80; cons. tng. program office of mgmt. studies Assn. of Rsch. Librs., 1979-80. Author: Writer's Research handbook, 1977, 2d edit., 1978; editor Utah Libraries jour., 1971-72; mem. editorial bd. RQ jour., 1980-84; contbr. articles to profl. jours. Fellow Council Library Resources, 1975-76; sr. fellow UCLA Grad. Sch. Library Info. Sci., 1985-86. Mem. ALA, Assn. Coll. Rsch. Librs., Wyo. Library Assn. (pres. 1998-99), Beta Phi Mu, Phi Kappa Phi. Republican. Mem. Ch. of Jesus Christ of Latter-day Saints. Avocations: bicycling, racing and touring; free-lance writer; gardening. Home: 1251 N 21st St Apt E-34 Laramie WY 82072 Office: U Wyo Libraries PO Box 3334 University Sta Laramie WY 82071

COTTEN, CATHERYN DEON, medical center international advisor; b. Erwin, N.C., Apr. 13, 1952; d. Ben Hur and Minnie Lee (Smith) C. BS in Anthropology, Duke U., 1975. Asst. internat. advisor Med. Ctr. Duke U., Durham, N.C., 1975-76; internat. advisor Med. Ctr. Duke U., Durham, 1976—. Editor and contbr. chpt. to Advisors Manual of Federal Regulations Affecting Foreign Students and Scholars. Key vol. City of Durham, 1990-91; pres. Durham County Lit. Coun., 1992-94. Recipient Cert. Recognition So. Regional Coun. Black Am. Affairs, Atlanta, 1985. Mem. Nat. Assn. Fgn. Student Affairs: Assn. Internat. Educators (gov. regulations adv. com. 1985-96, nat. chair 1991-94, chair Southeastern region 1989-90), Altrusa Club (pres. Durham chpt. 1987-89). Office: Duke U Med Ctr PO Box 3882 Durham NC 27710

COTTEN, SAMUEL RICHARD, former state legislator, fisherman; b. Juneau, Alaska, July 16, 1947; s. Samuel L. Cotten and Kathryn Russell; m. Martha Tillion, June 16, 1984; children: Samuel Tillion, Augustus O'Dwyer Russell. AA, U. Alaska, 1971. Rep. Alaskan Ho. Of Reps., Juneau, 1975-82, 85-90, speaker, 1989-91; senator Alaska State Senate, Juneau, 1991-93; chmn. Alaska Pub. Utilities Commn., 1995—; chmn. Spl. Com. on Oil and Gas, chmn. Natural Resources, 1991-93; spl. advisor Intergovtl. Consultative Com. to North Pacific Fisheries Adv. Bd., 1989-92; advisor Internat. North Pacific Fisheries Commn., 1984-90; bd. dirs. Fire Lake Recreational Ctr., Eagle River, Alaska. Co-chmn. Alaska Criminal Code Revision Commn., Juneau, 1976; mem. Anchorage Planning and Zoning Commn., 1983-84; candidate for Gov. Alaska, 1994—; apptd. commr. Alaska Pub. Utilities Commn., 1995—, chmn., 1996—. Recipient Nat. Def. award Vietnam Svc. (2); named Outstanding Vietnam Vet. No Greater Love Found., 1976. Mem. Cook Inlet Seiners Assn., Navy League, Elks, VFW (life), Anchorage Ski Club. Democrat. Avocations: fishing, skiing, bowling. Home: PO Box 770296 Eagle River AK 99577-0296

COTTEN-HUSTON, ANNIE LAURA, psychologist, educator; b. Oxford, N.C., Nov. 18, 1923; d. Leonard F. and Laura Estelle (Spencer) Cotten; children: Hollis W., Rebecca Ann, Laura Cotten. Diploma, Hardbarger Bus. Coll., 1944; AB, Duke U., 1945; MEd, U. Hartford, 1965; PhD, The Union Inst., 1979. Diplomate Am. Bd. Sexology. Asst. to pres. So. Meth. U., 1953; rsch. asst. Duke U., 1947-49; exec. sec. Ohio Wesleyan U., 1955-56, Conn. Coun. Chs., 1958-60; adj. prof. U. Hartford, 1976-78, 1976-78; clin. pastoral counselor Hartford Hosp., 1962-65; asst., then assoc. dir. social svcs. Hartford Conf. Chs., 1965-67; tchg. fellow U. N.C., 1970-71; assoc. prof. Ctrl. Conn. State U., New Britain, 1967-93, adj. prof., 1994—; adj. prof. St. Joseph Coll., 1986-96; clin. intern Montefiore Med. Ctr., 1995; dir. elderhostel programs Ctrl. Conn. State U., 1989-93, organizer ctr. adult learners, 1991-93; cons. Somers Correctional Ctr., Conn., 1980-81, instr./rschr., 1980-81; cons. Life Ins. Mktg. Rsch., 1981—; amb. to China, spring, 1986; presenter 3d Internat. Interdisciplinary Cong. on Women, 1987; vis. prof., scholar Duke U., 1989; adj. prof. health and human svcs. Ctrl. Ch. St. U., 1995—; vis. prof. Conn. Coll., New London, 1990; mem. clin. faculty, supr. Am. Bd. Sexology, 1994, 94; land developer N.C. Triangle, 1995—. *Annie Laura Cotten-Huston is currently teaching and training students in mental and family therapy in Connecticut. She has begun land development of worked property inherited from parents in Granville County, North Carolina (Triangle Area). She has published research in 1998-1999 in the fields of women's studies and human sexuality (mothers/daughters; anger management; contracting homophobia).* Organizer Elder Hostel Affiliate Network, 1991. Mem. AAUW, APA (chair divsn. 1987-91), Am. Assn. Marriage and Family Therapists (lic. 1987), Nat. Coun. Family Rels., Am. Assn. Sex Educators, Counselors and Therapists (cert. Outstanding Svc. 1996, Disting. Svc. award 1998), Conn. Psychol. Assn., Conn. Coun. Chs. (dir.), Sex Info. and Edn. Coun. of Conn. (bd. dirs. 1994—, Human Sexuality Leader of Yr. 1997), Hartford Women's Network. Home: 193 Westland Ave West Hartford CT 06107-3057 Office: Ctrl Conn State U Dept Psychology New Britain CT 06050

COTTER, CORNELIUS PHILIP, political scientist, educator; b. N.Y.C., Mar. 18, 1924; s. Cornelius Joseph and Charlotte F. (Keller) C.; m. Rose Marie Ackerl, 1946 (div. 1961); children: Cornelia, Lawrence, Charles, Steven; m. Beverly Blair Cook, 1966; children: Linda, C. Randall, Gary A., Scott. BA, Stanford U., 1949; MPA, Harvard U., 1951, PhD, 1953. Asst., then assoc. prof. Stanford (Calif.) U., 1953-61; asst. to chmn. (on leave from Stanford U.) Rep. Nat. Com., Washington, 1958-60; asst. dir. U.S. Commn. Civil Rights, Washington, 1960-63; prof. polit. sci. Wichita (Kans.) State U., 1963-66; prof. polit. sci. U. Wis., Milw., 1966-89, prof. emeritus, 1989—; instr. Columbia Univ., N.Y.C., 1953-54. Author: Government and Private Enterprise, 1960; co-author: Powers of President During Crises, 1960, Politics Without Power, 1964, Party Organizations in Am. Politics, 1984, others. Disting. Univ. Prof., Univ. Bologna, Fulbright Found., 1988. Mem. Am. Polit. Sci. Assn., Midwest Polit. Sci. Assn. Republican. Home: 9040 Junipero Ave Atascadero CA 93422-5210

COTTER, DANIEL A., diversified company executive; b. Duluth, Minn., Dec. 26, 1934. B.A., Marquette U., 1957; M.B.A., Northwestern U., 1960. With Truserv Corp., Chgo., 1959—, chmn., CEO. Office: Truserv Corp 8600 W Bryn Mawr Ave Chicago IL 60631-3579

COTTER, DENNIS JOSEPH, health services company executive; b. Boston, Dec. 25, 1946; s. Francis Henry and Esther (Milmore) C.; m. Mari Anne Hamilton, Oct. 23, 1982; children: Nicholas, Alexandra, Anastashia, Zachary. BS in Paper Engring./BSChemE, U. Lowell, Mass., 1969; MS in Chem./Biomed. Engring., Ariz. State U., 1974. Biomed. engr. Dept. Health Human Svcs./USPHS, Silver Spring, Md., 1976-79; dep. assoc. dir. Dept. Health Human Svcs./USPHS, Rockville, Md., 1979-82, sr. health policy analyst, 1982-83; co-founder Tech. Diffusion Assocs., Potomac, Md., 1983-84; health care tech. cons. Inst. for Health Policy, Washington, 1983-84; sr. health policy analyst ProPAC, Washington, 1984-85; staff assoc. Inst. for Health Policy, Washington, 1985-86; pres. Med. Tech. and Practice Pattern, Washington, 1986—; adj. prof. Georgetown U., Washington. Contbr. articles to profl. jours. U. Lowell Edwards scholar, 1965-69; VA grantee, 1976, USPHS grantee, 1982. Mem. AAAS, Assn. for Health Svcs. Rsch., Internat. Soc. Tech. Assessment of Health Care, Sigma Xi. Office: Med Tech & Practice Pattern Inst 4733 Bethesda Ave Ste 510 Bethesda MD 20814

COTTER, DOUGLAS ADRIAN, healthcare executive; b. Brockport, N.Y., Aug. 15, 1943; s. Adrian Edwards and Rita Elizabeth (Marshall) C.; m. Rosalyn DeVaughn, June 12, 1965 (div.); children: Elizabeth D., Anne R.; m. Anne Holmes Thompson, Oct. 4, 1986. BS, Duke U., 1965; MS, N.C. State U., 1967, PhD, 1970. Rsch. engr. Corning Glass Works, Raleigh, N.C., 1966-69, mgr. rsch. & devel., 1970-78; bus. devel. mgr. Corning Med. Europe, Halstead, Essex, England, 1978-80; portfolio mgr. Corning (N.Y.) Glass Works, 1980-83; dir. info. systems Corning Med., Medfield, Mass., 1984-85; pres. Healthcare Decisions Inc., Norwood, Mass., 1986-96; v.p. Decision Resources Inc., Waltham, Mass., 1996-98; pres. Healthcare Decisions, Inc., Walpole, Mass., 1998—; adj. prof. Boston U., 1985—, N.C. State U., 1973-76; dir. Respironics Inc., Murrysville, Pa., 1989—; dir. Applied Microbiology, Tarrytown, N.Y., 1995-96. Inventor/patentee in field. Mem. Inst. Elec. Engrs. (sr. mem.), Nat. Assn. Corp. Dirs., Licensing Exec. Soc. Avocations: sailing, tennis. Office: Healthcare Decisions Inc 1600 Providence Hwy Walpole MA 02081-2553

COTTER, JAMES MICHAEL, lawyer; b. Providence, May 12, 1942; s. James Henry and Marguerite Louise (Clark) C.; m. Melinda Irene Tighe, Feb. 6, 1971; children: Elizabeth, Heather, Kathryn. AB, Fairfield U., 1964; LLB, U. Va., 1967. Bar: N.Y. 1967. Assoc. Simpson Thacher & Bartlett, N.Y.C., 1967-75, ptnr., 1975—. Trustee Fairfield U., 1995—; bd. dirs. M.G.A. Found., 1990—, chmn., 1990-92. Mem. ABA, N.Y. State Bar Assn., N.Y. Law Inst. (bd. dirs. 1984—, chmn. exec. com. 1993—), Met. Golf Assn. (bd. dirs. 1974—, pres. 1990-92), Greenwich Conn. Country Club, Hudson Nat. Golf Club, Union League Club (N.Y.). Office: Simpson Thacher & Bartlett 425 Lexington Ave Fl 15 New York NY 10017-3954

COTTER, JOHN BURLEY, ophthalmologist, corneal specialist; b. Zanesville, Ohio, Sept. 14, 1946; s. John Burley and Evelyn Virginia (Ross) C.; m. Perrine Abauzit, Aug. 17, 1977; children: Neils John, Jeremy Pierre. BA, U. Kans., 1968; med. degree, U. Kans., Kansas City, 1968-72. Ophthalmology resident U. Mo., Kansas City, 1976-79; family practice Ashland (Kans.) Hosp., 1973-74; emergency room physician Providence-St. Margaret Hosp., Kansas City, Kans., 1974-75; family orthopedic practice Mountain Med. Assocs., Vail, Colo., 1975-76; ophthalmologist, pvt. practice Duluth, Minn., 1979-82; surgeon-chief out-patient clinic King Khaled Eye Specialist Hosp., Riyadh, Saudi Arabia, 1983-90, mem. exec. com., 1985-90; asst. clin. prof. King Saud U., Riyadh, Saudi Arabia, 1985-90; corneal splst., refractive surgeon in assn. Greensboro, N.C., 1990-98; seminar chmn. Status of Refractive Surgery, Riyadh, 1986; active Nat. Survey Eye Disease and Ea. Province Survey Coun., Saudi Arabia, 1984, 90. Author: (booklet) Radial Keratotomy, 1986; contbr. articles to profl. jours. Rsch. grantee Contact Lens Assn. of Ophthalmology, 1981, Lasers Steering Com. King Khalid Eye Hosp. at Hosp. Hotel Dieu, Paris, 1988; ORBIS fellow Baylor U., Houston, 1982. Fellow Am. Acad. Ophthalmology; mem. AMA, Internat. Assn. Ocular Surgeons, Internat. Soc. Refractive Keratoplasty, Societe Francaise D'Ophthalmologie, Saudi Ophthalmologisl Soc., Am. Soc. Cataract and Refractive Surgery. Independent. Avocations: wind surfing, scuba diving, running, math games. Office: 721 Green Valley Rd Greensboro NC 27408-7013

COTTER, JOSEPH FRANCIS, retired hotel and bank executive; b. Brockton, Mass., May 18, 1927; s. Joseph and Sarah (Thornell) C.; m. Catherine Sullivan, 1950 (dec.); m. Barbara Tribou Salter, 1986. BS cum laude, Boston Coll., 1949. CPA, Mass., N.Y. Accountant Price Waterhouse & Co., N.Y.C., 1949-67; v.p., contr. Howard Johnson Co., Braintree, Mass., 1967-70; exec. v.p., comptr., dir. Sheraton Corp., Boston, 1970-85, exec. v.p. planning and devel., 1985-87; ret., 1987-89; exec. Bank of Boston, 1989-95; ret., 1995. Former vice chmn. bd. trustees Boston Coll.; former chmn. bd. dirs. Greater Boston YMCA.; former v.p., bd. dirs. Greater Boston C. of C.; former trustee Dana-Farber Cancer Rsch. Inst.; former bd. dirs. United Way of Mass. Bay. Mem. AICPA, N.Y. Soc. CPAs, Mass. Soc. CPAs, Boston Coll. Alumni Assn. (past pres.), Jonathan's Landing Golf Club (pres.). Home: 15925 Westerly Ter Jupiter FL 33477-2304 Home (summer): 47 Peebles Point Rd Cape Elizabeth ME 04107

COTTER, LAWRENCE RAFFETY, management consultant; b. Albany, Calif., Aug. 13, 1933; s. Malcolm Thompson Cotter and Una Elyse Raffety. AA, U. Calif., Berkeley, 1953, BA in Astronomy, 1956; MS in Bus. Adminstrn., The George Washington U., 1967; PhD in Mgmt. Theory, UCLA, 1977. Commd. 2nd lt. USAF, 1956, advanced through grades to col., 1975, ret., 1982; orbital analyst, network controller Project Space Track USAF, Bedford, Mass., 1958-61; staff scientist Hdqs. N.Am. Air Def. Command, Colorado Springs, Colo., 1962-66, Hdqrs. USAF, Washington, 1967-70; dir. test and deployment DEF. Support program USAF, Los Angeles, 1975-76; commdr. detachment 1 Electronic Systems Div. USAF, Tehran, Iran, 1976-78; system program dir. Electronic Systems div. USAF, Bedford, Mass., 1978-79; dep. commdr. network plans and devel. AF Satellite Control Facility USAF, Sunnyvale, Calif., 1979-82; mgmt. cons. Berkeley, 1982—; adminstrv. asst. Arnold Air Soc., Washington, 1959-72. Co-author: The Arnold Air Soc. Manual, 1956; (computer program) SPACE, 1970; editor: The Arnold Air Soc. Manual 1964-72. Recipient Departmental Citation U. Calif. Berkeley, 1955, Citation of Honor, Arnold Air Soc., 1967. Mem. AF Assn., The Royal AF Club, Beta Gamma Sigma.

COTTER, MICHAEL WILLIAM, retired ambassador, business consultant; b. Madison, Wis., Aug. 1, 1943; s. Patrick William and Lois Katherine (Schaus) C.; m. Joanne Marie Miller, Aug. 30, 1974. BSFS, Georgetown U., 1965; JD, U. Mich., 1968; MS, Stanford U., 1976. Polit.-mil. affairs officer Am. Embassy, Ankara, Turkey, 1980-82; sr. Turkish desk officer U.S. Dept. State, Washington, 1982-84; polit. officer Am. Embassy, Kinshasa, Zaire, 1984-86, polit. counselor, 1986-88; mgmt. analyst sec. of mgmt. U.S. Dept. State, 1988-90, office dir. politico-military affairs, 1990-92; dep. chief of mission Am. Embassy, Santiago, Chile, 1992-95; U.S. amb. to Turkmenistan, 1995-98; internat. bus. cons., Washington, 1999—. Mem. Am. Fgn. Svc. Assn. (sec. 1989-91, bd. govs. 1988-89), Wis. Bar Assn. Home and Office: 4415 Springdale St NW Washington DC 20016-2715

COTTER, WILLIAM DONALD, state commissioner, former newspaper editor; b. Hartford, Conn., June 5, 1921; s. William Joseph and Alice I. (Murphy) C.; m. Alice K. Liller, Jan. 22, 1944; children: Carol A., Mary L., Alice E., William J., James D., Donald W. B.A., Fordham U., 1943; postgrad. polit. sci., St. John U., 1956-57, Syracuse U., 1958. Reporter L.I. Star-Jour., Long Island City, 1947-51; night city editor Nassau Rev., Rockville Centre, N.Y., 1952-53; night editor Jersey Jour., Jersey City, 1954; mag., Sunday editor L.I. Press, Jamaica, N.Y., 1955-58; city editor Syracuse Herald-Jour./Am., 1958-66, editor, 1966-83; chmn. N.Y. State Energy Research and Devel. Authority, 1983-92; commr. N.Y. State Energy Office, 1983-92, N.Y. State Public Svc. Commn., 1992-96; trustee N.Y. Power Authority, 1989-92; instr. journalism Syracuse U., 1960-66. Former bd. dirs. Community Gen. Hosp., Boys Town of Italy, Erie Canal Mus.; past chmn. communications com. LeMoyne Coll.; chmn. Onondaga County Energy Com., 1975-83. Served with USNR, 1943-46. Mem. N.Y. State Soc. Newspaper Editors (pres.), Auburn Golf and Country Club (dir.). Roman Catholic. Home: 55 Shadowwood Way Ballston Lake NY 12019-1213

COTTER, WILLIAM RECKLING, college president; b. Detroit, Mar. 9, 1936; s. Fred Joseph and Esther Jean (Reckling) C.; m. Linda Jane Kester, June 14, 1959; children: David Andrew, Deborah Anne, Elizabeth Anne. B.A. in Polit. Sci. magna cum laude, Harvard U., 1958, J.D. cum laude, 1961; LHD (hon.), Bowdoin Coll., 1987, West Brook Coll., 1995. Bar: N.Y. 1962, U.S. Supreme Ct. 1965. Law clk. to U.S. Fed. Judge, N.Y.C., 1961-62; M.I.T. fellow in Africa Nigeria, 1962-63; assoc. firm Cahill, Gordon, Sonnett, Reindell & Ohl, N.Y.C., 1963-65; White House fellow Washington, 1965-66; Ford Found. rep. to Colombia and Venezuela, 1966-70; pres. African-Am. Inst., N.Y.C., 1970-79, Colby Coll., 1979—. Contbr. articles on fgn. policy and edn. to profl. jours. Bd. dirs. Pvt. Agys. Collaborating Together, 1975-81, Waterville ARC, 1980-87, Kennebec Valley Regional Health Agy., 1982-88, Mid-Maine Econ. Devel. Corp.; chmn. bd. trustees Oyster Bay-East Norwich (N.Y.) Pub. Libr., 1975-79; trustee African-Am. Inst., 1970—; bd. dirs. Maine Pub. Broadcasting; chair bd. dirs. Waterville Regional Arts and Cmty. Ctr.; chair adv. com. Oak Found.; chmn. bd. visitors Baxter Sch. for the Deaf, 1982-87; chmn. com. for study ct. structure, probate and family law matters, 1985; bd. advisors Carrabassett Valley Acad., 1981-91; chair com. on pub. disclosure New Eng. Assn. Schs. and Colls., 1987; trustee Westbrook Coll., 1986-92; past mem. exec. com. South African Edn. Program; past mem. commn. on govt. rels. Am. Coun. on Edn.; commr. State of Maine Edn. Commn.; mem. Nat. Commn. on Responsibilities for Financing Postsecondary Edn., 1991-93; bd. visitors U. Maine Sch. Law; past chair and dir. Nat. Assn. Ind. Colls. and Univs. Named Educator of Yr. The Washington Ctr., 1993, Leader of Yr., Equity Inst. Maine, 1996, Disting. Citizen Waterville C. of C. 1998. Mem. Nat. Assn. Ind. Colls. and Univs. (past chair and dir.), Coun. Fgn. Rels., Harvard Club (N.Y.C.), Harvard Club (Boston). Office: Colby Coll Office of Pres Waterville ME 04901

COTTER-SMITH, CATHLEEN MARIE, art educator, artist; b. Dallas, 1950; d. Robert Jay and Betty Ann Cotter; 1 child, Ryan Patrick Holt; m.

Jack Glendon Smith, Jr., 1991. BS, East Tex. State U., 1974; MS, Tex. A&M U., Commerce, 1977. Freelance artist, Garland and Plano, Tex., 1976—; assoc. prof. art Grayson County Coll., Dennison, Tex., 1981-85; prof. art Collin County C.C., Plano, Tex., 1986—, coord. art dept., 1986-97; cons. on book Equine Images, 1992. One-woman Show Cultural Art Ctr., Plano, 1990, Collin County C. C. Gallery, Plano, 1994; exhibited in group show S.W. Watercolor Soc., Dallas, 1990; represented in permanent collection Farmerville C. of C. Mentor Boles Children's Home, Quinlan, Tex., 1996-99. Mem. S.W. Watercolor Soc. Republican. Mem. Ch. of Christ. Avocation: nature lover. Office: Collin County CC 2800 E Spring Creek Pky Plano TX 75074

COTTING, JAMES CHARLES, manufacturing company executive; b. Winchester, Mass., Oct. 15, 1933; s. Edward L. and Mary Ellen (Worrell) C.; m. Marjorie A. Kirsch, Feb. 8, 1963; children: James Charles, Steven Robert, Brenda Ann-Marie. BA cum laude, Ohio State U., 1955. Acctg. supr. U.S. Steel Corp., Pitts., 1959-61; mgr. profit analysis Ford Motor Co., Dearborn, Mich., 1961-63; mgr. devel. planning A.O. Smith Corp., Milw., 1963-66; asst. contr. Gen. Foods Corp., White Plains, N.Y., 1966-71; v.p. planning Internat. Paper Co., N.Y.C., 1971-76, v.p., contr., 1976-79; sr. v.p. fin. and planning, CFO Navistar Internat. Corp., Chgo., 1979-82, exec. v.p. fin., 1982-83, vice chmn., CFO, 1983-87, chmn., CEO, 1987-95, chmn. bd., 1995-96; mem. Pres. Reagan's Task Force on Mkt. Mechanisms; bd. dirs. ASARCO Inc., USG Corp., Chgo. Stock Exch. Dir. Jr. Achievement of Chgo.; trustee Adler Planetarium. Lt. USN, 1955-58. Mem. Comml. Club Chgo., Econ. Club Chgo., Montclair Golf Club, Barrington Hills Country Club, Chgo. Club, Phi Beta Kappa, Alpha Tau Omega.

COTTINGHAM, RICHARD SUMNER, paper company executive; b. Columbus, Ohio, May 7, 1941; s. Robert E. and Lee Alice (Gasaway) C.; B.A. in History, Ohio State U., 1964; m. Sheila L. Robertson, Dec. 20, 1980. Pres., Cottingham Paper Co., Columbus, Ohio, 1968—. Bd. dirs. Network Svcs. Co., 1984-90, chmn., 1986-88. Served as lt. (j.g.) USN, 1964-67; Vietnam. Recipient Ernst & Young Master Entrepreneur of Yr. award for Columbus and Ctr. Ohio, 1998. Mem. Nat. Paper Trade Assn. (young exec. com. 1976), Am. Mgmt. Assn., Nat. Assn. Wholesale Distbrs., Internat. Sanitary Supply Assn., Econ. Club Columbus, Columbus C. of C., Ohio C. of C. Worthington Country Club. Republican. Address: Cottingham Paper Co 324 E 2d Ave PO Box 163579 Columbus OH 43216-3579

COTTINGHAM, STEPHEN KENT, real estate development executive, researcher; b. Denver, Dec. 28, 1951; s. Miles Dixon and Ruth (Skeen) C.; m. Susan Kay Kelfer, Aug. 11, 1984. Student, So. Oreg. Coll., 1970-71; BBA, So. Meth. U., 1974; ThM, Dallas Theol. Sem., 1984. V.p. Cottingham Constrn. Co., Dallas, 1974-79; project mgmt. Avery Mays Constrn. Co., Dallas, 1981-82; asst. v.p. Pacific Realty Corp., Dallas, 1983-85, v.p., 1985-86, exec. v.p., 1986-88; v.p. Paragon Group, Dallas, 1988-91; regional v.p. The Prime Group Inc., San Antonio, Tex., 1991-93; pres. Brock Investment Group, Inc., San Antonio, 1993-95; chairman, pres. SKCI, Inc., San Antonio, 1995—; founder, chmn., pres. Theol. Edn. Found., Internat., 1996—; pres. Princeton Resources, Inc., 1992—; founder, chmn., pres. Cottingham Devel. Corp., San Antonio, 1997— ; adj. tchr. N.W. Bible Ch. Coll. Class, Dallas, 1981-83; student leader, counselor Young Life Internat., Dallas, 1974-76; chmn. Boyd Ministries, Norfolk, Va., 1996—; bd. dirs. Harvester Ministries, Plano, Tex. Charter mem. Rep. Nat. Com., Washington, 1985—; tchr. Christ Episcopal Ch., San Antonio, chmn. adult edn., exec. com.; founder, pres. Theol. Edn. Foun., Internat., San Antonio, 1996—. Named one of Outstanding Young Men of Am., Montgomery, Ala., 1986; So. Meth. U. Scholar, 1972-74. Mem. Urban Land Inst. (assoc.), Evang. Theol. Soc., Phi Gamma Delta (treas.), Phi Beta Lamda. Avocations: skiing, antique restoration, cycling, writing, travel, missionary work. Office: 9859 Ih 10 W Ste 225 San Antonio TX 78230-2295

COTTON, FRANK ALBERT, chemist, educator; b. Phila., Apr. 9, 1930; s. Albert and Helen (Taylor) C.; m. Diane Dornacher, June 13, 1959; children: Jennifer Helen, Jane Myrna. Student, Drexel Inst. Tech., 1947-49; AB, Temple U., 1951, DSc, 1963; PhD, Harvard U., 1955; Dr. rer. Nat. (hon.), Bielefeld U., 1979; DSc (hon.), Columbia U., 1980; D.Sc. (hon.), Northwestern U., 1981, U. Bordeaux, 1981, St. Joseph's U., 1982, U. Louis Pasteur, 1982, U. Valencia, 1983, Kenyon Coll., 1983, Technion-Israel Inst. Tech., 1983, U. Cambridge, 1986, Johann Wolfgang Goethe Universitât, 1989, U. S.C., 1989, U. Rennes, 1992, Lomonosov U., 1992, Fujian Inst. Rsch., Chinese Acad. Scis., 1993, U. Pisa, Italy, 1994, U. Zaragoza, 1994, Cleve. State U., 1995, U. Crete, 1996, Mich. State U., 1996, U. Pierre and Marie Curie, 1997. Instr. chemistry M.I.T., 1955-57, asst. prof., 1957-60, assoc. prof., 1960-61, prof., 1961-71; Robert A. Welch Distinguished prof. chemistry Tex. A&M U., 1971—, dir. Lab. for Molecular Stucture and Bonding, 1983—; Cons. Am. Cyanamid, Stamford, Conn., 1958-67, Union Carbide, N.Y.C., 1964—; Todd prof. U. Cambridge, 1985-86. Author: (with G. Wilkinson and P.L. Gaus) Basic Inorganic Chemistry, 3d edit., 1995, Chemical Applications of Group Theory, 3d edit., 1990, (with L. Lynch and C. Darlington) Chemistry, An Investigative Approach, (with G. Wilkinson) Advanced Inorganic Chemistry, 6th edit., 1999; editor: Progress in Inorganic Chemistry, Vols. 1-10, 1959-68, Inorganic Syntheses, Vol. 13, 1971, (with L.M. Jackman) Dynamic Nuclear Magnetic Resonance Spectroscopy, (with R.A. Walton) Multiple Bonds Between Metal Atoms, 2d edti., 1993 (with R.D. Adams) Catalysis by Di- and Polynuclear Metal Atom Clusters, 1998. Recipient Michelson-Morley award Case Western Res. U., 1980, Nat. Medal Sci., 1982, Paracelsus medal Swiss Chem. Soc., 1994, Polyhedron medal, 1995, Gold medal Am. Inst. Chemists; hon. fellow Robinson Coll., U. Cambridge. Mem. NAS (chmn. phys. scis. 1985-88, coun. 1991-94, gov. bd. NRC 1992-94, Cosepup 1992-94, chem. scis. bd. 1990, King Faisal Internat. prize 1990, Robert A. Welch award in chemistry 1994), Am. Soc. Biol. Chemists, Am. Chem. Soc. (awards 1962, 74, Baekeland medal N.J. sect. 1963, Nichols medal N.Y. sect. 1975, Pauling medal Oreg. and Puget Sound sect. 1976, Kirkwood medal N.Y. sect. 1978, Gibbs medal Chgo. sect. 1980, Richards medal N.E. sect. 1986, F.A. Cotton medal Tex. A&M sect. 1995, Priestley medal 1998), Am. Acad. Arts and Scis., N.Y. Acad. Scis. (life), Royal Soc. Chemistry (hon.), Royal Danish Acad. Scis. and Letters (hon.), Göttingen Acad. Scis., Societa Chimica Italiana (hon.), Indian Acad. Scis. (hon.), Indian Nat. Sci. Acad. (hon.) Royal Soc. Edinburgh (hon.), Am. Philos. Soc., Acad. Europea (hon.), Royal Soc. London (fgn.), Inst. de France (Acad. des Scis., fgn.). Home: 4101 Sand Creek Rd Bryan TX 77808-8337 Office: Tex A&M Univ Dept Of Chemistry College Station TX 77843

COTTON, JOHN PIERCE, principal; b. Winchester, Mass., Nov. 25, 1937; s. Dana Meserve and Geraldine (Pierce) C.; children: John E., Sarah P., Nathaniel C. H., Ethan S.; m. Tami Pleasanton, 1991. AB, Harvard U., 1960; MA, Colo. U., 1968. Trust asst. Old Colony Trust Co., Boston, 1962-64; head upper sch. Colo. Acad., Denver, 1964-68; headmaster Kimball Union Acad., Meriden, N.H., 1968-74, St. Andrew's Sch., Boca Raton, Fla., 1974-86; interim headmaster St. Stephen's Sch., Bradenton, Fla., 1986-87; prin. Francis W. Parker Sch., Chgo., 1987-93; headmaster Ransom Everglades Sch., Miami, Fla., 1993-98; trustee Gulfstream (Fla.) Sch., 1980-86. Lt. USNR, 1960-68. Mem. Fla. Coun. Ind. Schs. (pres., bd. dirs. 1976-86), Coun. Religion in Ind. Schs. (trustee 1980-87), Ind. Schs. Assn. Greater Chgo. (v.p. 1989-90, pres. 1990-93), Ind. Schs. Assn. Ctrl. States (bd. dirs. 1990-93). Homę: 633 Castilla Ln Boynton Beach FL 33435-6103

COTTON, JOYCE E. DOHERTY, mental health nurse; b. Stoneham, Mass., Sept. 4, 1952; d. Joseph Francis and Anne M. (Bickford) Doherty; m. Paul Briggs Cotton, Oct. 28, 1979; 1 stepchild, Charlotte; 1 child, Katherine Anne. Diploma, Lawrence Gen. Hosp. Sch. Nsg., 1973; BA in Psychology cum laude, Salem State Coll., 1978, MEd in Counseling, 1981. Cert. advanced practice RN, Maine, 1996. Team leader med.-surg. unit Lawrence (Mass.) Gen. Hosp., 1973-75; head nurse adolescent day treatment program Mass. Dept. Mental Health, Danvers (Mass.) State Hosp., 1976-78; psychiat. nurse, case mgr. adolescent aftercare program Greater Lawrence Area Office Mass. Dept. Mental Health, 1978-80, aftercare nurse day treatment ctr., 1980-81, coord. adult aftercare program, 1981-82; dir. aftercare clinic Greater Lynn (Mass.) Community Mental Health Ctr., 1982-85; psychiatric nurse Jackson Brook Inst., Maine, 1985-86; clin. nurse specialist Androscoggin Home Health Svcs., Auburn, Maine, 1986-87, clin. nurse specialist cons., 1987—; clin. nurse specialist Western Maine Counseling Svc., Brigton, 1987-90, clin. dir., 1990-91; asst. dir. nursing Jackson Brook Inst., South Portland, Maine, 1991-95, dir. nursing ambulatory care svcs., 1995-99; dir. clin. ops. Shoreline Cmty. Mental Health Ctr., Brunswick, Maine, 1999—; bd. dirs. Western Maine Counseling Svc., Solstice Adolescent Treatment Program, Office for Children in Lawrence. Recipient cert. of appreciation Greater Lynn Mental Health and Retardation Assn., 1984, North Shore Coll., 1985. Mem. ANA (cert. clin. nurse specialist in adult psychiat. and mental health nursing), Maine Assn. Clin. Nurse Speciialists, 1993—, Sigma Theta Tau. Home: 11 Countryfield Cir Kennebunk ME 04043 Office: Shoreline Cmty Mental Health Ctr 18 Pleasant St Brunswick ME 04011

COTTON, KAREN THERESA, audiologist; b. Detroit, Aug. 20, 1953; d. Arthur Russell Burgee and Shirley Rose Wilbert; m. Demetri Alexander Cotton, June 18, 1977 (div. 1985); 1 child, Aaron Alexander Cotton. BA, Mich. State U., 1975; MS, U. Oshkosh, 1991. Radiologic technologist Mich. Osteo. Med. Ctr., Detroit, 1980-88; audiologist Dr. Leslie Schier, Chgo., 1998, Dr. Antonio DeLeon, Chgo., 1992-98, Timbre Hearing Ctr., Columbia, Mo., 1998—. Office: Timbre Hearing Ctr 1504 E Broadway # 219 Columbia MO 65202

COTTON, LARRY, ranching executive. Pres. Cotton, Scheer & Assocs., Howell, Mich. Office: Cotton Scheer and Assocs 131 Robin Ct Howell MI 48843-8776*

COTTON, RICHARD, lawyer; b. Washington, July 1, 1944; s. Eugene and Sylvia Ruth (Glickstein) C.; m. Patricia B. Fellner, Oct. 11, 1981; children: Rachel, Jonathan. AB, Harvard Coll., 1965; LLB cum laude, Yale U., 1969. Bar: N.H. 1971, Calif. 1974, D.C. 1980, U.S. Ct. Appeals (D.C. cir.) 1984, U.S. Supreme Ct. 1980. Law clk. to judge J. Skelly Wright U.S. Ct. Appeals D.C. Cir., 1969-70; law clk. to justice Wm. J. Brennan Jr. U.S. Supreme Ct., 1970-71; mng. atty. N.H. Legal Assistance, Concord, 1972-73; staff atty. Nat. Resources Def. Coun., Palo Alto, Calif., 1974-77; exec. sec. U.S. Dept. HEW, Washington, 1978-79; ptnr. Califano, Ross & Heineman, Washington, 1981-83, Dewey, Ballantine, Washington, 1983-86; pres., chief exec. officer HCX, Inc., Washington, 1987-89; exec. v.p., gen. counsel NBC, N.Y.C., 1989—; chair bd. dirs. N.Y. Primary Care Devel. Corp., 1993—; lectr. in law U. Calif., Berkeley, 1973-74. Mem. Nat. Assn. Broadcasters (mem. exec. bd. 1995-96). Office: NBC 30 Rockefeller Plz Fl 52 New York NY 10112-0002*

COTTON, STACEY W., federal judge. Chief bankruptcy judge U.S. Bankruptcy Ct. (no. dist.) Ga., Atlanta. Office: 1415 US Courthouse 75 Spring St SW Atlanta GA 30303-3309

COTTON, W(ILLIAM) PHILIP, JR., architect; b. Columbia, Mo., July 11, 1932; s. William Philip and Frances Barbara (Harrington) C. AB, Princeton U., 1954; MArch, Harvard U., 1960. Registered architect, Mo., Ill. Pvt. practice architecture St. Louis, 1964—. Author (book) 100 Historic Buildings in St. Louis County, 1970. Treas. New Music Circle, St. Louis, 1968-96, Pub. Revenue Edn. Coun., St. Louis, 1977—; v.p. Music Diversions Soc., St. Louis, 1993—. Mem. AIA (Ctrl. States Spl. Honor award 1981, Rozier award for Hist. Preservation 1991), Valley Sailing Club (commodore 1985). Roman Catholic. Home: 5145 Lindell Blvd Saint Louis MO 63108-1221 Office: W Philip Cotton Jr Arch ste 1410 1221 Locust St Saint Louis MO 63103-2364

COTTON, WILLIAM ROBERT, dentist, retired; b. Miami, Fla., Nov. 29, 1931; s. Robert Lee and Mamie Bell (Daniel) C.; m. Marye Ruth Hartz; children: Caroline Ruth, William Robert Jr., David Michael, Lynn Cathryn. DDS, U. Md., 1955; MS, Northwestern U., Chgo., 1963; MA, Roosevelt U., 1973; EdS, George Washington U., 1980. With USN, 1955-81, commd. capt., 1973, ret., 1981; asst. dental officer Marine Corps Schs. and USS F.D. Roosevelt CVA 42, Quantico, Va. and Mayport, Fla., 1957-61; head exptl. pathology div. Naval Med. Rsch. Inst., Bethesda, Md., 1963-67; dental officer USS Fulton AS-11, New London, Conn., 1967-69; chief histopathology div. Naval Dental Rsch. Inst., Great Lakes, Ill., 1969-72, exec. officer, 1972-73, dep. comdg. officer, 1973-76; chmn. dental scis. dept. Naval Med. Rsch. Inst., Bethesda, Md., 1976-79; dir. Casualty Care Rsch. Program Ctr., Naval Med. Rsch. Inst., Bethesda, Md., 1979-81; assoc. prof. dept. operative dentistry Temple U., Phila., 1981-83; prof., chmn. dept. operative dentistry Georgetown U., Washington, 1983-90; pvt. practice Rockville, Md., ret.,, 1999; mem. spl. study sect. NIH, Washington, 1984, 87; mem. adv. com. Dental Tech. Program, So. Ill. U., Carbondale, 1976-85; cons. Naval Dental Rsch. Inst., Great Lakes, 1981-85, Dentsply Internat., York, Pa., 1984-88. Contbg. author: Biology Dental Cares, 1968, Dental Clinics of North America, 1986; editorial bd. Jour. Dental Rsch., 1976-86, 88, Jour. Operative Dentistry, 1986-92. Fellow Am. Coll. Dentists, Internat. Coll. Dentists; mem. ADA, D.C. Dental Soc. (bd. dirs. 1986-89). Democrat. Presbyterian. Home: 11816 Winterset Ter Potomac MD 20854-2846

COTTRELL, DAVID ALTON, school system administrator; b. Lima, Ohio, Sept. 8, 1941; s. Hiram David and Clara Marie (Williams) C.; m. Barbara Jean Campbell, Dec. 28, 1963; children: Richard, Deanna, Lynda. AA, Graceland Coll., 1961; BS in Edn., Bowling Green State U., 1964; MA, Kent State U., 1967; EdD, U. Akron, 1970. Cert. supt., Ohio. Social studies tchr. Fairview High Sch., Fairview Park, Ohio, 1964-68; curriculum rsch. specialist Geauga County Schs., Chardon, Ohio, 1968-70; asst. supt. Girard (Ohio) City Schs., 1970-75; supt. Northwood (Ohio) Local Schs., 1975-82, Newark (Ohio) City Schs., 1982-87, Berea (Ohio) City Schs., 1987—. Mem. Berea Cable TV Commn., 1987—; chair suburban schs. Greater Cleve. United Way, 1989. Mem. Am. Assn. Sch. Adminstrn., Buckeye Assn. Sch. Adminstrs. (chair profl. rights and responsibility com.), Mid-Am. Assn. Sch. Adminstrs. Avocations: sailing, jogging, golf, tennis. Office: Edn Dept 1717 Alum Creek Dr Columbus OH 43207-1708*

COTTRELL, FRANK STEWART, lawyer, manufacturing executive; b. Boulder, Colo., July 11, 1942; s. Frank Stewart Sr. and Dorris Mary (Payne) C.; m. Janet Anne Goode, Jan. 8, 1966; children: Kristin, Jeffrey, Steven. AB, Knox Coll., 1964; JD, U. Chgo., 1967. Bar: Ill. 1967. Atty. Deere & Co., Moline, Ill., 1967-77, internat. atty., 1977-80, sr. atty., 1980-82, asst. gen. counsel, 1982-87, assoc. gen. counsel, corp. sec., 1987-91, gen. counsel, sec., 1991-93, v.p., gen. counsel, sec., 1993-98, sr. v.p., gen. counsel, sec., 1998—. Mem. adv. bd. Butterworth Trust; trustee Knox Coll. Mem. ABA, Ill. Bar Assn., Assn. Gen. Counsel. Office: Deere & Co One John Deere Pl Moline IL 61265-8098

COTTRELL, G. WALTON, manufacturing executive; b. Auburn, N.Y., Sept. 26, 1939; s. George H. and Eleanor H. (Day) C.; m. Jean H. Springer, June 15, 1963; children: Lisa, Lori. BSME, Cornell U., 1962, MBA, 1963. Various positions Owens-Ill., Inc., Toledo, 1965-85, treas., 1980-83, v.p. corp. planning, 1984-85; dir. fin. Europe Owens-Ill. Internat., Geneva, 1976-80; v.p. fin. The Allen Group, Inc., Melville, N.Y., 1986; v.p., treas. Squibb Corp., Princeton, N.J., 1987-88; sr. v.p. fin., chief fin. officer Carpenter Tech. Corp., Reading, Pa., 1989—; dir. Andersen Labs., Inc., Bloomfield, Conn., 1992-98. Bd. dirs. Jr. Achievement N.W. Ohio, Toledo, 1980-86, Planned Parenthood N.W. Ohio, Toledo, 1982-86; mem. coun. Cornell U., 1985-95; bd. dirs. United Way Berks County, 1990-97. Lt. USNR, 1963-65. Mem. Fin. Execs. Inst. (bd. dirs. 1982-85), Nat. Assn. Corp. Treas. (pres. 1997-98, chair bd. dirs. 1998-99). Republican. United Ch. of Christ. Home: 4 Forest Rd Mohnton PA 19540-9300 Office: Carpenter Tech Corp 1047 N Park Rd Wyomissing PA 19610

COTTRELL, JANET ANN, controller; b. Berea, Ohio, Dec. 2, 1943; d. Carmen and Hazel (French) Volpe; m. Melvin M. Cottrell, Mar. 2, 1963; children: Lori A., Gregory C. Student, Los Angeles State Coll., 1961-63. Lic. ins. agt., Calif. Loan processing Eastern Lenders, Covina, 1962-64; asst. bookkeeper Golden Rule Discount Stores, Rosemead, Calif., 1964-66; acctg. supr. Walter Carpet Mills, Industry, Calif., 1967-69; co-owner Motorcycle Specialties Co., Industry, 1969-78, Covina (Calif.) Kawasaki, 1978-84; v.p., contr. M.C. Specialties Inc., Covina, 1984—; v.p., controller Aviation Communications Inc., Covina, 1992—; active various coms. relating to promotion, safety and advancement of the recreational vehicle and auto industry, So. Calif., 1981—. Mem. com. Miss Covina Pageant, 1986—, presdl. task force, nat., 1982—, Rep. nat. com., 1986—. Mem. Covina C. of C., Calif. Motorcycle Dealers Assn., Nat. Auto Dealers Assn., Internat. Jet Ski Boating Assn. Republican. Avocations: traveling, gourmet cooking. Office: Aviation Comm Inc 1025 W San Bernardino Rd Covina CA 91722-4106

COTTRELL, JEANNETTE ELIZABETH, retired librarian; b. Buffalo, Dec. 10, 1923; d. Benjamin Birch and Mary Jeannette (Ashdown) Milnes; m. William Barber Cottrell, Jan. 21, 1944 (dec.); children: Karen Jean, Susan Marie, William Milnes, Scott Barber, Stephen Ashdown. BA in Sociology, U. Tenn., 1970, MS, 1976; student, Alfred U., 1940-43. Cert. tchr. libr., Tenn. Nursery sch. tchr. Concord Meth. Ch., Knoxville, Tenn., 1964-65; libr. City Sch. System, Knoxville, Tenn., 1971-84, ret., 1984. Author: (with husband) An American Family in the 20th Century, 1987; recorder textbooks for the blind, 1983—. Libr. Concord United Meth. Ch., Knoxville, 1975—, curriculum chair spl. studies class, 1989—, reading chair Suzanna Wesley Circle. Mem. AAUW (chair contemporary lit.), Phi Kappa Phi, Beta Phi Mu. Republican. Methodist. Avocations: singing, bridge, cooking, travel, reading. Home: 308 Camelot Ct Knoxville TN 37922-2076

COTTRELL, THOMAS SYLVESTER, pathology educator, university dean; b. Chgo., Feb. 2, 1934; s. Sylvester Vincent and Cleo (Medley) C.; m. Jane Chichester, July 3, 1959; children: Matthew Thomas, Anne Medley, Sarah Jane. AB, Brown U., 1955; MD, Columbia U., 1965. Diplomate Am. Bd. Pathology. Asst. prof. N.Y. Med. Coll., Valhalla, 1968-79; assoc. prof. pathology SUNY Sch. Medicine, Stony Brook, 1979—, assoc. dean clin. affairs, 1979-88, exec. assoc. dean, 1988-97; interim exec. dir. U. Hosp. SUNY, Stony Brook, 1983-84, interim chmn. dept. ob-gyn. Sch. Medicine, 1991-92, interim chmn. dept. surgery Sch. Medicine, 1996, vice dean, 1997—. Lt. USNR, 1957-60. Scholar John and Mary R. Markle Found., 1969-73. Fellow Coll. Am. Pathologists, N.Y. Acad. Medicine; mem. AAAS. Home: PO Box 1292 3775 Skunk Ln Cutchogue NY 11935-1541 Office: SUNY Sch Medicine Office Of Dean Stony Brook NY 11794

COTTRILL, MARY ELSIE, family nurse practitioner; b. Charleston, W. Va., Sept. 17, 1939; d. Orville Hugh and Nancy Isabell (Fletcher) C. Diploma, RN, Sch. of Nursing, Chesapeake and Ohio Hosp., Clifton Forge, Va., 1964; diploma in Christian Edn., Appalachian Bible Coll., Bradley, W. Va., 1961; diploma in Spanish, Rio Grande Bible Inst. Missionary Lang., Edinburg, Tex., 1966; family nurse practitioner, Med. Sch. Nursing, U. Miami, Fla. Nurses asst. Thomas Meml. Hosp., S. Charleston, W. Va., 1953-58; RN Emmett Meml. Hosp., Clifton Forge, Va., 1961-64, Thomas Meml. Hosp., 1964-65; med. missionary Harvesters Internat. Mission, McAllen, Texas, 1965-74; primary care nurse Jackson Meml. Hosp., Miami, Fla., 1972-75; family nurse practitioner Martin Luther King Clinic, Homestead, Fla., 1975-98; ret., 1997. Asst. scout master Boy Scouts of Am., Miami, 1983—; den leader Cub Scouts of Am., Miami, 1983-97. Recipient Migrant Health Provider award Nat. Assn. of Community Health Ctrs., 1989, Wood Badge Boy Scouts Am., 1992, Dist. Award of Merit, 1989, Order of the Arrow, 1994, Dist. Chmn.'s award, 1995, Whitney Young award, 1996, Silver Beaver, 1999. Mem. Fla. Nurses Assn. Baptist. Avocations: hiking, camping, wood working, fishing, swimming. Home: 25510 SW 124th Ave Princeton FL 33032-5819

COUCH, DANIEL MICHAEL, healthcare executive; b. Chgo., July 1, 1937; s. Arthur Daniel and Helen Margret (Kreamer) C.; m. Marilee Hermon, Sept. 12, 1958; children: Laura Ann, Mark Allen, Kristina Lynn, Michelle Louise, Daniel Michael Jr. BS in Bus., Ind. U., 1958; MBA, Butler U., 1977. Field examiner Ind. State Bd. Accounts, Indpls., 1959-61; controller Community Hosp., Anderson, Ind., 1961-67; field rep. Am. Hosp. Assn., Chgo., 1967-68; treas./controller Health & Hosp. Corp. of Marion County, Indpls., 1968-71; assoc. adminstr. Winona Meml. Hosp., Indpls., 1971-78; pres. Huntington (Ind.) Meml. Hosp., 1978-80; dep. exec. dir. Truman Med. Ctr., Kansas City, Mo., 1980-99; bd. dirs. Nat. Pub. Health and Hosp. Inst., Washington, 1987-90, chmn., 1989. Bd. dirs., mem. exec. com. Labor-Mgmt. Coun., Kansas City, Mo., 1982—, co-chmn., 1991-97; bd. dirs. Greater Kansas City Mental Health Found., 1984-93, pres., 1992-93; bd. dirs. Kansas City Care Ctr., 1990—, Resource Devel. Inst., Kansas City, 1998—; vis. nurse Home Care Svcs., Kansas City, 1991-96, chmn., 1993-96. 1st lt. USAR, 1958-67. Fellow Am. Coll. Healthcare Execs. (nominating com. 1995-99); mem. Am. Hosp. Assn. (ho. of dels. and Regional Policy Bd. 7 1989-92, governing coun. sect. met. hosps. 1990-93, chmn. 1993), Nat. Assn. Pub. Hosps. (bd. dirs. 1981-99, chmn. 1989), Kansas City Area Hosp. Assn. (bd. dirs. 1990-96), Greater Kansas City C. of C. (various coms. 1985—), Healthcare Fin. Mgmt. Assn. (advanced), Kansas City Care Network (bd. dirs. 1995-99, pres. 1995-99), Family Health Ptnrs. (bd. dirs. 1995-99), Masons, Rotary. Episcopalian. Avocations: golf, bowling, reading. Office: 508 NE Sawgrass Ct Lees Summit MO 64064-1311
While into life a little rain must fall, I like to dwell on the fact that into every life a little joy must come.

COUCH, JAMES RUSSELL, JR., neurology educator; b. Bryan, Tex., Oct. 25, 1939; married; 2 children. BS, Texas A&M U., 1961; MD, Baylor U., 1965, PhD in Physiology, 1966; fellow, Lab of Neuropharmacology, NIMH, 1966-68; postgrad., Nat. Inst. Neurol. Diseases and Stroke, 1969-72. Diplomate Am. Bd. Psychiatry and Neurology; lic. physician, Tex., Md., Kans., Mo., Ill., Okla. Intern Barnes Hosp., St. Louis, 1966-67; resident in neurology Washington U. Sch. Medicine, St. Louis, 1969-72; mem. staff Kans. U. Med. Ctr., Kansas City, asst. prof. div. neurology, 1972-76, assoc. prof., 1976-79; prof., chief divsn. neurology So. Ill. U. Sch. Medicine, Springfield, 1979-92, acting chmn. dept. medicine, 1988-89; staff VA Hosp., Kansas City, Mo., Marion, Ill., Oklahoma City; staff St. Joseph (Mo.) Hosp., Kansas U. Med. Ctr., Atchison (Kans.) Hosp., Kansas City Gen. Hosp.; staff Meml. Med. Ctr., Springfield, dir. EEG lab., muscular dystrophy clinic, cons. speech and hearing lab., 1979-92; staff St. John's Hosp., Springfield; prof., chmn. dept. neurology Okla. U. Coll. Med. and Health Sci. Ctr., Oklahoma City, 1992—; staff Presbyn. Hosp., Oklahoma City, Univ. Hosp., Oklahoma City, Childrens Hosp. of Okla.; investigator Mental Retardation Rsch. Ctr. Kans. U. Med. Ctr., Kansas City, 1972-79; bd. dir. postgrad. neurology course Continuing Med. Edn.; examiner Am. Bd. Psychiatry and Neurology, 1975-77, 79, 84-85, 89-98, Am. Bd. Neurosurgery, 1977; cons. Richland Meml. Hosp., Olney, Ill., 1981-85, Abraham Lincoln Meml. Hosp., Lincoln, Ill., 1981-92; staff cons. Lincoln Devel. Ctr., Outpatient Clinics, Lincoln, 1981-92; vis. prof. Northwestern U., Chgo., 1982, 93, U. Nebr., 1992, Wayne State U. Med. Sch., 1992, Ind. U. Med. Sch., 1992, U. Rochester, 1992, U. Ala., Birmingham, 1994, U. W.Va., Morgantown, 1995, U. Mo., Columbia, Med. Sch. Kans. U., 1996, R.I. Hosp., Providence, 1996, Med. Coll. S.C., 1996, U. South Fla., 1996, 99, Med. Sch. Brown U., 1996, U. Md., 1997, U. Minn., 1997, U. North Tex., 1997, L.I. Jewish Hosp., 1998; presenter in field; com. mem. med. sch. Kans. U., 1972-79, So. Ill. U., 1980-92, 97, U. Nebr., Omaha, 1999. Mem. editorial bd. Headache, 1979-92; contbr. numerous articles to profl. jours. Mem. med. adv. bd. Lincoln Land Epilepsy Assn., 1980-92; mem. exec. bd., chmn. edn. com. Am. Soc. Neurorehab., 1990-95. Fellow Nat. Heart Inst., 1965-66, NIH, NIMH, 1967-69; recipient numerous grants for neurology rsch., 1969—. Fellow Am. Acad. Neurology (bd. dirs. asst. sec.-treas. 1984-86, sec.-treas. 1986-88, chmn. sect. neurorehab. 1996-98), Stroke Coun. of Am. Heart Assn.; mem. AMA, Am. Neurological Assn. (elected), Am. Assn. for Study of Headache (exec. com. ad hoc 1983-85, winter headache course, membership com. 1983-85, chmn., 1994-96, faculty continuing med. edn. courses 1983-99, edn. com. 1983-85, 86—, achievement recognition com., publs. com. 1986—, bd. dirs. 1983-85, 86-92, treas. 1992-94, sec. 1994-96, pres.-elect 1996-98, pres. 1998—), Am. Geriatric Soc., Am. Assn. Univ. Profs. Neurology (chmn. undergrad. edn. com, sec.-treas. 1992-96, chmn. VAMC com. 1997—) Am. Soc. Neurorehab. (chmn. edn. com. 1989-95, bd. dirs. 1990-98), Neurosci. Soc. (sec. Kansas City chpt. 1976-77, pres. 1977-78, pres. Sangamon County chptr. of Neurosci. 1982-92, pres. 1986-87), Ill. Med. Soc., Sangamon County Med. Soc., Okla. State Med. Soc., Okla. County Med. Soc., Baylor U. Med. Alumni Assn., Washington U. Med. Alumni Assn., Sigma Xi, Alpha Omega Alpha, Phi Eta Sigma, Phi Kappi Phi. Home: 1616 Queenstown Rd Oklahoma City OK 73116-5523 Office: U Okla Health Sci Ctr Dept of Neurology PPOB209 PO Box 26901 Oklahoma City OK 73190-3048

COUCH, JESSE WADSWORTH, retired insurance company executive; b. Atlanta, Mar. 2, 1921; s. Jesse Newton and Laura (Day) W.; m. Charlotte Lucretia Collins, Jan. 13, 1945 (dec.); children: Robert Collins (dec.), Laura W.; m. Charlotte H. Gran, Oct. 17, 1997. A.B., Princeton, 1947. With 1st Nat. Bank Houston, 1947-51; assoc. Wray Assocs., Houston, 1951-60; partner Wray, Couch & Elder, Houston, 1960-69; v.p. Marsh & McLennan,

Inc., 1969-83; pvt. cons., 1983-95. Mem. exec. bd. Episcopal Diocese of Tex., 1965-67, 68-71; trustee St. Luke's Episcopal Hosp., 1971-76; bd. dirs. Houston-Harris County YMCA, 1969-74, Houston Soc. Prevention Cruelty to Animals, 1974—; Bd. dirs. Tex. div. Am. Cancer Soc., mem. exec. com., 1982-91; chmn. Am. Cancer Soc. Greater Houston, 1981-83; trustee Mus. Fine Arts, Houston, 1970-74, Houston Arboretum and Nature Ctr., 1978—. Served to capt. USAAF, 1943-46. Mem. Houston C. of C. (aviation com. 1965-75), Eagle Lake, Rod & Gun Club, Houston Country Club, Bayou Club, Allegro Club, Argyle Club. Home: 6015 Pine Forest Rd Houston TX 77057-1431 Office: 800 Bering Dr Ste 303F Houston TX 77057-2131

COUCH, JOHN CHARLES, diversified company executive; b. Bremerton, Wash., May 10, 1939; s. Richard Bailey and Frances Harriet (Gilmore) C. BS in Engring., U. Mich., 1963, MS, 1964; MBA, Stanford U., 1976. With Ingalls Shipbldg. div. Litton Industries, 1967-74; asst. to sr. v.p. engring. and marine ops. Matson Navigation Co. subs. Alexander and Baldwin., San Francisco, 1976-78, v.p., 1978-84, exec. v.p., chief operating officer, 1984, pres., chief operating officer, 1985; pres., chief operating officer Alexander and Baldwin Inc., Honolulu, 1991—; pres., chief exec. officer Alexander and Baldwin, Inc., Honolulu, 1992-95, chmn., pres., CEO, 1995—; bd. dirs. A&B Devel. Co., Calif., A&B Properties, Inc., McBryde Sugar Co., Ltd., Kauai Coffee Co., Inc., WDCI Inc., Calif. and Hawaiian Sugar Co., First Hawaiian Bank, First Hawaiian Inc., Hawaiian Sugar Transp. Co., Inc., A&B Hawaii, Inc., Alexander & Baldwin, Inc., Kukuiula Devel. Co., Inc., Matson Navigation Co., Inc. Mem. Maui Econ. Devel. Bd., 1986—; mem. exec. bd. Aloha coun. Boy Scouts Am., 1986—; bd. dirs. Aloha United Way, 1988, campaign chmn., 1988, chmn. bd. dirs.; bd. dirs. Alexander & Baldwin Found., The Std. Steamship Owners' Protection and Indemnity Assn. (Bermuda) Ltd.; chmn. bd. trustees Bishop Mus., 1997—. Mem. Hawaii Maritime Ctr. (vice-chmn. 1988-89, 97—, chmn. 1990-97), Honolulu Club, Oahu Country Club, Plaza Club, Pacific Club, The Pacific-Union Club. Office: Alexander & Baldwin Inc PO Box 3440 822 Bishop St Honolulu HI 96813-3925

COUCH, LESLIE FRANKLIN, lawyer; b. Albany, N.Y., July 22, 1930; s. Leslie S. and Mary J. (Owens) C.; m. Joan Dunham, Dec. 29, 1951; children—Sharon DeBonis, Lawrence, Mark, Todd. LL.B., Union U., 1955, J.D., 1968. Bar: N.Y. 1955, U.S. Dist. Ct. (no. dist.) N.Y. 1955, U.S. Ct. Claims 1963, U.S. Ct. Appeals (2d cir.) 1962, U.S. Dist. Ct. (so. dist.) N.Y. 1979, U.S. Supreme Ct. 1979, U.S. Dist. Ct. Vt. 1987, U.S. Dist. Ct. D.C. 1997. Pvt. practice law, Albany, 1955-62; ptnr. Medwin & Couch, Albany, 1962-65, DiFabio & Couch, P.C., Albany, 1965-79, Couch & Howard, P.C., Albany, 1979-88, Couch, White, Brenner, Howard & Feigenbaum, 1988—; lectr. Am. Arbitration Assn., N.Y. State Bar Assn., others. Mem. North Colonie Sch. Dist., 1975-78. Mem. ABA, Am. Arbitration Assn. (nat. panel), Albany County Bar Assn. (com. on continuing legal edn. 1983—), N.Y. Bar Assn. (com. unlawful practice 1960-63, com. pub. info. 1969-72, com. media awards 1970-76, chmn. constrn. and surety law div. 1988-90), Capital Dist. Trial Lawyers Assn. Clubs: Fort Orange (Albany); Schuyler Meadows (Loudonville, N.Y.). Home: 20 Loudonwood East Loudonville NY 12211 Office: PO Box 22222 540 Broadway Albany NY 12207-2705

COUCH, ROBERT BARNARD, physician, scientist, educator; b. Guntersville, Ala., Sept. 25, 1930; s. Ezekiel Harvey and Frances Jane (Barnard) C.; m. Katherine Frances Klein, Apr. 23, 1955; children—Robert Steven, Leslie Ann, Colleen Frances, Elizabeth Lee. BA, Vanderbilt U., 1952, MD, 1956. Diplomate: Am. Bd. Internal Medicine. Intern Vanderbilt U. Hosp., Nashville, 1956-57; resident in medicine Vanderbilt U. Hosp., 1959-60, chief resident in medicine, 1960-61; clin. asso. NIH, Washington, 1957-59; sr. investigator NIH, 1961-65, head clin. virology sect., 1965-66; asso. prof. Baylor Coll. Medicine, Houston, 1966-71; dir. influenza research center Baylor Coll. Medicine, 1974—, prof. microbiology and immunology and medicine, 1971—, head infectious diseases sect. medicine, 1987-92, chmn. dept. microbiology and immunology, 1989—; mem. rsch. rev. panels infectious diseases; cons. NIH, Dept. Def., FDA. Contbr. articles to med. jours. Served to sr. surgeon USPHS, 1957-66. Mem. ACP, AAAS, Soc. Exptl. Biology and Medicine, Am. Soc. Microbiology, Infectious Diseases Soc. Am., Am. Assn. Immunologists, Am. Fedn. Clin. Rsch., Am. Soc. Clin. Investigation, So. Soc. Clin. Investigation, Am. Assn. Physicians, Am. Soc. Epidemiology, Am. Soc. Virology. Office: Baylor Coll Medicine 1 Baylor Plz Houston TX 77030-3411

COUCHMAN, ROBERT GEORGE JAMES, human services consultant; b. Toronto, Ont., Can., Feb. 21, 1937; s. Robert George and Mary (Bigelow) C.; m. Jane Barker (div. 1985); children: Barbara, Stephen; m. Carolyn Moore; 1 child, Michael. B.A., Queen's U., Kingston, Ont., 1965; M.Ed., U. Toronto, 1969. Tchr. Scarborough (Ont.) Bd. Edn., 1957-63; dir. student svcs. Etobicoke (Ont.) Bd. Edn., 1963-74; exec. dir. Family Svc. Assn. Met. Toronto, 1974-89; pres. Donner Can. Found., Toronto, 1989-93; assoc. Re Think Group, 1993; dir. Terra Nova, 1995-97; chmn. Outward Bound Can., 1989-95; found. cons. Atlin, 1995—; co-chmn. U.N. Can. Com. Internat. Yr. of Family, 1993-94; patron Outward Bound Can., 1995—. Contbr. 40 articles to profl. jours., 1984-87. Chmn. Outward Bound Wilderness Sch., 1987-88; pres. Can. Mental Health Assn., Ont., 1971-73; dir. White Ribbon Found. of Can.; bd. dirs. Addiction Rsch. Found., Ont., 1980-86, Metro Toronto Housing Co., 1982-88, United Way Metro Toronto, 1994-96; vice chmn. Vanier Inst. of the Family, 1988-90; chmn. parent adv. coun. Atlin Sch., 1996—; chmn. Atlin Big Water Soc.; gov., Grey Owl Nature Trust advisor Can. Arctic Resources Com. Mem. N.Am. Inst., Ont. Assn. Profl. Social Workers (hon.), Rotary (com. chmn.). Anglican. Fax: 250-651-0014. E-mail: couchmanmoore@ibm.net.

COUCOUZIS, DEMETRIOS A. See IAKOVOS

COUDERT, DALE HOKIN, real estate executive, marketing consultant; b. Chgo., Nov. 29, 1941; d. Sidney and Ruth (Brower) Manowitz; m. Frederic R. Coudert (div.); children Dana, Alexandra. BA, Northwester U., 1964. V.p. Cross & Brown, N.Y.C., 1975-86; dir., sec. First Women's Bank, N.Y.C., 1980-87; pres., head bus. devel. 1st N.Y. Bank for Bus., 1988-91; mktg. dir. Lafer Mgmt., N.Y.C., 1993-94; pres., CEO Coudert Assocs. Ltd., N.Y.C., 1991—; broker Brown Harris Stevens Palm Beach Real Estate, Pal, 1999—; dir. Hosp. Tak Co., Long Island, N.Y., 1979-98. Pub., editor: (book) Business and Pleasure, 1986-87. Bd. dirs. Women's Rep. Club, N.Y.C., 1994, N.Y. Drama League, N.Y.C., 1975—; mem. nat. bd. dirs. Aspen Art Mus.; trustee, treas. Zoo of the Palm Beaches at Dreker Park, 1996-98, bd. dirs., 1996—; regent St. John the Divine, N.Y.C., 1988. Mem. Internat. Womens Forum, Met. Opera Club, Internat. Women's Forum, Fla. Women's Forum. Avocations: piano, voice, dance, golf, tennis. Home: 485 Park Ave New York NY 10022-1228 also: 163 Seminole Ave Palm Beach FL 33480 Office: Coudert Assn Ltd 485 Park Ave Ste 7A New York NY 10022-1228 also: Brown Harris Stevens Palm Beach Real Estate Ste 329 340 Royal Poinciana Plz Palm Beach FL 33480

COUGHENOUR, JOHN CLARE, federal judge; b. Pittsburg, Kans., July 27, 1941; s. Owren M. and Margaret E. (Widner) C.; m. Gwendolyn A. Kieffaber, June 1, 1963; children: Jeffrey, Douglas, Marta. B.S., Kans. State Coll., 1963; J.D., U. Iowa, 1966. Bar: Iowa 1963, D.C. 1963, U.S. Dist. Ct. (we. dist.) Wash. 1966. Ptnr. Bogle & Gates, Seattle, 1966-81; vis. asst. prof. law U. Washington, Seattle, 1970-73; judge U.S. Dist. Ct. (we. dist.) Wash., Seattle, 1981-97, chief judge, 1997—. Mem. Iowa State Bar Assn., Wash. State Bar Assn. Office: US Dist Ct US Courthouse 1010 5th Ave Ste 609 Seattle WA 98104-1189

COUGHENOUR, KAVIN LUTHER, career officer, military historian; b. New Kensington, Pa., Mar. 1, 1947; s. Roy Edgar and Anna Louise (Coleman) C.; m. Kathryn Mary Domurat, May 17, 1969; 1 child, Stacey Anne. BA in Social Scis., Ind. U. of Pa., 1969; MA in Pers. Mgmt., Ctrl. Mich. U., 1979; diploma, U.S. Army War Coll., 1990. Commd. 2d lt. U.S. Army, 1969, advanced through grades to col., 1991; adj. U.S. Army, Ft. Meade, Md., 1973-75; adj. gen. 79th Res. Command U.S. Army, Willow Grove, Pa., 1976-79; adj. 5th Spl. Forces Group U.S. Army, Ft. Bragg, N.C., 1979-82; adj. gen. 3d Armored Divsn. U.S. Army, Frankfurt, Germany, 1985-86; commdg. officer U.S. Mil. Entrance Processing Sta., Dept. Defense U.S. Army, Chgo., 1986-88; tng. officer Spl. Forces Sch. U.S. Army, Ft. Bragg, 1988-89; spl. forces br. chief Pers. Command U.S. Army, Alexandria, Va., 1990-92; dep. comdr. Ctr. Mil. History U.S. Army, Washington, 1992-95; lic. battlefield guide Gettysburg (Pa.) Nat. Mil. Park, 1995—. Decorated Legion of Merit; recipient gold medal Nat. Hon. Soc. Pershing Rifles, 1968. Mem. Ret. Officers Assn., Spl. Forces Assn., Soc. Mil. History, U.S. Army Coll. Alumni Assn., Nepoleonic Soc. Am., Assn. Lic. Battlefield Guides. Republican. Methodist. Avocation: Civil War history. Home: Lake Heritage 964 Johnson Dr Gettysburg PA 17325-8970

COUGHLAN, GARY PATRICK, pharmaceutical company executive; b. Fresno, Calif., Feb. 14, 1944; s. Edward Patrick and Elizabeth Claire (Ryan) C.; m. Mary Cary Kelley, Dec. 21, 1967; children: Christopher, Sarah, Laura, Claire, Moira. B.A., St. Mary's Coll., 1966; M.A. in Econs., UCLA, 1967; M.B.A., Wayne State U., 1971. Sr. fin. analyst Burroughs Corp., Detroit, 1969-72; with Dart Industries, Los Angeles, 1972-81, group v.p. field services, 1978-81, v.p. ops. services, 1981; v.p. ops. services Dart & Kraft Inc., Northbrook, Ill., 1981-82, v.p. fin., controller, 1984-85, sr. v.p. fin. affairs, 1985-86, sr. v.p., chief fin. officer, 1986; v.p. fin. retail food group Kraft Inc., Glenview, Ill., 1982-84, sr. v.p., chief fin. officer, 1986-88; sr. v.p. fin. Kraft Gen. Foods, Glenview, 1989-90; sr. v.p. fin., chief fin. officer Abbott Labs., Abbott Park, Ill., 1990—; instr. prof. fin. ext. program UCLA, 1974-80; bd. dirs. Fort James Corp., Deerfield, Ill., Premark Internat., Inc., Deerfield, Chgo. Horticultural Soc., Glencoe, Ill.; mem. Chancellor's adv. bd., U. Ill., Chgo.; mem. adv. coun. DePaul U. Coll. Commerce, Coun. Fgn. Rels., Chgo. Com. Mem. Fin. Execs. Inst., The Conf. Bd. Inc., Coun. of Fin. Execs., Econ. Club Chgo. Republican. Roman Catholic. Home: 1135 Central Rd Glenview IL 60025-4432 Office: Abbott Labs 100 Abbott Park Rd Abbott Park IL 60064-3502

COUGHLAN, KENNETH LEWIS, lawyer; b. Chgo., July 8, 1940; s. Edward James and Mary Virginia (Lewis) C.; m. Therese Koziol, Oct. 11, 1981; 1 son, Kevin Edward. BA, U. Notre Dame, 1962; JD, Northwestern U., Chgo., 1966. Bar: Ill. 1967. Trust officer Am. Nat. Bank & Trust Co., Chgo., 1969-72; sec. bd., sr. v.p., gen. counsel, cashier Ctrl. Nat. Bank, Chgo., 1972-82; sec., gen. counsel Ctrl. Nat. Chgo. Corp., 1976-82; sr. v.p., gen. counsel Exch. Nat. Bank, Chgo., 1982-83; gen. counsel Exch. Internat. Corp., Chgo., 1982-83; chmn. bd., pres. Union Realty Mortgage Co., Inc., Chgo., 1981-83; ptnr. DeHaan & Richter P.C., 1983—. Capt. U.S. Army, 1966-68. Fellow Ill. Bar Found.; mem. ABA, Ill. State Bar Assn. (chmn. sect. on comml., banking and bankruptcy law 1981-82), Chgo. Bar Assn. (chmn. fin. instns. com. 1980-81, chmn. comml. fin. com. 1979-80), Law Club Chgo., Chgo. Athletic Assn. Office: DeHaan & Richter PC 55 W Monroe St Ste 1000 Chicago IL 60603-5089

COUGHLAN, PATRICK CAMPBELL, lawyer; b. Orange, N.J., May 28, 1940; s. Gerald Noel and Carter (Van Schaick) C.; m. Joyce Miskuf; children: Kimberly Campbell,Devon Gerald, Carter Turner. B.A., Duke U., 1962, J.D., 1965. Bar: Fla. 1965, U.S. Supreme Ct. 1968, Calif. 1974, Maine 1985. Assoc. Alley, Maass, Rogers & Lindsay, Palm Beach, Fla., 1969-72, ptnr., 1972-74; judge Municipal Ct., Ocean Ridge, Fla., 1970-72; assoc. firm Richards, Watson & Gershon, Los Angeles, 1974-75; ptnr. Richards, Watson & Gershon, 1975-84; city atty. City of Rancho Palos Verdes (Calif.), 1975-82, City of San Fernando (Calif.), 1977-82, City of Seal Beach, Calif., 1978-84; city atty. City of La Habra Heights, Calif., 1979-84, Avalon, Calif., 1981-84, Rolling Hills, Calif., 1981-84, Westlake Village, Calif., 1981-84; chair bd. appeals Raymond, Maine, 1985-98; pres. Kingsley Pines, Inc.; prin. Coughlan Assocs., 1987-88; pres. Resolve Disputes, Inc. N.Am., Portland, Maine, 1989-92, Conflict Solutions, Portland, 1992—. Pres. No. Pines, Inc., 1980-86; ptnr. Atlanean Ptnrs.; trustee, sec. Gulf Stream Sch. Found., Inc., 1970-85; bd. dirs. Mountains Restoration Trust, 1981-82; trustee North Yarmouth Acad., 1984-93, pres., 1985-89; treas., trustee Natural Resources Coun. Maine, 1989-93; pres. parish coun. Our Lady of Perpetual Help, 1983-85; pres. World Affairs Coun. of Maine, 1986-89, trustee, 1985-93; trustee Portland Stage Co., 1989-93, sec., 1990-91, v.p., 1991-92; trustee Maine Youth Camps Assn., 1989-96, sec., 1990, v.p., 1990-93, pres., 1993-95; trustee Susan Curtis Found., 1991-96; dir. Pvt. Adjudication Ctr. Duke U., 1994—, mediator 1998—; dir. The Club at La Peninsula, 1997-98. Capt. USAF, 1965-68. Fellow Internat. Acad. of Mediators; mem. ABA, State Bar Calif., Fla. Bar, Maine State Bar, Soc. Profls. in Dispute Resolution, Maine Assn. Dispute Resolution Profls. (pres. 1990-92), Internat. Acad. Mediators (dir. 1999—), Woodlands Country Club. Roman Catholic. Home: 30 Atlantic Reach Yarmouth ME 04096-5535 Office: Conflict Solutions 75 Pearl St Ste 370 Portland ME 04101-4101

COUGHLAN, WILLIAM DAVID, professional society administrator; b. Chgo., Feb. 21, 1946; s. Thomas Eugene and Helen Mildred (LaMalle) C.; m. Susan J. Moran, Aug. 16, 1965; children: William Sean, Richard Shannon, Michael Shane, Kristin Ann, Suzi Danielle, Joseph Thomas. BA in Philosophy, DePaul U., 1969, MA in Philosophy, 1973; MA in Health Adminstrn., Governors State U., Park Forest South, Ill., 1973; MPA, U. So. Calif., 1977. Survey and system analyst CNA Fin. Corp., Chgo., 1965-69; asst. dept. dir. AMA, Chgo., 1969-73; div. dir. Office Asst. Sec. for Health, HHS, Washington, 1973-78; dir. div. health and pub. policy ACP, Phila., 1978-79; dep. exec. v.p. Am. Coll. Cardiology, Bethesda, Md., 1979-87; exec. v.p., chief exec. officer Am. Phys. Therapy Assn., Alexandria, Va., 1987-93; pres., CEO Nat. Assn. for Med. Equipment Svcs., Alexandria, Va., 1995—; speaker, writer, facilitator, cons. in leadership on mgmt. strategies issue and topics, 1994. Contbg. editor Successful Meeting, 1987-91, Association Management, 1993, 94. Bd. dirs. Columbia (Md.) Coun. 1975-77, chmn. 1975-77. Fellow Am. Soc. Assn. Execs. (chmn. cert. com. 1988-89, bd. dirs. 1989-92); mem. Profl. Conv. Mgmt. Assn. (bd. dirs. 1989-93, v.p. 1993, initiator feed the needy program, chmn. task force on cultural diversity), Greater Washington Soc. Assn. Execs. (com. chmn. 1989-89). *

COUGHLIN, BERNARD JOHN, university chancellor; b. Galveston, Tex., Dec. 7, 1922; s. Eugene J. and Celeste M. (Ott) C. A.B., St. Louis U., 1946, Ph.L., 1949, S.T.L., 1956; M.S.W., U. So. Calif., 1959; Ph.D., Brandeis U., 1963; DHL (hon.), Seattle U., 1994. Joined S.J., Roman Cath. Ch., 1942, ordained priest, 1955; tchr., counselor chs. in Wis. and Kans., 1949-54; research asst. Los Angeles Juvenile Probation Project, 1959; social work ednl. cons. Guatemala City, summer 1960; mem. faculty St. Louis U., 1961-74; social work cons. Peru, Chile, 1967; Fulbright lectr. Colombia, 1970-71; prof. Sch. Social Service, 1970-74, dean, 1964-74; pres. Gonzaga U., Spokane, Wash., 1974-96, chancellor, 1996—; mem. program com. Nat. Conf. Cath. Charities, 1964-68, mem. com. legislation social justice, 1973-80, bd. dirs., 1973-80, mem. com. study and study cadre, 1970-72; mem. adv. com. social welfare service Model Cities, St. Louis, 1967-68; council social work edn. Commn. Internat. Social Work Edn., 1968-81, adv. com. project on integrative teaching and learning, 1968-69, adv. com. population dynamics and family planning, 1969-71, structure rev. com., 1970-71; bd. dirs. Health and Welfare Council Met. St. Louis, 1968-74, Shearson Fundamental Value Fund, Inc.; chmn. task force community planning Child Welfare League Am., 1967-69; chmn. Conf. Deans Schs. Social Work, 1972-73; chmn. nominating com. U.S. com. Internat. Council Social Work, 1973-79; cons. in field, del. internat. confs.; mem. Assn. Governing Bds., 1980-81, Council for Postsecondary Edn., 1979-85; mem. gov's. commn. on ethics in govt. and campaign practices. Author: Church and State in Social Welfare, 1965, also articles, revs., chpts. in books. Bd. dirs. United Way Spokane County, 1982-87; mem. Inland Empire council Boy Scouts Am., 1982—; mem. Nat. Conf. Cath. Charities, Washington Citizens' Commn. on Salaries for Elected Officials, 1987—; chmn. Northwest Citizens Forum Def. Waste, 1986-88; trustee St. Louis U., 1988—, Spokane Area Econ. Devel. Coun., 1991—; U.S. rep. to Internat. Coun. on Social Welfare, Study Commn. on Human Rights, Helsinki, Finland, 1968; mem. coun. on social work edn., Task Force on Structure and Quality in Social Work Edn., 1973-74; chmn. Northwest Citizens Forum on Nuclear Waste, 1986-88. Fulbright lectr. Colombia, 1970, 71; Grantee NIMH, 1963-68. Mem. Nat. Assn. Social Workers (chmn. cabinet div. profl. standards 1970-73), Internat. Assn. Schs. Social Work, Internat. Coun. Social Welfare, Nat. Conf. Social Welfare, Internat. Assn. Univ. Presidents (vice chmn. U.S. western regional coun. 1982—, mem. steering com. 1982—), Coun. Social Work Edn., Mo. Assn. for Social Welfare, Assn. Wash. Bus. (bd. dirs. 1991—), Spokane Area C. of C. (trustee 1979-81, vice chmn. 1987-88, chmn. 1988-89). Address: Gonzaga U 502 E Boone Ave Spokane WA 99258-1774*

COUGHLIN, CAROLINE MARY, library consultant, educator; b. Bronx, N.Y., Dec. 6, 1944; d. Daniel Anthony and Antoinette (Aponte) C.; m. William Martin Weinberg, Oct. 3, 1981; 1 child, Nora Harie Weinberg. BA, Mercy Coll., 1966; MLS, Emory U., 1967; PhD, Rutgers U., 1976. Reference libr. First Nat. City Bank, N.Y.C., 1967-68; instr. Emory U., Atlanta, 1968-71; teaching asst. Rutgers U., New Brunswick, N.J., 1971-74; children's libr. Phillipsburg (N.J.) Pub. Libr., 1972-73; asst. prof. libr. sci. Simmons Coll., Boston, 1974-78; asst. dir. libr. Drew U., Madison, N.J., 1978-86, dir., 1986-94, assoc. prof. bibliography and rsch., 1986-94; vis. lectr. Further Edn. Cen., Tampere, Finland, 1994, 96; cons. to librs., 1974—; team membership for site visits Mid. State Assn., 1979—; chair libr. dir.'s group Assn. Ind. Colls. and Univs. of N.J., 1987-92; bd. dirs. Ctr. for Rsch. Librs., Chgo., 1987-92; vis. faculty mem. Rutgers U., 1988, 90, 93—; vis. prof. Internat. Libr. Sch. U. Coll. Wales, 1992; evaluator HEA Office of Edn. and IMLR, 1987—. Co-author: Lyle's Administration of College Library Text. Bd. dirs. Women's Project of N.J., 1984—; mem. Women's Polit. Action Caucus, N.J., 1985—. Mem. ALA (councillor 1977-81), Assn. Libr. and Info. Sci. Edn. (various coms.), Archons of Colophon, N.J. Libr. Assn. (pres. coll. and univs. librs. sect. 1974-75, Disting. Svc. award 1993, Rsch. award 1993), Soc. for History of Authorship, Reading and Publ. (treas. 1994-96), Beta Phi Mu. Democrat. Avocations: reading, rug making, travel. Home: 304 Grant Ave Highland Park NJ 08904-1828

COUGHLIN, CORNELIUS EDWARD, accounting company executive; b. Boston, Sept. 9, 1927; s. Cornelius Stephen and Mabel Josephine (McMahon) C.; BBA with honors, Northeastern U., 1956; student Bentley Coll., 1948-50; m. Rosemarie Toppi, Sept. 5, 1954; children: William, Brian, Stephen, Christopher, Maureen, Michael. Office mgr. Trim Alloys, Inc., Boston, 1952-57; controller Form-A-Lite Inc., Northbridge, Mass., 1957-59; sales adminstr. Reiss Assos., Inc., Lowell, Mass., 1959-61; ops. mgr. GPS Instrument Co., Newton, Mass., 1961-65. Computer Products, Newton, 1965-67; partner McShane & Coughlin, Milton, Mass., 1967-74; owner, mgr. C.E. Coughlin & Co., Acton, Mass., 1974-78; pres. Coughlin, Sheff & Assocs., Acton, 1979—. Mem. auditcom. Town of Acton. Served with USN, 1945-48, 50-51. Mem. Mass. Soc. CPAs, Mass. Assn. Public Accts. (pres. 1989—), Am. Inst. CPAs, Inst. Mgmt. Accts., Small Business Assn. N.E. Democrat. Roman Catholic. Home: 98 Summer St Acton MA 01720-2223 Office: Coughlin Sheff & Assocs 40 Nagog Pk Acton MA 01720-3425

COUGHLIN, H. RICHARD, real estate broker; b. Quincy, Mass., Oct. 5, 1952; s. Thomas A. and Eva M. (Howard) C.; m. Cheryl Ann Swanson, May 26, 1974; children: Jaime Marie, Timothy Michael. Real estate agt. Century 21, Weymouth, Mass., 1983-91; pres. Coughlin & Co. Real Estate, Weymouth, Mass., 1991—. Mem. Fair Housing Commn., Weymouth, 1991-95; chmn. Weymouth Rep. Town Com., 1993-97; deacon South Shore Bapt. Ch., Hingham, Mass., 1996-97; With USAR, 1977-78, Mass. N.G. 1972-77. Mem. Mass. Assn. Realtors (dir. 1995—), South Shore Assn. Realtors (pres. 1997, dir. 1988-91, 97—, Realtor of Yr. 1997), Weymouth Music Parents Assn. (pres. 1994-96), Gideons Internat. (v.p. 1996-99, sec. 1999—), Lions. Republican. Baptist. Avocations: golf, canoeing, reading. Office: Coughlin & Co 122 Washington St Weymouth MA 02188-1704

COUGHLIN, JACK, printmaker, sculptor, art educator; b. Greenwich, Conn., Feb. 19, 1932; s. John J. and Gabrielle S. (Jones) C.; m. Joan M. Hopkins, July 5, 1958; children: Maura, Molly. Student, Art Students League, N.Y.C., 1950-52; B.F.A., R.I. Sch. Design, 1954, M.S., 1961. Asst. prof. art U. Mass., Amherst, 1964-68, assoc. prof., 1968-73, prof., 1973-94, prof. emeritus, 1994—. One-man shows include Hendriks Gallery, Dublin, Ireland, 1971, 74, 76, 78, 80, 83, 87, Harvard U., 1974, Associated Am. Artists, N.Y.C., 1977, Dublin Writers Mus., 1993, Brandeis U., 1995; group show include 17th Biennial Am. Printmaking, Bklyn., 1970, Davidson Nat. Print Show, 1973, NAD, 1974-97, numerous others; represented in permanent collections Met. Mus. Art, N.Y.C., Mus. Modern Art, N.Y.C., Nat. Collection Arts, Washington. Served with U.S. Army, 1954-56. Recipient numerous awards, prizes for work including award Nat. Inst. Arts and Letters, 1969, prize for drawing 158th Nat. Exhbn., NAD, 1983, 33d N.D. Print and Drawing Ann., 1991, 34th Nat. Print Exhbn., Hunterdon Art Ctr., Clinton, N.J. Mem. NAD (academician), Soc. Am. Graphic Artists. Home: N Leverett Rd Montague MA 01351-9538

COUGHLIN, JOAN HOPKINS, artist, educator; b. Jamaica, West Indies, July 4, 1936; parents Am. citizens; d. John Leroy and Marion (Baier) Hopkins; m. John J. Coughlin, July 5, 1958; children: Maura, Molly. BFA in Illustration, R.I. Sch. Design, 1958, BS in Art Edn., 1962; MFA in Painting, U. Mass., 1969. Painting tchr. Castle Hill Ctr. for the Arts, Truro, Mass., 1976—; dir. of family art gallery Golden Cod, Wellfleet, Mass., 1964—; curator Wellfleet Hist. Soc. Mus., 1990—. Recipient Gold medal for painting, Grumbacher, George Walter Smith Mus. Show, Springfield, Mass./ 67th Nat. Art League Exhbn. Episcopalian. Office: Wellfleet Hist Soc Main St Wellfleet MA 02667

COUGHLIN, KAREN A., health care company executive. Sr. v.p. Region II Humana Inc., Louisville; pres., CEO Physicians Health Svcs., Shelton, Conn., 1998—. Office: Physicians Health Sys Subs Found Health Sys One Far Mill Crossing Shelton CT 06484*

COUGHLIN, TOM, professional football coach; b. Waterloo, N.Y., Aug. 31, 1947; m. Judy Coughlin; children: Keli, Katie, Tim, Brian. BA Educ., Syracuse U.; MA Educ. Grad. asst. Syracuse U., 1969; head coach Rochester Inst. Tech., 1970-73; offensive backfield coach Syracuse U., 1974-76, offensive coord., 1977-80; offensive coord. Boston Coll., 1981-83; wide receivers coach Philadelphia Eagles, 1984-85; receivers coach Green Bay Packers, 1986-87, N.Y. Giants, 1988-90; head coach Boston Coll., 1991-93, Jacksonville Jaguars, 1994—. Reading, running, golf. Office: Jacksonville Jaguars One Alltel Stadium Place Jacksonville FL 32202*

COUGILL, ROSCOE MCDANIEL, mayor, retired air force officer; b. Charleston, Ill., Oct. 24, 1941; s. Oral Wilson and Malora Emaline (Vaughn) C.; m. Sallie Anne Carrow, Feb. 15, 1969; children: Christopher McDaniel, Andrew Ashby. BS in Edn., Ea. Ill. U., 1963; MS in Guidance and Counseling, Troy (Ala.) State U., 1976; postgrad., Air Command and Staff Coll., Maxwell AFB, Ala., 1976, Army War Coll., Carlisle, Pa., 1981. Commd. 2d lt. USAF, 1964, advanced through grades to brig. gen., 1989, ret., 1992; staff and exec. officer Hdqrs. USAF, Washington, 1976-80, dir., 1985-86, dep. asst. chief staff, 1988-89; comdr. 2179th Command Group, Patrick AFB, Fla., 1981-83; exec. officer internat. mil. staff NATO, Brussels, 1983-85; chief staff Air Force Communications Command, Scott AFB, Ill., 1986-88; dir. command and control, communications and computer systems Hdqrs. U.S. Cen. Command, MacDill AFB, Fla., 1989-92; mayor City of Charleston, Ill., 1993—. Decorated DSM, Legion of Merit, Def. Superior Svc. medal.

COUIG, MARY PATRICIA, federal agency administrator; b. Evanston, Ill.; d. J. Dalton Jr. and Patricia Mae Couig; m. Merton Vincent Smith II, May 26, 1991; children: M. Vincent, Madeline Mae. AS, Berkshire C.C., 1977; MSN, Fitchburg State Coll., 1979; MPH, Johns Hopkins U., 1986. RN, Mass. Clin. nurse emergency/outpatient dept. Phoenix Indian Med. Ctr., Indian Health Svc., 1981-84, quality assurance/infection control specialist, 1984-85; pub. health educator Wis. Dept. Health and Social Svcs., Madison, 1986; investigator FDA, Boston, 1986-88; assoc. dir. nursing affairs office health affairs FDA, Rockville, Md., 1989-98; dir. edn. and outreach MedWatch FDA, Rockville, 1999—; spl. asst. to chief nurse officer USPHS, Rockville, 1992-96; mem. RN stds. of practice com. Md. Bd. Nursing, Balt., 1998-99. Contbr. articles to profl. jours. Fellow Am. Acad. Nursing; mem. ANA (Nurses in Congress and Exec. Br. 1998), Md. Nurses Assn. (mem. HIV/AIDS task force 1993), Commd. Officers Assn. (pres. 1998-99), Sigma Theta Tau. Avocations: hiking, antiques. Fax: (301) 827-7241. E-mail: mcouig@oc.fda.gov. Office: FDA HF-2 5600 Fishers Ln Rockville MD 20857

COUKIS, PETER GEORGE, musician, composer; b. Waterbury, Conn., Jan. 15, 1955; s. George Peter and Antoinette (Kachulis) C.; m. Lucresia Monje, Aug. 20, 1998. BA, Western Conn. State U., 1978; AS, Mattatuck C.C., Waterbury, 1987. Musical arranger, composer Waterbury Children's Found., 1977-78; arranger, songwriter Youth Theatre Ensemble, Watertown, Conn., 1985-87; producer, performer Laurel Cablevision, Litchfield, Conn., 1988-91; solo recording artist Waterbury, Wallingford, Conn., 1990—; founder Blue Plum Records, 1993—. Composer, keyboardist The Nutmeg Ballet, Torrington, Conn., 1988; songwriter World Star Prodns., New Haven, 1988; keyboardist South Mich. Ave, Wolcott, Conn., 1980-86; synthesizer player Angels and Co. (Nunsense), N.Y.C. and Waterbury, 1989; artist, prodr. cable In Performance, 1988, Repertoire, 1989 (Laurel award 1989), Kaleidoscope, 1991, 13-week cable series, 1991, cable spl., 1992; released cassette single Girl, 1992; recording artist Stick Bride, 1994, Strange Beauty, 1995, Believe in Me, 1995, Midgetmajority, 1997, Tournament, 1997, Stephania in Orange, 1997, Blossoms of Beauty, 1999. Talk show guest Barbara Davitt's Coffee Break, Sta. WATR, Waterbury, 1990; feature guest Lifestyles with Dr. Kotler, Sta. WCAT-13, Waterbury, 1990. Mem. Conn. Songwriters Assn. (Three-year award 1985, Five-year award 1987), Nat. Acad. Recording Arts & Scis. (N.Y. chpt.). Democrat. Avocations: reading, traveling, outdoors, environmental awareness.

COULDWELL, WILLIAM TUPPER, neurosurgeon, educator; b. Vancouver, B.C., Can., Dec. 15, 1955; s. William John and Janet Mary (Tupper) C.; m. Marie Francoise Simard; children: Sandrine, Mitchell, Genevieve. MD, McGill U., 1984, PhD, 1991. Resident in neurosurgery U. So. Calif., L.A., 1984-89; fellow neuroimmunology Montreal Neurol. Inst., 1989-91, fellow epilepsy surgery, 1990; fellow neurosurgery CHUV, Lausanne, Switzerland, 1990-91; asst. prof. dept. neurol. surgery U. So. Calif., L.A., 1991-95, assoc. clin. prof., 1995-97; assoc. clin. prof. U. N.D., Minot, 1995-97; prof., chmn. dept. neurol. surgery N.Y. Med. Coll., Valhalla, 1997—. Contbr. articles to profl. jours. Recipient Preuss award Am. Assn. Neurol. Surgeons, 1991, Clinician Investigator award, 1993; Med. Rsch. Coun. Can. Centennial fellow, 1990; McGill U. scholar, 1984, Wood Gold medal. Fellow ACS; mem. Am. Assn. Neurol. Surgeons (joint sect. on tumors, joint sect. on cerebrovasc. disease 1991—), Congress of Neurol. Surgeons, N.Am. Skull Base Soc., Soc. Neurol. Surgeons, Neurol. Soc. Am. Office: NY Med Coll Munger Pavilion Dept Neurol Surgery Valhalla NY 10595

COULEHAN, JOHN LEO, physician educator, poet; b. Pitts., Sept. 26, 1943; s. Leo A. and Margaret J. Coulehan; m. Anne Leonard, July 9, 1966; children: Heather, Benjamin, Elizabeth. BA, St. Vincent Coll., 1965; MD, U. Pitts., 1969, MPH, 1972. Diplomate Am. Bd. Internal Medicine, Am. Bd. Preventive Medicine. Resident in medicine U. Pa., Phila., 1969-70; resident in comty. medicine U. Pitts., 1970-72; physician U.S. Indian Health Svc., Ft. Defiance, Ariz., 1972-74; resident in medicine N.C. Bapt. Hosp., Winston-Salem, 1974-75; from asst. prof. to assoc. prof. U. Pitts., 1975-91; prof. SUNY, Stony Brook, 1991—; dir. Inst. for Medicine in Contemporary Soc., Stony Brook, 1997—; cons. USPHS, Navajo area, 1975-90; cons., spkr. med. schs., 1980—. Author: (textbook) The Medical Interview, 1987, 97, (poetry) The Knitted Glove, 1991, First Photographs of Heaven, 1994; editor: (poetry book) Blood and Bone, 1998. Bd. Hospice Care Network, Westbury, N.Y., 1998—; bd. dirs. Walt Whitman Birthplace, West Hills, N.Y., 1998—. Surgeon USPHS, 1972-74. Fellow NEH, 1988, Pa. Coun. for Arts, 1989. Fellow ACP (Ann. Poetry award 1998); mem. Am. Assn. Humanities and Bioethics. Democrat. Roman Catholic. Avocations: hiking, running. E-mail: jcoulehan@uhmc.sunysb.edu. Office: SUNY Inst Med Contemporary Soc HSC L3-092 Stony Brook NY 11794

COULLARD, CHAD, information systems specialist; b. Bridgeport, Conn., Oct. 23, 1947; s. John B. and Elizabeth F. (Orfanello) C. BSc, Syracuse U., 1969; postgrad., U. Md.; MBA, Nichols Coll., 1986. Systems analyst Am. Chem. Soc., 1969-73; sr. programmer analyst Amherst (Mass.) Coll., 1973-77; programmer analyst, system analyst Spalding Div. Questor Corp., 1977-79; spl. projects coord. Gerber Scientific, Inc., Hartford, Conn., 1979-98; info. tech. mgr. Gerber Systems Corp., South Windsor, Conn., 1998—. Mem. Assn. Computing Machinery. Office: BARCO 30 S Satelitte Rd South Windsor CT 06074

COULMAN, GEORGE ALBERT, chemical engineer, educator; b. Detroit, June 29, 1930; s. William John Thompson and Mary (Dega) C.; m. Annette Marie Felder, Sept. 1, 1956; children: Karl, Paula. B.S., Case Inst. Tech., 1952, Ph.D. (Ford Found. fellow), 1962; M.S., U. Mich., 1958. Process devel. engr. Dow Corning Corp., Midland, Mich., 1954-57; mgr. devel. Am. Metal Products Co., Ann Arbor, Mich., 1958-60; asst. prof. chem. engring. U. Waterloo (Ont., Can.), 1961-64; mem. faculty Mich. State U., East Lansing, 1964-76; prof. chem. engring. Mich. State U., 1974-76; prof. chem. engring. Cleve. State U., 1976—, chmn. dept., 1976-85, interim dean engring., 1988-89, dean Coll. of Engring., 1989-96, prof. emeritus, 1996—; cons. in field. Author numerous papers in field. Served with AUS, 1952-54. Named Engr. of Yr., Nat. Engrs. Week Com., 1995. Mem. NSPE, Am. Chem. Soc., Am. Inst. Chem. Engrs., Am. Soc. Engring. Edn., Cleve. Engring. Soc. (bd. govs., 1st v.p.), Ohio Soc. Profl. Engrs. (outstanding engring. educator 1992), Cleve. Technical Soc. Coun. (Disting. Svc. award 1992). Office: 1963 E 24th St Cleveland OH 44115-2403

COULSON, ELIZABETH ANNE, physical therapy educator, state representative; b. Hastings, Nebr., Sept. 8, 1954; d. Alexander and Marilyn (Marvel) Shafernich; m. William Coulson, Feb. 14, 1986. Student, Wellesley Coll., 1972-73; BS in Edn., U. Kans., 1976; cert. in phys. therapy, Northwestern U., Chgo., 1977; MBA, Keller Grad. Sch. Mgmt., 1985; postgrad., U. Ill., 1991. Lic. phys. therapist, Ill. Assoc. prof. dept. phys. therapy Chgo. Med. Sch., North Chicago, Ill., chmn. dept. phys. therapy, 1993-96. Contbr. articles to profl. jours. Trustee Northfield Twp., Ill., 1993-97; Ill. state rep. 57th dist., 1997—. Mem. APHA, Am. Phys. Therapy Assn. (Ill. del. 1986-93, chief del. 1991-93), Ill. Phys. Therapy Assn. (chmn. jud. com. 1989-91). Home: 1701 Sequoia Trl Glenview IL 60025-2022

COULSON, JOHN SELDEN, retired marketing executive; b. Chgo., Aug. 14, 1915; s. Leonard Ward and Mabel (Selden) C.; m. Jane Eleanor Rinder, Nov. 28, 1943; children: Jane Greer Coulson Sherry, Nancy Allen Coulson Hobor, Ann Selden Coulson Hubbard, Sara Rinder Coulson Ellis. BA, U. Chgo., 1936; MBA, Harvard U., 1938. With Montgomery Ward & Co., Chgo., 1938-41, 45-48; sr. assoc. Joseph White & Assos., Chgo., 1948-50; rsch. supr. Leo Burnett Co., Inc., Chgo., 1950-55, mgr. rsch. dept., 1955-58, v.p. charge rsch., 1958-77; dir. Leo Burnett USA, Chgo., 1973-77; ptnr. Communications Workshop, Inc., Chgo., 1977-90, ret., 1990; lectr. U. Chgo., 1955, 78, Northwestern U., 1960-71, Columbia Coll., 1974-76, U. Ill., 1977. Mktg. Issues editor Jour. Mktg, 1960-81; mem. editorial bd. Jour. Advt, 1971-83; mem. policy bd. Jour. Consumer Research, 1972-79; Contbr. chpts. to On Knowing the Consumer, 1966, Handbook of Modern Marketing, 1970, Cognitive and Affective Responses to Advertising, 1988. Mem. citizens bd. U. Chgo., 1969-75; bd. mgrs. Lawson YMCA, Chgo., 1970-89; bd. govs. Chgo. Heart Assn., 1980-91; mem. community adv. bd. Sta. WBEZ, Pub. Radio, Chgo., 1980—; mem. publicity com. Art Inst. Chgo., 1972-87. Lt. comdr. USNR, 1941-45. Mem. Am. Statis. Assn. (past pres. Chgo. chpt.), Am. Mktg. Assn. (past pres. Chgo. chpt., nat. v.p.), Am. Assn. for Pub. Opinion Rsch. (exec. coun. 1969-72, 78-81), U. Chgo. Alumni Assn. (pres. 1969-73, Alumni medal 1987), Univ. Club, Harvard Bus. Sch. Club Chgo. (bd. dirs. 1976-82), Psi Upsilon, Alpha Kappa Psi. Home: 41 Knox Cir Evanston IL 60201-1912 Home (summer): 13610 N Wabigama Dr Rapid City MI 49676-9303

COULSON, ROBERT, retired association executive, arbitrator, author; b. New Rochelle, N.Y., July 24, 1924; s. Robert Earl and Abby (Stewart) C.; m. Cynthia Cunningham, Oct. 16, 1961; children: Cotton Richard, Dierdre, Crocker, Robert Cromwell, Christopher. BA, Yale U., 1949; LLB, Harvard U., 1953; DSc in Bus. Adminstrn. (hon.), Bryant U., 1985; LLD (hon.), Hofstra U., 1987. Bar: N.Y. 1954, Mass. 1954. Assoc. Whitman, Ransom & Coulson, N.Y.C., 1954-61; ptnr. Littlefield, Miller & Cleaves, N.Y.C., 1961-63; exec. v.p. Am. Arbitration Assn., N.Y.C., 1963-71; pres. Am. Arbitration Assn., 1971-94; ret., 1994; Cons. N.Y. State Div. Youth, 1961-63; pres. Youth Consultation Service of N.Y., 1970. Author: How to Stay Out of Court, 1968, Labor Arbitration: What You Need to Know, 1973, Business Arbitration: What You Need to Know, 1980, The Termination Handbook, 1981, Fighting Fair, 1983, Arbitration in Schools, 1985, Business Mediation, 1987, Alcohol and Drugs in Arbitration, 1988, Empowered at Forty, 1990, Police Under Pressure, 1993, ADR in America, 1994, Family Mediation, 1996; editor: Racing at Sea, 1958; contbr. articles to profl. jours. Bd. dirs. Fedn. Protestant Welfare Agys., pres., 1982-84, chmn. 1985-87; adv. com. Internat. Coun. for Comml. Arbitration. Mem. N.Y. Yacht Club, Cruising Club Am., Riverside Yacht Club. Avocations: sailing, travel, writing. Home: 9 Reginald St Riverside CT 06878-2522

COULSON, WILLIAM ROY, lawyer; b. Waukegan, Ill., Oct. 5, 1949; s. Robert E. and Rose (Stone) C.; m. Elizabeth A. Shafernich, Feb. 14, 1986. AB, Dartmouth Coll., 1969; JD, U. Ill., 1972. Bar: Ill. 1972, U.S. Dist. Ct. (no. dist.) Ill. 1974, U.S. Supreme Ct. 1976. Law clk. to judge U.S. Dist. Ct., East St. Louis, Ill., 1972-74, Chgo., 1975; asst. U.S. atty. U.S. Dept. Justice, Chgo., 1975-88, supr. criminal div., 1980-88; mng. ptnr. Cherry & Flynn, Chgo., 1988—; faculty Atty. Gens. Adv. Inst., Washington, 1980-88, Ill. Inst. for Continuing Legal Edn., Springfield, 1983-88, Fed. Law Enforcement Tng. Ctr., Glynco, Ga., 1983-86; co-chmn. U.S. Magistrate Merit Selection Panel, 1989-91. Author: Federal Juvenile Law, 1980; contbg. author Animation mag., 1993—. Served to 2d lt. Ill. N.G., 1965-66. Finalist U.S. Senate Jud. Selection Panel, 1996. Mem. ABA, Chgo. Bar Assn. (jud. evaluation com. 1987-89, vice chair 1990-91), Fed. Bar Assn. (pres. 1991-92), Dartmouth Club. Office: 30 N La Salle St Chicago IL 60602-2502

COULSON, ZOE ELIZABETH, retired consumer marketing executive; b. Sullivan, Ind., Sept. 22, 1932; d. Marion Allan and Mary Anne (Thompson) C. BS, Purdue U., 1954; AMP, Harvard U., 1983. Asst. dir. home econs. Am. Meat Inst., Chgo., 1954-57; acct. exec. J. Walter Thompson Co., Chgo., 1957-60; creative consumer dir. Leo Burnett Co., Chgo., 1960-64; mag. editor-in-chief Donnelley-Dun & Bradstreet, N.Y.C., 1964-68; food editor Good Housekeeping, N.Y.C., 1968-75; dir. G H Inst., 1975-81; corp. v.p. Campbell Soup Co., Camden, N.J., 1981-91, mktg. cons., 1991—. Author: Good Housekeeping Cookbook, 1972, Good Housekeeping Illustrated Cookbook, 1981. Trustee Cooper Hosp./Univ. Med. Ctr., 1982-91; elder Old Pine Presbyn. Ch., 1992-96; vol. exec. Internat. Exec. Svcs. Corp., 1998—. Named Disting. Alumni Purdue U., 1971. Mem. Women's Econ. Bus. Alliance (bd. govs. 1987-91), Food and Drug Law Inst. (food bd. dirs. 1979-81), Harvard Bus. Sch. Club (Phila. v.p. bidget 1994-95, mem. program com. 1993—), Soc. Hill Towns Assn. (mem. coun. 1997-99), Kappa Alpha Theta House Corp. (pres. U. Pa. chpt. 1992—). Republican. Avocation: Meso-Am. archaeology. Home: 220 Locust St Apt 18-b Philadelphia PA 19106-3931

COULSTON, STEPHEN BRETT, architect; b. Odessa, Tex., Oct. 4, 1967; s. Benny Carl Coulston and Barbara June (Townsend) Holt; m. Margaret Ann Fitzsimmons, July 1, 1995. BArch, Tex. Tech. U., 1992. Registered architect, Va. Intern Automall Design, Inc., Dallas, 1990, Masters & Assocs. Land Planners, Lubbock, Tex., 1991-92; project architect Einhorn Yaffee Prescott, P.C., Washington, 1992-96; dir. of bus. devel. Richter, Cornbrooks, Gribble, Inc., Balt., 1996—. Contbr. articles to profl. jours. Architect, engr. com. mem. Greater Balt. Com., 1996—; com. mem. Greater Balt. Com. Sch. Bus. Adv. Com., 1997—, Greater Balt. Com. Technology Com., 1997—. Mem. AIA (Young Architects Forum, Mid-Atlantic Regional Liaison 1997—, intern devel. program com. 1997—), Soc. for Coll. and Univ. Planning, Nat. Trust for Hist. Preservation. Home: 436 E Randall St Baltimore MD 21230-4644 Office: Richter Cornbrooks Gribble Inc 12th Fl 231 E Baltimore St Fl 12 Baltimore MD 21202-3410

COULTER, BORDEN MCKEE, retired management consultant; b. Casper, Wyo., Feb. 9, 1917; s. Borden McKee and Josephine Helen (Grother) C.; m. Emily Sawtelle, Aug. 23, 1950; children: Borden, Terry Lynn, Leigh, Richard. BS, UCLA, 1939, MBA, 1947. Rsch. analyst Australian Nat. R.R., 1939-40; indsl. engr. Lockheed Aircraft, 1940-47, staff indsl. engr., 1948-50; with div. indsl. engring. U.S. Steel Corp., 1947; mgr. prodn. control Bakewell Products, 1947; supr. orgn. and procedures Norris Industries, 1950-53; gen. mgr. Roed Engring. Assocs., 1943-45; prin., sr. v.p., dir. The Emerson Cons., Inc., 1960-88; mgmt. cons. N.Y.C., 1954-88; chmn. bd. Omega Cons. Inc., Atlanta, 1980-98. Contbr. articles to profl. jours. Fellow Inst. Dirs.; mem. Am. Inst. Indsl. Engrs. (pres. L.A. chpt.), Am. Mgmt. Assn. (Wall of Honor), Am. Inst. Plant Engrs., Nat. Assn. Accountants Am., Newcomen Soc., U.S. Naval Inst., Navy League U.S., Internat. Mgmt. Consultants, Nat. Petroleum Refiners Assn., Am. Arbitration Assn., Nat., Tex. Socs. Profl. Engrs., Assn. Mng. Cons., Houston Soc. Cons. Engrs. Blue Key, Kappa Kappa Psi, Alpha Kappa Psi, Tau Kappa Alpha, Phi Gamma Delta, Petroleum Club. Home: 12351 Escala Dr San Diego CA 92128-1208*

COULTER, CHARLES ROY, lawyer; b. Webster City, Iowa, June 10, 1940; s. Harold L. Coulter and Eloise (Wheeler) Harrison; m. Elizabeth Bean, Dec. 16, 1961; 1 child, Anne Elizabeth. BA in Journalism, U. Iowa, 1962, JD, 1965. Bar: Iowa 1965. Assoc. Stanley, Bloom, Mealy & Lande, Muscatine, Iowa, 1965-68; v.p. Stanley, Lande & Hunter, Muscatine, 1969—, also bd. dirs. County fin. chmn. Leach for Congress, 1980-96; county coord. George Bush for Pres. , 1980, 88, Reagan-Bush Campaign, 1984. Fellow Coll. of Law Practice Mgmt., Am. Bar Found., Iowa State Bar Found., Am. Coll. Trust and Estate Counsel; mem. ABA (mem. coun. law practice mgmt. sect. 1984-88, sec. 1988-89, vice chair 1989-90, chair 1991-92, chair coord. commn. legal tech. 1994-97, mem. standing com. on tech. and info. sys. 1997-98), Iowa Bar Assn., Muscatine County Bar Assn., Thirty-Three Club (pres. 1981), Rotary, Order of Coif. Episcopalian. Avocation: tennis. Office: Stanley Lande & Hunter 301 Iowa Ave Ste 400 Muscatine IA 52761-3881

COULTER, DAVID CRESWELL, research engineer; b. Fargo, N.D., Apr. 4, 1928; s. John Lee and Phoebe Frost Coulter; m. Winifred Alice Russell, Apr. 4, 1952; children: Douglas Lee, Ann Claire, James Russell. BS in Physics/Math., Am. U., Washington, 1951. Electronic scientist U.S. Naval Rsch. Lab., Washington, 1951-54, electronic engr., 1966-84; electronic engr. Melpar, Inc., Falls Church, Va., 1954-66; rsch. engr. Gallaudet U., Washington, 1987-90; prs. Coulter Assocs., Inc., Fairfax, Va., 1978—; co-founder Metavox, Inc., Fairfax, 1983—; CEO Metavox, Inc., Fairfax, Va., 1987-98; cons., engr. Gallaudet U., Washington, 1990-95. Contbr. articles to profl. jours. Deacon Grace Presbyn. Ch., Springfield, Va., 1956-58. Mem. IEEE (sr. mem.), Acoustical Soc. Am. Republican. Achievements include patents for method and apparatus for improving binaunal hearing, method and system for speech compression, system for determining consonant formant loci, frequency, amplitude, time plotter with simulated three dimensional display. Home: 9613 Pembroke Pl Vienna VA 22182-1443 Office: Coulter Assocs Inc 2821 Dorr Ave Ste R Fairfax VA 22031-1510

COULTER, ELIZABETH JACKSON, biostatistician, educator; b. Balt., Nov. 2, 1919; d. Waddie Pennington and Bessie (Gills) Jackson; m. Norman Arthur Coulter Jr., June 23, 1951; 1 child, Robert Jackson. A.B., Swarthmore Coll., 1941; A.M., Radcliffe Coll., 1946, Ph.D., 1948. Asst. dir. health study Bur. Labor Stats., San Juan, P.R., 1946; research asst. Milbank Meml. Fund, N.Y.C., 1948-51; economist Office Def. Prodn., 1951-52; research analyst Children's Bur.-HEW, 1952-53; from statistician to chief statistician Ohio Dept. Health, 1954-65; lectr. econs., then clin. asst. prof. preventive medicine Ohio State U., 1954-65; asst. clin. prof. biostats. U. Pitts. Sch. Pub. Health, 1958-62; assoc. prof. biostats. U. N.C., Chapel Hill, 1965-72, assoc. prof. econs., 1965-78, biostats. prof., 1972-90; adj. assoc. prof., hosp. adminstr. Duke U., 1972-79; assoc. dean undergrad. pub. health studies U. N.C., Chapel Hill, 1979-86, prof. biostats. emerita, 1990—. Contbr. articles to profl. jours. Mem. AAAS, AAUP, APHA (governing coun. 1970-72), Am. Econ. Assn., Am. Statis. Assn., Am. Acad. Polit. and Social Sci., Biometric Soc., Am. Evaluation Assn., Assn. for Health Svcs. Rsch., Sigma Xi, Delta Omega. Methodist. Home: 1825 N Lakeshore Dr Chapel Hill NC 27514-6734

COULTER, FREDRIK VLADIMIR, accountant, consultant; b. Glen Cove, N.Y., Apr. 30, 1958; s. Fred Profitt and Xenia Valerie (Bibicoff) C.; m. Lisa Kay Osterman, Sept. 24, 1988; children: Kathryn Victoria, Christina Marie. BBA in Acctg., Stetson U., 1994, BS in Computer Sci., 1994, M in Acctg., 1995. CPA, Fla.; cert. Novell adminstr.; cert. Internet bus. strategist; cert. mgmt. acct.; cert. internet bus. strategist; Microsoft Office user specialist, Excel 97 expert. Dir. billing Internat. Contract Furnishings, Orangeburg, N.Y., 1984-88, Sheft & Sheft, N.Y.C., 1988-90; staff acct. Morrison Brown Argiz & Co. LLP, Orlando, Fla., 1995-96; acct. Cuthill & Eddy LLP, Winter Park, Fla., 1996—. Mem. AICPA, Inst. Mgmt. Accts. (cert.), Fla. Inst. CPA (cert. of merit 1995), Greater Orlando NetWare Users Group. Libertarian. Avocations: music, hiking, reading, technology. Fax: 407 628-5277. E-mail: fcoulter@mpinet.net. Home: 916 N Boston Ave Deland FL 32724-2980 Office: Cuthill & Eddy LLP 1031 W Morse Blvd Ste 200 Winter Park FL 32789

COULTER, JAMES BENNETT, state official; b. Vinita, Okla., Aug. 2, 1920; s. Robert Leslie and Louise (Robinson) C.; m. Norma R. Brink, June 1, 1942; children: Linda Coulter Prandoni, James Bennett. BS in Civil Engring, U. Kans., 1950; MS, Harvard U., 1954; DSc (hon.), Washington Coll., 1979. Registered profl. engr., Md., Kans. Commd. officer USPHS, 1950-66; asst. commr. environ. health Md. Dept. Health, Balt., 1966-69; sec. Md. Dept. Natural Resources, Annapolis, 1969-82; mem. vis. com. Sch. Engring. and Applied Physics, Harvard U.; mem. adv. com. Sch. Engring., U. Kan., Civitan. Bd. dirs. Blue Shield Md.; trustee Chesapeake Research Consortium; mem. exec. bd. Md. Save Our Streams. Served with C.E. AUS, 1940-45. Decorated Bronze Star. Mem. NAE, Am. Acad. Environ. Engrs. (Gordon M. Fair award 1971, pres. 1978), Am. Public Health Assn., Am. Water Works Assn. (Fuller award 1987), Water Pollution Control Fedn., Tau Beta Pi, Sigma Tau. Home: 778 Eastern Point Rd Annapolis MD 21401-6945

COULTER, JEFFREY PHILIP, sociology educator, writer; b. Liverpool, Eng., May 25, 1948; s. Philip and Phyllis Mabel (Jones) C.; m. Lena Jayyusi, Sept. 12, 1970 (div. June 1990); 1 child, Jinan; m. Amal Almawi, Aug. 17, 1996. BA, Durham (Eng.) U., 1969; MA Econ., Manchester (Eng.) U., 1970, PhD, 1975. Faculty rsch. assoc. U. Manchester, 1970-71, lectr., 1971-74; vis. lectr. Boston U., 1974-75, asst. prof. sociology, 1975-81, chmn. dept. sociology, 1985-90, assoc. prof. sociology, 1989-93, chmn. dept. sociology, 1985-90, prof., 1993—; hon. sr. rsch. fellow, U. Lancaster, Eng., 1986—; Hon. Simon Vis. Prof., U. Manchester, 1993. Author: Approaches to Insanity, 1973, The Social Construction of Mind, 1979, Rethinking Cognitive Theory, 1983, Mind in Action, 1989; assoc. editor (jour.) Human Studies, 1978—. Avocations: 20th century history, politics, travel, comedy, movies, science fiction. Office: Boston U Dept Sociology 96 Cummington St Boston MA 02215-2407

COULTER, JOHN ARTHUR, academic administrator; b. Buffalo, N.Y., July 24, 1944; s. William David and Myra Elizabeth (Murray) C.; m. Ann Ahrens, July 4, 1966; children: Jennifer, Kelly, Amanda. BS, SUNY, Buffalo, 1967, MBA, 1975. Asst. to chmn. dept. physics SUNY, Buffalo, 1967-69, asst. dean Sch. of Pharmacy, 1969-73; asst. dean/adminstr./dir admissions SUNY, 1973-75; asst./assoc. dean medicine SUNY, Stony Brook, 1975-79; asst. v.p. health scis. U. Wash, Seattle, 1979-83, assoc. v.p. health scis., 1983-92; exec. dir, health scis adminstn./assoc. v.p. for med. affairs U. Wash., Seattle, 1992—. Bd. dirs. Cmty. Health Plan of Suffolk, N.Y., 1978-79, Wash. Assn. for Biomed. Rsch., Seattle, 1988-96, Nat. Assn. for Biomed. Rsch., 1996, Poison Control Ctr., Seattle, 1994—; active United Way Leadership Tomorrow, C. of C., Seattle, 1985. Mem. Am. Assn. Med. Colls., Assn. Acad. Health Scis. Ctrs. Avocations: sailing, skiing. Office: Univ Wash Health Scis Ctr PO Box 356355 Seattle WA 98195-6355

COULTER, JULIENNE ELLEN, secondary education educator, consultant; b. Peru, Ill., Jan. 24, 1943; d. Walter Harold and Pearl Grace (Baker) C. BS in Edn., Ill. State U., Normal, 1964, MS in English, 1977. English tchr. Gardner-South Wilmington Twp. H.S., Gardner, Ill., 1964—; mem. validation com. for Ill. Goal Assessment program Ill. State Bd. Edn., Springfield, 1985—;. Co-author: (manual) Write On, Illinois Training, 1986-87; co-author video. Mem. referendum com. Dwight Schs. Dist., 1988; mem. scholarship com. The Saints: Vols. for the Arts, Chgo., 1992-98. Finalist Ill. Tchr. Yr., 1995. Mem. NEA, Ill. Edn. Assn., Delta Kappa Gamma (v.p., pres. 1980-84). Avocations: reading, theater, gardening. Office: Gardner S Wilmington HS 500 E Main St Gardner IL 60424

COULTER, MYRON LEE, retired academic administrator; b. Albany, Ind., Mar. 21, 1929; s. Mark Earl and Thelma Violet (Marks) C.; m. Barbara Bolinger, July 21, 1951; children: Nan and Benjamin (twins). BS, Ind. State Tchrs. Coll., 1951; MS, Ind. U., 1956, EdD, 1959; HLD (hon.), Coll. Idaho, 1982. Tchr. English Reading (Mich.) Pub. Schs., 1951-52; tchr. elem. grades Bloomington (Ind.) Pub. Schs., 1954-56; instr. edn. Ind. U., Bloomington, 1958-59; asst. prof. Pa. State U., 1959-64, assoc. prof., 1964-66; vis. prof. U. Alaska, Fairbanks, 1965; assoc. dean edn., prof. edn. Western Mich. U., Kalamazoo, 1966-68, v.p. for adminstrn., prof. edn., 1968-76, interim pres., 1974; pres. Idaho State U., Pocatello, 1976-84; chancellor Western Carolina U., Cullowhee, N.C., 1984-94, chancellor emeritus, 1994—; del. Israeli Univs., 1976, Am. Assn. State Colls. and Univs. to People's Republic of China, 1981, Swaziland Coll. Tech., 1985, People's Republic China, 1985, 87, 88, 90, Jamaica, 1986, 89, 91, 94, Thailand, 1987, 90, The Netherlands, 1991; cons. in field. Author school textbooks. Bd. dirs. Kalamazoo C. of C., 1975-76, Pocatello Jr. Achievement; bd. dirs., chair N.C. Arboretum, 1994—; bd. dirs. WNC Pub. Radio, WNC Devel. Assn., WNC Tomorrow, Joint PVO/Univ. Rural Devel. Ctr., WNC Commn. Found.; lay leader Kalamazoo Meth. Ch., 1971-74; mem. Gov.'s Task Force on Aquaculture, 1988, N.C. Bd. Sci. and Tech., 1993—, Commn. for Competitive N.C., 1993—; chair N.C. Indian Gaming Cert. Commn., 1994—; trustee Bronson Hosp., Kalamazoo, 1975-76, N.C. Ctr. Advancement Teaching, C.J. Harris Community Hosp. With AUS, 1952-54. Named Disting. Alumnus, Ind. State U., 1975, Ind. U., 1994; recipient award Western Mich. U. Alumni Assn., 1974, resolution of tribute Mich. State Legislature, 1976. Mem. Internat. Reading Assn., Am. Assn. State Colls. and Univs. (bd. dirs. 1981-84, exec. com. 1981-84, sec.-treas. 1984-87, found. bd. dirs. 1987—, chmn. 1988-89), Nat. Soc. Study of Edn., N.C. Assn. Colls. and Univs. (bd. dirs.), Western Coll. Assn., Pocatello C. of C. (bd. dirs. 1977-80), Asheville C. of C. (bd. dirs. 1985-86), Cherokee Hist. Assn., Ind. U. Coll. Edn. Alumni Assn. (Disting. Alumnus award 1994), Phi Delta Kappa, Omicron Delta Kappa, Phi Kappa Phi, Beta Gamma Sigma. Office: Western Carolina Univ Office Chancellor Emeritus 61 Hunter Cullowhee NC 28723

COULTER, NORMAN ARTHUR, JR., biomedical engineering educator emeritus; b. Atlanta, Jan. 9, 1920; s. Norman Arthur and Carabelle (Clark) C.; m. Elizabeth Harwell Jackson, June 23, 1951; 1 child, Robert Jackson. B.S., Va. Poly. Inst., 1941; M.D., Harvard U., 1950; postdoctoral fellow, Johns Hopkins U., 1950-52. Instr. math. dept. Va. Poly. Inst., 1946; asst. to assoc. prof. physiology dept. Ohio State U., 1952-65; dir. biophysics div., physiology dept., 1962-65; assoc. prof. depts. surgery and physiology U. N.C., Chapel Hill, 1965-67; prof. U. N.C., 1967-90, prof. emeritus, 1990—, chmn. bioengring.-biomath. program, 1969-82, dir. grad. studies, 1982-90. *As an infantry officer, Coulter was thrilled by the atomic bomb. But he soon became convinced that the only sure way to prevent a nuclear holocaust was to abolish war itself. He began a long term project to develop a new mode of thinking called tracking which would generalize logical thinking to address beliefs and values in a scientific spirit. Tracking uses simple mental programs which promote synergy among mental and psychosocial processes. Coulter also became active in physicians for social responsibility. He served on its Board of Directors and received its Broad Street Pump and Peacemaker awards.* Author: Synergetics: An Adventure in Human Development, 1976; also articles in profl. jours. Served to maj. A.A. AUS, 1941-46. Mem. AMA, IEEE, Internat. Soc. Biorhel, Biophys. Soc., Am. Physiol. Soc., Biomed. Enging. Soc., Soc. Gen. Sys. Rsch., Physicians for Social Responsibility, Sigma Xi. Home: 1825 N Lakeshore Dr Chapel Hill NC 27514-6734

COULTER, PHILIP WYLIE, physicist, educator; b. Phenix City, Ala., Apr. 19, 1938; s. Leonard Alton and Winslow Lanae (Gullatt) C.; m. Peggy Jean Mullins, Nov. 23, 1960 (dec. Apr. 1986); children: Pippa, Kathryn; m. Lucinda Beth Hill, Nov. 8, 1986; 1 child, Eric. BS, U. Ala., 1959, MS, 1961; PhD, Stanford U., 1965. Research assoc. U. Mich., Ann Arbor, 1965-66; asst. prof. U. Calif., Irvine, 1967-71; assoc. prof. U. Ala., Tuscaloosa, 1971-76, prof. physics, 1976—, chmn. dept., 1981-91; cons. Oak Ridge (Tenn.) Nat. Lab., 1979-82. Contbr. articles to profl. jours. NSF fellow, 1961-64. Mem. Am. Phys. Soc., Phi Beta Kappa, Sigma Xi. Democrat. Office: U Ala Dept Physics and Astronomy Box 870324 Tuscaloosa AL 35487-0324*

COULTER, SHERRY PARKS, secondary education educator; b. Milw., May 11, 1950; d. Elizabeth (Humphrey) Parks; divorced; children: Thomas Lloyd, William Lloyd. BS in Edn., Framingham State Coll., 1972—; postgrad., Firchburg State Coll., 1994—. Head family & consumer scis. Gardner H.S., Gardner, Mass., 1972—; mem. adv. bd. Gardner H.S., 1990-95, mem. peer edn. adv. bd., 1991—; cons. Pampered Chef. pres. G.G. Jaycees, Gardner, 1979-80; incorporater Cath. of the Pines, Rinqe, N.H., 1983-88; hosp. aid Heywood Hosp., Gardner, 1995; mem. Teen Pregnancy Task Force, 1993—; chair Friendly Rememberabces Com., 1980. Named Tchr. of

Yr. Family Circle, 1980, Mass. Tchr. of Yr. Mem. Mass. Home Econs. Assn. (v.p. 1992-94), Gardner Edn. Assn. (bldg. rep. 1993-95, 96—), Worcester County Family and Consumer Scis. (pres. 1994-96, v.p. Worcester County 1996-99), Mass. Family & Consumer Sci. (v.p. 1992-94), Coll. Club. Avocations: skiing, camping, fishing, travel. Home: 47 Vine St Leominster MA 01453-2769 Office: Gardner High Sch 200 Catherine St Gardner MA 01440-2098

COUNCIL, TERRY RAY, military officer; b. Oakley, Kans., May 1, 1953; s. Dewey Junior and Phyllis Lorene (Hosley) C.; m. Ruth Louise Newman, Dec. 27, 1974; children: Charles R., Michael S., Lisa A., David A., Johnathan R., Sarah C. BSBA, Panhandle State U., 1975; MA in Procurement and Acquistion Mgmt., Webster U., 1994. Commd. 2d lt. U.S. Army, 1975, advanced through grades to lt. col.; ops. officer 10th ADA Group, Aviation Sec., Fed. Republic Germany, 1976-79; flight instr., combat skills 1st Bat./1st Aviation Bde, Ft. Rucker, Ala., 1980-81, flight comdr., combat skills, 1981-82; co. comdr. 12th Co., 1st Bat., 1st Avn Bde, Ft. Rucker, 1982-83; ops. officer 201st Assault Helicopter Co./17th Avn Bde, Republic of Korea, 1983-84; avn procurement officer AHIP, Avn systems Command, St. Louis, 1984-85; chief, OH-58 Procurement Sec. Avn Systems Command, St. Louis, 1985-86; bat. exec. officer 45th Aviation Bat., Tulsa, Okla., 1986-87; co. comdr. HHC, 1st Bat./245th Avn, Tulsa, 1987-89; co. comdr. maintenance co D Co, 1st Bat./245th Avn, 1989-91; bat. exec. officer 1st Bat./245th Avn, Tulsa, 1991-92, bat. comdr., 1992-94; aviation support facility comdr. AASF #2, Tulsa, 1991-96; sr. svc. coll. fellow U. Tex., Austin, 1996-97. Aviation support facility comdr. AASF #2, Tulsa, 1997—. Mem. Nat. Guard Assn., Army Aviation Assn. Republican. Avocations: golf, jogging, racquet ball. Home: 1829 N 14th St Broken Arrow OK 74012-9350 Office: AASF-Tulsa 4242 N Mingo Valley Expy Tulsa OK 74116-5001

COUNCILMAN, RICHARD ROBERT, product development engineer; b. L.A., Apr. 25, 1922; s. Frank Dwight and Gladys Vera (Clark) C.; m. Louise Perry Spalding (div.); children: Richard Martin, Robert Gordon; m. Barbara McCollough (div.); 1 child, Scott Richard; m. Shirley Ann DeVries, Apr. 25, 1964; 1 child, Marc Wayne. Chief draftsman USN, Pasadena & China Lake, Calif., 1944-49; engring. supr. USAF, Edwards AFB, Calif., 1949-51; sr. design specialist Bill Jack Scientific Inst., Solana Beach, Calif., 1951-52; head optical meche. rsch. Hughes Aircraft Flight Test, Culver City, Calif., 1952-56; group supr. rsch. & devel. LTV Elecs., Garland, Tex., 1956-64; sr. engring. specialist rsch. & devel. Conductron Divsn. McDonald Douglas, St. Louis, 1965-70; sr. project engr. Sr. Scientist Lab. Brunswick Corp., St. Louis, 1968-75; dir., chmn. bd. Imperial Gen. Life Ins. Co., St. Louis, 1970-75; sr. project rsch. & devel. Brunswick Corp., Tulsa, 1975-87; cons. product devel. pvt. practice, Collinsville, Okla., 1987—; cons. in field. Fellow Internat. Soc. Optical Engring., Soc. Photo-Optical Engrs. (pres. 1955-56). Achievements include patentee in field. Home: 17001 N 137th East Ave Collinsville OK 74021-4415

COUNSELL, PAUL S., advertising executive. CEO Cramer-Krasselt Co. Office: Cramer-Krasselt 733 N Van Buren St Fl 4 Milwaukee WI 53202-4799*

COUNSELMAN, ANNE, librarian; b. Silas, Ala., Oct. 5, 1940; d. Chester Arthur and Elva (Daniels) Martin; m. Terry J. Counselman; children: Daphne, Bruce, Phillip. BS, U. Montevallo, Ala., 1961; MA, U. Ala., Birmingham, 1979; EdS, U. Ala., Tuscaloosa, 1988. Tchr. Clarke County Bd. Edn., Grove Hill, Ala., 1966-69; libr. asst. Birmingham Pub. Libr., 1971-72, head bookmobile, 1972-73; project dir. Appalachian Adult Edn. Ctr., Birmingham, 1974-75; libr. Birmingham City Bd. Edn., 1975-76, Wallace State C.C., Selma, Ala., 1980-83, Marengo County Bd. Edn., Linden, Ala., 1984—; reader rsch. and rev. team Libr. Rsch. and Demonstration Div. Libr. Programs, Washington, 1974. Mem. Thomaston (Ala.) Planning and Zoning Bd., 1992, 93; active Thomaston Bapt. Ch. Linly Heflin scholar, 1958-61, scholar Columbus Sch. Speech Correction, 1960, Pacers scholar Program for Rural Svcs. and Rsch., 1987; fellow Coun. for Basic Edn., 1992. Mem. NEA, Am. Edn. Assn., Ala. Edn. Assn., Thomaston Study Club. Home: 122 Lake Cir Thomaston AL 36783-3030 Office: AL Johnson High Sch Coates Ave Thomaston AL 36783

COUNSIL, WILLIAM GLENN, electric utility executive; b. Detroit, Dec. 13, 1937; s. Glenn Dempsey and Jean Beverly (Rzepecki) C.; m. Donna Elizabeth Robinson, Sept. 10, 1960; children: Glenn, Craig. Student, U. Mich., 1955-56; BS, U.S. Naval Acad., 1960; Advanced Mgmt. Program, Harvard U., 1991. Ops. supr., asst. plant supt.. sta. supt. N.E. Nuclear Energy Co., Waterford, Conn., 1967-76; project mgr., v.p. nuclear engring. and ops. N.E. Utilities, Hartford, Conn., 1976-80, sr. v.p. nuclear engring. and ops., 1980-85; exec. v.p. nuclear engring. and ops., electric-generating div. Tex. Utilities Generating Co., 1985-88; vice chmn. Tex. Utilities Electric Co., 1989-93; mng. dir. Wash. Pub. Power Supply System, Richland, 1993-96. With USN, 1956-67. Recipient Outstanding Leadership award ASME, 1986. Republican. Presbyterian. *My goal has been to improve our quality of life first through service in the United States Navy and second by ensuring an adequate and safe energy supply for our country.*

COUNSILMAN, JAMES EDWARD, physical education educator; b. Birmingham, Ala., Dec. 28, 1920; s. Joseph Walter and Ottilia Lena (Schamburg) C.; m. Marjorie E. Scrafford, June 15, 1943; children: Cathy, James (dec.), Jill, Brian. B.S., Ohio State U., 1947; M.S., U. Ill., 1948; Ph.D., U. Iowa, 1951. Mem. phys. edn. faculty, swim coach Cortland (N.Y.) State U., 1952-57; mem. faculty Ind. U., Bloomington, 1957-90; prof. phys. edn. Ind. U., 1966-90, swim coach, 1957-90; pres. Counsilman Co., Inc. (film producers and publishers), 1971-90, Counsilman/Hunsaker and Assocs. (swimming pool constrn. cons.), 1971-89. Author: The Science of Swimming, 1969, rev. edit., 1994, The Complete Book of Swimming, 1977, Competitive Swimming Manual, 1977. U.S. Olympic Men's Team coach, 1964, 76; founding pres. Internat. Swimming Hall of Fame, 1963. Served as bomber pilot USAAF, 1943-45. Decorated Air medal with cluster, D.F.C. Ind. swim teams have won 20 consecutive Big Ten Swimming championships, 1961-80, 83, 84, 85; 6 consecutive NCAA championships, 1968-73. Fellow Am. Coll. Sports Medicine; mem. AAHPER, Am. Swim Coaches Assn. (past pres.), Coll. Swim Coaches Assn., English Channel Swim Assn. Home: 3602 William Ct Bloomington IN 47401-4487

COUNTRYMAN, DAYTON WENDELL, lawyer; b. Sioux City, Iowa, Mar. 31, 1918; s. Cleve and Susie (Schaeffer) C.; m. Ruth Hazen, Feb. 2, 1941; children—Karen, Joan, James, Kay. B.S., Iowa State Coll., 1940; LL.B., State U. Iowa, 1948, J.D., 1969. Bar: Iowa bar 1948. Since practiced in Nevada; ptnr. Hadley & Countryman, Nevada, Iowa, 1949-64; mem. Countryman & Zaffarano P.C., 1984-87, Dayton Countryman Law Offices, P.C., 1987—; county atty. Story County (Iowa), 1950-54; atty. gen. Iowa, 1954-56; Candidate for U.S. Senate, 1956, 1960, 68. Air Force Res. pilot USAAF, 1941-46. Mem. VFW, Am. Legion, Iowa State U. Alumni Assn. (pres. 1970-71), Am., Iowa, Story County bar assns., Iowa 2B Jud. Dist. Assn. Methodist. Clubs: Masons, Lions (pres. 1975-76). Office: PO Box 28, 1001 5th Street Nevada IA 50201-0028

COUNTRYMAN, EDWARD FRANCIS, historian, educator; b. Glens Falls, N.Y., July 31, 1944; s. Edward Francis and Agnes (Alford) C.; m. Evonne von Heussen, 1987; children: Karon Samantha, Kirstein Dawn; 1 son from previous marriage, Samuel Robert. BA, Manhattan Coll., 1966; MA, Cornell U., Ithaca, N.Y., 1969; PhD, Cornell U., 1971. Lectr. in history U. Canterbury (N.Z.), 1970-74; lectr. U. Warwick (Eng.), 1975-83, sr. lectr., 1983-88, reader, 1988-91; prof. So. Meth. U., Dallas, 1991—; vis. lectr. U. Cambridge (Eng.), 1979-80; vis. scholar NYU, N.Y.C., 1980-81; Cardozo vis. prof. Yale U., spring 1989. Cons. editor: Radical History Rev., 1982—; author: A People in Revolution, 1981 (Bancroft prize 1982), The American Revolution, 1985, (video) American Independence 1776, 1989, Americans: A Collision of Histories, 1996; co-author: Who Built America, 1990, Shane, 1999; editor: How Did American Slavery Begin?, 1998, What Did the Constitution Mean to Early Americans?, 1998. Active civil rights movement, U.S., 1965-68; spokesperson Anti-War Movement, N.Z., 1970-73; active Campaign for Nuclear Disarmament, Eng., 1981—. Woodrow Wilson fellow, 1966-67; Danforth fellow, 1966-71; Samuel Foster Haven fellow, 1983; Mellon vis. sr. scholar U. Cambridge, Eng., 1998. Home: 5454 Anita St Dallas TX 75206-5336 Office: So Meth U Dept History Dallas TX 75275

COUNTRYMAN, GARY LEE, insurance company executive; b. South Bend, Wash., July 30, 1939; s. William T. and Vernela K. (Stewart) C.; m. Sally Ann Mathews, Aug. 16, 1958; children: Christopher John, Susan Michelle, Sherry LeeAnn, Stefanie May. B.S., U. Oreg., 1961, M.S., 1963. With Liberty Mut. Ins. Co., Boston, 1963—, pres., 1981—, pres., chief exec. officer, 1986-91; chmn., pres., chief exec. officer Liberty Mut. Ins. Co., 1991-92, chmn., 1992—, chmn., CEO; bd. dirs. Liberty Mut. Ins. Group, Bank of Boston Corp., 1st Nat. Bank Boston, Boston Edison Co., Harcourt Gen., Inc., Alliance Am. Insurers; chmn. bd. dirs. Boston Mgmt. Consortium, Inc. Bd. dirs. Inst. Civil Justice, Jobs for Mass., Inc., Com. for Econ. Devel.; trustee Northeastern U., U. New Eng., Mus. Sci., Sudbury Valley Trustees; chmn. bd. Dana-Farber Cancer Inst.; bd. overseers Mass. Gen. Hosp. H.T. Miner fellow, 1962-63. Mem. NAM, Am. Inst. Property and Liability Underwriters (bd. dirs.), Algonquin Club. Office: Liberty Mut Ins Co 175 Berkeley St Boston MA 02116-5066

COUNTS, STANLEY THOMAS, aerospace consultant, retired naval officer, retired electronics company executive; b. Okfuskee County, Okla., July 3, 1926; s. Claud Curtley and Thelma (Thomas) C.; m. Bettejan Heft, Nov. 18, 1949; 1 child, Ashlie Heft. B.S., U.S. Naval Acad., 1949; B.S. in Elec. Engring, U.S. Naval Postgrad. Sch., 1954, M.S. in Elec. Engring, 1955. Commd. ensign U.S. Navy, 1949, advanced through grades to rear adm., 1972; comdg. officer USS Bronstein, 1963-64, comdg. officer USS Towers, 1966-68, project mgr. NATO Seasparrow Surface Missile System, 1968-70, comdg. officer USS Chgo., 1970-71; dir. ships, weapons, electronics and asso. systems Office Asst. Sec. Def. for Installations and Logistics Washington, 1971-73; dep. comdr. Naval Ordnance Systems Command, 1973-74; comdr. (Naval Ordnance Systems Command), 1974; vice comdr. Naval Sea Systems Command, 1974-76; comdr. Cruiser-Destroyer Group 5 San Diego, 1976-78; ret., 1978; exec. Hughes Aircraft Co., Fullerton, Calif., 1979-89; ret., 1989; aerospace cons., chief exec. officer Bjan Enterprises, La Jolla, Calif., 1989—; chmn. Seasparrow steering com. NATO, 1973-76. Bd. dirs. San Diego chpt. Freedoms Found. at Valley Forge, 1992-94, 97-98, greater La Jolla Meals on Wheels, Inc., 1998—. Decorated Legion of Merit with three oak leaf clusters, Bronze Star with combat distinguishing device. Mem. VFW, Surface Navy Assn. (life, bd. dirs. 1985-93), U.S. Naval Inst. (life), DAV (life), Ret. Officers Assn. (life), Navy League, Am. Legion, Rest and Aspiration Club San Diego. Home: 856 La Jolla Rancho Rd La Jolla CA 92037-7408

COUPER, RICHARD WATROUS, foundation executive, educator; b. Binghamton, N.Y., Dec. 16, 1922; s. Edgar W. and Esther (Watrous) C.; m. Patricia Pogue, Sept. 24, 1946; children: Frederick Pogue, Barrett Williams, Thomas Hayes, Margaret Couper Haskins. AB, Hamilton Coll., Clinton, N.Y., 1947, LLD (hon.), 1969; AM in Am. History, Harvard U., 1948; LLD (hon.), St. Joseph's Coll., 1982, Wesleyan U., 1986; LHD (hon.), NYU, 1974, William Paterson Coll., 1985, St. Lawrence U., 1986, Hartwick Coll., 1987. With Couper-Ackerman-Sampson, Inc. (and predecessor), Binghamton, 1948-62, treas., 1957-60, v.p., 1960-63; adminstrv. v.p. Hamilton Coll., 1962-65, v.p., 1965-66, acting pres., 1966-68, v.p., provost, 1968-69, charter trustee, 1967-92; life trustee, 1992—; dep. commr. higher edn. N.Y. State Edn. Dept., 1969-71; pres., chief exec. officer N.Y. Pub. Library, N.Y.C., 1971-81, pres. emeritus, 1981—; pres. The Woodrow Wilson Nat. Fellowship Found., Princeton, N.J., 1981-90, pres. emeritus, 1990—; bd. dirs. Archives Partnership Trust. Chmn. Episc. Fund for Human Needs. Capt. U.S. Army, 1942-46. Mem. Orgn. Am. Historians, Am. Hist. Assn., N.Y. State Hist. assn. (trustee 1979-97), Harvard Club, Century Assn., Lotos Club (N.Y.C.), Ft. Schuyler Club (Utica, N.Y.), Nassau Club, Grolier Club (N.Y.C.), Phi Beta Kappa Assocs. Office: Hamilton Coll Burke Libr Clinton NY 13323

COUPER, WILLIAM, banker; b. N.Y.C., May 3, 1947; s. John Lee and Margery (Beemer) C.; m. Elise Marie Palma, Oct. 4, 1969; children: Elise, Margery, Dorothy. BS in Commerce, U.Va., 1968; cert., Coll. Fin. Planning, 1986. Trainee Am. Security Bank, N.A., Washington, 1972, asst. treas., asst. br. mgr., 1972-76, asst. v.p., mgr. main office, 1976-77, v.p., regional mgr., 1977-80, v.p. strategic planning, 1981-83, v.p. retail banking devel., 1983-84, sr. v.p. retail banking, 1984-89; sr. v.p. Md. Nat. Bank, Greenbelt, 1989-92; vice chmn. Va. Fed. Savs. Bank, 1991-93; exec. v.p. Am. Security Bank, Md. Nat. Bank, Washington, 1993-94; pres. NationsBank, Balt., 1994—. Bd. dirs. Balt. Mus. Art, Balt. Symphony Orch., Balt. Children's Mus., United Way of Ctrl. Md., Md. C.of C., Md. Bankers Assn., Md. Comm. Ctr., Downtown Partnership of Balt. Mem. Ctr. Club Balt., Chartwell Golf and Country Club. Republican. Episcopalian. Home: 1114 Bellevista Ct Severna Park MD 21146-4846 Office: NationsBank 100 S Charles St Fl 1 Baltimore MD 21201-2791

COUPEY, SUSAN MCGUIRE, pediatrician, educator; b. Montreal, Que., Can., June 29, 1942; came to U.S., 1978; d. Clarence Herbert and Paulette (Lefevre) McGuire; m. Pierre M.L. Coupey, July 1964 (div. 1981); children: Marc M.R., Ariane S.; m. James R. English III, Nov. 23, 1988. BA, Queen's U., Kingston, Ont., Can., 1962; postgrad., McGill U., Montreal, 1962-63; MD, U. B.C., Vancouver, Can., 1975. Diplomate Am. Bd. Pediatrics, subboard in adolescent medicine. Devel. chemist Merck, Sharp & Dohme, Ltd., Montreal, 1963-64; rotating intern Montreal Gen. Hosp., 1975-76; resident in pediatrics Montreal Children's Hosp., 1976-78; fellow in adolescent medicine Montefiore Med. Ctr., Bronx, N.Y., 1978-79, attending pediatrician, 1980—; rsch. asst. Cancer Rsch. Ctr., U. B.C., 1967-72; instr., asst. prof. pediatrics Albert Einstein Coll. Medicine, Bronx, 1979-85, assoc. prof., 1985-93, prof., 1993—, assoc. dir. div. adolescent medicine, 1984—, course dir. introduction to clin. medicine, 1989—, mem. faculty senate, 1983-84, 88-90; attending pediatrician North Ctrl. Bronx Hosp., 1979-97; cons. in adolescent medicine Flushing (N.Y.) Hosp. and Med. Ctr., 1982-96; Maricopa-Pima vis. prof. U. Ariz., 1989; vis. prof. Children's Hosp. Ea. Ont., U. Ottawa and Ea. Can. chpt. Soc. for Adolescent Medicine, 1990; vis. prof. Philippine Children's Med. Ctr., U. Philippines Coll. of Medicine, 1997; chmn. health svcs. adv. com. Children's Aid Soc., 1985—, bd. trustees, 1993—; mem. adv. bd. Office Substance Abuse Ministry, Archdiocese of N.Y., 1983-85. Assoc. editor Adolescent Medicine: State of the Art Revs., 1990—, Jour. Devel. & Behavioral Pediatrics, 1992-96, editl. bd., 1996—; assoc. editor Jour. Pediat. & Adolescent Gynecology, 1992-98, editl. bd. 1998—; editl. bd. Jour. of Youth and Adolescence, 1998—; contbr. articles to med. jours., also chpts. to books and monographs. Fellow Am. Acad. Pediatrics (exec. com. sect. on adolescent health 1993-96); mem. Soc. for Adolescent Medicine (nominations com. 1984-85, chmn. jour. adv. com. 1987-97, program com. 1991-93, awards com. 1992-95, bd. dirs. 1997—), Am. Pediat. Soc., Soc. for Behavioral Pediatrics, N.Am. Soc. Pediat. and Adolescent Gynecology (bd. dirs. 1993-96, sec. 1996—, chair publs. com. 1996—), Ea. Soc. Pediat. Rsch., Soc. Rsch. in Adolescence, Sex Info. and Edn. Coun. U.S., Am. Acad. Physicians and Patients, Albert Einstein Coll. Medicine Alumni Assn. (v.p. pediatrics 1983-84, pres. 1984-85). Office: Albert Einstein Coll Medicine Montefiore Med Ctr 111 E 210th St Bronx NY 10467-2401

COUPLES, FREDERICK STEVEN, professional golfer; b. Seattle, Oct. 3, 1959. Student, U. Houston. mem. U.S. Ryder Cup golf team, 1989, 91, 93, 95. Named All-Am., 1978, 79; winner numerous golf tournaments including Kemper Open, 1983, Tournament Players Championship, 1984, Byron Nelson Golf Classic, 1987, French PGA, 1988, Nissan L.A. Open, 1990, 92, Tournoi Perrier de Paris, 1991, B.C. Open, 1991, Federal Express St. Jude Classic, 1991, Johnnie Walker World Championship, 1991, Nestle Invitational, 1992, The Masters, 1992, (with Jan Stephenson) J.C. Penney Classic, 1983, (with Mike Donald) Sazale Classic, 1990, (with Raymond Floyd) RMCC Invitational, 1990, Buick Open, 1994, World Cup, 1994, Dubai Desert Classic, 1995, Johnnie Walker Classic, 1995, The Player's Championship, 1996, Bob Hope chrysler Classic, 1998, Memorial Tournament, 1998; recipient Vardon trophy, 1991, 92; named PGA Player of Yr. Golf World Mag., 1991, 92, Golf Writers Assn., 1991, 92, PGA Tour Player of Yr, 1993, 94. Leading money winner PGA, 1992. Address: c/o PGA Tour 100 Ave of The Champions PO Box 109601 Palm Bch Gdns FL 33410-9601*

COURAGE, THOMAS ROBERTS, lawyer; b. New Haven, Conn., Apr. 22, 1947; s. Jack Haldane and Margaret Smith (Hirschberg) C.; m. Hollie Uong, May 27, 1972; children: Michael, Peter. AB, Harvard U., 1970; JD, U. Pa., 1973. Assoc. Hinckley, Allen, Salisbury & Parsons, Providence, 1973-79; ptnr. Hinckley, Allen & Snyder, Providence and Boston, 1979-98; v.p., gen. counsel Care New Eng. Health Sys., Providence, 1998—; trustee Hattie Ide Chaffee Home, East Providence, R.I., 1987—. Treas. Greater Providence Youth Hockey Assn., 1988-91; trustee Interfaith Healthcare Ministries, Providence, 1992-93. Mem. Am. Health Lawyer's Assn., Healthcare Fin. Mgmt. Assn., Univ. Club, Agawam Hunt, Harvard-Radcliff Club R.I. (pres. 1992-94). Avocations: golf, hiking, squash, photography. Office: Care New Eng Health Sys 45 Willard Ave Providence RI 02905-3218

COURANT, ERNEST DAVID, physicist; b. Goettingen, Germany, Mar. 26, 1920; came to U.S., 1934, naturalized, 1940; s. Richard and Nina (Runge) C.; m. Sara Paul, Dec. 9, 1944; children: Paul N., Carl R. BA, Swarthmore Coll., 1940; MS, U. Rochester, 1942, PhD, 1943; MA (hon.), Yale U., 1962; DSc (hon.), Swarthmore Coll., 1988. Scientist Atomic Energy Project, Montreal, Que., Can., 1943-46; rsch. assoc. physics Cornell U., 1946-48; staff Brookhaven Nat. Lab., 1947—, sr. physicist, 1960-89, disting. scientist emeritus, 1990—; Brookhaven prof. physics Yale U., 1962-67, vis. prof., 1961-62; prof. physics and engring. SUNY, Stony Brook, 1967-85; vis. asst. prof. Princeton, 1950-51; cons. Gen. Atomic divsn. Gen. Dynamics Corp., 1958-59; vis. physicist Nat. Accelerator Lab., 1968-69; vis. prof. U. Mich., 1989—; cons. Superconducting Supercollider Lab., Dallas, 1990-93; hon. prof. U. Sci. and Tech. of China, Hefei, 1994. Co-originator strong-focusing particle accelerators. Fulbright Research fellow Cambridge (Eng.) U., 1956; recipient Fermi award U.S. Dept. of Energy, 1986. Fellow Am. Phys. Soc. (R.R. Wilson prize 1987), AAAS; mem. Nat. Acad. Scis., N.Y. Acad. Scis. (Boris Pregel prize 1979). Home: 40 W 72nd St New York NY 10023

COURANT, PAUL NOAH, economist, educator, university official; b. Ithaca, N.Y., Jan. 5, 1948; s. Ernest David and Sara (Paul) C.; m. Katherine Olive Johnson, Sept. 21, 1969 (div. 1984); children: Ernest Mendel, Noah Albert; m. Marta Ann Manildi, Jan. 30, 1988; 1 child, Samuel Robinson Manildi. BA, Swarthmore Coll., 1968; MA, Princeton U., 1972, PhD, 1973. Jr. economist Coun. Econ. Advisers, Washington, 1969-70, sr. economist, 1979-80; asst. prof. econs., pub. policy U. Mich., Ann Arbor, 1973-78, assoc. prof., 1978-84, prof. econs. and pub. policy, 1984—, dir. Inst. Pub. Policy Studies, 1983-87, 89-90, chmn. econs. dept., 1995-97, assoc. provost, 1997—; mem. Task Force on Long-Term Econ. Growth, State of Mich., 1983-84; cons. Mich. Dept. Commerce, Lansing, 1984-85, Congl. Budget Office, Washington, 1988-89; bd. dirs. Mich. Future, Bingham Farms, 1991-97. Author: America's Great Consumption Binge, 1986; co-author: Economics, 1973, 11th edit., 1996; contbr. articles to profl. jours. Bd. dirs. Ctr. for Watershed and Cmty. Health, Eugene, Oreg., 1997—. Grantee NSF, 1976-77, 79-81, 94-97, Rockefeller Found., 1985-87, Nat. Cancer Inst., 1992-95. Mem. Am. Econ. Assn., Assn. Pub. Policy Analysis and Mgmt. (mem. policy coun. 1994-98), Nat. Tax Assn. Avocations: sailing, skiing, tennis, hiking, clarinet. Office: Univ Mich 3060 Fleming Bldg Ann Arbor MI 48109-1340

COURBIS, SARAH SHELBY, marine biologist; b. July 15, 1975. Student, U. N.C., 1993, Oreg. State U., 1998; BS in Marine Biology, Millersville U., 1996. Naturalist Marine Discovery Tours, Newport, Oreg., 1997; marine rsch. asst. Hatfield Marine Sci. Ctr., Newport, 1997-98, marine educator, 1997-98; aquatic toxicologist Northwestern Aquatic Scis., Newport, 1998; jr. staff scientist Dyanamc/EPA, Newport, 1998—. Email: dolphin-spice@hotmail.com.

COUREY, FRED SAMUEL, management consultant, former mayor; b. Lennox, S.D.; s. Samuel Thomas and Mabel (Salem) G.; student Lennox pub. schs. With Courey's Food Mart, Inc., Lennox, 1934-83, co-owner, 1946-83; city auditor, Lennox, 1948-50, mayor, 1960-80; with Fred Courey & Assocs., gen. cons., 1983—; news dir. Lennox Ind., 1983-97; past mem. Urbanized Devel. Commn., S.Eastern Criminal Justice Commn., S.Eastern Health Planning Council (all of S.E. Council Govts. S.D.); past mem. S.D. State Local Govt. Study Commn.; past mem. S.D. adv. council SBA, 1969-82, ACE mgmt. assistance counselor, 1969-84. Gen. chmn. Lennox Diamond Jubilee, 1954; past mem. parish council St. Magdalen Roman Cath. Ch., Lennox; project coordinator, program dir. Lennox Area Med. Center, 1975-83; past mem. bd. dirs. Lennox Area Devel. Corp. Served with AUS, 1941-45; PTO. Decorated Army Commendation medal. Mem. Am. Water Works Assn. (life), S.D. Water and Wastewater Conf. (past dir.), Am. Legion. Small Towns Inst., Smithsonian Instn., Nat. Wildlife Fedn., Lennox L.E.E. Com., Inc. (bd. dirs. 1983-87), VFW. Republican. Club: Lennox Comml. (past pres.), Nat. Travel, S.D. Auto, Amoco. Address: PO Box 56 Lennox SD 57039-0056

COURIC, KATIE (KATHERINE COURIC), broadcast journalist; b. Arlington, Va., 1957; m. Jay Monahan; 2 children, Elinor and Caroline. G-rad., with Am. Studies major, U. Va. Began career with reporting and producing jobs NBC affiliates, Miami, Washington; joined NBC Network News, 1989; former nat. corr. Today, NBC, Washington; co-anchor Today, NBC, 1991—; co-host Now with Tom Brokaw and Katie Couric, NBC, 1993-94. Address: NBC TV Today Show 30 Rockefeller Plz New York NY 10112-0002*

COURIER, JIM (JAMES SPENCER COURIER, JR.), tennis player; b. Sanford, Fla., Aug. 17, 1970; s. James and Linda Courier. Professional tennis player, 1989—. Winner tournaments including Orange Bowl, 1986, 87, Basel, 1989, French Open, 1991, 92, Indian Wells, 1991, 93, Key Biscayne, 1991, 93, Australian Open, 1992-93, Italian Open, 1991-93, Qator Mobile Open, 1997; finalist U.S. Open, 1991, quarterfinalist Wimbledon, 1991, semifinalist Australian Open, 1994, French Open, 1994; (with Stark) French Open Jr. doubles crown, 1987; ranked #1 in world, 1992; holder of the U.S. Jr. titles 16 hard court singles, 1985. Holder of Davis Cup record of 7-5 in singles. Address: Internat Mgmt Group 1 Erieview Plz Ste 300 Cleveland OH 44114-1715 also: US Tennis Assn 70 W Red Oak Ln White Plains NY 10604-3602*

COURNIOTES, HARRY JAMES, academic administrator; b. Chicopee Falls, Mass., Aug. 13, 1921; s. James Harry and Chrisanthe (Gardekas) C.; m. Annette R. Giguere, Sept. 4, 1945; children: James H., Gregory H. BS, Boston U., 1942; Indsl. Adminstr. with high distinction, Harvard U., 1943, MBA with high distinction, 1947; DCS, Western New Eng. Coll., 1976. CPA, Mass. Asst. prof. Am. Internat. Coll., Springfield, Mass., 1946-52; assoc. prof. Am. Internat. Coll., Springfield, 1952-58, prof., 1958-69, dean Sch. Bus. Adminstrn., 1960-69, v.p., 1964-69, pres., 1969-99; ret.; trustee, mem. investment com. Springfield Inst. Savs.; trustee Springfield Neighborhood Housing Svc., 1988-92; corporator Springfield Libr. and Mus. Assn., 1997—, former corporator, Springfield Boys Club, 1972-76. Mem. adv. bd. World Affairs Coun., 1970; corporator Springfield Girls Club, 1970—, Wing Meml. Hosp., 1976—; trustee Econ. Edn. Coun. Mass., 1971—; com. mem. United Negro Coll. Fund, 1971; mem. exec. com. Springfield Adult Edn. Coun., 1972-74; mem. exec. com., bd. dirs. Jr. Achievement Western Mass., 1975-76; bd. dirs. Springfield Ctrl. Bus. Dist., 1976-79; mem. bd. adv., N.E. Congl. Inst., 1980; trustee Econ. sponsor Laughing Brook project Mass. Audubon Soc. Lt. AUS, 1943-46. Named Acct. of Yr., Nat. Assn. Cost Accts., 1970; recipient Nat. Human Rels. award NCCJ, 1984, Henry A. Butova Meml. award Western Mass. chpt. Football Found. and Hall of Fame, 1989, Tree of Life award Jewish Nat. Fund, 1993, Disting. Citizen award Pioneer Valley Boy Scouts Am., 1998. Mem. AICPA, Mass. Soc. CPAs (Outstanding Educator for 1991), Fin. Exec. Inst. (chmn. edn. com. 1964-65), Assn. Ind. Colls. and Univs. Mass. (mem. exec. com. 1972-74, 81-84), Greater Springfield C. of C. (dir. 1974-77), Colony Club (Springfield), Harvard Club (Boston), Cranberry Valley Golf Club (Harwich, Mass.), Longmeadow Country Club (Mass.). Home: Cote Rd Monson MA 01057 Office: 1000 State St Springfield MA 01109-3151

COURSON, JOHN EDWARD, state senator, insurance company executive; b. Augusta, Ga., Nov. 21, 1944; s. James W. and Mary C. (Harris) C.; m. Elizabeth Poinsett Exum, Apr. 1973; children: James Poinsett, Elizabeth Boykin, Harris Russell. BA, U. S.C., 1968. Exec. v.p. Keenan Ins. & Fin. Svcs.. Fin. dir. S.C. Republican Party, 1969-75; sec., 1976-80, nat. committeeman for S.C. Rep. Nat. Committee, 1980-88; chmn. campaign '80 for S.C.; Presdl. elector Rep., 1980, 1984; mem. S.C. Senate, 1984—; co-chmn., treas. Re-elect Thurmond Com., 1990-95. Served with USMCR, 1968-74. Recipient Mounted Gold Elephant S.C. Republican Party, 1975, 80, 82; named Young Agt. of Yr., Ind. Ins. Agts. S.C., 1981; recipient Order of Palmetto. Mem. Am. Legion, Marine Corps League, Sigma Chi., Forest Lake Club,

Tarantella Club, Columbia Ball Club, Palmetto Club. Episcopalian. Avocations: tennis; politics. Office: 401 Gressette Senate Office Bldg PO Box 142 Columbia SC 29202

COURSON, MARNA B.P., public relations executive; b. Waynesboro, Pa., Feb. 22, 1951; d. Eugene Perry and Charlotte Mae (Sherman) Roschli; m. Sydney E. Courson, May 24, 1982; 1 child, Sydney Alexandra. BA, Franklin and Marshall Coll., 1973; postgrad., U. Kans., Kansas City. Reporter Beach Haven Times/The Beacon, Manahawkin, N.J., 1973-74, Dailey Observer Newspaper, Toms River, N.J., 1974-76; communications mgr. Frick India Ltd., New Delhi, 1976-77; reporter, dictationist UPI, Washington, 1978-80; reporter UPI, Richmond, Va.; reporter, editor AP, Balt., 1980-84; communications coord. St. Luke's Hosp. Found., Kansas City, Mo., 1986-88; exec. v.p. pub. rels. Spaw and Assocs., Inc., Overland Park, Kans., 1988-89; exec. v.p. CCI Pub. Rels. & Mktg. Comm., Inc., Shawnee Mission, Kans., 1990-92; pres. CCI Pub. Rels. & Mktg. Comm., Inc., Kansas City, Mo., 1992—. Mem. adv. bd. Wonderscope Children's Mus., Vol. Leadership Coun.; vol. bd. dirs. Ctr. for Mgmt. Assistance. Recipient Prism award for fund raising, numerous awards and honors for reporting, 1973-80; also pub. rels. awards, 1988-96. Mem. Internat. Assn. Bus. Communicators, Pub. Rels. Soc. of Am. (Pres.'s award with GKC), Nat. Assn. Women Bus. Owners, Nat. Soc. Fund Raising Execs., Silicon Prairie Tech. Assn. (bd. dirs., mem. exec. bd.), C. of C. Office: Kansas City Downtown Airport 250 NW Richards Rd Ste 269 Kansas City MO 64116-4275 *Every step in my career has been building on my accumulated experience skill and knowledge, providing the basis for creativity and learning for the next stage. In almost every case, I've found that for me the process is as important as achieving the goal.*

COURSON, WILLIAM A., association administrator; b. Oct. 15, 1952. Exec. dir. The Magnus Hirschfeld Ctr. for Human Rights, Upper Montclair, N.J. E-mail: crosswix@hotmail.com. Office: 551 Valley Rd Rm 169 Upper Montclair NJ 07043

COURT, LEONARD, lawyer, educator; b. Ardmore, Okla., Jan. 11, 1947; s. Leonard and Margaret Janet (Harvey) C.; m. JoAnn Dilleshaw, Sept. 2, 1967; children: Chris, Todd, Brooke. BA, Okla. State U., 1969; JD, Harvard U., 1972. Bar: Okla. 1973, U.S. Dist. Ct. (we. dist.) Okla. 1973, U.S. Dist. Ct. (no. dist.) Okla., 1978, U.S. Dist. Ct. (ea. dist.) Okla. 1983, U.S. Ct. Appeals (10th cir.) 1980, U.S. Ct. Mil. Appeals 1973. Assoc. Crowe & Dunlevy, Oklahoma City, Okla., 1977-81, shareholder, dir., 1981—; adj. prof. Okla. U. Law Sch., Norman, 1984-85, 88-89, 99, Okla. City U. Law Sch., 1998; planning com. Ann. Inst. Labor Law, S.W. Legal Found., Dallas, 1984—. Contbg. author: (supplement book) The Developing Labor Law, 1978, Corporate Counsel's Annual, 1974, Labor Law Developments, 1993, Employment Discrimination Law, 1998 Supplement. Chmn. bd. elders Meml. Christian Ch., Oklahoma City, 1980, 98-99; cubmaster Last Frontier coun. Boy Scouts Am., 1984, co-chmn. sustaining fund raising drive Oklahoma City Downtown YMCA, 1989, mem. bd. mgmt., 1994-96; participant Leadership Oklahoma City, 1987-88, bd. govs. Okla. State U. Found., 1990—; Oklahoma City Ronald McDonald House, 1990-93, mem. exec. com., 1991-93; co-chmn. ann. teleparty fundraising drive Am. Heart Assn., Okla. City, 1996-98, bd. dirs., 1996-98. Capt. USAF, 1973-77. Fellow Am. Coll. Labor and Employment Lawyer; mem. Am. Employment Law Coun. (charter), U.S. C. of C. (mem. labor rels. com. 1997—), Okla. State U. Bar Assn. (bd. dirs. 1980—), Oklahoma City C. of C. (mem. sports and recreation com. 1982-85, indsl. devel. com. 1986), Okla State U., Okla. State U. Alumni Assn. (nat. bd. dirs. 1989—, nat. exec. com., 1992-97, pres. 1995-96, long range planning com, alumni awards com., student recruitment com., pres. 1995-96, chmn. alumni ctr. task force 1998—, Disting. Alumni award 1998), Okla. County Alumni Assn. (bd. sec. 1987-88, treas. 1988-89, v.p. 1989-90, pres. 1990-91), Harvard Law Sch. Assn., ABA (labor and employment law sect. com. on devel. of law under Nat. Labor Relations Act, com. on EEO law, subcom. on substantive devels involving sex under Title VII, and subcom. of EEOC process Title VII coverage and multiple forums, litigation sect./employment and labor rels. law com.), Okla. Bar Assn. (labor and employment law sect. council 1978-83, 85-87, chmn. 1986), Okla. County Bar Assn., Fed. Bar Assn., U.S. Tennis Assn. (life). Office: Crowe & Dunlevy Mid America Tower 20 N Broadway Ave Ste 1800 Oklahoma City OK 73102-8273

COURTER, JEANNE LYNN, materials scientist; b. Flushing, N.Y., May 7, 1953; d. Harry Melvin Jr. and Ruth Jane (Rieben) C. B in Engring. Sci., SUNY, Stony Brook, 1975; PhD in Materials Sci., MIT, 1981. Rsch. scientist Am. Cyanamid Co., Stamford, Conn., 1981-83, materials section projects mgr., 1983-90, quality asst. to divsn. dir., 1990-94; sr. prin. rsch. scientist Cytec Industries, Inc., Stamford, 1994—. Inventor epoxy resin compound; patentee in field (with others), 1978-86. Pres., bd. dirs. Stamford Cross Road Residences, Inc. Recipient Elias Singer Best Paper award 23rd Ann. Internat. Waterborne, High Solids, and Powde Coatings Symposium, European Coatings award for best paper 5th Nürnberg Congress. Mem. ASTM, Am. Chem. Soc., N.Am. Guild Change Ringers, N.Y. Soc. for Coatings and Tech., Tau Beta Pi. Methodist. Avocation: perennial gardening. Office: Cytec Industries Inc PO Box 60 1937 W Main St Stamford CT 06902-4516

COURTER, ROBERT J., JR., career officer; b. N.J., Aug. 1, 1945. BS in Indsl. Engring., Rutgers U., 1968; student, Squadron Officer Sch., 1971; M in Indsl. and Bus. Mgmt., Ctrl. Mich. U., 1974; student, Air Command and Staff Coll., 1975, Air War Coll., 1978, Nat. Def. U., 1987, U. N.H., 1992. Registered profl. engr., Tex. Commd. 2d lt. USAF, 1968, advanced through grades to maj. gen., 1998; chief indsl. engring. 3510th Civil Engring. Squadron, Randolph AFB, Tex., 1968-70; command indsl. engr., dep. chief staff civil engring. Hdqs. Air Tng. Command, Randolph AFB, Tex., 1970-72; chief engring. and constrn. then chief ops. and maintenance 635th Civil Engring. Squadron, U-Tapao Airfield, Thailand, 1972-73; assoc. prof. and course dir. Sch. Engring. Air Force Inst. Tech., Wright-Patterson AFB, Ohio, 1973-77; engring. mgmt. officer ops. and maintenance div., others Hdqs. USAF, Washington, 1977-82; comdr. 67th Civil Engring. Squadron, Bergstrom AFB, Tex., 1982-84, 1st Civil Engring. Squadron, Langley AFB, Va., 1984-86; dir. readiness and force devel., dir programs Hdqs. Tactical Air Command, Langley AFB, Va., 1987-90, dep. chief staff engring. svcs., 1987-90; dep. chief staff civil engring. Hdqs. Air Force Logistics Command, Wright-Patterson AFB, 1990-92; command civil engr. Hdqs. Air Force Material Command, Wright-Patterson AFB, 1992-95, dir. plans and programs, 1997—; comdr. 37th Tng. Wing, Lackland AFB, Tex., 1995-97. Decorated Legion of Merit, Bronze Star with V device and oak leaf cluster, Rep. Vietnam Gallantry Cross with Palm, Rep. Vietnam Campaign medal. Fellow Soc. Am. Mil. Engrs. (former mem. nat. bd.). Office: USAF HQ AFMC/XP 4375 Chidlaw Rd Ste 6 Wright Patterson AFB OH 45433-5006

COURTÉS, JOSEPH JEAN-MARIE, humanities educator, writer, semiotician; b. Hérault, France, Feb. 6, 1936; s. Jean and Marthe (Carles) C.; m. Annie Joullié, June 22, 1974; children: Sophie, Jean-Noël, Benoît. Lic., Paris U., 1964, doctorate, 1965; doctorate, Paris U., 1971, Paris U., 1983. Dir. Internat. Ctr. Semiotics and Linguistics, Urbino, Italy, 1971-73; asst. prof. Ecole de Hautes Études en Scis. Soc., Paris, 1973-84; prof. semiotics Toulouse (France) U., 1985—; pres. of commn. of semiotics and linguistics Toulouse U., 1986-92, 98—; internat. cons. EHESS, 1985—; mem. Sci. Coms. of Revs., France, 1986—. Author: Lévi-Strauss et les contraintes de la pensée mythique, 1973, Introduction à la sémiotique narrative et discursive, 1976, Sémiotique, dictionnaire raisonné de la théorie du langage, vol. I, 1979, vol. II, 1986, Le conte Populaire: poétique et mythologie, 1986, Sémantiques de lénancé, 1989, Sémiotique du discours: de l'énoncé à l'énonciation, 1991, Du signifié au signifiant, 1992, Sémiotique narrative et discursive, 1993, Du lisible au visible: analyse sémiotique d'une nouvelle de Maupassant, d'une bande dessinée de B. Rabier, 1995, Éthnolittérature, rhétorique et sémiotique, 1995, Stratégies d'écriture et instabilité du sens, 1996, Des motifs ethno-litteraines aux to poi, 1997, L'énonciation comme acte sémiotique, 1998. Mem. Assn. for Devel. Semiotics (pres. 1988—), Semio-Linguistics Soc. Ctr. (pres. 1991-93). Office: Toulouse II Univ, 31058 Toulouse France

COURTHEOUX, RICHARD JAMES, management consultant; b. Rochester, N.Y., Mar. 25, 1949; s. David and Lillian (Altman) C.; m. Perri Orenstein, June 20, 1976; children: Suzanne Michele, Karen Lisabeth. BS, Yale U., 1972; MS, Weizmann Inst., Rehovot, Israel, 1975; MBA, U. Chgo., 1978. V.p. Kestabaum & Co., Chgo., 1978-86; pres. Precision Mktg., Northbrook, Ill., 1987-95; sr. v.p. Experian Direct Tech., Schaumburg, Ill., 1995—. Mem. editl. bd. Jour. Targeting, Measurement and Analysis for Mktg. Mem. Direct Mktg. Assn. (seminar instr. 1984—). E-mail: rick.courtheoux@experian.com.

COURTICE, KATIE, freelance writer and editor, office consultant; b. Des Moines, Oct. 4, 1942; d. Richard North and Janet E. (Walther) C.; m. Peter John Basquin, July 11, 1964. BA, Carleton Coll., 1964. Founding editor Virtuoso mag. Shacor Pub., Katonah, N.Y., 1980; freelance writer, ghostwriter, editor, Bklyn., N.J., 1977—. Co-author: Alzheimer's Disease: A Guide for Families, 1983. Mem. Editl. Freelancers Assn. Episcopalian. Avocations: bicycling, classical music, knitting, crocheting. Address: 60 Plaza St E Apt 5-K Brooklyn NY 11238-5033

COURTICE, THOMAS BARR, academic administrator; b. Dayton, Ohio, Oct. 31, 1943; s. Allyn J. and Mary Louise (Barr) C.; children: Heather, Ryan, Lindsey; m. Lisa Schweitzer. BS, U. Pitts, 1965; MBA, Ind. U., 1967; PhD, U. Minn., 1974; cert. Inst. Edn. Mgmt., Harvard U., 1977. Dir. placement, instr. Econs. Hamline U., St. Paul, 1967-69, asst. to pres., 1969-75, v.p. for univ. affairs, 1975-77; pres. Westbrook Coll., Portland, Maine, 1977-86, W.Va. Wesleyan Coll., Buckhannon, 1986-94, Ohio Wesleyan U., Delaware, 1994—; accreditation evaluator North Ctrl. and New Eng. Assn. Schs. and colls., 1980—; mem. exec. com. Found. for Ind. Higher Edn., 1994—, NCAA Pres. Commn. Divsn. III, 1998-2002; bd. dirs. Ednl. and Instnl. Ins. Adminstrs., Inc. Trustee Wayneflete Sch., Portland, 1980-86, Portland Symphony Orch, 1982-86, Delaware Cmty. Found., 1996—. Bush Found. summer fellow, St. Paul, 1977. Mem. Nat. Assn. Ind. Colls. and Univs. (bd. dirs. and exec. com. 1993), Nat. Assn. Schs. and Colls. of the United Meth. Ch. (bd. dirs., pres. 1996-97), Appalachian Coll. Assn. (pres. 1992-94). Home: 135 Oak Hill Ave Delaware OH 43015-2519 Office: Office of Pres Ohio Wesleyan Univ Delaware OH 43015

COURTISS, EUGENE HOWARD, plastic surgeon, educator; b. Boston, Jan. 18, 1930; s. Morris and Rosa (Grace) C.; m. Barbara Faith Block, June 9, 1957; 1 child, Linda. AB, Columbia U., 1951; MD, Boston U., 1955. Diplomate Am. Bd. Plastic Surgery (chmn. 1986-87). Intern U. Minn. Hosp., Mpls., 1955-56; jr. asst. resident Peter Bent Brigham Hosp., Boston, 1956-57; fellow in surgery U. Minn. Hosps., Mpls., 1960-61; jr. resident in plastic surgery Christ Hosp., Cin., 1961-62, chief resident in plastic surgery, 1962-63; clin. instr. Boston U., 1965-74, asst. prof. plastic surgery, 1974—; assoc. in surgery Univ. Hosp., Boston, 1964-83; chief plastic surgery Newton (Mass.)-Wellesley Hosp., 1969-93; assoc. prof. Harvard U., Boston, 1981—, U. Mass., Worcester, 1984-87; mem. cons. staff Waltham (Mass.) Hosp., 1977—; cons. Mass. Gen. Hosp., Boston, 1987—; vis. prof. U. Toronto, Ont., Can., Ohio State U., Columbus, U. Calif. San Diego, Baylor U., U. Tex., Pa. State U., Johns Hopkins U., U. Wis., Washington U., St. Louis, Chgo. Med. Coll., Brown U., Providence, Vanderbilt U., Nashville, U. Mich., Ann Arbor, McGill U., Montreal, Can., Emory U., Atlanta, Brigham and Women's Hosp., Boston, Oreg. Health Svcs., Portland; traveling prof. Am. Soc. for Aesthetic Plastic Surgery, 1980-81 (Best Presentation award 1982, Disting. Svc. award 1989). Editor: Aesthetic Surgery, 1978, Male Aesthetic Surgery, 1982; editor book revs. Plastic and Reconstructive Surgery, 1985-91; contbr. numerous articles to profl. jours. Served to capt. U.S. Army, 1957-60. Recipient Disting. Svc. award Plastic Surgery Ednl. Found. 1991. Fellow ACS; mem. Mass. Med. Soc. (consilor 1968-74), New Eng. Soc. Plastic Surgeons (pres. 1976-78), Northeastern Soc. Plastic Surgeons (pres. 1984), Am. Soc. Plastic and Reconstructive Surgeons (parliamentarian 1977-78, Ivy award 1976), Begg Soc. Republican. Avocations: skiing, golf. Office: Plastic Surgery Inc 60 Singletree Rd Chestnut Hill MA 02467-2827

COURTNEY, EDWARD, classics educator; b. Belfast, Northern Ireland, Mar. 22, 1932; came to U.S., 1982; s. George and Kathleen (Nicholson) C.; m. Brenda Virginia Meek, Dec. 18, 1962; children: Richard Marcus, Adam Matthew. BA, Trinity Coll., Dublin, Ireland, 1954; MA, Oxford U., 1957. Research lectr. Christ Ch., Oxford, 1955-59; lectr. in classics King's Coll., London, 1959-70, reader in classics, 1970-77, prof. Latin, 1977-82; prof. classics Stanford U., Calif., 1982-93, Ely prof. humanities, 1986-93; Gildersleeve prof. classics U. Va., Charlottesville, Va., 1993—. Author: Commentary on the Satires of Juvenal, 1980, The Poems of Petronius, 1991, The Fragmentary Latin Poets, 1993, Musa Lapidaria, A Selection of Latin Verse Inscriptions, 1995, Archaic Latin Prose, 1999; editor: Valerius Flaccus, Argonautica, 1970, Juvenal, The Satires, A Critical Text, 1985, Statius, Silvae, 1990; joint editor: Ovid, Fasti, 1978. Mem. Am. Philol. Assn. Avocation: chess. Office: U Va 401 New Cabell Hall Charlottesville VA 22903

COURTNEY, EUGENE WHITMAL, computer company executive; b. East St. Louis, Ill., Jan. 3, 1936; s. Eugene and Goldie Genell (Mitchell) C.; m. Barbara Ann Beckwith, Aug. 1, 1959; children: Kevin Eugene, Kyle Patrick. BSEE, Princeton U. with honors, 1957. Exec. v.p., gen. mgr., dir. Digital Sci. Corp., San Diego, 1970-75, pres., chief exec. officer, 1975-79; dir. Digital Sci./Europe, 1975-79; v.p. corp. devel. Topaz, Inc., San Diego, 1979; v.p. corp. devel. Nat. Computer Systems, Mpls., 1980-81, v.p., gen. mgr. scanning div., 1981-83, group v.p., 1983-88; exec. v.p., COO, dir. HEI Inc., Victoria, Minn., 1988-90, pres., CEO, 1990-99; dir., 1989—; prin. and dir. Triangle Tool and affiliates, 1988—; bd. dirs. DRS Data and Rsch. Svcs. plc, Milton Keynes, Eng., SFT Solutions From Tech., Mpls., Datakey, Inc., Mpls.; mem. Minn. Software Tech. Com., 1985-86. Contbr. articles to profl. jours. Trustee, v.p. engring. San Diego Hall of Sci., 1974-79; mem. State of Calif. gov.'s task force on edn. and industry, 1977-78; mem. Rancho Santa Fe (Calif.) Park and Recreation Bd., 1978; mem. tech. adv. bd. Minn. Dept. Corrections, Shakopee, 1985-86. Am. Electronics Assn. (nat. bd. dirs., chmn. San Diego coun. 1976-79, chmn. Minn. coun. 1993-96), Princeton Club (N.Y.C.). Republican. Avocation: print collecting. Home: 7312 Claredon Dr Minneapolis MN 55439-1722 Office: HEI Inc PO Box 5000 Victoria MN 55386-5000

COURTNEY, HOWARD PERRY, clergyman; b. Frederick, Okla., Dec. 20, 1911; m. Vaneda Harper, Mar. 21, 1932; 1 child, Howard Perry Jr. Grad., L.I.F.E. Bible Coll., 1932, D.D., 1944. Ordained to ministry Internat. Ch. of the Foursquare Gospel, 1933; pastor chs. Racine, Wis., 1932-34, Terre Haute, Ind., 1934, Portland, Ore., 1935-36, Riverside, Calif., 1936-39, Urbana, Ill., 1939; dist. supr. Great Lakes dist., Internat. Ch. of the Foursquare Gospel, 1940-44, gen. supr., dir. fgn. missions, 1944-50, v.p., 1953-80, gen. supr., 1953-74, gen. supr. emeritus, 1976—, bd. dirs. emeritus, 1993—; pastor Angelus Temple, L.A., 1950-53, 77-81; mem. faculty L.I.F.E. Bible Coll., 1937-39, 44-74; adv. com. Pentecostal World Conf., 1958-85; chmn. Pentecostal Conf., Jerusalem, 1961. Mem. Pentecostal Fellowship North Am. (chmn. 1953, 54, 65-66), Nat. Assn. Evangelicals (bd. mem. 1953-54, 59-60, 66-67, 69-77). Office: 1130 Sonora Ave Glendale CA 91201-1909

COURTNEY, JAMES EDMOND, real estate developer; b. Meadville, Pa., Dec. 28, 1931; s. Alexis James and Marian (Winans) C.; m. Eileen Patricia Alman, Nov. 2, 1970; children: Alison M., David E. AB in Econs., Dartmouth Coll., 1953, MBA in Fin. Analysis and Acctg., 1954; LLB, Harvard U., 1959. Bar: Ohio 1960. Assoc. Jones, Day, Reavis & Pogue, Cleve., 1959-62, ptnr., 1963-74; v.p. internat. M.A. Hanna Co., Cleve., 1974-78, sr. v.p. corp. devel., 1978-79, exec. v.p., 1981-90, also bd. dirs.; vice chmn. M.A. Hanna Co., 1989-90; pres. The Mariner Group, Ft. Myers, Fla., 1992-95; bd. dirs., 1994—; bd. dirs. United Dominion Industries, Ltd., Charlotte, N.C., First Cmty. Bank of S.W. Fla., Ft. Myers, Robb & Stuckey, Ltd., Ft. Myers; chmn., bd. dirs. The Mariner Group, Inc., Ft. Myers. Served to lt. USN, 1954-56. Mem. Sanctuary Golf Club. Home: 1779 Venus Dr Sanibel FL 33957-3427

COURTNEY, MARY E., writer, editor; b. Dallas, May 3, 1955; d. John Francis and Ellen Mary Courtney; m. Paul A. Messick, Nov. 22, 1990. BA in English, U. Tex., 1977; MEd in Internat. Edn., U. Mass., 1985; MA in English and Creative Writing, So. Meth. U., 1994. Tng. dir. Greater Dallas Coun. on Alcoholism and Drug Abuse, 1988-90; asst. event coord. Shakespeare World Congress, L.A., 1995-96; English instr., acad. dept. dir. Art Inst. L.A., 1997—, instr. writing, 1998—; website prodr., L.A., 1996—; freelance editor, writer, rschr., 1987—. Curator, author exhibit catalog Visionaries and Rebels: American Literature After the Atom Bomb, 1995. AIDS trainer in schs. AIDS Project L.A., 1996-97; bd. dirs. Celiac Found., Studio City, Calif., 1996-98. Avocations: scuba diving, folk dancing, cycling. Home: PMB 80 626 Santa Monica Blvd Santa Monica CA 90401-2538

COURTNEY, WILLIAM FRANCIS, food and vending service company executive; b. Altoona, Pa., July 3, 1914; s. W. Francis and Mary Edith (Hopkins) C.; m. Mary Jane Kelley, June 5, 1946 (dec. Dec. 1996); children: Sarah Ann, William Francis, Thomas Gerard, Richard Christopher; m. Mary G. Enterline, Jan. 17, 1998. Mgmt. staff W.T. Grant Co., 1933-37; sales mgr. Coca-Cola Co., 1937- 48; ptnr. Automatic Refreshment Service, 1948-60; v.p. Servomation Corp., Youngstown, Ohio, 1960-63, pres., 1963-71; pres. Serex Corp., Youngstown, 1971-97, chmn., 1997—; dir. emeritus Mahoning Nat. Bank, Youngstown. Past pres. Boys and Girls Club Youngstown. Served to capt., inf. AUS, 1945, PTO. Decorated Bronze Star. Mem. Nat. Automatic Merchandising Assn., Ohio Automatic Merchandising Assn. (past pres., dir.). Republican. Club: Youngstown. Lodge: Rotary (past pres. Austintown). Home: 725 Blueberry Hill Dr Canfield OH 44406-1037 Office: Serex Corp 55 Victoria Rd Youngstown OH 44515-2023*

COURTNEY, WILLIAM HARRISON, diplomat; b. Balt., July 18, 1944; s. Wilbur Harry Courtney and Mary Lee (Mitchell) Fleming; children: William Jr., Mary Alison. BA in Econs., W.Va. U., 1966; PhD in Econs., Brown U., 1980. Fgn. svc. officer Dept. State, Washington, 1972—; dep. exec. sec. NSC, The White House, Washington, 1987-88; dep. U.S. negotiator U.S.-Soviet Defense & Space Talks, Geneva, 1988-91; amb. Nuclear Testing & Nuclear Weapons Safety, Security, and Dismantlement,ACDA, Washington, 1991-92; amb. to Kazakhstan, 1992-95, amb. to Georgia, 1995-97; spl. asst. to pres. for Russia, Ukraine and Eurasia The White House, Washington, 1997-98; sr. advisor Fgn. Affairs Reorgn. U.S. Dept. State, Washington, 1998-99; sr. advisor U.S. Commn. Security & Coop. in Europe, 1999—. Mem. Coun. Fgn. Rels. Office: 3722 48th St NW Washington DC 20016 also: NSC Washington DC 20504

COURTNEY WESTFALL, CONSTANCE, lawyer; b. Plainview, Tex., Nov. 29, 1960; d. M.H. and Carolyn Courtney; m. Monte Jay Westfall, Jan. 3, 1998; 1 child, William Henry Westfall. BS, U. Tex., 1982, JD, 1985. Bar: Tex., U.S. Dist. Ct. (we. and no. dists.) Tex., U.S. Dist. Ct. (we. and ea. dists.) Ark., U.S. Dist. Ct. (we. dist.) Okla., U.S. Ct. Appeals (5th cir.) Tex. Com. clk. Natural Resources Com., Tex. Ho. of Rep., 1979; legis. staff to hon. Buck Florence Tex. Ho. of Rep., 1980-82; law clk. to hon. Jerre Williams U.S. Ct. Appeals (5th cir.), 1985-86; assoc. Thompson & Knight, Dallas, 1986-92, Brown McCarroll, Dallas, 1992-94; ptnr. Hutcheson & Grundy, Dallas, 1994-98, Strasburger & Price, Dallas, 1998—. Contbr. articles to profl. jours. Moderator So. Meth. U. Sch. Law Environ. Career Seminar, 1989—. Mem. ABA, State Bar Tex. (coll., chair outreach com. environ. sect. 1989-92, mem. law sch. com. 1988-97, chair law sch. com. 1997—, State Bar Coll., 1995—). Office: Strasburger & Price Ste 4300 901 Main St Ste 4300 Dallas TX 75202-3714

COURTOIS, BERNARD ANDRE, communications executive. BA, U. Mont., 1965, LLB, 1968. Bar: Que. 1969, Ont. 1984. Chief regulatory officer Bell Can., Montreal, Que. Office: Bell Canada, 105 Hotel de Ville Rm 600 S, Quebec, PQ Canada J8X 4H7

COURTRIGHT, JOHN R., information management specialist; b. Washington, June 3, 1939; s. John Graham Courtright and Ellen Reiss; m. Suzann Carolyn Davis, Mar. 15, 1960; children: Carolyn Denise Smith, Christine Marie Dolan. BSBA, Randolph-Macon Coll., 1962; MBA, George Washington U., 1969. Airline mgr. USAir, Washington, 1959-62; budget and pers. officer U.S. Dept. Health & Human Svcs., Washington, 1962-64; computer sys. analyst U.S. Dept. Navy, Washington, 1964-67; computer adminstr. U.S. Dept. Army, Washington, 1967-73; computer scientist, dir. FAA programs FAA/U.S. Dept. Transportation, Washington, 1973-87; sr. info. mgmt. specialist U.S. Army Spl. Staff, Washington, 1987-98; info. mgmt. cons., Y2K analyst Fin. Mgmt. Support, 1998—. Mem. Rotary Club Arlington. Catholic. Avocation: National Ski Patrol. Home: 3405 N Peary St Arlington VA 22207-5359 Office: Sec Army SAIS-C4A Pentagon Rm 1C660 Washington DC 20310-0107

COURTSAL, DONALD PRESTON, manufacturing company executive, financial consultant; b. New Haven, Dec. 30, 1929; s. Frederick Joseph and Viola (Schiffel) C.; m. Frances L. Chase, May 22, 1954; children: Lyle Donald, Charles Francis. B.S. in Mech. Engring. U.S. Coast Guard Acad., 1951; M.S. in Naval Architecture and Marine Engring, MIT, 1956. With shipbldg. div. Bethlehem Steel Co., Quincy, Mass., 1956-64; with Dravo Corp., 1965-85; gen. mgr. engring. works div., corp. v.p. Dravo Corp., Pitts., 1976-82, treas., corp. v.p., 1982-83; group officer mfg. group, sr. v.p. corp. Dravo Corp., 1983-85; fin. cons. Allegheny Fin. Ltd., 1986—; mem. ship research com. Nat. Acad. Scis., 1979-81. Author papers in field. Served with USCG, 1951-54. Mem. Soc. Naval Architects and Marine Engrs. (v.p. 1979-90, v.p. (hon.) 1991—, exec. com. 1974-77, 80-88, coun. 1974—, chmn. adv. pub. svc. com. 1978-88, chmn. audit com. 1991—). Unitarian. Club: Pymatuning Yacht. Home: 1208 Woodland Rd Pittsburgh PA 15237-4359 Office: Allegheny Fin Ltd 3000 Mcknight East Dr Pittsburgh PA 15237-6439

COUSAR, GLORIA, government official; b. Pitts.. BA, Vassar Coll.; MA in Urban Planning and Pub. Affairs, Princeton U.; postgrad., Am. U., Cairo. Ordained to ministry. Co-founder, exec. dir. Greater Washington Mut. Housing Assn., 1985-91; dep. rsch. dir. Joint Ctr. for Polit. Studies, Inc.; rural housing rsch. assoc. Housing Assistance Coun., Inc.; spl. asst. to sec., resident pub. policy fellow HUD, dep. for cmty. rels. and involvement, dep. asst. sec. for pub. and assisted housing delivery; HUD rep. 1st HUD-city partnership to turn around troubled pub. housing agy. Phila. Housing Authority. Former vol., prodr. and hostess for pub. affairs programming Sta. WPFW, Washington; vol. numerous nat. and cmty.-based bd. dirs. for non-profit orgns. dealing with homeless needs, rural land loss of so. minority farmers, investment lending for low and moderate income housing, promotion energy conservation, environ. problem solving and new techs. Office: HUD Office Pub and Indian Housing 451 7th St SW Washington DC 20410-0001

COUSAR, RONNY, city official; b. Newark, Sept. 20, 1957. BS in Natural Resource Mgmt., Rutgers U., 1980. Natural resource pk. ranger Gateway Nat. Recreation Area Nat. Pk. Svc., Sandy Hook, N.J., 1980-81; city forester, landscape architect engring. dept. City of Newark, 1981-83; city forester dept. pks. and recreation forestry divsn. City of Balt., 1983-91; city forester Dept. Pks. and Recreation forestry divsn. City of Colorado Springs, Colo., 1991-97; dir. neighborhood svcs. City of Colorado Springs, 1997—. Grad. Pikes Peak Leadership program; mem. Senate Bill 94 Juvenile Svcs. Com., Gov.'s Environ. Task Force, Md.; bd. dirs. Colo. Tree Coalition. Recipient cert. of recognition Nat. Pk. Svc. Mem. Alpha Phi Alpha. Office: Neighborhood Svcs City Adminstrn Bldg 30 S Nevada Ave Ste 302 Colorado Springs CO 80903-1825

COUSER, WILLIAM GRIFFITH, medical educator, academic administrator, nephrologist; b. Lebanon, N.H., July 11, 1939; s. Thomas Clifford and Winifred Priscilla (Ham) C. B.A., Harvard U., 1961, M.D., 1965; B.M.S., Dartmouth Med. Sch., 1963. Diplomate Am. Bd. Internal Medicine. Intern Moffitt Hosp./U. Calif. Med. Ctr., San Francisco, 1965-66, 66-67; resident Boston City Hosp., 1969-70; asst. prof. medicine U. Chgo., 1972-73; asst. prof. Boston U., 1972-77, assoc. prof., 1977-82; prof., head div. nephrology U. Wash., Seattle, 1982—; Belding Scribner prof.medicine U. Wash., 1995—; mem. sci. adv. bd. Kidney Found. Mass., Boston, 1974-82; mem. research grant com. Nat. Kidney Found., N.Y.C., 1981-86; mem. rev. bd. for nephrology VA, Washington, 1981-84; mem. exec. com. Council on Kidney in Cardiovascular Disease, Am. Heart Assn., Dallas, 1982-85; mem. pathology A study sect. NIH (chmn. 1988-89), subspecialty bd. in nephrology Am. Bd. Internal Medicine, 1988-92; dir. George M. O'Briend Kidney Rsch. Ctr., U. Wash., 1993. Co-editor: Immunologic Renal Diseases, 1997; contbr. numerous articles, chpts., abstracts to profl. publs.; mem. editl. bd. Kidney Internat., 1982-96, Am. Jour. Kidney Diseases, Am. Jour. Nephrology, Jour. Am. Soc. Nephrology. Served to capt. U.S. Army, 1967-69, Vietnam. Recipient Rsch. Career Devel. award NIH, 1975-80, Method to Extend Rsch. in Time award, 1991-97; fellow Nat. Kidney Found., 1971, NIH, 1973; grantee, 1974—. Fellow AAAS, ACP, Am. Soc.

Clin. Investigation (v.p. 1983-84), Am. Assn. Physicians, Am. Soc. Nephrology (coun. 1991-94, pres. 1996), Internat. Soc. Nephrology (coun. 1999), Am. Assn. Exptl. Pathology, Western Assn. Physicians (coun.). Avocation: boating. Office: U Wash Box 356521 1959 NE Pacific St Seattle WA 98195-0001

COUSINEAU, PHILIP ROBERT, writer, filmmaker; b. Columbia, S.C., Nov. 26, 1952; s. Stanley Horace and Rosemary Marie (La Chance) C.; 1 child, Jack Philip Blue Beaton-Cousineau. BA cum laude, U. Detroit, 1974. Writer-in residence Shakespeare and Co. Bookstore, Paris, 1987; script judge Bay Guardian Scriptwriting Contest, 1987-89; judge Nat. Ednl. Film and Video Festival, 1990; mem. adv. bd. Joseph Campbell Archives and Libr., 1991—; documentary film judge Emmy Awards, 1992; dir. mythological tours Joseph Campbell Found., 1993-96; documentary judge San Francisco Film Festival, 1993-95. Author: Deadlines, 1991, UFOs: Manual for the Millenium, 1995, German edit., 1997, Portugese edit., 1998, Soul Moments: Marvelous Stories from the World of Synchronicity, 1997, Spanish edit., 1998, The Book of Roads, 1998, The Art of Pilgrimage, 1998, in Portuguese, 1999 (Quality Paperback Book Club selection 1998); editor: The Hero's Journey: Joseph Campbell on His Life and Work, 1990, Portuguese edit., 1995, The Soul of the World, 1993 (Quality Paperback Book Club selection 1993, Book of Yr. award Contemporary Photography 1994), Soul: An Archaeology, 1994, Chinese edit., 1997, Turkish edit., 1999, Prayers at 3 A.M., 1995, Design Outlaws, 1997, Spanish edit., 1999, Riddle Me This: A World Treasury of Folk Riddles, 1999, The Soul A Flame, 1999; co-dir., screenwriter documentary films The Peyote Road, 1993 (best documentary award Gt. Plains Film Festival, Cine Golden Eagle award, Bronze Telly award, silver award Chgo. Film Festival, award Mill Valley Film Festival), The Red Road to Sobriety, 1995 (Cine Golden Eagle award 1995, Gold award Red River Film Festival 1998), Ecological Design, 1994 (Golden Gate award, Cine Golden Eagle award, Sundance Film Festival), Your Humble Serpent: The Legacy of Reuben Snake, 1996 (Silver Apple award Nat. Ednl. Film Festival, Gold award Red Earth Film Festival); co-writer The 1932 Ford V888, Silverado Prodns., 1986, The Presence of the Goddess, Balcorman Films, 1987, (film) Eritrea: A Portrait of the Eritrean People, 1989; co-writer video Wiping the Tears of Seven Generations, 1991 (Best Video award Am. Indian Film Festival, Silver Telly award, Gold Apple award Nat. Ednl. Film Festival; co-writer, assoc. prodr. The Hero's Journey: The World of Joseph Campbell, 1987 (Silver Apple award Ednl. Film and Video Festival); co-writer film Forever Activists: Stories from the Veterans of the Abraham Lincoln Brigade, 1990 (Acad. Award nomination, jury prize San Francisco Film Festival), also others. Trustee Native Land Found., 1993-96. Recipient award Nat. Assn. Ind. Pubs., 1991; fellow Calif. Inst. Integral Studies, 1991-95. Avocation: travel. Office: Harper San Francisco Pubs 353 Sacramento St San Francisco CA 94111-3620

COUSINO, JOE ANN, sculptor; b. Toledo, Nov. 17, 1925; d. George Carl and Lucille Caroline (Kocher) Bux; m. (div.); children: Paula Rene, Richard Nils. BA in Art, U. Toledo, 1947; stud., U. of Mex., 1948, U. Ill., 1953; attended, Internatl. Wkshp., Pietra Santa, Italy, 1980. Art tchr. Ctrl. YMCA & YWCA, Toledo, 1945-47; sculpture tchr. U. Tex. Jr. Coll., Gainesville, 1965, Defiance (Ohio) Coll., 1970, Bowling Green (Ohio) State Univ., 1971; profl. sculptor worldwide, 1963—; founder and pres. Toledo Potter's Guild, 1951-55; Ohio rep. Am. Craft Coun., N.Y.C., 1960-62; pres. Fedn. Art Socs. North Ohio, 1965-67; co-chair midwest Kefauver com. Art in the Embassies Program, Dept. of State, Washington, 1966. One-woman shows include Toledo Mus. Art, Frank Ryan Gallery, Chgo., Forsythe Gallery, Mich., Mount St. Joseph Gallery, Cin., Arndt Mus. Art, Elmira, N.Y., Button Gallery Ltd., Saugatuck, Mich., Bowling Green State Univ. Grad. Ctr. Gallery, Ohio State Gallery, Kent State Univ. Gallery, Exhbn. Bangkok, 1990; prin. sculptures include the John Leslie Stevens Meml., Oak Harbor, Ohio, Mame Gordon Meml., United Ch., Sylvania, Ohio, Greek Orthodox Holy Cathedral, Christ the King Ch., Toledo Hosp., Riverside Hosp., Univ. Toledo, Med. Coll. Ohio, Toledo Botanical Gardens, U. Toledo Student Union Bldg., Way Libr., Perrysburg, Ohio, 1986, Sister of St. Francis, Mother House Commons, Tiffon, Ohio, 1999; works featured in numerous mags. and jours. Sisters of Bunting Brass of U.S.A., Rngs. Soc. of Ohio, Vol. UNICEF, Madras, India, 1984; recipient Woman of Toledo civic award, 1987; bd. dirs. Toledo Arts Commn., 1978-84. Recipient Outstanding Svc. in Field of Art award Fedn. of Arts, Toledo, 1967. Mem. Internat. Sculpture Ctr., Pan Pacific S.E. Asia Women's Assn., Scandinavian Club of Toledo. Episc. Avocations: internat. travel, folk dancing, jazz, photography, lectr. on art. Home and Studio: 3717 Indian Rd Toledo OH 43606-2408

COUSINS, DERRYL, umpire; b. Fresno, Calif., Aug. 18, 1946; m. Shawna Cousins; children: Cas, Daryl-Lynne. Degree in Polit. Sci., El Camino (Calif.) C.C.; student, Umpire Devel. Program. Profl. baseball player Detroit Orgn., Cleve. Orgn.; former umpire Midwest League, Carolina League, Tex. League, Pacific Coast League, Dominican League, Puerto Rican Winter League; umpire maj. league baseball Am. League, N.Y.C., 1979—. Avocation: golfing. Office: Am League 350 Park Ave New York NY 10022

COUSINS, RICHARD FRANCIS, diversified financial services company executive; b. Oceanside, N.Y., Feb. 11, 1955; s. Richard Felix and Hedwig (Kobierec) C.; m. Alice Annette Arant, Sept. 3, 1977; 1 child, Kathryn. BA, Georgetown U., 1977; MBA in Acctg., NYU, 1987. Project analyst European div. Citibank, N.Y.C., 1977-78, fin. analyst, 1978-79, fin. mgr., 1979-80, project leader, bus. mgr., 1980-83; dir. opns. Merrill Lynch Hubbard, N.Y.C., 1983-85; sr. grad. asst. NYU Grad. Sch. Bus., N.Y.C., 1985-86; sr. systems cons. Am. Express, N.Y.C., 1986-88; mgr. strategic opns. Am. Express, Phoenix, 1988-92, project advisor, 1992-96, dir. of quality, 1996—. Home: 9998 Gyrfalcon Ct Sandy UT 84092-4074 Office: Am Express Stored Value Group 4315 S 2700 W Salt Lake City UT 84184-0001

COUSINS, ROBERT JOHN, nutritional biochemist, educator; b. N.Y.C., Apr. 5, 1941; s. Charles Robert and Doris Elizabeth (Sifferlen) C.; m. Elizabeth Anne Ward, Jan. 25, 1969; children: Sarah, Jonathan, Allison. BA, U. Vt., 1963; PhD, U. Conn., 1968. NIH postdoctoral fellow biochemistry U. Wis., 1968-70; asst. prof. nutrition Rutgers U., 1971-74, assoc. prof., 1974-77, prof. nutritional biochemistry, 1977-79, prof. II (disting. Prof.), 1979-82, dir. grad. program in nutrition, 1976-82, mem. grad. programs in biochemistry, nutrition and toxicology; Boston family prof. human nutrition and biochemistry U. Fla., Gainesville, 1982—; eminent scholar chair U. Fla., 1982—; dir. Nutritional Sci. Ctr., U. Fla., 1987—, grad. coun., 1990—; mem. nutrition study sect. NIH, 1980-84; mem. USDA Expt. Sta., dir. subcom. on human nutrition, 1987—; J.L. Pratt vis. prof. Va. Poly. Inst. and State U., 1980; Wellcome vis. prof. Auburn U., 1986; Mary E. Shorb lectr. nutrition U. Md., 1989, James Waddell Meml. lectr. U. Wis., Madison, 1989, Disting. lectr. biochemistry and molecular biology U. Wis., Milw., 1989; Hans Fisher lectureship Rutgers U., 1995; Lucille Hurley lectr. U. Calif., Davis, 1997; mem. NAS, Inst. of Med. Commn. on opportunities in nutrition and food scis., 1991-93, Food & Nutrition Bd., 1997—, Ad Hoc Bionutrition Commn., NIH, 1993. Assoc. editor Jour. Nutrition, 1990-96; mem. editl. com. Ann. Revs. Nutrition, 1985-90, 96—; contbg. editor Nutrition Revs., 1980-88; mem. editl. bd. FASEB Jour., 1994—, Biol. Trace Element Rsch.; contbr. articles in nutritional biochemistry to profl. jours., chpts. to books. Recipient Mead Johnson award in nutrition, 1979, Osborne and Mendel award for basic rsch. in nutrition, 1989, U. Conn. Disting. Alumnus award, 1991, Merit award NIH, 1992, Gamma Sigma Delta Sr. Faculty award U. Fla., 1993, Eric Underwood Lectureship award; Future Leader grantee Nutrition Found., Inc., 1973, NIH grantee, 1972—. Mem. AAAS, Am. Soc. Biochem. and Molecular Biology, Am. Soc. Nutrition Sci. (chmn. nominating com. elected officers 1983, coun. 1986-89, pres.-elect 1995-96, pres. 1996-97), Biochem. Soc. U.K., Soc. Exptl. Biology and Medicine (edit. bd. Proc. 1980-86), Am. Chem. Soc., Soc. Toxicology, Fedn. Am. Socs. Exptl. Biology (vice chmn. summer conf. 1985, chmn. summer conf. 1989, bd. dirs. 1989—, v.p. 1990-92, pres., chmn. bd. 1991-92, chmn. subcom. consensus conf. biomed. funding 1991-94, chmn. pub. affairs exec. com. 1992-93), Sigma Xi, Phi Kappa Phi, Gamma Sigma Delta (U. Conn. Disting. Alumni). Home: 4510 NW 20th Pl Gainesville FL 32605-3441 Office: U Fla Ctr for Nutritional Sciences 201 Food Sci & Human Nutr Bldg Gainesville FL 32611

COUSINS, WILLIAM LUKE, transportation administrator; b. Atlanta. BS in aviation mgmt., Embry Riddle Aero. U., Daytona Beach, Fla. Various positions Ga. Dept. of Transp., 1973-78, bur. chief of aero, 1978-91, adminstr., 1991—. Pres. Nat. Assn. of State Aviation Ofcls.; v.p. Met. Atlanta Aero Club; ex-officio mem. bd. dirs. Ga. Aviation Hall of Fame; with USAF, 1961-69. Office: Georgia Dept of Transp Intermodal Programs Office 276 Memorial Dr SW Atlanta GA 30303-3743

COUSINS, WILLIAM THOMAS, industrial engineer, educator; b. Ft. Bragg, N.C., Aug. 24, 1944; s. Thomas Jepson and Susan Virginia (Hill) C.; m. Marilyn Kay Bruch, Dec. 1, 1973; 1 child, Timothy. BA, BS in Indsl. Engring., U. Iowa, 1968, MS in Indsl. Engring., 1971; grad. exec. devel. program, Cornell U., 1983. Engr. Polaroid Corp., Cambridge, Mass., 1971-73; sr. engr. Polaroid Corp., Cambridge, 1973-76, gen. supr., 1976-77; mgr. quality assurance Polaroid Corp., Norwood, Mass., 1977-79; mgr. indsl. engring. Polaroid Corp., Waltham, Mass., 1979-83; tech. mgr. Polaroid Corp., Cambridge, 1983-96; mgr., v.p. QA/RA TREX Med., Broadview, Ill., 1996—; mem. adj. faculty Babson Coll., Wellesley, Mass., 1973-85, Lake Forest (Ill.) Bus. Coll., 1992-93; presenter confs. in field. Contbr. articles to profl. jours. Vol. Big Bros., Boston, 1972-81; soccer and baseball coach Darien (Ill.) Youth Club, 1995—. With U.S. Army, 1968-70. Decorated Bronze Star, U.S. Army, 1970. Mem. Am. Soc. Quality Control, Inst. Indsl. Engrs. Methodist. Avocations: golf, camping, jogging, teaching statistics, coaching youth sports. Home: 1821 Darien Club Dr Darien IL 60561-3663 Office: TREX Med 2000 S 25th Ave Broadview IL 60153-2828

COUTERMARSH, EVA MARINA, personnel executive; b. Salisbury, Md., Oct. 29, 1967; d. Ernest Richard Jr. and Marina (Hernandez) C. BA in English and Comms., Mass. Coll. Liberal Arts, 1997. Area coord. Experiment in Internat. Living, Brattleboro, Vt., 1992; adminstrv. asst. Nathan & Co., Pittsfield, Mass., 1992-93; personnel asst. Assoc. Staffing, Inc., Phoenix, 1993-94, staffing coord., 1994-95, sr. staffing coord., 1995-97; staffing mgr. Assoc. Staffing, Inc., Mesa, Ariz., 1997-98; sr. pers. cons. KNF&T, Boston, 1998—. Mem. Ariz. dist. 28 Republican Com., Scottsdale, 1997-98. Mem. NAFE, New Eng. Human Resources Assn., Mass. Assn. Pers. Cons. Republican. Roman Catholic. Avocations: reading, travel, entertaining, outdoors. Fax: (617) 574-8222. E-mail: EVA@KNFT.COM. Home: 35 D Richardson Ave Wakefield MA 01880 Office: KNF&T 133 Fed St Boston MA 02110

COUTO, NANCY VIEIRA, poet, literary consultant; b. New Bedford, Mass., June 11, 1942; d. Edward and Angelina (Vieira) C.; m. Joseph Anthony Martin, Aug. 13, 1988. BS in Edn., Bridgewater State Coll., 1964; MFA, Cornell U., 1980. Secondary rights asst. Cornell U. Press, Ithaca, N.Y., 1981-82; subsidiary rights mgr. Cornell U. Press, Ithaca, 1982-94; cons., proprietor Leatherstocking Literary Svcs., Ithaca, 1994—; juror literature fellowship program Pa. Coun. Arts, Harrisburg, 1994; mem. selection com. fellowships Am. Antiquarian Soc., Worcester, Mass., 1995. Author: The Face in the Water, 1990 (award), various poems; assoc. editor Epoch, 1979-82, The Laurel Review, 1992—. Artist ptnr. Cmty. Arts Partnership of Tompkins County. Creative Artists Pub. Svc. fellow N.Y. State, 1982-83, NEA fellow, 1987, 99, Creative Performing Artists and Writers fellow Am. Antiquarian Soc., 1995; Constance Saltonstall Found. for the Arts grantee, 1998; recipient Gettysburg Review award, 1994. Mem. Associated Writing Programs. Democrat.

COUTRAKON, BASIL H., federal judge; b. 1913. AB, Dartmouth Coll., 1936; LLB, U. Ill., 1939. Bar: Ill. Bankruptcy judge Springfield, Ill., 1946—. Served with USN, 1942-46. Office: 226 Federal Bldg 600 E Monroe St Springfield IL 62701-1626

COUTS, ROSE MARIE, medical radiographer, sonographer; b. Van Wert, Ohio, Nov. 18, 1951; d. David William and Peggy Jane (Gillespie) Hiller; m. Jed Dee Couts, June 20, 1970; children: Jeremy Joseph, Joshua Dee, Michelle Josette. AAS in Radiography with honors, Lima (Ohio) Tech. Coll., 1994. Radiographer Joint Twp. Dist. Meml. Hosp., St. Mary's, Ohio, 1993-98, sonographer, 1995-98; sonographer, vascular technologist St. Rita's Med. Ctr., LIma, Ohio, 1998—. 4-H advisor Ohio City Blue Ribbon Workers, Ohio City; mem. exec. com. 4-H coun. Ohio State U. Extension, Van Wert, 1995-97; candidate County Commr., Van Wert, 1988. Mem. Am. Soc. Radiologic Technologists, Soc. Diagnostic Med. Sonographers, Ohio Soc. Radiologic Technologists, Lima Soc. Radiologic Technologists (treas., pres. 1996—), Phi Theta Kappa, Alpha Beta Gamma. Democrat. Avocations: reading, crocheting, needlepoint, travel. Office: SRMC 730 W Market St Lima OH 45801-2494

COUTU, CHARLES ARTHUR, deacon; b. Central Falls, R.I., Oct. 3, 1927; s. Charles Arthur and Aldea Alma (Laliberte) C.; m. Yvette Rhea Dery, Nov. 26, 1953. AA, Our Lady of Providence Sem., 1949; Etudes Speciales de Philosophies, Sem. Philosophy, Montreal, Que., Can., 1951; A in Casualty Claims Law, Am. Ednl. Inst. N.J., 1966. Ordained deacon Roman Cath. Ch., 1978. Master of ceremonies Bishop Tracy, Lafayette, La., 1958-59; tchr. St. Teresa's High Sch., Decatur, Ill., 1964-65, Pitts., 1964-68, Holy Family Ch., Dale City, Va., 1971-97; ret., 1997; permanent diaconate commn. mem. St. Peter's Mission, Washington, Va., 1998; defender of the bond Tribunal, Arlington, Va., 1992; subrogation mgr. United Svcs. Automobile Assn., Reston, Va., 1976—; advocate Tribunal, Arlington, 1976—; chmn. Arbitration Com., Washington, 1975-88; mem. Diaconal Coun. Exec. Com., 1987-90; vice-chmn. Evangelization Commn., Diocese of Arlington, 1979-80. Religious emblem counselor Cath. Com. on Scouting and Campfire, 1990. Sgt. 1st class U.S. Army, 1952-55. Mem. KC. Home: 328 Pine Dr Amissville VA 20106 *I want to try to develop and nurture a deeper love and respect for God through His Mother, the Blessed Virgin Mary.*

COUTURE, JEAN G., retired surgeon, educator; b. Quebec City, Que., Can., July 1, 1924. Student, Jesuits Coll., Quebec City, 1936-44; MD, Laval U., 1944-49. Postgrad. New Rochelle Hosp., NYU, Bellevue Med. Ctr., N.Y.C., 1949-54; attending surgeon Hôpital du Saint-Sacrement, Que., 1954—, surgeon-in-chief, 1967-78, head dept. surgery, 1969-75, dir. oncology unit, 1981—; asst. prof. Faculty of Medicine, Laval U., Que., 1963-70, prof. surgery, 1970—, chmn. Dept. Surgery, 1981-89, mem. council Dept. Surgery, 1969-78, dir. postgrad. programs, 1973-79, asst. dean for postgrad. studies, 1975-79; v.p. med. bd. St. Sacrement Hosp., Que., 1967-68; med. advisor Regional Council for Health and Welfare, Quebec City, 1978-81; vis. prof. McGill U., 1977, Hôpital Henri Mondor, Paris, 1978, U. Ottawa, 1980, U. Calgary, 1984; mem. com. on accreditation Royal Coll., 1974-78, chmn. area 4 regional adv. com., 1977-80; bd. govs. Profl. Corp. Physicians and Surgeons Can., 1976—; lectr. in field. Mem. editorial bd. Can. Jour. Surgery, 1974-81; contbr. articles to profl. jours. Pres. Jesuits Coll. Alumni Assn., Que., 1957, Alumni Assn. Laval U., 1969-70. Named Alumni of Yr., Laval U., 1996. Fellow Royal Coll. Surgeons Can., ACS (bd. govs. 1980-86, exec. bd. govs. 1981-85, chmn. Que. Province adv. com. 1976-82), Australasian Coll. Surgeons (hon.), Coll. Surgeons South Africa (hon.), Royal Coll. Surgeons of Eng. (hon.), Order of Can. (hon.); mem. Royal Coll. Physicians and Surgeons Can. (bd. examiners 1958-66, pres. bd. examiners 1964-66, sci. program in surgery 1968-71, pres. program com. in surgery 1970-71, chmn. com. on accreditation 1980-82, chmn. com. on credentials 1982-84, council 1976-80, v.p. 1978-80, pres. 1984-86), Can. Assn. Gen. Surgeons (pres. Eastern div. 1985-86, chmn. edn. com. 1980-83, nat. pres. 1989-90), Can. Coun. on Health Facilities Accreditation (pres. 1992-93), Assn. Clin. Surgeons Can., Can. Med. Assn., Am. Surg. Assn., Assn. des Médecins de Langue Française du Can., Que. Surg. Soc. (sec. 1966-70, pres. 1972-73), Assn. Française de Chirurgie, Internat. Surg. Soc., Que. Med. Soc., James IV Assn. Surgeons, Internat. Surg. Group, l'Académie de Chirurgie de Paris, l'Assn. Française de Chirurgie (hon.). Office: Hosp du Saint Sacrement, 1050 Chemin Sainte Foy, Quebec, PQ Canada G1S 4L8

COUTURE, JEAN GUY, bishop; b. Quebec, Que., Can., May 6, 1929; s. Odilon and Eva (Drolet) C. B.A., Laval U., Quebec, 1949, B.Ph., 1949, L.Theol., 1953, L.Sc.Phys., 1959. Ordained priest Roman Cath. Ch., 1953; prof. math. and scis. St. Georges High Sch. and Coll., Beauce, Que., 1953-65; adminstr. coll. St. Georges High Sch. and Coll., 1961-68; mem. adminstrn. Roman Cath. Diocese Quebec, 1968-75; bishop of Hauterive Que., 1975-79, of Chicoutimi, 1979—. Mem. Order of Can. Home and Office: 602 E Racine, Chicoutimi, PQ Canada G7H 1V1

COUTURE, MAURICE, archbishop; b. Saint-Pierre-de-Broughton, Qué., Can., Nov. 3, 1926. Ordained priest Roman Cath. Ch., 1951; ordained titular bishop of Talattula and aux. bishop of Québec, 1982. Bishop Baie-Comeau, Qué., 1988-90; archbishop of Qué, primate of Can., 1990—. Home: CP 459 HV, 2 Port-Dauphin, Quebec, PQ Canada G1R 4R6 Office: Archdiocese of Québec, 1073 René-Levesque Ouest, Sillery, PQ Canada G1S 4R5*

COUTURE, RONALD DAVID, art administrator, design consultant; b. Ware, Mass., Dec. 1, 1944; s. Roy and Thelma Mary (Ledger) C.; m. Sandra Elaine Sharpe, Sept. 28, 1968; children: David, Meredith. Diploma, Butera Sch. Art, Boston, 1966. Graphic designer Sta. WGBH-TV Ednl. Found., Cambridge, Mass., 1970-73; promotion art dir. The Boston Globe, 1973-74, editorial design dir., 1974-77; asst. mng. art dir. N.Y. Times, 1977-78, assoc. mng. art dir., 1978-79, mng. art dir., 1979-84, dep. dir./editorial art, 1984-86, mng. dir./editorial art, 1986-88; owner, pres. Newsvision Inc., Mt. Kisco, N.Y., 1988-95; owner Riverbend Design, 1996—; design cons. for Web and corp. pub.; design cons. Met. Cultural Alliance, Boston, 1972-77, IBM Corp. Pubs., 1991-93; guest lectr. Boston U. Sch. Communications, 1977; judge 62d and 64th Ann Exhibit, The Art Dirs. Club of N.Y., 1983; internat. editorial design Internat. Editorial Design Forum, N.Y.C., 1983. Contbr. articles in field to profl. jours. Mem. Westborough Planning Bd., Mass., 1977; apptd. regional rep. Ctrl. Mass. Regional Planning Bd., Westborough, 1977; apptd. chmn. Archtl. Rev. Bd., Mount Kisco, N.Y., 1978, 81, 84, 86, 89, 92, 95; mem. task force Labor Market Info. Network of N.Y. Labor Dept. and N.Y.C. Dept. Employment, 1979. Recipient Gold medal set design New England Theater Conf., 1974; recipient Gold medal newspaper design Soc. Newspaper Design, 1980. Mem. Soc. Newspaper Design (Gold medal chart design 1981, bd. dirs., nat. conf. dir. 1987-90), Art Dirs. Club N.Y., Am. Inst. Graphic Artist, Art Dirs. Club Boston, Nat. Computer Graphics Assn., Soc. Publ. Design. Roman Catholic. Home: 44 Lake Rd Brookfield MA 01506-1812 Office: PO Box 537 9 S Maple St Brookfield MA 01506-1600

COVALT, ROBERT BYRON, chemicals executive; b. Chgo., Nov. 8, 1931; s. Byron L. and Thelma A. (Adams) C.; m. Virginia, Aug. 17, 1952; children: Karen Elizabeth Ryberg, David Byron. BSChemE, Purdue U., 1953, DEng (hon.), 1992; MBA, U. Chgo., 1967. Devel. engr. B.F. Goodrich Chem. Co., Avon Lake, Ohio, 1953-54; with Morton Chem. div. Morton Thiokol, Inc., 1956—; v.p. engring. and mfg. Morton Chem. div. Morton Thiokol, Inc., Chgo., 1973-78; group v.p. Morton Chem. div. Morton Thiokol, Inc., 1978-79, pres., 1979-87; pres. specialty chems. group, group v.p. Morton Thiokol, Inc., 1987-89; pres. splty. chems. group, group v.p. Morton Internat. Inc., 1989-90, exec. v.p., 1990-94; pres., CEO Sovereign Specialty Chems., Inc., 1994—; bd. dirs. CFC Internat. Trustee N. Cen. Coll., Naperville, Ill. Served as 1st lt. USAF, 1954-56. Recipient Disting. Engring. Alumnus award Purdue U. Mem. AIChE, Am. Chem. Soc., Soc. Chem. Industry, Chicagoland C. of C. (bd. dirs.). Home: 7517 Bull Valley Rd Mc Henry IL 60050-7493 Office: Sovereign Splty Chems LP 225 W Washington St Ste 2200 Chicago IL 60606-3418 *Success in business is truly based upon teamwork and the accomplishment of all members working in concert toward a common goal. In the end, it is the result of what you do with your people, not what you do to your people.*

COVAULT, CRAIG, editor; b. Dayton, Ohio, 1949. BS in Journalism, Bowling Green State U., 1971. Writer Urbana Citizen, 1971-72; sr. space editor Aviation Week & Space Tech., Washington, 1972-92, chief Paris bur., 1992-96; sr. editor Aviation Week & Space Tech., 1996—. Office: Aviation Week & Space Tech Cape Canaveral Bureau 449 Turtle Cir Satellite Bch FL 32937-3806*

COVAULT, LLOYD R., JR., retired hospital administrator, psychiatrist; b. Troy, Ohio, Feb. 3, 1928; s. Lloyd R. and Anne Marie (Grisez) C.; m. Janet Eileen Davidson, June 12, 1951; children: Sheryl Ann, Jane Helen, Michael Lee, Roger Ken. BA, Miami U., Oxford, Ohio, 1950; MD, Ohio State U., 1954. From extern to asst. supt. Orient (Ohio) State Inst., 1953-70; pvt. practice Columbus, 1968-75; psychiat. trainee Cen. Ohio Psychiat. Hosp., Columbus, 1966-68, psychiatrist, 1982-85; supt. Columbus State Inst., 1970-74; med. dir. North Cen. Cmty. Mental Health Ctr., Columbus, 1974-79, cons. psychiatry, 1985-90; assoc. prof. psychiatry Ohio State U. Med. Sch., 1975-76; cons. psychiatry North Cen. Community Mental Health Ctr., Columbus, 1985-90; from dir. to cons. psychiatrist S.E. Mental Health Ctr., Columbus, 1979-97, cons. psychiatrist, 1986-97; med. dir. Charles B. Milles Mental Health Ctr., Marysville, Ohio, 1989-95; psychiat. cons. Union Manor Nursing Home, Marysville, Ohio, 1996-99; ret.; mem. Franklin County Mental Health and Retardation Bd., 1970-74, Ohio Dept. Mental Health, ret. 1984; cons. psychiatrist Madison County Mental Health Ctr., London, 1984-85, Chillecothe VA Hosp., 1995-99; staff psychiatrist Ohio Correction Complex, Orient, 1988-89; 1st med. coord. Netcare Admission Unit Ctrl. Ohio Psychiat. Hosp., 1985-87; founding father Physicians Assn. Ohio Dept. Mental Health, 1956-68, pres. 1957; psychiatrist, cons. Buckeye Ranch for Children and Adolescents, Grove City, Ohio, 1998-99. Recipient Union County Pillar award, 1991; named Ohio's Disting. Rural Practitioner, Ohio State Dept. Health, 1993. Fellow Am. Assn. Mental Retardation (life, chmn. adminstrn. state chpt. 1974-75), Am. Psychiat. Assn. (life); mem. Ohio Psychiat. Assn., Neuropsychiat. Soc. Ctrl. Ohio (pres. 1973-74), Mental Health Supts. Assn. (pres. Ohio chpt. 1973-74). Home: 11092 Darby Creek Rd Orient OH 43146-9797 Office: Union Manor Nursing Home Rt 1 Marysville OH 43040 also: Chillicothe VA Hosp 17273 State Route 104 Chillicothe OH 45601-8608

COVELL, CHRISTOPHER GREENE, management executive; b. Providence, R.I., Apr. 14, 1947; s. Walter Howard and Harriette Francis (Tabakin) C. Founding pres. Ballet Who, Inc., N.Y.C., 1987—; resident fellow, ceo Abuse Rsch. Inst., N.Y.C., 1985—; pub. Music-To-Go, 1984—. Composer-lyricist various songs. Mem. ASCAP.

COVELLO, ALFRED VINCENT, federal judge; b. Hartford, Conn., Feb. 4, 1933; s. Frank and Bernadine (Neville) C.; m. Suzanne Rafferty, Sept. 6, 1958; children: Timothy J., Nancy J. AB, Harvard U., 1954; LLB, JD, U. Conn., 1960. Bar: Conn. 1960, U.S. Dist. Ct. Conn. 1960. Ptnr. Bieluch, Barry & Covello, Hartford, 1960-64, Gross, Hyde & Williams, Hartford, 1964-74; judge Conn. Cir. Ct., Hartford, 1974-75, Conn. Ct. Common Pleas, Hartford, 1975-78, Conn. Superior Ct., Hartford, 1978-87; assoc. justice Conn. Supreme Ct., Hartford, 1987-92; judge U.S. Dist. Ct., Dist. of Conn., Hartford, 1992—, now chief judge. With U.S. Army, 1955-57. Roman Catholic. Avocations: airline transport pilot, flight instructor. Office: US Dist Ct 450 Main St Fl 2 Hartford CT 06103-3010*

COVELLO, JOHN ANTHONY, water utility lobbyist; b. New Brunswick, N.J., Aug. 28, 1960; s. Gerald Robert Sr. and Elizabeth Ann (Conte) C.; m. Paula Anne Sollami, Oct. 9, 1994. Student, U. Md., 1978-80; BA in Polit. Sci., George Washington U., Washington, 1983; MA in Polit. Sci., Rutgers U., New Brunswick, N.J., 1991. Lic. real estate agt., N.J. Legis. aide Rep. Frank Thompson, Jr. (Dem.-N.J.), Washington, 1980, Rep. Elliott Levitas (Dem.-Ga.), Washington, 1981, Rep. Andy Ireland (Dem.-Fla.), Washington, 1981-82; legis. svcs. dir. Weil, Gotshal & Manges, Washington, 1984-90; sr. policy advisor N.J. Gen. Assembly Dem. Office, Trenton, 1991-96; regional field dir. N.J. Dem. State Coordinated Campaign, New Brunswick, 1996; mgr. govt. rels. United Water N.J., Harrington Park, 1997—; chmn. Bergen County Employer Legis. Com., Harrington Park, 1997—; bd. trustees N.J. Soc. Environ. & Econ. Devel., 1998—. Dist. Dem. committeeman Lawrence Twp., Lawrenceville, N.J., 1994-97; vice-chair Econ. Growth and Redevel. Adv. Com., Lawrenceville, 1996-97; mem. Zoning Bd. Adjustment, Lawrenceville, 1997; bd. trustee N.J. Seed, Trenton. Recipient grad. fellowship in politics and pub. policy Eagleton Inst. Politics, Rutgers U., New Brunswick, N.J., 1990-91. Mem. Nat. Assn. Water Cos., Am. Water Works Assn., N.J. Dem. Roundtable. Roman Catholic. Avocations: golf, tennis, travel, reading, political history. Office: United Water NJ 200 Old Hook Rd Harrington Park NJ 07640-1716

COVEN, ROBERT MICHAEL, secondary school educator, researcher, writer; b. Detroit, Aug. 9, 1959; s. Sorrel Maurice and Barbara Rose (Farber) C.; m. Caroline Mary Meenan, June 22, 1985; 1 child, Madeline Anne. BA, U. Calif., Berkeley, 1980; MArch, U. Wis., Milw., 1984; MA in History, U. Del., 1990; postgrad., U. Chgo., 1990—. Corp. energy mgr., assoc. store planner Ohrbach's, N.Y.C., 1981-82; design and project mgmt. cons. Wells Fargo Bank, San Francisco, 1984-85; office mgr. House & House Archs., San

Francisco, 1985-86; preceptor social scis. U. Chgo., 1993-95; chmn. dept. history and social scis. Foxcroft Sch., Middleburg, Va., 1996—; computer cons. U. Chgo., 1991-96; panelist regional planning com. Met. Planning Coun. Chgo., 1995. Co-author: America's History: Reader, 1993; editor AIA, 1985-86; contbr. articles to profl. jours.; presenter at profl. confs. Mem. William H. Ray Elem. Curriculum Com., Chgo., 1995-96. Fellow U. Chgo., 1995-96, U. Del., 1988-90. Mem. Am. Hist. Assn., Orgn. Am. Historians, Nat. Coun. for History Edn., Nat. Forensic League, Orgn. History Tchrs., Phi Kappa Phi. Democrat. Jewish. Avocations: photography, hiking, reading. Office: Foxcroft School PO Box 5555 Middleburg VA 20118-5555

COVENEY, RAYMOND MARTIN, JR., educator; b. Marlboro, Mass., Oct. 15, 1942; s. Raymond Martin and Rita Marie (Brani) C.; m. Anne Marie Keating, Feb. 22, 1965; children: Christine, Maureen, David. BS in Geology, Tufts U., 1964; MS in Geology, U. Mich., 1968, PhD in Geology, 1972. Asst. geologist N.J. Zinc Co., Hanover, N.Mex., 1968; geologist Dickey Exploration Co., Alleghany, Calif., 1969-70; grad. tchg. asst. U. Mich., Ann Arbor, 1966-70; from asst. prof. to prof. dept. geosci. U. Mo., Kansas City, 1971—, interim dean Coll. Arts and Scis., 1992-93, chair dept. geoscis., 1996—; cons. ProSo Co., Inc., Kansas City, 1986-92, Midwest Rsch. Inst., Kansas City, 1986-91, Woodward Clyde, Kansas City, 1981, Hunt Midwest, 1997. Contbr. articles to profl. jours. Lt. (j.g.) USNR, 1964-66. Rackham Predoctoral Rsch. fellow, U. Mich., 1970-71; NSF Rsch. grantee, 1981-85, 90-93, 95-98; recipient N.T. Veatch award, 1988. Fellow Geology Soc. Am., Soc. Econ. Geologists (councilor 1993-96, trustee 1992-96); mem. AAAS, Geol. Soc., Am. Geophys. Union. Roman Catholic. Achievements include research in metal-rich black shales and related deposits of molybdenum, zinc, platinum. Home: 5405 Locust St Kansas City MO 64110-2443 Office: U Mo 5100 Rockhill Rd Kansas City MO 64110-2446

COVER, THOMAS M., statistician, electrical engineer, educator; b. San Bernardino, Calif., Aug. 7, 1938; s. William Llewellyn and Carolyn (Merrill) C.; 1 child, William. BS in Physics, MIT, 1960; MS in EE, Stanford U., 1961, PhD in EE, 1964. Asst. prof. elec. engring. Stanford (Calif.) U., 1964-67, assoc. prof., 1967-71, assoc. prof. elec. engring. and statistics, 1972-73, prof., 1973—, lab. dir. info. systems elec. engring., 1989-96, Kwoh-Ting Li Prof. Engring., 1994; vis. assoc. prof. elec. engring. MIT, Cambridge, 1971-72. Author: Elements of Information Theory, 1991; editor: Open Problems in Communication and Computation, 1987; contbr. over 100 articles to profl. jours. Vinton Hayes fellow Harvard U., 1971-72. Fellow AAAS, IEEE (pres. info. theory soc. 1972, Claude E. Shannon award 1990, Outstanding Paper prize 1972, Jubilee Paper award 1998, Richard W. Hamming medal 1997), Inst. Math. Stats.; mem. Soc. for Indsl. and Applied Math., Nat. Acad. Engring. Office: Stanford U Dept Elec Engring & Stats Durand # 121 Stanford CA 94305

COVERDELL, PAUL DOUGLAS, senator; b. Jan. 20, 1939. BA in Journalism, U. Mo., 1960. m. Nancy Nally. Mem. Ga. Senate, 1970-89, minority leader, 1974-89, chmn. Fulton delegation, 1974-84; dir. Peace Corps., Washington, 1989-91; former pres., CEO Coverdell & Co., Inc., Atlanta; U.S. senator from Ga., 1993—, mem. senate fgn. rels. com., mem. senate agr. com., mem. senate small bus. com.; former pres., bd. dirs. Urban Study Inst. Ga., Ga. Health Found.; chmn. Ga. Rep. Party; former pres. Nat. Rep. Legis. Assn.; mem. sm. bus., nat. Rep. senatorial coms. Capt. USAR. Office: US Senate 200 Russell Senate Bldg Washington DC 20510-1004

COVERT, EUGENE EDZARDS, aerophysics educator; b. Rapid City, S.D., Feb. 6, 1926; s. Perry and Eda (Edzards) C.; m. Mary Solveig Rutford, Feb. 22, 1946; children: David H., Christine J., Pamela M., Steven P. BS, U. Minn., 1946, MS, 1948; ScD, MIT, 1958. Registered profl. engr., Mass.; chartered engr., U.K. Preliminary design group USNADC, Johnsville, Pa., 1948-52; mem. staff MIT Aerophysics Lab., 1952-63, assoc. dir., 1963-75, assoc. prof. aeronautics and astronautics, 1963-68, prof., 1968—, T. Wilson prof. aeronautics, 1993-96, head dept. aeronautics and astronautics, 1985-90; T. Wilson prof. of aeronautics emeritus, 1997—; cons. Bolt, Beranek & Newman, Inc., Govt. Israel, Pratt and Whitney Aircraft div. United Techs, Hercules, Inc., MIT Lincoln Lab., Sverdrup Tech., U.S. Army Research Office; chief scientist USAF, 1972-73; mem. panel Naval Aeroballistic Adv. Com., 1965-75; mem. NASA Aeronautical Adv. com., 1985-89, Aeronautics and Space Engring. Bd., 1986-92, chmn., 1992; mem., chmn. USAF Sci. Adv. Bd., 1975-86, 90-94; chmn. Power, Energetics and Propulsion panel Adv. Group for Aerospace Research and Devel. NATO, 1982-86; aero. policy com. Office Sci. and Tech. Policy, 1976-92; mem. Pres. commn. for investigation of space shuttle accident. Served with USNR, 1943-47. Recipient Exceptional Civilian Sci. award USAF, 1973, 86, 94, Univ. Educator of Yr. award, Am. Soc. Aerospace Edn., 1980, Tech. Leadership award U. Minn. Alumni Assocs., 1993, Pub. Svc. award NASA, 1991, von Karman medal Adv. Group for Aerospace R & D, 1980, Wright Brothers Lectureship Aeronautics AIAA, 1997. Fellow AAAS, Royal Aero. Soc.; hon. fellow AIAA (bd. dirs., Ground Testing award 1990, W.F. Durand lectureship for pub. svc. 1992, Wright Bros. lectr. 1997); mem. NAE, N.Y. Acad. Scis., Sigma Xi. Office: MIT 77 Massachusetts Ave Rm 9-466 Cambridge MA 02139-4307

COVERT, MICHAEL HENRI, healthcare facility administrator; b. Chgo., Apr. 7, 1949; s. Leonard and Shirley Gladys (Jeffe) C.; children: Jason, Tiffany, Brienn; m. Janie Sibley; children: Madison, J. Ben. BS in Bus., Washington U., St. Louis, 1970, M in Health Adminstrn., 1972. Adminstrv. asst. St. Agnes Hosp., White Plains, N.Y., 1969; adminstrv. resident Hillcrest Med. Ctr., Tulsa, 1971-72, asst. adminstr., 1972-73, adminstr., 1973-80; exec. v.p., chief operating officer St. Francis Regional Med. Ctr., Wichita, Kans., 1980-85; CEO Ohio State Univ. Hosps., Columbus, 1985-88; sr. v.p. Physician Corp. of Am., Wichita, Kans., 1988-89; ind. mgmt. cons. Wichita, 1989-91; acting dir. community health Wichita/Sedgwick County, Wichita, Kans., 1991-92; pres., CEO Sarasota (Fla.) Meml. Hosp., 1992—; pres.-elect Franklin County Hosp. Coun., Columbus, 1987-88; adj. faculty Ohio State U., 1985—, Washington U., St. Louis, 1992—. Bd. dirs. United Way Sarasota, 1993—, campaign chair, 1996-97, chair 1998-99; del. Am. Hosp. Assn., State of Fla., 1996. Fellow Am. Coll. Healthcare Execs. (mem. accreditation commn. grad. edn. in health care adminstrn. 1988-94, chair commn. 1991-94, regent west ctrl. Fla. ACHE 1997—); mem. Fla. Hosp. Assn. (bd. dirs. 1995-97), Assn. Cmty. Hosps. and Health Systems of Fla. (chair 1998-99), U. South Fla. Leadership Coun., Healthcare Alumni Assn. (chair Washington U., St. Louis 1994-95), Sarasota C. of C. (chair 1995-96), Univ. Club (v.p. 1996, chair-elect 1997-99). Home: 1258 Riegels Landing Dr Sarasota FL 34242-1780 Office: Sarasota Meml Hosp 1700 S Tamiami Trl Sarasota FL 34239-3555

COVEY, FRANK MICHAEL, JR., lawyer, educator; b. Chgo., Oct. 24, 1932; s. Frank M. and Marie B. (Lorenz) C.; m. Patricia Ann McGill, Oct. 7, 1961; children: Geralyn, Frank Michael III, Regis Patrick. BS with honors, Loyola U., Chgo., 1954, JD cum laude, 1957; SJD, U. Wis., Madison, 1960. Bar: Ill. 1957, U.S. Supreme Ct. 1965. Research assoc. Wis. Gov.'s Com. on Revision Law of Eminent Domain, 1958; law clk. Ill. Appellate Ct., 1959; assoc. Belnap, Spencer, Hardy & Freeman, Chgo., 1959-60; assoc. McDermott, Will & Emery, Chgo., 1960-64, ptnr., 1965-88, mem. exec. com., 1979-81, mgmt. com., 1979-82, of counsel, 1988—; instr. Northwestern U. Sch. Law, 1958-59, Loyola U. Coll., 1958-69, 79-80; prof. law Loyola U., Chgo., 1988—; faculty advisor Loyola Consumer Law Reporter, 1990—; sr. fellow Ctr. for Pub. Resources, N.Y.C., 1990-91; assoc. gen. counsel Union League Civic and Arts Found., 1967-69, v.p. 1969-72, 73-75, pres., 1972-73, dir., 1975-80, 1991-94, life trustee, 1994—; co-dir. Grant Park study team Nat. Commn. on Causes and Prevention of Violence, 1968; affiliate N. Shore Bd. Realtors, 1976-88. Author: Roadside Protection Through Access Control, 1960 (with others) Federal Civil Practice in Illinois, 1974, 8th edit., 1992, Business Litigation I: Competition and Its Limits, 1978, Class Actions, 1979, 5th edit., 1993, Architect and Engineer Liability: Claims Against the Design Professional, 1987, 2d edit., 1995; contbr. articles to profl. jours. Mem. bd. athletics Loyola U., 1970-72, mem. estate planning com., 1969-81, mem. com. on the future of the law sch., 1975-76, trustee, 1979-88, mem. citizens bd., 1979-95; bd. dirs. Chgo. Bldg. Congress, 1978-82, sec., 1982-84; mem. revenue adv. com. Chgo. City Coun., 1983-84; mem. Spl. Commn. on Adminstrn. Justice in Cook County, 1984-88, mem. Chgo. Crime Commn., 1991-94; arbitrator trainer Cir. Ct. Cook County Ct.-Annexed Mandatory Arbitration, 1990-93; chmn. bd. trustees St. Viator H.S., Arlington Heights, Ill., 1988-90, trustee, 1988-92; bd. dirs. Met. Chgo. Air Force Cmty. Coun., 1988-98, v.p. 1993-95, pres., 1995-96, Union League Boys and Girls Clubs Found., 1990—; bd. dirs. Chgo. Engrs. Found. of Union League Club, 1990—, v.p., 1991-93, 95-97, gen. counsel, 1993-95; mem. pres. task force St. Norbert Coll., 1991—; active Chgo. Architecture Found., Bus. Execs. for Econ. Justice, Landmarks Preservation Coun. of Ill., Classical Arts Soc., Les Aimes de Vitraux; docent St. James chapel, Quigley Prep. Sem., 1994—; mem. adv. bd. D'Arcy Gallery Medieval Art, 1995—. Decorated knight comdr. Equesterian Order of Holy Sepulchre of Jerusalem, 1991; recipient Conf. on Personal Fin. Law award, 1955, Founders Day award Loyola U., 1976, Disting. Service award Loyola U. Dept. Polit. Sci., 1979, Disting. Service award Loyola U. Dept. Socio-legal Studies, 1980, Excellence medal Loyola U. Law Sch., 1979, Lion award St. Viator High Sch., 1990; Frank M. Covey Jr. Loyola Lectures in Polit. Analysis named in his honor Loyola U., 1989; Frank M. Covey Jr. Award for Graduating Srs. established in his honor St. Viator High Sch., 1990. Fellow Ill. Bar Found. (charter), Chgo. Bar Found.; mem. Ill. State Bar Assn. (Lincoln award 1963, Bd. Govs. award 1986), Chgo. Bar Assn., Fed. 7th Circuit Bar Assn., Cath. Lawyers Guild, Chgo. Coun. Lawyers, Nat. Lawyers Assn. (hon. trustee 1995—), Am. Judicature Soc., Markey Wigmore Inn of Ct., Acad. Polit. Sci., Better Govt. Assn., The Federalist Soc., Internat. Assn. Defense Counsel, Def. Research Inst., Chgo. Architecture Found., Amici Thomas Mori, Ill. Hist. Soc., Air Force Assn., U.S. Navy League, U.S. Naval Inst., Nat. Strategy Forum, Assn. U.S. Army, Loyola U. Alumni Assn. (pres. 1965-66), Loyola U. Law Sch. Alumni Assn. (chmn. alumni fund campaign 1967-68, v.p. alumni 1968-69, pres. 1969-70, chmn. Thomas More Club 1973-75, award 1957), Western Soc. Engrs. (assoc.), Blue Key, Union League Club (bd. dirs. 1977-80, chmn. house com. 1977-80, 2d v.p. 1988-89, 1st v.p. 1989-90, pres. 1990-91), Legal Club, Law Club, Execs. Club Chgo., Rolling Green Country Club, Phi Alpha Delta, Alpha Sigma Nu, Pi Gamma Mu, Delta Sigma Rho (past chpt. pres.). Home: 400 N McClurg Ct Apt 1002 Chicago IL 60611-4323

COVI, LINO, psychiatrist; b. Trento, Italy, Mar. 19, 1926; came to U.S., 1956, naturalized, 1965; s. Giuseppe and Giuseppina (Mariotti) C.; m. Beverly A. Yeutsy, Dec. 30, 1958 (dec.); children: Lisa Martina, Michelle Peppina, Gina Albina, Tina Maria. Student in philosophy, U. Florence, Italy, 1945-47, Sch. Social Work, Trento and Rome, 1949-51; MD, U. Rome, 1955. Asst. U. Rome Neuropsychiat. Clinic, 1955-56; intern Albert Einstein Med. Ctr., Phila., 1956-57; resident fellow psychiatry Johns Hopkins Hosp., Balt., 1957-60, dir. outpatient clin. rsch. unit, 1968-83, dir. Cognitive Therapy Clinic, 1982-98, dir. treatment assessment rsch. unit, 1983-94; assoc. clin. prof. U. Md. Med. Sch., Balt., 1986-92; instr. psychiatry Johns Hopkins U., 1960-67, asst. prof., 1967-72, assoc. prof., 1972—; vis. psychiatrist Balt. City Hosp., 1960-80; vis. scientist Nat. Inst. Drug Abuse-Addiction Rsch. Ctr., Balt., 1988-94, guest rschr., 1996—; psychiatrist Francis Scott Key Med. Ctr.-Hopkins Bayview Med. Ctr., Balt., 1988—; med. dir. Friends Health Svcs., 1994-97; cons. Friends Rsch. Inst. Epoch Ctrs., Balt., 1997—; staff psychiatrist Patuxent Instn., Jessup, Md., 1960-62; chief out-patient dept. Gundry Hosp., Balt., 1962-86, pres. bd. dirs., 1972-84, rsch. dir., 1973-86; mem. bd. govs. Cen. Md. Health Systems Agy., 1978-83; rsch. psychiatrist NIMH Collaborative Studies, 1962-64, co-prin. investigator, 1964-65, prin. investigator, 1965-83, prin. investigator clin. trials of new drugs for depression and anxiety, 1970-94, studies of group cognitive therapy in depression, 1980-94; tchg. assoc. Sheppard and E. Pratt Hosp., 1973-79; cons. Pharm. Rsch. Labs., 1971-96, Centro Psicologia Clinica, Milan, 1981—. Editor: The Md. Psychiatrist, 1974-80, Today's Psychiatry, Md. Med. Jour., 1985-95; contbr. articles to profl. jours. Mem. human rights com. Coop. Studies Program, VA, 1981-84. Mem. AMA (prof. staff drug evaluation coun. on drugs 1968-71), Am. Coll. Neuropsychopharmacology (coms.), Md. Psychiat. Soc. (coms.), Am. Psychiat. Assn. (nat. coms., dep. rep. Md., Newsletter award 1977), Am. Soc. Clin. Psychopharmacology, World Fedn. Mental Health, Johns Hopkins Med. Soc., Assn. Advancement Behavior Therapy, Md. Med. Soc., Balt. Med. Soc. (chmn. coms.), Collegium Internat. Neuropsychopharmacologicum, Italian-Am. Hist. Assn. Democrat. Roman Catholic. Office: Friends Rsch Inst PO Box 10676 505 Baltimore Ave Baltimore MD 21204-4503

COVILLION, JANE TANNER, mathematics educator; b. Syracuse, N.Y., Aug. 20, 1956; d. Francis Duane and Barbara Ann (Zimmerman) Tanner; m. David Allen Covillion, Apr. 18, 1980 (dec. Sept. 1996). AB, Cornell U., 1978; MS, SUNY, Oswego, 1982; postgrad., SUNY, Syracuse, 1983-86. Cert. elem. and math. tchr., N.Y. Math. tchr. 7th grade Ray Jr. High Sch., Baldwinsville, N.Y., 1978-79; math. tchr. 6th/7th grades Zogg Mid. Sch., Liverpool, N.Y., 1979-81; tchr. math. Liverpool High Sch., 1981-82; prof. Onondaga C.C., Syracuse, 1982—; tchr. math. Lafayette (N.Y.) H.S., 1986; text reviewer in field. Co-author: Mathematics Teacher, 1978; contbr. articles to profl. jours. Mem. planning com. Syracuse Sci. Fair, 1982—. N.Y. State Regents scholar, 1974, James L. Sears Found. scholar, 1974. Mem. AAUW, Nat. Coun. Tchrs. Math., Assn. Math. Tchrs. N.Y. State, Math. Assn. Am., Assn. for Women in Math., N.Y. State United Tchrs., Am. Fedn. Tchrs., Onondaga County Math. Tchrs., N.Y. State Assn. Two-Yr. Colls., N.Y. State Math. Assn. Two-Yr. Colls. (pres. state scholarship chair), Am. Math. Assn. Two-Yr. Colls (prodn. mgr. AMATYC Rev.), Onondaga C.C. Fedn. Tchrs. (sec. 1987—), Embroiderers Guild Am., Am. Needlepoint Guild, Delta Kappa Gamma (rec. sec., pres. Beta Kappa chpt., state exec. sec.), Alpha Phi (house corp. bd. Delta chpt., sec., pres.). Republican. Avocations: traveling, crossword puzzles, reading, crafts. Home: 4129 Reddeer Rd Liverpool NY 13090-1605 Office: Onondaga Community Coll Math Dept Syracuse NY 13215

COVIN, CAROL LOUISE, computer consultant; b. Chgo., July 2, 1947; d. Raymond Lincoln and Elizabeth Day (Notley) Frederick; m. David William Covin, Jan. 24, 1968; children: David William Jr., Jonathan Michael. BA, George Washington U., 1972. Data base adminstr. USN, Alexandria, Va., 1973-77; cons. Data Base Mgmt., Inc., Springfield, Va., 1977-79, 82-87; pres. Covin Assocs., Falls Church, Va., 1987-90; cons. Electro-Tech. Internat., Annandale, Va., 1990-91, Abacus Tech., Chevy Chase, Md., 1991-93, Tech. Internat., Fairfax, Va., 1993-95; with Xybernaut Corp., Fairfax, 1995—. Author: The Computer Professional's Job Guide to Washington, D.C., 1989, Covin's New England Computer Job Guide, 1991, Covin's Washington Computer Job Guide, 1993, Covin's Midwest Computer Job Guide, 1995, Covin's Southeast Computer Job Guide, 1998. Mem. Assn. Systems Mgmt. (pres. 1990-92, v.p. 1992-93, treas. 1993-96), Data Adminstrn. Mgmt. Assn., Washington Apple Pi.

COVIN, THERON MICHAEL, psychotherapist; b. Repton, Ala., Feb. 27, 1947; s. Fisher Burt Covin and Doris (Salter) Hayes; m. Charlotte Covin, June 13, 1981; children: Caroline, Michelle. MS, Troy State U., 1971; Specialist in Edn., U. Ala., Tuscaloosa, 1973; D Edn., U. Sarasota, Fla., 1975. Diplomate Am. Bd. Med. Psychotherapists. Instr. psychology Troy (Ala.) State U., 1971-75, Lomax Hannon Jr. Coll., Greeville, Ala., 1975-78; asst. prof. Auburn U., Montgomery, Ala., 1978-80; staff psychologist S.E. Ala. Youth Svcs., Dothan, Ala., 1978-81; with Ctr. for Counseling and Human Devel., Ozark, Ala., 1981-96. Contbr. articles to profl. jours. Mem. Am. Counseling Assn., Am. Assn. Family and Marriage Therapy, Rotary (Paul Harris fellow 1987). Office: PO Box 1263 111 Katherine Ave Ozark AL 36360-1976

COVINGTON, ANN K., state supreme court justice; b. Fairmont, W.Va., Mar. 5, 1942; d. James R. and Elizabeth Ann (Hornor) Kettering; m. James E. Waddell, Aug. 17, 1963 (div. Aug. 1976); children: Mary Elizabeth Waddell, Paul Kettering Waddell; m. Joe E. Covington, May 14, 1977. BA, Duke U., 1963; JD, U. Mo., 1977. Bar: Mo. 1977, U.S. Dist. Ct. (we. dist.) Mo. 1977. Asst. atty. gen. State of Mo., Jefferson City, 1977-79; ptnr. Covington & Maier, Columbia, Mo., 1979-81, Butcher, Cline, Mallory & Covington, Columbia, Mo., 1981-87; justice Mo. Ct. Appeals (we. dist.), Kansas City, 1987-89; justice Mo. Supreme Ct., 1989-93, chief justice, 1993-95; now judge, 1995—; bd. dirs. Mid Mo. Legal Services Corp., Columbia, 1983-87; chmn. Juvenile Justice Adv. Bd., Columbia, 1984-87. Bd. dirs. Ellis Fischel State Cancer Hosp., Columbia, 1982-83, Nat. Ctr. for State Cts., 1998—; chmn. Columbia Indsl. Revenue Bond Authority, 1984-87; trustee United Meth. Ch., Columbia, 1983-86, Am. Law Inst., 1998—; bd. dirs. Nat. Ctr. State Cts., 1998—. Recipient Citation of Merit, U. Mo. Law Sch., 1993, Faculty-Alumni award U. Mo., 1993; Coun. of State Govt. Toll fellow, 1988. Fellow Am. Bar Found.; mem. ABA (jud. adminstrv. divsn., mem. adv. com. on Evidence Rules, U.S. Cts.), Mo. Bar Assn., Boone County Bar Assn. (sec. 1981-82), Am. Law Inst., Acad. Mo. Squires, Order of Coif (hon.), Mortar Bd. (hon.), Phi Alpha Delta, Kappa Kappa Gamma. Home: 1201 Torrey Pines Dr Columbia MO 65203-4825 Office: Mo Supreme Ct 101 High St Jefferson City MO 65102-0150

COVINGTON, FAITH HENRIETTA, health educator; b. Nov. 8, 1965. BS, Slippery Rock U., 1987. Health educator Balt. City Pub. Sch., 1989—.

COVINGTON, GAIL LYNN, nurse practitioner; b. N.J., Apr. 4, 1950; d. George and Ina May (Smith) Poole; m. Alexander Palmer Covington, May 20, 1972 (div. June 1979). BS in Nursing, East Carolina U., 1972; MS in Nursing, U. N.C., 1977, postgrad., 1993. Cert. color analyst, beauty cons., ACLS provider, childbirth educator. Instr. Stuart Circle Hosp. Sch. Nursing, Richmond, Va., 1972-73; instr. Richmond Meml. Hosp. Sch. Nursing, 1973-74, relief staff nurse, 1973-74; staff nurse Rex Hosp., Raleigh, N.C., 1974-76; coord. pediat. nursing Watts Hosp. Sch. Nursing, Durham, N.C., 1977-78; dir. clin. edn. Wake Med. Ctr., Raleigh, 1978-90; practice cons. N.C. Bd. of Nursing, Raleigh, 1990-92; FNP Hampton & Lewis, Ob-Gyn, Oxford, N.C., 1993-95, Ocracoke (N.C.) Health Ctr., 1994—, Montgomery Women's Health Svcs., Troy, N.C., 1995-99, Wendover Ob-gyn. and Infertility, Greensboro, N.C., 1999—; cons. in field. Editor: Pregnancy, 1976. Author: Post-Partum Exercises, 1977, 86. Coord. med. vols. Wake County Olympic Sports Festival, 1987; charge nurse ARC, N.C. State Fair, 1979-98; bd. dirs. Friends of Elizabeth II, 1990-92, crew mem., med. officer, 1986-92, Jamestown Sailing Vessels, 1991—. Mem. NAACOG (vice chmn. 1980-82, sec.-treas. 1984-87). Avocations: sailing, scuba diving, handcrafts. Home: 4123 Driftwood Rd Greensboro NC 27455 Office: Ste 400 301 E Wendover Ave Greensboro NC 27401

COVINGTON, GEORGE MORSE, lawyer; b. Lake Forest, Ill., Oct. 4, 1942; s. William Slaughter and Elizabeth (Morse) C.; m. Shelagh Tait Hickey, Dec.28, 1966 (div. May 1995); children: Karen Morse, Jean Tait, Sarah Ingersoll Covington; m. Barbara Schilling Trentham, Dec. 19, 1998. AB, Yale U., 1964; JD, U. Chgo., 1967. Assoc. Gardner, Carton & Douglas, Chgo., 1970-75, ptnr., 1976-95; atty. pvt. practice, Lake Forest, Ill., 1995—; lectr. in field. Contbr. articles to profl. jours. active Grant Hosp. of Chgo., 1974-95, chmn. of bd. 1990-95; bd. dirs. Grant Healthcare Found., 1995—; trustee Chgo. Acad. Sci., 1974-85, pres., 1980-82; trustee, chmn. Ill. chpt. Nature Conservancy, Chgo., 1974-88; bd. dirs. Latin Sch Chgo., 1979-80, Open Lands Project, Chgo., 1972-86, Chgo. Farmers, 1994-96; bd. dirs., sec. Lake Forest Open Lands Assn., 1984—; bd. dirs., sec., treas. Les Cheneaux Found., 1978—; bd. dirs. Student Conservation Assn., 1996—, Little Traverse Conservancy, 1998—; mem. Bd. Fire and Police Commrs., Village of Lake Bluff, Ill., 1991—. With U.S. Army, 1967-69. Mem. ABA, Ill. Bar Assn., Lake County Bar Assn., Chgo. Bar Assn., Univ. Club (bd. dirs. 1985-88), Commonwealth Club, Legal Club, Shoreacres (Lake Bluff, Ill.), Les Cheneaux Club (Cedarville, Mich.), Lambda Alpha. Office: 500 N Western Ave Ste 204 Lake Forest IL 60045-1955

COVINGTON, GERMAINE WARD, municipal agency administrator. BS in Social Work, Ind. State U., 1966; MA in Urban Studies, Occidental Coll., 1972. Budget analyst City of Seattle, Office Mgmt. and Budget, 1978-87; cmty. affairs mgr. City of Seattle, Engring. Dept., 1987-90, property and ct. svcs. mgr., 1990-91, dir. exec. mgmt., 1993-94, acting dir. drainage and wastewater utility, 1993-94; dep. chief staff City of Seattle, Mayor's Office, 1991-93; dir. City for Seattle, Office of Civil Rights, 1994—. Office: Seattle Office for Civil Rights 700 3rd Ave Ste 250 Seattle WA 98104-1849

COVINGTON, JAMES EDWIN, government agency administrator, psychologist; b. Wadesboro, N.C., June 26, 1943; s. James Edwin and Louise (Memory) C.; m. Linda Doreen Davis, May 31, 1971 (div. Feb. 1982); children: James Edwin III, Bradley Davis. BA, Duke U., 1965; MSc, N.C. State U., 1977, PhD, 1981. Lic. psychologist, N.C. Commd. 2d lt. U.S. Army, 1967, advanced through grades to col., 1989, served in Vietnam, ret., 1992; spl. advisor for arms control and chem. demilitarization Dept. of Def., Washington, 1993—; psychol. cons., Springfield, Va., 1992—; prof. mil. sci. Duke U., Durham, N.C., 1983; del. 1st U.S. visit to former Soviet Chem. Weapons Sites in Russia, 1990; mem. U.S. delegation for negotiation of worldwide Chem. Weapons Conv., Geneva, 1992; advisor U.S. Delegation to Chem. Weapons Preparatory Commn., The Hague, 1993; mem. oversight prog. to destroy all U.S. chem. weapons by year 2007. Decorated Def. Superior Svc. medal, Purple Heart with oak leaf cluster, Bronze Star, Air Medal with 7 oak leaf clusters, Army Commendation Medal with valor device, others; decorated for heroism at Hamburger Hill, Vietnam, 1969. Mem. APA, Va. Psychol. Assn. Methodist. Avocations: military history, music, physical fitness. Fax: 703-604-7797. E-mail: covingtj@sarda.army.mil. Home: 8620 Burling Wood Dr Springfield VA 22152-2316 Office: Office of Asst to Sec of the Army 2511 Jefferson Davis Hwy Arlington VA 22202-3926

COVINGTON, MARLOW STANLEY, retired lawyer; b. Langhorne, Pa., Apr. 25, 1937; s. Marlow O. and Madalyn L. (Johnson) C.; m. Laura Aline Wallace, Aug. 28, 1965; children: Lisa M., Scott, Eric (dec.). BS, Bloomsburg U., 1959; postgrad., Rutgers U., 1960; JD, Howard U., 1965. Bar: D.C. 1971, U.S. Dist. Ct. D.C. 1971, U.S. Supreme Ct. 1975, U.S. Dist. Ct. Md. 1981, Md. 1985. Tchr. Pub. Schs., Long Branch, N.J., 1959-62; referee N.J. Dept. Labor, Newark, 1965-66; claim examiner Allstate's Ins. Co., Verona, N.J., 1966-71; house counsel Allstate's Ins. Co., Washington, Greenbelt, Md., 1971-97; sr. trial atty. Allstate Ins. Co., Greenbelt, Md., 1989-96; ret., 1996; mem. adv. bd. Inverness Custom Plastics, Inc., Barrington, Ill., 1990—. Recipient cert. of recognition Balt.-Washington area Fellowship Christian Athletes, 1981. Mem. ABA (com. ins. negligence and compensation sect.), Md. Bar Assn., Montgomery County Bar Assn., D.C. Bar Assn. (com. ins. and compensation sect.), Nat. Bar Assn., Prince George's County Md. Bar Assn., Bloomsburg U. Alumni Assn. (bd. dirs. 1977-80), Sigma Delta Tau, Gamma Theta Upsilon. Avocation: collecting antique pocket knives. Fax: 301-421-4329. E-mail: SCoving104@aol.com. Home: 16001 Amina Dr Burtonsville MD 20866-1039

COVINGTON, ROBERT NEWMAN, law educator; b. Evansville, Ind., Sept. 9, 1936; s. George Milburn and Roberta (Newman) C.; m. Paula Anne Hattox, July 29, 1972. B.A., Yale U., 1958; J.D., Vanderbilt U., 1961. Bar: Tenn. 1961. Asst. prof. law Vanderbilt U., Nashville, 1961-64; assoc. prof. Vanderbilt U., 1964-69, prof., 1969—; chair faculty senate Vanderbilt U., 1988-89; vis. prof. U. Mich., 1971, U. Calif., Davis, 1975-76, U. Tex., 1983; Adminstrv. law officer Calif. Agrl. Labor Relations Bd., 1975-76; cons. Tenn. Dept. Labor, 1972, Tenn. Law Library Commn., 1965-75. Author works in field. Mem. Am. Bar Assn., Tenn. Bar Assn., Am. Arbitration Assn., Order of Coif, Phi Beta Kappa. Democrat. Episcopalian. Club: Univ. (Nashville). Home: 907 Estes Rd Nashville TN 37215-1008 Office: Vanderbilt U Sch Law 21st Ave S Nashville TN 37240

COVINGTON, STEPHANIE STEWART, psychotherapist, writer, educator; b. Whittier, Calif., Nov. 5, 1942; d. William and Bette (Robertson) Stewart; children: Richard, Kim. BA cum laude, U. So. Calif., 1963; MSW, Columbia U., 1970; PhD, Union Inst., 1982. Pvt. practice psychotherapy, co-dir. Inst. for Relational Devel., La Jolla, Calif., 1981—; instr. U. Calif., San Diego, 1981—, Calif. Sch. Profl. Psychology, San Diego, 1982-88, San Diego State U., 1982-84, Southwestern Sch. Behavioral Health Studies, 1982-84, Profl. Sch. Humanistic Psychology, San Diego, 1983-84, U.S. Internat. U., San Diego, 1983-84, UCLA, 1983-84, U. So. Calif., L.A., 1983-84, U. Utah, Salt Lake City, 1983-84; co-dir. Inst. Relational Devel.; cons. L.A. County Sch. Dist., N.C. Dept. Mental Health, Nat. Ctrs. Substance Abuse Treatment and Prevention, Nat. Inst. Corrections, others; designer women's treatment, cons. Betty Ford Ctr.; presenter at profl. meetings; lectr. in field; addiction cons. criminal justice sys. Author: Leaving the Enchanted Forest: The Path from Relationship Addiction to Intimacy, 1988, Awakening Your Sexuality: A Guide for Recovering Women and Their Partners, 1991, A Woman's Way Through the Twelve Steps, 1994, Helping Women Recover: A Program for Treating Addiction (with spl. edit. for criminal justice sys.), 1999; contbr. articles to profl. jours. Mem. NASW (diplomate), Am. Assn. Sex Educators, Counselors and Therapists, Am. Bd. Med. Psychotherapists (diplomate), Am. Bd. Sexology (diplomate), Am. Pub. Health Assn., Am. Assn. Marriage and Family Therapy, Assn. Women in Psychology, Calif.

Women's Commn. on Alcoholism (Achievement award), Ctr. for Study of the Person, Friends of Jung, Internat. Coun. on Alcoholism and Addictions (past chair women's com.), Kettil Brun Soc. (Finland), San Diego Soc. Sex Therapy and Edn., Soc. for Study of Addiction (Eng.). Avocations: reading, theater, raising orchids. Office: 7946 Ivanhoe Ave Ste 201B La Jolla CA 92037-4517

COVINGTON, TAMMIE WARREN, elementary education educator; b. Columbia, S.C., Dec. 20, 1960; d. Charles Larry and Betty Joyce (Collum) Warren; m. Terry Lee Covington, Dec. 22, 1979; 1 child, Matthew Lee. BA in Elem. Edn., U. S.C., 1982, M in Elem. Edn., 1989. Tchr. Ridge Spring (S.C.)-Monetta Elem. Sch., 1982-90, W. Wyman King Acad., Batesburg, S.C., 1991-92, North (S.C.) Elem. Sch., 1992-94, Batesburg (S.C.) Leesville Mid. Sch., 1994—. Mem. Delta Kappa Gamma. Office: Batesburg-Leesville Mid Sch 101 W Columbia Ave Batesburg SC 29006-2124

COVINGTON-KENT, DAWNA MARIE, chemical dependency counselor, continuing care and outpatient coordinator, writer; b. Russell, Kans., Mar. 28, 1948; d. James Don and Dorothy Louise (Bogue) Holt. BBA, Washburn U., 1973; postgrad., Grad. Sch. Am., Mpls. lic. ins. agt.; lic. realtor; lic. alcohol and drug abuse counselor; advanced cert. relapse prevention specialist; registered alcohol and other drug abuse counselor. Editorial cons. Josten's Am. Yearbook Co., Topeka, 1974-76, asst. product mgr., 1976-78; realtor assoc. Brosius and Slattery, Inc., Topeka, 1978-80, Valley, Inc., Topeka, 1980-82; ins. agt. State Farm Ins. Co., Topeka, 1982-86; dir. mktg. sales Castlewood Constrn., Inc., 1986-87; pres. Creative Patios of Topeka, 1986-87; profl. recruiter Stormont-Vail Regional Med. Ctr., Topeka, 1988-90; fin. planner N.Y. Life Ins. Co., 1990; sr. chem. dependency technician Women's Recovery Ctr., Topeka, 1990—, continuing care/outpatient program coord., 1992-94; pres. program dir. Relapse Prevention Counseling Inc, Topeka, 1994—. Author: The Journey No Place Sacred, 1994; Contbr. poem to lit. mag. Primary counselor Women's Recovery Ctr.; crisis counselor Battered Women's Task Force; mem. Mayor's Commn. Status on Women; mem. Topeka Shawnee County Alcohol and Drug Abuse Coun.; mem. Kans. Alcoholism and Drug Abuse Counselors Assn. (edn. chairperson 1995-97). Nat. Conv., Don Dougan, Hall of Fame. Mem. C. of C., Topeka Homebuilders Assn. Home: 1913 SW 29th Ter Topeka KS 66611-1953

COVINO, CHARLES PETER, chemicals executive; b. West New York, N.J., Dec. 9, 1923; s. Isaac L. and Rose (Luongo) C.; m. Sylvia A Covino, Dec. 27, 1947; 1 child, Candida. Student, U. Ala., 1941-43; BBA, Manhattan Coll., 1951; MBA, NYU; DHL (hon.), Philathea U., Can., 1963; DS (hon.), Manhattan Coll., 1995. Chmn. bd., CEO Gen. Magnaplate Corp., Linden, N.J.; mem. Hoover Inst. Coun. for Global Polit. and Econ. Transition, 1994; lectr. in field. Contbr. over 28 articles to profl. jours. Bd. dirs. Peoples Bankcorp, 1990. Recipient Air Force Assn. N.J. Wing award for space contbns., 1960, Royal Cross Austria Prince Rudolph, 1964, Eloy Alfaro Found. of Panama award, 1965, Manhattan Coll. Outstanding Alumni award, 1972, Vaaler award Chem. Engring. Inst., 1976, Indsl. Rsch. 100 award for Material Devels. of Yr., 1964, 68, 78, ASM award for Disting. Svc. and Contbns. to Metals Industry, 1967, Cookware Design of Yr. award Housewares Mfr.'s Assn., 1967, award of yr. Packaging Inst., 1967-68, Outstanding New Product award Popular Sci. mag., 1967, Packaging Design award Design Inst., 1968, Outstanding USA Design award U.S. Info. Agy., 1968, Italian-Am. Man of Sci. award 1978, Churchill Medal of Wisdom award, 1995, Heros of Chemistry award Am. Chem. Soc., 1996, Am. Chem. Soc. award, 1996; named to N.J. Inventors Hall of Fame, 1994-95, Manhattan Coll. Athletics Hall of Fame, 1998, N.J. Corp. Inventors Hall of Fame, 1999. Achievements include over 93 patents and trademarks; invention of non-destructive testing method for thick lead shielding in nuclear reactors, ultrasonic test method for nuclear tubing used for condensors, various metal surface enhancement processes; featured in Guinness World Book of Records for world's slipperiest solid lubricant. Office: Gen Magnaplate Corp 1331 Route 1 And 9 E Linden NJ 07036

COVINO, PAUL FRANCIS XAVIER, religious executive, college chaplain, consultant; b. Methuen, Mass., Aug. 3, 1958; s. Benjamin Gene and Lorraine Mary (Gallagher) C.; m. Anne Elizabeth Hallisey, Apr. 23, 1983. BA, Georgetown U., 1980; MA, U. Notre Dame, 1981. Mem. staff Diocesan Office for Worship, Worcester, Mass., 1980; assoc. dir. Georgetown Ctr. for Liturgy, Spirituality and Arts, Washington, 1981-89; pvt. practice liturgical resource cons., 1989—; asst. chaplain, dir. liturgy Coll. of Holy Cross, Worcester, Mass., 1993-97; assoc. chaplain, dir. liturgy Coll. of Holy Cross, Worcester, 1997—; dormitory min. in residence Georgetown U., Washington, 1981-83; mem. Rite of Christian Initiation of Adults steering com. Office of Permanent Diaconate adv. bd. ctrl. com. observance of millennium Diocese of Worcester; mem. Order of Marriage adaptations task force U.S. Bishops' Com. on Liturgy; mem. Cath. Common Ground Initiative com. Editor: Celebrating Marriage: Preparing the Wedding Liturgy, 1987, rev. edit., 1994; contbr. articles to profl. jours. Mem. Nat. Assn. Lay Ministry, N.Am. Acad. Liturgy, Nat. Conf. on Environ. and Art for Cath. Worship. Roman Catholic. Office: Coll of Holy Cross Office Coll Chaplains 1 College St # 16A Worcester MA 01610-2322

COVINO, WILLIAM ANTHONY, English language educator; b. Stamford, Conn., Sept. 16, 1951; s. Vito Anthony and Jeanette Sylvia (Tartaglia) C.; m. Deborah Caslav, Mar. 13, 1987; children: Christopher, Nicholas, Alexandra, Daniel. BA in English, UCLA, 1973; MA in English, Calif. State U., Northridge, 1975; PhD in English, U. So. Calif., 1981. Asst. prof. English San Diego State U., 1981-84, assoc. prof. English, 1984-88; assoc. prof. English U. Ill., Chgo., 1988-94, prof. English, 1994-98; prof., chair English Fla. Atlantic U., 1998—; consulting reader College English, College Composition and Communication, Rhetoric Rev., Jour. Advanced Composition, SUNY Press, Oxford U. Press, 1984—; contbg. edior The Writing Instr., L.A., 1994—; mem. editorial bd. Pre/Text: A Jour. of Rhetorical Theory, Arlington, Tex., 1994—; MLA exec. com. History of Rhetoric, 1999—. Author: The Art of Wondering, 1988, Forms of Wondering, 1990, Magic, Rhetoric and Literacy, 1994, The Elements of Persuasion, 1997. U. Ill. Chgo. scholar, 1991, Humanities Inst. fellow, 1993. Mem. MLA, Nat. Coun. Tchrs. of English, Internat. Soc. History of Rhetoric, Rhetoric Soc. Am., Assn. Tchrs. Advanced Composition.

COVINTREE, GEORGE E., retired physician; b. Camden, N.J., Apr. 18, 1913; s. Clarence C. and Jessie E. (Snyder) C.; m. Laura Claye Fraley, July 11, 1942; children: George Edward Jr., David Elwood, Ruth Ann. AB, Temple U., 1935; MD, Hahnemann U., 1941. Diplomate Am. Bd. Anesthesiology. Intern Deaconess Hosp., Cin., 1941-42; resident West Jersey Hosp., Camden, Berlin, Voorhees, 1947-49, mem. staff, 1956—, chief dept. anesthesiology, 1957-78, emeritus chief dept. anesthesiology, 1979—; fellow in anesthesiology Hahnemann Med. Coll., Phila., 1949-50; mem. staff Hahnemann Hosp., Phila., 1950-56; cons. anesthesiology Vets. Hosp., Phila., 1953-58; instr. anesthesiology Hahnemann Med. Coll., 1950-52, asst. prof. anesthesiology, 1952-56; founder Annual N.J. Postgrad. Anesthesia Seminar, 1959. With U.S. Army Med. Corps., 1942-46. Fellow Am. Coll. Anesthesiology; me. AMA, Am. Soc. Anesthesiology, Internat. Anesthesia Rsch. Soc., N.J. State Soc. Anesthesiologists (Disting. Svc. award 1981), N.Y. Acad. Scis.

COVITZ, CARL D., state official, real estate and investment executive; b. Boston, Mar. 31, 1939; s. Edward E. and Barbara (Matthews) C.; m. Aviva Habert, May 15, 1970; children: Philip, Marc. BS, Wharton Sch., U. Pa., 1960; MBA, Columbia U., 1962. Product mgr. Bristol-Myers Co., N.Y.C., 1962-66; dir. mktg. Rheingold Breweries, N.Y.C., 1966-68; nat. mktg. mgr. Can. Dry Corp., N.Y.C., 1968-70; v.p. mktg., dir. corp. devel. ITT/Levitt & Sons, Lake Success, N.Y., 1970-73; owner, pres. Landmark Communities, Inc., Beverly Hills, Calif., 1973-87, pres., 1989-91; undersec. HUD, Washington, 1987-89; sec. bus., transp. and housing State of Calif., Sacramento, 1991-93; pres. Landmark Capital, Inc. (formerly Landmark Communities, Inc.), 1993—; chmn. bd. Century Housing Corp., 1995—; bd. dirs. Arden Realty Group, chmn. acquisition com.; chmn. bd. Fed. Home Loan Bank, San Francisco, 1989-91, Century Housing Corp., 1995—. Exec. com. Presl. Commn. Cost Control and Efficiency (Grace Commn.); co-chmn. Dept. Def. Task Force; past chmn. ops. com. Mus. Contemporary Art Los Angeles; chmn. L.A. County Delinquency and Crime Commn.; dir. Columbia U. Grad. Bus. Sch. Alumni Assn. Mem. Young Pres. Orgn.; chmn. L.A. Housing Authority Commn., 1989-91; bd. trustees Kayne Anderson Mutual Funds, 1997—. Home: 818 Malcolm Ave Los Angeles CA 90024-3104 Office: 9595 Wilshire Blvd Beverly Hills CA 90212-2512*

COWAN, ANDREW GLENN, television writer, producer, performer; b. Phila., Dec. 24, 1951; s. Raymond Harold and Audrey Rene (Federman) C. BA in Psychology, The Am. U., 1973; MS in Broadcasting, Boston U., 1975. News reporter, writer Sta. WLYH-TV, Lancaster, Pa., 1975; announcer, news reporter Sta. WHUM, Reading, Pa., 1975; comedy performer various clubs, nationwide, 1976-81; talent coordinator, writer, performer, segment producer The Merv Griffin Show, Paris, L.A., N.Y.C., Atlantic City, and Las Vegas, 1981-86; freelance writer TV series Cheers Paramount, L.A., 1985-87; host, writer L.A. Singles, Group W Cable, L.A., 1985-86; freelance writer TV series Throb Taft Entertainment, L.A., 1986; story editor TV series Take Five Imagine Entertainment, CBS, L.A., 1987; freelance writer TV series Family Ties Paramount, L.A., 1988; staff writer, performer The Pat Sajak Show, CBS, L.A., 1988-90; staff writer Into the Night ABC, 1990; staff writer My Talk Show Second City Entertainment, 1990; freelance writer for Jay Leno The Tonight Show, NBC, L.A., 1990; Walt Disney Prodns., 1991; creator, writer TV pilot Howie Republic Pictures, L.A., 1991; freelance writer TV series Seinfeld Castle Rock Entertainment, L.A., 1994, then program cons., 1994-95; story editor TV series Double Rush Shukovsky-English Entertainment, L.A., 1994; exec. cons. TV series 3rd Rock from the Sun Carsey-Werner Co., L.A., 1995-96; exec. prodr., co-creator, writer, host tv pilot Evening Stew, 1996-97; writer, tv pilot Barley Fitz, 1999; vocalist various clubs and venues, L.A., 1987—; vocalist pilot theme song Life As We Know It, Second City Entertainment, 1990; voice-over announcer Aerospace Ednl. Svcs., L.A., 1985-89, Cutler Prodns., CBS Morning Zoo, L.A., 1990; host, writer, prodr., co-dir. video short Six Minutes, Showtime, The Movie Channel, Bravo, PBS, 1989-91. Voice-over actor Time-Warner Audio Books, Lucas Films, Star Wars-Dark Empire, The Audio Drama, 1994, Star Wars-Dark Empire 2, 1995;contbr. articles to profl. jours. Recipient CableAce award for best short-form programming spl., 1991; named one of 50 Creatives to Watch, Variety, 1996. Mem. AFTRA, Writers Guild Am. West. Avocations: cartooning, playing keyboards. *You're better off creating your own opportunities, rather than waiting for someone to create them for you. Ignore the naysayers. And if you listen to conventional wisdom, develop a serious case of amnesia afterwards.*

COWAN, BARTON ZALMAN, lawyer; b. Cleve., Mar. 3, 1934; s. Milton Jerome and Clara (Umans) C.; m. Teri Anne Thomas, June 25, 1961; children: Pamela B., Cynthia R., Susan L. Kraft AB with honors, U. Mich., 1955; JD cum laude, Harvard U., 1958. Bar: Ohio 1958, Pa. 1962, U.S. Dist. Ct. (we. dist.) Pa., U.S. Ct. Appeals (3d, 4th and D.C. cirs.), U.S. Supreme Ct. Assoc. Eckert Seamans Cherin & Mellott, Pitts., 1961-68; mem. Eckert Seamans Cherin & Mellott LLC, Pitts., 1968—; chmn. lawyers com., mem. policy com. Atomic Indsl. Forum, Washington, 1981-87; chmn. layers com. Nuclear Mgmt. and Resource Coun., Washington, 1988-90. Life trustee, mem. nat. coun. Am. Jewish Com., Pitts. chpt.; bd. govs. Hebrew Union Coll., Jewish Inst. Religion; bd. dirs. Pitts. Symphony Soc., bd. dirs. ARZA/World uinon N. Am., Am. Technion Soc./Pitts. chpt., Pitts.; pres. Rodef Shalom Cong., Pitts.; v.p. Pitts. chpt. Jewish Nat. Fund, Union Am. Hebrew Congregations, Pa. coun. 1st lt. USAF, 1958-61. Recipient Clyde A. Lilly award Atomic Indsl. Forum, Inc., 1985, Hebrew Inst. Pitts. award for leadership, 1991, Jewish Edn. Inst. award for dedication and commitment to Jewish edn., 1992, State of Israel bonds award, 1993., Am. Jewish Com. Human Rels. award, 1996. Mem. ABA (chmn. energy resources law com., tort and ins. practice sect. 1986-87), Pa. Bar Assn., Allegheny County Bar Assn., Am. Judicature Soc., Am. Nuclear Soc., Internat. Nuclear Law Assn., Duquesne Club, Concordia Club, Westmoreland Country Club. Republican. Office: Eckert Seamans Cherin & Mellott LLC 600 Grant St Ste 44th Pittsburgh PA 15219-2702

COWAN, CHARLES GIBBS, lawyer, corporate executive; b. Cannington, Ont., Can., Nov. 13, 1928; s. Charles Gibbs and Jean Clarke (Macfarlane) C.; m. Susan Mary Tidy, Sept. 24, 1954; children: Julia Mary Cowan Soong, James Charles Strathy, Stuart Philip Gibbs. Student, Upper Can. Coll.; BA, U. Toronto, 1950; LLB, York U., Toronto, 1954. Bar: Ont. 1954; apptd. Queen's Counsel 1966. Ptnr. Holden, Murdoch & Finlay, Toronto, Ont., 1960-90; sec. Hollinger Consolidated Gold Mines, Ltd., 1961; v.p., sec., bd. dirs. Hollinger Inc., Argus Corp. Ltd., The Ravelston Corp. Ltd. Maj. Queen's Own Rifles of Can., Militia, 1947-63. Recipient Can. Forces decoration; Armiger. Mem. Can. Bar Assn., Bd. Trade Met. Toronto, Toronto Club. Anglican. Home: 8 Powell Ave, Toronto, ON Canada M4W 2Y7 also Home: The Maples, Cannington, ON Canada L0E 1E0 Office: 10 Toronto St, Toronto, ON Canada M5C2B7

COWAN, DONALD DOUGLAS, mathematician, educator, computer scientist; b. Toronto, Ont., Mar. 11, 1938; 3 children. BA in Sci., U. Toronto, 1960; MSc, U. Waterloo (Can.), 1961, PhD in Applied Math., 1965. Fellow in math. U. Waterloo, 1960-62, lectr., 1961-65, from asst. to assoc. prof. computer sci., 1965-67, chmn. dept. applied analytical/computer sci. math. faculty, 1966-72, assoc. dean grad. studies, 1974-78, prof. math., 1975-96, prof. emeritus, 1996-99, dist. prof. emeritus, 1999—. Mem. IEEE, Assn. Computing Machinery, Soc. Indsl. and Applied Math., Can. Info. Processing Soc. Office: Dept Computer Sci, Univ Waterloo, Dept Computer Sci Davis Ctr, Waterloo, ON Canada N2L 3G1*

COWAN, EDWARD, journalist; b. Bklyn., Nov. 14, 1933; s. Marcy Hamilton and Jennie (Taleisnik) C.; m. Ann Louise Wrubel, July 1, 1962; children: Jeffrey Wrubel, Emily Martha, Rachel Jennifer. B.A., Columbia Coll., 1954; M.A. in Econs., Johns Hopkins U., 1960. With UPI, 1957-62; with N.Y. Times, 1962-86, banking reporter, 1963-65; Benelux corr. N.Y. Times, Brussels, Belgium, 1965-66; corr. London bur. N.Y. Times, 1966-67, corr. Toronto (Can.) Bur., 1967-72, Washington corr., 1972-83, Washington econs. editor, 1983-86; Washington mgr. Ried, Thunberg and Co., Inc., 1986—; instr. econs. Johns Hopkins, 1956-57; cons. U.S. Bur. Budget, 1963; co-founder Chronicle, Barton, Vt., 1974. Author: Oil and Water: The Torrey Canyon Disaster, 1968; contbr. to The Economist, 1977-90, op-ed pages Washington Post, L.A. Times, New Eng. Regional Rev., Jour. of Commerce. Treas., dir. Anne Frank House, 1987-90. Served with AUS, 1954-56. Fellow Knight Internat. Press; recipient Chanler Hist. Essay prize Columbia, 1954, Gerald R. Loeb Found. award for fin. reporting, 1971. Mem. Nat. Econs. Club (v.p. programs 1989-90, pres. 1990-91, chmn. 1991-93). Home: 3924 Harrison St NW Washington DC 20015-1938 Office: Ried Thunberg Co Inc 1725 K St NW Washington DC 20006-1401

COWAN, FAIRMAN CHAFFEE, lawyer; b. Wellesley Hills, Mass., Apr. 22, 1915; s. James Franklin and Hortense Victoria (Fairman) C.; m. Martha Logan Allis, Apr. 24, 1943; children: Douglas Fairman, Frederick Allis, Leonard Chaffee. AB magna cum laude, Amherst Coll., 1937; LLB, Harvard U., 1940; AMP, Harvard Bus. Sch., 1963. Bar: Mass. 1940. Assoc. Goodwin, Procter & Hoar, Boston, 1940-41; ptnr. Goodwin, Proctor & Hoar, 1952-54; gen. counsel, clk., sec., v.p., dir. Norton Co., 1955-79; counsel Bowditch & Dewey, Worcester, Mass., 1979-90. Mem. Citizen Plan E Assn. Worcester, 1957-87; vice chmn. Worcester Civic Ctr. Commn., 1977-79; chmn. Pvt. Industry Coun., Worcester Area CETA Consortium, 1979-83; bd. dirs. Legal Assistance Corp. of Ctr. Mass., 1982-86, Social Svc. Planning Corp., 1975-88, Worcester Mcpl. Rsch. Bur., Inc., 1986—, Mass. Job Tng. Inc., 1983-92, Elder Home Care Svcs. of Worcester, Inc., 1987-92, Daybreak, Inc., 1993-96; incorporator Alliance for Edn., 1986—, Worcester Dynamy, Inc., 1992—, Worcester Hist. Mus., 1995—, YOU, Inc., 1983—; mem. State Job Tng. Coordinating Coun., 1985-87, Worcester Housing Partnership, 1986-93; trustee Clark U., 1964-76, 79—, Meml. Hosp., Worcester, 1967-86; mem. bd. overseers Planned Parenthood League Mass., 1992—, adv. bd. Mass. Coastal Resource Bd., 1992—. Lt. USNR, 1942-45. Recipient Isaiah Thomas award, 1995. Mem. Am. Antiquarian Soc., Mass. Civic League (v.p. 1947), Worcester Club, Worcester Com. on Fgn. Rels., Phi Beta Kappa, Alpha Delta Phi. Home: 48 Berwick St Worcester MA 01602-1443

COWAN, FREDERIC JOSEPH, lawyer; b. N.Y.C., Oct. 11, 1945; s. Frederic Joseph Sr. and Mary Virginia (Wesley) C.; m. Linda Marshall Scholle, Apr. 28, 1974; children: Elizabeth, Caroline, Allison. AB, Dartmouth Coll., 1967; JD, Harvard U., 1978. Bar: Ky. 1978, U.S. Dist. Ct. (we. dist.) Ky. 1979, U.S. Ct. Appeals (6th cir.) 1984, U.S. Supreme Ct. 1989. Vol. Peace Corps, Ethiopia, 1967-69; assoc. Brown, Todd & Heyburn, Louisville, 1979-83; ptnr. Rice, Porter, Seiller & Price, Louisville, 1983-87; atty. gen. Commonwealth of Ky., 1988-92; counsel Lynch, Cox, Gilman & Manan, 1992—; Ky. State Rep., 32d legis. dist., 1982-87; chair Ky. Child Support Enforcement Commn., 1988-91, Ky. Sexual Abuse and Exploitation Prevention Bd., 1988-91; bd. dirs. Ky. Job Tng. Coordinating Council, Frankfort, Louisville Bar Found., 1986. Vice chmn. judiciary criminal com. Ky. Ho. of Reps., 1985-87; chmn. budget com. on justice Judiciary and Corrections Ky. Ho. of Reps., 1985-87, Leadership Ky., 1985; U.S. del. election mission to Namibia Nat. Dem. Inst. for Internat. Affairs, 1989; U.S. del. dem. instns. seminar Nat. Dem. Inst. for Internat. Affairs, Slovenia, 1992; electoral supr. Orgn. for Security and Cooperation in Europe, Bosnia and Herzogovina, 1996. Mem. ABA, Ky. Bar Assn., Louisville Bar Assn., Ky. Acad. Trial Attys. Methodist. Home: 1747 Sulgrave Rd Louisville KY 40205-1643 Office: 500 Meidinger Tower Louisville KY 40202*

COWAN, GEORGE ARTHUR, chemist, bank executive, director; b. Worcester, Mass., Feb. 15, 1920; s. Louis Abraham and Anna (Listic) C.; m. Helen Dunham, Sept. 9, 1946. BS, Worcester Poly. Inst., 1941; DSc, Carnegie-Mellon U., 1950. Research asst. Princeton U., 1941-42, U. Chgo., 1942-45; mem. staff Columbia U., N.Y.C., 1945; mem. staff, dir. rsch., sr. fellow Los Alamos (N.Mex.) Sci. Lab., 1945-46, 49-88, sr. fellow emeritus, 1988—; teaching fellow Carnegie Mellon U., Pitts., 1946-49; chmn. bd. dirs. Trinity Capital Corp., Los Alamos, 1974-95; pres. Santa Fe Inst., 1984-91; mem. The White House Sci. Coun., Washington, 1982-85, cons., 1985-90, Air Force Tech. Applications Ctr., 1952-88; chmn. Los Alamos Nat. Bank, 1965-94; bd. dirs. Title Guaranty, Inc., Universal Properties, inc. Contbr. sci. articles to profl. jours. Bd. dirs. Santa Fe Opera, 1964-79; treas. N.Mex. Opera Found., Santa Fe, 1970-79; regent N.Mex. Inst. Tech. Socorro, 1972-75; bd. dirs. N.Am. Inst., Santa Fe Inst., Coalition for Quality TV. Recipient E.O. Lawrence award, 1965, Disting. Scientist award N.Mex. Acad. Sci., 1975, Robert H. Goddard award Worcester Poly. Inst., 1984, Enrico Fermi award, Presdl. Citation, Dept. Energy, 1990. Fellow AAAS, Am. Phys. Soc.; mem. Am. Chem. Soc., Am. Acad. Arts and Scis., N.Mex. Acad. Sci., Sigma Xi. Avocations: skiing, fly-fishing. Home: 721 42nd St Los Alamos NM 87544-1804 Office: Santa Fe Inst 1399 Hyde Park Rd Santa Fe NM 87501-8943*

COWAN, IRVING, real estate owner, developer; b. Irvington, N.J., Apr. 27, 1932; s. Jospeh and Adele (Goldman) Cohen; m. Marjorie Friedland, Dec. 29, 1956; children: Debra Jean, Cynthia Ann, Jonathan David. Student, U. Miami, 1949-50. Owner Sea Air Towers, Presdl. Towers Assn., Hollywood, Fla., 1960—; gen. ptnr. Indian Trail Groves, West Palm Beach, Fla., 1959—; ptnr. Hasam Realty, Hollywood, 1991—; owner, breeder Cowan Thoroughbred Racing Stable, Hollywood; bd. dirs. City Nat. Bank, Miami, Fla.; owner Shelborne Hotel, South Miami Beach, Fla. Established Cowan Aviary Found., U. Ga. With USCG, 1950-53. Mem. Com. of 100, Founders Club Mt. Sinai Hosp. (Miami, Fla.), Capitol Club, 200 Club of Greater Miami. Jewish. Home: 1615 Diplomat Pky Hollywood FL 33019-2233 Office: Sea Air Towers 3725 S Ocean Dr Hollywood FL 33019-2926

COWAN, JERRY LOUIS, lawyer; b. Des Moines, May 18, 1927; s. William Lincoln and Avis I. (Spencer) C.; m. Lee Steel, June 11, 1955; children: Grant Spencer, Breck Martin. BA, Denison U., 1951; LLB, U. Va., 1956. Bar: Ohio 1956, U.S. Ct. Appeals (6th cir.) 1958, U.S. Dist. Ct. (so. dist.) Ohio 1958, U.S. Tax Ct. 1957, U.S. Claims Ct. 1966. Assoc. Frost & Jacobs, Cin., 1956-63, ptnr., 1963-94, counsel, 1994—. Contbr. articles to profl. jours. Trustee Big Bros./Big Sisters. Found. of Greater Cin., Inc., 1962-92; bd. dirs. Hoxworth Blood Ctr., Cin., 1986-92. With U.S. Army, 1945-46. Mem. ABA, Cin. Bar Assn. (chmn. tax com. 1962-64), Ohio Bar Assn., Greater Cin. C. of C. (gen. counsel 1972-84), Cin. Country Club, Univ. Club (Cin.). Republican. Episcopalian. Avocations: golfing, history. Home: 14 Spring Knoll Cincinnati OH 45227-3845 Office: Frost & Jacobs 2500 PNC Ctr 201 E 5th St Ste 2500 Cincinnati OH 45202-4182*

COWAN, MARK DOUGLAS, government relations executive, lawyer; b. Kankakee, Ill., Dec. 4, 1949; s. George Morterud and Esther (Shusterman) C.; m. Laura Macomber, June 26, 1981; children: Mattie Esther, John Gregory, Travis. BA, U. Minn., 1971; JD, Cath. U. Am., 1976. Desk chief ops. officer CIA, Washington, 1975-78, asst. legislative counsel, 1978-80; com. counsel Com. on Standards Ofcl. Conduct U.S. Ho. of Reps., Washington, 1980-81; dep. asst. sec. U.S. Dept. Labor, Washington, 1981-82, chief of staff, 1982-84; pres. G&HC Internat., Washington, London, Hong Kong offices; v.p. govt. rels. Golle & Holmes Cos., Washington, 1984-86; v.p., head fed. markets group Gray and Co., Pub. Comm. Internat., Washington, 1986-87; sr. v.p. Hill & Knowlton Pub. Affairs, worldwide, 1987; pres. The Jefferson Group, Washington, CEO and chmn., 1987-93; vice chmn. Cassidy and Assocs., 1993-96; pres. The Columbus Group, L.L.C., Washington, 1996—; pres. CEO Newmyer Assocs., Inc., Arlington, 1996—. Editor: Environ. Econ. Jour., 1982-84 . Commr. The Nat. Commn., Employment Policy, 1992-94; active Rep. Nat. Fin. Com., Coun. Excellence in Govt., Ptnrs. for Progress, Immanuel Presbyn., McLean, Va., 1985—; bd. dirs. Langley Sch., Am. Scores, Integral Resources, Inc., D.C. United, mgr. league soccer team; bd. advisors Va. Mil. Inst., Int. Rel. Capt. USAF, 1971-77. Mem. ABA (mem. OSHA com.), Am. League Lobbyists (bd. dirs.), Assn. Former Intelligence Officers, Va. State Bar, D.C. Bar, Minn. Alumni Assn. (pres. 1979-81, bd. dirs. 1978-84), U.S. C. of C. (labor rels. coun.), Washington Golf and Country Club, Four Seasons Club (Washington), Georgetown Club, Robert Trent Golf Club (Manassas, Va.), Phi Sigma Kappa. Republican. *In achieving success in any endeavor, there is no substitute for long hours and perseverance. Added to that is the basic belief that honesty must be a foundation for all one's dealings and that the maintenance of faith can help overcome any difficulty. The goal to return in small measure to this nation what it has given to me in ample quantity is what motivated me in government service and subsequently in assisting others to address their government.*

COWAN, ROBERT JENKINS, radiologist, educator; b. Greensboro, N.C., Apr. 22, 1937; s. John Columbus and Edith (Jenkins) C.; m. Leila Caroline Sikes, June 18, 1960; children: Caroline Cowan Morris, Barbara Haynes. AB, U. N.C., 1959, MD, 1963. Diplomate: Am. Bd. Radiology (guest examiner), Am. Bd. Nuclear Medicine. Intern in medicine Presbyn. Hosp., Columbia-Presbyn. Med. Center, N.Y.C., 1963-64; resident Presbyn. Hosp., Columbia-Presbyn. Med. Center, 1966-67; resident in radiology N.C. Bapt. Hosp., Winston-Salem, 1967-70; instr. radiology Bowman Gray Sch. Medicine, Wake Forest U., Winston-Salem, 1970-71; asst. prof. Wake Forest U. Sch. of Medicine, 1971-74, assoc. prof., 1974-79, prof., 1979-98; prof. emeritus Wake Forest U. Sch. Medicine, 1998—; dir. nuclear medicine N.C. Bapt. Hosp., Winston-Salem, 1977-98; med. dir. nuclear med. tech. tng. program Forsyth Tech. Coll., Winston-Salem, 1977-98. Contbr. articles to profl. jours. Adv. bd. Stone Mountain State Park, 1994—. Served to capt., M.C. U.S. Army, 1964-66. Decorated Bronze Star medal; Am. Cancer Soc. fellow, 1969-70; James Picker scholar, 1970-73; recipient James Quinn M.D. Teaching Excellence award, 1983, 97. Fellow Am. Coll. Radiology, Am. Coll. Nuclear Physicians; mem. AMA, Soc. Nuclear Medicine (coun. Southeastern chpt. 1972-84, pres. 1978, trustee 1983-84), Radiol. Soc. N.Am., N.C. Radiol. Soc., Med. Soc. N.C., Alpha Omega Alpha. Methodist. Office: Wake Forest U Sch Med Winston Salem NC 27157

COWAN, STUART MARSHALL, lawyer; b. Irvington, N.J., Mar. 20, 1932; s. Bernard Howard and Blanche (Hertz) C.; m. Marilyn R.C. Toepfer, Apr., 1961 (div. 1968); m. Eleanor Schmerel, June, 1953 (dec.); m. Jane Alison Averill, Feb. 24, 1974 (div. 1989); children: Fran Lori, Catherine R.L., Erika R.L., Bronwen P.; m. Victoria Yi, Nov. 11, 1989. BS in Econs., U. Pa., 1952; LLB, Rutgers U., 1955. Bar: N.J. 1957, Hawaii 1962, U.S. Supreme Ct. 1966. Atty. Greenstein & Cowan, Honolulu, 1961-70, Cowan & Fewy, Honolulu, 1970-89; pvt. practice, 1989—; of counsel Price Okomoto Himeno & Lum, 1993—; arbitrator Fed. Mediation & Conciliation Svc., Honolulu, 1972—, Am. Arbitration Assn., Honolulu, 1968—, Hawaii Pub. Employee Rels. Bd., 1972—. Bd. dirs. Honolulu Symphony; pres. Hawaii Epilepsy Soc., 1984-86; acquisition chair Hawaii Family Support Ctr., 1995-97. Lt. USN, 1955-61. Mem. ABA, Hawaii Bar Assn., Am. Judicature Soc., Assn. Trial Lawyers Am. (state committeeman for hawii 1965-69, bd. govs. 1972-75), Consumer Lawyers Hawaii, Hawaii Trial Lawyers Assn. (v.p. 1972-78), Japan-Hawaii Lawyers Assn., Soc. Profls. in Dispute Resolution, Inter Pacific Bar Assn., Honolulu Symphony Soc. (bd. dirs. 1989—), Hawaii Epilepsy soc. (pres. 1984-86), Royal Order of Kamehamehi, Order of St.

Stanislas, Waikiki Yacht Club, St. Francis Yacht Club, Hawaii Yacht Club, Plaza Club, Honolulu Club, Hawaii Scottish Assn. (chieftain 1983-88), St. Andrews Soc., Caledonian Soc. (vice chieftain 1983-85), Honolulu Pipes and Drums (sec.-treas. 1985-90), New Zealand Police Pipe Band, Masons (York Rite, Scottish Rite, Grand Lodge Hawaii, grand orator 1992, sr. grand steward 1993, jr. grand warden 1994, sr. grand warden 1995, grand master 1997), Red Cross of Constantine, Royal Order Scotland, Pearl Harbor (master 1971, chaplain 1992-96), Masada (#51 N.J.), Hawaiian Koolau, Elks, Chinese Acacia Club, Royal Hawaiian Ocean Rowing Club. Jewish. Home: 47-339 Mapumapu Rd Kaneohe HI 96744-4922 Office: 707 Richards St Honolulu HI 96813-4616 also: 47-653 Kamehameha Hwy # 202 Kaneohe HI 96744-4965

COWAN, WALLACE EDGAR, lawyer; b. Jersey City, Jan. 28, 1924; s. Benjamin and Dorothy (Zunz) C.; m. Ruth Daitzman, June 8, 1947; children: Laurie, Paul, Judith. BS magna cum laude, NYU, 1947; JD cum laude, Harvard U., 1950. Ptnr. Stroock, Stroock & Lavan, N.Y.C., 1950-93, of counsel, 1994—; dir. Ametek, Inc., Paoli, Pa., 1982-93, sec., 1969-93, sec. H.S. Stuttman, Inc., Westport, Conn., to 1996. Mem. Teaneck (N.J.) Adv. Bd. on Parks, Playgrounds and Recreation, 1966—, chmn., 1974—; pres. No. Valley Commuters Assn.; past pres., life trustee Congregation Beth Sholom, Teaneck; mem. Forum adv. bd. Sch.-Based Youth Svcs. Project, 1998—. 1st lt. USAF, 1942-45, ETO. Decorated Air medal with silver cluster; recipient Vol. in the Parks award Bergen County, N.J., 1993, Disting. Svc. award, 1994. Mem. Beta Gamma Sigma. Home: 499 Emerson Ave Teaneck NJ 07666-1927 Office: Stroock Stroock & Lavan 180 Maiden Ln New York NY 10038-4925

COWAN, WILLIAM MAXWELL, neurobiologist; b. Johannesburg, South Africa, Sept. 27, 1931; s. Adam and Jessie Sloan (Maxwell) C.; m. Margaret Sherlock, Mar. 31, 1956; children: Ruth Cowan Eadon-Rainer, Stephen Maxwell, David Maxwell. B.Sc., Witwatersrand U., Johannesburg, 1951, B.Sc. (hon.), 1952; D.Phil., Oxford U., 1956, BM, BCh, 1958, M.A., 1959; DSc (hon.), Emory U., 1995, Northwestern U., 1995. From demonstrator to univ. lectr. anatomy Oxford U., 1953-66; fellow Pembroke Coll., 1958-66; vis. prof. anatomy Washington U. Med. Sch., St. Louis, 1964-65; assoc. prof. U. Wis. Med. Sch., Madison, 1966-68; prof., chmn. dept. anatomy and neurobiology Washington U. Med. Sch., 1968-80; research prof., dir. Weingart Lab. Devel. Neurobiology, Salk Inst. Biol. Studies, La Jolla, Calif., 1980-86; v.p. Salk Inst. Biol. Studies, 1982-86; provost and exec. vice chancellor Washington U., St. Louis, 1986-87; v.p., chief sci. officer Howard Hughes Med. Inst., Chevy Chase, Md., 1988—; mem. Inst. Medicine, Nat. Acad. Scis., 1978; fgn. assoc. Nat. Acad. Scis., 1981; disting. adj. prof. neuroscience Johns Hopkins Sch. Medicine, 1988—. Editor-in-chief Jour. Neurosci., 1980-87; editor: Ann. Revs. Neurosci. Hon. fellow Pembroke Coll., Hertford Coll. Fellow Am. Acad. Arts and Scis., Royal Soc. (London); fgn. mem. Royal Soc. South Africa; mem. AAAS, Am. Philos. Soc., Anat. Soc. Gt. Britain and Ireland, Royal Micros. Soc., Am. Assn. Anatomists, Soc. Neurosci. (pres. 1977-78), Norwegian Acad. Sci. (fgn.), Sigma Xi, Alpha Omega Alpha, Phi Beta Kappa. Home: 6337 Windermere Cir Rockville MD 20852-3550 Office: Howard Hughes Med Inst 4000 Jones Bridge Rd Chevy Chase MD 20815-6789

COWARD, PATRICIA ANN, language educator; b. Oswego, N.Y., Nov. 2, 1954; d. Charles John and Ann Elizabeth (Daly) C.; m. Sanford J. MacMillen, Dec. 26, 1980; children: Emma Rose, Kathrine Daly, Therese Burns. BA, SUNY, Fredonia, 1976, MA, 1978; PhD, Bowling Green State U., 1990. Instr. SUNY, Oswego, 1979-81, Wayne (Nebr.) State Coll., 1981-84; grad. fellow Bowling Green (Ohio) State U., 1984-88, lectr., 1988-90; assoc. prof. Frostburg (Md.) State U., 1990—. Bd. dirs. Family Crisis Resource Ctr., Cumberland, Md., 1991-94. Mem. MLA (field bibliographer 1957—), Coll. Conf. on Composition and Comm., NCTE. Home: 843 Braddock Rd Cumberland MD 21502-2622 Office: Frostburg State U Frostburg MD 21532

COWART, GWEN, municipal official; b. Hagerstown, Md., 1953. BFA, U. Ga., 1975. TV engr. Tidewater C.C., Virginia Beach, Va., 1981-86; coord. joint cable ctr. City of Virginia Beach, 1986-92, dir. video svcs., 1992—. Mem. Nat. Assn. Telecom. Officers and Advisors. Office: City of Virginia Beach Video Svcs 2925 N Landing Rd Virginia Beach VA 23456-2405*

COWDEN, ROGER HUGH, II, systems engineer; b. Dayton, Ohio, Jan. 26, 1955; s. Roger Hugh and Beverly Eileen Cowden. BS in Systems Engring., Wright State U., 1979. Engr. Steve R. Rauch Inc., Dayton, 1979—; sec. Dayton Inventors Coun., 1994—. Mem. NSPE, Heartland Vintage Thunderbird Club (v.p.). Achievements include patent for secondary containment for underground storage tanks. Home: 9985 Ainsworth Ct Miamisburg OH 45342-4571 Office: 1550 Soldiers Home West Car Rd Dayton OH 45418-2146

COWDERY, ROBERT DOUGLAS, consulting geologist; b. Lyons, Kans., Aug. 20, 1926; s. Herman Rayburn and Blanche (Charles) C.; m. Mary Sue Barlow, Oct. 9, 1954; children:; Craig Douglas, Patricia Lynn. BS in Geology, Kans. State U., 1949; postgrad., U. Denver, 1953-54, Colo. Sch. Mines, 1963-64, U. Colo., 1963-71, Wichita State U., 1979-88. Geologist Cities Svc. Oil Co., Oklahoma City-Gt. Bend, Kans., 1949-51; staff geologist Petroleum Inc., Wichita, Kans., 1951-53; dist. geologist Petroleum Inc., Denver, 1953-56, div. geologist, 1956-57, Rocky Mountain exploration mgr., v.p., 1967-75; exploration mgr., v.p. Petroleum Inc., Wichita, 1975-85, pres., dir. exploration, 1985-88; ret., 1988; cons. geologist Wichita, 1988—. Pres. bd. dirs. Episcopal Social Svcs. S.W. Convocation, Wichita, 1989-90; bd. dirs. Breakthrough Club (serving mentally ill). Sgt. AUS, 1944-46. Recipient Disting. Svc. award Kans. State U. Coll. Arts and Scis., 1991; inducted into Kans. Oilmen's Hall of Fame. Mem. Am. Assn. Petroleum Geologists (cert., hon., v.p. 1983-84, v.p. divsn. profl. affairs 1987-88, pres.-elect 1990-91, pres. divsn. profl. affairs 1991-92, pres., Disting. Svc. award divsn. profl. affairs 1994, pres.-elect 1995-96, pres. 1996-97), Am. Inst. Profl. Geologists (cert.), Rocky Mountain Assn. Geologists (hon., pres. 1973), Kans. Geol. Soc. (hon., pres. 1986, Presdl. citation 1977, Spl. award 1998), Kans. Geol. Found. (pres. 1990—, bd. dirs. 1999—, Disting. Svc. award 1991, Pres.'s award 1993, Edn. award 1997), Soc. Ind. Profl. Earth Scientists (Kans. chpt. chmn., bd. dirs. 1995— nat. sec. 1996-97, v.p. natural resources 1997-98), Am. Geol. Inst. (rep. of AAPC on the mem. coun.), Archaeol. Assn. South Ctrl. Kans. (v.p. 1988-89, pres. 1990-93, program chair 1998-99), So. Am. Archaeologists, Wyo. Geol. Soc., Oklahoma City Geol. Soc., West Tex. Geol. Soc., Panhandle Geol. Soc., Petroleum Club (bd. dirs. 1988-91, sec. 1991), Phi Kappa Phi, Sigma Gamma Epsilon, Beta Theta Pi. Avocations: archaeology, karate (5th deg. black belt Tae Kwon Do). E-mail: sbc@southwind.net. Home: 7520 E 21st St N Unit 10 Wichita KS 67206-1086 Office: 107 N Market St Ste 1007 Wichita KS 67202-1811

COWELL, FULLER A., publisher; m. Christmas Cowell; 1 child, Alexis. BBA, U. Alaska Fairbanks. With McClatchy Newspapers, 1981—; pub. Gavilan Newspapers, Calif., 1987-91, Anchorage Daily News, 1993—; former pub. Cordova Times. Office: Anchorage Daily News PO Box 149001 Anchorage AK 99514-9001*

COWELL, MARION AUBREY, JR., lawyer; b. Wilmington, N.C., Dec. 25, 1934; s. Marion Aubrey and Alice Saunders (Hargett) C.; m. Norma Hearne; children: Lindsay G., Mark P., Kathryn Huffman, Graham Shannonhouse, Elizabeth Shannonhouse, Mary Robbins Whisnant. BSBA, U. N.C., 1958, LLB, 1964. Bar: N.C. 1964. Pvt. practice law Durham, N.C., 1964-72; assoc. Bryant, Lipton, Bryant and Battle, 1964-69, ptnr., 1971-72; pvt. practice law Durham, 1969-70; gen. counsel Cameron Brown Co., Raleigh, N.C., 1972-78; exec. v.p., gen. counsel, sec. First Union Corp., Charlotte, N.C., 1978—. Office: First Union Corp 1 First Union Ctr Charlotte NC 28288-0013

COWEN, DONALD EUGENE, retired physician; b. Ft. Morgan, Colo., Oct. 8, 1918; adopted s. Franklin and Mary Edith (Dalton) C.; BA, U. Denver, 1940; MD, U. Colo., 1943; m. Hulda Marie Helling, Dec. 24, 1942; children: David L., Marilyn Marie Cowen Dean, Theresa Kathleen Cowen Cunningham Byrd, Margaret Ann Cowen Koenigs. Intern, U.S. Naval Hosp., Oakland, Calif., 1944; gen. practice medicine, Ft. Morgan, 1947-52; resident internal medicine U. Colo. Med. Ctr., Denver, 1952-54; practice medicine specializing in allergy, Denver, 1954-90, ret., 1990; mem. staff Presbyn. Med. Ctr., Denver, Porter, Swedish hosps., Englewood, Colo.; clin. asst. prof. medicine U. Colo. Med. Center, 1964-91, ret., 1991; postgrad. faculty U. Tenn. Coll. Medicine, Memphis, 1962-82; cons. Queen of Thailand, 1973, 75, 77. Pres. Community Arts Symphony Found., 1980-82. Served to lt. M.C., USN, 1943-47. Fellow ACP, Am. Coll. Chest Physicians (vice chmn. com. on allergy 1968-72, 75-87, sec.-treas. Colo. chpt. 1971-77, pres. 1978-80), Am. Coll. Allergy and Immunology, Acad. Internat. Medicine, West Coast Allergy Soc., Southwest Allergy Forum, Am. Acad. Otolaryngic Allergy, Colo. socs. internal medicine, Colo. Allergy Soc. (past pres.), Ill. Soc. Opthalmology and Otolaryngology (hon.), Denver Med. Soc. (chmn. library and bldg. com. 1963-73), Arapahoe Med. Soc. (life emeritus mem.). Presbyterian (ruling elder 1956—). Club: Lions. Contbr. numerous articles to profl. jours. Home: 18560 Polvera Dr San Diego CA 92128-1120

COWEN, EDWARD S., lawyer; b. N.Y.C., Mar. 3, 1936; s. Michael and Edith (Cohen) C.; m. Lesley J. Hoffman, Nov. 16, 1958; children: Adriene, Justine. BS, Syracuse U., 1957; JD, NYU, 1961. Bar: N.Y. 1962, U.S. Dist. Ct. (so. dist.) N.Y. 1965, U.S. Ct. Appeals (2d cir.) 1965, U.S. Supreme Ct. 1967, U.S. Dist. Ct. (ea. dist.) N.Y. 1979. Law clk. to judge U.S. Dist. Ct. (so. dist.) N.Y., 1961-62; ptnr. Seligson & Morris, N.Y.C., 1963-69, Robinson, Silverman, Pearce, Aronsohn & Berman, N.Y.C., 1975-90, Kirkland & Ellis, N.Y.C., 1991-96; counsel Winthrop, Stimson, Putnam & Roberts, N.Y.C., 1996—; mem. faculty Practicing Law Inst. Author: Bankruptcy in Joint Venture Partnerships, Practicing Law Institute, 1985, Enforcing Liens Postpetition, Bankruptcy Strategist, 1998. With USAF, 1958. Recipient Honoree of Yr. awad UJA Fed. N.Y. Lawyers Divsn. Mem. ABA, N.Y. State Bar Assn., Assn. Bar City N.Y. (chmn. bankruptcy and corp. reorgn.), Harmonie Club. Home: 993 Park Ave New York NY 10028 Office: Winthrop Stimson Putnam & Roberts 34th Fl One Battery Park Plaza New York NY 10004

COWEN, EUGENE SHERMAN, broadcasting executive; b. N.Y.C., May 2, 1925; s. Jacob M. and Shirley (Sherman) C.; m. Phyllis L. Wallach, Jan. 29, 1948; children: James Sherman, Stephanie Jane. BA magna cum laude, Syracuse U., 1949, MA, 1954. Reporter Syracuse Herald-Jour., 1948-52, Newhouse News Bur., Washington, 1952-53; press sec. Rep. Frances P. Bolton, Washington, 1953-56; info. officer HEW, Washington, 1956-58; v.p. Standard Pub. Rels., Washington, 1958-59; asst. to Senator Hugh Scott, 1959-69; spl. asst., dep. asst. to pres. White House, 1969-71; v.p.-Washington Capital Cities/ABC, Inc., 1971-90; cons. in field Washington, 1990—. Legis. affairs dir. Svc. Corps Ret. Execs. With USAAF, 1943-46. Decorated Air medal. Mem. Phi Beta Kappa. Home: 2700 Calvert St NW # 713 Washington DC 20008-2621

COWEN, ROBERT E., federal judge; b. Newark, N.J., Sept. 4, 1930; s. Saul and Lillie (Selzer) C.; m. Toby Cowen, Dec. 21, 1973; children: Shulie, Eve. BS, Drake U., 1952; LLB, Rutgers U., 1958. Assoc. Schreiber, Lancaster & Demos, Newark, 1959-61; asst. prosecutor Essex County, N.J., 1969-70; dep. atty. gen. organized crime Criminal Justice Dept., N.J., 1970-72, dir. Div. Ethics and Profl. Svcs., 1972-78; magistrate U.S. Dist. Ct. N.J., Newark, 1978-85; judge U.S. Dist. Ct. N.J., Trenton, 1985-87; from judge to sr. judge U.S. Ct. Appeals (3d cir.), Trenton, 1987—; pvt. practice, Newark, 1961-69. Office: US Ct Appeals 3d Cir US Courthouse Rm 700 402 E State St Trenton NJ 08608-1507*

COWEN, ROY CHADWELL, JR., German language educator; b. Kansas City, Mo., Aug. 2, 1930; s. Roy Chadwell and Mildred Frances (Schuetz) C.; m. Hildegard Bredemeier, Oct. 6, 1956 (dec.); 1 son, Ernst Werner (dec.). B.A., Yale U., 1952; Ph.D., U. Gottingen, W.Ger., 1960. Instr. U. Mich., Ann Arbor, 1960-64, asst. prof., 1964-67, assoc. prof., 1967-71, prof., 1971—, chmn. dept. Germanic langs., 1979-85. Author: Christian Dietrich Grabbe, 1972, Naturalismus Kommentar zu einer Epoche, 1973, Hauptmann Kommentar zum dramatischen Werk, 1980, Hauptmann Kommentar zum nichtdramatischen Werk, 1981; Poetischer Realismus: Kommentar zu einer Epoche, 1985, Das deutsche Drama im 19. Jahrhundert, 1988, Christian Dietrich Grabbe—Dramatiker ungeloester Widersprueche, 1998. Served with USN, 1952-56. Decorated Sr. Officer's Cross Fed. Republic of Germany (Bundesverdienstkreuz I. Klasse); recipient Williams Teaching award U. Mich., 1967; sr. fellow NEH, 1972-73. Mem. MLA, Internationale Vereinigung fur Germanistik. Democrat. Methodist. Home: 2874 Baylis Dr Ann Arbor MI 48108-1764 Office: U Mich Dept Germanic Langs/Lits Ann Arbor MI 48109

COWEN, SCOTT S., university president; m. Marjorie Cowen; 4 children. BS, U. Conn.; MBA, George Washington U., PhD in Bus. Adminstrn. Faculty Case Western Res. U., Cleve., dean, Albert J. Weatherhead III prof. mgmt.; pres. Tulane U., New Orleans, 1998—, Seymour S. Goodman Meml. prof. bus., prof. econs. Faculty of Liberal Arts and Scis.; bd. dirs. Newell Rubbermaid Inc., Am. Greetings Corp., Jo-Ann Stores, Inc., Forest City Ent., Inc.; cons. in field. Co-author 4 books; contbr. articles to profl. jours. Recipient Torch of Learning, Hebrew U.; named George Washington U. Disting. Alumni Scholar, 1998-99; inductee Sch. of Bus. Administrn. Hall of Fame of U. Conn. Mem. Am. Assembly of Collegiate Schs. Bus. Fax: (504) 862-8777; email: scowen@mailhost.tcs.tulane.edu. Office: Tulane University Gibson Hall Ste 215 6823 St Charles Ave New Orleans LA 70118-5684*

COWEN, WILSON, federal judge; b. nr. Clifton, Tex., Dec. 20, 1905; s. John Rentz and Florence Juno (McFadden) C.; m. Florence Elizabeth Walker, Apr. 18, 1930; children: W. Walker, John E. LL.B., U. Tex., 1928. Bar: Tex. 1928. Pvt. practice Dalhart, Tex., 1928-34; judge Dallam County, Tex., 1935-38; Tex. dir. Farm Security Adminstrn., 1938-40, regional dir., 1940-42; commr. U.S. Ct. Claims, Washington, 1942-43, 45-59, chief commr., 1959-64, chief judge, 1964-77, sr. judge, 1977-82; sr. judge fed. cir. U.S. Ct. Appeals, Washington, 1982—; asst. adminstr. War Food Adminstrn., 1943-45; spl. asst. to sec. agr., 1945; mem. Jud. Conf. U.S., 1964-77. Mem. ABA, State Bar Tex., Fed. Bar Assn., Order of Coif, Cosmos Club (Washington), Delta Theta Phi. Presbyterian. Home: 2512 Q St NW Apt 205 Washington DC 20007 Office: US Ct Appeal Federal Circuit 717 Madison Pl NW Washington DC 20439-0002

COWGER, PHYLLIS, nurse; b. San Antonio, Sept. 12, 1944; d. Russell and Mildred Marie (Hamilton) Austin; m. Robert F. Cowger, Dec. 31, 1964; children: Rhonda, Teresa, Russell, Phillip, Robert II. Diploma in Nursing, Cochise Coll., Douglas, Ariz., 1985, AA in Gen. Studies, 1989. Lic. practical nurse, Ariz. Nurse Benson (Ariz.) Hosp., 1985-86; charge nurse Life Care Sierra Vista, Ariz., 1986-87; nurse Sierra Vista Care Ctr., 1987-89, Raymond W. Bliss Army Hosp., Ft. Huachuca, Ariz., 1989—. Com. mem. Sierra Vista council Boy Scouts Am. Nursing dept. grantee Cochise Coll., 1986. Democrat. Presbyterian. Avocations: reading, sewing, swimming. Home: 771 N Tacoma Pl Sierra Vista AZ 85635-1349

COWGILL, F(RANK) BROOKS, retired insurance company executive; b. Hungtington Park, Calif., Mar. 16, 1932; s. Frank H. and Henriette J. (Dickey) C.; m. Mary Lucena Hanna, Dec. 22, 1954; children: David B., Ann M. AB, Stanford U., 1954, MBA, 1956. Analyst treas.'s dept. Exxon Corp., N.Y.C., 1958-61; sr. analyst treas.'s dept. WR Grace Co., Cambridge, Mass., 1961-62; with New England Mut. Life Ins. Co., Boston, 1962-92; v.p., treas. New England Mut. Life Ins. Co., 1979-92; sr. devel. officer Harvard U., Cambridge, Mass., 1994-98. Active Boston Com. on Fgn. Rels. Served to 1st lt. U.S. Army, 1956-58. Mem. Inst. Chartered Fin. Analysts, Boston Security Analysts Soc., Boston Econs. Club, Treas. Club (Boston), Harvard Club (Boston). Home: 75 Lawson Rd Winchester MA 01890-3153

COWGILL, URSULA MOSER, biologist, educator, environmental consultant; b. Bern, Switzerland, Nov. 9, 1927; came to U.S., 1943, naturalized, 1945; d. John W. and Mara (Siegrist) Moser. A.B., Hunter Coll., 1948; M.S., Kans. State U., 1952; Ph.D., Iowa State U., 1956. Staff MIT, Lincoln Lab., Lexington, Mass., 1957-58; field work Doherty Found., Guatemala, 1958-60; research assoc. dept. biology Yale U., New Haven, 1960-68; prof. biology and anthropology U. Pitts., 1968-81; environ. scientist Dow Chem. Co., Midland, Mich., 1981-84; assoc. environ. cons. Dow Chem. Co., 1984-91; environ. cons., 1991—; mem. environ. measurements adv. com. Sci. Adv. Bd. EPA, 1976-80; Internat. Joint Commn., 1984-89. Contbr. numerous articles on ecology, biology and minerology to sci. publs. Trustee Carnegie Mus., Pitts., 1971-75. Grantee NSF 1960-78, Wenner Gren Found., 1965-66, Penrose fund Am. Philos. Soc., 1978; Sigma Xi grant-in-aid, 1965-66. Mem. AAAS, Am. Soc. Limnology and Oceanography, Internat. Soc. Theoretical and Applied Limnology. Home and Office: PO Box 1329 Carbondale CO 81623-1329

COWHER, BILL, professional football coach; b. Pitts., May 8, 1957; m. Kaye Cowher; children: Meagan Lyn, Lauren Marie, Lindsay Morgan. Degree in edn., N.C. State. Football player Cleve. Browns, 1980-82, spl. teams coach, 1985-86, secondary coach, 1987-88; football player Phila. Eagles, 1983-84; def. coord. Kansas City Chiefs, 1988-91; head coach Pitts. Steelers, 1992—. Office: 300 Stadium Cir Pittsburgh PA 15212-5729*

COWHERD, EDWIN RUSSELL, management consultant; b. Louisville, Mar. 12, 1921; s. Douglas Head and Katie (Martin) C.; m. Helen Marie Lammers , June 2, 1956; children: Douglas, Anne, Robert, Sarah, Joseph. B of Chem. Engring., U. Louisville, 1943; postgrad., MIT, 1944, U. Mich., 1948-57. Mgr. Dow Chem. Co., Midland, Mich., 1943-68; group v.p. GAF Corp., N.Y.C., 1968-71; pres. Cowherd Cons. Group., Darien, Conn., 1972—; bd. dirs. Congoleum Corp.; exec. v.p., pres. Congoleum Corp., Mercerville, N.J., 1988-93. Lt. USN, 1943-46, PTO. Served to lt. USN, 1943-46, PTO. Mem. AICE, Inst. Mgmt. Cons., Planning Forum. Republican. Home and Office: 106 Stephen Mather Rd Darien CT 06820-2233

COWHEY, PETER FRANCIS, international relations educator, consultant; b. Chgo., Sept. 28, 1948; s. Eugene F. and Vivien (High) C.; m. Mary Pat Williams, July 1973 (div. June 1978); m. M. Margaret McKeown, June 29, 1985; 1 child, Megan. BS in Fgn. Svc., Georgetown U., 1970; MA, PhD, U. Calif., Berkeley, 1976. Lectr. U. Calif., Berkeley, 1975-76; from asst. to assoc. prof. polit. sci. U. Calif. San Diego, La Jolla, 1976-88, prof. polit. sci. & internat. rels., 1989—; sr. counselor internat. econ. and competition policy FCC, Washington, 1994-97, chief internat. bur., 1997; market planner AT&T Internat., Basking Ridge, N.J., 1985-86; adv. Telemation Assocs., Washington, 1987-88; mem. telecom. adv. bd. A.T. Kearney, Chgo., 1988-91; co-dir. project on internat. and security affairs U. Calif., San Diego, 1990-94; rsch. scholar Berkeley Roundtable on the Internat. Economy, 1992-94; vis. prof. Juan March Inst., Madrid, 1992; rsch. prof. Inst. of Oriental Culture, U. Tokyo, 1993; U.S. del. G-7 Ministerial, 1995, U.S. del. Asian Pacific Econ. Cmty. Ministerial, 1995; mem. sec. gen. ITU Expert Group on Acctg. Rates, 1997-98; policy advisor Harris Wiltshire and Grannis, 1998—. Author: Problems of Plenty, 1985; co-author: Profit and the Pursuit of Energy, 1983, When Countries Talk, 1988, Managing the World's Economy, 1993; co-editor: Structure and Policy in Japan and the United States, 1994; mem. editl. bd. Internat. Orgn., 1989-94. Mem. adv. bd. Project Promothee, Paris, 1985-94, Ctr. on Telecom. Mgmt., Lincoln, Nebr., 1988-92; com. mem. NRC, 1992-93. Rockefeller Found. internat. affairs fellow, 1984-87. Mem. Am. Polit. Sci. Assn., Coun. Fgn. Rels. (internat. affairs fellow 1985-86), Internat. Studies Assn. Democrat. Home: 1522 40th Ave Seattle WA 98122-3510 also: Internat Bur FCC 2000 M St NW Fl 8 Washington DC 20036-3307

COWHILL, WILLIAM JOSEPH, retired naval officer, consultant; b. Bklyn., May 29, 1928; s. Joseph Henry and Lucy Rose (Foppiano) C.; m. Jennifer Jackson, Apr. 16, 1955; children Robin, Joseph, Beth, Michael, Douglas. BS, Northwestern U., 1950. Commd. ensign USN, 1950, advanced through grades to vice adm., 1979, comdg. officer USS Dace and USS Will Rogers, 1965-68, PCO instr., div. Naval Reactors, AEC, 1968-70, comdg. officer USS Holland, Rota, Spain, 1970-72, nuclear power program mgr. Bur. Naval Personnel, 1972, comdr. tng. command, U.S. Atlantic Fleet, 1973-75, asst. dep. chief naval ops. for submarine warfare, Office Chief Naval Ops., Washington, 1975-77, comdr. submarine force, U.S. Pacific Fleet, 1977-79, dep. chief ops. for logistics, office chief naval ops., 1979-83, dir. logistics, joint chiefs of staff, 1983-85, ret.; pvt. cons. Washington, 1985—. Decorated Def. D.S.M., Navy D.S.M., Legion of Merit. Home and Office: 1336 Elsinore Ave Mc Lean VA 22102-2753

COWIE, NORMAN EDWIN, credit manager; b. Balt., Nov. 24, 1958; s. Graham Norman Cowie and Jane Ardythe (Wertzler) Seekman; m. Sandra Jo Twaddle, Oct. 19, 1985; children: Samantha Lynn, Lauren Alexandra. AA, Kalamazoo Valley (Mich.) C.C., 1978; BBA magna cum laude, Western Mich. U., 1980. Cert. credit exec. Nat. Assn. Credit Mgmt. Mgr. Assocs. Fin. Co., Mich., Ill., 1980-85; region credit supr. Westinghouse Electric Supply, Elmhurst, Ill., 1985-89; v.p. fin., corp. credit mgr. Evergreen Oak Electric Sales and Supply, Crestwood, Ill., 1989—; chmn. Elec. Distbrs. Credit Group, Park Ridge, Ill., 1990-92; bd. dirs. Chgo. Midwest Credit Mgmt. Assn., Park Ridge, 1993-96; spkr. Nat. Elec. Contractors Assn., DuPage, Ill., 1991, Chgo. Plumbing & Heating Wholesalers Credit Group, Oak Brook, Ill., 1994; moderator Roundtable Discussion, Ill. Mechanic's Lien Law, Park Ridge, 1994, Ill. Mechanic's Lien Seminar, Rosemont, Ill., 1995; spkr. Understanding Constrn. Bonds and Mechanics Liens, Des Plaines, Ill., 1998, NACM/Chgo. Midwest Credit Leadership Conf. and Expo, 1999. Author: (comic) Short Circuit, 1992; contbr. articles to profl. jours. Mem. Nat. Assn. Credit Mgmt./Chgo. Midwest (collection activities task force com. 1996, nominating com. 1999), Am. Assn. Credit Mgmt. (nominating com., Chgo. Midwest, 1999), Improved Constn. Practices Com. (chmn. Ill. chpt. 1993—), Chgo. Midwest Credit Mgmt. Legis. Com. (chmn. 1992-95). Avocations: comic artist, volleyball. Home: 2822 Hawkshead Dr New Lenox IL 60451-2709 Office: Evergreen Oak Electric Supply 13400 Cicero Ave Crestwood IL 60445-1460

COWIN, STEPHEN CORTEEN, biomedical engineering educator, consultant; b. Elmira, N.Y., Oct. 26, 1934; s. William Corteen and Bernice (Reidy) C.; m. Martha Agnes Eisel, Aug. 10, 1956; children: Jennifer Marie, Thomas Burrows. BCE (Md. State scholar, Ambrose Howard Carner scholar), Johns Hopkins U., 1956, MCE (Univ. fellow), 1958; Ph.D. in Engring. Mechanics, Pa. State U., 1962. Registered profl. engr., La. Prof. mech. engring. Tulane U., 1969-77, prof. mechanics dept. biomed. engring., 1977-85, adj. prof. orthopedics, 1978-88, prof.-in-charge Tulane-Newcomb Jr. Yr. Abroad program, 1974-75, chmn. applied math. program, 1975-79, prof. applied stats., 1979-88, Alden J. Laborde prof. engring., 1985-88; Disting. prof. CUNY, 1988—; Sci. Research Council Gt. Brit. sr. vis. fellow U. Strathclyde, 1974, 80; vis. research prof. Instituto de Matematica, Estatistica e Ciencia de Computanao, Universidade Estadual de Campinas, Brazil, 1978; participant U.S. Nat. Acad. Scis. interacad. exchange program with Bulgaria, 1983; fellow Japan Soc. for the Promotion Sci., 1987. Editor: (with M. Satake) Continuum Mechanical and Statistical Approaches in the Mechanics of Granular Materials, 1978, Mechanics Applied to the Transport of Granular Materials, 1979, (with M.M. Carroll) The Effects of Voids on Material Deformation, 1976, Bone Mechanics, 1988; assoc. editor: Jour. Applied Mechanics, 1974-82, Jour. Biomech. Engring., 1982-88; editorial adv. bd. Handbook of Materials, Structures and Mechanics, 1981—, Handbook of Bioengineering, 1981, Acta Biomechanica, 1986—; editorial bd. Annals Biomed. Engring., 1985—; editorial cons. Jour. Biomechanics, 1988—. Served to capt. U.S. Army, 1957-64. Rsch. grantee NSF, NIH, NASA, U.S. Army Rsch. Office, Edward G. Schlieder Found.; sr. internat. rsch. fellow Fogarty Internat. Ctr., Amsterdam, 1996-97. Fellow AAAS, ASME (Melville medal 1993, Lissner medal 1999), Am. Inst. Med. and Biol. Engring., European Soc. Biomechanics (Rsch. award 1994), Am. Acad. Mechanics; mem. Orthopedic Rsch. Soc., Soc. Rheology, Soc. Natural Philosophy (treas. 1977-79), Soc. Engring. Sci., Math. Assn. Am., N.Y. Acad. Scis., Sigma Xi. Home: 107 W 86th St Apt 4F New York NY 10024-3409

COWLES, CHARLES, art dealer; b. Santa Monica, Calif., Feb. 7, 1941; s. Gardner and Jan (Streate) C. Student, Stanford, 1963. Assoc. pub. Artforum mag., San Francisco, 1964-65; pub., pres. Artforum, Inc., Los Angeles, 1965-67; pub., pres., chmn. Artforum, Inc., N.Y.C., 1967-79; chmn. Collegiate Press, N.Y.C., 1968-71; curator modern art Seattle Art Mus., 1975-79; pres., dir. Charles Cowles Gallery, N.Y.C., 1980—; Mem. Fine Arts Council Fla., 1972-75; Trustee Studio Mus. in Harlem, N.Y.C., 1967-75, Miami Art Ctr., 1973-75, San Francisco Art Inst., 1978-80, Cowles Charitable Trust, 1983—; mem. internat. council Mus. Modern Art, N.Y.C., 1967-79; chmn. bd. Jennifer Muller Dance Co., 1981-84. Trustee Wolfsonian, Miami Beach, 1995—, Lanmeier Sculpture Pk. St. Louis, 1996—, N.Y. Studio Sch., 1985—, chmn., 1987-95. With USCGR, 1962-70. Mem. Art Dealers Assn. Am. (bd. dirs. 1988-90, 93-96). Office: Charles Cowles Gallery 420 W Broadway New York NY 10012-3764*

COWLES, ELIZABETH HALL, program consultant; b. Wichita Falls, Tex., Aug. 27, 1936; d. Eugene DeWitt and Lorena (Perry) Hall; m. James Edgar Cowles, Dec. 26, 1957 (div. Jan. 1989); children: Gary Randall, Jan Alison Cowles Sendker, Richard Scott. BS in Edn., North Tex. State U., Denton, 1958; MAIS, U. Tex., Dallas, 1994. Elem. tchr. Long Beach (Calif.) Ind. Sch. Dist., 1958-59; tchr. 6th grade Austin (Tex.) Ind. Sch. Dist., 1960-62; statewide project dir. Rainbow Days, Inc., Dallas, 1989-90; LIFESPAN exec. dir. Dallas County Hosp. Dist., Dallas, 1990-94; Dallas Healthy Start exec. dir. Fed. Initiative Dallas County Hosp. Dist., Dallas, 1994-98; nat. cons. cmty. collaboration, program devel., resource devel. Concensus Bldg., 1999—; state pres. Tex. Coalition for Juvenile Justice, Dallas, 1983-84; mem. adv. com. Tex. Juvenile Probation Commn., Austin, 1987-88. Author: Early Influences on Development of English Language, 1994; initiated Listener Project, 1981. Pres. bd. dirs. Lone Star coun. Camp Fire, Dallas, 1986-87; mem. nat. steering com. Camp Fire, Inc., Kansas City, Kans., 1989; bd. dirs. United Way of Met. Dallas, 1988-89; pres. bd. dirs. Women's Coun. Dallas County, 1988-89; mem. pub. affairs com. Mental Health Assn.; mem. cmty. leaders forum Ctr. for Non-Profit Mgmt., 1996-97; mem. cmty. action com. Dallas Coun. on Alcohol and Drug Abuse, 1996-97; chair adminstrv. bd. Lovers Lane United Meth. Ch., 1997. Recipient Cmty. Advocacy award Dallas County Juvenile Dept., 1985, Gulick award for cmty. svc. Camp Fire, Inc., 1989, Women Helping Women award Women's Ctr. of Dallas County, 1995, Susan B. Anthony award United Meth. Ch., 1997, Award for Ednl. Excellence in Programming Planned Parenthood of Dallas, 1998. Mem. LWV (health edn. com.), Nat. Assn. Healthy Start (founding mem. bd. dirs. 1998). Avocations: travel, reading, swimming, tennis, family.

COWLES, ERNEST LEE, academic administrator, educator, consultant, researcher; b. Lead, S.D., Aug. 9, 1949; s. Leon Andrew and Freeda (Kaubisch) C.; m. Ellison Bell Fuller, Sept. 4, 1970. BA, U. So. Fla., 1971; MS, Rollins Coll., 1976; PhD, Fla. State U., 1981. Probation and parole officer I & II Fla. Probation Parole Commn., Central, Fla., 1971-76; psychologist Fla. Dept. Offender Rehab., Clearmont, 1976; asst. prof. Northeast Mo. State U., Kirksville, 1978-1984, assoc. prof., 1984-85; dir. div. classification and treatment Mo. Dept. Corrections and Human Svcs., Jefferson City, 1985-89; assoc. prof., prin. investigator Ctr. Study Crime Delinquency & Corrections So. Ill. U., Carbondale, 1989-94; dir. Ctr. Legal Studies U. Ill., Springfield, 1994—; cons. Ill. State Police, 1995—, Dept. Corrections, 1996—, Regional Inst. Cmty. Policing, 1996—; with Nat. Inst. Justice U.S. Dept. Justice, Washington, 1985—, Fed. Bur. Prisons, 1989, Bur. Justice Assistance, 1990—. Contbr. articles to profl. jours. and chpts. to books. Exec. bd. Lincoln Legal Papers, 1994—. Past mem. Gov.'s Task Force on Rape. Law Enforcement Asst. Adminstrn. fellow, 1976-78; mem. Inst. Pub. Affairs Cabinet & Exec. Com., 1998—, Coll. Pub. Adminstrs. Cabinet & Exec. Com., 1998—. Mem. Am. Soc. Criminology, Acad. Criminal Justice Scis., Am. Correctional Assn., Justice Rsch. & Stats. Assn. (exec. bd. 1993), Mensa. Home: 1312 Community Dr Springfield IL 62703-5363

COWLES, FLEUR (MRS. TOM M. MEYER), author, artist; m. Gardner Cowles, Dec. 27, 1946 (div. 1955); m. Tom Montague Meyer, Nov. 18, 1955. LLD, Elmira (N.Y.) Coll., 1954. Spl. cons. Famine Emergency Com., White House, Washington, 1946; assoc. editor, dir. spl. editorial depts. Look mag., 1947, fgn. corr., 1955-58; assoc. editor Quick mag., 1949; editor Flair mag., 1950-51, Flair Annual, 1952; fgn. dir. Cowles Mags., Inc.; cons. to chief of staff Hdqrs. USAF, 1950; mem. nat. adv. com. on women's participation Fed. Civil Def. Adminstrn., 1953-55; Spl. rep. Pres. Eisenhower (with rank of spl. ambassador) at coronation of Queen Elizabeth II of Eng.; founder Inst. Am. Studies Oxford (Eng.) Coll. Author: Bloody Precedent, 1952, The Case of Salvator Dali, 1959, The Hidden World of Hadhramoutt, 1963, Tiger Flower, 1968, Treasures of the British Museum, 1970, Lion and Blue, 1974, Friends and Memories, 1975, All Too True, 1981, The Flower Game, 1983, Flower Decorations, 1985, People as Animals, 1986, 87, An Artist's Journey, 1988, The Life and Times of the Rose, 1992, She Made Friends and KeptThem, 1995, The Best of Flair 1996—; exhibited paintings, London, 1959, 63, 66, 75, N.Y.C., 1960, 62, 64, 67, 73, Rome, 1961, Paris, 1962, Athens, 1966, Los Angeles, 1967, Madrid, 1967, Rio de Janeiro, 1966, 68, Dallas, 1969, 71, São Paulo, 1965, 66, 72, Seattle, 1970, San Francisco, 1973, Detroit, 1974, Kans., 1975, Dusseldorf, 1976, El Paso, 1985, Bermuda, 1986, Singer Mus., Holland, 1977, Cheekwood Mus., Nashville, 1978, Hammer Galleries, 1978, Partridge Gallery, London, 1978, 83, Gregg Juarez Gallery, 1980, Roelant Gallery, Amsterdam, 1980, S. L. Gallery, Dallas, El Paso Mus., 1985, Wako Galleries, Tokyo, 1988, Galeria de Arte Grife y Escoda, Barcelona, Spain, 1990, Chris Beetles Gallery, London, 1991, Portal Gallery, Chgo., 1991, Tiller Gallery, Dallas, 1992, Nat. Mus. Women in Arts, Washington, 1993, Red Fox Fine Art Gallery, Middleburg, 1993, The Alisan gallery, Hong Kong, 1995—, Galeria Montevideo. Pres. Leakey Trust, Europe; trustee LSB Leaky Found., Soc. Rehab. Facially Disfigured, SatelLife, Boston, Am. Mus. in Britain; chmn. Friends of Royal Geog. Soc. Decorated chevalier Legion of Honor (France), Queen's Coronation medal (U.K.), Order So. Cross (Brazil); comdr. Order So. Cross (Brazil), Order of Bienfaisence (Greece); La dama de Isabel Catolica (Spain); established Fleur Cowles Fellowships at U. Tex. at Austin. Fellow Royal Coll. Art (hon., founder), Inst. for Am. Studies Oxford U. Home: A5 Albany Piccadilly, London W1V 9RD, England

COWLES, FREDERICK OLIVER, lawyer; b. Steubenville, Ohio, Oct. 18, 1937; s. Oliver Howard and Cornelia Blanche (Regal) C.; m. Christina Monica Muller, Sept. 9, 1961; children: Randall, Eric, Gregory, Cornelius. AB magna cum laude, Yale U., 1959; JD, Harvard U., 1962. Bar: R.I. 1963, Mich. 1967, Ill. 1969, N.Y. 1998, Conn. 1998. Assoc. Hinckley, Allen, Salisbury & Parsons, Providence, 1962-67; internat. atty. Upjohn Co., Kalamazoo, Mich., 1967-69; chief internat. atty. Am. Hosp. Supply Crp., Evanston, Ill., 1969-71; internat. atty. Kendall Co., Boston, 1971-73; chief internat. counsel Colgate Palmolive Co., N.Y.C., 1973-86, assoc. gen. counsel, asst. sec., 1986-90, assoc. gen. counsel, asst. sec., v.p. legal ops., 1990-94, sr. assoc. gen. coun., asst. sec., v.p. legal ops., 1994-97, multinat. estate planning, 1997—; dir. various cos. Deacon South Salem Presbyn. Ch.; mem. com. Lewisboro Boy Scouts; co-founder Internat. House R.I. Inc.; group leader Operation Crossroads Africa, Gambia. Mem. ABA, Am. Corp. Coun. Assn., Internat. Bar Assn., Westchester Fairfield Corp. Csl. Assn., Yale Alumni Assn., Internat. Lawyers Assn., Phi Beta Kappa. E-mail: focowles@bestweb.net. FAX: 914-276-7853. Home: 111 Oscaleta Rd South Salem NY 10590-1003 Office: Multinational Estate Planning PLLC 358 Rte 202 Somers NY 10589

COWLES, JOE RICHARD, biology educator; b. Edmonson County, Ky., Oct. 29, 1941; s. Otis Wilson and Mamie E. (Rountree) C.; m. Barbara Sutton, June 5, 1965; children: Richard William, Daniel Morgan. BS, Western Ky. U., 1963; MS, U. Ky., 1965; PhD, Oreg. State U., 1968. Postdoctoral fellow Purdue U., West Lafayette, Ind., 1968-69, U. Ga., Athens, 1969-70; asst. prof. U. Houston, 1970-75, assoc. prof., 1976-81, chmn. biology dept., 1981-90, prof., 1982-90; prof., head biology Va. Tech. U., Blacksburg, 1990—. Contbr. more than 40 articles to profl. jours. Grantee NASA, NSF, Dept. Energy, USDA. Mem. Am. Soc. Plant Physiology, Sigma Xi. Democrat. Baptist. Avocations: sports. Office: Virginia Tech U Dept Biology Blacksburg VA 24061

COWLES, JOHN, JR., publisher, women's sports promoter; b. Des Moines, May 27, 1929; s. John and Elizabeth (Bates) C.; m. Jane Sage Fuller, Aug. 23, 1952; children: Tessa Sage Flores, John, Jane Sage, Charles Fuller. Grad., Phillips Exeter Acad., 1947; AB, Harvard U., 1951; LittD (hon.), Simpson Coll., 1965. With Cowles Media Co. (formerly Mpls. Star and Tribune Co.), 1953-83, v.p., 1957-68, editor, 1961-69, pres., 1968-73, 79-83, editorial chmn., 1969-73, chmn., 1973-79, dir., 1956-84; pres. Harper's Mag., Inc., 1965-68, chmn. bd., 1968-72; dir. Harper & Row, Pubs., Inc., N.Y.C., 1965-81; chmn. Harper & Row, Pubs., Inc., 1968-79; dir. Des Moines Register & Tribune Co., 1960-84, Farmers & Mechanics Savs. Bank, Mpls., 1960-65, Cowles Comms., Inc., N.Y.C., 1960-65, Equitable Life Ins. Co. Iowa, Des Moines, 1964-66, 1st Bank Systems, Inc., Mpls., 1964-68, A.P., N.Y.C., 1966-75, Midwest Radio-TV, Inc., Mpls., 1967-76; fitness instr. Sweatshop Fitness Ctr., St. Paul, 1989-93; guest artist Bill T. Jones/Arnie Zane & Co., 1990-92; vice chmn. Women's Pro. Softball League, Denver, 1994—. Mem. adv. bd. on Pulitzer Prizes, Columbia U., 1970-83; campaign chmn. Mpls. United Fund, 1967; bd. dirs. Guthrie Theatre Found., 1960-71, pres., 1960-63, chmn., 1964-65; trustee Phillips Exeter Acad., 1960-65; bd. dirs. Walker Art Ctr., 1960-69, 87-92, Minn. Civil Liberties Union, 1956-61, Urban Coalition Mpls., 1968-70, Mpls. Found., 1970-75, German Marshall Fund U.S., 1975-78; bd. dirs. Am. Newspaper Pubs. Assn., 1975-77, mem. govt. affairs com., 1976-79. Served to 2d lt. AUS, 1951-53. Named one of ten outstanding men of year U.S. Jr. C. of C., 1964. Mem. Greater Mpls. C. of C. (dir. 1978-81, chmn. stadium site task force 1977-78). Clubs: Minneapolis (Mpls.). Office: 123 N 3rd St # 804 Minneapolis MN 55401

COWLES, JOHN, III, management consultant, investor; b. Mpls., Nov. 1, 1953; s. John Jr. and Jane Sage (Fuller) C.; m. Elizabeth Page Knudsen, Sept. 8, 1984; children: Lucia, Colin, Maxwell. BA in Govt. cum laude, Harvard U., 1981, MBA, 1983. Pres., CEO Classic Printers, Prescott, Ariz., 1975-79, chmn., 1979-96; cons. Office Cable Comm. Boston City Hall, 1980-81; dir. planning Cowles Media Co., Mpls., 1985-88, vice chmn. bd. dirs., 1991-93, chmn. bd. dirs., 1993-98; dir. fin. analysis United Satellite Comm., Inc., N.Y.C., 1983-85; v.p. Sentinel Pub. (divsn. Cowles Media Co.), Denver, 1988-91, Book Ventures, Inc., Mpls., 1992-93; pres., CEO Women's Pro Softball, Mpls., 1993-95, chmn. bd., 1993—; bd. dirs. St. Paul Riverfront Corp., chmn., 1998—; bd. dirs. Capital City Partnership. Bd. dirs. Minn. Ctr. Book Arts, Mpls., 1991-98, chmn. bd. dirs., 1995-98, acting exec. dir., 1995-97; bd. dirs. Prescott Coll., 1976-82, Mpls. Found., 1987-88, Guthrie Theater, Mpls., 1993-98. Mem. Harvard Bus. Sch. Club. Minn., Mpls. Club, Minn. Club. Office: Ste 804 123 N 3d St Minneapolis MN 55401

COWLES, ROGER E., computer consultant; b. Boston, Feb. 9, 1950; s. S. Edwin C. and Irene M. Woodard. BA in Internat. Econs. with honors, Ohio Wesleyan U., 1974. Network cons. LAN Syss., Inc., N.Y.C., 1988-91, Network Alternatives, Inc., Washington, 1991-92; dir. network syss. Quad Microsystems, Inc., Southampton, Pa., 1992-93; network cons. Integrated Microcomputer Syss., Inc., Rockville, Md., 1993-95; sys. cons. Emtec, Inc., Mt. Laurel, N.J., 1995—; prin., owner Agora Devel. Corp., 1998—; cons. World Bank, Washington, 1992, Judge Tech. Svcs., Bala Cynwyd, Pa., 1997; sr. cons. Chem. Bank, N.Y.C., 1995-96; sr. network cons. Arco Chem. Co., 1998—; founder Transcend Media Corp., 1998, Agora Devel. Corp., 1998. Mem. IEEE, Assn. Sys. Mgmt. Avocations: reading, politics, economics, sports, travel. Home: 2101 Chestnut St Philadelphia PA 19103-3108

COWLES, RONALD EUGENE, church administrator; b. Ottumwa, Iowa, Jan. 30, 1941; s. Fred Howard and Bertha Ilela (Sammons) C.; m. Rowena Rae Miller, Apr. 30, 1959; children: Richard Eric, David Allen, Rebecca Ruth. BA, Ottawa (Kans.) U., 1963; BD, MDiv, Ctrl. Bapt. Theol. Sem., Kansas City, Kans., 1966; D of Ministry, U. Bibl. Studies, 1991. Pastor Dry Ridge Bapt. Ch., Uniontown, Kans., 1961-63, First Bapt. Ch., Easton, Kans., 1963-66, Renwick (Iowa)-Corwith Parish, 1966-72, First Bapt. Ch., Pella, Iowa, 1972-86; assoc. exec. min. S.D. Bapt. Conv., Sioux Falls, 1986-91; exec. min. Am. Bapt. Chs. Dakotas, Sioux Falls, 1991—; bd. trustees Sioux Falls Coll., Ctrl. Bapt. Theol. Sem., Kansas City. Mem. Lions (pres. 1971), Rotary (bd. dirs. 1980-82). Avocations: fishing, hunting, photography, canoe camping. Office: Am Bapt Chs 1524 S Summit Ave Sioux Falls SD 57105-1632

COWLES, SANDRA LYNNE, metallurgical engineer; b. Niagara Falls, N.Y., Mar. 4, 1949; d. Carl Edwin and Jessie Boone (McMurdo) Emerson; m. Robert C. Cowles, Jan. 12, 1974; 1 child, Michael Jason. BS, BA, Mich. Tech. U., 1971. Mfg., welding engr. GE, Cin., 1977-83; materials, welding engr. Copes-Vulcan/Jarecki Ind., Fairview, Pa., 1983-87; sr. quality engr. Olin Def. Corp., St. Petersburg, Fla., 1987-89; contract engr. St. Petersburg, 1989-92; sr. staff engr. Storz Ophthalmics, Clearwater, Fla., 1992—. Patentee in field. Pres. awards com. Booster Club Shorecrest Sch., St. Petersburg, 1994. mem. assn. for the Advancement of Med. Instrumentation (AAMI), 1998—. Republican. Avocations: horseback riding, reading. Home: 5500 16th Ln NE Saint Petersburg FL 33703-1716 Office: Bausch & Lomb Surg Storz Products 21 N Park Place Blvd Clearwater FL 33759-3917

COWLES, WALTER CURTIS, naval architect; b. Chgo., Aug. 25, 1919; s. Harry Samuel and Blanche Lee (Gates) C.; m. Betty Ann McDuff, July 28, 1945; children: Mark Allan, Garry Stephen, Kent Edward, Joy Elizabeth. BS in Engring., U. Mich., 1942. Draftsman Am. Ship Bldg. Co., Cleve., 1942-51, chief hull draftsman, 1951-57, naval architect, 1951-63; marine designer Esso/Exxon, N.Y.C. and Morristown, N.J., 1963-84; ret., 1984. Contbr. paper to Transactions of Soc. Naval Architects and Marine Engrs., 1980; coord. publ. of centennial hist. vol., 1993; pub. Antrim Steamers A Brief History of Steam Navigation on the Inland Lakes of Antrim County Michigan, 1997. Mem. Soc. Naval Architects (life), U.S. Naval Inst. (life), Am. Soc. Naval Engrs. Home: 55 Fieldstone Dr Morristown NJ 07960-2634

COWLES, WILLIAM STACEY, publisher; b. Spokane, Wash., Aug. 31, 1960; s. William Hutchinson 3rd and Allison Stacey C.; m. Anne Cannon, June 24, 1989. BA in Econs., Yale Coll., 1982; MBA in Fin., Columbia U., 1986. V.p., pub. The Spokesman Rev., Spokane, Wash. Office: Cowles Publishing Co PO Box 2160 Spokane WA 99210-2160

COWLEY, GERALD DEAN, architect; b. Great Bend, Kans., Oct. 2, 1931; s. Stone Oden and Elizabeth (Lillich) C.; m. Lois Ester Traudt, Aug. 10, 1957 (div. 1983); children: Tara Elizabeth, Craig Stone; m. Frances Leach, Dec. 28, 1986. BArch, Kans. State U., 1960. Lic. architect, Colo. Architect James H. Johnson Architect, Lakewood, Colo., 1963-74, James H. Johnson & Assocs. Architects, Lakewood, 1963-74; architect, ptnr., prin. Johnson Hopson & Ptnrs., Denver, 1974-82, JHP Architecture Interior Design and Planning, Denver, 1982—. Prin. works include Rocky Mountain Energy Headquarters Bldg., 1983, others. Sgt. USAF, 1951-55. Mem. AIA, Constrn. Specifications Inst. Republican. Avocations: golf, sailing, skiing, watercolor. Home: 645 E Yale Pl Englewood CO 80110-1673 Office: JHP Architecture 2505 Walnut St Ste 302 Boulder CO 80302-5744

COWLEY, JOHN MAXWELL, physics educator; b. Peterborough, South Australia, Feb. 18, 1923; came to U.S., 1970; s. Alfred Ernest and Doris (Milway) C.; m. Roberta Joan Beckett, Dec. 15, 1951; children—Deborah Suzanne, Jillian Patricia. BS, U. Adelaide, Australia, 1942, MS, 1945, DSc, 1957; PhD, Mass. Inst. Tech., 1949. Research officer Commonwealth Sci. and Indsl. Research Orgn., Melbourne, Australia, 1945-62; chief research officer, head crystallography sect. Commonwealth Sci. and Indsl. Research Orgn., 1960-62; prof. physics U. Melbourne, Australia, 1962-70; Galvin prof. physics Ariz. State U., Tempe, 1970-94, Regents' prof., 1988-94, regents prof. emeritus, 1994—; mem. U.S. Nat. Com. for Crystallography, 1973-78, 84-86. Author: Diffraction Physics, 1975; editor: (with others) Acta Crystallographica, 1971-80; contbr. (with others) articles to profl. jours. Fellow Australian Acad. Sci., Inst. Physics (London), Australian Inst. Physics, Royal Soc. (London), Am. Phys. Soc.; mem. Internat. Union Crystallography (mem. exec. com. 1963-69, chair commn. on electron diffraction 1987-93, Ewald Prize 1987), Am. Inst. Physics, Am. Crystallographic Assn., Electron Microscope Soc. Am. (dir. 1971-75). Home: 2625 E Southern Ave Unit C90 Tempe AZ 85282-7670 Office: Ariz State U Dept Physics and Astronomy Tempe AZ 85287-1504

COWLEY, JOSEPH GILBERT, editor, writer; b. Yonkers, N.Y., Oct. 9, 1923; s. Joseph Gilert and Gertrude Hersey Cowley; m. Ruth Muriel Wilson, Feb. 28, 1948 (div. Nov. 1983); children: Barbara, Charles, Jennifer, Joseph. BA with honors, Columbia U., 1947, MA, 1948. Ptnr. Writing-Editing Svcs., N.Y.C., 1946-47; instr. English, Cornell U., Ithaca, N.Y., 1948-49; salesman Allyn & Bacon, N.Y.C., 1949-54; sales promoter Home Life Ins. Co., N.Y.C., 1954-56; editor, then mng. editor Rsch. Inst. Am., N.Y.C., 1956-82; ret., 1982. Author: Executive Strategist, 1969, Three Novellas, 1998, (novel) Chrysanthemum Garden, 1981, (play) The Stargazers, 1991. 2nd lt. USAAF, 1943-45, ETO. Avocation: reading. Home: 69430 Main Rd Greenport NY 11944

COWLEY, ROBERT WILLIAM, editor, writer, lecturer; b. N.Y.C., Dec. 16, 1934; s. Malcolm and Muriel (Maurer) C.; m. Blair Phillips (div.); children: Elizabeth Blair Roberts, Miranda Phillips Heller; m. Edith Pray Lorillard, June 24, 1978; children: Olivia Lorillard, Savannah Caroline Lorillard. AB, Harvard U., 1956. Assoc. editor Am. Heritage, N.Y.C., 1956-64; mng. editor Sky, N.Y.C., 1964; asst. editor The Reporter, N.Y.C., 1965-66; articles editor, mng. editor Horizon, N.Y.C., 1966-72; co-editor The Saturday Review of the Arts, N.Y.C. and San Francisco, 1972-73; sr. editor, exec. editor Houghton Mifflin, Boston, 1973-77; sr. editor Random House, N.Y.C., 1977-84, Henry Holt, N.Y.C., 1984-88; founding editor, editor-in-chief MHQ: The Quarterly Journal of Military History, N.Y.C., 1988-98; cons., writer, 1998—. Author: The Rulers of Britain, 1982; editor, introducer: Experience of War, 1992; co-editor: (with Malcolm Cowley) Fitzgerald and the Jazz Age, 1966, (with Geoffrey Parker) The Reader's Companion to Military History, 1996; contbg. author: A Weekend with the Great War: Proceedings of the Fourth Annual Great War Inter-Conf. Sem., 1997; editor, contbr. What If?: The World's Foremost Military Historians Imagine What Might Have Been, 1999. Fellow Soc. Am. Historians; mem. Soc. Mil. History. Democrat. Episcopalian. Avocation: jazz collecting, military archaeology. Home: PO Box 268 Sherman CT 06784-0268 Office: Am Hist Publications 29 W 38th St New York NY 10018-5504

COWLING, COLIN DOUGLAS, JR., insurance executive; b. Aug. 28, 1946. BS, Barton Coll., 1973. Pvt. practice. Contbr. articles to local and regional newspapers. Chmn. Northampton County Rep. Party, Va., 1996—; regional vice-chair 1st Dist. Rep. Party, Va., 1996-98; sec. Commonwealth Adv. Commn., Va., 1998—. Home: PO Box 305 Eastville VA 23347-0305

COWLING, JUDY KATHLEEN, historic preservation consultant, nurse; b. Monroe, Mich., July 5, 1954; d. Fred Dietrich and Willie Evelyn (Thompson) Wohlers; m. William Eugene Cowling, May 13, 1974; 1 child, Andrew Robert. AS, Kettering Coll. Med. Arts, 1974; BSN, Ball State U., 1983; MSN, Ind. U., 1985; MS in Hist. Preservation, Ball State U., 1998. RN, Ind., Ohio; cert. Critical Care Nurses Assn. Charge nurse Loma Linda (Calif.) U. Med. Ctr., 1977-80; head nurse Kettering (Ohio) Med. Ctr., 1980-81, clin. sys. analyst, 1981; instr. Ball State U., Muncie, Ind., 1985-89, Ind. Wesleyan U., Marion, Ind., 1989-90; relief charge nurse Marion Gen. Hosp., Marion, Ind., 1990-93; pres., CEO Preservations by Cowling, Fairmount, Ind., 1994—; specialist in hist. preservation, Schmidt Assocs., Inc., 1995—; adv. bd. dirs. Ball State U., Muncie, 1995—. Author: (computer software) Spiritual Care for Nurses, 1987. Pres., bd. dirs. Hist. Fairmount, Inc., 1994—; instr., trainer CPR Am. Heart Assn., Marion, Ind.; vol. Park Elem. Sch., Fairmount, 1991—. Recipient scholarship Southold Restorations, 1995, Sustained Achievement in Preservation award Ball State U., 1998. Mem. Nat. Trust for Hist. Preservation, Royal Oak Soc., Hist. Landmarks Ind. (affiliate coun. 1995—), Sigma Theta Tau (by-laws chair 1988-89), Tau Sigma Delta, Sigma Pi Kappa. Avocations: bicycling, travel, reading, hiking, music. Home: 504 S Main St Fairmount IN 46928-1930 Office: Hist Fairmount Inc PO Box 257 Fairmount IN 46928-0257

COWLISHAW, MARY LOU, state legislator; b. Rockford, Ill., Feb. 20, 1932; d. Donald George and Mildred Corinne (Hayes) Miller; m. Wayne Arnold Cowlishaw, July 24, 1954; children: Beth Cowlishaw McDaniel, John, Paula Cowlishaw Rader. BS in Journalism, U. Ill., 1954; DHL, North Ctrl. Coll., 1999. Mem. editorial staff Naperville (Ill.) Sun newspaper, 1977-83; mem. Ill. Ho. of Reps., Springfield, 1983—, chmn. elem. and secondary edn. com., 1995—, vice-chmn. pub. utilities com., 1995—, mem. joint Ho.-Senate edn. reform oversight com., 1985—; mem. Ill. Task Force on Sch. Fin., 1990—; vice chmn. Ho. Rep. Campaign Com., 1990—; co-chair Ho. Rep. Policy Com., 1991—; chmn. edn. com. Nat. Conf. State Legislatures, 1993—; mem. Joint Com. Adminstrv. Rules, 1992—; commr. Edn. Commn. of the States, 1995—; chair, Ill. Women's Agenda Task Force, 1994—; mem. Nat. Edn. Goals Panel, 1996—, bd. govs. Lincoln Series for Excellence in Pub. Svc., 1996—. Author: This Band's Been Here Quite a Spell, 1983. Mem. Naperville Dist. 203 Bd. Edn., 1972-83; co-chmn. Ill. Citizens Coun. on Sch. Problems, Springfield, 1985—. Recipient 1st pl. award Ill. Press Assn., 1981, commendation Naperville Jaycees, 1986, Golden Apple award Ill. Assn. Sch. Bds., 1988, 90, 92, 94, Outstanding Women Leaders of DuPage County award West Suburban YWCA, 1990, Activator award Ill. Farm Bur., 1996, 1998, Bd. of Dirs. award Little Friends, Inc., 1998; named Best Legislator, Ill. Citizens for Better Care, 1985, Woman of Yr., Naperville AAUW, 1987, Best Legislator, Ill. Assn. Fire Chiefs, 1994, Outstanding Edn. Adv. Indian Prairie Sch. Dist. 204, 1994, Legislator of Yr., Ill. Assn. Pk. Dists., 1995; commr. Edn. Commn. of the States, 1994—; Mary Lou Cowlishaw Elem. Sch. named in her honor, 1997, Legislator of Yr., Ill. Assn. Mus., 1998. Mem. Am. Legis. Exch. Coun., Conf. Women Legislators, Nat. Fedn. Rep. Women, DAR, Naperville Rep. Women's Club (pres. 1994—), Jr. League of Greater DuKane (cmty. adv. bd. 1997—). Methodist. Avocation: the violin. Home: 924 Merrimac Cir Naperville IL 60540-7107 Office: 552 S Washington St Ste 119 Naperville IL 60540-6669

COWPERTHWAITE, JOHN MILTON, JR., architect, construction consultant; b. Bridgeport, Conn., Nov. 3, 1912; s. John Milton Sr. and Anna Emalia (Osterberg) C.; m. Eula Mae Lunny, Sept. 5, 1936; 1 child, John Milton III. Cert., U. Bridgeport, 1944; student, Yale U., 1945. Registered architect, N.Y., Pa., Conn. Project architect Ashiem & Wilkens, Bridgeport, Conn., 1946-47, Lyons & Mather, Bridgeport, 1947-48, Andrew Euston, New Haven, 1949-50, Schilling & Goldbecker, New Haven, 1950-51; co-owner Aubin & Cowperthwaite, Hartford, Conn., 1951-53, Eaton & Cowperthwaite, Stratford, Conn., 1953-55; designer Carl Segerberg, Middltown, Conn., 1955-56; assoc. William Cram, Norwalk, Conn., 1957-59; owner Stratford, 1960—; clk. of works City of Milford, Conn., 1974-76; owner, developer Milton Reed Assoc., Inc., Stratford, 1980—. Mem. Conservation Commn., Stratford, 1970, chmn., 1973-76; mem. Bd. Appeals Bldg. Dept., Stratford, 1975—. Mem. Conn. Soc. Genealogists. Republican. Episcopalian. Clubs: Classic Jaguar Assn. (Calif.) (chartered); Conn. Classic Jaguar Assn. Avocations: sailing, antique English cars. Home and Office: 941 E Broadway Stratford CT 06615-5909

COWSER, DANNY LEE, lawyer, mental health specialist; b. Peoria, Ill., July 7, 1948; s. Albert Paul Cowser and Shirley Mae (Donaldson) Chatten; m. Nancy Lynn Hatch, Nov. 11, 1976; children: Kimberly Catherine Hatch Cowser, Dustin Paul Hatch Cowser. BA, No. Ill. U., 1972, MS, 1975; JD, DePaul U., 1980. Bar: Ill. 1980, Wis. 1981, U.S. Dist. Ct. (no. dist.) Ill. 1981, U.S. Ct. Appeals (7th cir.) 1983, U.S. Dist. Ct. (ea. and we. dists.) Wis. 1984, U.S. Supreme Ct. 1984, Ariz. 1985, U.S. Ct. Appeals (9th cir.) 1987, U.S. Dist. Ct. Ariz. 1989, U.S. Tax Ct. 1990, U.S. Ct. Claims 1990. Adminstr. Ill. Dept. Mental Health, Elgin, 1972-76, psychotherapist, 1976-79; assoc. Slaby, Deda & Henderson, Phillips, Wis., 1982-83; ptnr. Slaby, Deda & Cowser, Phillips, 1983-86; asst. atty. City of Flagstaff, Ariz., 1986-88; pub. defender Coconino County, Flagstaff, 1988-89; pvt. practice Flagstaff, 1989-97; atty. City Park Falls, Wis., 1983-86; spl. dep. Mohave County capital def., 1989-90; instr. speech comms. No. Ariz. U., 1992-93; adminstrv. law judge Ariz. Dept. Econ. Security, 1997—. Bd. dirs. DeKalb County (Ill.) Drug Coun., 1973-75, Counseling and Personal Devel., Phillips, 1985-86, Northland YM-WYCA, 1990-91. Reginald Heber Smith fellow, 1980-81; C.J.S. legal scholar, 1979. Mem. ABA, Ariz. Bar Assn., State Bar Ariz. (cert. specialist in criminal law 1993-98), State Bar Wis., Ill. Bar Assn. Democrat. Avocations: skiing, photography, bicycling. Office: PO Box 22329 Flagstaff AZ 86002-2329

COX, ALBERT EDWARD, pastor; b. Turtle Creek, Pa., Oct. 30, 1935; s. Albert Earl and Naomi (Page) C.; m. Ruth Lynne Gray, July 5, 1958; children: Lynne Ellen Cox Chenot, Lisa Diane Brogardas. BS, Houghton, 1957; BS in Mission, St. Paul Bible, 1958. Ordained to ministry Christian and Missionary Alliance, 1966 and in United Meth. Ch., as deacon, 1971, as elder, 1983. Pastor C&MA, Pa., 1963-68, Cen. Pa. Conf. United Meth. Ch., 1968—. Republican. Home: HC 31 Box 396 Hillsgrove PA 18619

COX, ALBERT HARRINGTON, JR., economist; b. St. Louis, Oct. 13, 1932; s. Albert Harrington and Hildegarde (Raab) C.; m. Frances Marie French, Apr. 12, 1960; children: Cynthia, Bruce Harrington. *Son Bruce H. Cox is Senior Vice President, Investments with Prudential Securities in Atlanta. He and his wife Crystal are the proud parents of Connor (5 years old), Cort (3 years old) and Katherine (1 year old). Daughter Cynthia Cox Ogrey is the mother of Gregory (6) and Reilley (4). She is senior staffing specialist with the Atlanta office of DP Solutions, Inc., a software recruiting firm.* BBA, U. Tex., 1954, MBA, 1956; PhD, U. Mich., 1965. Asst. prof. finance So. Meth. U., Dallas, 1959; economist First Nat. City Bank, N.Y.C., 1960-61; sec. research com. Am. Bankers Assn., N.Y.C., 1962-64; v.p., economist First Nat. Bank, Dallas, 1965-68; spl. asst. to chmn. Pres.'s Council Econ. Advs., Washington, 1969-70; exec. v.p., chief economist, dir. Lionel D. Edie & Co., N.Y.C., 1970-75; sr. econ. adv. Merrill Lynch, Pierce, Fenner & Smith, Inc., N.Y.C., 1970-75; pres. Merrill Lynch Econs., Inc.,

N.Y.C., 1976-81, chmn., 1982-84; chief economist Merrill Lynch & Co., 1976-81; mng. dir. Merrill Lynch Capital Markets Group; dir. Merrill Lynch Capital Fund; mem. econ. adv. bd. Dept. Commerce, 1974-76; dir., sr. econ. adviser BIL Trainer, Wortham Inc. (Bank in Liechtenstein, A.G.), 1985-90; sr. econ. adviser Trainer Wortham, Inc., 1991; portfolio cons. The Seibels Bruce Ins. Cos., Columbia, S.C., 1993-94, dir., 1994-97; chief economist Investment Mgrs., Inc., Hilton Head, S.C., 1999—; mem. Pres.'s Inflation Policy Task Force, 1980; disting. lectr. in bus. and econs. U. S.C., Hilton Head, 1988-90. Author: Regulation of Interest Rates on Bank Deposits, 1966, Coast Business, 1997—; contbg. economist Bankers Monthly mag., 1970-88; bus. columnist Hilton Head News, 1990—; contbr. articles to profl. jours. Mem. Nat. Assn. Bus. Economists (past dir.), Securities Industries Assn. (chmn. econ. adv. com. 1979-80), Am. Econ. Assn., Beta Gamma Sigma, Beta Theta Pi, Phi Eta Sigma. Republican. Mem. Reformed Ch. Home: 2002 Claudette Cv Biloxi MS 39531-2426 Office: The Profl Bldg 2 Corpus Christie Ste 300 Hilton Head Island SC 29928

COX, ALBERT REGINALD, academic administrator, physician, retired; b. Victoria, B.C., Can., Apr. 18, 1928; s. Reginald Herbert and Marie Christina (Fraser) C.; m. Margaret Dobson, May, 1954; children—Susan, David John, Steven Fraser. B.A., U. B.C., 1950, M.D., 1954. Intern Vancouver Gen. Hosp., 1954-55, resident, 1955-59; fellow in cardiology U. Wash., 1959-61; asst. prof. medicine U. B.C., 1962-65, assoc. prof., 1966-69; prof., chmn. medicine Meml. U., St. John's, Nfld., Can., 1969-74, dean medicine, 1974-87, v.p. Health Scis. and Profl. Sch., 1988-90, v.p. acad., pro-vice chancellor, 1990-91; ret., 1991. Decorated mem. Order of Can. Fellow ACP, Royal Coll. Physicians and Surgeons Can., Am. Coll. Cardiology; mem. Nfld. Med. Assn., Can. Med. Assn., Can. Soc. Clin. Investigation, Assn. Can. Med. Colls. (pres. 1980-81), Coun. of Royal Coll. Physicians and Surgeons (v.p. medicine 1990-91), Alpha Omega Alpha. United Ch. Home: 1275 Campbell Rd, Cobble Hill, BC Canada V0R 1L0

COX, ALLAN JAMES, management consultant and sports executive; b. Berwyn, Ill., June 13, 1937; s. Brack C. and Ruby D. C.; m. Jeanne Begalke, 1961 (div. 1966); 1 child, Heather; m. Bonnie Lynne Welden, 1966 (div. 1990); 1 child, Laura; m. Cheryl Patric, 1991. B.A., No. Ill. U., 1961, M.A., 1962; postgrad., McCormick Theol. Sem., Chgo., 1962-63, Alfred Adler Inst. of Chgo., 1965-67, Gestalt Inst. of Chgo., 1994-96. Instr. Wheaton (Ill.) Coll., 1963-65; assoc. Case and Co., Inc., Chgo., 1965-66, Spencer Stuart & Assos., Inc., Chgo., 1966-68; v.p. Westcott Assos., Inc., Chgo., 1968-69; founder, pres. Allan Cox & Assocs., Inc., 1969-98, chmn., CEO, 1998—; chmn. Berryman Comm. Co., Chgo., 1994-98; chmn. of the bd. Amateur Baseball, Inc., Chgo., 1992-96, CEO, 1996-98; chmn., CEO All-Star Baseball, Inc., Chgo., 1996-98, Assn. for Internat. Youth Sports, Inc., Chgo., 1998—; adj. staff Ctr. for Creative Leadership, Greensboro, N.C., 1985-90; mem. vis. com. U. Chgo. Div. Sch. Author: Confessions of a Corporate Headhunter, 1973, Work, Love and Friendship, 1974, The Cox Report on the American Corporation, 1982, The Making of the Achiever, 1985, The Achiever's Profile, 1988, Straight Talk for Monday Morning, 1990, Redefining Corporate Soul: Linking Purpose and People, 1996; contbr. articles to profl. jours. Chmn. bd. Ctr. for Ethics and Corp. Policy, 1987-92; Elder Fourth Presbyn. Ch. of Chgo. Mem. Am. Sociol. Assn., N.Am. Soc. Adlerian Psychology, Midwest Human Resources Planners Group, Human Resources Planning Soc., Alpha Kappa Delta. Presbyterian. Club: Chgo. Office: 400 N Michigan Ave Ste 1016 Chicago IL 60611-4289

COX, AMIE C., publisher; b. 1956. BA, Auburn U., 1979; MA, U. West Fla., 1981. Editl. intern Nat. Geog. Soc., Washington, 1980; asst. to pub. Hyatt Regency Mag., New Orleans, 1981-82; assoc. editor Scuba Times Mag., Pensacola, Fla., 1982-83; graphic artist Dodson Craddock & Born Advt., Pensacola, 1983-85; mng. editor, art dir. Marlin Mag. of Marlin Internat., Pensacola, 1985-86; owner Pre-Press Svc. for Publs., Pensacola, 1986-87; art dir. Bassmaster Mag., Montgomery, Ala., 1987-89, Dutchess Mag. and Orange Mag. for Dutchess & Orange Counties, N.Y., 1989-92; owner VERSA Publs. and Coxswain Press, Hudson, N.Y., 1992—. Vol. coord. Cmty. Garden Horticulture Classes, Hudson, Environ. Rsch. Projects, Hudson. Recipient Columbia County N.Y. Good Earth Keeping award Environ. Mgmt. Coun. Mem. Sigma Tau Delta, Tau Sigma Delta. Office: VERSA Publs PO Box 739 Hudson NY 12534-0739 also: PO Box 30252 Pensacola FL 32503-1252

COX, ANNA LEE, retired administrative assistant; b. Knoxville, Tenn., Feb. 18, 1931; d. Carter Calloway and Fairy Belle (Byers) Bayless; m. William Smith Cox, Sept. 4, 1952; 1 child, Catherine Anne Cox Faust. Grad. high sch., Knoxville. Sec. Am. Mut. Liability Ins. Co., Knoxville, 1948-53; flight procedures clk. FAA, Atlanta, 1963-66; legal sec., paralegal U.S. Atty.'s Office for Dist. S.C., Greenville, 1972-79; sec. criminal investigation div. IRS, Knoxville, 1981-84; sec., adminstrv. asst. CIA, Knoxville, 1984-88; adminstrv. asst. U.S. Dept. Def., Knoxville, 1988-91, ret., 1991. Tutor Greenville Literacy Assn., 1977-79; founder, dir. NATO Womens Chorus, Izmir, Turkey, 1969-71; choir dir., pres. United Meth. Women, Stephenson Meml. United Meth. Ch., Greenville, 1972-79; bd. dirs. Fountainhead Conservatory Music, Knoxville, 1983-85, 92-95, sec. of bd. dirs., 1994-95; singer Knoxville Choral Soc., 1955-56, Atlanta Symphony Chorus, 1971, Greenville Civic Chorale, 1973-79; vol. Ch. and Knoxville Mus. Art, 1992—. Republican. Avocations: music, drama. Home: 619 Farragut Commons Dr Knoxville TN 37922-1673

COX, ARCHIBALD, lawyer, educator; b. Plainfield, N.J., May 17, 1912; s. Archibald and Frances Bruen (Perkins) C.; m. Phyllis Ames, June 12, 1937; children—Sally, Archibald, Phyllis. A.B., Harvard U., 1934, LL.B., 1937, LL.D. (hon.), 1975; LL.D. (hon.), Loyola U., Chgo., 1964, U. Cin., 1967, U. Denver, 1974, Amherst Coll., 1974, Rutgers U., 1974, Mich. State U., 1976, Wheaton Coll., 1977, Northeastern U., 1978, Clark U., 1980; L.H.D. (hon.), Hahnemann Med. Coll., 1980, U. Mass., 1981, Georgetown U., 1988. Bar: Mass. 1937. Gen. practice law Ropes, Gray, Best, Coolidge & Rugg, Boston, 1938-41; atty. Office of Solicitor Gen., U.S. Dept. Justice, 1941-43, solicitor gen., 1961-65; assoc. solicitor Dept. Labor, 1943-45; lectr. law Harvard U., 1945-46, prof. law, 1946-61, Williston prof. law, 1965-76, Carl M. Loeb U. prof., 1976-84, prof. emeritus, 1984—; vis. prof. Boston U., 1985-97; spl. investigator cases Mass. Legislature, 1972; dir. Office Watergate Spl. Prosecution Force, Washington, 1973; Co-chmn. Constrn. Industry Stblzn. Com., 1951-52; chmn. Wage Stablzn. Bd., 1952. Author: Cases on Labor Law, 1948, 12th edit., 1976, 11th edit. (with Derek C. Bok, Robert Gorman and Mathew W. Finkin), 1981, Law and the National Labor Policy, 1960, (with Mark DeWolfe Howe, J.R. Wiggins) Civil Rights, the Constitution and the Courts, 1967, The Warren Court, 1968, The Role of the Supreme Court in American Government, 1976, Freedom of Expression, 1981, The Court and the Constitution, 1987. Mem. bd. overseers Harvard U., 1962-65. Mem. ABA, Am. Acad. Arts and Scis., Common Cause (chmn. 1980-92), Health Effects Inst. (chmn. 1985—). Office: Harvard Law School Cambridge MA 02138

COX, ARCHIBALD, JR., investment banker; b. Wayland, Mass., July 13, 1940; s. Archibald and Phyllis (Ames) C.; m. Jean Inge, Aug. 20, 1977; children: Suzanne, Archibald III, Christopher. Pres., CEO The First Boston Corp., N.Y.C., 1990-93; chmn. Sextant Group, Inc., N.Y.C., 1993—; vice chmn., pres. Magnequench Internat., Inc., Anderson, Ind., 1995—; bd. dirs. Hutchinson Tech. Inc., Harris Chem. Group. Bd. dirs. Claremont McKenna Coll., 1992-97. Mem. Internat. Primary market Assn. (vice-chmn. 1984-86), Securities and Investments Bd. Ltd. (bd. dirs. 1986-88, Securities Industry Assn. (bd. dirs. 1990-93), N.Y. Yacht Club, Links Club N.Y.C. Avocations: bicycling, sailing. Office: c/o Magnequench 6435 Scatterfield Rd Anderson IN 46103-9606 Office: Sextant Group Inc 630 5th Ave Ste 3240 New York NY 10111-0100*

COX, BARBARA CLAIRE, costume designer, educator; b. Lock Haven, Pa., Apr. 4, 1939; d. Albert Clair and June Anna (Hutchins) Shultz; m. Richard Joseph Cox, Aug. 28, 1960 (div. 1970). BA, SUNY, Albany, 1961; student, Brandeis U., 1961, Cornell U., 1961-68; MFA, Carnegie-Mellon U., 1970. Mem. faculty Stanford U., Palo Alto, Calif., 1970-73; costume dir. Utah Shakespearean Festival, Cedar City, Utah, 1970-81; costume designer Alley Theatre, Houston, 1973-76; mem. faculty dept. theatre arts Calif. State U., Long Beach, 1976-81; costume designer South Coast Repertory Theatre, Costa Mesa, Calif., 1978-82; mem. faculty dance and theatre arts U. North Tex., Denton, 1988—; costume designer Dallas Shakespeare, 1991, Theatre L'Homme Dieu, 1997, Grand Canyon Shakespeare Festival, 1998; owner Barbara C. Cox Designs, 1978—. costume dir. Circle Theatre, Ft. Worth, 1989—. Bd. dirs. Denton Civic Ballet, 1997—, Denton Light Opera Co. Recipient Excellence in Costume Design award Los Angeles Drama Critics Circle, 1982, Costume Design awards Drama Logue, Los Angeles, 1982-88, LA Weekly, 1985-88. Mem. AAUP, AAUW, U.S. Inst. Theatre Tech., Costume Soc. Am., United Scenic Artists. Avocations: reading, gardening, needlework, photography, cats. Home: 716 Thomas St Denton TX 76201-2447 Office: Univ N Tex Dept Dance Theatre Arts Denton TX 76203

COX, BEVERLY E., educational researcher, educator; b. Dearborn, Mich.; d. Glenn F. and Mildred E. (Prosser) Griffin; m. Clifford E. Cox; children: Denise, Marc, Robert. AB, U. Mich., 1968; EdM, U. Rochester, 1974; PhD, Northwestern U., Evanston, Ill., 1987. Tchr. Dearborn (Mich.) Pub. Schs., 1968-69, West Irondequoit (N.Y.) Pub. Schs., 1969-72; tchr., team leader, coord. elem. Plano (Tex.) Pub. Schs., 1973-80; writer, cons. Ctr. for Study Reading U. Ill., Champaign, 1982-85; assoc. prof. Purdue U. Sch. of Edn., West Lafayette, Ind., 1987—; dir. Student Literacy Corps Project; sr. researcher Developing Literacy; primary investigator Funded Literacy Devel. Projects, 1991, 94-95. Contbr. chpts. to books and articles to profl. jours. Witty fellow, 1983-84. Mem. Nat. Reading Conf. (field coun. rep.), Am. Ednl. Rsch. Assn., Ind. Adult Literacy Coalition (rsch. coun.), Internat. Reading Assn., Nat. Coun. Rsch. English, Nat. Coun. Tchrs. English, Internat. Systemics Congress, Soc. for Sci. Study of Reading, Ind. State Reading Assn. (studies and rsch. com.), Kappa Delta Pi, Phi Kappa Phi, Alpha Upsilon Alpha. Office: Purdue U Sch Edn 1442 Liberal Arts Educ Bldg West Lafayette IN 47907-1442

COX, BOBBY (ROBERT JOE COX), professional baseball manager; b. Tulsa, Okla., May 21, 1941; m. Pamela Cox; children: Kami, Keisha, Skyla. Student, Reedley Jr. Coll., Calif. Player Calif. League, Reno, Nev., 1960, Northwest League, Salem, Oreg., 1961-62, Texas League, Albuquerque, 1963-64; player Pacific Coast League, Salt Lake City, 1965, Tacoma, Wash., 1966; player Internat. League, Richmond, Va., 1967, New York Yankees, N.Y.C., 1968-69, Internat. League, Syracuse, N.Y., 1970; player Fla. State League, Ft. Lauderdale, 1971, mgr., 1971; mgr. Ea. League, West Haven, Conn., 1972, Internat. League, Syracuse, 1973-76; 1st base coach New York Yankees, N.Y.C., 1977; mgr. Atlanta Braves, 1978-81, Toronto (Ont., Can.) Blue Jays, 1982-85, Atlanta Braves, 1990—. Named Maj. League Mgr. of Yr., Baseball Writers' Assn. Am., 1985, Nat. League Mgr. of Yr., 1991; Maj. League Mgr. of Yr. Sporting News, 1985, Nat. League Mgr. of Yr., 1991, 93. Mgr. Nat. League championship team, 1991-92, 95, World Series championship team, 1995. Office: care Atlanta Braves PO Box 4064 Atlanta GA 30302-4064*

COX, CAROL A., oncological nurse; b. N.C., Dec. 3, 1954. ADN, Miami (Fla.) Dade Community Coll., 1986; BSN, Fla. Internat. U., 1994. Fl. nurse Coral Reef Hosp., Miami; charge nurse, relief supr. Green Briar Nursing Ctr., Miami; charge nurse crisis unit CHI, Miami; supr. nursing Criticare Home Health, Miami; oncology staff nurse Bapt. Hosp., Miami, 1990—; nursing instr. part-time Miami Dade Cmty. Coll., 1995—; oncology staff nurse Bapt. Hosp., Miami, 1990-97; psychiat. nurse Doral Palm, Miami, 1998-99; emergency room nurse S. Miami Hosp., Miami, 1998—; instr. nursing Miami Dade C.C., 1995-99.

COX, CATHY, state official; b. Bainbridge, Ga.. A.Agr., Abraham Baldwin Agrl. Coll., 1978; BJ, U. Ga., 1980; JD with honors, Mercer U., 1986. Newspaper reporter The Times, Gainesville, Post-Searchlight, Bainbridge; police reporter Gainesville; atty. various firms Atlanta, Bainbridge, 1986-95; mem. Dist. 160 Ga. Gen. Assembly, 1993-96; asst. sec. of state State of Ga., Atlanta, sec. of state, 1999—. Editor Mercer U. Law Rev. Named Conservation Legislator of the Yr., Ga. Wildlife Fedn., 1994, Woman of Courage award Woman's Policy Group, 1995; recipient Ga. Press Assn. award for coverage of unsolved murder. Democrat. Methodist. Office: Office of Secretary of State State Capitol Rm 214 Atlanta GA 30334*

COX, CHAPMAN BEECHER, lawyer, corporate executive; b. Dayton, Ohio, July 31, 1940; s. Charles Benjamin and Jewel Lorene (Nicholson) C.; m. Jeannette Gail Korody, Aug. 28, 1964; children: Charles Benjamin, Andrew David. BA, U. So. Calif., 1962; JD, Harvard U., 1965. Bar: Calif. 1966, Colo. 1972, U.S. Ct. Mil. Appeals 1966, U.S. Supreme Ct. 1986. Assoc. Adams, Duque & Hazeltine, Los Angeles, 1968-72; assoc. Sherman & Howard, Denver, 1972-74, ptnr., 1974-80, mng. ptnr., 1980-81, ptnr., 1987-90; dep. asst. sec. U.S. Dept. Navy, Washington, 1981-83, asst. sec., 1983-84; gen. counsel Dept. Def., Washington, 1984-85; asst. sec. Dept. Def., 1985-87; pres., chief exec. officer United Svc. Orgns., Inc., 1990-96; sr. v.p. Lockheed Martin IMS, 1996—; vis. lectr. U. Colo. Sch. Law, Boulder, 1977-78; mem. def. policy bd. U.S. Dept. Def., 1988-90; mem. comml. space transp. adv. com. U.S. Dept. Transp., 1989-91; chmn. Colo. Commn. Space Sci. and Industry, 1988-90. Gen. counsel Colo. Reps., Denver, 1977-81; del. U.S. Dept. State cultural exch. mission to Syria and Jordan, 1979; ruling elder Presbyn. Ch., 1976—; bd. dirs. United Svc. Orgns., 1985-96, Colorado Springs Symphony Orch., 1988-90, MicroLithics Corp., 1989-91; bd. dirs. Presbyn. Ch. U.S.A. Found., 1990-99, Freedoms Found., 1994-99, Fund for Am. Studies, 1995—, New Covenant Trust Co., 1996-99, Presbyn. Lay Com., 1997—. Col. USMCR, 1962-93, ret. Fellow Am. Coll. Trust and Estate Counsel; m. ABA (standing com. law and nat. security 1988—), Calif. Bar Assn., Colo. Bar Assn. (bd. govs. 1977-79, chmn. probate and trust law sect. 1978-79), Army-Navy Club of Washington, Capitol Hill Club (Washington). Office: Lockheed Martin IMS 1200 K St NW Fl 11 Washington DC 20005-4029

COX, CHARLES C., economist; b. Missoula, Mont., May 8, 1945; m. Monica Lewis, 1984. BA magna cum laude, U. Wash., 1967; AM, U. Chgo., 1970, PhD, 1975. Asst. prof. econs. Ohio State U., Columbus, 1972-80; nat. fellow Hoover Instn., 1977-78; asst. prof. mgmt. Tex. A&M U., College Station, 1980-82; chief economist SEC, Washington, 1982-83, commr., 1983-89, acting chmn., 1987; prin., sr. v.p. Lexecon, Inc., Chgo., 1989—. Nat. fellow Hoover Institution, 1977-78. Mem. Am. Econ. Assn., United Shareholders Assn. (chmn. 1990-93), Mt. Pelerin Soc., Phi Beta Kappa. Office: Lexecon Inc 332 S Michigan Ave Ste 1300 Chicago IL 60604-4397

COX, CHARLES SHIPLEY, oceanography researcher, educator; b. Paia, Hawaii, Sept. 11, 1922; s. Joel Bean and Helen Clifford (Horton) C.; m. Maryruth Louise Melander, Dec. 23, 1951; children: Susan (dec.), Caroline, Valerie, Ginger, Joel. BS, Calif. Inst. Tech., 1944; PhD, U. Calif., San Diego, 1955. From asst. researcher to prof. U. Calif., San Diego, 1955—. Researcher in field. Fellow AAAS, NAS, Am. Geophys. Union (Maurice Ewing medal 1992), Royal Astron. Soc. Democrat. Office: U Calif San Diego Scripps Inst Oceanography Dept Oceanography La Jolla CA 92093-0230

COX, (CHARLES) CHRISTOPHER, congressman; b. St. Paul, Oct. 16, 1952; s. Charles C. and Marilyn A. (Miller) C.; m. Rebecca Gernhardt; children: Charles, Kathryn, Kevin. BA, U. So. Calif., 1973; MBA, JD, Harvard U., 1977. Bar: Calif. 1978, D.C. 1980. Law clk. to judge U.S. Ct. Appeals (9th cir.), 1977-78; assoc. Latham & Watkins, Newport Beach, Calif., 1978-82; lectr. bus. adminstrn. Harvard U., 1982-83; ptnr. Latham & Watkins, Newport Beach, Calif., 1984-86; sr. assoc. counsel to the Pres. The White House, Washington, 1986-88; mem. 101st-106th Congresses from 40th (now 47th) dist. Calif., Washington, 1986-87; mem. commerce com., steering com. U.S. Ho. of Reps., Washington, 1995—, chmn. select com. U.S. nat. security, mil./comml. concerns with the People's Republic of China, 1998—, chmn. house policy com., 1998—; mem. Bipartisan Commn. on Entitlement and Tax Reform, Washington, 1994—; prin., founder Context Corp., St. Paul, 1984-88. Editor Harvard Law Rev., 1975-77. Roman Catholic. Office: 1 Newport Place Dr Ste 420 Newport Beach CA 92660-2412 Office: US Ho of Reps 2402 Rayburn HOB Washington DC 20515-0547

COX, CLAIR EDWARD, II, urologist, medical educator; b. Lawrenceville, Ill., Sept. 2, 1933; s. Clair Edward and May E. (Judy) C.; m. Clarice Wicks, Aug. 23, 1958; children—Clair Edward III, Daniel Paul, Kevin Christopher, Kenneth Harold. Student, U. Mich., 1951-54, M.D., 1958. Diplomate: Am. Bd. Urology. Intern U. Colo. Med. Center, Denver, 1958-59; surg. resident U. Colo. Med. Center, 1959-60; resident urology U. Cal. Med. Center at San Francisco, 1960-63; mem. faculty Bowman Gray Sch. Medicine, Wake Forest U., Winston Salem, N.C., 1963-72; assoc. prof. Bowman Gray Sch. Medicine, Wake Forest U., 1967-70, prof. urology, 1970-72; prof., chmn. dept. urology U. Tenn. Med. Sch., Memphis, 1972—. Contbr. profl. jours. Fellow ACS; mem. AMA, Am. Assn. Genito-Urinary Surgeons, Am. Urol. Assn., Internat. Soc. Urology, N.Y. Acad. Scis., Infectious Disease Soc. Am., Soc. Univ. Urologists, Am. Assn. Med. Colls., Am. Soc. Microbiology. Achievements include research in urinary tract infectious disease. Home: 6011 Sweetbriar Cv Memphis TN 38120-2514

COX, CLIFFORD ERNEST, business executive former school administrator; b. Chgo., Apr. 28, 1942; s. Clifford Ernest and Beulah May (Lynn) C.; m. Scenobia Butler, June 20, 1964; children: Clifford, Fred, Sean. BA, U. Chgo., 1964, MBA, 1966; postgrad., No. Ill. U., 1988—. Cert. in data processing. Sr. systems engr. IBM, Chgo., 1966-69; v.p. MIS Golden Fifty Pharm., Chgo., 1969-71; sr. mgr. Arthur Andersen & Co., Chgo., 1971-79; pres. Cenox Systems, Inc., Chgo., 1979-81, 97—; chief info. officer Chgo. Pub. Schs., 1981-92; deputy supt. Detroit Pub. Schs., 1992-97; pres. Cenox Sys. Am., Cleve., 1998—; lectr. Keller Grad Sch. Mgmt., 1986-89; del. Ill. Regional White House conf., 1990. Contbr. articles to profl. jours. Bd. dirs. Assn. House, Chgo., 1991; mem. Chgo. Assembly. Home: 11457 Mayfield Rd Apt 1057 Cleveland OH 44106-5910 Office: Cenox Sys 11457 Mayfield Rd Ste 1058 Cleveland OH 44106-5910

COX, CLIFFORD LAIRD, university administrator, musician; b. New Kensington, Pa., Jan. 30, 1935; s. James Howard and Clara Pearl (Alderton) C.; m. Joanne Hill, Aug. 9, 1958; children: Lisa McKay, Bethany Jennings. BS in Music Edn., Indiana U., 1956, MEd, 1958, MusM, 1968; postgrad., SUNY, Buffalo, 1968-79. Tchr. Indiana Pub. Schs., 1956-68; prof. music U. Pa., Edinboro, 1968-82, dean sch. music, 1982-83, assoc. v.p., 1983-86, exec. asst. to pres., 1986—; bd. dirs. Nat. Bank NE, Pa., dir. N.E. Bankcorp Univ. Svcs. Inc., Edinboro; musician throughout U.S., 1956—; permanent guest conductor to Shandong Provincial Symphony Orch., Jinan, China. Composer: The Cynic (opera), 1956, PSI, 1961. Danforth Found. assoc., St. Louis, 1976; recipient Excellence in Teaching award Commonwealth of Pa., Harrisburg, 1979. Mem. Am. Fedn. Musicians. Republican. Presbyterian. Avocations: reading, aviation. Home: 222 Fairway Dr Edinboro PA 16412-2442 Office: U Pa Reeder Hall Edinboro PA 16444

COX, COURTENEY, actress; b. Birmingham, Ala., June 15, 1964; d. Richard Lewis and Courteney (Bass-Copland) C. Appearances include (music video) Bruce Springsteen's Dancing in the Dark, 1984; (TV series) Murder, She Wrote, 1984, Misfits of Science, 1985-86, Family Ties, 1987-88, Dream On, 1990, Seinfeld, 1990, The Larry Sanders Show, 1992, The Trouble with Larry, 1993, Friends, 1994—; (TV pilots) Sylvan in Paradise, 1986; (TV movies) If It's Tuesday, It Still Must Be Belgium, 1987, A Rockport Christmas, 1988, Roxanne: The Prize Pulitzer, 1989, Judith Krantz's Till We Meet Again, 1989, Curiosity Kills, 1990, Morton and Hays, 1991, Topper, 1992, Sketch Artist II: Hands That See, 1995; (feature films) Down Twisted, 1986, Masters of the Universe, 1987, Cocoon: The Return, 1988, Mr. Destiny, 1990, Blue Desert, 1990, Shaking the Tree, 1992, The Opposite Sex (and How to Live with Them), 1993, Ace Ventura, Pet Detective, 1994, Scream, 1996, Commandments, 1996, Scream 2, 1997, The Runner, 1999, Alien Love Triangle, 1999, Scream 3, 1999. Office: Creative Artists Agy care Brandt Joel 9830 Wilshire Blvd Beverly Hills CA 90212-1825*

COX, COURTLAND, minority business administrator; b. N.Y.C., Jan. 27, 1941; married; 1 child. Student, Howard U. Co-owner, mgr. Drum and Spear Bookstore, Drum and Spear Pubs.; spl. asst. to dep. mayor for econ. devel. D.C. Govt., dir. Minority Bus. Opportunity Commn., dir. Office of Internat. Bus.; spl. asst. to dep. asst. sec. for Africa, Near East and Sout Dept. of Commerce, Washington, 1993, dir. Office of Civil Rights,, 1994, dir. Minority Bus. Devel. Agy., 1998—; bus. con. drafting D.C. Small, Minority and Disadvantaged Bus. Legislation. Office: Dept of Commerce Minority Bus Devel Agy 14th and Coinstitution NW Washington DC 20230

COX, DANIEL T., management consultant; m. Mary Beth Cos; children: Daniel, Sandra, Christopher. BA in Econs. with highest honors, U. N.C.; MA in Econs., Vanderbilt U. Mgr. R&D Genesco, Inc.; pres. Cox, Black and Assocs.; mng. dir. William M. Mercer-Meidinger, Inc., Chgo.; exec. v.p. Aon Corp., Chgo., 1986—; chmn. Aon Cons. Worldwide; pres. Miller Mason & Dickenson, 1987—. Bd. dirs. Children's Meml. Hosp., Lincoln Park Zool. Soc.; bd. visitors Kenan-Flagler Bus. Sch. Corning Glass traveling fellow. Mem. Soc. Actuaries, Am. Acad. Actuaries. Office: Aon Cons Worldwide 123 N Wacker Dr Ste 1000 Chicago IL 60606

COX, DAVID ALAN, superintendent of schools; b. Kingsport, Tenn., Feb. 8, 1961; s. J. Ralph and Wilma Bernice (Blair) C.; m. Penny Kay Comer, Oct. 6, 1984; children: Andrew Ryan, Mary Kathryn. B in Music Edn., East Tenn. State U., 1984, MEd, 1987, EdD, 1994. Cert. sch. adminstr., Kans., Tenn., Va. Dir. choral music Appomattox County (Va.) H.S., 1984-85; dir. bands Rogersville (Tenn.) Mid. Sch., 1985-89; asst. prin. Church Hill (Tenn.) Mid. Sch., 1989-93; interim dir. bands Dobyns-Bennet H.S., Kingsport, 1993-94; prin. Linn Elem. Sch., Dodge City, Kans., 1994-97; asst. supt. for curriculum and instrn. Unified Sch. Dist. 443, Dodge City, 1997-99; supt. schs. Pulaski County Pub. Schs., Pulaski, Va., 1999—. Vestryman St. Cornelius Episcopal Ch., Dodge City, 1995-98; treas Hawkins County (Tenn.) Young Reps., 1988; bd. dirs. Dodge City Area Cmty. Found. Named one of Outstanding Young Men Am., 1986. Mem. ASCD, Internat. Reading Assn., Dodge City C. of C. (bus. edn. roundtable 1997), Am. Assn. Sch. Adminstrs., United Sch. Adminstrs., Optimists, Rotary, Phi Delta Kappa, Phi Mu Alpha Sinfonia (v.p., pres., collegiate province rep. 1979-97). Avocations: gardening, church choir, camping, cooking, fitness. Home: 1234 Collins Dr Pulaski VA 24301-3506 Office: Pulaski County Sch Bd 44 3d St Pulaski VA 24301

COX, DAVID JACKSON, biochemistry educator; b. N.Y.C., Dec. 22, 1934; s. Reavis and Rachel (Dunaway) C.; m. Joan M. Narbeth, Sept. 6, 1958 (dec. Oct. 8, 1982); children: Andrew Reavis, Matthew Bruce, Thomas Jackson; m. Tamara L. Compton, Nov. 26, 1983. B.A., Wesleyan U., 1956; Ph.D., U. Pa., 1960. Instr. biochemistry U. Wash., 1960-63; asst. prof. chemistry U. Tex., 1963-67, assoc. prof., 1967-73; prof., head dept. biochemistry Kans. State U., 1973-89; prof. chemistry Ind. U./Purdue U., Ft. Wayne, 1989—; vis. prof. U. Va., 1970-71; dean arts scis. Ind. U./Purdue U., Ft. Wayne, 1989-96. NSF predoctoral fellow, 1956-59; NSF sr. postdoctoral fellow, 1970-71. Mem. AAAS, Am. Soc. Biol. Chemists, Am. Chem. Soc., Phi Beta Kappa, Sigma Xi. Democrat. Presbyterian. Home: 5010 Tacoma Ave Fort Wayne IN 46807-3110 Office: Ind U Purdue U Dept Chemistry Fort Wayne IN 46805

COX, DAVID LEON, telecommunications company executive; b. Lima, Ohio, Sept. 8, 1952; s. Leon Hamiln and Mildred Marie (Johnson) C.; m. Carolle Marie Mallette, July 17, 1978; children: Paul David, Elizabeth Christine. BS in Chemistry, Mich. State U., 1975, BS in Computer Sci., 1976. Registered profl. engr., Va. Asst. v.p. engring. KollMorgan Corp., Newburgh, N.Y., 1975-76; staff mgr. AT&T, Bedminster, N.J., 1976-79; asst. v.p. Satellite Bus. Systems, McLean, Va., 1979-83; devel. mgr. MCI, Washington, 1983-84; chief engr. Harris Corp., Melbourne, Fla., 1984-95; asst. dir. GTE, Rockville, Md., 1997—; dir. GTE, Irving, Tex., 1998—; advisor Pres.'s Commn. on Critical Infrastructure Protection, 1996—; cons. Pres.'s Nat. Security Telecomm. Adv. Com., 1995—; mem. Pres.'s Commn. on Crit. Infrastructure Protection, advisor, 1996—, Pres.'s Nat. Security Telecomms. adv. com., cons., 1995—; bd. dirs. GTE, Irving, Tex. Contbr. articles to profl. jours. Active Friends of the Palm Bay (Fla.) Libr., Space Coast Sci. Ctr., 1000 Friends of Fla., Tallahassee, Turkey Creek Homeowners Assn., Turkey Creek Santuary Bd., Palm Bay PTA; vice chmn. pub. rels. Boy Scouts of Am., 1991—, dist. com. mem., 1991—, unit commr., 1990—, troop com. mem., 1992—, park com. mem., 1987—; mem. Comprehensive Plan Com., Palm Bay, Fla., 1986-87. Mem. IEEE, Am. Chem. Soc., Am. Inst. Plant Engrs., Mensa, Assn. for Computing Machinery, N.Y. Acad. Sci., Nat. Fire Protection Assn., Building Industry Cons. Svc. Internat., Am. Radio Relay League, Nat. Eagle Scout Assn. (life), Nat. Coun. Boy Scouts of Am., Mich. State U. Alumni Assn., Lyman Briggs Coll. Alumni Assn., Mason (3d deg.), Orlando Scottish Rite (32nd deg., Master of Royal Secret), Alpha Phi Omega (Beta Beta chpt.). Republican. Presbyterian. Achievements include 6 patents in Integrated Services Digital Network technology. Office: GTE

700 Hidden Ridge Irving TX 75038 Address: GTE-Romania 65 High Ridge Rd Stamford CT 06905-3806

COX, DENNIS E., photographer; b. Greencastle, Ind., Nov. 15, 1946; s. Paul E. and Mildred (Thompson) C.; m. Nancy Ruhl, Apr. 20, 1976 (div. Jan. 1991); children: Alicia, Colin; m. Jialin Nie Cox, Nov. 20, 1993; 1 child, Anqing Dong. BS, Western Mich. U., 1968. Owner D.E. Cox Photography, Ann Arbor, Mich., 1977—; owner/dir. D.E. Cox Photo Libr., Ann Arbor, 1993—, ChinaStock, Ann Arbor, 1993—, China Photo Workshop Tours, Ann Arbor, 1981-96, Photo Explorer Tours, Ann Arbor, 1996—. Author/photographer: Detroit Today, 1992; photographer: Michigan, Graphic Arts Center, 1993, China, The Child's World, 1998. Recipient Award of Excellence, Comm. Arts, 1984. Mem. Soc. Am. Travel Writers (Travel Photographer of the Yr. 1997), Am. Soc. of Media Photographers, Am. Soc. Picture Profls. Home and office: 2506 Country Vlg Ann Arbor MI 48103-6500

COX, DONALD CLYDE, electrical engineering educator; b. Lincoln, Nebr., Nov. 22, 1937; s. Elvin Clyde and C. Gertrude (Thomas) C.; m. Mary Dale Alexander, Aug. 27, 1961; children: Bruce Dale, Earl Clyde. BS, U. Nebr., 1959, MS, 1960, DSc (hon.), 1983; PhD, Stanford U., 1968. Registered profl. engr., Ohio, Nebr. With Bell Tel. Labs., Holmdel, N.J., 1968-84, head radio and satellite systems rsch. dept., 1983-84; mgr. radio and satellite systems rsch. divsn. Bell Comm. Rsch., Red Bank, N.J., 1984-91, exec. dir. radio rsch. dept., 1991-93; prof. elec. engring. Stanford (Calif.) U., 1993—, Harald Trap Friis Prof. Engring., 1994—, dir. telecomms., 1993—; em. commns. U.S. nat. com. Internat. Union of Radio Sci.; participant enbanc hearing on Personal Comm. Sys., FCC, 1991. Contbr. articles to profl. jours.; patentee in field. 1st lt. USAF, 1960-63. Johnson fellow, 1959-60; recipient Guglielmo Marconi prize in Electromagnetic Waves Propagation, Inst. Internat. Comm., 1983. Fellow IEEE (Morris E. Leeds award 1985, Alexander Graham Bell medal 1993), AAAS, Bellcore 1991, Radio Club Am.; mem. NAE, Comm. Soc. of IEEE (Leonard G. Abraham Prize Paper award 1992, Comms. Mag. Prize Paper award 1990), Vehicular Tech. Soc. of IEEE (Paper of Yr. award 1983), Antennas and Propagation Soc. of IEEE (elected mem. adminstrn. com. 1986-88), Sigma Xi. Achievements include rsch. in low-power wireless personal portable communication systems, cellular radio systems, radio propagation. Home: 924 Mears Ct Stanford CA 94305-1029 Office: Stanford U Dept Elec Engring Durand 305 Stanford CA 94305-9515

COX, DOUGLAS LYNN, financial corporation executive; b. Des Moines, Dec. 13, 1945; s. Carol Eugene and Maribelle (Harter) C.; m. Janice C. Kuchka, Nov. 15, 1969; children: David Michael, Kristen Anne. BS, U. Pa., 1968, MBA, 1973. With IU Internat. Corp., Phila., 1974-88, treas. assoc. long-term fin., 1974-76, sr. treas. assoc. internat. fin., 1976-77, mgr. internat. fin., 1977-79, dir. treas. planning, 1979-80, asst. treas., 1980-85, v.p., treas., 1985-88; sr. v.p. fin., CFO Elf Atochem N.Am., Phila., 1988-98; exec. v.p., CFO Opinion Rsch. Corp., Princeton, 1998—. Class gift com. U. Pa.; bd. dirs., treas. Big Bros./Big Sisters; treas. Old Pine St. Presbyn. Ch.; bd. govs. Pa. Econ. League; trustee Friends Select Sch., 1989—, pres. bd. trustees, 1992—; bd. dirs. Pa. Bus. Roundtable. With USCG, 1969-72. Decorated Gallantry Cross (Vietnam). Mem. Phila. Racquet Club, Phi Kappa Sigma. Home: 1220 Rodman St Philadelphia PA 19147-1130 Office: Opinion Rsch Corp PO Box 183 Princeton NJ 08542-0183

COX, EMMETT RIPLEY, federal judge; b. Cottonwood, Ala., Feb. 13, 1935; s. Emmett M. Cox, Jr. and Myra E. (Ripley) Stewart; m. Ann MacKay Haas, May 16, 1964; children: John Haas, Catherine MacKay. BA, U. Ala., 1957, JD, 1959. Bar: Ala. 1959, U.S. Ct. Appeal (5th, 8th and 11th cirs.), U.S. Supreme Ct. Assoc. Mead, Norman & Fitzpatrick, Birmingham, Ala., 1959-64; assoc. then ptnr. Gaillard, Wilkins, Smith & Cox, Mobile, Ala., 1964-69; ptnr. Nettles, Cox & Barker, 1969-81; judge U.S. Dist. Ct. (so. dist.) Ala., Mobile, 1981-88, U.S. Ct. Appeals (11th cir.), Mobile, 1988—; mem. def. svcs. com. Jud. Conf. U.S. Mem. Ala. Bar Assn., Mobile Bar Assn., Fed. Bar Assn., Maritime Law Assn. of the U.S., Omicron Delta Kappa, Phi Delta Phi, Alpha Tau Omega (past pres.). Office: US Courthouse 11th Circuit 113 Saint Joseph St Ste 433 Mobile AL 36602-3624

COX, ERIC FREDERICK, writer, book reviewer; b. Balt., July 20, 1932; s. Cecil Rhodes and Elvira Viola (Bile) C. BA, Dickinson Coll., 1954. In real estate bus. Cox and Co., Washington, 1954-66; exec. dir. Washington Metro. chpt. United World Federalists, 1966-68; radio program host WAMU-FM, Washington, 1966-68; projects. dir. Bronx Community Coll., Bronx, N.Y., 1969-72; cons. N.Y.C., 1972-74; exec. dir. Campaign for U.N. Reform, Wayne, N.J., 1975-76; exec. dir. Campaign for U.N. Reform, Washington, 1988—, legisl. dir., 1976-87; field dir. World Federalist Assn., Washington, 1975-90, dep. dir., 1990-91; faculty mem. Grad. Sch. USDA, 1994; nat. TV interviews Hearst, Fox stations, 1995; lectr. in field. Page writer guest columns St. Louis Dispatch, Cleveland Plain Dealer, Orlando Sentinel; editor newsletter Campaign for U.N. Reform, 1985-88; contbr. articles to profl. jours. Testified twice before Senate Fgn. Relations Com., D.C., 1964-65, before the Sub-com. on Poverty of the Senate Labor Com., 1965, before the House Com. on banking fin. and urban affairs, 1990; mem. Washington Crim Coun., 1965, Mayor's Vol. Coun., N.Y.C., 1972; chmn. fgn. relations com. Young Democrats U.S., 1964; publicity chmn Internat. Platform Assn., Washington, 1964. With AUS, 1954-56. Mem. Citizens for Clean Air (founder D.C. area), Metro. Athletic Assn. (founder 1963-66). Democratic. Unitarian. Fax: 202-234-4970. Home & Office: Apt 516 3133 Connecticut Ave NW Washington DC 20008-5107

COX, FRANK D. (BUDDY COX), oil company executive, exploration consultant; b. Shreveport, La., Dec. 20, 1932; s. Ohmer M. and Beulah O. (Scott) C.; m. Betty Jean Hand, June 19, 1956; children: Cynthia Dell, Carolyn Diane, Frank D. Jr. BS in Bus. Adminstrn., La. Tech. U., 1956; postgrad., Centenary Coll., 1958-59. Cert. profl. landman; lic. real estate, Fla. Various positions Exxon Corp., Houston, 1955-86, chief landman, v.p. coal resources, 1980-86; pvt. practice Houston, 1986-89; sr. v.p. Energy Exploration Mgmt. Co., Houston, 1989-94; v.p., mgr. T-Bar-X Ltd. Co., Houston, 1994—; v.p., dir. Power Exploration Internat., Houston, 1994—; ptnr. East Tex. Reef Fund, Ltd., 1994—; land mgr. Thomson-Barrow Corp., 1994—, Tecolotita, Inc., 1994—. Active Second Bapt. Ch., Houston. Capt. USAF, 1956-58. Named disting. mil. grad. La. Tech. U., Ruston, 1955. Mem. Am. Assn. Profl. Landmen, Houston Assn. Profl. Landmen, W. Houston Assn. Profl. Landmen, W. Houston Exxon Annuitant Club, 100 Club of Greater Houston, La. Tech. U. Found., Crimestoppers Inc., Pi Kappa Alpha Ednl. Found., Omicron Delta Kappa Found., Delta Sigma Pi. Republican. Avocations: golf, tennis, amateur radio. Home: 14830 Carolcrest St Houston TX 77079-6312 Office: T-Bar-X Ltd Co 5847 San Felipe St Ste 3830 Houston TX 77057-3011

COX, FREDERICK MORELAND, retired university dean, social worker; b. L.A., Dec. 8, 1928; s. Frederick Alfred Edward and Ethel (Moreland) C.; m. Gay Campbell, June 1951 (dec. June 1991); children: Lawrence, Elizabeth, Sherman; m. Judith Hance, June 1994. BA, UCLA, 1950, MSW, 1954; DSW, U. Calif., Berkeley, 1968. Caseworker child welfare Los Angeles Bur. Public Assistance, 1952-53; mental health counselor Los Angeles Superior Ct., 1953; caseworker Family Service Bur., Oakland, Calif., 1954-57; program dir. Easter Seal Soc., Oakland, 1957-60; asst. prof. to prof. social work U. Mich., Ann Arbor, 1964-76; prof., dir. Sch. Social Work, Mich. State U., East Lansing, 1976-80; prof., dean Sch. Social Welfare, U. Wis., Milw., 1980-89, ret., 1989. Sr. co-editor: collections of readings on community orgn. practice Community-Action Planning Development, A Casebook, 1974, Tactics and Techniques of Community Practice, 1977, 2d edit., 1984, Strategies of Community Organization, 4th edit, 1987; co-editor: Families in Trouble (5 vols.), 1988. Pres. Wis. Coun. Human Concerns, 1985-86. NIMH spl. research fellow, 1960-63. Mem. NASW (v.p. Wis. chpt. 1984-86), Acad. Cert. Social Workers, Nat. Deans and Dirs. Schs. Social Work (sec.-treas. 1985-87), Coun. Social Work Edn. (bd. dirs. 1985-89). Home: 11300 First Ave NE # 221 Seattle WA 98125-6038

COX, GEORGE SHERWOOD, computer science educator; b. McAllen, Tex., Jan. 12, 1963; s. Jerry Alton and Eldora (Chrismier) C. BA in Comm., Pan Am. U., 1985; MA in Religious Edn., Southwestern Bapt. Theol. Sem., Ft. Worth, 1988. Lic. to ministry So. Bapt. Conv., 1985, ordained, 1990. Assoc. min. edn. South Hills Bapt. Ch., Ft. Worth, 1987-88; min. youth, assoc. pastor Trinity Bapt. Ch., McAllen, 1989-91; account exec. radio Sta. KVTY, McAllen, 1991; mgr. Tex. Valley Computer, Weslaco, 1991-94; instr. computers South Tex. Vocat. Tech. Inst., McAllen, 1994—; dir. Bapt. Student Union, U. Tex., Brownsville, Bapt. Gen. Conv. Tex., Dallas, 1988-93. Republican. Home: 320 S Peking St Mcallen TX 78501

COX, GLENDA JEWELL, elementary school educator; b. Caruthersville, Mo., Mar. 6, 1938; d. Gladys Lee and Vera Lee (Malugen) Malone; m. Samuel Joseph Cox, Sept. 3, 1958; children: Cassandra Ann, Leslie Alexandria, Jonathan Paul, Peter Matthew. BS in Elem. Edn., Charleston (S.C.) So. U., 1975; MA, Maryville U., St. Louis, 1990. Cert. tchr., gifted, elem. edn. K-12, prin. Tchr, 2nd/3rd grade combination Midland Park Elem., Charleston, 1975-76; tchr. 2nd grade Summerville (S.C.) Sch. Dist. II, 1978; tchr. 2nd grade, 5th grade math. Mascoutah (Ill.) Dist. 19, 1980-82; 6th grade tchr. Francis Howell Sch. Dist., St. Charles, Mo., 1985-91, gifted facilitator, 1991-97, asst. prin. Ctrl. Elem. Sch., 1997-98, prin., 1998—; mem. curriculum com. Francis Howell Sch. Dist., St. Charles, 1989-90, pilot mentor/mentor, 1988—, dist. site support team, 1993-96; cooperating tchr. Becky-David Elem., St. Charles, 1986-88; site based team chmn./co-chmn., 1992-96, Odyssey of the Mind coord., 1991-96, tech. com., 1993—, cluster tchr. instr., 1993-97, prins. selection com., 1993. English conversation tchr. Bapt. Ch., Fuchu, Japan, 1969-71, vacation Bible sch. dir., 1970-71; PTA parent vol. chmn. Newington Elem., Summerville, 1977-78; chmn. Cystic Fibrosis Found., Summerville, 1977. Mem. NEA, Gifted Assn. Mo. (dist. A 1994-96, co-dir. 1994-96, dist. A registration chmn. 1992-94, state conf. registration chmn. 1995, 96), St. Louis Assn. Gifted Edn. Baptist. Avocations: bridge, bowling, learning. Home: 14344 Rainey Lake Dr Chesterfield MO 63017-2933 Office: Ctrl Elem Sch 4525 Central School Rd Saint Charles MO 63304-7113

COX, GLENN ANDREW, JR., petroleum company executive; b. Sedalia, Mo., Aug. 6, 1929; s. Glenn Andrew and Ruth Lonsdale (Atkinson) C.; m. Veronica Cecelia Martin, Jan. 3, 1953; children: Martin Stuart, Grant Andrew, Cecelia Ruth. BBA, So. Meth. U., 1951. With Phillips Petroleum Co., Bartlesville, Okla., 1956-91, asst. to chmn. oper. com., 1973-74, v.p. mgmt. info. and control, 1974-80, exec. v.p., 1980-85, dir., 1982-91, pres., COO, 1985-91; bd. dirs. BOK Fin. Corp., Bank of Okla., The Williams Co.'s, Inc., Helmerich and Payne, Tulsa, Union Tex. Petroleum Holdings, Houston, Therman Industries, Inc., San Marcos, Tex. Pres. Cherokee Area coun. Boy Scouts Am., 1977-82, South Ctrl. region, 1987-90, mem. nat. exec. bd., 1987-94; mem. bd. curators Ctrl. Meth. Coll., Fayette, Mo., 1984-88, 1997—; trustee Philbrook Mus. Art, 1987-92, So. Meth. U., Dallas, 1988-96; bd. dirs. Okla. United Meth. Found.; mem. Okla. State Regents for Higher Edn., 1990-96. Mem. Am. Petroleum Inst. (bd. dirs. 1982-91), Nat. Assn. Mfrs. (bd. dirs. 1985-91), Bartlesville Area C. of C. (pres. 1978), Hillcrest Country Club. Methodist. Office: Reda Bldg 401 S Dewey Ave Ste 318 Bartlesville OK 74003-3545

COX, HEADLEY MORRIS, JR., lawyer, educator; b. Mt. Olive, N.C., July 25, 1916; s. Headley Morris and Frank (English) C.; m. Irene Todd, June 26, 1940; children: John Morris, Deborah English, Thomas Headley; m. Elizabeth Shelton Smith, Dec. 30, 1994. AB, Duke, 1937, AM, 1939; postgrad., U. Colo., 1944-45; PhD, U. Pa., 1958; JD, U. S.C., 1984. Successively instr., asst. prof., assoc. prof., prof. English Clemson (S.C.) U., 1939-82, head dept., 1950-69, dean Coll. Liberal Arts, 1969-80; of counsel Olson, Smith, Jordan & Cox, P.A., 1984—; Sr. Fulbright lectr. in Am. lit. Universitat Graz, Austria, 1958-59. Served with USNR, 1944-46. Mem. Phi Beta Kappa. Methodist. Home: 213 Riggs Dr Clemson SC 29631-1427 Office: PO Box 1633 Clemson SC 29633-1633

COX, HELEN ADELAIDE (HOLLY COX), artist, writer; b. El Paso, Tex., Oct. 17, 1932; d. Eugene Bonfanti and Anna Margaret (Lind) Thurston; m. Sanford C. Cox Jr., Sept. 27, 1958; children: Sanford C. III, Christopher Thurston. BA, Tex. Western Coll., El Paso, 1954. Tchr. Chavez Acad., El Paso, 1954-56; tchr. art El Paso Pub. Schs., 1956-58; artist El Paso, 1958—. Co-author: Eugene Thurston, 1996, Index to Early El Paso Artists, 1998. Bd. dirs. Matrix Soc., U. El Paso, 1991-93, El Paso Mus. of Art Guild, 1988; com. chmn. Kermezaar Art Fair, El Paso, 1990-93; bd. dirs., libr. St. Clements Episcopal Ch., El Paso, 1975-80. Recipient McQuinn award Mesilla Valley Fine Arts, Las Cruces, N.Mex., 1995. Mem. Nat. Soc. Arts and Letters (bd. dirs., treas. 1996-98), Tex. Watercolor Soc., Tex. Fine Arts Assn., Internat. Assn. Visual Arts, El Paso Art Assn. (life, pres. 1971, 1st pl. 1997, Joseph A. Moore award 1994), Rio Bravo Watercolorists (signature, bd. dirs. 1994-95, Grumbacher award 1993). Avocations: collecting regional art, books. Home: 112 Vista Del Rey Dr El Paso TX 79912-4821

COX, HENRY, research company executive, research engineer; b. Phila., Mar. 7, 1935; s. Henry Robert and Helen (Kane) C.; m. Mary Ann Shaw, Sept. 3, 1960 (dec.); children: James, Daniel, Michael, Diane. BS, Coll. Holy Cross, 1956; ScD, MIT, 1963. Analyst Office Sec. of Def., 1970-72; research assoc. Scripps Instn. Oceanography, LaJolla, Calif., 1972-73; officer in charge Naval Underwater Systems Ctr., New London, Conn., 1973-76; div. dir. Def. Advanced Research Projects Agy., 1976-78; project mgr. Naval Electronic Systems Command, Arlington, Va., 1978-81; divisional v.p. BBN Systems and Tech. Corp., Arlington, 1981-91; chief scientist, sr. v.p. Orincon Corp., Arlington, 1991—. Contbr. articles to tech. jours. Served to capt. USN, 1956-81. Decorated Legion of Merit; decorated Meritorious Service medal, Navy Commendation medal; recipient Def. Superior Service medal Dept. Def., 1978. Fellow Acoustical Soc. Am., IEEE (Disting. Tech. Achievement award Oceanic Engring. Soc. 1991); mem. Am. Soc. Naval Engrs. (hon. Gold medal), Soc. Indsl. and Applied Math., U.S. Naval Inst. Roman Catholic. Home: 6513 Waterway Dr Falls Church VA 22044-1328 Office: Orincon Corp 4350 Fairfax Dr Arlington VA 22203-1695

COX, HERBERT BARTLE, natural gas company executive; b. Lynchburg, Va., Jan. 22, 1944; s. Arthur Hume and Margaret (Holberton) C.; m. Evelyn Crews King, Aug. 7, 1965; children: Richard Mark, Herbert David. BS in Engring., Va. Poly. Inst. and State U., 1966. Mktg. rep., systems engr. IBM, Roanoke and Lynchburg, 1966-78; v.p., corp. sec. Lynchburg Gas Co., 1978-88; dist. mgr. Pub. Svc. Co. N.C., Inc., Durham, 1988-90; sr. v.p. East ops. Raleigh, 1990-95; v.p. ops. svcs. Pub. Svc. Co. N.C., Inc., Gastonia, 1995-98; mgr. ops. Piedmont Textiles, Mooresville, 1999—. Mem. bd. advisors Salvation Army, Lynchburg, 1980-88; bd. dirs. United Way Cen. Va., Lynchburg, 1980-85. Mem. Am. Gas Assn., So. Gas Assn., Southeastern Gas Assn. (bd. dirs. 1985-88). Episcopalian. Home: 21226 Blakely Shores Dr Cornelius NC 28031-6608 Office: Piedmont Textiles PO Box 1422 476 S Main St Mooresville NC 28115

COX, HILLERY LEE, primary school educator; b. Akron, Ohio, Nov. 2, 1946; d. Ellwood Lester Jr. and Leonide Juanita (Williams) Cosper; m. William R. Cox Jr., Apr. 2, 1966; 1 child, Geoffrey William. Student, Ohio U., 1964-65; BS in Edn., U. Akron, 1967, MS in Edn., 1980. Cert. tchr., Ohio; cert. reading specialist, Ohio. Tchr. Copley (Ohio) Fairlawn Schs., 1967-69; presch. tchr. Northminster Coop. Nursery Sch., Cuyahoga Falls, Ohio, 1974-75; ednl. math. aide Stow (Ohio) City Schs., 1975-76; grad. tchg. asst. U. Akron, 1976-77; tchr. Cloverleaf Local Schs., Lodi, Ohio, 1977—; adj. prof. workshop presenter Ashland (Ohio) U., 1992—; cons. The ABC's of Whole Lang., Copley, 1988—; insvc. presenter various sch. sys. in Ohio, 1988—. Contbr. articles to profl. jours. Vol. Doggie Brigade, Children's Med. Ctr. of Akron, 1992—; driver substitute Mobile Meals, Copley, 1981-84; sec. Copley All Sports Boosters, 1984-88. Named Medina County Tchr. of Yr., 1993; grantee Ohio Dept. Edn., 1978-79, 79-80; Martha Holden Jennings Found. scholar, 1994. Mem. NEA, ASCD, Ohio Edn. Assn., Internat. Reading Assn. (pres. Lizotte coun. 1994-95, 97-97, spkr. Great Lakes conf. 1993), Ohio Coun. Tchrs. English and Lang. Arts (presenter 1987, 88, 89), Cloverleaf Edn. Assn. (bldg. rep. 1977—), Nat. Campers and Hikers and Family RVers (sec. local chpt. 1991—), Order of Ea. Star (adre officer Ellsworth chpt. 1991—, Worthy Matron 1996), Delta Kappa Gamma. Avocations: scuba diving, camping, crafts, traveling. Home: 649 S Medina Line Rd Copley OH 44321-1162 Office: Cloverleaf Local Schs Lodi Elem 301 Mill St Lodi OH 44254-1427

COX, HOWARD ELLIS, JR., venture capitalist; b. N.Y.C., Feb. 1, 1944; s. Howard Ellis and Anne Delafield (Finch) C.; m. Julia Bolton Dempsey, Oct. 31, 1970. BA, Princeton U., 1964; JD, Columbia U., 1967; MBA, Harvard U., 1969. Bar: N.Y. 1967. Co-mng. ptnr. Greylock, Boston, 1971—; bd. dirs. Amisys, Rockville, Md., Arbor Health Care, Lima, Ohio, Greylock Mgmt. Corp., Boston, Stryker, Kalamazoo, Pryon Corp., Milw., HPR, Boston, Centene, St. Louis, Landacorp, Chico, Calif., Vincam, Miami, Carinstone, Miami, Managed Comp., Boston. Bd. dirs. Preuss Found., San Diego, 1986—, Nat. Venture Capital Assn., Washington, 1997—; trustee Dana Farber Cancer Inst., 1987—; v.p., trustee Assn. Relief of the Elderly, N.Y.C. Capt. U.S. Army, 1969-71. Mem. New England Venture Capital Assn. (pres. 1986-88), Bus. Assocs. Club Boston (pres. 1979-80). Episcopalian. Home: 225 Sargent Rd Brookline MA 02445-7517 Office: Greylock 1 Federal St Boston MA 02110-2012

COX, J. ALLEN, physicist; b. Wilmington, N.C., Oct. 7, 1946; s. Samuel Clemens and Aileen Elizabeth (Mewborn) C.; m. Georgia Ann Manfredi, Mar. 4, 1977. BS cum laude, Wake Forest U., 1968; PhD, U. N.C., 1974. Praktikant Hahn-Meitner Inst., Berlin, 1970; rsch. scientist Honeywell Sys. Rsch. Ctr., Mpls., 1977-86; sr. rsch. fellow Honeywell Tech. Ctr., Mpls., 1986—. Contbr. articles to profl. jours.; patentee in field. Capt. U.S. Army, 1974-77. Mem. SPIE (program com. diffractive optics 1990-98), Am. Phys. Soc., Optical Soc. Am. (program chair diffractive optics 1994, 96, 98), Geol. Soc. Minn. (pres. 1991). Avocations: hiking, birdwatching, nature study, languages, skin diving. Office: Honeywell Tech Ctr 3660 Technology Dr Minneapolis MN 55418-1096

COX, J. ARTHUR, minister; b. Utica, N.Y., Aug. 5, 1940; s. James F. and Margaret (Craig) C.; m. Mahailie Tillson, Dec. 29, 1962; children: Deborah Jean, James Andrew. AAS, Mohawk Valley Community Coll., 1961; BTh, Concordia Sem., 1975; D Ministry, Faith Sem., Tacoma, 1991. Ordained to ministry Luth. Ch.-Mo. Synod, 1975. Pastor Grace Luth. Ch., Bradford, Pa., 1975—; del. Synodical Conv., Dallas, 1977; counselor Cattaraugus Cir., Bradford, 1978-82; chmn. Dist. Open House, Bradford, 1982, Dist. Extension Fund, Buffalo, 1982-85; chmn. ea. dist. Alive in Christ, bd. dirs., Mission Svcs., 1982-88, mem. evangelism com. ea. dist., 1992-97, bd. dirs.; chmn. dist. bd. Congl. Svcs., 1997—. Bd. dirs. Evergreen Hylands, 1979, Am. Cancer Soc., 1980, Vis. Nurse Assn., 1980-86, Bradford Hosp., 1985—. Mem. Rotary (bd. dirs. 1978-82, pres. 1982-83). Republican. Home: 465 Interstate Pky Bradford PA 16701-2733 Office: Grace Luth Ch 79 Mechanic St Bradford PA 16701-1241 *Life is a sequence of God-given opportunities to serve Him and His people. The excitement is derived from accepting His call to service and experiencing His magnificent power working through you to accomplish His purpose.*

COX, J. WILLIAM, retired physician, health services administrator; b. St. Louis, Aug. 31, 1928; s. William E. and Evelyn C.; m. Anne Maczewsk, June 11, 1949; 1 child, William E. Student, Washington U., St. Louis; MD, St. Louis U., 1952, PhD, 1953. Diplomate Am. Bd. Internal Medicine. Chief research labs. VA Hosps., St. Louis, 1953-54; commd. med. officer USN, 1954, advanced through grades to Vice Adm., ret., 1983; chief medicine, dir. clinics Naval Hosp., Subic Bay, Philippines, 1961-63; chief medicine, dir. rsch. Naval Hosp., Phila., 1965-69; dir. edn., tng. USN Med. Dept., Washington, 1971-77; comdg. officer Naval Regional Med. Ctr., San Diego, 1978-80; Surgeon Gen. USN, Washington, 1980-83, ret.; assoc. dir. Grad. Sch. Pub. Health San Diego State U., 1983-88; dir. Dept. Hlth. Svcs. County of San Diego, 1987-93; ret., 1994; cons. in pub. health, profl. rels. AMA, Chgo., 1983-87. Contbr. numerous tech. reports, articles to profl. jours. chmn. tech. adv. group San Diego County Bd. Suprs., 1986-93; chmn. spl. svcs. divsn. San Diego County coun. Boy Scouts Am., Access to Care Commn., San Diego County 1990-94, Commn. on Access to Health Care, San Diego, 1990-93. Decorated Legion of Merit; recipient Borden award for Med. Rsch., Borden Corp., St. Louis U., 1981, Svc. award Uniformed Svcs. Univ. Health Scis., Bethesda, Md. 1983, Diogenes award Pub. Rels. Soc. Am., Silver Beaver award Boy Scouts Am., 1986-90. Fellow ACP, Phila. Coll. Physicians, Am. Coll. Cardiology; mem. AMA (Spl. award for Meritorious Svc. 1983, ho. of dels. 1970-83, 86-94), Calif. Med. Assn. (ho. of dels. 1984-94), Rotary. Republican. Avocations: swimming, music.

COX, JAMES D., law educator; b. 1943. J.D., U. Calif. Hastings Sch. Law, 1969; LL.M., Harvard U., 1971. Bar: Calif. 1970. Atty.-adv. Office Gen. Counsel FTC, Washington, 1969-70; teaching fellow Boston U., 1970-71; asst. prof. U. San Francisco, 1971-74; assoc. prof. U. Calif. Hastings Sch. Law, 1974-75; vis. assoc. prof. Stanford U., 1976-77; prof. U. Calif. Hastings Sch. Law, 1977-79; vis. prof. Duke U. Sch. Law, spring 1979, prof., 1979—; mem. com. on corps. State Bar Calif., N.C. bus. corp. act. draft com., N.C. nonprofit corp. draft com.; E.T. Bost rsch. prof., fall 1980, 96; mem. legal adv. com. N.Y. Stock Exch., 1995—; mem. legal adv. bd. NASD, 1999—. Author: Financial Information, Accounting and the Law, 1980, Sum and Substance of Corporations, 5th edit., 1988, (with Hillman and Langevoort) Securities Regulation: Cases and Materials, 1997, 2d edit., (with Hazen and O'Neal) Corporations, 1995. Sr. Fulbright Rsch. fellow, Australia, 1989. Mem. Am. Law Inst., Order of Coif, Phi Kappa Phi. Office: Duke U Sch Law Durham NC 27706

COX, JAMES DAVID, art gallery executive; b. South Bend, Ind., Aug. 18, 1945; m. Mary Anna Goetz. Dir. Grand Central Art Galleries, N.Y.C., 1977-89; owner James Cox Gallery, Woodstock, N.Y., 1990—; bd. dirs. Grand Central Art Galleries Ednl. Assn.; co-chmn. Soviet-Am. Art Conf."Art Most", Moscow, 1989; dir. Tallix Mktg., Tallix Art Foundry, Beacon, N.Y., 1996—; advisor The Mus. Contemporary Impressionism, New Milford, Conn., 1997. Exec. editor: Illuminator, 1977. Mem. N.Y. Acad. Art (bd. dirs. 1983-85), Nat. Sculpture Soc., Woodstock Artists Assn., Woodstock Arts Bd., Nat. Arts Club, Salmagundi Club, Dutch Treat Club (N.Y.C.). Office: James Cox Gallery 4666 State Route 212 Willow NY 12495-5303

COX, JAMES MICHAEL, school district administrator, psychologist; b. Cedar Rapids, Iowa, Oct. 10, 1948; s. Richard Elmer and Betty Jo (Belknap) C.; children: Anthony Christopher, Angela Christine; m. Patricia Lynn Schnupp, June 25, 1983. BS in Edn., Millersville U., 1973, MS in Psychology, 1976; postgrad., Widener U., 1998. Cert. sch. psychologist N.J., Pa., cert. elem. and spl. ed. tchr., prin., supt., Pa. Spl. edn. tchr. Berks County Intermediate Unit, Reading, Pa., 1973-78; sch. Psychologist Schuylkill Intermediate Unit, Pottsville, Pa., 1978; sch. psychologist Lancaster-Lebanon Intermediate Unit, Lancaster, Pa., 1978-93; dir. spl. svcs. Eastern Lancaster County Sch. Dist., New Holland, Pa., 1993—; pres. Lancaster-Lebanon Psychologists Assn., Lancaster, 1990-91. Pres. Trinity Luth. Ch. New Holland, 1988-90, 93-95, Caernarvon Hist. Soc. Churchtown, Pa., 1988-94; mem. Churchtown Improvement Com., 1994-98; chmn. Caernarvon Twp. Zoning Hearing Bd., 1997—. With USN, 1966-69. Mem. AASPA, Nat. Assn. Sch. Psychologists (cert.), Pa. Assn. Sch. Psychologists, Pa. Assn. Pupil Personnel Adminstrs., Coun. for Exceptional Children, Assn. for Supervision and Curriculum Devel; Mem Mercedes Benz Club of Am. Democrat. Lutheran. Avocations: old house restoration, home brewing. Home: 2115 Main St Narvon PA 17555-9518 Office: Eastern Lancaster County Sch. Dist. 669 E Main St New Holland PA 17557-1409

COX, JAMES SIDNEY, physician; b. Homer, La., Nov. 17, 1950; s. Sidney and Rita (Haynes) C.; m. Judy Katherine Vickers, Oct. 21, 1984; children: Shannon Ruth, Sarah Anne, Megan Elizabeth. Student, La. State U., 1968-71; MD, Tulane U., 1971-75. Diplomate Am. Bd. Family Practice, Am. Bd. of Emergency Medicine. Intern, resident in family practice John Peter Smith Hosp., Ft. Worth, 1975-78; city health officer family practice City of Athens, Tex., 1978-84; pvt. practice Athens, 1978-84, Ft. Worth, 1984—; mem. staff Henderson County Meml. Hosp., Athens, vice chief med. staff, 1981-82; mem. staff Lakeland Med. Ctr., Athens, chief med. staff, dir., 1983-84; vice chief emergency medicine dept. Harris Meth. Hosp., Ft. Worth, 1988-91; dir. occupational medicine Harris Meth. Hosp., 1989—; chief emergency dept. Harris Meth. Hosp., Ft. Worth, 1992-93, 98—, sec. med. staff, 1994-95, sec. emergency medicine divsn., 1996-97; pres., chmn. bd. dirs. Occuhealth Physicians Group, P.A., Ft. Worth; mem. faculty U. Tex. Health Sci. Ctr.-Dallas Cmty. Medicine Dept., John Peter Smith Hosp., Ft. Worth, 1978-96, course dir. ACLS, 1989—, mem. affiliate faculty ACLS, 1991—, med. rev. officer for urine drug testing; med. bd. Harris Meth. Hosp., 1992-95, 98—; team chmn. emergency dept. redesign Rochester Inst. Tech. Coll. Bus., 1996; v.p. for physician affairs Emergency Medicine Cons., 1998—; med. dir. ACLS, Campbell Health Sys., 1997-98. Author: Intestinal Obstruction: A Programmed Text, 1975. Recipient Quality Cup award of Excellence, USA Today, 1996. Fellow Am. Acad. Family Physicians, Am. Coll. Emergency

Physicians; mem. AMA (Physician's Recognition award), Am. Coll. Occupl. and Environ. Medicine, Tex. Med. Assn. (alt. del. 1994-96), Tarrant County Med. Soc. (bd. dirs. 1994-96), Rotary (bd. dirs. Athens chpt. 1983-84), Alpha Epsilon Delta. Presbyterian. Avocations: reading, skiing, bonsai, horticulture, astronomy. Home: 3458 Lantern Holw Fort Worth TX 76109-2411 Office: Harris Meth Hosp Ft Worth Emergency Dept 1301 Pennsylvania Ave Fort Worth TX 76104-2122 also: Occuhealth Physicians Group #200 6451 Brentwood Stair Rd Ste 200 Fort Worth TX 76112-3200

COX, JAMES TALLEY, lawyer; b. Temple, Tex., Sept. 22, 1921; s. George Allan and Jane (Talley) C.; m. Alice Tarver, Jan. 12, 1945; children: Martha Cox Daniels, Louise Cox McGuire, Anne Cox, Allan. B.B.A., U. Tex., 1943; LL.B., 1947. Bar: Tex. 1947, U.S. Supreme Ct. 1951. Spl. atty. Justice Dept., Washington, 1947-48; staff atty. Tax Ct. U.S., Washington, 1948-50; trial atty. Treasury Dept., Phila., 1950-51; tax counsel Schlumberger Well Services, Houston, 1951-65; ptnr. Hoover, Cox & Shearer, Houston, 1965-86; sole practice Houston, 1986-90; pres. James T. Cox, P.C., Houston, 1990—, Advent Trust Co., 1991—; v.p., bd. dirs. Westchase Travels, Inc., 1972-82; bd. dirs. Paradigm Valve Svcs. Inc., Embedded Sys. Products Inc. Contbr. articles to profl. publs. Bd. dirs. Houston Met. YMCA, 1972-78, Pin Oak Charity Horse Show Assn., 1972—, Retina Research Found., 1977—. Served to lt. USNR, 1943-46. Mem. Am., Tex., Houston bar assns., Tax Research Assn. (exec. com. 1950-67), Delta Theta Phi, Phi Kappa Psi. Republican. Presbyn. Home: 11701 Forest Glen St Houston TX 77024-6433 Office: 6363 Woodway Dr Houston TX 77057-1735

COX, JAMES WILLIAM, newspaper executive; b. Waldron, Ark., Oct. 18, 1937; s. George T. and Louise M. (Harris) C.; m. Nichola F. Goudreau, Mar. 20, 1969 (div. Oct. 31, 1983); 1 son, James William; m. Cynthia Renée Moore, Apr. 25, 1986. B.B.A., U. Tex., Arlington, 1974. With Donrey Media Group, 1958-65, chief acct., 1960-65; bus. mgr. Las Vegas (Nev.) Rev.-Jour., 1960-65; contr. Palmer Media Group, 1965-69; with A.H. Belo Corp. (publisher Dallas Morning News), 1969—, internal auditor, then treas., 1969-79, v.p., contr., 1979-82, sr. v.p., contr., 1982-84, sr. v.p. adminstrn. and fin., 1985-93, sr. v.p. ops. and adminstrn., 1993-98, sr. v.p. pub. divsn., 1998—. Mem. budget com. Dallas County chpt. ARC, 1973-74; mem. planning com. Goals for Dallas, 1981, mem. membership com., 1990-91, chmn. job-scholarship com., 1990-91; bd. dirs. Dallas Alliance Bus., 1985-87, chmn., 1987-89; bd. dirs. Dallas BBB, 1986—, chmn. membership com., 1993—, mem. exec. com., 1993—; bd. dirs. Jr. Achievement Dallas, 1986-98, Mus. African-Am. Life and Culture, 1986—, Inroads, 1988-96, So. Prodn. Program, Inc., 1989—, United Way of Met. Dallas, 1996—, chmn. comms. unit, 1989-91. Mem. Fin. Execs. Inst., Tex. Daily Newspaper Assn., Las Colinas Country Club, Sigma Alpha Epsilon. Office: Dallas Morning News Communications Ctr PO Box 655237 Dallas TX 75265-5237

COX, JAMSON L., historic site director. M in History, Cooperstown Grad. Sch., 1967. Chief historian State of S.C., 1968-73; mgr. Charles Towne Landing 1670, Charleston, S.C., 1973-98; exec. dir. S.C. Cotton Mus, Bishopville, 1998—. Office: SC Cotton Mus 121 W Cedar Ln Bishopville SC 29010-6008*

COX, JEROME ROCKHOLD, JR., electrical engineer; b. Washington, May 24, 1925; s. Jerome R. and Jane (Mills) C.; m. Barbara Jane Lueders, Sept. 2,1951; children—Nancy Jane Cox Battersby, Jerome Mills, Randall Allen. S.B., Mass. Inst. Tech., 1947, S.M., 1949, Sc.D., 1954. Mem. faculty Washington U., St. Louis, 1955—, prof. elec. engring., 1961—, prof. biomed. engring. in physiology and biophysics, Sch. Medicine, 1965—, dir. Biomed. Computer Lab., 1964-75, chmn. computer labs., 1967-83, program dir. tng. program tech. in health care, 1970-78, chmn. dept. computer sci., 1975-91, prof. biomedicine, Inst. for Biomed. Computing, 1983—, Harold and Adelaide Welge prof. computer sci., 1989-98, sr. prof., 1999—, dir. Applied Rsch. Lab., 1991-95; v.p. Growth Networks, 1999—; co-chmn. computers in cardiology conf., 1974-88; cardiology adv. com. Nat. Heart and Lung Inst., 1975-78; mem. epidemiology biostatistics and bioengring. cluster Pres.'s Biomed. Rsch. Panel, 1975-76; chmn. Divsn. computer Rsch. and Tech. rev. com. NIH, 1983-96; mem. PROPHET adv. com. NIH, 1983-88; mem. adv. com. Harvard-MIT Health Scis. and Tech., Boston, 1988-92; mem. Nat. Neural Circuitry Database com. Inst. of Medicine, NAS, 1989-91; mem. Nat. Adv. Coun. Human Genome Rsch., 1990-95. Mem. editl. bd. Computers and Biomed. Rsch., 1967—, Applied Mathematics Letters, 1987-96; assoc. editor, IEEE, trans. biomed. engring., 1969-71. Mem. bd. mgrs. Ctrl. Inst. Deaf, 1993—. Served with U.S. Army, 1943-44. Fellow IEEE, Acoustical Soc. Am., Am. Coll. Med. Informatics; sr. mem. Inst. Medicine; mem. Assn. Computing Machinery, St. Louis Acad. Sci. (bd. dirs. 1997—), Sigma Xi, Eta Kappa Nu, Tau Beta Pi. Author, patentee air traffic control, computerized tomography, medical display technology. Office: Washington U Dept Computer Sci Campus Box 1045 One Brookings Dr Saint Louis MO 63130-4899

COX, JOHN CURTIS, healthcare and educational administrator; b. Lovington, N.Mex., July 27, 1947; s. Samuel Spurgeon and Monah LaJoyce (Perry) King; m. Mary Margaret King, May 27, 1967; children: Melissa Lynn Ewing, Melinda Leanne Field. BBA, Hardin-Simmons U., Abilene, Tex., 1969; MHA, Baylor U., 1978; PhD, Tex. A&M U., 1988. Commd. 2d lt. U.S. Army, 1969, advanced through grades to lt. col.; chief Ft. Hood Health Facility Project Office, Office Surgeon Gen., 1978-85; assoc. dir., mgr. field office, health facilities planning U.S. Army Med. Command, Stuttgart, Germany, 1988-89; dir. health facilities planning U.S. Army Med. Command, Heidelberg, Germany, 1989-90; chief programming div. Def. Med. Facilities Office, Office Asst. Sec. Def., Washington, 1990-91; ret. U.S. Army, 1991; adminstrv. asst. Garland (Tex.) Ind. Sch. Dist., 1991-93, exec. dir. sch. facilities, 1993-95; planning & cons. coord. HED Baylor Health Care Sys., 1995-98; adminstrv. dir. support svcs. Baylor Med. Ctr., Grapevine, Tex., 1997-98; project dir. Med. Cities Inc., Dallas, 1998—; dir. facility project Baylor Med. Ctr., Grapevine, Tex. Contbr. articles to profl. jours. Trustee Belton (Tex.) Ind. Sch. Dist., 1981-84; mem. pub. sch. bd. mems. adv. com. Tex. State Bd. Edn., 1982-84; fund raiser Garland br. Dallas YMCA, 1992-94. Decorated Legion of Merit, Bronze Star medal, Meritorious Svc. medal with 2 oak leaf clusters, Army Commendation medal, others; recipient Svc. Citation award Tex. Fellow Am. Coll. Healthcare Execs., Am. Soc. Healthcare Engrs., Phi Kappa Phi, Alpha Chi. Baptist. Avocations: woodworking, antiques, fitness.

COX, JOHN FRANCIS, retired cosmetic company executive; b. Chgo., Sept. 25, 1929; s. Roland Francis and Vera Pauline (Paisley) C.; m. T. Joanne Brown, Nov. 27, 1954; children: James O., Thomas B., Paul A. BJ, U. Ill., 1951; MS in English and Edn., Western Ill. U., 1954. Reporter Galesburg (Ill.) Register News, 1954-56; staff writer pub. rels. United Airlines, Chgo., 1956-58; press. rels. mgr. Kiekhaefer Corp., Fond du Lac, Wis., 1958-60, Internat. Minerals and Chems. Corp., Skokie, Ill., 1960-67; press rels. mgr. Heublein Inc., Hartford, Conn., 1967-69; v.p. pub. affairs Heublein Inc., Farmington, Conn., 1981-83; v.p. pub. rels. and advt. Warner Nat. Corp., Cin., 1969-72; v.p. franchising and pub. rels. Ky. Fried Chicken, Louisville, 1972-81; group dir. pub. rels. R. J. Reynolds Industries, Inc., Winston-Salem, N.C., 1983-84; sr. v.p. communications Avon Products, Inc., N.Y.C., 1984-91. Staff sgt. U.S. Army, 1951-53. Mem. Pub. Rels. Soc. Am., Sigma Delta Chi.

COX, JOHN MICHAEL, cardiologist; b. Toledo, June 21, 1952; s. William E. and Laura M. (Carroll) C.; m. Sandra Helen Kemner, Aug. 19, 1972 (div. Mar. 1978); 1 child, Justin Michael; m. Vickie Diane Humphreys, May 27, 1978; children: Sarah Elizabeth, Aaron Alexander, Gabriel John. BA magna cum laude, Westminster Coll., 1974; DO, Kirksville Coll. Osteo. Medicine, 1978. Cert. Am. Bd. Osteo. Cardiology, Internal Medicine. Rotating intern Riverside Hosp., Trenton, Mich., 1978-79, resident in internal medicine, 1979-81, fellow in cardiology, 1981-83; practice medicine specializing in cardiology Sedalia and Columbia, Mo., 1983-88, Joplin, Mo., 1988—; chmn. dept. internal medicine Bothwell Regional Health Ctr., 1985—, Oak Hill Hosp., 1991, 95; chmn. dept. internal medicine Freeman Hosp., 1992, med. dir. cardiac catheter lab., 1992—, vice chief staff, 1997, chief of staff, 1998—. Grantee Detroit Osteo. Hosp. Corp., Burroughs Wellcome Fellowship, Meade Johnson Fellowship. Fellow Am. Coll. Osteo. Internists, Am. Coll. Cardiology, Soc. for Cardiac Angiography and Interventions; mem. AMA, Am. Heart Assn., Am. Osteo. Assn., Mo. Assn. Osteo. Physicians and Surgeons (v.p. west cen. dist. 1985-87, pres. 1987), Am. Soc. Echocardiography, N.Am. Soc. Pacing and Electrophysiology, Psi Sigma Alpha, Sigma Sigma Phi. Methodist.

COX, JOHN THOMAS, JR., lawyer; b. Shreveport, La., Feb. 9, 1943; s. John Thomas and Gladys Virginia (Canterbury) C.; m. Tracey L. Tanquary, Aug. 27, 1966; children: John Thomas, III, Stephen Lewis. BS, La. State U., 1965; JD, 1968. Bar: La. 1968, U.S. Dist. Ct. (we., mid. and ea. dist.) La., U.S. Dist. Ct. (ea. dist.) Tex., U.S. Ct. Appeals (5th and 8th cir.), U.S. Tax Ct., U.S. Supreme Ct. Assoc. Sanders, Miller, Downing & Keene, Baton Rouge, 1968-70, Blanchard, Walker, O'Quin & Roberts, Shreveport, La., 1970-71; ptnr., 1971—; tchr. bus. law Centenary Coll. La. Served to lt. USAR, 1963-69. Lt. USAR, 1963-69. Recipient George Washington Honor medal Valley Forge Freedoms Found. Mem. ABA, La. Bar Assn., Caddo parish Bar Assn., Am. Assn. Def. Counsel, La. Assn. Def. Counsel, Shreveport Club. Presbyterian. Address: 555 Dunmoreland Dr Shreveport LA 71106-6124

COX, JOSEPH LAWRENCE, judge; b. Trenton, Mo., Dec. 7, 1932; s. Forrest Curtis and Lillian Judson (Ritzenthaler) C.; m. Lois Marie Hubble, May 20, 1956; children: Margaret Marie Cox Jarvis, Martha Mae Cox Anderson. BA, U. Mo., Kansas City, 1961, JD, 1965. Bar: Kans. 1965, U.S. Supreme Ct. 1970. Ptnr. Cox, Anderson & Covell, Mission, Kans., 1965-70; pvt. practice, Tonganoxie, Kans., 1968-90; city atty. of Tonganoxie, 1967-73, Linwood, Kans., 1972-78; mcpl. judge, Mission, 1969-80, Tonganoxie, 1983-90, Topeka, 1990—. With USAF, 1952-54. Mem. Kans. Bar Assn., Kans. Mcpl. Judges Assn. (bd. dirs. 1975-79, pres. 1977-78), Topeka Bar Assn., Masons, Shriners, Sertoma (pres. 1973-76, gov. Kans. dist. 1998-99), Topeka Evening Sertoma (pres. 1995-96). Avocations: photography, boating, travel. Home: 910 SE 43rd St Topeka KS 66609-1620 Office: 214 E 8th St Topeka KS 66603

COX, JOSEPH WILLIAM, academic administrator; b. Hagerstown, Md., May 26, 1937; s. Joseph F. and Ruth E. C.; m. Regina M. Bollinger, Aug. 17, 1963; children—Andrew, Matthew, Abigail. B.A., U. Md., 1959, Ph.D., 1967; Doctor (hon.), Towson State U., 1990. Successively instr., asst. prof., assoc. prof., prof. history Towson (Md.) State U., 1964-81, dean evening and summer programs, 1972-75, acting pres., 1978-79, v.p. acad. affairs and dean of univ., 1979-81; prof. history, v.p. acad. affairs. No. Ariz. U.,, Flagstaff, 1981-87; pres. So. Oregon U., Ashland, 1987-94; chancellor Oreg. Univ. Sys., Eugene, 1994—. Author: Champion of Southern Federalism: Robert Goodloe Harper of South Carolina, 1972, The Early National Experience: The Army Corps of Engineers, 1783-1812, 1979; mem. bd. editors Md. Hist. Mag., 1979-89; columnist So. Oreg. Hist. Mag., 1989-94; contbr. articles to profl. jours. Bd. dirs. Oreg. Hist. Soc., Oreg. Shakespearean Festival, 1989-95, So. Oreg. Econ. Deve. Bd., 1988-94, Jackson/Josephine Co., Western Book, 1993-97, Portland Ctr. Stage, 1999. Mem. AAUP, Am. Assn. Higher Edn., Am. Assn. State Colls. and Univs., Phi Kappa Phi, Omicron Delta Kappa. Episcopalian. Home: 2237 Spring Blvd Eugene OR 97403-1897 Office: Oreg Univ Sys Office of Chancellor PO Box 3175 Eugene OR 97403-0175

COX, KENNETH ALLEN, lawyer, communications consultant; b. Topeka, Dec. 7, 1916; s. Seth Leroy and Jean (Sears) C.; m. Nona Beth Fumerton, Jan. 1, 1943; children—Gregory Allen, Jeffrey Neal, Douglas Randall. B.A., U. Wash., 1938, LL.B., 1940; LL.M., U. Mich., 1941; LL.D., Chgo. Theol. Sem., 1969. Bar: Wash. bar 1941. Law clk. Wash. Supreme Ct., 1941-42; asst. prof. U. Mich. Law Sch., 1946-48; with firm Little, Palmer, Scott & Slemmons (and predecessor), Seattle, 1948-61; partner Little, Palmer, Scott & Slemmons (and predecessor), 1953-61; spl. counsel com. interstate and fgn. commerce charge TV inquiry U.S. Senate, 1956-57; chief broadcast bur. FCC, Washington, 1961-63; commr. FCC, 1963-70; counsel to communications law firm Haley, Bader & Potts, 1970—; sr. v.p., dir. MCI Communications Corp., 1970-87; cons. MCI, 1987—; lectr. U. Washington Law Sch., part-time 1954, 60; adj. prof. Georgetown U. Law Center, 1971, 72. Vice pres. Municipal League Seattle and King County, 1960, Seattle World Affairs Council, 1960; pres. Seattle chpt. Am. Assn. UN, 1957; chmn. one of five citizen subcoms. Legis. Interim Com. Edn., 1960; Bd. dirs. Nat. Pub. Radio, 1971-80; bd. dirs. Nat. Advt. Rev. Bd., 1971-74, chmn. bd., 1976-96 . Served to capt. Q.M.C. AUS, 1943-46, 51-52. Recipient Alfred I. duPont award in broadcast journalism Columbia U., 1970. Mem. Am., Fed. Communications, Wash. State, D.C. bar assns., Order of Coif, Phi Beta Kappa, Phi Delta Phi. Democrat. Conglist. Home: 5836 Marbury Rd Bethesda MD 20817-6076 Office: MCI Comm Corp 1801 Pennsylvania Ave NW Washington DC 20006-3606

COX, KEVIN MONTEREY, school administrator; b. New London, Conn., Nov. 30, 1965; s. Carroll Monterey and Barbara Freeman Cox. BS, U. S.C., Spartanburg, 1987; MEd, Converse Coll., 1990, EdS, 1993. Tchr. Clinton (S.C.) H.S., 1990-96, asst. prin., 1997—; asst. prin. Bell St. Mid. Sch., Clinton, 1996-97; state sponsor S.C. Beta Club, 1999—; adj. prof. Lander U., Greenwood, S.C., 1998—. Recipient S.C. Ambassador of Acad. Excellence award S.C. State Dept. Edn., 1992. Mem. ASCD, S.C. Sci. Coun., Exch. Club Clinton (pres. 1996-97), Phi Delta Kappa. Methodist. Avocations: movies, reading, music. E-mail: xmcox@laurens56.k12.sc.us. Home: 101 Teakwood Dr Clinton SC 29325 Office: Clinton HS 800 N Adair St Clinton SC 29325

COX, KIM CARROLL, lawyer, broadcaster; b. Chgo., Feb. 8, 1955; s. Carroll Thomas and Alice (Macqueen) C. BA, U. Ill., 1976; JD, Thomas Jefferson Sch. Law, San Diego, 1982. Bar: Calif., 1988, U.S. Supreme Ct., 1993, U.S. Ct. Appeals (7th, 9th & 10th cir.), 1993, 96, U.S. Dist. Ct. (so. dist.) Calif., 1988., U.S. Dist Ct. (so. dist.) Ill., 1996. Broadcaster KSDS-FM, San Diego, 1985—; sec. Calif. Electoral Coll., 1992, chair, 1996; assoc. Law Offices of Floyd Morrow, San Diego, 1989-95, Law Offices of Denise Moreno Ducheny, San Diego, 1996—; judge pro tem Calif. Mcpl. Ct., 1997-98, San Diego County Superior Ct., 1998—; mem. mediation panel San Diego County Superior Ct., 1995—. Chair Crawford County (Ill.) Young Dems., Robinson, 1974-76, San Diego County Dem. Party, 1990-95; field dir. Dukakis for Pres., San Diego, 1988; mem. exec. bd. Calif. Dem. Party, 1989-94. Mem. San Diego County Bar Assn. Avocations: jazz disc jockey, outdoor activities. Home: 2050 Emerald St Apt 3 San Diego CA 92109-3519 Office: Law Offices of Denise Ducheny 2168 Logan Ave San Diego CA 92113-2204

COX, LARRY D., airport terminal executive. With Memphis Internat. Airport, Tenn., 1973-84, pres., CEO, 1984. Office: Memphis Internat Airport Memphis-Shelby County Airport Authority 2491 Winchester Rd Ste 113 Memphis TN 38116-3856*

COX, LINDA SMOAK, real estate broker; b. Yonges Island, S.C., Sept. 5, 1943; d. Ryan Lanier Smoak and Frances Lapish Bock. Grad., Kings Coll., Charlotte, N.C., 1962. Lic. real estate broker, relocation specialist, new homes specialist. Exec. sec. Charlotte Observer Transp. Co., 1963-65; various positions Eastern Airlines, Charlotte, 1965-88; real estate salesperson Allen Tate Realtors, Charlotte, 1990—; program dir. Delta Investment, Charlotte, 1984-88; mem. Bd. Realtors, Charlotte, 1990—; mem. Bd. Realtors, Rock Hill, S.C., 1993—. Troop leader Girl Scouts U.S., Charlotte, 1964; mem., vol. U.S. Humane Soc., Charlotte, 1964, 96—; co-founder, vol. Midway Meth. Ch. Libr., Kannapolis, N.C., 1958; mem. coun. Riverhills Cmty. Ch., Lake Wylie, S.C., 1980-82, chair fellowship com., 1979-80, mem. edn. com., 1984-85; founding mem., vol. Stowe Bot. Gardens, Belmont, N.C., 1994—. Me. N.C. Assn. Realtors, Charlotte Regional Realtor Assn. Avocations: water sports, snow ski race team, sailing, gardening. Home: PO Box 240173 Charlotte NC 28224-0173

COX, LINDA SUSAN, allergist, immunologist; b. Oakland, Calif., Aug. 17, 1955; d. James Lee Dolan and Nancy Jane (Christie) C.; m. Robert Louis Wolfgram Jr.; children: Mary Elizabeth Cox, Christopher Alexander Cox-Wolfgram. BA cum laude, Boston U., 1978; postgrad., Harvard U., 1978-79, Hahnemann Med. Coll., 1979-80; MD, Northwestern U., 1985. Diplomate Am. Bd. Internal Medicine, Am. Bd. Allergy and Immunology. Intern in internal medicine Jackson Meml. Hosp., U. Miami, Fla., 1985-88; emergency room physician North Ridge Med. Ctr., Ft. Lauderdale, Fla., 1988-89; fellow in allergy and immunology Nat. Jewish Hosp., Denver, 1989-91; pvt. practice Allergy, Asthma and Clin. Immunology Ctr., Miami, Fla., 1991-92, Adult and Pediat. Allergy and Immunology, Ft. Lauderdale, 1992—; emergency rm. physician Imperial Point Med. Ctr., 1997—; part-time emergency room physician Fitzsimmons Med. Ctr., Aurora, Colo., 1989-91, Palmetto Gen. Hosp., 1992—; rschr. U. Miami Sch. Medicine Dept. Clin. Immunology, 1987, U. Colo. Sch. Medicine Dept. Allergy and Clin. Immunology, 1990-91; asst. clin. prof. medicine U. Miami Sch. Medicine, 1996—, also bd. dirs.; asst. clin. prof. medicine Nova Southeastern U. Ortho. Sch. Medicine. Fellow Am. Coll. Allergy and Immunology, ACP; mem. Am. Acad. Allergy and Immunology, Am. Coll. Chest Physicians, Fla. Allergy and Immunology Soc. (mem. exec. com. 1998—, sec. practice std. com., mem. edn. com.), Broward County Med. Assn. (bd. dirs. 1996—). Episcopalian. Avocations: ballet, skiing. Home: 5802 Poinsettia Ave West Palm Beach FL 33407-2536 Office: 5333 N Dixie Hwy Fort Lauderdale FL 33334-3414

COX, MARGARET STEWART, photographer; b. Indpls., Jan. 9, 1948; d. Douglass Falconer and Margaret Geraldine (Gates) Stewart; m. Herbert Leo Cox Jr., Dec. 21, 1977 (dec. Nov. 1985); 1 child, Matthew Michael. Student, Butler U., 1965-67. Real estate agt. Don Asher & Assocs., Orlando, Fla., 1972-80; real estate agt., appraiser Mary P. Logvin Real Estate, Orlando, 1987-90; freelance photographer Orlando, 1990—. Exhibited photographs in group shows at Marie Selby Gardens, 1993, 94, 98 (Merit awards), 1998 Exhibit, Orlando Artists Biennial Exhbn., 1992 (Merit award), Mt. Dora Ctr. for the Arts, 1994 (Merit award), others. Bd. dirs. Adult Literacy League, Inc., Orlando, 1987-95, pres., 1994; active Fla. Literacy Coalition, 1988-96; vice chair Orange County Devel. Adv. Bd., Orlando, 1993-94; active United Way Spkrs. Bur., 1994, 95; judge Chertok Nature Photo Contest, 1993, chairperson, 1995, 96, 98. Recipient Spl. Mission Recognition award United Meth. Women, 1985. Mem. High Country Art and Craft Guild, Nat. Audubon Soc., Fla. Audubon Soc. (bd. dirs. 1998—), Orange Audubon Soc. (bd. dirs. 1993-96, 97—, rec. sec. 1996, bd. pres. 1998-99). Democrat. Avocations: reading, boating, travel, wildlife art, gardening. Office: 9410 Oak Island Ln Clermont FL 34711-7304

COX, MARSHALL, lawyer; b. Cleve., Nov. 17, 1932; s. Marshall H.C. and Mary (Bateman) Mills; m. Nancy Huntley, Aug. 3, 1957 (div. Oct. 1994); 1 child, Vanessa; m. Nathalie Menapace, Jan. 3, 1997. BA, Vanderbilt U., 1954; JD, Ohio State U., 1958. Bar: D.C. 1974, N.Y. 1959. Assoc. Cahill Gordon & Reindel, N.Y.C., 1959-67, ptnr., 1968-97. Served to 1st. lt. U.S. Army, 1955-57, Korea. Republican. Episcopalian.

COX, MARY LINDA, maintenance industry executive; b. Alton, Ill., July 3, 1946; d. William M. and Helen (Winters) C. BA, McKendree Coll., 1970; MBA, So. Ill. U., 1977; postgrad. date St. Louis U., 1984—. Exec. dir. Girl Scouts U.S., 1969-76; instr. So. Ill. U., Edwardsville, 1976-80; mgr. Smith-Scharff, St. Louis, 1980-81; account exec. AT&T, Tulsa, 1981-82; pres. Mo. Disposable Products, St. Louis, 1982-91, Am. Comml. Cleaning, pres., CEO, 1987—; v.p. Devel. Family Svcs. and Vis. Nurse Assn., Alton, Ill., 1992-94. Media specialist Tenn. Rep. Party, 1974; bd. dirs., pub. rels. chmn. YWCA, Alton, 1st v.p., pres.; mem. fin. com., 1st v.p. Greater St. Louis coun. Girl Scouts U.S., pres., 1993; mem. youth panel United Way St. Louis; planning chmn., mem. Greene County Hist. Soc., City of Wood River planning commn., White House Com. on Librs.; active United Cerebral Palsy, 1994. Mem. Central Bus. Assn. (v.p. 1985), Am. Comml., Bus. Network Internat., Screenwriters Network, Romance Writers Am. (treas.), Beta Gamma Sigma (chpt. pres. 1978-79). Office: Am Comml Cleaning 4 E Lorena Ave Wood River IL 62095-1902

COX, MELVIN MONROE, lawyer; b. Omaha, Jan. 31, 1947; s. Monroe M. Cox and Wilma Grace (Prickett) McPherson. BA with high honors, U. Wyo., 1969; JD, Harvard U., 1972. Bar: Pa. 1972, U.S. Dist. Ct. (we. dist.) Pa. 1972, N.J. 1987, U.S. Dist. Ct. (N.J.) 1987. Assoc. Rose, Schmidt & Dixon, Pitts., 1972-78; atty. Chgo. Pneumatic Tool Co., N.Y.C., 1978-81, asst. sec., 1981-88; asst. gen. counsel Sun Chem. Corp., Ft. Lee, N.J., 1989-93, asst. gen. counsel and asst. sec., 1993-97, v.p., gen. counsel, sec., 1997—; adj. prof. engring. law The Cooper Union, N.Y.C., 1984-91; asst. sec. DIC Ams., Inc., Ft. Lee, 1993-97; mng. dir. Sun Chem. B.V., Soest, The Netherlands; bd. dirs. Polychrome Corp., Ft. Lee, Kemtek Imaging Sys. Ltd., Johannesburg, South Africa; bd. visitors U. Wyoming, Coll. Arts and Scis., 1997—, vice chmn., 1998—. Bd. dirs. Good Shepherd Cmty. Svcs., Inc., 1999—. Mem. ABA, Am. Corp. Counsel Assn., Phi Beta Kappa, Phi Kappa Phi. Office: Sun Chem Corp 222 Bridge Plz S Fort Lee NJ 07024-5703

COX, MITCHEL NEAL, editor; b. Portsmouth, Ohio, Sept. 8, 1956; s. Walter Eugene and Mary Agnes (Orlett) C.; m. Lisa Renee LaLonde, Sept. 8, 1979; children: Harmony, Leigh Ann, Katie. BS in Journalism, Ohio State U., 1985. Mng. editor The Puller, Columbus, Ohio, 1984-87; editor Bicycles Today, Columbus, 1985-87, Fur-Fish-Game, Columbus, 1987—. Contbr. monthly column to Fur-Fish-Game, 1987—. Mem. Outdoor Writers Assn. Am. Office: Fur-Fish-Game 2878 E Main St Columbus OH 43209-2698

COX, PAT, artist; b. Pasadena, Calif., Mar. 6, 1921; d. Walter Melville and Mary Elizabeth (Frost) Boadway; m. Dale William Cox Jr., Feb. 19, 1946; children: Brian Philip, Dale William III, Gary Walter. BA, Mills Coll., 1943, MA, 1944. Graphic artist Pacific Manifolding Book Co., Emeryville, Calif., 1944-45; tchr. art to adults China Lake, Calif., 1957-63; tchr. art to children Peninsula Enrichment Program, Rancho Palos Verdes, Calif., 1965-67; graphic artist Western Magnum Corp., Hermosa Beach, Calif., 1970-80; tchr. art workshop Art at Your Fingertips, Rancho Palos Verdes, 1994-95. One-woman shows include Palos Verdes Art Ctr., Rancho Palos Verdes, Calif., 1977, 79, 83, 92, Thinking Eye Gallery, L.A., 1988, Ventura (Calif.) Coll. Art Galleries, 1994, Mendenhall Gallery, Whittier (Calif.) Coll., 1995, The Gallery at Stevenson Union, So. Oreg. Coll., Ashland, 1996; two person exhibits Laguna Art Mus., Laguna Beach, Calif., 1971, Creative Arts Gallery, Burbank, Calif., 1993; group exhibits include Long Beach Mus. Art, Art Rental Gallery, 1979, L.A. County Mus. Art, Art Rental Gallery, 1979, Palm Springs Mus. Art, 1980, Laguna Art Mus., 1981, N.Mex. Fine Arts Gallery, 1981, Pacific Grove Art Ctr., 1983, Phoenix Art Mus., 1983, Riverside Art Mus., 1985, Laguna Art Mus., 1986, Zanesville Art Ctr., Ohio, 1987, The Thinking Eye Gallery, L.A., 1987, 89, Hippodrome Gallery, Long Beach, 1988, N.Mex. State Fine Arts Gallery, 1988, Long Beach City Coll., 1989, Newport Harbor Art Mus., 1988, Downey Mus. Art, 1990, 92, Rachele Lozzi Fine Art Gallery, L.A., 1991, Internat. Contemporary Art Fair L.A., 1986, 87, 88, 92, U. Tex. Health Sci. Ctr., 1992, Long Beach Arts, 1991, 92, 93, Young Aggressive Art Mus., Santa Ana, 1993, U. Ark. Fine Arts Gallery, Fayetteville, 1994, Laura Knott Art Gallery, Bradford Coll., Mass., 1994, Bridge Street Gallery, Big Fork, Mont., 1994, St. John's Coll. Art Gallery, Santa Fe, 1995, L.A. Harbor Coll., Calif., 1995, Walker Art Collection, Garnett, Kans., 1995, San Francisco State U., 1996, Coleman Gallery, Albuquerque, 1996, Loyola Law Sch., L.A., 1996, San Bernardino County Mus., 1996, Prieto Gallery, Mills Coll., Oakland, Calif., 1996, U. So. Calif. Hillel Gallery, L.A., 1997, Fresno Art Mus., 1998. Trustee L.A. Art Assn., 1972-79; bd. dirs. Palos Verdes Art Ctr., 1966-70, 87-89, chair exhbn. com., 1982-85, co-chair Art for Fun(d)s Sake, 1966; judge Tournament of Roses Assn., Pasadena, 1975; mem. strategic planning Palos Verdes Art Ctr., 1988; mem. Pacific Pl. Planning Commn. Percent for Art, San Pedro, Calif., 1989; juror Pasadena Soc. Artists, 1973, 81, Women Painters West, 1984-85. Recipient Silver Pin award Palos Verdes Art Ctr., 1988, Calif. Gold Discovery award V.I.P. Jury Panel, L.A., 1994. Mem. Nat. Watercolor Soc. (juror 1981, 1st v.p. 1980, 4th v.p. 1984), Nat. Mus. Women in the Arts, Oakland Mus. Art, Mus. Contemporary Art, L.A. County Mus. Art, Palos Verdes Cmty. Art Assn. (cert. appreciation 1981). Avocations: gardening, reading.

COX, RICHARD D., lawyer; b. Andrews, Tex., Jan. 6, 1951. AS, Christian Coll. Southwest, 1971; BA summa cum laude, U. Tex., Arlington, 1973; JD, So. Meth. U., 1976. Bar: Tex., U.S. Dist. Ct. (no., we. dist.) Tex., U.S. Ct. Appeals (5th cir.), U.S. Tax Ct. Ptnr. Brown McCarroll & Oaks Hartline, Dallas. Recipient Am. Jurisprudence award. Mem. Phi Delta Phi. Address: Brown McCarroll & Oaks Hartline 300 Crescent Ct Ste 1400 Dallas TX 75201-7855*

COX, RICHARD HORTON, civil engineering executive; b. Paia, Hawaii, Oct. 10, 1920; s. Joel B. and Helen Cliford (Horton) C.; m. Hester Virginia Smith, Dec. 12, 1942 (dec. Aug. 12, 1995); children: Millicent, Janet, Lydia, Evelyn, David, Samuel (dec.). BS, Calif. Inst. Tech., 1942, MS, 1946. Registered profl. engr., surveyor, Hawaii. Supr. rocket range Calif. Inst. Tech., Pasadena, 1942-46; civil engr. McBryde Sugar Co., Eleele, Hawaii, 1946-56; land mgr. Alexander & Baldwin, Honolulu, 1956-71, v.p., 1971-86; engring. cons. Honolulu, 1986—. Mem. State Commn. on Water Resource Mgmt., 1987-94, 95-99. Fellow ASCE; mem. AAAS, NSPE, Am. Geophys. Union. Mem. Soc. of Friends. Home and Office: 1951 Kakela Dr Honolulu HI 96822-2156

COX, RICHARD JOSEPH, former broadcasting executive; b. Bklyn., Aug. 21, 1929; s. Harry Joseph and Rosemary Magdelene (Broderick) C.; m. Ray Louise Bradley, Oct. 2, 1954 (dec. 1996); children: Christopher Bradley, Cynthia Anne, John Anthony, Claudia Claire. Student, Fordham U., 1947-49. With Young & Rubicam Inc., N.Y.C., 1949-66; v.p. in charge radio and TV Young & Rubicam Inc., 1963-66; v.p. in charge TV programming Doyle Dane Bernbach, 1966-71; v.p. in charge program devel. Tomorrow Entertainment Inc., 1971-73; pres. Y&R Ventures, Inc., N.Y.C., 1974-78; pres. subs. DCA Prodns. Inc., N.Y.C., 1974-78; owner, pres., exec. producer DCA TV, Inc., 1978-81; pres. CBS Cable div. CBS Inc., 1981-83; owner, pres. DCA TV Inc., 1983—. Co-producer off-Broadway play Orlando Furioso, 1970 (spl. Obie award 1971). Mem. Pres.'s Com. on Drug Abuse, 1969-70. Served with Psychol. Warfare Group, U.S. Army 1951-53. Republican. Roman Catholic. Clubs: Players, Burke Hollow, Vets of 7th Regt., Four Seasons. Home and Office: 135 Westport Tpke Fairfield CT 06430-1641

COX, ROBERT CLAUDE, retird educator and school system administrator; b. Milford, Conn., July 6, 1930; s. Claude Alphonso and Helen H. (French) C.; m. Rose Marie Madeline Babain, Aug. 11, 1962; children: Robert Brian, Marie Lynn. BA in History, U. Bridgeport, 1953, MS in Ednl. Adminstrn., 1956, MA in History, 1971. Cert. tchr., intermediate adminstr., Conn. Tchr. Milford Pub. Schs., 1955-73, K-12 supr. history, 1973-90; ret., 1990; exec. v.p. Conn. State Fedn. Tchrs., 1968-73; chmn. Conn. Tchrs. Cert. Bd., Hartford, 1965-73; presenter Yale Seminar in Russian Studies, 1981-97. Guest editor Yankee Forum, 1989; contbr. articles to various publs. Chmn. Milford Housing Authority, 1974-78; chmn. 3d dist. Milford Dem. Com., 1975-78. With U.S. Army, 1953-55. Recipient award for citizenship edn. Close-Up Found., 1986, 87, cert. of recognition Nat. Slavic Honor Soc., 1986; named Program in Internat. Ednl. Resources fellow in Russian studies Yale Ctr. for Inter-Area Studies, 1996. Mem. Ret. Tchrs. Conn. Roman Catholic. Avocations: writing, reading, travel, golf, classical music. Home: 139 Meadows End Rd Milford CT 06460-4228

COX, ROBERT GENE, management consultant; b. Liberal, Kans., June 3, 1929; s. Clarice Eldon and Margaret Verene (Jones) C.; m. Eileen Frances Hinshaw, July 10, 1953; children: Ann Rebecca Cox Taylor, Allan Robert. B.A. with honors, U. N.Mex., 1951, J.D., 1955; grad., Fgn. Service Inst., 1956, Harvard Bus. Sch., 1978, 79. Joined Fgn. Svc., 1956; 3d to 2d sec. Am. Embassy, Panama, 1956-58; Am. Consul, Caracas, Venezuela, 1959-61; Korea desk officer Dept. State, Washington, 1961-62; chief of staff mgmt. planning Dept. State, 1963-65, officer in charge Mission to Israel, 1965; staff asst. to President U.S. The White House, 1966-68; ptnr. William H. Clark Assos., N.Y.C. and Chgo., 1968-71; sr. staff officer UN Secretariat, Vienna and N.Y.C., 1971-72; pres. Hennes & Cox, Inc., N.Y.C., Washington and Los Angeles, 1972-75; prin., nat. dir. human resource systems Ernst & Ernst, Cleve., 1975-78; ptnr., mng. dir. Arthur Young & Co., N.Y.C., 1979-83; pres. PA Exec. Search Group, N.Y.C., 1983-86; chmn. PA Computers and Telecommunications NA, N.Y.C., 1985-86; mng. dir. A.T. Kearney, Inc., 1987-90, 93-96; exec. v.p. Oxford Analytica, Inc., N.Y.C., 1990-92; exec. dir. Oxford Analytica Ltd., Eng., 1990-92; pres. Nelson O'Connor & Cox, Tucson, Ariz., 1996—; mem. history faculty Fla. State U., 1958; cons. Commn. U.S.-Latin-Am. Rels., 1974; sr. advisor Commn. Orgn. of Govt. for Conduct of Fgn. Policy, 1974-75; expert witness on mil. value of Panama Canal U.S. Ho. of Reps., 1977; ITT lectr. Georgetown U., 1981. Author: Defense Department Diplomacy in Latin America, 1964, Choices for Partnership or Bloodshed in Panama, 1975, The Canal Zone: New Focal Point in U.S.-Latin American Relations, 1977, The Chief Executive, 1980, Planning for Immigration: A Business Perspective, 1981, Selection of the Chief Executive Officer, 1982. Mem. Pacific Coun. Internat. Policy; bd. dirs. cmty. drug control program, Glen Ridge, N.J., 1971-72, Unitarian-Universalist Christian Fellowship, 1987-90; dep. to county chmn. Albuquerque Dem. Party, 1954; advisor on exec. selection to transition staff of Pres.-elect Carter, 1976-77; mem. bd. advisors Georgetown U. Program in Bus. Diplomacy, 1985-95; bd. dirs. Coun. on Econ. Priorities, LeRoy Industries, Inc., 1984-87, 89-91, Alden Owners, Inc., 1986-88; trustee Meadville Theol. Sch. U. Chgo., 1986-92; gov. Manchester Coll. Oxford U., 1991-96, councillor, 1992-96, hon. gov. 1996—; trustee Unitarian Ch. of All Souls, N.Y.C., 1980-84, sec., 1979-80, pres., 1983-84, deacon, 1985-92; lay preacher Manchester Coll. Chapel, Oxford U., 1990—; mem. vestry St. Philip's Episc. Ch., Tucson, 1996—, sr. warden, 1997—. Mem. Jonesville (Mich.) Heritage Assn., Coun. Fgn. Rels. (chmn. study group on immigration and U.S. fgn. policy 1978), Royal Econ. Soc. (Eng.), Am. Soc. Internat. Law, Unitarian Hist. Soc. Eng., Martineau Soc. Eng., Internat. Assn. Religious Freedom, SAR. Episcopalian. Home: 2575 E Avenida De Posada Tucson AZ 85718-3055 Office: Ste 2010 5285 E Williams Cir Tucson AZ 85711

COX, ROBERT RIPLEY, JR., biology statistician; b. Mar. 1, 1959. BS in Forest Resources, U. Ga., 1987; MS in Fisherier and Wildlife, Utah State U., 1993; PhD in Wildlife and Fisherier Sci., La. State U., 1996. Ecologist No. Prarie Sci. Ctr., Jamestown, N.D., 1995-97, statistician, 1997—. Office: Northern Prarie Wildlife Rsch Ctr 8711 37th St SE Jamestown ND 58401

COX, RODY P(OWELL), medical educator, internist; b. New Brighton, Pa., June 24, 1926; s. Raymond James and Hazel (Powell) C.; m. Jane Beverly Birks, Sept. 5, 1953 (dec. Apr. 1995); children: Shelley Lea, Rody Powell, Sue Ellen; m. LaVaun Jeanne Sears, Mar. 1, 1997. Student Franklin and Marshall Coll., 1946-48; MD, U. Pa., 1952. Diplomate Am. Bd. Internal Medicine. Intern U. Mich., 1952-53, resident in medicine, 1953-54; resident in medicine U. Pa., Phila., 1953-57, asst. prof. medicine, 1957-60; rsch. assoc. U. Glasgow, Scotland, 1960-61; prof. medicine NYU, N.Y.C., 1961-79, prof. pharmacology, 1972-79, chief div. human genetics, 1972-79; prof., vice chmn. dept. medicine Case-Western Res. U., Cleve., 1979-88; chief med. svc. VA Med. Ctr., Cleve., 1979-88; dean Med. Sch. U. Tex. Southwestern Med. Ctr., Dallas, 1988-89, prof. internal medicine, 1988—; mem. metabolism study sect. NIH, 1970-74, chmn. genetics study sect., 1978-79, chmn. mammalian genetics study sect., 1979-81; mem. panel on clin. scis. NRC, 1976-86. Editor: Cell Communication, 1974; co-editor: Epithelial Cell Culture, 1981. Contbr. articles to profl. publs. Sgt. U.S. Army, 1944-46, NATOUSA. Fellow ACP; mem. Am. Soc. Clin. Investigation (emeritus), Assn. Am. Physicians, Cen. Soc. Clin. Research, John Morgan Soc. of U. Pa., Harvey Soc., Am. Clin. Climatol. Assn., Am. Soc. Human Genetics, Interurban Clin. Club, Alpha Omega Alpha (councillor NYU chpt. 1970-76). Home: 5 Connaught Ct Dallas TX 75225-2459 Office: U Tex Southwestern Med Ctr 5323 Harry Hines Blvd Dallas TX 75235-7208

COX, ROGER FRAZIER, lawyer; b. Phila., Sept. 11, 1939; s. Roger Newcomb and Ethel May (Frazier) C.; m. Lucy Jakstas, June 24, 1967. BA, Amherst Coll., 1962; LLB, U. Pa., 1966. Bar: D.C. 1967, Pa. 1967, Calif. 1970. Law clk. to presiding judge U.S. Dist. Ct., N.Y.C., 1966-67; asst. dist. atty. Phila. Dist. Atty.'s Office, 1967-69; staff atty. Alameda County Legal Aid Soc., Oakland, Calif., 1969-71; from assoc. to ptnr. Blank, Rome, Comisky & McCauley, Phila., 1971—. Mem. ABA, Am. Judicature Soc., Pa. Bar Assn., Phila. Bar Assn., Order of Coif. Home: 303 Delancey St Philadelphia PA 19106-4208 Office: Blank Rome Comisky & McCauley LLP One Logan Sq Philadelphia PA 19103-6998

COX, RONALD BAKER, engineering and management consultant, university dean; b. Chattanooga, Sept. 27, 1943; s. Fred T. and Mary A. (Baker) C.; m. Nancy C. Barger; children: Kathy, David, Sherry. BS in Mech. Engring., U. Tenn., 1965, MS, 1968; MBA, Vanderbilt U., 1980; PhD, Rice U., Houston, 1970. Registered profl. engr., Tenn. Design engr. duPont Co., 1965-66; dir. engring. Ind. Boiler Co., 1966-68; dir. engring. research U. Tenn., Chattanooga, 1972-74; dean engring. U. Tenn., 1979—; mng. dir. motor vehicle diagnostic demonstration program U.S. Dept. Transp., 1974-76; pres. Internat. Engring. and Mgmt., cons. firm., 1968—. Author articles, reports, columns in field. Deacon Signal Mountain (Tenn.) Bapt. Ch., 1972—. Named Engr. of Yr., Greater Chattanooga Area, 1982, Engr. of the Decade, 1990. Mem. ASME (chpt. pres. 1979-80), NSPE, Tex. Soc. Profl. Engrs., Tenn. Soc. Profl. Engrs., Am. Soc. for Engring. Mgmt. (nat. pres. 1994—), Am. Soc. Engring. Edn., Order Engring., Chattanooga C. of C. (com. chmn. 1976-77), Sigma Xi, Tau Beta Pi, Chattanooga Engrs. Club (pres. 1980). Office: U Tenn Sch Engring Chattanooga TN 37403

COX, SANDRA ANNETTE, economic developer; b. Oakland, Nebr., Dec. 10, 1961; d. David R. May and Marilyn R. (Hass) Fantz; m. Randall W. Huey, Apr. 25, 1981 (div. Aug. 1989); m. Jim B. Cox, Feb. 14, 1991; children: Ashley M., Tabitha L. and Tiffany L. (twins). Student, U. Mo., Kansas City, 1980-81, Ctrl. Mo. State U., Warrensburg, 1981, Mo. Valley Coll., Marshall, 1996—. Lic. life, health and property ins., Mo. Salesperson Readi Motors Inc., Clinton, Mo., 1983-85; bus. mgr., office mgr. Golden Valley Ford Tractor, Clinton, 1985-87; bus., fin., office mgr. Jim Raysik Chrysler, Clinton, 1987-90; ins. agt. Mike Keith Ins., Clinton, 1990-92; dist. mgr., info-ed specialist Saline Soil and Water Conservation Dist., Marshall, 1992-98; asst. dir. Marshall-Saline Devel. Corp., Marshall, Mo., 1998—; grant writer Saline Soil and Water Conservation Dist., 1995-98. Grad. Henry County Discover Leadership Program, 1988; gen. chair EXCEL Leadership Program, Marshall, 1993-95; mem. com. Mo. Envirothon Bd., Jefferson City, 1996-98; pres. Saline County Dem. Club, Marshall, 1996-97, Luth. Women's Missionary League, Marshall, 1995-97, North Ctrl. Region Dist. Employees Assn., 1993-95; bd. dirs. Marshall Pub. Schs., 1995— (bd. pres. 1998—), Mo. Sch. Bds. Sch. Improvement Com., Columbia, 1997-98, governance com. 1998—; mem. Partnership for Outstanding Schs., 1996—; sec. Saline County Dem. Ctrl. com., 1998—. Named Outstanding Dist. Mgr., Natural Resources Conservation Svc., Columbia, 1994. Mem. Nat. Conservation Dist. Employees Assn., Mo. Soil and Water Conservation Dist. Employees Assn. (Info-Ed Specialist of Yr. 1994). Avocations: bowling, reading. Home: 875 W Vest St Marshall MO 65340-1665 Office: Marshall-Saline Development Corp 261 W Washington St Marshall MO 65340

COX, SANFORD CURTIS, JR., lawyer; b. El Paso, Tex., July 31, 1929; s. Sanford Curtis Sr. and Iva M. (Richardson) C.; m. Helen A. Thurston, Sept. 27, 1958; children: Sanford Curtis III, Christopher Thurston. *Sanford Cox is a member of the ninth generation from Robert Cox of Massachusetts, born 1670. His great-grandfather, Reverend Leonard Cox, moved from Massachusetts to Charlotte Courthouse, Virginia, where grandfather, Edwin Peter Cox, and father were born. Wife Holly (Helen), a 3rd generation El Paso artist recognized for her research of early El Paso artists, is the granddaughter of artist Fern Thurston and daughter of artist Eugene B. Thurston. Son, Christopher Thurston Cox, JD 1993, is practicing law with his father. Elder son, S. Curtis Cox, III, JD 1996, is practicing law in Tacoma, Washington.* BA, Tex. Western Coll., 1951, MA, 1952; LLB, U. Tex., 1957. Bar: Tex. 1957, U.S. Dist. Ct. (we. dist.) Tex. 1960, U.S. Ct. Appeals (5th cir.) 1964, U.S. Ct. Appeals (D.C. cir.) 1975. Assoc. Andress, Lipscomb, Peticolas & Fisk, El Paso, 1957-61; ptnr. Lipscomb, Fisk & Cox, El Paso, 1961-74, Fisk & Cox, El Paso, 1974-79; sole practice El Paso, 1979-81; pres./shareholder Sanford C. Cox Jr. P.C., El Paso, 1981-93, mem., 1993—. Mem. bd. editors U. Tex. Law Rev. Mem. adv. bd. Booth Meml. Home, 1963-79, Pleasant View Home, 1979-91. Served with U.S. Army, 1952-54. Mem. ABA, Tex. Bar Assn. (admissions com. 17th dist. 1976), El Paso Bar Assn. (ethics com. 1965-69, fee arbitration com. 1973-75), Order of Coif, Phi Delta Phi. Republican. Episcopalian. Office: Coronado Tower Bldg Ste 220 6006 N Mesa El Paso TX 79912

COX, SHARON G., art educator. AA, Macon (Ga.) Coll., 1980; BA, Mercer U., 1982; MFA, U. Ga., 1983. Lectr. in art Mercer U., Macon, Ga., 1983-85; asst. prof. journalism Jackson (Miss.) State U., 1987-89, Lynchburg (Va.) Coll., 1989-91; art dept. head Jamestown (N.D.) Coll., 1992—. E-mail: http: cox@jc.edu. Home: PO Box 1559 Jamestown ND 58402-1559

COX, STEPHEN F., retired publishing company executive; b. Lyons, Kans., Apr. 2, 1939. BA, U. Okla., 1961; MA, U. Tenn., 1976. Fellow U. Okla. Press, 1961-62; asst. editor U. Tenn. Press, 1962-76; assoc. dir., exec. editor U. Nebr. Press, 1976-83; editor-in-chief, dir. U. Ariz. Press, Tucson, 1983-98; ret., 1998. Address: 5148 E 2d St Tucson AZ 85711*

COX, SUE, non-profit agency administrator; b. Sherman, Tex., Aug. 8, 1940; d. Cecil Elihu and Junia Launa (Cole) Green; m. Carl Bowen Cox, Aug. 12, 1961; 1 child, Cynthia Susan. BBA, Baylor U., 1961; MEd, Tex. Tech U., 1968. Tchr. Lamesa (Tex.) Ind. Schs., 1961-69, Caddo Parish Schs., Shreveport, La., 1970-74, Dallas Pub. Schs., 1974-82; cons. Sue Cox & Assocs., Dallas, 1982-92; exec. dir. Anti-Crime Coun. Tex., Dallas, 1984-87, Texans Who Care, Dallas, 1987-92, Tex. Coun. on Problem Gambling, Dallas, 1992—; bd. dirs. Gaming Entertainment Rsch. and Edn. Found., Washington, 1996—, Racetrack Chaplaincy of Tex., 1997—; mem. adv. bd. Nat. Coun. on Problem Gambling, Columbia, Md., 1992—, Nat. Ctr. for Responsible Gaming, Kansas City, Mo., 1996-97. Author pub. policy papers in field. Mem. State Dem. Exec. Com., Tex., 1978-84; del. Nat. Dem. Convention, N.Y.c., 1980; v.p. Dallas Dem. Forum, 1980-86; mem. Gov.'s Task Force on Illegal Gambling, 1997, Tex. Close Up Bd., 1978, Tex. Lottery Start-Up Commn., 1992, Baylor Bear Found., 1996—, Home for Home Com., 1997-98. Mem. Phi Beta Phi Alumnae Assn. (bd. dirs. 1993). Baptist. Avocations: piano, arts and crafts, reading, spectator sports, golf. Home: 4031 Willow Ridge Dr Dallas TX 75244-7360 Office: Tex Coun on Problem Gambling 770 N Coit Rd Richardson TX 75080-5426

COX, TERI P., public relations executive; b. Pitts., May 21, 1952; d. Meyer and Faye Helen (Tischler) Polack; m. William R. Cox, Jan. 1, 1982. BA, U. Pitts., 1974; MBA in Mktg., NYU, 1989. Info. dir. United Mental Health; prodr., host weekly PA radio program; pub. rels. dir. Atlanta Merchandise Mart; mktg. rsch., pub. rels. cons. Pfizer Inc., NYU Stern Sch. Bus.; acct. supr. Burson-Marsteller, Coleman & Pellet; mng. ptnr. Cox Comms. Ptnrs., Lawrenceville, N.J., 1992-98, sr. mng. ptnr., 1998—. Bd. dirs. Lupus Found. Am. N.J. chpt., N.J. divsn. Am. Cancer Soc., asst. sec., trustee. Recipient Capitol Dome award Nat. Am. Cancer Soc., 1997. Mem. Pub. Rels. Soc. Am., Am. Mktg. Assn., Healthcare Businesswomen's Assn. (bd. dirs., dir. of comm.). Office: Cox Comms Ptnrs 2 Roseberry Ct Lawrenceville NJ 08648-1058*

COX, TERRENCE GUY, manufacturing automation executive; b. Revere, Mass., Feb. 29, 1956; s. Thomas Ambrose and Jennie Constance (Meli) C.; m. Therese Marie Paone, Sept. 15, 1979. BS in Fin. cum laude, Babson Coll., 1976, MBA, 1977. Asst. to pres. Standard Bldg. Systems, Inc., Point of Rocks, Md., 1977-80; sr. fin. analyst Nortek, Inc., Cranston, R.I., 1980-82; mgr. new bus. devel. Compo Industries, Waltham, Mass., 1982-83; founder, v.p., chief fin. officer, treas. CAD/CAM Integration, Inc., Woburn, Mass., 1983—, also bd. dirs., 1983—; CFO, COO Industry Directions, Inc., Newburyport, Mass., 1997—. Author: (with others) Process/Industrial Instruments and Controls Handbook, 4th edit., The Color of Love; contbr. articles to profl. jours. Founder Revere track league, 1974, pres., 1974-77; coach Revere little league, 1969-77; bd. dirs. Revere Parks and Recreation Commn., 1972-74, Boy's Club of Revere, 1974-77; past treas., bd. dirs. Encode, Inc., Nashua, N.H. Roman Catholic. Avocations: reading, travel, diving. Office: CAD/CAM Integration Inc 76 Winn St Woburn MA 01801-2836

COX, VANDE LEE, critical care nurse; b. Takoma, Md., June 21, 1954; d. Vego Larkin and Lanette Lucille (Cunningham) Gooch; divorced; children: Andrea, Nathenial. Diploma, Deaconess Hosp. Sch. Nursing, 1976; BSN, U. Evansville, Ind., 1980, MSN, 1989; cert. family nurse practitioner, 1998. RN, Ind.; cert. family nurse practitioner; CEN, CCRN; cert. PALS, ACLS, TNCC, BTLS, ACLS instr. Nurse emergency rm. Deaconess Hosp., Evansville, 1976-77; clin. instr. Deaconess Hosp. Sch. Nursing, Evansville, 1980-85; clin. instr. ICU and med./surg. unit U. Evansville, 1989; critical care nurse Welborn Hosp., Evansville, 1989-90, emergency rm. nurse, 1990—; charge nurse Thunder on the Ohio, 1991-97; family nurse practitioner Cmty. Health Ctr., Evansville, 1999—; clin. instr. Ivy Tech., Evansville, 1992. Mem. Emergency Nurses Assn., Critical Care Nurses Assn., Sigma Theta Tau. Home: 3417 Koring Rd Evansville IN 47720-2612 Office: Welborn Hosp 501 John St Ste 12 Evansville IN 47713-1299

COX, WALTER THOMPSON, III, federal judge; b. Anderson, S.C., Aug. 13, 1942; s. Walter Thompson and Mary (Johnson) C.; m. Victoria Grubbs, Feb. 8, 1963; children: Lisa, Walter. BS, Clemson U., 1964; JD, U. S.C., 1967. Bar: S.C., 1967, U.S. Dist. Ct. S.C., 1967, U.S. Ct. Appeals (4th cir.), 1976, U.S. Ct. Appeals for Armed Forces, 1984, U.S. Supreme Ct., 1987. Commn. capt. U.S. Army, 1964, atty., 1964-73; ptnr. Jones, McIntosh, Threlkeld, Newman & Cox, Anderson, S.C., 1973-78; trial judge 10th cir. State S.C., Anderson, 1978-84; chief judge U.S. Ct. Appeal for Armed Forces, Washington, 1984—. Mem. ABA, FBA, Judge Advocate's Assn., S.C. Bar Assn. (del.), Army Navy Club, Wild Dune Golf & Racquet Club. Episcopalian. Office: US Ct Appeals Armed Forces Office of Chief Judge 450 E St NW Washington DC 20442-0001

COX, WARREN JACOB, architect; b. N.Y.C., Aug. 28, 1935; s. Oscar Sydney and Louise Bryson (Black) C.; m. Claire Christie-Miller, July 1, 1975; children: Alexandra Louise, Samuel Oscar. BA magna cum laude, Yale U., 1957, MArch, 1961. Ptnr. Hartman-Cox Architects, Washington, 1965—; vis. archtl. critic Yale, 1966, Cath. U. Am., 1967, U. Va., 1976; lectr. Works include master plan, dormitory and chapel, Mt. Vernon Coll., EURAM bldg. Nat. Perm. Bldg., Folger Shakespeare Libr. addition, Washington, Immanuel Presbyn. Ch., Nat. Humanities Ctr., Raleigh, Am. Embassy, Malaysia, HEB corp. hdqrs., San Antonio, Chrysler Mus. remodeling, Norfolk, Dumbarton Oaks remodeling, Monroe Hall addition, Charlottesville, Va., Sumner Sq., 1001 Pa. Ave., Market Sq., Franklin Sq., Georgetown U. Law Ctr. Libr. and Residence Hall, Washington, John Carter Brown Libr. addition, Providence, Winterthur New Exhbn. Bldg., Wilmington, Del., Tulane Law Sch., New Orleans, Law Sch. Libr. Univ. Conn., Hartford, Law Sch. Washington U., St. Louis, Libr. Case We. Res. U., Cleve., Fed. Courthouse, Corpus Christi, Tex., Concert Hall remodeling Kennedy Ctr. for Performing Arts, Washington, New Dist. and Cir. Courthouses, Lexington, Kennedy Warren Apts. addition, Lincoln and Jefferson Memls. restoration, Patent Office Bldg. renovation, Nat. Archives Bldg. renovation, Washington. Mem. Georgetown Commn. Fine Arts, 1971-75; chmn. Friends of Folger Shakespeare Libr., 1987-88; bd. dirs. Ctr. for Palladian Studies in Am., 1982—, D.C. Preservation League, 1987-89. Recipient over 100 nat. and regional design awards including Louis Sullivan Prize (1972), six AIA Nat. Honor awards, and the AIA Archtl. Firm award, 1988. Fellow AIA. Home: 3111 N St NW Washington DC 20007-3420 also: PO Box 1 Church Hill MD 21623-0001 Office: Hartman Cox Architects 1074 Thomas Jefferson St NW Washington DC 20007-3832

COX, WILFORD DONALD, retired food company executive; b. Marion, Ill., Sept. 5, 1925; s. James Roy and Mamie (Stahlhut) C.; m. Helen Eunice Turner, Sept. 8, 1945; 1 child, James Dexter. Grad. high sch., Crab Orchard, Ill. Asst. plant mgr. Standard Brands Inc., San Antonio, 1956-60; plant mgr. Dallas, 1960-64; asst. div. mgr. Kansas City, Mo., 1964-70; div. mgr. Kansas City, 1972-78; v.p. procurement N.Y.C., 1978-81; v.p. Cal-Maine Foods, Jackson, Miss., 1970-72; v.p. commodities Nabisco Brands Inc., East Hanover, N.J., 1981-84; v.p. oil procurement Kraft Inc., Glenview, Ill., then Memphis, 1984-90, ret., 1990. Mem. Nat. Inst. Oilseed Processors, Nat. Soybean Processors Assn., Nat. Assn. Purchasing Mgrs., Colonial Country Club (Memphis). Republican. Avocation: golf.

COX, WILLIAM ANDREW, cardiovascular thoracic surgeon; b. Columbus, Ga., Aug. 3, 1925; s. Virgil Augustus and Dale Jackson C.; m. Nina Recelle Hobby, Jan. 1, 1948; children: Constance Lynn Cox Rogers, Patricia Ann Cox Brown, William Robert, Janet Elaine Cox Sidewater. Student, Presbyn. Coll., 1942, Harvard U., 1944-45, Cornell U., 1945; BS, Emory U., 1950, MD, 1954; MS in Surgery, Baylor U., 1961. Diplomate Am. Bd. Surgery, Am. Bd. Thoracic Surgery. Active duty USN, 1943-46; lt. (s.g.) USNR, 1946-54; commd. 1st lt. M.C. U.S. Army, 1954, advanced through grades to col., 1969; intern Brooke Army Med. Ctr., San Antonio, 1954-55, resident gen. surgery, 1956-60; resident cardiovasc. thoracic surgery Walter Reed Army Med. Ctr., Washington, 1960-62, staff cardiothoracic surgeon, 1962; asst chief cardiothoracic surgery Letterman Gen. Hosp., San Francisco, 1962-65; chief dept. surgery and cardiothoracic surgery 121 Evaculation Hosp, Seoul, Korea, 1965-66; cons. cardiothoracic surgery Korean Theatre, 1965-66; asst. chief cardiothoracic surgery Brooke Army Med Ctr., 1966-69, chief, 1969-73, bd. dirs. thoracic surgery residency programs, 1966-73, ret., 1973; Brooke Tower, on call for Pres. Lyndon B. Johnson when he visited his Tex. Ranch, 1967-72; clin. prof. cardio-thoracic surgery U. Tex. Sch. Medicine, San Antonio, 1971—; practice specializing in cardiovasc. thoracic surgery, Corpus Christi, Tex., 1973-93; cons. cardio-thoracic surgery Brooke Army Med. Ctr., San Antonio, 1977—; chief staff Meml. Med. Ctr., 1980; dir. disaster med. care region 3A Tex. State Dept. Health, 1973-88; mem. Coastal Bend Coun. Gov.'s Emergency Med. Svc. Commn., 1979-88; mem. adv. bd. on congenital heart disease Tex. Dept. Health, 1980-88; participant joint confs. on cardiovasc. surgery and thoracic surgery Am. People Amb. Program, Leningrad, Moscow, Bucharest, Romania, Belgrade, Yugoslavia, Prague, Czechoslovakia, 1987; del. Vanderbilt U. Joint conf. vascular surgery Dublin, Ireland, Edinburgh, Scotland, London, 1986; participant joint confs. cardiovasc. surgery and thoracic surgery Am. Amb. People to People Program, Singapore, Kuala Lumpur, Malaysia, Hanoi, Vietnam, DaNang, Vietnam, Hue, Vietnam, Saigon, Vietnam, Hong Kong, 1992, People to People Am. Amb. Program, Eng., Scotland, Wales, 1996; spkr. symposium Controversies in Cardiology, Dr. Willis Hurst, Holland Am. Lines Veendam, 1997. Contbr. numerous articles to profl. jours. Ruling elder Presbyn. Ch., 1960—. Decorated Legion of Merit, Army Commendation medal; recipient A Prefix award Surgeon Gen. U.S. Army, commendation Surgeon Gen. South Korea, commendation Eighth U.S. Army Commdg. Gen. for Emergency Surgery on Adm. Blackburn U.S. Negotiator for Peace, Pan mun jom, North Korea; named hon. citizen Phila. by Mayor Edward G. Rendell, 1995. Fellow Am. Coll. Chest Physicians; mem. AMA, Soc. Thoracic Surgeons, Denton A. Coley Cardiovasc. Surgery Soc., Tex. Med. Assn. (del. conf. infectious diseases Bangkok, Hong Kong, Beijing, Shanghai, 1983), So. Thoracic Surgery Assn., Nueces County Med. Soc., Corpus Christi Surg. Soc., 38th Parallel Med. Soc., U.S. Power Squadron, People to People Internat., Internat. Platform, USN League (life), Retired Officers Assn. (life), Navy Meml. Yacht Club (past commodore presidio San Francisco), T-Bar-M Racquet Club, Corpus Christi Country Club, Corpus Christi Athletic Club, Corpus Christi Town, Ft. Sam Houston Officers Club. Republican. Home: 5214 Wooldridge Rd Corpus Christi TX 78413-3833

COX, WILLIAM FREDERICK, hospital executive; b. Richmond, Ind., Mar. 20, 1962; s. Leon Thompson and Donna Eloise (Mitchell) C.; m. Laurie Ann DeTore, July 25, 1992. BA, Earlham Coll., 1984; MD, Case Western Res. U., 1988. Diplomate Am. Bd. Psychiatry and Neurology. Gaughan fellow in forensic psychiatry Harvard Med. Sch., Cambridge, Mass., 1993-94; staff psychiatrist Carney Hosp., Boston, 1994-96; assoc. med. dir. Fuller Hosp., Attleboro, Mass., 1996-98; asst. prof. U. Mass. Med. Sch., 1999—; clin. preceptor Boston U. Sch. Medicine, 1994-96. Mem. Am. Psychiat. Assn., Am. Acad. Psychiatry and the Law. Republican. Avocations: bicycling, chess, basketball, canoeing.

COX, WILLIAM JACKSON, bishop; b. Valeria, Ky., Jan. 24, 1921; s. Robert Lee and Ora Ethel (Lawson) C.; m. Betty Drake, Dec. 20, 1941; children—Sharon Lee, William Richard, Michael Colin. Student, U. Cin., 1939-40, George Washington U., Washington, 1945-46, U. Md. overseas extension, London, 1951-53, Va. Theol. Sem., Alexandria, 1957; D.Div. (hon.), Va. Theol. Sem., Alexandria, 1974, Episcopal Theol. Sem. Ky., Lexington, 1980. Ordained priest Episcopal Ch., 1957. Pres., gen. mgr. McCook Broadcasting Co., McCook, Nebr., 1947-49; rector Church of the Holy Cross, Cumberland, Md., 1957-72; suffragan bishop of Md. Episcopal Ch., Frederick, Md., 1972-80; asst. bishop Okla. Episcopal Ch., Tulsa, 1980—; pres. Appalachian Peoples Service Orgn., Blacksburg, Va., 1974-80; chmn. Standing Com. on the Church in Small Communities, N.Y.C., 1976-82. Pres., Nursing Home Bd. of Allegany County, Cumberland, Md., 1965-72; pres. Episcopal Ministries to the Aging, Balt., 1973-80. Served to lt. col. U.S. Army, 1942-46, 1949-54; ETO. Avocation: private pilot. Home: 6130 S Hudson Pl Tulsa OK 74136-2703 Office: Diocese of Okla 501 S Cincinnati Ave Tulsa OK 74103-4801

COX, WILLIAM MARTIN, lawyer, educator; b. Bernardsville, N.J., Dec. 26, 1922; s. Martin John and Nellie (Fotens) C.; m. Julia Sebastian, June 14, 1952; children: Janice Cox Trautman, William Martin, Joann Cox Cahoon, Julieann Cox Allen. *Mr. Cox is a decendant of an English family which includes Sir Richard, Bishop of Ely (1559-1581). Isaac came to Elizabethtown NJ in 1690 following Whig predominance commencing in 1688, after which the Tories were eclipsed until the time of George III.*

Ancestors were essentially Tory and Anti-Federalist. Family seat has been Sussey Co. NJ since the early 18th century. Notwithstanding Tory sympathies during the Revolutionary War, John Cox served in the NJ General Assembly as early as 1810. AB, Syracuse U., 1947; JD, Cornell U., 1950. Bar: N.J., U.S. Dist. Ct. Mem. Dolan & Dolan, Newton, N.J., 1950—; mem. faculty, tchr. zoning admintrn. Rutgers U.; gen. counsel emeritus N.J. Planning Ofcls., bd. dirs. Newton Cemetary Assn., pres. N.J. Inst. Mcpl. Attys., 1982-84, mem. Land Use Law Drafting Com., 1970— (chmn. 1993-98), dir., sec. Equip, Inc., Marion, N.C. Author: Zoning and Land Use Administration in New Jersey, 18th edit., 1999. With U.S. Army, 1943-45. Recipient Resolution of Appreciation award N.J. Senate and Gen. Assembly, 1994,Pres.'s Disting. Svc. award N.J. League Municipalities, 1999. Mem. ABA, N.J. Bar Assn., Sussex County Bar Assn., Am. Planning Assn., Monarchist League, Rotary (Vocat. award 1996), Am. Legion, VFW. Baptist. Office: 1 Legal Ln Newton NJ 07860-1827

COX, WILLIAM WALTER, dentist; b. Abingdon, Va., Jan. 17, 1947; s. Walter Roy and Beatrice Ellen (Woodward) C.; m. Neva Duncan Herzog, Apr. 23, 1976 (div. Sept. 1985); 1 child, Lesley Ellen; m. Victoria Elizabeth Butt, May 25, 1996. BS in Chemistry, U. Richmond, 1969; DDS, Med. Coll. Va., 1973. Dentist Bisese, Kail & Cox, Inc., Portsmouth, Va., 1976—. Capt. U.S. Army, 1973-76. Settle scholar U. Richmond. Mem. Tidewater Dental Assn. (chmn. patient rels. com. 1984-96), Tidewater Dental Study Club, Portsmouth-Suffolk Dental Study Club (sec.-treas. 1990-91, pres. 1991-92). Republican. Methodist. Avocations: golf, snow skiing. Home: 2907 Scotsman Run Chesapeake VA 23321 Office: Bisese Kail & Cox 5717 Churchland Blvd Portsmouth VA 23703-3308

COXE, WELD, management consultant; b. Stamford, Conn., Nov. 6, 1929; s. Daniel Micheaux and Dorothy (Weld) C.; m. Georgia Mattison, Feb. 4, 1951 (div. 1977); children: Robin M., Sally M., Donald M.; m. Mary Chapman Hayden, July 4, 1985 (dec. July 1993). Student, Harvard Coll., 1947-49. Reporter Berkshire Eagle, Pittsfield, Mass., 1949-51; copy editor Ariz. Republic, Phoenix, 1952-63; writer Pa. Railroad, Phila., 1954-59; communications dir. Vincent G. Kling, Architect, Phila., 1960-67; prin. The Coxe Group, Inc., Seattle, 1967-95; adj. lectr. dept. architecture U. Pa., 1988, Rensesalear Poly. Inst., 1993—, U. Ariz., 1999. Author: Marketing Architectural and Engineering Services, 1972, 2d edit. 1983, Managing Architectural and Engineering Practice, 1982; co-author: Success Strategies for Design Profeesionals, 1987. Co-dir. Partnership for Profl. Devel., Phila., 1987-90; bd. dirs. Cathedral Village, 1980—, chmn., 1985-93; trustee Sophia G. Coxe Charitable Trust, Inc., 1988—; bd. dirs. Hist. Soc. Pa., 1993—; mem. Planning Bd., New Shoreham, R.I., 1995—; pres. Reed St. Settlement House, Phila., 1970-76; canon Cathedral Chpt. Episcopal Diocese of Pa., 1970-92. With U.S. Army, 1950-52. Mem. AIA (hon.), Inst. Mgmt. Cons. (cert.), Soc. Mktg. Profl. Services. Clubs: Racquet, Harvard. Home and Office: PO Box 515 Block Island RI 02807-0515

COXETER, HAROLD SCOTT MACDONALD, mathematician; b. London, Feb. 9, 1907; s. Harold Samuel and Lucy (Gee) C.; m. Hendrina J. Brouwer, Aug. 20, 1936; children—Edgar, Susan Coxeter Thomas. B.A., Trinity Coll., Cambridge (Eng.) U., 1929, Ph.D., 1931, rsch. fellow, 1931-35; hon. degrees, U. Alta., Acadia U., U. Waterloo, Trent U., U. Toronto, Carleton U., U. Giessen, McMaster U., York U. Rockefeller Found. fellow Princeton U., 1932-33, Procter fellow, 1934-35; asst. prof. math. U. Toronto, 1936-44, asso. prof., 1944-48, prof., 1948—; vis. prof. numerous univs. including Columbia U., 1949, U. Amsterdam, 1966, Calif. Inst. Tech., 1977, U. Bologna, 1978. Author: Non-Euclidean Geometry, 1942, Regular Polytopes, 1948, The Real Projective Plane, 1949, Introduction to Geometry, 1961, Projective Geometry, 1964, Twelve Geometric Essays, 1968, Regular Complex Polytopes, 1974, Kaleidoscopes, 1995. Fellow Royal Soc. London (Sylvester medal), Royal Soc. Can. (Tory medal); mem. K. Nederlandse Akademie Wetensch. (fgn.); hon. mem. Mathematische Gesellschaft, Wiskundig Genootschap, Edinburgh and London Math. Soc., Am. Acad. Arts and Scis. (fgn. hon.), Companion of Order of Can. Home: 67 Roxborough Dr, Toronto, ON Canada M4W 1X2 Office: U Toronto, Toronto, ON Canada M5S 3G3

COX-GERLOCK, BARBARA, academic administrator, consultant; b. N.Y.C., Oct. 9, 1943; d. George Linus and Madeline (Foody) B.; m. Glen G. Gerlock, July 31, 1992. BA, Mount St. Vincent, N.Y.C., 1965; MS, Fordham U., N.Y.C., 1967; PhD, Yeshiva U., N.Y.C., 1983. Asst. supt. Yonkers City Schs., Yonkers, N.Y., 1965-94; program planning dir. Dept. Children Families, 1996; project dir. PBC Health Care Dist., 1996-98; pres. Inner Dialogue Cons., 1998—; pres. Nat. Assn. Pupil Svcs. Admin., Alexandria, Va., 1994, Copso, N.Y., 1983-88, NYSA PSA, 1983-84. Vice chair Citizen's Adv. Bd., Palm Beach, 1997—, chair 1998-99; cmty. chair NCI Project Commit, N.Y., 1991-92. Named Adminstr. of the Yr. Rotary, 1988. Avocations: boating, yoga, needlework, reading, writing. Home: 2850 James River Rd West Palm Beach FL 33411-5754

COY, CHRISTOPHER HARTMANN, finance executive; b. Sagami-ono, Japan, May 7, 1966; came to U.S., 1966; s. Larry Lee Coy and Margaret Polk (Hartmann) Lohoff; m. Traci Raye Barger, July 27, 1996. BBA in Fin., U. Tex., Arlington, 1988; MBA, So. Meth. U., 1989. Fin. analyst Am. Airlines, Ft. Worth, 1989-90, sr. fin. analyst, 1990-95, mgr. fin., 1996—. Planning and zoning commr. City of Grapevine, 1996—, mem. bd. zoning adjustments, 1992-96; precinct chmn. Tarrant County Reps., Grapevine, 1990-96; del. state Rep. conv., Ft. Worth, 1996. With USN, 1984-85. ROTC scholar USN, 1984. Avocations: landscaping, gardening, travel, model railroading. Office: Am Airlines Dallas/Ft Worth Internat Airport PO Box 619616 Dallas TX 75261

COY, ELBA BOONE, retired real estate developer; b. Franklin, Ind., Oct. 19, 1924; s. Elba and Hazel Marie (Boone) C.; m. Maralee Thornburg, May 18, 1946 (div. 1966); children: Pamela Marie Coy Payne, Debra Diane Coy Reed, David Boone; m. Geraldine Knauff Reddick, Oct. 1, 1966; children: Steven Eugene, Kendra Joann Coy Kahn, Kristina Kay Coy Martin, Bruce Edward. BS, Ind. U., 1949, postgrad., 1949-50; student, Purdue U., 1943-44. Assoc. prof. econs. Wharton Sch. Fin., U. Pa., Phila., 1950-51; reg. mgr. Pilgrim Life Ins. Co., Indpls., 1956-60, Tower Group Cos./Channing Funds, Boston and Battle Creek, 1960-66; dir., pres. Jackson Std. Corp., Nat. Sec. Life Assurance, Universal Mort, Indpls., 1967-69; area dir. HUD, Indpls., 1969-71; dir. Urban Nat. Devel. Co., Houston, 1971-74; dir. devel. Monesson & Co., Dallas, 1974-75; exec. dir. Harris County Community Devel./Housing Authority, Houston, 1975-76; dir. devel. Good Samaritan Luth. Home, Houston, 1976-80, Caltex, Ltd., Houston, 1980-88. Author: Brief History of Whiteland, Indiana, 1956. Nat. bd. dirs. U.S. Jaycees, 1955; mem. Ind. Gen. Assembly, 1961-65. With USN, 1943-46, PTO. Mem. Am. Legion, VFW, Odd Fellows. Republican. Mem. Disciples of Christ. Avocations: bowling, fishing, travel. Address: 17602 Loring Ln Spring TX 77388-5745

COY, PATRICIA ANN, special education director, consultant; b. Beardstown, Ill., Apr. 2, 1952; d. Ben L. and Dorothy Lee (Hubbell) C. BS in Elem. and Spl. Edn., No. Ill. U., 1974; MS in Spl. Edn., Northeastern Ill. U., 1976, MA in Spl. Edn., 1978; MEd in Spl. Edn., Northeastern U., 1984; postgrad., No. Ill. U., 1988—. Cert. elem. and spl. edn. tchr.; cert. counselor. Mental health supr. Waukegan (Ill.) Devel. Ctr., 1974-77; ednl. therapist Grove Sch. and Residential Program, Lake Forest, Ill., 1977-78; dir. residential svcs. N.W. Suburban Aid for the Retarded, Park Ridge, Ill., 1978-83; exec. dir. The Learning Tree, Des Plaines, Ill., 1983—; dir. residential svcs. Augustanan Ctr. Luth. Social Svcs. of Ill., Chgo., 1984-86, dir. planning and evaluation, 1986-93, dir. community svc., 1993-95; exec. dir. Blare House Inc., Des Plaines, Ill., 1995—; behavior advisor Habilitative Systems, Inc., Chgo., 1985-88; program coord. Human Resource Devel. Inst., Chgo., 1986-89; project dir. Support Svcs. Ill., Inc., Chgo., 1987-91; dir. TranSteps Inc. Steps for Success for Adults with Learning Differences, 1991—. Contbr. articles to profl. jours. Mem. Coun. for Exceptional Children, Am. Assn. Mental Deficiency, Chgo. Assn. Behavioral Analysis, Behavior Analysis Soc. Ill., Assn. for Supervision and Curriculum Devel., Nat. Rehab. Assn., Coun. for Disability Rights, Assn. for Learning Disability, Profls. in Learning Disabilities, Cwens, Echoes, Mortar Bd., Kappa Delta Pi. Democrat. Mem. United Ch. of Christ. Home: 8936 N Parkside Ave Apt 118 Des Plaines IL 60016-5517 Office: 7144 N Harlem Ave Ste 344 Chicago IL 60631-1005 also: Blare House 960 Rand Rd Ste 216 Des Plaines IL 60016-2355

COY, WILLIAM RAYMOND, civil engineer; b. Omaha, Nov. 28, 1923; s. Vern Elmer and Edna Mae (Seymour) C.; m. Geraldine Petra Zaback, July 31, 1943; children: Carol Sue, William R. Jr., Russell B., Steven D., Marcus R. Student, Omaha Mcpl. U., 1944, 45. Registered profl. engr., N.D. Lab. technician U.S. Army CE, 1946-57; paving engr. CE, Albuquerque Dist., Roswell, N.Mex., 1958-61; chief materials testing CE Ballistic Missile Constrn., Minot and Grand Forks, N.D., 1961-65; engr.-in-charge CE Green River Dam, Campbellsville, Ky., 1965-68; chief concrete sect. CE Div. Lab., Omaha, 1968-78; chief materials engr. CE Missouri River Div., Omaha, 1978-87; assessor, constrn. technology Nat. Inst. Standards and Tech., Omaha, 1987-95. With USN, 1945-46. Mem. Soc. Am. Mil. Engrs., Am. Concrete Inst. Home: 3226 S 44th Ave Omaha NE 68105-3815

COYE, MOLLY JOEL, state agency administrator; b. Bennington, Vt., May 11, 1947; d. Robert Dudley Coye and Janet (Loper) Coye Nelson; m. Daniel Noah Lindheim, Sept. 22, 1974 (div. 1980); m. Mark Douglas Smith, Feb. 22, 1980; 1 child, Langston Matthew Coye. BA, U. Calif., Berkeley, 1968; MA, Stanford U., 1972; MPH, Johns Hopkins U., 1977, MD, 1977. Chief of occupational health clinic U. San Francisco, 1979-84; med. officer Nat. Inst. for Occupational Safety & Health, 1980-85; advisor health and environment Gov.'s Office of Policy & Planning, Trenton, N.J., 1985-86; dep. commr. N.J. Dept. Health, Trenton, 1986-87; v.p. strategic devel. Health Desk Corp., Berkely, Calif., 1988-98; sr. v.p. The Lewin Group, San Francisco, 1998—; chair adv. com. graduate program in pub. health U. Medicine and Dentistry of N.J., Newark, 1986—; mem. tech. bd. Milbank Meml. Fund, N.Y.C., 1986-88; mem. com. role of primary care physician in occupational/environ. medicine Nat. Acad. Scis, Inst. Medicine, Washington, 1986-88; mem. adv. com. AIDS U.S. Pub. Health Svc., Washington, 1989; mem. adv. coun. Nat. Inst. for Environ. Health Scis., Betheseda, Md., 1989. Co-author, editor: China: Inside the People's Republic, 1972, co-editor: China Yesterday and Today. Contbr. peer review articles to profl. jours. Recipient Virginia Apgar award March of Dimes, Plainsboro, N.J., 1988, Woman of the Yr. award Jersey Woman mag., 1989. Mem. AMA, Am. Coll. Preventive Medicine, Am. Pub. Health Assn. (chair exec. bd. 1988), Assn. for Health Svcs. Rsch., Assn. State and Territorial Health Officers (chair exec. bd. 1988—, mem. AIDS com. 1988—), Soc. for Occupational and Environ. Health (mem. governing coun. 1988—). Avocations: murder mysteries, cooking. Office: The Lewin Group 425 Market St 16th Flr San Francisco CA 94105*

COYLE, CHARLES A., marketing educator; b. Phila., June 13, 1931; s. Charles A. and Roseanne (McPeake) C.; m. Suzanne B. McCann, Sept. 28, 1963; children: Suzanne, Christopher, Kevin, Timothy. BSBA, LaSalle U., 1955; postgrad., U.S. Army Intelligence Ctr., 1956; MBA, Drexel U., 1967; EdD with distinction, Temple U., 1974; postgrad., Mary Immaculate Sem., 1990-95. Sales rep. IBM, SCM, Diebold, Inc., R.E. Lamb, 1958-67; spl. agt. U.S. Dept. Treasury; asst. prof. mktg. and mgmt. C.C. Phila., 1967-70; asst. prof. mktg. Phila. Coll. Textiles and Sci., 1970-74; tchr., coord. distributive edn. Middle Bucks (Pa.) AVTS, 1974-76; prof., chmn. mktg. Kutztown (Pa.) U., 1976—, dept. chmn.; chmn. mktg. adv. com. Lehigh Valley Vocat. Tech. Sch., 1984-94; adj. prof. Temple U., La Salle U., St. Josephs U., Allentown Coll.; presenter in field. Contbr. articles to profl. jours. Resource leader Nat. Conf. on New Strategies for Learning, 1969; permanent deacon Allentown Diocese; prefect min. St. Francis Order; mgr., coach soccer, baseball Warminster Little League, 1973-79, Grandlawn Baseball Assn., 1987-88; treas. Deerfield Cmty. Assn., 1983-85. With CIC, U.S. Army, 1956-58, PTO. Recipient award Dale Carnegie Found., Phila., 1967, Outstanding Svc. award Distributive Edn. Clubs Am., 1975, 86, 88, 91, award Lehigh Valley Vocat.-Tech. Sch. Adv. Com., 1993; Direct Mktg. fellow, 1989. Mem. AAUP, Am. Acad. Advt., Sales and Mktgs. Execs., Am. Mktg. Assn., Direct Mktg. Assn., Assn. Pa. Univ. Bus. and Econ. Faculty (bd. dirs. 1989-91), Sales and Mktg. Execs., Am. Mgmt. Assn., Cross Keys, KC (4th degree), Faculty and Adminstrn. Club (pres. Kutztown U. 1988-90, v.p. 1986-88, director mktg. fellow 1989—), Sons Union Vets. of the Civil War, Phi Delta Kappa, Phi Kappa Phi, Alpha Epsilon, Epsilon Delta Epsilon. Home: 1236 Buck Trail Rd Allentown PA 18104-2019 Office: Kutztown Univ Coll Bus DeFrancesco Rm 4 Kutztown PA 19530

COYLE, DENNIS PATRICK, lawyer; b. Detroit, Aug. 29, 1938; s. Myron Patrick and Vernice Beatrice (Smith) C.; children: Ian Patrick, Sean Patrick. B.A., Dartmouth Coll., 1960; J.D., Columbia U., 1964. Bar: N.Y. 1965, Fla. 1971. Assoc. Breed, Abbott & Morgan, N.Y.C., 1964-70; assoc. Courshon & Courshon, Miami Beach, Fla., 1970-74; mng. trustee First Mortgage Investors, Miami Beach, 1974-79; ptnr. Steel Hector & Davis, Miami, Fla., 1979-89; gen. counsel FPL Group, Inc., Fla. Power & Light Co., 1989—, dir. Fla. Power and Light Co., 1991—, Adelphia Comms. Corp., 1995—. Mem. ABA, Miami Beach C. of C. (hon. lifetime trustee). Home: 405 Eagleton Cove Way Palm Beach Gardens FL 33418-8464 Office: FPL Group Inc PO Box 14000 700 Universe Blvd North Palm Beach FL 33408-2657

COYLE, EDWARD J., physical education coordinator; b. Phila., July 8, 1949; s. Edward J. and Josephine (Orgilio) C. BS, West Chester U., 1973; MEd, Temple U., 1980; PhD, U. N.Mex., 1987. Cert. health edn. tchr., Pa.; cert. health, phys. edn. and recreation tchr., N.Mex. and Pa. Prog. dir. Sensitivity and Awareness progs. Phila. Sch. Dist., 1979-81; teaching asst. U. N.Mex., 1982-84; phys. edn. instr. Albuquerque Pub. Schs., 1982-88; cons. to phys. therapy dept. Grad. Health System, Phila., 1988-89; coord. adapted phys. edn. Norristown (Pa.) Area Sch. Dist., 1989—; coord. Sun Co.'s "Someone Spl. Prog.", Olympic Sports Prog., 1990; vol. conditioning coach, football, U. N.Mex., 1981-86; prog. coord. in gymnasium, Slaten Farmer's Sch., 1980, 82, 90, coord. spl. events, 1980-82; others. Named to Pa. Sports Hall of Fame, Delaware County, 1990; hon. capt. Del. County Hero Bowl Football Game, 1989; Delaware County Athletic Hall of Fame, Pa. chpt., 1988; named to Outstanding Young Men of Am., 1984; U.S. rep. to Olympic Games, two gold medals, 1 silver medal in weight lifting, 1972, 76, 80, 3 world championship gold medals, 1973, 74, 75, 4 Pan Am. gold medals, 1971, 73, 75, 79, 10 nat. champsionships,; recipient Father Washington medal for Outstanding Citizenship, Nat. Cath. War Vets. award, 1980, Rotary Achievement award, Balt. Pike/Clifton Heights, Pa., 1978; numerous other awards. Mem. Nat. Strength and Conditioning Assn., Internat. Olympic Com., U.S. Olympic Com., AAHPERD, Fedn. Internat. Edn. Physique, Nat. Corrective Therapy Assn., U.S. Master Swimming Assn., Am. Coll. Sports Medicine, N.Mex. Phys. Educators Assn., Amateur Athletic Assn., Internat. Fedn. Power Lifting, Pa. State Phys. Edn. Assn., lst Marine Div. Assn., 3rd Marine Div. Assn., British Officers Club of Phila., 5th and 14th Def. Bn. Assn., USMC, Marine Corps., Upland, Pa.; trustee Four Chaplains Assn., Phila., Pa., Sturzelecker Found. Westchester U., Delaware County Athletics Hall of Fame Commn.;. Home: 1078 Putnam Blvd Media PA 19086-6747

COYLE, FRANCIS SYLVESTER, III, management consultant; b. Orange, N.J.; s. Francis S. and Aileen M. (McCormack) C.; m. Mary E. Kellenberg, Sept. 12, 1959; children: Kevin, Kathleen, John, Christopher, Timothy, Maureen. BA, Bklyn. Coll., 1955; BS, Pa. State U., 1962; MBA, So. Ill. U., 1976; MPA, U. So. Calif., 1987. Cert. govt. fin. mgr. Programmer State of Del., Dover, 1977-78; tng. & staff devel. officer State of Del., Smyrna, 1978-79, dir. rsch. planning, 1979-80; asst. dir. ctrl. data processing State of Del., Dover, 1980-85, policy & fin. analyst, 1985-87, fin. mgmt. specialist, 1987-90, tng. adminstr., 1990-98; pres. Coyle Mgmt. Cons., Inc., Dover, 1998—. Bd. dirs. Thomas More Acad., Dover, 1988—, Holy Cross Edn. Found., Dover, 1985—. Maj. USAF, 1955-76. Mem. Am. Soc. Pub. Adminstrn., Am. Meteorological Soc., Assn. Govt. Accts., KC.

COYLE, GERALDINE ANNE, nursing administrator; b. Phila., Oct. 17, 1948; d. James J. and Jewell C. (McDermody) C.; divorced; children: Arthur E. Perkins III, Geraldine C. Perkins. RN, Lankenau Hosp., Phila., 1969; BSN, Pa. State U., State College, 1975; EdD, Temple U., 1985. RN, Pa., W.Va.; cert. RN practitioner, Nursing Adminstr. Nurse practitioner Phila. Vets. Affairs, 1975-79, clin. chief nursing svc., 1980-84; head nurse Wilkes Barre (Pa.) Vets. Affairs, 1979-80, nurse practitioner, 1991-94; coord. E.K. Long Hosp., Baton Rouge, 1990-91; assoc. chief nursing svc. Atlanta VA Med. Ctr., 1994-96; assoc. chief nurse Mountain Home VA Med. Ctr., 1996-98; assoc. dir. med. ctr. Martinsburg (W.Va.) VA Med. Ctr., 1999—; cons. State of La., Baton Rouge, 1991; restaurant owner, 1984-86. Fundraising, events organizer Baton Rouge Opera, 1988-90. Avocations: traveling, cooking, reading. Home: 1707 Meadowlark Ct Falling Waters WV 25419 Office: Martinsburg VA Med Ctr Rt 9 Charles Town Rd Martinsburg WV 25401

COYLE, JOSEPH THOMAS, psychiatrist; b. Chgo., Oct. 9, 1943; s. Joseph Thomas and Mercedes (Sartor) C.; m. Genevieve Sansoucy, Aug. 19, 1968; children: Andrew, Peter, David. AB, Coll. of the Holy Cross, 1965; MD, Johns Hopkins Sch. of Medicine, 1969; MA (hon), Harvard U., 1991. Diplomate Am. Bd. Psychiatry and Neurology. Asst. prof. pharmacology Johns Hopkins Sch. of Medicine, Balt., 1974-76, asst. prof pharmacology and psychiatry, 1976-78, assoc. prof pharmacology and psychiatry, 1978-80, prof of neurosci., psychiatry and pharmacology, 1980-91, dir. div. of child psychiatry, 1982-91, Disting. Svc. prof. of child psychiatry, 1985-91; Eben S. Draper prof. of psychiatry and neurosci. Harvard U., Boston, 1991—; chair consol. dept. psychiatry Harvard Med. Sch., Boston, 1991—; co-dir outpatient pharmacotherapy clinic Johns Hopkins Hosp., Balt., 1977-82; mem. sci. adv. bd. Pfizer Scholars Program, N.Y.C., 1989-94 John F. Merck Found., Boston, 1990—, Abbott Pharms., North Chgo. Ill., 1990—, Guilford Pharms., Balt., 1992-98. Contbr. articles to profl. jours. Mem. adv. bd. NIMH, Washington, 1990-94. Recipient AE Bennett award, 1978, Gold Medal award, 1991, EA Strecker award Inst. Pa. Hosp., 1991, McAlpin award, Mental Health Assn., Washington, 1992, Salamon Medal of N.Y. Acad. of Medicine, 1993. Fellow Am. Psychiat. Assn. (Found. Fund prize 1985, Adolph Meyer award 1994), Am. Acad. of Arts and Scis.; mem. Soc. Neurosci. (pres. 1991-92), Am. Coll. Neuropsychopharmacology (Efron award 1982), Am. Acad. Child and Adolescent Psychiatry, Am. Soc. Pharmacology and Exptl. Therapeutics (John Jacob Abel award 1979), Inst. of Medicine of the Nat. Acad. Sci. (Passrow Found. award 1997). Avocations: reading, fishing. Office: Harvard Med Sch Dept Psychiatry 115 Mill St Belmont MA 02478-1041

COYLE, MARTIN ADOLPHUS, JR., lawyer; b. Hamilton, Ohio, June 3, 1941; s. Martin Adolphus and Lucille (Baird) C.; m. Sharon Sullivan, Mar. 29, 1969 (div. Dec. 1991); children: Cynthia Ann, David Martin, Jennifer Ann; m. Linda J. O'Brien, July 31, 1993 (div. July 1996); m. Sandra C. Lund, July 1998. BA, Ohio Wesleyan U., 1963; JD summa cum laude, Ohio State U., 1966. Bar: N.Y. 1967. Assoc. Cravath, Swaine & Moore, N.Y.C., 1966-72; chief counsel securities and fin. TRW Inc., Cleve., 1972-73, sr. counsel, asst. sec., 1973-75, asst. gen. counsel, asst. sec., 1976, asst. gen. counsel, sec., 1976-80, v.p., gen. counsel, sec., 1980-89, exec. v.p., gen. counsel, sec., 1989-97, exec. v.p., 1997-99; sec. TRW Found., Cleve., 1975-80, trustee, 1980-88; sec. TRW Found., 1975-80, trustee, 1980—. Co-inventor voting machine. Pres. Judson Retirement Cmty., 1986-88, trustee, 1986-90; chmn., sec. Martin A. Coyle Found.; trustee Berea Coll. 1989—, Chautauqua Inst., 1990—; trustee Fairhill Inst. for the Elderly, 1990—, Ohioesleyan U., 1992—. Mem. ABA, Am. Soc. Corp. Secs. (pres. Ohio regional group 1978-80, nat. dir. 1981-87, nat. chmn. 1985-86), Assn. Gen. Counsel (exec. com. 1992—, pres. 1995-97), Ohio Bar Assn., Bar Assn. Greater Cleve., Shoreby Club, Union Club. Home: 5051 Overlook Ave Bemus Point NY 14712-9777 Office: TRW Inc 1900 Richmond Rd Cleveland OH 44124-3760

COYLE, PHILIP E., federal agency administrator, engineer. BA, Dartmouth Coll., 1956, MS in Mechanical Engring., 1957. With Lawrece Livermore (Calif.) Nat. Lab., 1959-79, 81-93, assoc. dir., 1981-84, lab. assoc. dir., dep. to lab. dir., 1987-93, ret., assoc. dir. emeritus, 1993; past prin. dep. asst. sec. for defense programs Dept. Energy; past sci. adv. on testing matters Nev. Ops. Office; past test dir. Nev. Test Site. Named commr. East Bay Conversion and Reinvestment Commn., 1991; mem. Alameda County Econ. Devel. Adv. Bd. Office: Dept of Defense Operational Test & Evaluation 1700 Defense Pentagon Washington DC 20301-1700

COYLE, ROBERT EVERETT, federal judge; b. Fresno, Calif., May 6, 1930; s. Everett LaJoya and Virginia Chandler C.; m. Faye Turnbaugh, June 11, 1953; children—Robert Allen, Richard Lee, Barbara Jean. BA, Fresno State Coll., 1953; JD, U. Calif., 1956. Bar: Calif. Ptnr. McCormick, Barstow, Sheppard, Coyle & Wayte, 1958-82; chief judge U.S. Dist. Ct. (ea. dist.) Calif., 1990-96, sr. judge, 1996—; former chair 9th Cir. Conf. of Chief Dist. Judges, chair 9th Cir. space and security com., mem. com. on state and fed. cts. Mem. Calif. Bar Assn. (exec. com. 1974-79, bd. govs. 1979-82, v.p. 1981), Fresno County Bar Assn. (pres. 1972). Office: US Dist Ct 5116 US Courthouse 1130 O St Fresno CA 93721-2201

COYLE, THOMAS, marketing executive. V.p. mktg. divsn. N.Am. grain Continental Grain Co., N.Y.C., v.p. origination. Office: Continental Grains 222 S Riverside Plz Chicago IL 60606-5808

COYNE, CHARLES COLE, lawyer; b. Abington, Pa., Dec. 3, 1948; s. James Kitchenman Jr. and Pearl (Black) C.; m. Paula J. Latta, May 15, 1976; 1 child, Anna Elizabeth. BS in Econs., U. Pa., 1970; JD, Temple U., 1973. Bar: Pa. 1973, U.S. Supreme Ct. 1982, N.J. 1985. Of counsel Hepburn, Willcox, Hamilton & Putnam, 1994—; dir., sec., chmn. fin. com. George S. Coyne Chem. Co., Inc., Croydon, Pa. Assoc. editor Temple Law Quar., 1972-73; columnist "Life In the Country", Ledger Newspaper Group, 1993—. Chester County (Pa.) rep. Delaware Valley Regional Planning Commn., 1982—; mem. Chester County Health and Edn. Facilities Authority, 1982—, chmn., 1996—; bd. suprs. East Fallowfield Twp., Chester County, 1982-83; mem. Panel of U.S. Bankruptcy Trustees, 1991-93; Chester County Pk. and Recreation Bd., 1998—. Mem. racing com. Pa. Hunt Cup, 1992—. AIESEC Exch. fellow, U. Melbourne, 1968; recipient Disting. Young Rep. award Greater Phila. Young Reps., 1976. Mem. ABA, Pa. Bar Assn., Phila. Bar Assn., Temple Law Sch. Alumni Assn. (chmn. 10th reunion com.), U. Pa. Gen. Alumni Soc. (exec. bd. organized classes, pres. Class of 1970). Clubs: Union League (Phila.), Capitol Hill Club (Washington), Lawyer's Club of Phila., Nat. Steeplechase Assn., Hartefeld Nat. Golf Club, Quaker City Farmers Club, Pa. Soc., Masons (master 1982), Kappa Alpha Soc. E-mail: cccoyne@aol.com. Home: Sycamore Run Farm PO Box 155 Unionville PA 19375-0155 Office: Hepburn Willcox Hamilton & Putnam 1100 One Penn Ctr 1617 John F Kennedy Blvd Philadelphia PA 19103-1979

COYNE, FRANK J., insurance industry executive; b. 1948. BS, U. Scranton, 1970; JD, Duquesne U., 1973. Trial atty. U.S. Dept. Treasury, 1973-77; v.p., asst. gen. counsel Lynn Ins. Group, 1977-80; assoc. gen. counsel Reliance Ins. Co., 1980-83; v.p., gen. counsel PMA Ins. Co., 1983-85; former sr. v.p., gen. counsel Gen. Accident Corp. of Am. and subs.; now pres., dir. Gen. Accident Corp. of Am. and subs., Phila.; also pres., chief oper. officer Gen. Accident Ins. Co. Ins. Am., Inc., Phila., also bd. dirs., resigned, 1998; exec. v.p. Kemper Ins., Long Grove, Ill., 1998-99; pres. Ins. Svcs. Office, Inc., N.Y.C., 1999—; pres., bd. dirs. Pa. Gen. Ins. Co., Potomac Ins. Co. Ill., Ga. Ins. Co. N.Y., PG Ins. Co. N.Y., Gen. Assurance Co.; bd. dirs. Silvey Cos., Hawkeye-Security Ins. Co., Oreg. Auto and North Pacific Ins. Cos., Pilot Ins. Co. (Can.), Mellon PSFS Bank, Ins. Fedn. Pa. Office: Insurance Services Office Inc 7 World Trade Ctr New York NY 10048-1199

COYNE, JAMES KITCHENMAN, III, association executive, congressman, aviator; b. Farmville, Va., Nov. 17, 1946; s. James Kitchenamn Jr. and Pearl Beatrice (Black) C.; m. Helen Biddle Mercer, Oct. 24, 1970; children: Alexander, Katherine, Michael. BS, Yale U., 1968; MBA, Harvard U., 1970; LLD (hon.), Spring Garden Coll., 1984. Pres. Coyne Chem. Co., Phila., 1981-83; mem. 97th Congress from 8th Pa. dist., 1981-83; spl. asst. to Pres. White House, Washington, 1983-85; chief exec. officer Am. Cons. Engring. Coun., Washington, 1985-86; pres., founder Am. Tort Reform Assn., Washington, 1986-88; v.p. regional mgr. Roy F. Weston, Inc., Washington, 1988-90; founder, pres. Ams. to Limit Congl. Terms, 1990-93; pres. Nat. Air Transp. Assn., 1994—; lectr. U. Pa., Phila., 1974-78; chmn. Energy Mgmt. Svcs., Phila., 1976-78; bd. dirs. P.B.&S. Chem. Co., Henderson, Ky., Rsch. and Mgmt. Found., Washington; vice chmn. Environ. Study Com., Washington, 1982. Contbr. articles to profl. jours. Del., mem. platform com. Rep. Nat. Conv., Dallas, 1984; bd. dirs. Gen. Aviation Team 2000; chmn. Gen. Aviation Action Plan Coalition, Aviation Svcs. and Suppliers Supershow. Recipient Boy Scout of Yr. award Boy Scouts Am., 1982, Outstanding Pvt. Sector award Am. Legion Exch. Coun., 1986, Disting. Svc. award Am. Tort Reform Assn., 1988. Mem. Former Mem. Congress Assn. (bd. dirs. 1984—), Union League Phila., World Affairs Coun. (bd. dirs. Phila. chpt. 1983-85), Yale Club, Washington Club, Pine Valley Country Club. Avocations: Skiing, tennis, golf. Office: Nat Air Transp Assn 4226 King St Alexandria VA 22302-1507

COYNE, NANCY CAROL, advertising executive; b. Washington, Mar. 14, 1946; d. John David and Gloria Louise (Davie) Druckenbrod; 1 child, Kathleen Louise. BS, NYU, 1968. Dir. visitor svcs. Lincoln Ctr., N.Y.C., 1968-71; dir. advt. Sta. WRVR Radio, N.Y.C., 1971-74; creative dir. Blaine Thompson Inc., N.Y.C., 1974-77; chief exec. officer Serino, Coyne Inc., N.Y.C., 1977—; adj. prof. Yale U., New Haven, Conn., 1980—; bd. dirs. Young Playwrights Inc, Theatre Devel. Fund. Recipient Clio awards, 1980, 82, Addy award, 1988, Big Apple Best Radio Spot of Ur. in N.Y.C. awards, 1980, 81, 84, 85, 88. Office: Serino Coyne Inc 1515 Broadway Fl 36 New York NY 10036-8901*

COYNE, PATRICK IVAN, physiological ecologist; b. Wichita, Kans., Feb. 26, 1944; s. Ivan Lefranz and Ellen Lucille (Brown) C.; m. Mary Ann White, Aug. 22, 1964; children: Shane Barrett, Shannon Renee. BS, Kans. State U., 1966; PhD, Utah State U., 1970. R & D coord. U.S. Army Cold Regions Rsch. and Engring. Lab., Hanover, N.H., 1970-72; asst. prof. forestry U. Alaska, Fairbanks, 1973-74; plant physiologist, environ. scientist Lawrence Livermore (Calif.) Nat. Lab., 1975-79, cons., 1980—; rsch. plant physiologist USDA/ Agrl. Rsch. Svc., Woodward, Okla., 1979-85; prof., head Agrl. Rsch. Ctr. Kansas State U., Hays, 1985-94, prof., head Western Kans. Agrl. Rsch. Ctrs., 1994—; mem. adv. coun. Kans. Geol. Survey, Lawrence, 1986-91. Contbr. 33 articles to profl. jours. Capt., U.S. Army, 1970-72. Mem. AAAS, Am. Soc. Agronomy, Soil Sci. Soc. Am., Crop Sci. Soc. Am., Soc. Range Mgmt., Coun. Agriculture Sci. and Tech., Hays Area C. of C. (bd. dirs. 1988-90), Rotary, Phi Kappa Phi, Gamma Sigma Delta, Sigma Xi. Republican. Mennonite Brethren Ch. Office: Kans State U Agrl Rsch Ctr 1232 240th Ave Hays KS 67601-9228

COYNE, THOMAS JOSEPH, economist, finance educator; b. Wheeling, W.Va., Dec. 24, 1933; s. Thomas Joseph and Mary Germaine (Fox) C.; Patricia Anne Smith, June 8, 1957 (div. June 1986); children: Kathleen, Karen, Kevin, Kenneth, Thomas. BBA, Marshall U., 1958; MBA, Kent State U., 1961; PhD, Case Western Res. U., 1967; postgrad. U. Chgo., 1968, U. Mich., summers 1972, 73. With B.F. Goodrich Co., Akron, Ohio, 1959-61, Robinson Clay Products Co., Akron, 1961-63, C&O-B&O Ry., Cleve., 1963-65; instr. econs. Kent State U., 1963-67; asst. prof. econs., chmn. dept. Marshall U., 1967-69; prof. bus. econs. U. Akron, 1969-81; prof. fin. John Carroll U., 1981-95; owner The Coyne Trust, 1986-91; pres. Coyne & Assocs., Inc., Akron, 1980—, Coyne Pub. Co., 1991—; pub. The Coyne Quar., 1990—; fin. mgmt., corp. valuations, acquisitions; cons. in field; presenter of seminar's in fin. engring. & mgmt., Zagreb, Croatia Stock Exch., 1993; leader first del. in fin. to USSR, 1989; arbitrator Am. Arbitration Assn., Fed. Mediation and Conciliation Service, 1968—, pres. 1979-81; pres. Summit Petroleum Corp., Akron. V.p. research Akron Regional Devel. Bd., 1975-78, chmn. taxation and legis. com., 1975-78; spkr. in field; candidate U.S. Senate, Ohio, 1994—; hosted half hour weekly Radio Show, 1994. Served with inf. U.S. Army, 1952-54; Korea. Nat. City Bank Cleve. fellow, 1963-65. Mem. Sigma Phi Epsilon. Roman Catholic. Author: Understanding Managerial Economics, 1975, Managerial Economics: Analysis and Cases, 5th edit., 1984, Readings in Managerial Economics, 5th edit., 1992, License To Lie, 1996; also articles and monographs. Home: 535 Haskell Dr Akron OH 44333-2810 *When God has given you a great deal, He expects a great deal of you.If you achieve everything you set out to achieve, you probably did not set out to achieve enough in the first place.*

COYNE, WILLIAM JOSEPH, congressman; b. Pittsburg, Pa., Aug. 24, 1936; s. Phillip and Mary (Ridge) C. BS, Robert Morris Coll., 1965. Mem. Pa. Ho. of Reps., 1970-72; mem. Pitts. City Council, 1973-80, 97th-105th Congresses from 14th Pa. dist., Washington, D.C., 1981—; mem. budget com., mem. ways and means com. With AUS, 1955-57. Democrat. Roman Catholic. Office: US Ho of Reps 2455 Rayburn Bldg Washington DC 20515-3814*

COYNER, KELLEY S., federal agency administrator; m. Tim Sears; 1 child. Bachelors Degree, U. Va.; LLM, Georgetown U. Law clk. U.S. Dist. Ct. So. Dist. Tex.; assoc. Arent, Fox, Kintner, Plotkin & Kahn, Washington; pro bono legal counsel Attention Deficit Disorder Assn., Va.; dir. Office Policy and Program Support U.S. Dept. Transp., Washington, 1994-96, dep. adminstr. Rsch. and Spl. Programs Adminstrn., 19969-97, acting adminstr. Rsch. and Spl. Programs Adminstrn., 1997-98, adminstr. Rsch. and Spl. Programs Adminstrn., 1998—; overseer Nat. Conf. to Highlight Transp. Edn. Programs, Knoxville, Tenn.; leader Tech. and Transp. Futures Program. Office: Dept Transp 400 7th St SW Washington DC 20590

COYOTE, PETER (PETER COHON), actor; b. N.Y.C., Oct. 10, 1941. Student, San Francisco Actors Workshop. Theater appearances include The Red Snake, True West, The Abduction of Kari Swenson, Baby Girl Scott, (also dir.) The Minstrel Show, (also co-writer) Olive Pits; film appearances include Die Laughing, Tell Me a Riddle, The Pursuit of D.B. Cooper, Southern Comfort, E.T.: The Extra Terrestrial, Endangered Species, Timerider, Cross Creek, Stranger's Kiss, Slayground, Heartbreakers, The Legend of Billie Jean, Troupers, Jagged Edge, Outrageous Fortune, Stacking, A Man in Love, Heart of Midnight, The Man Inside, Crooked Hearts, Keeper of the City, Bitter Moon, Kika, That Eye The Sky, Seeds of Doubt, Top of the World, Road Ends, Route 9, Last Call, Patch Adams, Sphere, Las Call, More Dogs Than Bones, The BAsket, Random Hearts; TV appearances include Alcatraz: The Whole Shocking Story, The People vs. Jean Harris, Isabel's Choice, Best Kept Secrets, Scorned and Swindled, The Blue Yonder, Child's Cry, Sworn to Silence, Echoes in the Darkness, Unconquered, A Seduction in Travis County, Living a Lie, Keeper of the City, Buffalo Girls, Moonlight and Valentino, Seduced by Madness, Unforgettable, 1996, Dalva, 1996, Two for Texas, 1998, Route 9, 1998, Execution of Justice, 1999, others, (TV mini-series) The West, 1996. Office: ICM care Jeff Danis 8942 Wilshire Blvd Beverly Hills CA 90211-1934 also: Ofcl Internat Peter Coyote Fan Club 3425 Knox Pl Bronx NY 10467-2009*

COZ, STEVE, editor-in-chief, publishing executive; b. Grafton, Mass., Mar. 26, 1957; s. Henry and Mary Coz; m. Valerie Virga, 1987. Honors degree, Harvard U., 1979. Freelance writer various U.S. publs., 1979-82; reporter Nat. Enquirer, Lantana, Fla., 1982—; Am. celebrity analyst BBC Radio, 1995-96. Named one of 25 Most Influential People in Am., Time Mag., 1997; recipient Edgar Hoover Meml. award for disting. pub. svc., 1996, Haven House Award of Excellence for outstanding reporting on domestic violence issues, 1996, Citation of Recognition, Mass. Senate, 1997; recognized for award winning news coverage N.Y. Times, 1994, Columbia Journalism Rev., 1995, L.A. Times Mag., 1995, MediaWeek, 1995, L.A. Times, 1997, ABC's Nightline. Mem. Harvard Club Palm Beach. Avocations: sport fishing, boogie boarding, scrimshaw collecting. Office: Nat Enquirer 600 East Coast Ave Lantana FL 33462

COZAD, JOHN CONDON, lawyer; b. Portland, Maine, Dec. 18, 1944; s. Francis E. and Arlyn Odell (Condon) C.; m. Linda Hickerson, Feb. 18, 1978. B.A. in Polit. Sci., Westminster Coll., Fulton, Mo., 1966; J.D., U. Mo.-Columbia, 1972. Bar: Mo. 1972. Assoc. & ptnr. Field, Gentry, Benjamin, & Robertson, Kansas City, Mo., 1972-83; ptnr. Morrison & Hecker, Kansas City, Mo., 1983—; chmn. Mo. Rep State Party, 1995-99. Chmn. Mo. Hwy. and Transp. Commn., 1985-91; mem. desegregation monitoring com. U.S. Dist. Ct. (we. dist.) Mo., 1989-91; bd. curators U. Mo. Sys., 1991-96; bd. trustees U. Kansas City, 1991—; mem. Rep. Nat. Com., 1995-99. Lt. USNR, 1967-69, Vietnam. Decorated Bronze Star. Navy Commendation medals, Presdl. Unit Citation. Mem. Mo. Bar Assn., Kansas City Bar Assn., Carriage Club. Republican. Mem. Disciples of Christ Ch. Avocations: politics, pheasant hunting, reading. Home: RR 2 Box 140 Platte City MO 64079-9805

COZAD, LYMAN HOWARD, city manager; b. Painesville, Ohio, May 22, 1914; s. William Howard and Ethyl (Phelps) C.; children: Bradford, Roberta, Kimberly. BSBA, Ohio State U., 1935, MS in Pub. Adminstrn., 1936; postgrad., Yale U., 1936-37, USC, 1948-57. Dir. exam City of L.A., 1939-42; personnel officer Nat. Housing Agy., Washington, 1942-43; personnel dir. UNRRA, Washington, 1944-47; So. Calif. mgr. Louis J. Kroeger & Assocs., L.A., 1947-56; city mgr. City of Colton, 1957-64; adminstrv. officer City of Beverly Hills, Calif., 1964-66; city mgr. City of Arcadia, Calif., 1966-77; So. Calif. mgr. League of Calif. Cities, 1977-84; ranger rider, 1985-98; v.p., So. Calif. rep. Pub. Svc. Skills Inc., Sacramento, 1986-98; instr. U. So. Calif., 1941-42, 48-58, U. Calif., Riverside, 1961-63, Calif. State U., Long Beach, 1974-77. Contbr. articles to profl. jours. With U.S. Army, 1943-44. Mem. ASPA, Internat. City Mgrs. Assn., City Mgrs. Dept. League of Calif. Cities (Sacramento pres. 1972, life), So. Calif. Pub. Pers. Assn. L.A. (pres. 1942), Rotary (Colton chpt. dir. 1961-62, Arcadia chpt. 1970-77). Avocation: gardening. Home: 952 Canyon View Dr La Verne CA 91750-1811

COZAN, LEE, clinical research psychologist; married, 1947. B.A., Am. U., 1948; M.A., George Washington U., 1951, Ph.D., 1964. Research psychologist U.S. Govt., Washington, 1954-64; pvt. practice psychology N.J., 1964-74; regional dir. Fla. Div. Mental Health, Ft. Lauderdale, 1974-76; mental hosp. adminstr. So. Fla. State Hosp., Hollywood, 1976-79; pres. Inst. Mental Health, Hollywood, 1979-81; dir. mental health program Fla. Dept. Health and Rehab. Services, Ft. Lauderdale, 1979-82; clin. psychologist Assocs. in Psychiatry, 1983-85; pres. Applied Psychology Corp., 1983-86, Children Residential and Day Treatment Ctr., Inc., 1987-96; health care cons. Fort Lauderdale, Fla., 1996—; adj. prof. Fla. Atlantic U., 1974-79, Nova U., 1979-80. Editor: Jour. Indsl. Psychology, 1961-65, Jour. Engring. Psychology, 1963-68; cons. editor: Jour. Schizophrenia, 1970-71. Mem. Broward County (Fla.) Republican Exec. Com., 1976-80. Served with U.S. Army, 1941-46. Mem. APA, AAAS, Nat. Geog. Soc., Human Factors Soc., Fla. Psychol. Assn., Children's Hosp. Internat. Greek Orthodox. Research, publs. in psychology.

COZBY, RICHARD SCOTT, electronics engineer, reserve army officer; b. Las Cruces, N.Mex., Apr. 13, 1961; s. Scott Dempsey and Elizabeth Ann (Carroll) C.; m. Maria (Jo) Blackwell, Dec. 28, 1984; children: Brenton Blackwell, Bradford Carroll. B in Engring., Vanderbilt U., 1983; postgrad., Ctrl. Mich. U., 1995—; diploma, U.S. Army Command Coll., 1994. Comm. engr. U.S. Army Signal Corps, 1983-88; electronics engr., chief, simulation and tech. divsn. Army Testing and Evaluation Command, Aberdeen Proving Ground, Md., 1988—, chief, simulation and tech. divsn., 1998—; major U.S. Army Res. Aberdeen Test Ctr., Aberdeen Proving Ground, 1988—; U.S. Army prin. Multi-Svc. Test Investment Rev. Com., Washington, 1990-95; bd. dirs. Northeast Md. Tech. Coun. Author: Army GPS Test Results, 1984, Aquila RPV Test Results, 1985. Mem. outreach com. St. Margaret Parish, Bel Air, Md., 1989-95; bd. dirs. Harford Leadership Alumni Assn., 1996—, v.p., 1997—, chmn. Hickory Recreation Coun., Bel Air, Md., 1998—. Mem. IEEE, Internat. Testing and Evaluation Assn. (chpt. pres. 1993, chpt. dir. 1994—). Roman Catholic. Avocations: stamp collecting. Office: HQ TECOM AMSTE-TM Aberdeen Proving Ground MD 21005

COZEN, LEWIS, orthopedic surgeon; b. Montreal, Aug. 14, 1911; came to U.S. 1922; AB, U. Calif., San Francisco, 1929, MD, 1934. Diplomate Am. Bd. Orthopedic Surgery. Intern San Francisco Hosp., 1933-34; resident orthopedic surgeron U. Iowa, 1934-35; resident and fellow orthopedic surgery San Francisco County Hosp., 1935-36, Children's Hosp. and Mass. Gen. Hosp., Boston, 1936-39; pvt. practice orthopedic surgery L.A., 1939-40, 45—; clin. prof. orthopedic surgery UCLA, 1965-93; assoc. clin. prof. emeritus Loma Linda Med. Sch., 1963—; attending orthopedic surgeon, emeritus Cedars Sinai Med. Ctr., 1939—, Orthopaedic Hosp., 1939—; chief orthopedic surgery City of Hope, 1948-67; sr. attending orthopedic surgeons, emeritus Unit One L.A. County Hosp., 1950-63; vis. lectr. U. Santo Tomas, Manila, U. Madrid, Spain; Far East Sch. of Medicine, Manila, 1994, Hadassah Med. Ctr., Jerusalem, 1994, U. Brussels; lectr. in field; vis. lectr., Brussels, U. London, Stammore, Eng., U. Guadalajara, Mexico, others. Author: Office Orthopedics, 1955, 4th edit. 1973, Operative Orthopedic Clinics (with Dr. Avia Brockway), 1960, Atlas of Orthopedic Surgery, 1966, Difficult Orthopedic Diagnosis, 1972, Plannings and Pitfalls in Orthopedic Surgery, Natural History of Orthopedic Disease, 1993, Supplement Book, 1996; mem. editl. bd. Resident & Staff Physician; contbr. numerous articles to profl. jours. Vol. physician Internat. Children's Program, Orthopedic Hosp., Mexicali, Mexico. Lt. col. U.S. Army, 1940-45. Fellow ACS, Internat. Coll. Surgeons, Am. Coll. Rheumatology, Royal Soc. Medicine; mem. Am. Rheumatism Assn., Internat. Orthopedic Assn., Am. Orthopaedic Assn. (sr.), Am. Acad. Orthopaedic Surgeons, So. Calif. Rheumatism Assn. (pres. 1979), Western Orthopaedic Assn., Phi Beta Kappa, Alpha Omega Alpha. Avocations: swimming, golf, dancing, travel.

COZZARELLI, NICHOLAS ROBERT, molecular biologist, educator; b. Jersey City, Mar. 26, 1938; s. Nicholas and Catherine (Meluso) C.; m. Linda Angela Ambrosini, July 28, 1967; 1 child, Laura Amelia. AB, Princeton U., 1960; PhD, Harvard U., 1966. Postdoctoral fellow dept. biochemistry Stanford U. Med. Sch., Palo Alto, Calif., 1966-68; asst. prof. dept. biochemistry U. Chgo., 1968-70, asst. prof. depts. biochemistry, biophysics and theoretical biology, 1970-74, assoc. prof., 1974-77, prof., 1977-82; prof. dept. molecular biology U. Calif., Berkeley, 1982-89, prof., div. biochemistry and molecular biology, dept. molecular and cell biology, 1989—, chmn. dept., 1986-89, dir. virus lab., 1986-90. Mem. editl. bd. Jour. Biol. Chemistry, 1988—, Cell, 1983-86; mem. editl. adv. bd. Biochemistry, 1982-86; contbr. articles to profl. jours. Mem. NAS (editor Procs. 1995—), AAAS, Am. Soc. for Microbiology, Am. Soc. for Biol. Chemistry. Democrat. Avocations: reading, theatre. Office: U Calif Biochem & Molecular Biol Dept Molecular/ Cell Biology 401 Barker Hall # 3204 Berkeley CA 94720-3204

COZZI, RONALD LEE, antiquarian book seller, rare book appraiser; b. Wellsville, N.Y., Dec. 29, 1943; s. Glenn Murray Cozzi and Almina (Rogers) Thornton; m. Marilee Ann Banas, Apr. 8, 1989; 1 child: Deborah Ann, stepchildren: Charles F. Banas III, William D. Banas. Diploma in acctg., Bryant Stratton Bus. Inst., Buffalo, 1972-73. Technician IBM, Buffalo, 1967-69, A-M Corp., Buffalo, 1969-71; with U.S. Post Office, Buffalo, 1971-75; owner, mgr. Old Editions Book Shop, Buffalo, 1976—. Active Buffalo and Erie County Hist. Soc. Decorated knight Imperial Constantinian Mil. Order of St. George, 1991. Mem. Antiquarian Booksellers Assn. Am., University Heights Bus. Assn. (bd. dirs. 1989—). Republican. Methodist. Avocations: chess, book collecting, travel. Office: Old Editions Book Shop 3124 Main St Buffalo NY 14214-1354

CRABB, BARBARA BRANDRIFF, federal judge; b. Green Bay, Wis., Mar. 17, 1939; d. Charles Edward and Mary (Forrest) Brandriff; m. Theodore E. Crabb, Jr., Aug. 29, 1959; children: Julia Forrest, Philip Elliott. A.B., U. Wis., 1960, J.D., 1962. Bar: Wis. 1963. Assoc. Roberts, Boardman, Suhr and Curry, Madison, Wis., 1962-64; legal rschr. Sch. Law, U. Wis., 1968-70, Am. Bar Assn., Madison, 1970-71; U.S. magistrate Madison, 1971-79; judge U.S. Dist. Ct. (we. dist.) Wis., Madison, 1979—, chief judge, 1980-96, dist. judge, 1996—; mem. Gov. Wis. Task Force Prison Reform, 1971-73. Membership chmn., v.p. Milw. LWV, 1966-68; mem. Milw. Jr. League, 1967-68. Mem. ABA, Nat. Assn. Women Judges, State Bar Wis., Dane County Bar Assn., U. Wis. Law Alumni Assn. Office: US Dist Ct PO Box 591 120 N Henry St Madison WI 53701-0591

CRABB, KENNETH WAYNE, obstetrician, gynecologist; b. Glendive, Mont.; s. Kenneth Willard and Marjorie Jane (Martin) C.; m. Gwen Aldean Wendelschafer; children: Kenneth Wendel, Richard David. BS with honors in Biochemistry, U. Iowa, 1971, MD, 1975. Diplomate Am. Bd. Ob-Gyn. Intern, then resident in ob-gyn St. Paul Ramsey Med. Ctr., 1975-79; practice medicine specializing in ob-gyn St. Paul, 1979—; clin. asst. prof. ob.-gyn. U. Minn., Mpls., 1981-89, clin. assoc. prof., 1989—; vice chmn. dept. ob.-gyn. United Hosp., St. Paul, 1984-86, 91-93, pharm. and therapeutics com., 1980-84, cancer com., 1995—; preceptor family practice resident St. John's Hosp., St. Paul, 1979—, maternal health com., 1979-88, cancer com., 1984-85; quality assurance com. St. Joseph's Hosp., St. Paul, 1981-83; mem. Med. Affairs Coun. for Health One, 1989-93; chmn. bd. dirs. ParaNatal Svcs., Inc., 1990-94; bd. dirs. Preferred One Physicians Assn., 1987—, pres. 1994-96, Prefered One PPO, 1987-98, Preferred One Mgmt. Co., 1994-96, Peak Adminstrv. Svcs., PACE Ins. Co., 1996—; physician advisor Medtrac. Health Mark, StratisHealth. With Actors Theatre of St. Paul, 1980-90, bd. dirs. 2d v.p., 1984-85; bd. trustees Minn. Med. Found., 1997—; mem. coun. Grace Luth. Ch., 1984-87; bd. dirs. Indianhead coun. Boy Scouts Am., 1986—, coun. advancement chair, 1996—. Recipient Appreciation award Am. Acad. Family Physicians, 1979-90. Fellow Am. Coll. Ob-Gyn. (jr. fellow dist. chmn. 1978-79, jr. fellow adv. coun. 1978-80, chmn. 1989 Dist. VI meeting, appreciation award 1978-79, chmn. higher edn. loan program com. 1989-91, adv. coun. Minn. sect. 1996-98), Am. Fertility Soc.; mem. AMA (Physicians Recognition award 1985, 88, 90, 93, 96), Ctrl. Assn. Obstetricians & Gynecologists, Am. Soc. Coloscopy & Cervical Pathology, Am. Assn. Gynecologic Laparoscopists, Minn. Med. Assn. (nominating com. 1986-87, legis. com. 1988-94, 97—, vice chmn. 1989-94, med. practice and planning com. 1995-96, vice chmn. 1995-96, alternate del. AMA 1997—), Minn. Obstetric and Gynecologic Soc. (program com. 1984), Ramsey Med. Soc. (bd. trustees 1993-94, med. practice com. 1982-87, del. 1983, 85-7, fin. com. 1984-89, med. svc. com. 1986-88, nominating com. 1992-93, polit. action com. 1988-94, pres.-elect 1995, pres. 1996), Assn. Profs. Ob-gyn., Found. Health Care Evaluation, Rotary (chmn. various coms. 1983-84, 87-88, bd. dirs. 1984-86, 89-91, v.p. 1991-92, pres. 1992-93, sgt. at arms 1986-7), Phi Beta Sigma, Omicron Delta Kappa, Phi Beta Phi (sec. U. Iowa chpt. 1972-73, 2d vice archon 1982-83, supreme sec. treas. 1984-89, supreme archon 1989-92). Avocations: volleyball, skiing, theatre, science fiction, sailing. E-mail: Kcrabb@advancedcape.com. Office: Advanced Specialty Care for Women 310 Smith Ave N Ste 390 Saint Paul MN 55102-2383

CRABBE, JOHN CROZIER, telecommunications consultant; b. Pomona, Calif., July 3, 1914; s. Arthur and Louise A. (Wiley) C.; m. Bobbin Gay Peck, June 17, 1940; children—John Crozier, William Charles, Barbara Gay. Student, Modesto (Calif.) Coll., 1931-34, Fresno (Calif.) State Coll., 1934-36; B.A., Coll. Pacific, 1937, M.A., 1940; postgrad., U. Iowa, 1938, N.Y. U., 1940, Stanford U., 1951, Ohio State U., 1951-52. Dir. broadcasting activities Coll. of Pacific, 1937-58; lectr. radio edn. Stanford U., summer 1951; asst., office radio-TV edn. Ohio State U., 1951-52; exec. sec. Delta-Sierra Ednl. TV Corp., 1953; dir. radio and TV Nat. Music Camp, Interlochen, Mich., 1954-55; program asso. Ednl. TV and Radio Center, Ann Arbor, Mich., 1955-56; exec. sec. Central Calif. Ednl. TV, 1955-58; gen. mgr. Sta. KVIE, 1958-69; spl. cons. radio edn., schs. central Calif.; chmn. TV Adv. Com. State Calif., 1967-69; cons. in broadcasting (East Africa) RTV Internat., N.Y., 1964; pres. Western Ednl. TV Network, 1967-69; mem. interim mgmt. group Corp. for Pub. Broadcasting Network Operation, 1969; cons. in pub. broadcasting, 1969-73; cons. Joint Com. on Telecommunications Calif. Legislature, 1973-74; asso. Arthur Bolton Assos., 1972-73; gen. mgr. Tel-Vue Stockton, Inc., Calif., 1972; dir. telecommunications, gen. mgr. KTSC-TV U. So. Colo., Pueblo, 1976-81, ret., 1981; cons., 1981—; bd. dirs. Rocky Mountain Corp. for Public Broadcasting; bd. govs. Pacific Mountain Network. Contbr. articles to profl. pubs. Served as lt. USNR, 1943-46. Mem. Assn. for Ednl. Radio-TV (pres. 1950-53), Western Radio TV Conf. Home: 1031 La Sierra Dr Sacramento CA 95864-5247 *I have always cherished a commitment to a concept that change is exciting and good. Keeping abreast of and adjusting to change - change in goals, thoughts, ideas, principles of conduct - keeps one flexible and demands continuing accommodation to new developments. Forecasting benchmarks of human conduct and, by indirection, leading others toward predictable behaviour makes me an active participant in the process of change. This preoccupation makes it impossible to become sedentary - physically or intellectually.*

CRABBS, ROGER ALAN, publisher, consultant, small business owner, educator; b. Cedar Rapids, Iowa, May 9, 1928; s. Winfred Wesley and Faye (Woodard) C.; m. Marilyn Lee Westcott, June 30, 1951; children: William Douglas, Janet Lee Crabbs Turner, Ann Lee Crabbs Menke. B.A. in Sci., State U. Iowa, 1954; M.B.A., George Washington U., 1965, D.B.A., 1973, M.Christian Leadership, 1978. Commd. 2nd lt. USAF, 1950, advanced through grades to lt. col., 1968, Ret., 1972; prof. mgmt. U. Portland, Oreg., 1972-79; prof. bus. George Fox Coll., Newberg, Oreg., 1979-83; pres. Judson Bapt. Coll., The Dalles, Oreg., 1983-85; pres. Host Pubs. Inc., pres., chmn. various corps., 1974-86; past chmn. nat. adv. bd. TRAVELHOST, Inc.; cons. to small bus. for Oreg. Econ. Devel., cons. to various orgns., corps. and agys. Author: The Infallible Foundation for Management-The Bible, 1978, The Secret of Success in Small Business Management-Is in the Short Range, 1983; co-author: The Storybook Primer on Managing, 1976. Past pres. English Speaking Union, 1994-96, bd. dirs., 1994-97; bd. dirs. Christ Cmty. Ch., Conf. and Vis. Bur. of Washington County, Oakhills Townhouse Assn., v.p., 1991-95; mem. Minority Conv. Tourism Adv. Coun., Oreg. Decorated Air Force Commendation medal with oak leaf cluster, Meritorious Service medal Dept. Def.; rated Command Air Force Missileman; recipient regional, dist. and nat. awards SBA. Mem. Acad. Mgmt., Am. Arbitration Assn., Svc. Corps Ret. Execs., Air Force Assn., Portland Officers Club, Rotary (past pres.), Masons, Kiwanis, Lang Syne Soc. of Portland, Alpha Kappa Psi, Delta Epsilon Sigma, Phi Mu Alpha. Republican. Office: Host Publs Inc PMB #173 822 NW Murray Blvd Portland OR 97229-5868 *A positive attitude, sincere interest in others and a sense of humility have been the building blocks of my personal philosophy. They have served me well through my three careers - professional military, university professor and publisher.*

CRABILL, LINDA JEAN, municipal government official; b. St. Albans, Vt., Oct. 12, 1954; d. Marvin Henry and Mildred Theresa (McKenney) Ladue; m. James Daniel Crabill, Sept. 17, 1977 (div. May 1991); 1 child, Krisanne Michele. AA, Evergreen Valley Coll., San Jose, Calif., 1985; student, San Jose State U., 1985-89, Boston Coll., 1998—. Analyst United Techs. Corp., Windsor Locks, Conn., 1973-75; cryptologic technician USN, San Vito dei Normanni, Italy, 1975-78; polit. aide to city coun. City of San Jose, Calif., 1984-89; asst. program coord. Foothill Coll., Los Altos, Calif., 1989-91; cmty. rels. coord. City of Sunnyvale, Calif., 1991—; master's cert. crisis com. State of Calif., 1998. Author, editor: Citizens Access Handbook, 1993 (3d place statewide Excellence in Comm. 1994). Chair Coord. Coun. United Way Santa Clara County (Coord. of Yr., Santa Clara County, 1993), San Jose, 1994—; state bd. dirs. Cmty. Health Charities Calif. (Person of Yr. 1995), Sacramento, 1996—; bd. mem. local affiliate Santa Clara County, San Jose, 1993— (Outstanding Campaign coord. 1993, 94, 95); com. mem. adv. bd. Am. Cancer Soc. of Santa Clara County, 1996—; mem. Dem. Senatorial Com., Washington, 1995—; mem. Olympic Torch Relay, Santa Clara County, 1996; bd. mem. Holy Family Ch. fin. com., San Jose, 1992-95. With USN, 1975-78, Italy. Recipient Disting. Grad. award, Evergreen Valley Coll., 1985. Mem. ASPA (bd. dirs. 1993-95, Pres.'s award 1995), Calif. Pub. Info. Officers Assn., South Bay Pub. Rels. Round Table (pres. 1994-95, v.p. 1993), Golden Key (life). Democrat. Roman Catholic. Avocations: showing Lhasa Apsos, camping, hiking, reading. Home: 4110 Wessex Dr San Jose CA 95136-1855 Office: City of Sunnyvale Office of City Mgr 603 All America Way Sunnyvale CA 94088-3707

CRABILL, MARK CLARE, agricultural specialist; b. Scottsbluff, Nebr.; s. Marion Wayne Crabill and Vivian Leola Daniels; m. Linda Louise Crabill, July 27, 1973; children: Aaron, Emerson, Jennifer. BS in Edn., Black Hills State U., 1974; MA, U. Nebr., 1983. Cert. tchr., S.D. Tchr. Woonona (Australia) H.S., 1975-76, Hyannis (Nebr.) H.S., 1977-86, Big Piney (Wyo.) Mid. Sch., 1986-87, Pinedale (Wyo.) H.S., 1988-89; lamb feeder Crabill Sheep Co., Belle Fourche, S.D., 1989—; dir. Nat. Live Stock and Meat Bd., Chgo., 1990-92. Mem. sch. bd. Belle Fourche Sch. Dist., 1994-97; bd. dirs. Belle Fourche Area Cmty. Ctr., 1996-97; chmn. Butte County Rep. Party, Belle Fourche, 1997-98. NEH grantee, 1985. Mem. Am. Sheep Industry Assn., Nat. Lamb Feeders Assn. (pres. 1992-93). Avocations: fishing, reading, writing, travel. E-mail: crabillm@dtgnet.com. Home: Rural Rte 1 Box 50 Belle Fourche SD 57717

CRABLE, JOHN V., chemist; b. New Castle, Pa., Sept. 14, 1923; s. Charles McDonough and Margaret Cecilia (O'Connor) C. Student, Geneva Coll., 1942-43, Va. Poly. Inst., 1943-44, U. Nancy, 1945; BS in Chemistry, Duquesne U., 1949; postgrad., U. Wis., 1949-50. Jr. fellow Mellon Inst. Indsl. Rsch., Pitts., 1950-57; rsch. chemist Gulf R&D, Pitts., 1957-62; rsch. chemist phys. & chem. analysis br. BOSH, Cin., 1962-69; chief phys. & chem. analysis br. Nat. Inst. Occupl. Health & Safety, Cin., 1970-76; chief measurements/methods rsch. br. NIOSH, Cin., 1976-90; cons., Cin., 1990—; mem. intersoc. com. ambient air sampling & analysis Am. Conf. Govt. Indsl. Hygiene, N.Y.C., 1969-80; mem. analytical chemistry com. Am. Indsl. Hygiene Assn., Fairfax, Va., lab. accreditation com., 1971-78; mem. Am. del. Internat. Orgn. Standardizaton, Geneva, 1972-86, tech. com. workplace atmospheres, 1979-85; project officer U. Alexandria, Egypt; temporary cons. Inst. Occupl. Health WHO, Beijing, 1984; chmn. subcom. biol. monitoring com. lab stds. and practices APHA, 1981-83. Co-editor Biol. Monitoring, 1983-88; editl. bd. Applied Indsl. Hygiene, 1985-90; contbr. articles to profl. jours. With U.S. Army, 1943-46, CIB, ETO. Decorated 3 Battle Stars, Bronze Star. Mem. Am. Chem. Soc. (emeritus), Am. Conf. Govtl. Indsl. Hygienists (emeritus), Am. Indsl. Hygiene Assn. (emeritus). Avocations: travel, reading, swimming, music, gardening. Home: 1146 Meriweather Ave Cincinnati OH 45208-2811

CRABTREE, BEN C., home health care agency administrator; b. Las Vegas, Sept. 11, 1964; s. Ben C. and Jaynelle (Felix) C.; m. Virginia Kathryn Vance, Feb. 7, 1988 (div. Nov. 1989); m. Tania Oylan Tason, May 5, 1992; children: Greta, Bryan. AS, Panama Canal Coll., La Boca, Rep. of Panama, 1993, Austin Peay State U., 1995; BBA, Our Lady of the Lake U., 1995. Cert. firearms instr., range officer. Software tech., adminstr. asst. Ace Personal Health Care, Inc., San Antonio, 1994-95; dir. info. systems River City Fin. Health Group/Home Health Care Solutions, San Antonio, 1995; chief fin. officer, alt. adminstr. A&E Quality Home Health Care, San Antonio, 1996—; pres. Oylan, Inc., San Antonio, 1997-99; profl. adv. com. Silver Days Home Health Care, San Antonio, 1996-97, Responsive Health Svcs., 1997-99. Mem. Dist. 128 State Budget Adv. Com., San Antonio, 1995. Ssgt. U.S. Army, 1984-92. Mem. U.S. Practical Shooting Assn., Tex. Action Shooting Club, Internat. Defensive Pistol Assn., Nat. Range Officers' Inst., Internat. Defensive Pistol Assn., Nat. Assn. Home Care. Avocations: practical shooting, web page design. Office: A & E Quality Home Health Care Inc Oylan Inc 10221 Desert Sands Ste 200 San Antonio TX 78216

CRABTREE, BEVERLY JUNE, retired college dean; b. Lincoln, Nebr., June 22, 1937; d. Wayne Uniack and Frances Margaret (Wibbels) Deles Dernier; m. Robert Jewell Crabtree, June 1, 1958; children: Gregory, Karen. BS in Edn., U. Mo., 1959, MEd, 1962; PhD, Iowa State U., 1965. Tchr. home econs. area pub. schs., Pierce City and Sarcoxie, Mo., 1959-61; mem. faculty home econs. Mich. State U., East Lansing, 1964-67; assoc. prof. U. Mo., Columbia, 1967-72, coord. home econs. edn., 1967-73, prof., 1972-73; assoc. dean home econs., dir. home econs. extension programs U. Mo., 1973-75; dean Coll. Home Econs. Okla. State U., Stillwater, 1975-87; dean Coll. Family and Consumer Scis. Iowa State U., Ames, 1987-97, ret., 1997; mem. faculty Family Impact Seminar Inst. Ednl. Leadership, George Washington U., 1976-82, Cath. U. Am., 1982-87; mem. nat. panel cons. for Vocat. Ednl. Pers. Devel., 1969-70; mem. nat. com. on future of coop. extension USDA and Nat. Assn. State Univs. and Land Grant Colls., 1982; mem. joint coun. on food and agrl. scis., 1987-91. Contbr. articles in field to profl. jours. Gen. Foods fellow, 1963-64; recipient Centennial Alumni award Coll. Home Econs. Iowa State U., 1971, Alumni Citation of Merit, Coll. Home Econs. U. Mo., 1976, Profl. Achievement award Iow State U., 1983. Mem. Am. Home Econs. Assn. (pres. 1977-78, chmn. adv. coun. Ctr. for Family 1982-83, mem. coun. profl. devel. 1980-83, a leader to commemorate 75th anniversary 1984, pres. found. 1987-88, chair Coun. for Certification 1991-92, chair Coun. for Accreditation 1997-98, Disting. Svc. award 1993), Okla. Home Econs. Assn. (Profl. Achievement award 1983), Nat. Assn. State Univs. and Land Grant Colls. (mem. commn. home econs. 1981-84), Assn. Tchr. Educators, Home Econs. Edn. Assn., Nat. Council of Adminstrs. of Home Econs., Am. Ednl. Research Assn., Am. Assn. Higher Edn., Nat. Assn. Tchr. Educators for Home Econs. (pres. 1969), Nat. Council on Family Relations, Mortar Bd., Golden Key, Omicron Nu, Phi Upsilon Omicron, Phi Delta Kappa, Omicron Delta Kappa, Pi Lambda Theta, Phi Kappa Phi, Gamma Sigma Delta. Methodist. Home: 3113 Rosewood Cir Ames IA 50014-4589

CRABTREE, BRUCE ISBESTER, JR., architect; b. Chattanooga, Sept. 1, 1923; s. Bruce Isbester and Anna Hunter (Kirkpatrick) C.; m. Dolly Nance Fischer, Mar. 31, 1948; children: Anna Hunter, Bruce Isbester III, Drucilla, Raymond, Thomas. Student, Vanderbilt U., 1942-43, Clemson Coll., 1943-44; BS, Va. Poly. Inst., 1948. Registered architect, Tenn., N.C., Va., S.C., Ga., Fla., Ala., Ky., Md., Wis., Mo., La., W.Va., Washington, Tex. Architect, designer Hart & McBryde, Nashville, 1948-52; ptnr. Taylor & Crabtree, Nashville, 1952-81; v.p. Taylor & Crabtree-Wiley & Wilson, Nashville, 1981-85; vice chmn. bd. Yearwood Johnson Stanton & Crabtree, Inc., Nashville, 1985-90; ptnr. Johnson, Johnson & Crabtree, P.C., Nashville, 1991—; archtl. columnist Nashville Banner. Architect works include Andrew Jackson State Office Bldg., 1974, Athletic and Convocation Ctr., Middle Tenn. State U., 1975, James K. Polk Performing Arts Ct., 1980, Graces Plaza Shopping Ctr., 1987. Bd. dirs. Nashville YMCA, 1968; mem. pub. adv. panel GSA, Atlanta, 1973-74; chmn. Belle Meade Bd. Zoning Appeals, Tenn., 1982-97, Belle Meade Bd. Codes Appeals, 1987-97; mem. Belle Meade Planning Commn., 1989-97, vice chmn., 1990-97; team leader and mem. of operating com. Mayor's Efficiency in Govt. Commn., Met. Govt. Nashville and Davidson County, Tenn., 1989; mem. commn. City of Belle Meade, 1988, vice-mayor, 1988-97. Served to tech. sgt. AUS, 1943-45, PTO. Recipient Tenn. Outstanding Achievement award State of tenn., 1983; Knight of the Sovereign Mil. Order of Temple of Jerusalem. Fellow AIA (pres. Middle Tenn. chpt. 1966); mem. Tenn. Soc. Architects (pres. 1967 Medal of Merit 1968, Spl. Service award 1984), Nat. Coun. Archtl. Registration Bds., Tau Beta Pi, Omicron Delta Kappa, Sigma Chi. Roman Catholic. Clubs: Cumberland, Exchange (Nashville), Belle Meade Country, Coffee House (sec. 1989-90, v.p. 1990-91, pres. 1992-93). Home: 424 Sunnyside Dr Nashville TN 37205-3414 Office: Johnson Johnson & Crabtree PC 4551 Trousdale Dr Nashville TN 37204-4513

CRABTREE, DAVIDA FOY, minister; b. Waterbury, Conn., June 7, 1944; Alfred and Davida (Blakeslee) Foy; m. David T. Hindinger Jr., Aug. 28, 1982; stepchildren: Elizabeth Anne, David Todd. BS, Marietta Coll., 1967; MDiv, Andover Newton Theol. Sch., 1972; D of Ministry, Hartford Sem., 1989. Ordained to ministry United Ch. of Christ, 1972. Founder, exec. dir. Prudence Crandall Ctr. for Women, New Britain, Conn., 1973-76; min., dir. Greater Hartford (Conn.) Campus Ministry, 1976-80; sr. min. Colchester (Conn.) Federated Ch., 1980-91; bd. dirs. Conn. Conf. United Ch. of Christ, Hartford, 1982-90; conf. min. So. Calif. Conf., United Ch. of Christ, Pasadena, 1991-96, Conn. Conf., United Ch. of Christ, Hartford, 1996—; rsch. assoc. Harvard Div. Sch., Cambridge, Mass., 1975-76. Author: The Empowering Church, 1989 (named one of Top Ten Books of Yr. 1990); editorial advisor Alban Inst., 1990—. Bd. dirs. Hartford region YWCA, 1979-82; trustee Cragin Meml. Libr., Colchester, 1980-91, Hartford Sem., 1983-91, Sch. of Theology at Claremont, 1993-96, Andover Newton Theol. Sch., 1997—; founder Youth Svcs. Bur., Colchester, 1984-89; pres. Creative Devel. for Colchester Inc., 1989-91; coun. Religious Leaders of L.A., 1991-96; v.p. Hope in Youth Campaign, 1992-96; dir. UCC Ins. bd., 1993—; bd. dirs. Amistad America, 1998—, Stowe-Day Found., 1998—. Recipient Antoinette Brown award Gen. Synod, United Ch. of Christ, 1977, Conf. Preacher award Conn. Conf. United Ch. of Christ, 1982, Woman in Leadership award Hartford region YWCA, 1987; named one of Outstanding Conn. Women, UN Assn., 1987, Somos Uno award United Neighborhood Orgn., 1995. Mem. Nat. Coun. Chs. (bd. dirs. 1969-81), Christians for Justice Action (exec. com. 1981-91).

CRABTREE, GERALD R., pathology and biology educator; b. Dec. 18, 1946. BS, Liberty State Coll., 1968; MD, Temple U., 1972. Asst. prof. pathology Dartmouth Coll. Sch. Medicine, 1979-82; sr. investigator NIH, 1982-84; assoc. prof. Stanford U. Sch. Medicine, 1985-93, prof. pathology and devel. biology, 1993—; assoc. investigator Howard Hughes Med. Inst., 1987-94, investigator, 1994—; mem. com. molecular and cellular biology. Mem. Nat. Acad. Sci.

CRABTREE, JOHN DAVID, manufacturing company executive; b. Evansville, Ind., Apr. 13, 1947; s. George B. and Lucille (Barnhart) C.; m. Teresa Jean Whitsitt, June 15, 1968; children: John David Jr., Katherine Suzanne. BS in Indsl. Econs., Purdue U., 1969. Tool and die engr. Willow Run Hydramatic, Ypsilanti, Mich., 1974-75, foreman, 1975-77, gen. foreman plant #3, 1977-78, supt. plant #3, 1978-80, gen. supt. mfg., 1980-83, gen. supt. maintenance and process engring., 1983-85; plant mgr. Toledo Powertrain div. GM Corp., 1985-91, plant mgr. Flint V8 engine, 1991—; mem. governing bd. Edison Indsl. Systems Ctr., Toledo 1987-88; coun. advisors ctr. for bus. and industry U. Toledo, 1988. Constable Saline Twp., 1985-88, mem. bd. tax rev., 1985-88; bd. dirs. Jr. Achievement, Toledo, 1986-88; governing bd. Working Coun. for Employee Involvement, NW Ohio, 1989, mem., 1990-91. Mem. Soc. Automotive Engrs., The Forum (Toledo), Toledo Leadership (com. of 100 1990-93), Am. Legion, Kiwanis. Republican. Methodist. Avocations: flying, pvt. pilot. Home: 2423 Pepperidge Trl Brighton MI 48114-8956

CRABTREE, LOREN WILLIAM, provost, academic administrator, history educator; b. Aberdeen, S.D., Sept. 2, 1940; s. Benjamin Forrest and Harriet Caroline (Zempel) C.; m. Sheila Ann Volz, Aug. 25, 1961 (div. May 1987); children: Christopher, Kathryn, Paul; m. Monica Sue Christen, 1987. BA, U. Minn., 1961, MA, 1965, PhD, 1969. Instr. Bethel Coll., St. Paul, 1965-67; from instr. to prof. history Colo. State U., Ft. Collins, 1967—, dean Coll. Liberal Arts, 1991-97, provost, acad. v.p., 1998—; vis. assoc. prof. U. Colo., Boulder, 1980; vis. prof., dean semester at sea program U. Pitts., 1986, 91; faculty affiliate Nat. Faculty, Atlanta, 1988—. Author: The Lion and the Dragon, 1970; co-author: Civilizations: A Cultural Atlas, 1994; contbr. articles to profl. publs. Trustee Am. Bapt. Ch., Ft. Collins, 1970-74; bd. deacons First Christian Ch., Ft. Collins, 1984-86. NDFL Chinese Lang. fellow Harvard U., 1964. Mem. Assn. for Asian Studies (pres. western conf. 1983-84), Coun. Colls. of Arts and Scis., Phi Beta Kappa, Phi Alpha Theta. Democrat. Avocations: hiking, mountain climbing, court sports, furniture building. Home: 2201 Grosvenor Ct Fort Collins CO 80526-5256 Office: Office of Provost Colo State Univ Fort Collins CO 80523

CRABTREE, TANIA OYLAN, home health nurse, administrator, consultant; b. Panama City, Panama, Sept. 8, 1942; d. German and Rosa America (Tason) Tortosa; m. Robert Crusoe, Feb. 27, 1969 (div. 1982); children: Greta, Bryan; m. Ben C. Crabtree II, May 5, 1992. Student, Radcliffe Coll., 1960; BSN, Ctrl. U., Quito, Ecuador, 1964. RN, Fla., Tex. Oper. rm. nurse Peter Bent Brigham Hosp., Boston, 1965-66; oper. rm. staff nurse Lakeland (Fla.) Gen. Hosp., 1966-69; surg. head nurse Miami (Fla.) Heart Inst., 1970-71; oper. rm. head nurse Mercy Hosp., Miami, 1971-74; staff nurse Gorgas Army Cmty. Hosp., Panama City, 1974-75, oper. rm. nurse, 1975-82, home health nurse practitioner, 1982-93; DON Ace Personal Health Care, Inc., San Antonio, 1993-95; cons., edn. coord. Precision Consulting, Inc., San Antonio, 1994-96; dir. profl. and clin. svcs. River City Fin. Health Group, San Antonio, 1995-96; adminstr., owner, dir. nurses A&E Quality Home Health Care, Inc., San Antonio, 1996—; geriatrics nursing cons. Hurley, Galvan and Assocs., Panama City, 1989-93. Mem. Tex. Nurses Assn. Roman Catholic. Avocations: dancing, karate, aerobics, swimming, dining. Office: A&E Quality Home Health Care Inc PO Box 791386 San Antonio TX 78279-1386

CRACCO, ROGER QUINLAN, medical educator, neurologist; b. Union City, N.J., June 1, 1934; s. Frederick A. and Ruby Ann (Quinlan) C.; m. Joan Marie Bender, June 9, 1962. A.B., Cornell U., 1956; M.D., N.J. Med. Sch., 1960. Diplomate Am. Bd. Psychiatry and Neurology, Am. Bd. Electrodiagnostic Medicine, Am. Bd. Clin. Neurophysiology (bd. dirs. 1984-88). Intern Phila. Gen. Hosp., 1960-61; resident in neurology Jersey City Med. Ctr., 1961-64; fellow in neurophysiology Mayo Grad. Sch., Mayo Clinic, 1964-66; asst. prof. neurology Jefferson Med. Coll., Phila., 1968-71, assoc. prof., 1971-73; prof. neurology SUNY Health Sci. Ctr. at Bklyn., 1973-80, prof., chmn. neurology, 1980—; head neurology service State U. Hosp.-Kings County Hosp. Ctr., Bklyn., 1980—; vice dean for acad. and sci. affairs Coll. Medicine SUNY Health Sci. Ctr., Bklyn., 1997—; mem. program project rev. com. Nat. Inst. Neurology, Communicative Disease and Stroke, NIH, USPHS, 1984-88, chmn. 1987-88. Editor: (with I. Bodis-Wollner) Evoked Potentials, 1986; mem. editorial bd. Ann. Neurology, Electroencephalography Clinical Neurophysiology, Muscle and Nerve jour., others.; contbr. articles to profl. jours. Served to capt. M.C., U.S. Army, 1966-68. NIH grantee, 1970-86. Fellow Am. Acad. Neurology; mem. Am. Neurol. Assn., Am. Electroencephalographic Soc. (pres. 1981-82), Eastern Assn. Electroencephalography (pres. 1979-80), Am. Assn. Electromyography and Electrodiagnosis, Am. Epilepsy Soc., Soc. for Neurosci., Assn. U. Profs. of Neurology, Am. Acad. Clin. Neurophysiology (pres. 1987-89), Alpha Omega Alpha. Office: SUNY Health Sci Ctr Bklyn Dept Neurology 450 Clarkson Ave Dept Brooklyn NY 11203-2056

CRACKEL, THEODORE JOSEPH, historian; b. Urbana, Ill., Sept. 10, 1938; s. Orville Lee and Aleta (Smith) C.; m. Kay Knight, Sept. 2, 1961 (div. 1972); children: Todd, Dana; m. Mai Thi Nguyen, Oct. 14, 1972 (div. 1991); children: John, Robert; m. Mary-Jo Kline, May 23, 1998. AB, U. Ill., 1962; MA, Rutgers U., 1971, PhD, 1985. Commd. 2nd lt. U.S. Army, 1962, advanced through grades to lt. col., 1978; tank unit comdr. U.S. Army, Germany, 1963-66; advisor U.S. Army, Vietnam, 1966-67, 71-72; weapons sys. analyst Combat Devels. Command, Ft. Knox, Ky., 1967-69; asst. prof. history U.S. Mil. Acad., West Point, N.Y., 1972-75, 78-81; instr. Dept. Stratoegy U.S. Army Command and Gen. Staff Coll., 1975-77; dir. mil. history and strategy studies U.S. Army War Coll., Carlisle Barracks, Pa., 1981-83, ret., 1983; sr. fellow The Heritage Found., Washington, 1983-85; sr. cons. GE Co., Washington, 1985-87; exec. dir. Papers of the Comdg. Gens., 1988-93; dir., editor Papers of the War Dept. 1784-1800, 1993—. Author: The Army Aditional Duty Guide, 1970, Mr. Jefferson's Army, 1987, The Illustrated History of West Point, 1991, History of the Civil Reserve Air Fleet, 1993, reprinted, 1999; contbr. articles on mil. and polit. history and def. orgn. reform to profl. jours. Mem. Assn. Documentary Editors, Orgn. Am. Historians, Soc. Historians of Early Am. Republic, Soc. Mil. History, Army and Navy Club (Washington), Chi Psi. Republican. Office: East Stroudsburg U Papers Of War Dept 1784-1800 East Stroudsburg PA 18301

CRACKETT, DELORES, womens bureau administrator. B in Psychology, Spelman Coll.; M in Guidance and Counseling, Atlanta U. Comm. and employment mgr. Avon Products, Inc.; dep. dir. Women's Bur., Dept. of Labor, Washington, 1993-96; field ops. mgr., regional adminstr. Region IV, Women's Bur., Dept. of Labor, Atlanta; acting dir. Women's Bur., Dept. of Labor, Washington. Office: Womens Bur 200 Constitution Ave NW Washington DC 20210-0001

CRACROFT, RICHARD HOLTON, English literature educator; b. Salt Lake City, June 28, 1936; s. Ralph and Grace Darling (White) C.; m. Janice Marie Alger, Sept. 17, 1959; children: Richard Alger, Jeffrey Ralph, Jennifer Cracroft Lewis. BA, U. Utah, 1961, MA, 1963; PhD in English and Am. Lit., U. Wis., 1969. Student instr. U. Utah, Salt Lake City, 1961-63; instr. English Brigham Young U., Provo, Utah, 1963-66; grad. instr. U. Wis., Madison, 1966-69; from asst. prof. English to assoc. prof. English Brigham Young U., Provo, 1969-74, prof. English, 1974—, dept. chair English, 1975-80, dean Coll. Humanities, 1981-86; dir. Ctr. for Study of Christian Values in Lit., Brigham Young U., Provo, 1993—; bd. judges David Evans Biography Prize, Logan, Utah, 1983—, Orton Prize for Mormon Letters, Salt Lake City, 1991—. Author: Washington Irving: The Western Works, 1974; co-editor: A Believing People: The Literature of the Latter-day Saints, 1974, 1979, 22 Young Mormon Writers, 1975, Voices From the Past: (LDS) Journals, Diaires, Autobiographies, 1980, My Soul Delighteth in the Scriptures, 1999; editor: Dictionary of Literary Biography: 20th Century American Writers, vols. 206, 212, 218, 1999, (jour.) Lit. and Belief, 1993—; founding assoc. editor: The Carpenter, 1966-70; assoc. editor: Dialogue, 1969-73, Western Am. Lit., 1973-86; mem. editl. bd.: BYU Studies, 1981-86, This People, 1996—; contbg author: Instruction and Delight, Critical Essays on Thomas Wolfe: A Literary History of the American West, Mark Twain Ency., Turning Hearts: Short Stories of Family Life, others; contbr. articles to profl. and popular jours. Bishop, stake pres., mission pres. LDS Ch. Democrat. Avocations: reading, writing, gardening, leading tours of Western Europe. Home: 770 E Center St Provo UT 84606-4950 Office: Brigham Young U Dept English 3146 Jesse Knights Hum Bldg Provo UT 84604-2724

CRADDICK, THOMAS RUSSELL, state representative, investor; b. Beloit, Wis., Sept. 19, 1943; s. Russell Francis and Beatrice Eleanor (Kowalik) C.; m. Nadine Nayfa, Sept. 6, 1969; children: Christi Leigh, Thomas Russell Jr. BBA, Tex. Tech. U., 1965, MBA, 1966. Owner Craddick Properties, Midland; owner, pres. Craddick Inc., Midland; sales rep. Mustang Mud, Midland; state rep. Tex. Legis., Austin, 1968—; chmn. Rep. Legis. Caucus, Austin, 1988—, ho. ways and means com., 1992, mem. legis. budget bd., Austin, 1992—, legis. audit com., 1992—. Bd. dirs. Tex. Tech. U. Found., Lubbock. Recipient Disting. Eagle Scout award Boy Scouts Am., 1990, Hats Off award Tex. Ind. Roy. Owners Assn., 1988; Paul Harris fellow Rotary Found., 1991. Mem. Lions Club. Republican. Roman Catholic. Avocations: sports, hunting, fishing. Home: 3108 Stanolind Ave Midland TX 79705-8240 Office: Craddick Properties 508 W Wall Ste 750 Midland TX 79701-5076*

CRADDOCK, (JOHN) CAMPBELL, geologist, educator; b. Chgo., Apr. 3, 1930; s. John and Bernice (Campbell) C.; m. Dorothy Dunkelberg, June 13, 1953; children: Susan, John, Carol. BA, DePauw U., 1951; MA, Columbia U., 1953, PhD, 1954. Geologist Shell Oil Co., N.Mex., Tex., Colo., Wyo., 1954-56; asst. prof. U. Minn., Mpls., 1956-60; assoc. prof. U. Minn., 1960-67; prof. geology U. Wis., Madison, 1967-96; prof. emeritus, 1996—; chmn. dept. U. Wis., 1977-80; leader Antarctic geologic field research programs, 1959-69, geologist, 1980; leader Alaskan geologic field research programs, 1968-81, Svalbard field research programs, 1977-86; cons. C.E., AUS, 1957-58, N. Star Research Inst., 1965-68, Dept. State, 1976, Phillips Petroleum Co., 1980, Texaco, 1985; vis. scientist N.Z. Geol. Survey, 1962-63; lectr. Nanjing and Beijing univs., China, 1981; chmn. panel polar geology and geophysics NRC, 1967-71, com. on polar rsch., 1967-71, polar rsch. bd., 1978-82; U.S. mem. working group on geology Sci. Com. on Antarctic Rsch., 1967-81, chmn. group, 1973-80; co-chief scientist Leg 35, Deep Sea Drilling Project, Antarctica, 1974; chmn. Antarctic panel Circum-Pacific Map Project, 1979-90. Editor: Antarctic Geoscience, 1982; co-editor: Geologic Maps of Antarctica, Folio 12, Antarctic Map Folio Series, 1970, Initial Reports of the Deep Sea Drilling Project, Vol. 35, 1976, Geology and Paleontology of the Ellsworth Mountains, Antarctica, Geol. Soc. of Am. Memoir 170, 1992; contbr. articles to profl. jours. Higgins fellow, 1951-52, NSF fellow, 1952-53; Rsch. grantee, 1957-95; recipient U.S. Antarctic Service medal, 1968, Bellingshausen-Lazarev medal Soviet Acad. Scis., 1970, Alumni citation DePauw U., 1976. Fellow AAAS (steering com. geology and geography sect. 1996-98), Geol. Soc. Am. (chmn. North Ctrl. sect. 1982-83, chmn. structural geology and tectonics divsn. 1983-84, books editor 1982-88, Disting. Svc. award 1988); mem. Internat. Union Geol. Scis. (commn. on structural geology 1968-76, mem. commn. on tectonics 1976-85, del. Sci. Com. on Antarctic Rsch. 1974-87, mem. commn. on geologic map of world 1974-91, commn. v.p. for Antarctica 1979-91), Am. Geophys. Union, Am. Assn. Petroleum Geologists, Groupe Francais d'Etude de Gondwana (hon.), Phi Beta Kappa, Sigma Xi. Office: U Wis Dept Geology and Geophysics 1215 W Dayton St Madison WI 53706-1600

CRAFORD, M. GEORGE, physicist, research administrator; b. Sioux City, Iowa, Dec. 29, 1938. BA, U. Iowa, 1961; MS, U. Ill., 1963, PhD in Physics, 1967. Mem. staff Monsanto, St. Louis, 1967-74, Palo Alto, Calif., 1974-79; mgr. R&D optoelec. divsn. Hewlett Packard, San Jose, Calif., 1979—. Mem. Nat. Acad. Engring. Office: Hewlett Packard Co 350-370 W Trimble Rd San Jose CA 95131-1008*

CRAFT, CHERYL MAE, neurobiologist, anatomist, researcher; b. Lynch, Ky., Apr. 15, 1947; d. Cecil Berton and Lillian Lovelle (Ellington) C.; m. Laney K. Cormney, Oct. 14, 1967 (div. Sept. 1980); children: Tyler Craft Cormney, Ryan Berton Cormney. BS in Biology/Chemistry/Math., Valdosta State Coll., 1969; Cert. in Tchg. Biol./Math., Ea. Ky. U., 1971; PhD in Human Anatomy/Neurosci., U. Tex., San Antonio, 1984. Undergrad. rsch. asst. Ea. Ky. U., Richmond, 1965-67; tchg. asst. dept. cell-structural biology U. Tex. Health Sci. Ctr., San Antonio, 1979-84; postdoctoral fellowship lab. devel. neurobiology NICHD and LMDB/NEI, Bethesda, Md., 1984-86; instr. dept. psychiatry U. Tex. Southwestern Med. Ctr., Dallas, 1986-87, asst. prof. dept. psychiatry, 1987-91; dir. lab. molecular neurogenetics Schizophrenia Rsch. Ctr. VA Med. Ctr., Dallas, 1988-94, Mental Health Clinic Rsch. Ctr., U. Tex. Southwestern Med. Ctr., Dallas, 1990-94; assoc. prof. dept. psychiatry U. Tex. Southwestern Med. Ctr., Dallas, 1991-94; Mary D. Allen prof. Doheney Eye Inst. U. So. Calif. Sch. Medicine, L.A., 1994—, chair dept. cell and neurobiology, 1994—; ad hoc reviewer NEI/NIH, Bethesda, 1993—; reviewer Molecular Biology, NSPB Fight for Sight Grants, 1991-94; STAR-sci. adv. bd. U. So. Calif./Bravo Magnet H.S., L.A., 1995—. Author: (chpt.) Melatonin: Biosyn., Physio. Effects, 1993; exec. editor Exptl. Eye Rsch. jour., 1993—. Recipient Merit award for rsch. VA Med. Ctr., 1992, 93, 94, nomination for Women in Sci. and Engring. award Dallas VA, 1992, 93; NEI fellow, 1986, NICHD/NIH fellow, 1986. Mem. AAAS, AAUW, Assn. for Rsch. in Vision and Ophthalmology (chair program planning com. 1991-94), Am. Soc. for Neurochemistry (Jordi Folch Pi Outstanding Young Investigator 1992), Sigma Xi (sec./treas. 1986-93, pres. 1993-94). Avocations: reading, travel. E-mail: ccraft@hsc.usc.edu. Home: 1191 Brookmere Rd Pasadena CA 91105-3301 Office: Univ So Calif Sch of Medicine 1333 San Pablo St Rm 401 Los Angeles CA 90033-1026

CRAFT, DOUGLAS DURWOOD, artist; b. Greene, N.Y., Oct. 20, 1924; s. Harry Benjamin and Phoebe (Hotchkiss) C.; m. Elizabeth Louise Harms, Sept. 8, 1951. BFA, U. Chgo. and Art Inst. Chgo., 1950; MA in Painting, U. N.Mex., 1953. Grad. asst. U. N.Mex., 1951-52; assoc. prof. fine arts Sch. Art Inst., Chgo., 1957-65, Carnegie-Mellon U., Pitts., 1966-69; prof. fine arts Coll. New Rochelle, N.Y., 1970-91; vis. artist in residence U. Ky., 1964, Cooper Union, N.Y.C., 1969-71, Sch. Visual Arts, N.Y.C., 1988; 1st Am. exch. prof., artist in residence Royal Coll. Art, London, 1964-65; guest artist curator Selected Women, Painters Castle Gallery, Coll. New Rochelle (N.Y.), 1982, Of Paper, Pigment and Glass, Castle Gallery, New Rochelle, 1987, bd. dirs. One-person shows include Kasha Heman Gallery, Chgo., 1963, 61, U. N.Mex., 1964, 52, U. Ky., 1964, Travers Festival Gallery, Edinburgh, Scotland, 1965, Royal Coll. Art, London, 1964, Carnegie Mellon U., 1968, Mus. Art, Carnegie Inst., Pitts., 1968, Fischbach Gallery, N.Y.C., 1973, Jersey City Mus., 1978, 55 Mercer Gallery, N.Y.C., 1980, Bratton Gallery, Inc., N.Y.C., 1989, Coll. Ctr. Art Gallery, Coll. New Rochelle, 1989, Rosefsky Studio Art Gallery SUNY Binghamton, 1993; two-person shows include Paul McCarron Gallery, N.Y.C., 1996; retrospective Butler Inst. Am. Art, Youngstown, Ohio, 1993, Paul McCarron Gallery, N.Y.C., 1995, Delaware Valley Arts Society, Narrowsburg, 1996, retrospective traveling exhbn. Makee Gallery, Canton, Mo., Gray Gallery, Quincy, Ill., Keokuk Art Ctr., Iowa, 1997; selected group exhbns. include Rose Fried Gallery, N.Y.C., 1968, Montclair (N.J.) Art Mus., 1984, Traverse Gallery, Edinburgh, Scotland, 1984, Studio K., Long Island City, N.Y., 1985, Castle Gallery, New Rochelle, N.Y., 1985-86, Jersey City Mus. and Montclair Art Mus., 1987, Robeson Gallery, Rutger's U., Newark, 1987, N.A.M.E. Gallery, Chgo., 1988, Bratton Gallery, Inc., 1988, Bratton Gallery, Inc., N.Y.C., 1989, Schick Art Gallery Skidmore Coll., 1995, Del. Arts Ctr. Gallery, 1995; represented in permanent collections Smithsonian Instn., Washington, Art Inst. Chgo., U. Ky., Mus. Modern Art, N.Y.C., Whitney Mus. Am. Art, N.Y.C., U. N.Mex., Gill Libr. Coll. New Rochelle, Butler Inst. Am. Art, Youngstown, Ohio, corp. collections; numerous pvt. collections in U.S.A, Can., Eng. Scotland, France, Saudi Arabia, Japan. Served with USNR, 1943-46. Recipient Logan bronze medal, prize Art Inst. Chgo., 1966, Harry Allison Logan meml. award Chautauqua Art Assn., 1963, jury award in painting Carnegie Inst., 1968; Carr scholar U. Iowa, 1942-43; Carl Loeb fellow Syracuse U., 1950; grantee Richard A. Florsheim Art Fund, 1993. Home: PO Box 245 Jeffersonville NY 12748-0245 Dealer: Penine Hart Antiques & Art 457 Broome St New York NY 10013-2681

CRAFT, EDMUND COLEMAN, automotive parts manufacturing company executive; b. Plainfield, N.J., Dec. 23, 1939; s. Edmund Coleman and Ruth Irene (Morrell) C.; m. Gail Christensen; children: Edmund Coleman III, Elisabeth Gordon, William Todd. BS, Lycoming Coll., 1963; postgrad., Syracuse U., 1963-64; grad. exec. program, U. Minn., 1984. With Borg-Warner Corp., Detroit; adminstrv. asst. to chmn. Borg-Warner Corp., Chgo., 1969-70; with Borg-Warner Ltd., Letchworth, Hertfordshire, Eng., 1970-75; v.p. hydraulics div. Borg-Warner, Wooster, Ohio, 1975-79; dir. hydraulics div. Donaldson Co. Inc., Mpls., 1979—, v.p., 1983—. Bd. dirs. Jr. Achievement of Upper Midwest Inc., 1993—, mem. exec. com., 1994—; divsn. chmn. United Way, Wooster, 1974. Mem. Automotive Filter Mfrs. Coun. (vice chmn. 1985-89, chmn. 1989-91, bd. dirs. 1991—), Decathlon Club. Republican. Presbyterian. Avocations: golf, power boating.

CRAFT, JEROME WALTER, plastic surgeon, health facility administrator; b. Erie, Pa., Oct. 20, 1932; s. Walter Sion and Elizabeth Mabel (Bowen) c.; divorced; children: Jerome Robert, Christine Anne, David William. MD, Case Western Res. U., 1948. Diplomate Am. Bd. Plastic and Reconstructive Surgery, Am. Bd. Forensic Examiners, Am. Bd. Forensic Medicine. Intern gen. surgery St. Vincent's Hosp., Erie, 1949, gen. surgery preceptee, 1949-52; flight surgeon USAF, 1952-54; resident gen. surgery, 1954-56; resident, clin. instr. plastic/reconstructive/hand surgery U. Rochester, N.Y., 1956-58; resident in head and neck surgery Roswell Pk. Cancer Inst., U. Buffalo, 1957-58; clin. practice in plastic and reconstructive surgery, head and neck surgery, surgery of hand Erie, 1958-66; chief Craft Surg. Ctr., West Palm Beach, Fla., 1966—; pres. Aesthetic Surgery Clinique Palm Beach, West Palm Beach, 1974—; acting head dept. Roswell Pk. Cancer Inst., U. Buffalo, 1977; mem. Senator Paula Hawkins Med. Adv. Com. to U.S. Congress, Fla., 1986-87; bd. dirs. Octagon Large Wild Animal Treatment Ctr., Ft. Myers, Fla. Author: Reconstruction Hypophanynx, 1959, Burn Cardiac Arrest, 1958, Cosmetic Surgery Book, 1987; rschr. Arterial Grafts, 1957; inventor in field. Med. advisor Congress, Washington, 1986. Capt. USAF, 1952-54. Mem. AMA, Am. Soc. Plastic & Reconstructive Surgeons, Am. Bd. Plastic

& Reconstructive Surgeons, Soc. Vascular Tech., Fla. Med. Soc., Palm Beach County Med. Soc. Republican. Avocations: drawings, photography, preservation wild animals, boating, wild cat pets. Office: Aesthetic Surgery Clinique 535 S Flagler Dr West Palm Beach FL 33401-5903

CRAFT, KAY STARK, real estate broker; b. Yoakum, Tex., Oct. 15, 1945; d. Jesse James and Leona Charlotte (Manchen) Stark; m. Michael Joseph Grogan IV, May 31, 1969 (div. June 1974); 1 child, Michael Joseph V; m. Roger Dale Craft, Apr. 1, 1983. AA, Victoria (Tex.) Coll., 1964; BS, S.W. Tex. State U., 1966; Broadway Sch. Real Estate, Hot Springs, Ark., 1985. Lic. real estate broker, Ark. Tchr. Victoria Ind. Sch. Dist., 1966-68, Pasadena (Tex.) Ind. Sch. Dist., 1968-85; real estate agt. Coldwell Banker, Hot Springs Village, Ark., 1985-88; prin. broker-owner Cross Roads Realty, Inc., Hot Springs Village, Ark., 1988—, pres., bd. dirs., 1991—, v.p., 1988-91; sec., bd. dirs. Craft Classic Homes, Inc., Hot Springs Village, Ark., 1987—; v.p., bd. dirs. Coronado Homes, Inc., Hot Springs Village, Ark., 1992-96. Mem. DAR, Colonial Dames of 17th Century, Nat. Soc. Magna Carta Dames, Nat. Assn. Realtors, Ark. Realtors Assn. (Million Dollar Club 1991—, Lifetime Million Dollar Prodr. award 1997, Multi Million Dollar Prodr. award 1993, 94, 96, 97, 98, cert. Grad. Realtors Inst. 1992), N.W. Garland Bd. Realtors (treas. 1992, Million Dollar Prodr. award 1990-98), Woman's Coun. Realtors, Residential Sales Coun. (cert. residential specialist 1993). Republican. Methodist. Avocations: genealogy, travel, reading. Home: 45 Gerona Way Hot Springs National Park AR 71909-2762 Office: Cross Roads Realty Inc 4136 N Highway 7 Hot Springs National Park AR 71909-9564

CRAFT, ROBERT HOMAN, JR., lawyer; b. N.Y.C., Sept. 24, 1939; s. Robert Homan and Janet Marie (Sullivan) C.; m. Margaret Jamison Ford, Feb. 6, 1971; children: Robert H. III, Gerard Ford. AB, Princeton U., 1961; BA, Oxford U., 1963; LLB, Harvard U., 1966. Bar: N.Y. 1973, U.S. Dist. Ct. (so. and ea. dists.) N.Y. 1977, U.S. Ct. Appeals (D.C. cir.) 1977, U.S. Dist. Ct. D.C. 1978, U.S. Ct. Appeals (2nd cir.) 1974, U.S. Supreme Ct. 1977. Assoc. Sullivan & Cromwell, N.Y.C., 1966-74; spl. asst. to under sec. of state for security assistance U.S. Dept. State, Washington, 1974-76; exec. asst. to chmn. SEC, Washington, 1976; ptnr. Sullivan & Cromwell, Washington, 1977—. Bd. trustees Washington Opera, 1978—, pres. 1998—; dir. Coun. for Excellence in Govt., 1989—. Mem. ABA, D.C. Bar Assn., N.Y. State Bar Assn., Assn. Bar City of N.Y., Am. Soc. Internat. Law, Met. Club (Washington), Chevy Chase (Md.) Club. Home: 5010 Millwood Ln NW Washington DC 20016-2620 Office: Sullivan & Cromwell 1701 Pennsylvania Ave NW Washington DC 20006-5866

CRAFT, SHERYL MCARTHUR, rehabilitation nurse; b. Pitts., Dec. 5, 1947; d. Edwin Ross Jr. and Virginia Wilma (Herchenroether) McA.; m. Bert Powell Craft, May 24, 1968 (div. June 1984); children: David Preston Craft, Kim Alissa Craft; m. Spencer Lesley Sprayberry, Apr. 21, 1990 (div.). BSN, U. Miss., Jackson, 1971, postgrad., 1974-75; MSN, U. Ala., 1978; cert. in exec. mgmt., So. Meth. U., 1987. RN, Tex. Staff nurse CCU, head nurse med.-surg. unit U. Miss. Med. Ctr., Jackson, 1971-74; clin. specialist, asst. DON, liaison nurse Miss. Meth. Rehab. Ctr., Jackson, 1974-85; clin. coord., rehab. clin. inpatient units Dallas Rehab. Inst., 1985-86, 86-88, asst. adminstr. nursing svcs., 1985-88; DON Houston Rehab. Inst., 1989-91; program cons. Rehab. Care Corp., St. Louis, 1991-95; dir. rehab. svcs. St. Joseph's Hosp. and Health Ctr., Paris, Tex., 1995-98; present SCCI, mng. dir. patient care Hosp. Victoria, 1998—; adj. instr. Alcorn State U., Natchez, Miss., 1981-82; adj. clin. instr. Sch. Nursing, U. Miss., 1978-85; clin. preceptor, guest instr. U. Tex., Arlington, 1985-88; clin. preceptor U. Tex., Houston, 1989-91; co-author, developer CEU courses, seminars, various nursing splty. presentations; lectr. in field. Mem. adv. bd. Crippled Children's Agy., Jackson, 1977; vol. med. asst. Tenneco Marathon, Houston, 1991. Mem. Nat. Assn. Rehab. Nurses (cert. CRRNA), S.E. Tex. Assn. Rehab., Sigma Theta Tau. Methodist. Avocations: painting, needle work, exercise, reading, ch. choir. Home: 6060 Westwood Victoria TX 77901

CRAFT, TERRY, umpire; b. Portsmouth, Ohio, Dec. 9, 1954; married; 1 child. Student, Shawnee State U. Former umpire Appalachian League, Carolina League, So. League, Internat. League, Dominican Winter League; umpire maj. league baseball Am. League, N.Y.C., 1993—; with Umpires Union, Phila. With U.S. Army. Avocations: biking, golfing. Office: Am League 350 Park Ave New York NY 10022 also: Umpires Union 1735 Market St Philadelphia PA 19103

CRAFT DAVIS, AUDREY ELLEN, writer, educator; b. Vanceburg, Ky., June 9, 1926; d. James Elmer and Lula Alice (Vance) Gilkison; m. Vernon Titus Craft, Nov. 5, 1943 (dec. Aug. 1979); children: James Vernon Craft, Alice Ann Craft Schuler; m. Louis Amzie Davis, Oct. 22, 1986. PhD, Ohio U., 1964; Dr. of Metaphysics, Coll. Divine Metaphysics, 1968; DD, Ohio U., 1971; postgrad., St. Petersburg Jr. Coll., 1975. Owner beauty salon Audrey Craft Enterprises, Tampa Bay, Fla., 1970-83; owner cosmetic co. Audrey Craft Enterprises, Portsmouth, Ohio, 1958-70; owner, distbr. Nightingale Motivation, Tampa Bay, 1960—; tchr., counselor Bus. Coll. U., Tampa Bay, 1965—; ins. staff Investors Heritage & Wabash, Portsmouth, 1967-70; ins. broker Jackson Nat. & Wabash, Tampa Bay, 1971-91; pres. The Gardens 107, Inc., Tampa Bay, 1987—; travel writer, counselor Cruises/Travel & Etc., Fla., 1981—. Author: (poetry) Pathways (1 Cert. awards), 1990, Metaphysical Techniques That Really Work, 1994, Metaphysical Encounters, 1992, How to Stay Secure in a Chaotic World, 1993, Metaphysics Encounters of a Fourth Kind, 1995, How to Safeguard Your World and Avoid Becoming a Target, 1996; contbr. articles to popular mags. Bd. dirs. The Gardens Domicurculums, Cmty. Coun., 1987—; bd. dirs. State Bd. Cosmetology, Columbus, Ohio, 1962-63, Bus. and Profl. Women, Portsmouth, 1967-69, Sci. Rsch., Portsmouth, 1965-69, Tampa Bay, 1972-74. Recipient Key to Miami, Office of Mayor Claude Kirk, 1969, Million Dollar trophy Lt. Gov. John Brown Ohio; commd. Ky. Col. by Gov. Edward T. Breathitt, 1968, Gov. Wendell Ford, 1969. Mem. AARP, S.E. Writers Assn., Christian Writers Guild, Writers Digest Book Club, Nat. Assn. Retired Fed. Employees (assoc.), Am. Heart Assn. (chmn. Seminole area 1994). Democrat. Avocations: writing, lectures, counseling, travel, meditation. Home and Office: 102 Saint Petersburg Dr W Oldsmar FL 34677-3620

CRAFTON-MASTERSON, ADRIENNE, real estate executive, writer, poet; b. Providence, Mar. 6, 1926; d. John Harold and Adrienne (Fitzgerald) Crafton; m. Francis T. Masterson, May 31, 1947 (div. Jan. 1977); children: Mary Victoria Masterson Bush, Kathleen Joan, John Andrew, Barbara Lynn Harrison. Student, No. Va. C.C., 1971-74; A in Biblical Studies, Christ to World Bible Inst., Jacksonville, Fla., 1992; A in Pastoral Leadership, Calvary Bible Inst., Jacksonville, Fla., 1993. Mem. staff Senator T.F. Green of R.I., Washington, 1944-47, 54-60; with U.S. Senate Com. on Campaign Expenditures Senator T.F. Green of R.I., 1944-45; asst. chief clk. Ho. Govt. Ops. Com., 1948-49; clk. Ho. Campaign Expenditures Com., 1950; asst. appointment sec. Office of Pres., 1951-53; with Hubbard Realty, Alexandria, Va., 1962-67; owner, mgr. Adrienne C. Masterson Real Estate, Alexandria, 1968-82; pres. Adrienne Investment Real Estate (AIRE) Ltd., Alexandria, 1982-91; devel. staff writer Calvary Internat., Jacksonville, Fla., 1992-93; Adrienne Crafton-Masterson Real Estate, Winchester, Va., 1993-94; owner, prin., broker Adrienne Crafton-Masterson Real Estate, Haymarket, Va., 1994—; pres. AIRE-Merkli developers, 1988-92; founder AIHRE USA, Inc., 1993—. Mem. adv. panel Fairfax County (Va.) Coun. on Arts, 1987-88; founder, pres. Mt. Vernon/Lee Cultural Ctr. Found., Inc. 1984-92; mem. Haymarket (Va.) Hist. Commn., 1994-95, 97—. Fellow Internat. Biog. Ctr. (dep. dir. gen.); mem. Internat. Orgn. Real Estate Appraisers (sr.), Nat. Assn. Realtors, No. Va. Assn. Realtors (chmn. comml. and indsl. com. 1982-83, cmty. revitalization com. 1983-84, pres. land comml. indsl. mems. 1985, v.p. land comml. and indsl. mems. 1989), Greater Piedmont Area Assn. Realtors, Fairfax Affordable Housing Inc. (sec. 1990-91), Haymarket-Gainesville (Va.) Busl. and Profl. Assn. (bd. dirs. 1996—, sec. 1998—), Alexandria C. of C., Mt. Vernon/Lee C. of C., Friends of Kennedy Ctr. (founder), Optimist Club Gainesville-Haymarket (charter, bd. dirs. 1997—), Haymarket Hist. Commn. FAX: 703-754-1170. E-mail: aihrecraft@earthlink.net. Office: Haymarket Profl Ctr PO Box 499 6611 Jefferson St Haymarket VA 20168-0499

CRAFT-ROSENBERG, MARTHA JANE, nursing educator; b. Downings, Mo., July 31, 1941; d. Harry R. and Emma (Bohi) Lewis; m. John Craft, Jan. 31, 1964 (deceased); 1 child, Jack; m. Guy Rosenberg, Oct. 24, 1993; children: Guy John, Gary Rosenberg. Diploma in nursing, Iowa Meth. Hosp. Sch. Nursing, 1962; BS, U. Iowa, 1970, MA, 1978, PhD, 1985. RN, Iowa. Staff/head nurse pediatrics U. Iowa Hosp./Clinics, Iowa City, 1962-64, asst. supr. pediatrics, 1964-66, supr. pediatrics, 1966-68, clin. nurse specialist, 1968-69, clin. nurse specialist neonatal, 1970-71; instr. Allen Meml. Hosp., Waterloo, Iowa, 1974-77; clin. nurse specialist II pediatrics U. Iowa Hosp./Clinics, Iowa City, 1977-80; asst. prof. nursing U. Iowa, Iowa City, 1980-86, assoc. prof. nursing, 1986-97, prof. nursing, 1997—. Editor: (two editions) Nursing Interventions for Infants and Children; contbr. articles to profl. jours. Robert Wood Johnson Found. grantee, 1987-88, Nat. Ctr. for Nursing Rsch. grantee, 1991-97. Fellow Am. Acad. Nursing; mem. ANA (bd. dirs. Iowa chpt. 1986-87, coun. nurse researchers 1988—), N.Am. Nursing Diagnosis, Midwest Nursing Rsch. Soc. (Rschr. award 1996), Am. Children Acad. Nursing (chair, expert panel 1998—), Sigma Theta Assn. Avocations: piano, reading. Office: U Iowa Coll Nursing 344 Nursing Building Iowa City IA 52242-1121

CRAGG, GORDON MITCHELL, government chemist; b. Cape Town, Cape, South Africa, Sept. 4, 1936; came to U.S., 1979; s. Ernest Lynn and Doris Jessie (Mitchell) C.; m. Jacqueline Claire Tuers, Dec. 30, 1966. BSc with honors, Rhodes U., Grahamstown, South Africa, 1956; D.Phil., Oxford U., England, 1963. Sr. lectr. U. South Africa, Pretoria, 1966-72, U. Cape Town, 1973-79; sr. rsch. chemist Cancer Rsch. Inst. Ariz. State U., 1979-80, asst. to dir. Cancer Rsch. Inst., 1980-84; expert natural products br. Nat. Cancer Inst., Bethesda, Md., 1984-87, chemist, 1988-89; chief natural products br. Nat. Cancer Inst., Frederick, Md., 1989—. Author: Organoboranes in Organic Synthesis, 1973; co-author: Biosynthetic Products for Cancer Chemotherapy, 1985; contbr. numerous articles to profl. jours. Recipient Merit award NIH, 1991. Mem. AAAS, Am. Chem. Soc., Am. Soc. Pharmacognosy (pres. 1998-99), Am. Assn. Advanced Scis., South African Chem. Inst., Internat. Soc. Econ. Botany. Achievements include patents for Prostratin, Michellamine B, Calanolides, Conocurvone; research in natural products isolation and structural elucidation with emphasis on novel antineoplastic and antiviral agents, development of policies for international collaborations in sustainable use of biological diversity in drug discovery and development. E-mail: cragg@dtpax2.ncifcrf.gov. Office: Nat Cancer Inst Natural Products Br Fairview Ctr Ste 206 Box B Frederick MD 21702-1201

CRAGIN, CHARLES LANGMAID, lawyer; b. Portland, Maine, Oct. 9, 1943; s. Charles Langmaid and Ruth (Meriam) C.; m. Maureen Patricia Ford, Oct. 8, 1994; children: Christine, Jean, Cathleen. BS, U. Maine, 1967, JD, 1970. Bar: Maine 1970, U.S. Dist. Ct. Maine 1970, U.S. Supreme Ct. 1974, U.S. Ct. Appeals (D.C. cir.) 1989, U.S. Ct. Vet. Appeals 1997. Assoc. Verrill & Dana, Portland, Maine, 1970-74, ptnr., 1974-90; chmn. U.S. Bd. of Vet.'s Appeals, Washington, D.C., 1991-97; counselor to undersec. U.S. Dept. VA, 1997, prin. dep. asst. sec. of def., Res. affairs, 1997-98, acting asst. sec. of def., res. affairs, 1998—. Contbr. articles to legal publs. Rep. candidate for gov. Maine, 1982; bd. dirs., v.p. Margaret Chase Smith Found., Skowhegan, Maine, 1986—, Potomac divsn. AAA, 1992—; chmn. budget com. Rep. Nat. Com., 1984-90; mem. MaineCommn. on Govt. Ethics and Elections, 1986-88, Def. Adv. Com. on Women in Svcs.,1986-88; bd. dirs. U.S. Navy Meml. Found., 1989—. Capt. USNR; ret. Named Outstanding Young Man Maine, Maine Jaycees, 1976; recipient Disting Svc. award, U. So. Maine Alumni Assn., 1986. Fellow Am. Acad. Hosp. Attys. (bd. dirs. 1979-82), Am. Acad. Matrimonial Lawyers; mem. Maine Bar Assn. (Disting. Svc. award 1986), Capitol Hill Club (Washington), The Univ. Club (Washington). Roman Catholic. Avocations: skiing, wine collecting, ham radio, gardening. Address: 331 11th St NE Washington DC 20002-6219 Office: Dept Defense The Pentagon Rm 2E520 Washington DC 20301-1500

CRAGLE, DONNA LYNNE, university administrator, researcher; b. Ft Knox, Ky., Oct. 14, 1953. BA in Biol. Scis., Ind. U., 1974; MS in Human Genetics, Med. Coll. Va., 1978; PhD in Environ. Epidemiology, U. N.C., 1984. Med. lab. technologist Blood Bank, N.C. Meml. Hosp., Chapel Hill, 1977-81; tchr. asst. dept. epidemiology U. N.C., Chapel Hill, 1979-80; epidemiologist Ctr. Epidemiol. Rsch., Oak Ridge Assoc. Univs., 1981082, epidmiology rsch. sect. leader, 1983-85, epidemiology rsch. sect. leader, dep. dir., 1986-91, epidemiology rsch. leder, dir., 1991—; dir. basic and applied rsch. Oak Ridge Assocs. Univs., 1998—; tchr. gen. genetics Pellissippi State Tech. C.C., 1993-96; cons. in field. Contbr. articles to profl. jours. Office: Oak Ridge Assoc Univs Oak Ridge Inst Sci and Edn Ctr Epid Rsch PO Box 117 Oak Ridge TN 37831

CRAGNOLIN, KAREN ZAMBELLA, real estate developer, lawyer; b. Boston, May 19, 1949; d. John T. Zambella and Corrine M. (Feeney) Zenga; m. Robert Louis Cragnolin, Sept. 8, 1974; 1 child, Nikki Josephine. BA, Georgian Ct. Coll., 1971; JD, New Eng. Sch. Law, 1974. Bar: N.Y. 1974, D.C. 1981. Sr. tax editor Prentice-Hall, Englewood Cliffs, N.J., 1974-76; dir. pub. affairs Am.-Arab Affairs Coun., Washington, 1981-83; founder, dir. Am. Bus. Coun., Dubai, United Arab Emirates, 1983-86; dir. River Link, Inc., Asheville, N.C., 1987—; bd. trustees Clean Water Mgmt. Trust Fund, WNC Tommorrow. Pres. Young Dems., Georgian Court, N.J., 1970-71; chair Greenway Commn., Asheville, N.C., 1990—; pres., bd. dirs. Leadership Asheville, 1993—, Asheville Area C. of C., 1992-96; bd. dirs. Hand Made Am., Asheville, 1994—, Handi-Skills, Asheville, 1986-90, chmn., 1986-88. Recipient Downtown Hero award Asheville Downtown Assn., 1991, Cir. Excellence Leadership Asheville, 1995, Friend of River award Land Regional Coun., 1995. Mem. D.C. Bar Assn., N.Y. Bar Assn. Avocations: gardening, cooking, paddling. Home: 7 Cedarcliff Rd Asheville NC 28803-2905 Office: RiverLink Inc PO Box 15488 Asheville NC 28813-0488

CRAGOE, JOHN HENRY, investment company executive; b. Washington, Dec. 12, 1944; s. John Henry and Carol (Cromelin) C.; m. Mary Elizabeth Andrews, Dec. 18, 1965; children: Christina, John H. III. BS in Comm., U. Va., 1967, MBA, 1973. CPA, CFA. Asst. to gen. mgr. Irwin Mgmt. Co., Columbus, Ind., 1973-75; pres. Irwin Union Corp., Columbus, 1975-85; ptnr. Greenwich (Conn.) Assocs., 1985-96; pres. SeaBridge Investment Advisors, LLC, Summit, N.J., 1996—; mem. adv. bd. McIntire Sch. of Comm., U. Va., Charlottesville, 1981-93. Lt. USNR, 1967-71. Recipient Hyde fellowship, Darden Sch. Faculty, U. Va., 1972. Office: Sea Bridge Investment Advs 450 Springfield Ave Summit NJ 07901-2611

CRAGON, HARVEY GEORGE, computer engineer; b. Ruston, La., Apr. 21, 1929; s. Miller M. and Lou Willie (Bond) C.; m. Henrietta Herbert, Sept. 2, 1950. B.S., La. Poly. Inst., Ruston, 1950. Engr. So. Bell Telephone, New Orleans, 1950-53, Hughes Aircraft, Los Angeles, 1953-57; mem. ARO Inc, Tullahoma, Tenn., 1957-58; sr. fellow Tex. Instruments Inc., Dallas, 1958-84; prof., Ernest Cockrell Jr. Centennial Chair in Engring. U. Tex., Austin, 1984—. Patentee in field. Trustee The Computer Mus., Boston, 1982—. Served with U.S. Army, 1951-52. Fellow IEEE (Emmanuel R. Piore award 1984, Eckert-Mauchly award 1986); mem. Nat. Acad. Engring., Assn. Computing Machinery, Charles Babbage Inst, IEEE Computer Soc. Office: U Tex Dept Elec & Computer Engring Austin TX 78712-1084*

CRAHAN, ANN TERESA, magazine editor; b. Alexandria, Va., Sept. 10, 1946; d. James Edward and Roberta Ann (George) C.; m. Donald Gordon Pedroja, Mar. 21, 1981 (dec. Feb. 1992). BA in English, Lang. and Lit., U. Mo., Kansas City, 1968. Editor-in-chief Capper's Mag., Topeka, Kans., 1984—. Editor: Heart Songs, 1986. Mem. 100 Good Women, Lawrence, Kans., 1996—, Lawrence Alliance, 1997—, Farm Bosses of Am., Lawrence, 1981—. Mem. Soc. Profl. Journalists, AP Mng. Editors, Ky. Cols. Avocations: gardening/landscaping, art, therapy dogs. Office: Ogden Publs 1503 SW 42nd St Topeka KS 66609-1214

CRAHAN, JACK BERTSCH, manufacturing company executive; b. Peoria, Ill., Aug. 24, 1923; s. John F. and Ann B. (Bertsch) C.; m. Peggy Furey, Sept. 9, 1944; children—Patrick Michael, Colleen Mary, Kevin Furey. BS, U. Minn., 1948. With Flexsteel Industries, Inc., Dubuque, Iowa, 1948—, plant mgr., 1950-54, gen. mgr., v.p., 1955-70, exec. v.p., 1970-84, pres., 1985-89, vice-chmn., chief ops. officer, 1989-90, chief exec. officer, 1990—, chmn. bd. dirs.; bd. dirs. Dubuque Bank and Trust Co., Dubuque Racing Assn.; trustee United Steel Workers Am. Pension Fund. Bd. regents Loras Coll., 1967-80, 81—; bd. dirs. Xavier Hosp., 1969-78, Boys Club Am., 1981—. Served with USNR, 1942-43; Served with USMC, 1943-46, 51-52. Decorated D.F.C. (2), Air medal (6). Mem. Am. Furniture Assn. (bd. dirs. 1974-80). Republican. Roman Catholic. Home: 1195 Arrowhead Dr Dubuque IA 52003-8594 Office: Flexsteel Industries Inc Brunswick Indsl Block PO Box 847 Dubuque IA 52004-0847

CRAIB, KENNETH BRYDEN, resource development executive, physicist, economist; b. Milford, Mass., Oct. 13, 1938; s. William Pirie and Virginia Louise (Bryden) C.; m. Gloria Faye Lisano, June 25, 1960; children—Kenneth Jr., Judith Diane, Lori Elaine, Melissa Suzanne. BS in Physics, U. Houston, 1967; MA in Econs., Calif. State U., 1982; postgrad. Harvard U., 1989. Aerospace technologist NASA, Houston, 1962-68; staff physicist Mark Systems, Inc., Cupertino, Calif., 1968-69; v.p. World Resources Corp., Cupertino, 1969-71; dir. resources devel. div. Aero Service Corp., Phila., 1971-72; dir. ops. Resources Devel. Assocs., Los Altos, Calif., 1972-80, pres., chief exec. officer, Diamond Springs, Calif., 1980-85; owner Sand Ridge Arabians, 1980—; chmn., dir. Resources Devel. Assocs., Inc., 1982-86, Devel. Support Internat. Inc., Placerville, Calif., 1981-86; pres., chmn., dir. RDA Internat., Inc., 1986-95, chmn., CEO, dir., 1995—; dir. Sierra Gen. Investments, 1985—, Transatlantic Fisheries, Inc., 1995—; adj. prof. Sacramento City Coll., 1996—, U. Phoenix, Sacramento, 1997—. Contbr. articles to profl. jours. Served with USAF, 1957-61. Recipient Sustained Superior Performance award NASA, 1966. NASA grantee, 1968. Mem. Am. Soc. Photogrammetry, Soc. Internat. Devel., Agrl. Research Inst., Calif. Select Com. Remote Sensing, Internat. Assn. Natural Resources Pilots, Remote Sensing Soc. (council), Am. Soc. Oceanography (charter), Aircraft Owners and Pilots Assn., Gulf and Caribbean Fisheries Inst., Placerville C. of C., Harvard Alumni Assn., Exptl. Aircraft Assn., Asian Fisheries Soc. Home: 6431 Mary Ann Ln Placerville CA 95667-8167 Office: RDA Internat Inc 801 Morey Dr Placerville CA 95667-4411 *What you do is not nearly so important as how you do it, and the people whose lives you touch in the process.*

CRAIG, CLIFFORD LINDLEY, orthopaedic pediatric surgery educator; b. Detroit, Mar. 25, 1944; s. Paul Forrest and Dorothy Madeline (Denhart) C.; m. Laura Ann Hackley, June 20, 1976; children: Paul Edward, Julia Marie. BS, Tufts U., 1965; MD, U. Mich., 1969. Diplomat Am. Bd. Orthopaedic Surgery. Asst. prof. orthopaedic surgery Tufts U. Sch. Medicine, Boston, 1979-94, assoc. prof. orthopaedic surgery, 1994-99; clin. assoc. prof. orthopedic surgery U. Mich. Med. Sch., Ann Arbor, 1999—. Fellow Am. Coll. Surgery; mem. AMA, Am. Acad. Orthopaedic Surgery, Am. Acad. Pediatrics, Am. Acad. Cerebral Palsy, Am. Assn. Clin. Anatomy, Pediatric Orthopaedic Soc. of N.Am. Office: Univ Mich Med Ctr Taubman Center 2912 Box 0328 Ann Arbor MI 48109-0328

CRAIG, DAVID CLARKE, financial advisor, instructor; b. Ft. Smith, Ark., Oct. 23, 1955; s. Earl Lewis Craig and Shirley Ann (Clarke) Shepherd; m. Dana Jane Thompson, Dec. 19, 1980; children: Lauren Elizabeth, Erin Jane. BBA, U. Ark., 1978, MBA, 1979; postgrad., U. Tex., 1983-88, U. Ark., 1988—. Registered fin. advisor. Mktg. officer Merchants Nat. Bank, Ft. Smith, 1979-81; instr. fin. and econs. Westark C.C., Ft. Smith, 1981—; faculty chairperson Westark C.C., Ft. Smith, 1987-88; asst. to pres. Richland Coll., Dallas, 1985; fin. advisor Oct. Money Mgmt., Inc., Ft. Smith, Ark., 1991—; adj. instr. John Brown U., 1995-97; bd. dirs., sec. Ark. Student Loan Authority, 1989-98, chmn. 1998—. Pres. Am. Cancer Soc. Ft. Smith, 1988-89, co-residential chmn. 1985-87, v.p. local bd. 1987-89, active Pub. Awareness Com. Ft. Smith, 1985-91; pres. Interfaith Comty. Ctr., Ft. Smith, 1982-84; vol. Ft. Smith Art Ctr. Auction, 1987, treas. 1995—; sponsor Harding U. Invitational Bus. Games, 1986-91; bd. dirs. Old Fort Mus., 1989-91; mem. class of 1990 Leadership Ft. Smith, elder, clk. of session 1st Presbyn. Ch., 1991-94; bd. ch. visitors U. Ozarks, Clarksville, Ark., 1996, 98; bd. dirs. Hobson Presch. and Kindergarten, 1993-95. Recipient Whirlpool Master Tchr. Awd., Westark Coll., 1999. Mem. Nat. Bus. Edn. Assn., Ark. Tchrs. of Bus. and Econs., Am. Inst. Banking (v.p. Ft. Smith chpt. 1981), Ark. Two Yr. Coll. Assn., East Side Baptist Ch., 1999—, Ft. Smith C. of C. (edn. com. 1987—), Blue Key, Kappa Delta Pi, Alpha Kappa Psi (sec. 1977-78), Phi Delta Kappa (Kappan of Month 1985), Phi Beta Lambda (co-advisor univ. ctr. 1986-95). Office: Westark CC 5210 Grand Ave Fort Smith AR 72904-7397 also: Oct Money Mgmt Inc 2220 S Waldron Rd Fort Smith AR 72903-3733

CRAIG, DAVID JEOFFREY, retired manufacturing company executive; b. Wyandotte, Mich., Sept. 29, 1925; s. Geoffrey F. and Catherine R. C.; m. Shirley M. Lemhagen, Mar. 3, 1945; children: Susan Craig Noyes, Janice, Sandra, Jeffrey Allan. B.S. in Physics, U. Detroit, 1950, M.S. summa cum laude, 1951; postgrad., U. Mich., 1952-53. With The BOC Group, Murray Hill, N.J., 1956-90; dir. corp. planning and devel., 1970-71, group v.p., 1971-79, dep. group mng. dir. BOC Group plc, Surrey, Eng., 1979-83, mng. dir. engring. and tech., 1983-90; dir. The BOC Group, Inc., BOC Group plc. Mem. Ticonderoga Country Club, Loblolly Pines Golf Club, Loblolly Bay Yacht Club, Northern Lake George Yacht Club, Hobe Sound Golf Club. Home: 7965 SE Golfhouse Dr Hobe Sound FL 33455-8013

CRAIG, DAVID W., judge, author; b. Pitts., Feb. 17, 1925; s. David and Ella (Williamson) C.; m. Ella Van Kirk, July 15, 1945; children: Linda Marie Craig Mooser, Muriel Jean Craig Lagnese. A.B., U. Pitts., 1948, J.D., 1950. Bar: Pa. 1950. Rsch. asst. U. Pitts. Law Sch., 1950-51; ptnr. Moorhead & Knox, Pitts., 1952-61; city solicitor City of Pitts., 1961-65, dir. pub. safety, 1965-69; ptnr. Baskin, Sachs & Craig, 1962-78; judge Commonwealth Ct. Pa., 1978-90, pres. judge, 1990-94; adj. prof. Carnegie-Mellon U., 1970-94; adj. asst. prof. U. Pitts., 1965-69; vis. lectr. Yale U., 1961-64. Author: Pennsylvania Building and Zoning Laws, 1951. Chmn. City Planning Commn., Pitts., 1960-61; mem. Home Rule Commn., Pitts., 1976. 1st lt. USAAF, 1943-45, ETO. Decorated D.F.C. Mem. Pa. Bar Inst. (pres. 1987-88), Am. Planning Assn. (pres. 1963-64), Inst. Jud. Adminstrn. (seminar faculty 1986-91). Avocations: sailing, running. Office: Ste 905 1812 Foxcroft Allison Park PA 15101-3261

CRAIG, DOUGLAS WARREN, food service industry executive; b. Woodbury, N.J., Nov. 22, 1942; s. John Galbraith Craig and Vivian (Rundquist) Morris; m. Carolyn Louise McCans, Nov. 22, 1964 (div. Oct. 1984); children: Carl Douglas, Jeffrey Alan, Eric John; m. Helen Mae Reisner, June 29, 1985; 1 child, Whitney Reisner. BA, Gettysburg Coll., 1964; MBA, Loyola Coll., Balt., 1982. Cert. foodsvc. mgmt. profl. Nat. Restaurant Assn. With Svc. Am. Corp., Stamford, Conn., 1960-75; regional v.p. Svc. Am. Corp., Stamford, 1972-75; pres. Food Svcs. Internat. Inc., Ft. Lauderdale, Fla., 1975-77; div. v.p. Marriott Corp., Washington, 1977-88; pres. Whitco Corp., Alexandria, Va., 1988-89, Am. Window and Bldg. Cleaning, Inc., Washington, 1989-90; sr. v.p. Scott's Mgmt. Svcs., Inc., Markham, Ont., Can., 1991-93; divsn. v.p. The Wood Co., Allentown, Pa., 1993-96; prin. Whitco Mgmt. Cons. Group, Allentown, 1996-98; mem. faculty Lehigh Carbon C.C., 1997-99; v.p. IQuest Solutions, Inc., Bethesda, MD., 1998—; bd. dirs. CFEP, Inc.; sec., treas., dir. Chesapeake Computer Solutions, Inc., Middleburg, Va., 1985-88. Fin. sec. Good Shepherd Luth. Ch., Reston, Va., 1983-85, treas., 1985-87; mem. Kutztown U. Bus. and Industry Coun.; bd. dirs. Pa. Shakespeare Festiva. Mem. Loyola Coll. Exec. Alumni Assn. (pres. 1985-88), Am. Philatelic Soc. Republican. Avocation: philately. Home: 227 Winter Walk Dr North Potomac MD 20878 Office: 85300 7200 Wisconsin Ave Bethesda MD 20814

CRAIG, ELIZABETH COYNE, marketing executive; b. N.Y.C., Jan. 7, 1956; d. John Thomas and Mary Ellen (O'Sullivan) Coyne; m. Charles Samuel Craig, Aug. 10, 1985; children: Mary Catherine, Caroline Elizabeth. BS in Occupl. Therapy, NYU, 1980, MBA, 1986. Occupl. therapist Jacobi Hosp., N.Y., 1980-81, St. Vincent's Hosp., N.Y., 1981-85; mktg. intern worldwide consumer banking Citibank U.S. and Europe Consumer Bank, Citicorp Ins., N.Y.C., 1985-86, mgmt. assoc., 1986-87, asst. mgr., 1987-88, mktg. mgr. new product devel., 1988-90, asst. v.p. life acquisitions and relationship mktg., 1990-93, v.p. life and health acquisitions and relationship mktg., 1993-94, v.p. 3d party direct response, retail ins. sales pilots, 1994-96, v.p. annuity product mgmt., 1996-98; v.p. investment and ins., product mgr. Citibank, Long Island City, N.Y., 1998—; bd. dirs. First Citicorp Life Ins. Co. Mem. Am. Occupl. Therapy Assn., Fin. Women's Assn., Direct Mktg. Assn. Avocations: antiques, bicycling. Office: Citibank One Court Sq Long Island City NY 11120

CRAIG, GEORGE DENNIS, economics educator, consultant; b. Sept. 14, 1936; s. George S. and Alice H. (Childs) C.; m. Lelah Price, Aug. 21, 1984;

children: R. Price Coyle, R. Nolan Coyle, Deborah L. Craig, W. Sean Coyle. BA, Wheaton Coll., 1960; MS, U. Ill., 1962, PhD, 1968. Asst. prof. econs. La. State U., Baton Rouge, 1965-69; assoc. prof. sch. bus. No. Ill. U., DeKalb, 1969-82; prof. econs., chmn. Oklahoma City U., 1982—; cons. AT&T, Oklahoma City, 1984—. Contbr. articles to profl. jours. Mem. Am. Econs. Assn., So. Econs. Assn., Nat. Assn. Bus. Economists, Internat. Inst. Forecasting. Avocation: tennis. Home: 6915 Avondale Ct Oklahoma City OK 73116-5008 Office: Oklahoma City U Dept Econs NW 23rd at N Blackwelder Oklahoma City OK 73106

CRAIG, GORDON ALEXANDER, historian, educator; b. Glasgow, Scotland, Nov. 26, 1913; came to U.S., 1925; s. Frank Mansfield and Jane (Bissell) C.; m. Phyllis Halcomb, June 16, 1939; children: Susan, Deborah Gordon, Martha Jane, Charles Grant. BA, Princeton U., 1936, MA, 1939, PhD, 1941, DLitt (hon.), 1970; BLitt (Rhodes Scholar), Oxford U., Eng., 1938; DPhil (hon.), Free U. Berlin, 1983; HHD (hon.), Ball State U., 1984; DHL (hon.), Wake Forest U., 1988. Instr. history Yale U., New Haven, 1939-41; from instr. to prof. history Princeton U., N.J., 1941-61; prof. history Stanford U., Calif., 1961—, J.E. Wallace Sterling prof. humanities, 1969-79, J.E. Wallace Sterling prof. humanities emeritus, 1979—; prof. history Free U. Berlin, 1962—. Author: The Politics of the Prussian Army, 1640-1945, 1955, From Bismarck to Adenauer: Aspects of German Statecraft, 1958, Europe Since 1815, 1961, Europe Since 1815, 6th edit., 1983, The Battle of Königgrätz, 1964, War, Politics and Diplomacy: Selected Essays, 1966, Treitschke's History of Modern Germany, 1975, Economic Interest, Militarism and Foreign Policy: Essays of Eckart Kehr, 1977, Germany, 1866-1945, 1978, The Germans, 1982, Force and Statecraft: Diplomatic Problems of Our Times, 1983, The End of Prussia, 1984, Geld und Geist: Zürich im Zeitalter des Liberalismus, 1830-1896, 1988, The Triumph of Liberalism: Zürich in the Golden Age 1830-1869, 1989, Die Politik der Unpolitischen: Deutsche Schriftsteller und die Macht, 1770-1870, 1993, The Politics of the Unpolitical: German Writers and the Problem of Power, 1770-1871, 1995, Ueber Fontane, 1997; assoc. editor, contbr.: Makers of Modern Strategy, 1943, Makers of Modern Strategy from Machiavelli to the Nuclear Age, 1986; joint editor, contbr.: The Diplomats, 1919-1939, 1953, The Diplomats, 1939-79, 1994; contbr. Geneva, Zurich, Basel: History, Culture and National Identity, 1994. Hon. mem. Berlin Hist. Commn., 1975—; polit. analyst Office Strategic Svcs., Dept. State, Washington, 1941-43; pub. mem. Fgn. Svc. Selection Bd., 1948-49; cons. U.S. Arms Control and Disarmament Agy., 1964-68; mem. adv. coun. USAF Acad., 1968-73; mem. adv. bd. USMC Hist. Sect., Washington, 1972-74. Served to capt. USMC, 1944-46. Recipient Historikerpreis, Stadt Münster, Fed. Republic Germany, 1982, comdr.'s cross Legion of Merit, Fed. Republic Germany, 1984, Goethe medal, Goethe Inst., Fed. Republic Germany, 1987, Polit. Book prize Ebert Stiftung, 1988, Max Geilinger prize Max Geilinger Found., Zurich, 1991; Guggenheim fellow, 1969-70, 82-83; named Hon. fellow Balliol Coll., Oxford U., 1989. Fellow Ctr. for Advanced Study in the Behavioral Scis., Brit. Acad.; mem. Am. Acad. Arts and Scis., Am. Philos. Soc., Am. Hist. Assn. (pres. 1983), Internat. Com. Hist. Scis. (1st v.p. 1975-85), Coun. of Scholars of Libr. of Congress, Order pour le Merite fur Wissenschaften und Kunste (Germany), Phi Beta Kappa. Democrat. Presbyterian. Home: 451 Oak Grove Ave Apt B-2 Menlo Park CA 94025-3269

CRAIG, GREGORY BESTOR, lawyer, government official; b. Norfolk, Va., Mar. 4, 1945; s. William Gregory and Lois (Bestor) C.; m. Margaret Davenport Noyes, July 27, 1974; children: William Eliot, Eliza Noyes, Margaret Bestor, Mary Duncan, James Gregory. AB magna cum laude, Harvard Coll., 1967; diploma in historical studies, Cambridge U., 1968; JD, Yale U., 1972. Bar: D.C. 1972, U.S. Ct. Appeals (D.C., 2d, 3d, 4th, 6th and 7th cirs.), U.S. Supreme Ct. Assoc. Williams Connolly & Califano, Washington, 1972-74; asst. fed. pub. defender U.S. Dist. Ct. Conn., 1974-76; assoc. Williams & Connolly, Washington, 1977-78, ptnr., 1979-84; sr. advisor on fgn. policy and def. Sen. Edward M. Kennedy, Washington, 1984-88; ptnr. Williams & Connolly, Washington, 1989—; dir. Office of the Policy and Planning staff, Dept. of State, 1997—; chmn. Internat. Human Rights Law Group, 1992-96; tchr. trial practice Yale Law Sch., 1975-76; mem. Mex. Am. Legal Def. and Edn. Fund, 1995—; chmn. Internat. Human Rights Law Group, 1989-96. Trustee Overseas Devel. Coun., 1993-96, Carnegie Endowment for Internat. Peace, 1990-97, Robert F. Kennedy Meml. Found., 1989-97, Fgn. Student Svc. Coun., 1990-96, Mexican-Am. Legal Def. and Edn. Fund, 1995-97. John Harvard scholar, 1967. Mem. ABA, Phi Beta Kappa. Avocations: mountain climbing, hiking. Office: Policy Planning Staff 2201 C St NW Washington DC 20520-0001*

CRAIG, HURSHEL EUGENE, agronomist; b. Chrisman, Ill., May 18, 1932; s. Thomas Hurshel and Letha Mae (Short) C.; m. Zada Pauline Honnold, Dec. 29, 1954; children: Toni Jane, Tina Jean. Student, Ea. Ill. U., 1951, Ill. State U., 1956; BS, U. Ill., 1958, MS, 1970, postgrad., 1974. Mgr. Lime Svc. Co., Chrisman, Ill., 1959-61; br. mgr. Remole Soil Svc., Inc., Potomac, Ill., 1961-64, home office mgr., 1966-67; ptnr., agronomist Harris Fertilizer, Inc., Farmer City, Ill., 1967-69; farm cons. Gifford (Ill.) State Bank, 1964-66; instr. agr. Danville (Ill.) Area Community Coll., 1970-80; agronomy cons. and ptnr. C & S Pro-Farm Svcs., Ridge Farm, Ill., 1977-80; agronomy cons. Ag-Vantage, Westerville, Ohio, 1980-85; soils analysis sales CLC Labs Ind., West Lafayette, 1985-90, agronomy cons., 1987—; soil and plant tissue analysis sales Cal-Mar Soil Testing Lab., West Lafayette, 1990—. Co-author: Career Awareness Test for Agriculture Students and Prospective Spouses, 1974. Chmn. adminstrv. coun. Bismarck (Ill.) United Meth. Ch., 1989-91. With U.S. Army, 1952-54. Mem. Ill. Fertilizer and Chem. Assn., Profl. Crop Cons. Ill. (pres. 1992), Ill. Soil Testing Assn. Methodist. Avocations: reading, gardening. Home and Office: 16916 E 2690 North Rd Danville IL 61834-6067

CRAIG, JAMES HICKLIN, fine arts consultant; b. Chester, S.C., July 23, 1937; s. John Edward and Una Bee (Martin) C. Student, U. S.C., 1955-56, Cin. Coll. Conservatory Music, 1956-59, Juilliard Sch. Music, 1960, Paris, 1960. Curator decorative arts N.C. Dept. Archives & History, Raleigh, 1962-64; grantee writing book on N.C. decorative arts Mus. So. Decorative Arts, 1964-65; prin. James Craig Fine & Decorative Arts, 1965-69; pres. Craig & Tarlton, Inc., Raleigh, 1969-85; fine arts cons. Independence, Va., 1985—; bd. dirs. Raleigh Chamber Music Soc., N.C. Chamber Opera Theater; cons. to N.C. Gov.'s Mansion bd.; adv. com. Mint Mus. Art, Charlotte, N.C. Author: The Arts and Crafts in North Carolina 1699-1840, 1965 (listed by Montgomery as part of 100 best in field). Avocations: collecting Am. art and antiques, violins and related material, gardening. Office: James Craig Fine Arts PO Box 397 Independence VA 24348-0397

CRAIG, JAMES LYNN, physician, consumer products company executive; b. Columbia, Tenn., Aug. 7, 1933; s. Clifford Paul and Maple (Harris) C.; m. Suzanne Anderson, July 20, 1957; children: James Lynn, Margaret; m. Roberta Anne, May 17, 1980. Ed., Mid. Tenn. State U., 1953; MD, U. Tenn., 1956; MPH, U. Pitts., 1963. Diplomate Am. Bd. Preventive Medicine, Am. Bd. Family Practice. Intern U. Tenn. Meml. Hosp., Knoxville, 1957; resident in occupl. medicine U. Pitts., 1962-64; resident in occupl. medicine TVA, Chattanooga, 1964-65, physician, 1966-69, chief med. officer, 1969-74; corp. med. dir. Gen. Mills Corp., Mpls., 1974-76, v.p. corp. med. dir., 1976-80, v.p., dir. health and human svcs., 1980-98; adj. clin. prof. U. Minn., Mpls., 1979—, chmn. cmty. adv. com. Ctr. for Environ. and Health Policy, 1994-97, mem. adv. coun. health in scis., 1992-95, chmn. adv. bd. Ctr. for Environ. and Health Policy, 1994-97; pres. Family and Preventive Health Svcs., Inc., Mpls., 1998—; clin. instr. U. Tenn., Memphis, 1970-74, Meharry Med. Sch., Nashville, 1972-74; bd. dirs. Inst. Rsch. and Edn. Health Sys. Minn.; mem. adv. bd. to dir. Ctr. Disease Control and Prevention. Contbr. articles to profl. jours. Bd. dirs. Mpls. Blood Bank, 1976-88, Minn. Bible Coll., Rochester, 1978-83, Minn. Safety Coun., 1981-90, Minn. Heart Assn., Mpls., 1976-87, Children's Heart Fund, 1976-88, Meth. Hosp. Found., 1979-87, Park Nicolett Med. Found., 1987-93, Altcare, 1983-95, Meth. Hosp. Health Assn., 1987-93, Minn. Wellness Coun., 1986-91, Health Sys. Minn. Assocs., 1993-94; bd. dirs. Health Systems Minn. Inst. for Rsch. and Edn., 1996—, chmn., 1997—. Recipient Physician Recognition award AMA, 1975, 78,81, 85, 89, 93, 96, Cmty. Svc. award Park Nicolett Med. Ctr., 1995. Fellow Am. Occupl. Medicine Assn. (bd. dirs. 1974-78), Am. Acad. Occupl. Medicine (treas. 1982-83, sec. 1983-84, v.p. 1984-85, prs. 1986-87), Health Achievement in Occupl. Medicine, Am. Acad. Family Practice; mem. AMA (alt. del. Ho. Dels. 1990-92, del. 1992-96), Occupl. Health Inst. (chmn. 1983-84), North Ctrl. Occupl. Medicine Assn. (pres. 1977), Mpls. Acad. Medicine (sec. 1983-85, pres. 1985-86), Emergency Physicians Assn. (bd. dirs. 1984-92). Home: 10008 S Shore Dr Minneapolis MN 55441-5011 Office: PO Box 270330 Minneapolis MN 55427 *The activities of my life are based on a balance between quality and acceptance.*

CRAIG, JAMES NORMAN, marketing executive, Internet consultant; b. San Pedro, Calif., Nov. 28, 1968; s. Russell T. and Phoebe Francis C.; m. Lisa Renee Collins. BA, U. Ariz., 1991. Promotions dir. Tucson Raceway Park, 1991-92; pub. rels. dir. Ad Dimensions, Tucson, 1992; sports corr. Albuquerque Jour., 1992-93; salesman Samon's Elec., Albuquerque, 1993, asst. mgr., 1993-94; comm. specialist N.Mex. Educators Fed. Credit Union, Albuquerque, 1994-96; comm. engr. N.Mex. Educators Federal Credit Union, Albuquerque, 1996-99; mktg. dir. IBM Tex. Employees Fed. Credit Union, Austin, 1999—. Vol. Greater Albuquerque Habitat for Humanity, 1996—, chair devel. com., 1995; bd. dirs. Austin Ad Fedn., 1999—. Recipient 1st place awards Internet Mktg., 1996, Newsletter 3 colors or less, CUNA Mktg., 1995, Credit Union Exec. Soc., 1995. Democrat. Avocations: woodworking, computers, biking. Home: 21602 Martin Ln Pflugerville TX 78660 Office: IBM Tex Employes Fed Credit Union PO Box 9926 Austin TX 78766

CRAIG, JAMES WILLIAM, physician, educator, university dean; b. West Liberty, Ohio, Jan. 23, 1921; s. J. Frank and Clara Helen (Scarborough) C.; m. Helen Catherine Lang, Sept. 18, 1948 (dec.); children: Maribeth, Jon, William, Barbara; m. Wendy Burnip Johnson, June 23, 1972; stepchildren: Steven, Barbara, Philip, Laura Johnson. BS, Western Res. U., 1943, MD, 1945. Intern, asst. resident in medicine Presbyn. Hosp., N.Y.C., 1945-46, 48-50; fellow in medicine Western Res. U. Sch. Medicine, Cleve., 1950-52; from instr. to assoc. prof. medicine Western Res. U. Sch. Medicine, 1952-72; assoc. dean Sch. Medicine U. Va., Charlottesville, 1972-89, prof. medicine, 1972-90, prof. emeritus, 1991—. Condr. research; contbr. articles on diabetes mellitus and intermediary metabolism to publs. Served with AUS, 1946-48. Recipient Lederle med. faculty award, 1962-64. Mem. Am. Inst. Nutrition, Ctrl. Soc. for Clin. Rsch., Med. Soc. Va., Phi Beta Kappa, Sigma Xi, Alpha Omega Alpha. Home: 101 Indian Spring Rd Charlottesville VA 22901-1019 Office: Univ Va Sch Medicine Charlottesville VA 22908

CRAIG, JENNY, weight management executive. From mgr. to nat. dir. ops. Body Contour, Inc.; pres., co-founder, vice chmn. Jenny Craig Weight Loss Prog., 1982—. Achievements include providing a comprehensive weight mgmt. prog. designed by registered dietitians, psychologsists and a med. adv. bd. to grow into one of the largest weigh mgmt. cos. in the world; only weight mgmt. co. listed on N.Y. Stock Exch. Office: Jenny Craig Inc 11355 N. Torrey Pines Rd PO Box 387910 La Jolla CA 92037*

CRAIG, JOAN CARMEN, secondary school educator, drama teacher; b. Sacramento, Calif., July 13, 1932; d. Frank Hurtado and Enid Pearl (Hogan) Alcalde; m. Elmer Lee Craig, Aug. 14, 1955 (dec. Jan. 1981); children: Shelley, Wendy, Cathleen, Scott; m. Donald E. Peterson, 1997. BA, San Jose State U., 1954, gen. secondary cert., 1955; postgrad. studies, various univs., 1956—. Cert. tchr. (life), Calif. Drama tchr. Willow Glen High Sch. San Jose (Calif.) Unified Sch. Dist., 1955-58, Kennedy Jr. High Sch. Cupertino (Calif.) Sch. Dist., 1968-93; cons. Cupertino Unified Sch. Dist., 1990—; coord. program activiy Growth Leadership Ctr., Mountain View, Calif., 1993; presenter Computer Use in Edn., 1990-93. Author, coord.: Drama Curriculum, 1971-93, Musical Comedy Curriculum, 1985-93, (Golden Bell, Calif. 1992). Dir. Nat. Multiple Sclerosis Soc., Santa Clara County, 1983-86. Recipient Spl. Svc. award Nat. Multiple Sclerosis Soc., Santa Clara, Calif., 1986, Hon. Membership award Nat. Jr. Honor Soc., 1990, Hon. Svc. award Calif. Congress Parents, Tchrs. and Students, Inc., 1992; named Tchr. of Year, Kennedy Jr. High, Cupertino Union Sch. Dist., 1993. Mem. AAUW, NEA, Calif. Tchrs. Assn., Cupertino Edn. Assn. (rep. 1982). Avocations: theater, hiking, biking, writing, swimming. Home: 3381 Brower Ave Mountain View CA 94040-4512

CRAIG, JOANNA BURBANK, historic site director; b. N.Y.C., Feb. 21, 1942; d. Robert DuBose and Jane (Maroney) Burbank; m. Douglas Wheelock Craig, Oct. 30, 1965 (div.); 1 child, Megan Southard. AA in Liberal Arts, Bennett Jr. Coll., Millbrook, N.Y., 1962; BA in Psychology, U. S.C., 1982. Asst. to pub. rels. dir. The New Yorker Mag., N.Y.C., 1963-68; co-owner The Corner Bookstore, Camden, S.C., 1975-80; mng. editor Sporting Classics Mag., Camden, S.C., 1982-87; pres. Craig & Vartorella, Inc., Camden, S.C., 1987—; dir. Hist. Camden Revolutionary War Site, Camden, S.C., 1989—. Editor: The Decorative Arts of Camden and Kershaw County, 1988 (Gold Addy 1988, Mead Top 60 award 1988). Commn. City of Camden Planning Comm., 1992—, Olde English Dist., Chester, S.C., 1993; bd. dirs. Kershaw County Accomodation Tax Comm., Camden, 1992-95, Camden Main St., 1991-95; mem. Kershaw County LWV, Camden, 1994—; bd. mem., past pres. Kershaw County Hist. Soc., 1980—. Mem. Am. Assn. Mus., Am. Assn. State and Local History, S.E. Mus. Conf., Rotary. Avocations: swimming, walking, touring historical sites, global travel, volunteering. Office: Hist Camden Rev War Site PO Box 710 Camden SC 29020-0710

CRAIG, JOHN CHARLES, educational researcher, consultant; b. Belvidere, Ill., Dec. 28, 1946; s. John George and Ruth Effie (Coan) C.; m. Mary Louise Loftus, Feb. 16, 1974; children: David Thomas, Jesse Lindsey. BS, No. Ill. U., 1969; PhD, Northwestern U., 1984. cert. edn. adminstr., tchr. Tchr. Rockford (Ill.) Pub. Sch., 1969-71; researcher, cons. Ill. State Bd. of Edn., Springfield, 1971—; bd. dirs., v.p. Ill. Fedn. Tchrs., 1987-93, pres. Ctrl. Ill. Area Coun., 1983-91, Ill. Fedn. of State Office Educators, Springfield, 1992—; cons. nat. ednl. std. setting activities, nat. geographic std. and assessment, nat. assessment; mem. design team Ill. Goal Assessment Program; designer Ill. Prairie State Achievement Test. Editor: Alternate Assessment, Social Sciences; contbr. articles to profl. jours. Prodr., broadcaster Sta. WSSR Radio, Springfield, 1976-87; leader Boy Scouts Am., Springfield, 1987—. Mem. Am. Acad. Polit. Sci., Nat. Assn. Geographic Edn., Am. Hist. Assn. Avocations: model railroads, woodworking. Office: Ill State Bd Edn 100 N 1st St Springfield IL 62702-5199

CRAIG, JON LEE, state environmental program administrator; b. Stratford, Okla., Aug. 17, 1945; s. Robert and Verl (White) C.; m. Lawanna Sue Warren, June 7, 1968; children: Benjamin, Daniel. BS in Biology, Chemistry, E. Ctrl. State U., Ada, Okla., 1967; MS in Environ. Sci., U. Okla., 1975. Cert. Sci. Tchr., Okla.; registered profl. sanitarian, Okla. Classroom sci. tchr. Maysville (Okla.) Sci. Tchr., Maysville, Okla., 1967-72; sanitarian Okla. State Dept. Health, Kingfisher, Okla., 1972-76; dir. water quality divsn. Dept. Environ. Quality, Okla. City, 1976—; bd. dirs. Assn. State Drinking Water Adminstrs., Washington, 1994-95; adj. biology instr. Redlands C.C., El Reno, Okla. Mem. Kingfisher Lions Club, 1972-76. Mem. Am. Water Works Assn. (S.W. sect.), Assn. State and Interstate Water Pollution Control Adminstrs. (v.p.), Am. Water Resources Assn. (Okla. sect.), Nat. Water Quality Monitoring Coun., Ground Water Protection Coun. (bd. dirs.), Assn. State Drinking Water Adminstrs., Okla. Soc. Profl. Sanitarians, Okla. Pub. Health Assn. Baptist. Avocations: reading, genealogy, collecting mil. artifacts. Office: State of Okla Dept Environ Quality 707 N Robinson Ave Oklahoma City OK 73102-6010

CRAIG, JUDITH, bishop; b. Lexington, Mo., June 5, 1937; d. Raymond Luther and Edna Amelia (Forsha) C. BA, William Jewell Coll., 1959; MA in Christian Edn., Eden Theol. Sem., 1961; MDiv, Union Theol. Sem., 1968; DD, Baldwin Wallace Coll., 1981; DHL, Adrian Coll., 1985, Otterbein Coll., 1993. Youth dir. Bellefontaine United Meth. Ch., St. Louis, 1959-61; intern children's work Nat. Coun. of Chs. of Christ, N.Y.C., 1961-62; dir. Christian edn. 1st United Meth. Ch., Stamford, Ct., 1962-66; inst. adult basic edn. N.Y.C. Schs., 1967; dir. Christian edn. Epworth Euclid United Meth. Ch., Cleve., 1969-72, assoc. pastor, 1972-76; pastor Pleasant Hills United Meth. Ch., Middleburg Heights, Ohio, 1976-80; conf. council dir. East Ohio Conf. United Meth. Ch., Canton, 1980-84; bishop United Meth. Ch., Mich. area, 1984-92, West Ohio area, 1992—; mem. United Meth. Gen. Coun. Mins., 1976-80, 88-92, United Meth. Commn. Status Role Women, 1984-88; gen. conf. del., 1980, 84; mem. United Meth. Publ. House Bd., 1992—; bd. dirs. U.S. Health Corp.; frequent lectr. and preacher; bd. trustees 27 institutions in West Ohio. Contbr. articles to ministry mags. Bd. dirs. YWCA, Middleburg Heights, 1976-80. Recipient Citation of Achievement William Jewell Coll., 1985, Woman of Achievement award YWCA, 1995. Office: United Methodist Church West Ohio Conf 32 Wesley Blvd Worthington OH 43085-3585

CRAIG, KARA LYNN, chief executive officer; b. Portland, Oreg., Nov. 29, 1962; d. Raymond L. and Donna J. (Telford) Spencer. BA in Communication, Boise State U., 1985; MA in Psychology, Pepperdine U., 1990. Office mgr. Ustick Chiropractic Clinic, Boise, 1983-85; comm. asst. First Interstate Bank of Idaho, Boise, 1985-87; dir. Golden Gate U., Irvine, Calif., 1988-91; adj. prof. Golden Gate U., Irvine, 1990-91; case mgr. Big Bros./Big Sisters of S.W. Idaho, Boise, 1992-94; CEO Children's Home Soc. of Idaho, Boise, 1994—; adj. prof. Boise State U., 1992—. Pub. rels. com. Sounds of Music (community choir), Boise, 1987-88; mem. Leadership Boise, 1996-97; bd. dirs. Children's Alliance of Idaho, 1998—; mem. S.W. Idaho Planned Giving Coun., 1996—, Internat. Platform Assn., 1999—. Mem. APA, SW Idaho Children's Mental Health Consortium (co-chmn. 1997—), Psi Chi. Avocations: playing piano and flute. Home: 12345 W Mercedes St Boise ID 83713-7100 Office: Children's Home Soc Idaho 740 Warm Springs Ave Boise ID 83712-6420

CRAIG, KAREN LYNN, accountant, controller; b. Detroit, Mar. 17, 1959; d. John and Corinne (Legel) C.; m. Robert A. Steshetz, May 3, 1986; children: Kamden, Kara. AS in Commerce, Henry Ford C.C., 1980; BS in Bus. and Acctg., Wayne State U., 1982. CPA, Mich., Calif. Cost and staff acct. Wilson Dairy Co., Detroit, 1982-83; sr. acct. Coopers & Lybrand, Detroit, 1984-85; supr. acct. Newport Beach, Calif., 1987-89; corp. controller J.F. Shea Co., Inc., Walnut, Calif., 1989—. Mem. Mich. Assn. CPA's, Calif. Soc. CPA's. Avocations: music, hockey, photography, baseball. Office: JF Shea Co Inc PO Box 489 Walnut CA 91788-0489

CRAIG, KENNETH DENTON, psychologist, educator, researcher; b. Calgary, Alta., Can., Nov. 21, 1937; s. William Denton and Wilhelmina Wylie (MacIntyre) C.; m. Sydney Grace Smith, Apr. 10, 1971; children: Kenneth Deane, Alexandra Grace, Christopher James, Daniel Smith (dec.). BA, Sir George Williams U., Montreal, Que., Can., 1958; MA, U. B.C., Vancouver, Can., 1960; PhD, Purdue U., 1964. Cert. clin. psychologist. Prof. psychology U. B.C., 1963—, assoc. dean Faculty Grad Studies, 1996—; assoc. prof. U. Calgary, 1969-71; dir. Banff Internat. Confs., 1981—, pres., 1994-96. Editor Can. Jour. Behavioural Sci., 1986-89; assoc. editor Pain, 1994—; contbr. articles to profl. jours. Nat. advisor first aid svc. Can. Red Cross Soc., 1987-90. Can. coun. Killam rsch. fellow 1992-94. Fellow APA, Can. Psychol. Assn. (pres. 1986-87); mem. Internat. Assn. for Study Pain (founding), B.C. Psychol. Assn. (pres. 1977), Social Sci. Fedn. Can. (treas. 1988-92), Can. Pain Soc. (pres. 1994-97). Office: U BC, Dept Psychology, Vancouver, BC Canada V6T 1Z4

CRAIG, L. CLIFFORD, lawyer; b. Ohio, Aug. 29, 1938. Student, Stanford U., 1957-59; BA, Duke U., 1961, LLB, 1964. Bar: Ohio. Ptnr. Taft, Stettinius & Hollister, Cin., 1971—. Fellow Am. Coll. Trial Lawyers; mem. ABA, Ohio Bar Assn., Cin. Bar Assn. Office: 1800 Star Bank Ctr Ste 1700 425 Walnut St Cincinnati OH 45202-3957

CRAIG, LARRY EDWIN, senator; b. Council, Idaho, July 20, 1945; s. Elvin and Dorothy Craig. B.A., U. Idaho; postgrad. George Washington U. Farmer, rancher Midvale area, Idaho; mem. Idaho Senate, 1974-80, 97th-101st Congresses from 1st Dist. Idaho, 1981-90; senator 102nd Congress from Idaho, 1990-97, mem. com. agr., nutrition and forestry, com. energy and natural resources, spl. com. on aging, chmn. com. Rep. policy, vets. affairs, appropriations, chmn. subcom. on forests and pub. land mgmt., chmn. subcom. energy rsch., devel., prodn. and regulation, subcom. water and power; senator 105th Congress from Idaho (now 106th Congress), 1996—; chmn. Idaho Rep. State Senate Races, 1976-78, chmn. senate steering com.; mem. joint econ. com., com. veterans' affairs, subcom. energy R & D. Pres. Young Rep. League Idaho, 1976-77; mem. Idaho Rep. Exec. Com., 1976-78; chmn. Rep. Central Com. Washington County, 1971-72; advisor vocat. edn. in public schs. HEW, 1971-73; mem. Idaho Farm Bur., 1965-79. Served with U.S. Army N.G., 1970-74. Mem. NRA (bd. dirs. 1983—), Future Farmers of Am. (v.p. 1965). Methodist. Office: US Senate 520 Hart Senate Office Bldg Washington DC 20510-1203

CRAIG, MARCI LYNNE, insurance claims administrator; b. June 22, 1969. BS in Edn., Kent State U., 1991, postgrad. Cosmetics mgr. Kaufmann's, Akron, Ohio; claims mgr. Ohio BWC, Akron, 1994-96, Kemper Ins., Akron, 1996—. E-mail: mcraig@kemperinsurance.com. Office: Kemper Ins 1366 Neptune Ave Akron OH 44301-2332

CRAIG, MARTHA ANN, retail store owner; b. Evansville, Ind., Oct. 31, 1952; d. Leonard Vincent and Bernice Gertrude (Deuser) Stratman; m. Gary Myron Craig, June 7, 1975; children: Grant, Adam. BEd, Ind. U., 1974; MEd, Ind. State U., 1976. Pharmacy technician Med. Arts Pharmacy, Evansville, Ind., 1969-71; tchr. Catholic Diocese of Evansville, 1974-79; owner, mgr. Classroom Paraphernalia, Evansville, 1978—; tchr. grades 6-8 Resurrection Sch., Evansville, 1996—; substitute tchr. Catholic Diocese Evansville, 1979-86; presenter workshops in field; mem. Slow, Hard Sci. Collaboration. Active Boy Scouts Am., Evansville, 1988—; Mem. Westside Cath. Consol. Sch. Bd., Evansville, 1988-91, v.p., 1990-91; co-chmn. fundraising com. Golfmoor Baseball Assn. Howard Hughes grantee, 1998. Mem. Nat. Sch. Supply Equipment Assn., Ednl. Dealers Suppliers Assn., Ind. U. Alumni Assn. (life), VFW Auxiliary, Evansville C. of C., Better Bus. Bur., Kennel Club. Roman Catholic. Office: Classroom Paraphernalia 2306 Division St Evansville IN 47711-6805

CRAIG, N(ORVELLE) WAYNE, secondary education educator; b. Newport News, Va., Aug. 22, 1944; s. Lawrence A. and Bertha C.; m. Candra J. McCoy, June 16, 1973. BS, Appalachian State Tchrs. Coll., 1966; MEd, U. Va., 1971. Cert. tchr., Va. Tchr. social studies Quantico (Va.) Dependents' Sch. Sys., 1966—; head dept. social studies Quantico H.S., 1984—, mem. task force, 1975-91; mem. evaluation com. So. Assn. Colls. and Schs., 1973-74, 79-80, 83-84, 90-91, 91-92, vis. com. Ea. Mennonite H.S., Harrisonburg, Va., 1979. Recipient Outstanding Am. History Tchr. of Yr. award Va. DAR, 1988. Mem. NEA, Fed. Edn. Assn., Orgn. Am. Historians, Va. Coun. Social Studies, Va. Edn. Assn., Quantico Edn. Assn. Home: 1600 Clover Dr Fredericksburg VA 22407-4823

CRAIG, PAUL MAX, JR., retired lawyer; b. Munich, Germany, Aug. 8, 1921; came to U.S., 1941; naturalized, 1944; s. Paul Max and Helen A. Craig; m. Leonie R. Hildebrand, June 26, 1962: children: Anthony P., Claudine A., Stephen P. BS in Elec. Engring., Worcester (Mass.) Poly. Inst., 1946; LLB, Georgetown U., 1950; LLM, George Washington U., 1952. Bar: D.C. 1950. Patent examiner U.S. Patent Office, Washington, 1946-50; patent advisor Office Chief Ordnance, Dept. Army, Washington, 1950-52; pvt. practice Washington, 1952—; ptnr. Craig & Antonelli (and predecessor firm), Washington, 1967-82, Craig & Burns, Washington, 1982-86, Barnes & Thornburg, Washington, 1986-88, Paul M. Craig, P.C., Washington, 1989-97; of counsel Dow, Lohnes & Albertson, 1989-92, affiliated with, 1992-95; of counsel Birch, Stewart, Kolasch & Birch, Falls Church, Va., 1995-97; pvt. practice Silver Spring, Md., 1998—. With USNR, 1944-46. Mem. Am., Inter-Am. bar assns., Am. Patent Law Assn., Assn. Internat. Pour la Protection de la Propriete Indsl., Licensing Execs. Soc., Am. Soc. Internat. Law, Assn. Trial Lawyers Am. Home: 207 Quaint Acres Dr Silver Spring MD 20904-2715

CRAIG, PETER STEBBINS, historian; b. Bklyn., Sept. 30, 1928; s. Clarence Tucker and Rena (Stebbins) C.; m. Lois Achor, June 9, 1950 (div. 1969); children: Stephen Tucker, Carolyn Alden, Jennifer Stebbins; m. Sally Love Banks, Feb. 14, 1970; 1 child, Katherine Love. BA, Oberlin (Ohio) Coll., 1950; JD, Yale U., 1953. Bar: D.C. 1953, U.S. Supreme Ct. 1959. Assoc. Covington & Burling, Washington, 1953-63; commerce counsel So. Rwy., Washington, 1964-67, gen. atty., 1969-84; asst. gen. counsel litigation U.S. DOT, Washington, 1967-69; assoc. gen. counsel Amtrak, Washington, 1984-89; historian 17th Century Scandinavian immigrants to Del. River, 1982—; speaker and cons. to various authors, mus., hist. socs. and geneal. socs. Author: The Stille Family in America, 1641-1772, 1986, 1693 Census of the Swedes on the Delaware, 1993, The Swedish Hulings Family, 1996; co-author: The Yocums of Aronomeck, 1983, Membership of Holy Trinity Church in Wilmington-1764, 1985, Membership of Swedish Lutheran

Churches at Raccoon and Penns Neck-1771, 1985; editor Gloria Dei Year 2000 Records Project; contbg. editor Swedish Am. Genealogist, 1989—; contbr. articles to profl. jours. Trustee Com. of 100 on the Federal City, Washington, 1965-85. Named Washingtonian of Yr., Washingtonian Mag., 1972; recipient Cert. Appreciation Swedish Nat. Com. of New Sweden, 1988, study grant to Sweden, Bicentennial Swedish-Am. Exchange Fund, 1991, Lifetime Achievement award Com. of 100 on Federal City, 1998. Fellow Am. Soc. Genealogists, Geneal. Soc. Pa.; mem. Am. Hist. Assn., Hist. Soc. Pa., Hist. Soc. Del., N.J. Hist. Soc., Md. Hist. Soc., Hist. Soc. of Washington, Swedish Colonial Soc., Del. Swedish Colonial Soc., Am. Swedish Hist. Found., Swedish Am. Hist. Soc., Am. Scandinavian Assn., Nat. Geneal. Soc., Del. Geneal. Soc., Geneal. Soc. N.J., Md. Geneal. Soc. Democrat. Soc. of Friends. Home and Office: 3406 Macomb St NW Washington DC 20016-3160

CRAIG, ROBERT GEORGE, dental science educator; b. Charlevoix, Mich., Sept. 8, 1923; s. Harry Allen and Marion Ione (Swinton) C.; m. Luella Georgine Dean, Sept. 29, 1945; children: Susan Georgine, Barbara Dean, Katherine Ann. BS, U. Mich., 1944, MS, 1951, PhD in Phys. Chemistry, 1955; MD (hon.), U. Geneva, Switzerland, 1989. Rsch. chemist Linde Air Products Co., 1944-50, Texaco, Inc., Beacon, N.Y., 1954-55; rsch. assoc. U. Mich. Engring. Rsch. Inst., 1955-57; faculty dept. dental materials Sch. Dentistry, U. Mich., Ann Arbor, 1957-87, asst. prof., 1957-60, assoc. prof., 1960-64, prof., 1964-87, chmn. dept., 1969-87, prof. biologic and material sci., 1987-93, Marcus Ward prof. dentistry, 1990-93, prof. emeritus, 1993—; dir. Specialized Materials Sci. Ctr. Nat. Inst. Dental Rsch., Ann Arbor, 1989-93; exec. com. Sch. Dentistry, U. Mich., Ann Arbor, 1972-75; budget priorities com. U. Mich., Ann Arbor, 1978-81; sci. adv. com. Dental Research Inst., U. Mich., Ann Arbor, 1980-89, chmn., 1984-89; cons. Walter Reed Army Hosp., 1969-75; assessor for Nat. Health and Med. Rsch. Coun., Commonwealth Australia. Author: Restorative Dental Materials, 10th edit., 1997; (with K.A. Easlick, S.I. Seger and A.L. Russell) Communicating in Dentistry, 1973; (with W.J. O'Brien, J.M. Powers) Dental Materials-Properties and Manipulation, 6th edit., 1996; (with J.M. Powers) Workbook for Dental Materials, 1979; (with J.M. Powers, J.C. Wataha) Dental Materials-Propertes and Manipulation, 7th edit., 1999; editor, contbr. Dental Materials Rev., 1977, Dental Materials-A Problem Oriented Approach, 1978; asst. editor Jour. Biomed. Materials Rsch., 1983-93; editl. assoc. Jour. Oral Rehab., 1995—; cons. editor Jour. Dental Rsch., 1971-73, 77-80, Jour. Dental Edn., 1971-76, Jour. Oral Rehab., 1974-94, Mich. State Dental Jour., 1973-77, Jour. Oral Implantology, 1988—; mem. adv. bd. Saudi Dental Jour., 1989—; contbr. articles to profl. jours. Prin. investigator specialized material Scis. Rsch. Ctr. (funded by Nat. Inst. Dental Rsch. 1989-94). Rsch. grantee Nat. Inst. Dental Rsch., 1965-76, 84-94, Nat. Scis. Res. Svc. Tng., 1976-93; Rsch. fellow E.I. du Pont, 1952-53. Mem. ADA (cons. coun. on dental materials and devices 1983-95), Am. Nat. Stds. Inst. (chmn. spl. com. 1968-77, subcom. with ADA on mouth protectors and materials 1996—), Internat. Assn. Dental Rsch. (pres.-elect dental materials group 1972-73, pres. 1973-74, Wilmer Souder award 1975), Am. Assn. Dental Schs. (chmn. biomaterials sect. 1977-79), Am. Chem. Soc., Soc. Biomaterials (Clemson award for basic rsch. in biomaterials 1978, program chmn. 1983, fellow 1994), Acad. Operative Dentistry (George Hollenbach Meml. prize 1991), Sigma Xi (sec. U. Mich chpt. 1978-81), Phi Kappa Phi, Phi Lambda Upsilon, Omicron Kappa Upsilon. Home: 1503 Wells St Ann Arbor MI 48104-3914 Office: U Mich Sch Dentistry Sch Dentistry 1011 N University Ave Ann Arbor MI 48109-1078

CRAIG, ROBERT MARK, III, lawyer, educator; b. Mpls., Sept. 21, 1948; s. Robert Mark Jr. and Shirley A. (Collier) C.; m. Suzanne Bartlett, Aug. 22, 1970; children: Shannon Michelle, Scott Collier. BA in Journalism, Tex. Christian U., 1970; JD, U. Va., 1973. Bar: Va. 1973, U.S. Ct. Mil. Appeals 1974, Tex. 1975, U.S. Dist. Ct. (no. dist.) Tex. 1976, U.S. Dist. Ct. (so. dist.) Tex. 1980, U.S. Dist. Ct. (we. dist.) 1985, U.S. Ct. Appeals (5th and 11th cirs.) 1981, U.S. Supreme Ct. 1981, U.S. Ct. Appeals (9th and 10th cir.) 1984. Assoc. Judin, Ellis & Barron, McAllen, Tex., 1979-80, ptnr., 1980-81; sr. atty. Tenneco Oil Co., Houston, 1981-88; sr. v.p., assoc. gen. counsel First City, Tex., Houston, 1988-93; assoc. gen. counsel Am. Gen. Corp., Houston, 1993—; staff atty. Presdl. Clemency Bd., Washington, 1975; mem. faculty Vernon Regional Jr. Coll., Sheppard AFB, 1975-76; instr. paralegal tng., Houston, 1982-85; instr. USAF Acad., 1976-77, asst. prof. law, 1977-79; councilman City of Oak Ridge North, Tex., 1988-94, also mayor pro tem; dir. Oak Ridge Mcpl. Utility Dist., 1994-96; pres. Oak Ridge Econ. Devel. Corp., 1994-96. Vice pres. Upper Rio Grande Valley Heart Assn., McAllen, 1980-81; ruling elder Timber Ridge Presbyn. Ch., 1983-88; pres. Montgomery County Assn. for Gifted and Talented, Conroe, Tex., 1985; chmn. Permanent Jud. Commn., New Covenant Presbytery, 1986-92; legal counsel Tex. Jaycees, 1981-82. Capt. USAF, 1973-79. Mem. ABA (co-chair subcom. on counsel retention com. on corp. counsel litigation sect.), Va. Bar Assn. (assoc.), Tex. Bar Assn. (coun. mem. antitrust and bus. litigation sect.), McAllen Jaycees (sec., bd. dirs. 1979-81). Republican. Avocations: youth coaching, golf, racquetball, softball. Home: 27122 Wells Ln Oak Ridge North TX 77385-9080 Office: Am Gen Corp Legal Div WT3-04 2727 Allen Pky Houston TX 77019-2197

CRAIG, SUSAN LYONS, library director; b. Barksdale Air Force Base, La., Feb. 23, 1948. BA, Trinity Coll., Washington, 1971; MSLS, Fla. State U., 1976; MBA, Rosary Coll., 1989. Pub. svcs. libr. St. Mary's Coll., Moraga, Calif., 1976-79; head pub. svcs. Hood Coll., Frederick, Md., 1979-85, Dominican U. (formerly Rosary Coll.), River Forest, Ill., 1985-87; dir. libr. Aurora (Ill.) U., 1987-97; dir. libr. and acad. info. svcs. Trinity Coll. Libr., Washington, 1997—; adj. assoc. prof Rosary Coll. Grad. Sch. Libr. and Info. Sci., 1990-97. Mem. ALA, Assn. Coll. and Rsch. Librs. (nat. adv. com., rep. Ill. chpt. 1991-95), Pvt. Acad. Librs. of Ill. (pres. 1994-96), Ill. Libr. Assn. (del. pre-White House Conf., Chgo., 1989-90), Beta Phi Mu, Phi Eta Sigma (hon.). Office: Trinity Coll Libr 125 Michigan Ave NE Washington DC 20017-1004

CRAIG, TRISHA ANN VARISH, secondary school teacher; b. Corry, Pa., Dec. 11, 1969; d. Edward James and Cathy Annette (McQueeney) Varish; m. William Kevin Craig, Aug. 12, 1995. BA in English Lit., U. Pitts., 1992, MEd in Adminstrv. and Policy Studies, 1998. Cert. secondary sch. tchr., secondary prin., cert. curriculum and instrn. supr. Tchr. Fort Cherry H.S., McDonald, Pa., 1993—. Adv. to literary mag. Few and Far Between, 1994, 95. Mem. NCTE, Assn. Supervision and Curriculum Devel. Office: Fort Cherry HS 110 Ft Cherry Rd Mc Donald PA 15057

CRAIG, WILLIAM EMERSON, lawyer; b. Springfield, Mass., July 6, 1942; s. W. Emerson and Vera L. (Platt) C.; m. Susan Hart Ryan; children: Lathrop B., Linsley G. BA, Dartmouth Coll., 1964; LLB, Yale U., 1967. Assoc. Wiggin & Dana, New Haven, 1967-73, ptnr., 1974-97, sr. counsel, 1997—; sec. HGT Fund, Inc., New Haven, 1972-90, pres., bd. dirs. 1990-93; sec. Pomperaug Woods, Inc., Southbury, Conn., 1986-91; sec. bd. dirs. Fairbank Corp., New Haven, 1975—. Mem. New Haven Rep. Town Com., 1969-75, New Haven Bd. Fin., 1976-81, New Haven Environ. Adv. Coun., 1988-91; bd. dirs., treas. Planned Parenthood Coun., 1988-93, Planned Parenthood Conn. Found., 1991-95. Fellow Conn. Bar Found. (bd. dirs. 1987-97, treas. 1987-91); mem. ABA, Conn. Bar Assn. (exec. com. of real property and banking law sects.), New Haven County Bar Assn., Quinniplack Club, The Quechee Club (Vt.). Congregationalist. Avocations: skiing, tennis, squash, bicycling. Home: PO Box 411 Quechee VT 05059-0411 Office: Wiggin & Dana One Century Tower New Haven CT 06508-1832

CRAIG, WILLIAM LAURENCE, lawyer; s. William Donald and Alicia (Harnecker) C.; m. Penelope Ann Hodge, Feb. 8, 1964; children: Geoffrey L., Benjamin K., Jennifer C. Student, Collegiate Sch., N.Y., 1950; BA, Williams Coll., 1954; JD, Harvard U., 1957; Doctorat, U. Paris, 1981. Bar: N.Y. 1957, D.C. 1961, U.S. Supreme Ct. 1961; avocat Paris bar 1973. Assoc. lawyer Covington & Burling, Washington, 1960-63; assoc. lawyer, ptnr. Coudert Frères, Paris, 1964—; U.S. mem. Ct. Arbitration Internat. C. of C., 1976-84; NATO Appeal bd., 1972-76; counsel over 100 Internat. C. of C. arbitrations. Co-author: International Chamber of Commerce Arbitration, 1984, 2d edit. 1990, International Commercial Arbitration, 1997; contbr. articles to profl. jours. Adv. coun. Internat. and comparative Law Ctr. Southwestern Legal Found., 1988—. Served to lt. USNR, 1957-60. Mem. Assn. d'Avocats Inscrits à un Barreau Etranger (pres. 1997—). Home: 42 rue Pierre Guérin, 75016 Paris France Office: Coudert Frères, 52 Ave des Champs-Elysées, 75008 Paris France

CRAIGE, DANNY DWAINE, dentist; b. Okla., Mar. 25, 1946; s. William and Ruby G. (Sinor) C.; m. Mary Ann Thompson, Dec. 22, 1970. BS in Math., Southeastern Okla. State U., 1967; MS, Okla. U., 1968, DDS, 1980. Tchr. Yuba (Okla.) Pub. Schs., 1968-69, Sherman (Tex.) Pub. Schs., 1971-73; asst. mgr. Thompson Book and Supply Co., Durant, Okla., 1973-76; pvt. practice Durant, 1980—; cons. Med. Ctr. of S.E. Okla., Durant, 1980—, Bryan County (Okla.) Nursing Homes, 1980—. Bd. dirs. Texoma chpt. Boy Scouts Am., Durant and Denison, Tex., 1983-90, chmn. sustaining membership drive, Durant, 1989, 90; bd. dirs. Durant Western Days Talent Contest, 1989, 90, 91. Capt. USNR. Okla. U. fellow, 1968. Mem. ADA, Okla. Dental Assn., Naval Res. Assn. (life), Naval Order U.S., Texoma Dental Study Club (chmn. 1980—), Lions (past chpt. pres. and bd. dirs.). Home: 601 W Pine St Durant OK 74701-3735 Office: 203 N 16th Ave Durant OK 74701-3607

CRAIGHEAD, FRANK COOPER, JR., ecologist; b. Washington, Aug. 14, 1916; s. Frank Cooper and Carolyn (Johnson) C.; m. Esther Melvin Stevens, Nov. 9, 1943 (dec. 1980); children: Frank Lance, Charles Stevens, Jana Catherine; m. Shirley Ann Cocker, July, 1987. AB, Pa. State U., 1939; MS, U. Mich., 1940, PhD, 1950. Sr. rsch. assoc. Atmospheric Scis. Rsch. Ctr., N.Y., 1967-77; wildlife biologist, cons. U.S. Dept. Interior, Washington, 1959-66; wildlife biologist U.S. Forest Svc., Washington, 1957-59; mgr. desert game range U.S. Dept. Interior, Las Vegas, 1955-57; cons. survival tng. Dept. Def., Washington, 1950-55; pres. Craighead Environ. Research Inst., Moose, Wyo., 1955—; research assoc. U. Mont., Missoula, 1959—, Nat. Geographic Soc., Washington, 1959—; lectr. in field. Author: Hawks in the Hand, 1937, How to Survive on Land and Sea, 1943, Hawks, Owls and Wildlife, 1956, A Field Guide to Rocky Mountain Wildflowers, 1963, Track of the Grizzly, 1979, For Everything There is a Season, 1994. Mem. Pryor Mountain Wild Horse Adv. Com., Dept. Interior, 1968; mem. Horizons adv. group Am. Revolution Bicentennial Commn., 1972. Recipient citation Sec. of Navy, 1947; recipient letter of commendation U.S. Dept. Interior, 1963, Disting. Alumnus award Pa. State U., 1970; alumni fellow Pa. State U., 1973; recipient John Oliver LaGorce Gold medal Nat. Geog. Soc., 1979, U. Mich. Sch. Natural Resources Alumni Soc. award for Disting. Service, 1984, Centennial award Nat. Geog. Soc., 1988. Mem. AAAS, Wilderness Soc., Wildlife Soc., Explorers Club, Phi Beta Kappa, Sigma Xi, Phi Sigma, Phi Kappa Phi. Home: PO Box 156 Moose WY 83012-0156 Office: Craighead Environ Rsch Inst PO Box 156 Moose WY 83012-0156

CRAIGHEAD, HAROLD G., physics educator. BS, U. Md., 1974; PhD, Cornell U., 1980. Mem. tech. staff Bell Telephone Labs., Holmdel, N.J., 1979-84; rsch. mgr. Bell Comms. Rsch., Red Bank, N.J., 1984-89; prof. Cornell U., Ithaca, N.Y., 1989—; dir. Sch. Applied and Engring. Physics, Cornell U., Ithaca, 1998—, 1998—; dir. Nat. Nanofabrication Facility, Ithaca, 1989-95. Contbr. articles to profl. jours. Office: Cornell U Dept Applied Physics Applied Physics Clark Hall Ithaca NY 14853

CRAIGHEAD, JOHN EDWARD, pathology educator; b. Pitts., Aug. 14, 1930; s. Samuel Judson and Madeleine Rose (Schmalz) C.; m. Dorothy Ellen Ford, July 29, 1957 (div. July 1992); 2 children; m. Christina Ann Canon, Aug. 29, 1992; 7 children. BS, U. Utah, 1952, MD, 1956. Diplomate Am. Bd. Pathology, Nat. Bd. Med. Examiners (mem. pathology com. 1978-81). Intern ward med. svc. Barnes Hosp., St. Louis, 1956-57; jr. asst. resident in pathology Peter Bent Brigham Hosp., Boston, 1960-61, sr. asst. resident, 1961-62, chief resident, 1962-65, assoc. in pathology, 1965-68; asst. prof. pathology Harvard U. Med. Sch., Boston, 1963-66, assoc. prof., 1966-68; assoc. prof. U. Vt. Coll. Medicine, Burlington, 1968-69, prof., 1969-72, chmn. dept. pathology, 1974-90; attending physician Med. Ctr. Hosp. Vt., Burlington, 1970-94, Fletcher Allen Health Care, Burlington, 1995—; Harry B. Harding meml. lectr. Evanston (Ill.) Hosp., 1981; 4th ann. Karl Sohlberg lectr. U. Ill., 1981; Finlayson seminar lectr. McGill U., Montreal, Que., Can., 1987; George Hoyt Whipple lectr. U. Rochester, N.Y., 1989; assoc. mem. Commn. Viral Infections, Armed Forces Epidemiol. Bd., 1966-68; mem. adv. com. on infectious diseases Nat. Inst. Allergy and Infectious Diseases, 1971-75; mem. pathology A study sect. NIH, 1984-86, mem. nat. adv. environ. health scis. coun., 1985-89; mem. adv. com. Registry Comparative Pathology, Armed Forces Inst. Pathology, 1993-96; mem. Vt. Regional Cancer Ctr., 1988-91; mem. med. sci. adv. bd. Juvenile Diabetes Found., 1978-80; mem. residency rev. com. for pathology Accreditation Coun. for Grad. Med. Edn., 1979-83, vice chmn., 1982-84; dir. sci. program, chmn. environ. pathology task force Univs. Assoc. for Rsch. and Edn. in Pathology, 1991-98; mem. pulmonary panel Am. Registry Pathology, 1992-98. Editor: The Pathology of Environmental and Occupational Disease, 1995; mem. editl. bd. Lab. Investigation, Archives Pathology and Lab. Medicine, Human Pathology, Am. Jour. Pathology, 1980-92; contbr. numerous articles and abstracts to med. jours., chpts. to books. Surgeon USPHS, 1957-60. Recipient David Rumbough sci. award, U. Ill., 1976, Moses Barron award, Twin Cities Diabetes Assn., 1977; spl. fellow NIH, 1963; travel fellow Royal Soc. Medicine, 1971. Mem. AAAS, AMA (mem. coun. sci. affairs, mem. adv. panel on asbestos related diseases, chmn. 1982-83), Am. Acad. Pathology, Am. Assn. for Cancer Rsch., Am. Assn. Pathologists, Am. Soc. Clin. Pathologists (mem. basic sci. rsch. symposium com. 1978-82, H.P. Smith Meml. award 1987), Am. Thoracic Soc., Assn. Pathology Chairmen (past sec.-treas., v.p., pres. 1981-82), Internat. Acad. Pathology (councillor 1980-84), Coll. Am. Pathologists (mem. environ. resource com. coun. on pathology practice 1980-81), Am. Soc. for Virology, New England Soc. Pathologists (pres. 1980-81), Mass. Soc. Pathologists (mem. exec. com. 1967), Vt. Med. Soc., Chittenden County Med. Soc. Avocation: horticulture. Office: Univ Vt Dept Pathology Burlington VT 05405

CRAIGHEAD, RODKEY, banker; b. Pitts., July 24, 1916; s. Ernest S. and Florence L. (Rodkey) C.; m. Carol M. Price, June 26, 1943 (dec. June 1978); children: Rodkey, Virginia, Corinne; m. La Verne Hastings, Mar. 1979. BS, U. Pitts., 1942; postgrad., Grad. Sch. Banking, U. Wis., 1959-61. With Mellon Nat. Bank, Pitts., 1936-41; with Detroit Bank & Trust Co., 1946—, v.p., 1961-67, sr. v.p., 1967-69, exec. v.p., 1969-73, dir., 1971—, pres., 1974—, chmn., chief exec. officer, 1977—; pres., dir. Detroitbank Corp., 1974-81, chmn., chief exec. officer, 1977-81. Bd. dirs. Alma Coll. Served to capt. AUS, 1942-46. Mem. Collier County Forum Club (bd. dirs.), Pelican Bay Club, Royal Poinciana Golf Club, Naples Athletic Club. Presbyterian. Home: 5555 Heron Point Dr Naples FL 34108-2708

CRAIGLOW, JAMES HAWKINS, graduate school official; b. Harrisburg, Pa., Nov. 21, 1941; s. James Hawkins and Jeanette (Sweeney) C.; m. Elizabeth Blatz, Aug. 31, 1964 (div. Nov. 1978); children: Alison, Hilary; m. Shelley Whittier, Aug. 22, 1981; 1 child, Brittany. BA, Lafayette Coll., 1963; MEd, Antioch N.E Grad. Sch., Keene, N.H., 1977. Secondary tchr. social studies Walton (N.Y.) Ctrl. Sch., 1963-66; elem. tchr. Transfiguration Day Sch., Freeport, N.Y., 1966-70; dept. chmn., adminstrv. intern Emma Willard Sch., Troy, N.Y., 1970-77; assoc. dean Antioch New England Grad. Sch., 1977-86, pres., CEO, 1986—; mgmt. cons.; presenter numerous confs. Contbr. numerous articles to profl. jours. Bd. dirs. Monadnock Children's Mus., Keene, 1987-91, Monadnock United Way, 1989-98, Monadnock Family Svcs., 1989-98, MonadNet Corp., 1994—; chair cmty. goals com. Mayor's Ct.; chair Ashuelot Park Adv. Bd. Mem. Nat. Assn. Coll. and Univ. Bus. Officers, Coun. for Adult and Experimental Edn., Coun. for the Advancement and Support Edn. (vice chair, exec. com. N.H. Campus Compact), Greater Keene C. of C. (bd. dirs. 1988-91). Democrat. Avocations: antique collecting, reading, baseball.

CRAIGO, GORDON EARL, quality systems consultant; b. Glasgow, W.Va., June 17, 1951. BS in Nuclear Engring., U. Fla., Gainesville, 1977; MS in Edn., Nat.-Louis U., 1995. Field engr. GE, Oak Brook, Ill., 1978-84; pres., owner Craigo Tech. Svc., Inc., 1984—. Office: Craigo Tech Svcs Inc Ste 12G 6S235 Steeple Run Dr Naperville IL 60540-3717

CRAIN, FRANCES UTTERBACK, retired dietitian; b. Crawfordsville, Ind., Dec. 28, 1914; d. Chelsey Chalmers and Margaret Myrtle (Henderson) Utterback; m. James William Crain, Sept. 13, 1937 (div. July 1944); children: James Michael, Patrick Desmond. BA, U. Ill., 1935; postgrad., Purdue U., 1945-46. Registered dietitian. Dietetic intern Indpls. City Hosp., 1935-36, therapeutic dietitian, 1936-37; dietitian Home Lawn Mineral Springs, Martinsville, Ind., 1937-38; WPA project dietitian Ill. Soldiers & Sailors Children's Home, Normal, 1939; chief dietitian Providence Hosp., Kansas City, Kans., 1939-40, Alexian Bros. Hosp., St. Louis, 1940-41; dietitian Ill. State Dept. Pub. Welfare, Springfield, 1943-45; exec. dir. Memphis Dairy Coun., 1947-61; program cons. Nat. Dairy Coun., Chgo., 1961-68; dietitian War on Poverty Com., Memphis, 1968-69, Shelby County Hosp., Memphis, 1969-74, Shelby County Penal Farm, Memphis, 1969-80; chief dietitian Oakville Health Care Ctr., Memphis, 1974-80; dietitian feeding programs Salvation Army, 1982-93. Writer food feature column. Comml. Appeal, 1952-61; author: To Your Taste-Butter, 1957. Mem. speakers and path. coms. Memphis in May Internat. Festival, 1983, 84, 85. Named Career Women of Yr., Pilot Club of Memphis, 1955; recipient Spl. Svcs. award Salvation Army, 1983. Mem. Am. Dietetic Assn., Tenn. Dietetic Assn. (pres. 1951-52, outstanding dietitian 1977), Memphis Dist. Dietetic Assn. (pres. 1949-50, editor bull. 1958-59), Memphis Area Nutrition Coun. (pres. 1973-74), Shelby County Retirees Orgn. (pres. 1987-89). Democrat. Avocations: reading, woodworking, cooking, scrabble. Home: 255 N Avalon St Memphis TN 38112-5101

CRAIN, GAYLA CAMPBELL, lawyer; b. Cleburne, Tex., June 13, 1950; d. R. C. and Marilyn Ruth (McFadyen) Campbell; m. Howard Leo Crain, May 27, 1978; 1 child, Robert Leo. BA, Baylor U., 1972, JD, 1974. Bar: Tex. 1974, U.S. Dist. Ct. (no., ea., we., and so. dists.) Tex., U.S. Ct. Appeals (5th cir.) 1988, U.S. Ct. Appeals (10th cir.) 1994, U.S. Ct. 1999, U.S. Supreme Ct. 1999. Asst. counsel Trailways, Inc., Dallas, 1975-79; counsel Schering Plough, Inc., Kenilworth, N.J., 1979-80, sr. counsel, 1980-81; assoc. Epstein Becker & Green, P.C., Ft. Worth, 1985-86; ptnr. Epstein Becker & Green, P.C., Dallas, 1986—. Contbg. author: State by State Guide to Human Resources Law, 1990, 91; editl. adv. bd. Employee Rels. Law Jour., Tex. Employment Law, 1998. Trustee Dallas Bapt. U., 1989-97, 98—. Office: Epstein Becker & Green PC 12750 Merit Dr Ste 1320 Dallas TX 75251*

CRAIN, JOHN KIP, school system administrator; b. Urbana, Ohio, June 14, 1956; s. William Frederick and Patricia Ann (Bumgardner) C.; m. Rebecca Ann Ireland, July 11, 1980; children: Amanda Ann, Tiffany Kay, Kelly Jo. BS in Edn. summa cum laude, Ohio State U., 1985, MA, 1987; postgrad., Bowling Green State U., 1992—. Cert. tchr., supr. dir., prin., asst. supt., supt., Ohio. Drafter, office mgr. Crain Bldgs., Mechanicsburg, Ohio, 1974-82; tchr. drafting Springfield (Ohio)-Clark County Joint Vocat. Sch., 1982-86; supr. Eastland Vocat. Schs., Groveport, Ohio, 1986-91; dir. Oregon (Ohio) City Schs., 1991—; bd. dirs. Ohio Indsl. Tng. Program, Toledo; co-chair skill olympics Ohio Vocat./Indsl. Clubs Am., Columbus, 1987-89; presenter in field. Author and editor catalog Eastland Vocat. Schs., 1987. Vol. St. Charles Hosp. Emergency Rm., 1991—; bd. dirs. Ea. Comty. YMCA, Toledo, 1992-94. Pres.'s sr. scholar Ohio State U., 1984. Mem. Am. Vocat. Assn. (life), Ohio Vocat. Assn. (life, N.W. Ohio chair), Ohio Vocat. Dirs. Assn. (exec. bd. 1996-99, pres. 1999—), Ohio Assn. Secondary Sch. Adminstrs., Bay Area Jr. C. of C. (state dir. 1991-94), Oregon Area C. of C., Kiwanis (bd. dirs. 1991-95, pres. 1995-96, 98-99, East Toledo chpt., Disting. Svc. award 1996), Ohio Vocat. Indsl. Club Am. (regional advisor 1984-86, asst. dir. summer leadership camp 1985-86, chmn. state skill olympics 1986-87, author and editor program guidelines 1985, local advisor notebook 1986), Phi Delta Kappa, Pi Lambda Theta, Omicron Tau Theta. United Methodist. Home: 2036 Coe Ct Perrysburg OH 43551-5600 Office: Oregon City Schs 5721 Seaman Rd Oregon OH 43616-2600

CRAIN, JOHN WALTER, historian; b. Amarillo, Tex., July 11, 1944; s. John Clyde and Roma (McDowell) C.; m. Mary Hemingway, Aug. 18, 1973; children: John Matthew, Sarah Hemingway, Margaret Aileen. BA, U. Tex., Austin, 1966; MA, S.W. Tex. State U., 1970; cert. arts adminstrn., Harvard U., 1975; cert. mus. mgmt., U. Calif.-Berkeley, 1979. Dir. Star of the Republic Museum, Washington-on-the-Brazos, Tex., 1971-76, Dallas Hist. Soc., 1976-90; chmn. Dallas County Hist. Commn., 1993-95; bd. dirs. Dallas County Hist. Found.; cons. in field, 1971—. Exec. dir. Summerlee Commn. on Tex. History, 1990-91; v.p. and bd. dirs. program History Summerlee Found., Tex., 1990—. Mem. Tex. State Hist. Assn. (hon., coun. 1994, exec. com.). Methodist. Office: 5956 Sherry Ln Ste 1414 Dallas TX 75225-8025

CRAIN, RICHARD CHARLES, school district music director; b. Christine, Tex., Apr. 22, 1934; s. Richard Clyde and Florence (Martin) C.; m. Gayle Ruth Albert, June 24, 1961; children: Richard Scott, Roy Christopher, Steven Guy. B in Music, Trinity U., San Antonio, 1956; postgrad., Vandercook Coll., 1958; MEd, U. N. Tex., 1969. Band dir. Mercedes (Tex.) H.S., 1956-60, Lamar Jr. H.S., Temple, Tex., 1960-64, Belton (Tex.) H.S., 1964-79, Spring H.S., Houston, 1979-81, Westfield H.S., Houston, 1981-82; dir. music Spring Ind. Sch. Dist., Houston, 1982—; coord. Nat. Concert Band Festival, Chgo., 1991—; bd. dirs. Midwest Internat. Band and Orch. Clinic, Chgo., 1991—. Mem. Tex. Bandmasters Assn. (Tex. Bandmaster of Yr. 1994), Nat. Fedn. Sch. Activities Assn. (Outstanding Music Educator award 1994), Univ. Interscholastic League (exec. sec. region IX 1994—), Phi Beta Mu Internat. Fraternity (exec. sec. 1977—). Home: 1111 Belaya Ln Houston TX 77090-1219 Office: Spring Ind Sch Dist 16717 Ella Blvd Houston TX 77090-4213

CRAINE, DIANE M., nursing educator; b. Canton, Ohio, Feb. 3, 1944; d. d. Richard Craine; children: Rick, Shari, Meg, Becky, Brett. BSN, Tex. Woman's U., 1966, MSN, 1973; PhD in Edn., Ga. State U., 1986. Critical care nurse and supv., 1966-72; instr. nursing Ga. State U., Atlanta, 1973-76, Gordon Coll., Barnesville, Ga., 1977-79; asst. prof. nursing Tift Coll., Forsyth, Ga., 1980-81; asst. prof. Macon Coll., 1982-88, prof., chmn. nursing dept., 1988—; rep. Regents Com. on Health Professions, 1988—; mem. Health Professions Subcom. on Nursing, 1988—; mem. adv. bd. Salvation Army; chmn. subcom. on nursing Univ. Sys. Health Professions. Contbr. articles to profl. jours. Mem. Ga. BSN Articulation Com., ANA, Ga. Nurses Assn., Nat. League Nursing, Ga. League for Nursing and Long Range Planning Com., Ga. Assn. Women in Edn., Bibb County C. of C., Sigma Theta Tau.

CRAINE, JOHN W., JR., career officer; b. Urbanna, Va.; m. Wendy Clarke Burchinal; children: David, Clark. BA, Randolph-Macon Coll., 1968; grad. with distinction, Air Command & Staff Coll., Maxwell AFB, 1978. Commd. 2d lt. USN, 1968, advanced through grades to rear admiral; pilot F-4 Phantoms Fighter Squadron 103, Vietnam; advanced tactics instr. Flight Squadron 101, Key West, Fla.; aide, flag lt. to Commdr. 2d Fleet, Commdr. Striking Fleet, 1975-77; ops., maintenance officer USS John F. Kennedy, 1978-80; fighter placement officer Air combat Placement Br. Naval Mil. Pers. Command, Washington, 1980-83; exec. officer USS Nimitz, 1983-84, commdr., 1984-85; air ops. officer to Commdr. Cruiser-Destroyer Group 8 USS Saratoga, 1985-88; spl. asst. flag officer mgmt. & distbn. Chief Naval Pers., Washington, 1988-92; commdg. officer Naval Air Sta. Oceana, Virginia Beach, Va., 1992-94; commdr. naval shore activities U.S. Atlantic Fleet, 1994-96; dir. assessment divsn. Office Chief Naval Ops., Washington, 1996-99, dir. naval tng., 1999—. Office: USN Rm 4E 536 2000 Navy Pentagon Washington DC 20350-2000*

CRAINE, THOMAS KNOWLTON, non-profit administrator; b. Utica, N.Y., Apr. 19, 1942; s. Donald Holmes and Marjorie (Knowlton) C.; m. Susan Lynda Moseley, Dec. 21, 1966; children: Matthew Moseley, Tish Marjorie. BA, U. Rochester, 1964; MEd, SUNY, Buffalo, 1966, EdD, 1972. Dir. architecture and planning SUNY, Buffalo, 1968-72, asst. to pres., 1972-76, clin. assoc. prof., 1975-83, asst. v.p. acad. affairs, 1976-79; exec. v.p., assoc. prof. D'Youville Coll., Buffalo, 1979-83; pres. Loretto Heights Coll., Denver, 1983-88; v.p. instl. advancement and planning Iliff Sch. Theology, Denver, 1988-98; pres./CEO YMCA Met. Denver, 1998—; evaluator North Cen. Assn. Instns. Higher Edn., 1984—, Assn. Theol. Schs., 1993—; cons. in strategic planning, bd. devel., fund raising. Mem. editl. bd. Jour. for Higher Edn. Mgmt. Mem. Newcomen Soc., Rotary. Office: YMCA of Met Denver 25 E 16th Ave Denver CO 80202-5195

CRAKE, ROGER F., general surgeon; b. Wilkes Barre, Pa., Dec. 24, 1952; s. Fred Alfred and Margaret Rose (Yuknavich) C.; m. Michele Robin Andreyko, June 3, 1978; children: Michael, Stephen. BS, U. Scranton, 1974; MD, Jefferson Med. Coll., 1978. Diplomate Am. Bd. Surgery, Nat. Bd. Med. Examiners. Staff Berwick (Pa.) Hosp., 1983—; chmn. div. surgery Berwick Hosp., 1987-89, sec.-treas. staff, 1991-93, v.p. staff, 1993, pres. staff, 1993-95, chmn. credentials, 1995—. Fellow Am. Coll. Surgeons; mem.

AMA, Soc. Am. Gastrointestinal Endoscopic Surgeons, Soc. Laparoscopic Surgeons, Pa. Med. Soc., Columbia County Med. Soc. Avocations: rock climbing, running, kayaking, inline skating, skiing. Home: 737 E Front St Berwick PA 18603-4917 Office: 695 E 16th St Berwick PA 18603-2320

CRAKES, GARY MICHAEL, economics educator; b. Southington, Conn., July 2, 1953; s. Harry Fremont and Frances Katherine (Koth) C.; m. Deborah Jean MacArthur, Aug. 14, 1976; children: Andrew David, Jeffrey Alan, Timothy Scott. BA in Econs., Cen. Conn. State U., 1975; MA in Econs., U. Conn., 1976, PhD in Econs., 1984. Rsch. asst. Health Ctr. U. Conn., Farmington, 1976-79, vis. prof. Health Ctr., Sch. Dental Medicine, 1988; instr. U. Conn., Hartford, 1979-80; asst. prof. So. Conn. State U., New Haven, 1980-85, assoc. prof., 1985-89, prof., 1989—, chmn. dept. econs. and fin., 1991-96; pres. Maher, Crakes & Assocs., Cheshire, Conn., 1987—; econ. expert witness. Contbr. articles to profl. jours. Mem. State of Conn. Sr. Economist Exam. Com., Hartford, 1987. Richard D. Irwin fellow Irwin Publ. Co., Homewood, Ill., 1983-84, U. Conn. fellow, 1983; recipient Univ. Tchr. of the Yr. award, 1987, Schs. of Bus. Outstanding Tchg. award, 1998. Mem. Am. Econ. Assn., Ea. Econ. Assn. Nat. Assn. Forensic Econ., AAUP, Omicron Delta Epsilon (chpt. advisor). Democrat. Avocations: family activities, golf, fishing. Home: 860 Ward Ln Cheshire CT 06410-3363 Office: So Conn State U 501 Crescent St New Haven CT 06515-1330

CRALEY, CAROL RUTH, art educator, academic administrator; b. Phila., Nov. 28, 1949; d. Amos B. and Ruth L. (Ehrig) C. BS, Pa. State U., 1972, MEd, 1975, prin. cert., 1993; postgrad. studies, Lehigh U., U. Mass., Dartmouth, 1990. Cert. tchr., elem. and secondary prin., Pa. Art tchr. Bensalem (Pa.) Twp. Sch. Dist., 1972-98, internal facilitator strategic planning, 1995—, visual art coord., 1990-94; art workshop and activities leader Activities Therapy Dept. Inst. of Pa. Hosp., Phila., 1986-87; curriculum coord. Sch. Dist. Haverford (Pa.) Twp., 1998—; cons., project leader Bucks County Schs., Doylestown, Pa., 1989-90, 92; v.p. arts edn. trust 1991—, visual art curriculum counsel, 1989-94. Bucks County Commr. Women's Adv. Coun., 1989-91, workshop leader adv. coun. for women, 1990-93; workshop leader Friends Gen. Conf., Boone, N.C., 1991. Recipient Artist in Edn. grant Pa. Coun. Arts, Harrisburg, 1985; George Bartol Arts in Edn. fellowship honoree, 1993, The Nat. Faculty Acad. fellowship, 1994. Mem. ACSD, NEA, Pa. Art Edn. Assn. (Outstanding Art Educator in Pa. 1983, bd. dirs, 1984-87; workshop leader 1983, 87, 91), Nat. Art Edn. Assn. (workshop leader 1981, 89-93), Pa. State Edn. Assn., Robert K. Greenleaf Ctr., Pi Lambda Theta (membership chair). Avocation: photography. Home: 320 Wallace Ave Bensalem PA 19020-7337 Office: Haverford Middle Sch 1701 Darby Rd Havertown PA 19083

CRALLEY, LESTER VINCENT, retired industrial hygienist, editor; b. Carmi, Ill., Mar. 27, 1911; s. John W. Cralley and Martha Jones; m. Gertrude E. Wilson, Aug. 24, 1940; 1 child, Agnes D. BS, McKendree Coll., 1933; PhD, U. Iowa, 1942. Res. officer USPHS, Bethesda, Md., 1941-45; chief indsl. hygienist Aluminum Co. of Am., Pitts., 1945-67, mgr. environ. health svcs., 1968-74; mem. Sec. of Labor's Nat. Safety Adv. Com., Washington, 1969-70. Co-editor: Theory and Rationale of Industrial Hygiene Practice, 1985, new edit., 1994, In Plant Practices for Job Related Health Hazards Control, 1989, Health and Safety Beyond the Workplace, 1990. Mem. Am. Indsl. Hygiene Assn. (hon., treas. 1953-56, pres. 1956-57, Cummings Meml. award 1971), Am. Acad. Indsl. Hygiene, Internat. Commn. on Occupational Health, Planetary Soc. Home: 1453 Banyan Dr Fallbrook CA 92028-1105

CRAM, BRIAN MANNING, school system administrator. AA, Dixie Jr. Coll., 1959; BA with honors, U. Utah, 1961; MA, Ariz. State U., 1962, EdS, 1964, EdD with Honors, 1967. Asst. prin. Clark (Nev.) High Sch., 1965-69, prin., 1969-73; asst. supt. Clark County (Nev.) Sch. Dist., 1973-78; supt. schs. Clark County (Nev.) Sch. Dist., 1989—; prin. Western High Sch., 1978-89; cons. Glendale Unified Sch. Dist., Whittier Sch. Dist., South Bay Union High Sch. Dist., Elk Grove Unified Sch. Dist., No. Ill. U., State of Hawaii; co-chairman Superintendent's Coun. Ednl. Tech., Coll. Prep Feasibility subcom.; mem. Speakers Bureau Pay as You Go Bond Plan, Disting. Scholar's com., Extended Day com., In-Svc. com., State Attendance Audit, Spl. Assistance Team, Computer Mgmt. Project, Prin. Attendance adv. com., Prin.'s Math Curriculum com; speaker in field. Contbr. articles to profl. jours. Bd. dirs. Boulder Dam Area Coun. Boy Scouts Am., Las Vegas Council PTA, United Way, Clark County Sch. Dist. Articulation Com., Nev. Assn. Handicapped, Nev. Devel. Authority, Nev. Inst. Contemporary Art, Animal Found., Las Vegas Mus. Nat. History, Southwest Regional Ednl. Lab., Nat. Coun. Christians and Jews; adv. bd. U. Nev. Las Vegas Spl. Svcs., U. Nev. Sch. Medicine, Clark County Community Coll. Mem. Nev. Assn. Secondary Sch. Prins. (past sec.), Nev. Educator Awards Selection Com., Clark County Assn. Sch. Administrs. (chmn. negotiations, past exec. coun., past sec., past pres.), Ariz. State U. Alumni Assn. (past pres. So. Nev. chpt.), Greater Las Vegas C. of C., Latin C. of C., Nev. Black C. of C., Rotary, Phi Delta Kappa. Home: 417 S Wallace Dr Las Vegas NV 89107-2559 Office: Clark County School District 2832 E Flamingo Rd Las Vegas NV 89121-5295*

CRAM, DONALD JAMES, chemistry educator; b. Chester, Vt., Apr. 22, 1919; s. William Moffet and Joanna (Shelley) C.; m. Jane Maxwell, Nov. 25, 1969. BS, Rollins Coll., 1941; MS, U. Nebr., 1942; PhD, Harvard U., 1947; PhD (hon.), U. Uppsala, 1977; DSc (hon.), U. So. Calif., 1983, Rollins Coll., 1988, U. Nebr., 1989, U. Western Ontario, 1990, U. Sheffield, 1991. Rsch. chemist Merck & Co., 1942-45; asst. prof. chemistry UCLA, 1947-50, assoc. prof., 1950-56, prof., 1956-90, S. Winstein prof., 1985-95, univ. prof., 1988-90, univ. prof. emeritus, 1990—; chem. con. Upjohn Co., 1952-88, Union Carbide Co., 1960-81, Eastman Kodak Co., 1981-91, Technicon Co., 1984-92, Inst. Guido Donegani, Milan, 1988-91; State Dept. exch. fellow to Inst. de Quimica, Nat. U. Mex., 1956; guest prof. U. Heidelberg, Fed. Republic Germany, 1958; guest lectr. S. Africa, 1967; Centenary lectr. Chem. Soc. London, 1976. Author: From Design to Discovery, 1990, (with Pine, Hendrickson and Hammond) Organic Chemistry, 1960, 4th edit., 1980, Fundamentals of Carbanion Chemistry, 1965, (with Richards and Hammond) Elements of Organic Chemistry, 1967, (with Cram) Essence of Organic Chemistry, 1977, (with Cram) Container Molecules and Their Guests, 1994; contbr. chpts. to textbooks, articles in field of host-guest complexation chemistry, carbanions, stereochemistry, mold metabolites, large ring chemistry. Named Young Man of Yr. Calif. Jr. C. of C., 1954, Calif. Scientist of Yr., 1974, Nobel Laureate in Chemistry, 1987, UCLA medal, 1993; recipient award for creative work in synthetic organic chemistry Am. Chem. Soc., 1965, Arthur C. Cope award, 1974, Richard Tolman medal, 1985, Willard Gibbs award, 1985, Roger Adams award, 1985, Herbert Newby McCoy award, 1965, 75, Glenn Seaborg award, 1989, Nat. Medal of Science, Nat. Sci. Found., 1993; award for creative rsch. organic chemistry Synthetic Organic Chem. Mfrs. Assn., 1965; Nat. Rsch. fellow Harvard U., 1947, Am. Chem. Soc. fellow, 1947-48, Guggenheim fellow, 1954-55. Fellow Royal Soc. (hon. 1989); mem. NAS (award in chem. scis. 1992), Am. Acad. Arts and Scis., Am. Chem. Soc., Royal Soc. Chemistry, Surfers Med. Assn., San Onofre Surfing Club, Sigma Xi, Lambda Chi Alpha. Office: UCLA Dept Chemistry Los Angeles CA 90095-1569

CRAM, REGINALD MAURICE, retired air force officer; b. Northfield, Vt., Apr. 29, 1914; s. Archie Rice and Beatrice (Cleveland) C.; m. Kathryn E. Mosher, June 29, 1937; children: Robin (Mrs. Paul Lualdi), Marilyn Jane (Mrs. Vcevold Strekalovsky). BS, Norwich U., 1936, D in Mil. Sci. (hon.), 1974; postgrad., Boston U. Law Sch., 1937-38, Air Force Intelligence Sch., 1943, U.S. Army Command and Gen. Staff Coll., 1944, Nat. Art Sch., 1949, Armed Forces Staff Coll., 1951, State Dept. Fgn. Service Inst., 1961; M.A., U. Md., 1963. With Office Adj. Gen. Vt., 1938-41; asst. U.S. property and disbursing officer State of Vt., 1946-47; commd. 2d lt. Cav., 1936; advanced through grades to maj. gen. USAF, 1968; with anti-submarine campaign USAAF, 1941-42; Asiatic-Pacific Theatre with USMC, 1943-45; plans and operations officer Hdqrs. USAF, 1947-51; sec. Can./U.S. Regional Planning Group, NATO, 1951-54; dir. plans 3d USAF, Eng., 1954-55; with Supreme Hdqrs. Allied Powers, Europe, 1955-57; comdr. Orientation Group USAF, 1957-61; with Orgn. Joint Chiefs of Staff, 1961-64; ret., 1964; dep. adj. gen. Vt., 1964-66, adj. gen., 1967-81. Past pres. Long Trail council Boy Scouts Am.; trustee Norwich U. Decorated D.S.M., USAF, Legion of Merit, USAF and U.S. Army, Air medals USN and U.S. Army, Joint Commendation medal, Army Commendation medal, Commendation medal, Selective Svc. Sys. Commendation medal USAF, Vt. WWII Victory medal; recipient Vt. Disting. Svc. medal. Mem. N.G. Assn. U.S. (Disting. Svc. medal, Am. Cancer Soc. St. George medal), Soc. Colonial Wars (war cross), Ret. Officers Assn. (dir.), VFW, Vt. Hist. Soc., The Hillard Soc., Theta Chi, Pi Sigma Alpha, Masons (32 deg.), Scottish Rite, Rotary Club (past dist. gov.). Congregationalist. Home: 936 S Prospect St Burlington VT 05401-6169

CRAM, RUSTY, basketball coach; m. Jana willie; children: Scott, Ryan. BS, La. Tech., 1985. Coach girl's basketball, softball, asst. football Cedar Creek H.S., Ruston, La., 1988; girl's basketball coach Sam Crow Acad., Oak Grove, La.; head coach Evangel Christian Acad., Mobile, Ala.; asst. coach Ga. So. U., Statesboro, 1990-96, head women's basketball coach, 1996—. Office: Georgia Southern Univ Women's Athletics Dept PO Box 8082 Statesboro GA 30460-1000

CRAMBLETT, HENRY GAYLORD, pediatrician, virologist, educator; b. Scio, Ohio, Feb. 8, 1929; s. Carl Smith and Olive (Fulton) C.; m. Donna Jean Reese, June 16, 1960; children: Deborah Kaye, Betsy Diane. BS, Mt. Union Coll., 1950; MD, U. Cin., 1953. Diplomate Am. Bd. Pediatrics, Am. Bd. Microbiology, Am. Bd. Med. Specialists. Intern in medicine Boston City Hosp., Harvard Med. Svc., 1953-54; resident in pediatrics Children's Hosp., Cin., 1954-55; clin. rsch. assoc. Nat. Inst. Allergy and Infectious Diseases, Clin. Center, Bethesda, Md., 1955-57; chief resident, instr. dept. pediatrics State U. Iowa, Iowa City, 1957-58, faculty, 1957-60, asst. prof., 1958-60; faculty Bowman Gray Sch. Medicine, 1960-64, prof. pediatrics, 1963-64, dir. virology lab., 1960-64; prof. pediatrics Ohio State U., Columbus, 1964-95; prof. med. microbiology Ohio State U., 1966-95, exec. dir. Children's Hosp. Research Found., 1964-73, chmn. dept. med. microbiology, 1966-73, dean Coll. Medicine, 1973-80, acting v.p. for med. affairs, 1974-80, v.p. health scis., 1980-83, Warner M. and Lora Kays Pomerene chair in medicine, 1982-95, assoc. to v.p. health services, to dean and prof. emeritus, 1984-95; mem. Ohio State U. bd. trustees Cancer Hosp. Oversight Com., 1991-96, mem. Ohio Med. Bd., sec. 1984-92, past pres.; hosp. surveyor Joint Com. on Accreditation of Health Care Orgns., 1985-95; chmn. com. on cert., subcert. and recert. Am. Bd. Med. Specialists; mem. coms. on written exam., comprehensive qualifying evaluation program Nat. Bd. Med. Examiners; mem. Accreditation Council Continuing Med. Edn., chmn., 1980-83, 93-94, also mem. fin. com., 1993—, mem. strategic plan implementation com., 1993—, mem. external monitoring com., 1993—; mem. adv. com. on undergrad. med. evaluation; mem. Fedn. State Med. Bds., pres., 1976-82 (mem. Flex bd. 1983-91, chmn. 1985-91), mem. fin. audit com., 1991; chmn. Fed. Exam. Bd., 1991-92, cons., 1992—; mem. composite com. Fedn. of State Med. Bds. and Nat. Bd. of Med. Examiners, U.S. Med. Licensing Exam., 1990-96; Fedn. of State Med. Bds. observer Clin. Skills Assessment Alliance, 1990-95; bd. dirs. Ohio State U. Hosp., 1979-80; dir. med. and postgrad. med. edn. King Faisal Specialist Hosp., Riyadh, Saudi Arabia, 1983-84; mem. strategic planning task force CSAA, 1992—; med. dir. Columbus Health Plan, 1995—. Trustee Children's Hosp. Research Found., 1973-84, Children's Hosp., 1973-84, Children's Hosp., Inc., 1982-84. Recipient Hoffheimer prize U. Cin., 1953, Eben J. Carey award in anatomy, 1950, Research Career Devel. award NIH, 1961-63. Fellow Am. Acad. Microbiology, AAAS; mem. So. Soc. Pediatric Research (past pres.), Soc. Pediatric Research, Am. Pediatric Soc., Am. Acad. Pediatrics, Midwest Soc. Pediatric Research, Soc. Exptl. Biology and Medicine, Am. Soc. Microbiology, Alpha Omega Alpha. Research, publs. on medical licensure, medical staff hospital standards, etiologic assn. virus infections in illnesses of infants and children, estimation of importance of various viruses in morbidity and mortality in pediatric age group. Home: 2480 Sheringham Rd Columbus OH 43220-4274 Office: Ohio State U 200 Meiling Hall 370 W 9th Ave Columbus OH 43210-1238

CRAMER, ALLAN P., lawyer; b. Norwich, Conn., Mar. 8, 1937; s. E.L. and Dorothy N. (Pasnik) C.; children—Peter Alden, Alison Jane. B.A. cum laude, U. Pa., 1958; J.D., U. Conn., 1964. Bar: Conn. 1964, U.S. Dist. Ct. Conn. 1965, U.S. Ct. Appeals (2d cir.) 1965. Atty. HEW, Washington, 1964-65; ptnr. Cramer & Ahern, Westport, Conn., 1966—. Chmn. Westport Democratic Town Com., 1972-73; J.P., Town of Westport, 1973-77; bd. dirs. Westport Pub. Library, 1975-82; mem. Westport Zoning Bd. Appeals, 1984-88 . Mem. Conn. Bar Assn., Westport Bar Assn. Home: Yankee Hill Rd Westport CT 06880 Office: Cramer & Ahern 38 Post Rd W Westport CT 06880-4207

CRAMER, BETTY F., life insurance company executive; b. Indpls., Dec. 9, 1920; d. Frank E. and Ethelyn L. (Jackson) C. B.A., Butler U., 1943. Sec. to head pers. dept., payroll acct. Am. United Life Ins. Co., 1943-51; Sec. to v.p. and treas. Indpls. Life Ins. Co., 1951-69, supr. bond and stock acctg., 1969-75, securities asst., 1975-81, sec.-treas., 1981-89, ret., 1989. Advisor Jr. Achievement, Indpls., 1959-60; campaign chmn. United Way, 1980. Mem. Nat. Assn. Corp. Treas., Life Ins. Women's Assn. Indpls. (past v.p., pres.). Republican. Roman Catholic. Avocations: swimming, reading, traveling. Home: 5158 N Central Ave Indianapolis IN 46205-1060

CRAMER, CHUCKIE, state senate official; b. Havre, Mont., Nov. 7, 1941. Sgt.-at-arms Mont. Ho. of Reps., Helena, 1985-88, Mont. State Senate, Helena, 1995—. Office: Sgt-at-Arms US Senate Mont State Capitol RM 366 Helena MT 59620

CRAMER, DALE LEWIS, economics educator; b. Dixon, Ill., June 25, 1924; s. Ray C. and Rebecca (Levan) C.; m. Hula Jean Bond, Aug. 30, 1946; children: Becky Cramer McCann, Craig Alan, Randall Scott. B.S., Bradley U., 1949, M.A., 1951; Ph.D., La. State U., 1958. Asst. prof. econs. La. State U., 1953-54; Asst. prof. econs. U. Tex.-El Paso, 1955-57, assoc. prof., 1957-58; assoc. prof. econs. U. Ala., 1958-63, prof., 1963-88, prof. emeritus econs., 1988—, head dept., 1968-72, acting head dept., 1981-82. Contbr. articles to profl. jours., books. Served with AUS, 1943-46. Earhart Found. fellow, 1954-55. Mem. Am., So. econ. assns., AAUP, Omicron Delta Epsilon, Beta Gamma Sigma. Home: 103 Riverdale N Tuscaloosa AL 35406-1818 Office: Econ Dept U Ala Tuscaloosa AL 35487-0224

CRAMER, EDWARD MORTON, lawyer, music company executive; b. N.Y.C., May 27, 1925; s. Israel and Elsie (Neuman) C.; m. Henrietta Pantel, 1973 (div.); children: Evin Joyce, Marjorie Sue Cramer Gmelin, Charles Harris; m. Ethel Metzger, June 13, 1982. BA, Columbia U., 1947; LLB with distinction, Cornell U., Ithaca, N.Y., 1950; LLM, NYU, 1953; HHD (hon.), Lincoln (Ill.) Coll., 1982; LHD (hon.), Five Towns Coll., N.Y., 1998. Bar: N.Y. 1950, U.S. Supreme Ct 1953. Teaching fellow NYU Sch. Law, 1950-51; assoc. Rosenman & Colin, N.Y.C., 1951-58; ptnr. Cramer & Hoffinger, N.Y.C., 1958-68; pres., CEO, Broadcast Music, Inc. (BMI), 1968-86; pvt. practice, N.Y.C., 1986—; treas. Copyright Soc. U.S., 1963-68, 78-79, bd. editors bull., 1953-63; former mem. Peabody Awards Selection Com. Trustee Congregation Adas Emuno; former trustee Tony Martell Found., Ford's Theater. lt. USNR, 1943-46. Recipient Spl. award Songwriters Guild Am., 1986, Spl. award Am. Composers Alliance, 1987, Spl. Peabody award, 1991; named Personality of Yr. Nat. Arts Club, 1972; Ed Cramer Day named in his honor, N.Y.C., 1979. Mem. ABA, Assn. Bar City N.Y., Nat. Music Coun. (v.p. 1968-86), Broadcast Pioneers (pres. 1984, officer, bd. dirs. 1984-97), Internat. Confedn. Authoral Socs. (adminstrv. coun.), Nat. Acad. Popular Music (trustee, bd. dirs. 1969-93, adv. com.), Practising Law Inst. (comm. and copyright law com.), B'nai B'rith (trustee, officer, pres. music and performing arts unit, pres. 1989-90, Man of Yr. award 1979), Order of Coif. Jewish. Home: 254 Chestnut St Englewood NJ 07631-3134 Office: 110 E 59th St New York NY 10022-1304 *I'm not a creatively talented person but working with people who are, has given me a sense that I have shared their accomplishments.*

CRAMER, EUGENE NORMAN, nuclear power engineer, computer educator; b. Arkansas City, Kans., Apr. 26, 1932; s. Norman Charles and Hulda Margaret (Maier) C.; m. Donna Marie Gagliardi, May 18, 1957 (dec. 1984); children: Lorene, Kristine, Eileen, Carla; m. Marlene McLean, Dec. 29, 1985. BS in Physics, Kans. State Coll., 1955, BS in Math., 1955; grad. Oak Ridge Sch. Reactor Tech., 1959; MA in Mgmt., Claremont Grad. Sch., 1976, MBA, 1985. Registered profl. engr., Calif. Jr. engr. Westinghouse Bettis, Pitts., 1955-57; devel. engr. Oak Ridge Nat. Lab., 1959-69; cons. examiner AEC, 1961-73; engr. advanced energy system So. Calif. Edison, Los Angeles, 1969-88, mgr. nuclear comm., 1988-95, pres., asst. to edn. 1995—; sec. task force on nuclear safety research Electric Research Council, 1969-74; chmn. Pub. Edn. Utility Nuclear Waste Mgmt. Group, 1978-81, Pub. Edn. Calif. Radioactive Waste Mgmt. Forum, 1982-97. Sect. editor Nuclear Safety jour., 1964-69. Contbr. articles to profl. jours. Mem. Capistrano Unified Sch. Dist. Edn. Found., 1994-96. Served as 1st lt. Signal Corps, U.S. Army, 1957-59. Fellow Inst. for Advancement Engring.; mem. Am. Nuclear Soc. (bd. dirs. 1978-81, Meritorious Service award 1981, pub. info. com. 1983—), Health Physics Soc., Soc. for Risk Analysis. Republican. Roman Catholic. Club: Sierra. Home and Office: 2176 Via Teca San Clemente CA 92673-5648

CRAMER, FRANK BROWN, engineering executive, combustion engineer, systems consultant; b. Long Beach, Calif., Aug. 29, 1921; s. Frank Brown and Clara Bell (Ritzenthaler) C.; m. Hendrika Van der Hulst, 1948 (div. 1962); children: Frieda Hendrika, Eric Gustav, Lisa Monica, Christina Elena; m. Paula Gil, Aug. 3, 1973; children: Alfred Alexander, Consuelo F., Peter M. BA, U. So. Calif., 1942, postgrad., 1942-43, 46-51. Rsch. fellow U. So. Calif., L.A., 1946-51; supr. engring. Rocketdyne, Canoga Park, Calif., 1953-63; pres. Multi-Tech, Inc., San Fernando, Calif., 1960-69; systems cons. Electro-Optical Systems, Pasadena, Calif., 1969-70, McDonnell-Douglas Astronautic, Huntington Beach, Calif., 1971-72; pres. Ergs Unltd. Inc., Mission Hills, Calif., 1973-89, Acquisition, Mission Hills, 1988—; instr. engring. stats. U. So. Calif., L.A., 1955-57, sys. cons. dept. medicine, 1959-68; sys. cons. Jet Propulsion Lab., Pasadena, 1964-68; mem. coun. Realtors Coun. Comml. and Investment Brokers. Author: Statistics for Medical Students, 1951, Combustion Processes/Liquid Rocket Engring., 1968; contbr. articles to profl. jours.; patentee in field. Committeeman Libertarian Party, San Fernando Valley, Calif., 1966, Rep. Party, Mission Hills, 1967-68; dir. realtor's com. on the air quality mgmt. plan So. Calif. Air Quality Control Dist., treas. realtor com. for air quality, 1994-95, vice chmn., 1996; pres. San Fernando Rep. Club, 1967-68; dir., mem. exec. com. Los Angeles County Bd. Realtors. Office: Acquisition 14800 Alexander St Mission Hills CA 91345-1210 *We, the children of the universe - glorify this relationship.To the laws of nature and the universe - we are accountable.Let us earn our bread each day.Let us admit to our ignorance - that we may learn.Let us hide, neither from ignorance nor accountability - that we may survive.*

CRAMER, HAROLD, lawyer; b. Phila., June 16, 1927; s. Aaron Harry and Blanche (Greenberg) C.; m. Geraldine Hassuk, July 14, 1957; 1 dau., Patricia Gail. AB, Temple U., 1948; LLB cum laude, U. Pa., 1951. Bar: Pa. 1951. Law clk. to judge Common Pleas Ct. No. 2, 1953; mem. law faculty U. Pa., 1954; assoc. firm Shapiro, Rosenfeld, Stalberg & Cook, 1955-56, ptnr., 1956-67; ptnr. Mesirov, Gelman, Jaffe & Levin, 1967-74, Mesirov, Gelman, Jaffe & Cramer, Phila., 1974-77; ptnr. Mesirov, Gelman, Jaffe, Cramer & Jamieson, Phila., 1977-89, of counsel, 1996—; CEO Grad. Health System, Phila., 1989-96; instr. Nat. Inst. Trial Advocacy, 1970—; pres. Jewish Exponent, 1987-89, Times., 1987-89. Co-author: Trial Advocacy, 1968; contbr. articles to profl. jours. Chmn. bd. Eastern Pa. Psychiat. Hosp., 1974-81, Grad. Hosp., 1975-91; trustee Fedn. Jewish Agys., Jewish Publ. Soc., pres., 1996-98. 1st lt. U.S. Army, 1951-53. Decorated Bronze Star. Fellow Am. Bar Found.; mem. ABA, Am. Law Inst., Pa. Bar Assn. (ho. of dels. 1966-75, 78—, bd. govs. 1975-78), Phila. Bar Found. (pres. 1988, trustee, pres. elect), Phila. Bar Assn. (bd. govs. 1967-69, chmn. 1969, vice chancellor 1970, chancellor 1972, editor The Shingle 1970-72), U. Pa. Law Alumni Soc. (bd. mgrs. 1959-64, pres. 1968-70), Order of Coif (past chpt. pres., nat. exec. com. 1973-76), Tau Epsilon Rho (chancellor Phila. grad. chpt. 1960-62), Philmont Country Club, Pyramid Club. Home: 728 Pine St Philadelphia PA 19106-4005 Office: Mesirov Gelman Jaffe Cramer & Jamieson 1735 Market St Ste 38 Philadelphia PA 19103-7501

CRAMER, HOWARD ROSS, geologist, environmental consultant; b. Chgo., Sept. 17, 1925; s. Don William and Esther Natalia (Johnson) C.; m. Ardis V. Lahann, Dec. 15, 1950 (dec. 1980); m. Themis Poulos, Dec. 5, 1982. B.S. (with honors), U. Ill., 1949, M.S., 1950; Ph.D., Northwestern U., 1954. Registered geologist, Ga. Mem. faculty Franklin and Marshall Coll., 1953-58; asst. prof. geology Emory U., Atlanta, 1958-62, assoc. prof., 1962-76, prof., 1976-87, chmn. dept., 1981-87; cons. geology Ga. State U., Atlanta, 1988-91; chmn. Ga. Bd. Registration Geologists, 1977-79; mem. Ga. Natural Areas Council, 1968-72. Contbr. articles to sci. jours., chpts. to books on geology. Served with AUS, 1943-46, to lt. USAR, 1948-53. Decorated Bronze Star; recipient Holgate prize Northwestern U., 1953, Cert. Commendation, Am. Assn. State and Local History, 1974, Honor award Am. Fedn. Mineralogy and Lapidary Socs., 1986. Fellow Geol. Soc. Am.; mem. Am. Assn. Petroleum Geologists, Paleontol. Soc., Nat. Assn. Geology Tchrs. (pres. Southeastern sect. 1971-73), Ga. Acad. Sci. (pres. 1964-65), Lambda Chi Alpha. Greek Orthodox. Lodge: Ahepa. Home: 2047 Deborah Dr NE Atlanta GA 30345-3917

CRAMER, JAMES PERRY, management consultant, publisher; b. Aberdeen, S.D., Aug. 7, 1947; s. Harry John and Carol B. (Bickel) C.; m. Corinne M. Aaker, Dec. 21, 1969; children: Ryan James, Austin Michael. BS, No. State U., Aberdeen, 1969; MA, St. Thomas U., St. Paul, 1974; planning cert., U. Minn., Mpls., 1976; bus. mgmt. cert., Wharton Sch. Bus., U. Pa., 1987. Dir., teaching faculty U. Minn., Mpls., 1974-76; dir. St. Louis Park Community Svcs., Minn., 1976-78; exec. v.p. Minn. Soc. Architects, Mpls., 1978-82; pres., chief exec. officer AIA Svc. Corp., Washington, 1982-86, also bd. regents; pres. Greenway Comms. Inc., 1994—; pres. Am. Archtl. Found. and Octagon Mus., Washington, 1986-89; CEO AIA, Washington, 1989-94; group pub. Architecture Mag., 1982-88, pub. chmn., 1990-94; with Archtl. Tech. Mag., 1983-89; chmn. The Greenway Group; pres. Greenway Comm. Inc., 1994—. Pres. Coun. Archtl. Components, Washington, 1980-81; pres. Greenway Civic Assn., McLean, Va., 1986-88; trustee Nat. Bldg. Mus., Washington, 1989-94; chmn. Washington div. United Way Assn., 1992; White House liaison, 1988-95. Recipient Disting. Alumnus award No. State U., 1992, medal of Distinction, U. Minn., 1994; Richard Upjohn fellow. Mem. AIA (hon.; chmn. 1981-82, chief exec. officer 1989—, Spl. award 1982), Am. Soc. Assn. Execs. (cert. assn. exec.), Mag. Pubs. Am., Octagon Soc. (life hon.), Am. Archtl. Found. (life; pres. 1986-89, regent 1981-82, 86—), Am. Design Coun. (founder, bd. dirs. 1988-95), Soc. Archtl. Historians (bd. dirs. 1994-97), Design Futures Coun. (chmn. 1994—). Avocations: gardening, tennis, antiquarian books, design. Home: 2320 Littlebrooke Dr Dunwoody GA 30338-3156 Office: Ste 200 30 Technology Pkwy South Norcross GA 30092

CRAMER, JOHN GLEASON, JR., physics educator, experimental physicist; b. Houston, Oct. 24, 1934; s. John Gleason and Frances Ann (Sakwitz) C.; m. Pauline Ruth Bond, June 2, 1961; children: Kathryn Elizabeth, John Gleason III, Karen Melissa. B.A., Rice U., 1957, M.A., 1959, Ph.D. in Physics, 1961. Postdoctoral fellow Ind. U., Bloomington, 1961-63, asst. prof., 1963-64; asst. prof. physics U. Wash., Seattle, 1964-68, assoc. prof., 1968-74, prof., 1974—, dir. nuclear physics lab., 1983-90; guest prof. W. Ger. Bundesministerium and U. Munich, 1971-72; mem. program adv. com. Los Alamos Meson Physics Facility, Los Alamos Nat. Lab., 1976-78, Nat. Superconducting Cyclotron Lab., 1983-87, TRIUMF (U. B.C.), 1985-88; program adviser-cons. Lawrence Berkeley Lab., Calif., 1979-82; mem. exec. coun. STAR Collaboration, 1991—, CERN Experiments NA 35 and NA 49, 1991—; guest prof. Hahn-Meitner Inst., West Berlin, 1982-83, Max-Planck-Inst. für Physik, Munich, Germany, 1994-95. Author: Twistor, 1989, Einstein's Bridge, 1997; columnist Analog Mag., 1983—; contbr. articles to physics and popular publs. Fellow AAAS, Am. Phys. Soc. (mem. panel on pub. affairs 1998—). Home: 7002 51st Ave NE Seattle WA 98115-6132 Office: U Wash Dept Physics PO Box 351560 Seattle WA 98195-1560 *When I was in about the eighth grade of junior high school I made the most important discovery of my life. I discovered that, for some reason, society was willing to pay respectable salaries to a certain group of people for doing what I would gladly do for free. These people were research scientists, and what they did was to discover how the universe really worked. From that point on I channeled all my effort into joining this select group, and I have been having a wonderful time ever since.*

CRAMER, JOHN MCNAIGHT, lawyer; b. Lewistown, Pa., Sept. 23, 1941; s. John Mumma and Elaine Elizabeth (McNaight) C.; m. Susan Oakman, Nov. 26, 1966 (div. Mar. 1989); children: Natalie, Daniel, Melinda; m. Kay Stephenson, Apr. 8, 1989; children: Julia, Maria. AB, Juniata Coll., 1963; LLB, Harvard Law Sch., 1966. Bar: Pa. 1968. Law clk. U.S. Dist. Ct. So. Dist. N.Y., 1966-67; assoc. Reed Smith Shaw & McClay, Pitts., 1967-76, ptnr., 1976—; advocacy fellow Dickinson Sch. Law, Pa. State U., Carlisle, Pa., 1987—. Mem. editorial staff: Harvard Law Rev. Trustee Juniata Coll., Huntingdon, Pa., 1981—, sec., 1983-96, vice chair 1996-97, chair, 1997—; bd. dirs. South Ctrl. Pa. Food Bank, 1996—. Mem. ABA, Pa. Bar Assn.,

Dauphin County Bar Assn., Cumberland County Bar Assn., Tuesday Club. Democrat. Presbyterian. Home: Box 17 Old Trail Rd New Buffalo PA 17069 Office: Reed Smith Shaw & McClay PO Box 11844 213 Market St Harrisburg PA 17108

CRAMER, JOHN SANDERSON, health care executive; b. Butte, Mont., Feb. 22, 1942; s. John Dale and Angela Rita (Sanderson) C.; m. Ellen E. McGrath, Apr. 15, 1968; children: Jennifer, Jon. BBA in Small Bus. Adminstrn., Adelphi U., 1964; MBA in Hosp. Adminstrn., George Washington U., 1969. Asst. to assocs. John G. Steinle and Assocs., Garden City, N.Y., 1960-64, jr. assoc., 1964-67, assoc., 1969-70; adminstrv. resident Harrisburg (Pa.) Hosp., 1968-69, asst. dir., 1970-73, dir. planning, 1973-78; v.p. corp. planning Capital Health System, Harrisburg, 1978-84, sr. v.p. corp. planning, 1984-88, pres., chief exec. officer, 1988-95; pres., CEO Pinnacle Health Sys., Harrisburg, 1996—. Author: (with others) Organizational Theory, Cases and Applications, 1990. Mem. Coun. for Pub. Edn.; Harrisburg, 1991-97; bd. dirs. Harrisburg Symphony Assn., 1992-95, mem. long range planning com., 1992-93; mem. adv. com. Harrisburg Acad., 1992-96; mem. Greater Harrisburg YWCA Adv. Com., 1994—; mem. Pa. Health Care Cost Containment Coun., 1993-97. Recipient Businessman of Yr. award City of Harrisburg, 1992. Fellow Am. Coll. Healthcare Execs. (Sr. Level award 1998); mem. Am. Hosp. Assn. (charter mem., soc. for healthcare planning and mktg., bd. dirs. 1990-93, nat. recognition award 1985, Pa. del., mem. regional policy bd. 2 1995-98), Hosp. and Health Sys. Assn. Pa. (blue ribbon vision 2000 panel 1990, bd. dirs. 1991-97, mem. exec. com., chmn. strategic planning com. 1993, 94, 98, ann. creative energy award 1981, chmn. bd. dirs. 1996, immediate past chmn. 1997, HAPAC/HAPAC fed. bd. dirs. 1994-97, mem. hosp. assoc. trust 1995, mem. policy rev. group 1990-91, chmn. policy rev. group 1995, mem. statewide med. assistance steering com. 1990-91, mem. nominating com. 1990), Health Alliance Pa. (bd. dirs. 1995—), Inst. Healthy Communities (bd. dirs. 1998—), Susquehanna Alliance (bd. dirs. 1998—), Vol. Hosps. Pa. (sec. 1991-93, bd. dirs. 1988—, officer, mem. exec. com. 1992—, membership com. 1997—, Judge Marriott Svc. Excellence award 1997), Capital Area C. of C. (bd. dirs. 1993-95), Capital Region Econ. Devel. Corp. (ambassador 1994—, bd. dirs. 1994-98), Colonial Country Club, Tuesday Club, Country Club of Harrisburg. Avocations: travel, reading, classical music, golf, hiking.

CRAMER, JOHN SCOTT, retired banker; b. Charlotte, N.C., Dec. 10, 1930; s. Stuart Warren Jr. and Julia (Scott) C.; m. Nancy Arnott, Aug. 9, 1952; children: Julia Baxter Smith, Alice Arnott Tolson. AB, U. N.C., 1953. With Wachovia Bank & Trust Co., Charlotte, 1955—; asst. v.p. Wachovia Bank & Trust Co., CHarlotte, 1958-61, v.p., 1961-64, sr. v.p., bd. mgrs., 1964-71; exec. v.p., head banking div. Wachovia Bank & Trust Co., Winston-Salem, N.C., 1971-74; vice chmn. bd., head fiduciary div. Wachovia Bank & Trust Co., Winston-Salem, 1974-88; also bd. dirs. Wachovia Bank & Trust Co., ret., 1989; vice chmn. bd., bd. dir. The Wachovia Corp., ret., 1989; exec. v.p. First Wachovia Corp., 1986, ret., 1989; pres. First Wachovia Trust Services, Inc., 1987-89, ret., 1989; dir. Linville Resorts, Inc. Trustee N. C. Sch. of the Arts, Salem Acad. and Coll., N.C. chpt. Nature Conservancy; active other civic, edn. and svc. orgns. Mem. Linville Golf Club (N.C.), Old Town Club, Twin City Club, Sigma Alpha Epsilon. Home: 16 Graylyn Pl Winston Salem NC 27106 Office: 420 A-2 West 4th St Winston Salem NC 27101

CRAMER, LAURA SCHWARZ, realtor; b. St. Louis, Aug. 13, 1925; d. Frederick William and Gertrude Margaret (Kipp) Schwarz; AB, Duke U., 1947; MA, Washington U., St. Louis, 1948; m. Robert R. Cramer, Oct. 29, 1949; children: Anne Randolph, Carol Parker, Laura Forster. Model, John Robert Powers Agy., N.Y.C., 1946; grad. asst. dept. psychology Washington U., St. Louis, 1947-48, instr., 1948-49; psychometrist Clayton (Mo.) pub. schs., 1961; dir. testing Columbia Sch., Rochester, N.Y., 1964-71; asst. registrar and counselor for women students St. John Fisher Coll., Rochester, N.Y., 1971-72, registrar, dean of women, 1972-76; sales exec. Sea Pines Real Estate Co., Hilton Head Island, S.C., 1976—; registered rep. Sea Pines Securities, 1983-88. Bd. dirs. Vol. Svc. Bur., St. Louis, 1960-61, Monroe County Hosp. Aux., 1974-76, St. Louis Cmty. Music Sch., 1959-61, Vol. Ctr., Hilton Head Island, 1992-–, chmn. 1998—; cmty. adv. bd. Hilton Head Hosp., 1995—; bd. dirs. St. Louis Inst., chmn., 1960; bd. visitors Hilton Head Prep. Sch, 1989-93; bd. dirs. Hilton Head Coll. Ctr., 1994—, Hilton Head Island Beach and Shore Commn., 1994—. Bd. dirs. United Way of Beaufort County, 1998—; trustee Tech. Coll. of Low Country Found., 1999—. Jesse M. Barr fellow, 1947-48; named Leading Sales Exec., 1981, 84, 86, 88, Leading Listing Exec., 1982, 83, 85, 86, 87, 88, 89. Mem. Hilton Head Island Bd. Realtors (Million Dollar Club, life), Jr. League Savannah, Phi Beta Kappa, Sigma Xi. Home: 9 Brown Pelican Rd Hilton Head Island SC 29928-5615 Office: Sea Pines Plantation Co Hilton Head Island SC 29928

CRAMER, MICHAEL WILLIAM, insurance executive; b. London, Feb. 14, 1924; came to U.S., 1939; s. William and Belle (Klauber) C.; m. Martha Lorena Deckman, Jan. 20, 1951; 1 child, Bruce Edward. BSBA, Washington U., St. Louis, 1947. CLU. Clk., group claims Gen. Am. Life Ins. Co., St. Louis, 1947-51; inventory control clk. Fred Campbell Auto Supply Co., St. Louis, 1951-55; sales and planning rep. Equitable Life Assurance Soc., St. Louis, 1955—. Active St. Louis Artists Guild, 1990; pres. Permanent Endowment Found., 1991-94, chmn. spl. funds com., 1994—, pres. council 1995—; bd. dirs. City of Univ. City (Mo.) C. of C. Recipient Distinguished Award of Merit for Keystone Dist., Greater St. Louis Coun., Boy Scouts Am., 1996. Mem. Life Underwriters Assn. St. Louis (bd. dirs. 1972-78, award 1987, nominee Life Underwriter of Yr. 1994), Estate Planning Coun. St. Louis, Assn. CLU and ChFC (bd. dirs. St. Louis chpt., chmn. student sponsorship com. through 1993, Meritorious Svc. award 1993), IW Club Varsity Athletics Alumni Washington U. (mem. exec. com. 1991—). Avocations: travel, hiking, photography, stamps, music. Home: 718 Audubon Dr Saint Louis MO 63105-2906 Office: 8182 Maryland Ave Ste 1000 Saint Louis MO 63105-3916

CRAMER, OWEN CARVER, classics educator; b. Tampa, Fla., Dec. 1, 1941; s. Maurice Browning and Alice (Carver) C.; m. Rebecca Jane Lowrey, June 23, 1962; children: Alfred, Thomas, Ethan, Benjamin. AB, Oberlin Coll., 1962; PhD, U. Tex., 1973. Spl. instr. U. Tex., Austin, 1964-65; instr. in classics Colo. Coll., Colorado Springs, 1965-69, asst. prof. classics, 1969-75, assoc. prof. classics, 1975-84, M.C. Gile prof. classics, 1984—, dir. comparative lit., 1993—; cons. humanist Colo. Humanities Program, Denver, 1982-83; vis. prof. U. Chgo., 1987-88; reader Advanced Placement Latin Exam., 1995—. Editorial asst. Arion, 1964-65; contbr. papers, articles on Greek lang. and lit. to profl. publs., 1974—; contbr. classical music revs. to Colorado Springs Sun, 1984-86. Chorus tenor Colo. Opera Festival, Colorado Springs, 1976-82; mem. El Paso County Dem. Ctrl. Com., Colo., 1968-88; ordained elder Presbyn. Ch., 1992. Hon. Woodrow Wilson fellow, 1962; univ. fellow U. Tex., Austin, 1962-64. Mem. Am. Philol. Assn. (campus adv. svc. 1989—, chmn. com. on smaller depts. 1979-80), Am. Comparative Lit. Assn., Classical Assn. Middle West and South, Modern Greek Studies Assn., Colo. Classics Assn., Round Table (Colorado Springs) Club,. Phi Beta Kappa. Home: 747 E Uintah St Colorado Springs CO 80903-2546 Office: Colo Coll Dept Classics Colorado Springs CO 80903

CRAMER, PHEBE, psychologist; b. San Francisco, Dec. 30, 1935; children: Mara, Julia. BA, U. Calif., Berkeley, 1957; PhD, NYU, 1962. Clin. psychologist Malmonides Hosp., Bklyn., 1962-63; asst. prof. Psychology Barnard Coll., N.Y.C., 1963-65; vis. asst. prof. Psychology U. Calif., Berkeley, 1965-70; assoc. prof. Psychology Williams Coll., Williamstown, Mass., 1970-73, prof. Psychology, 1973—; pvt. practice in clin. psychology, Williamstown, 1970—; chief psychologist Berkshire Mental Health Ctr., Pittsfield, Mass., 1978-86. Author: (books) Word Association, 1968, Understanding Intellectual Development, 1972, The Development of Defense Mechanisms, 1991, Story-telling, Narrative, and the Thematic Apperception Test, 1996; mem. editl. bd. Jour. of Personality, 1987-96, assoc. editor, 1991-96; mem. editl. bd. Jour. of Personality Assessment, 1989—. Judge U.S. Figure Skating Assn., 1989—. Mem. APA, Soc. For Personality Assessment. Office: Williams Coll Dept Psychology Bronfman Sci Ctr Williamstown MA 01267 Home: 20 Forest Rd Williamstown MA 01267-2029

CRAMER, RICHARD CHARLES, artist, educator; b. Appleton, Wis., Aug. 14, 1932; s. Joseph S. and Mildred (Kuck) C.; m. Carol Markel, Apr. 4, 1970. B.F.A., Layton Sch. Art, 1954; B.S., U. Wis.-Milw., 1960; M.S., U. Wis., Madison, 1961, M.F.A., 1962. Art instr. U.S. Army Spl. Services, Ft. Huachuca, Ariz., 1955-57; grad. instr. U. Wis., Madison, 1960-62; asst. prof. art Elmira Coll., N.Y., 1962-66; prof. painting Tyler Sch. Art, Temple U., Phila., 1966—; vis. artist SUNY-Oswego, 1982, U. Wis.-Milw., 1982, Washington U., St. Louis, 1986, U. N.Mex., Albuquerque, 1989. One-man shows Arnot Art Mus., Elmira, N.Y., 1964, Pa. Acad. Fine Arts, Ohila., 1978, New Gallery Contemporary Art, Cleve., 1980, Eric Makler Gallery, Phila., 1981, GHJ, N.Y.C., 1983, Space 504 N.Y.C., 1997; exhibited in group shows Contemporary Drawings, Phila. Mus. Art, 1979, Smithsonian, Inst. traveling exhibit, 1979, Phila. Coll. Art, 1980, Inst. Contemporary Art, Boston, 1981, Cranbrook Acad. Art Mus., 1981, Louis Meisel Gallery, N.Y.C., 1985, Steinbaum Krauss Gallery, N.Y.C., 1994, Glasgow (Scotland) Sch. Art, 1995. Recipient prize Munson-Williams Proctor Inst., 1965. Mem. AAUP, Coll. Art Assn. Home: Apt 5E 283 W 11th St New York NY 10014-2487 Office: Temple U Tyler Sch Art Beech And Penrose Ave Philadelphia PA 19126

CRAMER, ROBERT E., JR. (BUD CRAMER), congressman; b. Huntsville, AL, Aug. 22, 1947. BA, U. Ala., 1969, JD, 1972. Former dist. atty.; mem. 102nd-105th Congresses from 5th Dist. Ala., 1990—; mem. appropriations com. U.S. Ho. of Reps., subcom. on HUD, VA and IA, on the Interior. Democrat. Methodist. Office: US House of Reps 2350 Rayburn Bldg Washington DC 20515-0105

CRAMER, ROBERT VERN, retired college administrator, consultant; b. Fayetteville, Ark., Jan. 6, 1933; s. Paul and Fern (Way); m. M. Joan Sullivan, Sept. 6, 1953; children: Paula Jo, Melinda Kay, John Aaron. BA, Monmouth Coll., Ill., 1954; MA, U. Conn., 1964, PhD, 1965; LHD (hon.), Ill. Coll., 1985, Carroll Coll., 1988. Tchr. Monmouth Jr. High Sch., 1954-56; prin. Vandalia Elem. Sch., Ill., 1956-57; dir. publicity and publs. Monmouth Coll., 1957-59; dir. publs. and pub. information, also instr. journalism Millikin U., Decatur, Ill., 1959-61; v.p. Old Sturbridge Village, Mass., 1961-64; asst. dean, instr. Sch. Edn., U. Conn., 1964-65; v.p. Hanover Coll., Ind., 1965-68; pres. Northland Coll., Ashland, Wis., 1968-71; pres. Carroll Coll., Waukesha, Wis., 1971-88, pres. emeritus, 1988—; pres. Brunswick Pub. Charitable Found., Inc., Skokie, Ill., 1985-88; v.p. Wis. Found. Ind. Colls., 1969-71, pres., 1971-73, treas., 1973-76, sec., 1979-83; commr. Commn. Instns. Higher Edn., North Central Assn., 1972-76; v.p. Wis. Assn. Ind. Colls. and Univs., 1973-75, pres., 1985-87; bd. dirs. Payco Am. Corp., 1988-91; Council Ind. Colls, sec. 1979-88, vice chmn., 1981-83, chmn. 1983-85. Contbr. articles to profl. jours. Bd. dirs. Waukesha United Way, 1975-78, Waukesha Symphony, 1972-76, Waukesha Meml. Hosp., 1973-82, Lad Lake Residential Treatment Ctr. for Emotionally Disturbed Boys, 1974-78, Wis. Coun. on Econ. Edn., 1976-79; bd. dirs. Milw. chpt. ARC, 1973-81, vice chmn., 1978-80; mem. nexus com. Presbyn. Coll. Union, 1973-83; bd. dirs. Am. Coun. Edn., 1985-88; sec. Presbyn. Coll. Union, 1977-79, pres., 1979-81; trustee Columbia Coll. of Nursing, 1983-88, Hist. Preservation Soc. Durham, 1993-94; active Durham County Nursing Home Adv. Com., 1991-95, commr. Durham Hist. Preservation Com., 1992-97, Glaxo Welcome Instnl. Animal Care and Use Com., 1992—. Recipient Outstanding Young Alumnus award Monmouth Coll., 1968, Disting. Alumni award, 1980; named Ky. Col., 1975. Mem. Wis. Assn. Higher Edn. (exec. com., sec. 1972-73, pres. 1973-74), Delta Sigma Nu, Phi Delta Kappa, Theta Chi.

CRAMER, ROXANNE HERRICK, gifted and talented education educator; b. Albion, Mich., Apr. 24; d. Donald F. and Kathryn L. (Beery) Herrick; m. James Loveday Hofford, Jan. 29, 1955 (div.); children: William Herrick, Dana Webster, Paul Christopher; m. Harold Leslie Cramer, Apr. 20, 1967. Student, U. Mich., 1952-55; BA, U. Toledo, 1956; EdM, Harvard U., 1967; EdD, Va. Poly. Inst. and State U., 1990. Tchr. Wayland (Mass.) Pub. Schs., 1966-70, Fairfax County (Va.) Pub. Schs., 1970—; tchr./team leader Gifted and Talented program, 1975—; coordinating instr. Trinity Coll., Washington, 1978; nat. coord. gifted children programs Am. Mensa, Ltd., 1981-84. Editor newsletter Va. Assn. for the Edn. of Gifted, 1989-90; contbr. articles to profl. jours. Mem. NEA, Nat. Assn. Gifted Children, Fairfax County Assn. for the Gifted, Coalition for Advancement Gifted Edn. (bd. dirs. 1982-84), World Coun. Gifted and Talented Children, Intertel Found., Inc. (bd. dirs. 1986—), chmn. Hollingworth award com. 1984—, Fairfax County Assn. Gifted, Nat. Assn. Gifted Children, Va. Edn. Assn., Fairfax Edn. Assn., Mensa, Harvard Club, Phi Delta Kappa. Home: 4300 Sideburn Rd Fairfax VA 22030-3507 Office: Louise Archer Gifted Ctr 324 Nutley St NW Vienna VA 22180-4213

CRAMER, STANLEY HOWARD, psychology educator, author; b. N.Y.C., Oct. 1, 1933; s. Louis and Sophie (Zimmerman) C.; m. Rosalind Faber, Nov. 26, 1959; children: Elizabeth, Lauren, Matthew. BA, U. Mass., 1955; MA, SUNY, Albany, 1957; EdD, Columbia U., 1963. Prof. counseling psychology SUNY at Buffalo, Amherst, 1965—. Author: (with E.L. Herr) Critical Issues in the Helping Professions, 1987, Career Guidance and Counseling Through the Lifespan, 1972, 5th edit., 1996, (with J.C. Hansen and R.H. Rossberg) Counseling: Theory and Process, 1994. Mem. Am. Counseling Assn., Am. Psychol. Assn. Home: 39 Northwood Dr Lancaster NY 14043-4551 Office: SUNY Buffalo 423 Christopher Baldy Hall Amherst NY 14260

CRAMER, WALTER ELWOOD, II, educational administrator; b. Lancaster, Pa., Feb. 3, 1950; s. Walter Elwood and Evelyn Mae (Heiserman) C.; m. Mary Benson Greene, June 19, 1982; children: Blanche, Rebecca, Oliver, Charles. BA in Music, U. Pitts., 1972; MusM in Music, Ind. U., 1975; postgrad., Nova Southeastern U., 1994—. Coord. for performing arts Georgetown U., Washington, 1978-80, dir. student activities, 1980-82, asst. dean of students, 1982-87; dean of students Regent's Coll., London, 1987-90; dir. student svcs. Sch. for Internat. Tng., Brattleboro, Vt., 1991—; ednl. cons. Bloomsbury Ctr., London, 1990-91. Mem. chorus The Washington Opera Co., 1977-79, Austin (Tex.) Civic Opera, 1990-91; prodr., dir., actor 40 plays, musicals, operas, 1970—. Mem. sch. bd. St. Michael's Sch., Brattleboro, 1992-95, cantor, 1992—, dir. children's choir, 1992—. Mem. Nat. Assn. Student Pers. Adminstrs., KC, Sigma Alpha Mu, Alpha Sigma Nu. Democrat. Roman Catholic. Avocations: music, baseball, gardening. Home: 1 Moss Hollow Marlboro VT 05344 Office: Sch for Internat Tng Kipling Rd Brattleboro VT 05302

CRAMER, WILLIAM ANTHONY, biochemistry and biophysics researcher, educator; b. N.Y.C., June 11, 1938; s. Robert and Sylvia (Blumstein) C.; m. Hanni Aebersold, Sept. 11, 1964; children: Rebecca, Jean-Marc, Gabrielle, Nicholas. BS, MIT, 1959; MS, U. Chgo., 1960, PhD, 1965. NSF post doctoral fellow U. Calif., San Diego, 1965-67; research assoc. U. Calif., 1967-68; asst. prof. dept. biol. scis. Purdue U., West Lafayette, Ind., 1968-73; assoc. prof. Purdue U., 1973-78, prof., 1978—, assoc. head dept., 1984-86; Henry Koffler prof. biol. scis. Purdue U., West Lafayette, Ind., 1995—; head panel predoctoral fellowships in biophysics and biochemistry NSF, 1979, mem. molecular biology panel, 1980-82, mem. cellular biochemistry panel, 1989-91; mem. panel competitive grants USDA, 1983-84; chmn. Gordon Confs. on Photosynthesis, 1990, Bioenergetics, 2001; mem. phys. biochemistry study sect. NIH, 1991-95. Author textbook on bioenergetics; editor: Archives Biochemistry and Biophysics, 1979-91, Biochim. Biophys. Acta, 1983—, Photosynthesis Rsch., 1989-98, Jour. Bioenergetics Biomembranes, 1991—, Biophys. Jour., 1999—; contbr. articles to profl. jours. Recipient Rsch. Career Devel. awrd NIH, 1970-75, H.N.McCoy award for sci. achievement Purdue U., 1988, Charles F. Kettering award Am. Soc. Plant Physiologists, 1996; EMBO fellow U. Amsterdam, 1974-75, Alexander von Humboldt fellow Max-Planck Inst., Frankfurt, 1992, John Simon Guggenheim fellow, 1992-93. Mem. Am. Soc. Biol. Chemists, Protein Soc., Biophys. Soc. (chmn. bioenergetics subgroup 1989-92, organizing com. "Biophys. Discussions" 1992, program chair 40th annual meeting 1996, coun. 1997-01, exec. coun. 1999-01, rep. Fedn. Am. Socs. Exptl. Biology com. ethical issues genetic rsch. 1998, pub. policy com. 1999-01). Office: Purdue U Dept Biol Sci Lilly Hall of Life Sciences West Lafayette IN 47907

CRAMPTON, ESTHER LARSON, sociology and political science educator; b. Plainview, Nebr., Apr. 14, 1915; d. Charles W. and Anna Margrethe (Staugaard) Larson; m. Francis Asbury Crampton, Jan. 19, 1949 (dec.); children: Jacqueline, Edith. AB, Colo. Coll. of Edn., 1935; MA, U. Wis., 1937; PhD, Am. U., 1972. Observer, writer U.S. Weather Bur., Washington, 1942-48; interpreter Portuguese RFC Rubber Devel. Corp., Manaos, Brasil, 1943; tchr. Latin Glenn County High Sch., Willows, Calif., 1954-57; tchr. Latin/German Scottsdale (Ariz.) High Sch., 1957-62; tchr. Latin Natrona County High Sch., Casper, Wyo., 1962-64; tchr. social studies Bourgade High Sch., Phoenix, 1964-65; substitute tchr. Phoenix High Sch., 1965-66; instr. supr. We. N.Mex. U. Lab. Sch., Silver City, 1966-67; prof. sociology and polit. sci. Cochise C.C., Douglas, Ariz., 1967-77. Editor: Lily, Chinese Notes of the Late Frank Crampton, 1888-1961, 1990; copyright owner Deep Enough by Frank Crampton. Sec., v.p., bd. dirs. Easter Seal Soc. of Santa Cruz, 1979-81; active Nat. Women's Polit. Caucus Br., Santa Cruz, 1979; tutor reading Literacy Coun., San Luis Obispo, 1988. Grantee Amazonia Rsch. Orgn. of Am. States, 1970, Am. Coun. of Learned Socs., 1941. Mem. AAUW (chair 1977-81, internat. rels. group Santa Cruz br. mem.-at-large 1981—), Am. Assn. Women in Cmty. and Jr. Colls. (charter mem.). Avocations: Amazonia, genealogical research.

CRAMPTON, GEORGE HARRIS, neuroscientist, retired army officer; b. Spokane, Wash., Nov. 20, 1926. BS, Wash. State U., 1949, MS, 1950; PhD, U. Rochester, 1954. Enlisted U.S. Army Res., 1944; advanced through grades to col. U.S. Army M.S.C., 1969; ret. U.S. Army, 1971; prof. Wright State U., Dayton, Ohio, 1971-86, prof. emeritus, 1987—. Recipient Legion of Merit. Mem. Soc. for Neurosci. Home: 790 SW Dawnview Ter Oak Harbor WA 98277-8145

CRAMPTON, SCOTT PAUL, lawyer; b. Cleve., Sept. 1, 1913; s. Paul Scott and Mary Runnels (Fayram) C.; m. Harriet Yenne, Jan. 12, 1963; children: Don Paul, Scott Charles, Susan Runnels, Lucinda Lommasson Hanchin, Louis Harlan Lommasson. B.A. cum laude, Am. U., 1935; LL.B., George Washington U., 1939. Bar: D.C. 1938. Practiced with firm George E.H. Goodner, Washington, 1939-51; ptnr. firm Prince, Taylor & Crampton, Washington, 1951-61, Worth & Crampton, Washington, 1961-71; asst. atty. gen. tax div. U.S. Dept. Justice, Washington, 1971-76; ptnr. firm Hamel, Park, McCabe & Saunders, Washington, 1976-79; of counsel firm Bogan & Freeland, Washington, 1979-83; ptnr. Macdonald, McInerny, Guandolo, Jordan & Crampton, Washington, 1983-87; of counsel McCarthy & Durrette, Washington, 1987-88, Lalos & Keegan, Washington, 1988-92, Miller, Hamilton, Snider, Odom & Bridgeman, Washington, 1992-94; pvt. practice Washington, 1994—. Mem. ABA (past chmn. sect. taxation 1969-70), Met. Club (Washington), Kiwanis, Phi Alpha Delta. Home: 11701 River Dr Lorton VA 22079-4104 Office: 1815 H St NW Washington DC 20006-3604

CRAMPTON, STUART JESSUP BIGELOW, physicist, educator; b. N.Y.C., Nov. 3, 1936; s. Henry Edward and Harriet Elizabeth (Jessup) C.; m. Susan Harris, Dec. 29, 1961; children: David Stuart Jessup, Rebecca Lynn, Alexandra Lee. B.A., Williams Coll., 1958; B.A. with honors, Worcester Coll., Oxford (Eng.) U., 1960, M.A., 1965; Ph.D., Harvard U., 1964. NSF postdoctoral fellow Harvard U., 1964-65; mem. faculty Williams Coll., 1965—, prof. physics, 1975—, Barclay Jermain prof. natural philosophy, 1979—, chmn. dept. physics, 1970-77, chmn. dept. physics and astronomy, 1977-80; dir. Bronfman Sci. Ctr., 1988-90; vis. prof. U. Paris VI, 1982-83; bd. dirs. Rsch. Corp.; former cons. Hughes Rsch. Labs.; vice chair Coun. on Undergrad. Rsch., 1988-89, chair 89-90, pres. 1990-91; cons. Sherman Fairchild Scientific Equipment Program, Westat Inc.; mem. bd. assessment physics labs. Nat. Inst. Stds. & Tech., 1994—; provost Williams Coll., 1995-99. Author papers in field. Recipient NSF Faculty Profl. Devel. award, 1977-78; NATO sr. postdoctoral research fellow, 1975; grantee Nat. Bur. Standards; grantee NSF; grantee Office Naval Research; grantee NASA. Fellow Am. Phys. Soc. (councillor-at-large 1989-92, award for rsch. at undergrad. instn. 1989); mem. Am. Assn. Physics Tchrs., Sigma Xi, Sigma Phi. Episcopalian. Home: 54 Grandview Dr Williamstown MA 01267-2528 Office: Williams Coll Bronfman Sci Ctr Williamstown MA 02167

CRANDALL, DAVID LEROY, research scientist; b. Creston, Iowa, Sept. 1, 1952; s. Robert Miles and Margaret (Duncan) C.; m. Sarah Jane Scholl, June 12, 1982; children: Andrew, Elizabeth. B.S., Tulane U., 1974; M.S., Iowa State U., 1977, Ph.D., 1979. Research fellow Emory U., 1979-81; sr. research scientist Am. Cyanamid Co., Pearl River, N.Y., 1981-95, prin. scientist Wyeth Res., Princeton, N.J., 1995—; adj. asst. prof. dept medicine, SUNY; vis. lectr. N.Y. Med. Coll., Vahalla, 1985—; adj. asst. prof. SUNY Downstste Med. Ctr., 1987-88. Mem. editl. bd. Jour. Pharmacol. Exptl. Therapy; contbr. articles on biochem. and physiol. adaptations to obesity to profl. jours.; mem. editorial bd. Am. Jour. Physiology, Jour. Pharmacology. Bd. dirs. Union County Baseball League, Afton, Iowa, 1970-73. Mem. Am. Physiol. Soc., Am. Soc. Pharmacol. and Exptl. Therapy, Eastern Hypertension Soc., Sigma Xi. Roman Catholic. Avocations: jogging, golfing. Home: 181 Sunset View Dr Doylestown PA 18901-2762 Office: Wyeth Rsch CN 8000 Princeton NJ 08543

CRANDALL, IRA CARLTON, consulting electrical engineer; b. South Amboy, N.J., Oct. 30, 1931; s. Carlton Francis and Claire Elizabeth (Harned) C.; m. Jane Leigh Ford, Jan. 29, 1954; children—Elizabeth Anne, Amy Leigh, Matthew Garrett. BS in Radio Engring., Ind. Inst. Tech., 1954, BS in Elec. Engring., 1958; BS in Electronics Engring., U.S. Naval Postgrad. Sch., 1962; PhD, U. Sussex, 1964; MA, Piedmont U., 1967, DSc (hon.), 1968; LLB, Blackstone Sch. Law, 1970; DLitt, St. Matthew U., 1970; EdD, Mt. Sinai U., 1972; Assoc. Bus., LaSalle U., 1975, B in Computer Sci., 1986; D. Internat. Rels., Australian Inst. for Coordinated Rsch., 1991. Tchr. Madison Twp. Pub. Schs., N.J., 1954-55; commd. ensign U.S. Navy, 1955, advanced through grades to lt. comdr., 1965, released to inactive duty, 1972; engring. cons. Concord, Calif., 1972—; pres. 7C's Enterprises, Concord, 1972-96; v.p. Dickinson Enterprises, Concord, 1972-77, Williamson Engring., Inc., Walnut Creek, Calif., 1974-82; pres., chmn. bd. I.C. Crandall and Assocs., Inc., Concord and Westminster, Calif., Tigard, Oreg., 1976-82; pres. Internat. Rsch. Assocs., Concord, 1982—; v.p. Gayner Engring. Inc., San Francisco, 1982-92; sr. engr. Ajmani Assoc., San Francisco, 1992—. Vice pres. PTA, Concord, 1969; tribal organizer Mt. Diablo YMCA Indian Guide Program, 1971-74; pres. Mt. Diablo Unified Schs. Interested Citizens. Decorated Vietnamese Cross of Valor. Fellow Am. Coll. Engrs.; mem. U.S. Naval Inst. Am. Naval Assn., Assn. Elec. Engrs., IEEE, Am. Inst. Tech. Mgmt. (sr.), Soc. Am. Mil. Engrs., Nat. Model Ry. Assn., Assn. Old Crows, Concord Homeowners Assn., Concord Chamber Singers, Concord Blue Devils, SAR, Order of the Knights (knight), Templar of Jerusalem, Lofsensic Ursinius Order (knight commdr. 1991—), Pi Upsilon Eta, Gamma Chi Epsilon, Alpha Gamma Upsilon. Republican. Methodist (adminstrv. bd. ch. 1971-76). Clubs: Navy League, Century. Lodge: Optimists (pres.). Home: 5754 Pepperridge Pl Concord CA 94521-4821 Office: PO Box 3268 Walnut Creek CA 94598-0268

CRANDALL, JOHN LYNN, insurance consultant, retired insurance company executive; b. Chgo., Apr. 17, 1927; s. Paul Bertram and Olga (Bleich) C.; m. Irene Anze Ruenne, Dec. 26, 1973; children by previous marriage: Deborah Crandall Schmude, Jeffrey, Lynne Crandall Blais; stepchildren: George Ruenne, Helgi Ruenne Zentner. BS in Fire Protection Engring., Ill. Inst. Tech., 1951. CPCU; cert. in gen. ins. Highly protected risk inspector FIA, Chgo., 1951-53, asst. engring. supr., 1953-56, engring. supr., 1956-59, underwriting supr., special agt., 1959-65; HPR engr., underwriter Kemper Group, Chgo., 1965-67, HPR sales specialist, 1967-71; asst. to dir. underwriting Protection Mutual Ins. Co., Park Ridge, Ill., 1971-73, v.p. underwriting, 1973-78, v.p., dir. underwriting, 1978-90. Served with USN, 1945-46. Mem. Soc. Fire Protection Engrs. (charter), Soc. CPCU (chpt. pres. 1980-81, nat. dir. 1987-90, ethics com. 1990-97, sr. resource com. 1997—, v.p. ch. coun., 1992-95); sec. Ch. Coun., 1995-96. Home (summer): 10 Black Oak Trl Galena IL 61036-8518 also (winter): Cypress Lakes 10000 US Highway 98 N # 913 Lakeland FL 33809-8083

CRANDALL, NELSON DAVID, III, lawyer; b. Auburn, Calif., Aug. 8, 1954; s. Nelson David and Alice (Reimer) C.; m. Elizabeth L. Donovan, Aug. 25, 1984; children: Darren J., Colin M. Student, U. Calif., Irvine, 1974-76; AB with high honors, U. Calif., Berkeley, 1976; JD, U. Calif., Davis, 1979. Bar: Calif. 1979, U.S. Dist. Ct. (no. dist.) Calif. 1979, U.S. Dist. Ct. (ea. dist.) Calif. 1980. Ptnr. Hopkins & Carley Law Corp., San Jose, Calif., 1979-94; prin. Enterprise Law Group, Inc., Menlo Park, Calif., 1994—. Contbr. articles to profl. jours. Mediator, arbitrator Santa Clara County Neighborhood Small Claims Project, San Jose, 1980-92; bd. dirs. Ctrl. Calif. region ARC Blood Svcs., 1992-94, sec., 1992-94; active Santa Clara Valley chpt. ARC, San Jose, 1986-92, sec., 1987-90; trustee Jr. Statesman Found., 1987—; bd. dirs. Hope Rehab. Svcs., San Jose, 1985-88.

Mem. ABA, Calif. Bar Assn., Santa Clara County Bar Assn., Phi Beta Kappa. Republican. Avocations: travel, photography, backpacking, reading. Office: Enterprise Law Group Inc 4400 Bohannon Dr Ste 280 Menlo Park CA 94025-1071

CRANDALL, STEPHEN HARRY, engineering educator; b. Cebu, Philippines, Dec. 2, 1920; s. William Harry and Julia Josephine (Kuenemann) C.; m. Patricia Estelle Stickel, Jan. 21, 1949; children: Jane S., William S. M.E., Stevens Inst. Tech., 1942; Ph.D., MIT, 1946. Registered profl. engr. Mem. staff radiation lab MIT, Cambridge, 1942-43; instr. math MIT, 1944-46, asst. prof. mech. engring., 1947-51, assoc. prof., 1951-58, prof., 1958—, Ford prof. engring., 1975-91, prof. emeritus, 1991—, head div. applied mechanics, 1957-59, 61-67, head. div. mechanics and materials, 1968-71; vis. prof. Marseille, France, 1960, U. Nat. Autonoma Mex., Mexico City, 1967, Ecole Nat. Superieure de Mecanique, Nantes, France, 1978, Fla. Atlantic U., 1993, Korean Advanced Inst. Sci. and Tech., 1996; exch. prof. Imperial Coll., London, 1949; NSF sci. faculty fellow, vis. scholar U. Calif., Berkeley, 1964-65; hon. rsch. assoc. Harvard U., 1971-72; Lady Davis vis. prof. Technion, Israel, 1987. Author: Engineering Analysis, 1956, Random Vibration in Mechanical Systems, 1963, (with others) Dynamics of Mechanical and Electromechanical Systems, 1968; editor: Random Vibration vol. 1, 1958, Random Vibration vol. 2, 1963, (with others) Mechanics of Solids, 1959, author (with others), 3d edit., 1978; contbr. artcles to profl. jours. Recipient ASCE Von Karman medal, 1984, Freudenthal medal, 1996, Alexander von Humboldt sr. U.S. scientist award, 1989; Fulbright fellow, London, 1949. Fellow AAAS, ASME (Worcester Reed Warner medal 1971, v.p. 1978-80, hon. mem. 1988, Timoshenko medal 1990, Den Hartog award 1991), Am. Acad. Arts and Scis., Am. Acoustical Soc. (Trent-Crede medal 1978), Am. Acad. Mechanics (pres. 1997, Disting. Svc. medal 1993); mem. NAS, NAE, NSPE, Soc. Indsl. and Applied Math., Am. Math. Soc., Am. Soc. for Engring. Edn., Internat. Union Theoretical and Applied Mechanics (chmn. U.S. del. 1974). Home: 25 Tabor Hill Rd Lincoln MA 01773-2905 Office: MIT/3-360 Dept Mech Engring Cambridge MA 02139

CRANDALL, TERRENCE LEE, counselor; b. Watertown, S.D., Feb. 15, 1951; s. Howard Lee Crandall and Laurel Lynn (Overbaugh) Havelock; m. M. Catherine Dunn, Aug. 6, 1974; children: David, Caitlin, Alexander. BS, Dakota State U., 1974; MA, U. S.D., 1979. English tchr., seventh and eighth grades Irene (S.D.) Pub. Schs., 1975-78, counselor, K-12, 1978-80; counselor, 9-12 Yankton (S.D.) Sr. High, 1980—; supr. Ednl. Testing Svc., Princeton, N.J., 1985—. Mayor City of Yankton, 1993-96; commr. Yankton City Comm., 1986-96; pres., bd. dirs. Yankton Riverboat Days, 1987—, Yankton Centennial Bd.; pres. Fed. Prison Adv. Bd., Yankton, 1988-91. Named one of Outstanding Young Men of Am., 1981, 84, 89. Mem. ACA (cert., lic. profl. counselor), Am. Mental Health Counselors Assn., S.D. Counseling Assn. (pres. 1987-88, S.D. Counselor of Yr. 1992), S.D. Mental Health Counselors, NEA (outstanding young educator 1984), K.C., Elks (Outstanding Svc. award 1988, S.D. Elk of Yr. 1995, various offices), Phi Delta Kappa. Democrat. Roman Catholic. Avocations: music, politics, sports. E-mail: tcrandall@ysd.k12.sd.us. Home: 809 E 19th St Yankton SD 57078-2426 Office: Yankton Sr High 1801 Summit Yankton SD 57078-1872

CRANDALL HOLLICK, JULIAN BERNARD HUGH, radio producer; b. Oxford, Eng., Oct. 10, 1947; came to U.S., 1977; s. Harry Bernard and Margaret Francesca (Purcell) Hollick; m. Martine Lutece Crandall, Apr. 7, 1974; children: Jerome Francois, Margot Lutece. MS, London Sch. Econs., 1975. Lectr. New U. of Ulster, Coleraine, Northern Ireland, 1976; adminstr. Ministry of Defence, London, 1976-77; freelance journalist, Boston, 1977-80; radio prodr. for NPR, CBC, BBC, WBUR, Ind. Broadcasting Assocs., Inc., Littleton, Mass., 1980—. Author, producer: (radio shows) The World of Islam, 1984, The Fall of Berlin, 1985, United Nations at 40, 1985, Passages to India, 1987, 89, Living on the Edge, 1990, Imagining America, 1990, Islam Revisited, 1991, Letters From Jitvapur, 1992, Apna Street, 1995, 97, Trespass, 1996-98, Living Islam, 1995—, (BBC) Monsoon, 1997, others; exbhn. Gamv: Life in An Indian Village, Boston, 1985-90. Grantee NEH, 1981, 85, 89, 90, 97, 98—, Rockefeller Found., 1986, Carnegie Corp., 1987, Ford Found., 1987, 89, 93, 95, 98—; recipient Corp. for Pub. Broadcasting Radio award, 1985, 91, Cindy award, 1985, 89, 91, 92, 95, 97, 98, Nat. Coun. of Christians and Jews award, 1985, Armstrong award, 1986, 90, Gabriel award, 1989, 90, Ohio State award, 1989, 90, Presdl. End Hunger award, 1990, Grand prize N.Y. Internat. Radio Festival, 1991, 93, 94, 96, 98, Commonwealth award, 1995. Mem. Royal Inst. Internat. Affairs, Tocqueville Soc., Inst. Charles de Gaulle, WorldView Internat. Hindu. Avocations: classical music, squash, tennis. E-mail: Julian@ibaradio.org or Juluiuiba@aol.com. Home and Office: 111 King St Littleton MA 01460-1527

CRANDELL, DWIGHT SAMUEL, museum executive; b. Parke County, Ind., Nov. 30, 1943; s. Terence Wesley and Alice Ruth (Cox) C.; m. Rachel Louise Wentworth, June 14, 1965; children: Jeremy, Abigail, Joanna, Joshua. B.A., Principia Coll., 1965; M.A., SUNY-Oneonta, 1974. Asst. in research and adminstrn. Mt. Vernon (Va.) Ladies Assn. of the Union, 1965-66; exhibits coordinator, ednl. docent Children's Mus., Indpls., 1972-73, curator exhibits research and planning, 1973-77, collections dir., 1977-81; dir. devel., asst. dir. St. Louis Sci. Ctr., 1981-82, exec. dir., 1982-94, v.p. programs and ops., 1992-95, v.p. ops., 1996—; bd. dirs. Wild Canid Rsch. and Survival Ctr., 1983-88, 91-95. Served to capt. USAF, 1966-71. Nat. Mus. Act travel grantee, 1973. Mem. Am. Assn. Museums, Midwest Museums Conf., Mo. Museums Assocs. (v.p. 1983-85, pres. 1986-87, 94-95), Assn. Sci-Tech. Ctrs. (bd. dirs. 1983-85), St. Louis Area Mus. Collaborative, Rotary. Christian Scientist. Office: Saint Louis Sci Ctr 5050 Oakland Ave Saint Louis MO 63110-1460

CRANDELL, SARAH ALLEN, dean; b. Rockland, Maine, Mar. 10, 1944; d. Robert Meeks and Harriet Virginia (Snow) Allen; m. John Chester Crandell III, Dec. 19, 1964; children: Christopher H., Nathan A. BA, U. Maine, 1966; MEd, Bridgewater State U., 1981; CAGS, Suffolk U., 1987. Tchr. Boothbay Region High Sch., Boothbay Harbor, Maine, 1969-74; tchr., adminstr. Duxbury (Mass.) Pub. Sch., 1978-91; tchr. Killington Mountain Sch., Sherborne, Vt., 1993-95; dean students Poultney (Vt.) High Sch., 1995—. Chair Sch. Bd., Town of Plymouth, Vt., 1992—, also justice of the peace, mem. Bd. Civil Authority. Home: PO Box 83 Plymouth VT 05056-0083

CRANDLEMERE, ROBERT WAYNE, engineering executive; b. South Weymouth, Mass., Mar. 5, 1947; s. Robert Winton and Elizabeth Mildred (Smith) C.; m. Cynthia Robin Stoddard, May 18, 1980; children: Donna Marie, Raina Lee. A.E. in Chem. Tech., Franklin Inst. Boston, 1967; BS in Chemistry, Suffolk U., 1970, MS in Analytical Chemistry, 1975. V.p., chief chemist, lab. dir., dir. Briggs Engring. & Testing Inc., 1973-83; founder, prin., pres., CEO Cert. Engring. & Testing Co., Weymouth, Mass., 1983-92, R.W. Crandlemere & Assocs., Inc., Weymouth, Mass., 1993—; former instr. environmental and phys. chemistry Suffolk U. Contbr. articles to profl. jours. Memm. ASTM (comml. real estate transactions environ. due diligence subcom.), Nat. Inst. Bldg. Scis. (com. on asbestos ops. and mgmt. programs). Home: 423 S Franklin St Holbrook MA 02343-1855 Office: 549 Columbian St Ste 305 Weymouth MA 02190-1138

CRANE, BARBARA BACHMANN, photographer, educator; b. Chgo., Mar. 19, 1928; d. Burton Stanley and Della (Kreeger) Bachmann; children—Elizabeth, Jennifer, Bruce. Student, Mills Coll., 1945-48; B.A. in Art History, NYU, 1950; M.S. in Photography, Inst. Design, Ill. Inst. Tech., 1966. Prof. photography Sch. Art Inst. Chgo., 1967-93; vis. prof. Phila. Coll. Art, 1977, Sch. Mus. Fine Arts, Boston, 1979, Cornell U., Ithaca, N.Y., 1983; vis. prof. Bezalel Acad. Art and Design, Jerusalem, 1987. Author: (retrospective monograph) Barbara Crane: 1948-80, exhbn. catalogue Barbara Crane: The Evolution of a Vision, 1983; represented by Revolution Gallery, Ferndale, Mich., Lallak & Tom Gallery, Chgo., Troyer Gallery, Washington, Spl. Edits., Roslyn, Wash., N.C.E. Photographie Contemporaine, Paris, Stewart B. Baum Photography,. Photography fellow Nat. Endowment for Arts, 1975, 88, Guggenheim Meml. fellow in photography, 1979-80; Polaroid Corp. grantee, 1979—, Ill. Arts Coun. grantee, 1985. Recipient Honored Educator award, Soc. Photog. Edn., 1993. Mem. Soc. Photog. Edn., Friends of Photography (Carmel, Calif.) (trustee 1974-82). Studio: 1015 W Jackson Blvd Chicago IL 60607 *My work is my life's keel bringing enrichments discovered in the process. Many of my photographic ideas have grown from chance or accident, both visually and technically, or from a gift of the subject matter itself. I welcome an unaccountable occurrence stemming from combinations of shutter speed, subject changes, technical happenings, my mistakes, and whatever. When such unpredictable pictures appear, I try to harness the visual episode by taking pictures that will allow the new experience to happen with intent. Fortunately, this way of working seems to expand my ideas and to continuously generate new visual experiences.*

CRANE, BENJAMIN FIELD, lawyer; b. Holden, Mass., May 5, 1929; s. Frederick Turner and Gertrude (Stange) C.; m. Sarah Anne Molloy, Feb. 8, 1959; children: Michael Turner, Elizabeth Loring, Susan Field. B.A., U. Iowa, 1951; LL.B., NYU, 1954. Bar: N.Y. 1955. Assoc. Cravath, Swaine & Moore, N.Y.C., 1954-63, ptnr., 1963-94. Served with U.S. Army, 1946-47. Mem. Assn. of Bar of City of N.Y. Office: Cravath Swaine & Moore Worldwide Pla 825 8th Ave New York NY 10019-7475

CRANE, BONNIE LOYD, art gallery owner, director, author; b. Mpls., Aug. 24, 1930; d. Frank Riley and Evelyn (Davis) Loyd; m. David Alford, Oct. 23, 1954 (div. May 1992); children: Melinda Crane Engel, Matthew Loyd, Lauren Amanda. BA, Sweet Briar (Va.) Coll., 1950; MA, Bryn Mawr (Pa.) Coll., 1972. Lectr. Kinkaid Sch., Houston, 1975-76, Mus. Fin. Arts, Sch. of Arts, Houston, 1975-76, Rice U., Houston, 1976; tchr. Cairo Am. Coll., 1978-79; curator Clark Gallery, Lincoln, Mass., 1980-82; curatorial asst., dir. edn. Brockton (Mass.) Art Mus., 1982; freelance dealer Dedham and Dover, Mass., 1983-84; owner, dir. Crane Collection Gallery, Boston, 1985-96, Wellesla, MA, 1996—. Author: Blanche Ames, Artist & Activist, 1982, The Gentle Art of Still Life, 1989, Russian Light, 1995. Donor, mem. Channel 2 Auction, Boston, 1985—; active Newbury St. League, Boston, 1985—; tour guide Trinity Ch., Boston, 1988-89; spl. gifts solicitor United Way, Back Bay, Boston, 1988; bd. dirs. Handel and Haydn Soc., Boston, 1988—; v.p. bd. dirs. Friends of Art Sweet Briar Coll., 1992-97. Mem. Archives of Am. Art, Internat. Art Gallery Assn., New Eng. Appraisers Assn., St. Botolph Club. Episcopalian. Avocations: painting, traveling. Office: Crane Collection 564 Washington St Wellesley MA 02482-6409

CRANE, DAVID, producer. With Bright-Kauffman-Crane Prodns., Burbank, Calif. Creator, prodr. Dream On, 1990—; creator, exec. prodr. Friends, 1994— (Emmy nominee 1995, 96); creator, exec. producer Veronica's Closet, 1997—; exec. producer Jesse, 1998—. Office: Bright Kauffman Crane Prodns Bldg 160 Ste 750 4000 Warner Blvd Burbank CA 91522

CRANE, DAVID GOODRICH, psychiatrist, attorney, educator; b. Chgo., Jan. 11, 1937; s. George Washington and Cora Ellen (Miller) C.; m. Joan Leslee Brockman, Jan. 19, 1969; children: John Brockman, Douglas Macarthur Howard, Ethan Murray, Stephen David. AB, Hillsdale (Mich.) Coll., 1958; MD, Ind. U., 1962, JD, 1969. Bar: Ind. 1969; diplomate Am. Coll. Forensic Examiners. Dir. Mental Health Clinic, Bloomington, Ind., 1968-69; staff psychiatrist VA Hosp., Indpls., 1969-72; asst. prof. psychiatry Ind. U. Sch. Medicine, Indpls., 1969—; pvt. practice psychiatry and forensic psychiatry Bloomington and Indpls., 1970—. Co-author: Psychology Applied, 1982. Bd. dirs. fin. YMCA, Martinsville, Ind.; advisor Eisenhower Scholarship Found., Bloomington, 1981—; mem. county citizens adv. coun., Martinsville, 1996-97. Capt. U.S. Army, 1966-68. Decorated Bronze Star, U.S. Army, Vietnam, 1967; named Sagamore of the Wabash, Gov. of Ind., 1980. Mem. Am. Psychiat. Assn., Ind. Med. Assn., Ind. State Bar Assn., Ind. State Med. Assn. Republican. Methodist. Avocations: skiing, basketball, racquetball. Office: 802 S Washington St Bloomington IN 47401-4644

CRANE, EDWARD HARRISON, III, institute executive; b. Los Angeles, Aug. 15, 1944; s. Edward Harrison Jr. and Mary Barbara (Greene) C.; m. Kristina Knall; children: Geoffrey Harrison, Kathleen Wilder, Mary Adams. BS, U. Calif., Berkeley, 1967; MBA, U. So. Calif., 1968. Chartered fin. analyst. Portfolio mgr. Scudder, Stevens & Clark, Los Angeles, 1969-73; v.p. Alliance Capital Mgmt. Corp., San Francisco, 1973-75; nat. chmn. Libertarian Party, Washington, 1974-77; pres. Cato Inst., Washington, 1977—; bd. Nat. Taxpayers Legal Fund, 1978-82. Pub. Inquiry mag., 1977-81, Regulation mag., 1990—; editor: Beyond the Status Quo, 1984, An American Vision, 1988, Market Liberalism, 1993; contbr. articles to profl. jours. Bd. dirs. Inst. for Rsch. on the Econs. of Taxation, 1988-92, U.S. Term Limits, 1993—; bd. advisors Am. Inst. of Bus. and Econs. in Moscow. Inst. Chartered Fin. Analysts, Mont Pelerin Soc. Avocation: rowing. Home: 6213 Waterway Dr Falls Church VA 22044-1314 Office: Cato Inst 1000 Massachusetts Ave NW Washington DC 20001-5400

CRANE, FAYE, small business owner; b. Amery, Wis., Dec. 2, 1947; d. Vaemond Hall and Irene C. (L'Allier) C.; 1 child, Camille Mills Seifert. Grad. high sch., Milltown, Wis. Premiums statis. clk. State Farm Ins., St. Paul, 1968-73; pension adminstrn. asst. Mut. Svc. Ins., St. Paul, 1973-78; dist. dir. Avon Products, Inc., Morton Grove, Ill., 1978-79; sales rep. Midwest Bus. Sys., Duluth, Minn., 1979-84, REM's Inc., Grand Rapids, Minn., 1984; pres. prodn. Presto Print, Grand Rapids, 1984—. Mem. Grand Rapids Planning Commn., 1990-94; bd. dirs. Grand Rapids Econ. Devel. Authority, 1994—. Mem. NAFE, Nat. Fedn. Bus. and Profl. Women (treas. nat. conv. 1992, found. com. 1998-99, treas. nat. conv. 2000), Minn. Fedn. Bus. and Profl. Women (mem. promotion com. 1982-92, emblem chmn. 1982-83, found. chmn. 1983-84, exec. dir., chmn. 1984-85, editor 1987-90, v.p. 1992-93, pres.-elect 1993-94, pres. 1994-95), Grand Rapids Bus. and Profl. Women (pres. 1985-86), Minn. Bus. and Profl. Women's Found. (trustee 1995-96, leadership chmn. 1996-98), Nat. Mus. Women in Arts. Home: PO Box 404 Grand Rapids MN 55744-0404 Office: Presto Print 1235 Pokegama Ave Grand Rapids MN 55744-3820

CRANE, GLENDA PAULETTE, private school educator; b. Orlando, Fla., June 29, 1946; d. James Author and Elizabeth Lorine (Johnson) C. AA in Edn., Orlando Jr. Coll., 1966; BA in Elem. Edn., U. S. Fla., 1967; postgrad. So. Bapt. Theol. Sem., 1970; MEd, Rollins Coll., 1985. Tchr., Orange County Schs., Orlando, 1967-70, 79-80, Lake Highland Prep. Sch., Orlando, 1981—; tchr. Belle Glade (Fla.) Christian Sch., 1970-79, asst. prin., 1970-74, prin., 1975-79. State treas. Fla. Rainbow Girls., 1964; dir. Women's Missions and Ministries Greater Orlando Bapt. Assn.; bd. dirs. Christian Women's Job Corps. Mem. NEA, Fla. Edn. Assn., Fla. Council Tchrs. English, Orange County Tchrs. Assn., Assn. Supervision and Curriculum Devel., Internat. Reading Assn., Orange County Reading Council of Internat. Reading Assn., Fla. Reading Assn., Nat. Council for the Social Studies, Alumni Assn. U. South Fla., Alumni Assn. So. Bapt. Theol. Sem., Fla. Coun. Tchrs. of Math, Kappa Delta Pi. Democrat. Baptist. Clubs: Winter Park Pilot, Eastern Star, Winter Park Rainbow Girls. Home: 1705 E Harding St Orlando FL 32806-3100 Office: 1919 Delaney Ave Orlando FL 32806-3005

CRANE, HEWITT DAVID, science advisor; b. Jersey City, Apr. 27, 1927; m. Suzanne Gorlin, June 20, 1954; children: Russell Philip, Douglas Mitchell, Daniel Bruce. BSEE, Columbia U., 1947; PhD, Stanford U., 1960. With IBM, N.Y.C., 1949-51, Inst. for Advanced Study, Princeton, N.J., 1952-55, RCA Labs., Princeton, 1955-56; sr. scientific advisor SRI Internat., Menlo Park, Calif., 1956—; a founder Ridge Winery, Cupertino, Calif., 1959-86, Comm. Intelligence Corp., 1981. Author: (with D. Bennion and D. Nitzan) Digital Magnetic Logic, 1969, The New Social Marketplace: Notes on Effecting Social Change in America's Third Century, 1980; contbr. over 70 articles to profl. jours.; patentee in various fields. With USN, 1945-46. Recipient award NASA, 1970, numerous others. Fellow IEEE, Optical Soc. Am. Home: 25 Cordova Ct Menlo Park CA 94028-7908 Office: SRI Internat Sensory Scis and Tech Ctr 333 Ravenswood Ave Menlo Park CA 94025-3453

CRANE, HORACE RICHARD, physicist, educator; b. Turlock, Calif., Nov. 4, 1907; s. Horace Stephen and Mary Alice (Roselle) C.; m. Florence Rohmer LeBaron, Dec. 30, 1934; children—Carol Ann, Janet (dec.), George Richard. B.S., Calif. Inst. Tech., 1930, Ph.D., 1934. Research fellow Calif. Inst. Tech., 1934-35; mem. faculty U. Mich., Ann Arbor, 1935—; prof. physics U. Mich., 1946—, chmn. dept. physics, 1965-72, George P. Williams Univ. prof., 1972-78, emeritus, 1978—; Research asso. (radar) Mass. Inst. Tech., 1940-41; physicist Carnegie Inst. Washington, 1941; project dir., proximity fuze project U. Mich., 1941-43, atomic energy project, 1943-45; cons. NDRC, 1941-45; mem. standing com. on controlled thermonuclear research AEC, 1969-72; Vice pres. Midwestern Univs. Research Assn., 1956-57, pres., 1957-60; mem. policy bd. Argonne Nat. Lab., 1957-67; Bd. govs. Am. Inst. Physics, 1964-71, chmn., 1971-75; mem. Commn. on Human Resources, 1977-80, Council for Internat. Exchange of Scholars, 1977-80. Author: (monthly series) How Things Work in the Physics Teacher, 1983—, (books) How Things Work, 1992, Exhibits Guide, 1992, How to Build It, 1994; inventor, designer exhibits for hands-on type museums, 1981—; contbr. sci. articles to profl. mags. Recipient Davisson-Germer prize, 1967, Disting. Alumni medal Calif. Inst. Tech., 1968, Disting. Svc. award U. Mich., 1957, Nat. Medal of Sci., 1986, Can-Doer award Mich. Tech. Coun., 1993, Harris award of Rotary Internat., 1963; Henry Russel lectr., 1967. Fellow Am. Phys. Soc., AAAS, Am. Acad. Arts and Scis.; mem. Nat. Acad. Scis., Am. Assn. Physics Tchrs. (pres. 1965, Oersted medal 1977, Melba Newell Phillips award 1988), Sigma Xi. Clubs: Research Univ. of Mich. (pres. 1956-57); Science Research (U. Mich.) (v.p. 1946-47, pres. 1947-48). Inventor of Race Track, a modified form of synchrotron for nuclear studies, 1946; made early discoveries in field of artificially produced radioactive atoms, 1934-39; measurements of magnetic moment of free electron, 1950. Home: 830 Avon Rd Ann Arbor MI 48104-2738

CRANE, HUGH WINGATE, railroad executive; b. Evergreen Park, Ill., Dec. 25, 1941; s. Hugh B. and Grace May (Wesche) C.; m. Kathy Ann Jent, Sept. 27, 1975; children: Steven Henry, Katie R. Student, DeVry, 1964, Milw. Sch. Engring., 1969. Tchr., mem. faculty Milw. Sch. Engring., 1966-71; engring. instr. Control Data Tech. Inst., Chgo., 1971-72; founder, chmn. bd., pres., chief engring. officer ARH, Ltd. dba Crab Orchard & Egyptian R.R., Marion, Ill., 1972—; vice-chmn. Regional Econ. Devel. Corp., Marion; guest lectr. transp. and freight So. Ill. U., Carbondale, 1980. Author: (workbook) Engineering Descriptive Geometry, 1968, (textbook) Engineering Descriptive Geometry/Theory and Application, 1970. V.p. Lake Egypt Assn. Property Owners, Creal Springs, Ill., 1996-97. With ROTC, 1958-59. Recipient Sam Walton Cmty. Bus. Leader award, Marion, 1998; named Industrialist of Yr., Marion C. of C., 1993, Cert. of Appreciation, N.G. of Ill., 1995; transp. achievements recognized in U.S. congl. record U.S. Senator Paul Simon, 1994. Mem. Am. Rlwy. Engring. Assn., Am. R.R. Devel. Assn., Rotary. Avocations: boating, building large scale steam powered models. Office: Crab Orchard & Egyptian RR 514 N Market St Marion IL 62959-2300

CRANE, IRVING DONALD, pocket billiards player; b. Livonia, N.Y., Nov. 13, 1913; s. Scott W. and Laura (Stark) C.; m. Althea H. Sleight, Oct. 23, 1937; children—Irving Donald, Sandra. Student, Lima Jr. Coll., 1931, Hobart Coll., 1932. Cons., exhbn. player A.M.F., 1963-64; exhbn. player for U.S. Army Brunswick Co., 1944-47. Author: (with George Sullivan) The Young Sportsman's Guide to Pocket Billiards, 1964; contbg. author: (with George Sullivan) Sportsman's Ency., 1971; Short subject films Cue Men, 1942, Cue Tricks, 1946. Named Athlete of Year Rochester Press and Radio Club, 1970; recipient Pepsi-Cola Sports award Rochester (N.Y.) Profl. Salesman Assn., 1973; named to Hall of Fame Profl. Pool Players Assn., 1976, Hall of Fame Billiard Congress Am., 1978. Winner pocket billiards championships: World or Internat., 1942, 46, 55, 68, 69, 70, 72, U.S. Nat., 1950, 55, Eastern States Regional 3 Cushion, 1952, Tournament of Champions, 1963, U.S. Masters, 1964, Schaeffer Pocket Billiard Classic, 1965, Ballantine Invitational, 1965, U.S. Open, 1966, Salt City Open, 1970, U.S. Masters Classic, 1975, World Series of Pocket Billiards, 1978. Address: 270 Yarmouth Rd Rochester NY 14610-1454

CRANE, JAMESON, plastics manufacturing company executive; b. Columbus, Ohio, Mar. 14, 1926; s. Robert Sellers and Helen (Jameson) C.; m. Ann Burba, Sept. 17, 1948; children—Jameson, Jr., Elizabeth Crane Westwater, Michael S., Sarah Crane MacPhail. B.S., Ohio State U., 1947. Sales mgr. Columbus Coated Fabrics, 1948-60; pres. Crane Plastics Co., Columbus, 1970-96; chmn., CEO Crane Group Inc., Columbus, 1996—; bd. dirs. Bank One Columbus NA, Morgan Lumber Co. Bd. dirs. Ohio State U. Found. Bd., 1991—. Served with USN, 1944-45. Republican. Episcopalian. Clubs: Columbus, Columbus Country, The Golf (Columbus); Lyford Cay (Nassau, Bahamas). Home: 299 N Parkview Ave Columbus OH 43209-1437 Office: Crane Group Inc 2141 Fairwood Ave Columbus OH 43207-1753*

CRANE, JULIA GORHAM, anthropology educator; b. Mt. Kisco, N.Y., Nov. 8, 1925; d. Joseph Harold and Alma Evelyn (Reynolds) Crane. Student, Katharine Gibbs Sch., 1943-45; BS cum laude, Columbia U., 1959, PhD in Anthropology, 1966. Research asst. to Dr. Margaret Mead Am. Museum of Natural History, N.Y.C., 1956-59; asst. in anthropology Columbia U., N.Y.C., 1959-61; asst. prof. anthropology U. N.C., Chapel Hill, 1967-72; assoc. prof. U. N.C., 1972-76, prof., 1976-90. Author; Educated to Emigrate, 1971; co-author (with Michael Angrosino): Field Projects in Anthropology: A Student Handbook, 1974, 2d edit., 1984, 3d edit., 1992, Japanese edit., 1994, Korean edit., 1996, Saba Silhouettes, 1987, Statia Silhouettes, 1999. Recipient Prince Bernhard Fund award, The Netherlands, 1970; grantee NIH, 1961-66, U. N.C., 1970, 75, 85, 86, Cultural Cooperative Orgn. of Netherlands Antilles, 1985, 97; Tanner award for teaching excellence, 1986. Mem. So. Anthropol. Soc., Phi Beta Kappa. Office: U NC Dept Anthropology PO Box 3115 Chapel Hill NC 27515-3115

CRANE, KAREN R., director Alaska State Library. BA, Ind. U., 1970, MLS, 1971. Dir. Alaska State Libr., Juneau, 1986—. Office: Alaska State Libr PO Box 110571 Juneau AK 99811-0571 Other address: 333 Willoughby Ave Juneau AK 99801*

CRANE, LAURA JANE, research chemist; b. Middletown, Ohio, Nov. 2, 1941; d. David R. and Frances T. (Watkins) Scott; B.S., Carnegie Inst. Tech., 1963; M.S., Harvard U., 1964; Ph.D., Rutgers U., 1972; postdoctoral fellow Roche Inst. Molecular Biology, 1972-74, research asso., 1974-75; m. Robert K. Crane, Apr. 13, 1972. Analytical chemist Eastman Kodak Co., Rochester, N.Y., 1962; asst. scientist Warner-Lambert Co., Morris Plains, N.J., 1965, 67-68; English tchr. Am. Sch., Manila, 1966; assoc. scientist W. R. Grace & Co., Clarksville, Md., 1969; sr. scientist diagnostic enzymology Warner-Lambert Co., 1975, group leader coagulation research, 1976-79; mgr. lab. products research J. T. Baker Inc., Phillipsburg, N.J., 1979, asst. dir. research and devel., 1980-85, dir. research and devel., 1986-92; sr. dir., new product innovation, Schering-Plough Health Products, Inc., Memphis, 1992-93, sr. dir. adv. products rsch. and new product innovation, 1993—; mem. faculty Seton Hall U., 1979; participant profl. symposia. Mem. R&D Coun. N.J., state sci. adv. coun. Rutgers U. Armco Corp. scholar, 1959-63; Women's Dorm. Council scholar; William Connelly scholar; Nat. Merit scholar; NSF fellow; DuPont fellow; NDEA fellow, 1969-72; others. Mem. Am. Chem. Soc., AAAS, U.S. Dressage Fedn., Arabian Horse Registry Am., Al Khamsa Arabian Horse Breeders Assn. (pres.). Contbr., editor sci. articles and books. Home: 7155 Highway 194 Williston TN 38076-3511 Office: Schering-Plough Health Products Inc 3030 Jackson Ave Memphis TN 38112-2020

CRANE, LOUIS ARTHUR, retired labor arbitrator; b. Cleve., Apr. 15, 1922; m. Eleanor Darling, May 1979; children by previous marriage: Kevin A., Kathryn E., Julie E. B.B.A., U. Mich., 1945, M.B.A., 1947; LL.B., Wayne State U., 1950. Arbitrator, U.S. Rubber Co. and United Rubber, Cork, Linoleum and Plastic Workers Am., 1961-67; chmn. bd. arbitration Jones & Laughlin Steel Corp. and United Steelworkers Am., 1967-74; arbitrator Continental, Am. Can cos. and United Steelworkers Am., 1968-74; mem. system bd. adjustment Eastern Airlines Inc. and Internat. Assn. Machinists, 1967-85, Eastern Airlines Inc. and Air Line Pilots Assn., 1969-91; permanent arbitrator Gt. Lakes Steel Corp. and United Steelworkers Am., 1974-94; arbitrator Penn-Dixie Steel Corp. and United Steelworkers Am., 1973-83, Internat. Harvester Co. and United Automobile Aerospace and Agrl. Implement Workers, 1976-79; umpire Rockwell Internat. Corp. Automotive div. and U.A.W., 1976-94, Rockwell Internat. Corp. Automotive div. and United Steelworkers Am., 1976-82, Rockwell Internat. Corp. Aerospace div. and U.A.W., 1989-94; mem. system bd. adjustment United Airlines and Airline Pilots Assn., 1975-82, Continental Airlines and Airlines Pilots Assn., 1976-79, Flying Tiger Line and Airline Pilots Assn., 1982-92; Brit. Airways and IAM; arbitrator Budd Co. and UAW, 1976-94, Youngstown Sheet & Tube and United Steelworkers Am., 1977-84, Crucible Steel (Colt Industries) and United Steelworkers Am., 1984-86; permanent arbitrator Nat. Can Corp. and United Steelworkers Am., 1982-86; ret., 1994;

mem. Presdl. Emergency Bd. 164, 1964. Author: articles The Arbitrator and the Parties, 1958, Labor Arbitration and Industrial Changes, 1963, Labor Arbitration at the Quarter-Century Mark, 1972. Served to capt. AUS, 1943-46. Mem. State Bar Mich. (chmn. labor relations law sect. 1960-61), Nat. Acad. Arbitrators (gov. 1964-67), Phi Kappa Phi, Beta Gamma Sigma. Home: 3110 Glouchester Dr Troy MI 48084-2728

CRANE, MARK, lawyer; b. Chgo., Aug. 27, 1930; s. Martin and Ruth (Bangs) C.; m. Constance Bird Wilson, Aug. 18, 1956; children: Christopher, Katherine, Stephanie. AB, Princeton U., 1952; LLB, Harvard U., 1957. Bar: U.S. Dist. Ct. (no. dist.) Ill. 1957, U.S. Ct. Appeals (7th cir.) 1968, U.S. Ct. Appeals (9th cir.) 1972, U.S. Supreme Ct. 1978, U.S. Ct. Appeals (10th cir.) 1982, U.S. Ct. Appeals (fed. cir.) 1983, U.S. Ct. Appeals (6th cir.) 1995, U.S. Ct. Appeals (8th cir.) 1998. Assoc. Hopkins & Sutter, Chgo., 1957-63, ptnr., 1963—. Served to lt. (j.g.) USNR, 1952-54. Fellow Am. Bar Found., Am. Coll. Trial Lawyers (chmn. upstate Ill. com. 1997—); mem. ABA (chmn. antitrust sect. 1986-87), Ill. Bar Assn. (chmn. fed. jud. appointments com. 1978-79, chmn. antitrust sect. 1970), Chgo. Bar Assn., 7th Cir. Bar Assn. (pres. 1984-85). Republican. Episcopalian. Home: 520 Hoyt Ln Winnetka IL 60093-2623 Office: Hopkins & Sutter 3 1st National Plz Chicago IL 60602

CRANE, PETER ROBERT, botanist, geologist, paleontologist, educator; b. Eng., July 18, 1954; came to U.S., 1981; m. Elinor Margaret Hamer, 1986. BSc in Botany with honors, U. Reading, Eng., 1975, PhD in Botany, 1981. Lectr. dept. botany U. Reading, 1978-81; postdoctoral rsch. scholar dept. biology U. Ind., Bloomington, 1981-82; asst. curator paleobotany dept. geology Field Mus. Natural History, Chgo., 1982-85, assoc. curator paleobotany dept. geology, 1985-90, curator paleobotany dept. geology, 1990-92, chmn. dept. geology, 1991-92, v.p. acad. affairs, 1994—, dir., 1995—; Lectr. Com. on Evolutionary Biology, U. Chgo., 1984—; vis. prof. Botanischer Garten and Inst. Systematische Botanik, U. Zurich, Switzerland, 1987, Dept. Botany, U. Mass., Amherst, 1989; vis. rsch. fellow Dept. Botany The Natural History Mus., London, 1990-93; Mac Arthur curator The Field Mus., Chgo., 1992-94; sr. Mellon fellow, Smithsonian Instn., Washington, 1993-95; prof. dept. geophys. scis., U. Chgo., 1992—; chmn. dept. botany, Field Mus., 1993-96, dir. Ctr. for Evolutionary and Environ. Biology, Field Mus., 1994—, A Watson Armour III Curator, The Field Mus., Chgo.; mem. edtl. bds. Rev. of Palaeobotany and Palynology, Internat. Jour. Plant Sci., Plant Systematics and Evolution. Co-author: (with P. Kenrick) The Origin and Early Diversification of Land Plants, 1997; co-editor: (with others) The Origins of Angiosperms and Their Biological Consequences, 1987, The Evolution, Systematics and Fossil History of the Hamamelidae (Vols. I and II, 1989, Fifth North American Paleontological Convention, Abstract and Program, 1992; contbr. articles to profl. jours.; assoc. editor Botnical Jour. Linnean Soc., 1983-90; co-editor Paleobiology, 1984-86; mem. Rev. Panel, Kew Bull., 1987-91; editor Internat. Jour. Plant Scis. Grantee: NSF, 1984, 87, 88, 90, 91, 93, 96, Am. Chem. Soc., 1990. Fellow Royal Soc.; mem. Linnean Soc. London (Bicentenary medal 1984), Paleontological Soc. (pres. 1998—, Schuchert award 1993). Office: Field Museum Roosevelt Rd at Lake Shore Dr Chicago IL 60605

CRANE, PHILIP MILLER, congressman; b. Chgo., Nov. 3, 1930; s. George Washington III and Cora (Miller) C.; m. Arlene Catherine Johnson, Feb. 14, 1959; children: Catherine Anne, Susanna Marie, Jennifer Elizabeth, Rebekah Caroline, George Washington V, Rachel Ellen, Sarah Emma, Carrie Esther. Student, DePauw U., 1948-50; B.A., Hillsdale Coll., 1952; postgrad., U. Mich., 1952-54, U. Vienna, Austria, 1953, 56; M.A., Ind. U., 1961; Ph.D., 1963; LL.D., Grove City Coll., 1973, Nat. Coll. Edn., 1987; Doctor en Ciencias Politicas, Francisco Marroquin U., 1979. Advt. mgr. Hopkins Syndicate, Inc., Chgo., 1956-58; teaching asst. Ind. U., Bloomington, 1959-62; asst. prof. history Bradley U., Peoria, Ill., 1963-67; dir. schs. Westminster Acad., Northbrook, Ill., 1967-68; mem. 91st-106th Congresses, 12th (now 8th) Ill. Dist., 1969—, Ways and Means Com. Author: Democrat's Dilemma, 1964, The Sum of Good Government, 1976, Surrender In Panama: The Case Against the Treaty, 1978; contbr.: Continuity in Crisis, 1974, Crisis in Confidence, 1974, Case Against the Reckless Congress, 1976, Can You Afford This House?, 1978, View from the Capitol Dome (Looking Right), 1980, Liberal Cliches and Conservative Solutions, 1984. Dir. rsch. Ill. Goldwater Orgn., 1964; mem. nat. adv. bd. Young Ams. for Freedom, 1965—; bd. dirs. Am. Conservative Union, 1965-82, chmn., 1976; bd. dirs., chmn. Intercollegiate Studies Inst.; bd. advisors Ashbrook Ctr., Ashland U., 1983—, univ. trustee, 1988-93; founder Rep. Study Com., 1972—, chmn., 1984; commr. Commn. on Bicentennial U.S. Constn., 1986-91; trustee Hillsdale Coll. Recipient Distinguished Alumnus award Hillsdale Coll., 1968, Independence award, 1974, William McGovern award Chgo. Soc., 1969, Freedoms Found. award, 1973; named Ill. Statesman's Father Yr., 1979. Mem. ASCAP, VFW (award 1978), Am. Hist. Assn., Orgn. Am. Historians, Acad. Polit. Sci., Am. Acad. Polit. and Social Scis., Am. Legion, Phila. Soc., B'nai B'rith (award 1978), Phi Alpha Theta, Pi Gamma Mu. Office: US Ho of Reps 233 Cannon House Bldg Washington DC 20515-1308*

CRANE, R.H., poet, editor; b. Chgo., June 14, 1937; s. John and Helen Crane. BA in English, DePaul U., Chgo., 1972, MA in English, 1976. Founder, editor Veery, Chgo., 1991—. Author: Crossed Silver: Poems in Poetry, Drawing and Geometry, 1992. Mem. Am. Philos. Assn. Office: Veery 1 N Lasalle St Ste 2044 Chicago IL 60602-3908

CRANE, ROBERT KENDALL, engineering educator, researcher, consultant; b. Worcester, Mass., Dec. 9, 1935; s. Kendall Buck and Marjorie Armitage (Miller) C.; m. Emma Ruth Freeman, June 15, 1957; children: Garry Robert, Susan Emma Crane Jennings, Katherine Anne Crane Kulas, Cynthia Elizabeth Crane Murthy. BSEE, Worcester Poly. Inst., 1957, MSEE, 1959, PhD, 1970. Staff engr. MITRE Corp., Bedford, Mass., 1959-64; staff mem. Lincoln Lab. MIT, Lexington, 1964-76, cons., 1976-88; div. sr. scientist, dep. div. mgr. Environ. Rsch. and Tech., Inc., Concord, Mass., 1976-81; rsch. prof. Thayer Sch. Engring. Dartmouth Coll., Hanover, N.H., 1981-91; prof. meteorology, elec. engring. Coll. Geoscis. U. Okla., Norman, 1992—; cons. Raytheon Corp., Sudbury, Mass., 1981-87, Tech. Svc. Corp., Silver Spring, Md., 1988, Norden Sys., Melville, N.Y., 1988, Globalstar, San Jose, Calif., 1995-97, Applied Data Trends, Inc., 1996—, Teledesic Corp., 1997—. Contbr. over 100 tech. papers, reports to profl. jours. and other publs. Fellow IEEE (Disting. lectr. Antenna and Propagation Soc. 1988-91, adminstrv. com. 1985-87, wave propagation standards com. 1971-92, assoc. editor Trans. Antennas and Propagation 1972-74), Internat. Sci. Radio Union (chmn. commn. F. 1987-90, vice chmn. 1984-87); mem. Am. Meterorol. Soc. (cert. cons. meterorologist, com. on radar meteorology 1981-83), Sigma Xi, Eta Kappa Nu. Avocations: hiking, skiing, photography. Office: U Okla 100 E Boyd St Norman OK 73019-1000

CRANE, ROBERT MEREDITH, health care executive; b. Phila., Apr. 5, 1947; s. Frederick Barnard and Roberta Futhey (Philips) C.; m. Susan Gail Dewald, May 5, 1973; 1 child, Alexis Meredith. BA, Coll. of Wooster, 1969; M Pub. Adminstrn., Cornell U., Ithaca, N.Y., 1971. Health planning specialist U.S. Dept. Health, Edn. and Welfare, Rockville, Md., 1971-73, tech. assistance bur. chief, 1973-76, regulatory methods bur. chief, 1976-77; sr. staff assoc. U.S. Ho. of Reps., Washington, 1977-79; deputy commr. N.Y. State Health Dept., Albany, 1979-82; dir. N.Y. State Office Health Systems Mgmt., Albany, 1982-83; v.p. govt. rels. Kaiser Found. Health Plan, Oakland, calif., 1983-88, sr. v.p. nat. accts. and pub. rels., 1988-92; sr. v.p. quality mgmt. Kaiser Found. Health Plan, Oakland, Calif., 1992-94, sr. v.p., chief adminstrv. officer, 1994—. Campaign cabinet United Way Bay area, 1989-90; steering com. Bay Area Econ. Forum, 1988-94, Bay Area Coun., 1991—; selection judge, preceptor Coro Found., San Francisco, 1985-86; chmn. bd. Alpha Ctr., 1992-98; co-chair conf. bd. Coun. of Shared Bus. Svcs. Execs., 1996—. Sr. exec. fellow Harvard U., 1981. Mem. APHA (community health planning sect. chmn. 1983-84, bd. govs. 1979-81), Am. Health Planning Assn. (bd. dirs. 1986-92). Presbyterian. Avocations: tennis, golf. Office: Kaiser Found Health Plan 1 Kaiser Plz Oakland CA 94612-3610

CRANE, ROGER RYAN, JR., lawyer; b. Washington, Mar. 28, 1946; s. Roger Ryan Crane and Jeanette (Hurlbut) Rosar. AB, Coll. of Holy Cross, 1968; JD, Fordham U., 1973; LLM, NYU, 1980. Bar: N.Y. 1974; U.S. Dist. Ct. (so. and ea. dist.) N.Y. 1974; U.S. Ct. Appeals (2nd cir.) 1974, (1st cir.) 1994. Assoc. Dunnington Bartholow & Miller, N.Y.C., 1973-79, Trubin Sillcocks Edelman, N.Y.C., 1979-81; ptnr. Trubin Sillcocks Edelman, N.Y.C., 1981-84; ptnr., head litig. dept. Bachner Tally Polevoy & Misher, N.Y.C., 1984—. Contbr. articles to profl. jours. Mem. N.Y.C. Bar Assn. (prof. discipline com. 1996—), Univ. Club N.Y., Tuxedo Club. Avocations: golf, tennis, fly fishing, riding. Office: Bachner Tally Polevoy & Misher 380 Madison Ave New York NY 10017-2513

CRANE, STACEY LYNN, association executive; b. New Haven, July 3, 1960; d. Jacob and Nedra (Rosing) C. BA in Polit. Sci., Ind. U., 1982. From staff assoc. to assoc. dir. fin. divsn. State MH Dirs., Washington, 1982-85; legis. liaison Nat. Assn. State Treas., Washington, 1985-89; intergovt. liaison Coun. State Govts., Washington, 1985-89; asst. dir. office fed. affairs Nat. Assn. State Treas., Washington, 1989-90; exec. dir., CEO Mcpl. Treas. Assn. the U.S. & Can., Washington, 1990—; treas. Washington Mgmt. Cons., Inc., 1990—. Jewish.

CRANE, STEPHEN CHARLES, professional society administrator; b. Waterbury, Conn., Oct. 4, 1946; s. Homer and Edna Crane; m. Barbara Louise Baumberger, June 6, 1970; children: Russell, Elizabeth. BA, Princeton U., 1969; MPH, U. Mich., 1973, PhD, 1981. Legis. analyst, mgmt. intern Office of the Dir., NIH, Bethesda, Md., 1969; project dir. Columbia Rsch. Assocs., Inc., Cambridge, Mass., 1970; program analyst Office Asst. Sec. for Planning & Evaluation U.S. Dept. Health, Edn. and Welfare, 1972; grad. rsch. fellow Program Health Planning U. Mich.-Sch. Pub. Health, 1973, sr. rsch. assoc., rsch. assoc., grad. rsch. fellow, 1973-79, lectr. program and bur. hosp. adminstrn., 1979-80, asst. prof., lectr. dept. med. care orgn., 1980-83; asst. prof. Sch. Pub. Health Boston U., 1984-93, dep. chief health svcs. sect. Sch. Pub. Health, 1988, asst. acad. v.p. for health affairs, 1986-88, dir. ednl. programs Health Policy Inst., 1983-90; v.p. Assn. for Health Svcs. Rsch. & Found. for Health Svcs. Rsch., Washington, 1990-93; program dir. Robert Wood Johnson Found. Investigator Awards in Health, 1992-93; exec. v.p. Am. Acad. Physician Assts., Alexandria, Va., 1993—; investigator and presenter in field. Contbr. articles to profl. jours. Staff Mich. Pub. Health Statue Revision Project, 1975-78; cons. Spkr.'s Office, Mich. Ho. of Reps., Lansing, 1975-81; mem. adv. com. Mercy Coll. Physician Asst. Program, Detroit, 1979-83, Western Mich. Physician Asst. Program, Kalamazoo, 1981-85; staff Boston Mayor's Com. on Access to Health Care, 1984-86; mem. task force on access to health care Divsn. Alcoholism, Mass. Dept. Pub. Health, 1985-86; health care cons. Mass. Com. for the Medically Uninsured, 1985-86; cons. Gen. Assembly Task Force on Health Cost/Policies, Nat. Presbyn. Ch., 1985-91; corporator Milton Med. Ctr., 1988-90; mem. Commn. on Future of U. Detroit/Mercy. McConnell fellow Woodrow Wilson Sch., Princeton U., 1968; USPH Svc. fellow, 1972-73; Grad. Rsch. fellow Bur. Hosp. Adminstrn., Sch. Pub. Health, U. Mich., 1973-74; hon. fellow Mich. Acad. Physician Assts., 1977; recipient commendation Pub. Health Statue Revision Commn., 1979; Faculty Devel. grantee Ctr. for Rsch. on Learning and Teaching, U. Mich., 1982, John H. Romani Disting. Alumni award Mich. Sch. Pub. Health, 1996. Office: Am Acad Physician Assts 950 N Washington St Alexandria VA 22314-1534

CRANE, STEVEN, financial company executive; b. Los Angeles, Jan. 21, 1959; s. Roger D. and Violet (Heard) C.; m. Susan Jean Perea June 27, 1998; 1 child Allison Nicole. Grad. high sch. With Mobar Inc., Torrance, Calif., 1976-78; v.p. internat. Fluid Control Internat., Marina del Rey, Calif., 1978-79; pres. Energy Devel. Internat., Torrance, 1979-85; pres., chief exec. officer Kaempen USA, Inc., Anaheim, Calif., 1985-91; founding ptnr., chmn. Western Fin. Group, Inc., Redondo Beach, Calif., 1991-95; CEO, Artist Network, Huntington Beach, Calif., 1993-95; chmn., bd. dirs. CorpHQ Inc., Long Beach, 1995—; bd. dirs. Artist Network; chmn. bd. dirs. We. Finance Group, Inc.; bd. dirs. Source Capital Inc., 1999—. Mem. Avocations: kickboxing, photography, basketball, bird hunting. Office: CorpHQ Inc 110 W Ocean Blvd #604 Long Beach CA 90802-4430

CRANEFIELD, PAUL FREDERIC, physiology educator, physician, scientist; b. Madison, Wis., Apr. 28, 1925; s. Paul Frederic and Edna (Rothnick) C. Ph.B., U. Wis., 1946, Ph.D., 1951; M.D., Albert Einstein Coll. Medicine, 1964. Fellow biophysics Johns Hopkins U., 1951-53; from instr. to assoc. prof. physiology State U. N.Y. Downstate Med. Center, N.Y.C., 1953-62; research fellow psychiatry Albert Einstein Coll. Medicine, 1960-64; exec. sec. com. publs. and med. information, editor bull. N.Y. Acad. Medicine, 1963-66; adj. assoc. prof. pharmacology Columbia Coll. Physicians and Surgeons, 1964-75, adj. prof., 1975-96; assoc. prof. Rockefeller U., 1966-75, prof., 1975-96, prof. emeritus, 1996—. Author: (with Hoffman) The Electrophysiology of the Heart, 1960, Paired Pulse Stimulation of the Heart, 1968, (with C. McC. Brooks) The Historical Development of Physiological Thought, 1959, The Way In and the Way Out, 1974, The Conduction of the Cardiac Impulse, 1975, Claude Bernard's Revised Edition of his Introduction à L'Étude de la Médicine Expérimentale, 1976, (with Aronson) Cardiac Arrhythmias, The Role of Triggered Activity and Other Mechanisms, 1988, Science and Empire: East Coast Fever in Rhodesia and the Transvaal, 1991, Born Wanderer: The Life of Stanley Portal Hyatt, 1995; also numerous articles; editor: Two Great Scientists of the Nineteenth Century, 1982, Jour. Gen. Physiology, 1966-96; mem. editorial bd.: Circulation Research, Spl. Collections, Jour. of Electrocardiology; cons. editor: Internat. Microform Jour. Legal Medicine, 1969-77. Chmn. bd. dirs. LaMama Exptl. Theatre Club, 1965-69; chmn. bd. dirs. Circle Repertory Co., 1970-76, The Working Theatre; trustee Milton Helpern Library Legal Medicine. Recipient Einthoven medal U. Leiden, 1983, Disting. Scientist award N.Am. Soc. Pacing and Electrophysiology, 1994. Fellow N.Y. Acad. Medicine (medal 1988), Internat. Acad. History of Medicine; mem. Am. Physiol. Soc., Biophys. Soc., Am. Assn. History Medicine, Bibliog. Soc., Episcopal Actors Guild (mem. coun. 1990-92), Century Club, Players Club, Nat. Arts Club, Grolier Club, Coffee House Club, Cosmos Club (Washington), Savile Club (London). Home: 310 E 9th St New York NY 10003-7901

CRANEY, ROSE STIGLIANO, artist, sculptor; b. Bklyn., June 28, 1927; d. Joseph and Angelina (Rapanaro) Stigliano; m. Thomas Craney, Sept. 25, 1948; children: Angelique, Trudy, Thomas, Paul, Christine. BA, Newark State Coll., Union, N.J., 1971; postgrad., NYU, 1981. Tchr. pub. schs., Rumson/Middletown/Neptune, N.J., 1971-73; art instr. pvt. sector N.J., 1973-91; arts registry Monmouth County Arts Coun., Red Bank, N.J.; curator Art Alliance Monmouth County; county arts coord. Monmouth County Teen Arts Festival, Long Branch, N.J. Poet, Poets at Large, Monmouth County Libr., Shrewsbury, N.J.; commd. gallery and pvt.; one-woman shows include Georgian Ct. Coll., N.J., 1989; exhibited in group shows at Bell Lab, N.J., 1987, Art Alliance Monmouth County, N.J., 1988, Monmouth Coll., 1988, Sci. and Art Found., N.J., 1988, 97, Monmouth Mus., 97, 1989, Germans Van Eck, West Broadway, N.Y.C., 1989, Glassboro (N.J.) State Coll., 1990, City Without Walls, N.J., 1992, Phoenix Gallery, N.Y.C., 1992, Broome St. Gallery, N.Y.C., 1993, Georgian Ct. Coll., N.J., 1993, Lever House, N.Y.C., 1995-96, Polo Gallery, N.J., 1995-98, Noyes Mus., N.J., 1997. Mem. AAUW (orginator art history unit, cultural chairperson), Shore Area Art Edn. Assn. (pres. N.J.), Sculptors Assn. N.J. (pres. 1995-96), City Without Walls, Mus. Modern Art, Nat. Mus. Women in Arts, Smithsonian Inst. Home: 95 Deepdale Dr Middletown NJ 07748-3006

CRANFORD, JAMES BLEASE, retired real estate executive; b. Bethune, S.C., Oct. 22, 1950; s. Colel Blease and Olivia Ardel (Adams) C.; m. Virginia Sue Black, June 24, 1972; children: Chadwick Kyle (dec.), Shaun Welborn. BSBA, Western Carolina U., 1972. Mfg. supr. Deering Milliken, Inc., Lagrange, Ga., 1972-73, mfg. tng. mgr., 1973-74; mfg. tng. mgr. Burlington Industries, Hickory, N.C., 1974; mgmt. tng. mgr. Westinghouse Electric Corp., Winston-Salem, N.C., 1974-76; real estate property mgr. Chicora Devel., Inc., Myrtle Beach, S.C., 1977-81; pres., chief exec. officer Quadrant, Inc., Myrtle Beach, S.C., 1981-98; prin. Cranford Cons. Co., 1998—; bd. dirs. Nat. Shag Dance Championship. Bd. dirs. Grand Strand YMCA, Myrtle Beach, 1986-89; North-South High Sch. All-Star Game Com., Myrtle Beach, v.p. 1988, pres.-elect, 1989—, pres., 1990. Mem. Community Assns. Inst. (nat. trustee 1988-94, PCAM designee 1983, AMS designee 1990, Nat. Vol. of Yr. 1988, Pres. Club Hall of Fame 1989, Disting. Svc. award 1994), Cmty. Assn. Mgrs. (cert. 1996), Grand Strand Yacht Club, Tau Kappa Epsilon. Republican. Lutheran. Avocations: boating, bicycling, travel.

CRANFORD, PAGE DERONDE, lawyer, educator, executive; b. West Chester, Pa., Nov. 20, 1935; s. Joseph D. and Dorothy (Griffith) C.; m. Virginia Langen, Nov. 21, 1965; children: Elizabeth, Courtenay. BS, Washington and Lee U., 1958; JD, George Washington U., 1964; postgrad. in banking, Rutgers U., 1981. Bar: Md. 1964, D.C. 1965, Va. 1974, U.S. Ct. Appeals (D.C. cir.) 1965. Asst. v.p. Nat. Bank Washington, 1958-65; staff counsel U.S. Comptroller of Currency, Washington, 1965-66; regional adminstr. nat. banks U.S. Comptroller of Currency, Richmond, Va., 1966-72; sr. v.p., sec., gen. counsel Fidelity Am. Bank, Lynchburg, Va., 1972-75; assoc. Boothe, Prichard & Dudley, Fairfax, Va., 1975-76; corp. gen. counsel Va. Nat. Bankshares (now Sovran Fin. Corp.), Norfolk, Va., 1976-89; exec. v.p., gen. counsel Sorvan Fin. Corp, Norfolk, 1989-90, sr. exec. v.p., gen. counsel, 1990-91; sr. exec. v.p., gen. counsel, sec. C&S/Sovran Corp., Norfolk and Atlanta, 1990-92; ptnr. McGuire Woods Battle & Boothe, Norfolk, 1992—, ptnr. in charge, 1992-96; adj. prof. Sch. Law Regent U., Va. Beach, 1995—, Sch. Law Coll. William and Mary, Williamsburg, Va., 1997-98. Trustee Richmond Montessori Sch., 1970-72, Lynchburg Montessori Sch., 1972-75, James River Day Sch., Lynchburg, 1973-75, Va. Symphony, Norfolk, 1984—. Served to capt. U.S. Army, 1958-66. Recipient Arthur S. Fleming award Jaycees, 1972. Mem. ABA (banking law subcom, corp. counsel subcom., bus. law sect.), Va. Bar Assn., Md. Bar Assn., D.C. Bar Assn., Assn. Bank Holding Cos. (lawyers com.), Harbor Cub (Norfolk), Town Point Club (Norfolk). Republican. Episcopalian. Home: 1008 Chumley Rd Virginia Beach VA 23451-3735 Office: McGuire Woods Battle & Boothe PO Box 3767 Norfolk VA 23514-3767

CRANG, RICHARD FRANCIS EARL, plant and cell biologist, research center administrator; b. Clinton, Ill., Dec. 2, 1936; s. Richard Francis and Clara Esther (Cummins) C.; m. Linda L., Aug. 10, 1958 (div.); children—Steven E., Douglas E.; m. Nina V., Aug. 22, 1990; 1 stepson, Artyom N. B.S., Eastern Ill. U., 1958; M.S., U. S.D., 1962; Ph.D., U. Iowa, 1965. Asst. prof. biology Wittenberg U., 1965-69; assoc. prof. biol. sci. Bowling Green State U., 1969-74, prof., 1974-80; prof. plant biology U. Ill., Urbana-Champaign, 1980—, assoc. head dept. plant biology, 1995-97, faculty fellow in acad. adminstrn., 1997-99, dir. Ctr. Elec. Microsci., 1980-92; adj. prof. anatomy Med. Coll. Ohio, 1974-80; vis. scientist in botany Cambridge U., Eng., 1978-79, Komarov Bot. Inst., USSR, 1980, 88, 90, 93, Warsaw U., Poland, 1993; researcher, collaborator in fungal adhesion Kaohsiung Med. Coll., Taiwan, Republic of China, 1988-90; lectr. People's Republic of China, 1990. Rschr., contbr. numerous publs. in field of air pollution effects on plant, fungal, and lichen ultrastructure, 1967—; early developer asynchronous learning techs. by means of networked computers on World-Wide Web, 1995—. Mem. Statewide Democratic Support Group, Ill. Recipient Outstanding Faculty Rsch. Recognition awards Bowling Green State U., 1973, 75; grantee Paint Rsch. Inst., 1976-83, NSF, 1981-83, EPA, 1984-86, USDA, 1986-89, Internat. Plant and Pollution Lab., 1993-98; lifetime assoc. fellow Clare Hall, Cambridge, Eng. Mem. AAAS, Bot. Soc. Am., Internat. Soc. Environ. Botanists (advisor, life mem., inaugurated 1st internat. meeting, Lucknow, India, 1996), Microscopy Soc. Am. (nat. chmn. cert. bd. 1982-89, dir. USA local affiliates 1990-93, Disting. Svc. award 1994, Cecil Hall award for outstanding rsch. in biology with analytical microscopy 1994), Sigma Xi. Mem. Christian Ch. (Disciples of Christ). Home: 3901 Farhills Dr Champaign IL 61822-9305 Office: U Ill Plant Biology 505 S Goodwin Ave 155 Morrill Hall Urbana IL 61801-3707

CRANIN, ABRAHAM NORMAN, oral and maxillofacial surgeon, researcher, implantologist; b. Bklyn., June 17, 1927; s. Samuel Leonard and Henrietta C.; m. Marilyn Sunners, June 14, 1953; children: Jonathan, Andrew, Elizabeth. A.B., Swarthmore Coll., 1947; D.D.S., NYU, 1951; cert., Mt. Sinai Hosp., 1952, 53; DEng. (hon.) Rose-Hulman Inst. Tech., 1987. Assoc. attending oral surgeon Mt. Sinai Hosp., N.Y.C., 1961—; practice dentistry specializing in oral and maxillofacial surgery and implantology; chief oral surgery Greenpoint Hosp., Bklyn., 1961-63; attending oral surgeon Cmty. Hosp., Bklyn., 1962-72; assoc. clin. prof. Mt. Sinai Sch. Medicine, N.Y.C., 1974—; adj. prof. oral & maxillofacial surgery & hosp. dentistry Sch. Dental Medicine U. Pa., 1993—; clin. prof. oral and maxillofacial surgery NYU, 1975—, mem. curr. com., 1994—; dir., chmn. dental and oral surgery Brookdale U. Hosp. & Med. Ctr., Bklyn., 1965—, mem. med. exec. bd.; chmn. oral surgery Schachne S.N.F., Bklyn, 1995; cons. Nat. Patent Devel. Corp., N.Y.C., 1964-70, N.J. State Bd. Dental Examiners, 1989; pres. Internat. Congress Implantology and Biomaterials in Stomatology, 1988—; chmn. study sect. NIH Oral Biology and Medicine, 1982—, mem. study sect. Clin. Scis. Rev. Group Div. Research Group; clin. prof. oral and maxillofacial surgery U. Medicine and Dentistry N.J., 1987—, dir. dental implant ctr., 1987-91; hon. prof. Cirurgia BucoMaxilofacial Grupo Mogi das dos Cruzes, Brasil, 1996; cons. oral surgeon Bklyn. Devel. Ctr., 1973—, U.S. Surg. Corp., 1987-90, USPHS Gen Practice Residencies, 1995—. Author 6 books, including Atlas of Oral Implantology, 1992, 2d edit., 1999; editor-in-chief: Jour. Oral Implantology Quar, 1973 (Gold Key 1974), 1987—. Jour. Biomed. Materials Research, 1978-88 (cert. 1981, award Am. Assn. Pubs.); editor Brookdale Prof. Newsletter, 1982—; contbr. 121 articles to profl. jours., chpts. to textbooks. Pres. Informed Citizens Com. Hewlett Bay Park, N.Y., 1976. Ensign USNR, 1950-51. Recipient medal/plaque Univ. Mogi das Cruzes, Brazil, 1980, award of honor Met. Conf. Hosp. Dentists, 1982, cert. of honor Brit. Dental Implant Soc., 1989, Medal of Paris Mayor Jacques Chirac, 1989, medal Alpha Implant Group, 1989, Pierre Fauchard Acad., 1990, Pierre Fauchard medal, 1993; named Man of Yr. Fedn. of Jewish Philanthropies, Bklyn., 1973, Adm. Gt. Navy of Nebr., 1978, Tchr. of Yr. Internat. Coll. Oral Implantology, 1986, NYU, 1984, Outstanding Implantologist of Yr. Internat. Assn. Dental Rsch., 1990; AAID award Comm. 1st formal Implant Tng. Program, Pioneer's medal Implant Hall of Fame AAIP; honoree United Jewish Appeal, Brookdale Hosp., 1980; grantee USPHS, 1993-95; v.p. Am. Assn. Hosp. Dentists, Am. Assn. Dental Schs.; founder, dir. Brookdale Implant Maxicourse, 1988. Fellow Internat. Coll. Oral Implantology, Am. Acad. Implant Dentistry (founder, pres. 1972, Aaron Gershkoff award, 1986), Internat. Coll. Dentists, Am. Dental Soc. Anesthesiology, Royal Soc. Health, Am. Coll. Dentists, Brazilian Soc. Oral and Maxillofacial Surgery (hon., Rene Lefort medal 1980), Acad. Dental Materials, Soc. for Biomaterials (bd. dirs. San Antonio 1973—, pres. 1988-89, Clemson award 1976), Japanese Soc. for Biomaterials; mem. Am. Bd. Oral Implantology (founder, diplomate), Japanese Soc. Implant Dentistry (hon.; medal and plaque 1980), Argentina Soc. Implantology (hon.), Israeli Soc. Implantology Soc., Woodmere Bay Club (Bay Park, N.Y.), Woodmere (N.Y.) Club. Office: Brookdale U Hosp & Med Ctr One Brookdale Plz Brooklyn NY 11212

CRANKSHAW, JOHN HAMILTON, mechanical engineer; b. Canton, Ohio, Aug. 29, 1914; s. Fred. Weir and Mary (Lashels) C.; m. Wilma Chaffee Thurlow, June 5, 1940; children: Wilma Jean, John H., Geoffrey Thurlow. B.S. in Mech. Engring., MIT, M.S., 1940. Rotating engr. Gen. Electric Co., 1940-41, sect. engr., mech. design sect. Motor Engr. div. Locomotive Car Equipment, Erie, Pa., 1946-52; exec. engr. J.A. Zurn Mfg. Co., Am. Flexible Coupling Co., 1952-54; v.p. engring., 1954; exec. v.p., dir. Zurn Industries, Inc., mng. dir. Zurn Research and Devel. Div., until 1957; pres., dir. Dynetics, Inc., Erie, 1957—, Dynetic Systems, Inc., Erie, 1970—; expert witness numerous product liability cases. Mem. adv. council Gannon Coll.; chmn. Erie Sewer Authority. Served to maj. Ordnance Dept., AUS, 1941-46. Registered profl. engr., Pa. Mem. ASME, Soc. Automotive Engrs., Assn. Iron and Steel Engrs., Soc. Exptl. Stress Analysis, Soc. Naval Architects and Marine Engrs., Am. Soc. Metals, ASTM, Am. Soc. Lubricating Engrs. Erie Engring. Socs. Council (pres. 1955-57), Pa. Soc. Profl. Engrs., Sigma Xi. Clubs: MIT (N.Y.); Erie. Author several tech. papers. Achievements include 25 US and 5 foreign patents; invention and design of main propulsion couplings and clutches for nuclear powered submarines and Navy and Coast Guard surface ships. Home and Office: Dynetics Inc 439 Shawnee Dr Erie PA 16505-2433

CRANMER, THOMAS WILLIAM, lawyer; b. Detroit, Jan. 13, 1951; s. William Eugene and Betty Lee (Orphal) C.; m. Judy Kay Henson, Apr. 19, 1986; children: Jacqueline, Taylor, Chase. BA, U. Mich., 1972; JD, Ohio No. U., 1975. Bar: Mich. 1975, U.S. Dist. Ct. (ea. dist.) Mich. 1978, U.S. Ct. Appeals (6th cir.) 1978, U.S. Supreme Ct. 1982, U.S. Tax Ct. 1986. Asst. pros. atty. Oakland County, Mich., 1975-78; asst. atty. U.S. Dist. Ct. (ea. dist.) Mich., 1978-80, asst. chief criminal div., 1980-82; assoc. Miro, Miro & Weiner, Bloomfield Hills, Mich., 1982-84, ptnr., 1984—; mem. faculty Atty. Gen's. Adv. Inst., Washington, 1980-82, Nat. Inst. Trial Adv., Northwestern Chicago, Ill., 1987—, trial adv. workshop Inst. Continuing Legal Edn.,

1988—, local rules adv. com. U.S. Dist. Ct. (ea. dist.) Mich., 1989-92; hearing panelist Atty. Discipline Bd., 1987—. Fellow Oakland Bar-Adams Pratt Found. (charter, trustee 1994—), Mich. State Bar Found.; mem. ABA (chair litigation sect., Detroit graphic subcom. of com. on complex crimes litigation 1990), FBA (exec. bd. dirs. Detroit chpt. 1988—, pres. 1995—, Leonard R. Gilman award 1995), Am. Arbitration Assn. (mem. hearing panel 1990), Mich. Bar Assn. (rep. assembly 1986-92, mem. grievance com. 1990—, chair 1993-97, bd. commrs. 1998—), Oakland County Bar Assn. (chair CLE com. 1992, bd. dirs. 1994—, Disting. Svc. award 1996, chair membership com. 1997). Republican. Presbyterian. Home: 4249 Cherry Hill Dr Orchard Lake MI 48323-1607 Office: Miro Weiner & Kramer PC 500 N Woodward Ave Ste 100 Bloomfield Hills MI 48303-0908

CRANNEY, MARILYN KANREK, lawyer; b. Bklyn., June 18, 1949; d. Sidney Paul and Aurelia (Valice) Kanrek; m. John William Cranney, Jan. 22, 1970 (div. June 1975); 1 child, David Julian. BA, Brandeis U., 1970; MA in History, Brigham Young U., 1975; JD, U. Utah, 1979; LLM in Tax Law, NYU, 1984. Bar: N.Y. 1980, U.S. Dist. Ct. (so. and ea. dists.) N.Y. 1992. Assoc. Cravath Swaine & Moore, N.Y.C., 1979-81; 1st v.p., asst. gen. counsel Morgan Stanley Dean Witter Advisors Inc., N.Y.C., 1981—. Mem. Order of the Coif. Democrat. Jewish. Avocations: travel, reading. Home: 1830 E 23rd St Brooklyn NY 11229-1529 Office: Morgan Stanley Dean Witter Advisors Inc 2 World Trade Ctr New York NY 10048-0203

CRANSTON, ALAN, former senator; b. Palo Alto, Calif., June 19, 1914; s. William MacGregor and Carol (Dixon) C.; children: Robin MacGregor (dec.), Kim Christopher. Student, Pomona Coll., 1932-33, U. Mexico, 1933; A.B., Stanford, 1936. Fgn. corr. Internat. News Service, Eng., Italy, Ethiopia, Germany, 1936-38; Washington rep. Common Council Am. Unity, Washington, 1940-41; chief fgn. lang. div. Office War Info., Washington, 1942-44; exec. sec. Council for Am.-Italian Affairs, Inc., Washington, 1945-46; partner bldg. and real estate firm Ames-Cranston Co., Palo Alto, Calif., 1959-66; controller State of Calif., 1967-68; pres. Homes for a Better America Inc., 1967-68; v.p. Carlsberg Financial Corp., Los Angeles, 1968; mem. U.S. Senate from Calif., 1969-93; sr. internat. adv. Schooner Capital Corp., Boston, 1993-97; chmn. Gorbachev Found. USA, 1992-99, State of World Forum, 1995-99; chmn. U.S.-Kyrgiz Bus. Coun., 1993-96, hon. chmn., 1997-99. Author: The Big Story, 1940, The Killing of the Peace, 1945. Mem. exec. com. Calif. Democratic Central Com., 1954-60; pres. Calif. Dem. Council, 1953-57. Served with AUS, 1944-45. Mem. United World Federalists (nat. pres. 1949-52). Home and Office: 27080 W Fremont Rd Los Altos CA 94022-1900

CRANSTON, HOWARD STEPHEN, lawyer, management consultant; b. Hartford, Conn., Oct. 20, 1937; s. Howard Samuel and Agnes (Corvo) C.; m. Karen Youngman, June 16, 1962; children: Margaret, Susan. BA cum laude, Pomona Coll., 1959; LLB, Harvard U., 1962. Bar: Calif. 1963. Assoc. MacDonald & Halsted, L.A., 1964-68; ptnr. MacDonald, Halsted & Laybourne, L.A., 1968-82, of counsel, 1982-86; pres. Knapp Comm., L.A., 1982-87, S.C. Cons. Corp., 1987—; bd. dirs. Boys Republic, Mental Health Assn., L.A. Author: Handbook for Creative Managers, 1987. 1st Lt. U.S. Army, 1962-64. Mem. San Gabriel Country Club, Harvard Club (N.Y.). Republican. Episcopalian. Office: 1613 Chelsea Rd # 252 San Marino CA 91108

CRANSTON, JOHN WELCH, historian, educator; b. Utica, N.Y., Dec. 21, 1931; s. Earl and Mildred (Welch) C.; B.A., Pomona Coll., 1953; M.A., Columbia U., 1964; Ph.D., U. Wis., 1970. Asst. prof. history W. Tex. State U., 1970-74, U. Mo., Kansas City, 1970, Rust Coll., Holly Springs, Miss., 1974-80, assoc. prof., 1980-83; historian U.S. Army Armor Ctr., Ft. Knox, Ky., 1983-95; ret., 1995; adj. prof. history and govt. Elizabethtown C.C., Ft. Knox, 1988—. Served with U.S. Army, 1953-55. Nat. Endowment for Humanities fellow, summer 1976, summer 1981. Mem. Am. Hist. Assn., Orgn. of Am. Historians. Democrat. Episcopalian. Contbr. hist. articles to profl. lit. Home: PO Box 892 Radcliff KY 40159-0892

CRANSTON, ROBERT EARL, neurologist; b. West Palm Beach, Fla., June 21, 1955; s. Robert Jerrell and Carolyn Lucille (Shaw) C.; m. Barbara Jean Finger, June 11, 1977; children: Daniel, Sarah, Joanna. BA cum laude, Greenville Coll., 1977; MD, U. Ill., 1982. Diplomate Am. Bd. Psychiatry and Neurology, Am. Bd. Electroencephalography and Neurophysiology. Intern Valley Med. Ctr., Fresno, Calif., 1982-83; staff physician L.B.J. Tropical Med. Ctr., Pago Pago, American Samoa, 1983-85, Jay (Okla.) Meml. Hosp., 1985-87; resident U. Ariz., Tucson, 1987-90; staff neurologist Carle Clinic, Urbana, Ill., 1991—; clin. asst. prof. U. Ill. Coll. Medicine, Urbana-Champaign. Active layman Mattis Ave. Free Meth. Ch., Champaign, 1991—; trustee Greenville Coll. Recipient Recognition award LincolnLand Epilepsy Soc., 1993; Epilepsy fellow U. Minn., Mpls., 1990-91. Mem. Am. Epilepsy Soc., Am. Acad. Neurology. Republican. Avocations: reading, sports, friends. Office: Carle Clinic Divsn Neurosci 602 W University Ave Urbana IL 61801-2594

CRAPA, JOSEPH R., federal agency administrator; b. N.Y.C., Dec. 16, 1943. Assoc. adminstr. congl. and intergovtl. rels. EPA, Washington, 1997—. Office: EPA 401 M St MC 1301 Washington DC 20460

CRAPO, MICHAEL DEAN, senator, former congressman, lawyer; b. Idaho Falls, Idaho, May 20, 1951; s. George Lavelle and Melba (Olsen) C.; m. Susan Diane Hasleton, June 22, 1974; children: Michelle, Brian, Stephanie, Lara, Paul. BA Polit. Sci. summa cum laude, Brigham Young U., 1973; postgrad., U. Utah, 1973-74; JD cum laude, Harvard U., 1977. Bar: Calif. 1977, Idaho 1979. Law clk. to Hon. James M. Carter U.S. Ct. Appeals (9th cir.), San Diego, 1977-78; assoc. atty. Gibson, Dunn & Crutcher, L.A., 1978-79; atty. Holden, Kidwell, Hahn & Crapo, Idaho Falls, 1979-92, ptnr., 1983-92; mem. Idaho State Senate from 32A Dist., 1984-93, asst. majority leader, 1987-88; pres. Pro Tempore, 1989-92; congressman U.S. House of Reps., 2d Idaho dist., Washington, 1992-98; mem. commerce com., new mem. leader 103rd Congress, sophomore class leader 104th Congress, co-chair Congl. Beef Caucus, dep. whip western region U.S. House of Reps., Washington, vice chair energy and power subcom., strategic planning leader House Leadership 105th Congress, mem. house resources com., mem. commerce com., mem. resources com.; senator U.S. Senate, 1998—; precinct committeeman Dist. 29, 1980-85; vice chmn. Legislative Dist. 29, 1984-85; Mem. Health and Welfare Com., 1985-89, Resources and Environ. Com., 1985-90, State Affairs Com., 1987-92; Rep. Pres. Task Force, 1989. Leader Boy Scouts Am., Calif., Idaho, 1977-92; mem. Bar Exam Preparation, Bar Exam Grading; chmn. Law Day.; Bonneville County chmn. Phil Batt gubernatorial campaign, 1982. Named one of Outstanding Young Men of Am., 1985; recipient Cert. of Merit Rep. Nat. Com., 1990, Guardian of Small Bus. award Nat. Fedn. of Ind. Bus., 1990, 94, Cert. of Recognition Am. Cancer Soc., 1990, Idaho Housing Agy., 1990, Idaho Lung Assn., 1985, 86, 89, Friend of Agr. award Idaho Farm Bur., 1989-90, medal of merit Rep. Presdl. Task Force, 1989, Nat. Legislator of Yr. award Nat. Rep. Legislators Assn., 1991, Golden Bulldog award Watchdogs of the Treas., 1996, Thomas Jefferson award Nat. Am. Wholesale Grocers Assn.-Ind. Food Distbrs. Assn., 1996, Spirit of Enterprise award U.S. C. of C., 1993, 94, 95, 96. Mem. ABA (antitrust law sect.), Idaho Bar Assn., Rotary. Mormon. Avocations: sports, backpacking, hunting, skiing. Office: US Senate 111 Russell Senate Ofc Bldg Washington DC 20510

CRAPO, SHEILA ANNE, telecommunications company professional, artist; b. Elko, Nev., June 11, 1951; d. John Lewis and June Florene (Lani) C. BA, U. Nev., 1974. Various svc. positions Citizens Comm. (formerly Alltel-Nevada Inc.), Elko, 1974-78, svc. rep., 1978-84, bus. office supr., 1984-87, bus. supr. Nev. office, 1987-94, bus. supr., state pub. rels. coord., 1994-97; results coord., project mgmt. support person Citizens Comm. (formerly Alltel-Nevada Inc.), Elk Grove, Calif., 1997, supr. customer ops. escalations and exec. complaints, 1998—; active Citizens Ambassador program People to People Internat., 1995-98; writer, artist, 1974—; speaker in field. Contbg. author: Fence Post to Fiber, 1998. Officer, organizer Freedom Com., Elko, 1984; mem., treas. Elk Grove Cmty. Action Team, 1997-98. Mem. AAUW (editor newsletter Elko 1980-82, v.p. programs 1991-93, sec. 1995-96), Northeastern Nev. Hist. Soc., Soroptimist Internat. (treas. 1992-93, sec. 1993-94, v.p. 1995-96, pres. 1996-97). Office: Citizens Comm PO Box 340 Elk Grove CA 95759-0340

CRAPOL, EDWARD P., history educator; b. Buffalo, N.Y., Sept. 29, 1936; s. Paul H. and Emmi H. (klinger) C.; m. Jeanne Zeidler, Aug. 1, 1973; children: Heidi, Jennifer, Paul, Andrew. BA, SUNY, Buffalo, 1960; MS, Univ. Wis., 1964, PhD, 1968. Tchr. Amherst Ctrl. Jr. High Sch., Amherst, N.Y., 1961-63; instr. history Wis. State Univ., Eau Claire, Wis., 1966-67; asst. prof. history Coll. William and Mary, Williamsburg, Va., 1967-71, assoc. prof. history, 1971-77; exchange prof. history Univ. Exeter, Exeter, England, 1976-77; prof. history dept. Coll. William and Mary, Williamsburg, Va., 1978—, chmn. history dept., 1981-84, acting chmn. history dept., 1986-87; chancellor prof. history, 1994—; vis. faculty Utah State U., summer, 1972; reviewer grant proposals NEH, 1983-95; lectr. in field. Editor: Women and American Foreign Policy: Lobbyists, Critics, and Insiders, 1987, 1992, America for Americans: Economic Nationalism and Anglophobia in the Late Nineteenth Century, 1973; reviewer manuscripts for Diplomatic History, Journal of the Early Republic, Alfred A. Knopf, Scholary Recources, Greenwood Press, Kent State Univ. Press, D.C. Health, Univ. N.C. Press. William and Mary Alumni Summer Rsch. grant, 1970, 1981, William and Mary Summer Rsch. grant, 1973, Anheuser Busch Summer Rsch. grant, 1979, Va. Found. for Humanities and Pub. Policy grant, 1983, NEH grant, 1984, 1986, Internat. Studies Curriculum Devel. grant Coll of William and Mary, 1987; Univ. Humanities fellow Coll. William and Mary, 1988; Thomas A. Graves Jr. award for Sustained Excellence in Teaching William and Mary Coll., 1991, Thomas Jefferson award Coll. William and Mary, 1992. Mem. Soc. Historians Am. Fgn. Rels., Orgn. Am. Historians, Am. Hist. Assn., Soc. Historians Early Am. Republic. Home: 148 Mimosa Dr Williamsburg VA 23185-4004 Office: Coll William and Mary Dept History Williamsburg VA 23185

CRARY, MINER DUNHAM, JR., lawyer; b. Warren, Pa., Sept. 8, 1920; s. Miner D. and Edith (Ingraham) C.; m. Mary Chapman, Jan. 23, 1943; children: Edith Crary Howe, James G., Laura Crary Hall, Harriet Crary, Miner A. BA, Amherst Coll., 1942; MA, Harvard U., 1943, LLB, 1948. Bar: N.Y. 1949. Assoc. Curtis, Mallet-Prevost, 1949-61, ptnr., 1961-1996, coun., 1996—. Trustee Am. U. in Cairo, 1959—; trustee Heckscher Art Mus., Huntington, N.Y., 1968—; trustee Sterling and Francine Clark Art Inst., Williamstown, Mass., 1974—; bd. dirs. Robert Sterling Clark Found., N.Y.C., 1972—; chmn. exec. com. alumni coun. Amherst Coll., 1961-68; chmn. Huntington Bd. Edn. and Central Sch. Dist. 2, 1961-67; dep. village justice, Village of Asharoken, Northport, N.Y., 1987—. Lt. USNR, 1942-45. Mem. ABA (real property and probate com.), N.Y. State Bar Assn. (taxation and estate com. 1973), Assn. of Bar of City of N.Y. (surrogate ct. com. 1969-73). Clubs: Union League, Century Assn. (N.Y.C.); Huntington Country. Office: Curtis Mallet-Prevost Colt 101 Park Ave New York NY 10178

CRASEMANN, BERND, physicist, educator; b. Hamburg, Germany, Jan. 23, 1922; came to U.S., 1946, naturalized, 1955.; s. Pablo Joaquin and Hildegard Carlota (Vorwerk) C. A.B., UCLA, 1948; Ph.D., U. Calif.-Berkeley, 1953. With Lavadora de Lanas S.A., Viña del Mar, Chile, 1941-46; asst. prof. physics U. Oreg., Eugene, 1953-58; assoc. prof. U. Oreg., 1958-63, prof., 1963-89, prof. emeritus, 1989—, chmn. dept., 1976-84, dir. Chem. Physics Inst., 1984-87; Guest assoc. physicist Brookhaven Nat. Lab., Upton, N.Y., 1961-62; vis. prof. U. Calif., Berkeley, 1968-69, Université Pierre et Marie Curie, Paris, 1977; vis. scholar Stanford U., 1983; cons. Lawrence Radiation Lab., 1954-68, physicist, 1968-69; mem. com. on atomic and molecular sci. NRC/Nat. Acad. Scis., 1976-82; vis. scientist NASA Ames Research Center, 1975-76; mem. panel on radiation research NRC, 1985-87, chair bd. on assessment of NIST programs panel on atomic molecular and optical physics, 1989-90; chair exec. com. Advanced Light Source Users, 1984-88, sci. policy bd., 1989-92; chair adv. bd. Basic Energy Scis. Synchrotron Radiation Ctr. Argonne Nat. Lab, 1991-93; mem. U. Chgo. Review Com. for Argonne Nat. Lab. Physics Divsn., 1993-98; U.S. advisor in physics U.S.-Mex. Found. for Sci., 1994-97. Author: (with J.L. Powell) Quantum Mechanics, 1961; editor: Atomic Inner-Shell Processes, 1975, Atomic Inner-Shell Physics, 1985; editor Phys. Rev. A, 1992—; mem. editorial bd. Phys. Rev. C, 1978, Atomic Data and Nuclear Data Tables, 1982—; mem. publs. bd. Am. Inst. Physics, 1992—; contbr. articles to sci. jours. Mem. region XIV selection com. Woodrow Wilson Nat. Fellowship Found., 1959-61, 62-68. Recipient Ersted award for distinguished teaching U. Oreg., 1959; NSF research grantee, 1954-64; U.S. AEC grantee, 1964-72; NASA grantee, 1972-79; AFOSR grantee, 1979-86; NSF grantee, 1986—. Fellow AAAS, Am. Phys. Soc. (chmn. div. electron and atomic physics 1981-82, councillor 1983-86, mem. com. on internat. sci. affairs 1997—); mem. ACLU, Am. Assn. Physics Tchrs. (pres. Oreg. sect. 1956-57), Croatian Acad. Scis. and Arts (corr. mem.), Sierra Club, Phi Beta Kappa. Office: U Oreg Dept Physics Eugene OR 97403

CRASSWELLER, ROBERT DOELL, retired lawyer, writer; b. Duluth, Minn., Sept. 17, 1915; s. Arthur Hallifax and Mary Elizabeth (Doell) C.; m. Mildred Elizabeth Clarke, Mar. 21, 1942; children: Peter, Karen Farbman, Pamela Baldino. BA, Carleton Coll., 1937; LLB, Harvard U., 1941. Bar: Minn. 1941, N.Y. 1960. Pvt. practice Duluth, Minn., 1942-43; econ. warfare posts U.S. Dept. State, Washington, 1943-45; ptnr. McCabe, Gruber, Clure, Donovan & Crassweller, Duluth, Minn., 1946-51; mining exec. West Indies Mining Corp., San Juan, P.R., 1951-53; counsel Pan Am. Airways, N.Y.C., 1954-67; vis. fellow Coun. Fgn. Rels., N.Y.C., 1967-70; vis. prof. Bklyn. Coll., Sarah Lawrence, N.Y.C., 1969-70; staff atty. ITT, N.Y.C., 1970-74, gen. coun. Lat. Am., 1975-81. Author: Trujillo: Life and Times of a Caribbean Dictator, 1966, The Caribbean Community, 1972, Perón and the Enigmas of Argentina, 1986; reviewer (books) for Fgn. Affairs, 1968-81. Dir. Forum for World Affairs, Stamford, Conn., 1986-87. Mem. Internat. Assn. Torch Clubs (Chapel Hill Club v.p. 1994-95), Soc. Automotive Historians. Republican. Avocations: gardening, travel, reading, writing, antique cars. Home: 101 York Pl Chapel Hill NC 27514-6521

CRATER, TIMOTHY ANDREWS, physician; b. Winston-Salem, N.C., Aug. 27, 1966; s. John Lee Crater and Nancy Denton Hafner; m. Debra Marie Schuh, Feb. 14, 1992; children: Reed Brooks, Zoe Emerson. BA in History magna cum laude, Wake Forest U., 1989; student field arty. officers basic course, Ft. Sill Arty. Sch., Okla., 1990; officer's tng., U.S. Army Airborne Sch., Ft. Benning, Ga., 1990, 1st Infanty Divsn., 1991; MD, U. Kans., 1998. Commd. 2d lt. U.S. Army, 1989, advanced through grades to 1st lt., 1992; fire support officer hdqs. battery 1/5 field arty. U.S. Army, Ft. Riley, 1990-91, fire direction officer bravo battery 1/5 field arty., 1991-92, targeting officer hdqs. battery 1/5 field arty., 1992-93; resigned, 1993; resident in internal medicine U. Ala. Birmingham Hosp., 1998—; history of medicine fellow U. Kans., summer 1995. Capt. USAR, 1996-97. Decorated Bronze Star for combat action during Operation Desert Storm, Army Commendation medal with oak leaf clusters, Army Achievement medal with oak leaf cluster, Kuwait Liberation medal, Parachutist Badge. Mem. ACP, AMA, VFW, 5th Arty. Regtl. Assn., Am. Mensa, Am. Legion, Soc. of Big Red One, Phi Beta Kappa, Phi Alpha Theta, Alpha Omega Alpha. Republican. Avocations: reading, leading bible study group, running. Home: 3416 Cedar Crest Cir Hoover AL 35216-5361

CRAUN, JAMES, federal agency administrator; b. Balt., July 16, 1943. BA, U. Md., 1969; MA in Econs., George Washington U., 1982. Sr. economist Civil Aeronautics Bd. U.S. Dept. Transp., Washington, 1969-88, dep. aviation analysis, 1988-94, dir. aviation and internat. econs., 1994—. Recipient Silver award U.S. Dept. Transp., 1986, Gold award, 1995. Office: US Dept Transp Aviation and Internat Econs 400 7th St SW Washington DC 20590-0001*

CRAVEN, DONALD B., lawyer; b. Durham, N.C., Aug. 19, 1941. AB, U. N.C., 1963; LLB, Duke U., 1967; postgrad., Georgetown U. Bar: N.C. 1967, Va. 1973, D.C. 1975. Trial atty. tax divsn. U.S. Dept. Justice, 1968-73; assoc. asst. adminstr., acting asst. adminstr. Fed. Energy Adminstrn., 1974-75; mem. Miller & Chevalier Chartered, Washington. Mem. editorial bd. Duke Law Jour., 1966-67. Mem. ABA, N.C. Bar Assn., Va. Bar Assn., N.C. State Bar, Va. State Bar, D.C. Bar, Bar Assn. of D.C., Phi Delta Phi (magister 1966-67). Office: Miller & Chevalier Chartered 655 15th St NW Ste 900 Washington DC 20005-5799*

CRAVEN, GEORGE W., lawyer; b. Louisville, Mar. 11, 1951; s. Mark Patrick and Doris Ann Craven; m. Jane A. Gallery, Aug. 16, 1980; children: Charles, Francis. Student, Sophia U., Tokyo, Japan, 1970-71; BA, U. Notre Dame, 1973; JD, Harvard U., 1976. Bar: Ill. 1976, U.S. Dist. Ct. (no. dist.) Ill. 1976, U.S. Tax Ct. 1977. Assoc. Sidley & Austin, Chgo., 1976-80; ptnr. Ogden & Robertson, Louisville, 1980-81; assoc. Mayer, Brown & Platt, Chgo., 1981-82, ptnr., 1983—. Sec., United Way/Crusade of Mercy, Inc., 1997—. Mem. ABA (sect. taxation), Coun. on Fgn. Rels. (Chgo. com. 1996—). Roman Catholic. Office: Mayer Brown & Platt 190 S La Salle St Ste 3100 Chicago IL 60603-3441

CRAVEN, JAMES MICHAEL, economist, educator; b. Seattle, Mar. 10, 1946; s. Homer Henry and Mary Kathleen Craven; 1 child, Christina Kathleen Florindo-Craven. Student, U. Minn., 1966-68; BA in Sociology, U. Manitoba, Winnipeg, Can., 1971, BA in Econs., 1971, MA in Econs., 1974. Lic. pilot; cert. ground instr. Instr. econ. and bus. Red River C.C., Winnipeg, 1974-76; lectr. rsch. methods of stats. U. Manitoba, Winnipeg, 1977-78; instr. econ. and bus. Big Bend C.C., Moses Lake, Wash., 1980-81; planning analyst Govt. P.R., San Juan, 1984; prof. econs. and bus. Interam. U. P.R., Bayamon, 1984-85; instr. econs., lectr. history Green River C.C., Auburn, Wash., 1988-92; prof. dept. chair econs. Clark Coll., Vancouver, Wash., 1992—; vis. prof. St. Berchman's U., Kerala, India, 1981, 83, 86, 91; instr. econs. Bellevue (Wash.) C.C., 1988-92; cons. Bellevue, 1988—, Irwin Pubs., 1995—. Inventor in field; contbr. articles to profl. jours. Platform com. mem. Wash. State Dem., Seattle, 1992; cons. Lowry for Gov. Campaign, Seattle, 1992; mem. (assoc.) Dem. Party Nat. Com., 1994—; mem. Nat. Steering Com. for Re-election of Pres. Clinton, 1995-96; mem. Pres.'s Second Term Com., 1996—; tribunal judge Inter-Tribal Tribunal on Residential Schs. in Can., Vancouver, 1998; mem. Blackfoot Confederacy. With U.S. Army, 1963-66. Recipient pilot wings FAA, 1988-92; Govt. Can. fellow, 1973-74. Mem. Internat. Platform Assn., Assn. Northwest Econ. Educators, Wash. Edn. Assn., Assn. Nat. Security Alumni, Blackfoot Confederacy. Syrian Orthodox. Avocations: flying, languages, tennis, hiking. Home: 904 NE Minnehaha St Apt C9 Vancouver WA 98665-8732 Office: Clark Coll Dept Econs 1800 E Mcloughlin Blvd Vancouver WA 98663-3598

CRAVEN, RICKY, professional race car driver; b. Newburgh, Maine, May 24, 1966; m. Cathleen Craven; 1 child, Riley Diane. Professional race car driver NASCAR Winston Cup races, 1990—; winner Busch Pole award, 1990, winner 10 races, 6 poles, the Pole award, 1991, winner rookie title Busch Series, 1992, finished 2d in standings 1993, 94. Named NASCAR Rookie of Yr., 1990, recipient Most Popular Driver trophy, 1990, 1991; named MAXX Rookie of Yr., 1995. Office: c/o NASCAR PO Box 2875 Daytona Beach FL 32120-2875*

CRAVEN, ROBERTA JILL, educator in literature and film; b. White Plains, N.Y., Feb. 4, 1962; d. Robert James and Norma Eleanor (Page) C. BS in Math., U. N.C., 1984, PhD in Comparative Lit., 1999. Account systems engr. IBM Nat. Fed. Mktg., Bethesda, Md., 1984-86, account mktg. rep., 1986-89; telecomm. mktg. support rep. IBM, Research Triangle Park, N.C., 1990; instr. U. N.C., Chapel Hill, 1990-99; asst. prof. film Millersville U. of Pa., 1999—. T.J. Watson Nat. Merit scholar IBM, Armonk, N.Y., 1980, Hon. Regents scholar N.Y. Bd. Regents, 1980, Frank Porter Graham Grad. Hon. Soc., 1993, Dissertation fellow U. N.C., 1997, Sr. fellow, 1998. Mem. MLA, Southern Comparative Lit. Assn., Phi Beta Kappa, Phi Eta Sigma. Avocations: skiing, film, writing. Office: Dept English Chryst Hall PO Box 1002 Millersville U Pa Millersville PA 17551-0302

CRAVEN, WES, film director; b. Cleve., Aug. 2, 1939. writer, editor, dir. (films) Last House on the Left, 1972, The Hills Have Eyes, 1976; 2d editor You've Got To Walk It Like You Talk It or You'll Loose That Beat, 1973; co-writer, dir. Deadly Blessing, 1979; writer, dir. Swamp Thing, 1980, The Hills Have Eyes II, 1983, A Nightmare on Elm Street, 1984, Wes Craven's New Nightmare, 1994; co-writer Deadly Friend, 1986, The Serpent and the Rainbow, 1988; co-writer, co-exec. prodr. A Nightmare on Elm Street III, 1986; writer, dir., co-exec. prodr. Shocker, 1989, The People under the Stars, 1991; dir. Vampire in Brooklyn, 1995; co-writer (TV movies of week) A Stranger in Our House, 1978, Invitation to Hell, 1982; dir. Chiller, 1983, Casebusters, 1985, A Little Peace and Quiet, 1987, Wordplay, 1987, Chameleon, 1987, Her Pilgrim Soul, 1987, Shatterday, 1987, Dealer's Choice, 1987, The Road Not Taken, 1988; co-writer, dir., exec. prodr. Night Visions, 1990; exec. prodr. Nightmare Cafe, 1991. Mem. Dirs. Guild Am. Office: c/o Leslie Dart PMK 1775 Broadway Ste 701 New York NY 10019-1934*

CRAVEN, WILLIAM DONALD, internal auditor, consultant; b. Kennewick, Wash., Dec. 18, 1959; s. William Chester and Donna Marie (Wilson) C.; m. Sheri May Emery, Aug. 4, 1984; 1 child, Amanda Irene. BA in Polit. Sci., Wash. State U., 1985; BS in Acctg., Cen. Wash. U., 1987; postgrad., Wash. State U. CPA, Wash., Va.; cert. govt. fin. mgr.; cert. mgmt. acct. Photographer Tri-City Herald, Kenewick, 1976-78; mgr. ANDCO Corp., Seattle, 1983-84; auditor Def. Contract Audit Agy., Seattle, 1987-90, ops. auditor, 1990-91, sr. auditor, 1991-94; cost/price analyst Westinghouse Hanford Co., Richland, Wash., 1994-96, Fluor Daniel Hanford, Inc., Richland, 1996-97; internal audit mgr. Bechtel Hanford, Inc., Richland, 1998—. Bd. dirs. Richland Police Citizen Adv. Bd., 1995—, Richland Utility Adv. Bd., 1996—; chmn. Richland Utility Adv. Com., 1999—; treas. Sacajawea Elem. PTA, Richland, 1995-96; sec./treas. Deaf-Blind Svc. Ctr., Seattle, 1993-94. Mem. AICPA, Inst. Mgmt. Accts., Assn. Govt. Accts., Wash. Soc. CPAs (pres. Seattle chpt. 1992-93, dir. 1994-96, Outstanding Leadership award 1992, Chpt. Pres. of Yr. 1993), Inst. Internal Auditors, Nat. Contract Mgmt. Assn., MENSA, Kiwanis Club Three Rivers. Avocations: travel, photography, snow skiing, politics, reading. Home: 518 Doubletree Ct Richland WA 99352-1814 Office: Bechtel Hanford Inc 3350 George Washington Way Richland WA 99352

CRAVENS, RAYMOND LEWIS, retired political science educator; b. St. Bernard, Ohio, Dec. 5, 1930; s. R.L. and Ethel (Hammonds) C.; m. Ann Powell, Aug. 11, 1956; children—Andrea Lee, Alicia. A.B., Western Ky. State Coll., 1952, M.A., 1955; Haggin scholar, U. Ky., 1955-57, Ky. Research Found. fellow, 1957, Ph.D., 1958. Prof. govt. Western Ky. U., 1958—, dean of coll., 1959-64, dean of faculty, 1964-66, v.p. acad. affairs, dean faculties, 1966-77, dean pub. service and internat. programs, 1977-80, dir. Coop. Ctr. for Study in Britain, 1982-89; chmn. Ky. Council Acad. Vice Presidents; pres. Ky. Council on Internat. Edn., 1973-81; mem. adv. com. on tchr. edn. Ky. Council on Pub. Higher Edn. Served as 1st lt. USAF, 1952-54. Named one of 3 outstanding young men in state Ky. Jr. C. of C., 1964; named Ky. Internat. Educator of Yr., 1993. Mem. So. Acad. Deans, Am. Soc. Pub. Adminstrn., So. Assn. Colls. (commn. on colls., chmn. com. admissions to membership), Masons. Baptist. Home: 610 E Main St Bowling Green KY 42101-2228*

CRAVENS, STANLEY H., software development manager; b. San Francisco, Jan. 17, 1948; s. Homer A. and Virginia F. (Ference) C.; m. Debra Sargent, June 17, 1976. BA in History, U. N.H., 1974, MA in History, 1976. Project mgr. State of Wis., Madison, 1978—. Advisor: (film) A Vision Shaped in Stone, 1986. Sgt. U.S. Army, 1966-70. Decorated Bronze Star, U.S. Army, Viet Nam, 1970. Mem. Kiwanis (pres. Downtown Madison club 1990-91, lt. gov. 1992-93, gov. Wis. and Upper Mich. 1997-98). Home: 3814 Sunhill Dr Madison WI 53718-6283

CRAVER, CHARLES HENRY, illustrator; b. Eldon, Mo., Dec. 6, 1909; s. Charles Henry and Sylvia (John) C.; m. Nadia Aileen Palmer, Nov. 5, 1950. Student, St. Louis Sch. Fine Art, 1927-30, 34-36; AB, Washington U., 1933. Freelance mag. illustrator Capper Publs., Topeka, Kans., 1933-36; freelance mag. illustrator So. Agriculturist, Nashville, Tenn., 1936-42, Christian Bd. of Publ., St. Louis, 1945-1948; staff artist Mo. Dept. Health, Jefferson City, 1948-79, bur. chief, 1957; bur. chief Mo. Dept. Health Edn., Jefferson City, 1959; instr. art dept. Lincoln U., Jefferson City, 1991-94. Works include mural at Christian Ch., 1937, Bapt. Ch., 1945, exhibit at Am. Pub. Health, 1955 (2 awards), Mo. state seal, 1949, numerous landscapes, 1950-97. Mem. Capital City Coun. on the Arts, Jefferson City; advisor Nichols Ctr., Jefferson City. Staff Sgt. U.S. Air Corps, 1942-45, Africa. Recipient presdl. citation Mo. Pub. Health Assn., Jefferson City, 1984. Mem. St. Louis Artists Guild, Co. of Mil. Historians, Soc. for Army Hist. Rsch., Mil. Hist. Soc. Republican. Disciples of Christ. Home: 1305 Moreland Ave Jefferson City MO 65101-3734

CRAVER, JAMES BERNARD, lawyer; b. Morristown, N.J., July 20, 1943; s. Herbert Seward and Anne (Brady) C.; m. Elinor Ladd, Aug. 27, 1966; children: Elisabeth Ladd, Amy Richmond. AB cum laude, Harvard U.,

1965; JD, U. Pa., 1970. Bar: N.Y. 1970, Mass. 1974, Ohio 1980. Assoc. Sullivan & Cromwell, N.Y.C., 1970-73; asst. counsel, asst. sec. Mass. Fin. Svcs. Co., Boston, 1973-76; gen. counsel, sec. Anchor Corp., Elizabeth, N.J., 1976-79; sec., sr. corp. counsel B.F. Goodrich Co., Akron, Ohio, 1979-84; ptnr. Baker & Hostetler, Columbus, 1984-90; sr. v.p., gen. coun. Signature Fin. Group, Inc., Boston, 1991-95; mng. dir. Eagle Instl. Fin. Svcs., Inc., Dover, Mass., 1995—. Mem. N.Y. State Bar Assn., Mass. Bar Assn., Ohio Bar Assn., Columbus Bar Assn., Sakonnet Golf Club (Little Compton, R.I.), Harvard Club of Boston, Harvard Club of Akron, Dedham (Mass.) Country and Polo Club. Home: PO Box 811 Dover MA 02030-0811 Office: Eagle Instnl Fin Svcs Inc 42 Miller Hill Rd Dover MA 02030-2332

CRAVEY, PAMELA J., librarian; b. Washington, Mar. 6, 1945; d. Jack M. and Marjorie M.W. Bristow; m. G. Randall Cravey; 1 child, Christopher B. BA, Baldwin Wallace Coll., 1967; MS, Fla. State U., 1968; PhD, Ga. State U., 1989. Libr., instr. Fla. State U., Tallahassee, 1968-69, U. Ga., Athens, 1969-72; asst. then assoc. libr. U. Ctrl. Fla., Orlando, 1973-75; asst. then assoc. prof., libr. Ga. State U., Atlanta, 1975—. Contbr. articles to profl. jours. Libr. Svc. Enhancement Program grantee Coun. Libr. Resources; personal grantee Coun. Libr. Resources. Mem. ALA, Assn. Coll. Rsch. Librs., Southeastern Libr. Assn., Ga. Libr. Assn. Avocation: soccer. E-mail: libpjc@langate.gsu.edu. Home: 2413 Harrington Dr Decatur GA 30033 Office: Ga State U Pullen Libr 100 Decatur St SE Atlanta GA 30033

CRAW, FREEMAN (JERRY CRAW), graphic artist; b. East Orange, N.J.; s. Stanley Reston and Mildred (Godfrey) C.; m. Janet Secor Johnson; Children: Peter (dec.), Stephanie (dec.). Grad., Cooper Union, hon. degree, 1967. Artist Am. Colortype, Clifton, N.J., 1940-44; art dir. Tri-Arts Press, N.Y.C., 1944-65, art dir., v.p., 1956-65; prin. Freeman Craw Design, N.Y.C., 1965-81; mgr. graphics and prodn. Rockefeller U. Press, N.Y.C., 1981-86; prin. Freeman Craw, graphist, Millburn, N.J., 1986—. One-man shows include: Am. Type Founders, U. Ala., BBDO, N.Y.C., Carnegie-Mellon U., Cooper Union, Royal Coll. Art, London, Soc. Typog. Designers, London, Soc. Typog. Arts, Chgo., Rochester Inst. Tech., N.Y.; represented in permanent collections: Mus. Modern Art., N.Y.C., Cooper-Hewitt Mus., Smithsonian Instn., N.Y.C.; created 10 type faces. Mem. alumni adv. bd. Cooper Union, 1969-71. Recipient Goudy award Rochester Inst. Tech., 1981, Type Dirs. Club medal, 1988, Lernhardt award, 1966. Mem. Type Dirs. Club (bd. dirs. 1983-86), Art Dirs. Club, Guttenberg Mus. (hon.), Essex Skating Club (West Orange, N.J., hon.). Avocations: Japanese prints, lectures.

CRAW, NICHOLAS WESSON, motor sports association executive; b. Governor's Island, N.Y., Nov. 14, 1936; s. Demas Thurlow Craw and Mary Victoria Wesson. BA cum laude, Princeton U., 1959; MBA, Harvard U., 1982. Dir. ops. Project Hope, Washington, 1960-68; pres., CEO Scorpio Racing, Washington, 1968-80, Sports Car Club Am., Englewood, Colo., 1983—; pres. Sports Car Club Am. Found., Englewood, 1986—; chmn. Nat. Motorsports Coun., 1992—; bd. dirs. SCCA Pro Racing Ltd., SCCA Enterprises, Inc., USRRC, Rsch. Sys., Inc. Dir. Manpower divsn. VISTA, Washington, 1970-72; assoc. dir. ACTION, Washington, 1972-73; dir. U.S. Peace Corps, Washington, 1973-74. Office: Sports Car Club Am 9033 E Easter Pl Englewood CO 80112-2122

CRAWFORD, ANNMARIE, writer, model, actress, photographer; b. Chgo., Jan. 30, 1971; d. Timothy and Karen Jean (Graham) C. Student, John Casablancas Elite, 1994, Oakton C.C., 1994—. Model Kee Dept. Store, Chgo., 1979-83; actress P.G. Berland and Wallpaper TV comml., Chgo., 1984; model Mary Kay Cosmetics, Chgo., 1987-88; model, actress John Casablancas Elite, Chgo., 1994; model, demonstrator Revlon, Niles, Ill., 1994—. Author: The Disease of Alcoholism, 1996, The King of New England Street, 1997. Avocations: writing, plants, raising finches. Home: 450 W Palatine Rd Palatine IL 60067

CRAWFORD, BETTY ELIZABETH, English and computer science educator; b. Whittemore, Mich., Dec. 6, 1942; d. Kenneth Arnold and Ona Belle (Allen) St. John; m. Franklin Speaker Crawford, Dec. 29, 1968 (dec. Oct. 1994); 1 child, Tina. BS, Bob Jones U., 1965; MA in Tchg., Oakland U., 1980; cert. of journalism, Newspaper Inst., 1985. Cert. tchr., Mich. Computer coord., tchr. Faith Christian Schs., Clinton Twp., Mich., 1980—; English prof. Macomb C.C., Warren, Mich., 1988—; ESL instr. Lang. Masters, Southfield, Mich., 1999—; spkr. in field. Editor: Computer Science, 1990. Mem. Nat. Coun. Tchrs. English, Mich. Assn. Christian Schs., Am. Assn. Christian Schs. Avocations: reading, surfing the web, church, singing, piano. Office: Faith Christian Schools 23130 Remick Dr Clinton Township MI 48036-2735

CRAWFORD, BOB, state commissioner; b. Bartow, Fla., Jan. 26, 1948; m. Nancy Sue Caswall; children: Robert Bruce IV, Kristin Nicole. Degree in bus., U. Miami. Rep. Fla. House, 6 yrs.; senator Fla. Senate, 8 yrs., pres., 1988-90; commr. agriculture State of Fla., 1990—. Named Most Effective State Lawmaker, Miami Herald. Baptist. Office: Agrl and Consumer Services Plz Level 10 The Capit Tallahassee FL 32399*

CRAWFORD, BRUCE EDGAR, advertising executive; b. West Bridgewater, Mass., Mar. 16, 1929; s. Harry Ellsworth and Nancy (Morrison) C.; m. Christine Ameling, Feb. 1, 1958; 1 son, Robert Bosworth. B.S. in Econs., U. Pa., 1952. With Benton & Bowles, Inc., N.Y.C., 1954-58; v.p. Ted Bates & Co., N.Y.C., 1958-61; advt. dir. Chesebrough Ponds Inc., N.Y.C., 1961-63; with Batten, Barton, Durstine & Osborn, Inc., N.Y.C., 1963-85, pres., from 1978; pres. BBDO Internat., N.Y.C., 1975-83, chief exec. officer, 1977-85, chmn., 1985; dir. Met. Opera Assn., from 1976, v.p., 1981, pres., 1984-85, gen. mgr., 1986-88; pres., chief exec. officer Omnicom Group, N.Y.C., 1989-97; chmn. Omnicom Group, Inc., N.Y.C., 1997—. Served with U.S. Army, 1947-48. Republican. Clubs: Racquet and Tennis (N.Y.C.); Turf and Field. Office: Omnicom Group Inc 437 Madison Ave New York NY 10022-7001 Also: Met Opera Assn Lincoln Ctr New York NY 10023*

CRAWFORD, BRYCE LOW, JR., chemist, educator; b. New Orleans, Nov. 27, 1914; s. Bryce Low and Clara Hall (Crawford) C.; m. Ruth Raney, Dec. 21, 1940; children: Bryce, Craig, Sherry Ann. A.B., Stanford U., 1934, M.A., 1935, Ph.D., 1937; Nat. Research fellow, Harvard U., 1937-39. Instr. chemistry Yale U., 1939-40; asst. prof. U. Minn., Mpls., 1940-43; assoc. prof. U. Minn., 1943-46, prof. phys. chemistry, 1946-82, Regents' prof. chemistry, 1982-85, emeritus, 1985—, chmn. dept., 1955-60, dean grad. sch., 1960-72; Mem. Grad. Record Exam. Bd., 1968-72; chmn. Council Grad Schs. in U.S., 1962-63; pres. Assn. Grad. Schs., 1970; dir. research on rocket propellants under Div. 3 Nat. Def. Research Com., 1942-45. Editor: Jour. Phys. Chemistry, 1970-80. Trustee Midwest Research Inst., 1963-92. Guggenheim fellow, 1950-51, 72-73; Fulbright grantee Oxford, 1951; Fulbright grantee, Tokyo, 1966; recipient Presdl. Cert. of Merit. Fellow Optical Soc. Am. (Pitts. Spectroscopy award, Ellis Lippincott award), Am. Phys. Soc.; mem. Am. Chem. Soc. (bd. dirs. 1969-77, Priestley medal 1982), AAAS, AAUP, Nat. Acad. Scis. (council 1975-78, home. sec. 1979-87), Coblentz Soc., Am. Philos. Soc., Soc. for Applied Spectroscopy, Am. Acad. Arts and Scis., Phi Beta Kappa, Sigma Xi, Phi Lambda Upsilon, Alpha Chi Sigma. Episcopalian. Clubs: Campus, Cosmos. Specialist in molecular structure and molecular spectra. E-Mail: crawford@chemsun.chem.umm.edu. Home: 1666 Coffman St Apt 114 Saint Paul MN 55108-1326 Office: U Minn Dept Chemistry 207 Pleasant St SE Minneapolis MN 55455-0431

CRAWFORD, CARL BENSON, retired civil engineer, government research administrator; b. Dauphin, Man., Can., Oct. 2, 1923; s. Arthur Benson and Eileen Agnes (Einarson) C.; m. Adah May Shanks, Sept. 6, 1948; children: Nora, Henry, Margaret, Blair. B.Sc.E., Queen's U., Kingston, Ont., Can., 1949; M.Sc. in Soil Enging, Northwestern U., 1951; D.I.C. in Soil Enging, U. London, 1957; LL.D., Concordia U., 1984. Research officer soil mechanics sect. Bldg. Research div. Nat. Research Council Can., Ottawa, Ont., 1949-53; head soil mechanics sect. Bldg. Research div. Nat. Research Council Can., 1953-69, asst. dir., 1969-74, dir., 1974-85; ret., 1985; vis. prof. U. B.C., 1985—. Contbr. articles to tech. publs. Served with RCAF, 1943-45. Recipient Robert F. Legget award Can. Geotech. Soc., 1977, R.M. Quigley award, 1996. Fellow Can. Acad. Enging.; mem. ASTM (Hogentogler award 1961, Spl. Svc. award 1968, hon. mem. 1977—, dir. Inst. for Stds. Rsch., bd. dirs. 1990-92), ASCE, Enging. Inst. Can. (Julian C. Smith medal 1989), Internat. Soc. Soil Mechanics and Found. Enging. (v.p. N.Am. 1981-85), Stds. Coun. Can. (Jean P. Carriere award 1990), Assn. Profl. Engrs. Ont. Home: 108-2556 Highbury St. Vancouver, BC Canada V6R 3T3

CRAWFORD, CAROL L., opera company artistic director. Student, Julliard Sch., Mozarteum, Salzburg; PhD in music, Yale Univ. Assoc. condr. Memphis Symphony, Tenn.; condr. Memphis Youth Symphony, Tenn.; artistic dir. Tulsa Opera, Okla., 1993—, gen. dir.; music dir. Houston Grand Opera's Tex. Opera Theater, San Francisco Opera's Western Opera Theater, Ashlawn-Highland Festival, Charlottesville, Va.; assoc. music dir. Va. Opera. Condr.: (Tulsa Philharmonic) Madama Butterfly, 1991, Carmen, 1992; apprentice condr.: (documentary) Bernstein: Conductor, Teacher, Composer, 1984. Recipient first prize San Diego Opera Young American Opera Condrs. Competition, 1981. Office: Tulsa Opera Chapman Music Hall 1610 S Boulder Ave Tulsa OK 74119-4479*

CRAWFORD, CAROL TALLMAN, government executive; b. Mt. Holly, N.J., Feb. 25, 1943; m. Ronald Crawford; children: Timothy, Jeffrey, Richard. BA, Mt. Holyoke Coll., 1965; JD magna cum laude, Washington Coll. Law, Am. U., 1978. Bar: Va. 1978, D.C. 1979. Legis. asst. to Senator Bob Packwood Washington, 1969-75; assoc. firm Collier, Shannon, Rill & Scott, Washington, 1979-81; exec. asst. to chmn. FTC, Washington, 1981-83, dir. bur. consumer protection, 1983-85; assoc. dir. Office of Mgmt. & Budget, Washington, 1985-89; asst. atty. gen. legis. affairs U.S. Dept. Justice, Washington, 1989-90; commr. U.S. Internat. Trade Commn., 1991—; sr. advisor Reagan-Bush Transition Team, 1981. Trustee Barry Goldwater Chair of Am. Instns., Ariz. State U., Phoenix, 1983—; mem. dean's adv. coun. Wash Coll. of Law, 1995—; adv. com. Ind. Women's Forum, 1996—; v.p. The Hist. Georgetown Club; chair subcom. on trade and investment Federalist Soc., 1998—. Republican. Office: 500 E St SW Washington DC 20024-2760

CRAWFORD, CHARLES MCNEIL, winery science executive; b. Antioch, Calif., Sept. 23, 1918; s. Robert Elmer and Alice (Hust) C.; m. Sarah Katherine Glover, Aug. 19, 1940; children: Robert McNeil, Judith Lee. B.S., U. Calif. at Berkeley, 1940; M.S., Cornell U., 1941. Trainee Great Western Electro-Chem. Co., Pittsburg, Calif., 1939; research asst. N.Y. State Agrl. Expt. Sta., Geneva, N.Y., 1940; winemaker-chemist Urbana Wine Co., Hammondsport, N.Y., 1941; v.p., sec. E & J Gallo Winery, Modesto, Calif., 1942-; pres. Sub-Commn. II Nutrition and Health Office, Internat. de la Vigne et du Vin, Paris, 1995—; mem. Am. Soc. for Viticulture and Enology; sci. advisor Ernest Gallo Clinic and Rsch. Ctr., 1996—. Recipient Merit award, 1966, Am. Soc. Quality Control award, 1972, Am. Wine Soc. award, 1989; Cornell U. Research fellow, 1940-41. Mem. Am. Soc. Enologists (Merit award 1966), Am. Chem. Soc., Am. Inst. Chemists, Inst. Food Tech., Wine Inst. (tech. com., award for tech. excellence 1988), Nat., Calif. socs. profl. engrs., N.Y. Acad. Sci., Calif. Acad. Sci., AAAS, Alpha Zeta. Clubs: F.W. Ski Assn, Tahoe Yacht. Home: 417 The Bluff Modesto CA 95355 Office: PO Box 1130 Modesto CA 95353-1130

CRAWFORD, CINDY, model, actress; b. Dekalb, Ill., Feb. 20, 1966; d. Dan and Jennifer C.; m. Richard Gere, Dec. 12, 1991. Student, Northwestern U. Model for Victor Skrebneski, 1984-86; signed with Elite Modeling Agy., 1986; spokesperson Revlon, 1989—, JH Collectibles, Pepsi Cola, Kay Jewelers; host MTV's House of Style, 1989—. First featured on cover Vogue, 1986; exercise videos: Cindy Crawford's Shape Your Body Workout, 1992, The Next Challenge Workout, 1993; film appearances include: Fair Game, 1995. Office: Wolf-Kasteler 132 S Rodeo Dr Ste 300 Beverly Hills CA 90212-2414

CRAWFORD, DAVID L., astronomer; b. Tarenton, Pa., Mar. 2, 1931; s. William Letham and A. Blanche (Livingstone) C.; m. Mary Louise Meuller, Aug. 16, 1940; children: Christine, Deborah, Lisa. PhD, U. Chgo., 1958. Rsch. asst. Yerkes Obs., Chgo., 1953-57; asst. prof. Vanderbilt U., Nashville, 1957-59; staff astronomer Kitt Peak Nat. Obs., Tucson, 1960-96, emeritus astronomer, 1997—; rsch. asst. McDonald Obs., 1955-57; project mgr. Kitt Peak Nat. Obs., 1963-73, assoc. dir. rsch., 1970-73, head office univ. rels., 1984-85, head office of tech. transfer, 1993-95; exec. dir. Internat. Dark-Sky Assn., 1987—, pres. bd. dirs. GNAT, Inc., 1993—. Recipient outstanding svc. award Astron. League, 1992. Fellow AAAS (coun. 1986-89, com. on coun. affairs 1986-88), Illuminating Enging. Soc. N.Am. (roadway lighting com., outdoor environ. lighting impact com., sports lighting com.); mem. Am. Astron. Soc. (coun. 1972-75, Van Briesbrock award 1997), Astron. Soc. Pacific (bd. dirs. 1970-76, nominating com., publs. com.), Internat. Astron. Union (active numerous commns., exec. coms., past chmn. working group on amateur/profl. rels.). Avocations: travel, reading, teaching, trout fishing, photography. Office: NOAO Kitt Peak Nat Obs PO Box 26732 Tucson AZ 85726-6732

CRAWFORD, DEWEY BYERS, lawyer; b. Saginaw, Mich., Dec. 22, 1941; s. Edward Owen and Ruth (Wentworth) C.; m. Nancy Elizabeth Eck, Mar. 24, 1974. AB in Econs., Dartmouth Coll., 1963; JD with distinction, U. Mich., 1966. Bar: Ill. 1967, U.S. Dist. Ct. (no. dist.) Ill. 1969. Assoc. Gardner, Carton & Douglas, Chgo., 1969-74, ptnr., 1975—; adj. prof. law, ITT, Kent Sch. Law, 1992—. Contbr. articles to profl. jours. Chmn. Winnetka (Ill.) Caucus Coun., 1988-89. With U.S. Army, 1966-68, Vietnam. Mem. ABA, Chgo. Bar Assn., Am. Coll. Investment Counsel, Law Club Chgo., Legal Club Chgo. Republican. Congregationalist. Avocations: running, reading, music. Office: Gardner Carton & Douglas 321 N Clark St Ste 3000 Chicago IL 60610-4762

CRAWFORD, DONALD WESLEY, philosophy educator, university official; b. Berkeley, Calif., July 30, 1938; s. Arthur Loyd and Josephine (Gareffa) C.; m. Sharon Dee Messenger, Nov. 5, 1960; children: Kathryn, Alison. BA, U. Calif., Berkeley, 1960; PhD, U. Wis., 1965. Teaching asst. U. Wis., Madison, 1962-64, instr., 1965, asst. prof., 1968-70, assoc. prof., 1970-74, prof., 1974-79, chair dept. philosophy, 1973-76, 79-81, dean Coll. Letters and Sci., 1989-92; asst. prof. U. Sask., Saskatchewan, Can., 1965-68; vice chancellor acad. affairs U. Calif., Santa Barbara, 1992-93, exec. vice chancellor, 1993-98, dir. London Ctr. for Edn. Abroad program, 1998—. Author: Kant's Aesthetic Theory, 1974; editor Jour. Aesthetics and Art Criticism, 1989-93. Bd. dirs. Meriter Hosp., Madison, 1989-92, Santa Barbara Bot. Garden, 1993—, U. Calif. Santa Barbara Found., 1992—. NEH fellow, 1974. Mem. Am. Philos. Assn., Am. Soc. for Aesthetic, Brit. Soc. for Aesthetic. Office: U Calif 5105 Cheadle Hall Santa Barbara CA 93106*

CRAWFORD, EDWARD E., psychologist; b. Lawton, Ky., July 31, 1929; s. Thurmon Ray and Hazel Mae (Johnson) C.; m. Patricia Ann Dulin, Sept. 4, 1954; children: Scott, Susan. AB, W.Va. U., 1956, MA, 1958; postgrad., U. Pa., 1956-57; PhD, Cath. U. Am., 1969. Clin. psychologist Rosewood State Hosp., Owings Mills, Md., 1957-67; sr. staff psychologist Montrose Sch. for Girls, Reisterstown, Md., 1967-71; sr. psychol. cons. Md. Dept. Health and Mental Hygiene, Balt., 1971-74; dir. psychol. and developmental svcs. Md. Preventive Medicine Adminstrn., 1974-76; chief psychology programs Dept. Health and Mental Hygiene, 1976-80; chief psychology svcs. Md. Adminstrn. Chronically Ill and Aging, 1980-81; chief psychologist Henryton (Md.) Ctr., 1981-84; co-owner Psychol. Assessment & Therapy, 1984-86; pvt. practice psychology, 1984-98; psychol. cons. Wicomico County (Md.) Health Dept., 1958-60, Anne Arundel County (Md.) Pub. Schs., 1965-66, Kernan Crippled Children's Hosp., 1972, The Chimes, Inc., 1985-98. With AUS, 1948-52, VA trainee, 1956-57. Mem. APA, Masons, Scottish Rite, Shriners. Methodist. Office: 1005 Timber Trail Rd Baltimore MD 21286-1610

CRAWFORD, FELIX CONKLING, dentist; b. Jan. 11, 1938. DDS, U. Tex. Dental Br., Houston, 1963. Pvt. practice Plainview, Tex. Pres. Rotary, Plainview, 1971-72, Plainview Country Club, 1973-74, Plainview C. of C., 1984; chmn. Tex. Dental Found., 1990-92. Mem. ADA (vice-chmn. Coun. Govt. Affairs 1999—), Tex. Dental Assn. (chmn. DenPac 1982-85, pres. 1988). Office: 2615 W 24th St Plainview TX 79072

CRAWFORD, GERALD J. (JERRY CRAWFORD), umpire; b. Phila., Aug. 13, 1947; m. Carol Alessi, Feb. 24, 1968; children: Christopher, Alyson. Player Am. Legion Baseball, Connie Mack Baseball; former umpire Fla. State League, Carolina League, Ea. League, Internat. League; umpire maj. league baseball Nat. League, N.Y.C., 1976—; with Umpires Union, Phila. Avocations: HO trains, music. Office: Nat League 350 Park Ave New York NY 10022 also: Umpires Union 1735 Market St Philadelphia PA 19103

CRAWFORD, HAROLD BERNARD, publisher; b. Newark, N.J., Nov. 26, 1934; s. Harold Bernard and Florence Janet (Powers) Crappse; m. Eleanor Teresa Wrobleski, July 1, 1961 (div. 1973); children—Melanie Joyce, Allison Gail; m. Elizabeth Lucille Boehm, Aug. 18, 1973. B.A., NYU, 1956. Media buyer Lennen & Newell Advt., N.Y.C., 1956-60; asst. promotion dir. Am. Inst. C.P.A.s, N.Y.C., 1960-62; copy writer McGraw-Hill Book Co., N.Y.C., 1962-63, copy chief, 1963-66, product mgr., 1966-70, sr. editor, 1970-80, editor-in-chief tech. books profl. and reference divsn., 1980-97; instr. U. Chgo. Ctr. for Continuing Studies, instr. NYU Ctr. for Pub. Avocations: audio enthusiast; record collecting.

CRAWFORD, HOWARD ALLEN, lawyer; b. Stafford, Kans., Aug. 4, 1917; s. Perry V. and Kate (Allen) C.; m. Millie Houseworth, Oct. 9, 1948; children: Catherine, Edward. BS, Kans. State U., 1939; JD, U. Mich., 1942. Bar: Kans. 1942, Mo. 1943, U.S. Ct. Appeals (8th, 10th and D.C. cirs.), U.S. Supreme Ct. Mem. firm Lathrop and Gage, Kansas City, Mo., 1950-91; mng. ptnr. Lathrop and Norquist, Kansas City, Mo., 1970-85, ret., 1991; dir. various cos. Mem. coun. City of Mission Hills, Kans., 1965-70. Mem. Lawyers Assn. Kansas City, Kansas City Club, Mission Hills Country Club. Home: 3103 W 67th Ter Shawnee Mission KS 66208-1857 Office: Lathrop and Gage 25th Fl 2345 Grand Blvd Fl 25 Kansas City MO 64108-2603

CRAWFORD, HUNT DORN, JR., retired military officer, educator, diplomat; b. Louisville, Dec. 25, 1948; s. Hunt Dorn Sr. and Carrol Frank (Watson) C.; m. Kate Kerr Delano, Aug. 1, 1970; children: Scott Holden, Carolyn Hunt. BS, U.S. Mil. Acad., 1970; MA and MS, Stanford U., Palo Alto, Calif., 1978; MPh, Columbia U., 1980; MMAS, Command & Gen. Staff Coll., 1985. Commd. 2d lt. U.S. Army, 1970, advanced through grades to lt. col., 1987; staff officer, comdr. 1st Inf. Div. Forward, Augsburg, Germany, 1970-73; staff officer Hdqrs. III Corps, Ft. Hood, Tex., 1974-75; from instr. to asst. prof. U.S. Mil. Acad., West Point, N.Y., 1978-81; staff prin. 1st Inf. Div. Forward, Goppingen, 1981-84; instr. Command & Gen. Staff Coll., Ft. Leavenworth, Kans., 1985-88; strategic analyst U.S. Army Concepts Analysis Agy., Bethesda, Md., 1988-91; ret. U.S. Army, 1992; polit./mil. affairs advisor U.S. Arms Control & Disarmament Agy., Washington, 1991—; mem. NATO arms control analysts group SHAPE Tech. Ctr., Hague, Netherlands, 1988-90; mem. conv. arms control work group Ctr. for Strategic and Internat. Studies, Washington, 1989-90; mem. arms control ad hoc study group Carnegie Endowment for Internat. Peace, Washington, 1990-92; mem. conventional arms control project Ford Found., 1993-96; adj. prof. polit. sci. U. Louisville, 1995—. Author: Conventional Armed Forces in Europe (CFE): A Review and Update of Key Treaty Elements, ann. 1991—; contbr. articles to profl. jours. and books. Decorated ACDA Meritorious honor award, Def. Superior Svc. medal, 5 M.S.M. awards. Mem. AAAS, Am. Polit. Sci. Assn., Acad. Polit. Sci., Internat. Inst. Strategic Studies, Internat. Studies Assn., Mil. Ops. Rsch. Soc. (bd. dirs. 1991-98, exec. coun. 1995-98), Inst. Ops. Rsch and Mgmt. Scis., Phi Kappa Phi. Republican. Episcopalian. Avocations: racquetball, cycling, aquaria. Home: 932 Audubon Pkwy Louisville KY 40213-1365 Office: US Arms Ctl & Disarmament Agy 320 21st St NW Washington DC 20451-0003

CRAWFORD, JACKIE R., federal agency administrator; m. Frances Lindsey; children: Jessica, Andrea, Katrina. BBA, Fla. State U., 1967; M in Acctg., Bowling Green State U., 1974; postgrad., Fed. Exec. Inst., Charlottesville, Va., 1988, Harvard U., 1991. CPA, Fla. Auditor Air Force Audit Agy., Eglin AFB, Fla., 1967-72; audit mgr. Air Force Audit Agy., Wright-Patterson AFB, Ohio, 1972-77; supr. auditor Air Force Audit Agy., L.A. AFB, 1977-79, Robins AFB, Ga., 1980-82; assoc. dir. weapon sys. audits Air Force Audit Agy., Wright-Patterson AFB, Ohio, 1982-86, assoc. dir. acquisition, 1986-87, asst. auditor gen. acquisition and logistics audits, 1988-93; dir. acquisition support programs Dept. Def., Arlington, Va., 1987-88; auditor gen. of the Air Force The Pentagon, Washington, 1993—. Office: Dept Air Force 1120 Air Force Pentagon Washington DC 20330-1120

CRAWFORD, JAMES A., transportation authority executive; b. Yadon, Pa., Sept. 29, 1946; s. James and Regina (Connor) C.; m. Nola Nowicki, Apr. 22, 1946; children: Malia, Timothy. AB, St. Joseph's Coll., 1969; MS, U. So. Calif., 1974. Naval officer Pearl Harbor Naval Shipyard, Honolulu, 1971-74; from transportation planner to asst. commr. N.J. Dept. Transportation, Trenton, N.J., 1974-90; prin. JAC Cons., Bordentown, N.J., 1990-92; v.p. TAMS Cons., N.Y.C., 1992-94; exec. dir. South Jersey Trans. Auth., Hammonton, N.J., 1994—. Lt. USNR, 1970-74. Republican. Avocation: sailing. Office: South Jersey Transp Auth PO Box 351 Hammonton NJ 08037-0351*

CRAWFORD, JAMES DOUGLAS, lawyer; b. Phila., May 31, 1932; s. James A. and Katharine M. (Evenson) C.; m. Judith N. Dean, Apr. 29, 1977; 1 dau., Christopher Anne Crawford Samson. A.B., Haverford Coll., 1954; LL.B., U. Pa., 1962. Bar: Pa. 1963, D.C. 1979, U.S. Supreme Ct. 1968. Assoc. Montgomery, McCracken, Walker & Rhoads, Phila., 1962-66; asst. dist. atty. Phila., 1966-68; dep. dist. atty., chief appeals div., 1968-72; gen. counsel Redevel. Authority of City of Phila., 1972-74; ptnr. Schnader, Harrison, Segal & Lewis, Phila., 1974—; mem. adv. com. on appellate rules Pa. Supreme Ct., 1985-92; lectr. in law U. Pa., 1971-73; bd. dirs. Na. Assn. Law Placement, 1978-79; nat. chmn. annual giving U. Pa. Law Sch., 1985-87. Editor in chief U. Pa. Law Rev., 1961-62. Bd. dirs. ACLU, 1978—, v.p., 1985—, bd. dirs. Pa. chpt., 1962—, v.p., 1980-85, pres., 1985—; bd. dirs., mem. exec. com. ACLU Greater Phila., 1972—, v.p., 1983-85; bd. dirs. Pub. Interest Law Ctr. Phila., 1980-90; mem. adv. bd. Citizens Crime Commn. Phila., 1991—, bd. dirs., 1986-96; bd. dirs. Samuel S. Fleisher Art Meml., 1984—, v.p., 1994—; bd. dirs. Print Club Phila., 1983-85, v.p., 1984-96; mem. exec. com. Friends Phila. Mus. Art, 1980-86, fin. sec., 1981-82, co-chmn., 1982-84, mem. prints and drawing com., 1987—; treas. Hist. Soc. U.S. Ct. Appeals for 3d Cir., 1994—. With U.S. Army, 1955-57. Fellow Am. Bar Found., Am. Coll. Trial Lawyers, Am. Acad. Appellate Lawyers; mem. ABA, FBA, Pa. Bar Assn., Phila. Bar Assn. (gov. 1973-75, chmn. com. of censors 1972), Phila. Bar Found. (trustee 1987-93, sec. 1988-92), Am. Law Inst., Defender Assn. Phila. (bd. dirs. 1975—), Athenaem Club, St. Andrews Soc., Order of Coif, Phi Beta Kappa. Republican. Presbyterian. Home: 2018 Delancey St Philadelphia PA 19103-2563 Office: Schnader Harrison et al 1600 Market St Ste 3600 Philadelphia PA 19103-7240*

CRAWFORD, JAMES WELDON, psychiatrist, educator, administrator; b. Napoleon, Ohio, Oct. 27, 1927; s. Homer and Olga (Aderman) C.; m. Susan Young, July 5, 1955; 1 child, Robert James. A.B., Oberlin Coll., 1950; M.D., U. Chgo., 1954, Ph.D., 1961. Intern Wayne County Hosp. and Infirmary, Eloise, Mich., 1954-55; resident Northwestern U., Chgo., 1958-59, Mt. Sinai Hosp./Chgo. Med. Sch., 1959-60; practice medicine specializing in occupational psychiatry Chgo., 1961—; mem. staff Mt. Sinai Hosp., Chgo, Ravenswood Hosp. Med. Ctr., Chgo., St. Lukes-Presbyn. Med. Ctr.; clin. assoc. prof. dept. psychiatry Sch. of Medicine, U. Ill. at Chgo., 1970—; chair and assoc. prof. dept. psychiatry Ravenswood Hosp. Med. Ctr., 1973-79; chmn. J.W. Crawford Assocs., Inc., 1979-82; assoc. prof. depts. psychology and psychiatry Rush Med. Co.. Contbr. articles to profl. jours. Bd. dirs. Pegasus Player, Chgo., 1978—, chmn. bd. dirs., 1979-84; bd. dirs. Bach Soc., 1985—; del. to Russia and the Ukraine with People-to-People Internat., 1993, del. to Kenya, Africa, 1995, del. to China, 1998. NIH Inst. Neurol. Diseases postdoctoral fellow, 1955-59. Fellow Am. Psychiat. Assn. (life), Am. Orthopsychiat. Assn.; mem. AAAS, AAUP, ASsn. Am. Med. Colls., Nat. Coalition Mental Health Profls. and Consumers, Ill. Coalition Mental Health Profls. and Consumers (steering com.), Ill. Psychiat. Soc., Nat. Coun. on Family Rels., Sigma Xi. Lodge: Rotary. Home and Office: 2418 Lincoln St Evanston IL 60201-2151

CRAWFORD, JEAN ANDRE, clinical therapist; b. Chgo., Apr. 12, 1941; d. William Moses and Geneva Mae (Lacy) Jones; student Shimer Coll., 1959-60; BA, Carthage Coll., 1966; MEd, Loyola U., Chgo., 1971; postgrad. Nat. Coll. Edn., Evanston, Ill., 1971-77, Northwestern U., 1976-83; m. John N. Crawford, Jr., June 28, 1969; lic. prof. counselor; cert. sch. counselor Nat. Bd. Cert. Counselors, elem. edn., spl. edn. and pupil personnel services, Ill. Med. technologist, Chgo., 1960-62; primary and spl. edn. tchr. Chgo. Pub.

Schs., 1966-71, counselor maladjusted children and their families, 1971-88; counselor juvenile first-offenders, 1968-88, post-secondary vocat. counselor, 1988-93; tchr., transition coord. Cook County Dept. Corrections Alternative High Sch., Chgo., 1993-94; clin. therapist St. Mary of Nazareth Hosp. Ctr., Chgo., 1994—. Vol. Sta. WTTW-TV; vol. counselor deaf children and their families; counselor post-secondary students; vol., mem. community devel. bd. New City YMCA, 1987-92. Mem. scholarship com. Chgo. Urban League. Mem. AACD, Ill. Assn. Counseling and Devel., Am. Sch. Counselors Assn., Ill. Sch. Counselors Assn., Ill. Vocat. Counselors Assn., Am. Mental Health Counselor Assn., Ill. Mental Health Counselor Assn., IIll. Assn. Advancement Black Ams. in Vocat. Edn., Coun. Exceptional Children, Coordinating Coun. Handicapped Children, Shimer Coll. Alumni Assn. (sec. 1982-84), Phi Delta Kappa. Home: 601 E 32nd St Apt 1200 Chicago IL 60616-4205 Office: 2233 W Division St Chicago IL 60622-3043

CRAWFORD, JOHN EDWARD, geologist, scientist; b. Richmond, Va., June 6, 1924; s. James Henry and Loretta Ellen (Bankerd) C.; m. Mary Elizabeth Ayres, May 15, 1948; children: Michelle Lorraine, Caprice Lizette. B.A., Johns Hopkins, 1947. Reg. geologist, Calif. Geologist uranium exploration program U.S. Geol. Survey, 1948-51; nat. stockpile materials specialist Munitions Bd., Office Sec. Def., 1951-53; prodn. engr. AEC, 1953-54; specialist on source, feed, fissionable materials Bur. Mines, 1954-57, nuclear tech. adviser to dir., 1957-60, chief nuclear engr. for atomic research programs, 1960-63; dir. Marine Mineral Tech. Center, Tiburon, Calif., 1963-66; pres., founder Crawford Marine Specialists, Inc., San Francisco, also Suva, Fiji, 1966-76; pres. Earth Tech. Corp., San Rafael, 1973-77; mgr. geothermal research programs and Salton Sea sci. drilling project U.S. Dept. Energy Ops. Office, Oakland, Calif., 1977-89; mgr. ops. and prin. geologist Western Geologic Resources, Inc., San Rafael, Calif., 1989-90; cons. geothermal and environ. affairs, 1990—; assoc., regional mgr. Western Ops. Earth Resources Internat., L.C., Carson City, Nev., 1994—. Author: Facts Concerning Uranium Exploration and Production, 1956; contbr. articles to govt. and profl. jours., Leaders in Am. Sci. Vol. VIII, 1968-69. Mem. Calif. Gov.'s Commn. Ocean Resources, 1966-67, Calif. Gov.'s Small Hydro Task Force, 1981-82. Served with AUS, 1943-46. Mem. Internat. Marine Minerals Soc. (Moore medal for excellence in devel. of marine minerals 1998), Geol. Soc. Am., Geysers Geothermal Assn., Marine Tech. Soc. (past chmn. marine mineral resources com., past chmn. marine resources div.), Delta Upsilon. Home and Office: 1510 Valencia Ct Carson City NV 89703-2333

CRAWFORD, JOSEPH PATRICK, editor; b. Grand Rapids, Mich., Apr. 24, 1946; s. Thomas John and Evelyn Booth C.; m. Martha Louise Anderson, Aug. 20, 1971; children: Patrick Joseph, Thomas Paul, Mary Martha. BA, U. Notre Dame, 1968; postgrad., U. Md., 1971-72. Editl. writer The Grand Rapids Press, 1982-84, editl. page editor, 1984—. Recipient Editl. Writing award Inland Press Assn., Editl. Writing award Mich. Press. Assn., Editl. Writing award Mich. Associated Press. E-mail: jpcrawf@iserve.net. Office: The Grand Rapids Press 155 Michigan St NW Grand Rapids MI 49503

CRAWFORD, JUDY CAROL, energy services company executive; b. Lubbock, Tex., June 1, 1955; d. George Washington and Frances Louise (Hughes) Hopper; m. Joe Earl Crawford, May 31, 1975; children: Susan, Joshua. Pres. Nice Guy Registry, Crane, 1995-97; adminstrv. sec. County of Crane, Crane, Tex., 1996-98; v.p. Maranatha Energy Svcs., Crane, 1997—; county and dist. clk. County of Crane, Crane, Tex., 1999—. Mem. Family and Consumer Sci. Com., Crane, 1997—. Baptist. Home and Office: Maranatha Energy Svcs Inc PO Box 476 Crane TX 79731-0476

CRAWFORD, KATHRINE NELSON, special education educator; b. Springfield, Mass., June 5, 1954; d. Merrill William and Elizabeth (Hanor) Nelson; m. Michael David Crawford, June 19, 1993; 1 child, Cody M. BS in Phys. Edn. cum laude, U. N.C., Greensboro, 1979. Cert. tchr. phys. edn. K-12, learning disabled K-12, emotionally mentally handicapped K-12, Behavior emotionally handicapped K-12, N.C. Day care dir. Assn. for Retarded Citizens and United Way, Greensboro, 1979-82; behavioral self-contained instr. Guilford County Schs., Greensboro, 1982-88, EMH self-contained instr., 1988—, spl. olympic coach, 1988—; advisor for Action Mag., Scholastic, Inc., N.Y.C., 1999—. United Way campaign coord. Guilford County Schs., 1994-98. Recipient Cert. of Recognition for outstanding svc. BEH/Willie M., Guilford County Schs., 1987; Guilford County Schs. grantee, 1990, 96. Mem. Assn. for Retarded Citizens of Greensboro. Republican. Lutheran. Avocations: bowling, camping, cross-stitch, folk guitar, fishing. Home: 3257 Saw Mill Dr Elon College NC 27244-9576 Office: Eastern Guilford Middle Sch 435 Peeden Dr Gibsonville NC 27249

CRAWFORD, KENNETH CHARLES, educational institute executive, retired government official; b. Nokomis, Ill., Oct. 31, 1918; s. Charles Bryant and Blanche Dora (Gates) C.; m. Madge Marie Douglas, Aug. 23, 1942; 1 son, James Douglas. B.A., Ill. Coll., 1946, S.J.D. (hon.), 1970; J.D., U. Va., 1951; grad., Command and Gen. Staff Coll., 1957, Army War Coll., 1962; M.A., George Washington U., 1962. Bar: Va. 1951, Ga. 1967, Korean 1965, U.S. Supreme Ct. 1970, D.C. 1977. Commd. 2d lt. U.S. Army, 1942, advanced through grades to col., 1962; served in (F.A. and JAG Corps); tchr. legal subjects U. Md., U. Ga., Ga. State U., Nat. U., Washington, 1957-67; comdr. JAG Sch., 1967-70; ret., 1970; pres., CEO Ken Crawford Ednl. Inst., Inc., 1986-89. Editor: Laws of the Republic of Korea, 1964. Assoc. dir. edn. Southwestern Legal Found., Dallas, 1970-71, Atty. at Law, 1990-92; dir. edn. and tng. Fed. Jud. Ctr., Washington, 1971-86; cons. Fed. Jud. Ctr., 1986-87. Decorated Legion of Merit with 2 oak leaf clusters, Soldiers medal, Bronze Star, Belgian Fourragere, Disting. Citizen citation Ill. Coll., 1993. Mem. State Bar Va., State Bar Ga., D.C. Bar, Korean Bar, Order of Coif.

CRAWFORD, KEVAN CHARLES, nuclear engineer, educator; b. Salt Lake City, Utah, Jan. 26, 1956; s. Paul Gibson and Norma Irene (Christiansen) C. MS, U. Utah, 1983, PhD, 1986. Lic. Sr. reactor oper. U.S. NRC. V.p. Computer Mktg. Corp., Salt Lake City, 1977-81; sr. reactor engr. U. Utah Nuc. Engring. Lab., Salt Lake City, 1981-86; mgr. reactor ops. Tex. A&M U. Nuc. Sci. Ctr., College Station, Tex., 1986-88; prof. U. Utah, Salt Lake City, 1988-92, Idaho State U., Pocatello, 1991-94; pres. Precision Engring. Corp., Salt Lake City, 1994—; cons. Envirocare of Utah, Inc., Salt Lake City, 1989, Westinghouse Idaho Nuc., 1992-93, Belarussian Popular Front, 1996-97. Cadet Air Force Acad., 1974-75. S.S. Kisler scholar U. Utah, Salt Lake City, 1975-78; Fulbright prof. Minsk, Belarus, 1994-95. Mem. Am. Nuc. Soc., Am. Soc. Engring. Educators, Fulbright Assn., Phi Kappa Phi, Alpha Nu Sigma. Mormon. Achievements include research contributions in nuclear reactor dynamics and control, and neutron diffraction for use in beam condensers and neutron microscopes, and leading proponent for an honor code among nuclear scientists. Office: Precision Engring Corp 3781 S 3145 E Salt Lake City UT 84109-3744

CRAWFORD, LAWRENCE ROBERT, aviation and aerospace consultant; b. Ft. Lewis, Wash., May 4, 1936; s. Richard G. and Olive O. (Ericksen) C.; m. Yvonne G. Thompson, Nov. 8, 1957; children: Scott D., Robin L., Crawford Lafrankie. BS in Indsl. Engring., Ga. Inst. Tech., 1959; MS in Mgmt., Rensselaer Poly. Inst., 1965. Lic. comml. pilot. Commd. ensign USN, 1959, advanced through grades to lt. comdr., hon. discharge, 1968; airline pilot Pan Am, San Francisco, 1968-70; dir. corp. budgets Pan Am, N.Y.C., 1970-73; dir. methods and standards Am. Airlines, N.Y.C., 1973-75, sr. dir. reservations, 1975-79; v.p. mktg. Ransome Airlines, Phila., 1979-83; sr. v.p. mktg. and planning Empire Airlines, Utica, N.Y., 1983-85; founder, pres., CEO Avitas, Inc., Reston, Va., 1985-98; founder, chmn., CEO Avitas Engring., Inc., Miami, Fla., 1991-98; founder, pres., CEO Spectrum Aviation Svcs. Inc., Reston, 1998—; exec. adv. bd. EDS Fin. Corp., Dallas, 1987-90; v.p. Det Norske Veritas, Oslo, 1992-98. Contbr. articles to profl. jours. Bd. dirs. Internat. Aviation Found., 1996—. Mem. AIAA, Exptl. Aircraft Assn. (builder 1987), U.S. Ultralight Flying Assn., Am. Aero. Soc., Internat. Soc. Transport Aircraft Trading, Nat. Aeronautics Assn., Sr. Aerospace Execs. Assn., Stearman Restorers Assn., Wings Club, Washington Aero Club. Republican. Methodist. Achievements include devel. of the comml. aviation industry's first aircraft tech. monitoring product to ensure condition and value of leased aircraft; founded and devel. Avitas into world's largest appraiser and inspector of comml. aircraft. Home: 10031 Scenic View Ter Vienna VA 22182-1367 Office: Spectrum Aviation Svcs Inc 1801 Robert Fulton Dr Reston VA 20191-4347

CRAWFORD, LESTER MILLS, JR., veterinarian; b. Demopolis, Ala., Mar. 13, 1938; s. Lester Mills and Susan Doris (Mitchell) C.; m. Catherine Walker, July 27, 1963; children: Catherine Leigh, Mary Stuart. D.V.M., Auburn U., 1963; Ph.D., U. Ga., 1969; M.D.V. (hon.), Budapest U., Hungary, 1987. Pvt. practice vet. medicine Meridian, Miss. and Birmingham, Ala., 1963-64; research and devel. staff agrl. divsn. Am. Cyanamid Co., Princeton, N.J., 1964-66; cons. Am. Cyanamid Co.; assoc. dean Coll. Vet. Medicine, U. Ga., 1970-75, head dept. physiology-pharmacology, 1980-82; dir. Bur. Vet. Medicine, FDA, HEW, Rockville, Md., 1978-80, 82-85; assoc. adminstr. food safety and inspection service USDA, Washington, 1986-87, adminstr., 1987-91; exec. v.p. sci. affairs Nat. Food Processors Assn., Washington, 1991-93; exec. dir. Assn. Am. Vet. Med. Colls., Washington, 1993-97; dir. Ctr. Food and Nutrition Policy, Georgetown U., Washington, 1997—; cons. pharm. industry, agribus. FDA, WHO; mem. Health Professions Commn., Pew Meml. Trust, 1990-93; bd. dirs. Embrex Inc. Contbr. sci. articles to profl. jours. Vice chmn. Codex Alimentarius Commn., 1991-93; bd. dirs. Food and Drug Law Inst., 1988—; expert advisor food safety WHO com. scientific freedom & responsibility. Recipient A.M. Mills award, 1979, K.F. Meyer award, 1980, U.S. Presdl. Rank award of Meritorious Exec., 1988, Disting. Alumnus award Auburn U., 1989, Wooldridge Meml. medal Brit. Vet. Assn., 1991; Commrs. Spl. citation FDA, award of merit, 1983. Mem. AVMA (Aux. award), Nat. Acad. Practice, D.C. Vet Med. Assn., French Acad. Vet. (hon.), Fedn. Am. Sch. Hlth Professions (pres. 1997—), Cosmos Club (Washington), Sigma Xi, Phi Zeta, Phi Kappa Phi. Republican. Home: 5815 Highland Dr Chevy Chase MD 20815-5531 Office: Ctr Food Nutrition Policy Georgetown Univ 3240 Prospect St NW Washington DC 20007-3214 *I have always predicated my own life on the certain knowledge that God is still at work in the world. I believe that every person carries a divine spark, and that the function of leadership is to ignite that spark. I furthermore believe that a Franciscan love of and respect for animals is a prerequisite for membership in the human race. And I believe that the true rewards in life are to be found in communion with family, friends and colleagues.*

CRAWFORD, LEWIS CLEAVER, engineering executive; b. Salina, Kans., Dec. 7, 1925; s. Percival Wallace and Viva Estelle (Beichle) C.; m. Helen Alleyne Henry, May 28, 1950; children: Dorothy Caroline, Lewis Henry. B in Engring., Yale U., 1946. Registered profl. engr., Kans. Engr. Cemenstone Corp., Pitts., 1946-47; engr., then assoc. Wilson & Co. (engrs. and architects), Salina, 1947-67; ptnr. Wilson & Co. (engrs. and architects), 1967-87, Western Properties and Cenwest Partnerships, 1992—. Served with USNR, 1943-46. Fellow ASCE; mem. NSPE, SAR, Flagon and Trencher, Kans. Cons. Engrs. (past chmn.), Kans. Engring. Soc. (past. dir.), Salina Country Club. Republican. Methodist. Office: Board of Trade Bldg 631 E Crawford St Salina KS 67401-5101

CRAWFORD, LINDA SIBERY, lawyer, educator; b. Ann Arbor, Mich., Apr. 27, 1947; d. Donald Eugene and Verla Lillian (Schenck) Sibery; m. Leland Allardice Crawford, Apr. 4, 1970; children: Christina, Lillian, Leland. Student, Keele U., 1969; BA, U. Mich., 1969; postgrad., SUNY, Potsdam, 1971; JD, U. Maine, 1977. Bar: Maine 1977, U.S. Dist. Ct. Maine 1982, U.S. Ct. Appeals (1st cir.) 1983. Tchr. Pub. Sch., Tupper Lake, N.Y., 1970-71; asst. dist. atty. State of Maine, Farmington, 1977-79; asst. atty. gen. State of Maine, Augusta, Maine, 1979-95; prin. Litigation Consulting Firm, N.Y.C. & Hallowell, Maine, 1986-, Linda Crawford and Assoc. Law Firm, Hallowell, Maine, 1995—; legal adv. U. Maine, Farmington, 1975; legal counsel Fire Marshall's Office, Maine, 1980-83, Warden Svc., Maine, 1981-83, Dept. Mental Health, 1983-90, litigation divsn. 1990-95; mem. tchg. team trial advocacy Law Sch., Harvard U., 1987-; lectr. Sch. Medicine Harvard U., 1991; counsel to Bd. of Registration in Medicine, 1994-95; chmn. editl. bd. Mental and Physical Disability Law Reporter, 1993-95; arbitrator Am. Arbitration Assn., 1995-; facilitator Nat. Constrn. Task Force, St. Louis, 1995. Contbg. editor Med. Malpractice Law and Strategy, 1997—. Mem. Natural Resources Coun., Maine, 1985-90; bd. dirs. Diocesan Human Rels. Coun., Maine, 1977-78, Arthritis Found., Maine, 1983-88; atty. expert commn. experts UN War Crime Investigation in the former Yugoslavia, 1994. Named one of Outstanding Young Women of Yr. Jaycees, 1981. Mem. ATLA, ABA (com. on disability 1992-95), Maine Bar Assn., Kennebec County Bar Assn., Nat. Assn. State Mental Health Attys. (treas. 1984-86, vice chmn. 1987-89, chmn. 1989-91), Nat. Health Lawyers Assn. Home: 25 Winthrop St Hallowell ME 04347-1150 Office: PO Box 268 Hallowell ME 04347-0268 also: 20th Flr 45 Rockefeller Plz Fl 20 New York NY 10111-2099

CRAWFORD, MARC, professional hockey coach. Head coach Quebec Nordiques, 1994-95, Colo. Avalanche, 1995-97, Vancouver Canucks, Vancouver, 1998-. Recipient Louis A.R. Pieri Meml. award, 1992-93, Jack Adams award, 1994-95; named NHL Coach of Yr. The Sporting News, 1994-95. *

CRAWFORD, MARGARET JEAN BARNES, physical education educator, consultant; b. Wichita, Kans., Sept. 30, 1918; d. Emory Mark and Elizabeth (Flake) B.; m. Charles Clemmie Crawford, 1947 (dec. Sept. 1965). BS, Tuskegee Inst., 1941; MA in Edn., U. Mich., 1948. Tchr., coach Allen White High Sch., Whiteville, Tenn., 1941-42; prof., coach physical edn. Del. State Coll., Dover, 1947-52; physical edn. tchr. Phoenix Elem. Sch. Dist., 1953-79. Pres. Urban League Guild, Phoenix, 1982-83; worker Ariz. Jr. Olympics, Phoenix, 1982-83. Lt. USAF, 1942-46. Named to Athletic Hall of Fame, Tuskegee Inst., 1985, recipient Cleve. L. Abbott Civic and Community award, 1984. Fellow ASCD, Am. Alliance Health Physical Edn. and Dance, U.S. Olympic Soc., Alpha Kappa Alpha. Avocations: ceramics, athletics, organ.

CRAWFORD, MARIA LUISA BUSE, geology educator; b. Beverly, Mass., July 18, 1939; d. William Theodore Buse and Barbara (Kidder) Aldana; m. William A. Crawford, Aug. 29, 1963. B.A., Bryn Mawr Coll., 1960; postgrad., U. Oslo, 1960-61; Ph.D., U. Calif., 1965. Asst. prof. Bryn Mawr (Pa.) Coll., 1965-73, assoc. prof., 1973-79, prof., 1979-92, prof. environ. studies and sci., 1992—, William R. Kenan Jr. prof., 1985-92, chmn. dept. geology, 1976-88, 98—; mem. U.S. Nat. Com. Geology, 1994-97; chmn. women geoscientists com. Am. Geol. Inst., 1976-77; mem. U.S. Nat. Com. Geochemistry, 1980-82; organizing com. 28th Internat. Geol. Cong., 1987-89. MacArthur fellow, 1993-98; grantee NASA, 1973-76, NSF, 1967—. Fellow Geol. Soc. Am. (councillor 1982-85), Mineral Soc. Am. (councillor 1989-92);mem. Mineral Assn. Can. (councilor 1985-87), Am. Geophys. Union, Norwegian Geol. Soc., Phila. Geol. Soc., Assn. Women in Sci. Office: Bryn Mawr Coll Dept Geology Bryn Mawr PA 19010

CRAWFORD, MICHAEL, city council; married. BS in Computer Sci., Wright State U., 1988; law degree, U. Ariz., 1991. Clk. Ariz. Ct. Appeals; computer software cons.; vice chmn. Ariz. Common Cause; criminal def. atty. Pima County Pub. Defenders Office, 1994-98; with O'Connor, Cavanaugh, Malloy, Jones, Tucson, AZ, 1998—. Office: O'Connor Cavanaugh Malloy Jones 32 N Stone Ave Ste 2100 Tucson AZ 85702-1403

CRAWFORD, MURIEL LAURA, lawyer, author, educator; d. Mason Leland and Pauline Marie (DesIlets) Henderson; m. Barrett Matson Crawford, May 10, 1959; children: Laura Joanne, Janet Muriel, Barbara Elizabeth. Student, U. Calif., Berkeley, 1958-60, 67-69; B.A. with honors, U. Ill., 1973; J.D. with honors, Ill. Inst. Tech., 1977; cert. employee benefit specialist U. Pa., 1989. Bar: Ill. 1977, Calif. 1991, U.S. Dist. Ct. (no. dist.) Ill. 1977, U.S. Dist. Ct. (no. dist.) Calif. 1991, U.S. Ct. Appeals (7th cir.) 1977, U.S. Ct. Appeals (9th cir.) 1991; CLU; chartered fin. cons. Atty., Washington Nat. Ins. Co., Evanston, Ill., 1977-80, sr. atty., 1980-81, asst. counsel, 1982-83, asst. gen. counsel, 1984-87, assoc. gen. counsel, sec., 1987-89, cons. employee benefit specialist, 1989-91; assoc. Hancock, Rothert & Bunshoft, San Francisco, 1991-92. Author: (with Beadles) Law and the Life Insurance Contract, 1989, (sole author) 7th edit. 1994, Life and Health Insurance Law, 8th edit., 1998; co-author Legal Aspects of AIDS, 1990; contbr. articles to profl. jours. Recipient Am. Jurisprudence award Lawyer's Coop. Pub. Co., 1975, 2nd prize Internat. LeTourneau Student Med.-Legal Article contest, 1976, Bar and Gavel Soc. award Ill. Inst. Tech./Chgo.-Kent Student Bar Assn., 1977. Fellow Life Mgmt. Inst.; mem. Ill. Inst. Tech./Chgo.-Kent Alumni Assn. (bd. dir. 1983-89). Democrat. Congregationalist.

CRAWFORD, NATALIE WILSON, applied mathematician; b. Evansville, Ind., June 24, 1939; d. John Moore and Edna Dorothea (Huthsteiner) Wilson; m. Robert Charles Crawford, Mar. 1, 1969. BA in Math., UCLA, 1961, postgrad., 1964-67. Programmer analyst N.Am. Aviation Corp., El Segundo, Calif., 1961-64; mem. tech. staff RAND Corp., Santa Monica, Calif., 1964—; project leader, engring. tech., theater conflict and force employment programs RAND Corp., Santa Monica, 1975—; dir. Theater Forces Program, Santa Monica, 1988-90, Theater Force Employment Program, Santa Monica, 1990-92, Force Structure and Force Modernization Program, Santa Monica, 1992-93, Force Modernization and Employment Program, Santa Monica, 1993-95; assoc. dir. Project Air Force, Santa Monica, 1995-97, v.p.rand, dir. project, 1995-97; mem. Air Force Sci. Adv. Bd., 1988—, vice-chair, 1990-91, co-chair, 1996—; cons., joint tech. coordinating group munition effectiveness. Recipient Women's Bus. Coun. award Santa Monica C. of C., 1997, Clarence L. Kelly Johnson Meml. Lockheed Skunk Works award, 1999; named YWCA Woman of Yr., 1983; inducted into Santa Monica H.S. Hall of Fame, 1995. Mem. NDIA, USAF Assn. Republican. Home: 20940 Big Rock Dr Malibu CA 90265-5316

CRAWFORD, NORMA VIVIAN, nurse; b. Cleveland, Tex., Dec. 29, 1936; d. Ira Wesley and Lizzie Augusta (Godejohn) C.; m. Arthur B. Crawford, Sept. 20, 1956 (dec.); children: Pamela, Desiree. Lic. vis. nurse, Lee Jr. Coll., 1971-72; RN, Cumberland County Coll., 1977; BSN, U. Mary-Hardin Baylor, 1986. Charge nurse Patrick Henry Hosp., Newport News, Va., 1972-73; staff nurse Salem (N.J.) County Nursing Home, 1975-77, Nicholson Nursing Home, Penns Grove, N.J., 1977; nurse ICU, Metroplex Hosp., Killeen, Tex., 1977-79; dir. nurses Wind Crest Nursing Ctr., Copperas Cove, Tex., 1979-82; staff nurse supr., unit mgr. med./surg. unit, supr., home health nurse, dir. home health Metroplex Hosp., Killeen, Tex., 1979-87; dir. Metroplex Home Health Svcs., Killeen, Tex., 1988-91; dir. quality assurance, risk mgmt. Hill Country Home Health, Lampasas, Tex., 1991-93; clin. dir. Rollins Brook Home Health, Lampasas, 1993-95, Hill Country Home Health, Lampasas, 1995-97; dir. nurses Hill Country Home Health, Killeen, 1997—. Bd. dirs. Heart of Tex. Hospice, 1990-96. Mem. Order of Eastern Star. Baptist. Home: 604 Yucca Dr Copperas Cove TX 76522-3022 Office: 1010 W Jasper Dr Ste 1 Killeen TX 76542-1328

CRAWFORD, NORMAN CRANE, JR., academic administrator, consultant; b. Newark, Oct. 30, 1930; s. Norman Crane and Anna (Wares) C.; m. Garnette Bell, June 25, 1955; children: Sally Jean, Ellen Ann. BS in Edn., Rutgers U., 1951, MEd, 1957; PhD, Northwestern U., 1966. Dir. scholarships Nat. Merit Scholarship Corp., Evanston, Ill., 1957-62; asst. dean arts and sci., asst. to provost U. Del., 1962-66, 67-70; acting dir. exams. Coll. Entrance Exam. Bd., N.Y.C., 1966-67; pres. Salisbury (Md.) State Coll., 1970-80, Drury Coll., Springfield, Mo., 1981-83; v.p. ops. Council for Advancement and Support Edn., Washington, 1985-87; interim pres. U. Maine, Farmington, 1987-88; v.p. pub. affairs Thomas A. Edison State Coll., 1989-91; cons. higher edn. Berlin, 1992—. Lt. j.g. USN, 1951-55. Joint recipient Higher Edn. Leadership award Gov. Del., Gov. Md., Gov. Va., 1974; named hon. trustee Ward Found. Wildfowl Art Museum, 1977. Mem. Phi Delta Kappa. Episcopalian. Home and Office: 108 Ocean Pkwy Berlin MD 21811-1644

CRAWFORD, PAMELA J., critical care nurse; b. Houma, La., Aug. 10, 1957; d. Arthur Butler and Norma Vivien (Crawford) C.; children: Stephanie Pamela Cobb, Michele Anne Cobb. Assoc. of Legal Tech., Cumberland County Coll., Vineland, N.J., 1977; BSN, U. Mary Hardin-Baylor, Belton, Tex., 1987. Med. ICU-CCU staff nurse Scott and White Hosp., Temple, Tex., 1987-88; neuro ICU staff nurse Brooke Army Med. Ctr., San Antonio, 1989-91; case mgr. transplants, vendor negotiator, regional contact Traveler's Inc. Co., San Antonio, 1991-92; dir. quality control Brit-tex Home Health Svcs., 1992-94; dir. profl. svcs. Service Master Home Health, Houston, Tex., 1994-95, Columbia Home Health, Houston, 1995-96; field staff, clin. supr., staff devel. supr. First Am. Home Health, Houston, 1996; regional clin. mgr. IHS/First Am. Corp. Clin. Staff, Stafford, 1996-98; home health svcs., quality cons. appeal analyst Aetna, A US Healthcare Co., 1998—. Home Health Svcs., 1992-94; dir. Prof. Svcs., Svc. Master Home Health, Houston, 1994—. 1st lt. USAR, 1988—.

CRAWFORD, PATRICIA ALEXIS ANN, social justice and healthcare advocate, writer; b. N.Y.C., July 17, 1952; d. Alexander James and Dorothy Patricia (Mudzinski) C. BA in Polit. Sci., East Carolina U., 1974. With Naval Air Rework Facility, Dept. Navy, Norfolk, Va., 1973; news prodn. editor, fin. writer Media Gen. Fin. Weekly, Richmond, Va., 1974-75; editor, med. writer United Feature Syndicate, N.Y.C., 1975-79; asst. mng. editor United Feature Syndicate, Newspaper Enterprise Assn. and Ind. News Alliance, N.Y.C., 1979-86; bd. dirs. Integrity/N.Y., 1996—, v.p., 1998—. Mem. AIDS com. N.Y. Episc. Diocese. Recipient Spl. Achievement award Dept. of Navy, 1973. Mem. NGLTF, Anti-Violence Project, Soc. Profl. Journalists, Publishing Triangle, Episcopal Pub. Policy Network, Nat. Writers Union, Empire State Pride Agenda, Lambda Legal Def. and Edn., Human Rights Campaign, Anglican Soc., Episcopal Women's Caucus, Women's Alliance for Theology, Ethics and Ritual, Interfaith Alliance, Am. Scottish Found., African Wildlife Found., Nat. Assn. Individual Investors. Episcopalian. Avocations: public health, social justice. Address: PO Box 090-022 Brooklyn NY 11209

CRAWFORD, PATRICIA ANN, education educator; b. Pitts., Dec. 5, 1963; d. James F. and Patricia T. (Madden) C. BS in Elem. Edn., Indiana U. of Pa., 1986, MEd in Elem. Edn., 1991; PhD in Curriculum and Instrn., Pa. State U., 1995. Kindergarten and 1st grade tchr. Indiana (Pa.) Area Sch. Dist., 1986-91; grad. asst., instr. Pa. State U., University Park, 1991-94; asst. prof. elem. edn., literacy edn. U. Maine, Farmington, 1994-96; asst. prof. edn. U. Ctrl. Fla., Orlando, 1996—. Contb. editor Tchg. & Learning Lit., 1995-98. Tchr. edn. grantee Learning Disabilities Assn., 1997, faculty devel. grantee for tech. U. Ctrl. Fla., 1997. Mem. Nat. Coun. Tchrs. English, Internat. Reading Assn. (mem. editl. bd.), Nat. Assn. for Edn. of Young Children (mem. editl. bd. 1997—), Assn. for Childhood Edn. Internat. (mem. editl. bd. 1995—, editor internat. newsletter Focus 1997, column, column editor Tchg. and Learning Lit. 1995-98). Office: U Ctrl Fla Coll of Edu Dept of Instrl Progs Orlando FL 32816

CRAWFORD, PEGGY SMITH, design educator; b. Christiansburg, Va., Dec. 27, 1943; d. Andrew Morgan Smith and Margie Smith (Hill) Blakeslee; m. John Linnie Crawford, Jan. 12, 1963 (div. May 1979); children: John Christopher, James Andrew. Sec. Draper's Meadow EGA, Blacksburg, Va., 1983-85, 1999—; 2nd v.p. Draper's Meadow EGA, Blacksburg, 1989-90; com. mem. Smithfield Needlework Exhibit, Blacksburg, 1986-87, com. chairperson, 1987-88; pres. Blue Ridge Embroiderer's Guild, Roanoke, Va., 1989-90; regional rep. Brazilian Dimensional Embroidery Internat. Guild, Washington, 1991—, sec., 1996-97; tchr. Nat. Embroiderer's Guild Am., Inc. seminar, Greensboro, N.C., 1991, Reynolds Homestead, Critz, Va., 1993, Nat. Embroiderer's Guild Nat. Seminar, Williamsburg, Va., 1994, Brazilian Dimensional Embroidery Internat. Guild, Inc. seminars, 1994-97, Oreg., 1999. Author: Stitching the Wildflowers of Virginia., 1992. Mem. Am. Needlepoint Guild, Blue Ridge Embroiderer's Guild, Drapers' Meadow Embroiderer's Guild Am., Inc., Brazilian Dimensional Embroidery Internat. Guild. Avocations: needlework, sports, reading, hiking, music. Home: 206 Upland Rd Blacksburg VA 24060-5351 Office: Va Polytech and State U 1700 Pratt Dr Blacksburg VA 24060-6361

CRAWFORD, PHILIP STANLEY, bank executive; b. Wichita, Kans., Nov. 30, 1944; s. Carson Eugene and Elizabeth Ellen (Childs) C.; m. Carolyn Louise Stephenson, June 10, 1989. BA, Sterling Coll., 1967; MBA, Baruch Coll., 1973. Programmer, analyst City of N.Y., 1968-72; planning analyst Fed. Reserve Bank, Boston, 1972-74; cons. Index Systems, Cambridge, Mass., 1974-79; sr. cons. Ernst & Whinney, Los Angeles, 1979; v.p. Union Bank, Los Angeles, 1979—. Mem. Pres.'s Coun. Sterling Coll. Mem. Mgmt. Info. Continuing Seminar (pres. 1985), Assn. Computing Machinery. Republican. Avocations: photography, genealogy. Home: 3815 Olive Ave Long Beach CA 90807-3519 Office: Union Bank 1980 Saturn St Monterey Park CA 91755-7417

CRAWFORD, RAYMOND MAXWELL, JR., nuclear engineer; b. Charleston, S.C., July 28, 1933; s. Raymond Maxwell and Mary Elizabeth (Bates) C.; m. J. Denise LeDuc, Mar. 10, 1951; children: Denis, Michael,

Deborah, Peter, Elizabeth. B.S., Wayne State U., 1958, M.S., 1960; Ph.D., UCLA, 1969. Instr. Wayne State U., 1960-63; asst. prof. Calif. State U., Northridge, 1963-66; mem. tech. staff Atomics Internat., 1969-71; nuclear engr. Argonne Nat. Lab., Ill., 1971-74; assoc. and asst. head nuclear safeguards and licensing div. Sargent & Lundy, Chgo., 1974-80; v.p. Sci. Applications, Inc., Oak Brook, Ill., 1980-83; engring. dir. Nutech, Chgo., 1983-86; pres. Engring. Research Group, Naperville, Ill., 1986—; mgr. spl. projects Fluor Daniel, Inc., 1988—; tech. cons. Atomic Power Devel. Assn., 1962-63; summer fellow NASA Lewis Research Ctr., 1965-66. Contbr. articles to profl. jours. Scoutmaster, counsellor Boy Scouts Am., 1963-66; active YMCA, 1966-69, Recs. for Blind, 1964-65. Recipient numerous awards. Mem. Am. Nuclear Soc., Am. Inst. Chem. Engrs., Am. Chem. Soc., Nat. Soc. Profl. Engrs., Sigma Xi, Tau Beta Pi, Phi Lambda Upsilon. Home: 1005 Kennebec Ln Naperville IL 60563-1413*

CRAWFORD, RICHARD BRADWAY, biologist, biochemist, educator; b. Kalamazoo, Feb. 16, 1933; s. Kenneth and Alma (Smith) C.; m. Betty J. Jacobs, Jan. 30, 1954; children: Kathleen, Christine, Kevin, Nancy. A.B., Kalamazoo Coll., 1954; Ph.D. in Biochemistry, U. Rochester, 1959. Postdoctoral fellow U. Rochester, N.Y., 1959; instr. to assoc. prof. U. Pa., 1959-67; assoc. prof. to prof. biology Trinity Coll., Hartford, Conn., 1967-98; prof. emeritus Trinity Coll., Hartford, 1998—; chmn. dept. Trinity Coll., Hartford, Conn., 1978-87, resuming chmn., 1996-97; asst. dir., trustee Mt. desert Island Biol. Lab., Salsbury Cove, Maine, 1966-82; vis. scientist Jackson Lab., Bar Harbor, Maine, 1988; vis. prof. biology U. Warwick, Eng., 1988; vis. prof. marine biology U. Calif. San Diego, 1974; vis. prof. U. Edinburgh, 1996. Contbr. articles to profl. jours. Mem. Inlands, Wetlands and Water Courses Commn., Wethersfield, Conn., 1976-81, Wethersfield Conservation Commn., 1995-98. Mem. Rotary Club Hartford (pres. 1994-95), Mount Desert Island Rotary. Democrat. Baptist. Home: PO Box 826 Mount Desert ME 04660-0826

CRAWFORD, ROBERT ROY, rail company executive; b. S.I., N.Y., Apr. 6, 1939; s. Gustav and Ethel Elizabeth (Roy) C.; m. Arline Carolyn Altio, Mar. 12, 1960; children: Laura K. Danclovic, Robert B., Douglas R. BS in Metall. Engring., Lehigh U., 1960; MS in Metall. Engring./Solid State Phys., Poly. Inst. Bklyn., 1967; MBA in Corp. Fin./Internat. Bus., NYU, 1991. V.p. Dominick & Dominick, Inc., N.Y.C., 1971-75; vice chmn. Union Carbide Acquisitions, N.Y.C., 1975-81; pres. Poma of Am., Inc., Grand Junction, Colo., 1981-84; chmn. bd. Rio Costilla, Inc., Costilla, N.Mex., 1984-86; pres. Interstate B. Modal, Inc., Lyndhurst, N.J., 1987-90; chmn. bd. N.Y. Cross Harbor Rd., Bklyn., 1989—; pres. N.Y. Rail Corp., Bklyn., 1994-98, N.Am. Software Assocs., Iuka, Miss., 1999—; mem. N.Y. Transp. Adv. Bd., N.Y.C., 1993-96. Inventor in field. Bd. dirs. Colo. Tramway Bd., Denver, 1982-87. Capt. USAF, 1960-70. Named Outstanding Young Man of Am. Poly., 1970. Mem. Am. Soc. for Metals, Maritime Assn. N.Y. and N.J. (bd. dirs. 1997—), St. Andrews Soc. of N.Y. (bd. mgrs.), Bklyn. C. of C. (bd. dirs. 1990-95). Home: 225 Potter Ave Staten Island NY 10314-3050 Office: NAm Software Assocs 751 CR 929 Bldg 1000 Iuka MS 38852*

CRAWFORD, ROBERT W., JR., furniture rental company executive; b. Yonkers, N.Y., Oct. 19, 1938. BS, Dickinson Coll., 1960; MBA, U. Pa., 1963. Prin., owner Brook Furniture Rental, Inc., Arlington Heights, Ill. Active The Chgo. Council Foreign Rels., Art Inst. Chgo., Lyric Opera Chgo.; chmn. The Econ. Club Chgo.; adv. bd. Lake Forest Symphony; bd. dirs. Chicagoland C. of C., Greater Chgo. Home Bldrs. Assn.; governing mem. John G. Shedd Aquarium. Inductee into the Chicagoland Entrepreneurial Hall of Fame, 1998. Mem. National Recreation Found. (pres., bd. trustees), Internat. Furniture Rental Assn. (chmn., pres., bd. dirs., com. chmn.), The Chgo. Club, Union League Club, Exmoor Country Club, The CEO Club, Phi Kappa Sigma (Alumnus of Yr. award). Avocations: travel, athletics, reading, music, art. Office: Brook Furniture Rental Inc 2301 E Oakton St Arlington Heights IL 60005-4817

CRAWFORD, ROBERTA, association administrator; b. Richmond, Ind.; d. Melvin Lee and Vida Ellen (Halstead) Smith; m. Melvin Barfield, Dec. 3, 1940 (div.); 1 child, Stephen; m. Charles Britt, Feb. 2, 1949 (div.); 1 child, Alan; m. Vernon Crawford, Aug. 29, 1970 (dec.). Radio engr. WLBC, Muncie, Ind., 1942; announcer, engr. WMAN, Mansfield, Ohio, 1943; dispatcher WPDH, Richmond, 1944; continuity dir. WPTW, Piqua, Ohio, 1945, WCAV, Norfolk, Va., 1947; writer, announcer WKBV, Richmond, 1950; continuity dir., announcer WSAL, Logansport, Ind., 1951; continuity dir. WAVE-TV, Louisville, Ky., 1953; sales-svc. mgr. WPTV, Palm Beach, Fla., 1954; copywriter WQXT, Palm Beach, 1962; city desk asst. Palm Beach Times, West Palm Beach, 1971; women's editor The Stuart (Fla.) News, 1973-77; founder, pres. Iron Overload Diseases, North Palm Beach, Fla., 1980—. Author: The Iron Elephant, 1990, 2d edit., 1999, "tick... tick ... tick...", 1995. Avocation: barbershop singing. Office: Iron Overload Diseases 433 Westwind Dr No Palm Beach FL 33408-5123

CRAWFORD, RONALD MERRITT, history and geography educator; b. San Diego, Apr. 21, 1949; s. Leslie Merritt and Annie Louise (Briden) C. BA in History and Geography, UCLA, 1971, MA in History, 1972. Cert. standard secondary tchr. Tchr. social scis. divsn. Anchorage C.C., 1972-87; prof. Coll. Arts and Scis. U. Alaska Anchorage, 1987—, chmn. history/geography dept., 1988—; v.p. Anchorage C.C. Campus Assembly, 1985-87; 1st v.p. Faculty Senate U. Alaska Anchorage, 1987-89, 2d v.p., 1990-91; mem. Univ. Assembly, 1988-89; mem. Bartlett lectr. com. U. Alaska Anchorage, 1987-90, audio-visual adv. bd., 1989—, promotion and tenure appeals com., 1989-90; mem. exec. bd. Alaska C.Cs. Fedn. Tchrs., 1984—, Harry S. Truman scholarship com. Anchorage C.C., 1978-82; advisor Golden Key Honor Soc., 1993—, Campus Cinema Film Series, 1972—, Anchorage C.C. Student Assn., 1983-85; coord. history/geography discipline Anchorage C.C., 1979-87; columnist Anchorage Daily News, 1984-87; host Alaska Home and Gardens Program Sta. KAKM-TV, 1990. Host fund drives Sta. KAKM-TV, 1983—; guest speaker Anchorage Sch. Dist. Community Resource Ctr., 1972—, McLaughlin Youth Ctr., 1975—; advisor Friends of Libr. Film Program Loussac Libr., 1985—; presenter geography awareness programs Alaska Staff Devel. Network Summer Acad., 1990, 91, Alaska Geog. Alliance Inst., 1992, 93. Recipient Disting. Teaching Achievement award Alaska State Legislature, 1992, Disting. Teaching Achievement award Nat. Coun. Geog. Edn., 1992. Mem. Am. Fedn. Tchrs., Am. Film Inst., Nat. Coun. Geographic Edn., Alaska Geography Alliance, Assn. Pacific Coast Geographers, Univ. Film and Video Assn., Phi Alpha Theta. Avocations: travel, movie history, hiking, photography, videography. Home: PO Box 670572 Chugiak AK 99567-0572 Office: U of Alaska Dept Geography 3211 Providence Dr Anchorage AK 99508-4614*

CRAWFORD, ROY EDGINGTON, III, lawyer; b. Topeka, Dec. 23, 1938; s. Roy E. and Ethel Trula (Senne) C.; children: Michael, Jennifer. B.S., U. Pa., 1960; LL.B., Stanford U., 1963. Bar: Calif. 1964, U.S. Ct. Mil. Appeals 1964, U.S. Tax Ct. 1969, U.S. Dist. Ct. (no. dist.) Calif. 1971, U.S. Ct. Claims 1974, U.S. Supreme Ct. 1979. Assoc. Brobeck Phleger & Harison, San Francisco, 1967-73, ptnr., 1973—; bd. dirs. Sqauw Valley Ski Corp. Contbr. chpts. to books; bd. editors Stanford U. Law Rev., 1962-63. Served to capt. AUS, 1964-67. Recipient award of merit U.S. Ski Assn., 1980. Mem. ABA (chmn. com. on state and local taxes 1979-81), Calif. State Bar Assn., San Francisco Bar Assn., Calif. Trout (bd. dirs. 1970—, v.p. 1975-94, sec.-treas. 1994—), The Nature Conservancy of Idaho (bd. dirs. 1994—), Yosemite Inst. (bd. dirs. 1997—), Beta Gamma Sigma. Office: Brobeck Phleger & Harrison Spear St Tower 1 Market Plz Ste 341 San Francisco CA 94105-1193

CRAWFORD, SARAH CARTER (SALLY CARTER CRAWFORD), broadcast executive; b. Glen Ridge, N.J., Oct. 3, 1938; d. Raymond Hitchings and Katherine Latta (Gribbel) Carter; m. Joseph Paul Crawford III, Sept. 10, 1960 (dec. 1966). BA, Smith Coll., 1960. Media dir. Kampmann & Bright, Phila., 1961-64; sr. media buyer Foote, Cone & Belding, N.Y.C., 1964-69; assoc. media dir. Grey Advt., Los Angeles, 1969-75; account exec., research dir. Sta. KHJ-TV, Los Angeles, 1975-76; mgr. local sales Sta. KCOP-TV, Los Angeles, 1977-82; gen. sales mgr. Sta. KTVF-TV, Fairbanks, Alaska, 1982-96; nat. sales mgr. KTVF, KTVA, Fairbanks, 1996-97; gen. sales mgr. Sta. KYES-FM, Anchorage, 1997—; mem. adv. com. Golden Valley Electric Corp., Fairbanks, 1984-86; mem. coun. UAF Tanana County Campus, 1989-96, chair mktg. com. Chmn. Fairbanks Health and Social Svc. Commn., 1986-96; vice chmn. Fairbanks North Star Borough Health and Social Svc. Commn., 1993-96; pres. Fairbanks Meml. Hosp. Aux., 1988-90, creator trust fund, chmn. fin. com., 1990-94; bd. dirs. Fairbanks Downtown Assn., 1984-87; mem. FBKS Health Ctr. Coalition; mem. search com. UAF Tanana Valley Campus dir.; bd. dirs. Interior Regional Health Corp.; mem. Tesoro (Alaska) Citizens Adv. Coun.; pub. rels. chair Kids Vote Anchorage; mem. Gov.'s Coun. on Youth Substance Abuse Prevention. Mem. Alaska Broadcasters Assn. (bd. dirs., treas.), Alaska C. of C. (co-chair U. Alaska edn. com.). Episcopalian. Avocations: weightlifting, stock and real estate investments, running, motorcycling, ice hockey. Office: Sta KYES-FM 3700 Woodland Dr Anchorage AK 99517-2555

CRAWFORD, SUE ELLEN, elementary education educator; b. Fitzgerald, Ga., Dec. 16, 1958; d. Paul Gibbons and Mellie Mae (Roark) Chaudoin; m. Robert Emory Crawford, Dec. 5, 1992; 1 child, Katherine Ellen Coffey. BS, Ga. So. Coll., 1982, Cert. Early Childhood Edn., 1985. Kindergarten tchr. Lanier Elem. Complex, Pembroke, Ga., 1982-86; elem. tchr. Locust Grove (Ga.) Elem. Sch., 1986—; parent involvement coord. Locust Grove Elem., 1995-96, Title 1 Sch. Coord., 1994—. Actress The Henry Players, McDonough, Ga., 1992-97; dir. Cmty. Theatre. Mem. Internat. Reading Assn., Optimist. Avocations: acting, tchg. piano lessons. Office: Locust Grove Elem Sch 95 Griffen Rd Locust Grove GA 30248

CRAWFORD, SUSAN, library director, educator, author; b. Vancouver, B.C., Can.; d. James Y. and S. Young; m. James Weldon Crawford, July 5, 1955; 1 son, Robert James. BA, U. B.C., 1948; MA, U. Toronto, 1950, U. Chgo., 1954; PhD, U. Chgo., 1970. With bur. library and indexing service ADA, 1954-56; with office exec. v.p. AMA, Chgo., 1956-60; dir. div. library and archival services AMA, 1960-81; assoc. prof. Sch. Library Sci., Columbia U., N.Y.C., 1972-75; prof., dir. Sch. Medicine Library and Biomed. Communications Ctr. Washington U., 1981-92; adj. prof. U. Ill., Chgo., 1994—. Author over 150 books and sci. papers; mem. editl. bd. Med. Socioecon. Rsch. Sources, Index to Sci. Revs., Jour. Am. Soc. Info. Sci., Med. Libr. Assn. News, Health and Info. Librs. (Budapest), Health Librs. Rev. (London); assoc. editor Jour. Am. Soc. Info Sci., 1979-82, editor Med. Info. Sys., 1988-90; editor-in-chief Bull. of Med. Libr. Assn., 1982-88, 91-92. Bd. regents Nat. Library Medicine, NIH, 1971-75; mem. bd. overseers for univ. libraries Tufts U., 1988-89. Janet Doe hon. lectr., 1983; recipient Disting. Alumni award U. Toronto, 1987, Grad. medal U. Toronto, 1989. Fellow AAAS (chmn. coms.), Med. Libr. Assn. (life, Eliot award 1976, chmn. com. on surveys and stats. 1966-75, publs. panel 1977-80, chmn. consulting editors panel 1981-88, 91-92, spl. award to editor of bull. 1988, Noyes award 1992, pres.'s award 1992, Centennial award); mem. ALA, Soc. Social Studies of Sci., Assn., Acad. Health Scis. Libr. Dirs., Am. Soc. Info. Sci. (chmn. med. info. sys. 1987-88, outstanding specialty group award 1988, 89, bd. and program chair Chgo. chpt. 1993-95), Am. Med. Informatics Assn., Acad. Health Info. Profls. (disting. mem.), European Assn. Health and Info. Librs. (U.S. rep. 1989-94), Sigma Xi (chmn. coms.), Med. Libr. Assn. (100 Most Notable 1998). Home: 2418 Lincoln St Evanston IL 60201-2151

CRAWFORD, SUSAN JEAN, federal judge, lawyer; b. Pitts., Apr. 22, 1947; d. William Elmer Jr. and Joan Ruth (Bielau) C.; m. Roger W. Higgins; 1 child, Kelley S. BA, Bucknell U., 1969; JD, New Eng. Sch. Law, 1977. Bar: Md. 1977, D.C. 1980, U.S. Ct. Appeals for Armed Forces 1985, U.S. Supreme Ct. 1993. Tchr. history, coach Radnor (Pa.) H.S., 1969-74; assoc. Burnett & Eiswert, Oakland, Md., 1977-79; ptnr. Burnett, Eiswert and Crawford, Oakland, 1979-81; prin. dep. gen. counsel U.S. Dept. Army, Washington, 1981-83, gen. counsel, 1983-89; insp. gen. U.S. Dept. Def., Arlington, Va., 1989-91; judge U.S. Ct. Appeals for the Armed Forces, Washington, 1991—; asst. states atty. Garrett County, Md., 1978-79; instr. Garrett County C.C., 1979-81. Del. Md. Forestry Adv. Commn., Garrett County, 1978-81, Md. Commn. for Women, Garrett County, 1980-83; chair Rep. State Cen. Com., Garrett County, 1978-81; trustee Bucknell U., 1988—, New England Sch. Law, 1989—. Mem. FBA, Md. Bar Assn., D.C. Bar Assn., Edward Bennett Williams Am. Inn of Ct. Presbyterian. Office: US Ct Appeals Armed Forces 450 E St NW Washington DC 20442-0001

CRAWFORD, TOMMY F., career officer. AA, N.Mex. Mil. Inst., 1970; BA, N.Mex. State U., 1972; student pilot tng., Laughlin AFB, Tex., 1972-73; student, Squadron Officer Sch., 1976, Air Command and Staff Coll., 1978, Air War Coll., 1994; MS in Computer Info. Sys., Boston U., 1994. Commd. 2d lt. USAF, 1972, advanced through grades to brig. gen., 1998; pilot 390th Tactical Fighter Squadron, Mountain Home AFB, Idaho, 1973-75, various positions, 1977-81; pilot 429th Tactical Fighter Squadron, Nellis AFB, Nev., 1975-77; instr. pilot, weapons and tactics officer 4450th Tactical Group, Nellis AFB, Nev., 1981-84; air staff spl. projects officer Hdqs. USAF, Washington, 1984-88; stationed at RAF Lakenheath, Eng., 1988-91, Taif, Kingdom Saudi Arabia, 1990-91; chief spl. weapons sect., mil. asst. Supreme Allied Comdr. Europe Supreme Hdqs. Allied Powers Europe, Mons, Belgium, 1991-93; pilot, dir. combat ops. and dep. comdr. 607th Air Ops. Group, Osan Air Base, S. Korea, 1994-95, pilot, comdr., 1995-97; insp. gen. Hdqs. Pacific Air Forces, Hickam AFB, Hawaii, 1996-97; comdr. 354th Fighter Wing, Eielson AFB, Alaska, 1997—. Decorated D.F.C. with oak leaf cluster, Legion of Merit, Air medal with oak leaf cluster. Office: 354 FW/CC 3112 Broadway Ave Unit 19A Eielson AFB AK 99702-1899

CRAWFORD, WILLIAM DAVID, office equipment company executive; b. Tuscaloosa, Ala., Jan. 19, 1947; s. Clarence W. and Louise (Hatcher) C.; m. Elaine Randall, July 21, 1977; 1 child, John Samuel. BS in Indsl. Mgmt., U. Ala., 1971; MBA, Jacksonville State U., 1974. Prodn. supr. Goodyear Tire & Rubber Co., Gadsden, Ala., 1971-77; mgmt. instr. U. Ala., Gadsden, 1975-77; various positions Mead-Hatcher, Inc., Buffalo, 1977-85, v.p., 1985-91, pres., CEO, 1991—. Bd. dirs., treas. Christian Found. for Performing Arts, 1992—; bd. dirs. Athletes-in-Action, Buffalo, 1995—, Youth for Christ, Buffalo, 1996—; host com., Super Bowl XXXIV, Breakfast, Atlanta: coach Lou Gehrig Youth Baseball, Amherst, N.Y.; bd. dirs. Oakbrook Condominium, Williamsville, N.Y., 1978-80, 87-90, pres., 1989-90. With USNR, 1964-80, Vietnam, 1967-68. Mem. Bus. Products Industry Assn. (various coms. 1983—, treas. 1997, vice chair 1998, chair 1999, bd. dirs. 1994—), Office Products Mfrs. Assn. (bd. dirs. 1986-96, treas. 1990-91, v.p. 1992, pres. 1993-94), Sons of Amer. Revolution, U. Ala. Alumni Assn., Rotary. Republican. Protestant.

CRAWFORD, WILLIAM DAVID, real estate broker, consultant; b. Abbeville County, S.C., Aug. 13, 1945; s. Jesse David and Elizabeth Virginia (Ashley) C.; m. Gail Eileen Watkins, June 9, 1967 (div. Aug. 1985); 1 child, Merritt Caitlin; m. Dawn P. Lantz, June 10, 1995. BA, Wofford Coll., 1967; MS, Tex. A&M U., 1974; MBA, U. New Orleans, 1977. Lic. real estate broker, S.C., N.C., Ga., Tex., Tenn.; CCIM, CIPS; lic. comml. aircraft pilot. Gen. mgr. Ramada Inn, New Orleans, 1973-74; rschr. divsn. bus. and econ. rsch. U. New Orleans, 1975-77; exec. asst. to pres. LaSalle Properties, New Orleans, 1977-81; v.p. Doerring Devel. Co., Austin, Tex., 1981-84; project mgr. Street-Martin Cos., Austin, 1984; pres. TriSource Corp., San Antonio, 1985-86; v.p. Merritt Properties, Inc., Greenville, S.C., 1986-87; pres. Crawford & Assocs. LLC, Greenville, 1987—. Author: Louisiana Business Survey, 1977, Application of Travel Economic Impact Model to New Orleans, 1977. Chmn. Paris Mountain Water Dist., Greenville, 1990—. Capt. C.E., U.S. Army, 1968-71. Mem. Comml. Investment Real Estate Inst. (cert. comml. investment mem., cert. internat. property specialist internat. real estate sect.), Nat. Assn. Realtors (Internat. Real Estate sect.), Greenville Bd. Realtors, Comml. Bd. Realtors (dir.), Greenville C. of C., Gamma Sigma Delta, Beta Gamma Sigma. Mem. Unity Ch. Avocations: hiking, snow skiing, scuba diving, flying. Home and Office: 2 Persimmon Ln Greenville SC 29609-6511

CRAWFORD, WILLIAM F., corporate executive, consultant; b. Chgo., Apr. 11, 1911; s. William Wilberforce and Mona (Richards) C.; m. Ruth M. Fellinger, May 4, 1935; children: Judith Crawford Smith, Susan (dec.), Constance Crawford Dry, Barbara Crawford Boger, William Edwin. Student, Northwestern Mil. and Naval Acad., 1925-29, U. Chgo., 1929-31. Sec., Edward Valves, Inc. (formerly Edward Valve & Mfg. Co., Inc.), East Chicago, Ind., 1931-37; v.p. Edward Valves, Inc. (formerly Edward Valve & Mfg. Co., Inc.), 1937-41, pres., dir., 1941-63; pres. Republic Flow Meters Co., Chgo., 1957-61, Valve Products, Inc., Knox, Ind., 1950-63, W.E. Bowler Co., Phila., 1954-63; v.p., dir. Rockwell Mfg. Co., Pitts., 1945-72; chmn. fin. com. Rockwell Mfg. Co., 1963-73; emeritus dir. Rockwell Internat. Corp., Costa Mesa, Calif., 1973—; v.p., dir. Chgo. Fittings Corp.; chmn. W.F. Crawford & Assoc., Chgo. Contbr. articles to profl. jours. Trustee Crawford Found., Chgo., Ill. Inst. Tech.; mem. valve industry adv. com. WPB, 1941-45, 50-52. Mem. Valve Mfrs. Assn. (pres. 1959-61, 64-65, Silver Gavel award 1972), ASME, Newcomen Soc. N.Am., Art Inst. Chgo., Field Mus. Natural History (Chgo.), Delta Upsilon. Republican. Congregationalist. Clubs: Union League, Econ., Tavern (Chgo.), Duquesne (Pitts.), La Jaolla Country (Calif.). Home: 440 N Wabash Ave Apt 2809 Chicago IL 60611-3556 also: PO Box 1800 Sun Valley ID 83353-1800

CRAWFORD, WILLIAM REX, JR., former ambassador; b. Phila., Apr. 22, 1928; s. William Rex and Dorothy (Buckley) C.; m. Celia Faulkner Clevenger, Sept. 18, 1992; 1 child from previous marriage, Sarah Lowry. B.A. cum laude, Harvard, 1948; M.A., U. Pa., 1950. Joined U.S. Fgn. Service, 1951-79; fgn. service officer Jidda, 1951-53, Venice, 1954; Arabic lang. tng., 1955-57, consul in Aden, charge d'affaires Yemen, 1957-59; officer charge Arab-Israeli affairs State Dept., 1959-64, Morocco, 1964-67, Cyprus, 1968-72; ambassador to Yemen Arab Republic, 1972-74, Cyprus, 1974-78; prin. dep. asst. sec. state for Near Eastern and South Asian affairs, 1978-79; exec. dir. Nat. Com. to Honor 14th Centennial of Islam, 1979-82; pres. Eisenhower Exchange Fellowships, 1982-83, The Crawford Found., 1981-91. With USN, 1948-49. Recipient Dept. State Meritorious Service award, 1959; William A. Jump award for Disting. Fed. Svc., 1964; Woodrow Wilson fellow Princeton, 1967-68. Mem. Middle East Inst. Club: Hasty Pudding Inst., Dacor. Home: 3419 36th St NW Washington DC 20016-3147

CRAWFORD, WILLIAM WALSH, retired consumer products company executive; b. Clearwater, Fla., Oct. 7, 1927; s. Francis Marion and Frances Marie (Walsh) C. B.S., Georgetown U., 1950; LL.B., Harvard, 1954. Bar: N.Y. 1955, Ill. 1972. Assoc. Sullivan & Cromwell, N.Y.C., 1954-58; counsel Esso Standard Oil, N.Y.C., 1958-60; ptnr. Alexander & Green, N.Y.C., 1960-71; v.p., gen. counsel Internat. Harvester Co., Chgo., 1971-76; v.p., gen. counsel, sec. Internat. Harvester Co., 1976-80; sr. v.p. gen. counsel Kraft, Inc., Glenview, Ill., 1980-81; sr. v.p., gen. counsel, sec. Dart & Kraft, Inc., 1981-86; sr. v.p., gen. counsel, sec. Kraft, Inc., 1986-88, sr. v.p., sec., 1988-89, ret., 1989. Mem. ABA, Ill. Bar Assn., Assn. Bar City N.Y., Am. Judicature Soc., Am. Law Inst., Assn. Gen. Counsel, Chgo. Club, River Club (N.Y.C.), Beach Club, Everglades Club, Old Guard Soc. Palm Beach Golfers.

CRAWFORD-MASON, CLARE WOOTTEN, television producer, journalist; b. Durham, N.C., July 22, 1936; d. Charles Thomas and Clare (Erly) Wootten; m. Robert Watts Mason; children: Victor Lawrence Crawford Jr., Charlene Elizabeth Crawford; stepchildren—John Mason, Robert Mason 3d. B.A., U. Md., 1958. Reporter, columnist Washington Daily News, 1961-72; columnist Washington Star News, 1972-74; Washington bur. chief People mag., 1974-82; reporter, sr. producer NBC-TV, 1969-80; pres. CC-M Prodns. Inc., Washington, 1981—. Prodr. 1st network documentary on spouse abuse NBC-TV, 1975 (blue ribbon San Francisco Film Festival), 1st network documentary on child sexual abuse NBC, TV, 1977, People of the Year (CBS), 1982, If Japan Can, Why Can't We, 1980 (Dupont award Columbia U. Sch. Journalism), It's Up to the Women, 1984, The Issues Hit Home, 1986, Windows on Women, 1986, How To Fix Up a Little Old American Town, 1987, Work Worth Doing, 1987 (Golden Eagle award Coun. on Internat. Non-theatrical Events), The Deming Library: Vols. I-27, Implementing Deming, vols. 1-4; co-author: Thinking About Quality, Progress, Wisdom and the Deming Philosophy, 1994; prodr., dir. documentary series Quality of Else, 1991, W. Edwards Deming: The Prophet of Quality, 1994; co-author: Quality or Else: The Revolution in World Business, 1991. Recipient Bill Pryor Meml. award, 1st prize Washington Newspaper Guild, 1966; Disting. Pub. Affairs Reporting award Am. Polit. Sci. Assn., 1967; Nat. Assn. Broadcasters award, 1971, 2 Emmy awards Nat. Acad. TV Arts and Scis., 1972, award for broadcast investigative reporting AAUW, 1972, award for investigative reporting Chesapeake Press Assn., 1971, Douglas Southall Freeman award for pub. service Va. Assn. Press Broadcasters, 1972; Washington Newspaper Guild award, 1974, Blue Ribbon Am. Film Festival, 1977, 1st place award Nat. Edn. Film Festival, 1985, documentary award Am. Women in Radio and TV, 1986, Golden Eagle award, 1986, 87, Award of Excellence Soc. Tech. Communication, 1988. Mem. AFTRA, SAG. Democrat. Roman Catholic. Office: 8512 Cedar St Silver Spring MD 20910-4348

CRAWLEY, JOHN BOEVEY, publisher; b. N.Y.C., Y, Mar. 1, 1946; s. Charles John and Katherin Marie (Dowd) C.; m. Ann Auwerda, June 28, 1969; children: John, Mark, Brian, Jean. B.A., Coll. Santa Fe, 1968. Advt. salesman N.Y. Daily News, N.Y.C., 1968-73; L.I. (N.Y.) advt. mgr. N.Y. Daily News, 1973-75; western advt. mgr. N.Y. Daily News, Chgo., 1975-80; city circulation sales mgr. N.Y. Daily News, N.Y.C., 1980-81; advt. sales mgr. N.Y. Daily News, 1981-82; advt. sales rep. Time, Inc./People mag., N.Y.C., 1982-83; pub. Times Mirror Mags./Outdoor Life mag., N.Y.C., 1983-88; group pub. Times Mirror Mags., N.Y.C., 1988-98, v.p. pub., 1998—; cons., pres. J. Blair & Co., N.Y.C., 1981. Sgt. U.S. Army, 1967-68. Mem. N.Y. Athletic Club, Tokeneke Club (Darien, Conn.), Darien Country Club. Republican. Roman Catholic. Home: 10 Pheasant Run Darien CT 06820-4813 Office: Times Mirror Mags 2 Park Ave Fl 5 New York NY 10016-5695*

CRAWLEY, VERNON OBADIAH, academic adminstrator; b. Oct. 22, 1936; s. Joseph and Ruth (Adkins) C.; m. Betty W. Wood, July 9, 1966; children: V. Alan, Vonda, Keith. BS in Chemistry, Va. State U., 1958; postgrad., Coll. William and Mary, 1962, Am. U., 1964; MEd, U. Va., 1965; EdD, Pa. State U., 1971. Chemist Stuart Products Co., Richmond, Va., 1958-61; tchr. sci. and math. Ruthville (Va.) High Sch., 1961-64; asst. prof. sci. dept. Morgan State U., Balt., 1965-69; instr. phys. sci. Towson State Coll., Balt., 1969; assoc. prof. chemistry, chmn. sci., math. and technologies Dundalk C.C., Balt., 1971-74; assoc. dean acad. affairs Mercer County C.C., Trenton, N.J., 1974-78; pres. St. Louis C.C. at Forest Park, 1978-91, Moraine Valley C.C., Palos Hills, Ill., 1991—; acting dean James Kerney campus Mercer County C.C., Trenton, 1976-77; adminstrv. specialist in sci. NASA, Washington, summer 1966, 67, 68; cons. N. Cen. Assn., Coro Found. Adv. bd. mem. St. Francis Hosp., Blue Island, Ill.; fin. adv. com. mem. Ill. C.C. Bd.; chmn. Ill. Coun. C.C. Pres.; bd. dirs. Southwest YMCA, Alsip, Ill. Recipient Outstanding Svc. to Williams Community Sch. award 8th Dist. Police Community Youth Network Com., 1990, Assistance with Minority Tchr. Recruitment Program award St. Louis Area Pers. and Place Adminstrs., 1989, Outstanding Leadership award Nat. Coun. Black Am. Affairs, 1987, Citizenship award Wellston Sch. Dist., 1983, NSF Academic Yr. award, 1964-65, Southern fellowship, 1965. Mem. League for Innovation in C.C. (bd. dirs.), Expanding Leadership Opportunities for Minorities in C.C. (nat. adv. group), Am. Assn. C.C. (bd. dirs., exec. bd.), Nat. Coun. on Black Am. Affairs (bd. dirs.), Econ. Devel. Corp. for Southwest Suburbs (bd. dirs.), Rotary Club Oak Lawn, Moraine Valley C.C. Found. (bd. dirs.), Mo. Assn. Community and Jr. Colls. (bd. dirs.), Mo. Coun. C.C. Pres./Chancellors (chmn. 1986-87, v.p. 1985-86, sec. treas. 1984-85), Sigma Xi, Phi Theta Kappa. Avocations: travel, reading, gardening. Home: 7841 Sioux Rd Orland Park IL 60462-1894 Office: Moraine Valley CC 10900 S 88th Ave Palos Hills IL 60465-2175*

CRAWSHAW, RALPH, psychiatrist; b. N.Y.C., July 3, 1921. A.B., Middlebury (Vt.) Coll., 1943; M.D., N.Y. U., 1947. Diplomate: Nat. Bd. Med. Examiners, Am. Bd. Psychiatry and Neurology. Intern Lenox Hill Hosp., N.Y.C., 1947-48; resident Menninger Sch. Psychiatry, Topeka, 1948-50, Oreg. State Hosp., Salem, 1950-51; practice medicine specializing in psychiatry Washington, 1954; staff psychiatrist C.F. Menninger Meml. Hosp., Topeka, 1954-57; asst. chief VA Mental Hygiene Clinic, Topeka, 1957-60; staff psychiatrist Community Child Guidance Clinic, Portland, Oreg., 1960-63; founder, clinic dir. Tualatin Valley Guidance Clinic, Beaverton, Oreg., 1961-67; pvt. practice medicine, specializing in psychiatry Portland, 1960—; mem. staff Holladay Park Hosp., 1961—; lectr. dept. child psychiatry Med. Sch. U. Oreg., 1961-63, clin. prof. dept. psychiatry, 1976; lectr. Sch. Social Work, Portland State U., 1964-67; founder Benjamin Rush Found., 1968, pres., 1968—; founder Friends of Medicine, 1969, Ct. of Man, 1970, Club of Kos, 1974, Oreg. Health Decisions, 1983, Am. Health Decisions, 1989, Health Vol. Overseas, 1984; Sonian Machanic vis. prof. South African Coll. Medicine, 1993. Contbr. editor: AMA Jour. of Socio-Econs, 1972-75; Columnist: Prism mag, 1972-76, The Pharos, 1972—, Portland Physician, 1975, Western Jour. Medicine, 1980—; Contbr. articles to med. jours. Cons. Bur. Hearings and Appeals, HEW, 1964-90; cons. Albina Child Devel.

Center, Portland, 1965-75, HEW Region 8 Health Planning, 1979; mem. Inst. Medicine, Nat. Acad. Sci., 1978, Oreg. Health Coordinating Council, 1979; Mem. Gov.'s Adv. Com. on Mental Health, 1966-72; ad hoc com. Nat. Leadership Conf. on Am. Health Policy, 1976, Gov.'s Adv. Com. on Med. Care to Indigent, 1976—; trustee Millicent Found., 1964-67, Multnomah Found. for Med. Care, 1977; pres. Bull Run Heritage Found., 1996; vis. scholar Center for Study Democratic Instns., 1969, Jack Murdock Charitable Trust, 1977, U.S.-USSR exchange scholar, 1973; founder Bull Run Heritage Found., 1996. Served with AUS, 1943-46; to lt., M.C. USN, 1951-54. Named Oreg. Dr./Citizen of Yr., 1978; U.S.-USSR rsch. scholar, 1973, 79; recipient I.N. Piragou medal for humanitarian Svcs., Russian Govt., 1992; Ralph Crawshaw Ann. Lectr. in Civic Medicine named in honor by Oreg. Found. for Med. Excellence, 1987. Fellow Am. Psychiat. Assn.; mem. AMA, APA, AAAS, Nat. Med. Assn., Oreg. Med. Assn. (trustee 1972—), Multnomah County Med. Soc. (pres. 1975), Royal Soc. Medicine, Inst. of Medicine of NAS, North Pacific Soc. Neurology and Psychiatry, Soc. for Psychol. Study Social Issues, Western European Assn. Aviation Psychology, Am. Med. Writers Assn., Portland Psychiatrists in Pvt. Practice (pres. 1971), Russian Acad. Natural Scis. (fgn. mem.), Alpha Omega. Address: 2525 NW Lovejoy St Ste 404 Portland OR 97210-2865

CRAYMER, HELEN STOUGHTON, educator; b. Phila., Sept. 9, 1919; d. Walter S.and Helen P. (Anker) S.; widowed; children: R. Lee, John S., R. Lynne. BA, Temple U., 1953, MA, 1964. Tchr. Phila. Schs., 1943-52, Hatboro (Pa.) Schs., 1957-62, Centennial Schs., Warminster, Pa., 1961-67; sr. prof. Eastern Coll., St. Davids, Pa., 1967-98. Mem. ASCD, IRA, DVRA, Delta Kappa Gamma. Republican. Avocations: counted cross-stitch, sewing, dolls.

CRAYPO, CHARLES, labor economics educator; b. Jackson, Mich., Jan. 3, 1936; s. Norman Laverne and Ann Marie (Bogdan) C.; m. Mary Louise Vaclavik, Sept. 6, 1958; children: Jack, Carrie, Susan. BA in Econs., Mich. State U., 1959, MA in Econs., 1961, PhD in Econs., 1966. Asst. prof. econs. U. Maine, Orono, 1966-67; assoc. prof. Mich. State U., East Lansing, 1967-72, Pa. State U., University Park, 1972-78; assoc. prof. U. Notre Dame, Ind., 1978-82, prof., 1984—, prof., chmn. dept. econs., 1984-93; prof. Cornell U., Ithaca, N.Y., 1982-84; bd. dirs. Bus. Devel. Com., South Bend, Ind.; dir. Bur. Workers Edn., U. Maine, Orono, 1966-67, Higgins Labor Rsch. Ctr., U. Notre Dame, 1993; mem. acad. evaluating com. Labor Studies Ctr., Empire State Coll., SUNY, 1980; mem. labor studies dept. Ramapo Coll., 1981; mem. indsl. rels. dept. LeMoyne Coll., Syracuse, N.Y., 1983, Bur. of Labor Edn., U. Maine, Orono; lectr. in field; expert witness. Author: Economics of Collective Bargaining, 1986, Grand Designs, 1993; mem. editorial bd., bus. mgr. Labor Studies Jour., 1976-80, chmn. editorial bd., 1980-85; mem. editoral bd. Contbns. to Labor Studies, 1989—; internat. mem. editorial bd. Indsl. Rels. Jour., 1989—; contbr. articles to profl. jours. Mem. acad. adv. com. Div. Labor Studies Ind. U., 1978-82, 84-92, 95-96. Served with USMC, 1953-55. Grantee NEH, 1981; rsch. grantee Dept. Commerce, 1984, Lilly Endowment, 1992-93, D. Dority Labor Rsch. Fund. Mem. Indsl. Rels. Rsch. Assn. Home: 50600 Sorrel Dr Granger IN 46530-8506 Office: U Notre Dame Dept Econs Notre Dame IN 46556

CRAYTON, BILLY GENE, physician; b. Holden, Mo., May 15, 1931; s. John Reuben and Carrie Zona (Head) C.; student Central Mo. State Coll., 1948-49; BS, Stetson U., 1958; postgrad. U. Kansas City, summer 1955; MD, U. Mo., 1962. Intern, Mound Park Hosp., St. Petersburg, Fla., 1962-63; practice gen. medicine Latham Hosp., California, Mo., 1963-64, Kelling Clinic and Hosp., Waverly, Mo., 1964-88, vice chief of staff, 1980-88; preceptor in community health and med. practice U. Mo. Sch. Medicine, Waverly, 1968-88; sec., dir. Kelling Hosp., Inc., 1969-80; pres. Kelling Clinic, 1971-88; med. dir. Waverly Ambulance Co., 1985-86; pres. Riverview Heights, 1972-88. Adviser, Mo. chpt. Am. Assn. Med. Assts., 1973-79. Adviser, Explorer Post Boy Scouts Am., 1968-70. Served with AUS, 1952-54. Fellow Am. Acad. Family Physicians. Baptist. Home: 1231 W 69th Ter Kansas City MO 64113-2054

CREAGAN, JAMES FRANCIS, diplomat; b. Elyria, Ohio, Dec. 28, 1940; s. James Malcolm and Mareta Creagan; m. Cherry Gwyn Jonsson, Jan. 29, 1966; children: Kevin James, Sean Malcolm Alan. BA in History, U. Notre Dame, 1962; PhD in Polit. Sci., U. Va., 1965. Asst. prof. govt. St. Mary's U., San Antonio, 1965-66; asst. prof. polit. sci. Tex. A&M U., Bryan, Tex., 1970-71; joined fgn. svc. Dept. State, Washington, 1966; labor and polit. officer Am. Embassy, Mex., 1967-69; labor attache Am. Embassy, San Salvador, El Salvador, 1969-70; 2nd sec., labor officer Am. Embassy, Rome, 1971-74; 1st sec. Am. Embassy, Lima, Peru, 1974-77; U.S. consul Am. Consulate Gen., Naples, 1977-80; officer-in-charge, Italian and Vatican affairs U.S. Dept. of State, 1980-82; polit. counselor Am. Embassy, Lisbon, 1982-86, Brasilia, 1986-88; dep. chief of mission Am. Embassy to the Holy See, 1988-91; consul gen. Am. Consulate Gen., Sao Paulo, 1991-92; sr. advisor for Latin Am. U.S. Mission to UN, 1992; dep. chief mission Am. Embassy, Rome, 1993-96; Am. amb. to Honduras, 1996—. Mem. Am. Fgn. Svc. Assn., Cosmos Club, InterAm. Dialogue Club. Roman Catholic. Avocations: tennis, biking. Office: Am Embassy Tegucigalpa APO AA 34022

CREAGER, JOE SCOTT, geology and oceanography educator; b. Vernon, Tex., Aug. 30, 1929; s. Earl Litton and Irene Eugenia (Keller) C.; m. Barbara Clark, Aug. 30, 1951 (dec.); children: Kenneth Clark, Vanessa Irene; m. B. J. Wren, Sept. 5, 1987. B.S., Colo. Coll., 1951; postgrad., Columbia, 1952-53; M.S., Tex. A. and M. U., 1953, Ph.D., 1958. Asst. prof. dept. oceanography U. Wash., Seattle, 1958-61; assoc. prof. U. Wash., 1962-66, prof. oceanography, 1966-91, prof. geol. scis., 1981-91, prof. emeritus, 1991—, asst. chmn. dept. oceanography, 1964-65, assoc. dean arts and scis. for earth and planetary scis., 1966-95, assoc. dean for rsch., 1966-91, divisional dean emeritus, 1995—; program dir. for oceanography NSF, 1965-66; chief scientist numerous oceanographic expdns. to Arctic and Sub-arctic including Leg XIX of Deep Sea Drilling project, 1959-91; vis. geol. scientist Am. Geol. Inst., 1962, 63, 65; U.S. Nat. coord. Internat. Indian Ocean Expedition, 1965-66; vis. scientist program lectr. Am. Geophys. Union, 1965-72; Battelle cons., advanced waste mgmt., 1974; cons. to U.S. Army C.E., 1976, U.S. Depts. Interior and Commerce, 1975; exec. sec., exec. com., chmn. planning com. Joint Oceanographic Insts. Deep Earth Sampling, 1970-72, 76-78; mem. evaluation com. Northwest Assn. Schs. and Colls., 1989-99. Mem. editorial bd. Internat. Jour. Marine Geology, 1964-91; assoc. editor Jour. Sedimentary Petrology, 1963-76; asst. editor Quaternary Research, 1970-79; contbr. articles to profl. jours. Skipper Sea Scout Ship, Boy Scouts Am., Bryan, Tex., 1957; coach Little League Baseball, Seattle, 1964-71, sec., 1971; cons. sci. curriculum Northshore Sch. Dist., 1970; mem. Seattle Citizens Shoreline Com., 1973-74, King County Shoreline Com., 1980. Served with U.S. Army, 1953-55. Colo. Coll. scholar, 1949-51; NSF grantee, 1962-82; ERDA grantee, 1962-64; U.S. Army C.E. grantee, 1975-82; Office of Naval Research grantee; U.S. Dept. Commerce grantee; U.S. Geol. Survey grantee. Fellow Geol. Soc. Am., AAAS; mem. Internat. Assn. Quaternary Research, Am. Geophys. Union, Internat. Assn. Sedimentology, Internat. Assn. Math. Geologists, Soc. Econ. Paleontologists and Mineralists, Marine Tech. Soc. (sec.-treas. 1972-75), Sigma Xi, Beta Theta Pi, Delta Epsilon. Home: 6320 NE 157th St Kenmore WA 98028-4345 Office: U Wash PO Box 353765 Seattle WA 98195-3765

CREAMER, GERMAN GONZALO, bank executive, educator; b. Caracas, Venezuela, Oct. 31, 1960; arrived in Ecuador, 1978; s. Claudio Creamer and Maria Del Carmen Guillen; m. Maria Consuelo Botero, June 19, 1992; children: Mateo, Carolina. BA in psychology, Cath. U. Ecuador, 1985, BA in Sociology, 1986; MA, U. Notre Dame, 1989, PhD, 1993. Dir. human resource dept. Constructora Elepeve, Quito, Ecuador, 1985-86; econ. advisor President of Ecuador, Quito, 1990-91; econs. program officer UN, Quito, 1992-93; assoc. prof., econs. coord. FLACSO, Quito, 1993-95; mgr. Guayaquil (Ecuador) br. Ecuafactor (name now Bancomex), 1995-96; mgr. planning and econ. studies Banco del Pacifico, Guayaquil, 1995-97; prof. Catholic U, Guayaquil and Espol, 1995-97; vis. assoc. prof. of finance Bus. Sch., Tulane U., New Orleans, 1997-99; cons. UN, Equatorial Guinea, 1991, USAID, Quito, 1991, 94; Komex 1995. Author: Redistribution, Inflation, and Adjustment Policies, 1992; co-author: La desarticulacion del Mundo Andino, 1986, Las economias Andinas, 1993, The Ecuadorean Participation in the Andean Pact, 1996, Ecuador en la Economía Mundial, 1997, The Cost of Hospital Cholera Treatment in Ecuador, 1999. Fulbright scholar, N.Y., 1986, Inst. for Study of World Policies scholar, N.Y., 1988, MacArthur Found. scholar, U. Notre Dame, 1990, Kellogg Inst., 1989. Mem. Am. Econ. Assn., Am. Fin. Assn., Bus. Assn. of Latin Am. studies. Home: 31 McAlister Dr MRBox 5027 New Orleans LA 70118 Office: Tulane U Sch Bus 7 McAlister Dr New Orleans LA 70118

CREAMER, WILLIAM HENRY, III, insurance company executive; b. Narberth, Pa., Mar. 24, 1927; s. William Henry and Stella Elizabeth (McShane) C.; m. Anne Tyson Greer, Sept. 20, 1952 (dec. Mar. 1996); children: William Henry IV, Anne McSherry Creamer Devine, Mary Greer Conyack; m. Nancy Ann Falk, July 10, 1997. BS in Econ., Villanova U., 1951. C.L.U. With N.Y. Life Ins. Co., 1951-89; gen. mgr. N.Y. Life Ins. Co., Towson, Md., 1957-60; regional supt. tng. N.Y. Life Ins. Co., 1960-62; gen. mgr. N.Y. Life Ins. Co., Scranton, Pa., 1962-66, Arlington, Va., 1966-69; supt. agencies N.Y. Life Ins. Co., N.Y.C., 1969-70; regional v.p. N.Y. Life Ins. Co., Mpls., 1970-74; v.p. N.Y. Life Ins. Co., N.Y.C., 1974-83; sr. v.p. N.Y. Life Ins. Co., 1983-85; in charge office fed. affairs N.Y. Life Ins. Co., Washington, 1986-88; ret., 1988. Past chmn. Navisank River Municipality Com. Served with USN, 1945-46. Mem. Nat. Assn. Life Underwriters, Am. Soc. CLUs, U.S. Power Squadron (past comdr. Shrewsbury squadron), Estate Planning Coun. (past dir.), Shrewsbury River Yacht Club, George Town Club, Capital Hill Club, Root Beer and Checker Club (past pres.), Kiwanis (past pres. Scranton chpt., past dir.), K. of C. (past grand knight Red Bank coun.). Republican. Roman Catholic. Home: 3 Wardell Ave Rumson NJ 07760-1036

CREAN, JOHN C., retired housing and recreational vehicles manufacturing company executive; b. Bowden, N.D., 1925; married. Founder Fleetwood Enterprises, Inc., Riverside, Calif., 1950, pres., 1952-70, chmn., chief exec. officer, 1950-98, also dir. Served with USN, 1942; with U.S. Mcht. Marines, 1944-45. Office: PO Box 8449 Newport Beach CA 92658*

CREANY, CATHLEEN ANNETTE, television station executive; b. Johnstown, Pa., Jan. 14, 1950; d. Eugene Anthony and Winifred Nell (Sheridan) C. BA in Communication Arts, U. Notre Dame, 1972. Ptnr. Technivision, Inc., N.Y.C., 1972-75; producer commls. Innervision Prodns., St. Louis, 1975-76; film editor Sta. KPHO-TV, Phoenix, 1976-77, promotion asst., 1977-78, comml. and documentary photographer and producer, 1978-80; news photographer Sta. WTVH-TV, Syracuse, N.Y., 1980-81, field dir. PM Mag. show, 1981-82, exec. producer PM Mag. show, 1982-83, program dir., 1983-86, v.p., gen. mgr., 1986-92, Sta WTVH-TV, Syracuse; v.p., gen mgr. Sta. WFAA-TV, Dallas, 1993-94, pres., gen. mgr., 1994-97; sr. v.p. TV sta. group A.H. Belo Corp., 1997—; mem. bd. dirs. The Family Place, 1993—; Children's Med. Ctr. of Dallas, Children's Med. Found. Dallas, Better Business Bur. Dallas, adv. bd. of Jr. League, Dallas; mem. The Charter 100 of Dallas. Recipient Excellence in Photography award for PM Mag. show, 1982, Excellence in Story Producing award for PM Mag., 1983. Mem. Nat. Assn. TV Program Execs., Nat. Assn. Broadcasters, Am. Women in Radio and TV, Inc., ABC TV Affiliates Assn. (vice chair bd. govs.). Avocations: running, skiing, boating, gardening. Office: A H Belo Corp 400 S Record St Fl 14 Dallas TX 75202-4841

CREASE, ROBERT POOLE, JR., philosopher, writer, educator; b. Abington, Pa., Oct. 22, 1953; s. Robert Poole and Mary Augusta (Childs) C.; m. Susan Beth Schneider, Apr. 26, 1948 (div.); 1 child, India Augusta Schneider; m. Stephanie Laura Stein, Oct. 29, 1994; 1 child, Alexander Shael. BA, Amherst Coll., 1976; PhD, Columbia U., 1987. Historian Brookhaven Nat. Lab., Upton, N.Y., 1988—; asst. prof. SUNY, Stony Brook, 1988-94, assoc. prof., 1994—, dir. grad. program, 1997-99; vis. prof. philosophy SUNY, Stony Brook, 1987-88, Columbia U., 1988; contbg. corr. Science, Washington, 1989-95. Author: Making Physics: A Biography of Brookhaven National Laboratory, 1946-72, 1999, The Play of Nature: Experimentation as Performance, 1993, (with Charles C. Mann) The Second Creation: Makers of the Revolution in 20th Century Physics, 1986, 2d edit., 1996. Dancer, The Big Apple Lindy Hoppers, N.Y.C., 1985—. Fulbright grantee, 1979-80, Nat. Def. and Area Studies grantee, 1977-79. Mem. AAAS, Heidegger Conf., Soc. for Phenomenology and Existential Philosophy, N.Y. Swing Dance Soc. (co-founder, pres. 1990-94). Office: SUNY Stony Brook Dept Philosophy 213 Harriman Hall Stony Brook NY 11794

CREASEY, DAVID EDWARD, physician, psychiatrist, educator; b. Santa Barbara, Calif., Aug. 26, 1944; s. Edward Louis Aja and Ruth (Bryan) Creasey; m. Beverly Dewolfe, Apr. 8, 1972. BA cum laude, Tufts U., 1966, MD, 1970. Diplomate Am. Bd. Psychiatry and Neurology, Am. Coll. Forensic Medicine. Surgical intern, then OB/GYN resident Tufts-New England Med. Ctr., Boston, 1970-72; gen. med. officer Newport (R.I.) Naval Hosp., 1972-74; resident in psychiatry Boston VA Hosp., Boston, 1974-77; fellow in psychiatry Mt. Auburn Hosp., Cambridge, Mass., 1977-78; staff psychiatrist Westwood (Mass.) Lodge Hosp., 1978-79, Mass. Mental Health Ctr., Boston, 1979-97; psychiat. dir. New Eng. Psychiat. Rehab. Tng. program, Cambridge, Mass., 1978—; cons. Mass. Rehab. Com. and Com. for the Blind, Boston, 1984—; adj. assoc. prof. Boston U., 1986—; assoc., premed. adv. North House Harvard U., 1982—; ind. med. reviewer, Metlife, 1994—. Contbr. articles to profl. jours.; reviewer Am. Jour. Psychiatry, Hosp. and Cmty. Psychiatry, Jour. Clin. Neuropsychiatry; author interactive videodisc tchg. program, 1985; med. editor Ency. Disability and Rehab. Mem. various comty. orgns. Lt. cmdr. USN, 1972-74. Recipient Am. Psychiat. Assn. Physician's Recognition award, 1978, 82, 85, 88, 91, 94, Excellence in Media award Nat. Rehab. Assn., 1996. Avocations: hiking, raquetball, chess, marathoning, roadracing. Office: 1101 Beacon St Fl 8 Brookline MA 02446-5502

CREASEY, KATHERINE YVONNE, family nurse practitioner; b. McCrory, Ark., Jan. 24, 1961; d. Earnest E. and Mary A. (Stain) Tyler; m. Earnest Leon Creasey, June 3, 1995; 1 child, Stephanie K. AS, East Ark. Community Coll., 1981; BSN, U. Ark. for Med. Scis., 1996, MSN, 1998. RN, Ark. Staff nurse Crittenden Meml. Hosp., West Memphis, Ark., 1982; nurse ICU/CCU Bapt. Meml. Hosp., Forrest City, Ark., 1981-82, 82-86, nurse gastrointestinal and non-invasive vascular labs., 1986-87, surg. nurse gastrointestinal lab., 1987-91, mem. utilization rev., 1992-95, PRN CCU, 1995—. Mem. AACN. Home: PO Box 986 Mc Crory AR 72101-0986 Office: Bapt Meml Hosp PO Box 667 Forrest City AR 72336-0667

CREASIA, DONALD ANTHONY, toxicologist, researcher; b. Milford, Mass., Mar. 28, 1937; s. Dominic and Minnie (Bufalo) C.; m. Joan La Belle, June 29, 1963; children: Karen Joan, Tracey Dawn. BS in Biology, U. Vt., 1961; DSc, Harvard U., 1967; PhD, U. Tenn., 1981. Rsch. assoc. Sch. Pub. Health, Harvard U., Cambridge, Mass., 1963-69; toxicologist Oak Ridge (Tenn.) Nat. Lab., 1970-77; program dir. Frederick (Md.) Cancer Rsch. Ctr., 1977-83; rsch. chemist U.S. Army R&D, Frederick, 1983—; cons. toxicology, 1963—. Author: (chpts. in books with others) Internat. Symposium on the Biological Effects of Ozone and Related Photochemical Oxidents, 1983, Trycothecine Mycotoxicosis: Pathophysiological Efffects, 1989; contbr. over 120 articles to profl. jours. NSF scholar, 1965-67; NRC fellow, 1981-83. Mem. AAAS, Soc. Toxicology, Am. Coll. Toxicology, Soc. Govt. Toxicologists, Internat. Soc. Toxicology, Sigma Xi. Achievements include patents pending for use of castor bean protein as an immunological adjuvant, for nose-only and body plethismograph animal holder used in inhalation toxicology studies, and for discovery that insulin is equally effective in lowering blood glucose when inhaled into deep lung as when it is administered intramuscularly. Home: 6187 Viewsite Dr Frederick MD 21701-6750 Office: US Army R&D Ft Detrick Frederick MD 21702

CREASMAN, VIRENA WELBORN (RENE CREASMAN), retired elementary and secondary school educator, genealogist, researcher; b. Lebanon, Nebr., Feb. 10, 1909; d. Lawrence Morgan and Auretta Iva (Daffer) Welborn; m. Sam Doran Creasman, May 8, 1929 (dec. Jan. 1982); children: Gary W., Lee-Ellen Creasman Matzke. AA, McCook Jr. Coll., 1928; B in Edn., U. Nebr., 1962; postgrad., Kearney State Coll., 1967, Creighton U., 1968. Cert. elem., secondary tchr. Tchr. Rural Sch. grades 1-8, Red Willow County, Nebr., 1928-29; elem. tchr. McCook (Nebr.) City Schs., 1949-67, tchr. jr. high reading, English, 1968-76; tchr. genealogy, rschr. McCook Coll. and Southwest Nebr. Genealogy Soc., 1976—; rschr. state and local genealogy confs., 1976—. Vol., mem. Nebr. Hist. Soc. and Mus., High Plains Hist. Soc. and Mus., 1980—. Recipient Plaque of Appreciation from High Plains Hist. Soc. and Mus., 1990, Cert. of Appreciation from Nebr. State Hist. Soc. and Mus., 1989, Genealogist of Yr. cert. Southwest Nebr. Genealogy Soc., 1984, Appreciation of Svc. award as thrift shop coord. Congl. Ch., 1984-90. Mem. AAUW (chpt. leader 1962—), DAR (chpt. regent and registrar 1976—), NOW, LWV, UN Assn. U.S.A., Sierra Club, Arbor Day Found., Humane Soc., Assn. Retired Tchrs. (local pres. 1976—, nat., state), Delta Kappa Gamma (publicity com.), Eastern Star, Daus. of the Nile, Shriners Auxilliary, Genealogy Socs. (nat., local, state, libr. local chpt.). Democrat. Avocations: reading, genealogy, political events, gardening, bridge. Home: 8 Parkview Dr Mc Cook NE 69001-2248

CREASMAN, WILLIAM PAUL, lawyer; b. Washington, Dec. 6, 1952; s. Paul and Esther B. (Tucker) C.; m. S. Teresa Deese, Aug. 18, 1973; 3 children. BA, Johns Hopkins U., 1974; JD, Wake Forest U., 1977. Bar: N.C. 1977, U.S. Dist. Ct. (mid. dist.) N.C. 1978, Ark. 1992. Asst. trust officer First Citizen's Bank & Trust Co., Raleigh, N.C., 1977-78; atty. Wrangler div. Blue Bell Inc., Greensboro, N.C. and Brussels, Belgium, 1978-83; sr. corp. atty. Hardee's div. Imasco USA Inc., Rocky Mount, N.C., 1983-84; asst. gen. counsel Imasco USA Inc., Rocky Mount, N.C., 1985-87; gen. counsel Church's Fried Chicken, San Antonio, 1984-85; sr. v.p., gen. counsel TCBY Enterprises, Inc., Little Rock, Ark., 1987—; panelist Am. Arbitration Assn., Dallas, 1988—; adj. prof. U. Ark. Sch. Law, Little Rock, . Mem. N.C. Bar Assn., Ark. Bar Assn. Home: 12 Barber Dr Maumelle AR 72113-6481 Office: TCBY Enterprises Inc 1200 TCBY Tower Capitol And Broadway Little Rock AR 72201

CREATH, CURTIS JANSSEN, pediatric dentist; b. Lynwood, Calif., Mar. 10, 1958; s. Ronald J. and Madelyn W. (Chryst) C.; m. Deborah Ann Lipari, June 23, 1990; 1 child, Andrew. Student, UCLA, 1976-81; DMD, Oral Roberts U., 1985; MS, U. Ala., 1988. Asst. prof. Sch. Dental Medicine SUNY, Stony Brook, 1988-91, Sch. Dentistry U. Ala., Birmingham, 1991-94; staff pediat. dentist Family Cental Care Assocs., Cin., 1994-95; pvt. practice Milford, Ohio, 1995—; team leader dental mission trips to Mex., Jamaica, Peru, 1982-84. Contbr. chpt. to: Special and Medically Compromised Patients in Dentistry, 1989, Clark's Clinical Dentistry, Vol. 2, 1994; contbr. articles, revs. on tobacco control, pediat. dentistry, and preventive medicine to profl. jours. Semi-finalist E.H. Halton award Internat. Assn. Dental Rsch., 1985. Mem. ADA, Am. Acad. Pediat. Dentistry (mem. edn. com.), Am. Assn. Dental Schs. (v.p. 1986-88), Ala. Soc. Pediat. Dentistry (sec.-treas. 1992-94), Christian Med. and Dental Soc., Omicron Kappa Upsilon. Republican. Presbyterian. Avocations: vocal music, preaching, missionary work, woodworking, gardening. Home: 6514 Tulip Ct Middletown OH 45044-9726 Office: PO Box 267 1102 Main St Milford OH 45150-1706

CREAVEN, PATRICK JOSEPH, physician, research oncologist; b. Eng., Jan. 31, 1933. MB, BS, St. Mary's Hosp. Med. Sch., U. London, 1956, PhD, 1964. House surgeon Bedford Gen. Hosp.; also house physician Barnet Gen. Hosp., Eng., 1956-57; asst. lectr. biochemistry U. London, St. Mary's Hosp. Med. Sch., 1963-64, lectr., 1964-66; chief biochemistry Tex. Rsch. Inst. Mental Sci., 1966-69; chief, oncological pharmacology Nat. Cancer Inst., VA Med. Oncology Br., 1969-75; assoc. chief, cancer rsch. clinician Roswell Park Meml. Inst., Buffalo, 1975-79, chief cancer rsch. clinician, 1979—, chief dept. clin. pharmacology and therapeutics, 1979-89, chief div. clin. pharmacology and therapeutics, Dept. Medicine, 1989-91, sr. investigator dept. investigational therapeutics, 1991—; rsch. prof. medicine Dept. Medicine, SUNY, Buffalo, 1994—. Contbr. articles to profl. jours. Fellow Am. Coll. Clin. Pharmacology, Royal Soc. Health; mem. Am. Assn. Cancer Rsch., Am. Soc. Clin. Oncology, Am. Soc. Pharmacology and Exptl. Therapeutics, Am. Soc. Clin. Pharmacology and Therapeutics. Office: Roswell Park Cancer Inst Elm And Carlton St Buffalo NY 14263-0001

CREBS, P(AUL) TERENCE, lawyer; b. St. Louis, Apr. 14, 1938; s. Edward Rudd and Edith Ruth (Beppler) C.; m. Carol Ann Kring, June 17, 1961 (div. 1987); children: Paul T. Jr., Susan J.; m. Karen Charlotte Hensel, July 25, 1987. AB, Washington U., St. Louis, 1960, JD, 1962. Bar: Mo. 1962, U.S. Dist. Ct. (ea. dist.) Mo. 1962, U.S. Ct. Appeals (8th cir.) 1962, U.S. Ct. Appeals (7th cir.) 1977, U.S. Ct. Appeals (10th cir.) 1988, U.S. Dist. Ct. (so. dist.) Ill. 1989, U.S. Supreme Ct. 1990, U.S. Dist. (we. dist.) Mo., 1997. Ptnr. Fordyce & Mayne, St. Louis, 1962-76, Gallop, Johnson, Crebs & Neuman, St. Louis, 1976-81, Peper, Martin, Jensen, Maichel & Hetlage, St. Louis, 1981-87, Herzog, Crebs & McGhee, LLP, St. Louis, 1987—. Assoc. editor Washington U. Law Quar., 1961-62. Bd. dirs. North Ctrl. and South Ctrl. Regional Ctrs. for Deaf-Blind, Mpls. and Dallas, 1972-78; mem. Met. St. Louis Devel. Disability Coun., 1974-80, Presbyn. Children's Svcs., 1989-92. Mem. ABA (fin. officer coun., mem. tort and ins. practice sect. 1983-89), Internat. Assn. Def. Counsel (chair accident life and health com. 1979-80), Fedn. Ins. and Corp. Counsel (vice-chair bus. torts sect. 1990-94, vice chair life health and disability sect. 1993-94, chmn. employment litigation and civil rights sect. 1994-96, chmn. intellectual property sect. 1997—), Mo. Bar Assn., Mo. Orgn. Def. Lawyers, Bar Assn. Met. St. Louis, Trial Attys. Am. (v.p., dir. 1994—), Defense Rsch. Inst. Presbyterian. Office: Herzog Crebs & McGhee LLP 1 City Ctr 24th Fl 515 N 6th St Saint Louis MO 63101-1842

CRECENTE, BRIAN DAVID, writer, journalist; b. Washington, July 28, 1970; s. Joseph Wendell Crecente and Elizabeth Ann (Levato) Richeson. AA, Anne Arundel C.C., Arnold, Md., 1990; BA in English, U. Md., 1994, BA in Journalism, 1994. Edn. reporter Charles County (Md.) Times-Cresent, 1992-93; reporter Reuters, Balt., 1993-94; gen. assignment reporter Fort Worth Star Telegram, 1994-98; police reporter Palm Beach (Fla.) Post, 1998—. Avocation: fencing.

CREECH, HUGH JOHN, chemist; b. Exeter, Ont., Can., June 27, 1910; came to U.S., 1938, naturalized, 1945; s. Richard Newton and Edith (Sanders) C.; m. E. Marie Hearne, July 10, 1937; children: Richard Hearne, Joan Marie. B.A., U. Western Ont., 1933, M.A., 1935; Ph.D. (research fellow), U. Toronto, 1938; postgrad., Harvard U., 1938-41. Asst. prof. U. Md., 1941-43, asso. prof., 1943-45; lectr. Bryn Mawr (Pa.) Coll., 1945-47; immunochemist Inst. for Cancer Research and Lankenau Hosp. Research Inst., Phila., 1945-47, head dept. chemotherapy, 1947-57, chmn. div. chemotherapy, 1957-70, sr. mem., 1949—; chmn. adminstrv. com. Inst. Cancer Research, 1947-54; mem. U.S. nat. com. Internat. Union Against Cancer, 1957-60, 80-84; antimalarial research U. Md. with OSRD, Washington, 1943-45; expert cons. to Surgeon Gen. U.S. Army, 1947-49. Recipient numerous awards for research NIH, Am. Cancer Soc. Mem. Am. Assn. Cancer Research (hon., sec.-treas. 1952-77, v.p. 1977-78, pres. 1978-79, archivist 1983—). Home: 1135 Goodman Dr Fort Washington PA 19034-1752 Office: Am Assn Cancer Rsch Pub Ledger Bldg Ste 816 150 S Independence Mall W Philadelphia PA 19106-3413

CREECH, JOHN LEWIS, retired scientist, consultant; b. Woonsocket, R.I., Jan. 17, 1920; s. Edward and Bessie (Faulkner) C.; m. Amy Elizabeth Wentzel, Feb. 14, 1942 (dec. Apr. 1984); children: Diane, Victoria, John; m. Elaine E. Godden Innes, July 10, 1984. BS in Horticulture, U. R.I., 1941; MS in Horticulture, U. Mass., 1947; PhD in Botany, U. Md., 1953. Instr. horticulture U. Mass., Amherst, 1946-47; horticulturist Office Plant Exploration, Agrl. Rsch. Svc. USDA, 1947-50, asst. chief new crops rsch. br. Agrl. Rsch. Svc., 1958-66, chief br. Agrl. Rsch. Svc., 1966-72, scientist nat. program staff Agrl. Rsch. Svc., 1972-73; dir. U.S. Nat. Arboretum, Washington, 1973-80, N.C. Arboretum, 1987-88; sr. adviser Internat. Bd. for Plant Genetic Resources; negotiator Bicentennial gift of Nat. Bonsai Collection from people of Japan; developer Nat. Herb Garden; program dir. for conservation of plant genetic materials Internat. Biol. Program, NAS; mem. panel FAO, 1966-74; preparer U.S. position paper for Stockholm Conf. on the Environment; adj. prof. biology U. N.C., Asheville; bd. dirs. N.C. Arboretum, Asheville, interim dir., 1986-87; U.S. judge Internat. Flower & Garden Expo, Japan, 1990; leader 9 plant expeditions Japan, China, Taiwan, USSR, Nepal, 1955-78; co-chmn. Genetic Resource Team, China, 1974; rev. nat. gen. resource program USDA, NAS, 1988-92; cons. Time-Life Books for Children, 1993; cons. in horticulture; leader hort. tours. Co-author: Brocade Pillow, 1984, Garden Shrubs and Their Histories, 1992. Capt. U.S. Army, 1941-45, prisoner of war, ETO. Decorated Silver Star, Bronze Star; recipient Gold medal Scott Found., Gold medal Garden Club Am., Gold Seal medal Nat. Coun. State Garden Clubs, Thomas Roland medal Mass. Hort. Soc., Silver medal FAO-UN, Hort. medal Fedn. Garden Clubs N.Y., Norman J. Colman award Am. Nurserymans Assn., Hutchinson medal Chgo. Bot.

Garden/Chgo. Hort. Soc., 1987, Gold medal and cert. of merit City of Kurume, Japan, 1988, Veitch Meml. medal Royal Hort. Soc., U.K., 1992; grantee Merrill Found., 1976, Nat. Geog. Soc., 1978, Japan Found., 1982; selected to give Morrison Meml. lecture. Mem. Am. Genetics Assn. (bd. dirs., Meyer medal), Am. Hort. Soc. (pres. 1954-56, profl. citation, Liberty Hyde Bailey medal 1989), Internat. Dendrology Soc. (v.p. 1989—), Sigma Xi, Phi Kappa Phi, Pi Alpha Xi. Republican. Episcopalian. Achievements include introduction of several plant varieties.

CREECH, SHARON, children's author. BA, Hiram Coll.; MA, George Mason U. Editl. asst., indexer Congl. Quarterly, Washington; rschr. Libr. Congress. Author: The Recital, Nickel Malley, Walk Two Moons, 1994 (John Newbery medal 1995), Absolutely Normal Chaos, 1995, Pleasing The Ghost, 1996, Chasing Redbird, 1997. Office: care HarperCollins Children's Bks 10 E 53rd St New York NY 10022-5244*

CREECH, WILBUR LYMAN, retired career officer; b. Argyle, Mo., Mar. 30, 1927; s. Paul and Marie (Maloney) C.; m. Carol Ann DiDomenico, Nov. 20, 1969; 1 son, William L. Student, U. Mo., 1946-48; B.S., U. Md., 1960; M.S., George Washington U., 1966; postgrad., Nat. War Coll., 1966. Commd. 2d lt. U.S. Air Force, 1949; advanced through grades to gen.; fighter pilot 103 combat missions USAF, North Korea, 1950-51; pilot USAF Thunderbirds, 1953-56; comdr., leader Skyblazers, Europe aerial demo team USAF, 1956-60; dir. Fighter Weapons Sch., Nellis AFB, Nev., 1960-61; advisor to comdr. Argentine Air Force, 1962; exec., aide to comdr. Tactical Air Command, 1962-65; dep. comdr. fighter wing, 177 combat missions in F-100 fighters and asst. dep. chief staff for ops. 7th Air Force, Vietnam, 1968-69; comdr. fighter wings USAF in Europe, Spain and W.Ger., 1969-71; dep. for ops. and intelligence Air Forces Europe, 1971-74; comdr. Electronic Systems Div., Hanscom AFB, Mass., 1974-77; asst. vice chief of staff HQS Air Force, Washington, 1977-78; comdr. Tactical Air Command, Langley AFB, Va., 1978-85; lectr., internat. mgmt. expert; cons. in field. Author: The Five Pillars of TQM, 1994. Decorated D.S.M. with three oak leaf clusters, Silver Star medal, Legion of Merit with two oak leaf clusters, D.F.C. with three oak leaf clusters, Air medal with 14 oak leaf clusters, Air Force Commendation medal with two oak leaf clusters, Army Commendation medal; Spanish Grand Cross. Home and Office: 20 Quail Run Rd Henderson NV 89014-2147

CREED, ROBERT PAYSON, SR., retired literature educator; b. Phila., Apr. 22, 1925; s. Edward E. and Blanche H. (Southerland) C.; m. Catherine Hilton, Oct. 9, 1987; children from previous marriage: Mary Louise, Robert Payson. BA, Swarthmore Coll., 1948; MA, Harvard U., 1949, PhD, 1956. Instr. Smith Coll., Northampton, Mass., 1952-56; asst. prof. Brown U., Providence, 1956-61, assoc. prof., 1961-65; assoc. prof. SUNY-Stony Brook, 1965-67, prof., 1967-69; prof. English U. Mass., Amherst, 1969-97, prof. emeritus, 1997—, dir. grad. studies in English, 1969-72, prof. English and comparative lit., 1980-90, chmn. comparative lit. dept., 1980-85; cons. G&C Merriam Co., Springfield, Mass., 1955-56; featured storyteller 13th ann. nat. storytelling festival, Jonesborough, Tenn., 1985, 20th festival, 1992; disting. faculty lectr. U. Mass., Amherst, 1993-94; nat. vis. prof. Paul Valery U., Montpellier, France, spring 1987. Writer, chief performer: Beowulf, Sta. WNYC, pub. radio, 1979 (awards Corp. Pub. Broadcasting); author: Reconstructing the Rhythm of Beowulf, 1990; featured performer: Asheville (N.C.) Poetry Festival, 1994. Bd. dirs. Arcadia Players Baroque Orch., Chorus and Chamber Ensemble, Northampton, Mass., pres., 1995-98. Served to lt. (j.g.) USNR, 1943-46, 49. Guggenheim fellow, 1962-63; Nat. Endowment Humanities fellow Yugoslavia, 1976; Inst. Advanced Studies in Humanities fellow Edinburgh U., 1976; Am. Council Learned Socs. grantee, 1978. Mem. AAAS, Internat. Soc. Anglo-Saxonists, Internat. Soc. for Study of Time, N.Y. Acad. Scis., Nat. Storytelling Assn., Lang. Origins Soc., European Soc. for Study of Cognitive Sys., Archeol. Inst. Am. (exec. coun. Western Mass. soc. 1996—). Home: 5 Kinder Ln Shutesbury MA 01072-9762 *Though a professor of literature, I have become more and more deeply concerned with oral traditions. Behind surviving traditions-indeed, behind literature-lie tens of thousands of years of what we may call Memorable Speech, some of which survives embedded in early texts. Back of Memorable Speech lies the origin of human language. Through the study of (sound-) patterned Memorable Speech, I am trying to work back towards the beginning of language, our most adaptive and humanizing invention.*

CREEDON, JEREMIAH F., aeronautical research laboratory administrator. BSEE, U. R.I., 1961, MSEE, 1963, PhD in Elec. Engring., 1970; M Mgmt. Sci., Stanford U., 1983. Rsch. engr. navigation and guidance rsch. br. NASA Langley Rsch. Ctr., Hampton, Va., 1963-70, head control and info. sys. sect., 1970-79, asst. head avionics tech. rsch. br., 1979-82, chief flight control sys. divsn., 1982-85, head flight sys. directorate, 1985-94, dir. aeros. program group, 1994-96, dir. Airframe Sys. Program Office, 1996, dir. Ctr., 1996—; advisor to adminstr. on programs NASA. Contbr. articles to sci. jours. Recipient presdl. rank meritorious exec. in sr. exec. svc., 1989, disting. exec., 1995. Fellow AIAA. Office: NASA Langley Rsch Ctr Office of Dir Hampton VA 23681-0001*

CREEGAN, ROBERT FRANCIS, philosophy educator, writer; b. Battle Creek, Mich., Mar. 27, 1915; s. Charles Cole and Harriet (Stephenson) C.; m. Doris Ryan, Dec. 27, 1940; 1 child, Charles Louis. Student, Oberlin Coll., 1932-34; A.B., Marietta Coll., 1936; M.A., Duke, 1937, Ph.D., 1939. Asst. Coll. of William and Mary, 1939-40; asst. prof. Cumberland U., 1940-43, U. Miss., 1943-44, Bucknell U., 1944-45, Whitman Coll., 1945-47, Carleton Coll., 1947-48, Ohio U., 1948-52; prof. philosophy dept. SUNY-Albany, 1952-85, prof. emeritus, 1985—; vis. prof. No. Ill. U., summer 1948, No. Iowa U., summer 1952, Cen. Wash. State Coll., 1955, U. Ariz., summer 1970; mem. founding com. Soc. for Sci. Exploration, 1978—; mem. lectr. bur. Union of Concerned Scientists, 1987—; cons. in philosophy Aerial Phenomena Research Orgn. Author: The Shock of Existence, 1954, The Magic of Truth, 1980; contbr. articles to profl. jours., ednl. reports, press commentary, investigative reports on UFOs and other phenomena. Elder Presbyn. Ch. U.S.A., mem. global mission unit of Gen. Assembly, Presbyn. Ch. Mem. AAAS, APA, AAUP, Internat. Platform Assn., N.Y. Acad. Scis., Am. Philos. Assn., Internat. Phenomenological Soc., Soc. Advancement Edn. Home: 28 Wellington Rd Delmar NY 12054-3320 Office: SUNY Albany NY 12222

CREEKMORE, DAVID DICKASON, lawyer, educator; b. Knoxville, Tenn., Aug. 8, 1942; s. Frank Benson and Betsey (Beeler) C.; 1 child, Walton N.; m. Betty Jo Huffaker, May 1998; stepchildren: Seth Huffaker, Zach Hufaker, Christy White. LLB, U. Tenn., 1965, JD, 1966; grad., Judge Adv. Gen.'s Sch., 1979, Army Command Gen. Staff Sch., 1985. Bar: Tenn. 1966, U.S. Supreme Ct. 1970, U.S. Ct. Mil. Appeals 1985. Law clk. Gen. Session Ct. Knox County, Knoxville, Tenn., 1963-66; judge divsn. II, Gen. Sessions Ct. Knox County, Knoxville, 1972-86; asst. county atty. Knox County, Knoxville, 1966-70; ptnr. Creekmore, Thomson & Hollow, Knoxville, 1966-72, Walter, Regan & Creekmore, Knoxville, 1993-97; pvt. practice Knoxville, 1986-93, 97-98; dep. law dir. Knox County, Knoxville, 1998—; instr. criminal law and evidence Walters State Coll., Morristown, Tenn., 1974-80, U. Tenn., 1982-89. Committeeman Knox County Rep. Com., 1970—; active Tenn. Hist. Assn., Blount Mansion Assn. Lt. Col. JAGC, USAR, 1997. Mem. ABA, FBA, Tenn. Bar Assn., Tenn. Judges Conf. (v.p. 1976-78), Knox Bar Assn., Res. Officers Assn. (pres. 1989-91), Am. Legion (post judge adv. 1984-87), Studebaker Drivers Assn. (pres. 1992-97), Masons, Shriners, Elks, Eagles, Lions. Home: 11530 Midhurst Dr Knoxville TN 37922-4768 Office: Knox County Law Dept 612 City-County Bldg 400 Main St Knoxville TN 37902

CREEKMORE, VERITY VEIRS, media specialist; b. Cin., May 13; d. Noble L. and Maxine (Wright) Veirs; m. Kenneth L. Creekmore, Nov. 23, 1961; 1 child, Kenneth L. Jr. BS in Edn. magna cum laude, S.C. State U., 1975; MLS, U.S.C., 1978. Cert. libr. media specialist, S.C. Media specialist John Ford High Sch., St. Matthews, S.C., 1976-77, St. John High Sch., Cameron, S.C., 1977-82, St. John Elem./Mid. Sch., Cameron, 1982-86, Sheridan Elem. Sch., Orangeburg, S.C., 1986—; directed libr. U. S.C., Columbia, 1997—; adj. tech. instr. S.C. State Dept. Edn., 1997—. Rep. S.C. Sci. Hub. Sys. Operator Sheridan Sch. Local Area Computer Network: Trainer Laubach Literacy Program, Orangeburg, 1990—. Recipient IMAGEMAKER award SCASL, 1997. Mem. NEA, ALA, S.C. Assn. Sch. Librs., Nat. Assn. Storytelling, So. Assn. Colls. and Schs. (evaluator), S.C. Edn. Assn. (dist. rep. 1991-93, IPD rep. 1993-97), Hon. Order Ky. Cols., Order Ea. Star, Alpha Kappa Mu. Avocations: reading, church work, travel. Home: RR 6 Box 127 Saint Matthews SC 29135-9521 Office: Sheridan Elem Sch 139 Hillsboro St NE Orangeburg SC 29115-3305

CREEL, AUSTIN BOWMAN, religion educator; b. Alexandria, Va., Nov. 8, 1929; s. Benjamin Kemper and Bertha A. (Naff) C.; m. Patricia Ann Harrison, June 26, 1954 (dec. Aug. 1985); children: Stephen, Kathryn. BS, Northwestern U., 1950; BD, Colgate Rochester Div. Sch., 1954; MA, Yale U., 1957, PhD, 1959. Ordained to ministry Am. Bapt. Convs., 1952. Asst. chaplain U. Rochester Coll. for Men, 1950-52; del. ecumenical confs. in India, travel in Asia, 1952-53; student minister Calvary Presbyn. Ch., Rochester, N.Y., 1953-54; asst. prof. religion U. Fla., Gainesville, 1957-64, assoc. prof., 1964-77, prof., 1977-96, dir. Asian studies, 1973-75, chmn. dept. religion, 1977-90, interim dir. Ctr. for Jewish Studies, 1983-85; chmn. Humanities Council, 1987-89. Author: Dharma in Hindu Ethics, 1977; editor: A Larger View: Delton L. Scudder's Prayers and Addresses, 1973; co-editor: (with Vasudha Narayanan) Monasticism in the Christian and Hindu Traditions, 1990. Trustee Alachua Gen. Hosp., Gainesville, 1969-72, vice chmn., 1970-71. Recipient Sigmund Livington Interfaith prize Northwestern U., 1949, Agnes Crabtree Internat. Rels. award Fla. Coun. for the Social Studies, 1988; postdoctoral fellow in Asian religions Poona, India, 1965. Mem. ASCD (facilitator religion and pub. edn. network 1993-97), Am. Acad. Religion (bd. dirs. 1988-92, chmn. com. on edn. and study religion 1988-92, Ray Hart Svc. award), Am. Inst. Indian Studies (trustee 1974-95, v.p. 1990-91, exec. com. 1980-82, 89-91), Assn. Asian Studies (pres. S.E. conf. 1987-89), Soc. Asian and Comparative Philosophy, Nat. Coun. Religion and Pub. Edn. (exec. com. 1990-94, pres. 1992-94). Home: 7500 Woodmont Ave Apt 717 Bethesda MD 20814-5375 Office: U Fla Dept Religion Gainesville FL 32611-7410

CREEL, HAROLD JENNINGS, JR., federal commission administrator, lawyer; b. Florence, S.C., July 1, 1957; s. Harold Jennings Sr. and Dorothy Louise (Fenters) C. BA in Polit. Sci., Wofford Coll., 1979; JD, U. S.C., 1982. Bar: La. Assoc. Courtenay, Forstall, Grace & Hebert, New Orleans, 1982-83; atty./advisor NOAA, Washington, 1983-89; sr. counsel subcom. of com. on commerce, sci. and transp. U.S. Senate - Mcht. Marine Subcom., Washington, 1989-94; commr. Fed. Maritime Commn., Washington, 1994-96; chmn. Fed. Maritime Commn., 1996—. Mem. La. State Bar Assn. Democrat. Avocations: fishing, gardening. Office: Fed Maritime Commn Office of Chmn 800 N Capitol St NW Washington DC 20211

CREEL, LUTHER EDWARD, III, lawyer; b. Huntsville, Ala., Sept. 23, 1937; s. Luther Edward and June (Oldacre) C.; m. Nan Dee McHalek, Apr. 11, 1974; children by previous marriage: Scott Mitchell, Todd Oldacre. A.B. in Psychology, George Washington U., 1959; J.D., So. Methodist U., 1963. Bar: Tex. 1963. Pvt. practice law Dallas, 1963—; chmn. Creel & Atwood (and predecessors), Dallas, 1971-96; of counsel Malouf, Lynch, Jackson, Kessler & Collins, Dallas, 1996-98; chmn. Creel, Susman & Moore, Dallas, 1998—; bd. dirs. Capital Network, M-B Valuation Svcs., Inc., Internat. Tex. Longhorn Assn.; writer and lectr. in field of bankruptcy and reorgn. law. Contbr. articles to legal jours. Chmn. Ford Debtor Assistance Program, 1995-98. Mem. Dallas Bar Assn. (chmn. bankruptcy sect. 1972), State Bar Tex. (cert. bus. bankruptcy specialist 1989, chmn. bankruptcy com. 1979-81), Am. Bankruptcy Inst. (pres. 1982-87, vice chmn. 1987-96, bd. dirs. 1982—, chmn. 1996-98, chmn. emeritus 1998—), Am. Coll. Bankruptcy (co-founder, fellow, pres. 1996-97), Park Cities Club, GTG Tex. Longhorn Assn. (pres. 1998—), The Pines (adv. dir. 1997—). Republican. Baptist. Home: 7214 Desco Dr Dallas TX 75225-2003 Office: Creel Susman & Moore 5949 Sherry Ln Ste 525 Dallas TX 75225

CREEL, SUE CLOER, secondary education educator; b. Columbus, Miss., July 4, 1943; d. Ducler Cornelius Cloer and Verna Sarah (Shackelford) Cloer Mackie; children: Ricky (dec.), Ronny. *Sue Cloer Creel, working on Cloer geneology, believes a missing link connecting Cloer line back to 1630s Germany has been discovered. Cloer American ancestry dates back to 1717 Virginia, with connections to Hebron Lutheran Church, first one built in New World, still standing. If correct, German born Michael Cloer bore son George, who had a son, Michael, who moved to N.C. and had son Jacob Cloer, Sue's great-great grandfather. Her great grandfather is John Baldwin Cloer, Sr., grandfather is Jr. and father is Ducler Cornelius Cloer, 9th child of 10. Creel is still researching the American Indian connection with grandmother Elizabeth Caledonia Miller Cloer, born 1851.* BA, Harding U., 1982, MEd, 1986; specialty degree in edn., Jackson (Miss.) State U., 1996. Tchr. 8th grade English Alfh Jr. H.S., Searcy, Ark., 1982-87; part-time editor, writer for neurosurgery Miss. Med. Ctr., Jackson, 1987-89; adminstrv. asst. to dean of nursing U. Miss. Med. Ctr., Jackson, 1989-90; tchr. advanced placement English and creative writing Jackson Pub. Schs., 1990—; adj. instr. English Hinds C.C., Raymond, Miss., 1987-89; cons. Nat. Writing Project, 1985, Univ. Ctrl. Ark., Conway, Ark., Nat. Writing Project; session chair Writing-Across-the-Curriculum K-12, Charleston, S.C., 1997; tchr. long distance learning interactive video ETV, 1998-99, 00—. Contbg. poet: Moments in the Garden, 1998, Miss. Musings, Miss. Poetry Soc., 1997, The Drifting Sands, 1999. With USN, 1962-63. Grantee Entergy, Jackson, 1994-96; fellowship Jackson (Miss.) State U., 1996; recipient 2 Editor's Choice awards. Mem. AAUW, Nat. Coun. Tchrs. of English, Am. Acad. Poets, Miss. Poetry Soc., Magnolia Romance Writers, The Poetry Guild (poetry included Best Poems of the 90s, 1998), Poets Writers Inc., Beta Sigma Phi, Alpha Chi. Mem. Ch. of Christ. Avocations: reading, writing, theater, gardening, competitions. Home: 625 Choctaw Rd Jackson MS 39206-5325

CREEL, THOMAS LEONARD, lawyer; b. Kansas City, Mo., June 21, 1937; s. Thomas Howard and Elizabeth Alberta (Sharon) C.; m. Carol M. Plaisted, Nov. 26, 1992; children: Charles, Andrew, Andrea, Thomas. BS, U. Kans., 1960; LLB, U. Mich., 1963. Bar: Mich. 1963, N.Y. 1967, D.C. 1983, U.S. Supreme Ct. 1973, Ct. Mil. Appeals, 1964, U.S. Patent and Trademark Office 1965. Assoc. Kenyon and Kenyon, N.Y.C., 1966-74, ptnr., 1974-92; ptnr. Kaye, Scholer, Fierman, Hayes & Handler, N.Y.C., 1992—; faculty lectr. Columbia U. Sch. Law, N.Y.C., 1984—. Editor: Guide to Patent Arbitration, 1987. Capt., U.S. Army, 1963-66. Mem. ABA, Fed. Bar Coun., Intellectual Property Law Assn. (past pres.), Am. Intellectual Property Assn. Home: 104 Cedar Cliff Rd Riverside CT 06878-2606 Office: Kaye Scholer Fierman Hayes & Handler 425 Park Ave New York NY 10022-3506

CREELEY, ROBERT WHITE, author, English educator; b. Arlington, Mass., May 21, 1926; s. Oscar Slade and Genevieve (Jules) C.; m. Ann MacKinnon, 1946 (div. 1956); children: David, Thomas, Charlotte; m. Bobbie Louise Hall, Jan. 27, 1957 (div. 1976); children: Kirsten, Leslie, Sarah, Katherine; m. Penelope Highton, 1977; children: William, Hannah. BA, Black Mountain Coll., 1954; MA, U. N.Mex., 1960, LittD (hon.), 1993. Instr. Black Mountain Coll., 1954-55; vis. lectr. English U. N.Mex., Albuquerque, 1961-62, lectr., 1963-66, vis. prof., 1968-69, 78-80; vis. prof. SUNY, Buffalo, 1966-67, prof. English, 1967—, Gray prof. poetry and letters, 1978-89, Capen prof. poetry and humanities, 1989—, dir. poetics program, 1991-92; lectr. U. B.C., Vancouver, 1961-63; lectr. creative writing San Francisco State Coll., 1970-71; vis. prof. SUNY-Binghampton, spring 1985, 86; Bicentennial chair Am. studies, Fulbright award, U. Helsinki, Finland, 1988, Fulbright award U. Auckland, New Zealand, 1995. Author: Le Fou, 1952, The Immoral Proposition, 1953, The Kind of Act of, 1953, The Gold Diggers, rev. edit, 1965, All That is Lovely in Men, 1955, If You, 1956, The Whip, 1957, A Form of Women, 1959, For Love, Poems, 1950-60, 1962, The Island, 1963, Poems, 1950-65, 1966, Words, 1967, The Finger, rev. edit, 1970, The Charm, 1968, Numbers, 1968, Pieces, 1969, A Quick Graph, 1970, A Day Book, 1972, Listen, 1973, A Sense of Measure, 1973, Contexts of Poetry, 1973, Thirty Things, 1974, Backward, 1975, (with Marisol) Presences, 1976, Selected Poems, 1976, rev. edit., 1991, Mabel: A Story, 1976, Myself, 1977, Hello, 1978, Was That a Real Poem & Other Essays, 1979, Later, 1979, Robert Creeley and Charles Olson: The Complete Correspondence, Vols. 1 and 2, 1980, Vol. 3, 1981, Vol. 4, 1982, Vol. 5, 1983, Vol. 6, 1985, Vols. 7 and 8, 1987, Vol. 9, 1990, Vol. 10, 1996, Mother's Voice, 1981, Echoes, 1982, Collected Poems, 1945-1975, 1983, Mirrors, 1983, Collected Prose, 1984, Memory Gardens, 1986, The Company, 1988, Window, 1988, Collected Essays, 1989, (with Francesco Clemente) It, 1989, Windows, 1990, Places, 1990, Autobiography, 1990, The Old Days, 1991, Gnomic Verses, 1991, Tales Out of School, 1993, Echoes, 1994, Life & Death, 1998; I So There, poems, 1976-83, 1998, Day Book of a Virtual Poet, 1998; editor: Black Mountain Rev., 1954-59, New American Story, 1965, (with Donald M. Allen) The New Writing in the U.S.A, 1967, Selected Writings of Charles Olson, 1967, Whitman: Selected Poems, 1973; Robert Burns, The Essential Burns, 1989, Charles Olson, Selected Poems, 1993. With Am. Field Svc., 1944-45. Recipient Levinson prize Poetry mag., 1960, Blumenthal-Leviton award, 1965, Union League Civic and Arts Found. prize Poetry mag., 1967; D.H. Lawrence fellow, 1969; Guggenheim fellow, 1964, 71; Rockefeller grantee, 1965; Shelley Meml. award Poetry Soc. Am., 1981; Premis Speciale, Leone d'Oro, Venice, 1985; Frost medal Poetry Soc. Am., 1987; Walt Whitman citation of merit and named N.Y. State Poet by State of N.Y., 1989-91; Disting. prof. award SUNY, Buffalo, 1989, Horst Bienek Preis fur Lyrick, Munich, 1993, The America award for Poetry, Washington, 1995, Lila Wallace Reader's Digest Writers' award, 1996—; Bollingen Prize, 1999, Chancellor's medal, SUNY, Blffalo, 1999; NEA grantee, 1982, DAAD grantee, 1983, 87. Mem. AAAL. Office: SUNY/Buffalo 313 Clemens Buffalo NY 14260

CREENAN, KATHERINE HERAS, lawyer; b. Elizabeth, N.J., Oct. 7, 1945; d. Victor Joseph and Katherine Regina (Lederer) Petervary; m. Edward James Creenan; 1 child, David Heras. BA, Newark State Coll., 1968; JD, Rutgers U., 1984. Bar: N.J. 1984, Maine, 1996, U.S. Dist. Ct. N.J. 1984, U.S. Ct. Appeals (3d cir.), 1998. Various teaching positions including, Union and Stanhope, N.J., 1968-81; law clk. to presiding judge Superior Ct. of N.J. Appellate Div., Newark, 1984-85; assoc. Lowenstein, Sandler, Kohl, Fisher & Boylan, Roseland, N.J., 1985-88, Kirsten, Simon, Friedman, Allen, Cherin & Linken, Newark, 1988-89, Whitman & Ranson, Newark, 1989-93; sr. atty. Whitman Breed Abbott & Morgan LLP, Newark, 1993—. Mem. ABA, N.J. State Bar Assn., Union County Bar Assn., Essex County Bar Assn. Office: Whitman Breed Abbott Morgan 1 Gateway Ctr Newark NJ 07102-5311

CREGAN, FRANK ROBERT, financial executive, consultant; b. Jersey City, July 27, 1940; s. Frank Vincent and Maurie Geraldine (Kennedy) C.; m. Joan Marie Swancer, July 19, 1969; children: Christina Eileen, Darren Michael, Keith Francis. BBA, Manhattan Coll., 1962; MBA, St. John's U., Jamaica, N.Y., 1972. CPA, N.Y. Supr. KPMG Peat Marwick, N.Y.C., 1962-68; dir. taxes DuPont Glore Forgan, Inc., N.Y.C., 1968-73; v.p. taxes Marsh & McLennan Cos., Inc., N.Y.C., 1973-78; ptnr. Deloitte & Touche, Parsippany, N.J., 1978-83; v.p. fin. Madison Resources, Inc., N.Y.C., 1983-86; v.p., treas. WSGP Internat., Inc., Morristown, N.J., 1986-89; mng. dir. William E. Simon & Sons, L.L.C., Morristown, 1989—; fin. planning cons., Morristown, N.J., 1962—. Fundraiser, United Way of Essex and West Hudson Counties, Newark, 1978, Morristown-Beard Sch., 1990-92, Colonial Touchdown Club, Morristown, 1991—; bd. dirs. Better Bus. Bur. Greater Newark, 1981-83; team mgr. Morristown Nat. Little League, 1982-86; leader Boy Scouts Am., Morristown, 1984-95, fin. advisor Morris/Sussex coun., Denville, N.J., 1991-92; mem. adv. bd. St. Joseph Sch., Bronx, N.Y., 1991—, Resurrection Sch., N.Y.C., 1996—; treas. Morristown High Sch. Booster Club, 1992-94. Mem. AICPA, N.J. Soc. CPAs, Fin. Execs. Inst., Coun. N.J. Grantmakers, Kiwanis. Avocations: golf, camping. Home: 14 Kissel Ln Morristown NJ 07960-3613 Office: William E Simon & Sons LLC PO Box 1913 Morristown NJ 07962-1913

CREGER, DAVID LEE, financial planner, insurance executive; b. Bristol, Tenn., Mar. 20, 1957; s. Bobby Gene and Mary Nell (Goodman) C.; children: Joshua A., Sarah R. Student, Va. Highlands C.C., Abingdon, Va., 1975-76. Cert. agt./continuing edn. instr., Tenn., Va.; Life Underwriter Tng. Coun. fellow; registered fin. planner. Ins. agt. Home Beneficial Life Ins. Co., Bristol, Va., 1984-85, staff sales mgr., 1985-89; personal producing gen. agt./owner The David L. Creger Co., Bristol, 1989-91; agt. and mktg. svcs. mgr. Settlers Life Ins. Co., Bristol, 1991-96; pres. Pinnacle Fin. Svcs., Inc., Bristol, 1994—; v.p., gen. mgr. Ally-ance Mktg. Group, Inc., Bristol, 1996-97; disability income ins. course moderator Life Underwriter Tng. Coun., 1989-90; N.E. Tenn. (regional) Sales Conf. chmn. 1990; lectr. in field. Contbr. articles to profl. jours. Pres. Bristol affiliate Am. Heart Assn., 1993-95, chmn. bd., 1995-96, chmn. Queen of Hearts Fundraiser, 1992, 93; vol. Appalachia region March of Dimes, 1992-93; account exec. United Way of Bristol, 1992-93, team capt., 1994, bd. dirs., 1995—, treas., chair fin. com., 1996-97, investment com. chmn., 1996-97, v.p., pres.-elect 1998; Profl. Div. Campaign Chmn. 1998—, pres. bd. dirs. 1999; bd. dirs., The Janie Hammitt Meml. Children's Home, 1997; trustee, treas. Janie Hammitt Meml. Inc., 1998; mem. Tri-Cities Estate Planning Coun., 1998—; chmn. TALU Edn. Found. Com., 1997-98. Recipient Ernest E. Cragg Amb. award Life Underwriting Tng. Coun., 1994; named to Tri-Cities Bus. Jour. Regional 40 Under Forty, 1995, United Way of Bristol Vol. of Yr., 1996; named one of Outstanding Young Men of Am., 1998. Mem. Nat. Assn. Life Underwriters (polit. action com. 1989—), Tenn. Assn. Life Underwriters (N.E. Tenn. regional v.p. 1992-95, chair state profl. devel. com. 1994-95, sec. 1995-96, pres.-elect 1996-97, pres. 1997-98, past pres. 1998-99, state nat. committeeman 1999-2002), Bristol Assn. Life Underwriters (Queen of Hearts program com. 1986-97, pres. 1990, chair edn. com. 1991-93, exec. sec. 1993-94, chair state law and legis. com. 1993-95, sec. and treas., 1998-99, 2d v.p. 1999-2000, Louis I. Dubin Pub. Svc. award, Robert L. Rose Edn. and Assn. Achievment awards), Bristol C. of C. (VA legis. com. chair 1994, fed. issues com. chair 1995, govtl. rels. coun. vice-chair 1996, vice chair cmty. and govtl. rels. coun. 1997, exec. com. 1997, chmn. govtl. rels. divsn. 1998), vice-chmn. special events div. bd. dirs. exec. com., 1999, Assn. Health Ins. Agts. (charter), Internat. Assn. Fin. Planning, Inst. Cert. Fin. Planners, Registered Fin. Planners Inst., Tri-Cities Estate Planning Coun., Tri-Cities Regional Chamber Coalition (bd. dirs. 1998), Bristol C. of C. (bd. dirs. 1995-99). Republican. Avocations: reading, computers, billiards. Office: Pinnacle Fin Svcs Inc 624 Lawrence Ave Bristol VA 24201-3540

CREHAN, JOSEPH EDWARD, lawyer; b. Detroit, Dec. 8, 1938; s. Owen Thomas and Marguerite (Dunn) C.; m. Sheila Anderson, Nov. 6, 1965; children: Kerry Marie, Christa Ellen. A.B., Wayne State U., Detroit, 1961; J.D., Ind. U., 1965. Bar: Ind. 1965, Mich. 1966, U.S. Supreme Ct. 1984. Pvt. practice Detroit, 1966-68; assoc. Louisell & Barris (P.C.), 1968-72; ptnr. Fenton, Nederlander, Dodge, Barris & Crehan (P.C.), 1972-74, Barris & Crehan (P.C.), 1975-88; pvt. practice Bloomfield Hills, Mich. and Naples, Fla., 1977—. Mem. Am. Trial Lawyers Assn. Roman Catholic. Home and Office: 827 Bentwood Dr Naples FL 34108-8204

CREIGH, THOMAS, JR., utility executive; b. Evanston, Ill., Jan. 3, 1912; s. Thomas and Frances (Connor) C.; m. Dorothy Claire Weyer, July 17, 1948; children: Mary Elizabeth, Thomas III, John, James. Grad., Mercersburg (Pa.) Acad., 1929; A.B., Wabash Coll., 1933. With No. Natural Gas Co., 1933-36; with KN Energy, Inc. (formerly Kans.-Nebr. Natural Gas Co., Inc.), 1936-86; v.p. KN Energy, Inc., 1951-61, pres., 1961-78, chmn. bd., 1978-85, chmn. emeritus, 1985-93, also dir.; v.p., dir. Excelsior Oil Corp., 1955-68, pres., 1968-84; pres., dir. Western Gas Corp., 1967-84; v.p., dir. Helium, Inc., 1960-85; sec., dir. Western Plastics Corp., 1953-69; dir. Dunne Gardner Drilling Co., City Nat. Bank, Hastings, Western Alfalfa Corp., Cap-Con Internat Inc., Cape Constrn. Co., Energy Transmission System, Inc., Advanced Fuel Systems, Inc., Slurry Transport Assos.. Mem. Nebr. Gov.'s Task Force for Govt. Improvemenet, 1980-82, Nebr. Bd. Ednl. Lands and Funds, 1987-91; trustee Hastings Coll., Inst. Gas Tech., U. Nebr. Found., Nebr. State Hist. Found.; bd. dirs. Nebr. Art Collection, Nebr. chpt. Nature Conservancy, Nebraskans for Pub. TV; mem. Nebr. Hist. Preservation Bd., 1991—, Adams County Hist. Soc., Nebr. Ind. Coll. Found., Crane Meadows Nature Ctr. Mem. Am. Gas Assn. (dir. 1969-73), Midwest Gas Assn. (dir. 1965-68), Interstate Natural Gas Assn. (dir. 1967-71, 74-82), Nebr. Assn. Commerce and Industry (past pres.), Nebr. Coun. Econ. Edn. (chmn. 1967-70), Nebr. State Hist. Soc. (exec. bd. 1990-91). Presbyterian (trustee).

CREIGHTON, ELIZABETH GASTON, counselor; b. Pittsfield, Mass., May 23, 1953; d. Gilbert James and Elizabeth Lyde (Davis) Gaston; m. Robert Brigham Wood, Dec. 22, 1972 (div. Jan. 1978); m. Richard Guy Creighton, Aug. 4, 1979. BA in Psychology, U. So. Maine, 1993; MA in Counseling Psychology, Antioch New Eng. Coll., Keene, N.H., 1995. Lic. clin. profl. counselor, Maine. Pres. Village Florist, Inc., Yarmouth, Maine, 1976-87; pres., counselor Changing Perspectives, Inc., Portland, Maine, 1995-99. Mem. ACA, Am. Mental Health Counselors Assn., Maine State Florists

Assn. (hon., Edward Johnson award 1992), Altrusa (v.p. Portland 1997, pres. 1998), Psi Chi, Phi Kappa Phi. Avocations: gardening, travel, hiking, reading, cross-country skiing. Office: Cmty Concepts Inc 20 Maple St South Paris ME 04281

CREIGHTON, JOANNE VANISH, academic administrator; b. Marinette, Wis., Feb. 21, 1942; d. William J. and Bernice Vanish; m. Thomas F. Creighton, Nov. 9, 1968; 1 child, William. BA with honors, U. Wis., 1964; MA, Harvard U., 1965; PhD, U. Mich., 1969. From instr. to prof. English Wayne State U., Detroit, 1968-85, assoc. dean liberal arts, 1983-85; dean arts and scis., prof. English U. N.C., Greensboro, 1985-90; v.p. acad. affairs, provost, prof. English Wesleyan U., Middletown, Conn., 1990-94, interim pres., 94-95; prof. English, pres. Mt. Holyoke Coll., South Hadley, Mass., 1995—. Author: William Faulkner's Craft of Revision, 1977, Joyce Carol Oates, 1979, Margaret Drabble, 1985, Joyce Carol Oates: Novels of the Middle Years, 1992. Grantee Am. Coun. Learned Socs. Mem. Phi Beta Kappa, Phi Kappa Phi. Home: 45 College St South Hadley MA 01075-1403 Office: Mount Holyoke Coll Office of Pres 50 College St South Hadley MA 01075-1423

CREIGHTON, NEAL, foundation administrator, retired army officer; b. Ft. Sill, Okla., July 11, 1930; s. Neal and Charlotte (Gilliam) C.; m. Joan Hicks, Aug. 1, 1958; children: Linda, Lisa, Neal. B.S., U.S. Mil. Acad., 1953; student, U. Madrid, 1959-60; M.A., Middlebury Coll., 1961; grad., U.S. Army Command and Staff Coll., 1967, U.S. Army War Coll., 1970. Commd. 2d lt. U.S. Army, 1953; advanced through grades to maj. gen.; troop assignments U.S. Army, U.S., Germany, 1953-59; from instr. to asst. prof. fgn. lang. U.S. Mil. Acad., 1960-63; staff officer So. Command Panama, 1964-66; squadron comdr. Vietnam, 1967-68; mil. asst. Office of Sec. Army Washington, 1970-72; comdr. Combined Arms Tng. Center Germany, 1973-74, brigade comdr., 1974-76; dep. dir. Ops. and Readiness Directorate, Dept. Army, 1977-78; comdr. 1st Inf. Div. Germany, 1978-80; dep. chief of staff Allied Forces Central Europe, Brunssum, Netherlands, 1980; comdg. gen. 1st Inf. Div. Ft. Riley, Kans., 1982-84; ret. U.S. Army, 1984; administrator Robert R. McCormick Trust Founds., Chgo., 1985; pres., chief exec. officer R.R. McCormick Trust Found., Chgo., 1986—. Decorated Disting. Service Medal, Silver Star medal, Bronze Star medal, Air medal. Mem. Chgo. Coun. on Fgn. Rels., Nat. Strategy Forum. Episcopalian. Office: Robert R McCormick Founds 435 N Michigan Ave Chicago IL 60611-4066 also: Cantigny Found 1 S 151 Winfield Rd Wheaton IL 60187

CREMEANS, FRANK A., former congressman; b. Cheshire, Ohio, Apr. 5, 1943; m. Carol; 2 d., 1 s. BFA in Edn., U. Rio Grande, 1966; M in Edn., Ohio U., 1969. Tchr. Lorain County schs., 1966-67; tchr. Gallia schs., 1968-71, asst. supt., 1976; prin. Point Pleasant Jr. H. S., 1971-72; guidance couselor Kyger Creek local sch. dists., 1972-74, supt., 1975; founder, owner, oper., pres. Cremeans Concrete & Supply Co., Inc., 1974—; mem. 104th Congress from 6th Ohio dist., 1994-96. Home: 3417 Neighborhood Rd Gallipolis OH 45631*

CREMEANS, JAMES L., minister; b. Rayland, Ohio, Dec. 22, 1939; s. Leroy and Waneda (Montgomery) C.; m. Mary McCormick, Oct. 4, 1956; children: James, David, Jeffery, Diane, Janet. DD (hon.), Internat. Bible Sem., 1985. Ordained to ministry 1st Tabernacle Ch., Ironton, Ohio, 1967. Pastor City Mission Ch., Ironton, 1967—; exec. dir. City Welfare Mission, Ironton, 1967—; dir. corr. sch. Evangelistic Outreach, Pedro, Ohio, 1982—, v.p., 1975—, also bd. dirs. Mem. Lawrence County (Ohio) Welfare Adv. Bd., 1980-82, Home Health Care Bd., Ironton, 1980—, Lawrence County Youth Coun., 1988—. Named Citizen of Yr., Community Betterment Club, Lawrence County, 1979, Ironton Tribune, 1993. Mem. Lawrence County Ministerial Assn. (chmn. radio and TV 1975-80, sec.-treas. 1995—, chmn. chaplancy com. 1993—). Home: 365 Township Road 150 Pedro OH 45659-8928 Office: City Mission Ch 710 N 5th St Ironton OH 45638-1306

CREMER, LEON EARL, federal agent, lawyer; b. Cin., Dec. 30, 1945; s. Walter H. and Beatrice (Campbell) C. BS, Calif. State U., 1973; MA, George Washington U., 1976; JD, Rutgers U., 1982. Bar: Pa. 1982. Officer U.S. Secret Svc., Washington, 1975-77; spl. agt. U.S. Bur. Alcohol Tobacco and Firearms, U.S. Dept. Treasury, Phila., 1977-83, FBI, U.S. Dept. Justice, N.Y.C., 1983—. With U.S. Army, 1968-69. Mem. ABA, FBI Agts. Assn., Phila. Bar Assn., Pa. Bar Assn., Am. Trial Lawyers Assn., Internat. Platform Assn., Am. Mensa Soc. Avocations: yachting, aviation, skiing, tennis, long-distance running. Office: FBI 26 Federal Plz New York NY 10278-0127

CREMER, RICHARD ELDON, marketing professional; b. Detroit, Apr. 13, 1928; s. Eldon Grant and Mildred Odessa (Williams) C.; m. Bernadine Ann Beaugrand, Aug. 21, 1948; children: Susan Marie, David Grant. AA in Acctg., USMC Inst., 1947. Br. mgr. Household Fin. Corp., Detroit, 1948-51; collection mgr. Internat. Harvester Co., Detroit, 1951-53; credit mgr. Montgomery Ward Co. Inc., Detroit, 1953-54; dist. credit for Mich. Montgomery Ward Co. Inc., Livonia, Mich., 1954-56, store ops. mgr., 1956-61; corp. credit contr. Montgomery Ward Co. Inc., Chgo., 1961-64; regional credit mgr. east region Montgomery Ward Co. Inc., Balt., 1964-66; gen. credit mgr. Montgomery Ward Co. Inc., Chgo., 1966-72; pres., chief exec. officer The Signature Group (M.W. subs.), Schaumburg, Ill., 1970-85; exec. dir. consumer div. Bally Fitness Products Inc., Irvine, Calif., 1985-88; pres., chief exec. officer Richard E. Cremer and Assocs., Kerrville, Tex., 1985—. Entered the congressional record as tribute to free enterprise system, 1981. Exec. com. Columbia U. Arden House Cons. Credit Conf., 1965-75; spl. adviser Pres. Coun. Phys. Fitness and Sports, 1973-85, 92—, Ill. Gov.'s Coun. Health and Fitness, 1975-85; co-chmn. capital fund YMCA, Evanston, Ill., 1983. With USMC, 1945-48. Recipient Direct Marketer of Yr. award N.Y. Direct Mail Day, 1981. Mem. Direct Mktg. Assn. (bd. dirs. exec. com. 1974-80), Chgo. Assn. Direct Mktg. (Direct Marketer of Yr. award 1992), Econ. Club Chgo. Avocations: flying, yachting, running, skiing. Fax: 906-573-2806.

CREMER, THOMAS GERHARD, music educator; b. New Brunswick, N.J., May 23, 1961; s. Gerhard Josef and Lois Elaine (Cottrell) C.; m. Eva Almira Vivanco Vargas, Feb. 8, 1986. MusB magna cum laude, U. Mass., 1983; MusM, U. Ky., 1989. Cert. music tchr., Mass., N.Y., Va., Ky., Ga. Music tchr. Athol-Royalston (Mass.) Schs., 1983-84; music tchr., band dir. Am. Sch. Lima, Peru, 1984-87; instr. tuba, euphonium U. Ky., Lexington, 1988-89; hon. asst. conductor Fitchburg (Mass.) State Coll., 1989-90; dir. bands, music instr. Warwick Acad., Bermuda, 1990-95; dir. nat. band Columbia Columbia Inst. Culture, Bogota, 1995; low brass instr. Augusta State U., 1996—; brass instr. U. S.C., Aiken, 1998—; music dir. Jenkins County Middle Sch. and H.S., Millen, Ga., 1996-98; vis. prof. music, dir. faculty quintet Nat. Conservatory, Lima, 1985-87; tubist Nat. Symphony Peru, Lima, 1985-87; mem. Bermuda Secondary Sch. Curriculum Com., Warwick, 1991-94. Contbg. editor: Tuba Reference Guide, 1993; contbg. reviewer T.U.B.A. Jour., 1988, 94. Adv. All-City Music Fest, Lima, 1985-87. Recipient Diploma of Honor, West German Embassy in Peru, 1986; Acad. Excellence fellow U. Ky., 1988. Mem. Tubists Universal Brotherhood Assn., World Assn. Symphonic Bands Ensembles, Internat. Trombone Assn., Music Educators Nat. Conf., Masons, Phi Delta Kappa (Bermuda chpt., v.p., pres. 1992-94). Roman Catholic. Avocations: golf, reading, motorcycling, travel. Home: 3328 Tanglewood Dr Augusta GA 30909

CREMERS, CLIFFORD JOHN, mechanical engineering educator; b. Mpls., Mar. 27, 1933; s. Christian Joseph and Marie Hildegard C.; m. Claudette May Humble, Sept. 25, 1954; children: Carla Ann, Rachel Beth, Emily Therese, Eric John, Melissa Joan. BSME, U. Minn., 1957, MSME, 1961, PhD, 1964. Rsch. fellow in mech. engrng. U. Minn., 1959-61, instr. mech. engrng., 1961-64; asst. prof. Ga. Inst. Tech., Atlanta, 1964-66; assoc. prof. U. Ky., Lexington, 1966-71, prof., 1971-98, chmn. dept. mech. engrng., 1975-84, 94-95, prof. emeritus, 1998-99; cons. to industry, state and fed. agys., UNESCO; vis. prof. Imperial Coll. Sci. & Tech., London, 1973; Lady Davis prof. Technion, Haifa, 1986. Contbr. articles on heat transfer to profl. jours. With USNR, 1953-55. NSF grantee, 1965, 66, 69, 71, 76, 81, 86, NASA grantee, 1967, 68, 69, 70, 71, 72, 73, 94; Trane Co. fellow U. Minn., 1959, 60. Fellow ASME (past v.p. basic engrng.), AIAA (assoc.); mem. AAAS, Am. Soc. Engrng. Edn., Sigma Xi. Roman Catholic. Home: 3181 Lamar Dr Lexington KY 40502-2905 Office: Univ Ky Mech Engrng Dept Lexington KY 40506-0108

CREMIN, SUSAN ELIZABETH, lawyer; b. Chgo., July 2, 1947; d. William Amberg and Rosemary (Brennan) C. AB cum laude, Vassar Coll., 1969; JD, Northwestern U., Chgo., 1976. Bar: Ill. 1977. Assoc. Winston & Strawn, Chgo., 1976-83, ptnr., 1983-93, capital ptnr., 1993—. Co-author: Registration and Reporting Under the Exchange Act, 1995, 2nd edit., 1996. Trustee The Shedd Aquarium, Chgo., The Masters Sch., Dobbs Ferry, N.Y. Office: Winston & Strawn 35 W Wacker Dr Ste 4200 Chicago IL 60601-1695

CREMINS, BOBBY, college basketball coach; b. Bronx, N.Y., July 4, 1947; m. Carolyn Cremins; children: Liz, Suzie, Bobby III. BS in Mktg., U. S.C., 1970, MS in Guidance and Counseling, 1972. Basketball coach Point Park Coll., Pitts., 1971; asst. basketball coach U. S.C., Columbia, 1972-74; head basketball coach Appalachian State U., Boone, N.C., 1974-81; asst. basketball coach U.S. Olympic Dream Team, 1996; head coach Ga. Tech., Atlanta. Named ACC Coach of Yr., 1985, 95, Nat. Coach of Yr., Basketball Times, CBS-TV/Chevrolet, Al McGuire's NBC-TV Spl., 1985; named one of top 10 coll. recruiters, Sport mag., 1984. Office: Georgia Inst Tech/Athletic Assn 150 Bobby Dodd Way NW Atlanta GA 30313-2551*

CREMINS, WILLIAM CARROLL, lawyer; b. Virginia Beach, Va., Nov. 13, 1957; s. James Smyth and Mary Louise (Gallagher) C.; m. Kelly Robin Knapp, July 6, 1985; children: William Carroll Jr., Robert Gallagher. BA, BJ, U. Mo., 1980; JD, St. John's U., 1984. Bar: Tenn. 1984, N.Y. 1985, U.S. Dist. Ct. (ea. dist.) Tenn., U.S. Ct. Appeals (6th cir.). Assoc. Law Offices of J.D. Lee, Knoxville, Tenn., 1984-85; pvt. practice, Knoxville, 1986—. Dep. nat. organizer Ancient Order of Hibernians in Am., Inc., Tenn., 1985, pres. James Dardis divsn., 1997, 98; bd. dirs. Florence Crittenton Agy. of Knoxville, Inc., 1989-96, pres., 1995; Little League baseball coach, 1993-97, football coach, 1987, 1993-94, soccer coach, 1992, 1995. Recipient Pro Bono award Knoxville Bar Assn. Vol. Legal Assistance Program, 1992. Mem. ATLA (Advocate recognition 1994), ABA, Tenn. Bar Assn., Knoxville Bar Assn., Tenn. Trial Lawyers Assn. Roman Catholic. Fax: (865) 546-1394. Home: 710 Saint John Ct Knoxville TN 37922-1556 Office: 810 Henley St Knoxville TN 37902

CRENSHAW, ALBERT BURFORD, journalist; b. Lexington, Va., Oct. 4, 1942; s. Ollinger and Marjorie (Burford) C.; m. Margaret Alice Price, Aug. 11, 1973; children—David Ollinger, Caroline Abbey. A.B., Harvard U., 1964; M.S., U. Va., 1966; M.S. in Journalism, Columbia U., 1967. Reporter Washington Daily News, 1969-71, asst. city editor, 1971-72; asst. nat. editor Washington Post, 1972-76, night nat. editor, 1977-82, real estate editor, 1982-85, asst. fin. editor, 1985-88, fin. reporter, columnist, 1988—. Served with U.S. Army, 1967-69. Clubs: Harvard (N.Y.C.); Nat. Press (Washington). Home: 321 E Capitol St SE Washington DC 20003-3808 Office: Washington Post 1150 15th St NW Washington DC 20071-0002

CRENSHAW, BARCLAY MACBRIDE, film producer, writer; b. Cleve., July 7, 1971; s. David Kerry and Denise (Belcher) C. BA, U. Rochester, 1994. Freelance prodn. coord. Detroit, 1998, freelance assoc. prodr., 1999. Prodn. asst. The Relic, 1995-96, Beautician and the Beast, 1996; asst. location mgr. Polish Wedding, 1997; apprecntice editor The Jackal, 1997-98; freelance prodn. asst. The Truman Show, Con Air, Batman & Robin, Slums of Beverly Hills, Titanic, Jeans, 1995-97; screenwriter The Retirement Plan, 1997, Devastating, 1998; dir., prodr. (documentary) Road to Riches, 1999. Mem. Phi Beta Kappa. Avocations: music, running, computer programming, graphic art.

CRENSHAW, BEN, professional golfer; b. Austin, Tex., Jan. 11, 1952; m. Julie Ann; children: Katherine Vail, Claire Susan. Grad., U. Tex. Mem. U.S. World Amateur Cup Team, 1972; mem. U.S. Ryder Cup, 1981, 83, 87, 95; profl. golfer, 1973—; U.S. team capt. Kirin Cup, 1988. Winner San Antonio Open, 1973, Western Amateur open match and medal plan champion, 1973, Bing Crosby Nat. Pro-Am., Ohio Kings Island Open, Hawaiian Open, 1976, Colonial Nat. Invitational, 1977, NCAA Championship, 1971, 72, 73, Irish Open, 1976, Phoenix Open, 1979, Walt Disney World Team Championship, 1980, AnheuserOBusch Classic, 1980, Tex. State Open winner, 1980, Ryder Cup, 1981, 83, 87, Byron Nelson Classic, 1983, Masters tournament, 1984, PGA Sr. Event Jeremy Ranch Shoot-Out teameed with Miller Barber, 1985, Buick Open, 1986, Vantage Championship, 1986, USF&G, 1987, Doral Ryder Open, 1988, World Cup, 1988, Western Open, 1992, Masters winner Augusta Nat. Golf Club, 1995, Masters Tournament, 1995. Mem. Profl. Golfers Assn. Am. Office: 2905 San Gabriel St Ste 213 Austin TX 78705-3541*

CRENSHAW, CAROL, charitable organization administrator; b. Chgo., July 3, 1956. BS in Acctg., Fin., No. Ill. U., 1978. CPA, Ill. Auditor CPMG Peat Marwick, Chgo., 1978-83, asst. contr., 1983, contr., 1983-94; CFO The Chgo. Cmty. Trust, 1994—. Mem. fin. acting practice com. Com. for the Found. Sector, 1997—. Office: The Chicago Community Trust 222 N Lasalle St Ste 1400 Chicago IL 60601-1088*

CRENSHAW, FRANCIS NELSON, lawyer; b. Washington, Dec. 9, 1922; s. Russell Sydnor and Sally Nelson (Robins) C.; m. Jane Elizabeth Tresswell, Aug. 20, 1949 (dec. June 1993); children—Elizabeth, Page, Marian; m. Anne Bolling Alfriend, July 12, 1997. Grad., St. George's Sch., 1939; BA, U. Va., 1943, LLB, 1948. Bar: Va. 1948. Partner Baird, White & Lanning, Norfolk, 1952-55, Baird, Crenshaw & Lanning, Norfolk, 1955-60, Baird, Crenshaw & Ware, Norfolk, 1960-68, Crenshaw, Ware & Johnson, Norfolk, 1968-89, Crenshaw, Ware & Martin, Norfolk, 1989—; mem. Va. Bd. Bar Examiners, 1973-90, pres., 1983-90. Mem. Norfolk City Sch. Bd., 1955-64, chmn., 1962-64; bd. visitors Old Dominion U., 1968-76, rector, 1972-76; mem. bd. commrs., Eastern Va. Med. Authority, 1966-68. Served with USNR, 1943-46. Decorated Bronze Star. Fellow ABA, Va. Law Found.; mem. Va. Bar Assn., Va. State Bar, Norfolk-Portsmouth Bar Assn. (pres. 1967), Maritime Law Assn. Home: 923 W Princess Anne Rd Norfolk VA 23507-1217 Office: 1200 Nations Bank Bldg Norfolk VA 23510

CRENSHAW, JAMES FAULKNER, physician; b. Birmingham, Ala., Nov. 15, 1911; s. Faulkner Blevins and Mabel Bertha (George) C.; m. Peggie Ann O'Donnell; children: Jessica Crenshaw Copeland, James H., Peggie Ann. BS, Birmingham So. Coll., 1933; MD, Washington U., St. Louis, 1942. Diplomate Am. Bd. Internal Medicine. Med. resident St. Louis City Hosp., 1942-43; with mil. hosps., 25th divsn. 8th Gen. Hosp., 1944-46; physician Seale Harris Clinic, Birmingham, 1946-55, dir., 1955—; asst. prof. medicine U. Ala., Birmingham, 1946-70, clin. prof. med., 1970-89. Contbr. articles to profl. jours. Maj. U.S. Army, 1943-46, PTO. Decorated Bronze Star. Fellow Am. Geriatric Soc.; mem. ACP (life), AMA, Ala. Med. Assn., Mo. Med. Assn., Birmingham Country Club, The Club, Kiwanis, Alpha Tau Omega. Republican. Presbyterian. Avocation: golf. Office: Seale Harris Clinic 840 Montclair Rd Ste 500 Birmingham AL 35213-1946

CRENSHAW, PATRICIA SHRYACK, sales executive, consultant; b. Kansas City, Mo., Oct. 7, 1941; d. George Randolf and Velma Irene (Carroll) Shryack; m. Paul Burton, Mar. 24, 1961 (div. 1971); m. Peter Frederick Schmidt, Jan. 21, 1989. Student, William Jewell Coll., 1959-60, S.W. Mo. State U., 1960-61; BEd, U. Mo., 1967; postgrad., Cen. Mo. State U., 1971-73. Cert. tchr. secondary edn. and history, Mo. Tchr. Lillis High Sch., Kansas City, 1967-69, Park Hill High Sch., Kansas City, 1969-73; terr. mgr. Hollister, Inc., Kansas City, 1973-75, field trainer, 1974-75; sales edn. mgr. Hollister, Inc., Chgo., 1975; dist. sales mgr. Detroit Mich., 1976-81; regional sales mgr. Chgo., 1981-84; dir. contract sales Chgo. Serta, Inc., 1984-86, nat. dir. contract sales div., 1987-89, v.p. nat. contract sales, 1989-90; area v.p. B G Industries, Northridge, Calif., 1990-91, v.p. sales, 1992-95, v.p. internat. sales, 1995-97, v.p. clin. svcs., 1998—. Mem. women's com. Young Reps., Kansas City, 1962. Mem. NOW, NAFE, U.S. Golf Assn., Lake Barrington Shores (Ill.) Golf Club. Republican. Avocations: golfing, skiing, scuba diving, racquetball, reading, gardening. Home (winter): 101 E Ocean Dr Key Colony Beach FL 33051

CRENSHAW, TENA LULA, librarian; b. Coleman, Fla., Dec. 15, 1930; d. Herbert Joseph Crenshaw and Nellie (Wicker) Cox; BS, Fla. So. Coll., 1951; postgrad. U. Fla., 1952-55; MLS (Univ. scholar), U. Okla., 1960. Tchr. pub. schs., Coleman, Fla., 1952-55, St. Petersburg, Fla., 1955-57, Houston, 1957-59; tech. librarian Army Rocket & Guided Missile Agy., Redstone Arsenal, Huntsville, Ala., 1960-61; acquisitions librarian Martin Marietta Corp., Orlando, Fla., 1961-64; reader svcs. librarian John F. Kennedy Space Center, NASA, Fla., 1964-66; rsch. info. analyst, specialist, Lockheed Missiles and Space Co., Palo Alto, Calif., 1966-68; head svcs. to pub. A.W. Calhoun Med. Library, Emory U., Atlanta, 1969-78; dep. dir. Louis Calder Meml. Library, U. Miami (Fla.) Sch. Medicine, 1979-80; head edn. library U. Fla., Gainesville, 1980-84; librarian Westinghouse Electric Corp., Orlando, 1984-86; chief librarian tech info. ctr. U. Cen. Fla., Orlando, 1986-87, librarian contracts and grants, 1987-88; library cons. Coleman, Fla., 1988-89, sch. libr., 1989-90, libr. Kennedy Space Ctr., Fla., 1990-91, libr. Patrick Air Force Base, Fla., 1992-94; chmn. Fla. State adv. Council on Libraries. Mem. Spl. Libraries Assn. (treas. S. Atlantic chpt. 1970-72, chmn. membership com. 1973, v.p. 1973-74, pres. 1974-75, mem. resolutions com. 1975-76, nominating com. biol. scis. div. 1974-75, chmn. 1977-78), Med. Library Assn. (mem. conf. planning com. So. regional group 1973-74, membership com. 1977-79 by laws rev. com. 1979-80), Southeastern (mem. new directions com. 1972-74, chmn. spl. libraries sect. 1974), Ga. (careers in librarianship com. 1974-77), Fla. Library Assns., DAR, Alpha Delta Pi, Kappa Delta Pi. Democrat. Methodist. Home: PO Box 277 Coleman FL 33521-0277

CREPPEL, CLAIRE BINET, hotel owner; b. New Orleans, Nov. 30, 1936; d. Albert Leo and Leocadie (Dominique) Binet; m. Jacques Jules Creppel, Feb. 2, 1957; children: Ingrid, Foster, Collette and Gregg (twins), Lisa, Morgan. BA in English, U. Southwestern La., 1971; MEd in Guidance/Counseling Psychology, Loyola U., New Orleans, 1975; postgrad. adminstrn., mgmt., supervision, Tulane U., New Orleans, 1978. Instr. English and Spanish Booker T. Washington Sr. High Sch., 1972-74, instr. English and reading, 1974-76, guidance counselor, 1976-77; intervention counselor Sophie B. Wright Middle Sch., 1977-79; owner, gen. mgr. Columns Hotel, New Orleans, 1980—; owner Woodland Plantation, 1997—. New Orleans regional dir. La. Coun. on Child Abuse, 1985-87; mem. citizens adv. bd. Jo Ellen Smith Hosp.; mem. task force Ct. Appointed Spl. Advocate; bd. dirs. So. Repertory Theatre of New Orleans, New Orleans, Odyssey House, Bravo, Arts Coun.; bd. dirs. Overture to the Cultural Season, pres., 1997-98. Named one of Top Exec. Women New Orleans, 1990, one of Top Women New Orleans Bus. Owners, 1997. Mem. Am. Personnel and Guidance Assn., AAUW, La. Personnel and Guidance Assn., Orleans Sch. Counselors Assn., St. Charles Ave. Bus. Assn., Street Car Inns, Fgn. Rels. Assn. New Orleans, Kappa Delta Pi, Sigma Delta Pi. Republican. Roman Catholic. Avocations: preservation projects, real estate market, scuba diving, snow and water skiing, music. Home: 7927 St Charles Ave New Orleans LA 70118-2724 Office: Columns Hotel 3811 Saint Charles Ave New Orleans LA 70115-4681

CRERAR, KEN A., association executive; b. Binghamton, N.Y., Apr. 1, 1955; s. H. Kennard and Virginia M. Crerar. BA, Conn. Coll., 1977. Admission rep. Conn. Coll., New London, 1977-78; legis. asst. Office of U.S. Senator Chris Dodd, Washington, 1978-82; v.p. Footwear Industries Am., Washington, 1982-87; v.p. govt. affairs Coun. Ins. Agts. and Brokers, Washington, 1987-91, pres., 1991—; mem. U.S. Industry Sector Adv. Com. on Svcs., 1995—. Host Brokers World, Ins. Broadcasting Sys., 1997—. Mem. Internat. Brokers Assn. (dirs. com. 1995—), Conn. Coll. Alumni Assn. (v.p. 1996—), Capitol Hill Assn. of Merchants and Profls. (v.p. local chpt. 1996—). Office: Coun Ins Agt and Brokers S 750 701 Pennsylvania Ave NW Washington DC 20004-2608

CRESHEVSKY, NOAH EPHRIAM, music educator, composer; b. Rochester, N.Y., Jan. 31, 1945; m. Joseph and Sylvia (Goldman) Cohen; m. Marianna Rosett, May 31, 1969 (div. June 1975). BFA, SUNY, Buffalo, 1966; MS, Juilliard Sch., 1968. Mem. faculty Juilliard Sch., N.Y.C., 1968-70; prof. music Bklyn. Coll., CUNY, 1969—, dir. Ctr. for Computer Music, 1995—; vis. prof. Princeton (N.J.) U., 1987-88. Recordings include Circuit, In Other Words, Great Performances, Chaconne, Portrait of Rudy Perrez, Highway, Sonata, Celebration, Drummer, Strategic Defense Initiative, Man and Superman, Auxesis; compositions include Three Wordless Songs, 1988, Electric String Quartet, 1988, Memento Mori, 1989, Electric Partita, 1990, Talea, 1991, Cantiga, 1992, Borrowed Time, 1992, Private Lives, 1993, Twice, 1993, Coup d'etat, 1994, Gone Now, 1995, Who, 1995, Sha, 1996, Breathless, 1997, Independence Day, 1997 Ossi di morte, 1997, Chamber Concerto, 1998, Et Puis, 1998, Credo, 1999. Nat. Endowment for Arts fellow, 1981-82; grantee N.Y. State Coun. on ARts, Meet the Composer. Mem. ASCAP (composers award 1982—). Home: 301 W 45th St Apt 10L New York NY 10036-3831 Office: Bklyn Coll Conservatory of Music 2900 Bedford Ave Brooklyn NY 11210-2814

CRESIMORE, JAMES LEONARD, food broker; b. Statesville, N.C., Jan. 24, 1928; s. Fred Clayton and Cleo (Edison) C.; m. Mary Josephine Conrad, June 3, 1956; children: James Conrad, Jennifer Cheryl, Joel Clayton. BSBA, High Point U., 1949. Gen. mgr. Home Svc. Stores, Inc., High Point, N.C., 1948-50; co-founder, sec. Red Dot Food Stores, Inc., 1952-56; sec. Consol. Wholesale Corp., 1952-56; owner Village Super Market, High Point, 1953-56; co-owner Bunker Hill Packing Corp., Bedford, Va., 1964—; chmn. bd., CEO, co-owner Assoc. Brokers, Inc., Raleigh, N.C., 1956—; founding dir., chmn. bd. State Bank Raleigh; chmn. bd. Smithfield Cos. Inc., Va.; past chmn. United Carolina Bank, Raleigh; dir. United Carolina Bank N.C., chmn. fin. com.; bd. dirs. United Carolina Bancshares Corp; chmn. bd., CEO Allegiance Brokers, Inc., Charlotte, N.C., Associated Brokers, Inc.; bd. dirs., mem. fin. and pers. coms. N.C. Tech. Devel. Authority, Inc. Chmn. Mayor's Manpower Com., Raleigh., Wake County Republican Com., 1963—, del. nat. conv. San Francisco, 1964; 4th Congl. dist.; mem. platform com. Rep. Nat. Convention, Miami, Fla., 1968; mem. advisory bd. Salvation Army; trustee Pheiffer Coll., High Point U.; bd. trustees Raleigh Community Hosp., N.C. Citizens for Bus. and Industry, Bapt. Children's Homes of N.C. Served with U.S. Army, 1950-52. Recipient Hugh G. Ashcraft Jr. Leadership award N.C. Food Dealers Assn., 1995. Mem. Sales and Marketing Execs. Internat. (mem. bd., pres., v.p. Raleigh), N.C. Tech. Devel. Authority, Raleigh Food Brokers Assn. (past pres.), Nat. Food Brokers Asnn. (regional rep.), (lt. regional dir.) food brokers assns., Raleigh C. of C. (dir. 1973-74). Lodge: Rotary. Home: 3720 Williamsborough Ct Raleigh NC 27609-6358 Office: Associated Brokers Inc P O Bos 17743 1110 Wake Forest Rd Raleigh NC 27604-1380

CRESPI, IRVING, public opinion and market research consultant; b. Bklyn., May 8, 1926; s. Joseph and Esther (Crespi) C.; m. Joan Striefling, Aug. 4, 1968; children: Robert Joseph, Judith Shoshana. B.S.S., CCNY, 1945; M.A., State U. Ia., 1946; Ph.D., New Sch. for Social Research, 1955. Instr. sociology Triple Cities Coll., Endicott, N.Y., 1948-50; instr. sociology Harpur Coll., SUNY, 1950-51, 53-55, asst. prof. sociology, 1955-56; v.p. Gallup Orgn., Inc., Princeton, N.J., 1958-70; exec. v.p. Gallup Orgn., Inc., 1970-76; v.p. Mathematica Policy Research, 1976-77, sr. v.p., 1977-78, sr. fellow, 1978-79; v.p. Roper Orgn., 1979-81; owner Irving Crespi & Assos., Princeton, 1981-89; prof. mktg. Baruch Coll.-CUNY, 1986-88; dir. media and pub. affairs rsch. Total Rsch. Corp., 1989-91, v.p quality, 1991-94; part-time mkt. rsch. cons. Princeton, 1994—. Author: (with H. Mendelsohn) Polls, Television and New Politics, 1971; Pre-Election Polling: Sources of Accuracy and Error, 1988, Public Opinion, Polls and Democracy, 1989, The Public Opinion Process: How The People Speak, 1997; contbr. articles to profl. jours. Trustee Paul F. Lazarsfeld Fund, 1977-79. Served with USAF, 1951-53. Mem. Am. Assn. Pub. Opinion Research (v.p. 1975-76, pres. 1976-77, chmn. standards com. 1966-68, conf. chmn. 1970, award for exceptionally disting. achievement 1997), Am. Sociol. Assn., Am. Mktg. Assn. (dir. 1970-72), World Assn. for Pub. Opinion Research (v.p. 1974-76, pres. 1976-78), Market Research Council. Jewish. Home: 9 Orchard Cir Princeton NJ 08540-3025

CRESS, CECILE COLLEEN, retired librarian; b. Colorado Springs, Colo., Feb. 26, 1914; d. John Leo and Elizabeth Veronica (Rouse) Haley; m. Arthur Henry Cress, May 8, 1937 (div. 1960); children: Ronnie Lou Kordick, Dan, Elaine. BA, Adams State Coll., 1936; MA in English, Colo. Coll., 1964; MLS, Denver U., 1970. 5th grade tchr. Westcliffe (Colo.) Elem., 1953-56; English tchr. Penrose (Colo.) High Sch., 1956-59; English-social studies tchr. Excelsior Jr. High. Sch. Dist. 70, Pueblo, Colo., 1959-64; libr. Pueblo County High, Sch. Dist. 70, Pueblo, 1964-80, Nat. Coll./Pueblo Br., 1980-91; catatoger in library Pueblo C.C., 1992—. Tutor adult literacy program South Cen. Bd. Coop. Svcs., 1991. Recipient Ace of Clubs award Am. Contract Bridge League, 1988, 89. Mem. Pueblo Ret. Sch. Employees (v.p. 1990-92, pres. 1982-84, state bd. 1982-86, sec. 1995-97), Colo. Libr. Assn., Unit 367 Am. Contract Bridge Assn., Irish Club Pueblo (pres. 1995-96), Welsh Terrier

Club Colo., Alpha Delta Kappa (Pueblo chpt., pres. 1976-78, state historian 1980-82, state bd. 1980-82, rec. sec. 1994-98), Am. Contract Bridge League (v.p. unit 367 1998—). Democrat. Roman Catholic. Avocations: duplicate bridge, Welsh Terriers, travel. Home: 901 Jackson St Pueblo CO 81004-2425

CRESSEY, BRYAN CHARLES, lawyer; b. Seattle, Sept. 28, 1949; s. Charles Ovington and Alice Lorraine (Serry) C.; m. Christina Irene Petersen, Aug. 19, 1972; children: Monique Joy, Charlotte Lorraine, Alicia Lin. BA, U. Wash., 1972; MBA, Harvard U., 1976, JD, 1976. Bar: Wash. 1976, Ill. 1977. Sr. investment mgr. First Chgo. Investment Corp., Chgo., 1976-80; prin. Golder, Thoma, Cressey, Rauner, Inc., Chgo., 1980—, ptnr., Thoma, Cressey Equity Ptnrs., 1998—; chmn., bd. dirs. Cable Design Techs., Inc.; bd. dirs. Paging Network, Inc., Am. Habilitation, Inc., Houston, Assistive Tech., Ill., Clarion tech., Ill., Select Med., Harrisburg, Pa., Boston. Bd. dirs. Infant Welfare Soc., Chgo., 1984—, Jr. Achievement, Chgo., author, Explosions (thetrical play). Home: 500 W County Line Rd Barrington IL 60010-9629 Office: Thoma Cressey Equity Partners 4400 Sears Tower Chicago IL 60606

CRESSY, PETER HOLLON, university chancellor, retired naval officer; b. St. Augustine, Fla., Oct. 7, 1941; s. Norman Leo and Harriet (Northrup) C.; m. Sarah Anne Wilson, Apr. 18, 1964; children: Rebecca, Peter Hollon Jr. BA, Yale U., 1963; MS in Internat. Affairs, George Washington U., 1973; MBA, U. R.I., 1974; EdD in Orgnl. Devel., U. San Francisco, 1989; PhD in Orgnl. Devel (hon.), Pacific Grad. Sch. Psychology, 1990. Commd. ensign USN, 1963, advanced through grades to rear adm., 1988, various shore and ship duty assignments, 1963-78; commanding officer Patrol Squadron 5 USN, Moffett Field, Calif., 1978-80; exch. officer U.S. Dept. State USN, Washington, 1980-82, dir. naval legis. affairs for U.S. Ho. of Reps., 1982-84, dir. naval aviation tng. and manpower, 1987-89, dir. total force tng. and edn., 1989-90; commanding officer Patrol Wing 5 USN, Brunswick, Maine, 1984-86; commanding officer Tng. Group Atlantic USN, Norfolk, Va., 1986-87; comdr. fleet air Mediterranean USN, Naples, Italy, 1990-91; pres. Mass. Maritime Acad., Buzzards Bay, 1991-93; chancellor U. Mass., Dartmouth, 1993—; instr. U. San Francisco, 1976-78, U. Md., College Park, 1980-81, George Mason U., Fairfax, Va., 1981; vis. lectr. Bowdoin Coll., Brunswick, 1985. Bd. advisors Pacific Grad. Sch. Pyschology, Pala Alto, Calif. Decorated Legion of Merit with 2 oak leaf clusters, D.M.S., Meritorious Svc. medal. Mem. Assn. Naval Aviation. Roman Catholic. Office: U Mass Dartmouth 285 Old Westport Rd North Dartmouth MA 02747-2300

CRESWELL, DONALD CRESTON, management consultant; b. Mar. 28, 1932; s. Carroll Creston and Verna Moore (Taylor) C.; m. Terri Sue Tidwell; 1 child, Creston Lee. Student, Johns Hopkins U.; MBA, U. Dayton; postgrad., Stanford U. Cons. engr. A.D. Ring & Assocs., Washington; sales and mktg. mgr. Ampex Corp., Redwood City, Calif.; dir. mktg., magnetic products divsn. RCA Corp., N.Y.C.; staff v.p. sales and advt. Pan Am. World Airways, N.Y.C.; prin. mgmt. cons., dir. mktg. svcs. Stanford Rsch. Inst., Menlo Park, Calif.; v.p., gen. mgr. Decisions Sys.; dir. R & D Strategy Practice; gen. mgr., dir. strategy mktg. R & D Decisions quality Assoc.; with Strategic Decisions Group, Menlo Park, 1987—; mem. mgmt. com. Jets Cybernetics, 1987-94; lectr. planning and mktg. mgmt. Am. Mgmt. Assn., 1968-69; program chmn. Grad. Bus. Assn., 1965; rep. to Electronics Industries Assn., 1968-71, to Internat. Air Transport Assn., 1971-74. Bd. dirs. Peninsula Youth Soccer Club, 1981-82; nat. dir. referee assessment, mem. referee com. U.S. Soccer Fedn., 1986-88; regional chief referee San Carlos Am. Youth Soccer Orgn., 1981-85; state dir. assessment Calif. Soccer Assn., 1982-85; mem. L.A. Olympics Organizing Com., 1983-84; nat. referee assessor, 1987—; ofcl. N.Am. Soccer League, 1983-84, World Cup, 1994; sponsor Silicon Valley Roundtable. Mem. Am. Mktg. Assn. (exec. com.), Am. Theatre Organ Assn. (bd. dirs. 1978-79), Nat. Intercollegiate Soccer Ofcls. Assn. (World Cup video inspector 1994), Charles Lindbergh Fund, U.S. Soccer Fedn. (cert. nat. assessor, USSF referee inspector), Silicon Valley Roundtable, The Churchill Club, Stanford Jazz Com. Republican. Home: 8 Pyrola Ln San Carlos CA 94070-1532 Office: Strategic Decisions Group 2440 Sand Hill Rd Menlo Park CA 94025-6900

CRESWELL, DOROTHY ANNE, computer consultant; b. Burlington, Iowa, Feb. 6, 1943; d. Robert Emerson and Agnes Imogene (Gardner) Mefford; m. John Lewis Creswell, Aug. 28, 1965. AA, Burlington C.C., 1963; BA in Math., U. Iowa, 1965; MS in Math., Western Ill. U., 1970; postgrad., Iowa State U., 1974—. Cert. netware engr., Novell Corp. Computer programmer Mason & Hanger, Silas Mason Co., Inc., Burlington, 1965-74; systems programmer Contractor's Hotline, Ft. Dodge, Iowa, 1974; dir. data processing Iowa Cen. C.C., Ft. Dodge, 1975-80; systems programming mgr. Norand Corp., Cedar Rapids, Iowa, 1980-82; spl. svcs. mgr. Pioneer Hi-Bred Internat., Inc., Cedar Rapids, 1982-87; owner, pres. D.C. Cons., Inc., Ankeny, Iowa, 1987—; computers-in-edn. del. to China, People to People Internat., Kansas City, Mo., 1987. Contbr. articles, papers to profl. publs. Mem. Data Processing Mgmt. Assn. (bd. dirs. 1986-87, v.p. 1988, 91-93, pres. 1993-94), Adminstrv. Mgmt. Soc. (sec. 1985-86, v.p. 1986-90, Merit award 1987), Assn. Computing Machinery, Hawkeye Pers. Computer Users, DEC Users Group (v.p. Ea. Iowa chpt. 1981-82), Ind. Computer Cons. Assn. (mem. editl. bd. 1989-96, chpt. pres.-at-large 1993-95). Democrat. Methodist. Avocations: jogging, traveling. Office: DC Cons Inc PO Box 195 Ankeny IA 50021-0195

CRESWELL, NORMAN BRUCE, minister; b. Balt., Aug. 16, 1954; s. Norman Bruce and Ruth Lorraine (Hardin) C.; m. Carolyn Dale Main, June 9, 1979; children: Mary Elisabeth, Norman Bruce III, David Jeremiah, Gregory Frederick. Student, Balt. Sch. Bible, 1971; BA, Bob Jones U., Greenville, S.C., 1977. Ordained to ministry Ind. Bapt. Ch., 1980. Non-com leader Christian Svc. Brigade, Balt., 1969-72; asst. pastor Temple Bapt. Ch., Athens, Ga., 1974-78; tchr. Bible and U.S. history Cross Lanes Christian Sch., Charleston, W.Va., 1980-82; pastor Bellepoint Bapt. Ch., Hinton, W.Va., 1982-92; chaplain Summers County Hosp., Hinton, W.Va., 1983-92; chaplain, min. Hinton House, 1982-92; min. (local radio) Morning Light Program, 1984-89; missionary Scotland, 1985, 87, 91; pastor Faith Bible Ch., Mt. Crawford, Va., 1992—, (local radio) Gleanings From God's Word, 1993—. Bd. dirs., advisor Grace Bapt. Italian Mission. Recipient Herald of Christ award, Christian Svc. Brigade, Balt., 1972, Voice of Democracy award, VFW, 1972. Mem. Bapt. Std. Bearer Soc., Bob Jones U. Alumni Assn. Republican. Home: RR 620 Keezletown VA 22832-9999 Office: Faith Bible Ch PO Box 206 Mount Crawford VA 22841-0206 *The greatest purpose of life is to glorify God in walking in His Word and this is not done with sounding brass or clanging cymbals but by the heart of man who has been redeemed and cleansed by the shed blood of Jesus Christ.*

CRETAN, DONNA, neonatal nurse, lactation consultant; b. Mpls., May 18, 1939; d. Howard Robert and Frances E. (Warner) Bjerke; m. Nestor Nicholas Cretan, Jan. 24, 1959; children: Colette, John, Christopher, Bernadette. ADN, Contra Costa Coll., 1973; BSN, Sacred Heart U., Fairfield, Conn., 1986. RN, Conn. Nurse mgr., cons. St. Joseph Med. Ctr., Stamford, Conn., 1974-89; staff nurse Cmty. Hosp., Santa Rosa, Calif., 1989-93, Greenwich (Conn.) Hosp., 1993—; ESL tutor LVA, 1997—. Host parent A Better Chance, New Canaan, Conn., 1982-84, Am. Field Svc., 1983-84, Calif., 1991-93, Cultural Homestay, Cohasset, Mass., 1991-95, People Link, Petaluma, Calif.; sec. Hist. Soc., Sebastopol, Calif., 1989-92; vol. nurse Americares Free Clinic Norwalk, 1994—; literacy vol. ESL Inst., 1997-98. Mem. ANA, CCN, Assn. Women's Health, Obstetrics and Neonatal Nurses, Neonatal Network, Internat. Lactation Cons. Assn. (cert.). Avocations: lactation promotion, photography. Home: 126 Brushy Ridge Rd New Canaan CT 06840-4209 Office: Greenwich Hosp Perry Ridge Rd Greenwich CT 06840

CRETEKOS, GEORGE NICK, district assistant; b. Tampa, Jan. 26, 1947; s. Nick George and Frances (Gillas) C.; m. Carolyn Rose Farinola, Sept. 17, 1989. BA, Davidson Coll., 1969; MPA, U. Pitts., 1970. Congl. aide U.S. congressman Bill Young, Washington, 1971-75, 84-86, St. Petersburg, Fla., 1975-84, 86—. Greek Orthodox. Office: US Congressman Bill Young 360 Central Ave #1480 Saint Petersburg FL 33701-4396

CREUTZ, EDWARD CHESTER, physicist, museum consultant; b. Beaver Dam, Wis., Jan. 23, 1913; s. Lester Raymond and Grace (Smith) C.; m. Lela Rollefson, Sept. 13, 1937 (dec. Feb. 1972); children: Michael John, Carl Eugene, Ann Jo Carmel Creutz Cosgrove; m. Elisabeth B. Cordle, Oct. 5, 1974. B.S., U. Wis., 1936, Ph.D., 1939. Research assoc. Princeton U., 1939-40, instr. physics, 1940-41; physicist NDRC, 1941-42, Metall. Lab., U. Chgo., 1942-44, Manhattan Project, Los Alamos, 1944-46; assoc. prof. Carnegie Inst. Tech., Pitts., 1946-49, prof., head dept. physics, dir. Nuclear Research Ctr., 1948-55; dir. John Jay Hopkins Lab. for Pure and Applied Sci., 1955-59; dir. research Gen. Atomic Div. Gen. Dynamics Corp., San Diego, 1955-59; v.p. research and devel. Gen. Atomic div. Gen. Dynamics Corp., San Diego, 1959-67; v.p. research and devel Gulf Gen. Atomic, San Diego, 1967-70; asst. dir. NSF, Washington, 1970-77, acting dep. dir., 1976-77; dir. Bernice Pauahi Bishop Mus., Honolulu, 1977-84; cons. Bernice Pauahi Bishop Mus., 1984—; mem. sea water conversion com. Water resources Ctr., U. Calif.-Berkeley, 1958-68; adv. com. office Sci. Pers. NRC, 1960-63; mem. exec. coun. Argonne Nat. Lab. (1946-51); cons. NSF, 1950-68; scientist-at-large Project Sherwood div. research AEC, 1955-56; mem. com. sr. reviewers Dept. Energy, 1972-79, fusion power coordinating com., 1971-79; cons. Oak Ridge Nat. Lab., 1946-58; adv. panel gen. scis. Dept. Def., 1959-63; research adv. com. electrophysics NASA, 1964-71, tech. adv. com., 1971-77; adj. prof. physics and astronomy U. Hawaii, 1977-87; adj. prof. physics U. Calif., San Diego, 1987—. Co-editor: Handbuch der Physik, vols. 14, 15; mem. editorial bd. Ann. Rev. Nuclear Sci., 1961-66, 72-75, Handbook of Chemistry and Physics, 1961-71; mem. editorial bd.: Interdisciplinary Science Reviews, London, 1976—; editorial adv. com. ann. revs.: Nuclear Sci. and Engring., 1959-72. Bd. dirs. San Diego Hall Sci. and Planetarium, v.p., 1956-70; v.p. San Diego Industry-Edn. Council, 1956-65; mem. adv. council Dept. Edn. San Diego County. Fellow AAAS, Am. Phys. Soc. (NRC rep. 1956-57), Am. Nuclear Soc.; mem. NAS, Am. Assn. Physics Tchrs., Phys. Soc. Pitts. (pres. 1949), Am. Inst. Physics (dir.-at-large bd. govs. 1965-68). Home: PO Box 2757 Rancho Santa Fe CA 92067-2757

CREW, SPENCER, museum administrator; b. Poughkeepsie, N.Y., Jan. 7, 1949; s. R. Spencer and Ada Lee (Scott) C.; m. Sandra Lorraine Prioleau, June 19, 1971; children: Alika, Adom. BA, Brown U., 1971; MA, Rutgers U., 1973, PhD, 1979. Asst. prof. U. Md. Baltimore County, Catonsville, 1978-81; historian Nat. Mus. Am. History, Smithsonian Instn., Washington, 1981-87, curator, 1987-89, chmn. dept. social and cultural history, 1989-91, dep. dir., acting dir., 1991-94; dir., 1994—; commr. Md. Commn. on Afro-Am. History and Culture, Annapolis, 1990—; hist. cons. Nat. Civil Rights Mus., Memphis, 1987-91; cons. Civil Rights Inst., Birmingham, Ala., 1991-94; bd. dirs. Nat. History Day, 1994—. Exhbns. include Field to Factory: Afro-Am. Migration, 1915-40, 1987 (award 1988), Go Forth and Serve: Black Land Grant Colls., 1990. Bd. trustees Brown U., 1995—; adult leader Bapt. Youth Fellowship, St. John Ch., Columbia, Md., 1989-91; asst. coach Columbia Basketball Assn., 1990-92. Recipient Osceola award Delta Sigma Theta, 1988, Cert. award Smithsonian Instn., 1989, 90, 91, 92, Svc. award Assn. for Study of African Am. Life and History, 1994, Robert A. Brooks award Smithsonian Instn., 1994. Mem. African Am. Mus. Assn. (2d v.p. 1989-91), Orgn. Am. Historians (editl. bd. 1989-92), Am. Assn. Mus. (bd. dirs.), Nat. Coun. History Edn. (bd. trustees. 1995—), Am. Hist. Assn. (exhibit rev. co-editor 1990-95), Oral History in Mid Atlantic Region (exec. bd. 1987-90). Office: Smithsonian Instn Nat Mus Am History 14th & Constitution Ave Washington DC 20560*

CREWDSON, JOHN MARK, journalist, author; b. San Francisco, Dec. 15, 1945; s. Mark Guy and Eva Rebecca (Doane) C.; m. Prudence Gray Tillotson, Sept. 11, 1969; children: Anders Gray, Oliver McDuff. AB in Econs. with gt. distinction, U. Calif., Berkeley, 1970; postgrad. studies in politics, Oxford (Eng.) U., 1971-72. Reporter N.Y. Times, Washington, 1973-77; nat. corr N.Y. Times, Houston, 1977-82; nat. news editor Chgo. Tribune, 1982-83, met. news editor, 1983-84; west coast corr. Chgo. Tribune, L.A., 1984-90; sr. nat. corr. Chgo. Tribune, Washington, 1990-96, sr. writer, 1996—. Author: The Tarnished Door, 1983, By Silence Betrayed, 1988. Recipient Bronze medallion Sigma Delta Chi, 1974, Goldberg award N.Y. Deadline Club, 1977, Page One award N.Y. Newspaper Guild, 1977, Pulitizer prize for nat. reporting, 1981, Polk award for med. reporting L.I. U., 1990, William H. Jones award for investigative reporting, 1990, 95, 97, Peter Lisagor award Chgo. Headline Club, 1997. Office: Chgo Tribune 1325 G St NW Washington DC 20005-3104

CREWE, ALBERT VICTOR, physicist, artist, business executive; b. Bradford, Yorkshire, Eng., Feb. 18, 1927; came to U.S., 1955, naturalized, 1961; s. Wilfred and Edith Fish (Lawrence) C.; m. Doreen Blunsdon, Apr. 9, 1949; children: Jennifer, Sarah, Elizabeth, David. BS in Physics, U. Liverpool, Eng., 1947, PhD, 1951; hon. degrees, Lake Forest Coll., 1972, U. Mo., 1972, Elmhurst Coll., 1972. Asst. lectr. U. Liverpool, Eng., 1950-52; lectr. U. Liverpool, 1952-55; rsch. assoc. U. Chgo., 1955-56, asst. prof., 1956-58, assoc. prof., 1958-63; prof. dept. physics and Enrico Fermi Inst., 1963-71, dean phys. scis. div., 1971-81; also William Wrather Disting. Svc. prof. physics, 1958-61, emeritus, 1996—; dir. particle accelerator div. Argonne Nat. Lab., 1958-61, dir., 1961-66; pres. Orchid One Corp., 1987-90. Chmn. Chgo. Area Research and Devel. Council. Recipient Outstanding Local Citizen in Field of Sci. award Chgo. Jr. Assn. Commerce and Industry, 1961; Outstanding New Citizen of Year award Citizenship Council Chgo., 1962; award for outstanding achievement in field of sci. Immigrant's Service League, 1962; Man of Year in Research award Indsl. Research, Inc., 1970; Michelson medal Franklin Inst., 1977; Duddell medal Inst. of Physics, 1980. Fellow Am. Phys. Soc., Royal Microscopical Soc. (hon.), Chinese Electron Microscope Soc. (hon.); mem. NAS, Sci. Rsch. Soc. Am., Electron Microscopy Soc. Am. (Disting. Svc. award 1976), N.Y. Microscope Soc. (Abbe award 1979), Am. Acad. Arts and Scis., Palette and Chisel Acad. (artist mem.). Achievements include research on electron optics, design of electron microscopes. Avocations: sculptor, painter. Home: 8 Summit Dr Chesterton IN 46304-1024

CREWS, DAVID, protective services official; b. Oxford, Miss., Aug. 29, 1954. BA, U. of the South, 1972. U.S. Marshall for No. Dist. Miss. U.S. Cts./5th Cir., Jackson, 1994—. Office: US Marshall/Fed Bldg 911 Jackson Ave E Oxford MS 38655-3632*

CREWS, ESCA HOLMES, JR., utility company executive; b. Mecklenburg County, N.C., Apr. 4, 1922; s. Esca Holmes and Marie (Coffey) C.; m. Paralee Croy, May 16, 1942 (dec. June 1967); children: Edward E., Karen Crews; m. Dorothy Grice, Jan. 19, 1968; 1 child, Kelley Anne Crews Meyer. B.S.E.E., Va. Poly. Inst., 1943. Registered profl. engr., S.C. Cons. engr. Gilbert Assocs., Reading, Pa., 1946-62; with S.C. Electric & Gas Co., Columbia, 1962—; v.p. engring. services, constrn. and prodn. S.C. Electric & Gas Co., 1968-75, v.p., group exec., 1975-82, sr. v.p., power ops., 1982-85, exec. v.p., 1985—; pres., treas. Primesouth, Inc. of Scana Co., 1986-89; cons. power plant concepts, planning, constrn., ops., 1992—; pres., treas. Primesouth Inc.; advisor New Primesouth. Served to capt. U.S. Army, 1943-46, ETO. Mem. Austrian Alpine Soc., Greater Columbia C. of C., Nat. Audubon Soc., Soc. Am. Mil. Engrs., Tau Beta Pi. Republican. Presbyterian. *

CREWS, FREDERICK CAMPBELL, humanities educator, writer; b. Phila., Feb. 20, 1933; s. Maurice Augustus and Robina (Gaudet) C.; m. Betty Claire Peterson, Sept. 9, 1959; children: Gretchen Elizabeth, Ingrid Anna Crews Márquez. AB, Yale U., 1955; PhD, Princeton U., 1958. Faculty U. Calif., Berkeley, 1958—, instr. in English, 1958-60, asst. prof., 1960-62, assoc. prof., 1962-66, prof., 1986-94, vice-chair for grad. studies, 1988-92, chair dept., 1992-94; prof. emeritus, 1994—; mem. study fellowship selection com. Am. Coun. Learned Socs., 1971-73; mem. selection com. summer seminars Nat. Endowment for Humanities, 1976-77; Ward-Phillips lectr. U. Notre Dame, 1974-75, Dorothy T. Burstein lectr. UCLA, 1984; Frederick Ives Carpenter vis. prof. U. Chgo., 1985; Lansdowne visitor U. Victoria, 1987-88; John Dewey lectr., 1988, Nina Mae Kellogg lectr. Portland (Oreg.) State U., 1989; mem. exec. com. bd. dirs. Mark Twain Project, 1984—; faculty rsch. lectr. U. Calif., Berkeley, 1991-92; David L. Kubal Meml. lectr. Calif. State U., L.A., 1994; mem. sci. and profl. adv. bd. False Memory Syndrome Found., 1994—. Author: The Tragedy of Manners, 1957, E.M. Forster: The Perils of Humanism, 1962, The Pooh Perplex, 1963, The Sins of the Fathers, 1966, The Patch Commission, 1968, The Random House Handbook, 1974, 6th edit., 1992, Out of My System, 1975, Skeptical Engagements, 1986, The Critics Bear it Away, 1992; co-author: The Borzoi Handbook for Writers, 1985, 3d edit., 1993; prin. author: The Memory Wars, 1995; editor: The Red Badge of Courage (Crane), 1964, Great Short Works of Nathaniel Hawthorne, 1967, Starting Over, 1970, Psychoanalysis and Literary Process, 1970, The Random House Reader, 1981, Unauthorized Freud, 1998. Recipient Essay prize Nat. Endowment Arts, 1968, Disting. Tchg. award U. Calif., Berkeley, 1985, Spielvogel Diamonstein PEN prize, 1992; named Fulbright lectr. Turin, Italy, 1961-62; fellow Am. Coun. Learned Socs., 1965-66, Ctr. for Advanced Study in Behavioral Scis., 1965-66, Guggenheim Found., 1970-71, Am. Acad. Arts and Scis., 1992. Home: 636 Vincente Ave Berkeley CA 94707-1524 Office: U Calif Dept English Berkeley CA 94720-1030

CREWS, HARRY EUGENE, author; b. Alma, Ga., June 6, 1935; s. Ray and Myrtice (Haselden) C.; m. Sally Thornton Ellis, Jan. 22, 1960 (div.); children: Patrick Scott, Byron Jason. B.A., U. Fla., 1960, MSEd., 1962. English tchr. Broward Jr. Coll., Ft. Lauderdale, Fla., 1962-68; assoc. prof. English U. Fla. at Gainesville, 1968-74, prof. English. Author: The Gospel Singer, 1968, reprint, 1995, Naked in Garden Hills, 1969, This Thing Don't Lead To Heaven, 1970, Karate is a Thing of the Spirit, 1971, Car, 1972, The Hawk is Dying, 1973, The Gypsy's Curse, 1974, A Feast of Snakes, 1976, A Childhood: The Biography of a Place, 1978, Blood and Grits, 1979, The Enthusiast, 1981, Florida Frenzy, 1982, A Grit's Triumph, 1983, Two, 1984, All We Need of Hell, 1987, The Knockout Artists, 1988, Body, 1990, Madonna at Ringside, 1991, Scar Lover, 1992, Classic Crews: A Harry Crews Reader, 1993, The Mulching of America, 1995, Where Does One Go When There's No Place Left To Go?, 1998, Celebration: A Novel, 1998; columnist Esquire mag. Served with USMC, 1953-56. Recipient Am. Acad. Arts and Scis. award, 1972; Nat. Endowment for the Arts grantee, 1974. Office: Simon & Schuster Inc Ste C3-31 1230 Avenue Of The Americas Fl Concl New York NY 10020-1586*

CREWS, MARA LYNNE, writer; b. Shreveport, La., Aug. 12, 1957; d. Marlin E. Crews and Velma L. Brannon. Prodn. technician City of Shreveport, 1977-91; job coach Job Boost-Bossier Parish C.C., Bossier City, La., 1992-94; direct svc. worker II Evergreen Presbyn. Ministry, Bossier City, 1994-96. Author (anthologies): A Break in the Clouds, 1993, American Poetry Anthology, 1995, Dimensions of Thought, 1997, Best Poems of the 90s, 1998. Capt. Givens St. Neighborhood Watch, Bossier City, 1993-95; mem. N.W. La. Brain Injury Support Group, Shreveport, 1989—.

CREWS, WILLIAM EDWIN, lawyer; b. Cin., Oct. 29, 1944; s. Donald Luther and Mary Ruth (Gardiner) C. BA, Miami U., Oxford, Ohio, 1966; JD with honors, George Washington U., 1969. Bar: Ohio 1971, Ga. 1978, U.S. Dist. Ct. (no. dist.) Ga. 1978, U.S. Ct. Appeals (11th cir.) 1978. Assoc. Hausser & Atkinson, Marietta, Ohio, 1971-74; asst. counsel Union CommerceBank, Cleve., 1974-76; asst. corp. counsel Trust Co. Ga., Trust Co. Bank Atlanta, 1976-84; assoc. corp.counsel Trust Co. Ga., Trust Co. Bank, Atlanta, 1984-94; sr. atty. SunTrust Banks, Inc., Atlanta, 1994—. Mem. ABA, State Bar Ga. Home: 2460 Peachtree Rd NW Apt 1411 Atlanta GA 30305-4158 Office: SunTrust Banks Inc 25 Park Pl NE Atlanta GA 30303-2900

CREWS, WILLIAM ODELL, JR., seminary administrator; b. Houston, Feb. 8, 1936; s. William O. Sr. and Juanita (Pearson) C.; m. Wanda Jo Ann Cunningham; children: Ronald Wayne, Rhonda Ann Crews Bolei. BA, Hardin Simmons U., 1957, HHD, 1987; BDiv, Southwestern Bapt. Theol. Sem., 1964; DD, Calif. Bapt. Coll., 1987. Ordained to ministry Bapt. Ch., 1953. Pastor Grape Creek Bapt. Ch., San Angelo, Tex., 1952-54, Plainview Bapt. Ch., Stamford, Tex., 1955-57, 1st Bapt. Ch., Sterling City, Tex., 1957-60, 7th St. Bapt. Ch., Ballinger, Tex., 1960-65, Woodland Heights Bapt. Ch., Brownwood, Tex., 1965-67, Victory Bapt. Ch., Seattle, 1967-72, Met. Bapt. Ch., Portland, Oreg., 1972-77; dir. comm. N.W. Bapt. Conv., Portland, 1977-78; pastor Magnolia Ave Bapt. Ch., Riverside, Calif., 1978-86; pres. Golden Gate Bapt. Theol. Sem., Mill Valley, Calif., 1986—; pres. N.W. Bapt. Conv., Portland, 1974-76, So. Bapt. Gen. Conv. Calif., Fresno, 1982-84. Trustee Fgn. Mission Bd., Richmond, Va., 1973-78, Golden Gate Bapt. Theol. Sem., 1980-85, Marin Cmty. Hosp. Found., 1992-95; bd. dirs. Midway Seatac Boys Club, Des Moines, 1969-72. Mem. Marin County C. of C. (bd. dirs. 1987-95), Midway C. of C. (bd. dirs. 1968-72), Rotary (bd. dirs. San Rafael chpt. 1992—, pres. Portland club 1975-76, pres.-elect Riverside club 1984-85). Home: 157 Chapel Dr Mill Valley CA 94941-3168 Office: Golden Gate Bapt Theol Sem 201 Seminary Dr Mill Valley CA 94941-3197*

CRIBBET, JOHN EDWARD, law educator, former university chancellor; b. Findlay, Ill., Feb. 21, 1918; s. Howard H. and Ruth (Wright) C.; m. Betty Jane Smith, Dec. 24, 1941; children: Carol Ann, Pamela Lee. BA, Ill. Wesleyan U., 1940, LLD, 1971; JD, U. Ill., 1947. Bar: Ill. 1947. Pvt. practice in law Bloomington, Ill., 1947—; prof. law U. Ill., Urbana, 1947-67, dean. Coll. Law, 1967-79; chancellor Urbana-Champaign Campus, U. Ill., 1979-84, Corman prof. law, 1984-88, prof. emeritus, 1988—. Author: Cases and Materials on Judicial Remedies, 1954, Cases on Property, 7th edit., 1996, (with others) Principles of the Law of Property, 1975, (with Prof. Corwin Johnson), 3d edit., 1989; editor: U. Ill. Law Forum, 1947-55; contbr. articles to profl. jours. Chmn. com. on jud. ethics Il. Supreme Ct.; pres. United Fund Champaign County, (Ill.), 1962-63; trustee Ill. Wesleyan U.; mem. exec. com. Assn. Am. Law Schs., 1973-75, pres., 1979. Served to maj. AUS, 1941-45. Decorated Bronze Star; decorated Croix de Guerre. Mem. ABA, Ill. State Bar Assn., Champaign County Bar Assn., Order of Coif. Lodge: Rotary. Home: 306 E Sherwin Cir Urbana IL 61802-7137 Office: U Ill Coll of Law 504 E Pennsylvania Ave Champaign IL 61820-6909

CRIBBS, MAUREEN ANN, artist, educator; b. Marinette, Wis., Feb. 17, 1927; d. Roy Cecil Hubbard and Lillian Worner (Hubbard) Yeoman; m. James Milton Cribbs, Apr. 22, 1950; children: Cynthia, Valerie. BA, DePauw U., 1949; student, Sch. of Art Inst., Chgo., 1971-72, 79-81; MA, Govs. State U., 1973. Cert. secondary sch. tchr., Ill. Tchr. art Sch. Dist. 163, Park Forest, Ill., 1960-78; instr. humanities Sch. Dist. 227, Park Forest, 1978-79; artist, painter, printmaker Park Forest, 1979—; instr. painting Village Artists, Flossmoor, Ill., 1980-87; lectr. part-time Chgo. State U., 1980-81; adj. prof. Govs. State U., University Park, 1995; docent Nathan Manilow Sculpture Park, Govs. State U., 1996—; sec. Homewood-Flossmoor cmty. assocs. of woman's bd. Art Inst. Chgo., 1995-96, chair study group, 1989-95; artist-in-residence Ox Bow Sch. of Art; instr. art, art history Robert Morris Coll., Orland Park, Ill., 1996—; outreach presenter for Art Insights, Art Inst. of Chgo., 1995—; woodcut printing and presenter Sr. Celebrations, Art Inst. Chgo., 1998; participant printmaking Santa Clara Grafic Art Ctr., Florence, Italy, 1999, Tall Grass Gallery, Park Forest, Ill., 1999. Exhbns. include Recent Work South Suburban Cmty. Coll., Thornton, Ill, 1983, Augsburg Coll., Mpls., 1988, Matrix Gallery Ltd., 1992, Personal Spaces, Inside Art Gallery, Chgo., 1997, Union Street Gallery, Chicago Heights, 1998, Gov.'s State U., University Park, Ill., 1999, Ateljé Gallery, Geneva, Ill., 1999. Bd. dirs. Ill. Philaharm. Orch., Park Forest, 1981-83, Grace Migrant Day Care, Park Forest, 1981-85; adminstrv. chair Grace United Protestant Ch., Park Forest, 1984-94; lay mem. No. Ill. Ann. Conf. of United Meth. Ch., 1996—, mem. commn. on christian unity and interreligious concerns, 1996—. Monetary grantee to produce 15 works Freedom Hall, 1982; Artist-in-Residence Cmty. Arts Coun. Park Forest, 1983, Sch. of Art Inst. of Chgo., 1993. Mem. Mid-Am. Print Coun., Am. Print Alliance, Chgo. Artists Coalition. Methodist. Avocations: Reiki Master, studying herbs & wildflowers, reading, travel, swimming. Home: 74 Blackhawk Dr Park Forest IL 60466-2146 Studio: 266 Somonauk St Park Forest IL 60466-2241

CRICHTON, DOUGLAS BENTLEY, editor, writer; b. Petersburg, Va., Sept. 12, 1959; s. James Bentley and Marjorie Ulalier (Robertson) C.; m. Virginia Elizabeth Munsch, Sept. 5, 1981; children: Christopher Winfield, Alexander Douglas, William Perry, Susannah Elizabeth. BA in English, U. Va., 1981. Reporter Richmond (Va.) Times-Dispatch, 1982-84; reporter, editor AP, Dallas, 1984-88; mng. editor, then editor Am. Way Mag., Dallas, 1988-93; exec. editor, then editor, v.p. Cooking Light Mag., Birmingham, Ala., 1993—; judge Maggie awards Western Pub. Assn., L.A., 1989-93. Named Va. Young Journalist of Yr., UPI, 1983; recipient over 100 awards for editl. and artistic excellence Am. Way and Cooking Light Mags.; scholar James Hay Found., 1980. Mem. Am. Soc. Mag. Editors, Assn. Food Journalists. Office: Cooking Light PO Box 1748 Birmingham AL 35201-1748

CRICHTON, (JOHN) MICHAEL, author, film director; b. Chgo., Oct. 23, 1942; s. John Henderson and Zula (Miller) C. A.B. summa cum laude,

Harvard U., 1964, M.D., 1969. Postdoctoral fellow Salk Inst., La Jolla, Calif., 1969-70; vis. writer MIT, Cambridge, 1988; creator, co-exec. prodr. TV ER, 1994. Author: (as Jeffrey Hudson) A Case of Need, 1968 (Edgar award Mystery Writers of America 1968); (as John Lange) Odds On, 1966, Scratch One, 1967, Easy Go, 1968, Zero Cool, 1969, The Venom Business, 1969, Drug of Choice, 1970, Grave Descend, 1970, Binary, 1972; The Andromeda Strain, 1969, Five Patients, 1970 (Writer of the Year award Assn. American Medical Writers 1970), (with Douglas Crichton) Dealing: Or, The Berkeley to Boston Forty-Brick Lost-Bag Blues, 1971, The Terminal Man, 1972, The Great Train Robbery, 1975 (Edgar award Mystery Writers of America 1979), Eaters of the Dead, 1976, Jasper Johns, 1977, Congo, 1980, Electronic Life, 1983, Sphere, 1987, Travels, 1988, Jurassic Park, 1990, Rising Sun, 1992, Disclosure, 1994, Lost World, 1995, Airframe, 1996, Timeline, 1999; screenwriter, dir. film Westworld, 1973, Coma, 1978, The Great Train Robbery, 1979, Looker, 1981, Runaway, 1984; dir. film Pursuit, 1972, Physical Evidence, 1989; co-screenwriter Jurassic Park, 1993, Rising Sun, 1993; co-screenwriter, co-writer Twister, 1996; co-prodr. (film) Disclosure, 1994, Sphere, 1998, Eaters of the Dead, 1999. Recipient George Foster Peabody award ER, 1995, Emmy Best Dramatic series ER, 1996. Mem. Authors Guild, Writers Guild, Am. West, Dirs. Guild Am., Prodrs. Guild, PEN Am. Ctr. Acad. Motion Picture Arts and Scis., Harvard Bd. Overseers, Phi Beta Kappa. Office: Constant C Prodns 194 Katonah Ave # 246 Katonah NY 10536-2142

CRICK, FRANCIS HARRY COMPTON, science educator, researcher; b. June 8, 1916; s. Harry and Anne Elizabeth (Wilkins) C.; m. Ruth Doreen Dodd, 1940 (div. 1947); 1 son; m. Odile Speed, 1949; 2 daus. B.Sc., Univ. Coll., London; PhD, Cambridge U., Eng. Scientist Brit. Admiralty, 1940-47, Strangeways Lab., Cambridge, Eng., 1947-49; with Med. Rsch. Coun. Lab. of Molecular Biology, Cambridge, 1949-77; Kieckhefer Disting. prof. Salk Inst. Biol. Studies, San Diego, 1977—, non-resident fellow, 1962-73, pres., 1994-95; adj. prof. psychology U. Calif., San Diego; vis. lectr. Rockefeller Inst., N.Y.C., 1959; vis. prof. chemistry dept. Harvard U., 1959, vis. prof. biophysics, 1962; fellow Churchill Coll., Cambridge, 1960-61; Korkes Meml. lectr. Duke U., 1960; Henry Sidgewick Meml. lectr. Cambridge U., 1963; Graham Young lectr., Glasgow, 1963; Robert Boyle lectr. Oxford U., 1963; Vanuxem lectr. Princeton U., 1964; William T. Sedgwick Meml. lectr. MIT, 1965; Cherwell-Simon Meml. lectr. Oxford U., 1966; Shell lectr. Stanford U., 1969; Paul Lund lectr. Northwestern U., 1977; Dupont lectr. Harvard U., 1979, numerous other invited meml. lectrs. Author: Of Molecules and Men, 1966, Life Itself, 1981, What Mad Pursuit, 1988, The Astonishing Hypothesis: The Scientific Search for the Soul, 1994; contbr. papers and articles on molecular, cell biology and neurobiology to sci. jours. Recipient Prix Charles Leopold Mayer French Academies des Scis., 1961; (with J.D. Watson) Rsch. Corp. award, 1961, Warren Triennial prize, 1959, (with J.D. Watson & Maurice Wilkins) Lasker award, 1960, Nobel Prize for medicine, 1962; Gairdner Found. award, 1962, Royal Medal Royal Soc., 1972, Copley medal, 1975, Michelson-Morley award, 1981, Benjamin P. Cheney medal, 1986, Golden Plate award, 1987, Albert medal Royal Soc. Arts, London, 1987, Wright Prize VIII Harvey Mudd Coll., 1988, Joseph Priestly award Dickinson Coll., 1988, Order of Merit, 1991, Disting. Achievement award Oreg State U. Friends of Libr., 1995. Fellow AAAS, Univ. Coll. London, Royal Soc., Indian Nat. Sci. Acad., Rochester Mus., Indian Acad. Scis. (hon.), Churchill Coll. Cambridge (hon.), Royal Soc. Edinburgh (hon.), Caius Coll. Cambridge (hon.), John Muir Coll. U. Calif., San Diego (hon.), Tata Inst. Fundamental Rsch., Bombay (hon.), Inst. Biology London (hon.); mem. Acad. Arts Scis. (fgn. hon.), Am. Soc. Biol. Chemists (hon.), U.S. Nat. Acad. Scis. (fgn. assoc.), German Acad. Sci., Am. Philos. Soc. (fgn. mem.), French Acad. Scis. (assoc. fgn. mem.), Royal Irish Acad. (hon.), Hellenic Biochemical and Biophysical Soc. (hon.), Academia Europaea. Office: Salk Inst Biol Studies PO Box 85800 San Diego CA 92186-5800

CRIDER, ALLEN BILLY, English educator, novelist; b. Mexia, Tex., July 28, 1941; s. Billy and Frances Antoinette (Brodnax) C.; m. Judy Laverne Stutts, June 4, 1965; children: Angela Antoinette, Allen Blake. BA, U. Tex., Austin, 1963; MA, North Tex. State U., 1967; PhD, U. Tex., Austin, 1972. English tchr. Corsicana (Tex.) H.S., 1963-65; prof. English Howard Payne U., Brownwood, Tex., 1971-83; prof. English, chair dept. English Alvin (Tex.) C.C., 1983—. Author: (with Jack Davis) The Coyote Connection, 1981, Too Late to Die, 1986, 89, Shotgun Saturday Night, 1987, 89, Cursed to Death, 1988, 90, Keepers of the Beast, 1988, One Dead Dean, 1988, Ryan Rides Back, 1988, Time for Hanging, 1989, Blood Dreams, 1989, Death on the Move, 1989, 90, Dying Voices, 1989, Galveston Gunman, 1989, Goodnight, Moom, 1989, Evil at the Root, 1990, 91, Just Before Dark, 1990, Medicine Show, 1990, Rest in Peace, 1990, Vampire Named Fred, 1990, Blood Marks, 1991, Dead on the Island, 1991, Booked for a Hanging, 1992, Gator Kill, 1992, The Texas Capitol Murders, 1992, When Old Men Die, 1994, Murder Most Fowl, 1994, A Dangerous Thing, 1994, Mike Gonzo and the Almost Invisible Man, 1996, Mike Gonzo and the Sewer Monster, 1996, The Prairie Chicken Kill, 1996, Winning Can Be Murder, 1996, Mike Gonzo and the UFO Terror, 1997; contbr. short stories to publs. Recipient Anthony award for Best 1st Mystery Novel, Bouchercon, 1987. Mem. Tex. C.C. Tchrs.' Assn., Mystery Writers of Am., Pvt. Eye Writers of Am., Sisters in Crime, Western Writers of Am. Avocations: collecting old paperback books, running. Office: Alvin Cmty Coll 3110 Mustang Rd Alvin TX 77511-4807

CRIDER, ANDREW BLAKE, psychologist; b. Cleve., June 11, 1936; s. Blake and Doris (Towne) C.; m. Anne Horrocks, Apr. 25, 1964; children: Juliet Gage, Jonathan Andrew. BA, Colgate U., 1958; MS, U. Wis., 1960; PhD, Harvard U., 1964. Lic. psychologist, Mass. Research assoc. Harvard Med. Sch., Boston, 1964-68; asst., then assoc. prof. psychology Williams Coll., Williamstown, Mass., 1968-77, prof., 1977-84, Warren prof. psychology, 1984-94, chmn. dept., 1986-91, dir. Oxford program, 1991-93, prof. emeritus, 1994—; cons. Berkshire Med. Ctr. Psychiatry Dept., Pittsfield, Mass., 1979-85, Harvard Med. Sch. Dept. Psychiatry, Boston, 1996—; bd. dirs. Biofeedback Certification Inst. Am., 1994—. Author: Schizophrenia, 1979; (with others) Psychology, 1983; contbr. articles to profl. jours. Bd. dirs. No. Berkshire Mental Health Assn., 1982-91. Fulbright scholar U. Brussels, 1958-59; NIH research grantee, 1964-74. Mem. Am. Psychol. Assn., Soc. Psychophysiol. Research, Assn. for Applied Psychophysiol. and Biofeedback. Home: PO Box 234 Williamstown MA 01267-0234 Office: Williams Coll Dept Psychology Williamstown MA 01267

CRIDER, IRENE PERRITT, education educator, small business owner, consultant; b. Chatfield, Ark., Apr. 29, 1921; d. Dolphus France and Eula Allan (Springer) Perritt; m. Willis Jewel Crider, Aug. 3, 1945; 1 child, Larry Willis. BA, Bethel Coll., 1944; MA, Memphis State U., 1957; EdD, Fla. Atlantic U., 1977. Cert. elem., secondary tchr., administr., Tenn. Tchr. various schs., Tenn., 1941-57; dean girls Lake Worth (Fla.) Jr. High, 1957-65; dean women Lake Worth High Sch., 1965-73; gen. instructional supr. Palm Beach (Fla.) County Pub. Schs., 1973-75; asst. prin. Jupiter (Fla.) High Sch., 1975-76; supr. interns Fla. Atlantic U., Boca Raton, 1977-83, Palm Beach Atlantic Coll., West Palm Beach, Fla., 1982-84; cons. Paris, Tenn., 1984-87; owner, beauty sys. cons. Irene's Acad. Individual Image Improvement, 1991—; instr. edn. Bethel Coll., McKenzie, Tenn., 1987, prof. MEd Grad. Program; cons. in field. Contbr. articles to profl. jours. Founder, bd. dirs., charter mem. Palm Beach County Kidney Assn., 1973-93; chmn. citizens action com. Fla. Ch. Women United, 1982-84. Mem. Tallahassee Theatre Guild, Women's Club Tallahassee, Tallahassee Area C. of C., Zonta (Lake Worth, pres. 1969-70), Order Ea. Star, Delta Kappa Gamma (charter pres. Beta Xi-Mu 1968-70, chmn. state com., scholarship), Phi Delta Kappa, Beta Phi Mu. Democrat. Methodist. Avocations: gardening, reading, spectator sports, color analysis, Amera Natural nails cons. and beauty systems cons. Home and Office: 1606 N Meridian Rd Tallahassee FL 32303-5644

CRIDER, JEFFREY JOHN, public relations executive; b. Fontana, Calif., Oct. 16, 1962; s. Peter Roemer Crider and Barbara Jean (Matus) Wood; m. Michelle Marissa Strickland, July 20, 1991; children: Isabella Marissa, Maxwell Carl. Student, St. Louis U., Madrid, Spain, 1982-83; B of Spanish and European Studies, Loyola Marymount U., L.A., 1984; M of Hispanic and Internat. Studies, Monterey Inst. Internat. Studies, 1987. Reporter Imperial Valley Press, El Centro, Calif., 1987-91; bus. reporter The Desert Sun, Palm Springs, Calif., 1991-94, The Press-Enterprise, Riverside, Calif., 1994-98; pub. rels. mgr. U.S. Filter Corp., Palm Desert, Calif., 1998—. Mem. Latino adv. com. Cmty. Blood Bank, Rancho Mirage, Calif., 1993. Recipient award Calif. Newspaper Pubs. Assn. Mem. Soc. Profl. Journalists (bd. dirs. Inland Profl. chpt. 1996—), Sigma Delta Pi, Alpha Mu Gamma. Democrat. Roman Catholic. Avocations: photography, backpacking, cross-country skiing, study history and foreign languages. Office: US Filter Corp 40-004 Cook St Palm Desert CA 92211

CRIDER, ROBERT AGUSTINE, international financier, law enforcement official; b. Washington, Jan. 3, 1935; s. Rana Albert and Terasa Helen (Dampf) C.; student law enforcement U. Md., 1959-63; m. Debbie Ann Lee, Feb. 1960. Police officer Met. Police Dept., Washington, 1957-67; substitute tchr., bldg. trades instr. Maries R-1 Sch., Vienna, Mo., 1968-70; vets. constrn. tng. officer VA Dept. Edn., Mo., 1968-70; constrn. mgr. Tectonics Ltd., Vienna, 1970-79; owner, dir. R-A Crider & Assocs., St. Louis, 1979—; bd. dirs. TI-CO Investment Corp., Langcaster Corp. Served with USAF, 1952-56. Mem. Assn. Ret. Policemen, Internat. Conf. Police, Internat. Assn. Chiefs of Police, Nat. Police Assn., World Future Soc., Internat. Platform Assn., Mo. Police Chiefs Assn., Mo. Sheriff's Assn., Am. Correctional Assn., Law Enforcement Intelligence Assn., Internat. Drug Enforcement Assn., Nat. Assn. Fin. Cons., Internat. Soc. Financiers, Am. Legion, St. Louis Honor Guard. Roman Catholic. Clubs: Lions, K.C. (4th deg.). Home: PO Box 109 Vienna MO 65582-0109 Office: R-A Crider & Assocs PO Box 3459 2644 Roseland Ter Saint Louis MO 63143-2304

CRIGLER, B. WAUGH, federal judge; b. Charlottesville, Va., July 17, 1948; s. Bernard Weaver and Jayne (Waugh) C.; m. Anne Kendall, June 20, 1970; children: C. Kendall, Jason C., Anne Stuart. BA in History, Washington & Lee U., 1970; JD, U. Tenn., 1973. Bar: Tenn. 1973, U.S. Dist. Ct. (ea. dist.) Tenn. 1973, Va. 1974, D.C. 1974, U.S. Dist. Ct. (we. and ea. dists.) Va. 1975, U.S. Ct. Appeals (4th cir.) 1978, U.S. Supreme Ct. 1979. Law clk. to presiding judge U.S. Dist. Ct. Tenn., Knoxville, 1973-74; ptnr. Lea & Crigler, Culpeper, Va., 1974-75, Lea, Davies, Crigler & Barrell, Culpeper, 1975-79, Davies, Crigler, Barrell & Will, PC, Culpeper, 1979-81; magistrate judge U.S. Dist. Ct., Charlottesville, 1981—; instr. trial practice Sch. Law, U. Va., 1986—; mem. criminal rules adv. com. Jud. Conf. U.S., 1992-97; mem. Fed.-State Jud. Coun., Va., 1992—. Mem. ABA (criminal law com. young lawyers divsn. 1974-80), Thomas Jefferson Inn of Ct. (pres. 1991-92), Va. State Bar (standing com. on professionalism 1997—), Va. Bar Assn. (chmn. criminal law corrections young lawyers divsn. 1979-80), Tenn. Bar Assn., Order of Coif, Phi Kappa Phi. Avocations: landscaping, swimming, Biblical studies. Home: 100 Peterson Pl Charlottesvle VA 22901-3175 Office: US Magistrate Judge 255 W Main St Rm 328 Charlottesville VA 22902-5058

CRIHFIELD, PHILIP J., lawyer; b. Chgo., Ill., Oct. 3, 1945. BS with highest distinction, Purdue U., 1967; JD with honors, John Marshall Law Sch., 1971. Bar: Ill. 1971, U.S. Patents and Trademark Office 1972. Ptnr. Sidley & Austin, Chgo.; adj. prof. mktg. and pub. policy Northwestern U., 1986—. Mem. Chgo. Bar Assn. (chmn. law, sci., tech. com. 1975). Office: Sidley & Austin 1 First Natl Plz Chicago IL 60603-2003*

CRILLEY, JOSEPH JAMES, artist; b. Phila., Jan. 8, 1920; s. James John and Anna (Spoerl) C.; m. Marion Gertrude Haly, Jan. 31, 1948 (div.); children: Pamela, Geraldine, Candace, Joseph; m. Suzanne Corlette, Aug. 16, 1982. Student, Phila. Coll. Art, 1938-61. Art tchr. New Hope (Pa.)-Solebury High Sch., 1955-61; photographer William J. Keller, Inc., Buffalo, 1960-71. Photographer: New York, Island of Islands, 1965; one-man exhibn. Lambertville (N.J., 1976-80, 82-85, Coryell Gallery, Lambertville, 1981, Kiski Sch., Saltsburg, Pa., 1985, Genest Gallery, Lambertville, 1986-90, Phila. Sketch Club, 1990; exhibited in group shows at Nat. Acad. of Design, N.Y.C., Phila., Art and Alliance, Phila. Mus. of Art, Michener Art Mus., Doylestown, Pa., Mystic, Conn., others; represented in permanent collections at Kiski Sch., Atlantic Salmon Mus., Cape Breton, N.S., Can., Australia, France, others. Capt. AUS, 1942-45, ETO. Recipient 64 awards including Best of Show, 1983, New Hope Bar Seal, 1984, New Hope Arts Commn. Competition, 3 Gold medals, 1980-95, DaVinci Art Alliance Phila., Award of Excellence, 1991, 29th Mystic Internat., Conn., Anthony Cirino award 1992, Grumbacher Gold medal, 1996, Audubon Artists, N.Y., 15 awards 1962-95 Salmagundi Club, N.Y., 3 awards 1985-95, Phila. Sketch Club, Pa. Mem. Audubon Artists, Phila. Sketch Club, DaVinci Arts Alliance. Avocations: fly fishing, skiing.

CRILLY, EUGENE RICHARD, engineering consultant; b. Phila., Oct. 30, 1923; s. Eugene John and Mary Virginia (Harvey) C.; m. Alice Royal Roth, Feb. 16, 1952. ME, Stevens Inst. Tech., 1944, MS, 1949; MS, U. Penn., 1951; postgrad., UCLA, 1955-58. Sr. rsch. engr. N.Am. Aviation, L.A., 1954-57, Canoga Park and Downey, Calif., 1962-66; process engr. Northrop Aircraft Corp., Hawthorne, Calif., 1957-59; project engr., quality assurance mgr. HITCO, Gardena, Calif., 1959-62; sr. rsch. splist. Lockheed-Calif. Co., Burbank, Calif., 1966-74; engring. splist. N.Am. aircraft ops. Rockwell Internat., El Segundo, Calif., 1974-89. Author tech. papers. Mem. nat. com. 125th Anniversary Founding of Stevens Inst. Tech. in 1870. Served with USNR, 1943-46; comdr. Res. ret. Mem. Soc. for Advancement Material and Process Engring. (chmn. L.A. chpt. 1978-79, gen. chmn. 1981 symposium exhbn., nat. dir. 1979-86, treas. 1982-85, Award of Merit 1986), Naval Inst., ASM Internat., Naval Res. Assn., VFW, Mil. Order World Wars (adj. San Fernando Valley chpt. 1985, 2d vice comdr. 1986, commdr. 1987-89, vice comdr. West, Dept. Cen. Calif., 1988-89, comdr. Cajon Valley San Diego chpt. 1990-92, adj./ROTC chmn. region XIV 1990-91, comdr. Dept. So. Calif. 1991-93, vice comdr. regionXIV, 1992-93, dept. comdr. Gen. Staff Officer region XIV 1993-94, comdr. region XIV, 1994-95, Disting. Chpt. Comdr. Region XIV 1990-91, treas. region XIV 1998-99, treas. San Diego chpt. 1999—), Former Intelligence Officers Assn. (treas. San Diego chpt. one 1990-94), Ret. Officers Assn. (treas. Silver Strand chpt. 1992—, asst. treas. Convention 2000), Navy League U.S. (treas. Coronado coun. 1997—), Naval Order U.S., Naval Intelligence Profls. Assn., Brit. United Svc. Club L.A., Marines Meml. Club (San Francisco), Coronado Round Table, Hammer Club of San Diego, Sigma Xi, Sigma Nu. Republican. Roman Catholic. Home and Office: 276 J Ave Coronado CA 92118-1138

CRIM, GARY ALLEN, dental educator; b. Louisville, Ky., July 13, 1949; s. John W. Crim and Ruby M. Willis. DMD, U. Ky., 1974; MS in Dentistry, Ind. U., 1981. Asst. prof. U. Louisville Sch. Dentistry, 1981, assoc. prof., 1987-93, prof., chmn., 1993—. Contbr. articles to profl. jours. Mem. ADA, Internat. Assn. Dental Rsch., Am. Assn. Dental Schs., Acad. Operative Dentistry. Avocations: reading. Office: U Louisville Sch Dentistry 501 S Preston St Louisville KY 40202-1701

CRIMI, PAUL, artist; b. Boston, Dec. 22, 1943; s. Joseph Vincent and Mary Joyce Crimi; m. Mary Ellen Service, June 12, 1965; children: Christopher, Ellen, Jon Paul, Gina. Student, Boston Mus., 1963-65, 76-77. One-man shows include Marina Bay Gallery, Quincy, Mass., 1987, Heritage Plantation Mus., Boston, 1987, Sailor Valentine Gallery, Nantucket, Mass., 1988, Lonborg-Feeney Gallery, Scituate, Mass., 1989, Milton (Mass.) Art Mus., 1990, Bibl. Arts Ctr., Dallas, 1990, 92, Michael Allen Gallery, Brookline, Mass., 1992, Pyramid Gallery, Sarasota, Fla., 1993, The Eclipse Salon Gallery, Boston, 1997; group shows include Colors of the Morning Gallery, Palm Beach, Fla., 1986, Art Intentions Gallery, Hanover, Mass., 1987, Helene Gallery, Fairfax, Calif., 1989, The Frame it Center and Gallery, Milton, Mass., 1989, Yankee Book and Art Gallery, Plymouth, Mass., 1990, The Barn at Barnbook, Cohasset, Mass., 1992, Winthrop (Mass.) Art Assn., 1995, Agora Gallery, Soho, N.Y., 1995, Fuller Mus., Brockton, Mass., 1996, Art Store, W.Va., 1997; represented in permanent collections Adolph Bauer, Inc., Boston Globe, Ralston Purina, Inc., Patrica Cancannon, Kodak, N.Y., Marshfield Hills, Atty. Jack Atwood, Atty. F. Lee Bailey, Cardinal Medeiros, Boston, Sta. WGBH, Boston, among others. Recipient Winsor and Newton Aquamedia award, 1992, 2d Watercolor prize Carl Betz South Shore Art Ctr., 1992. Mem. Boston Print Makers. Studio: 185 Plain St Rt 139 Rockland MA 02339

CRIMINALE, WILLIAM OLIVER, JR., applied mathematics educator; b. Mobile, Ala., Nov. 29, 1933; s. William Oliver and Vivian Gertrude (Sketoe) C.; m. Ulrike Irmgard Wegner, June 7, 1962; children: Martin Oliver, Lucca. B.S., U. Ala., 1955; Ph.D., Johns Hopkins U., 1960. Asst. prof. Princeton (N.J.) U., 1962-68; asso. prof. U. Wash., Seattle, 1968-73; prof. oceanography, geophysics, applied math. U. Wash., 1973—, chmn. dept. applied math., 1976-84; cons. Aerospace Corp., 1963-65, Boeing Corp., 1968-72, AGARD, 1967-68, Lenox Hill Hosp., 1967-68, ICASE, NASA Langley, 1990—; guest prof., Can., 1965, France, 1967-68, Germany, 1973-74, Sweden, 1973-74, Scotland, 1985, 89, 91, Eng., 1990, 91, Stanford, 1990, Brazil, 1992, Italy, 1999; Nat. Acad. exch. scientist, USSR, 1969, 72. Author: Stability of Parallel Flows, 1967; Contbr. articles to profl. jours. Served with U.S. Army, 1961-62. Boris A. Bakmeteff Meml. fellow, 1957-58, NATO postdoctoral fellow, 1960-61, Alexander von Humboldt Sr. fellow, 1973-74, Royal Soc. fellow, 1990-91. Fellow Am. Phys. Soc.; mem. AAAS, Am. Geophys. Union, Fedn. Am. Scientists. Home: 1635 Peach Ct E Seattle WA 98112-3428 Office: U Wash Dept Applied Math Box 352420 Seattle WA 98195-2420

CRIMMINS, PHILIP PATRICK, metallurgical engineer, lawyer; b. Poughkeepsie, N.Y., Aug. 1, 1930; s. Philip Patrick and Eva (Booth) C.; m. Janet E. Ballou, Feb. 14, 1953; children: Lisa Jane, Philip Patrick, Michael Mathew. B.S., MIT, 1952; M.S., Wayne State U., 1959; J.D., U. Pacific, 1972. Registered profl. metall. engr. Metall. engr. Ford Motor Co., Livonia, Mich., 1954-58; dir. engring. Aerojet Space Boosters, Sacramento, 1958-95. Served with AUS, 1952-54. Recipient William Sparagen award Am. Welding Soc., 1968. Calif. Fellow Am. Inst. Chemists; mem. Am. Soc. Metals, Fed., Am., Calif. bar assns. Home: 9113 Rosewood Dr Sacramento CA 95826-4526

CRIMMINS, SEAN T(HOMAS), oil company executive; b. Pitts., Sept. 2, 1945; s. John Michael and Catherine Lucille (O'Malley) C.; m. Susan Davidson, June 24, 1989; children: Brendan, Angie, Tammy, Latisha. BA, U. Notre Dame, 1967, JD, 1972. Bar: Ill. 1972, Pa. 1978, Ky. 1985. Assoc. Mayer, Brown & Platt, Chgo., 1972-77; mgr. tax reorgn. Gulf Oil Co., Pitts., 1978-84; dir. tax planning Ashland (Ky.) Inc. (formerly Ashland Oil Inc.), 1984-88, v.p., gen. tax counsel, 1988-98; gen. tax counsel-oil products Shell Oil Co., Houston, 1998—. Mem. Ill. Bar Assn., Pa. Bar Assn., Ky. Bar Assn., Boyd County Bar Assn., Bellefonte Country Club. Avocation: golf. Home: 3401 Audubon Pl Houston TX 77006-4411 Office: Shell Oil Co PO Box 2463 Houston TX 77252*

CRINO, MARJANNE HELEN, anesthesiologist; b. Rochester, N.Y., Aug. 18, 1933; d. Michael Jay and Helen Barbara (Kennedy) C.; m. Michael Anthony La Iuppa, Nov. 12, 1960 (dec. Feb. 1996); children: James Michael, Barbara Anne, John Christopher. BS, Coll. St. Teresa, 1955; MD, Med. Coll. Wis., 1959; MA in Theology, St. Bernard's Inst., 1991. Diplomate Nat. Bd. Med. Examiners. House staff Genesee Hosp., Rochester, 1959-61; perinatal mortality rsch., resident in anesthesiology Jackson Meml Hosp.-U. Miami, 1962-65; attending staff in anesthesiology Genesee Hosp., Rochester, N.Y., 1969—; mem. exec. com., med. staff sec., 1980, 82; acting chmn. dept. anesthesiology Genesee Hosp., Rochester, N.Y., 1989, 91, chmn. pain control com., 1989-95; clin. instr. anesthesiology U. Rochester Sch. Medicine, 1983—; cons. anesthesiology Rochester Psychiat. Ctr., 1975-85; instr. anesthesiology U. Miami Sch. medicine, 1966, 67; attending staff anesthesiology Jackson Meml. Hosp., Miami, 1966, 67. Mem. adv. bd. Isaiah House Hosp., 1994—, com. Pittsford (N.Y.) Rep. Party, 1970's-80's; vol. chaplain Genesee Hosp. Mem. N.Y. State Soc. Anesthesiologists (bd. dirs., vice spkr. 1983-86, del. 1971-82, 87—), Am. Soc. Anesthesiologists (del. 1979-86, 97), AMA, N.Y. State Med. Soc., Med. Soc. County of Monroe, Rochester Acad. Medicine, Cath. Physicians Guild Rochester (bd.dirs., pres. 1988-89), Margaret Roper Guild (pres. 1975-76), Cath. Women's Club (Diocese of Rochester). Roman Catholic. Avocations: reading, gardening, music. Office: Genesee Hosp Dept Anesthesiology 224 Alexander St Rochester NY 14607-4055 *Whether you are dealing with a large group, a small gathering or a single person, don't worry about the impression you are making or how uncomfortable you are. Try to find some way to make the others comfortable. You will never go wrong.*

CRIPE, WYLAND SNYDER, veterinary medicine educator, consultant; b. Flora, Ind., Aug. 5, 1921; s. Ezra Cripe and Ruth (Olive) Snyder; m. Marnelle Filippini, June 20, 1943; children: Aline, Carra, Kirsti, Elizabeth, Anna. AB, Stanford U., 1946; BS, U. Calif., Davis, 1950, DVM, 1952. Vet. practitioner Elk Grove (Calif.) Vet. Ctr., 1952-68; dir. vet. medicine Chile-Calif. Univ. Program, Santiago, 1968-70; assoc. dean students U. Calif. Sch. Vet. Medicine, Davis, 1970-71; team leader UN program FAO, Barinas, Venezuela, 1971-73; asst. dean students and pub. svcs. U. Fla. Coll. Vet. Medicine, Gainesville, 1973-89; retirement cons. Micanopy, Fla., 1989—. Contbr. articles to profl. jours. Pres. sch. bd. Elk Grove Unified Sch. Dist., 1953-68, Sacramento County, 1965-67; pres. Micanopy Hist. Soc., 1995—. Comdr. USN, 1942-45. Recipient Aviation medal Forca Area Brasileira, Brasil, 1983, UCD Alumni Emil M. Mark Internat. award, 1994. Mem. AVMA (Internat. Vet. Congress prize 1987), Fla. Vet. Medicine Assn., Sacramento Valley Vet. Medicine Assn., Sacramento Valley Vet. Medicine Assn. (pres. 1966-68), Bovine Practitioner Assn., Internat. Buffalo Fedn. (standing com. 1985—, Internat. Sci. medal 1985, Honra Mérito 1994), Gammma Sigma Delta. Democrat. Avocations: fishing, aviation gliders. Home: 22859 NW 87th Avenue Rd Micanopy FL 32667-7443

CRIPPEN, RAYMOND CHARLES, chemist, consultant; b. Bklyn., Mar. 1, 1917; s. Charles H. and Betty B. (Brixner) C.; m. Helen L. Wolf, July 5, 1941; children: Lawrence J., Judith Ann Frisco. BS in Chemistry, Iowa State U., 1939; MS in Chem. Engring., Johns Hopkins U., 1948; PhD in Analytical Chemistry, St. Thomas Inst., 1970. Chemist Allied Chem., Chgo., 1939-41; chemist, group leader E. I. dupont de Nemours & co., Ft. Madison, Iowa, 1941-45; cons. rsch. and devel. Penniman and Browne, Inc., Balt., 1948-49; head of lab. Crippen Labs., Inc., Balt., 1949-61; group leader rsch. and devel. Atlas Chem. Industries, Inc., Wilmington, Del., 1961-66; section head Stauffer Chem. Co., Silicones, Adrian, Mich., 1966-68; head methods devel. dept. Richardson-Merrell Co., Cin., 1968-70; instr. North Ky. State U., Highland Heights, 1970-75; pres. Crippen Labs., Inc., 1975-87; cons. Cecon Group, Inc., Wilmington, 1987-95; pres. Crippen Consulting Co., Hockessin, Del., 1995—; mem. Tel-Tech Internat. Info Sci. Telephone Group. Author: ID of Organic Compounds, 1973, GC/LC Instr., Deriv. in ID Pollut., 1983, The Waste of Money (How to Avoid It), 1983; contbr. articles to profl. jours.; patentee in field. Inducted into Profl. and Exec. Hall of Fame, Orlando, Fla., 1967. Fellow Am. Inst. Chemists (cert. profl. com. pin 1983-87); mem. ASTM (com. mem. 1954—), Am. Chem. Soc. (editor/chemist Md. sect. 1949-61, asst. editor DelChem Bull. Del. sect. 1961-66), Soc. Appl. Spect. (chmn. 1964-65), Dickinson Theatre Organ Soc., St. Tropez Condo Owners Assn. Republican. Methodist. Achievements include patent for device for application to environment; development of Grecian Formula 16, Aspercreme, Charles Antell Hair Care Preparations. Home and Office: Oak Crest Village 4601 Hampton Pl 8800 Walther Blvd Baltimore MD 21234

CRIPPENS, DAVID LEE, broadcast executive; b. Nashville, Sept. 23, 1942; s. Nathaniel and Dorothy (Sharp) C.; m. Eloise Brown, Aug. 3, 1968; 1 child, Gerald Chinua. BA in Polit. Sci., Antioch Coll., 1964; MSW, San Diego State U., 1968. Vol. Peace Corps, Nigeria, 1964-66; assoc. dir. ednl. opportunities program San Diego State U., 1968-69; producer KPBS-TV, San Diego, 1969-71; staff producer, writer, newsperson WQED-TV, Pitts., 1971-73; dir. ednl. svc. KCET, L.A., 1973-77, v.p. ednl. svc., 1977-80, v.p., sta. mgr., 1980-83, v.p. nat. prodns., 1983-85, sr. v.p. ednl. enterprises, 1985—; Rufus Putnam vis. prof. Ohio U. Sch. Telecommunications, Athens, fall 1995. Exec. producer Count On Me, New American Work Force, Not the Way to Go/Get a Life, Begingin the Journey, Giving Care Taking Care, Community Under Siege, Mindworks; contbr. articles to profl. publs. Bd. dirs. Unite-LA, Inroads L.A.; mem. Editl. Projects in Edn. Bd.; mem. Gov.'s Sch.-to-Career Adv. Coun. Recipient Excellence in Edn. Commendation award Calif. Poly. Black Faculty and Staff Assn., 1991, Prin.'s Orgn. award Sr. High Sch. Prins., 1991, honor Assn. Adminstrs. L.A., 1988, Calif. Coalition for Pub. Edn., 1987, Nat. Assn. Media Women, 1986, Calif. Assembly Legis. Com., 1971, San Diego State Black Student Coun., 1971, named One of Pitts.' Most Influential Blacks, Pitts. Post Gazette, 1973, Outstanding Ednl. Leadership award Phi Delta Kappa, 1992, Nat. Citation award, 1993, Positive Image award Frank D. Parent PTA, 1992, John Senett award for outstanding coverage of educational concerns Calif. Tchrs. Assn., 1993, Martin award INROADS, L.A., Inc., 1996, award for outstanding coverage of pub. edn. Calif. Assn. Calif. Sch. Adminstrs., 1998. Home: 5252 W 64th St Inglewood CA 90302-1016 Office: KCET 4401 W Sunset Blvd Los Angeles CA 90027-6090

CRIPPS, KATHY HICKEY, public relations company official; b. Bklyn., Feb. 2, 1951; d. Thomas Joseph and Maureen (Kane) Hickey; m. Robert F. Cripps, Jan. 16, 1971. B.A., Queens Coll., 1973; M.B.A., Fordham U., 1983. Sr. home economist Nestle Co., N.Y.C., 1974-76; dir. product info. Farberware, Bronx, 1976-82; v.p., client service mgr. Burson-Marsteller, N.Y.C., 1982-99, pres., COO, 1999—. Mem. Home Economists in Bus. (controller 1980-82, NE region dir. 1984-86), Women in Communications. Home: 50 Parkview Dr Bronxville NY 10708-4608 Office: Sciens Worldwide 105 Madison Ave New York NY 10016-7418*

CRISCENTI, JOSEPH THOMAS, retired history educator; s. Salvatore Criscenti; m. Jacqueline L. Penez, Sept. 3, 1956; 1 child, Louise J. PhB, U. Detroit, 1942; MA, Harvard U., 1947, PhD, 1956. Assoc. prof. Boston Coll., Chestnut Hill, Mass., 1955-88; prof. emeritus Boston Coll., Chestnut Hill, 1988—; cons. CORE Collection, ALA, 1971-72; mem. case study Hispanic Divsn., Libr. of Congress, 1995-96. Author, editor: Sarmiento and His Argentina, 1993; contbg. editor Handbook of Latin American Studies, 1984-96; contbr. Encyclopedia of Latin American History and Culture, 1996. Tech. sgt. U.S. Army Adjutant Gen. Corps, 1942-46, PTO. Mem. Am. Hist. Assn., Conf. of L.Am. History (chmn. Robertson prize com. 1962, 73, Robertson prize 1962), New Eng. Coun. on L.Am. Studies (sec.-treas. 1972-93, sec.-treas. emeritus 1994—, Joseph T. Criscenti prize 1994). Home: 28 Richard Rd Needham MA 02492-4322

CRISCI, MATHEW G., marketing executive, writer; b. N.Y.C.; s. Mathew Anthony and Frances (Coscia) C.; m. Mary Ann, Nov. 14, 1968; children: Mathew Joseph, Mark David, Mitchell Justin. BS, Iona Coll. Sr. v.p. Young & Rubicam, Inc., N.Y.C. and Sydney, Australia, 1968-82; exec. v.p., COO, bd. dirs. Integrated Barter Internat., N.Y.C., 1982-85; sr. v.p., gen. mgr., bd. dirs. Chiat/Day Advt. Inc., San Francisco, 1986-90; exec. v.p. Ammirati Puris Lintas, N.Y.C., 1991-96; exec. v.p. Alton Entertainment Co., L.A. and Miami Beach, Fla., 1996—, also bd. dirs. Author: Observations of a Kind, 1998. Mem. Nat. Assn. H.S. Newspapers (mng. dir. 1996—, bd. dirs.). E-mail: mcrisci-orcapub@msw.com. Office: Alton 530 Lincoln Rd Miami Beach FL 33139-2985

CRISCIMAGNA, NED HENRY, mechanical engineer; b. Madison, Wis., Dec. 24, 1942; s. Frank Salvatore and Grace Mary Rose (Stancampiano) C.; m. Sandra Anne Kratina, June 19, 1965; children: Christine Marie Brent, Matthew Sean. BSME, U. Nebr., 1965; MS in Sys. Engring., Air Force Inst. Tech., 1970. Cert. reliability engr. Apprentice engr. Henningson, Durham & Richardson, Omaha, 1965; commd. 2d lt. USAF, 1965, advanced through grades to lt. col., 1981, ret., 1985; staff prin. engr. ARINC Rsch. Corp., Annapolis, Md., 1985-93; sr. engr. ITT Rsch. Inst., Lanham, Md., 1993—; mem. US TAG to IEC TC56, 1995—, chair Z-1 dependability subcom., 1997—. Co-author: Product Reliability, Maintainability, and Supportability Handbook, 1995. Treas. Homeowners Assn., Annapolis, 1995—; mem. Annapolis Chorale, 1990—; mem., lector St. Anne's Episcopal Ch., Annapolis, 1987—. Mem. Internat. Soc. Logistics (sr., cert.), Am. Soc. Quality (cert. reliability engr.), Soc. Automotive Engrs., Order Sons of Italy in Am. (v.p. 1997—). Avocations: college football, coin and stamp collecting, photography, music, computer simulation games. Home: 307 S Cherry Grove Ave Annapolis MD 21401-4234 Office: ITT Rsch Inst 4409 Forbes Blvd Lanham MD 20706-4328

CRISCUOLO, WENDY LAURA, lawyer, interior design consultant; b. N.Y.C., Dec. 17, 1949; d. Joseph Andrew and Betty Jane (Jackson) C.; m. John Howard Price, Jr., Sept. 5, 1970 (div. Apr. 1981); m. Ross J. Turner, July 23, 1988. BA with honors in Design, U. Calif., Berkeley, 1973; JD, U. San Francisco, 1982. Space planner GSA, San Francisco, 1973-79; sr. interior designer E. Lew & Assocs., San Francisco, 1979-80; design dir. Beier & Gunderson, Inc., Oakland, Calif., 1980-81; sr. interior designer Environ. Planning and Rsch., San Francisco, 1981-82; interior design cons. Rancho Santa Fe, Calif., 1982—; law clk. to Judge Spencer Williams U.S. Dist. Ct., San Francisco, 1983-84; atty. Ciros Investments, Rancho Santa Fe, Calif., 1984—. Author: (with others) Guide to the Laws of Charitable Giving, 3d rev. edit., 1983; staff mem. U. San Francisco Law Rev., 1983. Bd. dirs., v.p. and treas. Marin Citizens for Energy Planning, 1986-89; bd. dirs., pres. Calif. Ctr. for Wildlife, 1987-90; trustee Coyote Point Mus. for Environ. Edn., 1990-93. Mem. State Bar Calif. Episcopalian. Avocation: creative writing.

CRISER, MARSHALL M., lawyer, retired university president; b. Rumson, N.J., Sept. 4, 1928; s. Marshall and Louise (Johnson) C.; m. Paula Porcher, Apr. 27, 1957; children: Marshall III, Edward, Mary, Glenn, Kimberly, Mark. BBA, U. Fla., 1951, LLB, 1951 (replaced by J.D., 1967). Bar: Fla. 1951. Pvt. practice Palm Beach, 1953-84; ptnr. Gunster, Yoakley, Criser & Stewart, 1955-84; atty. Palm Beach County Sch. Bd., 1958-64; pres. U. Fla., Gainesville, 1984-89, pres. emeritus, 1989—; shareholder Mahoney, Adams & Criser, Jacksonville, Fla., 1989-97; of counsel McGuire, Woods Battle, & Boothe, LLP, Jacksonville, 1998—; bd. dirs. Flagler System, Inc., Perini Corp., FPL Group, Inc., CSR Am.; mem. pres.'s coun. NCAA, 1986-87; chmn. Installment Land Sales Bd., 1963-64, chmn. Acad. Task Force rev. tort and ins. law, Fla., 1986-88, The Emerald Funds; chmn. bd. trustees Emerald Fund, 1997-98. Bd. dirs. Shands at Jacksonville Hosp., 1999—, Shands Tchg. Hosp., Gainesville, Fla., pres., 1984-89, bd. govs., 1996—; bd. govs. Good Samaritan Hosp., West Palm Beach, pres., 1979-84; bd. dirs. Univ. Med. Ctr., Jacksonville, 1989-96; mem. Fla. Bd. Regents, 1965, 71-81, chmn., 1974-77, Bus.-Higher Edn. Forum, 1987-89; trustee Collins Ctr., 1989—, M.E. Rinker Found., 1998—; pres. Alliance for World Class Edn., Duval County, 1998—; chmn. Fed. Crt. Adv. Group Mid. Dist. of Fla., 1991-96. With U.S. Army, 1951-53. Fellow Am. Bar Found.; mem. Fla. Coun. 100 (chmn. 1979-80), ABA (ho. dels. 1968-72), Fla. Bar (gov. 1960-68, pres. 1968-69), Fla. Blue Key, Phi Delta Phi, Sigma Nu. Home: 4588 Swilcan Bridge Ln Jacksonville FL 32224 Office: McGuire Woods Battle Et Al 3400 Barnett Ctr Jacksonville FL 32201

CRISHAM, THOMAS MICHAEL, lawyer; b. Chgo., June 7, 1939; s. John and Ellen (Moore) C.; m. Catherine Marie Schaab, Oct. 2, 1965; children: Catherine Marie, Megan, Maura. BBA, Loyola U., 1962, JD cum laude, 1965. Bar: Ill. 1965, U.S. Dist. Ct. (no. dist.) Ill. 1965, U.S. Supreme Ct. 1971, U.S. Ct. Appeals (7th crct.) 1978. Ptnr. Hinshaw & Culbertson, Chgo., 1965-95; sr. ptnr. Quinlan & Crisham, Ltd., Chgo., 1996—; mem. editorial bd. Ins. Outlook, Colorado Springs, Colo., 1990; pres. Def. Rsch. and Trial Lawyers Inst., Chgo., 1989, chmn. bd., 1990; mem. advisors Expert Evidence Reporter, Colorado Springs, 1990. Contbg. author: Abortion and Social Justice, 1973, Human Life: Our Legacy and Our Challenge, 1975, Architect and Engineer Liability: Claims Against Design Professional, 1987, Prosecuting and Defending Insurance Claims, 1989. Bd. dirs. Wendy Will Case Cancer Rsch. Found., Boys' Hope Scholars. With USMCR, 1959-60. Fellow Am. Coll. Trial Lawyers, Internat. Soc. Barristers; mem. ABA, Am. Bd. Trial Advs. (diplomate), Def. Rsch. Inst. (pres. 1989-90, chair 1990-91), Internat. Assn. Def. Counsel, Ill. Bar Assn., Trial Lawyers Club Chgo. (pres. 1975-76), Soc. Trial Lawyers Ill., Appellate Lawyers Assn., Assn. Def. Trial Lawyers, Am. Inns of Ct. Roman Catholic. Office: Quinlan & Crisham Ltd 30 N LaSalle St Ste 2900 Chicago IL 60602

CRISLER, PAUL RICHARD, retired auditor; b. Dayton, Ohio, Feb. 13, 1938; s. Charles Author and Edwina Ann (Seibert) C.; m. Margaret Lynn Saaler, May 9, 1964 (div. Nov. 1991); children: David Vincent, Patrick Joseph. Assoc. Acctg., Miami Jacobs Coll., 1968; B Acctg., Sinclair Coll., 1972. Surg. asst. Miami Valley Hosp., Dayton, Ohio, 1957-64; acctg. clk. Sterling Rubber Products, Dayton, 1964-66; auditor, acct. Hooven-Allison Co., Xenia, Ohio, 1966-74; asst. state auditor State of Ohio, Dayton, 1974-98; ret., 1998. Mem. Internat. Assn. Cert. Fraud Examiners. Democrat.

CRISMAN, D'ETTA MARIE, nursing administrator, chemical dependency and psychiatric nurse; b. Chattanooga, Nov. 2, 1950; d. Bryan a. and Marie (Chambers) C. Student, David Lipscomb U., 1969-72, St. Joseph's Hosp. Sch. Nursing, 1973; BSN, Union U., 1977. RNC. Crisis support nurse, nurse therapist Whitehaven S.W. Mental Health Ctr.; nurse therapist Dr. C. Tom Rhodes, MD, Memphis; night tour coord. VA Med. Ctr., Memphis, 1983, 88-90; weekend supr. Parkwood Hosp., Olive Branch, Miss., 1991; evening charge nurse gero psychiatry Calif. Pacific Med. Ctr., San Francisco, 1991—; weekend charge nurse/adult mental health nurse, relief supr. Mid-South Hosp., Memphis, 1991-93; psychiat. nurse instr. Memphis State U., 1993—; charge nurse addiction unit Memphis Mental Health Inst. Dept. Mental Health, State of Tenn., Memphis, 1993—; disaster nurse Am. Red Cross; vol. RN mid south chpt. Nat. Multiple Sclerosis Soc., 1994—. Mem. ANA (cert. psychiat. and mental health nurse), Tenn. Nurse's Assn., Nat. Nurse's Soc. on Addiction. Home: 1025 Kings Park Rd Memphis TN 38117-5433 Office: The General Corp 4646 Poplar Ave Ste 327 Memphis TN 38117-4433

CRISMAN, MARY FRANCES BORDEN, librarian; b. Tacoma, Nov. 23, 1919; d. Lindon A. and Mary Cecelia (Donnelly) Borden; m. Fredric Lee Crisman, Apr. 12, 1975 (dec. Dec. 1975). BA in History, U. Wash., 1943, BA in Librarianship, 1944. Asst. br. librarian in charge work with children Mottet br. Tacoma Pub. Libr., 1944-45, br. librarian, 1945-49, br. librarian Moore br., 1950-55, asst. dir., 1955-70, dir., 1970-74, dir. emeritus, 1975—; mgr. corp. libr. Frank Russell Co., 1985-96, ret., 1997; chmn. Wash. Community Library Council, 1970-72. Hostess program Your Library and You, Sta. KTPS-TV, 1969-71. Mem. Highland Homeowners League, Tacoma, 1980—, incorporating dir. 1980, sec. and registered agt., 1980-82. Mem. ALA (chmn. mem. com. Wash. 1957-60, mem. nat. library week com. 1965, chmn. library adminstrn. div. nominating com. 1971, mem. ins. for libraries com. 1970-74, vice chmn. library adminstrn. div. personnel adminstrn. sect. 1972-73, chmn. 1973-74, mem. com. policy implementation 1973-74, mem. library orgn. and mgmt. sect. budgeting acctg. and costs com. 1974-75), Am. Library Trustee Assn. (legis. com. 1975-78, conf. program com. 1978-80, action devel. com. 1978-80), Pacific N.W. (trustee div. nominating com 1976-77), Wash. Library Assn. (exec. bd. 1957-59, state exec., dir. Nat. Library Week 1965, treas., exec. bd. 1969-71, 71-73), Urban Libraries Council (editorial sec. Newsletter 1972-73, exec. com. 1974-75), Ladies Aux. to United Transp. Union (past pres. Tacoma), Friends Tacoma Pub. Library (registered agt. 1975-83, sec. 1975-78, pres. 1978-80, bd. dir. 1980-83), Smithsonian Assocs., Nat. Railway Hist. Soc., U. Wash. Alumni Assn., U. Wash. Sch. Librarianship Alumni Assn. Roman Catholic. Club: Quota Internat. (sec. 1957-58, 1st v.p. 1960-61, pres. 1961-62, treas. 1975-76, pres. 1979-80) (Tacoma). Home: 6501 N Burning Tree Ln Tacoma WA 98406-2108 also: 9054 N 109th Ave Sun City AZ 85351-4676

CRISMAN CARLSON, RUTH MARIE, writer; b. Oak Park, Ill., June 16, 1914; d. John Henry and Ruth Ethel (Stiles) Thorup; m. James Lester Crisman July 7, 1941 (dec. 1992); children: Carol Ann, James Alan; m. Lennart Carlson, Feb. 6, 1993 (dec. 1998). BA in Elem. Edn., Calif. State Coll., L.A., 1966, MA in Elem. Edn., 1971, MA, 1976. Cert. tchr. reading, elem. edn. Dental asst. Dr. Bartram, L.A., 1931-41; dental clerk, typist, libr. clerk, 1954-65; tchr. L.A. City Schs., 1966-79. Author: The Mississippi Franklin Watts, 1984, Hot Off the Press, 1991, Thomas Jefferson, a Biography, 1992, Racing the Iditarod Trail, 1993; contbr. articles to newspapers, publs. Recipient PEN award. Mem. Soc. Children's Book Writers and Illustrators, Nat. League Am. PEN Women (pres. L.A. chpt. 1994-98), Calif. Fedn. Chaparral Poets, Calif. Writers Club, Pi Lambda Theta, Alpha Psi. Republican. Methodist. Avocations: line dancing, gardening.

CRISMOND, LINDA FRY, public relations executive; b. Burbank, Calif., Mar. 1, 1943; d. Billy Chapin and Lois (Harding) Fry; m. Donald Burleigh Crismond, 1965 (dec.). B.S., U. Calif.-Santa Barbara, 1964; M.L.S., U. Calif.-Berkeley, 1965. Cert. county libr., Calif., assn. exec. Reference librarian, EDP coordinator San Francisco Pub. Library, 1965-72, head acquisition, 1972-74; asst. univ. librarian U. So. Calif., Los Angeles, 1974-80; chief dep. county librarian Los Angeles County Pub. Library, Los Angeles, 1980-81; county librarian Los Angeles County Pub. Library, Downey, 1981-89; exec. dir ALA, Chgo., 1989-92; v.p. public rels. Profl. Media Svc. Corp., Chgo., 1992-98; nat. dir. sales, mktg. Follett Audiovisual Resources, Crystal Lake, Ill., 1999—; Western rep. quality control council Ohio Coll. Library Ctr., Columbus, 1977-80; mem. Am. Nat. Standards Inst., N.Y.C., 1978-80; bd. councillors U. So. Calif. Sch. Library and Info. Mgmt., 1980-83; adv. bd. mem. UCLA Library Sch., 1981-89; chmn. bd. dirs. Los Angeles County Pub. Library Found., 1982-85; mem. OCLC Users Coun., 1988-89; mem. exec. com. L.A. County Mgmt. Coun., 1986-88, pres., 1988; cons. libr. Trinity Coll., 1995—; prin. The Crismond Group, Inc., 1996—. Author: Directory of San Francisco Bay Area, 1968, Against All Odds, 1994; editor: Urban Librs. Coun. Exch., 1994—, The Charleston Report, 1996—. Bd. dirs. So. Meth. U. Libr., 1992-98. Named Staff Mem. of Year San Francisco Pub. Library, 1968. Mem. ALA, Calif. Library Assn. (council 1980-82), Calif. County Librarians Assn. (pres. 1984), L.A. County Mgmt. Assn. (pres. 1988). Home: 303 Mariner Dr Tarpon Springs FL 34689-5840

CRISONA, JAMES JOSEPH, lawyer; b. N.Y.C., Aug. 30, 1907; s. Frank and Rachel (Fantino) C.; m. Claire Peysson, July 8, 1934; children: Claire Mary, Cynthia. B.C.S., N.Y.U., 1928, LL.B., 1931. Sr. partner Crisona Bros., N.Y.C., 1945-57; gen. counsel, dir. Hudson & Manhattan R.R., 1948-54; v.p., gen. counsel, dir. Phoenix-Campbell Corp., 1951-57; pres. Boro of Queens, N.Y.C., 1957-59; supreme ct. justice State N.Y., 1959-76; bd. dirs. The Italy Fund, Inc., High Yield Fund, N.Y. Mcpls. Inc., Calif. Mcpls., Managed Mcpls. Inc., Calif. Tax Free Fund, others. Former assemblyman and state senator, N.Y. Mem. Queens County Bar Assn. Lodge: K.C. Home: 118 E 60th St New York NY 10022-1103

CRISP, FRED, publishing executive; m. Betty, Sept. 2, 1956; children: Michele Crisp Narron, Fred Durham III. Student, Mars Hill Coll., N.C.; BA, U. N.C. Advtg. salesman Charlotte (N.C.) Observer, 1957-59, Virginian Pilot and Ledger Star, Norfolk, Va., 1959-68; advtg. dir. The No. Va. Sun, Arlington, 1968-69; retail advtg. mgr. The News and Observer Publ. Co., Raleigh, N.C., 1969-76; advtg. dir. The News and Observer Publ. Co., Raleigh, 1976-85, dir. sales, mktg., 1985-87, v.p. sales, mktg., 1987-90, v.p. gen. mgr., 1990-96, assoc. publ., 1996, pres., publ., 1997—. Mem. First Presbyn. Ch. Raleigh; bd. dirs. N.C. Citizens for Bus. and Industry, United Way, Downtown Raleigh Alliance; past bd. dirs. Theatre in the Park, Wake County Boys' Club; past vice chmn. adv. bd. Salvation Army; mem. presdl. bd. advisors Mars Hill Coll.; bd. dirs. bd. vis. journalism and mass comm. U. N.C., v.p. Sch. Journalism and Mass Com. Found.; bd. trustees Peace Coll.; mem. Peace Coll. Found. Bd. Recipient Silver Medal awrd Am. Advtg. Fedn., 1979; inducted to N.C. Advtg. Hall of Fame, 1991. Mem. Am. Advtg. Fedn. (past gov. N.C.), Internat. Newspaper Advtg. and Mktg. Execs. (hon. life, past pres.), Mid-Atlantic Newspaper Advtg. and Mktg. Execs. (hon. life), N.C. Retail Merchant Assn. (bd. advisors), N.C. Press Assn. (past pres.), Newspaper Assn. Am. (past mem. exec. bd.), Distributive Edn. Clubs Am. (hon. life), Mid-Atlantic Newspaper Advtg. and Mktg. Execs. (past pres.), Triangle Advtsg. Fedn. (past pres.), Raleigh Sales and Mktg. Execs., Inc. (past bd. dirs.). Avocation: golf. Office: McClatchy Newspapers 215 S McDowell St PO Box 191 Raleigh NC 27602-9150

CRISP, JENNIFER ANN CLAIR, neurosurgical nurse; b. Bangalore, India, Aug. 30, 1943; came to U.S., 1959; d. Arthur E. Cleland and Pamela M.N. Ottley Hemming; m. Fred R. Crisp; 1 child, Karyn. RN diploma, Ind. Sch. Nursing, 1965; BSN, Greenville (Ill.) Coll., 1967. RN, Tex. Charge nurse thoracic surgery unit The Meth. Hosp. of Ind., Indpls., 1965-66; asst. head nurse orthop. unit Good Samaritan Hosp., Lexington, Ky., 1966-71; charge nurse, supr. relief hosp. nursing, charge nurse emerg Pardee Hosp., Hendersonville, N.C., 1971-76; charge nurse for skilled care unit, dir. insvc. edn. Carolina Village Inc., Hendersonville, 1976-78; staff nurse The Meth. Hosp., Houston, 1978-80, asst. head nurse, 1980-94, neurosurg. ICU nurse, 1994-97; patient care coord. neurosurg. ICU Meml. Hosp., Houston, 1997—. Home: Sea-lights PO Box 155 Gilchrist TX 77617-0155 Office: Methodist Hosp 6565 Fannin St Houston TX 77030-2707

CRISP, POLLY LENORE, psychologist; b. Atlanta, May 20, 1952; d. John Pershing and Dorotha Amelia (Hogan) C. BA, U. Tenn., 1976; MA, Mich. State U., 1981, PhD, 1984. Psychotherapist Arbours Ctr., London, 1983-85; clin. psychologist Kennebec Valley Mental Health Ctr., Augusta, Maine, 1987-90, Overlook Mental Health Ctr., Maryville, Tenn., 1990—. Contbr. articles to profl. publs. Mem. APA (membership com. div. clin. psychology 1990—), Brit. Psychol. Soc., Soc. Psychotherapy Rsch., N.Y. Acad. Scis., Phi Beta Kappa, Phi Kappa Phi, Alpha Lambda Delta. Avocations: woodworking, stained glass. Office: Overlook Mental Health 219 Court St Maryville TN 37804-5917

CRISP, SANDRA SUE, contract specialist; b. Jefferson City, Sept. 13, 1941; d. William Frederick and Marguerite Walters (Wilson) Meyer; m. Samuel Henry White, Sept. 20, 1965 (div. Feb. 1982); 1 child, Janelle Lynn; m. Richard Leslie Crisp, Apr. 26, 1982. BSBA, Lincoln U., 1963; MS in Mgmt., Naval Postgrad. Sch., 1996. Missile components buyer McDonnell/Douglas Corp., St. Louis, 1977-78; contract specialist U.S. Army Aviation R&D Command, St. Louis, 1978-80; contracting officer U.S. Army Aviation Materiel Command, St. Louis, 1980-82; chief facilities and materials br. U.S. Army-Europe, Frankfort, Germany, 1982-83, chief host nations br., 1983-85; spl. tech. asst. to dir. comml. activities Asst. Sec. of Army for Installations, Logistics & Environ., Arlington, Va., 1985-87; spl. tech. asst. to U.S. Army Competition Adv. Gen. Asst. Sec. of Army for Rsch., Devel. and Acquisition, Arlington, 1987-92; dep. chief of staff for procurement, prin. asst. contracting U.S. Army Depot Sys. Command, Chambersberg, Pa., 1992-95; chief ammunition procurement divsn. U.S. Army Indsl. Ops. Command, Rock Island, Ill., 1995—. Mem. Nat. Contract Mgmt. Assn. (pres. Monterey chpt. 1995-96, edn. chair Quad City chpt. 1997—), Nat. Def. Indsl. Assn. (bd. dirs. 1996—), U.S. Army Acquisition Corp. Avocations: volts marching, needlework, gardening. Home: 228 Longview Ct Geneseo IL 61254-9270 Office: US Army Indsl Ops Command Attn AMSIO-AC Rock Island IL 61299

CRISPI, MICHELE MARIE, lawyer; b. Neptune, N.J., Mar. 10, 1962; d. Michael and Mary (Vaccaro) C.; m. Lawrence J. Moloney. BS in Accountancy magna cum laude, Villanova U., 1984, JD, 1987, LLM in Taxation, 1989. Bar: N.J. 1988, U.S. Dist. Ct. N.J. 1988, D.C. 1989, U.S. Tax Ct. 1989. Assoc. Lampf, Lipkind, Prupis & Petigrow, West Orange, N.J., 1987-88, Lautman, Henderson & Wight, Manasquan, N.J., 1990-97; pvt. practice Sea Girt, N.J., 1997—. Mem. ABA (bus. law, real property, probate and trust law, taxation and gen. practice sects., solo and small firm and law practice mgmt. sects.), N.J. State Bar Assn. (corp. and bus. law, real property, probate and trust law, elder law, taxation and gen. practice sects.), D.C. Bar Assn. (taxation sect.), Monmouth County Bar Assn., Phi Kappa Phi, Beta Gamma Sigma, Gamma Phi. Republican. Roman Catholic. Avocations: tennis, swimming. Home: 32 Hunters Pointe Rd Middletown NJ 07748-5148 Office: 2164 Hwy 35 Bldg C Ste 8 PO Box 424 Sea Girt NJ 08750-0424

CRISPIN, ANDRE ARTHUR, international trading company executive; b. Brussels, Belgium, Aug. 23, 1923; came to U.S., 1947; naturalized Am. citizen; m. Sylvia Clevenger; 5 children. Ed., U. Louvain, Belgium, 1943. V.p. Am. Supply and Equipment Co., Houston, 1947-48; chmn. Crispin Co., Houston, 1949—; hon. consul-gen. Belgium. Past chmn. bd. trustees so. region Inst. Internat. Edn.; mem. Citizens Environ. Coalition; past pres. Music Guild Houston; chmn. bd. trustees Awty Internat. Sch., Houston; mem. external internat. bd. advs. Tex. A&M U., College Station. liaison officer with Belgian Army, 1940-46. Decorated officier Ordre de Leopold II, Civic Cross 1st class, officier Ordre de Leopold Ier (Belgium); chevalier Legion d'Honneur (France), Commdr.'s Cross Order of the Crown (Belgium), 1997; named one of 5 Outstanding Young Texans, 1953; recipient Houston Internat. Svc. award, 1986. Mem. Nat. Assn. Steel Pipe Distbrs. (past pres., bd. dirs.), Academie Internationale du Vin, Alliance Française de Houston (past pres., dir., exec. com.), Am. Inst. Imported Steel (past dir.), Commanderie de Bordeaux d'Amerique (grand maitre, gov.), Commanderie de Bordeaux du Texas à Houston (past maitre, commandeur), Commanderie du Bontemps, de Medoc et de Graves (France, commandeur d'honneur), German Wine Soc., Prodhomme, Jurade de St. Emilion Stylobate, Piliers Chablisiens, Compagnon de Loupiac, Echevin, Lussac Puisseguin St. Emilion, Lalande de Pomerol, Hospitaliers de Pomerol, Downtown Houston Assn., Belgian-Am. C. of C. (past bd. dirs.), French-Am. C. of C. (past pres. Houston chpt., dir.), Houston C. of C. (now named Greater Houston Partnership, bd. dirs. world trade divsn., internat. bus. com., past chmn.), World Trade Assn. (past pres., dir.), Petroleum Club of Houston (past dir., past 1st v.p.). Home: One Crestwood Dr Houston TX 77007 Office: Crispin Co 2929 Allen Pkwy Ste 2222 Houston TX 77019-7101

CRISPIN, JAMES HEWES, engineering and construction company executive; b. Rochester, Minn., July 23, 1915; s. Egerton Lafayette and Angela (Shipman) C.; m. Marjorie Holmes, Aug. 5, 1966. AB in Mech. Engring., Stanford U., 1938; MBA, Harvard U., 1941; grad., Army Command & Gen. Staff Sch., 1943. Registered profl. mech. engr., Calif. With C.F. Braun & Co. Alhambra, Calif., 1946-62; treas. Bechtel Corp., San Francisco, 1962-73, v.p., mem. fin. com., 1967-75, mgr. investment dept., 1973-75; retired, 1976; investment cons., Santa Barbara, Calif., 1978—. Trustee Santa Barbara Mus. Art, 1979-91, 97-98, pres., 1986-88, life. hon. trustee, 1992—. Lt. col. Ordnance Corps, AUS., 1941-46. Decorated Army Commendation medal with oak leaf cluster. Mem. Mil. Order World Wars, S.R., Soc. Colonial Wars, Colonial Wars Calif., Baronial Order Magna Carta, Mil. Order Crusades, Am. Def. Preparedness Assn., World Affairs Coun. No. Calif. (trustee 1968-75), Santa Barbara Mus. Art (trustee 1979-91, 97-98, pres. 1986-88, life hon. trustee 1992), Calif. Hist. Soc. (trustee 1979-86), Valley Club of Montecito (pres. 1987-90, bd. dirs. 1981-91), Calif. Club L.A., World Trade Club San Francisco (pres. 1977-78, bd. dirs. 1971-78), Santa Barbara Club (pres. 1995-96, bd. dirs. 1991-96), Pacific Union Club, San Francisco, Beta Theta Pi. Republican. Home Fax: 805-565-9077, Office fax: 805-966-2081. Home: 470 Eastgate Ln Santa Barbara CA 93108-2248 Office: La Arcada Bldg 1114 State St Ste 220 Santa Barbara CA 93101-6712

CRISPO, RICHARD CHARLES, artist, ethnologist, minister; b. Bklyn., Jan. 13, 1945; s. Frank C. and Irene M. (Lamont) C. M.F.A., Trinity Hall Coll., 1975; Ph.D., Collegii Romanii, Rome, 1976, Th.D., 1977. Instr. art Monterey Peninsula Coll., 1968-69, instr. ethnic studies, 1976; instr. art history Hartnell Coll.; coord. Arts in Corrections, Art Project, Soledad Prison, 1976-83; am. cultural specialist to Latin Am. for U.S.; vis. lectr. U. Calif., Santa Cruz, interdisciplinary studies dept. Porter Coll.; instr. pub. sch. art, Monterey, Calif., 1967-72; counselor Intrim, Inc., Monterey, 1976; founder Mus. on Wheels, 1973-74; founder World Folk Art Collection, Monterey, 1972; 53 murals and 63 one-man shows; executed half-mile-long mural at Soledad Prison; priest N. Am. Old Roman Catholic Ch. Recipient numerous awards including 1st prize Calif. State Fair, 1964; UNESCO award, 1971-73; Calif. Arts Council grantee. Mem. Artist Equity, Found. for the Community of Artists, Carmel Art Assn., Pacific Grove Art Center. Contbr. articles to art jours.

CRISS, CECIL M., chemistry educator; b. Wheeling, W.Va., Apr. 22, 1934; s. Cecil M. and Anna (Reece) C.; m. Laura Hopkins, Aug. 18, 1958; children: Cecil M. III, Laura Anna. AB, Kenyon Coll., 1956; PhD, Purdue U., 1961. Asst. prof. U. Vt., Burlington, 1961-65; asst. prof. U. Miami, Coral Gables, 1965-69, assoc. prof., 1970-75, prof., 1976—; vis. scientist U. Lund, Sweden, 1977-78; vis. prof. Calif. State Coll., San Diego, 1978; program officer NSF, Washington, 1982-83; dept. chmn. U. Miami, 1984-91; vis. scholar U. Del., 1992. Recipient Fla. award Fla. Sect. Am. Chem. Soc. Mem. AAAS, Am. Chem Soc., Sigma Xi, Phi Lambda Upsilon. Episcopalian. Home: 4910 San Amaro Dr Coral Gables FL 33146-1632 Office: Dept Chemistry U Miami Coral Gables FL 33124

CRISS, WILLIAM SOTELO, electronics company executive; b. Akron, Ohio, Oct. 14, 1949; s. Everett Robert and Lois Marie (Gill) C.; m. Celia P. Sotelo, Sept. 15, 1973; children: Celina, David. BS, Calif. Inst. Tech., 1971; MBA, U. Chgo., 1973. Sect. supr. car product devel. Ford Motor Co., Dearborn, Mich., 1973-78; gen. supt. Consol. Rail Corp., Phila., 1978-85; pres. Automated Laser System, Inc., Danville, Calif., 1985-89, gen. mgr. data display products, 1989-92, pres. data display products, 1992—; bd. dirs. Guardian Bancorp, L.A., 1995-96. Office: Data Display Products 445 S Douglas St El Segundo CA 90245-4630

CRIST, CHRISTINE MYERS, consulting executive; b. Harrisburg, Pa., Feb. 5, 1924; d. John Eyster and Eunice Horton (Ingham) Myers; m. Robert Grant Crist, June 25, 1949; children: Catherine Ingham Crist Marcson, Jessica Rogers Crist, Robert Jeffrey Myers Crist. BA, Dickinson Coll., 1946. Reporter The Patriot, Harrisburg, Pa., 1946-49; editor West Shore Times, Lemoyne, Pa., 1964-65; adminstr. arts in edn. Pa. Dept. Edn., Harrisburg, 1974-77, dir. leadership in arts edn., 1977-79; press sec. gov.'s office Pa. Commn. for Women, Harrisburg, 1980-83, dir. Gov.'s Commn. for Women, 1983-87; exec. dir. com. for women Evang. Luth. Ch. in Am., Chgo., 1987-90; ptnr. Crist and Crist Cons., Camp Hill, Pa., 1990—; mem. State Employees Retirement Bd., 1986-88; state coord. We the People Edn. Program. Editor: Song As A Measure of Man, 1975 (excellent pub. 1975). Mem. Camp Hill (Pa.) Sch. Bd., 1967-73, Capital Area Intermediate Bd.,

Lemoyne, Pa., 1970-73; pres. Camp Hill (Pa.) Civic Club, 1970-72; mem. coun. Trinity Congregation, 1991-94; mem. Harrisburg Choral Soc., Dickinson Alumni Coun., 1992—; bd. dirs. Women's Polit. Network Pa., Camp Hill Cmty. Found., 1996—; mem. candidacy bd. Lutheran Ch., 1992—; Pa. bd. Common Cause, 1997—. Mem. Monday Club, Cumberland County Fedn. Women's Clubs (pres. 1996—). Luthern. Home and Office: Crist and Crist 1915 Walnut St Camp Hill PA 17011-3854

CRIST, JUDITH, film and drama critic; b. N.Y.C., May 22, 1922; d. Solomon and Helen (Schoenberg) Klein; m. William B. Crist, July 3, 1947 (dec. Apr. 1993); 1 son, Steven Gordon. AB, Hunter Coll., 1941; tchg. fellow, State Coll. Wash., 1942-43; MSc in Journalism, Columbia, 1945; DHL (hon.), SUNY, New Paltz, 1994. Civilian instr. 3081st Army AFB Unit, 1943-44; reporter N.Y. Herald Tribune, 1945-60, editor arts, 1960-63, assoc. theater critic, 1957-63, film critic, 1963-66; film, theater critic NBC-TV Today Show, 1963-73; film critic World Jour. Tribune, 1966-67; critic-at-large Ladies Home Jour., 1966-67; contbg. editor and film critic TV Guide, 1966-88; film critic N.Y. mag., 1968-75, The Washingtonian, 1970-72, Palm Springs Life, 1971-75; contbg. editor, film critic Saturday Rev., 1975-77, 80-84, N.Y. Post, 1977-78, MD/Mrs., 1977—, 50 Plus, 1978-83, L'Officiel/USA, 1979-80; arts critic Sta. WWOR-TV, 1981-87; critical columnist for Coming Attractions, 1985-93; cons. editor Hollywood Mag., 1985-93; contbg. editor Columbia Mag., 1993-95; instr. journalism Hunter Coll., 1947, Sarah Lawrence Coll., 1958-59; assoc. journalism Columbia Grad. Sch. Journalism, 1958-62, lectr. journalism, 1962-64, adj. prof., 1964—. Author: The Private Eye, The Cowboy and the Very Naked Girl, 1968, Judith Crist's TV Guide to the Movies, 1974, Take 22: Moviemakers on Moviemaking, 1984, rev. edit., 1991; contbr. articles to nat. mags. Trustee Anne O'Hare McCormick Scholarship Fund. Recipient Page One award N.Y. Newspaper Guild, 1955; George Polk award, 1950; N.Y. Newspaper Women's Club award, 1955, 59, 63, 65, 67; Edn. Writers Assn. award, 1952; Columbia Grad. Sch. Journalism Alumni award, 1961; named to 50th Anniversary Honors List, 1963; Centennial Pres.'s medal Hunter Coll., 1970; named to Hunter Alumni Hall of Fame, 1973. Mem. Columbia Journalism Alumni (pres. 1967-70), N.Y. Film Critics Circle, Nat. Soc. Film Critics., Sigma Tau Delta. Office: 180 Riverside Dr New York NY 10024-1021 *Care about people-not things.*

CRIST, LEWIS ROGER, insurance company executive; b. Takoma Park, Md., Oct. 9, 1935; s. Howard Roger and Dorothy Ada (Massey) C.; m. Connie M. Combs, Mar. 29, 1980. Student, U. Md., 1953-54, 58-60. Cert. ins. examiner. Br. mgr. CNA Ins. Cos., St. Louis, 1961-85; dir. Mo. Div. Ins., Jefferson City, Mo., 1986-88; pres. The Bar Plan Ins. Co., St. Louis, 1988-93; chmn. bd. Cameron Mut. Ins. Co., Cameron Country Mut. Ins. Co., Cameron Life Ins. Co., 1968—; chmn. Inter-Co. Arbitration Com., Omaha, 1971, Spl. Arbitration Com., New Orleans, 1975; mem. Nat. Panel Consumer Arbitrators, New Orleans, 1975-76, Nat. Supplemental Health Ins. Panel, Washington, 1987-88; bd. dirs. Gateway Ins. Co. Mem. Alzheimers Task Force, Jefferson City, 1986-88. With U.S. Army, 1954-57. Mem. Ins. Inst. New Orleans (bd. dirs. 1976-78), La. Property Assn. (bd. dirs. 1974-77, Ins. Co. Execs. Assn. (pres. 1983), Ins. Regulatory Examiners Soc., Mo. Ins. Edn. Found. (bd. dirs. 1991—, pres. 1994). Republican. Episcopalian. Avocations: golf, gardening. Office: Crist & Assocs 175 Cherry Hills Meadows Dr Wildwood MO 63040-1649

CRIST, LYNDA LASSWELL, editor, historian; b. Bay City, Tex., Nov. 3, 1945; d. Jack and Elizabeth Lasswell; m. William Britton Crist, Sr., Apr. 2, 1977. BA, Rice U., 1967, MA, 1969; PhD, U. Tenn., 1980. Rsch. asst. Frank E. Vandiver, London and Paris, 1969, U. Tenn., Knoxville, 1973-76; assoc. editor The Papers of Jefferson Davis Rice U., Houston, 1976-79, editor, 1979—; cons. Beauvoir, Biloxi, Miss., 1997-98; book prize judge Mus. Confederacy, Richmond, Va. Editor: The Papers of Jefferson Davis, Vols. 4-10, 1983-99. Grad. fellow Rice U., 1967-69, grad. fellow U. Tenn., 1973-76, Mellon fellow Va. Hist. Soc., 1994; Centennial scholar, Mus. Confederacy, 1994, founders award Mus. Confederacy, 1997. Mem. So. Hist. Assn. (life mem.), So. Assn. Women Historians (mem. program com., book prize judge, life mem.), Assn. Documentary Editing, Houston Civil War Roundtable (pres., dir., Award of Merit 1982). Democrat. Presbyterian. Office: Rice Univ Jefferson Davis Assn PO Box 1892 MS43 Houston TX 77251-1892

CRIST, PAUL GRANT, lawyer; b. Denver, Sept. 9, 1949; s. Max Warren and Marjorie Raymond (Catland) C.; m. Christine Faye Clements, June 4, 1972; children: Susan Christine, Benjamin Warren, John Willis. BA, U. Nebr., 1971; JD cum laude, NYU, 1974. Bar: Ohio 1974, U.S. Ct. Mil. Appeals 1975, Calif. 1976, U.S. Dist. Ct. (no. dist.) Ohio 1979, U.S. Ct. Appeals (6th cir.) 1982. Assoc. Jones, Day, Reavis & Pogue, Cleve., 1974, 78-83, ptnr., 1984—. Rsch. editor NYU Law Rev., 1972-74. Capt. JAGC, USAF, 1974-78. Decorated Meritorious Svc. medal. Fellow Am. Coll. Trial Lawyers; mem. Ohio State Bar Assn., Cleve. Bar Assn., Order of Coif, Am. Inns of Ct. Democrat. Presbyterian. Home: 6565 Canterbury Dr Hudson OH 44236-3484 Office: Jones Day Reavis & Pogue N Point 901 Lakeside Ave E Cleveland OH 44114-1116

CRISTESCU, NICOLAIE DAN, engineering educator; b. Chelmenti, Romania, Feb. 17, 1929; married; 1 child. Diplomat, Bucharest U., Romania, 1951, docent, 1967; PhD, Romanian Acad., 1955. Asst. prof. U. Bucharest, Romania, 1951-55, lectr., 1955-57, assoc. prof., 1957-66, prof., 1966-92, dept. chmn., 1982-90, pres., 1990-92; vis. grad. rsch. prof. U. Fla., 1970-76; grad. rsch. prof. dept. aerospace engring. mechanics and engring. sci. U. Fla., Gainesville, 1992—; vis. prof. Johns Hopkins U., Balt., 1968-69, Drexel U., Phila., 1969; lectr. in field. Author: Dynamic Problems in Theory of Plasticity, 1958, The Mechanics of Extensible Strings, 1964, Dynamic Plasticity, 1967, 70 (in Japanese), Introduction to Rate-Dependent Plasticity (A Dynamic Approach), 1971, Rock Mechanics, 1983, 2d edit., 1984, supplemental 1988, Mechanics of Composite Materials, 1983, Rock Rheology, 1989, Rock Mechanics-Rheology Aspects, 1990, Rock Viscoplasticity, 1992, Viscoplasticity of Geomaterials, 1994, (with I. Suliciu) Viscoplasticity, 1976, 82, (with S. Cleja-Tigolu) Theory of Plasticity with Application to Metal Working, 1985, (with U. Hunsche) Time Effects in Rock Mechanics, 1998; contbr. articles to profl. jours.; sr. editor: Internat. Jour. Plasticity; mem. editl. bd. Internat. Jour. Mechanical Sci., Mechanics Rsch. Comm., Mechanics of Cohesive-Frictional Materials and Structures, others. Fellow Romanian Acad., Acad. Europaea; mem. ASME (Arpad L. Nadai award 1995), Soc. Scholars, Internat. Soc. Interaction of Mechanics and Maths. (founder), Am. Rock Mechanics Assn. (founder), Am. Acad. Mechanics, Soc. Exptl. Stress Analysis, Group Français de Rheology, Internat. Assn. Computer Methods and Advances in Geomechanics, Internat. Soc. Rock Mechanics, Tau Beta Pi, Sigma Xi. Achievements include research in mechanics of solid deformable bodies, theory of plasticity, rheology, rock and soil mechanics, mechanics of powder-like materials. Office: U Fla Dept Aerospce Engring Mech & Engring Sci Gainesville FL 32611-6250

CRISTIANO, MARILYN JEAN, speech communication educator; b. New Haven, Jan. 10, 1954; d. Michael William and Mary Rose (Porto) C. BA, Marquette U., 1975, MA, 1977; postgrad., Ariz. State U., 1977; EdD, Nova Southeastern U., 1991. Speech comm. instr. Phoenix Coll., 1977-87, Paradise Valley C.C., Phoenix, 1987—; presenter at profl. confs., workshops and seminars. Author tng. manual on pub. speaking, 1991, 92, 95, 97, 99; contbr. articles to profl. publs. Mem. Speech Comm. Assn., Western Speech Comm. Assn., Ariz. Comm. Assn. Avocation: tennis. Office: Paradise Valley CC 18401 N 32nd St Phoenix AZ 85032-1210

CRISTOL, A. JAY, federal judge; b. Fountain Hill, Pa., Feb. 25, 1929; s. Samuel and Mae (Stein) C.; m. Eleanor Rubin; children: Stephen Michael, David Alan. BA, U. Miami, 1958, LLB, 1959, PhD, 1997. Bar: Fla. 1959. Spl. asst. to Atty. Gen. of Fla. Tallahassee, 1959-65; sr. ptnr. Cristol, Mishan, Sloto, Miami, 1959-85; judge U.S. Bankruptcy Ct., Miami, 1985-93; chief judge, 1994—; trustee U.S. Bankruptcy Ct., Miami, 1982-84; adj. prof. U. Miami Law Sch.; bd. govs. 11th cir. Nat. Conf. Bankruptcy Judges; bankruptcy rules adv. com. Jud. Conf. of U.S., 1995; bankruptcy com. U.S. Ct. Appeals (11th cir.), 1996-98; tchr. bankruptcy law to judges in Czech Republic, Slovenia, Thailand, Russia, India, Malaysia, Hong Kong, South Africa. Bd. trustees U. Miami, 1988-90, Coral Gables; bd. dirs. ARC, Miami, 1989-97. Capt. USNR, 1951-89. Fellow Am. Coll. Bankruptcy; mem. ABA, Am. Bankruptcy Inst., Nat. Conf. Bankruptcy Judges, Fla. Bar Assn., Dade County Bar Assn. Avocations: water skiing, windsurfing, flying, reading. Office: US Bankruptcy Ct 1412 Fed Bldg 51 SW 1st Ave Miami FL 33130-1669

CRISTOL, STANLEY JEROME, chemistry educator; b. Chgo., June 14, 1916; s. Myer J. and Lillian (Young) C.; m. Barbara Wright Swingle, June 1957; children: Marjorie Jo, Jeffrey Tod. BS, Northwestern U., 1937; MA, UCLA, 1939, PhD, 1943. Rsch. chemist Standard Oil Co., Calif., 1938-41; rsch. fellow U. Ill., 1943-44; rsch. chemist U.S. Dept. Agr., 1944-46; asst. prof., then assoc. prof. U. Colo., 1946-55, prof., 1955—, Joseph Sewall Disting. prof., 1979—, chmn. dept. chemistry, 1960-62, grad. dean, 1980-81; vis. prof. Stanford U., summer 1961, U. Geneva, 1975, U. Lausanne, Switzerland, 1981; with OSRD, 1944-46; adv. panels NSF, 1957-63, 69-73, NIH, 1969-72. Author: (with L.O. Smith, Jr.) Organic Chemistry, 1966; editorial bd., Chem. Revs., 1957-59, Jour. Organic Chemistry, 1964-68; contbr. rsch. articles to sci. jours. Guggenheim fellow, 1955-56, 81, 82; recipient James Flack Norris award in phys.-organic chemistry, 1972, Alumni Merit award Northwestern U., 1987. Fellow AAAS (councilor 1986-92); mem. NAS, AAUP, Am. Chem. Soc. (chmn. organic chemistry div. 1961-62, adv. bd. petroleum rsch. fund 1963-66, coun. policy com. 1968-73), Colo.-Wyo. Acad. Sci., Phi Beta Kappa, Sigma Xi, Phi Lambda Upsilon. Home: 2918 3rd St Boulder CO 80304-3041 Office: U Colo Dept Chemistry & Biochemistry CB 215 Boulder CO 80309

CRISWELL, ANN, newspaper editor. Food editor Houston Chronicle. Office: Houston Chronicle 801 Texas Ave Houston TX 77002-2996*

CRISWELL, ELEANOR CAMP, psychologist; b. Norfolk, Va., May 12, 1938; d. Norman Harold Camp and Eleanor (Talman) David; m. Thomas L. Hanna. BA, U. Ky., 1961, MA, 1962; EdD, U. Fla., 1969. Asst. prof. edn. Calif. State Coll., Hayward, 1969; prof. psychology, former chair Calif. State U., Sonoma, 1969—; faculty adviser Humanistic Psychology Inst., San Francisco, 1970-77; dir. Novato Inst. Somatic Research and Tng.; editor Somatics jour.; cons. Venturi, Inc., Autogenic Systems, Inc.; clin. dir. Biotherapeutics, Kentfield Med. Hosp., 1985-90. Founder Humanistic Psychology Inst., 1970. Co-editor: Biofeedback and Family Practice Medicine, 1983; author: How Yoga Works, 1987, Biofeedback and Somatics, 1995. Mem. APA (pres.-elect), Biofeedback Soc. Calif. (dir.), Aerospace Med. Assn., Assn. for Transpersonal Psychology, Assn. for Humanistic Psychology (past pres.). Patentee optokinetic perceptual learning device. Office: Sonoma State U Psychology Dept 1801 E Cotati Ave Rohnert Park CA 94928-3609

CRITCHELL, SIMON JAMES, corporate executive; b. London, Feb. 28, 1946; came to U.S., 1979; s. Lionel James and Irene (Thomas) C.; m. Renee Francoise Roux, Sept. 6, 1969; children: David James, Vanessa Jane. BA with honors, King's Coll. London, 1968; MBA, Inst. European d'Adminstrn. des Affaires, France, 1972. V.p. mktg. Cosmair, Inc., N.Y.C., 1981-84; sr. v.p., gen. mgr. Lancome div. Cosmair, Inc., N.Y.C., 1985-90; pres., chief exec. officer Cartier, Inc., N.Y.C., 1990—. Office: Cartier Inc 653 5th Ave New York NY 10022-5902*

CRITCHLEY, JOHN J., JR., stock options trader; b. Mar. 15, 1967. BA, Dartmouth Coll., 1989. Mng. mem. J. Critchley & Co., L.L.C., N.Y.C., 1996—. Email: ja.critch@world.att.net. Home: 3 Dorset Way Edison NJ 08820

CRITCHLOW, CHARLES HOWARD, lawyer; b. Morristown, NJ, Nov. 23, 1950; s. George F. and Florence Critchlow; m. Mary Ellen Donnelly; children: Katharine F, Mary E.G. BA, Yale U., 1972; JD, Columbia U., 1975. Bar: N.Y. 1976, U.S. Dist. Ct. (so. and ea. dists.) N.Y. 1976, U.S. Ct. Appeals (2d cir.) 1982, U.S. Ct. Appeals (3d and 10th cirs.) 1991, U.S. Supreme Ct. 1993, U.S. Ct. Appeals (5th cir.) 1994, U.S. Ct. Appeals (4th cir.) 1995, U.S. Ct. Internat. Trade 1996, U.S. Ct. Appeals (Fed. Cir.) 1996. Assoc. Lord, Day & Lord, N.Y.C., 1975-85, ptnr., 1985-86; ptnr. Coudert Bros., N.Y.C., 1986—. Contbr. to Antitrust Law Developments, 3d edit., 1992; contbr. articles to profl. jours. Active Yale Alumni Fund; mem. Yale Alumni Schs. Com. Mem. ABA, N.Y.C. Bar Assn. Office: Coudert Bros 1114 Avenue Of The Americas New York NY 10036-7703

CRITCHLOW, DALE, electrical engineer; b. Harrisville, Pa., Jan. 6, 1932. BS, Grove City Coll., 1953; MS, Carnegie Inst. Tech., 1954; PhD, 1956. Engr. magnetic amplifiers Magnetics Inc., 1952-53; proj. engr. magnetic devices rsch. Carnegie Inst. Tech., 1953-56; assoc. prof. elec. engr., 1956-58; staff engr. IBM Corp., 1958-59, adv. engr., 1959-64; rsch. staff mem., 1964-80; sr. engr. Rsch. Ctr., 1980-86; sr. tech. staff, 1986-93; rsch. prof. Univ. Vermont, 1993—; cons. Magnetic Amplifiers Inc.; fellow IBM, 1986. Fellow IEEE; mem. Nat. Acad. Engr., Sigma Xi. Home: 260 Crescent Rd Burlington VT 05401-4125 Office: Univ Vt 317 Votey Bldg Burlington VT 05405-0156

CRITCHLOW, DONALD THOMAS, history educator; b. Pasadena, Calif., May 18, 1948; s. Patrick B. Critchlow and Anne Dawson Marchinton; m. Patricia Elizabeth Powers Feb. 18, 1978; children: Angieszka A., Magdalena D. BA magna cum laude, San Francisco State U., 1970; MA, U. Calif., Berkeley, 1972, PhD, 1978. Asst. prof. North Central Coll., Naperville, Ill., 1978-81, U. Dayton, Ohio, 1981-83; assoc. prof. Notre Dame U., South Bend, Ind., 1983-91; prof., dept. chair St. Louis U., Mo., 1991—; grad. dir. Phi Alph Theta, U. Dayton, U. Notre Dame; mem. Ill. steering com. OAH Conf. on the Promotion of History, Wesleyan U., Bloomington, Ill., 1980; program co-dir. Conf on Evolution of Fed. Social Policy, U. Notre Dame, South Bend, Ind.; guest scholar The Brookings Instn. 1976-77, Woodrow Wilson Internat. Ctr. Scholars/Guest Scholars, 1984-85, fellow 1996-97; vis. prof. U. Warsaw, 1988-89; summer fellow NEH, 1980, Rockefeller, 1983, 94. Author: (monographs) Brookings Institution 1916-1952 Expertise and Public Interest in a Democratic Society, 1985, Studebaker: The Life and Death of an American Corporation, 1852-1963, 1996, Intended Consequences: Birth Control, Abortion and the Federal Government in Modern America, 1999; co-author (with William Rorabaugh) America: A Concise History; editor: Socialism in the Heartland: The Midwestern Experience, 1986, A History of the United States I-V, 1995, The Politics of Abortion and Birth Control in Historical Perspective, 1996; co-editor (with Ellis Hawley), Federal Social Policy: The Historical Dimension, 1989, Poverty and Public Policy in Modern America, 1989, With Us Always: Private Charity and Public Welfare in Historical Perspective, 1998; contbr. chpts. to books and revs. and articles to profl. jours, presented papers at profl. confs., nat. and internat., 1981—; founding editor Jour. of Policy History; gen. editor Critical Issues in Policy History, Critical Issues in History. Named USIA Disting. Lectr., 1988-89, grantee, 1995; fellow Fulbright Scholars Program, 1997-98, USIA China Spkrs. Program, 1999. Home: 7175 Washington Ave University Cy MO 63130-4313 Office: St Louis U History Dept 221 N Grand Blvd Saint Louis MO 63103-2006

CRITCHLOW, EDITH HOPE, minister; b. Bklyn., N.Y., Feb. 23, 1964; d. Ruth K. C. Cert. in Christian Ministry, N.Y. Theol. Sem., 1989; postgrad., 1994—; BA in Psychology, CUNY, 1993. Ordained deacon and elder First AME Zion Ch., 1997. Supt. Sunday Ch. Sch. First AME Zion Ch., Bklyn., N.Y., 1994—, worship leader, 1995—; chaplain Young Adult Missionary Soc., Bklyn., N.Y., 1995—. Recipient Svc. award Women's History Mo., 1996. Mem. N.Y. Assn. Black Psychologists, Women's Home and Overseas Missionary Soc. (life, connectional). Democrat. Mem. AME Zion Ch. Avocations: good books, movies, plays, travel, nature walks. Office: First AME Zion Ch 54 Macdonough St Brooklyn NY 11216-2304

CRITCHLOW, PAUL, marketing and communications executive. Sr. v.p. mktg. and comm. Merrill Lynch & Co., Inc., N.Y.C. Office: Merrill Lynch & Co Inc World Fin Ctr N Tower 250 Vesey St New York NY 10281*

CRITELLI, MICHAEL J., lawyer, manufacturing executive; b. 1948. BA, U. Wis., 1970; JD, Harvard U., 1974. Bar: Ill. 1974, N.Y. 1982. Assoc. Ross & Hardies, Chgo., 1974-76, Schwartz & Freeman, Chgo., 1976-79; counsel Pitney Bowes, Inc., 1979-83, sr. counsel, 1983-84, asst. gen. counsel, 1984-86, assoc. gen. counsel, 1986-88, v.p., sec., gen. counsel, 1988, chief personnel officer, 1990-94, vice chmn., 1994—, chmn., CEO, 1996—. Office: Pitney Bowes Inc World Hdqrs Location 5001 1 Elmcroft Rd Stamford CT 06926-0700*

CRITES, STEPHEN DECATUR, religion educator; b. Elida, Ohio, July 27, 1931; s. Beryl Anderson and Martha Crites; m. Gertrud Elizabeth Bremer, Sept. 11, 1955 (div. June 1990); children: Dorothea, Stephanie, Lilian, Hannah; m. Ann Lindberg, Dec. 26, 1990. BA, Ohio Wesleyan U., 1953; BD, Yale U., 1956, MA, 1959, PhD, 1961; student, U. Heidelberg, Germany, 1959-60. Ordained to ministry United Meth. Ch., 1956. Minister Grace Meth. Ch., Southington, Conn., 1956-58; instr. philosophy and religion Colgate U., 1960-61; asst. prof. religion Wesleyan U., Middletown, Conn., 1961-66, assoc. prof., 1966-69; prof. Wesleyan U., Middletown, 1969—, prof. philosophy, 1991—. Author: In The Twilight of Christendom: Hegel vs. Kierkegaard on Faith and History, 1972, Dialectic and Gospel in the Development of Hegel's Thinking, 1998; translator: Kierkegaard, Crisis in the Life of an Actress and Other Essays on Drama, 1967; editor: Studies in Religion, Am. Acad. Religion monograph series, 1971-79. Mem. Am. Acad. Religion, Soc. for Values for Religion in Higher Edn. Home: 281 Beaver Brook Rd Lyme CT 06371-3203 Office: Philosophy Dept Wesleyan U Middletown CT 06457

CRITOPH, EUGENE, retired physicist, nuclear research company executive; b. Vancouver, B.C., Can., Mar. 29, 1929; s. Dennis Basil and Lillian Sarah Critoph; m. Mary Elizabeth Ivens, Feb. 9, 1952; children: Christopher Michael, Stephen Bard, Eugene Mark, Boyd. B in Applied Sci., U. B.C., 1951, M in Applied Sci., 1957. Physicist Chalk River (Ont., Can.) Nuclear Labs., Atomic Energy of Can. Ltd., 1953-67, br. head, reactor physics, 1967-75, dir. fuels and materials div., 1975-76, dir. advanced projects and reactor physics div., 1976-79, v.p., gen. mgr., 1979-86; v.p. strategic tech. mgmt. Atomic Energy of Can. Ltd. Research Co., Ottawa, Ont., 1986-92; mem., sec., chmn. European-Am. Com. on Reactor Physics, 1962-69. Co-author, coord. Canada Enters the Nuclear Age, 1997. Mem. Can. Nuclear Soc. (W.B. Lewis medal 1986).

CRITTENDEN, DANIELLE ANN, writer, journalist; b. Toronto, Ont., Can., Apr. 20, 1963; d. Maxwell John Crittenden and Yvonne Ann (Wilson) Worthington; m. David Jeffrey Frum, June 26, 1988; children: Miranda Ann, Nathaniel Saul. Reporter Toronto Sun, 1983-86; founding editor Women's Quar., Arlington, Va., 1994-99; columnist The Nat. Post, N.Y.C., 1999—. Author: What Our Mothers Didn't Tell Us: Why Happiness Eludes the Modern Woman, 1999. Jewish. Office: c/o Simon & Schuster 1230 Ave of the Americas New York NY 10020

CRITTENDEN, EUGENE DWIGHT, JR., chemical company executive; b. Syracuse, N.Y., Feb. 27, 1927; s. Eugene Dwight and Meltina Ester (Feldkamp) C.; m. Sarah Ann Rogers, June 23, 1951; children: Sarah Ann Crittenden D'Alonzo, Susan Gray Crittenden Chambers. BS, Purdue U., 1947; MS, U. Pa., 1949, PhD, 1951. With Hercules, Inc., 1951-92, sr. engr. Research Ctr., Wilmington, Del., 1951-53, asst. to dir. devel. Naval Stores Dept., 1953-55, sr. chem. engr., Brunswick, Ga., 1955-56, Wilmington, 1956-57, tech. asst. to devel. dir., 1957-60, sr. tech. rep., N.Y.C., 1960-62, asst. dir. devel. synthetics dept., Wilmington, 1962-63, asst. to gen. mgr. internat. dept., 1963-64, dir. Hercules Europe, Brussels, 1965-66, dir. sales organic chem. div., synthetics dept., Wilmington, 1966-67, asst. gen. mgr. synthetics dept., 1967-68, gen. mgr. new enterprise dept., 1968-72, indsl. systems dept., 1972-77, v.p. adminstrn. and pub. affairs, 1977-82, div. v.p. ops., corp. dir., mem. exec. and mgmt. com., 1982, corp. v.p. internat., 1983-87, pres. chief exec. officer, Aqualon Group, 1987-89, sr. v.p., 1982-92, ret.; corp. dir. Hercules Inc., Wilmington, 1982-92. Bd. dirs. City of Wilmington and New Castle County YMCA, 1968-92, pres. 1977-82; trustee, v.p., pres. Eleutherian Mills-Hagley Found., 1981—; bd. dirs. World Affairs Coun., 1981-92; trustee, bd. dirs. Med. Ctr. of Del., 1978-92, vice chmn. 1990—; Del. met. chmn. Nat. Alliance of Bus., 1981-82; mem. Gov.'s Internat. Trade Coun., 1984-92; mem. Del. and Eastern Pa. Dist. Export Council, 1984-92; del. Econ. and Fin. Adv. Coun., 1977—, chmn., 1989-93. Served with USN, 1945-46. Yerger fellow in chem. engring., 1949-51. Mem. AAAS, Am. Chem. Soc., Am. Inst. Chem. Engrs., Sigma Xi. Republican. Episcopalian. Clubs: Wilmington Country (bd. govs.), Wilmington, Vicmead Hunt, Pine Valley Golf, Ocean Forest Golf, Penn Club, N.Y., Sea Island Club, Sea Island Golf Club. Avocations: piano, golf, tennis. Home: 908 N Dupont Rd Wilmington DE 19807-2963

CRITTENDEN, GAZAWAY LAMAR, retired banker; b. Flushing, N.Y., Apr. 15, 1918; s. Jerome Parker and Paulina (Jones) C.; m. Gertrude Bramwell Shaw, Jan. 23, 1943; children: Gazaway Lamar, Penelope Shaw, Jane M. Grad., Phillips Exeter Acad., 1937; AB, Princeton U., 1941. With First Nat. Bank Boston, 1945-83, exec. v.p. charge investments div., 1967-83. Chmn. Fin. Adv. Bd. Mass., 1968-78; trustee, chmn. fin. com., treas. Mass. Gen. Hosp., 1968-90, hon. trustee, mem. investment com., 1990—; treas. Neurosci. Rsch. Found., 1974-81. Lt. comdr. USNR, 1941-45. Mem. Pub. Securities Assn. (govtl. securities com.), Dedham (Mass.) Country and Polo Club, The Country Club (Brookline, Mass.). Home: 80 Strawberry Hill St Dover MA 02030-2253

CRITTENDEN, KATHERINE LUCINA, nurse; b. Newport News, Va., Aug. 16, 1957; d. James Tyler III and Lucina Nan (Titlow) C. Diploma, York Acad., 1975; student, Longwood Coll., 1975-78; AS, John Tyler C.C., 1984. RN, Va., Wis.; CEN; cert. ACLS, PALS, Am. Heart Assn.; TNCC, CNPC.; cert. emergency nurse; cert emergency nurse in pediatric care. Nurse Med. Coll. Va., Richmond, 1985-94; dir. emergency and critical care svcs. Rappahannock Gen. Hosp., Kilmarnock, Va., 1994-96; nurse Bon Secours Hosp., Richmond, 1997—, Health South, Richmond, 1997—, John Randolph Hosp., Hopewell, Va., 1998—. Dir. nursing No. Neck Free Clinic, Lancaster, Va., 1995-97. Mem. Jamestown Soc., Va. Nurses Assn. Mem. Philippi Christian Ch. Avocations: golf, boating. Home: PO Box 581 Deltaville VA 23043-0581

CRITTENDEN, MARY LYNNE, science educator; b. Detroit, Oct. 27, 1951; d. William and Marie (Ryall) C. BS, Wayne State U., 1974; MS, U. Detroit, 1984; postgrad., Wayne State U., 1991—, 1997—. Tchr. sci. Detroit Bd. Edn., 1974-77, Highland Park (Mich.) C.C., 1980—; faculty rschr. Air Force program Wright Patterson AFB, Dayton, Ohio, 1991; speaker Mich. Ednl. Occupational Assn., 1989, Liberal Arts Network Devel., Lansing, Mich., 1990, 95; presider Qualities Edn. Minorities, Math., Sci. Engring. Conf., Detroit, 1996; adj. prof. U. Detroit, 1996-97. Author ednl. materials; contbr. to profl. publs. Mem. AAAS, Am. Chem. Soc. (outreach program 1992—), Civic Ctr. Optimist Club (bd. dirs. 1991-94, coord. scis. 1990-94), Mich. C.C. Biologists, Human Anatomy and Physiology Soc. Achievements include development of successful paradigm and teaching methods to make science palatable to urban community college students, modeling normal values in humans and some rodents applicable to physiologically-based pharmacokinetics. Home: 15386 Alden St Detroit MI 48238-2104 Office: Highland Park Schs 20 Bartlett St Highland Park MI 48203-3720

CRITTENDEN, SOPHIE MARIE, communications executive; b. Mansfield, Ohio, Apr. 14, 1926; d. Joseph S. and Mary Ellen (Hagerman) Wojcik; m. Robert Eugene Crittenden, Aug. 24, 1946 (dec. 1987); children: Robert J., Mark A., Christopher E., Laura Ann. Student, Coll. St. Francis, 1944-45, Ohio U., 1945-46, North Cen. Tech. Coll., 1976-78. Substitute tchr. Mansfield City Schs., 1956-62; lab. technician The Ohio Brass Co., Mansfield, 1962-68, draftsman, 1968, mgr. internal publs., 1969-78, mgr. advt., 1978-83, mgr. communications, 1983-88; cons. communications EFE N.Am., Inc., Mansfield, 1989-90; account coord. D & S Creative Advt., Inc., Mansfield, 1990—. Creator and shower of quilts. Com. chmn. United Way Campaign, Mansfield and Richland, Ohio, 1978; pub. relations chmn. Tribute to Women and Industry Project, Mansfield, 1986 (award 1985). Named Mrs. Mansfield Mrs. Am. Contest, 1961. Mem. Mktg. Club North Cen. Ohio (bd. dirs., sec. 1987-90), Altrusa (pres. 1976, internat. chmn. mktg. and pub. rels. 1991-93). Republican. Roman Catholic. Avocations: fiber arts, antiques. Home: 84 Wildwood Dr Mansfield OH 44907-1621 Office: 140 Park Ave E Mansfield OH 44902-1830

CRIVARO, JOHN PETE, family practice physician; b. Des Moines, Iowa, Nov. 25, 1922; s. Nick and Carmela (Leo) C.; m. Linda G. Iannaconne, Apr. 13, 1947; children: Alan J., Cynthia Ann Crivard Clinton. BA, U. Iowa, 1949, MD, 1953. Intern Seaside Hosp., Long Beach, Calif., 1953-54; surg. resident Seaside Hosp., Long Beach, 1954-55; family practice physician, 1955—; strategic planning chmn. Long Beach Meml. Med. Group, Inc., 1998—, Pro Health Ptnrs., 1998—; pres., founder Long Beach Shepherd's

Ctr.; clin. physician Rancho Los Amigos Hosp.; active staff Long Beach Meml. Hosp., Long Beach Children's Hosp.; sec., bd. dirs., pres., past pres. Long Beach Physicians Health Plan; chmn. utilization and rev. com., bd. dirs. Long Beach Med. Found. Bd. Dirs.; mem. bd. dirs., L.A. dist. mem. profl. edn. com. Am. Cancer Soc. Harbor Dist.; mem. ednl. com. So. Calif. Arthritic Found.; past mem. bd. dirs., mem. CPR com., dir. L.A. County, L.A. Heart Assn. Long Beach; mem. Long Beach Bd. Health, 1982—; mem. radiologic tech. cert. com. Dept. Health Svcs.-State of Calif., 1982—, others. Contbr. artidcles to profl. jours. 1st sgt. U.S. Army, 1942-46. Fellow Am. Acad. Family Practice (mem. clin. investigative and rsch. com., mem. com. on aging, chmn. com. on aging, others, Philanthropist of Yr. 1997); Calif. Acad. Family Practice (mem. bd. 1969-95, vice spkr. congress of dels., pres.-elect 1979-80, pres. 1980-81, past pres. 1981-82, mem. exec. com., mem. program com., others), L.A. Chpt. Calif. Acad. Family Practice (mem. bd. 1960—, sec., v.p., pres., med. edn. chmn., mem. student affairs com., program chmn., co-chmn. edn. program with L.A. County Heart Assn., John P. Crivaro Ann. Lecture, others), Calif. Med. Assn. (alt. del., chmn. adv. panel family practice, others), L.A. County Acad. Family Practice (med. edn. chmn., sec., v.p., pres. Long Beach sub-chpt.), L.A. County Med. Assn., Long Beach Med. Assn. (mem. exec. bd. 1974—, mem. legis. com., chmn. patients adv. com., treas., sec., pres.-elect, pres., others), L.A. Med. Assn. (mem. external rels. com., mem. joint liaison com.), Sons of Italy, KC. Office: ProHealth Ptnrs 2701 Atlantic Ave Long Beach CA 90806-2712

CRNCICH, TONY JOSEPH, retired pharmacy chain executive; b. Noranda, Que., Can., May 20, 1930; s. Anton and Zora (Pavacic) C.; m. Joanne Louise Potvin, May 11, 1957; children—Anne Marie, Diane, Christine, Anthony, Katherine, Robert. B.Sc. in Pharmacy, U. Toronto, 1953. Pharmacist Med. Art Dispensary, Windsor, Ont., Can., 1953-54; mgr. Wilkinsons Drug Store, Windsor, 1954-56; owner Lakeview Pharmacies, 1956-64; treas. Big V Pharmacies, Windsor, 1964-68, chmn., pres., chief exec. officer, 1968-84, chmn., 1984-91, also bd. dirs.; bd. dirs. AXA (Can.) Ins. Co., Robart Rsch. Inst. Mem. Green Shield Can. (life hon. bd. dirs.), Ont. Pharmacists Assn. (Pharmacist of Yr. 1969), Essex County Pharmacy Assn. (pres. 1967-69), Can. Pharm. Assn., Ont. Coll. Pharmacists (coun.) 1969-73), London Hunt and Country Club. Avocations: golfing; sailing; bridge. Home and Office: 75 Tetherwood Blvd, London, ON Canada N5X 3W3

CROAN, ROBERT JAMES, music critic, singer; b. N.Y.C., Apr. 30, 1937; s. Sydney Joseph and Sylvia (Zorn) C. BA, Columbia U., 1958, MA, 1959; PhD, Boston U., 1968. Prof. voice Duquesne U. Sch. of Music, Pitts., 1962—, chmn., 1983—; music critic Pitts. Post-Gazette, 1964—. Mem. Music Critics Assn. N.Am. (chmn. ednl. activities 1978-90, pres. 1997—), Nat. Assn. Tchrs. of Singing. Democrat. Avocations: travel, culinary arts. Office: Pitts Post-Gazette 34 Blvd Of The Allies Pittsburgh PA 15222-1204

CROAT, THOMAS BERNARD, botanical curator; b. Mar. 23, 1938; s. Oliver Theodore and Irene Mary (Wilgenbush) C.; m. Patricia Swope, Sept. 4, 1965; children: Anne Irene, Thomas Kevin. BA, Simpson Coll., 1962; MA, U. Kans., 1966, PhD, 1967. Tchr. sci. pub. schs. Virgin Islands and Iowa, 1962-64; rsch. botanist Mo. Bot. Garden, St. Louis, 1967-71, P.A. Schulze curator of botany, 1977—; vis. fellow Smithsonian Tropical Research Inst., Ancon, Canal Zone, 1968-71; adv. com. NSF Resources in Systematic Botany, 1972-74; faculty assoc. biology Washington U., St. Louis, 1970—; adj. faculty U. Mo., St. Louis, 1974—; adj. assoc. prof. St. Louis U., 1982—. author: Flora of Barro Colorado Island, 1978; contbr. articles to profl. jours. With U.S. Army, 1956-58. Recipient Rsch. award Soc. Sigma Xi, 1975; grantee NSF, 1972-99, Nat. Geog. soc., 1973, 83, 86, 89, 95, NEA, 1975, 79. Mem. am. Soc. Plant Taxonomists, Assn. Tropical Biology, Internat. Soc. Plant Toxonomist, Internat. Aroid soc. (hon. bd. 1978-84), bot. Soc. Am. Republican. Roman Catholic. Avocations: welding, electronics, auto repair, construction. Home: 5600 Hill View Dr Pacific MO 63069-3523 Office: Mo Bot Garden PO Box 299 Saint Louis MO 63166-0299

CROCE, ALAN J., government agency executive; m. Patricia Acampora; 4 children. BS in Criminal Justice, SUNY; grad., FBI Nat. Acad., Quantico, Va., Nat. Correctional Acad., Boulder, Colo. From dep. sheriff to sgt. dep. sheriff Suffolk County Sheriff's Dept., 1971-86, undersheriff, 1986-97; commr. and chmn. N.Y. State Commn. of Correction, 1997—. Mem. Suffolk County Police Assn. (past pres.). Office: State of NY Commn of Correction Four Tower Pl 2d Fl Albany NY 12203-3764

CROCE, ARLENE LOUISE, critic; b. Providence, May 5, 1934; d. Michael Daniel and Louise Natalie (Pensa) C. Student, Women's Coll., U. N.C., 1951-53; BA, Barnard Coll., 1955. Founder, editor Ballet Rev., 1965-78; dance critic New Yorker mag., 1973—; dance panelist Nat. Endowment for Arts, 1977-80. Author: The Fred Astaire & Ginger Rogers Book, 1972, Afterimages, 1977, Going to the Dance, 1982, Sight Lines, 1987. Recipient AAAL award 1979, award of Honor for Arts and Culture Mayor N.Y.C., 1979, Janeway prize Barnard Coll., 1955; Hodder fellow Princeton U., 1971; Guggenheim fellow, 1972, 86, NEH fellow 1992. Fellow Nat. Arts Journalism Program (sr.). Office: New Yorker Mag 20 W 43rd St New York NY 10036-7400

CROCE, PAT, sports team executive; m. Diane Croce; children: Kelly, Michael. Grad. cum laude, U. Pitts., 1977. Conditioning coach for Bobby Clarke Phila. Flyers, 1980; owner Sports Phys. Therapists, Inc., Broomall, Pa.; ptnr., pres. Phila. 76ers, 1996—; motivational spkr.; internat. karate champion. Contbr. articles to profl. jours. Vol. Sixers Slam Dunk Diabetes Family Festival, JDF Walk to Cure Diabetes; hon. chmn. Nat. Multiple Sclerosis Soc.; bd. dirs. Police Athletic League; instrumental in bringing 1999 NBA All-Star Weekend to Phila.. Office: Philadelphia 76ers First Union Ctr 3601 S Broad St Philadelphia PA 19148*

CROCETTI, GINO, elementary and secondary education educator; b. N.Y.C., Oct. 18, 1945; s. Guido M. and Annemarie F. Crocetti. AB in Philosophy, Columbia Coll., N.Y.C., 1970; BS in Psychology, SUNY, 1989; MA in Pub. Policy, Columbia Pacific U., 1989, PhD in Edn., 1989. V.p., gen. mgr. Douglas Books and Douglas Record, N.Y.C., 1971-73; one of organizers No. Manhattan Health Planning Project, N.Y.C., 1972-81; dir. Project on New Food Devel.-INFORM, N.Y.C., 1978-80; program dir. Sexton Edn. Programs Fairleigh Dickinson U., N.J., 1977—; sci. tchr., math. tchr. City and Country Sch., N.Y.C., 1980—; assoc. fellow Inst. Policy Studies, Washington, 1971; editorial cons. dept. psychiatry Johns Hopkins U., Balt., 1972-73; cons. survey data Coll. Medicine and Dentistry N.J., New Brunswick, 1974-75; instr. occupational and environ. health N.Y. State Sch. Ind. and Labor Rels., N.Y.C., 1979; instr. computer use Learning Annex, N.Y.C., 1984-88. Co-author: What's for Dinner Tomorrow: Corporate Views on New Food Product Development, 1980, Preparing for the LSAT, 1982, Preparing for GMAT, 1983, Preparing for the GRE, 1984; contbr. articles on health planning, computer use and mental hygiene to profl. jours. mem. N.Y. County Dem. Com., N.Y.C., 1974, N.Y. County Dem. Jud. Com., N.Y.C., 1974. Mem. AAAS, ASCD, Assn. Computers in Math. and Sci. Edn., Nat. Sci. Tchrs. Assn., Nat. Coun. Tchrs. Math., Am. Pub. Health Assn., CEDAM Internat. Avocations: diving, fish collecting, skiing, water sports. Office: City and Country Sch 146 W 13th St New York NY 10011-7802

CROCI, MARY ELLEN, artist, mental health specialist; b. Jan. 11, 1953. BFA, Coll. Art/Design, Detroit, 1990. Mental health specialist Oakwood United Hosps., 1992—. Exhibited art U.S. and Europe. Home: # 2 515 Chestnut St Wyandotte MI 48192

CROCK, STANLEY MILES, journalist; b. New Bedford, Mass., Apr. 6, 1950; s. Max and Lillian Rose (Kivowitz) C.; m. Pamela J. Brown, Mar. 21, 1987; children: Russell, Meryl. BA, Columbia Coll., 1972; MS in Journalism, Northwestern U., 1973; JD, Columbia U., 1977. Reporter AP, Chgo., 1973, Palm Beach Post, West Palm Beach, Fla., 1973-74, Wall St. Jour., Washington, 1978-82; cons. Worldwide Info. Resources Ltd., Washington, 1982-83; editor McGraw-Hill World News, Washington, 1983-86; news editor Bus. Week, Washington, 1986-95, chief diplomatic corr., 1995—. Bd. dirs. Rollingwood Citizens Assn., Chevy Chase, Md., 1991, pres., 1993-94; trustee Temple Sinai, Washington, 1997—. Jewish. Avocation: golf. Home: 7016 Western Ave Chevy Chase MD 20815-3111 Office: Bus Week # 1100 1200 G St NW Ste 1100 Washington DC 20005-3844

CROCKER, ALLEN CARROL, pediatrician; b. Boston, Dec. 25, 1925. Student, MIT, 1942-44; MD, Harvard U., 1948. Lab. house officer Children's Hosp., Boston, 1948-49, jr. asst. resident medicine, 1949-51, fellow pathology, 1953-56, from asst. to assoc. physician, 1956-62, rsch. assoc. pathology, 1956-60, assoc. medicine, 1962-66, sr. assoc., 1966—, dir. devel. evaluation ctr., 1967-93, program dir. Inst. for Cmty. Inclusion, 1993—; rsch. assoc. pathology Med. Sch., Harvard U., 1956-60, rsch. assoc. pediatrics, 1960-66, tutor med. sci., 1964-70, asst. prof., 1966-69, assoc. prof., 1969—, assoc. prof. maternal and child health Sch. Pub. Health, 1989—. Mem. Am. Assn. Mental Retardation (v.p. medicine 1980-82), Am. Assn. Univ. Affiliated Programs for Persons with Devel. Disabilities (pres. 1982-83), Nat. Down Syndrome Congress (v.p. 1984-85), Soc. Behavioral Pediatrics (pres. 1987-88). Achievements include research in pediatric metabolic diseases, biochemistry of the lipids, mental retardation. Office: Devel Evaluation Ctr Children's Hosp 300 Longwood Ave Boston MA 02115-5724

CROCKER, BARBARA JEAN, infection control practitioner; b. Worcester, Mass., Oct. 13, 1942; d. Roy A. and Mildred E. (Ewing) Benson; m. David L. Crocker, Aug. 29, 1964; children: Beth, Mark, Matthew. Diploma, Henry Heywood Meml. Hosp., Gardner, Mass., 1963; BS, Anna Maria Coll., Paxton, Mass., 1982, MS in Nursing, 1985. Cert. infection control nurse. Staff nurse Worcester Hahnemann Hosp., 1965-72, nursing supr., 1972-81, infection surveillance nurse, 1981-85; nurse epidemiologist The Med. Ctr.-Hahnemann, Worcester, 1985-92; infection control practitioner U. Mass. Meml. Health Care, 1992—. Mem. Assn. Profls. in Infection Control and Epidemiology, Inc., Henry Heywood Meml. Hosp. Alumnae Assn.

CROCKER, CHESTER ARTHUR, diplomat, scholar, federal agency administrator; b. N.Y.C., Oct. 29, 1941; s. Arthur M. and Clare V.; m. Saone Baron, Dec. 18, 1965; children—Bathsheba, Karena, Rebecca. B.A., Ohio State U., 1963; M.A. in Internat. Studies, Johns Hopkins U., 1965, Ph.D., 1969. News editor Africa Report, 1968-69; lectr. Am. U., 1969-70; staff officer Nat. Security Council, 1970-72; dir. M.S. in Fgn. Svc. program Georgetown U., Washington, 1972-78, dir. African studies Ctr. for Strategic-Internat. Studies, 1976-81, disting. prof. diplomacy Sch. Fgn. Svc., 1989—; asst. sec. state African affairs, 1981-89; chmn. bd. dirs. U.S. Inst. Peace, 1992—; cons. in strategy and negotiation; chmn. Africa working group Reagan campaign, 1980; coord. for Africa Bush campaign; bd. dirs. A.S.A. Ltd., Corp. Coun. on Africa, Henry-Dunant Ctr. for Humanitarian Dialogue, Nat. Def. U., Modern Africa Growth and Income Fund. Author: High Noon in Southern Africa, 1992, Managing Global Chaos, 1996, Herding Cats: Case Studies in International Mediation, 1999, also others; contbr. articles to profl. jours. Recipient Disting. Svc. award Sec. State, 1988, Presdl. Citizen's award, 1989. Mem. Coun. Fgn. Rels., Internat. Inst. Strategic Studies, Cosmos Club, Tahawus Club. Office: Georgetown U Sch Fgn Svc Intercultural Ctr Rm 813 Washington DC 20057

CROCKER, GEORGE A., career officer; b. Feb. 4, 1943. Commd. U.S. Army, advanced through grades to lt. gen., 1997.

CROCKER, JOY LAKSMI, concert pianist and organist, composer; b. San Antonio, June 12, 1928; d. Hugo Peoples and Anna Kathryn (Ball) Rush; m. Richard Lincoln Crocker, July 24, 1948 (div. July 1977); children: Nathaniel Homer, Martha Wells, David Laramie. MusB, Yale U., 1950; MS, Yale U., Berkeley, Calif., 1956; postgrad., Grad. Theol. Sem., 1978-81. Min. music First Congl. Ch., Branford, Conn., 1949-62; dir. music therapy West Haven (Conn.) VA Hosp.; min. music St. Stephen's Episcopal Ch./Sch., Orinda, Calif., 1963, First Bapt. Ch., Oakland, Calif., 1964-66, Greek Orthodox Cathedral, Oakland, 1969, San Quentin (Calif.) Protestant Chapel, 1976-78, Plymouth United Ch. of Christ, Oakland, 1977-84; pianist, assoc. dir. First Bapt. Ch., Managua, Nicaragua, 1984-94; organist, pianist Mills Grove Christian Ch., 1995; organist St. Andrews Presbyn. Ch., Pleasant Hill, Calif., 1996; prof. organ San Francisco Conservatory Music, 1962-69; chmn. piano dept. Nicaraguan Nat. Conservatory Music, 1984-93; founder-dir., prof. Bapt. Conservatory of Music, Managua, 1989—; instr. Yogalayam Yoga Ashram; creator, dir. diverse low-budget innovative music edn. programs, 1969—; mem. adjudicator Nat. Guild Piano Tchrs., Music Tchrs. Assn. Calif. Civic and legislation coord. Ch. Women United, Oakland unit and state unit, 1996—, chairperson for global concerns; pianist, organist Ch. Women United State Unit; San Francisco Bay area coord. for Hague Appeal for Peace. Named Woman of Yr., Bus. and Profl. Women's Club,, Inc., 1995; recipient prizes for compositions San Francisco Concerto Orch., 1997, Music Tchrs. Assn. Calif., 1998. Mem. Am. Guild Organists, Am. Coll. Musicians, Music Tchrs. Assn. Democrat. Mem. United Ch. of Christ. Avocation: traveling. Home: 3065 Monterey Blvd Oakland CA 94602-3559

CROCKER, KENNETH FRANKLIN, data processing consultant; b. Centralia, Wash., July 29, 1950; s. Earl Thomas and Mary Jane (Hamil) C.; m. Mary Louise Underwood, June 15, 1974 (div. Dec. 1987); children: Matthew A., Benjamin F., Jonathan C.; m. Sally Marlene Gammelgard, Dec. 21, 1987 (div. 1992). AS in Computer Programming and System Design, Control Data Inst., Long Beach, Calif., 1972. Programmer City of Greenville, S.C., 1973; computer operator Winn Dixie Stores, Greer, S.C., 1973-75; programmer Piedmont Industries, Greenville, S.C., 1975-78; systems engr. Micro-Systems, Greenville, 1978; sr. programmer Reeves Bros., Lyman, S.C., 1978-80; systems analyst Cryovac div. W.R. Grace Co., Duncan, S.C., 1980-84; sr. cons. Cap Gemini Am., San Francisco, 1984-85; prin. mem. tech. staff Citibank-FSB Calif., Oakland, 1985-91; sr. software engr. Lucky Stores Inc., Dublin, Calif., 1991-94; tech. cons. Lawrence Berkeley Labs., Berkeley, Calif., 1994-95, Delta-Net, San Francisco, 1995; plan architect, DBA technician Safeway, Walnut Creek, Calif., 1995—. Umpire Contra Costa Ofcls. Assn., 1990-96. Libertarian. Baptist. Avocation: children's sports activities. Home and Office: 1590 Thornwood Dr Concord CA 94521-1918

CROCKER, MYRON DONOVAN, federal judge; b. Pasadena, Calif., Sept. 4, 1915; s. Myron William and Ethel (Shoemaker) C.; m. Elaine Jensen, Apr. 26, 1941; children—Glenn, Holly. A.B., Fresno State Coll., 1937; LL.B., U. Calif. at Berkeley, 1940. Bar: Calif. bar 1940. Spl. agt. FBI, 1940-46; practiced law Chowchilla, Calif., 1946-58; asst. dist. atty. Madera County, Calif., 1946-51; judge Chowchilla Justice Ct., 1952-58, Superior Ct. Madera County, 1958-59; U.S. judge Eastern Dist. Calif., Sacramento, 1959—, now sr. judge. Mem. Madera County Republican Central Com., 1950—. Named Outstanding Citizen Chowchilla, 1960. Mem. Chowchilla C. of C. (sec.). Lutheran. Club: Lion. Office: US Dist Courthouse 1130 O St Rm 5007 Fresno CA 93721-2201*

CROCKER, RYAN C., ambassador; b. Spokane, Wash., June 19, 1949; married. BA, Whitman Coll., 1971; postgrad., Univ. Coll., Dublin, Ireland. Various positions with Am. embassies, Iran, Qatar, Tunis, Iraq, from 1971; chief polit. sect. Am. Embassy, Beirut, 1981-84; dep. dir. Office Israel and Arab-Israeli Affairs, Dept. State, Washington, 1985-87; polit. counselor Am. Embassy, Cairo, 1987-90; amb. to Lebanon, Am. Embassy, Beirut, 1990-93; amb. to Kuwait, Am. Embassy, Kuwait City, 1994-97; amb. to Syria, Am. Embassy, Damascus, 1998—. Office: Am Embassy Damascus c/o Dept State Washington DC 20521-6110

CROCKER, SAONE BARON, lawyer; b. Bulawayo, Zimbabwe, Jan. 11, 1943; came to U.S., 1963; d. Benjamin and Rachel (Joffe) Baron; m. Chester Arthur Crocker, Dec. 18, 1965; children: Bathsheba Nell, Karena Wynne, Rebecca Masten. BA, U. Cape Town, 1961, BA with honors, 1962; MA, Johns Hopkins U., 1966; JD cum laude, Georgetown U., 1983. Bar: D.C. 1983, U.S. Ct. Appeals (D.C. cir.) 1985, U.S. Dist. Ct. D.C. 1990, U.S. Supreme Ct. 1990, U.S. Ct. Appeals (7th cir.) 1991, U.S. Ct. Appeals (4th cir.) 1998. Adminstr. Guinea program African Am. Inst., Washington, 1965-66, author Africa Report, 1966; writer fgn. affairs div. Am. U., Washington, 1967-68; freelance writer Washington, 1968-80; atty. firm Wilmer, Cutler & Pickering, Washington, 1983-84; clk. to judge U.S. Ct. Appeals for D.C. Circuit, 1984-85; atty. firm O'Melveny & Myers, Washington, 1985-90, Beveridge & Diamond, Washington, 1990-92, Wright & Talisman, P.C., Washington, 1992—. Contbg. author: Zambia Handbook, 1967. AAUW fellow, 1963-65; Fulbright fellow, 1963; Johns Hopkins U. fellow, 1964-65; recipient Lawyers Coop. Pub. Co. awards, 1980. Mem. ABA, AAUW (state pres. 1992-94), Fulbright Assn. Office: Wright & Talisman PC 1200 G St NW Ste 600 Washington DC 20005-3082

CROCKER, STEPHEN L., federal judge. BA, Wesleyan U., 1980; JD, Northwestern U., 1983. Law clk. to Hon. Barbara Crabb U.S. Dist. Ct. (we. dist.) Wis., Madison, 1983-84; trial atty. D.O.J., 1984-86; asst. U.S. atty. No. Dist. Ill., 1986-90; assoc. Michael, Best & Fredrich, 1990-92; magistrate judge U.S. Dist. Ct. (we. dist.) Wis., Madison, 1992—. Office: US Courthouse 120 N Henry St Madison WI 53703-2559

CROCKER, THOMAS DUNSTAN, economics educator; b. Bangor, Maine, July 22, 1936; s. Floyd M. and Gloria F. (Thomas) C.; m. Sylvia Fleming, Dec. 31, 1961 (div. Sept. 1986); children: Sarah Lydia, Trena Elizabeth; m. Judith Powell, Sept. 9, 1989. AB, Bowdoin Coll., 1959; PhD, U. Mo., 1967. Asst. prof. econs. U. Wis., Milw., 1963-70; assoc. prof. U. Calif., Riverside, 1970-75; prof. U. Wyo., Laramie, 1975—, chairperson dept. econs. and fin., 1991-93, dir. Sch. Environment and Natural Resources, 1993-98; J.E. Warren distng. prof of Energy and Environment U. Wyo., 1997—; rsch. assoc. U. Calif., Berkeley, 1973, Pa. State U., 1974; cons. Asarco, Inc., 1985-89, Mathtech, Inc., Princeton, N.J., 1987-88, Indsl. Econs., Inc., Cambridge, Mass., 1998-99, Shea and Gardner, Washington, 1989, Arco, Inc., 1992, A. Coors Co., 1992, Eastern Rsch. Group, 1997; mem. sci. adv. bd. EPA, Washington, 1973-76; mem. panel on long range transport issues U.S. Congress, Washington, 1981; mem. Gov.'s Competition Rev. Com., State of Wyo. Co-author: Environmental Economics, 1971; author, editor: Economic Perspectives on Acid Deposition Control, 1984; editorial coun. Jour. Environ. Econs. and Mgmt., 1973-88, 95-99; contbr. articles to profl. jours. Mem. com. impacts pollution on agriculture Orgn. for Econ. Cooperation and Devel., Paris, 1987-88. Grantee NSF, 1968, 73, 81, EPA, 1971, 76-85, 97-99. Mem. Am. Econ. Assn., Assn. Environ. Resource Econs. (mem. awards structure com. 1981-83, contributed papers com. 1989), European Assn. Environ. Resource Econs., The Nature Conservancy. Republican. Avocations: skiing, bicycling, travel, trekking, rafting. E-mail: tcrocker@uwyo.edu. Office: Univ Wyo Dept Econs Laramie WY 82071-3985

CROCKER, VALERIE MARIAN, mechanical engineer; b. Annapolis, Md., July 21, 1962; d. Ernest O. and Virgina G. (Gleason) C.; m. Mark A. Young, May 18, 1991 (div. Apr. 1997). BS in Engrng./Bioengring., U. Vt., 1984; MS in Biomed. Engring., Duke U., 1986. Rehab. engr. Tufts U./New Eng. Med. Ctr., Boston, 1983; rsch. engr. Harvard Med. Sch., Southborough, Mass., 1987-88; project engr. surg. devices ETHICON Inc., Somerville, N.J., 1988-90; sr. mech. project engr. Abbott Labs., San Diego, 1990-92, supr. disposables mfg., 1992-94, mgr. mech. engring., R&D, 1994—. Contbr. articles to profl. jours. Avocations: triathlons, ocean swimming, marathons, biking, skiing, sail boat racing. Home: 12537 El Camino Real Unit C San Diego CA 92130-4044 Office: Abbott Labs 15330 Avenue Of Science San Diego CA 92128-3407

CROCKETT, CLYLL WEBB, lawyer; b. Preston, Idaho, Feb. 16, 1934; s. Frank Lee and Alta (Webb) C.; m. Nan Marie Mattice, June 27, 1958; children—Jeffrey Webb, Nicole, Karen, Cynthia. B.S., Brigham Young U., 1958; M.B.A. Northwestern U, 1959; LL.B., U. Ariz., 1962. Bar: Ariz. 1962, U.S. Supreme Ct. 1970. Clk. Ariz. Supreme Ct., 1962-63; ptnr. Fennemore Craig, Phoenix, 1968—; instr. eve. div. Mesa (Ariz.) C.C.; bd. dirs. S.W. Airlines Co. Mem. editorial bd. Ariz. Law Rev, 1961. Mem. charter rev. com., Scottsdale, Ariz., 1966-67; mem. bd. adjustment, Scottsdale, 1968-73, chmn., 1971-73; bd. dirs. Maricopa Mental Health Assn., 1976-78, Phoenix Cmty. Alliance, Valley Forward Assn.; mem. Mesa Crime Commn., 1980-82; mem. social scis. adv. bd. LDS Ch.; mem. State of Ariz. Gov.'s Regulatory Rev. Coun; mem. bd. of adjustment City of Mesa, 1996—. Mem. ABA, State Bar Ariz., Maricopa County Bar Assn., Am. Judicature Soc., Phoenix C. of C., Ariz. Acad. Republican. Home: 1510 N Gentry Cir Mesa AZ 85213-4001 Office: Fennemore Craig Ste 2600 3003 North Central Ave Phoenix AZ 85012-2913

CROCKETT, DODEE FROST, brokerage firm executive; b. Oklahoma City, Oct. 19, 1956; d. Carl S. Frost and Mikki (Matheny) Marcus; m. Billy Crockett. Postgrad., So. Meth. U., Perkins Sch. Theology. Gen. mgr. Keystone Readers Svc., Dallas, 1976-80; 1st v.p., sr. fin. cons. Merrill Lynch pvt. client, Dallas, 1980—. Bd. dirs. N. Dallas Shared Ministries, 1988-91, Mental Health Assn.; mem. adv. bd. EXCAP Ctr. for Prevention of Child Abuse, Ronald McDonald Children's Charities, 1992—; mem. investment com. Dallas Women's Found., 1991-94; bd. dirs. Dallas Opera, 1991—. Mem. Dallas Securities Dealers Assn., Nat. Assn. Securities Dealers (gen. securities prin., mcpl. securities rulemaking bd. prin., registered options prin., bd. arbitrators), NYSE (com. mem.), Merrill Lynch Cir. of Excellence, Park Cities Exch. Club (charter). Office: Merrill Lynch Pierce Fenner and Smith 2000 Premier Pl 5910 N Central Expy Ste 2000 Dallas TX 75206-5152

CROCKETT, DONALD HAROLD, composer, university educator; b. Pasadena, Calif., Feb. 18, 1951; s. Harold Brown and Martha Amy C.; m. Karen Anne Gallagher Crockett, Nov. 11, 1972 (div. 1986); 1 child: Katherine Jane Crockett; m. Vicki Lyn Ray, June 6, 1988. MusB, U. So. Calif., 1974, MusM, 1976; PhD, U. Calif., Santa Barbara, 1981. Composer-in-residence Pasadena Chamber Orch., 1984-86, L.A. Chamber Orch., 1991-97; asst. prof. U. So. Calif., L.A. 1981-84, assoc. prof., 1984-94,prof. 1994—; music dir., condr. U. So. Calif. Contemporary Music Ensemble, L.A., 1984—. Composer: Celestial Mechanics oboe and string quartet, 1990, Array string quartet number 1, 1987, Roethke Preludes for Orchestra, 1994, Concerto for Piano and Wind Ensemble, 1988, Island for concert band, 1998. Recipient Friedheim award Kennedy Ctr., Washington, 1991; Goddard Lieberson Fellowship Am. Acad. of Arts and Letters, N.Y.C., 1994; Nat. Endowment for the Arts grantee, Washington, 1993. Mem. BMI, Am. Music Ctr., Am. Composers Forum, Phi Kappa Phi. Avocations: reading, backpacking, skiing. Office: Univ of Southern California School of Music Los Angeles CA 90089-0851

CROCKETT, JAMES EDWIN, physician, educator; b. Kansas City, Kans., Oct. 20, 1924; s. John Edward and Orva Rose (Ramsey) C.; m. Martha Adam, June 8, 1949; children: Kevin, Brian, Cara. BA, Park Coll., 1945; MD, U. Kans., 1949. Diplomate Am. Bd. Internal Medicine and Cardiovascular Diseases. Intern U.S. Naval Hosp., Long Beach, Calif., 1949-50; resident U. Kans. Med. Ctr., Kansas City 1950-56; asst. prof. medicine U. Kans. Sch. Medicine, Kansas City, 1956-58, assoc. prof., 1958-63, dir. cardiology, 1960-63; clin. prof. medicine U. Mo.-Kansas City Sch. Medicine, 1972—; mem. adv. bd. Chinese Inst. Cardiology, Beijing, 1984—; co-founder, cons. cardiologist Mid-Am. Heart Inst., Kansas City, mem. adv. bd., 1980—. Author: Your Heart, 1983, 2d edit., 1990; contbr. articles to profl. jours. Bd. dirs. St. Lukes Hosp. Research Found., 1973-75. Served to lt. USN, 1949-57. Fellow ACP, Am. Coll. Cardiology (bd. trustees 1965-67, 71-73, treas. 1966-67, sec., bd. govs. 1972-74, assoc. editor Accel. 1969-81, Cummings Internat. Teaching award, 1967). Republican. Episcopalian. Clubs: River, Carriage. Avocations: music, reading, tennis. Home: 1015 Huntington Rd Kansas City MO 64113 Office: Cardiovascular Cons Office Pres 4320 Wornall Rd Kansas City MO 64111-3201

CROCKETT, JAMES GROVER, III, musician, former music publisher; b. San Francisco, Feb. 13, 1937; s. James Grover and Virginia (Adams) C.; m. Roberta Crockett; children: Chenoa Denelle, Doya Laurenne, Cordell Miller, Kessel Robinson; stepchildren: Devon, Susie. BA in Comms., Coll. of Pacific, 1958; MA in Comms., U. of Pacific, 1960. Various positions radio and TV stas. Stockton and Sacramento, Calif., Grants Pass, Oreg., Spokane, Wash., 1952-62; instr. radio-TV dept. U. Idaho, Moscow, 1961-63; concert producer, freelance writer, 1963-70; owner, mgr. Books Universal, Livermore, Calif., 1963-70; arts editor, columnist, writer Livermore Ind., 1968-70; asst. editor Guitar Player mag., 1970-71, editor, 1971, pub., 1971-89; v.p. GPI Corp., 1971-82, pres., 1982-89; also pub. Keyboard mag., Frets mag.; cons. to mag. industry., 1989—; news editor Radio Cayman, 1998—; bd. dirs., former CEO MusicWriter Inc., 1991-93; race car driver, 1987-93; gen. mgr., former owner Quabbin Dives, Grand Cayman, British West Indies, 1993-97; speaker various trade confs. Free-lance musician, writer, 1955—; pub. 1st non-objective coloring book for children, guitar repair manual, The Great White Shark, Why-To Book of Scuba Diving; pub. Autoracer's Monthly Newsletter, 1990-94. Mem. Alpha Epsilon Rho, Phi Mu Alpha. Office: Box 146 HELL, Grand Cayman Cayman Islands

CROCKETT, NOLUTHANDO PHYLLIS, communications executive; b. Chgo., July 14, 1950; d. Leo F. Crockett and Mae (Corbin) Williams; divorced; children: Adina Gittens-Smith, Andrew DuBois. BA, U. Ill.,

Chgo., 1972; MS in Journalism, Northwestern U., 1979. Free-lance reporter AP and UPI, Raleigh and Durham, N.C., 1978-80; news writer Sta. WTTG-TV, Washington, 1981-82; free-lance writer Pacific News Svc., San Francisco, 1984; producer, reporter, anchorperson Sta. WSOC, Charlotte, N.C., 1978-79, Stas. WFNC/WQSM, Fayetteville, N.C., 1979-80; exec. editor, talk show moderator Sheridan Broadcasting Network, Washington, 1980-81; reporter gen. assignments Nat. Pub. Radio, Washington, 1981-89, White House corr., 1989-91, sr. corr., 1991-94; pres. Chronicle Communications, Johannesburg, South Africa, 1994—; panelist CNN & Co., CNN's Internat. Corrs., CNN's Inside Politics, 1992-97, CNN's Both Sides with Jesse Jackson, Am.'s Black Forum, Washington, 1980-83; analyst C-Span Cable TV Network, Black Entertainment TV, Washington and Sta. WHMM-TV, Washington, 1987-97, Am. Urban Radio News Network, others; cons. Clark-Atlanta U., others, 1982-94; vis. instr. Fayetteville State U., 1980, Johnson C. Smith U., Charlotte, 1979; guest lectr. Howard U., U. D.C., Fairfax (Va.) Pub. Schs., 1980-94; media cons. South African Broadcasting Co., Radio 702, others. Contbg. author: Split Image: African-Americans in the Mass Media, 1990, 93; contbr. book reviews to N.Y. Times, 1988, 92, L.A. Times, 1989, Washington Post, 1994; pub. The Crockett Chronicle, 1984—. John S. Knight fellow Stanford U., 1990-91; recipient NEA award, 1988, Robert F. Kennedy award, 1990. Mem. Nat. Assn. Black Journalists (Frederick Douglass award 1984), Washington Assn. Black Journalists (v.p. 1982), Sigma Delta Chi. Baptist. Avocations: tennis, gardening, swimming, walking, movies. E-mail: info@chronicle.co.za. Office: PO Box 3257 Parklands, Johannesburg 2121, South Africa also: care Squire Padgett 1835 K St NW Ste 900 Washington DC 20006-1213

CROCKETT, PATRICIA JO FRY, psychiatric-mental health nurse; b. Cabell Countyy, W.Va., Nov. 25, 1966; d. Roger Lee and Patricia Lee (Queen) Fry; m. Virgil LeRoy Crockett, Mar. 18, 1989; children: Jennifer Lynn, Justin Lee. Student, Marshall U., 1985-86; diploma, St. Mary's Sch. Nursing, Huntington, W.Va., 1989. RN, W.Va.; cert. CPR instr.; cert. psychiat. mental health nurse. Nurse adolescent treatment unit St. Mary's Hosp., 1989—. Home: RR 2 Box 2324 Wayne WV 25570-9755

CROFT, HARRY ALLEN, psychiatrist; b. Houston, July 2, 1943; s. Louis and Ida (Kaplan) C.; m. Benay Bleacher, Dec. 27, 1964; children—Jamie Sue, Bradley Lane, Chasen Ashley. B.S., So. Meth. U., 1964; M.D., U. Tex. at Galveston, 1968. Intern Brackenridge Hosp., Austin, 1968-69; resident in obstetrics and gynecology U. Tex. Med. Br., 1969-70, resident in psychiatry, 1970-73; dir. methadone program Galveston County, Tex.; dir. sex therapy program U. Tex., Galveston, 1972-73; commd. capt. U.S. Army, 1973, advanced through grades to maj., 1975; chief (Mental Hygiene Service, Brooke Army Med. Center), Houston, 1973-76; pvt. practice, 1976—; clin. asst. prof. psychiatry and obstetrics and gynecology Med. Sch. San Antonio, 1973-75; columnist San Antonio Express-News, 1975-76; weekly contbr. Sta. KENS-TV (CBS) newscast; weekly radio talk show host PsychTalk, KENS Radio. Contbr. articles to profl. jours. Recipient physician's recognition award AMA, 1974, awards for med. TV work Nat. Healthcare Assn., 1988, Women in Comm., 1988; Meritorious Svc. medal U.S. Army, 1976, Ware 1st place audio-visual award Dept. Army, 1976, Gov.'s award State of Tex., 1991, award City of San Antonio, award Acad. Radio and TV Health Comm., Jules Bergman award-Broadcaster of Yr. award, 1995, Best Radio Show In U.S., Nat. Mental Health Assn., 1996. Mem. Am. Psychiat. Assn. (award 1991), Tex. Med. Assn. (award 1988), Am. Soc. Sex Educators, Counselors and Therapists, Am. Soc. Addiction Medince (cert. addictionist). Home: 12738 Hunters Chase St San Antonio TX 78230-1930 Office: 8038 Wurzbach Rd Ste 570 San Antonio TX 78229-3815*

CROFT, JANET BRENNAN, library director, fiber artist, costume designer; b. Pitts., May 5, 1961; d. Earl David and Marian (Maxwell) Brennan; m. Duane Shiffler, Aug. 11, 1984; 1 child, Sarah Gail. BA in English & Classical Civilization, Ind. U., 1982, MLS, 1983. Libr. Jenner and Block Law Firm, Chgo., 1983-84, Carnegie Libr. Pitts., 1985, Sewickley (Pa.) Pub. Libr., 1985-88, Moon Twp. Pub. Libr., Coraopolis, Pa., 1988-89, 90; libr. dir. Martin Meth. Coll., Pulaski, Tenn., 1993—, costume designer, 1997—. Contbr. articles to profl. jours. Mem. Mag. Club Pulaski. Avocations: quilting, wearable art. Office: Martin Meth Coll 433 W Madison St Pulaski TN 38478-2716

CROFT, KATHRYN DELAINE, business executive, consultant; b. Eastover, S.C., Jan. 13, 1944; d. Randolph and Ethel (Williams) Lloyd; m. Daniel Marranzini, June 26, 1987. BS, Wilberforce U., 1965; MS, Columbia U., 1982, New Sch. for Social Rsch., 1988. Cert. social worker, N.Y. Exec. dir. Family Dynamics, Inc., N.Y.C., 1987-92; asst. provost Columbia U., N.Y.C., 1992-94; commr. N.Y.C. Child Welfare Adminstrn., N.Y.C., 1994-96; dir. ops. Just One Break, Inc., N.Y.C., 1997—; cons. various nonprofit orgns., N.Y.C., 1996—. Chmn., bd. dirs. Artsgenesis, N.Y.C., 1993—; bd. dirs. Ackerman Inst., N.Y.C., 1997—. Recipient scholarships New Sch. for Social Rsch., 1985-88, Columbia U., 1978-82. Mem. NAFE, Assn. Black Women in Higher Edn. Avocations: travel, reading, photography.

CROFT, TERRENCE LEE, lawyer; b. St. Louis, Apr. 13, 1940; s. Thomas L. and Anita Belle (Brown) C.; m. Merry Patton, July 9, 1977; children: Michael, Shannon, Kimberly, Kristin, BethAnn, Katherine. AB, Yale U., 1962; JD with distinction, U. Mich., 1965. Bar: Mo. 1965, U.S. Dist. Ct. (ea. dist.) Mo. 1965, Ga. 1970, Fla. 1970, U.S. Dist. Ct. (no. dist.) Ga. 1970, U.S. Ct. Appeals (5th, 8th and 11th cirs.) 1970, U.S. Supreme Ct. Assoc. Coburn, Croft & Kohn, St. Louis, 1965-69, Hansell, Post, Brandon & Dorsey, Atlanta, 1969-73; ptnr. Huie, Sterne & Ide, Atlanta, 1973-78, Kutak, Rock & Huie, Atlanta, 1978-83; shareholder Griffin, Cochrane & Marshall, Atlanta, 1983-93; ptnr. King & Croft LLP, Atlanta, 1994—. Mem. ABA (ho. of dels. 1994—), ATLA, Atlanta Bar Assn. (pres., sec., treas. bd. dirs. 1986—, chmn., bd. dirs. litigation sect. 1982-86, pres. Alt. Dispute Resolution Lawyers sect. 1996-97), Atlanta Bar Found. (pres. 1998—), Ga. Trial Lawyers Assn., Lawyers Club Atlanta. Episcopalian. Avocations: hiking, shooting, motorcycling, reading. E-mail: tlc@king-croft.com. Fax: 404-577-8401. Home: 2580 Westminster Heath Atlanta GA 30327 Office: King & Croft LLP 707 The Candler Bldg 127 Peachtree St NE Atlanta GA 30303-1800

CROFTS, ANTONY RICHARD, biophysics educator; b. Harrow, Eng., Jan. 26, 1940; came to U.S., 1978; s. Richard Basil Iliffe and Vera Rosetta (Bland) C.; m. Paula Anne Hinds-Johnson, June 7, 1969 (div. 1981); 1 child, Charlotte Victoria Patricia; 1 adopted child, Rupert Charles; m. Christine Thompson Yerkes, Dec. 23, 1982; children: Stephanie Boynton, Terence Spencer. BA, U. Cambridge, Eng., 1961, PhD, 1965. Asst. lectr. dept. biochemistry U. Bristol, Eng., 1964-65, lectr., 1966-72, reader, 1972-78; prof. biophysics U. Ill., Urbana-Champaign, 1978—, prof. microbiology, 1992—, chmn. biophysics divsn., 1978-91, assoc. dean Coll. Liberal Arts & Scis., 1996-98, prof. biochemistry, 1998—; Mem. organizing com. 4th Internat. Congress Photosynthesis, Reading, Eng., 1977, 7th Internat. Congress Photosynthesis, Providence, 1986, Table Ronde, Rousel-UCLA Forum, Paris, 1985; vis. prof. Coll. de France, 1983; Melandri lectr. European BioEnergetics Conf., Lyon, France, 1982. Contbr. numerous articles, revs., etc., in area of biophysics, photosynthesis and bioenergetics; mem. editl. bd. Biochem. Jour., U.K., 1971-72, Biochimica Biophysica Acta, Holland, 1972-77, jour. Bacteriology, 1979-83, Archives Biochemistry and Biophysics, 1980-85. Major scholar nat. sci. U. Cambridge, 1958-61, U. Ill. scholar, 1989-92; grantee U.S. Dept. Energy, 1982-96, Guggenheim Found., 1985, NSF, NIH, U.S. Dept. Agr., 1979-98. Fellow AAAS; mem. Biophys. Soc., Am. Soc. Biochemistry and Molecular Biology, Am. Soc. Plant Physiologists (Charles F. Kettering award 1992). Avocations: windsurfing, skiing, fishing, sailing. Office: U Ill Ctr Biophysics 388 Morrill Hall 505 S Goodwin Ave Urbana IL 61801-3707

CROFTS, RICHARD A., academic administrator. PhD in Info., Duke U. Mem. faculty U. Toledo; assoc. v.p. rsch., dean Grad. Sch. E. Tenn. State U.; dep. commr. acad. affairs Mo. Univ. Sys., Helena, 1994-96; interim commr. higher edn. Mo. Univ. Sys., Helena, Mont., 1996-97, commr. higher edn., 1997—. Office: Mont Univ Sys PO Box 203101 2500 E Broadway St Helena MT 59620-3101

CROHAN, MARGARET ELIZABETH, communications educator, consultant; b. Boston, June 11, 1966. BS, Emerson Coll., 1988; MA, U. Del., 1990; postgrad., Tufts Med. U., 1997—. Project dir. Blue Cross/Blue Shield, Wilmington, Del., 1988-90; edn. coord. New Eng. Broadcasting Assn., Boston, 1990—; pres. Professionally Speaking, Framingham, Mass., 1990—; prof. Emerson Coll., Boston, 1990—; adj. prof. Northeastern U., Boston, 1990-96, Boston U., 1990—, Curry Coll., Milton, Mass., 1990—; cons. Phillips Acad., Andover, Mass., 1997, Am. Express, Boston, 1996, Pine St. Inn, Boston, 1995. Contbr. articles to profl. jours. Mem. geriat. com., health edn. com. Curry Coll., 1997; intercollegiate judge Green Line Forensics Soc., Boston, 1990—; coord. American Red Cross, Wilmington, 1989. Named Outstanding Tchr., Internat. Comm. Assn., 1990, Outstanding Young American, 1997. Mem. New Eng. Broadcasting Assn. (edn. coord. 1990—), Speech Comm. Assn., Mass. Pub. Health Assn. (chair women's health sect., chair women's health com.), Emerson Coll. Alumni Assn., U. Del. Alumni Assn. Avocations: tennis, reading, writing, hiking, travel. Office: Professionally Speaking PO Box 1171 Framingham MA 01701-1171

CROHN, MAX HENRY, JR., lawyer; b. Asheville, N.C., Feb. 4, 1934; s. Max Henry and Edith Pearl (Hoffman) C.; m. Barbara Jean Morris, Jan. 28, 1960; children: David Michael, Edith Ann, Randal Morris. B.A. in Polit. Sci, U. N.C., 1955; LL.B., Georgetown U., 1961. Bar: D.C. 1961, N.C. 1977, N.Y. 1986. Practiced in D.C., 1961-68; trial atty. Bur. Restraint of Trade, 1963-65; atty. adviser to chmn. FTC, 1965-66; asso. mem. firm Arnold & Porter, Washington, 1966-68; asso. counsel R.J. Reynolds Industries, Inc., Winston-Salem, N.C., 1968-75; asst. gen. counsel R.J. Reynolds Industries, Inc., 1975-78; sec. R.J. Reynolds Tobacco Co., 1971-81, gen. counsel, 1978-81; ptnr. Jacob, Medinger and Finnegan, 1981-95; former chmn. bd. dirs. Forsyth County Econ. Devel. Corp., 1975-78. Served to lt. (j.g.) USNR, 1955-58. Mem. ABA. Home: 517 Redbud Rd Chapel Hill NC 27514-1710

CROIS, JOHN HENRY, local government official; b. Chgo., Jan. 13, 1946; s. Henry F. and Dorothy M. (Priebe) C. BA, Elmhurst Coll., 1969; MA, U. Notre Dame, 1972. Asst. village mgr. Village of Oak Lawn, Ill., 1975-85; village mgr. Village of Westchester, Ill., 1985; dir. West Cook County Solid Waste Agy., 1990—; coord. Oak Lawn Swine Flu Immunization Program, 1976; bd. dirs. Ill. Met. Investment Fund. Mem. ASPA, West Ctrl. Mcpl. Conf. (chmn. intergovtl. com. 1991, exec. bd. 1991—), Ill. Met. Investment Fund (dir. 1996—), Chgo. Area Transp. Study Coun. Mayors (North Ctrl. region), Internat. City Mgmt. Assn., Ill. City Mgmt. Assn., Metro-Mgrs. Assn., St. Germaine's Men's Club. Home: 10233 Karlov Ave Oak Lawn IL 60453-4235 Office: 10300 W Roosevelt Rd Westchester IL 60154-2568

CROLAND, BARRY I., lawyer; b. Paterson, N.J., Jan. 11, 1938; s. Louis L. and Rae R. (Levine) C.; m. Joan Kohlreiter, Dec. 20, 1958; children: Richard, Heidi, Lizabeth, Jennifer. BA, Middlebury Coll., 1959; JD, Rutgers U., Newark, 1961. Bar: N.J. 1962, N.Y. 1983, U.S. Ct. Appeals (3d cir.) 1973. Law clk. to Hon. John Grimshaw N.J. Superior Ct., 1961, law clk. to Hon. Morris Pashman, 1961-62; assoc. Cole, Berman & Garth, Paterson, 1962-63, Shavick, Thevos, Stern, Schotz & Steiger, Paterson, 1963-68; ptnr. Shavick, Stern, Schotz, Steiger & Croland, Paterson, 1968-79, Stern, Steiger, Croland, Tanenbaum & Schielke, Paterson, 1979-95, Shapiro & Croland, Hackensack, N.J., 1995—; asst. bar examiner State of N.J., 1965-68; mem. Fed. Ethics Com., Dist. of N.J., 1975—; lectr. Inst. for Continuing Legal Edn., Trial Advocacy and Family Law, 1975—. Mem. bd. editors Rutgers Law Rev., 1959-61, case editor, 1960-61; sr. editor N.J. Family Lawyer. Fellow Am. Acad. Matrimonial Lawyers; mem. ABA (family law sect.), Am. Coll. Family Trial Lawyers (diplomate 1994—), Am. Inns of Ct. (master Morris Pashman 1990-95, pres.-master N.J. family law 1995—), N.J. State Bar Assn. (mem. exec. com. family law sect. 1981-95), Bergen County Bar Assn. (chmn. jud. and prosecutorial appts. com. 1983-95). Home: 243 Myrtle St Haworth NJ 07641-1137 Office: Shapiro & Croland 411 Hackensack Ave Hackensack NJ 07601-6328

CROLL, ROBERT FREDERICK, economist, educator; b. Evanston, Ill., Feb. 3, 1934; s. Frederick Warville and Florence (Campbell) C.; m. Sandra Elizabeth Bell, June 15, 1968; 1 child, Robert Frederick. BSBA, Northwestern U., 1954; MBA (Burton A. French scholar) with high distinction, U. Mich., 1956; DBA, Ind. U., 1969; DLitt, John F. Kennedy Coll., 1970. Instr. Ind. U. Sch. Bus., Bloomington, 1956, researcher in bus. econs., 1960-62; mng. dir. Motor Vehicle Industry Research Assocs., Evanston, 1962-63; personal asst. to speaker Ill. Ho. of Reps., 1963-65; asst. prof. bus. adminstrn. Kans. State U., 1965-66; asst. prof. Inst. Indsl. Relations, Loyola U. Chgo., 1966-70; assoc. prof. Sch. Bus. Adminstrn., Central Mich. U., 1970-76, prof., 1976—. Mem. platform committee Ind. Republican Com., 1958; Ind. del. Young Rep. Nat. Conv., 1959; nat. chmn. Youth for Goldwater Orgn., 1960-61; chmn. coll. clubs Young Rep. Orgn. Ill., 1960-62; treas. Young Rep. Orgn. Ill., 1963-65; asst. chief page Rep. Nat. Conv., 1964; mem. Mt. Pleasant City Charter Commn., 1973-76. Trustee estate of F.W. Croll, Chgo., 1959—; bd. govs. Clarke Hist. Library, 1986—. Recipient Grand prize Gov. of Ind., 1958. Accredited personnel diplomate Am. Soc. Personnel Adminstrn. Accreditation Inst. Mem. Soc. Automotive Engrs., Am. Inst. Mgmt., Soc. Advancement Mgmt., Am. Econ. Assn., Mt. Pleasant C. of C., Young Ams. for Freedom (founder 1960, vice chmn. 1962-63), Phila. Soc. (founder 1964), Beta Gamma Sigma, Delta Sigma Pi Key, Phi Delta Kappa, Phi Kappa Phi, Pi Sigma Alpha, Delta Mu Delta, Sigma Pi, Alpha Kappa Psi, Sigma Iota Epsilon, Phi Chi Theta, Pi Omega Pi., Phi Beta Delta. Episcopalian. Clubs: Little Harbor (Harbor Springs, Mich.); Mount Pleasant Country; Riomar Bay Yacht. Author: Fall of an Automotive Empire: A Business History of the Packard Motor Car Company, 1945-1958, others. Contbr. articles to profl. jours. Office: Ctrl Mich U Dept Mgmt Mount Pleasant MI 48859

CROM, JAMES OLIVER, professional training company executive; b. Alliance, Nebr., July 31, 1933; s. James Harvey and Evalyn Grace (Robinson) C.; m. Rosemary Vanderpool, Jan. 30, 1953 (dec. Aug. 1994); children: Michael Alexander, Marie Celeste, Brenda Leigh; m. Roselyn Maguire, Aug. 1996. B.S., U. Wyo., 1955. Sales rep. Investors Diversified Services, 1955-57; dist. supr. King Merritt and Co., 1957-59; field sales trainer Dale Carnegie and Assocs., Inc., Garden City, N.Y., 1959-60; asst. to v.p. ops. dept. Dale Carnegie and Assocs., Inc., 1960-62, dir. ops. sales course, 1962-64, dir. ops. all courses, 1964-67, v.p. field ops., 1967-74, exec. v.p., gen. mgr., 1974-78, pres., CEO, 1978—; chmn. bd. trustees emeritus Accrediting Coun. for Continuing Edn. and Tng., Inc. Pres. L.I. Ednl. TV Coun., Inc., 1977-79; former trustee Lincoln Meml. U., Harrogate, Tenn.; v.p. Dorothy Carnegie Found.; mem. adv. bd. Nassau County coun. Boy Scouts Am.; past pres. Huntington Men's Chorus; chmn. exec. com., trustee, v.p. Old Westbury Gardens. Recipient Pub. Svc. awards Momma's House honoree Garden City Epilepsy Ctr., L.I. Bus. News, L.I. Alzheimer's Found., Nassau County coun. Boy Scouts Am., L.I. Stage; named Outstanding Bd. Advisor, AIESEC-U.S. Mem. L.I. Assn., U.S. C. of C. Republican. Roman Catholic. Home and Office: 1475 Franklin Ave Garden City NY 11530-1662

CROMARTIE, ERIC ROSS, lawyer; b. Washington, Jan. 14, 1955; s. William Adrian and Dorothy Jane (Cann) C.; m. Lynn Prendergast, Sept. 12, 1981; children: William Ross, Morgan Nicole. BA, Amherst (Mass.) Coll., 1977; JD, Harvard U., 1980. Bar: Tex. 1980, U.S. Dist. Ct. (no. and ea. dists.) Tex. 1980, U.S. Tax. Ct. 1983, U.S. Ct. Appeals (5th and 11th cirs.) 1980, U.S. Ct. Appeals (8th and 10th cirs.) 1984, U.S. Supreme Ct. 1985. Assoc. Hughes and Luce, Dallas, 1980-85, ptnr., 1985-97. Mem. ABA, Dallas Bar Assn., Am. Law Inst. Home: 6724 Avalon Ave Dallas TX 75214-3703

CROMARTIE, ROBERT SAMUEL, III, thoracic surgeon; b. Fayetteville, N.C., Dec. 25, 1943; s. Robert Samuel Jr. and May Hunter (Cook) C.; m. Mary Elaine Collier; children: Robert Samuel IV, David Alan, Kimberly Elaine. AB in Chemistry, U. N.C., 1965, MD, 1969. Diplomate Am. Bd. Surgery, Am. Bd. Thoracic Surgery, Am. Bd. Laser Surgery. Intern in surgery U. Miami, 1969-70, resident in gen. surgery, 1972-74; resident in gen. surgery La. State U., New Orleans, 1974-76; resident in thoracic surgery Med. U. S.C., Charleston, 1976-78; asst. prof. surgery Ind. U. Med. Ctr., Indpls., 1978-80; thoracic and cardiovasc. surgeon Tampa (Fla.) Gen. Hosp., 1980-81, Meml. Hosp., Ormond Beach, Fla., 1981—; thoracic and cardiovasc. surgeon Columbia Med. Ctr., Daytona, Fla., 1981—, chief of surgery, 1996-97; thoracic and cardiovasc. surgeon, chief thoracic surgery Halifax Hosp., Daytona Beach, 1984—, Peninsula Med. Ctr., Ormond Beach, Fla., 1993—. Contbr. articles to profl. jours. Del. Fla. Med. Assn., 1992, 93, 94. Served to capt. U.S. Army, 1970-72. Decorated Bronze Star. Fellow ACS, Am. Coll. Cardiology, Am. Coll. Chest Physicians, Internat. Coll. Surgeons; mem. AMA, So. Thoracic Surg. Assn., Soc. Thoracic Surgeons, James D. Rives Surg. Soc., Am. Heart Assn., Soc. Critical Care Medicine. Avocations: snow skiing, racquetball, writing. Home: 236 John Anderson Dr Ormond Beach FL 32176-5706 Office: Coastal Cardiovasc & Thoracic Assocs 588 Sterthaus Ave Ormond Beach FL 32174-5128

CROMARTIE, WILLIAM JAMES, medical educator, researcher; b. Garland, N.C., May 19, 1913; s. Robert Samuel and Mary Blanche (Jester) C.; m. Josephine Colter Rule, Nov. 19, 1945; children: William James, Robert Colter, Mary Blanche, John Benjamin, Martha Anne. Student, Presbyn. Jr. Coll., 1929-30, U. N.C., 1931, U. Ala., 1931-33; MD, Emory U., 1937. Diplomate Am. Bd. Internal Medicine. Intern Emory U. divsn. Grady Hosp., Atlanta, 1937-38; resident Vanderbilt U. Hosp., Nashville, 1938-40; instr. pathology Vanderbilt U., 1939-41; asst. prof. bacteriology and medicine U. Minn., Mpls., 1949-50, assoc. prof., 1950-51; assoc. prof. bacteriology and medicine U. N.C., Chapel Hill, 1951-59, chief div. infectious diseases, dept. medicine N.C. Meml. Hosp., Chapel Hill, 1952-65, chief of staff, 1967-72; prof. microbiology-immunology-medicine U. N.C., Chapel Hill, 1959-85, prof. emeritus, 1985—; mem. adv. panel microbiology Office Naval Rsch., Washington, 1950-55; mem. Nat. Bd. Med. Examiners, Phila., 1966-68; mem. infectious disease adv. com. NIH, Bethesda, Md., 1971-75. Mem. bd. govs. Capital Health Planning Agy., Durham, N.C.; mem. exec. com. Regional Med. Program N.C., 1972-76. Maj. U.S. Army, 1942-46, ETO. Decorated Legion of Merit; named Alumni Disting. Prof. U. N.C., 1980. Fellow ACP, Am. Acad. Microbiology (chmn. bd. govs. 1974-75); mem. Soc. Am. Microbiologists (mem. coun. 1974-75), Am. Assn. Pathologists, Infectious Disease Soc. Am., U. N.C. Med. Alumni Assn. (Disting. Faculty award 1983, Disting. Svc. award 1989). Democrat. Home: Glendale 204 Weaver Rd Chapel Hill NC 27514-5947 Office: U NC Sch Medicine Dept Microbiology and Immunology 804 FLOB 23L-H Chapel Hill NC 27514

CROMBIE, DOUGLASS DARNILL, aerospace communications system engineer; b. Alexandra, N.Z., Sept. 14, 1924; came to U.S., 1962, naturalized, 1967; s. Colin Lindsay and Ruth (Darnill) C.; m. Pauline L.A. Morrison, Mar. 2, 1951. B.Sc., Otago U., Dunedin, N.Z., 1947, M.Sc., 1949. N.Z. nat. research fellow Cavendish Lab., Cambridge, Eng., 1958-59; head radio physics div. N.Z. Dept. Sci. and Indsl. Research, 1961-62; chief spectrum utilization div., chief low frequency group Inst. Telecommunications Scis., Dept. Commerce, Boulder, Colo., 1962-71, dir. inst., 1971-76; dir. Inst. Telecommunication Scis., Nat. Telecommunications and Info. Adminstrn., Boulder, Colo., 1976-80; chief scientist Nat. Telecommunication and Info. Agy., 1980-85; sr. engring. specialist Aerospace Corp., Los Angeles, 1985—. Served with N.Z. Air Force, 1943-44. Recipient Gold medal Dept. Commerce, 1970, citation, 1972. Fellow IEEE; mem. NAE, Union Radio Sci. Internat. Home: 524 Standard St El Segundo CA 90245-3039 Office: The Aerospace Corp PO Box 92957 Los Angeles CA 90009-2957

CROMER-CAMPBELL, TAMMY, commercial and fine art photographer; b. Longview, Tex., July 9, 1960; d. Bobby Wayne and Diana Cecilia (Hidalgo) Cromer; m. Scott Canterbury, Apr. 8, 1989. AA in Comml. Photography, Kilgore (Tex.) Coll., 1986. Photographer, fashion photographer Strictly Petites, Kilgore, 1987-89; sr. photographer awdNeedlecraft Shop, Big Sandy, Tex., 1989-96; owner Tammy Cromer-Campbell Photographs, Longview, 1987—; freelance photographer Longview; mem. adv. bd. photography dept. Kilgore Coll., 1992—. Photographer: (ann. awards books) Advertising Photographers of America, Book 1, 1991 (Disting. award 1991), Book 2, 1992 (1st award for still life 1992); contbr. photographs to: Pregnant Pictures. The Work of Women in the Age of Mechanical Reproduction, 1997. Named one of Top 100 Photographers, Ernst Haas Golden Light awards, N.Y.C., 1996, 98; recipient 3rd pl. award and hon. mention Photo Ams., Tulsa, 1997, various other awards. Mem. Tex. Photog. Soc. (bd. dirs. 1998—, 1st pl. Gov. Show 1996, 3rd pl. award 1997), Longview Mus. Fine Arts (PhotoView curator/coord. 1996—, bd. dirs. 1992—). Home: 200 Vinewood Ln Longview TX 75604-3233

CROMLEY, ALLAN WRAY, journalist; b. Topeka, Apr. 11, 1922; s. Frank George and Elsie May (Leedom) C.; m. Marian Minor, Jan. 30, 1949; children: Kathleen, Janet, Carter. B.S. in Journalism (Summerfield scholar 1940-43, 46), U. Kans., 1948. Reporter Kansas City Kansan, 1948-49, Oklahoma City Times, 1949-53; Washington bur. chief Daily Oklahoman and Oklahoma City Times, 1953-87; sr. corr. Washington bur. Daily Oklahoman, 1987-95; ret., 1995; sec. standing com. corrs. House and Senate Galleries, 1961. Bd. visitors U. Okla., 1970-72; active U. Okla. Found., 1994—; trustee William Allen White Found. U. Kans., 1978-90; bd. dirs. Nat. Press Found., 1987-99. With AUS, 1943-45, ETO. Mem. Soc. Profl. Journalists, Nat. Press Club (pres. 1968), Nat. Gridiron Club (v.p. 1977, pres. 1978, treas. 1981-88, sec. 1988-95). Home: 3320 Stoneybrae Dr Falls Church VA 22044-1222

CROMLEY, BRENT REED, lawyer, legal association administrator; b. Great Falls, Mont., June 12, 1941; s. Arthur and Louise Lilian (Hiebert) C.; m. Dorothea Mae Zamborini, Sept. 9, 1967; children: Brent Reed Jr., Giano Lorenzo, Taya Rose. AB in Math., Dartmouth Coll., 1963; JD with honors, U. Mont., 1968. Bar: Mont. 1968, U.S. Dist. Ct. Mont. 1968, U.S. Ct. Appeals (9th cir.) 1968, U.S. Supreme Ct. 1978, U.S. Ct. Claims 1988, U.S. Ct. Appeals (D.C. cir.) 1988. Law clk. to presiding justice U.S. Dist. Ct. Mont., Billings, 1968-69; assoc. Hutton & Sheehy and predecessor firms, Billings, 1969-77, ptnr., 1977-78; ptnr. Moulton, Bellingham, Longo & Mather, P.C., Billings, 1979—, also bd. dirs.; mem. Montana Ho. Reps., 1991-92; pres. State Bar Mont., 1998-99. Contbr. articles to profl. jours. Mem. Yellowstone Bd. Health, Billings, 1972—; chmn. Mont. Bd. Pers. Appeals, 1974-80. Mem. ABA (appellate practice com.), ACLU, Internat. Assn. Def. Counsel, State Bar Mont. (chmn. bd. trustees 1995-97, trustee 1991—, pres. 1998-99), Yellowstone County Bar Assn. (various offices), Internat. Assn. Defense Counsel, Christian Legal Soc., Internat. Brotherhood of Magicians, Kiwanis. Avocations: running, magic, pub. speaking. E=mail: Cromley@moultonlawfirm.com. Home: 235 Parkhill Dr Billings MT 59101-0660 Office: Moulton Bellingham Longo & Mather PC Ste 1900 Sheraton Plaza 27 N 27th St Billings MT 59101 also: State Bar Montana PO Box 577 Helena MT 59624

CROMLEY, JON LOWELL, lawyer; b. Riverton, Ill., May 23, 1934; s. John Donald and Naomi M. (Mathews) C. BS, U. Ill., 1958; JD, John Marshall Law Sch., 1966. Bar: Ill. 1966. Real estate title examiner Chgo. Title & Trust Co., 1966-70; pvt. practice, Genoa, Ill., 1970—; mem. firm O'Grady & Cromley, Genoa, 1970-96; bd. dirs. Citizen's First Nat. Bank, 1984-92, Kingston Mut. Ins. Co., Genoa Main St., Inc. Mem. ABA, Am. Judicature Soc., Am., Ill. State Bar Assn., Chgo. Bar Assn., DeKalb County Bar Assn. Home: 130 Homewood Dr Genoa IL 60135-1260

CROMLEY, RAYMOND AVOLON, syndicated columnist; b. Tulare, Calif., Aug. 23, 1910; s. William James and Grace Violet (Bailey) C.; m. Masuyo Marjorie Suto (dec. Apr. 1946); m. Helen Sue Holcomb (dec. July 1967); children: Donald Stowe, Helen Sue, Jessica Lynn, Linda Grace, william Holcomb, Mary Ann, John Austin. BS in Physics, Calif. Inst. Tech., 1933; student, Japanese Lang. Inst., Tokyo, 1936-39, Strategic Intelligence Sch., Washington, 1954. Reporter Pasadena (Calif.) Post, 1928-34, Honolulu Advertiser, 1934-35, Flintridge Sch., Pasadena, 1935-36; reporter, then financial editor Japan Advertiser, Tokyo, 1936-40; editor Trans Pacific (econ. and financial weekly), 1938-40; with Wall St. Jour., 1938-55; Far Ea. corr., 1938-47, Washington corr., 1947-55; sci. editor radio program Monitor, 1955-56; econ. and financial commentator NBC radio, 1956-57; asst. producer CBS Radio, 1957-58; mil. analyst Newspaper Enterprise Assn., 1958-64; pres. Cromley News-Features, 1976—; syndicated columnist, 1964—; Asst. logic, freshman English Calif. Inst. Tech., 1928-30; lectr. Air War Coll., 1952, 54, Dept. State Fgn. Service Inst., 1955, 65-67; cons. guerilla war, Asian politics, 1952—. Author: Veterans Benefits, 1966, 2d edit., 1970, 3d edit., 1973, rev. edit., 1975, Educational Benefits, 1968, Ariwara Narihira and Japanese Poetry of the Heian and Nara Periods. Chmn. dist. bds. charter rev. Boy Scouts Am., 1956-60; sec. bishop's com. pastoral benefits Va. Conf. Meth. Ch., 1967-68; organizer com. estatlishment Martha Washington Libr., Mt. Vernon, Va., 1954; chmn. Inter-ch. Coun. Teen Activities and Teen Clubs, Mt. Vernon, 1955-57, World Coun. Youth, 1932-35. Prisoner of war, 1941-42; col. AUS, 1943-46; comdg. officer U.S.

Mil. and Dept. State mission to Mao-Tse-tung's hdqs., Yenan, Communist China. Decorated Legion of Merit, Bronze Star medal. Mem. Nat. Trust for Historic Preservation, Asiatic Soc. Japan, State Dept. Corrs. Assn. (pres. 1954-55), White House Corrs. Assn., Ret. Officers Assn., Smithsonian Assocs., Nat. Archives Assn., Nat. Press Found., Am. Fgn. Svc. Assn., Nat. Press Club Washington, Assn.Corcoran Gallery Art, Sigma Delta Chi, Pi Kappa Delta. Republican. Methodist (lay speaker, Sunday sch. tchr.). Clubs: Tokyo Correspondents (exec. com. 1947); Overseas Writers (Washington). Home: Hollin Hills 1912 Marthas Rd Alexandria VA 22307-1952 Office: PO Box 46989 Washington DC 20050-6989 *All great religions have one common theme -- Do unto others as you would have them do unto you. Some express it, do not do unto others what you would not want them to do unto you. I have seen the power of these beliefs first hand among ordinary men and women in Japan, Korea, China, Vietnam, Laos, Thailand, Bangladesh, India, Cuba, Mexico.*

CROMPTON-MOORER, CASSANDRA, basketball player; b. Oct. 29, 1962; m. Roy Moorer. Degree in broadcast and film comm., Ala. State U. Basketball player Dallas Diamonds Women's Basketball League, 1983-84; basketball player Spain, Italy, Turkey; asst. coach Ala. State U., 1997; basketball player N.Y. Liberty Women's NBA, N.Y.C., 1997-98; asst. coach women's basketball team U. Ala., Tuscaloosa, 1998—. Named Western Conf. MVP, 1982. Office: U Ala PO Box 870393 Tuscaloosa AL 35487*

CROMWELL, ADELAIDE M., sociology educator; b. Washington, Nov. 27, 1919; d. John Wesley, Jr. and Yetta Elizabeth (Mavritte) C.; 1 son, Anthony C. Hill. AB, Smith Coll., 1940; MA, U. Pa., 1941; cert. social work, Bryn Mawr Coll., 1943; PhD, Radcliffe Coll., 1952; LHD (hon.), U. Southwestern Mass., 1972, George Washington U., 1989, Boston U., 1995. Mem. faculty Hunter Coll., 1942-44, Smith Coll., 1945-46; mem. faculty Boston U., 1951-85, prof. sociology, 1971-85, dir. Afro-Am. studies, 1969-88, prof. emerita sociology, 1985—; mem. adv. com. vol. fgn. aid AID, 1964-80; mem. NEH, 1968-70; adv. com. corrections Commonwealth Mass., 1955-68; mem. commn. instns. higher edn., 1973-74; adv. com. to dir. IRS, 1970-71, to dir. census, 1972-75. Bd. dirs. Wheelock Coll., 1971--74, Nat. Ctr. Afro-Am. Artists, 1971-80, African Am. Scholars Coun., 1971—, Nat. Fellowship Fund, 1974-75, Mass. Hist. Commn., 1993; bd. dirs. Sci. and Tech. for Internat. Devel., 1984-86; mem. exec. com. Am. Soc. African Culture, 1967; mem. Mass. Hist. Soc., 1997—. Mem. AAAS, African Studies Assn. (bd. dir. 1966-68), Am. Acad. of Arts and Scis., Am. Sociol. Assn., Council on Fgn. Affairs (bd. fgn. scholarships 1980-84), Mass. Hist. Soc., Phi Beta Kappa. Home: 51 Addington Rd Brookline MA 02445-4519 Office: Boston U 138 Mountfort St Brookline MA 02446-4039

CROMWELL, AMANDA CARYL, soccer player, coach; b. Washington, June 15, 1970. BS in Biology, U. Va., 1992. Head women's soccer coach U. Md.; mem. U.S. Women's Nat. Soccer Team, 1991—; mem. U.S. Team CONCACAF Qualifying Tournament, Haiti, 1991, Montreal, Can., 1994; mem. silver medal U.S. Team, 1993 World Univ. Games, Buffalo, N.Y.; alternate gold medal U.S. Olympic Team, 1996; mem. 3d place U.S. Team, 1995 FIFA Women's World Cup, Sweden; mem. Hammarby Soccer Club, Stockholm, 1994; mem. SA United Soccer Club of Fairfax (Va.), 1997. Named NSCAA All-Am. (twice); named Soccer Am. Freshman of Yr., h.s. Rookie of Yr., 1990. Office: US Soccer Fedn 1801-1811 S Prairie Ave Chicago IL 60616*

CROMWELL, EDWIN BOYKIN, architect; b. Manila, P.I., Nov. 13, 1909; s. James Ellis and Ada (Henley) C.; m. Henrietta Thompson, May 22, 1937; children: Gertrude Cromwell Levy, Mildred Cromwell Cooper, Patricia Ellis. A.B., Princeton U., 1931, postgrad., 1931-32. Archtl. planner Resettlement Adminstrn., Washington and Ark., 1935-36; chmn. emeritus Cromwell Truemper Levy Thompson & Woodsmall, Little Rock, 1941—. Projects include U. Ark. at Little Rock, Ark. Arts Center, Little Rock, Master Plan Ark. State Capitol, Ark. Children's Colony, Winrock Farms, Morrilton, Ark., Consul Gen. resident, Madras, India, Embassy Housing, New Delhi, Maumelle New Town, U. Ark., Little Rock; restoration of residential bldgs. Quapaw Quarter and historic Capital Hotel, Little Rock. Chmn. emeritus Ark. Territorial Restoration Commn. Recipient Westbrook award, 1984, Strawn award, 1984; S.I.R. (Skill-Integrity-Responsibility) award Ark. chpt. Assoc. Gen. Contractors, 1985; Paul Harris fellow award Rotary, 1996. Fellow AIA (Gold Medal award Ark. chpt. 1987). Episcopalian. Home: 1720 Beechwood Rd Little Rock AR 72207-5432

CROMWELL, FLORENCE STEVENS, occupational therapist; b. Lewistown, Pa., May 14, 1922; d. William Andrew and Florence (Stevens) C. BS in Edn., Miami U., Oxford, Ohio, 1943; BS in Occupational Therapy, Washington U., St. Louis, 1949; MA, U. So. Calif., 1952; cert. in health facility adminstrn., UCLA, 1978. Mem. staff, then supervising therapist Los Angeles County Gen. Hosp., 1949-53; occupational therapist Goodwill Industries, L.A., 1954-55; staff therapist Vis. Nurse Assn., Phila., 1955-56; rsch. therapist United Cerebral Palsy Assn., L.A., 1956-60; dir. occupational therapy Orthopaedic Hosp., L.A., 1961-67; coordinator occupational therapy Rsch. and Tng. Ctr. U. So. Calif. Med. Sch., L.A., 1967-70; assoc. prof. U. So. Calif., L.A., 1970-76, acting chmn. dept. occupational therapy, 1973-76, mem. adv. bd. project SEARCH, Sch. Medicine, 1969-72; founding editor Occupational Therapy in Health Care jour., 1984-88, editor emerita, 1988—; assoc. dir. L.A. Job Corps Ctr., 1977-78, cons. in edn. and program devel., 1976-95; free-lance editor, 1986—. Author: Manual for Basic Skills Assessment, 1960; also articles. Mem. scholarship com. Los Angeles March of Dimes, 1963-70; bd. dirs. Am. Occupational Therapy Found., 1965-69, v.p., 1966-69; bd. dirs. Nat. Health Council, 1975-78; mentor U. Tex.-Galveston Class 1990 Occupational Therapy. Served to lt. (j.g.) WAVES, 1943-46. Recipient Disting. Alumni award Washington U., 1978, Disting. Lectr. Calif. Occupational Therapy Found., 1986. Fellow Am. Occupational Therapy Assn. (pres. 1967-73, Pres.'s WLWest commendation AOTA-AOTF 1999); mem. Inst. Medicine NAS (sr. 1989), So. Calif. Occupational Therapy Assn. (pres. 1950-51, 75-76), Coalition Ind. Health Professions (chmn. 1973-74), Assn. Schs. Allied Health Professions (dir. 1973-74), Cwen, Mortar Bd., Kappa Delta Pi, Kappa Kappa Gamma.

CROMWELL, JAMES, actor; b. L.A., Jan. 27, 1942; s. John Cromwell and Kay Johnson; m. Julie Cobb. Student, Carnegie Inst. Tech. Appeared in films including Murder by Death, 1976, The Cheap Detective, 1978, The Man with Two Brains, 1983, Tank, 1984, Revenge of the Nerds, 1984, Oh, God! You Devil, 1984, The House of God, 1984, Explorers, 1985, Revenge of the Nerds II: Nerds in Paradise, 1987, The Rescue, 1988, The Runnin' Kind, 1989, Pink Cadillac, 1989, The Babe, 1992, Romeo is Bleeding, 1993, Babe, 1995 (Oscar award nominee for best supporting actor), Star Trek: First Contact, 1996, Eraser, 1996, Owd Bob, 1997, The People vs. Larry Flynt, 1996, The Education of Little Tree, 1997, L.A. Confidential, 1997, Snow Falling on Cedars, 1998, Deep Impact, 1998, Species II, 1998, Babe: Pig in the City, 1998, Winter, 1998; TV appearances include (TV series) All in the Family, 1971, Hot L. Baltimore, 1975, The Nancy Walker Show, 1976, The Last Precinct, 1986, Easy Street, 1986, Mama's Boy, 1988, (mini TV series) Once an Eagle, 1976, Dream West, 1986, (TV movies) The Girl in the Empty Grave, 1977, Deadly Game, 1977, A Christmas without Snow, 1980, The Rainmaker, 1982, Spraggue, 1984, Alison's Demise, 1987, China Beach, 1988, Christine Cromwell: Things That Go Bump in the Night, 1989, Miracle Landing, 1990, In a Child's Name, 1991, Revenge of the Nerds III: The Next Generation, 1992, The Shaggy Dog, 1994, Revenge of the Nerds IV: Nerds in Love, 1994; guest TV appearances include Little House on the Prairie, 1974, Three's Company, 1978, Star Trek: the Next Generation, 1987, The Client, 1995, The General's Daughter, 1999, RKO 281, 1999, The Green Mile, 1999. Office: c/o Arlene L Dayton Mgmt 10110 Empyrean Way Apt 304 Los Angeles CA 90067-3845*

CROMWELL, OLIVER DEAN, investment banker; b. Cleve., Sept. 19, 1950; s. Oliver and Mildred Jeanette (Galko) C.; m. Sheila Lea Terry, May 19, 1984; children: Ashley Melissa, Oliver Spencer. AB, Brown U., 1972; MBA, Harvard U., 1976. Chartered fin. analyst. Trust adminstr. Bankers Trust, N.Y.C., 1973-74; assoc. Donaldson, Lufkin & Jenrette, N.Y.C., 1976-79, v.p., 1980-84, sr. v.p., 1985-87; sr. v.p. Oppenheimer & Co. Inc., N.Y.C., 1987-88; 1st v.p. Paine Webber, N.Y.C., 1988-90; founder, sr. mng. dir. Bentley Assocs. L.P., N.Y.C., 1990—; sr. mng. dir. Bentley Securities Corp., N.Y.C., 1991—. Exec. com., bd. dirs. Assoc. Alumni Brown U., 1985-87, bd. govs., 1987-88, co-head class agt. ann. fund, 1983-87, steering com. 5-yr. reunion fund, 1976-77, 10-yr. reunion fund, 1985-87, co-chmn. 20-yr. reunion fund, 1991-92, co-chmn. 25-yr. reunion fund 1996-97; ann. fund exec. com., 1991-93, co-chmn. N.Y. met. area com. Brown Campaign, 1992-94; class '72 v.p. Brown U., 1997—; major gifts com. Harvard Bus. Sch. 20th Reunion, 1995-96. Recipient Alumni Svc. award Brown U., 1990. Mem. Assn. for Investment Mgmt. and Rsch., N.Y. Soc. Security Analysts, Securities Industry Assn. N.Y. (exec. com. 1987-90), Assn. Corp. Growth, Aston Martin Owners Club-East, Maserati Club Am., Rolls Royce Owners Club (bd. dirs. 1992-93), Bentley Drivers Club (U.K.), Brown U. Club N.Y.C. (bd. dirs. 1983-95, treas. 1984-89, v.p. 1989-91, pres. 1991-93), Harvard Bus. Sch. Club. N.Y. Home: 4 Eastway Bronxville NY 10708-4302 Office: Bentley Assocs LP 21st Fl 101 Park Ave New York NY 10178

CROMWELL, RONALD R., educator; b. Roswell, N.Mex., Aug. 5, 1952; s. Edward Charles and Theresa (Dominick) C. MA, U. Colo., 1982; MM, Seattle U., 1984, EdD, 1988. Prin. St. Raphael Sch., El Paso, Tex., 1981-84, Seattle Cath. Schs., 1984-90; dir.clin. experiences Ind. U., Richmond, 1990-92; dir. tchr. edn. Marist Coll., Poughkeepsie, N.Y., 1992-97; prof., chair edn. SUNY, Oneonta, N.Y., 1997-99; dean Sch. Edn. and Allied Studies, Bridgewater (Mass.) State Coll., 1999—. Co-author: (chpts.) Promising Practices, 1994, Theories of Learning, 1996. Mem. Assn. Ind. Liberal Arts Colls for Tchr. Edn. (exec.com. 1996-97). Avocations: walking, cooking, theater.

CRON, MARC C., secondary education educator; b. Atlanta, Aug. 10, 1967; s. John G. and Joy M. (Bach) C.; m. Martha L. Cron, July 20, 1991; children: Lauren Mary, Lindsay May. BS in Computer Sci. Edn., Miami U., Oxford, Ohio, 1990, BS in Biol. Sci. Edn., 1990, MAt in Biology, 1995. Sci. tchr. S.W. Local Schs., Harrison, Ohio, 1990—. Office: Harrison HS 9860 West Rd Harrison OH 45030-1929

CRON, THEODORE OSCAR, writer, editor, educator; b. Newton, Mass., June 20, 1930; s. Jacob and Anna Ruth (Siegel) C.; m. Rosalie Heilpern, Jan. 17, 1954 (dec. Dec. 1998); children: Elizabeth Daryl Koozmin, Adam David. AB, Harvard U., 1952, MAT, 1954. Asst. commr. FDA, Washington, 1965-68; cons., writer Cron Comm., Chevy Chase, Md., 1969-77, 91—; dir. info. FTC, Washington, 1977-79; speech writer Office of Surgeon Gen., Washington, 1979-89; dir. info. Nat. Assn. Elem. Sch. Prins., Alexandria, Va., 1989-91; editor Better Ways to Health, Chevy Chase, 1995-96; adj. prof. journalism George Washington U., Washington, 1979—; writer, editor NIH, Bethesda, Md., 1991—, Nat. Health Svc. corps., Bethesda, 1992—, NSF, Washington, 1993—, Cardiology Rsch. Found., Washington, 1995—, Nat. Acad. Scis., 1996—. Author: Portrait of Carnegie Hall, 1966; contbr. articles to profl. jours. Chmn. bd. dirs. Edn. Study Ctr., Washington, 1968-73; trustee Intermet, Washington, 1971-75; bd. dirs. Nat. Coalition Consumer Edn., Madison, N.J., 1989-94. Recipient Spl. award Assn. Am. Indian Physicians, 1985, Freedom Found. at Valley Forge award 1989. Mem. Washington Ind. Writers, D.C. Sci. Writers Assn. Avocation: watercolor painting. Home: 5517 Trent St Chevy Chase MD 20815-5511

CRONACHER, WARREN WILLIAM, consulting engineer; b. N.Y.C., June 14, 1934; s. Walter Leonard and Elsie Julianne Cronacher; m. Lola Ann Lee, Dec. 3, 1957 (div. Mar. 1982); m. Victoria Jean Koller, Mar. 12, 1983; children: Karen, Suzanne. BSCE, Northeastern U., 1957. Registered profl. engr., N.Y., Conn. Sales engr. Phillips Cooling Tower, Bklyn., 1957-65; ind. contractor Arthur Tauscher, Profl. Engr., Rockville Centre, N.Y., 1965-71, v.p., 1971-86; pres., owner Tauscher Cronacher, Profl. Engr., Rockville Centre, N.Y., 1986—; mem. adv. bd. Criterium Engrs., Portland, Maine, 1988—. Treas. Trinity Luth. Ch., New Hyde Park, N.Y., 1991-94, v.p., 1994—. Mem. Nat. Acad. Bldg. Inspection Engrs. (pres. 1994-96, v.p. 1990-94, co-founder 1989, diplomate), Nat. Acad. Forensic Engrs. (diplomate), Coalition of Profl. Engrs. in Bldg. Inspection (founder 1988), Port Washington Yacht Club (rear commodore). Avocation: sailing. Home: 35 Primrose Dr New Hyde Park NY 11040 Office: 265 Sunrise Hwy Rockville Centre NY 11570

CRONAS, PETER CHRIS, company executive; b. Bklyn., Jan. 16, 1945; s. Chris Peter and Caroline Rose (Battinelli) C.; m. Adrianne Marie Vigueras, June 22, 1968; children: Johanna, Chris. BA, St. John's U., Bklyn., 1968; cert. in systems and data processing, NYU, 1974, cert. in programming, 1977, cert. in telecomm. mgmt., 1993; cert. computer profl., Inst. Cert. Computer Profls. Underwriter USF & G, N.Y.C., 1968-69; office mgr. State Mut. Ins. Co., N.Y.C., 1969-71; systems analyst Marine Office Appleton & Cox, Inc., N.Y.C., 1971-74; mgr. systems and procedures Am. Fgn. Ins. Assn., Wayne, N.J., 1974-77; MIS project mgr. AIG Ins., N.Y.C., 1977-78; MIS project leader Gen. Reins. Corp., Greenwich, Conn., 1977-78, Pepsi-Cola Co., Purchase, N.Y., 1979-81; asst. v.p. MIS reins. div. Frank B. Hall & Co., Briarcliff Manor, N.Y., 1981-87; v.p., dir. MIS, Duncanson & Holt, Inc., N.Y.C., 1987-93; dir. IS N.Y. Shipping Assn., N.Y.C., 1993—; former bd. dirs. Rochdale Ins. Co., N.Y.C. EMT Monroe (N.Y.) Vol. Ambulance Corps, 1972-78; pres. Monroe Jaycees, 1975; cub scout master Pack 47, Westwood, N.J.; spkr. career day N.Y. City Coun. Boy Scouts Am., 1991, 92, 93; merit badge counselor, Boy Scouts Am. Bergen Coun., 1997-99. Mem. Soc. for Info. Mgmt., Smithsonian Inst., Assn. for Info. Tech. Profls., Assn. Computing Machinery. Avocations: driving, golf, reading, tennis, travel. Office: NY Shipping Assn Inc 2 World Trade Ctr New York NY 10048-0203

CRONE, JOHN ROSSMAN, pharmacist; b. Franklin, Pa., Apr. 11, 1933; s. Wilmer Jennings and Lydia Juanita (Rossman) C.; m. Shirley Mae Parker, July 27, 1955; children: Michael John, David Jennings, Alan Parker. BS in Pharmacy, U. Pitts., 1955. Pharmacist King's Drug Store, Clarion, Pa., 1955-56; pharmacist, mgr. Cowdrick's Drug Stores, Inc., Philipsburg, Pa., 1956-57; pharmacist Warren, Pa., 1959-80, pharmacist, mgr., 1980-88; prin., pharmacist Crone's Drug Store, Warren, 1988—. Mem. adv. bd. Salvation Army, Warren, 1984—; bd. dirs. Warren County United Way, 1983-97, pres. bd. dirs., 1993-95; chmn. Warren Bus. Group, 1990-92, Warren Bus. Dist. Coalition, 1998—; bd. dirs. Pa. Lions Eye Rsch. Found., 1970-79; bd. dirs. Pa. Lions Hearing Rsch. Found., 1980—, chmn. bd., 1994—; pres. bd. dirs. Warren Bus. Dist. Coalition, 1996—. Recipient Warren Lions Club Melvin Jones Fellow award, 1990, C. of C. Community Svcs. award, 1990. Mem. Am. Pharm. Assn., Pa. Pharm. Assn., Warren County Pharm. Assn., Nat. Cmty. Pharmacists Assn., Warren County C. of C. (bd. dirs. 1988-95, pres.-elect 1992-93, pres. 1993-94). Republican. Methodist. Avocation: photography. Home: 605 Madison Ave Warren PA 16365-2940 Office: Crones Drug Store 212-214 Liberty St Warren PA 16365-2347

CRONE, RICHARD ALLAN, cardiologist, educator; b. Tacoma, Nov. 26, 1947; s. Richard Irving and Alla Marguerite (Ernst) C.; m. Becky Jo Zimmerlin, Dec. 11, 1993. BA in Chemistry, U. Wash., 1969, MD, 1973. Intern Madigan Army Med. Ctr., Tacoma, 1973-74, resident in medicine, 1974-76, fellow in cardiology, 1977-79; commd. med. officer U.S. Army, Tacoma, Denver, San Francisco, 1972; advanced through grades to lt. col. U.S. Army, 1981; dir. coronary care unit Fitzsimons Army Med. Ctr., Denver, 1979-81; practice medicine specializing in cardiology Stevens Cardiology Group, Edmonds, Wash., 1981—, also dir. coronary care unit, cardiac catheter lab, 1982—; clin. assoc. prof. medicine U. Wash., Seattle, 1983—. Fellow Am. Coll. Angiology; mem. AMA, Am. Coll. Cardiology, Am. Heart Assn., Seattle Acad. Internal Medicine, Wash. State Soc. Internal Medicine, Wash. State Med. Assn. Republican. Roman Catholic. Avocations: skiing, wine collecting. Home: 10325 66th Pl W Mukilteo WA 98275-4559 Office: 21701 76th Ave W Ste 100 Edmonds WA 98026-7536

CRONENBERG, DAVID, film director; b. Toronto, Ont., Can., Mar. 15, 1943. Ed., U. Toronto. Dir.: (films) Stereo, 1969, Crimes of the Future, 1970, They Came From Within, 1976, Rabid, 1977, The Brood, 1979, Fast Company, 1979, Scanners, 1981, Videodrome, 1983, The Dead Zone, 1983, The Fly, 1986, Dead Ringers, 1988, Naked Lunch, 1992, M. Butterfly, 1993, Existenze, 1998; dir., writer, prodr., actor: Crash, 1997; actor: To Die For, 1995, Extreme Measures, 1996, The Stupids, 1996. Office: c/o William Morris Agy c/o John Burnham 151 S El Camino Dr Beverly Hills CA 90212-2704*

CRONENWETT, JACK LEMOYNE, vascular surgeon educator; b. Ludington, Mich., Dec. 13, 1946; s. Jack L. and K. Marie (Grundmark) C.; m. Linda R. Houk, 1969 (div. 1980); children: Sara, Molly; m. Debra A. Cote, Sept. 26, 1981. BS, U. Mich., 1969; MD, Stanford U., 1973. Diplomate Am. Bd. Surgery. Resident in gen. surgery U. Mich., Ann Arbor, 1973-79; resident in vacsular surgery U. Tenn., Memphis, 1979-80; asst. prof. surgery U. Mich., Ann Arbor, 1980-84; assoc. prof. surgery Dartmouth Coll., Hanover, N.H., 1984-89, prof. surgery, 1989—. Mem. Am. Surg. Assn., New Eng. Soc. Vascular Surgery (sec. 1991-96, pres. 1997-98), Soc. Vascular Surgery (recorder 1996—), Soc. Univ. Surgeons, Internat. Soc. for Cardiovascular Surgery, Ea. Vascular Soc., Midwestern Vascular Soc., New Eng. Surg. Soc., Assn. Program Dirs. in Vascular Surgery (sec.-treas. 1993-97). Office: Dartmouth-Hitchcock Med Ctr 1 Medical Center Dr Lebanon NH 03756-0002

CRONHOLM, LOIS S., biology educator; b. St. Louis, Aug. 15, 1930; d. Fred and Emma (Tobias) Kisslinger; m. James Cronholm, Sept. 15, 1965 (div. 1974); children: Judith Frances, Peter Foster; m. Stuart E. Neff, Apr. 11, 1975. BA, U. Louisville, 1962, PhD, 1966. Asst. prof. biology dept. U. Louisville, 1973-76, assoc. prof., 1976-80, dean arts and scis., 1979-85; prof. U. Louisville, 1980—, 1980-85; dean arts and scis., prof. Temple U., Phila., 1985-92; sr. v.p. acad. affairs, prof. Baruch Coll., CUNY, 1992-98, interim pres., 1998—; bd. dirs. J. History Ideas, 1987-93. Contbr. articles to profl. jours. Chmn. Human Relations Commn., Louisville, 1976-79; group capt. Dems., Valley Station, Ky., 1975-78; sec. Grass Roots Dem. Club, Valley Station, 1975; chmn. Southwestern Jefferson County Econ. Devel. Com., Valley Station, 1983-84; pres. Hampden-Booth Theater Libr., 1997—. Recipient Pre-Doctoral fellowship NIH, 1963-66, Post-Doctoral fellowship NIH, 1967-70. Mem. Nat. Assn. Land Grant and Urban Univs. (chmn. com. arts and scis. 1987-89, bd. dirs. divsn. urban affairs 1988-90, sec. bd. dirs. internat. divsn. 1991-92), Coun. Colls. Arts and Scis. (bd. dirs. 1987-90, pres.-elect 1989-90, pres. 1990-91, chair commn. on faculty recruitment ethics 1991-93), Players Club N.Y.C. (sec. bd. 1994). Democrat. Jewish. Avocations: gardening, cooking. Office: Baruch Coll CUNY 17 Lexington Ave New York NY 10010-5518

CRONIN, BONNIE KATHRYN LAMB, legislative staff executive; b. Mpls., Mar. 11, 1941; d. Edwin Rector and Maude Kathryn (MacPherson) Lamb; m. Barry Jay Cronin, Jan. 23, 1963 (div. Feb. 1972); 1 son, Philip Scott. BA, U. Mo., 1963, BS, 1964; MS, Ill. State U., 1970. Copywriter Neds & Wardlow Advt., Columbia, Mo., 1962-64; tchr. Columbia Sch. System, 1964-68, Normal (Ill.) Sch. System, 1968-69; asst. gen. mgr. Sta. WGLT, Normal, 1969-70; dir. devel. Radio Sta. WBUR, Boston, 1970-71; program dir. Radio Sta. WBUR, 1971-75, gen. mgr., 1975-78; dir. public relations Joy of Movement Center, 1978-80; dep. scheduler Anderson for Pres., 1980; scheduler Spaulding for Gov., 1980-81; dir. scheduling John Kerry Campaign, 1982; dir. of scheduling Mass. Lt. Gov.'s Office, dir. ops., 1983-84; dep. campaign mgr. Kerry for Senate Com., 1984; dir. ops. Senator John Kerry, Washington, 1985-86; dir. constituency outreach Senator John Kerry, Boston, 1986-92, exec. asst., 1992-95; chief staff to Senator John Kerry Boston, 1995-97; dir. devel. and public affairs Working Capital, 1997—. Mem. Nat. Pub. Radio (dir. 1974-77, chairperson devel. com.), Mass. Broadcasters Assn. (dir. 1973-78, chairperson scholarship com., pub. service com., adminstrv. oversight com.), Polymnia Choral Soc. Office: 99 Bishop Allen Dr Cambridge MA 02139-3425

CRONIN, DANIEL ANTHONY, archbishop; b. Newton, Mass., Nov. 14, 1927; s. Daniel George and Emily Frances (Joyce) C. S.T.L., Gregorian U., 1953, S.T.D. summa cum laude, 1956; LL.D., Suffolk U., Boston, 1969, Stonehill Coll., North Easton, 1971. Ordained priest Roman Cath. Ch., 1952; attache Apostolic Internunicature, Addis Ababa, Ethiopia, 1957-61, Secretariat of State, Vatican City, 1961-68; named Monsignor by His Holiness Pope John XXIII, 1962; named titular bishop of Egnatia and aux. bishop of Boston, 1968-70; Episcopal ordination from Richard Cardinal Cushing (archbishop of Boston), 1968; pastor St. Raphael Ch., Medford, Mass., 1968-70; bishop Fall River, Mass., 1970-92; archbishop of Hartford (Conn.), 1992—. Recipient Father Michael J. McGivney award K.C., 1999. Club: K.C. (4). Office: 134 Farmington Ave Hartford CT 06105-3723*

CRONIN, JAMES WATSON, physicist, educator; b. Chicago, Ill., Sept. 29, 1931; s. James Farley and Dorothy (Watson) C.; m. Annette Martin, Sept. 11, 1954; children: Cathryn, Emily, Daniel Watson. A.B., So. Methodist U. (1951); Ph.D., U. Chgo.; D (hon.), U. Paris, 1995, U. Leeds, 1996, Univ. Pierre & Marie Curie, 1994; DSc (hon.), U. Leeds, 1996. Asst. physicist Brookhaven Nat. Lab., 1955-58; asst. prof. Princeton, 1958-65, prof. physics, 1965-71; prof. physics and astronomy U. Chgo., 1971—, prof. emeritus physics and astronomy; Loeb lectr. physics Harvard U., 1967; participant early devel. spark chambers; co-discoverer CP-violation, 1964; lectr. Nashima Found., 1993. Recipient Research Corp. Am. award, 1967; John Price Wetherill medal Franklin Inst., 1976; E.O. Lawrence award ERDA, 1977; Nobel prize for physics, 1980; Sloan fellow, 1964-66; Guggenheim fellow, 1970-71, 82-83. Mem. Am. Acad. Arts and Scis., Nat. Acad. Sci. (council mem.), Am. Phys. Soc. Office: U Chgo Enrico Fermi Inst 5630 S Ellis Ave Chicago IL 60637-1433*

CRONIN, JOHN JOSEPH, airline pilot, poet, author; b. Bklyn., Feb. 1, 1961; s. John Joseph and Marian Grace (Walsh) C.; m. Terry Lynn Yourstone, Oct. 6, 1990; children: Kelly Ann, Courtney Beth. BS in Aviation Mgmt., Daniel Webster Coll., Nashua, N.H., 1983. Lic. airline transport pilot, flight engr. Flight instr. various flight schs., N.H., N.J., Mass., 1986-90; pilot, 1st officer Continental Express Airlines, Houston, 1990-94, pilot, capt. EMB 120, 1995-96; pilot, flight engr. B727 Continental Airlines, Houston, 1994-95, 1st officer B737-300/500, 1997—; admissions liaison officer USAF Acad., N.J., 1991—. Author: Your Flight Questions Answered--By a Jetliner Pilot, 1998; author of poems. Officer USAFR. Mem. Internat. Assn. Continental Pilots. Avocations: photography, coin collecting, genealogy. Office: PO Box 1204 Edison NJ 08818-1204

CRONIN, LAURA AILEEN, English language educator; b. Worcester, Mass., Aug. 20, 1973; d. Donald Gilbert and Joan Margaret (Friel) C. BA cum laude, Boston Coll., 1995; MEd, U. Mass., 1996. Tchr. English North Middlesex H.S., Townsend, Mass., 1996—; mktg. intern. Stratus Computer, Marlboro, Mass., 1996; class advisor North Middlesex H.S., Townsend, 1996—. Event chairperson Second Helping—Greater Boston Food Bank, Boston Coll., 1996; campaign vol. Peter Blute for Congress, 16th Congl. Dist., Mass., 1996. Mem. Nat. Coun. Tchrs. English, U.S. Figure Skating Assn., Boston Coll. Alumni Assn. (nominating com. 1996-97), Boston Coll. Young Alumni Club (exec. com., dir. 1996—). Avocations: figure skating, skiing. Home: 160 Crescent St Shrewsbury MA 01545-2834

CRONIN, MARY HAAG, real estate referral agent; b. Balt., June 1, 1925; d. Alfred Henry and Catherine (Hoover) Haag; m. Donald Everett Nork, Dec. 16, 1944 (div. 1958); m. John Paul Cronin, Jan. 12, 1963 (dec.). Cert. nurse asst., Sheridan Vocat. Tech. Ctr., 1975; cert. realtor, Chinelly Sch. Real Estate, 1982; cert. in eldercare, Fla. Internat. U., 1988. Nurse asst. Med. Pers. Pool, Hollywood, Fla., 1975-85; sales staff Chinelly Real Estate, Hollywood, Fla., 1982-84; referral real estate agt. Coldwell Banker Referral Network, Inc., Miami Lakes, Fla., 1991—. Patentee pot-pourri holder. Vol. nurse, Sunrise, 1988—; aux. mem. Meml. Hosp., Hollywood, 1970—. Mem. Ice Skating Club Am., Elks, Am. Legion (bd. dirs., co-dir. 1993—), Internat. Platform Assn., Inventors Soc. So. Fla., Inc., Nat. Congress Inventors Orgsn. Avocations: ice skating, bike riding, bowling, decorating, refurbishing. Address: PO Box 130071 Sunrise FL 33313-0001

CRONIN, PATTI ADRIENNE WRIGHT, state agency administrator; b. Chgo., May 25, 1943; d. Rodney Adrian and Dorothy Louise (Thiele) Wright; m. Kevin Brian Cronin, May 1, 1971; 1 child, Kevin. BA, Beloit (Wis.) Coll., 1965; JD with honors, U. Wis., 1983. Vol. Peace Corps, Turkey, 1965-67; recruiter Peace Corps, Washington, 1967-68; tchr. English Kamehameha III Sch., Lahaina, Hawaii, 1968-70, Evansville (Wis.) High Sch., 1972-77; tchr. math. and history Killian Sch., Hartford, Wis., 1977-78; tchr. English Kaiser High Sch., Honolulu, 1979-80; intern Wis. Ct. Appeals, Madison, 1983; exec. dir. waste facility siting bd. State of Wis., Madison, 1983—; founder, v.p., bd. dirs. Justice Ctr. Honolulu, 1979-82; sec., treas. Cronin Constrn. Co., Inc., Madison, 1986—. Editor: Internat. Law Jour., 1982. Bd. dirs. Neighborhood Bd., Honolulu, 1979-82; chmn. United Way, 1989—; active Parent Citizens Adv. Coun. Recipient Mayor's award of outstanding achievement, City of Honolulu, 1980. Mem. Soc. Profls. in Dispute Resolution, ABA, State Bar Wis. Avocations: family, real estate, travel. Office: Waste Facility Siting Bd 201 W Washington Ave Madison WI 53703-2727

CRONIN, PHILIP MARK, lawyer; b. Boston, July 21, 1932; s. Herbert Joseph and Elizabeth Ann (Sullivan) C.; m. Paula Cook Budlong, June 8, 1957; children—Thomas B., Philip S. A.B., Harvard U., 1953, LL.B., 1956. Bar: Mass. 1956. Sr. partner firm Withington, Cross, Park & Groden, Boston, 1956-89, Peabody & Arnold, Boston, 1989—; pres., pub. Harvard mag., 1971-78; city solicitor, Cambridge, Mass., 1968-72. Mng. editor: Mass. Law Rev, 1976-81; editor in chief, 1981-90; editor Mass. Legal History Jour., 1996—. Trustee Harvard Crimson, 1972—; pres. Cambridge Homes, 1991-94; overseer Mass. Supreme Jud. Ct. Hist. Soc., 1994—, editor jour., 1995—. Home: 3 Lincoln Ln Cambridge MA 02138-3351 Office: 50 Rowes Wharf Boston MA 02110-3339

CRONIN, RICHARD JAMES, university official, educator; b. Needham, Mass., Dec. 2, 1958; s. John Joseph and Margaret Mary (Healy) C. BS in Fgn. Svc., Georgetown U., 1980, JD, 1984. Bar: Mass. 1985. Asst. to dean Sch. Langs. and Linguistics, Georgetown U., Washington, 1980-84, asst. dean, 1984-92, assoc. dean, 1992-95, assoc. dean Georgetown Coll., 1995—, lectr. divsn. interpretation and translation, 1986-98. Mem. Mass. Bar Assn. Roman Catholic. Office: Georgetown U Coll Dean's Office Washington DC 20057

CRONIN, ROBERT LAWRENCE, sculptor, painter; b. Lexington, Mass., Aug. 10, 1936; s. Daniel Augustus and Eileen Ursula (Keating) C.; m. Constance Marie Nelson, June 27, 1964 (div. 1974). BFA, R.I. Sch. Design, 1959; MFA, Cornell U., 1962. Tchr. Mich. State U., East Lansing, 1965-66, Bennington (Vt.) Coll., 1967-68, Brown U., Providence, 1969-71; tchrs. Sch. Worcester (Mass.) Art Mus., 1972-80. One-man shows Mus. Art Carnegie Inst., Pitts., 1981, Sculpture Ctr. Gallery, N.Y.C., 1981, Gimpel Fils Gallery, London, 1982, Gimpel & Weitzenhoffer Gallery, N.Y.C., 1982, 84, 87, 89, Watson de Nagy Gallery, Houston, 1983, 86, Gimpel-Hanover Galerien, Zurich, 1983, Clark Gallery, Lincoln, Mass., 1983, 85, 87, Janet Steinberg Gallery, San Francisco, 1985, Galerie Esperanza, Montreal, 1985, 87, Klonaridis Gallery, Toronto, 1984, 85, 87, 88, 89, Galerie Keeser-Bohbot, Hamburg, Germany, 1987, 89, Alice Simsar Gallery, Ann Arbor, Mich., 1988, Yoh Art Gallery, Osaka, 1989, Gallery Hiro, Tokyo, 1989, Helander, Gallery, Palm Beach, Fla., 1990, Fitchburg (Mass.) Art Mus., 1990, Munson Gallery, New Haven, 1991, Sound Shore Gallery, Stamford, Conn., 1992, Virginia Lynch Gallery, Tiverton, R.I., 1996, 98, Dillon Gallery, N.Y.C., 1996, 99, Tremaine Gallery, Hotchkiss Sch., Lakeville, Conn., 1999; represented in permanent collections Bklyn. Mus., Mus. Fine Arts, Boston, Mus. Art, U. Okla., Mus. Art, Carnegie Inst., Mus. Art, R.I. Sch. Design, Nat. Air and Space Mus., Mus. Fine Arts, Springfield, Worcester Art Mus., Worcester Polytech. Inst., De Cordova Mus., Nat. Acad. Design, N.Y.C. Recipient 1st prize for painting Boston Fine Arts Festival, 1963; recipient awards Mass. Artists Found., 1975, 79; individual support grantee Adolph and Esther Gottlieb Found., 1991. Mem. Nat. Acad. Design. Home and Studio: PO Box 74 Falls Village CT 06031-0074

CRONIN, SUSAN GAYLE, county program coordinator; b. Bayonne, N.J., June 10, 1949; m. Brian E. Cronin, Oct. 14, 1972; children: Jennifer, Bridget. Svc. rep. Social Security Adminstrn., Jackson Heights, N.Y., 1967-74; collection mgr. trainee Carroll County Hosp., Westminster, Md., 1979-87; computer specialist Tandy Corp./Radio Shack, Westminster, 1987-88; county vol. program coord. Bur. of Aging, Westminster, 1989—; mem. Medigap nat. com. to preserve social security medicare State of Md. Area Office on Aging, Health Ins. Counseling, Balt., 1993; coord. Curb Abuse in Medicare and Medicaid Program, 1996—. Mem. campaign Dem. Election, Westminster, 1990. Recipient Carr County Commrs. Exceptional Svc. award, 1998. Avocations: computers, animals, swimming, art. Office: Westminster Sr Ctr 125 Stoner Ave Westminster MD 21157-5451

CRONIN, TIMOTHY CORNELIUS, III, computer manufacturing executive; b. Manchester, N.H., Sept. 26, 1927; s. Timothy Cornelius and Ann Frances (Meaney) C.; m. Gloria Mara, June 8, 1949 (dec. Sept. 1984); children: Gloria Ann, Constance, Timothy, Barbara, Mary, Thomas; m. A. Jeanine Wallis, June 15, 1991; children: Erik Wallis, Dana Wallis. BS, U.S. Mil. Acad., 1949; MBA, Ohio State U., 1952. Commd. 2d lt. USAF, 1949, advanced through grades to capt., 1956, resigned, 1956; mgr., v.p. Honeywell, Inc., Mpls. and Wellesley, Mass., 1956-71; v.p. Addressograph Multigraph, Cleve., 1971-74; chmn., chief exec. officer Inforex, Inc., Burlington, Mass., 1974-79; cons. in field Waltham, Mass., 1980-82; v.p. Wang Labs., Lowell, Mass., 1983-87; pres., chief exec. officer Wang Fin. Info. Services Corp., N.Y.C., 1987-90, Digitran, Inc., Englewood Cliffs, N.J., 1990-91; retired, pvt. investor, 1991. Decorated Legion of Merit. Mem. Computer Industries Assn. (exec. com. 1975-79), Assn. Industries Mass. (bd. dirs. 1976-79). Republican. Roman Catholic. Home: 31 Shaw Dr Bedford NH 03110-6050

CRONKITE, EUGENE PITCHER, physician, retired; b. Los Angeles, Dec. 11, 1914; s. Clarence Edgar and Anita (Pitcher) C.; m. Elizabeth Erna Kaitschuk, Aug. 17, 1940; 1 dau., Christina Elizabeth. AB, Stanford U., 1936, MD, 1940; DSc (hon.), L.I. U., 1962; MD (hon.), U. Ulm, Fed. Republic of Germany, 1987, U. Parma, Italy, 1991. Intern Stanford U. Hosps., San Francisco, 1939-40; resident in medicine Stanford U. Hosps., 1941-42; commd. lt. (s.g.) U.S. Navy, 1942, advanced through grades to rear adm., 1969, ret., 1954; head hematology Naval Med. Research Inst., Bethesda, Md., 1945-54; sr. scientist med. dept. Brookhaven Nat. Lab., 1954—, chmn., 1967-79; prof. medicine Health Sci. Center, SUNY, Stony Brook, 1979-92; doctor of medicine Health Ctr. U. Ulm, Fed. Republic Germany, 1987-93; ret., 1993. Contbr. articles to med. jours. Recipient Alfred Benzon award Denmark, 1969; Ludwig Heilmeyer medal Fed. Republic Germany, 1974; Semmelwiess award Hungary, 1975; Alexander von Humboldt sr. scientist award Fed. Republic Germany, 1977; deVilliers prize and medal Leukemia Soc. Am., 1989. Mem. Am. Soc. Hematology (pres. 1970), Internat. Soc. Exptl. Hematology (pres. 1976), U.S. Nat. Acad. Scis., Am. Soc. Clin. Investigation, Assn. Am. Physicians, Am. Soc. Hematology, Am. Assn. Physiologists.

CRONKITE, MARY SUE RIDDLE, journalist, fiction writer; b. Geneva, Ala., May 15, 1933; d. Simon Benjamin and Etta Udora (Mims) R.; m. Charlie Hubert Thomas, July 24, 1951 (div. Sept. 1962); children: Alda Ruth, Stephen Hubert, Mary Lynn. BS in English, Troy State U., 1995. Feature writer Fla. Times Union, Jacksonville, 1965-68; writer, editor Birmingham (Ala.) News, 1969-82; editor various newspaper cos., Fla., Ga., Ala., 1982-86; exec. editor Wiregrass Today, Dothan, Ala., 1986-87; pub., editor New Hope Press, Dothan, 1987-96; freelance writer Apalachicola, Fla., 1996—; corr. Life Mag., Time-Life News Bur., Atlanta, 1972-82; tchr. journalism Jefferson State Jr. Coll., Birmingham, 1970 (fall only), 1971-82 full sch. yr.; tchr. creative writing Wallace C.C., Dothan, 1987-95. Author short stories. Bd. dirs. Franklin County (Fla.) Sr. Citizens Coun., 1997, Friends Estuarine Res., Apalachicola, 1996—, Ret. Sr. Vol. Program, 1986-91, chmn. pub. rels. Named Best Weekly Newspaper, Ala. Press Assn., 1961; All-Am. scholar USA Today, 1996; recipient 1st Place Short Story award Fitzgerald Mus., 1994, State St. Rev., 1995, 96. Mem. Houston Arts and Humanities Coun. (chmn. pub. rels. 1991-95), Troy State U. Dothan Creative Writing Club (pres., v.p., chmn. pub. rels., sec., treas.), Creative Writing Club, Panhandle Writers Guild, Rotary, Philaco Woman's Club (bd. dirs., chmn. pub. rels.), Dem. Women's Club (chmn. pub. rels.). Mem. LDS Ch. Avocations: reading, walking, cooking, writing fiction. Home and Office: 108 9th St Apalachicola FL 32320-1602

CRONKITE, WALTER, radio and television news correspondent; b. St. Joseph, Mo., Nov. 4, 1916; s. Walter Leland and Helen Lena C.; m. Mary Elizabeth Maxwell, Mar. 30, 1940; children: Nancy Elizabeth, Mary Kathleen, Walter Leland III. Student, U. Tex., 1933-35; LL.D., Rollins Coll., 1966, Bucknell U., Syracuse U.; L.H.D., Ohio State U.; hon. degree, Am. Internat. Coll., Harvard U. News writer, editor Scripps-Howard, also UP, Houston, Kansas City, Dallas, Austin, El Paso, Tex., N.Y.C.; UP war corr., 1942-45, fgn. corr., reopening burs. in Amsterdam, Brussels, chief corr. Nuremberg war crimes trials, bur. mgr., Moscow, 1946-48, lectr., mag. contbr., 1948-49, CBS-News corr., 1950-81, spl. corr., 1981—; mng. editor CBS Evening News with Walter Cronkite, 1962-81; chmn. The Cronkite Ward Co., 1993—. Host spl.: Universe, CBS, The Holocaust: In Memory of Millions, The Discovery Channel, 1993 (Cable Ace award, Best Program Interviewer); anchor for: TV news spls. Vietnam: A War That Is Finished, 1975, In Celebration of US, 1976, Our Happiest Birthday, 1977, The President in China, 1975, Solzhenitsyn: 1984 Revisited; Author: Challenges of Change, 1971, A Reporter's Life, 1996; co-author: South by Southeast, North by Northeast, Westwind; producer/host: The Cronkite Reports (12-episode series for Discovery Channel), 1994-94, Cronkite Remembers (8-part series for CBS and Discovery Channel), 1996. Recipient Peabody award, 1962, 81, several Emmy awards; William A. White award for journalistic merit, 1969; George Polk Journalism award, 1971; Gold medal Internat. Radio and TV Soc., 1974; Alfred I. DuPont-Columbia U. award in Broadcast Journalism, 1978, 81; Presdl. medal of Freedom, 1981. Mem. Acad. Arts and Scis. (pres. nat. acad. N.Y. chpt. 1959, Govs. award 1979), Assn. Radio News Analysts, Nat. Press Club, Overseas Press Club, N.Y. Yacht Club, Explorers Club, Bohemian Club, Chi Phi. Office: CBS Inc 51 W 52nd St Ste 1934 New York NY 10019-6119*

CRONON, WILLIAM, history educator; b. New Haven, Sept. 11, 1954; m. Nancy Elizabeth Fey. BA in History, English with honors, U. Wis., 1976; MA in Am. History, Yale U., 1979, M of Philosophy in Am. History, 1981, PhD in Am. History, 1990; DPhil in Brit. History, Oxford U., 1981. Asst. prof. history Yale U., New Haven, 1981-86, assoc. prof., 1986-91, prof., 1991-92, mem. studies in environment program creation com., 1983-84, co-chair studies environment program, 1989-92, dir. grad. studies, history dept., 1990-92; Frederick Jackson Turner chair of history, geography, and environmental studies U. Wis., Madison, 1992—, dir. honors program Coll. Letters and Sci., 1996-98; found. fac. dir. Chadbourne Residential Coll., 1997—; asst. Am. sec. Rhodes Scholarship Trust, 1978-80, Wis. state sec., 1993-98; cons. in field; mem. adv. bd. The History Tchr., 1986—. Author: Changes in the Land: Indians, Colonists and the Ecology of New England, 1983 (Valley Forge honor cert. 1984, Soc. Colonial award citation of honor 1984, Francis Parkman prize 1984), Nature's Metropolis: Chicago and the Great West, 1991 (Chgo. Tribune Heartlaand prize 1991, Bancroft prize 1992, George Perkins Marsh prize 1993); editor: (with Miles and Gitlin) Under an Open Sky: Rethinking America's Western Past, 1992, Uncommon Ground: Toward Reinventing Nature, 1995, Uncommon Ground: Rethinking the Human Place in Nature, 1995; mem. bd. editors Forest and Conservation History, 1986-91; also articles. Bd. dirs. Conn. Fund for Environ., 1986-91, v.p., 1987-89; mem. adv. bd. TV series Am. Experience Sta. WGBH-TV; trustee Conn. Nature Conservancy, 1989-91; bd. dirs., mem. com. on problems and policy Social Sci. Rsch. Coun., 1991-96, chairperson com. on problems and policy, 1994-96. Rhodes scholar Oxford U., 1976-78; fellow Danforth Found., 1976-82, Newberry Libr., 1980, Mellon Found., 1982-83, Morse fellow Yale U., 1985-86, MacArthur Found., 1985-90, Whitney Humanities Ctr., 1987-89, fellow U. Calif. Humanities Rsch. Inst., 1994, Guggenheim fellow, 1995. Mem. AAAS, Am. Hist. Assn. (Robinson prize com. 1990), Am. Philos. Soc., Orgn. Am. Historians (chmn. Curti prize com. 1987-88), Forest History Soc. (bd. dirs.), Econ. History Assn., Agrl. History Soc., Ecol. Soc. Am., Western Hist. Assn. (conv. program com. 1987, chmn. 1991-92), Assn. Am. Geographers, Am. Studies Assn., Am. Anthrop. Assn., Am. Soc. for Ethnohistory, Chgo. Hist. Soc., Am. Antiquarian Soc., Soc. Am. Historians, Phi Beta Kappa (William C. DeVane award Yale chpt. 1988), Phi Kappa Phi, Phi Eta Sigma. Home: 2027 Chadbourne Ave Madison WI 53705-4046 Office: U Wis Dept History 3211 Humanities 455 N Park St Madison WI 53706-1405

CRONSON, CAROLINE MARY, financial executive; b. Cosford, Eng.; came to U.S., 1987; d. Charles Francis and Barbara Joan (Thompson) Milnes; m. Paul Christopher Cronson, Aug. 21, 1986; one son, Christopher Charles. BA with honours, Oxford U., 1984; MBA, Columbia U., 1989. Grad. trainee, exec. Charterhouse Bank, London, 1984-86; analyst Samuel Montagu, London, 1986-87; assoc. Shearson Lehman Hutton, Inc., N.Y.C., 1989-93; v.p. Lehman Bros., N.Y.C., 1993-95; assoc. dir. Larkspur Capital Corp., New York, 1995-97; CFO MetaStat Inc., New York, 1997—. Bd. dirs. Planned Parenthood of N.Y.C., Donald Byrd Dance Found., Sch. of Am. Ballet. Mem. Colony Club, Edgartown Yacht Club. Roman Catholic. Avocations: performing arts, riding, sailing. Home: 111 E 80th St Apt 5A New York NY 10021-0350 Office: MetaStat Inc Ste 2002 1370 Avenue Of The Americas New York NY 10019-4602

CRONSON, HARRY MARVIN, electronics engineer; b. Providence, May 31, 1937; s. George I. and Fay (Standel) C.; m. Ruth Marion Hyman, June 24, 1962; children: George F., Beth T. BSEE, Brown U., 1959, MS, 1961, PhD, 1963. Asst. prof. Poly. Inst. Bklyn., Farmingdale, N.Y., 1964-66; sr. scientist Avco Systems Div., Wilmington, Mass., 1966-68, Ikor Inc., Burlington, Mass., 1968-71; rsch. staff mem. Sperry Rsch. Ctr., Sudbury, Mass., 1971-83; group leader Mitre Corp., Bedford, Mass., 1983-90, prin. engr., 1990—. Contbr. articles to profl. jours., chpt. to book. Patentee in field. Oxford U. post doctoral fellow, Eng., 1963-64. Fellow IEEE (chmn. career maintenance and devel. com. 1983, USAB award 1980, Leadership in Career Planning award 1981), IEEE Instrument and Measurement Soc. (adcom mem. 1981-84), Internat. Union Radio Sci. (chmn. with U.S. nat. com. Commn. A-electromagnetic metrology 1986-87). Home: 1 Fulton Rd Lexington MA 02420-2317 Office: The Mitre Corp Mail Stop E090 202 Burlington Rd Bedford MA 01730-1420

CRONSON, ROBERT GRANVILLE, lawyer; b. Chgo., Dec. 23, 1924; s. Berthold A. and Ethel (Larson) C.; m. Agnes L. Diaz; children from previous marriage: Karen, Christopher, Keelyn, Morgan, Seth. A.B. in Econs., Dartmouth Coll., 1947; J.D., U. Chgo., 1950. Bar: Ill. 1950. Atty. Daily, Dines, Ross & O'Keefe, Chgo., 1951-53; partner DeBoice, Greening, Ackerman & Cronson, Springfield, Ill., 1957-60; asst. sec. of state of Ill. Springfield, 1958-64; sr. vp., sec. The Chgo. Corp., Chgo., 1965-73; assoc. prof. pub. adminstrn. Roosevelt U., 1973-74; adj. prof. adminstrn. Sangamon State U., 1983-87; auditor gen. State of Ill., 1974-92; retired, 1992; Mem. exec. com. post audit sect. Nat. Conf. State Legislatures, 1976-85, Nat. Assn. State Auditors, Comptrollers and Treasurers, 1979-81, and Nat. Intergovtl. Audit Forum, 1974-76; mem. Midwest Intergovtl. Audit Forum, 1974-92; adv. com. govt. acctg. standards Govt. Acctg. Standards Bd. 1984-85. Chmn. Midwest Vehicle Proration Compact, 1959-61, Ill. Securities Adv. Com., 1964-73; chmn. William H. Chamberlain Scholarship Fund, Sangamon State U., 1972-85. Cpl. USMCR, 1942-46. Recipient Fin. Mgmt. Improvement (Scantlebury) award U.S. Govt., 1980. Mem. Midwest Securities Commrs. Assn. (chmn. 1959-64), Securities Industry Assn. Am. (chmn. state legislation com. 1970-72), Nat. State Auditors Assn. (pres. 1980-81), Pi Alpha Alpha (hon.), Phi Kappa Psi.

CRONYN, HUME, actor, writer, director; b. London, Ont., Can., July 18, 1911; came to U.S., 1932; s. Hume Blake and Frances Amelia (Labatt) C.; m. Jessica Tandy, Sept. 27, 1942 (dec.); children: Susan Cronyn Tettemer, Christopher, Tandy. Grad., Ridley Coll., 1930; student, McGill U., 1930-31; grad., Am. Acad. Dramatic Art, 1934; LL.D. (hon.), U. Western Ont., 1974; LHD (hon.), Fordham U., 1985. Lectr. drama Am. Acad. Dramatic Arts, N.Y.C., 1938-39, Actors' Lab., Los Angeles, 1945-46; bd. govs. Stratford Festival, Can. Author: Rope (screen version), 1947, Under Capricorn (screen version), 1948, also various short stories and mag. articles; author (with Susan Cooper) play Foxfire and ABC teleplay The Dollmaker (Christopher and Writers Guild awards 1985), (autobiography) A Terrible Liar, 1991. First profl. theatre appearance, Nat. Theatre Stock Co., Washington, 1931; appeared in Hippers Holiday, N.Y.C., 1934, various plays, N.Y.C., including High Tor, Room Service, The Three Sisters, The Weak Link, Retreat to Pleasure, The Survivors (star); motion pictures include Shadow Of A Doubt, 1943, Life Boat, 1944, The Seventh Cross, 1944, The Postman Always Rings Twice, 1946, The Green Years, 1946, A Letter for Evie (star), 1945, Brute Force (star), 1947, Top O' The Morning, People Will Talk (star), 1951, Sunrise at Campobello, 1960, Cleopatra, 1963, Gaily Gaily, 1968, The Arrangement, 1968, There Was a Crooked Man, 1969, Conrack, 1974, Parallax View, 1974, Honky Tonk Freeway, 1980, The World According to Garp, 1981, Roll Over, 1981, Impulse, 1983, Brewster's Millions, 1985, Cocoon, 1985, Batteries Not Included, 1987, Cocoon: The Return, 1988, The Pelican Brief, 1993, Camilla, 1994, Marvin's Room, 1996; (TV moies) An African Love Story, 1996, 12 Angry Men, 1997; starred in ANTA touring prodn. of Hamlet, 1949; co-starred with Jessica Tandy in ANTA touring prodn. of The Little Blue Light, Brattle Theatre, Cambridge, Mass., 1950, The Fourposter, 1951-53, Madame Will You Walk, 1953-54, The Honeys; A Day by the Sea, 1955, The Man in the Dog Suit, 1958; dir.: ANTA touring prodn. of Portrait Of A Madonna, Los Angeles, 1946, Now I Lay Me Down To Sleep, 1949-50, Hilda Crane, 1950, The Egghead, 1957, all N.Y.C.; appears in major network dramatic shows TV, including Show of the Week; TV appearances include Foxfire, A Hallmark Prodn., 1987, Day One, 1988, Age Old Friends, 1988, Broadway Bound, 1991, Christmas on Division Street, 1991, To Dance with the White Dog, 1993 (Emmy award, Lead Actor - Special, 1994); appeared in: Big Fish, Little Fish, 1961, Tyrone Guthrie Prodns., Mpls., 1963; played Polonius in Hamlet, N.Y.C., 1964; producer: Slow Dance on the Killing Ground, 1964; produced and starred: (with Jessica Tandy) comedy prodn. The Marriage (a dramatic series), 1954, Triple Play, 1958, 59; appeared title role: (with Jessica Tandy) Richard III, 1965; in: (with Jessica Tandy) Cherry Orchard, 1965; as Harpagon in: comedy prodn. The Miser, Mpls., 1965; as Tobias in A Delicate Balance, 1966, 67; as Harpagon in: revival The Miser, Mark Taper Forum, Los Angeles, 1968; as Frederick William Rolfe in: revival Hadrian VII, Stratford Nat. Theatre Co., Can., 1969, tour, 1969-70; as Capt. Queeg in: Caine Mutiny Court Martial, Los Angeles, 1971-72; appeared in: Promenade All, N.Y.C., 1972; dir., appeared in tour, 1972-73; appeared in: (with Jessica Tandy) Samuel Beckett Festival, Lincoln Center, N.Y.C., 1972; and tour Krapp's Last Tape in Samuel Beckett Festival, Toronto, Washington, other cities, 1973, (with Jessica Tandy) Noel Coward in Two Keys, 1974, tour, 1975, Many Faces of Love, 1974, 75, 76; appeared as Shylock in The Merchant of Venice; as Bottom in: (with Jessica Tandy) A Midsummer Night's Dream, Stratford (Ont., Can.) Festival, 1976; co-producer: (with Mike Nichols and star) The Gin Game (Pulitzer prize 1978), Golden Theatre, N.Y.C., 1977; tour The Gin Game, U.S., Can., Eng., USSR, 1978-79; star: tour Foxfire, Stratford (Ont.) Festival, 1980, Guthrie Theatre, Minn., 1981, Ethel Barrymore Theatre, N.Y.C., 1983; Traveler in the Dark, Am. Repertory Theatre, Loeb Drama Ctr., Cambridge, 1984; limited run of Foxfire, Ahmanson Theatre, Los Angeles, 1985; (with Jessica Tandy) The Petition, Golden Theatre, N.Y.C., 1986. Decorated Order of Canada; recipient Comodedia Matinee Club award for Fourposter, 1952, Barter Theatre award for outstanding contbn. to theatre, 1961, Delia Austria medal N.Y. Drama League for Big Fish, Little Fish 1961, Antoinnette Perry (Tony) award, also Variety N.Y. Drama critics poll of performance as Polonius, 1964, 9th ann. award Am. Acad. Dramatic Art 1964, Straw Hat award for best dir. 1972, Obie award for outstanding achievement, disting. performance Krapp's Last Tape 1973, Brandeis U. Creative Arts award 1978, nominee Tony award for The Gin Game 1979, winner Los Angeles Critics award 1979, named to Theatre Hall of Fame 1979, Nat. Press Club award 1979, Commonwealth award for disting. service in dramatic arts, 1983, Humanitas Prize, 1985, Kennedy Ctr. Honors, 1986, Alley Theatre award, 1987, Franklin Haven Sargent award Am. Acad. Dramatic Arts as disting. alumnus for quality of acting, 1988, Nat. Medal of Arts, 1990; Emmy award supporting actor Broadway Bound, 1992, Antoinette Perry Lifetime Achievement Award, 1994 (with Jessica Tandy). Mem. AFTRA, Screen Actors Guild, Writers Guild Am., Actors Equity Assn., Soc. Stage Dirs. and Choreographers, Dramatists Guild. Office: 63-23 Carlton St Rego Park NY 11374-2826 also: ICM 8942 Wilshire Blvd Beverly Hills CA 90211-1934*

CROOG, ROSLYN ZEPORAH, senior systems engineer; b. New Haven, July 14, 1942; d. Herbert Bernard and Belle (Brown) Croog; children: Bradley Jordan Paul, Katie Miriam Paul. AS, Quinnipiac Coll., 1962; BS, Fla. Internat. U., 1982. Analyst, programmer DBA Systems, Inc., Melbourne, Fla., 1982-84; system mgr. DBA Systems, Inc., Fairfax, Va., 1984-86; mem. tech. staff MRJ, Inc., Fairfax, Va., 1986-98; sr. sys. engr. AverStar, Inc., Vienna, Va., 1998—. Avocations: photography, sailing, cross-country skiing. Office: AverStar Inc 1595 Spring Hill Rd Vienna VA 22182-2228

CROOK, BARBARA COENSON, marketing and sales professional; b. Phila., Dec. 20, 1956; d. Martin and Rita (Cassel) Coenson; m. Steve L. Crook, Mar. 6, 1994. BS, U. Fla., 1978; M in Mgmt., Fla. Inst. Tech., 1996. Mng. editor Heritage Fla. News, Fern Park, Fla., 1978-82; freelance photographer and writer Altamonte Springs, Fla., 1982-89; campaign mgr. Pearlman for Congress, Orlando, Fla., 1990; mktg. mgr. AAA Travel Pub., Orlando, 1991-96, AAA Ptnr. Sales, Orlando, 1996-97; mktg. cons. AAA Internat. Pub. Co., 1997, Pathfinder Mortgage and Investments, Inc., 1997; nat. sales mgr. AAA Partnership Programs and AAA Car and Travel mag., 1997-98, AAA Nat. Hdqrs., Heathrow, Fla.; v.p. Affinity Mktg., HardwareStreet.com, Inc., Reno, Nev., 1999—. Author: Tom and Jerry, 1989; contbr., editor articles to various pubs. Del. Fla. Rep. Conv., 1990; campaign mgr. Fla. State rep. Frank Stone, 1990; vol., advisor White House advance staff for Pres. Bush's visit to Fla., 1990. Recipient 7 Press awards Fla. Press Assn., 1980. Mem. Hadassah Club. Avocations: piano, tennis, travelling.

CROOK, DONALD MARTIN, lawyer; b. Wichita, Kans., Dec. 18, 1947; s. Leroy R. and Audrey E. (Mattiason). BA in History with honors, U. Kans., 1970; JD, U. Chgo., 1973. Bar: N.Y. 1974, Tex. 1982. Assoc. Kramer, Levin, Nessen, Kamin & Frankel, N.Y.C., 1973-75, Layton & Sherman, N.Y.C., 1975-80; counsel LTV Corp., Dallas, 1980-85; chief counsel corp. affairs Kimberly-Clark Corp., Dallas, 1985—, v.p., sec., 1986—. Mem. ABA, Dallas Bar Assn. (chmn. corp. counsel sect. 1986-87), Am. Soc. Corp. Secs. (securities law com.). *

CROOK, FREDERICK W., economist; b. Fallon, Nev., Feb. 15, 1940; s. Royal Don and Willmuth (Witt) C.; m. Elizabeth Jean Fletcher, June 5, 1964; children: Sarah, Stephen, Daniel, Rachel, Rebecca, Peter. BA, Brigham Young U., 1964; MA, Tufts U., 1965, PhD, 1970. Prof. Dana Hall Sch., Wellesley, Mass., 1966-67; economist Dept. Commerce, Washington, 1967-70, Dept. Treas., Washington, 1970-71, USDA/Econ. Rsch. Svcs., Washington, 1971-74; mem. fgn. svc. USDA/Fgn. Agrl. Svc., Hong Kong, 1974-76; economist Econ. Rsch. Svc., Washington, 1976-77, 80—; ch. adminstr. LDS Ch., Taiwan, 1977-80; pres. China Shop, Great Falls, Va., 1982—. Author: Chinese English Pocket Dictionary, 1980, Planning and Statistical System in China, 1983, Agricultural Statistics of the Peoples Republic of China 1949-90, 1993, The Future of China: Grain Market, 1996; editor: (China report) Econ. Rsch. Svc., 1985—. Scoutmaster Boy Scouts Am., Alexandria, 1980-84, advisor, Great Falls, 1984-86, LDS chmn. Nat. Capital Area Coun., 1992-96, mem. exec. bd. dirs., 1994-96. Mem. Am. Agrl. Econs. Assn., Assn. for Asian Studies. Avocations: camping, sailing. Home: 770 Carol Ct Great Falls VA 22066-2932

CROOK, PENNY LORAINE, investment broker; b. Gettysburg, S.D., Feb. 20, 1968; d. Paul E. and Phyllis J. (Clark) Daneau; m. Marshall Keith Crook, Sept. 6, 1986; 1 child, Zachary Patrick. AS, Pensacola Jr. Coll., 1991; degree, Am. Inst. of Banking, 1993; student, U. West Fla., 1993—. Lic. ins. rep., lic. investment broker. Bank teller AmSouth Bank, Pensacola, 1991, sr. teller, 1991-92, customer svc. rep., 1992-93, fin. svcs. rep., 1994-95, br. mgr., 1995-97, asst. v.p., 1996—; investment broker AmSouth Investment Svcs., Pensacola, 1997-99, v.p., 1999—; rep. Mary Kay Cosmetics. Mem. fund raising com. Sacred Heart Children's Hosp., Pensacola, 1995—; sec. facilities com. Milestone HomeOwners Assn., Pensacola, 1996—; vol. Emerald Coast Classic Golf Tournament, Pensacola, 1994—. Mem. Nat. Assn. Female Execs., Kiwanis. Avocations: SCUBA diving, softball, water-sports, bargain shopping, computers. Home: 728 Rockland St Cantonment FL 32533-6561

CROOK, ROBERT WAYNE, mutual funds executive; b. Hartford, Conn., Apr. 6, 1936; s. William Gregor and Laura Foster (Keenan) C.; m. Leslie C. Rischer, Oct. 22, 1988; children from previous marriage: Robert Wayne, Laura Sigrid. A.B., Harvard U., 1959; postgrad., U. Va. Sch. Law, 1962. With White, Weld & Co., Inc., Boston, 1961-78; v.p. White, Weld & Co., Inc., 1971-75, 1st v.p., 1975-78; pres., dir. White Weld Money Market Fund, Boston, 1974-78, White Weld Govt. Fund, Boston, 1977-78; with Merrill Lynch Asset Mgmt., Inc., Boston, 1978—, v.p., 1981-89, sr. v.p., 1989—; pres. Merrill Lynch Funds Distbr., Inc., 1978-89, sr. v.p., 1989—; pres., trustee Merrill Lynch Funds for Instns. Series, Boston, 1978—, Merrill Lynch Tax-Exempt Fund, 1983—, Merrill Lynch Intermediate Gov. Bond Fund, 1986—; mng. dir. Merrill Lynch Mercury Asset Mgmt., 1997—. Served with U.S. Army, 1960. Office: 1 Financial Ctr Fl 23 Boston MA 02111-2621

CROOK, SEAN PAUL, aerospace systems program director; b. Pawtucket, R.I., July 6, 1953; s. Ralph Frederick and Rosemary Rita (Dolan) C.; m. Mary Wickman, June 10, 1978; children: Kimberly Anne, Kelly Dolan, Erin

Webster, Mary Katherine. BSME, U.S. Naval Acad., 1975; MBA, U. So. Calif., 1991. Commd. ensign USN, 1975, advanced through grades to lt., 1979, resigned, 1981; sr. systems engr. space div. Gen. Electric Co., Springfield, Va., 1982-84; sr. aerospace systems engr. Martin Marietta Aero. Def. Systems, Long Beach, Calif., 1984-87; sr. aerospace system engring. mgr. Martin Marietta Aero Def. Systems, Long Beach, Calif., 1987-93; chief engr. GDE Sys. Inc., A Tracor Co., San Diego, 1993-96, program mgr., 1996-99; program dir. Marconi Integrated Systems, San Diego, 1999—; sec., bd. dirs. Guardian Minerals Inc. Commdr. USNR, 1992—. Mem. Am. Mgmt. Assn., U. So. Calif. Exec. MBA Alumni Assn. (bd. dirs.), U.S. Naval Acad. Alumni Assn. Avocation: fin. planning. Home: 23565 Via Calzada Mission Viejo CA 92691-3625 Office: Marconi Integrated Systems PO Box 509008 San Diego CA 92150-9008

CROOK, STEPHEN RICHARD, sales and marketing management consultant; b. Madison, Wis., Apr. 20, 1963; s. Richard John and Marcia Jane (Monroe) C.; m. Laura Ann Nabhan, Sept. 10, 1988. AS in Computer Sci. with highest honors, Purdue U., 1985, BS in Indsl. Engring., 1985; MS in Ops. Rsch., Stanford U., 1986; MBA, Northwestern U., 1992. Systems engr. AT&T Bell Labs. Inc., Naperville, Ill., 1985-88; design engr. Smart House Venture, Upper Marlboro, Md., 1986-88; product mgr. new product devel. planning AT&T Network Systems Inc., Lisle, Ill., 1989-90; product mgr. intelligent network bus. planning AT&T Network Systems Inc., Naperville, Ill., 1990-92; assoc. strategy discipline Gemini Consulting, Chgo., 1992-93; mgr. ZS Assocs., Evanston, Ill., 1993—. Inventor Smart House telephone gateway. Mem. Alpha Sigma Phi, Tau Beta Pi, Alpha Pi Mu. E-mail: scrook@zsassociates.com. Office: ZS Assocs 1800 Sherman Ave Evanston IL 60201-3777

CROOKE, ROBERT ANDREW, media relations executive; b. Bklyn., Apr. 17, 1947; s. Henry A. and Theresa E. (Dougherty) C.; m. Angela Keller Lynch, Sept. 13, 1969; 1 child, Sean Peter. BA in English, Providence Coll., 1969; MA in English, Fordham U., 1974. Sports reporter, columnist L.I. Press, Jamaica, N.Y., 1969-75; assoc. editor Mag. Age, N.Y.C., 1979-81; reporter, contbg. editor L.I. Bus. Newsweekly, Ronkonkoma, N.Y., 1981-86; sr. acct. exec. Howard J. Rubenstein, N.Y.C., 1986-87; dir. media rels. Reuters Am., Inc., N.Y.C., 1987-94; v.p. comm. Reuters New Media, N.Y.C., 1994-95; v.p. media rels. Reuters Am. Holdings, Inc., N.Y.C., 1995-98; lectr. Sch. Journalism U. Nebr., 1998—; adj. prof. pub. affairs NYU, 1998—. Author of poems and books; contbr. articles to profl. jours. Bd. dirs. Walt Whitmen Birth Place Assn., Huntington, N.Y., 1985-87; bd. corp. trustees The Vanderbilt Mus., Centerport, N.Y., 1984-87. Office: Reuters Am Holdings Inc 1700 Broadway 2nd Fl New York NY 10019-5945

CROOKE, STANLEY THOMAS, pharmaceutical company executive; b. Indpls., Mar. 28, 1945; m. Nancy Alder (dec.); 1 child, Evan; m. Rosanne M. Snyder. BS in Pharmacy, Butler U., 1966; PhD, Baylor Coll., 1971, MD, 1974. Asst. dir. med. rsch. Bristol Labs., N.Y.C., 1975-76, assoc. dir. med. rsch., 1976-77, assoc. dir. R&D, 1977-79, v.p. R&D, 1979-80; v.p. R&D Smith Kline & French Labs., Phila., 1980-82; pres. R&D Smith Kline French, Phila., 1982-88; chmn. bd., chief exec. officer ISIS Pharms., Inc., Carlsbad, Calif., 1989; chmn. bd. dirs. GES Pharms., Inc., Houston, 1989-91; adj. prof. Baylor Coll. Medicine, Houston, 1982, U. Pa., Phila., 1982-98; chmn. bd. dirs. GeneMedicine, Houston, 1996—; bd. dirs. Calif. Healthcare Inst., Indsl. Biotech. Assn., Washington, Idun Pharms., San Diego, Epix Med., Cambridge, Mass., BIO, Washington; mem. sci. adv. bd. SIBIA, La Jolla, Calif.; adj. prof. pharmacology UCLA, 1991, U. Calif. San Diego, 1994. Mem. editl. adv. bd. Molecular Pharmacology, 1986-91, Jour. Drug Targeting, 1992; editl. bd. Antisense Rsch. and Devel., 1994; sect. editl. bd. for biologicals and immunologicals Expert Opinion on Investigational Drugs, 1995. Trustee Franklin Inst., Phila., 1987-89; bd. dirs. Mann Music Ctr., Phila., 1987-89; children's com. Children's Svcs., Inc., Phila., 1983-84; adv. com. World Affairs Coun., Phila. Recipient Disting. Prof. award U. Ky., 1986, Julius Stermer award Phila. Coll. Pharmacy and Sci., 1981, Outstanding Lectr. award Baylor Coll. Medicine, 1984. Mem. AAAS, Am. Assn. for Cancer Rsch. (state legis. com.), Am. Soc. for Microbiology, Am. Soc. Pharmacology and Exptl. Therapeutics, Am. Soc. Clin. Pharmacology and Therapeutics, Am. Soc. Clin. Oncology, Indsl. Biotech. Assn. (bd. dirs. 1992-93). Achievements include numerous patents in field. Office: ISIS Pharms Inc 2292 Faraday Ave Carlsbad CA 92008-7208*

CROOKER, JOHN H., JR., lawyer; b. Houston, Oct. 26, 1914; s. John H. and Marguerite (Malsch) C.; m. Kay Berry; children: Carolyn (Mrs. W.E. Schwing), John H. III, Linda (Mrs. Barry Hunsaker, Jr.), Tara (Mrs. Alec Mize), Allison (Mrs. David R. Margrave). B.A. with distinction, Rice U., 1935; LL.B. with highest honors, U. Tex., 1937. Bar: Tex. 1937, D.C. 1953. Practice law Houston and Washington, 1937-67, 70—; chmn. CAB, 1968-69. Chmn. bd. dirs. U. St. Thomas, Tex., 1974-78. Served to lt. comdr. USNR, 1941-45. Decorated Bronze Star. Mem. ABA, State Bar Tex. (past chmn. corp. sect.), Am. Law Inst. (life), Houston Bar Found. (chmn. bd. dirs. 1984), Houston C. of C. (chmn. bd. dirs. 1978-79). Home: 3711 San Felipe St Unit 5A Houston TX 77027-4047 Office: 1301 Mckinney St Ste 5100 Houston TX 77010-3031

CROOKS, DORENA MAY (DEE CROOKS), administrative assistant, social worker; b. Center Point, W.Va., Sept. 15, 1938; d. Paul Jefferson and Ruby Catherine (Lasure) Ashcraft; m. William H.D. Crooks, June 27, 1956 (div. Nov. 1975); children: Charles Jefferson, Kimberly May, Raechelle Dee. Grad., W.Va. State Police Acad., 1977; BA, Glenville State Coll., 1992. Lic. social worker, W.Va. Legal sec. Hickel, Wilson & Hill, Attys., Parkersburg, W.Va., 1963-65, Robert T. Goldenberg, Atty., Parkersburg, W.Va., 1965-68; exec. sec. W.Va. State Rd., Parkersburg, 1968-70; dep. sheriff Wood County Sheriff Dept., Parkersburg, 1973-79; legal sec. George W. Hill, Atty., Parkersburg, 1984-88; Vista vol. Wood County Sr. Citizens Assn., Parkersburg, 1990-91, adminstrv. asst., social worker, 1991—; coord. of Widowed Persons Svc., sr. companion program and Sr. Health Ins. Network, Wood County; sec./treas. Mid Ohio Valley Social Workers Networking Group. Avocations: golf, swimming, reading, pinochle. Office: Wood County Citizens Assn 925 Market St Parkersburg WV 26101-4736

CROOKSTON, R. KENT, agronomy educator; b. Magrath, Alta., Can., Mar. 8, 1943; s. Bryan Grant and Lisadore (Brown) C.; m. Gayle Loraine Jones, June 22, 1966; children: Rebecca, Casey, Polly, Daniel, Elizabeth, Emily, Sadie. BS, Brigham Young U., 1968; MS, U. Minn., 1970, PhD, 1972. Postdoctoral fellow Agr. Can., Lethbridge, Alta., 1972; rsch. assoc. Cornell U., Ithaca, N.Y., 1972-74; from asst. prof. to prof. U. Minn., St. Paul, 1974-98, dir. sustainable agr. program Coll. Agr., 1988-92, head dept. agronomy, 1990-98; adj. prof. Inst. Agronomique Et Veterinaire Hassan II, Rabat, Morocco, 1984—; dean Coll. Biology and Agr., Brigham Young U., Provo, Utah, 1998—. Author rsch. manuscripts. With Can. armed forces, 1962. Fellow Am. Soc. Agronomy, Crop Sci. Soc. Am.; mem. Coun. Agrl. Sci. and Tech. Avocations: oil painting, woodworking, writing, photography. Home: 1055 N 1100 E Orem UT 84097 Address: College of Biology and Agriculture 301 WIDB Brigham Young Univ Provo UT 84602-5250

CROOM, CHARLES EDWARD, JR., brigadier general United States Air Force. BS in Elec. Engring., Rutgers U., 1973, BA in Econs., 1973; MBA, Webster Coll., 1977; disting. grad., Squadron Officer Sch., Maxwell AFB, Ala., Air Command and Staff Coll., Maxwell AFB, Ala., 1985, Nat. War Coll., Maxwell AFB, Ala., 1985; completed exec. devel. program, Cornell U., 1996. Commd. 2d lt. USAF, 1973, advanced through grades to brigadier gen., 1998; tech. evaluation chief Hdqs. Air Force Comm. Command, Richards-Gebaur AFB, Mo., 1974-77; elec. engr. Hdqs. Aif Force Comm. Command, Scott AFB, Ill., 1977-79; from comm. systems engr. to exec. officer Defense Comm. Agy., Washington, 1980-83; cmmdr. detachment 25 2187th Comm. Group USAF, Monte Limbara, Sardinia, Italy, 1983-84; chief plans and policy br., systems for C4S Hdqs. USAF, Washington, 1985-88; chief comm. drawdown br., cmmdr. data svcs ctr. Hdqs. U.S. European Command, Stuttgart, Germany, 1989-92; from cmmdr. 438th comm. group to cmmdr. 438th support group Hdqs. 21st Air Force, McGuire AFB, N.J., 1992-94; dir. comm. Hdqs. Air Mobility Command, Scott AFB, Ill., 1994-96; dir. mission systems, dep. chief of staff comm. Hdqs. USAF, Washington, 1996-97; dir. command, control, comm. systems Hdqs. U.S. European Command, Stuttgart-Vaihingen, Germany, 1997—. Decorated Defense Superior Svc. medal, Legion of Merit, Meritorious Svc. medal with 3 oak leaf clusters, Air Force Commendation medal, Defense Meritorious Service medal. Office: HQ USEUCOM/ECJ6 Unit 30400 Box 1000 APO AE 09128

CROOM, FREDERICK HAILEY, college administrator, mathematics educator; b. Lumberton, N.C., Aug. 6, 1941; s. Robert DeVane and Anna Rosalyn (Currie) C.; m. Henrietta Brown, Aug. 17, 1963; children: Elizabeth Bonner, Frederick Hailey. BS, U. N.C., 1963, PhD, 1967. Asst. prof. math. U. Ky., Lexington, 1967-71; asst. prof. math. U. of the South, Sewanee, Tenn., 1971-74, assoc. prof., 1974-81, prof., 1981—, dir. Summer Sch., 1980-88, assoc. dean, 1984-88, provost, 1989—; bd. dirs. Regions Bank of Franklin County, Tenn. Author: Basic Concepts of Algebraic Topology, 1978, Principles of Topology, 1989. Bd. dirs. St. Andrews-Sewanee Sch., 1981-86, Found. Ind. Colls., 1996-99; trustee U. of the South, 1983-85. Woodrow Wilson fellow, 1963; NSF fellow, 1963-67. Mem. AAUP, Am. Math. Soc., Math. Assn. Am., Tenn. Colls. Assn. (pres. 1999—), Sigma Xi. Episcopalian. Office: U South University Ave Sewanee TN 37383-1000

CROOM, JOHN HENRY, III, utility company executive; b. Fayetteville, N.C., Dec. 12, 1932; s. John Henry and Mary Dalice (Howard) C.; m. Verna Arlene Willetts, June 21, 1953; children: Mary, Karen, Elizabeth, John. BS in Mech. Engring., N.C. State Coll., 1954. Engr. United Fuel Gas Co., Charleston, W.Va., 1954-69; indsl. sales mgr. Charleston Group Cos., 1969-73; indsl. utilization mgr. Columbia Distbn. Cos., Columbus, Ohio, 1973-74; v.p. engring. and planning Columbia Distbn. Cos., Columbus, 1974-79; sr. v.p. Columbia Gas System, Wilmington, Del., 1979-80; exec. v.p., dir. Columbia Gas System, Wilmington, 1981-82, pres., 1982-84, chmn., pres., CEO, 1984-95; ret., 1995; bd. dirs. Associated Electric & Gas Ins. Svcs., Med. Ctr. Del., N.E. region Del-Mar-Va Coun. Boy Scouts Am., past pres. Former bd. dirs., pres. Del-Mar-Va Coun., Boy Scouts Am. With AUS, 1954-56, Korea. Mem. NSPE, Del. Roundtable (bd. dirs., past chmn.), Nat. Eagle Scout Assn. (bd. regents). Home: 5 Seafarer's Cir Savannah GA 31411-3112

CROPP, LINDA W., city official; m. Dwight S. Cropp; children: Allison, Christopher. BA, Howard U., MA. Past pub. sch. tchr. and guidance counselor; city councilwoman at large Washington, 1990-98, chmn. city councilwomen, 1999—; past chair human svcs. com., past mem. regional authorities, pub. svc. and youth affairs, govt. ops. and self-determination coms. Rep. Ward 4 Bd. Edn., 1979, past v.p., pres.; past mem. Washington Met. Area Transit Authority; active Rock Creek Civic Assn., Travelers Aid Soc., Girl Scouts Nation's Capital, Jr. Achievement; mem. adv. bd. United Negro Coll. Fund. Office: 441 4th St NW Ste 704 Washington DC 20001-2714*

CROPPER, ANDRÉ DOMINIC, research scientist; b. Port-of-Spain, Trinidad and Tobago, Aug. 4, 1961; came to U.S., 1978; s. Anthony and Vilma V. (Skinner) C. BSEE, Howard U., 1984, MSEE, 1987; PhD, Va. Tech., 1995. Instr. Norfolk (Va.) U., 1989-91, asst. prof. elec. engring., 1991-92; rsch. assoc. Morgan State U., Balt., 1993-95; rsch., tchr. asst. Va. Tech., 1992-95; lectr. U. West Indies, St. Augustine, Trinidad, Trinidad, 1995-96; project engr. Process, Measurements and Controls, Corning, N.Y., 1996-98; sr. rsch. scientist Active Materials and Device Directorate, Corning Inc.; cons. Advance Controls and Equipment Svcs., Freeport, Bahamas, summer 1990, 96—; dir. engring. enrichment program NASA/Morgan State U., Balt., summer 1990, 92; mem. CISE Infrastructure Planning Task Force, Norfolk, 1989-95; tech. reviewer, presenter in field. Contbr. articles to profl. publs. Mem. Trinidad and Tobago Nat. Swim Team, 1972-84; spkr. St. Paul's H.S., Freeport, 1991; mem. worship com. Christ the King Ch., Norfolk, 1991-92; v.p. Black Grad. Student Assn., Va. Tech., 1993-94. Mem. IEEE, Nat. Soc. Black Engrs., Am. Indian Sci. and Engring. Soc., Internat. Soc. Hybrid Microelectronics, Tidewater Water Polo Club, Alpha Phi Alpha, Tau Beta Pi, Beta Kappa Chi. Roman Catholic. Home: 24 Thayer St Rochester NY 14607-2824

CROPPER, SUSAN PEGGY, veterinarian; b. N.Y.C., Feb. 11, 1941; d. Eli and Ruth (Rader) Abrahams; divorced; 1 child, Tracy Lynn. BS, Kans. State U., 1962, DVM, 1964. Assoc. veterinarian Asbury Park (N.J.) Animal Hosp., 1964-65; instr. in Vet. Sci. Kans. State U., Manhattan, 1965-66; owner, veterinarian Markle (Ind.) Vet. Clinic, 1966-71, Meisels Animal Hosp. Clinic, Elmwood Park, N.J., 1971-73, Ridgewood (N.J.) Animal Hosp., 1973-75, Cropper House Call Practice, Wyckoff, N.J., 1975—; editor Nat. Assn. Women Vets., 1966-68; mem. Audibon Soc. Mus. Natural History. Co-author: Loving and Losing a Pet; editor WJMA Jour., 1973; photographer: Best Diving Spots in Western Hemisphere, 1987. Leader Brownie troop Girl Scouts U.S., Glen Rock, N.J., 1976-77, Wyckoff, 1977-83; chairperson No. Jersey Tridents, Ridgefield, N.J., 1985-86. Mem. AVMA, Soc. Aquatic Vet. Medicine (treas.), No. N.J. Vet. Med. Assn. (pres. 1972-73), Met. Vet. Med. Assn., N.Y. Zool. Soc., Van Saun Zool. Soc., N.J. Acad., Ski and Scuba Club of Westwood, North Jersey Tridents Club (Ridgefield, chair 1985-86). Avocations: scuba diving, underwater photography, travel, racquetball, markmanship practice. Office: 310 Newtown Rd Wyckoff NJ 07481-2608

CROPSEY, JOSEPH, political science educator; b. N.Y.C., Aug. 27, 1919; s. Gustave and Margaret (Dirnfeld) C.; m. Lilian Crystal Levy, Nov. 4, 1945; children—Seth, Rachel Cropsey Simons. A.B., Columbia U., 1939, A.M., 1940, Ph.D., 1952; DHL (hon.), Colo. Coll., 1989. Tutor, asst. prof. CCNY, 1946-57; instr. polit. sci. New Sch. Social Research, N.Y.C., 1949-54; asst. prof. U. Chgo., 1958-64, assoc. prof., 1964-70, prof., 1970-85, Disting. Service prof., 1985-89, prof. emeritus, 1989—. Author: Polity and Economy, 1957, Political Philosophy and the Issues of Politics, 1977, Plato's World, 1995; editor: Ancients and Moderns, 1964; co-editor, co-author: History of Political Philosophy, 1963. Served to 1st. lt. U.S. Army, 1941-46, PTO, ETO. Republican. Jewish. Office: U Chgo 5828 S University Ave Chicago IL 60637-1515

CRORY, ELIZABETH L., former state legislator; b. Gardner, Mass., Sept. 12, 1932; d. James Quaiel and Mary (Reilly) Lupien; m. Frederick E. Crory, Aug. 21, 1954; children: Thomas, David, Ellen, Ann, Edward, Stephen. AB, U. Mass., 1954; MALS, Dartmouth Coll., 1975. Tchr. Amherst (Mass.) Schs., 1954, Lyme (N.H.) Schs., 1972-76; mem. N.H. Ho. of Reps., 1977-87, 92-96, mem. commerce/consumer affairs com., 1977-87, 93-96, mem. spl. com. on med. malpractice, 1984; exec. dir. Children's Ctr. of Upper Valley, 1986-90; bd. dirs. Mascoma Savs. Bank. Mem. assembly of overseers Mary Hitchcock Meml. Hosp., 1987-98; mem. character and fitness com. N.H. Supreme Ct., 1987-98, mem. profl. conduct com., 1998-99; mem. N.H. Health Svcs. Planning and Rev. Bd., 1998—. Roman Catholic. Home: 40 Rip Rd Hanover NH 03755-1614

CROSBIE, ALFRED LINDEN, mechanical engineering educator; b. Muskogee, Okla., Aug. 1, 1942; s. Alfred Henry and Jacquetta Hope (Stoneburner) C.; M. Ann Frances Cirou, July 18, 1963; children: Mark, Jacqueline. BSME, U. Okla., d1964; MSME, Purdue U., 1966, PhD, 1969. Asst. prof. U. Mo., Rolla, 1968-72, assoc. prof., 1972-75, prof., 1975-91, curators' prof., 1991—. Editor: Aerothermodynamics and Planetary Entry, 1981, Heat Transfer and Thermal Control, 1981; editor-in-chief Jour. Thermophysics and Heat Transfer, 1986—; assoc. editor Jour. Quantitative Spectroscopy and Radiative Transfer, 1979—; mem. editl. bd. Heat Transfer-Recent Contents, 1996—; contbr. over 70 articles on radiative heat transfer to profl. jours. Fellow AIAA (chmn. thermophysics com. 1984-86, tech. program chmn. 15th Thermophysics Conf. 1980, assoc. editor AIAA Jour. 1981-83, Thermophysics award 1987, Tech. Contbn. award, 1988), ASME (heat transfer com. on theory and fundamentals 1983—, heat transfer com. on numerical heat transfer 1993—, Heat Transfer Meml. award 1990), AAAS; mem. Optical Soc. Am., Phi Eta Sigma, Sigma Pi Sigma, Tau Beta Pi, Pi Tau Sigma, Sigma Tau, Pi Mu Epsilon, Sigma Xi. Lutheran. Avocation: fishing. Home: 8 Mcfarland Dr Rolla MO 65401-3805 Office: U Mo 233 Mech Engring Rolla MO 65401

CROSBIE, MICHAEL JAMES, architect, writer, educator; b. Denville, N.J., Aug. 10, 1956; s. Leo P. and Viola Marie (Nicolicchia) C.; m. Sharon Ann Maher, Oct. 5, 1985; children: Sean, Christopher, Brigit Rose. BS in Architecture, Cath. U., 1978, MArch, 1980, PhD, 1983. Lic. architect, Conn. Editor Architecture Mag., 1982-92; with Centerbrook Architects, 1987-92; editor Progressive Architecture Mag., 1993-96; assoc. Steven Winter Assocs., Norwalk, Conn., 1996—; adj. prof. architecture Roger Williams U., 1992—, U. Hartford, 1993-94; vis. lectr./critic Yale U., U. Penn, Columbia U., U. Calif., Berkeley, N.Y. Inst. Tech., U. Md., U. Utah, Moscow Archtl. Inst., others; speaker and panelist in field. Author: The Jersey Devil Design/Build Book, 1985, Centerbrook: Reinventing American Architecture, 1993, Architecture Counts, 1993, Architecture Colors, 1993, Architecture Shapes, 1993, Color and Context, 1995, Architecture Animals, 1995, Cesar Pelli: Recent Themes, 1998, others; author introductions to several books; contbg. editor Constrn. Specifier mag., 1996—; asst. editor Faith and Form mag., 1998—; contbr. several hundred articles to Archtl. Record, Domus, Historic Preservation, Landscape Architecture, New Shelter, Town and Country, others. Bd. dirs. Yestermorrow Design/Build Sch., 1990-97. Recipient Neal award for editl. achievement, 1990, 94, William H. Donaldson award for editorial achievement, Henry Adams medal and cert. AIA, others. Mem. Boston Soc. Architects, Tau Beta Pi, Sigma Psi. Episcopalian. Home: 47 Grandview Ter Essex CT 06426-1004 Office: 50 Washington St Norwalk CT 06854-2710

CROSBY, DAVID, musician. Mem. music groups Beefeaters, 1964, The Byrds, 1964-67, Crosby, Stills, Nash, 1968-70, Crosby and Nash, Crosby, Stills, Nash and Young; albums with Crosby and Nash If I Could Only Remember My Name, Oh Yes I Can, Wind On The Water, with Crosby, Stills and Nash CSN, Daylight Again, Live it Up, 1990, Replay, So Far, with Crosby, Stills, Nash and Young American Dream, 1989, Deja Vu, Four Way Street; solo recordings include Thousand Roads, 1993, It's All Coming Back Now, 1995, King Biscuit Flower Hour, 1996. Inducted into Rock and Roll Hall of Fame, 1991. Office: care Atlantic Records 75 Rockefeller Plz New York NY 10019-6908

CROSBY, ELLEN LOUISE, counselor; b. Edenville, Mich., July 9, 1944; d. Donald Wellington and Gladys Leona (Fowler) Marsh; m. James A. Crosby, Mar. 15, 1964; children: Angela Louise, Andrew James, Allen Jackson, James Alvin, JoAnne Marie. BA, So. Coll., 1987; MEd, U. Tenn., Chattanooga, 1990; postgrad., Andrews U., 1997—. Cert. Nat. Bd. Cert. Counselors; lic. profl. counselor.; cert. tchr. N.Am. Divsn. Office Edn. Counselor Advent Youth Ranch, Calhoun, Tenn., 1989-92; dir., supr., founder Young Women's Prep. Home, Macon, Mo., 1992—; pres. Christian Family Learning Ctrs., Inc., McDonald, Tenn., 1992—. Mem. Am. Assn. Christian Counselors, Adventist-Laymen's Svcs. and Industries, Toastmasters (sec. 1992-94). Republican. Seventh-Day Adventist. Avocations: writing articles, writing a book, gardening, grandchildren. Home: 6818 White Oak Cir McDonald TN 37353 Office: Christian Family Learning Ctrs Inc PO Box 2153 Collegedale TN 37315-2153

CROSBY, FRED MCCLELLAN, retail home and office furnishings executive; b. Cleve., May 17, 1928; s. Fred Douglas and Marion Grace (Naylor) C.; m. Phendalyné D. Tazewell, Dec. 23, 1958; children: Fred, James, Llionicia. Grad. high sch. Vice pres. Seaway Flooring & Paving Co., Cleve., 1959-63; chmn., CEO Crosby Furniture Co., Inc., Cleve., 1963—; vice chmn. bd. First Bank Nat.; bd. dirs. Cleve. Auto Systems, Greater Cleve. Growth Assn.; dir., chmn. First Intercity Banc Corp.; trustee Better Bus. Bur. Bd. dirs. Forest City Hosp. Found., Cleve. State U. Found., Greater Cleve. Growth Assn., 1971-90, 93—, Coun. Smaller Enterprise, 1973-80, Goodwill Industries, 1973-80, 97—, Woodruff Hosp., 1975-82, Cleve. Devel. Found., Pub. TV, Surveyors Telecom., Inc., Sta. WVIZ-TV, Cleve.-Cuyahoga Port Authority, 1986-90; dir. adv. coun. Ohio Bd. Workmen's Compensation, 1974-82; chmn. Minority Econ. Devel. Corp., 1972-83; chmn. bd. dirs. Glenville YMCA, 1973-76; trustee BBB, 1995—, Cleve. Play House, 1979-87, Eliza Bryant Health Care Ctr., 1984-86, Cleve. Small Bus. Incubator, 1986-90; bd. dirs., treas. Urban League Cleve., 1971-78; mem. adv. coun. Small Bus. Assn.; mem. adv. bd. Salvation Army, 1980; commr. Ohio State Boxing Commn., 1984-94, Pvt. Industry Coun., 1985, Nat. Small Bus. Adv. Coun., 1980; bd. advs. Antioch Coll.; county commrs. appointee to Cmty. Adv. Bd., 1987—; mem. Cleve. Opera Coun., 1987-89, Forest City Hosp. Found., 1985—; trustee Ohio Motorist, 1993—; Gov. Voinovich appointee to minority devel. fin. adv. bd., 1996—. With AUS, 1950-52. Recipient award bus. excellence Dept. Commerce, 1972; Presdl. award YMCA, 1974; Gov. Ohio award community action, 1973; First Class Leadership Cleve., 1977. named Family of Yr. Cleve. Urban League, 1971. Mem. Cleve. C. of C., NAACP (v.p. Cleve. 1969-78, exec. dir.), Ohio Coun. Retail Mchts. (chmn. 1991-93), Ohio Home Furnishings and Appliance Assn. (pres. 1981-87), Exec. Order Ohio Commodore, Am. Auto Assn. (corp. mem.), Mid-Day Club, Cleve. Play House, Harvard Bus. Sch. Club, Clevelander, Bratenahl Club, Univ. Club (Cleve.), Rotary. Clubs: Mid-Day, Cleve. Play House, Harvard Bus. Sch., Clevelander, Bratenahl, Univ. (Cleve.). Lodge: Rotary. Home: 2530 Richmond Rd Cleveland OH 44122-1767 Office: 12435 Saint Clair Ave Cleveland OH 44108-2013

CROSBY, GEORGE MINER, former state legislator; b. St. Johnsbury, Vt., Nov. 24, 1916; s. Fred Morant and Susan Julia (Miner) C.; m. Gertrude Roderick, Dec. 21, 1944; children: Susan, Peter, William. Grad. pvt. sch., St. Johnsbury. Printer Cowles Press, Inc., St. Johnsbury, 1934-41; asst. advt. mgr. Caldeonian-Record newspaper, St. Johnsbury, 1946-50; sales rep. Gen. Foods Corp., St. Johnsbury, 1950-53, Lever Bros. Co., St. Johnsbury, 1953-80, French and Bean Co., St. Johnsbury, 1980-95; mem. Vt. Ho. of Reps., Montpelier, 1990-94; elderhostel lectr. St. Johnsbury Acad. Contbr. articles to history publs. Pres. St. Johnsbury Athenaeum, 1974-76; trustee Vt. Hist. Soc., Montpelier, 1989-96; chmn. State House Adv. Bd., Montpelier, 1988-95. With USNR, 1942-46. Recipient Citizen of Yr. award St. Johnsbury C. of C., 1984, Legis. award Lyndon State Coll., 1986, Alummni Svc. award St. Johnsbury Acad., 1989. Mem. VFW (legis. officer 1985), Am. Legion (post fin. officer 1973-74). Republican. Roman Catholic. Avocations: history, stamp and coin collecting. Home: 7 Cliff St Saint Johnsbury VT 05819-1001*

CROSBY, GLENN ARTHUR, chemistry educator; b. nr. Youngwood, Pa., July 30, 1928; s. Edwin Glenn and Bertha May (Ritchey) C.; m. Jane Lichtenfels, May 29, 1950; children: Brian, Alan, Karen. B.S., Waynesburg Coll., 1950; Ph.D., U. Wash., 1954. Research assoc. Fla. State U., Tallahassee, 1955-57; vis. asst. prof. physics Fla. State U., 1957; asst. prof. chemistry U. N. Mex., Albuquerque, 1957-62; assoc. prof. chemistry U. N. Mex., 1962-67; prof. chemistry and chem. physics Wash. State U., Pullman, 1967—; chmn. chem. physics program Wash. State U., 1977-84; mem. adv. com. Rsch. Corp., Tucson, 1981-88, 90-92; vis. prof. phys. chemistry U. Tübingen, Fed. Republic Germany, 1964; vis. prof. physics U. Canterbury, Christchurch, N.Z., 1974; Humboldt sr. scientist, vis. prof. phys. chemistry U. Hohenheim, Fed. Republic Germany, 1978-79; mem. commn. on life scis. NRC, 1991-96. Author: Chemistry: Matter and Chemical change, 1962; also numerous sci. and sci.-related articles. Recipient U.S. Sr. Scientist award Humboldt Found., Fed. Republic Germany, 1978-79, Catalyst award Chem. Mfrs. Assn., 1979, Disting. Alumnus award Waynesburg Coll., 1982, Faculty Excellence award Wash. State U., 1984, Pub. Svc. award Wash. State U., 1989, Disting. Prof. award Wash. State U. Mortar Bd., 1990, Pres.'s medallion Waynesburg Coll. for disting. lifetime sci. and ednl. achievement, 1998; named Prof. of Yr., U. N.Mex., 1967; NSF fellow U. Wash., Seattle, 1953-54; Rsch. Corp. Venture grantee, 1960; Fulbright fello2, 1964. Fellow AAAS; mem. Am. Chem. Soc. (numerous activities including chmn. div. chem. edn. 1982, chmn. com. on edn. 1990-91, We. Conn. sect. Vis. Scientist award 1981, nat. award in chem. edn. 1985, bd. dirs. 1994—, Harry and Carol Mosher award Santa Clara Valley sect. 1998), Am. Phys. Soc., Inter-Am. Photochem. Soc., Nat. Sci. Tchrs. Assn., Wash. Sci. Tchrs. Assn. (Outstanding Coll. Sci. Tchr. award 1975), Sigma Xi, Phi Kappa Phi, Sigma Pi Sigma. Home: 1825 NE Valley Rd Pullman WA 99163-4628 Office: Wash State U Dept Chemistry Pullman WA 99164-4630

CROSBY, JACQUELINE GARTON, newspaper editor, journalist; b. Jacksonville, Fla., May 13, 1961; d. James Ellis and Marianne (Garton) C.; m. Robert Edward Legge, Jr., Oct. 19, 1985. ABJ, U. Ga., 1983; MBA, U. Cen. Fla., 1987. Staff writer Macon Telegraph & News, Ga., 1983-84; copy editor Orlando Sentinel, Fla., 1984-85; dir. spl. projects Ivanhoe Communications, Inc., Orlando, Fla., 1987-89; producer spl. projects Sta. KSTP-TV, Mpls., 1989-94; asst. news editor Star Tribune Online, Mpls., 1994—. Recipient award for best sports story Ga. Press Assn., 1982; award for best series of yr. AP, 1985, Pulitzer prize, 1985. Mem. Quill. Avocations: competing in triathlons, playing electric bass, tutoring, reading. Home: 5348 Drew Ave S Minneapolis MN 55410-2006 Office: Star Tribune Online 425 Portland Ave Minneapolis MN 55488-0001*

CROSBY, JAMES EARL, newspaper publisher; b. Staunton, Va., Sept. 17, 1935; s. Lee Marvin and Mildred Lillian (Jones) C.; m. Ruth Anne Southwell, Apr. 27, 1956 (div. Mar. 1980); children: Lee Jepson, Peter William, Lynn Jeannette; m. Patsy Marie Shiflett, July 31, 1981; children: Ashley Blair, Avery Beth. Student, U. Del., 1957, U. Md., 1958. News photographer Staunton News-Leader, 1950-54, News-Jour. Co., Wilmington, Del., 1956-60; freelance photographer Unique Photo, New Castle, Del., 1960-62; devel. dir. Ocean City, Md., 1962-65; travel dir. State of Del., Dover, 1965-70, Shenandoah Valley, Inc., Staunton, 1970-71; pres. Motivation Rsch., Inc., Staunton, 1971-72; asst. to supt. Miller Sch., Va., 1973-80; pres., pub. Bulletin, Inc., Crozet, Va., 1980-94; pres. Md. Travel Coun., Annapolis, 1964-65. First aid chmn. Del. chpt. Red Cross, Wilmington, 1968-69; vice chmn. Cen. Va. chpt. Red Cross, Charlottesville, 1984; founder Western Albemarle Rescue Squad, Crozet, 1978, Albemarle County Fair, Inc., Crozet, 1981; boating instr. boating safety com. Va. Dept. Game & Inland Fisheries, Richmond, 1991—. With USN, 1954-56. Named Outstanding Citizen, City of Staunton, 1970. Mem. Soc. Profl. Journalists, USCG-Aux. (flotilla comdr. 1990-91, divsn. capt. 1994-95, Outstanding Vessel Operator 1990, Outstanding Mem. Achievement 1989, 90, 91, 92), Lake Anna Boating Safety, Inc. (pres. 1990-92), Rivanna Rifle & Pistol Club. Avocations: recreational boating, ham radio operator. Home and Office: 5571 Brookwood Rd Crozet VA 22932-9370

CROSBY, JANICE CELIA, language and literature educator; b. Chambersburg, Pa., July 23, 1962. BA English & Philosophy magna cum laude, Mercer U., 1984; MA in Brit. and Am. lit., Kent State U., 1987; PhD, La. State U., 1994. Grad. tchg. asst. Kent State U., 1985-87; instr. So. U., Baton Rouge, 1991-95, asst. prof., 1995—; pres. Mid. Ea. Dance Artists of Baton Rouge, 1996-99; presenter in field. La. State U. Alumni Fedn. fellow, 1987-91. Mem. MLA, Popular Culture Assn., Phi Kappa Phi. E-mail: drjcrosby@aol.com. Home: Apt D 10203 Ballina Ave Baton Rouge LA 70815 Office: So U Dept English Baton Rouge LA 70813

CROSBY, JOHN O'HEA, conductor, opera manager; b. N.Y.C., July 12, 1926; s. Laurence Alden and Aileen Mary (O'Hea) C. Grad., Hotchkiss Sch., 1944; BA, Yale U., 1950, DFA (hon.), 1991; LittD (hon.), U. N.Mex., 1967; MusD (hon.), Coll. of Santa Fe, 1968, Cleve. Inst. Music, 1974; LHD (hon.), U. Denver, 1977. pres. Manhattan Sch. Music, 1976-86. Accompanist, opera coach, condr., N.Y.C., 1951-56, gen. dir., mem. conducting staff Santa Fe Opera, 1957—; guest condr. various opera cos. in U.S. and Can. and Europe, 1967—; condr. U.S. stage premiere Daphne, 1964; U.S. profl. premier Friedenstag, 1988; world premiere Wuthering Heights, 1958. With inf. AUS, 1944-46, ETO. Recipient Nat. Medal of Arts, 1991, Verdienstkreuz 1st klasse Bundesrepublik, Deutschland, 1992. Roman Catholic. Clubs: Metropolitan Opera (N.Y.C.), Century Assn. (N.Y.C.), University (N.Y.C.). Office: Santa Fe Opera PO Box 2408 Santa Fe NM 87504-2408

CROSBY, JULIE LYNNE, theater industry executive, educator; b. Midland, Mich., Mar. 5, 1964; d. Wayne W. Crosby and Janet (Cuddie) Snyder. BA, Mich. State U., 1985; MA, Columbia U., 1994, MPhil, 1996. Company mgr. Black & Blue, N.Y.C., 1988-91; mgr. Lincoln Ctr. Theater, N.Y.C., 1992-97; preceptor Columbia U., N.Y.C., 1998—; company mgr. On The Town, N.Y.C., 1998-99, Laurie Anderson's Moby Dick, 1999; assoc. gen. mgr. Carrie, N.Y.C., 1988; company mgr. Andre Heller's Wonderhouse, N.Y.C., 1991, Tango Pasión, N.Y.C., 1993, Black & Blue European Tour, 1996; fundraising cons. Joffrey Ballet Sch., N.Y.C., 1990-95; founder Midland-Joffrey Summer Dance Project, Midland, Mich., 1994. Assoc. prodr.: Black & Blue, 1991; dir.: Killing of the Children, 1995, Last Judgment, 1996, Mankind, 1997. Pres. fellow Columbia U., 1994—, Judith D. Lipsey fellow Disting Studies in Humanities Columbia U. Alumni Assn. Bd., 1999; Milton Weintraub scholar Assn. Theatrical Press Agts., 1994-96. Mem. MLA, Assn. Theatrical Press Agts. and Mgrs, Medieval Acad. Am.

CROSBY, KATHRYN GRANDSTAFF (GRANT CROSBY), actress; b. Houston, Nov. 25, 1933; d. Delbert Emery and Olive Catherine (Stokely) Grandstaff; m. Harry L. (Bing) Crosby, Jr., Oct. 24, 1957 (dec. Oct. 1977); children—Harry Lillis III, Mary Frances, Nathaniel Patrick. BFA, U. Tex., 1955; RN, Queens of Angles Sch. Nursing, Los Angeles, 1964; attended, UCLA; teaching credential, Immaculate Heart Coll., L.A., 1965. Actress: in plays including Sunday in New York, 1963, Pygmalion, Sabrina Fair, 1964, Peter Pan, 1965, Arms and the Man, 1965, Mary, Mary, 1966, The Guardsman, 1967, The Prime of Miss Jean Brodie, 1969, Same Time Next Year, 1977-78; films include Rear Window, Unchained, Reprisal, Operation Mad Ball, 1958, others; hostess daily TV talk show, Sta. KPIX, San Francisco; TV appearances Bing Crosby Christmas Specials, Suspense Theater, Ben Casey; Author: Bing and Other Things, 1967; also column Texas Gal in Hollywood, 1952-54. Mem. advisory com. arts State Dept.; Co-chmn. bd. trustees Immaculate Heart Coll.; trustee Eisenhower Med. Center. Named Distinguised Alumae U. Tex., 1969, Rodeo Queen Houston Fatstock Show, 1950. Mem. Am. Conservatory Theatre. Roman Catholic. Address: care Sta KPIX 855 Battery St San Francisco CA 94111-1503*

CROSBY, (CLAIRE) MARENA LIENHARD, retired college administrator; b. Shreveport, La., Mar. 2, 1948; d. John Joseph and Clara Curtis (Lawton) L.; m. H.W. Patrick Obrien, Sept. 23, 1977; m. John L. Crosby, Nov. 23, 1997. MEd, U. New Orleans; JD, Loyola U., New Orleans. Bar: La. 1971; lic. profl. counselor, La. Instr. Delgado C.C., New Orleans, 1973-80, counselor, 1980-86, coord. testing, 1986-88, dir. admissions, 1988-90, dir. counseling and mktg., 1990-97, asst. to v.p. student affairs, 1997-98; dir. degree audit program Delgado C.C., 1993-97, ret., 1998. Mem. DAR, FBA, ACA, Am. Psychotherapy Assn., Inst. Noetic Scis., Family Mediation Coun., La. Bar Assn., La. Notary Assn., La. Assn. Spiritual and Religious Values in Counseling, New Orleans Bar Assn., New Orleans Womens Opera Guild, Colonial Dames, Magna Charta Dames. Republican. Avocations: reading, piano.

CROSBY, NORMAN LAWRENCE, comedian; b. Boston, Sept. 15, 1927; s. John and Ann (Lansky) C.; m. Joan Crane Foley, Nov. 1, 1966; children: Daniel Joseph, Andrew Crane. Student, Mass. Sch. Art, Boston. Ind. comedian, entertainer, 1947—; nat. spokesman Anheuser-Busch Natural Light Beer. Began work as comedian in New England clubs, fraternity and polit. dinners, numerous civic and charity functions; N.Y.C. debut Latin Quarter; several appearances London Palladium, regular appearances at all major hotels in Las Vegas, numerous other night clubs, concert halls, theaters, TV variety and panel shows; host: (syndicated TV series) Norm Crosby's Comedy Shop; nat. co-host on Jerry Lewis Muscular Dystrophy Assn. Telethon. Nat. hon. chmn. better Hearing Inst., Washington; trustee Hope for Hearing Found., UCLA; sponsor Norm Crosby Ann. Celebrity Golf Tournament benefitting City of Hope. With USCG, 1945-46. Recipient Jack Benny Comedy award Authors and Celebrities, 1981, Star on Hollywood (Calif.) Walk of Fame, Hollywood C. of C., 1982, Lifetime Achievement award in Entertainment, Touchdown Club, Washington, 1988, Victory award, Kennedy Ctr. PRes. George Bush, 1991; named Internat. Variety Clubs Man of Yr., 1986. Mem. Friars Club (N.Y.C., L.A.; 15th term Internat. Amb. of Good Will for City of Hope), Masons, Shriners. Jewish.

CROSBY, PETER ALAN, management consultant; b. Santa Barbara, Calif., Oct. 20, 1945; s. Harold Bartley and Margaret Maida (Peterson) C.; m. Stephanie Jay Ellis, Dec. 20, 1969; children: Kelly Michelle, Michael Ellis. BS in Engring., U. Calif., Berkeley, 1967; MS in Ops. Rsch., Stanford U., 1969; ED, Stanford Bus. Sch., 1971. Cert. mgmt. cons. Logistics inventory analyst Ford Motor Co., Palo Alto, Calif., 1967-71; corp. ops. planning analyst FMC Corp., San Jose, Calif., 1972; assoc. mgmt. cons. A.T. Kearney, Inc., San Francisco, 1972-75; mgr. materials mgmt. cons. svcs. Coopers & Lybrand, Los Angeles, 1976-78; ptnr. gen. cons. unit (Case & Co.) Towers Perrin Forster & Crosby, L.A., 1978-81; prin. Crosby, Gustin, Rice & Co. (CGR Mgmt. Cons.), 1981—; dir. Carbide Products Internat. Co. Mem. adv. bd. dirs. Stanton Chase. Mem. Coun. Logistic Mgmt., Inst. Mgmt. Cons., Assn. for Corp. Growth, Turnaround Mgmt. Assn., Phi Gamma Delta. Office: CGR Mgmt Consultants Ste 2000 1901 Avenue Of The Stars Los Angeles CA 90067-6021*

CROSBY, RALPH WOLF, communications executive; b. Annapolis, Md., Dec. 16, 1933; s. Raymond Thomas and Lillian Sylvia (Wolf) C.; m. Carlotta Stafford, June 16, 1958; children: Laura Crosby Avallone, Raymond, Belinda Crosby Butler. BS in Journalism, U Md., 1956. Reporter, editor Balt. News-Am., 1956-60; bur. editor Iron Age Mag., Washington, 1960-65, Med. Econs. mag., Washington, 1966-67; assoc. editor Kiplinger's Changing Times, Washington, 1967-70; exec. v.p. Annapolis Harbour House, Inc., 1970-86; pres. Crosby Mktg. Communications, Annapolis, 1972—; owner Severn Valley Racquet Club, Millersville, Md.; bd. dirs. Annapolis Bank and Trust Co. Editor (book) Person to Person Management, 1966; contbr. articles to numerous mags. including N.Y. Times Mag. Recipient Jesse H. Neal editorial award, 1966. Mem. Md. Direct Mktg. Assn., Advt. Assn. Balt., Greater Annapolis C. of C. (pres. 1975-76), Annapolis Bus. Coalition (pres. 1983-84), U. Md. Colonnade Soc. (nat. chair 1994-95), Nat. Press Club, Annapolis Touchdown Club (pres. 1976), U. Md. Dean's First Edit. Club (chmn. 1986—), Annapolitan Club. Democrat. Avocation: tennis. Home: 139 Wallace Manor Rd Edgewater MD 21037-1205 Office: Crosby Mktg Comms 705 Melvin Ave Ste 200 Annapolis MD 21401-1544

CROSBY, THOMAS MANVILLE, JR., lawyer; b. Mpls., Oct. 9, 1938; s. Thomas M. and Ella (Pillsbury) C.; m. Eleanor Rauch, June 12, 1965; children: Stewart, Brewster, Grant, Brooke. BA, Yale U., 1960, LLB, 1965. Bar: Minn. 1965. Assoc. Faegre & Benson, Mpls., 1965-72, ptnr., 1965—. Served to lt. USNR, 1960-62. Office: Faegre & Benson 2200 Norwest Ctr 90 S 7th St Ste 2200 Minneapolis MN 55402-3901

CROSBY, THOMAS W., computer scientist; b. Boston, Apr. 17, 1942; s. Thomas W. and Dorothy Crosby. AA, Dean Jr. Coll., 1962; BA, Mich. State U., 1964; MBA, Babson Coll., 1980. From software engr. to mgr. corp. advanced tech. lab. Data Gen., Westboro, Mass., 1974—. Mem. IEEE, VFW, Vets of Vietnam. Office: Data General Corp 4400 Computer Dr Westborough MA 01580-0001

CROSBY, WILLIAM DUNCAN, JR., lawyer; b. Louisville, Sept. 1, 1943; s. William Duncan and Lucille (Edwards) C.; m. Constance Elaine Frederick, June 2, 1973; children: William Duncan III, Lelia Margaret. BA, Yale U., 1965; JD, Columbia U., 1968. Bar: Ky. 1968, U.S. Dist. Ct. D.C. 1971, U.S. Supreme Ct. 1977. Minority chief counsel Com. on Rules U.S. Ho. of Reps., Washington, 1972-94, chief counsel Com. on Rules, 1995-99; v.p., COO The Solomon Group, Washington, 1999—. Chmn. Dranesville Dist., Fairfax County (Va.) Rep. Party, 1987-89; mem. Fairfax County Rep. Com., 1981—. Lt. (j.g.) USNR, 1968-71. Mem. ABA, FBA, Ky. Bar Assn., D.C. Bar, Columbia Law Sch. Alumni Assn. of Washington (pres. 1987-89). Baptist. Avocation: swimming. Home: 920 Mackall Ave Mc Lean VA 22101-1618 Office: The Solomon Group Ste 750 801 Pennsylvania Ave NW Washington DC 20004

CROSER, MARY DOREEN, educational association executive; b. N.Y.C., June 22, 1944; d. Charles William and Rita Mary (Lalor) C. BS, SUCNY, Buffalo, 1969; MS, Va. Commonwealth U., 1975. Cert. spl. edn., vocat. rehab. counseling tchr. Spl. educator Hampton (Va.) City Schs., 1971-73, dean of students, 1973-75; dir. devel. disabilities svcs. Community Svc. Bd., Portsmouth, Va., 1975-79; assoc. dir. Welfare Rsch. Inc., N.Y.C., 1979-83; asst. dir. Md. Dept. Health and Mental Hygiene, Balt., 1983-88; exec. dir. Am. Assn. on Mental Retardation, Washington, 1988—; free-lance cons. on disabilities; lectr. on nat. disabilities issues; active Gov.'s Coun. on Devel. Disabilities, 1993—. Contbr. articles to profl. jours. Mem. Gov.'s Com. on Employment of the Handicapped, 1987-88, Pres.'s Com. on Employment of People with Disabilities, 1989-93, adv. com. Pres.'s Com. on Mental Retardation, 1990-91. Fellow Am. Assn. on Mental Retardation (pres. Md. chpt. 1988); mem. Am. Soc. Assn. Execs. Avocations: sailing, photography, music, art, travel. Office: Am Assn on Mental Retardation 444 North Capitol St NW Washington DC 20001-1512

CROSIER, JOHN DAVID, trade association administrator; b. North Adams, Mass., Apr. 21, 1937; s. Walter Schuster and Felicie (Strickland) C.; m. Judith Decker, Sept. 6, 1969; children: John Jr., Michael. BA in Econs., Hamilton Coll., 1959. With mktg. dept. Crompton & Knowles Corp., Worcester, Mass., 1959-70; v.p. mktg. David Gessner Co., Worcester, 1971-72; v.p., gen. mgr. Am. Steel & Aluminum, Auburn, Mass., 1972-74; dir. employment security Commonwealth of Mass., 1974-77; commr. of commerce Commonwealth of Mass., Boston, 1978; exec. v.p. Jobs for Mass., Boston, 1979-80; pres. Mass. Bus. Roundtable, Boston, 1980-88, Bus. and Industry Assn. N.H., Concord, 1988—. Commr. Nat. Commn. on Unemployment Compensation, Washington, 1979-80; vice chair N.H. Charitable Found., 1994-98; treas. N.H. Pub. Policy Ctr., 1996-98; trustee U. Sys. N.H., 1998—. With U.S. Army, 1959-61. Episcopalian. Home: 10 New Castle St Concord NH 03301-2209 Office: Bus & Industry Assn 122 N Main St Concord NH 03301-4917

CROSLEY, POWEL A., physician; b. Cin., Nov. 2, 1963; s. Lewis L. and Georgine Griswold Crosley. BS in Bus., U. Tampa, 1987; MD, St. Georges U., 1999. Doctor Jersey Shore Med. Ctr., Neptune, N.J.; seat owner Chgo. Bd. Trade-Midam; nat. trading advisor Checkmate Fin. Ltd., Northbrook, Ill. E-mail: lampacmd@aol.com. Office: Jersey Shore Med Ctr 1945 State Rt 33 Neptune NJ 07753-9919

CROSMAN, ROBERT TRUE, English language educator; b. Feb. 18, 1940. BA, U. Calif., Berkeley, 1963; PhD, Columbia U., 1971. Asst. prof. English, Williams Coll., Williamstown, Mass., 1969-73; assoc. prof. English, U. Alaska, Anchorage, 1985—. E-mail: afrd@uaa.alaska.edu. Home: 7123 Henderson Loop Anchorage AK 99507-2542 Office: U Alaska Dept English 3211 Providence Dr Anchorage AK 99508-4614

CROSS, ALEXANDER DENNIS, business consultant, former chemical and pharmaceutical executive; b. Leicester, Eng., Mar. 29, 1932; came to U.S., 1970; s. Arthur Lewis and Gladys Mary Tryphena (Narracott) C.; m. Antonia Inez Szilas, Dec. 15, 1973; children: Guy Tibor Boscoe, James Tristan. BS, U. Nottingham, Eng., 1952, PhD in Organic Chemistry, 1955, DSc, 1966. With research div. Syntex Corp., 1961-66, v.p. research, 1967, v.p. comml. relations, 1967-70, v.p. chems. div., 1967-72, pres. internat. pharm. div., 1974-78, pres. Syntex Scientific Systems, 1970-76, sr. v.p. corp. econ. and strategic planning, 1978-79, chmn. mktg. com., chmn. mgmt. com., mem. bd. fin. com.; exec. v.p. Zoecon Corp., 1979-83, pres., chief exec. officer, 1983-85; founder, chmn. bd. dirs., chief exec. officer Cytopharm, Inc., 1987—; chmn. bd. dirs., CEO Pharmetrix Corp., 1987-92, bd. dirs., 1992-94; bd. dirs. Ligand Pharm. Corp., Myelos Corp. Author: (book) Introduction to Infrared Spectroscopy; patentee in field. Fellow Royal Soc. Chemistry; mem. Am. Chem. Soc., Licensing Exec. Soc.

CROSS, ALVIN MILLER (AL CROSS), political columnist, writer; b. Knoxville, Tenn., Apr. 24, 1954; s. Perry Martin and Winnie Cook (Miller) C.; m. Patricia Hodges, June 19, 1976. BA in Mass Communications, Western Ky. U., 1978; postgrad., Poynter Inst. Media Studies, 1999. Sports reporter Clinton County News, Albany, 1967-71; announcer WANY Radio, Albany, Ky., 1968-75; advt. mgr., reporter, editor College Heights Herald, Bowling Green, Ky., 1973-74; reporter, editor The Reporter, Monticello, Ky., 1974-75; asst. mng. editor Logan Leader & News-Democrat, Russellville, Ky., 1975-77; editor Leitchfield (Ky.) Gazette, Grayson County News Gazette, 1977-78; reporter Courier-Journal, Louisville, 1978-88, polit. writer, 1989—. Rep. acad. coun. Associated Student Govt. We. Ky. U., 1972-73. Recipient Founder's award Foothills Festival Inc., Albany, 1989, Outstanding Print Journalist in Ky. and Adjoining States award journalism dept. Western Ky. U., 1995, Deadline Reporting award Metro Louisville Journalism, 1989, 92, Column Writing award, 1989, Continuing Coverage award, 1992, 95. Mem. Soc. Profl. Journalists (regional dir. 1987-89, v.p. Louisville chpt. 1983-84, pres. 1984-85, chmn. nat. com. Project Watchdog 1995—, Outstanding Newspaper in Region 5 award 1974), Ky. Hist. Soc., Western Ky. U. Alumni Assn. Baptist. Avocations: reading, gardening, boating, touring. Home: 123 W Todd St Frankfort KY 40601-2825 Office: Courier-Jour Bur 614B Shelby St Frankfort KY 40601-3460

CROSS, APRIL LEE, geriatrics nurse, nursing educator; b. Columbus, Ohio, Aug. 9, 1956; d. Jack Lutzweit and Dixie Warner (Faulkner) Warner; m. Jeffrey David Cross, June 14, 1980; children: James Lee, Elizabeth Lee. BSN, U. Cin., 1978, MSN, 1982; nursing home administr. cert., George Washington U., 1985. RN, Ohio; cert. nursing home adminstr., Ohio; cert. program coord., Ohio. Dir., asst. dir., cons. Cmty. Multicare Ctr., Fairfield, Ohio, 1979-82; nursing supr. Oak Pavilion, Cin., 1980-81; asst. DON Villa Homes West, Monclova, Ohio, 1983-84; charge nurse Arlington Ct., Columbus, 1985; DON Westminster Thurber Cmty., Columbus, 1985-86; adminstr. Athena Manor Nursing Ctr., Newark, Ohio, 1986-92, Gaulden Manor Nursing Ctr., Balt., 1986-93; faculty Mt. Carmel Coll. Nursing, Columbus, 1993—; mem., support group facilitator Alzheimer's Assn., Newark, 1986-92; mem. task force Task Force on Aging, Newark, 1986-92. Reviewer: OBRA A Challenge and an Opportunity for Nutrition Care, 1992. Vol. ch. nursery Linworth United Meth., Worthington, Ohio, 1988—. Mem. Nat. League Nursing, Ohio Health Care Assn., Sigma Theta Tau. Avocations: piano, gardening, reading. Home: 1392 Kinnards Pl Columbus OH 43235-5131

CROSS, AUREAL THEOPHILUS, geology and botany educator; b. Findlay, Ohio, June 4, 1916; s. Raymond Willard and Myra Jane (Coon) C.; m. Christina Aleen Teyssier, Mar. 11, 1945; children: Timothy Aureal, Christina Avonne Cross Read, Jonathan Ariel, Cheryl Aleen (Mrs. Richard M. Bowman), Christopher Charles. BA, Coe Coll., 1939; MS in Botany, U. Cin., 1941, PhD in Botany and Paleontology, 1943. Instr. to asst. prof. U. Notre Dame, 1943-46; NRC fellow in geology, 1943-44; paleobotanist, Central Expt. Sta., U.S. Bur. Mines, Pitts., 1945; asst. prof. dept. geology U. Cin., 1946-49, asst. prof. dept. botany, 1948-49; part-time geologist Geol. Survey Ohio, 1946-51; coal geologist and paleobotanist W.Va. Geol. and Econ. Survey, 1949-57; asso. prof. to prof. dept. geology U. W.Va., 1949-57; sr. research engr. Pan Am. Petroleum Corp. Research Center, Tulsa, 1957-61; supr. tech. group and research group Pan Am. Petroleum Corp. Research Center, 1959-61; prof. dept. geology Mich. State U., East Lansing, 1961-86; prof. dept. botany and plant pathology Mich. State U., 1961-86; prof. emeritus Mich. State U., East Lansing, 1987—; prof. ecology U. Alaska, 1971; research palynologist U. So. Calif., 1972; Morton vis. prof. Ohio U., Athens Ohio, 1981; Nathaniel S. Shaler Disting. lectr. U. Ky., 1991; UNESCO adviser U. grants commn. India Coal Programs, 1983; Calcutta adviser geology dept. Jadavpur U., India, 1983. Editor: Palynology in Oil Exploration, 1964, Compte Rendu 9th Internat. Congress Carboniferous Stratigraphy and Geology, vol. 4, Econ. Geology: Coal, Oil and Gas, 1985; co-editor: Coal Resources and Research in Latin America, 1978, World Class Coal Deposits, Internat. Jour. Coal Geology, 1993; assoc. editor: Fossil Spores and Pollen, 41 vols, 1956-87; contbr. numerous articles, abstracts and revs. to profl. jours. Chmn. citywide rally Fellowship Christian Athletes, Tulsa, 1960; mem. nat. council U.P. Men, 1966-68, 74-84; active Boy Scouts Am., YMCA, others. Named Seward Meml. lectr. Sahni Inst. Palaeobotany, 1985, J. Sen Meml. lectr., 1985; named Disting. lectr. Am. Assn. Petroleum Geologists, 1964, Outstanding Educator Am. Assn. Petroleum Geologists Ea. Sect., 1987; recipient Gordon H. Wood Jr. Meml. award, 1993, John T. Galey medal, 1995. Mem. Am. Assn. Stratigraphic Palynologists (hon.), Bot. Soc. Am. (chmn. paleobotany sect. 1953, 77, grantee 1954, Disting. Svc. Paleobotany award 1985), Geol. Soc. Am. (Gilbert H. Cady Coal Geology award 1987, chmn. coal geology divsn. 1966, chmn. North Ctrl. sect. 1969-70, exec. sec. sect. 1971-80, grantee 1951), Soc. Econ. Paleontologists and Mineralogists (chmn. rsch. com. 1961-62, councillor in paleontology 1971-73, numerous other internat., nat. and regional profl. assns. Presbyn. E-mail: cross1@pilot.msu.edu. Fax: 517-353-8787. Home: 529 N Harrison Rd East Lansing MI 48823-3015 Office: Mich State Univ Dept Geol Scis East Lansing MI 48824

CROSS, BETTY FELT, small business owner; b. Newcastle, Ind., Jan. 8, 1920; d. Frank Ernest and Olive (Shock) Felt; m. Paris O. Cross, July 14, 1939 (div.); children: Ernest, Betty J., Robert D., Paris, Toni, Frank; m. John B. Gatlin, 1976 (dec. Oct. 1995). Owner, mgr. Salon D'Or, Indpls., 1956-74; owner Bejon, Madison, Ind., 1974-78, Brass & Things, Madison, 1978-81; pres. Felts Mfg. Inc., 1966-74, Black Angus, Inc., 1991, Job Rock I and II, Inc., 1994-97; owner Silver City U.S.A., 1981-97; small business owner; b. Newcastle, Ind., Jan. 8, 1920; d. Frank Ernest and Olive (Shock) Felt; m. Paris O. Cross, July 14, 1939 (div.); children: Ernest, Betty J., Robert D., Paris, Toni, Frank; m. John B. Gatlin, 1976 (dec. Oct. 1995). Owner, mgr. Salon D'Or, Indpls., 1956-74, owner Bejon, Madison, Ind., 1974-78, Brass & Things, Madison, 1978-81; pres. Felts Mfg., Inc., 1966-74, Black Angus, Inc, 1991, Job Rock I and II, Inc., 1994-97. Mem. Nashville C. of C. Avocations: collecting dolls, gold and silver coins, art objects, gold antique jewelry, silver sterling. Mem. Nashville C. of C. Avocations: collecting dolls, gold and silver coins, art objects, gold antique jewelry, silver sterling.

CROSS, BRIAN GREGORY, internist; b. Phila., Dec. 13, 1967; s. Milton Harold and Joyce Eileen (Volchok) C. BA, Emory U., 1990; MD, Georgetown U., 1994. Resident in internal medicine N.C. Bapt. Hosp., Winston Salem, 1994-97; gen. internist Internal Medicine of Griffin, Ga., 1997—. Mem. AMA, ACP. Avocations: computers, film, music, literature.

CROSS, CHARLOTTE LORD, social worker; b. Andalusia, Ala., Dec. 1, 1941; d. Roy Olice and Laura Emily (Smith) Lord; m. Jack Allen Cross, May 5, 1960; children: Jack Allen III, James Duane, Jeffrey Miles. BA in English, Auburn U., Montgomery, Ala., 1979, MS in Psychology, 1980, MS in Secondary Edn./English, 1993. Social worker dept. human resources State of Ala., Andalusia, 1980—; tchr. in English conversation to Nat. Cancer Inst. research scientists, Tokyo, 1965-66; adj. instr. psychology Lurleen B. Wallace State Jr. Coll, 1988-98, Troy State U., Fort Rucker, 1991; owner Capriccio's Coffee Shop and Gifts; portrait artist. Recipient Dept. of Human Resources Commr.'s Merit award, 1989. Mem. Visual Arts League of Andalusia, Am. Soc. Portrait Artists. Baptist.

CROSS, CHESTER JOSEPH, lawyer, accountant; b. June 16, 1931; s. Chester Walter and Stephanie (Nowaczyk) Krzyzaniak. Student, Northwestern U., 1950-56, DePaul U., 1958-59; LLB, U. Ill., 1962. Bar: Ill. 1963, U.S. Dist. Ct. (no. dist.) Ill. 1963; CPA, Ill. Sr. acct. S.D. Leidesdorf & Co., Chgo., 1954-57, Hall, Penny, Jackson & Co., Chgo., 1957-58; contr. Comml. Discount Corp., Chgo., 1958-59; pvt. practice Oak Park and Chgo., Ill., 1963—; corp. dir. The Protectoseal Co. Mem. AICPA, Ill. State Bar Assn., Chgo. Bar Assn. (probate practice com., real property law com.), Ill. CPA Soc., East Bank Club (Al Lipman Black Shoe award 1989), East Bank Club (Al Lipman Black Shoe award). Home: River's Edge at Sauganash 5320 N Lowell # 301 Chicago IL 60630 Office: PO Box 30339 Chicago IL 60630

CROSS, CHRISTOPHER T., association executive; b. Lakewood, Ohio, May 30, 1940; s. Sterling Leonard and Virginia Mae (Taylor) C.; m. Constance Heatherly Woods, Aug. 26, 1961 (div. 1981); children: H. Allyson (dec.), Dana M., Charles M.B.; m. Diane Stricklan DeRoche, June 11, 1982; 1 child, Charles. BA in Polit. Sci., Whittier Coll., Calif., 1962; MA, Calif. State Coll., L.A., 1969. With Dept. HEW, Washington, 1969-70, dep. asst. sec. for legislation, 1970-73; sr. ednl. cons. U.S. Ho. of Reps., Washington, 1973-77, Rep. staff dir., com. on edn. and labor, 1977-78; dir. Washington Office ops. Abt Assocs., Inc., 1978-80; mktg. mgr. fed. govt. Westinghouse Info. Svcs., Washington, 1980-82, mgr. fed. svcs., 1982-83; pres., chief operating officer Univ. Rsch. Corp., Chevy Chase, Md., 1983-89; asst. sec. for ednl. rsch. and improvement U.S. Dept. Edn., Washington, 1989-91; dir. Am. Inst. Rsch., 1993—; exec. dir., edn. initiative The Bus. Roundtable, 1991-9 4; pres. Coun. for Basic Edn., 1994—; mem. Nat. Edn. Commn. on Time and Learning, 1992-94; mem. Md. State Bd. Edn., 1993-97, pres. 1994-97. Contbr. articles to profl. jours. Mem. Profl. Svc. Coun. (exec. com. 1981-86, trustee), Coun. Excellence in Govt. Congregationalist. Home: 4721 Cumberland Ave Chevy Chase MD 20815-5457 Office: Coun for Basic Edn 1319 F St NW # 900 Washington DC 20004

CROSS, DAVID R., farmer, livestock raiser; b. Larned, Kans., July 25, 1952; s. Charles Rusk and Mary Helen (Gatterman) C.; m. Linda Rae Wheeler, Nov. 3, 1974; children: Aaron R., Carolyn R., Aimee E. BS in Agr., Fort Hays State U., 1974; AI Tech. Course, Kans. State U., 1988. Ptnr. Cross Bros., Lewis, Kans., 1974-94; bd. dirs. Home State Bank, Lewis, 1979-94, chmn. of the bd., 1991-94; bd. dirs. Star Alfalfa, Inc., Lewis, 1986—; pres. Cross Bros., 1994—; mem. adv. bd. Kennedy & Coe, LLC, Pratt, Kans., 1996—, class II grad. Wheat Industry Leaders of Tomorrow, St. Louis, 1998-99; panelist Kans. Farmer Mag., 1996—. Mem. sch. bd. United Sch. Dist. 503, Lewis, Kans., 1986-88; cub master Boy Scouts Am., Cub Pack 238, Lewis, Kans. 1987-89; mem. com. Troop 238 Boy Scouts Am., Lewis, 1989-96; trustee United Meth. Ch., 1994—; precinct com. Ctrl

Com. Kans. Reps., Edwards County, Kans., 1984-91, chmn. 1996—; first dist. alt. del. Kans. Rep. Party, Topeka, 1999; chmn. Edwards County Leadership, Kinsley, Kans., 1995-98. Recipient 20th N.Am. Big Game award, Boone and Crockett Club, 1987; owner Res. Champion Live, Heifer Beef Empire Days, Garden City, Kans., 1988. Mem. Nat. Cattleman's Beef Assn. (agr. policy com. 1995—), Kans. Livestock Assn. (bd. dirs. 1978-80, water com. 1994—, vice chmn. 1996—, policy and resolutions com., 1997—, cow, calf stocker coun. exec. com. 1999—), Kans. Assn. Wheat Growers (Edwards County chmn., 1994-95, bd. dirs. 1996—), Masons (master). Avocations: hunting, collecting western memorabalia. E-mail: crossbro@ruraltel.net. Home: Rt 1 Box 22 Lewis KS 67552

CROSS, DOLORES EVELYN, university administrator, educator; b. Newark, Aug. 29, 1938; d. Charles and Ozie (Johnson) Tucker; children: Thomas E., Jane E. BA in Elem. Edn., Seton Hall U., 1963; MS, Hofstra U. 1968; PhD in Higher Edn. Adminstrn., U. Mich. 1971; hon. doctorates Marymount Coll., Skidmore Coll., Hofstra U., Elmhurst Coll. Asst. prof. edn. Northwestern U., Evanston, Ill. 1971-74; assoc. prof. Claremont Grad. Sch., Calif., 1974-78; vice chancellor CUNY, 1978-81; prof. Brooklyn Coll., 1978-81; pres. N.Y. State Higher Edn. Service Corp., Albany, 1981-88; assoc. provost, assoc. v.p. academic affairs U. Minn., Mpls., 1988-90; pres. Chgo. State U., 1990—; pres. Gen. Electric Fund, 1996-99; pres. Morris Brown Coll., Atlanta, 1999—; bd. dirs. Coll. Bd., Campus Compact, 1997—, Assn. Black Women in Higher Edn., No. Trust Co.; sr. cons. South Africa's Historically Black Colls. Editor: Teaching in a Multicultural Society, 1978; bd. dirs. Field Mus., Chgo. Urban League, Leadership for Quality Edn., Chgo. Area Fulbright Scholars Program; Tosney award, Amer. Assn. of Univ. Admin., 1995. Mem. NAACP (life), Am. Edn. Research Assn., Am. Assn. Higher Edn. (chair-elect 1997—), Am. Council on Edn. (bd. dirs.), Women Execs. in State Govt. (adv. bd.), Commercial Club (Chgo.). Avocations: running, hiking, bicycling, theater, writing.*

CROSS, EASON, JR., architect; b. Bisbee, Ariz., Nov. 14, 1925; s. Eason and Olive (Hardwick) C.; m. Diana Johnson, June 17, 1950; children: Ben, Becca, Amy, Susan. BA, Harvard U., 1949, MArch, 1951. With Prentiss Huddleston & Assos., Tallahassee, Fla., 1950-51, W.D. Compton, Cambridge, Mass., 1951-52, Deigert & Yerkes, Washington, 1952; assoc. Charles M. Goodman, Washington, 1952-59, Keyes, Lethbridge & Condon, 1959-61; ptnr. Cross & Adreon, Arlington, Va., 1961-87, pres. Va. Architects Accord P.C., Alexandria, 1989—; prin. Cross Assocs., Alexandria, Va., 1987—. Pres. Hollin Hills Cmty. Assn., 1978; chmn. Fairfax County Appeals Bd., 1970-80; pres. Old Dominion DESA, 1997-98, Purysburg Preservation Found., 1998—. With USNR, World War II. Recipient Ware prize, 1950, Washington Bd. Trade design award, 1965, Bethesda-Chevy Chase C. of C. design awards, 1966, 67; House and Home awards A.I.A., 1965-66; Mid-Atlantic Region design awards, 1967, 69; Nat. Honor award, 1968; Nat. Honor award Am. Inst. Steel Constrn., 1967; 4 awards H.U.D.-Washington Center Urban Studies furniture competition, 1971; Fairfax County Exceptional Design award, 1985, 87, N.V. CAA Design award, 1991. Fellow AIA (Housing Competition ADPSR award 1993); mem. Va. Soc. AIA (bd. dirs. 1985-87, Energy award 1979, 87, design award 1986, Noland medal 1994, Frameworks Home Design Merit award 1995), Harvard Club, Fox Club, Ga. Salzburger Soc. Episcopalian. Patentee fastenings and furniture. Home: 2309 Glasgow Rd Alexandria VA 22307-1821 Office: Va Architects Accord PC 8808H Pear Tree Ct Alexandria VA 22309-4221

CROSS, FRANK MOORE, JR., foreign language educator; b. Ross, Calif., July 13, 1921; s. Frank Moore and Mary (Ellison) C.; m. Elizabeth A. Showalter, June 20, 1947; children: Susan E., Ellen M., Priscilla Rachel. AB, Maryville Coll., 1942; BD, McCormick Theol. Sem., 1946; PhD, Johns Hopkins, 1950; MA (hon.), Harvard U., 1957; LittD, Maryville Coll., 1968; DPhil (hon.), Hebrew U. Jerusalem, 1984; DSc (hon.), Lethbridge U., 1990; DHL (hon.), Miami U., 1992; LHD (hon.), Albright Coll., 1994; D in Jewish Letters (hon.), Jewish Theol. Sem., 1997; DHL (hon.), U. Pa., 1998. Hancock prof. Hebrew and Oriental langs. Coll. Arts and Scis., Harvard U., Cambridge, Mass., 1957-92; Hancock prof. emeritus Coll. Arts and Scis., Harvard U., 1992—; also curator Semitic Mus., 1958-61, dir., 1974-87, chmn. dept. neareastern langs., 1958-65; ann. prof. Am. Sch. Oriental Research, Jerusalem, 1953-54; mem. internat. staff for editing Dead Sea Scrolls, 1953—; co-dir. archaeol. expdn. to Judaean Buge'ah, 1955; prin. investigator Am. Schs. Oriental Rsch., Harvard U., U. Mich. expdn. to Carthage, 1975-80; archaeol. dir. Hebrew Union Coll., Jerusalem, 1963-64. Author: (with David N. Freedman) Early Hebrew Orthography, 1952, The Ancient Library of Qumran, 3rd ed. 1995; (with D.N. Freedman) Studies in Ancient Yahwistic Poetry, 2nd ed., 1997; Canaanite Myth and Hebrew Epic, 1973; From Epic to Canon, 1998; Qumran Cave 4:XII Genesis to Number 1994; editor: (with Michael Stone) Scrolls from the Wilderness of the Dead Sea, 1965, (with S. Talmon) Qumran and the History of the Biblical Text, 1975, Magnalia Dei, 1976; editor: Harvard Semitic Studies, 1968-92, Harvard Semitic Monographs, 1968-92; assoc. editor: Harvard Theol. Rev, 1963-74, Bull. of Am. Schs. Oriental Rsch., 1969-91, contbg. editor, 1992—; contbr. articles to profl. jours. Trustee Am. Schs. Oriental Rsch., 1973-91, pres., 1974-76, hon. trustee, 1992—. Recipient Percia Schimmel award Israel Mus., 1980, Inst. for Advanced Studies fellow Hebrew U., Jerusalem, 1978-79, Medalla De Honor De La Universidad Complutense (Univ. Madrid), 1991; Am. Council Learned Socs. fellow, 1971-72. Fellow Am. Acad. Arts and Scis.; mem. Am. Philos. Soc., Am. Oriental Soc., Soc. Bibl. Lit. (pres. 1973-74, William Foxwell Albright award 1980), Bibl. Colloquium, Israel Exploration Soc. (hon.), British Soc. for Study Old Testament (hon.), Phi Beta Kappa. Home: 31 Woodland Rd Lexington MA 02420-2015 Office: Harvard Semitic Mus 6 Divinity Ave Cambridge MA 02138-2020

CROSS, GEORGE ALAN MARTIN, biochemistry educator, researcher; b. Cheadle, Cheshire, Eng., Sept. 27, 1942; s. George Bernard and Beatrice Mary (Horton) C.; m. Nadia Maria Nogueira, Feb. 26, 1986; 1 child, Julia Elizabeth. BA, Cambridge (Eng.) U., 1964, PhD, 1968. Scientist Med. Research Council, Cambridge, 1970-77; dept. head Wellcome Found. Research Labs., Kent, Eng., 1977-82; Andre and Bella Meyer prof. molecular parasitology Rockefeller U., N.Y.C., 1982—, dean grad. and postgrad. studies, 1995—; cons. Wellcome Found., Eng., 1982-87, World Health Orgns., Geneva, 1983-87, New Eng. Biolabs., Beverly Mass., 1985—. Contbr. articles to profl. jours. Recipient Paul Ehrlich prize, 1984, Chalmers medal Royal Soc. of Tropical Medicine, 1983; named Fleming Lectr. Soc. for Gen. Microbiology, 1978. Fellow The Royal Soc. (Leeuwenhoek Lectr. 1998). Office: The Rockefeller Univ 1230 York Ave New York NY 10021-6399

CROSS, HAROLD DICK, physician; b. Wellington, Kans., Apr. 2, 1930; married, 1947; four children. BA, Colby Coll., 1953; MD, Yale Y., 1957. Intern Eastern Maine Med. Ctr., 1957-58, prof., physician, 1958-91; pvt. practice, 1958-91; clin. assoc. prof. medicine and family practice U. Vt., Elizabethtown, N.C., 1971-84; emergency rm. physician Johnston Meml. Hosp., Smithfield, N.C., 1971-98, Naval Hosp., Beaufort, S.C., 1998—. Mem. Inst. Medicine, Nat. Acad. Sci.

CROSS, HAROLD ZANE, agronomist, educator; b. Portales, N.Mex., Dec. 25, 1941; s. Guy Edner and Hagabelle (Lawson) C.; m. Glenda Faye Wilhoit, Nov. 24, 1961; children: Carter Dale, Carson Lee, Curtis Don, Cathryn Faye. BS with honors, N.Mex. State U., 1965, MS, 1967; PhD, U. Mo., 1971. Rancher Elida, N.Mex., 1965-67; grad. rsch. asst. N.Mex. State U., Las Cruces, 1965-67; NDEA fellow U. Mo., Columbia, 1967-71; asst. prof. N.D. State U., Fargo, 1971-77, assoc. prof., 1977-82, prof., 1982-98; prof. emeritus N.D. State U., 1998—; cons. Agrl. Inst. Osijek, Yugoslavia, 1984, CIMMYT, Mexico City, 1984, Eli Lilly Co., Indpls., 1987, N.D. State U., Fargo, 1998—. Contbr. numerous articles to profl. jours.; 9 plant variety patents pending. Crops judge N.D. Winter show, Valley City, 1973-98. Santa Fe Rwy. scholar, 1961-62; NDEA fellow, 1967-71; recipient Outstanding Sr. Rsch. award N.D. State U. Coll. Agr., 1992. Mem. Crop Sci. Soc. Am. (editor for maize germplasm 1989-92), Am. Soc. Agronomy, Sigma Xi, Phi Kappa Phi, Gamma Sigma Delta, Alpha Zeta. Achievements include development and release of 51 inbred parental lines of maize and 39 synthetic varieties of maize; 12 plant variety patent applications; development of maize breeding procedures to genetically improve grain drying rates, procedures to improve leaf growth rates, kernel growth.

CROSS, HARRY MAYBURY, retired law educator, consultant; b. Ritzville, Wash., Aug. 23, 1913; s. James Leman and Mary Rosella (Maybury) C.; m. Mylinn A. Gould, Dec. 25, 1935; children: Harry Maybury, BruceMichael, Kim Judson. B.A., Wash. State U., 1936; J.D., U. Wash., 1940. Bar: Wash. 1941. Reporter Yakima (Wash.) Morning Herald, 1937; abstracter, title examiner Wash. Title Ins. Co., Seattle, 1937-40; Sterling fellow in law Yale U., 1940-41; atty. U.S. Treasury Dept., Washington, 1941-42, TVA, Chattanooga, 1942-43; asst. prof. law U. Wash., Seattle, 1943-45; assoc. prof. U. Wash., 1945-49, prof., 1949-84; prof. emeritus U. Wash., Seattle, 1984—; assoc. dean U. Wash. (Sch. of Law), 1975-78, acting dean, 1978, 79; vis. prof. Columbia U., 1956-57, NYU, 1964, U. Mich., 1972. Contbg. editor: Community Property Deskbook, 2d edit., 1989. Recipient Law medal Gonzaga U., 1994, Don Palmer award U. Wash. Alumni, 1997. Mem. Wash. State Bar Assn. (Honor and Merit award 1984), ABA, Nat. Collegiate Athletic Assn. (pres. 1969, 70), U. Wash. Retirement Assn. (pres. 1987-88), Order of Coif, Crimson Circle, Oval Club, Phi Beta Kappa, Phi Kappa Phi, Sigma Delta Chi, Phi Alpha Delta, Kappa Sigma. Home: 10125 NE 126th St Kirkland WA 98034-2855 Office: U Wash Law Sch JB 20 Seattle WA 98105

CROSS, J. BRUCE, lawyer; b. Sharon, Pa., Oct. 6, 1949; s. John Lantz and Agnes (Bruce) C.; children: Lantz Davis, Heather Lynn. BA, U. Notre Dame, 1971; JD, U. Ark., 1974. Bar: Ark. 1974, U.S. Ct. Appeals (8th cir.) 1979, U.S. Supreme Ct. 1980. Ptnr. House, Holmes and Jewell, Little Rock, 1974-90, Cross and Gunter, P.A., Little Rock, 1990, McGlinchey Stafford Lang, Little Rock, 1991-97, Cross, Gunter, Witherspoon & Galchus, P.C., Little Rock, 1997—; chpt. atty. Ark. Subcontractors Assn., Little Rock, 1987-90; mem. young execs. coun. Associated Gen. Contractors, 1989. Contbr. to profl. publs. Active Big Bros. Ark., Little Rock, 1976-87; pres., bd. dirs. Ark. divsn. Nat. Soc. to Prevent Blindness, 1987-90; bd. dirs. Urban League Ark., 1989; nat. bd. dirs. Associated Builders & Contractors Am., 1999—; bd. dirs. Ark. Constrn. Edn. Found., 1999; active Leadership Hot Springs; active Habitat for Humanity, Youth Home. Recipient Pres.'s award Nat. Soc. to Prevent Blindness. Mem. Ark. Hospitality Assn. (bd. dirs. 1988-89), Ark. Subcontractors Assn., Assoc. Bldrs. and Contrs. (pres. 1999), Ark. Ready Mixed Concrete Assn., Little Rock C. of C. (ptnrs. in edn. com. 1989-90), ABA (sect. labor and employment law com. on labor arbitration and the law of collective bargaining agreements 1981—), Greater Hot Springs C. of C., Notre Dame Club Ark. (pres.). Roman Catholic. Office: Cross, Gunter, Witherspoon & Galchus PC 500 E Markham St Ste 200 Little Rock AR 72201-1747

CROSS, JOHN WILLIAM, foreign language educator; b. Franklin, Pa., June 1, 1943; s. William Robert and Madaline Ann (Maurin) C.; m. Beverly Jean Boor; 1 child, Catherine Elizabeth. BA, W.Va. U., 1965, MA, 1967; PhD, U. Conn., 1974. Instr. French U. N.C., Asheville, 1967-68; asst. Lycee Louis-Le-Grand, Paris, 1972-73; instr., asst. prof. French SUNY, Geneseo, N.Y., 1969-75; asst. prof. SUNY-Potsdam Coll., 1976-84, chair modern langs., 1985-86, 90-91, 93—, assoc. prof., 1984-91, prof. modern langs., 1991; dir. for lang. programs MLA of Am., N.Y.C., 1991-93; advanced placement reader Ednl. Testing Svc., Princeton, N.J., 1983-87; cons. in field. Editor Assn. Depts. of Fgn. Langs. Bull.; contbr. articles and revs. to profl. jours. Recipient French Govt. scholarship Svcs. Culturels Francais, 1990; grantee NEH, 1977, 85, 88, Office des Universites, 1972-73. Mem. MLA of Am., Am. Assn. Tchrs. French, N.Y. State Assn. Fgn. Lang. Tchrs., Societe d'Analyse de la Topique du Roman, Internat. Courtly Lit. Soc. Avocations: music appreciation, performance, recreational sports, poetry translation. Home: 36 Pierrepont Ave Potsdam NY 13676-2111 Office: SUNY Dept Modern Langs Potsdam NY 13676

CROSS, JUNE CREWS, retired music educator; b. Creedmoor, N.C., Oct. 7, 1935; d. David Reid and Virginia Frances (Bullock) Crews; m. Joel Allen Cross, June 26, 1965; children: Dhedra Frances, Allen Reid. BS in Music, Reading, East Carolina U., 1957; MS in Recreation Adminstrn., U. N.C., Chapel Hill, 1964. Cert. tchr., N.C. Tchr. music Mecklenburg County Schs., Charlotte, N.C., 1957-58; tchr. music Granville County Schs., Oxford, N.C., 1958-60, 65-66, tchr. reading, music, 1977-97, lead tchr., 1989-90; pvt. tchr. piano, voice, Creedmoor, 1966-74. Choir dir. Creedmoor United Meth. Ch., 1988-99; asst. dir. Sparkle, Granville County Show Choir; accompanist The King and I prodn. Granville Little Theatre, Oxford, 1997. Named Tchr. of Yr. Butner (N.C.) -Stem Elem. Sch., 1993-94. Mem. Delta Kappa Gamma, Sigma Alpha Iota. Methodist. Avocation: reading. Home: 701 Forest Ln Creedmoor NC 27522-8196

CROSS, KATHRYN PATRICIA, education educator; b. Normal, Ill., Mar. 17, 1926; d. Clarence L. and Katherine (Dague) C. BS, Ill. State U., 1948; MA, U. Ill., 1951, PhD, 1958; LLD (hon.), SUNY, 1988; DS (hon.), Loyola U., 1980, Northeastern U., 1975; DHL (hon.), De Paul U., 1986, Open U., The Netherlands, 1989. Math. tchr. Harvard (Ill.) Community High Sch., 1948-49; rsch. asst. dept. psychology U. Ill., Urbana, 1949-53, asst. dean of women, 1953-59; dean of women then dean of students Cornell U., Ithaca, N.Y., 1959-63; dir. coll. and univ. programs Ednl. Testing Svc., Princeton, N.J., 1963-66; rsch. educator Ctr. Rsch. and Devel. in Higher Edn. U. Calif., Berkeley, 1966-77; rsch. scientist, sr. rsch. psychologist, dir. univ. programs Ednl. Testing Svc., Berkeley, 1966-80; prof. edn., chair dept. adminstrn., planning & social policy Harvard U., Cambridge, Mass., 1980-88; Elizabeth and Edward Conner prof. edn. U. Calif., Berkeley, 1988-94, David Pierpont Gardner prof. higher edn., 1994-96; mem. sec. adv. com. on automated personal data sys. Dept. HEW, 1972-73; del. to Soviet Union, Seminar on Problems in Higher Edn., 1975; vis. prof. U. Nebr., 1975-76; vis. scholar Miami-Dade C.C., 1987; spkr., cons. in field. Author: Beyond the Open Door: New Students to Higher Education, 1971, (with S. B. Gould) Explorations in Non-Traditional Study, 1972, (with J. R. Valley and Assocs.) Planning Non-Traditional Programs: An Analysis of the Issues for Post-secondary Education, 1974, Accent on Learning, 1976, Adults as Learners, 1981, (with Thomas A. Angelo) Classroom Assessment Techniques, 1993, (with Mimi Harris Steadman) Classroom Research, 1996; contbr. articles, monographs to profl. publs., chpts. to books; mem. editl. bd. to several ednl. jours.; cons. editor ednl. mag. Change, 1980—. Active Nat. Acad. Edn., 1975—, Coun. for Advancement of Exptl. Learning, 1982-85; trustee Bradford Coll., Mass., 1986-88, Antioch Coll., Yellow Springs, Ohio, 1976-78; mem. nat. adv. bd. Nat. Ctr. of Study of Adult Learning, Empire State Coll.; mem. nat. adv. bd. Okla. Bd. Regents; mem. higher edn. rsch. program Pew Charitable Trusts; mem. vis. com. Harvard Grad. Sch. Edn., 1998—; bd. dirs. Elderhostel, 1999—; trustee Berkeley Pub. Libr., 1999—, Carnegie Found., 1999—. Mem. Am. Assn. Higher Edn. (bd. dirs. 1987—, pres. 1975, chair 1989-90), Am. Assn. Comty. and Jr. Colls. (vice chair commn. of future comty. colls.), Carnegie Found. Advancement of Tchg. (adv. com. on classification of colls. and univs.), Nat. Ctr. for Devel. Edn. (adv. bd.), New Eng. Assn. Schs. and Colls. (commn. on instns. higher edn. 1982-86), Am. Coun. Edn. (commn. on higher edn. and adult learner 1986-88). Office: U Calif Sch Edn 3659 Tolman Hall Berkeley CA 94720

CROSS, LESLIE ERIC, electrical engineering educator; b. Leeds, Eng., Aug. 14, 1923; came to U.S., 1961; s. Charles Eric and Alice Emily (Plant) C.; m. Lorna Lucilla Fish, Apr. 1, 1950; children: Peter Charles, Matthew John, Daniel Eric, Rebecca Lorna, Rachel Jean, Elizabeth Mary. B.Sc., Ph.D., Leeds U.; D.Sc. (hon.), Xian Jiaotong U. ICI fellow Leeds U., 1951-54; research scientist Elec. Research Assn., Eng., 1954-61; assoc. prof. Pa. State U., University Park, 1961-65, Evon Pugh prof. elec. engring., 1965—, formerly dir. Materials Research Lab. Recipient John Jeppson medal, 1984; Ross Coffin Purdy award, 1985, MRS medal, 1992. Fellow Am. Inst. Physics, Am. Ceramics Soc. (electronics award 1968), IEEE, Optical Soc. Am.; mem. Japan Phys. Soc., Nat. Acad. Engring. Office: Pa State U Materials Rsch Lab Rm 187 University Park PA 16802

CROSS, RALPH EMERSON, mechanical engineer; b. Detroit, June 3, 1910; s. Milton Osgood and Helen (Heim) C.; m. Eloise Florence Fountain, June 18, 1932; children: Ralph Emerson, Carol (Mrs. Peter G. Wodtke), Dennis W. Student, MIT, 1933; D.Eng. (hon.), Lawrence Inst. Tech., 1977. V.p. Cross Co., Fraser, Mich., 1932-67, pres., gen. mgr., 1967-79, chmn., 1979-82; chmn. bd. Cross & Trecker, Bloomfield Hills, Mich., 1979-82, chmn. emeritus, dir., 1982-86; chmn. bd., chief exec. officer Intelitec Corp., Grosse Pointe Farms, Mich., 1982-89; chmn. bd., pres. Cross Internat. A.G., Fribourg, Switzerland, 1965-68; pres. Cross Export Corp., 1972-80; spl. cons. to asst. sec. Air Force for Material, 1955-59; mem. corp. Econ. Devel. Corp. Greater Detroit, 1968-73, Mich. Blue Shield, 1969-74; mem. corp. devel. com. MIT, 1970—; mem. Am. Iranian Joint Bus. Coun., 1975-76; trustee Lawrence Inst. Tech., 1979—; pres. SME Edn. Found., 1979-84, chmn. emeritus, dir., 1984—. Recipient Engring. citation Am. Soc. Tool Engrs., 1956, Corp. Leadership award MIT, 1976; elected to Machine Tool Hall of Fame, 1992. Mem. NAE, Nat. Machine Tool Builders Assn. (pres. 1975), Soc. Automotive Engrs., Soc. Mfg. Engrs. (hon.), Engring. Soc. Detroit, Lochmoor Club, Quail Ridge Country Club, Delray Beach Club, Detroit Athletic Club. Home: 22 Windemere Pl Grosse Pointe MI 48236-3079

CROSS, RICHARD JAMES, physician, educator; b. N.Y.C., Mar. 31, 1915; m. Margaret W. Lee, June 28, 1939; children—Richard James, Margaret Lee, AlanWhittemore, Anne Redmond, Jane Randolph. Grad., Groton Sch., 1933; B.A., Yale, 1937; M.D., Columbia, 1941, Med. Sc.D., 1949. Intern Presbyn. Hosp., N.Y.C., 1941-42; asst. resident Presbyn. Hosp., 1946-48; instr. medicine Columbia, 1947-49, asso. medicine, 1951-57, asst. prof., 1957-59, asst. dean, 1957-59; asso. dean, asst. prof. medicine U. Pitts. Sch. Medicine, 1959-63; dean faculty medicine U. Ghana, West Africa, 1963; asso. prof. medicine Temple U., 1963-64; asst. to exec. dir. Assn. Am. Med. Colls., 1964-65; lectr. Northwestern U. Sch. Medicine, 1965; prof. medicine Rutgers Med. Sch., Coll. Medicine and Dentistry of N.J., 1965-85, asso. dean, 1965-70, prof. community medicine, 1970-85, prof. emeritus, 1985—, chmn. dept., 1970-80; NRC fellow Pub. Health Research Inst., N.Y.C., 1949-51; bd. dirs. Sex Info. and Edn. Council U.S. Mem. Fair Lawn (N.J.) Bd. Edn., 1951-54. Served to capt., M.C. AUS, 1942-46. Decorated Bronze Star, Purple Heart. Mem. AMA, Assn. Am. Med. Colls., Am. Public Health Assn., Am. Soc. for Sci. Study of Sex, Am. Assn. Sex Educators, Counselors and Therapists. Home: 210 Elm Rd Princeton NJ 08540-2506

CROSS, RICHARD JOHN, banker; b. Denver, May 22, 1929; s. Arthur Chester and Gertrude Eva (Ryan) C.; m. Mildred Louise Mouton, Jan. 19, 1957; children: John Charles, Carolyn Louise, Paul Arthur. B.S., U. Colo., 1950; M.B.A, Wharton Sch. Finance U. Pa., 1955. With Lloyds Bank Calif., 1962-81, exec. v.p., 1974-81; sr. v.p. Fidelity Fed. Savs. & Loan, Glendale, Calif., 1981-83; vice chmn. Fidelity Nat. Trust, Glendale, Calif., 1981-83; mng. ptnr. Cross Investment Co., 1971—; dir. bus. program Woodbury U., L.A., 1985-87; adj. prof. fin. and mgmt., 1987—; cons. Higgins, Marcus & Lovett, L.A., 1988; chmn. bd. Highland Fed. Bank, 1993—; adv. bd. Archdiocese of L.A. Dept. Detention Ministries, 1991-97. Mem. regents council Mt. St. Mary's Coll., Los Angeles; regional bd. Cath. Social Service; councilman, Boulder, 1959-62; bd. dirs. Glendale Symphony Assn.; trustee Flintridge Prep. Sch. Served with USN, 1950-53. Fellow Royal Soc. Arts; mem. Calif. Bankers Assn., So. Calif. Trust Officers Assn., Delta Tau Delta, Phi Epsilon Phi. Democrat. Roman Catholic. Clubs: Sutter (Sacramento); Jonathan (Los Angeles); Oakmont Country (Glendale, Calif.). Home: 1430 Greenbriar Rd Glendale CA 91207-1256

CROSS, RITA FAYE, librarian, early childhood educator, writer; b. Franklin, Va., Apr. 4, 1957; d. Alonza Riddick and Earleen (Smith) C.; m. Cameron Michael Moody. BS in Early Childhood Edn., Elizabeth City State U., 1979; MA in Libr. Sci., U. D.C., 1993. Tchr. kindergarten Great Mt. Zion Day Care, Washington, 1979-86, Woodridge Elem. Sch., Washington, 1986-92; libr. Ea. Sr. H.S., Washington, 1992—. Avocations: writing poetry, horseback riding, boating, concerts, theater. Home: 10207 Fort Hills Ct Fort Washington MD 20744-3913

CROSS, ROBERT CLARK, journalist; b. Cheboygan, Mich., May 12, 1939; s. Warren Clark and Meryle M. (Allaire) C.; m. JuJu Lien; children: Gabriel Francis, Amy Lien. B.A. in Journalism, Wayne State U., 1962. Writer, researcher Newsweek mag., 1962; reporter, editor Chgo. Tribune, 1962-66, 67-82, assoc. editor mag., 1973-82, writer, 1982—; reporter Newsday, 1966-67; travel writer, 1992—. Recipient Gold and Silver Lowell Thomas awards Soc. of Am. Travel Writers. Office: 435 N Michigan Ave Chicago IL 60611-4066

CROSS, ROBERT FRANCIS, city official; b. Port Jervis, N.Y., Dec. 17, 1950; s. Francis Stuart and Rita Clotilde (Beilman) C.; m. Sheila Lynne Cochrane, Sept. 24, 1983. AA, Orange County Coll., Middletown, N.Y., 1971; BS, SUNY, Albany, 1973; MA, SUNY, New Paltz, 1976. Reporter, photographer The Union-Gazette, Port Jervis, 1974-76; Albany (N.Y.) bur. chief Ottaway News Svc., 1976-78; Albany corr. The Wall St. Jour., 1976-78; sci. editor N.Y. State Dept. Environ. Conservation, Albany, 1978-83, spl. asst. to commr., 1983-85, exec. asst. to commr., 1985-87, asst. commr., 1987-95; commr. City of Albany Dept. of Water, 1996—. Contbr. articles to profl. publs. Mem. N.Y. State Gov.'s Task Force on the Del. Water Gap Nat. Recreation Area, 1973; chmn. People United to Restore the Environment, Orange County Coll., 1970-71, Mayor's Task Force on Water Resources; commr. Albany Port Dist. Commn.; mem. Albany City Planning Bd., 1995-96; mem. Minisink Valley Hist. Soc., Albany Inst. History and Art, N.Y. State Hist. Assn., Nantucket Hist. Assn., Dorflinger-Suydam Wildlife Sanctuary. Mem. Am. Philatelic Soc., Nantucket Wharf Rat Club, Pacific Club Nantucket. Democrat. Roman Catholic. Avocations: writing on historical topics, reading American history and presidential biographies. Home: 977 Washington Ave Albany NY 12206-1431 Office: City of Albany Dept Water Supply 35 Erie Blvd Albany NY 12204-2593

CROSS, ROBERT LAWRENCE, retired surgeon; b. Chesterville, Ont., Can., July 29, 1929. MD, U. Ottawa, Can., 1955. Diplomate Am. Bd. Surgery. Intern U. Ottawa Hosp., 1954-55; sr. rotating resident Ottawa Civic Hosp., 1955-56; resident in surgery Harper Hosp., Detroit, 1956-57; resident in pathology Hurley Hosp., Flint, Mich., 1957-58, resident in surgery, 1958-59; resident in surgery McLaren Hosp., Flint, 1959-60, chief resident, 1960-61, mem. staff, 1961-97; ret.; asst. clin. prof. surgery Mich. State U.; mem. courtesy staff Hurley Hosp., St. Joseph Hosp. Recipient Silver award Am. Coll. Pathology and Clin. Pathology for Original Investigation, 1959. Fellow ACS (rsch. award 1959); mem. AMA, Genesee County Med. Soc. (bd. dirs. 1975-86), Pan-Pacific Surg. Assn., Mich. State Med. Soc., Lic. of Med. Coun. Can.

CROSS, ROBERT WILLIAM, lawyer, venture capital executive; b. Balt., Oct. 9, 1937; s. Rosamond and Mildred (Fowler) C.; m. Deanna Louise Deerr, Feb. 7, 1965; children Ann Elizabeth, Robert William II. BSBA, Washington U., St. Louis, 1962; JD, Washington U., 1964. Bar: N.Y. 1964. Assoc. Winthrop, Stimson, Putnam & Roberts, N.Y.C., 1964-68; gen. counsel Electronic Data Systems Corp., Dallas, 1968-69; pres. R.W. Cross & Co., Dallas and N.Y.C., 1970-90; chmn., CEO Cross Tech. Inc., Chgo., also Solebury, Pa., 1990—; pres., CEO Nanophase Tech. Corp., Burr Ridge, Ill., 1993-98; pres., COO Venture Capital Online LLC, Chgo., 1998—, also bd. dirs.; bd. dirs. Ill. Coalition, Chgo. With USMC, 1957-63. Mem. Assn. of Bar of City of N.Y., University Club, Down Town Assn., Omicron Delta Kappa. Republican. Home: PO Box 200 Solebury PA 18963-0200 Office: Cross Tech Inc 6475 Upper York Rd Solebury PA 18963

CROSS, RONALD, musicologist, educator; b. Fort Worth, Feb. 18, 1929; s. John Butler and Verna (Bailey) C. BA, Centenary Coll. La., 1950; MA, NYU, 1953, PhD, 1961; Fulbright scholar, U. Florence, U. Vienna, 1955-57. Mem. faculty Notre Dame Coll., S.I., 1958-68; assoc. prof. music Wagner Coll., S.I., 1968-75, prof., 1975—, chmn. music dept., 1981-84; dir. Collegium Musicum, S.I., 1968—; chair Kurt & Auguste Reimann, 1984—. Organist, choirmaster various chs.; recorded and directed Songs and Dances of the Renaissance (Lieder und Tänze der Renaissance) Collegium Pro Musica FSM Pantheon, 1984; author: Mathaeus Pipelare: Opera Omnia, 3 vols., 1966-67; reviewer Renaissance recs. for Music Quar., 1971-76; video: The Harpsichord Today: An Interview With Ronald Cross, 1991; contbr. articles to profl. jours. Am. Coun. Learned Socs. grantee, 1954, performance grantee Staten Island Coun. on the Arts, 1986, 87, 88, 89, 90, 91, 92, grantee to present harpsichord recitals, N.Y. State Coun. on Arts, 1986-99; recipient Founders Day award NYU, 1962, Alumni Achievement award, 1988, Faculty award Omicron Delta Kappa, 1996. Mem. Am. Guild Organists (asso.), Internat., Am. Musicol. Socs., Coll. Music Soc., Soc. for Ethnomusicology. Home: 221 Ward Ave Staten Island NY 10304-2140

CROSS, ROSE MARIE, school administrator; b. Memphis, Jan. 3, 1936; d. Anselmo Joseph and Lillie Mae (Crabb) Barrasso; m. Robert Edwin Cross. BA magna cum laude, Siena Coll.; MEd magna cum laude, U.

Memphis. English chair Immaculate Conception H.S., Memphis; career ladder in edn. English chair Fayette Ware H.S., Somerville, Tenn., chair theater arts. Author: (play) A Time for Talking; composer; actress regional theater prodns. Campaign mgr. for local city coun. Dem. Party, Memphis. Roman Catholic. Office: Fayette Ware H S PO Box 409 Somerville TN 38068-0409

CROSS, RUEL PARKMAN, state legislator; b. Guildord, Maine, Sept. 27, 1926; s. Hugo Silas and Eveline (Snow) C.; m. Jacqueline Joyce Jenkins, July 19, 1947; children: Jeffrey P., Judith L. Student, U. Maine. Store owner Guilford, Maine, 1948-65; hotel owner Guilford, 1953-77; prodn. control mgr. Guilford Industries, 1968-77; selectmen Town on Guilford, 1977-79; life ins. salesmen Modern Woodmen of Am., Guilford, 1977-80; town mgr. Monson, Maine, 1980-92; state rep. State of Maine, Augusta, 1992—. Treas., pres. Kiwanis, Guilford, 1954-84; scoutmaster Boy Scout of Am., 1958-68; exec. com. Maine Mcpl. Assn., Augusta, 1989-92, legis. policy com., 1982-92. With USN, 1944-47. Mem. Kiwanis (hon., treas., pres. 1954-84). Republican. Home: 56 W Main St Dover Foxcroft ME 04426-1027*

CROSS, STEVEN JASPER, finance educator; b. Hohenwald, Tenn., Apr. 19, 1954; s. Thomas Edward and Eula Mae Cross; m. Patricia Aldas, Jan. 6, 1995. BS, Mid. Tenn. State U., 1976, MAT, 1980, DA, 1984. Sales rep. Univ. Ford Inc., Murfreesboro, Tenn., 1976; ins. underwriter Continental Ins., Inc., Nashville, 1976-77; credit rep. SunAm. Inc., Murfreesboro, 1977-78; instr. mgmt. Dyersburg (Tenn.) State C.C., 1980-81, Motlow State C.C., Tullahoma, Tenn., 1981-83; asst. prof. econs. Motlow State C.C., Tullahoma, 1983-85; assoc. prof. fin. Delta State U., 1985-88, prof. fin., chmn. divsn. econs. and fin., 1988-91; dean Sch. Bus., prof. bus. Troy State U., Dothan, Ala., 1991-97; prof. fin. Troy State U., Dothan, 1997—. Contbr. articles to profl. jours. Mem. AAUP, NEA, Am. Fin. Assn., Am. Econ. Assn., Acad. Econs. and Fin., Delta Mu Delta. Home: 112 Wentworth Dr Dothan AL 36305 Office: Troy State U Sch Bus PO Box 8368 Dothan AL 36304-0368

CROSS, THEODORE LAMONT, publisher, author; b. Newton, Mass., Feb. 12, 1924; s. Gorham Lamont and Margaret Moore (Warren) C.; m. Sheilah Burr Ross, Sept. 16, 1950 (div. 1972); children: Amanda Burr, Lisa Warren; m. Mary Warner, 1974. Grad., Deerfield Acad., 1942; AB, Amherst Coll., 1946; LLB, Harvard U., 1950. Bar: Mass. 1950, N.Y. 1953. With Hale and Dorr, Boston, 1950-52; chmn. bd., chief exec. officer, dir. Warren, Gorham & Lamont, Inc., 1980-83; chmn. Faulkner & Gray, Pubs., 1985-92, Hanover Pub., Inc., 1985—; editor in chief Bus. and Soc. Rev., 1971—; editor Jour. of Blacks in Higher Edn., 1993—; cons. HEW, Fed. Office Econ. Opportunity, 1964-69; pub. gov. Am. Stock Exchange, 1972-77; bd. dirs. Inst. for Sci. Info., 1988—; lectr. on inner city econs. and minority econ. devel. Harvard, Cornell U., U. Va. Author: Black Capitalism: Strategy for Business in the Ghetto (McKinsey Found. book award 1969), (with Mary Cross) Behind the Great Wall, 1979, The Black Power Imperative, 1984, Birds of the Sea, Shore and Tundra, 1989; founder: Atomic Energy Law Jour., 1959; editor Harvard Law Rev., 1948-50. Trustee Amherst Coll., chmn. investment com., 1976-88; trustee Folger Shakespeare Libr., Princeton U. Press, Inst. Advanced Study, Nat. Humanities Ctr., John Simon Guggenheim Meml. Found.; mem. Coun. Fgn. Rels.; dir. Legal Def. Fund, NAACP, Century Assn., N.Y.C. With USNR, 1945-46. Mem. Coun. on Fgn. Rels. (treas.), Am. Philos. Soc. Home: 233 Carter Rd Princeton NJ 08540-2104 Office: 200 W 57th St New York NY 10019-3211

CROSS, THOMAS GARY, executive search consultant; b. Bayonne, N.J., July 17, 1947; s. Louis F. Jr. and Muriel B. (Burnett) C.; m. Lynda A. Armitage, June 15, 1968; children: Brian T., Jason S., Jonathan A. BA, Seton Hall U., 1969. CLU; ChFC. Mgmt. trainee Chem. Bank, N.Y.C., 1969-70; sales mgr. Met. Life Ins., Hillside, N.J., 1970-74; employee benefits cons. Corroon & Black, N.Y.C., 1974-77; asst. v.p. Bayley Martin & Fay, N.Y.C., 1977-78; mktg. specialist Merrill Lynch, N.Y.C., 1978; sr. v.p., corp. life specialist Rollins Burdick Hunter, Roseland, N.J., 1978-87; v.p. exec. planning svcs. Alexander & Alexander, N.Y.C., 1987-88; pres. Cross & Assocs., Inc., Long Valley, N.J., 1988-91; mgr. brokerage sales Prin. Fin. Group, Old Bridge, N.J., 1992-96; sr. bus. planning cons. IIG Case Devel., Prudential, Berkeley Heights, N.J., 1996—. Asst. coach Long Valley (N.J.) Soccer Assn., 1982-84. Served with U.S. Army, 1969-75. Avocations: camping, weight tng., reading. Home: 15 Falcon Ln Long Valley NJ 07853-3345

CROSS, W. THOMAS, investment company executive; b. Knoxville, Tenn., Sept. 1, 1949; s. Joseph Eugene and Wanda (Price) C.; children: Joseph, Victoria. BS, U. Tenn., 1971; CLU, Am. Coll., Bryn Mawr, Pa., 1983, ChFC, 1987. Sales rep. John Hancock Fin. Svcs., Knoxville, 1971-72, sales mgr., 1972-78; regional supr. John Hancock Fin. Svcs., Washington, 1978-79; agy. mgr. John Hancock Fin. Svcs., Appleton, Wis., 1979-84, Memphis, 1984-95; v.p. ins. mktg. Securities Am., Inc., Omaha, 1995—; pres. Fin. Dynamics Am., Inc., Omaha, 1997—. Chair troop com., scoutmaster Boy Scouts Am., Germantown, Tenn., 1991-95. Mem. Am. Soc. CLU and ChFC (bd. dirs. 1992-95), Am. Health Ins. Assn., Gen. Agts. and Mgrs. Assn. (pres. Appleton chpt. 1977-78, pres. Memphis chpt. 1988-89, pres. 1993-94), Memphis Life Underwriters (bd. dirs. 1985-88). Avocations: golf, scouting. Office: Securities Am Inc 7100 W Center Rd Ste 500 Omaha NE 68106-2798

CROSS, WILBUR LUCIUS, writer, editorial consultant; b. Scranton, Pa., Aug. 17, 1918; s. Wilbur Lucius and Alice Elizabeth (Sanderson) C.; m. Gabrielle Jane Wilkinson, May 3, 1952; children: Candace, Melissa, Alison, Jennifer. BA, Yale U., 1941. Copy writer, chief Benton & Bowles, N.Y.C., 1946-53; editor Life Mag., N.Y.C., 1953-62; pres. Cross, Hinshaw & Lindberg, Stamford, Conn., 1962-69; editl. dir. Conoco, Stamford, 1969-80; owner, editl. dir. Wilbur Cross Assocs., Ltd., Bronxville, N.Y., 1980—, Hilton Head, S.C., 1980—. Author: Choices With Clout: How to Make Things Happen By Making the Right Decisions Every Day of Your Life, 1995, Encyclopedia Dictionary of Business Terms, 1996, The Complete Idiot's Guide to Grandparenting, 1998. Officer Am. Soc. Journalists and Authors, N.Y.C., 1962-94. Capt. U.S. Army, 1941-46, PTO. Home and Office: Wilbur Cross Assocs Ltd 27 Royal Crest Dr Hilton Head Island SC 29928-5506

CROSS, WILLIAM DENNIS, lawyer; b. Tulsa, Nov. 7, 1940; s. John Howell and Virginia Grace (Ferford) C.; m. Peggy Ruth Plapp, Jan. 30, 1982; children: William Dennis Jr., John Frederick. BS, U.S. Naval Acad., 1962; JD, NYU, 1969. Bar: N.Y. 1970, U.S. Dist. Ct. (so. and ea. dists.) N.Y. 1970, U.S. Ct. Appeals (2d cir.) 1970, U.S. Supreme Ct. 1974, Calif. 1977, U.S. Dist. Ct. (ctrl. dist.) Calif. 1977, U.S. Ct. Appeals (9th cir.) 1977, U.S. Ct. Appeals (5th, 10th and 11th cirs.) 1981, Mo. 1982, U.S. Dist. Ct. (we. dist.) Mo. 1982, U.S. Ct. Appeals (8th cir.) 1989, U.S. Ct. Appeals (fed. cir.) 1992, U.S. Dist. Ct. Ariz. 1997, U.S. Dist. Ct. Colo. 1997, U.S. Dist. Ct. Kans. 1998. Commd. ensign USN, 1962, advanced through ranks to lt., 1965, resigned, 1966; assoc. Cravath, Swaine & Moore, N.Y.C., 1969-76, Lillick, McHose & Charles, L.A., 1976-77; asst. gen. counsel FTC, Washington, 1977-82; of counsel Morrison & Hecker, Kansas City, Mo., 1982-83; ptnr. Morrison & Hecker, 1983—. Staff mem. NYU Law Rev., 1967-69, editor, 1968-69. Mem. ABA (vice-chair sports, labor and entertainment com., antitrust sect.), Calif. Bar Assn., Mo. Bar Assn., Assn. Bar City N.Y., Kansas City Bar Assn., Lawyers Assn. Kansas City. Home: 1223 Huntington Rd Kansas City MO 64113-1347 Office: Morrison & Hecker 2600 Grand Blvd Kansas City MO 64108-4606

CROSSAN, JOHN ROBERT, lawyer; b. Buchannon, W.Va., May 31, 1947; s. Thomas Benjamin Jr. and Margaret Windsor (Hicks) C.; m. Monique Margaretha Scheen, Dec. 22, 1973; children: Ashley Margaret, Aubry Kelly. BS with honors, U. Va., 1969; JD, U. Chgo., 1974. Bar: Ill. 1974, U.S. Dist. Ct. (no. dist.) Ill. 1974, (ctrl. dist.) Ill. 1998, U.S. Ct. Appeals (4th and 10th cirs.) 1978, U.S. Ct. Appeals (7th cir.) 1979, U.S. Ct. Appeals (fed. cir.) 1983, U.S. Supreme Ct. 1985, U.S. Ct. Appeals (6th cir.) 1989. Staff atty. Ill. Task Force N.E. Ill. Pub. Transp., Chgo., 1972-73; assoc. Hill, Van Santen, Steadman, Chiara, Chgo., 1973-77; assoc., then ptnr. Cook, Wetzel and Egan, Ltd., Chgo., 1978-88; counsel Willian, Brinks, Hofer, Gilson and Lione, Chgo., 1989-90; ptnr. Brinks, Hofer, Gilson & Lione, Chgo., 1991-97, Chapman and Cutler, Chgo., 1998—; dir. Va. Engring. Found., 1996—, v.p. 1998—. Author: Quick Guide to the Patent Law, 1994; contbr. articles to profl publs. Pres. aux. bd. Chgo. Architecture Found., 1983-85. Mem. Am. Intellectual Property Lawyers Assn., Chgo. Yacht Club. Home: 2825 N Cambridge Ave Chicago IL 60657-6018 Office: Chapman and Cutler 111 W Monroe St Chicago IL 60603

CROSSEN, JOHN JACOB, radiologist, educator; b. Chgo., Mar. 28, 1932; s. John Shelly and Viola Catherine (Geis) C.; divorced; children: John, Pamela, Gregory, Terrence; m. Esther Aileen Cowie, Aug. 4, 1972. BS, U. Ill., 1953; MD, Loyola U., Chgo., 1957. Diplomate Am. Bd. Radiology, Nat. Bd. Med. Examiners. Intern Mercy Hosp., Buffalo, 1957-58; resident in radiology Cook County Hosp., Chgo., 1960-63; radiologist San Pedro and Long Beach, Calif., 1963-79; attending radiologist Harbor Hosp. of UCLA, Torrance, 1964-69; radiologist Tacoma, 1979-82; radiologist United Hosp. Ctr., Clarksburg, W.Va., 1982-93, dir. diagnostic radiology, 1992-93; asst. clin. prof. W.Va. U. Med. Sch., Morgantown, 1982-93; pres. Clarskburg Radiology Group Inc., 1992-94; diagnostic radiologist Columbia E Hosp. and Diagnostic Ctr., El Paso, Tex., 1993—. Capt. M.C., USAF, 1958-60. Recipient tchr. recognition Am. Acad. Family Practice, 1983-91. Fellow Am. Coll. Radiology; mem. AMA, Radiol. Soc. N.Am., Tex. Radiology Soc., El Paso County Med. Soc., Coronado Country Club, El Paso Club, Lancer's Club, Baja Bush Pilots Club. Democrat. Roman Catholic. Avocations: aviation, skiing. Home: 804 Pintada Pl El Paso TX 79912-1805

CROSSEN, SHANI KATHRYN, secondary school educator, tax preparer; b. Emporia, Kans., Sept. 24, 1945; d. Leon Arthur and Clara Irene (Keen) Wooton; married, May 11, 1968; children: Erin, Aidan. BS, U. Kans., 1967; MS, Ft. Hays State U., 1985. Cert. tchr., Kans. Mem. claims staff Aetna Life Ins., 1967-68; English tchr. Osseo Schs., Minn., 1975-78; ESL tchr. Robbinsdale Sch., Minn., 1978-79, Shawnee Mission (Kans.) Schs., 1980—. Mem. NEA, Kans. Edn. Assn., Kans. TESOL, TESOL. Avocations: reading, golf, swimming, boating. Home: 8918 W 64th Pl # 204 Shawnee Mission KS 66202

CROSSER, CARMEN LYNN, marriage and family therapist, clinical social worker, consultant; b. Iowa Falls, Iowa, Jan. 17, 1970; d. Gary Laverne Sr. and Karen Dorothy (Ulrich) C.; m. Trent K. Klomhaus, July 22, 1995. AA, Ellsworth C.C., 1990; BS, Iowa State U., 1993; MSW, U. Iowa, 1995; postgrad., U. Chgo., 1998—. Lic. clin. social worker, marriage and family thrapist, Ill.; cert. brief therapist, ACSW. Grad. teaching asst. U. Iowa, Iowa City, 1994-95; mental health therapy intern Mid-Eastern Cmty. Mental Health Ctr., Iowa City, 1994-95; clin. social worker Sinnissippi Ctrs., Inc., Dixon, Ill., 1995-97, Ctr. for Counseling, DeKalb, Ill., 1997—; cons. sexual abuse svcs. Sinnissippi Ctrs. Inc., 1997-98; rsch. asst. U. Chgo., 1998—. *Carmen L. Crosser is currently a Doctoral Student at the University of Chicago: School of Social Service Administration. She also maintains a clinical outpatient therapy practice, specializing in marital, child and family therapy. Crosser's therapeutic philosophy embodies personal empowerment, promotes self-respect and is grounded in the belief that therapy is a collaborative process. In addition, she is a member of the Institutional Review Board (IRB) at Northern Illinois University. The IRB is a federally mandated university committee whose responsibility it is to oversee and review all research projects involving the use of human subjects.* Mem. DeKalb Area Women's Ctr., 1997—; mem. instnl. rev. bd. No. Ill. U., DeKalb, 1997—. All-Am. scholar, 1995. Mem. ACA, NASW, NOW, Am. Soc. Prevention Cruelty Animals (voting mem.), Am. Assn. Marriage and Family Therapy (clin. mem.), Am. Coll. Counselors, Internat. Assn. Marriage and Family Counselors, Ill. Soc. Clin. Social Work, Assn. Play Therapy, Nat. Fedn. Socs. for Clin. Social Work, Golden Key, Phi Kappa Phi, Phi Alpha. Office: Ctr for Counseling 14 Health Svcs Dr Dekalb IL 60115

CROSSFIELD, ALBERT SCOTT, aeronautical science consultant, pilot; b. Berkeley, Calif., Oct. 2, 1921; s. Albert Scott and Lucia (Dwyer) C.; m. Alice Virginia Knoph, Apr. 21, 1943; children: Becky Lee, Thomas Scott, Paul Stanley, Anthony Scott, Sally Virginia, Robert Scott. B.S. in Aero. Engring., U. Wash., 1949, M.S. in Aero. Sci., 1950; D.Sc. (hon.), Fla. Inst. Tech., 1982. Lic. pilot. Mem. U. Wash. staff charge wind tunnel operation, 1946-50; aerodynamicist, project engr., also pilot research airplanes X-1, X-4, X-5, D-558-I and II, X-F-92, F-102, F-100, F-86, NACA, 1950-55; participation proposal, design, 1st pilot X-15 research aircraft, design specialist, also chief engring. test pilot Los Angeles div. N.Am. Aviation, Inc., 1955-61, dir. test and quality assurance, space and info. systems div., 1961-66, tech. dir. research and engring., space and info. systems div., 1966-67; v.p. flight research and devel. div. Eastern Air Lines, Miami, Fla., 1967-71; staff v.p. transp. systems devel. Eastern Air Lines, Washington, 1971-74; sr. v.p. Hawker Siddeley Aviation Inc., Washington, 1974; tech. cons. House Com. on Sci. and Tech., Washington, 1977-93; spl. work on the WS-131b, Apollo, Saturn S-II, Paraglider programs. Author: Always Another Dawn, 1960; also articles. Mem. aviation and space hist. preservation com. Calif. Mus. Found., mem. Aerospace Walk of Honor, City of Lancaster, 1990. Lt. USN, 1942-46, WWII, USNR. Recipient Aerospace Laureate for 1997, Aviation Week & Space Tech., Lawrence Sperry award Inst. Aeronautical Sci., 1954, Octave Chanute award, 1958, Flight Achievement award Am. Astronautics Soc., 1959, Astronautics award Am. Rocket Soc., 1960, Commendation award County L.A. Bd. Suprs., 1960, Internat. Clifford B. Harmon Trophy, 1961, Achievement award Nat. Aeronautics Assn., 1961, Collier Trophy, 1961, Charter award, 1963, Elder Statesman of Aviation award, 1983, Godfry Cabot award Aero Club New England, 1961, John J. Montgomery award Nat. Soc. Aerospace Profls., 1962, Kitty Hawk Meml. award City of L.A., 1969, Al J. Engel award Western Res. Hist. Soc., 1983, Meritorious Svc. to Aviation award Nat. Bus. Aircraft Assn., 1984, Disting. Alumnus award U. Wash., 1986, Crown Cir. award Nat. Congress Aviation and Space Edn., 1988, A. Scott Crossfield Elem. Sch. award Fairfax County Sch. Bd., 1988, Bernt Balchin Trophy, N.Y. State Air Force Assn., 1988, Glenn A. Gilbert Meml. award Air Traffic Control Assn., 1990, Aerospace Walk of Honor, City of Lancaster, Calif., 1990, Disting. Pub. Svc. medal NASA, 1993, Cert. of Appreciation, FAA, 1993, Ho. of Reps., 1993, Gold Air medal Fedn. Aeronautique Internat., Sun City, South Africa, 1995, Ray Lien award Internat. Sport Aviation Mus. and Sun 'N Fun, 1999; inducted into Nat. Aviation Hall of Fame, 1983, Internat. Aerospace Hall of Fame, 1963, Internat. Space Hall of Fame, 1988, Va. Aviation Hall of Fame, 1998. Fellow AIAA (chmn. flight test tech. com. 1963-64, Disting. lectr. 1987, 88, 89), Soc. Exptl. Test Pilots (co-founder; chmn. East Coast sect. 1976-77, past exec. advisor, Ivan C. Kincheloe award 1960, Ray E. Tenhoff award 1978), Inst. Aerospace Scis., Aerospace Med. Assn. (hon.); mem. Am. Soc. Qualtiy Control (sect.; chmn. L.A. 1964-66, Outstanding Contbn. to Quality Control award 1967), Flying Physicians Assn. (hon. mem., Man of Yr. 1961), Exptl. Aircaft Assn. (hon., Svc. to Sport Aviation award 1979, Cert. Appreciation 1982), Fedn. Aeronautique Internat. (Gold Air medal 1995), First Flight Soc. (life), Sterman Alumnus Club, Mustang Pilot Soc. (charter), OX-5 Club, Nat. Aviation Club (pres. 1983, gov. emeritus, Achievement award 1960), Nat. Space Club (Dr. Wernher von Braun Space Flight trophy), Order of Daedalians (hon.), Sigma Xi, Tau Beta Pi. Republican. Episcopalian. Home: 12100 Thoroughbred Rd Herndon VA 20171-2009

CROSSLAND, ANN ELIZABETH, retired psychotherapist; b. Cambridge, Ohio, Apr. 24, 1940; d. H. Stewart and Laura Geraldine (Geese) Hastings; m. Eugene Joseph Szmuc, Nov. 30, 1963 (dec. Oct. 1976); m. Richard Ray Crossland, July 16, 1988; children: Rae Ann, Nancy, Carol. BS in Edn., Kent State U., 1965; MSEd in Counseling, U. Akron, 1981. Third grade tchr. Bertha Bradshaw Elem. Sch., Rootstown, Ohio, 1963-64; substitute tchr. Kent (Ohio) City Schs., 1967-84, Portage County Schs., Ravenna, Ohio, 1979-84; assoc. tchr. severely behaviorally handicapped Portage County Schs., Ravenna, 1984-88, H.S. tchr. severe behavior handicap, 1988-92; therapist Child & Adolescent Svc. Ctr., Canton, Ohio, 1992-98. Bd. dirs., facilitator Oncology Support Group, Akron, 1977-81; bd. dirs., vol. trainer, counselor WomanShelter, Ravenna, 1980-87; organizer, group facilitator Portage County Cancer Group, Ravenna, 1982-83; mem. steering com. Portage County Adolescent Network, Ravenna, 1987-92. Mem. ACA, Am. Mental Health Counselors Assn., Delta Kappa Gamma (Theta chpt.). Democrat. Unitarian Universalist. Avocations: choir, piano, amateur acting, skiing.

CROSSLEY, FRANCIS RENDEL ERSKINE, engineering educator; b. Quarndon Derby, Eng., July 21, 1915; came to U.S., 1937, naturalized, 1957; s. Erskine Alick and Edith Mary (Helme) C.; m. Mary Eleanore De Lacy Bernadotte Coyne, Aug. 23, 1941 (dec. May, 1998); children: Phyllis De Lacy Mervine, Michael Francis Erskine Crossley. BA in Mech. Scis., Cambridge (Eng.) U., 1937; MA, Cambridge U., Eng., 1941; DEng, Yale U., 1949. Asst. prof. mech. engring. Yale U., New Haven, 1944-55, fellow Branford Coll., 1948-65, assoc. prof., 1955-65; vis. fellow U. Manchester (Eng.) Inst. Sci. and Tech., 1965; prof. mech. engring. Ga. Inst. of Tech., Atlanta, 1966-69; prof. mech. engring. U. Mass., Amherst, 1970-78, prof. civil engring., 1978-80, prof. civil engring. emeritus, 1980—; adj. prof. mech. engring. Rensselaer Poly. Inst., Troy, N.Y., 1978-79, U. Fla., Gainesville, 1988-91; Fulbright lectr. Technische Hochschule Munich, 1962-63, Tech. U. Bucharest, Romania, 1976; mem. U.S. del. forestry energy divsn. Internat. Energy Agy., Ottawa, Helsinki, Dublin, 1977-79; initiated talks with Soviet Acad. Scis. for U.S.-USSR exch. of info. on space flight, 1970; staff scientist Conn. State Legislature, Hartford, 1981-83. Author: Dynamics in Machines, 1954; editor-in-chief Mechanism and Machine Theory, 1971-73; founder, editor Jour. Mechanisms, 1966-71; designer mech. robot's 3-fingered hand for NASA Space Flight Ctr., 1973-74. Chmn. solid waste mgmt. commn. Town of Branford, Conn., 1985-86, bd. edn., 1987-92; chmn. land mgmt., 1995-96, trustee Branford Land Trust, 1996-99. Recipient sr. scientist award von Humboldt Found., Germany, 1975-76. Fellow ASME (life, chmn. mechanisms conf. Atlanta 1968, legis. fellow 1981-83, Centennial medal 1980, Machine Design award 1991), Am. Soc. Engring. Edn.; mem. Verein Deutscher Ingenieure (hon. corr.), Internat. Fedn. for Theory Machines and Mechanisms (hon., founding com., author constn., 1st v.p. 1967-75). Episcopalian. Home: Evergreen Woods 88 88 Notch Hill Rd Apt 230 North Branford CT 06471

CROSSLEY, FRANK ALPHONSO, former metallurgical engineer; b. Chgo., Feb. 19, 1925; s. Joseph Buddie and Rosa Lee (Brefford) C.; m. Elaine J. Sherman, Nov. 23, 1950; 1 child, Desne Adrienne. BSChemE, Ill. Inst. Tech., 1945, MS in Metall. Engring, 1947, PhD in Metall. Engring, 1950. Instr. Ill. Inst. Tech., Chgo., 1948-49; sr. scientist Ill. Inst. Tech. Rsch. Inst., 1952-66; prof. foundry engring., head dept. foundry engring. Tenn. Agrl. and Indsl. State U., 1950-52; sr. mem. rsch. lab. Lockheed Missiles & Space Co., Palo Alto, Calif., 1966-74, mgr. dept. producibility and standards, 1974-78, mgr. dept. missile body mch. engring., 1978-79; cons. engr. missile systems div. Lockheed Missiles & Space Co., Sunnyvale, Calif., 1979-86; dir. rsch. propulsion materials Aerojet Propulsion Rsch. Inst., 1986-87, rsch. dir. materials applications, 1987-90; tech. prin. Aerojet Propulsion div. GenCorp, Sacramento, 1990-91. Contbr. articles to metall. jours. and symposia. Served to ensign USNR, 1944-46, PTO. Recipient GenCorp Aerojet 1990 R.B. Young Tech. Innovation award. Fellow Am. Soc. for Metals Internat.; mem. AIAA (mem. materials tech. com. 1979-81), Minerals, Metals and Materials Soc. of AIME (chmn. titanium com. 1974-75), Sigma Xi. Congregationalist. Achievements include patent on Transage titanium alloys and grain refiner for titanium alloy castings; research in titanium alloys; diffusion bonding of metals and alloys. Home: 44 Goodnow Ln Framingham MA 01701-5505 *Choose well how your time is spent. Time spent doing one thing is time that cannot be spent doing something else.*

CROSSMAN, HAROLD G., JR., former state legislator; b. Claremont, N.H., Mar. 18, 1922; m. Janette Crossman; 2 children. BS, U. N.H., 1948; MS, Colby Coll., 1973. Formerly N.H. state rep. Dist. 32; ret. sci. tchr. Ret. capt. USAR. Mem. Masons (past master St. John's Lodge # 1 F&AM 1998), St. John's Masonic Assn., Bektash Temple Shrine, Portsmouth Shrine Club (past pres.), Shrine Patrol Club (past pres.). Address: 52 Sherburne Rd Portsmouth NH 03801-4747

CROSSMAN, WILLIAM WHITTARD, retired wire cable and communications executive; b. Mineola, N.Y., Aug. 10, 1927; s. Homer Danforth and Emily May (Whittard) C.; m. Mary DeJesu, Dec. 6, 1952; children: William Whittard Jr., Lindsay Maria, Michael DeJesu. BS in Engring. Sci., U. Miami, 1949. West coast mgr., gen. mgr. HiTemp Wires div. Simplex Wire & Cable Co., 1955-69; pres. surprenant divsn. ITT Corp., 1969-74; pres. royal electric div. ITT Corp., Pawtucket, R.I., 1974-77; group gen. mgr. ITT Corp., N.Y.C., 1977-85, v.p., 1979-87; chmn. and group exec. communications and info. svcs. ITT Corp., Secaucus, N.J., 1985-88; sr. v.p. ITT Corp., Secaucus, 1987-88; ret. ITT Corp., 1988. With USNR, 1945-46, USAF, 1951. Republican. Episcopalian. Clubs: Owls Head Harbor, San Remo, N.E. Wire and Cable. Home: 24 White Oak Shade Rd New Canaan CT 06840-6829

CROSSON, FREDERICK JAMES, former university dean, humanities educator; b. Belmar, N.J., Apr. 27, 1926; s. George Leon and Emily (Bennett) C.; m. Mary Patricia Burns, Sept. 5, 1953; children: Jessica, Christopher, Veronica, Benedict, Jennifer. BA, Cath. U. Am., 1949, MA, 1950; postgrad., U. Paris, 1951-52; PhD, U. Notre Dame, 1956. Instr. U. Notre Dame, 1953-56, asst. prof., 1956-62, assoc. prof., 1962-66, prof., 1966—; dean Coll. Arts and Letters, 1968-76, O'Hara Disting. prof. philosophy, 1976-84, Cavanaugh Disting. prof. humanities, 1984—. Author: The Modeling of Mind, 1963, Philosophy and Cybernetics, 1967, Science and Contemporary Society, 1967; Editor: Review of Politics, 1976-83. With USNR, 1943-46. Mem. Am. Philos. Assn., North Cen. Assn. (exec. commr. 1984-89), Phi Beta Kappa (senator 1982—, v.p. 1994-97, pres. 1997—). Home: 51997 Heather Cv South Bend IN 46635-1074 Office: Coll Arts and Letters U of Notre Dame Notre Dame IN 46556

CROSSON, JOHN ALBERT, advertising executive; b. L.A., Oct. 5, 1961; s. Albert J. and Virginia (Kienzle) C.; m. Carolyn Stevens, Oct. 3, 1992. BA, Loyola Marymount U., 1983; MBA, U. So. Calif., 1984. Exec. v.p. Dailey & Assocs. Advt., L.A., 1984-98; exec. v.p., mng. dir. L.A., Grey Advt., 1998—; lectr. Loyola Marymount U., L.A., 1986-89. Avocations: tennis, golf.

CROTEAU, DENIS, bishop; b. Thetford Mines, Que., Can., Oct. 23, 1932. Ordained priest Roman Cath. Ch., 1958. Bishop Diocese MacKenzie/Ft. Smith, Yellowknife, N.W.T., Can., 1986—. Office: Evêché, 5117 52d St, Yellowknife, NT Canada X1A 1T7

CROTEAU, GERALD A., JR., school system administrator; b. Millbury, Mass., Aug. 6, 1937; s. Gerald A. Sr. and Flora Ann (Nash) C.; m. Eleanore Majewski, Sept. 5, 1959; children: Gerald A. III, Catherine Macone, Robert, André. AB, Assumption Coll., 1959; MEd, U. Mass., 1966, CAGS, 1968, EdD, 1979. Cert. supt. of schs. History tchr. The Arnold Sch., East Pembroke, Mass., 1961-64; French tchr. Hopkins Acad., Hadley, Mass., 1964-66; asst. pers. mgr. Kowlmorgen Corp., Northampton, Mass., 1966-68; adminstrv. intern Eastchester (N.Y.) H.S., 1968-69; supervising prin. Marlborough (N.H.) Pub. Schs., 1969-72; asst. supt. Supervisory Union 53, Suncook, N.H., 1972-74; supt. of schs. Supervisory Union 53, Suncook, 1974-81, Taunton (Mass.) Sch. Dept., 1981—; ptnr. J.W. & Assocs., North Dartmouth, Mass., 1994—; developer curriculum Instrumental Enrichment. Exec. bd. mem. Boy Scouts Am., Taunton, 1984-95, ARC, Taunton, 1986-94; trustee Morton Hosp., Taunton, 1987-95. Recipient Leadership for Learning award Am. Assn. Sch. Adminstrs., 1995. Mem. Taunton C. of C. (dir. 1984-91, v.p. 1987-89), Taunton (Mass.) Rotary Club (dir. 1986-90, pres. 1989-90). Avocations: family activities, reading, sailing, traveling, probability and stats. Home: Taunton Sch Dist 157 Fremont St Taunton MA 02780 Office: Taunton Sch Dept 50 Williams St Taunton MA 02780-2710*

CROTEAU, JOAN M., nursing administrator, educator; b. Lawrence, Mass., Oct. 24, 1935; d. John B. and Stella M. (Kostrzewa) Piekarski; m. Gerald J. Croteau, May 22, 1956; children: Gerald J., John E., Mark A., Paul M., Marie C., David P. BSN, Boston Coll., 1956; MS in Biology, Rivier Coll., Nashua, N.H., 1974; MS in Nursing Adminstrn., U. Lowell, 1989. Cert. coun. of staff devel. Mass. Long Term Care Found. Instr. nursing St. Joseph Hosp. Sch. Practical Nursing, Nashua, Rivier Coll.-St. Joseph Sch. Nursing, Nashua; staff devel. coord. MI Nursing/Restorative Ctr., Lawrence. Contbg. author: Maternity and Pediatric Nursing, Introduction to Maternity and Pediatric Nursing, 1990. Mem. N.H. Coun. Vocat.-Tech. Nurse Educators, N.H. Coalition of Action for Nursing. Mem. ANA, Mass. Nurses Assn., New Eng. Cath. Hosp. Assn., Nurses for Laughter, Sigma Theta Tau.

CROTHERS, DONALD MORRIS, biochemist, educator; b. Fatehgarh, India, Jan. 28, 1937; came to U.S., 1939; s. Morris K. and Eunice F.C.; m. Leena Kareoja, June 24, 1960; children: Nina H., Kirstina A. BS, Yale U., 1958; BA, Cambridge U., 1960; PhD, U. Calif., San Diego, 1963.

Postdoctoral fellow Max Planck Inst., Gottingen, Germany, 1963-64; asst. prof. Yale U., New Haven, 1964-68, assoc. prof., 1968-71, prof. chemistry and molecular biophysics and biochemistry, 1971—, chmn. dept. chemistry, 1971-81, 93-99; chmn. biophysics, biophys. chemistry B study sect. NIH, 1972-76; co-chmn. nucleic acids Gordon Conf., 1975. Author: Physical Chemistry of Nucleic Acids, 1974, Physical Chemistry with Application to the Life Sciences, 1979; mem. editorial bd. Jour. Molecular Biology, 1971-75, Nucleic Acids Research, 1973-82, Biochemistry, 1975-78, Biopolymers, 1977-90; contbr. articles to profl. jours. Recipient Sci. and Engring. award Yale U., 1977; Alexander von Humboldt Sr. Scientist award, 1981; Mellon fellow Clare Coll. Cambridge U., 1958-60; Guggenheim fellow, 1978. Fellow AAAS, Am. Acad. Arts and Scis.; mem. NAS, Am. Soc. Biol. Chemists, Biophys. Soc. (coun. 1979-82). Office: Yale Univ Dept of Chemistry PO Box 208107 New Haven CT 06520-8107

CROTTI, ROSE MARIE, special education educator; b. Scranton, Pa., Aug. 29, 1952; d. Frank Joseph and Cecelia Ann (Bossi) Leitza; m. John Anthony Crotti, Sept. 26, 1975; children: Annette Michelle, Joseph Francis, John Michael. BA, Marywood U., 1974, MS, 1984; student, U. Scranton, 1979-80. Cert. elem. and secondary prin. Program dir. St. Joseph's Ctr., Dunmore, Pa., 1974-75; instr. Northeastern Ednl. Intermediate Unit #19, Scranton, 1976-80, 1980-83; tchr. Learning Disabilities Northeastern Ednl. Intermediate Unit #19, Montdale, Pa., 1983-86; cons. Learning Disabilities Northeastern Ednl. Intermediate Unit #19, Carbondale, Pa., 1988-89; cons., state validator Instrnl. Support Pa. Dept. Edn., Harrisburg, Pa., 1990—; instr. spl. edn. undergrad. and grad. dept. Marywood U., 1994—; asst. sec. prin. Lakeland Sch. Dist., Jermyn, Pa., 1998—; presenter Northeastern Ednl. Intermediate Unit #19, Scranton, 1988—; appeared on PBS, An Apple a Day, 1991, 92; coord., trainer peer tutors Carbondale Sch. Dist., 1992-93, peer mediators, 1993-94. Co-author: Parent-to-Parent Handbook on Drugs and Alcohol Abuse Among Teenagers, 1993. Active Parent Tchrs. Guild, Clarks Summit, Pa.; chmn. Lackawanna County Handicapped Awareness Day, 1990; co-chmn. Children Without a Conscience Sch. Conf., 1990; coord. Students Against Driving Drunk, 1992-94; chair family festival Marywood Coll., 1993; chair reorgn. PTA Lakeland Elem. Sch., 1993; chairperson Bus. Cmty.-Non-Alcoholic Mix-Off, 1993; bd. govs. Scranton Prep. Sch., v.p., 1992; mem. lead tchr. governing bd., lead tchr. adv. coun., adv. bd. Bishop O'Hara H.S., 1994, pres. PTO, 1996—. Named Northeast Woman of Pa. Scranton Times Newspaper, 1989. Mem. Coun. for Exceptional Children (local chpt. bd. dirs. 1989—), Platform Speakers Assn. Roman Catholic. Avocations: cooking, reading, crafts, broadway shows, shopping. Home: 24 Green Grove Rd # 1 Olyphant PA 18447 Office: Lakeland Sch Dist 1593 Lakeland Dr Jermyn PA 18433-3140

CROTTY, ROBERT BELL, lawyer; b. Dallas, Aug. 16, 1951; s. Willard and Betty (Bell) C.; m. Sarah Smith, Mar. 8, 1980; children: Robert Edwin, Rebecca Bell. BA, Va. Mil. Inst, 1973; JD, U. Tex., 1976. Bar: Tex. 1976, U.S. Dist. Ct. (no. dist.) Tex. 1977, U.S. Ct. Appeals (5th cir.) 1978. Assoc. Akin, Gump, Strauss, Hauer & Feld, Dallas, 1976-82, ptnr., 1983-92, hiring ptnr., 1988-91; prin. McKool Smith, P.C., Dallas, 1992-94; ptnr. Crotty & Johansen, L.L.P., Dallas, 1995—; bd. visitors Va. Mil. Inst., 1995—. Mem. Leadership Dallas, 1981; dir. Salesmanship Club, 1989-90, 94-95, Va. Mil. Inst. Alumni Assn., 1991-95, Highland Park Ind. Sch. Dist. Edn. Found., 1991-97, pres. 1997—; chmn. GTE Byron Nelson Classic, 1995; pres. Dallas Bus. League, 1983, Big Bros./Big Sisters Met. Dallas, 1987-88; deacon North Dallas Bible Ch., 1989-95. 1st lt. U.S. Army, 1976, USAR, 1973-81. Fellow Tex. Bar Found. (life), Dallas Bar Found.; mem. Dallas Bar Assn., Tex. Law Rev. Assn. (life), State Bar Tex. Avocations: golf, reading, rock climbing, hiking. Office: Crotty & Johansen LLP 2311 Cedar Springs Rd Ste 250 Dallas TX 75201-7810

CROTTY, WILLIAM, political science educator; b. Somerville, Mass., Apr. 14, 1936. BA in Govt. with honors, U. Mass., 1958; MA, U. N.C., 1960, PhD in Polit. Sci., 1964. Asst. prof. polit. sci. U. Ga., Athens, 1963-65; asst. prof. Ctr. for Higher Edn. U. Oreg., 1965-66; asst. prof. polit. sci. Northwestern U., Evanston, Ill., 1966-69, assoc. prof., 1970-73, prof., 1974-95; Thomas P. O'Neill Chair in Pub. Life, prof. polit. sci., di. Ctr. Comparative Democracy, Northeastern U., Boston, 1995—; co-dir. task force on polit. assassination Nat. Commn. on Causes and Prevention Violence, Washington, 1968-70; project dir. Am. polit. parties project Nat. Mcpl. League, 1972-74; guest scholar Woodrow Wilson Internat. Ctr. for Scholars, summer 1971; prin. on broadcast Bill Moyers' Jour. Pub. TV Network, 1980, CBS-TV Spl. Program, 1980; cons. permanent community sample and community action program study Nat. Opinion Research Ctr.; dir. Ctr. for Comparative Democracy, Northeastern U., Boston, 1995—. Author: Approaches to the Study of Party Organization, 1968, Assassinations and the Political Order, 1972, Political Reform and American Experiment, 1977, Decision for the Democrats, 1978, Party Reform, 1983, Party Game, 1985; co-author: books, including American Parties in Decline, 1980, 2d edit., 1984, Presidential Primaries and Nominations, 1985, Political Parties in Local Areas, 1987, Post-Cold War Policy, 2 vols., 1995, The Politics of Presidential Selection, 1996; co-author, editor: Paths to Political Reform, 1980, Comparative Political Parties, 1985, Public Opinion and Politics, 1990, America's Choice, 1995; editor, contbg. author: books, including The Party Symbol, 1980; editor Policy Studies Jour., 1972-74; mem. editl. bd. Am. Jour. Polit. Sci., 1988-92, Nat. Polit. Sci. Rev., 1988—, Political Participation and American Democracy, 1991, Political Science: Looking to the Future, 4 vols., 1992, Policy Studies Rev., 1992—, America's Choice: The Election of 1992, 1993; co-author, editor: The Democrats Must Lead; co-author, co-editor: The Election of 1996, Ireland and the Politics of Change, 1998; contbr. articles to profl. publs. Exec. dir. Freedom To Vote Task Force, Washington, 1969-70; exec. dir. Task Force on Campaign Financing, 1970; nat. bd. dirs. DISARM, Ams. for Democratic Action 1972; mem. Conv. Reform Task Force, Democratic Party Accountability Commn., 1980-84, Com. To Observe Honduran Election, 1981, Com. to Observe Argentine Elections, 1983, Com. to Observe Election in El Salvador, 1984, Com. to Observe Nicaraguan Election, 1984, Com. to Observe Haitian Election, 1987, Latin Am. Studies Assn., Commn. to Observe Nicaragua Election, 1990; mem. exec. bd. com. on party accountability Dem. Party, 1981-84. Fellow Ctr. for Higher Edn. U. Oreg., 1965-66; Am. Polit. Sci. Assn. fellow Dem. Nat. Com., 1969-70. Mem. Policy Studies Orgn. (pres. 1990-91), Am. Polit. Sci. Assn. (pres. polit. oorgns./parties orgn. sect. 1983-87, Pres.'s award 1991, Samuel J. Eldersveld Lifetime Achievement award 1991), Midwest Polit. Sci. Assn., Policy Studies Assn. (pres. 1990-91, Pres.'s award 1991, Herbert H. Humphrey award, 1993), Internat. Soc. Polit. Psychology, Am. Assn. Pub. Opinion Analysts, Midwest Assn. Pub. Opinion Research, Latin Am. Studies Assn., Americans for Democratic Action (nat. bd. 1980—, exec. com. 1999—), Progressive Polit. Scientists Assn. (nat. chair 1994—). Office: Northeastern U Dept Polit Sci Boston MA 02115

CROUCH, DIANNE KAY, secondary school guidance counselor; b. Campbellsville, Ky., Apr. 28, 1954; d. James Edgar and Imogene (Bailey) Gabbert; m. Thomas Frederick Crouch, June 6, 1987. BA, Campbellsville Coll., 1976; MS, U. Ky., 1984, EdS, 1991. Cert. tchr. English, psychology, counselor, secondary schs., Ky. Tchr. English Grayson County High Sch., Leitchfield, Ky., 1976-78, Jessamine County Jr. High Sch., Nicholasville, Ky., 1978-83, Jessamine County High Sch., Nicholasville, 1983-89, Tates Creek Jr. High Sch., Lexington, Ky., 1989-90; guidance counselor Tates Creek High Sch., Lexington, 1990—; mem. pub. rels. com. Tates Creek H.S.; mem. task force on grouping/tracking Fayette County; selected Inst. Women in Sch. Adminstrn. Ky. Active Calvary Bapt. Ch., Lexington, 1991—; active Fayette County Task Force on Grouping Trucking. Named Jessamine County Tchr. of Yr., Jessamine County Bd. Edn., Nicholasville, Ky., 1986-87, Outstanding Tchr. 5th Dist., Campbellsville Coll., 1988; sponsor of Jr. High newspaper Tates Creek Clarion named 1 of top 5 in U.S Nat. Jr. Beta Club. Mem. Ky. Assn. Secondary and Coll. Admission Counselors, Ky. Counseling Assn. (bd. dirs.), Ctrl. Ky. Counseling Assn. (pres.), Kappa Delta Pi. Avocations: piano, dog tng., walking, exercising, travel. Home: 716 Keene Way Ct Nicholasville KY 40356

CROUCH, PAUL FRANKLIN, minister, church official; b. St. Joseph, Mo., Mar. 30, 1934; s. Andrew Franklin and Sarah Matilda (Swingle) C.; m. Janice Wendell Bethany, Aug. 25, 1957; children—Paul F., Matthew W. B.Th., Central Bible Coll. and Sem., Springfield, Mo., 1955. Ordained to ministry, 1955; dir. fgn. missions film and audio visual dept. Assemblies of God, 1955-58; assoc. pastor 1st Assembly of God, Rapid City, S.D., 1958-60, Central Assembly of God, Muskegon, Mich., 1960-62; gen. mgr. TV and film prodn. center Assemblies of God, Burbank, Calif., 1962-65; gen. mgr. Sta. KREL, Cornona, Calif., 1965-71, Sta. KHOF, KHOF-TV, Glendale, Calif., 1971-73; founder, pres. Sta. KTBN-TV, Trinity Broadcasting Network, Los Angeles, 1973—. Recipient Best Religious film award Winona Lake Film Festival, 1956. Mem. Nat. Assn. Religious Broadcasters, Western Religious Broadcasters Assn., Assn. Christian TV Stas. (founder). Office: Trinity Broadcasting Network 2442 Michelle Dr Tustin CA 92780-7015*

CROUCH, ROBERT P., JR., prosecutor; b. Mar. 28, 1948; s. Robert and Rosa Crouch; m. Clara Johnson Sept. 2, 1973; 1 child, Emily. BA, U. Md., 1971; MPA, U. N.C., 1982; JD, U. Va., 1988. Bar: Va. 1988. Aide to William B. Spong U.S. Senate, 1971-73; asst. mgr. employee benefits Fieldcrest Mills, 1973-75; adminstrv. asst. Patrick Henry Comm. Coll., 1975; adj. prof. Ferrum Coll., 1984-85; clerk cir. ct., 1976-85; assoc. McGuire, Woods, Battle & Boothe, 1988-89, Young, Haskins, Mann & Gregory, 1989-93; atty. U.S. Dept. Justice, Roanoke, Va., 1993—. Mem. bd. trustees Va. Mus. Nat. History, 1989-95, pres. bd. dirs., 1990-93; mem. edn. found. Patrick Henry C.C., 1984-93; mem. bd. visitors George Mason U., 1983-91; vice chmn. Dem. Party Va., 1989-93, state party sec., 1985-89, 5th dist. com. chmn., 1981-85; chmn. statewide Wilder-Beyer-Terry Campaign Com., 1989. Mem. Va. Bar Assn., Va. Trial Lawyers Assn. Democrat. Presbyterian. Office: Thomas B Mason Bldg 105 Franklin Rd SW Ste 1 Roanoke VA 24011-2305*

CROUCH, TONI L., association executive, educator; b. Roswell, N.Mex., Sept. 7, 1948; d. Harry Baker Jr. and Dorothy Jean (Hamme) C. BA, Vassar Coll., 1970; MEd, Salem State Coll., 1972. Cert: tchr. and prin., Mass.; cert. assn. exec. Tchr. Revere (Mass.) Pub. Schs., 1970-74; elem. and mid. sch. counselor Singapore Am. Sch., 1974-76; elem. and mid. sch. prin. Asociacion Escuclas Lincoln, Buenos Aires, Argentina, 1979-83; Eastern European regional coord. Internat. Sch. Belgrade, Yugoslavia, 1983-85; asst. dir. edn. Am. Phys. Therapy Assn., Alexandria, Va., 1986-88; v.p. Found. for Phys. Therapy, Alexandria, Va., 1988-92; exec. dir. Counseling and Human Devel. Fedn., Alexandria, Va., 1992-94; regional rep. Johns Hopkins Inst. for Policy, Budapest, Hungary, 1994-95; assoc. exec. dir. Character Edn. Partnership, Washington, 1995-98; dir. edn. Am. Soc. Assn. Execs., Washington, 1998—; exec. cons. Assn. for Specialized Accreditation, Alexandria, 1991-92. Youth leader Revere Cmty. Ctr., 1971-74; v.p. Lee Oaks Bd., Falls Church, Va., 1989-97. Mem. Am. Soc. Assn. Execs. (Final Project award 1991), Am. Counseling Assn., Am. Sch. Counselors Assn. Avocations: gardening, photography, writing. Office: Am Soc Assn Execs 1575 I St NWNW Ste 501 Washington DC 20005

CROUCHET, KATHLEEN HUNT, elementary educator, reading educator; b. Dec. 30, 1946; d. Abram Davis Sr. and May (Botsay) Hunt; m. Courtland Adam Crouchet, Sr., Feb. 5, 1966; children: Chantelle C. McInerney, Courtland Adam. BS in Elem. Edn., Our Lady of Holy Cross, New Orleans, 1983; MEd in Curriculum and Instrn., U. New Orleans, 1990, PhD in Curriculum and Instrn., 1998. Cert. reading specialist, supr. student tchg., parish and city sch. supervision of instrn. tchr. assesment, elem. and secondary prin., La. Tchr. Archdiocesan Schs., Arabi, La., 1965-84, Orleans Parish Schs., New Orleans, 1984-94, St. Bernard Parish Schs., Chalmette, La., 1994-97; reading instr. Nunez C.C., Chalmette, 1996—; lectr., cons. Our Lady of Holy Cross Coll., New Orleans; adj. asst. prof. U. New Orleans; participant Model Career Option program State of La., New Orleans, 1991-92; tchr. assesor State of La., St. Bernard, 1994—; curriculum writer St. Bernard Parish Schs., 1997; cooperating tchr. U. New Orleans, 1989-90, 94; insvc. lectr. Co-author: Teacher Professionalism and Leadership in Louisiana, 1992. Moderator, 4-H Cleanest Parish Competition, St. Bernard, 1995. Mem. ASCD, Internat. Reading Assn., Nat. Coun. Tchrs. English, La. Middle Sch. Assn., Phi Delta Kappa, Kappa Delta Pi (historian, sec.). Avocations: reading, travel, gardening. Home: 4429 Colony Dr Meraux LA 70075-2286 Office: Nunez CC 3700 La Fontaine St Chalmette LA 70043-1249

CROUCH-SMOLAREK, JUDITH ANN, community health nurse; b. Fond du Lac, Wis., Jan. 28, 1953; d. Halley and Helen (Golichnik) C.; m. Mike Smolarek, Apr. 1995; step-children: Gretchen, Kristopher, Olivia. BSN, U. Wis., Madison, 1975; MSN, U. Wis., 1990. RN, Wis. Staff nurse hematology and gastrointestinal unit U. Hosp., Madison; staff nurse cardiac step-down unit Appleton (Wis.) Med. Ctr.; pub. health nurse City of Neenah (Wis.) Dept. Pub. Health Nursing, dir. pub. health, health officer, 1991—. Mem. adv. com. Neenah Joint Sch. Dist. Human Growth & Devel.; mem. alcohol and drug abuse prevention core team Neenah Joint Sch. Dist., mem. health curriculum com; pres., bd. dirs. Neenah Community Action Com. for Alcohol and Drug Abuse Prevention. Named Outstanding Young Alumnus, U. Wis.-Oshkosh, 1992. Mem. Appleton Dist. Nurses Assn. (bd. dirs., chairperson by-laws com., past pres., treas. pub. rels. and membership coms., Nurse of Yr. 1990), Wisconsin Nurses' Assn. (bd. dirs. 1992—), Neenah Rotary Club (bd. dirs., chmn. youth exchange com., grants com., immunization com.), Sigma Theta Tau (Eta Pi chpt.). Address: 1601 Meadowbreeze Cir Neenah WI 54956-4479

CROUGH, DANIEL FRANCIS, lawyer, insurance company executive; b. Syracuse, N.Y., Feb. 2, 1936; s. Vincent Leo and Sarah Jane (McMahon) C.; m. Domenica Dolores Cappadozy, July 27, 1957; children: Sara, Deborah, Maura, Deanne, Daniel. BA, LeMoyne Coll., 1957; JD, Syracuse U., 1960. Bar: N.Y. 1961, Pa. 1969, U.S. Supreme Ct. 1981. Sole practice Syracuse, 1961-63; staff atty. Reliance Ins. Co., Phila., 1963-69, asst. gen. counsel, 1969-71, sec., assoc. gen. counsel, 1971-72; v.p., gen. counsel Colonial Penn Ins. Co., Phila., 1972-74; v.p., corp. counsel Colonial Penn Group, Inc., Phila., 1975-78, sr. v.p., sec., gen. counsel, 1978-83, pres., 1983-86, chief exec. officer, 1985-86; pres., chief exec. officer, trustee The Mutual Assurance Co., Phila., 1988—; bd. dirs. Green Tree Ins. Co., Am. Loyalty Ins. Co., Old Dominion Ins. Co., Ins. Soc. Phila., chmn. 1990-92. Bd. dirs. Citizens Crime Commn. of Delaware Valley, YMCA of Phila. Mem. ABA, N.Y. State Bar Assn., Pa. Bar Assn., Phila. Bar Assn., Aronimink Golf Club. Republican. Roman Catholic. Office: The Mutual Assurance Co 414 Walnut St Ste 1 Philadelphia PA 19106-3737

CROUSE, CAROL K. MAVROMATIS, elementary education educator; b. Phila., Nov. 27, 1950; d. George and Helen (Captis) Mavromatis; m. David Crouse (dec.). BS in Edn., Temple U., 1972, MEd, 1981. Elem. tchr. grades 1 and 3-5 Upper Darby (Pa.) Sch. Dist., 1974—; cert. NASA Lunar Rock Edn. Program, 1993; tchr. adv. bd. Phila. Zoo, 1995—; mem. writing and evaluation team Schuylkill Valley Nature Ctr., 1993-94; coord. cmty. svc. Learn and Serve Bldg., 1999. Recipient Howard W. McComb award Temple U. Phi Delta Kappa, 1981. Mem. ASCD, NSTA, Delaware County Sci. Tchrs. Assn., Pa. Sci. Tchrs. Assn., Upper Darby Recreation Tennis Players (tournament co-dir. 1983-92).

CROUSE, FARRELL R., lawyer; b. Portsmouth, Va., Dec. 23, 1963; s. Farrell Rondall and Grace Alice (Kenworthy) C. BA in History and Sociology, Bucknell U., Lewisburg, Pa., 1986; JD, Widener U., Wilmington, Del., 1989, LLM in Taxation, 1992. Bar: N.J. 1989, Pa. 1989, U.S. Dist. Ct. N.J. 1989. Assoc. Law Offices John William Neef, Carneys Point, N.J., 1990-91; pvt. practice Woodstown, N.J., 1991—. Mem. ABA, N.J. Bar Assn., Pa. Bar Assn. Avocations: auto racing, travel, collecting auto racing books and memorabilia. Home and Office: 317 Auburn Rd # A Pilesgrove Township NJ 08098

CROUSE, JOHN OLIVER, II, journalist, publisher; b. El Paso, Tex., Jan. 16, 1931; s. John Oliver Sr. and Helen Claire (Oliver) O.; divorced; 1 child, John Oliver III. Student, U.S. Naval Acad., 1950-51, U. Fla., 1954-56; BA, U. Miami, 1957. Sportswriter Miami (Fla.) Daily News, 1957-58, boating editor, 1958; sports editor Hollywood (Fla.) Sun Tattler, 1958; editor, pub. Key Biscayne (Fla.) Jour., 1958; owner John Crouse Assocs. Pub. Rels. Agy., Miami, 1960—; assoc. editor Powerboat Mag., Van Nuys, Calif., 1968-91; founder, owner Crouse Publs., Miami, 1969—; owner antique stores, Homestead, Fla., 1989—; dir. Homestead Auto Show, 1996-97. Author: Searace: A History of Offshore Powerboat Racing, 1989. Address: 20740 SW 248th St Homestead FL 33031-1502

CROUSE, LINDSAY, actress; b. N.Y.C., May 12, 1948; d. Russel and Anna (Erskine) C. BA, Radcliffe Coll., 1970. Appearances include: (films) All the President's Men, 1976, Between the Lines, 1977, Slapshot, 1977, Prince of the City, 1981, The Verdict, 1982, Daniel, 1983, Iceman, 1984, Places in the Heart, 1984 (Acad. award nomination 1985), House of Games, 1987, Communion, 1989, Desperate Hours, 1990, Being Human, 1993, Bye Bye Love, 1995, Indian in the Cupboard, 1995, The Juror, 1996, The Arrival, 1996, Prefontaine, 1997, The Progeny, 1999, Man of the People, 1999, Stranger in My House, 1999; (TV movies) Eleanor and Franklin, 1976, Eleanor and Franklin: The White House Years, 1977, Reunion, 1980, Paul's Case, 1980, Summer Solstice, 1981, Lemon Sky, 1987, Chantilly Lace, 1993, Final Appeal, 1993, Parallel Lives, 1994, Out of Darkness, 1994, Between Mother and Daughter, 1995 (Emmy award nomination), Norma Jean and Marilyn, 1996, If These Walls Could Talk, 1996, Beyond the Prairie: The True Story of Laura Ingalls Wilder, 1999; (TV series) Hill Street Blues, Murder She Wrote, Columbo, Law and Order, Lifestories, The Equalizer, Civil Wars, L.A. Law, Traps, ER, NYPD Blue, Millenium, Brimstone, Batman: The Animated Series. Recipient Obie award for Reunion, 1980, Theater World award for The Homecoming, 1992. *

CROUSE, ROGER LESLIE, information analyst, quality consultant, facilitator; b. Medford, Mass., Mar. 24, 1944; s. Mahlon Dale and Doris Mabel (Butman) C.; m. Judy Avis Wiley, May 10, 1969; children: Alison, Erin. BS, U. Mass., 1966; MS, U. Vt., 1977. Programmer, analyst positions IBM, Essex Junction, Vt., 1966-77; adv. systems analyst IBM, 1977-80, devel. mgr., 1980-82, adv. edn. analyst, 1982-83, adv. info. ctr. analyst, 1983-91, distributed computing cons., 1991-92, quality focus mgr., team facilitator, 1992-94, provisional ISO 9000 assessor, 1993-96; dir. info. tech. svcs. Trinity Coll. of Vt., Burlington, 1996—; ptnr. in edn. Burlington (Vt.) Area Vocat. Ctr., 1986-88; pub. software specialist IBM, Burlington, 1988-89; adj. prof. U. Vt., 1990—. Contbr. articles to profl. jours. Treas. N.G. Assn. Vt., Burlington, 1980-86; bd. dirs. Lake Iroquois Actions Commn., Hinesburg, Vt., 1980—; 10-gallon blood donor ARC, Burlington, 1966—; bd. dirs. Make-A-Wish Found. of Vt., Burlington, 1989-97, 98—, pres., 1994-97; nat. trainer Make-A-Wish Found. Am., 1992—, mem. nat. tng. com., 1995-97, mem. nat. nominating com., 1997—. Col Vt. Air NG, 1967-95 (ret.). Mem. Masons (worshipful master local chpt. 1976-77). Avocations: jogging, swimming, cross-country skiing, music, acting, writing. Office: Trinity Coll Vt 208 Colchester Ave Burlington VT 05401-1470

CROUT, J(OHN) RICHARD, physician, pharmaceutical researcher; b. Portland, Oreg., Dec. 30, 1929; s. John Shaw and Georgia (Jacobs) C.; m. Carol Jean Keith, June 19, 1954; children: Linda Jane, Keith Richard, Andrew Richard. AB, Oberlin Coll., 1951; MD, Northwestern U., 1955, MS, 1956; DMed (hon.), U. Uppsala, Sweden, 1977. Intern Passavant Meml. Hosp., Chgo., 1955-56; asst. resident in internal medicine VA Rsch. Hosp., Chgo., 1956-57; clin. asso. Nat. Heart Inst., Bethesda, Md., 1957-60; asst. resident in Medicine NYU-Bellevue Med. Ctr., N.Y.C., 1960-61; USPHS fellow, instr. pharmacology Harvard U., 1961-63; asst. prof. pharmacology and internal medicine U. Tex. Southwestern Med. Sch., Dallas, 1963-65; assoc. prof. U. Tex. Southwestern Med. Sch., 1965-70; prof. pharmacology and medicine Mich. State U., 1970-71; dep. dir. Bur. Drugs FDA, Rockville, Md., 1971-72; dir. office sci. evaluation Bur. Drugs FDA, 1972-73, dir. Bur. Drugs, 1973-82; dir. Office of Med. Applications of Rsch. NIH, 1982-84; v.p. med. and sci. affairs Boehringer Mannheim Pharms., 1984-94; scholar in residence Inst. Medicine, 1994-95; pres. Crout Cons., Bethesda, 1994—; mem. drug rsch. bd. NAS-NRC; cons. WHO, 1974-84; trustee U.S. Pharmacopeia, 1985-95; mem. com. Inst. Medicine, 1990, 92, 93; mem. bd. Genetics Inst., Inc., Cambridge, Mass., 1994-96; bd. dirs. GelTex Pharm., Waltham, Mass., Trimeris, Durham, N.C., Genelabs Techs., Redwood City, Calif. Contbr. articles to profl. jours. Served to sr. asst. surgeon USPHS, 1957-60; asst. surgeon gen. 1976-84. Recipient Dist. Svc. award USPHS, 1977, Spl. Citation Commr. of FDA, 1981, 82, Disting. Career award Drug Info. Assn., 1994, Oscar B. Hunter award in Therapeutics, Am. Soc. for Clin. Pharm. and Therapeutics, 1997; Burroughs Wellcome scholar in clin. pharmacology, 1965-70. Fellow ACP; mem. Am. Fedn. Clin. Rsch., Am. Soc. Pharmacology and Exptl. Therapeutics, Am. Soc. Clin. Investigation, Am. Soc. Clin. Pharmacology and Therapeutics, Heart Assn., Soc. Clin. Trials, Phi Beta Kappa, Alpha Omega Alpha. Home and Office: 5300 Alta Vista Rd Bethesda MD 20814-1629

CROUTER, RICHARD EARL, religion educator; b. Washington, Nov. 2, 1937; s. Earl Clinton and Neva J. (Crain) C.; m. Barbara Jean Williams, Jan. 30, 1960; children—Edward, Frances. A.B., Occidental Coll., 1960; B.D., Union Theol. U., N.Y.C., 1963, Th.D., 1968. Asst. prof. religion Carleton Coll., Northfield, Minn., 1967-73, assoc. prof., 1973-79, prof., 1979-92, Bryn-Jones disting. tchg. prof. humanities, 1993-96, Musser prof. religious studies, 1997—. Translator, editor: On Religion (F. Schleiermacher), 1988, 96; co-editor Jour. for the History of Modern Theology, 1993—. Chmn. parents adv. council Greenvale Sch. Northfield, 1977-78; resident dir. A Better Chance Program, Northfield, 1968-70. Fulbright scholar, 1976-77, 87, 91-92; Am. Council Learned Socs. fellow, 1976-77. Mem. Am. Acad. Religion (steering com. 19th century theol. group 1982-92, chmn. 1987-92), Hegel Soc. Am., Troeltsch Soc., German Studies Assn., Kierkegaard Soc., Schleiermacher Gesellschaft. Democrat. Avocations: hiking, travel, biking, piano. Home: 808 2d St E Northfield MN 55057-2307 Office: Carleton Coll Dept Religious Studies Northfield MN 55057

CROUTHAMEL, THOMAS GROVER, SR., editor; b. Berkeley, Calif., Sept. 10, 1930; s. Martin Luther and Elizabeth (Grover) C.; m. Madalene Donati, Sept. 6, 1954; children: Thomas Grover Jr., Annalise. BS, Thiel Coll., 1953. Sr. drug investigator FDA, L.A. and Edison, N.J., 1958-81; pres. Thomas G. Crouthamel, Inc., Bradenton, Fla., 1981—; ptnr. Crouthamel & Crouthamel, Bradenton, 1983-93; treas. Crouthamel Enterprises, Inc., Liberty Hill, Tex., 1986-92; sr. editor Keystone Press, Bradenton, 1982—. Author: Auditing EtO, 1982, It's OK, 1986, A History of Trailer Estates, 1987; When the Unthinkable Happens, 1995; contbr. articles to profl. jours. Cubmaster Boy Scouts Am., Pomona, Calif., 1963, committeeman, Spotswood, N.J., 1968-76, adult adviser Explorer Post, 1976-79; trustee Spotswood Libr. Bd., 1970-79; co-leader Compassionate Friends, Sarasota, Fla., 1984-90, chpt. advisor, facilitator, Englewood, Fla., 1989-91. With U.S. Army, 1953-55. Mem. Parenteral Drug Assn., Internat. Narcotics Officers Assn., The Authors Guild, AAAS, Toastmasters (pres. 1969-71), Masons (high priest local chpt. 1967). Avocations: travel, reading, fishing. Office: PO Box 6163 Bradenton FL 34281-6163

CROW, EDWIN LOUIS, mathematical statistician, consultant; b. Browntown, Wis., Sept. 15, 1916; s. Frederick Marion and Alice Blanche (Cox) C.; m. Eleanor Gish, June 13, 1942; children: Nancy Rebecca, Dorothy Carol Crow-Willard. B.S. summa cum laude, Beloit Coll., 1937; Ph.M., U. Wis., 1938, Ph.D., 1941; postgrad., Brown U., 1941, 42, U. Calif.-Berkeley, 1947, 48, Univ. Coll., London, 1961-62. Instr. math. Case Sch. Applied Sci., Cleve., 1941-42; mathematician Bur. Ordnance Dept. Navy, Washington, 1942-46, U.S. Naval Ordnance Test Sta., China Lake, Calif., 1946-54; cons. statistics Boulder Labs., U.S. Dept. Commerce, Boulder, Colo., 1954-73, Nat. Telecommunications and Info. Adminstrn., Boulder, Colo., 1974—; statistician Nat. Ctr. Atmospheric Research, Boulder, Colo., 1975-82; instr. math. extension div. UCLA, China Lake, 1947-54; adj. prof. math. U. Colo., Boulder, 1963-81; lectr. stats. Met. State Coll., Denver, 1974. Co-author: Statistics Manual, 1960; co-editor: Lognormal Distributions, 1988; assoc. editor: Communications in Statistics, 1972-98, Jour. Am. Statis. Assn., 1967-75, Current Index to Stats., 1981—; contbr. articles to profl. jours. Survey statistician Boulder Valley Sch. Dist., 1971-72; founder, pres. Boulder Tennis Assn., 1967-69, pres., 1982. Recipient Outstanding Publ. award Nat. Telecommunications and Info. Adminstrn., 1980, 82; Bronze medal U.S. Dept. Commerce, 1970, Editor's award Am. Meteorol. Soc., 1987. Fellow Royal Statis. Soc., Am. Statis Assn. (coun. mem. 1959-60, 68-69, Outstanding Chpt. mem. 1989), AAAS; mem. Am. Math. Soc., Math. Assn. Am., Inst. Math. Stats., Bernoulli Soc. for Math. Stats. and Probability, Soc. Indsl. and Applied Math., U.S. Tennis Assn., Sigma Xi, Phi Beta Kappa. Democrat. Unitarian. Clubs: Colo. Mountain, Harvest House Sporting Assn. (Boulder). Achievements include theory and applications of mathematical statistics in ordnance, radio standards, radio propagation, communication systems, weather modification, and ranking data. Home: 605 20th St Boulder CO 80302-7714 Office: Nat Telecommunications and Info Adminstrn ITS N3 325 Broadway Boulder CO 80303-3337

CROW, ELIZABETH SMITH, publishing company executive; b. N.Y.C.; d. Harrison Venture and Marlis (deGreve) Smith; children: Samuel Harrison, Rachel Venture, Sarah Gibson. BA, Mills Coll.; postgrad., Brown U. Exec. editor New York mag., N.Y.C.; editor in chief Parents mag., N.Y.C.; pres., editorial dir., CEO Gruner & Jahr USA Pub.; editor-in-chief Mademoiselle Mag., N.Y.C., 1993—; free-lance book reviewer N.Y. Times Book Rev.;

judge Nat. Mag. awards. Mem., bd. trustees March of Dimes; bd. dirs. N.Y. Revels; bd. dirs., exec. com. Met. Opera Guild; mem. N.Y. steering com. Women's Studies in Religion Program, Harvard Divinity Sch.; advisor Ctr. for the Study of Women and Soc., CUNY Grad. Ctr.; with Intersch. Orchestras of N.Y. Recipient Nat. Mag. award for gen. excellence, 1988. Mem. Am. Soc. Mag. Editors, Cosmopolitan Club, Century Assn. Democrat. Office: Mademoiselle Mag Condé Nast Publs 350 Madison Ave New York NY 10017-3704

CROW, HAROLD EUGENE, physician, family medicine educator; b. Farber, Mo., Jan. 17, 1933; s. Leslie J. and Laura L. (Sparks) C.; m. Mary Kay Krenke, July 5, 1974; children: Janet L., Jason P. MD, U. Mo., 1963. Diplomate Am. Bd. Family Practice, Am. Bd. Med. Examiners. Intern E.W. Sparrow Hosp., Lansing, Mich., 1963-64; pvt. practice medicine specializing in family practice Lansing, 1964-70; dir. family practice residency E.W. Sparrow Hosp., Lansing, Mich., 1970-82; chmn. dept. family and community medicine Sch. Medicine U. Nev., Reno, 1982-87, dir. office Rural Health Sch. Medicine, 1984-87; med. dir. S.W. Med. Assocs., Reno, 1987-88; dir. Lynchburg (Va.) Family Practice Resident Program, 1988-96; dir. Outer Banks Project East Carolina U. Sch. of Medicine, Nags Head, N.C., 1996-98, ret., 1998; dir. Outer Banks Edn. and Program Devel. Project. Developer non-rotational residency model for family practice tng., tng. model for rural med. practice; innovator computerized health info. systems for family physicians. Numerous civic activities. With U.S. Army, 1955-57. Mem. Am. Coll. Phys. Exec., numerous profl. assns. Presbyterian. Home: 408 Stoneham Dr Sun City Center FL 33575-5841 *Not being hampered by Dogma, but being freed up by curiousity. Not being a heavy handed teacher, but a caring helper of learning; that's the essense of a successful innovator and educator.*

CROW, JACK E., physics administrator; b. N.Y., Aug. 17, 1939. BES, Cleve. State U., 1962; PhD in Physics, U. Rochester, 1967. Assoc. and asst. physicist Brookhaven Nat. Lab., 1967-73; assoc. prof., prof. and chmn. Temple U., 1973-89; dir. Ben Franklin Superconductivity Ctr. Temple U., Drexel U., U. Pa., 1988-89; dir. Ctr. Material Rsch. and Tech. Fla. State U., 1990-91; dir. Nat. High Magnetic Field Lab., Tallahassee, Fla., 1991—; dir. solid state physics program NSF, 1984-86. Fellow AAAS, Am. Phys. Soc.; mem. Materials Rsch. Soc., Am. Cryogenic Soc., Sigma Xi. Achievements include research in experimental condensed matter physics, superconductivity, magnetism, high correlated metallic system-Heavy fermion, kondo and kondo lattice systems. Office: Nat High Magnetic Field Lab 1800 E Paul Dirac Dr Tallahassee FL 32310-3706

CROW, JAMES FRANKLIN, retired genetics educator; b. Phoenixville, Pa., Jan. 18, 1916; s. H. Ernest and Lena (Whitaker) C.; m. Ann Crockett, Aug. 9, 1941; children—Franklin, Laura, Catherine. A.B., Friends U., 1937; Ph.D., U. Tex., 1941; DSc. (hon.), U. Chgo., 1991. Instr., then asst. prof. zoology Dartmouth U., 1941-48; faculty U. Wis., 1948—, prof. genetics, 1954-86, chmn. dept. med. genetics, 1958-63, 65-71, acting dean sch. medicine, 1963-65, prof. emeritus, 1986—; Chmn. genetics study sect. NIH, 1965-68. Author: Genetics Notes, 8th edit, 1983, Introduction to Population Genetics Theory, 1970, Basic Concepts in Population, Quantitative and Evolutionary Genetics, 1986, also articles. Chmn. mammalian genetics study sect. NIH, 1985-88. Mem. Nat. Acad. Scis. (chmn. com. genetic effects atomic radiation 1960-63, 70-72, chmn. com. chem. environ. mutagens 1980-83), Japan Acad. (fgn. mem.), Genetics Soc. Am. (pres. 1960), Am. Soc. Human Genetics (pres. 1963). Home: 24 Glenway St Madison WI 53705-5206*

CROW, LAURA JEAN, design educator, costume designer; b. Hanover, N.H., Sept. 29, 1945; d. James Franklin and Rebecca Ann (Crockett) C.; m. Daniel Caine, Apr. 28, 1980 (div. Mar. 1987); children: Sarah Katherine, Matthew Jordan Caine. BFA, Boston U., 1967; MFA, U. Wis., 1969; postgrad., U. London, 1969-70, Courtauld Inst., 1969-70. Lectr. Brandeis U., Waltham, Mass., 1985; vis. assoc. prof. U. Mass., Amherst, 1986-87; assoc. prof. of design U. Mich., Ann Arbor, 1987-94; prof. of design U. Conn., Storrs, 1994—; active NEA Theatre Comms. Group, Washington and N.Y.C., 1998; adjudicator young designer's forum U.S. Inst. for Tech. Theatre, 1988-98; cons. profl. tng. Nat. Assn. Schs. of Theatre, Rutgers U., 1993; resident designer Greenwich Theater, London, 1971-73, Acad. Festival Theatre, Chgo., 1973-76, Cir. Repertory Co., N.Y.C., 1977-90. Costume designer: (Broadway prodns.) Warp, Sweet Bird of Youth, The Water Engine, Fifth of July, Burn This, The Seagull, Redwood Curtain, (off-Broadway prodns.) The Farm, Winter Signs, Hamlet, A TAle Tole, Orchards, Brilliant Traces, Raft of Medusa, Cakewalk, Sympathetic Magic, others, (films) Harry and the Hendersons, Fifth of July, The Lathe of Heaven, Charlie Smith & the Fritter Tree; designer regional theaters including Seattle Rep, ACT, Goodman Theatre, Milw. Rep., Bukeley Rep., Ariz. Theatre Co., Mark Tapere Forum, Arena Stage, Alley Theatre, Long Wharf Theatre, Hartford Stage, Old Globe Theatre, Asolo Theatre, Ctr. Stage. Recipient Drama Desk award N.Y. Drama Critics, 1973, Joseph Jefferson award Jeff Com., Chgo., 1975, 76, 77, 78, 88, Obie award Village Voice, 1980, Am. Theatre Wing award, 1980, 97, Dramalogue award L.A. Drama Critics, 1988, 97, Backstage West award Backstage Newspaper, 1997, San Francisco Bay Area Critics award, 1998, Zoni award Phoenix Drama Critics, 1998. Mem. United Scenic Artists, U.S. Inst. Theatre Tech. Fax: (860) 486-3110. E-mail: laura.crow.@uconn.edu. Home: 88 Hillyndale Rd Storrs Mansfield CT 06268-1802 Office: U of Conn Dept Dramatic Arts 802 Bolton Rd Storrs Mansfield CT 06269-1127

CROW, LYNNE CAMPBELL SMITH, insurance company representative; b. Buffalo, Oct. 13, 1942; d. Stephen Smith and Jean Campbell (Ruggles) Hall; m. William David Crow II, Apr. 16, 1966 (div. Dec. 1989); children: William David III, Alexander Fairbairn, Margaret Campbell. BA, Sweet Briar (Va.) Coll., 1964; postgrad., Am. Coll., 1986. CLU; ChFC. Claims rep. Liberty Mut. Ins. Co., Bklyn. and N.Y.C., 1964-66; with McGraw-Hill Corp., N.Y.C., 1966-67; claims rep. Liberty Mut. Ins. Co., East Orange, N.J., 1967-68; sales assoc. Realty World/Allsopp Realtors, Millburn, N.J., 1981-82; field rep. Guardian Life Ins. Co., 1982—. Bd. dirs. Jr. League Oranges and Short Hills, Millburn, 1979-80, 95-96, Millburn LWV, 1979-80; campaign chair, bus. chair, bd. dirs. United Way Millburn/Short Hills, 1981-88, 90-96, sec., 1990-91. Named Life Underwriter of Yr., 1996. Mem. Nat. Assn. Life Underwriters (Nat. Quality award 1988, 91, 95, Nat. Health Achievement award 1988, 90), Am. Soc. Fin. Svc. Profls. (bd. dirs. 1994-99), N.J. Assn. Life Underwriters (dir. region II 1993-95, health chair 1995—, sec. 1998-99, 2d v.p., 1999—). Newark Assn. Life Underwriters (pres. 1993-94, bd. dirs. 1986-94, 96-98, sec. 1987-88, treas. 1988-89, 3d v.p. 1989-90,, 2d v.p. 1990, pres.-elect 1991-92, pres. 1992-93, health chair 1995-98, Life Underwriter of Yr. 1996), Women's Life Underwriter Confedn., Million Dollar Round Table (life), Knight of Round Table, Assn. Health Ins. Agts., Nat. Assn. Security Dealers, Racquets Club Short Hills (bd. dirs. 1982-84), Chatham (Mass.) Beach and Tennis Club, LeTip of Millburn. Republican. Episcopalian. Avocations: travel, sailing, reading, hiking. Home: 22 Winding Way Short Hills NJ 07078-2530 Office: 1150 Raritan Rd Cranford NJ 07016-3369

CROW, NANCY REBECCA, lawyer; b. Ridgecrest, Calif., Nov. 3, 1948; d. Edwin Louis and Eleanor Elizabeth (Gish) C.; 1 child, Rebecca Ann Carr; m. Mark A.A. Skrotzki, Apr. 4, 1987. BA, Antioch Coll., 1970; JD, U. Colo., 1974; LLM in Taxation, NYU, 1977. Bars: Colo. 1974, Calif. 1977. Atty., advisor IRS, N.Y.C., 1975-77; assoc. Brawerman & Kopple, Los Angeles, 1977-80; prof. Sch. Law, U. Denver, 1980-81; of counsel Krendl & Netzorg, Denver, 1981-84; shareholder Krendl & Krendl, Denver, 1984-92, Pendleton, Friedberg, Wilson & Hennessey, P.C., Denver, 1992—. Editor estate and trust forum Colorado Lawyer, 1992-93, bd. editors, 1993—; contbr. chpts. to books. Bd. dirs. Centennial Philharm. Orch., 1998—. Mem. ABA (chmn. Welfare Benefits subcom. of personal svcs. orgns. com. com., tax sect. 1987-92), Colo. Bar Assn. (exec. coun. tax sect. 1990-93, sec. tax sect. 1993-94, chair-elect 1994-95, chair 1995-96, bd. govs. 1996-98), Colo. Women's Bar Assn. (chair pub. policy com. 1982-83), Denver Bar Assn., Denver Tax Assn., Denver Tax Inst. Planning Com., Alliance of Profl. Women, Women's Estate Planning Coun. (bd. dirs. 1996-98), U.S.-Mex. C. of C. (bd. dirs. Rocky Mountain chpt., sec. 1998—), Sierra Club. Democrat. Unitarian. Avocations: skiing, backpacking, cello, running. Home: 1031 Marion St Denver CO 80218-3016 Office: Pendleton Friedberg Wilson & Hennessey PC 303 E 17th Ave Ste 1000 Denver CO 80203-1263

CROW, PAUL ABERNATHY, JR., clergyman, religious council executive, educator; b. Birmingham, Ala., Nov. 17, 1931; s. Paul Abernathy and Beulah Elizabeth (Parker) C.; m. Mary Evelyn Matthews, Sept. 11, 1955; children: Carol Ann, Stephen Paul, Susan Margaret. BS, U. Ala., 1954; BD, Lexington Theol. Sem., 1957; MST, Hartford Sem. Found., 1958, PhD, 1962; postdoctoral studies, Oxford U., 1967-68, U. Geneva, Ecumenical Inst. Bossey, 1981, 87; DD, Phillips U., 1983, Bethany Coll., 1983, Yale U., 1986, Va. Theological Sem., 1987, Lynchburg Coll., 1997. Ordained to ministry Disciples of Christ, 1957. Minister in various Disciples congregations Ala., Ky., 1955-57; min. First Congl. Ch., Hadley, Mass., 1957-61; assoc. prof. ch. history Lexington Theol. Sem., 1961-66, prof., 1966-68; Am. Assn. Theol. Schs. vis. fellow Oxford U., 1967-68; gen. sec. Consultation on Ch. Union, Princeton, N.J., 1968-74; pres. Coun. on Christian Unity, Indpls., 1974-98; vis. lectr. Princeton Theol. Sem., 1969-76; affiliate prof. Christian Theol. Sem., 1974—; Mem. cen. com. World Coun. Chs., exec. com., plenary faith and order commn., 1975-98; vice moderator Faith and Order Commn., 1992-98; del. faith and order confs., St. Andrews, Scotland, 1960, Montreal, Que., Can., 1963, Bristol, Eng., 1967, Louvain, Belgium, 1971, Accra, Ghana, 1974, Bangalore, India, 1978, Lima, Peru, 1982, Stavanger, Norway, 1985, Budapest, Hungary, 1989, Santiago de Compostela, Spain, 1993, Moshi, Tazania, 1996; del. World Coun. Chs. assembly Uppsala, Sweden, 1968, Nairobi, Kenya, 1975, Vancouver, Can., 1983, Canberra, Australia, 1991, Harare, Zimbabwe, 1998; del. ch. union confs., Limuru, Kenya, 1970, Toronto, Ont., Can., 1975, Colombo, Sri Lanka, 1981, Potsdam, German Democratic Republic, 1987, WCC World Missionary Conf., San Antonio, Tex., 1989, Ocho Rios, Jamaica, 1995; mem. exec. com. Consultation on Ch. Union; chmn. Disciples of Christ del., mem. exec. com., mem. gen. bd. Nat. Coun. Chs.; co-chmn. Disciples of Christ-Roman Cath. Internat. Bilaterals; co-chmn. Disciples-Russian Orthodox Internat. Bilateral, co-chmn. Disciples-Reformed Internat. Bilateral, Disciples-Finnish Luth.; vis. prof. Princeton Theol. Sem., 1968-78; affiliate prof. Christian Theol. Sem., 1974—; gen. sec. Disciples Ecumenical Consultative Coun., 1975-98; vis. lectr. Princeton Theol. Sem., 1969-76. Author: Where We Are in Church Union, 1965, The Ecumenical Movement in Bibliographical Outline, 1965, No Greater Love: The Gospel and Its Imperatives, 1967, Church Union at Mid-Point, 1972, Christian Unity: Matrix for Mission, 1982, The Anatomy of a Nineteenth Century United Church, 1983, The Vision of Christian Unity: Essays in Honor of Paul A. Crow, Jr., 1997; contbr. over 300 articles to maj. scholarly jours. and ency.; editor: Mid-Stream: An Ecumenical Jour., 1974-99. Bd. dirs., moderator Ecumenical Inst., Bossey, 1974-83; trustee Disciples of Christ Hist. Soc. Jacobus fellow Hartford Sem. Found., 1958; Recipient Disting. Alumni award Hartford Sem. Found., 1986, Nat Ecumenical Svc. award, 1998, Focolare Internat. Luminos (Light) of Christian Unity award, 1998. Mem. Nat. Assn. Ecumenical Officers (pres. 1988-93), Am. Soc. Ch. History, North Am. Acad. Ecumenists, Societas Oecumenica, Nassau Club (Princeton, N.J.), Indianapolis Athletic Club, Omicron Delta Kappa, Theta Phi. Democrat. Fax: 317-585-0015. Home: 7215 Vauxhall Rd Indianapolis IN 46250-2737

CROW, SAM ALFRED, federal judge; b. Topeka, May 5, 1926; s. Samuel Wheadon and Phyllis K. (Brown) C.; m. Ruth M. Rush, Jan. 30, 1948; children: Sam A., Dan W. BA, U. Kans., 1949; JD, Washburn U., 1952. Ptnr. Rooney, Dickinson, Prager & Crow, Topeka, 1953-63, Dickinson, Crow, Skoog & Honeyman, Topeka, 1963-70; sr. ptnr. Crow & Skoog, Topeka, 1971-75; part-time U.S. magistrate, 1973-75, U.S. magistrate, 1975-81; judge U.S. Dist. Ct. Kans., Wichita, 1981-92; sr. judge U.S. Dist. Ct. Kans., Topeka, 1992—; lectr. Washburn U. Sch. Law; participant adv. com. on criminal rules Jud. Conf., 1990-96; mem. 10th Cir. Jud. Coun., 1987-88; pres., 1992-94; criminal rules adv. com.'s liaison Ct. Adminstrn. and Case Mgmt. Com.'s Subcom. on Criminal Case Mgmt., 1994-96; bd. dirs. Riverside Hosp., Wichita, 1986-92; mem. The Honorable Sam A. Crow Am. Inn of Ct.; lectr. in field. Bd. rev. Boy Scouts Am., 1960-70, cubmaster, 1957-60; mem. vestry Grace Episcopal Ch., Topeka, 1960-65; chmn. Kans. March of Dimes, 1959, bd. dirs. 1960-65; bd. dirs. Topeka Council Chs., 1960-70; mem. Kans. Hist. Soc., 1960—; pres., v.p. PTA.; bd. govs. Washburn Law Sch. Alumni Assn., 1993—. Col. JAGC, USAR, ret. Fellow Kans. Bar Found.; mem. ABA (del. Nat. Conf. Spl. Ct. Judges 1978, 19), Kans. Bar Assn. (trustee 1970-76, chmn. mil. law sect. 1965, 67, 70, 72, 74, 75), Kans. Trial Lawyers Assn. (sec. 1959-60, pres. 1960-61), Nat. Assn. U.S. Magistrates (com. discovery abuse), Topeka Bar Assn. (chmn. jud. reform com., chmn. bench and bar com., chmn. criminal law com.), Wichita Bar Assn., Topeka Lawyers Club (sec. 1964-65, pres. 1965-66), Am. Legion, Shawnee Country Club, Delta Theta Phi, Sigma Alpha Epsilon. Office: US Dist Ct 444 SE Quincy St Topeka KS 66683

CROW, SHERYL, singer/songwriter, musician; b. Kennett, Mo., 1963. Degree in classical piano, U. Mo., 1984. Backup singer Bad tour Michael Jackson, 1987; backup singer The End of the Innocence tour Don Henley, 1989; also backup singer George Harrison, Joe Cocker, Stevie Wonder, Rod Stewart; singer, songwriter Tuesday Night Music Club, 1992—. Albums include Tuesday Night Music Club, 1993, Sheryl Crow, 1996, The Globe Sessions, 1998; singles include Leaving Las Vegas, All I Wanna Do (Grammy awards for Record of Year and Female Pop Vocal, 1995), Strong Enough; participant Lilith Fair, 1998, 99. Recipient Grammy award for Best New Artist, 1995. Address: care A&M Records 1416 N La Brea Ave Hollywood CA 90028-7506*

CROWDER, BARBARA LYNN, judge; b. Mattoon, Ill., Feb. 3, 1956; d. Robert Dale and Martha Elizabeth (Harrison) C.; m. Lawrence Owen Taliana, Apr. 17, 1982; children: Paul Joseph, Robert Lawrence, Benjamin Owen. BA, U. Ill., 1978, JD, 1981. Bar: Ill. 1981. Assoc. Louis E. Olivero, Peru, Ill., 1981-82; asst. state's atty. Madison County, Edwardsville, Ill., 1982-84; ptnr. Robbins & Crowder, Edwardsville, 1985-87, Robbins, Crowder & Bader, Edwardsville, 1987-88, Crowder, Taliana, Rubin & Buckley, 1988-98; assoc. judge 3d Jud. Cir. of Madison County, Ill., 1999—; spkr. Continuing Legal Edn. Seminars Family Law Update, 1993-99. Co-editor ISBA Family Law Newsletter, 1993; co-author chpts. in ISBA Family Law Handbook, 1995, Maintenance Chapter Ill. Family Law, 1998; contbr. articles to profl. jours. Chmn. City of Edwardsville Zoning Bd. Appeals, 1986-87; committee woman Edwardsville De, Precinct 15, 1986-98; mem. City of Edwardsville Planning Commn., 1985-87; bd. dirs. Madison-Bond County Workforce Devel. Bd., 1995-96, 96-97. Named Best Oral Advocate, Moot Ct. Bd., 1979, Outstanding Young Career Woman, Dist. XIV, Ill. Bus. and Profl. Women, 1986; recipient Alice Paul award Alton-Edwardsville NOW, 1987, Outstanding Working Woman of Ill. Ill. Fed. of Bus. and Profl. Women, 1988-89, Woman of Achievement YWCA, 1996; recipient Athena award Edwardsville/Glen Carbon C. of C., 1991. Fellow Am. Acad. Matrimonial Lawyers; mem. ABA, Ill. Bar Assn. (family law coun. sect. 1990-99, chair 1997-98, co-editor family law newsletter 1993, vice chair 1996-97), Ill. Fedn. Bus. and Profl. Women (parliamentaria dist. XIV 1991-92), Women Lawyers Assn. Met. East (pres. 1986), Edwardsville Bus. and Profl Women's Club (pres. 1988-89, 95-96, treas. 1989-90, Woman of Achievement award 1985, Jr. Svc. award 1987), Ul Ill. Alumni Assn. (v.p. met.-east club 1994-95, bd. dirs. 1995-97). Democrat. Office: Madison County Courthouse 155 N Main St Edwardsville IL 62025

CROWDER, BONNIE WALTON, small business owner, composer; b. Lafayette, Tenn., Apr. 14, 1916; d. Edward Samuel Bailey and Nannie Elizabeth (Goad) Walton; m. Reggie Ray Crowder, Nov. 19, 1936; 1 child, Rita Faye. Grad., Nashville Beauty Coll. Owner, operator Bonnie's Beauty Salon, Tampa, Fla. Composer: A Man of Faith, 1988, This Miracle, 1988, (with Willard E. Walton) God Bless Our President, 1988, Awake, Arise America, 1989, Touching My Jesus, 1990, (with Willard E. Walton) Muscle Jerky Boogie, 1992. Mem. ch. choir, Tampa; mem. Bus. and Profl. Women's Chorus, 1960's and 70's, U. South Fla. Community Chorus, 1973-81. Mem. Beta Sigma Phi. Home: 266 Oak Knob Rd Lafayette TN 37083-4137

CROWDER, HENRY ALVIN, military officer; b. Panama City, Fla., Aug. 30, 1953; s. Henry Ford and Margaret Ann (Bland) C.; m. Beth Marie Burlingame, Apr. 16, 1977; children: Heather Elizabeth, Jeremy Allen. G-rad. high sch., Beckley, W.Va.; student, various univs., 1975-94, various mil. edn. programs; grad., U. Md., 1995. Enlisted U.S. Army, 1974, advanced through grades to chief warrant officer IV, 1995; order of battle analyst 502d Army Security Agy. Group, Augsburg, Fed. Republic Germany, 1974-75; combat intelligence analyst 856th ASA Co. 3d Armored Div., Frankfurt, Fed. Republic Germany, 1975-77; intelligence analyst, hdqrs. U.S. Army Field Artillery Ctr. and Sch., Ft. Sill, Okla., 1977-79; non-commd. officer in charge intelligence ctr. 2d M.I. 2d Inf. Div., Korea, 1979-80; team non-commd. officer in charge intelligence prodn. 504th M.I. Group III Corps, Ft. Hood, Tex., 1980-81; order of battle technician 9th Inf. Div., Ft. Lewis, Wash., 1981-84, 1st Armored Div., Ansbach, Fed. Republic Germany, 1984-87; all source intelligence technician 513th Mil. Intelligence Bridgade/3rd U.S. Army/U.S. Forces Cen. Command, Ft. Monmouth, N.J., 1987-90; sr. all source intelligence technician Ops. Desert Shield, Desert Storm U.S. Army ARCENT/U.S. Forces CENTCOM, Saudi Arabia, 1990-91; sr. all source intelligence technician 513th Intel Support Element/3d U.S. Army/U.S. Forces CENTCOM, Ft. McPherson, Ga., 1991-96; ops. officer Advanced Studies Br. U.S. Army Warrant Officer Career Ctr., Ft. Rucker, Ala., 1996-97; chief joint intel support element Spl. Ops. Commd. Ctrl., MacDill AFB, Fla., 1997—; ops. officer Desert Thunder, Desert Fox, Kuwait, 1998. Asst. pack leader, asst. scoutmaster, active Atlanta coun. Order of the Arrow Boy Scouts Am. Decorated Bronze Star; named Outstanding Young Man of Am. U.S. Jaycees, 1982. Mem. U.S. Army Warrant Officers Assn. (sec. Ansbach chpt. 1984-87, ways and means chmn. European region 1986-87, ways and means chmn. Jersey Shore-Ft. Monmouth chpt. 1989-91, greater Atlanta chpt. 1992-96, pres. Ft. Rucker chpt. 1996-97). Office: Spl Ops Commd Ctrl SOC J2 Attn CW 4 Crowder 7115 S Boundary Blvd MacDill AFB FL 33621-5101

CROWDER, JO ANNE CORKRAN, certified public accountant; b. Cambridge, Md., Jan. 13, 1957; d. Robert William and Joan (Barth) Corkran; m. Glenn Scott Crowder, Sept. 7, 1991; 1 child, Lauren Hayley. BS, Towson State U., 1980. From staff to mgr. Beatty, Satchell & Co., LLC, Easton, Md., 1980-92; partner Beatty, Satchell & Co., LLC, Easton, 1992—. Vol. Waterfowl Festival, Easton, Md., 1981-96; bd. dirs. Hopkins Scholarship Fund, 1994—. Mem. Chesapeake Women's Network (treas., 1996—), Md. Assn. CPAs (peer review com., 1997—), Am. Inst. CPAs, Tred Avon Yacht Club (sec., 1995-97, treas. 1998—). Office: Beatty Satchell PO Box 1187 Easton MD 21601-1187

CROWDER, JULIAN ANTHONY, optometrist; b. Asheville, N.C., May 7, 1950; s. Olfa N. and Helen (Roberts) C.; m. Paula Herda; children: Heidi Michelle, Winston Roberts. AB in Chemistry, U. N.C., 1972; OD, So. Coll. Optometry, 1978. Pvt. practice optometry Candler, N.C., 1979—; mem. Channel 13 News Med. Adv. Bd., Asheville; mem. cmty. adv. panel BASF, Enka, N.C.; mem. nat. adv. bd. The Laser Ctr., Inc., Toronto, 1994—, Piedmont Laser Ctr., Greenville, S.C., 1995-96. Mem. Am. Optometric Assn., N.C. State Optometric Soc. (trustee 1990-93, v.p. 1993-95, exec. coun. 1979-81, 89—, pres. 1996-97), Mountain Dist. Optometric Assn. (pres. 1989-93), So. Coun. Optometrists, Enka-Candler Bus. Assn. (pres. 1986). Republican. Methodist. Avocations: photography, sound recordings, classic car collecting. Home: 172 Weston Rd Arden NC 28704-3109 Office: 1431 Smoky Park Hwy Candler NC 28715-0399

CROWDER, LENA BELLE, retired special education educator; b. Winston-Salem, N.C., Apr. 4, 1931; d. Henry Lee and Janie (Woods) Thomas; m. Raymond Crowder, June 12, 1954; 1 child, Rayonette Janease. BS in Edn., Winston Salem State U., 1952; MS in Edn., Agrl. and Tech. Coll., 1959. Cert. elem. edn. tchr., N.C. Tchr. 1st grade Early County Sch. System, Blakely, Ga., 1953-56; tchr. kindergarten Thomas-Anderson Kindergarten, Winston-Salem, 1956-57, 58-60, 61-62; tchr. 1st grade Beaufort (S.C.) County Schs., 1957-58; tchr. Chapel Hill (N.C.) City Sch. System, 1960-61, Forsyth County Sch. System, Winston-Salem, 1961-62, 1962-67; tchr. Winston-Salem/Forsyth County Schs., 1967-93, ret., 1993. Precinct election recorder Winston-Salem/Forsyth County Election Bd., 1961; rec. fin. sec. Mt. Zion Bapt. Ch. Sunday Sch., Winston Salem, 1977, 90-91, 95—; supporter Crisis Control Ministry, Winston-Salem, 1982—; participant neighborhood watch system Winston-Salem Police Dept.; chairperson sch. involvement projects ARC, 1991-92. Mem. NEA, Nat. Assn. Univ. Women, Coun. Exceptional Children, Nat. Women of Achievement (rec. sec. 1991-98 Winston-Salem chpt.), Assn. Classroom Tchrs. Democrat. Home: 1140 Rich Ave Winston Salem NC 27101-3432

CROWDER, LILLIE MAE BROWN, retired architectural engineer; b. Georgetown, S.C., May 31, 1936; d. Moses and Maude (Session) Brown; m. Charles Lamar Crowder, Apr. 15, 1960 (div. Feb. 1972); children: Barney, Frederick. BS in Archtl. Engring., S.C. State U., 1958; postgrad., Tuskegee Inst., 1960, Inst. Design and Constrn., 1961, 63; diploma in archtl. drafting, CUNY, 1971; MA in Urban Edn., L.I. U., 1981. Rated aero. engr./jr. archtl. engr. U.S. Civil Svc. Commn. Draftperson David Byrd Assoc., Washington, 1958-59; tchr. Choppee H.S., Georgetown, 1958-60; draftperson Big 6 Press, N.Y.C., 1960-62; sr. warrant officer N.Y. Telephone Co., N.Y.C., 1963-64; chief draftsperson Wilbur Smith & Assoc. C.E., Manhattan, N.Y., 1964-67; asst. architect sch. planning and rsch. Bklyn. Bd. Edn., 1967-71, edn. facility coord. facilities planning divsn., 1971-84, archtl. faculty coord. divsn. spl. edn., 1984-90, sr. project liaison divsn. sch. facilities, 1990-98; jr. engr. N.Y.C. Resignalization Study, 1959-60; organized 1st mech. drawing dept. at Choppee H.S. Spkr: Women History Month, 1998, Bus. and Profl. Women, N.Y.C.; Author: Essence of a Dream (featured in Sotheby's 8th Annual exhbn. of art by N.Y.C. pub. sch. tchrs. and students, 1998; contbr. poems to profl. publs. Trustee Salem United Meth. Ch., N.Y.C., 1972; bd. dirs. Lewis H. Latimer Fund, Inc., Flushing, N.Y., 1982—, Human Resource Ctr./St. Albans, Queens, N.Y., 1984; mem. adv. com. Black Am. Heritage Found. Music History Arch. York Coll., 1995—; women's com. Local 375, Architects and Engrs.; borough pres. Bklyn. Citation Achievement Field Edn. & Arch., Queens Black History Month-Mary McLeod Bethune Celebration; guest spkr. Women History Program, 1998, fed. women's com. Social Security Adminstrn. Recipient Disting. Alumni award S.C. State U., 1981, Nat. Assn. Equal Oppty. Higher Edn., 1982, Quarter Century award Black Am. Heritage Found., 1993, Positive Image award Key Women of Am.; L.B. Crowder Day proclaimed borough pres., city coun., Queens, 1993 (cited in Jet Magazine and Congl. Record 1993, 94), award Borough Pres. of Queens; 1st woman in N.Y.C. to receive archl. drafting license; architecture achievement citation Borough Pres. of Brooklyn, N.Y.; Black history month citation Borough Pres., Queens. Mem. New Yorkers for Inclusive Edn. Curriculum, United Fedn. Tchrs., S.C. State U. Club (exec. bd., sec. 1976-81), Delta Sigma Theta Sorority, Inc. Democrat. Avocations: painting, piano, poetry, composing, writing lyrics. Home: PO Box 401 91 W Bartlett Rd Middle Island NY 11953

CROWDER, RICHARD MORGAN, pilot; b. Wurzburg, Bavaria, Germany, July 22, 1963; (parents Am. citizens); s. Richard Thomas and Margaret Taylor (Rainey) C. BS, U. Minn., 1986; postgrad., U. Colo., 1995—. Pilot Classic Aviation, Mpls., 1985-87, Air South, Homestead, Fla., 1987, AVAir, Raleigh, N.C., 1987-88, Am. Eagle, Dallas, 1988-89, USAir, Arlington, Va., 1989-92, United Airlines, Chgo., 1992—. Republican. Methodist. Avocations: reading, running, hunting, trap shooting.

CROWDER, ROBERT GEORGE, psychology educator; b. Waterloo, Iowa, Sept. 16, 1939; s. Louis Lomelino and Lucille (Burrell) C.; m. Julie Anne Butterfield, Apr. 22, 1962; children: Edward, Bruce, Lorial. BA in Psychology, U. Mich., 1960, PhD in Psychology, 1965. Instr. Yale U., New Haven, 1965-66, asst. prof., 1966-69, assoc. prof., 1969-75, prof., 1975—. Author: Principles of Learning & Memory, 1976, The Psychology of Reading, 1982. Fellow Am. Psychol. Assn.; mem. Psychonomic Soc. Office: Yale U PO Box 11A New Haven CT 06520

CROWDUS, GARY ALAN, film company executive; b. Lexington, Ky., Jan. 2, 1945; s. Charles Dallas and Bess May (Rice) C. BFA, NYU Inst. Film and TV, 1969. Founding editor Cineaste mag., N.Y.C., 1967—; assoc. editor Film Society Review, N.Y.C., 1968-72; v.p. Tricontinental Film Ctr., N.Y.C., 1972-79, Unifilm Inc., N.Y.C., 1979-80; gen. mgr. The Cinema Guild, Inc., N.Y.C., 1981—; mem. U.S. Conf. on Alternative Cinema, N.Y.C., 1978-79; mem. internat. adv. com. Internat. Documentary Film Week, 1989. Co-author: (with others) Quinze and de Cinema Mondial, 1975, The Documentary Tradition, 1979, The Cineaste Interviews, 1983, New Challenges for Documentary, 1988, Film and Politics in the Third World, 1988, Celluloid Power: Social Film Criticism from The Birth of a Nation to Judgement at Nuremberg, 1992, The Political Companion to American Film, 1994. Mem. Assn. Ind. Video and Filmmakers, Internat. Documentary Assn., N.Y. Film/Video Coun. Home: 116 Saint Marks Pl Apt 8 New York NY 10009-5856 Office: The Cinema Guild 1697 Broadway Rm 506 New

York NY 10019-5904 also: Cineaste Mag Art Politics Cinema 200 Park Ave S New York NY 10003-1503

CROWE, CAMERON, screenwriter, film director; b. Palm Springs, Calif., July 13, 1957. Student, Calif. State U., San Diego. Writer Rolling Stone mag., N.Y.C. Scripts include Fast Times at Ridgemont High, 1982, The Wild Life, 1984; screenwriter, dir.: Say Anything, 1989, Singles, 1992, Jerry Maguire, 1996; actor: American Hot Wax, 1978; creative cons.: (TV series) Fast Times, 1986. Office: care Columbia Tristar 10202 Washington Blvd Culver City CA 90232-3119*

CROWE, CAMERON MACMILLAN, chemical engineering educator; b. Montreal, Que., Can., Oct. 6, 1931; s. Ernest Watson and Marianne (Macmillan) C.; m. Jean Margaret Gilbertson, Feb. 15, 1969. Student, Royal Mil. Coll., 1948-52; B.Eng., McGill U., 1953; Ph.D., Cambridge (Eng.) U., 1957. Sr. devel. engr. DuPont of Can., Maitland, Ont., 1957-59; mem. faculty dept. chem. engring. McMaster U., Hamilton, Ont., 1959—; assoc. prof. McMaster U., Hamilton, 1964-70, prof., 1970-96, prof. emeritus, 1996—, chmn. dept., 1971-74. Author: (with others) Chemical Plant Simulation, 1971; Assoc. editor: Canadian Jour. Chem. Engring, 1975-81. C.D. Howe Meml. fellow Rice U., Houston, 1967-68; Athlone fellow, 1953-55. Fellow Chem. Inst. Can.; mem. Am. Inst. Chem. Engrs., Can. Soc. Chem. Engring. (bd. dirs. 1984-87, v.p. 1990-91, pres. 1991-92). Home: 821 Glenwood Ave, Burlington, ON Canada L7T 2J8 Office: Chem Engring Dept, McMaster U, Hamilton, ON Canada L8S 4L7

CROWE, HAL SCOTT, chiropractor; b. Atlanta, Apr. 19, 1953; s. Hugh Lee and Dorothy Elizabeth (Cooke) C.; m. PiHsiou Hsu, Mar. 29, 1980; children: Hal Scott Jr., Colleen Jao. Student, Johns Hopkins U., 1971-72, Ga. State U., 1973-76, 78-80; D of Chiropractic, Life Chiropractic Coll., 1983; post D. in Chiropractic Neurology, Logan Chiropractic Coll., 1992. Diplomate Nat. Bd. Chiropractic Examiners; cert. chiropractic orthospinologist, cert. chiropractic neurologist Logan Chiropractic Coll.; cert. advance open water scuba diver, cavern diver. Radiol. technician Crowe Chiropractic Offices, College Park, Ga., 1979-83; chiropractic practitioner Crowe Chiropractic Offices, College Park and Brunswick, Ga., 1983—; clin. rschr. Sweat Found., Atlanta, 1984—; resident in neurology Am. Coll. of Chiropractic Neurology, 1989-92; mem. postgrad. faculty Life Chiropractic Coll.; interim chmn. Acad. Upper Cervical Chiropractic Orgn., 1994, pres., 1995-97; preceptor faculty mem. Palmer Chiropractic Coll.; participant 4th through 13th Ann. Upper Cervical Confs., 1987-96; mem. Dolphin Project Rsch. Program. Contbr. articles to profl. jours.; 2d chair trombonist Jekyll Island Big Dance Band, 1985-94, condr., 1993-95. Host Columbus Ship Replica exhibit, 1992; missionary United Meth. Ch., Petite Goave, Haiti, 1986; mem. coun. on ministries McKendree United Meth. Ch., Brunswick, 1986-87. Recipient Appreciation award Grostic Study Club, Life Chiropractic Coll., 1985. Mem. Internat. Chiropractors Assn., Ga. Coun. Chiropractic, Soc. Chiropractic Orthospinologists (cert. doctor, instr.), Chiropractic Atlas Orthogonists, Nat. Upper Cervical Chiropractic Assn., Acad. Upper Cervical Chiropractic Orgns. Inc., Reef Environ. Edn. Found., Nat. Speleological Soc. (cave diving sect.), Lions (bd. dirs. 1986-88, Lion Tamer 1986-87, presdl. appreciation award 1986, pres. 1988-89, Tail Twister 1991), Diver's Alert Network, Ian Fleming Found. Avocations: golf, water sports, Caribbean history, archaeology, music. Home: 792 S Beachview Dr Jekyll Island GA 31527-0919 Office: Crowe Chiropractic Offices 2321 Parkwood Dr Brunswick GA 31520-4720

CROWE, JAMES JOSEPH, lawyer; b. New Castle, Pa., June 9, 1935; s. William J. and Anna M. (Dickson) C.; m. Joan D. Verba, Dec. 26, 1959. BA, Youngstown State U., 1958; JD, Georgetown U., 1963. Bar: Va. 1963, Ohio 1966. Atty. SEC, Washington, 1964-65, Gen. Tire & Rubber Co., Akron, Ohio, 1965-68; sr. atty. Eaton Corp., Cleve., 1968-72; sec., gen. counsel U.S. Shoe Corp., Cin., 1972-95, v.p., 1975-95; ptnr. Kepley, Gilligan & Eyrich, Cin., 1996—. Chmn. divsn. Fine Arts Fund, 1976; trustee Springer Ednl. Found., 1978-84, Cin. Music Festival Assn., 1980-86, 96—; group chmn. United Appeal, 1980; mem. pres.'s coun. Coll. Mt. St. Joseph, 1985-88; trustee Tennis for Charity Inc., 1986—, Playhouse in the Park, 1990-96, Greater Cin. Ctr. for Econ. Edn., 1992-96, Leadership Cin., Class 1990-91; trustee Cin. Nature Ctr., 1993—, chmn. 1996-98; bd. visitors U. Cin. Coll. Law, 1993—; trustee Invest in Neighborhoods, 1982-89, pres. 1984-86; trustee Cin. Hort. Soc., 1996—. 2d lt. U.S. Army, 1958-59. Mem. Ohio Bar Assn., Va. Bar, Cin. Bar Assn., Am. Soc. Corp. Secs., Cin. Country Club, Queen City Club, Cin. Tennis Club, Met. Club.

CROWE, JAMES WILSON, university administrator, educator; b. Churubusco, Ind., June 27, 1934; s. James A. and Ruth Crowe; m. Barbara Jones; children: Michael James, Monica Sue Crowe Black. BS, Purdue U., 1959; MS, U. Fla., 1960; Dir. Degree, Ind. U., 1970, EdD, 1979. Grad. asst. in health and safety edn. U. Fla., Gainesville, 1959-60; health edn. tchr., coach, dir. driver edn. program Edinburg (Ind.) Cmty. H.S., 1960-65; dir. health and safety edn. Atterbury Job Corps Ctr., Columbus, Ind., 1965-66; asst. prof. applied health sci. Ind. U., Bloomington, 1966-80, assoc. prof. applied health sci., 1980-96; prof., 1996—; dir. Ctr. for Health and Safety Studies Ind. U., Bloomington, 1992—, co-dir. Inst. for Drug Abuse Prevention, 1992—, acting chair dept. applied health sci., 1992-93, chair dept. applied health sci., 1993—. Bd. dirs. Monroe County chpt. ARC, 1991-94. Recipient Svc. award ARC, 1986, 87, 88, 89, Instr. of Yr. award ARC, 1985, 87, 88, Outstanding Tchg. award Amoco, 1977. Mem. AAHPERD (v.p. cmty./safety divsn. Midwest dist. 1989-90), Am. Assn. Active Lifestyles and Fitness (bd. dirs. 1994—), Am. Driver and Traffic Edn. Assn. (Visions of Tomorrow award 1992), Am. Sch. Health Assn., Nat. Safety Coun. (mem.-at-large ednl. rsch. sect. 1993, cert. in recognition of outstanding contbn. 1994), Sch. and Cmty. Safety Soc. Am. (bd. dirs. 1991—, pres.-elect 1992-94, pres. 1994-96, past pres. 1996-98, scholar award 1996, C.P. Yost Disting. Svc. award 1998). Office: Ind U HPER 116 Bloomington IN 47405

CROWE, JOHN T., lawyer; b. Cabin Cove, Calif., Aug. 14, 1938; s. J. Thomas and Wanda (Walston) C.; m. Marina Protopapa, Dec. 28, 1968; 1 child, Erin Aleka. BA, U. Santa Clara, 1960, JD, 1962. Bar: Calif. 1962, U.S. Dist. Ct. (ea. dist.) Calif. 1967. Lawyer Visalia, Calif., 1964—; ptnr. Crowe, Mitchell & Crowe, 1971-85; bd. dirs. World Parts Industries, Willson Ranch Co., pres. 1997—; referee State Bar Ct., 1976-82; gen. counsel Sierra Wine, 1986—. Bd. dirs. Mt. Whitney Area Coun. Boys Scouts Am., 1966-85, pres., 1971, 72; bd. dirs. Visalia Associated In-Group Donors (AID), 1973-81, pres., 1978-79, Tulare County Libr. Found.; mem. Visalia Airport Commn., 1982-90. 1st lt. U.S. Army, 1962-64; mem. Army Res. Forces Policy Com., 1995-99, chmn., 1997-99. Decorated D.S.M. with Oak Leaf Cluster, Legion of Merit with oak leaf cluster, Meritorious Svc. Medal with 3 oak leaf clusters, Army Commendation Medal; named Young Man of Yr., Visalia, 1973; Senator Jr. Chamber Internat., 1970; recipient Silver Beaver awrd Boy Scouts Am., 1983. Mem. ABA, Tulare County Bar Assn., Nat. Assn. R.R. Trial Counsel, State Bar Calif., Visalia C. of C. (pres. 1979-80), Rotary (pres. 1980-81). Republican. Roman Catholic. Home: 3939 W School Ave Visalia CA 93291-5514

CROWE, ROBERT WILLIAM, lawyer, mediator; b. Chgo., Aug. 20, 1924; s. Harry James and Miriam (McCune) C.; m. Virginia C. Kelley, Mar. 25, 1955 (dec. Feb. 1976); children—Robert Kelley, William Park; m. Elizabeth F. Roenisch, Oct. 22, 1977. A.B., U. Chgo., 1948, J.D., 1949. Bar: Ill. 1949. Practice in Chgo., 1949-57; with R.R. Donnelley & Sons Co., Chgo., 1957-83; sec. R.R. Donnelley & Sons Co., 1965-83, v.p., 1970-83; chmn. Resolve Dispute Mgmt. Inc., Chgo., 1983-92; pres. Dearborn Inst. for Conflict Resolution, Chgo., 1992-94; dir. Peoria Jour. Star, Inc., 1972-95. Bd. dirs. Chgo. Child Care Soc., 1963—; trustee Christian Century Found., 1966—; vis. com. U. Chgo. Divinity Sch. Served to 1st lt. USAAF, 1943-45. Decorated Air medal with 5 oak leaf clusters. Mem. ABA, Chgo. Bar Assn., Law Club (Chgo.), Legal Club (Chgo.), Econ. Club (Chgo.), Univ. Club (Chgo.). Presbyterian. Home and Office: 1228 Westmoor Rd Winnetka IL 60093-1845 *Cultivate a sense of gratitude as an approach to all of life, for the gift of life itself and for the potential for finding something joyful, empowering or at least instructive in every circumstance. These are the seeds for sharing the best of one's life with others.*

CROWE, RUSSELL, actor; b. Wellington, New Zealand, Apr. 7, 1964. Appeared in films The Crossing, 1993, The Quick and the Dead, 1995, Proof, 1995, Romper Stomper, 1995, Rough Magic, 1995, Virtuosity, 1995, Under the Gun, 1995, Heaven's Burning, 1997, Breaking Up, 1997, L.A. Confidential, 1997, Gladiator, 1999, Mystery Alaska, 1999, Man of the Peoples, 1999. Office: ICM 8942 Wilshire Blvd Beverly Hills CA 90211-1934*

CROWE, SHELBY, educational specialist, consultant; b. Irvine, Ky., July 5, 1935; s. Claude and Lena (Clem) C.; m. Ina House, May 22, 1961 (div. 1977); children: Craig, Cara; m. Bonnie Wohlslagel, Aug. 6, 1977; children: Tyler, Trisha, Matthew. BA in Edn., Ea. Ky. U., 1958; MEd, Miami U., Oxford, Ohio, 1961; PhD in Ednl. Founds., Ohio State U., 1980. Cert. permanent spl. K-12 art edn. tchr., Ohio. Tchr. Cin. Pub. Schs., 1958-66; tchr. McGuffey Lab. Sch. Miami U., Oxford, Ohio, 1966-70; prof. edn. Wright State U., Dayton, Ohio, 1970-88, U. Dayton, 1988-90; ednl. specialist Dorothy Lane Markets, Dayton, 1990—; cooperating tchr. U. Cin., 1960-66; instr. Ohio U., 1966; instr. Morehead (Ky.) State U., summers 1964-65; adj. prof. Union for Experimenting Colls. and Univs., Cin., 1982; condr. insvc. workshops, presenter in field local, regional, state and nat. level. Contbr. book revs. to various publs. Recipient Teaching Excellence award Wright State U. Coll. Edn., 1981, 82, Wright State U. Alumni Assn., 1982, Faculty Mem. of Yr. award Wright State U. Student Govt., 1985,. Mem. NEA, ASCD, AAUP, Nat. Coun. for Scoial Studies Edn., Ohio Confedn. Tchr. Edn. Orgns., Ohio Edn. Assn., Nat. Art Edn. Assn. (Students Best Educator award 1973), Ohio Art Edn. Assn., Phi Delta Kappa. Home: 412 Corona Ave Dayton OH 45419-2605

CROWE, THOMAS LEONARD, lawyer; b. Amsterdam, N.Y., Aug. 3, 1944; s. Leonard Hoctor and Grace Agnes (O'Malley) C.; m. Barbara Ann Hauck, Aug. 2, 1969; children: Patrick, Brendan. AB, Georgetown U., 1966, JD, 1969. Law clk. to chief judge U.S. Dist. Ct. (no. dist.), Elkins, W.Va., 1969-70; trial atty. U.S. Dept. Justice, Washington, 1970-72; asst. U.S. atty. Balt., 1973-78; chief of criminal div. U.S. Atty.'s Office, Balt., 1977-78; ptnr. Cable, McDaniel, Bowie & Bond, Balt., 1979-91, McGuire, Woods, Battle & Boothe, Balt., 1991-95; of counsel Monshower & Miller, LLP, Columbia, Md., 1996-98; pvt. practice Balt., 1998—; mem. jud. conf. U.S. Ct. Appeals for 4th Cir. Fellow Md. Bar Found.; mem. ABA, Fed. Bar Assn. (pres. Balt. chpt. 1981-82), Md. Bar Assn., Barristers Club (pres. 1990-91),. Democrat. Roman Catholic. Home: 11 Osborne Ave Baltimore MD 21228-4935 Office: Law Offices of Thomas L Crowe 1622 The World Trade Ctr 401 E Pratt St Baltimore MD 21202

CROWE, WILLIAM JAMES, JR., diplomat, think tank executive; b. La Grange, Ky., Jan. 2, 1925; s. William James and Eula (Russell) C.; m. Shirley Mary Grennell, Feb. 14, 1954; children: William Blake, James Brent, Mary Russell. BS, U.S. Naval Acad., 1946; MA in Edn., Stanford U., 1956; PhD in Politics (Harold W. Dodds fellow), Princeton U., 1965. Commd. ensign U.S. Navy, 1946, advanced through grades to adm.; comdg. officer U.S.S. Trout, 1960-62; comdr. Submarine Div. 31 San Diego, 1966-67; sr. adviser Vietnamese Navy, 1970-71; dep. to Pres.'s Spl. Rep. for Micronesian Status Negotiations, 1971-73; dep. dir. strategic plans CNO Staff, 1973-75; dir. East Asia and Pacific region Office of Sec. of Def. Washington, until 1976; comdr. Middle East Force Bahrain, 1976-77; dep. chief naval ops. plans and policy Washington, 1977-80; comdr.-in-chief Allied Forces So. Europe, 1980-83, comdr.-in-chief Pacific, 1983-85; chmn. Joint Chiefs of Staff, 1985-89; prof. geopolitics U. Okla., Norman, 1989-94; chmn. Fgn. Intelligence Adv. Bd., Washington, DC, 1993-94; U.S. amb. to U.K. London, 1994-97; counselor Ctr. for Strategic and Internat. Studies, Washington, 1989-94; prof. U. Okla., 1989-94. Author: Line of Fire, 1993; co-author: Reducing Nuclear Danger: The Road Away from the Brink, 1993; author supr. ops. plan for repatriation of U.S.S. Pueblo crew. Decorated Defense DSM with three oak leaf clusters (Dept. Def.), Navy DSM with two oak leaf clusters (USN), DSM (U.S. Army, USAF, USCG), Legion of Merit, Bronze Star with combat V, Air medal with six oak leaf clusters. Mem. U.S. Naval Inst., Am. Polit. Sci. Assn., Internat. Studies Assn., Coun. on Fgn. Rels., Washington Inst. Fgn. Affairs, Phi Gamma Delta, Phi Delta Phi. Office: Global Options Ste 1350 1615 L St NW Washington DC 20036-5610

CROWE, WILLIAM JOSEPH, librarian; b. Boston, Feb. 27, 1947; s. William J. and Mary (Dawley) C.; m. Nancy P. Sanders, June 10, 1978; children: Katherine. BA in European history with highest honors, Boston State Coll., 1968; MLS, Rutgers U., 1969; PhD in Adminstrn. Acad. Librs., Ind. U., 1986. Cataloger Boston Pub. Libr., 1969-70, asst. to acquisitions libr., 1970-71; coord. processing Ind. U. Librs., Bloomington, 1971-76, asst. to dean univ. librs., 1977-79; mgmt. intern U. Mich. Libr., Ann Arbor, 1976-77; asst. to dir. librs. Ohio State U., Columbus, 1979-83, asst. dir. librs. adminstrn. and tech. svcs., 1983-90; dean librs. U. Kans., Lawrence, 1990-96, vice chancellor, 1996-99, libr. Spencer Rsch. Libr., 1999—; cons. Newberry Libr., Chgo., 1989; alternate del. Ind. Gov.'s Conf. Librs. and Info. Svcs., 1978; co-prin. investigator Am. fiction 1901-25 Dept. Edn., 1983-85; tech. mgr. project Am. fiction 1901-25 NEH, 1988-90; trustee Online Computer Lit. Ctr., 1996—. Contbr. articles to profl. jours. Sr. fellow UCLA, 1991. Mem. ALA, Kans. Libr. Assn., Beta Phi Mu, Phi Alpha Theta. Home: 910 E 850th Rd Lawrence KS 66047-9578 Office: U Kans Office Vice Chancellor Info Svcs Spencer Rsch Libr Lawrence KS 66045-2800 *We must work to expand the next generation's opportunity for education--to foster greater equality of intellectual privilege.*

CROWELL, CRAVEN H., JR., federal agency administrator; b. Nashville, Aug. 27, 1943; s. Craven H. and Addie Ailene (Cooper) C.; m. Fredricka Friedli, Nov. 27, 1970; 1 child, Stephanie Kaye. BA, Lipscomb U., 1965. Reporter, city editor Nashville Tennessean, 1964-77; press sec. Senator Jim Sasser, 1977-80, chief of staff, 1989-93; dir. info. Tenn. Valley Authority, 1980-87, v.p. govtl. and pub. affairs, 1987-89, chmn. bd. dirs., 1993—; bd. dirs., mem. exec. com. Nuclear Energy Inst.; vice chair bd. dirs., mem. exec. com. Electric Power Rsch. Inst. Hon. pres. Pohai U., China, 1997. With USMC, USNR. Recipient Nat. Headliner award, 1969; named Alumnus of Yr. Lipscomb U., 1995. Mem. Econ. Club of N.Y., Pi Delta Epsilon. Mem. Ch. of Christ. Office: Tennessee Valley Authority 400 W Summit Hill Dr Knoxville TN 37999-0002

CROWELL, JOHN B., JR., lawyer, former government official; b. Elizabeth, N.J., Mar. 18, 1930; s. John B. and Anna B. (Trull) C.; m. Rebecca Margaret McCue, Feb. 13, 1954; children—John P., Patrick E., Ann M. A.B., Dartmouth Coll., 1952; LL.B., Harvard U., 1957. Bar: N.J. bar 1958, Oreg. bar 1959. Law clk. to Judge Gerald McLaughlin U.S. Ct. Appeals, Newark, 1957-59; atty. Ga.-Pacific Corp., Portland, Oreg., 1959-72; gen. counsel La.-Pacific Corp., Portland, 1972-81; asst. sec. for natural resources and environment Dept. Agr., Washington, 1981-85; ptnr. Lane Powell Spears Lubersky, Portland, 1986—. Served with USN, 1952-54. Mem. ABA, Am. Ornithologists Union, Wilson Ornithol. Soc., Cooper Ornithol. Soc., Soc. Am. Foresters, Soil Conservation Soc. Am. Republican. Presbyterian. Club: Univ. (Portland). Home: 1185 Hallinan Cir Lake Oswego OR 97034-4970 Office: Lane Powell Spears Lubersky 520 SW Yamhill St Ste 800 Portland OR 97204-1383

CROWELL, JOHN C(HAMBERS), geology educator, researcher; b. State College, Pa., May 12, 1917; s. James White and Helen Hunt (Chambers) C.; m. Betty Marie Bruner, Nov. 22, 1946; 1 child, Martha Lynn Crowell Bobroskie. BS in Geology, U. Tex., 1939; MA in Oceanographic meteorology, Scripps Inst. Oceanography UCLA, 1946; PhD in Geology, UCLA, 1947; DSc (hon.), U. Louvain, Belgium, 1966. Geologist Shell Oil Co., Inc., Ventura, Calif., 1941-42; from instr. to prof. geology UCLA, 1947-67, chmn. dept., 1957-60, 63-66; prof. geology U. Calif., Santa Barbara, 1967-87, prof. emeritus, 1987, rsch. geologist Inst. for Crustal Studies, 1987—; chmn. Office of Earth Scis., NRC, Nat. Acad. Scis., 1979-82. Served to capt. U.S. Army USAAF, 1942-46. Fellow Geol. Soc. Am. (Penrose medal 1995), Am. Acad. Arts and Scis.; mem. Am. Assn. Petroleum Geologists, Am. Geophys. Union, AAAS, Am. Inst. Profl. Geologists, Nat. Acad. Scis. Spl. research structural geology, tectonics, interpretation sedimentary rocks, studies Andreas fault system, tectonics Calif. ancient glaciation, continental drift. Home: 300 Hot Springs Rd Montecito CA 93108-2038 Office: U Calif Inst for Crustal Studies Santa Barbara CA 93106

CROWELL, KENNETH E., lawyer, chemical engineer; b. Kearny, N.J., Dec. 29, 1957; s. Earl L.S. and Moira Parker (Foster) C.; m. Liliana Mino, June 24, 1990. BS in Biology, Allegheny Coll., 1979; BSChemE, N.J. Inst. Tech., 1984, MS in Chem. Engring., 1992; JD, Rutgers U., 1997. Registered profl. engr., N.J.; bar: N.J., N.Y. Tech. sales rep. Armak divsn. Akzo N.V., Chgo., 1979-82; prodn. mgr. Drew Chem. divsn. Ashland Oil, Kearny, N.J., 1984-87; sr. chem. engr. Jacobs Engring. Group, Mountainside, N.J., 1987-92; sr. environ. engr. Schering Plough Corp., Union, N.J., 1992-94; assoc. Milbank, Tweed, Hadley & McCloy LLP, N.Y.C., 1997—. Author: Handbook of Biotechnology, 1997. Mem. ABA, AIChE, N.Y. State Bar Assn., Essex County Bar Assn., Bar Assn. of City of N.Y., Order of the Coif, Tau Beta Pi. Avocation: fly fishing. Home: 40 Mitchell Rd Gillette NJ 07933-1428 Office: Milbank Tweed Hadley and McCloy LLP 1 Chase Manhattan Plz Fl 47 New York NY 10005-1413

CROWELL, RICHARD LANE, microbiology educator; b. Springfield, Mo., Sept. 27, 1930; s. Thomas Rolla and Addie Malinda (Lane) C.; m. Arlene Mildred Prell, June 27, 1953; children: Steven Richard, Kathleen Margaret Crowell Miller, Barbara Lane, Wendy Jane. BA, U. Buffalo, 1952; MS, U. Minn., 1954, PhD, 1958. Instr. microbiology U. Minn. Med. Sch., Mpls., 1958-60; asst. prof. Allegheny U. (formerly Med. Coll. Pa. and Hahnemann U. Sch. Medicine, Phila., 1960-64, assoc. prof., 1964-71, prof., 1971—, chmn. microbiology and immunology, 1979-95, emeritus prof., 1995—; rsch. cons. Smith Kline Corp., Phila., 1975-77, Lehn and Fink Co., Montvale, N.J., 1976-80; ad hoc reviewer NIH, Bethesda, Md., 1966—. Editor: Tumor Virus Infections and Immunity, 1976; Virus Attachment and Entry into Cells, 1986, Innovations in Antiviral Development and the Detection of Virus Infections, 1992; assoc. editor Jour. Microbial Pathogenesis, 1985-91, mem. editl. bd., 1991—. Recipient Lindback award Hahnemann U. Sch. Medicine, 1967-68; NIH rsch. career devel. awardee, 1962-72. Fellow Am. Acad. Microbiology; mem. Am. Soc. Virology, Am. Soc. Microbiology (pres. 1991-92, pres. eastern Pa. br. 1974-76), Found. for Microbiology (lectr. 1994-96), Assn. Med. Sch. Microbiology Chairmen (pres. U.S. and Can. 1986), Am. Assn. Immunologists, Phi Beta Kappa, Sigma Xi. Democrat. Presbyterian. Avocations: camping; fishing. Home: 407 Hutchins Dr Ambler PA 19002-2822

CROWELL, SAMUEL MARVIN, JR., education educator; b. Lexington, N.C., May 8, 1949; s. Samuel Marvin and Margaret Louise (Riddle) C.; m. Deborah Jane Costolo, Jan. 1, 1987; 1 child, Chesley Carole. BA, Carson-Newman Coll., 1971; MS, Radford U., 1975; EdD, U. Va., 1992. Tchr. elem. edn. Carroll County Sch. Dist., Hillsville, Va., 1971-73; dir. career opportunities program Carroll County Schs., Hillsville, 1973-75, prin., 1975-78; dir. elem. edn., dir. ednl. adminstrn. U. Redlands, Calif., 1982-87; prof. Calif. State U., San Bernardino, 1987—; coord. elem. edn. Calif. State U., San Bernardino, 1987-89, dir. Ctr. for Rsch. in Integrative Studies, 1989—. Author: Mindshifts, 1994, Reenchantment of Learning, 1997; contbr. chpts. and articles to profl. publs. Mem. Idyllwild (Calif.) Environ. Group, 1993—, Idyllwild Poetry Readings, 1995—. Mem. ASCD, Phi Beta Delta, Phi Delta Kappa. Avocations: poet, naturalist, Tai Chi. Home: PO Box 1511 Idyllwild CA 92549-1511 Office: 5500 Univ Pky San Bernardino CA 92407

CROWL, JOHN ALLEN, retired publishing company executive; b. Winchester, Va., Aug. 10, 1935; s. John Decatur and Cora Elizabeth (LLoyd) C.; m. Dana Jane Bernasek, Aug. 27, 1960 (div. 1986); 1 son, Patrick Joseph; m. Gaal Shepherd, Feb. 10, 1988. B.A., U. Md., 1957, M.A., 1961; LhD (hon.), Lebanon Valley Coll., 1993. Instr. Staunton (Va.) Mil. Acad., 1958-59; asst. dir. public relations Johns Hopkins U., Balt., 1961-64; asso. dir. Editorial Projects for Edn., Inc., Balt. and Washington, 1964-75; v.p. Editorial Projects for Edn., Inc., 1975-78; asso. editor Chronicle of Higher Edn., Washington, 1966-72; mng. editor Chronicle of Higher Edn., 1972-79, pub., 1978-91, v.p., 1979-92. Contbg. editor Vermont Mag., 1995—. Trustee Vt. Folklife Ctr., 1994—, Vt. Arts Coun., 1994-98; trustee Planned Parenthood of No. New Eng., 1994—, chair 1997-99. With U.S. Army, 1958. Recipient Edn. Writers award AAUP, 1971. Home: Thistle Hill North Pomfret VT 05053

CROWL, SAMUEL RENNINGER, former university dean, English language educator, author; b. Toledo, Oct. 9, 1940; s. Lester Samuel and Margaret Elizabeth (Renninger) C.; m. Susan Richardson, Dec. 29, 1963; children: Miranda Paine, Samuel Emerson. AB, Hamilton Coll., 1962; MA, Ind. U., 1969, PhD, 1970. Resident lectr. Ind. U., Indpls., 1967-69; asst. prof. English, Ohio U., Athens, 1970-75, assoc. prof., 1975-80, prof., 1980—, dean Univ. Coll., 1981-92, trustee prof. Eng., 1992—; cons. NEH, Washington, 1980—; observer Royal Shakespeare Co. Mem. Ohio Humanities Coun., 1985-91, Ohio Student Loan Commn., 1985-88. Author: Shakespeare Observed: Studies in Performance on Stage and Screen, 1992; co-author: Ohio University's Educational Plan, 1977-78; contbr. articles to profl. and Shakespearian jours. Recipient O'Bleness award for pub. broadcasting Ctr. Telecommunications, Ohio U., 1976, several awards disting. teaching. Fellow Royal Soc. Arts (London); mem. Nat. Assn. Univ. and Gen. Coll. Deans (pres. 1991—), Nat. Humanities Faculty, Ohio Shakespeare Assn. (founding mem.), Ohio U. Alumni Assn. (hon.), Univ. Club (Chgo.), Phi Kappa Phi. Avocations: Royal Shakespeare Co., Detroit Tigers. Office: Ohio U Eng Dept Ellis Hall Athens OH 45701

CROWLEY, ANNA AVRA, secondary education educator, historian; b. Chgo., June 13, 1957; d. Samuel Harry and Theresa (Coroneos) Tzakis; m. James F. Crowley, July 25, 1982; children: Theresa Maria, Michael James. BA, Northwestern U., 1973; postgrad., Lake Forest Coll., 1994—. Cert. bus., English, social studies tchr., Ill. State Bd. Edn. Adminstr. asst. Water Reclamation Dist. Greater Chgo., 1973-80; adminstr. asst. to mid. east regional dir. Lockwood Greene Inc., Athens, Greece, 1980-81; tchr. Elgin (Ill.) H.S., 1982-85; specialist writing tutor Coll. Lake County, 1993-94; libr. asst., rsch. asst. Deerfield H.S., 1994-96; tchr. Holy Trinity H.S., Chgo., 1996-97, Regina Dominican H.S., Wilmette, Ill., 1997—; asst. spl. events coord., adminstr. asst. Comdisco Inc., Rosemont, Ill, 1979, 81; sec., treas. North Shore Videos To Go, Lake Forest, Ill, 1982-95; pres., resident historian Am. Aristocracy Inc., Bannockburn, Ill., 1992—. Writer, prodr.: (TV show) Windy City Castles, 1996. Scholar State Ill. Edn. Dept, 1969, Ahepa Orgn., 1969. Mem. Nat. Trust Hist. Preservation, Lake Forest/Lake Bluft Hist. Soc., Preservation Found. Lake Forest/Lake Bluff, Hellenic Women's Philanthropic Assn. (recording sec. 1982-97),. Eastern Orthodox. Avocations: writing music, historical research. Home: 1497 W Fork Dr Lake Forest IL 60045-3540

CROWLEY, CYNTHIA JOHNSON, secondary school educator; b. Summit, N.J., June 28, 1930; d. Theodore Eames and Frances Lysett (Wetmore) J.; m. Robert J. Crowley, Sept. 6, 1952 (dec.); children: David Cochrane II, Cynthia Wetmore. BA, U. Pa., 1952; MA, Fairleigh-Dickinson U., Rutherford, N.J. Cert. English tchr., N.J. Tchr. econs. and reading St. Mary's Sch., Peekskill, N.Y., 1952-53; tchr. humanities Henry Hudson Regional Sch., Highlands, N.J., 1969-92, coord. gifted program, 1983-92; pres. Associated Ednl. Svcs.; active N.J. Curriculum Revision Project; adv. bd. mem. Women's Athletics U. Pa., N.J. Council U.S. Congressional Awards Program; ednl. cons.; cons., lectr. creative writing workshops; mem. secondary sch. admissions com. U. Pa. Prodr. TV Tutor Series for Home and Schs. Former mem. Atlantic Highlands (N.J.) Bd. Edn., also past pres.; chair women's athletic bd. U. Pa., 1992—; mem. exec. com. Monmouth County Sch. Bds. Assn. Team Room named in her honor U. Pa., 1997; elected U. Pa. Hall of Fame, 1998. Mem. ASCD, Nat. Coun. Tchrs. English, Nat. Acad. TV Arts and Scis. (N.Y. chpt.), Gifted Educators (exec. com. 1986—), Shore Consortium for Gifted and Talented, Alumni Pres.'s Coun. Ind. Secondary Schs. (life, past pres.), Phi Delta Kappa. Home: 125 E Mount Ave Atlantic Highlands NJ 07716-1549

CROWLEY, DANIEL FRANCIS, JR., transportation and logistics executive; b. Yonkers, N.Y., Oct. 23, 1949; s. Daniel F. and Margaret M. (Murphy) C.; m. Karen E. Williams, Dec. 18, 1982; children: Daniel, Ryan. BA in Lit., Columbia U., 1971, MBA in Fin., 1973. Mem. audit staff Arthur Andersen & Co., N.Y.C., 1973-78; audit mgr. Arthur Andersen & Co., London, 1978-81; dir. internal audit IMS Internat. Inc., London, 1981-82, contr. pharmacy svcs. divsn., 1982-83; exec. v.p., bd. dirs. Pharmassist, Inc., Dallas, 1983-84; sr. mgr. Coopers & Lybrand, N.Y.C., 1985-90; v.p. audit Grand Met. Food Sector, Mpls., 1990-91; v.p., contr. Grand Met./Green Giant USA, Mpls., 1991-92; v.p., ops. contr. Grand Met./Pillsbury, Mpls., 1992-93, v.p. reengring., 1993-95; v.p., contr. food sector Grand Met, London, 1995; dir. Pearle Vision, Inc., 1995-97; sr. v.p., CFO, Pearle Vision/Grand Met, Dallas, 1995-97; v.p. planning Frito-Lay Internat., Plano, Tex., 1997-98; exec. v.p., CFO BAX Global/Pittston, 1998—; bd. dirs. Pearle

Vision, Inc., 1995-97; treas. Grand Met/Pearle Found., Dallas, 1995-97. Treas. Grand Met/Pillsbury Found., Mpls., 1991-93. Mem. AICPA. Home: 3815 Vista Azul San Clemente CA 92672 Office: BAX Global 16808 Armstrong Ave Irvine CA 92606-4936

CROWLEY, GEOFFREY THOMAS, airline executive; b. St. Catherines, Ont., Can., Oct. 8, 1952; came to U.S., 1959; s. Douglas Geoffrey and Joan Margaret (Ratley) C.; m. Linda Anne Buckelew, Jan. 30, 1986; 4 children. BS in Engring., Purdue U., 1974; MBA, Xavier U., 1977. Sr. cons. Booz, Allen & Hamilton TCD, Cin., 1974-77; dir. customer svc. quality assurance Tex. Internat. Airlines, Houston, 1977-80; gen. mgr. People Express Airlines, Newark, N.J., 1980-85; sr. v.p. mktg. and planning Presdl. Airways, Washington, 1985-89; v.p. sales and svc. Trump Shuttle, Inc., N.Y.C., 1989-91; v.p. mktg. alliances Northwest Airlines, Inc., St. Paul, Minn., 1991-93; chmn., pres., CEO Air Wisconsin Airlines Corp., Appleton, 1993—. Mem. Regional Airline Assn. (chmn. 1995-96, dir. 1994—), Wings Club (gov. 1995—). Office: Air Wisconsin Airlines Corp W6390 Challenger Dr Ste 203 Appleton WI 54915-9119*

CROWLEY, JAMES PATRICK, hematologist, medical educator; b. Birmingham, Eng., Oct. 13, 1943; came to U.S., 1947; s. Francis Michael and Rose Ann (Donaghy) C.; m. Carol Ann Crowley, Dec. 6, 1943; children: Jason W.F., James M. AB, Providence Coll., 1965; MD, Georgetown U., 1969; MA, Brown U., 1981. Intern Boston City Hosp./Harvard Med. Sch., 1969, resident, 1970; resident Mass. Gen. Hosp., Boston, 1971, Peter Bent Brigham Hosp., Boston, 1974; instr. medicine Harvard Med. Sch., Boston, 1974; asst. prof. medicine Brown U., Providence, 1975-81, assoc. prof., 1981-92, prof., 1992—; dir. hematology R.I. Hosp./Brown U., Providence, 1992—; bd. dirs. Providence Ambulatory Health Care Found., Inc.; cons. Naval Blood Rsch. Program, USN, 1977—; adj. prof. medicine Tufts U. Sch. Vet. Medicine, 1986—. Author: Principles of Transfusion Medicine, 2nd edit., 1995; contbr. articles to profl. jours. Mem. Retirement Bd. City of Providence, 1993—; physician Camp Yawgoog Boy Scouts Am., 1992—. Capt. USNR, 1971-95, ret. Recipient Transfusion Medicine Acad. award NIH, 1984-89, award R.I. Blood Banking Soc., 1986. Mem. Am. Soc. Hematology, R.I. Med. Soc. (pres. 1992-93), Providence Med. Assn., (pres. 1992-92), Mt. Tom Club (v.p. 1994). Democrat. Roman Catholic. Achievements include important contbns. to the devel. of successful system for freezing blood and deglycerolizing blood for transfusion on Navy hosp. ships, successful demonstration that erythropoeitin could enhance autologous pre-donation prior to orthopedic surgery and the immunosuppressive effects of passenger leukocytes during allogeneic transfusion. Office: RI Hosp 593 Eddy St Providence RI 02903-4971

CROWLEY, JAMES WORTHINGTON, retired lawyer, business consultant, investor; b. Cookville, Tenn., Feb. 18, 1930; s. Worth and Jessie (Officer) C.; m. Laura June Bauserman, Jan. 27, 1951; children: James Kenneth, Laura Cynthia; m. Joyce A. Goode, Jan. 15, 1966; children: John Worthington, Noelle Virginia; m. Carol Golden, Sept. 4, 1981. BA, George Washington U., 1950, LLB, 1953. Bar: D.C. 1954. Underwriter, spl. agt. Am. Surety Co. of N.Y., Washington, 1953-56; adminstrv. asst., contract adminstr. Atlantic Rsch. Corp., Alexandria, Va., 1956-59; mgr. legal dept., asst. sec., counsel Atlantic Rsch. Corp., 1959-65, sec., legal mgr., counsel, 1965-67; sec., legal mgr., counsel Susquehanna Corp. (merger with Atlantic Rsch. Corp.), 1967-70; pres., dir. Gen. Communication Co., Boston, 1962-70; v.p., gen. counsel E-Systems, Inc., 1970-95, sec., 1976-95; ret., 1995; ind. cons. bus. and fin., investor Dallas, 1995—; v.p., asst. sec., dir. Cemco, Inc.; v.p., dir. TAI, Inc., Serv-air, Inc., Greenville, Tex., Engring. Rsch. Assocs., Inc., Vienna, Va., HRB Systems, Inc., State Coll., Pa.; mem. adv. bd. sec. Internat. and Comparative Law Ctr.; v.p., sec., dir. Advanced Video Products, 1992-95; v.p., sec., gen. counsel E-Systems Med. Electronics, Inc., 1992-95. Mem. Am. Soc. Corp. Secs. (pres. Dallas regional group 1988-89, nat. dir. 1989-92), Inf. Mus. Assn., Nat. Security Indsl. Assn., Mfrs.' Alliance for Productivity and Innovation (mem. law coun.), Omicron Delta Kappa, Alpha Chi Sigma, Phi Sigma Kappa. Republican. Baptist. Home and Office: 16203 Spring Creek Rd Dallas TX 75248-3116

CROWLEY, JEROME JOSEPH, JR., investment company executive; b. South Bend, Ind., Sept. 18, 1939; s. Jerome J. and Rosaleen C.; m. Carol Ann Ellithorn, June 23, 1962; children: Michael, Karen, Brian, Colleen. BS, U. Notre Dame, 1961; MBA, U. Chgo., 1967. With O'Brien Corp., Mountain View, Calif., 1965—, pres., 1975—. With USMC, 1961-65. Roman Catholic. Office: O'Brien Corp 2483 Old Middlefield Way Mountain View CA 94043-2359

CROWLEY, JOHN CHARLES, academic director; b. Batavia, N.Y., Sept. 4, 1941; s. Bernard Joseph and Margaret Mae Crowley; m. Ellen Maureen McCarthy, May 25, 1968; children: Kathleen, Michael. BS, St. John Fisher Coll., 1963; MPA, Syracuse U., 1967, PhD, 1977. Asst. dir. admissions St. John Fisher Coll., Rochester, N.Y., 1965-66; assoc. Cresap, McCormick and Paget, Mgmt. Cons., N.Y.C., 1967-70; asst. exec. sec. Assn. Am. Univs., Washington, 1972-74, assoc. exec. sec., 1974-78, dir. fed. rels. for sci. rsch., 1978-83, v.p., 1983-91; spl. asst. to pres., dir. Washington office MIT, Cambridge, Mass., 1991—; cons. U.S. Dept. Transp., Washington, 1971-72, Am. Coun. on Edn., Washington, 1972. Bd. dirs. Nat. Assn. Ind. Colls. and Univs., Washington, 1993-96; pres. parish coun. Holy Trinity Ch., Washington, 1984-86. With U.S. Army, 1964-70. Recipient Mid-Career award Soc. Nat. Security and Def. Adminstrn., 1990, Disting. Svc. award Assn. Am. Univs., 1991. Fellow AAAS. Avocations: travel, history, family. E-mail: jcrowley@mit.edu. Office: MIT Washington Office 410 820 1st St NE Washington DC 20002

CROWLEY, JOHN CRANE, real estate developer; b. Detroit, June 29, 1919; s. Edward John and Leah Helen (Crane) C.; m. Barbara Wenzel Gilfillan, Jan. 12, 1945; children: F. Alexander, Leonard, Philip, Eliot, Louise, Sylvia. BA, Swarthmore Coll., 1941; MS, U. Denver, 1943. Asst. dir. Mcpl. Finance Officers Assn., Chgo., 1946-48; So. Calif. mgr. League Calif. Cities, Los Angeles, 1948-53; mgr. City of Monterey Park, Calif., 1953-56; founder, exec. v.p. Nat. Med. Enterprises, L.A., 1968; pres. Ventura Towne House (Calif.), 1963-96; mem. faculty U. So. Calif. Sch. Pub. Adminstrn., 1950-53; bd. dirs. Regional Inst. of So. Calif., The L.A. Partnership 2000, Burbank-Glendale-Pasadena Airport Authority. Trustee Pacific Oaks Friends Sch. and Coll., Pasadena, 1954-57, 92-98, Swarthmore Coll., 1987—; bd. dirs. Pasadena Area Liberal Arts Ctr., 1962-72, pres., 1965-68; bd. dirs. Pacificulture Found. and Asia Mus., 1971-76, pres., 1972-74; bd. dirs. Nat. Mcpl. League, 1986-92, AAF Rose Bowl Aquatics Ctr., 1997—; chmn. Pasadena Cultural Heritage Commn., 1975-78; city dir. Pasadena, 1979-91; mayor City of Pasadena, 1986-88; bd. dirs. Western Justice Ctr., 1992—, v.p., 1995—, LA County Commn. on Efficiency and Economy, 1994—. Sloan Found. fellow, 1941-43; recipient Arthur Nobel award City of Pasadena. Mem. Am. Soc. Pub. Adminstrn. (local chpt., Winston Crouch award 1990), Internat. City Mgmt. Assn., Nat. Mcpl. League (nat. bd. 1980-92, Disting. Citizen award, 1984), Inst. Pub. Adminstrn. (sr. assoc.), Phi Delta Theta. Democrat. Unitarian. Home: 615 Linda Vista Ave Pasadena CA 91105-1122

CROWLEY, JOHN FRANCIS, III, university dean; b. New Haven, Jan. 29, 1945; s. John Francis Jr. and Anna Cecil (Elliott) C.; m. Alice Ann Kennedy, Dec. 26, 1970; children: John Francis IV, Sarah Ann. BA in History, Art History, U. Okla., 1970, MA in Regional and City Planning, 1973, PhD in Urban Geography, 1977. Planner Lawton Urban Renewal Authority, Okla., 1971-72; dir. planning City of Seminole, Okla., 1972-73; chief planner Okla. Divsn. State Parks, Oklahoma City, 1973-74; asst. prof. environ. design U. Ga., Athens, 1974-78, dean Sch. Environ. Design, 1996—; exec. dir. Tulsa Metro Area Planning Commn., 1978-80; v.p., devel. Williams Realty Corp., Tulsa, 1980-87; pres. Urbantech Inc., Tulsa, 1987—; dir. Okla. Dept. of Transp., Oklahoma City, 1993-95. Bd. dirs. Downtown Tulsa Unltd., 1983-89; chmn. Sales Tax Overview Com., Tulsa, 1988-90; sec. bd. trustees Tulsa County Pub. Facilities Authority, 1983-96. 1st lt. U.S. Army, 1965-69. Sara Moss faculty fellow U. Ga., 1976. Mem. Am. Soc. Landscape Architects, Am. Inst. Cert. Planners, Am. Planning Assn., Nature Conservancy, Urban Land Inst. Democrat. Roman Catholic. Avocations: art, sports, travel. Home: 335 Crystal Ct Athens GA 30606-3245

CROWLEY, JOHN W(ILLIAM), English language educator; b. New Haven, Dec. 27, 1945; s. John Adam and Mary T. (McKenna) C.; m. Sheila A. Myers, Mar. 17, 1967 (div. 1977); children: Matthew, Anne; m. Susan Wolstenholme, May 27, 1978; children: Raphael, Mary. BA, Yale U., 1967; MA, Ind. U., 1969, PhD, 1970. Asst. prof. English Syracuse (N.Y.) U., 1970-74, assoc. prof., 1974-79, prof., 1979—, dir. humanities doctoral program, 1985-88, 96—, dir. grad. studies, 1986-89, chair, 1989-92. Author: George Cabot Lodge, 1976, The Black Heart's Truth, 1985, The Mask of Fiction, 1989, The White Logic, 1994, The Dean of American Letters, 1999; editor: New Essays on Winesburg, Ohio, 1990, Genteel Pagan, 1991, The Sunnier Side, 1996, The Rise of Silas Lapham, 1996, Drunkard's Progress, 1999; co-editor: The Haunted Dusk, 1983. Hon. Woodrow Wilson fellow, 1967; NDEA fellow, 1967-70; Nat. Endowment for Humanities summer stipend, 1975. Mem. Phi Beta Kappa. Democrat. Home: 66 E Lake Rd Skaneateles NY 13152-1321 Office: Dept of English Syracuse U Syracuse NY 13244-1170

CROWLEY, JOSEPH, congressman; b. Queens County, N.Y., Mar. 16, 1962. BA, Queens Coll., 1985. Mem. N.J. Gen. Assembly, 1987-98, U.S. Congress from 7th N.Y. dist., Washington, 1998—; standing com. in banking N.J. State Assembly, elec. law com., consumer affairs com., labor & housing com., chmn. racing & wagering com; mem. Com. on Internat. Rels., Com. Resources. Mem. Cavan Men's Assn., VFW, K. of C. Office: US Ho of Reps 1517 Longworth HOB Washington DC 20515

CROWLEY, JOSEPH MICHAEL, electrical engineer, educator; b. Phila., Sept. 9, 1940; s. Joseph Edward and Mary Veronica (McCall) C.; m. Barbara Ann Sauerwald, June 22, 1963; children: Joseph W., Kevin, James, Michael, Daniel. B.S., MIT, 1962, M.S., 1963, Ph.D., 1965. Vis. scientist Max Planck Inst., Goettingen, W.Ger, 1965-66; asst. prof. elec. engring. U. Ill., Urbana, 1966-69, assoc. prof., 1969-78, prof., dir. applied electrostats. research lab., 1978-88; pres. JMC Inc., 1981-91, Electrostatic Applications, 1986—; Piercey Disting. prof. chem. engring. U. Minn., 1993; adj. prof. U. Ill., 1988-94; cons. to several corps. Contbr. articles to profl. jours.; patentee ink jet printers. Pres. Champaign-Urbana Bd. Cath. Edn., 1978-80. Recipient Gen. Motors scholarship, 1958-62; AEC fellow, 1962-65; NATO fellow, 1965-66. Fellow IEEE, Electrostats. Soc. Am. (pres. 1992-95), Am. Phys. Soc., Soc. Inf. Display, Mensa. Roman Catholic.

CROWLEY, JOSEPH NEIL, university president, political science educator; b. Oelwein, Iowa, July 9, 1933; . James Bernard and Nina Mary (Neil) C.; m. Johanna Lois Reitz, Sept. 9, 1961; children: Theresa, Neil, Margaret, Timothy. BA, U. Iowa, 1959; MA, Calif. State U., Fresno, 1963; PhD (Univ. fellow), U. Wash., 1967. Reporter Fresno Bee, 1961-62; asst. prof. polit. sci. U. Nev., Reno, 1966-71, asso. prof., 1971-79, prof., 1979—, chmn. dept. polit. sci., 1976-78, pres., 1978—; bd. dirs. Citibank Nev.; policy formulation officer EPA, Washington, 1973-74; dir. instl. studies Nat. Commn. on Water Quality, Washington, 1974-75. Author: Democrats, Delegates and Politics in Nevada: A Grassroots Chronicle of 1972, 1976, Notes From the President's Chair, 1988, No Equal in the World: An Interpretation of the Academic Presidency, 1994; editor: (with R. Roelofs and D. Hardesty) Environment and Society, 1973. Mem. Commn. on Colls., 1980-87; mem. adv. comn. on mining and minerals rsch. U.S. Dept. Interior, 1985-91; mem. coun. NCAA, 1987-92, mem. pres.' commn., 1991-92, pres., 1993-95; bd. dirs. Nat. Consortium for Acads. and Sports, 1992—; mem. Honda Awards Program Adv. Bd., 1994—; bd. dirs., campaign chmn. No. Nev. United Way, 1985, 97—. Recipient Thornton Peace Prize U. Nev., 1971, Humanitarian of Yr. award NCCJ, 1986, Alumnus of Yr. award Calif. State U., 1989, ADL Champion of Liberty award, 1993, Disting. Alumni award U. Iowa, 1994, Giant Step award Ctr. for Study of Sport in Soc., 1994, William Anderson award AAHPERD, 1998; Nat. Assn. Schs. Pub. Affairs and Adminstrn. fellow, 1973-74. Mem. Nat. Assn. State Univs. and Land Grant Colls. (bd. dirs. 1998—). Roman Catholic. Home: 1265 Muir Dr Reno NV 89503-2629 Office: U Nev Office of Pres Reno NV 89557-0095

CROWLEY, JOSEPH R., bishop; b. Ft. Wayne, Ind., Jan. 12, 1915. Student, St. Mary's Coll., St. Mary, Ky., St. Meinrad (Ind.) Sem. Ordained priest Roman Cath. Ch., 1953. Ordained titular bishop of Maraguia and aux. bishop of Ft. Wayne-South Bend, Ind., 1971-90. Editor: Our Sunday Visitor, 1958-67. Office: 1240 Honan Dr South Bend IN 46614-2172*

CROWLEY, M. THERESE, broadcaster, singer, songwriter; b. Chgo., Sept. 30, 1958; d. Robert William and Cecelia (Smith) C. BS in Radio and TV, So. Ill. U., 1979. Program host WCIL AM/FM, Carbondale, Ill., 1977-79; news dir./program host KOPA AM/FM, Scottsdale, Ariz., 1979; anchor/corr. RKO Radio Networks, 1980-88; mng. editor/anchor United Stas. Radio Networks, 1988; vice pres. news and sports Unistar Radio Networks, N.Y.C., 1989; afternoon anchor/host WCBS Newsradio, N.Y.C., 1990—; vocalist nightclub bands, Chgo., 1974-77. Vocalist, Lyric Opera of Chgo. Children's Chorus, including Tosca and Werther, 1970-72; voiceover HBO original movies: Hostages, Doomsday Gun, 1993-94, CBS Television Network; backing vocals: Vineyard Sound 2, 1995; producer, singer/songwriter My Obsession, 1996. Recipient Nat. Headliner award, 1991, Best Spot News awards N.Y. Deadline Club, 1991, 93, Outstanding Spot News award N.Y. State Broadcasters Assn., 1991, 94, 95, RTNDA Regional Spot News award, 1994, AP Best Radio Spot News award for World Trade Ctr. bombing, 1993. Office: WCBS-Newsradio 51 W 52nd St New York NY 10019-6119*

CROWLEY, MARY ELIZABETH (MARY ELIZABETH CROWLEY-FARRELL), journalist, editor; b. Hackensack, N.J., Nov. 7, 1956; d. Jeremiah Christopher and Charlotte Mary (Keith) C.; m. William Christopher Farrell, Sept. 1, 1979; children: Eliza Carolyn Farrell, Luke Jeremiah Farrell. BA in Polit. Sci. & Comm. magna cum laude, Rutgers U., 1978; MA, U. Pa., 1980; postgrad., Trinity Coll., Dublin, Ireland. Reporter various local newspapers, 1974-77; regional corr. Capitol Hill News Svc., Washington, 1977; Washington corr. Thomson Newspapers, 1978-83; dep. mng. editor Comm. Daily, Washington, 1983-92; Washington bur. chief Stevens Pub. Corp., 1992; exec. editor, v.p. editl. Bus. Pubs., Inc., Silver Spring, Md., 1992-94; group editl. dir. news and info. svcs. Phillips Bus. Info., Inc., Potomac, Md., 1995—; lectr., speaker in field. Contbr. articles to profl. publs., chpts. to books. Active many profl. and local civic orgns. Phila. Advertisers Soc. fellow, 1978, Annenberg fellow, 1978-80, Rotary Internat. fellow for profl. journalists, 1980-81, Found. Am. Comms. econs. fellow, 1996; recipient Outstanding Newswriting award N.J. Press Assn., 1976, N.Y. Bldg. and Trades Assn. award, 1976, Spot News/Exclusive Story award Newsletter Pubs. Found., 1999. Mem. Am. Soc. Bus. Editors, Soc. Profl. Journalists (past pres. Washington chpt., Outstanding Newswriting award (2), Outstanding Profl. Chpt./Large award), Investigative Reporters and Editors, Soc. Environ. Journalists, Quill Big Inch Club, Nat. Press Club (v.p. speakers com., mem. awards com., Outstanding Newsletter Journalism 1st Place award 1987), Newsletter Pub. Assn., Reporters Com. for Freedom of the Press (steering com., Apex award 1997), D.C. On-Line Users Group, Pi Sigma Alpha, Sigma Delta Chi (past vice chmn. Found., Apex award 1997). Avocations: furniture refinishing, landscape gardening, performing on recorder. Office: Phillips Bus Info 1201 Seven Locks Rd Potomac MD 20854-2931

CROWLEY, MICHAEL RYAN, real estate appraiser/analyst, educator; b. Spring Valley, Ill., Oct. 18, 1943; s. William P. and Mary T. (Bergagna) C.; m. Diane T. Kujawa, Sept. 29, 1962; children: Michael R. Jr., Mary Frances. BA, U. Chgo., 1968, MBA, 1971. Exec. v.p. 1st Savs. and Loan, Spring Valley, 1963-77; owner Real Estate Cons., Spring Valley, 1977—; part-time faculty Ill. Valley C.C., Oglesby, 1980—; sr. resdl. appraiser, resdl. mem. Appraisal Inst., Chgo., 1981—; presenter seminars on touring Walt Disney World. Recipient Appreciation award St. Bede Acad., Peru, Ill., 1991. Mem. Ill. Assn. Real Estate Educators (charter), Illini Valley Realtors (affiliate), Ill. Valley Appraisers (past pres.). Home: 511 Ladd Rd Spring Valley IL 61362-1107

CROWLEY, ROBERT KENAN, radio station executive; b. Dec. 22, 1955. Student, U. Houston, 1973, Trinity U., San Antonio, 1977. Radio announcer radio stations, Tex./La., 1973-78; radio prodr., radio mass Archdiocese of San Antonio, 1979-80; announcer Sta. KENS-TV, San Antonio, 1979-82; news dir. Sta. KSAQ, San Antonio, 1984-85, Sta. KRNN, San Antonio, 1985, Sta. KPEZ-FM, Austin, 1987-93; news reporter Sta. WOAI, San Antonio, 1985-87; news announcer Stas. KVET-AM-FM and KASE-FM, Austin, 1993-99; radio cons. Lower Colo. River Auth. KWTR, 1994; news dir. Stas. KVET-AM-FM and KASE-FM, Austin, 1998-99; radio news announcer TXN The news of Texas, Austin, 1999—. Bd. dirs. Teach the Children, Austin, 1988, Austin Cmty. TV, 1988-89. Bd. dir. Any Baby Can, Austin. Home: 2506 Friar Tuck Ln Austin TX 78704-5612

CROWLEY, THOMAS B., JR., water transportation executive; b. 1966. BS in Fin., U. Wash. With Crowley Maritime Corp., Oakland, Calif., 1987—, chmn., CEO, 1994—. Office: Crowley Maritime 155 Grand Ave Oakland CA 94612-3758*

CROWLEY-KIGGINS, MARGARET LOUISE, artist; b. Mar. 26, 1960. BS in Comml. Design, Appalachian U., 1985. Artist Boca Raton, 1990—. Featured in Am. Artist's Watercolor mag., 1995, Best of Watercolor II., 1997. Mem. Fla. Watercolor Soc., Mensa, Intertel. E-mail: mckiggins@aol.com. Please give exhibits and galleries for your works with dates. Give your office address (not for publication).

CROWN, DAVID ALLAN, criminologist, educator; b. Long Beach, N.Y., Sept. 13, 1928; s. John and Florence (Coe) C.; m. Maria Braml, Feb. 13, 1954; children: Ingrid, Eric. BS, Union Coll., 1948; M in Criminology, U. Calif., 1960, D in Criminology, 1969. Spl. agt. CIC, 1951-53; asst. dir. San Francisco Indentification Lab., U.S. Postal Inspection Service, 1957-67; dir. Questioned Document Lab., Records Analysis Group, Dept. Army, Washington, 1967-72, Questioned Documents Staff, INR/DDC, U.S. Dept. State, Washington, 1972-77; chief Questioned Documents Lab., Office of Tech. Services, 1977-82; lectr. Chabot Coll., Hayward, Calif., 1966-67, Georgetown U., Washington, 1973; adj. prof. Am. U., Washington, 1971-80; professorial lectr. George Washington U., 1973-77, Antioch Sch. Law, 1977-1981; guest lectr. FBI Acad., Quantico, Va.; pres. Crown Forensic Labs., Inc.; chmn. recert. com. Am. Bd. Forensic Document Examiners. Author: The Forensic Examination of Paints and Pigments, 1968; co-author: Forensic Science, 1982, Legal Medicine, 1985, Forensic Handwriting Examination, 1993; contbr. articles to profl. publs.; mem. editl. bd.: Jour. Forensic Scis., 1971-73, Internat. Jour. Forensic Document Examiners; book rev. editor, 1973-74, assoc. editor, 1974-84. Pres. Temple Bat Yam, Sanibel, Fla., 1996-98. Mem. Am. Acad. Forensic Scis. (chmn. questioned document sect. 1969-70, exec. com. 1970-74, pres. 1974-75), Am. Soc. Questioned Document Examiners (chmn. accreditation com. 1969-70, sec.-treas. 1976-78, pres. 1980-82), ASTM (chmn. questioned document com. 1970-71, vice chmn. 1972), Forensic Sci. Found. (dir. 1971-72, trustee 1973-75), Am. Coll. Document Examiners (dir. 1970—), Ft. Myers Officers Club. Home: 3344 Twin Lakes Ln Sanibel FL 33957-5528

CROWN, JAMES SCHINE, investment executive; b. Chgo., June 25, 1953; s. Lester and Renée (Schine) C.; m. Paula Ann Hannaway, July 27, 1985; children: Victoria, Hayley, Andrew. BA, Hampshire Coll., 1976; JD, Stanford U., 1980. Bar: Ill. 1980. V.p. Salomon Bros. Inc., N.Y.C., 1980-85; gen. ptnr. Henry Crown and Co., Chgo., 1985—; bd. dirs. Gen. Dynamics Corp., Falls Church, Va., Bank One Corp., Sara Lee Corp. Trustee U. Chgo., Mus. Sci. and Industry, Orchestral Assn. Mem. Ill. State Bar Assn. Office: Henry Crown and Co 222 N La Salle St Chicago IL 60601-1003

CROWN, LESTER, manufacturing company executive; b. Chgo., June 7, 1925; s. Henry and Rebecca (Kranz) C.; m. Renee Schine, Dec. 28, 1950; children: Steven, James, Patricia, Daniel, Susan, Sara, Janet. BS in Chem. Engring., Northwestern U., 1946; MBA, Harvard U., 1949. Instr. math. Northwestern U., 1946-47; v.p., chem. engr. Marblehead Lime Co., 1950-56, pres., 1956-66, also bd. dirs.; v.p. Material Svc. Corp. subs. Gen. Dynamics Corp., Chgo., 1953-66, pres., 1970-83, chmn., 1983—, also bd. dirs.; chmn. exec. com. Gen. Dynamics Corp., 1982—, also bd. dirs.; pres. Henry Crown & Co., Chgo., 1969—, also bd. dirs.; bd. dirs. Maytag Corp.; ptnr. N.Y. Yankees Partnership, from 1973. Trustee Aspen Inst. Humanistic Studies, Northwestern U., Michael Reese Found.; bd. dirs. Lyric Opera Corp., Children's Meml. Med. Ctr., Jewish Theol. Sem., Jerusalem Found.; mem. bd. advisors Chgo. Zool. Soc.; mem. bd. govs. Weizmann Inst. of Sci./Tel Aviv U. Mem. Lake Shore Country Club, Northmoor Country Club, Standard Club, Econ. Club (dir. 1972), Chgo. Club, Comml. Club, Mid-Am. Club (Chgo.), John Evans Club of Northwestern U., Tau Beta Pi, Pi My Epsilon, Phi Eta Sigma. Office: Material Svc Corp 222 N La Salle St Chicago IL 60601-1002 also: Gen Dynamics Corp 3190 Fairview Park Dr Falls Church VA 22042-4510

CROWN, NANCY ELIZABETH, lawyer; b. Bronx, N.Y., Mar. 27, 1955; d. Paul and Joanne Barbara (Newman) C.; children: Rebecca, Adam. BA, Barnard Coll., 1977, MA, 1978; MEd, Columbia U., 1983; JD cum laude, Nova Law Sch., 1992. Cert. tchr.; Bar: Fla. 1992. Tchr. Sachem Sch. Dist., Holbrook, N.Y., 1978-82; v.p. mail order dept. Haber-Klein, Inc., Hicksville, N.Y., 1984-88; mgr. mdse., dir. ops. Sure Card Inc., Pompano Beach, Fla., 1988-89; legal intern Office U.S. Trustee/Dept. Justice, 1992; assoc. John T. Kinsey, P.A., Boca Raton, Fla., 1993-95; pvt. practice Nancy E. Crown, P.A., Boca Raton, Fla., 1995—. Recipient West Pub. award for acad. achievement, 1992. Mem. NAFE, Fla. Bar Assn., South Palm Beach County Women's Exec. Club, Phi Alpha Delta. Democrat. Jewish. Avocations: theatre, walking, reading, jazz.

CROWNER, DEE KAY, library administrator; b. Spirit Lake, Jan. 15, 1946; d. Harold Raymond Crowner and Kathryn Margaret Louise Hinkey. BA in Libr. Sci., U. No. Iowa, 1969. Media specialist Nashua (Iowa) Pub. Schs., Alden (Iowa) Pub. Schs., Berkley & Co., Spirit Lake, Iowa, Stylecraft Furniture, Milford, Iowa, Nat. Computer Sys., Iowa City, AT&T, Cedar Rapids, Iowa, MCI, Cedar Rapids; libr. dir. North Liberty (Iowa) Cmty. Libr., 1987—; past mem. conf. planning com. State Libr. Iowa, mem. accreditation com. Author: (monthly news column) Bookends; newsletter editor Iowa Pub. Libr. Forum. Mem. Big Bros./Big Sisters. Mem. ALA, Iowa Small Libr. Assn. (pres., newsletter editor), Iowa Libr. Assn. (membership com., past mem. govtl. affairs com., children's and young people's roundtable and conf. planning com.), Pub. Libr. Assn., Iowa Libr. Adminstrn. and Mgmt. Assn., Johnson County Pub. Libr. Assn. (chair), North Liberty Optimists. Avocations: reading, theater, restaurants, movies, traveling. E-mail: nlcl@zeus.ia.net. Office: North Liberty Cmty Libr 520 W Cherry St North Liberty IA 52317

CROWSON, JAMES LAWRENCE, lawyer, financial company executive, academic administrator; b. Duncan, Okla., Aug. 3, 1938; s. George L. and Emry Elifair (McKee) C.; children from previous marriage: James Lawrence Jr., Jason, Donna Kristan Nickel; m. Linda Sue Crowson, Mar. 2, 1986; stepchildren: Chadwick Lanier Johnson, Kim Johnson Osborn. BA in English Lit., U. Okla., 1960; LLB, So. Meth. U., 1963. Bar: Tex. 1963. Legis. counsel Tex. Legis. Coun., Austin, 1966-67; dir. hearings Tex. Water Quality Bd., Austin, 1967-68, chief legal officer, 1967-68, dir. hearings and enforcement, 1969-70; adminstrv. asst. Office of Gov., Austin, 1968-69; univ. atty. U. Tex. System, Austin, 1970; asst. to pres. U. Tex., Austin, 1970-71; asst. to pres. U. Tex., Dallas, 1971-74, v.p., 1974-77, exec. v.p., 1977-80; vice chancellor, gen. counsel U. Tex. System, Austin, 1980-87; sr. v.p., gen. counsel Lomas Fin. Group, Dallas, 1987-94, exec. v.p., 1994-95; pvt. investment practice Dallas, 1995-96; dep. chancellor Tex. Tech. Univ. System, Austin, 1996—; sec. Tex. Higher Edn. Found., 1988—, Higher Edn. Legis. Polit. Action Com., 1987—; vice chmn. HCB Enterprises Inc., 1995—; bd. dirs. KOHM Pub. Radio Sta., Market Lubbock, Inc., 1997—, v.p. 1999. Trustee Alliance for Higher Edn., 1991-96, Dallas Edn. Ctr., 1995-96. Capt. U.S. Army, 1963-66. Mem. Mortgage Bankers Assn. Am. (mem. legal issues com., mem. legis. com.), U.S. C. of C. (mem. edn. employment and tng. com., mem. labor rels. com., mem. S.W. pub. affairs task force). Office: PO Box 42013 Lubbock TX 79409-2013

CROWSTON, WALLACE BRUCE STEWART, management educator; b. Toronto, Ont., Can., Jan. 28, 1934; s. Arthur William and Clara Helena (Donnelly) C.; m. Taka Ohkubo, Sept. 15, 1961; children: Kevin, Cathy, Clare. BA Sc, U. Toronto, 1956; SM, MIT, 1958; MSc, Carnegie Mellon U., 1965, PhD, 1968. Asst. prof. U. Alta., 1960-62; asst. prof. MIT, 1966, assoc. prof., 1969-72; prof., faculty adminstrv. studies York U., 1972-87, dean, 1976-84; dean faculty mgmt. McGill U., Montreal, Que., Can., 1987—. Mem. Univ. Club (Montreal). Office: McGill U Faculty Mgmt, 1001 Sherbrooke St W, Montreal, PQ Canada H3A 1G5

CROWTHER, ANN ROLLINS, dean, political science educator; b. Zanesville, Ohio, Aug. 29, 1950; d. Walter Edmund and Norma Lucille (Rollins) C. BA in English, Rollins Coll., 1972; M. EdS, U. Fla., 1975; D in Pub. Adminstrn., U. Ga., 1988. Dir. residence hall Ga. Southern U., Statesboro, 1975-78; asst. to head personnel and staff devel. dept. coop. ext. svc. U. Ga., 1978-80, acad. advisor Franklin Coll. Arts & Scis., 1980-81, grad. teaching asst. dept. polit. sci., 1981-84, instr. evening classes program, 1982-85, coord. acad. advising Franklin Coll. Arts & Scis., 1984-89, asst. dean, adj. asst. prof. polit. sci. Franklin Coll. Arts & Scis., 1989-93, assoc. dean, adj. asst. prof. polit. sci. Franklin Coll. Arts & Scis., 1993—. Mem. Am. Polit. Sci. Assn., Am. Soc. Pub. Adminstrn., Ga. Assn. Women in Edn., Nat. Acad. Advising Assn., Nat. Assn. Women in Edn., Nat. Assn. Acad. Affairs Afminstrs. Avocations: travel, theatre, golf. Home: 375 Ponderosa Dr Athens GA 30605-3321 Office: Univ Ga Franklin Coll Arts & Scis 212 New College Athens GA 30602-1732

CROWTHER, G(EORGE) RODNEY, III, television production company executive, writer, photographer; b. Asheville, N.C., Jan. 11, 1927; s. G. Rodney Jr. and Martha Maria (Lewis) C. Grad., Boys' Latin Sch., Balt., 1944; student, Sch. Modern Photography, N.Y.C., 1949-50. Fashion photographer Amos Parrish & Co., N.Y.C., 1950-53; ind. comml. photographer Chevy Chase, Md., 1956-61; free-lance writer Washington, 1962—; pres. The Carrollian Age, Washington, 1987—. Author: Surname Index to Sixty-Five Volumes of Colonial and Revolutionary Pedigrees, 1964; contbr. articles to Nat. Geneal. Soc. Quar., 1962—; photograph Sputnik and the Big Dipper in Modern Mus. Art, N.Y.C., Echo I satellite in Smithsonian Inst., Where 'KONG' Stood, UN, N.Y.C., 1951. Served with USN, 1945-46, PTO. Episcopalian. Avocations: miniature gardening, audio-video editing. Office: PO Box 369 Ben Franklin Sta Washington DC 20044

CROWTHER, JAMES EARL, radio and television executive, lawyer; b. Cleve., Jan. 2, 1930; s. Byron Scott and Leota Belle (Frye) C.; m. Nancy Louise Swanner, Nov. 28, 1953; children: Richard Scott, Robert Phillip, Paul William. BA, Ohio Wesleyan U., 1956; JD, U. Mich., 1958. Bar: Tex. 1959. Assoc. Butler, Binion, Rice, Cook & Knapp, Houston, 1959-67; v.p. Channel Five TV Co., Nashville, 1975-86, Channel Two TV Co., Houston, 1970-86; v.p., gen. counsel Houston Post Co., 1967-76, exec. v.p., gen. counsel, 1976-83; v.p. Channel Four TV Co., Tucson, 1982-86, Channel Eleven TV Co., Meridian, Miss., 1981-84, KPRC Radio Co., Houston, 1983-86, WESH-TV, Inc., Daytona Beach, Fla., 1985-86, KCCI-TV, Inc., Des Moines, 1985-86; sec. H & C Comm., Inc., Houston, 1979-83, pres., 1983-94; gen. counsel U. Houston Sys., 1995-96, dep. chancellor, gen. counsel, 1996-97; adj. prof. law South Tex. Law Sch., Houston, 1974-75. Pres. Briargrove Park Property Owners, Inc., 1969-70; bd. dirs. Uptown Houston, 1990-94, Post Oak YMCA, 1991-93. With USAF, 1951-55. Mem. Tex. Bar Assn., Houston Bar Assn., Galleria Area C. of C. (bd. dirs. 1988-92). Methodist.

CROWTHER, RICHARD LAYTON, architect, consultant, researcher, author, lecturer; b. Newark, Dec. 16, 1910; s. William George and Grace (Layton) C.; m. Emma Jane Hubbard, 1935 (div. 1949); children: Bethe Crowther Allison, Warren Winfield, Vivian Layton; m. 2d Pearl Marie Tesch, Sept. 16, 1950. Student, Newark Sch. Fine and Indsl. Arts, 1928-31, San Diego State Coll., 1933, U. Colo., 1956. Registered architect, Colo. Prin. Crowther & Marshall, San Diego, 1946-50, Richard L. Crowther, Denver, 1951-66, Crowther, Kruse, Landin, Denver, 1966-70, Crowther, Kruse, McWilliams, Denver, 1970-75, Crowther Solar Group, Denver, 1975-82, Richard L. Crowther FAIA, Denver, 1982—; vis. critic, lectr. U. Nebr., 1981; holistic energy design process methodology energy cons. Holistic Health Ctr., 1982-83; adv. cons. interior and archtl. design class U. Colo., 1982-83, Cherry Creek, Denver redevel., 1984-88, Colo. smoking control legislation, 1985, interior solar concepts Colo. Inst. Art, 1986, Bio-Electro-Magnetics Inst., 1987-88; mentor U. Colo. Sch. Architecture, 1987-88. Author Sun/Earth, 1975 (Progressive Architecture award, 1975), rev. edit., 1983, reprint, 1995, Affordable Passive Solar Homes, 1983, reprint, 1996, Paradox of Smoking, 1983, Women/Nature/Destiny: Female/Male Equity for Global Survival, 1987, (monographs) Context in Art and Design, 1985, Existence, Design and Risk, 1986, Indoor Air: Risks and Remedies, 1986, Human Migration in Solar Homes for Seasonal Comfort and Energy Conservation, 1986, 88, Ecologic Architecture, 1992, Ecologic Digest, 1993, Ecologic Connections, 1996, Colorado Architect Monographs on Environmental Themes, 1998, others. NSF grantee, 1974-75. Fellow AIA (commr. research, edn. and environ. Colo. Central chpt. 1972-75, bd. dirs. chpt. 1973-74 AIA Research Corp. Solar Monitoring Program contract award, spkr. and pub. Colo. Ecologic Connections open forum 1996). Achievements include bio-toxic and bio-electromagnetic research. *Inner awareness, relevancy, persistence and adaptiveness are all that we have in a world of vanity, variety and change.*

CROXFORD, LYNNE LOUISE, social services administrator; b. Schenectady, N.Y., Nov. 9, 1947; d. Frederick William and Elizabeth Elger (Irish) C.; BA, Kalamazoo Coll., 1969; MPA, Wayne State U., 1975; m. Daniel Roderick Talhelm; 2 children, Alan Frederick, Thomas Arthur. Caseworker dept. social svc. County of Calhoun, Battle Creek, Mich., 1969-70; caseworker, supr. County of Oakland, Pontiac, Mich., 1970-76; program specialist Mich. Dept. Social Svcs., Lansing, 1976-78; exec. coord. for programming Mich. State Planning Coun. for Devel. Disabilities, 1978-79; staff coord. Gov. Com. on Unification of Pub. Mental Health System, Lansing, 1979-80; dir. dept. social svc. County of Ingham, Lansing, 1980-90; dir. fin. control Mich. Dept. Social Svcs., 1990-91, dir. office payment systems, 1991-97, dir. office of sys. internal control and security, 1997—; adv. Mich. Assn. Non-Profit Residential Facilities, 1976-78; incorporating dir. Mich. Pub. Mgmt. Inst., 1990; co-chair Mich. Pub. Mgmt. Inst., 1992, chair, 1995-97. Trustee, Unitarian Universalist Ch. of Greater Lansing, 1979-82, v.p., 1980-82; bd. dirs. Coun. for Prevention Child Abuse and Neglect, 1980-83; mem. Lansing Tri-County Pvt. Industry Coun., 1980-90; chair Pvt. Industry Coun. Steering Com., 1987-90. Mem. ASPA (nat. coun. 1986-92, Mich. Pub. Svc. award, 1993), Am. Pub. Welfare Assn., Michigan County Social Svcs. Assn. Club: Zonta (charter Mich. Capitol area, v.p. 1991-92, pres. 1992-93). Recipient Disting. Alumnus award Wayne State U. Grad. Program in Pub. Adminstrn., 1988, Spl. Recognition award Mich. Pub. Mgmt. Inst., 1994. Contbr. in field. Home: 750 Pebblebrook Ln East Lansing MI 48823-2140 Office: 235 S Grand PO Box 30037 Lansing MI 48909-7537

CROXTON, DOROTHY AUDREY SIMPSON, speech educator; b. Las Vegas, N.Mex., Feb. 29, 1944; d. Clyde Joseph and Audrey Shirley (Clements) Simpson; m. Gary Alan Beimer, May 13, 1972 (div. Apr. 1986); children: Laura Lea Beimer Nelson, Rose Anne Colleen Beimer; m. Ian B. Croxton, Dec. 27, 1992 (div. Oct. 1993). BA, N.Mex. Highlands U., 1965; MS, U. Utah, 1968; EdD, U. N.Mex., 1989. Cert. secondary edn., N.Mex. Tchr. West Las Vegas (N.Mex.) H.S., 1966-67, Santa Rosa (N.Mex.) H.S., 1968-71, Questa (N.Mex.) Consol. Schs., 1972-73; prof. speech comm. N.Mex. Highlands U., Las Vegas, 1975—. Author: Hovels, Haciendas, and House Calls: The Life of Carl H. Gellenthien, M.D., 1986, Speaking for Life: A Speech Communication Guide for Adults, 1990, Wreck of the Destiny Train, 1993. Active Calvary Bapt. Ch., Las Vegas, 1959—. Recipient Educator of Yr. award Pub. Svc. Co. of N.Mex., Albuquerque, 1990. Mem. P.E.O. Republican. Avocation: writing. Home: PO Box 778 Las Vegas NM 87701 Office: NMex Highlands Univ Communication Arts Dept Las Vegas NM 87701

CROYLE, BARBARA ANN, health care management executive; b. Knoxville, Tenn., Oct. 22, 1949; d. Charles Evans and Myrtle Elizabeth (Kellam) C. BA cum laude in Sociology, Coll. William and Mary, 1971; cert. corp. tax and securities law Inst. Paralegal Tng., 1971; JD, U. Colo., 1975; cert. program mgmt. devel. Colo. Women's Coll., 1980; MBA, U. Denver, 1983. Bar: Colo. 1976. Paralegal Holland & Hart, Denver, 1972-73; law clk. Colo. Ct. Appeals, Denver, summer 1976; assoc. firm Shaw Spangler & Roth, Denver, 1976-77; mgr. acquisitions/lands Petro-Lewis Corp., Denver, 1977-85; mgr. strategic planning Westinghouse, Transp. Div., 1985-87; mng. dir. Benefit Resource Mgmt. Group (subs. Blue Cross We. Pa.), 1987-92; COO and v.p. D.T. Watson Rehab. Hosp., 1992-93; v.p. ambulatory care svcs., compliance officer Franciscan Med. Ctr., Dayton campus, Ohio, 1994—; tchr. oil and gas law Colo. Paralegal Inst., 1978, 79; arbitrator Am. Arbitration Assn.; mediator Dayton Mediation Ctr. Mem. NAFE, ABA, Pa. Bar Assn., Inst. Noetic Scis., Am. Coll. Healthcare Execs. Home: 329 Monteray Ave Dayton OH 45419-2652 Office: Franciscan Med Ctr Dayton Campus 601 S Edwin C Moses Blvd Dayton OH 45408-1424

CROYLE, DOUGLAS EUGENE, career officer; b. Tripoli, Lioya, Africa, Feb. 6, 1956; s. James Armin and Rose Travis (Bradley) C.; m. Susan Bernice Blomeley, Dec. 27, 1974; children: Alexa Virginia, Bethany Rose, abigail Lynn. A. in Telecom. Sci., USN TechTraCen, San Diego, 1991. Commd. USCG, 1974—; advanced through grades; watchstander COMMSTA USCG, Kodiak, Alaska, 1982-86; watchstander Group Grand Haven USCG, Grand Haven, Mich., 1986-89; watch supr. USCG, Guam, 1989-91; radioman in chg. Yocona (WMEC 168) USCG, Kodiak, 1994-96, commSysTech/watch supr., 1991—; with BNGI, Miami, Fla., 1979-82; loadmaster Emery Airfreight, Miami, 1980-82; fin. cons. Gen. Fin. corp., Miami, 1978-79. Author poetry in jours. Sec. Kodaik Rodeo and State Fairgrounds, 1992-93, Kodiak Rodeo and State Fair, 1995-96. Mem. Acad. Am. Poets (assoc.), Chief Petty Officers assn., N.Am. Hunting Club. Republican. Avocations: gemology, military miniatures, rare coins, writing, painting. Home: 1217A Selief Ln Kodiak AK 99615-6222

CROYLE, ROBERT HAROLD, physician assistant; b. Dayton, Ohio, Aug. 28, 1955; s. Allen Paul and Mary Alice (Okpealuk) C.; m. Cynthia Ann McConnell, May 10, 1975; children: Elizabeth Anne-Marie, Robert Harold Jr., Kirsten Louise. AA, Am. River Coll., 1983; primary care assoc. program, Stanford U., 1987. Cert. physician asst. Nat. Commn. on Certification of Physician Assts. Physician asst. Yolo County Jail Med. Program, Woodland, Calif., 1988-90, PHS/IHS Hosp., Rapid City, S.D., 1990-91, Rapid Care Med. Ctr., Rapid City, 1991-94, Custer (S.D.) Comty. Hosp., 1994-95, Neurosurg./Spinal Surg. Assocs., Rapid City, 1995-97, Trav Corps, Malden, Mass., 1997-99, Health S., Rapid City, 1999—. Contbr. articles to newsletters. Mem. Am. Acad. Physician Assts., High Plains Drifters Balloon Club. Republican. Avocations: hot air balloon pilot, hunting, fishing. Home: # 97 840 N Spruce St Lot 97 Rapid City SD 57701-1355

CROZIER, LORNA, poet, educator; b. Swift Current, Sask., Can., May 24, 1948; d. Emerson and Margaret (Ford) C.; m. Patrick Lane, 1978. BA, U. Sask., 1969; MA, U. Alta., Can., 1980. Cert. tchr. High sch. tchr. English Glaslya, Sask., 1970-72; high sch. tchr. English, guidance counsellor Swift Current, 1972-78; dir. comm. Govt. of Sask., Regina, 1983-85; assoc. prof. dept. writing U. Victoria, B.C., Can., 1990-97; prof. dept. writing U. Victoria, Can., 1997—. Author: The Weather, 1983, The Garden Going on Without Us, 1985, Angels of Flesh, Angels of Silence, 1988, Inventing the Hawk, 1992, (Gov. Gen.'s Poetry award Can. Coun. 1992, Can. Authors Assn. award 1992, Pat Lowther award League Can. Poets 1992), Everything Arrives at the Light, 1995 (Pat Lawther award 1996), A Saving Grace, 1996, What the Living Won't Let Go, 1999. Mem. ACTRA, League Can. Poets, Writer's Union Can. Avocations: reading, cross-country skiing, gardening, cycling, bird watching. Home: 1886 Cultra Ave, Saanichton, BC Canada V8M 1L7

CROZIER, WILLIAM MARSHALL, JR., bank holding company executive; b. N.Y.C., Oct. 2, 1932; s. William Marshall and Alice (Parsons) C.; m. Prudence van Zandt Slitor, June 20, 1964; children: Matthew Eaton, Abigail Parsons, Patience Wells. B.A. in Econs., Yale U., 1954; M.B.A. with distinction, Harvard U., 1963. With Hanover Bank, N.Y.C., 1954-61; asst. sec. Hanover Bank, 1959; with BayBanks, Inc., Boston, 1964—, asst. treas., 1965, asst. v.p., 1968, v.p., sec., 1969, sr. v.p., sec., 1973, chmn. bd., chief exec. officer, 1974-96, pres., 1977-96, dir., 1974-96; chmn. bd. dirs. BankBoston Corp., 1996-97, chmn. emeritus, 1997—. Trustee Boston Symphony Orch.; overseer Boston Mus. Fine Arts. Served with U.S. Army, 1955-57. Episcopalian. Clubs: Comml.-Mchts. (Boston), Union (Boston), Harvard (Boston); Yale (N.Y.C.).

CRUDEN, ROBERT WILLIAM, botany educator; b. Cleve., Mar. 18, 1936; m. Diana Benedict Loeb, Dec. 21, 1967; children: Nathalie Rebecca, Lyda Marie; m. Diana Ruth Gannett, July 1996. AB, Hiram (Ohio) Coll., 1958; MS, Ohio State U., Columbus, 1960; PhD, U. Calif., Berkeley, 1967. Asst. prof. U. Iowa, Iowa City, 1967-71, assoc. prof., 1971-78, prof., 1978—; acting dir. Iowa Lakeside Lab., Wahepton, 1989-94, past asst. dir. Editor Ecol. Soc. Am., 1983-86; editorial bd. Madrono; contbr. numerous articles to profl. jours. Mem. pres.'s coun. on sci. initiatives Hiram Coll., 1994—. Mem. AAAS, AM. Soc. Plant Taxonomists, Bot. Soc. Am., Ecol. Soc. Am., Brit. Ecology Soc., Soc. for the Study of Evolution, Assn. for Tropical Biology, New Eng. Bot. Soc., Iowa Acad. Sci. Home: 10 Spring Valley Dr NE Iowa City IA 52240-9186 Office: U Iowa Dept Biol Scis Iowa City IA 52242

CRUESS, LEIGH SAUNDERS, financial executive; b. N.Y.C., Jan. 5, 1958; s. Richard Leigh and Sylvia (Robinson) C.; m. Susan Andrews, July 11, 1981. BA with honors, Queens U., Kingston, Ont., Can., 1979; MBA, Dartmouth Coll., 1981. Analyst Cargill, Inc., Mpls., 1981-84; account mgr. Cargill Leasing Corp., Chgo., 1984-86; asst. v.p. Citicorp N.Am., Leveraged Capital Group, Chgo., 1986-88; v.p. AT Comml. Corp. (subs. Ameritrust), Chgo., 1988-89; mng. dir. MASI Ltd., Chgo., 1990-95; v.p. corp. devel. Utilicorp United Inc., Kansas City, Mo., 1996—. Chmn. Hinsdale Village Caucus, 1994-95; bd. elders Union Ch. of Hinsdale, 1992-95, bd. worship Union Ch., 1997—. Avocations: tennis, skiing, cooking, music. Home: 2511 W 70th Ter Shawnee Mission KS 66208-2743 Office: UtiliCorp United Inc 20 W 9th St Kansas City MO 64105

CRUESS, RICHARD LEIGH, surgeon, university dean; b. London, Ont., Can., Dec. 17, 1929; s. Leigh S. and Martha A. (Peever) C.; m. Sylvia Crane Robinson, May 30, 1953; children: Leigh S., Andrew C. B.A., Princeton U., 1951; M.D., Columbia U., 1955. Diplomate Am. Bd. Orthopedic Surgery. Intern Royal Victoria Hosp., Montreal, Que., 1955-56; resident surgery Royal Victoria Hosp., 1956-57; resident surgery N.Y. Orthopedic Hosp., 1959-60, asst. resident orthopedic surgery, 1960-61, resident orthopedic surgery, 1961-62, Annie C. Kane fellow orthopedic surgery, 1961-62; research asso. depts. orthopedic surgery and biochemistry Columbia U., N.Y.C., 1962-63; John Armour Travelling fellow, 1962-63, Am.-Brit.-Can. Travelling fellow, 1967; practice medicine specializing in orthopedic surgery Montreal, 1963—; orthopedic surgeon Royal Victoria Hosp., orthopedic surgeon-in-charge, 1968-81, asst. surgeon-in-chief, 1970-81; chief surgeon Shriner's Hosp. for Crippled Children, Montreal, 1970-82; prof. surgery McGill U., Montreal, 1970—, chmn. div. orthopedic surgery, 1976-81, dean faculty medicine, 1981-95, prof. Ctr. for Med. Edn., 1995—; bd. dirs. Carter-Wallace, Inc., N.Y.C.; hon. cons. orthopedic surgery Queen Elizabeth Hosp., 1972—; mem. clin. grants com. Med. Rsch. Coun., 1972-75, mem. coun., 1980-86, mem. exec., 1983-86. Contbr. articles on surgery to profl. jours.; mem. editl. bd. Jour. Internat. Orthopedics, 1976-85, Jour. Bone and Joint Surgery, 1977-83, Current Problems in Orthopedics, 1977-83, Jour. Orthopaedic Rsch., 1986-88. Served to lt. M.C., USN, 1957-59. Fellow Royal Coll. Physicians and Surgeons Can. (chief examiner orthopedic surgery 1970-72), ACS, Am. Acad. Orthopedic Surgeons, Royal Soc. Can.; mem. Order of Can., Can. Orthopedic Assn. (sec. 1971-76, pres. 1977-78), Can. Orthopedic Rsch. Soc. (pres. 1971-72), Am. Orthopedic Rsch. Soc. (pres. 1975-76), Am. Orthopedic Assn., Ann. Orthopedic Surgeons Province Que. (treas. 1971-72), Société Française de Chirurgie Orthopedique (hon.), McGill Osler Reporting Soc., Assn. can. Med. colls. (pres. 1987-89). Home: Apt 903, 2333 Sherbrooke St W, Montreal, PQ Canada H3H 2TG Office: McGill U, 3655 Drummond St, Montreal, PQ Canada H3G 1Y6

CRUIKSHANK, JOHN W., III, life insurance underwriter; b. Sharon, Pa., Aug. 22, 1933; s. John W. and Jeannette Sprague (Lane) C.; m. Myrna Jean Wright, Nov. 25, 1960; children—Nancy Lynn, David Wright. BA, Princeton U., 1955. CLU. Group ins. sales rep. Conn. Gen. Life Ins. Co., Hartford, also Chgo., 1955-56; spl. agt. Northwestern Mut. Life Ins. Co., Chgo., 1959—, pres. Spl. Agts., Inc., 1983-84, faculty mem. advanced planning sch., 1978—; pres. Assn. of Agts. Northwestern Mut. Life, 1994-95; pres. Million Dollar Round Table Found., 1988-89; divisional v.p. Million Dollar Round Table, 1976-77, 86-87, 92-93, exec. com., 2d v.p., 1994-95, 1st v.p., 1995-96, pres., 1996-97, immediate past pres., 1997-98. Elder United Presbyn. Ch. in U.S.A., 1975—, mem. gen. assembly mission coun., 1972-78; pres. Nat. Coun. United Presbyn. Men, 1971-72; chmn. mission div. Presbytery of Chgo., also mem. gen. coun., 1966-67, 80-84; bd. dirs. Vocation Agy., Presbyn. Ch. in U.S.A., 1982-87, Life and Health Ins. Found. for Edn., 1998—; trustee Pikeville (Ky.) Coll., 1969-75. Mem. Assn. for Advanced Life Underwriting. Home: 1412 Ridge Rd Northbrook IL 60062-4628 Office: Northwestern Mut Life Ins Co 102 Wilmot Rd Ste 130 Deerfield IL 60015-5106

CRUIKSHANK, MARGARET LOUISE, humanities educator, writer; b. Duluth, Minn., Apr. 26, 1940; d. George Patrick and Louise Wimmer C. PhD, Loyola U., 1969; BA, Coll. St. Scholastica, Duluth, 1962; MA, San Francisco State U., 1992. Prof. City Coll., San Francisco, 1981-97; adj. prof. U. Maine, 1997—; prof. U. Maine, Orono, summers 1994, 95. Author: Thomas Babington Macaulay, 1978, The Gay and Lesbian Liberation Movement, 1992 (award Myers Ctr. for Human Rights, 1993); editor: The Lesbian Path, 1980, Lesbian Studies, 1982, New Lesbian Writing, 1984, Fierce with Reality (an anthology of literature about aging), 1995. Affiliate scholar U. Calif., Berkeley, 1996-97, Stanford Ctr. for Rsch. on Women, 1981-88. Mem. Nat. Women's Studies Assn. Avocations: hiking, canoeing. Office: U Maine Women's Studies Fernald Hall Orono ME 04469

CRUIKSHANK, STEPHEN HERRICK, physician, consultant; b. Parkersburg, W.Va., Dec. 4, 1950; s. Dwight Phelps and Clara Louise (Trissler) C.; m. Britt-Marie Siegert, June 13, 1998; children: Nathan, Sara. BA in Chemistry, W.Va. Wesleyan Coll., 1972, BA in Psychology, 1972; MD, Bowman Gray-Wake Forest U., Winston-Salem, N.C., 1980; MBA, Calif. Coast U., Santa Anna, 1993. Diplomate Am. Bd. Obstetrics/Gynecology. Asst. prof. Mich. State U., Grand Rapids, Mich., 1980-82, U. Mo., Kansas City, 1982-83; prof., vice chair U. Minn., Mpls., 1986-93; chmn. dept. Ob/Gyn Hennepin County Hosp., Mpls., 1986-93; prof., chair, program dir. Wright State Sch. Medicine, Dayton, 1993—; dir. gynecologic surg. WVa. U. Sch. Medicine, Morgantown, 1983-86; cons. U.S. Air Force, Dayton, Ohio, 1993—; pvt. legal cons., 1986—; mem. adv. bd. Soc. Reconstructive Surgeons, 1996—,. Author: (book) Gynecology For Home, 1993, Drug Use in Gynecology, 1994; contbr. numerous articles to jours. in field. Mem. fin. com. Mpls. Christian Sch., Mpls. 1991-92; mem. bd. dirs. Big Brothers, Big Sisters, Dayton, 1996. Mem. Soc. Gynecologic Surgeons, Cen. Assn. Ob/Gyn (sec.-treas. 1994—). Republican. Mem. Christian Missionary Alliance. Avocations: exercise, hunting, flying. Office: 128 E Apple St Ste 3800 Dayton OH 45409-2902

CRUIKSHANK, THOMAS HENRY, energy services and engineering executive; b. Lake Charles, La., Nov. 3, 1931; s. Louis James and Helene L. (Little) C.; m. Ann Coe, Nov. 17, 1955; children: Thomas Henry, Kate Martin, Stuart Coe. B.A., Rice U., 1952; postgrad., U. Tex. Law Sch., 1952-53, U. Houston Law Sch., 1953-55. Bar: Tex.; C.P.A., Tex. Accountant Arthur Andersen & Co., Houston, 1953-55, 58-60; mem. firm Vinson & Elkins, Houston, 1961-69; v.p. Halliburton Co., Dallas, 1969-72, sr. v.p., 1972-80, exec. v.p., 1980, pres., chief exec. officer subs. Otis Engring. Corp., 1980-81, pres., 1981-83, pres., chief exec. officer, 1983-89, chmn., CEO, 1989-95, dir., 1977-95; bd. dirs. Goodyear Tire & Rubber Co., Williams Cos., Inc., Seagull Energy, Inc., Lehman Bros. Holdings Inc.; former mem. Nat. Petroleum Coun., policy com. Bus. Roundtable. Pres. Jr. Achievement, Dallas, 1974-76, chmn., 1976-78, mem. nat. bd. dirs., 1976-95, chmn. 1989-90; bd. dirs. Up With People, chmn., 1998—; trustee Calif. Inst. Tech., 1991-96 Lt. (j.g.) USNR, 1955-58. Mem. ABA, Tex. Bar Assn., Am. Petroleum Inst., Dallas Country Club (bd. govs. 1977-79, 86-88), River Oaks Country Club (Houston), Pine Valley Golf Club (N.J.), Haig Point Country Club (S.C.), Preston Trail Golf Club, Plantation Golf Club (Calif.), Grandfather Golf and Country Club (N.C.), Eldorado Country Club (Calif.). Home: 3508 Marquette St Dallas TX 75225-5015 Office: 5949 Sherry Ln Dallas TX 75225-6532*

CRUISE, TOM (TOM CRUISE MAPOTHER, IV), actor; b. Syracuse, N.Y., July 3, 1962; s. Thomas C. III and Mary Lee Mapother; m. Mimi Rogers, May 9, 1987 (div. 1990); m. Nicole Kidman, Dec. 24, 1990; adopted children: Isabella Jane Kidman, Connor Antony Kidman. Grad. high sch., Glen Ridge, N.J. Actor: stage prodn. Godspell; feature film appearances include Endless Love, Taps, 1981, Losin' It, 1981, The Outsiders, 1983, Risky Business, 1983, All the Right Moves, 1983, Top Gun, 1986, Legend, 1986, The Color of Money, 1986, Cocktail,1988, Rain Man, 1988, Born on the Fourth of July, 1989 (Acad. award nominee for best actor 1990, Golden Globe award Best Actor Drama, Chgo. Film Festival Critics award, Best Actor), Days of Thunder, 1990, Far and Away, 1992, A Few Good Men, 1992, The Firm, 1993, Interview with the Vampire, 1994, Mission Impossible, 1996, Jerry McGuire, 1996 (MTV Movie award Best Male Performance, Golden Globe award Best Performance Comedy/Musical, Blockbuster Entertainment award Favorite Actor-Comedy/Romance, nominated Oscar award Best Actor), Eyes Wide Shut, 1998, Mission Impossible 2, 1999, Magnolia, 1999. *

CRUM, ALBERT BYRD, psychiatrist, consultant; b. Omaha, Nov. 17, 1931; s. J. Rufus and Alberta (McCreary) C.; m. Rosa Maria Hennessy y Sinclair; children: Rosa Maria Crum O'Brien, Elsie Crum McCabe, Alberta Crum Fousek. BS, U. Redlands, Calif., 1953; MD, Harvard U., 1957; MS, NYU, 1987; DS (hon.), U. Redlands, 1974. Med. intern Columbia U. div. Bellevue Med. Ctr., N.Y.C., 1957-58; rsch. fellow, psychiat. resident Creedmoor Inst. for Psychol. Studies, Queens Village, N.Y., 1958-59; chief, neuropsychiatric svcs., Continental Air Command USAF Hosp., 1959-61; psychiat. resident Columbia U. Psychiat. Inst. of Columbia-Presbyn. Hosp., N.Y.C., 1961-63; pvt. practice Brooklyn Heights, N.Y., 1963—; active attending staff Gracie Sq. Hosp., N.Y.C., 1963—; med. dirs. Psychiatric Svcs. Internat. P.C., Brooklyn Heights, 1980—; ednl. dir. med. and health seminars Internat. Inst. for Human Behavior, Inc., Brooklyn Heights, 1983—; advisor Office of Tibet, N.Y.C., 1984—; clin. prof. behavioral scis. NYU, N.Y.C., 1987—; pres., dir. behavioral scis. Way of Life/N.Y., Ltd., Brooklyn Heights, 1989—; pres. Y.F. One/N.Y., Ltd., Brooklyn Heights, 1991—, Y.F. Nationwide, Inc., Brooklyn Heights, 1991—, Immune Advantage Internat., Inc., Brooklyn Heights, 1995—; chmn., mem. Immune Products, L.L.C., Brooklyn Heights, 1996; co-chmn. U.S. Coordinating Commn. for Nomination of His Holiness the Dalai Lama of Tibet for the Nobel Peace Prize, Brooklyn Heights, 1986—; adj. prof. anatomy and neuroanatomy, NYU, 1987—; ptnr. Burdick Assocs. Investment Firm, Brooklyn Heights, 1976—; pres. Burdick Assocs. Owners Corp., Brooklyn Heights, 1983—; chmn. Human Behavior Found., Brooklyn Heights, 1968—; chmn. selection com. Human Behavior Found.'s Albert Schweitzer Humanitarian Award, Brooklyn Heights, 1986—. Author (chpt.) The Triumphant Person, 1989. Bd. dirs. Albert Schweitzer Fellowship, N.Y.C., 1982—; chmn. William James Found., Brooklyn Heights, 1989—; bd. dirs. Burdick Internat. Ancestry Library, Sarasota, Fla., 1985—; mem., chn., bd. advisors NYU's Coll. of Dentistry, N.Y.C., 1988—; mem. Brooklyn Heights Assn., 1970—. Capt. USAF, 1959-61. Recipient Disting. Svc. award Bklyn. Jr. C. of C., 1966, Bicentennial award Nat. Jogging Assn., 1976. Fellow Royal Coll. Physicians and Surgeons in Psychiatry; mem. Pan Am. Med. Assn., Nat. Bd. Med. Examiners, Med. Coun. of Can., Am. Acad. Clin. Psychiatrists, Am. Orthopsychiatric Assn., Am. Psychiat. Assn., AMA, Med. Soc. State of N.Y., Kings County (N.Y.) Med. Soc., World Med. Assn., World Fedn. Mental Health, Am. Physicians Art Assn., Harvard Med. Soc., English Speaking Union, Harvard Club of N.Y., Bklyn. Club, Heights Casino and Racquet Club, MENSA (life, nat. coord. 1980-84), Phi Beta Kappa (councillor 1981-84). Avocations: jogging, studying world religions, history, leadership. Home and Office: Psychiat Svcs Internat PC 77 Remsen St Brooklyn NY 11201-3401

CRUM, BECKY SUE, supervisor, educator; b. Rushville, Ill., July 27, 1956; d. William Ashwood and Hazel Ruth (Vogler) C. BS in Edn., Greenville (Ill.) Coll., 1978. Cert. basketball, volleyball and softball ofcl., Ill.; cert. basketball and softball ofcl., Calif. Tchr. phys. edn. and health, coach Hartsburg (Ill.) Unit Dist., 1978-79; tchr. phys. edn., coach Eswood Community Consol. Grade Sch., Esmond, Ill., 1979-80, Thomasboro (Ill.) Grade Sch., 1980-81, Urbana (Ill.) High Sch., 1981-84; supr. holding room, coach Cen. High Sch., Champaign, Ill., 1985-90; substitute tchr., official Chaffey Joint Union High Sch., Ontario, Calif., 1990-91; holding rm. supr. Centennial High Sch., Champaign, Ill., 1991-98; health tchr., jr. high sci. tchr. Rushville H.S./Middle Sch., 1998—, middle sch. basketball/volleyball coach, H.S. softball coach; Supr. T-ball Urbana Park Dist., 1985-90; ofcl. Ill. High Sch. Assn., Champaign, 1985-91, Calif. Interscholastic Fedn., 1990-91. Mem. AAHPER and Dance, Ill. Athletic Assn., Ill. Edn. Assn., Nat. Assn. Sports Officials. Mem. Vineyard Christian Fellowship. Home: RR 1 Box 37 Rushville IL 62681-9719 Office: Centennial High Sch Champaign IL 61821

CRUM, DENNY (DENZEL EDWIN CRUM), collegiate basketball coach; b. San Fernando, Calif., Mar. 2, 1937; s. Alwin Denzel and June (Turner) C.; m. Joyce Elaine Lunsford, Feb. 11, 1977; children—Cynthia Lynne, Steven Scott, Robert Scott. BA, UCLA, 1959; secondary teaching cert., San Fernando Valley State Coll., 1960. Asst., then head basketball coach Pierce Coll., Los Angeles, 1962-67; asst. coach UCLA, 1968-70; head basketball coach U. Louisville, 1971—; coach champion team NCAA Basketball Tournament, 1980, 86; coach U.S. basketball team Pan Am. Games, 1987. Author articles in field. Named Mo. Valley Conf. Coach of Year, 1973, 75, Coll. Coach of Year, 1974, Metro Conf. Coach of Year, 1979, 83, Coach of Yr. Sporting News mag., 1983, 86, Playboy mag., 1986; named to UCLA Hall of Fame, 1990. Mem. Nat. Assn. Basketball Coaches (bd. dirs. 1989). Coached U. Louisville team to 10 Metro Conf. titles and 8 Metro Conf. Tournament championships. Earned 400th career coaching victory, Feb. 3, 1988. Office: Univ of Louisville Belknap Campus 2301 S 3rd St Louisville KY 40292-0001*

CRUM, HENRY HAYNE, lawyer; b. Denmark, S.C., Oct. 1, 1914; s. J. Wesley Jr. and Priscilla (Hart) C.; m. Mary Bass, July 27, 1946; children: Elizabeth, J. Wesley III, H. Hayne III. AB, Wofford Coll., 1935; LLB, U. S.C., 1939. Bar: S.C. 1939, U.S. Ct. Appeals (4th cir.) 1953, U.S. Dist. Ct. S.C. 1959, U.S. Tax Ct. 1963, U.S. Supreme Ct. 1953. Ptnr. Crum & Crum Attys., Denmark, 1939-40, 45—; mem. S.C. Supreme Ct. Grievance and Discipline Com., 1978-81, S.C. Supreme Ct. Specialization Adv. Bd. for Taxation, 1982-84, S.C. Bar Resolution of Fee Disputation Bd., 1983-84; city atty. City of Denmark, 1946-76. With AUS, 1940-45, ETO, Col. USAR ret. Decorated Bronze Star, ETO Ribbon with 5 Campaign Stars, Bronze Arrowhead. Democrat. Methodist. Avocations: golf, tennis, reading. Home: 277 N Palmetto Ave Denmark SC 29042-1107 Office: Crum & Crum Attys PO Box 12B Denmark SC 29042-0012

CRUM, JOHN KISTLER, chemical society director; b. Brownsville, Tex., July 28, 1936; s. John Mears and Mary Louise (Kistler) C. B.S., U. Tex., 1960, Ph.D., 1964; grad. Advanced Mgmt. Program, Harvard U., 1975. Research fellow Robert A. Welch Found., 1962-64; asst. editor Am. Chem. Soc., Washington, 1964-65; assoc. editor Am. Chem. Soc., 1966-68, mng. editor, 1969-70, group mgr. jours., 1970, dir. books and jours. div., 1971-75, treas., chief fin. officer, 1975-80, dep. exec. dir. and chief operating officer, 1981-82, exec. dir., 1983—; chmn. bd. Centcom Ltd., chmn. governing bd. Chemical Abstracts Svc., 1991—; chmn. bd. Sci. Info. Internat., Ltd., 1995—; mem. U.S. nat. com. Internat. Union Pure and Applied Chemistry; mem. Nat. Com. for Edn. in Space; regular mem. Con. Bd.; bd. dirs. Consumers Union of U.S., 1991-93. Mem. editorial adv. bd. Am. Men and Women of Sci.; contbr. articles to profl. jours. Fellow Washington Acad. Scis.; mem. Royal Chem. Soc. (London), Am. Chem. Soc., Am. Soc. Assn. Execs., Coun. Engring. and Sci., Soc. Execs., Assn. Sci. Soc. Editors, N.Y. Acad. Scis., Chem. Soc. Washington, Cosmos CLub, City Club, Univ. Club (Washington), Chemists Club (N.Y.), Sigma Xi, Phi Theta Kappa. Republican. Home: 1701 N Kent St Arlington VA 22209-2112 Office: Am Chem Soc 1155 16th St NW Washington DC 20036-4800*

CRUM, LAWRENCE LEE, banking educator; b. Brownsville, Tex., July 25, 1933; s. John Mears and Mary Louise (Kistler) C. B.B.A. with highest honors (Alpha Kappa Psi scholar 1954), U. Tex., Austin, 1954, M.B.A., 1956, Ph.D., 1961; postgrad., Carnegie-Mellon U., 1962, Harvard U., 1965. Ayres fellow Am. Bankers Assn., 1966; asst. prof., then assoc. prof. U. Fla., 1959-65; mem. faculty U. Tex., Austin, 1965—, prof. fin., 1969-82, Tex. Commerce Bancshares Centennial prof. comml. banking, 1982-94, Tex. Commerce Bancshares Centennial prof. emeritus, 1994—, chmn. dept. fin., 1969-76, fellow, Ben F. Love chair in bank mgmt., 1991-93, dir. banking program, 1980-92; chmn. bd. dirs. San Antonio br. Fed. Res. Bank, Dallas, 1980-86; cons. in comml. banking field; mem. loan com. Franklin Lindsay Student Aid Fund, 1980-94. Author: Time Deposits in Present Day Commercial Banking, 1964, Transition in the Texas Commercial Banking Industry, 1970; co-author: The Development of State-Chartered Banking in Texas, 1978, Competition for the Commercial Banking Industry in the Establishment and Operation of an Electronic Payments System, 1971 contbr. articles to profl. jours. Ford Found. fellow, 1963-64. Mem. Am. Fin. Assn., Am. Econ. Assn., Fin. Mgmt. Assn., Beta Gamma Sigma, Phi Kappa Phi. Republican. Presbyterian. Home: 3920 Sierra Dr Austin TX 78731-3912 Office: CBA 6.464 U Tex Austin TX 78712

CRUMB, GEORGE HENRY, composer, educator; b. Charleston, W.Va., Oct. 24, 1929; s. George Henry and Vivian (Reed) C.; m. Elizabeth May Brown, May 21, 1949; children: Elizabeth Ann, David Reed, Peter Stanley. B.Mus., Mason Coll., 1950; M.Mus., U. Ill., 1952; postgrad. (Fulbright fellow), Hochschule für Musik, Berlin, Germany, 1955-56, Berkshire Music Center, Tanglewood, Mass., summer 1955; D.Mus. Arts, U. Mich., 1959. Instr. theory Hollins Coll., Va., 1958-59; asst. prof. composition and piano U. Colo., 1959-64; creative asso. composition State U. N.Y. at Buffalo, 1964-65; asst. prof. composition U. Pa., Phila., 1965-66; asso. prof. U. Pa., 1966-71, prof., 1971—, Annenberg prof., 1983—. Composer: String Quartet, 1954, Sonata; for solo violincello, 1955; Variazioni; for large orch., 1959; Five Pieces; for piano, 1962, Night Music I; for soprano, keyboard and percussion, 1963; Four Nocturnes Night Music II; for violin and piano, 1964; Madrigals, Books I and II; for solo voice and instruments, 1965; Eleven Echoes of Autumn; for violin, alto flute, clarinet and piano, 1966; Echoes of Time and the River, 1967 (Pulitzer prize 1968); for orch. Songs, Drones and Refrains of Death for baritone and electric instruments; U. Iowa commn., 1968, Madrigals, Books III and IV; for soprano and instruments, 1969; Night of the Four Moons; for alto and instruments, 1969; Black Angels (Thirteen Images from the Dark Land); for electric string quartet, U. Mich. commn., 1970; Ancient Voices of Children; for soprano and instruments, Coolidge Found. commn., 1970; Vox Balaenae; for electric flute, electric cello and electric piano, 1971; Lux Aeterna; for soprano, sitar, bass flute and two percussionists, 1971; for amplified piano Makrokosmos, Vol I, 1972, Vol. II, 1973; Makrokosmos, Vol. I Music for a Summer Evening; for 2 amplified pianos and percussion, Fromm Found. commn., 1974; Dream Sequence; for violin, cello, piano, percussion and glass-harmonica, 1976; Star-Child: A Parable; for Solo Soprano, Antiphonal Children's Voices, Bell Ringers and Large Orch., Ford Found. Commn., 1977; Celestial Mechanics, Cosmic Dances; for Amplified Piano, 4-Hands, 1979; Apparition; elegiac songs and vocalises for soprano and amplified piano, 1979; A Little Suite for Christmas, A.D. 1979, 1980, Gnomic Variations for Piano, 1981, Pastoral Drone for Organ, 1982, Processional for piano, 1983, A Haunted Landscape for Orchestra, 1984, The Sleeper for Soprano and Piano, 1984, An Idyll for the Misbegotten for Flute and Drums, 1985; Federico's Little Songs for Children for Soprano, Flute and Harp, 1986, Zeitgeist for two amplified pianos, 1987, Easter Dawning for Carillon, 1991; also commns. Koussevitzky Found., 1964, Bowdoin Coll., 1965, U. Chgo., 1966; Quest, 1994 for guitar and chamber ensemble, Mundus Canis for Guitar and Percussion, 1997. Edward MacDowell Colony medal, Peterborough, 1995. Mem. B.M.I., Nat. Inst. Arts and Letters, German Acad. Arts (hon.), Bavarian Acad. Fine Arts, Am. Acad. Arts and Scis., Pi Kappa Lambda, Phi Mu Alpha. Office: U Pa Music Bldg Philadelphia PA 19104

CRUMB, ROBERT, cartoonist; b. Phila., Aug. 30, 1943; s. Charles Sr. C.; m. Dana Morgan (div. 1977); m. Aline Kominski, 1978. Colorist Am. Greetings Corp., 1963-67; cartoonist Fantagraphics Books, Seattle, 1967—. Creator: (comic book) Zap, 1968; founder, cartoonist: (mag.) Wierdo, 1981-89; author: The Complete Crumb Comics, (with Aline Kominski) My Troubles with Women, 1991, Wierdo Art of R. Crumb: His Early Period 1981-85, 1992, Crumb's Complete Dirty Laundry Comics, 1993; illustrator: The Monkey Wrench Gang by Edward Abbey, 1985; frequent contbr. to comic mags.; subject of documentary film: Crumb, 1994; creator cartoon character Fritz the Cat. Office: Fantagraphics Books 7563 Lake City Way NE Seattle WA 98115-4218*

CRUMBAUGH, JAMES CHARLES, psychologist; b. Terrell, Tex., Dec. 11, 1912; s. Charles Miller and Hallie Virginia (Dansby) C.; m. Edna Mae Bailey, 1938 (dec. 1946); 1 child, Charles; m. Teresa Amanda Croteau, June 14, 1975 (dec. Feb. 1989); m. Lois Dickson Hicks, Nov. 10, 1992. AB, Baylor U., 1935; AM, So. Meth. U., 1938; PhD, U. Tex., 1953. Lic. psychologist, Miss.; cert. logotherapist. Psychologist, tchr. Memphis State U., 1947-56; chmn. Dept. Psychology MacMurray Coll., Jacksonville, Ill., 1957-59; rsch. dir. Bradley Ctr., Inc., Columbus, Ga., 1959-64; staff psychologist VA Med. Ctr., Augusta, Ga., 1964-65, Gulfport, Miss., 1965-80; so. regional dir. Inst. Logotheraphy, Berkeley, Calif., 1980—; rsch. cons. Internat. Graphoanalysis Soc., Chgo., 1968—. *James Charles Crumbaugh is senior author (with L.T. Maholick, M.D.) of Purpose-in-life Test. Based on Viennese psychiatrist Viktor E. Frankl's book Logotheraphy, it has been translated into at least eight languages, and has been used over the world in more than 150 research studies, mostly MA theses or Doctoral dissertations, and is still in wide use 30 years after publication. He is a diplomate in psychotherapy with the American Board of Psychological Specialties and a diplomate and fellow of the Viktor E. Frankl Institute of Logotherapy.* Author: Counseling for Graphoanalysts, 1970, Everything to Gain, 1973; co-author: Logotherapy, 1980; co-editor: Primer of Projective Techniques, 1990. With U.S. Army air Corps, 1941-45. Rsch. fellow Duke U., 1954-55. Mem. APA, Miss. Psychol. Assn. (Kinlock Gill award 1989), Southeastern Psychol. Assn., So. Soc. Philosophy and Psychology, Psi Chi. Roman Catholic. Avocation: writing. Home: 140 Balmoral Ave Biloxi MS 39531-4701

CRUMBLEY, DONALD LARRY, accounting educator, writer, consultant; b. Kannapolis, N.C., Jan. 18, 1941; s. Carl Donald and Velvia Luetta (Kelly) C.; m. Donna Darlene Loflin, Aug. 31, 1963; children: Stacey Lynn, Dana Lea, Heather Ann. BS cum laude, Pfeiffer U., 1963; MS, La. State U., 1965, PhD, 1967. CPA, N.C. Grad research asst. La. State U., Baton Rouge, 1963-65, teaching asst., 1965-66; asst. prof. acctg. Pa. State U., State College, 1967-69; staff acct. Arthur Andersen & Co., N.Y.C., 1969-70; adj. asst. prof. NYU Grad. Sch. Bus., spring 1970; faculty resident Laventhol & Horwath, summer 1972; assoc. prof., dir. M. Bus. Taxation program U. So. Calif., Los Angeles, 1973-74, U. Fla., Gainesville, 1970-73, 74-75; prof. Tex. A&M U., College Station, 1975-97, Shelton prof. taxation, 1984-97; KPMG Peat Marwick prof. La. State U., Baton Rouge, 1997—; newspaper and mag. columnist; creator Soc. for a Return to Acad. Stds., 1993—. Author: Financial Management of Your Coin-Stamp Estate, 1978, Practical Guide to Preparing a Federal Gift Tax Return, 1981, Readings in Selected Tax Problems of the Oil Industry, 1982, Handbook of Accounting for Natural Resources, 1986, Handbook of Estate Planning, 1988, Handbook of Governmental Accounting and Finance, 1988, 1992, Handbook of Financial Management for Banks, 1988, The Ultimate Rip-off: A Taxing Tale, 1988, Accosting the Golden Spire, 1989, Handbook on Financial Aspect of Divorce and Separation, 1989, Keys to Understanding the Financial News, 1989, Keys to Estate Planning and Trusts, 1989, Keys to Personal Financial Planning, 1991, Keys to Surviving a Tax Audit, 1991, Handbook of Natural Gas Accounting, 1991, Keys to Understanding Social Security Benefits, 1992; co-author: Donate Less to the IRS, 1981, Readings in Oil Industry Accounting, 1980, Estate Planning: A Guide for Advisers and Their Clients, West's Federal Taxation, 4 vols., Trap Doors and Trojan Horses, 1991, Financial Analysis, 1994, How To Manage Corporate Cash, 1994, Costly Reflections in a Midas Mirror, 1995, Barron's Guide to Tax Terms, 1995, Activity Based Costing, 1995, Deadly Art Puzzle: Accounting for Murder, 1996, The Bottom Line is Betrayal, 1995, Non-profit Sleuths: Follow the Money, 1997, Simon the Incredible: A Novel, 1998, Chemistry in Whispering Caves, 1998, Computer Encryptions in Whispering Caves, 1999; contbr. chpts. to books, articles to profl. publs.; editor Oil, Gas & Energy Quar., 1977—, Jour. Forensic Acctg., 1999—; co-editor Tex. Tax Services, 1983—; cons. editor Lawyers and Judges Pub. Co., Tucson; contbg. editor Hard Facts and Tax Angles; mem. editorial bd. Jour. Petroleum Acctg., Jour. Managerial Issues, Jour. East-West Bus., Acctg. Rev.; mem. editl. adv. bd. Advances in Acctg. Named to Alumni Hall of Fame, A.L. Brown High Sch., 1972; recipient Contbn. to Community award Sta. WRUF, 1972; Coll. Bus. Adminstrn. Research award Tex. A&M U., 1982; Ford Found. grantee, 1966-67; Disting. Alumni award Pfeiffer Coll., 1972; Arthur Young research grantee, 1984-85. Mem. Am. Taxation Assn. (pres. 1974-75, trustee 1975-77, founder), Am. Inst. CPA's, Am. Acctg. Assn., Nat. Taxation Assn., Am. Tax Assn. (founding pres.), Govt. Fin. Officers' Assn., Tex. Soc. CPA's, Numis. Lit. Guild, Order of Sundial, Phi Kappa Phi, Beta Gamma Sigma, Beta Alpha Psi. Methodist. Office: La State U Dept Acct 3101 Ceba Bldg Baton Rouge LA 70803

CRUMBLEY, ESTHER HELEN KENDRICK, realtor, retired secondary education educator; b. Okeechobee, Fla., Oct. 3, 1928; d. James A. and Corrine (Burney) Kendrick; m. Chandler Jackson, Oct. 24, 1949 (dec.); children: Pamela E., Chandler A., William J. BS in Math. Edn., Ga. So. Coll., 1966; M in Math., Jacksonville (Fla.) U., 1979. Cert. secondary edn. tchr., Ga. Secondary edn. tchr. Camden County Bd. Edn., St. Mary's, Ga., 1958-92, ret.; realtor Watson Realty, St. Mary's, 1985-98; valedictorian H.S., 1946, dept. chairperson Camden H.S., St. Mary's, 1966-72; pres., sec., treas. Camden GMA, St. Mary's, 1976-78. Area contact person Max Cleand U.S. Senator, Ga., Atlanta, 1982-90; councilwoman Cityof St. Mary's, 1979-86, mayor pro tem, 1981-86. Named Star Tchr., 1972, Camden GMA, 1979-88. Mem. Camden Ga. Assn. Educators (pres. 1976, sec.-treas. 1977-78, star tchr. 1972), PAGE (biog. com. rep. 1984-92, 1992 retired, named outstanding 8th dist. bldg. rep.), Camden Gen. Mcpl. Assn. (pres., sec.-treas. 1979-88), fin. and budget coms.), Math. Assn., Internat. Platform Assn. Internat. Dictionary Ctr., ABI. Republican. Baptist. Avocations: reading, art. Home: RR 3 Box 810 Folkston GA 31537-9729 *Hard work, perseverance and determination will get you to any goal in life. Put God first, country and family in that order. Can't should not be in your vocabulary.*

CRUMBLEY, PAUL JAMES, English language educator; b. Montevideo, Uruguay, Sept. 26, 1952; came to U.S., 1956; s. T. A. and Janet (Christly) C.; m. Phebe Clare Jensen, June 14, 1986; children: Nell Clare, Emma Rose. MA, Sch. Theology at Claremont, 1976; MA in Teaching Lang. Arts, Reed Coll., 1978; MA, Bread Loaf Sch. English, Middlebury, Vt., 1986; PhD, U. N.C., 1993. Tchr. English Helen Bush Sch., Seattle, 1980-86, chair English dept., 1984-86; lectr. English U. N.C., Wilmington, 1986-87; tchg. asst. English U. N.C., Chapel Hill, 1987-93, dir. writing ctr., 1990-92; asst. prof. English Niagara U., N.Y., 1993-95, Utah State U., Logan, 1995—; faculty cons. Ednl. Testing Svc., 1992—. Author: Inflections of the Pen: Dash and Voice in Emily Dickinson, 1996, (chpt.) The Emily Dickinson Handbook, 1997. Mem. MLA, Am. Lit. Assn., Am. Studies Assn., Emily Dickinson Internat. Soc. (sec. 1995—). Office: Utah State U Dept English Logan UT 84322-3200

CRUMLEY, DAVID OLIVER, publisher, author, foundation executive; b. New Orleans, May 18, 1949; s. David Shiffer III and Martha Ann (Carey) C. BA, Tulane U., 1974. Sec., editor The Social Dir. of Greater New Orleans, Inc., 1975-77, pres., pub., 1977-92; pres. Laser Documentation Inc. Author, historian: Reflection of Life in New Orleans: Architecture & Interior Decoration as Historical, Social & Cultural Commentary, 1970; pub., author: Mardi Gras in New Orleans 1971, 1971; researcher Town & Country, 1979. Historian hist. marker Ashland Plantation, 1969, La Maison Blanche Plantation, 1974; co-founder Soc. Huguenot A Nouvelle, New Orleans, 1973, The Grand Priory of the South, The Mil. and Hospitaller Order of St. Lazarus of Jerusalem, New Orleans, 1976; vestry Mt. Olivet Episc. Ch., 1971-90, jr. warden of vestry, 1976-88, sr. warden of vestry, 1989. Internat. Rels. scholar Tulane U., 1974. Mem. Sons of the Revolution (genealogist La chpt. 1974-88), Societe Huguenot A Nouvelle Orleans (bd. dirs. 1973—), Soc. of the War of 1812 (vice-genealogist La. chpt. 1974-80), Royal Soc. of St. George (bd. dirs. New Orleans chpt. 1974-76), Soc. Colonial Wars (dep. genealogist La. chpt. 1974-77, 79-88, genealogist La. chpt. 1977-79), SAR (genealogist George Washington chpt. 1986-87), La. Hist. Soc., Masons. Avocation: reading. Office: Social Dir of Greater New Orleans Inc 4403 Maple Leaf Dr New Orleans LA 70131-7455

CRUMLEY, JAMES ROBERT, JR., retired clergyman; b. Bluff City, Tenn., Mar. 30, 1925; s. James Robert and Ida Frances (Fine) C.; m. Sara Annette Bodie, May 26, 1950; children: Frances Crumley Holman, James Robert, Jeanne Crumley Lindeman. BA, Roanoke Coll., 1948, DD (hon.), 1973; MDiv, Luth. Theol. So. Sem., Columbia, S.C., 1951; DD (hon.), Newberry (S.C.) Coll., 1971, Augustana Coll., 1982, Muhlenberg Coll., Allentown, Pa., 1983; LLD (hon.), Susquehanna U., Selinsgrove, Pa., 1977; LHD (hon.), Lenoir-Rhyne Coll., Hickory, N.C., 1979; LittD (hon.), Bethany Coll., 1981; LHD (hon.), Manhattan Coll., 1984, U. S.C., 1987. Ordained to ministry Luth. Ch., 1951. Pastor chs. in Greenville and Oak Ridge, Tenn., Savannah, Ga., 1951-74; sec. Luth. Ch. in Am., N.Y.C., 1974-78, bishop, 1978-88; vis. prof. ecumenism Luth. Theol. So. Sem., Columbia, S.C., 1988, ret., 1993. Home: 362 Little Creek Dr Leesville SC 29070-9379

CRUMLEY, MARTHA ANN, company executive; b. New Orleans, Aug. 8, 1910; d. Mark Oliver and Mary Elizabeth (Schroder) Carey; m. David Shiffer Crumley III, May 7, 1947; 1 child, David Oliver. Grad., Tulane U., New Orleans, 1974. Pres., chief exec. officer Westbank Acad., Gretna, La., 1953-68; sr. v.p. The Social Directory Greater New Orleans, Inc., 1975-92, pres., 1992-94. Pres. Algiers Little Theatre, New Orleans, 1930; tchr. speech and drama YWCA, New Orleans, 1938-39, producer, dir. plays, 1938-39; prs. Krewe of Aparamest, New Orleans, 1938; chmn. fundraising New Orleans Philharmonic Symphony, New Orleans, 1967; mem. women's vol. com. New Orleans Mus. Art, 1967-68; dir. sr. and jr. choir Mt. Olivet Episcopal Ch., New Orleans, 1922-83, mem. altar guild, 1922-83; pres. Mt. Olivet's Women Aux., New Orleans, 1950; mem. women's guild New Orleans Philharmonic; pres. Social Directory of Greater Ne Orlenas, 1992-94. Mem. DAR, English Speaking Union, La. Landmark Soc., Friends of the Cabildo, Children of the Am. Revolution (sr. prs. 1969), Colonial Dames XVII Century (pres. La. chpt. 1977). Home: 4403 Maple Leaf Dr New Orleans LA 70131-7455

CRUMLEY, ROGER LEE, surgeon, educator; b. Perry, Iowa, Oct. 8, 1941; s. Dwight Moody and Helen Ethelwyn (Anderson) C.; m. Janet Lynn Conant, Nov. 13, 1987; children: Erin Kelly Helen, Danielle Nicole. BA, Simpson Coll., 1964; MS, U. Iowa, 1975, MD, 1967. Diplomate Am. Bd. Otolaryngology (dir. 1992—). Intern L.A. County Gen. Hosp., 1967-68; resident in surgery Highland-Alameda Hosp., Oakland, Calif., 1968-69; battalion surgeon 1st Marine Div., Vietnam, 1968-69; resident in otolaryngology U. Iowa, Iowa City, 1971-75; chief otolaryngology San Francisco Gen. Hosp., 1975-81; assoc. prof., then prof. U. Calif., San Francisco, 1981-87; prof., chief otolaryngology-head and neck surgery U. Calif., Irvine, 1987—; guest prof. Humboldt U., East Berlin, 1982, M.S. McLeod vis. prof. S. Australian Postgrad. Edn. Ctr., Adelaide, 1988; treas., pres. Am. Acad. Facial Plastic Surgeons, 1994-95; McBride lectr. U. Edinburgh, 1998. Contbr. articles and book chpts. to profl. publs. With USN, 1969-71, Vietnam. Recipient Alumni Achievement award Simpson Coll., 1984. Fellow ACS, Am. Acad. Otolaryngology (treas., bd. dirs. 1988—, award 1989); mem. Soc. Univ. Otolaryngologists, Bohemian Club (San Francisco), Center Club (Costa Mesa, Calif.). Republican. Methodist. Avocations: music, piano, jazz flügelhorn, running, skiing. Office: U Calif-Irvine Med Ctr Dept Otolaryngology/Head/Neck 101 The City Dr S Orange CA 92868-3201

CRUMMETT, WARREN BERLIN, analytical chemistry consultant; b. Moyers, W.Va., Apr. 4, 1922; s. Elmer and Virginia Maude (Smith) C.; m. Elizabeth Ann Stathers, Feb. 28, 1948; children: Allan Warren, Daniel David. *Pioneer Christopher Crummett arrived in Philadelphia 1752 and established his homestead on Crummett Run in Shenandoah Mountains of Virginia by 1787. A community developed around a one-room school and rustic church. There two sixth-generation descendants, Elmer and Virginia Maude Smith Crummett, certified teachers and devout Christians, married and gave life to Warren Berlin Crummett. Warren married Elizabeth Ann Strathers, removed to Midland, Michigan, and fathered Allan Warren (psychologist), who married Carrie Ann Bristow and fathered Warren Luke and Autumn Leah; and Daniel David (physician), who married Bobbi Dee Price. Their children are Elisabeth Hannah, Carrianne Strathers, and Samuel Christopher.* BA, Bridgewater (Va.) Coll., 1943; PhD, Ohio State U., 1951. Control chemist Solvay Process Co., Hopewell, Va., 1943-46; chemist Dow Chem. Co., Midland, Mich., 1951-55, lab. supr., 1955-61, asst. lab. dir., 1961-71, rsch. scientist, 1971-84, rsch. fellow, 1984-88; cons. chemist, Midland, 1988—; mem. sci. adv. bd. EPA, Washington, 1976-78, cons., 1980; cons. USAF, Washington, 1981. Contbr. articles to sci. jours. Recipient H.H. Dow medal, 1980, Disting. Alumnus award Bridgewater Coll., 1983. Mem. Am. Chem. Soc. (chmn. analytical div. 1983, Midland sect. award 1987), Rsch. Soc. Am., N.Y. Acad. Scis. Achievements include research on hypothesis of trace chemistries of fire. Home and Office: 808 Crescent Dr Midland MI 48640-3434

CRUMP, JOHN, lawyer; Exec. dir. Nat. Bar Assn., Washington. Office: Nat Bar Assn 1225 11th St NW Washington DC 20001-4217*

CRUMP, LISA M., rehabilitation nurse; b. St. Louis, Mar. 26, 1963; d. James J. and Sheila A. (Busch) Gilliam; married. ADN, Maryville Coll., St. Louis, 1984, BSN, 1987; MSN, U. Mo., St. Louis, 1999. Cert. rehab. nurse. Nurse clinician rehab. unit St. John's Mercy Med. Ctr., St. Louis.

CRUMP, RONALD CORDELL, lawyer; b. Washington, Nov. 2, 1951; s. Robert Callwell and Marie Evangeline (Greene) C. BS, U. Ariz., 1974; JD, U. Notre Dame, 1979. Bar: D.C. 1980, U.S. Dist Ct. D.C. 1980, U.S. Ct. Appeals 1980, U.S. Ct. Claims 1980, U.S. Tax Ct. 1980, U.S. Ct. Mil. Appeals 1980, U.S. Ct. Appeals (4th cir.) 1981, U.S. Supreme Ct. 1984. Intern Law Revision Counsel U.S. Ho. of Reps., Washington, 1978; law clk. to assoc. judge D.C. Ct. Appeals, Washington, 1979-80; gen atty. VA, Washington, 1980-86; asst. atty. Office of U.S. Atty., Washington, 1986-90; atty. com. on stds. ofcl. conduct U.S. Ho. of Reps., Washington, 1990-93, atty. com. on internat. rels., 1995—; pvt. practice, 1993-95. Mem. FBA (bd. dirs. 1984—), Washington Bar Assn. (pres. 1995-97), D.C. Bar Assn., Notre Dame Club, Sigma Delta Tau. Republican. Roman Catholic. Home: 3819 Kansas Ave NW Washington DC 20011-5709

CRUMP, SPENCER, publisher, business executive; b. San Jose, Calif., Nov. 25; s. Spencer M. and Jessie (Person) C.; m. Cynthia Fink, 1992; children by previous marriage: John Spencer, Victoria Elizabeth Margaret. B.A., U. So. Calif., 1960, M.S. in Edn, 1962, M.A. in Journalism, 1969. Reporter Long Beach (Calif.) Ind., 1945-49; freelance writer Long Beach, 1950-51; travel columnist, picture editor Long Beach Ind.-Press-Telegram, 1952-56; pres. Crest Industries Corp., Long Beach, 1957-58; editor suburban sects. Los Angeles Times, 1959-62; editorial dir. Trans-Anglo Books, Los Angeles, 1962-73, pub., 1973-81; pub. Zeta Pubs. Co., Corona Del Mar, Calif., 1981—; mng. dir. Person-Crump Devel. Co. (formerly Person Properties Co.), Justiceburg, Tex., 1951—; chmn. dept. journalism Orange Coast Coll., 1966-84; chmn. bd. Zeta Internat., 1976—; cons. Queen Beach Press, 1974-87, Flying Spur Press, 1976—, So. Pacific Transp. Co., 1979-80, Interurban Press/Trans-Anglo Books, 1981-87; bd. dirs. Zeta Britain, Zeta Internat.; chmn. bd. T & S Publs. Group, Inc., Canyon Lake, Calif., 1988-89. Author: Ride the Big Red Cars, 1962, Redwoods, Iron Horses and the Pacific, 1963, Western Pacific-The Railroad that Was Built Too Late, 1963, California's Spanish Missions Yesterday and Today, 1964, Black Riot in Los Angeles, 1966, Henry Huntington and the Pacific Electric, 1970, Fundamentals of Journalism, 1974, California's Spanish Missions—An Album, 1975, Suggestions for Teaching the Fundamentals of Journalism in College, 1976, The Stylebook for Newswriting, 1979, Newsgathering and Newswriting for the 1980s and Beyond, 1981, Riding the California Western Skunk R.R., 1988, Durango to Silverton by Narrow Gauge Rail, 1990, Riding the Cumbres & Toltec Railroad, 1992, Rails to the Grand Canyon, 1993, Route 66: America's First Main Street, 1994. Mem. Los Angeles County Democratic Central Com., 1961-62. Mem. Book Pubs. Assn. So. Calif., Fellowship Reconciliation, Soc. Profl. Journalists. Unitarian-Universalist. Office: Zeta Pubs Co PO Box 38 Corona Del Mar CA 92625-0038

CRUMPACKER, MARGERY ANN, educator; b. Hammond, Ind., Aug. 15; d. Frederick Charles and Mary Windle C. BA in European History, U. Mich., 1946; PhD in French, CUNY, 1997. Rsch., media asst. advt. agys., Chgo., 1946-53; recreation dir., supr. Dept. Army Civilian Spl. Svcs., Germany, France, 1954-58; legal sec. Nestle Alimentana Co., Vevey, Switzerland, 1961, Belg. Am. Bank, N.Y.C., 1961-71; freelance legal sec. temp. agys., N.Y.C., 1972-53; rschr. CUNY, 1994-97. Author of poems. Travel rsch. grantee, Henri Peyre Inst., Paris, 1996. Mem. Modern Lang Assn., Northeast Modern Lang Assn. Presbyterian. Avocations: dogs, hiking, writing. Home: 165 E 35th St 5-D New York NY 10016

CRUMPACKER, REX K., anesthesiologist; b. Lindsborg, Kans., Apr. 13, 1964; s. John Edward and Shirley Jane (Heidebrecht) Dornberger; m. Katherine J. Jones Crumpacker, Apr. 28, 1990; children: Kristen Jane, Michael Curtis. BA in Life Sci., Kans. State U., 1986; MD, U. Kans., 1990. Diplomate Am. Bd. Anesthesiology. Intern U. Nebr., Omaha, 1990-92, resident, 1992-95; attending anesthesiologist Freeman Hosp., Joplin, Mo., 1995—. Mem. AMA, Am. Soc. Regional Anesthesiologists, Internat. Anesthesia Rsch. Soc., Soc. Cardiovascular Anesthesiologists. Republican. Presbyterian. Home: 602 Seville Cir Joplin MO 64804-4568 Office: 3333 Mc Intosh Cir Ste 6 Joplin MO 64804-3681

CRUMPLER, HUGH ALLAN, author; b. Rolla, Mo., Mar. 14, 1918; s. Hugh Dinsmore and Addye Adelle (Alexander) C.; m. Dorothy Carter, May 28, 1945; children: Hugh III, Shelley Ann Hexom, Joan Carter Gross. B of Journalism, U. Mo., 1941. Journalist N.Y. Herald Tribune, 1941-43; field cashier Am. Field Svc. Motor Ambulance, Burma and India, 1943-44; war correspondent United Press, China, Burma, India, Philippines, Okinawa, Japan and Korea, 1944-45; coll. instr. Mo. Sch. of Mines and Metallurgy, Rolla, 1946-49; lectr. U. Minn., Mpls., 1949-50; asst. attache, press officer Am. Embassy, Karachi, Pakistan, 1950-52; attache, press officer Am. Embassy, Ankara, Turkey, 1952-54; counsul, pub. affairs officer Am. Consulate Gen., Istanbul, Turkey, 1955-56; country pub. affairs officer Am. Embassy, Amman, Jordan, 1957-58; attache, pub. analyst Office of Rsch. and Intelligence, U.S. Info. Agy., Washington, 1958-60; v.p., Washington rep. Dean Internat., Inc., Long Beach, Calif., 1960-65, Global Van Lines, Inc., Anaheim, Calif., 1965-67; v.p. advt., pub. rels. Four Winds Internat., Inc., Washington and San Diego, 1967—; lectr. Continuing Edn. Ctr. San Diego State U., Rancho Bernardo, Calif., 1992—; v.p., dean Indpls. Racing Team, 1963-65; columnist San Diego Union-Tribune, 1975—, How's Your CBI IQ, 1979—, Ex-CBI Roundup, 1979—; adv. bd. San Diego Union-Tribune, 1994—; comml. lectr. WWII, world deserts, desert wildflowers, classic poets, Himalayan kingdoms. Author: On the Trail of the Desert Wildflower, 1994, The Last Patrol: A Correspondent's Journey to the War in Asia and the Pacific, 1997; author, co-editor: (with Theodore Wertheim) Communist Propaganda: A Fact Book, 1957-58. Decorated Burma star (Great Britain), Medal of Freedom Fighters (China), U.S. Pacific campaign ribbons. Mem. Assn. Former Intelligence Officers, Sigma Nu. Home: 17205 Montero Rd San Diego CA 92128-2339

CRUMPLEY, CHARLES ROBERT THOMAS, journalist; b. Kansas City, Mo., July 2, 1953; s. Charles Walter and Patricia (Greeley) C.; m. Susan Kay Childs, Aug. 3, 1974; children: Brian D., Benton G.B., Elliott Maxwell, Michael R.T. BS in English and Journalism, U. Mo., Kansas City, 1976. Reporter met. staff Kansas City Times, 1976-81, bus. writer, 1981-90; sr. fin. writer Kansas City Star, 1990—; mem., chmn. Fulbright judging com. Com. for Internat. Exch. Scholars, 1991-97. Recipient award for consumer journalism Nat. Press Club, 1987, award for fin. writing, Pannell Kerr Forster, 1989, John Hancock Ins. Co., 1989; Fulbright rsch. scholar, Tokyo, 1990-91. Office: Kansas City Star 1729 Grand Blvd Kansas City MO 64108-1458

CRUMRINE, PATRICIA K., physician, educator; b. Jan. 19, 1942. BS, Marietta Coll., 1964; MD, Med. Coll. Pa., 1968. Prof. pediatrics and neurology U. Pitts./Children's Hosp., 1975—. E-mail: pkc@med.pitt.edu. Office: 3705 5th Ave Pittsburgh PA 15213-2583

CRUNDWELL, DUNCAN JAMES, electronics executive; b. Maidstone, Kent, Eng., Mar. 18, 1957; s. James Stanley and June (Reid) C.; m. Bridgette Grieve, Dec. 24, 1983 (div. Jan. 1995); 1 child, Ben; m. Natasha Shankova, May 12, 1995. BS in Mech. Engring., Brunel U., London, 1979; MBA, Henley Mgmt. Coll., Eng., 1996. Chartered Engr. Student engr. Dowty Group, Cheltenham, Eng., 1975-79; chief engr. Yamco, London, 1979-80; tech. mgr. Bandive, London, 1980-84; custom projects mgr. Solid State Logic, Oxford, Eng., 1984-86; systems mgr. Solid State Logic, 1986-88, product group mgr., 1988-90; mng. dir. Solid State Logic Organ Systems, Brandon, Eng., 1990-95; CEO, pres. Solid State Logic Organ Systems, Detroit, 1995—; tchr. Opening Windows on Engring., Oxford Schs., 1988-91. Prodr.: (radio program) Glad to Be Gay or Not?, 1977 (UK Local Radio award 1977); client/project mgr. new hdqs. bldg. Solid State Logic (Royal Inst. Brit. Architects award 1989); inventor in field. Recipient Dir. Gen.'s cert. Engring. Coun., London, 1990. Mem. Instn. Mech. Engrs. (chmn. YM panel 1988-89, sec. 1987-88, Outstanding Project Work award 1979), Assn. MBAs. Anglican. Avocations: photography, architecture, music, fine art. Home: Apt 3224 1766 Grant St Birmingham MI 48009-2036 Office: Solid State Logic Organ Sys 37545 Schoolcraft Rd Livonia MI 48150-1009

CRUSE, ALLAN BAIRD, mathematician, computer scientist, educator; b. Birmingham, Ala., Aug. 28, 1941; s. J. Clyde and Irma R. Cruse. AB, Emory U., 1962, PhD, 1974; postgrad. (Woodrow Wilson fellow) U. Calif., Berkeley, 1962-63, MA, 1965; tchg. fellow Dartmouth Coll., 1963-64. Instr., U. San Francisco, 1966-73, asst. prof. math., 1973-76, assoc. prof., 1976-79, prof., 1979—, chmn. math. dept. 1988-91; vis. instr. Stillman Coll., summer 1967; vis. assoc. prof. Emory U., spring 1978; prof. computer sci. Sonoma State U., 1983-85; cons. math edn. NSF fellow, 1972-73. Mem. Am. Math. Soc., Math. Am. Math. Soc., Math. Assn. Am. (chmn. No. Calif. sect. 1995-96), Assn. Computing Machinery, U. San Francisco Faculty Assn., Sigma Xi (Dissertation award 1974). Author: (with Millianne Granberg) Lectures on Freshman Calculus, 1971; research, publs. in field. Office: U San Francisco Harney Sci Ctr San Francisco CA 94117

CRUSE, DENTON W., marketing and advertising executive, consultant; b. Washington, May 21, 1944; s. Denton W. Sr. and Frances Rankin (Moore) C.; m. Susan Costello, June 11, 1988; 1 child, Thomas Moore. BS, Va. Commonwealth U., 1966; MBA, So. Ill. U., 1977. Media supr. Procter & Gamble Co., Cin., 1967-73; assoc. media dir. Ralston Purina Co., St. Louis, 1973-78; dir. advt. Armour-Dial Co., Phoenix, 1978-81; mktg. dir. Valentine Greeting Inc., Phoenix, 1981-82; dir. mktg. svcs. J. Walter Thompson/USA, L.A., 1982-83; cons. L.A., 1983-86; dir. advt. svcs. Mattel Inc., L.A., 1986-88; cons. C and O Assocs., L.A., 1988—; instr. UCLA, 1986—; spkr. internat. mktg. seminar Tech. Tng. Corp., 1993—. Editor-in-chief: Cobblestone, 1965. Marathon monitor L.A. Olympic Organizing Com., 1984; bd. dirs. Old Hometown Fair. Mem. Mktg. Club L.A., Beta Gamma Sigma, Pi Sigma Epsilon. Republican. Presbyterian.

CRUSE, JULIUS MAJOR, JR., pathologist, educator; b. New Albany, Miss., Feb. 15, 1937; s. Julius Major and Effie (Davis) C. BA, BS with honors, U. Miss., 1958; DMS with honors, U. Graz, Austria, 1960; MD, U. Tenn., 1964, Ph.D. in Pathology (USPHS fellow), 1966, USPHS postdoctoral fellow, 1964-67; DD (hon.), Gen. Theol. Sem., 1999. Mem. faculty U. Miss. Med. Sch., 1967—; prof. immunology, biology Grad. Sch., 1967-74, prof. pathology, 1974—, asso. prof. microbiology, 1974—, dir. grad. studies program in pathology, 1974—, dir. clin. immunopathology, 1978—, dir. immunopathology sect., 1978—, dir. tissue typing lab., 1980—, assoc. prof. medicine, 1989—; lectr. pathology U. Tenn. Coll. Medicine, 1967-74; aj. prof. immunology Miss. Coll., 1977—; mem. sci. adv. bd. Immuno Tech. Corp., L.A.; active FDA Expert Panel on Alternatives to Silicone Breast Implants, 1994—. Author: Immunology Examination Review Book, 1971, rev. edit., 1975, Introduction to Immunology, 1977, Principles of Immunopathology, 1979; editor-in-chief Immunologic Rsch., 1981—, Pathology and Immunopathology Rsch., 1982-90, Concepts in Immunopathology, 1985—, The Year in Immunology, 1984—, Pathobiology: Jour. Immunopathology, 1990—, Molecular and Cellular Biology, 1990, Transgenics: Biological Analysis Through DNA Transfer; contbns. to Microbiology and Immunology; editor Immunomodulation of Neoplasia, Antigenic Variation: Molecular and Genetic Mechanisms of Relapsing Disease, 1987, Autoimmunoregulation and Autoimmune Disease, 1987; The Year in Immunology, vol. 1, 1984-85, vol. 2, 1985-86, The Year in Immunology, vol. 3, 1987, The Year in Immunology, vols. 4, 5, 1988, vol. 6, 1989-90, Genetic Basis of Autoimmune Disease, 1988, Cellular Aspects of Autoimmunity, 1988, Therapy of Autoimmune Diseases, 1989, B Lymphocytes: Function and Regulation, Conjugate Vaccines, 1989, Molecules and Cells of Immunity, 1990, Immunoregulation and Autoimmunity, 1986, Organ-Based Autoimmune Diseases, 1985, Autoimmunity: Basic Concepts, Systematic and Selected Organ-Specific Diseases, 1985, Clinical and Molecular Aspects of Autoimmune Diseases, 1990, Immunoregulatory Cytokines and Cell Growth, 1989, Complement Profiles, 1992; co-editor: Self-Nonself Discrimination in the Immune System, 1992, Complement Profiles, vol. 1, 1992, Illustrated Dictionary of Immunology, 1995, Atlas of Immunology, 1998; contbr. chpts. to books and articles to profl. jours. Recipient Pathologists award in continuing edn. Coll. Am. Pathologists-Am. Soc. Clin. Pathologists, 1976; Julius M. Cruse collection in immunology established in his honor Middleton Med. Libr., U. Wis., Madison, 1979, Julius M. Cruse collection of T.S. Eliot's works, St. Mark's Libr., Gen. Theol. Sem. (Episcopal), N.Y.C.; Wilson Found. grantee, 1990-95, 93-94, 95-98; B.S. Guyton lectr. on history of medicine, 1998. Fellow AAAS, Royal Soc. Promotion Health, Am. Acad. Microbiology, Am. Soc. for Histocompatibility and Immunogenetics (chmn. publs. com. 1987-95, councillor 1997—), Intercontinental Biog. Assn.; mem. AMA (Physicians Recognition award 196-75), Clin. Immunology Soc., Am. Inst. Biol. Scis., Am. Soc. Clin. Pathologists, Can. Soc. Microbiologists, N.Y. Acad. Scis. Exptl. Biology and Medicine, Soc. Francaise d'Immunologie, Reticuloendothelial Soc., Transplantation Soc., Electron Microscopy Soc. Am., Am. Assn. History Medicine, The Paul Ehrlich Soc., Am. Assn. Pathologists, Am. Chem. Soc., Brit. Soc. Immunology, Can. Soc. Immunology, Am. Soc. Microbiology, Internat. Acad. Pathology, Am. Assn. Immunologists (historian 1990—), Sigma Xi, Phi Kappa Phi, Phi Eta Sigma, Alpha Epsilon Delta, Gamma Sigma Epsilon, Beta Beta Beta. Episcopalian. Office: U Miss Med Ctr Dept Pathology 2500 N State St Jackson MS 39216-4500

CRUSEMANN, F(REDERICK) ROSS, advertising agency official; b. Ft. Worth, Nov. 9, 1953; s. Frederick Ross and Louise (Russell) C. BA, Austin Coll., 1975; MBA, Tex. Christian U., 1977. Supr. Ben E. Keith Co., Ft. Worth, 1977-78; project dir. Parmer Cos., Ft. Worth, 1978-80; mktg. mgr. Shoreline Products, Ft. Worth, 1980-85; mktg. cons. Dallas, 1986; mgr. programs visibility FW divsn. Gen. Dynamics, Ft. Worth, 1986-89; dir. mktg. Motel 6, Dallas, 1989-94; v.p. Peter A. Mayer Advt., Baton Rouge, 1994—. Sponsor Spl. Olympics Internat., Washington, 1992-94, Dallas Symphony Assn., 1992—, Sta. KERA-PBS Affiliation, Dallas, 1993—. Recipient Commendation award Radio Advt. Bur., N.Y.C., 1993; named Am. Advt. Assn. Ad Person of Yr., New Orleans Ad Club, 1998. Mem. Am. Mktg. Assn. (Tomy award 1989), Assn. Nat. Advertisers (com. chmn. 1989—), Travel Industry Assn. (com. mem. 1992—, nat. conf. planning com. 1992—, POW WOW internat. planning com. 1993—), Am. Hotel and Motel Assn. (comms. com. 1991—), Hotel Sales and Mktg. Assn. Internat. (Adrian award 1989—). Avocations: skiing, water-skiing, bicycling, cooking. Home: 6403 Ellsworth Ave Dallas TX 75214-2723 Office: Peter A Mayer Advt 5757 Corporate Blvd Ste 300 Baton Rouge LA 70808-2559

CRUSTO, MITCHELL FERDINAND, lawyer, educator; b. New Orleans, Apr. 22, 1953. BA magna cum laude, Yale U., 1975; BA, Oxford U., Eng., 1980, MA, 1985; JD, Yale U., 1981. Bar: La. 1982, Mo. 1984, Ill. 1985. Law clk. to Hon. John M. Wisdom U.S. Ct. Appeals (5th cir.), New Orleans, 1981-82; assoc. Jones, Walker, Waechter, Pointevent, Carrere & Denegre, New Orleans, 1982-84; sr. v.p., gen. counsel, asst. corp. sec. Stifel, Nicolaus & Co., Inc., St. Louis, 1984-88; CEO Crusto Capital Resources, Inc., St. Louis, 1988-89; assoc. dep. adminstr. for fin., investment and procurement U.S. Small Bus. Adminstrn., Washington, 1989-91; dir. corp. environ. policy Monsanto Co., St. Louis, 1991-93; sr. mgr. Arthur Andersen Environ. Svcs., Chgo., 1993-95; assoc. prof. Loyola Sch. Law, New Orleans, 1995—; mem. faculty Washington U., St. Louis, 1985-89, St. Louis U. Law Sch., 1987-88, Webster U., St. Louis, 1986; securities advisor to sec. of state State of Mo., 1986-89; lectr. legal divsn. Securities Industry Assn., 1986-88; mem. Pres. Clinton transition team natural resource cluster EPA, 1992. Contbr. articles in newspapers, mags., jours. Mem. ABA, La. Bar Assn., Mo. Bar Assn., Ill. Bar Assn., Middle Temple (London). Home: 3443 Esplanade Ave Apt 361 New Orleans LA 70119-2954 Office: Loyola U Sch Law 7214 Saint Charles Ave # 901 New Orleans LA 70118-3538

CRUTCHER, DIMETREC ARTEZ, electronics technician; b. Gallatin, Tenn., June 27, 1964; s. James Davis and Lavenia Ann (Turner) C.; m. Kimolin Gilbert, Aug. 1, 1992; chhildren: Dimitria Kim, Kyanna D'ar. AS in Electronic Engring., ITT Tech. Inst., 1984. Audio-visual specialist Allied Audio-Visual Svcs., Nashville, 1985-88; field svc. tech. Spectradyne Inc., Nashville, 1988-94; field svc. supr. Spectradyne Inc., Louisville, Ky., 1990-94; co-owner Urbannetic Comms., 1994-96; project mgr. ICS Comm., 1996—; lead technician Spectravision by Oncommand, 1996-98; GPS/network adminstr. White House Utility Dist., 1998—; audio-visual cons., engr. Key Meth. Ch., Gallatin, 1988—. Recipient 1st Place award Queen City Bodybldg. Championship, 1985, Southeastern Bodybldg. Championship, 1987, Light Heavy Weight Mr. Tenn., 1998. Mem. Nat. Physique Com. Democrat. Methodist. Avocations: bodybuilding, amateur photography, video and satellite repair. Home: 887 Green Wave Dr Gallatin TN 37066-3685

CRUTCHFIELD, CAROLYN ANN, physical therapy educator; b. New Castle, Colo., Apr. 2, 1942; d. Leland Arnold and Josephine Kathyrn (Leppink) C. BA, Western State Coll., 1964; cert. phys. therapy, Duke U., 1965; MS in Anatomy, West Va. U., 1970, EdD, 1976. Lic. phys. therapist, Ga. Dir. Rockingham Crippled Children's Ctr., Harrisonburg, Va., 1967-68; staff therapist Woodrow Wilson Rehab. Ctr., Fisherville, Va., 1966-67, West Va. U. Hosp., Morgantown, Va., 1968-70; asst. prof., asst. dir. Dept. Phys. Therapy, West Va. Sch. Medicine, Morgantown, 1970-75, assoc. prof., dir., 1975-78, prof., acting chair, 1978-80; prof., dir. grad. studies Dept. Phys. Therapy, Ga. State U., Atlanta, 1980—, disting. prof., 1983; chair Am. Bd. Phys. Therapy Specialties, Alexandria, Va., 1978-90; sec. Soc. for Behavioral Kinesiology, 1977-79. Author: The Muscle Spindle, 1972, Reflexes in Motor Development, 1978, Patient at Home, 1970, 84, Reflex and Vestibular Aspects of Motor Control, Motor Learning, Motor Development, 1990, Peripheral Components of Motor Control, 1984, Motor Control and Motor Learning in Rehabilitation, 1993, others; contbr. numerous chpts. to book and articles to jours. Chair ushers North Decatur Presbyn. Ch., Decatur, Ga., 1990, co-treas., 1991—. Recipient Cert. of Merit award Am. Bd. Phys. Therapy Specialties, 1990. Mem. Am. Phys. Therapy Assn. (chair neurology sect. 1983-85, treas. 1989-91, pres. West Va. chpt. 1978-79, Baethke-Carlin Teaching award 1984, Lucy Blair Svc. award 1991, Catherine Worthingham fellow 1996, Svc. to Neurology Sect. award 1999), Assn. Clin. Electrophysiology. Avocations: poet, amateur archaeologist, model maker. Home: 3127 W Roxboro Rd NE Atlanta GA 30324-2541

CRUTCHFIELD, EDWARD ELLIOTT, JR., banking executive; b. Detroit, July 14, 1941; s. Edward Elliott and Katherine (Sikes) C.; m. Nancy Glass Kizer, July 27, 1963; children: Edward Elliott, III, Sarah Palmer. BA, Davidson Coll., 1963; MBA, U. Pa., 1965. With First Union Nat. Bank, Charlotte, N.C., 1965—, head retail bank services group, 1970-72, exec. v.p. gen. adminstrn., 1972-73, pres., 1973-84, vice chmn., from 1984; pres. First Union Corp. (parent), Charlotte, 1983-86, chief exec. officer, 1984—, now also chmn., bd. dirs.; bd. dirs. Bernhardt Industries, Inc., Charlotte, 1983—. Bd. deacons Myers Park Presbyn. Ch.; bd. dirs. United Community Services, Salvation Army, Charlotte Bd., Charlotte Latin Sch.; trustee Mint Mus. Art, N.C. Nature Conservancy; bd. mgrs. Charlotte Meml. Hosp.; bd. visitors Davidson Coll. Mem. Charlotte C. of C., Assn. Res. City Bankers, Am., N.C. bankers assns., Am. Textile Mfrs. Assn., Young Pres.'s Orgn. Clubs: Charlotte City, Charlotte Country, Linville (N.C.) Golf. Office: 1st Union Corp One First Union Center 301 S College St Charlotte NC 28202-6000*

CRUTCHFIELD, ROBERT ALAN, computer scientist; b. Houston, Nov. 1, 1962; s. Joseph Everitt and Marilyn Louise (Colliver) C. Student, San Jacinto Coll., 1982-84, U. Houston, 1984-86; certificate in paralegal, S.W. Paralegal Inst., 1988; DD (hon.), First Internt. Church of the Web, 1998; grad., The Leadership Inst., 1998, 99. Paralegal, legal clerk Houston, 1988-90; reporter, photographer Arcane Pub., Houston, 1990; sales assoc. Computer City, Houston, 1991, 95; sales rep. Radio Shack, Houston, 1993-94; treas., press sec. Eide for Congress, Houston, 1994-95; demo specialist Channel Reps. Inc., Houston, 1996; customer support rep. Matrix Mktg., Houston, 1996-98; comm. dir. Cottar for Congress, Baytown, Tex., 1998; ind. tech. cons. hand techs., 1998—. Chmn. pub. rels. Harris County Rep. Party, Houston, 1992-94; chmn. 6th Senate Dist. Rep. Party, Houston, 1994-96; v.p. recreation bd. City of Galena (Tex.) Park, 1996—; bd. dirs., admissions bd. Christian Acad. Theol. Studies, Tallahasse, Fla. Recipient Tex. Yellow Rose award ARC, 1983, 100 Fathoms Group award, 1990; Named Hon. Adm., Tex. Navy, 1986. Mem. Houston Area League PC Users (mem. com. 1995-99), Rep. Nat. Comm. (life mem.), Navy League of U.S., Biblical Archaeology Soc. Assembly of God. Avocations: boating, writing, politics. Home and Office: 12414 Ledger Ln Houston TX 77015-6628

CRUTCHFIELD, WILLIAM RICHARD, artist, educator; b. Indpls., Jan. 21, 1932; s. William C. and Vera Eleanor (Wiggam) Neidlinger; m. Barbara Jean Seaman, June 14, 1964. B.F.A., Herron Sch. Art, Ind. U., 1956; M.F.A., Tulane U., 1960. Instr. Herron Sch. Art, Ind. U., Indpls., 1963-65; asst. prof. Mpls. Coll. Art and Design, 1966-67, chmn. found. studies, 1966-67. Author: Owl Feathers, 1975, (film) William Crutchfield, Sage of Machine Wit, 1973, Crutchfield, A Recollection of the Future, 1977; principal works include Alphabet Spire, Corbins Corner, Conn., 1974, Countdown, Short Hills, N.J., 1980, Punctuation Spire, Los Angeles, 1982, Wish, Glen Burnie, Md., 1986, The Importance of Being A Bubble, Ft. Lauderdale/Hollywood Internat. Airport, Ft. Lauderdale, Fla., 1989, Fifty Years of Flight, SAS Hdqs., Stockholm, 1996. Served with U.S. Army, 1957-59. Recipient Mary Milliken award Herron Sch. Art, 1956, Mayor's award for outstanding achievement in arts, L.A., 1988; Fulbright scholar, 1961; named Disting. Artist of Los Angeles 100 Club, Music Center, 1982. Home: 2011 S Mesa St San Pedro CA 90731-5515

CRUTZEN, PAUL JOSEF, research meteorologist, chemist; b. Amsterdam, The Netherlands, 1933. PhD in Meteorology, Stockholm U., 1973; hon. degree, York U., Can., Tel Aviv U., Oreg. State U., U. Bourgogne, Dijon, France, U. Leige, Belgium, U. Cath., Louvain-le-Neuve, Belgium, Aristotelian U., Thessaloniki, Greece. Prof. Max-Planck-Inst. fur Chemie, Mainz, Germany. Recipient Nobel Prize for Chemistry, 1995. Mem. NAS (fgn. assoc.), Russian Acad. Scis. (fgn. assoc.), Royal Swedish Acad. Scis., Royal Swedish Acad. Engring. Scis., Academia Europea.

CRUZ, B. ROBERT, academic administrator; m. Guadalupe Rojas; children: Roberto, Marco Antonio, Fernando Rey. BA in Edn., Wichita State U., 1964; MA in Edn., U. Calif., Berkeley, 1968, PhD in Policy, Planning and Administrn., 1971. Asst. prof. Sch. Edn. St. Mary's Coll., 1972-74; lectr. Sch. Edn. Stanford (Calif.) U., 1978-79; pres. Nat. Hispanic U., San Jose, Calif., 1981—; apptd. nat. adv. coun. dealing with edn. lang. minority students; exec. dir. non-profit ednl. orgn. 5 sch. dist. consortium. Contbr. articles to profl. jours. Recipient numerous awards and honors including Legis. Recognition award in Bilingual Edn., 1974, Cmty. Appreciation award Bakersfield Parent Bd., 1975, Appreciation award Asian Edn. Assn. San Francisco, 1977, Outstanding Leadership award in Edn. U. Calif. Berkeley Chpt. Phi Delta Kappa, 1977, Meritorious award Edn. Limited and Non-English Speaking Students, 1977, Edn. Excellence award Operation Push, 1983; inducted Hispanic Hall of Fame, 1987. Mem. Nat. Assn. Bilingual Edn. (past pres.), Calif. Assn. Bilingual Edn. (past pres., Leadership award 1978). Office: The Nat'l Hispanic U Office of the Pres 14271 Story Rd San Jose CA 95127-3889*

CRUZ, JAVIER F., architect; b. Havana, Cuba, Sept. 1, 1947; came to U.S., 1961; s. Javier Francisco and Rosa Ana (Freire) C.; m. Elodia Degaray, Jan. 26, 1973; children: Anna, Laura. AA, Miami-Dade C.C., Miami, Fla., 1967; BArch, U. Miami, 1972; BSin Environ. Engring., Fla. Internat. U., 1977. Registered architect, Fla. Ptnr. Devel. Cons. Svcs., Miami, 1973-79; prin. Lopez-Cantera & Cruz, Inc., Miami, 1973-79; ptnr. Filer, Hammond, Cruz and Assocs., Coral Gables, Fla., 1979-83; owner Javier Cruz Architects, Miami, 1982—. Com. mem. Met. Dade County Bldg. and Zoning Rev. Com., Miami, 1977-82; advisor architect intern devel. program State of Fla. Bd. Arch., 1984-92; mem. A/E adv. com. Dade County Sch. Bd., 1986-87; mem. adv. bd. for accreditation Fla. Internat. U., 1986-89; dir. Dade County Employs the Handicapped Com., 1988-90, chmn. accessibility com., 1988-90; com. mem. Hurricane Andrew Archtl. Recovery Ctr., 1992; team mem. City of Coral Gables Disaster Assessment Team, 1981-91; exhibit designer Miami Youth Mus., 1989; dir. Bus. Coalition for Ams. with Disabilities, 1990-94; mem. Miami Youth Mus. Bldg. Devel. Com., 1990-91, others. Recipient Grand Orden Martiana, Liceo Cubano, 1977, Grand Orden del Bicentenario, Cuban Liceum, 1976. Mem. AIA (Miami chpt. dir. 1997—, Silver medal 1996), Fla. Assn. of AIA (state dir. 1997—), U. Miami Sch. Arch. Alumni Assn. (sec. 1998). Roman Catholic. Office: Javier Cruz Architects 3400 SW 105th Ct Miami FL 33165-3738

CRUZ, JOSE BEJAR, JR., engineering educator; b. Bacolod City, The Philippines, Sept. 17, 1932; came to U.S., 1954, naturalized, 1969; s. Jose P. and Felicidad (Bejar) C.; m. Stella E. Rubia; children by previous marriage: Fe E. Cruz Langdon, Ricardo A., Rene L., Sylvia C. Cruz Loebach, Loretta C. Cruz Spray. BSEE summa cum laude, U. Philippines, 1953; MS, MIT, 1956; PhD, U. Ill., 1959. Lic. profl. engr., Ill., Ohio. Instr. elec. engring. U. Philippines, Quezon City, 1953-54; rsch. asst. MIT, Cambridge, 1954-56, vis. prof., 1973; from instr. to assoc. prof. U. Ill., Urbana-Champaign, 1956-65; prof. elec. engring. U. Ill., 1965-86, assoc. mem. Ctr. Advanced Study, 1967-68; rsch. prof. Coordinated Sci. Lab., 1965-86; prof. dept. elec. and computer engring. U. Calif., Irvine, 1986-92, chmn. dept., 1986-90; prof. elec. engring. Ohio State U., Columbus, 1992—, dean Coll. Engring., 1992-97, Howard D. Winbigler chair in engring., 1997—; vis. assoc. prof. U. Calif., Berkeley, 1964-65; vis. prof. Harvard U., 1973; pres. Dynamic Sys.; mem. theory com. Am. Automatic Control Coun., 1967; gen. chmn. Conf. on Decision and Control, 1975; mem. profl. engring. exam. com. State of Ill., 1984-86; mem. Nat. Coun. Engring. Examiners, 1985-86; mem. project adv. group on engring. and sci. edn. project Dept. Sci. and Tech., Republic of The Philippines, 1993-98. Author: (with M.E. Van Valkenburg) Introductory Signals and Circuits, 1967, (with W.R. Perkins) Engineering of Dynamic Systems, 1969, Feedback Systems, 1972, translated into Chinese, 1976, Polish, 1977, System Sensitivity Analysis, 1973, (with M.E. Van Valkenburg) Signals in Linear Circuits, 1974, translated into Spanish, 1978; Assoc. editor: Jour. Franklin Inst, 1976-82, Jour. Optimization Theory and Applications, 1980—; series editor Advances in Large Scale Systems Theory and Applications; contbr. articles on network theory, automatic control systems, system theory, sensitivity theory of dynamical systems, large scale systems, dynamic games and dynamic scheduling in mfg. systems to sci., tech. jours. Recipient Purple Tower award Beta Epsilon U., Philippines, 1969, Curtis W. McGraw Rsch. award Am. Soc. for Engring. Edn., 1972, Halliburton Engring. Edn. Leadership award, 1981, Most Outstanding Alumnus award U. of the Philippines Alumni Assn. Am., 1989, Most Outstanding Overseas Alumnus Coll. Engring., U. of the Philippines Alumni Assn., 1990, Richard E. Bellman Control Heritage award Am. Automatic Control Coun., 1994. Fellow AAAS (sect. com. for sect. on engring. 1991-94, sec. 1998—), IEEE (chmn. linear sys. com., group on automatic control 1966-68, assoc. editor Trans. on Circuit Theory 1962-64); mem. Control Sys. Soc. (adminstrv. com. 1966-75, 78-80, v.p. fin. and adminstrv. activities 1976-77, pres. 1979, chmn. awards com. 1973-75, ednl. activities bd. 1973-75, editor Trans. on Automatic Control 1971-73, mem. tech. activities bd 1979-83, chmn. 1982-83, v.p. tech. activities 1982-83, edn. med. com. 1977-79, dir. 1980-85, vice-chmn. publs. bd. 1981, chmn. 1984-85, chmn. panel of tech. editors 1981, chmn. TAB periodicals com. 1981, chmn. PUB. Soc. publs. com. 1981, v.p. publ. activities 1984-85, exec. com. 1982-85, Richard M. Emberson award 1989), Philippine Engrs. and Scientists Orgn., Am. Soc. Engring Edn. (awards policy com.), U.S. Nat. Acad. Engring. (mem. peer com. for electronics engring. 1982, com. on nat. agenda for career-long edn. for engrs. 1986-88, membership com. 1987-90, acad. adv. bd. 1994-97), Philippine-Am. Acad. Sci. and Engring. (founding mem. 1980, pres. 1982, chmn. bd. dirs. 1998), Internat. Fedn. Automatic Control (chmn. theory com. 1981-84, vice-chmn. tech. bd. 1984-87, policy com. 1987-93, vice-chmn. 1993, chmn. 1996, congress internat. program com.), Philippine Engrs. and Scientists Orgn., Sigma Xi, Phi Kappa Phi, Eta Kappa Nu. Achievements include introduction of concept of comparison sensitivity in dynamical feedback systems, of leader-follower strategies in hierarchical engineering systems; development of synthesis methods for time-varying systems. Office: Ohio State U Dept Elec Engring Columbus OH 43210-1272

CRUZ, LUCY, city councilwoman; b. Bayamon, P.R.; m. Orlan do Cruz; children: Christopher, Iliana, Brandon. Dist. mgr. Bronx. Cmty. Bd.; exec. aide to Dep. Mayor Herman Badillo; mayoral liaison Off Neighborhood Svc., -83; mem. Cmty. Sch. Bd., -90; city councilwoman Dist. 18, N.Y.C., 1992—; mem. edn., youth, state and fed. legis., aging coms.; dir. cmty. affairs Bronx Mcpl. Hosp., -91. chair civil svc. and labor, Bronx, 1998—; mem. youth and aging coms., Bronx, 1998—. Office: 1967 Turnbull Ave Bronx NY 10473-2519*

CRUZ, WILFREDO VARGAS, software safety and reliability consultant; b. Metro-Manila, The Philippines, Nov. 27, 1942; came to U.S., 1967; s. Alfredo Cordova and Presentacion (Vargas) C.; m. Florita Vedoya Salandanan, July 30, 1979; children: John Christopher, Charles Wesley. BSEE, U. the East, Manila, 1964. Cons. Braun Global Svcs. Inc., Arabian Am. Oil Co., Dharan, Saudia Arabia, 1977-83, Lockheed Space Ops. Co., Titusville, Fla., 1984-89, Lockheed Engring. and Scis. Co., Moffett Field, Calif., 1989, Westinghouse Marine Divsn., Sunnyvale, Calif., 1989-91, Ralph M. Parsons Co., Pasadena, Calif., Boeing Aerospace Ops., Inc., Moffett Field, 1994, Hernandez Engring., Inc., Moffett Field, 1995, Lockheed Martin Def. Sys., Pittsfield, Mass., 1996, United Def. LP, Mpls., 1996, Boeing Def. and Space

Co., Chatsworth, Calif., 1996-98, Hunterskil Howard Internat. Ltd., London, 1998—. CEO, founder Euro-Asian-Am. Found., Hengelo, The Netherlands, 1998. Specialist 5 U.S. Army, 1967-70. Mem. Sys. Safety Soc. E-mail: will.cruz@wxs.nl; wvcruz1227@aol.com. Home: 17895 Calle Barcelona Rowland Heights CA 91748 also: Castorweg 189, 7557 KK Hengelo The Netherlands Office: Hollandse Singallapparaten, PO Box 42, 7550 GD Hengelo The Netherlands

CRUZ, WILHELMINA MANGAHAS, nephrologist educator; b. Bulacan, Philippines, July 20, 1942; d. Rectorino Bernardo and Mercedes Correa (Manganas) C.; m. Antonio I. Lee, May 28, 1977; children: Richard Anthony, Alexander Victor. AA, U. Santo Tomas, Philippines, 1960, MD, 1965. Diplomate Am. Bd. Internal Medicine, Am. Bd. Nephrology (spl. qualifications in critical care medicine). Intern Meml. Hosp., Albany, N.Y., 1967-68; resident in internal medicine Coney Island Hosp., Bklyn., 1968-71; fellow in nephrology VA Hosp., Bronx, 1971-72, Downstate Med. Ctr., Bklyn., 1972-73; staff physician King's County Hosp. Ctr., Bklyn., 1973-76; coord. in medicine Kingsbrook Jewish Med. Ctr., Bklyn., 1976—; assoc. medical dir. ICU, Doctor's Community Hosp., Lanh am, Md., 1977—; clin. asst. prof. SUNY, Downstate Med. Center, Bklyn., 1977—. Mem. ACP, Med. And Chirurg. Soc. Md., Prince George's Med. Soc., Am. Soc. Nephrology, Soc. Critical Care Medicine, Philippine Med. Assn. Washington. Roman Catholic. Office: 7700 Old Branch Ave Ste D205 Clinton MD 20735-1611

CRUZAN, CLARAH CATHERINE, dietitian; b. Cushing, Okla., Mar. 17, 1913; d. Ulysses Grant and Mamie Amanda (Montgomery) C. BS, Okla. State U., 1941; MS, U. Iowa, 1942. Lic. dietitian, Okla., 1984. Instr. household sci. Okla. State U., Stillwater, 1942-43, instr. home econs. edn., 1947-49; cons. dietitian Rest Haven Nursing Home, Cushing, Okla., 1967-91. Sec. Cushing Sr. Citizens Steering Coun., 1972-91; reporter Okla. Pioneer club, Cushing, 1973-85; precinct election judge, 1989-94. 1st lt. U.S. Army, 1943-46, ETO. Decorated Bronze Star. Mem. AAUW (life, treas. 1970-72, pres. 1974-75), Am. Dietetic Assn., Okla. Heritage Assn., Iris Garden Club (pres. 1971-73), Eastside Garden Club (reporter 1970-75), Omicron Nu, Phi Kappa Phi. Republican. Presbyterian. Home: RR 4 Box 2445 Cushing OK 74023-9123

CRUZE, ALVIN M., research institute executive; b. Maryville, Tenn., Apr. 18, 1939; s. Gifford G. and Kathryn B. (McNutt) C.; children: Sidney, Warren; m. Karen H. Winton, Aug. 8, 1991. B.S., U. Tenn., 1961; M.S., Rutgers U., 1962; Ph.D., N.C. State U., 1972. Economist Research Triangle Inst., Research Triangle Park, N.C., 1965-70, 71-75, ctr. dir., 1975-83, v.p., 1983-88, exec. v.p., 1989-98; interior pres. Research Triangle Inst., Research Triangle Park, 1998—; lectr. U. N.C., Chapel Hill, 1970-71; bd. dirs. N.C. Biotech. Corp. Served to lt. U.S. Army, 1963-65. Mem. Nat. Inst. Stat. Sci. Democrat. Methodist. Avocations: golf, gardening. Home: 211 Bank Dr Cary NC 27511-8992 Office: Rsch Triangle Inst PO Box 12194 Durham NC 27709-2194*

CRUZE, KENNETH, retired surgeon; b. Takoma Park, Md., Oct. 10, 1927; s. Conrad Ellis and Claudia Eleanore (Carpenter) C.; B.A., Columbia Union Coll., 1949; M.D., Loma Linda U., 1955; m. Jean Anna Hansen, June 13, 1948; children: Wendy Jean, Lori Ann, Barbara Lee. Diplomate Am. Bd. Gen. Surgery, Am. Bd. Thoracic Surgery. Intern L.A. County Gen. Hosp., 1955-56; resident in surgery Wadsworth Gen. Med. and Surg. Hosp., West Los Angeles, 1956-60; resident in pediatric surgery Children's Hosp. Los Angeles, 1958-59; fellow in thoracic and cardiovascular surgery U. Fla., Gainesville, 1960-62; practice medicine specializing in thoracic and cardiovascular surgery, Takoma Park, Md., 1962-89; mem. staff Washington Adventist Hosp., Takoma Park, 1962-89, dir. open heart surgery program, 1970-89; ret. Mem. exec. com., bd. trustees D.C. Blue Shield, Columbia Union Coll., Takoma Park. Served to capt. M.C., U.S. Army, 1956-63. Fellow ACS, Am. Coll. Chest Physicians, Am. Coll. Angiology; mem. Am. Thoracic Soc., Am. Trauma Soc., Med. and Chirurg. Faculty Md., Md. Heart Assn., Soc. Thoracic Surgeons. Republican. Club: Civitan. Mem. editorial bd. Md. State Med. Jour., 1972-77; contbr. articles to med. jours. Home: 919 Brick Manor Cir Silver Spring MD 20905-3818

CRUZ-ROMO, GILDA, soprano; b. Guadalajara, Jalisco, Mexico; came to U.S., 1967; d. Feliciano and Maria del Rosario (Diaz) C.; m. Robert B. Romo, June 10, 1967. Grad., Colegio Nueva Galicia, Guadalajara, 1958; student, Nat. Conservatory of Music of Mexico, Mexico City, 1962-64. Tchr. voice U. Tex., Austin, 1990—; assoc. prof., coach, voice tchr. U. Tex., Austin, 1990—. With, Nat. and Internat. Opera, Mexico City, 1962-67, toured, Australia, N.Z., S.Am., with, Dallas Civic Opera, 1966-68, N.Y.C. Opera, 1969-72, Lyric Opera Chgo., 1975, Met. Opera debut as Madama Butterfly, 1970, leading soprano, 1970—, appeared in U.S. and abroad including, Covent Garden, La Scala, Vienna State Opera, Rome Opera, Paris Opera, Florence Opera, Torino Opera, Verona Opera, Portugal, Buenos Aires, others, concert appearances in, U.S., Can., Mexico; U.S. rep., World-Wide Madama Butterfly Competition, Tokyo, 1970; La Scala rep. in: Aida, USSR, 1974; appeared on radio, TV; filmed and recorded: Aida, with Orange Festival, France, 1976; roles include Aida, Madama Butterfly, Suor Angelica, Tosca, Odabella in Attila; Manon Lescaut, Leonora in Il Trovatore; Norma; Maddelena in Andrea Chenier; Desdemona in Otello; Donna Anna in Don Giovanni; Santuzza in Cavalleria Rusticana; (title role) La Gioconda; Adriana Lecouvreur; Luisa Miller; Elisabetta in Don Carlo; Margherite in Faust; Venus in Tannhauser; Giorgetta in Il Tabarro; also roles in Macbeth, Turnadot, Norma, Medea. Winner Met. Opera Nat. Auditions, 1970; recipient Critics award Union Mexicana de Cronistas de Teatro y Musica, 1973, Minerva al Arte award, Mexico, 1991, Minerva al Arte, Mexico, 1991, Silver Bird award, Govt. of Jalisco, Mex.; named Best Singer, 1976-77; season Cronistas de Santiago de Chile, 1976.

CRUZ-SÁENZ, MICHÈLE FRANCES SCHIAVONE DE, educator, researcher; b. Mt. Vernon, N.Y., Jan. 5, 1949; d. Sebastian Joseph and Rosa Antonia (Greco) Schiavone; m. Gonzalo Francisco Cruz-Sáenz, June 5, 1971 (div. Nov. 1991); children: Sebastian Francis, Gonzalo Edward Cruz-Schiavone. AB, Conn. Coll., New London, 1971; MA, U. Pa., 1974, PhD, 1976. Cert. secondary tchr., Conn., N.Y., Pa. Teaching fellow Ohio U., Athens, 1971-72, U. Pa., Phila., 1972-74; instr. Haverford (Pa.) Coll., 1974-75; lectr. U. Pa., Phila., 1973-75, Swarthmore (Pa.) Coll., 1974-76; asst. prof. Beaver Coll., Glenside, Pa., 1976-78, George Washington U., Washington, 1978-82; tchr. Wallingford (Pa.)-Swarthmore Sch. Dist., 1982—; cons. ETS-A.P. Program, 1985—, rev. Tchrs'. Guide for A.P. Lang. Course ETS, 1992; mem. com. Middle States Evaluation, 1987, 89. Author: The Life of St. Mary of Egypt, 1979, El Romancero tradicional de Costa Rica, 1986, Resource Guide: Medieval Ballads of Hispania, 1990, Manuscript of the Biblioteca Escorial III-K-4, 1993, Traditional Spanish Ballads of Aragon, 1995. Recipient award for excellence in tchg. Bus. Week, 1990; grantee: Am. Philos. Soc., 1975, 79. 83, NEH, 1990, Ludwig Vogelstein Found., 1985, Spanish Ministry of Culture, 1994, 95. Mem. MLA, N.E. MLA, Am. Assn. Tchrs. Spanish and Portuguese (pres. Delaware Valley chpt. 1991-97, treas. 1998—), Asociación Internacional de Hispanistas, Medieval Acad. Roman Catholic. Avocations: opera and classical music, mystery and suspense novels, soccer. Home: 739 Windsor Pl Wallingford PA 19086-6730

CRYER, DENNIS ROBERT, pharmaceutical company executive, researcher; b. Dearborn, Mich., Mar. 30, 1944; s. Earl Wilton and Marguerite Gladys (Root) C.; children: Jonathan Eric, Catherine grace, Laura Rose. BA in Biology, Johns Hopkins U., 1968; MD, Albert Einstein Coll. Medicine, 1977. Intern Children's Hosp. Phila., 1977-78, resident, 1978-79, 80-81; fellow in pathology and molecular biology U. Pa. Sch. Medicine, Phila., 1979-80; fellow in human genetics Sch. Medicine U. Pa., Phila., 1981-84, clin. asst. prof. pediatrics Sch. Medicine, 1983-84, asst. prof. pediatrics Sch. Medicine, 1984-87; assoc. clin. rsch. dir. E.R. Squibb and Sons, Princeton, N.J., 1987-89; assoc. med. devel. dir. Squibb U.S. Pharm. Group, Princeton, 1989-90, med. ops. dir., 1990-91, med. dir., 1991-94; sr. med. dir. cardiovascular/metabolism Women's Healthcare, 94-96, v.p. cardiovascular/metabolics, 1996; v.p. cardiovascular/metabolic advocacy programs Bristol Myers Squibb U.S. Pharm., Princeton, N.J., 1996—; corp. rep., corp. affairs com. Am. Soc. Hypertension, 1991—; mem. internat. adv. bd. XII Internat. Symposium on Drugs Affecting Lipid Metabolism, 1993-95; corp. rep. Pharm. Round Table, 1997—; mem. sci. edn. policy com. Liberty Sci. Ctr., N.J., 1998—. Author: with others Cold Spring Harbor Symposium on Quantitative Biology, 1974, Methods in Cell Biology, 1975; contbr. articles Jour. of Molecular Biology, Jour. Lipid Rsch., Jour. Clin. Investigation. Grantee Nat. Heart, Lung, and Blood Inst., NIH, 1986, Am. Heart Assn., 1987; recipient Merck Faculty Devel. award Merck, Sharp, and Dohme, 1984. Fellow Am. Heart Assn. (arteriosclerosis coun., corp. rep. Pharm. Round Table, 1997—); mem. AAAS, Am. Diabetes Assn., Am. Fedn. Med. Rsch., Am. Soc. Human Genetics, Am. Soc. Hypertension (corp. rep., corp. affairs com.), Endocrine Soc., Internat. Atherosclerosis Soc., Molecular Medicine Soc., N.Y. Acad. Scis., Alpha Epsilon Delta. Achievements include pioneering development of evidence that eukaryotic chromosomes contain a single, double-stranded DNA molecule; demonstration of a gene dosage effect for mitochondrial DNA (using mating strains of yeast); development of methods using stable isotopes and gas chromatography-mass spectrometry to study human lipoprotein metabolism; demonstration of accurate measurement of hepatic lipoprotein synthesis using these methods; demonstration of a powerful autosomal dominant human gene which lowers cholesterol in a family with coexistent familial hypercholesterolemia. Home: 530 Aspen Woods Dr Yardley PA 19067-6377 Office: Bristol-Myers Squibb Co PO Box 4500 Princeton NJ 08543-4500

CRYER, GRETCHEN, playwright, lyricist, actress; b. Indpls., Oct. 17, 1935; d. Earl William and Louise Gerladine (Niven) Kiger; m. Donald David Cryer, June 7, 1958 (div. June 1970); children: Robin, Jon, Shelly. BA, DePauw U., 1957; MAT, Harvard U., 1960; ArtsD (hon.), Ea. Mich. U., 1986. Cert. tchr. Writer and lyricist N.Y.C., 1967—; founder, owner The Extended Family, N.Y.C., 1991—; founder, pres. The Extended Family. Writer, lyricist (with Nancy Ford) Off-Broadway and Broadway musicals Now Is the Time for All the Good Men, 1967, The Last Sweet Days of Isaac, 1970 (Obie award 1970), Shelter, 1973, Booth Is Back in Town, 1981, I'm Getting My Act Together and Taking it on the Road, 1978, Hang on to the Good Times, 1984, The American Girls Revue, 1998; (with Doug Dyer and Peter Link) The Wedding of Iphigenia and Iphigenia in Concert, 1971; theater appearances in Little Me, 1962, 110 In The Shade, 1963, Now is the Time For All Good Men, 1967, I'm Getting My Act Together and Taking it on the Road, 1978, A Circle of Sounds, 1978, Blue Plate Special, 1983, To Whom It May Concern, 1985-86, Alterations, 1986, The Fabulous Party, 1996, The American Girls Review, 1999; film appearances include Hiding Out, 1987; author, singer: (albums) Cryer and Ford, 1976, You Know My Music, 1977; author: (musical) Booth is Back in Town, 1981, Eleanor, 1984; playwright: The House That Goes On Forever, 1988. Recipient Ind. Arts award Gov. of Ind., 1982. Mem. Dramatists Guild (council), Actors Equity Assn., Screen Actors Guild. Democrat. Avocations: playing the piano. Home and Office: 885 W End Ave New York NY 10025-3501

CRYER, PHILIP EUGENE, medical educator, scientist, endocrinologist; b. El Paso, Ill., Jan. 5, 1940; s. Clifford Eugene and Carol Ruth (Cherry) C.; m. Susan Odette Shipman, Dec. 23, 1963 (div. May 1990); children: Philip Clifford, Justine Laurel; m. Carolyn Elizabeth Havlin, Sept. 16, 1994. BA, Northwestern U., 1962, MD, 1965. Diplomate Am. Bd. Internal Medicine, diplomate Am. Bd. Endocrinology and Metabolism. Intern Barnes Hosp., St. Louis, 1965-67; fellow in endocrinology Barnes Hosp./Washington U., 1967-68, resident in medicine, 1968-69, 71-72; investigator Naval Med. Rsch. Inst., Bethesda, Md., 1969-71; from instr. to assoc. prof. Washington U. Sch. Medicine, St. Louis, 1971-80, prof., 1981—, Irene E. and Michael M. Karl prof. endocrinology/metabolism, 1995—, dir. gen. clin. rsch. ctr., 1978—, dir. div. endocrinology, diabetes and metabolism, 1985—; Connaught-Novo lectr. Can. Diabetes Assn., 1987; Pimstone lectr. Soc. Endocrinology, Metabolism and Diabetes, South Africa, 1989; Kellion lectr. Australian Diabetes Soc., 1992; Plenary lectr. Japan Diabetes Soc., 1994, plenary lectr. Argentine Diabetes Assn., 1998. Author: Diagnostic Endocrinology, 1976, 2d edit., 1979, Hypoglycemia, 1997, also 66 book chpts.; editor: Diabetes; mem. editl. bd. Jour. Clin. Investigation, Am. Jour. Physiology, Jour. Clin. Endocrinology and Metabolism; contbr. over 275 articles to profl. jours. Recipient Rorer Clin. Investigator award Endocrine Soc., 1988, Rumbough Sci. award Juvenile Diabetes Found., 1989, Banting medal Am. Diabetes Assn., 1994, Excellence in Clin. Rsch. award NIH, 1994, Am. Diabetes Clin. Rsch. grantee, 1996, NIH Rsch. grantee, 1980—. Fellow ACP; mem. Am. Fedn. Clin. Rsch. (councilor 1979-80), Am. Soc. Clin. Investigation (v.p. 1985-86), Assn. Am. Physicians, Am. Diabetes Assn. (pres. 1996-97), Phi Beta Kappa, Alpha Omega Alpha. Office: Washington U Sch Medicine 660 South Euclid Ave PO Box 8127 Saint Louis MO 63156-8127

CRYER, RODGER EARL, educational administrator; b. Detroit, Apr. 2, 1940. AB in Fine Arts, San Diego State U., 1965; MA in Edn. Adminstrn., Stanford U., 1972; PhD in Psychol. Services Counseling, Columbia-Pacific U., 1985. Cert. tchr., N.J., Calif.; cert. gen. adminstrn., Calif. Spl. asst. to commissioner N.J. State Dept. Edn., Trenton, 1967-68; cons. N.J. Urban Sch. Devel., Trenton, 1969-70; mgmt. cons. Rodger E. Cryer, Co., Pinole, Calif., 1970-73; adminstrv. asst. Franklin McKinley Sch. Dist., San Jose, Calif., pres. Chief Exec. Tng. Corp., San Jose, 1981-82; prin. McKinley Sch., 1986-91, prin. Hellyer Sch., 1991-96; bd. instl. rev. Calif. State Dept. Edn. Accreditation Commn., 1996—; adj. prof. Nat. U., San Jose, 1996—; ptnr. Guided Learning Enterprises; bd. dirs., Commonwealth Cen. Credit Union, 1989—, Our City Forest, Inc., 1994—, Bd. dirs. Friends of San Jose Beautiful, Inc., 1994-95; adv. com. City of San Jose Bicycle, 1994-95. Mem. Nat. Sch. Pub. Rels. Assn. (sec. 1975—), Calif. Sch. Pub. Rels. Assn. (pres.). Contbr. articles to profl. jours. Commr. Home: 3529 Milburn St San Jose CA 95148-2250

CRYMBLE, JOHN FREDERICK, chemical engineer, consultant; b. N.Y.C., Oct. 18, 1916; s. Hugh and Hannah (Knecht) C.; B.A., Columbia U., 1938; B.S., 1939, Chem. E., 1940; m. Mary Alenda Smith, June 24, 1944; 1 dau., Joanne Lee (Mrs. Donald L. Gilmore). Prodn. supr. E.I. duPont de Nemours and Co., Chambers Works, Deepwater, N.J., 1940-73, sr. prodn. engr., 1973-76; cons., 1977—. Past pres. Salem City Bd. Edn., also rep. N.J. Sch. Bds. Assn.; bd. dirs. Salem Free Libr. Mem. Am. Chem. Soc., Am. Inst. Chem. Engrs., John Jay Assos. Columbia, Thomas Egleston Assocs. Columbia Sch. Engring. and Applied Sci., Columbia U. Alumni Assn. (alumni medalist 1988), Sigma Xi, Phi Lambda Upsilon, Tau Beta Pi. Methodist (trustee, past lay leader). Clubs: DuPont Country (Wilmington, Del.); Columbia U. Alumni (past exec. com., v.p. Phila.). Home and Office: 65 W Broadway Salem NJ 08079-1329

CRYMES, MARY COOPER, secondary school educator; b. Abilene, Tex., Oct. 27, 1950; d. James Travis and Mary Francis (Chapple) Cooper; m. David Stuart Crymes, Dec. 25, 1970. BS, U. Tex., 1974. Tchr. govt. Midland (Tex.) Ind. Sch. Dist., 1974-80, Abilene (Tex.) Ind. Sch. Dist., 1980—. Author: (poem) Young America Sings, 1970; co-author: County Records Inventory, 1974. Recipient Teaching Excellence in Free Enterprise 1st prize award West Tex. C. of C., 1980, Martha Washington medal SAR, 1990; named Taft Sr. fellow Taft Inst., 1993. Mem. NEA, Tex. State Tchrs. Assn., Abilene Educators Assn., Nat. Coun. for Social Studies, Tex. Coun. for Social Studies, Abilene Coun. for Social Studies (pres. 1984-86), Daus. of Republic of Tex. (treas. 1990-95, v.p. 1995—), West Tex. Geneal. Soc. Avocation: genealogical research. Office: Abilene High Sch 2800 N 6th St Abilene TX 79603-7190

CRYSTAL, BILLY, comedian, actor; b. Long Beach, N.Y., Mar. 14, 1947; s. Jack and Helen C.; m. Janice Goldfinger; children: Jennifer, Lindsay. Student, Marshall U., Nassau Community Coll; BFA in TV & Film Direction, N.Y.U., 1970. House mgr. for play You're a Good Man Charlie Brown, 1971; mem. group 3's Company; later solo appearances as stand-up comedian; TV appearances in (series) Soap, 1977-81, The Billy Crystal Comedy Hour, 1982, Saturday Night Live, 1984-85; exec. prodr., writer Midnight Train to Moscow, 1989 (Emmy award outstanding writing 1989), HBO series Sessions, 1991; TV films include SST-Death Flight, 1977, Human Feelings, 1978, Breaking Up Is Hard to Do, 1979, Enola Gay, The Men, The Mission, The Atomic Bomb, 1980; motion pictures include Rabbit Test, 1978, (voice) Animalympics, 1979, This Is Spinal Tap, 1984, Running Scared, 1986, The Princess Bride, 1987, Goodnight Moon, 1987, Throw Momma from the Train, 1987, (also prodr., co-screenwriter) Memories of Me, 1988, When Harry Met Sally..., 1989 (Am.Comedy award funniest actor in a motion picture 1989) , (also exec. prodr., story) City Slickers, 1991 (Golden Globe nomination best actor 1991, Am. Comedy award 1991), (also dir., writer, prodr.) Mr. Saturday Night, 1992, City Slickers II: The Legend of Curley's Gold, 1994, (also dir., prodr., writer) Forget Paris, 1995, Hamlet, 1996, Father's Day, 1997, Deconstructing Harry, 1997; host (HBO) Comic Relief, 1986, (TV host) Grammy Awards, 1988, 89, Acad. Awards, 1990-93, 96, (Emmy award outstanding performance in special events 1989, Emmy award outstanding writing 1991, Emmy award outstanding individual performance 1991); author: (with Dick Schaap) Absolutley Mahvelous, 1986; recording You Look Mahvelous, 1985. Office: CAA 9830 Wilshire Blvd Beverly Hills CA 90212-1825 also: Wilkinson/Lipsman Pub Rels 8170 Beverly Blvd Ste 205 Los Angeles CA 90048-4524

CRYSTAL, BORIS, artist; b. nr. Warsaw, Poland, Dec. 25, 1931; came to U.S., 1968, naturalized, 1974; s. Shea and Bronislawa (Blumenfeld) C.; m. Dalia Gilad, Oct. 6, 1961; children: Julius S., Byron R. Student, Plocer's Sch. Fine Arts, 1962-63, Acad. Fine Arts Israel, 1963-64. One-man exhbns. include, Katz Art Gallery, Tel Aviv, 1964, Art Gallery 97, Tel Aviv, 1965-66, Journalist House Art Gallery, Tel Aviv, 1967, Lerner Art Gallery, N.Y.C., 1968, Herzl Inst., N.Y.C., 1969, Roerich Mus., N.Y.C., 1970, Crystal Art Gallery, N.Y.C., 1972-76, group exhbns. include, Katz Art Gallery, 1964-68, Mus. Israel, Tel Aviv, 1964-68, Lerner Art Gallery, 1968-76, Roerich Mus., 1968-76, Jewish Mus., N.Y.C., 1968-76, Mus. Modern Art, N.Y.C., 1968-76, LaGalerie Mouffe, Paris; represented in permanent collections, Katz Art Gallery, Mus. Israel, Art Gallery 97, Journalist House, Continental Gallery, Crown Art Gallery, Herzl Inst., Lerner Art Gallery, Roerich Mus., Jewish Mus., Mus. Modern Art. Recipient Gold medal Accademia Italia delle Arti e del Lavoro, 1980; Contbns. to Arts award Am. Biog. Inst., 1981. Mem. Artists Equity Assn. Address: 70-20 108th St Forest Hills NY 11375-4449

CRYSTAL, JAMES WILLIAM, insurance company executive; b. N.Y.C., Oct. 9, 1937; s. I. Frank and Evelyn G. Crystal; m. Jean Crystal; children: James F., Sanford F., Jonathan F. BS, Trinity Coll., 1958. With Royal Globe Ins. Group, N.Y.C., 1956; underwriter Home Ins. Co., N.Y.C., 1957; spl. agt. Home Ins. Co., San Francisco, 1958-59; chmn., chief exec. officer Frank Crystal & Co. Inc., N.Y.C., 1960—; chmn. bd. F.F.H. Ins. Co., Northeast Inst. Co., 879 Park Ave. Corp.; bd. dirs. Atlantic Internat. Ins. Co., Donkenny, Inc. Bd. dirs. Auto Resources, Inc., Inst. for East-West Studies, Inc., Internat. Space Brokers; trustee Mt. Sinai NYU Health Orgn. and Mt. Sinai Med. Sch. Mem. Nat. Assn. Casualty and Surety Agts., Harmonie Club, N.Y. Stock Exch. Lunch Club, India Ho. Club N.Y., Century Country Club, Wings Club N.Y. Republican. Home: 875 Park Ave New York NY 10021-0341 Office: Frank Crystal & Co 40 Broad St New York NY 10004-2315

CRYSTAL, JONATHAN ANDREW, executive recruiter; b. New Rochelle, N.Y., May 18, 1943; s. Robert Garrison and Luella (Peters) C.; m. Pamela Paterson, July 31, 1965; children: Alexandra, Laura, Elizabeth, Matthew. BSBA, Northwestern U., 1965; MBA in Fin., Columbia U., 1971. Mktg. rep. Texaco, Inc., 1965-66; trainee Chase Manhattan Bank, 1971; assoc. corp. fin. Drexel Burnham & Lambert, Inc., 1971-73; acct. officer Citicorp, N.Y.C., 1973-77, asst. v.p., 1975-77; v.p., regional treas. mgr. Citicorp, Houston, 1977-80; prin. Russell Reynolds & Assocs., Houston, 1980-88; prin. SpencerStuart, Houston, 1988—, chmn. audit com., 1997—; speaker numerous trade convs., 1980—. Contbr. articles to profl. jours. Mem. adv. bd. Ctr. for Bus. Ethics U. St. Thomas, 1998—. Lt. (j.g.) USN, 1966-69. Named one of Top 200 Recruiters in the U.S. The Career Makers, 1990. Mem. Houston Forum (bd. govs. 1992—, exec. com. 1995—), Spring Branch Edn. Found. (bd. dirs. 1993—, exec. com. 1994—, vice chmn., 1999—), Univ. Club, Petroleum Club (Houston). Home: 14419 Broadgreen Dr Houston TX 77079-6635

CRYSTALL, JOSEPH N., communications company executive; b. Bklyn., Dec. 19, 1922; s. Samuel H. and Frances (Eiten) C.; m. Martha Jane Ladson, Feb. 23, 1957; 1 child, Bonnie Leigh. Student, Bklyn. Coll., 1939-42, U. Pitts., 1942-43. Radio performer Sta. KOPO, Tucson, 1951-54; advt. agy. exec. The Wiener Co., Tucson, 1955-59; sta. mgr., TV performer Sta. KOLD-AM-TV, Tucson, 1959-69; gen. mgr. Sta. KOPO, Tucson, 1969-73, Stas. KEVT, KWFM, Tucson, 1974-81; pres., gen. mgr. Sta. KGVY, Green Valley, Ariz., 1981—; pres. Crystal Sets, Inc., Tucson, 1981—; instr. U. Ariz., Tucson, 1968-69. Author two books; contbr. articles, TV scripts, short stories to various publs., 1955—. Pres. Better Bus. Bur. So. Ariz., Tucson, 1983. Served as 1st lt. USAF, 1943-45, ETO, MTO. Decorated DFC, Air medal with three clusters. Mem. Ariz. Broadcasters Assn. (pres. 1966-67), Tucson Broadcasters Assn. (pres. 1971-72), Nat. Assn. Broadcasters, Tucson Advt. Club (pres. 1968-69, 73-74, named to Advt. Hall of Fame 1987), Am. Advt. Fedn. (Silver medal 1989, named to Ariz. Broadcasters Hall of Fame 1996), Green Valley C. of C. (bd. dirs., v.p. 1988—), Tucson Press Club (pres. 1967, 71, 72, Broadcaster of Yr. 1981), Lions (pres. 1974-75), Rotary (pres. 1989-90), Sigma Delta Chi. Avocations: writing, public speaking, cruising, big band music, traveling. Home: 3147 E Pima St Tucson AZ 85716-3131 Office: Sta KGVY PO Box 767 Green Valley AZ 85622-0767

CSAR, MICHAEL F., lawyer; b. Chgo., May 26, 1950; s. Frank J. and Rosaria (Motto) C.; m. Anne E. Taylor, Mar. 7, 1954; children: Cordelia, Christian. BA, Yale U., 1972, Kings Coll., Cambridge, 1974; JD, Yale U., 1977. Bar: Ill. 1977, U.S. Dist. Ct. (no. dist.) Ill. 1977. Assoc. Wilson & McIlvaine, Chgo., 1977-83; ptnr. Quarles & Brady (formerly Wilson & McIlvaine), Chgo., 1983—. Office: Quarles & Brady 500 W Madison St Chicago IL 60661-2511*

CSENDES, ERNEST, chemist, corporate and financial executive; b. Satu-Mare, Szatmár-Németi, Romania, Mar. 2, 1926; came to U.S., 1951, naturalized, 1955; s. Edward O. and Sidonia (Littman) C. m. Catharine Vera Tolnai, Feb. 7, 1953; children: Audrey Carol, Robert Alexander Edward. BA, Protestant Coll., Hungary, 1944; BS, U. Heidelberg (Ger.), 1948, MSc, 1950, PhD summa cum laude, 1951. Rsch. asst. chemistry U. Heidelberg, 1950-51; rsch. assoc. biochemistry Tulane U., New Orleans, 1952; rsch. fellow chemistry Harvard U., 1952-53; rsch. chemist organic chems. dept. E. I. Du Pont de Nemours and Co., Wilmington, Del., 1953-56, elastomer chems. dept., 1956-61; dir. rsch. and devel. agrl. chems. div. Armour & Co., Atlanta, 1961-63; v.p. corp. devel. Occidental Petroleum Corp., L.A., 1963-64, exec. v.p. rsch., engring. and devel., mem. exec. com., 1964-68; COO, exec. v.p., dir. Occidental Rsch. and Engring. Corp., L.A., London, Moscow, 1963-68; mng. dir. Occidental Rsch. and Engring. (U.K.) Ltd., London, 1964-68; pres., CEO TRI Group, London, Amsterdam, Rome and Bermuda, 1968-84; chmn., CEO Micronic Techs., Inc., L.A., 1981-85; mng. ptnr. Inter-Consult Ltd., Pacific Palisades, Calif.; internat. cons. on tech., econ. feasibility and mgmt., 1984—; pres., CEO, chief tech. officer Gen. Grinding Corp., L.A., 1991—; chmn., CEO Eden Mgmt. Ltd., L.A. and London, 1993—. Contbr. 250 articles to profl. and trade jours., studies and books. Recipient Pro Mundi Beneficio gold medal Brazilian Acad. Humanities, 1975; Harvard U. fellow, 1953. Fellow AAAS, Am. Inst. Chemists, Royal Soc. Chemistry (London); mem. AIAA, IEEE, SMME, AIChE, Am. Chem. Soc., German Chem. Soc., N.Y. Acad. Sci., Am. Concrete Inst., Am. Water Works Assn., AMS Internat., Acad. Polit. Sci., Nat. Def. and Indsl. Assn., Sigma Xi. Achievements include 39 patents; rsch. in area of elastomers, rubber chemicals, adhesives, dyes and intermediates, organometallics, organic and biochemistry, high polymers, antioxidants, superphosphoric acid and ammonium polyphosphates, plant nutrients, pesticides, process engineering, design of fertilizer plants, sulfur, potash, phosphate and iron ore mining and metallurgy, coal burning and acid rain, coal utilization, methods for aerodynamic grinding of solids, particles technology, advanced building materials, petrochemicals, biomed. engring., consumer products; also acquisitions, mergers, internat. fin. related to leasing investments and loans, trusts and ins., new Eurodollar instruments; regional indsl. devel. related to agr. and energy resources; projects in western Europe, no. Africa, Russia, Japan, Saudi Arabia, India, China and the Philippines. Home: 514 N Marquette St Pacific Palisades CA 90272-3314

CSERE, CSABA, magazine editor; b. Cleve., June 16, 1951; s. Zoltan and Theresa (Balazs) C.; m. Mary Patricia O'Brien, July 6, 1975; 1 child, Madeline Christine. SB, MIT, 1975. Design engr. Data Gen. Corp., Southboro, Mass., 1975-77, Ford Motor Co., 1978-80; tech. editor Car and Driver mag., 1980-87, tech. dir., 1987-93, editor-in-chief, 1993—. Mem. Soc. Automotive Engrs., Am. Soc. Mag. Editors. Office: Car and Driver Hachette Filipacchi Mags Inc 2002 Hogback Rd Ste 1 Ann Arbor MI 48105-9795*

CSERR, ROBERT, psychiatrist, physician, hospital administrator; b. Perth Amboy, N.J., May 29, 1936; s. Frank Joseph and Helen (Bodzany) C.; m. Helen Fitzgerald, May 28, 1962; 1 dau., Ruth. AB magna cum laude, Harvard U., 1958, MD, 1962. Med. intern U. Va. Hosp., 1962-63; resident, fellow in psychiatry Mass. Gen. Hosp., Harvard Med. Sch., 1963-66; alcohol coordinator Mass. Gen. Hosp., 1967-68, clin. assoc. psychiatry, 1968—; asst. supt. Medfield State Hosp., Harding, Mass., 1968-70, supt., 1970-74, area program dir., 1970-74; dir. Outlook Psychiat. Facility, Hampstead, N.H., 1974-76; med. dir. Charles River Hosp., Wellesley, Mass., 1976-80; psychiatrist-in-chief Charles River Hosp., 1980-87, Hahnemann Hosp., Boston, 1982—; med. dir. Taunton Hosp. and Regional Svc. Ctr., 1990-92; assoc. med. dir. psychiatry PHCS, Lexington, Mass., 1991-93; v.p., med. dir. mental health svcs. PHCS, Waltham, Mass., 1993-96; v.p. clin. affairs Cmty. Care Systems Inc., 1979-86, sr. cons., 1986—; asst. clin. prof. psychiatry Boston U. Sch. Medicine, 1968-74, assoc. clin. prof., 1979—; asst. psychiatrist Beth Israel Hosp., 1970—; lectr. in psychiatry Harvard Med. Sch., 1972-89; cons. Med. Mgmt., Managed Care Programs, 1986—. Pres. Medfield Found.; bd. overseers Mt. Desert Island Biol. Lab. Served with AUS, 1966-68. Mem. Am. Coll. Mental Health Adminstrn., Mass. Med. Soc., BCN Med. Soc. Home: Green Acres North Dighton MA 02764 Office: Chase St North Dighton MA 02764

CSIZA, CHARLES KAROLY, veterinarian, microbiologist; b. Pacsony, Hungary, Apr. 4, 1937; came to U.S., 1966; s. Istvan and Anna (Nemeth) C.; m. Colette Marcoux, Sept. 5, 1964; children: Andrew, Kathleen, Stephen. DVM, U. Toronto, Ont., Can., 1963; PhD, Cornell U., 1970. Rsch. asst. Connaught Med. Rsch. Lab. U. Toronto, 1963-66; teaching asst. dept. microbiology N.Y. State Vet. Coll./Cornell U., Ithaca, 1966-70; rsch. scientist Wadsworth Ctr. Labs. and Rsch. N.Y. State Dept. Health, Albany, 1970—. Author: Pathogenisis of Feline Panleukopenia Virus, 1971, Myelin Deficient Mutation in Rats, 1979, Lipid Class Analysis of Myelin Deficient Rats, 1982. Mem. AVMA, Am. Coll. Vet. Microbiologists, N.Y. Acad. Sci., Conf. Rsch. Workers in Animal Diseases, Albany Curling Club. Roman Catholic. Office: Wadsworth Ctr Labs/Rsch NY State Dept Health ESP Albany NY 12201-0509

CSÖRGÖ, MIKLÓS, mathematics and statistics educator; b. Egerfarmos, Hungary, Mar. 12, 1932; came to Can., 1957, naturalized, 1962; s. Miklós and Ilona (Veres) C.; m. Anna Eszter Tóth, Aug. 10, 1957; children: Adria, Lilla. BA, Karl Marx U. Econs., Budapest, Hungary, 1955; MA, McGill U., 1961, PhD, 1963. Instr., postdoctoral fellow Princeton U., N.J., 1963-65; asst. prof. McGill U., Montreal, Que., Can., 1965-68, assoc. prof., 1968-71; vis. prof. U. Vienna, Austria, 1969-70; assoc. prof. math. and stats. Carleton U., Ottawa, Ont., Can., 1971-72, prof., 1972—, co-dir. Lab. for Research in Stats. and Probability, 1983—; vis. prof. U. Utah, 1991-92. Author: (with P. Révész) Strong Approximations in Probability and Statistics, 1981; Quantile Processes with Statistical Applications, 1983; (with others) An Asymptotic Theory for Empirical Reliability and Concentration Processes, 1986, (with L. Horváth) Wieghted Approximations in Probility and Statistics, 1993, Limit Theorems in Change-Point Analysis; assoc. editor The Annals of Probability, 1979-81; mem. editl. bd. Stats. and Decisions, 1981—, Jour. of Multivariate Analysis, 1986-87. Fellow Can. Council, 1969-70, 76-77; Killam sr. research fellow, 1978-79, 79-80. Fellow Inst. Math. and Stats., Royal Soc. Can.; mem. Am. Math. Soc., Can. Math. Soc., Statis. Soc. Can., Bernoulli Soc. for Math. Statistics and Probability, Internat. Statis. Inst., Hungarian Acad. Sci. (fgn. mem.). Office: Carleton U Lab Rsch in Stats, 1125 Colonel By Dr, Ottawa, ON Canada K1S 5B6

CUA, ANTONIO S., philosophy educator; b. Manila, Philippines, July 23, 1932; came to U.S., 1953, naturalized, 1971; s. Oh and Chio (So) C.; m. Shoke-Hwee Khaw, June 11, 1956; 1 dau., Athene K. B.A., Far Eastern U., Manila, 1952; M.A., U. Calif.-Berkeley, 1954; Ph.D., 1958. Instr., asst. prof. Ohio U., 1958-62; prof., chmn. dept. philosophy SUNY Coll. at Oswego, 1962-69; prof. philosophy Catholic U. Am., Washington, 1969-96; prof. emeritus Cath. U. Am., Washington, 1996—; vis. prof. U. Mo.-Columbia, spring 1974-75, U. Hawaii, fall 1976-77. Author: Reason and Virtue: A Study in the Ethics of Richard Price, 1966, Dimensions of Moral Creativity: Paradigms, Principles, and Ideals, 1978, The Unity of Knowledge and Action: A Study in Wang Yang-ming's Moral Psychology, 1982, Ethical Argumentation: A Study in Hsün Tzu's Moral Epistemology, 1985, Moral Vision and Tradition: Essays in Chinese Ethics, 1998; co-editor Jour. Chinese Philosophy; assoc. editor Internat. Jour. Philosophy Religion; mem. editorial bd. Am. Philos. Quar., Philosophy East and West; contbr. articles to profl. jours.; lectr. on Confucian Ethics, 1998. Mem. Am. Philos. Assn., Internat. Soc. for Chinese Philosophy (pres. 1984-86), Soc. for Asian and Comparative Philosophy (pres. 1978-79). Office: Cath U Am Sch Philosophy Washington DC 20064

CUA, CHRISTOPHER LEE, thoracic surgeon; b. Harrisburg, Pa., May 1, 1959; s. Cicero and Rosita Cua; m. Elizabeth Johnson, Apr. 25, 1987; children: Lily, Christopher. BA, Ind. U., 1978, MD, 1982. Diplomate Am. Bd. Surgery, Am. Bd. Thoracic Surgery, Am. Bd. Surgery Critical Care. Intern U. Ill., Chgo., 1982-84; resident U. Mass., Worcester, 1984-87; fellow Northwestern U., Chgo., 1987-89; thoracic surgeon pvt. practice, 1989—. Office: 1153 Center St Ste 4990 Boston MA 02130

CUA, FLORENCE, consultant; b. Manila, Philippines, Aug. 3, 1953; came to the U.S., 1975; d. Jose P. and Petra T. Cua; m. Edward A. Christman, July 21, 1979. BS in Physics magna cum laude, Coll. of the Holy Spirit, Manila, 1973; MS in Radiol. Sci., Rutgers U., 1978, MS in Environ. Sci., 1991; MS in Bionucleonics, Purdue U., 1981. Health physics assoc. Marshall Islands Radiol. Program, Brookhaven Nat. Lab., Upton, N.Y., 1977-80; ptnr. Christman Cua and Assocs., Kendall Park, N.J., 1980—; health physics trainee Purdue U. Radiol. Control Office, West Lafayette, Ind., 1978; rsch. asst. NYU Environ. Medicine, Longmeadow, Tuxedo, N.Y., 1992. Contbr. articles to profl. jours.; author numerous manuals and monographs. Mem. Assn. for Women in Sci. (co-founder N.J. chpt.), Third World Orgn. Women in Sci., Health Physics Soc., Internat. Assn. Dental Rsch., Am. Assn. Dental Rsch., Bone and Tooth Soc. N.Y., Philippine-Am. Acad. Scis. and Engring., N.Y. Acad. Scis. Democrat. Roman Catholic. Avocations: science-by-mail, singing, fishing, boating. Office: Christman Cua & Assocs 59 Eleanor Dr Kendall Park NJ 08824-1815

CUADRA, CARLOS ALBERT, information scientist, management executive; b. San Francisco, Dec. 21, 1925; s. Gregorio and Amanda (Mendoza) C.; m. Gloria Nathalie Adams, May 3, 1947; children: Mary Susan Cuadra Nielsen, Neil Gregory, Dean Arthur. A.B. with highest honors in Psychology, U. Calif., Berkeley, 1949, Ph.D. in Psychology, 1953. Staff psychologist VA, Downey, Ill., 1953-56; with System Devel. Corp., Los Angeles, Calif., 1957-78; mgr. library and documentation systems dept. System Devel. Corp., 1968-70, mgr. edn. and library systems dept., 1971-74; gen. mgr. SDC Search Service, 1974-78; founder Cuadra Assos., L.A., 1978—. Contbr. articles to profl. jours.; Editor: Ann. Rev. of Info. Sci. and Tech, 1964-75. Mem. Nat. Commn. Libraries and Info. Sci., 1971-84. Served with USN, 1944-46. Recipient Merit award Am. Soc. Info. Sci., 1968, Best Info. Sci. Book award, 1969; named Disting. Lectr. of Year, 1970; received Miles Conrad award Nat. Fedn. Abstracting and Info. Services, 1980, hon. fellow, 1997. Mem. Info. Industry Assn. (bd. dirs., Hall of Fame award 1980), Chem. Abstracts Soc. (governing bd. 1991-96), Am. Chem. Soc. (governing bd. pub.). Home: 13213 Warren Ave Los Angeles CA 90066-1750 Office: Cuadra Associates 11835 W Olympic Blvd Ste 855 Los Angeles CA 90064-5033

CUATRECASAS, PEDRO MARTIN, research biochemist, pharmaceutical executive; b. Madrid, Sept. 27, 1936; came to U.S., 1947; s. Jose and Martha C.; m. Carol Zies, Aug. 15, 1959; children: Paul, Lisa, Diane, Julia. AB, Washington U., St. Louis, 1958, MD, 1962; DSc honoris causa, U. Barcelona, 1984, Mt. Sinai Sch. Medicine, 1985, U. Buenos Aires, 1990, U. Naples, Italy, 1990. Intern, then resident in internal medicine Osler Svc. Johns Hopkins Hosp., 1962-64, asst. physician, 1972-75; clin. asso., clin. endocrinology br. Nat. Inst. Arthritis and Metabolic Diseases, NIH, 1964-66; spl. USPHS postdoctoral fellow Lab. Chem. Biology, 1966-67, med. officer, 1967-70; professorial lectr. biochemistry George Washington U. Med. Sch., 1967-70; assoc. prof. pharmacology and exptl. therapeutics, assoc. prof. medicine, dir. div. clin. pharmacology, Burroughs Wellcome prof. clin. pharmacology Johns Hopkins U. Med. Sch., 1970-72, prof. pharmacology and exptl. therapeutics, assoc. prof. medicine, 1972-75; v.p. rsch., devel. and med. Wellcome Rsch. Labs.; dir. Burroughs Wellcome Co., Research Triangle Park, N.C., 1975-86; sr. v.p. R&D Glaxo Rsch. Labs., Glaxo Inc., 1986-89; also bd. dirs. Glaxo Rsch. Labs., Glaxo Inc., Glaxo Internat. Rsch., Ltd., London, 1986-89; pres. pharm. rsch. divsn., and co. v.p. Warner-Lambert Co., Ann Arbor, Mich., 1989-97; ind. pharm. rsch. cons. Rancho Santa Fe, Calif., 1997—; prof. dept. medicine & pharm. U. Calif., San Diego, 1997—; adj. prof. Duke U. Med. Sch., 1975-89; adj. prof., mem. adv. com. cancer rsch. program U. N.C. Med. Sch., 1975-90; adj. prof. dept. pharm. and medicinal chemistry, U. Mich., 1990-97; bd. dirs. Mitokor Inc., Alliance Pharms., Metabolex Inc.; mem. FDA sci. bd., 1996—. Editor: Receptors and Recognition Series, 1975, Jour. Solid-Phase Biochemistry, 1975-80; editorial bd.: Jour. Membrane Biology, 1973, Internat. Jour. Biochemistry, 1973, Molecular and Cellular Endocrinology, 1973-77, Biochimica Biophysica Acta, 1973-79, Life Scis., 1978—, Neuropeptides, 1979—, Jour. Applied Biochemistry, 1978-91, Cancer Research, 1980-81, Jour. Applied Biochemistry and Biotech., 1980—, Toxin Revs., 1981—, Biochem. Biophys. Research Communications, 1981-94; contbr. articles to profl. jours. Active Am. Diabetes Assn., 1972—, PMA Commn. on Drugs and Rare Diseases, 1982-89; bd. dirs. Burroughs Wellcome Fund, 1975-86. Recipient John Jacob Abel prize, 1972, Laude prize Pharm. World, 1975, Beerman award Soc. Investigative Dermatology, 1981, Isco award U. Nebr., 1985, Dupont Splty. Diagnostics award Clin. Ligand Assay Soc., 1986, Alumni Achievement award Washington U. Sch. Medicine, 1987, Wolf Found. prize in medicine, 1987, N.C. Gov.'s medal award in sci., 1988; FDA Commr.'s Spl. citation, 1997, City of Medicine award (disting. achievement in medicine), 1998; inducted into Johns Hopkins Soc. Scholar, 1990. Fellow Am. Acad. Arts. and Scis.; mem. Am. Soc. Biol. Chemists, Nat. Acad. Scis., Inst. Medicine of Nat. Acad. Scis. (governing council 1988—), Am. Soc. Pharmacology and Exptl. Therapeutics (Goodman and Gilman award 1982), Am. Soc. Clin. Investigation, Am. Soc. Clin. Research, Spanish Biochem. Soc., Md. Acad. Scis. (Outstanding Young Scientist of Year 1970), Am. Cancer Soc., Endocrine Soc., Am. Chem. Soc., Am. Diabetes Assn. (Eli Lilly award 1975), Am. Diabetes Assn., Sigma Xi.

CUBAS, JOSE M(ANUEL), advertising agency executive; b. Matanzas, Cuba, Mar. 1, 1930; came to U.S., 1960; s. Jose M. and Luisa M. (Ruiz) C.; m. Edith Perez, Apr. 26, 1952; children: Mercedes, Alina. Student, U. Havana Law Sch. Pres. Publicidad Siboney, S.A., Havana, 1953-60, San Juan, P.R., 1962-84; pres. Internat. Mktg. and Advt. Services Corp., Fla., 1979-84; pres., CEO Foote Cone & Belding-Latin Am., N.Y.C., 1985-86, pres., 1987-97; chmn., CEO Siboney USA, Miami, Fla., 1998—. Mem. Internat. Advt. Assn., U.S.-Hispanic C. of C. (recipient awards). Republican. Roman Catholic. Avocations: travel, swimming, tennis. Office: FCB Latin Am/Siboney 1401 Brickell Ave Ste 1100 Miami FL 33131-3506*

CUBBAGE, ALAN KENNETT, academic administrator; b. Hammond, Ind., Dec. 10, 1952; s. Jerome Kennett and Marion Jane Cubbage; m. Charlotte Strader; children: Kennett, Geoffrey. BA in Comm., Grinnell Coll., 1975; MS in Journalism, Northwestern U., Evanston, Ill., 1978, MS in Advt., 1987; JD, Drake U., 1998. Reporter, editor Newspapers Iowa County, Marengo, 1975-76; editor Pella (Iowa) Chronicle, 1976-77; reporter, editor Daily Herald, Arlington Heights, Ill., 1978-84; divsn. mgr. comm. and cmty. rels. Pace Suburban Bus Svc., Chgo., 1984-88; divsn. mktg. and comm. Drake U., Des Moines, 1988-93, assoc. v.p. instnl. advancement, 1993-96; v.p. univ. rels. Northwestern U., Evanston, 1997—. Avocations: reading, bicycling. E-mail: a-cubbage@nwu.edu. Office: Northwestern U Dept Univ Rels 555 Clark Evanston IL 60208

CUBBAGE, ELINOR PHILLIPS, English language educator; b. Milford, Del., Apr. 4, 1948; d. Thomas Allen and Katheryn Augusta (Schaeffer) Phillips; m. James Stephenson, July 11, 1970; children: Kate Allen, Benjamin David. BA, U. Del., Newark, 1970; MS, Ea. Conn. State Coll., 1975; EdD, U. Md., 1993. Tchr. English Vernon (Conn.) H.S., 1971-75; prof. English Wor-Wic C.C., Salisbury, Md., 1977—, chairperson honors program, 1997—, chief writer Middle States Report, 1994-95, 99—; adj. prof. Salisbury State U., 1975, 99; rsch. coord. Nat. Ctr. for Devel. Edn., 1990-91. Editor-in-chief Student Creative Arts Mag., 1987—; contbr. articles, poetry to profl. jours. Sec.-treas. Wesley Fellowship Class, Hebron, Md., 1995—; mem. ch. choir Rockawalkin United Meth. Ch., Hebron, 1994—. NEH grantee, 1994-95. Mem. Nat. Coun. Tchrs. English, Tchrs. of English in the Two-Yr. Coll. (sec. of exec. bd. 1985-97). Avocation: creative writing. Home: 7180 Rockawalkin Rd Hebron MD 21830-1177 Office: Wor-Wic Cmty Coll 32000 Campus Dr Salisbury MD 21804-1485

CUBBISON, CHRISTOPHER ALLEN, editor; b. Honolulu, Dec. 22, 1948; s. Donald Cameron and Mary (Pritchett) C.; m. Linda Cicero, Jan. 3, 1976; children: Genevieve, Cameron. BJ, U. Mo., 1971. Reporter N.Y. Daily News, N.Y.C., 1971-72; reporter St. Petersburg (Fla.) Times, 1972-76, asst. city editor, 1976-78; editor various locations including The Miami Herald, 1978-89; asst. mng. editor Rocky Mountain News, Denver, 1989-90, mng. editor projects, 1990—. Avocations: golf, skiing. Home: 11 Sycamore Ln Littleton CO 80127-3525 Office: Rocky Mountain News 400 W Colfax Ave Denver CO 80204-2694*

CUBILLOS, ROBERT HERNAN, church administrator, philosophy educator; b. Long Beach, Calif., Sept. 16, 1957; s. Roberto Hernan and Jacqueline Lee (Smith) C.; m. Deborah Sue Forbes, June 21, 1986; children: Robby, Kelli. BS, Calif. State U., Carson, 1983; cert. in human rights, Internat. Inst. Human Rights, Strasbourg, France, 1984; MA in Apologetics, Simon Greenleaf Sch. of Law, Orange, Calif., 1985; MA in Theology, Fuller Theol. Sem., Pasadena, Calif., 1986; postgrad. studies, Claremont (Calif.) Grad. Sch., 1987.; MA in Social Ethics and Religion, U. So. Calif., 1996. Ch. bus. adminstr. The Harbor Ch., Lomita, Calif., 1983-87, Rolling Hills Covenant Ch., Rolling Hills Estates, Calif., 1987—; asst. prof., co-editor Law Review Simon Greenleaf Sch. of Law, Orange, Calif., 1987—; thesis sec., dean of students Simon Greenleaf Sch. of Law, Orange, 1988—. Contbr. articles to religious and philos. jours. Mem. Am. Acad. Religion, Christian Mgmt. Assn., Evangel. Theol. Soc., Soc. Bibl. Lit., Pi Delta Phi. Office: Rolling Hills Covenant Ch 2222 Palos Verdes Dr N Palos Verdes Peninsula CA 90274-4220

CUBIN, BARBARA LYNN, congresswoman, former state legislator; b. Salinas, Calif., Nov. 30; d. Russell G. and Barbara Lee (Howard) Sage; m. Frederick William Cubin, Aug. 1; children: William Russell, Frederick William III. BS in Chemistry, Creighton U., 1969. Chemist Wyo. Machinery Co., Casper, Wyo., 1973-75; social worker State of Wyo.; office mgr. Casper, Wyo.; mem. Wyo. Ho. Reps., 1987-92, Wyo. Senate, 1993-94; pres. Spectrum Promotions and Mgmt., Casper, 1993-94; congresswoman, Wyo., at large U.S. House Reps., Washington, 1995—; mem. fin. & Hazardous materials, health & environment, commerce com., resources com., chmn., energy and mineral subcom., mem. com. Nat. Coun. State Legislators, San Francisco, 1987—, Lexington, Ky., 1990—. Mem. steering com. Exptl. Program to Stimulate Competitive Rsch. (EPSCOR); mem. Coun. of State Govts.; active Gov.'s Com. on Preventive Medicine, 1992; vice chmn. Cleer Bd. Energy Coun., Irving, Tex., 1993—; chmn. Wyo. Senate Rep. Conf., Casper, 1993—; mem. Wyo. Rep. Party Exec. Com., 1993; pres. Southridge Elem. Sch. PTO, Casper, Wyo. Toll fellow Coun. State Govts., 1990, Wyo. Legislator of Yr. award for energy and environ. issues Edison Electric Inst., 1994. Mem. Am. Legis. Exch. Coun., Rep. Women. Avocations: duplicate bridge, golfing, singing, reading, hunting. Office: US House Reps Office House Mem 1114 Longworth HOB Washington DC 20515*

CUBITTO, ROBERT J., lawyer; b. Globe, Ariz., Aug. 1, 1950; s. Claude A. and Arizona C. (DiMario) C. BA, U. Ariz., 1972, BSBA, 1974; JD, Harvard Law Sch., 1976. Bar: Mass. 1977, N.Y. 1979, U.S. Dist. Ct. (so. and ea. dists.) N.Y. 1979, U.S. Tax Ct. 1979. Cons. Boston Cons. Group, 1976-78; assoc. Debevoise & Plimpton, N.Y.C., 1978-84, ptnr., 1985—. Mem. ABA, N.Y. State Bar Assn. (exec. com. tax sect. 1987-88), Assn. of Bar of City of N.Y., Harvard Club N.Y.C. (asst. treas. 1985-89, bd. mgrs. 1990-93), The Club of Turtle Bay (treas. 1994-97, pres. 1998—). Office: Debevoise & Plimpton 875 3rd Ave Fl 23 New York NY 10022-6256

CUCCARO, RONALD ANTHONY, insurance adjusting company executive; b. Utica, N.Y., Dec. 14, 1944; s. Pasquale and Rose (Pepe) C.; m. Sheila Jane McCarthy, Apr. 1, 1967; children: Stephanie Ann, Elizabeth Ann. BS, Syracuse U., 1966. Cert. sr. profl. pub. adjuster. Adjuster, br. mgr. Gen. Adjustment Bur., Utica and Plattsburg, N.Y., 1966-71; pres. Basloe, Levin & Cuccaro, Ltd., Utica, 1971—; pres., chief exec. officer Adjusters Internat., Utica, 1985—; cons. Govt. Kuwait for UN claims program for Iraqi war reparations; mem. Gov.'s Task Force for Assessment of Oklahoma City Bombing. Pub. Adjusting Today; contbr. articles to profl. jours. Pres. Oneida County Assn. Retarded Citizens, 1976-79, JCI senator Utica Jaycees, Ctrl. N.Y. Cmty. Arts Coun.,1 982-85, Friends in Deed of the Retarded Found., 1991; bd. dirs. BBB, Utica, 1980-81, Downtown Utica Devel. Assn., 1991; founder Cmty. Coalition for Progress, 1993; mem. Utica-Oneida County Fin. Partnership Bd.; mem. bd. trustees Utica Coll. Recipient Chpt. Service award Oneida County Assn. Retarded Citizens, 1979, Coll. Services award Utica Coll., 1983; named Dirs. Emeritus, Cen. N.Y. Arts Council, 1986, Top 40 Alumni of Achievement, Utica Coll., 1987. Mem. N.Y. Assn. Pub. Adjusters, Nat. Assn. Pub. Ins. Adjusters (v.p. 1985-90, pres. 1990-91), Ft. Schuyler Club, Yanundasis Golf Club, Alpha Phi Delta Alumni (pres. 1971-72). Roman Catholic. Avocations: running, boating, sculpture, antique boat restoration. Home: 2230 Douglas Cres Utica NY 13501-5907 Office: Adjusters Internat PO Box 90 Utica NY 13503-0090

CUCCO, JUDITH ELENE, international marketing professional; b. Summit, N.J., Aug. 9; d. Louis John and Patricia T. (Procaccini) C. BS in Internat. Rels. and Spanish, Am. U., 1973; MBA, U. Md., 1983. Prof. English Universidad Nacional Autonoma de Mex., Mexico City, 1971-72; tchr. Spanish, ESL Montgomery (Md.) County Pub. Schs., 1973-81; acct. exec., industry cons. AT&T Comms., Parsippany, N.J., 1983-87; mgr. internat. mktg. support ctr. AT&T, Morristown, N.J., 1987-89; dir. market devel. internat. ops. divsn. AT&T, Caracas, Venezuela, 1989-91; mgr. global product line Sch. Bus. AT&T, Somerset, N.J., 1991-93; regional mgr. market mgmt. Latin Am., Network Wireless Systems Bus. Unit AT&T, Whippany, N.J., 1994-95; bus. devel. dir. Asia/Pacific and Caribbean/L.Am. AT&T Global Bus. Multimedia Svcs., 1995-96; Ams. regional mgr. AT&T Internat. Product Mgmt., 1996-97; market analysis and bus. planning AT&T Internat. Traffic Mgmt., Morristown, N.J., 1997—. Sponsor Child Reach, Warwick, R.I., 1984—, Friends of India, 1995—; mem. Small Faith Cmty., Bridgewater, 1992-98; vol. Interfaith Hospitality Network, Bridgewater, 1993—; mem. Womyn Included, 1994—. Mem. HISPA, U. Md. Alumni Assn., Am. U. Alumni Assn. Avocations: scuba diving, sailing, reading, traveling. Home: 308 Greenfield Rd Bridgewater NJ 08807-3714 Office: AT&T Rm N524 412 Mount Kemble Ave Morristown NJ 07960-6617

CUCCO, ULISSE P., obstetrician, gynecologist; b. Bklyn., Aug. 19, 1929; s. Charles and Elvira (Garafalo) C.; m. Antoinette DeMarco, Aug. 31, 1952; children—Carl, Richard, Antoinette Marie, Michael, Frank, James. B.S. cum laude, L.I. U., 1950; M.D., Loyola U., Chgo., 1954. Diplomate Am. Bd. Ob-Gyn. Intern Nassau County Hosp., Hempstead, N.Y., 1954-55; resident in ob-gyn Lewis Meml. Mercy Hosp., Chgo., 1955-58; practice medicine specializing in ob-gyn Des Plaines, Ill., 1960—; mem. staff N.W. Cmty. Hosp., Arlington Heights, Ill.; past pres. med. staff, ch mn. dept. ob-gyn Holy Family Hosp., Des Plaines, Ill.; clin. asst. prof. Stritch Sch. Medicine, Loyola U. Contbr. articles to med. jours. Mem. ACS, Am. Fertility Soc., Ctrl. Assn. Ob-Gyn., Ill. Med. Soc., Chgo. Med. Soc., Chgo. Gynecol. Soc. (past pres.), Chgo. Inst. Medicine, Sunset Ridge Country Club. Roman Catholic. Home: 665 Midfield Ln Northbrook IL 60062-5507 Office: Holy Family Med Ctr 100 N River Rd Des Plaines IL 60016-1209

CUCINA, VINCENT ROBERT, retired financial executive; b. Balt., Mar. 31, 1936; s. Anthony James and Josephine (Lazzaro) C.; m. Rosemary Warrington, Apr. 24, 1965; children: Victor, Gregory, Russell. BS in Acctg. magna cum laude, Loyola Coll., Balt., 1958; MS in Fin. Mgmt., George Washington U., 1967. CPA, Calif. Auditor Haskins & Sells, CPAs, Balt., 1958, 61-63; acctg. mgr. books and reports Chesapeake & Potomac Telephone Co. (AT&T), Cockeysville, Md., 1964-68; mgr. fin. controls ITT, N.Y.C., 1968; contr. ITT World Directories, N.Y.C., 1969-70; v.p. fin. analysis and planning Dart Industries, Inc., L.A., 1970-82; v.p. fin., chief fin. officer Epson Am., Inc., Torrance, Calif., 1984-87; cons. Westlake Village, Calif., 1988-95; lectr. planning and fin. Calif. Luth. U., 1991-95. Capt. U.S. Army, 1959-60, USAR, 61-64. Mem. AICPA, Fin. Execs. Inst. Roman Catholic. Avocations: travel, reading, target shooting. Home: 32305 Blue Rock Rdg Westlake Village CA 91361-3912

CUDAHY, RICHARD D., federal judge; b. Milwaukee, Wisc., Feb. 2, 1926; s. Michael F. and Alice (Dickson) C.; m. Ann Featherson, July 14, 1956 (dec. 1974); m. Janet Stuart, July 17, 1976; children: Richard D., Norma K., Theresa E., Daniel M., Michaela A., Marguerite L., Patrick G. BS, U.S. Mil. Acad., 1948; JD, Yale U., 1955; LLD (hon.), Ripon Coll., 1981, DePaul U., 1995, Wabash Coll., 1996, Stetson U., 1998. Bar: Conn. 1955, D.C. 1957, Ill. 1957, Wis. 1961. Commd. 2d. lt. U.S. Army, 1948, advanced through grades to 1st lt., 1950; law clk. to presiding judge U.S. Ct. Appeals (2d cir.), 1955-56; asst. to legal adv. Dept. State, 1956-57; assoc. firm Isham, Lincoln & Beale, Chgo., 1957-60; pres. Patrick Cudahy, Inc., Wis., 1961-71, Patrick Cudahy Family Co., 1968-75; ptnr. firm Godfrey & Kahn, Milw., 1972; commr., chmn. Wis. Pub. Service Commn., 1972-75; ptnr. Isham, Lincoln & Beale, Chgo., 1976-79; judge U.S. Ct Appeals (7th cir.), Chgo., 1979-94, sr. judge, 1994—; lectr. law Marquette U. Law Sch., 1961-66; vis. prof. law U. Wis., 1966-67; prof. lectr. law George Washington U., Washington, D.C., 1978-79, DePaul U. Coll. Law, 1996-99; adj. prof. DePaul U., 1996-99. Commr. Milw. Harbor, 1964-66; pres. Milw. Urban League, 1965-66; trustee Environ. Def. Fund, 1976-79; chmn. DePaul Human Rights Law Inst., 1990-98; chmn. Wis. Dem. party, 1967-68; Dem. candidate for Wis. atty. gen., 1968. Mem. ABA (spl. com. on Energy Law 1978-84, 90-96, pub. utility/sect. coun. group), Am. Law Inst., Wis. Bar Assn., Milw. Bar Assn., Chgo. Bar Assn., Fed. Judges' Assn. (bd. dirs.), Am. Inst. for Pub. Svc. (bd. selectors), Cath. Theol. Union (trustee), Law Club Chgo. (pres. 1992-93, spl. divsn. D.C. cir. for appt. ind. counsel 1998—). Roman Catholic. Office: US Ct Appeals 219 S Dearborn St Chicago IL 60604-1702

CUDD, J. EARL, federal judge; b. 1930. LLB, U. Minn., 1954. Bar: Minn. Pvt. law practice Mpls., 1956-61, 65-67; asst. U.S. atty. for Minn., Dept. Justice, 1961-63, first asst. U.S. Atty. for Minn., 1967-73; solicitor gen. State of Minn., 1963-65; part-time magistrate judge U.S. Dist. Ct. Minn., Mpls., 1973—. Office: 586 US Courthouse 300 S 4th St Minneapolis MN 55415-1320

CUDDIHY, ROBERT VINCENT, JR., marketing executive; b. Rochester, N.Y., July 15, 1959; s. Robert Vincent Sr. and June Marie (Tuck) C.; m. Michele Pittenger; children: Brendan, Shea, Tara. BA in Acctg., Franklin and Marshall Coll., Lancaster, Pa., 1981. CPA, N.Y. Sr. mgr. KPMG Peat Marwick, N.Y.C., 1981-87; pres., chief fin. officer, chief operating officer, sec. HMG Worldwide Corp., N.Y.C., 1987—, bd. dirs., 1988—, chief oper. officer, 1989—, pres., 1990—; cons. in field. Mem. Am. Inst. CPA's, N.Y. State Soc. CPA's, Nat. Assn. Accts. Republican. Avocations: home improvements, golf, reading. Office: HMG Worldwide Corp 475 10th Ave New York NY 10018-1120

CUDDY, BRIAN GERARD, neurosurgeon; b. Syracuse, N.Y., July 13, 1959; s. Edward Michael and Mary Elizabeth (O'Brien) C. BS in Biology, SUNY, Albany, 1981; MS in Physiology, Albany Med. Coll., 1983, MD, 1987. Asst. prof. neurosurgery Med. U. S.C., 1994—, Med. Coll. Wis., 1993-94. Contbr. articles to profl. jours. Mem. Am. Assn. Neurol. Surgeons, Sigma Xi. Roman Catholic. Office: Med U of SC Dept Neurosurgery 171 Ashley Ave Charleston SC 29425-0001

CUDDY, DANIEL HON, bank executive; b. Valdez, Alaska, Feb. 8, 1921; s. Warren N. and Lucy C.; m. Betty Puckett, Oct. 6, 1947; children: Roxanna, David, Gretchen, Jane, Lucy, Laurel. BA, Stanford U., 1946. Bar: Alaska 1948. Pvt. practice Anchorage, 1948-53; pres. First Nat. Bank Anchorage, 1951—, chmn. bd. With U.S. Army, World War II, ETO. Office: First Nat Bank 101 W 36th Ave Anchorage AK 99503-5904

CUDE, REGINALD HODGIN, architect; b. Greensboro, N.C., May 9, 1936; s. Ernest Hodgin and Ann Smith (Hodgin) C.; m. Nancy Virginia Worrall, Dec. 31, 1966; children: Jonathan Christopher, Jennifer Elizabeth. BArch, N.C. State U., 1959. Cert. Nat. Coun. Archtl. Registration Bds. Intern McMinn, Norfleet & Wicker, Architects, Greensboro, N.C., 1959-60; with Abraham W. Geller, N.Y.C., 1961, Marcel Breuer Assocs.,

N.Y.C., 1962; architect I.M. Pei & Ptrns., N.Y.C., 1962-65; assoc. Mariani & Assocs., Washington, 1966-68, prin., v.p., 1968-84, exec. v.p., 1984-92; prin. Mariani Archs./Planners (formerly Mariani & Assocs.), Washington, 1992—; cons. Dept. Justice, Washington, 1983; cons. architect Mt. St. Mary's Coll., Emmitsburg, Md., 1982-90. Prin. works include J.V. Dahlgren Med. Libr., Georgetown U., 1968, Paul Robeson Sch., Washington, 1975, Nevils Student Apts., Georgetown U., 1983, Village "C" Student Residence, Georgetown U., 1986, Fine Arts Complex, U. D.C., 1977, Beall Office Bldg., Alexandria, Va., 1983, Protoype Metrobus Facility, Rockville, Md., 1983, Master Plans, Mt. St. Marys Coll., 1985, Cath. U. Am., 1990, Univ. Bookstore and Ctrl. Grounds Parking Facility, U. Va., 1993, numerous others. Mem. Arlington County Landmark Rev. Bd., Va., 1983-88, chmn. design rev. com., 1987-88; mem. Arlington Schs. Capital Improvement Task Force, 1989; pres. Waycroft-Woodlawn Civic Assn., Arlington, 1980. With U.S. Army, 1960. Mem. AIA (chpt. design awards 1980, 83, 84, regional design award 1983, Washingtonian Residential Design award 1984, Masonry Inst. Design award 1987). Methodist. Office: Mariani Archs/Planners 1350 Connecticut Ave NW Washington DC 20036-1722

CUDKOWICZ, LEON, medical educator; b. Lodz, Poland, Jan. 18, 1923; came to U.S., 1956; s. Mauryce and Masza (Malynski) C.;m. Margaret Chandler, Mar. 14, 1950 (div. July 1981); children: Alexander, Penelope; m. Teresa Cuiza de Alfaro, Jan. 18, 1986. BS, U. London, 1946, MD, 1951. James Hudson fellow Yale U. Sch. Medicine, 1956-58; registrar St. Thomas Hosp., U. London, 1958-59; asst. prof. then assoc. prof. medicine Dalhousie U., Halifax, N.S., Can., 1960-69; prof. medicine Thomas Jefferson U., Phila., 1970-74; prof., chmn. Wright State U., Dayton, 1974-79, King Faisal U., Dammam, Saudi Arabia, 1979-81; prof. medicine U. Cin., 1981-95, prof. emeritus, 1995—. Author: Human Bronchial Circulation, 1970; contbr. 107 articles to profl. jours. Capt. RAMC, 1946-49. Capt. RAMC, 1946-49. Fellow RCP, Nat. Pediat. Soc. Bolivia (hon.), NIH (sr.). Avocations: writing, mountaineering, gardening, travel. Home: Yonder Hill Farm Highland OH 45132 Office: U Cin Sch Medicine 253 Bethesda Ave Cincinnati OH 45229-2827

CUDNOHUFSKY, WALTER LEE, landscape architect; b. Pontiac, Mich., July 15, 1940; s. Walter and Gertrude (Degroot) C.; m. Irene K. Koster, June 4, 1964 (div. 1975); children: Craig William, Niels Walter; m. Susan H. Willett, Aug. 9, 1986. BS in Landscape Architecture with honors, Mich. State U., 1962; MLA with honors, Harvard U., 1965. Registered landscape architect, Mass., Conn. Designer East Detroit (Mich.) Pub. Works, 1960-62; landscape architect Sasaki Strong Assn., Toronto, Ont., Can., 1962-63, 65-66, The Architects Collaborative, Cambridge, Mass., 1963-66; ptnr. landscape architecture Rsch. Planning and Design Assocs., Amherst, Mass., 1966-72; landscape architect Conway, Mass., 1972-80; ptnr., landscape architect Conway Design Assocs., 1980-90; prin. Walter Cudnohufsky Assocs., Conway, 1990—; founder, dir. Conway Sch. Landscape Design, 1972-92; asst. prof. grad. faculty U. Mass., 1966-72; vis. prof. critic programs landscape architecture throughout U.S. and Can., 1966-76, guest critic, workshop participant landscape architecture programs for students, faculty, 1976—; co-dir. S.E. New Eng. Study, 1972; co-dir. visual and social subproject on study of freshwater wetlands in Mass., 1969-72; workshop leader Hariot Watt U., Edinburgh, Scotland, 1982; cons. Regional Mayors Inst. on City Design, Nat. Endowments Arts-MIT, 1992, 93; invited cons. Internat. Countryside Stewardship Exch., Pike County, Pa., June 1995. contbr. articles, editorials to profl. publs.; several solo art exhbns., 1995. Chmn. Conway Long Range Planning Com., 1983-86; mem. Greenfield C.C. Found., 1984-86, Conway Bd. Health, 1970-73; mem. Ashfield Planning Bd., 1992, chmn., 1994; co-founder Deerfield (Mass.) Land Trust, 1990-91; steering com. Ft. Devens Charrette, 1992-93; bd. trustees Community Land Trust So. Berkshires, 1991-93; mem. coms. Berkshire Bot. Garden, Stockbridge, 1993-94; commr. Mass. Hist. Commn., 1994, adv. panel Vegetation Mgmt. Plans, Pesticide Bur., Mass. Dept. Food and Agrl., 1998-99. Recipient Regional award for Outstanding Comprehensive Planning, Am. Planning Assn., 1991, Regional award for Planning Implementation, Am. Planning Assn., 1991, Merit awards for Landscape Planning, Boston Soc. Landscape Architects, 1991, AIA Regional Honor award, 1982, Award of Excellence, Design and Environment Mag., 1973, Jacob Weidenman Traveling fellowship, 1965; named Outstanding Educator in Conservation, 1981; faculty growth and faculty rsch. grantee U. Mass., Amherst, 1966-67; Citizen Activist of Yr. award Environmental League of Mass., 1998. Mem. Am. Soc. Landscape Architects. Avocation: art, sketching and water color. Office: Walter Cudnohufsky Assocs 455 Bug Hill Rd Ashfield MA 01330-9742

CUELLO, AUGUSTO CLAUDIO GUILLERMO, medical research scientist, author; b. Buenos Aires, Argentina, Apr. 7, 1939; came to Can., 1985; s. Juan Andres and Rita Maria (Sagarra) Cuello-Freyre; m. Martha Maria J. Kaes, Mar. 10, 1967; children: Paula Marcela, Karina Rosa. MD, U. Buenos Aires, 1965; MA (hon.), Oxford (Eng.) U., 1978, DSc, 1986; hon. degree, U. Fed. do Ceará, 1991. Asst. prof. Sch. Biochemistry, U. Buenos Aires, 1974-75; scientist MRC Neurochem. Pharmacology, Cambridge, Eng., 1975-78; lectr. depts. pharmacology and human anatomy U. Oxford, 1978-85; med. tutor, E.P. Abraham sr. research fellow Lincoln Coll., Oxford, 1978-85; chmn., prof. pharmacology and therapeutics McGill Univ., Montreal, Que., Can., 1985—; cons. Seralab Ltd., Sussex, Eng., 1981-85, Sandoz Ltd., Basel, Switzerland, 1982-84, Medicorp-Immunocorp, Montreal, 1985—, Synthelabo, Paris, 1977-78, Fidia Rsch. Labs., 1991-93, UN Inst. Biotech. and Genetic Engring., Italy, 1993; internat. advisor Cajal Inst., Madrid, 1983-88; mem. sci. adv. bd. A.I. virtanen Inst., Kuopio, Finland, 1997—. Editor: Co-Transmission 1, 1982, Immunohistochemistry, 1983, Brain Microdissection Techniques, 1983, Substance P and Neurokinins, 1987, Pain and Mobility, 1987, Neuronal Cell Death and Repair, 1993, Cholinergic Function and Dysfunction, 1993, Immunohistochemistry II, 1993, Pharmacological Sciences: Perspectives For Research and Therapy in the Late 1990's, 1995, NeuroReport, 1990—, Jour. Chem. Neuroanatomy, 1987-93; mem. editl. bd. profl. jours. Recipient Estela A. de Goytia prize Argentinian Assn. Advancement Sci., 1968, Prof. A. Rosenblueth award Grass Found., 1979, Robert Feulgen prize Gesellschaft für Histochemie, 1981; NIH Postdoctoral fellow, 1970-72; named Hon. Prof. faculty of Pharmacy and Biochemistry, Buenos Aires U., 1992, Norman Bethune U. Med. Scis., China., Hon. Citizen of New Orleans, 1992, Heinz Lehman award Can. Coll. Neuropsychopharmacology, 1995, Novartis Sr. Rsch. award Pharmacological Soc. Can., 1997. Fellow Royal Soc. of Can.; mem. Brit. Pharm. Soc., Can. Coll. Neuropsychopharmacology, Am. Soc. Neurochemistry, European Neurosci. Assn., Internat. Soc. Neuroendocrinology, Soc. for Neurosci., Assn. Med. Sch. Pharmacology, Can. Assn. Neurosci., Internat. Soc. Neurochemistry, Can. Assn. Acad. Pharm., Internat. Brain Rsch. Orgn., World Health Orgn., Am. Soc. Pharmacology and Exptl. Therapeutics, Oxford Soc., Physiol. Soc. Gt. Britain, Pharm. Soc. of Can., Gesellschaft fur histochemie, Corr. Pharma. Soc. of Argentina, Can. Fed. of Bio. Sci., Collegium Internat. Neuro-Psychopharma Cologiaine, Oxford and Cambridge United Club, Univ. Club Montreal. Avocations: tennis, reading, theatre, history, Spanish and Latin American literature. Office: McGill U Dept Pharmacology, 3655 Drummond St, Montreal, PQ Canada H3G 1Y6

CUELLO, JOEL L., biosystems engineer, educator; b. San Pablo City, Philippines, Nov. 20, 1962; s. Vicente Reyes and Gertrudis B. (Lansigan) C. BSin Agrl. and Biol. Engring., U. Philippines, 1984; MS in Agrl. and Biol. Engring., Penn State U., 1990, PhD in Agrl. and Biol. Engring., 1994, MS in Plant Physiology, 1999. Instr. U. Philippines, Los Baños, 1984-88; grad. rsch. asst. Pa. State U., University Park, 1988-93; rsch. assoc. U.S. NRC, NASA Kennedy Space Ctr., Cape Canaveral, Fla., 1994; asst. prof. U. Ariz., Tucson, 1995—. Mem. editl. bd. Life Support and Biosphere Sci. Internat., Jour. for Earth and Space; contbr. articles to profl. jours.; inventor cellular biochem. electroelicitation process. Rsch. grantee USDA, 1996, 97, 98, 99, NASA, 1997, 98, 99. Mem. Am. Soc. Agrl. Engring. (chmn. biol. engring. exec. com. 1998-99, plant biol. engring. com. 1995, pres. 1999, Ariz. chpt. 1997-98, advisor Ariz. student br. 1996—, Best Paper award 1992), Inst. Biol. Engring. (councilor 1998-99), Am. Soc. Engring. Edn., Nat. Honor Soc. Agr., Nat. Honor Soc. Engring., Honor Soc. Agrl. and Biol. Engring. (pres. Pa. chpt. 1993). Avocations: reading, hiking. Office: U Ariz Dept Agrl and Biosystems Engring 507 Shantz Bldg Tucson AZ 85721

CUETTER, ALBERT CAYETANO, neurologist; b. Cartagena, Colombia, Aug. 7, 1938. MD, Med. U. Cartagena, Colombia, 1963. Diplomate Am. Bd. Neurology. Internist Hosp. Santa Clara, Cartagena, Colombia, 1963-64; res. neur. Northwestern U., 1965-68, fellowship in electromyography, 1968-69; prof. neurology Tex. Tech. U. Health Scis. Ctr., 1990.

CUEVAS, DAVID, psychologist; b. Mt. Vernon, Ohio, Sept. 28, 1947; s. Robert Myron Ryan and Wanda Mae Carter; m. Belia Cuevas, Apr. 1, 1980; 1 child, Angela Marie. AA in Gen. Edn., Lassen Coll., 1975; BS in Psychology, U. Md., 1984; MA in Psychology, Webster U., 1986; PhD in Psychology, Columbia Pacific U., 1989. Drafted USN, 1964-67; enlisted U.S. Army, 1971, advanced through ranks to sgt., specialist behavioral sci., 1966-86, ret., 1986; faculty El Paso (Tex.) Community Coll., 1986-92; cons. Cuevas Cons. Svcs., El Paso, 1986-98; sch. dir. Computer Career Ctr., El Paso, 1987-89; speaker conf. Fed. Women's Assn., Ft. Bliss, Tex., 1990; sch. adminstrn. & assessment cons. Computer Labs Inc., 1995—, Am. Inst. English, 1998—. DAV. Mem. APA, ASCD, VFW (life), Spl. Forces Nat. Assn. (life). Avocations: boating, camping, travel, flying, scuba diving. Home and Office: 11640 Lake Erie Dr El Paso TX 79936-4054 Office: El Paso Community Coll 11640 Lake Erie Dr El Paso TX 79936-0500

CUFFE, ROBIN JEAN, nursing educator; b. Frankfurt, Sept. 8, 1951; d. Russell Bates and Jean May (Clark) Preuit; m. Ronald Frederick Cuffe, Mar. 9, 1974; 1 child, Matthew David. Diploma, Richmond Meml. Hosp., 1973; BSN, Marymount U., 1982; MS in Edn., Va. Technol. and State U., 1990. RNC; cert. in cardiac rehab. nursing AACN; cert. health edn. specialist. Staff nurse Fairfax Hosp., Falls Church, Va., 1973-75; asst. head nurse, staff nurse, supr. ICU Arlington (Va.) Hosp., 1975-78, asst. coord. cardiac rehab., 1978-81, coord. cardiopulmonary rehab., 1981—. Bd. dirs. Am. Heart Assn., Northern, Va., 1982-91; jr. high youth group leader Ch. of the Holy Comforter, Vienna, Va., 1988-90, mem. adult edn. commn., 1990—. Fellow Am. Assn. Cardiovasc. and Pulmonary Rehab. (chmn. stds. and reimbursement com. 1991—, pres.-elect 1994-95, pres. 1995-96, treas. 1996-98), Va. Assn. Cardiovasc. and Pulmonary Rehab., Sigma Theta Tau (pres. chpt. 1984-86). Episcopalian. Home: 1804 Cloverlawn Ct Mc Lean VA 22101

CUFFE, STAFFORD SIGESMUND, automotive engineer, consultant; b. Kingston, Jamaica; s. Edwin Syndey and Leida C. (Sasso) C.; m. Dorothy Cummings, Sept. 15, 1973; children: Keisha, Kendra. AAS, N.Y.C. Community Coll., 1975; BS in Engring. Tech., CCNY, 1977; MS in Adminstrn., Ctrl. Mich. U., 1993; PhD in Adminstrn./Mgmt., Walden U., 1995. Project engr. PPG Inds. Inc., Wichita Falls, Tex., 1977-79; mfg. engr. Ford Motor Co., Tulsa, 1979-85; sr. mfg. engr. Ford Motor Co., Lincoln Park, Mich., 1985-90; sr. mfg. engr. Glass Tech. Ctr. Ford Motor Co., Dearborn, 1992-95, sr. mfg. engr. Rsch. & Engring. Ctr., 1996; pres. Cuffe & Assocs., Bloomfield Hills, Mich., 1996—; mem. Dearborn (Mich.) plant modernization team (Japanese venture), 1990-92; adj. prof. Nova Southeastern U., Sch. Bus. and Entrepreneurship-MBA program, 1996—, Oakland U., Sch. Mgmt. and Mktg., Bus. Adminstrn.-MBA program, 1997—;. Bd. dirs. Tulsa Jaycees, 1981; tech. advisor Boy Scouts Am., Tulsa, 1982; exec advisor Jr. Achievement of S.W. Mich., 1986; fund raiser United Way Found. of Mich., 1988. Mem. IEEE (nat. chmn. glass industry com. 1990—), Soc. Mfg. Engrs., Rotary (Southfield Mich. chpt.). Democrat. Roman Catholic. Avocations: golf, tennis, cross-country skiing. Fax: (248) 557-5144. E-mail: caimmts@aol.com. Office: Cuffe & Assocs Inc PO Box 7123 Bloomfield Hills MI 48302-7123

CUFFIE, KEVIN LAMONT, academic administrator, educational consultant; b. Balt., Aug. 23, 1955; s. James Joslin and Christine (Alston) C.; m. Deborah Hearst. AB in Med. Care Planning and Sociology, Wash. U., 1986; MSEd in Higher Edn., So. Ill. U., 1992. Mental health counselor Provident Hosp., Balt., 1980-85; asst. dir. Frostburg (Md.) State U., 1986-88; assoc. dir. Coppin State Coll., Balt., 1988-89; asst. dir. Essex C.C., Balt., 1989-90, Advocates for Children and Youth, Balt., 1992-93; instr. Frederick (Md.) C.C., 1994, coord., 1993—; cons. Frederick County Pub. Schs., 1995—, Frederick Job Tng. Agy., 1995—, Morgan State U., Balt., 1993-94; co-founder Collegiate Black Male Summit, Balt., 1995—; organizational facilitator Johns Hopkins U., 1998—. Co-author: When School Isn't Special, 1992. Mem. Liberty Cmty. Action Plan, Baltimore County, 1997; bd. dirs. Druid Hill YMCA, 1992-95. Recipient Svc. award USDA, 1994; Dean's fellow So. Ill. U., 1990-92; rsch. fellow Upjohn Corp., 1981-83. Mem. Internat. Mentoring Assn., Nat. Assn. Student Pers. Adminstrs., Md. Multicultural Coalition (bd. dirs. 1997—). Avocations: jazz music, martial arts, coaching youth sports. Home: 4028 Cedar Mills Rd Randallstown MD 21133-4400 Office: Frederick CC 7932 Opossumtown Pike Frederick MD 21702-2964

CUGGINO, MICHAEL JOSEPH, financial executive; b. Cambridge, Mass., Feb. 9, 1963; s. Joseph Anthony Jr. and Christine Adele (Dabrowski) C. Ed., Bentley Coll., 1985. CPA, Mass., Calif.; CISA. With Ernst & Young, Boston, 1985-91; pvt. practice Petaluma, Calif., 1991—; treas., dir. Permanent Portfolio Family of Funds, Inc., Petaluma, 1993—; treas. World Money Securities, Inc., Petaluma, 1993-96, Bullion Security Corp., Petaluma, 1993—, Passport Fin., Inc., 1993—. Mem. AICPA (pvt. cos. practice sect., mgmt. cons. practice sect., pers. fin. planning practice sect., tax practice sect.), Mass. Soc. CPAs, Calif. Soc. CPAs, EDP Auditors Assn. Home: 2201 Pacific Ave Apt 703 San Francisco CA 94115-1440 Office: 625 2nd St Ste 102 Petaluma CA 94952-5120

CUGNINI, ALDO GODFREY, electrical engineer; b. Buenos Aires, Apr. 26, 1956; came to U.S., 1956; s. Aldo Mario and Cecilia (Heitner) C.; m. Helen Van Zobler, Oct. 25, 1987; children: Charlotte, Elizabeth. BS, Columbia U., 1977, MS, 1979. Product specialist RCA Broadcast Sys., Camden, N.J., 1979-80; sr. project engr. CBS Labs., Stamford, Conn., 1980-87; dir. rsch. Broadcast Tech., Greenwich, Conn., 1987-89; from rsch. staff to prin. mem. Philips Labs., Briarcliff Manor, N.Y., 1989-96, head advanced TV rsch. dept., 1996-98; hardware design mgr., project mgr., digital video group Philips Consumer Electronics, Briarcliff Manor, N.Y., 1998—; specialist group mem. ATSC Tech. Group on Distbn., Washington, 1994-97; tech. oversight group Grand Alliance, 1994-97; bd. dirs. Advanced TV Tech. Ctr., Washington. Contbr. articles to profl. jours. Mem. IEEE, Audio Engring. Soc., Eta Kappa Nu. Achievements include 5 patents in field. Avocation: astronomy. Office: Philips CE 345 Scarborough Rd Briarcliff Manor NY 10510-2027

CUI, KE-HUI, embryologist, obstetrician, gynecologist; b. Guangzhou, Guangdong, China, May 15, 1948; arrived in Australia, 1989; s. Shen-Zhi and Zi-Jian (Chen) C.; m. Ling-Jia Wang, Dec. 31, 1982; children: Jing, Yong-Yan. MD, Sun Yat-sen U. Med. Scis., Guangzhou, 1982; PhD, U. Adelaide, Australia, 1993. Tech. officer 1st Affiliated Hosp. Sun Yat-sen U. Med. Scis., 1976-78, resident in ob-gyn., 1982-86; postdoctoral fellow U. Fla., Gainesville, 1986-89; scientist in charge preimplantation diagnosis U. Adelaide, 1993-96; dir. molecular and preimplantation genetics The Ctr. For Human Reproduction, Chgo., 1996-97; lab. dir. Midwest Fertility Ctr., Chgo., 1998—; honorable assoc. prof. Sun Yat-sen U. Med. Scis., Guangzhou, China, 1995—. Referee Human Fertilisation and Embryology Authority, London, 1995; mem. panel assessors Nat. Health and Med. Rsch. Coun., Australia, 1995—. Mem. Fertility Soc. Australia (Marion Merrell Dow prize 1991, 94), European Soc. Human Reprodn. and Embryology. Achievements include patent for book indexing system; determined that human X sperm are statistically larger and longer than Y sperm, sperm prefertilization diagnosis, multiplex polymerase chain reaction (PCR) amplification in single cells, amplification of whole B-globin gene from single cells by PCR, precise sex determination and safety diagnosis in mice preimplantation diagnosis, routine preimplantation diagnosis in humans, invention of culture medium for human blastocyst and hatching embryos. Avocation: shopping. Address: 1537A N Clybourn Ave Chicago IL 60610-1009

CUIFFO, FRANK WAYNE, lawyer; b. Houston, Oct. 13, 1943; s. Richard and Helen (Giaco) C.; m. Barbara Joyce Streeter, Nov. 26, 1966; children: Karen, Deborah, Richard, Steven. BS, U. Notre Dame, 1964; JD, Fordham U., 1967. Bar: N.Y. 1967. Assoc. Pennie & Edmonds (formerly Pennie, Edmonds, Morton, Taylor & Adams), N.Y.C., 1967-69; sr. assoc. Emmet, Marvin, & Martin, N.Y.C., 1969-74, Golenbock & Barell, N.Y.C., 1974-78; mng. ptnr. Carro, Spanbock, Kaster & Cuiffo, N.Y.C., 1978-93; chmn. real estate dept., exec. com. Donovan, Leisure, Newton & Irvine, N.Y.C., 1993-98; ptnr. McDermott, Will & Emery, N.Y.C., 1998—. Mem. ABA, U.S. Patent Bar, N.Y. State Bar, Siwanoy Country Club, South Seas Club. Office: McDermott Will & Emery 50 Rockefeller Plz Fl 12 New York NY 10020-1605

CULBERSON, GARY MICHAEL, hotel manager; b. Jackson, Miss., Sept. 16, 1955; s. William James and Peggy Ann (Pickett) C.; m. Mary Lee Yadron, May 8, 1986; children: Ashley Victoria, Brent Michael. Student, Miss. State U., 1973-78. Cert. hotel adminstr. Resident mgr. Kingston Plantation, Myrtle Beach, S.C.; exec. asst., mgr. Brown Palace Hotel, Denver; mng. dir. Tremont Hotel, Chgo., 1991; gen. mgr. Embassy Suites Hotel, Denver, 1996-97; hotel mgr. Casino Magic Hotel, Biloxi, Miss., 1997—. Mem. Confrerie De La Chaine Des Rotisseurs (Maitre of Table Restaurateur 1991-92), Miss. Gulf Coast Hotel and Motel Assn. (v.p. 1998—), Mensa. Avocations: snow skiing, golf.

CULBERSON, JAMES O., retired rehabilitation educator; b. Floyd County, Ga., Apr. 5, 1932; s. John T. and Willie Mae (Colston) C.; m. Janice May Jaquith, Jan. 11, 1958; children: Pamela, John, Sarah, James Jr. BS, Bob Jones U., 1953; MEd, U. S.C., 1960; EdD, U. Ga., 1970. Prin., tchr. Bur. Ind. Affairs, Juneau, Alaska, 1960-62; English tchr. Floyd County, Rome, Ga., 1962-67; high sch. counselor Gordon County, Calhoun, Ga., 1967-68; prof. counseling psychology U. So. Miss., Hattiesburg, 1970-95, dir. undergrad. rehab. svcs. edn., 1972-95, prof. emeritus of psychology, 1996—. Mem. editorial bd. Rehab. Counseling Bull., 1980-83; contbr. articles to profl. jours. Mem. Nat. Coun. Rehab. Edn., S.E. Coun. Rehab. Edn., Am. Rehab. Counseling Assn. (cert. recognition outstanding svc. 1987). Office: PO Box 17377 Hattiesburg MS 39404-7377

CULBERSON, WILLIAM LOUIS, botany educator; b. Indpls., Apr. 5, 1929; s. Louis Henry and Lucy Helene (Hellman) C.; m. Chicita Forman, Aug. 24, 1953. BS, U. Cin., 1951; Diplome d'Etudes Supérieures, U. de Paris, 1952; PhD, U. Wis., 1954. NSF postdoctoral fellow Harvard U., Cambridge, Mass., 1954-55; instr. Duke U., Durham, N.C., 1955-58, asst. prof., 1958-64, assoc. prof., 1964-70, prof., 1970-84, Hugo L. Blomquist prof., 1984-95; vis. research prof. Mus. Nat. d'Histoire Naturelle, Paris, 1980. Author over 100 rsch. papers. Dir. Sarah P. Duke Gardens at Duke U., Durham, 1978-98. Grantee NSF, 1957-93. Mem. Am. Bryological and Lichenological Soc. (pres. 1987-89), Bot. Soc. Am. (pres. 1991-92), Am. Soc. Plant Taxonomists, Mycol. Soc. Am. Avocations: greenhouse gardening. Office: Duke U Dept Botany Durham NC 27708-0338 Home: 5501 George King Rd Durham NC 27707-9043

CULBERT, PETER VAN HORN, lawyer; b. San Antonio, July 27, 1944; s. Robert William and Dorothy Fairfax (Kift) C.; m. Elizabeth Tamara Spagnola, July 12, 1980; children: Michael, Daniel, Robert, David, William. BA, Cornell U., 1966; MA, SUNY, Buffalo, 1969; JD, U. N.Mex., 1977. Bar: N.Mex. 1977, U.S. Dist. Ct. N.Mex. 1977, U.S. Ct. Appeals (10th cir.) 1977. Law clk. to Hon. Mack Easley N.Mex. Supreme Ct., Santa Fe, 1977-78; sr. ptnr. Jones, Snead, Wertheim, Wentworth & Jaramillo, Santa Fe, 1978-98; pvt. practice Santa Fe, 1998—. Mem. adv. bd., legal counsel Desert Chorale, Santa Fe, 1991—, bd. dirs., 1986-91. Recipient hon. cert. Strathmore Registry Bus. Leaders, 1995-97. Mem. ABA, ATLA, N.Mex. Trial Lawyers Assn., Canyon Assn., Alpha Delta Phi (life). Avocations: flamenco guitarist, bicycling, horticulture, camping. E-mail: pvculbert@law-sf.com. Office: 911 Old Pecos Trail Santa Fe NM 87501

CULBERTSON, FRANCES MITCHELL, psychology educator; b. Boston, Jan. 31, 1921; d. David and Goldie (Fishman) Mitchell; m. John Mathew Culbertson, Aug. 27, 1947; children: John David, Joanne, Lyndall, Amy. BS, U. Mich., 1947, MS, 1949, PhD, 1955. Diplomate Am. Bd. of Profl. Psychology; lic. psychologist, Wis. Clin. child psychologist Wis. Diagnostic Ctr., Madison, 1961-65; chief clin. psychologist dept. child psychiatry U. Wis., Madison, 1965-66; resident rsch. psychologist NIMH, Berkeley, Calif., 1966-67; psychologist Madison Pub. Schs., 1967-68; prof. psychology U. Wis., Whitewater, 1968-88, prof. emeritus, 1988—; psychologist Mental Health Assocs., Madison, 1987—; clin. psychologist Counseling and Psychotherapy Assn., Madison, 1982-87; clin. hypnotherapy cons. Family Achievement Ctr., Oconomowoc, Wis., 1984-89. Author: Voices in International School Psychology, 1985; contbr. chpts. to books, articles to profl. jours. Mem. Dane County Mental Health Bd., Madison, 1980-82. Recipient APA Disting. Contbn. award for Internat. Achievement, 1994. Fellow APA (pres. sect. clin. psychology women 1991-92, bd. conv. affairs 1990-94, chair membership com. 1998-99, coun. rep. liaison and bd. mem. internat. psychology divsn. 1997-98, coun. rep. psychol. hypnosis divsn. 1998-99, coun. rep. internat. psych. divsn. 1999—); mem. Internat. Assn. Applied Psychology Divsn. A pplied Gerontology (pres.-elect 1994-98, pres. 1998—, exec. bd. mem. 1995—), Internat. Soc. Clin. Psychology (founding co-chair 1997-98, treas. 1997—), Internat. Coun. Psychologists (pres. 1979), Wis. Psychol. Assn. (pres. divsn. psychol. hypnosis 1991-99), Madison Hypnotherapy Soc. (pres. 1986-94), Brazilian Soc. Clin. Psychology (hon. pres. 1979), Sigma Xi, Pi Lambda Theta, Phi Kappa Phi. Avocations: skiing, walking, hiking, reading, gardening. Home: 5305 Burnett Dr Madison WI 53705-4609 Office: U Wis Dept Psychology N Prairie Whitewater WI 53190 also: Mental Health Assocs 20 S Park St # 408 Madison WI 53715-1348

CULBERTSON, JACK ARTHUR, education educator; b. Nickelsville, Va., July 16, 1918; s. Otto Cecil and Lola Kate (Fuller) C.; m. Mary Virginia Pond, Aug. 12, 1952; children: Karen Anne Hasselo, Margaret Lynn. AB in Edn., Emory and Henry Coll., 1943; MA in German, Duke U., 1946; PhD in Ednl. Adminstrn., U. Calif., Berkeley, 1955. Cert. tchr., sch. adminstr., Va., Calif. Tchg. prin. Scott County Sch. Sys., Gate City, Va., 1937-41, Jewell Ridge (Va.) Sch. Sys., 1941-42, Tazewell (Va.) County Sch. Sys., 1947-49; H.S. tchr. Mineral Springs (N.C.) Sch. Sys., 1943-44; tchr. jr. h.s. El Centro (Calif.) Sch. Sys., 1949-51; sch. supt. Ellwood Sch. Dist., Goleta, Calif., 1951-53; prof. U. Oreg., Eugene, 1955-59; exec. dir. Univ. Coun. for Ednl. Adminstrn., Columbus, 1959-81; prof. Ohio State U., Columbus, 1981-86, emeritus prof., 1986—; cons. W.K. Kellogg Found., Battle Creek, Mich., 1968, Ford Found., N.Y.C., 1967; advisor Edn. Commn. States, Denver, 1967, Pan Am. Union, Washington, 1968; founder 1st Internat. Intervisitation Program in Ednl. Adminstrn., 1966; spkr. OAS, Brasilia, Brazil, 1968, Australian Coun. for Ednl. Rsch., Sydney, 1967, German Assn. for Tng. Sch. Adminstrs., 1975. Author: Building Bridges, 1995; co-author: Administrative Relationships, 1960, Preparing Educational Leaders for the Seventies, 1969. Recipient Commonwealth Fellow award Commonwealth Coun. for Ednl. Adminstrn., 1978, Roald F. Campbell Lifetime Achievement award Univ. Coun. for Ednl. Adminstrn., 1993. Mem. Am. Ednl. Rsch. Assn. (v.p. 1964-66), Am. Assn. Sch. Adminstrs. (adv. commn. 1974-76), Nat. Coun. for Profs. of Ednl. Adminstrn. (exec. com. 1957-60), Nat. Soc. for Study of Edn. (co-editor yearbook 1986). Avocations: reading, television, card playing. Home: 145 Montrose Way Columbus OH 43214-3634

CULBERTSON, JAMES THOMAS, psychologist; b. Scranton, Pa., Dec. 25, 1911; s. Walter Edwards and Katharine (Evans) C.; m. Jean Herman, Nov. 1, 1941; children—Elizabeth, Hazel, Jamie, Samuel. B.A., Yale U., 1934, Ph.D., 1940. Sterling Research fellow Yale U., 1941; research assoc. in math. and biology U. Chgo., 1946-49; prof. philosophy U. So. Calif., Los Angeles, 1949-51; math. rsch. assoc. Rand Corp., Santa Monica, Calif., 1951-53; prof. math. and computer sci. Calif. Poly. State U.-San Luis Obispo, 1953-65, chmn. philosophy dept., 1968-78; rsch. prof. psychology UCLA, 1965-68; freelance theoretical brain rschr., San Luis Obispo, 1978—. Author: Consciousness and Behavior, 1950; Mathematics and Logic for Digital Devices, 1958; A Student's Survey of the Mind-Body Problem, 1960; The Minds of Robots, 1963; Sensations, Memories and the Flow of Time, 1976; Consciousness: Natural and Artificial, 1982; Achievements include contributions to early work on neural nets and designs for any input-output; helped develop RAND robots; contbr. book chpts. and articles to profl. jours. Mem. nat. bd. advisers Inst. Advanced Philos. Research. Mem. IEEE, AAAS, Am. Math. Soc., Am. Philos. Assn., Philosophy of Sci. Assn., Soc. Philosophy and Psychology. Mind Assn. Home: 115 Del Norte Way San Luis Obispo CA 93405-1507

CULBERTSON, JANET LYNN, artist; b. Greensburg, Pa., Mar. 15, 1932; d. Joseph F. and Helen C. (Moore) Culbertson; m. Douglas I. Kaften, Sept. 30, 1964. BFA, Carnegie Inst. Tech., 1953; MA, NYU, 1963. Instr. art Pace Coll., N.Y.C., 1964-68, Pratt Art Inst., Bklyn., 1973; assoc. prof. Southampton Coll., 1976; drawing instr. Parrish Art Mus., 1979. Exhibited one-woman shows 20th Century West Gallery, N.Y.C., 1967, Molly Barnes Gallery, L.A., 1970, Midtown Gallery, Atlanta, 1971, Lerner-Misrachi Gallery, N.Y.C., 1971, Lerner-Heller Gallery, N.Y.C., 1973, 75, 77, Tower Gallery, Southampton, N.Y., 1976, Benson Gallery, Bridgehampton, N.Y., 1978, 81, 89, Interart Gallery, N.Y.C., 1979, Harriman Coll., N.Y., 1980, Nardin Gallery, N.Y.C., 1981, Aronson Gallery, Atlanta, 1982, Harrisburg State Mus. Pa., 1988, Women Artists Series Rutgers U., N.J., 1988, Carnegie Mellon U., Pitts., 1991, Acme Art Co., Columbus, Ohio, 1992, Islip (N.Y.) Mus., 1992, Suffolk Coll., Riverhead, N.Y., 1996, Stone Quarry Art Park, Cazenovia, N.Y., 1996, Wave Hill, Bronx, N.Y., 1997, Atelier A/E Gallery, N.Y.C., 1997, Nat. Acad. of Sciences in Wash. D.C., 1998, Hoyt Mus., New Castle, PA, 1998; two-women shows Women's Art Ctr., San Francisco, 1975, U. Conn., Bridgport, 1999; four-women show Heckscher Mus., Huntington, N.Y., 1980; group exhbns. include Carnegie Mus., Pitts., 1953, ann. drawing Bucknell U., 1966-68, Palos Verdes (Calif.) Mus., 1970, 16th ann. all Calif. purchase L.A. Art Assn., 1969-70, nat. drawing ann. San Francisco Mus., 1970, Princeton Gallery Fine Arts, 1972, drawing show Fleisher Meml., Phila., 1974, Am. Acad. Arts and Letters, N.Y.C., 1975, Kingpitcher Gallery, Pitts, 1976, West Broadway Galley, N.Y.C., 1976, Bronx Mus., 1976, Guild Hall, East Hampton, N.Y., 1976, 79, 82, 89, (invitational) 94 (Abstract award 1979, Mixed Media award 1992), Orgn. Ind. Artists, N.Y.C., 1978, Parrish Mus., Southampton, N.Y. Meml. Art Gallery, Rochester N.Y., 1979, Western Carolina U., Cullowhee, Phoenix Mus, Tucson Mus., 1980, The Arsenal, N.Y.C., 1981, 50 nat. women artists Edison Coll. Art Gallery, Ft. Myers, Fla., 1982, Norton Art Gallery, W. Palm Beach, Fla., 1985-86, Easthampton (N.Y.) Ctr. Contemporary Arts, 1988, Newport (R.I.) Art Mus., 1988, 91, Trabia Macafee Gallery, N.Y.C., 1988, Vered Gallery, Easthampton, 1989, 90, 92, Hillwood Mus., Brookville, N.Y., 1990, Islip Art Mus., N.Y., 1990, Ucross Wyo. (invitational), 1990, Women's Caucus for Art, Dallas, 1990, Wash., 1991, Benton Gallery, Southampton, N.Y., 1991, 92, 93, Ark. Arts Ctr. (invitational), Little Rock, 1991, Arlene Bujese Gallery, East Hampton, N.Y., 1994, Hillwood Art Mus., L.I. U., Brookville, N.Y., 1994, Hamilton Coll., Clinton, N.Y., 1995, Stony Brook U., N.Y., 1995, others; Babcock Gallery traveling exhibit, 1993-94, Art and the Law traveling exhbn., 1995-97, Anita Shapolsky Gallery, N.Y.C., 1995, Gerald Peters Gallery, 1996-97, ("Women Realists") Ringling Sch. Art and Design, Sarasota Fla., Nabi Gallery, Sag Harbor, 1997; contbr. collage to Attica Book, 1972; contbr. articles to profl. jours., prodr. and contbr. Heresies #13 mag. Creative Artists Pub. Service grantee, 1979. Recipient Shirk Meml. award for oil painting Nat. Assn. Women Artists, Inc., 1993, first place award Notorious L.I. exhibit Hillwood Art Mus., Brookville, N.Y., 1994, Purchase award Hoyt Art Inst., 1995, Purchase award Nassau County Mus. Art, 1997; fellow Ossabaw Found., 1981, Dorland, 1983, Ucross Found., 1989, 99, Blue Mt. Found., 1991, 94, 96, VCCA Ctr. Found., 1992. Home: PO Box 455 Shelter Island NY 11964-0455

CULBERTSON, KATHERYN CAMPBELL, lawyer; b. Tom's Creek, Va., Aug. 14, 1920; d. Robert Fugate and Mary Campbell (Leonard) C. B.S., East Tenn. State U. (1940); B.S. in L.S, George Peabody Library Sch., 1942; J.D., YMCA Night Law Sch., Nashville, 1968. Bar: Tenn. 1969. Librarian Bur. Ships Tech. Library, U.S. Navy Dept., Washington, 1945-49, 51-53; librarian Lincoln Elementary Sch., Kingsport, Tenn., 1949-50, 51, Regional Library, Tenn. State Library and Archives, Johnson City, 1953-61; dir. extension services library Met. Govt. Nashville and Davidson County, Tenn, 1961-71; state librarian and archivist State of Tenn., Nashville, 1972-82; pvt. practice law Nashville, 1982—; mem. library com. Pres.'s Com. on Employment of Handicapped, 1966-86; Nat. Bus. and Profl. Women's Found., 1968-70; pres. Tenn. Fedn. Bus. and Profl. Women's Clubs, 1974-75. Contbg. author: Encyclopedia of Education, 1966; Editor: YMCA Alumni Assn. Bull, 1970-71. Named One of Five Women of Yr. Nashville Banner-Davidson County Bus. and Profl. Women's Club, 1979. Mem. Tenn. Bar Assn., Nashville Bar Assn., Nashville Bus. and Profl. Women's Club (past pres.). Republican. Home and Office: 800 Glen Leven Dr Nashville TN 37204-4305

CULBERTSON, PHILIP EDGAR, SR., aerospace company executive, consultant; b. Colfax, Wash., Aug. 19, 1925; s. Julian L. and Lucia Culbertson; m. Shirley E. Coskey, Aug. 19, 1950; children: Camden E. Culbertson Gooch, Philip E. Jr. BS in Aero. Engring., Ga. Inst. Tech., 1946; MS, U. Mich., 1949. Mem. research staff U. Mich., 1948-52; aerodynamicist Convair divsn. Gen. Dynamics Corp., 1952-56, chief project engr. Atlas space launch vehicles, 1958-65; head aerodynamics and propulsion Bendix Sys. Divsn., 1956-57; project mgr. Apollo Applications/Skylab, 1969-73; dir. payload integration and mission analysis Office Manned Space Flight, 1973-76, asst. adminstr. planning and program integration, 1976-78, dep. assoc. adminstr. space transp. systems, 1979-81; assoc. dep. adminstr. NASA, 1981-84, assoc. adminstr. space sta., 1984-85, gen. mgr., 1985-87, assoc. adminstr. policy and planning, 1987-88; exec. dir. President's Com. Sci. and Tech., 1976-77; pres. Lew Evans Found., Washington, 1988-96; sr. v.p., bd. dirs. Space Destinations Svcs., Inc., Boulder, 1995-98; mem. v.p.'s space policy adv. bd., 1992-93; bd. dirs. Ctr. for Space and Advanced Tech., NASA Alumni League; bd. govs. Krafft A. Ehricke Inst. for Space Devel.; mem. bd. advisors Luna Corp.; lectr. in field. Served with USNR, World War II. Fellow AIAA, Am. Astron. Soc.; mem. Internat. Acad. Astronautics, NASA Alumni League. *We grow and improve by seeking and accepting challenge. Whatever the job - give it the best you have in a way that you can take pride in it. Work with integrity and live with honesty. Never give up curiousity and the desire to learn.*

CULICK, FRED ELLSWORTH CLOW, physics and engineering educator; b. Wolfeboro, N.H., Oct. 25, 1933; s. Joseph Frank and Mildred Beliss (Clow) C.; m. Frederica Mills, June 11, 1960; children—Liza Hall, Alexander Joseph, Mariette Huxham. Student, U. Glasgow, Scotland, 1957-58; SB, MIT, 1957, PhD, 1961. Rsch. fellow Calif. Inst. Tech., Pasadena, 1961-63, asst. prof., 1963-66, assoc. prof., 1966-70, prof. mech. engring. and jet propulsion, 1970-97, Richard L. and Dorothy M. Hayman prof. mech. engring., 1997—, prof. jet propulsion, 1997—; cons. to govt. agys. and indsl. orgns. Fellow AIAA; mem. Internat. Acad. Astronautics, Internat. Fedn. Astronautics, Am. Phys. Soc. Home: 1375 Hull Ln Altadena CA 91001-2620 Office: Calif Inst Tech Caltech 205-45 207 Guggenheim Pasadena CA 91001

CULKIN, CHARLES WALKER, JR., trade association administrator; b. Arlington, Va., Aug. 22, 1947; s. Charles Walker and Helen Elizabeth (Wilson) C.; m. Carolyn DeWayne Franklin, Apr. 5, 1974; children: David Laurence Franklin, Kimberly Anne Franklin. Assoc. in Bus. Adminstrn., Benjamin Franklin U., 1968, BA in Comml. Sci., 1970. Asst. auditor United Va. Bank, Vienna, 1967-70; sr. asst. dir. U.S. GAO, Washington, 1970-97; exec. dir. Assn. of Govt. Accts., 1997—; chmn. Pacific Emerging Issues Conf., Honolulu, 1982; speaker confs. and seminars. Pub. The Govt. Accts. Jour.; contbr. articles to profl. jours. Founder, incorporator Reston Commuter Bus., Inc., 1971, treas., dir., 1971-78. Recipient RCB Bd. Dirs. award 1978, Outstanding Achievement award Fairfax County (Va.) Bd. Suprs., 1978. Mem. Am. Assn. for Budget Program Analysis, Inst. Internal Auditors (sec. no. Va. chpt. 1984-86), Assn. Govt. Accts (dir. Hawaii chpt. 1981-84, conf. mgr. fed. leadership conf. 1994, No. Va. chpt. 1991—, Nat. AGA Spl. Recognition award 1988, 90, 93, President's award 1992, 95-96, Outstanding Mem. award 1983, nat. treas.-elect, 1995-96, nat. treas. 1996-97, Edn. award, 1994), Nat. Assn. Accts. (no. Va. Chpt. dir. 1977-78, v.p. 1979-80), Benjamin Franklin U. Alumni Assn. (pres. 1988-92, Outstanding Leadership award 1991, Bd. Govs. Svc. award 1992, Disting. Alumni award, 1995), George Washington U. Gen. Alumni Assn. (dir. 1991-92, Vol. of Yr. award 1992). Roman Catholic. Home: 11293 Silentwood Ln Reston VA 20191-4138 Office: AGA 2208 Mount Vernon Ave Alexandria VA 22301-1314

CULKIN, MACAULAY, actor; b. N.Y.C., Aug. 26, 1980; s. Christopher "Kit" and Pat C. Student, St Joseph's Sch. of Yorkville, N.Y.C., George Balanchine's Sch. of Ballet, N.Y.C. Appeared in TV commercials; films include Rocket Gibraltar, 1988, Uncle Buck, 1989, See You In The Morning, 1989, Jacob's Ladder, 1990, Home Alone, 1990, My Girl, 1991, Only the Lonely, 1991, Home Alone 2: Lost In New York, 1992, The Good Son, 1993, George Balanchine's The Nutcracker, 1993, Getting Even With Dad, 1994, The Pagemaster, 1994, Richie Rich, 1994; appeared in Michael Jackson's Black or White video, 1991; voice of Nicholas McClary on Wishkid cartoon, 1991-92. *

CULL, JOHN JOSEPH, novelist, playwright; b. Ogdensburg, N.Y., Oct. 4, 1925; s. John Joseph and Adah Jane (Hyde) C.; m. Carol June Andrews (dec. Dec. 1992); stepchildren: Cathy Andrews Jordan, Michael R. Andrews. Cert., U. Buffalo, 1952. Office clk. N.Y. State Electric & Gas Corp., Lockport, 1956-76; creative writing instr. Genesee C.C., Batavia, N.Y., 1984-86; writer Lockport, 1986—; facilitator Write Touch, Lockport, N.Y., 1997. Author: (novels) Windweir, 1999, Haven House, 1991, Out of the Night, 1994, In Silent Hours, 1994, Of Gnarled Roots, 1997, (play) The Late Mark Jordan, 1984, Of Gnarled Roots, 1997, A Call to Valor, 1997, (poetry) The Hedgerow Chapbook, 1988; author numerous short stories and poems. Recipient Non-Fiction Book award Am. Soc. Writers, 1977, Golden Poetry award World of Poetry, 1987, Genesee Arts Coun. award, 1985, 87, Editor's Choice award Nat. Libr. of Poetry, 1989. Avocations: symphony concerts, opera, live theatre, films, classic novels. Home: 546 Birchwood Dr Lockport NY 14094-9160

CULL, ROBERT ROBINETTE, electric products manufacturing company executive; b. Cleve., Sept. 24, 1912; s. Louis David and Wilma Penn (Robinette) C.; m. Gay Cornwell, Oct. 4, 1986. B.S. in Physics, M.I.T., 1934. Supr. Eastman Kodak Co., Rochester, N.Y., 1934-39; asst. to gen. mgr. Cleve. Chain & Mfg. Co., 1940-45; partner Tenna Mfg. Co., Cleve., 1945-56; pres. Tenatronics Ltd., Newmarket, Ont., Can., 1956—, Sterling Mfg. Co., Cleve., 1960—. Trustee Garden Center Greater Cleve., 1975-80, pres., 1979-80; trustee Musical Arts Assn. of Cleve. Orch., 1976—. Mem. IEEE, Cleve. Engring. Soc., Sigma Psi. Clubs: Hermit, Union. *

CULLARI, SALVATORE SANTINO, clinical psychologist, educator, writer; b. Caroniti, Calabria, Italy, Apr. 1, 1952; came to U.S., 1955; s. Carmelo and Carmela (Cullari) C.; m. Kathryn Plesce, Apr. 26, 1985; children: Catherine, Dante. *Dr. Cullari's grandfather Salvatore left Italy in 1922, leaving a pregnant wife behind. Because of the discriminatory practices of the United States against Southern Europeans, the only way to come to America was as an illegal alien. In 1929, he was arrested due to his illegal alien status, and just as he was about to be deported, a federal law was passed, that protected people who had been in this country for more than five years, without criminal activity. Shortly after he became an American citizen. Unfortunately, The Great Depression, World War II and The Immigration Quota System prevented him from bringing his wife and son to this country until 1955. It had been 32 years since he had last seen his family.* BA, Kean Coll., 1974; MA, Western Mich. U., 1976, PhD, 1981. Lic. psychologist, Pa., W.Va. Dir. psychology White Haven (Pa.) Ctr., 1982-83; psychologist Danville (Pa.) State Hosp., 1983-84; coord. of psychology Harrisburg (Pa.) State Hosp., 1984-86; prof., chair dept. psychology Lebanon Valley Coll., Annville, Pa., 1986—; cons. Bur. Disability Determination, Harrisburg, 1987—. Author questionaire acad. social evaluation scales, 1990, Treatment Resistance, 1996; editor Found. of Clin. Psychology, 1998; contbr. numerous articles to profl. jours. Mem. APA, Assn. Advancement of Behavior Therapy, Pa. Psychol. Assn., Soc. for the Exploration of Psychotherapy Integration. Office: Lebanon Valley Coll Psychology Dept Annville PA 17003

CULLEN, BRUCE F., anesthesiologist; b. Iowa City, May 6, 1940. MD, UCLA, 1966. Intern Blodgett Meml. Hosp., Grand Rapids, Mich., 1966-67; resident in anesthesiology U. Calif., San Francisco, 1967-70; chief anesthesiologist Harborview Med. Ctr., Seattle; prof. U. Wash. Office: U Wash HMC Anesthesiology 325 9th Ave Seattle WA 98104-2420*

CULLEN, CHARLES THOMAS, historian, librarian; b. Gainesville, Fla., Oct. 11, 1940; s. Spencer L. and Blanche J. Cullen; m. Shirley Harrington, June 13, 1964; children: Leslie Lanier, Charles Spencer Harrington. BA, U. of South, 1962; MA, Fla. State U., 1963; PhD, U. Va., 1971; HHD (hon.), Lewis U., 1987; DLitt (hon.), U. South, 1994; LLD (hon.), John Marshall Law Sch., 1995. Asst. prof. history Averett Coll., 1963-66; assoc. editor Papers of John Marshall Inst. Early Am. History and Culture, Williamsburg, Va., 1971-74, co-editor, 1974-77, editor, 1977-79; lectr. history Coll. William and Mary, 1971-79; sr. research historian, editor Papers of Thomas Jefferson Princeton (N.J.) U., 1979-86; pres., librarian Newberry Library, Chgo., 1986—; mem. N.J. Hist. Commn., 1985-86, Nat. Hist. Publs. and Records Com., 1990—. Nat. Hist. Publs. and Records Commn. fellow, 1970-71. Mem. Assn. Documentary Editing (pres.), Orgn. Am. Historians, Am. Hist. Assn., Am. Antiquarian Soc., Heartland Lit. Soc. (pres. 1994—), Modern Poetry Assn. (trustee 1987—, v.p. 1998—), Caxton Club, Grolier Club. Office: Newberry Libr 60 W Walton St Chicago IL 60610-3380

CULLEN, EDWARD PETER, bishop; b. Phila., Mar. 15, 1933. Student, St. Charles Borromeo Sem., Overbrook, Pa.; MSW, U. Pa., 1970; M in Edn., LaSalle U., 1971; MDiv, St. Charles Borromeo Sem., 1974. Ordained priest Roman Cath. Ch., 1962. Asst. pastor St. Maria Goretti Ch., Hatfield, St. Bartholomew Ch., Phila.; chaplain to Sisters of Mercy Merion Motherhouse; chaplain St. Edmond's Home for Children, See of Allentown; titular bishop Diocese of Paria, Proconsolare, 1994—; auxiliary bishop Diocese of Phila., 1994-99; bishop Diocese of Allentown, Pa., 1998—; with Cath. Social Svcs. Named Hon. Prelate to His Holiness Pope John Paul II, 1982. Office: Diocese of Allentown PO Box F Allentown PA 18105*

CULLEN, FRANK W., government relations consultant; b. Bklyn., June 29, 1926; s. Robert J. F. and Mae E. Cullen; m. Mary Anne Cullen, Sept. 8, 1951 (dec. May 1995); children: Peter J., Frank W. Jr. BS in Bus. Adminstrn., Coll. of the Holy Cross, 1952. Pres. Cullen Pub. Affairs Co., N.Y.C., 1952-59, L.A., 1959-61; campaign asst. Gov. Edmund G. "Pat" Brown, L.A., 1962-63; asst. legis. sec. Gov. Edmund G. "Pat" Brown, Sacramento, 1964-66; chief of staff Calif. Gov. Edmund G. "Pat" Brown, Beverly Hills, 1967-96; pres. FCA Co., Santa Monica, Calif., 1967—; founder, bd. advisors, former vice chmn. The Edmund G. "Pat" Brown Inst. Pub. Affairs, Calif. State U., L.A., 1979—; pres., co-founder Indonesian-U.S. Bus. Alliance, L.A., 1979-84. Author: The 80 Proof Cookbook, 1982; commentator (radio/TV) Talking Politics, 1995—. Neighborhood commr. Crescent Bay Area Coun., Boy Scouts Am., 1961-65; commr. State Calif. Econ. Devel. Commn., Sacramento, 1982-91; advisor Dem. Senate Campaign Com., Washington, 1982-92; western regional dir. Harry S. Truman Presdl. Libr., Independence, Mo., 1994-96. With USAF, 1943-46. Recipient Merit award Union U., L.A., 1979, Svc. award Palmer Drug Abuse Program, L.A., 1985, Eagle Outstanding Svc. award Calif. State U., L.A., 1991. Mem. Am. Philatilec Soc. Democrat. Roman Catholic. Avocations: stamp collecting, political items collecting, presidential collecting. E-mail: cullen@shoptheworkshop.com. Fax: 310-828-0427. Office: FCA Co Ste 702 2118 Wilshire Blvd Santa Monica CA 90403

CULLEN, JACK SYDNEY GEORGE BUD, federal judge; b. Creighton Mine, Ont., Can., Apr. 20, 1927; s. Chaffey Roi and Margaret Evelyn (Leck) C.; m. Nicole Chenier; 6 children. B.A., U. Toronto, 1950; LL.B., Osgoode Hall Law Sch., Toronto, 1956. Bar: Called to bar 1956. Barrister-at-law Sarnia, Ont., 1956-68; mem. Ho. of Commons Sarnia-Lambton, 1968-79, 80-84; minister of nat. revenue, 1975-76, of employment and immigration, 1976-79, mem. Privy Council, 1975—; judge Fed. Ct. of Can. trial div. Ottawa, 1984—. First pres. Sarnia Edn. Authority, 1962; mem. Sarnia Sch. Bd., 1959. Mem. Lambton Law Assn. (past pres.), Sarnia and Dist. Assn. Mentally Retarded. Kinsmen Club of Sarnia (life). Liberal. Mem. United Ch. Can. Club: Sarnia Kinsmen (life). Office: Fed Ct of Can, Supreme Ct Bldg, Ottawa, ON Canada K1A OH9

CULLEN, JAMES D., lawyer; b. St. Louis, May 18, 1925; s. James and Frances C. Cullen; m. Joyce Marie Jackson, Aug. 19, 1950; children: Mary Lynn Cullen Walsh, James D., Michael Parnell, Carol Cullen Bernstein. LLD, St. Louis, 1948. Bar: Mo. 1948. Assoc. Spalding & Cullen, St. Louis, 1950-99; pvt. practice law St. Louis. Bd. dirs. Marygrove, Gen. Protestant Children's Home; counsel Dismas House of St. Louis, Richard Greene Co. 1st lt. USAF, 1943-45. Mem. ABA, Mo. Bar Assn., St. Louis Bar Assn., Lawyers Assn. St. Louis, MAC Club. Roman Catholic. Home: 16 Berkshire Dr Saint Louis MO 63117-1030

CULLEN, JAMES DOUGLAS, banker, finance company executive; b. N.Y.C., Jan. 26, 1945; s. Eugene Richard and Anna Marie (Constantine) C.; m. Wendy Stephens, May 24, 1969; children: John W., Anne T. BSBA, U. Denver, 1968. Mgmt. trainee Wells Fargo Bank, San Francisco, 1968-69, credit officer, 1969-72, asst. v.p., 1972-77, v.p., 1977-82; v.p. Rainier Nat. Bank (now Seattle First Nat. Bank), Seattle, 1982, sr. v.p., 1982-85, sr. v.p., mgr. internat. divsn., mem. mgmt. com., 1985, exec. v.p., mgr. internat. divsn., 1986, exec. v.p., mgr. corp. banking divsn., 1987; exec. v.p. Comml. Markets Group Seattle 1st Nat. Bank, 1992-93; mng. dir. J.D. Cullen and Co., Inc., Seattle, 1993-94; sr. v.p. and mgr. internat. divsn U.S. Bancorp, Seattle, 1995-96, exec. v.p., 1996-98; sr. v.p., regional mgr. Nat. Bank Alaska, Seattle, 1999—; pres. Nat. Bank of Alaska Internat. Trustee Seattle Opera; dir. Trade Devel. Alliance. Clubs: Rainier, Seattle Yacht, Seattle Tennis, Tanglin, Cricket (Singapore); Royal Hong Kong Yacht, Ladies Recreation (Hong Kong). Avocations: running; skiing; travel. Home: 1320 Lexington Way E Seattle WA 98112-3712

CULLEN, JAMES G., telecommunications industry executive; b. 1942; Married. B.A., Rutgers U., 1964; Postgrad., M.I.T. With N. J. Bell Telephone Co. Bell Telephone Co., Newark, N.J., 1964; pres., chief. exec. officer N.J. Bell Telephone Co., Newark, N.J., 1989-95; vice chmn. Bell Atlantic Corp., Phila., 1995-96, 1996-98, pres., CEO Telecom, 1998—. Office: Bell Atlantic Corp 1310 N Court House Rd Ste 1 Arlington VA 22201-2586*

CULLEN, PAULA BRAMSEN, author; b. May 12, 1942. BS in English, Washington U., 1967. Self-employed author Princeton, N.J., 1968—; pres. Opportunity Found., Princeton, 1992—; co-owner Spraying Sys. Co., Wheaton, Ill., 1989—. Author: Journey of Storms, 1994; author of poetry; contbr. articles to publs.

CULLEN, RICHARD, lawyer, former state attorney general; b. N.Y.C., Mar. 10, 1948; m. Agnes Tullidge; children: Thomas, Anne Gray, Elizabeth, Richard. BS, Furman U., 1971; JD, U. Richmond, 1977. Bar: Va. Ptnr. McGuire, Woods, Battle and Boothe, Richmond, 1977-97, 98—; atty. gen. Commonwealth of Va., 1997-98; spl. counsel Senate Iran-Contra Investigation, 1987; U.S. atty. for ea. dist. Va., 1991-93. Editor-in-chief U. Richmond Law Rev., 1976-77. Mem. Juvenile Criminal Commn.; mem. Va. Criminal Sentencing Commn.; co-chmn. Gov.'s Commn. on Parole Abolition and Sentencing Reform. Office: McGuire, Woods, Battle & Boothe One James Ctr 901 E Cary St Richmond VA 23219-4057

CULLEN, ROBERT JOHN, publishing executive, financial consultant; b. York, Pa., Feb. 14, 1949; s. John Joseph and Florence Susanne (Staab) C.; m. Elizabeth Maule, Oct. 20, 1984; 1 child, Michael Joseph. BA, Winona (Minn.) State U., 1972. CFP; registered investment advisor. Editor-in-chief Overseas Life, Leimen, Fed. Republic of Germany, 1978-80; feature editor L.A. Daily Commerce, 1980-83; pres. HighTech Editorial, L.A., 1983—; fin. planner Cullen Fin. Svcs., Rancho Cucamonga, Calif., 1989—; computer editor Plaza Communications, Irvine, Calif., 1984-91. With U.S. Army, 1974-78, ETO. Mem. Inst. of Cert. Fin. Planners, Calif. Advs. Nursing Home Reform. Avocations: golf, chess, creative writing, public speaking.

CULLEN, THOMAS JOSEPH, history educator; b. Trenton, N.J., Jan. 26, 1934; s. James Augustus and Anna Merrick (Matlack) C.; m. Ruth Enck, Aug. 22, 1959; children: Randall Richard, Lauren Cullen Radick, Amy Alyse. BS, Coll. N.J., 1959; MA, Montclair U., 1967. Educator Bergenfield (N.J.) H.S., 1959-99; ret., 1999; staff rels., Bergenfield H.S., 1965—, chairperson scholarship com., 1960-95, class advisor, 1959-65. With U.S. Army, 1954-56. Avocations: travel, reading. Home: 12 Shadow Rd U Saddle Riv NJ 07458-1918

CULLEN, VALERIE ADELIA, secondary education educator; b. Northampton, Mass., May 28, 1948; d. Stanley Walter and Wanda Mary (Rup) Helstowski; m. Lawrence Joseph Cullen, June 26, 1982; 1 child, Shanna Valerie. BA, Westfield (Mass.) State Coll., 1970; MALS, SUNY, Stony Brook, 1975. Cert. secondary math. tchr., N.Y., Mass. Tchr. math. Brentwood (N.Y.) Pub. Schs., 1970-71, Center Moriches (N.Y.) Jr.-Sr. High Sch., 1971-88, BOCES I, Alternative High Sch. and Adolescent Pregnancy Program, Riverhead, N.Y., 1988-90, Ctr. Moriches (N.Y.) Jr.-Sr. High Sch., 1990—. Mem. Nat. Coun. Tchrs. Math., N.Y. State United Tchrs., N.Y. Math. Tchrs. Assn., Smithsonian Assocs. Home: 4 Keswick Dr East Islip NY 11730-2808 Office: Center Moriches Jr/Sr HS Frowein Rd Center Moriches NY 11934

CULLEN, WILLIAM ZACHARY, lawyer; b. Stamford, Conn., Feb. 15, 1955; s. John Cornelius and Ann D. (Woytowicz) C. BA, U. Conn., 1977; JD, New Eng. Sch. Law, 1980. Bar: Ala. 1989, U.S. Dist. Ct. (no. dist.) Ala. 1989, U.S. Ct. Appeals (11th cir.) 1989. Legal asst. Birmingham (Ala.) Legal Svcs., 1980-82; legal asst. Cooper, Mitch, Crawford, Kuykendall & Whatley, Birmingham, 1983-89, atty., 1989-98; atty. Sexton, Cullen & Jones P.C., Birmingham, 1998—. Office: Sexton Cullen and Jones PC 3021 Lorna Rd Ste 310 Birmingham AL 35216-4500

CULLEN-DUPONT, KATHRYN, writer; b. N.Y.C., June 29, 1956; d. Martin F. and Arlene Frances (Collins) Cullen; m. Joseph F. DuPont, Aug. 14, 1977; children: Melissa Cullen-DuPont, Jesse Cullen-DuPont. BA, NYU, 1987. Cons. on womens issues Grolier's New Book of Knowledge Encyclopedia, Hawleyville, Conn., 1992—; mem. adv. bd. Primary Source Media CD-ROM, Woodbridge, Conn., 1994; frequent guest lectr. in ednl. instns. Author: American Journey: Women in America, Elizabeth Cady Stanton and Women's Liberty, 1992 (N.Y. Pub. Libr. Best Book for the Teen Age award 1994), The Encyclopedia of Women's History in America, 1996 (History Book Club Selection 1996, N.Y. Pub. Libr.'s Outstanding Reference Book award 1997); co-author: Women's Suffrage in America, 1992, Women's Rights on Trial, 1997. Mem. Am. Soc. Journalists and Authors. Office: 352 9th St Brooklyn NY 11215-4008

CULLER, ARTHUR DWIGHT, English language educator; b. McPherson, Kans., July 25, 1917; s. Arthur Jerome and Susanna (Stover) C.; m. Helen Lucile Simpson, Sept. 14, 1941; children: Jonathan Dwight, Helen Elizabeth. B.A., Oberlin Coll., 1938; Ph.D., Yale U., 1941. Instr. English Cornell U., 1941-42; instr., then asst. prof. Yale U., 1946-55; prof. English, 1958-85, chmn. English dept., 1971-75; assoc. prof. English U. Ill., 1955-58. Author: The Imperial Intellect; A Study of Newman's Educational Ideal, 1955; Editor: (J.H. Newman) Apologia pro Vita Sua, 1956, (with G.P. Clark) Student and Society, 1959, Poetry and Criticism of Matthew Arnold, 1961, Imaginative Reason: The Poetry of Matthew Arnold, 1966, The Poetry of Tennyson, 1977, The Victorian Mirror of History, 1986. Fulbright fellow in Eng., 1950-51; Guggenheim fellow, 1961-62, 76; NEH fellow, 1979-80. Mem. Am. Acad. Arts and Scis., MLA, Phi Beta Kappa. Home: 80 Tokeneke Dr North Haven CT 06473-4347

CULLER, JONATHAN DWIGHT, English language educator; b. Cleve., Oct. 1, 1944; s. Arthur Dwight and Helen Lucille (Simpson) C.; m. Cynthia Chase, Dec. 27, 1976. BA, Harvard U., 1966; BPhil, St. John's Coll., Oxford, 1968, DPhil, 1972. Fellow Selwyn Coll. Cambridge U., Eng., 1969-74; fellow Brasenose Coll., lectr. French Oxford U., Eng., 1974-77; vis. prof. French and comparative lit. Yale U., 1975; prof. English and comparative lit. Cornell U., Ithaca, N.Y., 1977—, chair dept. comparative lit., 1993-96, chmn. dept. English, 1996-99; dir. Soc. for the Humanities, Cornell U., 1984-93. Author: Flaubert: The Uses of Uncertainty, 1974, Structuralist Poetics: Structuralism, Linguistics and the Study of Literature, 1975 (James Russell Lowell prize MLA 1975), Ferdinand de Saussure, 1976, The Pursuit of Signs: Semiotics, Literature, Deconstruction, 1981, On Deconstruction: Theory and Criticism after Structuralism, 1982, Roland Barthes, 1983, Framing the Sign: Criticism and Its Institutions, 1988, Literary Theory: A Very Short Introduction, 1997; translator: Jacques Derrida's Memoires for Paul de Man, 1986; editor: The Harvard Advocate, Centennial Anthology, 1966; adv. editor: New Literary History, 1972—, PTL, 1976-79; mem. adv. bd. Publs. Modern Lang. Assn., 1978-81; mem. editl. bd. Diacritics, 1974—, Poetics Today, 1979—, editor, 1994—. Rhodes scholar, 1966-69; Guggenheim fellow, 1979-80; NEH fellow, 1987-88. Mem. Semiotic Soc. of Am. (v.p. 1987, pres. 1988), MLA (exec. coun. 1985-88, 90-91), Am. Comparative Lit. Assn. (v.p. 1997-99, pres. 1999—). Office: Cornell U Dept English Lit Ithaca NY 14853

CULLER, ROBERT RANSOM, furniture designing and product development company executive; b. High Point, N.C., Nov. 16, 1950; s. Roy Braxton and Dorthey Faye (Pegram) C.; m. Heidi Miller Maas, Feb. 24,

1969; children: Robert Ransom, John Byron, Kathrine Marie. Profl. degree in furniture design and interior design Kendall Sch. Design, Grand Rapids, Mich., 1974. Head of design La-Z-Boy Chair Co., Monroe, Mich., 1974-76; pres. R.R. Culler Assoc., High Point, 1976—, RCR Devel. Corp., High Point, 1978—; dir. The Color Works, Greensboro, N.C. Mem. Am. Furnitire Designers Assn., Am. Soc. Interior Designers. Democrat. Baptist. Club: Triad World Trade. Avocation: scuba diving. Office: RCR Devel Corp 1009 Finch Ave High Point NC 27263-1625

CULLEY, JUNE ELIZABETH, clinical reviewer, quality improvement specialist; b. Valley Station, Ky., July 22, 1933; d. Wilbur W. and Elizabeth Piper (Dodge) C. Diploma, Ky. Bapt. Hosp., Louisville, 1954; BSN, Case Western Res. U., 1963; MPH, Johns Hopkins U., 1970, ScD, 1981. Dir. nursing State Tb Commn., Louisville; dir. nursing svcs. Louisville/Jefferson County Dept. Pub. Health; dir. nursing, long-term care svcs. City Health Dept., Balt.; quality mgmt. analyst VA Med. Ctr., Ft. Howard, Md.; coord. Pallatine Care ProgramFt. Howard divsn. Va./Md. Health Care Sys. Mem. AAUW, VA Nat. Nurses Rsch. Coun., VA Regional Nurses Rsch. Com., Sigma Theta Tau, Delta Omega (nat. award).

CULLEY, PETER WILLIAM, lawyer; b. Dover-Foxcroft, Maine, Oct. 17, 1943; s. William Redfern and Kathryn (Boyle) C.; children: Courtney Little, Jonathan Redfern. BA, U. Maine, 1965; JD, Boston U., 1968. Bar: Maine 1969, U.S. Dist. Ct. Maine 1969. Asst. atty. gen. Dept. of Atty. Gen. State of Maine, 1969-72, chief, criminal div., 1971-72; ptnr. Hewes, Culley and Beals, Portland, Maine, 1972-85, Pierce Atwood, Portland, 1985—. Chmn. Falmouth (Maine) Town Coun., 1986-87. Fellow Am. Coll. Trial Lawyers (state chmn. 1990-92); mem. ABA, Maine State Bar Assn., Internat. Assn. Def. Counsel, Def. Rsch. Inst. (state chmn. 1978-87), No. New England Def. Counsel (pres. 1985-86), Am. Bd. Trial Advocates. Home: 406 Chandlers Wharf Portland ME 04101-4653 Office: Pierce Atwood One Monument Sq Portland ME 04101

CULLEY-FOSTER, ANTHONY ROBERT, international business consultant; b. Londonderry, No. Ireland, July 31, 1947; came to U.S., 1971; s. Allen Foster and Eileen Louisa Culley; children: Joshua, Daniel, Valentina. Diploma, Reading U., 1969, Coll. Preceptors, U.K., 1971; BA magna cum laude, Roosevelt U., Chgo., 1973, MA, 1981. Cert. tchr., U.K. High sch. tchr. London, 1969-71; dir. Boys & Girls Clubs of Chgo., 1971-77; personal asst. to chmn. Combined Internat. Corp., Chgo., 1977-81; founding dir., chief exec. officer The Congl. Award, Washington, 1981-85; pres. Culley-Foster & Co. Internat., Washington, 1985—; cons. W. Clement Stone Enterprises, Chgo., 1978-86, Brit. and Am. Multinat. Corps., 1985—. Nat. organizer Run Across Am. program Am. Bicentennial Com., 1976, Run for Ireland program Olympic Coun., Ireland, 1980; co-founder Congl. Award U.S., 1979, Pres.'s Award for Youth, Ireland, 1983; founding chmn. No. Ireland Partnership U.S., 1990, No. Ireland-U.S. C. of C. Inc., 1993; mem. Nat. Boys Club U.K., 1966—; trustee Internat. Fedn. Keystone Youth orgns., World Meml. Fund for Disaster Relief, Boys and Girls Clubs Washington, Boys and Girls Clubs No. Ireland, Boys and Girls Clubs-Chgo. Alumni Assn. Recipient Duke of Edinburgh's Gold Award, 1966, Pub. Service commendations Office of Pres. of U.S., 1976, 79, 83, 91, 96, Congl. award U.S. Congress, 1981, Nat. Achievement award Pres.'s Council on Phys. Fitness and Sports, 1976, Nat. Achievement award Olympic Council Ireland, 1980. Mem. Brit.-Am. C. of C., C. of C. of the U.S., French-Am. C. of C., Brit.-Am. Bus. Assn. Washington D.C., Irish Rowing Union (hon. life), Royal Automobile Club (U.K.). Office: Culley-Foster & Co Internat PO Box 17370 Washington DC 20041-0370

CULLIGAN, JOHN WILLIAM, retired corporate executive; b. Newark, Nov. 22, 1916; s. John J. and Elizabeth (Kearns) C.; children: Nancy, Mary Carol, Elizabeth, Sheila (dec.), Jack, Neil. With Am. Home Products Corp., N.Y.C., 1937—, also bd. dirs. emeritus, chmn. bd. dirs., CEO, 1981-86, chmn. exec. com., 1988-90; chmn. bd. dirs. Scios Inc., 1987-93. Bd. dirs. pres. Valley Hosp. Found., Ridgewood, N.J.; mem. adv. bd. St. Benedict's Prep. Sch., Newark; chmn. Archbishop's Com. of Laity, Newark. Wtih AUS, 1942-46. Mem. Non-Prescription Drug Mfrs. Assn. (hon. v.p.), N.Y. Athletic Club, Sky Club, Union League Club (N.Y.C.), Hackensack Golf Club (pres.), Knights of Malta, Knights of St. Gregory, Knights of Holy Sepulchre, Friendly Sons of St. Patrick. Office: Am Home Products Corp 685 3rd Ave New York NY 10017-4024

CULLINA, WILLIAM MICHAEL, lawyer; b. Hartford, Conn., July 22, 1921; s. Michael Stephen and Margaret (Carroll) C.; m. Gertrude Evelyn Blasig, Apr. 29, 1961; children: William Gregory, Kevin Michael, John Stephen, Susan Margaret. AB, Catholic U. Am., 1942; LLB, Yale U., 1948. Bar: Conn. bar 1948. Assoc. Murtha, Cullina, Richter & Pinney, Hartford, 1948—, ptnr., 1952-91, of counsel, 1992—. Bd. dirs. St. Francis Hosp. and Med. Ctr.; trustee St. Joseph Coll., 1986-98, trustee emeritus, 1998—; bd. govs. The Hartford Club, 1984-89, chair, 1987-88. Served with USNR, 1942-46. Fellow Am. Bar Found.; mem. ABA, Conn. Bar Assn., Hartford County Bar Assn., Hartford Tennis Club, Country Club of Farmington, Knight of St. Gregory, Phi Beta Kappa. Roman Catholic. Office: Murtha Cullina Richter & Pinney City Pl 185 Asylum St Ste 29 Hartford CT 06103-3469

CULLINAN, BERNICE E(LLINGER), education educator; b. Hamilton, Ohio, Oct. 12, 1926; d. Lee Alexander and Hazel (Berry) Dees; m. George W. Ellinger, June 5, 1948 (div. 1966); children: Susan Jane, James Webb; m. Paul Anthony Cullinan, June 9, 1967 (div. 1994). BS, Ohio State U., 1948, MA, 1951, PhD, 1964. Cert. elem. educator, Ohio, N.Y. Tchr. Maple Pk. Elem. Sch., Middletown, Ohio, 1944-46, Trotwood (Ohio) Elem. Sch., 1946-47, Columbus (Ohio) Pub. Schs., 1948-50, Upper Arlington (Ohio) Pub. Schs., 1950-52; instr. Ohio State U., Columbus, 1959-64, asst. prof., 1964-67, Charlotte Huck prof. children's lit., 1997; assoc. prof. NYU, N.Y.C., 1967-72, prof., 1972-97, prof. emeritus, 1998—; editor-in-chief Wordsong Books, Honesdale, Pa., 1990—; adv. bd. The Reading Rainbow, 1979—, WGBH-TV, 1989—; chair selection com. Ezra Jack Keats New Writer award, 1984—; exec. sec. English Standards Project, 1993-94. Author: (with Lee Galda) Literature and the Child, 1989, 4th edit., 1998, Children's Literature in the Classrom: Weaving Charlotte's Web, 1989, 2d edit., 1994, Read to Me: Raising Kids Who Love to Read, 1992, 2nd edit., 1999, Let's Read About: Finding Books They'll Love to Read, 1993, (with Brod Bagert) Helping Your Child Learn to Read, 1993, (with L. Galda and D. Strickland) Language, Literacy and the Child, 1993, 2d edit., 1997, (with Marilyn Scala and Virginia Schroder) Three Voices: Invitation to Poetry Across the Curriculum, 1995, 75 Authors and Illustrators Everyone Should Know, 1994, Future Poets Guide, 1999, (with D. Harrison) Poetry Lessons that Dazzle and Delight, 1999, Poetry for All Ages, 1999, (with David Harrison) Poetry Lessons That Dazzle and Delight, 1999, Future Poets Guide, 1999, Poetry for All Ages, 1999; editor: Children's Literature in the Reading Program, 1987, Invitation to Read: More Children's Literature in the Reading Program, 1992, Black Dialects and Reading, 1974, Fact and Fiction: Literature Across the Curriculum, 1993, Children's Voices, 1993, Pen in Hand, 1993, A Jar of Tiny Stars, 1996; author, editor: (with M. Jerry Weiss) Books I Read When I Was Young, 1980, (with Carolyn Carmichael) Literature and Young Children, 1977, Children's Literature in the Classroom: Extending Charlotte's Web, 1993; mem. editl. bd. The New Advocate, 1987—, The New Advocate, 1987-99; adv. bd. Ranger Rick Mag., 1992—; contbr. articles to profl. jours. Editorial bd. Nat. Coun. Tchrs. English, Champaign, 1973-76; selection com. Caldecott Award Am. Libr. Assn., Chgo., 1982-83; trustee Highlights for Children Found., 1993—. Recipient Arbuthnot award for Outstanding Tchr. Children's Lit., Internat. Reading Assn., 1989, Ind. U. Citation Outstanding Contbn. to Literacy, 1995; named Charlotte Huck prof. of children's lit., 1997; inducted into the Ohio State U. Coll. of Edn. Hall of Fame, 1995, Reading Hall of Fame, 1989 (pres. 1998-99). Mem. Internat. Reading Assn. (chair Tchrs. Choices 1988-91, pres. 1984-85, bd. dirs. 1979-84), Internat. Reading Found. (trustee 1984-91, Jeremiah Ludington award 1992). Avocations: tennis, reading for pleasure, poetry. E-mail: BerniceCullinan@Worldnet.att.net. Home and Office: Tudor Ln Sands Point NY 11050-6250

CULLINEY, JOHN JAMES, radiologist, educator; b. N.Y.C., Oct. 17, 1955; s. Michael and Marion (Dakowski) C.; m. Margaret Mary Steinhardt, Oct. 11, 1986. BS, Rutgers U., 1977, MS, 1981; MD, U Medicine and Dentistry N.J., 1984. Diplomate Am. Bd. Radiology, Nat. Bd. Med. Examiners. Intern physician Med. Coll. of Pa. Hosp., Phila., 1984-85; resident physician U. Medicine & Dentistry N.J., Newark, 1985-89; fellow body imaging, instr. diagnostic radiology Hahnemann U. Hosp., Phila., 1989-90, asst. prof. clin. diagnostic radiology, 1990-92; asst. prof. clin. diagnostic radiology, chief uroradiology U. Med. and Dentistry N.J., Newark, Pa., 1990-92; clin. instr. diagnostic radiology, chief cross-sect. imaging Mercy & Moses Taylor Hosps. affiliates Temple Med. Sch., Scranton, Pa., 1992—; pres. Radiol. Cons. Inc., 1999—; chief uroradiology U. Med. and Dentistry N.J., Newark, 1990-92; pres. Radiol. Cons., Inc., Dunmore, Pa., 1994—; co-dir. Phoenix Vascular Lab.; dir. radiology Mercy Hosp. Scranton, Clin. Vascular Lab. Mem. AMA, AAUP, Am. Coll. Radiology, Am. Soc. Breast Imagers, Roentgen Soc. N.Am., KC. Roman Catholic. Avocations: amateur radio technician class, skiing. Home: 318 Stevenson Rd Clarks Summit PA 18411-9261 Office: Radiol Cons Inc 751 Keystone Industrial Park Dunmore PA 18512-1530

CULLINGFORD, HATICE SADAN, chemical engineer; b. Konya, Turkey, June 10, 1945; d. Ahmet and Emine Harmanci. Student, Mid. East Tech. U., 1962-66; BS in Chem. Engring. with high honors, N.C. State U., 1969, Engring. Honors Cert., 1969, PhD, 1974. Registered profl. engr., Tex.; cert. mgr. Statis. clk. Rsch. Triangle Inst., 1966; reactor engr. AEC, Washington, 1973-75; spl. asst. ERDA, Washington, 1975; mech. engr. U.S. Dept. Energy, Washington, 1975-78; staff mem. Los Alamos (N.Mex.) Nat. Lab., 1978-82; sci. cons. Houston, 1982-84; environ. control and life support systems test bed mgr. Johnson Space Ctr., NASA, Houston, 1984-85, sr. project engr. advanced tech. dept., 1985-86, sr. staff engr. divsn. solar system exploration, 1986-88, asst. divsn. advanced devel., 1988-90; sr. system engr. Exploration Programs Office NASA, Houston, 1990-92; engring. and mgmt. cons. Houston, 1992—; founder Peace U., 1993; mem. internal adv. com. Ctr. for Nonlinear Studies Los Alamos Nat. Lab., 1981; organizer tech. workshops, sessions at soc. meetings; lectr. in field; docent Mus. Fine Arts, Houston. Editor, author tech. reports; contbr. articles to profl. jours.; patentee in field. Mem. curriculum rev. com. U. N.Mex., Los Alamos, 1980. Recipient Woman's badge Tau Beta Pi, 1968, ERDA Spl. Achievement award, 1976, Inventor award Los Alamos Nat. Lab., 1982, Group Achievement award NASA Johnson Space Ctr., 1987, Outstanding Performance award NASA Johnson Space Ctr., 1987, 89, Superior Performance award NASA Johnson Space Ctr., 1987, 89, Cert. of Recognition for Inventions, NASA, 1988, 89, 90, 92, 93. Mem. AIAA (organizer, 1st chmn. human support com. Houston chpt. 1988-93), AIChE (organizer, 1st chmn. No. N.Mex. club 1980-81, organizer and chmn. low-pressure processes and tech. 1981-89), Am. Nuclear Soc. (sec.-treas. fusion energy divsn. 1982-84, vice chmn. South Tex. sect. 1984-86, mem. local sects. com. 1986-88), Am. Chem. Soc., Soc. for Risk Analysis (organizer, sec. Lone Star chpt. 1986-88, chmn. soc. publicity 1990-93), No. N.Mex. Chem. Engrs. Club, Engrs. Coun. Houston (councilor, sec. energy com.), Sierra Club, Houston Orienteering Club, Phi Kappa Phi, Pi Mu Epsilon.

CULLINGWORTH, LARRY ROSS, residential and real estate development company executive; b. Toronto, Ont., Can., Sept. 26, 1939; s. Allan Joyce and Ethel Alexandra (Davis) C.; m. Betty Kathleen Hughes, July 9, 1966; children: Lisa, Kevin. B.A.Sc., U. Toronto, 1963, P. Eng., 1965; M.B.A., York U., Toronto, 1972. Cons. engr. Proctor & Redfern, Toronto, 1963-68; regional mgr. George Wimpey Can. Ltd., Toronto, 1968-72; mgr. corp. devel. Brookfield Homes Ltd. (formerly Coscan Devel. Corp.), Toronto, 1973-74, v.p. fin., sec., 1975-78, sr. v.p., chief fin. officer, sec., 1979, exec. v.p., CFO, sec., 1980-83, pres., COO, 1983-85, pres., CEO, 1986-94, chmn., 1994-97; vice chmn. Brookfield Properties Corp., Toronto, 1997-98; bd. dirs. Brookfield Homes Ltd. Bd. dirs. Brookfield Properties Corp., Brookfield Homes Ltd., Toronto Hydro. Mem. Assn. Profl. Engrs. Ont., Bayview Club, Granite Club (Toronto). Home: 23 York Valley Crescent, Willowdale, ON Canada M2P 1A8 Office: Brookfield Homes Ltd, 181 Bay St Ste 4300, Toronto, ON Canada M5J 2T3

CULLIS, CHRISTOPHER ASHLEY, dean, biology educator; b. Harrow, Eng., Nov. 20, 1945; s. Jack Douglas Bungard and Isette Sarah (Cullis) Giles; m. Margaret Angela Webb, Sept. 4, 1971; children: Benjamin, Oliver, Thomas, Bethia, Tristan, Camilla. BS, London U., 1966; MS in Biophysics, U. East Anglia, Norwich, Eng., 1968, PhD, 1971. Higher sci. officer John Innes Inst., Norwich, 1971-73, sr. sci. officer, 1973-81, prin. sci. officer, 1981-85; prof. biology Case Western Res. U., Cleve., 1986—, dean, math. and natural scis., 1989-93; Francis Hobart Herrick prof. biology U. Cleve., 1994—; vis. prof. Case Western Res. U., 1985-86, Stanford U., Palo Alto, Calif., 1982-83; adj. prof. plant biotech. ctr. Bond U., Queensland, Australia, 1990-93; founder, gen. ptnr. Novomark Technols. LLC.; mem. rsch. com. Holden Arboretum, 1992—. Editor: The Nucleolus, 1981, John Innes Symposium, 1983; author chpts. in books. Cubmaster Boy Scouts Am., Winding River, 1988, 89, com. chair, 1990-94. Nuffield and Leverhulme fellow Civil Svc. Commn., 1982-83; Assn. Commonwealth Univs. scholar, 1967-70. Mem. AAAS, Genetical Soc. Am., Bot. Soc. Am., Soc. for Plant Molecular Biology, Soc. for Exptl. Biology (coun. 1979-81, chair com. for cell biology 1980-81). Avocations: sports, reading. Office: Case Western Res U 2040 Adelbert Rd Cleveland OH 44106-2623

CULLISON, ALEXANDER C. (DOC CULLISON), mediator, arbitrator; b. Balt., May 24, 1951; m. Diana Cullison; children: Alexander Paul, Holly. BS, USNY, 1987; BA in Labor Studies, Antioch U., 1983; MA in Labor and Policy Studies, SUNY, Empire, 1988; PhD in Labor Rels. and Conflict Resolution, Union Inst., 1997. Cert. mediator, Fla., Va. Union rep. dist. 1 Marine Engrs. Benficial Assn., 1978-93, nat. pres., 1992-93; founder, pres. Soc. for AIDS Prevention, Humanitarianism, and Edn., Fairfax, Va., 1993—; panel mem. Am. Arbitration Assn., 1991. Mem. SAR; bd. advisers Dem. Leadership Coun.; mgn. trustee Dem. Nat. Com., del., 1992; del. Fla. Dem. Conv., 1991, Tex. Dem. Conv., 1988. With USAFR, 1969. Named Outstanding Labor Leader of Yr. Plantation (Fla.) Dem. Club, 1991, Outstanding Labor Leader of Yr. Dania (Fla.) Dem. Club, 1992. Mem. Am. Income Life Labor Adv. Bd., Soc. Naval Architects and Marine Engrs., Acad. Family Mediators. Home: 9341 Tovito Dr Fairfax VA 22031-3824

CULLMAN, HUGH, retired tobacco company executive; b. N.Y.C., Jan. 27, 1923; s. Howard S. and Elsie (Gottheil) C.; m. Nan Alva Ogburn, May 12, 1951; children: Katherine Victoria, Hugh Jr., Alexandra Miriam. B.S., U.S. Naval Acad., 1945. With Benson & Hedges, 1949-54, mgr. research, 1952-54; with Philip Morris Inc., 1954—, treas., 1959-60, v.p., asst. chief ops., 1960-64, exec. v.p. ops., 1966—, also bd. dirs.; exec. v.p. Philip Morris Internat., 1965, pres., 1967-78, also bd. dirs.; group exec. v.p. Philip Morris Inc., 1978-84; chief exec. officer Philip Morris U.S.A., 1978-84; vice chmn. Philip Morris Cos. Inc., 1985-88. Sr. trustee U.S. Coun. for Internat. Bus.; gov. Beaufort Hist. Assn., Inc.; mem. Tryon Palace Commn.; bd. dirs. Carolina Cmty. Found.; trustee The Kellenberger His. Found. Lt. USN, 1945-47, PTO, 1951-52, Europe. Address: 821 Front St Beaufort NC 28516-2230

CULLMAN, JOAN, theatrical producer. adv. bd. dirs. Musical Theatreworks; bd. dirs. Bay Street Theatre; vice chmn. Lincoln Ctr. Theatre, Inc. Co-prodr. plays Carmelina, One Night Stand, Oh, Brother!, The Rink, Mademoiselle Colombe, Eating Raoul, Orphans, Anything Goes, Cole, Art (Tony award best play 1998). Office: c/o Royale Theatre 242 W 45th St New York NY 10036-3901*

CULLOM, WILLIAM OTIS, trade association executive; b. Huntsville, Ala., Mar. 20, 1932; s. Otis McKinley and Elna (Reese) C.; m. Caryl James, May 26, 1956; children: Cheryl Ann Cullom Stewart, Jennifer James Cullom Barksdale. BS, Fla. State U., 1958. Finger-print expert FBI, 1950-52; asst. bus. mgr. Fla. State U., 1954-64; with Ryder Truck Rental Inc., Miami, Fla., 1964-79; exec. v.p. mktg., to Ryder Truck Rental Inc., 1979; pres., chief operating officer Jartran, Inc., Coral Gables, Fla., 1979-81; pres. Greater Miami C. of C., 1981—; v.p. Orange Bowl Com., 1992—. Sec., bd. dirs. Miami-Dade Coll. Found.; mem. cabinet exec. com. Beacon Coun. United Way, Miami, 1974-80; trustee Bethune Cookman Coll., Daytona Beach, Fla., Barry U., St. Thomas U., Miami-Dade C.C. Found.; past chmn. bd. trustees Fla. State U; chmn. adminstrv. bd. Kendall Meth. Ch.; mem. pres.'s adv. com. Fla. Meml. Coll., Miami; bd. dirs. Bapt. Hosp. Found., Coconut Grove Playhouse, Goodwill Industries, Salvation Army; v.p. Orange Bowl Com.; chmn. bd. trustees Fla. State U. Found., 1994-95; chmn. Greater Miami Chamber Coalition. With U.S. Army, 1952-54. Recipient Miami Black Bus. Cmtys. Econ. Unity award, 1984, Anti Defamation League Human Rels. award, 1992, Disting. Cmty. Svc. award, 1998, Cedars Found. Concern award, 1994, NCCJ Humanitarian award, 1995, Silver Medallion award Greater Miami NCCJ, Citizen of Yr. award Greater Miami Rotary Club; named South Fla. Scout of Yr., Scouts Internat. in South Fla., 1997. Mem. Am. Trucking Assn., Truck Leasing and Renting Assn. (pres. Fla. chpt. 1972-73), Fla. State U. Nat. Alumni Assn. (pres.), Miami Hist. Assn., Brickell Club, Univ. Club, Riviera Country Club, City Club, Bankers Club, Ocean Reef Yacht Club, Gov.'s Club (Tallahassee), Dearing Bay Yacht Club, Biscayne Bay Yacht Club, Mountain Air Country Club (Burnsville, N.C.), Rotary. Democrat. Methodist. Home: 8445 SW 151st St Miami FL 33158-1961 Office: Greater Miami C of C 1601 Biscayne Blvd Miami FL 33132-1224

CULLUM, COLIN MUNRO, psychiatry and neurology educator; b. Freeport, Tex., Mar. 28, 1959. BA, Pacific Luth. U., 1981; PhD, U. Tex., 1986. Diplomate in clin. neuropsychology Am. Bd. Profl. Psychology/Am. Bd. Clin. Neuropsychology. Postdoctoral fellow U. Calif., San Diego, 1986-88, asst. rsch. neuropsychologist, 1988-89; asst. prof. psychiatry and neurology U. Colo. Sch. of Medicine, Denver, 1989-94; assoc. prof. psychiatry and neurology, dir. neuropsychology U. Tex. Southwestern Med. Ctr., Dallas, 1994—. Assoc. editor Neuropsychology Review 1996-98; mem. editl. bd. Archives Clin. Neuropsychology, Jour. Internat. Neuropsychol. Soc. Fellow APA, Nat. Acad. Neuropsychology (exec. dir. 1992-98, pres. 1999); mem. Am. Psychol. Soc., Assn. Med. Sch. Profs. of Psychology, Internat. Neuropsychol. Soc., Nat. Acad. Neuropsychology. Achievements include research in neuropsychology of memory disorders, neuropsychological functions in aging and dementia, neuropsychological and neuroimaging correlates in neurological and psychiatric disorders. Office: U Tex Southwestern Med Ctr Neuropsychology Program 5323 Harry Hines Blvd Dallas TX 75235-8898

CULLY, SUZANNE MARÍA, modern language educator; b. Albuquerque, N. Mex., Mar. 15, 1957; d. Jack Francis and Martha (Crittenden) C.; m. Rex Smith, Jr., May 10, 1986 (div. Jan. 1991); 1 child, Maria Makenna Smith. BA, U. N. Mex., 1980, MA in French Lit., 1993; Cert. des Études Politiques, U. Aix, Marseilles, France, 1981. Tchr. French U. N. Mex., Albuquerque, 1991-93; tchr. Spanish Albuquerque Pub. Schs., 1994, tchr. Spanish, French, 1994-95, tchr. French Lit., 1995-96, prin. mid. sch., 1999; grant writing cons. N. Mex. Agy. on Aging, Santa Fe, 1992-93, Albuquerque Pub. Schs., 1995-96. Mem. Jr. League of Albuquerque, 1987—; bd. dirs. Nat. Coun. on Alcoholism, 1996—. U. N.Mex. grad. fellow, 1991-93; Ctr. for Tchg. Excellence grantee, 1996; Danforth fellow, 1997-98. Mem. bd. dirs. Alburquerque Mus. Associates, 1998-99. Democrat. Roman Catholic. Avocations: skiing, soccer, golf, fiction writing. Office: 1101 Pennsylvania St NE Albuquerque NM 87110-7407

CULNON, SHARON DARLENE, reading specialist, special education educator; b. Balt., Apr. 20, 1947; d. Clayton Claude and Ann (McIntyre) Legg; m. Allen William Culnon, July 9, 1975. BA in Elem. Edn., U. Mich., 1972; MAT in Reading Edn., Oakland U., 1980; Learning Disabilities Cert., Ariz. State U., 1983. Cert. K-8 edn., K-12 reading specialist, K-12 learning disabilities specialist. Tchr. Mt. Morris (Mich.) Consolidated Schs., 1972-77; reading specialist Paradise Valley Schs., Phoenix, 1978-87, learning disabilities specialist, 1987-90, tchr., 1990—. Mem. Kachina Jr. Women's Club, Phoenix, 1980-83, sec., 1981-82. Recipient Learning Leader/dist. award Paradise Valley Bd. of Edn., Phoenix, 1986. Mem. Phi Delta Kappa (historian 1987-88). Presbyterian. Avocations: travel, wildlife viewing and study, reading, pets, photography. Home: 9035 N Concho Ln Phoenix AZ 85028-5318

CULP, BARBARA JUNE, secondary school educator; b. Hallettsville, Tex., Nov. 1, 1944; d. Arthur William and Marion A. (Vick) Clark; m. Charles Linden Culp, Aug. 27, 1966; children: John David, Brian Clark. BS in Biology, Psychology and Math., Stephen F. Austin State U., Nacogdoches, Tex., 1966, MS in Biology, 1969, cert. mid-mgmt., 1985. Tchr. Horace Mann Jr. High, Baytown, Tex., 1966-80; tchr. gifted Cedar Bayou Jr. High, Baytown, 1980-82; tchr., dept. chmn. Gentry Jr. High, Baytown, 1982-85; tchr. Ross S. Sterling High Sch., Baytown, 1985-97; Lee Coll., Baytown, 1992—; mem. Goose Creek Consol. Ind. Sch. Dist. Recovery Com. for Dropouts; mem. gifted and talented adv. coun. GATE program for Goose Creek Consol. Ind. Sch. Dist., 1980-82, math./sci. fair coord., 1983-84, ednl. adv. coun., 1987-89, TAAS math. coord., 1994—; state textbook advisor Tex. State Textbook Com., Baytown, 1984, 89; number sense and math. coach U. Interscholastic League R.S. Sterling H.S., 1984—, sponsor student coun., 1992—; math. coord. pre-kindergarten to 12th grade Goose Creek C.I.S.D., Baytown, 1997—. Pres., treas. Tri-Cities DeMolay Mothers Club, Baytown, 1983-88; youth educator Grace United Meth. Ch., Baytown, 1978-79; mem. Caring Adults Reaching Everyone team R.S. Sterling High Sch., 1989. Nominee for Presdl. Award of Excellence for Math. Teaching, 1990. Mem. NEA, Nat. Coun. Tchrs. Math. (conf. presenter 1991, 92), Nat. Coun. Suprs. Math, Tex. State Tchrs. Assn., Tex. Classroom Tchrs. Assn. (com. chmn., conv. del. 1980-84), Tex. State Tchrs. Math., Tex. Assn. Suprs. Math, Baytown Edn. Assn. (treas., com. chair 1980-84), Baytown Classroom Tchrs. Assn. (chmn., Tchr. of Yr. 1985), Delta Kappa Gamma (pres. 1990-92). Methodist. Avocations: puzzles and games, collecting antiques, kaleidoscopes and seashells, fishing, cooking. Home: 4905 Saint Andrews Dr Baytown TX 77521-3017 Office: 300 W Baker Rd Baytown TX 77521-2301

CULP, CHARLES ALLEN, financial executive; b. Birmingham, Ala., Oct. 23, 1930; s. William Newton and Winifred Evelyn (Orr) C.; m. Elsie Gayle Trechsel Hall, Oct. 7, 1960; children: Charles Allen, Stephen Andrew; stepchildren: John C., Edward P., David G. B.S., U. Ala., 1952; M.B.A., Samford U., Birmingham, 1969. CLU. With So. Life & Health Ins. Co., 1950-52, 54-72, v.p., dir., 1965-72; sr. v.p., dir. Investors Fidelity Ins. Co., Birmingham, 1972-74; dir. agys. Gulf Life Ins. Co., Jacksonville, Fla., 1975-76, pres., 1980-85, also bd. dirs.; exec. v.p., then pres. Interstate Life Ins. Co., Chattanooga, 1976-80, also bd. dirs., 1976-80; pres. Interstate Fire Ins. Co., 1976-85, dir., 1976-85; chmn. Culp Investment Group, 1985—; bd. dirs. REDC Co., Invesco Co., Gulf United Corp., Equitable Life Ins. Co. Va., Utility Tool Co., Fin. Computer Svcs., Life Care Inc., French Country Stores de Provence; mem. exec. com. Life Insurers Conf. Area chmn. March of Dimes, Birmingham, 1961; chmn. Southside YMCA, 1959-60; bd. dirs. Valley Theatre, 1960, Met. YMCA, 1965-72, United Fund Greater Chattanooga, 1979-80. Served to 1st lt. USAF, 1952-54. Fellow Life Office Mgmt. Assn., Life Mgmt. Inst.; mem. Am. Soc. CLUs, Sawgrass Club, Mountain Brook Club, Ponte Vedra Club, Cedar Creek Racquet Club, Phi Eta Sigma, Sigma Alpha Epsilon. Republican. Episcopalian. Home (winter): 4326 Kennesaw Dr Birmingham AL 35213-3312 Office: Culp Investment Group 4326 Kennesaw Dr Birmingham AL 35213-3312

CULP, FAYE BERRY, former state legislator; b. Kilmichael, Miss., Dec. 6, 1939; d. Otis Milton and Drapa (Clark) Berry; m. James H. Culp, Dec. 28, 1966; children: James Jr., David. BS in Bus. Edn., Miss. U. for Women, 1961; postgrad., Ga. State U., 1965-66; M, U. South Fla., Tampa, 1993. Tchr. Atlanta Pub. Schs., 1961-66; ednl. svcs. rep. IBM, San Francisco, 1966, Poughkeepsie, N.Y., 1967-68; real estate salesperson Yates Realty, Tampa, 1975-79; mem. sch. bd. Hillsborough County, Tampa, 1988-92; mem. Fla. Ho. of Reps., Tallahassee and Tampa, 1994-98, majority whip, 1994-98; chair Joint Ho. and Senate Com. for Legis. Info. Tech. Resources/Procedural Coun., mem. edn., appropriations, tourism coms.; mem. State Task Force for Tech. Fla. Sch. Bds. Assn.; chmn. legis. subcom. on spl. legislation, chmn. bylaws com. Fla. Sch. Bds. Assn.; mem. State Instrnl. Coun. Textbook Selection. Asst. dir. Theatre Atlanta prodns.; dir., prodr. musicals First United Meth. Ch., Tampa. Mem. Govs. Task Force for Prevention Teen-Age Suicides; del. Fla. Fedn. Rep. Women's Conv.; 1st pres. Child Abuse Coun. Aux.; pres. Hillsborough Women's Rep. Club, Tampa Realistic Artists, Inc., United Meth. Women, 1st United Meth. Ch., Tampa, Plant High Sch. Parent Student Tchrs. Assn.; v.p. various PTAs; area v.p. Hillsborough County Coun.; juvenile protection chmn. Hillsborough PTA County Coun.; youth coord., bd. trustees First United Meth. Ch.; bd. mem. Nat. Coun. Christians and Jews, Coun. Downtown Chs.; treas. West State Archaeol. Soc.; chmn. internat. affairs Tampa Civic Assn.; leader, den mother Cub Scouts; chmn. Just Friends Mentoring Program; bd. mem., officer Friends of Pub. Edn.; chmn. Masterpiece Morning. Named Woman of Distinction Girl Scouts Am., Tampa, Pacesetter in Ky. So. Women in Pub. Svc., 1997, Disting. Alumni of Yr. U. South Fla. Coll. Fine Arts, Tampa, 1997, Legislator of Yr. Internat. Coun. Shopping Ctrs., Orlando, Fla., 1997, One of Top

40 Legislators, Fla. C. of C., 1997, Legislator of Yr. Fla. Sch. Bds. Assn., 1997; recipient over 150 awards in photography, 40 awards in painting, 3 awards in poetry, others. Mem. LWV, Nat. Order Women Legislators (stakeholder, regional dir. nat. conf.), PEO (chpt. historian), Miss. U. for Women Alumni Assn. (pres. Suncoast chpt.), Hillsborough County Pres. Roundtable, Greater Tampa C. of C. (mem. edn. coun.), South Tampa C. of C., Greater Town n' Country C. of C., Lamplighters, Red Cross Angels, Friends of the Arts, Fla. Orch. Guild, Port Tampa Civic Assn., Alpha. Republican. Methodist. Avocations: photography, painting, travel. E-mail: culp@gte.net.

CULP, GORDON CALVIN, retired lawyer; b. Auburn, Wash., Feb. 17, 1926; s. Norman and Cara Virl (Carter) C.; widowed, 1996. BS, U. Wash., 1950, JD, 1952. Assoc. Ferguson & Burdell, Seattle, 1952-55; pvt. practice Seattle, 1955-57; counsel subcom. on territories and insular affairs U.S. Senate, Washington, 1957-58; ptnr. Culp, Dwyer & Guterson, Seattle, 1959-60; asst. to chmn. Dem. Nat. Com., Washington, 1960-61; ptnr., of counsel Culp, Dwyer, Guterson & Grader, Seattle, 1961-91; ret., 1991; scheduling officer Henry M. Jackson for Pres. Campaign, Washington, 1972. Bd. regents U. Wash., Seattle, 1977-89, U. Wash. Med. Ctr., Seattle, 1989-98, Cancer Care Alliance, Seattle, 1998—. With USN, 1944-46. Mem. ABA, Seattle-King County Bar Assn. Democrat. Avocations: fly fishing, travel.

CULP, GORDON LOUIS, consulting engineer; b. Topeka, Dec. 30, 1939; s. Russell Louis and Dorothy Marion (Wilson) C.; m. Bette Marline DeWalt, June 6, 1961 (div.); m. Mary Kay Moelker, Sept. 11, 1979 (div.); children: David, Steven, Ivan; m. Rosemary Anne Smith, Apr. 7, 1991. BS in Civil Engring., U. Kans., 1961, MS in Environ. Health Engring., 1962, MA in Applied Psychology, U. Santa Monica, 1991. Registered profl. engr., 21 states. San. engr. USPHS, Cin., 1962-64, CH2M/Hill Engrs., Corvallis, Oreg., 1964-66; rsch. engr. Neptune Microfloc, Corvallis, 1966-70; rsch. mgr. Battelle N.W., Richland, Wash., 1970-71; regional mgr. CH2M/Hill Engrs., Reston, Va., 1971-73; pres. Culp, Wesner Culp (acquired by HDR Engring. 1986), Cameron Park, Calif., 1973-93, Smith Culp. Consulting, 1993—. Author: New Concepts in Water Purification, 1974; Handbook of Advanced Wastewater Treatment, 1978; Managing People (Including Yourself) for Project Success, 1991, others; assoc. editor Jour. Engring. Mgmt. Mem. ASCE (chmn. urban wastewater com.), Am. Water Works Assn., Water Pollution Control Fedn., Am. Acad. Environ. Engrs., Rotary (pres. 1977-78). Office: Smith Culp Consulting 653 Ravel Ct Las Vegas NV 89128-8628

CULP, JOE C(ARL), electronics executive; b. Little Rock, July 23, 1933; s. Charles Carl and Doris Evelyn (Jackson) C.; m. Norma Carol Kennan, Jan. 26, 1954; 1 dau., Karen Gay Culp Ashorn. BSEE, U. Ark., 1955. Staff asst. to exec. v.p. Collins Radio, Dallas, 1967-68; with Rockwell Internat., Dallas, 1968-88, dir. data sys. mktg., 1968-71, dir. mktg. transp. sys. divsn., 1971-78, v.p. Latin Am. divsn., 1978-80, v.p., gen. mgr. transp. sys. divsn., 1980-82, pres. telecomm. group, 1982-88; pres., CEO Lightnet, Rockville, Md., 1988-89; exec. v.p. Communications Transmission Inc., Austin, Tex., 1989—; pres. Culp Comm. Assocs. Inc., Austin, 1990—; bd. dirs. IXC Comms. Inc.; vice chmn. Fast Lane Techs., Crosskeys Corp.; mem. chmn. exec. coun. Newbridge Networks Corp. Chmn. engring. bd. U. Tex., Arlington, 1984; bd. advisors Coll. Engring. U. Ark., Fayetteville, 1982. Named Disting. Grad., Coll. Engring. U. Ark., 1981, Disting. Engr., U. Tex., Arlington, 1984. Mem. Electronic Industry Assn. (bd. govs. 1984-88), U.S. Telephone Suppliers Assn. (dir. 1984-88), Ind. Telephone Pioneers. Republican. Methodist. Office: Culp Communications Assocs Inc 5 Hedge Ln Austin TX 78746-3208

CULP, KRISTINE ANN, dean, theology educator. B in Gen. Studies with distinction, U. Iowa, 1978; MDiv, Princeton Theol. Sem., 1982; PhD in Religion, U. Chgo., 1989. Vis. instr. theology St. Paul Sch. Theology, Kansas City, Mo., 1985-86, instr. theology, 1986-89, asst. prof. theology, 1990-91; dean Disciples Div. House U. Chgo., 1991—, sr. lectr. theology Div. Sch., 1991—. Contbr. articles to profl. jours. Office: U Chgo Disciples Divinity House 1156 E 57th St Chicago IL 60637-1536 also: The Divinity Sch-U Chgo Swift Hall S-406 1025 E 58th St Chicago IL 60637-1509*

CULP, MICHAEL BRONSTON, securities company executive, research director; b. N.Y.C., June 17, 1952; s. Robert Walter and Anna Lee (Filtzer) C. BA in Econs. magna cum laude, CUNY, 1973; CFA, U. Va. Securities analyst Standard & Poor's, N.Y.C., 1974-79; v.p., securities analyst E. F. Hutton & Co., Inc., N.Y.C., 1979-82; v.p., sr. securities analyst Prudential Securities Inc., N.Y.C., 1982-86, sr. v.p., mng. dir. rsch., 1986-94, sr. v.p., dir. global rsch., 1994-97, bd. dirs., 1986-91, oper. coun., 1991-97, chmn. stock selection com., 1989-97, chmn. equity devel. com., 1991-97, equity transactions bd., 1994-97, investment banking com., 1994-97; mem. investment com. Roman Arch Fund, 1996-97; mng. dir., dir. rsch., mem. oper. com. PaineWebber Inc., N.Y.C., 1997—, also bd. dirs., 1997—. Mem. N.Y. Soc. Security Analysts, Fin. Analysts' Fedn., Inst. CFA's, Internat. Soc. Fin. Analysts, Assn. for Investment Mgmt. and Rsch., Mensa, Phi Beta Kappa, Omicron Delta Epsilon. Home: 3 Lincoln Ctr New York NY 10023 Office: 1285 Ave of Americas New York NY 10019

CULP, MILDRED LOUISE, corporate executive; b. Ft. Monroe, Va., Jan. 13, 1949; d. William W. and Winifred (Stilwell) C. BA in English, Knox Coll., 1971; AM in religion and literature, U. Chgo., 1974, PhD The Com. on History of Culture, 1976. Mem. faculty, adminstr. Coll., 1976-81; dir. Exec. Résumés, Seattle, 1981—; pres. Exec. Directions Internat., Inc., Seattle, 1985—; mem. MBA mgmt. skills adv. com. U. Wash. Sch. Bus. Adminstrn., 1993; spkr. in field; contract rschr. U.S. Army Recruiting Command, 1997. Author: Be WorkWise: Retooling Your Work for the 21st Century, 1994; columnist Seattle Daily Jour. Commerce, 1982-88; writer Singer Media Corp., 1991-95, WorkWise syndicated column, 1994—, Universal Press Syndicate, 1997—, syndicated to newspapers, online svcs. and mags. in U.S. and The Philippines with several million subscribers, WorkWise Registered, 1992 (radio), 96 (print); featured on TV and radio; contbr. articles and book revs. to profl. jours.; presenter WorkWise Report, Sta. KIRO, 1991-96. Admissions counselor U. Chgo., 1981—; mem. Nat. Alliance Mentally Ill, 1984—, bd. dirs., 1987, mem. adv. bd., 1988; mem. A.M.I. Hamilton County, 1984—; founding mem. People Against Telephone Terrorism and Harassment, 1990. Recipient Alumni Achievement award Knox Coll., 1990, 8 other awards; named Hon. Army Recruiter. Mem. Knox County Alumni Network, U. Chgo. Puget Sound Alumni Club (bd. dirs. 1982-86). Office: Exec Directions Internat Inc 3313 39th Ave W Seattle WA 98199-2530

CULP, NATHAN CRAIG, lawyer; b. Camden, Ark., 1965; s. Harold Lloyd and Carole Culp; m. Clara M. Graves, 1995. BA, La. Tech. U., 1988; JD, U. Ark., 1991. Bar: Ark. 1991, U.S. Dist. Ct. Ark. 1992. Law clk. Walker, Roaf, Campbell, Ivory and Dunkin, Little Rock, 1989-91, assoc., 1991-94; staff atty. Pub. Employee Claims divsn. Ark. Dept. Ins., Little Rock, 1994—. Mem. Ark. Bar Assn. Methodist. Avocations: computers, reading. Office: Ark Dept Ins Pub Employee Claims Divsn 1200 W 3rd St Ste 201 Little Rock AR 72201-1904

CULP, ROBERT, actor, writer, director; b. Oakland, Calif., Aug. 16, 1930; m. Nancy Wilner (div. 1967); 4 children; m. France Nuyen (div. 1969). Student, Coll of Pacific, Washington U., St. Louis, San Francisco State Coll. Play appearances include He Who Gets Slapped (Obie award), The Prescott Proposals, A Clearing In the Woods; film appearances include PT 109, 1963, Sammy, 1963, The Raiders, 1964, Sunday in New York, 1964, Rhino, 1964, The Hanged Man, Bob & Carol & Ted & Alice, 1969, The Grove, Hannie Caulder, 1972, Hickey and Boggs, 1972, Sky Riders, 1976, The Great Scout and Cathouse Thursday, 1976, Breaking Point, 1976, Inside Out, 1976, Turk 182, 1985, Big Bad Mama II, 1987, Silent Night, Deadly Night III, Better Watch Out, The Pelican Brief, 1993, Panther, 1995, National Lampoon's Favorite Deadly Sins, 1995, Spy Hard, 1996, Most Wanted, 1997, Wanted, 1999, Unconditional Love, 1999, Farewell, My Love, 1999; acted in TV series Trackdown, 1957, I Spy, 1965-68, The Greatest American Hero, 1981-83, Columbo, 1990; appeared in numerous TV movies including: Cry for Help, 1975, Strange Homecoming, 1974, Flood!, 1976, A Cold Night's Death, 1973, Outrage, 1973, Houston, We've Got a Problem, 1974, Her Life As a Man, 1984, The Key to Rebecca, 1985, Combat High, 1986, Voyage of Terror: The Achile Lauro Affair, 1990, I Spy Returns, 1994, Mercenary, 1997, Big Guns Talk: The Story of the Western, 1997; appeared in 7-part TV series From Sea to Shining Sea, 1974-75; numerous other TV appearances. Office: Hillard Elkins 8306 Wilshire Blvd Ste 438 Beverly Hills CA 90211-2382*

CULPEPPER, JO LONG, librarian; b. Franklin, Va., Mar. 10, 1945; d. Sidney Earl and Fannie Lou (Flythe) Long; m. Britton Barclay Culpepper, Jr., Aug. 19, 1967; children: Britton B. III, Edmond Scott, Lou Ann. BS, Radford (Va.) U., 1967; MS, Old Dominion U., 1983. Min. of activities Westmoreland Bapt. Ch., Huntington, W.Va., 1967-70; libr. Walter Cecil Rawls Libr. and Mus., Courtland, Va., 1971-79, Hunterdale Elem. Sch., Franklin, Va., 1979—. Dir. Sunday sch. Franklin Bapt. Ch., 1988-98, bd. deacons, 1994-97; trustee Walter Cecil Rawls Libr. and Mus., 1985-89; troop leader Boy Scouts Am. Mem. Va. Ednl. Media Assn., Franklin/Southampton Reading Coun., Va. Reading Coun., Delta Kappa Gamma Internat. Avocations: scouting, reading, bowling, camping. Home: 401 Trail Dr Franklin VA 23851-2909 Office: Hunterdale Elem Sch 23190 Sedley Rd Franklin VA 23851-3848

CULPEPPER, MABEL CLAIRE, artist; b. St. Louis, Mo., June 20, 1936; d. John Raymond and Mabel Lorene (Hardy) Bondurant; m. James William Culpepper, Dec. 24, 1957; children: Julie Ann, James Jeffrey, John William. AA, Columbia Coll., 1956; BS in Edn., Mo. U., 1958, MEd, 1965. Represented by Artel Gallery, Emmitsburg, Md., 1987-88, Nob Hill Artisans, Albuquerque, 1993-94, Amapola Gallery, Albuquerque, 1995-98; art tchr. Twinbrook BApt., Rockville, Md., 1972-75. One woman exhbn. Artel Gallery, 1987; group exhbns. Rockville (Md.) Art League, 1987, N. Mex. Watercolor Soc., 1989-96. Host parent, officer Am. Field Svc., Damascus, Md., 1978-80; program chmn. Albuquerque Newcomers, 1989-91; docent Albuquerque Mus., 1990-94. Recipient First Prize Rockville Art League, 1987. Mem. Nat. Mus. Women in the Arts, Nat. League Am. Penwomen (pres. Yucca Br. 1998), N. Mex. Watercolor Soc. (pres. 1992-93, First Prize 1990, 1998, Best of Show 1993, 99), Frederick County Art Assn. (pres. 1988), Delta Gamma, Mortar Bd. Avocations: hiking, singing in church choir, crafts, Bible study, travel. Home: 3208 Casa Bonita Dr NE Albuquerque NM 87111-5610

CULSHAW, ROBERT NICHOLAS, British diplomat; b. London, Dec. 22, 1952; s. Ivan and Edith Marjorie Jose (Barnard) C.; m. Elaine Ritchie Clegg, Mar. 19, 1977; 1 child, Robin Alexander. BA with honourse 1st class in Classics, Cambridge (Eng.) U., 1974, MA with honours in Classics, 1977. With Brit. Diplomatic Svc., 1977—; 3d sec. Brit. Embassy, Muscat, Oman, 1977-79; 2d sec. Brit. Embassy, Khartoun, Sudan, 1979-80; 1st sec. Brit. Embassy, Rome, 1980-84; pvt. sec. Fgn. Office, London, 1985-88; dep. head mission Brit. Embassy, Athens, 1988-93; head news and chief spokesman Fgn. Office, 1993-95; min.-counselor Brit. Embassy, Washington, 1995—. Mem. Washington Bach Consort. Decorated Royal Victorian Order (U.K.). Fellow Royal Soc. Arts; mem. Univ. Club Washington. Avocations: singing, skiing, poetry. Office: British Embassy 3100 Massachusetts Ave NW Washington DC 20008-3688

CULTON, PAUL MELVIN, retired counselor, educator, interpreter; b. Council Bluffs, Iowa, Feb. 12, 1932; s. Paul Roland and Hallie Ethel Emma (Paschal) C. BA, Minn. Bible Coll., 1955; BS, U. Nebr., 1965; MA, Calif. State U., Northridge, 1970; EdD, Brigham Young U., 1981. Cert. tchr., Iowa. Tchr. Iowa Sch. for Deaf, Council Bluffs, 1956-70; ednl. specialist Golden West Coll., Huntington Beach, Calif., 1970-71, dir. disabled students, 1971-82, instr., 1982-88; counselor El Camino Coll., Via Torrance, Calif., 1990-93, acting assoc. dean, 1993-94; counselor El Camino Coll., Via Torrance, Caif., 1994-97; interpreter various state and fed. cts., Iowa, Calif., 1960-90; asst. prof. Calif. State U., Northridge, Fresno & Dominguez Hills, 1973, 76, 80, 87-91; vis. prof. U. Guam, Agana, 1977; mem. allocations task force, task force on deafness, trainer handicapped students Calif. C.C.s, 1971-81. Editor: Region IX Conf. for Coordinating Rehab. and Edn. Svcs. for Deaf proceedings, 1970, Toward Rehab. Involvement by Parents of Deaf conf. proceedings, 1971; composer Carry the Light, 1986. Bd. dirs. Iowa NAACP, 1966-68, Gay and Lesbian Cmty. Svcs. Ctr., Orange County, Calif., 1975-77; founding sec. Dayle McIntosh Ctr. for Disabled, Anaheim and Garden Grove, Calif., 1974-80; active Dem. Cent. Com. Pottawattamie County, Council Bluffs, 1960-70; del. People to People N.Am. Educators Deaf Vis. Russian Schs. & Programs for Deaf, 1993. League for Innovation in Community Coll. fellow, 1974. Mem. Registry of Interpreters for Deaf, Congress Am. Instrs. Deaf, Am. Deafness and Rehab. Assn., Calif. Assn. Postsecondary Educators Disabled, Am. Fedn. Tchrs., Nat. Assn. Deaf. Mem. Am. Humanist Assn. Avocations: vocal music, languages, community activism, travel, politics. Home: 2567 Plaza Del Amo Apt 203 Torrance CA 90503-8962

CULTON, SARAH ALEXANDER, psychologist, writer; b. Burwell, Nebr., Nov. 12, 1927; d. James Claude and Frances Ann (Evans) Alexander;m. Verlen Ross Culton, June 19, 1949; children: James Verlen, Sarah Ann. BA in Edn., Ea. Wash. U., 1953, MA in Edn., 1956; EdD in Psychology, U. Idaho, 1966. Tchr. pub. schs. Kennewick, Northport, Wash., Potlatch, Idaho, 1946-56; prof. Lewis-Clark U. of Idaho, Lewiston, 1956-59, North Idaho Jr. Coll., Coeur d'Alene, 1961-66; sch. psychologist Sch. Dist. 81, Spokane, Wash., 1966-67; prof. psychology Spokane Falls Community Coll., 1967-88; author Colville, Wash., 1988—; sch. psychologist Adna (Wash.) Spl. Edn. Coop., 1994; mid. sch. counselor Soda Springs (Idaho) Sch. Dist., 1994-98; sch. psychologist Canyon-Owyhee Spl. Svc. Agy., Caldwell, Idaho, 1998—; sch. psychologist, sch. counselor vol. Northport Schs., 1989-92; presenter convs. in field. Author: Psychology of Stress and Nutrition, 1991, The Psychology of Stress and Nutrition, 1992. Doctoral fellow Wash. State U., 1959, U. Idaho, 1964; recipient Faculty Achievement award Burlington No. Found., 1988. Fellow Am. Inst. Stress; mem. NEA, APA, Internat. Coun. Psychologists, Internat. Stress Mgmt. Assn. (newsletter editor), Nat. Stroke Assn., Western Psychol. Assn., Am. Counseling Assn. (writer invitation 1992), Nat. Assn. Sch. Psychologists, Alpha Delta Kappa. Avocations: travel, painting, photography, genealogy, writing. Address: PO Box 713 Wilder ID 83676 also: 717 Prouty Corner Loop Colville WA 99114

CULVAHOUSE, ARTHUR BOGGESS, JR., lawyer; b. Athens, Tenn., July 4, 1948; s. Arthur Boggess and Ruth Webb (Wear) C.; children: Sarah Abbott, Arthur Boggess, Elizabeth Louise, Anne Pierce. BS, U. Tenn., 1970; JD, NYU, 1973. Bar: Tenn. 1973, Calif. 1977, D.C. 1977. Chief legis. asst. to U.S. Sen. Howard Baker Washington, 1973-76; assoc. O'Melveny & Myers, Washington, 1976-81, ptnr., 1982-84, 89—; ptnr. Vinson & Elkins, Washington, 1984-87; counsel to the Pres. The White House, Washington, 1987-89. Recipient Presdl. Citizen's medal, 1989, Def. Dept. Disting. Svc. medal. 1992. Republican. Episcopalian. Office: 555 13th St NW Ste 500 Washington DC 20004-1109*

CULVER, CHESTER J., state official. Office: Office of Secretary of State State House Des Moines IA 50319*

CULVER, DAN LOUIS, federal agency administrator; b. Savannah, Ga., Dec. 7, 1957; s. Louis Harry and Jean Marie Culver. BS in Mktg., U. Tenn., 1981; postgrad., Air Force Acad., 1982, Cornell U., 1985; BS in Edn. and Tng., U. West Fla, 1995; MEd in Orgnl. Devel. and Leadership, U. West Fla., 1998. Cert. tchr., Fla. Hotel gen. mgr. U.S. Govt., Ft. Walton Beach, Fla., 1982-85, asst. dir. food and lodging, 1985-86; mgmt. assoc. Barnett Bank, Ft. Walton Beach, 1987-89; loan officer SBA, Atlanta, 1989—; promoter for profl. lectrs., entertainers, and authors. Pioneered automation of air force support ops., 1982-84. Served on bd. of dirs. to business and nonprofit organizations. Vol. disaster relief for victims of Hurricane Hugo, Charleston, S.C., 1989, Hurricane Andrew, Miami, Fla., 1992, Miss. River flood, 1993, L.A. earthquake, 1994. With USAF, 1982-86. Recipient Commander-in-Chief's Spl. Recognition for Excellence award, Pres. Ronald Reagan, 1986. Mem. Internat. Platform Assn., Asia Soc., U. Tenn. Alumni Assn., Phi Kappa Phi, Sigma Phi Epsilon. Avocations: flying, skiing, sailing. Office: PO Box 5453 Fort Walton Beach FL 32549-5453

CULVER, JOHN BLAINE, minister; b. Urbana, Ill., Nov. 3, 1938; s. Lawson Blaine and Sunray Lillian (Cooper) C.; m. Rosa Bertha Diaz-Mori, Feb. 28, 1970; children: Janice Lillian, John Manuel, Edward Blaine. BA, U. Ill., 1962, MA, 1964; MDiv cum laude, Chgo. Theol. Sem., 1972; postgrad., Escuela de Idiomas, Sociedad de Santiago Apostol, Pontifical U., Lima, Peru, 1969-70. Ordained to ministry United Ch. of Christ, 1973. Pastor, adminstr. Winnebago Indian Mission, United Ch. of Christ, Black River Falls, Wis., 1972-75; pastor Bethany United Ch. of Christ, San Antonio, 1975-78, Bethany Congl. Ch., San Antonio, 1978-96 (ret.); interim pastor Pilgrim Congl. Ch., San Antonio, 1978, Iglesia Unida de Cristo Betania, San Antonio, 1982-83; pastor emeritus Bethany Congregational United Ch. of Christ, San Antonio, 1998—; adj. instr. history San Antonio Coll., 1978-96; bd. dirs. South Ctrl. Conf. United Ch. of Christ, Austin, Tex., 1982, 84-87, 90-92, gen. synod del., 1997; mem. exec. com., sec.-registrar South Tex. Assn. United Ch. of Christ, 1982-90, 94-96, moderator, 1982, 90-92. Bd. dirs., program chmn. Illini Young Reps., Urbana, Ill., 1963; bd. dirs. Greater San Antonio Community of Chs., 1976-80, San Antonio Urban Coun., 1984-86, 88; sec. Tobin Hill Neighborhood Assn., San Antonio, 1978-79. Mem. Masons (chaplain 1981-82, 90-92, tiler 1980-81, 84-85), Scottish Rite, York Rite. Home: 102 Shadywood Ln San Antonio TX 78216-7334 *For the Christ Disciple the most important thing is to live out of that core of faith within in order to become a vehicle of God's love, peace and salvation in the world and to minister to others in their need as an instrument of Christ's presence and compassion.*

CULVERN, JULIAN BREWER, retired chemist, educator; b. July 23, 1919; m. Shirley Bowman, 1946; children: Janine Amelia, David Bowman, Linda Hazel. BS, N.C. State U., 1942; MSc, Ohio State U., 1948; postgrad., U. Tenn., 1970-72. Assay chemist Haile Gold Mine, 1940-41; shift supr. Anhydrous Ammonia Plant TVA, Wilson Dam, Ala., 1942-44; asst. mgr. Chem. & Microscopical Lab., 1949-61; sr. process engr. Am. Enka Corp., Lowland, Tenn., 1961-69; instr. gen. chemistry, earth and space sci., environ. sci. Morristown (Tenn.) Coll., 1969-76, chmn. div. natural sci., 1969-73.; condr. libr. rsch. in field sci. and religion Sir John M. Templeton Found., 1970; chemist atomic bomb project Corps of Engrs., Manhattan Dist., Oak Ridge, Tenn., 1944-46. Columnist Daily Gazette-Mail, Morristown, 1960-74; contbr. articles to Sci. of Mind mag., others. Chmn. Cherokee dist. Boy Scouts Am., 1962-63, 91, 92, exec. bd. Great Smoky Mountain coun., 1991-98; ruling elder 1st Presbyn. Ch., Morristown, Tenn., Marshall, N.C.; sci. judge Sou. Appalachian Sci. and Engring. Fair, U. Tenn., Knoxville, 1995-98. Mem. AAUP, Am. Chem. Soc., Tenn. Acad. Scis., Gamma Sigma Epsilon, Phi Lambda Upsilon. Home: Birdsong Hill 2832 Indian Trl Morristown TN 37814-5824

CULVERWELL, ALBERT HENRY, historian; b. Portland, Oreg., Jan. 28, 1913; s. John Albert and Nettie L. (Kingery) C.; m. Ethel E. Klein, Aug. 17, 1941 (dec.); children: Cheryl Evelyn, John Albert; m. Eleanor M. Liere, May 6, 1986. Scholarship student in stagecraft, color and design, Cornish Sch., Seattle, 1935-36; B.A., U. Wash., Seattle, 1936, M.A., 1941; postgrad., Am. U., Wash. State U. Mem. faculty Whitworth Coll., Spokane, Wash., 1941-42, 46-50; civilian U.S. Naval Air Sta., Seattle, 1942-45; safety engr., asst. dir. personnel Pacific Car & Foundry Co., Renton, Wash., 1945-46; instr. social sci. Wash. State U., Pullman, 1949-50; asst. prof. history Western Wash. State Coll., Bellingham, 1950-53; historian, supr. interpretation Wash. State Parks, Olympia, 1953-62; chief br. interpretive services Region 4, U.S. Forest Service, Ogden, Utah, 1962-68; dir. Eastern Wash. State Hist. Soc., Spokane, 1968-82; pres. Wash. Art Consortium, 1979-82; mem. Wash. Archives Adv. Bd., 1977-82, Adv. Coun. Preservation of Hist. Sites and Bldgs., 1968-78, com. to develop Hist. Interpretive Ctr., Wash. State Capitol Bldg., 1983-84; mem. design com. Main St. Program, San Jacinto, Calif., 1988-91; vol. art assoc. in support and adminstrn. Fine Arts Gallery, Mt. San Jacinto Coll., 1988-98; vol. history assoc. in preservation and interpretation of Estudillo Mansion in San Jacinto, 1993-98, pres. Resident Coun. SunWest Village, Hemet, CA, 1998—. Author articles in field, also, film and TV scripts. Elder United Presbyn. Ch. U.S.A., 1942—; adminstrv. adv. com. Sheldon Jackson Jr. Coll., Sitka, Alaska, 1961-63; bd. dirs. Westminster Found., 1961-62; mem. Woodway (Wash.) Planning Commn., 1961-63, Wash. Gov.'s Adv. Coun. on Observance Civil War Centennial, 1961; Gov. Wash. Coun. Boundary Survey Centennial, 1961. Recipient cert. of commendation Am. Assn. State and Local History, 1965. Mem. Am. Assn. Museums (pres. Western regional conf. 1969-71), Orgn. Am. Historians, Pacific N.W. Hist. Soc., Idaho Hist. Soc., Utah Hist. Soc., Westerners, Phi Sigma Kappa, Pi Sigma Alpha. Club: Rotary. *In my life I have striven to achieve something positive in whatever I have done. Success depends on faith in myself as well as in someone greater than I, and, to an extent, with those with whom I have worked. This has brought a measure of patience to me which has made it possible to accept setbacks which make achievement slow. But when one has gained confidence and patience, success is often achieved.*

CULWELL, CHARLES LOUIS, retired manufacturing company executive; b. Putnam, Tex., Apr. 26, 1927; s. Willie and Ila Alberta (Crosby) C.; m. Virginia Green, June 10, 1949; children—Andrew Scott, Perry Neal, Curtis Austin, Travis Lee. B.S. in Elec. Engring, U.S. Naval Acad., 1949; M.S. in Mgmt, U.S. Naval Postgrad. Sch., 1969. Commd. ensign U.S. Navy, 1949, advanced through grades to capt., 1969; service in Korea and Vietnam; comdg. officer Naval Supply Center, Oakland, Calif., 1975-76; ret., 1976; asst. to pres., then v.p. Purex Corp., 1976-79; group v.p., gen. mgr. indsl., instl. and comml. products Purex Industries, Inc., Lakewood, Calif., 1979-84; v.p., asst. to chief exec. officer Purex Industries, Inc., Carson, Calif., 1984-86; v.p., asst. to chief exec. officer Purex Industries Liquidation, Carson, Calif., 1986-87, retired, 1987. Decorated Legion of Merit, Bronze Star with combat V, Meritorious Service medal. Mem. U.S. Naval Acad. Alumni Assn. Republican. Presbyterian.

CUMBER, SHERRY G., psychotherapist, research consultant; b. Dallas; d. Jessie Ray and Dorothy Mae (Weeden) Wilford; 1 child Brooke Dawn Thrash Willis. BA, U. Colo., Colorado Springs, 1993; MA, Chapman U., Colorado Springs, 1997; postgrad., Walden U. Cert. profo. hypnotherapist. CEO CSI, Inc., Tulsa, 1975-87; bus. cons. ind. contractor, Costa Mesa, Calif., 1987-90; rschr. U. Colo., Colorado Springs, 1990-93; bus. cons. Colorado Springs, 1993-95; psychotherapist in pvt. practice, Colorado Springs, 1995—. State legis. candidate Dem. Party, Okla., 1978, legis. and congl. campaign coord., 1978-86; lobbyist NRA, Oklahoma City, 1983. Recipient Contbn. award NRA, 1983, Participation award Okla. Pub. Sch. Sys., 1984-87. Mem. ACA, Assn. for Drug and Alcohol Addiction. Avocations: kickboxing, scuba diving, parasailing, skiing, sculpting.

CUMBERLAND, WILLIAM EDWIN, lawyer; b. Washington, Sept. 11, 1938; m. Clare Hogan, Aug. 17, 1973; children: Lisa, Joseph, Kara. AB, Georgetown U., 1960; LLB, Harvard U., 1963. Bar: D.C. 1963, Va. 1963. Law clk. to judge U.S. Dist. Ct. D.C., Washington, 1963-64; from assoc. to ptnr. Cefaratti & Cumberland, Washington, 1964-71; atty. HUD, Washington, 1971-72; counsel Mortgage Bankers Assn. Am., Washington, 1972—, gen. counsel, sr. v.p., 1988—. Office: Mortgage Bankers Assn Am 1125 15th St NW Ste 500 Washington DC 20005-2766

CUMING, PAMELA, marketing professional, author; b. Denver, Oct. 13, 1944; d. John Gerald and Rosemary (Miller) C.; m. Terrence C. Shea, June 18, 1966 (div. 1973); m. William I. Bechard, June 23, 1974 (dec. July 1979); m. David Druetzer Gregory, Dec. 9, 1989; children: Monica Cuming, Melissa Cotter. BA, Smith Coll., 1966. Ins. underwriter Chubb & Son, N.Y.C., 1966-69; orgn. devel. specialist Am. Express, N.Y.C., 1969-71; orgn. devel. cons. Ednl. Systems & Designs, Westport, Conn., 1971-73; v.p. Dialectics Inc., Stamford, Conn., 1973-79; pres. Dialectics Inc., Stamford and Encinitas, Calif., 1979-93; sr. mng. dir., dir. mktg. Bear, Stearns & Co., Inc., N.Y.C., 1993—; developer computerized expert systems. Author: The Power Handbook, 1982, Turf and Other Corporate Power Plays, 1987; contbr. articles to profl. jours. Avocations: writing fiction, tennis, travelling. Office: Bear Stearns & Co Inc 245 Park Ave New York NY 10017-2500

CUMINGS, BRUCE, history educator, writer; b. Rochester, N.Y., Sept. 5, 1943; s. Edgar C. and Eleanor (Sharts) C.; m. Bonnie Limpus, July 9, 1966 (div. Sept. 1984); 1 child, Jacqueline; m. Meredith Woo, Aug. 10, 1988; children: Ian Benjamin. BA, Denison U., 1965; PhD, Columbia U., 1975. Steelworker Rep. Steel, Cleve., summers 1963-66; vol. Peace Corps, Seoul, Korea, 1967-68; asst. prof. Swarthmore (Pa.) Coll., 1975-77; from asst. prof. to prof. U. Wash., Seattle, 1977-87; prof. East Asian and internat. history U. Chgo., 1987-94; Norman and Edna Freehling prof. history U. Chgo., Ill., 1994—; John Evans prof. internat. history and politics Northwestern U., Evanston, Ill., 1994-97; cons. Carnegie Endowment, MacArthur Found., Soc. Sci. Rsch. Coun., Econ. Strategy Inst.; advisor Asia panel Am. Friends Svc., Phila., 1997—. Author: The Origins of the Korea War, 1981 (John King

Fairbank award Am. Hist. Assn. 1983), Origins of the Korea War, Vol. 2, 1990 (Quincy Wright book award 1992), War and Television, 1992 (finalist for George Orwell book awrad 1993), Korea's Place in the Sun, 1997 (finalist for the Kiriyama Pacific Rim book prize 1997); editor, advisor Bull. Concerned Asian Scholars, 1970—. Human rights activist for various orgns. including Amnesty Internat., the Am. Friends Svc., 1973—. Recipient Disting. Alumnus award Denison U., 1996, Human Rights award Korean Inst. for Human Rights, 1984. Mem. Assn. for Asian Studies (N.E. Asia coun. 1987-90), Am. Hist. Assn., Coun. Fgn. Rels. (Chgo. com.). Democrat. Avocations: classic cars, basketball, baseball. Office: U Chgo Dept History 1125 E 59th St Chicago IL 60637

CUMMER, WILLIAM JACKSON, former oil company executive, investor; b. Drumheller, Alta., Can., July 6, 1922; s. John Wellington and Laurine Lila (Jackson) C.; m. Barbara Louise Nadeau, Apr. 7, 1942 (div. 1949); 1 child, William Allen; m. Marion Emma Murray, Sept. 9, 1950; children: Donald John, Marion Diane, Denise Mary Elizabeth, Dean Frederick William. Grad., Banff Sch. Advanced Mgmt., Alta., 1957. Controller, treas., dir. Gen. Petroleums Drilling Ltd., Calgary, Alta., Can., 1943-66; treas. Westburne Petroleum Services Ltd., Calgary, 1966-69; treas. Westburne Internat. Industries Ltd., Calgary, 1969-76, pres., dir., 1977-82, vice chmn., dir., 1982-84; treas., exec. v.p., pres. Westburne Internat. Drilling Ltd., Hamilton, Bermuda, 1976-84; dir. Getty Copper Corp., Vancouver, B.C. Sgt. Can. Army, 1941-43. Mem. Calgary Petroleum Club. Progressive Conservative.

CUMMIN, SYLVIA ESTHER, secondary education educator; b. N.Y.C., Mar. 15; d. Harry and Sarah (Josephson) Smolok; BS, NYU, 1946, MA, 1947; m. Alfred S. Cummin, Mar. 24, 1946; 1 dau., Cynthia Katherine. Mktg. adminstr. Ayerst Labs. div. Am. Home Products, N.Y.C., 1946-55; tchr. Queensbury (N.Y.) High Sch., 1955-57, Corfu (N.Y.) Central Sch., 1957-59, Brookline (Mass.) High Sch., 1959-63; tchr. bus. Westfield (N.J.) Secondary Sch., 1963-90, Edison (N.J.) Jr. H.S., 1990—. Active, Westfield PTA, 1963—, YWCA, 1966—; sponsor, committeewoman Nat. Debutante Assembly, N.Y.C., 1972—, Internat. Debutante Ball, N.Y.C., 1973—, Debutante Cotillion, Washington, 1973—, Ball of the Silver Rose, Vienna, Austria, 1973—; Cert. tchr., Mass., N.Y., N.J. Mem. NEA, N.J. Edn. Assn., Mass. Tchrs. Assn., N.Y. Educators Assn., Eastern Bus. Tchrs. Assn., Nat. Bus. Edn. Assn., N.Y. U. Alumni Assn., N.Y. U. Faculty Wives Assn., Am. Platform Assn., Internat. Bus. Edn. Assn. Clubs: Westfield Coll. Women's, Glens Falls Country, Garden. Contbr. articles to profl. jours. Home: 2 Naworth Pass Westfield NJ 07090-3715 Office: Edison Jr H S Rahway Ave Westfield NJ 07090

CUMMING, ALAN, actor; b. Perthshire, Scotland, Jan. 27, 1965. Actor (movies): Prague, 1992, Second Best, 1994, Circle of Friends, 1995, GoldenEye, 1995, Burn Your Phone, 1996, Emma, 1996, Spice World, 1997, For My Baby, 1997, Romy and Michele's High School Reunion, 1997, Buddy, 1997, Urban Folk Tales, 1999, Flintstones in Viva Rock Vegas, 1999, Company Man, 1999, Plunkett & MacLeane, 1999, Eyes Wide Shut, 1999, Titus, 1999; (tv) The Last Romantics, 1991, Bernard and the Genie, 1991, Airzone Solution, 1993, Micky Love, 1993, That Sunday, 1994, (tv series) The High Life, 1994; voice of Black Beauty in Black Beauty, 1994; guest appearances include: Mr. Bean, 1993, Have I Got News for You, 1995. Winner Tony award for Cabaret, 1998. Office: c/o SAG 1515 Broadway 44th Flr New York NY 10036*

CUMMING, GEORGE ANDERSON, JR., lawyer; b. Washington, Apr. 16, 1942; s. George Anderson and Gene (Chapman) C.; m. Linda Lucille Harder, Aug. 25, 1963; children: Mary Elizabeth, Andrew Gordon. AA, Coll. San Mateo, 1962; AB magna cum laude, San Francisco State U., 1963; JD, U. Calif., Berkeley, 1967. Bar: Calif. 1967, U.S. Dist. Ct. (no. dist.) Calif. 1967, U.S. Ct. Appeals (9th cir.) 1967, U.S. Supreme Ct. 1974. Assoc. Brobeck, Phleger & Harrison, San Francisco, 1967-75, ptnr., 1975-98; spl. trial counsel antitrust divsn. U.S. Dept. Justice, Washington, 1996-97; with Brobeck Phleger, San Francisco, 1998—. Fellow Am. Coll. Trial Lawyers; mem. ABA, San Francisco Bar Assn., Order of Coif. Avocation: model railroading. Office: Brobeck Phleger Antitrust Divsn One Market Spear St Tower San Francisco CA 94105*

CUMMING, GLEN EDWARD, art museum director; b. Calgary, Alta., Can., July 23, 1936; s. Alexander Edward Brown and Johanna Maria Christina (Van Der Doorn) C. Diploma fine arts, Alta. Coll. Art, 1963. Asst. to dir. Edmonton (Alta.) Art Gallery, 1963-64; dir. expressive arts City of Edmonton Parks and Recreation Dept., 1965-67; curator Regina (Sask.) Public Library Art Gallery, 1967-69; dir. Kitchener-Waterloo Art Gallery, Kitchener, Ont., 1969-72, Robert McLaughlin Art Gallery, Oshawa, Ont., 1972-73, Art Gallery of Hamilton, Ont., 1973-89, 49th Parallel Gallery for Contemporary Can. Art, N.Y.C., 1989-92, Art Gallery of North York, Ont., Can., 1993-98, Mus. Contemporary Can. Art, 1998—; bd. dirs. Hamilton and Region Arts Council, 1987-89, Art Mag., Toronto, 1977-80; chmn. art adv. com. Mohawk Coll. Applied Arts and Tech., 1979-89; adv. Ont. Coll. Art, 1979-83; mem. adv. bd. Sir Sandford Fleming Coll., 1973. Editor: Town Talk, 1965-66. Mem. Can. Soc. Decorative Arts (nat. coun. 1986-88), Can. Art Mus. Dirs. Orgns. (pres. 1981-82), Ont. Assn. Art Galleries (pres. 1974), Internat. Assn. Art Critics, Internat. Coun. Mus., Can. Club. Home: 40 Homewood Ave PH-2, Toronto, ON Canada M4Y 2K2 Office: Art Gallery of North York, Mus Contemporary Can Art, 5040 Yonge St, North York, ON Canada M2N 6R8

CUMMING, MARILEE, apparel company executive; b. Columbus, Nebr.; m. Andrew Cumming; 1 child, Melissa. BA in Psychology, Rosemont Coll., 1969. Buyer trainee children's divsn. J.C. Penney, Inc., N.Y.C., 1975, asst. and assoc. buyer positions in children's and women's, 1975-82, catalog dress buyer, 1982-84, sr. buyer misses blouses, 1984-86, merchandise mgr. men's accessories and furnishings, 1986-87, merchandise mgr. women's, misses and updated apparel, 1987-90, dir. women's merchandise dept., 1990, dir. merchandising women's divsn., 1990-93, pres. home and leisure divsn., 1993-96, pres. women's apparel divsn., 1996-99; pres. merchandising J.C. Penney Stores and Catalog, 1999—. Campaign vice chmn. Met. Dallas United Way Campaign, 1996—; mem. NWCA N.Y., Acad. Women Achievers. Avocations: health and fitness, family activities. Office: JC Penney Co Inc 6501 Legacy Dr Plano TX 75024-3698*

CUMMING, ROBERT EMIL, editor; b. Lincoln, Nebr., June 2, 1933; s. Eugene Earl and Christiana (Jensen) C. Student, U. Nebr., 1955; Music Ed. (Presser Found. scholar), Nebr. Wesleyan U., 1956. With Music Jour. mag., N.Y.C., 1958-75; editor in chief Music Jour. mag., 1964-75; with Weekly Reader Corp. (formerly Xerox Edn. Publs. and Field Publs.), 1977-97; founder, pres. Conn. Singers Agy., 1997—. Theater editor Middlesex mag., 1995—, The Trumpeter, 1997—, critic, 1994—; critic, condr., singer, stage dir. Village Light Opera Group, Hunter Coll., N.Y.C., Cmty. Opera, Little Orch. Soc.; founder-mem. Singing Editors, nationally concertized, 1974-76; toured U.S. and Can. as stage dir. Naughty Marietta, Little Orch. Concerts, 1976; compiler, editor: The Power of Music by Dmitri Shostakovich, 1968, They Talk About Music, 1971-72; editor Spl. Librs. Assn. Bull., Publ. Divsn., 1989—, Life is a Poem, 1999; composer children's operettas Rumpelstiltskin, 1952, Song of Andorra, 1953; songs: God Is My Salvation, 1954, How Sly, 1954, Ya Gotta Have Love, 1955, The Hills of Sand, 1969; ann. music report for Living History of the World, 1967-68; contbr. articles to profl. jours. Mem. East Haddam Hist. Soc., 1977—, pres. 1998—; dir. East Lyme Arts Coun., 1990—, U. Conn. Gilbert and Sullivan Summer Prodns., 1985-88. Mem. N.Y. Gilbert and Sullivan Soc. (pres. 1967-69), Conn. Gilbert and Sullivan Soc. (founder, dir. 1980—), Conn. Sinfonia Soc. (founder), So. Conn. Libr. Coun. (bd. dirs. 1986-89). Episcopalian. Home: PO Box 196 East Haddam CT 06423-0196 Office: PO Box 294 Moodus CT 06469-0294 *I have developed an awareness of the need for: enough strength to overcome loneliness; enough ego to communicate well; enough vision to perceive the need; enough ambition to overcome laziness; enough drive to complete what is begun; enough compassion to wish to help; enough insight to grow humility; enough talent to be grateful; enough intelligence to remain practical; enough wisdom to be open; enough sensitivity to be myself; enough pain to keep in balance; enough pleasure to retain my humor; enough culture to be knowing; enough honesty to admit ignorance; enough love to appreciate symbols; enough religion to sense God.*

CUMMING, ROBERT HUGH, artist, photographer; b. Worcester, Mass., Oct. 7, 1943; s. Robert H. and Evelyn (Schold) C. B.F.A., Mass. Coll. Art, 1965; M.F.A., U. Ill., 1967. Lectr. UCLA Extension, 1974-77, Otis Art Inst., Los Angeles, 1975-76, Calif. Inst. Arts, Valencia, 1976-77; asst. prof. U. Calif.-Irvine, 1977-78; assoc. prof. U. Hartford, West Hartford, Conn., 1978-86; juror, cons. U.S. Eye Exhibit Winter Olympics, Lake Placid, N.Y., 1979; vis. artist Polaroid Corp., Cambridge, Mass., 1979, traveling retrospective through Australian Gallery Dirs. Council, Sydney, Australia, 1979. Exhibited retrospective show, Friends of Photography, Carmel, Calif., 1979, Travelling retrospective show, Brisbane, Sydney, Melbourne, Adelaide, and Burney, Australia, 1979, one man shows, Castelli Gallery, N.Y.C., 1982, 85, 86, 88, 91, Werkstatt fur Photographie, Berlin, 1982, Whitney Mus. Am. Art, 1986, Hirshhorn Mus., Washington, 1988; retrospective exhbns. include San Diego Mus. of Contemporary Art, Boston Mus. of Fine Arts, Houston Contemporary Arts Mus., 1993-94. Recipient awards in visual arts, Winston-Salem, N.C., 1984, creative arts award Brandeis U., 1985; grantee Nat. Endowment for Arts, 1972, 75; John S. Guggenheim fellow, 1980; fellow Japan-U.S. Friendship Commn., 1981.

CUMMING, THOMAS ALEXANDER, stock exchange executive; b. Toronto, Ont., Can., Oct. 14, 1937; s. Alison A. and Anne B. (Berry) C.; m. E. Mary Stevens, Mar. 12, 1965; children: Jennifer, Allison, Katy. BAS, U. Toronto, 1960. Registered profl. engr., Can. With Bank of Nova Scotia, 1965-88; spl. rep. Toronto, 1965-68; br. mgr. Dublin, Ireland, 1969-71, London, 1971-75; v.p. Calgary, Alta., Can., 1975-80; sr. v.p. Calgary, Alta., Can., 1980-85, Toronto, 1986-88; pres., chief exec. officer Alta. Stock Exchange, Calgary, 1988—. Mem. Assn. Profl. Engrs., Calgary C. of C. (pres. 1991), Calgary Golf and Country Club, Calgary Petroleum Club. Home: 2906 10th St SW, Calgary, AB Canada T2T 3H2 Office: Alberta Stock Exch, 300 5th Ave SW 10th Fl, Calgary, AB Canada T2P 3C4

CUMMINGS, BARTON, musician; b. Newport, N.H., July 10, 1946; s. C. Barton and Ruth (Ricard) C.; m. Florecita L. Lim, July 23, 1983;. BS in Music Edn., U. N.H., 1968; MusM, Ball State U., Muncie, Ind., 1973. Dir. music Alton (N.H.) Pub. Sch., 1971-72; lectr. San Diego State U., 1974-79; instr. music Point Loma Coll., San Diego, 1976-79; instr. San Diego Community Coll. Dist., 1977-79, Delta State U., Cleveland, Miss., 1979-82; supr. Clarksdale Separate Sch. Dist., 1982-84; dir. music Walnut (Calif.) Creek Concert Band, 1985—, Richmond Unified Sch. Dist., 1988—, Golden Hills Concert Band, 1990—; condr. Devil Mountain Symphony, 1991—; tuba player Vallejo Symphony Orch., 1988—, Concord Pavilion Pops Orch., 1985—, Brassworks of San Francisco, 1985—, Solano Dixie Jubilee. Author: The Contemporary Tuba, 1984, The Tuba Guide, 1989, Teaching Techniques for Brass Instruments, 1989; composer over 6 dozen pub. compositions; recorded on Capra, Coronet and Crystal, Channel Classics, Mark labels. Mem. ASCAP, NACUSA, T.U.B.A., Am. Fedn. of Musicians, Conductor's Guild, Phi Mu Alpha Sinfonia. Avocations: traveling, cooking, writing, composing, reading. Home: 550 Cambridge Dr Benicia CA 94510-1316

CUMMINGS, BRIAN THOMAS, public relations company executive; b. Pitts., Aug. 31, 1945; s. John Patrick and Edith E. (Gailey) C.; m. Maureen Ellen Decewicz, July 8, 1967; children: Kimberly, Carey, Brian T. Jr. BA, Duquesne U., Pitts., 1968. Reporter Pitts. Press, 1968; editor Rockwell Internat., Pitts., 1972-74, mgr. employee communications, 1974-78, dir. communications, 1978-84; sr. v.p., gen. mgr. Burson Marsteller, Pitts., 1984-88; pres., CEO Bloom Pub. Rels., Inc., Dallas, 1988-92; chmn., CEO Publicis Pub. Rels., Dallas, 1992-97; bd. dirs., chmn. The Worldcom Group, Inc.; pres. BTC Pub. Rels., Dallas, 1997-99; chmn. Cummings, McGlone & Assocs., 1999—. Bd. dirs., past chmn. Dallas divsn. Am. Heart Assn.; bd. dirs. Lee Purle & Arlington Hall Conservancy, 1998—. Served to capt. U.S. Army, 1968-72, Vietnam. Decorated Bronze Star; recipient Cornelius McCarthy Disting. Alumni award Duquesne U., 1985. Roman Catholic.

CUMMINGS, CAROLE EDWARDS, special education educator; b. Dover, Ohio, June 17, 1942; d. John T. and Dorothy M. (Plotts) Edwards; children: Kimberly Cummings Pfister, Rebecca Cummings Berry. BS, Kent State U., 1964; MA, Ohio State U., 1986. Cert. elem. tchr., learning disabilities tchr., spl. edn. supervision., Ohio. Elem. tchr. Dover Pub. Schs., 1965-66, 70-71; mid. sch. tchr. South-Western City Schs., Grove City, Ohio, 1971-74, tutor, 1974-76; elem. and high sch. tutor Hamilton Local Sch., Columbus, Ohio, 1976-77, elem. tchr. learning disabilities, 1978-85; high sch. tchr. learning disabilities Southwest Licking Local Schs., Kirkersville, Ohio, 1985-86; cons. Cen. Ohio Spl. Edn. Regional Resource Ctr., Columbus, 1987-91, Lincoln Way Spl. Edn. Regional Resource Ctr., Louisville, Ohio, 1991-93; supr. Stark County Sch. Dist., Canton, Ohio, 1993—. Mem. Coun. for Exceptional Children, Coun. for Adminstrs. Spl. Edn., DAR, Order Ea. Star, Phi Delta Kappa. Office: Stark County Sch Dist 2100 38th St NW Canton OH 44709-2312

CUMMINGS, CHARLES WILLIAM, physician, educator; b. Boston, Nov. 16, 1935; s. Harry Blanchard and Madge (Frey) C.; m. Jane Drake Cummings, July 1, 1983; children—Charles William, Lee Blanchard, Evelyn Howard. A.B., Dartmouth Coll., 1957; M.D., U. Va., 1961. Intern Mary Hitchcock Meml. Hosp., Hanover, N.H., 1961-62; resident otolaryngology Harvard U. Med. Sch., 1965-68; assoc. prof. otolaryngology Upstate Med. Sch., SUNY, Syracuse, 1976-78; prof., chmn. dept. otolaryngology-head and neck surgery U. Wash. Med. Sch., Seattle, 1978-91, Johns Hopkins Hosp. and Med. Ctr., Balt., 1991—; chief staff Johns Hopkins Hosp., 1996-98; bd. dirs. Am. Bd. Otolaryngology. Author: Atlas of Laryngeal Surgery; co-author: Comprehensive Text of Otolaryngology-Head and Neck Surgery; contbr. sci. articles to profl. jours. Served to capt., M.C. USAF, 1963-65. Mem. ACS (chmn. adv. coun.), Soc. Head and Neck Surgeons, Am. Soc. for Head and Neck Surgery (sec., pres.), Soc. Univ. Otolaryngologists, Assn. Acad. Depts., Otolaryngology (past pres.), Triological Soc., Laryngological Soc., Bronchoesophagological Soc. (past pres.), Am. Acad. Otolaryngology-Head and Neck Surgery (bd. dirs., past pres.). Episcopalian. Office: Johns Hopkins U Dept Otolaryngology/Head/Neck/Surgery 601 N Caroline St Baltimore MD 21287-0006

CUMMINGS, CONSTANCE, actress; b. Seattle; d. Dallas Vernon and Kate Logan (Cummings) Halverstadt; m. Benn Wolfe Levy, 1933; children: Jonathan, Jemima. Chmn. Young People's Theatre Panel; mem. Arts Council, 1963-69. Broadway debut Treasure Girl, 1928; London debut Sour Grapes, Repertory Players, 1934; film debut Movie Crazy, 1932; appeared on radio, TV, films, theatre; joined Nat. Theatre Co., 1971; appeared in London stage prodns.: Madame Bovary, 1937, Romeo and Juliet, 1939, Saint Joan, 1939, The Petrified Forest, 1942, Return to Tyass, 1950, Lysistrata, 1957, The Rape of the Belt, 1957, Who's Afraid of Virginia Woolf?, 1964, Justice is a Woman, 1966, Fallen Angel, 1967, Nat. Theatre Co., A Long Day's Journey Into Night, 1972, The Cherry Orchard, 1973, The Circle, 1975, Mrs. Warren's Profession, Vienna, 1976, Wings, U.S., 1978, London, 1979 (Tony award 1979), Hay Fever, 1980, The Golden Age, 1981, The Chalk Garden, N.Y.C., 1982, The Glass Menagerie, N.Y.C., London, 1982, (one woman show) Fanny Kemble, 1986, Crown Matrimonial, 1987, Tête a Tête, Mass., 1989, The Chalk Garden, London, 1992, Uncle Vanya, Chichester Theatre, 1996, others; performed in Claudel-Honnegar oratorio St. John at the Stake, Albert Hall, London, 1949, Peter and the Wolf, Albert Hall, 1955, Wings on Am. pub. TV; dir. Royal Ct. Theatre. Recipient Obie award, 1979, Drama Desk award, 1979; decorated Comdr. Brit. Empire. Mem. Brit. Actors Equity (mem. council), Royal Soc. for Encouragement of Arts and Commerce. Mem. Labour Party. Club: Chelsea Arts. *

CUMMINGS, DAROLD BERNARD, aircraft engineer; b. Batavia, N.Y., June 27, 1944; s. Bernard Laverne and Doris Helen (Klotzbach) C.; children from a previous marrage: Carla, Bret; m. Karen Jean Cacciola, Dec. 19, 1992; children: Kyle, Scott. BS in Indsl. Design, Calif. State U., Long Beach, 1967. Engr. aircraft design Rockwell Internat., L.A., 1967-82; chief engr. Boeing, Long Beach, Calif., 1988—; chief designer advanced design Northrop Corp., Hawthorne, Calif., 1982-88; lectr. Calif. State U., Long Beach, 1969-73; pres. Matrix Design, Hawthorne, 1967—; tech. fellow Boeing, 1997. Author: What Not to Name Your Baby, 1982; cons., actor (movie) Search for Solutions, 1979; multiple patents in field. Mem. AIAA, Air Force Assn. Republican. Avocations: prospecting, hunting. Home: 5320 W 124th Pl Hawthorne CA 90250-4154 Office: Boeing Long Beach CA 90807

CUMMINGS, DAVID WILLIAM, artist, educator; b. Okmulgee, Okla., July 15, 1937; s. Harold Raymond and Mildred Delores (Smith) C.; m. Marcia Mills Laging, June 20, 1964 (div. 1970); m. Beatrice M. Mady, Oct. 2, 1981. BFA, Kansas City Art Inst., 1963; MFA, U. Nebr., 1967. Prof. SUNY, New Paltz, 1964-70; adj. instr. Wagner Coll., S.I., N.Y., 1970-71; prof. CUNY, 1971-89; adj. prof. St. Peter's Coll., Jersey City, 1985—; vis. prof. NYU, 1980-82, SUNY, Purchase, 1984, Rochester (N.Y.) Inst. Tech., 1983, U. N.D., Grand Forks, 1982, Colo. Mountain Coll., Vail, 1975-84. One-man shows include Katz Galleries, N.Y.C., 1970, Henri Gallery, Washington, 1969-70, Allan Stone Gallery, N.Y.C., 1974-77, Gallery Alexandra Monett, Brussels, 1975, 77, 78, Sebastian/Moore Gallery, Denver, 1978, Ericson Gallery, N.Y.C., 1981, U. N.D., Grand Forks, 1981, Shahin Requicha Gallery, Rochester, N.Y., 1983, La Petite Galeria, Bayonne, N.J., 1986, Gallery Jupiter, Little Silver, N.J., 1987, A.M.B. Galleries, Hoboken, N.J., Cabrillo Coll. Gallery, Aptos, Calif., 1991, Clin. Ctr. Galleries, NIH, Bethesda, Md., 1993, Rabbet Gallery, New Brunswick, N.J., 1996. Served with U.S. Army, 1957-59. Wood Found. fellow, 1966-67, N.J. State Coun. of Arts fellow, 1985, 91; Ford Found. grantee, 1963.

CUMMINGS, ELIJAH E., congressman; b. Balt., Jan. 18, 1951; m. Joyce Cummings. BS, Howard U., 1973; JD, U. Md., 1976. Bar: Md. 1976. Atty. Md. Gen. Assembly, 1982; mem. Md. Ho. of Dels., Annapolis, 1983-94, 95—, vice chmn. constl. and adminstrv. law com., 1987—, chmn. com. econ. devel., 1996, vice chmn. house econ. matters com., 1994—; mem. transp. subcom. for coast guard and maritime transp., mem. transp. subcom. for water resources and environ. 104th-106th Congress from 7th Md. dist., 1996—, 105th Congress, 1997—; mem. transp. subcom. for aviation and subcom. for surface transportation. Chmn. Md. Legis. Black Caucus; chmn. Gov.'s Commn. on Black Males, 1990—; pres. Bancroft Lit. Soc., Congressional Black Caucus Found. (bd. dirs.) 1998. Named Outstanding U.S. Student Govt. Leader award Royal Arts Soc. of London. Mem. Md. Bar Assn. Office: US Ho of Reps 1632 Longworth Bldg Washington DC 20515-2007*

CUMMINGS, ERIKA HELGA, business consultant; b. Offenbach, Germany; came to U.S., 1978; d. Erwin and Edith (Trunski) Maier; 1 child, Marisa Anne. BSBA, Calif. State U., Bakersfield; MM in Internat. Mgmt., Am. Grad. Sch. Internat. Mgmt., Glendale, Ariz., 1983. Cert. fin. planner. Inflight supr. TWA, Paris; internat. ops. mgr. Cooper LaserSonics, Santa Clara, Calif., 1983-85; bus. cons. Suncoast Bus. Industries, Sarasota, Fla., 1985-89; cert. fin. planner Am. Express Fin. Advisors, Sarasota, 1989-94; bus. cons., 1994—; Peace Corps. vol. City Adminstrn. of Vladimir, Russia, 1994-96; internat. cons. Solutions Internat., Sarasota, Fla., 1996—. Mem. Toastmasters, Beta Gamma Sigma. Avocations: travel, tennis, reading, langs. Home: 5294 Huntingwood Ct Sarasota FL 34235

CUMMINGS, ERWIN KARL, information technology executive; b. Toledo, June 19, 1954; s. Idell and Mae Sue (Jones) C. AS in Electronic Engring., U. Toledo, 1976, BS in Bus. Svcs., 1981; postgrad., Bowling Green State U., 1990-96. Computer ops. analyst Owens-Ill. Inc., Toledo, 1972-73, telecomms. analyst, 1975-78, ops. and planning analyst, 1978-81, software systems analyst, 1981-83, sr. data comms. analyst, 1983-86, lead data comms. analyst, 1986-89, mgr. voice and data comms., 1989-97, mgr. infrastructure and comms., 1997—. Pres. Christian Youth Fellowship, Phillips Temple, 1971-72, young adult tchr., 1971-79, supt. Sunday sch., 1979-81, asst. supt., 1983-87, sec. steward bd., 1983-93, head basketball coach, 1986-87, chmn. budget com., 1988-89; bd. dirs. Rosa Morgan Enrichment Ctr., 1988-92, chmn. fin. com., 1989-92, treas., 1990-92; mem. Christian Appalachian Project, 1989—. Mem. NAACP (life), DAV (Comdrs. Club 1985—), YMCA Century Club, Nat. Assn. Systems Programmers, Black Data Processing Assocs., Sacred Heart Automobile League, TV30/FM91, United Way Comdrs. Club, Handymen of Am. Club (life). Democrat. Methodist. Avocations: personal computing, roller skating, basketball, bicycling, bowling. Home: 1180 Berabh Pky Toledo OH 43615-6742 Office: Owens-Ill Inc 1 Seagate Toledo OH 43604-1558

CUMMINGS, FRANK, lawyer; b. N.Y.C., Dec. 11, 1929; s. Louis and Florence (Levine) C.; m. Jill Schwartz, July 6, 1958; children: Peter Ian, Margaret Anne. BA, Hobart Coll., 1951; MA, Columbia U., 1955, LLB, 1958. Bar: N.Y. 1959, D.C. 1963. Adminstrv. asst. to U.S. Senator Javits, 1969-71; minority counsel com. labor and pub. welfare U.S. Senate, 1965-67, 71-72; assoc. Cravath, Swaine & Moore, N.Y.C., 1958-63, Gall, Lane & Powell, Washington, 1967-68; ptnr. Gall, Lane & Powell, Washington, 1972-75, Marshall, Bratter, Greene, Allison & Tucker, Washington, 1976-82, Nossaman, Krueger & Knox, 1982-83, Cummings & Cummings, P.C. and predecessor firm (Cummings & Kershaw, P.C.), 1983-86, LeBoeuf, Lamb, Greene & MacRae, L.L.P., Washington, 1986—; lectr. law Columbia U. Law Sch., 1970-74; adj. prof. Georgetown U. Law Sch., 1983-86; chmn. Am. Law Inst.-ABA Ann. Course Employee Benefits Litigation, 1989—, Employment and Labor Rels. Law for Corp. Coun. and Gen. Practitioner, 1978—; mem. pub. adv. coun. employee welfare and pension benefit plans Dept. Labor, 1972-74; mem. adv. bd. Pension Reporter Bur. Nat. Affairs. Author: Capitol Hill Manual, 1976, 2nd edit., 1984, Pension Plan Terminations-Single Employer Plans, 2nd edit., 1994, Multiemployer Plans, 2nd edit., 1986; articles editor Columbia U. Law Rev., 1957-58. Mem. ABA (chmn. com. pension, welfare and related plans 1976-79), Am. Law Inst.; Bar Assn. D.C. (chmn. com. labor rels. law 1972-73), Cosmos Club, Phi Beta Kappa. Articles editor Columbia U. Law Rev., 1957-58. Home: 4305 Bradley Ln Chevy Chase MD 20815-5232 Office: LeBoeuf Lamb Greene & MacRae LLP 1875 Connecticut Ave NW Washington DC 20009-5728

CUMMINGS, HENRY SAVAGE CHASE, manufacturing executive; b. Middlefield, Mass., June 17, 1928; s. Henry S.C. and Dorothy S. (Smith) C.; m. Barbara Siegars, Apr. 3, 1950; children: David, Stephen, Janet. BSME, Worcester Polytech. Inst., 1950. Engr. Singer Mfg. Co., Bridgeport, Conn., 1950-51; chmn. Lowell Corp., West Boylston, Mass., 1954—; mem. Pres. Adv. Coun., Worcester, 1968—. Author: Cummings Heritage, 1991, Sinclair Families in America, 1990, Sinclair's Expedition to America, 1995, Geneaology of Prince Henry, 1997. Treas., trustee Becker Coll., Worcester, 1980—; genealogist Clan Sinclair, Duluth, Minn., 1989—; v.p., bd. dirs. Boy Scouts Mohegan Coun., Worcester, 1962-95; chmn. Worcester Heart Assn., 1960-64. Mem. Worcester Rotary Club, Brookline Lodge Masons, SAR. Congregationalist. Avocations: carpentry and woodworking, genealogy, writing, country music. Office: Lowell Corp 65 Hartwell St West Boylston MA 01583-2407

CUMMINGS, JAMES M., urology educator; b. Chattanooga, Mar. 20, 1956; s. James M. and Judith Ann (Mason) C.; m. Toni Rae St. Clair, Aug. 20, 1983; children: Caron, Andrew, Bryant. BS with honors in Chemistry, U. Ala., Tuscaloosa, 1978; MD, U. South Ala., 1982. Diplomate Am. Bd. Urology. Mem. staff Magnolia Hosp., Corinth, Miss., 1987-92, chief surgery, 1989, chief staff, 1991; resident in gen. surgery St. Louis U. Hosps., 1982-84, resident in urology, 1984-87, mem. staff, 1992-97; asst. prof. St. Louis U. Sch. Medicine, 1992-97; assoc. prof. U. South Ala. Coll. Medicine, Mobile, 1997—; mem. staff Knollwood Park Hosp., 1997—, U. South Ala.-Children's and Women's Hosp., 1997—; mem. staff St. Mary's Health Ctr., Cardinal Glennon Children's Hosp., Bethesda Gen. Hosp., 1992-97; presenter in field. Mem. editl. bd., clin. reactor Contemporary Urology; contbr. articles and abstracts to med. jours., chpt. to book. Grantee Am. Found. for Urologic Diseases, SWOG. Mem. Am. Urol. Assn., Am. Assn. Clin. Urologists, Southeastern Sect. Am. Urol. Assn., Med. Assn. State Ala., Urodynamics Soc., Phi Beta Pi. Presbyterian. Avocations: tennis, bicycling, Civil War history. Home: 6705 Ridgeland Rd Mobile AL 36695 Office: U South Ala Med Ctr 2451 Fillingim St Mobile AL 36617-2238

CUMMINGS, JOHN PATRICK, lawyer; b. Westfield, Mass., June 28, 1933; s. Daniel Thoams and Nora (Brick) C.; m. Dorothy June D'Ingianni, Dec. 27, 1957 (div. May 1978); children: John Patrick, Mary Catherine, Michael Brick, Kevin Andrew, Colleen Elise, Erin Christine, Christopher Gerald; m. Marilyn Ann Welch, May 23, 1980. BS, St. Michael's Coll., 1955; PhD, U. Tex., 1969; JD, U. Toledo, 1973, MCE, 1977. Bar: Ohio 1973, U.S. Mil. Appeals 1974, U.S. Dist. Ct. (no. dist.) Ohio 1979. Mgr. Hamilton Mgmt., Inc., Austin, Tex., 1962-68; scientist Owens Ill., Toledo, 1968-73, risk mgr., 1974-76, staff atty., 1977-80, mgr. legis. affairs, 1981-84; pres. Hansa World Cargo Svc., Inc., Oakland, Calif., 1984-86; in-house counsel Brown Vence & Assocs., San Francisco, 1987-88; gen. counsel Pacific

Mgmt. Co., Sacramento, 1986-88; pres. John P. Cummings & Assoc., Fremont, Calif., 1988—; cons. Glass Packaging Inst., Washington, 1970-83, EPA, Washington, 1970-74. Contbr. articles to profl. jours.; patentee in field. With USAF, 1955-62, 68-69, 75-76, 84-85, col. Res. ret. 1986. USPHS fellow, 1963-66. Fellow Royal Chem. Soc.; mem. ABA, VFW, Am. Chem. Soc., ASTM (chmn. 1979), Am. Ceramic Soc. (chpt. chmn. 1973), Res. Officers Assn. (legis. chmn. 1979-85), Am. Legion, KC (4th degree). Roman Catholic. Avocations: reading, travel, coin and stamp collecting. Home: 843 Barcelona Dr Fremont CA 94536-2607 Office: PO Box 2847 Fremont CA 94536-0847

CUMMINGS, JOHN WILLIAM, JR., logistician, systems analyst; b. Washington, Apr. 5, 1942; s. John William Sr. and Helen Gerhold (Schanberger) C.; m. Carol Fron King, July 12, 1964; children: Kathleen Ellen Cummings Maloney, Elizabeth Nan Cummings MacBride, Abigail Helen Cummings Sidell, John William III. BA, Am. U., 1964; MA, U. N.Mex., 1971. Ordained elder, Sunday Sch. supt. Presbyn. Ch. Commd. 2d lt. USAF, 1964, advanced through grades to lt. col., 1980; dep. sys. program mgr. USAF, Warner Robins, Ga., 1984-87; ret., 1987; sys. simulation mgr. Riverside Rsch. Inst., Arlington, Va., 1987-92; mem. tech. staff Analytic Scis. Corp., Arlington, 1992; missile def. program mgr. Dynamics Rsch. Corp., Arlington, 1992—. Asst. editor Logistics Spectrum, 1996—; contbr. articles to profl. jours. Mem. AIAA, Soc. Logistics Engrs. (sr.; chpt. vice chair, Pres.'s award 1996), Air Force Assn., VFW, Ret. Officers Assn. Republican. Avocations: Sunday school teaching and administration, gardening. Home: 17006 Horn Point Dr Gaithersburg MD 20878-2086 Office: Dynamics Rsch Corp 1755 Jefferson Davis Hwy Arlington VA 22202-3509

CUMMINGS, JOSEPHINE ANNA, writer; b. Gainesville, Fla., July 12, 1949; d. Robert Jay and Marcella Dee (Mount) Cummings. A.B.J./Design cum laude, U. Ga., Athens, 1971. Copywriter William Cook, Jacksonville, Fla., 1971-73; creative dir. Leo Burnett, Chgo., 1973-76; sr. v.p., group creative dir. D. D. B. Needham, Chgo., 1976-84; sr. v.p., creative dir. Saatchi-Saatchi, N.Y.C., 1984; sr. v.p., sr. creative dir. Ted Bates, N.Y.C., 1984; exec. v.p., chief creative officer Tracy-Locke, Dallas, 1985-87; exec. v.p., exec. creative dir. Bozell, Chgo, 1989; exec. v.p., creative dir. Y&R, N.Y.C., 1990-92; pres. The Joey Co., N.Y.C., 1992—. Author: (play) Azaleas, 1988, (short story collection) Crimes of Passion, 1988, (childrens' book) The Hospital is a Funny Place, 1988, (short film) Night Magic, 1989. Named as creator One of Hundred Best TV Commls. Advt. Age, 1978-79, one of Advt. 100 Best Advt. Age, 1986, one of People to Watch Fortune mag., 1986, Ad Age one of Best and Brightest, N.Y. Mem. Amelia Earhard, Ninety Niners Club, N.Y. Women in Film. Avocations: reading, writing, juggling. Office: The Joey Co 133 W 19th St Fl 5 New York NY 10011-4117

CUMMINGS, KAREN SUE, corrections classification administrator; b. Ft. Wayne, Ind., July 15, 1939; d. Floyd Henry and Mary Emma (Wolfe) Kneller; m. Oswald Wade Cummings, Feb. 16, 1962; children: Ruth Marie Cummings Everett, John Phillip. BA, Bethal Coll., 1976; MA, Webster U., 1989; grad., Corrections Mgmt. Sch., La., 1991. Sub. tchr. various sch., Mishawaka, Ind., La., 1978-82; classification dir. Work Tng. Facility North La. Dept. Corrections, Pineville, La., 1978-82; eligibility worker Office of Family Security, Alexandria, La., 1982-84; classification officer Work Tng. Facility North La. Dept. Corrections, Pineville, 1984-92, classification dir. Work Tng. Facility North, 1992—. Big sister Big Bros./Big Sisters, Mishawaka, 1974-76, Pineville, 1990-91. With USAF, 1957-62. Mem. Am. Correctional Assn., So. States Corrections Assn. Republican. Baptist. Avocation: travel. Office: Work Tng Facility North 1453 15th St Pineville LA 71360-8718

CUMMINGS, KENNETH ILA, writer, retired dermatologist; b. Athens, La., Mar. 14, 1936; s. Otto L. and Idelle (James) C.; m. (div. 1981); children: Alison, Courney, Kurt, Emily. BS in Liberal Arts, La. Tech. U., 1958; MD, La. State U., New Orleans, 1962; M in Dermatology, Tulane U., 1966. Diplomate Am. Acad. Dermatology. Intern Confederate Meml. Med. Ctr., Shreveport, La., 1962-63; resident Tulane U. Charity Hosp. of La., New Orleans, 1963-66; chief res. dermatology La. State U. Sch. Med., New Orleans, 1965-66; clin. prof. dermatology La. State U. Med. Sch., Shreveport, 1968-87; chief res. dermatology Tulane U. Med. Sch., New Orleans, 1965-66, Charity Hosp. La., New Orleans, 1965-66; instr. U.S. Naval Aerospace Med. Inst., Pensacola, Fla., 1966-68; pvt. practice Shreveport, La., 1968-87; coroner, med. examiner Bienville Parish, Arcadia, La., 1987-96; fed. referee disability cases U.S. Govt., Shreveport, 1972—. Author: (novel) Poppies in the Field, 1998; contbr. articles to profl. jours. Lt. comdr. USNR, 1966-68. Recipient Award for Surg. Treatment for Baldness Tex. Med. Assn., 1967, Peterkin prize La. Dermatol. Soc., 1966. Mem. SAG, Am. Acad. Dermatology, La. State Med. Soc., Shreveport Med. Soc., La. Coroners Assn., Screen Writers Guild. Democrat. Episcopalian. Avocations: nusmismatics, fiction writing, movie acting, freelance work. Home: 3072 Hazel St Arcadia LA 71001-4100

CUMMINGS, KEVIN BRYAN, minister; b. Lake Charles, La., Dec. 8, 1967; s. Kenneth Richard and Sharon Elaine (Kinchen) C.; m. Terri Lynn Pickering, June 11, 1988; children: Brent Andrew, Ashley Lynn. BS cum laude, Liberty U., 1989; M in Biblical Sci., Phila. Coll. Bible, 1995. Ordained to ministry Bapt. Ch., 1989. Camp counselor Milldale Bapt. Teen Retreat, Zachary, La., 1985-86; youth pastor Tamuning (Guam) Bapt. Ch., 1986-87; dir. campus club Thomas Rd. Bapt. Ch., Lynchburg, Va., 1987-88; youth worker Temple Bapt. Ch., Madison Heights, Va., 1988-89; pastor youth and Christian edn. Ch. of the Open Door, Ft. Washington, Pa., 1989-93; asst. pastor Second Cape May Bapt. Ch., Marmora, N.J., 1993-97; sr. pastor Fincastle (Va.) Bapt. Ch., 1997—. Republican. Office: Fincastle Bapt Ch PO Box 707 Fincastle VA 24090-0707 *When all you can do is pray, you have done all you can do!.*

CUMMINGS, LUCILLE MAUD, geriatrics, psychiatric mental health nurse; d. Adrian and Mabel Fuller; m. Elbert Cummings, Mar. 31, 1956. Diploma in nursing, Middlewood Hosp., Shefield, Yorkshire, Eng., 1960; BS in Gerontology cum laude, Mercy Coll., Dobbs Ferry, N.Y., 1981; MS in Gerontology, Coll. of New Rochelle, 1983. RN, Fla. Staff nurse med. psychiat. unit Montefiore Hosp. Med. Ctr., Bronx, N.Y., 1969-71, clin. nurse, 1971-72, coord. patient care, 1972-85; staff nurse gerontology unit Bronx VA Med. Ctr., 1985-86; staff nurse med.-surg. units Humana Mobile Nurse Inc., Louisville, 1986-88; traveling nurse ORMC, Orlando, Fla., 1989; staff nurse Flagler Hosp., St. Augustine, Fla., 1989-90. Mem. Am. Assn. Ret. Persons.

CUMMINGS, LUIS EMILIO, anesthesiologist, consultant; b. Mayagüez, P.R., Nov. 2, 1954; s. Luis and Gladys (Carrero) C.; m. Hazel Ruiz, 1993; 1 child, Luisito. MD, U. P.R., 1979; postgrad., U. Miami, 1983. Diplomate Am. Bd. Anesthesia. Intern U. P.R., 1979-80; resident in anesthesiology Jackson Meml. Hosp., Miami, Fla., 1980-83; cardiovasc. anesthesiologist St. Luke's Episcopal Hosp., Ponce, P.R., 1983—. Mem. P.R. Soc. Anesthesia (pres. 1995—), Caribbean Anesthesia Soc. (bd. dirs. 1992—). Roman Catholic. Avocations: skiing, fishing. Home: Vista Point B-23 Ponce PR 00731 Office: Caribbean Anesthesia Soc PO Box 1790 Ponce PR 00733-1790

CUMMINGS, MARTIN MARC, medical educator, physician, scientific administrator; b. Camden, N.J., Sept. 7, 1920; s. Samuel and Cecelia (Silverman) C.; m. Arlene Sally Avrutine, Sept. 27, 1942; children: Marc Steven, Lee Bernard, Stuart Lewis. BS, Bucknell U., 1941, DS, 1969; MD, Duke U., 1944; DHL (hon.), Georgetown U., 1971; DS. (hon.), Duke U., 1985; DSc, U. Nebr., Emory U.; MD (hon.), Karolinska Inst., 1972, U. Lvov, 1975; DHL, Georgetown U., 1976. Diplomate Am. Bd. Microbiology. Intern, resident Boston Marine Hosp., 1944-46; resident Tb Grasslands Hosp., Valhalla, N.Y., 1946-47; dir. Tb evaluation lab. Communicable Disease Ctr., USPHS, Atlanta, 1947-49; instr. medicine Emory U. Sch. Medicine, 1948-50, assoc. medicine, 1950-52, asst. prof., 1953; chief Tb sect., also dir. Tb research lab. VA Hosp., Atlanta, 1949-53; dir. research services VA Cen. Office, Washington, 1953-59; prof. microbiology, chmn. dept. Okla. U. Sch. Medicine, 1959-61; chief Office Internat. Research, NIH, USPHS, 1961-63; dir. Nat. Library of Medicine, 1964-84, dir. emeritus, 1984—; cons. Council on Library Resources, 1984—; chmn., bd. dirs. Coun. on Libr. Resources, 1994-96; assoc. dir. for research grants NIH, 1963-64; chmn. com. med. research Nat. Tb Assn., 1958-59; chmn. panel Sarcoidosis NRC-Nat. Acad. Scis., 1958-60; dist. prof. community medicine Georgetown U. Sch. Medicine, 1986-90. Author: (with Dr. H.S. Willis) Diagnostic and Experimental Methods in Tuberculosis, 1952, The Economics of Research Libraries, 1986; contbr. chpt. on Tubercle Bacilli, Diagnostic Procedures and Reagents, 1950; editor: Influencing Change in Research Libraries, 1989. Served with AUS, 1943-44. Recipient Exceptional Service award VA, 1959; Distinguished Service award HEW, 1968; Rockefeller Pub. Service award, 1973; Disting. Achievement award Modern Medicine, 1976; Disting. Service award Am. Coll. Cardiology, 1978; John C. Leonard award Assn. Hosp. Med. Edn., 1979. Fellow AAAS (dir.), Royal Soc. Medicine, Med. Libr. Assn., N.Y. Acad. Medicine (hon.), Phila. Coll. Physicians; mem. Am. Soc. Clin. Investigation (sr. mem.), Am. Fedn. Clin. Rsch., Inst. Medicine, Nat. Acad. Scis. Home: 605 Sutton Pl A-402 Longboat Key FL 34228

CUMMINGS, MAXINE GIBSON, elementary school educator; b. Tupelo, Miss., Oct. 7, 1940; d. T. Ruben and Maggie (Ruff) Gibson; m. Willie B. Cummings, Aug. 15, 1964; 1 child, Stanley. BS, Barber-Scotia Coll., Concord, N.C., 1962; MA, Northeastern Ill. U., Chgo., 1974. Cert. tchr., N.C., Ill. Tchr. Walter Reed Elem. Sch., Chgo., 1963-75, reading tchr., 1975-82, social studies tchr., 1982-85; reading resource tchr. Arna Bontemps Sch., Chgo., 1985-91, ESEA lab. tchr., 1991—; mentor tchr. Tchrs. for Chgo. Program, Arna W. Bontemps Sch. Site, 1996—; counselor Westside YWCA, Chgo., 1963-68; chmn. reading com. Bontemps Sch., 1986-92, chmn. activity com., 1992-93; mentor tchr. Bontemps Tchrs. for Chgo. Program; mem. staff devel. team Reading Tchrs. Acad. for Profl. Growth, Chgo. Bd. Edn. Contbr. articles to profl. jours. Mem. Vol. Edna White Century Garden; sec. S.W. Morgan Parkk Civic Assn., Chgo., 1990-92; block rep. Neighborhood Watch Program, Chgo., 1989-90; trustee Morgan Park Presbyn. Ch., peace and justice com., mem. choir; Great Books Discussion leader Walker Br. Libr. Grantee Chgo.-Incentive, 1987, NEH, 1984, Northeastern Ill. U., 1980; recipient Regional Cmty. Gardening award, Morgan Park Neighborhood, Chgo., 1998 May Daley's Landscpae Improvement Program award, 1999. Mem. Minority Students of Chgo. Area (recruiter), Barber-Scotia Alumni Club (sec. 1989-92), Pi Lambda Theta. Avocations: biking, walking, reading, travel, gardening. Home: 11116 S Longwood Dr Chicago IL 60643-4043 Office: Bontemps Elem Sch 1241 W 58th St Chicago IL 60636-1994

CUMMINGS, MELVIN O'NEAL, educator elementary school, administrator; b. Mubane, N.C., Apr. 8, 1954; s. Fred and Dorothy C. BS, Okla. City Schs., 1980; MA, Jersey City State Coll., 1986. Cert. elem. tchr., supr., prin. N.J. Basic skills tchr. Orange Twp. Pub. Schs., Orange, N.J., 1986-89; tchr. Newark Pub. Schs., 1989-93; supr. Camden (N.J.) City Pub. Schs., 1993—. Mem. N.J. State Commn. to Adopt African-Am. children, 1993-96. Sgt. USAF, 1972-76. Mem. ASCD, Internat. Reading Assn., N.J. Prins. and Suprs. Assn., Nat. Alliance Black Sch. Educators, N.J. Alliance Black Sch. Educators (v.p. 1994-95), Kappa Alpha Psi (asst. keeper of records 1995-99). Baptist. Avocation: golf. Office: Camden City Pub Schs 201 N Front St Camden NJ 08043

CUMMINGS, NICHOLAS ANDREW, psychologist; b. Salinas, Calif., July 25, 1924; s. Andrew and Urania (Sims) C.; m. Dorothy Mills, Feb. 5, 1948; children: Janet Lynn, Andrew Mark. AB, U. Calif., Berkeley, 1948; MA, Claremont Grad. Sch., 1954; PhD, Adelphi U., 1958. Chief psychologist Kaiser Permanente No. Calif., San Francisco, 1959-76; pres. Found Behavioral Health, San Francisco, 1976—; chmn., CEO Am. Biodyne, Inc., San Francisco, 1985-93, Kendron Internat., Ltd., Reno, Nev., 1992-95; chmn. Nicholas & Dorothy Cummings Found., Reno, 1994—; chmn., pres. U.K. Behavioural Health, Ltd., London, 1996-98; Disting. prof. U. Nev., 1997—; chmn., CEO DynaMed Integrated Care, Inc., 1998—; co-dir. South San Francisco Health Ctr., 1959-75; pres. Calif. Sch. Profl. Psychology, L.A., San Francisco, San Diego, Fresno campuses, 1969-76; chmn. bd. Calif. Cmty. Mental Health Ctrs., Inc., L.A., San Diego, San Francisco, 1975-77; pres. Blue Psi, Inc., San Francisco, 1972-80, Inst. for Psychosocial Interaction, 1980-84; mem. mental health adv. bd. City and County San Francisco, 1968-75; bd. dirs. San Francisco Assn. Mental Health, 1965-75; pres., chmn. bd. Psycho-Social Inst., 1972-80; dir. Mental Rsch. Inst., Palo Alto, Calif., 1979-80; pres. Nat. Acads. of Practice, 1981-93. Served with U.S. Army, 1944-46. Fellow Am. Psychol. Assn. (dir. 1975-81, pres. 1979); mem. Calif. Psychol. Assn. (pres. 1968). Office: Nicholas & Dorothy Cummings Found 561 Keystone Ave PMB 212 Reno NV 89503-4331

CUMMINGS, PATRICIA ANN (FELICIA MARGARITA CRUZ), writer, journalist, poet; b. El Paso, Tex., Nov. 19, 1963; d. Herman Charles Cummings and Felicia Cruz. Diploma, Inst. Children's Lit., 1989, 92, 96. Cert. associated journalist. Poet World Poetry, L.A., 1980-85; poet, editor Poets Inc., El Paso, 1985-88; pvt. practice El Paso, 1993—; instr. poetry Cath. Ch., El Paso, 1992—, instr. writing, 1993—. Author: I Will Sail My Vessel, 1993 (1st Pl. 1994); author numerous poems. Recipient Golden Poet award Poetry World, 1985, 86, Silver Poet award Poetry World, 1989; named Outstanding Journalist, City News Svc., 1992. Mem. Am. Acad. Poets (contbg. mem.), Poetry Soc. Am. (contbg. mem.). Democrat. Roman Catholic. Avocations: motocross, arenacross, supercross. Home: 6231 Trowbridge El Paso TX 79905

CUMMINGS, PATRICK HENRY, manufacturing executive; b. Cleve., May 3, 1941; s. Henry Patrick and Ruth (Farrell) C.; m. Sharon Lynn Slama; children: Dawn, Kelly, Patrick. BS in Indsl. Engring., GMI Engring. and Mgmt. Inst., 1964. Prodn. analyst Euclid (Ohio) Div. Gen. Motors Corp., 1964-65; methods engr. Euclid Div. Gen. Motors Corp., Hudson, Ohio, 1965-68, supr. parts, methods and warehouse Terex div., 1968-71, gen. supr., prodn. planning Terex div., 1972; parts mgr. Lorain div. Koehring Co., Chattanooga, 1973-74, material control mgr. Lorain div., 1974-77; materials mgr. Robbins div. Joy Mfg. Co., Birmingham, Ala., 1977-80; materials mgr. Unit Rig and Equipment Co., Tulsa, 1980-85; data processing mgr. Kendavis Holding Co., Ft. Worth, 1985-87; info. svcs. mgr. Stratoflex Aerospace & Mil. Connectors div. Parker Hannifin, Ft. Worth, 1987-89, materials mgr., 1990—. Republican. Roman Catholic. Home: 5716 Guadalajara Dr Fort Worth TX 76180-6122 Office: Parker Hannifin Stratoflex Aero/Mil Connecters Div PO Box 10398 Fort Worth TX 76114-0398

CUMMINGS, RALPH WALDO, soil scientist, educator, researcher; b. Reidsville, N.C., Dec. 13, 1911; s. William and Sarah Elizabeth (Huffines) C.; m. Mary Parrish, June 22, 1936 (dec. mar. 1989); children: Ralph Waldo, Walter B., William K., Mary Ann; m. Eunice Perkinson, Oct. 16, 1993. BS, N.C. State U., 1933; PhD, Ohio State U., 1938, DSc (hon.), 1992; DSc (hon.), Nehru U., India, 1967, Punjab U., India, 1970, Pant U., India, 1971, N.C. State U., 1968; EdD, Ohio State U., 1992. From asst. prof. soil tech. to assoc. prof. Cornell U., Ithaca, N.Y., 1937-42; prof., head dept. agronomy N.C. State U., Raleigh, 1942-47, prof. emeritus, 1977—; from assoc. dir. to dir. N.C. Agrl. Expt. Sta., 1948-54; chief N.C. Agrl. Rsch. Mission to Peru USAID, 1955-56; field dir., prin. rep. Rockefeller Found., India, 1957-66; assoc. dir. for agrl. scis. Rockefeller Found., N.Y.C., 1964-68; adminstrv. dean for rsch. N.C. State U., Raleigh, 1969-71; program adviser in agrl. for Asia and the Pacific Ford Found., 1971-72; chmn. tech. adv. com. Internat. Agrl. Rsch., 1977-82; acting dir. gen. Internat. Irrigation Mgmt. Inst., 1983-84; asst. dir. N.C. Agrl. Expt. Sta., 1945-47; adj. prof. N.C. State U., Raleigh, 1971-74; dir. Internat. Rice Rsch. Inst., 1972, Internat. Crops Rsch. Inst. for the Semi-Arid Tropics, 1972-77; many missions in connection with U.S. aid to third world countries, including: chmn. Agrl. Univs. Commn., Govt. India; mem. Task Force for Devel. Recommendations for Establishing S.E. Asian Ctr. for Rsch. and Postgrad. Studies in Agr.; vice chmn. NAS Study Team on Agrl. Tsch. Capabilities for Africa. Recipient Centennial award for svc. to agr. Ohio State U., Presdl. End Hunger award U.S. AID and State Dept., 1988, Disting. Svc. award Soil Sci. Soc. Am., 1992, Ohio State U. Alumni Assn. Medalist award for disting. svc., 1993, Watauga medal, N.C. State U., 1995; named Jenkatreddy Venkat Reddy Meml. lectr., 1976, Lal Bahadur Shastri Meml. lectr., New Delhi, 1979, Kellogg Meml. lectr. Am. Assn. State Colls. and Univs., 1980; Cummings Lab in Indian Agrl. Rsch. Inst. named in his honor. Fellow Am. Soc. Agronomy, Am. Acad. Arts and Scis.; mem. Rotary Club (v.p. Raleigh chpt. 1952-53, pres. 1953-54). Democrat. Presbyterian. Home: 812 Rosemont Ave Raleigh NC 27607-6924

CUMMINGS, RICHARD J., otologist; b. Topeka, Nov. 18, 1932; s. John Edward and Mary J. (Harrington) C.; m. Laura Roberta Herring, Dec. 21, 1956; children: Thomas, Anne, William, John. BA, U. Kans., 1954, MD, 1957. Intern St. Benedict Hosp., Ogden, Utah, 1957-58; resident U. Okla. Med. Ctr., Oklahoma City, 1959-62; practice medicine specializing in ear, nose, throat Colorado Springs Med. Clinic, Colo., 1961-62; practice medicine specializing in otology Wichita (Kans.) Ear Clinic, 1962—; clin. asst. prof. U. Kans. Sch. Medicine; pres. med. staff St. Francis Hosp., Wichita, 1974-75; mem. med. staff St. Joseph Hosp., Wichita, pres., 1990-91; host M.D. Radio program, Wichita, 1978-79. Contbr. articles to med. jours. Bd. dirs. Kans. State Bd. of Healing Arts, 1981-83, Kans. Commn. for Deaf and Hearing Impaired, 1988-91, Newman U., 1995—; mem. Kans. tissue transplantation com. ARC, 1990-94; chmn. St. Joseph Charity Classic Tournament, 1981; physician's group chmn. United Way Campaign, 1968, 69, 77, 84; mem. U. Kans. Athletic Bd., 1991-95. With USPHS, 1958-59. Fellow ACP, ACS, Am. Acad. Otolaryngology; mem. AMA, Am. Audiol. Soc., Kans. Med. Soc., Kans. Ear Nose Throat Soc. (pres. 1975), Wichita Surg. Soc. (pres. 1989), Sedgwick County Med. Soc. (pres. 1978), Otosclerosis Study Group, Hearing Conservation Assn., Pan Am. Soc. Otolaryngology, Wichita Cochlear Implant Program (bd. dirs.), Rotary (bd. dirs. Wichita chpt. 1978-79), U. Kans. Nat. Alumni Assn. (bd. dirs. 1979-84, vice chmn. 1994-95, chmn. 1995-96). Home: 1258 Burning Tree Dr Wichita KS 67230-1410 Office: 427 N Hillside St Wichita KS 67214-4917

CUMMINGS, SAM R., federal judge; b. 1944. BBA with high honors, Tex. Tech. U., 1967; JD cum laude, Baylor U., 1970. With Culton, Morgan, Britain & White, Amarillo, Tex., 1970-87; dist. judge No. Dist. Tex., Lubbock, 1987—. Com. chmn. Troop 86, Boy Scouts Am., Amarillo; trustee Presbyn. Children's Home, Amarillo, Howard Payne U., Brownwood, Tex. Recipient Wall St. Jour. award, Am. Jurisprudence award; Judge Hunter D. Barrow Meml. scholar Baylor U. Sch. Law. Mem. Kiwanis (v.p. South Amarillo club). Office: US Dist Ct 1205 Texas Ave Rm 210C Lubbock TX 79401*

CUMMINGS, VIRGINIA (JEANNE), retired real estate company executive; b. Greenwood, S.C., June 24; d. Samuel Barksdale and Alma Virginia (Davis) Jones; m. John W. Cummings, Nov. 7, 1938; children: John W. Jr., Martha (Cummings) Wells. Student, U. Miami; PhD (hon.), Colo. State Christian Coll., 1973. Sec. Pine Crest Pvt. Sch., Ft. Lauderdale, Fla.; founder Cummings Realty Inc., Ft. Lauderdale, 1962-85; v.p. Magic Carpet Travel, Ft. Lauderdale, 1975-89; pres. Women's Coun. Ft. Lauderdale Bd. Realtors, 1961; freelance writer. Feature writer Fla. Living Mag.; contbr. articles to profl. jours. Bd. dirs., past chmn. Ch. of Religious Sci., Ft. Lauderdale. Mem. Opera Soc., DAR. Democrat. Avocations: piano, languages, travel, reading, dancing. Home: 4300 N Ocean Blvd Apt 19a-b Fort Lauderdale FL 33308-5944

CUMMINGS, WILLIAM ROBERT, JR., business executive; b. Detroit, July 13, 1937; s. William Robert Sr. and Geraldine Alberta (Leffel) C.; children: William, Michael. B of Gen. Studies in Math., U. Nebr., 1970. Commd. 2nd lt. USAF, 1959, advanced through grades to lt. col., 1975, ret., 1978; owner Bill's Shell Svc., Ft. Wayne, Ind., 1980-97, Cummings Shell Svc., Ft. Wayne, 1980-96; owner Cummings Shell Svc. II, Ft. Wayne, 1993-97, ret., 1997; bd. dirs., vice chmn. Northeastern Rural Electric Mgmt. Coop., Columbia City, 1986; bd. dirs. Wabash Valley Power Assn. Arbitrator Better Bus. Bur., Ft. Wayne; ward chmn. Rep. Party. Decorated Air medal with thirteen oak leaf clusters, Meritorious Svc. medal with oak leaf clusters, Cross of Gallantry with Palm. Mem. Air Force Assn. (life, state pres. Ind.), Order of Daedalians (life). Republican. Home: 12031 Mahogany Dr Fort Wayne IN 46804-4513

CUMMINGS PERSELLIN, DIANE Y., music education educator; b. Jamestown, N.D., June 4, 1952; d. Kent Barber and Floyce Delores (Smith) Cummings; m. Robert H. Persellin, June 14, 1986. BS in Edn., U. N.D., 1974, MS in Edn., 1977; EdD, Ariz. State U., 1981. Music educator Elk River (Minn.) Sch. Dist., 1974-76; instr. music Mayville (N.D.) State U., 1977-78, Ariz. State U., Tempe, 1978-81; prof. music Trinity U., San Antonio, Tex., 1981—; edn. cons. San Antonio Symphony, 1992-95; mem. adv. bd. San Antonio Boys Choir, 1991-94; conducted many nat. and internat. presentations on music edn. Assoc. editor: Strategies for Teaching College Music Methods, 1997; mem. editl. bd. Jour. Music Tchr. Edn., 1993—; chair rev. com. Southwestern Musician, 1991-97; author numerous profl. articles and book chpts. Bd. dirs. San Antonio Women's Hall of Fame, 1998—; chair edn. com. San Antonio Symphony, 1998—. Named to San Antonio Women's Hall of Fame, 1997. Mem. Tex. Coalition for Music Edn. (pres. 1997-98), Tex. Music Educators Conf. (pres. 1998—), Ctrl. Tex. Orff Assn. (coll. liaison 1994-97), Music Educators Nat. conf. (S.W. divsn. bd. dirs. 1998—), Tex. Music Educators Assn., San Antonio Chamber Music Soc. (bd. dirs. 1984-87, faculty senate sec. 1986-90). Avocations: running, church organist. Office: Trinity U Dept Music 715 Stadium Dr San Antonio TX 78212-3104

CUMMINGS-SAXTON, JAMES, chemical engineer, consultant, educator; b. Pitts., Dec. 5, 1936; s. James Allen and Margaret Mary (Helsel) Saxton; m. Carolyn Cummings, Aug. 22, 1959; children: Megan Caitlin Cummings-Krueger, James Cummings Saxton, Jennifer Aine. B Engring. Sci. in Chem. Engring., Johns Hopkins U., 1959; PhD in Chem. Engring., U. Calif., Berkeley, 1966. Registered profl. engr., D.C. Supr. Bellcomm, Washington, 1964-71; sr. v.p. Internat. Rsch. & Tech., Washington, 1971-79; dep. tech. dir. internat. energy program Argonne (Ill.) Nat. Lab., 1979-83; prin. Indsl. Econs., Inc., Cambridge, Mass., 1983—; instr. chem. engring. Cath. U. Am., Washington, 1974-75, Ill. Inst. Tech., Chgo., 1979-80; rsch. assoc. prof. Clark U., Worcester, Mass., 1994—. Mem. AIChE (pres. Boston sect. 1993-94), Lions (pres. Nahant, Mass. 1993-95). Unitarian. Avocations: hiking, biking, reading. Home: 40 Summer St Nahant MA 01908-1437 Office: Indsl Econs Inc 2067 Massachusetts Ave Cambridge MA 02140-1340

CUMMINS, CHARLES FITCH, JR., lawyer; b. Lansing, Mich., Aug. 19, 1939; s. Charles F. Sr. and Ruth M. Cummins; m. Anne Warner, Feb. 11, 1961; children: Michael, John, Mark. AB in Econs., U. Mich., 1961; LLB, U. Calif., Hastings, 1966. Bar: Calif. 1966, Mich. 1976. Assoc. Hall, Henry, Oliver & McReavy, San Francisco, 1966-70, ptnr., 1971-75; ptnr. Cummins & Cummins, Lansing, Mich., 1976-82, Pitto & Ubhaus, San Jose, Calif., 1982-85; prin. Law Offices Charles F. Cummins Jr., San Jose, 1985-87; ptnr. Cummins & Chandler, San Jose, 1987-92; prin. Law Offices of Charles F. Cummins, Jr., San Jose, 1992—. Bd. dirs., officer various civic orgns., chs. and pvt. shcs. Lt. (j.g.) USNR, 1961-63. Mem. Kiwanis. Office: 4 N 2nd St Ste 1230 San Jose CA 95113-1307

CUMMINS, DELMER DUANE, academic administrator, historian; b. Dawson, Nebr., June 4, 1935; s. Delmer H. and Ina Z. (Arnold) C.; m. Darla Sue Beard, Oct. 6, 1957; children: Stephen Duane, Cristi Sue, Caroline Renee. BS, Phillips U., Enid, Okla., 1957; MA, U. Denver, 1965; PhD, U. Okla., 1974; LLD, Williams Woods Coll., 1979; HHD (hon.), Phillips U., 1983; DLitt (hon.), Chapman U., 1996. Tchr., Jefferson County Pub. Schs., Denver, 1956-67; mem. faculty Oklahoma City U., 1967-77, Darbeth-Whitten prof. history, 1974-77, curator George Shirk Collection, 1977; chmn. dept. history Oklahoma City U., 1969-72; dir. Robert A. Taft Inst. Govt., 1972-77; pres. div. higher edn. Christian Ch., 1978-88; pres. Bethany (W.Va.) Coll., 1988—; bd. dirs. Wesbanco Bank and Trust. Author: The American Frontier, 1968, 3d edit., 1978, Origins of the Civil War, 1971, 2d edit., 1978, The American Revolution, 1968, 3d edit., 1978, Contrasting Decades, 1920's and 1930's, 1972, 2d edit., 1978, Consensus and Turmoil, 1972, William R. Leigh: Biography of a Western Artist, 1980, A Handbook for Today's Disciples, 1981, 2d edit., 1991, (with D. Hohweller) An Enlisted Soldier's View of the Civil War, 1981, (with others) Seeking God's Peace in a Nuclear Age, 1985, The Disciples Colleges: A History, 1987, The Search for Indentity, Disciples Of Christ-The Restructure Years, 1987; editor The Disciples Theol. Digest, 1986-88; contbr. articles to profl. jours. Trustee Culver-Stockton Coll., 1978-88, Tougaloo Coll., 1978-88, vice chmn., 1985-88; Danforth assoc., 1976-78; moderator, active multiple nat. bds. and task forces Christian Ch., 1993-95; mem. Pitts. Opera Bd., 1996—. Mem. Okla. Council Humanities (grantee 1974), Phillips U. Alumni Assn. (pres. 1975-76), Nat. Assn. Ind. Colls. and Univs. (secretariat, policy commn. 1990-94), chair pres.'s athletic conf. 1990-92), W.Va. Assn. Ind. Colls. (chair 1994-97, chair east ctrl. coll. consortium 1997-98), Co. of Ind. Colls. (bd. dirs. 1998—).

Home: Bethany Coll Pendleton Heights Bethany WV 26032 Office: Bethany Coll Old Main Bethany WV 26032

CUMMINS, HERMAN ZACHARY, physicist; b. Rochester, N.Y., Apr. 23, 1933; s. Louis H. and Rhoda Edith (Kitay) C.; m. Marsha Z. Hirsch, Aug. 18, 1963. B.S., M.S., Ohio State U., 1956; Diplome d'Etudes Superieures (Fulbright fellow), U. Paris, 1957; Ph.D., Columbia U., 1963; D honoris causa, U. P. et M. Curie, 1999. Research asso. Columbia U., N.Y.C., 1963-64; asst. prof. physics Johns Hopkins U., Balt, 1964-67; asso. prof. Johns Hopkins U., 1967-69, prof., 1969-71; prof. physics N.Y..U., 1971-73; distinguished prof. physics City Coll., CUNY, 1973—. Guggenheim fellow, 1984-85; Sloan fellow, 1969-72; recipient von Humboldt Sr. Rsch. award, 1998. Fellow Am. Phys. Soc., N.Y. Acad. Scis.; mem. NAS. Research in laser light scattering physics, phase transititions and critical phenomena, solid state and biophysics. Office: City Coll CUNY Dept Physics New York NY 10031

CUMMINS, HOWARD WALLACE, lawyer; b. Portland, Oreg., May 4, 1937; s. Robert Vinton and Lenore Ethel (Lindholm) C.; m. Susan Roberta Smith, Dec. 21, 1969 (div. Apr. 1982); children: Mark, Jason. BA, Stanford U., 1959; JD, Golden Gate U., 1964; MA, U. Oreg., 1968, PhD, 1972. Asst. prof. U. Alta., Edmonton, 1969-74, assoc. prof., 1974-78; legis. liaison Bd. Commrs., Lane County, Oreg., 1979; adminstrv. asst. Congressman Jim Weaver 4th Dist. Oreg., 1984-86; CEO, rsch. dir. Profiles Northwest, Portland, 1980-92; rsch. dir., adj. rsch. dir. Portland State U., 1987—; dir. Radlaw, Washington, 1992-95; mng. ptnr. Cummins & Brown, Washington, 1995-99; pres. Cummins & Assoc., Washington, 1999—; pres., CEO Environ. Svcs. Group Internat., Inc., Washington, 1999—; host, commentator Radio Noon Show, CBC/Radio Can., Edmonton, 1972-76, freelance interviewer pub. affairs divsn., 1970-73; guest commentator CTV and ITV TV Networks, Edmonton, 1971-73; v.p. Garneau Cmty. League, 1974-75; jour. referee Sage Profl. Papers in Internat. Studies, 1974, Gonzaga Law Rev., 1995; mem. panel Can. Inst. Internat. Affairs, Edmonton, 1970; spkr. Christian Fellowship Conf., Edmonton, 1970, Hinton Citizens Conf., Edmonton, 1970, Can. Inst. Internat. Affairs, Calgary, 1972, U. Alta., Edmonton, 1972, Hinton Citzens Edn. Coun., 1971, U. Alta., 1972; dir. Western Regional Symposium on Instrnl. Simulations, Edmonton, 1971; mem. planning commn. Athabasca U., Edmonton, 1972, mem. seminar on human cmty. studies program, 1972; chmn. panel Western Polit. Sci. Assn., L.A., 1978; keynote spkr. Nat. Assn. Radiation Survival Nat. conf., Seattle, 1991, Nat. Assn. Atomic Vets. Nat. conf., Orlando, Fla., 1991, Hanford Concerns of Wash. conf., Spokane, 1992, Healing Global Wounds conf., Las Vegas, Nev., 1992; mem. univ. coll. health phsyics adv. bd. U. Md., 1992—. Contbr. articles to profl. jours. Bd. dirs. Centennial Montessori Sch., 1973-76; treas. Oregonians for McCarthy, 1968-69. Capt. U.S. Army, 1962-66. Mem. ABA (criminal law sect., task force on proposed protocols for future war crimes tribunal), ATLA, Am. Polit. Sci. Assn., Pa. Bar Assn. Avocations: travel, fitness, writing. Office: Cummins & Brown 5039 Connecticut Ave NW Washington DC 20008-2056

CUMMINS, JAMES DUANE, correspondent, media executive; b. Cedar Rapids, Iowa, Mar. 11, 1945; s. Dewey Homer and Dorothy Marie (Colgan) C.; m. Constance Marie Driscoll, July 27, 1968; children: Kimberly, Christine, Douglas, John, Molly, Bill. BS in journalism, Northwestern U., 1967, MS in journalism, 1968. News reporter Sta. KGLO-TV, Mason City, Iowa, 1969-70, Sta. WOOD-TV, Grand Rapids, Mich., 1970-73, Sta. WTMJ-TV, Milw., 1973-75, Sta. WMAQ-TV, Chgo., 1975-78; corr. NBC News, Chgo., 1978-89; corr./bur. chief NBC News, Dallas, 1989—. Corr. (news reports) Civil War-El Salvador, 1981, Korean Airline Disaster, 1983, Hurricane Hugo, 1989, Waco Standoff, 1993, Calif. Earthquake, 1994, Okla. City Bombing, 1995. Recipient Nat. News Emmy award for "Floods", 1993, Emmy award Chgo. TV Acad., 1976. Mem. Northwestern U. Sch. Journalism Alumni Assn., Northwestern U. N Men's Club, Sigma Delta Chi (journalism soc.). Roman Catholic. Avocations: reading, swimming, golf, fishing. Home: 5815 Flintshire Ln Dallas TX 75252-5132 Office: NBC News 3100 Mckinnon St Dallas TX 75201-7003

CUMMINS, JOHN STEPHEN, bishop; b. Oakland, Calif., Mar. 3, 1928; s. Michael and Mary (Connolly) C. A.B., St. Patrick's Coll., 1949. Ordained priest Roman Catholic Ch., 1953; asst. pastor Mission Dolores Ch., San Francisco, 1953-57; mem. faculty Bishop O'Dowd High Sch., Oakland, 1957-62; chancellor Diocese of Oakland, 1962-71; rev. monsignor, 1962, domestic prelate, 1967; exec. dir. Calif. Cath. Conf., Sacramento, 1971-77; consecrated bishop, 1974; aux. bishop of Sacramento, 1974-77; bishop of Oakland, 1977—; Campus minister San Francisco State Coll., 1953-57, Mills Coll., Oakland, 1957-71; Trustee St. Mary's Coll., 1968-79. Home: 634 21st St Oakland CA 94612-1608 Office: Oakland Diocese 2900 Lakeshore Ave Oakland CA 94610-3614*

CUMMINS, KENNETH BURDETTE, retired science and mathematics educator; b. New Washington, Ohio, July 27, 1911; s. Royal Clinton and Pearl (Rittenour) C. A.B., Ohio Wesleyan U., 1933; M.A., Bowling Green State U., 1939; Ph.D., Ohio State U., 1958. Tchr. sci. and math. Sulphur Springs (Ohio) High Sch., 1933-40; tchr. sci. and math. New Washington High Sch., 1941-57; asst. prof. math. Kent State U., 1957-59, assoc. prof., 1959-64, prof., 1964-81, emeritus prof., 1981—; chmn. dept., 1964-65; Dir. Math. Inst., NSF, 1959-73. Author: Teaching of Mathematics, 1970; Contbr. articles to profl. jours. Recipient alumni award for distinguished teaching Kent State U., 1968, 76, President's medal, 1981; Christofferson-Fawcett Math. Edn. award Ohio, 1981. Mem. Math. Assn. Am., Nat. Coun. Tchrs. Math., Cen. Assn. Sci. and Math. Tchrs., Ohio Acad. Sci., Mortar Board, Phi Beta Kappa, Sigma Xi, Sigma Pi Sigma, Pi Mu Epsilon, Kappa Delta Pi. Home: 421 S Center St New Washington OH 44854-9711 Office: Math Dept Kent State U Kent OH 44242*

CUMMINS, PAUL ZACH, II, insurance company executive; b. Fitchburg, Mass., May 1, 1936; s. Paul Z. and Camille M. (Hook) C.; children: Paul Zach III, Colleen Elizabeth. BS, U.S. Naval Acad., 1958, MS, 1964. Mgr., engring. liaison Carrier Corp., Syracuse, N.Y., 1969-73; mgr. systems, mfg. group Republic Steel Corp., Youngstown, Ohio, 1973-74, mgr., bus. planning, 1974-76; dir. adminstrn. planning Republic Builders Products Corp., Atlanta, 1976-77; dir. corporate strategy and devel. Blue Cross/Blue Shield of Md., 1978-89, cons. internal ops., 1989-92; ind. cons., 1992—; instr. U.S. Naval Acad., Annapolis, 1964-65. Stratex Study mem. Dept. Def., 1967-68; past chmn., mem. Md. Gov.'s Vietnam and Disabled Vets. Bus. Resource Coun., SBA Adv. Bd. Balt. Dist. With USN, 1958-69. Decorated Joint Svc. Commendation medal. Mem. U.S. Naval Acad. Alumni Assn., Am. Legion, Kiwanis (past pres. Liverpool, N.Y., past pres. Camillus, N.Y.). Methodist. Home: 16933 Flickerwood Rd Parkton MD 21120-9767

CUMMIS, CLIVE SANFORD, lawyer; b. Newark, Nov. 21, 1928; s. Joseph Jack and Lee (Berkie) C.; m. Ann Denburg, Mar. 24, 1956; children: Andrea, Deborah, Cynthia, Jessica. A.B., Tulane U., 1949; J.D., U. Pa., 1952; LL.M., N.Y. U., 1959. Bar: N.J. 1952. Law sec. Hon. Walter Freund, Appellate Div., Superior Ct., 1955-56; partner firm Cummis & Kroner, Newark, 1956-60; chief counsel County and Mcpl. Law Revision Commn., State of N.J., Newark, 1959-62; partner firm Schiff, Cummis & Kent, Newark, 1962-67, Cummis, Kent, Radin & Tischman, Newark, 1967-70; sr. v.p., dir. Cadence Industries, N.Y.C., 1967-70; dir. Plume & Atwood Industries, Stamford, Conn., 1969-71; chmn. Sills Cummis Radin Tischman Epstein & Gross, Newark, 1970—; dir. Essex County State Bank, Financial Resources Group; instr. Practising Law Inst. Chief counsel County and Mcpl. Revision Commn., 1959-62, N.J. Pub. Market Commn., 1961-63; counsel Bd. Edn. of South Orange and Maplewood, 1964-74, Town of Cedar Grove, 1966-70, Bd. Edn. of Dumont, 1968-72; mem. com. on rules and civil practice N.J. Supreme Ct., 1975-78. Assoc. editor NJ. Law Jour., 1961—. Trustee Newark Beth Israel Med. Ctr., 1965-75, Northfield YM-YWHA, 1968-70, U. Medicine and Dentistry N.J., 1980-84, Newark Mus., N.J. Performing Arts Ctr., Blue Cross and Blue Shield N.J.; gen. coun. N.J. Turnpike Authority, 1990-94; mem. bd. overseers U. Pa. Law Sch.; mem. bd. govs. Daus. of Israel Home for Aged, 1968-70; mem. N.J. Commn. on Statue of Liberty; mem. pres.'s coun. Tulane U., 1992—; pres. bd. dirs. Tulane Assocs., 1994-96; mem. Pres.'s commn. on White House Fellows, 1993—; dir. N.J. Regional Planning Assn. Recipient 1st Ann. Judge Learned Hand award Am. Jewish Com., 1994. 'ellow Am. Bar Found.; mem. ABA, Am. Law Inst., Am. Judicature Soc., U. Pa. Law Sch. Alumni Soc. (pres.), N.J. Bar Assn., Essex County Bar Assn., City Athletic Club (N.Y.C.), Greenbrook County Club (North Caldwell, N.J.), Stockbridge Golf Club (Mass.). Democrat. Jewish. Office: Sills Cummis Radin Tischman Epstein & Gross One Riverfront Pl Newark NJ 07102

CUMMISKEY, J. KENNETH, former college president; b. Boston, Nov. 18, 1928; s. Joseph K. and Helen F. (Penney) C.; m. Joan Lydia Ross, Aug. 13, 1953; children: Lynn Anne, David Ross. BS., Springfield Coll., 1952; M.Ed., Oreg. State U., 1953; Ph.D., Stanford U., 1963. Tchr., coach Sweet Home (Oreg.) High Sch., 1953-55; asso. prof. edn. phys. edn., coach Oreg. Coll. Edn., 1955-65; asso. dir. Peace Corps, Morocco, 1965-66; supr. edn. programs Tng. Corp. Am.; dir. headstart tng. programs Territory of Guam, Islands of Trust Territories, 1966-68; dir. community services project Am. Assn. Jr. Colls., 1968-71; exec. dir. Nat. Council Community Services, 1970-72; v.p. acad. affairs New Eng. Coll., Henniker, N.H., 1971-73; pres. New Eng. Coll., 1973-81, pres. emeritus, 1981—; fin. cons., 1988—; mem. N.H. Postsecondary Edn. Commn., 1978-84; auditor Henniker, 1977-80; mediator N.H. Public Employee Labor Relations Bd., 1977-81; steering com. N.H. Common Cause, 1975-81; bd. advisers Merrimack Valley Coll., 1981-84; mem. N.H. Commn. to Study Impact of Tax-Exempt Non-Fed. Instl. Property on Localities, 1979-81; mem. exec. com. New Eng.-China Consortium, 1981-84. Author works in field; mem. adv. bd.: Community Edn. Jour., 1970-73; editorial bd.: Jour. Edn, 1971-73. Served with U.S. Army, 1946-48, 51-54. Fellow Royal Soc. Arts; Mem. NEA, Am. Psychol. Assn., Nat. Council Community Services and Continuing Edn., Am. Assn. Higher Edn., N.H. Coll. and Univ. Council (pres. 1979-81), Phi Delta Kappa. Unitarian. Clubs: Univ. (N.Y.C.); Arundel Yacht. Home: Rust Island 39 Ye Old County Rd Gloucester MA 01930-2115 Office: New England Coll 7 Main St Henniker NH 03242-3202 ADDRESS: P O BOX 103B SAN DIEGO CA 92112-0103*

CUMMISKEY, RAYMOND VINCENT, academic administrator; b. Apr. 24, 1958. BA, Park Coll., 1980; MA, U. Mo., 1981, EdS, 1986, PhD, 1993. Assoc. prof. comm. arts, chair divsn. humanities Park Coll., Parkville, Mo., 1987-91; assoc. v.p. Neosho County C.C., Ottawa, Kans., 1991-97; v.p. acad. affairs Jefferson C.C., Steubenville, Ohio, 1998—. Home: 1805 Hamilton Pl Steubenville OH 43952-1327

CUNDEY, PAUL EDWARD, JR., cardiologist; b. Phila., Sept. 9, 1936; s. Paul Edward and Ann Elizabeth (Morris) C.; m. Katharine Zerbey, Aug. 1, 1959; children: Richard David, Paul Edward III, Heath John, Elizabeth Ann. BA, LaSalle U., 1958; MD, Temple U., 1962. Intern Temple U. Med. Ctr., Phila., 1962-63; resident in cardiology Med. Coll. Ga., Augusta, 1965-69; assoc. prof. medicine Med. Coll. Ga., 1968-70, prof. medicine, 1978—; practice medicine specializing in cardiology Univ. Hosp., Augusta, 1970—; bd. dirs. East Cen. Ga. Emergency Med. Systems, Augusta, 1989. Contbr. numerous articles and abstracts to profl. publs. Mem. exec. com. Richmond County div. Am. Heart Assn., 1972-84. Capt. U.S. Army, 1963-65. Rsch. fellow, Nat. Heart Inst., 1967-79, NIH, 1967-69. Fellow ACP, Am. Coll. Angiology, Am. Coll. Cardiology. Office: Cardiology Assocs 818 Saint Sebastian Way Ste 312 Augusta GA 30901-2651

CUNDIFF, EDWARD WILLIAM, marketing educator; b. Long Beach, Calif., Sept. 28, 1919; s. Harry Thomas and Martha Magdalene (Koltes) C.; m. Margaret Wallace Stroud, Sept. 8, 1956; children: Richard Wallace, Gregory Edward, Geoffrey William. B.A., Stanford, 1940, M.B.A., 1942; Ed.D., 1952; Ford Fellow, Harvard Sch. Bus. Adminstrn., 1956. Retailing exec., 1946-48; instr. mktg. San Jose State Coll., 1949-52; asst. prof., later asso. prof. mktg. Syracuse U., 1952-58, asst. dean, 1954-58; prof. mktg., chmn. dept. mktg. adminstrn. U. Tex., 1958-73, assoc. dean Grad. Sch. Bus., 1973-76; L.J. Buchan distinguished vis. prof. U. Tex. at San Antonio, 1976-77; Charles C. Kellstadt prof. mktg. Emory U., 1977-87; John A. Beck Centennial prof. comm. U. Tex., Austin, 1987-94, John A. Beck emeritus prof. comm. dept. advt., 1994-96, emeritus prof. mktg., 1996—; vis. prof. mktg., Fontainebleau, France, Palermo, Sicily, 1960-61. Author: (with R.R. Still) Sales Management: Decisions, Policies and Cases, 5th edit., 1988, Basic Marketing: Concepts, Environment, and Decisions, 1964, rev. edit., 1970, Essentials of Marketing, 1966, 3d edit., 1986, (with R.R. Still and N.A.P. Govoni) Fundamentals of Modern Marketing, 3d edit, 1980, (with Marye Hilger) Marketing in the International Environment, 2d edit., 1988; editor: Jour. Mktg, 1973-76. Served to lt. (s.g.) USNR, World War II. Mem. Am. Mktg. Assn. (v.p. 1980—), So. Mktg. Assn. (pres. 1967-68), Beta Gamma Sigma, Delta Sigma Pi, Theta Chi. Home: 7802 Deer Ridge Cir Austin TX 78731-1502 Office: U Tex Coll Communication Austin TX 78712

CUNDIFF, JERRY H., secondary music educator, church choir director; b. Abilene, Kans., Dec. 9, 1939; s. John Verl and Bernice C. Cundiff. BS, Kans. State U., Manhattan, 1961, MS, 1969. Music educator Norton (Kans.) Cmty. H.S., 1961-65, Junction City (Kans.) Schs., 1965-68, Topeka Pub. Schs., 1968-73, Chapman (Kans.) Unified Sch. Dist., 1973-79, Turner Unified Sch. Dist. 202, Kansas City, Kans., 1979-99. Composer Consider the Lillies, 1987, Come Share With Me, 1979. Mem. Am. Choral Dirs. Assn., Kans. Music Educators, Kans.-NEA (pres. Chapman 1975-76, chair govt. rels. 1978-79). Republican. Mem. UCC Ch. Avocations: farming, travel, gardening, fitness. Home: 9965 Edelweiss Cir Shawnee Mission KS 66203 Office: Country Club Congl Ch Brookside at 65th St Kansas City MO 64113-1841

CUNDIFF, KATHLEEN JEAN, business executive; b. Hawthorne, Calif., Nov. 7, 1958; d. Raymond Leslie Cundiff and Betty Jean Williams; m. Dennis Alan F'Mayer, July 16, 1980 (div. Aug. 1996). AS magna cum laude, Riverside City Coll., 1985; BS cum laude, Calif. Poly., 1988. CPA, Calif. Supervising sr. auditor KPMG Peat Marwick, Costa Mesa, Calif., 1988-92; sr. auditor The Walt Disney Co., Anaheim, Calif., 1992-94; sr. internal auditor Bowater Inc., Greenville, S.C., 1994-95; contr. Haynsworth, Marion, McKay & Guerard, LLP, Greenville, 1995-97, COO, CFO, 1997—. Mem. AICPA, Assn. Legal Adminstrs., Inst. Mgmt. Accts., S.C. Assn. CPA, Jr. League Greenville. Republican. Office: Haynsworth Marion McKay & Guerard LLP 11th Fl 75 Beattie Pl Ste 11 Greenville SC 29601-2130

CUNEO, DENNIS CLIFFORD, automotive company executive; b. Ridgway, Pa., Jan. 12, 1950; s. Clifford Francis and Erma Theresa (Nissel) C.; m. Bonnie Frances Mish, Aug. 18, 1972; children: Corinne, Kyle, James. BS, Gannon U., 1971; MBA, Kent State U., 1973; JD, Loyola U., New Orleans, 1976. Bar: D.C. 1977. Trial atty. U.S. Dept. Justice, Washington, 1976-80; assoc. Arent, Fox, Kintner, Plotkin & Kahn, Washington, 1980-84; gen. counsel New United Motor Mfg. Inc. joint venture GM-Toyota, Fremont, Calif., 1984-88, v.p. legal and govt. affairs, 1988-90, v.p. corp. planning and legal affairs, 1990-92, v.p. corp. planning and external affairs, corp. sec., 1992-96; v.p. legal, environ., external affairs Toyota Motor Mfg. N.Am., 1996—; chmn. Calif. Workside Rsch. Com., Sacramento, 1988-96; lectr. exec. program U. Calif., Davis, 1988-95; lectr. internat. motor vehicle program MIT, Berlin and Beijing, 1994; mem. Gov. Pete Wilson Trade Mission to Asia, 1993; bd. dirs. Toyota Motor Corp. Svcs., Inc., 1996—. Campaign chmn. United Way, Alameda County, 1993-95; co-chmn. Blue Ribbon com. to Save the Oakland A's, 1994; vice chmn. Alameda County Econ. Devel. Bd., Oakland, 1990-96, Team Calif., Sacramento, 1994; bd. visitors Loyola Law Sch., 1987-95; mem. Calif. Select Com. on Jud. Retirement, 1993; mem. steering com. Bay Area Coun., San Francisco, 1990-95, Bay Area Dredging Coalition, San Francisco, 1991-96; mem. Statewide Pupil Assessment Rev. Panel, Sacramento, 1996-97; bd. dirs. Oakland-Alameda County Coliseum, 1995-97, Cin. United Way, 1997—, Nat. Assn. Mfrs., 1998—, Bay Area Regional Tech. Alliance, Oakland, 1994-96; mem. flood relief cabinet ARC, 1997; mem. Gov.'s Task Force on Child Devel., Frankfort, Ky., 1999— . aem. ABA, Calif. Mfrs. Assn. (vice chmn. 1994—, pres. Calif. manufactures svcs. corp. 1996-97), Oakland Football Mktg. Assn. (pres. 1995-96), No. Ky. C. of C. (bd. dirs. 1997-98), Greater Cin. C. of C. (bd. dirs. 1998—), Metro. Club (bd. dirs. 1999—), Assoc. Industries Ky. (bd. dirs. 1999—). Avocations: skiing, model trains. Office: Toyota Motor Mfg NAm 25 Atlantic Ave Erlanger KY 41018-3188

CUNEO, DONALD LANE, lawyer, educator; b. Alameda, Calif., Apr. 19, 1944; s. Vernon Edmund and Dorothy (Lane) c.; m. Frances Susan Huze, Aug. 8, 1981; children: Kristen Marie, Lane Michael. BA, Lehigh U., 1966; JD, Columbia U., 1970, MBA, 1970. Bar: N.Y. 1971, D.C. 1992, U.S. Claims Ct. 1972, U.S. Tax Ct. 1972, U.S. Dist. Ct. (so. dist.) N.Y. 1973, U.S. Dist. Ct. (no. dist.) 1978, U.S. Dist. Ct. D.C. 1992, U.S. Ct. Appeals (2nd cir.) 1979, U.S. Ct. Appeals (D.C. cir.) 1992, U.S. Ct. Internat. Trade 1979, U.S. Ct. Appeals (fed. cir.) 1979, U.S. Supreme Ct. 1979. Assoc. Shearman & Sterling, N.Y.C., 1971-79, ptnr., 1979-93; pres., CEO Internat. House, 1993—; sec./trustee Internat. House, N.Y.C., 1977-93. Author: (with others) Prevention and Prosecution of Computer and High Technology Crime, 1988; contbr. articles to profl. jours. Reginald Heber Smith Community Lawyer fellow U.S. Govt., N.Y.C., 1970-71. Mem. Coun. Fgn. Rels. Avocations: sports, travel. Home and Office: Internat House 500 Riverside Dr New York NY 10027-3916*

CUNEO, JACK ALFRED, real estate investment executive; b. Bklyn., Dec. 7, 1947; s. Alfred Louis and Elvira Clementina (Landolphi) C.; m. Barbara Rose Kenig, May 9, 1970 (div. Nov. 1981); 1 child, Andrew; m. Renee Joan Savastano, May 26, 1984; children: Matthew, Christina. BA in Psychology, CCNY, 1969; postgrad., U. Mass., 1969-72. Rschr. Continental Rsch. Inst., N.Y.C., 1967-70; lectr. U. Mass., Amherst, Mass., 1970-72; ptnr. Skera-Retail Craft, Northampton, Mass., 1972-77; broker Town and Country Realtors, Amherst, Mass., 1972-74; pres. New England Real Vest, Amherst, 1974-75; account exec. Merrill Lynch Pierce Fenner and Smith, Springfield, Mass., 1975-77; sr. dept. rep. Merrill Lynch Investment Banking, N.Y.C., 1977-78; v.p. real estate investment Merrill Lynch Hubbard, N.Y.C., 1978-86, sr. v.p., chief investment officer, 1986-97, chmn., CEO, 1997—; bd. dirs. MLH Properties, N.Y.C., MLH Income Realty I-VI, N.Y.C., ML Real Estate Recovery Fund, N.Y.C.; founding investor Nat. Bank of Calif., L.A., 1984—. Fellowship Nat. Inst. Mental Health, 1969. Mem. Urban Land Inst., Ctr. for Real Estate and Urban Econs. U. Calif. (policy adv. bd.), MIT (real estate ctr.), 200 Club, Nat. Italian Am. Found. Avocations: golf, fishing, military aircraft, shooting. Office: Merrill Lynch Hubbard World Fin Ctr S Tower New York NY 10080

CUNHA, MARK GEOFFREY, lawyer; b. Lexington, Mass., Sept. 26, 1955; s. John Henry and Dolores (DeRosas) c.; m. Viviane Sirotto; children: Celine Yvonne, Nicholas Brian. AB magna cum laude, Cornell U., 1977; JD, Stanford U., 1980. Bar: N.Y. 1981, U.S. Dist. Ct. (so. and ea. dists.) N.Y. 1981, U.S. Ct. Appeals (2nd cir.) 1991, U.S. Tax Ct. 1992, U.S. Supreme Ct. 1996. Intern The White House, Washington, 1979-80; assoc. Simpson Thacher & Bartlett, N.Y.C., 1980-88, ptnr., 1989—; mediator comml. divsn. N.Y. State Supreme Ct., N.Y. County, 1996—; bd. dir. legal svcs. for N.Y.C., 1997—. Bd. dirs. N.Y. Lawyers for Pub. Interest, 1989—; trustee Inst. for Ednl. Achievement, 1995—, Lycee Francais N.Y., 1998—. Recipient Outstanding Vol. Lawyers award Legal Aid Soc., 1990, Pro Bono award N.Y. County Lawyers Assn., 1991. Mem. ABA, Internat. Bar Assn., N.Y. State Bar Assn. (exec. com. on comml. and fed. litigation sect.), Assn. Bar City N.Y. (chmn. com. on legal assistance, chmn. of del. to N.Y. State Bar Assn. Ho. of Dels., steering com. on legal assistance), Phi Beta Kappa. Democrat. Home: 1150 Fifth Ave Apt 3A New York NY 10128-0724 Office: Simpson Thacher & Bartlett 425 Lexington Ave New York NY 10017-3954

CUNINGGIM, WHITTY DANIEL, educator; b. Oxford, N.C., Aug. 18, 1918; d. Ethel Jenkins and Annie Penelope (Whitty) Daniel; m. Merrimon Cuninggim, June 10, 1939 (dec.); children: Lee C. Neff, Penny, Terry (dec.). BA, Duke U., 1938. Founder, chmn. Reading Is Fun-damental, St. Louis, 1970-76; bd. of edn. Spl. Sch. Dist. St. Louis County, St. Louis, 1970-75; pres. Spl. Sch. Dist. St. Louis County, 1975-76; chmn. Adv. Coun. for Exceptional Children, Winston Salem, N.C., 1976-82; Bd. dirs. Nat. Citizens' Com. for Support of Pub. Schs., 1970-76, Nat. Sch. Vol. Program, Alexandria, Va., 1976-83, White House Conference on Edn. Co-founder Catalyst Assocs., St. Louis, 1974; chmn. Forsyth County N.C. 2000, 1982; pres. Women's Forum, N.C., 1985-86, Art Coun., Winston-Salem, 1982-83; mem. N.C. Pub. Edn. Policy Coun., 1983-84; bd. assocs. N.C. Child Advocacy Inst., 1987-89; mem. Md. Edn. Coalition, Balt., 1989—, mem. exec. bd., 1991-95, Leadership Coun., 1995—; v.p. Broadmead, 1990-92, trustee, 1998—; mem. exec. com. N.C. Dems., 1980-84, co-chmn. edn. com. League of Women Voters of Baltimore County, 1995-99. Recipient Duke U. Alumni award, Duke U. Alumni Assn., Winston Salem, 1982, award for Community Svc., League of Women Voters, N.C., 1989; named Woman of Achievment, St. Louis Globe-Democrat, 1968, Nat. Sch. Vol of Year, Nat. Sch. Vol. Program, 1979. Mem. AAUW, Nat. Women's Dem. Club, LWV (bd. dirs.), Phi Beta Kappa, Phi Delta Kappa. Democrat. Avocations: art history, rug hooking, tennis. Home: 13801 York Rd Apt 9E Cockeysville MD 21030-1837

CUNIO, MARIA T. MUÑOZ, psychologist; b. San Juan, P.R., Sept. 19, 1971; d. Lorenzo Muñoz Franco and Hilda I. (Ruiz) Muñoz; m. Christopher J. Cunio, Aug. 10, 1996. BA, Coll. of the Holy Cross, 1993; MS, U. Mass., 1995, PhD, 1998. Mem. rsch. team U. Mass., Amherst, 1993-96, therapist, mem. clin. team Psychology Svcs. Ctr., 1993-96; mem. rsch. team divsn. on aging Harvard Med. Sch., Boston, 1996-97; mem. geriatric consulting team River Valley Counseling Ctr., Holyoke, Mass., spring 1996; clin. psychology intern VA Med. Ctr., Brockton and West Roxbury, 1997-98; therapist New England Geriatrics; rsch. team mbr. Wellesley College Ctr for Women; post-doctoral fellow in Geropsychology Brockton/West Roxbury VA Med. Ctr. Harvard Med. Schl., 1998-99; psychologist behavioral neurology unit Beth Israel Deaconess Med. Ctr., 1999—; presenter Gerontol. Soc. Am., 1992, 93, Ea. Psychol. Assn., 1995. Co-author: (book chpt.) The Psychology of Adversity, 1996. Office of Minority Grad. Student fellow U. Mass., 1993-94. Mem. APA (Minority fellow 1995-96, 96-97. Roman Catholic. Avocations: camping, biking, hiking, sailing. Home: 370 Oak St Marshfield MA 02050-6229

CUNNANE, PATRICIA S., medical facility administrator; b. Clinton, Iowa, Sept. 7, 1946; d. Cyril J. and Corinne Spain; m. Edward J. Cunnane, June 19, 1971. AA, Mt. St. Clare Coll., Clinton, Iowa, 1966. Mgr. Eye Med. Clinic of Santa Clara Valley, San Jose, Calif. Mem. Med. Adminstrs. Calif. Polit. Action Com., San Francisco, 1987. Mem. Med. Group Mgmt. Assn., Am. Coll. Med. Group Adminstrs. (nominee), Nat. Notary Assn., NAFE, Exec. Women Internat. (v.p. 1986-87, pres. 1987—), Profl. Secs. Internat. (sec. 1979-80), Am. Soc. Ophthalmic Adminstrs., Women Health Care Execs., Healthcare Human Resource Mgmt. Assn. Calif. Roman Catholic. Avocations: calligraphy, golf. Home: 232 Tolin Ct San Jose CA 95139-1445 Office: Eye Med Clinic of Santa Clara Valley 220 Meridian Ave San Jose CA 95126-2903

CUNNEEN, SALLY MCDEVITT, English language educator, editor, writer; b. Providence, July 9, 1926; d. John Newman and Marguerite O'Callaghan McDevitt; m. Joseph E. Cunneen, Nov. 19, 1949; children: Michael, Peter, Paul. BA, U. Toronto, Can., 1947; MA, Fordham U., 1964; PhD, Columbia U., 1978; hon. doctorate, The Elms, Chicopee, Mass., 1981, Coll. New Rochelle, 1981, Kings Coll., 1991, Coll. of Holy Cross, 1991, St. Mary's Coll., 1995, St. Bernard's Sem., Rochester, N.Y., 1996. From instr. to prof. English Rockland C.C. (SUNY), 1970-93; evaluator cultural arts component Project on Religion and Urban Culture, Indpls., 1996-98. Author: Sex: Female; Religion: Catholic, 1968, A Contemporary Meditation on the Everyday God, 1976, Mother Church: What Contemporary Women Are Teaching Her, 1991, In Search of Mary: The Woman and the Symbol, 1996 (Coll. Theology Soc. Book award 1997); contbr. articles to profl. jours.; cofounder, editor: (rev.) Cross Curents, 1950—. Mgr. Ch. Women United, 1971-73; program chair Nat. Coun. Cath. Women, 1973-75; mem. U.S. Cath. Bishops Ofc. Consultation with Reformed Orthodox Chs. Coolidge fellow Assn. for Religion and Higher Edn., 1992. Roman Catholic. Home: 103 Vanhouten Flds West Nyack NY 10994-2529

CUNNIFF, PATRICK FRANCIS, mechanical engineer; b. N.Y.C., Oct. 25, 1933; s. Martin and Della (McDonald) C.; m. Patricia McCann, June 18, 1960; children: Brian, John, Elizabeth, Christopher. B.C.E., Manhattan Coll., 1955; M.S., Va. Poly. Inst., 1956, Ph.D., 1962. Research engr. U.S. Naval Research Lab., 1960-63; mem. dept. mech. engring. U. Md., 1963—, prof., 1969—, acting assoc. dean grad. studies, 1988-91; assoc. dean Coll. Engring., 1994—; cons. vibration and noise control. Author: (with D. Anand) Engineering Mechanics—Statics and Dynamics, 1973, Environmental Noise Pollution, 1977. Served with USPHS, 1956-58. U.S. Steel Found. fellow, 1959-60. Fellow ASME, Am. Soc. Engring. Edn. Republican. Roman Catholic. Office: Univ Md Office of Grad Studies Coll Engring College Park MD 20742*

CUNNINGHAM, ANDREA LEE, public relations executive; b. Oak Park, Ill., Dec. 15, 1956; d. Ralph Edward and Barbara Ann C.; m. Rand Wyatt Siegfried, Sept. 24, 1983. BA, Northwestern U., 1979. Feature writer Irving-Cloud Pub. Co., Lincolnwood, Ill., 1979-81; account exec. Burson-Marsteller Inc., Chgo., 1981-83; group account mgr. Regis McKenna Inc., Palo Alto, Calif., 1983-85; founder, owner, pres. Cunningham Communication Inc., Santa Clara, Calif., 1985—. Mem. Am. Electronics Assn., U.S. C. of C., Young Pres.' Orgn., Software Pubs. Assn., Boston Computer Soc., Leadership Calif., U.S. Cambridge C. of C. Republican. Avocations: running, roller skating, aerobics, racquetball. *

CUNNINGHAM, ATLEE MARION, JR., aeronautical engineer; b. Corpus Christi, Aug. 17, 1938; s. Atlee Marion and Carlos Dean (Shepherd) C.; m. Diana Wahl Bonelli, July 17, 1976; children by previous marriage: Christopher Atlee Acie, Scott Patrick, Sean Michael. BS in Mech. Engring., U. Tex., 1961, MS in Mech. Engring., 1963, PhD, 1966. Rsch. scientist Def. Research Lab., Austin, Tex., 1965; engring. staff specialist Gen. Dynamics Corp., Ft. Worth, 1965-93, Lockheed Corp., Ft. Worth, 1993-95, Lockheed Martin, 1995—; vis. indsl. prof. So. Meth. U. Inst. Tech., Dallas, 1969-70; vis. assoc. prof. aero. engring. U. Tex., 1978—; lectr. in aeroelasticity Nat. Cheng Kung U., Taiwan, 1984, U. Tex., Arlington, 1990—; cons. NASA, USAF, USN, U. Tex. Vice pres. Tex. Fine Arts Assn., Fort Worth, 1972. Served with USN, 1962-64. Welding Rsch. Assn. fellow, 1961-62; NATO fellow, 1964-65; recipient NASA Cert. of Recognition for tech. publ., 1980, Extraordinary Achievement award Gen. Dynamics, 1980, 83, 89. Fellow AIAA (assoc.; tech. reviewer jours.); mem. Sigma Xi. Contbr. articles to profl. jours. and AGARD publs.; innovator in subsonic, transonic and supersonic steady and oscillatory aerodynamics method; developer new methods for predicting high angle of attack aerodynamics in subsonic and supersonic flows. Major contbr. to aeroelastic developments and improvements for Gen. Dynamics F-16 and F-111 aircrafts. Pioneer in new technology development for unsteady separated flows and buffeting on aircraft maneuvering at high angle of attack involving support of Air Force, Navy, NASA, National Aerospace Laboratory (Netherlands), General Dynamics, Lockheed and University of Texas at Austin. Developer of steady and unsteady force testing techniques for aerodynamic investigations using water tunnels, new concepts and methods for nonlinear aeroelasticity. Home: 4932 Black Oak Ln Fort Worth TX 76114-2936

CUNNINGHAM, BRUCE ARTHUR, biochemist; b. Winnebago, Ill., Jan. 18, 1940; s. Wallace Calvin and Margaret Wright (Clinite) C.; m. Katrina Sue Susdorf, Feb. 27, 1965; children—Jennifer Ruth, Douglas James. B.S., U. Dubuque, 1962; Ph.D., Yale U., 1966. NSF postdoctoral fellow Rockefeller U., N.Y.C., 1966-68; asst. prof. biochemistry Rockefeller U., 1968-71, assoc. prof., 1971-77, prof. molecular and devel. biology, 1978-92; prof. dept. neurobiology The Scripps Rsch. Inst., San Diego, 1992—. Editorial bd.: Jour. Biol. Chemistry, 1978-82, Jour. Cell Biology, 1992-96. Camille and Henry Dreyfus Found. grantee, 1970-75; recipient Career Scientist award Irma T. Hirschl Trust, 1975-80. Mem. AAAS, Am. Soc. Biol. Chemists, Am. Soc. Cell Biology, Protein Soc., Am. Chem. Soc., Harvey Soc., Am. Gynecol. Obstet. Soc. (hon.), Sigma Xi. Research on structure and function of molecules on cell surfaces. Office: Scripps Rsch Inst 10550 N Torrey Pines Rd La Jolla CA 92037-1000

CUNNINGHAM, BRUCE L., plastic and reconstructive surgeon, educator; b. Phila., Feb. 18, 1949; m. Marie Christensen. BA in English, Trinity Coll., Hartford, Conn., 1971; MD, Northwestern U., 1975; MS, U. Minn., 1983. Bd. cert. plastic surgery. Chief plastic surgery St. Paul Ramsey Med. Ctr., 1980-85; instr. surgery U. Minn., Mpls., 1980-84, asst. prof. surgery, 1984-88, assoc. prof. surgery, 1988-94, prof. surgery, 1994—, dir. residency tng. program plastic surgery, 1990—. Mem. Am. Bd. Plastic Surgery (bd. dirs. 1997—), Am. Soc. Plastic Reconstructive Surgeons (bd. dirs. 1997—). Avocations: sailing, distance running. E-mail: wnni001@maroon.tc.umn.edu. Office: Univ Minn PO Box 122 420 Delaware St SE Minneapolis MN 55455

CUNNINGHAM, CHARLES BAKER, III, manufacturing company executive; b. St. Louis, Oct. 1, 1941; s. Charles Baker C. and Mary Blythe (Cunningham); m. Georganne Rose, Sept. 17, 1966; children: Margaret B., Charles B. IV. B.S., Washington U., St. Louis, 1964; M.S., Ga. Inst. Tech., 1966; M.B.A., Harvard U., 1970. Dir. fin. The Cooper Group, Raleigh, N.C., 1972-75, v.p. adminstrn., 1975-77; v.p. devel. Cooper Industries Inc., Houston, 1977-79, v.p. ops., 1980-82, exec. v.p., 1982-93; pres. Indsl. Equipment Group Cooper Industries Inc., 1979-80; chmn., pres., CEO Belden Inc., 1993—. Served to 1st lt. U.S. Army, 1966-68, Iran. Decorated Army Commendation medal. Office: Belden Inc 7701 Forsyth Blvd Ste 800 Saint Louis MO 63105-1861

CUNNINGHAM, FRANK ROBERT, humanities educator, researcher; b. Phila., Aug. 15, 1937; s. Frank A. and Mildred F. (McCrosson) C.; m. Mara Lemanis, Aug. 5, 1976. AB in English, Villanova U., 1960, MA in English, 1962; PhD in English, Lehigh U., 1970. Asst. prof. English Franklin & Marshall Coll., Lancaster, Pa., 1968-69, Fordham U., Bronx, N.Y., 1970-71, Kans. State U., Manhattan, 1971-73; asst. prof. English San Jose (Calif.) State U., 1973-76, asst. prof. writing Sch. Bus., 1977-78; assoc. prof. English U. S.D., Vermillion, 1978-84, prof. English, 1984—; cons. Oxford U. Press, N.Y.C., 1990, World Book Ency., Chgo., 1990, U. Ky. Press, Lexington, 1992—, U. Ga. Press, Athens, 1994; writer, radio commentator jazz edn. program KUSD Radio, Vermillion, 1982-84; Fulbright sr. lectr. U. Cracow, Poland, 1976-77. Author: (pamphlet) Clifford Odets, 1981, (books) Sidney Lumet: Film and Literary Vision, 1991, Sidney Lumet's Fail Safe, 1999; contbr. some 40 articles to profl. jours.; mem. editl. bd. Lit./Film Quar., 1988—, Eugene O'Neill Rev., 1989—. Parkhurst fellow Lehigh U., 1969-70, vis. fellow Sterling Libr. Yale U., 1999. Mem. MLA, Assn. Lit. Scholars and Critics (curriculum com. 1996-97), Eugene O'Neill Soc. (bd. dirs. 1988—, editl. bd. rev. 1988—). Avocations: jogging, jazz percussion, book reviewing. Office: U SD Vermillion SD 57069

CUNNINGHAM, GARY H., lawyer; b. Grand Rapids, Mich., Jan. 11, 1953; s. Gordon H. and Marilyn J. (Lookabill) C.; m. Arlene M. Marcy, Apr. 23, 1983; children: Stephanie M., Gregory H. B.Gen. Studies, U. Mich., 1975, MA, 1977; JD, Detroit Coll. Law, 1980. Bar: Mich. 1980, U.S. Dist. Ct. Mich. 1983, U.S. Ct. Appeals (6th cir.) 1986, U.S. Ct. Appeals (Fed. cir.) 1990. Law clk. and estate adminstr. U.S. Bankruptcy Ct., Ea. Dist. Mich., Detroit, 1980-83; assoc./ptnr. Schlussel, Lifton, Simon, Rands, Galvin & Jackier, Southfield, Mich., 1983-90; ptnr./shareholder Kramer Mellen, P.C., Southfield, Mich., 1990-95; prin. shareholder Strobl Cunningham Caretti & Sharp, P.C., Bloomfield Hills, Mich., 1995—. Sr. staff mem. Detroit Coll. of Law Rev., 1978-80; contbr. articles to profl. jours. Mem. ABA (bus. law sect.), Fed. Bar Assn. (chmn. bankruptcy sect. 1989-91), Oakland County Bar Assn. (bus. law com.), State Bar of Mich. (mem. corp., fin. and bus. law sect.), Am. Bankruptcy Inst. (sponsor), Comml. Law League of Am., Detroit Econ. Club, Detroit Inst. Arts, Delta Theta Phi. Avocations: sailing, skiing, tennis. Home: 2959 Cedar Ridge Dr Troy MI 48084-2613 Office: Strobl Cunningham Caretti & Sharp PC 300 E Long Lake Rd Ste 200 Bloomfield Hills MI 48304-2376

CUNNINGHAM, GEORGE WOODY, federal official, metallurgical engineer; b. Union City, Tenn., Dec. 3, 1930; s. Mose Marshall and Zula Ethel (Easterwood) C.; m. Patricia G. Pate, Dec. 31, 1954; children: John, Ann. BSChemE, U. Tenn., 1954, MS in Metallurgy, 1955; PhD in Metall. Engring., Ohio State U., 1960. Prin. metall. engr. Battelle Meml. Inst., Columbus, Ohio, 1955-62, chief materials thermodynamics div., 1965-66; mem. fuel and materials br. div. reactor devel. and tech. AEC, Washington, 1966-70, chief liquid metal products br., 1970-73, asst. dir. engring. and tech., 1973-75; dep. dir. tech. ERDA, Washington, 1975-76; dir. div. waste mgmt., program dir. for nuclear energy Dept. Energy, Washington, 1977-78, counselor atomic energy U.S. mission to Internat. Atomic Energy Assn., Vienna, 1978-79; asst. sec. for nuclear energy Dept. Energy, 1980-81; dir. nuclear studies Mitre Corp., McLean, Va., 1981-84, dir. Mitre Inst., 1984-90; tech. dir. Def. Nuclear Facilities Safety Bd., Washington, 1990—; Am. del. Internat. Working Group on Fast Reactors, 1976; chmn. U.S.-U.K. Libby-Cockcroft Exchange of Ceramic Fuels, 1967, U.S. Fast Breeder Reactor Team, Japan, 1971, U.S.-USSR Coordinating Com. on Fast Reactors, 1976. Contbr. articles to profl. jours. Mem. Am. Soc. Metals, Sigma Xi, Tau Beta Pi, Lamda Chi Upsilon, Alpha Chi Sigma. Home: 4601 North Park Ave Apt 804 Chevy Chase MD 20815 Office: Def Nuclear Facilities Safety Bd 625 Indiana Ave NW Washington DC 20004-2923

CUNNINGHAM, GILBERT EARL, business owner; b. Fort Worth, Tex., May 4, 1930; s. George Alvin and Lillian Louise (Fogg) C. Student, Benz-Floral Design, 1948. Designer Balche's Flowers, Ft. Worth, Tex., 1948-53; owner, tchr. Ft. Worth Sch. of Floral Design, 1953-61; mgr. Cheri's Flowers, Tucson, Ariz., 1961-68; owner Ariz. Sch. of Floral Design, Tucson, 1961-68, Buddy's Distinctive Flowers and Gifts, Mesa, Ariz., 1968—; pres. Ariz. unit Teleflora, Inc., Mesa, 1976-78; instr. western U.S.A. Teleflora Nat. Conf., Cleve., 1968; instr. Florists Transworld Del., Phoenix, 1982. With U.S. Army, 1953-56. Mem. Am. Inst. Floral Desingers, Mesa Merchants Assn. Republican. Baptist. Avocations: interior design, antiques, gourmet cooking. Home: 8508 E Orange Blossom Ln Scottsdale AZ 85250-7427

CUNNINGHAM, GLENN DALE, protective services official; b. Jersey City, N.J., Sept. 16, 1943; m. Sandra B. Cunningham. BS, Jersey City State Coll., 1974. With Jersey City Police Dept., 1967-92; dir. public safety Hudson County, N.J., 1992-96; U.S. marshal Dist. of N.J., 1996—. Pres. City Coun., City of Jersey City, 1981-89; mem. Bd. Chosen Freeholders, 1975-78; mem. Jersey City Alcohol Beverage Control Commn., 1992-93. Office: US Marshal Svc ML King Jr Fed Courthouse 50 Walnut St Newark NJ 07102-3506

CUNNINGHAM, GORDON ROSS, financial executive; b. Toronto, Nov. 15, 1944; s. Wendell Carson and Catherine Ann C.; m. Patricia Dorothy Westheuser, Dec. 22, 1966; children: Kristyn Catherine, Kaleigh Ann, James Gordon. BA, U. Toronto, 1966, LLB, 1969; LLD (hon.), U. Victoria, 1995. Bar: Ont. 1971. With Tory, Tory, DesLauriers & Binnington, Toronto, 1971-76; ptnr. Toronto, 1977-84; exec. v.p., chief oper. officer Trilon Fin. Corp., Toronto, 1984-88, pres., chief operating officer, 1988-89, bd. dirs.; pres., chief exec. officer London Life Ins. Co. and London Ins. Group Inc., 1989-96; pres. Cumberland Asset Mgmt. Corp., 1997—; pres., dir. Fairmoor Holdings Inc.; bd. dirs. D.C. Diagnosticare Inc., Intertape Polymer, Inc. Former nat. corp. campaign chmn. Diabetes Can. Mem. Can. Bar Assn., Can. Life and Health Ins. Assn. (past chmn.), Bus. Coun. Nat. Isues, Upper Can. Law Soc., Rosedale Golf Club, Univ. Club, Devil's Glen Ski Club, Mad River Golf Club, Portmarnock Golf Club (Dublin), Ristigouche Salmon Club. Avocations: golf, squash, fishing, tennis, skiing. Office: Cumberland Asset Mgmt Corp, M99 Yorkville Ave, Toronto, ON Canada M5R 3K5

CUNNINGHAM, GUNTHER, professional football coach; m. Rene Cunningham; children: Natalie, Adam. Grad., U. Oreg. Football coach U. Oreg., 1969-71, U. Kar., 1972, Stanford (Calif.) U., 1973-76, U. Calif., 1977-80; coach defensive line, linebackers CFL's Hamilton Tiger Cats, 1981; defensive line coach Balt. Colts, 1982-84; mentor defensive line San Diego Charters, 1985-90; coach linebackers Oakland Raiders, 1991, defensive coord., 1992-93, tutor defensive line, 1994; defensive coord. Kansas City Chief, 1995-98, coach, 1999—. Office: c/o Kansas City Chiefs One Arrowhead Dr Kansas City MO 64129*

CUNNINGHAM, JAMES GERALD, JR., transportation company executive; b. Morristown, N.J., Aug. 5, 1930; s. James Gerald and Kathryn Virginia (Cannon) C.; m. Marilyn Swanson, Sept. 22, 1956; children: Kathleen, Jean Marie, Barbara, James Gerald, III, Carl. B.S. in Civil Engring, Newark Coll. Engring., 1952. Civil engr. Pa. R.R., 1952-54; trainmaster Erie-Lackawanna R.R., 1956-62; div. mgr., dir. transp. Consol. Freightways, Menlo Park, Calif., 1962-69; sr. v.p., dir. REA Express, Inc., N.Y.C., 1969-75; also dir. REA Holding Corp.; pres., dir. Gateway Transp. Co., La Crosse, Wis., 1976-78; gen. mgr. intermodal ops. Consol. Rail Corp., Phila., 1978-79; pres., chief exec. officer PTL Transp. Svcs. Inc., Phila., 1980—. Served with Transp. Corps AUS, 1953-55. Mem. Am. Trucking Assn. (chmn. met. planning orgn. task force, exec. com.), Equipment Interchange Assn. (exec. com., past pres.), Intermodal Transp. Assn. (exec. com., past pres.), N.Y. Athletic Club, Aronimink Country Club, Pablo Creek Club. Home: 3505 Saint Davids Rd Newtown Square PA 19073-1417 Office: PTL Transp Svcs Inc 1100 E Hector St Ste 222 Conshohocken PA 19428-2378

CUNNINGHAM, JAMES WILLIAM, literacy education educator, researcher; b. Chattanooga, Jan. 22, 1947; s. Ernest James and Ann Louise Katherine (Martin) C.; m. Patricia M. Cunningham, Aug. 24, 1974; 1 child, David Ernest. BA in English, U. Va., 1970; MA in Reading Edn., U. Ga., 1973, PhD in Reading Edn., 1975. Classroom tchr. South Pittsburg (Tenn.) Elem. Sch., 1970-72; project coord. Right-to-Read Project, Athens, Ga., 1972-74; asst. prof. edn. U. N.C., Chapel Hill, 1975-80, assoc. prof., 1980-93, prof., 1993—, dir. literacy studies, 1991-96. Contbr. numerous articles to profl. jours. and chpts. to books; co-author 9 textbooks, including: Developing Readers and Writers in the Content Areas: K-12, 3nd edit., 1998, Reading and Writing in Elementary Classrooms, 3rd edit., 1995. Mem. Internat. Reading Assn., Nat. Reading Conf. (bd. dirs. 1997—), Nat. Conf. on Rsch. in Lang. and Literacy (fellow). Home: 811 Leigh Dr Gibsonville NC 27249-2734 Office: 304 Peabody Hall Cb 3500 U Nc Chapel Hill NC 27599

CUNNINGHAM, JEFFREY MILTON, publishing executive; b. Rome, Aug. 25, 1952; s. Allen Hamilton and Nina (Gertzovsky) C.; m. Elizabeth Anne Moir, Sept. 17, 1983; children: Kimberly Anne, James Hamilton, Benjamin William, Elizabeth Anne. BA, Binghamton U., Binghamton, 1974; student Wharton Sch. Exec. Program, U. Pa., 1992. Auditor Bus. Pubs. Audit Bur., N.Y.C., 1974-76; dist. mgr. McGraw-Hill Pubs., N.Y.C., 1976-80; mgr. agy. relations Forbes mag., N.Y.C., 1980-85; regional advt. dir. Bus. Week, N.Y.C., 1985-86; pub. Am. Heritage mag., N.Y.C., 1986-88; sales dir. worldwide advt. Forbes Mag., N.Y.C., 1990-93, pub., 1993-97, group pub., 1997—. Bd. dirs. Nat. Policy Assn., Global Econ. Coun., Internat. Ctr. N.Y., Jr. Achievement Found., Am. Swiss Foun., Greenwich Japanese Sch. Mem. Econ. Club N.Y., Blind Brook Club (Purchase, N.Y.), Laurel Valley Golf Club (Ligonier, Pa.), Belle Haven Club, Clove Valley Rod and Gun Club (La Grangeville, N.Y.), Internat. Ctr. N.Y. (pres., bd. dirs.), Links Club, Knickerbocker Club. Republican. Mem. Dutch Reformed Ch. Office: Forbes Mag 60 5th Ave New York NY 10011-8802*

CUNNINGHAM, JOEL DEAN, lawyer; b. Seattle, Feb. 19, 1948; s. Edgar Norwood and Florence (Burgunder) C.; m. Amy Jean Radewan, Oct. 1, 1970; children: Erin Jane, Rad Norwood. BA in Econs., U. Wash., 1971, JD with high honors, 1974. Lawyer, ptnr. Williams, Kastner & Gibbs, Seattle, 1974-95; ptnr. Luvera, Barnett, Brindley, Beninger & Cunningham, Seattle, 1995—. Fellow Am. Coll. Trial Lawyers, Am. Bd. Profl. Liability Attys., Internat. Soc. Barristers; mem. Am. Bd. Trial Attys. (pres. Washington chpt. 1994), Damage Attys. Round Table, Order of Coif. Avocations: fishing, cycling, boating. Office: Luvera Barnett Brindley Beninger & Cunningham 6700 Columbia Ctr 701 Fifth Ave Seattle WA 98104-7016

CUNNINGHAM, JOEL LUTHER, university president; b. Mooresville, N.C., Jan. 11, 1944; s. Elbert Claxton and Ruth Morton (Journey) C.; m. Trudy Bender, June 12, 1965; children: Nancy Elizabeth, Susan Ruth. BA, U. Tenn., Chattanooga, 1965; MA, U. Oreg., 1967, PhD, 1969. Asst. prof. math. U. Ky., Lexington, 1969-74; dean continuing edn. U. Tenn., Chattanooga, 1974-79; acad. v.p. Susquehanna U., Selinsgrove, Pa., 1979-84, pres., 1984—. Bd. dirs. Sunbury (Pa.) Hosp., 1984—, v.p., 1992—; bd. dirs. Pa. Campus Compact, 1987-92, Tressler Luth. Svcs., 1995—. Woodrow Wilson fellow, 1965, Am. Council on Edn. fellow, 1976-77. Mem. Am. Math. Soc., Math. Assn. Am., Am. Assn. for Higher Edn., Soc. for Values in Higher Edn. (bd. dirs. 1992—, v.p. 1994-95, pres. 1995—), Susquehanna Valley C. of C. (bd. dirs. 1985-95), Sigma Xi, Sigma Chi (chmn. bd. leadership tng. 1977-87, treas. 1987-89, v.p. 1989-91, pres. 1991-93, Internat. Balfour award 1965). Lutheran. Home: RR 1 Box 48 Winfield PA 17889-9607 Office: Susquehanna U Office of Pres Selinsgrove PA 17870-9989*

CUNNINGHAM, JOHN RANDOLPH, systems analyst; b. Alexandria, La., July 17, 1954; s. John Adolphus and Zelma Audrey (Cox) C.; m. Teresa Ellen Toms, Jan. 22, 1977. BS in Computer Sci., La. Tech. U., 1976. Customer support specialist South Ctrl. Bell Tel. Co., New Orleans, 1977-81; data communication designer Weyerhaeuser, Tacoma, 1981-87, acct. rep., 1987-89, planning mgr., 1989-92, EDI project leader, 1992—; mem. adv. bd. U. Wash., Seattle, 1989-94; spkr. fin. EDI confs. Contbr. articles to profl. jours. Vol. Big Bros., Tacoma, 1989-99, Wash. State First Responder, 1989—; instr. CPR, 1990—, neighborhood emergency tng., 1999—. Mem. Computer and Automated Systems Assn. (treas. 1991-95, pres. 1995-99), Project Mgmt. Inst., Indsl. Computing Soc., Instrument Soc. Am., Toastmasters Internat., Upsilon Pi Epsilon. Republican. Baptist. Home: 319 SW 328th St Federal Way WA 98023-5645

CUNNINGHAM, JOHN THOMAS, science educator. BA in Biology, Hofstra U., 1973; MA in Liberal Studies and Anthropology, NYU, 1991. Forensics instr. John Jay High Sch., Bklyn., 1989—. Fellow Rockefeller U. Sci. Outreach Program; mem. N.Y. Acad. Scis., N.Y. Biology Tchrs. Assn. (v.p. 1998—). E-mail: slypig@prodigy.net. Home: 40 Prospect Park W Apt 6J Brooklyn NY 11215-2356

CUNNINGHAM, JOSEPH NEWTON, JR., cardiothoracic and vascular surgeon; b. Selma, Ala., Mar. 10, 1940; s. Joseph N. and Velma (Greenfield) C.; m. Bonnie Halper; children: Teri, Lori, Stephanie, Jessica, Gaynor, Joseph, Daniel. BS, U. Ala., 1962; MD, Med. Coll. Ala., 1966. Attending surgeon divsn. thoracic surgery NYU Med. Ctr., N.Y.C., 1974-82, Bellevue Hosp., N.Y.C., 1974-82, Manhattan VA Hosp., N.Y.C., 1974-82, Beekman-Downtown Hosp., N.Y.C., 1977-83, St. Vincent's Hosp. and Med. Ctr., N.Y.C., 1977-90; chmn. dept. surgery Maimonides Med. Ctr., Bklyn., 1982—, chief divsn. cardiothoracic surgery, 1982-88, 99—; attending surgeon dept. surg. svcs. Coney Island Hosp., Bklyn., 1982—, Bklyn. VA Hosp., 1982—, Kings County Hosp., Bklyn., 1985—; attending surgeon, dir. divsn. cardiothoracic surgery SUNY Health Sci. Ctr., Bklyn., 1985—. Contbr. numerous chpts. to textbooks in field. rsch. fellow in surgery Parkland Meml. Hosp./U. Tex. Southwestern Med. Sch., Dallas, 1966-72; dir. Berg Lab. for Cardiothoracic Rsch. NYU Med. Ctr., N.Y.C., 1975-82; dir. lab. for surg. rsch. Edward Neimeth Inst. Med. Rsch. Maimonides Med. Ctr., 1982—. Grantee USPHS, 1966-72, NIH, 1981-84, 93-96, Maimonides Med. Ctr. R&D Found., 1990-93, 94-95, N.Y. Cardiac Ctr., 1993-96. Fellow ACS (mem. com. on applicants L.I. dist.), N.Y. Acad. Medicine; mem. Am. Heart Assn., Soc. Thoracic Surgeons, Am. Surg. Assn., Am. Coll. Chest surgeons, Am. Assn. Thoracic Surgery, Internat. Soc. Cardiovascular Surgery, Am. Soc. Artificial Internal Organs, N.Y. Acad. Scis., N.Y. Surg. Soc., N.Y. Cardiovascular Soc., N.Y. Cardiol. Soc., N.Y. Heart Assn. Coun. on Rsch., N.Y. Soc. Thoracic Surgery (pres. 1990), N.Y. Soc. Surgeons, Bklyn. Surg. Soc. (pres. 1989). Office: Cardiothoracic Surg Assoc 4802 10th Ave Brooklyn NY 11219-2916

CUNNINGHAM, JUDY MARIE, lawyer; b. Durant, Okla., Sept. 7, 1944; d. Rowe Edwin and Margaret (Arnott) C. BA, U. Tex., 1967, JD, 1971; postgrad., Schiller Coll., Heidelberg, Fed. Republic Germany, 1976. Bar: Tex. 1972. Quizmaster U. Tex. Law Sch., Austin, 1969-71; researcher Tex. Law Rev., Washington, 1970; staff atty. Tex. Legis. Coun., Austin, 1972-75; adminstrv. law judge, dir. sales tax div., assoc. counsel Comptroller of Pub. Accounts, Austin, 1975-85; owner, editor J.C. Law Publs., Austin, 1986—; pvt. practice Austin, 1986—. Author: (with others) Texas Tax Service, 1985; pub., editor, contbr. (newsletter) Tex. State Tax Update, 1986—; contbr. articles to Revenue Adminstrn.; assoc. editor Tex. Law Rev., 1968-71. State del. Dem. Party, Ft. Worth, 1990, county del., Austin, 1972, 88, 90, 92; vol. numerous Dem. campaigns, Austin, 1972-90. Mem. Nat. Tax Assn., Industry Practitioners Liaison Group (comptr. pub. accts.), State Bar Tex. (taxation sect.), Travis County Bar (bus. corp. and taxation sect.), Tex. Taxpayers and Rsch. Assn. Avocations: traveling, cooking, reading mysteries, photography, swimming. Office: 4905 W Park Dr Austin TX 78731-5535

CUNNINGHAM, JULIA WOOLFOLK, author; b. Spokane, Oct. 4, 1916; d. John George and Sue (Larabie) C. Grad., St. Anne's Sch., Charlottesville, Va., 1933. Author: (juveniles): The Vision of Francois the Fox, 1960, Dear Rat, 1961, Macaroon, 1962, Candle Tales, 1964, Dorp Dead, 1965 (Children's Spring Book Festival award), Violet, 1966, Onion Journey, 1967, Burnish Me Bright, 1970, Wings of the Morning, 1971, Far in the Day, 1972, The Treasure Is the Rose, 1973, Maybe, A Mole, 1974, Come to the Edge, 1977 (Christoper award 1978), Tuppenny, 1978, A Mouse called Junction, 1980, Flight of the Sparrow, 1980 (Commonwealth Club Calif. award, Honor Book award Boston Globe), The Silent Voice, 1981, Wolf Roland, 1983, Oaf, 1986. Mem. Authors Guild. Home: 122 W Valerio St Apt A Santa Barbara CA 93101-2945

CUNNINGHAM, KAREN LEE, marketing professional; b. St. Louis, Sept. 23, 1949; d. Everett R. and Madelyn Marie (Restivo) Saddler; m. David G. Cunningham, May 4, 1970 (div. 1974). Attended, Ind. State U., 1967-69, Butler U., 1975. Cmty. affairs rep. Am. Fletcher Nat. Bank, Indpls., 1969-80; owner Corporate Art Cons., Indpls., 1980-83; dir. pub. rels. and spl. events L.S. Ayres & Co., Indpls., 1983-85; dir. pub. rels. and promotions Drum Corps Internat., Lombard, Ill., 1986; dir. bus. devel. Schmidt Assocs. Archs. Inc., Indpls., 1987-90; dir. mktg., bus. devel. and pub. rels. Eden Design Assocs., Inc., Carmel, Ind., 1990-97; dir. mktg. bus. devel. and pub. rels. MD Rowe Constrn., Inc., Indpls., 1998—. V.p. bd. dirs. Cathedral Arts, Inc., Indpls., 1978-86; mem. adv. coun. Humana Hosp., Indpls., 1983-85; mem. steering com. Eiteljorg Mus., Indpls., 1988-89; city govt. liaison Arts Coun. Indpls., 1989; mem. numerous coms. Meth. Hosp. Task Core, Indpls., 1987-96, 500 Festival Assocs., Indpls., 1989-96; bd. dirs. Ind. State Mus., Indpls., 1990-97; mem. adv. bd. Ind. State U., Terre Haute, 1994—; Mem. Pub. Rels. Soc. Am., Ind. Soc. Pub. Rels. Profls., Internat. Facility Mgmt. Assn. (bd. dirs., Affiliate Member of Yr. 1993), Soc. Mktg. Profl. Svcs. (bd. dirs.), Network Women in Bus. (bd. dirs. 1978-82, Networker of Yr. 1984). Avocations: fitness walking, travel, hiking. Home: 8516 Hague Rd Indianapolis IN 46256-3441 Office: MD Rowe Constrn Inc 8739 Castle Park Dr Indianapolis IN 46256-1272

CUNNINGHAM, KEVIN JAMES, internist; b. Davenport, Iowa, Sept. 10, 1951; s. Glenn Donald and Grace Trinetta (Kinnavey) C.; m. Jeanne Anne Naughton, May 10, 1980; children: Kelly, Emily, Erin, John. BS with high honors, U. Notre Dame, 1973; MD, U. Iowa, 1977. Diplomate Am. Bd. Internal Medicine, Am. Bd. Geriat. Medicine; CLU. Intern, resident Iowa Meth. Med. Ctr. U. Iowa, Des Moines, 1977-80; med. dir. Amerus Life, Des Moines, 1985—, Farm Bur. Life, West Des Moines, Iowa, 1988—; med. dir. Iowa Clinic, Des Moines, 1994—, N.Y.C., 1996-98; chief of staff Iowa Luth. Hosp., Des Moines, 1989-90, Iowa Meth. Med. Ctr., Des Moines, 1993-94. Bd. dirs. Homestead, Des Moines, 1995-96; mem. telemedicine com. State of Iowa, 1996—. Fellow ACP; mem. AMA, Iowa Med. Soc. (legis. chair 1994—). Avocations: jogging, skiing, computers. Office: Iowa Clinic 6800 Lake Dr Ste 185 West Des Moines IA 50266-2504

CUNNINGHAM, LEAH VOTA, medical/surgical nursing educator; b. Pitts., July 19, 1948. BSN, Duquesne U., 1970, MEd, 1973; M in Nursing Edn., U. Pitts., 1976, postgrad., 1990—. Staff nurse Forbes Hospice, Pitts.; assoc. chair BSN program Duquesne U. Sch. Nursing, Pitts. Mem. Oncology Nursing Soc., Transcultural Nursing Soc., Nat. Hospice Orgn., Sigma Theta Tau (newsletter editorial bd.). Home: 107 Cherry Valley Rd Pittsburgh PA 15221-3625

CUNNINGHAM, LEON WILLIAM, biochemist, educator; b. Columbus, Ga., June 9, 1927; s. Leon W. and Annie (Bussey) C.; m. Jean Swingle, Aug. 21, 1948; children: Hugh, Pamela, Sue Ellen. BS, Auburn U., 1947; MS, U. Ill., 1949, PhD, 1951. Research fellow protein chemistry U. Wash., Seattle, 1951-53; asst. prof. biochemistry Sch. Medicine, Vanderbilt U., Nashville, 1953-60, assoc. prof., 1960-65, prof., 1965-94, Branscomb Disting. prof., 1989-94, chmn. dept. biochemistry, 1973-88, assoc. dean Sch. Medicine, 1967-73; prof. emeritus Vanderbilt U., Nashville, 1994; vis. staff Nat. Inst. for Med. Rsch., London, 1976; vis. prof. physiol. chemistry U. Utrecht, Netherlands, 1980, 85, 91. Served with USNR, 1945-46. USPHS spl. fellow Netherlands Nat. Def. Orgn., 1961-62. Mem. AAAS, N.Y. Acad. Sci., Chem. Soc., Am. Soc. Biochemistry and Molecular Biology. Home: 105 Longwood Pl Nashville TN 37215-1926

CUNNINGHAM, MERCE, dancer; b. Centralia, Wash.. Student, Cornish Sch.; PhD (hon.), U. Ill.; DFA (hon.), Wesleyan U., 1995. Own dance co., 1953—; tchr. Sch. Am. Ballet, 1948-51; propr. own dance sch. N.Y.C., 1959—. Soloist Martha Graham Co., 1939-45; 1st solo concert, 1944, many tours including U.S. and Europe, 1949, 58, 60, 66, 69-70, 72, 76-77, 79—, world tour 1964, S.Am., 1968, 76, 82, 88, Mideast, 1972, 76, Australia, 1976, Japan, 1964, 76, 87, 94, 98, Far East, 1984, India, 1964, 84, 90; prin. works choreographed include The Seasons, 1947, Sixteen Dances for Soloist and Company of Three, 1951, Septet, 1953, Minutiae, 1954, Suite for Five, 1956, Nocturnes, 1956, Rune, 1959, Crises, 1960, Aeon, 1961, Story, 1963, Winterbranch, 1964, Variations V, 1965, How to Pass, Kick, Fall and Run, 1965, Place, 1966, Canbield, 1969, Tread, 1970, Second Hand, 1970, Signals, 1970, Landrover, 1972, Changing Steps, 1975, Solo, 1975, Un Jour ou Deux, 1973, Sounddance, 1975, Rebus, 1975, Torse, 1976, Squaregame, 1976, Travelogue, 1977, Inlets, 1977, Fractions, 1977, Exchange, 1978, Locale, 1979, Duets, 1980, Channels/Inserts, 1981, Trails, 1982, Quartet, 1982, Coast Zone, 1983, Roaratorio, 1983, Pictures, 1984, Doubles, 1984, Phrases, 1984, Native Green, 1985, Arcade, 1985, Points in Space, 1986, Fabrications, 1987, Shards, 1987, Five Stone Wind, 1988, Cargo X, 1989, August Pace, 1989, Polarity, 1990, Neighbors, 1991, Trackers, 1991, Beach Birds, 1991, Loosestrife, 1991, Change of Address, 1992, Touchbase, 1992, Enter, 1992, Doubletoss, 1993, CRWDSPCR, 1993, Breakers, 1994, Ocean, 1994, Ground Level Overlay, 1995, Windows, 1995, Rondo, 1996, Installations, 1996, Scenario, 1997, Pond Way, 1998, BIPED, 1999, Occasion Piece, 1999. Decorated comdr. Order of Arts and Letters, Legion of Honor (France); recipient Gold medal Internat. Festival Dance, 1966, Grand prix Belgrade Internat. Theatre Festival, 1972, Creative Arts award Brandeis U., 1973, Capezio award, 1977, Samuel H. Scripps/Am. Dance Festival award, 1982, N.Y.C. Mayor's award of honor for arts and culture, 1983, Kennedy Ctr. honors, 1985, Laurence Olivier award, 1985, Meadows award for Excellence in the Arts, So. Meth. U., 1987, Nat. Medal of Arts, 1990, Digital Dance Premier award, 1990, Wexner prize, Wexner Ctr. for the Arts, Columbus, Ohio, 1993, Golden Lion award Venice Biennale, 1995; MacArthur Found. fellow, 1985, Nellie Cornish Arts Achievement award Cornish Coll. of the Arts, Seattle, 1996, medal of Distinction, Barnard Coll., 1997, Grand prix SACD, France, 1997, Belknap award in Humanities, Princeton U., 1998, Key to City of Montpellier, Mayor of Montpellier, France, 1999, Bagley Wright Fund Established Artists award, Seattle, Isadora Duncan award for Lifetime Achievement in Dance, Nat. Dance Week, San Francisco, 1999. Mem. Am. Acad. and Inst. Arts and Letters (hon.). Office: Cunningham Dance Found 55 Bethune St New York NY 10014-2010

CUNNINGHAM, MICHAEL, author, educator. BA, Stanford U., 1975; MA, U. Iowa, 1980. Adj. asst. prof. Creative Writing Ctr., Columbia U., N.Y.C. Author: Golden States, A Home at the End of the World, Flesh and Blood, The Hours; contbg. author: The Penguin Book of Gay Short Stories; contbr. to Atlantic Monthly, Redbook, Paris Rev., New Yorker, WigWag. Office: Columbia U Creative Writing Ctr 612 Lewisohn Hall 2970 Broadway New York NY 10027-6902

CUNNINGHAM, MICHAEL GERALD, composer, music educator; b. Warren, Mich., Aug. 5, 1937; s. Edmund John and Mary Ann (Etienne) C. MusB, Wayne State U., 1959; MusM, U. Mich., 1961; MusD, Ind. U., 1973. Accompanist, music dir. dance dept. Wayne State U., Detroit, 1961, 64-67, instr. music dept., 1967-69; teaching asst. Ind. U. Sch. Music, Bloomington, 1969-71; lectr. music theory U. Kans. Sch. Fine Arts, Lawrence, 1972; asst. prof. Conservatory Music, U. Pacific, Stockton, Calif., 1973; prof. music theory and composition U. Wis., Eau Claire, 1973—. Author: The Inner World of Traditional Theory, 1989; composer numerous compositions. With U.S. Army, 1962-63. Mem. ASCAP (ann. stipend 1969—), Wis. Alliance Composers, Sigma Alpha Iota. Office: U Wis Music Dept Eau Claire WI 54702

CUNNINGHAM, MILAMARI ANTOINELLA, anesthesiologist; b. Cody, Wyo., Oct. 4, 1949; d. Milo Leo and Mary Madeline (Haley) Olds; m. Michael Otis Webb, June 4, 1970 (div. Feb. 1971); m. James Kenneth Cunningham, June 14, 1975. BA with honors, U. Mo., 1971, MD, 1975. Diplomate Am. Bd. Anesthesiologists. Intern and resident U. Mo., Columbia, 1975-78; jr. ptnr. Anesthesiologist, Inc., 1979-82, ptnr., 1982-86; owner Cunningham Anesthesia, 1986—; dir. anesthesia dept. Ellis Fischel Cancer Ctr., 1991-92; acting chief anesthesia Harry S. Truman Meml. Vets. Hosp., 1994-95; mem. med. staff Columbia Regional Hosp., Boone Hosp. Ctr., Columbia U. Mo. Hosp. and Clinics, Columbia; cons. staff Audrain Med. Ctr., Mexico, Mo. Active Mo. Med. Polit. Action Com., 1991—, Friends of Music, Friends of Libr., Boone County Fair, 1978-94, with ham breakfast divsn., 1978-85, with draft horse and mule show, 1978-86; bd. dirs. A Call to Serve Mo., 1996. Fellowship Am. Coll. Anesthesiologists, 1977. Mem. AMA (physicians recognition award 1978, 85, 87, 91, 95), Am. Soc. Regional Anesthesia, Am. Med. Women's Assn., Internat. Anesthesia Rsch. Soc., Mo. Soc. Anesthesiologists (v.p. 1986-87, pres. elect 1987-88, pres. 1988-89, Am. Soc. Anesthesiologists del. 1989—), Boone County Med. Soc. (alt. del. 1986, del. 1987-89, 97, membership chair 1982-84, sec.-treas. 1996—, pres. 1988-98, bd. dirs. 1996-99), Mo. State Med. Assn. (commn. econs. third party payors 1986—, chair 1989), Vis. Nurses Assn. (bd. dirs. 1982-89, chair 1984-86, adv. bd. 1989-93), Phi Beta Kappa. Home: 8202 S Bennett Dr Columbia MO 65201-9178 Office: PO Box 1301 Columbia MO 65205-1301

CUNNINGHAM, PAUL GEORGE, minister; b. Chgo., Aug. 27, 1937; s. Paul George Sr. and Naomi Pearl (Anderson) C.; m. Constance Ruth Seaman, May 27, 1960; children: Lori, Paul, Connie Jo. BA, Olivet Nazarene U., 1960; BDiv., Nazarene Theol. Sem., 1964; DD, Mid Am. Nazarene Coll., 1975. Sr. pastor Coll. Ch. of the Nazarene, Olathe, Kans., 1964-93; gen. supt. Internat. Ch. of the Nazarene, 1993—; adv. bd. Kansas City Dist. Ch. of the Nazarene, Overland Park, Kans., 1971—; trustee Mid Am. Nazarene Coll., Olathe, 1971—; chmn. book com. Nazarene Pub. House, Kansas City, Mo., 1974-90; pres. gen. bd. Internat. Ch. of the Nazarene, Kansas City, 1985—. Police chaplain Olathe (Kans.) Police Dept., 1975—; adv. bd. Good Samaritan Ctr., Olathe, 1990—. Recipient Disting. Svc. award Jaycees, Olathe, 1967, Paul Harris fellow Rotary Internat., Olathe, 1989. Mem. Nat. Assn. Evangelicals, Rotary. Home: 12543 S Hagan Ln Olathe KS 66062-6075 Office: Ch of the Nazarene 6401 Paseo Blvd Kansas City MO 64131-1213

CUNNINGHAM, PAUL RAYMOND GOLDWYN, surgery educator; b. Jamaica, July 28, 1949; came to U.S., 1974; s. Winston Pommells and Sylvia Fenella (Marsh) C.; m. Bridget Ann Mulvany, 1974 (div. 1985); children: Rachel Louise, Lucinda Jane; m. Sydney Louise Keniston, Feb. 14, 1987. MB, BS, Univ. West Indies, Jamaica, 1972. Diplomate Am. Bd. Surgery. Commd. maj. U.S. Army Res. Med. Corp., 1990; resident surgeon Mt. Sinai Hosp., N.Y.C., 1974-78, chief resident surgery, 1978-79, clin. instr., 1978-81; asst. dir. surgery and joint diseases North Gen. Hosp., N.Y.C., 1979-81, instr., 1981-84; attending surgeon Bertie County Meml. Hosp., Windsor, N.C., 1981-84, vice chief of staff, 1981-84; clin. instr. surgery East Carolina U. Sch. Medicine, Greenville, N.C., 1981-84, asst. prof. surgery Dept. Surgery, 1984-89, assoc. prof. and tenure, 1989-93, prof., 1993—; med. dir. Pitt County Meml. Hosp. Trauma Svc., Greenville, 1986—, chief of staff, 1991, various coms.; mem. N.C. Com. on Trauma, 1985—; cons., mem. Bertie County Dept. Health, Windsor, 1982-84. Contbr. articles to profl. jours. Mem. AMA, Am. Coun. on Transplantation, N.C. Med. Soc., Pitt County Med. Soc. A. Trauma Soc. (pres. N.C. chpt. 1989-91). Avocations: nature appreciation, reading, music, painting, photography. Office: Pitt County Meml Hosp PO Box 6028 Greenville NC 27835-6028

CUNNINGHAM, R. JOHN, retired financial consultant; b. Detroit, May 1, 1926; s. Richard John and Mary Gladys (Lahey) C.; m. Dorothy A. Clair, Nov. 29, 1947; children—Karen A., Richard J., William J., Patricia A., Cathy A., Kevin P., Maryann. *1997 was the Golden Wedding Anniversary Year. His 7 children have given him a combined 17 grandchildren.* PhB in Commerce, U. Notre Dame, 1950; MBA, N.Y. U., 1954. Sr. v.p. Midwest Stock Exch., Chgo., 1966-68; exec. v.p. New York Stock Exch., 1968-71; dir. fin. svcs. Arthur Young & Co., N.Y.C., 1971-76; sr. v.p. Federated Dept. Stores, Inc., Cin., 1976-81; cons. Arthur D. Little, Inc., Cambridge, Mass., 1981-88, Horwitz & Assocs., Inc., Northbrook, Ill., 1988—; chmn. adv. com. SEC Report Coordinating Group, 1974-76. Mem. pres.'s coun. U. Notre Dame, 1968-75; mem. parents coun. St. Marys Coll., South Bend, Ind., 1972-74. With AUS, 1944-47. Recipient cert. of appreciation U.S. SEC, 1975, cert. of appreciation SEC Report Coordinating Group, 1976; named Man of Year Chgo. Assn. Investment Bankers, 1967. Home: 68 Diana Rd # 428 Portage IN 46368-8702

CUNNINGHAM, R. WALTER, venture capitalist; b. Creston, Iowa, Mar. 16, 1932; s. Walter Wilfred and Gladys (Backen) C.; m. Dorothy League, Dec. 27, 1997; children: Brian Keith, Kimberly Ann. B.S. in Physics, UCLA, 1960, M.A., 1961; advanced mgmt. program, Harvard Grad. Sch. Bus., 1974. Research asst. Planning Research Corp., Westwood, Calif., 1959-60; physicist RAND Corp., Santa Monica, Calif., 1960-64; astronaut NASA, 1964-71; crew member of first manned Apollo spacecraft Apollo 7; sr. v.p. Century Devel., 1971-74; pres. Hydrotech Devel. Co., Houston, 1974-76; sr. v.p. 3D/Internat., Houston, 1976-79; founder The Capital Group, Houston, 1979-86; mng. ptnr. Genesis Fund, 1986—; bd. dirs. numerous tech. based cos.; chmn. Tex. Aerospace Commn. Author: The All American Boys, 1977. Judge Rolex awards for enterprise, 1984. With USNR, 1951-52, fighter pilot USMCR, 1952-74, col. ret. Recipient NASA Exceptional Service medal, also; Haley Astronautics award; Profl. Achievement award U. Calif. at Los Angeles Alumni, 1969; Spl. Trustee award Nat. Acad. Television Arts and Scis., 1969; medal of valor Am. Legion, 1975; Outstanding Am. award Am. Conservative Union, 1975; named to Internat. Space Hall of Fame, Houston Hall of Fame, Astronaut Hall of Fame, 1997. Fellow Am. Astronautical Soc.; mem. Soc. Exptl. Test Pilots, Am. Inst. Aeros. and Astronautics, Assn. Space Explorers-U.S.A., Am. Geophys. Union, Sigma Pi Sigma. Office: 2425 W Loop South Ste 200 Houston TX 77027 Office: 2425 West Loop S Ste 200 Houston TX 77027-4207

CUNNINGHAM, RANDALL, professional football player; b. Santa Barbara, Calif., Mar. 27, 1963; s. Samuel and Mabel Cunningham. Student, U. Nev., Las Vegas. With Phila. Eagles, 1985-95; analyst Turner Network TV, Atlanta, 1996-98; backup quarterback Minn. Vikings, 1998—; player NFL Pro Bowl, 1988, 89, 90. Named N.F.L. Player of Yr., 1991, punter The Sporting News Coll. All-Am. Team, 1984. Office: care Minn Vikings 9520 Viking Dr Eden Prairie MN 55344-3825*

CUNNINGHAM, RANDY, congressman; b. L.A., Dec. 8, 1941; m. Nancy Jones; 3 children. BA, U. Mo., MA; MBA, Nat. U. Mem. 102nd-105th Congresses from Calif. dist. 44 (now 51), 1991—, mem. nat. security com., mem. appropriations com. Republican. Christian. Office: US Ho of Reps 2238 Rayburn HOB Washington DC 20515*

CUNNINGHAM, RAYMOND LEO, research chemist, retired; b. Easton, Ill., Jan. 5, 1934; s. Raymond J. and Minnie G. (Vaughn) C. BA, St. Ambrose U., Davenport, Iowa, 1955. Phys. sci. aid in chemistry Nat. Ctr. Agrl. Utilization Rsch USDA Agrl. Rsch. Svc., Peoria, Ill., 1957-61, chemist Nat. Ctr. Agrl. Utilization Rsch., 1961-78, rsch. chemist Nat. Ctr. Agrl. Utilization Rsch., 1978-97; ret., 1997. Contbr. articles to profl. jours. With U.S. Army, 1958. Co-recipient R&D 100 award R&D mag., 1988. Mem. AAAS, Am. Chem. Soc., Ill. State Acad. Sci. Home: 1108 W MacQueen Ave Peoria IL 61604-3310

CUNNINGHAM, ROBERT D., lawyer. BA, Occidental Coll., Calif., 1971; JD, UCLA, 1975. Bar: Calif. 1975. Assoc. Lawler, Felix & Hall, L.A., 1975-78; atty. Buena Vista Pictures Distbn., Inc., Burbank, Calif., 1978-84, v.p., sec., gen. counsel, 1984-96; sr. v.p., sec., gen. counsel Buena Vista Pictures Distbn., Inc. (now Walt Disney Pictures & TV), Burbank, Calif., 1996—. Office: Walt Disney Pictures & TV 500 S Buena Vista St Burbank CA 91521*

CUNNINGHAM, ROBERT JAMES, lawyer; b. Kearney, Nebr., June 27, 1942; m. Sara Jean Dickson, July 22, 1967. BA, U. Nebr., 1964; JD, NYU, 1967, LLM in Taxation, 1969. Bar: N.Y. 1967, Ill. 1969, U.S. Dist. Ct. (no. dist.) Ill. 1969, U.S. Ct. Claims 1970, U.S. Tax Ct. 1970, U.S. Ct. Appeals (D.C. cir.) 1972, U.S. Ct. Appeals (9th cir.) 1975, U.S. Ct. Appeals (7th cir.) 1979, U.S. Ct. Appeals (fed. cir.) 1982. Instr. law NYU, N.Y.C., 1967-69; assoc. Baker & McKenzie, Chgo., 1969-74, ptnr., 1974—; spkr. in field. Contbr. articles to profl. jours. Mem. ABA, Ill. Bar Assn., Chgo. Bar Assn. Office: Baker & McKenzie One Prudential Plz 130 E Randolph Dr Ste 3700 Chicago IL 60601-6342

CUNNINGHAM, RON, choreographer, artistic director; b. Chgo., Sept. 15, 1939; m. Carrine Binda, June 12, 1982; children: Christopher, Alexandra. Student, Allegro Ballet, 1961-65, Am. Ballet Theatre, 1968-70; studies with Merce Cunningham, N.Y.C., 1968-70; BS in Mktg., Roosevelt U., 1966. Dancer Allegro Am. Ballet Co., Chgo., 1962-66; artistic dir. Ron Cunningham Contemporary Dance Co., Chgo., 1966-68; dancer Lucas Hoving Dance Co., 1968-72, Lotte Goslar Pantomime Circus, 1968-72, Daniel Nagrin Dance Co., 1968-72; prin. dancer, resident choreographer Boston Ballet, 1972-85; artistic dir. Balt. Ballet, 1985-86; artistic assoc. Washington Ballet, 1986-87; ind. choreographer, 1987-88; artistic dir. Sacramento Ballet, 1988—; panelist various regional and state art councils, 1979—; dir. Craft of Choreography, 1985; adjudicator, master tchr. Nat. Assn. Regional Ballet, 1985—, Am. Coll. Dance Assn., 1986. Dancer, choreographer 40 original internat. ballets, 1972—, 4 ballets Nat. Choreography Plan, 1978—, Cinderella, Peoples Republic of China, 1980. Nat. Endowment Arts fellow, 1977, 86, Mass. Art Council fellow, 1984, Md. Arts Council fellow, 1988. Mem. Nat. Assn. Regional Ballet, Dance/U.S.A. Avocation: archeology--bronze age cultures. *

CUNNINGHAM, STANLEY LLOYD, lawyer; b. Durant, Okla., Feb. 7, 1938; s. Stanley Ryan and Hazel Dell (Dillingham) C.; m. Suzanne Yerger, Sept. 18, 1960; children: Stanley William, Ryan Yerger. BS in Geology, U. Okla., 1960, LLB, 1963. Bar: U.S. Dist. Ct. (we. dist.) Okla. 1963; U.S. Ct. Appeals (10th cir.) 1965; U.S. Supreme Ct. Okla. 1963. Atty. Phillips Petroleum Co., Oklahoma City, 1963-64, Bartlesville, Okla., 1964-71; assoc. McAfee, Taft, et al., Oklahoma City, 1971-73; mem. McAfee & Taft, Oklahoma City, 1973—; lecturer U. Okla. Coll. Law, Norman, 1977, 79, S.W. Legal Found., Dallas, 1986, 89. Contbr. articles to profl. jours. Layreader All Souls' Episcopal Ch., Oklahoma City, 1972-75. 1st lt. USAFR, 1963-72. Harry J. Brown scholar, U. Okla., 1960-63. Mem. ABA, Fed. Energy Bar Assn., Am. Soc. Internat. Law, Geological Soc. Am., Alumni Adv. Coun., U. Okla. Assoc., Oklahoma City Golf & Country Club, Order of Coif, Phi Alpha Delta, Sigma Gamma Epsilon. Republican. Episcopalian. Avocations: golf, reading. Office: McAfee & Taft 2 Leadership Sq Fl 10 Oklahoma City OK 73102

CUNNINGHAM, TERENCE THOMAS, III, hospital administrator; b. Bell, Calif., Feb. 13, 1943; s. Terence Thomas and Leone (Downey), C.; m. Mary Katherine Kasarda, Apr. 22, 1967; children: Wendy Victoria C., Terence Thomas IV. BS in Microbiology, Calif. State U., Long Beach, 1967; MA in Hosp. Adminstrn., George Washington U., Washington, 1974. Commd. 2d lt. USAF, 1967, advanced through grades to col., 1989; adminstrv. resident MacDill Hosp., Tampa, Fla., 1973-74; adminstr. Rhein-Main Clinic, Frankfurt, Germany, 1974-79; hosp. cons. Air Force Med. Inspection Ctr., San Bernardino, Calif., 1979-81; CFO David Grant Med. Ctr., Fairfield, Calif., 1981-82; adminstr. Torrejon Hosp., Madrid, 1982-85; chief fin. and materials officer Office Command Surgeon, Hdqrs. Mil. Airlift Command, Bellville, Ill., 1985-87; adminstr. Wright Patterson Med. Ctr., Dayton, Ohio, 1987-92, Wilford Hall Med. Ctr., San Antonio, 1992-94; v.p. adminstrn. Johns Hopkins Hosp., Balt., 1994—; instr. grad. program health care adminstrn. Chapman Coll., Calif., 1981-82; preceptor grad. students in hosp. and health care adminstrn. Xavier U., Cin., 1987—, Baylor U., San Antonio, 1988—, George Washington U., Washington, 1995—, Johns Hopkins U., Balt., 1995—; asst. clin. prof. Wright State U. Sch. Medicine, Dayton, Ohio, 1990—; assoc. prof. Dept. Health Policy and Mgmt. Johns Hopkins U. Sch. Pub. Health and Hygiene; cons. Surgeon Gen. USAF, 1986—. Book reviewer Hosps. and Health Svcs. Adminstrn., Jour. Quality Assurance, Mil. Medicine; editorial bd. Frontiers of Health Svcs. Mgmt. Fellow Am. Coll. Healthcare Execs. (various coms., regent to U.S. Air Force); mem. Ohio Hosp. Assn. (chmn. accreditation com.), Greater Dayton Area Hosp. Assn. (bd. dirs.), Tex. Hosp. Assn. (mem. edn. com.), Assn. Mil. Surgeons U.S. (Young Fed. Health Care Adminstr. of Yr. 1983, Fed. Health-care Adminstr. of Yr. 1989, Sr. Fed. Healthcare Adminstr. of Yr. 1992), Interagy. Inst. Fed. Health Care Alumni Assn. Avocations: bicycling, photography, sailing, reading, scouting. Office: Johns Hopkins Hosp Adminstrn Bldg Rm 107 600 N Wolfe St Baltimore MD 21287-0005

CUNNINGHAM, THOMAS JUSTIN, lawyer; b. Hinsdale, Ill., Feb. 27, 1968; s. Thomas J. and Diane (Carlton) C.; m. Paula J. Friant, Sept. 9, 1989; children: Thomas Justin, Nicholas Joseph. BS, Ariz. State U., 1989; JD, DePaul U., 1993. Bar: Ill. 1993, U.S. Dist. Ct. (no. dist.) Ill. 1993, U.S. Ct. Appeals (7th cir.) 1993, U.S. Dist. Ct. (ctrl. dist.) Ill. 1996, U.S. Supreme Ct. 1996, Trial bar 1997. Dep. clk. U.S. Bankruptcy Ct., Chgo., 1989-90; law clk. Burke, Smith & Williams, Chgo., 1990-93; assoc. Smith, Lodge & Schneider, Chgo., 1993-98, Hopkins & Sutter, Chgo., 1998—. Contbr. articles to profl. jours. Pres. Ill. Dist. 58 Bd. Edn. Mem. Chgo. Bar Assn. (chair moot ct. com. 1995, co-editor in chief YLS jour.). Republican. Presbyterian. Avocations: hunting, fishing. Home: 5135 Fairview Ave Downers Grove IL 60515-5211 Office: Hopkins & Sutter 3 First Nat Pla Ste 4100 Chicago IL 60602

CUNNINGHAM, WALTER JACK, electrical engineering educator; b. Comanche, Tex., Aug. 21, 1917; s. Walter Jack and Percy Adele (Moore) C.; m. Barbara Virginia Lynch, Feb. 26, 1944; children: Lawrence Bradford, John Hartwell. AB, U. Tex., 1937, AM, 1938; PhD, Harvard U., 1947. Instr. physics and communication engring. Harvard, 1939-46; part-time research OSRD, in acoustics and electric circuits, 1939-46; asst. prof. elec. engring. Yale U., 1946-50, assoc. prof., 1950-56, prof. engring. and applied sci., 1956-81, prof. elec. engring., 1981-88, assoc. chmn. dept. engring. and applied sci., 1969-72, prof. emeritus, 1988—. Author: Introduction to Nonlinear Analysis, 1958, Engineering at Yale, 1992; bd. editors Am. Scientist, 1955-81, 83-90, Jour. Franklin Inst., 1962-75; also articles. Mem. IEEE, Acoustical Soc. Am., Sigma Xi (bd. editors, chmn. com. on publs. 1983-87). Home: 200 Leeder Hill Dr Apt 326 Hamden CT 06517-2798 Office: Yale U Becton Ctr New Haven CT 06520-8284

CUNNINGHAM, WILLIAM FRANCIS, JR., English language educator, university administrator; b. Holyoke, Mass., Feb. 9, 1931; s. William Francis and Constance Emma (Cox) C.; m. Eleanor Mary Bissonette, Dec. 27, 1956; children—Margaret Ann, William John, Mary Elizabeth. A.B., Holy Cross Coll., 1954; M.A., Boston Coll., 1956; Ph.D., U. Pitts., 1961; DHL honoris causa, Le Moyne Coll., 1994. Asst. prof. English, Duquesne U., 1955-63; prof. Le Moyne Coll., 1963-78; prof. English Creighton U., 1978—, dean Coll. Arts and Scis., 1978-87, acting v.p. for acad. affairs, 1986-87, v.p. acad. affairs, 1987-93, spl. asst. to pres., 1993-96; dean emeritus, 1994—, ret., 1997; Danforth assoc., 1974—. Contbr. articles on 18th-century Brit. lit. to profl. jours. Mem. Coll. Bd. (council on coll.-level services, exec. com. Midwestern regional assembly 1980-84), Am. Soc. 18th-century Studies.

CUNNINGHAM, WILLIAM HENRY, retired food products executive; b. Oxnard, Calif., Dec. 2, 1930; s. William Henry and Carrie Edna (Wilson) C.; m. Carmen Nelson Alden, Jan. 19, 1957; children: Nelson, Clifford, Cynthia. BA, U. Calif., Santa Barbara, 1952; B of Foreign Trade, Am Grad. Sch. Internat. Mgmt., 1958. With Colgate-Palmolive Internat., N.Y. and Colombia, El Salvador, 1958-63; mktg. cons. Anderson, Clayton Co., Mexico City, Buenos Aires and Lima, 1963-66; mgr. consumer div. Cyanamid, Buenos Aires, 1966-69; dir. mktg. and sales Alimentos Kraft, Caracas, Venezuela, 1969-74; gen. mgr. Panama and Cen. Am. Panama and Ctrl. Am. Kraft Foods, Inc., 1974-80; pres. Alimentos Kraft Alimentos Kraft Foods, Inc., Venezuela, 1980-86; v.p., dir. Kraft Foods, Inc. Kraft Gen. Foods, Walt Disney World, Fla., 1986-92; v.p., dir. The Land, Epcot Ctr., Walt Disney World, Fla. Stewartship chmn. St. Lukes Meth., Windermere, Fla., 1991-92; vol. Inter Exec. Svc. Corp. for assignment in L.Am. to help local industry, 1993, assignment to Bogota Colombia, 1994, Ctrl. Russia, 1996; vol. Second Helping. Sgt. U.S. Army, 1952-54. Recipient Tribute Appreciation award U.S. State Dept., 1980, Order of Vasco Nunez de Balboa, Govt. Panama, 1980, First Class Work Merit award Govt. Venezuela, 1985, Jonas Mayer Disting. Alum award Thunderbird Grad. Sch. for Internat. Mgmt., 1997. Mem. Am. C. of C. (pres., founder Panama City chpt. 1979, sec. Caracas 1986), Am. Soc. (pres. Panama City chpt. 1977), Walt Disney World Participant Assn. (pres. 1990-91), U. Calif. Alumni Assn. (bd. dirs. Santa Barbara 1992-98, chair awards), Bear Creek Golf Club, Hilton Head. Democrat. Methodist. Avocations: golf, tennis, skiing. Home: 11 Bear Creek Dr Hilton Head Island SC 29926-1904

CUNNINGHAM, WILLIAM HUGHES, academic administrator, marketing educator; b. Detroit, Jan. 5, 1944; married; 1 child. BA, Mich. State U., 1966, MBA, 1967, PhD, 1971, LLD (hon.), 1993. Mem. faculty U. Tex., Austin, 1971—, assoc. prof. mktg., 1973-79, prof., 1979—, assoc. dean grad. programs, 1976-82, Foley/Sanger Harris prof. retail merchandising, 1982-83, acting dean Coll. Bus. Adminstrn. and Grad. Sch. Bus., 1982-83, dean, 1983-85, pres., 1985-92, Centennial Chair Bus. Edn. Leadership, 1983-85, Regents Chair Higher Edn. Leadership, 1985-92, Lee Hage and Joseph D. Jamail Regents Chair Higher Edn. Leadership, 1992—, James L. Bayless Chair for Free Enterprise, 1988—; chancellor U. Tex. System, Austin, 1992—; bd. dirs. Jefferson-Pilot Corp., John Hancock Funds, Golfsmith Internat. Inc.; mem. Corp. of the Conf. Bd. Author: (with W.J.E. Crissy and I.C.M. Cunningham) Selling: The Personal Force in Marketing, 1977, 2d edit. (with D.W. Jackson and Cunningham), 1988, Effective Selling, 1977, Spanish edit., 1980, (with S. Lopreato) Consumers' Energy Attitudes and Behavior, 1977, (with Cunningham) Marketing: A Managerial Approach, 1981, 2d edit. (with Cunningham and C. Swift), 1988, (with R. Aldag and C. Swift) Introduction to Business, 1984, 3d edit. (with R. Aldag and S. Block), 1992, 4th edit. (with R. Aldag and M. Stone), 1995, (with B. Verhage and Cunningham) Grondslagen van het Marketing Management, 1984, (with R. Aldag and S. Block) Business in a Changing World, 1992, also monographs and articles; editor Jour. Mktg., 1981-84. Bd. dirs. Houston Area Rsch. Coun., 1984; mem. Mental Health/Mental Retardation Legis. Oversight Com., 1984; mem. adv. bd. Found. for Cultural Exch./The Netherlands-U.S.A.; bd. dirs. Lyndon Baines Johnson Found. Recipient Teaching Excellence award Coll. Bus. Adminstrn., U. Tex., 1972, Alpha Kappa Psi, 1975, Hank and Mary Harkins Found., 1978, Disting. Scholastic Contbn. award Coll. Bus. Adminstrn. Found. Adv. Council, 1982, Disting. Alumnus award Coll. and Grad. Sch. Bus., Mich. State U., 1983, 93, Tree of Life award Jewish Nat. Fund, 1992; named among top 20 profs. Utmost Mag., 1982; research grantee Univ. Research Inst., 1971, 72-73, Latin Am. Inst., 1972, So. Union Gas Energy, 1975-76, ERDA, 1976. Mem. Am. Inst. for Decision Scis., Am. Mktg. Assn., Assn. Consumer Research, So. Mktg. Assn., S.W. Social Sci. Assn., Phi Kappa Phi, Omicron Delta Kappa. Office: U TX System Office Chancellor 601 Colorado St Austin TX 78701-2904

CUNNINGHAME, DONNA HOLT, former government official; b. Sunnyside, Wash., Sept. 6, 1939; d. Roy Emerson and Genevieve Gilberta (Gwynne) Holt; m. Ferguson Todd Cunninghame (dec. July 1998); children: Christina Gwynne, Todd Samuel. BBA in Acctg., U. Mo., 1974; MGA, U. Md., 1992. CPA, Mo. Sr. acct. KPMG Peat Marwick, Kansas City, Mo., 1975-78; dir. fin. Kansas City Area Transp. Authority, 1978-81; v.p. fin. Isis Foods, Kansas City, 1981-82; asst. treas. Higher Edn. Mgmt. and Resources Found., Overland Park, Kans., 1982-85; CFO, assoc. vice chancellor U. Md., Adelphi, 1985-93; CFO, Resolution Trust Corp., Washington, 1993-96, Corp. for Nat. Svc., Washington, 1996-98, IRS, Washington, 1998-99. Mem. fin. com. Episcopal Diocese West Mo., Kansas City, 1984-85; bd. dirs. Assn. Clay County Dems., 1980-85; bd. dirs., treas. Clay County Indsl. Devel. Authority, 1980-85; bd. dirs., v.p. Northland Youth-Adult Project Com., North Kansas City, 1978-85, German Orphan Home, Upper Marlboro, Md., 1987-93; mem. Md. Higher Edn. Commn., 1996—. Mem. Md. Pub. Fin. Officers Assn. (bd. dirs. 1989-93, chmn. continuing edn. com. 1989-93). Home: 1116 Windmill Ln Silver Spring MD 20905-6040 Office: IRS 1111 Constitution Ave NW Washington DC 20224-0001

CUNO, JAMES, art museum director; b. St. Louis, Apr. 6, 1951; married; 2 children. BA in History, Willamette U., 1973; MA in History of Art, U. Oreg., 1978; AM in Fine Arts, Harvard U., 1980, PhD in Fine Arts, 1985. Asst. curator prints Fogg Art Mus. Harvard U., Cambridge, Mass., 1980-83, dir. Univ. Art Mus., 1991—; asst. prof. dept. art Vassar Coll., Poughkeepsie, N.Y., 1983-86; dir. Grunwald Ctr. for Graphic Arts UCLA, 1986-89; dir. Hood Mus. Art Dartmouth Coll., Hanover, N.H., 1989-91; trustee Mus. Fine Arts, Boston; panelist NEH, NEA; mem. pub. grant adv. com. Getty Grant Program, 1991-96. Author, editor exhbn. catalogues (with others) Foirades/Fizzles: Echo and Allusion in the Art of Jasper Johns, 1987, Politics and Polemics: French Caricature and the Revolution, 1789-1799, 1988, Scenes and Sequences: Recent Monotypes by Eric Fischl, 1990, Jonathan Borofsky: Prints and Multiples, 1982-91, 1991, The Popularization of Images: Visual Culture Under the July Monarchy, 1994; contbr. articles to profl. jours. Mem. Coll. Art Assn. (nat. com. history of art), Print Coun.

Am., Assn. Art Mus. Dirs. Office: Harvard U Art Mus 32 Quincy St Cambridge MA 02138-3845

CUOMO, ANDREW, federal agency administrator. BA, Fordham U., 1979; JD, Albany Law Sch., 1982. Asst. dist. atty. Dist. Atty's Office, Manhattan; ptnr. Blutrich, Falcone and Miller, N.Y.C.; chmn. N.Y.C. Commn. on the Homeless, 1991-93; asst. sec. comty. planning and devel. U.S. Dept. Housing and Urban Devel., Washington, 1993—, sec. Campaign mgr. Mario M. Cuomo for Gov. N.Y., 1982; founder, pres. H.E.L.P., 1986, founder Genesis, 1992. Recipient Good Neighbor award ARC, Outstanding Comty. Svc. award Latin Soul, 1988, Man of the Yr. award Coalition of Italian Am. Orgns., 1988, Ed Sulzberger award, Our Town newspaper, 1989, Pub. Svc. award Coun. of Jewish Orgns., 1989, Disting. Comty. Svc. award NYU, 1991, Bard award, 1992, Albert Einstein award, 1993, Encore Heart to Heart award, 1994, Innovation Am. Govt. award John F. Kennedy Sch. Govt. Harvard U., 1996. Office: Sec HUD 451 7th St SW Washington DC 20410-0001*

CUOMO, DONNA FOURNIER, state legislator. Rep. Mass. Ho. of Reps., 1993-98; dir. health & safety Commonwealth Mass. Exec. Off. of Elder Affairs, Boston, 1999—. Office: 1 Ashburton Pl Boston MA 02108

CUOMO, MARIO MATTHEW, lawyer, former governor; b. Queens County, N.Y., June 15, 1932; s. Andrea and Immaculata (Giordano) C.; m. Matilda Raffa, June 5, 1954; children: Margaret Cuomo Maier, Maria Cuomo Cole, Madeline Cuomo O'Donoghue, Christopher. B.A. summa cum laude, St. John's Coll., 1953; LL.B. cum laude, St. John's U., 1956. Bar: N.Y. 1956, U.S. Dist. Ct. (no. dist.) N.Y. 1957, U.S. Supreme Ct. 1960, U.S. Dist. Ct. (ea. dist.) N.Y. 1962, U.S. Ct. Appeals (2d cir. 1967). Confidential legal asst. to Hon. Adrian P. Burke, N.Y. State Ct. Appeals, 1956-58; assoc. Corner, Weisbrod, Froeb and Charles, Bklyn., 1958-63; ptnr. Corner, Cuomo & Charles, 1963-75; sec. of state State of N.Y., 1975-79, lt. gov., 1979-83, gov., 1983-94; ptnr. Wilkie Farr & Gallagher, N.Y.C., 1995—; mem. faculty St. John's U. Sch. Law, 1963-73; counsel to community groups, including Corona Homeowners, 1966-72; charter mem. First Ecumenical Commn. of Christians and Jews for Bklyn. and Queens, N.Y. Author: Forest Hills Diary: The Crisis of Low-Income Housing, 1974, Diaries of Mario M. Cuomo, Campaign for Governor, 1982; co-author: Lincoln on Democracy, 1990, More Than Words, 1993, The New York Idea: An Experiment in Democracy, 1994; contbr. articles to legal publs. Speaker keynote address Dem. Nat. Conv., San Francisco, 1984, nominating address Dem. Nat. Conv., New York City, 1992. Recipient Rapallo award Columbia Lawyers Assn., 1976, Dante medal Italian Govt.-Am. Assn. Tchrs. Italian, 1976, Silver medallion Columbia Coalition, 1976, Pub. Adminstr. award C.W. Post Coll., 1977; Theodore Roosevelt award Internat. Platform Assn., 1984. Mem. Am., N.Y. State Bar Assn., Bklyn. Bar Assn., Nassau Bar Assn., Queens County Bar Assn., Assn. of Bar of City of N.Y., Am. Judicature Soc., St. John's U. Alumni Fedn. (chmn. bd. 1970-72), Cath. Lawyers Guild of Queens County (pres. 1966-67), Skull and Circle. Home: 50 Sutton Pl S New York NY 10022-4167 Address: Wilkie Farr & Galler 787 7th Ave New York NY 10019-6018*

CUOZZO, STEVEN DAVID, newspaper editor; b. N.Y.C., Jan. 17, 1950; s. Joseph and Lillian (Picini) C.; m. Jane Hershey, Nov. 29, 1980. BA in English, SUNY, Stony Brook, 1971. Arts and leisure editor N.Y. Post, N.Y.C., 1978-80, asst. mng. editor features, 1980-91, mng. editor, 1991-93, exec. editor, 1993—. Author: It's Alive: How America's Oldest Newspaper Cheated Death and Why It Matters, 1996. Office: NY Post 1211 Avenue Of The Americas New York NY 10036-8701

CUPANI, JEAN EVELYN MORGAN, elementary education educator; b. Wilkinsburg, Pa., Apr. 4, 1950; d. Elmer Herbert and Bernice Gladys Morgan; m. Joseph Frank Cupani, June 16, 1973; children: Jennifer Rose, Christina Bernice. BS in Edn., Bloomsburg State Coll., 1972, MS in Edn., reading specialist cert., 1975. Cert. elem. edn. grades 1-8, reading specialist grades K-12, Pa., Md. 4th grade tchr. Waynesboro (Pa.) Sch. Dist., 1972-73; reading specialist Bloomsburg (Pa.) Sch. Dist., 1974-76; 5th grade tchr. Queene Anne's County Sch. Sys., Centreville, Md., 1976-77; title I resource tchr. Queene Anne's County Sch. Sys., Centreville, 1977-79, reading helping tchr., 1979-81, 1st grade tchr., 1985-90, 2nd grade tchr., 1990-98, tchr. specialist, 1998—; GED instr. Columbia County Prison, Bloomsburg, 1974-76; writer Md. Assessment Consortium, Frederick, 1994, 95; scorer MD sch. performance assessments State Bd. Edn., Centreville, Md., summer 1997; presenter in field. Sunday sch. and bible sch. tchr. Calvary-Asbury Meth. Ch., Sudlersville, Md., 1981-86; mem. PTA and Band Booster Orgn., Queen Anne's County Schs., 1984-99; leader Caravan-Ch. Scouting Group, Ch. of Nazarene, Chestertown, Md., 1987-91, asst. ch. youth group, 1990-92, mem. SWAT hwy. trash pick-up, 1990-92. Recipient 1st pl. student slide/tape presentation Md. State Student Media Festival, Towson, 1991, 2nd pl. student slide/tape presentation Internat. Student Media Festival, Washington, 1992; Fulbright Meml. Fund scholar Japanese Govt./JUSEC, Tokyo, 1998. Mem. ASCD, NEA, Md. Tchrs. Assn., Upper Shore Reading Coun. Republican. Avocations: walking, reading, skiing. E-mail: jmc@dmv.com. Office: Queen Annes County Bd Edn Chesterfield Ave Centreville MD 21617

CUPINI, MARIELLEN LOUISE, school district administrator; b. Bethlehem, Pa., Dec. 30, 1952; d. John Joseph and Verna Louise (Rhoads) Mikatavage; m. Richard August Cupini; children: Alison, Kimberly, John. BS, Nazareth Coll., Rochester, N.Y., 1974, MS, 1977; Cert. Advanced Study, Brockport U., 1993. Cert. sch. dist. adminstr.; lic. speech pathology tchr., tchr. speech and hearing handicapped, N.Y. Lang. coord. Conv. Hosp. for Child, Rochester, 1974-79; speech pathologist Rochester City Sch. Dist., 1988-90; pvt. practice speech pathology Rochester, 1979-90; dir. presch. spl. edn. program Rochester Childrens Nursery, 1990-94; founder, dir. spl. edn./nursery sch. Stepping Stones Learning Ctr., Rochester, 1994—; speech pathology cons., Lifetime Assistance, Rochester, 1988; nursery sch. adv. bd. Fairport Montessori, Fairport, N.Y., 1982-86. Developer Innovative Inclusion Nursery Sch. Program, 1994. Founding task force mem. ECICMC, Rochester, 1992—. Mem. Preschool Providers, Genesee Valley Speech and Hearing Assn. (ethical practice chmn. 1988-92), Am. Speech, Lang. and Hearing Assn., Rochester Area Early Childhood Assn. Avocations: children, boating, reading. Home: 23 Park Square Ln Pittsford NY 14534-1064

CUPIT, JIM (THOMAS), county official; b. Allen, Miss., July 21, 1943. BS, U. So. Miss., 1964. Dri. inventory, property, mfg. and quality Textron Corp., Nashville, 1966-96; dir. Met. Farmers Market, Nashville, 1997—. Office: Met Farmers Market 900 8th Ave N Nashville TN 37208-2622

CUPOLO, JOSEPH, periodical editor; b. Astoria, N.Y., Apr. 18, 1946; s. Gennaro Joseph and Mildred Mary (Cardone) C.; m. Cynthia Van Nostrand, Feb. 23, 1991; 1 child, Scott. BA, St. John's U., Jamaica, N.Y., 1967; MA, Syracuse U., 1968; MS, SUNY, Stony Brook, 1976. Cert. tchr., N.J., N.Y.; cert. coach, N.Y. Tchr., coach Holy Trinity High Sch., Hicksville, N.Y., 1968-77, Warren Hills High Sch., Washington, N.J., 1977-79; instr. comm. East Stroudsburg (Pa.) U., 1979-80; sr. editor Physics Today publ. Am. Inst. Physics, Bull. Am. Physical Soc., Woodbury, N.Y., 1979-80; exec. editor Pharmacy Times publ. Romaine Pierson Pub., Port Washington, N.Y., 1981-92; editor U.S. Pharmacist publ. Jobson Pub., N.Y.C., 1993—; v.p., pharmacy cons. Consumer Edn. Publ., Pittsfield, Mass., 1996-97; head baseball coach Holy Trinity High Sch., 1975-77; moderator, speaker, facilitator various health-related assns. and orgns., 1985—. Author, editor: Mediquiz 2, 1985, Inside Pharmacy: The Anatomy of a Profession, 1998; contbr. articles to profl. jours. and mag. Mem. Bus. Press Edn1. Found., Am. Bus. Press, Assn. Med. Pubs., Am. Med. Writers Assn., Am. Soc. Bus. Press Editors. Avocations: baseball, football, writing. Office: US Pharmacist 100 Avenue Of The Americas New York NY 10013-1689

CUPP, DAVID FOSTER, photographer, journalist; b. Derry Twp., Pa., Feb. 4, 1938; s. Foster Wilson and Elizabeth (Erhard) C.; m. Catherine Lucille Lum, Nov. 20, 1965; children: Mary Catherine, David Patterson, John. B.A. in Journalism, U. Miami (Fla.), 1960. Staff photographer Miami News, 1960-63, Charlotte (N.C.) Observer, 1963-66; photographer, writer Internat. Harvesters, Chgo., 1966-67; picture editor Nat. Geog. Mag., Washington, 1967; photographer Nat. Geog. Mag., 1967-69; picture editor Detroit Free Press, 1969; writer, photographer Denver Post, 1969-77; freelance writer, photographer, 1977-88; dir. photography Press-Enterprise, Riverside, Calif., 1988-90; instr. photojournalism, dept. journalism U. Mo., Columbia, 1990; instr. Sch. Vis. Communication Ohio U., Athens, 1991-92; working book author Cupp Design, Inc., Atlanta, 1993; graphics editor Ft. Lauderdale (Fla.) Sun-Sentinel, 1993-94; freelance writer & photographer Hilliard, Ohio, 1994—; pres., creative dir. Photos Online, Inc., Hilliard, OH, 1995—; tchr. jr. and sr. high sch.-adult classes, including Journalist-in-the-schs., pilot program, Aurora, Colo., 1974-76, Nat. Endowment Arts poet-in-residence 5 Colo. schs.; photography aboard Voyager Spacecraft. Co-author Search and Rescue Dogs, 1988; contbg. author: Nat. Geog. books; co-author: Cindy, a Hearing Ear Dog, The Animal Shelter, All Wild Creatures Welcome; contbr. article, photographs to popular mags. Bd. dirs. Friends of Children of Vietnam, adoption agy., 1973. Mem. Nat. Press Photographers Assn. (recipient numerous awards, citations, including, named Nat. runner-up Photographer of Year 1965, 72, named Regional Photographer of Year 1974, recipient 2nd Place News Picture Story award 1974, 3rd Place Sports Picture Story award 1974, McWilliams award for picture story 1974, McWilliams award for single picture 1974, 75, 2d Home, Family Picture Story award 1972, co-chmn. nat. conv.), Colo. Press Photographers Assn. (v.p.), Am. Soc. Mag. Photographers. Home: 4508 Swenson St Hilliard OH 43026-3811 *I don't think it's possible to sum life up in a few sentences, life is too complex, but if I were to try, I would have to say that I try to live my life in such a way that my children have pride in me, what I do, and how I do it. I don't feel I can tell my children to be honest, then I be dishonest, or tell them to have compassion, while I have none. I cannot punish a child for doing something at night, that I do during the day. In short, I try to be the person that I would want my children to be.*

CUPP, HORACE BALLARD, surgeon, educator; b. Bristol, Va., Nov. 30, 1930; s. Horace Ballard and Laura Reece Cupp; m. Ann Miller, Dec. 3, 1958; children: Robert Ballard, Laura Cupp Oliva. BA, U. Tenn., 1951; MD, Duke U., 1955. Resident neurosurgery Duke U., Durham, N.C., 1958-64; pvt. practice Johnson City, Tenn., 1964-93; clin. prof. of surgery East Tenn. State U. Coll. of Medicine, Johnson City, 1980—; bd. dirs. Johnson City Med. Ctr. Hosp., 1990—. Past comdr. Johnson City Power Squadron, 1965—. Lt. comdr. USNR, 1956-58. Fellow ACS; mem. AMA, Congress of Neurol. Surgeons, Assn. of Neurol. Surgeons, So. Neurol. Soc., Coral Lodge #142. Seventh-Day Adventist. Avocations: travel, photography, fly fishing. Home: 604 E Holston Ave Johnson City TN 37601 Office: Appalachian Neurosurg Clinic 408 State of Franklin Rd Johnson City TN 37604

CUPP, MARILYN MARIE, sales executive; b. Coleman, Tex., Feb. 22, 1953; d. Kellum and Jean (Sheppard) Guthne: Johnson; m. David Allan Coyle (div. Aug. 1981); 1 child, Daniel Steven Jr. BBA, So. Meth. U., Dallas, 1976. Buyer Kelly's Childrens Shop, Dallas, 1982-90; sales rep. ATC, Addison, Tex., 1995—. Albums include I'm Walking On Sunshine; producer Nat. Dem. Conv., Stas. ABC, CBS and NBC, 1992. Mem. DeSoto Bapt. Ch. Recipient Grammy award as best singer of yr., 1996. Mem. So. Meth. U. Alumni Assn., 500, Inc. Democrat. Methodist. Avocations: swimming, gardening, exercising, reading. Home: 1024 Inez St Early TX 76802-2516

CUPP, ROBERT ERHARD, golf course architect, land use planner; b. Lewistown, Pa., Dec. 27, 1939; s. Foster Wilson and Elizabeth (Erhard) C.; m. Glenda Dell, Aug. 26, 1962 (div. 1983); children: Robert E. II, Caren E., Laura G.; m. Pamela Patricia Amy, Dec. 27, 1986. BA, U. Miami, Coral Gables, Fla., 1962; MA, U.S. Army, Anchorage, 1966. Art dir. Jefferson, Inc., Miami, 1966-67; golf profl. Colonial Palms Country Club, Miami, 1967-68, Crooked Creek Country Club, Miami, 1968-69; pvt. practice golf course architect Miami, 1969-72; golf course architect Golden Bear Enterprises, North Palm Beach, Fla., 1972-84; pvt. practice golf course architect Atlanta, 1984—; sr. designer Jack Nicklaus Design, North Palm Beach, 1972-84; pres. Cupp Design, Inc., Atlanta, 1984—. Designed East Sussex (Eng.) Nat. Golf Club, site of 1993-94 European Open Championship (Best New Golf Course, Golf Monthly), Pumpkin Ridge Golf Club, Portland, Oreg., Greystone Country Club, Birminham, Ala., permanent site of Bruno Meml. Classic, PGA Tours Seniors, Old Waverly Golf Club, West Point, Miss. (Top 100 Golf Course in U.S., Golf Digest), Settindown Creek Golf Club, Atlanta, site of U.S. Nike Tour Ann. Championship, 1995, 96, Pumpkin Ridge, Ghost Creek, 1992 (Best New Course, Golf Digest), Western Gales, Osceola, Mich., 1993, Indianwood, Lake Orion, Mich., 1988 (Runner up Best New Course, Golf Digest), Pumpkin Ridge, Witch Hollow, Portland, 1992, Old Waverly, West Point, 1989, Big Sky Country Club, Pemberton, B.C., Can., 1994, Crosswater Golf Club, Sunriver, Oreg., 1995 (Best New Course 1995). Served to capt. U.S. Army, 1963-66. Named Golf World/Golf Digest Designer of Yr., 1992. Office: Cupp Design Inc 5457 Roswell Rd NE Ste 103 Atlanta GA 30342-1900

CUPP, ROBERT RICHARD, state senator, attorney; b. Bluffton, Ohio, Nov. 9, 1950; s. William Henry and Pearl Margaret (Keifer) C.; m. Lisbeth Ann Cochran, July 29, 1978; children: Matthew R., Ryan W. BA, Ohio Northern U., 1973, JD, 1976. Bar: Ohio. Prosecutor, asst. city law dir. City of Lima, Ohio, 1976-80; county commr. Allen County, Lima, 1981-84; ptnr. Cupp and Smith, Attys., Lima, 1983-86; mem. Ohio Senate, 1985—; ptnr. Cupp and Jenson, Attys., Lima, 1986-93; pres. Bd. County Commrs., Allen County, Ohio, 1981, 82, 84; chmn. Gilmor Commn. Sch. Funding, 1987-88; commerce and labor com. chmn. Ohio Senate 1989-94; com. chmn. Fin. Instns. Ins. and Commerce, 1995-96; majority whip Ohio Senate, 1995-96, pres. pro tem, 1997—. Co-author: Ethics and Discipline in Ohio, 1977. Co-chmn. Midwest Fedn. Coll. Reps., 1974; exec. bd. Black Swamp coun. Boy Scouts Am.; chmn. League of Coll. Republican Clubs, 1972-73. Mem. Allen County and Ohio State Bar Assn. Methodist. Office: 2021 Allentown Rd # 3 Lima OH 45805-1850

CUPPAGE, FRANCIS EDWARD, retired physician, educator; b. Cleve., Aug. 17, 1932; s. Frank Edward and Eunice Agnes (Bartels) C.; m. Virginia Lee Bartch, Aug. 18, 1956; children: Lisa Kay, Peter John, Sharon Elizabeth. BS, Case Western Res. U., 1954; MD, Ohio State U., 1959, MS in Pathology, 1959. Diplomate Am. Bd. Pathology. Intern U. Hosps. of Cleve., 1959-60, resident in pathology, 1960-64, instr. pathology, 1964-65; asst. prof. pathology Ohio State U. Sch. Medicine, Columbus, 1965-67; asst. prof. U. Kans. Med. Ctr., Kansas City, 1967-95, prof., 1973-95; prof., chmn. pathology, 1984-85, 90-92; cons. in field. Contbr. articles to profl. jours. Mem. com. Civic Arts Commn. City of Shawnee, Kans., 1970-73; lay leader Luth. Ch. Orgns., 1967-97; bd. dirs. Trinity Manor Nursing Home, Merriam, Kans., 1980-89, Bethany Coll., Lindsborg, Kans., 1983-91. Teaching award, U. Kans., 1972; NIH grantee, 1967-75; Fogarty Internat. fellow, 1979. Mem. Am. Assn. Pathologists, Kansas City Soc. Pathologists (pres. 1980-81), Am. Soc. Nephrology, Internat. Acad. Pathologists, AAUP, Group for Rsch. in Pathology Edn. Avocations: woodcarving, hiking, canoeing, photography, ship building. Home: 4740 Black Swan Dr Shawnee Mission KS 66216-1235 Office: U Kans Med Ctr Dept Pathology 3901 Rainbow Blvd Kansas City KS 66160-0001

CUPPO CSAKI, LUCIANA, foreign language educator, writer; b. Trieste, Italy, May 30, 1941; came to U.S., 1965; d. Bruno Cuppo and Nerina Dimini. BA in German, U. Heidelberg, Germany, 1962; MA in German, U. Kans., 1970; PhD in Latin, Fordham U., 1995. Adj. prof. Manhattanville Coll., Purchase, N.Y., 1989-91, CUNY, 1991-95; adj. prof. SUNY, Westchester, 1996—, Albany, 1997-98. Author: The Vivarium Monastery of Cassiodorus After the Year 575 A.D., 1998. E-mail: vivario@geocities.com.

CURBOY, ROBERT EDWARD, aviation safety consultant; b. Southbridge, Mass., Jan. 4, 1928; s. William Joseph and Rosetta (Lariviere) C. BS, St. Louis U., 1952; MS, Embry-Riddle, Daytona Beach, Fla., 1987. Cert. FAA airman. Aviation safety rep. North Am. Aviation, Inc., Columbus, Ohio, 1955-57; Pacific area rep. North Am. Aviation, Inc., Kaneohe, Hawaii, 1957-59; test program dir. North Am. Aviation, Inc., Columbus, Ohio, 1960-63; team leader North Am. Aviation, Inc., Sanford, Fla., 1963-67; base mgr. Rockwell Internat. Corp., Sanford and Key West, 1967-78; Middle East rep. Rockwell, Sabreliner Div., Amman, Jordan, 1978-79; Southeastern U.S. regional rep. Rockwell, Sabreliner Div., Ft. Lauderdale, Fla., 1979-83; project mgr. Rockwell Internat. Corp., El Segundo, Calif., 1983-89; cons., owner Aviation Safety Sci., Lake Mary, Fla., 1989—; adj. prof. Embry-Riddle Aero. U., Riverside, Calif., 1987-89, alumni corp. rep., 1988-89; citizen ambassador People to People, Peoples Rep. of China, 1988. Contbr. articles to profl. jours.; editor: (tng. manual) Aircraft Systems, 1953. Dir. Home Owners Assn., Key West, 1974-76; pres. Home Owners Assn., Lake Mary, Fla., 1995—; pres. Condo Owners Assn., Winter Springs Ctr. Recipient Boss of Yr. award, City of Albany, Ga., 1973. Mem. AIAA, Am. Soc. Safety Engrs., Internat. Soc. Air Safety Investigators (mem. standards and policy rev. bd. 1991—), Nat. Space Soc., Exptl. Aircrafts Assn. (bd. dirs. chpt. 949, 1992—), Ret. Naval Officers Assn. (bd. dirs. Sanford area 1991—), People to People Internat., Phi Alpha Chi (pres. St. Louis chpt. 1951-52). Avocations: water sports, sports aircraft, photography, sculpture. Home and Office: Aviation Safety Sci PO Box 951524 Lake Mary FL 32795-1524

CURCIO, CHRISTOPHER FRANK, city official; b. Oakland, Calif., Feb. 3, 1950; s. Frank William and Virginie Theresa (Le Gris) C. BA in Speech/Drama, Calif. State U., Hayward, 1971; MBA in Arts Adminstrn., UCLA, 1974; MPA in Pub. Policy, Ariz. State U., 1982. Intern John F. Kennedy Ctr. for Arts, Washington, 1973; gen. mgr. Old Eagle Theatre, Sacramento, 1974-75; cultural arts supr. Fresno (Calif.) Parks and Recreation Dept., 1975-79; supr. cultural and spl. events Phoenix Parks, Recreation and Libr. Dept., 1979-87, budget analyst, 1987, mgmt. svcs. adminstr., 1987-97, dep. dir., 1997—; mgmt. and budget analyst City of Phoenix, 1985; grants panelist Phoenix Arts Commn., 1987, Ariz. Commn. on Arts, 1987-88; voter Zony Theatre Awards, 1991-92; freelance theater critic, 1987-89; theater critic Ariz. Republic, 1990—, PHX Downtown, 1997—, CityAZ, 1997-98, Ariz. Foothills Mag., 1998—, Sunday Showtunes, 1998—. Active Valley Leadership Program, Phoenix, 1987—, Valley Big Bros./Big Sisters, 1980-94; chair allocation panel United Way, 1990-92; sec. Los Olivos Townhome Assn., Phoenix, 1986-92. Mem. Am. Soc. Pub. Adminstrn., Nat. Recreation and Park Assn., Am. Theatre Critics Assn., Internat. Theater Critics Assn., Ariz. Park and Recreation Assn. Republican. Avocations: theater history, writing, reading, cooking, gardening. Office: Phoenix Parks Recreation Libr Dept 200 W Washington St Fl 16 Phoenix AZ 85003-1611

CURETON, BRYANT LEWIS, college president, educator; b. Hammonton, N.J., July 3, 1938; s. Charles Ladd and Laurie Evelyn (Harrell) C.; m. Jeanette Elaine Smith, Aug. 14, 1967; children: Elizabeth Ladd, Sarah McDaniel. BA, Maryville Coll., 1960; MA, Am. U., 1964; PhD, U. Pa., 1976. Customer relations asst., internat. div. Irving Trust Co., N.Y.C., 1964-65; tchr. Bordentown (N.J.) Military Inst., 1965-67; instr. Hartwick Coll., Oneonta, N.Y., 1971-73, asst. prof., 1973-78, assoc. prof. polit. sci., 1978-89, prof., 1989-94, assoc. dean, 1978-80, v.p., dean of coll., 1980-86, provost, 1986-94; pres., prof. polit. sci. Elmhurst (Ill.) Coll., 1994—; vis. scholar Harvard U. Div. Sch., 1988. With USMCR, 1963-68. Mem. Am. Polit. Sci. Assn., Am. Assn. Higher Edn. Office: Elmhurst Coll Office of Pres 190 Prospect Ave Elmhurst IL 60126-3271*

CURETON, CLAUDETTE HAZEL CHAPMAN, biology educator; b. Greenville, S.C., May 3, 1932; d. John H. and Beatrice (Washington) Chapman; m. Stewart Cleveland, Dec. 27, 1954; children: Ruthye, Stewart II, S. Charles, Samuel. AB, Spelman Coll., 1951; MA, Fisk U., 1966; DHum (hon.), Morris Coll., Sumter, S.C., 1996. Tchr. North Warren High Sch., Wise, N.C., 1952-60; tchr. Sterling High Sch., Greenville, 1960-66, Wade Hampton High Sch., Greenville, 1967-73; instr. Greenville Tech. Coll., 1973-95, ret., 1995; bd. dirs. State Heritage Trust, 1978-91; commr. Basic Skills Adv. Program, Columbia, 1990—; mem. adv. bd. Am. Fed. Bank, NCNB Bank, Greenville, 1991—. Mem. Greenville Urban League, NAACP, S.C. Curriculum Congress; v.p. Woman's Bapt. E.& M. Conv. of S.C.; mem. S.C. Commn. on Higher Edn. Com. for Selection of the 1995 Gov.'s Prof. of the Yr.; mem. Gov.'s Task Force on Juvenile Crime, S.C., Gov.'s Juvenile Justice Task Force, 1997, S.C., Gov.'s Juvenile Justice Youth Coun., S.C., 1996—, Best Chance Network Task Force of Am. Cancer Soc., 1995—. Recipient Presdl. award Morris Coll., 1987, 91, Svc. award S.C. Wildlife and Marine Dept., 1986, Outstanding Jack and Jill of Am. citation, 1986, Excellence in Tchg. award Nat. Inst. for Staff and Orgnl. Devel., U. Tex., Austin, 1992-93, Educator of Yr. award Greenville chpt. Am. Cancer Soc., 1994, Outstanding Svc. award Best Chance Network/Am. Cancer Soc., 1994, Citation S.C. House of Reps., 1995; named Unsung Hero of the Cmty. for Outstanding Svc. to Humankind Greenville Tech. Coll., 1999. Mem. AAAS, AAUW, Nat. Assn. Biology Tchrs., S.C. Curriculum Congress, Nat. Coun. Negro Women, Inc., Higher Edn. S.C. Com. for Selection Prof. of Yr. 1995, Delta Sigma Theta (past v.p. Greenville chpt. alumnae). Home: 501 Mary Knob Greenville SC 29607-5242

CURFMAN, DAVID RALPH, neurological surgeon, musician; b. Bucyrus, Ohio, Jan. 2, 1942; s. Ralph Oliver and Agnes Mozelle (Schreck) C.; m. Blanche Lee Anderson, June 6, 1970. Student, Capital U., 1960-62; AB, Columbia Union Coll., 1965; MS, George Washington U., 1967, MD, 1973. Diplomate Nat. Bd. Med. Examiners. Asst. organist, choirmaster Peace Luth. Ch., Galion, Ohio, 1956-62; bus. mgr. Mansfield/Galion Ambulance Svc., Galion, Ohio, 1962-66; with news divsn. Sta. WTOP-TV, Washington, 1965; choirmaster, assoc. organist Grace Luth. Ch., Washington, 1966-73, historian, curator, 1969—; teaching fellow in anatomy George Washington U., Washington, 1966-67, gen. surgery intern, 1973-74, resident in neurol. surgery, 1974-78; resident in neuropathology Armed Forces Inst. Pathology, Washington, 1975; resident in pediatric neurol. surgery Children's Hosp. Nat. Med. Ctr., Washington, 1976; teaching fellow in anatomy Georgetown U., Washington, 1967-69, clin. instr. neurol. surgery, 1978—, neurol. surgeon, 1978—; chief divsn. neurol. surgery Jefferson Hosp., Alexandria, Va., 1989-93, Wash. Hosp. Ctr. Soc., 1992—, operating room com. 1998—; vice-chmn. bylaws com. Providence Hosp., 1987-95; panelist ann. meeting ethical issues in neurol. surgery Am. Assn. Neurol. Surgery; guest spkr. Nat. Youth Leadership Forum, 1996—. Chmn., chief author: Physician's Reference Guide for Medicolegal Matters, 1982. Elected mem. D.C. Rep. Com., 1988-94; bd. dirs., historian The Christmas Pageant of Peace, Inc., Washington, The Leo Sowerby Found.; pres., bd. govs. Washington Columbus Celebration Assn. Hon. mem. Quiz Kid Show, 1953. Mem. AMA (Phys. Recognition award 1983—), Assn. Am. Med. Colls. (nat. student chmn. rules and regulations com. 1971-73), Am. Soc. Law, Medicine and Ethics, Med. Soc. D.C. (chmn. medicine and religion com. 1981-83, chmn. medico-legal com. 1986-88), Pan Am. Med. Soc. (mem. exec. bd. 1993-97, pres. 1997—), Congress Neurol. Surgeons (joint section on neurotrauma and critical care), Am. Coll. Legal Medicine, Washington Acad. Neurosurgery, Assn. Mil. Surgeons U.S. (Continuing Edn. Neurosurgery award 1993—), Galion Hist. Soc. (charter), Children Am. Revolution (pres. Ohio 1963-64, hon. pres.), Sr. Nat. Officers' Club, SR, bd., N.Y./D.C. Socs., 1997—, bd., Sons of the Amer. Revolution, Washington, 1996, U.S. Capitol Hist. Soc. (founding supporting mem., trust mem., mem. bd. 1997—), Nat. Cathedral Assn., Cathedral Choral Soc. (v.p. bd. trustees 1981-83, pres. 1984-86, repertoire chmn. 1981-92), Am. Guild Organists (dean D.C. chpt. 1974-76, publicity chmn. nat. conv. 1982, state chmn. 1984-91, nat. com. long-range devel. 1990-96), Internat. Congress Organists (Washington program chmn. 1977), Royal Sch. Ch. Music (Eng.), St. Andrew's Soc. Washington D.C.- 1760, Soc. War 1812 (Md. chpt., 1st v.p. D.C. chpt.), Pilgrim Soc. (Plymouth chpt.), Hymn Soc. Am., Order Three Crusades (1096-1192), Mil. Hospitaller Order Saint Lazarus Jerusalem, Sovereign Mil. Order Temple of Jerusalem (grand chirurgeon), Sons & Daughters of Colonial & Antebellum Bench & Bar, Mil. Order Loyal Legion U.S., Sons of Union Vets. Civil War (chmn. historic Memorial Day observances), Hospitaller Order of St. John (knight), Crawford County Coin Club (charter mem.), Am. Polit. Items Collectors Assn., George Washington U. Club, Elks (Galion Lodge No. 1191, hon. founder Elks Nat. Found.), Ordo Sancti Constantini Magni, Sons/Daus. of the Pilgrims (historian gen.), Continental Soc. Sons Indian Wars, Order of Indian Wars in the U.S. (historian gen.), Soc. Colonial Wars (surgeon 1997—), Sons Am. Colonists (surgeon gen. 1997—), Nat. Soc. Children Am. Colonists (v.p. gen.), Colonial Order of the Acorn N.Y., Order of Wash., Vet. Corps Artillery State N.Y., Am. Revolution Soc., Soc. of 1812, Hereditary Order Descendants of the Loyalists and Patriots of the Am. Revolution, Sigma Xi (pres. chpt. 1981-82), Phi Delta Epsilon. Home: 4201 Massachusetts Ave NW Washington DC 20016-4701 Office: 3301 New Mexico Ave NW Ste 210 Washington DC 20016-3622

CURFMAN, LAWRENCE EVERETT, retired lawyer; b. Champaign, Ill., Apr. 13, 1909; s. Lawrence Everett and Winifred (Williams) C.; m. Margaret Sylvia Baldwin, May 1, 1937; children: Lawrence Everett III, Elizabeth Ann (Mrs. Peter Koch), John Edward. A.B., U. Mich., 1930, J.D., 1932. Bar: Kans. 1932. Since practiced in Wichita; ptnr. Curfman, Harris, Rose, Weltz

& Smith, Wichita, 1940-95. Contbr. articles to legal jours. Pres. Wichita Pub. Libr. Bd., 1954, 57, 58. Mem. ABA (chmn. sect. urban, state and local govt. law 1970- 71), Wichita Bar Assn. (pres. 1956), City Attys. Assn. Kan. (pres. 1953). Club: University (Wichita) (pres. 1965-66). Home: 7373 E 29th St N Wichita KS 67226-3405*

CURFMAN, WALTER L., school system administrator; b. Todd, Pa., Mar. 10, 1946; s. Walter L. and Grace O. Curfman; m. Florence Carol Ammon, July 15, 1978; children: Keith W. R., Megan. BS in Edn., Shippensburg U., 1968, MEd, 1970; EdD, Pa. State U., 1979. Tchr. Tuscarora Schs., Mercersburg, Pa., 1967-68; tchr. Tussey Mt. Schs., Saxton, Pa., 1968-73, asst. supt., 1977-84, supt., 1984—; prin. Forbes Rd. Schs., Waterfall, Pa., 1973-75, supt., 1975-77. Bd. dirs. Home Nursing Agy., Huntingdon, Pa., 1990—; chairperson United Family Svc. Sys., Bedford, Pa., 1998-99. Mem. NEA, Pa. State Edn. Assn., Pa. Assn. Sch. Adminstrs., Pa. Assn. Rural and Small Schs., Phi Delta Kappa. Republican. Methodist. Avocation: reading. Office: Tussey Mt Sch Dist 199 Front St Saxton PA 16678-8610

CURIE, EVE, writer, lecturer; b. Paris, Dec. 6, 1904; d. Pierre (Nobel prize winner for work in radium 1903) and Marie (Sklodowska) (Nobel prize winner in radio-active substances, 1903, in chemistry 1911) Curie; m. Henry Richardson Labouisse, Nov. 1954 (dec. 1987). B.S., Ph.B., Sevigne Coll.; D.H.L. (hon.), Mills Coll., 1939, Russell Sage Coll., 1941; Litt.D. (hon.), U. Rochester, 1941; Hartwick Coll., 1983. Took up study of music and gave first concert as pianist, Paris, 1925; later concerts in France and Belgium; mus. critic for Candide (weekly jour.) for several years; also wrote articles on motion pictures and the theater; made first visit to U.S. with mother, 1921; on 2d visit lectured in 10 U.S. cities (speaks English, French and Polish), 1939; witnessed fall of France, 1940, went to London to work for cause of Free France; came to U.S., 1941, lectured on war in France and Eng.; because of pro-ally activities deprived of French citizenship by Vichy Govt., 1941. Served in Europe with Fighting French as officer in Women's div. of army; one of pubs. Paris Presse (daily), resigned to return to ind. writing, 1949. Spl. adviser Sec. Gen., NATO, 1952-54. Decorated Chevalier Legion of Honor (France), 1939; Polonia Restituta (Poland), 1939; Croix de Guerre (France), 1944. Author: Madame Curie (selection of Lit. Guild, Jr. Guild, Book-of-the-Month Club, Scientific Book of the month; Nat. book award for non-fiction), 1937; Journey Among Warriors (Lit. Guild Selection), 1943. Home: 1 Sutton Pl S New York NY 10022-2471

CURL, EILEEN DEGES, nursing educator; b. Oakley, Kans., Sept. 28, 1954; d. Leonard and Dorothea Anna (Engel) Deges; m. Donald Dewane Curl, Aug. 7, 1982. BSN summa cum laude, Marymount Coll. Kans., 1976; MS, U. Colo. Health Sci. Ctr., 1977; PhD, U. Tex., Austin, 1992. Staff nurse Hadley Regional Med. Ctr., Hays, Kans., 1976; dist. nurse cons. Kans. Dept. Health and Environ., Hays, 1979-81; prof. nursing Ft. Hays State U., Hays, 1981—; apptd. mem. Kans. State Bd. Nursing, 1994-98. Grantee Nurse Traineeship, Wagner Fellowship. Mem. Kans. Nurses Assn. (mem. editl. bd., state bd. dirs., 2nd v.p.), Sigma Theta Tau (Region 2 Dissertation award 1995). Office: Fort Hays State U Dept Nursing 600 Park St Bldg 1 Hays KS 67601-4099

CURL, ROBERT FLOYD, JR., chemistry educator; b. Alice, Tex., Aug. 23, 1933; s. Robert Floyd and Lessie (Merritt) C.; m. Jonel Whipple, Dec. 21, 1955; children: Michael, David. BA, Rice U., 1954; PhD, U. Calif., Berkeley, 1957; D (hon.), U. Buenos Aires, 1997. Rsch. fellow Harvard U., Cambridge, Mass., 1957-58; asst. prof. chemistry Rice U., Houston, 1958-63, assoc. prof., 1963-67, prof., 1967—, chmn. dept. chemistry, 1992-96, Harry C. and Olga K. Wiess prof. natural scis., 1996—; master Lovett Coll., 1968-72; vis. rsch. officer NRC Can., 1972-73; vis. prof. Inst. for Molecular Sci., Okazaki, Japan, 1977, U. Bonn, 1985. Contbr. articles profl. jours. Fellow NSF, Alfred P. Sloan fellow, 1961-63; NATO postdoctoral fellow, 1964; recipient Clayton prize Instn. Mech. Engrs., London, 1958, Internat. New Materials prize Am. Phys. Soc., 1992, Alexander von Humboldt sr. U.S. scientist award, 1984, Order of Golden Plate, 1997, Achievement Carbon Sci. award Am. Carbon Soc., 1997, co-recipient Nobel prize in chemistry, 1996, Tex. Disting. Scientist award, 1997, Johannes Marcus Marci award in spectroscopy, 1998, Madison Marshall award, 1998, Space Act award, 1998. Fellow Am. Optical Soc., Am. Acad. Arts and Scis.; mem. NAS, Am. Chem. Soc., European Acad. Scis., Arts and Letters (titulaire mem.), Phi Beta Kappa, Sigma Xi. Methodist. Home: 1824 Bolsover St Houston TX 77005-1728 Office: Rice University PO Box 1892 6100 Main St Houston TX 77005-1892

CURL, SAMUEL EVERETT, university dean, agricultural scientist; b. Ft. Worth, Dec. 26, 1937; s. Henry Clay and Mary Elva (Watson) C.; m. Betty Doris Savage, June 6, 1957 (div.); children: Jane Ellen, Julia Kathleen, Karen Elizabeth; m. Mary Behrends Reeves, Sept. 11, 1993; stepchildren: Ryan Andrew, Shelly Lyn. Student, Tarleton State Coll., 1955-57; BS, Sam Houston State U., 1959; MS, U. Mo., 1961; PhD, Tex. A&M U., 1963. Mem. faculty Tex. Tech U., Lubbock, 1961, 63-76, 79-97, tchr., researcher animal physiology and genetics, 1963-76, asst., assoc. and interim dean Coll. Agrl. Sci., 1968-73, assoc. v.p. acad. affairs, prof., 1973-76, dean Coll. Agrl. Scis., prof., 1979-97; pres. Phillips U., Enid, Okla., 1976-79; agrl. cons., 1964-76; dean and dir. Divsn. of Agrl. Scis. and Natural Resources Okla. State U., Stillwater, 1997—; vice-chmn. adminstrv. heads sect. So. Assn. Agrl. Scientists; bd. dirs. Okla. Ctr. for the Advancement of Sci. and Tech.; bd. dirs., chmn. Mid Am. Internat. Agrl. Consortium; ; mem. Gov.'s Task Force on Agrl. Devel. in Tex., 1982-83, 88; mem. Tex. Crop and Livestock Adv. Com., 1985-91; mem. Tex. Agrl. Resources Protection Authority, 1989-97, Tex. Agribus. Rsch. Promotion Coun., 1995-97; del. Eisenhower Consortium for Western Environ. Forestry Rsch., 1979-84; mgmt. com. S.W. Consortium on Plant Genetics and Water Resources, 1984-97, chmn., 1989-95; mem. USDA Nat. Planning Com. on Hispanic Minority Recruitment, 1988-93; trustee Consortium for Internat. Devel., 1979-97, mem. exec. com., 1981-84, 86-87, 89-90; former mem. High Plains Rsch. Coord. Bd.; former mem. So. Regional Coun., U.S. Joint Coun. Food and Agrl. Scis.; former trustee Water Inc.; chmn. agrl. and natural resources program rev. task force Sam Houston State U., 1982-83; mem. adv. com. Sch. Agr. Angelo State U., 1989-95; mem. 1995 farm bill task force Tex. Dept. Agr., 1994-95. Author: (with others) Progress and Change in the Agricultural Industry, 1974, Food and Fiber for a Changing World, 1976, 2d edit., 1982; contbr. 95 articles to profl. jours. Pres. Lubbock Econ. Coun., 1982; bd. dirs. Market Lubbock Econ. Devel. Corp., 1995-97; former mem. bd. overseers Ranching Heritage Assn.; mem. Goals for Lubbock: A Vision into the 21st Century Com., 1995-96; elder Westminster Presbyn. Ch., Lubbock, 1994-97; mem. First United Meth. Ch., Stillwater, 1997—. 2d lt. U.S. Army, 1959, capt. USAR. Danforth Assn. fellow, 1964-76, Am. Coun. Edn. fellow, 1972-73; recipient Disting. Alumnus award, Faculty-Alumni Gold medal U. Mo., 1975, Outstanding Agr. Alumnus award Sam Houston State U., 1986, Disting. Alumnus award, 1993, Tex. Citation for Outstanding Svc. award Tex. 4-H Found., 1987, Tex. 4-H Alumni award, 1993, Disting. Svc. award Vocational Agrl. Tchrs. Assn. Tex., 1987, Blue and Gold Meritorious Svc. award Tex. Future Farmers of Am., 1988, Tex. State degree Future Farmers Am., 1988, Area Disting. Svc. award Vocat. Agr. Tchrs., 1987. Mem. Am. Soc. Animal Sci. (program com. Biennial Symposium on Animal Reprodn. 1972-76, reviewer Jour. Animal Sci.), Am. Assn. Univ. Agrl. Adminstrs., Assn. U.S. Univ. Dirs. Internat. Agrl. Programs, So. Assn. Agrl. Scientists, Nat. Assn. State Univs. and Land-Grant Colls. (exec. com. bd. agr. 1994-97), Coun. Adminstrv. Heads of Agr., Profl. Agrl. Workers Tex. (bd. dirs., Disting. Svc. to Tex. Agr. award 1984), Okla. State U. Alumni Assn., Sirloin Club Okla., Centennial Rotary (hon.), Century Club, West Tex. C. of C. (bd. dirs., chmn. agrl. and ranching com.), Lubbock C. of C. (bd. dirs. 1988-92, chmn. agr. task force, chmn. rsch. com. 1981-86, water com., legis. affairs com., agr. com., gubernatorial appointments task force), Rotary (bd. dirs., 1st. v.p. Lubbock club), Farmhouse Frat. (assoc.), Omicron Delta Kappa, Sigma Xi, Phi Kappa Phi, Gamma Sigma Delta. Home: 32 Yellow Brick Dr Stillwater OK 74074-1726 Office: Office Dean & Dir Divsn Agrl Scis & Natural Resources Okla State U Stillwater OK 74078

CURLE, ROBIN LEA, computer software industry executive; b. Denver, Feb. 23, 1950; d. Fred Warren and Claudia Jean (Harding) C.; m. Lucien Ray Reed, Feb. 23, 1981 (div. Oct. 1984). BS in Bus. Comm., U. Ky., 1972. Systems analyst 1st Nat. BAnk, Lexington, Ky., 1972-73, SW BancShares, Houston, 1973-77; sales rep. Software Internat., Houston, 1977-80; dist. mgr. UCCEL, Dallas, 1980-82; v.p. and gen. mgr. Southeastern region Info. Sci., Inc., Atlanta, 1982-83; v.p. sales and mktg. TesserAct, San Francisco, 1983-86, Foothill Rsch., San Francisco, 1986; pres., founder Curle Cons. Group, San Francisco, 1986-89; mgr. strategic mktg. MCC, Austin, Tex., 1989-90; founder, exec. v.p. Evolutionary Tech., Inc., Austin, 1991—; bd. dirs. Evolutionary Techs. Internat., Austin Software Coun., Tex. Property and Casualty, Journal Software; dir. adv. bd. Life Savs. Bank, U. Tex. Engring. Sch.; adv. bd. SWTS U. Recipient Ma Ferguson award Exec. Women Internat. 1997, Grad of Yr. award Nat. Bus. Incubator Assn. 1996, X/Open Software award 1997; feature in Forbes Mag., 1996, Entrepreneur Mag., 1997; profile documentary Entrepreneurial Revolution, 1997, Inc 500 List, 1997, 98. Mem. U. Ky. Alumni Assn., Women in Tech., Women of Austin, Software Exec. Com., Inc. 500 Cos., Austin C. of C., Delta Gamma (pres. 1969). Republican. Avocations: scuba diving, running, skiing, cooking. Home: 7009 Quill Leaf Cv Austin TX 78750-8306

CURLEY, EDWIN MUNSON, philosophy educator; b. Albany, N.Y., May 1, 1937; s. Julius Edwin and Gertrude E.; m. Ruth Helen Snyder, Dec. 12, 1959; children: Julia Anne, Richard Edwin. BA, Lafayette Coll., 1959; PhD, Duke U., 1963. Asst. prof. philosophy San Jose State Coll., 1963-66; research fellow Australian Nat. U., Canberra, 1966-68; fellow Australian Nat. U., 1968-72, sr. fellow, 1972-77; prof. philosophy Northwestern U., 1977-83, U. Ill.-Chgo., 1983-93, U. Mich., 1993—. Author: Hellenistic Philosophy, 1965, Spinoza's Metaphysics, 1969, Descartes Against the Skeptics, 1978, The Collected Works of Spinoza, vol. 1, 1985, Behind the Geometrical Method, 1988, A Spinoza Reader, 1994, Hobbes' Leviathan, 1994; Am. co-editor Archiv für Geschichte der Philosophie, 1979-95; contbr. articles to profl. jours. Fellow AAAS; mem. Am. Philos. Assn. (v.p. cen. div., 1989-90, pres. 1990-91). Home: 2645 Pin Oak Dr Ann Arbor MI 48103-2370 Office: U Mich Dept Philosophy 2215 Angell Hall Ann Arbor MI 48109

CURLEY, JOHN FRANCIS, JR., mutual fund executive; b. Wollaston, Mass., July 24, 1939; s. John Francis and Ann (Omar) C.; m. Loretta Mae O'Keeffe, Oct. 20, 1962; children: William Laurance, Edward Reid, David Neil. Grad., Phillips Acad.; AB, Princeton U., 1960; MBA, Harvard U., 1962. With Paine, Webber, Jackson & Curtis, Inc., N.Y.C., 1964—, gen. ptnr., 1969-72, exec. v.p., 1972-77, pres., 1977-80, chmn. fin. com., 1980-82; vice-chmn. bd. Legg Mason, Inc., Balt., 1982-98, Legg Mason Wood Walker, Inc., Balt., 1982-98; pres., bd. dirs. Legg Mason Value Trust, Inc., 1982—; chmn. bd. dirs. other Legg Mason Mutual Funds; bd. govs. Investment Co. Inst., ICI Mut. Ins. Co., 1994-98, Sellinger Sch. Bus., 1995-98. 1st lt. AUS, 1962-64. Mem. Securities Industry Assn. (dir., exec. com. 1978-80), Investment Assn. N.Y. (past pres.), Princeton Club (N.Y.C), Center Club, L'Hirondelle Club, Maryland Club. Office: Legg Mason Wood Walker Inc 100 Light St Ste B2 Baltimore MD 21202-1099

CURLEY, JOHN J., diversified media company executive; b. Dec. 31, 1938; m. Ann Conser; two sons. BA, Dickinson Coll., 1960; MS, Columbia Univ., 1963. Reporter, editor AP, 1961-66; with Gannett Co., Inc., Arlington, Va., 1969—; pres. Mid-Atlantic newspaper group Gannett Co., Inc., Washington, 1980-82; sr. v.p. Gannett Co., Inc., Washington, 1983-84, pres., 1984-97, chief operating officer, 1984-86, chief exec. officer, 1986—, chmn., 1989—, also bd. dirs. Lt. U.S. Army, 1960-62. Office: Gannett Co Inc 1100 Wilson Blvd Ste 2100 Arlington VA 22209-2299

CURLEY, JOHN PETER, sports editor; b. N.Y.C., Apr. 12, 1952; s. James J. and Jean (Lyons) C.; children: Jordan, Lindsay. Student, Fairfield U., 1970-72, Boston U., 1972-74. Reporter Ridgewood (N.J.) News, 1975-76; reporter Paterson (N.J.) News, 1976-78, columnist, 1978-79; news editor L.A. Herald Examiner, 1979-81; copy editor San Francisco Chronicle, 1981-87, sports editor, 1987-97, asst. mng. editor news desk, 1997—. Mem. AP, Sports Editors Assn. Roman Catholic. Avocations: softball, basketball, skiing, tennis. Office: San Francisco Chronicle 901 Mission St San Francisco CA 94103-2905*

CURLEY, ROBERT AMBROSE, JR., lawyer; b. Boston, June 5, 1949; s. Robert Ambrose and Terese M. (O'Hara) C.; m. Kathleen M. Foley, June 10, 1972; children: Christine, Elizabeth, Margaret. AB cum laude, Harvard U., 1971; JD, Cornell U., 1974. Bar: Mass. 1974, U.S. Dist. Ct. Mass. 1975, U.S. Ct. Appeals (1st. cir.) 1976. Prin. Curley & Curley, P.C., Boston, 1974—, pres.; lectr. Mass. Continuing Legal Edn., Mass. Def. Attys., Mass. Acad. Trial Attys., Flaschner Judicial Inst., Nat. Bus. Inst. Mem. ABA, Internat. Assn. Def. Counsel, Mass. Bar Assn. (lectr., chmn. civil trial practice sect., civil litig. com. 1990-91, Mass. Def. Lawyers Assn. (co-chmn. products liability sects. 1994-96, bd. dirs. 1996—, sec. 1998—), Nat. Bus. Inst., Def. Rsch. Inst., Trial Lawyers Assn. (assoc.), Harvard Club (Hingham, treas. 1983-84, v.p. 1984-85, pres. 1985-86), Clover (Boston). Roman Catholic. Office: Curley & Curley PC 27 School St Ste 600 Boston MA 02108-4391

CURLEY, SARAH SHARER, federal bankruptcy judge; b. Oak Park, Ill.; d. Robert F. Sharer and Marian Elizabeth (White) Fitzgerald; m. Roger D. Curley; 1 child. BA, Mount Holyoke Coll., 1971; JD cum laude, N.Y. Law Sch., 1977. Bar: N.Y. 1978, Wis. 1983, Ariz. 1986, U.S. Dist. Ct. (so., ea. dists.) N.Y., U.S. Dist. Ct. Ariz., U.S. Ct. Appeals (2nd cir.). Law clk. U.S. Dist. Ct., N.Y.C., 1977; atty. Fogelson, Fogelson & Collins, N.Y.C., 1978, Otterbourg, Steindler, Houston & Rosen, N.Y.C., 1979-82; asst. counsel First Wisconsin Corp., Milw., 1982-86; atty. Ayers & Graham, Phoenix, 1986; U.S. bankruptcy judge Dist. of Ariz., Phoenix, 1986—. Contbr. articles to profl. jours.; exec. editor: Bankruptcy Bar Bulletin, 1978. Fellow Ariz. Bar Found., Nat. Assn. Women Judges; mem. Nat. Conf. Bankruptcy Judges, Ariz. State Bar, Maricopa County Bar Assn., Ariz. Women's Lawyers Assn., State Bar of Wis., Am. Bar Assn., Soroptimists, Mount Holyoke Club (v.p.). Avocations: skiing, swimming, flying. Address: US Bankruptcy Ct PO Box 34151 Phoenix AZ 85067-4151

CURLEY, THOMAS, newspaper executive; b. Easton, Pa., July 6, 1948; s. John Joseph and Emily Dixon (Sprague) C.; m. Marsha Stanley, Sept. 14, 1974; children: Laura Stanley, Melinda Burke. BA in Polit. Sci., La Salle U., 1970; MBA, Rochester Inst. Tech., 1977. Reporter The News Tribune, Woodbridge, N.J., 1967, 68, reporter, copy editor, 1970-72; night city/ suburban editor The Times-Tribune, Rochester, N.Y., 1972-76; dir. info. Gannett Co., Inc., Rochester, 1976-80, dir. research, 1980-82; editor Norwich (Conn.) Bulletin, 1982-83; pub. The Courier-News, Bridgewater, N.J., 1983-85; exec. v.p. USA Today, Washington, 1985-86, pres., 1986-89, pres., chief operating officer, from 1989, now pres., pub.; trustee La Salle U., Phila., 1987—; trustee Rochester Inst. Tech. Pres. Ctrl. Jersey C. of C., Plainfield, N.J., 1984-85; exec. v.p. United Way Somerset Valley, Bridgewater, 1985; bd. dirs. Assn. for Retarded Citizens, Manville, N.J., 1983-85. Pub. Opinion Rsch. fellow Northwestern U., 1976; recipient Alumnus of Yr. award Rochester Inst. Tech., 1986. Office: USA Today 1000 Wilson Blvd Ste 600 Arlington VA 22229-3905*

CURLEY, WALTER JOSEPH PATRICK, diplomat, investment banker; b. Pitts., Sept. 17, 1922; s. Walter Joseph and Marguerite Inez (Cowan) C.; m. Mary Walton, Dec. 18, 1948; children: Margaret Cowan, Walter Joseph, Patrick III, John Walton, James Mellon (dec. 1994). Grad., Phillips Acad., Andover, Mass., 1940; BA, Yale U., 1944; cert., U. Oslo, 1948; MBA, Harvard U., 1948; LLD (hon.), Trinity Coll., Dublin, Ireland, 1976. Mgr. Caltex Oil Co., India, 1948-52, Italy, 1952-55, N.Y.C., 1955-57; v.p. San Jacinto Petroleum, 1957-60; ptnr. J.H. Whitney Co., 1961-75; bd. dirs. various U.S. and internat. cos. including Sotheby's, N.Y., France Growth Fund, N.Y.C.; commr. pub. events, chief protocol City of N.Y., 1973-74; amb. to Ireland, 1975-77, amb. to France, 1989-93; prin. W.J.P. Curley, 1978-89; pres. Curley Land Co., Pitts., 1993—. Author: Letters From The Pacific, 1965, Monarchs in Waiting, 1974. Trustee Buckley Sch., 1960-75, Miss Porter's Sch., Farmington, Mass., 1965-74, Barnard Coll., 1966-75, N.Y. Pub. Libr., 1972-75, The Frick Collection, 1993—; hon. chmn. French-Am. Found., N.Y., 1993—. Decorated Bronze Star; Cloud and Banner (Republic of China); comdr. French Legion of Honor. Mem. Coun. Fgn. Rels., Yale Club, Knickerbocker Club, Links Club, Racquet and Tennis Club, Rolling Rock Club (Ligonier, Pa.), Kildare St. Club (Dublin), Bedford Golf Club, St. Stephen's Green Club (Dublin), Traveller's Club (Paris), Golf Morfontaine (France). Office: 450 Park Ave Ste 2104 New York NY 10022-2605

CURLIN, WILLIAM G., bishop; b. Portsmouth, Va., Aug. 30, 1927. Student, Georgetown U., St. Mary's Sem., Balt. Ordained priest Roman Catholic Ch., 1957. Titular bishop Rosemarkie and aux. bishop Washington, 1988-93; bishop diocese of Charlotte Pastoral Ctr, Charlotte, N.C., 1994—. Office: Chancery Office PO Box 36776 Charlotte NC 28236-6776

CURLOOK, WALTER, management consultant; b. Coniston, Ont., Can., Mar. 14, 1929; s. William and Stephanie (Acker) C.; m. Jennifer Burak, May 28, 1955; children: Christine, William Paul, John Michael, Andrea. BA in Sci., U. Toronto, 1950, MA in Sci., 1951, Ph.D., 1953; D.Sc. (hon.), Laurentian U., 1983. Postdoctoral fellow Imperial Coll. Sci. and Tech., London, 1954; rsch. metallurgist Inco, Sudbury, Ont., Can., 1954-59; supr. rsch. sta. Inco, Port Colborne, Ont., 1959-60; supr. rsch. Inco, Copper Cliff, Ont., 1960-64, asst. to gen. mgr., 1964-69; dir. tech. COFIMPAC, Paris, 1969-72; v.p. adminstrv. and engring. svcs. Inco, Copper Cliff, 1973-74; v.p. Inco, N.Y.C., 1974-77; sr. v.p. prodn. Inco Metals Co., Toronto, 1977-80, pres., chief exec. officer, 1980-82; exec. v.p. Inco Ltd., Toronto, 1982-91, vice chmn., 1991-94; dir. Inco Ltd., 1989-94; pres. Inco Gold Co., Toronto, 1987-89; pres. commr. P.T. Inco, Indonesia, 1990-93; pres., dir. gen. Goro Nickel, S.A., Noumea, New Caledonia, 1992-97; mem. Nat. Adv. Com. Mining Industry, 1980-94; mem. Premier's Coun. Econ. Renewal, 1991-94. Patentee in field. Bd. dirs. Foundation Cambrian Found., Sudbury, 1983; first chmn. bd. Cambrian Coll. Applied Arts and Tech., Sudbury, Ont., 1980. Recipient Mc Charles prize U. Toronto, 1989; inducted into Can. Mining Hall of Fame, 1997. Fellow Can. Acad. Engring.; mem. Assn. Profl. Engrs. of Ont., Metall. Soc. of Can. Inst. Mining and Metallurgy (Airey 1979, Platinum medal 1994), Mining Assn. Can. (bd. dir. and past chmn.), Sci. North (hon. life Sudbury chpt. 1988), Ont. Mining Assn. (past pres.), Order of Can. Home and OfficY: 25 Cluny Dr, Toronto, ON Canada M4W 2P9

CURNOW, KATHY, art historian, educator. BA in Art History magna cum laude, Pa. State U., 1974; MA in Art History, Ind. U., 1980, PhD in Art History, African Studies, 1983. Prin. lectr. dept. design Nigerian TV Coll., Jos Plateau State, 1983-85; head dept. gen. studies, sr. lectr. Nigerian TV Coll., 1985-88; exec. asst. Am. Found. Negro Affairs, Nat. Edn. Rsch. Fund, Phila., 1988-89; vis. asst. prof. dept. art Cleve. State U., 1990-91, asst. prof., 1991-94, assoc. prof., 1995—; grad. asst. Ind. U., Bloomington, 1978-80; adj. asst. prof. U. Pa., Phila., 1989-91; vis. asst. prof. dept. art Lincoln U., Pa., 1989-90, dept. humanities U. Arts, Phila., 1990; lectr. Met. Mus. Art, N.Y.C., 1990; vis. Fulbright assoc. prof. U. Benin, Benin City, Nigeria, 1997-98. Author: (chpt.) Communications Training and Practice in Nigeria, 1987, Kulte, Kunstler, Könige in Afrika, 1997; contbr. articles to profl. jours. Recipient Nigerian Learning Materials award, 1987, Nat. Merit award Nigerian Festival TV Programming, 1987; Westinghouse scholar, 1973; Ind. U. fellow, 1977-80; grantee Rsch. Challenge, 1992, Social Sci. Rsch. Coun., 1993, NEH, 1993-98, Fulbright award, 1997-98. Mem. African Studies Assn. (arts coun., textbook writing com. 1991-93, bd. dirs. 1993-97, chair book prize com. 1994-95, sec.-treas. 1995-97), African Studies Assn., Coll. Art Assn., Delta Studies Assn., Midwest Art Historians Assn., Sierra Leone Studies Assn. Avocation: writing fiction. Office: Cleve State U Art Dept 111 AB Cleveland OH 44115

CUROL, HELEN RUTH, librarian, English language educator; b. Grayson, La., May 30, 1944; d. Alfred John and Ethel Lea (McDaniel) Broussard; m. Kenneth Arthur Curol, June 25, 1967 (div. 1988); children: Edward, Bryan. BA, McNeese State U., 1966; postgrad., L.I. U., 1969-70; MLS, La. State U., 1987. Tchr., libr. Cameron Parish Schs., Grand Lake, La., 1966-67; media specialist Brentwood (N.Y.) Sch. Dist., 1967-69; sch. libr. Patchogue (N.Y.) H.S., 1969-70;, 1976-95; reference libr., mgr. circulation dept. McNeese State U., Lake Charles, La., 1976-96; test adminstr. Edn. Testing Svc., Princeton, N.J., 1987-95, Curol Consulting, Lake Charles, 1995—; asst. prof. McNeese U., 1989-95; owner Curol Consulting, Lake Charles, 1995—; head adult svcs. Laman Pub. Libr., North Little Rock, Ark., 1996; rschr. Boise Cascade, DeRidder, La., 1987-88, Vidtron, Dallas, 1990-92, Nat. Archives, Washington, 1989; cons. Cmty. Housing Resource Bd., Lake Charles, 1988-93, Boyce Internat. Engrs., Houston, 1988-89, La. Pub. Broadcasting, Baton Rouge, 1989; devel. cons. Calcasieu Women's Shelter, 1988-92; reference cons. Calcasieu Parish Pub. Libr., 1990-95; presenter conf. at Tulane U., South Ctrl. Women's Assn., 1994. Sr. arbitrator Better Bus. Bur., Lake Charles, 1986-95; local facilitator La. Com. for Fiscal Reform, Lake Charles, 1988; state bd. dirs. PTA, Baton Rouge, 1981-83, LWV La., Baton Rouge, 1983-85; chairperson budget panel com. United Way S.W. La., Lake Charles, 1992-94, bd. dirs., 1995-96; judge La. region IV Social Studies Fair, 1979-89; program spkr. region IV tng. conf. HUD, El Paso, 1992. Named Citizen of the Day, Sta. KLOU, 1978; grantee La. Endowment for Humanities, 1987, La. Divsn. Arts, 1989, Fair Housing Initiative Program, 1990, HUD, 1992, La. Ctr. Women and Govt. of Nicholls State U., 1993. Mem. ALA (sec. coun. 1988-90, chairperson coun. 1990-91), AAUW (chairperson intellectual freedom com. 1988-89), La. Libr. Assn. (chairperson reference group 1988-90), La. Assn. Coll. and Rsch. Librs. (chairperson 1995-96), Ark. Libr. Assn., McNeese U. Alumni Assn., S.W. La. C. of C. (mem. legis. com. 1992), Krewe du Feteurs (Mardi Gras Ct. Duchess 1992), Beta Sigma Phi (pres. Lake Charles chpt. 1983-84), Beta Phi Mu. Democrat. Lutheran. Office: La Grange Media Ctr 3420 Louisiana Ave Lake Charles LA 70605 Address: 1005 Cherryhill St Lake Charles LA 70607-4911

CURPHEY, GERALDINE CASTERLINE, church musician, retired; b. Cleve., Jan. 6, 1921; d. Charles and Lyla Mae (Overmyer) Casterline; m. Clifford L. Curphey, Mar. 31, 1943 (div. Sept. 1971); children: Denis Hall, Devon Scott. Assoc. in Fine Arts, Assoc. in Music, Stephens Coll., 1940; MusB, Sherwood Music Sch., 1942; postgrad., Fla. State U., 1954, Acad. Music, Vienna, 1969-73. Pvt. tchr. piano and voice, 1942—; organist, dir. Holy Trinity Episcopal Ch., Chgo., 1945-48; min. of music First Bapt. Ch., Ft. Lauderdale, Fla., 1949-63; dir. of music Christ United Meth. Ch., Ft. Lauderdale, 1963-72; piano instr. Broward C.C., Ft. Lauderdale, 1969-95; organist, dir. St. Clement Cath. Ch., Ft. Lauderdale, 1972-75; organist, dir. St. Andrew's United Methodist, Ft. Lauderdale, 1978-89, ret., 1989; founding conductor Ft. Lauderdale Symphony Chorus, 1951-56; pres. Soroptimist Club, 1952-54. Composer: Song Cycle, 1941, Suite for Orchestra, 1942, Choral: The Mother's Name Was Mary, 1942, Choral: The Lord of Glory is My Light, 1968. Recipient 1st pl. honors Am. Composer's Clinic, 1941. Mem. Am. Guild Organists (past dean Ft. Lauderdale chpt. 1963-64), Music Tchrs. Nat. Assn., Fla. State Music Tchrs. Assn., Broward County Music Tchrs. Assn. (pres. 1970-72), Morning Musicale Federated Music Club (pres. 1955-56), Nat. League Am. Pen Women (Fla. state first pl. award 1972). Home: 220 Thorn Apple Ct Royal Palm Beach FL 33411

CURRAN, BARBARA ADELL, retired law foundation administrator, lawyer, writer; b. Washington, Oct. 21, 1928; d. John R. and Beda (Parkins) Curran. BA, U. Mass., 1950; LLB, U. Conn., 1953; LLM, Yale U., 1961. Bar: Conn. 1953. Atty. Conn. Gen. Life Ins. Co., 1953-61; mem. rsch. staff Am. Bar Found., Chgo., 1961-93, assoc. exec. dir., 1976-86, rsch. atty., 1986-93, rsch. fellow emeritus, 1993—; vis. prof. U. Ill. Law Sch., 1965, Sch. Social Svc., U. Chgo., 1966-68, Ariz. State U., 1980; cons. in field. Author of eight books in field; contbr. articles to profl. jours. Mem. Ill. Gov.'s Consumer Credit Adv. Com., 1962-63; consumer credit adv. com. Nat. Conf. Commns. on Uniform State Laws, 1964-70; credit legis. subcom. Mayor Daley's Com. on New Residents, 1966-69; cons. Pres.'s Commn. on Consumer Interests, 1966-70, Ill. Commn. on Gender Bias in the Cts., 1987-92. Mem. ABA, Pi Beta Phi. Address: Am Bar Found 750 N Lake Shore Dr Chicago IL 60611-4403

CURRAN, BARBARA SANSON, lawyer; b. Wiesbaden, Fed. Republic of Germany, Jan. 25, 1955; came to U.S., 1973; d. Allan David and Gertrude Maria (Trendl) S.; m. Stephen P. Curran, Sept. 15, 1990; 1 child, Catherine L. Student, U. London, 1975-76; AB, Bryn Mawr Coll., 1977; JD, Dickinson Sch. Law, 1980. Bar: Pa. 1980, U.S. Dist. Ct. (ea. dist.) Pa. 1981. Law clk. Lehigh County Ct., Allentown, Pa., 1980-82; assoc. Duane Morris & Heckscher, Phila., 1982-84; atty. ICI Americas Inc., Wilmington, Del., 1984-90, corp. sec., 1991—. Mem. ABA, Pa. Bar Assn. Avocation: ice skating. Home: 105 Montana Dr Chadds Ford PA 19317-9284 Office: ICI Ams Inc 3411 Silverside Rd Ste 101 Wilmington DE 19810-4837

CURRAN, CHRISTOPHER, economics educator; b. Washington, Nov. 5, 1943; s. Charles Daniel and Virginia (Wray) C.; m. Nannette Carter, June 10,

1978; children: John Fredrick, Christianne Michelle. BA in History, Rice U., 1967; MS in Econs., Purdue U., 1969, PhD in Econs., 1972. Grad. instr. econs. Purdue U., 1967-70; asst. prof. econs. Emory U., Atlanta, 1970-77, sr. acad. assoc. Law and Econs. Ctr., 1983-86, sr. acad. assoc. law and econs., 1986—, assoc. prof. econs., 1977—, dir. undergrad. studies, 1994-96; Fulbright lectr., Peru, 1976. Contbr. articles and book revs. to profl. jours. Bd. mem. Lullwater Sch., Atlanta, 1975; v.p. Virginia Hill Condo Assn., Atlanta, 1993, pres. 1994, treas. 1995. Krannert rsch. grantee, 1969-70, grantee Emory U., 1972, 75, 79, Emory Bus. Sch., 1978-80, 82. Mem. Am. Econ. Assn., So. Econ. Assn., Am. Law and Econs. Assn., European Assn. Law and Econs. (assoc.). Avocation: tennis. Home: 578 N Superior Ave Decatur GA 30033-5402 Office: Emory U Dept Econs Atlanta GA 30322-1009

CURRAN, DARRYL JOSEPH, photographer, educator; b. Santa Barbara, Calif., Oct. 19, 1935; s. Joseph Harold and Irma Marie (Schlagel) C.; m. Doris Jean Smith, July 12, 1968. A.A., Ventura Coll., 1958; B.A., UCLA, 1960, M.A., 1964. Designer, installer UCLA Art Galleries, 1963-65; mem. faculty Los Angeles Harbor Coll., 1968-69, UCLA Ext., 1972-79, Sch. Art Inst. Chgo., 1975; prof. art Calif. State U., Fullerton, 1967—; chmn. art dept. Calif. State U., 1989—; curator various shows, 1971—; bd. dirs. Los Angeles Center Photog. Studies, 1973-77, pres., 1980-83; juror Los Angeles Olympics Photog. Commns. Project, 1983. One-man shows include U. Chgo., 1975, U. R.I., 1975, Art Space, L.A., 1978, Photoworks Gallery, Richmond, Va., 1979, Alan Hancock Coll., Santa Maria, Calif., 1979, G. Ray Howkins Gallery, L.A., 1981, Portland (Maine) Sch. Art, 1983, Grossmont Coll., San Diego, 1982, (retrospectives) Chaffey Coll., Alta Loma, Calif., L.A. Ctr. for Photographic Studies, 1984, U. Calif. Ext. Ctr., San Francisco, 1986, Cuesta Coll., San Luis Obispo, Calif., 1992, Cypress Coll., 1993, Tex. Woman's U., Denton, 1997, Irvine Valley Coll., 1997; two-person show No. Ky. U., 1995; group exhbns. include Laguna Mus. Art, San Francisco, 1992, Friends of Photography, San Francisco, 1993, U.S. Info. Agy. Empowered Images, 1994—, USIA, Jan Abrams Gallery, L.A., 1995; group exhibns. include Mt. St. Mary's Coll., 1997, Ranch Santiago Coll., 1997; represented in permanent collections Mus. Modern Art, Royal Photog. Soc., London, Nat. Gallery Can., Ottawa, Mpls. Inst. Art, Oakland Mus., U. N.Mex., UCLA, Seagram's Collection, N.Y.C., Mus. Photog. Arts, San Diego, Phila. Mus. Art, J. Paul Getty Mus., Phila. Mus. Art, San Francisco Mus. Art. Bd. dirs. Cheviot Hills Home Owners Assn., 1973. Served with U.S. Army, 1954-56. Recipient Career Achievement award Calif. Mus. Photography, 1986; NEA Photographers fellow, 1980; Honored Educatior award Soc. Photographic Edn., 1996. Mem. Soc. Photog. Edn. (dir. 1975-79, honored educator 1996). Home: 10537 Dunleer Dr Los Angeles CA 90064-4317 Office: Calif State Univ Chmn Dept Art 800 N State College Blvd Fullerton CA 92831-3547 *I am an artist with abstract expressionist sympathies who chooses to use the photographic medium in its broadest definition.*

CURRAN, DAVID BERNARD, JR., real estate executive; b. New Haven, June 6, 1959; s. David Bernard Sr. and Helen Rita (Healey) C.; m. Nancy Manier Nickey, Mar. 19, 1988; children: David Bernard III, George Nickey, Sarah Elizabeth. BBA, So. Meth. U., 1981. Ptnr., exec. v.p. Fults Realty Corp., Dallas, 1981—; bd. trustees bldgs. and grounds com. So. Meth. U. Fundraiser Am. Heart Assn., Dallas, 1982—, Boy Scouts Am., Dallas, 1983; vol. Big Bros. Dallas, 1985. Mem. North Tex. Comml. Assn. of Realtors, Northwood Country Club. Republican. Roman Catholic. Avocations: golf, travel, people. Home: 3541 Colgate Ave Dallas TX 75225-5010 Office: Fults Realty Corp 9400 N Central Expy Fl 5 Dallas TX 75231-5027

CURRAN, EMILY KATHERINE, museum director; b. Boston, Mar. 27, 1960; d. George Morton and Gloria Rose (Martino) C.; m. John Vincent Callahan, Oct. 8, 1989. AB in Fine Arts, Bard Coll., 1982; MS in Mus. Leadership, Bank Street Coll., 1992. Sr. developer The Children's Mus., Boston, 1982-88; dir. edn. The Old South Meeting House, Boston, 1988-92, exec. dir., 1992—; vis. community artist Great George's Project, Liverpool, Eng., 1983. Author: Science Sensations, 1989, An Architectural History of the Old South Meeting House, 1995. Bd. dirs. Freedom Trail Found., Boston, 1992-97; elected mem. Colonial Soc. Mass., 1996—; mem., exec. com. mem. cmty. adv. bd. WGBH, Boston, 1996-99, vice chair, 1998-99. Mus. edn. fellow Bank Street Coll., 1989-91. Mem. Am. Assn. Mus., Am. Assn. State and Local History, New Eng. Mus. Assn., Boston Mus. Educators' Roundtable (chair steering com. 1989-91). Office: Old South Meeting House 310 Washington St Boston MA 02108-4616

CURRAN, GEOFFREY MICHAEL, lawyer; b. Tarrytown, N.J., Mar. 20, 1949; s. Geoffrey C. and Marjorie May (Barnes) C.; m. Rose Marie Strong, June 5, 1970 (div. Feb. 1981); children: Christopher, Sarah, Deborah; m. Karol Ann Chumchal, Feb. 9, 1985; 1 child, Brandon. BBA, U. Tex., 1971; JD, St. Mary's U., San Antonio, 1973. Bar: Tex. 1974, U.S. Dist. Ct. (so. dist.) Tex. 1975, U.S. Dist. Ct. (no. dist.) Tex. 1984, U.S Ct. of Appeals, (5th cir.) 1991, U.S. Dist. Ct. Ariz, 1992. Briefing atty. First Ct. of Appeals, Houston, 1974; lawyer Vinson & Elkins, Houston, 1975-82, Axelrod, Smith, Komiss & Kirshbaum, Houston, 1983, Sheinfeld, Maley & Kay, Dallas, 1984-87; ptnr. Akin, Gump, Strauss, Hauer & Feld, Dallas, 1988—; Contbr. articles to profl. jours. Office: Akin Gump Strauss Hauer & Feld LLP 1700 Pacific Ave Ste 4100 Dallas TX 75201-4675

CURRAN, J. JOSEPH, JR., state attorney general; b. West Palm Beach, Fla., July 7, 1931; s. J. Joseph Sr. and Catherine (Clark) C.; m. Barbara Marie Atkins, 1959; children: Mary Carole, Alice Ann, Catherine Marie, J. Joseph III, William A. (dec.). LLB, U. Balt., 1959. Bar: Md. 1959, U.S. Dist. Ct. Md., U.S. Supreme Ct. 1987. State senator from Md., 1963-83; lt. gov. State of Md., 1983-86; atty. gen. State of Md., Balt., 1987—; mem. Md. Regional Planning Council, 1963-82. Mem. Md. Bar Assn., Balt. Bar Assn. Office: Office of Atty Gen 200 Saint Paul Pl Baltimore MD 21202-2004*

CURRAN, JAMES W., epidemiologist, educator, academic administrator; b. Monroe, Mich., Sept. 16, 1944; married; two children.; BS, U. Notre Dame, 1966; MD, U. Mich., 1970; MPH, Harvard U., 1974. Rsch. instr. dept. preventive and cmty. medicine U. Tenn. Med. Sch., 1971-73; career devel. tng. Ctr. Disease Control, USPHS, 1973-75; asst. commr. health med. svc. Columbus (Ohio) City Health Dept., 1975-78; chief oper. rsch. br. Venereal Disease Control Ctr. Disease Control and Prevention, 1978-82; dir. Acquired Immune Deficiency Syndrome Activ, 1982-84; chief AIDS br. Divsn. Viral Diseases, Ctr. Infectious Diseases, 1984-85; dir. WHO Referal Ctr. AIDS & Retroviruses, 1985-92; assoc. dir. human immunodeficiency virus/AIDS Ctr. Disease Control and Prevention, 1992-95; dean Rollins Sch. Pub. Health Emory U., Atlanta, 1995—; L. Vernon Scott lectr. U. Okla. Health Sci. Ctr., 1985, Verna & Mars lectr. Baylor Coll. Medicine, 1988, Oliver Cope lectr. Mass. Gen. Hosp., 1988; clin. rsch. investigator Venereal Disease Br., Ctr. Disease Control, 1971-73; med. dir. Influenza Immunication Program, Franklin County, 1976-77; clin. rsch. investigator, coord. Oper. Rsch. Br., Venereal Disease Control Divsn., Ctr. Disease Control, 1975-78; clin. asst. prof. dept. preventive and cmty. medicine, Coll. Medicine, Ohio State U., 1976-79; John Forbes fellow infectious disease Fairfield Hosp., Melbourne, Australia, 1985; vis. prof. Coll. Medicine, U. Ill., 1988; asst. surgeon gen. USPHS, 1991. Recipient William C. Watson Jr. award, 1987. Fellow Infectious Disease Soc. Am., Am. Coll. Preventive Medicine, Am. Epidemiol. Soc.; mem. AAAS, Inst. Medicine-NAS, Am. Venereal Disease Assn., Sigma Xi. Office: Emory U Rollins Sch Pub Health 1518 Clifton Rd NE Atlanta GA 30329-4218

CURRAN, JANET S., advertising executive; b. Detroit, Aug. 22, 1953; d. Donald Arvid and Marilyn Jeanne (Carso) Bergdahl; m. Mark Randall Curran, Nov. 29, 1980. BA, Mich. State U., 1975. Art dir. Rogers & Bell Advt., Birmingham, Mich., 1975-79, Leo Burnett Advt., Southfield, Mich., 1979-80; v.p. creative group head Foote, Cone & Belding, L.A., 1980-87, Campbell Wagman, L.A., 1987-88; v.p., creative dir. Klein and La Brucherie, L.A., 1988-91; pres., exec. creative dir. Curran — Co., 1991—. Recipient Internat. Film and TV awards, 1986, 87, Belding award 1987, Internat. Broadcast award, 1988. Avocations: skiing, graphic design. Home: 528 15th St Manhattan Beach CA 90266-4803

CURRAN, JOHN MARK, military career officer; b. West Palm Beach, Fla., Jan. 27, 1952; m. Cindy Templon; children: Jennifer, Jessica, Julia. Grad., Fla. So. Coll.; M in Mil. Arts and Scis.; grad., Command & Gen. Staff Coll., Nat. War Coll. Commd. officer U.S. Army, advanced through grades to brig. gen., 1998; evaluation officer 1st ROTC region U.S. Army, Ft. Bragg; armored cavalry platoon leader, trans sect. leader, officer U.S. Army, Ft. Bliss, Tex.; hdqrs. co. exec. officer, aeroscout platoon leader, bn. S1 U.S. Army, Germany; flight comdr., ops. officer, br. comdr., dept. flight tng. U.S. Army; tng. devel. officer dept. combined arms tactics, co. comdr. U.S. Army, Ft. Rucker, Ala.; G3 air, attack bn. exec. officer Aviation Brigade S3 U.S. Army, Ft. Campbell, Ky.; dep. aviation brigade comdr. 101st Airborne Divsn. U.S. Army, Ft. Campbell; dept. of the Army programs, priorities & requirements divsn. Office Dep. Chief Staff for Ops. and Plans, Force Devel.; comdr. aviation brigade 2nd Inf. Divsn. U.S. Army, Republic of Korea; dep. chief staff ops. USAREUR Forward, U.S. Army, Heidelberg, Germany; asst. divsn. comdr. for support 1st Inf. Divsn. U.S. Army; dep. commdg. gen. Combined Arms Ctr.-Combined Arms Tng. U.S. Army, Ft. Leavenworth, Kans., 1998—. Decorated Bronze Star, Legion of Merit with oak leaf cluster, Meritorious Svc. medal with three oak leaf clusters, Army Commendation medal, two Air medals, Army Achievement medal, Nat. Def. Svc. medal, NATO medal, Kuwait Liberation medal Govts. of Saudi Arabia and Kuwait. Office: Combined Arms Ctr Combined Arms Tng Ft Leavenworth KS 66027-1327

CURRAN, JOSEPH PATRICK, lawyer; b. Providence, Apr. 25, 1951; s. Joseph Patrick and Susan (Donohue) C.; m. Sheila Jane McGowan, July 14, 1974; children: Christopher, Peter. BA, Holy Cross Coll., 1973; MA, London Sch. Econs., 1974; JD, U. Mich., 1978. Bar: R.I. 1978. Spl. asst. to gen. counsel Office of Sec. USN, Washington, 1978-81; assoc. Hinckley, Allen & Snyder, Providence, 1981-86; ptnr. Hinckley, Allen & Snyder, Providence, 1986—. Editor U. Mich. Law Rev., 1976-78. Pres. Improvise Inc., Providence, 1989—; v.p. Nickerson Community Ctr., Providence, 1986—. Lt. USN, 1978-81. Mem. ABA, R.I. Bar Assn., Order of Coif. Home: 232 Taber Ave Providence RI 02906-3351 Office: Hinckley Allen Snyder 1500 Fleet Ctr Providence RI 02903-2319

CURRAN, MAURICE FRANCIS, lawyer; b. Yonkers, N.Y., Feb. 20, 1931; s. James F. and Mary (O'Brien) C.; m. Deborah M., May 7, 1960; children: James, Maurice, Amy, Bridget, Ceara, Sara. Student Cathedral Coll., 1950; BA in Philosophy, St. Joseph Coll. and Sem., 1952; LLB, Fordham U., 1958. Bar: N.Y. 1958, U.S. Dist. Ct. (so. and ea. dists.) N.Y. 1960, U.S. Ct. Appeals (2d cir.) 1982, U.S. Supreme Ct. Assoc. Kelley, Drye, Newhall & Maginnes, N.Y.C., 1958-60; assoc. Wilson & Bave, Yonkers, 1960-65; div. counsel Merck & Co., Rahway, N.J., 1965-67; asst. gen. counsel E. R. Squibb & Sons, Inc., N.Y.C., 1967-70; corp. counsel, chief law dept. City of Yonkers, 1970-72; ptnr. Bleakley, Platt, Schmidt & Fritz, White Plains, N.Y., 1972-83, Banks, Curran & Keefe, Mt. Kisco, N.Y., 1983—. Past trustee, vice chmn. Westchester C.C. Capt. USMC, 1952-58. Mem. Fed. Bar Coun., N.Y. State Bar Assn., Assn. Bar City N.Y. Roman Catholic. Home: 388 Bronxville Rd Bronxville NY 10708-1233 Office: 61 Smith Ave Mount Kisco NY 10549-2813

CURRAN, M(ICHAEL) SCOT, lawyer; b. Dayton, Ohio, Feb. 7, 1952; s. John J. Curran and Patricia (Ludwig) Curran Schaffner; m. Ellen L. O'Leary, Apr. 22, 1978; children: Allison M., Scot Michael. BA, Washington & Jefferson U., 1974; JD, U. Pitts., 1977. Bar: Pa. 1977, U.S. Dist. Ct. (we. dist.) Pa. 1977, U.S. Ct. Appeals (3d cir.) 1977. Assoc. Lawrence R. Zewe Law Office, Washington, Pa., 1977-80; ptnr. Clarke & Curran, Washington, Pa., 1980-83, Saxton & Curran, Washington, Pa., 1983-86, M. Scot Curran & Assocs., Washington, Pa., 1986—. Bd. dirs. Mental Health/Mental Retardation, Washington, 1983-85; chmn. Civil Rights Com., Washington, 1988, mem., 1989-98; co-chmn. Profl. Awareness Com., Washington, 1989—. Fellow Washington County Acad. Trial Lawyers, SW Pa. Acad. Trial Lawyers (past pres. 1997); mem. Pa. Bar Assn., Pa. Trial Lawyers Assn., Washington County Bar Assn. Avocations: reading, golf. Office: M Scot Curran & Assoc 11 S College St Washington PA 15301-4821

CURRAN, MICHAEL WALTER, management scientist; b. St. Louis, Dec. 6, 1935; s. Clarence Maurice and Helen Gertrude (Parsons) C.; m. Jeanette Lucille Rawizza, Sept. 24, 1955 (div. 1977); children: Kevin Michael, Karen Ann, Kathleen Marie (dec.), Kimberly Elizabeth; m. Mary Jane Lemanek, Aug. 18, 1981. BS, Washington U., St. Louis, 1964. With Monsanto Co., St. Louis, 1953-65; supervisory positions dept. adminstrv. services Monsanto Co., 1956-64, research technician inorganic chems. div., 1964-65; sr. ops. research analyst Pet Inc., St. Louis, 1965-68; pres. Decision Scis. Corp., St. Louis, 1968—; also dir. Decision Scis. Corp. Co-author: Handbook of Budgeting, 1981, 3d edit., 1993, Effective Project Management Through Applied Cost and Schedule Control, 1996; editor: Professional Practice Guide to Risk, Vols. 1-3; contbr. articles to profl. jours.; developer theories of bracket budgeting and range estimating. Adviser Jr. Achievement, St. Louis, 1958-59; active United Way, 1958-62. Mem. Inst. Mgmt. Scis. (chmn. St. Louis chpt. 1971-72), Ops. Research Soc. Am., Am. Assn. Cost Engrs. (chmn. risk mgmt. com. 1991—), Project Mgmt. Inst., Soc. Cost Estimating and Analysis, Internat. Platform Assn., Mensa, Intertel, Sigma Xi, Alpha Sigma Lambda. Office: Decision Scis Corp PO Box 28848 Saint Louis MO 63123-0048

CURRAN, ROBERT, councilman. City councilman Balt., 1995—. Office: City Hall 100 Holliday St Ste 504 Baltimore MD 21202-3417*

CURRAN, ROBERT EMMETT, history educator; b. Balt., May 23, 1936; s. Joseph Francis and Marie Anna (Mahrenholz) C. AB, Coll. of Holy Cross, 1958; MA, Fordham U., 1965; PhD, Yale U., 1974. Lectr. Georgetown U., Washington, 1972-74, asst. prof., 1974-77, assoc. prof., 1977-97, prof., 1997—. Author: Michael Augustine Corrigan and the Shaping of a Conservative Catholicism in America, 1978, The Bicentennial History of Georgetown, 1993; editor: American Jesuit Spirituality, 1988. Bd. dirs. St. Joseph's U., Phila., 1979-85, Coll. of the Holy Cross, 1988-96, Worcester, Mass., Loyola Coll., Balt., 1991-97. Mem. Am. Hist. Assn., Orgn. Am. Historians, Am. Cath. Hist. Assn. (nominating com.), Am. Soc. Ch. History, Immigration History Soc., So. Hist. Assn. Democrat. Roman Catholic. Avocation: running. Home: 1919 Youngblood St McLean VA 22101 Office: History Dept Georgetown U 37th and O Sts NW Washington DC 20057

CURRAN, THOMAS, molecular biologist, educator; b. Broxburn, West Lothian, Scotland, Feb. 14, 1956; came to U.S., 1982; s. Thomas and Jane Holden (McGovern) C.; m. Frances Ko-Fang Yao, Dec. 27, 1979; 1 child, Sean Philip. BS, U. Edinburgh, Scotland, 1978; PhD, U. Coll. London, 1982. Postdoctoral fellow Salk Inst., San Diego, 1982-84; sr. scientist Hoffman-La Roche Inc., Nutley, N.J., 1984-85; asst. mem. Roche Inst. Molecular Biology, Nutley, 1985-86, assoc. mem., 1986-88, full mem., 1988-95, head dept., 1989-92, assoc. dir., 1991-95; adj. prof. Columbia U., N.Y.C., 1989-95; mem. and chmn. dept. devel. neurobiology St. Jude Children's Rsch. Hosp., Memphis, 1995—; mem. adv. bd. study sect. NIH, Washington, 1991-94, Damon Runyan/Walter Winchell Cancer Rsch. Fund, N.Y.C., 1992—96 Merton F. Utter Meml. lectr. Case Western Res. U., 1992. Editor: The Oncogene Handbook, 1988, Origins of Human Cancer, 1991; contbr. over 150 articles to sci. jours. and books. Recipient Young Scientist award Passano Found., 1992, Rita Levi Montalcino Lecture award Fidia Rsch. Found., 1992, Glasgow U.-Tenovus-Scotland medal, 1992, Litchfield Lecture award Oxford U., 1994, Golgi award Italian Acad. Neurosci. and Camillo Golgi Found., 1994.; Imperial Cancer Rsch. Fund grantee. Fellow AAAS, Am. Acad. Microbiology; mem. Am. Assn. for Cancer Rsch. (Rhoads award 1993, pres.-elect 1999), Am. Soc. for Cell Biology, Am. Soc. Biochemistry and Molecular Biology, Soc. for Neurosci., Harvey Soc. Roman Catholic. Achievements include discovery and characterization of fos oncogene which causes bone tumors in mice; demonstration that fos gene expression is increased rapidly in many cell types treated with agents associated with mitogenesis, differentiation and stimulation of neurons, fos encodes DNA binding protein that functions in transcriptional regulation in association with the product of the jun oncogene, identification of gene responsible for the mouse, neurodevelopmental mutation reeler. Office: St Jude Childrens Rsch Hosp 332 N Lauderdale St Memphis TN 38105-2729

CURRAN, THOMAS J., federal judge; b. 1924. B of Naval Scis., Marquette U., 1945, LLB, 1948. Ptnr. Curran, Curran and Hollenback, Mauston, Wis., 1948-83; judge U.S. Dist. Ct. (ea. dist.) Wis., Milw., 1983—, now sr. judge; mem. Gov's Commn. on Crime and Law Enforcement, State of Wis. With USN, 1943-46. Mem. ABA, Am. Coll. Trial Lawyers. Office: US Dist Ct 250 US Courthouse 517 E Wisconsin Ave Milwaukee WI 53202-4500*

CURRAN, WILLIAM P., lawyer; b. Mpls., Feb. 27, 1946; s. William P. and Margaret L. (Killoren) C.; m. Jean L. Stabenow, Jan. 1, 1978; children: Patrick, Lisa, John. BA, U. Minn., 1969; JD, U. Calif., Berkeley, 1972. Law clk. Nev. Supreme Ct., Carson City, 1973-74, state ct. adminstr., 1973-74; assoc. Wiener, Goldwater & Galatz, Las Vegas, Nev., 1974-75; chief dept. dist. atty. Clark County Dist. Atty.'s Office, Las Vegas, 1975-79; county counsel Clark County, Las Vegas, 1979-89; pvt. practice Las Vegas, 1989-94; ptnr. Curran & Parry, Las Vegas, 1994—. Co-author: Nevada Judicial Orientation Manual, 1974. Mem. Nev. Gaming Commn., Carson City, 1989-99, chmn., 1991-99. Recipient Educator Yr. award UNLV Internat. Gaming Inst., 1998. Mem. ABA (state del. 1994—), Internat. Assn. Gaming Regulators (chmn. 1992-94), Nat. Assn. County Civil Attys. (pres. 1984-85), State Bar Nev. (pres. 1988-89). Democrat. Roman Catholic. Office: Curran & Parry 601 S Rancho Dr Ste C-23 Las Vegas NV 89106-4825

CURRERI, JOHN ROBERT, mechanical engineer, consultant; b. N.Y.C., July 20, 1922; s. Girolomo and Genoveffa (Dasaro) C.; m. Margaret McHugh, June 2, 1946 (dec.); children: Eileen, Ellen, Joan; m. Ann Jurgensen, Oct. 1, 1976. BME cum laude, Bklyn. Poly. Inst., 1944; MME, Poly. U., Bklyn., 1948. Registered profl. engr., N.Y. Assoc. prof. Bklyn. Poly. Inst., 1948-55; head dynamics sect. ARMA Corp., Garden City, N.Y., 1955-57; prof. Poly. U., Bklyn., 1957-64, head mech. dept., 1964-74, prof., 1974-90; vis. prof. CUNY, 1990-91; prof. emeritus Poly. U., Bklyn., 1992—; cons. Brookhaven Nat. Lab., Upton, N.Y., 1974-90, Sperry, Great Neck, N.Y., 1966-70. Author: (textbook) Vibration of Structures, 1961; co-author: (textbook) Vibration Control, 1958; contbr. articles to more than 60 profl. jours. Recipient Sci. Faculty fellowship NSF, 1963. Mem. ASME, NSPE, Am. Soc. Engring. Edn., N.Y. Soc. Profl. Engrs., Sigma Xi, Tau Beta Pi, Pi Tau Sigma. Home and Office: John R Curreri 2506 Bentley Dr Palm Harbor FL 34684-1845

CURREY, MELODY ALENA, state legislator; b. Margaretsville, N.Y., Dec. 17, 1950; m. Donald Currey; children: Rebecca, Jeffrey, Matthew. Student, SUNY, Cobleskill. Tchr. St. Mary's Ch.; mem. from dist. 10 Conn. State Ho. of Reps., 1993—, dep. spkr. Mem. Dem. Town Com., Hartford, Conn., 1984—, mem. fin. com., 1988; mem. rules com. Hartford Town Conv., 1989, 90; chmn. 5th Dem. Dist. Com., 1988-92, also sec.; issues chmn. Com. to Elect John Larson, 1990; canvass chmn. Rosemary Moynihan for State Rep., 1990, mem. steering com., 1990; coord. Com. to Re-elect Congresswoman Barbara Kennelly, East Hartford, Conn., 1990; scheduling dir. DelPonte for Mayor Com., 1991; leader Girl Scouts U.S.; mem. Student at Risk Com., 1988. Mem. Nat. Sch. Vol. Am., Supts. Adv. Coun., Dem. Women's Club (former sec.), Sci. Ctr. Conn. (leadership coun.). Address: 14 Martin Cir East Hartford CT 06118-1119 Office: Conn Ho of Reps State Capitol Hartford CT 06106

CURREY, RICHARD, writer; b. Parkersburg, W.Va., Oct. 19, 1949; s. Allen E. and Mary K. Currey; m. Aiko Allen (div. Sept. 1997); 1 child, Asia Devon. BA, W.Va. U., 1974; MA, Howard U., 1979. Disting. vis. writer Wichita (Kans.) State U., 1993; vis. prof. U. N.Mex., Albuquerque, 1993-94; artist in residence State of W.Va., Charleston, 1994, 97; writer in residence Chesterfield Film Co., L.A., 1996—; lectr. Nat. Pub. Radio, U. Calif., Berkeley, U. Calif., Santa Cruz, Harvard U., NYU, San Francisco State U., others, 1984—; fiction judge Ill. Arts Coun. Artists Fellowship Program, 1993. Author: Crossing Over: The Vietnam Stories, 1980, re-issue, 1993 (nominated Pulitzer Prize, Best of the Yr. Libr. Jour. 1981), Fatal Light, 1988, re-issue, 1997, (Spl. citation Ernest Hemingway Found., Enoch Pratt Libr. award, Excellence Arts award Vietnam Vets. Am. 1989), The Wars of Heaven, 1990, re-issue, 1991 (O. Henry award 1988, Pushcart prize 1990), Lost Highway, 1997, re-issue, 1998(Daugherty award, N.Mex. Arts Alliance award 1997); contbg. editor Pushcart Prize series, 1989-96; contbr. short stories to periodicals. Recipient Poetry prize Sante Fe Festival Arts, 1979, Associated Writing Programs Short Fiction prize, 1984; named Best Am. Writers Esquire Mag., 1989; D. H. Lawrence fellow, 1981; NEA fellow, 1982, 87; Western States Arts Fedn. grantee, 1993. E-mail: rcurrey@swcp.com. Office: 160 Washington SE # 185 Albuquerque NM 87109

CURRI, JOANNE M., pharmaceutical company executive; b. Bridgeport, Conn., June 24, 1940; d. Cosmo Daniels and Flora Frances (Aurilio) C. Regulatory affairs mgr. Hi-Tech Pharmacal Co. Inc., Amityville, N.Y. Home: 568 S 8th St Lindenhurst NY 11757 Office: Hi-Tech Pharmacal Co Inc 369 Bayview Ave Amityville NY 11701

CURRIE, BARBARA FLYNN, state legislator; b. LaCrosse, Wis., May 3, 1940; d. Frank T. and Elsie R. (Gobel) Flynn; AB cum laude, U. Chgo., 1968, AM, 1973; m. David P. Currie, Dec. 29, 1959; children: Stephen Francis, Margaret Rose. Asst. study dir. Nat. Opinion Rsch. Ctr., Chgo., 1973-77; part time instr. polit. sci. DePaul U., Chgo., 1973-74; mem. Ill. Ho. of Reps., 1979—, chmn. House Dem. Study Group, 1981-83, asst. majority leader, 1993, asst. minority leader, 1995, majority leader, 1997. Mem. adv. bd. Harriet Harris YWCA; v.p. Chgo. LWV, 1965-69; mem. ACLU, Hyde Park-Kenwood Cmty. Conf., Ind. Voters of Ill.-Ind. Precinct Orgn., Hyde Park Coop. Soc., Ams. for Dem. Action. Named Best Legislator, Ind. Voters of Ill., 1980, 82, 84, 86, 88, 90, 92, 94, 96, 98, Best Legislator, Ill. Credit Union League, Outstanding Legislator, Ill. Hosp. Assn., 1987; recipient Leon Despres award, 1991, Ill. Environ. Coun. award, Ill. Cmty.Action Agys. award, Ill. Women's Polit. Caucus Lottie Holman O'Neill award, Susan B. Anthony award, honor award Nat. Trust Historic Preservation; awards Welfare Rights Coalition of Orgns., Ill. Pub. Action Coun., Chgo. Heart Assn.; named Legislator of Yr., Ill. Nurses Assn., 1984, Nat. Assn. Social Workers, 1984, Ill. Women's Substance Abuse Coalition, 1984; recipient BEST BETS award Nat. Ctr. Policy Alternatives, 1988, Svc. award Nat. Ctr. For Freedom of Info. Studies, 1989, Beautiful Person award Chgo. Urban League, 1989, Friend of Labor award Ill. AFL-CIO, 1990, Ill. Maternal and Child Health Coalition award, 1990, Ill. Hunger Coalition award, 1991, Cert. of Appreciation SEIU Local 880, 1989, March of Dimes, 1988, Chgo. Tchrs. Union, Ill. Hosp. Assn., Ptnr. Vision award Families' and Children's AIDS Network, Woman of Vision award Womens' Bar Assn. Ill., 1997, Nat. Elected Pub. Offcl. award Nat. Assn. Social Workers, 1997, Outstanding Working Woman of Ill. award Ill. Fedn. Bus. and Profl. Women. Mem. ACLU (bd. dirs. Ill.), Ill. Conf. Women Legislators, Nat. Order Women Legislators. Contbr. article to publ. Office: Ill Gen Assembly 300 S State House Springfield IL 62706-1757

CURRIE, BRUCE, artist; b. Sac City, Iowa, Nov. 27, 1911; s. Malcolm and Clara Mabel (Austin) C.; m. Ethel Magafan, June 30, 1946; 1 dau., Jenne Magafan. Student, Northwestern U., 1930-32, U. Chgo., 1932-33. One-man shows include Am. embassy, Athens, Greece, 1952, Ganso Gallery, N.Y.C., 1953, 54, Roko Gallery, 1958, 60, Albany Inst. History and Art, 1958, Ulster County Community Coll., Kingston, N.Y., 1967, Joseloff Gallery, U. Hartford, 1968, Schenectady Mus., 1970, Jacques Seligmann Galleries, N.Y.C., 1978, Midtown Galleries, N.Y.C., 1980, 83, retrospective exhbn. Woodstock (N.Y.) Artists Assn., 1993; represented in permanent collections SUNY-Albany, Dwight Art Meml., Mt. Holyoke Coll., Colorado Springs Fine Arts Ctr., Butler Inst. Am. Art, Kalamazoo Inst. Arts, N.A.D., Ulster County Community Coll., Kingston, Berkshire Community Coll. Served with USAAF, 1942-45, ETO. Decorated European - African - Middle Ea. Theater ribbon with 1 Silver and 1 Bronze Battle Star; recipient Purchase award Henry Ward Ranger Fund, N.A.D., 1964, 75, Clarke prize, 1966, Benjamin Altman figure prize, 1979, Gold medal of honor Nat. Arts Club, 1964; Albany Inst. History and Art award, 1967, Berle award Berkshire Art Assn., 1967, purchase award, 1973, Soletsky award Nat. Soc. Painters in Casein and Acrylic, 1973, Grumbacher award, 1974, John J. Newman Meml. award, 1976, Wallach Meml. award, 1980, Wright Meml. prize Cooperstown Art Assn., 1978, grand prize, 1981, also others. Mem. NAD (acad.), Audubon Artists (Medal of Honor 1963, 82, Joseph Raskin Meml. award 1987, Ralph Fabri Medal of Honor 1989, Emily Lowe award 1990), Am. Watercolor Soc. (Silver medal 1958, Emily Lowe award 1968, Whitney award 1975, Winsor-Newton award 1981, Mario Cooper award 1985, Elsie and David WU Ject-Key Meml. award 1997, Audubon Artists Silver Medal 1998), Adirondack Nat. Exhbn. of Am. Watercolors (Martin award 1988, Smith Packing Co. award 1990), Conn. Acad. Fine Arts (Conn. Acad. prize for Painting, 1965, The Charles Noel Flagg Meml. prize 1968). Home: 120 Boggs Hill Rd Woodstock NY 12498-2712

CURRIE, CAMERON MCGOWAN, judge; b. 1948. BA, U. S.C., 1970; JD with honors, George Washington U., 1975. Tchr. Moultrie H.S., Mt. Pleasant; law intern to magistrate judge Hon. Arthur L. Burnett U.S. Dist. Ct. D.C., 1973-74; atty. Arent, Fox, Kintner, Plotkin & Kahn, Washington, 1975-78; asst. U.S. Atty. Office U.S. Atty., Washington, 1978-80, Columbia, S.C., 1980-84; magistrate judge U.S. Dist. Ct. S.C., Columbia, 1984-86; pvt. practice Columbia, 1986-89; chief dep. atty. gen. Office Atty. Gen., State of S.C., Columbia, 1989-94; judge U.S. Dist. Ct. S.C., Florence, 1994—; adj. prof. in trial advocacy Sch. Law U. S.C., 1986-89. Assoc. editor SEC No Action Letters Index, 1972-73. Bd. dirs. Wings, Inc., 1986-94, sec., 1992-94. Mem. ABA, S.C. Bar, D.C. Bar, S.C. Women Lawyers Assn. Office: US Dist Ct PO Box 2617 Florence SC 29503-2617

CURRIE, CONSTANCE MERSHON, investment services professional; b. Missoula, Mont., June 22, 1950; d. Alan Clark Van Horn and Saralee (Neumann) Visscher; m. R. Hector Currie, Aug. 14, 1986 (div. 1997). BA in Art with highest hons., Mont. State U., 1977; MFA in Painting, U. Cin., 1981, MA in Arts Adminstrn., 1988; grad., Tsukuba Daigaku, Ibariki, Japan, 1977-78. Bus. mgr. Fort Peck Summer Theatre, Glasgow, Mont., 1983; asst. telemarketing mgr. Cin. Symphony Orchestra, 1984, telemarketing mgr., 1985; mem. coord. Cin. Mus. of Natural History, 1986-88; mktg. cons. Currie Consulting, Cin., 1988-98; investor info. rep. The Vanguard Group, Scottsdale, Ariz., 1998—; lectr. fine art Raymond Walters Coll. U., Cin., 1988-96, instr., 1996-97, asst. prof., 1997-98. Exhbns. include SUNY, Binghamton, 1983, Tangeman Gallery/U. Cin., 1981, Miami U., 1981, No. Rockies Regional Exhbn./Sheridan (Wyo.) Coll., 1981, Bell Art Competition, Cin., 1981 (Purchase award, 1981), Wilmington Coll., 1979, Mont. State U., 1976, 77 (Printmaking Purchase award 1976, 77), Yellowstone Ehbn., Billings, Mont., 1977 (Printmaking Purchase award 1977), others. Trustee Good Harvest Cooperative, Middletown, Conn., 1974-75, Methuen & Gertrude Currie Found., 1986—; bd. dirs. Bozeman (Mont.) Film Festival, 1982-83; vol. Cin. Chamber Orchestra, 1985-87, Cin. Mus. Natural History, 1988-90; capt. Green-Up Day, Rawson Woods Bird Preserve, 1996, 97. Mem. Beta Gamma Sigma, Tau Pi Phi, Phi Kappa Phi. Address: 21824 N 48th Pl Phoenix AZ 85054-6702

CURRIE, DAVID PARK, lawyer, educator; b. Macon, Ga., May 29, 1936; s. Gillette Brainerd and Elmyr (Park) C.; m. Barbara Suzanne Flynn, Dec. 29, 1959; children: Stephen Francis, Margaret Rose. BA, U. Chgo., 1957; LLB, Harvard U., 1960. Bar: Ill. 1963. Law clk. to Hon. Henry J. Friendly U.S. Ct. Appeals (2d cir.), N.Y.C., 1960-61; to Hon. Felix Frankfurter U.S. Supreme Ct., Washington, 1961-62; asst. prof. law U. Chgo., 1962-65, assoc. prof., 1965-68, prof., 1968—, now Edward H. Levi Disting. Svc. prof., 1991—; vis. prof. Stanford (Calif.) U. Law Sch., 1965, U. Mich. Law Sch., Ann Arbor, 1964, 68, U. Hanover, Germany, 1981, U. Frankfurt, Germany, 1986, U. Heidelberg, Germany, 1989, U. Tubingen, Germany, 1996, U. Aix-Marselle, France, 1998; coord. environ. quality State of Ill., Chgo., 1970; chmn. Ill. Pollution Control Bd., Chgo., 1970-72. Author: Cases and Materials on Federal Courts, 1968, 4th edit., 1990, On Pollution, 1975, (with R. Cramton, L. Kramer and H. Kay) On Conflict of Laws, 1968, 5th edit., 1994, Federal Jurisdiction in a Nutshell, 1976, 81, 90, Air Pollution: Federal Law and Analysis, 1981, Constitution in the Supreme Court, (2 vols.) 1985, 1990, Constitution of the Federal Republic of Germany, 1994, Constitution in Congress, 1997. Mem. Am. Acad. Arts and Scis. Office: U Chgo Law Sch 1111 E 60th St Chicago IL 60637-2776*

CURRIE, EARL JAMES, transportation company executive; b. Fergus Falls, Minn., May 14, 1939; s. Victor James and Calma (Hammer) C.; m. Kathleen P. Phalen, June 3, 1972; children: Jane, Joseph. BA, St. Olaf Coll., 1961; cert. in transp., Yale U., 1963; P.M.D., Harvard U., 1974. With Burlington No. Inc., 1964-85; asst. v.p. St. Paul, 1977-78, Chgo., 1978-80; v.p., gen. mgr. Seattle, 1980-83; sr. v.p. Overland Park, Kans., 1983-85; pres. Camas Prairie R.R., Lewiston, Idaho, 1982-83, Longview Switching Co., Wash., 1982-83, Western Fruit Express Co., 1984-85; exec. v.p. ops. Soo Line R.R. Co. & Rail Units, 1986-89; v.p. engring. CSX Transp. Co., Jacksonville, Fla., 1989-92, v.p., chief transp. officer, 1992-95; v.p. planning, chief safety officer Wis. Ctrl. Ltd., 1996—; bd. dirs. Belt Ry. Co. Chgo., Terminal R.R. Assn. St. Louis, Norfolk and Portsmouth Ry. Co. Bd. dirs. United Way, King County, Wash., 1980-83, Corp. Council for Arts, Seattle, 1980-83, Jr. Achievement, 1980-82, Lake Superior Mus. Transp., 1986-89, 1999—, North Shore Scenic Railroad, 1999—; trustee St. Martins Coll., Lacey, Wash., 1982-83; mem. Mpls. Neighborhood Employment Network. Mem. Am. Rlwy. Engring. Assn. (bd. dirs. 1989-92), Am. Rlwy. Engring. and Maintenance Assn., Am. Assn. R.R. Supts. (bd. dirs. 1979-80), Seattle C. of C. (bd. dirs. 1980-83), St. Olaf Coll. Alumni Assn. (bd. dirs. 1993—), Internat. Assn. of Railroad Operating Officers, Roadmasters Assn. Home: 8 Graystone Ct Barrington IL 60010-6957 Office: Wis Ctrl Ltd 6250 N River Rd Rosemont IL 60018-4247

CURRIE, EDWARD JONES, JR., lawyer; b. Jackson, Miss., May 23, 1951; s. Edward J. and Nell (Branton) C.; m. Barbara Scott Miller, June 26, 1976; children: Morgan E., Scott E. BA, U. Miss., 1973, JD, 1976. Bar: Miss. 1976, U.S. Dist. Ct. (no. and so. dists.) Miss. 1976, U.S. Ct. Appeals (5th cir.) 1978, U.S. Supreme Ct. 1979. Assoc. Wise, Carter, Child, Steen & Caraway, Jackson, 1976-80; ptnr. Steen, Reynolds, Dalehite & Currie, Jackson, 1980-94, Currie Johnson Griffin Gaines & Myers, Jackson, 1994—; adj. prof. Miss. Coll. Sch. Law, Jackson, 1977-81, 84-86. Bd. dirs. Miss. chpt. Am. Diabetes Assn., Jackson, 1980-82. Mem. FBA (pres. Miss. chpt. 1989), Internat. Assn. Def. Coun. (trial acad. faculty 1992), Nat. Inst. Trial Advocacy, Nat. Lawyers Assn. (chmn. ins. sect. 1998-99), Nat. Lawyers Assn. Found. (bd. dirs. 1998-99), Miss. Jud. Coll. (model civil jury instrn. com. 1991), Miss. Def. Lawyers Assn., Miss. Bar Assn. (bd. dirs. young lawyers sect. 1981-82, chmn. litigation/gen. practice sect. 1992), Miss. Bd. Bar Commrs., Jackson Young Lawyers (bd. dirs. 1980-81), Hinds County Bar Assn., Phi Delta Phi, Sigma Alpha Epsilon (pres. Ctrl. Miss. alumni 1981), Omicron Delta Kappa. Presbyterian. Home: 50 Moss Forest Cir Jackson MS 39211-2905 Office: Currie Johnson Griffin Gaines & Myers PO Box 750 Jackson MS 39205-0750

CURRIE, FERGUS GARDNER, performing arts educator; b. Chgo., June 29, 1931; s. Neill Roswell and Ruth (Anderson) C. BS, Davidson Coll., 1953; MA, U. Mo., 1957; EdD, Columbia U., 1963. Instr. Columbia U., N.Y.C., 1957-61; instr. CUNY, 1961-64, asst. prof. speech and theatre, 1966-69; asst. exec. sec. Speech Assn. Am., N.Y.C., 1964-66; dir. theatre Ga. Inst. Tech., Atlanta, 1970-72, Emory U., Atlanta, 1972-82; pres. Atlantis Prodns., Inc., Atlanta, 1977-86; coord. arts mgmt. U. So. Fla., Tampa, 1985-86; ctrl. regional dir. Actor's Equity Assn., Chgo., 1986-96; ptnr. Theatre Mgmt. Assocs., Chgo., 1996—; prof. theatre, chair dept. theatre Ill. State U., 1997—; assoc. producer Centauri Films, Washington, 1983-84; guest dir. Okla. Theatre Ctr., Oklahoma City, 1982, Fort Wayne Civic Theatre, 1984, Kanahwa Players, Charleston, W.Va., 1984; artist in residence Ga. Council for Arts, Atlanta, 1982-84. Creator musical revues: From Harlem to Broadway, 1981; Harlem Nocturen, 1983, Sweet Auburn, 1985. V.p. DeKalb Coun. for Arts, Decatur, Ga., 1980-82; bd. dirs. Ill. Arts Alliance, 1988—. 1st lt. inf. U.S. Army, 1954-56. Gregory scholar, 1956. Mem. Screen Actors Guild (pres. Ga. br. 1983-85), Actors' Equity Assn., AFTRA (Atlanta chtp. pres. 1983-85, nat. merger com. 1982-87), Am. Coun. of the Arts, Ill. Arts Alliance, Assn. of Theatre in Higher Edn. (gov. bd. conf. chair, 1996-97), Nat. Assn. Schs. Theatre (chair ethics com. 1999—), Nat. Theatre Conf., Mid-Am. Theatre Conf. (pres. 1999—), Ill. Theatre Assn. (chair conf. 1999), Phi Gamma Delta (treas. 1952-53). Democrat. Presbyterian. Avocations: writing, golfing.

CURRIE, JACKIE L., city clerk; married; 4 children. Student, AM&N Coll., Pine Bluff, Ark., Wayne County C.C., Mercy Coll.; grad., Wayne State U.; postgrad., U. Mich. Commr. Wayne County, Mich., 1973-93; city clk. City of Detroit, 1993—. Bd. dirs. SHAR House, Detroit East, Inc.; vice chair Polly Johnson Cancer Found. Mem. Internat. Inst. Mcpl. Clks., Internat. Assn. Clks., Recorders, Election Ofcls. and Treasurers, Mich. Mcpl. Clks. Assn., Mich. Mcpl. League, The Election Ctr., Mich. Assn. Clks. Office: Office of City Clk City-County Bldg 2 Woodward Ave Detroit MI 48226-3437*

CURRIE, JOHN THORNTON (JACK CURRIE), retired investment banker; b. Houston, Aug. 4, 1928; s. John Felix and Irma Lillian (Haxthausen) C.; m. Dorothy Lee Peek, May 30, 1959; children: Harriss Thornton, Laura Tucker. BA, U. Tex., 1949, BBA, 1950. Salesman Harris, Upham & Co., N.Y.C. and Houston, 1950-52; ptnr. Moreland, Brandenberger & Currie, Galveston, Tex., 1955-60; pres., bd. dirs. Moroney, Beissner & Co., Inc., Houston, 1960-74; sr. v.p., bd. dirs. Rotan Mosle Inc., Houston, 1974-81, chmn., 1981-83; vice chmn. Rotan Mosle Fin. Corp., Houston, 1984; mng. dir. Mason Best Co., Houston, 1984-86; bd. dirs. Stewart & Stevenson Svcs., Inc., Houston, Am. Nat. Growth Fund, Am. Nat. Income Fund, Triflex Fund, Galveston, Am. Indemnity Fin. Corp., Galveston; Internat. Exec. Svc. Corps rep. Muslim Comml. Bank, Karachi, Pakistan, 1992, Govt. of Lithuania, Vilnius, 1993, Capital Ptnrs., Bratislava, Slovakia, 1997. Trustee Holly Hall, Hosuton, 1968-73, Harris and Eliza Kempner Fund, Galveston, Tex., 1975—; mem. devel. bd. U. Tex. Health Sci. Ctr., Houston, 1978-89, U. Tex. Med. Br., Galveston, 1992—; mem. Chancellor's Coun. U. Tex. System; established Mary Tucker Currie Professorship, Tex. A&M u. 1st lt. U.S. Army, 1952-54. Mem. Houston Country Club, Galveston Artillery Club, Krewe of Momus Galveston (pres. 1990-91), The Yacht Club (Galveston). Republican. Episcopalian. Avocations: sailing, hunting, history. Home: 323 Longwoods Ln Houston TX 77024-5615 Office: 515 Post Oak Blvd Ste 750 Houston TX 77027-9495 *The acquisition of material goods makes life comfortable. Love received and given is the only real hallmark of a successful life.*

CURRIE, LARRY LAMAR, insurance company executive; b. Rome, Ga., Dec. 30, 1946; s. Kaylor and Mary R. (Lee) C.; m. Linda Marie Warner, Nov. 9, 1968; children: Kristin Denise, Jeremy Scott, Matthew Lamar. Student, U. N.D., 1968-69, Gadsden State Coll., 1972-73; MS in Mgmt., Am. Coll., 1997. CLU, 1987; cert. facilitator Covey Leadership. Agt. State Farm Ins., Millbrook, Ala., 1974-81; agy. mgr. State Farm Ins., Alexandria City, Ala., 1981-88; agy. dir. State Farm Ins., Birmingham, Ala., 1988-96, agy. field exec., 1996—; mem. adv. bd. East Tallapuosa County Med. Ctr., Dadeville, Ala., 1987-88. Editor: Multiline Family Practice, 1995-98. Adv. bd. U. Ala.-Birmingham, Golden 100 Club, 1993-94; high sch. econs. cons. Jr. Achievement, 1996-98; mem. adv. bd. Project Kids in Distress, 1997-98; bd. dirs. Kid One Transport, 1998—; exec. com. mem. Shelby County Rep. Party, 1998—. Mem. Nat. Assn. Life Underwriters, Autauga-Elmore County Life Underwriters (pres. 1978-79), Birmingham Assn. Life Underwriters (bd. dirs. 1996-97), Internat. Assn. for Fin. Planning, Soc. Fin. Svc. Profls. (chair leadership and mgmt. sect.), Pres.'s Cir. Am. Coll., Porsche Club Am. Republican. Roman Catholic. Avocations: jogging, sailing. Home: 5513 Afton Dr Birmingham AL 35242-4202 Office: State Farm Ins 100 Concourse Pkwy Ste 165 Birmingham AL 35244

CURRIE, LEAH RAE, special education educator; b. Chgo., Feb. 14, 1942; d. Raymond Carl and Esther Dorthea (Hansen) Strahl; m. William W. Currie, June 15, 1963; children: Raymond, Robert (dec.), Christopher. BS, Nat. Coll. Edn., 1979, MEd, 1989. Cert. elem., spl. edn. tchr., Ill. Learning disabilities tchr. Sch. Dist. 81, Schiller Park, Ill., 1979-80; resource tchr. Sch. Dist. 5, Fox River Grove, Ill., 1980-85; learning disabilities, behavior disorders tchr. Sch. Dist. 84, Franklin Park, Ill., 1985—; cons., interdistrict learning disabilities guide Leyden Area Spl. Edn. Coop., 1987. Mem. ASCD, Coun. for Exceptional Children, Ill. Divsn. for Learning Disabilities, Ill. Reading Coun., Barrington Assn. for Citizens with Learning Disabilities, Learning Disabilities Assn. Ill. Avocation: fashion design. Home: 275 Surrey Ln Barrington IL 60010-3400 Office: Hester Jr High Sch 2836 Gustav St Franklin Park IL 60131-2987

CURRIE, MALCOLM RODERICK, aerospace and automotive executive, scientist; b. Spokane, Wash., Mar. 13, 1927; s. Erwin Casper and Genevieve (Hauenstein) C.; m. Sunya Lofsky, June 24, 1951; children: Deborah, David, Diana; m. Barbara L. Dyer, Mar. 5, 1977. AB, U. Calif., Berkeley, 1949, MS, 1951, PhD, 1954. Research engr. Microwave Lab., U. Calif. at Berkeley, 1949-52; elec. engring. faculty microwave lab. U. Calif., Berkeley, 1953-54; lectr. UCLA, 1955-57; rsch. engr. Hughes Aircraft Co., 1954-57, v.p., 1965-66; head electron dynamics dept. Hughes Rsch. Labs., Culver City, Calif., 1957-60; dir. physics lab. Hughes Rsch. Labs., Malibu, Calif., 1960-61, asso. dir., 1961-63, v.p., dir. rsch. labs., 1963-65, v.p., mgr. R & D divsn., 1965-69; v.p. R & D Beckman Instruments, Inc., 1969-73; undersec. rsch. and engring. dept. Office Sec. Def., Washington, 1973-77; pres. missile sys. group Hughes Aircraft Co., Canoga Park, Calif., 1977-83, exec. v.p., 1983-88, CEO, chmn. bd. dirs., 1988—, also bd. dirs.; pres., CEO Delco Electronics Corp., 1986-88; chmn., CEO Hughes Aircraft Co., 1988-92, chmn. emeritus, 1992—; CEO Currie Technologies Inc., 1997—; bd. dirs. Unocal Corp., Investment Co. Am., LSI Logic Corp., SM & A Corp., Moltech Corp., Inamed Corp.; mem. Def. Sci. Bd. Contbr. articles to profl. jours.; patentee in field. Mem. adv. bd. U. Calif., Berkeley, UCLA, Galaxy Edn. Inst., Calif. Coun. Sci. and Tech.; chmn. bd. trustees U. So. Calif., 1989; trustee Howard U., 1989-92, UCLA Found.; bd. dirs. western region United Way, 1987; coord., head U.S. Savs. Bond Dr., So. Calif., 1991. With USNR, 1944-47. Decorated comdr. Legion of Honor France; named Nation's Outstanding Young Elec. Engr. Eta Kappa Nu, 1958, one of 5 Outstanding Young Men of Calif. by Calif. Jr. C. of C., 1960; recipient Nat. Achievement medal Am. Elec. Assn. 1992, Goddard Astronautics award AIAA, Chester Nimitz award U.S. Navy League, 92, Thomas White award USAF, 1992. Fellow IEEE (Founders award 1995), AIAA (pres. 1994, Goddard Astronautics award), AAAS, Royal Aeroantuics Soc., Am. Acad. Arts and Scis.; mem. NAE, Am. Phys. Soc., Berkeley Fellow, Commn. on Competitiveness, Calif. Coun. on Sci. and Tech. (co-chair project Calif.), Cosmos Club, Phi Beta Kappa, Sigma Xi, Lambda Chi Alpha. Home: 28780 Wagon Rd Agoura Hills CA 91301-2732

CURRIE, PHILIP JOHN, research paleontologist, museum curator; b. Toronto, Ont., Can., Mar. 13, 1949; children: Tarl, Devin, Brett. BSc, U. Toronto, 1972; MSc, McGill U., 1975, PhD in Biology, 1981. Curator paleontology Provincial Mus. Alta., Edmonton, 1976-81; mus. curator Paleontology Mus. and Rsch. Inst., Drumheller, Alb., Can., 1981-82; asst. dir. rsch. Tyrrell Mus. Paleontology, Drumheller, Alta., 1982-89, head dinosaur rsch., 1989—; sec. Alta. Paleontology Adv. Com., 1977-89; treas. Palaeont Can., 1981-84. Author: Flying Dinosaurs, 1991, Dinosaur Renaissance, 1994; co-author: The Great Dinosaurs, 1994, 101 Questions About Dinosaurs, 1996, Troodon, 1997, Albertosaurus, 1998, Centrosaurus, 1998; co-editor: Dinosaur Systematics, 1990, Dinosaur Encyclopedia, 1997, Newest and Coolest Dinosaurs, 1998; contbr. articles to profl. pubrs.; featured in numerous articles and programs. Recipient Commendation medal 125th Anniversary of Govt. of Can., 1993, Sir Frederick Haultain award Govt. of Alta., 1988, Michel Halbouty award Am. Assn. Petroleum Geologists, 1999. Mem. Soc. Vertebrate Paleontology (program officer 1985-87, conf. chmn. 1988, conf. chmn. Mesozoic Terrestrial Ecosystems 1987), Paleontol. Soc., Can. Soc. Petroleum Geologists, Am. Soc. Zoologists, Royal Soc. Can., Sigma Xi. Achievements include research in fossil reptiles including Permian Sphenacodonts from Europe and United States; Permian eosuchians from Africa and Madagascar; Jurassic and Cretaceous dinosaurs from Canada and Asia and their footprints. Office: Royal Tyrrell Mus Palaeontology, Box 7500, Drumheller, AB Canada T0J 0Y0

CURRIE, ROBERT EMIL, lawyer; b. Jackson, Tenn., Oct. 10, 1937; s. Forrest Edward Currie and Mary Elizabeth (Nuckolls) Empson; m. Brenda Ray Eddings, July 2, 1960; children: Cheryl Lynn, Forrest Clayton, Kristin Emil. BS with distinction, U.S. Naval Acad., 1959; LLB cum laude, Harvard U., 1967. Bar: Calif. 1967, U.S. Ct. Appeals (9th cir.) 1970, U.S. Supreme Ct. 1979. Assoc. Latham & Watkins, L.A., 1967-75; ptnr. Latham & Watkins, Costa Mesa, Calif., 1975—, mng. ptnr., 1993-97; dir. Constl. Rights Found., Orange County, Calif., 1986-91; lawyer rep. 9th Cir. Jud. Conf., 1991-93. Mem. exec. com. Orange County coun. Boy Scouts Am., Costa Mesa, 1982-95. Capt. USNR, 1955-83. Recipient Silver Beaver award Boy Scouts Am., Orange County coun., 1991. Fellow Am. Coll. Trial Lawyers; mem. Orange County Bar Assn. (dir. 1984-91), U.S. Supreme Ct. Hist. Soc. (so. Calif. chmn. 1992-93). Home: 24 Pinehurst Ln Newport Beach CA 92660-5229 Office: Latham & Watkins 650 Town Center Dr Ste 2000 Costa Mesa CA 92626-7135*

CURRIE, STEPHEN, educator, writer; b. Chgo., Sept. 29, 1960; s. David Park and Barbara (Flynn) C.; m. Amity Elizabeth Smith, July 3, 1983; children: Irene Elizabeth, Nicholas David. BA, Williams Coll., 1982. Primary tchr. Poughkeepsie (N.Y.) Day Sch., 1982—; Saturday enrichment tchr. various schs. and orgns., Poughkeepsie, 1988-92; freelance ednl. writer, 1992—; pvt. tutor, Poughkeepsie, 1982—; workshop leader/presenter, 1986—; materials reviewer Nat. Coun. Tchrs. Math. Author: Music in the Civil War, 1992, Birthday a Day, 1996, We Have Marched Together, 1997, Life in a Wild West Show, 1998, numerous others. Bd. dirs., performer Hudson Valley Gilbert and Sullivan Soc., Poughkeepsie, 1983-92; youth soccer coach Town of Poughkeepsie Soccer Club, 1993-94. Mem. Nat. Assn. for Edn. of Young Children, Nat. Coun. Tchrs. Math. Avocations: singing, swimming, reading. Home: 14 Oakwood Blvd Poughkeepsie NY 12603 Office: Poughkeepsie Day Sch 140 Boardman Rd Poughkeepsie NY 12603

CURRIE, STEVEN RAY, artist; b. Flint, Mich., Sept. 1, 1954; s. Richard Lee and Gwen Laurie (Cummings) C.; m. Annette Marie Davidek, July 27, 1985. BFA, U. Mich., 1977; MFA, Yale U., 1984. One man show includes Borgenicht Gallery, N.Y.C., 1988, 90, 92, 93, Ctr. Contemporary Art, Chgo., 1989, 91, Weatherspoon Art Gallery, Greensboro, N.C., 1995, Revolution Gallery, Detroit, 1995, Littlejohn Contemporary, N.Y.C., 1997; group shows include Boise (Idaho) Art Mus., 1994; represented in various mus. collections including Bklyn. Mus., Modern Art Mus. Ft. Worth, Walker Art Ctr., Mpls., Met. Mus. Art, N.Y.C., Albright-Knox Art Gallery, Buffalo. NEA fellow, 1988, N.Y. Found. Arts fellow, 1990, 97.

CURRIER, DAVID P., retired state legislator; b. Boston, July 26, 1944; m. Teresa Currier. BA, New Eng. Coll., 1972; postgrad., Antioch Coll. Del. Constnl. Conv., 1975—; N.H. state rep., 1977-78; selectman Town of Henniker, N.H., 1976-88; alt. del. Rep. Nat. Conv., 1980, 88, 92; chmn. N.H. Emergency Med. Svc. Coord. Bd., 1986-91; N.H. state senator Dist. 7, 1989-97, asst. majority leader, 1991-92; chmn. Exec. Depts. Coms., Joint Com. Adminstrn. Rules; vice chmn. Econ. Devel. Com., Edn. Com.; former mem. Fiscal Com.; chair Fin. Com.; vice-chair Rules and Enrolled Bills Com.; mem. Fish and Game Transp. and Ways and Means Com.; ret., 1997; pres. Bound Tree Corp., 1982—. Mem. N.H. Mcpl. Assn. (mem. exec. com., past 1st v.p.), N.H. Ski Area Assn. (exec. sec. 1975—), Am. Legion, Vietnam Vets., Gun Owners of N.H., Henniker Lions club (past pres.). Address: PO Box 926 Henniker NH 03242-0926

CURRIER, DOUGLAS GILFILLAN, II, urban planner; b. Chelsea, Mass., Jan. 11, 1960; s. Douglas G. and Anita Louise Currier. BA, U. South Fla., 1987. Assoc. planner Tampa Bay Regional Planning Coun., St. Petersburg, Fla., 1985-90; resource planner West Coast Regional Water Supply Authority, Clearwater, Fla., 1990-96; city planner City of Dade City, Fla., 1996—. Mem. Am. Planning Assn., Hillsborough Literacy Coun. (sec. 1994—), 1000 Friends of Fla., U. South Fla. Alumni Assn., Phi Kappa Phi (hon.). Avocations: adult literacy, environment causes, traveling, reading. Office: City of Dade City 38020 Meridian Ave Dade City FL 33525-3836

CURRIER, ROBERT DAVID, neurologist; b. Grand Rapids, Mich., Feb. 19, 1925; s. Frederick Plummer and Margaret (Hoedemaker) C.; m. Marilyn Jane Johnson, Sept. 1, 1951; children: Mary Margaret, Angela Maria. AB, U. Mich., 1948, MD, 1952, MS in Neurology, 1956; postgrad., Nat. Hosp., U. London, 1955; postgrad. Medico-Social Research Bd, Dublin, Ireland, 1972. Intern, then resident in neurology Univ. Hosp., Ann Arbor, 1952-56; from instr. to asso. prof. U. Mich. Med. Sch., 1956-61; mem. faculty U. Miss. Med. Ctr., Jackson, 1961—, prof. neurology, 1971—, chief div., 1961-77, chmn. dept., 1977-90, H.F. McCarty prof., 1987-94, prof. emeritus, 1994—; mem. adv. bd. Nat. Ataxia Found., rsch. dir., 1985-93; mem. clin. adv. coun. Amyotrophic Lateral Sclerosis Soc. Am., 1979-85; mem. Ataxia com. World Fedn. Neurology, 1981-95, sec., 1985-93. Co-editor; Yearbook of Neurology and Neurosurgery, 1981-88, editor, 1989-92; co-editor (jour.) Key Quar. Neurology and Neurosurgery, 1986-92; asst. editor for history Archives of Neurology, 1983-97; assoc. editor Jour. Neuroscis., 1990-95; contbr. articles to med. jours. Served with USAAF, 1943-45, ETO. Decorated Air medal with 2 oak leaf clusters; NIH grantee, 1961-74. Fellow Am. Acad. Neurology (chmn. history com. 1980-82, treas. 1991-95); mem. Am. Neurol. Assn., Ctrl. Soc. Neurol. Rsch. (pres. 1971), Sigma Xi, Alpha Omega Alpha. Home: 5529 Marblehead Dr Jackson MS 39211-4249 *It has been interesting.*

CURRIER, RUTH, dancer, choreographer and educator; b. Ashland, Ohio, Jan. 4, 1926; d. Elmer MacDonald and Zada (Holliman) Miller. Student, Black Mountain Coll., 1942-44, NYU, 1944-45. Soloist José Limón Dance Co., N.Y.C., 1949-63, artistic dir., 1973-77; asst. to Doris Humphrey, 1950-58; prin. Ruth Currier and Dance Co., N.Y.C., 1957-68; asso. prof. dance, dir. Am. Dance in Repertory, Ohio State U., Columbus, 1968-73; freelance choreographer N.Y.C., 1978-81; dir. Ruth Currier Dance Studio, N.Y.C., 1981-90; adj. mem. faculty Bennington Coll., 1958-63; guest tchr., choreographer numerous colls., dance cos. Choreographer over 50 mus. prodns.

CURRIER, SUSAN ANNE, computer software company executive; b. Melbourne, Victoria, Australia, Nov. 20, 1949; d. David Eric and Irene Bruce-Smith; m. Kenneth Palmer Currier, Feb. 16, 1974. Student, Melbourne U., 1967-70. Fashion model Eileen Ford Model Agy., N.Y.C., 1971-74, Wilhelmina Models, N.Y.C., 1974-82; owner Softsync Inc., N.Y.C., 1981-91; pres. Expert Software, Coral Gables, Fla., 1989—. Home: 201 Crandon Blvd Apt 1141 Key Biscayne FL 33149-1525 Office: Expert Software North Tower 800 S Douglas Rd Ste 600 Coral Gables FL 33134-3125*

CURRIS, CONSTANTINE WILLIAM, university president; b. Lexington, Ky., Nov. 13, 1940; s. William C. and Mary (Kalpakis) C.; m. Roberta Jo Hern, Aug. 9, 1974. BA, U. Ky., 1962, EdD, 1967; MA, U. Ill., 1965. Vice pres., dean of faculty Midway (Ky.) Coll., 1965-68; dir. ednl. programs W.Va. Bd. Edn., Charleston, 1968-69; dean student personnel programs Marshall U., Huntington, W.Va., 1969-71; v.p., dean of faculty W.Va. Inst. Tech., Montgomery, 1971-73; pres. Murray (Ky.) State U., 1973-83, U. No. Iowa, 1983-95, Clemson U., 1995—; exec. com. Am. Humanics, Inc., 1995; chmn. Am. Assn. State Colls. and Univs., 1995. Trustee Midway Coll., Allen Coll. Nursing; charter mem. adv. coun. Nat. Small Bus. Devel. Ctr. Recipient Algernon S. Sullivan medallion U. Ky., 1962; named outstanding young man in Ky., Jaycees, 1974. Mem. Phi Beta Kappa, Omicron Delta Kappa, Sigma Chi. Greek Orthodox. Club: Rotary. Office: Clemson University 201 Sikes Hall Clemson SC 29634 *I am very grateful for what America has given me. As the son of a Greek immigrant who possessed neither education nor a command of the English language, I am keenly aware of the opportunities a government of and for the people affords its citizens. If there is any quality to which I attribute what success I have achieved it would be that of an abiding devotion to the "public interest" rather than allowing my decisions to be determined by vested or parochial interests.**

CURRIVAN, BRUCE JOSEPH, electronics engineer; b. Nicosia, Cyprus, Nov. 14, 1950; father Am. citizen; s. Eugene Ambrose and Rachel (Marash) C.; m. Annamaria Panunzio, Nov. 12, 1978; children: Joseph, Jean Anne, Peter. BS in Elec. Engring., Cornell U., 1972; MS in Engring., Princeton U., 1976. Assoc. engr., Astro-Electronics Div. RCA, Princeton, NJ, 1972-76; comms. sys. design engr. Stanford Telecom., Sunnyvale, Calif., 1977-81, 84-94, tech. dir., 1995-97; ingénieur d'études Thomson-CSF, Gennevilliers, France, 1982-83; tech. dir. modern devel. WaveSpan Corp., Mountain View, Calif., 1997-98; dir. cable and satellite sys. engring. Broadcom Corp., Irvine, Calif., 1998—. Presenter in field; contbr. articles to profl. jours; patentee in field. Natural Law candidate for U.S. Ho. of Reps., 1996; chmn. Natural Law Party Central Com., Santa Clara County, Calif., 1996-98. Mem. IEEE (sr., chmn. 802.14 cable modem phys. layer subcom. 1995-97). Office: Broadcom Corp 16205 Alton Pkwy Irvine CA 92618-3616

CURRIVAN, JOHN DANIEL, lawyer; b. Paris, Jan. 15, 1947. s. Gene and Rachel (Marash) C.; m. Patrice Salley; children: Christopher, Melissa. BS with distinction, Cornell U., 1968; MS, U. Calif.-Berkeley, 1969, U. West Fla., 1971; JD summa cum laude, Cornell Law Sch., 1978. Bar: Ohio 1978. Mng. ptnr. Southwest Devel. Co., Kingsville, Tex., 1971-76; note editor Cornell Law Review, Ithaca, N.Y., 1977-78; prosecutor, Naval Legal Office, Norfolk, Va., 1978-79, chief prosecutor, 1979-81; sr. atty. USS Nimitz, 1981-83; trial judge Naval Base, Norfolk, 1983-84; tax atty. Jones, Day, Reavis & Pogue, Cleve., 1984-88, ptnr., 1989—; adj. prof. law Case Western Res. U. Sch. Law, 1997—. Comdr. USN, 1969-84. Author: (with Rickert) Ohio Limited Liability Companies, 1999. Recipient Younger Fed. Lawyer award FBA, 1981. Mem. ABA, Nat. Assn. Bond Lawyers, Order of Coif, Tau Beta

Pi, Eta Kappa Nu, Phi Kappa Phi. Home: 12700 Lake Ave Ste 2105 Lakewood OH 44107-1506 Office: Jones Day Reavis & Pogue 901 Lakeside Ave E Cleveland OH 44114-1116

CURRY, ALAN CHESTER, insurance company executive; b. Columbus, Ohio, Oct. 15, 1933; s. Harold E. and Martha (Dew) C.; children: Diane, Thomas, Timothy, Jeffrey. Student, U. Ill., 1951-52; EdB, Ill. State U., 1957. Various actuarial positions State Farm Mut. Automobile Ins. Co., Bloomington, Ill., 1952-70, v.p., actuary, 1970-97; bd. dirs. State Farm Gen. Ins. Co. Mem. bd. indsl. advisors Rose-Hullman Inst. Tech. Fellow Casualty Actuarial Soc. (dir. 1970-73, 87-90); mem. Am. Acad. Actuaries (dir. 1977-80), Midwestern Actuarial Forum (pres. 1972-73), Shriners, Pi Gamma Mu, Pi Omega Pi, Kappa Delta Pi. Home: 7 Canterbury Ct Bloomington IL 61701-3401

CURRY, ALTON FRANK, lawyer; b. Dallas, Aug. 21, 1933; s. William Hadley and Myrtle Estelle (Posey) McKinney; m. Carole B. Piepgrass, Feb. 14, 1960 (div. Nov. 1979); children: Robyn, Mark, John; m. Ann O. Williams, Apr. 12, 1980. BA, Baylor U., 1958, LLB, 1960. Bar: Tex. 1960. Assoc. Fulbright & Jaworski, Houston, 1960-70, ptnr., 1970-78; spl. asst. to Atty. Gen. of Tex., 1964-65, 71-72. Trustee Found. for Bus., Politics and Econs., 1979-92, A.A. White Inst.; chmn. adminstrv. bd. Methodist Ch. Cpl. U.S. Army, 1953-55. Mem. ABA, Tex. Bar Assn., Houston Bar Assn., Baylor Law Alumni Assn. (dir. 1977-79, pres. 1979-80), Phi Alpha Delta, Houstonian Club (trustee 1980-83), Coronado Club, Masons. Home: 2707 Weslayan St Houston TX 77027-5123 Office: Fulbright & Jaworski 1301 Mckinney St Houston TX 77010-3031

CURRY, ANN, correspondent, anchor; b. Agana, Guam, Nov. 19, 1956; d. Robert Paul Hiroe (Nagase) C.; m. Brian Wilson Ross, Oct. 21, 1987; children: Anna McKenzie, William Walker. Student, U. Oreg. Journalism Sch., 1974-78. Reporter Sta. KTVL-TV, Medford, Oreg., 1978-81; reporter, weekend anchor Sta. KGW-TV, Portland, Oreg., 1981-84; reporter Sta. KCBS-TV, L.A., 1984-90; corr., anchor NBC News at Sunrise NBC News, N.Y.C., 1990-97; news anchor Today Show, 1997—. Recipient Golden Mike award RTNA, 1986, 87, 89, Cert. Excellence award AP, 1987, 88, Cert. Excellence award Greater L.A. Press Club, 1987, Superior Reporting award NAACP, 1989, Emmy award Acad. TV Arts and Scis., 1987, 89, Emmy nominations, 1985, 86, 87, 88. Avocation: art history. Office: NBC News 30 Rockefeller Plz # 374E New York NY 10112-0002

CURRY, BEATRICE CHESROWN, retired English educator; b. Lakefork, Ohio, Jan. 14, 1932; d. Tod Shields and Sadie Irene (Springer) C.; m. Elton Wheeler Curry, Sept. 9, 1967 (div. 1988); 1 child, James Christopher. BA, Ashland (Ohio) Coll., 1954; MA, Western Res. U., 1965. English tchr. Hamilton Jr. High Sch., Houston, 1954-58, Oliver Hazard Perry Jr. High Sch., Cleve., 1958-59, Glenville High Sch., Cleve., 1959-60; tchr. English, head dept. Fonville Jr. High Sch., Houston, 1960-66; prof. English, Columbia (Tenn.) State Community Coll., 1967-98; ret. Bd. dirs. Child Care Svc., Columbia, 1973-76; panel moderator So. Festival of Books and Authors, 1991. NEA grantee, 1979, Mellon grantee, 1981, 82; co-recipient Paragon award for Best Coll. Promotional Video, Nat. Coll. Coun. Mktg. and Advt., 1993. Mem. Maury County Creative Arts Guild (literary chmn. 1984-86), Alpha Delta Kappa (Beta Alpha chpt. pres. 1990-92). Home: 810 Barrow Ct Columbia TN 38401-3115

CURRY, BERNARD FRANCIS, former banker, consultant; b. N.Y.C., Aug. 8, 1918; s. John F. and Mary F. (McKiernan) C.; m. Lorraine Vocco Kelly, Sept. 10, 1947; 1 dau., Catherine V. AB, Coll. Holy Cross, 1939; JD, Columbia U., 1942. Bar: N.Y. 1946. Sec. to Surrogate Delehanty, New York County, 1946-47; assoc. Davis Polk Wardwell, Sunderl & Kendl, N.Y.C., 1947-55; with Morgan Guaranty Trust Co. N.Y., N.Y.C., 1955-84; sr. v.p. Morgan Guaranty Trust Co. N.Y., 1970-82; pres. Morgan Trust Co., Fla., 1982-84, dir., 1984-91; dir. J.P. Morgan, Fla., 1994—; adv. council Labor Dept., 1976-79. V.p., bd. dirs. Dom Mocquereau Found., N.Y.C., 1967-96; trustee W. Alton Jones Found., Flower Hosp., 1979-82, W. Alton Jones Cell Soc. Ctr., 1980-97, Harry I. Etelman Found., 1985—, Mary Alice Fortin Child Care Found.; bd. dirs. Ireland Am. Arts Exch., 1984-95, Young Broadcasting Inc., 1994—. With AUS, 1942-46. Mem. Assn. Bar City N.Y., N.Y. State Bar Assn., Am. Bankers Assn. (pres. trust div. 1979-80). Club: Knight of Malta. Home: 350 S Ocean Blvd Palm Beach FL 33480-4408 Office: 109 Royal Palm Way Palm Beach FL 33480-4249

CURRY, CARLTON E., corporate executive, city councilman; b. Lizton, Ind., Mar. 4, 1935; m. Ann Merritt, 1957. BS, Purdue U., 1958. Program adminstr. Allison Gas Turbine divsn. GM, 1966-79, staff systems analyst, 1979-83, mgr. mktg. program, 1983-85, dir. logistics support, 1985-90; cons., 1990-93; pres. SaniServ, Inc., 1990-96, Curry Inc., 1997—; chmn. Cable Franchise Bd., 1996—. City councilman, Indpls., 1983—. With USN, 1958-66, USAR, 1956-63. Mem. AIAA, Soc. Logistics Engrs., Lions. Republican. Baptist.

CURRY, CLIFTON CONRAD, JR., lawyer; b. Tampa, Fla., July 8, 1957; s. Clifton C. and Louise (Owens) C.; m. Teresa D. Cox, Dec. 22, 1979; children: Mary Beth, Clifton C. III, Colton Cox. BS, Fla. State U., 1979; JD, Stetson U., 1981. Bar: Fla. 1982, U.S. Dist. Ct. (mid. dist.) Fla. 1982. Assoc. Mark R. Horwitz, P.A., Orlando, Fla., 1981-83; pres. Tittsworth and Curry, P.A., Brandon, Fla., 1984—, Curry and Assocs., P.A., Brandon, 1991—. Bd. dirs. Kiwanis Children's Clinic, 1988-90; vol. Missing Children's Help Ctr.; bd. dirs. Big Bros./Big Sisters, 1985-88, Rough Riders, 1987—, Brandon Outreach Clinic; chmn. Brandon Walk, March of Dimes Birth Defects Found., 1989; gen. coun. Grand Lodge of Fla. Masons, Egypt Temple Shrine, Tampa, Fla., 1996-97; active various polit. campaign coms. Recipient Alice Be. Thompkins Community Svc. award, 1991; named hon. mayor City of Brandon, 1985-86; recipient svc. award Brandon Lions Club, 1985. Mem. ABA, Assn. Trial Lawyers Am., Fla. Bar Assn., Hillsborough County Bar Assn., Brandon Bar Assn., Acad. Fla. Trial Lawyers, Brandon C. of C. (pres. 1989, bd. dirs. 1987-91, chmn. exec. bd. 1990-91, Small Bus. Leader of Yr. 1990), Kiwanis Club Brandon (past bd. dirs., pres. 1988-89), Krewe of Venus King's Guard (bd. dirs.), Fla. State Alumni Assn., Brandon Yacht Club, Ducks Unlimited, YMCA Century Club, Masons, Shriners, Scottish Rite, York Rite. Office: Curry and Assocs PA 750 W Lumsden Rd Brandon FL 33511-6217

CURRY, DALE BLAIR, journalist; b. Memphis, May 30, 1941; d. Hamilton Minter and Doris (Terry) Blair; m. Douglas Hester Curry, Dec. 21, 1963; children: Jennifer, Elizabeth. BA, U. Miss., 1963. Reporter The Commercial-Appeal, Memphis, 1962-63, Atlanta Constn., 1963-65, The States-Item, New Orleans, 1969-72, The Morning Advocate, Baton Rouge, 1974-76, 82-84; food editor The Times-Picayune, New Orleans, 1984—. Elder St. Charles Avenue Presbyn. Ch., New Orleans, 1984-87, 91-94. Recipient award AP, UPI, New Orleans Press Club; named among Top 50 alumni 50th Anniversary U. Miss. Sch. Journalism, 1998. Mem. Assn. Food Journalists (pres. 1994-96), Theta Sigma Phi (Alumni of Yr. U. Miss. chpt.). Office: The Times-Picayune 3800 Howard Ave New Orleans LA 70125-1429

CURRY, DANIEL ARTHUR, judge; b. Phoenix, Mar. 28, 1937; s. John Joseph and Eva May (Wills) C.; m. Joy M. Shallenberger, Sept. 5, 1959; children: Elizabeth, Catherine, Peter, Jennifer, Julia , David. B.S., Loyola U., Los Angeles, 1957, LL.B., 1960; postgrad., U. So. Calif. Law Center, 1964-65; postgrad. exec. program, Grad. Sch. Bus., Stanford U., 1980. Bar: Calif. 1961, Hawaii 1972, N.Y. 1988, U.S. Dist. Ct. (cen. dist.) Calif. 1961, U.S. Ct. Appeals (9th cir.) 1961, U.S. Ct. Mil. Appeals 1963, U.S. Customs Ct. 1968, U.S. Dist. Ct. Hawaii 1972, U.S. Dist. Ct. (no. dist.) Calif. 1983 . Assoc. Wolford, Johnson, Pike & Covell, El Monte, Calif., 1964-65, Demetriou & Del Guercio, Los Angeles, 1965-67; counsel, corporate staff divisional asst. Technicolor, Inc., Hollywood, Calif., 1967-70; v.p., sec., gen. counsel Amfac, Inc., Honolulu, 1970-78; sr. v.p., gen. counsel Amfac, Inc., Honolulu and San Francisco, 1978-87; v.p., gen. counsel Times Mirror, L.A., 1987-92; judge Superior Ct. of State of Calif., 1992-98; assoc. justice Calif. Ct. Appeal 2d dist., L.A., 1998—; bd. regents Loyola Marymount U., Chaminade U. (hon.). Served to capt. USAF, 1961-64. Mem. ABA (hon., com. corp. law depts.), L.A. County Club, Sigma Rho, Phi Delta Phi. Office: Calif Ct of Appeal 2d Dist 4th Fl North Tower 300 S Spring St Los Angeles CA 90013

CURRY, DANIEL FRANCIS MYLES, filmmaker; b. N.Y.C., Sept. 22, 1946; s. John Joseph Jr. and Florence Cecelia (Rattler) C.; m. Ubolvan Chaiwatana, July 27, 1972; children: Devin, Daniel. BA, Middlebury Coll., 1968; MFA, Humboldt State U., 1979. Vol. community devel. U.S. Peace Corps, Khon Kaen, Thailand, 1969-71; writer-dir. ednl. TV Ministry of Edn., Govt. of Thailand, Bangkok, 1971-72; freelance filmmaker/artist/designer various clients Bangkok, 1972-74; instr. fine arts Cape Cod Community Coll., West Barnstable, Mass., 1974-77; instr. film and theatre Humboldt State U., Arcata, Calif., 1977-79; visual effects artist Universal Studios Hartland Facility, North Hollywood, Calif., 1979-80; art dir. Modern Film Effects, Hollywood, Calif., 1980-85; v.p., dir. creative svcs. Cinema Rsch. Corp., Hollywood, 1985-88; visual effects producer-dir. Star Trek, the Next Generation, Paramount Pictures, Hollywood, 1987—; pres. O.M.R. Prodns., Manhattan Beach, Calif., 1989—. Supr., title designer Star Trek IV, Top Gun, Flash Dance, Fatal Attraction, Cujo, The Blob, Rocky IV, Cobra, Staying Alive, Tootsie, Risky Business, Amadeus, The Right Stuff, Mommie Dearest, Uncommon Valor, Pure Luck, Back to School, Raging Bull, Class, Cool World, Captured, Christine, Body Double, Flashpoint, Tiger Town, Invasion U.S.A., Fast Forward, Bolero, Wild Thing, Pray for Death, Days of Thunder, Indiana Jones & The Temple of Doom, Star Trek, Generations; visual effects prodr. 6th season Star Trek, The Next Generation (best spl. visual effects Emmy award 1992), Star Trek Deep Space Nine, 1993—, Star Trek Voyager, 1995— (Emmy award). Recipient Emmy award for spl. visual effects Acad. TV Arts and Scis., 1992, 94, nominations, 1989, 90, Internat. Monitor award, 1996. Mem. Acad. TV Arts and Scis., Soc. Motion Picture and TV Engrs., Am. Film Inst., Am. Soc. Cinematrographers. Avocations: painting, sculpture, world travel. Office: Paramount TV Group 5555 Melrose Ave Hollywood CA 90038-3197*

CURRY, DAVID, guidance staff developer; b. Bklyn., Feb. 12, 1940; s. David and Ella (Washington) C.; m. Mary Elaine Cuthrell, Nov. 17, 1962; 1 child, Anjorin Sebastian. *Spouse, Mary Cuthrell Curry, BS 1967 from Virginia University, MS 1970 from The New School for Social Research, PhD 1991 from the Graduate Center at CUNY. She is presently an Assistant Professor of Sociology at the University of Houston, Sociology Department. Her publications include: Making the Gods in New York: The Yoruba Religion in the African American Community, New York and London, Garland 1997; "From West Africa to Brooklyn: Yoruba Religion Among African Americans" in Religion in a Changing World, edited by Madeline Cousineau, Praeger, Connecticutand London, 1998.* BA in Polit. Sci./Econs., CCNY, 1972; MS in Edn., Bklyn. Coll., 1990, adv. cert. in guidance and counseling, 1990. Cert. elem. tchr., N.Y. Asst. offic mgr. Elmo Roper & Assocs., N.Y.C., 1964-70; accounts investigator Citibank, N.Y.C., 1970-72; rsch. assoc. Nat. Urban League, N.Y.C., 1972-76; adminstrv. dir. Edn. Unltd., Bklyn., 1978-82; guidance counselor N.Y.C. Bd. of Edn., Bklyn., 1982—. County com. Polit. Club; area policy bd. #3 Community Devel. Agy. City of N.Y.; mem. Unity Dem. Club; mem. block assn. With USAF, 1963. Impact II grantee N.Y.C. Bd. Edn., 1984, 86; N.Y. State Dept. Labor fellow, 1995; recipient Cmty. Svc. award HPD of N.Y.C., 1992, William F. Boyland Edn. award, 1996; named Father of Yr. Sisterhood of Single Black Mothers, 1984. Mem. ASCD, ACA, ASCA, Alpha Phi Alpha. Yoruba. Avocations: trombone, barritone horn, camping, writing. Home: 519 Macdonough St Brooklyn NY 11233-1511 Office: Cmty Sch Dist # 16 1010 Lafayette Ave Brooklyn NY 11221-2303

CURRY, DEBBIE HARTLEY, secondary education educator; b. Mobile, Ala., June 7, 1954; d. Dewey Louis and Lou Jean (Killcrease) H.; m. Donald Stanley Peterson, Nov. 22, 1977 (div. Feb. 1986); m. Alexander Edward Curry, III, July 22, 1989. AA, Faulkner State Jr. Coll., 1974; BS, Troy State U., 1977. Cert. tchr., Ala. Tchrs. aide Baldwin County Bd. Edn., Bay Minette, Ala., 1977-79; tchr. Baldwin County Bd. Edn., Bay Minette, 1979—. Mem. NEA, Ala. Edn. Assn., Baldwin County Edn. Assn. (Coach of Yr. 1982). Democrat. Avocations: walking, dogs, fishing, reading. Home: 2701 Scarlet Dr Bay Minette AL 36507-6204 Office: Perdido Elem Sch 23589 County Rd 47 Perdido AL 36562

CURRY, DENISE, university women's basketball coach. BS, UCLA, 1982, MA in Humanities, 1985. Asst. coach Calif., San Jose Lasers, 1996; head coach Calif. State Fullerton, 1997—. Named to Naismith Meml. Basketball Hall of Fame, French Profl. Player of the Decade 1980's, Three-time Kodak All-Am.; recipient Olympic gold medal. Office: Women's Athletic Dept Calif State Fullerton PO Box 6810 Fullerton CA 92834-6810*

CURRY, DIANNE SWETZ, school nurse; b. Hazleton, Pa., Mar. 12, 1946; d. Anthony Lawrence and Mary Ellen (Kakalecik) Swetz; m. Richard Paul Curry, Feb. 12, 1970; children: Christopher, Elizabeth. Diploma, Wilkes Barre Gen. Hosp., 1966; BSN, Coll. Misericordia, 1987, MSN, 1992. Rn, Pa.; cert. sch. nurse. Staff nurse med.-surg. VA, West L.A., 1970-71, Corona (Calif.) Community Hosp., 1973-74; supr., asst. DON Little Flower Manor, Wilkes Barre, Pa., 1985-87; sch. nurse Wilkes-Barre Area Sch. Dist., 1987—; mem. test devel. com. for sch. nurses ANCC, 1995—, mem. bd. cert. cmty. health, 1997—; chairperson Sch. Nurse Test Devel. Com., 1999—. Com. mem. Wilkes-Barre Dem., 1985-88. Mem. Luzerne County Nurses Assn. (sec. 1987-94, legis. chmn. 1988—), Pa. Nurses Assn. (vice treas. 1991-92, chmn. govt. rels. com. 1992-93), Pa. State Edn. Assn. (pres. dept. pupil svcs. sch. nurse sect. northeastern region 1994—, state v.p., chair profl. devel. 1996-98), Luzerne County Safe Kids, Pa. Sch. Nurses and Practitioners, Sigma Theta Tau. Roman Catholic. Avocations: reading, gardening, cooking. Home: 148 S Meade St Wilkes Barre PA 18702-6332 Office: Dr David Kistler Elem 301 Old River Rd Wilkes Barre PA 18702-1507

CURRY, DONALD ROBERT, lawyer, oil company executive; b. Pampa, Tex., Aug. 7, 1943; s. Robert Ward and Alleith Elizabeth (Elliston) C.; m. Carolyn Sue Boland, Apr. 17, 1965; 1 son, James Ward. BS, West Tex. State U., 1965; JD, U. Tex., 1968. Bar: Tex. 1968, U.S. Dist. Ct. (no. dist.) Tex. 1970, U.S. Tax Ct. 1973. Assoc., Day & Gandy, Ft. Worth, 1968-69, ptnr., 1970-72; pvt. practice, Ft. Worth, 1972—; mng. ptnr. Curry & Thornton Oil, 1981—; lectr. in field. Bd. regents West Tex. State U., Canyon, 1969-77, sec., mem. exec. com., 1972-75; mem. exec. bd. Longhorn council Boy Scouts Am., 1970—, dist. chmn., 1970-75 (recipient Silver Beaver award 1994); precinct chmn. Tarrant County (Tex.) Democratic Party, 1982-98, election judge, 1982-94; aviation adv. bd. City of Ft. Worth, 1990-95, vice chmn. bd., chmn. bd. dirs., 1994-95. Jamed E. West fellow, 1997. Fellow Tex. Bar Found.; Mem. ABA, State Bar Tex., Ft. Worth-Tarrant County Bar Assn., Ft. Worth Bus. and Estate Council, Tex. Ind. Producers and Royalty Owners Assn., Phi Alpha Delta, Phi Delta Theta. Methodist. Clubs: YMCA Century, Ft. Worth, Petroleum of Ft. Worth. Home: 3800 Tulsa Way Fort Worth TX 76107-3346 Office: 905 Ft Worth Club Bldg Fort Worth TX 76102-4911

CURRY, EVERETT WILLIAM, JR., minister; b. Glendale, Calif., Mar. 7, 1942; s. Everett William and Sylvia Pauline (Burkholder) C.; m. Barbara Kay Orman, June 13, 1964; children: Kimberly Suzanne Curry McSwain, Kevin Everett. BA, Calif. State U., Northridge, 1964; MDiv, Am. Bapt. Sem., Berkeley, Calif., 1967; cert. pub. rels., UCLA, 1971; Doctor of Ministry, San Francisco Theol. Sem., San Anselmo, Calif., 1977. CFP; chartered mutual fund counselor. Minister to youth First Bapt. Ch., San Fernando, Calif., 1960-62; assoc. pastor Valley Park Bapt. Ch., Sepulveda, Calif., 1962-66; dir., media ministries Coachella Valley Bapt. Found., Thermal, Calif., 1966-68; pastor Lakeview Terrace Bapt. Ch., Lakeview Terrace, Calif., 1968-71; dir., media ministries L.A. Bapt. City Mission Soc., 1971-74; pastor Community Bapt. Ch., Pearl Harbor, Hawaii, 1974-78, First Bapt. Ch., Coos Bay, Oreg., 1978-86; planned giving counselor Am. Bapt. Found., Valley Forge, Pa., 1986-98; assoc. exec. min. Am. Bapt. Chs. Oreg., Portland, 1998—. Chmn., bd. dirs. Coos Bay Sch. Dist., Coos Bay, 1988-89; chief, chaplain corps, Coos Bay Police Dept., 1979-85; pres. Hawaiian Islands Pub. Radio, Honolulu, 1977-78; bd. dirs. Rosevilla Found., 1998—. Named Alumnus of Yr., Am. Bapt. Sem. of the West, 1995. Mem. Am. Bapt. Ministers Coun. (sen. 1983-87, 92, 94-95), Western Commn. on Ministry (sec. 1988-91, chair 1992-94), Coos-Bay North Bend Rotary (Outstanding Citizen award 1985). Republican. Baptist. Avocations: amateur radio, backpacking, genealogy, travel. Home: 1546 NE Greensword Dr Hillsboro OR 97124-6139 *The test of my generation is found in whether we pass along values in faith and democracy for adoption by the new generation—to be adopted by them for their world.*

CURRY, GEORGE EDWARD, journalist; b. Tuscaloosa, Ala., Feb. 23, 1947; s. Homer Lee Curry and Martha Lee (Harris) Burks; m. Dina Ann Johnson, Apr. 15, 1995; 1 child, Edward DuBois. Student, Harvard U., summer 1968, Yale U., summer 1969, Knoxville Coll., 1970. Reporter Sports Illustrated, N.Y.C., 1970-72, St. Louis Post-Dispatch, 1972-83; reporter Chgo. Tribune, 1983-84, Washington corr., 1984-89, N.Y. bur. chief, 1989-93; editor-in-chief Emerge Mag., Washington, 1993—; founding dir. St. Louis, Washington and N.Y.C. Minority Journalism Workshops; TV appearances include The Today Show, The MacNeil/Lehrer Newshour, Washington Week in Review, America's Black Forum, Lead Story, C-Span and Speaking of Everything. Author: Jake Gaither: America's Most Famous Black Coach, 1977; writer, chief corr. TV documentary Assault on Affirmative Action, PBS, 1986. Chmn. bd. dirs. Youth Comm. (nat. teenage news svc.), 1990. Recipient Top Annual award Assn. for Edn. in Journalism and Mass Comm., 1989, Disting. Svc. award So. Press Inst., Savannah State Coll., 1989, Unity in Media award, Lincoln U., 1990, 94, 95; named Journalist of Yr. Washington Assn. Black Journalists, 1995. Avocations: reading, racquetball, tennis. Office: 1 Bet Plz 1900 W Pl NE Washington DC 20018-1230*

CURRY, HUGH ROBERT, tennis player; b. Neptune, N.J., July 13, 1948; s. Beatrice Fernanda (Wartli) C.; m. Linda Marie Boutin, June 16, 1991. BA, U. Pa., 1970. Profl. tennis player ITP, Salisbury, Md., 1970—; dir. tennis, Breakers Hotel, Palm Beach, Fla., 1970-90, Dublin (N.H.) Lake Club, 1993—; owner, operator Tumblin Falls House, Purling, N.Y., 1993—; adv. com. mem. Spaulding Sporting Goods, 1980-90, Wilson Sporting Goods, 1965-85. Recipient U.S. Nat. Tennis Champ, 1961, Can. Nat. Champ, 1960, 50 State Titles in U.S., 1950-90; named Top Ten Most Popular Tennis Players Martini-Rossi and World Tennis, 1962; named Outstanding Athlete U. Pa., 1970, #1 Coll. Tennis Player in the east, E. Coast Athletic Conf., 1968-69. Avocations: canoeing, philately, photography.

CURRY, JACK, magazine editor. BA in English, Le Moyne Coll., 1974; MA in Journalism, Syracuse U., 1976. Former asst. Sunday entertainment editor N.Y. Daily News; critic, reporter USA Today, 1983-87, dep. mng. editor, 1987-90; mng. editor TV Guide, 1990—. Author: Woodstock: The Summer of Our Lives, 1989; contbr. articles to popular periodicals. Office: News America Pub Inc TV Guide 1211 Avenue Of The Americas Fl 4 New York NY 10036-8701*

CURRY, JANE LOUISE, writer; b. East Liverpool, Ohio, Sept. 24, 1932; d. William Jack and Helen Margaret (Willis) C. Student, Pa. State U., 1950-51; BS, Indiana U. of Pa., 1954; postgrad., UCLA, 1957-59; AM, Stanford U., 1962, PhD, 1969; student, U. London, 1961-62, 65-66. Tchr. art East Liverpool schs., 1955, L.A. schs., 1956-59; teaching asst. dept. English Stanford (Calif.) U., 1959-61, 64-65, acting instr., 1967-68, instr., 1983-84, lectr., 1987; storyteller, 1962—. Author: Down from the Lonely Mountain, 1965, Beneath the Hill, 1967, The Sleepers, 1968, The Change-Child, 1969, The Daybreakers, 1970, Mindy's Mysterious Miniature, 1970, Over the Sea's Edge, 1971, The Ice Ghosts Mystery, 1972, The Lost Farm, 1974, Parsley Sage, Rosemary and Time, 1975, The Watchers, 1975, The Magical Cupboard, 1976, Poor Tom's Ghost, 1977, The Birdstones, 1977, The Bassumtyte Treasure, 1978, Ghost Lane, 1979, The Wolves of Aam, 1981, Shadow Dancers, 1983, The Great Flood Mystery, 1985, The Lotus Cup, 1986, Back in the Beforetime, 1987, Me, Myself and I, 1987, The Big Smith Snatch, 1989, Little Little Sister, 1989, What the Dickens?, 1991, The Great Smith House Hustle, 1993, The Christmas Knight, 1993, Robin Hood and his Merry Men, 1994, Robin Hood in the Greenwood, 1995, Moon Window, 1996, Dark Shade, 1998, Turtle Island, 1999, A Stolen Life, 1999. Office: Simon & Schuster Children's Publ Divsn 1230 Ave of Ams New York NY 10020

CURRY, JOHN JOSEPH, professional organization executive; b. Brooklyn, Feb. 6, 1936; s. John and Maude (Smith) C.; m. Claire Degnan (div. Apr. 1987); children: Claire, Julianne, Marie; m. Elizabeth Keiser, Dec. 9, 1989. BA, CCNY, 1958. Pers. mgr. Royal Globe Ins. Co., Phila., 1960-70; dept. adminstr. Thomas Jefferson U. Hosp., Phila., 1970-75; dir. Phila. office Am. Coll. Radiology, 1975-84, exec. dir., Reston, Va., 1984—. Capt. inf. U.S. Army. Mem. Am. Soc. Assn. Execs. Office: Am Coll Radiology 1891 Preston White Dr Reston VA 20191-5431

CURRY, JOHN MICHAEL, investment banker; b. Buffalo, N.Y., Dec. 30, 1942; s. John Vincent and June (Eisele) C.; m. Thea Adrian KIrk, July 12, 1969 (div. 1982); children: John Adrian, James Prescott; m. Margaretta Buckley, Mar. 17, 1990; 1 child, Michael Jeremiah. BA, U. San Francisco, 1968; MBA, Harvard U., 1970; postgrad., Suffolk U., 1971. Cert. property mgr.; registered rep. and gen. securities rep.; registered fiduciary and investment adviser, registered securities prin. Developer Devel. Corp. Am., Boston, 1970-73; founder, chmn. APT Fin. Svcs., Inc., Boston, 1977—, APT Asset Mgmt., Boston, 1992—, Am. Properties Team, APT Asset, Boston, 1987—; chmn. Am. Devel. Team, 1985-92, Am. Realty Team, Fla., 1994—, Infrastructure Repair Technologies, 1998—; bd. dirs. six corps.; Boston rep. Taylor Woodrow PLC, London, 1983-85. Vol. various fed., state, local polit. orgns. and campaigns. Sgt. U.S. Army, 1961-64. Recipient Modernization award Building Mag., 1980-81, Outstanding Restoration award Lowell C. of C., 1981, Nat. Jewish Life award, 1987. Mem. Harvard Club (Boston), various securities firms orgns. Avocations: scuba diving, karate, golf. Home: 211 Commodore Dr Jupiter FL 33477-4006 Office: Apt Group Cummings Park Ste 6000 Bldg 500 26 Woburn MA 01810

CURRY, JOHN PATRICK, insurance company executive, management consultant; b. Logan, W.Va., May 3, 1934; s. Albert Bruce and Mary Naomi (Shugert) C.; m. Patricia Jean Blessington, Oct. 26, 1956; children: Joseph Patrick, Mary Patricia, Kathleen Anne, Carmen Frances, John Gregory. Student St. Charles Coll., Catonsville, Md., 1949-52; B.A., U. Notre Dame, 1956; M.S. in Ops. Research, Western Mich. U., 1976. Lic. profl. cons., Mich. Agt., Conn. Mut. Life Ins. Co., 1959-65; gen. agt. Occidental Life Ins. Co., Los Angeles, 1965-66; pres. Investment Assocs. Inc., 1966-69; gen. agt. Fed. Life Ins. Co., Peoples Home Life Ins. Co. and Home Assurance Cos., 1969-71; actuarial cons. Am.-Brit. Ins. & Annuity Co., Ltd. (Bermuda), Battle Creek, Mich., 1979-87; mgmt. cons., 1971-88; owner, mgr. Nat. Search Cons., exec. search firm, Kalamazoo; owner, operator Curry Supply Co., Portage, Mich., 1978-83; pres. The Consulting Group, Inc. (Del.), Kalamazoo, 1985—; pres. The Pilot Co., Turks and Caicos Islands, 1985-90; dir. Anglo-Am. Ins. Co., Ltd. (Bermuda), 1979-87. Served with U.S. Army, 1957-59. U. Notre Dame scholar, 1952-55; Pat O'Brien scholar, 1956. Republican. Roman Catholic. Clubs: Sertoma (charter dir. 1961-64) (Kalamazoo). Home: 7226 Rockford St Kalamazoo MI 49024-4122 Office: The Consulting Group Kalamazoo MI 49024

CURRY, KIMBERLY M., communications consultant; b. San Diego, Nov. 30, 1960; d. Harry Graham and Jessica Caroline Lois (Selby) Martin; m. Adrian E. Curry, June 17, 1983; children: Dana P., Craig A. Assoc. in Bus., Pa. State U., 1980. Trainer Gallatin Nat. Bank, Uniontown, Pa., 1980-89; teller PNC Bank, Uniontown, 1989-91; cons. Bell Atlantic PA, Uniontown, 1991—; mem. Pier One Adv. Bd., Fort Worth. Sec. St. Paul's AME Ch., Uniontown, 1986—. Mem. Smeal Coll. Bus., Pa. State U. Alumni. Avocations: religion, reading, crafts. Home: 135 Lenox St Uniontown PA 15401-3041

CURRY, MARY EARLE LOWRY, poet; b. Seneca, S.C., May 13, 1917; d. Ullin Sidney and Mary Sloan (Earle) Lowry; m. Peden Gene Curry, Dec. 25, 1941; children: Eugene Lowry, Mary Earle (dec.). Student, Furman U., Greenville, S.C., 1944-45. Author: (poetry books) Looking Up, 1949, Looking Within, 1961, reprinted, 1980, Hymn, 1973; contbr. to Yearbook of Modern Poetry, Poets of Am., Poetic Voice of Am., We the People, Poetry Digest, Poetry Anthology of Verse, Internat. Anthology on World Brotherhood and Peace, Parnassas of World Poets, others; weekly poetry columns in Inman Times, Fountain Inn Times, Fort Mill Times, Laurens Advertiser, Ware Shoals Life, others. Recipient World award for culture Centro Studi E Ricerche Delle Naioni, Italy, 1985. Mem. Centro Studi Scambi Internat. Roma, United Meth. Women's Orgns., United Meth. Ministers' Wives Clubs, various cmty. clubs. Methodist. Avocations: music, photography, reading. Home: 345 Curry Dr Seneca SC 29678-1907

CURRY, NANCY ELLEN, educator, psychoanalyst, psychologist; b. Brockway, Pa., Jan. 26, 1931; d. George R. and Mary F. (Covert) C. BA, Grove City Coll., 1952; MEd, U. Pitts., 1956, PhD, 1972; grad., Pitts. Psychoanalytic Inst., 1988, grad. child analytic program, 1992. Lic. psychologist, Pa. Tchr. public schs. East Brady and Oakmont, Pa., 1952-55; presch. demonstration tchr. Arsenal Family and Children's Center, U. Pitts., 1955-79, assoc. dir., 1971-79; from instr. in psychiatry to prof. child devel. Sch. Social Wk U. Pitts, 1957-93; prof. emeritus Sch. Social Work, U. Pitts., 1993—; also mem. faculty U. Pitts Sch. Medicine, Sch. Edn., Sch. Health Related Professions.; pvt. practice in psychanalysis and psychotherapy; Fulbright exchange tchr. North Oxford Nursery Sch., Oxford, Eng., 1957-58; vis. prof. Oreg. State U., summer, 1964, Ariz. State U., summer, 1969; assoc. dir. early childhood project Edn. Professions Devel. Act, U.S. Office of Edn., 1970-74; cons. in field. Co-producer 12 films on children's play; co-author Beyond Self-esteem, 1990; editor The Feeling Child; author numerous articles on child devel. Mem. Am. Psychol. Assn., Am. Psychoanalytic Assn., Assn. Child Psychoanalysis. Home: 149 Shadow Ridge Dr Pittsburgh PA 15238-2133 Office: II Fox Chapel Pl 1326 Freeport Rd Pittsburgh PA 15238-3131

CURRY, RAVENEL BOYKIN, investment manager; b. July 8, 1941. BA, Furman U., 1963; MBA, U. Va., 1967. Pres. Eagle Capital Mgmt., N.Y.C., 1988—. Address: 435 E 52nd St New York NY 10022-6445

CURRY, ROBERT FURMAN, JR., educator, academic advisor; b. Anderson, S.C., Dec. 13, 1953; s. Robert Furman and Mary Lenora (Russell) C. BA cum laude, Furman U., 1975; MEd, U. Ga., 1976; Edn. Specialist, Coll. of William and Mary, 1993, EdD, 1997. Residence hall dir. Abraham Baldwin Agrl. Coll., Tifton, Ga., 1976-78, counselor, 1978-79; acad. counselor, instr. Old Dominion U., Norfolk, Va., 1979-86, asst. dir. advising svcs., 1986-94, site dir., 1994-95, coord. corp. sites, asst. prof., 1995—; presenter at confs. in field. Contbr. articles to journs. Mem. Nat. Acad. Advising Assn. (presenter 1988, 97, 99, student rsch. award 1997), Old Dominion U. Assn. Univ. Adminstrs. (treas. 1989-93, 98-99, pres. 1999—), Kappa Delta Pi. Democrat. Episcopalian. Home: 775 W 49th St Norfolk VA 23508-2029 Office: Old Dominion U Norfolk VA 23508

CURRY, ROBERT LEE, lawyer; b. Lamont, Wis., May 10, 1923; s. Irving Gregg and Emma (Zimmerman) C.; m. Muriel Clapp, July 29, 1950; children—Robert Lee J., Laura Lynne, Melinda Ann. B.S., Lawrence U., 1948; LL.B., U. Wis., 1953. Bar: Wis. bar 1953. Assoc. firm Boardman, Suhr, Curry & Field, Madison, Wis., 1953-56; sr. partner Boardman, Suhr, Curry & Field, Madison, 1956-73, of counsel, 1989-94; v.p., gen. counsel CUNA Mut. Ins. Group, Madison, 1964-73, pres., 1973-88, bd. dirs., 1972-88, dir. emeritus, 1988—; dir. CUNA Credit Union, 1965-70, pres., 1968-69; bd. dirs. Cumis Ins. Soc., 1972-88, pres., 1973-88; bd. dirs. Cumis Ins. Group Can., 1972-88; pres., dir. Cudis Ins. Soc., Inc., 1972-88, C.M.C.I. Corp. Chmn., United Way of Dane County, Wis., 1981. Served with USAAF, 1942-46. Mem. Am. Law Inst., U. Wis. Law Alumni Assn. (dir. 1967-70, pres. 1969-70), Order of Coif. Home: 4805 Fond Du Lac Trl Madison WI 53705-4814

CURRY, THOMAS FORTSON, electronics engineer, defense industry executive; b. Thomasville, Ga., Nov. 22, 1926; s. Bostick Underwood and Bertie Eugenia (Cook) C.; m. Mary Ann Kemper, July 2, 1949; children: Bostick U., Thomas Lee, Ruthann, David C.K., Laurie F., Clinton M. BEE, Ga. Inst. Tech., 1949; MSEE, Pa. State U., 1954; PhDEE, Carnegie-Mellon U., 1959. Registered profl. engr., Pa., Va. Rsch. fellow elec. engring. dept. Carnegie-Mellon U., Pitts., 1955-57; mem. tech. staff Bell Telephone Labs., Murray Hill, N.J., 1957-58; lab. dir. Syracuse (N.Y.) U. Rsch. Corp., 1959-64; chmn. bd. dirs. Curry, McLaughlin & Len Inc., Syracuse, 1964-65; dept. mgr., chief engr. Melpar, Inc., Falls Church, Va., 1966-70; product line dir. LTV-Electrosystems, Inc., Garland, Tex., 1970-71; tech. advisor to pres. Melpar, Divsn., E-Systems, Inc., Falls Church, 1971-74; v.p., dir. Microwave Systems, Inc., Syracuse, 1974-76; asst. dir. Signals Intelligence, Office Sec. of Def., Washington, 1976-80; assoc. dep. asst. sec. of Navy, Office Sec. of Navy, Washington, 1980-83; pres., dir. C-Systems, Inc., Oakton, Va., 1983—; chief scientist E-Systems, Inc., Fairfax, Va., 1983-93; chief engr. C-Systems, Inc., Oakton, Va., 1993—; mem., dir. Navy Intelligence Cons. Group, Office of Navy Ops., 1983-86; mem. tech. working group 9F Crit. Techs. Rev., Office Strategic Def., 1988-93. Contbr. articles to profl. jours. Pres. Kemper Park Civic Assn., Fairfax County, Va., 1972-73; treas. Centerville Coun. Civic Assn., Fairfax County, 1973-74; mem. trustees vis. com. elec. engring. dept. Carnegie-Mellon U., 1972-74. 1st lt. U.S. Army, 1944-47, 50-52. Named Fellow in Elec. Communications, Bell Telephone Labs., Murray Hill, N.J., 1956-57. Fellow IEEE (chmn. No. Va. sect. 1973, Centennial award 1984); mem. Assn. Old Crows (life; pres. Capitol Club 1972, nat. dir. 1976-85); mem. Security Affairs Support Assn., Assn. Energy Engrs., Hunter Mill Swim and Racquet Club (bd. dirs. 1979-83), Sigma Xi, Tau Beta Pi, Eta Kappa Nu, Alpha Tau Omega. Office: C-Systems Inc PO Box 310 Oakton VA 22124-0310

CURRY, THOMAS JAMES, manufacturers representative; b. New Brunswick, N.J., Sept. 8, 1921; s. Thomas Christopher and Leanore Margaret (Craven) C.; m. Mary Louise Bisaccio, Apr. 1, 1945. *Great-grandfather Thomas Curry left County Cavan, Ireland, in 1850, for New York City. He enlisted in the Union Army in 1863, and was mustered into Company D of the 83rd New York Volunteer Infantry Regiment. On May 5-6, 1864, at the battle of Wilderness, Virginia, he was wounded and taken prisoner. His regiment was decimated in this bloody battle, and surviving remnants were assigned to the 97th New York. He died on December 20, 1864, in the notorious Andersonville Prison Camp, Andersonville, Georgia. He left two male children. Recent family genealogical work shows he has over four hundred descendants.* BA, Rutgers U., 1944. Export sales traffic mgr. Am. Cyanamid Corp., Bound Brook, N.J., 1945-47; sales coord. Interchemical Corp., Bound Brook, 1948-52; sales rep. Sun Chem. Corp., N.Y.C., 1953-67; pvt. practice mfrs. rep. Pa., 1968—. Pres. coun. Rutgers U. Mem. Col. Henry Rutgers Soc. Avocations: golf, geneaology, photography, history. Home: 10 Crestline Rd Wayne PA 19087-2607

CURRY, TIM, actor; b. Cheshire, Eng., Apr. 19, 1946. Attended, U. Birmingham, Eng. Stage performances include A Mid-Summer Night's Dream, The Rocky Horror Show, Amadeus, The Pirates of Penzance, Me and My Girl, My Favorite Year; films The Rocky Horror Picture Show, 1975, The Shout, 1980, Times Square, 1980, Annie, 1982, The Ploughman's Lunch, 1984, Clue, 1985, Legend, 1986, Pass the Ammo, 1988, The Hunt for Red October, 1990, Oscar, 1991, (voice) Ferngully...The Last Rainforest, 1992, Passed Away, 1992, Home Alone 2: Lost in New York, 1992, Loaded Weapon 1, 1992, The Three Musketeers, 1993, The Shadow, 1994, Congo, 1995, Lovers' Knot, 1995, (voice) The Pebble and the Penguin, 1995; TV appearances Oliver Twist, 1982, Stephen King's It, 1990, (voice) Peter Pan and the Pirates, 1991 (Emmy award), (voice) Fish Police, 1992, Tales From the Crypt (Death of Some Salesman), 1993 (Emmy nomination, Guest Actor - Drama, 1994), Earth 2, 1994, Superhuman Samurai Syber-Squad (TV series voice), 1994, Aaahh!! Real Monsters, 1994, The Mask, 1995, Toonstruck, 1996, Story of Santa Claus, 1996, (voice) Quack Pack, 1996, Mighty Ducks, 1996, Lexx: The Dark Zone, 1996, (series voice) Jumanji, 1996, Bruno the Kid, 1996, Muppet Treasure Island, 1996, Titanic, 1996, Doom Runners, 1997, Beauty and the Beast: The Enchanted Christmas, 1997, McHale's Navy, 1997, Over the Top, 1997, Addams Family Reunion, 1998, Gabriel Knight: Blood of the Sacred, Blood of the Damned, 1998, (voice) Rugrats Movie, 1998, The Titanic Chronicles, 1999, Pirates of the Plain, 1999, Four Dogs Playing Poker, 1999; albums: Read My Lips, 1978, Fearless, 1979, Simplicity, 1981, The Best of Tim Curry, 1989. Office: UTA c/o Elyse Scherz 9560 Wilshire Blvd Ste 500 Beverly Hills CA 90212-2427*

CURRY, TONI GRIFFIN, counseling center executive, consultant; b. Langdale, Ala., June 23, 1938; d. Robert Alton and Elsie (Dodson) Griffin; m. Ronald William Curry, June 13, 1959 (div. 1972); children: Christopher, Catherine, Angela. BA, Ga. State U., 1962; MSW, U. Ga., 1981. Lic. clin. therapist; cert. addictions counselor. Tchr. DeKalb County Bd. Edn., Atlanta, 1962-63; counselor Charter Peachford Hosp., Atlanta, 1974-79; dir. aftercare, 1976-79; dir. aftercare and occupational svcs. Ridgeview Inst., Atlanta, 1979-82; owner, dir., adminstr., counselor Toni Cury and Assocs., Inc., Atlanta, 1982—; cons., lectr. to numerous cos. and orgns.; mem. adv. bd. Peachford Hosp., Atlanta, 1982-87, Rockdale House, Conyers, Ga., 1981—, Outpatient Addictions Clinics Am., 1983-85; bd. dirs. Employee Assistance Programs Inst.; lectr. local, nat. and internat. confs. Cloud's House, Wilshire, Eng., 1986; founder Internat. Recovery Ctr., Cannes, France, 1990; founder, bd. dirs. Anchor Hosp., 1985-93; seminars on addiction in Italy and Switzerland; pres., mem. exec. bd. Ga. Employee Assistance Programs Forum, Atlanta, 1981-86; appointed to Gov.'s Advisory Coun. on Mental Health, Mental Retardation and Substance Abuse, 1984, Gov.'s Commn. Drug Awareness and Prevention, 1986; chairperson Ga. Gov.'s Driving Under Influence of Alcohol Assessment Task Force; adv. bd. Hawthorne House; presenter European Conf. Drugs and Alcohol, Edinburgh, Scotland; faculty Southeastern Conf. Alcohol and Drugs, 1996; annual presenter So. Coastal Conf., Jekyll Is., Ga., 1996—; mem. steering com. personnel programs Delta Air Lines, 1992—. Vol. My Sister's Ho. Mem. Nat. Assn. Social Workers, Ga. Addiction Counselors Assn. (dir. 1982-86), Ga. Citizens Coun. Alcoholism, Employee Assistance Programs Assn., Assn. Behavioral Therapists, Nat. Assn. Alcoholism and Drug Abuse Counselors, Mems. Guild of High Mus. Art, Kappa Alpha Theta. Home: 7245 Chattahoochee Bluff Dr Atlanta GA 30350-1071 Office: 4546 Barclay Dr Atlanta GA 30338-5802

CURRY-CARLBURG, JOANNE JEANNE, elementary education educator; b. Cleve., Oct. 11, 1947; d. James Michael and Joan Marie (Bukky) Curry; m. Stan R. Carlburg. BS, Villa Maria Coll., Erie, Pa., 1973; MEd, Edinboro U. Pa., 1975; EdD, SUNY, Buffalo, 1987. Cert. tchr., reading specialist, Pa. Tchr. Erie Diocese, 1966-76; reading specialist N.W. Tri-County Intermediate Unit 5, Edinboro, Pa., 1976—; cons. Erie Diocese Cath. Schs., 1990—; adj. faculty Gannon U., Erie, 1991—. Author: Pseudoword Phonics Test, 1986. Active Flagship Niagara League, Erie, Erie Zool. Soc. Recipient Friends of Edn. award Gannon U., 1993; finalist Elem. Sch. Tchr. of Yr. 1995, Commonwealth of Pa., Disting. Alumni award Gannon U., 1998. Me. ASCD, AAUW, NEA, Pa. State Edn. Assn., Internat. Reading Assn. (Celebrate March 1998 Literacy award, with Erie Reading Coun.), Keystone Reading Assn., U. Buffalo Alumni Assn., Grad. Sch. Edn. Alumni Assn. U. Buffalo, Gannon U. Alumni Assn. Avocations: outdoor activities, golf, walking, photography, reading. Office: Northwest Tri-County Intermediate Unit 5 252 Waterford St Edinboro PA 16412-2373

CURSCHMANN, MICHAEL JOHANN HENDRIK, German language and literature educator; b. Cologne, Germany, Jan. 11, 1936; came to U.S., 1963; s. Fritz Heinrich and Hanna Regine (Schinnerer) C.; m. Beryl G. Davies, Jan. 14, 1961; children: Jane, Paul (dec. 1982). Student, Munich U., 1954-56, 58-62, London U., 1957-58; Phd, Munich U., 1962. Asst. prof. Munich U., 1961-63; asst. prof. dept. Germanic langs. and lit. Princeton U., 1963-65, assoc. prof., 1965-69, prof., 1969—, chmn. dept., 1979-82, 86-89, dir. program in medieval studies, 1993—; vis. prof. Munich U., 1985-86, Tübingen U., 1990, Fribourg U., 1996. Author works on German and European medieval literature, literature and other arts. Guggenheim fellow, 1970-71, Inst. for Germanic Studies, U. London fellow. Mem. Bavarian Acad. Sci. (corres.). Home: 134 Sycamore Rd Princeton NJ 08540-5325 Office: Princeton U 230 E Pyne Princeton NJ 08544

CURSON, THEODORE, musician; b. Phila., June 3, 1935; s. Leroy and Reava (Paige) C.; m. Marjorie N. Goltry, Apr. 1, 1967; children: Charlene, Theodore II. Student, Mastbaum Sch., Granoff Music Conservatory, Phila., 1952-53. Mem. Charles Mingus' Jazz Workshop, 1959-60; guest instr. U. Vt. Festival of Contemporary Music, 1968; instr. music Warsaw U.; pres. Nosruc Pub. Co., Jersey City, from 1961. Trumpeter with Max Roach, Philly Joe Jones, Cecil Taylor, Eric Dolphy, 1960-63; appeared radio, TV, clubs, also jazz festivals including Tallinn, Estonia, Vienne, France; NorthSea, The Hague, Nice, Jazz Yatra, India, Antibes, Aix en Provence, Lugano, Bologna, Macerata, Prague, Bled, Warsaw, Molde, Kongsberg, Ahus, Laren, Pori, Caracas, Amsterdam, 1964—, U.S. festivals New Music Across America, Portland, Maine; Birdland, Monterey, Newport/N.Y., Newport Rebels Festival, univ. concerts including Princeton, N.J., U. Wis., Platteville, Baton Rouge, Columbia, N.Y.U., Hobart Coll., Western Wash. Coll., Grinnell Coll., U. Calif., Santa Monica, U. Calif., Berkeley, U. Vt., toured India, Middle East and North Africa for State Dept., 1980; toured Siberia, 1996; guest soloist Norddeutscher Rundfunk TV, star P.B.S. TV show Jazz Set, 1972, Last Date (jazz video) with NOS (Dutch TV); composer Nosruc Waltz, 1960, Flatted Fifth, 1960, Straight Ice, 1965, Typical Ted, 1970, The Leopard, 1964, Reava's Waltz, Airi's Tune, Searchin for the Blues, Lost Her, 1987; rec. artist: Plenty of Horn, 1961, Fire Down Below, 1963, Tears for Dolphy, 1976, New Thing and Blue Thing, 1965, Urge, 1966, Ode to Booker Ervin, 1970, Pop Wine, 1972, Quicksand, 1975, Jubilant Power, 1976, Blue Piccolo, 1976, Flip Top, 1977, Typical Ted, 1977, The Trio, 1979, I Heard Mingus, 1980, Snake Johnson, 1981, Round Midnight, 1990, Cattin' Curson, 1993, Tears for Dolphy, 1994, Traveling On, 1997; music for films include Teorema, 1968, Notes for a Film on Jazz, 1968; dir. Blue Note Open Jam, 1984-93. Named New Star Montery Jazz Festival 1962, winner Trumpet sect. Down Beat Internat. Critics Poll, 1966, Ted Curson & Co. winner Down Beat Reader's Poll, 1978, named New Jazz Artist Jazz Podium, Germany; recipient L.I. Musicians Soc. award 1970, Pori (Finland) City Standard 1978, Keys to City, 1998, Paul Robeson Community Arts award Jersey City Pub. Libr., 1994. Mem. Am. Fedn. Musicians.

CURT, DENISE MORRIS, artist, limner, photographer; b. New Haven, Nov. 15, 1936; d. Bertrand and Anna Geraldine (Fiak) Rocheleau; m. John Morris, Oct. 4, 1954 (dec.); children: Tyler John, Cynthia Leigh Morris Bell; m. Albert A. Curt, 1973 (div. 1981). Student of Louis Crescenti, Orange, Conn., 1950-52; student, Whitney Sch. Art, New Haven, 1950, Luchetti Sch. Art, New Haven, 1951, Paier Sch. Art, Hamden, Conn., 1951. Dir. Meet The Artists and Artisans, Milford, Conn., 1962—; interior designer State of Conn., Hartford, 1972-75. One-woman shows Gull Gallery, Provincetown, Mass., Chapelle Jean Cocteau, Villefranche Sur Mer, France, Garfield Galleries, Orange, Conn., Yale U., Stratford Gallery, Stevenson (Md.) Galleries, also others; represented in numerous pvt. and pub. collections throughout world. Lectr. to numerous civic orgns.; mem. Vis. Artists in Schs., 1970—; commr. Conn. Commn. on Arts, 1974-79; photography chmn. Milford Fine Arts Coun., New Haven Arts Coun.; bd. dirs. Milford Hosp. Aux.; mem. Literacy Vols., Milford. Recipient award Mystic Art Festival, 1969, Sterling House Art Show, 1985, Glastonbury Art Guild, 1988. Mem. Guilford Art League (bd. dirs. 1975-80), Nat. League Am. Pen Women (category painting, bd. dirs. Fairfield chpt., art chair), Conn. Classic Arts, Milford Hist. Soc., Yale U. Gallery, Met. Mus. Art. Republican. Congregationalist. Avocations: Renaissance and baroque music, antiques, foreign travel. Fax: 203-876-2322. E-mail: ctlimner@snet.net. Home and Studio: 41 Green St Milford CT 06460-4709

CURTHOYS, NORMAN P., biochemistry educator, consultant; b. Buffalo, Apr. 29, 1944; s. Albert J. and Emily M. (Ellman) C.; m. Linda H. Harriger, July 22, 1967; children: Paul, Michele. B.S. in Chemistry, Clarkson Coll., Potsdam, N.Y., 1966; Ph.D. in Biochemistry, U. Calif.-Berkeley, 1970. Postdoctoral fellow Washington U., St. Louis, 1970-72; asst. prof. biochemistry U. Pitts., 1972-77, assoc. prof., 1977-82, W.S. McEllroy prof., 1982-89; prof. biochemistry Colo. State U., Ft. Collins, 1989—, chmn. dept., 1989—; vis. prof. U. Tubingen, Fed. Republic Germany, 1977, Case-Western Res. U., 1987, U. Zürich, 1996, U. Innsbruck, Austria, 1997; mem. med. biochemistry study sect. NIH, 1982-85, gen. medicine B. study sect., 1991-93.d. Mem. editl. bd. Archives of Biochemistry and Biophysics, 1977-82, Jour. Biol. Chemistry, 1991-95, Biochem. Jour., 1992—; contbr. chpts. to books and articles to profl. jours. Recipient Rsch. Career Devel. award NIH, 1976-81; Am. Cancer Soc. postdoctoral fellow, 1970-72; vis. fellow Alexander von Humboldt Found., 1977; Fogerty Sr. Internat. fellow, 1996-97; rsch. grantee NIH, 1973—. Mem. Am. Physiol. Soc., Am. Soc. Biochemistry and Molecular Biology, Am. Soc. Nephrology. Office: Colo State U Dept Biochemistry Fort Collins CO 80523

CURTIN, BRIAN JOSEPH, ophthalmologist; b. N.Y.C., July 25, 1921; s. James Joseph and Julia Margaret (Smith) C.; m. Claire Margaret Flood, June 18, 1955; children: Edward Brian, James Martin, Thomas Hayes, Deirdre Claire. BS, Fordham U., 1942; MD, NYU, 1945. Intern St. Vincent's Hosp., N.Y.C., 1945-46; resident surgeon Manhattan Eye, Ear and Throat Hosp., 1950-53, asst. attending surgeon, asso. attending surgeon, 1953-74, surgeon dir., 1974-89, surgeon dir. emertus, 1990—, pres. med. bd., 1977-79, vice chmn. dept. ophthalmology, 1983-89, med. dir., 1989-91; attending ophthalmologist, chief svc. Misericordia-Lincoln Affiliated Hosps., 1958-79; attending ophthalmologist N.Y. Hosp., 1969-84; assoc. attending ophthalmologist Columbia Presbyn. Med. Ctr., 1985-92; asst. prof. clin. ophthalmology NYU, 1954-70; assoc. prof. clin. ophthalmology Cornell Med. Coll., 1970-84, Columbia U. Coll. Physicians and Surgeons, 1985-98; med. adv. bd. Eye Bank for Sight Restoration, N.Y.C., 1978-90, chmn., 1988-90; attending ophthalmologist, chmn. dept. St. Clare's Hosp. and Health Ctr., 1978-81. Author: The Myopias: Basic Science and Clinical Management, 1985; mem. editorial bd. Cornea, 1981-85; contbr. chpts. to textbooks, articles to med. jours. With U.S. Navy, 1946-48. Recipient Achievement award Fordham U., 1976. Mem. ACS, AMA, AAAS, Am. Ophthalmol. Soc., N.Y. State Med. Soc., N.Y. County Med. Soc., N.Y. Acad. Medicine, N.Y. Acad. Scis., Am. Acad. Ophthalmology, N.Y. Ophthal. Soc. (v.p. 1981-82, pres. 1982-83), Am. Eye Study Club, Siwanoy Country Club, Knights of Malta. Home: 50 Columbus Ave Tuckahoe NY 10707

CURTIN, DANIEL JOSEPH, JR., lawyer; b. San Francisco, Jan. 7, 1933; s. Daniel Joseph and Nell Helen (Lenihan) C.; m. Myrtle Rose Wanke, Feb. 7, 1959; children: Kathleen, Mary, Patricia, Thomas, Carol. AB in Polit. Sci., U. San Francisco, 1954, JD, 1957. Bar: Calif. 1958. Asst. sec. State Senate Calif., Sacramento, 1959; cons., counsel Assembly Com. on Local Govt., Sacramento, 1959-60; dep. city atty. Richmond, Calif., 1961-65; city atty. Walnut Creek, Calif., 1965-82; with Williams, Caploe, Robbins & Curtin, Benicia, Calif., 1983-84; ptnr. McCutchen, Doyle, Brown & Enersen, Walnut Creek, 1984—; mem. bd. advisors environ. affairs Boston Coll. Sch. of Law, 1987—; mem. State Sen. Housing Adv. Task Force, 1983-84, State Sen. Subcom. on the Redevel. of Antiquated Subdivs., 1986; instr. continuing edn. of the bar, 1975, 82, 88, U. San Francisco Sch. of Law, 1988-92, Golden Gate U. Sch. of Law, 1979-82, U. Calif. Extension, 1973—, John F. Kennedy U. Sch. of Law, Walnut Creek, 1983-90; mem. adv. com. Alcohol and Drug Abuse Coun., Pleasant Hill, Calif. Contbr. articles to profl. jours. Lt. U.S. Army, 1958, 56-64. Recipient Nat. Disting. Leadership awards Am. Planning Assn., 1987; named City Atty. of Yr., 1971 and others. Mem. ABA (sect. on state and local govt. law, coun. sec. 1992—, chmn. land use, planning and zoning com. 1976-78), Calif. State Bar Assn. (mem. exec. com., real property law sect. 1988-91, mem. com. on environ. 1977-80), Nat. Inst. Mcpl. Law Officer (chmn. zoning and planning com. 1969-79, regional v.p. 1979-82, Lifetime Achievement in Mcpl. Law Charles S. Rhyne award), Calif. Pk. and Recreation Soc., League of Calif. Cities (pres. city atty.'s dept. 1973-74), Lambda Alpha, others. Democrat. Roman Catholic. Avocations: pub. speaking, gardening. Office: McCutchen Doyle Brown & Enersen PO Box V 1331 N California Blvd Walnut Creek CA 94596-4537

CURTIN, GARY LEE, air force officer; b. Washington, Apr. 24, 1943; s. Thomas Francis and Lois Sarah (Hall) C.; m. Karen Marcella Reinmann, Nov. 26, 1966; children: Jennifer Lynne, Scott Marshall. BS in Aerospace Engring., U. Md., 1965; MS in Econs., S.D. State U., Ellsworth AFB, 1970. Commd. 2d lt. USAF, 1965, advanced through grades to maj. gen., 1992; launch officer 44th Strategic Missile Wing, Ellsworth AFB, 1965-70; intelligence officer Pacific Air Forces, Udorn, Thailand, Hickam AFB, Hawaii, 1971-75; internat. polit. affairs staff officer Hdqrs. USAF/Dep. Chief of Staff, Plans Pentagon, Washington, 1976-80; comdr. 400th Strategic Missile Squadron, Warren AFB, Wyo., 1980-82; dir. Intercontinental Ballistic Missile requirements Hdqrs. Strategic Air Command, Offutt AFB, Nebr., 1983-86; comdr. 90th Strategic Missile Wing, Warren AFB, Wyo., 1986-88; dir. comd. control Hdqrs. SAC, Offutt AFB, 1988-90; Joint Chiefs of Staff rep. to START negotiations Joint Staff, Geneva, 1990-91; dep. dir. for internat. negotiations Joint Staff/J-5/Pentagon, Washington, 1991-93; dir. of intelligence U. S. Strategic Command, Offutt AFB, Neb., 1993-95; dir. Def. Nuclear Agy./Def. Spl. Weapons Agy., Alexandria, Va., 1995—; sr. v.p. for strategic devel. Defense Gp. Inc. Mem. Air Force Assn., Tau Beta Pi, Omicron Delta Epsilon. Avocations: jogging, travel, reading, model aircraft. Office: Defense Gp Inc 2034 Eisenhower Ave Ste 115 Alexandria VA 22314*

CURTIN, JANE THERESE, actress, writer; b. Cambridge, Mass., Sept. 6, 1947; d. John Joseph and Mary Constance (Farrell) C.; m. Patrick F. Lynch, Apr. 31, 1975. A.A., Elizabeth Seton Jr. Coll., 1967; student, Northeastern U., 1967-68. Appeared in plays The Proposition, Cambridge and N.Y.C., 1968-72, Last of the Red Hot Lovers touring co., 1973; Broadway debut in Candida, 1981; author, actress Off-Broadway mus. rev. Pretzels, 1974-75; star TV series NBC Saturday Night Live, 1975-79, Kate & Allie, 1984-88, Working It Out, 1990, 3rd Rock from the Sun, 1996—; appeared in films including Mr. Mike's Mondo Video, 1979, How to Beat the High Cost of Living, 1980, O.C. and Stiggs, 1987, Coneheads, 1993, Antz, 1998; TV films include Divorce Wars-A Love Story, 1982, Suspicion, 1988, Maybe Baby, 1988, Common Ground, 1990, Tad, 1995, Christmas in Washington, 1996, AN/3, 1999; TV guest appearance Recess, 1997. Recipient Emmy nomination, 1977, 87; Emmy awards for outstanding actress in comedy series, 1984, 85. Mem. Screen Actors Guild, Actors Equity, AFTRA. Office: ICM care Boaty Boatwright 40 W 57th St New York NY 10019-4001*

CURTIN, JOHN JOSEPH, JR., lawyer; b. Englewood, N.J., Mar. 12, 1933; s. John Joseph and Marion (Walsh) C.; m. Mary Daly, Sept. 27, 1958; children: Kevin Joseph, Catherine Mary, Joseph Patrick, Ann Mary, Daniel Joseph. AB magna cum laude, Boston Coll., 1954, JD, 1957; LLM, Georgetown U., 1959. Bar: Mass. 1957, D.C. 1959, U.S. Supreme Ct. 1961. Atty. Dept. Justice, Washington, 1957-59; assoc. firm Hogan and Hartson, Washington, 1959-61; atty. Office of U.S. Atty., Boston, 1961-64; chief civil divsn., 1963-64; assoc., ptnr. Bingham, Dana & Gould, Boston, 1964—; instr. Boston Coll. Law Sch., 1965—; lectr. Harvard U. Law Sch., 1977-82; bd. dirs. Nat. Consumer Law Ctr., 1994—. Trustee Regis Coll., 1977-83, Newton Coll. Sacred Heart, 1973-75; mem. local govt. adv. com. Commonwealth of Mass., 1978; mem. Town Mtg., Wellesley, Mass., 1970-79, moderator, 1979-84, chmn. adv. com., 1974-75, chmn. town improvements coordinating com., 1977-79, chmn. capital budgeting and investment com., 1979-80; chmn. bd. advisors Boston Coll. Law Sch., 1997—; exec. com. mem. Ctr. for Public Resources, 1994—. Recipient numerous awards and hon. degrees. Mem. ABA (chmn. sect. litigation 1984-85, pres. 1990-91, chmn. working group state justice initiatives, 1994—), Boston Bar Assn. (pres. 1979-81, chmn. task force profl. fulfillment, 1996—), Am. Bar Found., Am. Law Inst., Greater Boston Legal Svcs. (bd. dirs. until 1990), Boston Coll. Alumni Assn. (v.p., pres. 1975-76), Mass. Assn. Town Fin. Fin. Com. (pres. 1978), Nat. Assn. Pub. Interest Law, Fellowships for Equal Justice (pres. 1992-95), Nat. Legal Aid and Defender Assn. (bd. dirs. 1990—). Home: 2 Woodchester Rd Wellesley MA 02481-1417 Office: Bingham Dana & Gould 150 Federal St Fl 15 Boston MA 02110-1726*

CURTIN, JOHN T., federal judge; b. Buffalo, Aug. 24, 1921; s. John J. and Ellen (Quigley) C.; m. Jane R. Good, Aug. 9, 1952; children: Ann Elizabeth, John James, Patricia Marie, Eileen Jane, Mary Ellen, Mark Andrew, William Joseph. BS, Canisius Coll., 1945; LLB, U. Buffalo, 1949. Bar: N.Y. 1949. Pvt. practice law Buffalo, 1949-61; formerly U.S. atty. for Western Dist. N.Y., 1961-67; judge U.S. Dist. Ct. for Western N.Y., Buffalo, 1967—; previously chief judge U.S. Dist. Ct. for Western N.Y.; now sr. judge U.S. Dist. Ct. for Western N.Y., Buffalo. Served to lt. col. USMC, 1942-45, USMCR, 1952-54. Mem. ABA, N.Y. State Bar Assn., Erie County Bar Assn. Democrat. Roman Catholic. Office: US Dist Ct 624 US Courthouse 68 Court St Buffalo NY 14202-3405*

CURTIN, LAWRENCE N., lawyer; b. Glen Ridge, N.J., Apr. 29, 1950. BS with honors, Fla. State U., 1972, JD with honors, 1976. Bar: Fla. 1976, U.S. Dist. Ct. (no. dist.) Fla., U.S. Ct. Appeals (4th, 5th, 11th and D.C. cirs.). Law clerk to Hon. William Stafford U.S. Dist. Ct. (no. dist.) Fla., 1976-78; mem. Holland & Knight, Tallahassee. Co-author: Surface Water Pollution Control, vol. 1, 1986-96. Mem. ABA, Fla. Bar (chmn. energy law com. 1983-84), Tallahassee Bar Assn., Beta Gamma Sigma, Sigma Iota Epsilon. Office: Holland & Knight PO Drawer 810 315 S Calhoun St Ste 600 Tallahassee FL 32301-1897

CURTIN, LEAH LOUISE, publisher, editor, author, nurse; b. Chgo., Mar. 8, 1942; d. Jean Wilson and Veronica Eloise (Dunst) Sutter; m. Peter Joseph Curtin, Apr. 15, 1966 (div. May 1990); children: Peter James, Rose Mary, Christopher Charles, Joseph Wilson. Diploma in nursing, Good Samaritan Hosp. Sch. Nursing, Cin., 1965; BS in Community Health Planning, U. Cin., 1976, MS in Health Planning and Adminstrn., 1977; MA in Philosophy, Athenaeum of Ohio, 1977; DSc (hon.), SUNY, Utica, 1990. RN, Ohio.

Staff nurse Vets. Hosp., Cin., 1965-66, Vis. Nurses' Assn., Cin., 1966-67; instr. No. Ky. U., Highland Heights, 1974-76; asst. prof. Coll. Mt. St. Joseph-On-The-Ohio, Cin., 1976-80; editor Nursing Mgmt. Springhouse Corp., Phila., 1979-98; ptnr. Metier Cons., Cin., 1990—; adj. faculty U. Cin., 1984—; organizational cons. Franciscan Sisters of Poor Health System, N.Y.C., 1987-96; cons. on nursing ethics Nurse Corps, USAF, Washington, 1991—. Author: Nursing Ethics: Theories and Pragmatics, 1982 (Am. Jour. Nursing Book of Yr. award 1982), DRGS: The Reorganization of Health, 1984, Curtin Calls, 1986, Cornerstones of Healthcare in the '90s, 1991; contbr. articles to profl. jours; editor, publisher Curtain Call, On The Front Lines, Prism. Recipient Disting. Nurse award Virginia Mason Med. Ctr., 1986, recognition Med. Coll. Ohio, 1988, Mary Hammer Greenwood award Ohio Nurses Assn., 1990, Outstanding Svc. award Franciscan Sisters of Poor Health System, 1991; Am. Acad. Nursing fellow, 1983. Mem. ANA, Am. Nurses Assn., Internat. Acad. Nursing Editors, Nat. League for Nursing, Am. Acad. Polit. and Social Scis., Hastings Ctr., Sigma Theta Tau. Home: 5932 Rapid Run Rd Cincinnati OH 45233-4852 Office: Metier Pub PO Box 11054 Cincinnati OH 45211-0054

CURTIN, MICHAEL FRANCIS, editor; b. Columbus, Ohio, Oct. 23, 1951; s. Robert Edward and Marie (Cummins) C.; m. Sharon Rhodes, May 26, 1976; children: Matthew, Christy. BA in Journalism, Ohio State U., 1973. Reporter The Columbus (Ohio) Dispatch, 1973-85, pub. affairs editor, 1985-94, exec. mng. editor, 1994-95, editor, 1995—; bd. dirs. The Columbus Dispatch, Ohio Mag. Author: (book) The Ohio Politics Almanac, 1996. Bd. dirs. YMCA, Columbus, 1996-97, Prevent Blindiness/Ohio, Columbus, 1997. Mem. Soc. Profl. Journalists, Athletic Club. Roman Catholic. Office: The Columbus Dispatch 34 S 3rd St Columbus OH 43215-4241

CURTIN, PHYLLIS, music educator, former dean, operatic singer; b. Clarksburg, W.Va.; d. E. Vernon and Betty R. (Robinson) Smith; m. Eugene Cook, May 6, 1956 (dec.); 1 child, Claudia Madeleine. BA, Wellesley Coll., 1943. Prof. Yale Sch. Music, New Haven, 1974-83; master Branford Coll. Yale U., New Haven, 1979-83; dean Sch. Arts, prof. music Boston U., 1983-91, prof. music, 1983—, dean emerita, prof. music, 1991—; artist-in-residence Tanglewood Music Ctr., Tanglewood, Lenox, Mass., 1965—; former mem. Nat. Coun. on the Arts; named Amb. for the Arts; tchr. master classes U.S., Can., Beijing, Moscow. Made recital debut Town Hall, N.Y.C., 1950, opera debut, N.Y.C. Opera in U.S. premiere of The Trial, 1953, recitals throughout, U.S. and fgn. countries; soprano soloist leading symphony orchestras; performer, tchr., Aspen Mus. Festival, 1953-57, appeared as Cressida in, Walton's Troilus and Cressida in, N.Y. premiere, 1955; title role in Floyd's: Susannah, world premiere, Tallahassee, 1955; title role in: Darius Milhaud's Medea, U.S. premiere, Brandeis U., 1955; world premiere Floyd's opera Wuthering Heights, 1958, Floyd's Passion of Jonathan Wade, 1959, Flower and Hawk, 1971; leading soprano: Vienna Staatsoper, 1960, 61; debut as Fiordiligi in Cosi Fan Tutte, Met. Opera Co., 1961; debut, La Scala Opera, Milan, 1962; U.S. premiere Benjamin Britten's War Requiem, 1963; world premiere of Darius Milhaud's opera La Mére Coupable, Geneva, 1966; U.S. premiere Dimitri Shostakovitch's Symphony No. 14, with Phila. Orch., 1971. Home: 9 Seekonk Rd Great Barrington MA 01230-1558

CURTIN, THOMAS LEE, ophthalmologist; b. Columbus, Ohio, Sept. 9, 1932; s. Leo Anthony and Mary Elizabeth (Burns) C.; m. Constance L. Sallman; children: Michael, Gregory, Thomas, Christopher. BS, Loyola U., L.A., 1954; MD, U. So. Calif., 1957; cert. navy flight surgeon, U.S. Naval Sch. Aerospace Med., 1959. Diplomate Am. Bd. Ophthalmology. Intern Ohio State U. Hosp., 1957-58; resident in ophthalmology U.S. Naval Hosp, San Diego, 1961-64; practice medicine specializing in ophthalmology Oceanside, Calif., 1967—; mem. staff Tri City, Scripps Meml. hosps.; sci. adv. bd. So. Calif. Soc. Prevention Blindness, 1973-76; bd. dirs. North Coast Surgery Ctr., Oceanside, 1987-96; cons. in field. Trustee Carlsbad (Calif.) Unified Sch. Dist., 1975-83, pres., 1979, 82, 83; trustee Carlsbad Libr., 1990-99, pres., 1993, 98. Officer, MC, USN, 1958-67. Mem. AMA, Calif. Med. Assn., San Diego County Med. Soc., Am. Acad. Ophthalmology, Aerospace Med. Assn., San Diego Acad. Ophthalmology (pres. 1979), Calif. Assn. Ophthalmology (bd. dirs.), Carlsbad Rotary, El Camino Country Club. Repubican. Roman Catholic. Office: 3231 Waring Ct Ste S Oceanside CA 92056-4510

CURTIN, TIMOTHY JOHN, lawyer; b. Detroit, Sept. 21, 1942; s. James J. and Irma Alice (Sirotti) C.; m. B. Colleen Lindsey, July 11, 1964; children: Kathleen, Mary. BA, U. Mich., 1964, JD, 1967. Bar: Ohio 1968, Mich. 1970, U.S. Dist. Ct. (no. dist.) Ohio 1968, U.S. Dist. Ct. (we. dist.) Mich. 1970, U.S. Dist. Ct. (ea. dist.) Mich. 1980, U.S. Ct. Appeals (6th cir.) 1968. Assoc. Taft, Stettinius & Hollister, Cin., 1967-70, McCobb, Heaney & Van't Hof, Grand Rapids, Mich., 1970-72; ptnr. Schmidt, Howlett, Van't Hof, Snell & Vana, Grand Rapids, 1972-83, Varnum, Riddering, Schmidt & Howlett, Grand Rapids, 1983—. Contbr. articles to legal publs. Treas. Kent County Dem. Com., 1976-78, chmn. 3rd Dist. Dem. Com., 1993—. Mem. ABA, Mich. Bar Assn., Grand Rapids Bar Assn., Fed.. Bar Assn., Am. Bankruptcy Inst., Egypt Valley C.C. Roman Catholic. Avocations: travel, fishing. Home: 448 Cambridge Blvd SE Grand Rapids MI 49506-2807 Office: Varnum Riddering Schmidt & Howlett Box 352 1700 Bridgewater Pl Grand Rapids MI 49501-0352*

CURTIS, ALLAN CRAIG, video and film production executive, consultant; b. Dodge City, Kans., Sept. 8, 1925; s. Allan Smith and Hazel Susan (Craig) C.; m. Suzanne Wallschlaeger, June 12, 1953; children: Fritz, Jonathan, Allan, Bradford. AB cum laude, U. So. Calif., 1950, postgrad. Editor, cameraman KTTV-TV (CBS), L.A., 1950-52; supervising editor recording dept. NBC, Hollywood, Calif., 1952-68; supr. editorial, rec., lab. & libr. NBC, Hollywood & Burbank, Calif., 1968-79, mgr. editorial, rec., lab. & libr., 1979; dir. recording & post-prodn. NBC, Burbank, Calif., 1980-89; cons. Curtis Group, Glendale, Calif., 1989—. Editor (TV) The Julie Andrews Show, 1965 (Emmy award), Lorne Greene spl., 1965 (Emmy nomination), Ezio Pinza in Capistrano, 1952, Another Evening with Fred Astaire, Danny Thomas spls., 1964-65, Shirley Temple's Storybook series, 1962-63; supervising editor Laugh-In, 1968-73, Bob Hope series spls., 1964-65, Red Skelton, Flip Wilson, Dean Martin, others, 1952-89; established 1st motion picture editorial procedures for TV, multi-track audio editing for TV; copatentee Double Frame 35mm RV Recorder. Chmn., leader Boy Scouts Am., Glendale, 1965-76; assoc. coach YMCA, Glendale, 1976-80; sec. bd. dirs. Our Saviour Ctr., El Monte, Calif., 1988-90; mem. adv. com. UCLA, 1988—, Pasadena C.C., 1975—, Glendale C.C., 1989—; bd. dirs. Chevy Chase Estates, 1997—. With USCG, 1943-46. Fellow Soc. Motion Picture & TV Engrs. (life, bd. govs. 1986-87, 89-90, chmn. edn. com., chmn. Hollywood sect. 1979, sec. & treas. 1978, bd. dirs. 1974-78, co-chair nat. conf. 1983, Eastman Kodak Gold Medal award 1985); mem. Acad. TV Arts and Scis. (bd. dirs. 1995—), Soc. TV Engrs. Republican. Episcopalian. Avocations: boating, hiking, travel, photography. Home: 1534 Belleau Rd Glendale CA 91206-1307

CURTIS, ALTON KENNETH, film company executive, clergyman; b. June 14, 1939; s. Alton T. and Althea A. Curtis; m. Dorothy Stevenson, Aug. 27, 1961; children: William Kenneth, Karen Althea. BA, Gordon Coll., 1961; MDiv, Gordon Conwell Theol. Sem., 1964, DD, 1987; PhD, Walden U., 1976; postgrad., Boston U., 1966-69, Pa. State U., 1971. Ordained to ministry Am. Bapt. Chs., 1964. Dir. comms. City Mission Soc., Boston, 1967-68; media cons. Am. Bapt. Chs., 1968-70; gen. mgr. Creative Venture Assocs., Valley Forge, Pa., 1970-72; pres. Gateway Films, Inc., Worcester, Pa., 1972—; chmn. Curtis Mark Comms., Lansdale, Pa., 1980-85, Vision Video, Inc., Worcester, 1981—; adj. faculty mem. Gordon Conwell Theol. Sem., Boston Theol. Inst., Harvard Div. Sch., 1965-67; adj. faculty Ea. Coll., St. Davids, Pa., 1974—; adj. faculty, prof. ch. history Ea. Bapt. Theol. sem., Pa., 1986-87, chmn., pres. Friends of the Libr., 1991-95; vis. prof. Inst. Youth Ministries, Colorado Springs, Colo., 1991; cons. Stratetic Careers Project, 1990-95. Author: Dates with Destiny, 1991, 92, From Christ to Constantine, 1991; founder, pub., editor Christian History mag., 1982-89, sr. editor, 1990—; editor, pub. (periodicals) Glimpses, Pastor's Notes, 1990—; writer, prodr. (film) First Fruits, 1982; prodr., dir., author The Good Seed, 1985; assoc. prodr. Shadowlands, 1986 (Internat. Emmy); writer, prodr. Comenius, 1987, (TV documentary series) The Trial and Testimony of the Early Church, 1989 (Gold medal Houston Internat. Film Festival, Chris award Columbus Film Festival, Angel award Religion in Media, Best Series award Christian Visual Media Internat.), (TV series) Discovering the Bible, 1995; prodn. assoc., cons. (TV documentary series) Mine Eyes Have Seen the Glory, 1992; prodr., host Refamation Overview, 1994; prodr., dir. (video documentary series) Jesus The New Way (Gold award Flagstaff Internat. Film Festival 1998, Chris award Columbus Internat. Film Festival); exec. prodr. (film) Candle in the Dark, 1998 (Gold award Christian Broadcasting Commn. of U.K. 1998, Gold award Worldfest Houston, 1999); co-prodr. film So Who Is This Jesus?; editl. dir. Pocket Classics; contbr. articles on mass media and religion to mags. Mem. adv. bd. Episcopal Radio-TV Found., 1991-96; bd. dirs. Martin Luther Acad., Wittenberg, Germany, Christianity Today Inc. v.p. Internat. Christian Visual Media Assn., 1993-94; sr. pastor Lower Providence Bapt. Ch., Collegeville, Pa., 1977-80; pres. Christian History Inst., 1983—; instr. YMCA Handicapped Persons Swimming Program, Lansdale, Pa., 1986-97. Recipient Best Screenplay of Yr. award and Best Film of Yr. award Acad. Christian Cinemagraphic Arts, 1983, Chris award Columbus Film Festival, Gold award Houston Internat. Film Festival, Silver award Charleston Internat. Film Festival, Best Series award Internat. Christian Visual Media. Mem. Montgomery County Bar Assn. Found. (bd. dirs. 1988—), Phi Alpha Chi. Office: Gateway Films Inc PO Box 540 Worcester PA 19490-0540

CURTIS, ARNOLD BENNETT, lumber company executive; b. Astoria, Oreg., May 5, 1940; s. Arnold Bennett and Irja Virginia (Thompson) C.; m. Erica Katherine Mitchell, Dec. 23, 1985; children: Braden Thomas, Bryce Bennett. BS, Oreg. State U., 1962. Brewing chemist Gen. Brewing, San Francisco, 1962-67; v.p. N.W. Hardwoods, Inc., Portland, Oreg., 1967-71, pres., 1971-80, also bd. dirs.; pres. N.W. Hardwoods divsn. Weyerhauser Co., Federal Way, Wash., 1980-97, v.p. Hardwood Bus. Group, 1990-98; bd. dirs. Puyallup Internat. Inc., Weyerhaeuser New Zealand Ltd. Mem. adv. bd. Ctr. Retail and Bus. Market Strategy. Mem. Hardwood Mfrs. Assn. (dir., exec. com. 1985-95, pres. 1993). *When you commit yourself to an answer it's best to always tell the truth - then you never have to worry about remembering what you said.*

CURTIS, CARL THOMAS, former senator; b. Minden, Nebr., Mar. 15, 1905; s. Frank O. and Alberta Mae (Smith) C.; m. Lois Wylie-Atwater, June 6, 1931 (dec. Sept. 1970); children: Clara Mae (Mrs. James A. Hopkins) (dec.), Carl Thomas; m. Mildred Genier Baker, Dec. 1, 1972. Ed., Nebr. Wesleyan U. Bar: Nebr. 1930. Tchr. Minden Schs.; practiced in Minden; county atty., 1931-34; mem. 76th to 83d congresses from 1st Nebr. dist.; U.S. senator from Nebr., 1955-79. Author: To Remind, Forty Years Against the Tide. Mem. Nebr. Bar Assn., Masons, Odd Fellows, Elks, Theta Chi. Republican. Presbyterian. Home: 1300 G St Lincoln NE 68508-3705

CURTIS, CAROLINE A. S., community health and oncology nurse; b. Salem, Mass., June 7, 1941; d. Lawrence A. and Celestine L. (Wyman) Sager; m. John S. Curtis, July 31, 1981; children: Richard H. Smith, Craig A. Smith. Diploma, Lynn (Mass.) Hosp., 1962. Cert. oncology nurse. Head nurse, developer inpatient oncology unit Atlanticare Med. Ctr., Lynn, 1981-86; hospice nurse Greater Lynn Vis. Nurses Assn., Lynn, 1986-87; case manager Bon Secours Home Health, Englewood, Fla., 1988—; terminal care coord., oncology & pain cons., 1992—, terminal care coord.; bd. dirs., guest spkr. support group Am. Cancer Soc.; mem. pain mgmt. task force Bon Secours health Sys., 1996—. Mem. Care of the Dying. Mem. Oncology Nursing Soc., Internat. Soc. Nurses in Cancer Care, Home Health Nursing Assn., Am. Pain Soc., Am. Soc. Pain Mgmt. Nurses. Home: #201 6610 Gasparilla Pines Blvd Englewood FL 34224-7517

CURTIS, CHARLES EDWARD, Canadian government official; b. Winnipeg, Man., Can., July 28, 1931; s. Samuel and May (Goodison) C.; m. Hilda Marion Simpson, Oct. 30, 1954; 1 dau., Nancy Maude. C.A., U. Manitoba, 1955. Chartered acct. Dunwoody & Co., Winnipeg, 1949-54; chief assessor nat. revenue, income tax bd. Province of N.B., Can., 1954-67; asst. dep. minister budget fin. and adminstrn. Province of Man., Winnipeg, 1967-75, dep. minister, 1976-96; past CEO Man. Energy Authority; acting CEO MTX subs. Man. Telephone Sys.; mem. Man. Hydro-Electric Bd.; mem. investment coms. Superannuation Bd.; fin. advisor Min. of Fin.; exec.-in-residence faculty of mgmt. U. Man.; dir. Indsl. Bank of Japan (Can.). Fellow Can. Inst. Chartered Accts. (past chmn. pub. sector acctg. and audit standards com.); mem. Man. Inst. Chartered Accts. (pres. 1975-76), Law Soc. of Man. (lay bencher), Rotary (hon. treas. 1974—), Manitoba Club. Home: 596 South Dr, Winnipeg, MB Canada R3T 0B1 Office: Provincial Govt Province of Manitoba, 109-450 Broadway Ave, Winnipeg, MB Canada R3C 0V8

CURTIS, CHESTER HARRIS, lawyer, retired bank executive; b. Montgomery, Ala., Mar. 21, 1913; s. Chester Dare and Jennie Mae (Harris) C.; m. Katherine Fletcher Parchman; children: Chester H. Jr. BA, U. Miss., 1935, LLB, 1937. Ptnr. Holcomb & Curtis, Clarksdale, Miss., 1937-69; vice chmn. bd., sec. United Southern Bank, Clarksdale, 1969-89; of counsel Holcomb-Dunbar Law Firm, Clarksdale, Miss., 1990—; pres. Miss. State Bar Assn., 1968-69. Pres. Coahoma County C. of C., Clarksdale, Miss., 1974. Served to lt. USNR, 1942-45, PTO. Recipient Silver Beaver award Nat. Council Boy Scouts Am., 1953. Mem. U. Miss. Alumni Assn. (pres. 1959, named to Hall of Fame 1985). Republican. Presbyterian. Lodge: Rotary (local pres. 1953-54) (Paul Harris fellow 1984). Avocations: golf, tennis, hunting. Office: Holcomb-Dunbar Law Firm 152 Delta Ave Clarksdale MS 38614-4212

CURTIS, CHRISTOPHER BRYAN, secondary education educator; b. Three Rivers, Mich., May 6, 1967; s. Jon Lee and Susan Kay (Gearhart) C.; m. Laura Cameron Lyon, June 22, 1996. BA, Ea. Mich. U., 1995, MA, 1999. Cert. secondary edn. tchr., Mich. Police comm. officer Ypsilanti (Mich.) City Police, 1987-88, Ea. Mich. Univ. Police, Ypsilanti, 1987-91; security officer Washtenaw C.C., Ann Arbor, 1992-94; retail detective Marshalls Inc., Ann Arbor, 1991-94; tchr. Redford (Mich.) Union Schs., 1995; tchr. project edn. Ann Arbor Pub. Schs., 1995—; instr. BLS Huron Valley Ambulance, Ann Arbor, 1997—. Stream adoption mem. Huron River Watershed Coun., Ann Arbor. Mem. Nat. Coun. Tchrs. of English, BMW Motorcycle Owners Am., Mich. Alternative Edn. Assn. Democrat. Presbyterian. Avocations: motorcycles, fishing, dog training, weightlifting, writing. Home: 315 Cambridge Dr Dexter MI 48130-2506 Office: Project Edn Ann Arbor Pub Schs 2800 Stone School Rd Ann Arbor MI 48104-7434

CURTIS, DAVID LAMBERT, rheumatologist, educator; b. Salt Lake City, Oct. 31, 1945; s. David Haws and Rosetta (Egli) C.; m. Nora C. Blay, May 25, 1980; 1 child, Andrew Blay. BA, Colgate U., 1968; MD, Columbia U., 1972. Diplomate Am. Bd. Internal Medicine, Am. Bd. Rheumatology. Internship in medicine Johns Hopkins Hosp., Balt., 1972-73, residency in medicine, 1973-75; med. dir. French Hosp. Health Plan, San Francisco, 1978-83; pvt. practice, San Francisco, 1983—; asst. clin. prof. medicine U. Calif., San Francisco. Fellow Am. Coll. Rheumatology. Office: Pacific Rheumatology Assocs Med Group 2100 Webster St Ste 112 San Francisco CA 94115-2374

CURTIS, DOUGLAS HOMER, small business owner; b. Jackson, Mich., July 19, 1934; s. Homer K. and Luella D. (Hall) C.; m. Jean A. Breaux; children: Rebecca, Linda, Colleen, Robert. BA, Park Coll., Parkville, Mo., 1956. With Gen. Electric Co., 1958-69, mgr. Boston region Gen. Electric Supply Co. div., 1967-69; v.p. fin. and adminstrn. internat. Data Corp., Boston, 1969; v.p. fin. Franklin Electric Co. Inc., Bluffton, Ind., 1969-80; pres. Curtis Assocs., Inc., Bluffton, 1980-82; pres., chief operating officer Satelco, Inc., San Antonio, 1983-84; v.p. adminstrn. Lyall Electric Co., Kendallville, Ind., 1984-86; pres., owner Flexible Personnel Group of Cos., Inc., Ft. Wayne, Ind., 1987-97, Nat. On-Site Pers., 1991—, HR America, 1992—; bd. dirs. Wabash Valley Mfg., Inc., Silver Lake, Ind.; pres. Wells County (Ind.) Hosp. Authority, 1974-75. Served to capt. USMCR, 1956-58. Mem. Nat. Assn. Securities Dealers (vicechmn. fin. 1980, chmn. fin. com. 1980), Fin. Execs. Inst. (chpt. dir. 1975). Home: 3206 Covington Lake Dr Fort Wayne IN 46804-2516 Office: 1833 Magnavox Way Fort Wayne IN 46804-1539

CURTIS, GARNISS HEARFIELD, geology educator; b. San Rafael, Calif., May 27, 1919; s. Chester Alphonse Kemp and Elizabeth Garniss (Hearfield) C.; m. Dorette D. Davis, May 15, 1942 (dec. Oct. 1987); children: Penelope, Ann, Robin. BS, U. Calif., Berkeley, 1942, PhD, 1951. Registered geologist, Calif. Mining engr. Christmas (Ariz.) Copper Corp., 1942-45; geologist Shell Oil Co., Ventura, Calif., 1945-46; prof. geologist and geophysics U. Calif., Berkeley, 1951-89, prof. emeritus, 1989—, chair dept. geology and geophysics, 1971-72; dir. Geochronology Ctr. Inst. Human Origins, Berkeley, 1985-91, dir. geochronology, 1986-91, sr. scientist, 1991-94; sr. geochronologist Berkeley Geochronology Ctr., 1994—; chair 8th Internat. Conf. on Geochronology, Berkeley, 1990-94. Author: A Guide to Dating Methods, 1981, (with others) Milestones in Human Evolution, 1993; co-author: The Sutter Buttes of California, 1977; contbr. articles to profl. jours. Recipient Berkeley Citation award, 1989; Miller Inst. fellow, 1958, 60. Fellow Calif. Acad. Scis. (Fellows Medal 1995), AAAS (Newcomb Cleveland award 1963, fellow, 1998); mem. Am. Geophys. Union. Avocations: music, travel, camping. Home: 10 Saint James Ct Orinda CA 94563-1114 Office: Berkeley Geochronology Ctr 2455 Ridge Rd Berkeley CA 94709-1211*

CURTIS, GEORGE CLIFTON, psychiatry educator, clinical research investigator; b. St. Petersburg, Fla., Dec. 10, 1926; s. George Clifton and Anne Mildred (Perry) C.; m. Marion Margaret Johnson, Sept. 24, 1955; children: Paul Jefferson, Andrew Warren, Brian Ross. BA, Lambuth Coll., 1950; MD, Vanderbilt U., 1953; MSc, McGill U., Montreal, Que., Can., 1959; grad., Phila. Psychoanalytic Inst., 1968. Diplomate Am. Bd. Psychiatry and Neurology. From assoc. in psychiatry to assoc. prof. psychiatry U. Pa., Phila., 1959-72; prof. psychiatry U. Mich., Ann Arbor, 1972-97, acting chmn. psychiatry, 1983-84, chief of adult psychiatry, 1984-87, prof. emeritus, 1997—; External reviewer NIMH, Bethesda, Md., 1985, 86, 89. Guest editor: Psychiatric Clinics of North America, 1985; manuscript reviewer for many sci. jours.; mem. editl. bd. Anxiety Jour., 1994-97, Depression and Anxiey Jour., 1997—. With USN, 1945-46. Fellow Am. Psychiat. Assn. (life, mem. revision com. DSM-III-R, cons. work group Diagnostic and Stats. Manual of Mental Disorders IV); mem. AAAS, Am. Psychosomatic Soc. (coun. 1969-72, mem. program com. 1969), Soc. Biol. Psychiatry, Anxiety Disorders Assn. Am. (bd. dirs. 1981-91, chmn. sci. adv. com. 1985-91, chmn. nominating com. 1989-91), Am. Acad. Psychiatry and the Law. Avocations: golf, fishing, skiing, history. Home: 2206 Rivenoak Court Ann Arbor MI 48103 Office: Univ Mich Dept Psychiatry 1500 E Medical Center Dr Ann Arbor MI 48109-0005

CURTIS, GEORGE WARREN, lawyer; b. Merrill, Wis., Sept. 24, 1936; s. George Gregory and Rose E. (Zimmerman) C.; m. Judith Olson, 1956 (div. 1966); m. Mary Pelman, 1967 (dec. 1973); children: George, Catherine Edwall, Eric, Greg, Paul, David; m. Mary Ruth Kersztyn, Dec. 27, 1973 (div. 1999); children: Emily, Benjamin; m. Suzette Bigler Whyte, July 10, 1999. BA, U. Minn., 1959; JD, U. Wis., 1962. Bar: Wis. 1962, Fla. 1968. Assoc. Russell & Curtis, Merrill, 1962-68; ptnr. Nolan, Engler, Yakes & Curtis, Oshkosh, Wis., 1968-74, Curtis, MacKenzie, Haase & Brown, Oshkosh, 1974-83, Curtis, Wilde & Neal, Oshkosh, 1984-96, Curtis & Neal, Oshkosh, 1997—. Mem. ATLA, Am. Coll. Trial Lawyers, Am. Bd. Trial Advocates (pres. Wis. chpt.), Wis. Acad. Trial Lawyers (bd. dirs. 1978-83, treas. 1984, sec. 1985, v.p. 1986, pres. 1987), Assn. Trial Lawyers Am. (bd. govs.), Internat. Soc. Barristers. Democrat. Avocations: conservationist, dog trainer. Home: 7361 Canary Rd Pickett WI 54964-9724 Office: Curtis Law Offices 2905 Universal St Oshkosh WI 54904-6341

CURTIS, JAMES C., cultural organization administrator/history educator. Dir. Winterthur Program in Early Am. Culture, Newark, Del.; prof., history U. Del., Newark. Office: University of Delaware Winterthur Prg Early Am Culture 304 Old College Newark DE 19716

CURTIS, JAMES THEODORE, lawyer; b. Lowell, Mass., July 8, 1923; s. Theodore D. and Maria (Souliotis) Koutras; m. Kleanthe D. Dusopol, June 25, 1950; children: Madelon Mary, Theodore James, Stephanie Diane, Gregory Theodosius, James Theodore Jr. BA, U. Mich., 1948; JD, Harvard U., 1951; ScD (hon.), U. Mass., 1972. Bar: Mass. 1951. Assoc. Adams & Blinn, Boston, 1951-52; legal asst., asst. atty. gen. Mass., 1952-53; pvt. practice law, Lowell, 1953-57; sr. ptnr. firm Goldman & Curtis, and predecessors, Lowell and Boston, 1957—. Chmn. Lowell and Greater Lowell Heart Fund, 1967-68; mem. adv. bd. Salvation Army, sec., 1956-58; mem. Bd. Higher Edn. Mass., 1967-72; elected mem. Lowell Charter Commn., 1969-71; del. Dem. Party State Convs., 1956-60; trustee U. Mass., Lowell, 1963-72, chmn. bd., 1968-72; bd. dirs. U. Mass. Rsch. Found., Lowell, 1965-72, Merrimack Valley Health Planning Coun., 1969-72. Served with US Army, 1943-46, special agent Counter Intelligence Corps, 1945-46. Decorated Knight Order Orthodox Crusade Holy Sepulcher. Mem. ABA, ATLA, Mass. Bar Assn., Middlesex County Bar Assn., Lowell Bar Assn., Mass. Trial Lawyers Assn., Mass. Acad. Trial Lawyers, Am. Judicature Soc., Harvard Law Sch. Alumni Assn., U. Mich. Alumni Assn., Lowell Hist. Soc., DAV, Delta Epsilon Pi, Harvard Club of Lowell (pres. 1969-71, bd. dirs.), Masons. Democrat. Greek Orthodox. Home: 111 Rivercliff Rd Lowell MA 01852-1471 Office: Goldman & Curtis 144 Merrimack St Lowell MA 01852-1713

CURTIS, JAMIE LEE, actress; b. L.A., Nov. 22, 1958; d. Tony Curtis and Janet Leigh; m. Christopher Guest; 1 child. Student, U. of the Pacific. Actress: (films) Halloween, 1978, The Fog, 1980, Prom Night, 1980, Terror Train, 1980, Halloween II, 1981, Road Games, 1981, Love Letters, 1983, Trading Places, 1983, Grandview USA, 1984, Adventures of Buckaroo Banzai, 1984, Perfect, 1985, Amazing Grace and Chuck, 1987, Un Homme Amoreux, 1987, Dominick and Eugene, 1988, A Fish Called Wanda, 1988, Blue Steel, 1990, Queens Logic, 1991, My Girl, 1991, Forever Young, 1992, Mother's Boys, 1994, My Girl 2, 1994, True Lies, 1994 (Golden Globe award Best Actress - Musical or Comedy), House Arrest, 1996, Ellen's Energy Adventure, 1996, Fierce Creatures, 1996, Halloween U2O, 1998, Homegrown, 1998, Daddy and Them, 1999, Virus, 1999; (TV pilots) Callahan, She's in the Army Now, 1981, Tall Tales, (TV series) Operation Petticoat, 1977-78, Anything but Love, 1990-93, (TV movies) Death of a Centerfold: The Dorothy Stratten Story, 1981, Money on the Side, 1982. As Summers Die, 1982, The Heidi Chronicles, 1995, Nicolas' Gift, 1997; author: When I Was Little, 1993; dir.: Anything But Love, 1989. Office: CAA care Rick Kurtzman 9830 Wilshire Blvd Beverly Hills CA 90212-1804*

CURTIS, JESSE WILLIAM, JR., retired federal judge; b. San Bernardino, Calif., Dec. 26, 1905; s. Jesse William and Ida L. (Seymour) C.; m. Mildred F. Mort, Aug. 24, 1930; children: Suzanne, Jesse W., Clyde Hamilton, Christopher Cowles. AB, U. Redlands, 1928, LLD, 1973; JD, Harvard Law Sch., 1931. Bar: Calif. 1931. Pvt. practice, 1931-35; mem. firms Guthrie & Curtis, San Bernardino, 1935-40, Curtis & Curtis, 1946-50, Curtis, Knauf, Henry & Farrell, 1950-53; judge Superior Ct. of Calif., 1953-62; judge U.S. Dist. Ct. (cen. dist.) Calif., 1962-90, ret., 1990; with Jud. Arbitration and Mediations Svc., L.A., 1990-95; rep. dist. ct. on Jud. Council U.S., 1972-74. Chmn. San Bernardino Sch. Bd., 1942-46, mem., 1946-49; mem. Del Rosa Bd. Edn., 1950-53; chmn. San Bernardino County Heart Fund; dir., past pres. YMCA; bd. dirs. GoodWill Industries, Crippled Children's Soc., Arrowhead United Fund; adv. bd. Community Hosp. Mem. ABA, Calif. State Bar, Orange County Bar Assn., Am. Judicature Soc., Am. Law Inst., Newport Harbor Yacht Club, Phi Delta Phi. Democrat. Congregationalist. Home: 19191 Harvard Ave Apt 337A Irvine CA 92612-4650

CURTIS, JOHN BARRY, archbishop; b. June 19, 1933; s. Harold Boyd and Eva B. (Saunders) C.; m. Patricia Emily Simpson, 1959; four children. BA, U. Toronto, 1955, LTh, 1958; student, Theol. Coll., Chichester, Sussex, Eng.; DD (hon.), Trinity Coll., 1985, U. Toronto, 1985. Ordained to deacon The Anglican Ch. of Can., 1958, priest, 1959. Asst. curate Holy Trinity, Pembroke, Ont., 1958-61; rector Parish of March, Kanata, Ont., 1961-65, St. Stephen's Ch., Buckingham, Que., 1965-69, All Saints (Westboro), Ottawa, Ont., 1969-78; program dir. Diocese of Ottawa, 1978-80; rector Christ Ch., Elbow Park, Calgary, Alta., 1980-83; bishop Diocese of Calgary, 1983-99; archbishop Calgary-Met. of Rupert's Land, 1994-99. Mem. Ranchmen's Club (Calgary). Office: Diocese Calgary, 3015 Glencoe Rd SW, Calgary, AB Canada T2S 2L9

CURTIS, JOHN J., medical educator; b. Rochester, N.Y., Jan. 16, 1944; s. John Joseph and Mabel (Leatherman) C.; m. Vicky Burleson, Oct. 2, 1987. BS, U. Scranton, 1966; MD, Georgetown U., 1970. Diplomate Am. Bd. Internal Medicine, Am. Bd. Nephrology. Asst. prof. medicine U. Ky. Med. Ctr., Lexington, Ky., 1974-79; assoc. prof. medicine U. Ala., Birmingham, 1979-85, prof. medicine, 1985—, prof. surgery, 1991—, dir. The Transplant Ctr., 1999—; program dir. Gen. Clin. Rsch. Ctr., Birmingham,

1988-98; mem. med. adv. bd. Ala. Kidney Found., Birmingham, 1989—. Asst. editor Am. Jour. Kidney Diseases, 1987-92; transplantion editor (book) Yearbook of Nephrology, 1992-96. 1st lt. USAR, 1970-72. Mem. Am. Soc. Nephrology, Internat. Soc. Nephrology, The Transplantation Soc., Am. Soc. Transplant Physicians, European Dialysis & Transplant Assn. Office: U Ala Birmingham Divsn Nephrology THT 643 1900 University Blvd Birmingham AL 35294-0006

CURTIS, JOHN JOSEPH, lawyer; b. Fairmont, W.Va., Nov. 23, 1942; s. John Joseph and Marie Francis (Christopher) C.; m. Shirley Ann Slater, Oct. 15, 1971 (div. June 1993); children: Christopher, Kevin. AB, U. W.Va., 1964, JD, 1967. Bar: W.Va. 1967, Ill. 1972, Calif. 1979. Pvt. practice law South Charleston, W.Va., 1967-68; chief counsel, asst. dir. W.Va. Tax Dept., Charleston, 1968-71; tax atty. Sears, Roebuck & Co., Chgo., 1971-73; chief tax counsel, dir. taxes Pacific Lighting, L.A., 1973-87; ptnr. Baker & Hostetler, L.A., 1987-93, Law Offices of John Curtis, L.A., 1994—. Com. mem. Pasadena Tournament Roses, 1978-93. Lt. comdr. USNR, 1968-80. Mem. ABA, L.A. County Bar Assn. (chmn. com. 1989), Calif. Bar Assn., Inst. Property Tax, So. Calif.Tax Found. (pres. 1990-96), L.A. Taxpayers Assn. (pres. 1990-95), Calif. Taxpayers Assn. (pres. 1987-88). Avocations: skiing, scuba, fishing. Office: 2 Arado Rancho Santa Margarita CA 92688-2749

CURTIS, LEGRAND R., JR., lawyer; b. Ogden, Utah, Aug. 1, 1952. BA summa cum laude, Brigham Young U., 1975; JD cum laude, U. Mich., 1978. Bar: Utah 1978, U.S. Ct. Appeals (10th cir.) 1985, U.S. Ct. Claims 1986, U.S. Supreme Ct. 1987. Ptnr. Manning, Curtis Bradshaw & Bednar, LLC, Salt Lake City, 1997—. Mem. Utah State Bar, Salt Lake County Bar Assn. Office: Manning Curtis Bradshaw & Bednar LLC 370 E South Temple Ste 200 Salt Lake City UT 84111-1259

CURTIS, LORETTA O'ELLEN, retired construction executive; b. Washington, Pa., Apr. 5, 1937; d. Monroe and Mildred (Carr) Bogan; m. Joseph H. Dudley (div. Oct. 1964); children: Ronald S., Joseph T., Mildred M.; m. Wayne J. Curtis (dec. 12/98). AS, Franklin U., 1983, BS, 1989; Grad., Columbus Leadership Program, 1991; grad., Premier Sch. of Travel, 1996. With Bur. Employment Svcs., Columbus, Ohio, 1962-87, examiner, equal employment opportunity officer, 1983-87, ret., 1987; v.p. Aries Constrn., Inc., Columbus, 1988-91, pres., 1991-96; ret., 1996; mediator small claims divsn. Franklin County; tour leader GLAMER; chmn. Sch. of Ushering ICUA (Interdenominational Church Ushers Assn.), Columbus, substitute tchg., Columbus Pub. Schs., 1999—. Mem. Interdenominational Ch. Ushers Assn. Columbus. Recipient Plaque ICUA of Dayton, 1989, ICUA of Columbus, 1991. Mem. NAFE, Nat. Assn. Parliamentarians (registered parliamentarian), Nat. United Ch. Ushers Assn., Ohio Assn. Colored Women (treas. 1990-94), Ohio Assn. Parliamentarians (pres. 1989-90), ICUA of Columbus (pres. 1977-84), Mayme Moore Club (pres. 1990-93, cert. 1989). Avocations, cooking, reading, golf, volunteer work. Home: 2257 Century Dr Columbus OH 43211-1919 Office: Aries Constrn Inc 983 E Main St # 7014 Columbus OH 43205-2342

CURTIS, MARVIN VERNELL, music educator; b. Chgo., Feb. 12, 1951; s. John Wesley Jr. and Dorothy Marva Curtis. MusB, North Park Coll., 1972; MA, Presbyn. Sch. Christian Edn., 1974; EdD, U. of Pacific, 1990. Asst. prof. music Calif. State U.-Stanislaus, Turlock, 1988-91; assoc. prof. music Va. Union U., Richmond, 1991-94, Lane Coll., Jackson, Tenn., 1995-96, Fayetteville (N.C.) State U., 1996—; music advisor In Harmony series Richmond Symphony, 1996—. Composer City on the Hill written for 1st Inauguration of Pres. Clinton, 1993; contbr. articles to profl. jours. Bd. dirs. Fayetteville Symphony, 1998—, Cmty. Concert Series, 1998—. Recipient Key to City, Savannah, Ga., 1992, Medallion of City of Richmond, Mayor's Office, 1993, Outstanding Rsch. award Nat. Assn. for Equal Opportunity, 1992. Mem. Music Educators Nat. Conf., Nat. Coun. for Black Studies, Am. Choral Dirs. Assn. Democrat. E-mail: mcurtis@chi1.uncfsu.edu. Home: 4911 Cooper Rd Fayetteville NC 28311

CURTIS, MARY C., journalist; b. Balt.; d. Thomas Eugene and Evelyn Cecelia (Thomas) C.; m. Martin F. Olsen, Oct. 16, 1976; 1 child, Zane Anthony Curtis-Olsen. BA, Fordham U., N.Y.C. Copy editor, wire editor The Arizona Daily Star, Tucson, 1981-83; asst. features editor, travel editor The Baltimore Sun, 1983-84, features editor, arts & entertainment, 1984-85; copy editor, culture & style The New York Times, N.Y.C., 1985-88, asst. editor, The Living Arts, 1988-90, editor, The Living Arts, 1990-92, editor The Home Section, 1992-93, edn. life editor, 1993-94; features editor The Charlotte Observer, 1994—; editor The Maynard Inst. Editing Program for Minority Journalists, U. Ariz., 1981; Cmty. Journalism Wkshp., Poynter Inst., St. Petersburg, 1996. Recipient Excellence award Internat. Assn. Bus. Comms., 1979, recipient, Excellence in Feature Writing awd., 2d place, commentary, Amer. Assn. of Sunday and Feature Editors, 1995. Mem. Nat. Assn. Black Journalists, Am. Assn. Sunday & Feature Editors, Soc. Profl. Journalists. Avocations: reading, theater, music, fitness. Office: The Charlotte Observer 600 S Tryon St Charlotte NC 28202-1842

CURTIS, MARY ELLEN (MARY CURTIS HOROWITZ), publishing company executive; b. Paragould, Ark., Oct. 24, 1946; d. Lloyd E. and Jean (Cain) C.; m. Irving Louis Horowitz, Oct. 30, 1979. AB cum laude, Washington U., St. Louis, 1968. Editl. dir. Transaction Pubs., New Brunswick, N.J., 1968-74, exec. v.p., 1987-97, pres., 1997—, chmn. bd. dirs., 1994-97; editor in chief Praeger Pubs. subs. CBS Ednl. Pub., N.Y.C., 1974-79; v.p., pub. periodicals John Wiley and Sons, N.Y.C., 1979-87; v.p. Scripta Techica subs. John Wiley and Sons, Washington, 1984-87; mem. mgmt. bd. MIT Press, 1998—; vice chair, trustee Irving Louis Horowitz Found. for Social Policy, 1998—; chair adv. com. Serials Industry Systems, 1985-88; dir. Transaction Pubs. (U.K.) Ltd.; lectr. in field. Contbr. articles to profl. jours. Mem. Soc. Scholarly Pubs. (bd. dirs. 1984-88), Assn. Am. Pubs. (Freedom to Read com.). Jewish.

CURTIS, ORLIE LINDSEY, JR., lawyer; b. Hutchinson, Kans., Feb. 27, 1934; s. Orlie Lindsey and Lillian Esther (Barnes) C.; m. Idella Mae Krueger, June 5, 1955; children: Elizabeth, Victoria. BA with distinction, Union Coll., Lincoln, Nebr., 1954; MS, Purdue U., 1956; PhD, U. Tenn., 1961; JD, U. So. Calif., 1977. Bar: Calif. 1977. Group chief Oak Ridge Nat. Lab., 1956-63; lab. dir., sci. fellow Northrop Corp., Hawthorne, Calif., 1963-77; ptnr. firm Kroloff, Belcher, Smart, Perry & Christopherson, 1980—; vis. lectr. physics U. Calif., Berkeley, 1970-71; adv. bd. physics dept. U. Ky., 1970-73; lectr. Nat. Symposia Products Liability and Ins. Law. Author: Point Defects in Solids, 1975; contbr. articles to profl. jours. Bd. dirs. So. Calif. Conf. Seventh-day Adventists, 1970-74, Newbury Park Acad., 1970-74, Lodi Acad., 1979-84, No. Calif. Conf. Seventh-day Adventists, 1980-86, 95—, Dameron Hosp. Found., 1985—, N.Am. Divsn. Seventh-day Adventists, 1997—. Fellow Am. Phys. Soc., IEEE (chmn. radiation effects com. 1970-73); mem. Assn. Def. Coun. No. Calif., Def. Rsch. Inst., State Bar Calif., San Joaquin County Bar Assn., Adventist Attys. Assn. (pres. 1983-84), Internat. Assn. Def. Counsel, Order of Coif, Am. Bd. Trial Advocates. Patentee in field. Home: 5530 El Greco Dr Stockton CA 95212-9228

CURTIS, PAUL JAMES, mime; b. Boston, Aug. 29, 1927; s. Lawrence D. and Madeleine Maria (Schwager) C. Studied directing with Erwin Piscator, New Sch. for Social Rsch., 1947-49. Dir. Deal Conservatory Theatre, 1948; actor in film, TV, theatre Paris, 1949-52; founder, dir. Am. Mime Theatre, N.Y.C., 1952—; founder Am. Mime, Inc., N.Y.C., 1970—, Internat. Mimes & Pantomimists, 1972-74; chmn. mime dept. Am. Acad. Dramatic Arts, N.Y.C., 1956-71; sr. lectr. Cornell U., Ithaca, N.Y., 1969-89; instr. mime Bennington (Vt.) Coll., Jacob's Pillow Dance Festival, Mass., Ohio U., Austin Coll., Goodman Sch. Drama, Chgo., Pace U., N.Y.C., Hunter Coll., N.Y.C., Met. Opera Ballet Sch., N.Y.C., New Sch. Social Rsch., N.Y.C., Gene Frankel Theatre Workshop, N.Y.C., Guggenheim Mus., N.Y.C., Johns Hopkins U., Balt., Am. Conservatory Theatre, San Francisco, Circle in Sq. Theatre Sch., N.Y.C., Sarah Lawrence Coll., N.Y., D'Youville Coll., N.Y., Lincoln Sch., Calif., Fairleigh Dickinson U., N.J., Stockton State Coll. N.J., Rutgers U., New Brunswick, N.J., The Leonardo's, Paris; Am. mime course established at Salle Pleyel, Paris, 1998. With USN, 1944-46. Author: (textbook) American Mime, the Medium, 1952, (plays) The Pinball Machine, 1953, Fate, 1953, The Tell Tale Heart, 1953, Escapade, 1953, The Demon Lover, 1953, Of Identity, 1953, Once Upon An Island, 1954, Monolotry, 1954, The Triple Goddess, 1954, The Western, 1954, Improvisation, 1955, Presentation, 1955, Eden, 1956, Abstraction, 1956, Commedia, 1956, Dreams I, 1958, The Scarecrow, 1962, Dreams II, 1962, The Godstuff, 1962, The Lovers, 1963, Birds, 1965, Female, 1967, Light, 1968, Hurly-Burly, 1969, Evolution, 1973, Sludge, 1974, Six, 1975, Work in Progress, 1976, Abstraction, 1977, The Unitaur, 1982, Peepshow, 1988, Pageant, 1989, Music Box, 1991, Couplings, 1999. Mem. AEA, AFTRA, Nat. Movement Theatre Assn. Avocations: antique collector, ultralight pilot. E-mail: Am-Mime@aol.com. Office: Am Mime Theatre 61 4th Ave Fl 2 New York NY 10003-5204

CURTIS, PAULA ANNETTE, elementary and secondary education educator; b. Natrona Heights, Pa., Apr. 16, 1953; d. Stephen John and Josephine Kathleen (Killian) C. BS In Edn., Geneva Coll., 1974; postgrad., U. Vt., 1975, Pa. State U., New Kensington, 1978. Cert. religious edn. tchr., Pitts. Diocese. Tchr. Transfiguration Sch., Russellton, Pa., 1979—, dir. religious edn., 1995-98; tchr. continuing edn. C.C. of Allegheny County, Pitts., 1992—, Pa. State U., New Kensington, 1988—; tchr. O'Mara Driving Sch., Lower Burrell, Pa., 1976—, Lenape Votech., 1990—; CCD tchr. Transfiguration Sch., Russellton, 1995—, head tchr., head fine arts dept., 1995—; chmn. vision and values in Pitts. Diocese, Transfiguration Sch., 1980—; CCD tchr. St. Clement Parish, Tarentum, Pa., 1986-92, dir. religious edn., 1987-92; dir. religious edn. St. Joseph Parish, Natrona, Pa., 1992-93; product tester Nat. Family Opinion Poll, 1987—; model Van Enterprises, Cranberry, Pa., 1989-92; tchr. driver edn. Plum (Pa.) Sr. H.S., 1996-98. Vol. Help Beautify the Cmty. with Art, Russellton. Mem. Nat. Cath. Educators Assn., Nat. English Tchrs. Assn. Democrat. Roman Catholic. Avocations: craft designs, needle work, collecting reptiles, collecting and breeding tropical birds, breeding Shih-Tzus. Home: 211 W 9th Ave Tarentum PA 15084-1241 Office: Transfiguration Sch CCD Office 100 Mckrell Rd Russellton PA 15076-1100

CURTIS, PHILIP KERRY, real estate developer; b. Mineola, N.Y., Nov. 6, 1945; s. William Kerry and Cherry (Smith) C.; m. Janet McDowell, Sept. 9, 1970; 1 child, Kerry Bowen. AB, Dartmouth Coll., 1968; JD, Harvard U., 1971, MBA, 1974. Bar: N.Y. 1971, Ga. 1974. Assoc. White & Case, N.Y.C., 1971-72, Hansell & Post, Atlanta, 1975-76; counsel, asst. to pres. Wiggins & Assocs., Atlanta, 1976-82; exec. v.p. Coers, Steinemann & Co., Atlanta, 1982-84; exec. v.p., ptnr. Western Devel. S.E., Atlanta, 1984-87; ptnr., sr. v.p. Charter Properties, Inc., Atlanta, 1987-93; exec. v.p. JDN Realty Corp., 1994-96; pres. Habersham Ptnrs., Inc., Atlanta, 1996-98; sr. developer AIG Baker Shopping Ctr. Properties, Inc., Atlanta, 1998—; vis. lectr. real estate Kennesaw Coll. Grad. Bus. Sch., 1992-93. Elder Peachtree Presbyn. Ch., Atlanta, 1983-86; dir. Met. Arts Found., Atlanta, 1983-87. 1st lt. U.S. Army, 1971-78. Mem. German Club (pres. 1986), Harvard Club of Ga., Cherokee Town & Country Club, Buckhead Rotary, Dartmouth Club of Ga. (pres. 1982-84, Club of the Yr. 1984), Harvard Bus. Sch. Club of Atlanta (pres. 1982-83), SAR, Sigma Chi Club Atlanta (bd. dirs. 1985-86). Republican. Home: 3111 Arden Rd NW Atlanta GA 30305-1916 Office: 3400 Peachtree Rd NE Ste 111 Atlanta GA 30326-1107

CURTIS, R. CRAIG, political science educator; b. Meridian, Miss., July 8, 1960; s. D.L. and Jeanne Claire Curtis; m. Leah E. Adams, May 16, 1982; children: Anna Chimene, Galen Russell. BA, Millsaps Coll., 1982; JD, U. of Pacific, 1985; MA, Wash. State U., 1987, PhD, 1991. Rsch. asst. McGeorge Sch. Law, Sacramento, Calif., 1983-85; tchg. asst. Wash. State U., Pullman, 1986-90; local govt. specialist Wash. State Coop. Ext., Pullman, 1990-91; asst. prof. polit. sci. Bradley U., Peoria, Ill., 1991-97, dir. adminstrn. criminal justice program, 1996-99, assoc. prof. polit. sci., 1997—. Mem. ASPA (pres. chpt. 1995-96, 98-99), Am. Polit. Sci. Assn., Acad. Criminal Justice Scis., Midwest Polit. Sci. Assn. Avocations: folk music, tennis, home brewing. E-mail: rcc@bradley.edu. Office: Bradley Univ Dept Polit Sci 1501 W Bradley Ave Peoria IL 61625

CURTIS, RICHARD EARL, former naval officer, former company executive, business consultant; b. Beckley, W.Va., Nov. 17, 1930; s. Herbert Earl and Lizzie Belle (Ramsey) C.; m. Martha Rhodes Lancaster, June 6, 1953; children: Steven Andrew, Richard Earl, Elizabeth Graham. B.S. in Elec. Engring., U.S. Naval Acad., 1953; M.B.A., Harvard U., 1961; grad., Indsl. Coll. Armed Forces, 1972. Commd. ensign U.S. Navy, 1953, advanced through grades to rear adm., 1980; logistics mgr. Strategic Systems Project Office, Washington, 1972-76; comdg. officer Naval Supply Center, Charleston, S.C., 1976-78; asst. for logistic project Naval Material Command, Washington, 1978-79; dep. dir. policy, programs, projects and systems Naval Supply System Command, Washington, 1979-81; vice comdr. Naval Supply System Command, 1981-82, ret., 1982; v.p. U.S. Elevator Co., Spring Valley, Calif., 1982-85; v.p. adminstrn. Cubic Corp., San Diego, 1985-86. Leader, dist. commr. Boy Scouts Am. Decorated Legion of Merit, Bronze Star with combat V, Navy-Marine Corps medal for heroism. Republican. Episcopalian. Home: 5130 Choc Cliff Dr Bonita CA 91902-2538

CURTIS, RICHARD LEWIS, pastor; b. Indpls.; s. Lewis Richard and Patricia Ellen (Scribner) C.; m. Mayetta Eloise Wirth, Dec. 30, 1983; children: Nathaniel, Rebekah, Phillip. BA, Cen. Bible Coll., 1985; MDiv, Assemblies of God Theol. Sem., 1988. Ordained to ministry Assemblies of God, 1988; ordained to ministry N.Am. Bapt. Conf., 1997; lic. pastoral counselor. Pastor March (Mo.) Assembly of God, 1986, Renault (Ill.) Assembly of God, 1987-89; pastor First Assembly of God, Clay Center, Kans., 1989, Watonga, Okla., 1990-92; pastor First Bapt. Ch., Durham, Kans., 1994—; Christian edn. prof. Ill. Dist. Coun. Assemblies of God, Carlinville, Ill.; moderator Kans. Fellowship, 1996-98; staff counselor Victory Village, 1997—. With U.S. Army, 1975-78; with USN, 1978-80. Decorated Meritorious Achievement. Mem. Nat. Christian Counselors Assn. Republican. Home: PO Box 92 Durham KS 67438-0092 Office: First Bapt Ch PO Box 92 Durham KS 67438-0092 *A personal relationship with God cannot insure you against the crisis of loss, poverty, illness, or disaster. It can, however, help you to overcome your trials, rather than succumb to them.*

CURTIS, ROBERT KERN, lawyer, physics educator; b. N.Y.C., June 11, 1940; s. Sargent Jackson and Phyllis (Kern) C.; m. Beverley Meadows, Dec. 26, 1971; 1 child, Phyllis. AB in Physics, Fordham U., 1964, MS in Edn., 1970; Lic. in Philosophy, Woodstock Coll., 1965; JD, Seton Hall U., 1985. Tchr. Bklyn. Prep. Sch., 1965-67; dir. Jesuit Sem. and Mission Bur., N.Y.C., 1967; tchr. Xavier High Sch., N.Y.C., 1967-69, Hackensack (N.J.) High Sch., 1969—; sole practice Hackensack, 1985—; tchr. law Hackensack Evening Sch., 1980, law for tchrs. Hackensack Pub. Schs., 1986. Mem. Am. Phys. Soc., Assn. Trial Lawyers Am., ACLU, N.Y. Acad. Scis., Am. Assn. Physics Tchrs., Math. Assn. Am., Hackensack Edn. Assn. (pres. 1979-81, 97—). Home and Office: 287 Hamilton Pl Hackensack NJ 07601-3614

CURTIS, ROSANNE JEANNE, medical facility administrator; b. N.J., Mar. 7, 1952; d. George F. and Helen (Novick) Sigler; m. Ralph S. Curtis, Mar. 27, 1982; children: Victoria Ashley, Justine Elyse. BSN magna cum laude, Mount St. Mary's Coll., 1979; M in Nursing, UCLA, 1983; EdD, Pepperdine U., 1997. RN, Calif.; cert. pub. health nurse. Nurse oncology St. John's Hosp. and Health Ctr., Santa Monica, Calif., 1979-80, charge nurse med./surg., 1980-81; nurse oncology Encino (Calif.) Hosp., 1981-82; clin. nurse specialist oncology, med./surg. educator Holy Cross Hosp., Mission Hills, Calif., 1982-84; clin. care specialist oncology Johnson and Johnson Home Health Care, Inc., Long Beach, Calif., 1984; nurse editor Williams and Wilkins/Nurseco, Pacific Palisades, Calif., 1984-85; instr. Mount St. Mary's Coll., L.A., 1985-86; nurse per diem St. John's Hosp. and Health Ctr., Santa Monica, Calif., 1985-86; clin. educator Kaiser Permanente, Panorama City, Calif., 1986-87; asst. dir. edn. Kaiser Found. Hosp., Panorama City, Calif., 1987-89; dir. edn. Kaiser Found. Hosp., Panorama City, 1989-94—, leader/mem. nursing exec. team, 1994-96, asst. hosp. adminstr., 1996-98—; asst. clin. prof. UCLA, 1987—, asst. med. group adminstr., 1998—; mem. adj. clin. faculty Mount St. Mary's Coll., 1989—. Past bd. dirs. Calif. divsn. Am. Cancer Soc. Recipient Career award March of Dimes, 1978. Mem. Valley Nursing Edn. Coun., Nurse Resource Coalition, Assn. Calif. Nurse Leaders, Calif. Strtegic Planning Com. for Nursing (adv. com. mem.), Sigma Theta Tau. Office: Kaiser Permanente 13652 Cantara St Panorama City CA 91402-5497

CURTIS, SUSAN GRACE, lawyer; b. N.Y.C., Apr. 24, 1950; d. Henry G. and Helen Curtis; m. Robert Y. Pelgrift Jr., June 8, 1974; children: Robert III, Henry, Victoria. A.B., Yale Coll., 1971; J.D., Columbia U., 1974. Bar: N.Y. 1975, U.S. Ct. Appeals (2d cir.) 1975. With Lord, Day & Lord, N.Y.C., 1974-79, Shearman & Sterling, N.Y.C., 1979-84, Proskauer, Rose, 1984-87, 93-98; ptnr. Epstein, Becker & Green, N.Y.C., 1987-93; of counsel White & Case, N.Y.C., 1998—; adj. asst. prof. law NYU Sch. Law, 1995-98; mem. faculty Practising Law Inst., 1990—. Contbg. editor: Jour. Pension Planning and Compliance, 1991—; mem. editorial adv. bd. BNA Pension Reporter, 1993—, tax mgmt. adv. bd., 1993—; contbr. articles to profl. jours. Mem. ABA (com. employee benefits), N.Y. State Bar Assn. (com. employee benefits), Assn. Bar City N.Y. (sec. com. employee benefits 1987-90). Home: 55 E 72nd St New York NY 10021-4149 Office: White & Case Bldg Ll 1155 Avenue Of The Americas New York NY 10036-2787

CURTIS, TONY (BERNARD SCHWARTZ), actor; b. N.Y.C., June 3, 1925; s. Manuel and Helen (Klein) Schwartz; m. Janet Leigh, June 4, 1951 (div. 1963); children: Kelly, Jamie Leigh; m. Christine Kaufmann, Feb. 8, 1963 (div. 1967); children: Alexandra, Allegra; m. Leslie Allen, Apr. 20, 1968 (div.); children: Nicholas, Benjamin; m. Lisa Deutsch, Feb. 28, 1993. Student drama, New Sch. Social Rsch. Films include Criss Cross, 1948, City Across the River, 1949, Flesh and Fury, 1952, Houdini, 1953, Black Shield of Falworth, 1954, Six Bridges to Cross, 1955, So This is Paris, 1954, Trapeze, 1956, Mister Cory, 1957, Sweet Smell of Success, 1957, Midnight Story, 1957, The Vikings, 1958, Defiant Ones, 1958 (Acad. award nomination for best actor), Some Like It Hot, 1959, Perfect, Furlough, 1958, Spartacus, 1960, The Great Imposter, 1960, Pepe, 1960, The Outsider, 1961, Taras Bulba, 1962, Forty Pounds of Trouble, 1962, Paris When it Sizzles, 1964, The List of Adrian Messenger, 1963, Captain Newman, 1963, Wild and Wonderful, 1964, Sex and the Single Girl, 1964, Goodbye Charlie, 1964, The Great Race, 1965, Boeing, Boeing, 1965, Arriverderci, Baby, 1966, Not with My Wife, You Don't, 1966, Don't Make Waves, 1967, Boston Strangler, 1968, Lepke, 1975, The Bad News Bears Go to Japan, 1978, The Manitou, 1978, Sextette, 1978, Little Miss Marker, 1980, The Mirror Crack'd, 1980, Venom, 1982, Brainwaves, 1983, Insignificance, 1985, Club Life, 1986, The Last of Philip Banter, 1988, Midnight, 1989, Lobster Man from Mars, 1990, Prime Target, 1991, Center of the Web, 1992, Naked in New York, 1994, The Immortals, 1995, The Celluloid Closet, 1995, Louis et Frank, 1997, Brittle Glory, 1997; star TV series The Persuaders, 1971-72, McCoy, 1975-76, Vegas, 1978-81; TV films include The Users, 1978; Moviola: The Scarlet O'Hara War, 1980, The Million Dollar Face, 1981, The Second Girl on the Right, 1985, Mafia Princess, 1986, Christmas in Connecticut, 1992; author: (novel) Kid Andrew Cody and Julie Sparrow, 1977, (with Barry Paris) Tony Curtis: An Autobiography, 1993. Office: William Morris Agy 1325 Avenue of the Americas New York NY 10019*

CURTIS, WILLIAM EDGAR, conductor, composer; b. Aberdeen, Scotland, Mar. 11, 1914; came to U.S., 1940; s. William Alexander and Florence (Malseed) C.; m. Doris Gray Schauffler, June 20, 1942; children: Michael Gray, Julie Malseed Curtis, Annie Curtis Chittenden. MusB magna cum laude, U. Edinburgh, 1935, MA magna cum laude, 1936; studies with Rudolph Serkin,, Adolph and Fritz Busch, 1936-39; postgrad., Curtis Inst., 1940-42, Cleve. Orch. Condrs. Workshop, 1956. Condr., founder Curtis String Orch., Boston, 1942-44; mem. faculty Boston Conservatory and Boston U., 1946-48; music dir., condr. Albany (N.Y.) Symphony Orch., 1948-67; dir. music, chmn. dept art, music, drama Union Coll., Schenectady, N.Y., 1955-72; founder, condr. Northeastern N.Y. Student Orch., Schenectady, 1965—, Northeastern N.Y. Philharm., Schenectady, 1966—; guest condr., composer, 1979—; Guest condr. Boston Symphony Orch., 1944, BBC, Swiss Radio, Zürich, Switzerland, Oslo (Norway) Philharm., Brabant Orkest, Holland, others. Composer: Suite for contralto, viola and orch, 1966, Concerto for organ, 1967, Three Piano Pieces, 1968, Suite for solo flute, 1969, Double Exposure for String Quartet and Prerecorded Tape, 1969, music for film To Open Eyes, 1968, Music for Brass, 1973, Sonata for Two (flute and guitar), 1974, Brass Quintet, 1976, Music for Dance Perhaps, retitled Music in Search of a Choreographer (1 piano, 4 hands), 1976, Music for Chamber Orch., 1985, Sonata for Unaccompanied Violin, 1989-90, Music for Carillon, 1993; Essays: What Is Music About?, 1991—. Served with USN, 1944-46. Recipient Mark Twain award Mark Twain Soc., 1971; Title III U.S. Govt. grantee, 1967. Mem. Am. Fedn. Musicians (award 1952). Avocations: hiking, traveling. Home: Kimball Farms 235 Walker St Apt 251 Lenox MA 01240-2749 *Two lifelong convictions remain clear: that music, and each of the arts, is directly accessible to any person whose early exposure was a happy one; and that a piece of music, a painting. . . approached as an art work, reveals itself to the mind; but approached as an experience to be shared, enters into the whole person. For these reasons, teaching and learning is, in any field, a shared artistic experience, no less than the composing, conducting or performing of music. We need, in Josef Albers' phrase, "To teach the young more search, less research."*

CURTISS, CAROL PERRY, nursing consultant; b. Worcester, Mass., Dec. 9, 1946; d. Joseph Anthony and Marjorie Ruth (Riedle) Perry; m. Jack Daniel Curtiss, Feb. 8, 1970; children: Paul Daniel, Jennifer Perry. Diploma in nursing, Mass. Gen. Hosp. Sch. Nursing, Boston, 1967; BS, Am. Internat. Coll., Springfield, Mass., 1978; MSN, Yale U., 1981. RN, Mass.; cert. Oncology Nursing Cert. Corp. Staff nurse Franklin Med. Ctr., Greenfield, Mass., 1970, Greenfield Ob-Gyn. Assocs., 1972-74, Greenfield Vis. Nurses, 1974-75; instr. Slim Living Program YMCA, Greenfield, 1977-78; instr. nursing Greenfield C.C., 1978; asst. prof. nursing Elms Coll., Chicopee, Mass., 1981-84; oncology program mgr. Franklin Med. Ctr, Greenfield, 1986-93; cancer care cons. Greenfield, 1981—; mem. faculty Greenfield C.C., 1985-87; vis. lectr., clin. instr. Fitchburg (Mass.) State Coll., 1985-86; vis. lectr. Elms Coll., Chicopee, Mass., 1984-85; mem. adj. faculty SUNY, 1987-90, U. Mass., Amherst, 1989—; mem. U.S. com. Internat. Union Against Cancer, NRC, 1992—, mem. nursing project, 1992-95; peer reviewer Agy. for Health Care Policy and Rsch., Cancer Pain Guidelines, Health & Human Svcs., 1993; presenter numerous instns., U.S. and fgn. countries, 1981—. Co-author: Cancer Doesn't Have to Hurt, 1997; guest editor Oncology Nursing Forum, 1993; contbr. articles to profl. jours. Bd. dirs. Franklin County, Am. Cancer Soc., Greenfield, 1979-95, mem. nurse and social work scholarship com., 1988-96, nursing com. liaison, 1990—; mem. steering com. Mass. Cancer Pain Initiative, 1988-90, liaison, 1990-97; trustee Oncology Nursing Found., 1995—. Mem. Oncology Nursing Soc. (mem. numerous sub coms. 1987—, bd. dirs. 1991—, pres. elect 1991-92, corp. adv. bd. 1991-93, Oncology Nursing Press pres. 1992-94, co-chair conf. on pain 1994, pres. 1993-94), Internat. Union Against Cancer (U.S. com. 1992—, nursing project 1992-94), Sigma Theta Tau. Avocations: biking, skiing, tennis, carpentry. Home: 73 James St Greenfield MA 01301-3607

CURTISS, CHARLES FRANCIS, chemist, educator; b. Chgo., Apr. 4, 1921; s. Ralph Charles and Camille (Guthormsen) C.; m. Lois Pauline Hruska, Mar. 23, 1946; children: Larry A., Glenn D., Ned S. B.S., U. Wis., 1942, Ph.D., 1948. Faculty U. Wis., 1949—, prof. chemistry, 1960-89, emeritus, 1989—. Author: (with others) Molecular Theory of Gases and Liquids, 1954, Dynamics of Polymeric Liquids, 1977, 87; also research papers. Fellow Am. Phys. Soc., AAAS; mem. Am. Chem. Soc. Home: 6317 Keelson Dr Madison WI 53705-4368

CURTISS, ELDEN F., bishop; b. Baker, Oreg., June 16, 1932; s. Elden F. and Mary (Neiger) C. B.A., St. Edward Sem., Seattle, M.Div., 1958; M.A. in Ednl. Adminstrn, U. Portland, 1965; postgrad., Fordham U., U. Notre Dame. Ordained priest Roman Cath. Ch., 1958; campus chaplain, 1959-64, 65-68; supt. schs. Diocese of Baker (Oreg.), 1962-70; pastor, 1968-70; pres./rector Mt. Angel Sem., Benedict, Oreg., 1972-76; mem. bd. regents Mt. Angel Sem., Benedict, 1976-93; bishop of Diocese of Helena (Mont.), 1976-93; archbishop Diocese of Omaha, 1993—; mem. ecumenical ministries State of Oreg., 1972; mem. pastoral services com. Oreg. State Hosp., Salem, 1975-76; bishop Diocese Helena, Mont., 1976-93, Archdiocese of Omaha, 1993; chmn. bd. Boys Town USA, Cath. Mut. Relief Soc. Am.; mem. Pontifical Coun. for Family (Rome); Episcopal advisor Serra Internat. Mem. Nat. Cath. Ednl. Assn. (Outstanding Educator 1972, bishops and pres's com. coll. dept.). Office: Archdiocese of Omaha 100 N 62nd St Omaha NE 68132-2702*

CURTISS, HOWARD CROSBY, JR., mechanical engineer, educator; b. Chgo., Mar. 17, 1930; s. Howard Crosby and Susan (Stephenson) C.; m. Betty Ruth Cloke, Mar. 24, 1956 (dec. June 1985); children: Lisa Crosby, Jonathan Cloke; m. Elizabeth M. Fenton, May 22, 1988. B.Aero.Engring., Rensselaer Poly. Inst., 1952; Ph.D., Princeton U., 1965. Mem. research staff dept. aerospace and mech. scis. Princeton U., 1956-65, mem. faculty, 1965—, prof., 1970-98; mem. Army. Sci. Bd., 1978-82; prof. emeritus Princeton U., 1998—; mem. Army Sci. Adv. Panel, 1972-77; mem. Naval Research Adv. Com., 1978-80; hon. prof. Nanjing Aero. Inst., Nanjing, China, 1985—. Author: (with others) A Modern Course in Aeroelasticity, 1978; Editor: (with others) Jour. of Am. Helicopter Soc, 1972-74. Served with USN, 1952-54. Mem. Am. Helicopter Soc. (dir. 1978-79), AIAA, Sigma Xi, Tau Beta Pi. Clubs: Metedeconk River Yacht. Home: 24 Chestnut St Princeton NJ 08542-3806 Office: Princeton Univ Dept Mech and Aerospace Engring Princeton NJ 08544

CURTISS, JEFFERY STEVEN, organizational development executive; b. Victoria, Tex., Oct. 18, 1958; s. Gary Oran and Mary Elizabeth (Haschke) C.; m. Annette Fay Hyatt, Nov. 19, 1983. B of Mus. Edn. cum laude, Oral Roberts U., 1981; MA summa cum laude, Regent U., 1983; PhD, U. South Fla., 1994. Cert. K-12 adminstr., K-12 music tchr. Asst. adminstr. Glade Valley (N.C.), 1983-84; adminstr. Good Shepherd Sch., Owensboro, Ky., 1984-86, Faith Acad., Orlando, Fla., 1986-90; pers. adminstr. Winter Park (Fla.) Meml. Hosp., 1991-92; found. assoc. Orlando Regional Healthcare Found., 1994-95; adj. prof. Mercer U., 1995—, Nat. Louis U., 1996—; dir. orgnl. devel. Promina DeKalb Med. Ctr., 1996—. Vol. Give Kids the World, Kissimmee, Fla., 1993, Orlando Regional Healthcare Found., 1993. Mem. Nat. Soc. Fundraising Execs., Phi Kappa Phi. Republican. Avocations: instrumental and vocal music, figure skating, ice dancing, golf, beach and water activities. Home: 3461 Sunderland Cir NE Atlanta GA 30319-1949

CURTISS, RICHARD HOLDEN, magazine editor; b. Grand Rapids, Mich., June 13, 1927; s. Fred Adelbert and Alma Clement (Holden) C.; m. Donna Jean Bourne, June 18, 1950; children: Diana Ruth Sreenby, Delinda Louise Hanley, Andrew Bourne, Raymond Holden. BA in Journalism, U. So. Calif., L.A., 1949. Reporter OMGUS Observer, Berlin, Germany, 1946-47; editor/reporter Whittier (Calif.) Star Reporter, 1949-50; newsman UP, L.A., 1950-51; pubs. officer U.S. Embassy, Djakarta, Indonesia, 1951-53; press attache U.S. Embassy, Ankara, Turkey, 1957-59, Baghdad, 1963-66; pub. affairs officer U.S. Embassy, Damascus, Syria, 1966-67; counselor for pub. affairs U.S. Embassy, Beirut, 1973-76; info. officer Am. Consulate Gen., Stuttgart, Germany, 1954-56; newswriter USIA, Washington, 1959-62, program coord. Near East, South Asia, 1967-69, dep. asst. dir. Near East, North Africa, 1976-78, chief inspector, 1979-80; dir. Voice of Am. Program Ctr., Rhodes, Greece, 1970-73; exec. dir. Am. Edn. Trust, Washington, 1981—; exec. editor Washington Report on Mid. East Affairs, 1983—; founding dir. Mid.-East Policy Coun., Washington, 1981-82, Coun. for Nat. Interest, Washington, 1985-86. Author: A Changing Image: American Perceptions of the Arab-Israel Dispute, 1982, 2d edit., 1986, Stealth Pacs: Lobbying Congress for Control of U.S.-Mid. East Policy, 1990, 4th edit., 1996; co-editor: Seeing the Light: Personal Encounters with the Middle East and Islam, 1997; contbr. numerous articles to profl. jours. Recipient Edward R. Murrow award for excellence in pub. diplomacy Fletcher Sch. for Law and Diplomacy, 1976, Superior Honor award USIA, 1976, Lifetime Achievement award Am.-Arab Anti-Discrimination Com., 1992, Achievement award Ptnrs. for Peace, 1993, Dedicated Svc. award Islamic Assn. for Palestine in N.Am., 1994, Lifelong Dedication award United Muslims of Am., 1994, Cert. of Appreciation The Jerusalem Fund for Edn. and Cmty. Devel. and Ctr. for Policy Analysis on Palestine, 1995, They Dared to Speak Out award Coun. for Nat. Interest, 1995. Mem. Nat. Press Club. Avocations: archaeology, paleontology, environmental protection, human rights. Office: American Educational Trust 1902 18th St NW Washington DC 20009-1707

CURTISS, ROY, III, biology educator; b. May 27, 1934; m. Josephine Clark, Dec. 28, 1976; children: Brian, Wayne, Roy IV, Lynn, Gregory Clark, Eric Garth, Megan Kimberly. B.S. in Agr., Cornell U., 1956; Ph.D. in Microbiology, U. Chgo., 1962. Instr., research asst. Cornell U., 1955-56; jr. tech. specialist Brookhaven Nat. Lab., 1956-58; fellow microbiology U. Chgo., 1958-60, USPHS fellow, 1960-62; biologist Oak Ridge Nat. Lab., 1963-72; lectr. microbiology U. Tenn., 1965-72; lectr. Grad. Sch. Biomed. Scis. U. Tenn., Oak Ridge, 1967-69; prof. U. Tenn. (Grad. Sch. Biomed. Scis.), 1969-72, assoc. dir., 1970-71, interim dir., 1971-72; Charles H. McCauley prof. microbiology U. Ala., Birmingham, 1972-83; sr. scientist Inst. Dental Research, 1972-83, Comprehensive Cancer Center, 1972-83; dir. molecular cell biology grad. program, 1973-82; dir., sr. scientist Cystic Fibrosis Research Center, 1981-83; prof. cellular and molecular biology Sch. Dental Medicine Washington U., St. Louis, 1983-91; George William and Irene Koechig Freiberg prof. biology Wash. U., St. Louis, 1984—, chmn. dept. biology, 1983-93, dir. Ctr. Plant Sci. and Biotech., 1991-94; mem. Ctr. for Infectious Disease, Wash. U., St. Louis; vis. prof. Instituto Venezolana de Investigaciones Cientificas, 1969, U. P.R., 1972, U. Católica de Chile, 1973, U. Okla., 1982; Mem. NIH Recombinant DNA Molecule Program Adv. Com., 1974-77, NSF Genetic Biology Com., 1975-78; mem. NIH Genetic Basis of Disease Rev. Com., 1979-83, chmn., 1981-83. Editor: Jour. Bacteriology, 1970-76, Infection and Immunity, 1985-92, Escherichia coli and Salmonella: Cellular and Molecular Biology, 1993-96. Mem. Oak Ridge City Coun., 1969-72, Cystic Fibrosis Found. (rsch. devel. program rev. com. 1984-89), Conf. Rsch. Workers on Animal Diseases, Heiser Found. Scientific Adv. Bd., 1996—; bd. dirs. Am. Type Culture Collection, 1989—, Whitfield Sch., 1997—; founder, dir. and sci. adv. MEGAN Health, Inc., 1992—, v.p. rsch., 1998—. Named Mo. Inventor of Yr., 1997. Fellow AAAS, Am. Acad. Microbiology; mem. Genetics Soc. Am. (chmn. genetics stock ctrs. com. 1987-89), Am. Assn. Avian Pathologists, Internat. Soc. Mucosal Immunology, Soc. Gen. Microbiology, Am. Soc. Microbiology (Parliamentarian 1970-75, dir. 1977-80, 89-94, editorial bd. ASM News 1987—), N.Y. Acad. Scis., Coun. Advancement Sci. Writing (dir. 1976-82, v.p. 1978-82), World Health Orgn. (steering com. immunology of Tb 1982-85), Acad. Sci. St. Louis, Internat. Soc. Vaccines, Gateway Strikers Soccer Club (founder, pres. 1995—), Sigma Xi. Home: 6065 Lindell Blvd Saint Louis MO 63112-1009 Office: Washington U Dept Biology Saint Louis MO 63130

CURTRIGHT, ROBERT EUGENE, newspaper critic and columnist; b. Kansas City, Mo., Aug. 27, 1944; s. Leslie Odean and Wilma Jean (Kraus) C. BA in Journalism, U. Kans., 1966, MA in Journalism, 1968. Reporter Coffeyville (Kans.) Jour., 1969-74; reporter Wichita (Kans.) Eagle-Beacon (name changed to The Wichita Eagle 1990), 1974-76, spl. bicentennial editor, 1976, movie critic, 1976—, TV columnist, 1981—. Mem. TV Critics Assn. (sec. 1993-95, newsletter editor 1993—, v.p. 1995-97, pres. 1997—). Office: Wichita Eagle 825 E Douglas Ave Wichita KS 67202-3594

CURWEN, RANDALL WILLIAM, journalist, editor; b. Hazel Green, Wis., Apr. 18, 1946; s. Charles William and Theda (Hillary) C. BS, U. Wis., 1968. Reporter Rockford (Ill.) Morning Star, 1968-69, copy editor/asst. city editor, 1969-72; copy editor Chgo. Today, 1972-74; copy editor/asst. sect. editor Chgo. Tribune, 1974-80, assoc. features editor, 1980-91, co-editor evening edit., 1992, travel editor, 1992—. Recipient 1st place headline writing award Ill. UPI, 1977, Johnrae Earl award Chgo. Tribune, 1979, 96, Soc. Am. Travel Writers Ctrl. States award for best travel sect., 1994, Lowell Thomas award for best travel sect., 1995, 97. Mem. Soc. Am. Travel Writers, Nat. Lesbian and Gay Journalists Assn. Avocations: travel, baseball, video. Home: 930 W Roscoe Rear Coachhouse Chicago IL 60657 Office: Chgo Tribune Co 435 N Michigan Ave PO Box 25340 Chicago IL 60625-0340

CURZON, SUSAN CAROL, university administrator; b. Poole, Eng., Dec. 11, 1947; came to U.S., 1952.; d. Kenneth Nigel and Terry Marguerite (Morris) C. AB, U. Calif., Riverside, 1970; MLS, U. Wash., 1972; PhD, U. So. Calif., 1983. Spl. libr. Kennecott Exploration, San Diego, 1972-73; various positions L.A. County Pub. Libr., 1973-89; dir. libr. Glendale (Calif.) Pub. Libr., 1989-92; dean univ. libr. Calif. State U., Northridge, 1992—, 1992—; cons. Grantsmanship Ctr., L.A., 1981-83; vis. lectr. Grad. Sch. Libr. and Info. Sci. UCLA, 1986-92. Author: Managing Change, Managing the Interview. Librarian of the Year, Library Journal, 1994. Mem. ALA, Calif. Libr. Assn. Democrat. Avocations: history, horseback riding. Office: Calif State U Libr Office Dean 18111 Nordhoff St Northridge CA 91330-0001

CUSACK, JOAN, actress; b. N.Y.C., Oct. 12, 1962; d. Richard and Nancy C. Student, U. Wis. Stage appearances include Road, 1988, Brilliant Traces, 1989, Cymbeline, 1989; TV appearances include (series) Saturday Night Live (regular 1985-86 season), (movies) The Mother, 1994; film appearances include My Bodyguard, 1990, Sixteen Candles, 1984, The Allnighter, 1987, Broadcast News, 1987, Married to the Mob, 1988, Working Girl, 1988 (Acad. award nominee best supporting actress 1989), Say Anything, 1989, Men Don't Leave, 1989, My Blue Heaven, 1990, The Cabinet of Dr. Ramirez, 1991, Hero, 1992, Toys, 1992, Addams Family Values, 1993, Corrina, Corrina, 1994, Nine Months, 1995, Two Much, 1996, Mr. Wrong, 1996, A Smile Like Yours, 1997, In and Out, 1997, Grosse Pointe Blank, 1997, Arlington Road, 1999, Runaway Bride, 1999, Toy Story 2, 1999. Office: Care Tracy Jacobs ICM 8942 Wilshire Blvd Beverly Hills CA 90211-1934*

CUSACK, JOHN, actor; b. Chgo., June 28, 1966; s. Richard and Nancy C. Former mem. Piven Theatre Workshop. Actor: (film) debut Class, 1983, Sixteen Candles, 1984, Grandview USA, 1984, The Sure Thing, 1985, Journey of Natty Gann, 1985, Better Off Dead, 1985, Stand By Me, 1986, One Crazy Summer, 1986, Broadcast News, 1987, Hot Pursuit, 1987, Eight Men Out, 1988, Tapeheads, 1988, Say Anything, 1989, Fatman and Little Boy, 1989, The Grifters, 1990, True Colors, 1991, Shadows and Fog, 1992, Roadside Prophets, 1992, The Player, 1992, Map of the Human Heart, 1992, Bob Roberts, 1992, Money for Nothing, 1993, Bullets Over Broadway, 1994, The Road to Wellville, 1994, City Hall, 1995, Anastasia, 1997, Con Air, 1997, Hellcab, 1997, Midnight in the Garden of Good and Evil, 1997, This is My Father, 1998, The Thin Red Line, 1998, Pushing Tin, 1998; actor, dir., writer Grosse Pointe Blank, 1997; prodr., actor Arigo, 1998; actor, writer High Fidelity, 1997, The Cradle Will Rock, 1999. Office: care Gaby Margeman William Morris Agy 151 S El Camino Dr Beverly Hills CA 90212-2704*

CUSACK, JOHN THOMAS, lawyer; b. Oak Park, Ill., June 22, 1935; s. Thomas Jr. and Clare (Hock) C.; m. Mary Louise Coughlin, Nov. 1, 1969; children: John, James, Mary Helen, Cathleen. AB cum laude, U. Notre Dame, 1957; JD, U. Mich., 1960; postgrad., Harvard U., 1961-62. Bar: Ill. 1960, U.S. Dist. Ct. (no. dist.) Ill. 1961, U.S. Dist. Ct. (no. dist.) Ind. 1983, U.S. Tax Ct. 1984, U.S. Ct. Appeals (7th cir.) 1973, U.S. Ct. Appeals (5th and 9th cirs.) 1975, U.S. Ct. Appeals (3d cir.) 1986, U.S. Ct. Appeals (10th cir.) 1987, U.S. Ct. Appeals (11th cir.) 1988, U.S. Supreme Ct. 1966. Trial atty. antitrust div. U.S. Dept. Justice, 1962-70; assoc. Gardner, Carton & Douglas, Chgo., 1970-74, ptnr., 1974—, chmn. litigation dept., 1978-86, chmn. antitrust practice group, 1986—. Contbr. articles to legal jours. Trustee Fenwick H.S. 1st lt. JAGC, USAR, 1963-67. Mem. ABA (antitrust and litigation sect., health law com. 1960—), Chgo. Bar Assn., Law Club City Chgo., Oak Park Country Club. Roman Catholic. Avocations: running, tennis, golf. Home: 1030 Franklin Ave River Forest IL 60305-1340 Office: Gardner Carton & Douglas 321 N Clark St Ste 3400 Chicago IL 60610-4795

CUSACK, THOMAS JOSEPH, retired banker; b. N.Y.C., Aug. 12, 1938; s. Thomas Joseph and Josephine (Mingalone) C.; m. Elizabeth Mary McAuliffe, June 4, 1960; children: Thomas, Elizabeth, Bridget. BBA, St. Francis Coll., 1968; grad., Stonier Grad. Sch. Banking, New Brunswick, N.J. Asst. v.p. Irving Trust Co., N.Y.C., 1959-79; v.p., sr. ops. mgr. Mellon Bank Internat., N.Y.C., 1979-83, gen. mgr., 1983-85; v.p., sr. ops. mgr. Creditanstalt, Greenwich, Conn., 1985-90, v.p. planning and devel., 1990-93, v.p., COO, 1993-94, sr. v.p., COO, 1995-98; ret., 1998; U.S. rep. Swift Documentary Credit Working Group, Brussels, Belgium, 1983-85; mem. Payments and Settlement Systems Com., Bankers Assn. Fgn. Trade, 1983-85. Mem. fin. com. St. Vincent DePaul Roman Cath. Ch., Elmont, N.Y., 1988—. Mem. U.S. Council on Internat. Banking (chmn. 1987-88), K.C. (4th deg.). Avocations: camping, touring. Home: 10 John Ave Elmont NY 11003-1916 *If we all would realize that the only lasting thing we leave in this world is our reputation, what a better world this would be.*

CUSANO, CRISTINO, mechanical engineer, educator; b. Sepino, Italy, Mar. 22, 1941; s. Crescenzo and Carmela (D'Anello) C.; m. Isabella Pera, Aug. 7, 1974. B.S., Rochester Inst. Tech., 1965; M.S., Cornell U., 1967, Ph.D., 1970. Asst. prof. mech. engring. U. Ill., Urbana, 1970-74; assoc. prof. U. Ill., 1974-83, prof., 1983—; cons. Mattison Machine Works, Whirlpool Corp. Contbr. articles to profl. jours. NSF fellow, 1965-69, ASME fellow; recipient Capt. Alfred E. Hunt award, Al Sonntag award, Xerox award. Mem. Soc. Tribologists and Lubrication Engrs., Am. Soc. Engring. Edn., Sigma Xi, Phi Kappa Phi, Pi Tau Sigma. Roman Catholic. Home: 1303 Belmeade Dr Champaign IL 61821-5027 Office: Univ Ill Dept Mech Engring 1206 W Green St Urbana IL 61801-2906

CUSHING, GEORGE LITTLETON, lawyer; b. Boston, Mar. 24, 1943; s. George Marston and Mary Margaret (Loring) C.; m. Elizabeth Hope, June 12, 1967; children: George L. Jr., Matthew S. BA, Harvard Coll., 1965, JD, 1970. Bar: Mass. 1970, U.S. Dist. Ct. Mass. 1971. Assoc. Hill & Barlow, Boston, 1970-75; assoc. Foley, Hoag & Eliot, Boston, 1975-79, ptnr., 1980-89; ptnr. Day, Berry & Howard, Boston, 1989—. Co-author: Massachusetts Practical Probate, 1985, rev. edit., 1987. Lt. (j.g.) USN, 1965-67. Fellow Am. Coll. Trust and Estate Counsel; mem. ABA, Boston Bar Assn. (regent 1999—), Phi Beta Kappa Alpha (treas. Harvard U. 1979-95). Avocations: sailing, reading, swimming, photography. E-mail: glcushing@dbh.com. Office: Day Berry & Howard 260 Franklin St Ste 21 Boston MA 02110-3112

CUSHING, HARRY COOKE, IV, investment banker; b. N.Y.C.; s. Harry Cooke and Cathleen (Vanderbilt) C.; m. Ruth Swift Dunbar, Jan. 14, 1961 (div.); 1 son, Harry Cooke V.; m. Laura Alvarez, Jan. 23, 1976 (div.). Student, Cornell U., 1945. Adviser for European ops. to chmn. bd. Ventures Ltd., 1955-59; pvt. adviser individuals and corps., 1959—; ltd. partner Hallgarten & Co., N.Y.C., 1966-74. Chmn. polo com. People-to-People Sports Com., 1962—. Served with AUS, 1942-46. Decorated commendatore Order Crown of Italy. Mem. S.R. Clubs: Turf (London), White's (London); Travellers (Paris), Polo (Paris); Polo (Rome), Golf (Rome); Hurlingham (Buenos Aires, Argentina); Racquet and Tennis (N.Y.C.), Brook (N.Y.C.); Corviglia (St. Moritz, Switzerland); Palm Beach Polo and Country, Malta Polo. Address: c/o Edmonds and Co PC 420 Fifth Ave New York NY 10018-2729

CUSHING, MICHAEL, federal agency administrator; b. Bangor, Maine, Sept. 9, 1947. BA, Harvard U., 1969, JD, 1974. Pvt. practice; with pvt. asset mgmt. co.; assoc. dir. Presdl. Pers. White House; mng. dir. Nat. Transp. Safety Bd.; chief of staff, dir. Ctr. for Labor-Mgmt. Rels. U.S. Office Pers. Mgmt.; mng. dir. mgmt. svcs. Overseas Pvt. Investment Corp., Washington, 1997—. Office: Overseas Pvt Investment Corp 1100 New York Ave NW Washington DC 20527

CUSHING, RALPH HARVEY, chemical company executive; b. Buffalo, Nov. 3, 1922; s. Benjamin Ralph and Ella Mabel (Lukens) C.; m. Edith Elizabeth Smith, Nov. 27, 1947; children: Sharonrose, Paul Ralph. BS ChemE, Drexel U., 1952. Chem. engr. Bristol Labs., Syracuse, N.Y., 1952-60; project engr. Mobay Chem. Co., Pitts., 1960-63; sr. project engr. Gulf Research Co., Harmarville, Pa., 1963-65; sr. researcher, mgr. engring., dir. coordinated computer services, sr. cons. Enron Corp. (formerly No. Nat. Gas Co.), Omaha, 1965-86; pres. CISSCO, Inc., Omaha, 1968—. Patentee corrosion protection of pipelines; contbr. articles to profl. jours. Lay minister Meth. Ch., Pitts., 1960-63. Served to cpl. U.S. Army, 1944-46. CBI. Mem. Am. Inst. Chem. Engrs., Am. Assn. Cost Engrs., Nat. Assn. Corrosion Engrs. (corrosion specialist 1978—). Republican. Avocations: photography, computer art.

CUSHMAN, DAVID WAYNE, research biochemist; b. Indpls., Nov. 15, 1939; s. Wayne B. and Mildred M. (Coffin) C.; m. Linda L. Kranch, July 31, 1964; children: Michael, Laura. B.A., Wabash Coll., 1961; Ph.D., U. Ill., 1966. Rsch. investigator Squibb Inst. Med. Rsch., Princeton, N.J., 1966-69, sr. rsch. investigator, 1969-73, rsch. fellow, 1973-78, sr. rsch. fellow, 1978-83, asst. dept. dir., 1983-87, prin. scientist, 1987-91, disting. rsch. fellow, 1991-93; ret., 1994. Co-inventor antihypertensive drug Captopril. Recipient CIBA award, 1983, Discoverers award Pharm. Mfrs. Assn., 1990, Warren Alpert award Harvard U. Med. Sch., 1991, discovery award N.J. affiliate Am. Heart Assn., 1996; NSF fellow, 1961-63. Mem. Am. Soc. Pharmacology and Exptl. Therapeutics, Am. Chem. Soc. (Alfred Burger award in medicinal chemistry 1982, Thomas Alva Edison patent award 1983, Creative Invention award 1991), AAAS, N.Y. Acad. Sci., Am. Soc. Biol. Chemists, Phi Beta Kappa, Delta Phi Alpha, Sigma Xi. Home: 20 Lake Shore Dr Trenton NJ 08648-4906

CUSHMAN, HELEN MERLE BAKER, retired management consultant; b. Perth Amboy, N.J.; d. Ivan F. and Lucile (Atkinson) Baker; m. Robert Arnold Cushman, June 2, 1945; children—Lucinda Ann, Robert Rorem. A.B. in History, Barnard Coll., 1942; postgrad., NYU, 1944. Route analyst intelligence divsn. Air Transport Command, Washington, 1943-44; personnel asst. Gen. Cable Corp., N.Y.C., 1944-45; sr. staff asst. to chmn. bd. Trans World Airlines, N.Y.C., 1945-50; pres. H.M. Baker Assocs., Westfield, N.J., 1958-93; ret., 1993; past archivist-historian N.J. chpt. Am. Records Mgmt. Assn. Author: ARMA-New Jersey, The Founding Years, 1972, A History of Shreve, Cramp and Low, 1974, Butterick and the Story of Sewing, 1975, The Anniversary Manual, 1976, Gears, Machines, Systems, 1978, Mountainside Chapel: Yesterday, Today, Tomorrow, 1981, Serving Westerly Since 1800, 1985, The Mill on the Third River, 1992, From Seed to Harvest, 1993, The Church at the Crossroads, 1999; editor, pub. Ministry Press, The Bus. History Letter; contbr. to Am. Archivist. Recipient Lit. award Am. Records Mgmt. Assn., 1972. Mem. Newcomen Soc., various hist. socs., Barnard Coll. Club of North Cen. N.J. (past pres.). Address: 266 E Dudley Ave Westfield NJ 07090-3102

CUSHMAN, KAREN LIPSKI, writer; b. Chgo.; married; 1 child, Leah. BA in English/Greek, Stanford U., 1963; MA in Human Behavior, USIU, 1977; MA in Mus. Studies, JFK U., 1987. Faculty mus. studies dept. John F. Kennedy U., San Francisco. Author: Catherine, Called Birdy, 1994, The Midwife's Apprentice, 1995 (John Newbery award 1996), The Ballad of Lucy Whipple, 1996. Address: 5480 CollegeaAve Oakland CA 94618

CUSHMAN, MARGARET JANE, home care executive, nurse; b. Pahokee, Fla., Nov. 17, 1948; d. Edmund Francis and Mary Margaret (Adams) C. Diploma in nursing, Johns Hopkins Hosp., 1969; BSN, U. Pa., 1972; MSN, Yale U., 1976. Asst. dir. nursing St. Joseph's Hosp., Phila., 1972-74; asst. dir. Regional Vis. Nurse Agy., North Haven, Conn., 1976-78; exec. dir. Waterbury (Conn.) Vis. Nurse Assn., 1978-82; exec. v.p. VNA Health Care, Inc., Plainville, Conn., 1982-86; pres. Vis. Nurse And Home Care, Inc. (name changed to VNA Health Care, Inc.), Plainville, Conn., 1986-98; CEO Home Care U. Nat. Assn. for Home Care, Washington, 1998—; chief adminstrv. officer Nat. Assn. Home Care, Washington, 1999—; asst. clin. prof. Yale U. Sch. Nursing, New Haven, 1978—, U. Tex. Sch. Nursing, San Antonio, 1990-97; cons. U. S.C. Sch. Nursing, 1987-89, U. Tex. Sch. Nursing, San Antonio, 1989-90; corporator Am. Savs. Bank, 1993-98, Hartford Hosp., 1993—, Hosp. for Special Care, 1994-98; bd. dirs. St. Mary's Hosp., Waterbury, Conn.; bd. dirs. HealthTech Svcs. Corp. Contbg. author: (chpt.) Home Health Adminstration, 1988; editl. adv. bd. Home Healthcare Nurse, 1988-95; contbr. articles to profl. jours. Mem. Conn. Gov.'s Blue Ribbon Com. to Investigate Nursing Home Industry in Conn., Hartford, 1975-77; mem. nat. adv. com. Ctr. for Health Policy Rsch., Denver, 1989-94; mem. Conn. Award for Excellence Health Adv. Task Force, 1993-94; sec. Found. for Hospice and Home Care, 1989-95; mem. joint adv. coun. and pub. health adv. coun. Conn. Dept. Pub. Health and Addiction Svcs., 1994-95. Robert Wood Johnson/Nat. League for nursing fellow, 1975, fellow Found. for Hospice and Home Care, 1992; recipient Andrew Veckerelli prize Yale U. Sch. Nursing, 1976, Disting. Alumni award, 1986, Creative Thinking Assn. Tribute, 1990, Leadership award Conn. Assn. for Home Care, 1995. Mem. ANA, ASTD, Creative Thinking Assn., World Future Soc., Nat. League for Nursing (nat. adv. coun. home health outcome study 1989-93), Nat. Assn. Home Care (chmn. 1986-88, sec. 1984-86, 91-94, vice chair 1995-98, Mem. of Yr. award 1984, 97, Virginia Henderson award for excellence in nursing 1997), Conn. Assn. Home Care (sec. 1981-85), U.S. Distance Learning Assn., Greater Hartford C. of C. (women execs. com. 1990-98), Alumni Assn. Leadership Greater Hartford, Sigma Theta Tau. Avocations: herb gardening. Home: 638 C St NE Washington DC 20002-6002 Office: Home Care U 228 7th St SE Washington DC 20003

CUSHMAN, ROBERT FAIRCHILD, political science educator, author, editor; b. Champaign, Ill, Nov. 28, 1918; s. Robert Eugene and Clarissa White (Fairchild) C.; m. Rhea Lillian Casterline, June 3, 1917; children: Leslee Cushman Myers, Linda Cushman Ruth. AB, Cornell U., 1940, MA, 1948, PhD, 1949. Grad. teaching asst. Cornell U., Ithaca, N.Y., 1946-49; instr. polit. sci. Ohio State U., Columbus, 1949-53, asst. prof., 1952-53; assoc. prof. NYU, N.Y.C., 1953-69, prof. govt., 1969-84, ret., 1984. Contbr. articles to law revs.; editor, contbg. author: Leading Constitutional Decisions, 10th and all subsequent revised edits., Cases in Constitutional Law, 1st and all subsequent revised edits., 1958—, Cases in Civil Liberties, 1st and all subsequent revised edits., 1968—. Served to sgt. AC, U.S. Army, 1942-46, India. Democrat. Quaker. Home: 19191 Harvard Ave Apt 149B Irvine CA 92612-4646

CUSHMAN, VALERIE JEAN, athletic director; b. Rome, N.Y., Oct. 25, 1962; d. Robert Harley and Peggy Ann C. BS in Edn., SUNY, Cortland, 1984; MS in Edn., East Stroudsburg U., 1988. Tchr. John Coleman H.S., Kingston, N.Y., 1984-87; tchr., coach Vassar Coll., Poughkeepsie, N.Y., 1988-97; athletic dir. Randolph Macon Woman's Coll., Lynchburg, Va., 1997—. Mem. Nat. Assn. Collegiate Women Athletic Adminstrs. (nominating com. 1996-97), Nat. Collegiate Athletic Assn. (nominating com. 1997—). Home: 105 Mullbury Pl Lynchburg VA 24502 Office: Randolph Macon Womans Coll 2500 Rivermont Ave Lynchburg VA 24503

CUSHWA, WILLIAM WALLACE, retired machinery parts company executive; b. Youngstown, Ohio, Aug. 15, 1937; s. Charles Benton Jr. and Margaret Elizabeth (Hall) C.; m. Anna Jean Schuler, Feb. 4, 1961; children: Elizabeth Ann, William W. Jr., Margaret Louise, David Frederick, Anne Jennifer. BA in English, U. Notre Dame, 1959; MBA, Case Western Res. U., 1975. Systems analyst Comml. Shearing, Inc., Youngstown, Ohio, 1960-67, asst. to sec.-treas., 1967-77, asst. treas., 1969-966, dir. corp. planning, 1977-81, v.p. planning, 1981-96, also bd dirs. Pres. Youngstown Area Urban League, 1975-78; trustee St. Elizabeth Hosp. Med. Ctr., Youngstown, 1975-95, treas., 1986-92; chmn. fund drive United Negro Coll. Fund, Youngstown, 1978; treas. Hospice of Youngstown, 1980-87. Roman Catholic.

CUSIMANO, ADELINE MARY MILETTI, educational administrator; b. Jamestown, N.Y., Apr. 18, 1939; d. Joseph and Rose (Bivona) Miletti; m. John Leo Cusimano, Sept. 24, 1960; children: Judith Ann Cusimano Pancio, John Anthony Cusimano. BS, Elmira Coll., 1961, MS, 1976. Cert. reading specialist, N.Y., Pa. Tchr. Horseheads (N.Y.) Sch. Dist., 1961-62; diagnostician, clinician Horseheads, 1962-76; reading specialist Elmira Heights Schs., N.Y., 1976-78; dir. Achievement Ctr., Horseheads, 1978-95; presenter ednl. N.Y. St. Reading Conf., Kiamesha Lake, N.Y., 1982, Bd. Coop. Ednl. Svcs. Tchrs. Tng., Horseheads, 1978-80; researcher learning disabilities, Horseheads, 1962—. Author: Achieve Visual Memory Teaching Material, 4 Vols., 1980. Mem. pub. affairs edn. home life Chemung Valley Jr. Women's Club, 1968-78, 1st v.p., 1971-72; asst. treas. Horseheads Women's Club, 1983-85; fundraiser com. Lansdale Pub. Libr. Recipient Outstanding Jr. Women's Club award, 1975. Mem. Nat. Assn. Learning Disabilities, N.Y. State Head Injury Assn., Chemung Valley Reading Assn., Horseheads Women's Club (asst. treas. 1983, corr. sec. 1990-91), Welcome Wagon Club (2d v.p. North Pa. chpt. 1997-99). Republican. Roman Catholic. Avocations: reading, needlework, golf, swimming, bridge, genealogy. Office: 1216 Scobee Dr Lansdale PA 19446-6508

CUSIMANO, CHERYLL ANN, nursing administrator; b. New Orleans, Oct. 5, 1946; d. Raymond M. and Bernadette R. (Rich) Schroeder; m. Richard C. Cusimano, Aug. 27, 1967; children: Richard C. Jr., Beth Ann, Mark Allen. Diploma, Mercy Hosp. Sch. Nursing, New Orleans, 1967; cert. vocat. tchr., La. State U., 1979; student, U. New Orleans. RN, La.; cert. in ACLS, med. surg. nursing ANCC. Various nursing positions, 1967-76; asst. head nurse pediatric unit East Jefferson Hosp., 1976-77; instr. allied health field Jefferson Parish Vocat.-Tech. Sch., 1977-79; instr. med.-surg. nursing Charity Hosp., New Orleans, 1979-80; dir. operating room Marion County Gen. Hosp., Columbia, Miss., 1981; night house supr. Children's Hosp., New Orleans, 1984; asst. supr. progressive care unit Northshore Regional Med. Ctr., Slidell, La., 1985-87; pediatric staff nurse pediatric unit Touro Infirmary, New Orleans, 1982-85, charge nurse med.-surg. unit, 1987-91; nursing supr. Touro Infirmary Ctr. Chronic Pain, Rehab., New Orleans, 1992-94, program coord., 1994—. Mem. nursing com. East Jefferson chpt.

ARC; ; former vol. classroom asst. Roudolph Matas Elem. Sch.; former mem. adv. bd. Project Head Start; guest speaker Am. Cancer Soc.; bd. dirs. Northshore Hospice, 1986-87, Charity Hosp. Sch. Surg. Tech., 1980. Nursing scholar Am. Legion. Mem. Am. Soc. Pain Mgmt. Nurses (mem. planning com.), So. Pain Soc. (chair awards com.), New Orleans Dist. Nurses Assn. (award Great Nurses of 1999). Office: Touro Infirmary Chronic Pain Unit 1401 Foucher St New Orleans LA 70115-3593

CUSSLER, CLIVE ERIC, author; b. Aurora, Ill., July 15, 1931; s. Eric E. and Amy (Hunnewell) C.; m. Barbara Knight, Aug. 28, 1955; children: Teri, Dirk, Dana. Student, Pasadena City Coll., 1949-51; PhD in Maritime History, N.Y. State Maritime Coll., 1997. Owner Bestgen & Cussler Advt., Newport Beach, Calif., 1961-65; creative dir. Darcy Advt., Hollywood, Calif., 1965-67; chmn. Nat. Underwater and Marine Agy. Author: (novels) The Mediterranean Caper, 1973, Iceberg, 1975, Raise the Titanic!, 1976, Vixen 03, 1978, Night Probe, 1981, Pacific Vortex, 1982, Deep Six, 1984, Cyclops, 1986, Treasure, 1988, Dragon, 1990, Sahara, 1992, Inca Gold, 1994, Shock Wave, 1995, Sea Hunters, 1996, Flood Tide, 1997, Clive Cussler & Dirk Pitt Revealed, 1998, Atlantis Found, 1999. Served in USAF, 1950-54. Recipient numerous advt. awards. Fellow Nat. Soc. Oceanographers, N.Y. Explorers Club (Lowell Thomas Underwater Explorers award), Royal Geog. Soc. London, Classic Car Club Am. Discoverer over 60 historic shipwrecks. Address: 5539 E Sanna St Paradise Valley AZ 85253-1622

CUSTER, CHARLES FRANCIS, lawyer; b. Hays, Kans., Aug. 19, 1928; s. Raymond Earl and Eva Marie (Walker) C.; m. Irene Louise Macarow, Jan. 2, 1950; children: Shannon Elaine, Charles Francis, Murray Maxwell, Kelly Sue. AB, U. Chgo., 1948, JD, 1958. Bar: Ill. 1958, U.S. Dist. Ct. (no dist.) Ill. 1971, U.S. Supreme Ct. 1991. Assoc. Meyers & Matthias, Chgo., 1958-72; pvt. practice Chgo., 1972-78; ptnr., arbitrator, mediator Vedder, Price, Kaufman & Kammholz, Chgo., 1978-98, of counsel, 1998—; lectr. continuing legal edn. Bd. dirs. Family Care Svcs., Chgo., 1959-81. Mem. ABA (mem. fed. regulation of securities and devels. in investment svcs. coms., dispute resolution sect.), Chgo. Bar Assn. (mem. securities law com., mem. investment cos. subcom., alternative dispute resolution com.), Chgo. Coun. Lawyers, Law Club Chgo., Cliff Dwellers (treas. 1980-83, bd. dirs. 1992-95). Avocations: music, theater. Home: 5210 S Kenwood Ave Chicago IL 60615-4006 Office: Vedder Price Kaufman & Kammholz 222 N La Salle St Chicago IL 60601-1003

CUSTER, JOHN CHARLES, investment broker; b. Chgo., Aug. 30, 1934; s. John Howard and Irene Lillian (McGovern) C.; m. Barbara Ann Welcher, Sept. 5, 1959 (dec. Sept. 1996); 1 child, John Thomas. AB, Ind. U., 1956; MHA, U. Minn., 1966; grad., Harvard U., 1975. Asst. adminstr. Johns Hopkins Hosp., Balt., 1966-67; clin. adminstr. Kaiser Permanente Med. Care Program, Oakland, Calif., 1967-69, dir. materials, 1969-70; mgr. health plan Cleve., 1970-74; v.p., health plan mgr., 1974-79; v.p. Kaiser Permanente Adv. Services, Oakland, 1979-84; pres., chief exec. officer Keystone Health Plan, Camp Hill, Pa., 1984-85; pres. chief exec. officer Custer & Assocs., Hummelstown, Pa., 1986-92; investment broker Legg Mason Wood Walker, Inc., 1992—; lectr. U. Minn. Grad. Sch. of Pub. Health, Mpls., 1981-85, Harvard U. Grad. Sch. of Pub. Health, Boston, 1977-80. Chmn. Pa. Assn. HMO's, Harrisburg, 1984-86. 1st lt. U.S. Army, 1956-58, col. USAR. Mem. Am. Coll. Health Care Execs., Am. Pub. Health Assn., Am. Hosp. Assn., Med. Group Mgmt. Assn., Internat. Fedn. of Employee Benefit Plans, Pa. State C. of C. (health care cost contain com.), Pa. State Dept. of Pub. Welfare (health care adv. subcom. 1984-85), Country Club Hershey, Delta Upsilon. Episcopalian. Clubs: Cosmos (Washington), Army-Navy (Washington). Lodge: Elks. Home: 589 Lovell Ct Hummelstown PA 17036-9156 Office: 214 Senate Ave Ste 700 Camp Hill PA 17011-2336

CUSUMANO, JAMES ANTHONY, pharmaceutical company executive; b. Elizabeth, N.J., Apr. 14, 1942; s. Charles Anthony and Carmella Madeline (Catalano) C.; m. Jane LaVerne Melvin, June 15, 1985; children: Doreen Ann, Polly Jean. BA, Rutgers U., 1964, PhD, 1967; grad. Exec. Mktg. Program, Stanford U., 1981, Harvard U., 1988. Mgr. catalyst rsch. Exxon Rsch. and Engring. Co., Linden, N.J., 1967-74; pres., chief exec. officer, founder Catalytica Inc., Mountain View, Calif., 1974-85, chmn., 1985—, also bd. dirs.; pres., CEO, bd. dirs. Catalytica Fine Chems., Inc., Mountain View, Calif., 1993-97; chmn., CEO, bd. dirs. Catalytica Pharms., Inc., 1997—; lectr. chem. engring. Stanford U., 1978, Rutgers U., 1966-67, Charles D. Hurd lectr. Northwestern U., 1989-90, Jean Day hon. lectr. Rutgers U.; advisor Fulbright scholar progam Inst. Internat. Edn.; mem. dean's adv. bd. Rutgers U., 1997—; speaker in field; mem. com. on catalysts and environ. NSF; exec. briefings with Pres. George Bush and Cabinet mems., 1990, 92, plenary lectr. in field; bd. dirs. Catalytica Advanced Techs., Inc. Author: Catalysis in Coal Conversion, 1978, (with others) Critical Materials Problems in Energy Production, 1976, Advanced Materials in Catalysis, 1977, Liquid Fuels from Coal, 1977, Kirk-Othmer Encyclopedia of Chemical Technology, 1979, Chemistry for the 21st Century, Perspectives in Catalysis, 1992, Science and Technology in Catalysis 1994, 1995; contbr. articles to profl. jours., chpts. to books; founding editor Jour. of Applied Catalysis, 1980; rec. artist with Royal Teens and Dino Take Five for ABC Paramount, Capitol and Jubilee Records, 1957-67; single records include Short Shorts, Short Shorts Twist, My Way, Hey Jude, Rosemarie, Please Say You Want Me, Lovers Never Say Goodbye; albums include The Best of the Royal Teens, Newies But Oldies; appeared in PBS TV prodn. on molecular engring., Little by Little, 1989. Recipient Surface Chemistry award Continental Oil Co., 1964; Henry Rutgers scholar, 1963, Lever Bros. fellow, 1965, Churchill Coll. fellow Cambridge Univ., 1992. Mem. AIChE, Am. Chem. Soc. (plenary lectr. to chem. educators nat. meeting 1994), Am. Phys. Soc., N.Y. Acad. Scis., Soc. Organic Chems. Mfrs. (bd. dirs. 1996), Am. Mus. Natural History, Pres.'s Assn., Smithsonian Assocs., Sigma Psi, Phi Lambda Upsilon. Republican. Roman Catholic. Achievements include 20 patents in catalysis and surface science; avocations: mountain climbing, skiing, hiking, sailing, swimming, travel. Home: 620 McNell Rd Ojai CA 93023 Office: Catalytica Inc 430 Ferguson Dr Ste 3 Mountain View CA 94043-5272

CUSUMANO, PHILIP ANTHONY, physician; b. Bedford, Ohio, Aug. 9, 1950; s. Philip A. and Mary A. (Famiano) C.; m. Barbara Stockdale Cusumano, May 6, 1978; children: Laura, Christy, Katy, Chelcie. BS in Pharmacy, Ohio No. U., 1973; MD, Wright State U., 1983. Diplomate Am. Bd. Internal Medicine. Intern, resident Cleve. Met. Gen. Hosp., 1983-86; assoc. clin. prof. Case Western Res. U. Med. Sch., 1986—; staff St. Luke's Med. Ctr., 1986-97; physician Outreach Profl. Svcs. Inc., Beachwood, 1990-97; physician dept. regional medicine Cleve. Clin. Found., 1997—; med. review officer Centerior Elec. Co., Cleve., 1987-92; staff Meridia Hillcrest Hosp., 1994—; quality assurance com. St. Luke's Med. Ctr., resident tng. com., bus. adv. com. 1993, primary care task force, 1993, profl. rels. appellate review com., 1995; mem. Med. Leadership Coun., Washington, 1995—. Mem. Valley Christian Acad. Sch. Bd., 1991-93; mem. N.E. Ohio Roundtable. Recipient Achievement award Upjohn, 1973. Fellow Am. Coll. Physicians (Preceptorship award 1996); mem. AMA, Christian Med. Soc., Phi Eta Sigma, Phi Kappa Phi, Omicron Delta Kappa, Rho Chi, Sigma Phi Epsilon. Avocations: tennis, golf, raising children, church related work. Office: 551 E Washington Chagrin Falls OH 44022

CUTCHEN, J. THOMAS, physicist; b. Dothan, Ala., Apr. 9, 1938; s. Oliver M. Barnabas and Clara Belle (Bullard) C.; m. Glenda Rose Morrill, Sept. 9, 1961; children: Tina Lyn, Lisa Anne, Carrie Lee, Robert Glenn, Suzanne Elizabeth. B in Engring. Physics, Auburn U., 1960, MS in Physics, 1961; PhD in Physics, U. Va., 1970. Registered profl. engr., N.Mex. Mem. tech. staff Sandia Nat. Labs., Albuquerque, 1961-65, 70-79, divsn. supr., 1980-85, dept. mgr., 1985-96, dep. dir., 1996—. Contbr. articles to profl. jours. Scout, scoutmaster Boy Scouts Am., N.Mex., Va., 1962-90; pres., bd. mem. Osuna Sch. PTA, Albuquerque, 1971-85; bd. mem., participant N.Mex. Chords and Duke City Chorus, Albuquerque, 1994—; treas. Sunset Hills Estates Homeowners Assn., Albuquerque, 1997—. Recipient Silver Beaver award Boy Scouts Am., Albuquerque. Mem. IEEE (sr., pres.-elect ferroelectrics com. 1998-99), Am. Phys. Soc., Am. Vacuum Soc., Am. Electrochem. Soc., Optical Soc. Am., Tau Beta Pi, Sigma Pi Sigma, Sigma Xi, Pi Mu Epsilon, Phi Kappa Phi. Republican. Mem. LDS Ch. Achievements include patent for ferroelectric type optical filter. Avocations: gardening, music, woodwork, barbershop harmony singing, camping. E-mail: jtcutch@sandia.gov. Office: Sandia Nat Labs Energy Components/Metrology PO Box 5800 Albuquerque NM 87185-0953

CUTCHINS, CLIFFORD ARMSTRONG, III, banker; b. Southampton County, Va., July 12, 1923; s. Clifford Armstrong Jr. and Sarah (Vaughan) C.; m. Ann Woods, June 21, 1947; children: Clifford Armstrong IV, William Witherspoon, Cecil Vaughan. BSBA, Va. Poly. Inst. and State U., 1947; grad., Stonier Grad. Sch. Banking, 1953. From asst. cashier to pres., dir. Vaughan & Co. Bankers, Franklin, Va., 1947-62; pres., cashier dir. Tidewater Bank & Trust Co., Franklin, 1962-63; sr. v.p., bd. dirs. Tidewater Bank & Trust Co. (merged with Va. Nat. Bank 1963), Norfolk, 1963-65; exec. v.p. Va. Nat. Bank, Norfolk, 1965-69, pres., 1969-80, chmn. bd., CEO, dir., 1980-83; chmn. bd., CEO, dir. Sovran Bank, N.A., Norfolk, 1983-86; CEO, dir. Sovran Fin. Corp., Norfolk, 1983-90, chmn. bd., 1983-89, ret. chmn. bd., 1989; rector Va. Poly. Inst. and State U., 1989-91; bd. dirs. Franklin Equipment Co. Bd. dirs. Camp Found., Franklin, 1962—, Tidewater Scholarship Found.; bd. dirs., trustee Sentara HealthCare, Va. Retirement System; bd. visitors Va. Poly. Inst. and State U., 1965-70, 87-91; mem. Future of Hampton Rds., Inc.; bd. dirs. Greater Norfolk Corp., Olympia Devel. Corp., German Club Alumni Found., Inc., Va. Tech. Found.; trustee Va. Hist. Soc.; mem. adv. coun. Va. Tech. Bus. Coun.; active Va. Inst. Marine Sci. and Marine Sci. Devel. Coun. Mem. Va. Tech. Alumni Assn. (hon. bd. dirs.). Presbyterian. Home: 5906 Ocean Front Virginia Beach VA 23451-2137 Office: NationsBank Ctr 6th Flr One Commercial Pl Norfolk VA 23510-2100

CUTCHINS, CLIFFORD ARMSTRONG, IV, lawyer; b. Norfolk, Va., May 13, 1948; s. Clifford Armstrong III and Ann (Woods) C.; m. Jane McKenzie, Aug. 14, 1971; children: Sarah Helen, Ann Woods. BA, Princeton U., 1971; JD, MBA, U. Va., 1975. Bar: Va. 1975, U.S. Dist. Ct. (ea. dist.) Va. 1975, U.S. Ct. Appeals (4th cir.) 1975. Ptnr. McGuire, Woods, Battle & Boothe, Richmond, Va., 1975-90; sr. v.p., gen. counsel, sec. James River Corp. Va., Richmond, 1990-97, Ft. James Corp., Deerfield, Ill., 1997—; bd. dirs. Ft. James Europe N.V., Ft. James Operating Co. Bd. dirs. Arts Coun. Richmond, 1980-86, Richmond Heart Assn., 1980-83, St. Catherine's Sch., Richmond, 1983-86, Richmond Ballet, 1986-88, Richmond Children's Mus., 1986-94, Richmond on the James, 1986-88, Henrico Drs. Hosp., 1986—, Hist. Richmond Found., 1990-94, Richmond Met. Blood Svc., 1995-97, Kohl Children's Mus., Wilmette, Ill., 1998—, United Way Deerfield, 1999—; chmn. Fort James Found., 1997—. Mem. ABA, Va. Bar Assn., Country Club Va. (bd. dirs. 1990-93), Commonwealth Club (bd. dirs. 1983-86, 97—). Republican. Baptist. Avocations: golf, travel, photography. Home: 118 Tempsford Ln Richmond VA 23226-2319 Office: Fort James Corp PO Box 89 1650 W Lake Cook Rd Deerfield IL 60015

CUTERI, FRANK R., JR., automotive executive; married; 2 children. BA cum laude, Waynesburg Coll., 1975. Auto. sales rep. North Hills Chrysler-Plymouth, Inc., Pitts., 1974-75; dist. sales mgr. Chrysler Corp., 1975-77; gen. sales mgr. Dodge City Inc., Morgantown, W.Va., 1977-80, Ted McWilliams Volkswagen, Monroeville, W.Va., 1980-83; gen. mgr. Ted McWilliams Porsche-Audi-Toyota, Monroeville, W.Va., 1983-86, West Hills Motors, Inc. Pontiac-Nissan-Jeep Eagle, Coroapolis, W.Va., 1986-91; pres., gen. mgr. Brown's Volvo-Subaru-Hyundai, Alexandria, Va., 1991-92, Brown's Fairfax (Va.) Nissan, 1992; exec. v.p. sales ops. Mid-Atlantic Cars, 1992-95; pres. Mid-Atlantic Cars, Fairfax, 1996—, Dulles Auto Pk, Ashburn, Va., 1998—. Avocations: golf, basketball, rollerblading. Office: Dulles Auto Park 20245 Ordinary Pl Ashburn VA 20147-3314*

CUTHBERT, ROBERT LOWELL, product specialist; b. Bay City, Mich., June 28, 1939; s. Lowell Robert and Katherine Ann (Popp) C.; m. Carol Ann Barcia, Apr. 23, 1960; children: Steven Robert, Douglas Brian, Kristi Ann. Student, Bay City Jr. Coll., 1957-59, Saginaw Vly. State U., 1990-94; AAS, Delta Coll., 1999. Lab. tech. coatings Dow Corning Corp., Midland, Mich., 1964-70, silicone acrylic rsch., 1970-72, electronic tech., 1972-78, solar cell rsch., 1978-81, electrical prodn. tech. rep., 1981-88, masonry products tech. rep., 1988-90, product specialist, 1990—. Contbr. articles to profl. jours. With USAF, 1959-63. Mem. Am. Soc. Testing and MAterials, Am. Radio Relay League, Elks. Democrat. Methodist. Achievements include patents for masonry water repellent compositions and research in field. Office: Dow Corning Mail C02230 Midland MI 48686

CUTHBERTSON, GILBERT MORRIS, political science educator; b. Warrensburg, Mo., Nov. 20, 1937; s. Gilbert and Marion Darlington (Morris) C. BA, U. Kans., 1959; PhD, Harvard U., 1963. Asst. prof. Rice U., Houston, 1963-68, assoc. prof., 1968-77, prof., 1977—; resident assoc. Will Rice Coll., Houston, 1964—. Author: (book) Political Myth and Epic, 1975, (monographs) Political Power, 1968, Myth, Power, Value, 1982; co-author: Teacher Immortal, 1984. Mem. curator's bd. Mus. of Printing History. Recipient George R. Brown lifetime award for excellence in teaching, 1993; Summerfield scholar U. Kans., 1955-59; Woodrow Wilson fellow Harvard U., 1959-63; Wilson C. Morris fellow. Mem. Am. Polit. Sci. Assn., Scottish Heritage Found. (bd. dirs. Great Scot award), River Oaks Rotary (bd. dirs., Paul Harris fellow), Knife and Fork Club, Phi Beta Kappa (past pres. chpt.), Pi Sigma Alpha, Sigma Tau Gamma, Delta Phi Alpha. Democrat. Presbyterian. Avocation: bridge. Office: Rice U Rice U Dept Polit Sci 6100 Main St Houston TX 77005-1892

CUTHRELL, CARL EDWARD, lawyer, educator, clergyman; b. Norfolk, Va., Aug. 13, 1934; s. Cecil Edward and Edna Catherine (Kirby) C.; m. Naomi Lorene Marshall, Dec. 23, 1960; children: Byron Eugene, Benjamin Dean. LLB, LaSalle U. Law Sch., Chgo., 1959; diploma Egyptian studies, Oriental Inst., U. Chgo., 1960; BD, Brantridge Forest Sch., Eng., 1970; MA in Med. History, Sussex (Eng.) Coll. Tech., 1972; MA in Classical Studies, Christ Ch. Coll., Oxford, Eng., 1973; diploma Germanic langs., Heidelberg (Fed. Republic Germany) U., 1975; BA, Upper Iowa U., 1979; MA, Covington Theol. Sem., 1982; BRE, Cen. Bapt. Bicle Coll., 1989. Pvt. practice Hampton; ordained to ministry Evang. Friends Ch., 1972; pastor Rescue (Va.) Friends Ch., 1968-96; mem. faculty dept. theology, Norfolk extension Washington Bible Coll., Lanham, Md., dept. spl. programs/history Coll. William and Mary, Williamsburg, Va., dept. secular studies Cen. Bapt. Bible Coll., Hampton, Va. Author: Ancient Mummies, 1967, Paul's Voyage, 1971; Contbr.: lit. criticisms to Times Herald Newspaper; also numerous short stories. Bd. dirs. Nat. Philatelic Inst.; trustee Quincy Coll., 1970, Nat. Coll. Surgeons Hall of Fame, 1972. Served with M.C. AUS, 1950-57, Korea. Decorated Silver Star; recipient Scouter's award medal Boy Scouts Am., 1956, Silver Beaver award, 1976, Nat. Tchrs. medal Freedoms Found., 1973, Peace medal UN, 1973, Good Citizenship medal SAR, 1976. Mem. U.S. Capital, Nat. hist. socs., SR, Sons Confederate Vets., Christian Educators Assn., Va. Herpetological Soc., Mil. Order Stars and Bars. Republican. Home: 307 Agusta Dr Newport News VA 23601-1436

CUTINO, BERT PAUL, restaurant co-founder, chef; b. Carmel, Calif., Aug. 7, 1939; m. Bella Manigiapane; children: Marc, Bart. AA in Bus., Monterey Peninsula Coll., 1964; D of Culinary Arts (hon.), Johnson and Wales Coll., 1988; D of Food Svc. (hon.), N.Am. Assn. Edn. Equipment Found. Cert. exec. chef. Various restaurant positions Monterey, Calif.; co-founder Sardine Factory, Monterey, 1968—, Cannery Row Co., Monterey, 1976—; with Pacific Hospitality, Inc., 1983—; protocol chmn. 1992 USA Nat. Culinary Team (recipient gold medals in culinary competitions, 1966, 67); formation of Western Region Culinary Team to 1988 Culinary Olympics, Frankfurt; founder Culinary Arts Program at local community coll., 1981; hospitality amb. internat. teams to Am. Culinary Classic, 1991; bd. trustees Antonin Careme Soc., 1997; bd. dirs. Calif. Culinary Acad., San Francisco; nat. chmn. Am. acad. of Chefs 1996-99; chmn. Disting. Restaurants of N. Am., DiRona, 1997; spkr. and lectr. in field. Contbr. articles for hospitality industry publs. and profl. jours.; featured in TV commls. for Am. Express; Chef and Host Chef TV show Celebrated Chefs; guest on TV shows including Good Morning Am.; featured in Blue Diamond Almond ad for Nat. Food Svc. mag., 1998, on Radio Show, Cooking with Chef John Folse, 1998, on KXCI's Radio Show Chef Robert Shell's VIP Kitchen Tips, 1999; participant in Monterey County Wine Festival (annual event). V.p. Monterey Peninsula C. of C., 1984-88; mem. Sheriff's Adv. Com., Monterey County; hon. judge March of Dimes Gourmet Gala, 1985-92; dir. Found. to Support Monterey Peninsula Schs., 1984-86. With USNR, 1959-67. Recipient numerous awards including Disting. Restaurants N.Am., Mobil Guide, Nat. Restaurant News Hall of Fame, Calif. Top 10 Restaurants, Town and Country, local Cal. State and Nat. Chef of Yr. awards, Lobo Hall of Fame Alumni award Monterey Peninsula Coll., Chef Hermann G. Rusch Humanitarian award; one of 50 restaurants in Am. selected to serve at Pres. Reagan's Inauguration, 1981, 85; recipient Alumni award Calif. C.C., 1982, Antonin Careme Soc. medal Chefs Assn. of Pacific Coast, 1987, Medal of Honor, Escoffier Soc., 1986, Presdl. Medallion, Les Toques Blanches Internat., 1989, 1st Soviet-Am. Culinary Exchange Medallion, 1988, Medallion of World Trade Ctr., Moscow, 1988; named Chef of Yr., Monterey Peninsula Chefs Assn., 1983, Humanitarian of Yr., Boy Scouts Am., 1996; named to Les Toques Blanches Internat. Hall of Fame, 1993, named 1st nat. pres. U.S.A., 1994, Nations Restaurant News top 50 hospitality preferred in U.S.; inducted into Calif. Tourism Hall of Fame, Calif. Trade and Commerce Agy., 1997; recognized by local, state, U.S. Congress by Hon. Leon Panetta; asst. to Calif. Assemblyman Sam Farr for Culinary Art Bill 1850-51. Mem. Am. Culinary Fedn. (life, cert. exec. chef, western region v.p. 1985-89, bd. dirs. The Chef and the Child Found. 1989, accreditation team 1987, Pres.'s medal 1982, 89, Pres. Recognition award 1994), Am. Acad. Chefs (nat. chmn. 1995—), Am. Acad. of Restaurant Scis., Am. Inst. of Wine and Food (founding), Knights of Vine (master knight), Wine Inst., Soc. for Am. Cuisine (founding), bd. mem. Calif. Culnary Acad., San Francisco, Calif. Restaurant Assn. (Chef of Yr., 1984), Nat. Restaurant Assn., Guild of Sommeliers Eng., Am. Inst. Food and Wine, Les Amis d'Escoffier Soc. N.Y. (amb.-at-large), Internat. Assn. Cooking Profls., Soc. Advancement of Food Svc. Rsch., Italian Restaurant Soc., Calif. Culinary Acad. (adv. bd. 1990—), L'Ordre Mondial Des Gourmets Degustateurs (spl. medal of honor, 1991), Confrerie de la Chaine Des Rotisseurs (bailli 1995, Bronze medal, 1990), Assn. Des Maitres Conseils en Gastronomie Francaise (comdr.), Les Toques Blanches Internat. Club (France, founder Monterey chpt., mem. internat. bd., 1st nat. pres., Presdl. Medallion). Travel Industry Assn. (F. Norman Clark Entrepreneur award 1992), Monterey Peninsula C. of C. (v.p.), Disting. Restaurants of N.Am. (nat. chmn. 1996-97), Euro Toque European Cooks in U.S. Office: Restaurants Central 765 Wave St Monterey CA 93940-1016

CUTLER, ALEXANDER MACDONALD, manufacturing company executive; b. Milw., May 28, 1951; s. Richard Woolsey and Elizabeth (Fitzgerald) C.; m. Sarah Lynn Stark, Oct. 11, 1980; children: David Alexander, William MacDonald. BA, Yale U., 1973; MBA, Dartmouth Coll., 1975. Fin. analyst Cutler-Hammer, Milw., 1975-77, bus. group controller, 1977-79; controller custom distbn. and control div. Eaton Corp., Atlanta, 1979-80, plant mgr. custom distbn. and control div., 1981-82, mgr. custom distbn. and control div., 1982-83; mgr. power distbn. div. Eaton Corp., Milw., 1984-85, gen. mgr. indsl. control and power distbn., 1985-86; pres. controls group Eaton Corp., Cleve., 1986-91, exec. v.p. ops., 1992-93, exec. v.p., COO controls, 1993-95, pres., COO, bd. dirs., 1995—. Bd. dirs. United Way Svcs. Cleve., NE Ohio Coun. on Higher Edn., 1993-97; Class agt. alumni fund Loomis Chaffee Sch., Windsor, Conn., 1969—; bd. dirs. alumni fund Yale U., New Haven, 1974-89; trustee The Cleve. Play House, 1987-94, 95—, Gt. Lakes Mus., Inc., 1988-91, Mus. Natural History, Cleve., 1989-97; mem. bd. overseers Amos Tuck Sch. Bus. Dartmouth Coll. Mem. Nat. Elec. Mfrs. Assn. (bd. govs. 1987—, indsl. automation divsn. 1986-90, treas. 1993-95, bd. govs. 1996—), Elec. Mfrs. Club (bd. dirs.), Yale U. Alumni Assn. (pres. Cleve. chpt. 1991-93, exec. com. of vis. com. Weatherhood Sch. Mgmt. 1993—), Chagrin Valley Hunt Club. Avocation: tennis. Office: Eaton Corp 1111 Superior Ave Eaton Ctr Cleveland OH 44114-2584*

CUTLER, ARNOLD ROBERT, lawyer; b. New Haven, Mar. 20, 1908; s. Max Nathan and Kate (Harder) C.; m. Hazel Lourie, Apr. 8, 1942; 1 son, David. B.A., Yale U., 1930, J.D., 1932; LLD (hon.), Brandeis U., 1984. Bar: Conn. 1932, Mass. 1946. Mem. staff Office Gen. Counsel Pub. Works Adminstrn., Washington, 1933-36; chief counsel Pub. Works Adminstrn. State of Wash., 1937-38; spl. asst. to chief counsel IRS, 1939-44, trial counsel New Eng. div., 1945-47; ptnr. Lourie & Cutler, Boston, 1947—; lectr. on taxation. Contbr. to books, articles to legal jours. Trustee Beth Israel Hosp.; trustee emeritus Brandeis U.; trustee, past mem. exec. com. Combined Jewish Philanthropies Greater Boston; past. bd. dirs. Nat. Jewish Welfare Bd.; past pres. Brookline, Brighton and Newton Jewish Community Ctr.; past. treas. Associated Jewish Community Ctrs. of Greater Boston; past chmn. bd. Yale Law Sch. Fund; past chmn. bequest com. Yale Law Sch. Lt. comdr. USCG, 1942-45. Fellow Am. Coll. tax Counsel, Mass. Bar Found.; mem. ABA (com. on govt. submissions 1987—, past chmn. spl. adv. exempt orgns. com. tax sect.), Mass Bar Assn., Boston Bar Assn. (past chmn. fed. tax com., former coun. mem.), Am. Law Inst., New Century Club (past pres.), Greater Boston Brandeis Club (past pres.), Yale Club, Harvard Club, Rotary (past bd. dirs.). Office: Lourie & Cutler 60 State St Boston MA 02109-1800*

CUTLER, BERNARD JOSEPH, editor-in-chief, writer; b. N.Y.C., May 26, 1924; s. Joseph Louis and Sophie (Appel) C.; m. Carol Ann Rataic, Mar. 6, 1948. BSME, Pa. State Coll., 1945. Reporter Pitts. Press, 1945-51; reporter N.Y. Herald Tribune, 1951-56, Moscow corr., 1956-58, chief Paris bur., 1958-60; mng. editor European edition N.Y. Herald Tribune, Paris, 1960; editor European edition N.Y. Herald Tribune, 1961-66; European corr. Scripps-Howard Newspapers, Paris, 1966-69; fgn. editorial writer Scripps-Howard Newspapers, Washington, 1969-72; chief editorial writer Scripps-Howard Newspapers, 1972-80, editor-in-chief, 1980-89, fgn. affairs columnist, 1989-95. Author: Reactionary! Sgt. Lloyd W. Pate's Story, 1956. Recipient Disting. Alumni award Pa. State U., 1972. Clubs: Gridiron, National Press. Office: 2735 P St NW Washington DC 20007-3065

CUTLER, CAROL ANN, food writer, consultant; b. Pitts.; d. John Michael and Stella (Kope) Rataic; m. B.J. Cutler, Mar. 6, 1948. Student, U. Pitts., 1945-46, Hunter Coll., 1953, U. Paris-Sorbonne, 1959-60, Le Cordon Bleu, Paris, 1962-66; diploma, Ecole des 3 Gourmandes, Paris, 1967. Art critic Paris Herald Tribune, 1959-69; European corr. Art in Am., N.Y.C., 1963-71; cons. Nat. Gallery Art, Washington, 1970, Met. Mus. Art, N.Y.C., 1971; food columnist Washington Post, 1971-73; pub. affairs officer Nat. Portrait Gallery, Washington, 1974-78; chief food cons. Time-Life Books, Alexandria, Va., 1978-86; syndicated columnist Copley News Service, San Diego, 1986—; restaurant critic, Dossier, Washington, 1988. Author 8 cookbooks including The Six-Minute Souffle and Other Culinary Delights, 1976 (Tastemaker award); freelance author and food cons. Mem. Am. Wine Soc., Am. Inst. Wine and Food, Les Dames d'Escoffier (pres. 1983-84), Le Cercle des Goumettes. Avocations: music, touring architectural sites. Home and Office: 2735 P St NW Washington DC 20007-3065

CUTLER, CASSIUS CHAPIN, physicist, educator; b. Springfield, Mass., Dec. 16, 1914; s. Paul A. and Myra B. (Chapin) C.; m. Virginia Tyler, Sept. 27, 1941; children: (Cassius) Chapin, William (Urban) (dec.), Virginia Cutler Raymond. B.Sc., Worcester Poly. Inst., 1937, D.Eng. (hon.), 1975. With Bell Telephone Labs, 1937-78; asst. dir. electronics and radio research Bell Telephone Labs, Murray Hill, N.J., 1959-63; dir. electronic and computer systems research lab. Bell Telephone Labs, Holmdel, N.J., 1963-78; prof. applied physics Stanford U., 1979-96. Contbr. articles to profl. jours. Mem. 1st Ch. of Christ Scientist, Keyport, N.J., 1966-78, Menlo Park, Calif., 1979-96 , reader, chmn. bd., Plainfield, N.J., 1946-66. Recipient Robert H. Goddard Disting. Alumni award Worcester Polytechnic Inst., 1982. Fellow IEEE (Edison medal 1981, Centennial medal 1984, Alexander Graham Bell medal 1991), AAAS; mem. Nat. Acad. Engring. Nat. Acad. Scis., Sigma Xi. Patentee numerous devices. Home: PO Box 94 1 Rice Rd Waterford ME 04088*

CUTLER, JOHN CHARLES, physician, educator; b. Cleve., June 29, 1915; s. Glenn Allen and Grace Amanda (Allen) C.; m. Eliese Helene Strahl, Nov. 21, 1942. B.A., Western Res. U., 1937, M.D., 1941; M.P.H., Sch. Hygiene and Pub. Health, Johns Hopkins U., 1951. Diplomate: Am. Bd. Preventive Medicine and Pub. Health. Commd. asst. surgeon (lt. j.g.) USPHS, 1941, advanced through grades to asst. surgeon gen. (rear adm.), 1958; intern USPHS Hosp., Staten Island, N.Y., 1941; venereal disease investigations Pub. Health Service Venereal Disease Research Lab., Stapleton, N.Y., 1943-46; venereal disease rsch. and demonstration Guatemala, 1946-48; assigned WHO, 1949-50; with venereal disease div. USPHS, 1951-54; program office Bur. State Svcs., 1954-57; asst. dir. Nat. Inst. Allergy and Infectious Diseases, 1958; asst. surgeon gen. for program, 1958-59; health officer Central dist. Allegheny County Health Dept., 1959-61; dep. dir. Pan Am. San. Bur., regional office for Americas WHO, 1961-68; prof. internat. health, dir. population program Grad. Sch. Public Health, U. Pitts., 1968-79, chmn. dept. health svcs. adminstrn., 1979-80, assoc. dept. chmn., prof. internat. health, 1980-85, prof. emeritus, 1985—; pres. Family Planning Council Southwestern Pa., 1971-72; sec. Am. Social Health Assn., 1972-76; pres. Internat.

Health Soc., 1972-73, Am. Assn. World Health, 1973-75, Assn. Voluntary Sterilization, 1977-83; sec.-treas. World Fedn. Health Agys. for Advancement Vol. Surg. Contraception, 1975-81, pres.-elect., 1981-85, pres. 1985-87. Contbr. articles to med. publs. Pres. UN Assn., Pitts., 1988-90. Fellow Am. Pub. Health Assn.; mem. Phi Beta Kappa. Home: 210 S Dallas Ave Pittsburgh PA 15208-2626 Office: U Pitts Grad Sch Pub Health Pittsburgh PA 15261

CUTLER, JOHN EARL, landscape architect; b. Houston, Nov. 21, 1943; s. John Cecil and Dorothy Evelyn (Hewett) C.; m. Paula Helene Murdy, Dec. 27, 1969; children: Christian Hewett, Leigh Helene. BS in Landscape Architecture, Tex. A&M U., 1967. Registered landscape architect, Tex. Landscape arch. Caudill Rowlett Scott, Houston, 1968-69, Marmon Mok Green, Houston, 1969-70; campus landscape arch. U. Houston, 1970-74; ptnr., landscape arch. Office of George Porcher, Houston, 1974-79; prin., landscape arch. The SWA Group, Houston, 1979—. Bd. dirs. Trees for Houston, 1984—. Fellow Am. Soc. Landscape Architects. Avocations: sailing, Checker automobiles, ice cream scoops. Home: 2235 Bartlett St Houston TX 77098-5201 Office: The SWA Group 1245 W 18th St Houston TX 77008-3392

CUTLER, KENNETH BURNETT, lawyer, investment company executive; b. Muskegon Heights, Mich., June 19, 1932; s. Stanley and Lucile (Miles) C.; m. Cecelia Bilsly, Mar. 9, 1967; children: Kenneth Burnett, Randall Miles, Cynthia Bilsly, Robert Appleby, Jeffrey Lamont Derrick. BBA, U. Mich., 1954, JD, 1957. Bar: Mich. 1957, N.Y. 1960. Assoc. Dewey Ballantine, Bushby, Palmer & Wood, N.Y.C., 1957-66; v.p., sec. The Lord Abbett Managed Funds, N.Y.C., 1966-97; gen. counsel Lord, Abbett & Co., N.Y.C., 1966-97, ptnr., 1972-97; bd. govs. ICI Mut. Ins. Co. Former pres. Bronxville Scout Com., Inc. Mem. Investment Co. Inst. (past mem. bd. govs.), Met. Club (N.Y.C.) (bd. govs.), Winged Foot Golf Club, Bronxville Field Club, Delta Tau Delta, Phi Delta Phi. Avocations: golf, tennis, skiing. Home: 10 Westway Bronxville NY 10708-4311

CUTLER, LAUREL, advertising agency executive; b. N.Y.C., Dec. 8, 1926; d. A. Smith and Dorothy (Glaser) C.; m. Stanley Bernstein, July 3, 1952 (div. 1983); children—Jon Cutler, Amy Sarah, Seth Perry. B.A., Wellesley Coll., 1946. Reporter Washington Post, 1946—; copywriter J. Walter Thompson, N.Y.C., 1947-50; copy chief Wesley Assocs., 1950-56; v.p. Fletcher, Richard, Calkins & Holden, N.Y.C., 1956-63; sr. v.p., creative dir. McCann Erickson, N.Y.C., 1963-72; sr. v.p. Leber Katz Ptnrs., N.Y.C., 1972-80, exec. v.p., dir. mktg. planning, 1980-84, vice chmn., 1984—; vice chmn. FCB/Leber Katz Ptnrs., N.Y.C., 1986—; v.p. consumer affairs Chrysler Corp., Highland Park, Mich., 1988-91; global dir. mktg. and planning Foote Cone & Belding Comms., Chgo., 1991-98; dir. Fallon McElligott, N.Y.C., 1998—; spkr. to orgns. including Assn. Nat. Advertisers, Am. Mktg. Assn., Produce Mktg. Assn., Grocery Mfrs. Am., Conf. Bd.; bd. dirs. True North Comms., Inc., Hannaford Bros. Co., Quaker State Corp., Domino's Mktg. Adv. Bd. Recipient Matrix award Women in Communications, 1985, Achievement award Wellesley Alumni Assn., 1990; named Ladies Home Jour. One of Am.'s Fifty Most Powerful Women, 1990, Advt. Industry Man of Yr., 1995. Mem. Fashion Group (bd. dirs.), N.Y.C. Partnership, Com. of 200, Cosmopolitan Club, Womens' Forum Inc. Avocations: reading, antiques, art. Home: 180 E 79th St New York NY 10021-0437 also: 14 John St Sag Harbor NY 11963-2620 Office: Fallon McElligott 79 5th Ave New York NY 10003-3034

CUTLER, LAURENCE STEPHAN, architect, urban designer, advertising executive, educator; b. New Haven, Conn., Aug. 27, 1940; s. Herman Shepard and Doris Winifred C.; m. Sherrie Stephens, Jan. 24, 1967 (div. 1992); children: A. Macmilian S., Zachary wold S.; m. Judy Goffman, Feb. 7, 1995; stepchildren: Jennifer Paige, Andrew Douglas. BA, U. Pa., 1962; MArch, Harvard U., 1966, MArch in Urgan Design, 1967. Nationally cert. architect. Founder, co-prin. Ecodesign, Cambridge, 1966; with Ecodesign subs. Combustion Engring., Inc., 1972-79; founder C-E Tec Internat., Inc., 1972-79, Ecidesign/SPC Internat., 1979-82; with Architects Collaborative, Ero Saarinen & Assocs.; group dir. Lodigiani U.S.A. Ltd., 1985-87, also bd. dirs.; prof. MIT, 1967-72, Harvard U., 1965-73, R.I. Sch. Design, 1965-68; group dir. N.Am. Gold Greenless Trott (USA) Holdings, Inc., London, 1988-91. Prin. archtl. works include Chase Manhattan Bank Hdqrs. for Caribbean, St. Thomas, Ballys Park Pl. Casino Hotel, Sugarloaf/USA Ski Area, Maine, fire and police complex, Westford Mass., Lockhart Gardens Shopping Ctr., U.S. Virgin Islands, Am. Embassy housing, Lagos, Nigeria; author: (with Albert G.H. Dietz) Industrialized Building Systems for Housing, 1971, (with Sherrie Steohens Cutler) Recycling Cities for People: The Urban Design Process, 1976, 3d edit., 1983, Handbook of Housing Systems for Designers and Developers, 1974, (with Judy Goffman) Maxfield Parrish & Poetry, 1995, Maxfield Parrish: A Retrospective, 1996, (with Judy Cutler) Treasures of Art: Maxfield Parish, 1999. Inmcorporator Cambridge Sch. Weston; founder, trustee The Woodbridge Found.; adv. dir. Am. Illustrators Gallery, N.Y.C., 1984—, founder, chair ARTShows and Products, Corp., 1993—, Maxfield Parrish Family Trust, officer The Cezanne Family Licensing Corp., Nat. Mus. Am. Illustration, Newport, R.I., 1999—. Recipient Alpha-Rho Chi Gold medal Harvard U., 1966, Engring. Excellence award Colo. Cons. Engrs. Coun., 1973, Design and Environment award, 1975, Design Arts Program award NEA, 1980; Milton Fund grantee, Harvard U., 1966, Fulbright-Hays grantee, India, 1968. Mem. AIA (Regional Honors award 1974, 75), Royal Inst. Brit. Architects, Am. Soc. planning Ofcls., Nat. Coun. Archtl. Registration Bds., Harvard Club N.Y., Art Dirs. Club N.Y., Nat. Arts Club. Home: Tallwood PO Box 687 Rte 3 Shepard Hill on Squam Lake Holderness NH 03245 also: 18 E 77th St Apt 2A New York NY 10021-1700 and: Vernon Ct Bellevue Ave Newport RI 02840

CUTLER, LEONARD SAMUEL, physicist; b. Los Angeles, Jan. 10, 1928; s. Morris and Ethel (Kalech) C.; m. Dorothy Alice Pett, Feb. 13, 1954; children: Jeffrey Alan, Gregory Michael, Steven Russell, Scott Darren. BS in Physics, Stanford U., 1958, MS, 1960, PhD, 1966. Chief engr. Gertsch Products Co., Los Angeles, 1948-56, v.p. research and devel., 1956-57; with Hewlett-Packard Co., Palo Alto, Calif., 1957—, dir. physics research lab., 1969-85, dir. instruments and photonics lab., 1985—, dir. superconductivity lab., 1987-89; disting. contbr., 1989—; mem. adv. panels Nat. Bur. Standards; cons. Kernco, Inc., Danvers, Mass., 1982—, others. Patentee in field. Served with USNR, 1945-46. Recipient Achievement award Indsl. Rsch. Inst., 1990, Industrial Applications prize Am. Inst. of Physics, 1993. Fellow IEEE (Morris Leeds award 1984, Rabi award 1989), Am. Phys. Soc.; mem. AAAS, NAE, Sigma Xi. Home: 26944 Almaden Ct Los Altos CA 94022-4349 Office: Hewlett-Packard Co PO Box 10350 Palo Alto CA 94303-0867

CUTLER, LLOYD NORTON, lawyer, company director; b. N.Y.C., Nov. 10, 1917; s. Aaron Smith and Dorothy (Glaser) C.; m. Louise W. Howe, 1941 (dec. July 1988); children: Deborah Norton (Mrs. James Notman Jr.), Beverly Winslow (Mrs. Mark Weaver), Lloyd Norton Jr., Louisiana Winslow (Mrs. Lamar Johnson); m. Rhoda Winton Kraft, 1989. AB cum laude, Yale U., 1936, LLB magna cum laude, 1939, LLD (hon.), 1983; LLD (hon.), Princeton U., 1994. Bar: N.Y. 1940, D.C. 1946. Pvt. practice N.Y.C., 1940-42, Washington, 1946—; prin. Wilmer, Cutler & Pickering, 1962-79, 81-90, sr. counsel, 1990—; counsel to Pres. of U.S., 1979-81, 94; sec. Lawyers Com. Civil Rights Under Law, 1963-65, co-chmn., 1971-73; chmn. D.C. Com. on Adminstrn. Justice under Emergency Conditions, 1968; exec. dir. Nat. Commn. on the Causes and Prevention of Violence, 1968-69; President's spl. rep. for maritime boundary and resource negotiations with Can., 1977-79; sr. cons. Pres.'s Commn. on Strategic Forces, 1983; vis. lectr. Yale U. Law Sch., 1973-76, Yale U. Sch. Orgn. and Mgmt., 1977-79, All Souls Coll., Oxford (Eng.) U., 1983, Nuffield Coll., Oxford, 1986; mem. U.S. Group to Permanent Ct. Arbitration, The Hague, 1984-93; mem. Quadrennial Commn. on Legis., Exec. and Jud. Salaries, 1984, chmn., 1989; mem. Pres.'s Commn. on Fed. Ethics Law Reform, 1989. Hon. trustee Brookings Instn.; chmn., mem. coun. Yale U., 1966-71, 89-94, chmn. devel. bd., 1972-77, chmn. campaign for Yale U., 1978-79; exec. bd. dirs. Met. Opera Assn., 1974-79; chmn. Salzburg Seminar, 1984-94. Recipient Jefferson medal in law U. Va., 1995, Marshall-Wythe Sch. Law medal Coll. William and Mary, 1998. Mem. Am. Law Inst. (coun.), ABA, Coun. on Fgn. Rels. (bd. dirs. 1977-79), Am. Acad. Arts and Scis., Mid. Temple of London (Hon., Bencher). Clubs: Metropolitan, Chevy Chase (Washington), Century Assn. (N.Y.C.). Home: 3115 O St NW Washington DC 20007-3117 Office: Wilmer Cutler & Pickering 2445 M St NW Ste 500 Washington DC 20037-1487

CUTLER, MAXINE GORDON, French language and literature educator; b. N.Y.C., Sept. 15, 1927; d. Milt and Ciel (Blacker) Gordon; m. Cy Cutler, Mar. 29, 1950; children: Robert, Sara. AB, Bryn Mawr-Barnard Coll., 1949; PhD, Columbia U., 1967. Asst. prof. French Barnard Coll., N.Y.C., 1967-71; faculty New Sch. for Social Rsch., N.Y.C., 1981-95; adj. prof. humanities Sch. of Continuing Edn., NYU, 1996—. Author: Evocations of the Eighteenth Century in French Poetry 1800-69, 1967; author, editor: Voltaire, The Englightenment and the Comic Mode, 1990; gen. editor Teaching Language Through Literature, 1971-87. Mem. MLA (hon.).

CUTLER, PHILIP EDGERTON, lawyer; b. Evanston, Ill., Mar. 18, 1948; s. John A. and Catherine (Hedman) C.; m. Barbara Anne Phippen, Oct. 27, 1948; children: David, Nathanael, Andrew. AB in History, Georgetown U., 1970; JD with honors, Northwestern U., 1973. Assoc. Perkins Coie, Seattle, 1973-79; ptnr. Sax and MacIver, Seattle, 1979-85; ptnr., shareholder Sax and MacIver merged Karr Tuttle Campbell, Seattle, 1986-89; shareholder, pres. Cutler & Nylander, Seattle, 1990—, also bd. dirs.; ct.-approved arbitrator King County Superior Ct., 1982—, U.S. Dist. Ct. (we. dist.) Wash., 1992—; mediator U.S. Dist. Ct. (we. dist.) Wash., 1982—; judge pro tem King County Superior Ct., 1993—; mem. comml. arbitration panel Am. Arbitration Assn., 1992—, mediator, 1997—; lectr., program chmn. numerous continuing legal edn. programs; mem. arbitration panel Nat. Assn. Securities Dealers, 1996—. Co-founder Country Dr. Comty. Legal Clinic, Seattle, 1974—; co-pres. parents club St. Joseph Sch., Seattle, 1984-86, mem. sch. adv. bd., 1985-88; dir. St. Joseph Endowment Fund, 1986—, St. Joseph Parish Sch. Fund, 1990—, St. George Sch. Endowment Found., Seattle, 1994—, sec., 1996—; mem. sch. adv. bd. Blanchet H.S., Seattle, 1991—, mem. devel. com., 1992—; chair Georgetown Alumni Admissions Interviewing Program, 1975—; active St. Patrick Parish, Seattle, 1974-82, St. Joseph Parish, Seattle, 1982—, Cursillo Movement, 1975-85, Cath. Archdiocese of Seattle, 1979-82, YMCA Indian Guides/Indian Princesses program, 1980-84, chief of Husky Nation, 1982-84. Mem. ABA (antitrust and litigation sects., civil practice and procedure com. antitrust sect. 1980-90), FBA (chair ct. congestion/alt. dispute resolution com. 1985—, mem. spl. alt. dispute resolution task force 1994 western dist. Wash.), Wash. State Bar Assn. (consumer protection, antitrust and unfair bus. practices sect., litigation sect., alt. dispute resolution sect.), St. Thomas More Soc. Seattle (pres. 1993-95), Georgetown Alumni Assn. (bd. dirs. 1977-80, alumni sen. 1980—), King County Bar Assn. (numerous coms.), Rainier Club, Wash. Athletic Club, Georgetown Club Wash. (pres. 1980-86, mem. exec. com. 1986—). Roman Catholic. Avocations: swimming, downhill skiing, gourmet cooking, reading, furniture-making and woodworking. Office: Cutler & Nylander 999 3rd Ave Ste 3150 Seattle WA 98104-4035

CUTLER, RICHARD WOOLSEY, lawyer; b. New Rochelle, N.Y., Mar. 9, 1917; s. Charles Evelyn and Amelia (MacDonald) C.; m. Elizabeth Fitzgerald, Oct. 18, 1947; children: Marguerite Blackburn, Alexander MacDonald, Judith Elizabeth. BA, Yale U., 1938, LLB, 1941. Bar: Conn. 1941, N.Y. 1942, Wis. 1950, D.C. 1975, U.S. Supreme Ct. 1980. Practiced in N.Y.C., 1941-49, Milw., 1949-87; assoc. Donovan, Leisure, Newton & Lumbard, 1941-42; atty. Legal Aid Soc., 1946-47, RCA Communications, Inc., 1947-49; ptnr. Quarles & Brady (and predecessor firms), 1954-87; gen. ptnr. Sunset Investment Co., Milw. Author: Zoning Law and Practice in Wisconsin, 1967. Chmn. Milw. br. Fgn. Policy Assn., 1951-53; pres. Childrens Service Soc. Wis., 1961-63, Neighborhood House, 1971-74; sec. Southeastern Wis. Regional Planning Commn., 1960-84, Yale Devel. Bd., 1973-79; bd. dirs. Wis. Dept. Resource Devel., 1967-68; Met. Milw. Study Commn., 1957-61; bd. dirs. Milw. Innovation Ctr., 1985-89, pres., 1984-85, exec. v.p., 1985-89; bd. dirs. Greater Milw. Com., 1982-89. Capt. USAAF, 1943-46 and OSS, 1944-46. Recipient Disting. Leadership award Am. Planning Assn., 1992. Mem. ABA, Wis. Bar Assn., Milw. Club, Milw. Country Club, Town Club, Phi Beta Kappa. Republican. Presbyterian. Home: 938 W Shaker Cir Mequon WI 53092-6032 Office: 411 E Wisconsin Ave Milwaukee WI 53202-4461

CUTLER, RONNIE, artist; b. N.Y.C.; d. Leo and Sarah (Saks) C.; m. Mar. 1, 1951 (dec. May 1990). Student, Columbia U., 1955-56, Bklyn. Mus. Art, 1958, Art Students League, N.Y.C., 1959-60. Exhibited in group shows Whitney Mus. Am. Art, N.Y.C., 1954, Am. Watercolor Soc. 132nd Ann. Internat., 1999, Delgado Mus. Art, New Orleans, 1955, Berkshire Mus. Art, Pittsfield, Mass., 1955, 56, Bklyn. Mus., 1956, 58, Riverside Mus. Art, N.Y.C., 1957, Springfield (Mass.) Mus. Art, 1957, Nat. Acad. Art, N.Y.C., 1958, Provincetown (Mass.) Art Assn. and Mus., 1993. Recipient Sherwood prize in oil Silvermine Guild Artists, 1955, 1st prize Riverside Mus. Art, 1957, alumni purchase award Art Students League, 1960, 1st prize in oil So. Berkshire Assn., 1979, 80, Painters and Sculptors Soc., 1955. Mem. Salgamundi Club. Home and Studio: 175 W 12th St Apt 11J New York NY 10011-8206

CUTLER, STEPHEN JOEL, sociologist; b. Lawrence, Mass., Jan. 1, 1943; s. Lewis J. and Minnie C.; m. Karan Elizabeth Davis, Apr. 25, 1968; children: Ellen Min, Timothy Spence. BA, Dartmouth Coll., 1964; MA, U. Mich., 1965, PhD, 1969. Mem. faculty Oberlin Coll., Ohio, 1969-84; prof. sociology-anthropology Oberlin Coll., 1979-84, chmn. dept., 1979-82; prof. sociology, Bishop Robert F. Joyce Disting. Prof. gerontology U. Vt., Burlington, 1984-93, dir. Ctr. Study of Aging, 1993-96; sr. fellow Center Study Aging and Human Devel., Duke U., 1975-76; adv. bd. nat. data program social scis. Nat. Opinion Research Center, 1980-85; mem. human devel. and aging study sect. NIH, 1979-84, 88-92, chmn., 1990-92. Co-author: Middle Start: An Experiment in the Educational Enrichment of Young Adolescents, 1978; co-editor: Major Social Problems: A Multidisciplinary View, 1979, Promoting Successful and Productive Aging, 1995; assoc. editor Gerontol. Monographs, 1976-82; mem. editl. bd. Internat. Jour. Aging and Human Devel., 1980—, Jour. Gerontology, 1981-86, Rsch. on Aging, 1982—; editor Jour. Gerontology: Social Scis., 1990-93. Woodrow Wilson fellow, 1965; grantee NIMH, NSF, NIH, Alzheimer's Assn. Fellow Gerontol. Soc. Am. (mem. exec. com. behavioral and social scis. sect. 1979-81, chmn. 1987, mem. coun. 1986-88, pres.-elect 1997, pres. 1998); mem. Am. Sociol. Assn. (coun. sect. on aging 1982-84, chair-elect 1993-94, chair 1994-95), Assn. for Gerontology in Higher Edn. (bd. dirs., mem. exec. com. 1985-87, 95-97). Home: 54 Sleepy Hollow Rd Essex Junction VT 05452-2722 Office: U Vt Dept Sociology Burlington VT 05405

CUTLER, WALTER LEON, diplomat, foundation executive; b. Boston, Nov. 25, 1931; s. Walter Leon and Esther Dewey (Bradley) C.; m. Sarah G. Beeson, Mar. 16, 1957 (div. 1981); children: Allen Bradley, Thomas Gerard.; m. Isabel K. Brookfield, Nov. 28, 1981. BA, Wesleyan U., Middletown, Conn., 1953; MA, Fletcher Sch. of Law & Diplo., 1954. Joined U.S. Fgn. Service, 1956; vice consul Am. consulate Yaounde, Cameroon, 1957-59; fgn. affairs officer Dept. State, Washington, 1959-60; staff asst. to sec. of state Dept. State, 1960-62; 2d sec. Am. Embassy Algiers, Algeria, 1962-65; prin. officer Am. Consulate Tabriz, Iran, 1965-67; polit. officer, 1st sec. Am. Embassy Seoul, Korea, 1967-69, Saigon, Vietnam, 1969-71; spl. asst. for Vietnam Peace Negotiations U.S. Dept. State, 1971-73; mem. Sr. Seminar in Fgn. Policy, 1973-74; dir. Office Ctrl. African Affairs, 1974-75; amb. to Zaire, 1975-79; amb.-designate to Iran, 1979; prin. dep. asst. sec. for congl. rels. Dept. State, Washington, 1979-81; amb. to Tunisia, 1982-84, Saudi Arabia, 1984-87, 1988-89; rsch. prof. diplomacy Georgetown U., Washington, 1987-88; pres. Meridian Internat. Ctr., Washington, 1989—; spl. emissary for sec. gen. UN, N.Y.C., 1994. Served with U.S. Army, 1954-56. Recipient Disting. Alumnus award Wesleyan U., 1983, King Abdul Aziz award Saudi Arabia, 1986, Presdl. Performance award, 1986, 87, Wilbur J. Carr award U.S. Dept. State, 1989, Dir. Gen.'s Cup award, 1993; decorated Order of the Leopard, Zaire, 1979. Mem. Coun. Fgn. Rels., Am. Fgn. Svc. Assn., Am. Acad. Diplomacy (bd. dirs.), Washington Inst. Fgn. Affairs (bd. dirs.), Mid. East Inst., Am. Tunisian Assn. (hon. com. The Am. Coms. on Foreign Rels.), Met. Club. Office: Meridian Internat Ctr 1630 Crescent Pl NW Washington DC 20009-4004

CUTLIP, RANDALL BROWER, retired psychologist, college president emeritus; b. Clarksburg, W.Va., Oct. 1, 1916; s. M.N. and Mildred (Brower) C.; m. Virginia White, Apr. 21, 1951; children: Raymond Bennett, Catherine Baumgarten. AB, Bethany Coll., 1940; cert. indsl. pers. mgmt., So. Meth. U., 1944; MA, East Tex. U., 1949; EdD, U. Houston, 1953; LLD, Bethany Coll., 1965, Columbia Coll., 1980; LHD, Drury Coll., 1975; ScD, S.W. Bapt. U., 1978; LittD, William Woods U., 1981. Tchr. adminstr. Tex. pub. schs., 1947-50; dir. tchr. placement U. Houston, 1950-51, supr. counselling, 1951-53; dean students Atlantic Christian Coll., Wilson, N.C., 1953-56, dean, 1956-58; dean personnel, dir. grad. div. Chapman U., Orange, Calif., 1958-60; pres. William Woods Coll., Fulton, Mo., 1960-81, pres. emeritus, 1981—; trustee William Woods U., Fulton, Mo., 1981-85, 92—; chmn. bd. dirs. Mo. Colls. Fund, 1973-75; chmn. Mid-Mo. Assn. Colls., 1972-76; bd. dirs. Marina del Sol, bd. pres., 1985-90, 92-95. Mem. visitors' bd. Mo. Mil. Acad., 1966-90, chmn., 1968-72; trustee Schreiner Coll., Kerrville, Tex., 1983-92, Amy Shelton McNutt Charitable Trust, 1983—, Permanent Endowment Fund, 1987-96, Scholarship Found. and Res. Fund of Christian Ch., 1992-96, Christian Found., 1990—; bd. dirs. Univ. of the Americas, 1984-96, exec. v.p., 1985-96; bd. dirs. Tex. State Aquarium, 1994, exec. com., 1994—, pres. 1998; elder Life Christian Ch., bd. dirs., exec. com. Recipient McCubbin award, 1968, Delta Beta Xi award, 1959. Mem. Am. Personnel and Guidance Assn., Alpha Sigma Phi, Phi Delta Kappa, Kappa Delta Pi, Alpha Chi. Address: 1400 Ocean Dr Corpus Christi TX 78404-2109

CUTNAW, MARY-FRANCES, emeritus communications educator; b. Dickinson, N.D., June 15, 1931; d. Delbert A. and Edith (Calhoun-Pritchard) C. BS, U. Wis., 1953, MS, 1957, postgrad., to 1968. Life tchg. license in speech, English and French, Wis. Vol. tchr. Vocat. Sch. for World War II Displaced Persons, Stevens Point, Wis., 1951-52; speech tchr. Pulaski H.S., Milw., 1953-55; tchg. asst. dept. speech U. Wis., Madison, 1956-57, spl. asst. Sch. Edn., summer 1957; instr. speech U. Wis.-Stout, Menomonie, 1957-58, dean of women, 1958-59, asst. prof. speech, 1959-64, assoc. prof. speech, 1964-74, prof. emeritus, 1974—; comm. and pers. cons., St. Paul, 1974—; writer, editor, pub. New Legal Press, 1995—. Author: How to Settle a Living Trust, 1996. Organizer, past advisor Young Dems., Menomonie, 1959—; founder Edith and Kent Cutnaw Scholarship, U. Wis., Stevens Point, 1960—; bd. dirs. Blaisdell Place, Mpls., 1980-85. Hon. scholar U. Wis., Madison, 1959-60, 67-68. Mem. ACLU, NOW, Internat. Platform Assn., Wis. Acad. Arts and Scis., Wis. Women's Network, Progressive Roundtable (Mpls.), Calhoun Beach Club (Mpls.), Amnesty Internat., World Jewish Congress (charter), U. Club St. Paul, Greenpeace, Dunn County Humane Soc., Soc. for Prevention of Cruelty to Animals, Gamma Phi Beta, Phi Beta, Sigma Tau Delta, Pi Lambda Theta. Roman Catholic. Avocations: ecology, civil rights, animal rights, consumer protection, health and wellness. Office: New Legal Press PO Box 282 Menomonie WI 54751-0282

CUTRONE, DEE T., retired elementary education educator; b. Islip, N.Y., Jan. 7, 1942; d. Joseph August and Victoria Harriet (Scepaniak) Boesel; m. Nick J. Cutrone, July 11, 1996; children: Kevin McAllister, Brian J. McAllister, Victoria R. McAllister. BS in Elem. Edn. and Spl. Edn., Marywood Coll., Scranton, Pa., 1963; postgrad., L.I.U., 1983-86. Cert. elem. tchr., N.Y., lic. real estate. Tchr. Our Lady of Good Counsel Parochial Sch., Inwood, N.Y., 1963-64, Elmont (N.Y.) Sch. Dist., 1964; tchr. Middle County Sch. Dist., Centereach, N.Y., 1968-97, ret., 1997; union rep. MCTA, Centereach, 1969-70. Recipient Jenkins award N.Y. Congress of Parents and Tchrs., 1997. Mem. Audubon Soc., Mus. Nat. History, Nat. Geographic Soc., NCTM, Internat. Platform Assn., N.Y. State United Tchrs. Avocations: traveling, playing piano, reading, photography, bird watching, breeding English Budgies. Home: PO Box 370757 Las Vegas NV 89137-0757 Office: Elem Sch North Coleman Rd Centereach NY 11720

CUTRONE, LAWRENCE GARY, school system administrator, consultant, writer; b. Washington, Pa., Oct. 7, 1947; s. Lawrence James and Ruth (Neebling) C.; m. Jean Valene Osment, Feb. 14, 1982; children: Christopher, Carly, Anthony. BA, Doane Coll., 1969; MPA, Ind. U., 1976. Editor, writer Ind. U., Bloomington, 1976-77; econ. devel. planner San Carlos (Ariz.) Apache Tribe, 1978-80; planning dir. Pascua Yaqui Tribe, Tucson, 1981-88, cons., 1988-89; asst. dep. coord. Tohono O'Odham Nation, Tucson, 1988-89; contract mgr. Tucson Unified Sch. Dist., 1990-97, Oreg. State U., 1997-98; program mgr. Pima County, 1998-99, contracts mgr., 1999—. Contbr. articles to profl. jours. Denmaster Boy Souts Am., Tucson, 1993-95; v.p. PTA, Tucson, 1994-95. Fellow Ind. U., 1976, U. Ariz., 1981. Mem. Nat. Contract Mgmt. Assn. (cert. profl. contracts mgr.), Assn. Sch. Bus. Ofcls. Internat. Democrat. Avocations: biking, swimming, walking, reading, volunteering. Home: 1507 E Manlove St Tucson AZ 85719-6125

CUTSCHALL, JOHN RAY, hospital administrator; b. Bicknell, Ind., Oct. 18, 1937; s. Robert Jacob and Jessie Myrtle (Durnil) C.; m. Connie Kaye Nicholson, Oct. 24, 1958; children: John Robert, Stewart Alan, Howard Ray. Student, Cin. Coll. Music, 1956, Ind. U. S.E., New Albany, 1972-74. Staff announcer WTAY Radio, Robinson, Ill., 1956, WJCD Radio, Seymour, Ind., 1957-58, WRAY Radio, Princeton, Ind., 1958-59, WAOV Radio, Vincennes, Ind., 1959-62, WORX Radio, Madison, Ind., 1962-65; agt. Farm Bur. Ins., Madison, 1965-69; program dir. WORX Radio, Madison, 1969-71; TV prodr. Madison State Hosp., 1971—, cmty. svcs. dir., 1980—. Prs. Jefferson County Farm City Com., Madison, 1965-66. Named to Outstanding Young Men of Am., 1966. Republican. Christian. Avocations: reading, woodworking, do-it-yourself projects, grandfathering. Home: 4850 E Pleasant Ridge Rd Madison IN 47250-8672 Office: Madison State Hosp 711 Green Rd Madison IN 47250-2199

CUTSHALL, JANET MARIE, educator; b. Sioux Falls, S.D., July 26, 1946; d. Ove Arland and Doris May (Rider) Nerison; m. Don Arden Cutshall, Aug. 10, 1968; children: Cynthia Alison, Jeffrey Hayes, Anne Elizabeth. AA, Cottey Coll., 1966; BS, U. Nebr., 1968, MEd, 1970. Elem. tchr. Lincoln (Nebr.) Pub. Schs., 1968-72; reading instr. Rathmichael Nat. Sch., Dublin, 1982-84; instr. Sussex County C.C., Newton, N.J., 1987-91, asst. prof., 1991-96, assoc. prof., 1996—, divsn. area coord. devel. studies program, 1987—; mem., chair Keogh-Dwyer Correctional Facility GED Adv. Com., N.J., 1990-96; vice chair Basic Skills Adv. Com. Acad. Affairs, N.J., 1995-96. Bd. dirs., sec. Literacy Vols. Am., Sussex County, 1989-98—; pres. Am. Internat. Women's Club, Dublin, 1983-85; mem., officer P.E.O. Sisterhood, Nebr. & N.J., 1967—; mem. allocations com. United Way Sussex County, 1995—. Mem. Nat. Assn. Devel. Educators, Nat. Coun. Tchrs. English, Mid-Atlantic C.C. Reading Assn., N.J. Assn. Devel. Educators, Internat. Reading Assn. Avocations: tennis, reading, cooking. Office: Sussex County C C 1 College Hill Rd Newton NJ 07860-1149

CUTSHALL, JON TYLER, aerospace engineer, researcher; b. Texas City, Tex., July 15, 1964; s. Gerald Clayton and Susan Florine (Davis) C.; m. Wiede Marie Koop, July 1, 1989. BS in Aerospace Engring., U. Tex., 1988. Registered profl. engr., Tex. Rsch. asst. U. Tex., Austin, 1986-88; engr. The Dee Howard Co., San Antonio, 1988-89; sr. rsch. engr. S.W. Rsch. Inst., San Antonio, 1989—. Bd. dirs. SABEST. Mem. AIAA. Avocations: tennis, archery, billiards, reading. Home: 7207 W Beverly Mae Dr San Antonio TX 78229-4945 Office: SW Rsch Inst 6220 Culebra Rd San Antonio TX 78238-5100

CUTSHALL-HAYES, DIANE MARION, elementary education educator; b. Pitts., Jan. 15, 1954; d. William Edward and Irma Delores (Marion) Snowden; m. John Steven Baran, Jan. 11, 1975 (div. 1982); 1 child, Allison Rae; m. Dean F. Cutshall, Dec. 17, 1989. BA, Eureka Coll., 1975; BS, Ind. U., Ft. Wayne, 1986. First grade tchr. Hoover Elem. Sch., Schaumburg, Ill., 1976-79, Indian Meadows Elem. Sch., Ft. Wayne, Ind., 1979-80, 82-86, Perry Hill Elem. Sch., Ft. Wayne, 1981-82; second grade tchr. Indian Meadows Elem. Sch., Ft. Wayne, 1986—; tchr. rep. State Ill. Rsch. Adv. Coun., 1991; active ISTEP Blue Ribbon Commn., Ill., 1989, State Ill. Lang. Arts Adv. Commn., 1988, Project REAP Adv. Bd., 1988. Spl. events chair Greater Ft. Wayne (Ind.) Crime Stoppers, 1992-95; active YMCA Camp Potawotami, Ft. Wayne, 1993—, Eureka Coll. Alumni Assn., 1992—, pres., 1995—. Christa McAuliffe fellow State of Ind., 1987; recipient Excellence in Edn. award Inst. Copy Corp., 1988, Outstanding Young Alumna award Eureka Coll., 1990, Armstrong Tchr. Educator award, 1998; named Ind. State Elem. Tchr. of Yr., 1993. Mem. Nat. Coun. Tchrs. Math., Internat. Reading Assn., Tchrs. Applying Whole Langs. Lutheran. Avocations: inline skating, racquetball, reading, walking. Home: 5809 Eagle Creek Dr Fort Wayne IN 46804-3207 Office: Indian Meadows Elem Sch 4810 Homestead Rd Fort Wayne IN 46804-5461*

CUTSHAW, KENNETH ANDREW, lawyer; b. Knoxville, Tenn., Sept. 2, 1953; s. Harvey Audley and Frankie Janelle (Temple) C.; m. Diane Dracos. BA, U. Tenn., 1975, JD, 1978; LLM, Am. U., 1987. Bar: Tenn. 1978, D.C. 1987, U.S. Dist. Ct. (mid. dist.) 1978, Tenn., (ea. dist.) 1978, Tenn. Supreme Ct. 1978, U.S. Supreme Ct. 1987, U.S. Fed. cir., 1991. Sr. atty. State of Tenn. Legis., Nashville, 1979-80; sr. atty. The 1982 World's Affair, Knoxville, 1980-83, cons., 1984; campaign mgr. for candidate U.S. Senate, 1983-84; asst. dep., asst. sec. import adminstrn. Dept. Commerce, Washington, 1985-87, chief of staff export adminstrn., 1987-89, dep. asst. sec. export enforcement, 1989-91; ptnr. Miller & Steuart, Washington, 1991-93; pres. Global Trading Ptnrs., Inc., Washington, 1991-93; of counsel Troutman Sanders, LLP, Atlanta, 1993-95, Smith Gambrell & Russell, LLP, 1995—; mem. U.S. Govt. Industry Adv. Com. on Customs and Trade, 1994-96; adj. fellow Houston Inst. Author: Criminal Law Statutes, 1980, Doing Business in China, 1995; contbr. articles to profl. jours. Vice chmn., exec. com. Tenn. Rep. Party, 1982-85; internat. chmn. Boy Scouts Am., Atlanta; mem. Bretton Woods Com.; co-chmn. Awakening Weekend. Roddy Acad. scholar U. Tenn., 1971-72. Mem. ABA, Tenn. Bar Assn. (com. chmn. 1983-84), D.C. Bar Assn., Am. Coun. Young Polit. Leaders (bd. dirs., co-chmn.), Coun. on Fgn. Rels., Atlanta Round Table (chmn.), World Trade Club, Elks, Sigma Chi. Baptist. Avocations: flying, skiing, hiking, cultural events. Home: 4417 Dunmore Rd Marietta GA 30068-4224 Office: Smith Gambrell & Russell LLP 1230 Peachtree St NE Ste 3100 Atlanta GA 30309-3592

CUTTER, CHARLES ROSS, historian, educator; b. Berkeley, Calif., Sept. 22, 1950; s. Donald Colgett and Charlotte Leona (Lazear) C.; m. Maryann Williams, Aug. 8, 1976 (div. Aug. 1989); children: Francisco, Casandra; m. Susan Curtis, Jan. 11, 1992. BA, U. N.Mex., 1976, MA, 1984, PhD, 1989. Vis. asst. prof. Lewis & Clark Coll., Portland, Oreg., 1987-88; vis. asst. prof. Purdue U., West Lafayette, Ind., 1988-91; asst. prof. Purdue U., 1991-95, assoc. prof., 1995—, asst. head, dir. grad. studies Dept. of History, 1998—. Author: The Legal Culture of Northern New Spain, 1700-1810, 1995 (Presidio La Bahia award 1996, Fray Francisco Atanasio Dominguez award 1996), The Protector de Indios in Colonial New Mexico, 1659-1821, 1986; editor and introduction: Libro de los Principales Rudimentos Tocante a Todos Juicios, Criminal, Civil y Executivo, 1764, 1994. Recipient Fulbright Sr. Scholar award, 1993-94, Fulbright-Hays/Spanish Govt. Rsch. grant, 1985-86, Purdue Rsch. Found. Summer Faculty grant, 1992, 96, Dorothy Woodward Meml. fellowship U. N.Mex., 1985. Mem. Instituto Internacional de Historia del Derecho Indiano (elected 1992); Am. Hist. Assn., Conf. on Latin Am. History, Western History Assn., Am. Soc. for Legal History, Phi Alpha Theta (treas. Sigma chpt. 1982-83, pres. 1983-84). Avocations: basketball, gardening, woodworking, guitar playing. Home: 492 Littleton St West Lafayette IN 47906-3013 Office: Dept History Purdue U West Lafayette IN 47907-1358

CUTTER, CURTIS CARLY, consulting company executive; b. Sacramento, Oct. 27, 1928; s. Curtis Harold and Leita (Carly) C.; m. Christiane Kühne, Jan. 29, 1965; children: Colette, Curtis Brooks, Lucho Antonio, Kai Kirsten, Sasha Christiana, Knut Carly. AB, U. Calif., Berkeley, 1951; cert. U. Geneva, 1955; MA, Stanford U., 1969. Consular officer Am. Embassy, Phnom Penh, Cambodia, 1957-59; mem. U.S. del. to UN and Trusteeship Coun., 1959-62; polit. officer Am. embassy, Lima, Peru, 1962-65; chief Office Peruvian Affairs, State Dept., Washington, 1965-67; mem. U.S. del. OAS, 1967-68; prin. officer Am. Consulate, Porto Alegre, Brazil, 1969-70; polit. officer Am. Embassy, Madrid, 1970-72; prin. officer, consul gen. Am. Consulate Gen., Seville, Spain, 1972-75; dep. dir. Office UN Polit. Affairs, 1975-77; acting dep. asst. sec. for congl. rels., 1977-78; pres. Interworld Cons., 1978-93, chmn. 1994—; pres. ChinaMetrik, 1989-98; dir. IMS ChinaMetrik, 1998—; sr. cons. Nat. Dem. Inst. Bd. dirs. China Med. Tribune; dir. AMS Found. Capt. AUS, 1951-53. Recipient State Dept. award for heroism, 1970, State Dept. Meritorious Honor award, 1971, Woodrow Wilson fellow, 1983-94. Mem. Am. Fgn. Svc. Assn., Union League (N.Y.C.), Nat. Press Club (Washington), Alpha Delta Phi. Address: 175 Commonwealth Ave Boston MA 02116-2215

CUTTER, DAVID L., advertising specialty executive; b. Waltham, Mass., Mar. 10, 1941; s. Howell G. and Marion E. (Nickerson) C.; m. Kathryn Ann Pombriant, July 31, 1965; children: Mary C., Susan Beth. BSBA, Ohio State U., 1963. Cost acct. Honeywell Info. Systems, Waltham, Mass., 1969-70; cost acct., pers. mgr. Geiger Bros., Lewiston, Maine, 1970-76, data processing mgr., pers. mgr., 1976-83, v.p. human resources and mgmt. info. systems, 1983—. Bd. dirs. United Way, Lewiston, 1985-90; bd. dirs. Pathways, Inc., Auburn, Maine, 1977-84, 96—, mem. pers. com., 1977-97; mem. Citizens Evaluation Comm., Lewiston, 1986-87. Lt. USN, 1963-69. Office: Geiger Bros Mount Hope Ave Lewiston ME 04241

CUTTER, DAVID LEE, pharmaceutical company executive; b. Oakland, Calif., Jan. 3, 1929; s. Robert Kennedy and Virginia (White) C.; m. Nancy Lee Baugh, Sept. 14, 1950; children: David Lee, Jr., Thomas White, William Baugh, Steven Kennedy, Michael Lee. Student, U. Calif.-Berkeley, 1947; A.B., Stanford U., 1950, M.B.A., 1952. C.P.A., Calif. Staff accountant Webb & Webb, C.P.A.'s, San Francisco, 1952-54; with Cutter Labs., Inc., 1954-84, pres., 1967-74, chmn., 1974-80, vice-chmn., 1980-82; sr. cons., 1982-84; dir. Chad Therapeutics, Inc., Chatsworth, Calif., 1983—, Civic Bancorp, Civic Bank of Commerce, Oakland, 1984—. Active various community drives; mem. Citizens Com. to Study Discrimination in Housing, Berkeley, 1961-62; troop committeeman Boy Scouts Am., 1964-74; v.p. Mt. Diablo Coun., 1975-77, pres., 1978-80, bd. dirs., 1975—; bd. dirs. Golden Gate Scouting, 1978-90, pres. 1980-84; bd. dirs. Park Hills Homes Assn., 1961-63, HEALS, Emeryville, Calif., 1980-87, Alameda County (Calif.) Taxpayers Assn., 1967-69, Insts. Med. Scis., San Francisco, 1974-76, San Francisco Bay Area Coun., 1968-84, pres. Cutter Found., 1967-86; trustee United Way of Bay Area, 1981-86, Miles Found., 1986-92; mem. adv. bd. Herrick Hosp., 1968-76, trustee, 1976-84, pres. bd. trustees, 1978-84; mem. Accrediting Commn. on Edn. in Health Svcs. Adminstrn., 1982-88, adv. coun. Sch. Bus., San Francisco State Coll., 1966-70; bd. dirs. Alta Bates Health Sys., 1984-95, Alta Bates Med. Ctr., 1988-95, chmn., 1991-95, East Bay Community Found., 1984-89, Hosp. Coun. No. Calif., 1983-89, Pathology Inst., 1986-90; bd. dirs. Acute Care Affiliates, 1987-89, chmn. 1988-89, Calif. Healthcare System, 1992-95; bd. govs. Vol. Trustees Not-for-Profit Hosps., 1989-95, vice chmn. 1990-92, treas. 1993-95. Recipient Silver Beaver award Boy Scouts Am., 1982. Mem. AICPA, Stanford Alumni Assn., Berkeley C. of C. (dir. 1977-83, v.p. 1978-83), Rotary (Paul Harris fellow 1990), Delta Upsilon. Office: Bayer Corp 4th and Parker Sts PO Box 1986 Berkeley CA 94701-1986

CUTTER, GARY RAYMOND, biostatistician; b. St. Louis, Feb. 18, 1948; s. Daniel and Mildred (Mandel) C.; m. Sharon R. Gornek, Aug. 24, 1969; children: Corey N., Scott J., Todd J. BA in Math., U. Mo., 1970; MS in Biometry, U. Tex., Houston, 1971, PhD in Biometry, 1974. Asst. prof. biometry U. Tex. Sch. Pub. Health, Houston, 1974-78; expert, cons. Nat. Cancer Inst., Bethesda, Md., 1978-79; assoc. prof. biostats. U. Ala., Birmingham, 1979-89; prof. pub. health St. Jude Children's Rsch. Hosp., Memphis, 1979-89, chair biostats and info. sys., 1989-91; pres. Pythagoras, Inc., Birmingham, 1991—; chmn. Ctr. for Rsch. Methodology and Biometrics AMC Cancer Rsch. Ctr., Denver, 1994—; adj. prof. U. Colo. Health Sci. Ctr., Denver, 1994—, U. Denver, 1996—. Author: A Module of Math., 1972, (with others) Evaluation of Health Education and Promotion Programs: Principles, Guidelines and Methods for the Practitioner, 1984, 2d edit., 1994; contbr. numerous articles to profl. jours. Bd. dirs. Legal Environ. Assistance Found., Birmingham, 1986-89, Temple Emanu El, Birmingham, 1987-89, Jewish Cmty. Ctr., Birmingham, 1984-88, Fair Share for Health, Denver, 1994-96. Grantee NIH, NHLBI, NIDDK, NCI, Multiple Sclerosis Soc., others. Mem. Am. Pub. Health Assn., Am. Statis. Assn., Am. Biometric Soc., Soc. Clin. Trials, Am. Optometric Assn., Mtn. Brook Soccer Club (bd. dirs. 1983-94), Mtn. Brook Athletic Assn. (bd. dirs. 1986-88). Office: AMC Cancer Rsch Ctr 1600 Pierce St Denver CO 80214-1897

CUTTER, JEFFREY S., secondary education educator, music educator; b. Royal Oak, Mich., July 20, 1956; s. George E. and Joy G. (Dolby) C. MusB with distinction, Wayne State U., 1978, MEd, M in Ednl. Leadership/Administrn., 1994. Cert. tchr., Mich. Performing arts facilitator Warren (Mich.) Consol. Community Edn., 1980—; student activities dir. Warren High Sch., 1987-92, auditorium mgr., 1987-92, dir. bands, 1985-92; dir. bands Fuhrmann Middle Sch., 1982—. Vice chmn. Warren Cultural Commn. Mem. Mich. Sch. Band and Orch. Assn. (pres. dist. XVI). Home: 32774 McConnell Ct Warren MI 48092-3111 Office: Fuhrmann Mid Sch 5155 E 14 Mile Rd Sterling Heights MI 48310-6534

CUTTER, JOHN MICHAEL, dentist; b. Columbus, Ohio, May 28, 1952; s. John Raymond and Betty Mae (Paripovich) C.; m. Alice May Mcquitty, Aug. 6, 1977 (div. May 1984); 1 child, John David Benjamin; m. Linda Ann Hovis-Smith, Oct. 20, 1990 (div. Jan. 1997). BA, Ohio State U., 1974, DDS, 1976. Pvt. practice family dentistry and laser-assisted care Fairfield, Ohio, 1976—, Loveland, Ohio, 1993-96; assoc. staff dental outpatient dept. Jewish Hosp. Cin., 1977-80, courtesy staff mem. 1980-84; also dental outpatient rep. to med. records and ambulatory care com.; instr. radiology div. dental hygiene U. Cin., 1977, supervising dentist clin. affairs; clin. dentist Rockdale Elem. & Condon Schs. for Handicapped, 1977-79; founding mem., trustee DenCare, 1986-89. Contbr. articles to profl. jour. Sr. clin. dentist Cin. Bd. Edn.; mem. programming com. Southwestern Ohio chpt. Am. Heart Assn., 1983; co-chmn. fin. com., ch. bd. Lindenwald United Meth. Ch., 1982;. Mem. ADA, Ohio Dental Assn., Acad. Gen. Dentistry (nat. spokesdentist in laser-assisted dentistry), Am. Endodontic Soc., Internat. Acad. Laser Dentistry, Cin. Dental Soc. (assoc.), Keely Dental Soc. (co-chmn. programming com. 1980, chmn. continuing edn. 1979-82, editor Keely Bull. 1982-85, mem.-at-large coun. 1982), Psi Omega. Republican. Avocations: cross-country bicycling, collecting antique banks and toys, skiing. Office: 1251 Nilles Rd Fairfield OH 45014-7205

CUTTING, COURT BALDWIN, plastic surgeon, computer graphics researcher; b. N.J., June 26, 1949; s. Richard Park and Holly Cutting; m. Sherry Cutting. BS, Pa. State U., 1971; MD, U. Chgo., 1975. Diplomate Am. Bd. Plastic Surgery, Am. Bd. Otolaryngology. Intern in surgery Yale U. Hosp., New Haven, Conn., 1975; head and neck surgery resident U. Iowa, Iowa City, 1976-80; craniofacial rsch. fellow N.Y. Med. Ctr., N.Y.C., 1980, plastic surgery resident, 1981-83, craniofacial surgery fellow, 1984, assoc. prof. surgery, 1984—; dir. cleft lip and palate program, N.Y.C., 1984—. Office: Court Cutting MD PC 333 E 34th St IK New York NY 10016

CUTTING, HEYWARD, designer, planner; b. N.Y.C., Dec. 3, 1921; s. Heyward and Constance (Roberson) C.; m. Jeremy Hohenstein, 1948 (div. 1978); children: Heyward, Francis Brockholst, William Bayard; m. Joan Faulkner Randell, Nov. 3, 1979; Stepson, Thomas William Randell. Grad., Eton, 1939; student, Harvard, 1939-41; B.Sc., Ill. Inst. Tech., 1953. Partner Chermayeff & Cutting (architects and indsl. designers), 1954-56; pvt. practice architecture Cambridge, 1957; mem. Geometrics, Inc. (architects, engrs. and cons. specialized structures), Cambridge, 1958-68, 73-86; pvt. practice cons., 1986—; asst. dir. adminstrn. Mus. Fine Arts, Boston, 1968-73, trustee, 1961-68, 73-78. Former trustee Mt. Auburn Hosp., Cambridge; past mem. vis. com. dept. archaeology, also dept. fine arts Harvard U. Served to maj. KRRC, 60th Rifles Brit. Army, 1941-45, Egypt, Italy. Mentioned in despatches. Club: Tavern (Boston). Home and Office: 377 Main St Concord MA 01742-2340

CUTTING, ROBERT THOMAS, army officer, physician; b. Winchendon, Mass., Oct. 28, 1929; s. Leon Louis and Albina Agnes (Duquette) C.; m. Frances Clark Smith, May 16, 1992; children from previous marriage: Mary Beth, Jeanne, Jonathan, Rosemary, Paul, Eileen, James. BS, Holy Cross Coll., 1951; MD, Boston U., 1955; MPH, Harvard U., 1959. Diplomate: Am. Bd. Preventive Medicine. Commd. officer U.S. Army, advanced through grades to brig. gen.; chief preventive medicine research div. U.S. Army Med. Research and Devel. Command, 1965-69; chief med. research team Vietnam, 1969-70; dir. div. surgery Walter Reed Army Inst. Research, 1970-72; chief preventive medicine div. Office of the Surgeon Gen., Washington, 1972-75; command surgeon U.S. Army Materiel Devel. and Readiness Command, 1976-80; dir. health care ops. Office of the Surgeon Gen., Washington, 1980-82; comdg. gen. Dwight David Eisenhower Army Med. Ctr., Ft. Gordon, Ga., 1982-84; Westinghouse, Aiken, S.C., 1984—. Contbr. articles to profl. jours. Decorated Legion of Merit (2), Bronze Star (2), Air Medal (3), D.S.M. Fellow Am. Coll. Preventive Medicine; mem. AMA, Am. Pub. Health Assn., Assn. Mil. Surgeons, Am. Soc. Tropical Medicine and Hygiene, Aerospace Med. Assn. Republican. Roman Catholic. Home: 752 Westport Rd Augusta GA 30907-9531 Office: Savannah River Plant Med Dept Aiken SC 29808

CUTTS, CHARLES EUGENE, civil engineering educator; b. Sioux Falls, S.D., May 15, 1914; s. Charles Clifford and Ethel May (Gardner) C.; m. Jane Bebensee, Mar. 16, 1946; children: George Gardner, Elizabeth Anne. B.C.E., U. Minn., 1936, M.S. in Civil Engring, 1939, Ph.D., 1949. Registered profl. engr., Minn., Fla., Mich. Instrumentman Milw. R.R., 1936- 38; teaching asst. dept. civil engring. U. Minn., 1938-39, instr., asst. prof., 1946-50; engr. C.F. Haglin & Sons, summer 1939; asst. prof. dept. civil engring. Robert Coll., Istanbul, Turkey, 1939-42; engr. Braithwaite Co., Ltd., Iskenderun, Turkey, summer 1942, 43; asso. prof., asso. research engr. U. Fla., 1950-53; engr. Engring. Scis. Program NSF, Washington, 1953-56; profl. lectr. civil engring. George Washington U., 1955-56; prof., chmn. dept. civil engring. Mich. State U., 1956-69, prof., 1969-84, prof. emeritus, 1984—; cons. U. Minn. Morocco Project, 1986. Author: Structural Design in Reinforced Concrete, 1954, other tech. publs. Served to maj. C.E. AUS, 1943-46; lt. col. Res. ret. Mem. Nat. Acad. Scis. (fellowship com. 1961-63), ASCE (chmn. com. on mech. properties of materials 1965, pres. Mich. sect. 1967, chmn. com. on engring. edn. 1969-70), Am. Concrete Inst., Am. Soc. Engring. Edn. (chmn. civil engr. div. 1965-66, v.p. 1970—, chmn. constn. and bylaws com. 1981-83), Engrs. Council Profl. Devel. (chmn. region 5 1972-73), Nat. Soc. Profl. Engrs., Column Research Council, Tau Beta Pi, Chi Epsilon. Home: 4599 Ottawa Dr Okemos MI 48864-2028 Office: Civil Engring Mich State Univ East Lansing MI 48824

CUZZETTO, CHARLES EDWARD, accountant, financial analyst, educator; b. Tacoma, Wash., Nov. 1, 1954; s. Edward Ralph and Bernice Almira (Schmidt) C.; m. Susan Lynne Race, June 15, 1991; 1 child, Shandey Race Cuzzetto. AA, Tacoma Community Coll., 1975; BA in Acctg., U. Wash., 1977; MBA, City U., Bellevue, Wash., 1982. CPA, Wash.; cert. internal auditor; cert. mgmt. acct.; cert. fraud examiner; cert. govtl. fin. mgr. Auditor Chevron Corp., San Francisco, 1977-79, Union Oil Corp., Seattle, 1980-83; owner, operator Cuzzetto Enterprises Restaurant, Tacoma, 1981-83; auditor Alaska Airlines, Seattle, 1983-85; dir. auditing Tacoma Pub. Schs., 1985—; mgmt./fiscal analyst Pierce County Coun., Tacoma, 1991; instr. bus. and acctg. City U., 1985—; adj. faculty U. Puget Sound, 1995—. Author: Internal Auditing in School Districts, 1993; contbr. articles to profl. jours. Hon. mem. Seattle Ind. Comedy Co-Op, 1983—; chmn. supervisory com. Ednl. Employees Credit Union, 1987-93; vice chmn. bd. dirs. Rainier Pacific Credit Union, 1996—. Mem. Inst. Internal Auditors (Internat. Gold medal 1986), Christopher Columbus Soc. (treas. 1983-92). Avocations: genealogy, wine making, boating. Home: 2614 88th Street Ct NW Gig Harbor WA 98332-9546

CVENGROS, JOSEPH MICHAEL, manufacturing company executive; b. Pana, Ill., Oct. 8, 1931; s. Joseph John and Mary Bernice (Sturgeon) C.; m. Mary Elizabeth Ainsworth, Feb. 11, 1956; children: Joseph J., Mary E., Andrew T., Katherine A., J. Michael, Robert A., David L., Susan M. BABS, Washington U., St. Louis, 1955; MBA, Northwestern U., 1960. Pers. mgr. Continental Baking Co., Chgo., 1956-57; asst. to chmn. bd. dirs. Automatic Canteen Co. divsn. ITT, Chgo., 1957-65; cons. Spencer Stuart and Assoc., Chgo., 1965-68; investor High Tech., Inc., Chgo., 1968—; chmn. bd. dirs., CEO Anaconda Metal Hose divsn. Anamet, Inc., Glen Ellyn, Ill., 1984—. Fellow Econ. Club Chgo. Office: Anamet Inc 739 Roosevelt Rd Ste 204 Glen Ellyn IL 60137-5873

CVETANOVICH, DANNY L., lawyer; b. Wheeling, W.Va., Oct. 2, 1952; s. Louis J. and Nila J. (Hall) C.; m. Sharon M. Smith, Sept. 8, 1979; children: Gregory L., Steven W. BA, West Liberty State Coll., 1974; JD, Harvard U., 1977. Bar: Ohio 1977, U.S. Dist. Ct. (so. dist.) Ohio 1978, U.S. Ct. Appeals (6th cir.) 1980, U.S. Dist. Ct. (no. dist.) Ohio 1984, W.Va. 1985, U.S. Dist. Ct. (so. dist.) W.Va. 1985, U.S. Ct. Appeals (4th cir.) 1986, U.S. Dist. Ct. (we. dist.) Tex. 1998. Assoc. Bricker & Eckler, Columbus, Ohio, 1977-82, ptnr., 1983-87; ptnr. Arter & Hadden LLP, Columbus, 1987—. Mem. ABA, Ohio State Bar Assn., W.Va. Bar Assn., Columbus Bar Assn. Democrat. Avocations: hunting, fishing, golf. Office: Arter & Hadden LLP One Columbus 10 W Broad St Columbus OH 43215-3422

CWERENZ-MAXIME, VIRGINIA MARGARET, primary educator, secondary education educator; b. Chgo., Aug. 30, 1937; d. John B. and Bessie (Mayworm) Cwerenz; m. Daniel S. Maxime, June 19, 1988; stepchildren: Lisa, Brian, Mark. BS, Alverno Coll., 1968; MS, No. Ill. U., 1974. Cert. tchr., Ill., Nev. Tchr. grades 1st thru 6th St. Joseph Catholic Sch., Richmond, Ill., 1959-66; tchr. grades 6th thru 8th St. Matthew Sch., Glendale Heights, Ill., 1966-69, St. Teresa Sch., Kankakee, Ill., 1969-70; tchr. art Edison Jr. High Sch., Wheaton, Ill., 1971-78, Wheaton Ctrl. High Sch., 1979-83, Edison Jr. High Sch., Wheaton, 1980-83, Edison Mid. Sch., Wheaton, Ill., 1983-94; chair dept. fine and applied art Edison Mid. Sch., Wheaton, Ill., 1981-92; adult educator Wheaton Warrenville Dist. 200, 1973-78, 91-94; art tchr. various elem. schs., 1993-94; co-author art program; art tchr. Gwendolyn Woolley and Cox Elem., Las Vegas, 1994—, G. Woolley & Cox Elem., 1994-96, G. Woolley & L. Creig, 1996-97, G. Woolley, 1997-98, Edith Gareheim, 1998—; exhibitor Educators as Artists of Southern Nevada, 1997, 98; A tchr. Las Vegas Channel 13, 1995; grant participant Getty Found. Discipline Base Art Edn., Cin., 1992. One-woman show includes Hawthorn Bank, Wheaton, 1984; exhibited in group shows at No. Ill. U., DeKalb, 1970-71, various places, Wheaton, 1973-94; tile mural designer, installer Ganechime Elem. Sch., 1999; multicultural mural designer, dir., 1994-95. Mem. art gallery coun. Coll. DuPage, Glen Ellyn, Ill., 1975-76; fund raiser 10M-Fund, Jerry's Kids, ERA Realtors, Wheaton, 1979-83; mem. Las Vegas Art Mus., 1994—; judge various art shows, DuPage. Recipient blue and gold ribbons Ill. State Town and Country, 1970; study grants to Eng., France, Holland, Belgium, Greece and Austria. Mem. NEA, Ill. Edn. Assn., Nat. Art Edn. Assn., Ill. Art Edn. Assn. (v.p. student chpt. 1970-71), Wheaton Warrenville Edn. Assn., DuPage Art League, Clark County Classroom Tchrs. Assn., Nev. State Edn. Assn. and Southern Nevada Art educators. Roman Catholic. Avocations: water colors, choir. Home: 5121 Thousand Palms Ln Las Vegas NV 89130-3606

CWIKLA, RICH I., secondary education educator. Secondary tchr. West Fargo (N.D.) High Sch. Recipient Tchr. Excellence for N.D. award Internat. Tech. Edn. Assn., 1992. Office: West Fargo High Sch 801 9th St E West Fargo ND 58078-3100*

CYGANOWSKI, MELANIE L., bankruptcy judge; b. Chgo., June 8, 1952; d. Daniel F. and Sophia A. C.; married, 1989. AB in anthropology, Grinnell Coll., 1974; postgrad. in urban devel., Cornell U., 1975; JD magna cum laude, SUNY, Buffalo, 1981. Coord. program planning, planner, cons. dept. community devel. and human resources City of Buffalo, N.Y., 1974-78; dir. individual referral program Broadway-Fillmore Area Coun., Inc., Buffalo, 1978-79; summer assoc. Hodgson, Russ, Andrews, Wood & Goodyear, Buffalo, 1980; law clerk to Hon. Charles L. Brieant U.S. Dist. Ct. (so. dist.) N.Y., 1981-82; litigation assoc. Sullivan & Cromwell, N.Y.C., 1982-89; sr. atty. Milbank, Tweed, Hadley & McCloy, 1989-93; judge U.S. Bankruptcy Ct. (ea. dist.) N.Y., Happauge, 1993—; Bar: N.Y. 1982, U.S. Supreme Ct., U.S. Ct. Appeals (2nd. cir.), U.S. Dist. Ct. (so., ea. and we. dists.) N.Y. Contbr. articles to legal jours. Mem. ABA, N.Y. State Bar Assn., N.Y.C. Bar Assn. Roman Catholic. Avocations: bicycling, gardening, fishing. Office: US Bankruptcy Ct 601 Veterans Memorial Hwy Hauppauge NY 11788-2903

CYLKE, FRANK KURT, librarian; b. New Haven, Feb. 13, 1932; s. Frank Anton and Helen Mary (Callahan) C.; m. Mary Elizabeth Newhouse, Dec. 28, 1962; children: Frank Kurt, Mary Amanda, Virginia Ann. B.A., U. Conn., 1954; M.L.S., Pratt Inst., 1957; postgrad., Fairfield U., Am. U., Georgetown U. Libr. Graham-Eckes Sch., Palm Beach, Fla., 1957-58; reference libr. Bridgeport (Conn.) Pub. Libr., 1958-62; head pub. svc. New Haven Pub. Libr., 1962-65; asst. libr. Providence Pub. Libr., 1965-68; chief libr. rsch. U.S. Office Edn., 1968-69; exec. dir. fed. libr. com. Libr. of Congress, 1970-73; dir. nat. libr. svc. for blind, physically handicapped Library of Congress, 1973—; instr. Grad. Libr. Sch. U. R.I., 1967-68; instr. Grad. Libr. Sch. Cath. U. Am., 1974—, bd. visitors, 1980—; exec. sec. panel edn. & tng. Com. Sci. and Tech. Inst.; chmn. librs. tech. com. Met. Washington Coun. Govts., 1970-71; sec. U.S. Book Exch., 1972-74; sec.-treas. Joint Venture Pub. Activity, 1970-74; mem. E. Greenwich (R.I.) Free Libr. Corp., 1967—; adv. bd. Ednl. Resources Info. Ctr./Clearinghouse Libr. and Info. Sci., 1970-72; bd. visitors Grad. Sch. Libr./Info. Sci., Pratt Inst., 1980—. Editor: Captains Shelf, 1964-66, FLC Newsletter, 1970-73, Library Service for the Blind and Physically Handicapped: An International Approach, 1979,. Recipient Va. Cultural Laureate, 1992, Dayton M. Forman Meml. award, 1996 (Can. Nat. Inst. for the Blind); grantee U.S. Office Edn., 1972. Mem. ALA (F.J. Campbell medal 1982, Joseph W. Lippincott award 1994), Spl. Librs. Assn. (chpt. pres. 1975-76), Am. Soc. Info. Sci. (sec. 1974-75), Pvt. Librs. Assn., World Blind Union, Internat. Fedn. Libr. Assns. (founder, chmn. sect. for blind), Friends of Librs. for Blind in N.Am. (founder, ex-officio bd. dirs.), Shenandoah Natural History Assn., Manuscript Soc., Crow's Nest, Ancient Order Hibernians. Roman Catholic. Home: PO Box 192 Great Falls VA 22066-0192 Office: Libr of Congress Nat Libr Svc 1291 Taylor St NW Washington DC 20542-0002

CYMBLER, MURRAY JOEL, corporate professional; b. Germany, July 20, 1948; came to U.S., 1949; s. Harry and Adele C.; m. Carol Horowitz, Nov. 23, 1972; children: Adam, Robyn. BA, Hunter Coll., 1970. Tchr. N.Y. Bd. Edn., Bronx, 1970-71; contract analyst The Equitable Life Assurance Soc., N.Y.C., 1972-86; chmn., chief exec. officer Astro-Stream Corp., Levittown, N.Y., 1986-91; mgr. fin. Landmark Plaza Properties Corp., Sayville, N.Y., 1991—. Inventor Orbi Sport-toy, 1985. Office: Orbico Inc 133 Ronni Dr East Meadow NY 11554-1330

CYMROT, MARK ALAN, lawyer; b. Queens, N.Y., Oct. 8, 1947; s. Irwin Maurice and Anne (Kipnis) C.; children: Isaac, Erin. BA, George Washington U., 1969; JD, Columbia U., 1972. Bar: D.C. 1973. Trial lawyer civil div. U.S. Dept. of Justice, Washington, 1972-77; sr. litigator Consumers Union of U.S. Inc., Washington, 1977-79; special litigation counsel civil div. U.S. Dept. of Justice, Washington, 1979-83; ptnr. Cole Corette & Abrutyn, Washington, 1983-91, Baker & Hostetler, Washington, 1991—. Contbr. articles to profl. jours. Named one of 50 Best Lawyers in Washington by Washingtonian Mag., 1992. Avocations: photography, golf. Office: Baker & Hostetler 1050 Connecticut Ave NW Washington DC 20036-5304

CYNADER, MAX SIGMUND, psychology, physiology, brain research educator, researcher; b. Berlin, Feb. 24, 1947; arrived in Can., 1951; s. Samuel and Maria (Kraushar) C.; m. Moira Elizabeth Langton, May 30, 1985; children: Madeleine Maria, Rebecca Kay, Alexandra Josephine. BSc, Mc Gill U., Montreal, Que., Can., 1967; PhD, MIT, 1972. Fellow neuroanatomy Max-Planck Inst. Psychiatry, Munich, 1972-73; asst. prof. psychology Dalhousie U., 1973-77, assoc. prof., 1977-81, assoc. prof. physiology, 1979-84, prof. psychology, 1981-84, Killam rsch. prof., 1984-88, prof. physiology, 1984-88; prof. psychology U. B.C., 1988—, prof. physiology, 1988—, prof., dir. rsch. dept. ophthalmology, 1988—; dir. brain & spinal cord rsch. ctr. U. B.C. & Vancouver Gen. Hosp., 1997—; mem. pres.'s workshop on five yr. plan strengthening sci. support in Can. Natural Scis. and Engring. Rsch. Coun. Can., 1984, workshop for Steacie fellows, 1988; mem. task force on curriculum devel. in Can. neurosci., 1984; mem. spl. adv. panel on rsch. preparedness USAF, 1985; rep. Internat. Human Frontiers Sci. program Med. Rsch. Coun. Can., 1988; mem. grants com. behavioural scis. Med. Rsch. Coun. Can., program grants com. 1989—; referee senate rev. grad. program in neurosci. U. Western Ont., 1989; mem. math., computational and theoretical spl. rev. com. NIMH, 1989—; external reviewer Med. Rsch. Coun. Can., Alta. Heritage Fund Med. Rsch., NIH, NSF, USAF Office Sci. Rsch., Multiple Sclerosis Soc. Can., Vancouver Found., March of Dimes, Fight for Sight. Mem. editorial bd. jours. Behavioral Brain Rsch., Clin. Vision Scis., Concepts in Neurosci., Devel. Brain Rsch., Exptl. Brain Rsch., Neural Networks, Visual Neurosci.; mem. adv. bd. series Rsch. Notes in Neural Computing; contbr. articles to profl. jours. Recipient Killam Rsch. prize U. B.C., 1989—; E.W.R. Steacie fellow Natural Sci. and Engring. Rsch. Coun. Can., 1979; Can. Inst. Advanced Rsch. fellow, 1986—; grantee Med. Rsch. Coun. Can., 1973—, Natural Sci. and Engring. Rsch. Coun. Can., 1975—, NIH, 1978-81. Fellow Can. Inst. Advanced Rsch., Royal Soc. Can.; mem. Soc. Neurosci. (Halifax chpt., pres. 1985, edn. com. 1986-89), Can. Assn. Neurosci. (pres. 1986), Assn. Rsch. Otolaryngology,

Assn. Rsch. in Vision and Opthalmology, Can. Physiol. Soc., Internat. Brain Rsch. Orgn., Internat. Soc. Devel. Neurosci., Internat. Strabismol. Assn., World Fedn. Neuroscientists. Semifinalist Can. Astronaut program, 1983. Office: U of BC Dept Ophthalmology, 2550 Willow St, Vancouver, BC Canada V5Z 3N9

CYPERT, JIMMY DEAN, lawyer; b. Springdale, Ark., May 24, 1934; s. Burl Irvin and Ora Opal (Sisco) C.; m. Gaye Annette Warren, Aug. 26, 1956; children: Julie Jan, Jamie Ann. BS, U. Ark., 1956, LLB, JD, 1959. Bar: Ark. 1959. Assoc. Crouch, Jones & Blair, Springdale, 1959-60; ptnr. Crouch, Blair, Cypert & Waters, Springdale, 1960-91, Cypert, Crouch, Clark & Harwell, Springdale, 1991—; bd. dirs., pres. Westwood Inc., Indsl. Leasing Inc., TC Investments; bd. dirs. 1st Nat. Bank. Pres. Washington County Young Democrats, 1962; bd. dirs. United Fund, 1962; pres., bd. dirs. Springdale Bd. Edn., 1966-73; bd. dirs. Washington County Sch. for Retarded Children, 1967-70; mem. hon. coun. U. Ark. Sch. Law., 1958; trustee Springdale Meml. Hosp., 1976—. Capt. U.S. Army, 1956-58. Recipient Disting. Svc. award Springdale Jaycees, 1963; named one of Outstanding Young Men of Am., U.S. Jaycees, 1963. Mem. ABA (Outstanding Lawyer-Citizen award 1985-86), Ark. Bar Assn. (exec. com., ho. of dels. 1976-78, chmn. exec. com. 1978, pres. 1981-82), Washington County Bar Assn., Internat. Platform Assn., Ark. Young Lawyers Assn. (pres. 1962), Springdale C. of C. (dir. 1964-70, pres. 1966, Outstanding Svc. award 1968, Outstanding Citizen award 1984), Elks, Kiwanis, Sigma Nu, Alph Kappa Psi. Methodist (chmn. bd.). Home: 109 Woodcliff Cir Springdale AR 72764-3603 Office: 111 S Holcomb St Springdale AR 72764-4441

CYPESS, RAYMOND HAROLD, bioscience organization executive. BS, Bklyn. Coll., 1961; DVM, U. Ill., 1967; PhD, U. N.C., 1970. From asst. to assoc. prof. microbiology and epidemiology U. Pitts. Sch. Pub. Health, 1970-76; chmn., dir. diagnostic lab. N.Y. State Coll. Vet. Medicine, 1977-87; prof. microbiology and immunology U. Tenn., Memphis, 1988-93, vice-provost for rsch. and rsch. tng., dean, 1988-93; pres., CEO Am. Type Culture Collection, Manassas, Va., 1993—; chmn. dept. preventive medicine N.Y. Staet Coll. Vet. Medicine, 1978-84; adj. prof. U. Pitts. Sch. Pub. Health, 1977; chmn. nominating com. Am. Coll. Epidemiology, 1987-89; mem. U.S.-Spain coop. program devel. and coord. symposium on control infectious disease Inst. Nat. Investigation Agrarias, 1985-87; bd. dirs. MD-IPA Corp. Mem. editl. bd. Jour. Parasitology, 1979-82, Exptl. Parasitology, 1983-89; contbr. over 60 revs. and articles to profl. jours., chpts. to books. Gov. appointee Va. Biotech. Authority, 1995—. Fellow Fogarty Internat., Mexico, 1975; recipient Career Devel. award NIH, 1975-79. Mem. Am. Soc. for Microbiology (com. on internat. affairs pub. and sci. affairs bd. 1995—). Fax: 703-365-2725. Office: Am Type Culture Collection 10801 University Blvd Manassas VA 20110-2204*

CYPHERS, STEVE, reporter; b. July 22, 1955. BA, MA, Colo. State U., 1978. Sports dir. Sta. KTVG-TV, Helena, Mont., 1981; weekend sports anchor Sta. KELO-TV, Sioux Falls, S.D., 1981, Sta. WGUN-TV, Tucson, 1982; weeknight sportscasts anchor Sta. WVTH-TV, Syracuse, 1983-85; anchor/reporter Sta. KSL-TV, Salt Lake City, 1985—; corr. SportsCenter ESPN, 1990—; profiled numerous sports personalities including Nolan Ryan, Buster Douglas, Earnest Byner, Boomer Esiason, Lou Pinella, and Dwight Gooden; covered major events including the 1992 Summer Olympics, the Ky. Derby, the Cotton Bowl, Major League Baseball League Championship series, NFL playoffs, NFL draft, and the NCAA Basketball Championship, among others. Named Utah's Sportscaster of Yr. Nat. Sportscasters and Sportswriters Assn., 1988, Rocky Mountain Emmy award. Office: c/o ESPN ESPN Pla Bristol CT 06010*

CYPHERT, STACEY TODD, health facilities administrator; b. Torrance, Calif., Mar. 14, 1959; s. Frederick Ralph and Lois Florence Cyphert; m. Rosemary Wilmoth, July 25, 1992. BS, Ohio State U., 1981, MHA, 1983; PhD, U. Iowa, 1990. Fellow Duke U. Med. Ctr., Durham, N.C., 1983-84; coord. prospective payment U. Cin. Hosp., 1984-86; rsch. and tchg. asst. U. Iowa, Iowa City, 1986-89, program assoc., 1989-92, adminstrv. assoc. statewide health, 1993-95, asst. to v.p. for statewide health, 1995-97, asst. v.p. for statewide health, asst. dir. hosps. and clinics, 1997—; asst. dir. Iowa Hosp. Quality Assessment and Enhancement Inst., Iowa City, 1992-93; reviewer Hosp. and Health Svc. Adminstrn., 1988-92; adj. lectr. U. Iowa, 1990—. Contbr. articles to jours. in field. Vol. Iowa Spl. Olympics, Iowa City, 1995—; mem. State of Iowa Med. Assistance Adv. Coun., 1991—, vice chair, 1995, chair, 1996, 97; mem. State of Iowa Welfare Reform Adv. Group, 1996-98; mem. Assn. of Iowa Hosp. and Health Systems Coun. on Representation and Advocacy, 1997—; mem. adv. com. Iowa Plan, 1998—. Mem. Assn. Health Svcs. Rsch., Nat. Speleological Soc., Am. Coll. Healthcare Execs., Am. Hosp. Assn., Iowa City C. of C. (health and human svcs. subcom. 1994—), Iowa Rural Health Assn. (bd. dirs. 1998—), Optimists (bd. dirs. 1996—). Avocations: photography, volleyball, caving, tennis. Home: 316 Monroe St Iowa City IA 52246-1614 Office: U Iowa Hosps and Clinics 200 Hawkins Dr Iowa City IA 52242-1009

CYR, ARTHUR I., political science and economics educator; b. L.A., Mar. 1, 1945; s. Irving Arthur and Frances Mary Cyr; m. Betty Totten (div.); children: David Arthur, Thomas Harold, James Price. BA, UCLA, 1966, MA, 1967; AM, Harvard U., 1969, PhD, 1971. Teaching fellow Harvard U., 1970-71; program officer internat. and edn.-research divs. Ford Found., 1971-74; asst. prof. polit. sci., adminstr. UCLA, 1974-76; program dir. Chgo. Coun. Fgn. Rels., 1976-81, v.p., 1981-96; pres., CEO, World Trade Ctr. Assn., Chgo., 1996-98; Clausen prof. polit. econ. and world bus. Carthage Coll., Kenosha, Wis., 1998—. Author: Liberal Politics in Britain, 1977, rev. edit., 1988, British Foreign Policy and the Atlantic Area, 1979, U.S. Foreign Policy and European Security, 1987, After the Cold War—American Foreign Policy, Europe and Asia, 1997, rev. edit., 1999; contbr. articles to profl. jours. With USAR 1966-73. Mem. Internat. Inst. Strategic Studies, Am. Polit. Sci. Assn., Coun. Fgn. Rels., Century Assn., Econ. Club, Phi Beta Kappa. Office: Carthage Coll Chair Polit Econ World Bus Kenosha WI 53140-1994

CYR, CONRAD KEEFE, federal judge; b. Limestone, Maine, Dec. 9, 1931; s. Louis Emery and Kathleen Mary (Keefe) C.; m. Judith Ann Pirie, June 23, 1962 (dec. Mar. 1985); children: Keefe Clark, Jeffrey Louis Frederick; m. Diana Kathleen Sanborn, Sept. 25, 1987. BS cum laude, Holy Cross Coll., 1953; JD, Yale U., 1956; LLD (hon.), Husson Coll., 1991, Husson Coll., 1991. Bar: Maine 1956. Pvt. practice Limestone, 1956-59; asst. U.S. atty., Bangor, Maine, 1959-61; judge U.S. Bankruptcy Court, Bangor, 1961-81; judge U.S. Dist. Ct., Bangor, 1981-83, chief judge, 1983-89; judge U.S. Fgn. Intelligence Surveillance Ct., 1987-89; judge U.S. Ct. Appeals (1st cir.), Boston, 1989-97, sr. judge, 1997—; standing spl. master U.S. Dist. Ct., Maine, 1974-76; chief judge Bankruptcy Appellate Panel Dist., Mass., 1980-81; mem. Jud. Council for the 1st Circuit, 1987—, com. on adminstrn. of the bankruptcy system Jud. Conf. U.S., 1987—. founder, editor-in-chief Am. Bankruptcy Law Jour., 1970-81; contbg. author, editor: Collier on Bankruptcy, Vol. 10. Treas. Limestone Republican Com., 1958; chmn. Town of Limestone Budget Com., 1959; mem. steering com. U.S. AID Project for Assisting Bankruptcy and Reorgn. Procedures in Ctr. and Ea. Europe. Recipient cert. of appreciation Kans. Bar Assn., 1979, U. Maine, 1983; Nat. Judge's Recognition award Nat. Conf. Bankruptcy Judges, 1979; Key to Town Limestone, 1983; named one of Outstanding Young Men of Maine, 1963. Fellow Maine Bar Found. (charter), Am. Coll. Bankruptcy; mem. Maine Bar Assn., Penobscot Bar Assn., Nat. Conf. Bankruptcy Judges (prs. 1976-77), Nat. Bankruptcy Conf. (exec. bd. 1974-77), Am. Juticature Soc., Limestone C. of C. (pres.). Roman Catholic. *

CYR, J. V. RAYMOND, telecommunications company executive; b. Montreal, Que., Can., Feb. 11, 1934; s. Armand and Yvonne (Lagace) C.; m. Marie Bourdon, Sept. 1, 1956; children: Helene, Paul Andre. Student, Ecole Poly.; BASc., U. Montreal, 1958; postgrad. studies in engring., Bell Labs., N.J., Nat. Def. Coll., 1972-73; LLD (hon.), Concordia U., Montreal, 1988. With Bell Can., 1992-96, BCE, Inc., 1987-93; engr. Bell Can., 1958-65; staff engr. Bell Can., Montreal, 1965-70; chief engr. Bell Can., Quebec City, 1970-73; v.p. ops. staff region Bell Can., Montreal, 1973-75, v.p., 1975; exec. v.p. Bell Can., Quebec, 1975-79, v.p. adminstrn., 1979-83; pres. Bell Can., Montreal, 1983-85, chmn., pres., chief exec. officer, 1985-87; chmn., 1992-96; chmn. bd. Bell Can., Montreal, 1987-89; pres. BCE Inc. (formerly Bell Can. Enterprises), Montreal, 1987-88; pres., chief exec. officer BCE, Inc. (formerly Bell Can. Enterprises), Montreal, 1988-89, also bd. dirs., chmn., pres., chief exec. officer, 1989-90, chmn., chief exec. officer, 1990-92; chmn. BCE, Inc. (formerly Bell Can. Enterprises), 1992-93, dir., sr. advisor to chmn.'s office, 1993-97; chmn. Montreal Trust, 1989-90; bd. dirs. Can. Nat., Air Can., SR Telecom, ART Advanced Rsch. & Techs. Inc., Polyvalor Inc., Cognicase Inc., G.T.C. Transcontinental Ltd., Manitex Inc., Cable Satisfaction Internat. Inc., CESCOM Inc., Cable Satisfaction Internat. Inc., Transp. Can. Pipelines, chmn. bd., 1989-92; chmn. Telesat Can., 1992-98, TMI Comm., 1994-97, Geomatics Internat. Inc., 1995—, VISTAR Telecomms. Inc., 1998-99, Polyvalor Inc., 1997—; vice chmn. Domtar Inc., 1994-96, Aerospace Advanced and Techs., 1998—. Mem. assoc. gov. U. Montreal; past chmn. Jr. Achievement Can., Montreal Mus. Contemporary Art, Opera de Montreal; bd. dirs. Ecole Poly. de Montreal, Old Port of Montreal Corp. Inc. Decorated Officer Order of Can., 1988; recipient Can. Engrs. Gold Medal award, 1987, Ordre du Mérite des Diplômes, U. Montreal, 1988, Laureate of Prix des comm. du Que., 1990, Mgmt. Achievement award McGill U., 1991, Great Montrealer award, 1991, Commemorative medal for 125th ann. of Confedn. of Can., 1992, Personnalité du 125e Anniversaire de l'Ecole Poly, 1998; chair in mgmt. of tech. named in his honor Ecole Poly, named Laureate Personnalite du 125e Anniversaire de l'Ecole Polytechnique, 1998. Mem. Can. Acad. Engring. (founding), St. Denis Club, St. James Club, Mt. Bruno Golf Club, Islemere Club. Roman Catholic. Avocations: golf, swimming. Office: Bell Canada, 1050 Beaver Hall Hill 19th, Montreal, PQ Canada H2Z 1S4

CYR, JULIETTE MARY, molecular biology researcher; b. Bristol, Conn., Aug. 12, 1965; d. Raoul Joseph and Rita (Castonguay) C. BS cum laude, Coll. New Rochelle, 1988; MS in Comparative Physiology, U. Conn., 1995, postgrad., 1995—. Grad. rschr. in psychopharmacology Sch. Pharmacy, U. Conn., Storrs, 1988-90, tchg. asst., 1989-90; asst. rsch. scientist Nathan Kline Inst. Psychiat. Rsch., Orangeburg, N.Y., 1990-91; clin. rsch. assoc. Nat. Med. Rsch. Assn., Hartford, Conn., 1991-94; pres. Grad. Student Senate U. Conn., Storrs, 1996-97, tchg. asst. dept. biolg. scis. and devel. biology, 1993—, rsch. asst. dept. molecular and cell biology, 1995—; chair exec. com. Grad. Student Senate, Storrs, 1996-97; mem. various univ. coms. U. Conn., Storrs, 1996—. Prodn., host Celtic Voyage, WHUS Radio, Storrs, 1995-96. Sales dir. WHUS Radio, Storrs, 1994-95, celtic music dir., 1994—. Mem. AAAS, Am. Physiol. Soc., Fedn. Am. Socs. Exptl. Biology, Assn. Women in Sci. Democrat. Roman Catholic. Avocations: celtic and folk music, computers. Home: 15-2 Kent Ct Ashford CT 06278-1536 Office: U Conn Dept Molecular & Cell Biol 125 N Eagleville Rd # Storrs Mansfield CT 06269-9011

CYR, KAREN D., lawyer. Gen. counsel Nuclear Regulatory Commn., Fockville, Md. Office: Nuclear Regulatory Commn 11555 Rockville Pike Rockville MD 20852-2738*

CYS, RICHARD L., lawyer; b. Boulder, Colo., Oct. 9, 1944. BS with honors, U. Colo., 1966; JD, Georgetown U., 1969. Bar: D.C. 1969. Law clk. to Hon. John Pratt D.C., 1969-70, asst. U.S. atty. D.C., 1970-77; mem. Davis Wright Tremaine LLP, Washington. Mem. ABA, D.C. Bar, Bar Assn. D.C. Office: Davis Wright Tremaine LLP 1155 Connecticut Ave NW Ste 700 Washington DC 20036-4313

CYWAR, ADAM WALTER, management engineer; b. Kearny, N.J., Mar. 14, 1937; s. Adam Benjamin and Sophie Julia (Kurak) C.; m. Gloria Ella Beresford, Mar. 29, 1956 (div. May 1973); children: Victoria Fumagalli, Douglas A., Sophia; m. Rose Barter Tubb, May 11, 1973. BSME, N.J. Inst. Tech., Newark, 1960, MSMgtE, 1965. Design engr. Colgate-Palmolive, Jersey City, N.J., 1956-60; indsl. engr. Lionel Corp., Hillside, N.J., 1960-63; sr. engr. IBM Corp., Boca Raton, Fla., 1963-93; pres. Adam Cywar Indsl. Engr., Austin, Tex., 1993—; v.p. info. sys. RPM Assocs., Georgetown, Tex., 1993-97; founder IBM Worldwide Activity Based Mgmt. Competency Ctr. Author: Handbook of Industrial Engineering, 1982 (IBM Achievement award 1983). Chmn. Town of Poughkeepsie Rep. Com. to Elect Jim Buckley, 1968. Mem. ASME (sr. mem.), Inst. Indsl. Engrs. (sr., treas. 1975-90, dir. honors and awards 1970-75, Disting. Svc. award 1977). Avocations: writing, industrial engineering research. Home and Office: Adam Cywar Indsl Engr 4307 Las Palmas Dr Austin TX 78759-5062

CZAJKA, JAMES VINCENT, architect; b. Lackawanna, N.Y., Dec. 6, 1950; s. Joseph Martin and Livia Maria (Jengo) C. BS in Art and Design, MIT, 1972, MArch, 1975. Registered architect, N.Y. Asst. prof. architecture SUNY, Buffalo, 1975-79; architect Ehrenkrantz Group Architects and Planners, N.Y.C., 1979-84; architect Beyer, Blinder, Belle Architects and Planners, N.Y.C., 1984-91, assoc., 1987-91, studio dir., 1988-91; pvt. practice N.Y.C., 1991-92; prin. Allanbrook Benic Czajka Architects & Planners, N.Y.C., 1993—. Prin. works include Baird Point Amphitheater, SUNY, Buffalo, 1978, Social Security Adminstrn. Bldg., Queens, N.Y., 1982, Paul Klapper Hall, Queens Coll., 1986, N.Y. Hall Sci. Master Plan, Manhattan, 1992, Am. Acad. Arts and Letters Master Plan, 1994, St. Joseph Parish Master Plan, Queens, 1994, World Monuments Fund Hdqrs., Manhattan, 1995, Loyola Sch. Sci. Ctr. renovation, Manhattan, 1996, Rutgers Ch. renovation, Manhattan, 1997, Bklyn. Conservatory of Music renovation, 1998, Blue Heron Arts Ctr., Manhattan, 1999. Mem. AIA, Nat. Coun. Archtl. Registration Bds. (cert.). Avocation: piano. Home: 303 E 84th St Apt 2F New York NY 10028-4435 Office: 611 Broadway Rm 817 New York NY 10012-2608

CZAJKOWSKI, EVA ANNA, aerospace engineer, educator; b. New Britain, Conn., Sept. 4, 1961; d. Jan Wiktor and Weronika Janina (Nadolny) C. Student, Yale U., 1978; BS in Aero. Engring. cum laude, Rensselaer Poly. Inst., 1983, M in Aero. Engring., 1983; SM in Aeronautics and Astronautics, MIT, 1985; PhD in Aerospace Engring., Va. Poly. Inst. and State U., 1988. Registered profl. engr., N.Y. Student trainee U.S. Govt., Washington, 1981-82; intern N.Y. State Assembly, Albany, 1983; teaching asst. Rensselaer Poly. Inst., Troy, N.Y., 1983, rsch. asst. U.S. Army Rsch. Office Ctr. Excellence, 1982-83; engring. analyst Pratt & Whitney Aircraft, West Palm Beach, Fla., 1984; rsch. asst. Gas Turbine and Plasma Dynamics Lab., Cambridge, 1984-85; rsch. asst., tchg. asst. dept. aerospace & ocean engring. Va. Poly. Inst. and State U., Blacksburg, 1985-88, aerospace engr., 1988-91, sr. aerospace engr., 1991-94, prin. aerospace engr., 1994—; participant U.S. dels. to seven European nations, 1991-92, 96-99. Author: Russian Aeronautical Test Facilities, 1994; contbr. papers to confs., articles to profl. jours. and ency. Vol. New Britain Gen. Hosp., 1977-79. Assoc. mem. Nat. Air and Space Mus., Am. Mus. Natural History. Recipient Bausch & Lomb medal hon. sci. award, 1978, Commemorative Medal of Honor, 1987, Decree of Internat. Letters for Cultural Achievement ABI, 1997, Joseph B. Platt award, 1997; named Woman of Yr., 1990, 96; Internat. Woman of Yr., 1991-92, 96-97; Amelia Earhart fellow Zonta Internat., 1983-85; scholar Am. Helicopter Soc. Vertical Flight Found., 1983, Unico Nat., 1979-80; fellow Prat Presdl. Engring. Program, 1985-88. Mem. AIAA, NAFE, N.Y. Acad. Scis., Am. Astronaut. Soc., Am. Helicopter Soc., Polish Rotorcraft Assn., The Planetary Soc., Internat. Platform Assn., World Found. Successful Women, Nat. Space Soc., Confederation Chivalry (named dame commandeur Ordre Souverain et Mil. Milice du St. Sepulcre 1990), Sigma Xi, Sigma Gamma Tau, Tau Beta Pi, Phi Kappa Phi, Gamma Beta Phi. Avocations: art, horseback riding, piano, flying pvt. plane, sailing. Home: 170 Carlton St New Britain CT 06053-3106

CZAJKOWSKI-BARRETT, KAREN ANGELA, human resources management executive; b. Bklyn., Sept. 13, 1957; d. Frank Henry and Cecilia (Artowicz) Czajkowski; div. Mar. 1992; children: Jennifer Marie, Michael Joseph. BSBA, Fairfield U., 1979; MBA, Sacred Heart U., 1984. Office systems analyst Union Trust Co., Stamford, Conn., 1979-80, sr. office systems analyst, 1980-81; ops. analyst Homequity, Inc., Wilton, 1981-82, project leader human rels. dept., 1982-85, organization devel. cons., 1985-87; tng. and devel. cons. People's Bank, Bridgeport, Conn., 1987-90; mgr. human resource planning and devel. Pitney Bowes Mgmt. Svcs., Stamford, 1990-93, dir. human resources planning and devel., 1993-98; regional learning mgr. Hewitt Assocs. LLC, Rowayton, Conn., 1998—; adj. instr. Sacred Heart U., Bridgeport, 1987. Sec. Cub Scouts Adv. Com., 1991-92; mem. regional bd. Conn. Fedn. Cath. Sch. Parents, 1993-94; treas. St. Theresa Sch.-Home Sch. Assn., 1994-96. Recipient award Nash Engring., 1979; named Bus. Advisor of Yr., INROADS/Fairfield-Westchester Counties, Inc., 1993. Mem. ASTD, Am. Mgmt. Assn., Human Resource Planning Soc. Home: 28 Wendover Rd Trumbull CT 06611-1530 Office: Hewitt Assocs LLC 40 Highland Ave Norwalk CT 06853-1599

CZAPLEWSKI, LYNN MARIE, intravenous nurse, educator; b. Milw., Feb. 18, 1950; m. Richard J. Czaplewski Sr., Aug. 8, 1970; children: Richard J. Jr., Amy, John. Diploma, Milw. County Gen. Hosp. Sch. Nursing, 1971; BSN, Regents Coll., 1999. RN, Wis.; cert. in intravenous therapy. Pres. IV Tng. Cons., Inc., Franklin, Wis., 1991—; IV cons. in field. Recepient CRNI yr. award, 1999. Mem. Nat. Nurses in Bus., Oncology Nurses Soc. (cert.), League of IV Therapy Edn., Nat. Assn. Vascular Access Network, IV Nurses Soc., Mil. County Gen. Hosp. Sch. Nursing Alumni Assn. Home: 6440 S Carroll Cir Franklin WI 53132-1124

CZARNECKI, ANTHONY J., correction administrator, educator; b. Mt. Vernon, N.Y., Aug. 28, 1948; s. Stanley and Lucy (Calabrese) C.; m. Lorraine Portman, Oct. 9, 1971; children: David, Pamela. BA, Iona Coll., 1970; MA, John Jay Coll., 1975; MPA, Pace U., 1990. Probation officer, sr. probation officer, tng. dir. Westchester County Probation Dept., White Plains, N.Y., 1970-83; spl. asst. to commr. Westchester County Correction Dept., Valhalla, N.Y., 1983—; adj. prof. criminal justice Westchester C.C., Valhalla, 1976—, Iona Coll., New Rochelle, N.Y., 1981—. Editor-in-chief Jour. Probation and Parole, 1980-82; contbr. articles to profl. jours. Mem. Am. Correctional Assn., Am. Probation & Parole Assn. (Probation officer Yr. award 1981), Am. Soc. Pub. Adminstrn., Middle Atlantic States Correctional Assn. (pres. 1997-99, bd. trustees 1979—, Achievement award 1989, Leadership award 1997), N.Y. State Probation Officers Assn. (pres. 1978-80). Roman Catholic. Office: Westchester County Correcton Dept PO Box 389 Hdq Bldg Valhalla NY 10595-0389

CZARNECKI, GERALD MILTON, investment banking and venture capital; b. Phila., Mar. 22, 1940; s. Casimir M. and Rose-Mary (Grajek) C.; m. Lois Rae DiJoseph, July 9, 1965; 1 dau., Robyn Alexandra. BS, Temple U., 1965; MA, Mich. State U., 1967; LHD (hon.), Nat. U., 1994. C.P.A., Ill., Tex. With Continental Bank, Chgo., 1968-79, v.p., operating gen. mgr. trust ops. and gen. mgr. corp. services, 1971-78; pres. Fla. Computing Services, 1979; exec. v.p. Houston Nat. Bank, 1979-82; sr. v.p. fin. Republic Bank Corp., 1982-83, exec. v.p., 1983-84; pres., chief exec. officer Altus Bank, 1984-87; chmn., chief exec. officer Bank of Am. Hawaii, Honolulu, 1987-93; sr. v.p. human resources and adminstrn. IBM Corp., Armonk, N.Y., 1993-94; pres. UNC Inc., Annapolis, Md., 1994-95; chmn. Deltennium Group, Inc., Annapolis, 1995—; mem. faculty DePaul U., Chgo., 1975-78; adj. prof. econs. Houston Bapt. U., 1980-82; mem. faculty Bank Adminstrn. Inst., 1978-85, Grad. Sch. Banking, U. Wis., 1979-86; chmn. bd. dirs. Inroads, Inc./Chgo., 1977-79, Inroads, Inc./Houston, 1981 vis. prof. Jones Sch. Bus., Rice U., 1980; adj. prof. policy and strategy So. Methodist U., 1983-84; mem. adv. com. Banking Center, Tex. So. U., 1980-82; chmn. securities processing sub-com. Am. Nat. Standards Inst., 1974-79, mem. Tuskegee Inst. State Adv. Council, 1984-87; treas., mem. exec. com., bd. dirs. Nat. Council Savs. Instns., 1984-90; pres. thrift adv. council Fed. Res. Bd., 1986-90; bd. dirs. State Farm Ins. Cos., Rollingpin Kitchen Emporium, Inc.; chmn. bd. dirs. Great Clips Mid-Atlantic, Inc., 1997—, Deltennium Corp., 1996—. Contbr. articles to profl. publs. Bd. dirs., treas. Hawaii Theatre Ctr., 1988-93; bd. dirs. Honolulu Econ. Devel. Corp., 1988-93, Nature Conservancy Hawaii, 1988-93, U. Hawaii Pres.' Coun., 1988-93, Aloha United Way, 1988-93; mem. Bus. Roundtable of Hawaii, 1989-93; chmn. Mil. Affairs Coun., 1992-93; mem. exec. and policy coms. Bus. Coun. N.Y. State, 1993-94; mem. adv. bd. Corp. Leadership Coun., 1993-94; nat. bd. dirs. Jr. Achievement, 1993—; bd. trustees Nat. U., 1994—. Mem. AICPA, Am. Bankers Assn. (chmn. securities processing com. 1974-77, trust ops. com. 1978, mem. exec. com. ops. and automation div. 1980-83, rsch. com.), Am. Econ. Assn., Tex. Soc. CPAs, Fin. Execs. Inst., Consumer Bankers Assn. (bd. dirs. 1986-89), N. Am. Soc. Corp. Planners (bd. dirs. Dallas Chpt. 1982-83), Assn. for Corp. Growth, Orgn. Resource Counselors, Inc., Hawaii C. of C. (bd. dirs. 1988-89, chmn. bd. 1990-92), Omicron Delta Epsilon, Alpha Delta Phi. E-mail: gmczar@deltennium.com. Fax: (410)573-5551.

CZARNECKI, WALTER P., truck rental company executive. Exec. v.p. Penske Corp., Detroit, 1978—. Office: Penske Corp 13400 W Outer Dr Detroit MI 48239-1309*

CZARRA, EDGAR F., JR., lawyer; b. Langhorne, Pa., Oct. 4, 1928; s. Edgar F. and Mary Agnes (Copeland) C.; m. Doris Catharine Lane, June 14, 1952; children: Penelope L., Edgar F. III, Jonathan C., Melanie A. BS, Yale U., 1949, LLB, 1952. Bar: U.S. Dist. Ct. D.C. 1954, U.S. Ct. Appeals (D.C. cir.) 1954, U.S. Supreme Ct. 1959. Assoc. Covington & Burling, Washington, 1952, 55-63, ptnr., 1963-97, ret., 1997; chmn. Global View Prodns., Inc. Served to lt. (j.g.) USN, 1952-55. Mem. ABA, D.C. Bar Assn., Fed. Communications Bar Assn. Office: Covington & Burling PO Box 7566 1201 Pennsylvania Ave NW Washington DC 20044-7566

CZERWIEC, IRENE THERESA, gifted education educator; b. Holyoke, Mass., Dec. 1, 1948; d. Stanley John and Pauline Martha (Zerek) Matuszek; m. Stanley Joseph Czerwiec, Jan. 24, 1970; children: Keith John, Daniel Paul. BS, U. Mass., 1969, MEd, 1987, EdD, 1992. Cert. secondary math. tchr., Mass. Math., physics tchr. Holyoke Cath. High Sch., 1969-71; substitute tchr. Chicopee (Mass.) Pub. Schs., 1979-85; gifted tchr. Bellamy Mid. Sch., Chicopee, 1985-90, math., gifted tchr., 1990-92, tchr. computer, gifted, 1992—; coach Future Problem Solving Program, Chicopee, 1985—; evaluator State of Mass., 1986—, cons., 1988—; presenter World Future Soc. Conf., Cambridge, 1994, Mass. Future Problem Solving Conf., Harvard, 1994, Worcester, 1996, NSTA conv., Boston, 1992, 2d Ann. Conf. on Gifted and Talented Edn., Worcester, Mass., 1996, New Eng. Future Problem Solving Fall Tng. Conf., Sturbridge, Mass., 1998; presenter New Eng. League of Middle Schs.-Unified Arts Conf., Sturbridge, Mass., 1997; participant current students, future scientists, and engrs. workshop, Smith Coll., 1993. Coord. looking forward program Chicopee Centennial, 1990. Recipient Merit award Chicopee Coun. Parents and Tchrs., 1990, cert. of recognition for excellence in coaching a team Internat. Future Problem Solving Conf., Ann Arbor, Mich., 1987, 88, Ednl. Leaders in Math., 1987, 88, Cert. of Merit Mass. Bar Assn., 1988, 89; SpaceMet fellow NSF, 1990-91. Mem. NEA, AAUW, ASCD, World Future Soc., Coun. Exceptional Children, Mass. Tchrs. Assn., Nat. Space Soc., Hampden County Tchrs. Assn., Chicopee Edn. Assn. Roman Catholic. Avocation: reading, gardening. Home: 4 Plainville Cir South Hadley MA 01075-2664 Office: Bellamy Mid Sch 314 Pendleton Ave Chicopee MA 01020-2135

CZERWINSKI, EDWARD JOSEPH, foreign language educator; b. Erie, Pa., June 6, 1929; s. Joseph and Anna (Branecka) C. BA, Grove City Coll., 1951; MA in Drama and English, Pa. State U., 1955; postgrad., Emory U., 1955-57, Ind. U., 1960-61; MA in Russian, U. Wis., Madison, 1964, PhD in Russian and Polish, 1965. Instr. English Ga. Tech. Inst., Atlanta, 1957-59; asst. prof. English and drama McNeese State Coll., La., 1959-60; assoc. prof. Russian and Polish lits. U. Pitts., 1965-66, SUNY at Buffalo, 1966-67; assoc. prof. Russian and Polish U. Kans., Lawrence, 1967-70; prof. Russian and comparative lit. SUNY, Stony Brook, 1970-93, prof. emeritus, 1993—; ofcl. translator from Polish into English Interpress Pubs., Warsaw; founder, exec. and artistic dir. Slavic Cultural Center, Port Jefferson, N.Y., 1970—, pres. bd. trustees, 1970—. Editor: (with J. Piekalkiewicz) The Soviet Invasion of Czechoslovakia: The Effects on East Europe, 1972; editor, translator Pieces of Poland: Four Polish Dramatists, 1983, (with Mario Suško) Twenty Yugoslav Poets: the Meditative Generation, 1982, Bogdan Suchodolski's A History of Polish Culture, 1986, Bogdan Grzelonski's America Through Polish Eyes, 1988; editor: Alternatives: An Anthology of Slavic and East European Drama, 1983, (with Mario Susko) The Mythmakers: An Anthology of Contemporary Yugoslav Short Stories, 1984, (with Nicholas Rzhevsky) The Dramaturg and Dramaturgy, 1986, Chekhov Reconstructed: New Translations of Chekhov's Plays, 1987, Satire Cum Poesis: Three Bulgarian Plays, 1987, Contemporary Polish Theater and Drama (1956-84), 1988, (with Czeslaw Hernas) Alter-Altar Art: A Revolution of Silence in Contemporary Polish Art, 1989, Tadeusz Rozewicz's Bas-Relief and Other Poems, 1992, A Dictionary of Polish Literature, 1994; author numerous articles and revs.; mem. editorial bd. Books Abroad (now World Lit. Today), 1968—, 20th Century Lit., Comparative Drama, spl. editor, 1969-70; editor: Slavic and East European Arts Jour., 1982—, Polish lit. sect. Ency. Brit, 1975-78, 88-96; area editor ea. Europe Theatre Companies of the World, 1986—. Tour sponsor Poland's Studio Theatre, 1973, 76. Served to 2d lt.

USAF, 1951-53. Kosciuszko Found. grantee, 1962-64; Wanda Rohr Found. grantee, 1963, Internat. Dimensions grantee, 1966, Fulbright grantee Yugoslavia, 1968-69; Inter-Univ. travel grantee USSR, 1968-69, Inter-Univ. travel grantee Czechoslovakia, 1969; Internat. Rsch. and Exch. Bd. fellow, Yugoslavia, 1983-84, summer seminar grantee, Bulgaria, 1985, IREX grantee Poland, 1987, 90-91; recipient Disting. Alumni award Grove City Coll., 1973, Chancellor's Excellence in Teaching award SUNY, 1973-74; Amicus Poloniae award Poland, 1974, Disting. Prof. award N.Y. State Tchrs. of Fgn. Langs., 1975; named Man. of Yr. in Culture and Arts, Am. coun. Polish Cultural clubs, 1986. Mem. MLA (exec. com. Slavic-Western lit. rels. 1970-72), AAUP, Polish Acad. Arts and Scis. Am., Am. Assn. Tchrs. of Slavic and East European Langs., Am. Assn. Advancement of Slavic Studies, PEN Am. Ctr. Home: 341 W 47th St Apt 4R New York NY 10036-2429

CZERWINSKI, SALLY HUFFMAN, information systems manager; b. New Orleans, Dec. 6, 1949; d. Robert Lee and Lula Sarah (Motley) Huffman; m. Michael Henry Czerwinski, June 12, 1971; children: Jill Alison, Sarah Ann. BS in Merchandising, La. State U., 1971. Saleswoman, asst. buyer, buyer D.H. Holmes, New Orleans, 1970-74, MIS mgr., 1982-84; buyer, mgr. MIS, Godchaux's, $, 1974-82; cons., Baton Rouge, 1984-87, 91-97; v.p. Maison Blanche, Baton Rouge, 1987-91; mgr. sys. support Merc. Credit Svcs., Baton Rouge, 1997-98; gift card mgr., corp. trainer Dillard's Baton Rouge, 1998—; PRJ sys. cons., San Francisco, 1991-92, 96. Leader Brownie troop Girl Scouts U.S.A., Kenner, La., 1984-85; bd. dirs., sec. UpLIFTD (La. Industries for the Disabled), Baton Rouge, 1991—; youth counselor United Meth. Youth Fedn., Baton Rouge, 1992-94; bd. dirs. Episcopal Parent's Guild, Baton Rouge, 1994-95; bd. dirs., 2d v.p., membership chmn. Baton Rouge Symphony League, 1992—. Mem. PRJ User Group (pres. 1987-91), Krewe of Romany, Bengal Belles, Order of Omega, Zeta Tau Alpha (v.p. nat. coun. 1995-98, nat. sec.-treas. 1998—, cert. of merit 1981, honor ring 1984). Republican. Avocations: reading, sailing, skiing, gardening, sewing. Office: Dillards 1450 Main St Baton Rouge LA 70802-4663

CZESTOCHOWSKI, JOSEPH STEPHEN, museum administrator; b. Bklyn., Aug. 6, 1950; s. Joseph Stephen and Julia (Skowron) C.; m. Debra J. Nicholson, Nov. 18, 1972; 1 child, J. F. Stefan Parker. Diploma, Jagiellonian U., Poland, 1971; BA, U. Ill., 1971, MA, 1973. Curator of collections Brooks Mus. Art, Memphis, 1973-75; dir. Decker Gallery, Md. Inst., Balt., 1975-78; exec. dir. Cedar Rapids (Iowa) Mus. Art, 1978-94; dir. The Dixon Gallery and Gardens, Memphis, 1994—; sr. examiner Accreditation Commn. of the AAM; field reviewer Inst. Mus. Svcs.; govt. and art com. Assn. Art Mus. Dirs. Monographs include The Pioneers, 1977, Polish Posters, 1979, The Combined Works of Arthur B. Davies, 1980, Prints by Childe Hassam, 1980, John S. Curry and Grant Wood - A Portrait of Rural America, 1981, The American Landscape Tradition 1738-1965, 1982, Marvin D. Cone - An American Tradition, 1985, Arthur B. Davies - Catalogue Raisonne of Prints, 1988. Mem. adv. bd. Krannert Art Mus. Fellow Vatican Mus. and Smithsonian Inst., 1976, Smithsonian Instn., 1977-79; recipient first Nancy Hanks Meml. award for profl. excellence Am. Assn. Mus., 1985. Mem. Am. Assn. Mus. Dirs., Internat. Coun. Mus., The Kosciuszko Found. (trustee 1988-96), The Polish Inst. Arts and Scis. in Am., Inc. (trustee 1986—), Ctr. for the Study of the Presidency (trustee), Coll. Liberal Arts and Scis. U. Ill. Alumni Assn. (trustee 1994—), Rotary Internat. Office: The Parker Corp 319 Goodwyn St Memphis TN 38111-3311

CZNARTY, DONNA MAE, secondary education educator; b. Bridgeport, Conn., Aug. 17, 1950; d. Richard W. and Dorothy Mae (Kosturko (Oefinger); m. William C. Cole, Jr., July 11, 1970; 1 child, Michael William Cole; m. Thomas Robert Cznarty, Apr. 29, 1983. BS in Edn., So. Conn. State U., 1973, MS in Edn., 1977. Lang. arts tchr. Shelton Bd. Edn., Conn., 1973-82; English tchr. Millbrook Bd. Edn., N.Y., 1985-86; sec., bd. dirs. Hopewell Precision, Inc., Hopewell Junction, N.Y., 1986—, CFO, 1997—; bd. dirs. Dutchess Arts Coun. Mem. NAFE. Republican. Avocations: interior design, antiques, travel, boating. Home: Field Haven Stanfordville NY 12581 Office: Hopewell Precision Inc Ryan Dr Hopewell Junction NY 12533

CZUJ, CHESTER FRANCIS, JR., food service professional; b. Greenfield, Mass., Apr. 28, 1955; s. Chester Francis and Mary Theresa (O'Sullivan) Matthews; m. Joanne M. Divece, Nov. 25, 1989; children: Chester Francis III, Matthew Joseph, Elizabeth Marie. B in Math., Worcester State Coll., 1978. Food svc. mgr. Dining and Kitchen Adminstrn. Inc., Wakefield, Mass., 1973-81; asst. food svc. adminstr. Quincy (Mass.) City Hosp., 1981-84; owner, operator Parkar Bros. Inc., Weymouth, Mass., 1984-86; food svc. mgr. Seiler Corp., Waltham, Mass., 1986-88; resident dist. mgr. Seiler Corp., Phila., 1988-90; dist. mgr. All Seasons Svcs., Inc., Mid-Atlantic, 1990-94, Chester F. Czuj, Jr., food svc. mgmt. cons., Broomall, Pa., 1994—; food svc. dir. Brock & Co., Malvern, Pa., 1995-97; dist. mgr. Brock & Co., Malvern, 199-99, Wood Co., Allentown, Pa., 1999—; instr. Quincy (Mass.) Jr. Coll., 1985-86. Democrat. Roman Catholic. Avocations: golf, darts. Home and Office: 314 Langford Rd Broomall PA 19008-2811

CZUJKO, ROMAN, psychologist, survey researcher; b. Regensburg, Germany, June 24, 1948; s. Stefan and Kateryna (Balash) C.; m. Nancy Ruth Grace, June 1, 1985; children: Stephen Paul, Alexander John. BS, Rutgers U., 1975; MA, U. Oreg., 1980. Rsch. assoc. Am. Inst. Physics, N.Y.C., 1980-85, asst. mgr., 1985-92; mgr. Am. Inst. Physics, College Park, Md., 1992—; commr. Commn. on Profls. in Sci. and Tech., 1988—, bd. dirs. With U.S. Army, 1968-70. Grantee NSF, 1990, 97, Alfred P. Sloan Found., 1994, 99. Mem. Am. Assn. Pub. Opinion Rschrs., Am. Phys. Soc., Nat. Acad. Scis. (adv. panels 1993, 97), Am. Geol. Inst. (adv. com. 1994—), N.Y. Acad. Scis. Office: Am Inst Physics One Physics Ellipse College Park MD 20740

CZUSZAK, JANIS MARIE, former credit company official, researcher; b. Greensburg, Pa., Aug. 3, 1956; d. Charles Clyde and Olga (Plica) C. BS, Indiana U. of Pa., 1978; MBA, U. Pitts., 1985, PhD, 1995. Supervising sr. acct., computer audit specialist KPMG Peat Marwick, Pitts., 1979-81; fin. analyst Westinghouse Credit Corp., Pitts., 1981-83, staff analyst, 1983-84, fin. and computer auditor, 1984-86, real estate financing rep., 1986-88, assoc. investment mgr., 1988-91, investment mgr., 1991-93; asst. v.p. Mellon Bank, Pitts., 1993-98; mgr. Ernst & Young, LLP, Pitts., 1998—. Mem. Greater Pitts. Commn. for Women, 1989—. Mem. Nat. Comml. Fin. Assn., NAFE. Avocations: reading, snow skiing, golf, aerobics, swimming. Office: Ernst & Young LLP 1 Oxford Ctr Pittsburgh PA 15219-6403

DAAB-KRZYKOWSKI, ANDRE, pharmaceutical and nutritional manufacturing company administrator; b. Warsaw, Poland, May 16, 1949; came to U.S., 1973, naturalized, 1981; s. Aleksy Czeslaw crest Polkozic and Zofia (Dyszkiewicz crest Kudrys) Krzykowski; m. Susan Elizabeth Read, June 26, 1987; 1 child, Cecylia. MSChemE, Tech. U. Warsaw, 1973; MBA, Memphis State U., 1979. Research chemist Schering-Plough, Memphis, 1974-77; process control mgr. Ralston Purina Co., Memphis, 1977-80; dir. pharm. projects Bristol-Myers Squibb Co., Mayaguez, P.R., 1980-90; process tech. mgr. R & D Ross Labs. divsn. Abbott Labs., 1990—. Holder patents. Served to 2d lt. Polish Army Res. Mem. Am. Mgmt. Assn., Am. Chem. Soc. Republican. Lutheran. Club: Toastmasters (pres. local chpt. 1986). Avocations: sailing, scuba diving, karate. Office: Ross Labs 625 Cleveland Ave Columbus OH 43215-1724

DAANE, JAMES DEWEY, banker; b. Grand Rapids, Mich., July 6, 1918; s. Gilbert L. and Mamie (Blocksma) D.; m. Blanche M. Tichenor, Apr. 28, 1941 (div. 1952); 1 dau., Elizabeth Marie Daane Mallek; m. Onnie B. Selby, Jan. 23, 1953 (dec. Dec. 1961); m. Barbara W. McMann, Feb. 16, 1963; children—Elizabeth Whitney, Olivia Quartel. AB magna cum laude, Duke U., 1939; M in Pub. Adminstrn., Harvard U., 1946, D in Pub. Adminstrn. (Littauer fellow), 1949. With Fed. Res. Bank, Richmond, Va., 1939-60, asst. v.p., 1953-57, v.p., 1957-60, also cons. to pres. bank; adviser to pres. Fed. Res. Bank, Mpls., 1960; asst. to sec. treasury, 1960-61, dep. undersec. treasury for monetary affairs, 1961-63; mem. bd. govs. Fed. Reserve System, Washington, 1963-74; vice chmn. bd. dirs. Commerce Union Bank, Sovran Bank/Cen. South, Nashville, 1974-78; chmn. internat. policy com. Commerce Union Corp., 1978-87; dir. Nat. Futures Assn., Ill., 1983—; chmn. internat. policy com Sovran Fin. Corp., Nashville, 1988; chmn. money market com. Commerce Union Bank, 1974-87; chmn. money market com. cen. S. Sovran Bank, 1988-90; assoc. economist Fed. Open Market Com., 1955-56, 58-59; chief IMF Fiscal Mission to Paraquay, 1950-51; vice chmn. Tennessee Valley Bancorp. Inc., 1975-78; Rank K. Houston prof. banking and fin. Owen Grad. Sch. Mgmt., Vanderbilt U., 1974-85, Valere Blair Potter prof. banking and fin., 1985-89, Frank K. Houston prof. emeritus, 1989—, Alan R. Holmes prof. econs. Middlebury Coll., 1991-93; bd. dirs. Chgo. Bd. of Trade, 1979-82. Editor: (with David C. Colander) The Art of Monetary Policy. Bd. advisers Patterson Sch. Diplomacy and Internat. Commerce, U. Ky. Mem. J.F. Kennedy Sch. Govt. Assn. of Harvard U., Am. Econ. Assn., Am. Finance Assn. Home: 102 Westhampton Pl Nashville TN 37205-3439 Office: Vanderbilt U Owen Grad Sch Mgmt 401 21st Ave N Nashville TN 37203

DAANE, KATHRYN D., retired nursing administrator; b. Faith, S.D., Mar. 18, 1935; d. Vernon Floyd and Evelyn May (Armour) Donnenwirth; m. Robert D. Daane, Aug. 17, 1957; children: Janelle, James, Jeffrey. Diploma in nursing, St. John's McNamara Sch. Nursing, 1956; BSN, S.D. State U., 1960; MSN, Tex. Woman's U., 1981. Staff and head nurse VA Med. Ctr., Ft. Meade, S.D., 1957-69, nursing instr., 1969-74, clin. supr., 1974-75, asst. chief nurse, 1975-84, chief nurse, 1984-86; chief nurse Harry S. Truman Meml. VAH, Columbia, Mo., 1986-88, assoc. DON, 1988-91; chief nurse Edward Hines (Ill.) VA Hosp., 1992-95; v.p., bd. dirs. Community Meml. Hosp., Sturgis, S.D., 1980-86; mem. Regional Planning Bd., VA Cen. Region, 1987-95, chief nursing adv. bd., 1990-95, chairperson Regional Tech. Adv. Group for Women Vets., 1992-95. Adj. asst. prof. S.D. State U., Brookings, 1984-86; adj. faculty U. Mo., Columbia, 1987-91. Mem. ANA (cert.), Nurses Orgn. Vets. Affairs, Sigma Theta Tau. Roman Catholic. Home: 1918 Davenport St Sturgis SD 57785-2415*

DAANE, MARY CONSTANCE, English language educator; b. Sheboygan, Wis., Dec. 14, 1946; d. Julian Winfred and Julia Constance (Westermeyer) D.; children: Peter Daane Cirasella, Jill Cariffe Cirasella. BA, Upsala Coll., 1969; MA in Edn., Seton Hall U., 1979; PhD, NYU, 1989. Cert. English and reading tchr., N.J. Adj. instr. Union County Coll., Cranford, N.J., 1979-83, 86-90; asst. prof. English Union County Coll., Cranford, 1990-91; preceptor Writing Ctr. NYU, N.Y.C., 1984-86; asst. prof. English Waycross (Ga.) Coll., 1991-92, assoc. prof., chair divsn. developmental studies, 1992-97; dir. acad. founds. Hudson County C.C., Jersey City, 1997—; vis. rschr. U. Calif. Berkeley, summer 1996; reading cons., tchr. trainer Ware County Bd. Edn., Waycross, 1996-97; editl. adv. bd. Jour. Adolescent and Adult Literacy, 1997, 98; presenter in field. Contbr. articles and revs. to profl. jours. Chair scholarship com. Ga. Assn. for Women in Edn., Waycross, 1997; coord. postsecondary readiness enrichment program Waycross Coll., 1997, chair Take Our Daughters to Work Day, 1997. Mem. Internat. Reading Assn. (pres. Okefenokee Coun. Reading 1995), Nat. Coun. Tchrs. English, Nat. Assn. Developmental Educators. Office: Hudson County CC 25 Journal Sq Jersey City NJ 07306-4012

DABBAGH, MOHAMED ABDUL-HAY, financial economist, oil-capital flow researcher; b. Tripoli, Lebanon, Nov. 22, 1932; s. Haj Abdul-Hay and Karia Abdeen; m. Marsha Beth Dabbah, Mar. 7, 1961 (dec. July 1974); children: Omar, Randa, Nadia; m. Theresa Lynn Dabbagh, Apr. 18, 1977; children: Liala, Tarek, Tallal, Aida. AA, Coll. of San Mateo, Calif., 1961; BA, San Jose (Calif.) State U., 1963; MA, U. Calif., Riverside, 1965; PhD, St. Louis U., 1974. Instr. J.J. Pershing Coll., Beatrice, Nebr., 1966-71; tchg. fellow St. Louis U., 1971-74; asst. prof. Elmira (N.Y.) Coll., 1974-76; assoc. prof. Union Coll., Barbourville, Ky., 1976-78; rschr. Arab Monetary Fund, Abu Dhabi, United Arab Emirates, 1978-81; fin. economist Abu Dhabi Investment Authority, 1981-97; prof. fin. Ea. Ky. U., Corbin; vis. prof. dept. bus. Union Coll., 1998—. Author: The Monetary System and the Role of the Central Bank in Lebanon, 1977. Mem. Am. Econ. Assn., So. Econ. Assn., Missouri Valley Econ. Assn., Western Econ. Assn. Moslem. Avocations: tennis, basketball, swimming, pool, travel. Home: 2765 McNeil Hallow Rockholds KY 40759 Office: Union Coll PO Box 812 Barbourville KY 40906-0812

DABBS, HENRY ERVEN, television and film producer, educator; b. Clover, Va., Oct. 15, 1932; s. Charles E. and Gertrude (Hudson) D.; m. Loretta D. Young, Jan. 9, 1957. B.F.A., Pratt Inst., 1955. Book designer Berton Wink, Inc., N.Y.C., 1958-62; pres., owner Henry Dabbs Prodns. (A Total Communication Complex), 1978—; partner Henry Dabbs Prodns. (DAK Communications div.), 1980—; instr. cinema Jersey City State Coll., 1977—. Art dir.-prodr.: Dancer, Fitzgerald Sample, N.Y.C., 1963—; editor, prodr., dir.: motion picture Joshua, 1975-76; prodr., dir.: documentary film The Movers, 1978; original paintings depicting famous Afro-Americans in Am. history in permanent collection Smithsonian Instn., Washington; creator: Afro-American History Fact Pack, 1968; author: Afro-American History Highlights, 1968, Black Brass, 1983, 2d edit. 1996 (NAACP Humanitarian award 1995), Black Generals and Admirals in the Armed Forces of the United States; audio video series The ABC's of Black History, 1983; prodr., dir., writer: comprehensive black history video program, 1990, Afro-Centric Black Videos including: African Homeland, Black American Women, The World's Great Black Men and Women and the Great Ones, 1991,. Served with AUS, 1955-58. Mem. NAACP.

DABBS RILEY, JEANNE KERNODLE, retired public relations executive; b. Corsicana, Tex., 1922; d. Robert and Anne (Forrest) McCluer; m. John David Kernodle, June 27, 1942 (div. 1968); 1 child, Elizabeth Kernodle Cabell; m. Jack Autrey Dabbs, Feb. 14, 1981 (dec. 1992); m. James J. Riley, Jr., June 28, 1997. BS in Sociology, Tex. Woman's U., 1970. Supr., writer pub. rels. St. Paul's Hosp., Dallas, 1974-76; dir., v.p. mktg. svcs. Fidelity Union Life Ins. Co., Dallas, 1976-81, ret., 1981. Author poetry book and greeting cards. Mem., comm. com. Mental Health Assn., Austin, Tex., 1991—; pres. aux. Seton Med. Ctr., Austin, 1985-86; mem. Dallas Civic Chorus, Austin Choral Union. Recipient Editorial medal Freedoms Found. Valley Forge, 1973, Eddy award Internat. Assn. Bus. Communicators, 1974, 76, 79, Matrix award Women in Comm., Inc., 1975, Best of Show award Life Ins. Advts. Assn., 1980, Sr. Vol. award Retirees Coordinating Bd., 1989. Mem. Tex. Women's U. Alumnae Assn. (pres. Capital Area chpt. 1987-89), Tuesday Book Club Austin (pres. 1986), Austin Poetry Soc. Methodist. Avocations: book reviewer, singing. Home: 2806 Cherry Ln Austin TX 78703-2820

DABDOUB, PAUL OSCAR, academic administrator; b. La Lima, Honduras, July 7, 1946; came to U.S., 1955; s. Jacob Abraham and Helen (McNabb) D.; m. Lorrie Suzanne Shell, Aug. 9, 1993; children by previous marriage: Desiree, John Kelly, Paul Jacob. B of Bible, Open Bible Coll., 1983; student, Liberty U., 1979; M of Theology, Andersonville Bapt. Sem., 1996, D of Pastoral Theology, 1996. Fin. mgr. 3d Nat. Bank, Nashville, 1973-78; min. Mooring Bapt. Ch., Tiptonville, Tenn., 1978-79, Kinfolks Ridge Bapt. Ch., Caruthersville, Mo., 1979-80; min., founder Victory Bapt. Ch., Caruthersville, 1980-91; min. Victory Bapt. Ch., Caruthersville, Mo., 1980-91; adminstr., founder Victory Bapt. Acad., Caruthersville, 1984-91; min. Victory Bapt. Ch., Caruthersville, Mo., 1980-91, Victory Bapt. Acad., Caruthersville, 1984-91, Ridge Meml. Bapt. Ch., Slidell, La., 1991—; sci. instr. Northlake Christian Sch., Covington, La., 1991; founder, pres., instr. Slidell Bapt. Sem., 1994—. Avocation: wild turkey hunting. Home: PO Box 7 Slidell LA 70459-0007

DABERKO, DAVID A., banker; b. Hudson, Ohio, 1945. BA, Denison U., 1967; MBA, Case Western Res. U., 1970. Mgmt. trainee Nat. City Bank, Cleve., 1968-72, asst. v.p., 1972-73, v.p. bank investment divsn., dept. head met. lending divsn., 1973-80, sr. v.p. corp. banking, 1980-82, pres., 1987-93; exec. v.p. corp. banking Nat. City Corp., Nat. City Bank, Cleve., 1982-85; pres., bd. dirs. Nat. City Bank (formerly BancOhio Nat. Bank), Columbus, 1985-87; dep. chmn. Nat. City Corp., Cleve., 1987-93, pres., CEO, 1993-95, chmn., COO, 1995—; dir. Fed. Res. Bank, Cleve. Trustee Cleve. Tomorrow, Greater Cleve. Growth Assn., Case Western Res. U., Hawken Sch., Neighborhood Progress, Univ. Cir. Inc., Univ. Hosp. Health Sys.; co-chair Harvest for Hunger Campaign, 1992, 93. Mem. Bankers Roundtable. Office: Nat City Corp National City Center 1900 E 9th St Cleveland OH 44114-3401

DABERKOW, DAVE, historic site director; b. Windam, Minn., Nov. 16, 1945. BS, S.D. State U., 1968. Park mgr. Richmond & Mina Recreation Area, Aberdeen, S.D., 1971-86; dist. park mgr. Ft. Sisseton State Park, Lake City, S.D., 1986—. Office: Fort Sisseton State Hist Park 11545 Northside Dr Lake City SD 57247-9704

DABICH, ELI, JR., insurance company executive; b. Chgo., June 7, 1939; s. Eli and Helen (Radakovich) D.; m. Eileen Dabich, June 8, 1963; children: Michael, Charles, Mary, Kathleen. BS, U.S. Naval Acad., 1963; MS, George Washington U., 1970. Mktg. rep. IBM, Balt., 1970-74; sr. v.p. adminstrn. Sun Life, Atlanta, 1974-82; sr. exec. v.p. adminstrn. and fin. Md. Casualty Co., Balt., 1982-88; nat. dir. ins. cons. Coopers & Lybrand, N.Y.C., 1988-90; sr. v.p. Nationale Nederlanden, Washington, 1990-93; sr. v.p., chief adminstrv. officer TIG Ins. Co., 1993-95; pres. Synergy 2000 Inc., 1995—; bd. dirs. Ivans. Pres. Oak Hill Elem. Sch., PTA, Severna Park, Md., 1970; sec. U.S. Naval Acad., Annapolis, Md., 1963-70; bd. dirs. Ins. Tech., Securities Software & Cons. Capt. USN, 1963-85. Home: 2815 Cox Neck Rd Chester MD 21619-2345

DABKOWSKI, JOHN, electrical engineering executive; b. Chgo., Feb. 15, 1933; s. John and Harriet (Sierakowski) D.; m. Mary A Walkosz, Aug. 15, 1959 (dec. Apr. 1973); 1 child, Colette A.; m. Cecilia Klonowski, June 26, 1976; 1 child, Katherine A. BSEE, Ill. Inst. Tech., 1955, MSEE, 1960, PhD in Elec. Engring., 1969. Sr. rsch. engr. Ill. Inst. Tech. Rsch. Inst., Chgo., 1957-79; ops. mgr. Sci. Applications Internat. Corp., Hoffman Estates, Ill., 1979-85, dir. EM effects rsch., 1985-87, div. mgr., 1987-88; pres. Electro Scis., Inc., 1988—; instr. Grad. Sch., Ill. Inst. Tech., Chgo., 1962-79. Author rsch. publs. in field. With U.S. Army, 1955-57. Mem. IEEE (sr.), Nat. Assn. Corrosion Engrs., Sigma Xi. Republican. Roman Catholic. Home: 7021 Foxfire Dr Crystal Lake IL 60012-1641 Office: Electro Scis Inc PO Box 1438 Crystal Lake IL 60039-1438

DABNEY, H. SLAYTON, JR., lawyer; b. Charlottesville, Va., Sept. 14, 1949; s. Hovey S. and Patricia S (Schmidt) D.; m. Donna C. Warns, Jan. 14, 1983; children: Slayton, Kate, Andrew. BA, U. Va., 1971, JD, 1974. Bar: Va. 1974, U.S. Dist. Ct. (ea. and we. dists.) Va., U.S. Bankruptcy Ct. (ea. and we. dists.) Va., U.S. Ct. Appeals (4th cir.), U.S. Dist. Ct. D.C., U.S. Bankruptcy Ct. Md. Ptnr. McGuire, Woods, Battle & Boothe, Richmond, Va. Mem. ABA, Am. Bankruptcy Inst., Va. Bar Assn., Richmond Bar Assn. (chmn. bankruptcy sect. 1990-91). Office: McGuire Woods Battle & Boothe One James Ctr 901 E Cory St Richmond VA 23219-3229*

D'ABO, OLIVIA, actress; b. London, Jan. 22, 1967. Appeared in films Conan The Destroyer, 1984, Bolero, 1984, Into The Fire Legend of Wolf Lodge, 1987, Really Weird Tales, 1987, Bullies, 1986, Bank Robber, 1993, Greedy, 1994, Clean Slate, 1994, Live Nude Girls, 1995, The Big Green, 1995, The Last Good Time, 1995, Kicking and Screaming, 1995, Hacks, 1997, The Velocity of Gary, 1998, It Had to Be You, 1998, Seven Girlfriends, 1999; TV appearances (series) The Single Guy, 1996-97, National Lampoon's Dad's Week Off, 1997, Party of Five (2 episodes) 1998, 99. Office: ICM 8942 Wilshire Blvd Beverly Hills CA 90211-1934*

DABROWSKI, ALBERT S., federal judge; b. 1944. BS, U. Conn., 1967; JD, Suffolk U., 1970. Bar: Conn. 1970. With U.S. Dept. Justice, 1970-73, asst. U.S. atty. for dist. Conn., 1973-91, U.S. atty. for dist. Conn., 1991-93; bankruptcy judge for Conn., U.S. Bankruptcy Ct., New Haven, 1993—. Office: US Bankruptcy Ct Conn Fin Ctr 18th Fl 157 Church St New Haven CT 06510-2100

DABROWSKI, DORIS JANE, lawyer; b. Paterson, N.J., May 20, 1950. BA, Rutgers U., 1972, JD, 1975. Bar: Pa. 1975, U.S. Dist. Ct. (ea. dist.) Pa. 1976, U.S. Ct. Appeals (3d cir.) 1977, N.J. 1979, U.S. Dist. Ct. N.J. 1979, U.S. Ct. Appeals (fed. cir.) 1985. Staff atty. Delaware County Legal Assistance, Chester, Pa., 1975-77; assoc. Tabas, Horwitz & Furlong (later Tabas, Furlong & Roser), Phila., 1977-83; pvt. practice Phila. and Moorestown, N.J., 1983—; arbitrator Nat. Assn. Securities Dealers, Am. Arbitration Assn., Phila. and N.J.; participant Nat. Pension Assistance Project; mem. adv. coun. 18th Police Dist., 1997—. Mem. editorial bd. Women's Rights Law Reporter, 1974-75. Dir. Well Woman, Phila., 1983-87, Pa. Pro Musica, Phila., 1983-84; mem. adv. bd. Clara Bell Duvall Edn. Fund, Phila.; mem. gov. bd. Health Systems Agy., S.E. Pa., 1980-86; mem. 18th Police Dist. Adv. Coun. Recipient Cert. of Achievement Bus. Women's Network, Phila., 1984. Mem. Nat. Employment Lawyers' Assn. (pres. Ea. Pa. chpt. 1992-98), Nat. Assn. Women Lawyers (amicus com., bd. dirs. 1994-95), Phila. Bar Assn. (mem. evidence task force 1992-93, chair support subcom. of small firm and sole practice com. 1992), Assn. for Union Democracy, Nat. Police Def. Found. (hon.), Am. Guild Organists. Office: 1308 Spruce St Philadelphia PA 19107-5812 also: 1930 Marlton Pike E Ste 148 Cherry Hill NJ 08003-4105

DABROWSKI, EDWARD JOHN, television technical director; b. Chgo., Nov. 16, 1957; s. Edward J. and Justina J. (Grilc) D. BS in Elec. Engring., Ill. Inst. Tech., Chgo., 1979. Engr. Sta. WMAQ-TV, Chgo., 1976-83, tech. dir., 1983—; enrg.-in-charge The Jenny Jones Show, 1995. Tech. dir. (NBC afternoon spl.) The Sixth Street Kids, 1984, (WMAQ-TV docu-drama) Fast Break to Glory: Dusable Panthers, 1988, Chgo. Sisslin (Chgo. Emmy award 1989), Chgo. Bears Pre-Season football, 1993, Engring. Devel. Group, 1996—. Emmy nomination, Chgo. Chpt., 1998. Mem. IEEE, Soc. Broadcast Engrs., NATAS (Emmy nominations Chgo. chpt. 1986), Nat. Assn. Broadcast Employees and Technicians (steward Chgo. chpt. 1981-87, mobilization coord. Chgo. 1994-95), Natl. Assn. of Broadcast Employees and Technicians, Broadcasting and Cable Television Workers Sector of the Communications Workers of Amer., AFL-CIO Steward and Exec. Bd. Mem. Chgo. Local 41 1999—, Am. Radio Relay League (life), Chgo.-Suburban Radio Assn., Mus. Broadcast Comm. (charter), Am. Fraternal Union, Slovene Nat. Benefit Soc. (rec. sec. lodge 449). Democrat. Roman Catholic. Avocations: amateur radio, photography. Office: Sta WMAQ-TV NBC Tower 454 N Columbus Dr Chicago IL 60611-5501

DABROWSKI, THADDEUS E., educator, painter; b. Bronx, N.Y., July 17, 1945; s. Theodore J. and Wanda K. (Curylo) D.; m. Althea M. Smith, May 17, 1970; children: Veronika M., Sibyl T. BBA, U. Mass., 1968, MFA, 1970, MEd, 1972. Tech. specialist U. Mass., Amherst, 1972-78, adminstrv. asst., 1978-95, textbook adminstr., 1995—, adj. lectr. art, 1981—; pres., v.p., treas. Leverette (Mass.) Artists and Craftsmen, 1982—; mem. Pub. Arts Commn., Amherst, 1990-94. One man shows include Campus Cinema, Hadley, Mass., 1968, U. Mass. Student Union Gallery, Amherst, 1970, Leverett (Mass.) Crafts and Art Ctr., 1990, Burnett Gallery, Jones Libr., Amherst, 1995; showcase artist New Eng. Arts Festival, U. Mass., 1983. Loaned exec., mem. cabinet United Way of Hampshire, Amherst, 1987—. Recipient Milton Bradley award Springfield (Mass.) Art League, 1976. Mem. Mass. Assn. for Ednl. Tech. (charter), Rotary Club of Amherst (sec. 1989-91, v.p. 1991-92, pres. 1992-93, Paul Harris fellow 1984—). Avocations: classic automobile preservation, piano, computer systems. Home: 9 Squire Ln Amherst MA 01002-3232 Office: U Mass Dept Art Amherst MA 01003

D'ACCONE, FRANK ANTHONY, music educator; b. Somerville, Mass., June 13, 1931; s. Salvatore and Maria (DiChiappari) D'A. Mus. B., Boston U., 1952, Mus.M., 1953; A.M., Harvard U., 1955, Ph.D., 1960. Asst. prof. music SUNY at Buffalo, 1960-63, assoc. prof., 1964-68; prof. music UCLA, 1968-94, chmn. dept., 1973-76; chmn. faculty UCLA (Coll. Fine Arts), 1976-79; chmn. dept. musicology UCLA, 1989-93; vis. prof. music Yale U., 1972-73. Author: The History of a Baroque Opera, 1985, The Civic Muse, 1997; editor: Music of the Florentine Renaissance, vols. 1-12, 1967-94; gen. editor Corpus Mensurabilis Musicae, 1986—; co-editor Musica Disciplina, 1990—; contbr. articles to profl. jours. Fellow Am. Acad. Rome, 1963-64, Fulbright Found., 1963-64, NEH, 1975; recipient G.K. Delmas Venetian Studies award, 1977, J.S. Guggenheim Found. award, 1980, Internat. Galilei prize, Pisa, 1997. Fellow Am. Acad. of Arts and Scis.; mem. Am. Musicol. Soc. (dir. 1973-74), Internat. Musicol. Soc. Home: 725 Fontana Way Laguna Beach CA 92651-4010 Office: U Calif Dept Music Los Angeles CA 90024

DACE, TISH, drama educator; b. Washington, Sept. 13, 1941; d. Edward Durnford and Claude Marshall (Russell) Skinner; children: Hal, Ted. AB, Sweet Briar (Va.) Coll., 1963; MA, Kans. State U., 1967, PhD, 1971. Instr. Kans. State U., Manhattan, 1967-71; asst. prof. John Jay Co. CUNY, 1971-74, dep. chmn. speech and theatre, 1974-79, assoc. prof., 1975-80, chmn. speech and theatre, 1979-80; dean Coll. Arts & Scis. U. Mass. Dartmouth, North Dartmouth, 1980-86; prof. English U. Mass. Dartmouth, North Dartmouth, 1986-97, chancellor prof. English, 1997—; chmn. Am. Theatre Wing Design Awards, N.Y., 1986—; mem. adv. bd. Contemporary Dramatists, London, 1986—. Author: LeRoi Jones (Imamu Amiri Baraka): A Checklist of Works by and About Him, 1971, Langston Hughes: The Contemporary Reviews, 1997; co-author: Modern Theater and Drama, 1973, Black American Writers, 1978; New Eng. editor Stages, 1986-88; assoc. editor Shakespearean Rsch. & Opportunities, 1971-75; theatre critic several thousand play reviews; contbr. 150 articles to newspapers, mags., profl. jours. and books. Recipient research stipend, NEH, 1987; named Scholar of Yr., 1997. Mem. Outer Critics Circle (exec. com. 1980-83), Am. Theatre Critics Assn. (exec. com. 1994—, v.p. found., 1995—), Drama Desk, Am. Soc. Theatre Rsch., Phi Beta Kappa (pres. Kans. Alpha assn. 1969-70). Democrat. Office: English Dept U Mass Dartmouth North Dartmouth MA 02747-2300

DACEY, BRIAN FRANCIS, real estate executive; b. Boston, Dec. 12, 1951; s. John Morrissey and Mary Elizabeth (Mullin) D.; m. Beth Ann DiBuono, Sept. 19, 1976; children: Ann, Sara. BA in Polit. Sci., Boston Coll., 1974; MBA, Boston U., 1984. Asst. to v.p. Sverdrup Corp., Boston, 1974-75; staff dir. Mass. State Senate, Boston, 1975-76; project mgr. Mass. Lt. Gov., Boston, 1976-77; dep. dir., then dir. fed. regulations Mayor's Office, City of Boston, 1977-79; dir. Econ. Devel. and Indsl. Corp. of Boston, 1979-84; exec. v.p. Combined Properties, Inc., Boston, 1984-89, The Drew Co., Boston, 1989—; mng. dir. Trade Ctr. Mgmt. Assocs., 1995—; bd. dirs. Boston Local Devel. Corp., founder revolving loan fund for local businesses, 1980; bd. dirs. Boston Pvt. Industry Coun., 1980-84. Bd. dirs. Morgan Meml. Goodwill Industries, 1986-96, chmn., 1991-93; sub-com. chair Artery Bus. Com., Boston, 1989—; trustee The Boston Harbor Assn., 1994—; subcom. chmn. Greater Boston C. of C., 1993—. Mem. Greater Boston Real Estate Bd. (mem. fin. div.), Urban Land Inst. Avocations: tennis, golf. Office: The Drew Co World Trade Ctr Boston MA 02210

DACEY, EILEEN M., lawyer; b. N.Y.C., Dec. 15, 1948; d. Gabriel A. and Mary (Breen) D.; m. Kinchen C. Bizzell, Jan. 1, 1984. BA in Sociology, SUNY, Stony Brook, 1970; JD, St. John's U., 1975. Assoc. Mendes & Mount, N.Y.C., 1976-80, jr. ptnr., 1980-88; ptnr. Adams, Duque & Hazeltine, N.Y.C., 1988-94, Morrison Mahoney & Miller, N.Y.C., 1994-96, Querrey & Harrow, N.Y.C., 1996-98. Vol. Lawyers for the Arts, Jewish Braille Inst.; mem. elderly project Vols. of Legal Svc. Mem. ABA (chair subcom. fed. regulation of ins. co. investment sect.), N.Y. State Bar Assn., Assn. of Bar of City of N.Y. (com. profl. discipline class of 1996), Practicing Law Inst. (ins. law adv. bd.). Home: 71 Park Ave New York NY 10016-2507

DACEY, GEORGE CLEMENT, retired laboratory administrator, consultant; b. Chgo., Jan. 23, 1921; s. Clement Anthony Dacey and Helyn MacLachlan; m. Anne Zeamer, June 20, 1954; children: Donna Lynn, John Clement, Sarah Anne. B.S. in E.E, U. Ill., 1942; Ph.D. in Physics, Calif. Inst. Tech., 1951. Research engr. Westinghouse Research Labs, East Pittsburgh, 1942-45; mem. tech. staff transistor research Bell Telephone Labs, 1952-55, head transistor devel., 1955-58, dir. solid state electronics research, 1958-61, exec. dir. telephones div., 1963-68, v.p. customer equipment devel., 1968-70, v.p. transmission systems, 1970-79, v.p. ops. systems, 1979-81; pres. Sandia Nat. Labs., 1981-86; v.p. research Sandia Corp., Albuquerque, 1961-63; bd. dirs. Milliken & Co. Contbr. articles on transistor physics, lasers to tech. jours. Mem. exec. bd. Monmouth council Boy Scouts Am., 1970-75; bd. dirs. Monmouth Mus., 1972-81. Recipient distinguished alumnus award U. Ill. Elec. Engring. Alumni Assn., 1970. Fellow IEEE, Am. Phys. Soc.; mem. Nat. Acad. Engring., Sigma Xi, Phi Kappa Phi, Tau Beta Pi, Eta Kappa Nu. Patentee transistors. Home: 3171 Laurel Ridge Ct Bonita Springs FL 34134-2663

DACEY, KATHLEEN RYAN, judge; b. Boston; m. William A. Dacey (dec. Aug. 1986); 1 child, Mary Dacey White. AB with honors, Emmanuel Coll., 1941; MS in L.S., Simmons Coll., 1942; JD, Northeastern U., 1945; postgrad., Boston U. Law Sch., 1945-46; LLD (hon.), Suffolk Law Sch., 1990, Emmanuel Coll., 1992. Bar: Mass. 1945, U.S. Supreme Ct. 1957. Practiced in Boston, 1947-75; asst. dist. atty. Suffolk County, Mass., 1971-72; asst. atty. gen., chief civil bur. Mass. Dept. Atty. Gen., Boston, 1975-77; law clk. to justices Mass. Supreme Jud. Ct., 1945-47; U.S. adminstrv. law judge Boston, 1977—; auditor, master Commonwealth of Mass., 1972-75, Suffolk and Norfolk Counties, Mass., 1972-75; asst. dist. atty. Suffolk County, Mass., 1971-72; mem. panel def. counsel for indigent persons U.S. Dist. Ct. Dist. Mass.; lectr., speaker in field. Contbr. articles to profl. jours. Bd. dirs. Mission United Neighborhood Improvement Team, Boston; mem. Boston Sch. Com., 1945-46, chmn., 1946-47. Recipient Silver Shingle award Boston U. Sch. Law, 1980; named Alumnae Woman of Yr., Northeastern U. Law Sch. Assn., 1976. Mem. ABA (ho. of dels. 1982—, exec. com. conf. of adminstrv. law judges jud. adminstrn. div. 1987—), Internat. Bar Assn., Mass. Bar Assn., Boston Bar Assn., Norfolk Bar Lawyers Assn., Nat. Assn. Women Lawyers (pres.), Mass. Assn. Women Lawyers, Internat. Fedn. Women Lawyers, Boston U. Law Sch. Alumni Assn. (corr. sec. 1974-76), Boston U. Nat. Alumni Council. Office: SSA-OHA 10 Causeway St Rm 417 Boston MA 02222-1047

DACH, LESLIE ALAN, public relations company executive; b. N.Y.C., Apr. 17, 1954; s. Joseph and Edith (Lipsyzc) D.; m. Mary Ann Dickie, Nov. 19, 1983; children: Jonathan Alexander, Eliza May. BS in Biology, Yale U., 1975; MPA, Harvard U., 1981. Staff scientist Environ. Def. Fund., Washington, 1977-79; mem. scheduling staff Kennedy for Pres., Washington, 1979-80; assoc. dir. Nat. Audubon Soc., Washington, 1981-84, legis. dir., 1984-87; dir. scheduling Mondale-Ferraro campaign, Washington, 1984; spl. asst. to chmn. U.S. Senate Agr. Com., Washington, 1987; dir. communications Dukakis for Pres., Boston, 1987-88; sr. v.p. Edelman Pub. Rels., Washington, 1989-90, exec. v.p., 1990-96, vice chmn., 1996—. Office: Edelman Pub Rels 1420 K St NW Washington DC 20005-2500

DACHOWSKI, PETER RICHARD, manufacturing executive; b. Hillingdon, Middlesex, Eng., June 2, 1948; came to U.S., 1969; s. Teodor and Mary (Stracey) D.; m. Victoria Kaplan Ortiz, May 1, 1977. MA in Econs. with first class honors, Queens' Coll., Cambridge, Eng., 1969; MBA, U. Chgo., 1971. Fin. analyst Exxon Corp., 1971-73; mgr. Boston Cons. Group, 1973-76; asst. treas. CertainTeed Corp., Valley Forge, Pa., 1976-78; asst. to chief exec. officer CertainTeed Corp., 1979-80; v.p. planning and devel. CertainTeed Co., Valley Forge, Pa., 1980-81, v.p., treas., 1981-83, v.p., compt., 1983-85; v.p., pres. Roofing Products Group, 1985-90, Vinyl Bldg. Products Group, Valley Forge, 1987-90; sr. v.p., pres. Exterior Products Group, 1990-93; exec. v.p., 1994—; mem. corp. devel. staff Saint Gobain, Paris, 1978-79; chmn. Isover St. Gobain, Brit. Gypsum-Isover, Gullfiber AB; pres. Worldwide Insulation Saint-Gobain, 1996—; bd. dirs. Grundzweig und Hartmann AG, Ecophon AB. Trustee Internat. House of Phila., 1994-96. Recipient Wall St. Jour. award Dow Jones-Chgo., 1971. Mem. World Pres. Orgn., Bri.-Am. C. of C., Alliance Francaise Phila. (trustee 1994-96), U. Chgo. Grad. Sch. Bus. Alumni Assn. (bd. dirs. 1986-88), Union League Phila., Beta Gamma Sigma. Avocations: tennis, travel, listening to live music, sailing. Home: 321 Woodmont Cir Berwyn PA 19312-1431 Office: CertainTeed Corp PO Box 860 Valley Forge PA 19482-0860

DACHS, ALAN MARK, investment company executive; b. N.Y.C., Dec. 7, 1947; s. Sidney and Martha (Selz) D.; m. Lauren B. Dachs, June 23, 1973. BA, Wesleyan U., Middletown, Conn., 1970; MBA, NYU, 1978. Account officer Chem. Bank, N.Y.C., 1971-74; various positions Bechtel Group, Inc., San Francisco, 1974-81; v.p., CFO Dual Drilling Co., Wichita Falls, Tex., 1981-82; sr. v.p., mng. dir. Bechtel Investments, Inc., San Francisco, 1982-89; pres., dir., mem. exec. com. and CEO Fremont Group, L.L.C., San Francisco, 1989—; bd. dirs. Bechtel Enterprises, Inc., ESCO Corp., Portland, Oreg., Sequoia Ventures Inc., San Francisco. Charter trustee Wesleyan U., 1991—, vice chair bd.; bd. trustees The Brookings Instn. Mem. Young Pres. Orgn. Office: Fremont Group LLC 50 Fremont St Ste 3700 San Francisco CA 94105-2230*

DACKAWICH, S. JOHN, sociology educator; b. Loch Gelley, W.Va., Jan. 31, 1926; s. Samuel and Estelle (Jablonski) D.; m. Shirley Jean McVay, May 20, 1950; children—Robert John, Nancy Joan. B.A., U. Md., 1955; Ph.D., U. Colo., 1958. Instr. U. Colo., 1955-57; instr. Colo. State U., 1957-59; prof., chmn. sociology Calif. State U., Long Beach, 1959-70; prof. sociology Calif. State U., Fresno, 1970-94, chmn. dept., 1970-75, prof. sociology emeritus, 1994—; pvt. practice survey research, 1962—. Contbr. articles and rsch. papers to profl. publs. Mem. Calif. Dem. Ctrl. Com., 1960-62; co-dir. Long Beach Ctrl. Area Study, 1962-64, Citizen Participation Study, Fresno. With USMCR, 1943-46, U.S. Army, 1950-53. Mem. Am., Pacific sociol. assns. Home: 5841 W Judy Ct Visalia CA 93277-8601 Office: Calif State U Dept Sociology 5340 N Campus Dr Fresno CA 93740-8019

DACKO, MARNIE, coach. BS, So. Conn. State U., 1978. Asst. coach U. Wis., Madison, 1978-79; asst. basketball coach, head softball coach St. John's U., Jamaica, N.Y., 1979-83; asst. coach Northwestern U., Evanston, Ill., 1984-95; head coach women's basketball Cornell U., Ithaca, N.Y., 1995—; asst. coach Big Tenn all-star Squad, 1993; head coach North Shore Women's Open Team, 1988 Prairie State Games; dir. Carol Blazejowski Basketball Camp, Montclair, N.J., 1982-86; co-dir. Calvin Murphy, Hamden, Conn., Pocono (Pa.) Invitational, Pine Tree Clinic, Waterville, Maine, Conn. Girl's basketball camps, Fairfield. Inducted into So. Conn. State U. Hall of Fame, 1996. Office: Cornell U Womens Athletics Dept Teagle Hall Campus Rd Ithaca NY 14853-6501

DACKOW, OREST TARAS, insurance company executive; b. Wynyard, Sask., Can., Sept. 17, 1936; s. Luke Dackow and Irene Stacheruk; m. Florence Dorothy Waples, Sept. 20, 1958; children: Trevor Wade, Heather Lynn, Donna Louise. B.Commerce with honors, U. Man., Winnipeg, Can., 1958; Grad. Advanced Mgmt. Program, Harvard U., 1976. Enrolled actuary. V.p. individual ops. Great-West Life Ins. Co., Winnipeg, Man., Can., 1976-78, sr. v.p. individual ops., 1978-79, sr. v.p. U.S., 1979-83; exec. v.p., chief operating officer U.S. Great-West Life Assurance Co., Denver, 1983-88; exec. v.p. corp. fin. and control Great-West Life Assurance Co., Winnipeg, 1988-90, pres., 1990-94, dir., 1992—; pres., CEO, dir. Great-West Lifeco Inc., 1992—; bd. dirs. London Life, 1997—. Bd. dirs. Met. YMCA, Winnipeg, 1971-80, pres., 1979-80; bd. dirs. Met. YMCA, Denver, 1981-84, Colo. Alliance of Bus., 1986-87, Nat. Jewish Ctr. for Immunology and Respiratory Medicine, 1985—, Health Scis. Centre Rsch. Found., 1990-94, Instrumental Diagnostics Devel. Office, 1992-94. Fellow Soc. Actuaries, Can. Inst. Actuaries; mem. Am. Acad. Actuaries. Avocation: sailing.

DACLES-MARIANI, JENNIFER SAMSON, engineering educator; b. Quezon City, Philippines, June 28, 1959; came to U.S., 1972; d. Simplicio and Anita (Samson) Dacles; m. Peter William Mariani, Aug. 18, 1990. BS in Engring., Calif. State U., Northridge, 1982; MSChemE, U. Mich., 1984, MSME, 1985; PhD, U. Calif., Davis, 1990. Jr. engr. Rockwell Internat., Santa Susana (Calif.) Lab., 1981; mem. tech. staff Rocketdyne divsn. Rockwell Internat., Canoga Park, Calif., 1984; rsch. engr. KMS Fusion, Ann Arbor, Mich., 1985; rsch. assoc. Nat. Rsch. Coun., NASA Ames Rsch. Ctr., Moffett Field, Calif., 1991-94; asst. rsch. prof. U. Calif., Davis, 1994—; rsch. assoc. U. Calif. Davis, 1986-91; rsch. asst. U. Mich., 1983-85. Contbr. articles to profl. jours. Patricia Harris fellowship award U. Calif., 1987-90; Getty Oil scholarship Calif. State U., 1982. Mem. AIAA, Soc. of the Divine Savior. Democrat. Roman Catholic. Acheivements include research on assesment of a accurate computational simulation of a wingtip vortex flowfield; co-investigator on project which uses a computational fluid dynamics as a tool to study and numerically simulate the interaction of cosmic dust, gases and turbulence in the solar nebula. Office: NASA Ames Rsch Ctr MS T27B-1 Moffett Field CA 94035

DACOSTA, EDWARD HOBAN, plastics and electronics manufacturing company executive; b. Phila., Sept. 19, 1918; s. Robert C. and Edna (Hoban) DaC.; m. Joyce Jehl, Oct. 7, 1944 (dec. 1946); 1 child, Stephen Edward; m. Elizabeth Brendlinger, Feb. 26, 1949 (dec. 1968); 1 child, David Hoban; m. Sarah McDonnell Kratz, Dec. 28, 1968; stepchildren: Carolyn Ann Borlo, Beverly Randolph. Student, Villanova U., 1936-38, Wharton Sch. of U. Pa., 1946-47. With Synthane Taylor Corp., Valley Forge, Pa., 1938-76; gen. mgr. Western div. LaVerne, Calif., 1953-56; v.p. mktg. Valley Forge, 1956-61; pres., chief exec. officer, 1961-69, chmn., chief exec. officer, 1969-75; dir. C-W Industries, Inc., Southampton, Pa., 1972—, v.p., 1977-82; pres. C-W Properties, Inc., 1977—; mng. dir. Alco Std. Corp., 1969-72; chmn. Beaumont Retirement Cmty. Inc., Bryn Mawr, Pa., 1995-99. Pres. Pa. United Fund, Harrisburg, 1964-67; pres. bd. trustees Norristown State Hosp., 1963-75; mem. adv. bd. Bryn Mawr Coll. Grad. Sch., 1963-85; bd. dirs. Community Services Planning Council, v.p., 1974-78, pres., 1978-80; trustee The Eye Disease Fedn., Wills Eye Hosp., Phila. Served as pilot USAAF, 1942-46. Mem. Nat. Elec. Mfg. Assn. (dir., chmn. insulating materials div. 1963-70). Episcopalian. Home: 73 Pasture Ln Bryn Mawr PA 19010-1763 Office: CW Industries Inc Southampton PA 18966

DACUNHA, SUSAN ELIZABETH, school nurse; b. Bronx, N.Y., July 27, 1948; d. Joseph Stephen and Eleanor Mary Taubner; m. Carlos Almeida DaCunha, May 28, 1972; children: Carlos Joseph, Diana Marie. BS, Western Conn. State U., 1970. Dir. health svcs. The Gunnery, Inc., Washington, Conn.; office mgr. Dr. Andrew Ragona/Oral & Maxillofacial Surgery Associates, Danbury, Conn.; staff nurse med./surg. unit Danbury Hosp.; staff nurse CCU/med. unit The Valley Hosp., Ridgewood, N.J. Mem. Ind. Sch. Health Assn., Nat. Assn. Sch. Nurses, Conn. Residential Sch. Nurses Assn., Assn. Sch. Nurses Conn., Conn. Assn. for Sch. Health. Home: 214 Danbury Rd New Milford CT 06776-4311

D'ADAMO, NICHOLAS C., city councilman; b. Jan. 14, 1958; s. Nicholas C. and Grace D'A.; m. Susan Moorefield. Mem. State Ctrl. Com. Balt. City Coun., 1986—, city councilman, 1987—, mem. Budget and Appropriations Com., mem. Policy and Planning Com. and Econ. Devel., 1998—; chair budget and appropriations com. Balt. City Coun., 1998—; owner Shocket's Discount Store. Mem. Sons of Italy, Polish Am. Congress. Office: City Hall 100 Holliday St Rm 523 Baltimore MD 21202-3417*

D'ADDARIO, ALICE MARIE, school administrator; b. N.Y.C., Feb. 9, 1942; d. Ralph and Rose Marie (Ventigmiglia) DeMartino; m. Joseph L. D'Addario, June 27, 1964; children: Joseph R., Paul T. BS in Social Studies, St. John's U., 1962, MS in Secondary Edn., 1963; MA in Liberal Studies, NYU, 1981. Cert. sch. adminstr., secondary educator of English and Social Studies, N.Y. Tchr. social studies So. Huntington Schs., Huntington Station, N.Y., 1963-83; dept. chair Walt Whitman H.S., Huntington Station, 1983—; adj. prof. Adelphi U., Garden City, N.Y., 1989—; tchg. adv. panelist, program reviewer America, Pathways to the Present, Prentice Hall, 1998, program reviewer, tchr. adv. panel World History, Connections to Today, 1999; counselor Ind. Coll., 1988—. Author: Writing Across the Curriculum, 1988, Participationin Government-A Guide for Teachers I, 1989, II, 1991, Asian Studies Elective Curriculum. PTA pres. P.S. 144 Queens, 1981-83, Russell Sage Jr. High Sch. 190, Queens, 1983-85, Parents Assn. Hillcrest H.S., Queens, 1986-88, Queen's Confederation of Parents, 1987-88. Recipient Parent Svc. award Hillcrest H.S., Queens, 1986-88, Profl. Recognition award Bd. Edn. South Huntington Schs., 1983, Tchr. of Yr. award Walt Whitman H.S. Parent Assn., 1984, Spl. Tchrs. Are Recognized award Cornell U., 1992, Dartmouth Coll. Freshman Tchr. Recognition award, 1994, Outstanding Social Studies Supr. award L.I. Coun. for the Social Studies, 1997. Mem. L.I. Council for the Social Studies, Assn. Sch. Adminstrs., So. Huntington Chairperson Assn. (v.p. 1985-87, pres. 1987—). Democrat. Roman Catholic. Avocations: reading, theater, art museums, cycling, jogging. Home: 68-47 Harrow St Flushing NY 11375-5157 Office: Walt Whitman High Sch West Hills Rd West Hills Rd Huntington NY 11746

DADDARIO, DIANE KAY, nurse, educator; b. Sunbury, Pa., July 21, 1959; d. Marlin Glenn and Irene Leona (Jarrett) Fetter; m. Dwayne Andrew Daddario, Apr. 24, 1982; children: Jeffrey Andrew, Jonathan Michael. LPN, Danville (Pa.) Sch. PN, 1978; RN, Geisinger Sch. Nursing, Danville, 1982; BS in Nursing, Pa. State U., 1997. Med.-surg. nurse, Am. Nurses Credentialing Ctr.; RN, Pa. Staff nurse Geisinger Med. Ctr., Danville, 1980-90, Evang. Cmty. Hosp., Lewisburg, Pa., 1990—; part-time health asst. tchr., Snyder-Union-Northumberland Area Career and Tech. Ctr., New Berlin, Pa., 1986—; mem. test devel. com. Nat. Coun. Licensure Exam. Mat. Bd. Nursing. Mem. Mifflinburg (Pa.) Area Mid. Sch. adv. group, 1996—. Mem. Am. Nurses Assn., Pa. State Nurses Assn., Geisinger Sch. Nursing Alumni Assn., Pa. State U. Sch. Nursing Alumni Assn., Pa. State U. Coll. Health and Human Devel. Alumni Assn., Pa. State Alumni Assn.

DADDARIO, EMILIO QUINCY, lawyer; b. Newton Centre, Mass., Sept. 24, 1918; s. Attilio Dante and Julia (Ciovacco) D.; m. Berenice Mary Carbo, Oct. 20, 1940; children: Edward, Stephen, Richard. B.A., Wesleyan U., 1939; LLB, U. Conn, 1942; DSc, Wesleyan U., 1967; LLD, Rensselaer Polytech. Inst., Troy, N.Y., 1967, Phila. Coll. Osteo. Medicine, 1976. Bar: Conn., Mass., D.C., 86th-91st Congresses from 1st Conn. dist. Judge Mcpl. Ct., Middletown, Conn., 1948-50; mem. 86th, 87th, 88th, 89th, 90th and 91st Congresses, from 1st Conn. dist., 1958-71; dir. Office Tech. Assessment, Washington, 1973-77; mem. Wilkes, Artis, Hedrick & Lane, Washington, 1977-87; vis. prof. MIT, Cambridge, 1970-71; co-chmn. ABA-AAAS Conf. of Lawyers and Scientists, Washington, 1976-88. Contbr. articles on sci. policy to profl. publs. Mayor, City of Middletown, Conn., 1946-48; mem. Commn. on Sci., Engring. and Pub. Policy, Nat. Acad. Scis., Washington, 1981—; trustee Wesleyan U., 1962—; adv. bd. Georgetown U. Sch. of Nursing. Served to maj., inf. U.S. Army, 1942-45, 50-52, ETO, PTO, Korea. Decorated Legion of Merit; Medaglia D'Argento (Italy). Mem. Silver Anniversary All-Am. Football Team, 1964; recipient Ralph Coats Roe award ASME, 1974; honor award and medal Stevens Inst. Tech., 1975; Pub. Welfare award Nat. Acad. Scis., 1976; Disting. Svc. award Nat. Sci. Found., 1990, W.R. Grace award Am. Cham. Soc., 1992. Mem. ABA, AAAS (pres. 1977, chmn. 1978, chmn. governance com. 1989-90), Inst. Medicine (bd. health sci. policy 1991-97), D.C. Bar Assn., Oak Ridge Associated Univs. (bd. dirs. 1991-97), Nat. Acad. Sci. (com. nat. forum on sci. and tech. goals 1995), Vets of OSS (v.p. 1990—). Democrat. Roman Catholic. Club: Cosmos (Washington). Home: #1027 3133 Conncticut Ave NW Washington DC 20008-5112

DADISMAN, JOSEPH CARROL, newspaper executive; b. Statesboro, Ga., May 24, 1934; s. Howard Dean and Mary Lou (Moore) D.; m. Mildred Jean Sparks, Aug. 19, 1956; children: David Carrol, Ellen Clarice. AB, U. Ga., 1956. Reporter, editorial writer, mng. editor Augusta (Ga.) Chronicle, 1956-66; editor Marietta (Ga.) Daily Jour., 1966-72; mng. editor Macon (Ga.) News, 1972-74; exec. editor, v.p. Columbus (Ga.) Ledger-Enquirer, 1974-80; gen. mgr. Tallahassee Democrat, 1980-81, pub., pres., 1981-97; Knight Internat. Press fellow to Russia, 1998. Pres. adv. bd. U. Ga. Sch. Journalism, 1979-81, Fla. A&M U. Sch. Journalism, 1988-90; pres. Jr. Achievement of Columbus-Phenix City, 1977-78, United Way of Leon County, 1985-86, Ga. AP Assn., 1976-77; pres. Cmty. Found. of North Fla., 1997—. Served with AUS, 1957-59. Recipient Pub. Svc. award Cobb County C. of C., 1968, Fearless Editl. award Ga. Press Assn., 1963, Outstanding Alumnus award U. Ga. Sch. Journalism, 1994, Disting. Leader award Tallahassee Area C. of C., 1995, meritorious achievement award Fla. A&M U., 1996, Knight-Ridder excellence award in cmty. svc., 1997; named Young Man of Yr., Augusta Jaycees, 1962. Mem. Am. Soc. Newspaper Editors, Fla. Press Assn. (bd. dirs. 1984-86, v.p. 1986-87, pres. 1987-88), So. Newspaper Pubs. Assn. (bd. dirs. 1989-92), Econ. Club Fla. (pres. 1993-94, chmn. 1995-97), Orange Bowl Com., Governors Club, Killearn Country Club, Capital Tiger Bay Club, Rotary. Methodist. Home: 1235 Live Oak Plantation Rd Tallahassee FL 32312-2509

DADMEHR, NAHID, neurologist; b. Mashhad, Khorasan, Iran, May 8, 1953; came to U.S., 1983, naturalized; d. Hussein Dadmehr and Hajar Behkish; m. Hojjat Adeli, Feb. 1979; children: Anahita, Amir, Mona, Cyrus Dean. MD, U. Tehran, Iran, 1979. Diplomate Am. Bd. Psychiatry and Neurology. Rsch. fellow Ohio State U., Columbus, 1986, clin. instr. medicine, 1986-87, clin. instr. neurology, 1987-90, fellow clin. instrn. neurology, 1990-91; pvt. practice Westerville, Ohio, 1991—; clin. asst. prof. dept. neurology Ohio State U., Columbus, 1993—. Mem. editorial bd. Heuristics Jour. Knowledge Engring.; contbr. articles to profl. jours. Mem. Am. Acad. Neurology, Movement Disorder Soc., Internat. Conf. on Intelligent Info. Systems (internat. program com.). Achievements include fundamental contributions to field of neurological movement disorder; research in neurology, clinical electroencephalography. Office: 555 W Schrock Rd Ste F Westerville OH 43081-8717*

DADRIAN, VAHAKN NORAIR, sociology educator; b. Istanbul, Turkey, May 26, 1926; came to U.S., 1947, naturalized, 1961; s. Hagop and Mayreni (Der Garabedian) D. Ed. (Alexander von Humboldt fellow), U. Berlin, Germany, U. Vienna, Austria; ed. (scholar), U. Zurich, Switzerland; M.A., Wayne State U., 1950; Ph.D. (Reynolds fellow), U. Chgo., 1954. Asst. prof. sociology Washington Coll., Chestertown, Md., 1955-56, Boston U., 1957-59; research fellow Harvard Center for Middle Eastern Studies, 1961-62; sr. analyst dept. strategic studies div. missiles and space Raytheon, 1962-63; lectr. Boston Coll., 1963-65; asso. prof. Wis. State U., Superior, 1965-67; asso. prof. Fla. Atlantic U., 1967-68, prof., 1968-70; prof. SUNY, Geneseo, 1970-91; dir. genocide study project H.F. Guggenheim Found., Conesus, N.Y., 1991—; Vis. scholar Mass. Inst. Tech. Center Internat. Studies, 1960-61; guest researcher Inst. for Research on Soviet Union, Munich, Germany, summer 1962; participant, Am. Sociol. Assn. grantee 6th World Congress of Sociology, Evian, France, fall 1966; vis. prof. Duke, summer 1971; dir. genocide study project NSF, 1977—; lectr. at univs., confs. and on TV in, U.S., Europe, Soviet Union, S.Am. Contbg. author: World Book Ency., 1972—; Cons. editor: Internat. Jour. Contemporary Soc; translator, editor: United and Independent Turania (Zarevand), 1971; Contbr. articles to profl. jours., newspapers. Harvard Lab. Social Relations grantee, 1959; Am. Philos. Soc. grantee, 1961; Am. Com. Travel grantee-in-aid, 1962; Wenner-Gren Found. Anthropol. Research grantee, 1963, 65; Am. Council Learned Socs. grantee, summer 1966; recipient Wis. U. Bd. Regents award, 1966, St. Vardan medal for scholarship in field of Soviet nationalities Cardinal Aghadjanian, Rome, 1968; NSF grantee, 1968, 73, 76; State U. N.Y. grantee-in-aid, 1974; H.F. Guggenheim Found. grantee, 1990-91. Mem. Delta Tau Kappa (hon.). Home: PO Box 99 Conesus NY 14435-0099 Office: Guggenheim Rsch Project PO Box 99 Conesus NY 14435-0099

DADURIAN, MEDINA DIANA, pediatric dentist, educator; b. Landstuhl, Germany, Apr. 12, 1964; came to U.S., 1964; d. John Gulbenc Jr. and Alice Nartouhi (Vosgeritchian) D.; m. Gregory Sarkis Kinoian, July 3, 1993; 1 child, Melissa Marie. BS, Allegheny Coll., Meadville, Pa., 1986; DMD, U. Medicine and Dentistry N.J., Newark, 1991. Resident in hosp. gen. practice dentistry Hackensack (N.J.) Med. Ctr., 1991-92; tng. in pediatric dentistry Columbia U. Sch. Dental and Oral Surgery, N.Y.C., 1994-96; assoc. dentist pvt. practices, 1992-93, Assocs. for Dental Care, Hackensack, 1993-95; assoc. dental specialist Denville (N.J.) Dental Assocs., 1997; owner, pediatric dentist in pvt. practice, Rochelle Park, N.J., 1996—; assoc. clin. prof. Hackensack U. Med. Ctr., 1993—; dental adminstr. Hackensack Bd. Edn., 1993-95. Author in field. Dental dir. Bergen County Head Start, Englewood, N.J., 1993-95. Cerebral Palsy fellow United Cerebral Palsy Found., 1995-96; Gulbenkian Found. grantee, 1983-86. Fellow Acad. Gen. Dentistry; mem. ADA, Am. Acad. Pediatric Dentistry, Am. Armenian Dental Soc. Mem. Armenian Apostolic Ch. Avocations: reading, cooking, horseback riding, martial arts, needlework. E-mail: mdadurian@aol.com. Home: 377 Elliot Pl Paramus NJ 07652-4647 Office: 315 Rochelle Ave Rochelle Park NJ 07662-3916

DADY, ROBERT EDWARD, lawyer; b. N.Y.C., Nov. 11, 1936; s. Edward Joseph and Florence (Scheidt) D.; m. Mollie D. Richman; children: Michael, Andrew, Rachel. BA, Queens Coll., 1958; LLB, Fordham U., 1961. Bar: N.Y. 1962, Fla. 1974. Asst. gen. counsel The Equity Corp., N.Y.C., 1962-66; gen. atty. ITT-Levitt and Sons, Inc., Washington and Lake Success, N.Y., 1966-70; sr. v.p.-legal First Realty Investment Corp., Miami Beach, Fla., 1970-71; v.p.-legal, sec. Cavanagh Communities Corp., Miami, Fla., 1971-75; ptnr. Mann & Dady, P.A., Miami, 1975-80, Mann, Dady, Corrigan & Zelman, P.A., 1980-83, Dady, Siegfried & Kipnis, P.A., 1984-85, pvt. practice, 1985-87; ptnr. Kimbrell and Hamann, P.A., 1987-89; shareholder Popham, Haik, Schnobrich, & Kaufman, Ltd, 1990-96; of counsel, Fieldstone, Lester and Shear, 1996—; past adj. prof. law U. Miami Sch. Law.; bd. dirs. Spectrum Programs, Inc., pres., 1984-86, Spectrum Found., Inc., pres. 1988—. Bd. dirs., exec. comm. Miami Coalition for a Safe and Drug Free Cmty., 1992-99; vice chair Childrens Home Soc. Found. Miami, 1993-96, bd. dirs., 1993—; appointed to (by gov.) Fla. Jud. Nom. Com., 1995-98. Mem. Nat. Land Coun. (pres. 1974-81, bd. dirs. 1973—), Builders Assn. So. Fla. (gen. counsel 1982—), ABA (environ. law com., timesharing and recreation law com.), Fla. Bar Assn. Republican. Author: Land Acquistion and Development, 1975. Home: 8440 SW 143rd St Miami FL 33158-1457 Office: Fieldstone Lester & Shear First Union Fin Ctr 2100 200 S Biscayne Blvd Ste 2100B Miami FL 33131-5337

DAEHN, GLENN STEVEN, materials scientist; b. Chgo., July 4, 1961; s. Ralph Charles and Beverly S. (Shanske) D.; m. Margaret A. Burkhart, Oct. 25, 1987; children: Andrew Joseph, Katrin Ellen, Matthew Charles. BS, Northwestern U., 1983; MS, Stanford U., 1985, PhD, 1988. Rsch. asst. Stanford U., Palo Alto, Calif., 1983-87; asst. prof. dept. materials sci. and engring. Ohio State U., Columbus, 1987-92, assoc. prof. dept. materials sci. and engring., 1992-96, Fontana prof. dept. materials sci. and engring., 1996—; v.p. BFD, Inc., 1992—. Co-editor: Modeling the Deformation of Crystalline Solids, 1991. Named Nat. Young Investigator, NSF, 1992; recipient Young Investigator award Army Rsch. Office, 1992, R.L. Hardy Gold medal TMS, 1992, Marcus Grossman award ASM Internat., 1990. Mem. ASM Internat., Am. Ceramic Soc., Materials Rsch. Soc., Minerals, Metals and Materials Soc. Achievements include description and practical applications of how temperature changes accelerate the deformation of composite materials; co-development of new class of ceramic-metal composites; development of hyperplasticity --practical application of extended metal ductility observed at high velocity. Home: 2076 Fairfax Rd Upper Arlngtn OH 43221-4319 Office: Ohio State U Materials Sci Dept 2041 N College Rd Columbus OH 43210-1124

DAENZER, BERNARD JOHN, insurance company executive, legal consultant; b. N.Y.C., Jan. 15, 1916; s. Bernard Cornelius and Amelia Catherine (Heinze) D.; m. Valerie Antoinette Lee, June 8, 1941; children—Peter, Jean Daenzer Aiken, John, Richard (dec.). A.B., Fordham Coll., 1937, LL.D., 1942; LL.D., Coll. Ins. N.Y.C., 1981. Spl. agt. Loyalty Group, Westchester, N.Y., 1937-43; with Security-Conn. Group, 1943-57, exec. v.p., 1955-57; pres. Wohlreich & Anderson Ltd., Cranford, N.J., 1957-81; bd. dirs. RLI Ins. Co. Ltd., Hamilton, Bermuda; dir. Alexander Howden Group Ltd., London, 1968-81; underwriter Lloyds of London, 1968—; dir. RLI Corp., Peoria, Ill., 1972—. Columnist: Weekly Underwriter, 1964-86; Author publs. in field. Trustee Ocean Reef Chapel, Loman Found., Malvern, Pa. Served with USNR, 1944-46. Mem. Coll. Ins. N.Y.C. (past chmn. bd.), Soc. Chartered Property and Casualty Underwriters (past pres. Conn. chpt., past pres. nat. assn.), Ocean Reef Club, Card Sound Country Club, Racquet Club, Springlake Country Club. Republican. Roman Catholic. Office: Ocean Reef 29 Angelfish Cay Dr Key Largo FL 33037-5271

DAFERMOS, CONSTANTINE MICHAEL, applied mathematics educator; b. Athens, Greece, May 26, 1941; came to U.S., 1964; s. Michael Constantine and Sophia (Raptarchis) D.; m. Stella Theodoracopoulos, Sept. 6, 1964; children: Thalia, Michael. Diploma, Athens Nat. Tech. U., 1964; PhD, Johns Hopkins U., 1967. Fellow Johns Hopkins U., 1967-68; asst. prof. Cornell U., 1968-71; assoc. prof. Brown U., 1971-76, prof. applied math., 1976—, Univ. prof., 1988—, dir. Lefschetz Ctr. for Dynamical Systems, 1988-94. Mem. editl. bd. Archive for Rational Mechanics and Analysis, 1972—, Jour. of Thermal Stresses, 1978—, Quar. Applied Math., 1985—, Math. Modeling and Numerical Analysis, 1986-96, Proc. Royal Soc. Edinburgh, 1987—, Advances Math. Applied Sci., 1989—, Math. Models and Methods, 1990-97, Communications on Applied Nonlinear Analysis, 1995—, Computer Math. and its Applications, 1995—, Ricerche di Matematica, 1997—, Jour. Am. Math. Soc., 1999—; contbr. articles to profl. jours. NSF grantee, 1970—, Office Naval Rsch. grantee, 1972-80, 92—, USAF grantee, 1972-73, U.S. Army grantee, 1973-96. Mem. Soc. Natural Philosophy (treas. 1975-76, chmn. 1977-78), Am. Math. Soc., Acad. of Athens. Office: Brown U Lefschetz Ctr Dynamical Sys 182 George St Providence RI 02912-9056

DAFFORN, GEOFFREY ALAN, biochemist; b. Cunningham, Kans., Feb. 4, 1944; s. Francis Elston and Anna Elizabeth Dafforn; m. Gail McLaughlin, July 14, 1973; 1 child, Christine Elizabeth. BA cum laude, Harvard U., 1966; PhD, U. Calif., Berkeley, 1970. Postdoctoral fellow U. Calif., Berkeley, 1973; asst. prof. U. Tex., Austin, 1974; from asst. prof. to assoc. prof. Bowling Green (Ohio) State U., 1974-81; sr. chemist Syva Co., Palo Alto, Calif., 1982-87, rsch. fellow, 1987—. Author articles and abstracts; patentee in field. Grantee Army Rsch. Office, 1979-82, Am. Chem. Soc., 1975-80. Mem. AAAS, Am. Chem. Soc., Sierra Club. Office: Dade Behring 3403 Yerba Buena Rd San Jose CA 95135-1500

DAFFRON, MARYELLEN, librarian; b. Richmond, Va., Nov. 12, 1946; d. William Charles and Ellen (Ahern) D. BA, Coll. Mt. St. Joseph on Ohio, Cin., 1968; MLS, Drexel U., 1970. Libr. Richmond Pub. Libr., 1969-73, FMC, Washington, 1973-93; with U.S. Immigration and Naturalization Svc. Office of Gen. Counsel, Washington, 1993—. Vol. No. Va. Hotline, Arlington, 1974-79. City of Richmond fellow, 1968. Mem. Law Libr. Soc. Washington, Beta Phi Mu. Roman Catholic. Office: US Immigration Naturalization Svc Office Gen Counsel 425 I St NW Rm 6100 Washington DC 20536-0001

DAFFRON, SANDRA RATCLIFF, professional society administrator; b. Washington, May 2, 1944. BS in Home Econs., Ea. Ill. U., 1965; MS in Spl. Edn., So. Ill. U., 1969; EdD in Adult and Continuing Edn., No. Ill. U., 1985. Mgr. restaurant Stix, Baer and Fuller Dept. Store, St. Louis, 1965-66; tchr. spl. edn. Mascoutah (Ill.) H.S., Highland (Ill.) H.S., 1966-74; instr., chair dept. spl. edn. Forest Park (Ga.) Sr. H.S., 1974-76, Louisville (Ga.) H.S., 1976-77; instr. adult basic edn. Venice (Ill.) Lincoln Tech. Ctr., 1977-80; assoc. dir. No. Area Adult Edn. Svc. Ctr., No. Ill. U./Ill. Bd. Edn., DeKalb, 1980-84; asst. dir. instrnl. svcs. Ill. Inst. Continuing Legal Edn., Chgo., 1984-87; cons. Cir. Ct. Cook County, Chgo., 1984-88; asst. dean, dir. continuing Edn. Ill. Inst. Tech., Chgo.-Kent Coll. Law, 1987-88; asst. exec. dir. programs Am. Judicature Soc., Chgo., 1988-93, project dir., 1992-93, exec. v.p., dir., 1997—; adj. prof. Va. Commonwealth U., Richmond, 1993-96; constn. activities com. Ill. Supreme Ct., 1985-86; project coord., rschr. Med. Coll. Va., 1993-94; coord. train-the-trainers program Nat. Inst. Corrections Acad./Va. Dept. Correctional Edn., 1993-94; cons., presenter in field. Contbr. articles to profl. jours. Named One of 100 Women Shaping Future of Chgo., Today's Chgo. Woman, 1988. Mem. Assn. Continuing Legal Edn. Adminstrs., Am. Assn. Adult Continuing Edn. (chair commn. continuing profl. edn. 1985-88, bd. dirs. 1988—), Nat. Assn. Adult Continuing Edn., Chgo. Soc. Assn. Execs., Am. Judicature Soc. Office: Am Judicature Soc 180 N Michigan Ave Ste 600 Chicago IL 60601-7454*

DAFOE, DONALD CAMERON, surgeon, educator; b. Appleton, Wis., Nov. 22, 1949. BS in Zoology, U. Wis., 1971, MD, 1975. Diplomate Am. Bd. Surgery. Intern Hosp. of U. of Pa., Phila., 1975-76, resident, 1976-80, Measey rsch. fellow, 1978-80, chief resident, 1980-81, clin. fellow, Culpeper Found. fellow, 1981-82; asst. prof. surgery U. Mich., Ann Arbor, 1982-87; dir. clin. pancreas transplantation program u. Mich., Ann. Arbor, 1984-87; assoc. prof. surgery U. Mich., Ann Arbor, 1987; assoc. prof. surgery, chief divsn. transplantation Hosp. of U. of Pa., Phila., 1987-91; assoc. prof. surgery, chief divsn. transplantation Stanford (Calif.) U. Med. Ctr., 1991-99, dir. kidney/kidney pancreas program, 1999—. Reviewer various publs.; mem. editorial bd. Transplantation Sci., 1992, The Chimera, 1993; contbr. over 100 articles to profl. jours; also numerous book chpts. Mem. ACS, Am. Surg. Assn., Am. Diabetes Assn., Am. Soc. Transplant Surgeons, Assn. for Acad. Surgery, Soc. Internat. de Chirurgie, The Transplantation Soc., Pacific Coast Surg. Assn., Ctrl. Surg. Assn., Frederick A. Coller Surg. Soc., Soc. Univ. Surgeons, Surg. Biology Club II, Ravdin-Rhoads Surg. Soc., United Network for Organ Sharing, Calif. Transplant Donor Network, Western Assn. Transplant Surgeons. Office: 750 Welch Rd Ste 200 Palo Alto CA 94304*

DAFOE, WILLEM, actor; b. Appleton, Wis., July 22, 1955; s. William Dafoe; 1 child, Jack. Student, U. Wis. Mem. Theatre X theatrical co., 1975, Wooster Group theatrical co., N.Y.C., 1977—. Actor (feature films) The Loveless, 1983, The Hunger, 1983, New York Nights, 1984, Roadhouse 66, 1984, Streets of Fire, 1984, To Live and Die in L.A., 1985, Platoon, 1986 (Acad. award nomination 1987), The Last Temptation of Christ, 1988, Off Limits, 1988, Mississippi Burning, 1988, Triumph of the Spirit, 1989, Born on the Fourth of July, 1989, Cry-Baby, Flight of the Intruder, Wild at Heart, 1990, White Sands, 1992, Light Sleeper, 1992, Body of Evidence, 1992, Far Away So Close, 1993, The Night and the Moment, 1994, Clear and Present Danger, 1994, Tom and Viv, 1995, The English Patient, 1996, Basquiat, 1996, Speed 2: Cruise Control, 1997, Affliction, 1997, Victory, 1995, Lulu on the Bridge, 1998, eXisten Z, 1998, American Psycho, 1999. *

DAGA, ANDREW WILLIAM, architect, inventor, space technology researcher; b. N.Y.C., July 18, 1957; s. Lorenzo Mario and Gloria Valentine (Bloom) D. BArch magna cum laude, Spring Garden Coll., 1985. Lectr. Spring Garden Coll., Phila., 1985—, Pa. State U., 1992—; promoter Internat. Space U., Cambridge, Mass., 1987; pub. speaker, lectr. on future of manned space program and tech. implications. Inventor system for forming structural concrete, lunar base architecture, novel architecture for undeveloped nations, inertially-based surveying instrument, concrete bladdercasting technique.

DAGDIGIAN, PAUL JOSEPH, chemistry educator; b. Phila., Oct. 18, 1945; s. Vahan P. and Shirley (Sirabonian) D.; m. Sandra Gilluly, Aug. 20, 1967; children: Elizabeth, David. AB, Haverford Coll., 1967; PhD, U. Chgo., 1972. Postdoctoral fellow Columbia U., N.Y.C., 1972-74; from asst. prof. to assoc. prof. chemistry Johns Hopkins U., Balt., 1974-81, prof. chemistry, 1981—, chmn. dept. chemistry, 1998—. Camille and Henry Dreyfus Found. scholar, 1977-82; Fannie and John Hertz Found. fellow, 1968-69, Alfred P. Sloan Found. rsch. fellow, 1976-80. Fellow Am. Physical Soc. (chair divsn. chemical physics 1989-91). Office: Johns Hopkins U Dept Chemistry 3400 N Charles St Baltimore MD 21218-2680*

DAGEFORDE, MARY L., technical writer, software designer; m. Thomas J. Wills, June 12, 1994. BA in French, Stanford U., 1976, BS in Math. Scis., 1976; MS in Computer Sci., 1985. Software designer, developer Stanford U., 1976-80; designer computer lang. and software Xerox Corp., Palo Alto, Calif., 1980-88; team leader software devel. Xerox Corp., Sunnyvale, Calif., 1988-90; owner Dageforde Consulting, Santa Clara, Calif., 1990—; founder Xidak, Inc., 1979. Contbr. online books. Mem. Soc. Tech. Comm. Avocations: tennis, running.

DAGENAIS, MARCEL GILLES, economist, educator; b. Montreal, Que., Can., Feb. 22, 1935; s. Emilien and Antoinette (Girard) D.; m. Denyse Laberge, July 5, 1958; children—Danielle, Michel, Jean-Francois. BA, Coll. Jean de Brébeuf, 1952; MA, U. Montreal, 1958, Yale U., 1960; PhD, Yale U., 1964. Asst. prof. U. Montreal, 1961-66; vis. prof. Ecole de Hautes Etudes Commerciales de Montreal, 1966-67, assoc. prof., 1967-70, prof., 1970-72; vis. prof. U. Montreal, 1972-73, prof., 1973-97, research fellow cen. rech. et devel. econ., 1987—; rsch. dir. Ctr. for Interuniversity Rsch. and Analysis on Orgns., 1994—; prof. emeritus U. Montreal, 1997—; cons. econometrician Amstec Inc., 1998—; spl. prof. Sir George Williams U., 1969-73; assoc. dir. Internat. Inst. Quantitative Econs., 1969-74; dir. Centre d'econometrie, 1968-72; tech. mgr. econ. rsch., dir. Automatec Inc., Montreal, 1965-67; pres. Rotec Inc., 1967-69; invited prof. McGill U., 1998—, U. Bourgogne, 1998. Book rev. editor Canadian Jour. Econs., 1969-74; assoc. editor Jour. of Econometrics, 1980—, Revue Canadienne de Statistique, 1980-84; mem. editorial bd. Advanced Studies in Theoretical and Applied Econometrics, 1982—; adv. com. on systems of nat. accounts Statistics Can., 1984—. Mem. steering com. on audit of nat. accts. INSEE, France. Woodrow Wilson hon. fellow, 1958, Can. Coun. fellow, 1958-60, Imperial Oil Grad. Rsch. fellow, 1958-61, Killam Rsch. fellow, 1987-89, Prix du statisticien d'expression française, Soc. Statistique de Paris, 1990, Prix Marcel-Vincent Assn. Can. Française pour L'Avancement des Sci., 1991, Bourse de chercheur de haut niveau du Ministère de l'education nationale de France, 1995-96. Fellow Royal Soc. Can., Jour. Econometrics; mem. Can. Econ. Assn. (v.p. 1980-82), Econometric Soc., Sociètè canadienne de science economique (pres. 1980-81, award 1982), Cons. on Rsch. in Income and Wealth, Assn. de Comptabilité nationale, Assn. d'econométrie appliquée. Home: 60 Berlioz, Apt 1002, Ile des Soeurs, PQ Canada H3E 1M4

DAGENHART, BETTY JANE MAHAFFEY, nursing educator, administrator; b. Welch, W.Va.; d. Charley F. and Edith L. (Lucas) Mahaffey; divorced; 1 child, Cynthia Leigh. BA in Health Care Adminstrn., Mary Baldwin, Staunton, Va., 1991; postgrad., St. Joseph's Coll. RN, Va.; cert. nursing adminstr., ANA. Nurse mgr. ortho. and emergency svcs. Cmty. Hosp. of Roanoke (Va.) Valley, 1967-77, asst. dir. nursing svcs., 1977-83, coord. quality mgmt., dir. occupl. health svcs., dir. emergency svcs., 1983-92, dir. med./surg. nursing, 1992-94; dir. nursing edn. City of Salem (Va.) Sch. Sys., 1994—; mem. disaster planning coun. City of Roanoke, 1980-90, prehosp. care providers, 1982-88, chmn. pers. com.: organized free standing clinic Cmty. Hosp. Roanoke, 1986; dir. med. office asst. program Dominican Coll., Roanoke, Va., 1997—. Bd. dirs. Emergency Med. Svcs. Western Va., 1979-92; mem. pers. com. Cave Spring Bapt. Ch., Roanoke, 1991-92. Mem. ANA, Va. Orgn. Nurse Execs., Exec. Females, Health Occupation Educators. Avocations: golf, walking, crafts, cooking, ednl. endeavors. Home: 2638 Southwoods Dr Roanoke VA 24018-2523 Office: Dominion Coll Ste B 5372 Fallowater Ln Roanoke VA 24014

DAGENHART, LARRY JONES, lawyer; b. Taylorsville, N.C., July 20, 1932; s. Luther Jones and Louise (Icenhour) D.; m. Sarah Katheryne Petty, June 23, 1956; children: Katie Dagenhart Satterwhite, Mary Louise Dagenhart Culpepper, Larry Jones Jr. B.S., Davidson (N.C.) Coll., 1953; LL.B., NYU, 1958. Bar: N.C. 1958. Pvt. practice Charlotte, 1958—; ptnr. Smith Helms Mulliss & Moore; bd. dirs. So. Webbing, J.A. Jones. Cannon med. rsch. ctr.1994—. Trustee Davidson Coll., 1970—, chmn., 1998—; trustee U. N.C., Wilmington, 1997—. Kate B. Reynolds Trust, 1990-96; chmn. Ben Craig Incubator Ctr., 1998—; bd. dirs. N.C. Citizens for Bus. and Industry, 1995—; past chmn. Charlotte C. of C., 1983, Charlotte Arts and Scis. Coun., 1976-77, Mecklenburg County Bar Assn., 1974-75, Charlotte United Way, 1978, Found. for the Carolinas, 1987-89, Charlotte Country Day Sch., 1985-87, Charlotte City Club, 1979, Charlotte World Affairs Coun., 1996-98. George F. Baker scholar, 1949-53, Root-Tilden scholar, 1953-58; fellow Am. Bar Found., 1970—. Mem. ABA, Am. Law Inst. Democrat. Lutheran. E-mail: larryúdagenhart@shmm.com. Home: 1601 Biltmore Dr Charlotte NC 28207-2611 Office: Smith Helms Mulliss & Moore PO Box 31247 Charlotte NC 28231-1247

DAGGETT, BEVERLY CLARK, state legislator; b. Florence, S.C., Sept. 9, 1945; d. John and Beth Clark; m. Thomas A. Daggett, May 8, 1971; children: John, Page, Paul. BS in Biology, Hillsdale Coll., 1967. Mem. Maine Ho. of Reps., Augusta, 1987-96; chair commn. to study biotech. and genetic engring., 1995—, house chair joint standing com. on state and local govt., 1995-96; mem. Maine State Senate, 1996—; chair joint standing com. on legal and vets. affairs Maine State Senate, mem. taxation com.; mem. Substance Abuse Svcs. Commn. Coun. State Govts. Toll fellow, 1990; Flemming fellow, 1997. Democrat. Home: 16 Pine St Augusta ME 04330-5340

DAGIT, CHARLES EDWARD, JR., architect, educator; b. Phila., July 1, 1943; s. Charles E. and Janet (Donnelly) D.; m. Alice M. Murdoch, June 3, 1967; children: Charles Edward, J. Murdoch. B.A., U. Pa., 1965, B.Arch., 1967, M.Arch., 1968. Registered architect, Pa., N.Y., N.J., Conn., Va., Md., Ohio. Designer Henry D. Dagit & Sons, Phila., 1965-68, Mitchell, Giurgola Assocs., Phila., 1968-69; project designer Henry D. Dagit & Sons, Phila., 1969-70; ptnr. Dagit Saylor Architects, Phila., 1970—; adj. asst. prof. Sch. Arch. and Engring., Temple U., 1973-80; adj. prof. dept. arch. Phila. Coll. Art, 1979-80; vis. prof. U. Pa., 1980; prof. dept. arch. Drexel U. Prin. works include Peale House of Pa. Acad. Fine Arts, Agrl. Arena at Pa. State U., Spring Garden Health Ctr. (runner-up for Rudi Brunner award), Phoenix City Ctr. for Arts (NEA grant), 1983, Cumberland Union Bldg. Shippensburg U. (Phila. chpt. AIA Design award 1992, Design award PSA 1992), Bartram's Garden (Pa. Mus. and Hist. Commn. Preservation award 1993), Campus Ctr. Bldg. Haverford Coll. (Phila. chpt. AIA Design award 1994, Design award PSA 1994, F.W. Olin Bldg. (Phila. chpt. AIA Design award 1992, Design award PSA 1992), Pa. Ballet (Design award PSA 1989), Gwynedd Mercy Coll. Lourdes Libr. Addition (Phila. chpt. AIA Design award 1986), Magee Rehab. Hosp. (Phila. chpt. Design award 1984), Logan Mus. Anthropology, Beloit Coll. (Phila. chpt. AIA Design award 1995, Internat. Illumination Design award, Preservation award WI Preservation Trust 1995). Pres. Gladwyne Civic Assn., 1981-82; pres. Friends of St. Christopher's Hosp., Phila., 1977-78; trustee Bryn Mawr. (Pa.) Country Day Sch., 1975-79; bd. dirs. Phila. Zool. Soc., 1979-87; pres. bd. trustees Gladwyne Libr. Bd., 1990-91; trustee Acad. Cmty. Music, 1997—. Recipient Design award Progressive Architecture, 1974, 40 Under 40 award A&U Mag., Japan, 1977, View of World Contemporary Architecture award Japan Architect, 1977; winner nat. design competition Cultural Arts Pavillion, Newport News, Va., 1985. Fellow AIA (Silver medal Phila. chpt. 1976, Gold medal 1978, pres.-elect Phila. chpt. 1989, pres. Phila. chpt. 1990, chair Nat. Design Conf. commn. on architecture for arts and recreation, Cin. 1976, chair Nat. Design Conf. commn. on design, Louis I. Kahn & Phila. Sch. 1991, chmn. designate commn. on design 1992, vice chmn. commn. design, 1993, chmn. commn. design 1994); mem. Pa. Soc. AIA (Silver medal 1985), Soc. Coll.and U. Planners, Facilities Planning Acad., Downtown Club Phila. (bd. dirs. 1986-89), Merion Golf Club (Ardmore, Pa.), Mask and Wig Club, U. Pa. Spinx Sr. Soc. (bd. dirs. 1973-76), The Carpenter's Co. Republican. Roman Catholic. Home: 381 Williamson Rd Gladwyne PA 19035-1618 Office: Dagit Saylor Architects 100 S Broad St Ste 1100 Philadelphia PA 19110-1023

DAGLEY, MARK, artist; b. Washington, Dec. 7, 1957; s. John Charles and Billie (Burg) D.; m. Lauri Bortz, June 10, 1995. Student, Corcoran Mus. Sch., Washington, 1976, Boston Mus. Sch., 1977. Exhibited in some 20 gallery exhbns. in U.S. and Europe. Home: 116 Spring St Newton NJ 07860-2009

DAGLI, CIHAN HAYREDDIN, engineering educator; b. Ankara, Turkey, Oct. 18, 1949; came to U.S., 1985; s. Kenan and Zuhre (Kavlakoglu) D.; m. Refia Oner, Nov. 3, 1975; children: Cagri, Ediz. BS in Indsl. Engring., Middle East Tech. U., Ankara, 1971, MS in Indsl. Engring., 1972; PhD in Engring. Prodn., U. Birmingham, Eng., 1979. Cert. engr., Turkey. From tchg. asst. to instr. Middle East Tech. U., Ankara, 1972-76, from asst. to assoc. prof., 1979-85; Brit. coun. rsch. fellow U. Birmingham, 1976-79; assoc. prof. U. Mo., Rolla, 1988-95, prof., 1995—; vis. assoc. prof. Wichita (Kans.) State U., 1985-88; indsl. and engring. dept. chmn. Middle East Tech. U., Ankara, 1979-82; cons. UN Indsl. Devel., Ankara, 1980, AT&T Bell Labs., N.J., 1989. Editor: Artificial Neural Networks for Intelligent Manufacturing; co-editor: Intelligent Engineering Systems Through Artificial Neural Networks, Vol. 1, 1991, Vol. 2, 1992, Vol. 3, 1993, Vol. 4, 1994, Vol. 5, 1995, Vol. 6, 1996, Vol. 7, 1997, Vol. 8, 1998, Intelligent Systems in Design and Manufacturing, 1994; editor-in-chief Internat. Jour. Smart Engring. System Design; contbr. articles to profl. jours. Aspirant lt. Turkish Army, 1975. Brit. Coun. Rsch. fellow, 1976-79; Ed Smith Rsch. grantee U. Mo., Rolla, 1989, 90. Mem. Internat. Neural Network Soc., Internat. Found. for Prodn. Rsch. (bd. dirs. 1987—), Inst. Indsl. Engring. (chmn. Wichita chpt. 1987-88). Home: 401 Greenbriar Dr Rolla MO 65401-3694 Office: Univ Missouri 229 Engineering Management Rolla MO 65401

D'AGNESE, JOHN JOSEPH, sanitation, public health and pest management consultant; b. N.Y.C., Apr. 2, 1920; s. Michele and Liberata (Cucolo) D'A.; m. Helen DeSantis, Oct. 29, 1942; children: John Jr., Linda, Diane, Michele, Helen, Gina, Paul. BS, CCNY, 1946; student, U. San Francisco, 1953-54. Lic. pest mgmt., Fla., Ga.; lic. chief purser USCG. Chief purser U.S. Merchant Marine, 1942-46; quarantine officer USPHS, Staten Island, N.Y., 1946-53; supervisory quarantine officer USPHS, San Francisco, 1953-62; Mexican border supervisory quarantine officer USPHS, El Paso, Tex., 1962-68; chief program ops. quarantine div. Ctr. Disease Control USPHS, Atlanta, 1968-80, dir. quarantine div., 1980-81; ret. USPHS, 1981; dir. Cruise Ship Consultation Svc., Fernandina Beach, Fla., 1981—. Contbr. sci. and health-related articles to nat. mags. and jours. including Pest Control Tech., Jour. Environ. Health, Jour. Milk Food Tech., Pest Control Jour. Mag. Bd. dirs. Nat. Coun. Aging, 1986-90. Recipient United Fund Leadership award El Paso Tex., 1966-67. Fellow Nat. Sanitation Found.; mem. Am. Pub. Health Assn., Fla. Pest Control Assn., Ga. Pest Control Assn., Nat. Assn. Fed. Ret. Employees. Democrat. Roman Catholic. Avocations: music, tennis, fencing, chess, fishing, cooking. Home: 3240 S Fletcher Ave Fernandina Beach FL 32034-4378

DAGNON, JAMES BERNARD, human resources executive; b. St. Paul, Jan. 31, 1940; s. James Lavern and Margaret Elizabeth (Coughlin) D.; m. Sandra Ann McGinley, June 4, 1960; children: Sheri T. Dagnon Tice, Terry J., Laurie M., Diana L. BS in Bus. with distinction, U. Minn., St. Paul, 1979, cert. in indsl. rels., 1978. Various clerical positions No. Pacific Ry. Co., St. Paul, 1957-70; supr., then mgr. pers. rsch. and stats. Burlington No. R.R. Co., St. Paul, 1970, mgr. manpower planning, 1970-78, dir. compensation and organizational planning, 1978-81; asst. v.p. compensation and benefits Burlington No. Inc., Seattle, 1981-84; from v.p. labor rels. to exec. v.p. employee rels. Burlington No. Inc., Ft. Worth, 1984-95; sr. v.p. employee rels. Burlington No. Santa Fe Ry Co., Ft. Worth, 1995-97; sr. v.p. people The Boeing Co., Seattle, 1997—; bd. dirs. Electro-No. Inc., Ft. Worth, Inroads Inc., Seattle Inroads, Inc. Pres. Cath. Evang. Outreach, Seattle, 1981-84; chmn. Corp. Champions, Ft. Worth, 1994-96; bd. trustees Cook-Ft. Worth Children's Med. Ctr., 1995-97; bd. dirs. United Way Met. Tarrant County, 1995-97, Wash. State Gov.'s Commn. on Higher Edn. in 2020. Capt. USAR, 1957-70. Mem. Beta Gamma Sigma. Republican. Avocations: flying, scuba diving, photography. Home: 1237 Evergreen Point Rd Medina WA 98039-3136 Office: The Boeing Co 7755 E Marginal Way S Seattle WA 98108-4000

DAGOGO-JACK, SAMUEL E., medical educator, physician scientist, endocrinologist; b. Abonnema, Rivers, Nigeria, Mar. 17, 1954; came to U.S., 1990; s. Karibi Jim and Titty (Biribota) D.-J.; m. Agbani Ibinabo Iyalla, May 28, 1983; children: Karibi, Ibi, Alali, Tari. MBBS, U. Ibadan (Nigeria), 1978, MD, 1994; MSc, U. Newcastle Upon Tyne (U.K.), 1988. Diplomate Am. Bd. Internal Medicine, Am. Bd. Endocrinology, Am. Bd. Diabetes and Metabolism. Rsch. assoc. U. Newcastle Upon Tyne (U.K.), 1983-85; cons. physician U. Port Harcourt (Nigeria), 1985-89; chief resident endocrinologist King Faisal Specialist Hosp., Riyadh, Saudi Arabia, 1989-90; rsch. fellow Washington U. Sch. Medicine, St. Louis, 1990-92, instr. medicine, 1992-93, asst. prof. medicine, 1993-97, assoc. prof. medicine, 1998—; assoc. chief internal medicine svc. Barnes-Jewish Hosp., St. Louis, 1996—; lectr. St. Louis Acad. Scis., 1995, The Ethical Soc., 1996; lectr. Nat. Diabetes Edn. Initiative, 1997—; reviewer for numerous scientific jours.; extra-mural rschr. diabetes drugs devel. programs for Amgen, Hoechst-Marion-Roussel, Bristol-Myers Squibb Pharms., others; chair Excellence Diabetes Mgmt. Symposium, 1998-99. Author: The Diabetes Guide, 1992, (with others) The Washington Manual, 1995, The Uncomplicated Guide to Diabetes Complications, 1999; internat. editl. adv. bd. Kuwait Med. Jour., 1995-98; contbr. over 100 articles to profl. jours. Diabetes Prevention grantee NIH, 1994—, Diabetes Rsch. & Tng. Ctr. grantee, 1999—; recipient Young Investigator Travel award Internat. Soc. Endocrinology, 1987; grantee Diabetes Rsch. Tng. Ctr., 1999-2000. Fellow ACP (co-dir. workshop urban health 1998), Royal Coll. Physicians (London), Am. Fedn. Clin. Rsch.; mem. AAAS, Am. Diabetes Assn. (sec. St. Louis chpt. 1997-98, pres. St. Louis chpt. 1998-99, Rsch. fellow 1990-91, Clin. Rsch. award 1997—), Endocrine Soc., Am. Fedn. for Med. Rsch. Achievements include extra-mural research, diabetes drugs development programs for AMGEN, Hoechst-Marion-Roussel, Bristol-Myers Squibb Pharms., others. Avocations: squash racquets, world travel, poetry. Office: Washington U Sch Medicine PO Box 8127 Saint Louis MO 63156-8127

D'AGOSTINO, JAMES SAMUEL, JR., financial executive; b. Balt., July 4, 1946; s. James Samuel and Betty Ann (List) D'A.; m. Diane Martin Greener, Sept. 25, 1971; children: James Martin, Ann Diestel. BS in Econs., Villanova U., 1968; JD, Seton Hall Sch. Law, Newark, 1974; postgrad., Harvard U., 1993. Bar: N.J. 1974, Tex. 1979. Trust officer Fidelity Union Trust Co., Newark, 1968-73; asst. treas. The Chase Manhattan Bank, N.A., N.Y.C., 1973-76; v.p. Citibank/Citicorp, Houston, 1976-86; v.p., treas. Am. Gen. Corp., Houston, 1986-90, sr. v.p. investor rels., 1990-91, sr. v.p. adminstrn., 1991-93, exec. v.p. adminstrn., 1993; pres., CEO Am. Gen. Life and Accident Ins. Co., Nashville, 1993-95, chmn., CEO, 1995-97; pres. Am. Gen. Corp., Houston, 1997—. Republican. Presbyterian. Office: Am Gen Corp 3435 Piping Rock Houston TX 77027-2197*

D'AGOSTINO, MATTHEW PAUL, bakery executive; b. Yonkers, N.Y., Apr. 15, 1948; s. Paul Francis and Mary Cristina D'A.; m. Kathleen Marie Karpinski, July 18, 1951; children: Carolyn, Paul. BA in English, Polit. Sci., Nathaniel Hawthorne Coll., Antrim, N.H., 1970. Bakery mgr. Pathmark Supermarkets, Woodbridge, N.J., 1971; gen. mgr. La Bonbonniere Bake Shoppes, Edison, N.J., 1972-83, CEO, 1983—. Mem. Am. Soc. Bakery Engrs., Tri-County Bakers Assn. (pres. 1986-88), N.J. Bakers Bd. Trade (pres. 1988-90), Retail Bakers Am. (dir.-at-large 1988, mem. exec. com. 1990-97, v.p. 1992-95, N.J. dir. 1990-94, pres. 1995-96). Roman Catholic. Avocations: golf, photography, computer programming. Home: 16 Huntington

Rd Edison NJ 08820-3109 Office: La Bonbonniere Bake Shoppes PO Box 981 Edison NJ 08818-0981

D'AGOSTINO, RAYMOND, city manager; b. Phila., Sept. 3, 1966; s. Raymond and Susan (Scibilia) D'A.; m. Memory Lynne Smith, July 7, 1990; children: Anthony John, Janae Rayelle. BS in Edn., Shippensburg U., 1988, MPA, 1991. Codes compliance officer Twp. of Hampden, Mechanicsburg, Pa., 1990-91; asst. borough mgr. Borough of Palmyra, Pa., 1991-94; borough mgr. Borough of Mt. Joy, Pa., 1994—; authority adminstr. Mt. Joy Borough Authority, 1994—; mem. governing bd. Lancaster (Pa.) County Sys. Reform, 1996-98. Mem. exec. bd. PSAB, 1998; mem. adv. bd. LTAP, 1999—. With USNR, 1986-94; sgt. Pa. Army N.G., 1994—. Recipient Emma Guffey Miller award James A. Finnegan Found., Harrisburg, Pa., 1987. Mem. Assn. for Pa. Mcpl. Mgmt., Govt. Fin. Officers Assn., Pa. Local Govt. Secs. Assn., Mt. Joy Area C. of C. (bd. dirs. 1995—). Lutheran. Avocations: cooking, traveling, family activities. Office: Borough of Mount Joy 21 E Main St Mount Joy PA 17552-1415

D'AGOSTINO, STEPHEN IGNATIUS, bottling company executive; b. N.Y.C., Oct. 23, 1933; s. Nicholas J. and Josephine D'Agostino; m. Mary Egan, July 2, 1955; children: Mary Jo D'Agostino Razook, Joseph, Christopher, Gregory, Elizabeth Anne Ross, Sarah D'Agostino Christensen, Constance. BA, Holy Cross Coll., 1955. With D'Agostino Supermarkets, New Rochelle, N.Y., 1955-82; controller D'Agostino Supermarkets, 1960-78, chmn., CEO, 1978-82; pres., COO, JTL Corp., Chattanooga, 1982—; pres., chief operating officer Gt. Western Coca-Cola Bottling Co., Chattanooga, 1982-87; mng. ptnr. CSD Investments, 1987-88; chmn. Lord Capital Corp., N.Y.C., 1988-92; pres., CEO D'Agostino Enterprises Inc., Hobe Sound, 1992—; bd. dirs. Catalina Mktg., St. Petersburg, Fla., Supervalu Stores, Mpls. Mem. Food Mktg. Inst. (past chmn., hon. bd. mem.), N.Y. State Food Mchts. (past chmn.).

D'AGUSTO, KAREN ROSE, lawyer; b. Phila., Jan. 4, 1952; d. Les and Anne Heilenman; m. Stephen Joseph Bernasconi, Aug. 21, 1976; children: Lesley Anne D. Bernasconi, Stephanie Kalena D. Bernasconi. BA in History cum laude, Immaculata Coll., 1974; JD, U. San Diego, 1977; postgrad., U. So. Calif., 1983—. Bar: Conn. 1977, Hawaii 1978, S.C. 1986. Tng. coord. Protection and Advocacy, Honolulu, 1978, adv. coord., 1979, staff atty., 1980-81, assoc dir., 1982, project dir., 1983—; regional coord. S.C. Protection and Adv. System, 1986-88; dep. dir. Hawaii Protection and Advocacy, 1989-91; pvt. practice law Mililani, Hawaii, 1980—; instr. Hawaii Pacific Coll., Honolulu, 1982-84; dir. Harmon-Johnson Inst., Honolulu, 1983—; adj. prof. Immaculata Coll., 1998-99. Author: Legal Rights of Handicapped, 1980; author, editor curriculum Vol. I Guardians Ad. Litem, 1983; editor Jour. Comparative Legis. Analysis of Protection and Advocacy System, 1991. Pres. Cen. Oahu Mental Health Ctr., Pearl City, Hawaii, 1981-82; officer Kings Grant Assn., Summerville, S.C., 1988; rep. St. Andrews Priory Parent-Tchr. Fellowship Bd., 1990-91; mem. John B. Dey PTA, mem. bd. dirs., chair legis. com.; leader Girl Scouts Am., svc. unit mgr., trainer, cons. Cape Henry Svc. unit, Colonial Coast coun.; mem. PTA legis. com.; vol. Great Neck Mid. Sch.; co-chair Tower Hill Camp Fair, 1998-99; chair family appeal Brandywine Valley Girl Scout Svc. Unit, 1996-99. Recipient Exceptional Achievement award, 1989-90, Disting. Contbn. to Civil Rights of Persons with Disabilities award, 1991, Outstanding Svc. to Hawaiis Disabled Citizens award, 1982, Outstanding Vol. of Yr. award Colonial Coast coun. Girl Scouts U.S., 1995, Vol. of Yr. award Great Neck Middle Sch., 1996; named Outstanding Adv., 1985. Mem. ABA, Hawaii State Bar Assn., S.C. Bar Assn., Hawaii Lawyers Care, Am. Assn. Counsel for Children Counsel, Wimbledon on the Bay Homeowners Assn. (v.p. 1992-93, chair by-laws com. 1993-94).

DAHIYA, JAI BHAGWAN, chemist; b. Badhkhalsa, Haryana, India, June 1, 1956; came to U.S., 1978; s. Vijai Singh Dahiya and Lachhmi (Antil) Devi; m. Sharda Grewal Dahiya, June 30, 1982; children: Anita, Vicki, Neil. BS, Kurukshetra U., India, 1977, East Tex. State U., 1982; MS, East Tex. State U., 1985. Rsch. asst. East Tex. State U., Commerce, 1979-80, rsch. scholar, 1980-81; lab. asst. Wesleyan Coll., Buckhannon, W.Va., 1983; mgr. Texmart Inc., Commerce, 1984-86; chemical analyst E-Systems Inc., Greenville, Tex., 1987-89; technologist in Chemistry Barnes Hosp. Washington U. Med. Ctr., St. Louis, 1990-91; chemist Internat. Tech. Corp., St. Louis, 1991-94; technologist SmithKline Beecham, Dallas, 1994-96; quality engr. Raytheon Systems Co., Greenville, Tex., 1996—. Robert A. Welch Rsch. Scholar East Tex. State U., 1980-81. Mem. Am. Chem. Soc. Avocations: tennis, jogging, swimming, reading, photography. Home: 1608 Fannin Cir Plano TX 75025-2800

DAHIYA, RAJBIR SINGH, mathematics educator, researcher; b. Rattangarh, Haryana, India, Dec. 3, 1940; came to U.S., 1968; s. Ram S. and Kesar (Devi) D.; m. Krishna Tavathia, Dec. 11, 1966; children: Madhu, Ranjan. PhD, Birla Inst. Sci. and Tech., Pilani, India, 1967. Lectr. Birla Inst. Sci. and Tech., 1967-68; asst. prof. math. Iowa State U., Ames, 1968-72, assoc. prof., 1972-78, prof., 1978—; reviewer math. revs. Zentrallblat; referee applied math. jours. Contbr. over 140 rsch. papers on delay and advanced differential equations, transform theory and spl. functions to U.S., European and Australian profl. jours. Mem. Am. Math. Soc. Democrat. Hindu. Home: 3144 Sycamore Rd Ames IA 50014-4510 Office: Iowa State U Dept Math Ames IA 50011

DAHL, ANDREW WILBUR, health services executive; b. N.Y.C., Feb. 19, 1943; s. Wilbur A. and Margret L. Dahl; BS, Clark U., 1968; MPA, Cornell U., 1970; ScD, Johns Hopkins U., 1974; m. Janice White, Sept. 4, 1965; children: Kristina, Jennifer, Meredith. Staff asst. Md. Comprehensive Health Planning Agy., Balt., 1970-72; dir. planning St. John Hosp., Detroit, 1972-79; exec. v.p., COO St. John Health Corp., Detroit, 1979-85; pres., CEO United Health System, Detroit, 1983-88; v.p. devel. Hosp. Corp. Am. Mgmt. Co., 1988-90; pres., CEO IVF America Inc., Greenwich, Conn., 1990-94; pres., CEO HealthNet, Kansas City, 1994—; instr. U. Mich. Bur. Hosp. Adminstrn., 1981-88. Bd. dirs. Detroit Sci. Ctr., 1984-91; mem. Nat. Com. for Quality Health Care, Washington, 1984-89; bd. dirs. Forum Health Care Planning Kansas City (Mo.) Mus., 1995—. Served with USN, 1965-67. Recipient Disting. Service award Mich. Jaycees, 1977, Outstanding Contbns. to Profl. Mgmt. award, Cornell U., 1980. Fellow Am. Coll. Healthcare Execs.; mem. AAAS, APHA, Am. Hosp. Assn. (rehab. sect. bd.), Am. Assn. Health Plans, Internat. Health Econs. and Mgmt. Inst., Hallbrook Country Club, Cornell Club N.Y. Methodist. Office: 2300 Main St Ste 700 Kansas City MO 64108-2417

DAHL, ARLENE, actress, author, designer, cosmetic executive; b. Mpls., Aug. 11, 1928; d. Rudolph and Idelle (Swan) D.; m. Marc A. Rosen; children: Lorenzo Lamas, Carole Christine Holmes, Stephen Andreas Schaum. Student, U. Minn., 1943-44, Mpls. Inst. Art, 1945, Minn. Coll. Music, 1944, Minn. Bus. Coll., 1944. Pres. Arlene Dahl Enterprises, 1952-67; v.p. Kenyon & Eckhart, 1967-72; pres. Woman's World divsn. Kenyon & Eckhart Advt. Agy., 1967-72; nat. beauty and health advisor Sears Roebuck Co., 1970-75; internat. dir. Sales and Mktg. Execs. Internat., 1972-75; fashion dir. O.M.A., 1975-78; pres. Dahlia Parfums, Inc., 1975-80, Dahlia Prodns., Inc., 1978-81, Dahlmark Prodns., 1981—, Scandia Cosmetics, Ltd., 1978-80; pres., chmn. Lasting Beauty Ltd., 1986—. Author: Always Ask a Man, 1965, 12 Beautyscope books, 1968, rev. edit., 1978, Arlene Dahl's Secrets of Hair Care, 1969, Arlene Dahl's Secrets of Skin Care, 1972, Beyond Beauty, 1980, Arlene Dahl's Lovescopes, 1983, Arlene Dahl's Astro Forecast, 1991, 92, 93, 94, 95, 96, 97, Arlene Dahl's Hollywood Horoscope internat. syndicated weekly column, 1994—; actress: (Broadway plays) including Mr. Strauss Goes to Boston, Questionable Ladies, Cyrano de Bergerac, Applause (Tony award musical), (films) including (debut) My Wild Irish Rose, The Bride Goes Wild, Reign of Terror, A Southern Yankee, Ambush, The Outriders, Three Little Words, Watch the Birdie, Scene of the Crime, Inside Straight, No Questions Asked, Desert Legion, Slightly Scarlet, Sangaree, Caribbean Gold, Jamaica Run, Diamond Queen, Here Come the Girls, Bengal Brigade, Kisses for My President, Woman's World, Journey to the Center of the Earth, Wicked as They Come, She Played with Fire, Les Poneyettes, Du Blé Enliases, The Land Raiders, The Way to Kathmandu, Fortune Is a Woman, The Big Bank Roll, Who Killed Maxwell Thorn?, Midnight Warrior, 1991, (TV shows) Lux Video Theatre, 1952-53, guest starring appearances on The Love Boat, Fantasy Island, Love American Style, One Life to Live, 1981-84, Night of 100 Stars, 1983, Happy Birthday Hollywood, 1987, All My Children, 1995, Renegade, 1995, 96, 97, Air America, 1999; hostess (TV series): Pepsi-Cola Theatre, 1954, Opening Night, 1958, Arlene Dahl's Beauty Spot, 1966, Arlene Dahl's Starscope, 1979-80, Arlene Dahl's Lovescope, 1980-82; played throughout U.S. in One Touch of Venus, The Camel Bell, Blithe Spirit, Liliom, The King and I, Roman Candle, I Married an Angel, Bell, Book and Candle, Applause, Marriage Go Round, Pal Joey, A Little Night Music, Forty Carats, Life with Father, Murder Among Friends, Dear Liar; nightclub acts Flamingo Hotel, Las Vegas, Latin Quarter, N.Y.C., musical stage appearances: Carnegie Hall, 1997, London Paladium, 1992, 1998, Salute to MGM Musicals; internat. syndicated beauty columnist Chgo. Tribune/ N.Y. News Syndicate, 1950-70, Arlene Dahl's Lucky Stars Column, Globe Communications, 1988-90, Arlene Dahl's Starscope Mag., 1991, 92, 93, 94, 95, 96, 97; designer sleepwear for A.N. Saab & Co., 1952-57, In Vogue with Arlene Dahl (Vogue Patterns), 1980-85, Arlene Dahl Pvt. Collection Jewelry, 1989-94, Arlene Dahl's Jewels of Fortune Home Shopping Network, 1996. Hon. life mem. Father Flannagan's Boys Town; internat. chair Pearl Buck Found.; bd. dirs. Hollywood Mus. Recipient 10 Laurel awards Box Office mag., Hollywood Walk of Fame Star, 1952, Coup de Chapeau Deaville Film Festival award, 1982, 92; named Best Coiffed, Heads of Fame awards, 1967-72, 80, award Scandinavian Hall of Fame, 1997; named Woman of the Yr., Advt. Club of N.Y.C., 1969, Mother of the Yr., 1982, Lifetime Achievement award WorldFest, 1994, Leadership in the Arts, 1997. Mem. NATAS (trustee), Acad. TV Arts and Scis. (bd. govs., v.p.), Acad. Motion Picture Arts and Scis. (vice chair N.Y. spl. events), Author's Guild, Commanderie de Bontemps du Medoc et Graves, Commanderie de Bordeaux, Internat. Platform Assn., Nat. Trust for Hist. Preservation, Sierra Club, Vesterheim Norwegian/Am. Found., Film Soc., Smithsonian Assocs., UNIFEM. Office: Dahlmark Prodns PO Box 116 Sparkill NY 10976-0116

DAHL, ARTHUR ERNEST, former manufacturing executive, consultant; b. Alexis, Ill., Sept. 16, 1916; s. Ernest Victor and Emma P. (Olson) D.; m. Dorothy Evelyn Peterson, Sept. 10, 1944 (dec. Jan. 1994); children: John Arthur, Robert Alan. Student, Augustana Coll., Rock Island, Ill., 1935-39. Head planning div. Home-O-Nize Co., Muscatine, Iowa, 1947-50; v.p., gen. mgr. The Prime Mover Co., Muscatine, 1950-70; chmn. bd. The Prime Mover Co., 1982, 83; sr. v.p. HON Industries Inc., Muscatine, 1970-81; dir. Bank of Alexis, 1979-83, pres., 1983; cons., 1981—. Bd. dirs. Augustana Coll., 1976-82, mem. exec. com., 1979-82; mem. Iowa State Investment Adv. Bd., 1975-81; mem. council Grace Lutheran Ch., Muscatine. Served with U.S. Army, 1942-43. Republican. Home: 421 Parkington Dr Muscatine IA 52761-5533

DAHL, CURTIS, English literature educator; b. New Haven, July 6, 1920; s. George and Elizabeth Eudora (Curtis) D.; m. Mary Huntington Kellogg, Nov. 15, 1952; children: Julia Curtis (dec.), Winthrop Huntington Kellogg. B.A., Yale U., 1941, M.A., 1942, Ph.D., 1945. Dir. fellowships, asst. to editor Dodd, Mead & Co., 1944-46; instr. English, U. Tenn., 1946-48; mem. faculty Wheaton Coll., Norton, Mass., 1948—; prof. Wheaton Coll., 1958-91, Samuel Valentine Cole prof. English lit., 1966-91, Samuel Valentine Cole prof. emeritus, 1991—; vis. prof. So. Ill. U., 1964, 66, 70, U. Wash., 1967, Brown U., 1970; vis. lectr. in English Bridgewater State Coll., 1992-98. Author: Robert Montgomery Bird, 1963; editor: There She Blows: A Narrative of a Whaling Voyage, 1971; contbr. articles to profl. jours. Fenceviewer Town of Norton, 1964-77, 1989—, selectman, 1970-73; chmn. Norton Historic Dist. Commn., 1975-87, 1990—, Norton Hist. Commn., 1976-80. Carnegie fellow Harvard U., 1954-55; Guggenheim fellow, 1957-58; Fulbright prof. U. Oslo, 1965-66. Mem. MLA, Nat. Assn. of Scholars, Melville Soc., Boston Browning Soc., Presbyn. Hist. Soc. Republican. Home: 189 N Washington St Norton MA 02766-1801 *Too few people today know the difference between "uninterested" and "disinterested."*

DAHL, GARDAR GODFREY, JR., geologist, consultant; b. Hood River, Oreg., May 27, 1946; s. Gardar Godfrey Sr. and Margaret Jean (North) D.; m. Margarette Yvonne Berryman Goodwin. BS in Geol. Engring., Mont. Coll. Mineral Sci. and Tech., 1969, MS in Geol. Engring., 1971. Registered profl. geologist. Asst. geologist Burlington No., St. Paul, 1971-72; mining geologist Burlington No., Seattle, Wash. and Billings, Mont., 1972-75; mgr. coal exploration and devel. Burlington No., Billings, 1975-79; dir. resource devel. Peabody Coal Co., Flagstaff, Ariz., 1979-81; chief geologist Cyprus Coal Co., Englewood, Colo., 1981-85, mgr. geology, 1985-88; mgr. tech. services Cyprus Shoshone Coal Co., Hanna, Wyo., 1988-90; sr. cons. geologist Cyprus Coal Co., Englewood, Colo., 1990-92; contract geologist Dahl & Assocs., 1992—; mng. dir. MEC Resources, Ltd., 1993—; sec. KF7 Explorations Ltd., 1994-98; exec. v.p. Ky. Favorite Ventures, Inc., 1994-98; dir. mining ventures Chartwell Internat., Inc., 1995-97. Mem. AIME, AAAS, Rocky Mountain Coal and Mining Inst., Am. Assn. Profl. Geologists, Mont. Mining Assn., Colo. Mining Assn., Denver Coal Club. Lutheran. E-mail: gardahl@aol.com. Home: 8008 S Newport Ct Englewood CO 80112-3121 Office: 8008 S Newport Ct Ste 100A Englewood CO 80112-3121

DAHL, GERALD LUVERN, psychotherapist, educator, consultant, writer; b. Osage, Iowa, Nov. 10, 1938; s. Lloyd F. and Leola J. (Painter) D.; m. Judith Lee Brown, June 24, 1960; children: Peter, Stephen, Leah. BA, Wheaton Coll., 1960; MSW, U. Nebr., 1962; PhD in psychotherapy (Hon.), Internat. U. Found., 1987; cert. diplomate Am. Psychotherapy Assn., 1998. Juvenile probation officer Hennepin County Ct. Svcs., 1962-65; cons. Citizens Coun. on Delinquency and Crime, Mpls., 1965-67; dir. patient svcs. Mt. Sinai Hosp., Mpls., 1967-69; clin. social worker Mpls. Clinic of Psychiatry, 1969-82, G.L. Dahl & Assocs., Inc., Mpls., 1983—; assoc. prof. social work Bethel Coll., St. Paul, 1964-83; spl. instr. sociology Golden Valley Luth. Coll., 1974-83; pres. Strategic Team-Makers, Inc., 1985—; adj. prof. U. Wis., River Falls, 1988-90. Founder Family Counseling Svc., Minn. Baptist Conf., bd. stewards, 1994—; bd. dirs. Edgewater Baptist Ch., 1972-75, chmn., 1974-75; vice-chmn. bd. stewards Minnetonka Bapt. Ch., 1995. Mem. AAUP, Am. Assn. Behavioral Therapists, Pi Gamma Mu. Author: Why Christian Marriages Are Breaking Up, 1979; Everybody Needs Somebody Sometime, 1980, How Can We Keep Christian Marriages from Falling Apart, 1988, The Sandwich Family, 1995; contbr. articles to profl. jours. Office: 4825 Highway 55 Ste 140 Minneapolis MN 55422-5155

DAHL, JOHN, film director; b. Billings, Mont., 1956. Dir., writer: Kill Me Again, 1989, Red Rock West, 1992 (nominated Ind. Spirit awards for best dir., best screenplay, 1995); dir.: (TV movie) The Last Seduction, 1994, Unforgettable, 1996, Rounders, 1998 (nominated Golden Lion award Venice Film Festival, 198); dir., prodr.: Striking Back: A Jewish Commando's War Against the Nazis, 1998; writer: Meltdown, 1999. Recipient New Generation award L.A. Film Critics Assn., 1994. Office: c/o DGA 7920 Sunset Blvd Los Angeles CA 90046*

DAHL, JOYLE COCHRAN, lawyer; b. Oakland, Calif., Oct. 5, 1935; s. Carl Arthur and Jane Virginia (Cochran) D.; m. Dawn Adele Wood, Aug. 16, 1959; children: Brenda Loreen, Peter Carl. BS, U. Oreg., 1957, LLB, 1959; LLM, NYU, 1964. Bar: Oreg. 1959, U.S. Supreme Ct. 1963. Trial atty. tax div. Dept. Justice, Washington, 1960-63; ptnr. Duffy, Georgeson, Dahl et al, Portland, Oreg., 1964-76, Dahl, Zalutsky, Nichols et al, Portland, 1976-79, Tonkon, Torp, Galen et al, Portland, 1979-85; sr. ptnr. Schwabe Williamson & Wyatt, Portland, 1985—; bd. dirs. Portland Fixture Ltd. Partnership, Peter Jacobsen Prodns., Portland. Contbr. numerous articles on taxation to profl. jours. Bd. dirs. Portland Youth Philharmonic, 1989-90, Oreg. Sports Hall of Fame, Delauney Mental Health Ctr., Portland, 1974-80; adv. bd. Salvation Army. Fellow Am. Coll. Trust and Estate Counsel; mem. Oreg. Bar Assn. (chmn. tax sect. 1972), Estate Planning Coun. Oreg., Waverley Country Club (Portland, v.p. 1984), Thunderbird Country Club (Rancho Mirage, Calif.), Oreg. Golf Club (West Linn, pres. 1994-95), Multnomah Athletic Club (Portland, v.p. 1979), Arlington Club (Portland). Republican. Presbyterian. Avocation: golf. Home: 1111 SW Myrtle Dr Portland OR 97201-2270 Office: Schwabe Williamson & Wyatt 1211 SW 5th Ave Ste 1800 Portland OR 97204-3718

DAHL, LAUREL JEAN, human services administrator; b. Chgo.; d. James Edward and Gladys Uarda (Boquist) Findlay; m. Philip Nels Dahl, Aug. 29, 1970; children: Eric Nels, John Philip. BA, Trinity Coll., 1970; MS in Human Svcs., Nat. Louis U., 1992. Cert. sr. alcohol and other drug preventionist. Tchr. Grove Sch., Lake Forest, Ill., 1971, Little Bear Child Care Ctr., Waukegan, Ill., 1975-77; sec. to dir. Strang Funeral Home, Antioch, Ill., 1981-87; comptroller, office mgr. Village of Antioch, 1987-92; prevention specialist Lake County Dept. of Health: Mental Health Div., 1992; community coord. Fighting Back Project of Lake County, Round Lake, Ill., 1992-94; prevention adminstr. No. Ill.Coun. on Alcoholism and Substance Abuse, Lake, 1994—; adj. faculty Nat. Louis U., 1996. Mem. Antioch Comty. H.S. Bd. Edn., 1987-95, pres., 1991-95, sec., 1989-91; mem. Antioch Comty. H.S. Drug Task Force, MADD; past pres. PTO; mem. adv. bd. WAY; bd. dirs. COURAGE; vice chair Human Svc. Coun., 1994-96, chmn., 1996-98; mem. peer rev. com. Ill. Alcohol and Other Drug Abuse Profl. Cert. Assn., 1996—; mem. women's bd. No. Ill. Coun. on Alcoholism and Substance Abuse, 1996—, v.p. for programs, 1997—; bd. govs. Timber Lee Christian Ctr., 1998. Recipient commendation for Gt. Lakes Naval Tng. Ctr. for Drug Edn. for Youth, 1994-95, Disting. Svc. award Ill. chpt. Nat. Sch. Pub. Rels. Assn., Enrique Camarena "One Person Can" award, 1995, State Prevention Leadership award Ill. Alcoholism and Drug Dependence Assn., 1996, Individuals in the Forefront for Lake County award, 1998. Mem. Alliance Against Intoxicated Motorists, Ill. Student Assistance Profls., Ill. Assn. for Prevention. Home: PO Box 613 Antioch IL 60002-0613

DAHL, LAWRENCE FREDERICK, chemistry educator; b. Evanston, Ill., June 2, 1929; s. Lawrence Gustave and Anne (Stuessy) D.; m. June Lomnes, Sept. 1, 1956; children: Larry, Eric, Christopher. BS in Chemistry, U. Louisville, 1951; PhD, Iowa State U., 1956; DSc (hon.), U. Louisville, 1991. Postdoctoral fellow Ames (Iowa) Lab. AEC, 1957; from instr. to assoc. prof. chemistry U. Wis., Madison, 1957-64, prof., 1964—, R. E. Rundle chair, 1978—, Hilldale chair and prof., 1991—; Brotherton rsch. prof. U. Leeds, 1983. Recipient Inorganic Chemistry award Am. Chem. Soc., 1974, Disting. Alumnus award U. Louisville Coll. Letters and Sci., 1983, Sr. U.S. Scientist Humboldt award Alexander von Humboldt Stiftung, 1985, R.S. Nyholm medal Royal Soc. Chemistry, 1985, P. Chini medal Italian Soc. Chemistry, 1989, J.C. Bailar Jr. medal U. Ill., 1990, F. Basolo medal Northwestern U., 1995, Hilldale award in phys. scis. U. Wis., 1994; named to Hon. Order Ky. Cols., 1982; Alfred P. Sloan fellow, 1963-65, U. Louisville Coll. Letters and Sci. fellow, 1990. Fellow AAAS, N.Y. Acad. Sci., Am. Acad. Arts and Scis.; mem. NAS. Home: 4817 Woodburn Dr Madison WI 53711-1345 Office: Univ of Wis Dept of Chemistry 1101 University Ave Madison WI 53706-1322

DAHL, LOREN SILVESTER, retired federal judge; b. East Fairview, N.D., Mar. 1, 1921; s. William T. and Maude (Silvester) D.; m. Pamela B. Miller, Mar. 16, 1995; children by previous marriage: Candy, Walter Ray. AA, Coll. of Pacific, 1940; LLB, JD, U. Calif., San Francisco, 1949. Bar: Calif., 1950, U.S. Supreme Ct., 1957. Pvt. practice law Sacramento, 1950; sr. ptnr. Dahl, Hefner, Stark & Marois, Sacramento, 1950-80; chief judge U.S. Bankruptcy Ct. (ea. dist.) Calif., Sacramento, 1980, 86-94; chief judge emeritus, 1994—; Chmn. Conf. Chief Judges, 9th Cir., 1992. Pres. Golden Empire Coun. Boy Scouts Am., Sacramento, 1955-56, chmn. bd. trustees, 1956, exec. com. region 12, 1958, regional chmn. 1968-70, nat. exec. bd. 1968-70; Sacramento County Juvenile Justice Comm.; mem. bd. visitors McGeorge sch. law U. Pacific, 1987—; bd. dirs. Salvation Army, Sacramento, 1954-57; Sacramento Symphony Assn., 1958-59, Sacramento Safety Coun. With USAAF, 1942-46. Recipient Disting. Svc. award Jaycees, 1957, Silver Beaver award, Boy Scouts Am., 1957, Silver Antelope award, Boy Scouts Am., 1963, Disting. Eagle Scout award, Boy Scouts Am., Judge of Yr. award Sacramento County Bar Assn., 1993. Mem. U. of Pacific Alumni Assn. (pres. 1974-78, bd. regents 1980—, Disting. Alumnus award 1979), ABA, Calif. Bar Assn. (lectr. bankruptcy, continuing edn.), Am. Judicature Soc., Phi Delta Phi. Club: Del Paso Country. Lodge: Masons, Shriners, Lions (dir. Sacramento club 1952-53). Home: 842 Lake Oak Ct Sacramento CA 95864-6154

DAHL, REYNOLD PAUL, applied economics educator; b. Willmar, Minn., Feb. 19, 1924; s. Paul Efrain and Margaret Elizabeth (Peterson) D.; m. Alyce Rosalind Druskis, Sept. 11, 1948; children—John, Ann. Student, North Park Coll., Chgo., 1942-43; B.S., U. Minn., 1949, M.S., 1950, Ph.D., 1954. Instr. agrl. econs. U. Minn., St. Paul, 1950-54, asst. prof., 1954-58, assoc. prof., 1958-63, prof., 1963-94; prof. emeritus U. Minn., St. Paul, Tunisia, 1994—; chief of party, economist U. Minn., Tunis, Tunisia, 1967-70; agrl. economist Soybean Council of Am., Brussels, 1962-63; dir. Mpls. Grain Exchange, 1972-80; agrl. economist U.S. AID, Port-au-Prince, Haiti, 1972, 74. Contbr. articles to profl. jours., chpt. to book. Served with USAAF, 1943-46; PTO. Mem. Am. Agrl. Econs. Assn., Am. Inst. Coop. (trustee 1981-84), Xi Sigma Pi, Alpha Zeta. Roman Catholic. Avocations: gardening; fishing; outdoor activities. Home: 1666 Coffman St Apt 326 Saint Paul MN 55108-1344 Office: U Minn Dept Applied Econs 1994 Buford Ave Saint Paul MN 55108-6038

DAHL, ROBERT ALAN, political science educator; b. Inwood, Iowa, Dec. 17, 1915; s. Peter Ivor and Vera (Lewis) D.; m. Mary Louise Bartlett, 1940 (dec. 1970); children: Ellen Kirsten, Peter Bartlett (dec.), Eric Lewis, Christopher Robert; m. Ann Goodrich Sale, 1973. AB, U. Wash., 1936; PhD, Yale U., 1940; LLD (hon.), U. Mich., 1985, U. Alaska, 1987; D of Philosophy (hon.), U. Oslo, 1994; LLD (hon.), Law Sch. for Social Rsch., 1996, Harvard U., 1998. Mgmt. analyst USDA, 1940; economist Office Prodn. Mgmt., Office Price Adminstrn. and Civilian Supply, War Prodn. Bd., 1940-42; faculty Yale U., 1946—, Eugene M3yer prof. polit. sci., 1955-64, Sterling prof. polit sci., from 1964, Ford Rsch. prof., 1957-58, chmn. dept. polit. sci., 1957-62; lectr. polit. sci., Flacso, Santiago, Chile, 1967; pres. Am. Polit. Sci. Assn., 1967. Author: Congress and Foreign Policy, 1950, (with E. Browne) Domestic Control of Atomic Energy, 1951, (with C.E. Lindblom) Politics, Economics and Welfare, 1952, A Preface to Democratic Theory, 1956, (with Haire and Lazarsfeld) Social Science Research on Business, 1959, Who Governs?, 1961, Modern Political Analysis, 1963, Political Oppositions in Western Democracies, 1966, After the Revolution?, 1970, Polyarchy: Participation and Opposition, 1971, Regimes and Oppositions, 1972, Democracy in the United States, 1972, (with E.R. Tufte) Size and Democracy, 1973, Dilemmas of Pluralist Democracy, 1982, A Preface to Economic Democracy, 1985, Controlling Nuclear Weapons, 1985, Democracy, Liberty and Equality, 1986, Democracy and the Critics, 1989, The New American Political (Dis) Order, 1994, Toward Democracy: A Journey Reflections: 1940-1997, 1997, On Democracy, 1999. With U.S. Army, 1943-45. Decorated Bronze Star with cluster; Cavaliere of Republic of Italy, 1988; recipient Woodrow Wilson prize, 1963, 90, Talcott Parsons prize, 1977, Wilbur Lucius Cross medal, 1986, Elaine and David Spitz award, 1991; Guggenheim fellow, 1950, 78, fellow Ctr. for Advanced Study in Behavioral Scis., 1955-56, 67. Fellow Am. Acad. Arts and Scis. (Talcott Parsons prize 1977); mem. NAS, Am. Philos. Soc., Am. Polit. Sci. Assn. (pres. 1966-67, Woodrow Wilson prize 1963, James Madison prize 1978, Gladys Kammerer award 1983, Benjamin Lippincott award 1989, Johan Skytte prize 1995), New Eng. Polit. Assn. (pres. 1951), ACLU, Brit. Acad., Phi Beta Kappa. Home: 17 Cooper Rd North Haven CT 06473-3001

DAHLBERG, ALBERT EDWARD, biochemistry educator; b. Chgo., Sept. 19, 1938; s. Albert Archer and Thelma Elizabeth (Ham) D.; m. Pamela Kathy Voth, June 29, 1963; children—Albert Andrew, Krista Katherine. Paul Eric. B.S., Haverford Coll., 1960; M.D., U. Chgo., 1965, Ph.D. in Biochemistry, 1968. Rsch. assoc. Nat. Cancer Inst.-NIH, Bethesda, Md., 1967-70; European Molecular Biology Orgn. fellow Molecular Biol. Inst., U. Aarhus, Denmark, 1970-72; prof. biochemistry Brown U., Providence, 1972—, chmn. dept. biochemistry, 1985, 87; vis. prof. U. Wis., Madison, 1978-79; v.p. rsch. Mora Pharms., Inc., Miami, Fla., 1983—; bd. dirs. Milkhaus Lab. Inc., Delanson, N.Y., 1993—; mem. bd. sci. counselors divsn. cancer biology diagnosis and ctrs. Nat. Cancer Inst., 1992-95; mem. Corp. of Haverford Coll., 1995—. Contbr. articles to profl. jours., chpts. to books. NIH grantee, 1972—; recipient USPHS Research Career Devel. award NIH, 1975-80. Mem. Am. Soc. Biochemistry and Molecular Biology, The Monroe Inst. Mem. Society of Friends. Home: 554 Wayland Ave Providence RI 02906-4723 Office: Brown U Dept Biochemistry Box G Providence RI 02912

DAHLBERG, ALFRED WILLIAM, electric company executive; b. Atlanta, 1940. Grad., Ga. State U., 1970. Chmn., pres., CEO Southern Co., Atlanta, 1999—; pres. Allen Franklin, Atlanta, 1999—; bd. dirs. So. Co., So. Co. Svcs., Inc., So. Electric Generating Co., Protective Life Corp., Electric Power Rsch. Inst., Trust Co. Ga., Trust Co. Bank; pres., dir. Piedmont-Forrest Corp.; mem. Southeastern Electric Exch., Edison Electric Inst. Office: Southern Co 270 Peachtree St NW Ste 2200 Atlanta GA 30303-1205*

DAHLBERG, BURTON FRANCIS, real estate corporation executive; b. Ashland, Wis., Dec. 14, 1932; s. Oscar A. and Estelle (Bratton) D.; m. Gloria Dahlberg, Aug. 23, 1957 (div. Nov. 1982); children: Michael, Andrea, David; m. Sandy Sieverson, Jan. 22, 1985. BA, U. Minn., 1960. Cert. property mgr. Property mgr., leasing Oneida Realty, Duluth, Minn.; real estate analyst Control Data Corp., Bloomington, Minn., 1965-68; v.p., real estate mgr. Kraus-Anderson Realty Co., Bloomington, 1968-84, pres., 1984—; bd. dirs. Am. State Bank, Bloomington, 1985-94. Bd. dirs. Minn. Taxpayers Assn., 1984—. Mem. Minn. C. of C. (bd. dirs. 1994—), Bloomington C. of C. (bd. dirs. 1983-80), Nat. Assn. Office and Indsl. Parks (bd. dirs.), Mpls. Bldg. Onwers and Mgrs. Assn. (past pres.), Internat. Council Shopping Ctrs. (bd. dirs.), Inst. Real Estate Mgmt. Club: Decathlon Athletic (Bloomington, bd. dirs. 1983-86). Avocations: racquetball, hunting, cooking, race horses. Office: Kraus-Anderson Inc 4210 W Old Shakopee Rd Bloomington MN 55437-2995

DAHLBERG, CARL FREDRICK, JR., entrepreneur; b. New Orleans, Aug. 20, 1936; s. Carl Fredrick and Nancey Erwin (Jones) D.; m. Constance Weston, Dec. 30, 1961; children: Kirsten Erwin Dahlberg Turner, Catherine Morgan. BSCE, Tulane U., 1958; MBA, Harvard U., 1964. Registered profl. engr., La., land surveyer, La. Regional mgr. bond dept. E.F. Hutton & Co., Inc., New Orleans, 1965-67; chmn. exec. com. Dahlberg, Kelly & Wisdom, Inc., New Orleans, 1967-71; pres. St. Mary Galvanizing Co., Inc., New Orleans, 1971—; co-organizer, dir. Charter Med. Corp., 1969-72; adv. dir. Rathborne Cos., 1985-91; with Internat. Trade Mart, 1974-89, mem. exec. com., 1981-84, treas., 1983-84; consul gen. of Monaco, New Orleans, 1981-98; treas. Consul Corps of New Orleans, 1990-94. Co-author: Hydrochloric Acid Pickling, 1979. Trustee Metairie Park Country Day Sch., New Orleans, 1976-85, treas., 1980-82, chmn., 1982-84; trustee Eye, Ear, Nose and Throat Hosp., New Orleans, 1980-96, mem. exec. com., 1980-83; trustee Eye, Ear, Nose and Throat Found., 1980-83, U. South, Sewanee, Tenn., 1984-90; bd. dirs. New Orleans Tech. Coun., 1993-98; vestryman Christ Ch. Cathedral, New Orleans, 1981-85. With U.S. Army, 1958-59. Mem. ASCE, Am. Soc. Venerable Order Hosp. of St. John of Jerusalem, Mil. and Hospitaller Order St. Lazarus, Order of Merit of Italian Republic, Order of Grimaldi (Monaco), New Orleans Country Club, Pickwick Club, City Energy Club, S. La. Gun Club, Army and Navy Club (Washington); bd. dirs. Nat. Assn. Mfrs., 1997—. Republican. Episcopalian. Home: 199 Audubon Blvd New Orleans LA 70118-5538 Office: 201 St Charles Ave Ste 2531 New Orleans LA 70170

DAHLBERG, JAMES E(RIC), biochemist, molecular biologist; b. Chgo., May 30, 1940; m. E. Lund, 1978; children: Caroline, Maria. BA, Haverford Coll., 1962; PhD in Biochemistry, U. Chgo., 1966. Rsch. assoc. Med. Rsch. Coun. Lab Molecular Biology, Cambridge, England, 1966-68, U. Genava, Lab Biophysics, 19687-69; asst. prof. to assoc. prof. U. Wis., Med. Sch., Madison, 1969-74, prof. biomolecular chemistry, 1974—; mem. Am. Cancer Soc. Study. Fellow Romnes, 1976, Macy, 1979, Fairchild fellow Calif. Inst. Tech., 1986. Fellow AAAS; mem. NAS, Am. Soc. Microbiology, Am. Soc. Biochemistry and Molecular Biology, Am. Chemical Soc. (Eli Lilly award in Biology Chemistry, 1974), Am. Acad. Arts and Sci. Office: Univ Wis Dept Biomolecular Chemistry 1300 University Ave Madison WI 53706-1510*

DAHLBERG, THOMAS ROBERT, author, attorney, educator, software company executive; b. Pitts., Nov. 28, 1961; s. J. Robert and Patricia Ann (McSweeney) D.; m. Teresa Marie Dorr, Aug. 21, 1981 (annulled 1992); 1 child, Mary Katherine; m. Jeanne Marie Henderson, July 19, 1992 (dec. 1994). BS, Pa. State U., 1984, postgrad, 1982-84; AM, Georgetown U., 1986; JD, U. Notre Dame, 1987; PhD, Stanford U., 1994. Legis. asst. U.S. Senate, Washington, 1985; dir. fin. Ctr. Judical Studies, Washington, 1986; fgn. svc. officer U.S. Dept. State, Reston, Va., 1987-88; assoc. various firms, 1988-90; columnist, screenwriter, author Sacramento, 1991—; instr. U. Calif. at Berkeley, 1996—; adj. prof. U. Notre Dame Law Sch., 1997—; CIO Precept Software Inc., Palo Alto, Calif., 1997-98, Virtuosi, Inc., 1998—. Author: Drug Crazy, 1993, Literary Transaction Guide, 1993, (screenplay) Sequential Monogamy, 1992, (screenplay) Spooks and Loggers, 1992, (screenplay) Whippers and Slippers, 1992, (screenplay) Trauma Drama, 1993; editor Benchmark, Washington, 1986-87; Notre Dame Law Sch. editorial group, Harvard Jour. Law & Public Policy, editor, 1985-86, sr. editor, 1986-87; contbr. articles to profl. jours. and mags. Bd. dirs., chair strategic planning com. Boulder Vol. Connection, 1994-95, Rocky Mountain Wolf Sanctuary, 1994-96, Frontier Airlines, 1995-96; spkr. Sacramento AIDS Found., 1991-92; caticical min. 1998—. Capt. USAR, 1979-90, Ctrl. Am., Europe. Decorated knigh most gallant corss Order of Bath; nominee Pulitzer prize for Disting. Commentary, 1993; recipient Exceptional Svc. medallion CIA, 1987. Mem. Federalist Soc. for Law and Pub. Policy Studies (past pres. Notre Dame chpt. 1985-87), Assn. Trial Lawyers Am., Nat. Assn. Criminal Defense Lawyers (com. on prosecutorial misconduct, com. to free the innocent imprisoned, death penalty project), Writers Guild Am. (west), Amnesty Internat. (lawyer's com.). Avocations: travel, reading. Office: 15466 Los Gatos Blvd # 109-324 Los Gatos CA 95032

DAHLBURG, JOHN-THOR THEODORE, newspaper correspondent; b. Orange, N.J., Apr. 30, 1953; s. Donald Russell and Madeline (Blackadore) D.; m. Yvonne Michelle Bastien, Nov. 18, 1980; children: Cecile, Charlotte. BA summa cum laude, Washington and Lee U., 1975; LLD with highest honors, U. Toulouse, France, 1980. Reporter, pub. affairs dir. Sta. WLUR-FM, Lexington, Va., 1971-75; stringer Lynchburg (Va.) News, 1974-75; news clk., intern Time Mag., Paris, 1974; reporter, editor Boca Raton (Fla.) News, 1980-81; newsman AP, Miami, Paris, 1981-83; editor, fgn. desk AP, N.Y.C., 1984-86; corr. AP, Moscow, 1986-90, L.A. Times, Moscow, 1990-93; bur. chief L.A. Times, New Delhi, 1993-96, Paris, 1996—. Journalistes en Europe fellow, 1983-84; recipient George Polk award L.I. U., 1993, Excellence citation Overseas Press Club Am., 1993, Hal Boyle award, 1996, Cert. of Merit AP News Execs. Coun., 1993, Robert F. Kennedy Journalism award, 1996, Soc. Profl. Journalists award for internat. reporting, 1997; named finalist Pulitzer Prize in internat. reporting, 1992, 93. Office: LA Times, 10 Boulevard Malesherbes, 75008 Paris France Office: LA Times Care Foreign Desk Times Mirror Sq Los Angeles CA 90053

DAHLE, JOHANNES UPTON, academic administrator; b. Ada, Minn., Nov. 28, 1933; s. Upton Emmanuel and Marte (Goli) D.; m. Arlene Isabel Powell, Dec. 27, 1956; children—Randall Douglas, Lisa Johanna. B.S., U. Minn., 1956, M.A., 1966. Choral dir. U. Minn., Mpls., 1960-62, 63-66; dir. choirs Macalester Coll., St. Paul, 1962-63; dir. student activities and univ. programs U. Wis.-Eau Claire, 1966-71, dir. univ. ctrs., 1971-84, dir. devel., 1984-95, ret., 1995. Pres., dir. Eau Claire Conv. Tourism Bur., 1979-84; v.p., dir. Eau Claire Regional Arts Council, 1982-84; bd. dirs. United Way of Eau Claire. Served to capt. USAF, 1956-60. Mem. Internat. Assn. Coll. Unions, Council for Advancement and Support Edn., Phi Kappa Phi (sec. 1982-84), Omicron Delta Kappa (sec. 1981-84), Phi Mu Alpha Sinfonia. Mem. United Ch. of Christ. Lodge: Kiwanis (pres. Eau Claire chpt. 1975-76). Home: 1929 Hunter Hill Rd Hudson WI 54016-5818

DAHLGREN, CARL HERMAN PER, educator, arts administrator; b. N.Y.C., July 2, 1929; s. Harry W.A. and Ester Florence (Carlson) D.; m. Ella Kate Bowes, Oct. 8, 1960; children: Robert C., John L., Per M., Eva B. MusB, Westminster Choir Coll., Princeton, N.J., 1954. Project dir. Benson & Benson, Princeton, 1954-55; asst. head spl. research and analysis Gallup & Robinson, Princeton, 1956-57; v.p., artist mgr. Columbia Artists Mgmt., Inc., N.Y.C., 1958-68, dir., 1962-68; v.p. Hurok Concerts, Inc., N.Y.C., 1968-70, assoc., 1970-74; pres. Dahlgren Arts Mgmt., Inc., Denver, 1970-78; sr. ptnr. Dahlgren, Schiffmann & Assocs., N.Y.C., 1978-80; assoc. prof. arts adminstrn. U. Cin., 1978—, acting head broadcasting div., 1979-80; dir. masters program in arts adminstrn. Coll. Conservatory of Music, 1978—, prof., 1989—, prof. emeritus, 1992; prin. Dahlgren & Yaffe, Arts Cons., 1992; acting exec. dir. Assn. for Advancement of Arts Edn., Cin., 1995-96; mem. faculty senate U. Cin., 1988-90. *Carl H.P. Dahlgren joined the market research firm of Benson & Benson Inc. in Princeton, 1954. In 1956 he joined the Princeton firm of Gallup and Robinson Inc. He was a filed representative for Columbia Artists Management Inc. in 1958. He joined Judson, O'Neal and Judd, which managed some of the most established artists of the day, in 1959. In 1970 he began Dahlgren Arts Management Inc. in Denver. In 1978 he became Director of Arts Administration at the College-Conservatory of Music at the University of Cincinnati. He is now Professor Emeritus and he continues his interest in the University's program and the arts community.* Co-founder, exec. dir. Westminster Choir Coll. Alumni Fund Assn., 1954-59; mgr. Princeton Symphony Orch., 1957-59; gen. mgr., dir. Central City (Colo.) Opera House, 1970-72; bd. dirs. Gilpin County Arts Assn., 1970-76; bd. dirs., sec. Colo. Celebration of Arts, 1974-76; pres. Classic Choral, 1975-78, Cin. Chamber Orch., 1982-91; trustee Westminster Choir Coll., 1967-74. With AUS, 1947-49. Decorated knight 1st Class Order of Lion, Finland; recipient Merit award Westminster Choir Coll. Mem. AAUP (v.p. U. Cin. chpt. 1990-92), Assn. Arts Adminstrn. Educators (trustee 1988, pres. 1990), Am. Assn. Mus., Faculty Club U. Cin. Episcopalian.

DAHLGREN, DOROTHY, museum director; b. Coeur d'Alene, Idaho; m. Robert Eagan, 1985; 1 child, Ivan. BS in Museology and History, U. Idaho, 1982; M in Orgnl. Leadership, Gonzaga U., 1998. Dir. Mus. N. Idaho, Coeur d'Alene, 1982—; grant reviewer gen. operating support grants Inst. Mus. and Libr. Svcs., 1993—; mem. Kootenai County Historic Preservation Commn. Author: (with Simone Carbonneau Kincaid) In All the West No Place Like This; A Pictorial HIstory of the Coeur d'Alene Region, 1996. mem. Idaho Heritage Trust com. N. region. Office: Mus N Idaho PO Box 812 Coeur D Alene ID 83816-0812

DAHLIN, DENNIS JOHN, landscape architect, environmental consultant; b. Ft. Dodge, Iowa, June 12, 1947; s. Fred E. and Arlene (Olson) D.; m. Jeanne M. Larson, Mar. 2, 1969 (div. 1990); 1 child, Lisa. BA, Iowa State U., 1970; M in Landscape Architecture, U. Calif., Berkeley, 1975. Lic. landscape arch., Calif. Assoc. planner San Luis Obispo County, Calif., 1971-73; prin. Dennis Dahlin Assocs., Modesto, Calif., 1975-90; pres. WPM Planning Team, Inc., Sacramento, 1991—; bd. dirs. El Porvenir Found., Sacramento, 1991—. Contbg. author: The Energy Primer, 1976, Restoring Our River, 1997. Bd. dirs. Ecology Action Ednl. Inst., Modesto, 1984-85, Econ. Conversion Coun., San Diego, 1988-89; pres. San Joaquin Habitat for Humanity, Stockton, Calif., 1986-87. Ferrand fellow U. Calif., 1974, Kearney fellow Harvard U., 1975. Mem. Am. Planning Assn., Am. Soc. Landscape Architects (bd. dirs. Sierra chpt. 1993-95). Methodist. Avocations: canoeing, travel, folk music. Office: PO Box 261 Sacramento CA 95812-0261

DAHLIN, DONALD C(LIFFORD), academic administrator; b. Ironwood, Mich., June 18, 1941; married; 2 children. BA magna cum laude in history, Carroll Coll., 1963; PhD in Govt. (Univ. Departmental fellow), Claremont Grad. Sch., 1969; fellow in ct. mgmt., Inst. Ct. Mgmt., 1980. Asst. prof. govt. U. S.D., Vermillion, 1966-70, assoc. prof., 1970-75, prof., 1975—, dir. criminal justice studies program, 1972-75, 78-89, chmn. dept. polit. sci., 1978-89, 95-98, fellow Pres.'s office, 1984-85, interim v.p. acad. affairs, 1988-90, acting dean continuing edn., 1995, v.p. acad. affairs, 1997—; mgmt. analyst Law Enforcement Assistance Adminstrn., Dept. Justice, Washington, 1970-71; sec. S.D. Dept. Public Safety, Pierre, 1975-78; lectr., cons. in field; mem. S.D. Human Resource Cabinet Sub-Group, 1975-78, chmn., 1977-78; mem. S.D. Planning Commn., 1975-78; adv. bd. Criminal Justice Statis. Analysis Center, 1975-78; chmn. S.D. Criminal Justice Commn., 1976-78; mem. U. So. Calif. Criminal Justice Tng. Center Planning Com., 1977-79, U. S.D. Research Inst. Adv. Panel, 1978-80, Gov.'s Corrections Task Force, 1987; mem. acad. resource council S.D. Planning Agy., 1978-79; chmn. S.D. County Commr.'s Juvenile Justice Com., 1986-89; chmn. S.D. Youth Advocacy Project; mem. Commn. on Advancement of Fed. Law Enforcement, 1997—. Author: Models of Court Management, 1986; contbr. articles to profl. publs. Recipient Sustained High Performance award Law Enforcement Assistance Adminstrn., 1971, Disting. Safety Service award S.D. Auto Club, 1978, Disting. Faculty award U. S.D., 1980, Friend of Law Enforcement award S.D. Peace Officers, 1983; Haynes Found. research fellow, 1965-66; Am. Soc. Public Adminstrn. fellow, 1970-71; Bush Leadership fellow, summer 1975; Law Enforcement Edn. Program grantee, 1972-75; S.D. Criminal Justice Commn. grantee, 1972-74, 72-75; Criminal Justice Standards and Goals for S.D. grantee, 1974-75; Criminal Justice Data Collection grantee, 1974-75. Mem. Am. Soc. Public Adminstrn. (pres. Siouxland chpt. 1980-81, exec. bd. dirs. and sec./treas. criminal justice adminstrn. sect.), Am. Polit. Sci. Assn., Am. Judicature Soc. Home: 608 Poplar St Vermillion SD 57069-3529 Office: U SD Acad Affairs Vermillion SD 57069

DAHLSTEN, DONALD LEE, entomology educator, university dean; b. Clay Center, Nebr., Dec. 8, 1933; s. Leonard Harold and Shirley B. (Courtright) D.; m. Reva D. Wilson, Sept. 19, 1959 (div.); children: Dia Lee, Andrea; m. Janet Clair Winner, Aug. 7, 1965; stepchildren: Karen Rae, Michael Allen. BS, U. Calif., Davis, 1956; MS, U. Calif., Berkeley, 1960, PhD, 1963. Asst. prof. Los Angeles State Coll., 1962-63; asst. entomologist U. Calif., Berkeley, 1963-65, lectr., 1965-68, asst. prof., 1968-69, assoc. prof., 1969-74, prof. entomology, 1974—, chmn. div. Biol. Control, 1980-88;, 1990-91; chmn. dept. cons. and resource studies U. Calif., Berkeley, 1989-91, dir. lab. biol. control, 1992-94; assoc. dean instrn. and student affairs Coll. Natural Resources, U. Calif., Berkeley, 1996—; vis. prof. Yale Sch. Forestry and Environ. Studies, 1980-81, Integrated Pest Mgmt. Team People's Republic China, 1980, 81.. Mem. AAAS, Am. Inst. Biol. Scis. (vis. prof., lectr. 1970-71), Entomol. Soc. Am., Entomol. Soc. Can., Soc. Am. Foresters. Office: U Calif Ctr for Biol Control 201 Wellman Hall Berkeley CA 94720-3112

DAHLSTROM, DONALD ALBERT, former chemical-metallurgical engineering educator; b. Mpls., Jan. 16, 1920; s. Raymond Estin and Dora Adina (Bloomgren) D.; m. Betty Cordelia Robertson, Dec. 4, 1942; children: Mary Elizabeth, Donald Raymond, Christine Dora, Stephanie Lou, Michael Jeffrey. Student, Macalester Coll., 1937-39; BSChemE, U. Minn., 1942; PhD, Northwestern U., 1949. Petroleum engr. Internat. Petroleum Co., Ltd., Negritos, Peru, 1942-45; from instr. to assoc. prof. chem. engring. Northwestern U., 1946-56; with Eimco Corp., Palatine, Ill., 1952-69; v.p., dir. research and devel. Eimco Corp., 1960-80, also dir.; v.p. research and devel. Envirotech Corp., Salt Lake City, 1969-84; v.p., dir. Erco-Environtech, 1974-84; sr. v.p. research and devel. Eimco Process Equipment Co., 1981-84; rsch. prof. chem., metall. and fuels engring. U. Utah, Salt Lake City, 1984-97; ret., 1998; dir. Process Engrs., Inc.; Am. mem. internat. sci. com. 6th Internat. Mineral Processing Congress, 1963; mem. adv. council on engring. NSF. Contbr. to handbooks. Mem. State Air Conservation Com. State Utah, 1971-78, vice chmn., 1977-78, Mem. sch. bd. dist. 110, Deerfield, Ill., 1959-61; pres. Riverwoods Residents Assn., 1962-63; chmn. bd. Northwestern YMCA, 1950-52; trustee Village of Riverwoods, 1966-69. Served with USNR, 1945-46. Recipient Merit award Northwestern U., 1965. Mem. Am. Inst. Chem. Engrs. (dir. 1960-62, v.p. 1963, pres. 1964-65, chmn. environ. div. 1971, Founders award 1972, Environ. award 1977, One of 30 Eminent Chem. Engrs at 75th anniversary), AIME (disting. mem., hon. mem., chmn. minerals benefication div. 1963-64, bd. dirs. soc. mining engrs. 1965-67, pres. soc. mining engrs. 1974-75, dir. 1973-76, Rossiter W. Raymond award 1952, Richards award 1976, Krumb lectr. 1980, Taggart award 1983, Presdl. citation 1988), Am. Chem. Soc. (hon.), Nat. Acad. Engring., The Am. Filtration Soc., Mining and Metall. Soc. Am. (dir. Engrs. Council Profl. Devel.), Am. Soc. Engring. Edn., Nat. Acad. Engrs., Sigma Xi (Holgate award Northwestern U. chpt. 1949), Phi Lambda Upsilon, Tau Beta Pi (nat. pres. 1958-62). Presbyterian. Home: 5340 Cottonwood Ln Salt Lake City UT 84117-7606 Office: Univ Utah Dept Chem and Fuels Engring Salt Lake City UT 84112

DAHLSTROM, WILLIAM GRANT, psychologist, educator; b. Mpls., Nov. 1, 1922; s. Arthur William and Elizabeth Priscilla (Baker) D.; m. Leona Erickson, Sept. 3, 1948; children: Amy Louise, Eric Lee. Student, UCLA, 1940-41; B.A. cum laude, U. Minn., 1944, Ph.D. in Psychology, 1949. Instr. psychology U. Minn., 1946-48, Ohio Wesleyan U., 1948-49; vis. asst. prof. State U. Iowa, 1949-53, research assoc., summer 1957; assoc. prof. psychiatry and psychology, dir. psychol. services Meml. Hosp. U. N.C., Chapel Hill, 1953-56; assoc. prof. psychology U. N.C., 1956-60, research assoc. psychiatry, 1956-60, prof. psychology, 1960-87, Kenan prof. psychology, 1987-93, Kenan prof. emeritus, 1993—, clin. prof. psychology in dept. psychiatry, 1960—; research prof. Inst. for Research in Social Sci., 1960—, chmn. dept., 1971-76; vis. scholar U. Calif., Berkeley, 1968, 76-77; field dir. Child Study Center U. N.C., 1962-63; chmn. mental health study sect. NIH, 1966-67. Author: (with G.S. Welsh) An MMPI Handbook, 1960, rev. edit. (with G.S. Welsh and L.E. Dahlstrom) Vol. I, 1972, Vol. II, 1975, (with E.E. Baughman) Negro and White Children, 1968, (with L.E. Dahlstrom) Basic Readings on the MMPI, 1980, (with D. Lachar and L.E. Dahlstrom) MMPI Patterns of American Minorities, 1986. Co-editor: (with J.W. Thibaut) Jour. Personality, 1959-60; Cons. editor: Jour. Cons. Psychology, 1964-78, Jour. Abnormal Psychology, 1964-70, Psychosomatic Medicine, 1982—; Contbr. articles to profl. jours. NIMH sr. postdoctoral fellow Menninger Found., Topeka, Kans., 1967-68; Co-recipient Anisfield-Wolf award for outstanding contbn. to race relations Sat. Rev. Lit., 1968; Hargrove award N.C. Found. for Research in Mental Health, 1987. Fellow Soc. Personality Assessment, APA (Disting. Profl. Contbn. to Knowledge award 1991), AAAS, N.Y. Acad. Scis.; mem. Am. Psychosomatic Soc.; Sigma Xi. Democrat. Home: 750 Weaver Dairy Rd Apt 188 Chapel Hill NC 27514-1441 Office: U NC Dept Psychology Chapel Hill NC 27599-3270

DAHMANN, ROSEMARY GAISER, librarian; b. Cin., Apr. 6, 1948; d. William Harmon and Mary Elizabeth (Klosterman) Gaiser; m. James Donald Dahmann, June 8, 1985. BMus, U. Cin., 1970; MLS, U. Ky., 1971. Libr. Pub. Libr. Cin. and Hamilton County, 1971—; head libr. for blind Cin. and Hamilton County Libr., 1973-76, head sci. and tech. dept., 1977-92, head pers. svc., 1992—. Mem. ALA, Nat. Human Resources Assn., Soc. Human Resource Mgmt., Ohio Libr. Coun. Avocations: music, hiking, travel, reading, cooking. Office: Pub Libr Cin & Hamilton County Pers Svcs 800 Vine St Cincinnati OH 45202-2009

DAHN, CARL JAMES, aerospace engineer; b. Chgo., June 22, 1936; s. Carl E. and Genevieve (Bardon) D.; BS in Aero. Engring., U. Minn., 1959; m. Rose E. Kucenski, May 25, 1974. Cert. chem. engr.; registered profl. engr. Rocket propulsion devel. engr. Aerojet Gen. Corp., Azusa, Calif., 1959-61, propulsion and explosives devel. engr., 1962-63; chief engr. Omega Ordanace Co., Azusa, 1961-62; propulsion and explosives specialist Honeywell, Inc., Mpls., 1963-68; system safety rsch. engr. IIT Rsch. Inst. Systems Hazard Analysis, Chgo., 1968-74; hazards engring. specialist Polytechnic, Inc., Chgo., 1974-77; pres. Safety Cons. Engrs., Inc., Schaumburg, Ill., 1977—; instr. explosives, guns and ballistics, engring. hazards analysis, electrostatics hazard; cons. in same field; researcher dust explosions. Patentee in explosives field. Asst. scout master Mpls. St. Paul coun. Boy Scouts Am., 1962; area dir. Parents Without Partners, 1973; ward chmn. Rep. Com., 1964; ward chmn. Dem. Com., 1973. Mem. Am. Soc. Safety Engrs., ASTM (com. sec.), System Safety Soc., Soc. Explosives Engrs., Nat. Soc. Profl. Engrs. Democrat. Roman Catholic. Rschr. dust explosion potentials. Home: 2704 George Ct Rolling Meadows IL 60008 Office: 2131 Hammond Dr Schaumburg IL 60173-3811

DAHN, JEFF RAYMOND, physics educator; b. Bridgeport, Conn., Jan. 9, 1957; arrived in Can., 1970; s. Raymond Charles and Margery (Halsted) D.; m. Katherine Mary Lillian MacDonald, July 1, 1987; children: Hannah, Tara, Jackson. BSc in Physics with honors, Dalhousie U., Halifax, N.S., Can., 1978; MSc in Physics, U. B.C., Vancouver, Can., 1980, PhD in Physics, 1982. Rsch. assoc. Nat. Rsch. Coun. Can., Ottawa, Ont., 1982-83, mem. continuing staff, 1983-85; project leader materials sci. Moli Energy Ltd., Vancouver, 1985-87, rsch. dir., 1987-90; assoc. prof. physics Simon Fraser U., Burnaby, B.C., 1990-94, prof. physics, 1994-96; prof. physics and chemistry Dalhousie U., Halifax, N.S., Can., 1996—; cons. Moli Energy (1990) Ltd., 1990-96, 3M Co., 1996—. Contbr. over 165 sci. papers to profl. jours. Recipient Medal for Innovation in Physics from Can. Assn. Physicists, 1987, Herzberg medal Can. Assn. Physicists, 1996, Gold medal B.C. Sci. Coun., 1996. Mem. Am. Phys. Soc., Electrochem. Soc. (Lash Miller award Can. sect. 1993, Battery divsn. Rsch. award 1996), Internat. Battery Materials Assn. (Rsch. award 1995). Avocations: woodworking, basketball, hiking in mountains. Office: Dalhousie U, Dept Physics, Halifax, NS Canada B3H 3J5

DAHOOD, ROGER, English literature educator; b. N.Y.C., Dec. 21, 1942; s. Michel A. and Sophie Dahood; m. Karen Jeanne Helberg, May 3, 1980; children: Gregory, Ann, Thomas Fisher. BA, Colgate U., 1964; MA, Stanford U., 1967, PhD, 1970. Asst. prof. English U. Ariz., Tucson, 1970-76, assoc. prof., 1977-84, prof., 1985—. Editor: The Avowing of King Arthur, 1984; co-editor: (with R.W. Ackerman) Ancrene Riwle: Introduction and Part One, 1984; contbr. chpt. to book, articles to profl. jours.; mem. editl. bd. Medieval and Renaissance Texts and Studies, on-line jour. Prolepsis. Trustee St. Gregory Coll. Prep. Sch., Tucson, 1991-96; mem. adv. bd. Ariz. Ctr. for Medieval and Renaissance Studies, Tempe, 1994—. Mem. Medieval Acad. Am., Medieval Assn. of the Pacific, New Chaucer Soc., Internat. Arthurian Soc. Office: U Ariz Dept English Modern Lang Bldg Tucson AZ 85721

DAHOTRE, NARENDRA BAPURAO, materials scientist, researcher, educator; b. Poona, India, Dec. 2, 1956; came to U.S., 1981; s. Bapurao B. and Latika B. Dahotre; m. Anita Thangan, Dec. 6, 1984; children: Shreyas, Shruti, Sanket. BS in Metall. Engring., U. Poona, 1980; MS in Metallurgy, Mich. State U., 1983, PhD in Materials Sci., 1987. Instr. metallurgy and materials sci. Mich. State U., East Lansing, 1985-86; postdoctoral fellow, instr. materials sci. U. Wis., Milw., 1987-88; rsch. metallurgist U. Tenn. Space Inst., Tullahoma, 1988-91, adj. asst. prof. engring. sci. and mechanics, 1991-95, adj. asst. prof. materials sci. and engring., 1995-96; rsch. assoc. prof. materials sci. and engring., 1996-99, assoc. prof. of materials sci. and engring., 1997-99, prof. materials sci. & engring., 1999—; vis. rsch. fellow Electrotech. Lab., Agy. Indsl. Sci. and Tech., Ministry Internat. Trade and Industry, Tsukuba, 1995; hon. tech. cons. Ascan Tribology Ctr., Manila, 1996—; tech. advisor Ctr. for Laser Processing of Materials, NFTDC, Hyderabad, India, 1996—. Prin. editor: Elevated Temperature Coatings: Science and Technology-I, 1995, Elevated Temperature Coatings: Science and Technology-II, 1996, Elevated Temperature Coatings: Science and Technology-III, 1998; mem. internat. editl. bd. Indsl. Laser Handbook, 1992-94; editor: Lasers in Surface Engineering, 1998; reviewer Jour. Meall. Transactions, 1991—, Jour. Materials and Mfg. Processes, 1991—; contbr. articles to profl. jours. and conf. procs. Rsch. grantee Internat. Lead Zinc Rsch. Orgn., 1990-91, Energy Conversion Program, U. Tenn. Space Inst., 1992—, NASA Marshal Flight Ctr., 1990-91, NASA Godard, 1994—, Dept. Energy, 1993—, Dept. Defense, 1994—; recipient rsch. award Aluminum Co. of Am. Found., 1997—. Mem. Am. Soc. for Metals, The Metall. Soc. of AIME, Laser Inst. Am. Materials Rsch. Soc., Am. Ceramic Soc., Soc. Mfg. Engrs., Sigma Xi. Achievements include rsch. on laser processign of composites, ceramics and intermetallic compounds, phase transformations, characterization of materials using analytical techniques. E-mail address: ndahotre@utsi.edu. Office: U Tenn Space Inst BH Goethert Pkwy Tullahoma TN 37388

DAHSE, KENNETH WILLIAM, educator, photojournalist; b. Teaneck, N.J., May 3, 1949; s. William Charles Dahse and Dorothy Devine; m. Carol Salminen (div.); 1 child, Lisa; m. Linda Jewell, Feb. 23, 1974; 1 child, Shannon. BA, Montclair State U., 1972, MA, 1977. Secondary educator Bogota (N.J.) Pub. Schs., 1977—; adj. instr. Bergen C.C., Paramus, N.J., 1991—. Author: RVing America's Backroads, 1989, The Hellriders, 1995; contbr. articles to jours. including Am. Legion, Trailer Life, Motorcycle Tour & Cruiser, Motor/Home. Environ. activist C.L.E.A.N., Inc., Ringwood, N.J. Mem. N.J. Edn. Assn., Bogota Edn. Assn. (pres., 1995—), Sierra Club, Appalachian Mt. Club. Avocations: motorcycle riding, backpacking, hiking, swimming.

DAIDONE, LEWIS EUGENE, financial services company executive; b. Perth Amboy, N.J., Aug. 6, 1957; s. Eugene John and Gertrude Rose (Sawyer) D.; m. Kathleen Eleanor Ward, May 11, 1985; children: Eugene Joseph, Brittany Nicole, Lewis Peter. BA, Rutgers U., 1979, MBA, 1980. CPA, N.Y., N.J. Sr. acct. Ernst & Young, N.Y.C., 1980-82; asst. controller Reserve Group, N.Y.C., 1982-84; mgr. commodity acctg. Dean Witter Reynolds, N.Y.C., 1984; v.p., treas., sec. Cortland Distbrs., Inc., Hackensack, N.J., 1984-89; sr. v.p., chief fin. officer Cortland Fin. Group, Inc., Hackensack, N.J., 1984-89; also bd. dirs. Cortland Distbrs., Inc., Hackensack, N.J.; mng. dir., chief fin. officer mutual funds Salomon Smith Barney, Inc., N.Y.C., 1990—; sr. v.p., dir. Mutual Mgmt. Corp., N.Y.C., 1990—; sr. v.p., treas. Smith Barney Funds., Inc., N.Y.C., 1990—, Smith Barney Money Funds, Inc., N.Y.C., 1990—, Smith Barney Muni Funds, N.Y.C., 1990—, Smith Barney Tax-Free Money Fund, N.Y.C., 1990—, Smith Barney Intermediate Mcpl. Fund, N.Y.C., 1992—, Smith Barney Mcpl. Fund, Inc., N.Y.C., 1992—, Smith Barney High Income Opportunity Fund, Inc., N.Y.C., 1992—; chmn. Global Horizon Investment Series, Brit. West Indies, 1992—, Smith Barney Internat. Funds, Luxembourg, 1993—; and exec. of 150 other investment cos. with Salomon Smith Barney; head global funds adminstrn. SSB Citi Asset Mgmt., 1998—; v.p., treas. Cortland Trust, Inc., Hackensack, 1984-89; cons. in field. Trustee Wyndmoor Condominium Assn., Woodbridge, N.J. Named one of Outstanding Young Men Am., U.S. Jaycees, 1979. Fellow N.J. State Soc. CPAs; mem. AICPA, N.Y. State Soc. CPAs, Beta Gamma Sigma. Avocations: golf, racquetball. Office: Salomon Smith Barney Inc 388 Greenwich St New York NY 10013-2339

DAIGLE, CYNTHIA COFFEY, speech and language pathologist; b. Rayville, La., Aug. 22, 1957; d. Henry Anderson and Rosa Lee (Minor) Coffey; divorced; children: Jazzelynn Moné, Chester Joseph III. BA, Northeastern La. U., 1979; postgrad., Lamar U., 1987-88. Pvt. practice speech pathology, Lake Charles, La.; mem. La. Bd. Examiners Speech Pathologists and Audiologists, Baton Rouge, 1979—. Charter Black Heritage Festival La., Lake Charles, 1987—; membership chmn. Oak Park Mid. Sch. PTO, Lake Charles, 1996—; parent adv. chmn. Youth Black Achievers, Foreman-Reynaud YMCA, Lake Charles, 1997—. Mem. NEA, Am. Speech, Hearing and Lang. Assn. (cert. clin. competence), La. Ednl. Assn., Speech Pathologists and Audiologists in La. Schs., Calcasieu Assn. Educators, Alpha Kappa Alpha (pub. rels. com., scrapbool chmn. Zeta Psi Omega chpt. 1992—). Avocations: writing poems, biking, swimming. Home: 1609 Oregon St Lake Charles LA 70607 Office: Speech Pathology Svcs PO Box 210 Lake Charles LA 70607

DAIL, JOSEPH GARNER, JR., judge; b. Elloree, S.C., June 15, 1932; s. Joseph Garner and Esther Vernette (Harbort) D.; m. Martha E. MacReynolds; children: Edward Benjamin, Mary Holyoke. BS, U. N.C., 1953, JD with honors, 1955. Bar: N.C. 1955, D.C. 1959, Va. 1976. Pvt. practice Washington, 1959-76, McLean, Va., 1976-87; ptnr. Croft, Dail & Vance (and predecessor), 1966-76; counsel Gabeler, Ward & Griggs, 1983-87; judge U.S. adminstrv. law Fresno, Calif., 1987-94, San Francisco, 1994-97; judge U.S. adminstrv. law Tampa, 1997-99, sr. U.S. adminstrv. law judge, 1999—. Assoc. editor: N.C. Law Rev, 1954-55. Lt. USNR, 1955-59; capt. Res. (ret.). Mem. FBA, N.C. Bar Assn., D.C. Bar Assn., Transp. Lawyers Assn. (Disting. Svc. award 1976), Order of Coif, Phi Beta Kappa. Republican. Home: 103 Masters Ln Safety Harbor FL 34695-3722 Office: Times Bldg 1000 N Ashley Dr Ste 200 Tampa FL 33602-3719

DAILEY, ALICE BEATRICE, postmaster; b. Pekin, Ill., Apr. 14, 1943; d. Herbert and Lillian Beatrice (Wilkins) Read; m. Larry Lee Dailey, Jan. 7, 1962. Grad. h.s., Morton, Ill. Clk., officer, teller various cos. Peoria, Ill., 1961-65; coops., data entry Computer Mgmt. Svcs., Peoria, 1965-85; clk. Mapleton (Ill.) Post Office, 1968-85, postmaster, 1985—. Village clk. Village Govt., Mapleton, 1969—; bd. trustees Mapleton Ch., 1980. Democrat. Avocations: bird and animal watching, traveling, fishing, quilting, woodworking. Home: 7725 W 1st St Mapleton IL 61547-9620 Office: Mapleton Post Office 8607 W Main St Mapleton IL 61547

DAILEY, BENJAMIN PETER, chemistry educator; b. San Marcos, Tex., Sept. 1, 1919; s. Benjamin Peter and Anna Clementine (Waldo) D.; m. Beverly Elizabeth Holmes, June 30, 1945; children: Peter, William, Stephen. B.S., Southwest Tex. State U., 1938; M.A., U. Tex.-Austin, 1940, Ph.D., 1942. Group leader Nat. Def. Research Com., Pitts., 1942-45; postdoctoral fellow Harvard U., Cambridge, Mass., 1946-47; instr. to assoc. prof. chemistry Columbia U., N.Y.C., 1947-57, prof. chemistry, 1957-88, prof. emeritus, 1989—. Contbr. articles to profl. jours.; patentee in field. Recipient Presdl. Cert. of Appreciation, 1946; Sloan fellow, 1957-60; Adams fellow, 1962-63; NSF sr. postdoctoral fellow, 1962-63; Guggenheim fellow, 1970-71. Fellow Am. Acad. Arts and Scis., Am. Phys. Soc., Chem. Soc. (London), Faraday Soc. Home: 440 Riverside Dr New York NY 10027-6828 Office: Columbia Univ Dept Chemistry New York NY 10027*

DAILEY, COLEEN HALL, lawyer, judge; b. East Liverpool, Ohio, Aug. 10, 1955; d. David Lawrence and Deloris Mae (Rosensteel) Hall; m. Donald W. Dailey Jr., Aug. 16, 1980; children: Erin Elizabeth, Daniel Lester. Student, Wittenberg U., 1973-75; BA, Youngstown State U., 1977; JD, U. Cin., 1980. Bar: Ohio 1981, U.S. Dist. Ct. (no. dist.) Ohio 1981. Sr. library assoc. Marx Law Library, Cin., 1979-80; law clk. Kapp Law Office, East Liverpool, 1979, 1980-81, assoc., 1981-85; sole practice East Liverpool, 1985-95; magistrate Columbiana County, Ohio, 1995—; spl. counsel Atty. Gen. Ohio, 1985-92. Pres. Columbiana County Young Dems., 1985-87; bd. dirs. Big Bros./Big Sisters Columbiana County, Inc., Lisbon, Ohio, 1984-87, Planned Parenthood Mahoning Valley, Inc., 1993-97; trustee Ohio Women Inc., 1991-95; mem. Columbiana County Progress Coun., Inc. Mem. ABA, Ohio Bar Assn. (Ohio Supreme Ct. Joint Task Force on Gender Fairness), Ohio Assn. Magistrates (chmn. domestic rels. sect. 1998—), Columbiana County Bar Assn., East Liverpool Bus. and Profl. Women's Assn., Ohio Women's Bar Assn. (trustee 1997-99). Democrat. Lutheran. Office: Columbia County Common Pleas Court 105 S Market St Lisbon OH 44432-1255

DAILEY, DANIEL OWEN, artist, educator, designer; b. Phila., Feb. 4, 1947; s. David Bireley and Barbara Tarleton (Tricebock) D.; m. Linda MacNeil, Aug. 19, 1977; children: Allison MacNeil, Owen MacNeil. B.F.A., Phila. Coll. Art, 1969; M.F.A., R.I. Sch. Design, Providence, 1972. Tchr., fellow MIT Ctr. for Advanced Visual Studies, Cambridge, 1975-80; founder, prof. glass program Mass. Coll. Art, Boston, 1973-89; mem. faculty Pilchuck Glass Sch., Stanwood, Wash., 1974—; designer, artist Cristallerie Daum, Paris and Nancy, France, 1975—; designer Steuben Glass, Corning, N.Y., 1982—; tchr. glass R.I. Sch. Design, 1970-72, Haystack Mountain Sch. Crafts, Deer Isle, Maine, 1976—; owner Dan Dailey Inc. Studio, Kensington, N.H., 1977—; mem. faculty Mass. Coll. Art, 1989—; bd. dirs. Glass Art Ctr. Bradford (Mass.) Coll. One-man shows throughout U.S. and Europe, 1970—, numerous nat. and internat. group shows, 1970—; represented in permanent collections Renwick Gallery, Smithsonian Inst., Washington, Toledo Mus. Art, J.B. Speed Mus., Louisville, Creative Glass Ctr. Am., Millville, N.J., Morris Mus., Morristown, N.J., Royal Ont. (Can.) Mus., Met. Mus. Art, N.Y.C., Smithsonian Inst., Washington, Corning (N.Y.) Mus. Glass, Huntington (W.Va.) Mus., New Indian Mus., Flagstaff, Ariz., Les Archives Daum, Nancy, France, U. Ill. Art Gallery, Normal, Brockton (Mass.) Art Mus., Nat. Gallery Victoria, Melbourne, Australia, Nat. Mus. Modern Art, Kyoto, Japan, St. Louis Mus. Art, High Mus. Art, Atlanta, Phila. Mus. Art, Kestner Mus., Hannover, Fed. Republic Germany, Mus. Art, Darmstatt, Fed. Republic Germany, Indpls. Mus. Art, Am. Craft Mus., N.Y.C., L.A. County Mus. Art, Musée des Arts Decoratifs, Paris, Boston Mus. Fine Arts, Detroit Inst. Art, Yokohama Mus. Art, Japan, Musée des Arts Decoratifs, Lausanne, Switzerland, L.A. Folk and Craft Art Mus., Wheaton Mus., Millville, N.J., Milw. Mus. Art, Boca Raton (Fla.) Mus. Art, Royal Ontario Mus., Toronto, Can., Renwick Gallery, Smithsonian Inst., Washington; major exhibitions of 53 works, 1972-87, Renwick Gallery, 1987, Smithsonian Inst., 1987, Mus. Am. Art, 1987; numerous arctl. commns. include sculptural installation: 5 abstract hdqs., Jasper's Restaurant, Boston, 3 cast glass murals for Dreyfus Corp. Hdgrs., Pan Am Bldg., N.Y.C., 3 cast glass murals, The Children's Hosp., Boston, cast glass mural for No. Essex County Courthouse, Newburyport, Mass., illuminated (cast) glass mural, Rockefeller Ctr., Rainbow Room, N.Y.C., 9 cast glass murals Commonwealth Energy Svcs. Corp. Hdqrs., Cambridge, Mass., cast glass mural and street lamps for the Town of Vail, Colo., 1992—, cast glass mural, L.A. County Mus., 1993, cast and fabricated bronze 3-story stair railing, pvt. residence, Zurich, Switzerland, 26 vases, Boca Raton (Fla.) Mus. Art, 1 cast glass mural 92d St. YMCA, N.Y.C., 1998; 15 yr. retrospective Renwick Gallery, Smithsonian Inst., 1987; represented in pvt. collections. Trustee Haystack Mountain Sch., Deer Isle, Maine, 1983-92; mem. nat. adv. bd. U. Arts, Phila., 1989—, Renwick Gallery, Smithsonian Instn., Washington. Fulbright Hayes fellow Venice, Italy, 1972, 73; NEA glass fellow, 1979, Masters fellow Creative Glass Ctr. Am., 1989, Mass. Council for Arts, 1980, 85-87, MIT Ctr. Advanced Visual Studies fellow, 1975-79, grad. teaching fellow RISD, 1970-72. Fellow Am. Craft Coun.; mem. Glass Art Soc. (pres., chmn. bd. dirs. 1980-82, hon. life), N.Y. Exptl. Glass Workshop (bd. dirs. 1979-88). Office: Dailey Inc 2 North Rd Exeter NH 03833-5605

DAILEY, DAWN ELAINE, public health service official; b. Berkeley, Calif., Feb. 2, 1965; d. Stanley Wilfred Sr. and Mercedes Anderson; m. Kenneth Lamar Dailey, Apr. 19, 1986; 1 child, Mariana. BSN, U. San Francisco, 1988; MSN, Samuel Merritt Coll., 1997. RN, CNS, Calif.; bd. cert. Clin. Nurse Specialist, Calif., Clinical Specialist in Cmty. Health Nursing. Nurse Alta Bates Hosp., Berkeley, 1988-91; home health nurse Kaiser Permanente, Martinez, Calif., 1992-94; coord. Contra Costa SIDS Program, Martinez, 1995—, Fetal Infant Mortality Review Program, Martinez, 1998—; pub. health nurse Contra Costa County, Martinez, 1989—; cons. Calif. SIDS Program, Fair Oaks, 1994-98; mem. Calif. SIDS Adv. Coun., Sacramento, 1996—, pres. No. Calif. Regional SIDS Adv. Coun., Berkeley, 1993-98; mem. Contra Costa Immunization Coalition, Martinez, 1996-97, Childhood Injury Prevention Coalition, Contra Costa County, 1993—; bd. mem. Fetal and Infant Mortality Rev. Bd., Berkeley; coord. fetal infant mortality review program, 1997-98; v.p. Assn. of SIDS and Infant Mortality Program. Bd. dirs. Child Abuse Prevention Coun. Contra Costa County. Shirley C. Titus scholarship Calif. Nurses Assn., 1995, Nursing Edn. scholarship, 1996; recipient Contra Costa County award of Excellence, 1998. Mem. APHA, AMA, Assn. SIDS and Infant Mortality Programs (v.p.), Assn. SIDS Program Profls., Calif. Pub. Health Nursing Assn., Sigma Theta Tau, Chi Eta Phi (Basileus 1997, Omicron Phi chpt.). Avocations: boating, quilting. Home: 898 Sage Dr Vacaville CA 95687-7391

DAILEY, DIANNE K., lawyer; b. Great Falls, Mont., Oct. 10, 1950; d. Gilmore and Patricia Marie (Linnane) Halverson. BS, Portland State U., 1977; JD, Lewis & Clark Coll., 1982. Assoc. Bullivant, Houser, Bailey, et. al., Portland, Oreg., 1982-88, ptnr., 1988—. Contbr. articles to profl. jours. Mem. ABA (vice chair tort and ins. practice sect. 1995-96, chair-elect tort and ins. practice sect. 1996-97, chair tort and ins. practice sect. 1997-98, governing coun. 1992—, property ins. law com., ins. coverage litigation com., comm. com., chair task force on involvement of women 1990-93, liaison to commn. on women 1993-97, chair task force CERCLA reauthorization, litigation sect., standing com. environ. law 1996—, chair officers conf. sect. 1998—), Wash. Bar Assn., Oreg. State Bar, Oreg. Assn. Def. Counsel, Multnomah Bar Assn. (bd. dirs. 1994-95), Internat. Assn. Def. Counsel, Def. Rsch. Inst., Fedn. Ins. and Corp. Counsel. Office: Bullivant Houser Bailey 300 Pioneer Tower 888 SW 5th Ave Ste 300 Portland OR 97204-2089

DAILEY, DONALD HARRY, adult education educator, volunteer; b. Sommerville, Mass., Mar. 26, 1949; s. Walter Merle Dailey and Shirley Esma (Clarke) Davidson; m. Janet Lynn Johnson, May 25, 1974; children: Catherine Shirley, Amanda Margaret. AS in Behavioral Scis., SUNY, Albany, 1978, BS in Liberal Arts, 1987; M in Public Adminstrn., Ball State U., 1991, M in Adult Edn., 1995. Substitute Tchrs' Cert., Ind. Career noncommissioned U.S. Army, 1968-88; field enumerator U.S. CENSUS Dept., Indpls., 1990; course developer Veteran's Upward Bound, Indpls., 1994; demographic cons. DataSource, Indpls., 1985—; com. mem. at large INCONJUCTION; spokesman Parents Adv. Coun. Author, critical reviews: Sherlock Holmes Review, 1990—; author, editor: Media Newsletter INTERCOM: 1705, 1983-88 (Best in Orgn. 1983-85). Polit. cons. Ind. State Senate, Indpls., 1994-95. With U.S. Army, 1968-88. Recipient Appreciation Plaque INCONJUNCTION, Indpls., 1991, 94, Cert. of Appreciation Salvation Army, Indpls., 1990-94. Mem. VFW, Mensa. Republican. Lutheran. Avocations: newsletter editing/pub., media fan orgns., lit. history. Home: 8003 Maple Grove Dr Georgetown IN 47122-9047

DAILEY, FRANKLYN EDWARD, JR., electronic image technology company executive, analyst, consultant; b. Rochester, N.Y., Feb. 5, 1921; s. Franklyn Edward and Isabel Louise (Lasher) D.; m. Marguerite Virginia Parker, Apr. 1, 1944; children: Franklyn III, Michael, Philip, Elizabeth, John, Paul, Thomas, Vincent. BS, U.S. Naval Acad., 1942; BSEE, U.S. Naval Postgrad. Sch., 1950; MS in Applied Physics, UCLA, 1951. Commd. ensign USN, 1942, advanced through ranks to capt.; mgr. planning and engrng. ops. Stromberg-Carlson Co., Rochester, N.Y, San Diego, 1956-61; treas. Stati-Systems Inc., Springfield, Mass., 1962-65; dir. mfg. Tecnifax Corp., Holyoke, Mass., 1965-66; asst. dir. rsch. The Plastic Coating Corp., South Hadley, Mass., 1966-67; asst. v.p. mktg. Scott Graphics Inc., South Hadley, 1967-68, v.p. new bus. devel., 1968-70, v.p. rsch., 1970-76; cons. Image Tech. & Application, Wilbraham, Mass., 1977—; prin. Daily Internat. Pub., 1996—; pres. Photon Chroma Inc., Westfield, Mass., 1982, 84; image cons. McGraw-Hill, N.Y.C., 1978, Isomet Corp., Springfield, Va., 1980; v.p. mfg. Coulter System Corp., Bedford, Mass., 1981; chmn. Electronic Imaging Conf., Boston, Anaheim, 1985-90; speaker in field. Author: Joining the War at Sea, 1939-45, 1998, 2nd edit., 1999. Pres. Pioneer Valley chpt. Am. Diabetes Assn., 1986-88. Roman Catholic. Avocations: tennis, biking. Home and Office: 19 Brookside Cir Wilbraham MA 01095-2102

DAILEY, GARRETT CLARK, publisher, lawyer; b. Bethesda, Md., Mar. 22, 1947; s. Garrett Hobart Valentine and Margaret (Clark) Dailey; m. Carolynn Farrar, June 21, 1969; children: Patrick, Steven. AB, UCLA, 1969; MA, Ariz. State U., 1974; JD, U. Calif., Davis, 1977. Bar: Calif. 1977, U.S. Dist. Ct. (no. dist.) Calif. 1959. Assoc. Stark, Stewart, Simon & Sparrowe, Oakland, Calif., 1977-80; ptnr. Davies & Dailey, Oakland, 1980-85, owner, 1986-90; ptnr. Blum, Davies & Dailey, Oakland, 1985-86; pres., pub. Attys. Briefcase, Inc., Oakland, 1989—, pres., CEO, 1989—; lectr. U. Calif. Davis Sch. Law, 1988-90, Golden Gate U. Grad. Sch. Taxation, San Francisco, 1986—. Co-author: Attorney's Briefcase, Calif. Family Law, 1990-99, Calif. Evidence, 1993-99, Children and the Law, 1992-99, Calif. Pre/Post Marital Agreements, 1997-99, Calif. Divorce Guide, 1997-99. Bd. dirs. Amigos de las Americas, San Ramon Valley, Calif., 1980-85, Rotary 517 Found., Oakland, 1985, Kid's Turn, 1993. Recipient Hall of Fame award Calif. Assn. Cert. Family Law Specialists, 1995. Fellow Am. Acad. Matrimonial Lawyers; mem. Assn. Cert. Family Law Specialists (Hall of Fame award 1995). Democrat. Congregationalist. Home: 1651 W Livorna Rd Alamo CA 94507-1018 Office: Attys Briefcase Inc 519 17th St Fl 7 Oakland CA 94612-1527

DAILEY, IRENE, actress, educator; b. N.Y.C., Sept. 12, 1920; d. Daniel James and Helen Therese (Ryan) D. Student of, Uta Hagen, N.Y.C., 1951-61, Herbert Berghof, N.Y.C., 1951-61. Cons. for Am. Nat. Theatre and Acad., 1965-68; cons. and coach for various theatre groups and individual artists, 1956—; guest artist and tchr. various univs. in, U.S., 1965—; founder Sch. of the Actors Co., N.Y.C., 1961, artistic dir., 1961-72, mem. faculty, 1961-72. Appeared in: films Daring Game, 1967, No Way to Treat A Lady, 1968, Five Easy Pieces, 1970, The Grissom Gang, 1970, The Last Two Weeks, 1977, The Amityville Horror, 1978, Stacking, 1986; Broadway plays Andorra, 1962, The Subject Was Roses, 1964-65, Rooms, 1966-67 (Drama Desk award), You Know I Can't Hear You When the Water's Running, 1968, (off-Broadway) The Loves of Cass Maguire, 1982; appeared as Jasmin Adair in Tomorrow With Pictures (London Mag. Critics award), Duke of York's, London, 1960; appeared in The Effect of Gamma Rays on Man-In-the-Moon Marigolds, Chgo., 1970 (Sarah Siddons award), The House of Blue Leaves, Chgo., 1972 (Joseph Jefferson nomination), Lost in Yonkers, 1993, If We Are Women, Syracuse, 1993, (off-Broadway) Edith Stein, 1993-94, The Last Adam, Syracuse, 1994-95, (broadway) The Father, 1995-96; appeared in Another World, NBC-TV, 1973— (Emmy award 1980); appeared in (plays) Desire Under the Elms, Princeton, N.J., 1961, The Sea Gull, 1973; author: play Waiting for Mickey and Ava, 1978. Mem. Actors Equity Assn., Screen Actors Guild, Nat. Acad. TV Arts and Scis., Am. Ednl. Theatre Assn., AFTRA. Unitarian.

DAILEY, JANET, novelist; b. Storm Lake, Iowa, May 21, 1944; d. Boyd and Louise Haradon; m. William Dailey; 2 stepchildren. Student pub. schs., Independence, Iowa. Sec. Nebr., Iowa, 1963-74. Author: No Quarter Asked, 1976, After the Storm, 1976, Boss Man From Ogallala, 1976, Savage Land, 1976, Land of Enchantment, 1976, Fire and Ice, 1976, The Homeplace, 1976, Dangerous Masquerade, 1977, Night of the Cotillion, 1977, Valley of the Vapors, 1977, Fiesta San Antonio, 1977, Show Me, 1977, Bluegrass King, 1977, A Lyon's Share, 1977, The Widow and the Wastrel, 1977, Giant of Mesabi, 1978, The Ivory Cane, 1978, The Indy Man, 1978, Darling Jenny, 1978, Reilly's Woman, 1978, To Tell the Truth, 1978, Sonora Sundown, 1978, Big Sky Country, 1978, Something Extra, 1978, Master Fiddler, 1978, Beware of the Stranger, 1978, The Matchmakers, 1978, For Bitter or Worse, 1979, Green Mountain Man, 1979, Six White Horses, 1979, Summer Mahogany, 1979, Touch the Wind, 1979, Strange Bedfellow, 1979, Low Country Liars, 1979, Sweet Promise, 1979, For Mike's Sake, 1979, Sentimental Journey, 1979, A Land Called Deseret, 1979, The Bride of the Delta Queen, 1979, Tidewater Lover, 1979, Lord of the High Lonesome, 1980, Kona Winds, 1980, The Boston Man, 1980, The Rogue, 1980, Bed of Grass, 1980, The Thawing of Mara, 1980, The Mating Season, 1980, Southern Nights, 1980, Ride the Thunder, 1980, Enemy in Camp, 1980, Difficult Decision, 1980, Heart of Stone, 1980, One of the Boys, 1980, Wild and Wonderful, 1981, A Tradition of Pride, 1981, The Traveling Kind, 1981, The Hostage Bride, 1981, Dakota Dreamin', 1981, For the Love of God, 1981, Night Way, 1981, This Calder Sky, 1981, Lancaster Men, 1981, Terms of Surrender, 1982, With a Little Luck, 1982, Wildcatter's Woman, 1982, Northern Magic, 1982, That Carolina Summer, 1982, This Calder Range, 1982, Foxfire Light, 1982, The Second Time, 1982, Mistletoe and Holly, 1982, Stands a Calder Man, 1983, Separate Cabins, 1983, Western Man, 1983, Calder Born, Calder Bred, 1983, Best Way to Lose, 1983, Leftover Love, 1984, Silver Wings, Santiago Blue, 1984, The Pride of Hannah Wade, 1985, The Glory Game, 1985, The Great Alone, 1986, Heiress, 1987, Rivals, 1989, Masquerade, 1990, Aspen Gold, 1991, Tangled Vines, 1992, Riding High, 1994, The Proud and The Free, 1994, Touch the Wind, 1994, Summer Mahogany, 1995, Legacies, 1996, Homecoming, 1997, Illusions: A Novel, 1997, The Prodigal Daughter, 1998, This Calder Sky, 1999. Recipient Golden Heart award Romance Writers Am., 1981, Romantic Times Contemporary award, 1983. Office: Harper Collins Publs Inc 10 E 53rd St New York NY 10022*

DAILEY, MICHAEL DENNIS, painter, educator; b. Des Moines, Aug. 2, 1938; s. Malcolm Nelson and Lois Marjorie (Rider) D.; children: John, Susanne. BA, U. Iowa, 1960, MFA, 1963. Prof. Sch. of Art U. Wash., Seattle, 1963-98, prof. emeritus, 1998—. Mem. Phi Beta Kappa. Office: Francine Seders Gallery 6701 Greenwood Ave N Seattle WA 98103-5294

DAILEY, THOMAS HAMMOND, retired surgeon; b. Orange, N.J.; s. Louis Bird and Evelyn (Hammond) D.; m. Denise Benzacar Dailey, Aug. 22, 1959; children: Andrea, Erika, Seth. AB, Princeton U., 1957; MD, Cornell U. Med. Coll., 1961. Assoc. prof. clin. surgery Columbia U. Coll. Phys. and Surg., N.Y.C., 1991; sr. attending dept. surgery St. Luke's-Roosevelt Hosp. Ctr., N.Y.C., 1982, dir. div. colon and rectal surgery, 1990-96, chief med. officer, 1996-99; clin. prof. surgery Columbia U. Coll. Phys. and Surg., N.Y.C., 1997-99; ret., 1999; pres. med. bd. St. Luke's-Roosevelt Hosp., N.Y.C., 1989-91; v.p. Rsch. Found. of Am. Soc. Colon and Rectal Surgeons, pres., 1995-98. Pres. Am. Soc. Colon and Rectal Surgeons Rsch. Found., 1995—. Capt. M.C., U.S. Army, 1966-68, Vietnam. Mem. Med. Strollers, Physician's Sci. Soc., N.Y. Soc. of Colon and Rectal Surgeons (pres. 1979-81).

DAILY, EILEEN M., state legislator; b. Boston; d. Mary and Jim Meade; m. Jim Daily; children: Jeff, Amy. Student, Northestern U., Cambridge Coll. Mem. staff dept. revenue svc. Commr.'s Office, State of Conn., 1990-91; mem. Conn. State Senate, 1993—, asst. minority leader; asst. pres. Senate, 1997-98; chair Legis. Environ. Com.; vice-chair Fin., Revenue and Bonding Com.; ranking mem. Program rev. and Investigations Com.; mem. Edn. and Legis. Mgmt. Coms.; mem. L.I. Sound Bi-State commn., New England Recycling Coun.; Conn. vice-chair, New England dir. Order of Women Legislators. Mem. Westbrook (Conn.) Dem. Town Com.; chair pers. com. Westbrook Bd. Edn., 1977-83; first selectman Town of Westbrook, 1983-89, mem. bd. selectman, 1989-91; chmn. Lower Valley Selectmen's Assn., 1985-89; mem. exec. com. Coun. Small Towns, 1985-89; bd. dirs. Conn. Conf. Municipalities, 1987-89; mem. Friends of Libr.; hon. chair March of Dimes Walk-a-thon, 1997. Recipient Govs. Vol. Svc. award Conn. Alcohol and Drug Abuse Commn., award for outstanding svc. Coun. of Small Towns, award for svc. to boating industry Conn. Marine Trade Assn. Mem. C. of C., Soroptomists, Westbrook Grange. Office: Conn State Senate State Capitol Hartford CT 06106 also: 103 Cold Spring Rd Westbrook CT 06498-3511

DAILY, FAY KENOYER, retired botany educator; b. Feb. 17, 1911; d. Frederick and Camellia (Thea) Neal Kenoyer; m. William Allen Daily, June 24, 1937. AB, Butler U., 1935, MS, 1952. Lab. technician Eli Lilly & Co., Indpls., 1935-37, Abbott Labs., North Chicago, Ill., 1939, William S. Merrell & Co., Ohio, 1940-41; lubrication chemist Indpls. Propellor divsn. Curtiss-Wright Corp., 1945; lectr. botany Butler U., Indpls., 1947-49, instr. immunology and microbiology, 1957-58, lectr. microbiology, 1962-63, mem. herbarium staff, 1949-87, curator cryptogamic herbarium, 1987-95. Grantee Ind. Acad. Sci., 1961-62. Mem. Bot. Soc. Am., Phycol. Soc. Am., Internat. Phycol. Soc., Ind. Acad. Sci., Sigma Xi, Phi Kappa Phi, Sigma Delta Epsilon. Republican. Methodist. Co-author book on sci. soc. history; contbr. articles on fossil and extant charophytes (algae) to profl. jours. Home: 5884 Compton St Indianapolis IN 46220-2653

DAILY, FRANK J(EROME), lawyer; b. Chgo., Mar. 22, 1942; s. Francis Jerome and Eileen Veronica (O'Toole) D.; m. Julianna Ebert, June 23, 1996; children: Catherine, Eileen, Frank, William, Michael. BA in Journalism, Marquette U., 1964, JD, 1968. Bar: Wis. 1968, U.S. Dist. Ct. (ea. dist.) Wis. 1968, U.S. Dist. Ct. (we. dist.) Wis. 1971, U.S. Dist. Ct. (ctrl. dist.) Ill. 1990, U.S. Dist. Ct. (ea. dist.) Mich. 1994, U.S. Ct. Appeals (7th cir.) 1977, U.S. Ct. Appeals (3d and 5th cirs.) 1985, U.S. Ct. Appeals (4th, 6th, 8th, 9th, 10th, 11th cirs.) 1990, U.S. Supreme Ct. 1998, U.S. Dist. Ct. (no. dist.) Ill. 1999. Assoc. Quarles & Brady, Milw., 1968-75, ptnr., 1975—; lectr. in product liability law and trial techniques Marquette U. Law Sch., U. Wis., Harvard U. and seminars sponsored by ABA, State Bar Wis., State Bar S.D., State Bar S.C., Product Liability Adv. Coun., Chem. Mfrs. Assn., Wis. Acad. Trial Lawyers, Trial Attys. Am., Marquette U., Southeastern Corp. Law Inst., Risk Ins. Mgmt. Soc. Inc.; mem. bd. visitors Wake Forest U. Law Sch. Author: Your Product's Life Is in the Balance: Litigation Survival-Increasing the Odds for Success, 1986, Product Liability Litigation in the 80s: A Trial Lawyer's View from the Trenches, 1986, Discovery Available to the Litigator and Its Effective Use, 1986, The Future of Tort Litigation: The Continuing Validity of Jury Trials, 1991, How to Make an Impact in Opening Statements for the Defense in Automobile Product Liability Cases, 1992, How Much Reform Does Civil Jury System Need, 1992, Do Protective Orders Compromise Public's Right to Know, 1993, Developments in Chemical Exposure Cases: Challenging Expert Testimony, 1993, The Spoliation Doctrine: The Sword, The Shield and The Shadow, 1997, Trial Tested Techniques for Winning Opening Statements, 1997, Litigation in the Next Millennium -- A Trial Lawyer's Crystal Ball Report, 1998, What's Hot and What's Not in Non-Daubert Products Liability In the Seventh Circuit, 1998. Life mem. Pres.'s Coun., Marquette U. Fellow Internat. Acad. Trial Lawyers; mem. ABA (past co-chair discovery com. litigation sect., vice chmn. products, gen. liability and consumer law com. of sect. tort and ins. practice, litigation sect. and mfrs. liability subcom.), ATLA, AAAS, Trial Atty. of Am., Wis. Bar Assn., Chgo. Bar Assn., Milw. Bar Assn., 7th Cir. Bar Assn., Am. Judicature Soc., Def. Rsch. Inst., Supreme Ct. Hist. Soc., Indsl. Truck Assn. (lawyers com.), Am. Law Inst., Product Liability Adv. Coun., Am. Agrl. Law Assn., Wis. Acad. Trial Lawyers, Assn. for Advancement of Automotive Medicine (life), Nat. I-Club U. Iowa, U. Ala. Nat. Alumni Assn., Circle of Champions. Roman Catholic. Office: Quarles & Brady 411 E Wisconsin Ave Ste 2550 Milwaukee WI 53202-4497

DAILY, FRED L., ; m. Rita Dailey; children: Dawn, Shawn, Calley. BA in Polit. Sci. and History, Anderson U., Ind.; MPA, Ball State U. Formerly rodeo cowboy and amateur mountaineer; with Ind. Dept. Corrections; later with U.S. Treasury; dir. Ind. Divsn. Agr., 1975-82; exec. v.p. Ohio Beef Coun., 1982-91; exec. sec. Ohio Cattlemen's Assn., 1982-91; dir. Ohio Dept. Agr., 1991—. Served with U.S. Army, Viet Nam. Recipient numerous awards include Agri-Marketer of Yr., Industry svc. awards, golden Boot award. Mem. Nat. Assn. State Depts. Agr. (chmn. food regulation and nutrition com.), Midwest Assn. State Depts. Agr. (pres.), Mid-Am. Internat. Agri-Trade Coun. Office: Ohio Dept Agr Divsn Comms 8995 E Main St Reynoldsburg OH 43068

DAILY, JAMES L., JR., retired financial executive; b. Houston, Dec. 2, 1929; m. Virginia Teinert, Jan. 31, 1953; children: Kathy, Jimmy, Ricky. B.A. in Bus. Adminstrn, Rice U., 1951. C.P.A., Tex. Jr. accountant Tenneco, Inc., Houston, 1956-57; accountant Tenneco, Inc., 1957-58, sr. accountant, 1958-59, acctg. supr., 1959-61, acctg. mgr., 1961-71, asst. controller, 1971-75, controller, 1975-78, v.p., controller, 1978-87. Served to 1st lt. USAF, 1953-56. Mem. Tex. Soc. CPAs, Houston Soc. CPAs. Lutheran. Home: 4907 Candleleaf Dr Houston TX 77018-1418

DAILY, JEAN A., marketing executive, spokesperson; b. Bloomington, Ill., Nov. 20, 1949; d. William H. and Niola N. (Thompson) D.; m. Ronald R. Willis, June 14, 1968 (div. 1972); m. Rodger D. Melick, Aug. 15, 1981. BS, Ill. State U., 1975. Sr. acctg. clk. Country Cos., Bloomington, 1976-78;

owner, mgr. Danvers (Ill.) Motor Co., 1979-85; office mgr., ops. mgr. Goods Carpet, Bloomington, 1986-87; dir. mktg. Westminster Village Inc., Bloomington, 1987—. Chair Com. to Elect Judge Prall, Bloomington, 1996; publ. chair Danvers Days, 1982-85; bd. dirs., publ. rels. & devel. advisor Twin Cities Ballet, Bloomington, 1994-96; bd. dirs. ARC, 1991-94; pres. Chestnut Health Sys. Aux., 1995-97, treas., 1997—; vol. Arthritis Telethon, St. Jude's Golf Tournament; publicity chair Gardenwalk 97; mem. adv. bd. Arthritis Found., 1997—; apptd. cabinet bd. Ill. Life Svcs. Network Assisted Living, 1997-99, sec., 1997-99. Mem. Women in Comms., Nat. Soc. Fund Raising Execs. (co-editor chpt. newsletter 1989-91). Avocations: reading, crafts, golf, photography, country dance. Office: Westminster Village 2025 E Lincoln St Bloomington IL 61701-5995

DAILY, JOHN CHARLES, executive recruiting company executive; b. Washington, May 5, 1943; s. Edwin Francis and Elta Katherine (Waters) D.; m. Barbara Lucille Kissling, Mar. 1, 1969; children: Craig Alexander, Leigh Christina. BA in Psychology, Dartmouth Coll., 1966; MBA in Mktg., Columbia U., 1968. Various exec. and mgmt. positions IBM, Armonk, N.Y., 1968-91; sr. v.p. mktg. Systems Ctr., Inc., Reston, Va., 1992, pres., CEO, 1993; pres., CEO, Image Bus. Systems, N.Y.C., 1994; exec. v.p. info. tech. practice Handy HRM Corp., N.Y.C., 1995-97; v.p., prin. Christian & Timbers, N.Y.C., 1997—; chmn. bd. Proginet Corp. Avocations: golf, tennis, squash, mountain biking. Office: Christian & Timbers 570 Lexington Ave New York NY 10022-6837

DAILY, LOUIS, ophthalmologist; b. Houston, Apr. 23, 1919; s. Louis and Ray (Karchmer) D.; B.S., Harvard U., 1940; M.D., U. Tex. at Galveston, 1943; Ph.D., U. Minn., 1950; m. LaVerl Daily, Apr. 5, 1958; children: Evan Ray, Collin Derek (dec.). Intern, Jefferson Davis Hosp., Houston, 1943-44; resident in ophthalmology Jefferson Davis Hosp., 1944-45, Mayo Found., Rochester, Minn., 1947-50; individual practice medicine, specializing in ophthalmology, Houston, 1950—; assoc. prof. ophthalmology U. Tex.-Houston, 1972-86, Baylor Med. Sch., Houston, 1950—. Vice pres. bd. dirs. Mus. Med. Sci., 1973-85, pres., 1980-82. Served as lt. (j.g.) USNR, 1945-46. Diplomate Am. Bd. Ophthalmology. Fellow A.C.S., Internat. Coll. Surgeons; mem. Soc. Prevention of Blindness (med. chmn. Tex. 1968-70), Contact Lens Assn. Ophthalmologists (exec. bd. 1976-78), Tex. Ophthal. Assn. (pres. 1963-64), Houston Ophthal. Soc. (pres. 1970-71), numerous other med. socs., Sigma Xi, Alpha Omega Alpha. Jewish. Clubs: Doctors, Harvard (dir. 1965-66) (Houston). Editorial bd. Jour. Pediatric Ophthalmology, 1964-68; asso. editor Eye, Ear, Nose and Throat Monthly, 1962-65, Jour. Ophthalmic Surgery, 1970; contbr. numerous articles to profl. publs., also contbr. to books. Home: 2523 Maroneal St Houston TX 77030-3117 Office: 1517 Med Towers 1709 Dryden Rd Houston TX 77030-2400

DAILY, THOMAS V., bishop; b. Belmont, Mass., Sept. 23, 1927. Student, Boston Coll., St. John's Sem., Brighton, Mass. Ordained priest Roman Cath. Ch., 1952; missionary Peru as mem. Soc. St. James the Apostle; ordained titular bishop of Bladia and aux. bishop Boston, 1975-84; first bishop Palm Beach, Fla., 1984-90; bishop Diocese of Bklyn., 1990—. Address: Chancery Office PO Box C 75 Greene Ave Brooklyn NY 11202*

DAISLEY, WILLIAM PRESCOTT, lawyer; b. Washington, Aug. 11, 1935; s. Gordon Walford and Augusta Greenleaf (Prescott) D.; m. Linda L. Thelin, Nov. 3, 1962; children: William Prescott Jr., Susan DeLeon. B.A., Randolph Macon Coll., 1959; LL.B., George Washington U., 1962. Bar: D.C. 1962, Md. 1968, U.S. Supreme Ct. 1978. Law clk. firm King & Nordlinger, Washington, 1960-62, assoc., 1963-69, ptnr., 1969-90; prin. McChesney, Duncan & Dale, Washington, 1991-93; pres., chief exec. officer, chmn. of bd. William P. Daisley, Esq., P.C., Kensington, Md., 1993—; mem. Montgomery County (Md.) Juvenile Ct. Com., 1970-73; guest lectr. law George Washington U., 1972-76, 79; bd. dirs., trustee McLeod, Strasbaugh Scholarship Fund, 1984—; bd. dirs. Citizens Bank Washington (formerly McLachlen Nat. Bank), 1982-97, chmn. audit com., 1992-94; mem. audit com. Citizens Bank of Md., 1994-97. Trustee, St. Andrew's Episc. Sch., Bethesda, Md., 1985-87. Mem. Md., Am., Montgomery County, D.C. bar assns., Phi Delta Theta, Phi Delta Phi. Republican. Episcopalian. Club: Columbia Country (bd. govs. 1983-86). Home and Office: 9817 Gartrell Pl Kensington MD 20895-3743 *Success, though rarely achieved with utter perfection, is a goal not to be eschewed, but rather one sought with diligent preparation. Those who achieve a fair modicum of success are often called "lucky". The lucky people I have known have one quality in common—they are invariably the best prepared.*

DAJANI, BADR MUSTAFA, neurologist; b. Beirut, Lebanon, Sept. 24, 1961; came to U.s., 1991; 1 child, Mustafa Adam. MD, Am. U. Beirut, 1989. Intern U. Tenn., Memphis, 1991-92; resident neurology U. Ala., Birmingham, 1992-95, fellow in neurophysiology, 1997-98; pvt. practice neurology Coral Springs, Fla., 1998—. Avocations: weightlifting, jogging. Office: 1725 University Dr # 350 Coral Springs FL 33071

DAJANI, ESAM ZAPHER, pharmacologist; b. Jaffa, Palestine, May 30, 1940; came to U.S., 1958; s. Zapher Rageb and Mamdouha (Dajani) D.; m. Najwa Said Beidas, July 16, 1964; children: Mona, Zapher, Noura. BS in Pharmacy, U. Mo., 1963; MS in Pharmacology and Med. Chemistry, Auburn U., 1966; PhD in Pharmacology, Purdue U., 1969. Sr. pharmacologist Rohm and Hass Co., 1968-72; sr. rsch. investigator G.D. Searle and Co., Chgo., 1972-74, group leader, 1974-80, chmn. G.I. diseases, 1974-80, sect. head, 1980, asst. dir., 1980-82, assoc. dir., 1982-85, dir. Cytotec sci. and med. affairs, 1985-87, dir. clin. rsch., 1987-93; pres. Internat. Drug Devel. Cons. Corp.-IDDC, Long Grove, Ill., 1993—; editl. adv. bd. Drug Devel. Rsch., Dallas, 1983-93, Jour. Assn. Acad. Minority Physicians, Bklyn., 1992—, Jour. Physiology and Pharmacology, Krakow, Poland, 1993—; adj. prof. medicine UCLA, 1984-95; adj. prof. medicine Loyola U., Chgo., 1995—, adj. prof. pharmacology Chgo. Med. Sch., 1983-90; scientific adv. bd. Atlantic Pharm., Inc., C.V. Therapeutics, Inc.; presenter in field. Editor: Gastrointestinal Cytoprotection, 1987; author: (with others) Prostaglandins and GI Mucosa, 1987, Pharmacology of Misoprostol, 1989, Prostaglandins and Esophagus, 1991, Pharmaceutical Industry Perspective, 1991, Prevention and Treatment of Ulcers induced by NSAIDS, 1995, EGF Prevents Esophogeal Ulcers Induced by Sclerotherapy, 1995, 3rd edit., 1997, Drug Induced Ulcers, 1998, Gastrointestinal Toxicity of Over the Counter Analgesics, 1998; contbr. articles to profl. jours.; patentee in field. Mem. Arab-Am. Anti-discrimination Com., Washington, 1972, Arab-Am. U. Grads., Washington, 1991. Recipient Edgar M. Queeny award, Monsanto Corp., 1991; named Disting. Alumnus Purdue U., 1991. Fellow Am. Coll. Gastroenterology; mem. Am. Soc. Pharmacology and Exptl. Therapeutics, Am. Gastroent. Assn., Gastroenterology Rsch. Group, Soc. Exptl. Biology and Medicine, Drug Info. Assn., Am. Pharm. Assn., European Soc. Gastroenterology and Endoscopy, Assn. Acad. Minority Physicians (bd. dirs.), N.Y. Acad. Sci., Chgo. Biotech Network (founder, bd. dirs.), Rho Chi, Phi Kappa Phi. Achievements include 9 patents; co-discovery and development of Cytotec, the first commercial prostaglandin anti-ulcer drug; directed pre-clinical and clinical research at multinational pharmaceutical companies; considerable expertise in worldwide drug development. Office: IDDC Corp 1549 RFD Long Grove IL 60047-9532

DAJANI, VIRGINIA, arts administrator; b. Chgo., Jan. 19, 1936; d. Philip Linden Boddy and Lillian (McArdle) O'Brien; m. Majed Dajani (div. 1968); children: Magda, Tarek, Najeeb, Nadia. Student, Loyola U., Chgo., 1953-55, Am. U., Cairo, 1961, Am. U., Beirut, 1963-67; postgrad., Harvard U., 1980-81. News editor Archtl. Forum mag., N.Y.C., 1968-72, Architecture Plus mag., N.Y.C., 1972-74; asst. George Nelson, Architect, N.Y.C., 1975-76; editor The Livable City, quar. of Mcpl. Art Soc., N.Y.C., 1976-89; dir. spl. projects Mcpl. Art Soc., N.Y.C., 1977-89; exec. dir. Am. Acad. Arts and Letters, N.Y.C., 1990—; dir. archtl. competition Mcpl. Art Soc., N.Y.C., 1985, 87; competition advisor Bronx Mus. Arts, N.Y.C., 1989, Mcpl. Art Soc., N.Y.C., 1991—; lectr. Harvard U. Grad. Sch. Design, 1980-87. Author: Juror's Guide to Lower Manhattan, 1984, rev. edits., 1985, 87, 90; contbr. articles to profl. archtl. jours. Recipient Citation for editing design mus. catalogue Am. Inst. Graphic Artists, 1975, award for editing The Livable City, AIA, 1982; Loeb fellow Harvard U., 1980-81. Mem. Century Assn. Office: Am Acad Arts and Letters 633 W 155th St New York NY 10032-7501*

DAJANY, INNAM, academic administrator; b. American Fork, Utah, Oct. 9, 1951; d. Fuad Wafa and Doris Dean (Ault) Dajany; divorced; 1 child, Nadia Marina Fenton. BS, SUNY, Cortland, 1973; MEd, U. Idaho, 1985. Cert. elem. and secondary English tchr., Idaho, Wyo., N.Y. Tchr. Converse County Sch. Dist., Douglas, Wyo., 1973-75; newspaper reporter Casper (Wyo.) Star Tribune, 1974-76; rsch. asst. edn. dept. U. Idaho, Moscow, 1978-81, asst. dir. Early Childhood Learning Ctr., 1980-84, dir. Early Childhood Learning Ctr., 1984-90, cons., coord. Early Childhood Inst., 1989-91; mktg. and sales dir. Golden Arrow Hotel, Lake Placid, N.Y., 1990-92; continuing edn. asst. SUNY, Clinton C. C., 1992-94; coord. Riverview Acad., 1993-95; owner An Original Idea, Crown Point, N.Y., 1996; cons. Gov.'s Commn. Children and Youth, Boise, Idaho, 1988-90, child devel. specialist region II coun., 1986-90; conf. coord. U.S. Agy. Internat. Devel., 1988-90; independent grant writer, 1993—; ind. real estate agent, patent writer, invention marketer; speaker in field; instr. English, writing SUNY-North County C.C., 1998—. Author: Building Your Child's Self Esteem During Home Reading, 1985, (booklet) You, Your Child, and Reading, 1986, (brochure) Help Arrest Child Abuse, 1982. Tchr., project coord. North Country Women at Work, 1993-95; advisor child care licensing laws City of Moscow, advisor HUD grant; coord. Parents in Action, Moscow, 1989, 90; co-pres. Moscow Swim Team, 1989, 90; leader Bluebirds, Moscow; active N.W. Found. grant, Ford Found. grant with KAID-TV. Mem. Nat. Assn. for Edn. Young Children (state pres. 1989-90, conf. chair 1985-87, leadership trainer and presenter 1981—), Internat. Reading Assn. (state pres. 1987-88, nat. com. literacy devel. 1987-89, nat. com. reading and arts 1985-87, leadership trainer and presenter 1981—), Phi Delta Kappa, Kappa Delta Phi. Avocations: hiking, reading, travel, learning, writing children's and young adult books. Home: PO Box 277 Crown Point NY 12928-0277 Office: Noteco Inc PO Box 533 Crown Point NY 12928-0533 also: SUNY-North County CC Saranac Lake NY 12983

DAKE, MARCIA ALLENE, retired nursing educator, university dean; b. Bemus Point, N.Y., May 22, 1923; d. Earl B. and Bernice DeLeo (Haskin) D. Diploma, Crouse Irving Hosp., 1944; BS, Syracuse U., 1951; MA, Columbia U., 1955, EdD, 1958. RN. Sch. nurse tchr. various locations, 1946-48; chmn. health dept. SUNY, Oneonta, 1982-56; dean coll. nursing U. Ky., Lexington, 1958-72; dir. dept. nursing edn. Am. Nurses Assn., Kansas City, 1972-74; project dir. program devel. nursing ARC, Washington, 1975-79; dir. nursing edn. James Madison U. Coll. Nursing, 1981-88; prof. dean Coll. Nursing, 1981-88; ret., 1988. Mem. Ky. Bd. Nursing Edn. Nurse Registration, 1969-72, pres., 1970-72; pres. Va. Coun. Deans of Baccalaureate Nursing Programs, 1981-84; nurse officer Civil Def. Otsego County, N.Y., 1953-56; mem. Def. Adv. Com. on Women in Svcs., 1963-65; mem. Ky. Comprehensive Health Planning Coun., 1968-71; pres. Ky. League for Nursing, 1961-65; bd. dirs. Cmty. Ch. Coll., Sun City Ctr., Fla., 1989-92, Sun City Ctr. Guardianship Found., 1990-98; trustee United Cmty. Ch., Sun City Ctr., 1993-96, chmn. personnel com., 1994-96, fin. com., 1994-95, vice chmn. bd. trustees, 1995-96, stewardship com., 1996, mem. pastoral rels. com., 1996—, mem. long range planning com., 1996-97, chmn. pastoral rels. com., 1998—; sec. Caloosa Women's Golf Assn., Sun City Ctr., 1991-92; treas. Greater Sun City Ctr. Disaster Coun., 1992-94. 1st lt. U.S. Army Nurse Corps, 1945-46. Fellow Nat. League Nursing; mem. ANA, Va. Nurses Assn. (pres. dist. 9 1983-85), Va. Soc. Profl. Nurses (treas. 1983-88), Va. Assn. Colls. of Nursing (sec. 1980-82, pres. 1982-85), Alliance of Nursing Orgns. (chmn. Va. 1985-88), LWV, Delta Kappa Gamma, Kappa Delta Pi, Pu Lambda Theta. Address: PV 222 7442 Spring Village Dr Springfield VA 22150-4333

DAKE, TERRENCE R., career officer; m. Sue Long; children: Jana, Joshua. AA, Coll. of Ozarks; BA, U. Ark.; MA, Pepperdine U.; grad., Officer Candidate Sch. Commd. 2nd lt. USMC, 1966, advanced through grades to gen., 1996; naval aviator for CH-53A HMH-462, 1968-69; forward air contr. 1st Bn. 9th Marines; stationed with HMH-461, New River, N.C., HMM-164, Okinawa; aircraft comdr. in the CH-46, UH-1 and VH-3, exec. aircraft HMX-1, exec. officer; helicopter pilot for the Pres., 1983-85; ops. officer Marine Aircraft Group 36, Okinawa, 1986; dir. joint tng. and doctrine Staff of the Comdr.-in-Chief of the Atlantic Command, Norfolk, Va., 1987-90; asst. chief of staff for ops. 3rd Marine Aircraft Wing, 1990; chief of staff 3rd Marine Aircraft Wing, El Toro, Calif., comdg. gen., 1995-96; asst. dep. chief of staff for aviation, 1992-94. Decorated Legion of Merit, Air medal with Combat V with the numeral 2. Office: USMC Asst Commandant Marine Corps Washington DC 20380-1775 also: Hdqs Marine Corps Divsn Pub Affairs Washington DC 20380-1775

DAKIN, CHRISTINE WHITNEY, dancer, educator; b. New Haven, Aug. 25, 1949; d. James Irving, Jr. and Jean Evelyn (Coulter) Crump; m. Robert Ford Dakin, June 21, 1969 (div. Sept. 1982); m. Stephen J. Mauer, Aug. 1, 1985. Student, U. Mich., 1967-71; D of Arts (hon.), Shenandoah U., 1996. Performer, teacher Ann Arbor Dance Theater, Mich., 1965-71; tchr. Ann Arbor Pub. Schs., 1967-70, Lincoln Ctr. Inst., N.Y.C., 1978, Guanajuato U., Mex., 1982; vis. artist USIA Vladivastock, Vladivastock, Russia, 1992; Art-sLink grantee, vis. artist Vladivastock, 1996; tchr., faculty advisor Ballet Nacional de Mex., 1993—; vis. artist USIA Ballet Contemporaneo, Buenos Aires, 1993; prin. dancer Martha Graham Dance Co., N.Y.C., 1976—; dancer, rehearsal dir. Pearl Lang. Dance Co., 1972-76, Kazuko Hirabayashi Dance Co., 1974-76; faculty Martha Graham Sch., 1972—, Juilliard Sch., 1992—, Alvin Alley Am. Dance Ctr., 1989-93. Appeared in: It's Hard to Be a Jew, 1972, The Dybuk, 1975; appeared (with Martha Graham Dance Co.) Covent Garden, London, 1976, Met. Opera, 1980, Bklyn. Acad. Music, 1994, Sta. WNET Dance in Am. Series, 1979; Young Artist in Performance at The White House, Sta. WNET, 1982, (with Rudolph Nureyev) Paris Opera, Berlin Opera, 1984, N.Y. State Theater, 1985; NHK Film, Japan, 1990, Paris Opera Film, 1991, (documentary film) Les Printemps du Sacre, 1993; assoc. founder Buglisi/Foreman Dance, 1994, (with Buglisi/Foreman Dance) Runes of the Heart, Kennedy Ctr., 1997; assoc. artistic dir. Martha Graham Dance Co., 1997. Am. Dance Festival scholar, 1969, Garcia-Robles Sr. scholar Fulbright Found., 1999; recipient award Dance Mag., 1994; grantee Rockefeller U.S.-Mex. Fund for Culture, 1997-98. Mem. Am. Guild Mus. Artists (life, bd. govs.). Office: Martha Graham Dance Co 316 E 63rd St New York NY 10021-7702

DAKOFSKY, LADONNA JUNG, radiation oncologist, educator; b. N.Y.C., Oct. 30, 1960; d. George S. and Kay (Han) Chung. BA magna cum laude, Columbia U., N.Y.C., 1982; MD, NYU, 1987. Bd. cert. radiation oncologist. Rsch. asst. dept. neurology UCLA, 1980-81, Harvard U., Boston, 1982; tchr. chemistry St. Ann's Sch., Brooklyn Heights, N.Y., 1982-83; resident in internal medicine Lenox Hill Hosp., N.Y.C., 1987-88; resident in radiation oncology Hosp. of U. Pa., Phila., 1988-91; instr. in radiation oncology New Eng. Med. Ctr., Boston, 1991-92; attending physician Norwalk (Conn.) Hosp., 1992—; clin. asst. prof. radiation oncology Yale U., 1994—; prin. investigator RTOG cancer rsch. Norwalk Hosp., exec. com. hosp. staff, IPA chair of quality improvement subcom. Mem. jr. com. Boys Club N.Y.; sponsor Mus. City of N.Y.; mem. com. Vocat. Found., N.Y.C.; mem. Jr. League of Stamford-Norwalk. Marine Biol. Lab. scholar, 1981. Mem. AMA, Assn. Therapeutic Radiology and Oncology, Fairfield County Med. Assn. (Melville Magida award 1998, Best Younger Physician in Fairfield County 1998), New Eng. Cancer Soc., Met. Breast Cancer Group. Presbyterian. Avocations: writing, sailing, voice. Office: Norwalk Hosp Radiation Oncology PO Box 5050 Norwalk CT 06856-5050

DAKS, PETER A., telecommunications company executive. Pres. GTE Fla. Inc., Tampa. Office: GTE Fla Inc PO Box 110 Tampa FL 33601-0110

DALAMBAKIS, CHRISTOPHER A., workplace performance consultant; b. Dayton, Ohio, Mar. 11, 1960; s. Angelo George and Irene D.; m. Judy Ann Schneider, July 28, 1984. BS in Biology, U. Cin., 1983. Asst. mgr. Brendamour's, Dayton, 1976-79; asst. to dir. U. Cin. Alumni Assn., 1982-83; service rep. United Technologies Otis, Chgo., Cin., 1983-84; new equipment rep. United Technologies Otis, Cin., 1984-86; dist. mgr. Steelcase, Inc., Cin., 1986-97; workplace performance cons., 1997-98. Mem. exec. com. bd. govs. U. Cin. McMicken Coll., 1987-93; trustee U. Cin., 1981-82; bd. dirs., chmn. com. Cin. Art Mus. Friends Assn., 1989-94; trustee Cin. Fire Mus., 1994—, mem. exec. com., 1998—; trustee Nat. Hemophilia Found., 1995—, Leukemia Soc., 1999—; active Nat. Trust for Hist. Preservation, 1990-94. Named Outstanding Young Man of Am., Jaycees, 1982. Mem. Metro Men's Spirit (hon. 1980—), Am. Student Assn. (nat.dir. 1981-83), Cincinnatus (hon. 1980-83), U.S. Senatorial Club, Sigma Sigma (pres. 1982-83, social chmn. 1990—). Republican. Greek Orthodox. Avocations: gardening, foreign cars, antique swords, skeet shooting. Home and Office: 3759 Old Heritage Ct Loveland OH 45140-5506

DALBECK, RICHARD BRUCE, insurance executive; b. Cambridge, Mass., May 17, 1929; s. Harold Lewis and Elizabeth (Kessell) D.; m. Shirley Carolyn Wells, Apr. 7, 1956; children: Barbara Jane, Elizabeth Ann, Bruce Wells. AB, Dartmouth Coll., 1952, MBA, 1953. With GE, Lynn, Mass., Lynchburg, Va., 1956-62; with A.T. Kearney & Co., Inc., Chgo. and N.Y.C., 1962-69; from v.p. to first sr. v.p. Union Mut. Life Ins. Co., Portland, Maine, 1969-84; first sr. v.p. Unionmutual Life Ins. Co., Portland, 1984-86; exec. v.p. Unum Corp., Portland, Maine, 1987-91; bd. dirs. 1st Unum Life Ins. Co., N.Y.C., 1972-91, Unuim Life Ins. Co. of Am., Portland, Maine, 1988-91; commr. Maine Health Care Fin. Commn., 1991-96, Maine Blue Ribbon Commn. on Workers Compensation, 1992; councilor Town of Cape Elizabeth, Maine, 1992-95; trustee Maine Mcpl. Assn. Property and Casualty Pool, 1995-98. Trustee Camp O-At-Ka, 1996—, Camp Bishopswood, 1975-96, Masterton Found. for Tech. Edn., 1988-93, Maine Maritime Mus., 1991—; trustee Sweetser Children's Svcs., 1996—, treas., 1997—; trustee Park Danforth Home for Aged, Portland, 1981-91, pres., 1988-90; bd. dirs. United Way Greater Portland, 1980-83, campaign chmn., 1985; former warden St. Albans Episc. Ch.; active Episcopal Diocese Maine. Lt. Supply Corps, USNR, 1953-56. Mem. Greater Portland C. of C. (bd. dirs., exec. com., 1985-92, vice chmn. 1988-90, chmn. 1990-92), Phi Beta Kappa. Episcopalian (lic. lay reader). Home: 17 Spoondrift Ln Cape Eliz ME 04107-2934 Office: 17 Spoondrift Ln Cape Eliz ME 04107-2934

DALE, CHUCK, landmark staff member; b. Dayton, Ohio, June 13, 1947. BA, Thomas Edison Coll., 1977. Ranger Shennandoah (Va.) River Nat. Park, 1975-79; dist. ranger Isle Royal (Mich.) Nat. Park, 1979-82, Ozark (Ark.) Nat. Scenic Riverway, 1982-89; chief ranger Virgin Isles Nat. Park, 1989-92, Ft. Matanzas Nat. Monument and Castillo de San Marcos, St. Augustine, Fla., 1992—. Office: Ft Matanzas Nat Monument and Castillo de San Marcos 1 S Castillo Dr Saint Augustine FL 32084*

DALE, CYNTHIA LYNN ARPKE, educational administrator, retired; b. Plymouth, Wis., Jan. 11, 1942; sd.; children: robert S., Peter D., Kimberly A. (Dale) Keaveny. BS, Wis. State U., Oshkosh, 1964; M degree, U. Ctrl. Fla. Cert. tchr., Wis., Fla. Tchr. Omro (Wis.) Sch. Sys., 1964, West Allis (Wis.) Sch. Sys., 1965-68; substitute tchr. Brevard County Sch. Sys., Melbourne, Fla., 1972-68; early edn. tchr. various schs. Melbourne, Fla., 1980-88; supr. site coord. for S. Brevard County Sch. Sys. Child Care Assn., Melbourne, Fla., 1988-93. Contbg. author: (poetry) A Far Out Place, 1994 (merit award), Forgetfulness, 1995 (merit award), Ickey Poo, A Special Birthday and Beth, 1996, Eh?, Beein' Around, Bad Habits, Memories, Ever Have One of Those Nights?, 1997. Mem. PTA various schs. sys.; mem. choir, Christian edn. com., Sunday sch. tchr. Palmdale Presbyn. Ch., Melbourne; cub scout den mother Boy Scouts Am., Melbourne; soccer mother, coach, asst. Little League, Melbourne, swimming instr.; mem. homeowner's assn. Groveland Mobile Home Park, Melbourne. Mem. AARP, ASCD, Audubon Soc., Internat. Soc. Poets. Republican. Avocations: writing, reading, swimming, hand sewing, dachsunds. Home: 523 Wavecrest Ct Melbourne FL 32934

DALE, DAVID C., physician, medical educator; b. Knoxville, Tenn., Sept. 19, 1940; s. John Irvin and Cecil (Chandler) D.; m. Rose Marie Wilson, June 22, 1963. BS magna cum laude, Carson-Newman Coll., 1962; MD cum laude, Harvard U., 1966. Intern and resident Mass. Gen. Hosp., 1966-68; resident U. Wash. Hosp., Seattle, 1971-72; clin. assoc. NIH, 1968-71; prof., assoc. chmn. dept. medicine U. Wash., Seattle, 1976-82, dean Sch. of Medicine, 1982-86. Contbr. numerous articles to profl. jours. Served to comdr. USPHS, 1968-70, 72-74. Mem. Am. Soc. Hematology, Assn. Am. Physicians, Am. Soc. for Clin. Investigation, ACP. Avocations: woodworking; gardening; backpacking; sports. Office: U Wash Sch of Medicine RG-22 PO Box 356422 Seattle WA 98195-6422

DALE, DAVID WILSON, English educator, poet; b. Helena, Mont., May 24, 1937; s. Arbie Myron and Dona Wilson Dale; m. Donna Jean Smatlan, Feb. 13, 1960; children: David Matthew, Erich Arbie, James Wilson. BA, Mont. State U., 1962; MA in English, U. Mont., 1969, MFA in Creative Writing, 1991. Cert. tchr. Tchr. English-Spanish Granger (Wash.) H.S., 1964-68; tchr. English Dawson Coll., 1969-70; tchr. English-Spanish Ronan (Mont.) H.S., 1970-75, 76—; mem. exec. coun. Mont. Fedn. of Tchrs., Butte, 1978-82. Author: What We Call Our Own, 1991, The Way on Bear Is, 1994, Montanta Primer, Skating Backwards. With USMC, USN, 1954-59. Mem. Mont. Edn. Assn. Democrat. Avocations: fishing, reading, music. Home: Box 257 Big Arm MT 59910

DALE, ERIC MICHAEL, philosopher of religion; b. Texarkana, Tex., May 25, 1972; s. James Wesley and Rose Marie Dale. MusB in Vocal Music, U. Ctrl. Ark., 1995; MA in Theology, Southwestern Sem., 1997. Tchr. English and French, Victory Christian Sch., Little Rock, 1995-96. Author: (poetry) Antechamber, 1996; tenor Porgy and Bess, Opera Memphis, 1993, Susanna, 1993, Turandot, Shreveport Opera, 1994. Recipient Howard Groth Performer award U. Ctrl. Ark., 1995. Mem. Brothers and Sister of Charity (Franciscan domestic), Am. Acad. Religion/Soc. Bibl. Lit., Soc. Buddhist Christian Studies, Soc. Continental Philosophy Theology, Coun. Soc. Study Religion, Maria Kannon Zen Ctr., Amnesty Internat., Sierra Club. Avocations: mountain climbing, gardening, composing, travel. Office: HermitMusic No 102 4316 Baldwin Ave Fort Worth TX 76115

DALE, ERWIN RANDOLPH, lawyer, author; b. Herrin, Ill., July 30, 1915; s. Henry and Lena Bell (Campbell) D.; m. Charline Vincent, Aug. 27, 1955; children: Allyson Ann (Mrs. Earl A. Samson III), Kristan Charline (Mrs. Victor L. Zimmerman). BA, U. Tex., El Paso, 1937; JD, U. Tex., 1943. Bar: Tex. 1943, D.C. 1953, Mich. 1956, N.Y. 1960. Atty. IRS, 1943-56, chief reorgn. and dividend br., 1954-56; legal staff Gen. Motors Corp., 1956-57; ptnr. firm Chapman, Walsh & O'Connell, N.Y.C. and Washington, 1957-59, Hawkins, Delafield & Wood, N.Y.C., 1959-84; of counsel Hutchison, Price, Boyle & Brooks, Dallas, 1985-86, Jenkens, Hutchison & Gilchrist, Dallas, 1986, Hutchison, Price, Boyle & Brooks, Dallas, 1986-87; lectr. tax matters; dir. Md. Electronics Mfg. Corp., 1948-58; dir., treas. The Renaissance Corp., 1968-72; dir., asst. treas. Shancom Reconstrn. Corp., 1968-72, Newhaven Corp., 1968-72. Author numerous articles on fed. tax matters; bd. editors: Tex. Law Rev., 1941-42, 42-43. Mem. ABA (chmn. com. consol. returns sect. taxation 1959-60), Tex. Bar Assn., Mich. Bar Assn., N.Y. State Bar Assn. (chmn. corp. tax com. tax sect. 1967-68, mem. exec. com. 1968-70), Tax Inst. Am. (bd. dirs. 1967-69, treas. 1966), Assn. of Bar of City of N.Y., Nat. Tax Assn., Nat. Assn. Bond Lawyers, Am. Coll. Tax Counsel, Ex-Students Assn. U. Tex., Ex-Students Assn. U. Tex., El Paso, Bronxville Field Club (N.Y.), Masons. Home: 10 Holly Ln Darien CT 06820-3303

DALE, JIM, actor; b. Rothwell, Northamptonshire, Eng., Aug. 15, 1935; s. William and Miriam Smith; m. Julie Schafler; children by previous marriage—Belinda, Murray, Adam, Toby. Actor Nat. Theatre Co., Old Vic, Eng.; plays The Card, Taming of the Shrew, Scapino, N.Y.C., Scapino, Barnum (Tony award 1980), Joe Egg (Tony nomination), Me and My Girl (1986-89), Privates on Parade, 1989 (Tony nomination), Travels with My Aunt, Long Wharf Theatre, 1994, UK Radio "The Music Man", 1994, Oliver, 1995, Candide, 1997; films: Raising the Wind, Carry On Spying, Carry On Cleo, Carry On Cowboy, Lock Up Your Daughter, The National Health, Digby, Joseph Andrews, Pete's Dragon, Scandalous, 1985, Adventures of Huckleberry Finn (TV), 1985, Carry On Columbus, 1992, (voice) Lincoln, 1992, The American Clock, 1993, The Hunchback, 1997; comedian (debut) solo, Savoy, London, 1951; songwriter Georgy Girl; host TV spl. Ringling Bros. Barnum and Bailey Circus, 1985; guest appearances on The Equalizer, 1985, The Ellen Burstyn Show, 1986, TV guest appearances, 1987-90. Office: care Sendroff & Assocs PC 1500 Broadway Ste 2001 New York NY 10036-4015*

DALE, JOHN SORENSEN, investment company executive, portfolio manager; b. Mpls., Sept. 30, 1945; s. John Sorensen and Ruth Elaine (Bergstrom) D.; m. Cheryl Lee Woolley, June 19, 1965; children: John, Christopher. BA in Mktg. and Humanities, U. Minn., 1968. CFA. Securities analyst, portfolio mgr. Norwest Corp., Mpls., 1968-78, v.p., sr. trust investment strategist, 1978-84, sr. v.p., mgr. equity advisors, 1984-87; sr.

v.p., sr. portfolio mgr. Peregrine Capital Mgmt., Mpls., 1987—. Fellow Inst. Chartered Fin. Analysts; mem. Assn. Investment Mgmt. and Rsch., Twin Cities Soc., Security Analysts, Internat. Soc. Fin. Analysts. Avocations: travel, fishing, hunting. Office: Peregrine Capital Mgmt LaSalle Plz Ste 1850 8th and LaSalle Minneapolis MN 55402-2018

DALE, JUDY RIES, religious organization administrator; b. Memphis, Dec. 13, 1944; d. James Lorigan and Julia Marie (Schwinn) Ries; m. Eddie Melvin Ashmore, July 12, 1969 (div. Dec. 1983). BA, Rhodes Coll., 1966; M in Religious Edn., So. Bapt. Theol. Sem., 1969, Grad. Specialist in Religious Edn., 1969. Cert. tchr. educable mentally handicapped, secondary English, adminstrn. and supervision in spl. edn. EMH tchr., curriculum writer, tchr. trainer Jefferson County Bd. Edn., Louisville, 1969-88, ednl. cons., 1988-90; dist. coord. Gt. Lakes dist. Universal Fellowship Met. Community Chs., Louisville, 1990—; lectr. Jefferson C.C., Louisville, 1987-93, U. Louisville, 1976-77, 87-90; mem. faculty Samaritan Inst. for Religious Studies, 1992-98; mem. program adv. com. Internat. Conf. Spl. Edn., Beijing, 1987-88. Editor, writer: (handbook) Handbook for Beginning Teachers, 1989, A Manual of Instructional Strategies, 1985; author: (kit) Math Activities Cards, 1978. Bd. sec. Com. of Ten, Inc., Louisville, 1987-91; v.p. GLUE, 1988-92, pres., 1992-94; mem. Universal Fellowship of Met. Cmty. Chs., programs and budget divsn., 1990-97, mem. gen. coun., 1990—, mem. core team, 1993—, chair, 1997—, active Women's Secretariat steering com., 1991-95; dist. coord. Gt. Lakes Dist. (parliamentarian 1987-89); mem. membership com. Cmty. Health Trust, 1991-94; trustee Samaritan Inst. Religious Studies, 1992-98, chair acad. affairs com., 1996-97. Recipient Honorable Order of Ky. Cols., 1976; named Outstanding Elem. Tchr. Am., 1975. Mem. AAUW, NOW, ACLU, Nat. Gay & Lesbian Task Force, Parents, Family & Friends of Lesians & Gays, Nat. Ctr. for Lesbian Rights, Lambda Legal Def. & Edn. Fund, Gay & Lesbian Assn. Anti-Defamation, Coun. Exceptional Children (keynote speaker 1984-88, internat. pres. 1986-87, exec. com. 1984-88, bd. govs. 1981-88), Ky. Coun. Exceptional Children (bd. dirs. 1976-90, Mem. of Yr. 1987), Internat. Platform Assn., Women's Alliance, Phi Delta Kappa. Democrat. Avocations: people, church work, reading, handwork. Home and Office: 1300 Ambridge Dr Louisville KY 40207-2410

DALE, KATHY GAIL, rehabilitation rheumatology nurse; b. Evansville, Ind., Sept. 28, 1954; d. Albert Joseph and Doris Maxine (Dunning) D. ADN, U. Evansville, 1975, BSN, 1986; MS in Health Svcs. Adminstrn., Coll. of St. Francis, Joliet, Ill., 1992. RN, Tenn., Ind.; cert. rehab. registered nurse. Staff nurse St. Mary's Med. Ctr., Evansville, Ind., 1975-86, Vanderbilt Med. Ctr., Nashville, 1986-87; head nurse St. Thomas Hosp., Nashville, 1987-89; referral coord. Edgefield Rehab. Ctr., Nashville, 1989-90; nurse educator Arthritis and Osteoporosis Care Ctr. at Bapt. Hosp., Nashville, 1990—. Contbr. articles to profl. jours. Mem. Assn. Rehab. Nurses, Tenn. Assn. Rehab. Nurses (pres.-elect 1990, 94, pres. 1991, 95, bd. dirs. 1992, 96), Am. Assn. Neurosci. Nurses. Avocations: reading, football. Home: 8300 Sawyer Brown Rd Apt F-301 Nashville TN 37221-7625 Office: Arthritis and Osteoporosis Care Ctr Bapt Hosp-Med Office Bldg 300 20th Ave N Ste G-1 Nashville TN 37203-2132

DALE, KENNETH RAY, computer executive; b. Garnett, Kans., Aug. 22, 1948; s. Earnest Kenneth and Dorothy Mae (Root) D.; m. Sheila Rae Talbott, June 23, 1979; children: Anne Marie Camp, Carolee Talbott. BA, Washburn U., 1978. Programmer trainee Kans. Power and Light Co., Topeka, 1978-79, programmer, 1979-80, sr. programmer, 1980-81, programmer, analyst, 1981-82, sr. programmer, analyst, 1982-83, systems analyst, 1983-85; programmer, analyst Vol. Shoe Corp., Topeka, 1985-86, sr. programmer, analyst, 1986-87, computer ops. shift mgr., 1987-88, lead programmer, analyst, 1988-91; pvt. practice cons. Overbrook, Kans., 1991-92; staff analyst Profl. Resources Inc., Shawnee Mission, Kans., 1992; tech. svcs. cons. CAP Gemini Am, Overland Park, Kans., 1992-97; cons. Maximgroup Info. Systems Cons., Overland Park, Kans., 1997—. With USN, 1967-70. Mem. Am. Mgmt. Assn., Data Processing Mgmt. Assn., Masons. Democrat. Home: PO Box 444 Overbrook KS 66524-0444

DALE, MADELINE HOUSTON MCWHINNEY, banker; b. Denver, Mar. 11, 1922; d. Leroy and Alice Barse (Houston) McWhinney; m. John Denny Dale, June 23, 1961; 1 son, Thomas Denny. BA, Smith Coll., 1943; MBA in Fin, NYU, 1947. With Fed. Res. Bank N.Y., 1943-73; pres. First Women's Bank, N.Y.C., 1974-76; vis. lectr. NYU Grad. Sch. Bus., 1976-77; pres. Dale, Elliott & Co., Inc., N.Y.C., 1977-97; dir. Carnegie Corp. N.Y., 1974-82, vice chmn. bd., 1980-82; asst. dir. Whitney Mus. Am. Art, 1983-86; mem. adv. bd. NYU Grad. Sch. Bus. Adminstrn., 1974-85, U. Denver Grad. Sch. Bus. and Pub. Adminstrn., 1974-86; dir. Atlantic Energy Inc., 1983-93. Adv. bd. Banking Law Jour., 1973-83. Trustee Retirement Sys. Fed. Res. Banks, 1955-58, Mgrs. Funds, 1983—, Inst. Internat. Edn., 1976—, treas., 1979-85, 88-96; bd. dirs. Investor Responsibility Rsch. Ctr., 1975-80, Charles F. Kettering Found., 1975-93, chmn., 1987-91; mem. Pres.' Commn. on White House Fellows, 1975-77; bd. govs. Am. Stock Exch., Inc., 1977-81; commr. N.J. Casino Control Commn., 1980-82; mem. adv. com. profl. ethics N.J. Supreme Ct., 1983-98; mem. N.J. Com. for Humanities, 1988-93; trustee Monmouth Mus., 1995—, Jersey Vis. Nurses Assn., 1995—. Recipient medal Smith Coll., 1971, Alumni Achievement award N.Y. U., 1971. Mem. Am. Fin. Assn. (dir. 1955-57), Alumni Assn. NYU Grads. Bus. Adminstrn. (pres. 1957-59), Money Marketeers (pres. 1960-61), Women's Bond Club, Soc. Meml. Ctr., Phi Beta Kappa. Home: PO Box 458 Red Bank NJ 07701-0458

DALE, MARTIN ALBERT, investment banking executive, retired; b. Newark, Jan. 3, 1932; s. Philip D. and Lucie M. (Mintz) D.; m. Joan Clements, Apr. 3, 1954 (div. 1977); children: Charles, W. Gregory, Pamela, Eric; m. Berteline Baier, Nov. 21, 1980. BA cum laude, Princeton U., 1953; postgrad., U. Strasbourg, France, 1953-54; MA in Internat. Econs. with honors, Tufts U., 1955. Fgn. svc. officer U.S. Dept. State, 1955-60; pvt. counsellor, econ. advisor Prince Rainier III of Monaco, 1960-64; v.p., exec. asst. to pres. Grand Bahama Port Authority Ltd., Freeport, 1965-67; sr. v.p. fin., adminstrn. and ops. Revlon Internat. Corp., N.Y.C., 1967-72; corp. sr. v.p., dir. office strategic projects W.R. Grace & Co., N.Y.C., 1972-82; strategic planning cons. Henkel KGaA, Duesseldorf, Germany, 1983-93; vice chmn. Hill Thompson Capital Markets, Duesseldorf, 1993-97. Trustee, chmn. emeritus Lycée Francais N.Y. Decorated knight Order of Nat. Merit, France; Fulbright fellow, 1953-54. Mem. Princeton Club N.Y., N.Y. Athletic Club, Sarasota Yacht Club, Phi Beta Kappa. Republican. Home: 455 Longboat Club Rd Longboat Key FL 34228-3850

DALE, ROBERT GORDON, business executive; b. Toronto, Ont., Can., Nov. 1, 1920; s. Gordon McIntyre and Helen Marjorie (Cartwright) D.; m. Mary Austin Babcock, Apr. 3, 1948; children: Robert Austin, John Gordon. Ed., U. Toronto Schs., 1930-39, Trinity Coll.; student, U. Toronto, 1939-40. Cert. in bus. adminstrn., 1946. With Maple Leaf Mills, Ltd., Toronto, 1947—; plant mgr. Maple Leaf Mills, Ltd., 1957-61, gen. product mgr., 1961-65, asst. to pres., 1965-67, exec. v.p., 1967-68, chmn., pres., chief exec. officer, 1968-86, dir., cons., 1986-95; chmn. Upper Lakes Group Inc., Toronto, 1995-97; dep. chmn. Upper Lakes Group, Inc., Toronto, 1997—; pres. Pinedale Investments Inc., Toronto, 1994—. Hon. pres. Air Cadet League Can.; past chmn. Ont. Provincial Com.; trustee United Comty. Fund Greater Toronto; chmn. bd. govs. Can. Corps Commissionaires; bd. dirs. Sunnybrook Med. Ctr. With RCAF, 1940-45. Decorated D.F.C., Can. Forces Decoration, Disting. Service Order. Mem. Can. Nat. Millers Assn. (dir., past chmn.), Phi Kappa Pi. Conservative. Anglican. Clubs: Rosedale Golf, Nat, Badminton and Raquet, Bd. of Trade, Empire. Office: Upper Lakes Group Inc, 49 Jackes Ave, Toronto, ON Canada M4T 1E2

DALE, SAM E., JR., retired educational administrator; b. Harmon, La., July 10, 1921; s. Sam E. and Willie Edith (Parr) D.; B.S. in Vocat. Agr., La. State U., Baton Rouge, 1947, M.S. in Vocat. Agr., 1954, Ph.D. in Vocat. Agr., 1972; m. Cathleen Trichel; 1 child, Cathy Sue. With Catahoula Parish Sch. Bd., Jonesville, La., 1948-85, supervising prin., 1969-72, dir. career and vocat. edn., 1973-79, supt., 1979-85. Mem. adv. council La. State U.; mem. supts. council La. Bd. Elem. and Secondary Edn; chmn. bd. trustees Catahoula Hosp. Dist. #2; mem. County agrl. stabilization and conservation com. Mem. La. Vocat. Assn., La. Agr. Tchrs. Assn., Am. Vocat. Assn., La. Supts. Assn., La. Ret. Tchrs. Assn., Gideons, Am. Legion, Phi Delta Kappa. Baptist. Home: PO Box 56 Sicily Island LA 71368-0056

DALE, WESLEY JOHN, chemistry educator; b. Milw., Aug. 8, 1921; s. Colin B. and Irma P. (Pohl) D.; m. Pattie Surine, Aug. 20, 1949; 1 dau., Claudia. B.S. in Chemistry with highest honors, U. Ill., 1943; Ph.D., U. Minn., 1949. Teaching asst. U. Minn., 1943; research chemist Govt. Synthetic Rubber Research Program, 1943-46; mem. faculty U. Mo. at Columbia, 1949-66, prof. chemistry, 1958-66, chmn. dept., 1961-64; asst. to dean U. Mo. at Columbia (Coll. Arts and Scis.), 1954-55; staff assoc. sci. facilities evaluation group, div. instl. programs NSF, 1964, sr. staff asso. sci. devel. evaluation group, div. instl. programs, 1964-66; dean Sch. Grad. Studies, U. Mo. at Kansas City, 1966-72, prof. chemistry, 1966-85, univ. research adminstr., 1969-72, acting provost and dean faculties, 1971, provost, 1972-79, acting chancellor, 1976-77; prof. chemistry and chmn. dept. Principia Coll., Elsah, Ill., 1985-89; cons. long range academic planning; chmn. Midwest Conf. Grad. Study and Research, 1970-71. Contbr. articles to profl. jours. Bd. dirs. Sci. Pioneers, Kansas City, Mo., 1967-78, Inst. Community Studies, 1970-73; trustee Mid-Continent Regional Ednl. Lab., Kansas City, 1972-73; mem. adv. com. U.S. Army Command and Gen. Staff Coll., Fort Leavenworth, Kans., 1973; bd. dirs. Harry S. Truman Library Inst., 1977, Kansas City Mus., 1976-77, The Principle Found., 1993-99. Fellow Am. Inst. Chemists; mem. AAAS, Am. Chem. Soc., Sigma Xi, Phi Kappa Phi, Phi Eta Sigma, Phi Lambda Upsilon, Pi Mu Epsilon, Gamma Alpha, Alpha Chi Sigma.

D'ALEMBERTE, TALBOT (SANDY D'ALEMBERTE), academic administrator, lawyer; b. Tallahassee, June 1, 1933; m. Patsy Palmer; children: Gabrielle Lynn, Joshua Talbot. BA in Polit. Sci. with honors, U. South, 1955; postgrad., London Sch. Econs. and Polit. Sci., U. London, 1958-59; JD with honors, U. Fla., 1962. Assoc. Steel Hector & Davis, Miami, Fla., 1962-65, ptnr., 1965-84, 89-93; prof. Fla. State U., 1984—, dean, 1984-89, pres., 1994—; lectr. U. Miami Coll. Law, 1969-71, adj. prof., 1974-76; reader Fla. Bd. Bar Examiners, 1965-67; mem. jud. nominating commn. Fla. Supreme Ct., 1975-78; chief counsel Ho. Select Com. for Impeachment of Certain Justices, 1975; mem. Fla. Law Revision Coun., 1968-74; chmn. Fla. Constl. Revision Commn., 197-778. Contbr. articles to profl. jours.; articles editor U. Fla. Law Rev. Mem. Fla. Ho. Reps., 1966-72, chmn. com. on ad valorem taxation, 1969-70, chmn. judiciary com., 1971-72, mem. various coms.; chmn. Fla. Commn. on Ethics, 1974-75; trustee Miami-Dade Community Coll., 1976-84. Served with USN, 1955-58; to lt. USNR. Recipient award Fla. Acad. Trial Lawyers, 1972, 93, Fla. Patriots award Fla. Bicentennial Commn., 1976, Disting. Alumnus award U. Fla., 1977, Nelson Poynter award Fla. Civil Liberties Union, 1984, Gov.'s Emmy award Nat. Acad. TV Arts and Scis., 1985, 1st Amendment award Nat. Sigma Delta Chi/Soc. Profl. Journalists, 1986, Medal of Honor award Fla. Bar Found., 1987, Juris prudence award Anti-Defamation League of S. Fla., 1990, Fla. Acad. of Criminal Def. Lawyers Annual Justice award, 1993, Acad. of Fla. Trial Lawyers Perry Nichols award, 1993, Nat. Coun. of Jewish Women's Hannah G. Soloman award, 1996, Am. Judicature Soc. Justice award, 1996; named Outstanding First Term House Mem., 1967, Most Outstanding Mem. of House, Capital Press Corps; Rotary Found. fellowship. Mem. ABA (pres. 1991-92, chmn. spl. com. on election reform 1973-76, chmn. spl. com. on resolution of minor disputes 1976-79, chmn. spl. com. on med. malpractice 1985-86, state del. from Fla. 1980-89, commn. on governance 1983-84, rules and calender com. ho. of dels. 1982-84, commn. on women in profession 1987, chair com. rule of law project for Haiti 1993, chair nom. com. sect. dispute res. 1993, individual rights and responsibilities com., co-founder Ctrl. and East European Law Initiative, World Order Under Law award 1998, Robert J. Kutak award sect. legal edn. 1998), Fla. Bar Assn. (bd. govs. 1974-82), Dade County Bar Assn. (pres. young lawyers sect. 1965-66, bd. dirs.), Am. Judicature Soc. (pres. 1982-84), U. Fla. Law Ctr. Assn. (trustee 1967—), Order of Coif, Omicron Delta Kappa, Phi Beta Kappa. Office: Office of Pres Fla State U 211 Westcott Bldg Tallahassee FL 32306-1470

DALEN, JAMES EUGENE, physician, educator; b. Seattle, Apr. 1, 1932; s. Charles A. and Muriel E. (Joanise) Robinson. BS, Wash. State U., 1955; MA, U. Mich., 1956; MD, U. Wash., 1961; MPH, Harvard U., 1972. Intern and asst. med. resident Boston City Hosp., 1961-63; sr. resident New Eng. Med. Ctr., Boston, 1963-64; research fellow in cardiology Peter Bent Brigham Hosp., Boston, 1964-67, asso. dir. cardiovascular lab., 1967-75; instr., asst. prof., asso. prof. medicine Harvard Med. Sch., 1967-75; chmn. dept. cardiovascular medicine U. Mass. Med. Sch., 1975-77, prof., chmn. dept. medicine, 1977-88; physician-in-chief U. Mass. Hosp., 1977-88; acting chancellor U. Mass. at Worcester, 1986-87; dean, vice provost med. affairs U. Ariz. Coll. of Medicine, Tucson, 1988-95; dean, v.p. health scis. U. Ariz. Coll. Medicine, Tucson, 1995—. Contbr. articles to med. jours.; editor: Archives of Internal Medicine, 1987—. Served with USN, 1951-53. Mem. A.C.P., Assn. Univ. Cardiologists, Am. Coll. Cardiology, Am. Coll. Chest Physicians (pres. 1985-86), Am. Fedn. Clin. Research. Home: 5305 N Via Velazquez Tucson AZ 85750-5989 Office: U Ariz Coll Medicine Tucson AZ 85724-5018

D'ALENE, ALIXANDRIA FRANCES, human resources professional; b. Buffalo, Oct. 21, 1951; d. Fern (Hill D'A. BA, Canisius Coll., Buffalo, 1973, MS, 1975, MBA, 1980. Tchr. Buffalo pub. schs., 1973-76; pers. cons. Sanford Rose Assocs., Williamsville, N.Y., 1976-78; mgr. benefits adminstrn. Svc. Sys. Corp., Clarence, N.Y., 1978-80; mgr. employee rels. Del. Monte Corp., Walnut Creek, Calif., 1980-82; human resource mgmt. cons. H.R.S., Inc., Winston-Salem, N.C., 1982-87; corp. pers. specialist Advance Stroes Co., Inc., Roanoke, Va., 1987-90; pers. dir. Alfred (N.Y.) U., 1990-94; dir. human resources Framtone Connectors USA, Inc., Norwalk, Conn., 1994—; mgr. Lord Corp., Shelton, Conn., 1994-96; dir. human resources Energy Scis., Inc., Wilmington, Mass., 1999—. Mem. Assn. Pers. Adminstrs., Indsl. Pers. Soc., Coll. and U. Pers. Assn., Phi Alpha Theta. Episcopalian. Address: 250 Lynnfield St # A Peabody MA 01960-4921 Office: 42 Industrial Way Wilmington MA 01887

D'ALEO, PENNY FREW, special education educator, consultant; b. Willimantic, Conn., Jan. 15, 1961; d. Hurlburt Harrison and Bettie Jane (Bovee) Frew; m. John Francis D'Aleo, June 25, 1983; children: Gregory, Shelly. BS, So. Conn. State U., 1983; MEd, Westfield State Coll., 1987. Cert. spl. edn. tchr. pre-K and kindergarten; registered edn. tchr., adult edn. tchr., Conn. Learning disabilities specialist Suffield (Conn.) Bd. Edn., 1983-92, 94—, Enfield (Conn.) Adult Edn., 1992-94; sch. liaison Greater Suffield Learning Disabilities Assn., 1988-89; trained mentor for Conn. BEST program, 1988; conducted pvt. self-esteem workshops for exceptional children, 1992; presenter in field. Mem. adminstrv. bd. United Meth. Ch., Hazardville, Conn., 1984-87, 95—. Paul Harris fellow Rotary Internat., 1988. Mem. NEA, Coun. Exceptional Children, Learning Disabilities Assn. Am., KC Aux. (pres. 1987-88, KC Woman of Yr. 1987), Johnson Meml. Hosp. Aux. Republican. Avocations: water skiing, reading, writing, tennis, golf. Home: 41 Grant Rd Enfield CT 06082 Office: Suffield High Sch Mountain Rd Suffield CT 06078

DALEO, ROBERT, communications executive. Sr. v.p. fin. bus. devel. Thompson Corp., Stanford, Conn., 1998, exec. v.p., CFO, 1998—. Office: Thompson Corp Metro Ctr One Sta Pl Stamford CT 06902*

DALE RIIKONEN, CHARLENE BOOTHE, international health administrator; b. Washington, June 10, 1942; d. John Edward and Frances Elizabeth (Jett) Boothe; m. Esko Riikonen, 1989; children: Cynthia Lee, Anthony John, Jennifer Elizabeth. AA with high honors, Howard C.C., 1977; BA magna cum laude, U. Md., 1979. Asst. dir. univ. rels., alumni dir. U. Md., Catonsville, 1977-81; assoc. dir. univ. rels. and devel. U. Md., College Park, 1982-83; sr. devel. officer Internat. Ctr. Diarrhoeal Disease Rsch., Dhaka, Bangladesh, 1984-86; exec. v.p. Child Health Found. (formerly Internat. Child Health Found.), Columbia, Md., 1985-97; pres. Cera Products, LL., Jessup, Md., 1997—, mng. dir., CEO; cons. to organize symposium oral rehydration therapy Nat. Coun. Internat. Health, Washington, 1987; organizer internat. symposium on food-based oral rehydration therapy Aga Khan U., Pakistan, 1989; organizer consensus conf. cereal-based oral rehydration therapy, Columbia, Md., 1993. Author: (tng. manual) Prevention and Treatment of Childhood Diarrhea with Oral Rehydration Therapy, Nutrition and Breastfeeding, 1992; editor procs. Oral Rehydration Therapy Symposia, 1987, 89, 93, 94; editor Child Health News, 1993—; contbr. articles to profl. jours. Pub. affairs chmn. United Way, Washington Capital Area, Prince Georges County, 1981-83; v.p. Waterfowl Assn.; pres. Windstream Assn., 1988-89; v.p. Waterfowl Terrace Assn., 1994—; mem. pub. rels. com. Md., Del. Cable TV Assn., Balt., 1981-83. Mem. APHA (internat. maternal-child health com.), AAUW, Nat. Coun. Internat. Health Assn., U. Md. Balt. County Alumni Assn. (bd. dirs. 1979-83), Women's Internat. Pub. Health Network. Democrat. Club: Columbia Assn. Athletic (Md.) (capt. women's traveling racquetball team 1979-83). Avocations: racquetball, windsurfing, skiing, oil painting. Fax: 410-792-8671. E-mail: criikonen@ceralyte.com.

DALES, SAMUEL, microbiologist, virologist, educator; b. Warsaw, Poland, Aug. 31, 1927; emigrated to Can., 1948, naturalized, 1953; s. James and Helen (Ochs) D.; m. Laura L.R.J. Fischer, Dec. 28, 1952 (dec.); children: Adam Charles, Pamela Ann. B.A. with honors, U. B.C., 1951, M.A., 1953; Ph.D., U. Toronto, 1956. Postdoctoral fellow Nat. Cancer Inst. Can., 1957-60; research assoc., asst. prof. Rockefeller U., N.Y.C., 1960-66; assoc. mem., mem., chief cytobiology Public Health Research Inst. City of N.Y., Inc., 1966-76; prof. U. Western Ont., Can.; prof. U. Western Ont., London, Can., 1975-93, prof. emeritus, 1993—; chmn. microbiology and immunology U. Western Ont., 1975-80; research prof. NYU Med. Sch., 1969-75; mem. adv. bd. spl. virus cancer program Nat. Cancer Inst., NIH, 1969-73; mem. virology study sect. NIH, 1971-75, ad hoc, 1977, 79; mem. sci. adv. bd. Banting Research Found., 1978-80; mem. rev. panels virology and cancer USPHS, Med. Research Council Can.; adj. prof. Rockefeller U., 1996—. Author: Biology of Poxviruses, 1981; mem. editorial bd. Virology, 1963—, Jour. Cell Biology, 1973-76, Intervirology, 1973-91, Virus Rsch., 1983-92, Microbial Pathogenesis, 1985—, Jour. Virology, 1989-97, Ency. Virology, 1990-95; contbr. sci. articles and revs. to profl. publs. Fellow Royal Soc. Can.; Macy Found. scholar, 1981-82; research grantee USPHS; research grantee Med. Research Council Can.; research grantee Multiple Sclerosis Soc. Mem. Fedn. Am. Socs. for Exptl. Biology, Harvey Soc., Am. Soc. Cell Biology, N.Y. Soc. Electron Microscopy (council 1968-70), Amyotrophic Lateral Sclerosis Soc. An. (sci. adv. bd.). Home: 262 Central Park W Apt 4C New York NY 10024-3512

D'ALESANDRO, PAUL J., legislative staff member. BS, Robert Morris Coll., 1976. Bus. owner, 1984-94; caseworker Rep. Michael F. Doyle, 1994-95, cmty. rep., 1996, dist. dir., 1997—. Office: Office Rep Michael F Doyle 11 Duff Rd Penn Hills PA 15235*

D'ALESANDRO, PHILIP ANTHONY, parasitologist, immunologist, retired educator; b. Bound Brook, N.J., Apr. 2, 1927; s. Philip and Antoinette Ann (Vaccaro) D'A.; m. Rosemary Natale Falzarine, Nov. 25, 1961. BSc, Rutgers U., 1952, MSc, 1954; PhD, U. Chgo., 1958. Rsch. assoc. U. Chgo., 1958-59; assoc. prof. Rockefeller U., N.Y.C., 1959-75; assoc. prof., acting head divsn. tropical medicine Columbia U., N.Y.C., 1975-92, emeritus prof., 1992—; chmn. tropical medicine and parasitology study sect. NIH, Bethesda, Md., 1976-80. Author: (with others) Immunity to Parasitic Animals, 1970, Pathogenicity of Trypanosomes, 1979, Parasitic Protoza, Vol. 1, 1991; editor Jour. Protozoology, 1980-88; contbr. articles to profl. jours. Sgt. U.S. Army Air Corps, 1945-46. Grantee NIH, 1972-90, 79-82. Fellow AAAS; mem. Phi Beta Kappa. Avocations: antique cars, model railroading, photography.

DALESIO, WESLEY CHARLES, former aerospace educator; b. Paterson, N.J., Mar. 26, 1930; s. William James and Sarah (Sheets) Delison; m. Dorothy May Zellers, Nov. 17, 1951; children: Michael Kerry, Debra Kaye Dalesio Weber. Student, Tex. Christian U., 1950, U. Tex., Arlington, 1957. Enlisted USAF, 1948, advanced through grades to sr. master sgt., 1968; aircraft engine mech., mgmt. analyst USAF, worldwide, 1948-70; ins. agt. John Hancock Ins., Denver, 1970-71; office mgr. Comml. Builder, Denver, 1972-73; aerospace educator Sch. Dist. 50, Westminster, Colo., 1973-93; dir. aerospace edn. CAP, Denver, 1982-86, 94—. Mem. Crimestoppers, Westminster, 1988-91, Police and Citizens Teamed Against Crime, Westminster, 1992-93. Lt. col. CAP, 1981—. Mem. Nat. Assn. Ret. Mil. Instrs. (charter mem.), Westminster Edn. Assn., 7th Bomb Wing B-36 Assn., Internat. Platform Assn., Nat. Aeronautic Assn., Acad. Model Aeronautics, Arvada Associated Modelers (life). Episcopalian. Avocations: antique collecting, leatherwork, flying miniature aircraft, model car collecting. Home: 2537 W 104th Cir Westminster CO 80234-3507

D'ALESSANDRI, ROBERT M., dean; b. N.Y.C., June 26, 1945. BA, Fordham U., 1967; MD, N.Y. Med. Coll., 1971. Diplomate Am. Bd. Internal Medicine, Am. Bd. Infectious Diseases. Intern Dept. Medicine, Met. Hosp., N.Y.C., 1971-72; fellowship Divsn. Infectious Diseases, U. Fla., Gainesville, 1974-76; resident Dept. Medicine, U. Fla., Gainesville, 1976-77; instr., chief resident Dept. Medicine, W.Va. U. Sch. Medicine, 1977-78, asst. prof., 1978-81, assoc. prof., 1981-84, prof., 1985—, chief sect. of comprehensive medicine, 1979-87, assoc. dean ambulatory svcs., 1987-90, dean Sch. of Medicine, 1989—; v.p. for health scis. W.Va. U., 1992—; bd. dirs. Nat. Bank of W.Va., Morgantown, MountainView Regional Rehab. Hosp., W.Va. U. Rsch. Corp., Chestnut Ridge Psychiat. Hosp., W.Va. U. Hosps., W.Va. U. Med. Corp., Morgantown HealthRight Clinic, Morgantown Hospice; commentator Sta. WNPB, W.Va. Pub. Radio; host weekly Doctors on Call; weekly med. corr. Sta. WCHS-TV, Charleston, Sta. WDTV, Clarksbur, Sta. WTRF, Wheeling; elected shc. medicine rep. Univ. Faculty Senate, 1980-84; chair credentials com. W.Va. Hosps., 1984-85, med. exec. bd. chair 1985-86, chair infection control com., 1985-86, exec. com. chair 1986-87, mem. 1983-87, chair hosp. med. records com., 1986-87, chair hosps. patient care rev. com., 1986-87, chair ambulatory care bldg. com., 1987-89, chair dean's com. VA Med. Ctr., Martinsburg, 1991—, Clarksburg, 1989—; chair sch. of medicine ednl. adv. coun. W.Va. U. Health Scis. Ctr., 1989—, chair sch. of medicine exec. faculty, 1989—, chair health scis. ctr. exec. com., 1992—; coord. intro. clin. medicine dental studies, 1979-84, coord. intro. to clin. medicine, phys. diagnosis course, 1979-84; spl. lectr. Guiyang (China) Med. Coll., 1988, Hangzhou (China) Red Cross Hosp., 1988. Contbr. numerous articles to profl. jours. Bd. dirs. Monongalia Arts Ctr., Morgantown, 1989—. Mem. AMA, Am. Coll. of Physicians, Infectious Diseases Soc., Soc. for Gen. Internal Medicine, Nat. Rural Health Assn., W.Va. State Med. Assn., Monongalia County Med. Soc. Office: 1150 Health Sciences North RC Byrd Health Scis Ctr PO Box 9000 Morgantown WV 26506-9000*

D'ALESSANDRO, DANIEL ANTHONY, lawyer, educator; b. Jersey City, Oct. 10, 1949; s. Donato Marino D'Alessandro and Rose Teresa (Casamassimo) Drennan; m. Beth Anne Lill, Sept. 2, 1978; children: Daniel Patrick, Eric Charles. BA, St. Peter's Coll., 1971; JD, Seton Hall U., 1974; LLM in Criminal Justice, NYU, 1981. Bar: N.J. 1975, U.S. Dist. Ct. N.J. 1975, N.Y. 1982, U.S. Supreme Ct. 1985, U.S. Dist. Ct. (so. dist.) N.Y. 1989. Law clk. to presiding judge Juvenile and Domestic Relations Ct., Hudson County, N.J., 1974-75; pub. defender City of Jersey City, 1975-76; prosecutor Town of Secaucus, N.J., 1976-77; prin. D'Alessandro & Assocs., Jersey City, 1977-82; ptnr. D' Alessandro & Tutak, Jersey City, 1982-90; pres. D'Alessandro, Tutak & Aschoff, P.C., Jersey City, 1990-92; ptnr. D'Alessandro & Aschoff, P.C., Jersey City, 1993-94; pvt. practice Jersey City, 1994—; adj. prof. Middlesex County Coll., Edison, N.J., 1981-83, St. Peter's Prep., 1981-83; arbitrator automobile arbitration program N.J. Supreme Ct.; mem. ethics com. N.J. Supreme Ct. Dist. VI; counsel Employees Retirement System of Jersey City, 1985-89; vice-chair fee arbitration com. Supreme Ct. N.J. Vol. probation officer Hudson County Probation Dept., 1977; pro bono counsel Anthony R. Cucci Civic Assn., Jersey City, 1981-89; pro bono counsel Battered Women's Shelter, Jersey City, 1982; pro bono counsel Mayor's Task Force for Handicapped, Jersey City, 1985-89; v.p. Jersey City Boys Club, 1991, pres., 1993—, also trustee; baseball coach Jersey Shore Thunderbirds, N.J. AAU, 1993-99. Named Prof. of Yr., Secaucus (N.J.) Patrolmen's Benevolent Assn., 1980; recipient Disting. Svc. award Jersey City Police Dept., 1988, Cert. of Merit, N.J. Supreme Ct., Meritorious Pub. Svc. award, 1990, Outstanding Bd. Mem. award N.J. Boys Clubs Coun., 1991, Outstanding Bd. Mem. award Boys and Girls Clubs of Hudson County, 1998. Mem. ABA, N.J. State Bar Assn., Hudson County Bar Assn. (past chmn., mem. various coms., trustee, treas. 1991, sec. 1992, v.p. 1994, 95, pres-elect 1996, pres. 1997—, Outstanding Bd. Mem. award 1998). Democrat. Roman Catholic. Avocations: renovating old homes, sports, photography. Office: 3279 John F Kennedy Blvd Jersey City NJ 07306-3418

D'ALESSANDRO, DAVID FRANCIS, financial services company executive; b. Utica, N.Y., Jan. 6, 1951; s. Dominick Vincent and Rosemary (Pallaria) D'A.; children: Michael, Andrew. BA, Utica Coll. of Syracuse U., 1972. Account supr. Daniel J. Edelman Inc. Pub. Rels., 1972-74; info. programs mgr. svc. bur. Control Data Corp., 1974-77, communications mgr.

data svcs., 1977-79, gen. mgr. comml. credit, 1980-84; asst. v.p. Citibank Communications Svcs., 1979-80; v.p. John Hancock Fin. Svcs., Boston, 1984-85, sr. v.p., 1985-88, pres. corp. sector, mem. mgt. com., 1988-91, sr. exec. v.p. retail sector, 1991—, pres., 1996, also bd. dirs. Trustee, mem. exec. com. Wang Ctr. for Performing Arts, Boston, 1989—; chmn. Harvard U. Kennedy Sch. Govt., 1990—; bd. trustees Syracuse U., 1990—, Utica (N.Y.) Coll., 1988—. Office: John Hancock Fin Svcs 200 Clarendon St Boston MA 02116-5021*

D'ALESSANDRO, DIANNE MARIE, public defender; b. N.Y.C., Apr. 20, 1952; d. Frank and Marie A. D'A.; m. John P. Foley, July 24, 1977; children: Maria, James. BA in Psychology, Upsala Coll., East Orange, N.J., 1974; JD, N.Y. Law Sch., 1981. Bar: N.J. 1981, N.Y. 1990, U.S. Dist. Ct. N.J. 1981. Staff atty. Bergen City Legal Svc., Hackensack, N.J., 1981-83; sr. trial atty. Office Pub. Defender, Hackensack, 1983—; dist. II B ethics com., Office of Atty. Ethics of the Supreme Ct. of N.J., 1992-95; bd. dirs. Bergen County Legal Svc. Recipient citation from Susan Reisner, pub. advocate, for work done on State vs. Harris. Mem. Assn. Criminal Def. Lawyers, Women Lawyers in Bergen County. Avocations: reading, hiking, historic preservation. Office: Office of Pub Advocate/Pub Defender 60 State St Hackensack NJ 07601-5451

D'ALESSANDRO, DOMINIC, financial executive; b. Italy, Jan. 18, 1947; arrived in Can., 1954; 3 children. BSc., Loyola Coll., 1967; postgrad., McGill U., 1971. Acct. Coopers & Lybrand, 1968-75, dep. mgr. Paris office, 1970-71; asst. controller GenStar, Ltd., 1975; from dir. fin. to gen. mgr. GenStar, Saudi Arabia, 1976-79; v.p. Materials and Constrn. Group, San Francisco, 1979-81; dep. comptroller Royal Bank of Can., Toronto, 1981, v.p. and comptroller, 1982, sr. v.p., 1983-87, exec. v.p. fin., 1987; pres., CEO Laurentian Bank of Can., 1988, Manulife Fin., Toronto, 1994—; also bd. dirs. ManuLife Fin., Toronto; bd. dirs. Hudson's Bay Co.; adv. bd. Schroder Can., Ltd., Willis Corroon Melling, Inc.; vice-chmn. Canadian Life and Health Ins. Assn.; bd. dirs. Am. Coun. of Life Ins., Washington, TransCan. Pipelines. Mem. Bus. Coun. on Nat. Issues; chmn. United Way of Greater Toronto, 1998. Fellow Inst. Chartered Accts. (chartered). Office: Manulife Financial, 200 Bloor St E, Toronto, ON Canada M4W 1E5

D'ALESSIO, DAVID WESLEY, communications educator; b. Glen Head, N.Y., May 7, 1956; s. John Joseph and Helen (Munn) D'A. BS in Comm., Rensselaer Poly. Inst., 1978, MS in Comm., 1980; PhD in Comm., Mich. State U., 1997. Chemist Schenectady Chems., Nyskayuna, N.Y., 1978-80; grad. asst. Mich. State U., East Lansing, 1980-85; instr. Albion (Mich.) Coll., 1985-86, Grand Valley State U., Allendale, Mich., 1986-88; ops. mgr. GRTV, Grand Rapids, Mich., 1989-91; adj. prof. Lansing (Mich.) C.C., 1991-93; asst. prof. comm. Richard Stockton Coll., Pomona, N.J., 1993-97, U. Conn., Stamford, 1997—. Animator (film) The Three Penny Operation, 1990 (Philo award 1991); contbr. articles to profl. jours. Ops. dir. Galloway (N.J.) TV, 1995-97. Named Bd. Mem. of Yr. Jaycees, Grand Rapids, 1990. Mem. Internat. Comm. Assn. (reviewer 1995—), Nat. Comm. Assn., N.J. Comm. Assn., Assn. Internat. du Film d'Animation. Avocations: reading, golf, model trains.

DALESSIO, DONALD JOHN, physician, neurologist, educator; b. Jersey City, Mar. 2, 1931; s. John Andrea and Susan Dorothy (Minotta) D.; m. Jane Catherine Schneider, Sept. 4, 1954 (dec. Mar. 1998); children: Catherine Leah, James John, Susan Jane. BA, Wesleyan U., 1952; MD, Yale U., 1956. Diplomate Am. Bd. Internal Medicine. Intern in medicine N.Y.C. Hosp., 1956-57, asst. resident in medicine and neurology, 1959-61; resident in medicine Yale Med. Ctr., 1961-62; pres. med. staff Scripps Clinic, La Jolla, Calif., 1974-78; chmn. dept. medicine Scripps Clin., La Jolla, Calif., 1974-89, chmn. emeritus, 1989—, cons., 1982—, pres. med. group, 1980-81; clin. prof. neurology U. Calif., San Diego, 1973—; physician in chief Green Hosp., La Jolla, 1974-89; Musser-Burch lectr. Tulane U., 1979, Kash lectr. U. Ky., 1979; pres. Am. Assn. Study Headache, Chgo., 1974-76, Nat. Migraine Found., Chgo., 1977-79; chmn. Fedn. Western Soc. Neurology, Santa Barbara, Calif., 1976-77. Author: Wolff's Headache, 6th edit., 1993, Approach to Headache, 1973, 5th edit., 1992; editor: Headache jour., 1965-75, 79-84, Scripps Clinic Personal Health Letter; mem. editorial bd.: Jour. AMA, 1977-87; columnist San Diego Tribune. Capt. U.S. Army, 1957-59. Recipient Disting. Alumnus award Wesleyan U., Middletown, Conn., 1982. Fellow ACP; mem. Am. Acad. Neurology (assoc.), World Fedn. Neurology (Am. sec. 1980-90, rsch. group on migraine), La Jolla Country Club, La Jolla Beach/Tennis Club. Republican. Roman Catholic. Avocations: tennis, squash, piano. Home: 8891 Nottingham Pl La Jolla CA 92037-2131 Office: Scripps Clinic & Rsch Found 10666 N Torrey Pines Rd La Jolla CA 92037-1092

D'ALESSIO, FREDERICK D., telecommunications company executive. BSEE, N.J. Inst. Tech., MS in Engring.; MBA, Rutgers U. With N.J. Bell, from 1971; v.p. ops. and engring. Bell Atlantic Corp., 1990-91; pres., CEO, Bell Atlantic-Md., Inc., 1991-95; pres. Bell Atlantic-Consumer Svcs., Arlington, Va., 1995—. Bd. govs. Nat. Aquarium, Balt.; bd. dirs. Balt. Symphony Orch., Greater Balt. Com., Inc., Kennedy Krieger Inst.; trustee Goucher Coll. Office: Bell Atlantic-Consumer Svcs 1310 N Court House Rd Ste 1 Arlington VA 22201-2586*

DALEY, ARTHUR JAMES, retired magazine publisher; b. St. Paul, Aug. 15, 1916; s. John and Mary (Mayer) D.; m. Lorayne Mary Mongan, June 7, 1941; children—Michael, Kay. Student pub. schs., Fond du Lac, Wis. Advt. salesman Fond du Lac Commonwealth Reporter, 1936, sports editor, 1937-40; sports writer Green Bay (Wis.) Press-Gazette, 1941-43, sports editor, 1946-68, telegraph, picture editor, 1968-78; pub. Green Bay Packer Yearbook, 1960-83, assoc. pub., 1984-88, ret., 1988; columnist Green Bay Packer Report, 1974—. Mem. Wis. Hall of Fame Com. Served with AUS, 1943-46, ETO. Inducted into Green Bay Packer Hall of Fame, 1993. Mem. Pro Football Writers Am., Nat. Football League Alumni Assn. Club: Oneida Golf and Riding. Home: 1146 Highview Ln Green Bay WI 54304-2222

DALEY, ARTHUR STUART, retired humanities educator; b. Osceola, N.Y., Sept. 16, 1908; s. Kieran A. and Mary (Adams) D.; m. Jean Abendroth, Aug. 29, 1942; 1 child, Arthur Stuart. AB with honors in English, Syracuse U., 1932; postgrad., Harvard U., 1932-33; PhD, Yale U., 1942. Instr. English Syracuse (N.Y.) U., 1935-37, Ind. U., 1946-47, UCLA, 1947-49; asst. prof. English U. Nev., 1949-54; prof., chmn. dept. Coe Coll., 1954-59; prof. Drake U., Des Moines, 1959-76, chmn. dept., 1959-67, coord. humanities div., 1967-75, prof. emeritus, 1976—. Co-author: Private Charity in England, 1747-57, 1938; contbr. articles, especially on Shakespeare, to profl. jours.; contbr. articles to rev. Norton crit. edit. Wuthering Heights (Emily Bronte), Shakespeare Studies XXI, The Upstart Crow XIV. Served to lt. col. AUS, 1941-46, 51-53; lt. col. AUS ret. Decorated Bronze Star; hon. grant of English armorial bearings, 1978; mem. by right Ancient and Hon. Arty. Co. Mass. Mem. MLA, Soc. Mayflower Descs., Shakespeare Assn., Brontë Soc., Theta Alpha Phi, Sigma Nu. Home: 2705 Barnson Pl San Diego CA 92103-6103

DALEY, CHARLES MIKE, vehicle recovery company executive; b. Boston, June 7, 1936; s. Francis Daniel and Kathleen (Gillin) D.; m. Janet Marie Richards, Aug. 24, 1957; children: Stephen M., Kevin F., Thomas P., Mary E. BS, Boston Coll., 1958. With S.S. Kresge Co., Boston and Burlington, Vt., 1958-59; sales staff Libby McNeill & Libby, Chgo., 1960-63; account exec. J. Daren & Sons, Norwich, Conn., 1963-66; CEO, pres., treas. Daley Care Mgmt. Co., Boston, 1966-88; CEO, chmn., treas. Lojack Corp., Dedham, Mass., 1986—; bd. dirs., v.p., pres., chmn. Mass. Fedn. Nursing Homes, Boston; v.p., pres. Mass. Health Coun., Boston; trustee, vice chmn., chmn. Emmanuel Coll., Boston. Pres. Norwich (Conn.) Jaycees; v.p. Conn. Jaycees; state chmn., v.p., nat. dir., pres., chmn. Mass. Jaycees, 1966-72. Named Man of Yr., Norwich C. of C., 1965, Disting. Nursing Home Adminstr., Boston chpt. Am. Coll. Nursing Home Adminstrs. Mem. Boston Coll. Club (founder), Boston Coll. Alumni Assn., Oyster Harbors Club, Bonita Bay Country Club. Roman Catholic. Avocations: music, walking, art and antique collecting, boating. Home: 60 Elm St Canton MA 02021-1230 Office: Lojack Corp 333 Elm St Dedham MA 02026-4549

DALEY, JOHN TERENCE, priest; b. Birkenhead, U.K., Jan. 5, 1918; came to U.S., 1992; s. William Joseph and Teresa (Baker) D. Cert., Cotton Coll., U.K., 1936; lic. philosophy, Gregorian U., Rome, 1939; lic. theology, Gregorian U., 1943; grad., Ven. Coll. English, Rome, 1943. Ordained priest Roman Cath. Ch., 1943. Curate Roman Cath. Diocese, Shrewsbury, U.K., 1943-57; pastor St. Thomas' Tarporley, Cheshire, U.K., 1957-62; pastor Our Lady's Warrington, Cheshire, 1962-91, pastor emeritus, 1991; assoc. Holy Spirit Ch., New Hyde Park, N.Y., 1994—. Home: 500 Jericho Tpke New Hyde Park NY 11040-4511

DALEY, LAURANA BUSH, elementary education educator; b. Lowville, N.Y., May 27, 1951; d. Phillip M. and Shirley F. (Secor) Bush; m. Bernard S. Daley, Apr. 22, 1972; children: Greg David, Andrea Lynne. BS in Phys. Edn., SUNY, Brockport, 1972; MS in Elem. Edn., SUNY, Potsdam, 1980; CAS in Ednl. Adminstrn., SUNY, Oswego, 1996. Permanent tchg. cert., permanent sch. dist. adminstr. cert., N.Y. Substitute tchr. Lowville, Beaver River, South Lewis Dists., 1972; tchr. grade 5 Beaver River Ctrl. Sch., Beaver Falls, N.Y., 1972-73; tchr. title 1 math. Jefferson-Lewis Bd. Coop. Ednl. Svcs., Lowville, 1974-75, 77-81; intermediate classroom tchr. Lowville Acad. and Ctrl. Sch., 1981—, adminstrv. intern, 1995-96, spl. projects coord., 1996—, K-12 tech. chair, model schs. site adminstr., 1997—; coach, advisor Synchronized Swim Club, Lowville, 1974—; workshop instr. Jefferson-Lewis Bd. Coop. Ednl. Svcs., Watertown, N.Y., 1996—; faculty adv. com. Nat. Honor Soc., Lowville, 1996—. Mem. ASCD, Lowville Tchrs. Assn. (v.p. 1994—, liaison chairperson 1995—), Phi Delta Kappa (nat. founds. chair 1996—, ednl. found. chair, chairperson/newsletter editor). Avocations: swimming, basket-weaving, silver jewelry making, reading, crafts. Home: RR 2 Box 245E Lowville NY 13367-9577 Office: Lowville Acad and Ctrl Sch 7668 State St Lowville NY 13367

DALEY, PAMELA, lawyer; b. Springfield, Mass., Oct. 1, 1952; d. Edward Murray and Elizabeth Bloom Daley; m. Randall Lee Phelps, Aug. 26, 1995. AB summa cum laude in Romance Langs. and Lit., Princeton U., 1974; JD magna cum laude, U. Pa., 1979. Bar: Pa. 1979, N.Y. 1991. Lectr. partnership taxation law U. Pa., Phila., 1982-89; assoc. tax sect. Morgan, Lewis & Bockius, Phila., 1979-86, ptnr., 1986-89; tax counsel GE, Fairfield, Conn., 1989-91, v.p., sr. counsel for transactions, 1991—; bd. outside advisor Va. Tax Review assn., 1982-92. Editor-in-chief U. Pa. Law Review; contbr. articles to profl. jours. Trustee MacDuffie Sch., Springfield, 1986-92; bd. govs. Pa. Economy League, 1986-89; mem. bd. overseers Law Sch. U. Pa., 1999—; bd. dirs. G.E. Fund, 1999—. Teaching fellow Salzburg Seminar on Am. Law and Legal Instns., 1986; named to Acad. Women Achievers YWCA, 1992. Mem. Am. Corp. Counsel Assn., Order Coif, Phi Beta Kappa. Office: GE 3135 Easton Tpke #W3A Fairfield CT 06431-0002

DALEY, PAUL PATRICK, lawyer; b. Boston, July 10, 1941; s. Patrick Joseph and Catherine Josephine (Ford) D.; m. Barbara Sabin, May 24, 1980; 1 child, Patrick. AB, Boston Coll., 1963; MBA, Harvard U., 1973, JD, 1973. Bar: Mass. 1973, N.Y. 1983, U.S. Supreme Ct., U.S. Ct. Appeals (1st cir.) 1974, U.S. Ct. Appeals (5th cir.) 1980, U.S. Ct. Appeals (2d cir.) 1998. Assoc. Hale and Dorr, Boston, 1973-78, jr. ptnr., 1978-82, sr. ptnr., 1982—; lectr. CLE programs. Contbr. articles to profl. jours. Trustee Mass. Sch. Profl. Psychology, Boston, 1985—, chair, 1994—; trustee St. Sebastians Sch., Boston, 1981, Naval War Coll. Found., 1996—; bd. dirs. Am. Sail Train Assn., Newport, R.I., 1982-86. Capt. USNR, 1965-67, Vietnam. Decorated DFC, Air Medals (16). Fellow Am. Coll. Bankruptcy; mem. ABA, Mass. Bar Assn. (chmn. bus. bank com., bus. law sect.), Boston Bar Assn. (coun.), Am. Bankruptcy Inst., Nat. Def. U. Found., U.S. Naval Inst., Naval Res. Assn., Comml. Law League, Windsor Club (Waban, Mass.), Braeburn Country Club, Wardroom Club. Democrat. Roman Catholic. Avocations: flying, scuba diving, running, reading, theater. E-mail: paul.daley@haledorr.com. Home: 9 Crofton Rd Waban MA 02468-1931 Office: Hale and Dorr 60 State St Boston MA 02109-1816

DALEY, PETER EDMUND, business and human resources company executive; b. Washington, Mar. 28, 1943; s. Edmund Frances and Marie (Herbert) D.; BS, Wheeling Coll., 1966; MBA, U. Md., 1968; JD, U. Balt., 1975; m. Alexandra Stanish, June 27, 1970; children: Peter, Gina, Melissa, Angela, Thomas, Paul, Alexis, Kara, Nikos. With Westinghouse Electric Co., Balt., 1970-75, Pitts., 1975-77; corp. mgr. compensation benefits PHH Group, Hunt Valley, Md., 1977-78, corp. mgr. human resources, 1978-79, dir. human resources, 1979-81; dir. employee relations Fairchild Industries, 1981-83; v.p. human resources and adminstrv. services Fairchild Space and Fairchild Communications and Electronics Cos., 1983-84; pres., CEO P.M.A. Inc., 1985-90; dir. Washington Hosp. Ctr., Washington, 1991-95; pres. Harbor Consulting Group, 1995-97; v.p. human resources and adminstrn. Digex, Inc., 1997—. Bd. dirs. Girl Scouts U.S. Central Md., 1978-81; mem. exec. adv. com. indsl. relations and labor studies U. Md., mem. Naval Indsl. Facilities Adv. Panel. Mem. ABA, Am. Mgmt. Assn., Am. Assn. Personnel Adminstrs., Md. Bar Assn., Greater Balt. Personnel Assocs., Am. Compensation Assn. Home: 411 Deacon Brook Cir Reisterstown MD 21136-2228

DALEY, RICHARD MICHAEL, mayor; b. Chgo., Apr. 24, 1942; s. Richard J. and Eleanor (Guilfoyle) D.; m. Margaret Corbett, Mar. 25, 1972; children: Nora, Patrick, Elizabeth. B.A., DePaul U., Chgo., 1964, J.D., 1968. Bar: Ill. 1969. Ptnr. Simon and Daley, Chgo., 1970-72, Daley, Riley & Daley, Chgo., 1972-80; mem. Ill. State Senate, 1973-80, chmn. Judiciary I Com., 1975, 77; state's atty. Cook County, Ill., 1980-89; mayor Chgo., 1989—. Bd. dirs. Little City Home; mem. Citizens Bd. U. Chgo.; mem. adv. bd. Mercy Hosp., Chgo.; bd. mgrs. Valentine Boys Club; active Nativity of Our Lord Parish, Chgo. Recipient Golden Rule plaque Chgo. Boys Club Am.; named Outstanding Legislator of Yr., Lt. Gov's. Sr. Legis. Forum, 1979, Outstanding Leader in Revision of Ill. Mental Health Code, Ill. Assn. Retarded Citizens, 1979, Outstanding Leader, Ill. Assn. Social workers, 1978. Mem. Chgo. Bar Assn., Ill. State Bar Assn., ABA, Cath. Lawyers Guild. Democrat. Roman Catholic. Office: Office of the Mayor City Hall Rm 507 121 N La Salle St Chicago IL 60602-1202*

DALEY, ROBERT EMMETT, foundation executive, retired; b. Cleve., Mar. 13, 1933; s. Emmett Wilfred and Anne Gertrude (O'Donnell) D.; m. Mary Bernieta Fredericks, June 7, 1958; children: Marianne Fredericks, John Gerard. BA in English, U. Dayton, 1955; MA in Polit. Sci., Ohio State U., 1968, MA in Pub. Adminstrn., 1976. Local govt. reporter, Washington corr., fin. editor Jour. Herald, Dayton, Ohio, 1957-65, pub. affairs reporter, 1967; staff writer Congressional Quarterly, Inc., Washington, 1966; pub. affairs reporter Dayton Daily News, Dayton, 1969; dir. pub. affairs & communications Charles F. Kettering Found., Dayton, 1977-94, ret., now assoc., 1994—; part-time copy boy, sports reporter Jour. Herald, Dayton, 1953-55. Past pres., bd. trustees St. Joseph Home for Children; former mem. adv. bd. Ctr. for Religious Telecomms., U. Dayton; traveling press sec. sen. candidate John J. Gilligan, 1968, for gubernatorial candidate, 1970-71, asst. to Gov. Gilligan, 1971-75; media rels. dir. Nat. League of Cities, Washington, 1976-77; mem. Montgomery County Hist. Soc.; past mem. Ind. Sector Pub. Info. & Edn. Com. With U.S. Army, 1955-57. Mem. Pub. Rels. Soc. Am., Soc. Profl. Journalists, Nat. Press Club, KC, Ancient Order Hibernians. Roman Catholic. Home: 888 Cranbrook Ct Dayton OH 45459-1525 Office: Charles F Kettering Found 200 Commons Rd Dayton OH 45459-2788

DALEY, RON (RONALD EUGENE DALEY), playwright, poet, director, producer; b. Washington, Sept. 24, 1945; s. Russell Eugene and Dorothy Sybil (Krouse) D.; m. Virginia Ann Bean, Nov. 7, 1986; children: Jackson Phillip Wesley, Bryan Augustin, Geoffrey Eugene. BA in Philosophy, North Park Coll., 1967; MA in English with honors, Roosevelt U., 1968; MA in Drama, Syracuse U., 1975. Instr. English/Philosophy Malcolm X C.C., Chgo., 1968-70, Orange County C.C., Middletown, N.Y., 1970-73; English N.Y.C. C.C., Bklyn., 1975-78; dir./designer many theatre companies, 1978-80; producer Jerron Prodns., N.Y.C., 1980-81; assoc. artistic dir. New World Theatre, N.Y.C., 1981-82; artistic dir. Nat. Shakespeare Co., N.Y.C., 1982-85; resident dir./producer Riverside Shakespeare Co., N.Y.C., 1986; exec. dir. RED Prodns., Argyle, Wis., 1985—; guest dir. Broom St. Theatre, Madison, 1987-94, Classic Theatre, N.Y.C., 1979-84, AMDA Studio One, N.Y.C., 1977-78, Camden (Maine) Shakespeare Festival, 1979, Mercury Players, Madison, 1994—. Author of plays off Broadway including Beyond the Veil, Damphools and Wowsers, Argyle Wisconsin 53504, In the Matter of John David Hutchins, It's Gotta Be the Shoes, Nobody Dies, 5:45, Badger Orpheus, The Third Blackhawk War, Journeys with Nanabozo, The Abrazo, The Knight of the Burning Pestle, The Red Palace; editor Amphibious Maneuvers. Prodr. Free Shakespeare in the Parks, N.Y.C., 1986. Mem Soc. of Stage Dirs. and Choreographers, Dramatists Guild, Chgo. Area Playwrights, U.S. Holocaust Meml. Mus., ACLU. Avocations: fishing, gardening, carpentry. Home: 17740 River Rd Argyle WI 53504-9726

DALEY, SANDRA, retired artist, filmmaker, photographer; b. Fargo, N.D., Feb. 28, 1940; d. Cecil Raymond and Margaret (Anderson) D. AB cum laude, Oberlin Coll., 1961; MFA with high distinction, Calif. Coll. Arts and Crafts, 1965. Artist, photographer show (with Nicholas Quennell) Dwan Gallery, L.A., 1965; prodr., dir. film: (with Sally Potter) London Mysteries, 1964, (with Robert Mapplethorpe and Patti Smith) Robert Having His Nipple Pierced, 1970, (with Patti Smith, Sam Shepard and Vali) Patti Having Her Knee Tattooed, 1971. Avocations: writing, drawing. Home: 504 Marlborough Rd Brooklyn NY 11226-6516

DALEY, VETA ADASSA, educational administrator; b. St. Elizabeth, Jamaica, Jan. 14, 1953; came to U.S., 1981; d. Waldemar and Princess (Bartley) Solomon; m. Vincent Daley, Jan. 27, 1973; children: Yuland, Angelo. Cert. in edn., U. W.I., Jamaica, 1978; BS, Westfield (Mass.) State Coll., 1987, MEd in Adminstrn., 1991. Tchr. Ministry Edn., Jamaica, 1972-81, Forest Park Jr.-Mid. Sch., Springfield, Mass., 1987-92; grad. asst. Westfield State Coll., 1988-90; asst. prin. Duggan Mid. Sch., Springfield, 1992-94; prin. John F. Kennedy Mid. Sch., Springfield, 1994—; Mem. Mass. Curriculum Adv. Commn., Malden, 1992—. Advisor Jamaica Festival Commn., Mandeville, 1973-80, Jamaica 4-H Clubs, 1970-76; vice chmn. adminstrv. bd. Wesley United Meth. Ch., Springfield, 1988—, pres. Meth. Women, 1991-93; chmn. Liberian Christian Fund, Springfield, 1990, New Eng. Conf. United Meth. Women, 1994; mem. African Task Force-R.I., 1991—. Recipient Outstanding Achievement award Jamaica 4-H Clubs, 1975, Outstanding Achievement in Edn. award Jamaican Cmty., Springfield, 1992, citation Mass. Ho. of Reps., 1992. Mem. New Eng. League Mid. Schs., Springfield Adminstrv. Assn., Jack and Jill Am. (pres. Springfield chpt. 1992—, Disting. Mother of Yr. award ea. region 1994). Home: 81 Embury St Springfield MA 01109-1847 Office: John F Kennedy Mid Sch 1385 Berkshire Ave Indian Orch MA 01151-1360

DALEY, VINCENT RAYMOND, JR., real estate executive, consultant; b. Evanston, Ill., June 21, 1940; s. Vincent R. and Carole V. (Johnson) D.; m. Viola Elizabeth Bursiek, May 6, 1967; children: Kathleen Marie, Colleen Patricia. *Wife Vi Daley, was elected Alderman of the City of Chicago 43rd Ward (Lincoln Park, Gold Coast Area). The 43rd Ward in the city represents 63,000 people, has a direct paid staff of 5 plus a Street & Sanitation section of 15. His youngest daughter Colleen (25) is the Chief of Staff for Illinois State Representative John Fritichy. Daughter Kathleen (27) is a freelance graphic designer specializing in election campaigns (Presidential, State of Illinois, and Local Government).* AA, Lincoln Coll., 1961; BS, Loyola U., Chgo., 1963; student in real estate, Roosevelt U., 1964. From salesman to store mgr. Sears Roebuck & Co., Chgo., 1962-73; v.p., cons. Kencoe Corp., Des Plaines, Ill., 1973-74; pres. Daley & Assocs., Chgo., 1974—; chmn. Wacker Real Estate Svcs., Chgo., 1997—; chmn. Wacker Mgmt. Corp., Chgo. Mem. Econ. Devel. Com., State of Ill., Springfield, 1985-88; legis. asst. 8th Legis. Dist., Chgo., 1985-93. Men. Chgo. Bd. Realtors (life) (bd. dirs.), Nat. Assn. Realtors (bd. regents), Ill. Assn. Realtors (bd. dirs.), Realtors Land Inst. (bd. govs.), Realtors Nat. Mktg. Inst. (CCIM), Internat. Real Estate Fed. (sr. cert. valuerer, registered internat. mem., cert. investment financier). Democrat. Roman Catholic. Avocation: traveling. Home: 1807 N Orleans St Chicago IL 60614-5325 Office: Daley & Assocs 400 N Michigan Ave Ste 415 Chicago IL 60611-4129 also: Wacker Real Estate Svcs 400 N Michigan Ave Ste 415 Chicago IL 60611-4129

DALEY, WILLIAM M., federal government official; m. Loretta Daley; 3 children. BA, Loyola U.; LLB, John Marshall Law Sch., Chgo., LLD (hon.). Bar: Ill. 1975. With Daley and George, Chgo.; ptnr. Mayer, Brown & Platt; vice chmn. Amalgamated Bank, Chgo., 1989, pres., COO, 1990-93; sec. Dept. Commerce, Washington, 1997—; spl. counsel to Pres. for NAFTA. Recipient St. Ignatius award fro Excellence in the Practice of Law, 2995, World Trade award World Trade Ctr., Chgo., 1994. Office: Dept Commerce Herbert C Hoover Bldg Rm 5854 14th St and Constitution Ave NW Washington DC 20230*

D'ALFONSO, MARIO JOSEPH, lawyer, consultant; b. Phila., Nov. 3, 1951; s. Albert Carmine and Yolanda (Zanfrisco) D'A.; m. Rita F. Borrelli, Apr. 26, 1975; 1 child, Mario C. BA, Villanova U., 1973; JD, Widener U., 1979. Bar: Pa. 1979, N.J. 1979, U.S. Dist. Ct. (ea. dist.) Pa. 1979, U.S. Dist. Ct. N.J. 1979, U.S. Ct. Appeals (3rd dist.) 1980, U.S. Supreme Ct. 1983, U.S. Ct. Appeals (5th cir.) 1989. Assoc. Avena, Hendren & Friedman, Camden, N.J., 1979-81; ptnr. Avena, Hendren, Friedman & D'Alfonso, 1981-84, D'Alfonso & Camacho, P.A., Haddon Heights, N.J., 1984—; cons. Marbert Construction, Haddon Heights, N.J., 1982—. Mem. Am. Arbitration Assn. (Service award 1984), Assn. Criminal Def. Lawyers, Camden County Bar Assn., N.J. Trial Lawyers Assn., Phi Delta Phi (pres. 1978), Phi Kappa Phi. Roman Catholic. Home: 64 Lady Diana Cir Marlton NJ 08053-3705 Office: 304 White Horse Pike Haddon Heights NJ 08035-1705

DALINKA, MURRAY KENNETH, radiologist, educator; b. Bklyn., May 13, 1938; s. Joseph and Gertrude (Cohen) D.; m. Janice L. Kolber, Feb. 28, 1982; 1 son, Bradford Gordon; children by previous marriage: Ilene, Ian Scott. BS, U. Mich., 1960, MD, 1964. Diplomate Am. Bd. Radiology. Intern Pa. Hosp., Phila., 1964-65; resident in radiology Montefiore Hosp., N.Y.C., 1965-68; instr. radiology Harvard Med. Sch., 1970-71; from asst. prof. to assoc. prof. radiology Thomas Jefferson U. Hosp., Phila., 1971-76, prof., 1976—; chief orthop. radiology Hosp. U. Pa., 1976—; chief diagnostic radiology Thomas Jefferson U. Hosp., Phila., 1974-76; . cons.hila. Naval Hosp., 1974-79, Walson Hosp., Ft. Dix Army Base, 1972-77. Author: Arthography, 1980, Symposium on Orthopedic Radiology, 1983; mem. editorial bd. Bone Syllabus IV, 1982—, Skeletal Radiology, 1982—, Conversations in Radiology, 1977-79; guest editor Emergency Medicine Clinics of North America, Vol. 3, 1985; editor: (with J.J. Kaye) Radiology in Emergency Medicine Clinics in Emergency, Vol. 3, 1984, (with J. Edeiken and D. Karasick) Edeiken's Roentgen Diagnosis of Diseases of Bone, 4th edit. Served to capt. USAF, 1968-70. James Picker research fellow, 1972-73. Mem. Internat. Skeletal Soc. (past pres.), Radiol. Soc. N.Am., Am. Coll. Radiology, Phila. Roentgen Ray Soc. (past pres.). Home: 318 S 21st St Philadelphia PA 19103-6531 Office: U Pa Hosp Dept Radiology 3400 Spruce St Philadelphia PA 19104-4204

DALIS, IRENE, mezzo-soprano, opera company administrator, music educator; b. San Jose, Calif., Oct. 8, 1925; d. Peter Nicholas and Mamie Rose (Boitano) D.; m. George Loinaz, July 16, 1957; 1 child, Alida Mercedes. AB, San Jose State Coll., 1946; MA in Teaching, Columbia U., 1947; MMus (hon.), San Jose State U., 1957; studied voice with, Edyth Walker, N.Y.C., 1947-50, Paul Althouse, 1950-51, Dr. Otto Mueller, Milan, Italy, 1952-72; MusD (hon.), Santa Clara U., 1987. Prin. artist Berlin Opera, 1955-65, Met. Opera, N.Y.C., 1957-77, San Francisco Opera, 1958-73, Hamburg (Fed. Republic Germany) Staatsoper, 1966-71; prof. music San Jose State U., Calif., 1977—; founder, gen. dir. Opera San Jose, 1984—; dir. Met. Opera Nat. Auditions, San Jose dist., 1980-88. Operatic debut as dramatic mezzo-soprano Oldenburgisches Staatstheater, 1953, Berlin Staedtische Opera, 1955; debut Met. Opera, N.Y.C., 1957, 1st Am.-born singer, Kundry Bayreuth Festival, 1961, opened, Bayreuth Festival, Parsifal, 1963; commemorative Wagner 150th Birth Anniversary; opened 1963 Met. Opera Season in Aida; premiered: Dello Joio's Blood Moon, 1961, Henderson's Medea, 1972; rec. artist Parsifal, 1964 (Grand Prix du Disque award); contbg. editor Opera Quarterly, 1983. Recipient Fulbright award for study in Italy, 1951, Woman of Achievement award Commn. on Status of Women, 1983, Pres.'s award Nat. Italian Am. Found., 1985, award of merit People of San Francisco, 1985, San Jose Renaissance award for sustained and outstanding artistic contbn., 1987, Medal of Achievement Acad. Vocal Arts, 1988; named Honored Citizen City of San Jose, 1986; inducted into Calif. Pub. Edn. Hall of Fame, 1985, others. Mem. Beethoven Soc. (mem. adv. bd. 1985—), San Jose Arts Round Table, San Jose Opera Guild, Am. Soc. Univ. Women, Arts Edn. Week Consortium, Phi Kappa Phi, Mu Phi Epsilon. Office: Opera San Jose 2049 Paragon Dr San Jose CA 95131

DALIS, JOHN S., federal judge; b. 1952. Chief bankruptcy judge U.S. Bankruptcy Ct. (so. dist.) Ga., Augusta, 1987—. Office: 150 US Bankruptcy Ct 827 Telfair St Augusta GA 30901-2209

DALIS, PETER T., athletic director. BS in Phys. Edn., UCLA, 1959, MS in Edn., 1963. Dir. Cultural & Recreational Affairs Dept. UCLA, 1963-83, athletic dir., 1983—; capital project cons. U. Conn., U. New South Wales, Australia; spl. events com. Pacific-10 Conf., chair TV com. Mem. L.A.-Athens Sister City Com., L.A. Sports Coun., Rose Bowl Mgmt. Com.; bd. dirs. So. Calif. Com. Olympic Games. Named Axios Sportsman of Yr., 1987-88. Office: UCLA Dept Athletics PO Box 24044 Los Angeles CA 90024*

DALKEY, FREDRIC DYNAN, artist; b. Sacramento, Calif., Feb. 22, 1943; s. Frank Ferdinand and Susan Gwendolyn (Dynan) D.; m. Victoria Lucille Sellick, Sept. 10, 1966; 1 child, Emile Sellick. BA, Calif. State U., Sacramento, 1966, MA, 1969. Tchg. asst. dept. art Calif. State U., Sacramento, 1966-69, lectr. honors dept., 1969-71, instr. art dept., 1972-73; art dept. chair Sacramento City Coll., 1980-81, prof., 1969—. One-man shows include Calif. State U., Sacramento, 1966, Crocker Art Mus., Sacramento, 1969, 72, Art Co., 1970-71, Artists Contemporary Gallery, 1973-74, 77-78, 81, 83, 85-86, 90, 93, Open Ring Gallery, Sacramento, 1976, Weinstock's, Sacramento, 1980, Kondos Gallery, 1980, 86, Sierra Coll., 1984, Campbell-Thiebaud Gallery, San Francisco, 1992, 94, 97, 99, Thomas Babeor Gallery, La Jolla, Calif., 1995, 96; exhibited in group shows at Calif. State Fair Exhibition, 1963 (1st place watercolors), 65, Lytton Ctr. Visual Arts, L.A., 1967, Crocker Art Mus., 1968, 69, 75, 83, 88, 91, U. Calif., 1979, Artists Contemporary Gallery, 1980, 84, 90, 93, Pence Gallery, 1981, Am. River Coll., 1986, Charles Campbell Gallery, 1987, Sierra Coll., 1989, Southern Pacific Warehouse, 1991, Am. Acad. Arts and Letters, 1992, M.M. de Young Meml. Mus., 1997, Crocker Art Mus., 1997, Crown Point Press, San Francisco, 1997, Christopher Winfield Gallery, Carmel, Calif., 1998, Artists Contemporary Gallery, Sacramento, Solomon Duknik Gallery, Sacramento; represented in permanent collections Calif. State Fair, Calif. State U., City Sacramento, Crocker Art Mus., Hyatt Regency Hotel, Lytton Industries, Sacramento City Coll., Nat. Gallery Art, Washington, Achenbach Found., San Francisco. Founding mem. ad hoc com. Sacramento Met. Arts Commn., 1978; founding mem. adv. bd., artist in crisis fund Sacramento Regional Coun., 1985. Recipient Inst. award Am. Acad. Arts and Letters, 1992. Avocations: muscial instrument repair and making, playing violin. Home: 2164 35th St Sacramento CA 95817-1306 Office: Sacramento City Coll Dept Humanities & Fine Arts 3835 Freeport Blvd Sacramento CA 95822-1318

DALL, PETER ANDREW, management and organizational consultant; b. Nashville, Dec. 5, 1951; s. David George and Agnes Mariah (Suggs) D.; m. Mary Lou Boudrie, Apr. 26, 1980; 1 child, David George II. BS in Edn., Tenn.-Wesleyan Coll., 1976. Cert. power exec. Gen. mgr. VIP Placement & Counseling Svc., Hixson, Tenn., 1978-79; dir. edn., tng. and conf. Tenn. Valley Pub. Power Assn., Chattanooga, 1979-87; dep. chief mgmt. tng. and devel. TVA, Chattanooga, 1987-88; asst. to pres.-chief exec. officer Cobb Electric Membership Corp., Marietta, Ga., 1988-92; nat. sales mgr. John-Michaels Enterprises, Inc., 1992—; bd. dirs. Greater Atlanta Electric League. Active Chattanooga Big Bors. and Big Sisters Assn., 1980-84, 86-88; mem. state tech. com. Ga. Bd. Tech. and Adult Edn., Atlanta, 1989-90, state v.p.; asst scoutmaster Troop 172, Boy Scouts Am., 1994-96. Mem. Nat. Safety Mgmt. Soc. (state v.p.), Nat. Utility Tng. and Safety Edn. Assn., Internat. Assn. for Continuing Edn. and Tng. (pres. 1990-92, bd. dirs.), N.Am. Hunting Club, Highland Sportsman Club (bd. dirs. 1987-88), Rotary (pres. North Cobb chpt. 1990-91). Presbyterian. Avocations: big game hunting, camping, travel, hand blending pipe tobacco, pipe collecting. Home: Tall Pines Estates Box 16 9218 Dayton Pike Soddy Daisy TN 37379-4825

DALL, SASHA RAOUL XOLA, evolutionary ecologist, researcher; b. Ndola, Copper Belt, Zambia, June 29, 1970; s. Frank Patrick and Barbara Jane (Denham) D. BSc in Zoology with honors, U. Bristol (U.K.), 1991, PhD in Zoology, 1996. Lectr. behavioral ecology U. Bristol (U.K.), 1996-97; postdoctoral rsch. fellow U. Louisville, Fla. State U., Tallahassee, 1997—; biol. cons. The Bristol Exploratory, 1993; sec., postdoctoral com. mem. Behavioral Biology Group, Ctr. Behavioral Biology, U. Bristol, 1994-97. Contbr. articles to profl. jours. Rsch. fellow Royal Soc. London, 1997-98. Mem. Assn. Study Animal Behavior (Postgrad. Conf. grantee 1993), Internat. Soc. Behavioral Ecology. Avocation: ultimate frisbee. Office: Fla State U Dept Math Tallahassee FL 32306

DALLAGER, JOHN R., career officer. BS in Mech. Engring., USAF Acad., 1969; disting. grad. pilot tng., Craig AFB, Ala., 1970; student F-4 replacement tng., Davis-Monthan AFB, Ariz., 1970-71; MBA, Troy State U., 1978; student, Air Command and Staff Coll., 1983, Nat. Def. U., 1983, U.S. Army War Coll., 1988. Commd. 2d lt. USAF, 1969, maj. gen., 1997, various pilot assignments, 1971-74; air staff tng. officer, legis. liaison Pentagon, Washington, 1974-75; flight comdr., chief wing aircrew tng. 347th Tactical Fighter Wing, Moody AFB, Ga., 1975-76; air liaison officer 601st Tactical Air Support Group, Gelnhausen, W. Germany, 1976-77; instr. Air and Ground Ops. Sch. USAF Europe, Sembach Air Base, W. Germany, 1977-79; A-10 weapons and tactics instr. then exec. officer 355th Tactical Tng. Squadron/Wing, Davis-Monthan AFB, 1979-82; mgr. tactical flying hour programs, other positions Hdqs. USAF, Pentagon, Washington, 1983-85; stationed at Davis-Monthan AFB, 1985-87; various comdr. positions USAF, 1988-92, 94-98; dep. dir. logistics and security asst. then dep. chief staff Hdqs. U.S. Ctrl. Command, MacDill AFB, Fla., 1992-94; asst. chief staff ops. and logistics Supreme Hdqs. Allied Powers Europe, 1998—; dir. ops. Joint Guard Bosnia, Joint Guarantor Bosnia, Mons, Belgium, 1998—. Decorated D.S.M., Legion of Merit with oak leaf cluster, D.F.C. with two oak leaf clusters, Air medal with 15 oak leaf clusters, Rep. Vietnam Gallantry Cross with Palm, Rep. Vietnam Campaign Medal. Office: 13 AF/CC Unit 14033 APO AP 96543-4033

DALLARA, CHARLES H., think tank executive, financial analyst; b. Spartanburg, S.C.; m. Carolyn Gault; children: Stephen, Emily. BS in Econs., U. S.C., 1970; MA, Tufts U., 1975, MA in Law and Diplomacy, 1976, PhD, 1986; LLD (hon.), U. S.C., 1990. Various positions Dept. Treasury; U.S. alt. exec. dir. IMF, 1982-83, dep. asst. set. treas., 1983-85, exec. dir., 1984-89, sr. dep. asst. sec. treasury internat. econ. policy, 1985-88, asst. sec. treasury for policy devel., sr. adv. policy, 1988-89; mng. dir. J.P. Morgan & Co., 1991-93; mng. dir. Inst. Internat. Fin., 1993—, also bd. dirs. With USN, 1970-74. Office: IIF Ste 8500 200 Pennsylvania Ave NW Washington DC 20006*

DALLAS, DANIEL GEORGE, social worker; b. Chgo., June 8, 1932; s. George C. and Azimena P. (Marines) D.; B.A., Anderson (Ind.) Coll., 1955; B.D., No. Bapt. Theol. Sem., 1958; M.S.W., Mich. State U., 1963; M.Div., No. Bapt. Theol. Sem., 1972, D.Min., 1981; m. G. Aleta Leppien, May 26, 1956; children—Paul, Rhonda. Mem. faculty Mich. Dept. Corrections, Mich. State U., 1963-66; med. social adminstr. Med. Services div. Mich. Dept. Social Services, 1966-68; cons. Outreach Center of DuPage County, 1976—, also dir. social service Meml. Hosp. of DuPage County, Elmhurst, Ill., 1968—; therapist, lectr. Traffic Sch., Elmhurst Coll.; pvt. practice; indsl. cons. Mem. Elmhurst Sr. Citizen Commn., 1976—. Recipient Outstanding Service award Mental Health Assn. Ill., 1978. Mem. Nat. Assn. Social Workers, Soc. Hosp. Social Work Dirs., Am. Hosp. Assn., Nat. Registry of Health Care Providers, Mental Health Assn. Chgo. Club: Rotary. Contbr. articles to profl. jours. Office: 242 N York St Ste 203 Elmhurst IL 60126-2747

DALLAS, DONALD EDWARD, JR., corporate executive; b. East Cleveland, Ohio, Sept. 17, 1931; s. Donald Edward and Zella Gwynn (Rogers) D.; m. Marianne Mock, May 25, 1968 (dec. 1981); children: Susan, Benjamin. BS, U. Cin., 1954; postgrad., MIT, 1958-61. Rsch. engr. Ludlow Corp., Needham Heights, Mass., 1961-63; sales rep. J. M. Huber Corp., Westwood, Mass., 1963-69; mktg. mgr. J. M. Huber Corp., Edison, N.J., 1969-73; pres. D.E. Dallas & Assocs. Inc., Balt., Wellesley, Mass. and Freeport, Maine, 1962—; mktg. mgr. Allis-Chalmers Corp., West Allis, Wis., 1974-87; pres. Hoult Engring. & Mfg. Co., Wayland, Mass., 1987-88; mktg. mgr. Allis Mineral Systems (formerly Boliden Allis, Inc.), West Allis, Wis., 1987-92; pres., CEO Electro/Magnetic Solutions, Inc., Denver, 1992-95, Advanced Environ. Sys., Inc., South Freeport, Maine, 1995-96; vice-chmn. AES Tech. Corp., South Freeport, 1996—; pres., COO AES Technologies, Inc., South Freeport, 1996—, AES R&D, Inc., South Freeport, 1997—; lectr. mktg. MIT, 1988-92. Contbr. articles to profl. jours. With USNR, 1954-64. Mem. ASME, Engrs. Soc. Western Pa.

DALLAS, SANDRA, correspondent, writer; b. Washington, June 11, 1939; d. Forrest Everett and Harriett (Mavity) Dallas; m. Robert Thomas Atchison, Apr. 20, 1963; children: Dana Dallas, Povy Kendal Dallas. BA, U. Denver, 1960. Asst. editor U. Denver Mag., 1965-66; editorial asst. Bus. Week, Denver, 1961-63, 67-69, bur. chief, 1969-85, 90-91, sr. corr., 1985-90; freelance editor, 1990—; book reviewer Denver Post, 1961—, regional book columnist, 1980—. Author: Gaslights and Gingerbread, 1965, rev. edit., 1984, Gold and Gothic, 1967, No More Than 5 in a Bed, 1967, Vail, 1969, Cherry Creek Gothic, 1971, Yesterday's Denver, 1974, Sacred Paint, 1980, Colorado Ghost Towns and Mining Camps, 1985, Colorado Homes, 1986, Buster Midnight's Cafe, 1990, reissued 1998, The Persian Pickle Club, 1995, The Diary of Mattie Spenser, 1997; editor: The Colorado Book, 1993; contbr. articles to various mags. Bd. dirs. Vis. Nurse Assn., Denver, 1983-85, Hist. Denver, Inc., 1979-82, 84-87. recipient Wrangler award Nat. Cowboy Hall of Fame, 1980, Lifetime Achievement award Denver Posse of Westerners, 1996, disting. svc. award U. Colo., 1997; named Colo. Exceptional Chronicler of Western History by Women's Library Assn. and Denver Pub. Library Friends Found., 1986; finalist Spur award We. Writers of Am., 1998. Mem. Women's Forum Colo., Denver Woman's Press Club, Western Writers Am., Women Writing the West. Democrat. Presbyterian. Home and Office: 750 Marion St Denver CO 80218-3434

DALLAS, SATERIOS (SAM), aerospace engineer, researcher, consultant; b. Detroit, May 9, 1938; s. Peter and Pauline (Alex) D.; m. Athena Ethel Spartos, July 12, 1964; children: Gregory Dean, Paula Marie. BS in Aero. Engring., U. Mich., 1959, BS in Engring. Math., 1960; MS in Astrodynamics, UCLA, 1963, PhD in Engring., 1968. Rsch. engr. astrodynamics dept. Jet Propulsion Lab., Pasadena, Calif., 1965-78, supr. tech. group mission design, 1978-82, flight engring. office mgr. Voyager Project, 1982-84; sci. and mission design mgr. Magellan Project Jet Propulsion Lab., Pasadena, 1984-89, tech. mgr. spacecraft analysis, 1989-90, mission mgr. Mars Observer Project, 1990-93, mission mgr. Mars Global Surveyor Project, 1994-97, mission mgr. space interferometry mission, 1997—; instr. Pepperdine U., Malibu, Calif., 1973-75; lectr. on space missions Kennedy Space Ctr., Cape Canaveral, Fla., 1988, Australian Dept. Industry, Tech. and Commerce, Canberra, 1988, USAF-CAP-PLR Ctr. Aerospace Edn., Las Vegas, Neb., 1991. Author: Progress in Astronautics and Aeronautics, 1964, Natural and Artificial Satellite Motion, 1979; contbr. articles to sci. jours. Coach Glendale (Calif.) Little League, 1979-82; com. mem. troop 125 Boy Scouts Am., Glendale, 1980. Recipient Apollo achievement award NASA, 1969, cert. of recognition, 1974, Laurels award Aviation Week, 1989, 94. Mem. AIAA, Am. Astron. Soc. (astrodynamics tech. com. 1970-80). Republican. Greek Orthodox. Avocations: snow skiing, hiking, woodworking, tennis, computer applications development. Home: 3860 Karen Lynn Dr Glendale CA 91206-1218 Office: Jet Propulsion Lab 4800 Oak Grove Dr Pasadena CA 91109-8001

DALLAS, WILLIAM MOFFIT, JR., lawyer; b. Cedar Rapids, Iowa, May 7, 1949; s. William Moffit and Winifred Mae (Lillie) D.; m. Lynne Louise Russo, July 30, 1977 (div. July 1984); m. Janet Neustaetter, Apr. 19, 1985; children: Sarah Anne, Steven Kurt. AB, Oberlin Coll., 1971; JD, Harvard U., 1974. Bar: N.Y. 1975, U.S. Dist. Ct. (so. and ea. dists.) N.Y. 1975, U.S. Ct. Appeals (2d cir.) 1976, U.S. Ct. Appeals (3d cir.) 1983, U.S. Ct. Appeals (8th cir.) 1984. Assoc. Sullivan & Cromwell, N.Y.C., 1974-82, ptnr., 1982—; fed. mediator U.S. Dist. Ct., 1995—. Contbr. articles on antitrust issues to law revs., 1978—, chpt. to book. Served to lt. USN, 1971-77. Mem. ABA, Assn. of Bar of City of N.Y. (chmn. com. on judicial admin., 1999—, sec. judiciary com. 1977-80, chmn. com. jud. adminstrn. 1999—), N.Y. County Lawyers' Assn. (chmn. com. on trade regulation 1978-81), India House Club (N.Y.C.). Office: Sullivan & Cromwell 125 Broad St Fl 28 New York NY 10004-2489

DALLA-VICENZA, MARIO JOSEPH, steel company executive; b. Sudbury, Ont., Can., Oct. 30, 1938; s. Mario Valentino and Cecilia (Bonaldo) D.-V.; m. Deanna Karen Leblanc, July 15, 1961; children: Janice, Peter, Mark. Grad. in acctg., Queens U., Kingston, Can., 1962, McMaster U., Can., 1969; MBA, Lake Superior State U., 1983. Chartered acct., Can.; cert. mgmt. acct., Can. Acct. Tessier, Massicotte & Co., Sault Ste Marie, Ont., 1957-63; with Algoma Steel Corp., Sault Ste Marie, 1963-83, gen. mgr. corp. acctg. svcs., 1981-83; treas. IPSCO Inc., Regina, Sask., Can., 1983-87, v.p., chief fin. officer, 1987-88, sr. v.p., chief fin. officer, 1988-96, sr. v.p. corp. affairs, 1996-97; pres. Demar Enterprises, Calgary, Alta., Can., 1998—. Pres., bd. dirs. Sault Ste Marie C. of C., 1974-79; chmn. econ. devel. coun. City of Sault Ste Marie, 1981-83. Fellow Inst. Chartered Accts. (nat. coun., nat. exec. com. 1994-95, provincial coun. 1990-96, pres. 1996); mem. Soc. Mgmt. Accts. (pres., coun. 1984-88, fellow 1993, nat. bd. 1989-90), Fin. Execs. Inst. (bd. dirs. Regina chpt. 1985-90, chpt. pres. 1989-90), Ranch Ehrlo Soc. (bd. dirs. 1992—, chmn. 1997—). Office: IPSCO Inc PO Box 1670, Regina, SK Canada S4P 3C7

DALLEK, ROBERT, history educator; b. Bklyn., May 16, 1934; s. Rubin and Esther (Fisher) D.; m. Ilse F. Shatzkin, Nov. 20, 1959 (dec. Oct. 1962); m. Geraldine R. Kronmal, Aug. 22, 1965; children: Matthew J., Rebecca R. BA, U. Ill., 1955; MA, Columbia U., 1957, PhD, 1964. Lectr. history CCNY, 1959-60; instr. history Columbia U., N.Y.C., 1960-64; from asst. prof. to prof. UCLA, 1964—, vice-chmn. dept. history, 1972-74; prof. history Boston U., 1996—; rsch. assoc. So. Calif. Psychoanalytic Inst., L.A., 1981-85; Commonwealth Fund lectr. Univ. Coll., London, 1984; Thompson lectr. U. Wyo., Laramie, 1986; Charles Griffin lectr. Vassar Coll., Poughkeepsie, N.Y., 1987; George W. Littlefield lectr. U. Tex., Austin, 1990; vis. Harmsworth prof. Oxford (Eng.) U., 1994-95; cons. ABC, N.Y.C., 1981-82, Ednl. Film Ctr., Annandale, Va., 1988, Sta. KCET-TV, L.A., 1988, Sta. KERA-TV, Dallas, 1989-91. Author: Democrat and Diplomat: The Life of William E. Dodd, 1968, Franklin D. Roosevelt and American Foreign Policy, 1932-1945, 1979, The American Style of Foreign Policy: Cultural Politics and Foreign Affairs, 1983, Ronald Reagan: The Politics of Symbolism, 1984, Lone Star Rising: Lyndon Johnson and His Times, 1908-1960, 1991, Hail to the Chief: The Making and Unmaking of American Presidents, 1996, Flawed Giant: Lyndon Johnson and His Times 1961-73, 1998; editor 3 books; contbr. articles to profl. jours. Mem. adv. com. on diplomatic documents Dept. State, Washinton, 1985-88; mem. adv. com. to Mayor Tom Bradley, L.A., 1986, adv. com. on ethics L.A. City Coun., 1989-90. John Simon Guggenheim fellow, 1973-74, sr. fellow NEH, 1976-77, Humanities fellow Rockefeller Found., 1981-82, Am. Coun. Learned Socs. fellow, 1984-85; rsch. grantee Eleanor Roosevelt Inst., 1976-77, Lyndon B. Johnson Found., 1984-85, 88-89. Fellow Soc. Am. Historians, Am. Acad. Arts and Scis.; mem. Am. Hist. Assn., Soc. for Historians of Am. Fgn. Rels., Com. on History Second World War. Home: 2138 Cathedral Ave NW Washington DC 20008-1502 Office: Boston U Dept History Boston MA 02215

DALLEN, RUSSELL MORRIS, JR., investment company executive, lawyer; b. Biloxi, Miss., Jan. 20, 1963; s. Russell Morris and Faye Annette (Werner) D.; m. Claire Lucia Hodgson, May 27, 1995; 1 child, Allegra Julia Faye. BA in Econs. and Polit. Sci., U. Miss., 1985; M in Internat. Affairs, Columbia U., 1987; Diploma in Internat. Law, Nottingham (Eng.) U., 1988; BA in Jurisprudence, Oxford (Eng.) U., 1990, MA in Law, 1994. Fgn. corres. Newsweek, London, 1990-91; sr. fellow, dir. UN Assn.-USA, N.Y.C., 1991-93; assoc. Morgan Stanley & Co., Inc., N.Y.C., 1994-96; ptnr. Stires, O'Donnell & Co., Inc., 1996—. Author: Revitalizing The United Nations, 1993; (with others) Issues Before the United Nations, 1989, A Global Agenda, 1992; contbr. articles to profl. jours. Mem. bd. govs. Harold W. Rosenthal Fellowship, Washington, 1985—; mem. exec. com. Manhattan coun. Boy Scouts Am., N.Y.C., 1992—; vol. Big Bros./Big Sisters, N.Y.C., 1992—. Recipient Ner Tamid Leadership award Nat. Jewish Com. on Scouting, 1979, Kluwer Internat. Law award, 1990, Article of Yr. award Common Market Law Rev.; named Century III Leader, 1981; Harry S. Truman scholar, 1983, U.K. Fgn. and Commonwealth Office scholar, 1987; Harold Rosenthal fellow, 1985, Am. fellow European Communities, 1986, Ctr. fellow Ctr. for Study of Presdy., 1985. Mem. N.Y. State Bar Assn., N.Y. County Lawyers Assn. (chmn. sub-com. 1992—), Oxford and Cambridge Club, Squadron A Club, Cornell Club, Landsdowne Club. Avocations: sailing, flying, riding. Home: PO Box 3340 New York NY 10185-3340

DALLENBACH, WALLY, professional race car driver; b. May 23, 1963; m. Robin Dallenbach; children: Jacob, Wyatt, Katie. Driver Team Sabco, 1998, Hendrick Motorsports, 1999—; SCCA Trans-Am champion, 1985, 86, IMSA GTO Series runner-up, 1988-89; NASCAR Winston Cup Series debut, 1991; 2d place, 1993 Bud at the Glen, 1995 MBNA Pontiac. Avocation: hunting. *

DALLER, WALTER E., JR., banking executive; b. Parkesburg, Pa., Mar. 31, 1939; s. Walter E. and Edna (Miller) D.; m. Ruth Ann Tennant; children: Walter III, Gregory, Susan. BSBA, Lafayette Coll., 1961. With Harleysville (Pa.) Nat. Bank, 1962—, pres., chief exec. officer, 1981-98, also bd. dirs., chmn., CEO, 1999—; bd. dirs. Harleysville Nat. Corp., Citizens Nat. Bank, Lansford, Pa., Security Nat. Bank, Pottstown, Pa.; rep. 3d dist. adv. coun. Fed. Res. Bank, 1996, 97, 98; mem. mktg. devel. com., nominating com. IBAA Bank Svcs., 1994—; Visa nat. bd. Merchant Bank Svcs., 1993—; founding bd. dirs. TCM Bank. Bd. dirs. Lower Salford Hist. Soc., Harleysville, 1991, North Penn United Way, Kulpsville, Pa., 1991. Mem. Ind. Bankers Assn. Am. (exec. com. 1990—), Pa. Bankers Assn. (governing coun. 1989-91), Cmty. Bankers Pa. (past pres. 1987-88), Lions (past pres. Limerick, Pa. club), Masons. Republican. Avocations: hunting, golf. Office: Harleysville Nat Bank/Trust PO Box 195 483 Main St Harleysville PA 19438-2311

DALLES, JOHN ALLAN, minister; b. Pitts., Sept. 13, 1954; s. John Samuel and Patricia (Yolton) D.; m. Judith Ann Taylor; children: John Taylor, Anne Elizabeth. MDiv, Lancaster Theol. Sem., 1982; D Ministry, Pitts. Theol. Sem., 1994. Ordained minister Donegal Presbytery, 1982. Assoc. pastor First Presbyn. Ch., South Bend, Ind., 1982-86, Fox Chapel Presbyn. Ch., Pitts., 1986-97; pastor Wekiva Presbyn. Ch., Longwood, Fla., 1997—. Contbr. articles to profl. jours.; author over 250 hymn texts, appearing in the Presbyn. Hymnal, New Century Hymnal, Worship Together, Come, O Spirit, Moravian Book of Worship, In Life and in Death We Belong to God, Covenant Hymnal, Book of Praise (Canadian), Australian Book of Praise, others. Mem. area coun. of various religions orgns.; bd. dirs., awards chmn. St. Joseph County Scholarship Found.; mem. worship task force, mem. com. on discipleship and ch. life Wabash Valley Presbytery; chmn. theology and worship com. Ctrl. Fla. Presbytery, Ctrl. Fla. Presbyn. Ch.; founding Notre Dame Civitan, South Bend Habitat for Humanity. Paul Harris fellow Rotary Internat. Mem. Hymn Soc. Presbyterian. Office: 211 Wekiva Springs Ln Longwood FL 32779-3601

DALLEY, GEORGE ALBERT, lawyer; b. Havana, Cuba, Aug. 25, 1941; s. Cleveland Ernest and Constance Joyce (Powell) D.; m. Pearl Elizabeth Love, Aug. 1, 1970; children: Jason Christopher, Benjamin Christian. A.B., Columbia U., 1963, J.D., 1966, M.B.A., 1966. Bar: N.Y. 1966, D.C. 1971, U.S. Supreme Ct. 1972. Asst. to pres. Met. Applied Research Center, N.Y.C., 1967-69; counsel The Children's Found., Washington, 1970-71; assoc. counsel Stroock and Stroock and Lavan, Washington, 1970-71, Com. on Judiciary, U.S. Ho. of Reps., Washington, 1971-72; adminstrv. asst. to Rep. Charles B. Rangel, N.Y.C., Washington, 1973-77, counsel, staff dir., 1985-89; dep. asst. sec. for human rights and social affairs Bur. Internat. Orgns. Affairs Dept. State, Washington, 1977-80; mem. CAB, 1980-82; dep. dir. Mondale for Pres. Com., Washington, 1983-84; counsel, staff dir. Congressman Charles B. Rangel, U.S. Ho. of Reps., Washington, 1985-89; sr. v.p. Neill and Co., Washington, 1989-93; ptnr. Neill, Dalley, Carroll, Nealer and Assevero, Washington, 1992-93; sr. ptnr. Holland and Knight, Washington, 1993—; adj. prof. Am. U. Sch. Law. Mem. legal adv. com. Dem. Nat. Com., 1975-76; bd. dirs. Africare, TransAfrica; Joint Ctr. for Polit. and Econ. Studies Internat. Inst., Jamaica Nats. Devel. Found. Mem. ABA, Nat. Bar Assn., Fed. Bar Assn., Nat. Conf. Black Lawyers, Cosmos Club, Coun. Fgn. Rels., Coun. Ams. Presbyterian. Home: 1706 Crestwood Dr NW Washington DC 20011-5334 Office: 2100 Pennsylvania Ave NW Washington DC 20037-3202

DALLMAN, MARY F., physiology educator. BA in Chemistry, Smith Coll., 1956; PhD in Physiology, Stanford U., 1967; postgrad., Swedish Royal Vet. Sch., 1968, U. Calif., San Francisco, 1969-70. Lectr. U. Calif. Dept. Physiology, San Francisco, 1970-72, asst., 1972-76, assoc. prof., 1976-81, prof., 1981—, vice-chair, 1987—. Assoc. editor: Am. Jour. Physiol.: Endocrinology and Metabolism, 1979-85, Steroids, 1985-87, Am. Jour. Physiol.: Regulatory, Integrative and Comparative Physiology, 1990-92; contbr. articles to profl. jours. Recipient Am. Diabetes Rsch. award, 1996. Mem. NIH (mem. endocrine study sect. 1977-81, mem. diabetes, digestive, kidney grants rev. subcom. 1988-92, chair 1992-93), Women in Endocrinology (pres. 1993-95), Internat. Soc. Neuroendocrinology (pres. 1996). Office: U Calif Dept Physiology Box 0444 HSIR W 47 513 Parnassus Ave Rm S-762 San Francisco CA 94122-2722*

DALLMAN, ROBERT E., lawyer; b. Shawano, Wis., Apr. 16, 1947. BA, Valparaiso U., 1970; JD, U. Kans., 1973; LLM, Georgetown U., 1977. Bar: Kans. 1973, U.S. Tax Ct. 1973, U.S. Supreme Ct. 1978, Wis. 1980. Chief counsel IRS, Washington, 1973-77, Milw., 1977-80; atty. Reinhart, Boerner, Van Deuren, Norris & Rieselbach S.C., Milw.; instr. corp. tax planning, real estate taxation, advanced real estate tax planning, U. Wis., Madison, 1981-86, 96—; cons. to chief counsel IRS, Washington, 1980. Co-author: Tax Planning for Real Estate Transactions, 1983; contbr. articles to profl. jours. Mem. ABA, State Bar Wis., Milw. Bar Assn. Office: Reinhart Boerner Van Deuren Norris & Rieselbach PO Box 92900 1000 N Water St Ste 2100 Milwaukee WI 53202-3197*

DALLMANN, DANIEL F., artist, educator; b. St. Paul, Mar. 21, 1942. B.S., Minn. State U., 1965; M.A., U. Iowa, 1968, M.F.A., 1969. Prof. Tyler Sch. Art, Phila., 1969—. One-man shows include Schoelkopf Gallery, N.Y.C., 1980, 84, 87, J. Rosenthal Fine Arts, Ltd., Chgo., 1989, Tatischeff Gallery, N.Y.C., 1993, Davidson Gallery, Seattle, 1994, Payne Gallery of Moravian Coll., Bethlehem, Pa., Kendall Gallery of Miami-Dade Coll., Miami, Fla., 1997, Dartmouth Coll. Hanover N.H., Lied Art Gallery, Creighton U., Omaha, 1998; exhibited in group shows, including Allan Frumkin, N.Y.C., 1982, Berkshire Mus., Pittsfield, Mass., 1983, Hudson River Mus., Yonkers, N.Y., 1984, 86, San Francisco Mus. Modern Art, 1985, Orlando (Fla.) Mus. Art at Loch Haven, 1986, NAD, N.Y.C., 1988, NAS, Washington, 1989, Md. Inst., Balt., 1990, So. Alleghenies Mus. Art, Loretto, Pa., 1992, 93, Forum Gallery, N.Y.C., 1994, Smith Coll., Northampton, Mass., 1996; represented in permanent collections Woodmere Art Mus., Phila., J.B. Speed Mus., Louisville, Nat. Mus. Am. Art, Washington, Art Inst. Chgo., also corp. collections.

DALLOS, PETER JOHN, neurobiologist, educator; b. Budapest, Hungary, Nov. 26, 1934; came to U.S., 1956, naturalized, 1962; s. Ernest and Maria Dallos; m. Joan Usis, Aug. 18, 1977; 1 child by previous marriage, Christopher. Student, Tech. U. Budapest, 1953-56; BS, Ill. Inst. Tech., 1958; MS, Northwestern U., 1959, PhD, 1962. Research engr. Am. Machine and Foundry Co., 1959; cons. engr., 1959-60; mem. faculty Northwestern U., 1962—, prof. audiology and elec. engring., 1969—, prof. neurobiology and physiology, 1981—, chmn., 1981-84, 86-87, assoc. dean Coll. Arts and Scis., 1984-85, John Evans prof. neurosci., 1986—, Hugh Knowles prof. audiology, 1994—; vis. scientist Karolinska Inst., Stockholm, 1977-78; chmn. behavioral and neurosci. rev. panel No. 5 Nat. Inst. Neurol., Communicative Disorders and Stroke, NIH, 1982-85, mem. nat. adv. council, 1984-87. Author: The Auditory Periphery: Biophysics and Physiology, 1973; contbr. articles to profl. jours. Recipient 12th ann. award Beltone Inst. HEaring Rsch., 1977, Internat. prize Amplifon Rsch. and Study Ctr., 1984, Senator Jacob Javits Neurosci. Investigator award, 1984, Honors of Assn. award Am. Speech-Lang.-Hearing Assn., 1994, Bekesy medal of Acoustical Soc. Am., 1995, Sigma Xi Disting. Nat. lectr., 1997-98; Acta Otolaryngologica Internat. prize, 1997; Guggenheim fellow, 1977-78; McKnight sr. fellow, 1997—. Fellow IEEE, AAAS, Acoustical Soc. Am.; mem. Am. Acad. Arts and Scis., Soc. for Neurosci., Assn. for Rsch. in Otolaryngology (pres. 1992-93, award of merit 1994), Collegium Otolaryngologicum Amicitae Sacrum, Sigma Xi, Tau Beta Pi, Eta Kappa Nu. Office: Frances Searle Bldg Northwestern U 2299 N Campus Dr Evanston IL 60208

DALLURA, SAL ANTHONY, physician; b. Flushing, N.Y., Nov. 7, 1960; s. Russ and Mayann (Taranto) D.; m. Donna Ann Baldassare, Aug. 6, 1983 (div. Mar. 1993); children: Christopher Anthony, Corinne Elizabeth; m. Stacy Elizabeth Carberry, July 1, 1995 (div. Jan. 1999); 1 child, Matthew Anthony. BS, U. Notre Dame, 1982; DO, N.Y. Coll. Osteo. Medicine, 1986. Diplomate Am. Acad. Family Physicians. Mng. ptnr. Flashner Med. Ptnrship., Babylon, N.Y., 1989-91; assoc. physician Moriches Med. Care, Center Moriches, N.Y., 1989-91, Digiovanna, Massepequa Park, N.Y., 1991-92; physician Tippecanoe Family Physicians, Tipp City, Ohio, 1992-98; physician mng. ptnr. After Hours Family Care, Tipp City, 1994-98; physician Milton Union Med. Ctr., West Milton, Ohio, 1998—, Upper Valley Profl. Corp., 1994—. Mem. Am. Osteo. Assn., Am. Coll. Family Practice, Am. Coll. Legal Medicine, Ohio Osteo. Assn., Ohio State Med. Assn. Republican. Roman Catholic. Avocations: model railroading, coin collecting, bowling, golf, reading. Office: 751 S Miami St West Milton OH 45383-1303

DALLWEIN, EDWARD K., controller; b. Warren, Mich., Nov. 16, 1967. B of Accountancy, Walsh Coll. Accountancy/Bus., Troy, Mich., 1996. CPA, Mich. Teller Huntington Banks of Mich., Warren, 1986-89, internal auditor, 1989-90; internal auditor Blockbuster Entertainment, Garden City, Mich., 1990-91; staff acct. Addison & Addison, P.C., Grosse Pointe Woods, Mich., 1992-96; asst. contr. Speedring Systems, Rochester Hills, Mich., 1996-97; sr. internal auditor Compuware Corp., Farmington Hills, Mich., 1997-98; contr. CareTech Solutions, Dearborn, Mich., 1998—. Mem. AICPA, Mich. Assn. CPAs (William A. Paton award 1996). Avocations: computers, golf, woodworking, movies, books.

DALLY, JAMES WILLIAM, mechanical engineering educator, consultant; b. Sardis, Ohio, Aug. 2, 1929; s. William Hiram and Martha (Siebert) D.; m. Anne Evangeline Tziritas, Dec. 22, 1955; children: Lisa, William, Michelle. BSME, Carnegie Mellon U., 1951, MSME, 1953; PhD, Ill. Inst. Tech., 1958. Registered profl. engr., Md. Asst. dir. research Armour Research Found., Chgo., 1961-64; prof. Ill. Inst. Tech., Chgo., 1964-71; prof., chmn. dept. U. Md., College Park, 1971-79; dean Coll. Engring. U. R.I., Kingston, 1979-82; mgr. mech. devel. IBM, Manassas, Va., 1982-84; prof. mech. engring. U. Md., College Park, 1984-97; Disting. vis. prof. USAF Acad., 1995-96. Author: Experimental Stress Analysis, 1965, 3d edit., 1991, Photoelastic Coatings, 1977, Engineering Measurements, 1984, 2d edit., 1993, Packaging Electronic Systems, 1990, Introduction to Engineering Design, 1997, Product Engineering and Manufacturing, 1998; contbr. numerous tech. articles to profl. jours.; patentee in field. Recipient Boeing Outstanding Educator award, 1996. Fellow ASME, Am. Acad. Mechanics (bd. dirs. 1984-88, pres. 1990-91), Soc. Exptl. Mechanics (hon.; pres. 1970-71, Murray lectureship 1979, Past Pres. award 1971, M.M. Frocht award 1976, Hetenyi award 1995); mem. Nat. Acad. Engring., U.S. Nat. Com. Theoretical and Applied Mechanics (chmn. 1982-84, vice chmn., 1984-86). Avocation: sailing.

DALMAN, GISLI CONRAD, electrical engineering educator; b. Winnipeg, Man., Can., Apr. 7, 1917; s. Conrad Fred and Valgerdur (Thorsteinsdottir) D.; m. Catherine Stewart, Dec. 24, 1941; children: Diana Dalman Dotson, Kristine, Karen, Conrad. B.E.E., Coll. City N.Y., 1940; M.E.E., Poly. Inst. Bklyn., 1947, D.E.E., 1949. Mfg. engr. RCA, 1940-45; mem. tech. staff Bell Telephone Labs., 1945-47; engring. sect. head Sperry Gyroscope Co., Great Neck, N.Y., 1949-56; mem. faculty Cornell U., Ithaca, N.Y., 1956—; prof. elec. engring. Cornell U., 1956-87, prof. emeritus, 1987—; acting dir. Sch. Elec. Engring., 1972-73, dir., 1975-80; adj. prof. Poly. Inst. Bklyn., 1954-56; cons. to industry, 1956—; cons. on millimeter wave amplifiers to TRW, Redondo Beach, Calif., 1980-81. Author articles on microwave solid state devices; co-author two textbooks; holder 5 U.S. patents. Project mgr. UN Spl. Fund China Project, Chiao Tung U., Hsinchu, Taiwan, 1962-63. Fellow IEEE, AAAS; mem. Sigma Xi, Tau Beta Pi, Eta Kappa Nu. Home: 506 Hanshaw Rd Ithaca NY 14850-2214

DALPHOND-GUIRAL, MADELEINE, member of Canadian parliament; b. Monteal, Quebec, Can., June 6, 1938. BS in Nursing. Mem. parliament from Laval Centre Parliament of Canada, Ottawa, 1963—, dep. whip, 1996—. Office: House of Commons, Rm 528 N Ctr Block, Ottawa, ON Canada KIA 086*

DALPINO, IDA JANE, secondary education educator; b. Newhall, Calif., Oct. 20, 1936; d. Bernhardt Arthur and Wahneta May (Blyler) Melby; m. Gilbert Augustus, June 14, 1963 (div. 1976); 1 child, Nicolette Jane. BA, Calif. State U., Chico, 1960; postgrad., Sacramento State, 1961-65, Sonoma State, 1970-71; MA, U. San Francisco, 1978. Cert. community counselor, learning handicapped, community coll. instr., exceptional children, pupil pers. specialist, secondary tchr., resource specialist. Tchr. Chico High Sch., 1959-60; counselor Mira Loma High Sch., Sacramento, 1960-66; tchr. ESL Phoenix Ind. High Sch., 1968-69; resource specialist Yuba City (Calif.) High Sch., 1971—; English tchr. Rough Rock Demonstration Sch., summers, 1975, 76. Office sec. Job's Daus., North Bend, Oreg., 1953—; active Environ. Def. Fund, Centerville Hist. Assn., Chico, 1991—. Mem. NEA, Calif. Tchrs. Assn., Chico State Alumni Assn., Sigma Kappa Alumni. Democrat. Mem. Science of the Mind Church. Avocations: reading, ecology, genealogy. Home: 4676 Cable Bridge Dr Chico CA 95928-8840 Office: Yuba City Unified Sch Dist 850 B St Yuba City CA 95991-4926

DALRYMPLE, CHERYL, online information company executive. CFO LEXIS-NEXIS, Dayton, Ohio, 1997-98, CFO, sr. v.p., 1998—. Office: LEXIS-NEXIS 9443 Springboro Pike Miamisburg OH 45342-4425*

DALRYMPLE, CHRISTOPHER GUY, chiropractor; b. Beaumont, Tex., Sept. 2, 1958; s. Guy H. and Betty Jane (Williams) D.; m. Angela Hackley, Dec. 15, 1979; children: Sarah E., William C., Clayton G. Student, Baylor U., 1976-78; D in Chiropractic Medicine, Tex. Chiropractic Coll., 1982. Diplomate Nat. Bd. Chiropractic Examiners, Tex. Bd. Chiropractic Examiners; ordained Baptist Deacon, 1988. Chiropractor Brassard Chiropractic Clinic, Beaumont, 1982-85; chiropractic physician, adminstr. Brenham (Tex.) Chiropractic Clinic, 1985—; host Back Talk, 1987-88; cons., lectr. in field. Author: Brenham & Masonry...150 Years Together, 1995; contbr. articles to profl. jours. Team chiropractor track team Blinn Coll., Brenham, 1987-94, Tex. track and field participants Olympics, 1992; Sunday sch. dir. First Bapt., 1986-87, 90-93, Sunday sch. tchr., 1987-89, bd. trustees Calvary Bapt. Ch., Brenham, 1992-94, Sunday sch. tchr. youth, 1993-94, actor, playwright ch. pageants, 1993-94, 96, 98, 99, deacon, chmn., 1994-98, chmn. pers. com., 1995-98, chmn. long range planning com., 1995-98, adult Sunday sch. tchr., 1995-99; treas. Brenham Ind. Sch. Devel.-PAC, 1994; participant Health Occupation Students of Am. Program, Brenham H.S., 1992—. Recipient State Sweepstakes Winner "Jake", Tex. Jaycees, 1984, Outstanding Officer, 1984. Mem. Am. Chiropractic Assn., Tex. Chiropractic Assn. (state com., labor rels. 1983, membership com. 1994-95, dist. 9 sec. 1983-84, chmn. publ. com. 1987—, editor-in-chief 1987—, dist. 8 state dir. 1996-99, state sec. 199—, Young Chiropractor award 1997, Pres.'s award 1999), Christian Chiropractors Assn., Tex. Chiropractic Coll. Alumni Assn., Baylor Alumni Assn. (life), Royal Arch, Gideons Internat. (bible chmn. 1994—), Graham Masonic Lodge (various offices), Delta Sigma Chi (sec. 1981, bd. dirs. 1982). Republican. Baptist. Avocations: computers, reading, sevice work, arts, drama. Office: Brenham Chiropractic Clinic PO Box 2350 Brenham TX 77834-2350

DALRYMPLE, GARY BRENT, research geologist; b. Alhambra, Calif., May 9, 1937; s. Donald Inlow and Wynona Edith (Pierce) D.; m. Sharon Ann Tramel, June 28, 1959; children: Stacie Ann, Robynne Ann Sisco, Melinda Ann Dalrymple McGurer. AB in Geology, Occidental Coll., 1959; PhD in Geology, U. Calif., Berkeley, 1963; DSc (hon.), Occidental Coll., Los Angeles, 1993. Rsch. geologist U.S. Geol. Survey, Menlo Park, Calif., 1963-81, 84-94, asst. chief geologist we. region, 1981-84; dean, prof. coll. oceanic and atmospheric sci. Oregon State U., Corvallis, 1994—; vis. prof. sch. earth scis. Stanford U., 1969-72, cons. prof., 1983-85, 90-94; disting. alumni centennial spkr. Occidental Coll., 1986-87. Author: Potassium-Argon Dating, 1969, Age of Earth, 1991; contbr. chpts. to books and articles to profl. jours. Fellow NSF, 1961-63; recipient Meritorius Svc. award U.S. Dept. Interior, 1984. Fellow Am. Geophys. Union (pres.-elect 1988-90, pres. 1990-92), Am. Acad. Arts and Scis., Geol. Soc. Am.; mem. AAAS, NAS (chair geology sect. 1997—), Am. Inst. Physics (bd. govs. 1991-97), Consortium for Oceanographic Rsch. & Edn. (bd. govs. 1994—), Joint Oceanographic Inst. (bd. govs. 1994—, chair 1996-98). Achievements include discovery that the earth's magnetic field reverses polarity and determination of time scale of these reversals for the past 3.5 million years; development of ultra-fast high-sensitivity thermoluminescence analyzer for studying lunar surface processes; development and refinement of K-Ar and 40 Ar/39 Ar dating methods and instrumentation, continuous laser probe for determining ages of microgram-sized mineral samples; research on volcanoes in the Hawaiian-Emperor volcanic chain, chronology of lunar basin formation, development and improvement of isotopic dating techniques and instrumentation, geomagnetic field behavior, plate tectonics of the Pacific Ocean basin, evolution of volcanoes, various aspects of Pleistocene history of the western U.S. Home: 1847 NW Hillcrest Dr Corvallis OR 97330-1859 Office: Oregon State U Coll Oceanic and Atmospheric Sci Corvallis OR 97331-5503

DALRYMPLE, JOHN, federal agency administrator; b. Waterloo, Iowa. BS in econs. and history, U. No. Iowa, Cedar Falls, 1974; IRS exec. devel. program, 1990. Revenue officer Balt. dist. IRS, 1975-80; supervisory revenue officer IRS, Cheyenne, Wyo., 1980-83; chief collection divsn. field br. IRS, Sacramento, Calif., 1983-87; asst. chief collection divsn. Laguna Niguel Dist. IRS, 1987-88, chief collection divsn. Laguna Niguel Dist., 1988-90, asst. to dir. Laguna Niguel Dist., 1990-91, asst. dist. dir. Hartford Dist., 1992-93, asst. dist. dir. L.A. Dist., 1993-94; dist. dir. North Ctrl. Dist. St. Paul, 1995-96; dep. chief ops. officer Washington, 1996-98, chief ops. officer, 1998—. Office: Chief Operation 1111 Constitution Ave NW Washington DC 20224-0001*

DALRYMPLE, THOMAS LAWRENCE, retired lawyer; b. Wellsburg, W. Va., May 20, 1921; s. Lawrence Chester and Ethel May (Taylor) D.; m. Marjorie May Keeler; children: Bruce Lawrence, Dale Brian. A.B., U. Mich., 1943, J.D., 1947. Bar: Ohio 1947, U.S. Supreme Ct. Practiced in Toledo, 1947-96; assoc. Williams, Eversman & Morgan and successor firms, 1947-50, Welles, Kelsey, Fuller, Harrington & Seney and successor firms, 1950-52; ptnr. Fuller & Henry and predecessor firms, 1953-96. Mem. Trout Unltd., Toledo Mus. Art. Served to capt. inf. AUS, 1943-46. Decorated Combat Inf. badge, Silver Star medal, Purple Heart. Fellow Am. Coll. Trial Lawyers, Am. Bar Found., Ohio Bar Found.; mem. Order of Coif, Phi Beta Kappa. Home: 4307 Stannard Dr Toledo OH 43613-3636

DAL SANTO, DIANE, judge, writer; b. East Chicago, Ind., Sept. 20, 1949; d. John Quentin Dal Santo and Helen (Koval) D.; m. Fred O'Cheskey, June 29, 1985. BA, U. N.Mex., 1971; cert., Inst. Internat. and Comparative Law, Guadalajara, Mex., 1978; JD, U. San Diego, 1980. Bar: N.Mex. 1980, U.S. Dist. Ct. N.Mex. 1980. Ct. planner Met. Criminal Justice Coordinating Coun., Albuquerque, 1973-75; planning coord. Dist. Atty.'s Office, Albuquerque, 1975-76, exec. asst. to dist. atty., 1976-77, asst. dir. atty. for violent crimes, 1980-82; chief dep. city atty. City of Albuquerque, 1983; assoc. firm T.B. Keleher & Assocs., 1983-84; judge Met. Ct., 1985-89, chief judge, 1988-89; judge Dist. Ct., 1989—; mem. faculty Nat. Jud. Coll., 1990-95, 97—, bd. trustees, 1995-96. Columnist Albuquerque Jour., 1996-98. Bd. dirs. Nat. Coun. Alcoholism, 1984, S.W. Ballet Co., Albuquerque, 1982-83; mem. Mayor's Task Force on Alcoholism and Crime, 1987-88, N.Mex. Coun. Crime and Delinquency, 1987-97, bd. dirs., 1992-94, Task Force Domestic Violence, 1987-94; pres. bench, bar, media com., 1987, pres. 1992, rules of evidence com. Supreme Ct., 1993-96, chair com. access to pub. records Supreme Ct., 1988; steering com. N.Mex. Buddy Awards, 1995—; mem. Metro. Criminal Justice Coordinating Coun., 1998—. U. San Diego scholar, 1978-79; recipient Women on the Move award YWCA, 1989, Disting. Woman award U. N.Mex. Alumni Assn., 1994, Outstanding Alumnus Dept. Sociology U. N.Mex., 1995; named Woman of Yr. award Duke City Bus. and Profl. Women, 1985. Mem. ABA (Nat. Conf. State Trial Judges Jud. Excellence award 1996), LWV, AAUW, Am. Judicature Soc., N.Mex. Women's Found., N.Mex. State Bar Assn. (silver gavel award 1997), N.Mex. Women's Bar Assn. (bd. dirs. 1991-92), Albuqrque Bar Assn., Nat. Assn. Women Judges, Greater Albuquerque C. of C. (steering com. 1989), N.Mex. Magistrate Judges Assn. (v.p. 1985-89), Dist. Judges Assn. (pres. 1994-95), Pennies for Homeless. Office: Dist Ct 415 Tijeras Ave NW Albuquerque NM 87102-3252

DALTAS, ARTHUR JOHN, management consultant; b. Mpls., Aug. 5, 1945; s. John Howard Locken and Adella Marie (DeChaney) D.; stepfather, John Paul Daltas; m. Ivy Valerie Schram, Dec. 22, 1970 (div. Oct. 1974); m. Suzanne Elizabeth Drury, May 20, 1977 (div. Oct. 1994); children: Alexander, Andrew, Elizabeth. BA, Coll. St. Thomas, 1968; MBA with high honors, Boston U., 1973. Tchr. U.S. Dept. Def., Frankfurt, Germany, 1970-71; treas., dir. Cambridge (Mass.) Comm. Group, Inc., 1973-78; v.p. The MAC Group/Gemini Inc., Cambridge, 1978-84; founder, pres. The Mgrs. Group, Concord, Mass., 1984-87; prin., chmn. Concord Cons. Group, 1987—; pres. Exec. Advisors Corp., 1997. Contbg. author: Implementing Strategy, 1982, Marketing Management, 1991; contbr. articles to various publs. Mem. fin. com. Carlisle (Mass.) Castle Playground, 1987-88; bd. dirs. Make a Wish Boston, 1991-96. With U.S. Army, 1968-70. Mem. Nat. Alumni Coun. Boston U., SMG Alumni Bd. Dirs. Boston U., 1st Religious Soc. (parish com. 1991-94), Beta Gamma Sigma. Avocations: skiing, hiking, golf. Office: Concord Consulting Group 30 Monument Sq Ste 215 Concord MA 01742-1895

DALTON, ANNE, lawyer; b. Pitts., Dec. 6, 1951; d. Thomas John and Mary Olive (Paul) D.; m. Oliver E. Martin, Dec. 26, 1987. BA in Polit. Sci., NYU, 1973; JD, Fordham U., 1977. Bar: N.Y. 1978, U.S. Dist. Ct. (so. and ea. dists.) N.Y. 1979, Pa. 1987, Fla. 1990. Assoc. Mendes & Mount, N.Y.C., 1979-80; atty. news div. ABC, N.Y.C., 1980-85; TV news producer ABC Network, N.Y.C., 1985-86; sr. atty. Radio City Music Hall Prodns., Inc., N.Y.C., 1986-87; pvt. practice Stroudsburg, Pa., 1987-91; asst. county att., asst. port authority atty. Lee County, Ft. Myers, Fla., 1991-94; pvt. practice Ft. Myers, 1994—; family law mediator Fla., 1994—, cir. civil mediator, 1995—; spl. hearing master 20th Jud. Cir., Fla., 1991—, ct. Commr., gen. master family civil and probate divsn., 1995—; adj. prof. Edison C.C., Ft. Myers, Barry U., Ft. Myers; family, cir. civil mediator, 1995. Recipient Clio award Internat. Clio Award Com., 1978. Mem. Pa. Bar Assn., Fla. Bar Assn., N.Y. Bar Assn., Lee County Bar Assn. Roman Catholic. Avocations: reading, gardening, swimming. Office: 2044 Bayside Pkwy Fort Myers FL 33901-3102

DALTON, CARYL, school psychologist; b. Mineral Wells, Tex., Aug. 8, 1949; d. Pat Francis Dalton and Yvonne (Ridings) Erwin. BA, U. Tex., 1970, MEd, 1977, PhD, 1987. Tchr. Brown Schs., Austin, San Marcos, Tex., 1971-73; homebound tchr. Rochester (N.Y.) City Schs., 1974-75; asst. dir. Big Buddies, Austin, Tex., 1975-77; ednl. cons. Edn. Svc. Ctr. XIII, Austin, Tex., 1978-79, pvt. practice, Austin, Tex., 1979-84; asst. instr. U. Tex., Austin, Tex., 1983-86; from doctoral intern to sch. psychologist Balcones Special Svcs. Coop., Austin, Tex., 1986-93; psychologist pvt. practice Austin, Tex., 1989—; cons. Edn. Svc. Ctr. XIII, Austin; adj. prof. U. Tex., Austin, 1990. Mem. YMCA, Austin, Tex., bd. dirs. Austin (Tex.) Rape Crisis Ctr. Mem. APA, Tex. Psychol. Assn. (pub. info. chmn. 1995-96), Audubon Soc. Office: 5750 Balcones Dr Ste 201 Austin TX 78731-4269

DALTON, CLAUDETTE ELLIS HARLOE, anesthesiologist, educator, university official; b. Roanoke, Va., Jan. 18, 1947; d. John Pinckney and Dorothy Anne (Ellis) Harloe; m. Henry Tucker Dalton, May 17, 1973 (div. 1979); 1 child, Gordon Tucker. BA, Sweet Briar Coll., 1969; MD, U. Va., 1974. Resident in anesthesiology U. N.C., Chapel Hill, 1974-77; med. edn. Lenoir County Meml Hosp./East Carolina U., Kinston, N.C., 1978-80; med. edn. in intensive care Presbyn Hosp., Charlotte, N.C., 1981-82; practice anesthesiology Charlotte Eye, Ear, Nose and Throat Hosp., 1982-85, Medivision of Charlotte and Orthopedic Hosp. of Charlotte, 1985-89; asst. dean alumni affairs U. Va., Charlottesville, 1989-92; instr. anesthesiology U. Va. Health Scis. Ctr., Charlottesville, 1997, asst. prof., 1998—, adminstrv. dir. Pre-Admission Assessment Ctr., 1997—, cmty. preceptor coord., 1992-94, asst. prof. med. edn., 1992—; dir. Office of Cmty. Based Med. Edn., Charlottesville, 1994—. Author developer patient edn. materials for illiterate patients, 1979—, emergency med. svc. tng. program, 1981. Bd. dirs. Charlottesville Family Svcs., Family Svcs. Albemarle County, 1992-93, Coun. on Aging, Lenoir County C.C., Am. Cancer Soc.; exec. dir. Cmty. Involvement Coun. Lenoir County, Kinston, 1979; county coord. Internat. Yr. of Child, Kinston, 1979; mem. sch. medicine com. on women U. Va. Med. Sch.; also others. Recipient Gov.'s award State of N.C., 1980, cert. of merit for svc. to children N.C. Dept. Human Resources, Outstanding Teaching award U. Va. Sch. Medicine, 1993; named Commencement speaker U. Va. Sch. Medicine Graduation, 1993. Mem. Va. Med. Soc. (editor med. news. Va. Med. Quar., mem. legis. com., mem. health access com., mem. strategic planning and implementation com., mem. women's com., Va. del. to AMA, bd. dirs. Va. Health Quality Coun. 1995-97, chair ad hoc com. on telemedicine 1996-99, chair scope of practice com. 1999—, del. to ann. meeting, reference com., 2nd v.p. 1998-99), Albemarle County Med. Soc. (sec.-treas. 1995-98, v.p. 1998-99, pres. 1999—), Va. Soc. Anesthesiology, U. Va. Med. Alumni Assn. (assoc. bd. dirs. 1989-92, chair women in medicine leadership conf. 1998-99), Alpha Omega Alpha. Avocations: natural history, environment, dancing, writing, gardening. Office: U Va Med Sch Box 325 Charlottesville VA 22908-0325

DALTON, DAN R., college dean. PhD, U. Calif. Mem. staff Gen. Telephone & Electronics; dean Kelley Sch. Ind. U., Bloomington, Ind. Contbr. over 160 articles to profl. jours.; cons. editor Jour. Applied Psychology; editor Jour. Mgmt. Recipient of 25 awards and citations for excellence in tchg.; nat. recognized by Bus. Week for excellence in tchg. E-mail: dalton@indiana.edu. Fax: 812-855-8983. Office: Indiana Univ Kelley School Business 1309 E 10th St Bloomington IN 47405-1701*

DALTON, DEBORAH WHITMORE, dean; b. Cleve., Dec. 30, 1951. BA in Landscape Architecture, U. Pa., 1974, MLA, 1976. Registered landscape architect, Calif., N.C. Staff lancscape designer Skidmore, Owings and Merrill, Chgo., 1976-78; assoc. The Planning Collaborative, Inc., San Francisco, 1978-80; staff landscape architect Brown/Heldt ASsocs., Inc., San Francisco, 1980-81; assoc. prof. landscape architecture N.C. State U., 1981-92, Temple U., 1992-94; dean Coll. of Architecture U. Okla., Norman, 1994-97, prof. landscape architecture, 1994—. Contbr. articles to profl. jours. Mem. pub. art subcom. City of Raleigh Arts Commn., 1991-92. Recipient Recognition award N.C. ASLA, 1992, Gold award Soc. Environ. Graphic Designers, 1991; grantee U.S. Dept. Edn., 1993. Mem. Am. Soc. of Landscape Architects. E-mail: dalton@ou.edu. Office: Coll. of Architec. U. Okla. Carn Rm 336 Norman OK 73019-6140*

DALTON, DENNIS GILMORE, political science educator; b. Morristown, N.J., Mar. 12, 1938; s. Andrew John and Emily Snow (Smith) D.; m. Sharron Louise Scheline, May 22, 1961; children: Kevin Andrew, Shaun Michael. B.A., Rutgers U., 1960; M.A., U. Chgo., 1962; Ph.D., U. London, 1965. Lectr. politics U. London, 1965-69; Ann Whitney Olin prof. polit. sci. Barnard Coll., Columbia U., N.Y.C., 1969—. Author: Indian Idea of Freedom, 1982, Mahatma Gandhi: Nonviolent Power in Action, 1993; editor: States of South Asia, 1983, Mahatma Gandhi: Selected Political Writings, 1996. Mem. War Resisters League, N.Y.C., 1969—. Recipient Emily Gregory Disting. Teaching award, 1978; Am. Coun. Learned Socs. grantee, 1975, Am. Philos. Soc. grantee, 1975; Am. Inst. Indian Studies fellow, 1974; Fulbright scholar to Nepal, 1994-95. Home: 390 Riverside Dr Apt 3e-1 New York NY 10025-1867 Office: Columbia Univ Barnard Coll 606 W 120th St New York NY 10027-5706 *My research for the last three decades on the life and thought of Mahatma Gandhi has convinced me that his example carries universal implications for the study of conflict resolution. The theory and practice of nonviolence offer us today a system of values and a hope for the future that should serve to inspire humanity.*

DALTON, DON, principal. Prin. Canyon Vista Middle Sch., Austin, Tex., 1984—. Recipient Blue Ribbon Sch. award U.S. Dept. Edn., 1990-91. Office: Canyon Vista Mid Sch 8455 Spicewood Springs Rd Austin TX 78759-6099*

DALTON, FRANCES MARLENE, business consultant; b. Clarksburg, W.Va., Mar. 8, 1953; d. Russell Lynwood and Wanta (Biggs) D.; m. Bary Lynn Kuhn, Oct. 17, 1997. BS, U. Balt., 1982; MAS, Johns Hopkins U., 1988. Dir. U.S. mktg. Tate Access Floors, Jessup, Md., 1986-91; founder, pres. Dalton Alliances, Inc., Balt., 1991—; adj. faculty mem. U. Md., Balt., 1995—; entrepreneurial cons. Indsl. Video Magic, Balt., 1993—; cons., presenter seminars in field. Author, presenter video The Chameleon's Edge, 1993. With U.S. Army, 1972-77. Mem. Am. Soc. Assn. Execs., Soc. for Human Resource Mgmt., Chesapeake Human Resources Assn. Republican. Presbyterian. Avocations: wilderness retreats, dogs, Bible study. Home and Office: 1203 Watervale Ct Pasadena MD 21122-2366

DALTON, HOWARD EDWARD, retired accounting executive; b. N.Y.C., June 28, 1937; s. Edward R. and Josephine J. Dalton; m. Elizabeth J. Jeronimus; children: Kevin, Kathleen. BSBA, Holy Cross, 1959. CPA. Ptnr. KPMG Peat Marwick, Mpls., 1959-87; sr. v.p., chief acctg. officer St. Paul Cos., Inc., 1987-98. Treas., dir. Cath. Charities, Mpls., 1978—. Avocations: golf, travel. Address: 11551 E Bronco Trail Scottsdale AZ 85255

DALTON, JAMES EDGAR, JR., health facility administrator; b. Gretna, Va., Sept. 17, 1942; married. Bachelors degree, Randolph-Macon Coll., 1964; Masters degree, Va. Commonwealth U., 1966. Adminstrv. resident Lynchburg (Va.) Gen. Hosp., 1965-66, adminstrv. asst., 1966-69, asst. adminstr., 1969-70; adminstr. Princeton (W.Va.) Community Hosp., 1970-72; regional adminstr. Humana Inc., Dallas, 1972-73; regional v.p. Humana Inc., Tampa, Fla., 1973-76; dir. hosp. svcs. Am. Medicorp Inc., Atlanta, 1976-77, Dallas, 1977-78; v.p. Hosp. Corp. Am., Nashville, 1978-79, Arlington, Tex., 1979-87; v.p. HealthTrust, Inc., Arlington, 1987-89, Nashville, 1989-90; pres., CEO Quorum Health Group, Inc., Brentwood, Tenn., 1990—. Home: 6505 Edinburgh Dr Nashville TN 37221-3707 Office: Quorum Health Group 103 Continental Pl Brentwood TN 37027-5014

DALTON, JENNIFER FAYE, accountant; b. Maryville, Tenn., May 1, 1959; d. James Theodore Teffeteller and Melody (Potts) Allison; m. Robert Byron Dalton, Dec. 15, 1979. Student, U. Tenn., 1977-79, Coastal Carolina Community Coll., 1980-81, 84-86; BS in Mgmt., Golden Gate U., Camp Lejeune, N.C., 1982. Bookkeeper, with accounts payable dept. McMar Too, Inc., Jacksonville, N.C., 1980-83; acctg. technician City of Jacksonville, 1983-89; acctg. mgr., corp. sec. treas. Bankers Mortgage Corp., Louisville, 1989-92; sr. acct., payroll officer City of Louisville, 1992-96; sr. acct. Louisville Zoo, 1996—. Alcoa Found. scholar, 1977. Mem. Amateur Radio Transmitting Soc., Inst. Mgmt. Accts., Gamma Beta Phi. Republican. Baptist. Avocations: amateur radio, pistol shooting, sailing, water skiing, swimming. Home: 827 Markham Ln Louisville KY 40207-4444

DALTON, JOHN HOWARD, Former Secretary of the Navy, financial consultant; b. New Orleans, Dec. 13, 1941; s. William Carl and Jaunice Dalton (Davenport) Winterrowd Dalton; m. Margaret; children: John Jr., Chris. BSCum Laude, U.S. Naval Acad., 1964; MBA, U. Pa., 1971. Commd. ensign USN, 1964, advanced through grades to lt., resigned, 1969; investment bank trainee Goldman, Sachs & Co., N.Y.C., 1971-72; with security sales sect. Goldman, Sachs & Co., Dallas, 1972-77; pres. Govt. Nat. Mortgage Assn., Washington, 1977-79; nat. treas. Carter/Mondale Presdl. Campaign, Washington, 1979; chmn., mem. Fed. Home Loan Bank Bd., Washington, 1979-81; pres. real estate div. Gill Cos., San Antonio, 1981-84; chmn., pres. Seguin Savs. Assn., San Antonio, 1984-88; chmn., chief exec. officer Freedom Capital Corp., San Antonio, 1984-88; Secretary of the Navy, 1993-98; pres. Stephens, Inc. San Antonio; managing dir. Best Assocs. & Mason Best Co., Houston/Dallas; chmn. fin. inst. adv. com. Fed. Res. Bank Dallas; bd. dirs. Capstead Mortgage (formerly Lomas Mortgage Corp.); Lt. Commander, U.S. Naval Reserve. Trustee Ecumenical Ctr. Religion and Health, San Antonio, 1983—, Mental Health Assn. Tex., Austin, 1986-88, YMCA, San Antonio, 1984-89; chmn. World Affairs Coun., San Antonio, 1987-89. Democrat. Episcopalian. Lodge: Elks. Finalist, Rhodes Scholarship Competition. *

DALTON, JOHN JOSEPH, lawyer; b. N.Y.C., Feb. 7, 1943; s. John Henry and Anna Veronica (Chiusano) D.; m. Martha E. Dalton, Feb. 24, 1968; children: Martha G., J. Michael, W. Brian. BBA, Fairfield U., 1964; JD, Northwestern U., 1967. Bar: Ill. 1967, Ga. 1970, U.S. Dist. Ct. (no. and mid. dists.) Ga., U.S. Dist. Ct. (no. dist.) Ill., U.S. Ct. Appeals (2d, 4th, 5th, 7th, 10th and 11th cirs.), U.S. Tax Ct., U.S. Supreme Ct. Atty. Clausen, Miller, Gorman, Caffrey & Witous, Chgo., 1967-69; ptnr. Troutman Sanders (formerly Troutman, Sanders, Lockerman & Ashmore), Atlanta, 1970—. Chmn. bd. Atlanta Vol. Lawyers Found., 1993. With U.S. Army, 1968-69.

Fellow Am. Coll. Trial Lawyers, Am. Bar Found.; mem. Atlanta Bar Assn. (dir.), Piedmont Driving Club, Peachtree Golf Club. Office: Troutman Sanders 600 Peachtree St NE Ste 5200 Atlanta GA 30308-2216

DALTON, LARRY RAYMOND, chemistry educator, researcher, consultant; b. Belpre, Ohio, Apr. 25, 1945; s. Leonard William Henry and Virginia (Maylee) D.; m. Nicole A. Boand. BS with honors, Mich. State U., 1965, MS, 1966; AM, PhD, Harvard U., 1971. Asst. prof. chemistry Vanderbilt U., Nashville, 1971-73; assoc. prof. Vanderbilt U., 1973-77, research prof. biochemistry, 1977-98; assoc. prof. SUNY-Stony Brook, 1976-81, prof., 1981-82; prof. U. So. Calif., Los Angeles, 1982-94, Harold Moulton prof. chemistry, 1994-98, sci. co-dir. Loker hydrocarbon rsch. inst., 1994-98; prof. materials sci. and engring. U. So. Calif., 1994-98; prof. chemistry U. Wash., 1998—; cons., IBM Corp., Yorktown, N.Y., IBM Instruments Co., Danbury, Conn., 1977-85, Celanese Rsch. Corp., 1987—, Lockheed Missiles and Space Co., 1988—, Maxdem Inc., 1990; cons. rev. of NIH sickle cell ctrs. USPHS, 1981-82; mem. parent com. for rev. of comprehensive sickle cell ctrs. Nat. Heart, Lung, Blood Inst.-NIH, 1987, 92; panelist for presdl. young investigator awards NSF, Washington, 1983, 89, panelist for presdl. faculty fellow awards, 1986, mem. materials rsch. adv. com., 1984-90, mem. high magnetic field panel, 1987; bd. dirs. Key Mgmt., Inc., Bomans, Inc.; mem. NAS-NRC panel for selection of NSF predoctoral fellows, 1989—; mem. panel for selection DOD predoctoral fellows. Editor-author: EPR and Advanced EPR Studies of Biological Systems, 1985. Recipient Burlington No. Found. Faculty Achievement award, 1986, U. So. Calif. Assocs. award, 1990, Profl. Achievement award Spring Arbor Coll., 1993; Camille and Henry Dreyfus tchr./scholar, 1975-77; rsch. career devel. grantee NIH, 1976-81; Alfred P. Sloan Found. fellow, 1974-77. Mem. Am. Chem. Soc. (Richard C. Tolman medal 1996), Sigma Xi. Avocations: skiing; hiking. Office: U Wash Dept Chemistry Box 351700 Seattle WA 98195-1700

DALTON, LINDA CATHERINE, university administrator; b. Seattle, May 5, 1945; d. Chester Carlton and Dorothy Catherine (Salladay) Little; m. Thomas Barron Fitzpatrick, June 10, 1967 (div. 1983); children: Pandora Catherine, Benjamin Lawrence; m. Thomas Carlyle Dalton, Aug. 16, 1984. AB magna cum laude, Radcliffe Coll., 1967; M.Urban Planning, U. Wash., 1974, PhD in Urban Planning, 1978. Archtl./historic preservation staff Boston Redevel. Authority, 1967-68; long-range campus planner MIT, Cambridge, Mass., 1969-71; environ. impact analyst Kelly Pittelko Fritz & Forssen Cons., Seattle, 1974-76; lectr. Seattle U., 1976-78, asst. prof., 1978-82, assoc. prof., 1982-83; assoc. prof. Calif. Poly. State U., San Luis Obispo, 1983-87, prof. city and regional planning, 1987—, dept. head city and regional planning, 1989-95; interim assoc. v.p. acad. resources Calif. Poly. State U., 1995-97, vice provost for instnl. planning, 1997—. Contbr. articles to profl. jours.; mem. editl. bds. profl. jours. Mem. Citizen Transp. Adv. Com., San Luis Obispo, 1990-94; mem. vis. com. Coll. Arch. and Urban Planning, U. Wash., Seattle, 1982-83; mem., vice chair, chair Seattle City Planning Commn., 1979-83; mem. Planning Accreditation Bd., 1992-97, chair, 1993-97. Am. Coun. on Edn. fellow, 1994-95; Nat. Merit scholar, 1963-67. Mem. Am. Inst. Cert. Planners (cert.), Am. Planning Assn., Assn. Collegiate Sch. of Planning (exec. com. 1990-97), Calif. Planning Found. (v.p. 1995-98, pres. 1998—). Avocation: wildflowers. Office: California Poly State Univ San Luis Obispo CA 93407

DALTON, MATT, retired foundry executive; b. Chgo., June 27, 1922; s. Donald J. and Jessie (Shrimplim) D.; children: D. J., J. B., Katherine A.; m. Frances Walter, Jan. 1, 1994. Student, Pomona Coll., Claremont, Calif., Butler U.; grad. advanced mgmt. program, Harvard U., 1956. Pres. Dalton Foundries, Inc., Warsaw, Ind., 1959-68, chmn. bd., 1968-91, chmn. emeritus, 1992-94. Founder Warsaw Jr. Achievement, 1953; charter mem. bd. dirs. Warsaw Devel. Corp., 1973; mem. Warsaw Community Sch. Bd., 1962-68, Kosciusko County Coun., 1981-84—; trustee Ind. Vocat. Tech. Coll., 1964-70; chmn. Gov. of Ind. Com. on Youth Employment, 1979-82; pres. Lake Tippecanoe Property Owners Assn., 1979-82; founder, chmn. Kosciusko Econ. Devel. Corp., 1984, Kosciusko Leadership Acad., 1981; mem. Ind. Econ. Devel. Coun., 1984-88, Ind. Commn. on Vocat. and Tech. Edn., 1988-89; del. Ind. Gov.'s Far East Tour, 1987. With AUS, 1943-45. Mem. Ind. State C. of C. (chmn. 1982-84), Warsaw C. of C. (chmn., found. Indsl. Div. 1959). Office: PO Box 181099 Coronado CA 92178

DALTON, ROBERT EDGAR, mathematician, computer scientist; b. Boston, May 2, 1938; s. Robert Evelyn and Mildred Louise (Zoellick) D.; m. Sally Turner, Sept. 12, 1961 (div. 1977); children: Stephen Howard, Alena Lynn; m. Judith Eyges, July 17, 1993. BS in Math., U. Chgo., 1959; MS in Applied Math., N.C. State U., 1961, PhD in Applied Math., 1964; MS in Computer Sci., Fla. State U., 1982. Systems analyst RCA Svc. Co., Cocoa Beach, Fla., 1964-65; mem. tech. staff TRW Systems Group, Cocoa Beach, 1965-71; ops. rsch. analyst Naval Underwater Systems Ctr., West Palm Beach, Fla., 1971-79; grad. teaching asst. Fla. State U., Tallahassee, 1980-81; asst. prof. Am. U., Washington, 1981-83; mem. tech. staff Mitre Corp., Greenbelt, Md., 1983-85; prin. investigator Vitro Corp., Silver Spring, Md., 1985-93; sr. software devel. engr. Raytheon Co., Tewksbury, Mass., 1995—; adj. prof. Fla. Inst. Tech., 1964-68, Fla. Atlantic U., 1979. Contbr. chpts. to books, articles to jours. Sec. U.S. Jaycees, Boynton Beach, Fla., 1974; chmn. U. Chgo. Alumni Fund, Palm Beach County, Fla., 1975-79. Recipient Spl. Achievement award Naval Underwater Sys. Ctr., 1974, 76. Mem. IEEE, Am. Assn. Artificial Intelligence. Achievements include research in knowledge acquisition and learning, computer games, pattern recognition, knowledge-based system development, and decision support with fuzzy logic. Home: 26 Crescent Rd Winchester MA 01890-2814

DALTON, ROBERT ISSAC, JR., textile executive, consultant, researcher; b. Charlotte, N.C., Apr. 2, 1921; s. Robert I. and Edith (Gossett) D.; m. Gwin Barnwell, Nov. 16, 1946; children—Millie, Edith. B.S. in Textile Engring., N.C. State U. Vice pres. sales Whitin Machine Works, Whitinsville, Mass., 1946-67; pres. Cocker Machine and Foundry, Gastonia, N.C., 1967-70, Tech-Tex Inc., Charlotte, 1970—, Gossett-Dalton Co., Charlotte, 1973—, dir., 1955—; bd. dir. Cadmus Communication Co., Richmond, Va., 1983-96, Am.-Truetzschler, Charlotte, 1976-97, N.C. Nat. Bank, Charlotte, 1962-94. Pres. Charlotte Symphony Orch., 1979-80; mem. bd. edn. Mecklenburg County, Charlotte, 1957-58; chmn. nat. bd. dirs. Handicapped Orgn. Women, Inc., 1986; chmn. bd. trustees Brevard Coll, 1987-93, Brevard Music Ctr., 1998—. Served to maj. U.S. Army, 1943-46, ETO. Mem. Phi Psi. Methodist. Clubs: Charlotte City (pres. 1980-81), Charlotte Country. Avocations: tennis; photography. Home: 318 S Canterbury Rd Charlotte NC 28211-1838

DALTON, RONNIE THOMAS, theology educator; b. Dayton, Ohio, Apr. 25, 1953; s. Merl Thomas and Luttie (Scrimager) D.; m. Martha Gomer, Oct. 15, 1977; children: John Thomas, James Douglas, Stephen Wade. AA, Mt. Vernon Nazarene Coll., 1973; BA, Trevecca Nazarene Coll., 1975; MDiv, Nazarene Theol. Sem., 1979; D Ministry, Vanderbilt U., 1984. Ordained to ministry Ch. of Nazarene, 1983. Pastor Ch. of Brethren, St. Joseph, Mo., 1977-78; assoc. pastor Grace Nazarene Ch., Chattanooga, 1979-80; v.p. Nazarene Youth Internat., Dist. E. Tenn., 1982-84; teaching asst. Vanderbilt Div. Sch., Nashville, 1983-84; pastor West View Nazarene Ch., Lebanon, Tenn., 1980-85, Montana Ave Nazarene Ch., Cin., 1985; assoc. prof. practical theology Olivet Nazarene U., Kankakee, Ill., 1993—, dir. Ch. Growth Rsch. & Resource Ctr., 1995—, chair master of pastoral counseling and master of ch. mgmt. programs, 1996—, chair master of min., dir. Inst. Pastoral Leadership, 1996—; adj. prof. religion Mt. Vernon Nazarene Coll.; dir. mins. tng. seminars Antioch U. Mem. Am. Acad. of Religion, Religious Rsch. Assn., Wesleyan Theol. Soc. Avocations: computer programming and design, golf, antique auto rebuilding. Home: 1454 Westminster Ln Bourbonnais IL 60914-1636 Office: Olivet Nazarene U PO Box 592 Kankakee IL 60901-0592 *The challenge of holiness is to reconcile our experiences of Being in the World and those of Being in Christ. It is an ethic which is both personal and social, attained by both personal struggle and Divine gift.*

DALTON, THOMAS GEORGE, paralegal, social worker, legal consultant; b. Hoonah, Alaska, Mar. 13, 1940; s. George and Jessie K. (Starr) D.; m. Hazel Hope, Nov. 1960 (div. Sept. 1965); children: Roderick O., Rhoeda J. Garcia, Pamela Y. Masterman; m. Kathy Pelan, Sept. 1972 (div. Feb. 1980); children: Deirdra J. (dec.), Thomas L., Michael G. AAS, Shoreline Community Coll., Seattle, 1981; BA, Seattle Pacific U., 1984. Paralegal, social worker Pub. Defender's Assn., Seattle, 1983—; client advocate in criminal justice system Seattle, 1984—; legal cons., Seattle; tchr. Tlingit Culture and Lang., Northwest Indian Coll., Bellingham, Wash. Elder United Presbyn. Ch., Hoonah, 1973—; pres. Alaska Native Brotherhood, Seattle, 1984—, Nat. Am. Community Coun., Seattle, 1990—; pres. Seattle chpt. Tlinget and Haida Indians Alaska; bd. dir. LANCE (Leading Am. Native for Excellence), 1996—. Recipient Founder's award Alaska Native Brotherhood, 1989. Democrat. Home: 7009 10th Ave NW Seattle WA 98117-5242 Office: Ctrl Bldg 8th fl 810 3rd Ave Seattle WA 98104-1655

DALTON, TIMOTHY, actor; b. Wales, Mar. 21, 1944. Actor appearing in films in Eng., France, Spain and U.S.; The Lion in Winter, 1968, Cromwell, 1970, Wuthering Heights, 1970, Mary, Queen of Scots, 1971, Lady Caroline Lamb, 1972, Permission to Kill, 1975, El Hombre Que Supo Amar, 1975, Sextette, 1978, Agatha, 1979, Glash Gordon, 1980, Chanel Solitaire, 1981, Mistral's Daughter, 1984, Florence Nightingale, 1985, The Doctor and the Devils, 1985, Sins, 1986, The Living Daylights, 1987, Licence to Kill, 1989, Hawks, 1989, La Putain du roi, 1990, The Rocketeer, 1991, Brenda Starr, 1992, Naked in New York, 1994, Scarlett, 1994, Beautician and the Beast, 1997; TV films Five Finger Exercise, 1970, The Flame is Love, 1979, The Master of Ballantrae, 1984, The Emporer's New Clothes, 1984, Florence Nightingale, 1985, The Tradgedy of Antony and Cleopatra, 1989, Framed, 1993, Lie Down With Lions, 1994; TV series Sat'day While Sunday, 1966, Centennial, 1978, Jane Eyre, 1983, The Mistral's Daughter, 1984, Sins, 1986, Scarlett, 1994, Cleopatra, 1999. Office: Internat Creative Mgmt 8943 Wilshire Blvd Beverly Hills CA 90211-1907*

DALTON, WALLER LISLE, obstetrician and gynecologist; b. Louisville, July 19, 1944; s. Roscoe Rueben and Mary Dorothy (Baker) D.; m. Katherine Headley Vance, July 14, 1971; children: Waller Lisle Jr., Charles Vance, Robert Rodes. BA, Williams Coll., Williamstown, Mass., 1966; MD, U. Ky., 1975. Lic. MD, Ky. Internship U. Ky., 1975-76, residency, 1976-79; ob-gyn Lexington (Ky.) Clinic, 1979—. Bd. dirs. Ctrl. Ky. Blood Ctr., Lexington, 1997-98; mem. vestry Christ Ch. Episc., Lexington, 1991-94. Lt. (j.g.) USN, 1966-69. Fellow ACOG (state chmn. jr. fellows 1978-79); mem. Fayette County Med. Soc. (pres. 1998-99), Lexington Ob-Gyn. Soc., John Greene Jr. Soc., Idle Hour Country Club , Iroquois Hunt Club. Avocations: golf, skiing, woodwork, boating, horseback riding. Home: 1409 Essex Park Lexington KY 40502-2814 Office: Lexington Clinic 100 N Eagle Creek Dr Lexington KY 40509-1805

DALY, CECILY A., author, educator; b. Spanish Town, Jamaica, May 15, 1938; d. Wilfred Anderson Reece and Daisy Lucinda (Price) Reece-Batten; divorced; children: Hilary, Nadine. BEd, West Indies Coll., Mandeville, Jamaica, 1972; MA, Western Carolina U., Cullowhee, N.C., 1979; EdD, U. Ala., Tuscaloosa, 1994. Tchr. Northestern Conf., N.Y.C., 1982-85, Jamaica, 1958-80; adj. instr. edn./reading Ala. A&M U., Normal, 1988-97; assoc. prof. dept. English Oakwood Coll., Huntsville, Ala., 1985—, reading specialist Ctr. for Acad. Advancement, 1985—; initiator, sponsor Oakwood Lit. Guild, Huntsville, 1989—; rschr. Oakwood Ctr. for Acad. Advancement, 1990-94. Author: Memba de Culcha, 1997; lead author: An Interactive Reading Manual, 1998, Accompanying Instructors Manual, 1998. Counselor, Boys and Girls Club, Huntsville, 1989-90. Mem. Internat. Reading Assn., Nat. Assn. for Devel. Edn., Ala. Assn. for Devel. Edn., Nat. Coun. Tcrs. English, Rev. and Herald Authors Guild, Kappa Delta Pi. Home: 3903 Nelson Dr NW Huntsville AL 35810-3919

DALY, CHARLES ARTHUR, health services administrator; b. Hartford, Conn., Aug. 22, 1945; s. Robert William and Josephine Frances (Gustafson) D.; m. Leslie Jane Lane, Nov. 5, 1967; children: Cheryl, Christopher. BA, Yale U., 1967; MHA, U. Mich., 1974. Mgr. Blue Cross and Blue Shield of Mich., Detroit, 1974-83; v.p. Del. Valley Hosp. Coun., Phila., 1984-96, Health Visions, Inc., Pennsauken, N.J., 1996-97, South Ctrl. Health Planning Coun., Brick, N.J., 1997-98; Bd. dirs. Health Strategy Network, Phila., Phila. AIDS Consortium, Phila. Health Mmgt. Corp.; mem. Phila. Emergency Med. Svcs. Coun., 1984-96. Lt. USN, 1967-72. Fellow Am. Coll. Healthcare Execs. Avocations: swimming, golf, baseball. Home: 304 Bickmore Dr Wallingford PA 19086-6856

DALY, CHARLES ULICK, foundation executive; b. Dublin, May 29, 1927; came to U.S., 1934, naturalized, 1940; s. Ulick deBurgh and Violet (Sealy-King) D.; m. Mary Larmonth, June 11, 1949 (dec.); children: Michael, Douglas; m. Christine Sullivan, Nov. 5, 1988; children: Charles, Kevin. B.A. Internat. Relations, Yale U., 1949; M.S. Journalism, Columbia U., 1959. Mgr. then v.p. Mexican subs. Pacific Molases Co., San Francisco, 1949-50, 52-58; congl. fellow Am. Polit. Sci. Assn., 1959-60; editor Stanford U., Calif., 1961; staff asst. Pres. Kennedy and Pres. Johnson, 1962-64; v.p. U. Chgo., 1964-71; v.p. govt. and cmty. affairs Harvard U., Cambridge, Mass., 1971-76; editor Media and the Cities, The Quality of Inequality, Urban Violence; pres. Joyce Found., Chgo., 1978-86; dir. John F. Kennedy Found., Boston, 1988—; mem. Lloyd's of London, 1976—; freelance writer, 1958—. Mem. Commn. on Adminstrv. Rev., U.S. Ho. of Reps.; chmn. Donor's Forum, Chgo., 1980; bd. dirs. Am. Ireland Fund, Joint Ctr. for Polit. Studies, Princes Holdings, Ireland. With USNR, 1945-46; USMCR, 1950-52. Decorated Silver Star, Purple Heart. Mem. Bantry Golf Club (Ireland), Bantry Sailing Club (Ireland), St. Botolph Club (Boston), Hibernian Club (Dublin), Boca Grande Club (Fla.). Office: John F Kennedy Libr Found Columbia Pt Dorchester MA 02125

DALY, CHERYL, broadcast executive; b. Providence, Apr. 20, 1947; d. Francis Patrick and Mary Ann (Wallis) D.; m. Arthur James Generas, July 18, 1970; 1 child, Caroline. BA, Rutgers U., 1969; postgrad., New Sch. for Social Rsch., 1975-78. Account exec. Phil Dean Assocs., N.Y.C., 1969-72; dir. pub. rels. Kirkland Coll., Clinton, N.Y., 1972-75; mgr. press svcs. CBS Radio, N.Y.C., 1976-80; assoc. dir. internal comm. CBS, Inc., N.Y.C., 1980-81, dir. corp. info., 1981-83; v.p. pub. rels. Group W Satellite Comm., N.Y.C., 1984-95, sr. v.p. pub. rels., 1995-97; sr. v.p. pub. rels. CBS Cable, N.Y.C., 1997—; examiner Westinghouse Quality Awards, Pitts., 1990. Recipient Best Co. Communication award Cable TV Bus., 1986, mktg. award Westinghouse Broadcasting Co., 1991. Mem. Cable TV Pub. Affairs Assn. (bd. dirs. 1985-87), Media Mommies (co-founder 1987). Democrat. Roman Catholic. Home: 1 W 67th St New York NY 10023-6200 Office: CBS Cable 685 3rd Ave Fl 17 New York NY 10017-4024

DALY, CHRISTOPHER BURKE, journalist, educator; b. Boston, July 7, 1954; s. John Edward and Mary Gertrude (Duggan) D.; m. Anne K. Fishel, Sept. 9, 1955; children: Gabriel, Joseph. BA magna cum laude, Harvard U., 1976; MA, U. N.C., 1982. Statehouse bur. chief AP, Boston, 1986-89; contbg. editor New England Monthly, Haydenville, Mass., 1987-90; instr. Harvard U., Cambridge, Mass., 1994-97; lectr. Brandeis U., Waltham, Mass., 1995; New England corr. Washington Post, Boston, 1989-97; contbg. writer Commonwealth Mag., Boston, 1995—; vis. assoc. prof. journalism Boston U., 1997-98, now assoc. prof. journalism, 1998—; cons. Trellix Corp., Waltham, 1996-97. Co-author: Like a Family, 1987 (Taft & Beveridge award 1988); contbr. articles to various mags. Waddell fellow U. N.C., Chapel Hill, 1980-82. Mem. Nat. Writers Union, Soc. Profl. Journalists. Avocations: gardening, birding. E-mail: cdaly@bu.edu. Office: Boston Univ Dept Journalism 640 Commonwealth Ave Boston MA 02215-2422

DALY, CHUCK (CHARLES JEROME DALY), sports commentator, professional basketball coach; b. St. Mary's, Pa., July 20, 1930; m. Terry Daly; 1 child, Cydney. Student, St. Bonaventure U., 1948-49, Bloomsburg State Coll., 1949-52; MA, Pa. State U. Asst. coach Duke U., Durham, N.C., 1963-69; coach Boston Coll., 1969-71, U. Pa., Phila., 1971-77; asst. coach Phila. 76ers, 1977-81; coach Cleve. Cavaliers, 1981-82, Detroit Pistons, 1983-92, N.J. Nets, 1992-94; sports commentator TNT, 1995-97; head coach Orlando Magic, 1997-99, cons., 1999—; coach, 1992 U.S. Olympic basketball team. Coached team to NBA Championship, 1989, 90; elected to Basketball Hall of Fame, 1994. *

DALY, DONALD F., engineering company executive; b. Morristown, N.J., Jan. 10, 1933; s. John F. and Sophie E. (Podeski) D.; m. Bennie L. London, Nov. 2, 1963; children: Stephen, David, Eric. ME, Stevens Inst. Tech., 1955. Equipment engr. Corning (N.Y.) Glass Works, 1955-56; sales engr. Mundet Cork, 1958-60; process engr. Thiokol Chem. Corp., 1961-65; dir. engring. Syntex Corp., 1966-78; v.p., project mgr. Indsl. Design Corp., 1978—; dir. Tech. Design & Constrn. Co., Portland, Oreg., 1992-94. Republican. Avocations: golf, skiing, horse ranching. Home: 15596 SW Midway Rd Hillsboro OR 97123-9431 Office: Industrial Design Corp 2020 SW 4th Ave Fl 3 Portland OR 97201-4953

DALY, DONALD FRANCIS, investment counsel; b. Bridgeport, Conn., Aug. 6, 1928; s. Christopher M. and Anne F. (Kelleher) D.; m. Magdalene Johnston, July 10, 1953 (div. 1975); children: Candace, Jacqueline, Elizabeth, Patrick; m. Susan S. Coyle, Mar. 21, 1976 (div. 1984); 1 child, Jennifer (dec.); m. Sandra R. Godfrey, Apr. 19, 1985; 1 child, Samuel. AB, Yale U., 1950. Account exec. Hemphill Noyes, N.Y.C., 1957-63; v.p. Scudder Stevens & Clark, N.Y.C., 1963-78; ptnr. Brundage Story & Rose, N.Y.C., 1978-95; sr. v.p. Mellon Bank Pvt. Asset Mgmt., Phila., 1995-96; dir. acquisitions Mellon Pvt. Asset Mgmt., 1996-98; cons. Mellow Pvt. Asset Mgmt., 1998—; pres. Brundage Story & Rose Mut. Funds, 1990-95; adv. bd. Charles Schwab & Co., 1993-94; dir. Mellon Trust of N.Y., 1996-98. Mem. Korean Meml. Commn., 1989-91; pres. Diocesan Trust, Episc. Diocese of N.Y., 1990-94. Capt. U.S. Army, 1950-57. Decorated Disting. Svc. Cross, Bronze Star medals (2), Purple Heart (2), Gold Medal of Valor, Greece, Chung Mu Disting. Svc. Cross, Korea. Fellow N.Y. Soc. Security Analysts; mem. Am. Inst. Investment Mgrs., Investment Counsel Assn. (former gov.), Phila. Estate Planning Coun., Order of St. John of Jerusalem, Yale Club N.Y., Church Club N.Y., Point O'Woods Club, The Pilgrims. Republican. Home: 321 S Roberts Rd Bryn Mawr PA 19010 Office: Mellon Bank Pvt Asset Mgmt 1735 Market St Philadelphia PA 19103-7501

DALY, GEORGE GARMAN, college dean, educator; b. Painesville, Ohio, Oct. 5, 1940; s. George Ferdinand and Helen May (Garman) D.; m. Barbara Leigh Anthony, Mar. 13, 1977. A.B., Miami U., Oxford, Ohio, 1962; M.A., Northwestern U., 1965, Ph.D., 1967. Asst. then assoc. prof. Miami U., Oxford, 1965-69; asst. prof. U. Tex., Austin, 1969-70; asst. prof., then prof. U. Houston, 1971-77, dean Coll. Social Sci., 1979-83; dean Coll. Bus. U. Iowa, Iowa City, 1983-93; dean Stern Sch. Bus. NYU, N.Y.C., 1993—; sr. economist Exec. Officer Pres., Washington, 1974; economist Fed. Energy Agy., Washington, 1975-76; adv. bd. Ctr. Pub. Policy, Houston. Mem. Am. Econs. Assn., Public Choice Soc., Phi Beta Kappa, Beta Gamma Sigma. Home: 29 Washington Sq W Apt 10A New York NY 10011-9128 Office: Mgmt Edn Ctr NYU 44 W 4th St New York NY 10012-1106*

DALY, GERALD, accountant; b. Montreal, Que., Can., Apr. 1, 1948; s. Paul and Rejane (De RePentigny) D.; m. Danielle Raymond, Dec. 20, 1969 (div. 1978); m. Nicole Huot, June 17, 1994. BA, U. Mont., 1969; MS in Comm., U. Sherbrooke, 1973. CA, cert. info. systems auditor, cert. mgmt. cons., fraud examiner. Mgr. Coopers & Lybrand, Montreal, 1973-80; ptnr. Raymond, Chabot, Grant, Thornton, Montreal, 1980—. Mem. Inst. Internal Auditors (gov. 1989-92), EDP Auditors Assn. (v.p., sec. 1983-86). Office: Raymond Chabot Martin & Pare, 600 Rue Gauchietiere Quest, Bureau 1900, Montreal, PQ Canada H3B 4L8

DALY, JAMES JOSEPH, bishop; b. Bronx, N.Y., Aug. 14, 1921; s. Thomas and Catherine (Cass) D. Grad., Immaculate Conception Sem., Huntington, 1948; LL.D., Molloy Coll., Rockville Centre, N.Y., St. John's U., Jamaica, N.Y., 1979. Ordained priest Roman Catholic Ch., 1948; priest Our Lady of Snow, Blue Point, N.Y., 1948-51, Holy Child Jesus, Richmond Hill, 1951, St. William the Abbot, Seaford, 1951-58; procurator Immaculate Conception Sem., Huntington, 1958; dir. Priests' Personnel Bd., 1968-72; pastor St. Boniface, Elmont; aux. bishop of Rockville Centre, 1977—; vicar gen. Diocese of Rockville Centre, 1989—, now aux. bishop, vicar gen. Address: 25 Lanes End Blue Point NY 11715-2003

DALY, JOE ANN GODOWN, publishing company executive; b. Galveston, Tex., Aug. 7, 1924; d. Elmer and Jessie Fee (Beck) Godown; m. William Jerome Daly, Jr., Jan. 25, 1958 (dec.). BA in Journalism, U. Okla., 1945, BA in Piano, 1952. Asst. editor house organ Southwestern Bell Telephone, St. Louis, 1945-47; sec. to city mgr. Okla. Daily News, Oklahoma City, 1947-49; pvt. piano tchr. Alva, Okla., 1952-54; sec. to editor Prentice-Hall, Inc., N.Y.C., 1954-55, asst. to children's book editor, 1955-58; asst. editor children's books Dodd, Mead & Co., N.Y.C., 1963, dir. children's books, 1965-88, asst. v.p., assoc. pub. children's books, 1986-88; editorial dir. Cobblehill Books affiliate Dutton Children's Books, N.Y.C., 1988-97, ret., 1997; mem. Children's Book Council, N.Y.C., 1963, treas., 1969; mem. CBC/LA Com., N.Y.C., 1980, CBC/Prelude Com., N.Y.C., 1983. Active Bklyn. Heights Assn., 1976—; friend Carnegie Hall, N.Y. Philharm.; mem. Met. Opera Guild, Mus. Modern Art, Mus. Natural History. Mem. Phi Beta Kappa, Sigma Delta Chi, Theta Sigma Phi, Mu Phi Epsilon. Democrat. Methodist. Home: 80 Cranberry St Brooklyn NY 11201-1726

DALY, JOHN, professional golfer; b. Dardanelle, Ark., 1966. Student, U. Ark. Winner golf tournaments including PGA Championship, 1991, B.C. Open, 1992, Bell South Classic, 1994, British Open, 1995. Address: care PGA Am 100 Avenue Of Champions Palm Bch Gdns FL 33418-3653*

DALY, JOHN NEAL, investment company executive; b. Washington, Nov. 14, 1937; s. John Charles, Jr. and Margaret Criswell (Neal) D.; m. Barbara Claire Krueger, Apr. 2, 1966; children: John Gorman, Cristina Reed. BA, Yale U., 1959, postgrad. Law Sch., 1959-60; AMP, Harvard Bus. Sch., 1979. With E.F. Hutton & Co., Inc., N.Y.C., 1960-83; exec. v.p., dir. E.F. Hutton & Co., Inc., to 1983; v.p. Salomon Bros. Inc., N.Y.C., 1983-87, 89, Salomon Bros Internat. Ltd., London, 1987-89; pres. RS&A Cons. Inc., 1990-93; mng. dir. Spears Benzak Salomon & Farrell, N.Y.C., 1993-98, Trainer, Wortham & Co., Inc., 1999—; exch. ofcl. Am. Stock Exch., 1979; trustee Culinary Inst. Am., 1992—, treas., 1993—; dir. Hist. Soc. of the Town of Greenwich, 1991-97. Mem. Bond Club N.Y. (sec. 1973-74, gov. 1975-78), Securities Industry Assn. (chmn. nat. syndicate com. 1978-78), Comex Clearing Assn. (dir. 1981-87), Burning Tree Club, Yale Club N.Y., Mark's Club, Knickerbocker Club, Round Hill Club, The Sky Club. Home: 338 Stanwich Rd Greenwich CT 06830-3530 Office: Trainer Wortham & Co Inc 845 Third Ave New York NY 10022

DALY, JOHN W., chemistry research administrator. Chief of pharmacoduinmics Nat. Inst. of Diabetes and Digestive and Kidney Disases, Division of Intramural Reaearch Lab. of Bioorganic Chemistry, Bethesda, Md., 1992—. Mem. Am. Chem. Soc. (Hillebrand prize 1977), AAAS, Internat. Soc. Neurochemists. Office: Nat Inst Diabetes and Digestive Bldg 8 Rm 1A-17 9000 Rockville Pike Bethesda MD 20892-0001

DALY, PATRICK F., real estate executive, architect; b. Chgo., Jan. 25, 1949; s. John F. and Margaret M. (Gleason) D.; m. Shirley J. Kumis, June 25, 1971; children: Sean P., James P. BArch with honors and distinction, U. Ill., Chgo., 1972, BA in Archtl. History with honors and distinction, 1972. Cert. arch., Ill. Prin. Patrick F. Daly Archs. & Engrs., Chgo., 1975-77; chmn. bd. Armanco, Inc., Chgo., 1977—, PFDA, Inc., Chgo., 1975—, DEI, Inc., Chgo., 1980—, Dalan Devel. Corp., Chgo., 1986—; pres. Dalan/Jupiter, Inc., Chgo., 1987—; mng. ptnr. Rising Sun Riverboat Casino and Resort, LLC, Chgo., 1995—; chmn. The Daly Group LLC, 1995—; bd. dirs. Internat. Marine & Gaming, Inc. (chmn. bd.) Empire Cruise Lines, Inc. Contbr. articles to profl. jours. Chmn. Ill. Ambs., Chgo., 1990-98; vice chmn. Met. Pier & Expn. Authority, Chgo., 1985—; commr. Nat. Adv. Commn. U.S. Dept. Labor, Washington, 1991-93; trustee Fund Am. Studies, 1993—, Univ. Ill. Found., 1993—, Inst. Cmty. Empowerment, 1991—; chmn. Chancellor's Corp. adv. com. U. Ill., Chgo., 1995—; adv. bd. mem. Ind. Univ. Ctr. Real Estate Studies, 1994—; dir. U.S. Com. for UNICEF, 1996—; pres. U. Ill. Alumni Assn., 1997-99; leadership com. United Way, 1998, dir., US Com. for Unicef, 1996—. Recipient Alumni Achievement award U. Ill., 1993. Mem. Pres.'s Club, Chgo. Coun. on Fgn. Rels., Arts Club Chgo., Alpha Rho Chi. Office: The Daly Group 20 N Wacker Dr Ste 1500 Chicago IL 60606-2903

DALY, ROBERT ANTHONY, former film executive; b. Bklyn., Dec. 8, 1936; s. James and Eleanor D.; children: Linda Marie, Robert Anthony, Brian James. Student, Bklyn. Coll. From dir. bus. affairs to v.p. bus. affairs, to exec. v.p. CBS TV Network, 1955-80; pres. CBS Entertainment Co., from 1977; chmn., co-CEO Warner Bros., Burbank, Calif., 1981-99, Warner Music Group Inc. -99; bd. dirs. Am. Film Inst. Trustee Am. Film Inst. Mem. NATAS, Acad. Motion Picture Arts and Scis., Motion Picture

Pioneers, Hollywood Radio and TV Soc. Roman Catholic. Club: Bel Air Country. Office: Warner Bros & Warner Music Group 4000 Warner Blvd Burbank CA 91522 Office: Warner Bros & Warner Music Group 75 Rockefeller Plz New York NY 10019-6908*

DALY, ROBERT W., psychiatrist, medical educator; b. Watertown, N.Y., Oct. 1, 1932; s. Robert Joseph and Margaret Florence (Ward) D.; m. Elizabeth Mary McCarthy, July 4, 1958; children: Kendra, Lauren, Robert, John, Erik. BS, St. Lawrence U., 1957; MD, SUNY, Syracuse, 1957. Diplomate Am. Bd. Psychiatry and Neurology, Nat. Bd. Med. Examiners. Resident in psychiatry SUNY, Syracuse, 1958-60, chief resident in psychiatry, 1960-61; chief Dept. Psychiatry & Neurology, Barksdale AFB, Bossier City, La., 1961-63; asst. prof. psychiatry SUNY Upstate Med. Ctr., Syracuse, 1963-69, assoc. prof. psychiatry, 1969-75; visiting scholar U. Cambridge, England, 1969-70; sr. fellow Nat. Endowment for the Humanities, 1974-75; prof. psychiatry SUNY Upstate Med. Ctr., Syracuse, 1975—; adj. prof. philosophy Syracuse U., 1980—; prof. med. humanities, dir. program in med. humanities SUNY Health Sci. Ctr., Syracuse, 1984—; exec. dir. Syracuse Consortium for the Cultural Found. of Medicine, 1978—; chmn. bd., pres. Inst. for Ethics in Health Care, Inc., 1995—; examiner Am. Bd. Psychiatry and Neurology, 1980-90; pvt. practice psychiatry, Syracuse, 1963—; cons. to hosps., govt. agencies, religious orgns., law firms, 1964—. Contbr. articles to profl. jours.; co-editor: The Cultures of Medicine, Vol. 8 of Literature and Medicine. Mem. mental health adv. bd., County Onondaga, N.Y., 1976-77. Capt. USAF, 1961-63. Rsch. fellow N.Y. State Dept. Mental Hygiene, 1969-70; recipient award in recognition of svcs. Ctrl. N.Y. Eye Bank & Rsch. Corp., 1985. Fellow Am. Psychiat. Assn. (life; pres. Onondaga dist. bd. 1968-69); mem. N.Y. State Med. Soc., Internat. Soc. for Comparative Study Civilization (coun. 1977-80), Soc. Health and Human Values, Assn. Faculty in Med. Humanities (program chmn. 1986-87, pres., program dir. sect. 1995-96), Assn. for Advancement of Philosophy and Psychiatry, Soc. for Bioethics and Humanities. Democrat. Roman Catholic. Avocations: fishing, tennis, gardening, furniture design and building. Home: 101 Revere Rd Syracuse NY 13214-1938 Office: SUNY Health Sci Ctr 750 E Adams St Syracuse NY 13210-2399

DALY, SIMEON PHILIP JOHN, librarian; b. Detroit, May 9, 1922; s. Philip T. and Marguerite I. (Ginzel) D. BA, St. Meinrad Coll., 1945; Licentiate in Sacred Theol., Cath. U., 1949, MLS, 1951; MDiv, St. Meinrad Sch. Theol., 1985. Joined Benedictines, 1943, ordained priest Roman Cath. Ch., 1948. Libr. dir. St. Meinrad (Ind.) Coll. and St. Meinrad Sch. Theol., 1951—; pres. Four Rivers Area Libr. Svcs. Authority, Ind., 1974-75, Am. Theol. Libr. Assn., St. Meinrad, 1979-81; exec. sec. Am. Theol. Library Assn., St. Meinrad, 1985-90. Mem. ALA, Ind. Library Assn., Am. Theol. Library Assn. (bd. dirs., pres., exec. sec.), Am. Benedictine Acad. Home: St Meinrad Archabbey Saint Meinrad IN 47577 Office: St Meinrad Sch Theology Archabbey Libr Saint Meinrad IN 47577

DALY, SUSAN MARY, lawyer; b. White Plains, N.Y., Dec. 12, 1963; d. J. Spencer and Mary E. (Kramer) D. Student, U. Madrid, 1983-85; BA, St. Lawrence U., 1985; JD, Bklyn. Law Sch., 1990. Bar: Conn. 1990, N.Y. 1991, Fla. 1991. Legal asst. Skadden, Arps, Slate, Meagher & Flom, N.Y.C., 1986-89; counsel Gilbride, Tusa, Last & Spellane, N.Y.C. and Greenwich, Conn., 1990-95, Gunster, Yoakley, Valdes-Fauli & Stewart, Ft. Lauderdale, Fla., 1995-99; trademark counsel Sundbeam Corp., 1999—. Chmn. Comm. Rev. and Project Devel., Jr. League Indian River, Vero Beach, 1997, Jr. League, Ft. Lauderdale, 1998; chmn. profl. com. United Way Indian River, 1997. Mem. ABA, Free Trade Am. (chairperson), Internat. Trademark Assn. (treaty analysis com. 1998—), Phi Beta Alpha, Kappa Kappa Gamma. Home: Unit 1 2004 Riverside Pl Wilton Manors FL 33305

DALY, TIMOTHY, actor; b. N.Y.C., Mar. 1, 1956; s. James Daly and Hoep Newell; m. Any Van Nostrand; 1 child, Sam. BA, Bennington Coll. Theatre appearances include Fables For Friends, 1984, Oliver, Oliver, 1985 (Boradway debut), Coastal Disturbances, 1987 (Theatre World award 1987); films include Diner, 1982, Just the Way You Are, 1984, Made In Heaven, 1987, Spellbinder, 1988, Love or Money, 1989, Year of the Comet, 1992, Dr. Jekyll and Ms. Hyde, 1995, Witness to the Execution, 1994, Caroline at Midnight, 1994, Dr. Jekyll and Ms. Hyde, 1995, Denise Calls Up, 1995, The Associate, 1996; TV appearances include (series) Ryan's Four, 1983, Almost Grown, 1988, Wings, 1990—, Superman, 1996; (movies) I Married A Centerfold, 1984, Mirrors, 1985, Red Earth, White Earth, 1989, In The Line of Duty: Ambush in Waco, 1993, Dangerous Heart, 1994, (TV mini series) Alex Haley's Queen, 1993. Office: Gersh Agency, Inc 232 N Canon Dr Beverly Hills CA 90210-5302

DALY, TOM, mayor; m. Debra Daly; children: Anna, Ryan. BA, Harvard U., 1976. Elected mem. City Council of Anaheim, 1988, elected mayor, 1992-94, 94—. mem. bd. trustees Anaheim Union Hish Sch. Dist., 1985—; active Anaheim Library Bd., 1985—; mem. adv. bd. Anaheim Boys and Girls Club; mem. bd. dirs. cmty. support group Anaheim Meml. Hosp.; mem. bd. dirs. Orange County Transp. Authority, Urban Water Inst.; mem. El Toro Citizens Adv. Commn.; chair regional adv. planning coun. Orange County, 1992—. Office: Office of the Mayor/City Council City Hall 7th Fl 200 S Anaheim Blvd Anaheim CA 92805-3820*

DALY, TYNE, actress; b. Madison, Wis., Feb. 21, 1946; d. James Daly and Hope Newell; m. Georg Stanford Brown (div.); children: Alyxandra, Kathryne, Alisabeth. Student, Brandeis U., Am. Music and Dramatic Acad. Performed at Am. Shakespeare Festival, Stratford, Conn.; appeared on Broadway in Gypsy, 1990, 91 revivals, The Seagull, 1992; films include Angel Unchained, 1970, The Enforcer, 1976, The Entertainer, 1976, Speed Trap, 1977, Telefon, 1977, Zoot Suit, 1982, The Aviator, 1985, Movers and Shakers, 1985; made TV debut in series The Virginian; guest appearances in various TV series, starring role in Cagney & Lacey, 1982-88 (Emmy awards 1983, 84, 85, 88); TV films include In Search of America, 1971, A Howling in the Woods, 1971, Heat of Anger, 1972, The Man Who Could Talk to Kids, 1973, Larry, 1974, Intimate Strangers, 1977, Better Late Than Never, 1979, The Women's Room, 1980, A Matter of Life and Death, 1981, The Great Gilly Hopkins, 1981, Your Place or Mine, 1983, Kids Like These, 1987, Stuck With Each Other, 1989, The Last to Go, 1990, Face of a Stranger, 1991, On the Town, 1993, Scattered Dreams, 1994, Christy, 1994 (Emmy award 1996), Colombo: Bird in the Hand, 1994, Columbo: Undercover, 1994, The Forget-Me-Not Murders, 1994, Cagney and Lacey: The Return, 1994, Cagney and Lacey: Together Again, 1995, A Perfect Mother, 1996, Tricks, 1997, The Perfect Mother, 1997, Vig, 1998, Execution of Justice, 1999. Recipient Tony award for Mama Rose role in Gypsy, 1990, Emmy award, 1996. *

DALY, WALTER JOSEPH, physician, educator; b. Michigan City, Ind., Jan. 12, 1930; s. Walter Hayes and Nellie Martha (Stipp) D.; m. Joan Brown, June 12, 1953; children: Lois Kay, Alice Louise. AB, Ind. U., 1951, MD, 1955, ScD, 1998. Diplomate Am. Bd. Internal Medicine. Intern Ind. U., 1955-56, resident, 1956-57, 59-62, instr. medicine, 1962-63, asst. prof., 1963-65, assoc. prof., 1965-68, prof., 1968-77, John B. Hickam prof., 1977-80, J.O. Ritchey prof., 1980-95, J.O. Ritchey prof. emeritus, 1995—; chmn. dept. medicine, 1970-83, dean Sch. Medicine, 1983-95; dean emeritus Ind. U., 1995—; dir. Regenstrief Inst. Health Rsch., 1976-83. Capt. M.C., U.S. Army, 1957-59. Master ACP (gov. 1980-84), Am. Physiol. Soc., Cen. Soc. Clin. Rsch. (pres. 1980-81), Am. Soc. Clin. Investigation, Am. Clin. and Climatol. Assn., Assn. Am. Physicians. Home: 2064 Oak Run N Dr Indianapolis IN 46260 Office: Ind U Sch Medicine 1120 South Dr Indianapolis IN 46202-5135

DALY, WILLIAM JAMES, retired health industry distributing company executive; b. Lawrence, Mass., Aug. 29, 1917; s. James W. and Alice Gertrude Daly; m. Cornelia Mahony, July 18, 1942 (dec. 1997); children: Jane, Cornelius, James, William James, Christopher. B.S. in Elec. Engring, U.S. Naval Acad., 1941. With James W. Daly, Inc. (health care distbn.), Lynnfield, Mass., 1946-87; pres. James W. Daly, Inc. (health care distbn.), 1967-87. Served to comdr. U.S. Navy, 1941-46, 50-52. Mem. Nat. Wholesale Druggists Assn., Health Industry Distbrs. Assn. (past chmn.), Nat. Assn. Wholesalers, Am. Mgmt. Assn. Clubs: Salem Country, Lanam.

DALY, WILLIAM JOSEPH, lawyer; b. Bklyn., Mar. 19, 1928; s. William Bernard and Charlotte Marie (Saunders) D.; m. Barbara A. Longenecker, Nov. 19, 1955; children: Sharon, Nancy, Carol. B.A., St. John's U., 1951, J.D., 1953. Bar: N.Y. 1954, U.S. Dist. Ct. (so. and ea. dists.) N.Y. 1958, U.S. Ct. Mil. Appeals 1969, U.S. Ct. Claims 1969, U.S. Tax Ct. 1969, U.S. Supreme Ct. 1973. Assoc. Garvey & Conway, Esquires, N.Y.C., 1954-55, Wing & Wing, Esquires, N.Y.C., 1955-58; ptnr. Daly Lavery & Hall, Esquires and predecessors, Ossining, N.Y., 1958—; adj. prof. law Mercy Coll., Dobbs Ferry, N.Y. V.p. Legal Aid Soc., Westchester County, N.Y., 1983—; mem. 9th Jud. Dist. Grievance Com., 1981-89, chmn. 1988-89; spl. referee in disciplinary proceedings; trustee Supreme Ct. Libr. at White Plains, 1985—. With U.S. Army, 1946-48; ret. col. JA-AUS, 1978. Fellow Am. Bar Found., N.Y. Bar Found.; mem. ABA, N.Y. State Bar Assn. (ho. of dels. 1977-89, 90-96, exec. com. 1983-89, 90-96, v.p. 1985-89, 90-96), Westchester County Bar Assn. (pres. 1979-81, dirs. coun. 1981—), Westchester County Bar Inst. (bd. dirs. 1982-98), Ossinging Bar Assn. (pres. 1966-67), Assn. Trial Lawyers Am., N.Y. State Trial Lawyers Assn., Res. Officers Assn. U.S., Assn. U.S. Army, Skull and Circle, Phi Delta Phi. Roman Catholic. Home: 232 Hunter Ave Sleepy Hollow NY 10591-1317 Office: 73 Croton Ave Ste 209 Ossining NY 10562-4971

DALZELL, JEFFREY ALEXANDER, agent, musician; b. Pittsfield, Mass., Apr. 14, 1956; s. David Rudolf and Jeanne (Alexander) D. Student, U. Wis., 1974-75. Bassist Ray Griff, Nashville, 1982, Jeannie C. Riley Enterprises, Nashville, 1982-85; bassist, road mgr. Jeannie C. Riley, Nashville, 1985—. Bassist for TV and studio including Seasons in the Sun, 1985, Silk Cut Festival Live, 1985, Jeannie C. Riley, 1983, Grand Ol Opry Live, 1986. Recipient Cert. Recognition Non-Commissioned Officers Assn., 1989, 1st Pl. Finisher in Div. Miss. Track Club, 1988, Product Endorsement S.I.T. Strings, Inc., 1990—. Mem. Am. Fedn. Musicians. Episcopalian. Avocations: running, drawing, tennis. Home: PO Box 158332 Nashville TN 37215-8332 Office: J C R Enterprises PO Box 23256 Nashville TN 37202-3256

DALZELL, ROBERT FENTON, JR., historian; b. Cleve., Apr. 28, 1937; s. Robert Fenton and Lucile (Cain) D.; m. Lee Baldwin, June 18, 1960; children: Frederick, Jeffery, Victoria, Alex. BA, Amherst Coll., 1959; MA, Yale U., 1962, PhD, 1966. Instr. history Yale U., New Haven, 1962-66, asst. prof., 1966-70; assoc. prof. history Williams Coll., Williamstown, Mass., 1970-75, prof., 1975-77, Ephraim Williams prof. Am. history, 1977—; chmn. Am. civilization program, 1980-91; dep. coll. marshal, 1984-87, coll. marshal, 1987-95; vis. prof. U. Va., 1985-86; trustee Hist. Deerfield, 1983—; mem. mass. Found. Humanities and Pub. Policy, 1982-89, v.p. 1987-88. Author: American Participation in the Great Exhibition of 1851, 1960, Daniel Webster and the Trial of American Nationalism, 1973, Enterprising Elite: The Boston Associates and the World They Made, 1987, (with Lee B. Dalzell) George Washington's Mount Vernon: At Home in Revolutionary America, 1998. Morse fellow, 1968-69, Guggenheim fellow, 1973-74, Charles Warren fellow, 1973-74, Williams Coll. Ctr. for Humanities and Social Scis., 1990. Mem. Orgn. Am. Historians, Mass. Hist. Soc., Colonial Soc. Mass., Am. Studies Assn., Berkshire County Hist. Soc. Home: 148 South St Williamstown MA 01267-2822 Office: Williams Coll Stetson Hall Williamstown MA 01267

DALZELL, STEWART, federal judge; b. Hackensack, N.J., Sept. 18, 1943; s. Stewart V. and Jeannette (Johnson) D.; m. Kathleen Regan, Mar. 28, 1981; children: Rebecca, Andrew. BS in Economics, U. Pa., 1965, JD, 1969. Bar: Pa. 1970, U.S. Dist. Ct. (ea. dist.) Pa. 1970, U.S. Ct. Appeals (11th cir.) 1979, U.S. Ct. Appeals (9th cir.) 1977, U.S. Ct. Appeals (Fed. cir.) 1983, U.S. Ct. Appeals (5th cir.) 1984, U.S. Ct. Appeals (2d cir.) 1986, U.S. Ct. Appeals (3d cir.) 1991, U.S. Supreme Ct. 1975. Fin. analyst NBC, N.Y.C., 1965-66; assoc. Drinker, Biddle & Reath, Phila., 1970-76, ptnr., 1976-91; judge U.S. Dist. Ct. (ea. dist.) Pa., 1991—; vis. lectr. law Wharton Sch. U. Pa., 1969-70. Contbr. articles to law revs. and profl. jours. Recipient Speiser award. Mem. Beta Gamma Sigma. Episcopalian. Avocations: movies, music. Office: US Dist Cts US Courthouse Rm 5614 601 Market St Philadelphia PA 19106-1713*

DAM, KENNETH W., lawyer, law educator; b. Marysville, Kans., Aug. 10, 1932; s. Oliver W. and Ida L. (Hueppelsheuser) D.; m. Marcia Wachs, June 9, 1962; children: Eliot, Charlotte. BS, U. Kans., 1954; JD, U. Chgo., 1957; LLD (hon.), New Sch. Social Rsch., 1983. Bar: N.Y. State 1959. Law clk. to justice U.S. Supreme Ct., 1957-58; assoc. Cravath, Swaine & Moore, N.Y.C., 1958-60; faculty U. Chgo. Law Sch., 1960-82, prof., 1964-71, 74-82, Harold J. and Marion F. Green prof., 1976-82, provost, 1980-82; dep. sec. of state Dept. State, 1982-85; v.p. law and external rels. IBM Corp., 1985-92; pres., CEO United Way Am., 1992; Max Pam prof. of Am. and fgn. law U. Chgo. Law Sch., 1992—; asst. dir. nat. security and internat. affairs Office Mgmt. and Budget, 1971-73; exec. dir. Coun. Econ. Policy, 1973; vis. prof. U. Freiburg, Germany, 1964; adv. bd. BMW of N.Am., 1990-95; bd. dirs. Alcoa Corp. Author: The GATT: Law and International Economic Organization, 1970, Oil Resources: Who Gets What How?, 1976, The Rules of the Game: Reform and Evolution in the International Monetary System, 1982; co-author: Federal Tax Treatment of Foreign Income, 1964, Economic Policy Beyond the Headlines, 1977, 2d edit., 1998; co-editor: Crytography's Role in Securing the Information Society, 1996; chair bd. advisors Fgn. Affairs jour. Bd. dirs. Am. Coun. on Germany, 1986-95, Am.-China Soc., Coun. on Fgn. Rels., Chgo. Coun. on Fgn. Rels.; trustee Brookings Inst.; co-chmn. Aspen Strategy Group; chmn. German-Am. Acad. Coun.; panelist Am. Arbitration Assn. Mem. ABA, Coun. Fgn. Rels., Am. Acad. Arts and Scis., Am. Acad. Diplomacy, Am. Law Inst., Chgo. Coun. Fgn. Rels., Met. Club (Washington), Quadrangle Club. Office: Univ Chgo Law Sch 1111 E 60th St Chicago IL 60637-2786

DAMADIAN, RAYMOND VAHAN, biophysicist; b. N.Y.C., Mar. 16, 1936; s. Vahan and Odette (Yazedjian) D.; m. Elizabeth Donna Terry, June 4, 1960; children: Timothy, Jevan, Kiera. BS in Math., U. Wis., 1956; MD, Albert Einstein Coll. Medicine, 1960. Univ. rsch. fellow in biophysics Harvard U., Cambridge, Mass., 1963-65; sr. investigator Sch. Aerospace Medicine, USAF, 1965-67; asst. prof. SUNY, Bklyn., 1967-71, assoc. prof., 1971-80; pres., chmn. Fonar Corp., Melville, N.Y., 1978—; career investigator Health Rsch. Coun., City of N.Y., 1967-72. Capt. USAF, 1963-65. Recipient Lawrence Sperry award, 1984, Nat. Medal of Tech., 1988. Mem. AAAS, Am. Chem. Soc., Biophys. Soc., Sigma Xi. Office: Fonar Corp 110 Marcus Dr Melville NY 11747-4292*

DAMAN, ERNEST LUDWIG, mechanical engineer; b. Hannover, Germany, Mar. 14, 1923; came to U.S., 1940, naturalized, 1944; s. Fritz and Ruth Edith (Meyer) Dammann; m. Jan. 20, 1945 (div.); children: Diane Cathrine, Cynthia Ruth, Bruce Hershey; m. Dorothy Russo, June 21, 1980; stepchildren: Christopher Walsweer, Jonathan Walsweer. B.S. in Mech. Engring, Poly. Inst. Bklyn., 1943. With Foster Wheeler Corp., Livingston, N.J., 1947—; dir. rsch. Foster Wheeler Energy Corp., Livingston, N.J., 1960-73, v.p., 1973-81, sr. v.p., 1981-88; chmn. Foster Wheeler Devel. Corp., Livingston, N.J., 1977-88, chmn. emeritus, 1988—; chmn., chief exec. officer HDS Fibers Inc., 1986-89; technology exec. Exec. Office of Pres., The White House, Washington, 1995-97; chmn. Nat. Materials Property Data Network, Inc., 1986-94; mem. sci. and tech. info. bd. NRC, 1989-91; lectr. in field. Patentee in field. Chmn. Westfield (N.J.) Democratic Com., 1956-60, Westfield Area Com. for Human Rights, 1962-68; mem. Westfield Charter Study Commn., 1964. Served with U.S. Army, 1944-46. Decorated Bronze Star. Fellow AAAS, ASME (pres.-elect 1987, pres. 1988-89); mem. NAE, Welding Rsch. Coun. (chmn. 1985), Am. Assn. Engring. Socs. (bd. dirs., chmn.-elect engring. roundtable 1992, chmn. 1993), United Engring. Trustees (bd. dirs. 1989-92, trustee 1989—), Westfield Tennis Club, Pi Tau Sigma. Achievements include development of advanced naval propulsion machinery, fluidized bed combustion, fast breeder reactor steam generators and intermediate heat exchangers; 19 patents in energy conversion processes and heat system. E-mail: ernieüdaman@fwc.com. Home: 7 Mountainview Dr Mountainside NJ 07092-2510 Office: Foster Wheeler Corp 12 Peach Tree Hill Rd Livingston NJ 07039-5701 *As a naturalized citizen my life has been influenced by my strong admiration for American Democracy and all that it implies.*

DAMAN, HARLAN RICHARD, allergist; b. N.Y.C., Nov. 1, 1941; s. D. Leon and Frances (Weissler) D.; AB cum laude, Harvard U., 1963; MD, Albert Einstein Coll. Medicine, 1967. Diplomate Am. Bd. Pediatrics, Am. Bd. Allergy and Immunology. Intern, then resident Yale-New Haven Hosp./Med. Ctr., 1967-69; fellow in allergy and clin. immunology Nat. Jewish Hosp. Research Ctr./U. Colo. Med. Ctr., Denver, 1971-73, instr., 1974-81; clin. asst. prof. pediatrics Albert Einstein Coll. Medicine, N.Y.C., 1981—; dir. pediatric allergy clinic Bronx Mcpl. Hosp. Ctr., 1982-92; mem. Mt. Sinai Med. Ctr./Sch. Medicine, 1976-90. Co-editor: Psychobiologic Aspects of Allergic Disorders, 1986; contbr. chpt. to Outpatient Medicine, 1980; contbr. articles on pulmonary function testing in asthmatic disorders. Served to maj. M.C., USAF, 1969-71. Fellow Am. Acad. Pediatrics, Am. Coll. Allergy, Asthma, and Immunology, Am. Coll. Chest Physicians, Am. Acad. Asthma, Allergy, and Immunology; mem. N.Y. Allergy Soc., Westchester Allergy Soc. (ednl. program dir. 1978-89, treas. 1980-81, pres. 1982-83), Westchester Acad. Medicine. Office: 769 Kimball Ave Yonkers NY 10704-1534

DAMASIO, ANTONIO R., physician, neurologist; b. Lisbon, Portugal, Feb. 25, 1944; came to U.S., 1975; m. Hanna Damasio. MD, U. Lisbon, 1969, DMS, 1974. Intern U. Hosp., Lisbon, 1969-72; prof. auxiliar in neurology Med. Sch., U. Lisbon, 1971; assoc. prof. dept. neurology U. Iowa, Iowa City, 1976-80, prof. neurology, 1980-86, prof. neurology, head dept., 1986—, M.W. Van Allen Disting. prof., 1989—, chief div. behavioral neurology and cognitive neurosci., 1977—; adj. prof. Salk Inst., San Diego, 1989—; mem. planning subcom. Nat. Adv. Neurol. Disorders Stroke Coun.; mem. adv. bd. The Neuroscientist. Author: Lesion Analysis in Neuropsychgology, 1989 (award Assn. Am. Pubs. 1990); mem. editorial bd. Trends in Neuroscis., 1986-91, Behavioral Brain Rsch., 1988—, Cerebral Cortex, 1990—, Jour. Neurosci., 1990, Cognitive Brain Rsch., Learning and Memory, spl. brain issue Sci. Am, 1992; contbr. articles to profl. jours. Recipient Disting. prof. award U. So. Calif., 1985, Nelson Urban Rsch. award Mental Health Assn. Iowa, 1990, Dr. William Beaumont award AMA, 1990, Pessoa prize Portuguese govt., 1992. Fellow Am. Acad. Neurology, Am. Neurol. Assn.; mem. NAS Inst. Medicine, Soc. for Neurosci., Acad. Aphasia (pres. 1983), Behavioral Neurology Soc., (pres. 1985), Royal Soc. Medicine Belgium (elected), European Acad. Arts and Scis. (elected), Am. Acad. Arts and Scis. Office: U Iowa Hosp & Clinic Dept Neurology 200 Hawkins Dr Iowa City IA 52242-1009*

DAMASKA, MIRJAN RADOVAN, law educator; b. Brezice, Slovenia, Oct. 8, 1931; came to U.S., 1972; s. Radovan and Ljerka (Tkalcic) D.; m. Marija Brkoevic, Aug. 10, 1960. LL.M., U. Zagreb, Croatia, 1956; D.Jurisprudence, Ljubljana Law Sch., 1960; LL.M., U. Zagreb, Croatia, 1956. Prof. law U. Zagreb, 1960-72, acting dean Law Sch., 1970-71; prof. law U. Pa. Law Sch., Phila., 1972-76; Ford Found. prof. law Yale U. Law Sch., New Haven, 1976-95, Sterling prof. law, 1996—; cons. Author: Position of the Criminal Defendant, 1962, Faces of Justice and State Authority, 1986, (with Schlesinger, Baade & Herzog) Comparative Law, 1988, Evidence Law Adrift, 1997; contbr. articles to profl. jours. Nat. Found. for Study of Humanities fellow, 1978-79. Fellow Am. Acad. Arts and Scis.; mem. Am. Assn. for Comparative Study of Law, Internat. Acad. Comparative Law.

D'AMATO, ALFONSE M., lawyer, former senator; b. Bklyn., Aug. 1, 1937; m. Penelope Ann Collenburg, 1960 (div. 1995); children: Lisa, Lorraine, Daniel, Christopher. BS, Syracuse U., 1959, JD, 1961. Bar: N.Y. 1962. Adminstr. Nassau County, N.Y., 1965-68; receiver of taxes Town of Hempstead, L.I., N.Y., 1971-77, presiding supr., vice chmn. county bd. suprs., 1977-80; U.S. senator from N.Y., 1981-98; lawyer Fox News, 1999—; chmn. banking, housing and urban affairs com., mem. fin. com., caucus on internat. narcotics control; co-chmn. U.S. Commn. on Security and Cooperation in Europe. Mem. Island Park Vol. Fire Dept. Mem. Lions, Sons of Italy, KC. Roman Catholic. Avocations: reading, piano. Office: George Publ Co 1633 Broadway 41st Fl New York NY 10019*

D'AMATO, ANTHONY ROGER, recording company executive; b. N.Y.C., Jan. 21, 1931; s. Agostino and Luisa (Galiani) D'A.; m. Gabrielle Hilton, June 26, 1958; children—Luisa, Jennie, Tania, Joanna, Antonia. B.A. in Music and English Lit. cum laude (Founders Day award 1956), N.Y. U., 1956; MI.A. (teaching fellow), Brandeis U., 1957. Artist and repertoire dir. stereophonic div. Decca Record Co., Ltd., Eng., 1958-78; pres. TDA Prodns. Ltd., N.Y.C., 1978—; exec. dir. Winnipeg (Man., Can.) Symphony Orch., 1979-80; v.p. artist and repertoire AudioFidelity Enterprises, N.Y.C., 1980-81; mng. dir. Mantovani Prodns., Mantovani Orch., N.Y.C., 1982—; mng. cons. Leopold Stokowski, 1964-72. Served with USMCR, 1951-53. Recipient Grand Prix du Disque, Charles Cros award rec., 1969. Mem. Assn. Cultural Execs. Can., Winnipeg C. of C., Phi Beta Kappa.

DAMAZ, PAUL F., architect; b. Portugal, Nov. 8, 1917; came to U.S., 1947, naturalized, 1953; s. Pierre L. and Maria A. (Leite) D.; m. Solange Guillon, Dec. 26, 1981. B.A. in Architecture, Ecole Speciale d'Architecture, 1941; M. Town Planning, U. Paris, Sorbonne, 1946. Archtl. designer UN Hdqrs., N.Y.C., 1948-51, Harrison & Abramowitz, N.Y.C., 1951-53; chief designer Cajetan Baumann, N.Y.C., 1953-61; partner Damaz & Weigel, N.Y.C., 1962-76; pres. Adasco Tech Internat., N.Y.C., 1976-81; prin. Paul Damaz Assos., East Hampton, N.Y., 1981—; design critic Columbia, 1953; writer, critic, lectr. maj. univs. and TV. Dir. N.Y. Fine Arts Fedn.; Mem. nat. panel arbitrators Am. Arbitration Assn. Author: Art in European Architecture, 1956, Art in Latin American Architecture, 1962. Served as capt. French Army, 1941-45. Fellow A.I.A.; mem. French Ordre des Architectes, Archtl. League N.Y. (past v.p.), Arnold W. Brunner award 1958), Municipal Arts Soc., French-Am. Soc., Am. Inst. Planners. Office: 218 Old Stone Hwy East Hampton NY 11937-1621

D'AMBOISE, JACQUES JOSEPH, dancer, choreographer; b. Dedham, Mass., July 28, 1934; s. Andrew Ahearn and Georgette d'A.; m. Carolyn George, Jan. 1, 1956; children: George Jacques, Christopher R., Charlotte Lorraine and Catherine Liza (twins). With N.Y.C. Ballet Co., 1949-84; prin. Dancer, 1953-84; instr. Sch. Am. Ballet; prof., dean SUNY Sch. Dance, Purchase, 1977-80. Founder Nat. Dance Inst., N.Y.; motion pictures include Seven Brides for Seven Brothers, 1954, The Best Things in Life are Free, 1956, Carousel, 1956, Off Beat, 1986, He Makes Me Feel Like Dancin, 1983 (Acad award best documentary 1983); co-author: Teaching the Magic of Dance, 1983; choreographer: Scherzo Opus 42, Valse-Scherzo Concert Fantasy, Celebration, The Chase, Twschaikovsky Suite (No. 2), Sarabande and Danse II, Quatouor, Prologue and Saltarelli. MacArthur fellow, 1990; recipient Paul Robeson award, 1988, Capezio award, 1990, Disting. Svc. to Arts. award Am. Acad. Arts and Letters, 1993, Kennedy Ctr. Honors, 1995, Nat. Medal of Arts award U.S. Pres., 1998, Dance mag. award, 1999. Office: Nat Dance Inst Inc 594 Broadway Rm 805 New York NY 10012-3257

D'AMBROSIO, VINNI MARIE, writer; b. N.Y.C.; d. Melvin Mix and Lucille DeMarco Aguanno; (div. 1962): 1 child, Cynthia Johnson. BA, Smith Coll., Northhampton, Mass.; PhD, NYU, 1981. Prof. CUNY, 1972-94; v.p. T.S. Eliot Soc., 1990-93, pres., 1993-96; assoc. prof. San Diego State U., 1981. Author: Life of Touching Months, 1971, Eliot Possessed, 1989, Mexican Gothic, 1995, (Pen and Brush, Inc. award 1998). Fellow Va. Ctr. for Creative Arts, Sweet Briar, 1994, 96. Mem. AAUW (bd. mem.), Pen and Brush Inc. (pres. 1994-98, v.p. 1998—), PEN-Am. Ctr., Poetry Soc. Am., Am. Assn. U. Women Bd. Greenwich Village Hist. Assn.

DAME, CATHERINE ELAINE, acupuncturist; b. Holyoke, Mass., Oct. 1, 1951; d. Josaphat Charles and Lillian Geneva (Archer) Boulanger; m. William Henry Dame, Jan. 9, 1970; 1 child, Cristinna Lian. Acupuncture Diplomate, N.E. Sch. Acupuncture, Watertown, Mass., 1992; student, Ind. U., 1988-93; MEd, Cambridge Coll., 1994. Lic. acupuncturist, Mass.; nat. bd. cert. in acupuncture. Dept. mgr. Zayre Dept. Store, Chicopee, Mass., 1969; retail sales clk. Woodward & Lothrop Store, Alexandria, Va., 1971-72; dept. mgr. Steiger Dept. Store, Enfield, Conn., 1972-73; retail sales clk. Point Dept. Store, Ft. Walton Beach, Fla., 1973-74; assembly, repair mfg. Texas Instruments, Ft. Walton Beach, 1974-75; tller Third Nat. Bank, Springfield, Mass., 1975-81, customer svc. rep., 1981-82; teller Bank of N.E./Fleet Bank, Springfield, 1990-93; owner, mgr. Acupuncture Svcs., Chicopee, 1994—; cons. Cambridge Coll., Springfield, Mass., 1994-95; bus. office liaison Cambridge Coll., 1995-98. Mem. Am. Assn. Oriental Medicine, Nat. Commn. for Cert. of Acupuncturists Directory, Bus. and Profl. Trade Exch., Acupuncture Soc. Mass., Granby Regional Horse Coun., Kings Bridge Equine Rescue, Inc., Chicopee C. of C. Office: Acupuncture Svcs Chicopee 665 Prospect St Chicopee MA 01020-3064

DAME, LAUREEN EVA, nursing administrator; b. Framingham, Mass., Mar. 15, 1947; d. Irving Lawrence Jr. and Cora Justina (Wells) Dame; children: Daryl Lawrence, Jeffrey Lee. Diploma, Dartmouth-Hickock Med. Ctr., Hanover N.H., 1968; BSN, Clayton State Coll., Morrow, Ga., 1996; MSN, Emory U., 1997; doctoral student, Ga. State U. RN, Ga.; cert. profl. in healthcare quality. Staff nurse, charge nurse, team leader maternity and surgical nursing various hosps., N.H., Boston, St. Louis, 1968-69, 80-83; sch. nurse practitioner Dept. Pub. Health, Bedford, Mass., 1983-85; perioperative nurse, 1st asst. South Fulton Hosp., East Point, Ga., 1985-86; nurse, first asst., plastic surgery John Munna M.D., Atlanta, 1986-90; resource nurse, intake coord. Shallowford Hosp., Atlanta, 1989-91, staff educator, quality assurance coord. dept. surg. svcs., 1991-92; quality improvement coord., nursing South Fulton Med. Ctr., East Point, Ga., 1992; nurse coord. quality assurance Kaiser Permanente, Atlanta, 1992-93, dir. quality assurance, 1993-95; mgr. coord. care Egleston Children's Hosp., Emory U., Atlanta, 1995-96; mgr. quality mgmt. Egleston Pediat. Group, Decatur, Ga., 1996-97; dir. dept. surgery Emory U. Hosp., Atlanta, 1997-98; dir. regulatory and quality mgmt. MATRIA Healthcare, Inc., 1998-99. Mem. NAACOG (charter; chmn. steering com. 1972), AORN (chmn. hospitality com. 1992, mem. workshop and publicity coms. 1983), NAFE, Am. Soc. Plastic and Reconstructive Surg. Nurses, Nat. Assn. Quality Profls., Ga. Assn. Quality Profls., Ga. North Ctrl. Dist. Quality Profls., Am. Acad. Disting. Students, Am. Needlepoint Guild (life), Embroiderers Guild Am. (life), Sigma Theta Tau. Lutheran. Avocations: fiber artist (nat. cert. judge), needlepoint, embroidery. Home: 8726 Twin Oaks Dr Jonesboro GA 30236-5152

DAME, THOMAS MICHAEL, radio astronomer; b. Winthrop, Mass., Oct. 16, 1954; s. Chester Thomas and Claire J. (White) D.; m. Geraldine Ann Healey, Aug. 23, 1985. BA, Boston U., 1976; PhD, Columbia U., 1983. Rsch. assoc. Goddard Inst. for Space Studies NASA, N.Y.C., 1983-84; rsch. assoc. Columbia U., N.Y.C., 1985-86; radio astronomer Smithsonian Astrophys. Obs., Cambridge, Mass., 1986—; lectr. astronomy Harvard U., Cambridge, 1989—. Contbr. articles to Astrophys. Jour., Sky and Telescope Mag., NASA Publ. NAS fellow, 1983-84. Mem. Am. Astron. Soc. Achievements include publication of first and only complete maps of molecular gas in the Milky Way and Andromeda galaxies; catalogued largest molecular clouds in Milky Way; calibrated conversion from CO intensity to molecular mass. Home: 40 Magoun St Cambridge MA 02140-1617 Office: Ctr for Astrophysics 60 Garden St Cambridge MA 02138-1516

DAMÉ-SHEPP, DIANE, art management administrator; b. Berkeley, Calif., Nov. 1, 1946; d. Paul David and Eleanor June Ingraham; children: Josette Laura, Criselle Lynn, Castiel Armanda, Zia Felice. BA, U. Calif., Berkeley, 1977, cert. Mus. Mgmt. Inst. Am. Fedn. Arts, 1982; cert., Grantsmanship Tng. Ctr., San Francisco, 1984; cert. Leadership Inst., Calif. Arts Coun., Sacramento, 1988. Teaching asst., video co-prodr., writer art dept. Los Medanos Coll., Pittsburg, Calif., 1974-78; asst. security supt., spl. events coord. Univ. Art Mus., Berkeley, Calif., 1976-82, exec. dir. Univ. Art Mus. Coun., 1982-83; asst. devel. dir. Univ. Art Mus., U. Calif., Berkeley, 1983-85; exec. dir. Napa (Calif.) County Arts Coun., 1985-88, Solano County Arts Alliance, Fairfield, Calif., 1993-95; pub. rels. coord. The Oxbow Sch., Napa, Calif., 1998—; founding bd. dirs., past pres. Calif. Assembly Local Arts Agys., San Francisco, 1986-92; mem. leadership com. Nat. Assembly Local Arts Agys., Washington, 1987-91; art mgmt. cons. Calif. Arts Coun., Mono County Arts, Nevada County Arts, Napa Landmarks, Calif., River Sch., Napa, Calif., Magical Moonshine Theatre, Calif., Calif. Maritime Acad., 1988—; guest speaker Nat. Fedn. Flyfishers, Livingston, Mont., 1996. Artist/sculptor Sacramento Met. Arts Commn.-Light Rail Project Starfire Sta., 1984-87; exhibited in group shows at Weiss Gallery, San Francisco, 1984-85, Zaks Gallery,Chgo., 1982-87, San Francisco Airport, 1987-88, San Francisco Mus. Modern Art Coun. Auction, 1988, New Langston Arts, San Francisco, 1990, Headlands Art Ctr., Marin, Calif., 1993, Clos Pegase Winery, St. Helena, Calif., 1994, Sonoma State U., 1986, 88-91, 94, Oakland Mus. Collectors Gallery, 1994, Falkirk Cultural Ctr., San Rafael, Calif., 1995. Founding bd. dirs., v.p., fundraising sec./treas. Napa Valley Opera House, Inc., 1985-97; mem. faculty Leadership Napa, 1986-90; founding bd. mem., sec. Napa Valley Film Festival; sight coord. Internat. Sculpture Conf., Oakland, 1982. Recipient Calif. State Scholarship, 1976, Scholarship AAUW, 1975-77, Mus.Mgmt. Inst. Scholarship Art Mus. Assn., Berkeley, 1982. Avocations: sculptor, fly fishing. Home and Office: PO Box 2398 Yountville CA 94599-2398

DAMGARD, JOHN MICHAEL, trade association executive; b. Ottawa, Ill., Dec. 7, 1939; s. Theodor Miller and Dorothy (Oughton) D.; m. Darcy Mead, Oct. 23, 1965 (div.); children: Michael Theodor, Julie Mead. B.A., Knox Coll., Galesburg, Ill., 1964; student, U. Munich, Ger., 1962, U. Va., 1960. Chair, CEO Ill. Valley Investment Co., Dwight, Ill., 1966-70, dir., pres., 1976—; asst. to Vice Pres. U.S. White House, 1971-74; dep. asst. sec. U.S. Dept. Agr., Washington, 1974-77; v.p. ACLI Internat., Washington, 1977-82; pres., dir., exec. com. Futures Industry Assn., Washington, 1982—; president Futures Industry Assn., present. Adv. Republican Heritage Group, 1976; mem. Rep. Nat. Com. Policy Group; bd. dirs. Washington Internat. Horse Show, 1975-81. Mem. Futures Industry Inst. (trustee), Am. Soc. Assn. Execs., Met. Club (Washington), Racquet Club (Chgo.), Meadow Club (Southampton, N.Y.), Farmington Country Club (Charlottesville, Va.). Home: 2439 Tracy Pl NW Washington DC 20008-1628 Office: Futures Industry Assn 2001 Pennsylvania Ave NW Washington DC 20006-1850

DAMIANOS, SYLVESTER, architect, sculptor; b. McKeesport, Pa., Dec. 31, 1933; s. Tsambikos and Melanie (Barboteau) D.; m. Eva Lu Spears, Dec. 28, 1957; children: Lynne Lucille, Laurie Elizabeth, Leigh Ann. BArch, Carnegie Inst. Tech., 1956; postgrad., Tech. Inst. Delft, Netherlands, 1957. Registered architect, Pa. Assoc. ptnr. Celli-Flynn, McKeesport, Pa., 1960-67; prin. Damianos & Pedone, Pitts., 1967-79; pres. Damianos & Assocs., Pitts., 1979-89; chmn. Damianos Brown Andrews Inc., Pitts., 1989-95; pres. Damianos & Anthony, Pitts., 1995—; pres. Pitts. Plan for Art, 1960-82; bd. dirs. Action-Housing, Inc. Architect bldg. renovation, 601 Grant St. Office Bldg. (Design 1993); exhibited works of sculpture, Mus. Art Carnegie Inst., 1975, Westmoreland County Mus. Art, 1966, N.Y.C., London. Chmn. planning com. Borough of Edgewood, Pa., 1976-77, mem. coun., 1977-81; bd. dirs. Met. Pitts. Pub. Broadcasting, Am. Wind Symphony, Pitts., 1975-76; sec. Pitts. Art Commn., 1970-78; chmn. bd. regents Am. Archtl. Found., 1991-94; chair pub. art adv. com. Pitts. Cultural Trust, 1994—. Fulbright grantee USIS, Netherlands, 1956. Fellow AIA (regional dir. 1985-87, v.p. 1988, 1st v.p. 1989, nat. pres. 1990, pres. Pitts. chpt. 1980, Kemper award 1996, Medal of Distinction, Pa. chpt. 1997), Fedn. Architects Republic Mex. (hon.), Royal Can. Inst. Architects (hon.), Japan Inst. Architects (hon.); mem. Pa. Soc. Architects (bd. dirs., v.p. svcs.), Pitts. Archtl. Club (pres. 1963-64), Soc. Sculptors (dir. 1977-79), Assoc. Artists Pitts. (pres., dir. 1963-65, 93—), Edgewood Club (pres., dir. 1969-75). Greek Orthodox. Home: 328 Locust St Pittsburgh PA 15218-1457 Office: Damianos & Anthony 4617 Winthrop St Pittsburgh PA 15213-3718

DAMICO, DEBRA LYNN, college official, English and French educator; b. Passaic, N.J., Apr. 15, 1956; d. Nicholas Biagio and Eleanore Lorraine (Hugle) D. BA, Montclair State U., 1978, MA, 1989. Cert. tchr., N.J, reading specialist. Tchr. St. Francis Sch., Hackensack, N.J., 1978-79, Saddle Brook (N.J.) H.S., 1979-80, St. Dominic Acad., Jersey City, 1980-84; tchr. adult basic edn., gen. edn devel. and ESL, Montclair State U., 1974—, coord. EXCEL program, 1993—; internat. student advisor Manhattan Coll., Bronx, N.Y., 1984—, ESL instr., 1986—, instr. French, 1998—; instr. Writing Inst. Adult Edn. Resource Ctr., Jersey City State Coll., 1987—; Outstanding Internat. Student advisor, 1989—. Mem. Dist. Wide Curriculum Council, Lodi, N.J., 1977-78; ch. cantor and musician. Nat. Assn. for Foreign Student Affairs grantee, 1985-86; named Outstanding Young Woman Am., 1986. Mem. Nat. Assn. Tchrs. of English as a Fgn. Lang., N.Y. Tchrs. of ESL, Nat. Assn. Fgn. Student Affairs-Assn. of Internat. Educators, Metro-Internat., Am. Assn. Tchrs. French, YMCA Internat. Student Svc., Kappa Delta Pi, Pi Delta Phi. Democrat. Roman Catholic. Avocations: singing, playing and teaching guitar, cantor and musician at church. Fax: 718-862-8016. E-mail: ddamico@manhattan.edu. Office: Manhattan Coll 4513 Manhattan College Pkwy Bronx NY 10471-4004

DAMICO, NICHOLAS PETER, lawyer; b. Chester, Pa., June 29, 1937; s. Ralph A. and Mary C. (Ametrane) D.; m. Patricia Ann Swatek, Aug. 26, 1967; children: Christine, Gregory. BS in Acctg., St. Joseph's U. 1960, LLB, U. Pa., 1963; LLM, Georgetown U., 1967. Bar: Pa. 1963, D.C. 1967, Md. 1986. Tax law specialist IRS, Washington, 1963-66; assoc. Silverstein and Mullens, Washington, 1966-72, ptnr. 1972-76; prin. Damico & Assocs., Washington, 1976—; adj. prof. Georgetown U. Law Ctr., Washington, 1973-75. Mem. ABA. Office: 1101 17th St NW Ste 820 Washington DC 20036-4704

D'AMICO, THOMAS F., economist, educator; b. N.Y.C., Aug. 20, 1948; s. Lawrence J. and Anita (Mingione) D'A.; m. Franca Paola Paniccia, Sept. 1970; children: Diana Christina, Gina Maria. BA, Fordham Coll., 1970; MA, NYU, 1979, MPhil, 1981, PhD, 1983. Econ. analyst Con Edison, N.Y.C., 1970-72; program dir. East Harlem Community Corp., N.Y.C., 1972-75; instr. St. Peter's Coll., Jersey City, N.J., 1975-78, from assoc. prof. to prof. econs., 1981—, chair dept. econs., 1989—; asst. prof. Manhattan Coll., Riverdale, N.Y., 1978-81; cons. various pvt. firms and non-profit agys., N.Y. Met. area, 1975—. Author: The Economics of Market and Non-Market Racial Discrimination, 1983; contbr. articles to scholarly jours.; referee various scholarly jours. Mem. AAUP, Am. Econ. Assn., Ea. Econ. Assn., Assn. Social Econs. Roman Catholic. Office: St Peter's Coll Dept Econs Jersey City NJ 07306

DAMIN, DAVID E., technology integration company executive; b. Tell City, Ind., Jan. 29, 1947; s. Earl Louis and Emma Louise (Gilliland) D; m. Mary James Greenfield, Nov. 28, 1970. BS in Elec. Engring., Auburn U., 1973; MA in Mgmt., Webster U., 1980. Electronics technician U.S. Navy, various locations, 1965-73, advanced through grades to lt. comdr., 1973-85; founder/v.p. Ind. ops., gen. mgr. Sci. Applications Internat. Corp., San Diego, 1985—; founder, coord. Winter Harbor Ctr., N.H. Coll., 1974; mem. mfg. com. Ind. BMT Corp., Skip Barber race driver. Mem. Gov.'s task force Mfg. Excellence Modernization; bd. advisors Ind. State U. Sch. of Tech.; mem. St. Lawrence Ch., Salvation Army Assn., Habitat for Humanity. Decorated Naval Commendation medal, Meritorious Svc. medal, Joint Svc. Commendation medal; recipient U.S. Naval Inst. award, 1973; named one of Outstanding Young Men of Am., 1975. Mem. Naval Cryptologic Vets. Assn., Auburn Alumni Assn. (pres. Indy Club), St. Meinrad Sem. Alumni Assn., Am. Soc. Naval Engrs., Ind. Chamber Com., Hudson Inst. Agenda for Am. Mfg. Competitivesness Task Force, Indpls. Rotary, Sports Car Club Am. (driver), Mid-Am. Electric Vehicle Consortium, Nat. Electronics Mfg. Productivity Ctr., Hoosier Auto Racing Fans, U. S. Auto Club, 500/400 Festival Assn., Soc. Old Crows, Ind. Electrical Mfgs. Assn. (bd. dirs.), Ind. Software Assn. Democrat. Home: 10635 Chesapeake Dr N Indianapolis IN 46236-8508 Office: SAIC 6330 Castleplace Dr Indianapolis IN 46250-1902

DAMJANOV, IVAN, pathologist, educator; b. Subotica, Yugoslavia, Mar. 31, 1941; came to U.S., 1967; s. Milenko and Ana (Pavkovic) D.; m. Andrea Zivanovic, Jan. 18, 1964; children: Nevena, Ivana, Milena. MD, U. Zagreb (Croatia), 1964, PhD, 1971. Lic. physician, Croatia; diplomate Am. Bd. Pathology. Intern Gen. Hosp., Zagreb, 1964-65; resident in pathology U. Zagreb, 1966-67; intern in pathology Cleve. Met. Gen. Hosp., 1967-68; resident in pathology Mt. Sinai Hosp., N.Y.C., 1968-69; asst. in pathology U. Zagreb, 1969-71; postdoctoral fellow Fels Rsch. Inst., Temple U., Phila., 1971-72; asst. prof. pathology U. Zagreb, 1972-73; from asst. prof. to assoc. prof. U. Conn., Farmington, 1973-77; from assoc. prof. to prof. Hahnemann Med. Coll. and Hosp., Phila., 1977-86; prof. pathology Jefferson Med. Coll. of Thomas Jefferson U., Phila., 1986-94; prof. pathology, chmn. U. Kans. Sch. Med., Kansas City, 1994-98; cons. pathologist VA Hosp., Newington, Conn., 1975-77, Cancer Info. Dissemination and Analysis Ctr. for Virology, Immunology and Cancer-Related Biology, Franklin Inst., Phila., 1977-82; mem. group for rsch. in pathology edn. U. Iowa, 1977-82; ad hoc reviewer, mem. site vis. teams and study sects. NIH, Bethesda, Md., 1978—; mem. basic sci. merit award bd. VA, 1989-92; mem. Croatian Acad. Arts and Scis., 1992. Mem. editl. bd. Ultrastructural Pathology, 1985-96, Virchows Archiv, 1986—, In Vivo, 1988—, Hosp. Physician, 1990-96, Human Pathology, 1991—, Lab. Investigation, 1994—; assoc. editor Lab. Investigation, 1982-94; regional editor N.Am. Differentiation, 1985-96; co-editor Anderson's Pathology, 10th edit., 1996. Recipient Christian R. and Mary F. Lindback award for disting. teaching Jefferson Med. Coll., Phila., 1988. Mem. Am. Assn. Pathologists, Am. Assn. for Cancer Rsch., Internat. Acad. Pathology, Internat. Soc. Differentiation, Developmental Biology Soc. Office: U Kansas Sch of Med Dept Pathol & Lab Med 3901 Rainbow Blvd Kansas City KS 66160-0001

DAMMANN, JULIE ANN, legislative staff member; married; two children. BA in Econs. and Polit. Sci., U. Minn. Legis. asst. U.S. Senator Rudy Boschwitz, Washington, 1982-87; legis. dir. U.S. Senator Christopher Bond, Washington, 1987-96, chief of staff, 1996—. Office: 274 Russell Senate Office Washington DC 20510-2503

DAMON, EDMUND HOLCOMBE, retired plastics company executive; b. St. Louis, Aug. 5, 1929; s. Ralph Shepard Damon and Harriet (Dudley) Holcombe; m. Florence Elizabeth Drake, Apr. 14, 1956; children: Elizabeth, Leslie. BA, Amherst Coll., 1951; MA, U. Bridgeport, 1991. Contr., treas. Strategic Materials Corp., N.Y.C., 1955-63; ops. analyst Norton Co., Troy, N.Y., 1964-65; v.p. corp. devel. Singer Co., Stamford, Conn., 1965-82; pres., chief exec. officer Pantasote Inc., Greenwich, Conn., 1983-89; bd. dirs. The Bombay Co., Inc., Ft. Worth. Elder First Presbyn. Ch., Greenwich, 1970-88; bd. dirs. Child Guidance Ctr., Stamford, 1983-84, Fairfield County Cmty. Found., exec. com., 1991-97; pres. Greenwich United Way, 1986-92, Greenwich Cmty. Fund, 1992-97; bd. dirs., vice chmn. Greenwich chpt. ARC, 1989-92; mem. ARC N.E. regional commn., 1992-93; chmn. adminstrv. coun. First Ch. of Round Hill, Greenwich, 1989-97; bd. dirs. United Way, York County, Maine, 1998—, Brick Store Mus., Kennebunk, Maine, 1998—; trustee Ch. on Cape, Cape Porpoise, Maine. Mem. Webhannet Golf Club (Kennebunk, Maine). Home: 5 Annies Way Kennebunk ME 04043-7533

DAMON, MATTHEW PAIGE, actor; b. Cambridge, Mass., Oct. 8, 1970. Actor (films): Mystic Pizza, 1988, School Ties, 1992, Geronimo: An American Legend, 1993, Courage Under Fire, 1996, Glory Daze, 1996, Chasing Amy, 1997, The Rainmaker, 1997 (nominated Blockbuster Entertainment award Favorite Actor-Drama), Rounders, 1998, Saving Private Ryan, 1998 (nominated SAG award Outstanding Performance by a Cast), The Talented Mr. Ripley, 1999, Dogma, 1999, All the Pretty Horses, 1999; actor, writer (film): Good Will Hunting, 1997 (nominated SAG award Outstanding Performance by a Male Actor in a Leading Role, MTV Movie awards Best Kiss, Best Male Performance, Best On-Screen Duo, ALFS award London Critics Circle Actor of Yr., Screenwriter of Yr., Writers Guild Am. Screen award Best Screenplay written directly for screen, Golden Satellite award Best Action in Motion Picture, Golden Globe award Best Performance by an Actor in a Motion Picture-Drama, 3d place Boston Soc. Film Criics award Best Screenplay, Blockbuster Entertainment award Favorite Actor-Video, Oscar award Best Actor; recipient Nat. Bd. Rev. USA Spl. Achievement in Filmmaking award, Golden Satellite award Best Motion Picture Screenplay, Golden Globe award Best Screenplay-Motion Picture, Fla. Film Critics Cir. award Newcomer of Yr., Chgo. Film Critics Assn. award Most Promising Actor, BFCA award Breakthrough Artist, Berlin Internat. Film Festival Silver Berlin Bear award Outstanding Single Achievement, Oscar award Best Writing, Screenplay Written Directly for Screen). Office: Creative Artists Agy Wilshire Blvd 9830 Beverly Hills CA 90212*

DAMON, WILLIAM VAN BUREN, developmental psychologist, educator, writer; b. Brockton, Mass., Nov. 10, 1944; s. Philip Arthur and Helen (Meyers) D.; m. Wendy Obernauer (div. 1982); children: Jesse Louis, Maria; m. Anne Colby, Sept. 24, 1983, 1 child, Caroline. BA, Harvard U., 1967; PhD, U. Calif., Berkeley, 1973. Social worker N.Y.C. Dept. Social Svcs., 1968-70; prof. psychology Clark U., Worcester, Mass., 1973-89; dean Grad Sch. Clark U., Worcester, 1983-87, chmn. dept. edn., 1988-89; Disting. vis. prof. U. P.R., 1988; prof., chair edn. dept. Brown U., Providence, 1989-92, prof., Mittlemann Family dir. Ctr. for Study of Human Devel., 1993-98; univ. prof., 1997-98; fellow Ctr. for Advanced Study in the Behavioral Scis., 1994-95; prof., dir. Ctr. on Adolescence Stanford (Calif.) U., 1997—; mem. study sect. NIMH, Bethesda, Md., 1981-84; cons. State of Mass., 1976, State of Calif., 1978, Allegheny County, Pa., 1979, Pinellas County, Fla., 1990, Com. of Va., 1993, Hawaii, 1995, Children's TV Workshop, 1991—, Annenberg Adv. Coun. on Excellence in Children's TV, 1996—; mem. nat. adv. bd. Fox Family TV Network, 1998—. Author: Social World of the Child, 1977, Social and Personality Development, 1983, Self-Understanding in Childhood and Adolescence, 1988, The Moral Child, 1988, Child Development Today and Tomorrow, 1989, Some Do Care, 1992, Greater Expectations, 1995 (Parent's Choice Book award 1995), The Youth Charter, 1997; editor: New Directions for Child Devel., 1978—, Handbook of Child Psychology, 1998. Trustee Bancroft Sch., Worcester, Mass., 1982-84; mem. adv. bd. Ednl. Alliance, 1991—. Grantee Carnegie Corp., N.Y.C., 1975-79, 97—, Spencer Found., 1980, 92-96, 98—, N.Y. comty. Trust, 1984-88, Inst. Noetic Scis., 1988-90, MacArthur Found., 1990-95, Pew Charitable Trusts, 1990-95, 98—, Ross Inst., 1996—, Hewlett Found., 1997—, The Templeton Found., 1998—. Mem. APA, Jean Piaget Soc. (bd. dirs. 1983-87), Am. Ednl. Rsch. Assn., Soc. for Rsch. in Child Devel. Republican. Office: Stanford U Ctr on Adolescence Cypress Bldg C Stanford CA 94305-4145
Learn to thrive on the risks and challenges themselves rather than merely on the prospects of winning; expect that every right and privilege must be vigorously defended; and through it all never give up the principle of common decency.

DAMOOSE, GEORGE LYNN, lawyer; b. Grand Rapids, Mich., Feb. 2, 1938; s. George G. and Geneva J. (Joseph) D.; m. Carol Sweeney, Dec. 7, 1968; children: Alison Dana, George Christopher. AB cum laude, Harvard U., 1959, JD cum laude, 1965. Bar: Calif. 1966, U.S. Tax Ct., 1973. Assoc. O'Melveny and Myers, L.A., 1965-72; ptnr. Jennings, Engstrand, Henrikson, P.C., San Diego, 1972-76, Procopio, Cory, Hargreaves, and Savitch, San Diego, 1976—. Bd. dirs. San Diego Civic Light Opera Assn., 1984-90, 92; trustee The Bishops Sch., LaJolla, 1987-90, La Jolla Chamber Music Soc., 1988-89; commr. San Diego Crime Commn., 1987-90. Served to lt. (j.g.) USN, 1959-62. Mem. Am. Bar Found., San Diego County Bar Assn. (chmn. tax sect. 1974-75, 86-87), Calif. Bar Assn. (ind. inquiry and rev. panel, program for certifying legal specialists 1986-87), State Bar Calif. (exec. com., taxation sect. 1990-95, chair 1994-95, chair CEB joint adv. com. taxation 1996-98), San Diego C. of C. (bd. dirs. 1994-96), La Jolla Country Club, La Jolla Beach and Tennis Club. Republican. Episcopalian. Avocations: tennis, bicycling, music, golf. Home: 208 Avenida Cortez La Jolla CA 92037-6502 Office: Procopio Cory et al 530 B St Ste 2100 San Diego CA 92101-4496

DAMORA, ROBERT MATTHEW, architect; s. Matthew Robert and Giacinta (Volonnino) d'Amora; m. Sirkka Heikkinen, Feb. 27, 1950; children: Jesa Sirkka, Matthew Robert. BArch., Yale U., 1953. Registered architect, N.Y., Conn., Mass., Vt., Fla.; cert. Nat. Council Archtl. Reg. Bds. Archtl. journalist-photographer, designer, 1935—, architecture, tech., communications cons. to industry, 1947—, practice architecture, 1955—; assoc. prof. architecture, design critic Columbia U., 1963-64; creator programs of archtl. research, devel., communications, mktg. Knoll Assocs., U.S. Plywood Corp., Pitts. Plate Glass Corp., Am. St. Gobain Glass Corp., STO Industries Inc., others; pres., Archtl. Photographers Assn., 1947-49; dir. Seeds for Architecture program Universal Atlas Cements div. U.S. Steel Corp., including design of prototype concrete hangar for corp. airport and prototype 100-story free-span concrete office bldg., 1956-58. Prin. works in affordable housing design include prefabricated interchangeable concrete components system for tract housing, Cape Cod, Mass., 1962, prefabricated custom house constructed of 3 reduplicated concrete components, Ft. Lauderdale, Fla., 1967, low-cost housing community built with light-weight sprayed concrete on panel forms, Nassau, Bahamas, 1968, prefabricated interchangeable glu-lam and stressed-skin plywood components house, Westchester, N.Y., 1970, curvilinear house, Hillsdale, N.Y., 1974; exhibited in Visionary Architecture show, Mus. Modern Art, 1960, Work featured on various TV programs, in numerous profl. jours. and newspapers. Served to lt. (j.g.), Spl. Devices Div. Bur. Research and Invention USNR, 1943- 46. Recipient 1st prize Portland Cement Assn. Horizon Homes, 1962; Record House of Year, Archtl. Record, 1962; Merit award AIA/House & Home, 1962; 1st prize AIA Conv. Products Exhibit, 1963, 64; Gold medal archtl. photography AIA, 1965; Honor award in architecture, AIA, 1965; Guggenheim Fellow in archtl. research, 1966-67; Nat. Endowment for the Arts Fellow in archtl. design, 1977-78. Fellow AIA (chmn., dir. affordable housing program, 1992—); mem. Westchester 2000 (affordable housing com. 1986-87). Home: Pound Ridge Rd Bedford NY 10506*

D'AMORE, VICTOR, director, choreographer, dance educator; b. Bronx, N.Y., May 31, 1943; s. Victor and Angela (Cavolina) D.; m. Donna Marie Apple, Oct. 12, 1968. BA, Adelphi U., 1976. Pres., Vic D'Amore Studio Dance, Deer Park, Coram, Patchogue, N.Y., 1976—. Dir./choreographer 60 mus. comedy prodns.; choreographer 5 ballets, 300 short works, CLUBJAM. Served to sgt. U.S. Army, 1964-68. Mem. Soc. Stage Dirs. and Choreographers, Dance Masters Am. (bd. dirs.), Dance Educators Am. (bd. dirs., treas.), Brookhaven Theatre Dance Guild (v.p.). Roman Catholic. Home: 122 Woodbury Rd Hauppauge NY 11788-4728 Office: Vic D'Amore Studio of Dance 721 Acorn St Deer Park NY 11729-3202 also: 30 Grove Ave Patchogue NY 11772-4112

DAMOUDE, DENISE ANN, postal worker; b. West Point, Nebr., Oct. 27, 1953; d. Dean Welch and Ella Marie (Knobel) DaM. BS in Edn., Chadron State Coll., 1976; MA in Cmty. Mental Health, Regent U., 1996. Cert. tchr., Nebr. Tchr. phys. edn. and health, coach Pine Ridge (S.D.) Mid. Sch., 1977-79; dorm supr. and counselor U.S. Forest Svc., Chadron, Nebr., 1980-81; city carrier U.S. Postal Svc., Chadron, 1981-83, clk., 1983-92; city carrier U.S. Postal Svc., Portsmouth, Va., 1993—; mem. women's program com. U.S. Postal Svc., North Platte, Nebr., 1986-90; mental health counselor; facilitator for boundaries, divorce care and sexual brokeness groups. Bd. dirs. Guilding Star coun. Girl Scouts U.S.A., Ogallala, Nebr., 1981-83, 90-92, day camp dir. Chadron coun., 1978, sr. troop leader Chadron coun., 1977-79; mem. Community Chorus, Chadron; co-chmn. Christian edn. com. Chadron Community Ch., 1987-88, supt. Christian edn., 1988-91, active with coll. students and single parent households, 1983-92; com. mem. Fellowship of Christian Adult Singles, West Nebr., 1986-92. Mem. Nat. Food Coop. (bd. dirs., sec. 1984-86), Christian Assn. Psychol. Studies, Am. Assn. Christian Counselors, Cardinal Key, Sigma Delta Nu. Republican. Mem. Evangelical Presbyn. Ch. Avocations: gardening, travel, tole painting, reading. Home: 941 Josephine Cres Virginia Beach VA 23464-3916 Office: US Postal Svc 933 Broad St Portsmouth VA 23707-2099

D'AMOUR, DONALD H., supermarket chain executive; b. Holyoke, Mass., 1943. Diploma, Assumption Coll., 1964, Univ. Notre Dame, 1971. Sr. v.p., CEO Big Y Foods, Sprinfield, Mass.; chmn., CEO Big Y Foods, Springfield, 1998—. Office: Big Y Foods PO Box 7840 Springfield MA 01102-7840*

D'AMOURS, NORMAN EDWARD, lawyer, former congressman; b. Holyoke, Mass., Oct. 14, 1937; s. Albert L. and Edna (Laplant) D'A.; m. Helen E. Manning, Sept. 4, 1965; children: Danielle Ann, Susan Ellen, Norman Manning. A.B., Assumption Coll., 1960; LL.B., Boston U., 1963. Bar: N.H. 1964. Practiced in Manchester, from 1969; asst. atty. gen. State N.H., 1966-69; city prosecutor Manchester, 1970-72; mem. 94th-98th Congresses from 1st N.H. dist.; of counsel McLane, Graf, Raulerson & Middleton, Manchester, 1985-93; chmn. Nat. Credit Union Adminstrn., Alexandria, Va., 1993—; instr. Anselm's Coll., 1971-73; chmn. Nat. Credit Union Adminstrn. Bd. Bd. dirs. N.H. Child and Family Svcs., 1993-94. Democrat. Clubs: Optimists (Manchester) (treas. 1965-67), Elks (Manchester), Richelieu (Manchester). Office: Nat Credit Union Admn 1775 Duke St Alexandria VA 22314-3428*

DAMP, GEORGE EDWARD, music educator; b. Ithaca, N.Y., Sept. 20, 1943; s. Russell Salter and Jessica Patricia (Parker) D.; m. Alice Muriel Bancroft, Dec. 28, 1969. BA, Cornell U., 1964, MA, 1966; D of Mus. Arts, Eastman Sch. Music, 1973. Asst. prof. Whitworth Coll., Spokane, Wash., 1969-71, Carleton Coll., Northfield, Minn., 1973-75, Wake Forest U., Winston-Salem, N.C., 1975-76, Ithaca (N.Y.) Coll., 1977-84; prof. Lawrence U., Appleton, Wis., 1984—; vis. instr. Oreg. State U., Corvallis, 1967-68, Williams Coll., Williamstown, Mass., 1968-69; vis. fellow Cornell U., Ithaca, 1991; organist, choirmaster Trinity Episcopal Ch., Geneva, N.Y., 1971-72, Grace Episcopal Ch., Utica, N.Y., 1976-77, St. John's Episcopal Ch., Ithaca, 1977-84, Grace Episcopal Ch., Sheboygan, Wis., 1995-97. Organist: (compact discs) From Byrd to Britten, 1992, Last Works: Brahms, Franck, 1994, Brombaugh, Op. 33, 1996, Meditations from Grace, 1998. Recipient German Govt. award Deutsche Academische AustaUschdienst, 1965, Summer Seminar award NEH, 1984, 87. Mem. Am. Guild Organists, Assn.

Anglican Musicians. Democrat. Episcopalian. Avocations: astronomy, aviation, ornithology. Office: Lawrence U Conservatory of Music Appleton WI 54912

DAMPHOUSSE, VINCENT, professional hockey player; b. Montreal, Ont., Can., Dec. 17, 1967. Left wing/center Edmonton (Can.) Oilers, 1991-93; left wing Montreal Canadiens, 1993-99, San Jose (Calif.) Sharks, 1999—; mem. Stanley Cup championship team, 1993. Shares NHL All-Star single-game record for most goals (4), 1991. Office: San Jose Sharks San Jose Arena 525 W Santa Clara St San Jose CA 95113*

DAMRELL, FRANK C., JR., judge. BA, U. Calif., Berkeley, 1961; JD, Yale U., 1964. Judge U.S. Dist. Ct. (ea. dist.) Calif., 1997—. Office: 650 Capitol Mall Sacramento CA 95814

DAMROW, RICHARD G., marketing executive; s. Donald C. and V. June (Miller) D.; m. Mary Jen Bear, Sept. 1, 1995; children: Andrew, Anthony, Adam, Deborah, Scott. BA cum laude, Hastings Coll., 1970; postgrad. Creighton U., 1970-72. Cert. bus. communicator. Pub. rels. assoc. Western Electric Co., Omaha, 1970-71; mgr. employee and pub. rels. Gate City Steel Corp., Omaha, 1971-72; advt. mgr. Ag-tronic, Inc., Hastings, Nebr., 1972-74; v.p. Fletcher/Mayo Assocs., St. Joseph, Mo., 1974-80; pres. Mark Morris & Co., Mpls., 1980-82; sr. v.p., mng. dir. Carmichael Lynch Advt., Mpls., 1982-86, exec. v.p., 1989-92; exec. v.p. Miller Meester Advt., Mpls., 1986-89, CMF&Z, Cedar Rapids, Iowa, 1992-94; founding ptnr. Contract Mktg. Assocs., 1994-95; exec. v.p., chief mktg. officer The AdTrack Corp., Cedar Rapids, Iowa, 1995-97; chief mktg. officer, Davis, Jones, Lamb Ins., Cedar Rapids, 1997, Net Worth Advisors, 1998—. Mem. M.W. Direct Mktg. Assn., Bus. Mktg. Assn., Nat. Agrimktg. Assn., Direct Mktg. Assn. Republican. Presbyterian. Home: 2700 Granite Ct NE Cedar Rapids IA 52402-3324 Office: Net Worth Advisors PO Box 10260 Cedar Rapids IA 52410-0260

DAMSGAARD, KELL MARSH, lawyer; b. Darby, Pa., May 16, 1949; s. Kjeld and Dorothy (Fanck) D.; m. Katherine Elizabeth Stark, June 17, 1972; children: Peter Kjeld, Christopher William, David Zentner. BA cum laude, Yale U., 1971; JD, U. Pa., 1974. Bar: Pa. 1974, U.S. Dist. Ct. (ea. dist.) Pa. 1975, U.S. Ct. Appeals (3d cir.) 1984, U.S. Ct. Appeals (D.C. cir.) 1989, U.S. Ct. Appeals (8th cir.) 1990, U.S. Ct. Appeals (10th cir.), 1991, U.S. Supreme Ct. 1991. Law clk. to judge Superior Ct. of Pa., Phila., 1974-75; assoc. Morgan, Lewis & Bockius LLP, Phila., 1975-81; ptnr. Morgan, Lewis & Bockius, Phila., 1981—, firm adminstrv. ptnr., 1996—, co-chair product liability and toxic tort practice group. Mem. ABA, Phila. Bar Assn. Avocations: skiing, jogging, tennis, antiques. Home: PO Box 141 Birchrunville PA 19421-0141 Office: Morgan Lewis & Bockius LLP 1701 Market St Philadelphia PA 19103

DAMSKY, ROBERT PHILIP, communications executive; b. Boston, May 19, 1921; s. Mark and Ann (Wisser) D.; m. Rose Hollender, Jan. 18, 1955 (div. 1985); children: Marla Markley, Lori Diana. Cert., MIT, 1939, Tex. A&M U., 1944; diploma, Spartan Sch. Aero., Tulsa, 1946. Indsl. editor Spartan Aircraft Co., Tulsa, 1946-47; with Transocean Airlines, Hartford, Conn., 1947; chief pilot MIT, Beverly, Mass., 1947-48; sr. check pilot Civil Air Patrol, Beverly, 1948; airport mgr. Hartport, Inc., Bellfontaine, Ohio, 1948-49; airline pilot Slick Airlines and U.S. Overseas Airlines, Burbank, Calif. and Wildwood, N.J., 1949-55; founder Flight Edn. Assn., Santa Ana, Calif., 1955-80; pub., editor, pres. Aeromedia Nat. Syndicate, L.A., 1980—. Aviation editor: Beverly News, Mass., Gen. Aviation News. With U.S. Army Air Corps, 1940-45. Decorated Purple Heart, 1941. Mem. Airline Pilots Assn., Aircraft Owners and Pilots Assn., Silver Wings, VFW, Am. Legion, Pearl Harbor Survivors Assn. Avocations: flying, hiking, reading. Home: PO Box 2704 Costa Mesa CA 92628-2704

DAMSON, BARRIE MORTON, oil and gas exploration company executive; b. N.Y.C., Jan. 29, 1936; s. Harry and Ethel (Brody) D.; m. Joan Selig, Feb. 29, 1972; children: Blair, Laura, Bethany. AB, Harvard U., 1956; LLB, NYU, 1959. Bar: N.Y. 1959. Pres. Damson Petroleum Corp., N.Y.C., 1963-69, Bronco Oil Corp., Midland, Tex., 1965-69, Delta Minerals Inc., Lake Charles, La., 1967-69; pres., chmn. bd. Damson Oil Corp., N.Y.C., 1969-91; pres., chmn. bd. First Crescent Corp.; chmn. Crescent Natural Resources, Inc.; bd. dirs., chmn. nominating com. Am. Stock Exch., 1981-91, also bd. govs., chmn. audit com.; chmn. Damson Natural Resources, Inc., 1991, Damson Investment Group, Inc., 1991, European Am. Oil Co., Inc., 1991-94; chmn. Stagebill, 1993; bd. dirs. United Gas Holding Corp., 1993-97. Chmn. bd. mem. N.Y.C. Econ. Devel. Corp., 1992-96; bd. dirs. Queens West Devel. Corp., 1993-97; dir. Robert Steel Found. for Pediatric Cancer Rsch., 1995; mem. Dean's Coun. Harvard Sch. Pub. Health; mem. Am. Bus. Conf., 1980-94. Mem. Bar Assn. N.Y., Harvard Club. Address: 1095 Pequot Ave Southport CT 06490-1421

DAMTOFT, WALTER ATKINSON, editor, publisher; b. Asheville, N.C., June 1, 1922; s. Walter Julius and Dorothy (Atkinson) D.; m. Janet Russell, Mar. 31, 1951; children—Russell Walter, Lisa. Student, Yale U., 1940-41; B.S. in Commerce, U. N.C., Chapel Hill, 1947. Salesman Sta. WKIX, Columbia, S.C., 1947; reporter Ark. Gazette, Little Rock, 1947-50; reporter, city editor Asheville (N.C.) Citizen, 1950-55; city editor Charlotte (N.C.) Observer, 1956-58, N.C. editor, 1958-60, Carolinas editor, 1960-62; writer Nat. Observer, Silver Spring, Md., 1962-69, news editor, 1969-72, sr. editor, 1972-77; editor, pub. Am. Way mag., Ft. Worth, 1977-85; editor, pub. AA Mag. Publs., 1985-86, editor-in-chief, 1986-87; mag. cons., 1987—; seminar leader Am. Press Inst., 1957. Editor: The Consumer's Handbook II, 1971, Here's Help, 1974. Pres. Garrett Park (Md.) Citizen's Assn., 1969-70; mem. Garrett Park Town Council, 1972-76. Served with USNR, 1943-46. Mem. Soc. Profl. Journalists, Men's Garden Club Asheville, RiverLink, Phi Delta Theta. Democrat. Home and Office: 65 Edgemont Rd Asheville NC 28801-1543

DAMUS, PAUL SHIBLI, cardiac surgeon; b. San Bernardino, Calif., Dec. 14, 1942; s. Shibli Shibl and Margaret Joan (Salia) D.; m. Karla Hilda Kuder, Aug. 28, 1971; children: Robert, Michael. BA, U. Colo., 1964; MD, UCLA, 1968. Intern, resident in gen. surg. UCLA, 1968-70; rsch. fellow Harvard U., Boston, 1970-72; resident in cardiothoracic surgery Columbis-Presbyn. Hosp., N.Y.C., 1979-80; resident in pediatric heart surgery Hosp. for Sick Children, Toronto, Ont., Can., 1979-80; dir. infant cardiac surgery St. Francis Hosp., Roslyn, N.Y., 1980-92, dir. cardiac thoracic surgery, 1992—. Creator cardiac operation Damus Procedure. Maj. USAF, 1975-77. Fellow ACS; mem. Soc. Thoracic Surgeons. Avocations: fly fishing, ancient history. Office: St Francis Hosp 100 Port Washington Blvd Roslyn NY 11576-1348*

DAMUS, ROBERT GEORGE, lawyer, government official; b. San Bernardino, Calif., June 24, 1945; s. Shibli and Margaret (Saliba) D.; m. Pamela Claire Aldridge, Aug. 28, 1976; children: David Alexander, Elizabeth Anne. BA magna cum laude, Harvard U., 1967, JD cum laude, 1972; BA, MA (1st class scholar), St. John's Coll., Cambridge U. (Eng.), 1969. Bar: Calif. 1972. Teaching fellow dept. econs. Harvard Coll., Cambridge, Mass., 1970-71; lectr. law U. Warwick, Coventry, Eng. 1972-73; assoc. McCutchen, Black, Verleger & Shea, L.A., 1973-80; gen. trial atty. fed. programs br., civil div., U.S. Dept. Justice, Washington, 1980-82, asst. dir., 1982-85; asst. gen. counsel Office Mgmt. and Budget, Exec. Office of Pres. of U.S., 1985-87, acting gen. counsel, 1987-88, 89-94, gen. counsel, 1994—, dep. gen. counsel, 1988-89. Recipient Spl. Achievement awards Dept. Justice, 1981, 83, Wright prize in Econs., Cambridge U. (Eng.), 1972, Sr. Exec. Svcs. Presdl. Rank Merit award of meritorious exec., 1994, disting. exec., 1995. Club: Harvard Varsity. Office: Office Mgmt & Budget Old Executive Office Bldg Washington DC 20503

DAMUTH, JOHN ERWIN, marine geologist; b. Dayton, Ohio, Nov. 22, 1942; s. Jason Donald and Sarah Maxine (Simpson) D.; m. Patricia Jane Keenan, Oct. 8, 1971 (div. July 1990). BS in Geology, Ohio State U., 1965; MA in Geology, Columbia U., 1968, PhD in Geology, 1973. Grad. rsch. asst. Lamont-Doherty Geol. Obs., Columbia U., 1965-73, rsch. scientist, 1973-74, rsch. assoc., 1974-82, sr. rsch. assoc., 1982-83; rsch. geologist Dallas Rsch. Lab. Dallas Rsch. Lab., Mobil R & D Corp., 1983-84, sr. rsch. geologist, 1984-92; sr. rsch. scientist Earth Rsch. and Environ. Ctr., U. Tex., Arlington, 1992—; adj. sr. rsch. scientist Lamont-Doherty Earth Obs., Columbia U., 1996—; adj. prof. dept. geology U. Tex., Arlington, 1996—; adj. rsch. scientist Lamont-Doherty Geol. Obs., Columbia U., 1983-91; instr. ecology adult edn. N.J. H.S., 1977-83; mem. Nat. Site Assessment Com. Subseabed Disposal High-Level Nuc. Waste, 1978-83; lectr. in field. Contbr. articles to profl. jours. Texaco scholar, 1964-65; Eugene Higgins fellow, 1965-66, Pan Am. Oil Co. fellow, 1967, Pres.'s fellow, 1968-69, Nat. Lord Britton fellow, 1967-68. Fellow Geol. Soc. Am.; mem. Am. Assn. Petroleum Geologists, Soc. Econ. Paleontologists and Mineralogists, Am. Geohphys. Union, Sigma Xi. Avocations: fishing, skiing, travel, exercise. E-mail: damuth@uta.edu. Office: Univ Tex Dept Geology PO Box 19049 Arlington TX 76019

DANA, F(RANK) MITCHELL, theatrical lighting designer; b. Washington, Nov. 14, 1942; s. John Daskum Mitchell and Elizabeth Francis (Woods) D.; m. Wendy Karen Bensinger, Dec. 31, 1967; children: Scott Cameron, Ian Michael. B.F.A., Utah State U., 1964; M.F.A., Yale U., 1967. Asst. to Jo Mielziner N.Y.C., 1968-69; tech. dir. Yale Drama Sch., New Haven, Conn., 1970-71; assoc. lighting dir. Ferd Manning, N.Y.C., 1978-88; guest lectr. U. Wash., So. Meth. U., San Francisco State U.; lectr. Rutgers U., 1982-97, asst. prof., 1997. Prodn. mgr.: Stratford Festival, Pitts. Civic Light Opera; prodn. supr. Yale Repertory Theatre; lighting designer: Broadway Plays include The Freedom of the City, 1974, Once in a Lifetime, 1978, Inspector General, 1978, Man and Superman, 1978, The Suicide, 1980 (Drama Logue award), Mass Appeal, 1981, Monday After the Miracle, 1982, The Babe, 1984, Oh Coward, 1986; off-Broadway Plays include Three Acts of Recognition, 1982, A Coupla White Chicks, 1980, Mass Appeal, 1980, Oh Coward, 1981, Calling in Crazy, 1969, Songs My Mother Never Sang Me, 1982, Husbandry, 1984, A Hell of a Town, 1984, The Ninth Step, 1984, Daughters, 1986, Cold Sweat, 1988, Other People's Money, 1989, King Fish, 1991, Lust 1995, PaPa 1996; operas World Premier of Harriet: The Woman Called Moses, Orphee, Patricia II, Tempest 94, Turandot, Royal Opera, Covent Garden, 1984, Olympic Arts Festival, 1984, La Rondine, N.Y.C. Opera, 1984, Magic Flute, 1985, Merry Widow, 1986, Cleve. Symphony, Un Ballo in Maschera Va. Opera, 1985, Opera Festival of N.J., 1989-98 Turandot, Royal Opera/Covent Garden at Wembly Arena, 1991, Carmen for L.A. Opera and Seville Expo92, La Traviata for Barcelona's Gran Licieu, 1992; Makropolous Case, Traviata, Midsummer Night's Dream, 1992, Elgato Montez, Madama Butterfly, Faust, Electra, Don Giovanni, L.A. Opera, 1994; also Pitts. Civic Light Opera, 1973-74, 79, 84-87; tours Hello Dolly, 1981, Mass Appeal, 1982, Guys and Dolls, 1984, George M., Jesus Christ Superstar, 1985, Stop the World, 1986, Other People's Money, Okla., 1990; regional theaters Am. Conservatory Theatre, 1972-80, BAM Theatre Co., 1977, 78, 80, 81, Goodman Theatre, 1973-82, McCarter Theatre, 1969-71, 82, 86-90, Nat. Arts Ctr., Ottawa, 1982-84, others including Mark Taper Forum, Paper Mill Playhouse, Phila. Drama Guild, Va. Mus. Theatre, Crossroads Theatre Co., Geva Theater, Folger Theater, Hartford Stage Co., Ala. Shakespeare Co., Cin. Playhouse, Syracuse Stage, 1984, 87, 96, Seattle Repertory, Stratford Shakespeare Festival, Studio Arena Theatre, Stratford Festival Theatre, Roundabout Theatre, 1987, 88, George Street Playhouse, Interact Theatre Co., Derby Playhouse (U.K.). Mem. Internat. Alliance Theatrical Stage Employees, United Scenic Artists (exec. bd. 1970-72, 96—). Republican. Office: 221 W 82d St New York NY 10024-5406

DANA, HOWARD H., JR., state supreme court justice. Assoc. justice Supreme Judicial Ct. of Maine, Portland, 1993—. Office: Supreme Judicial Court 142 Federal St PO Box 368 Portland ME 04112-0368*

DANA, LAUREN ELIZABETH, lawyer; b. Hollywood, Calif., Sept. 30, 1950; d. Franklin Eugene and Margaret Elizabeth (Nixon) D.; m. Andrew Russell Willing, May 25, 1986; 1 child, Matthew Barkan Willing. BA cum laude, Calif. State U., Northridge, 1973; JD cum laude, Southwestern U., 1982. Bar: Calif. 1982, U.S. Dist. Ct. (cen. dist.) Calif. 1983, U.S. Ct. Appeals (9th cir.) 1983, U.S. Supreme Ct. 1987. Assoc. Law Office Andrew R. Willing, Los Angeles, 1982-84; dep. atty. gen. Calif. Dept. Justice-Atty. Gen., Los Angeles, 1984—; temporary judge L.A. Mcpl. Ct. Assoc. editor legal update Police Officer Law Report, 1986-87. Recipient Am. Jurisprudence Book award Lawyers Coop. Pub. Co., 1980, Am. Jurisprudence Book award in Evidence, 1980. Mem. ABA, Fed. Bar Assn., Am. Judicature Soc., Constitutional Rights Found., Selden Soc., U.S. Supreme Ct. Hist. Soc., L.A. County Bar Assn. (conf. of delegates 1998, 99), Women Lawyers Assn. L.A., L.A. World Affairs Coun., Alliance for Children's Rights, Town Hall, Phi Alpha Delta, The Da Camera Soc. Avocations: music, collecting books on English history, reading, traveling. Office: Calif Dept Justice 300 S Spring St Los Angeles CA 90013-1230

DANA, RICHARD L., painter, arts administrator; b. Orange, N.J., Nov. 8, 1952; s. William D. Jr. and Emma Joy (Linen) D. BA in Soviet Studies, U. N.C., 1975; MA in Internat. Rels., Johns Hopkins U., 1977. Soviet affairs expert to Chief of Staff, Air Force Intelligence, Pentagon, Washington, 1980-84; tchr. art and graphics St. Albans Sch., Washington, 1988-91; co-dir. Art of Work, Work of Art Project, Washington, 1995—; juror Reaching Across Our Borders, Virginia Beach (Va.) Ctr. for the Arts, 1996; guest curator 3 Painters from Morocco, Nat. Mus. Women in the Arts, Washington, 1996; pres. Touchstone Gallery, Washington, 1987; exec. dir. Washington Area Arts Consortium, Washington, 1988-94; pres. bd. dirs. Arlington (Va.) Arts Ctr., 1994-96, co-chair exhbns. com., 1996—. One-man shows include A-3 Gallery, Moscow, 1993, Troyer, Fitzpatrick Lassman Gallery, Washington, 1995, Juniata Coll., Huntingdon, Pa., 1996, IMF, Washington, 1996, Antitesi Gallery, Rome, 1998; exhibited in group shows at Corcoran Gallery of Art, Washington, 1994, Chrysler Mus., Norfolk, Va., 1996, Taipei Fine Arts Mus., Taiwan, 1997, others. Recipient Individual Artist award Md. State Arts Coun., 1996. Avocations: fly fishing, soccer. Office: 925 1/2 F St NW Washington DC 20004-1405

DANAHAR, DAVID C., academic administrator, history educator; b. Dobbs Ferry, N.Y., Sept. 29, 1941; s. Walter Vincent and Catherine Marie (Charles) D.; m. Cecelia Upritchard, Aug. 24, 1985; children: Deirdre, Rebecca, Michael. BA, Manhattan Coll., Bronx, N.Y., 1963; MA, U. Mass., 1965, PhD, 1970. Instr. U. Mass., Amherst, 1969-70; asst. prof. SUNY, Oswego, 1970-73, assoc. prof., 1973-84, prof., 1984-85; dean Coll. Arts and Scis., prof. history Fairfield (Conn.) U., 1985-92; provost, acad. v.p. Loyola U., New Orleans, 1992—; vis. prof. U. Pisa, Italy, 1971-72. Contbr. articles on Habsburg and Austrian history to profl. jours. Mem. Fairfield 2000, 1985-88; bd. trustees New Orleans Mus. of Art, 1993-95. Univ. fellow U. Mass., 1966-69, rsch. fellow Am. Coun. Learned Socs., 1975-76; grantee SUNY Rsch. Found., 1971-73, NEH, 1983-88, also numerous others from U.S. Govt., Founds. and Corps. including Hilton Found., Monroe Found., HUD, DOE, Culpeper Found., Keck Found., IBM, GE, 1985—. Mem. Am. Hist. Assn., Am. Conf. Acad. Deans, Coun. Colls. Arts and Scis., Conf. on Cen. European History, Am. Assn. Higher Edn. Advocation: travel, sailing. Office: Loyola U Marquette 221C Box 007 6363 Saint Charles Ave New Orleans LA 70118-6195

DANAHER, FRANK ERWIN, transportation technologist; b. Montclair, N.J., Mar. 5, 1936; s. Frank E. and Mildred (Acquino) D.; m. Joan Marie Donovan, Apr. 12, 1986; children: Maria, Frank, Heather (dec.). BA in Math., Rutgers U., 1961; MBA, Fairleigh Dickinson, 1982. Supr. programming ITT, Paramus, N.J., 1961-66; mgr. systems Lummus, Bloomfield, N.J., 1966-83; rsch. specialist Dun & Bradstreet, Basking Ridge, N.J., 1983-87; technologist Met. Transp. Auth., N.Y.C., 1987—; cons. in field. Contbr. articles to profl. publs. Area gov. Toastmasters, N.Y.C., 1984-85, chpt. pres., 1993; pres. Fairleigh Early Birds, 1982, 94; spkr. in field. With U.S. Army, 1959. Urban Mass Transit Authority grantee, 1988, 90. Mem. Assn. for Sys. Mgmt. (pres. 1983, 95), Geog. Info. Sys. Users (chmn. 1990-99), Computer Aided Design and Drafting, User Group Met. Transp. Auth. (chmn. 1990-99), Radio User Group Met. Transp. Auth. (chmn. 1996), Rock Spring Country Club, Delta Mu Delta. Republican. Roman Catholic. E-mail: fdanaher@mtahq.org. Home: 454-147 Prospect Ave West Orange NJ 07052-4103 Office: Met Transit Auth 341 Madison Ave New York NY 10017

DANAHER, JAMES WILLIAM, retired federal government executive; b. St. Marys, Ohio, Feb. 20, 1929; s. William Louis and Cora Caroline (Hausfeld) D.; m. Ellen Serena Martin, Feb. 5, 1972; children—Patrick Brendan, Kathryn Annette. BS in Econs., Villanova U., 1952; MA in Psychology, Ohio State U., 1958; grad., Fed. Execs. Inst., 1978. Lic. comml. pilot. Rsch. assoc. Courtney & Co., Phila., 1958-62; v.p., rsch. scientist Matrix Rsch. Corp., Arlington, Va., 1962-70; chief human factors divsn. Nat. Transp. Safety Bd., Washington, 1970-76, from chief operational factors divsn. to dir. bur. techn., 1976-85, chief operational factors and human performance divsn., 1985-98; ret., 1998; aviation safety cons., 1998—. Contbr. articles to profl. jours. Bd. dirs. Alexandria Soccer Assn., Va., 1983-86; v.p. Charles Barrett Sch. PTA, Alexandria, 1983-84. Capt. USNR, 1952-76. Mem. Human Factors and Ergonomics Soc., Internat. Soc. Air Safety Investigators, Assn. Aviation Psychologists, Naval Res. Assn. (life). Roman Catholic. Lodge: K.C. Avocations: long distance running; skiing; golf. Home: 717 S Overlook Dr Alexandria VA 22305-1215

DANAS, ANDREW MICHAEL, lawyer; b. Redwood City, Calif., Apr. 25, 1955; s. Michael George and Marjorie Jean (Bailey) D. BA in Polit. Sci. and History, U. Conn., 1977; JD, George Washington U., 1982. Bar: D.C. 1982, U.S. Dist. Ct. (D.C. cir.), U.S. Dist. Ct. Md., U.S. Ct. Appeals (D.C., 2d, 3d, 4th, 6th, 11th and fed. cirs.), U.S. Ct. of Claims, U.S. Supreme Ct. Atty. Assn. Am. R.R.s, Washington, 1983-84; assoc. Grove Jaskiewicz & Cobert, Washington, 1984-90, Ptnr., 1991—. Contbg. author: Freewheeling; author legal column Intermodal Reporter, 1986-94; contbr. articles to profl. jours. Mem. exec. com. Friends Assisting the Nat. Symphony, Washington, 1996-97. Mem. Transp. Law Inst. (chair 1993-94), Transp. Lawyers Assn. (chair legis. com. 1995-98, co-chair 1999, Disting. Svc. award 1996), Phi Alpha Theta, Mensa. Avocations: skiing, music, travel. Home: 1400 20th St NW Apt 506 Washington DC 20036-5992 Office: Grove Jaskiewicz and Cobert 1730 M St NW Ste 400 Washington DC 20036-4579

DANBOM, DAVID BYERS, history educator; b. Denver, Mar. 29, 1947; s. Raymond Carl and Rowene Caroline (Byers) D.; m. Karen Renee Poor, June 19, 1971; children: Elizabeth Poor, Mark Raymond. BA, Colo. State U., 1969; MA, Stanford U., 1970, PhD, 1974. Prof. history N.D. State U., Fargo, 1974—, faculty lectr., 1998; editor N.D. Inst. for Regional Studies, Fargo, 1981-92. Author: The Resisted Revolution, 1979, The World of Hope, 1987, Our Purpose is to Serve, 1990, Born in the Country, 1995; editor: Publicly Sponsored Agricultural Research, 1988. Sec. bd. dirs. Red River Valley Heritage Soc., Moorhead, Minn., 1987-92; mem. Fargo Hist. Preservation Commn., 1990—. Named N.D. Prof. of Yr., Coun. Advancement and Support of Edn., 1990, Disting. Prof., Fargo C. of C., 1990; recipient Faculty Achievement award Burlington No., 1990. Mem. Agrl. History Soc. (bd. dirs. 1990-94, pres. 1990-91), Orgn. Am. Historians (membership com. 1990-95), Soc. Historians of the Gilded Age and Progressive Period. Office: ND State U Dept History Fargo ND 58105

DANCE, FRANCIS ESBURN XAVIER, communication educator; b. Bklyn., Nov. 9, 1929; s. Clifton Louis and Catherine (Tester) D.; m. Nora Alice Rush, May 1, 1954 (div. 1974); children: Clifton Louis III, Charles Daniel, Alison Catherine, Andrea Frances, Frances Sue, Brendan Rush; m. Carol Camille Zak, July 4, 1974; children: Zachary Esburn, Gabriel Joseph, Caleb Michael, Catherine Emily. BS, Fordham U., 1951; MS, Northwestern U., 1953, PhD, 1959. Instr. speech Bklyn. Adult Labor Schs., 1951; instr. humanities, coordinator radio and TV U. Ill. at Chgo., 1953-54; instr. Univ. Coll., U. Chgo., 1958; asst. prof. St. Joseph's (Ind.) Coll., 1958-60; asst. prof., then assoc. prof. U. Kans., 1960-63; mem. faculty U. Wis., Milw., 1963-71, prof. communication, 1965-71, dir. Speech Communication Center, 1963-70; prof. U. Denver, 1971—, John Evans prof., 1995—; content expert and mem. faculty adv. bd. to Internat. U. on Knowledge Channel, 1993-95; cons. in field. Author: The Citizen Speaks, 1962, (with Harold P. Zelko) Business and Professional Speech Communication, 1965, 2d edit., 1978, Human Communication Theory, 1967, (with Carl E. Larson) Perspectives on Communication, 1970, Speech Communication: Concepts and Behavior, 1972, The Functions of Speech Communication: A Theoretical Approach, 1976, Human Communication Theory, 1982, (with Carol C. Zak-Dance) Public Speaking, 1986, Speaking Your Mind, 1994, 2d edit., 1996; editor Jour. Comm., 1962-64, Speech Tchr., 1970-72; adv. bd. Jour. Black Studies; editl. bd. Jour. Psycholinguistic Rsch; contbr. articles to profl. jours. Bd. dirs. Milw. Mental Health Assn., 1966-67. 2d lt. AUS, 1954-56. Knapp Univ. scholar in communication, 1967-68; recipient Outstanding Prof. award Standard Oil Found., 1967; Master Tchr. award U. Denver, 1985, University Lectr. award U. Denver, 1986. Fellow Internat. Communication Assn. (pres. 1967); mem. Nat. Communication Assn. (pres. 1982), Psi Upsilon. Office: U Denver Dept Human Comm Studies Denver CO 80208 *Life should include a personal commitment to excellence with a corresponding humane tolerance for failure in self or in others. A belief in the progressive acquisition of autonomy can help guide both personal and professional decisions.*

DANCE, MAURICE EUGENE, college administrator; b. Bismarck, N.D., Jan. 14, 1923; s. Alvin Cecil and Jennie (Brown) D.; m. Margaret Thorstenson, Mar. 25, 1944; (dec. Apr. 1964); children—Muriel, Maurice, Marcia, Mark, Michelle, Michael, Myles; m. Anita Ruth Bell, Apr. 10, 1965; children—Jennifer, Kristina. B.A., U. Wash., 1947; M.S., U. Wis., 1949, Ph.D., 1953. Asst. prof. econs. Los Angeles State Coll., 1950-56; with San Fernando Valley State Coll., Northridge, Calif., 1956-69; prof. econs. San Fernando Valley State Coll., 1956-69, chmn. dept., 1956-64, asst. to v.p. for acad. affairs, 1964-65; dean Sch. of Letters and Scis., 1965-69; provost, v.p. acad. affairs Calif. State U., Hayward, 1969-91, provost emeritus, v.p. acad. affairs emeritus, 1991—; Econs. cons. Office: Calif State U 25800 Carlos Bee Blvd Hayward CA 94542*

DANCEWICZ, JOHN EDWARD, investment banker; b. Boston, Mass., Feb. 12, 1949; s. John Felix and Teresa Sophia (Lewandowski) D.; m. Barbaragail Jarrett, Jan. 23, 1971; children: John Lawrence, Jill Elizabeth, Jenna Gail. BA in Econs., Yale U., 1971; MBA, Harvard U., 1973. Project adminstr., cons. Nat. Shawmut Bank Boston, 1972-73; v.p., mgr. U.S. investment banking Continental Ill. Nat. Bank Chgo., 1973-82; sr. mng. dir., mgr. corp. fin. Bear Stearns & Co. Inc., Chgo., 1982-96; founder, mng. ptnr. DN Ptnrs. L.L.C., 1996—; chmn. bd. dirs. Aztec Outdoor Advt. Co. Contbr. articles to profl. jours. Active Yale U. Schs. Com., Spl. Gifts Com. (chmn. 25th Reunion Fundraising, sec. Yale class 1971); sec. Harvard Bus. Sch. sect.; mem. spl. gifts com. Harvard Bus. Sch. Fund. Mem. Mid. Am. Com., Scholarship and Guidance Assn. (bd. dirs., v.p. 1982—), Lake Forest H.S. Hockey Assn. (pres.), Harvard Bus. Sch. Club Chgo. (bd. dirs.), Econ. Club, Univ. Club, East Bank Club, Mid-Am. Club. Home: 969 Spring Ln Lake Forest IL 60045-2302 Office: 3 First Nat Plz Chicago IL 60602

DANCEY, CHARLES LOHMAN, newspaper executive; b. Pekin, Ill., Nov. 28, 1916; s. Albert Duane and Bertha (Lohman) D.; m. Nina Evelyn Manker, Dec. 10, 1944; children: Richard, Burt Lee, Clinton Dancey. BS, U. Ill., 1938. Reporter Peoria (Ill.) Star, 1938-40, Peoria Jour., 1946-50; editor Peoria Jour. Star, 1958-80, asst. pub., 1980-87, cons., 1987-96, dir., 1993-96; dir., exec. bd. Dirksen Congrl. Rsch. Ctr., 1994—; owner rep., mgmt. bd. WTVH-TV, Peoria, 1956-58. Ill. state comdt. Marine Corps League, 1947; City councilman, commr. fire and police, Pekin, 1946-50. Col. USMCR, 1941-46, 50-51. Recipient Peoria chpt. B'nai B'rith Citizenship award, 1964. Mem. Inter-Am. Press Assn. (dir., exec. bd.), Am. Soc. Newspaper Editors. Club: Mason. Home: 419 Haines Ave Pekin IL 61554-4229

DANCO, LÉON ANTOINE, management consultant, educator; b. N.Y.C., May 30, 1923; s. Leon A. and Alvira T. (Gomez) D.; m. Katharine Elizabeth Leck, Aug. 25, 1951; children—Suzanne, Walter Ten Eyck. AB, Harvard, 1943, MBA, 1947, PhD, Case We. Res. U., 1963. Asst. to div. pres. Interchem. Corp., N.Y.C., 1947-50; sales promotion mgr. Risdon Mfg. Co., Waterbury, Conn., 1950-55; mgmt. cons. Cheshire, Conn., 1955-57; prof., asso. dir. mgmt. program Case Inst. Tech., Cleve., 1957-58; lectr. Case Inst. Tech., 1959—; mgmt. cons. L.A. Danco & Co., 1957—; lectr. John Carroll U., Cleve., 1959-66; prof., dir. mgmt. confs. John Carroll U., 1966—; vis. prof. econs. Cleve. Inst. Art, 1966-69, Kent State U., 1966-67; exec. dir. Univ. Svcs. Inst., Cleve., 1967-69, pres., 1969—, chmn., 1989—; pub. The Family in Business (newsletter), 1978—; pres. Center for Family Bus., 1978—, chmn.Center for Family Bus., 1991. Author: Beyond Survival—A Business Owners Guide for Success, 1975, Inside the Successful Family Business, 1979, Outside Directors in the Family Owned Business, 1981, Someday It'll All Be...Whose?, 1990, (in French) L'Entreprise Familiale, 1998, (in Spanish) La Empresa Familiare, 1998; syndicated columnist: It's Your Business, 1973—. Served to lt. (j.g.) USCG, 1942-46, PTO. Mem. Am. Econ. Assn. Home: 28230 Cedar Rd Pepper Pike Cleveland OH 44124

Office: Ctr for Family Bus PO Box 24219 Cleveland OH 44124-0219 *Whatever success we may achieve in this life will come from the purpose to which we put God's priceless gift of time.*

DANCYGER, ALAIN, performing company executive; b. Limoges, France. Student, Guildhall Sch. Music and Drama, London, 1977-78; MMus, Juilliard Sch., N.Y.C., 1984; MBA, Ecole Superieure des Scis. Economiques et Commerciales, Paris, 1987. Founding mem. Viri Duo, Iris Trio; with Jeunesses Musicales, Yugoslavia; acting internal cons. Soc. Nat. des Chemins de Fer Francais, Paris, 1987, 88; with sales and mktg. depts. Frenchrail, N.Y., 1988-91; asst. dir. Saidye Bronfman Ctr. for the Arts, Quebec, 1991-93, dir., 1993-96; dir. gen. Les Grands Ballets Canadiens, Montreal, Que., Can., 1996—, mem. exec. com., bd. dirs. Regroupement Quebecois de la danse; apptd. to Commission des arts de la scene, 1996. performer various summer festivals and Capitol Hill, Washington. Office: Les Grands Ballets Canadiens, 4816 rue Rivard, Montreal, PQ Canada H2J 2N6*

DANDO, PAT, city official. City coun. San Jose, Calif. Office: 801 N 1st St Rm 600 San Jose CA 95110-1704*

DANDOY, MAXIMA ANTONIO, education educator emeritus; b. Santa Maria, Ilocos, Sur., Philippines; came to U.S., 1949, naturalized, 1951; d. Manuel and Isidra (Mendoza) Antonio. Teaching cert., Philippine Normal Coll., 1938; A.B., Nat. Tchrs. Coll., Manila, 1947; M.A., Arellano U., Manila, 1949; Ed.D. (John M. Switzer scholar, Newhouse Found. scholar), Stanford U., 1951, postgrad. (Calif. Fedn. Bus. and Profl. Women's Club scholar), 1952. Tchr. elem. sch. Philippines, 1927-37; lab. sch. tchr. Philippine Normal Coll., Manila, 1938-49; instr. Arellano U., Manila, 1947-49; lab. sch. prin. U. of East, Manila, 1953-54; assoc. prof. U. of East, 1952-55; prof. edn. Calif. State U., Fresno, 1956-82, prof. edn. emeritus, 1982—; curriculum writer, gen. office supr. Manila Dept. Edn., 1944-45; Mem. com. for the selection social studies textbooks for state adoption Calif., 1970-71; vis. prof. UCLA, 1956; Floro Crisologo Meml. lectr. U. No. Philippines, 1977. Author: Teaching Competencies, A Workbook and Log, 1985. Mem. Friends of the Stanford (Calif.) U. Sch. Edn., 1993, Sch. of Edn. and Human Devel. Alumni and Friends, Calif. State U., Fresno, 1992-93; mem. Calif. Gov.'s Conf. on Traffic Safety, 1962, Calif. Gov.'s Conf. Delinquency Prevention, 1963. Named Disting. Woman of Year, Fresno Bus. and Profl. Women's Club, 1957, Woman of Achievement, 1973, Outstanding Filipino, 1982, 98; recipient Higher Edn. and Internat. Understanding award Philippine Normal Coll. Alumni Assn., 1986, One Moment in Time award Calif. Fedn. Bus. and Profl. Women, 1997-98. Mem. AAUW (liaison Calif. State U. Fresno 1970-71, bridge gen. coord. 1995-99), Nat. Coun. Social Studies (chmn. sec. internat. understanding, nat. conv. 1966), Calif. Fedn. Bus. and Profl. Women's Clubs (state chmn. scholarships 1961-63, treas. Fresno), Calif. Tchrs. Assn., Orgn. Filipino-Am. Educators Fresno (pres. 1977-95), Filipino-Am. Women's Club (adv. 1969-74), Internat. Platform Assn., Phi Delta Kappa, Pi Lambda Theta, Kappa Delta Pi (counselor 1972-79, nat. com. attendance and credentials 1975, nat. com. regional confs. 1966). Home: 1419 W Bullard Ave Fresno CA 93711-2324

DANDOY, SUZANNE EGGLESTON, physician, academic administrator, educator; b. Los Angeles, Jan. 2, 1935; d. Leonard Lester and Catherine (Wheelwright) Eggleston; m. Jeremiah Richard Dandoy, June 14, 1958; children: Kevin, Bret, Jolyn. BA, UCLA, 1956, MD, 1960, MPH, 1963. Diplomate: Am. Bd. Preventive Medicine. Intern, Los Angeles Harbor Gen. Hosp., Torrance, Calif., 1960-61; resident Los Angeles Health Dept., 1961-62, 63-64; epidemiologist San Diego Dept. Pub. Health, 1967-68; bur. chief Ariz. Dept. Health Service, Phoenix, 1970-72; asst. commr. Ariz. Dept. Health Service, 1973-74, asst. dir., 1974-75, dir., 1975-80; prof. health adminstrn. Ariz. State U., Tempe, 1981-85; exec. dir. Utah Dept. Health, Salt Lake City, 1985-92; dep. commr. Va. Dept. Health, Richmond, 1992-94; dir. Va. Beach Health Dept., 1994-97; dir. pub. health grad. program, prof. Eastern Va. Med. Sch., 1997—; adj. prof. U. Utah; bd. dirs. Pub. Health Found. Chair editl. bd. Am. Jour. Pub. Health; contbr. articles to profl. jours.; assoc. editor: Am. Jour. Preventive Medicine, 1996-97. Chair Nat. Vaccine Adv. Com., HHS; adv. com. on immunization practices HEW; pres. Utah Women's Forum. Recipient award Ariz. Dietetic Assn., 1976; award Maricopa County Med. Soc., 1980. Fellow APHA, Am. Coll. Preventive Medicine (pres. 1991-93, Disting. Svc. award 1995); mem. Nat. Assn. County and City Health Ofcls., Assn. State Health Officers (pres. 1990-91), Phi Beta Kappa, Delta Omega. Democrat. Mormon. Home: 1321 Botetourt Gdns Norfolk VA 23517-2203 Office: Ea Va Med Sch Grad Program in Pub Health PO Box 1980 Norfolk VA 23501-1980

D'ANDREA, FRANCES MARY, special education educator; b. Southampton, N.Y., Nov. 17, 1960; d. John and Margaret (Faye) D'A.; m. Stephen F. Cox, June 23. BS, George Peabody Coll. Tchrs., Nashville, 1982; MEd, Ga. State U., 1996. Tchr. of visually impaired Utah Sch. for the Blind, Ogden, 1982-87, Salt Lake City, 1982-87; tchr. of visually impaired Fulton County Schs., Atlanta, 1987-94; dir. Nat. Literacy program Am. Found. for the Blind, Atlanta, 1995—, rep. to Braille Authority of N.Am., dir. S.E. office, 1998—; mem. adv. com. Ga. Deafblind Project, Atlanta, 1995—. Co-author, editor Instructional Strategies for Braille Literacy, 1997 (Best Title in Category award Assn. Am. Pubs. 1997); contbr. articles to profl. publs. Bd. dirs. Atlanta chpt. Nat. Audubon Soc., 1991-92; sec. Wilson Woods Garden Club, Decatur, Ga., 1997-98; active Atlanta Regional Folders, 1987—, Choral Guild Atlanta, 1987-95. Mem. Assn. for Edn. and Rehab. of Blind and Visually Impaired (pres. Ga. chpt. 1991-93, 97-99, divsn. 16 chair elect 1998—, editor 1990-94, Bennett Baxley award for Outstanding Svc. 1991), Internat. Reading Assn., Coun. Exceptional Children (divsn. visual impairments), Omicron Delta Kappa. Office: Am Found for the Blind 100 Peachtree St NW Ste 620 Atlanta GA 30303-1909

D'ANDREA, MARK, radiation oncologist; b. Palos Park, Ill., May 24, 1960; s. Anthony E. and Adriene D'Andrea. BA in Chemistry, Religion, and Biology, Luther Coll., 1981; MD, Ponce (P.R.) Sch. Medicine, 1985. Diplomate Am. Acad. Pain Mgmt., Am. Bd. Radiology in Radiation Oncology. Resident in internal medicine Cabrini Med. Ctr., N.Y.C., 1985-86; resident in radiation oncology Meth. Hosp., Bklyn., 1986-89; radiation oncologist East Tex. Cancer Ctr., Tyler, 1989-94, Mother Frances Hosp., Tyler, Med. Ctr. Hosp., Tyler, U. Tex. Health Ctr., Tyler, St. Josephs Hosp., Paris, Tex., McCuistion Hosp., Paris, Tex., Longview (Tex.) Radiation Oncology Ctr.; resident U. Tex. Med. Branch, Galveston, 1991-92; dir. radiation oncology Bayshore Hosp., Pasadena, Tex., 1994-98; med. dir. radiation oncology Gulf Coast Cancer Ctr., Pasadena, Tex., 1998—; prin. investigator Radiation Therapy Oncology Group, Bayshore Cancer Ctr., 1995—; prof. radiation biology Tyler Jr. Coll., 1990-91; chief resident in radiation oncology Meth. Hosp., Bklyn., 1988-89; cons. Longview Regional, Good Shepherd Hosp., 1989-94, pres., chmn. bd. Danhul Corp., 1992, 96. Patentee diagnostic marking catheter system and intracavitary catheter for use in radiation diagnosis procedures. Chmn. Com. Pub. health Kings and Bklyn. County, N.Y., 1988-89. Named One of Outstanding Young Men Am., 1987; recipient Outstanding award Ill. Jr. Acad. Sci., 1978. Fellow Am. and Internat. Coll. Angiology, InterAm. Coll. Physicians and Surgeons; mem. Am. Inst. Chemists (ethics com.), Am. Chem. Soc., Am. Soc. Clin. Oncology, Am. Soc. Therapeutic Radiology and Oncology, AMA, Radiol. Soc. N.Am., Med. Soc. N.Y. State, Kings County Med. Soc., Acad. Medicine Bklyn., Smith County Med. Soc., Tex. Med. Assn., Circilo de Radioterapeutas ibero Latino Americanos. Office: Gulf Coast Cancer Ctr Dept Radiation Oncology PO Box 7894 Pasadena TX 77508-7894

DANDRIDGE, WILLIAM SHELTON, orthopedic surgeon; b. Atoka, Okla., May 21, 1914; s. Theodore Oscar and Estelle (Shelton) D.; m. Pearl Sessions, Feb. 3, 1941 (dec. Apr. 1993); m. Eva Thurman, Dec. 2, 1994; children: Diana Dawn, James Rutledge. B.A., U. Okla., 1935; M.D., U. Ark., 1939; M.S., Baylor U., 1950. Intern, St. Paul's Hosp., Dallas, 1939-40; surg. residence Med. Arts Hosp., Dallas, 1940; commd. 1st lt. USAF, advanced through grades to lt. col., 1950; chief reconditioning svc. and reconstructive surgery Ashburn Gen. Hosp., McKinney, Tex., 1945-46; neurosurg. resident Brooke Army Med. Center, San Antonio, 1946-47; orthopedic surg. resident, 1947-50; chief orthopedic svc. and gen. surgery Francis E. Warren AFB, Cheyenne, Wyo., Travis AFB, Susan, Calif., 1950-51; chief orthopedic svc. and gen. surgery Shepherd AFB, 1951-52; comdg. officer, chief orthopedic svc., chief gen. surgery Craig AFB Hosp., Selma, Ala., 1952-53; pvt. practice medicine specializing in orthopedic surgery, Muskogee, Okla., 1954-69, 72-94. Exec. mem. Eastern Okla. council Boy Scouts Am. Fellow ACS, Internat. Coll. Surgeons; mem. AMA, Am. Fracture Assn., Nat. Found. (adviser 1958-61), N.Y. Acad. Scis., Okla. State, Pan-Am., So., Aerospace Med. Assns., So. Orthopaedic Assn., Garfield County Med. Soc., S.W. Surg. Congress, Am. Rheumatology Soc., Air Force Assn. (life), Okla. Med. Assn. (life). Republican. Methodist. Masons, K.T. Shriners, Jesters, Lions, Club of Enid. Contbr. articles to profl. jours.; research and evaluation of various uses of refrigerated homogenous bone. Home: 5801 N Oakwood Rd # 130 Enid OK 73703-9306

DANE, MAXWELL, former advertising executive; b. Cin., June 7, 1906; s. Abraham and Sophie (Sall) D.; m. Belle Sloan, Apr. 4, 1933 (dec. 1985), 1 child, Henry; m. Esther Levine, 1986. Advt. dept. Stern Bros., N.Y.C., 1928-32; retail promotion mgr. Evening Jour., 1933-36; account exec. Dorland Internat., 1937-39; advt. promotion mgr. Look mag., 1939-41; sales promotion mgr., radio sta. WMCA, 1941-44; pres. Maxwell Dane, Inc. (advt.), N.Y.C., 1944-49; founder, exec. v.p., sec.-treas. Doyle Dane Bernbach, Inc., N.Y.C., 1949-71; dir. Doyle Dane Bernbach, Inc., 1971-86. Chmn. advt. and pub. div. UJA/Fedn., 1976-81, chmn. exec. com. Jewish Week, N.Y.C., 1976-81, pres., 1982-92; trustee Ctrl. Synagogue, N.Y., 1995—, Haverford Coll., 1967-80, emeritus, 1981—; exec. com. Nat. Com. for Effective Congress, 1979. Recipient Karl Menninger award Fortune Soc., 1983. Fellow Met. Mus. Art (life), N.Y. Civil Liberties Union (vice chmn. 1960-66, treas. 1966-89), Anti-Defamation League (chmn. nat. program com. 1969-76, hon. vice-chmn. 1976—), Fedn. Jewish Philanthropies (trustee, chmn. pub. rels. com. 1971-76), Am. Arbitration Assn. (arbitrator 1972-85), Internat. League Human Rights (treas. 1973-84), Am. Assn. Advt. Agys. (chmn. EEO com. 1970-72), City Athletic Club (N.Y.C.), Old Oaks Club (Purchase, N.Y.), Canyon Country Club (Palm Springs, Calif.). Home: 650 Park Ave New York NY 10021-6115 Office: 437 Madison Ave New York NY 10022-7001

DANE, STEPHEN MARK, lawyer; b. Chillicothe, Ohio, Mar. 27, 1956; s. Clyde and Rita M. (Murray) D.; m. Kim P. Piatt, July 7, 1979; children: Tara, Adam, Shannon, Alexandra, Courtney. BS with honors, U. Notre Dame, 1978; JD magna cum laude, U. Toledo, 1981. Bar: Ohio 1981, U.S. Ct. Appeals (6th and 10th cirs.) 1982, U.S. Dist. Ct. (no. dist.) Ohio 1983, U.S. Dist. Ct. (no. dist.) Tex. 1983, U.S. Ct. Appeals (5th cir.) 1984, U.S. Supreme Ct. 1985, U.S. Ct. Appeals (7th cir.) 1993. Law clk. U.S. Ct. Appeals (6th cir.), Cin., 1981-82; ptnr. Cooper, Walinski & Cramer, Toledo, 1986—; judge pro tempore Perrysburg Mcpl. Ct., 1990—. Mem. Charter Rev. Commn., Perrysburg, Ohio, 1988; pres. Perrysburg Dem. Club, 1987-88; mem. exec. com. Wood County Dem. Party, Bowling Green, Ohio, 1986-90; pres. St. Rose Peace and Justice Com., Perrysburg, 1987-92, St. John's H.S. Alumni Assn., 1988-89; chmn. Human Rights Commn. of Diocese of Toledo, 1991-93. Recipient Fair Housing award HUD, 1996, Spirit of Wood County award, 1988; named Lawyer of Yr. Lawyers Weekly, 1998; named to St. John's Jesuit H.S. Hall of Fame, 1991. Mem. ABA, Ohio State Bas Assn., Toledo Bar Assn. (chmn. fed. ct. com. 1987-89), Wood County Bar Assn.. Roman Catholic. Home: 501 Hickory St Perrysburg OH 43551-2206 Office: Cooper Walinski & Cramer 900 Adams St Toledo OH 43624-1505

DANE, STEVEN HOWARD, neurologist, educator; b. N.Y.C., May 28, 1960. BA, Columbia Coll., N.Y.C., 1982; MD, N.Y. Med. Coll., 1986. Diplomate Am. Bd. Psychiatry and Neurology. Rotating intern St. Vincent's Hosp., N.Y.C., 1986-87; resident in neurology Mt. Sinai Hosp., N.Y.C., 1987-90, fellow in clin. neurophysiology, 1990-91; clin. instr. dept. neurology Mt. Sinai Sch. Medicine, N.Y.C., 1991—.

DANES, CLAIRE, actress; b. N.Y.C., Apr. 12, 1979; d. Chris and Carla Danes. TV role as Angela Chase in series My So-Called Life, ABC, 1994-95 (nominee Emmy award for Best Lead in Drama Series 1995, Golden Globe award for Best Actress ina Drama 1995); appeared in HBO spl. More Than Friends: The Coming Out of Heidi Leiter, 1994, also guest appearances on TV series Law and Order; film appearances include: Dreams of Love, 1992, 30, 1993, Little Women, 1994, Dead Man's Jack, 1994, How to Make an American Quilt, 1995, Home for the Holidays, 1995, I Love You No, 1996, To Gillian on Her 37th Birthday, 1996, as Juliet in William Shakespeare's Romeo and Juliet, 1996, U-Turn, 1997, The Rainmaker, 1997, Les Misérables, 1998, Polish Wedding, 1998, The Mod Squad, 1998, Brokedown Palace, 1999. Address: care Susan Geller & Assocs 335 N Maple St Ste 254 Beverly Hills CA 90210*

DANFORTH, ARTHUR EDWARDS, finance executive; b. Cleve., Jan. 23, 1925; s. Arthur Edwards and Jane (Hillyard) D.; m. Elizabeth Wagley, Mar. 17, 1956; children: Hillyard Raible, Nicholas Edwards (dec.), Jonathan Ingersoll, Elizabeth Wagley, Michael Stowe. B.A., Yale, 1949. With Hayden Miller Co., Cleve., 1949-54, First Nat. City Bank (predecessor to Citibank N.A.), N.Y.C., 1954-63; asst. mgr. Buenos Aires office First Nat. City Bank (predecessor to Citibank N.A.), 1959-61; treas. Bunge Corp., N.Y.C., 1963-65; sr. v.p., treas. Colonial Bank & Trust Co., Waterbury, Conn., 1965-70; chmn., chief exec. officer Farmers Bank of Del., Wilmington, 1970-76; prin. Danforth Group, New Canaan, Conn., 1976-98; ret., 1998. Former bd. dirs. United Way of Del., Boys Club of Wilmington, Grand Opera House Inc. of Del., NCCJ, Audubon Soc. Conn., Greater Wilmington Devel. Council. Served as ensign USNR, 1945-46. Mem. Sankety Head Golf Club, Nantucket Yacht Club, Yale Club. Home: 230 Bermuda Bay Ln Vero Beach FL 32963-3421

DANFORTH, DAVID NEWTON, JR., physician, scientist; b. N.Y.C., June 25, 1942; s. David Newton and Gladys Margaret (Blaine) D.; m. Anne Walker Nickson, Apr. 13, 1985. BA, Northwestern U., Evanston, Ill., 1965; MD, Northwestern U., Chgo., 1971; MS, U. N.Mex., Albuquerque, 1967. Diplomate Am. Bd. Surgery. Intern, then resident Cornell Med. Ctr., N.Y.C., 1971-74, 77-79; clin. assoc. NIH, Bethesda, Md., 1974-77; surg. fellow M.D. Anderson Hosp., Houston, 1979-80; sr. staff fellow NIH, Bethesda, 1980-82; sr. investigator Nat. Cancer Inst., NIH, Bethesda, 1982—. Editor: Diagnosis and Management of Breast Cancer, 1988; contbr. articles to profl. jours. Served to lt. comdr. USPHS, 1974-76. Fellow Am. Cancer Soc., 1979-80. Fellow ACS, Soc. Surg. Oncology, Am. Soc. Clin. Oncology, Am. Assn. Cancer Research, Endocrine Soc. Republican. Episcopalian. Avocations: travel, sports, reading. Home: 7301 Meadow Ln Chevy Chase MD 20815-5009 Office: Nat Cancer Inst Surgery Br Bldg 10 Rm 2B38 Bethesda MD 20892

DANFORTH, ELLIOT, JR., medical educator; b. Bainbridge, N.Y., Oct. 21, 1933; s. Elliot and Ellen (Roberts) D.; m. Joan C. Garrett, Dec. 26, 1959; children: Kimberly H., Noel, Peter E. AB, Dartmouth Coll., 1956; MS, Ohio State U., 1958; MD, Albany (N.Y.) Med. Coll., 1962. Resident Dartmouth Affliated Hosps., Hanover, N.H., 1962-65; instr. Dartmouth Med. Sch., Hanover, 1965-66; rsch. internist Walter Reed Army Inst. Rsch., Washington, 1966-70; asst. prof. U. Vt. Coll. Medicine, Burlington, 1970-74, assoc. prof., 1974-79, prof., 1979-94, prof. emeritus, 1993—, dir. clin. rsch. ctr., 1980-93, chief divsn. endocrinology, metabolism and nutrition, 1990-93; dir. Sims Obesity/Nutrition Rsch. Ctr., 1992-93; exec. dir. cardiovasc. metabolic rsch. Lederle Labs., Am. Cyanamid Co., 1993-95; med. cons. to pharm. industry, 1996—; pres., CEO Beartown Pharma, Underhill, Vt., 1998—; cons. Walter Reed Gen. Hosp. Mem. editl. bd. J. Clin. Endocrinology and Metabolism, Jour. Gerontology, Obesity Rsch., Jour. Gerontology: Biol. Scis.; contbr. articles to profl. jours. Served to cpt. U.S. Army, 1966-68. NIH grantee, Washington, 1970-94. Mem. AAAS, Endocrine Soc., Am. Diabetes Assn., Am. Thyroid Assn., Am. Fedn. Clin. Rsch., Soc. Exptl. Biology and Medicine (mem. editl. bd. procs., coun. mem.), Internat. Assn. for Study of Obesity, N.Y. Acad. Scis., N.Am. Assn. Study Obesity. Avocations: travel, farming, fishing. Home and Office: 84 Beartown Rd. Underhill VT 05489-9365

DANFORTH, GLENN R., magazine publisher; b. Boston, Sept. 5, 1957; s. Robert C. and Evelyn M. (Thibeau) D.; m. Kelly Danforth; children: Jeremy R., Nicole R., Dylan T. Student, U. Fla., 1998—. Agt. Prudential Ins., Lancaster, Pa., 1980-82; sales agt. Faulkner Oldsmobile/BMW, Lancaster, 1982-85; corp. sales trainer Nat. Bedrooms/Nat. Livingrooms, Pa., N.J. and Md., 1985-90; cons. for furniture cos. Fla., 1990-94; pub., editor Space Coast Rev. Mag., Brevard County, Fla., 1994-96; mng. editor, photo editor, designer Capsule newspaper, Brevard County, 1996—; contbg. editor Nat. Lampoon mag., 1994-95; Co-author: Fightin'Irish, 1997; contbr. articles to profl. publs. Ofcl. vol. Spl. Olympics of Fla., Brevard County, 1995—. Recipient Best Coll. Newspaper award Fla. Leader, 1996-97. Mem. ACLU (bd. dirs., chmn. intake com. Brevard chpt. 1997—), Soc. Profl. Journalists, Fla. Mid-Coast Ofcls. Assn., Nat. Press Photographers Assn., Am. Mensa Soc., Phi Theta Kappa, Psi Beta (historian), Kappa Tau Alpha. Avocations: photography, writing, graphic arts, tennis, golf. Home: 298 Diamond Village Apt 9 Gainesville FL 32603

DANFORTH, JOHN CLAGGETT, former senator, lawyer, clergyman; b. St. Louis, Sept. 5, 1936; s. Donald and Dorothy (Claggett) D.; m. Sally B. Dobson, Sept. 7, 1957; children: Eleanor, Mary, Dorothy, Johanna, Thomas. BA with honors, Princeton U., 1958; BD, Yale U., 1963, LLB, 1963, MA (hon.); LHD (hon.), Lindenwood Coll., 1970, Ind. Central U.; LLD (hon.), Drury Coll., 1970, Maryville Coll., Rockhurst Coll., Westminster Coll., Culver-Stockton Coll., St. Louis U.; DD (hon.), Lewis and Clark Coll.; HHD (hon.), William Jewell Coll.; STD (hon.), Southwest Bapt. Coll.; hon. deg., Va. Theol. Sem., 1990, Holy Cross Coll., 1992, Harris Stowe Coll., 1992, Wash. U., 1995, U. Mo., 1995. Bar: N.Y. 1964, Mo. 1966, D.C. 1994. With firm Davis Polk Wardwell Sunderland & Kiendl, N.Y.C., 1964-66; ptnr. Bryan, Cave, McPheeters and McRoberts (now Bryan Cave LLP), St. Louis, 1966-68, 95—; atty. gen. State of Mo., 1969-76; U.S. senator from Mo., 1976-94; ordained deacon Episc. Ch., 1963, priest, 1964; asst. rector N.Y.C., 1963-66; assoc. rector Clayton, Mo., 1966-68, Grace Ch., Jefferson City, 1969; hon. assoc. St. Alban's Ch., Washington, 1977-94; chmn. Mo. Law Enforcement Assistance Council, 1973-74; asst. chaplain Meml. Sloan-Kettering Cancer Ctr. of N.Y.C.; asst. rector Ch. of Epiphany in N.Y.C., Ch. of St. Michael and St. George, Clayton, Mo.; hon. canon Christ Ch. Cathedral, St. Louis. Republican nominee U.S. Senate, 1970; assoc. rector Ch. of the Holy Communion, Univ. City, Mo., 1995—. Recipient Disting. Svc. award St. Louis Jr. C. of C., 1969, Disting. Missourian and Brotherhood awards NCCJ, Presdl. World Without Hunger award, 1985, Disting. Lectr. award Avila Coll., Chancellors medal UMKC, 1995; named Outstanding Young Man Mo. Jr. C. of C., 1968, St. Louis Man of Yr., 1994; Alumni fellow Yale U., 1973-79. Mem. Mo. Acad. Squires, Alpha Sigma Nu (hon.). Republican.

DANFORTH, WILLIAM HENRY, retired academic administrator, physician; b. St. Louis, Apr. 10, 1926; s. Donald and Dorothy (Claggett) D.; m. Elizabeth Anne Gray, Sept. 1, 1950; children: Cynthia Danforth Prather, David Gray, Maebelle Danforth Reed, Elizabeth D. Sankey. A.B., Princeton U., 1947; M.D., Harvard U., 1951. Intern Barnes Hosp., St. Louis, 1951-52; resident Barnes Hosp., 1954-57; now mem. staff; asst. prof. medicine Washington U., St. Louis, 1960-65, assoc. prof., 1965-67, prof., 1967—; vice chancellor for med. affairs Washington U., 1965-71, chancellor, 1971-95; chmn., bd. trustees Washington U., St. Louis, 1995—; pres. Washington U. Med. Sch. and Assoc. Hosps., 1965-71; program coord. Bi-State Regional Med. Program, 1967-68; dir. Ralston Purina Co., Ralcorp Holdings. Trustee, chmn. bd. Danforth Found.; trustee Am. Youth Found., 1963—, Princeton U., 1970-74; pres. St. Louis Christmas Carols Assn., 1958-74, chmn., 1975—; co-chair Barnes/Jewish Hosp., 1996—; bd. dirs. BJC Health Systems, 1996—. Named Man of Yr. St. Louis Globe-Democrat, 1978. Fellow AAAS, Am. Acad. Arts and Scis.; mem. Inst. Medicine. Home: 10 Glenview Rd Saint Louis MO 63124-1308 Office: Washington U West Campus Campus Box 1044 7425 Forsyth Blvd Ste 262 Saint Louis MO 63105-2161

DANFORTH-MORNINGSTAR, ELIZABETH, obstetrician/gynecologist; b. Sioux Falls, S.D., July 3, 1951; d. George Jonathan and Mina (Schumacher) Danforth; m. John Wesley Morningstar III, May 29, 1976; children: John Wesley Morningstar IV, George Danforth, Charles Alexander. BA, Grinnell (Iowa) Coll., 1973; MD, Med. Coll. Va., Richmond, 1976. Intern Strong Meml. Hosp.-U. Rochester, 1976-77, resident ob/gyn, 1977-80; MD Genesee Hosp., Rochester, N.Y.; clin. assoc. prof. U. Rochester Sch. Medicine; pres. Women Gynecology and Childbirth Assocs., 1989—; adv. bd. Rochester Individual Practice Assocs. Adv., mem. Monroe County Bd. for Infant Mortality, Rochester, N.Y. Mem. Monroe County Med. Soc., Am. Coll. Obstetricians/Gynecologists. Home: 55 Babcock Dr Rochester NY 14610-3304

DANG, CHI VAN, hematology and oncology educator; b. Saigon, Vietnam, Nov. 2, 1954; came to U.S., 1967; s. Chieu Van and Nga Ngoc (Nguyen) D.; m. Mary Doreen Seeley, May 18, 1985; children: Eric Van, Vanessa Marie. BS in Chemistry, U. Mich., 1975; PhD in Chemistry, Georgetown U., 1978; MD, Johns Hopkins U., 1982. Diplomate Am. Bd. Internal Medicine, Am. Bd. Med. Oncology. Resident in internal medicine Johns Hopkins Hosp., Balt., 1982-85; fellow in hematology and oncology U. Calif., San Francisco, 1985-87; asst. prof. medicine Johns Hopkins U., 1987-91, assoc. prof., 1991-97, assoc. prof. oncol., pathology, molecular biology & genetics, 1995-97, dir. hematology, 1993-99, prof. medicine, oncology, and pathology, 1997—, dep. dir. basic rsch., dept. medicine, 1996-99, co-dir. immunology and hematopoiesis, oncology, 1998—; mem. oncological scis. path B NIH, Bethesda, Md., 1993-97; cons. Novartis, East Hanover, N.J., 1993—, Genentech, South San Francisco, Calif., 1995; scientific adv. bd. Lion Pharm. Corp., Balt. Contbr. articles to Nature, Molecular and Cellular Biology, Genes and Devel.; mem. editl. bd. Jour. Clin. Invest., 1998—, Neoplasia, 1999—. Scholar Leukemia Soc. Am., 1992-97, Stohlman scholar award Leukemia Soc. Am., 1996, Merit award NIH/NCI, 1999. Mem. Assn. Am. Physicians, Am. Soc. for Clin. Investigation, Phi Beta Kappa, Alpha Omega Alpha, Phi Lambda Upsilon. Avocations: India ink sketching, poetry. E-mail: ovdang@welchlink.welch.jhu.edu. Home: 217 Upnor Rd Baltimore MD 21212-3425 Office: Johns Hopkins U Sch Med Ross 1025 720 Rutland Ave Baltimore MD 21205-2109

D'ANGELO, ANDREW WILLIAM, retired civil engineer; b. Bklyn., Jan. 23, 1924; s. William and Filomena (Soviero) D'A.; m. Filomena Margaret Loiero, June 26, 1949; children: Carol Lorraine Mauch, William Andrew. BSCE, Bklyn. Poly. Inst., 1952, MCE, 1956. Lic. engr., N.Y., N.J., Pa., Md., Conn., Mass., Fla. Project engr. D.B. Steinman, N.Y.C., 1952-56, Merritt Chapman & Scott Corp., N.Y.C., 1956-67; v.p. engring. Murphy Pacific Marine Salvage Co., N.Y.C., 1967-74; chief engr. Internat. Underwater Contractors, City Island, N.Y., 1974-76; cons. self-employed N.Y.C., 1976-77; pres. D'Angelo, Schoenewaldt Assoc. Inc., Floral Pk., N.Y., 1977-85; project mgr. North Star Contracting, New Rochelle, N.Y., 1985-88; project engr. Yonkers Contracting Co. Inc., Yonkers, N.Y., 1988-97; cons. marine salvage, 1998—; cons. in field. Author: Salvage of Coastwise #1, 1975. Sgt. U.S. Army, 1943-45. Recipient Bronze star U.S. Army, 1945, Commendation USN, 1965. Mem. ASCE, NSPE, Soc. Naval Architects and Marine Engrs., The Moles. Republican. Roman Catholic. Achievements include patent for Mooring Apparatus. Home: 7751 Olympia Dr West Palm Beach FL 33411-5786

D'ANGELO, ARTHUR E., advertising agency executive. Pres. Saatchi & Saatchi Mktg. Svcs. Group, Wilmington, Del., 1993—. Office: Saatchi & Saatchi Mktg Svcs Group 1105 N Market St Wilmington DE 19801-1216*

D'ANGELO, BEVERLY, actress; b. Columbus, Ohio, Nov. 15, 1954. cartoonist Hanna-Barbera Studios, Hollywood, Calif., former singer with Rompin' Ronnie Hawkins. Performances include (feature films) The Sentinel, 1977, Annie Hall, 1977, First Love, 1977, Every Which Way but Loose, 1978, Hair, 1979, Coal Miner's Daughter, 1980, Honky Tonk Freeway, 1981, Paternity, 1981, National Lampoon's Vacation, 1983, Finders Keepers, 1984, National Lampoon's European Vacation, 1985, Big Trouble, 1986, Maid to Order, 1987, In the Mood, 1987, Aria, 1988, Trading Hearts, 1988, High Spirits, 1988, National Lampoon's Christmas Vacation, 1989, Daddy's Dying...Who's Got The Will?, 1990, Pacific Heights, 1990, The Miracle, 1991, The Pope Must Die, 1991, Man Trouble, 1992, Lonely Hearts, 1992, Lighting Jack, 1994, Widow's Kiss, 1994, Eye for an Eye, 1995, The Crazysitter, 1995, Vegas Vacation, 1997, Nowhere, 1997, Love Always, 1997, With Friends Like These. . ., 1998, Illuminata, 1998, American History X, 1998, Sugar Town, 1999, The Red Door, 1999, Jazz Night, 1999, others; (stage prodns.) Rockabye Hamlet, Hey, Marilyn, The Zinger, Simpatico; (TV movies) A Streetcar Named Desire, 1984, Doubletake, 1985, Hands of a Stranger, 1987, Trial: The Price of Passion, 1992, A Child Lost Forever, 1992, Judgement Day: The John List Story, 1993, Menendez: A Killing in Beverly Hills, 1994, Jonathan Stone: Threat of Innocence, 1994,

Sweet Temptation, 1996, Lansky, 1999; prodr. Pterodactyl Woman from Beverly Hills, 1994; TV guest appearances Tall Tales and Legends, 1985, The Simpsons, 1989, Tales from the Crypt, 1989, Frasier, 1993. Recipient CMA award 1981, Golden Globe award, 1981, Golden Reed award, 1981, Emmy award Nomination, 1985.

D'ANGELO, ERNEST EUSTACHIO, brokerage house executive; b. Jersey City, Jan. 21, 1944; s. Eustachio and Catherine (Valentino) D'A.; m. Carol Abramowitz, Apr. 23, 1966; 1 child, Ernest E. Jr. BS in Acctg., Rutgers U., 1972. Contract officer N.Y. State Urban Devel. Corp., N.Y.C., 1972-75; fin. dir. Cen. Essex Health Plan, Orange, N.J., 1975-79, New Community Corp., Newark, 1979-81; first v.p. corp. services Prudential Securities, Inc., N.Y.C., 1981-95; v.p. adminstrv. svcs. Prudential Ins. Co., Newark, 1995—. Active Worldwide Marriage Encounter, Montclair, N.J., 1975-81; bd. dirs. United Scleroderma Found., Watsonville, Calif., 1987. Mem. Nat. Assn. Accts., Nat. Purchasing Mgrs. Assn., Assn. Corp. Travel Execs. (bd. govs.). Roman Catholic. Home: 57 Eastern Dr Kendall Park NJ 08824-1321 Office: Prudential Securities One New York Pla New York NY 10292-0804

DANGELO, EUGENE MICHAEL, elementary education educator; b. Greensburg, Pa., Oct. 6, 1955; s. Louis Anthony and Dolores Joan (Sylvester) D. BS in Music Edn., Duquesne U., 1977, MusM in Composition, 1979; PhD in Tchr. Devel., U. Pitts., 1985. Cert. music edn. grades K-12, elem. sch. prin. grades K-8, Pa. Music educator, choral & orch. dir. The Winchester-Thurston Sch., Pitts., 1985-88; music educator, choral dir. Mt. Pleasant (Pa.) Area Sch. Dist., 1988—; musical dir., prin. condr. Greensburg (Pa.) Musical Soc. Philharmonic Winds, 1990-95; adj. asst. prof. grad. edn. Seton Hill Coll., Greensburg, Pa., 1995—. Composer: All That I Might Be, 1987, Centennial Suite, 1987, The B. Cool Jingle, 1992. Dir. liturgical music St. Paul Ch., Greensburg, Pa., 1989-92, voting mem. parish coun., 1986-87; dir. music and liturgy St. Bede Ch., Bovard, Pa., 1993-98; dir. music St. Pius X Ch., Mt. Pleasant, 1998—; voting mem. St. Paul Elem. Sch. Bd. Edn., Greensburg, Pa., 1991-95; Westmoreland County Labor Conf. rep. Am. Fedn. Musicians Local 339, Greensburg, Pa., 1992; mem. devel. adv. bd. Holy Cross Elem. Sch., Youngwood, Pa., 1998; mem. adv. bd. exemplary tchr. database U.S. Dept. Edn., 1998—. Mem. ASCD, Am. Choral Dirs.' Assn., U. Pitts. Doctoral Assn. Educators (life), Pa. Music Educators' Assn., Music Educators' Nat. Conf. (dsignation as nat. registered music educator, 1991—), Pi Lambda Theta,. Democrat. Roman Catholic. Avocations: genealogy, numismatics, philately, radio communications, astronomy, antique auto restoration. Home: 260 Wyoming Ave Greensburg PA 15601-3980 Office: Mt Pleasant Area Sch Dist RR 4 Mount Pleasant PA 15666-9804

D'ANGELO, JOSEPH FRANCIS, publishing company executive; b. Astoria, N.Y., July 4, 1930; s. Frank and Matilda (Oliveri) D'A.; m. Marcia Elaine Mackie, Mar. 4, 1965; children: Elena, Joseph Francis. BBA, St. John's U., 1952; PhD (hon.), St. John's U., William Penn Coll. Mem. Haskins & Sells CPAs, N.Y.C., 1952-61; treas., contr. internat. operations Borden Co., Panama and P.R., 1961-65; from v.p. to pres. King Features Syndicate divsn. Hearst Corp., N.Y.C., 1973-96; chmn. King Features Syndicate divsn. Hearst Corp., 1997—; resident contr., 1965-73, bus. mgr., 1968-73, gen. mgr., 1973-75; pres., dir. King Features Syndicate, Inc., 1973-97; pres., bd. dirs. Cowles Syndicate Inc., 1986-97, NAS, Inc., 1987-97; chmn. King Features Syndicate, Inc., Cowles, Inc., NAS, Inc., 1997—. Mem. Com. of 300 Archdiocese of N.Y.; bd. dirs. Alcoholism Coun. Greater N.Y.; trustee Emerson Coll., Boston, North Shore Univ. Hosp., pres. Mus. Cartoon Art and Hall of Fame, Boca Raton, Fla., Bd. of Trade. Mem. Artists and Writers Assn., Nat. Cartoonists Soc., Newspaper Features Coun., N.Y. Newspaper Pubs. Assn., N.Y. State Soc. Newspaper Editors, So. Newspaper Pubs. Assn., Sigma Delta Chi, Dutch Treat Club, Friars Club, N.Y. Athletic Club, Overseas Press Club, Wheatley Hills Golf Club, Knights of Malta. Republican. Roman Catholic. Office: King Features Syndicate Inc 235 E 45th St Fl 2 New York NY 10017-3367

D'ANGELO, ROBERT WILLIAM, lawyer; b. Buffalo, Nov. 10, 1932; s. Samuel and Margaret Theresa Guercio D'A.; m. Ellen Frances Neary, Sept. 17, 1959; children: Christopher Robert, Gregory Andrew. B.B.A., Loyola U. Los Angeles, 1954; J.D., UCLA, 1960. Bar: Calif. 1960; cert. specialist taxation law. Practiced in L.A., 1960-89; mem. firm. Myers & D'Angelo, Pasadena, Calif., 1967—; adj. prof. law, taxation Whittier Coll. Sch. of Law., 1981. Served to capt. USAF, 1954-57. Mem. ABA, AICPA, State Bar Calif., Los Angeles County Bar Assn., Wilshire Bar Assn., Pasadena Bar Assn., Calif. Soc. CPAs, Am. Assn. Atty. CPAs, Calif. Assn. Atty. CPAs (pres. 1980), Phi Delta Phi, Alpha Sigma Nu. Home: 1706 Highland Ave Glendale CA 91202-1265 Office: 301 N Lake Ave Ste 800 Pasadena CA 91101-4108

D'ANGELO, VICTORIA SCOTT, entrepreneur, writer; b. Phila., June 5, 1964; d. George Anthony and Antonia (Billett) D'A. BA, U. Va., 1981; MBA, Columbia U., 1986. Cert. attendance Sorbonne/Sorbonne Nouvelle, Paris, 1980, Inst. Scis. Politiques, Paris, 1980, Brit. Am. Acting Acad., London, N.Y.C., 1982. Fin. cons., broker deals, cons. on bus. negotiations healthcare project Victory Angel Enterprises, Santa Monica, Calif., 1987—, CEO, 1990—; exec. v.p. Northeastern U.S. Acad. Gymnastics, Northampton, N.H., 1995—. Dir. (documentary) Leslie Clark—Nomad Painter, 1995; prodr., actor (TV situation comedies) Dinette, 1996, The Crasher (based on Victoria's short story, The Crusher), 1996. Vol. Permanent Charities Com., Hollywood Women's Polit. Com.; fundraiser Breast Cancer Rsch. Mem. Am. Film Inst. (3d decade coun.), Hollywood Radio and TV Soc., U.S. Field Hockey Assn. (videographer), Athenaeum. Episcopalian. Avocations: umpiring, sports, adventure travel, reading, theater. Home: PO Box 5132 Santa Monica CA 90409-5132

D'ANGIO, GIULIO JOHN, radiologist, educator; b. N.Y.C., May 2, 1922; s. Carlo and Rosa (Calderazzo) D'A.; m. Jean Chittenden Terhune, Aug. 27, 1955; children: Carl, Peter. AB, Columbia U., 1943; MD, Harvard U., 1945; D. Medicine and Surgery (hon.), U. Bologna, 1983. Diplomate: Am. Bd. Radiology, Am. Bd. Therapeutic Radiology. Surg. intern Children's Hosp., Boston, 1945-46, tng. in pathology, 1948-49; resident in radiology Boston City Hosp., 1949-53; also mem. staff; radiation therapist Children's Hosp., Boston, 1956-62; researcher Donner Lab., also Lawrence Radiation Lab., U. Calif., Berkeley, 1962-63; dir. div. radiation therapy U. Minn. Med. Sch., 1964-68; chmn. dept. radiation therapy Meml. Hosp., N.Y.C., 1968-76; dir. children's cancer rsch. ctr. Children's Hosp., Phila., 1976-89; prof. radiation oncology Hosp. of U. Pa., Phila., 1976-92, vice chmn., clin. dir. dept. radiation oncology, 1989-92, prof. emeritus, 1992—; prof. pediatric oncology U. Pa. Med. Sch., Phila., 1976-92; chmn. Nat. Wilms Tumor Study Com., 1968-91; past chmn. cancer clin. investigation rev. com. Nat. Cancer Inst. Editor-in-chief Med. and Pediat. Oncology, 1996—; contbr. numerous articles to med. jours. Capt. M.C. AUS, 1946-48. Decorated Commendation medal; recipient ann. award Am. Cancer Soc., 1978, Heath Meml. award M.D. Anderson Tumor and Cancer Inst., 1979. Fellow Royal Coll. Radiology, Am. Acad. Pediatrics; mem. Am. Acad. Pediatrics (past chmn. sect. oncology-hematology), AAAS, Am. Assn. Cancer Rsch., Am. Coll. Radiology, Am. Soc. Therapeutic Radiologists, Mass. Med. Soc., Pa. Med. Soc., Royal Soc. Medicine, Internat. Soc. Pediatric Oncology (pres. 1987), Radiol. Soc. N.Am., Am. Radium Soc., Soc. Pediatric Radiology, Phi Beta Kappa. Episcopalian. Home: 518 Cedar Ln Swarthmore PA 19081-1105 Office: U Pa Hosp Dept Radiation Oncology 3400 Spruce St Philadelphia PA 19104-4204

DANGOND, FERNANDO, neurologist, educator; b. Nov. 5, 1962. MD, Javeriana U., Colombia, 1987. Neurology resident Brigham and Women's Hosp., Boston, 1990-94; neuroimmunology fellow Harvard Med. Sch., Boston, 1994-97; assoc. neurologist Brigham and Women's Hosp., Boston, 1997—; instr. neurology Harvard Med. Sch., Boston, 1994—. E-mail: fdangond@rics.bwh.harvard.edu. Office: Unit F 412 Parker St Newton MA 02459

DANGOOR, DAVID EZRA RAMSI, consumer goods company executive; b. Teheran, Iran, Aug. 3, 1949; arrived in sweden, 1950, came to U.S., 1987; s. Selim Eliaho and Ruth (Lehr) D.; m. Ida (Ide) Weitzen, May 24, 1992; children: Rebecca Frances, Diana Katherine, Louisa Faye. Civilekonom (MBA), Stockholm Sch. Econs., Sweden, 1973. Asst. dir. Scandinavian Supplies AB, Stockholm, 1970-74; asst. corp. treas. AGA Group AB, Stockholm, 1974-76; asst. to. v.p. Philip Morris Europe, Middle East & Africa, Lausanne, Switzerland, 1976; dept. mktg. dir. Philip Morris Co. Germany, Munich, Fed. Republic Germany, 1977-80; area dir. No. Europe Seven Up Internat., London, 1980-84; pres. Benson & Hedges Can. Inc., Philip Morris Internat., Montreal, Que., Can., 1984-86; sr. v.p. mktg. Philip Morris USA, N.Y.C., 1987-92; exec. v.p. Philip Morris Internat., Rye Brook, N.Y., 1992—; bd. dirs. Rothmans, Benson & Hedges, Inc., Toronto, 1987—; mem. bd. dirs. and exec. com. Swedish Am. C. of C., N.Y., 1996—, chmn., 1998—; bd. dirs. Fgn. Policy Assn. N.Y., 1997—. Exec. v.p. Student Assn. Palmgrenska Samskolan, Stockholm, 1966-68; bd. dirs. Student Assn. Stockholm Sch. Bus. Adminstrn. and Econs., 1969-72; officer Royal Swedish Coast Art; exec. bd. dirs. Raoul Wallenberg Com. of U.S., 1990-93; trustee Arthur F. Burns Fellowships, 1997—; mem. internat. devel. com. Internat. Fedn. Multiple Sclerosis Socs., 1993-95. Fellow Amaranten, Sweden, 1971. Mem. Swedish Am. C. of C. (bd. dirs. exec. com. 1996—), Sallskapet Club (Stockholm), Hurlingham Club (London), Hillside Tennis Club (Montreal). Avocations: squash, tennis, sailing, bridge. *

D'ANGORA, KENDRA MARIE, artist, preschool educator; b. Plymouth, Mass., July 4, 1968; d. Robert Joseph D'Angora and Marcia Leigh Nickerson; m. Christopher Michael Schopp, Sept. 26, 1998. BFA in Ceramics, Mass. Coll. Art, 1992; student, Aquinas Coll., 1997. Cert. lead tchr., Mass. Nanny Plymouth, Mass., 1985-87; clerical worker Charette Corp., Boston, 1990-95; freelance artist Allston, Mass., 1992—; preschool tchr. Clinton Path Preschool, Brookline, Mass., 1995—. Recipient Blue Ribbon, Boston Globe Scholastic Art, 1985, 86. Mem. Am. Craft Coun., Plymouth Art Guild (blue ribbon, 1985, 1986), Provincetown Art Assn., United South End Artists, Mus. of Fine Arts. Avocations: hiking, exercise, dancing, reading, skating. Home: 38 Brainerd Rd Apt 1R Allston MA 02134

DANGREMOND, DAVID W., museum administrator, educator; b. Norristown, Pa., June 8, 1952; s. James L. and Joan O. (Kross) D.; m. Mary Plant Spivy, Oct. 18, 1980; children: Saumel Plant Chapin, Augustus Welles Ewing. BA cum laude, Amherst Coll., 1974; MA, U. Del., 1976, Yale U., 1987; MPhil, Yale U., 1990. Dir. Webb-Deane-Stevens Mus., Wethersfield, Conn., 1976-80, Bennington Mus., Vt., 1980-86; adj. prof. fine arts Trinity Coll., 1996—; adj. prof. art history U. Hartford, Conn., 1977-80; tutor Historic Deerfield, Mass., 1975; trustee Williamstown (Mass.) Regional Art Conservation Lab., 1981-86, Florence Griswold Mus., Old Lyme, Conn., 1987—, v.p., 1992—; trustee Conn. Humanities Coun., 1997—; mem. adv. bd. Gunston Hall Plantation, Lorton, Va., 1985—, Nat. Trust Hist. Preservation; dir. Attingham Summer Sch., Shropshire, Eng., 1980—; profl. adv. bd. Victoria Mus., Portland, Maine, 1985—; bd. overseers Strawbery Banke Mus., Portsmouth, N.H., 1987—, v.p., 1988-90; mem. exec. com. Yale U. Art Gallery Assocs., 1987-93; mus. cons. various mus., 1995—; vis. lectr. Trinity Coll., Hartford, Conn., 1996—. Foreword author: Heritage Houses: the American Tradition in Connecticut 1660-1900, 1979; contbr. articles to jours. Bd. dirs. Hartford Architecture Conservancy, 1978-80; mem. adv. bd. Deacon John Grave Found.; mem. art and antiques coun. Conn. Pub. TV, Hartford, 1977-80; mem. concert com. Vt. Symphony Orch., 1980-86; trustee Musical Masterworks, 1992—, v.p. 1998—; div. head United Way Bennington County, 1982-84; del. Gov.'s Conf. on Future of Vt.'s Heritage, Montpelier, 1982; sr. warden St. Peter's Episcopal Ch., 1985—; bd. govs. Hill-Stead Mus., Farmington, 1990—; trustee Wadsworth Atheneum, Hartford, 1991—, exec. com., 1995—, chmn. curatorial com., 1995—, chmn. ethics com. 1996—, v.p. 1998—; trustee Conn. Hist. Soc., 1989—. Fellow Historic Deerfield, 1973; Winterthur fellow H.F. duPont Winterthur Mus., 1974-76; Sir George Trevelyan scholar Attingham summer sch., Shropshire, Eng., 1976. Mem. Am. Assn. for State and Local History (state awards chmn.), New Eng. Mus. Assn. (exec. com. 1985-86), Am. Assn. Mus. (accreditation vis. com., mus. assessment program cons.), Vt. Mus. and Gallery Alliance (pres. 1983-86), Greater Hartford Assn. of Historic Houses (bd. dirs.), Decorative Arts Soc., Am. Ceramics Circle, Coll. Art Assn., Soc. Archtl. Historians, Century Assn. (N.Y.C.), Knickerbocker Club (N.Y.C.), Grolier Club (N.Y.C.), Hartford Club, Old Lyme Country, Yale Club N.Y.C., Lawn Club (New Haven), Dauntless Club (Essex), Newport Reading Rm. Episcopalian. Office: PO Box 910 Old Lyme CT 06371-0910*

DANGUE REWAKA, DENIS, diplomat. Permanent rep. of Gabonese Republic UN, N.Y.C. Office: UN Permanent Mission Gabon 18 E 41st St Fl 9 New York NY 10017-6222*

DANHEISER, RICK LANE, organic chemistry educator; b. N.Y., Oct. 12, 1951. BA, Columbia Coll., 1972; MA, Harvard U., 1975, PhD in Chemistry, 1978. From asst. to assoc. prof. MIT, 1978-89, prof. chemistry, 1989—, assoc. head dept. chemistry, 1995—. Recipient Excellence in Chem. Rsch. award Stuart Pharmaceutical, 1985, Arthur C. Cope Scholar award Am. Chem. Soc., 1995. Fellow AAAS, Japan Soc. Prom. Sci.; mem. Am. Chem. Soc., Chem. Soc. Britain, Swiss Chem. Soc. Office: MIT 77 Massachusetts Ave Cambridge MA 02139-4307*

DANHOF, VICKI SPICHER, maternal/women's health nurse; b. Havre, Mont., Jan. 10, 1949; d. Ralph David and Arlette Anne (Johnson) Spicher; m. Charles Richard Danhof, Dec. 17, 1987; 1 child, Kevin Michael. Student, Coll. of Gt. Falls, Mont., 1973; BSN, Mont. State U., 1985, postgrad., 1999. RN, Mont.; cert. in neonatal resuscitation. Staff nurse oncology unit Kalispell (Mont.) Regional Hosp.; nurse labor-delivery Bozeman (Mont.) Deaconess Hosp., 1985, nurse intensive care nursery, 1986-88, nurse outpatient surgery, 1988—, surg. coord., 1989—, ACLS, 1994—, parish nurse, 1998—. Mem. ch. choir, Sunday sch. tchr., organist. Mem. Am. Women in Computing, Mont. Nurses Assn., Sigma Theta Tau.

DANIEL, ARLIE VERL, speech education educator; b. Spencer, Iowa, May 15, 1943; s. Arlie Verl and Eleanor Marie (Grover) D. AA, Iowa Lakes C.C., 1963; BA, Morningside Coll., 1965; MA, U. Iowa, 1978; PhD, U. Nebr., 1981. High sch. tchr. Missouri Valley (Iowa) Pub. Schs., 1965-68, Clinton (Iowa) Pub. Schs., 1971-78; dir. speech edn. East Cen. U., Ada, Okla., 1981—. Co-author: Project Text for Public Speaking, 6th edit., 1991; co-author chpt. in Basic Communication Course Annual, 1994; editor: Activities Integrating Oral Communication Skills for Students in Grades K-8, 1992; contbr. chpt. to Teaching and Directing the Basic Communication Course, 1993. 1st lt. U.S. Army, 1968-71. Mem. AAUP, Assn. Tchr. Educators, Internat. Comm. Assn., Okla. Speech Theatre Comm. Assn. (pres. 1986-87, exec. sec. 1989-92, Outstanding Comm. Educator award 1985, Josh Lee Svc. award 1992, Spl. award for Contbns. to Profession 1994), Ctrl. States Comm. Assn. (life, exec. dir. 1994-97, v.p., 1997-98, pres. elect, 1998-99, pres. 1999—, Outstanding Young Speech Tchr. award 1985), Nat. Comm. Assn. (life), Rotary Internat. (chairperson youth com. Ada chpt. 1994—, Dist. 5770 1995—), Pi Kappa Delta. Democrat. Methodist. Avocations: golf, bowling, wine making. Home: RR 6 Box 1395 Ada OK 74820-9273 Office: East Cen U Communication Dept Ada OK 74820-6899

DANIEL, AUBREY MARSHALL, III, lawyer; b. Monks Corner, S.C., May 16, 1941; s. Aubrey Marshall and Laura D.; m. Carolyn H. Williams, June 16, 1984; children: Laura E., Anne Meade. BA, U. Va., 1963; LLB, U. Richmond, 1966. Assoc. Atty. Minor, Savage, Richmond, Va., 1966-67; ptnr. Williams & Connolly, Washington, 1971—. Active ABA Task Force on War Crimes, 1993—. Capt. JAGC, U.S. Army, 1967-71. Recipient Outstanding Svc. award Nat. Dist. Attys. Assn., 1971. Mem. Assn. Trial Lawyers Am., Va. Bar Assn., D.C. Bar Assn., Md. Bar Assn., Am. Coll. Trial Lawyers, Farmington Golf and Country Club, Talbot Golf and Country Club. Methodist. Office: Williams and Connolly 725 12th St NW Washington DC 20005-3901*

DANIEL, BARBARA ANN, elementary and secondary education educator; b. LaCrosse, Wis., Mar. 22, 1938; d. Rudolph J. and Dorothy M. (Farnham) Beranek; m. David Daniel; children: Raychelle, Clarence, Bernadette, Brenda. BS in Edn. cum laude, Midwestern U., Wichita Falls, Tex., 1967; postgrad., U. Alaska, Fairbanks, Anchorage, Juneau, U. Alaska, Bethel. Cert. tchr., Alaska. Primary tchr. Bur. Indian Affairs, Nunapitchuk and Tuntutuliak, Alaska, 1967-70; tchr., generalist, English, reading, English lang. devel. grades 6-12 Lower Kuskokwim Sch. Dist., Tuntutuliak, 1981—; English language leader grades k-12 Lower Kuskokwim Sch. Dist., Tuntutuliak, 1995—; mem. lang. arts curriculum revision task force Lower Kuskokwim Sch. Dist., 1990; mem. state bd. Academic Pentathlon, Alaska; acad. decathlon, pentathlon coach, 1980's. Rsch. video recording of elders in Alaskan village. Mem. NEA, Lower Kuskokwin Edn. Assn., Alaska Coun. Tchrs. English. Home: 25 West Circle PO Box Wtl-8048 Tuntutuliak AK 99680

DANIEL, BETH, professional golfer; b. Charleston, S.C., Oct. 14, 1956; d. Robert and Lucia D. Grad., Furman U., 1978. Profl. golfer Ladies Profl. Golf Assn. tour, 1979—; Winner U.S. Amateur Title, 1975, 77; youngest mem. S.C. Hall of Fame, 1979. Winner 31 LPGA events including Patty Berg Classic, 1979, World Ladies, Japan, 1979, World Series Women's Golf, 1980, 81, Columbia Savs. Classic, 1980, 82, Patty Berg Classic, 1980, Golden Lights, 1980, J.C. Penney Classic, 1981, 90 (with Davis Love III), Lady Citurs, 1981, Bent Tree Classic, 1982, Sun City Classic, 1982, Birmingham Classic, 1982, J & B Putting Championship, 1982, 85, WUI Classic, 1982, McDonald's Kids Classic, 1983, Kyocera Inamori Classic, 1985, Rail Charity Classic, 1989, 90, Konica San Jose Classic, 1989, Greater Washington Open, 1989, Safeco Classic, 1989, LPGA Championship, 1990, Orix Hawaiian Open, 1990, Kemper Open, 1990, Centel Classic, 1990, Northgate Classic, McDonald's Championship, Phar Mor Classic, 1990, 91, Corning Classic, 1994, Oldsmobile Classic, 1994, Big Apple Classic, 1994; Mazda Series winner, 1982; named Rookie of Yr., Ladies Profl. Golf Assn., 1979, Player of Yr., 1980, 94, Golfer of Yr., Seagrams Seven Crown Royal, 1981. Leading money winner LPGA, 1980, 81, 90. Office: care Pros Inc 9 S 12th St Richmond VA 23219-4032*

DANIEL, CATHY BROOKS, tutor, educational consultant; b. Nashville, Sept. 1, 1946; d. Conway William and Alliene Marie (Gilliam) B.; m. James Newton Daniel Jr., Dec. 29, 1967 (div. July 1988; children: Laura Marie, James Newton III. Student, Memphis State U., 1964-66; BS, George Peabody Coll., 1968, MA, 1971. Cert. elem. tchr., special edn. tchr., learning disabilities and behavior disorders. Tchr. Fairview (Tenn.) Elem. Sch., 1968-69; special edn. tchr. Ross Elem. Sch., Nashville, 1969-70, Rosebank Elem. Sch., Nashville, 1970-71, Graymar Elem. Sch., Nashville, 1971-73, Norman Binkley Elem. Sch., Nashville, 1973-74; cons. ednl. and family counseling, ednl. testing Franklin, Tenn., 1976—. Methodist. Avocation: tennis. Home and Office: 2203 Springdale Dr Franklin TN 37064-4962

DANIEL, CHARLES DWELLE, JR., consultant, retired army officer; b. San Antonio, Oct. 30, 1925; s. Charles Dwelle and Jean Elizabeth (Stormont) D.; m. Ann Meredith Carter, June 7, 1946; children: Charles Dwelle III, Peter C. BS, U.S. Mil. Acad., 1946; MS, Tulane U., 1961, PhD, 1968; BA in Studio Art, Am. U., 1987. Joined U.S. Army; advanced through grades to maj. gen.; F.A. battery comdr. U.S. Army (3d inf. div.), Korean War, 1950-52; adviser Ky. N.G., Louisville, 1953-55; F.A. missile officer 7th U.S. Army Europe, 1956-59; physicist Def. Atomic Support Agy Washington, 1963-66; F.A. bn. and div. artillery comdr. 1st inf. div. Viet Nam, 1966-67; div. chief, dir. Office of Chief of U.S. Army Research and Devel., 1968-71; comdg. gen. I Corps, Arty., Korea, 1971; dep. comdg. gen. Korean Support Command, 1971-72; dir. army research Dept. Army, Washington, 1972-74; dir. combat support systems Dept. Army, 1974; dep. comdt. Nat. War Coll., Ft. McNair, Washington, 1974-75; spl. asst. to comdg. gen. U.S. Army Materiel Command, Alexandria, Va., 1975-77; comdg. gen. U.S. Army Electronics Research and Devel. Command, Adelphi, Md., 1977-79; ret., 1979; dir. target acquisition BDM Corp., McLean, Va., 1979-80; cons. Burdeshaw Assocs., 1981—; bd. dirs. Microwave Semicondr. Corp. 1983-89. Decorated D.S.M., Silver Star, Legion of Merit with oak leaf cluster, D.F.C., Bronze Star with 4 oak leaf clusters, Air medal with 16 oak leaf clusters, Joint Service Commendation medal, Army Commendation medal U.S.; Vietnamese Cross of Gallantry with Silver Star. Mem. Assn. U.S. Army, Assn. Grads. U.S. Mil. Acad., S.A.R. Home: 4904 Baltan Rd Bethesda MD 20816-2404 Office: Burdeshaw Assocs Ltd 4701 Sangamore Rd Bethesda MD 20816-2508

DANIEL, CHARLES TIMOTHY, transportation engineer, consultant; b. N.Y.C., Aug. 3, 1958; s. John Carl and Eleanor (Sauer) D.; m. Melissa J. Sanft, Mar. 4, 1995. BA in Engring., Lafayette Coll., 1980; MS in Transp., MIT, 1982; MBA, NYU, 1991. Staff engr. George Beetle Co., Phila., 1983-84; project engr. Transamerica Leasing, Purchase, N.Y., 1984-87; mgr. tech. svcs. Transamerica Leasing, White Plains, N.Y., 1987-89, engring. cons., 1989—; treas. Midtown Daniel Corp., 1990—, pres., 1995—; mem. domestic freight container stds. subcom. Internat. Standardization Orgn. Tech. Com. on Freight Containers, 1986-88. Mem. alumni bd. Rutgers Preparatory Sch., Somerset, N.J., 1985—; county committeeman Middlesex County (N.J.) Dem. Orgn., 1992—. Mem. ASCE, Sigma Xi, Beta Gamma Sigma. Lutheran. Achievements include development of code structure for electronic data interchange of freight container chassis repair data. Home: 33 North Dr East Brunswick NJ 08816-1124 Office: Midtown Daniel Corp 20th Fl 645 Madison Ave New York NY 10022-1010

DANIEL, COLDWELL, III, economist, educator; b. New Orleans; s. Coldwell Jr. and Josephine Agnes (Weick) D.; children: Anne Alexis, Coldwell IV. BBA, Tulane U., 1949; MBA, Ind. U., 1950; PhD, U. Va., 1959; postdoctoral, U. Chgo., 1964-65. Instr. stats. U. Va., 1955-56; instr. econs. Pomona Coll., 1956-57; prof. econs., dept. chmn. U. So. Miss., 1958-65; prof. econs. U. Houston, 1965-70, U. Memphis, 1970—; rsch. coord. So. Calif. Rsch. Coun., 1956-57; vis. prof. La. State U., 1959; sr. Fulbright prof. econs. Dacca U., Bangladesh, 1961-62; project dir. Miss. Test Facility Econ. Impact Study NASA, 1963; prin. The Anwell Co., Memphis, 1974—. Author: Mathematical Models in Microeconomics, 1970; reader Jour. Econ. and Bus., 1991—, Social Sci. Jour., 1988—, Am. Jour. Econs. and Sociology, 1990—; founder, chmn. bd. editors, The Southern Quarterly, 1962-64; co-founder and manuscript review editor Jour. Econs. and Fin., 1977-91, mem. editl. bd., 1991-94; assoc. editor for econs. Social Sci. Quarterly, 1968-70, mem. editl. bd., 1972-84; contbbr. articles to profl. jours. Trustee Christ United Meth. Ch. With USAF, 1945-46; 1st lt. U.S. Army, 1951-53. NSF Sci. Faculty fellow, 1964-66. Mem. Am. Econ. Assn., Pakistan Econ. Assn. (life), Southwestern Econs. Assn., Acad. Econs. and Fin. (co-founder, pres. 1977-78, area coord. Indsl. Orgn. and pub. Policy, 1990-94, Disting. Svc. award 1979, Cert. Appreciation 1981), Mo. Valley Econs. Assn. (pres. 1984-85, Meritorious Svc. award 1986), So. Econ. Assn., Atlantic Econ. Soc. (exec. com. 1991-94, area coord. Indsl. Orgn. and Pub. Policy 1989-94), The Raven Soc., Sigma Xi, Beta Gamma Sigma, Omicron Delta Kappa, Pi Kappa Pi, Omicron Delta Epsilon, Pi Gamma Mu, Delta Tau Kappa, Pi Sigma Epsilon, Delta Sigma Pi, Sigma Xi. Office: U Memphis Dept Econs Memphis TN 38152

DANIEL, DAVID RONALD, management consultant; b. Hartford, Conn., Feb. 26, 1930; s. David Richard and Marion (Ingalls) D.; m. Lise C. Scott; children: David, Peter, Stephen. AB, Wesleyan U., Middletown, Conn., 1952; MBA, Harvard U., 1954; LHD (hon), Wesleyan U. Assoc. McKinsey & Co. Inc., N.Y.C., 1957-63, prin., 1963-68, dir., 1968—, mng. dir. N.Y. office, 1970-76, mng. dir. firm, 1976-88. Contbr. articles to profl. jours. Chmn. emeritus Wesleyan U.; mem. corp. and bd. overseers, treas. Harvard U.; chmn. Harvard Mgmt. Co.; chmn. bd. fellows Harvard Med. Sch.; bd. dirs., mem. exec. com. Brookings Instn.; bd. dirs. Markle Found.; trustee Nat. Trust for Hist. Preservation, Rockefeller U., Thirteen/WNET, N.Y. Mem. Coun. on Fgn. Rels. Home: 580 Park Ave New York NY 10021-7313 Office: McKinsey & Co Inc 55 E 52nd St Fl 18 New York NY 10055-0183

DANIEL, DOROTHY ISOM, nurse specialist, consultant; b. El Paso, Tex., Aug. 13, 1943; d. Charles Dandridge Isom Jr. and Joyce Marie (Mayo) Fisher; m. Marshall E. Daniel Jr., June 20, 1987; children: Michael P. Taylor, Julia D. Taylor, Laura A., Keith R., Craig C. BSN, U. N.C., 1965. RN, Va., Mo., N.C.; cert. diabetes educator, med.-surg. nursing, cardiopulmonary resuscitation. Staff nurse maternal-child health Rex Hosp., Raleigh, N.C., 1974-78; staff nurse rehab. unit St. John's Mercy Med. Ctr., St. Louis, 1983-84; staff nurse med.-surg., diabetes resource nurse Alexandria (Va.) Hosp., 1980-83, 84-87, diabetes nurse specialist, 1987—; expert witness; developer, educator tng. diabetes care and mgmt.; diabetes case mgr. for inpatients and outpatients; cons. diabetes edn. programs; lectr. in field; mentor 1st Internat. Diabetes Edn. Mentor Program, 1993; adv. bd. Eli Lilly Lispro, 1994-96. Chair advanced practice coun. Alexandria Hosp., 1991-92. Mem. Am. Assn. Diabetes Educators (exec. bd. 1987-91, treas. 1989-91, pres. 1992-93, past pres. 1993-95, ADA liaison 1995—, hon. chpt. Diabetes Educator of Yr., 1995-96, No. Va. chpt. James M. Moss award 1996), Sigma Theta Tau. Home: 5245 Pumphrey Dr Fairfax VA 22032-2627 Office: Alexandria Hosp 4320 Seminary Rd Alexandria VA 22304-1592

DANIEL, ELBERT CLIFTON, journalist; b. Zebulon, N.C., Sept. 19, 1912; s. E. Clifton and Elvah Thomas (Jones) D.; m. Margaret Truman (dau. 33d Pres. of U.S.), Apr. 21, 1956; Clifton, William, Harrison, Thomas. AB, U. N.C., 1933, DLitt (hon.), 1970. Assoc. editor Daily Bull., Dunn, N.C., 1933-34; reporter, columnist News and Observer, Raleigh, N.C., 1934-37; reporter, war corr., editor AP, N.Y.C., Washington, Bern (Switzerland), London, 1937-44; corr. N.Y. Times, London, Bonn, Cairo, Moscow, 1944-55; various editorial assignments N.Y. Times, N.Y.C., 1955-63, mng. editor, 1963-69, assoc. editor, 1969-77; Washington bur. chief N.Y. Times, 1973-77; cons. N.Y.C., 1977-86; editor in chief ECAM Publs., Inc., Mt. Kisco, N.Y., 1986-88, editorial dir., 1989-90. Author: Lords, Ladies and Gentlemen, 1984. Recipient award for fgn. corr. from Moscow, Overseas Press Club, 1956. Mem. Century Assn. Democrat. Baptist. Avocations: reading, travel.

DANIEL, GARY WAYNE, motivation and performance consultant; b. Wendall, Idaho, June 22, 1948; s. Milan Chauncey Daniel and Ila Fay (Cox) Harkins. AA, Boise Bus. Coll., 1969; PhD in Psychology, Westbrook U., 1994. Cert. master practitioner Neuro Linguistic Programming. Pres., chief exec. officer Victory Media Group, Santa Rosa, Calif., 1985—; gen. mgr. Victory Record Label, 1986—; also bd. dirs.; bd. dirs. Bay City Records, San Francisco; pres. Lightforce Music Pub., Santa Rosa, 1987—; mktg. cons. Fienze Records, San Francisco, 1987—, Capital Bus. Sys., Napa, Calif., 1986-91. Author: Concert Operations Manual, 1987; devel. of the Neuro Achievement System. Named Top Radio Personality Idaho State Broadcasters Assn., 1971. Mem. ASCAP, NARAS, Ind. Record Mfrs. and Distbrs., Am. Coun. Hypnotist Examiners, Hypnotist Examiners Coun. Calif., Am. Assn. Behavioral Therapists, Internat. Assn. Neuro Linguistic Programming. Office: Neuro Achievement Ctr 55 Maria Dr Ste 844 Petaluma CA 94954-3563

DANIEL, GEORGE EMMETT, academic administrator. BS in history, Ga. Southwestern State U., 1980; BS in Gen. Bus., U. Tenn., 1981, MS in Agrl. Econs., 1983, EdD, 1993. Dir. student activities/housing Cumberland U., Lebanon, Tenn., 1983-89, assoc. v.p. acad. affairs, 1990-94, v.p. instutional rsch., 1995-98, interim v.p. acad. affairs, 1999—. Home: 919 Malquin Dr Nashville TN 37216

DANIEL, J. REESE, lawyer; b. Sanford, N.C., Dec. 24, 1924. AB, U. S.C., 1949, JD cum laude, 1956. Bar: S.C. 1955, U.S. Dist. Ct. S.C. 1956, U.S. Tax Ct. 1959, U.S. Cr. Appeals (4th cir.) 1959. Sr. ptnr. Daniel & Daniel, Litchfield, S.C.; mem. S.C. Supreme Ct. Bd. Commrs. on Grievances and Discipline, 1970-73, Columbia Zoning Bd. of Adjustment, 1970-79. Contbg. author 7 South Carolina Law Quarterly; contbr. articles to profl. jours. With USNR, 1943-46. Mem. ABA, S.C. Bar Assn. (assoc. editor S.C. Bar Assn. News Bull. 1957, editor 1958-59), Phi Delta Phi. E-mail: reesedaniel@email.msn.com. Office: Daniel & Daniel PO Box 857 10B Pawleys Sta Hwy 17 S Pawleys Island SC 29585

DANIEL, JAMES, curator, business executive, writer, former editor,; b. Davidson County, N.C., June 6, 1916; s. James Manly and Bert (Fletcher) D.; m. Ramona Teijeiro, Apr. 15, 1939; children: Jane Clare, Ramona Nina. A.B., U. N.C., 1937; Nieman fellow, Harvard, 1942-43. Reporter Raleigh (N.C.) News & Observer, 1937-40; reporter Washington Daily News, 1941, city editor, 1946-47; with Office War Info., CBI, 1943-45; Washington corr. Scripps-Howard Papers, 1948-56; contbg. editor Time mag., 1957-60; roving editor Reader's Digest, 1961-81; pres. Healing Springs Properties, Inc.; curator Weston (Conn.) Town Hall Art Collection, 1992—. Author: (with J. G. Hubbell) Strike in the West, The Complete Story of the Cuban Crisis, 1963; editor: Private Investment, The Key to International Development, 1958. Club: Harvard (N.Y.C.). Home: 183 Good Hill Rd Weston CT 06883-2312

DANIEL, JAMES RICHARD, accountant, computer company financial executive; b. Chgo., June 26, 1947; s. Elmer Alexander and June B. (Bush) D.; m. Marsha Ruth Stone, Nov. 8, 1969; children: Jennifer Rae, Michael James. BS in Acctg., U. Ill., 1970; MBA, Loyola U., 1974. CPA, Ill., La. Dir. fin. Baxter Travenol Labs., Chgo., 1974-79; corp. controller Bio-Rad Labs. Inc., Richmond, Calif., 1979-81; v.p., treas., controller Lykes Bros. Steamship Co. Inc., New Orleans, 1981-84; cfo SCI Systems Inc., Huntsville, Ala., 1984-91; sr. v.p., chief fin. officer Dell Computer Corp., Austin, Tex., 1991-93; sr. v.p., cfo, pres. hdqrs. support, treas. MicroAge, Inc., Tempe, 1993—; mem. issuer affairs com. NASDAQ, 1996-97. With U.S. Army, 1970-73. Recipient Outstanding Alumnus award Loyola U. Grad. Sch. Bus., 1995. Mem. AICPA. Republican. Home: 3858 E Cholla Ln Phoenix AZ 85028-5023

DANIEL, JAMES RICHARD, surgeon, oncologist. MD, Tulane U., 1978. Surg. oncologist Mary Washington Hosp., Fredericksburg, Va., 1989—. Home: 7 Aiken Rd Fredericksburg VA 22405-3341 Office: 1101 Sam Perry Blvd Ste 311 Fredericksburg VA 22401-4466

DANIEL, JANIS SUE, women's health nurse; b. Frederick, Okla., May 29, 1947; d. O. Frank and Dorothy Jean (Grayson) Gouchie; married; children: Christopher Elmore, Randle Elmore, Stanley Elmore, Garron Elmore. Diploma, Greenville Vocat. Nursing Sch., 1978; AAS, Grayson County Coll., 1989, Assoc. Nursing, 1989; student, U. Houston, East Tex. State U. Cert. in inpatient obstet. nursing. Office nurse Sherman (Tex.) Ob/Gyn Assocs., 1984-87; staff nurse Wilson N. Jones Hosp., Sherman, 1981-84; charge nurse Med. Pla. Hosp., Sherman, 1989-91; nurse, women's care unit Poudre Valley Hosp., Ft. Collins, Colo., 1991-93; with Apothecare, Inc. Wound Care Liasion, Ft. Collins, 1993-95; dir. Maxim Home Care, Ft. Collins, 1996-98; nurse educator Ft. Collins Surg. Assocs., 1998—; instr. maternal nutrition Med. Plaza Hosp., preceptor orientation ob-gyn.; asst. in devel. 1st ann. perinatal conf., North Tex., So. Okla. Mem. com. March of Dimes. Mem. Home Health Nurse Assn., Pottsboro Bus. and Profl. Women (past pres.), Phi Eta Sigma. Home: 1200 Harris Dr Fort Collins CO 80524-1025

DANIEL, SIR JOHN SAGAR, academic administrator, metallurgist; b. Banstead, U.K., May 31, 1942; s. John Edward and Winifred (Sagar) D.; m. Kristin Anne Swanson, July 30, 1966; children—Julian, Anne-Marie, Catherine. BA, Oxford U., Eng., 1964, MA, 1969; MA, Concordia U., Montreal, Can., 1995; DSc in Metallurgy, U. Paris, 1969; DLitt (hon.), Deakin U., Australia, 1985; DSc (hon.), Royal Mil. Coll., St. Jean, Can., 1988, Open U., Sri Lanka, 1994; DEd (hon.), Coun. for Nat. Acad. Awards, UK, 1992; A in Theology, Thorneloe Coll., 1992; LLD (hon.), U. Waterloo, 1993; DUniv, U. Humberside, 1996; D.Litt (hon.), Amer. Internat. U. of London, 1997, Athabasca U., 1998. From asst. prof. to assoc. prof. Ecole Polytechnique, Montreal, Que., Can., 1969-73; dir. etudes Télé-univ. U. Quebec, 1973-77; v.p. learning svcs. Athabasca U., Alberta, Can., 1978-80; v.p. acad. affairs Concordia U., Montreal, 1980-84; pres. Laurentian U., Sudbury, Ont., 1984-90; vice-chancellor Open U. U.K., 1990—; pres. Open U. of U.S., 1998—; mem. adv. bd. Xerox Can. Author: Learning at a Distance: A World Perspective, 1982, Mega-Univ. and Knowledge Media, 1996; contbr. articles to profl. jours. Bd. govs. Commonwealth of Learning, 1988-90; mem. Coun. of Found., Internat. Baccalaureate, 1992—, v.p., 1997—; mem. Brit. N.Am. Com., 1995—; trustee Carnegie Foun. Advancement of Tchg., 1993—; active Higher Edn. Quality Coun., U.K., 1993-94, mem. University for Industry Brd., U.K., dir. (non-exec) Blackwell's Publishing; mem. coun. Open U. of Hong Kong. Decorated officer de l'Ordre des Palmes Acadèmiques (France), Knight Bachelor (U.K.); Forum fellow World Econ. Forum, Davos, 1998; recipient Individual excellence award Commonwealth of Learning, 1995. Fellow St. Edmund Hall (U. Oxford, Eng., hon.); mem. Internat. Coun. for Distance Edn. (pres. 1982-85), Can. Soc. Study Higher Edn. (disting. mem. 1992, Coun. Open Learning Inst., Inst. Mgmt. U.K. Mem. Anglican Ch. Home: Wednesden House, Aspley Guise, Milton Keynes MK17 8DQ, England Office: Open Univ, Off of Vice Chancellor, Milton Keynes MK7 6AA, England

DANIEL, KENNETH RULE, former iron and steel manufacturing company executive; b. Milford, Conn., Oct. 13, 1913; s. Cullen Coleman and Margaret Estelle (Elliott) D.; m. Virginia Moody Simpson, June 11, 1938; children: Kenneth Rule, Cullen Coleman, Robert Tennent Simpson, William Francis McKemie. B.S., U. Ala., 1936, Profl. Degree in Mech. Engring., 1957, D.Sc., 1980. Registered profl. engr. Ala. With Am. Cast Iron Pipe Co., Birmingham, Ala., 1936-78; chief engr. Am. Cast Iron Pipe Co., 1948-55, v.p. engring., 1955-59, v.p. engring. and purchases, 1959-61, exec. v.p., 1961-63, pres., 1963-78, also dir., dir. various subsidiaries, 1963-78; vice chmn. bd. 1st Ala. Bank of Birmingham, 1977-86; Sesquicentennial hon. prof. U. Ala., 1981; bd. dirs. L&N R.R., Seaboard Coast Line R.R., CSX R.R. Mem. Ala. Bd. of Registration for Profl. Engrs. and Land Surveyors, 1967-87; mem. regional adv. council Conf. Bd., 1967-78, Ala. Export Council, 1966-69; bd. dirs. Community Chest, 1965-78, Jr. Achievement, 1964-78, Birmingham Centennial Corp., 1968-73, Warrior Tombigbee Devel. Assn., 1963-78, L and N RR-Seaboard Coast Line RR-CSX RR, 1969-78; gen. co-chmn. United Appeal, 1964, chmn. indsl. div., 1958; chmn. Radio Free Europe, Birmingham, 1966; mem. Jefferson County Judicial Commn., 1967-72; chmn. adv. bd. Salvation Army, 1968-69, mem. adv. council home and hosp., mem. nat. adv. council, 1976—; trustee Foundry Ednl. Found. (pres. 1964-65); trustee, mem. exec. com. So. Research Inst.; chmn. bd. trustees Jefferson County Cooper Green Hosp.; bd. visitors Berry Coll., Mt. Berry, Ga., 1968-78. Served to lt. col. AUS, 1941-46, ETO. Decorated Bronze Star, Legion of Merit; Croix de Guerre France; recipient Gold Knight of Mgmt. award Nat. Mgmt. Assn., 1965, William Booth award Salvation Army, 1967, Henry Laurence Gantt medal Am. Mgmt. Assn. and ASME, 1977, Exec. of the Yr. award Nat. Mgmt. Assn., 1978; named Engr. of the Yr., Birmingham Engring. Coun., 1967, Paladium medal Am. Engring. Soc. and Nat. Audubon Soc., 1986; elected to Ala. Acad. Honor, 1982, Nat. Mgmt. Assn. Hall of Fame, 1987, Ala. Engring. Hall of Fame, 1989. Fellow ASME (chmn. Birmingham sect. 1950-51, hon. mem. 1984); mem. NAM (dir. 1967-70), Am. Iron and Steel Inst. (bd. dirs. 1968-78), Assn. Industries Ala. (bd. dirs. 1963-78), Birmingham Area C. of C. (pres. 1969), Assn. Iron and Steel Engrs. (chmn. Birmingham Sect. 1954, nat. dir. 1955), Am. Ordnance Assn. (pres. Birmingham post 1964), Am. Foundrymen's Soc. (Thomas W. Pangborn Gold Medal award 1974), Am. Soc. for Engring. Edn., Engring. Soc. Birmingham, Newcomen Soc. N. Am., Birmingham Country Club, The Club, Mountain Brook Club, Masons (knight comdr. Ct. of Honor), Kiwanis, Sigma Alpha Epsilon, Theta Tau, Tau Beta Pi. Methodist. Office: PO Box 2727 Birmingham AL 35202-2727

DANIEL, LEON, journalist, newspaper columnist, editor; b. Etowah, Tenn., Aug. 8, 1931; s. Oscar Leon and Mary Nancy (Cook) D.; m. Carobel Heidt Calhoun, Oct. 26, 1963 (div.); 1 child, Lillian Fant. Student, U. Tenn., 1949-56. Reporter UP, Nashville, 1956-58; bur. mgr. UPI, Knoxville, Tenn., 1958-61; reporter UPI, Atlanta, 1961-66; corr. UPI, Saigon, 1966-67, Tokyo, 1967-70; mgr. for Thailand UPI, Bangkok, 1970-72; chief corr. for South Asia UPI, New Delhi, 1972-74; chief corr. for East Asia UPI, Manila, 1974; editor for Asia, Hong Kong UPI, Hong Kong, 1974-77; editor for Europe UPI, London, 1977-80; nat. reporter UPI, Washington, 1980-87, mng. editor, internat., 1987-88, sr. editor, columnist, 1989-93; cons., columnist The Ind., Dhaka, Bangladesh, 1995. With USMC, 1950-53, Korea. Decorated Purple Heart. Mem. Phi Gamma Delta, Sigma Delta Chi. Democrat. Episcopalian. Home: 956 Manchester Ct Charlottesville VA 22901-1781

DANIEL, LORI EDWARDS, assistant principal; b. Fort Dix, N.J., Feb. 3, 1969; d. Dennis Elmer and Susan Lorraine (Lewis) Edwards; m. Martin Cleve Daniel, Dec. 18, 1993; 1 child, Madeline Lane. BS in English Edn., East Carolina U., 1991; M in Sch. Adminstrn., U. N.C., Greensboro, 1997. Cert. tchr. adminstrn., N.C. English tchr. Bartlett Yancey H.S., Yanceyville, N.C., 1991-95; asst. prin. South Elem. Sch., Roxboro, N.C., 1997—. Bd. vis. East Carolina U., Greenville, 1995—. Fellow N.C. Prins. Program, 1995-97. Mem. ASCD, NEA, N.C. Edn. Assn., Pirate Club, Gamma Beta Phi. Democrat. Methodist. Avocations: reading, antique shopping, floral design. Home: 113 Yarboroughs Mill Rd Milton NC 27305-9272 Office: South Elem Sch 1333 Hurdle Mills Rd Roxboro NC 27573-3731

DANIEL, MARILYN S., lawyer; b. Tulsa, Okla., July 30, 1940; d. Basil M. and Kathryne (Shannon) Stewart; m. John A. Daniel, June 15, 1962; 1 child, John S. BA, Rhodes Coll., 1962; JD, U. Ky. Coll. of Law, 1976. Bar: Ky. Sec. math. tchr. Ky., N.J., 1962-71; legal clerk U.S. Dist. Judge, Lexington, Ky., 1977; asst. U.S. atty. U.S. Dept. Justice, Lexington, 1978-81; gen. counsel Mason & Hanger Corp., Lexington, 1982—, v.p. adminstrn., 1992-96, sr. v.p., 1996—; dir. Mason Techs. Inc., 1988—, The Mason Co., Lexington, 1990—, Ky. Bar Assn. for Women, 1991-93. Mem. Fayette County Bd. Edn., 1985-88; trustee Transylvania Presbytery, 1985—; elder Maxwell St. Presbyn. Ch., 1993—. Recipient Women of Achievement award YWCA, 1993. Mem. ABA, KBA (CLE chair ann. conv. 1992), Fayette County Bar Assn. (Henry T. Duncan award 1994. Avocations: gardening, cooking, hiking, quilting, handwork. Office: Mason & Hanger Corp 2355 Harrodsburg Rd Lexington KY 40504-3307*

DANIEL, MICHAEL EDWIN, insurance agency executive; b. Indpls., Sept. 8, 1948; s. Richard E. and Margret A. (Phillips) D.; m. Jeanne L. Nobbe, Sept. 29, 1979; children: Whitney Marie, Lindsay Michelle, Tyler Edwin. BA, Principia Coll., Elsah, Ill., 1970; German lang. degree, Dept. Def., Monterey, Calif., 1971. Sales mgr. Mr. Ins. of Ind., Indpls., 1973-77; pres. Ind. Ins. Svcs., Inc., Greenwood, 1977—, Ins. Svc., Inc., 5, 1990—; v.p. Brown County Water Utility, Helmsburg, Ind., 1982-85. Leader Johnson County 4-H, 1993—. With U.S. Army, 1970-73. Mem. Ind. Ins. Agts. Assn., Profl. Ins. Agt. Assn. (treas. Indpls. region 1990), Ind. Trail Riders Assn., BMW Motorcycle Owners Am. Christian Scientist. Avocations: Appaloosa and quarter horses, camping. Office: Ind Ins Svcs 3115 Meridian Parke Dr Ste P Greenwood IN 46142-9414

DANIEL, RICHARD NICHOLAS, fabricated metals manufacturing company executive; b. Bklyn., Sept. 18, 1935; s. Louis V. and Jean (D'Andrea) D.; m. Elaine E. Sherman, Sept. 24, 1966; children: Matthew, Jeffrey. B.B.A., St. John's U., 1957; M.B.A., U. Pa., 1959. C.P.A., Tex. Planning assoc. Mobil Oil Corp., N.Y.C., 1962-70; v.p. fin. Laird Enterprises Inc., N.Y.C., 1970-71; v.p. ops. Wheelabrator-Frye, N.Y.C., 1971; v.p., controller Handy & Harman, N.Y.C., 1971-76, v.p.-fin., 1977-78, group v.p., 1978-79, pres., COO, 1979-83, pres., CEO, 1983-87, chmn., pres., CEO, 1988-92, chmn., CEO, 1992-98; ind. bus. cons., 1998—. Home: 91 Hawthorn Pl Briarcliff Manor NY 10510-2226 Office: 555 Madison Ave 17th Fl New York NY 10022-3301

DANIEL, ROBERT MICHAEL, lawyer; b. Rocky Mount, N.C., Aug. 21, 1947; s. Harvey Derby and Edna Lois (McCullen) D.; m. Kaye Ruth Coates, Aug. 31, 1968; children: Robert M. Jr., John Matthew. AB in Econs., U. N.C., 1968, JD, 1971. Bar: N.C. 1971, Pa. 1976; U.S. Dist. Ct. (we. dist.) Pa. 1976; U.S. Tax Ct. 1979. Judge adv. U.S. Marine Corps., 1971-74; ptnr. Smith & Daniel, Pittsboro, N.C., 1974-75; trust officer Mellon Bank, N.A., Pitts., 1975-78; assoc. Buchanan Ingersoll, Pitts., 1978-82, ptnr., 1982—. Pres. Greater Pitts. coun. Boy Scouts Am., 1996-99, bd. dirs. N.E. region. Col. USMCR, 1966-98, ret. Fellow Am. Coll. Trust and Estate Coun.; mem. Pa. Bar Assn. (probate and trust law sect. 1998-99, chmn. real property, probate and trust law sect. 1998, chmn. 1998—), Duquesne Club. Democrat. Presbyterian. Avocations: running, reading military history. Home: 1491 Redfern Dr Pittsburgh PA 15241-2956 Office: Buchanan Ingersoll 301 Grant St Ste 20 Pittsburgh PA 15219-1408

DANIEL, THOMAS L., zoology educator; b. N.Y.C., Aug. 21, 1954. BS in Anthropology and Engring., U. Wis., 1976, MS in Zoology and Engring., 1978; PhD in Zoology, Duke U., 1982; postgrad., Calif. Inst. Tech. Myron A. Bantrell postdoctoral fellow in sci. and engring. Calif. Inst. Tech., 1982-84; asst. prof. dept. zoology U. Wash., Seattle, 1984-88, assoc. prof. dept. zoology, 1988-92, prof. dept. zoology, 1992—; external grad. faculty Oreg. State U., 1987—; mem. various coms. at U. Wash. including chair grad. admissions dept. zoology, 1989-91, chair grad. program dept. zoology, 1991-94, dir. math. biology tng. program, 1993—; panel mem. physiol. processes NSF, 1991—; presenter in field. Mem. editl. bd. Jour. Exptl. Biology, Cambridge U., 1988-90, 93—; contbr. articles to profl. jours. Grantee NSF, 1984-87, 88-91, 91-93, 93, U. Wash., 1987-88, J. Fluke Co., 1988, Reticon, Inc., 1988, Am. Soc. Zoologists Symposium on Efficiency in Organisms, 1988-89, Whitaker Found. for Biomed. Rsch., 1988-91, Howard Hughes Found., 1989-94, M.J. Murdock Meml. Trust, 1989-94, Apple Computer, 1991; recipient MacArthur fellow, 1996. Office: U Wash Dept Zoology PO Box 351800 Seattle WA 98195-1800*

DANIEL, WILEY Y., lawyer; b. Louisville, Sept. 10, 1946; m. Ida S. Daniel; children: Jennifer, Stephanie, Nicole. BA in History, Howard U., JD. Atty. Gorsuch, Kirgis, Campbell, Walker & Grover, Denver, 1995; shareholder Popham, Haik, Schnobrich & Kaufman Ltd., Denver, 1995; judge U.S. Dist. Ct. Colo., Denver, 1995—. Trustee Iliff Sch. Theology, Denver. Mem. Colo. Bar Assn. (pres. 1992-93), Denver Bar Assn., State Bd. Architecture. Democrat. Office: US District Court of Colorado Byron White US Courthouse 1929 Stout St C 218 Denver CO 80294-0001

DANIELEWICZ, CLAUDIA ANNE, quality assurance engineer; b. Niagara Falls, N.Y., Aug. 8, 1964; d. Chester Albert and Florence Carolyn (Pasek) D. AS in Engring., Erie C.C., 1984; BS in Engring., Rochester Inst. Tech., 1987, MS in Engring., 1993. Cert. quality assurance/mech./process engr. Farm equipment oper. Danielewicz Dairy Farms, Sanborn, N.Y., 1984-93; intern mech. engring. Sohio Electro Mineral, Niagara Falls, N.Y., 1984-85, Vets. Hosp., Batavia, N.Y., 1985-86; sales assoc. Gold Circle, Niagara Falls, 1987-88; asst. planner Cambridge Instruments, Buffalo, N.Y., 1988; engr. mfr., quality Par Foam Products, Buffalo, N.Y., 1988-92; engr. quality assurance Avm (Arvin/Gabirel), Marion, S.C., 1992; quality assurance engr. GenCorp Automotive, Batesville, Ark., 1993-94; process/quality assurance engr. Courtaulds Thatcher Tubes, Woodstock, Ill., 1994-95; quality assurance engr. Statis. Resource Quality Network GM Corp., Pontiac, Mich., 1995—. Mem. ASME, Am. Soc. Quality, Nat. Soc. Profl. Engrs. Avocations: bowling, motorcross, stock car racing, farming, reading. Home: 4286 Saunders Settlement Rd Sanborn NY 14132-9411 Office: General Motors Corp Truck Grp Code 483-511-7K5 2000 Centerpoint Pkwy Pontiac MI 48341-3146

DANIELEWSKI, DONNA KRYSTYNA, secondary school educator; b. Poland, Jan. 4, 1942; came to U.S., 1947; d. Walter and Alice Wojec; m. George L. Danielewski, June 7, 1969; children: Eva, Christopher, Paul. BA, Beaver Coll., 1963; MA, Temple U., 1966. Cert. tchr., Pa. Classroom tchr. Upper Dublin Sch. Dist., Dresher, Pa., 1963-77; classroom tchr., scholars bowl coach Pennsbury H.S., Fairless Hills, Pa., 1989—; instr. Holy Family Coll., Phila., 1993. Cub scout den leader Boy Scouts Am. Mem. AAUW, Polish Heritage Soc. Phila. (pres. 1996), Delta Kappa Gamma. Avocations: reading, research, travel, skiing, family. Home: 1775 Autumn Leaf Ln Huntingdon Valley PA 19006-1514

DANIELL, HERMAN BURCH, pharmacologist; b. Cadwell, Ga., May 25, 1929; s. Walter and Ruby Florence (Burch) D.; m. Lorraine Smith, June 30, 1957; children: Kimberley Ann, Anthony Burch, Walter Herman. B.S. in Pharmacy, U. Ga., 1951, M.S. in Pharmacology, 1964; Ph.D. in Pharmacology; USPHS trainee 1964-66, Med. Coll. S.C., Charleston, 1966. Owner-operator retail pharmacies Savannah, Ga., 1953-62; instr. U. Ga., 1962-64; mem. faculty Med. U. S.C., 1966-92, prof. pharmacology, 1978-92; prof. emeritus, 1992—. Author papers in field. Served to capt. Med. Service Corps, AUS, 1951-53. Grantee USPHS, 1966-85, S.C. Heart Assn., 1966-73. Mem. Am. Soc. Pharmacology and Exptl. Therapeutics, Sigma Xi, Rho Chi, Kappa Sigma. Episcopalian. Home: 1549 Burningtree Rd Charleston SC 29412-2630 Office: 171 Ashley Ave Charleston SC 29425-0001

DANIELL, JERE ROGERS, II, history educator, consultant, public lecturer; b. Millinocket, Maine, Nov. 28, 1932; s. Warren Fisher and Mary (Holway) D.; m. Sally Ann Wellborn, Dec. 1955 (div. 1969); children: Douglas, Alexander, Matthew; m. 2d Elena Lillie, July 19, 1969; stepchildren: Breena Daniell, Clifford Brodsky. AB, Dartmouth Coll., 1955; MA, Harvard U., 1962, PhD, 1964. Asst. prof. history Dartmouth Coll., 1964-69, assoc. prof., 1969-74, prof., 1974—, chmn. dept., 1979-83; class of 1925 prof., 1984—; head tutor Heritage Found., Old Deerfield, Mass., 1960-64. Author: Experiment in Republicanism: N.H. Politics and the American Revolution, 1970, Colonial N.H.: A History, 1981; bd. editors: Univ. Press of New England, 1978-86. Served to lt (j.g.) USN, 1955-58. Mem. Colonial Soc. Mass., N.H. Hist. Soc., Vt. Hist. Soc., Maine Hist. Soc., Mass. Hist. Soc. Home: 11 Barrymore Rd Hanover NH 03755-2401 Office: Dartmouth Coll Dept History Hanover NH 03755

D'ANIELLO, DANIEL, merchant banker; b. Pitts., Sept. 14, 1946; s. Beatrice V. (Laconi) D'A.; m. Gayle V. Yanicky, Oct. 9, 1976; children: Dana F., Bethany A. BS, Syracuse U., 1968; MBA, Harvard U., 1974. Sr. fin. analyst Trans World Airlines, N.Y.C., 1974-76; dir. planning Pepsico, Purchase, N.Y., 1976-80; v.p. corp. fin. planning Marriott Corp., Washington, 1980-86; CFO, v.p. devel. Marriott Inflite, Washington, 1986-87; co-founder, mng. dir. The Carlyle Group, Washington, 1987—; bd. dirs. CB Comml., Elgar Electronics Corp., GTS Duratek, Internat. Tech., Inc., Pharm. Rsch. Assocs., Inc., Baker & Taylor Inc., vice chmn. Author: A Model for Airline Route Analysis, 1973, (case study) Braniff International, 1974. Bd. dirs. Fight for Children, Inc., 1992—; vice chmn. events U.S. Holocaust Meml. Found., Washington, 1992; selection com. Pres.' Commn. White Ho. Fellow, Washington, 1993. Lt. (j.g.) USN, 1968-71. Fellow Teagle Found., 1973; named Disting. Grad. Butler (Pa.) Area High Sch., 1993. Mem. City Club Washington. Avocations: golf, reading, opera. Office: The Carlyle Group 1001 Pennsylvania Ave NW Washington DC 20004-2505*

DANIELS, ARLENE KAPLAN, sociology educator; b. N.Y.C., Dec. 10, 1930; d. Jacob and Elizabeth (Rathstein) Kaplan; m. Richard Rene Daniels, June 9, 1956. B.A. with honors in English, U. Calif., Berkeley, 1952; M.A. in Sociology, 1954, Ph.D. in Sociology, 1960. Instr. dept. speech U. Calif., Berkeley, 1959-61; rsch. assoc. Mental Rsch. Inst., Palo Alto, Calif., 1961-66; assoc. prof. sociology San Francisco State Coll., 1966-70; chief Center for Study Women in Soc., Inst. Sci. Analysis, San Francisco, 1970-80; mem. faculty Northwestern U., Evanston, Ill., 1975-95; prof. dept. sociology Northwestern U., 1975-95, dir. Women's Studies, 1992-94, prof. emerita; vis. prof. dept. sociology U. Calif., Berkeley, 1997—; cons. NIMH, 1971-73, NEH, 1975-80, Nat. Inst. Edn., 1978-82. Editor: (with Rachel Kahn-Hut) Academics on the Line, 1970; co-editor: (with Gaye Tuchman and James Benét) Hearth and Home: Images of Women in the Mass Media, 1978, (with James Benét) Education: Straightjacket or Opportunity?, 1979, (with Rachel Kahn-Hut and Richard Colvard) Women and Work, 1982, (with Alice Cook and Val Lorwin) Women and Trade Unions in Eleven Industrialized Countries, (with Teresa Odendahl and Elizabeth Boris) Working in Foundations, 1985, Invisible Careers, 1988, (with Alice Cook and Val Lorwin) The Most Difficult Revolution: Women in the Trade Union Movement, 1992; editor: Jour. Social Problems, 1974-78; assoc. editor: Contemporary Sociology, 1980-82, Symbolic Interaction, 1979-84, Am. Sociol. Rev., 1987-90. Trustee Bus. and Profl. Women's Rsch. Found. Bd., 1980-85, Women's Equity Action League Legal and Ednl. Def. Fund, 1979-81; mem. Chgo. Rsch. Assoc. Bd., 1981-87. Recipient Social Sci. Rsch. Council Faculty Rsch. award, 1970-71; Ford Found. Faculty fellow, 1975-76; grantee Nat. Inst. Edn., 1978-79, 1979-80, NSF, 1974-75, NIMH, 1973-74. Mem. Inst. Medicine NAS. Sociologists Women in Soc. (pres. 1975-76), Am. Sociology Assn. (coun. 1979-81, chmn. occupations and orgns. 1987, chmn. pubs. com. 1985-87, sec. 1992-95, Jessie Bernard award 1995), Soc. Study Social Problems (v.p. 1981-82, pres. 1987 Lee Founders award 1988), Soc. Study Symbolic Inter-Action.

DANIELS, ASTAR, artist; b. Fostoria, Ohio, Nov. 27, 1920; d. Alfred Henry and Edna Mae (Roush) Shultz; m. Bert Franklin Daniels, May 17, 1942 (div. Sept. 1976); children: Larry Bert, Cheri Hogue-Daniels, N. Dana Rahbar-Daniels. Honor grad., Art Instrn., Inc., Mpls., 1952; student, Toledo Mus. Sch. Design, 1950-52; studied with, Emerson C. Burkhart, 1952-54; student, Thomas Moore Coll., 1971-73; grad. summa cum laude, U. Cin., 1977; student, Ohio U., 1984-85. Tchr. art pvt. adult and youth art classes Forest and Cin., Ohio, 1950-57; portrait demonstrator numerous galleries, colls., mus., TV nationwide, 1951-79; dir. art, tchr. Defiance (Ohio) Coll., 1956-57; tchr. art and drama Meth. Ch. Camp, Sabina, Ohio, 1960-64; lectr. on liturgical art Hyde Park Comty. Ch., Cin., 1960-79; tchr. art and drama Fairview Arts Ctr., Cin., 1977-78; tchr. art Losantiville Summer Sch. Disadvantages Youth, 1996; judge, mem. jury art shows, 1956-70; gallery guide Contemporary Art Ctr., Cin., 1972-73; costume designer Girl Scout Symphony Music Hall, Cin., 1960, 62, 66; dir. art Ohio State Fair, Columbus, 1955-57; nat. art dir. Sr. Girl Scout Round-up, Button Bay, Vt., 1962; founder, chairperson Fine Arts Com. Ecclesia, Cin., 1960-79. Exhibited in one woman portrait shows mus., colls., galleries, 1954-72; exhibited glass sculpture Schaff Gallery, Cin., 1996; commns. include Richard Nixon, Dr. A. B. Graham, James Arness; author, illustrator: (book) Aiming in His Direction, 1971; illustrator: (book) Woman Spirit Bonding, 1983. Art therapist Christ Hosp. Psychiat. Ward, Cin., 1959-61; youth liturgical dance dir.

Hyde Park Comty. Ch., Cin., 1959-66; citizen diplomat Soc. for Positive Future, 1986. Recipient Scouters award for tng. leadership Boy Scouts Am., Forest, 1957, Cert. of Achievement, Charlotte R. Schmidlapp Found., Cin., 1977, Exptl. Inst. for Human Devel. award Hyde Park Comty. Ch., 1976. Mem. Soc. for Universal Human (founding mem. 1996). Avocations: world travel, exploring Incan and Mayan sites, mentoring young women, reading, metaphysical phenomena. Home and Office: Daniels Portrait Studio 3740 Drakewood Dr Cincinnati OH 45209-2327

DANIELS, BARBARA ANN, non-profit organization executive; b. Middletown, Ohio, Apr. 8, 1968; d. Benjamin Franklin and Hazel May (Dorsey) Lewis; m. Kevin Wilson Daniels, Oct. 8, 1988; children: Kara Marie, Kaitlyn Brooke. Student, U. Phoenix, 1999—. Acctg. intern AC&D Bus. Svcs., Inc., Mesa, 1989, Switzer's Corp., Phoenix, 1991; accts. payable clk. Rockford Fosgate Corp., Tempe, 1989-91; office asst., sr. cons. Ariz. State U., Tempe, 1992, bus. cons. deans office Coll. of Bus., 1992-93; pres. Daniels Bus. Svcs., Mesa, 1992—; dir. mem. svcs. Greater Phoenix Leadership, 1993—. Chair GPL Adminstrv. Assts. Network, Phoenix, 1995—. Mem. NAFE, Profl. Secs. Internat. (chair publicity team Tempe chpt. 1995, chair cmty. svc. com. 1993-94), Nat. Trust for Hist. Preservation, Valley Citizens League, Exec. Women Internat. (Phoenix Chpt., bd. dirs., program dir.). Republican. Avocations: family, education, physical fitness, community involvement. Home: 6035 E Ivyglen St Mesa AZ 85205-3653 Office: Greater Phoenix Leadership Inc 201 N Central Ave Fl 3 Phoenix AZ 85073-0073

DANIELS, CHERYL LYNN, pediatrics nurse, case manager; b. Paterson, N.J., June 15, 1951; d. Nathan and Frances Avonna (Bradshaw) D. RN, Martland Hosp. Sch. Nursing, Newark, 1971; AAS in Health and Community Svc., NYU, 1984, BA in Journalism, 1987. Cert. pediat. nurse, ANCC. Evening charge nurse Martland Hosp. Unit, Newark, 1971-73; staff nurse Heal Econs. Advancement League, Paterson, N.J., 1972-74; neonatal intensive care nurse St. Joseph's Hosp. & Med. Ctr., Paterson, N.J., 1973-77, 1977-79, charge, staff nurse ICN, 1979-89, intensive care nurse, pediatric HIV outpatient nurse, 1989-90; rsch. outpatient HIV case mgmt. nurse Aids Clin. Trial Group, 1990—; case mgr. outpatient pediat. HIV Clinic, 1989—. Mentor Career Beginning Program, Paterson, 1988-90. Recipient Gobetz award, NYU, 1984. Mem. ARC, ANA, AACN (cert. pediat. nursing), Alpha Sigma Lambda. Baptist. Avocations: clarinet, swimming, reading, writing, oil painting. Home: 721 14th Ave Paterson NJ 07504-1531 Office: Saint Joseph Hosp 703 Main St Paterson NJ 07503-2691

DANIELS, CINDY LOU, space agency executive; b. Moline, Ill., Sept. 24, 1959; d. Ronald McCrae and Mary Lou (McLaughlin) Guthrie; m. Charles Burton Daniels, June 19, 1982. Student, Augustana Coll., Rock Island, Ill., 1977-78; BS cum laude, No. Mich. U., 1981. Field engr. Ford Aerospace, Houston, 1982-83; engr. flight ops. McDonnell Douglas Corp., Houston, 1983-85; electronics engr. Johnson Space Ctr. NASA, Houston, 1985-89; project mgr. multiple program control ctr. NASA, 1989-90; project mgr. NASA, Houston, 1989-91, mission control ctr. upgrade project mgr., 1990-91; mgr. program control office NASA, 1991-93; mgr. ground facilities Space Sta. Program Office NASA, Houston, 1993-94; engrng. and ops. mgmt., space sta. program NASA Hdqrs., Washington, 1994-96; spl. assessments and acquisition mgr. NASA Langley Rsch. Ctr., Hampton, Va., 1996—; dynamics contr. NASA Johnson Space Ctr., 1982-83; payload data engr. NASA, 1983-84, earth radiation budget satellite joint ops. integration plan mgr., 1984; mem. payload assist module team NASA-McDonnell Douglas Corp., 1984-85. Avocation: skiing. Home: 900 N Randolph St Apt 321 Arlington VA 22203-1988 Office: NASA Langley Rsch Ctr 12 W Taylor Ave Hampton VA 23663-2206

DANIELS, DIANA M., lawyer; b. Dillon, Mont.. BA, Cornell U., 1971; JD, Harvard U., 1974; M of City Planning, MIT, 1974; diploma, U. Edinburgh, Scotland, 1976. Bar: N.Y. 1975, U.S. Dist. Ct. (ea. and so. dists.) N.Y. 1975, U.S. Ct. Appeals (2d cir.) 1975, D.C. 1978, U.S. Supreme Ct. 1988. Assoc. Cravath, Swaine & Moore, N.Y.C., 1975-78; asst. counsel Washington Post newspaper, 1978-79, gen. counsel Washington Post Co., 1988-89, v.p., gen. counsel, 1989-91, v.p., gen. counsel, sec., 1991—; v.p., counsel Newsweek, N.Y.C., 1979-85, v.p., gen. counsel, 1985-88. Trustee Cornell U., 1995—, ABA Mus. of Law, 1997, Appleseed Found., 1998—, Ctr. for Study of Presidency, 1997—. Office: Washington Post Co 1150 15th St NW Washington DC 20071-0002

DANIELS, ELIZABETH ADAMS, English language educator; b. Westport, Conn., May 8, 1920; d. Thomas Davies and Minnie Mae (Sherwood) Adams; m. John L. Daniels, Mar. 21, 1942; children: John L., Eleanor B. (dec.), Sherwood A., Ann S. A.B., Vassar Coll., 1941; A.M., U. Mich., 1942; Ph.D., N.Y. U., 1954. From instr. to prof. English Vassar Coll., Poughkeepsie, N.Y., 1948-85; dean freshmen Vassar Coll., 1955-58, dean studies, 1965-73, chmn. dept. English, 1974-76, 81-84, acting dean faculty, 1976-78, chmn. self-study, 1978-80, Vassar historian, 1985—. Author: Jessie White Mario, Risorgimento Revolutionary, 1972, Main to Mudd, Bridges to the World, 1994, Main to Mudd, and More, 1996; also articles. Bd. dirs. Alzheimer's Assn. Mid-Hudson Valley. Recipient Grad. award Alumnae Assn. N.Y. U., 1954; Vassar fellow, 1941; Nat. Endowment Humanities summer stipend, 1981. Mem. MLA, AAUP, Phi Beta Kappa. Democrat. Club: Poughkeepsie Tennis. Home: 10 Squires Gate Poughkeepsie NY 12603-3647 Office: Vassar Coll PO Box 74 Poughkeepsie NY 12602-0074 *Growing up with intellectual ambitions, I was able to work out a very satisfactory career combining teaching, college administration, scholarship, family life, and a good marriage slightly forerunning the feminist movement of the late nineteen-sixties. I owe much of this to Vassar College, the first endowed woman's college in the U.S.*

DANIELS, FRANK ARTHUR, JR., newspaper publisher; b. Raleigh, N.C., Sept. 7, 1931; s. Frank Arthur and Ruth (Aunspaugh) D.; m. Julia Bryan Jones, June 4, 1954; children: Frank Arthur III, Julia Graham Nowell. A.B., U. N.C., 1953. With News and Observer Pub. Co., Raleigh, 1953-97; pres., pub. News and Observer Pub. Co., 1971-97; trustee Commonwealth Fund, N.Y.C., 1994—; chmn. Associated Press, 1992-97; bd. dirs. Landmark Comm.; chmn. So. Pines Pilot newspaper, Philanthropy Jour., Koz, Inc. Internet pub. aggregator, Total Sports. Bd. dirs., mem. exec. com., campaign chmn. Raleigh United Way, 1964, pres., 1974-75; bd. dirs. Greater Triangle Community Found.; former trustee Peace Coll., St. Mary's Coll.; former chmn. Rex. Hosp.; chmn., former pres. Am. Newspaper Pub. Assn. Found.; former mem. Raleigh-Durham Airport Authority; past trustee Woodberry Forest Sch.; past bd. visitors U. N.C.; bd. dirs. Smithsonian Inst., 1996—; campaign chmn. Triangle United Way, 1996; chmn. Josephus Duvals Found.; trustee U. N.C. Health Care Sys. With USAF, 1954-55. Named Outstanding Young Man of Yr. Raleigh Jaycees, 1963. Mem. So. Newspaper Pubs. Assn. (chmn. bd. 1973-74, pres. 1972-73, dir.), Am. Newspaper Pubs. Assn. (past bd. dirs., treas.), N.C. Press Assn. (past pres.), Greater Raleigh C. of C. (bd. dirs.), Carolina Motor Club (dir.), Country Club of N.C., Capital City Club, Carolina Country Club, Sphinx Club, Univ. Club (N.Y.C.), Coral Beach Club (Bermuda), Delta Kappa Epsilon. Democrat. Presbyn. Office: KOZ Inc Ste 600 133 Fayetteville Street Mall Raleigh NC 27601-2911

DANIELS, FRANK ARTHUR, III, publishing executive; b. Raleigh, N.C., Mar. 7, 1956; s. Frank Arthur Jr. and Julia Bryan (Jones) D.; m. Teresa Ann Davison, Apr. 12, 1980; children: Kimberly, Frank A. IV, Joseph. BA, Duke U., 1978. Reporter St. Joseph (Mo.) News-Press/Gazette, 1978-79, The Ledger Star, Norfolk, Va., 1979-81; circulation mgr., advt. rep., then asst. to controller The News and Observer Pub. Co., Raleigh, 1981-85, asst. gen. mgr., 1985-87, dir. ops., 1989-90, v.p., exec. editor, 1990-95; pres., pub. Nando-net, Raleigh, 1995-96; chmn., CEO Koz Inc., 1996-98, chmn., 1998—; pres. The Josephus Group, Raleigh, 1996—; chmn., CEO Total Sports, Raleigh, 1997—; vis. lectr. Duke Univ., 1996; pub. Bus. N.C. mag., 1987-89; bd. dirs. Cadmus Comms. Corp., Exploris. Bd. dirs. Gov.'s Task Force on Rail Passengers, 1988-91, N.C. 1st Amendment Found.; mem. bd. visitors Sanford Inst. Policy Scis., Duke U., Durham, N.C., 1988—; mem., bd. dirs. New Directions for the News, 1993—; mem. adv. bd. Woodberry Forest Sch.; chmn. New Media Fedn. Newspaper Assn. Am., 1996. Recipient Ozzie award Mag. Design and Prodn., 1987, 88, Pulitzer Prize gold medal for pub. svc. journalism, 1995, New Media Pioneer Newspaper Assn. of Am., 1996. Office: Total Sports PO Box 10708 Raleigh NC 27605-0708*

DANIELS, IRISH C., principal; b. Miami, Fla.; children: Irisha, Jessica. BS, Fla. A&M U., 1964, MEd, 1974; postgrad., Fla. State U., 1978. cert. adminstrn., supervision, early childhood, elem. edn., reading gifted edn., health. Tchr. Gadsden County Sch. Bd., Quincy, Fla.; tchr. Leon County Sch. Bd., Tallahassee, asst. prin.; grade level chmn.; sch. SACS chmn.; originator, coord. vocat. incentive program Hartsfield Sch., 1988-90; establisher, coord. Help Ctr. for grades 3-5, 1991; organizer, coord. Parent Tutorial Program, 1993-94; presenter Am. Assn. Colls. tchr. Edn. Conv., 1994, Assn. Tchr. Edn. Conv., 1996; coord. sch. renewal process Pineview Elem., 1997-98. Named Disting. Black Educator from Hartsfield, 1991, Disting. Educator of Minorities, 1992. Mem. Asst. Prins. Facilitator or Sch. Improvement (chair), Phi Delta Kappa, Kappa Delta Pi. Home: 2605 Vence Dr Tallahassee FL 32312-3239

DANIELS, JAMES DOUGLAS, academic administrator; b. Harmony, N.C., Nov. 14, 1935; m. Marie Brown, Oct. 6, 1957; children: Christopher James, Gregory John, Susan Marie. AB, Davidson Coll., 1957; MA, U. N.C., 1962, PhD, 1968. Exec. tng. program Deering-Milliken Textile Corp., Gainesville, Ga., 1957-58; history instr. Hargrave Military Acad., Chatham, Va., 1961-62, chmn., divsn. social sci., 1962-65, dean students, summer sch., 1964-65; asst. prof. history Valdosta (Ga.) State Coll., 1968-71, assoc. prof. history, 1971-78, history prof., 1978, dean, sch. arts, sci., 1970-80; pres., prof. history Coker Coll., Hartsville, S.C., 1981—; bd. dirs. Byerly Hosp., 1981-85; Sunday sch. tchr. First Presbyn. Ch. Hartsville, 1981—. Adv. bd. Nations Bank, 1988—, Pee Dee Heritage, 1982—, Darlington County Mental Health Citizens, 1987—; mins. search com. First Presbyn. Ch. Hartsville, 1984-85; com. on ministry Pee Dee Presbytery of S.C., 1985—, moderator, 1985. With U.S. Army, 1958-60. NDEA fellow, U. N.C., 1966-68; recipient Man and Boy award Valdosta Boys' Club Bd. Dirs., 1970. Mem. Greater Hartsville C. of C. (bd. dirs. 1982-88, v.p. 1986, pres. 1987, chmn. bd. 1988), Hartsville High Sch. Acad. Boosters Club and Band Boosters, Rotary (bd. dirs. 1982-99, Citizen of Yr. award 1989), Omicron Delta Kappa. Presbyterian. Avocations: reading, fishing. Home: 222 E Home Ave Hartsville SC 29550-3714 Office: Coker Coll 300 E College Ave Hartsville SC 29550-3742

DANIELS, JAMES MAURICE, physicist; b. Leeds, Eng., Aug. 26, 1924; emigrated to Can., 1953, naturalized, 1971; came to U.S., 1984, naturalized, 1992.; s. Bernard and Mary Mahala (Proctor) D.; married; children—Ian Nicolas James, Maurice Edward Bruce. BA, Oxford (Eng.) U., 1945, MA, 1949, D.Phil., 1952. Exptl. asst. Radar R & D Establishment, Malvern, Eng., 1944-46; tech. officer explosives div. Imperial Chem. Industries, Ardeer, Scotland, 1946-47; rsch. fellow Clarendon Lab., Oxford (Eng.) U., 1952-53; asst. prof. physics U. B.C., Vancouver, Can., 1953-56, assoc. prof., 1956-60; UNESCO expert U. Buenos Aires, Argentina, 1958-59; prof. U. Toronto, Can., 1961-87, prof. emeritus, 1987—, chmn. dept. physics, 1969-73; chmn. dept. stats. U. Toronto, 1983-84; vis. prof. Instituto de Fisica, S.C. de Bariloche Artentina, 1960-61, Helsinki U. Tech., 1974, Columbia U., 1978-79, Princeton U., 1984-85, Ecole Normale Superieure Paris, 1985-86, Nat. Tsing Hua U., Hsinchu, Republic of China, 1990, 91-92; vis. disting. prof. Oakland U., Rochester, Mich., 1994-95; pres. U. Toronto Faculty Assn., 1976-77; v.p. Can. Assn. Univ. Tchrs., Ottawa, 1979-80; sec., treas. Can. Inst. Particle Physics, Ottawa, 1970-73. Author: Oriented Nuclei, Polarized Targets and Beams, 1965; contbr. numerous articles to profl. jours. Alfred P. Sloan fellow, 1962-65, Guggenheim fellow, 1978-79. Fellow London Phys. Soc., London Inst. Physics (chartered physicist), London Royal Soc. Arts, Royal Soc. Can.; mem. Can. Assn. Physicists, Am. Phys. Soc., N.Y. Acad. Scis., Can. Inst. Particle Physics (sec-treas. 1971-73), Can. Assn. Univ. Tchrs. (v.p. 1977-78). Achievements include patent for Doppler Radar; first successful production of spatially oriented atomic nuclei, of compressed spin-polarized 3 He; application of the Mossbauer effect for determining spin arrangements in magnetic materials.

DANIELS, JAMES WALTER, lawyer; b. Chgo., Oct. 13, 1945; s. Ben George and Delores L. (Wolanin) D.; m. Gail Anne Rihacek, June 14, 1969; children: Morgan, Abigail, Rachel. AB, Brown U., 1967; JD, U. Chgo., 1970. Bar: Calif. 1970, U.S. Dist. Ct. (ctrl. dist.) Calif. 1970, U.S. Tax Ct., 1972, U.S. Supreme Ct. 1979. Assoc. firm Latham & Watkins, L.A. and Newport Beach, Calif., 1970-77, ptnr., 1977—; arbitrator Orange County Superior Ct., Santa Ana, Calif., 1978-88, judge pro tem, 1979-87. Fin. dir. St. Elizabeth Ann Seton Parish, Irvine, Calif., 1975-82; sec. Turtlerock Tennis Com., Irvine, 1981-83, 86—, pres., 1985-86; bd. dirs. Turtlerock Terr. Homeowners Assn., 1983-85, 87-89. Mem. ABA, Internat. Coun. Shopping Ctrs., Center club, Irvine Racquet Club, Palm Valley Country Club. Democrat. Roman Catholic. Home: 19241 Beckwith Ter Irvine CA 92612-3503 Office: Latham & Watkins 650 Town Center Dr Ste 2000 Costa Mesa CA 92626-7135

DANIELS, JEFF, actor; b. Ga., Feb. 19, 1955. Student, Cen. Mich. U. Apprentice Circle Repertory Co., N.Y.C.; exec. dir. Purple Rose Theatre Co. Actor: (stage prodns.) The Farm, 1976, My Life, 1977, Brontosaurus, 1977, Feedlot, 1977, Lulu, 1978, Slugger, 1978, The Fifth of July, 1978, 79, 80-81, Johnny Got His Gun, 1982 (Obie award), Three Sisters, 1982-83, The Golden Age, 1984, Short-Changed Review, Redwood Curtain, 1993, (feature films) Ragtime, 1981, Terms of Endearment, 1983, The Purple Rose of Cairo, 1985, Marie, 1985, Heartburn, 1986, Something Wild, 1986, Radio Days, 1987, The House on Carroll Street, 1988, Sweet Hearts Dance, 1988, Grand Tour, 1989, Checking Out, 1989, Arachnophobia, 1990, Welcome Home, Roxy Carmichael, 1990, Love Hurts, 1990, The Butcher's Wife, 1992, Gettysburg, 1993, Speed, 1994, Dumb and Dumber, 1994, Fly Away Home, 1996, 2 Days in the Valley, 1996, 101 Dalmations, 1996, Trial and Error, 1997; (TV movies) A Rumor of War, 1980, An Invasion of Privacy, 1983, The Caine Mutiny Court Marshall, 1988, No Place Like Home, 1989, Disaster in Time, 1992, Redwood Curtain, 1995; playwright: Shoeman, 1991, The Tropical Pickle, 1992, The Vast Difference, 1993, Thy Kingdom's Coming, 1994, Escanaba in da moonlight, 1995.

DANIELS, JOHN DRAPER, lawyer; b. Bklyn., Feb. 11, 1939; s. Draper L. and Louise Parker-Lux (Cort) D.; m. Sara Josephine Sears, Dec. 27, 1962; children: Stephen Draper, Elizabeth Marie, Rebecca Cort. AB, Princeton U., 1961; JD, U. Chgo., 1964. Bar: Ill. 1964, U.S. Dist. Ct. (no. dist.) Ill. 1967. Assoc. Jacobs & McKenna, Chgo., 1964-70, Law Offices Dale L. Schlafer, Chgo., 1970-73; assoc. then ptnr. Jacobs, Williams & Montgomery, Chgo., 1973-87; ptnr. Sanchez & Daniels, Chgo., 1987—; Arbitrator Cir. Ct. of Cook County. Mem. admissions screening panel Princeton Alumni Council. Capt. U.S. Army, 1964-66. Mem. ABA, Ill. Bar Assn. (chmn. ins. sect. coun.), Chgo. Bar Assn., Am. Arbitration Assn. (arbitrator 1977—), Internat. Assn. Def. Counsel, Soc. Trial Lawyers (bd. dirs. 1990, '92), Am. Bd. Trial Advs., Ill. Assn. Defense Trial Counsel, Trial Lawyers Club of Chgo., Tower of Chgo. Club (bd. trustees. 1985-87), East Bank Club. Roman Catholic. Avocations: guitar, musical composition, tennis, fishing, golf. Home: 1611 Wilmette Ave Wilmette IL 60091-2424 Office: Sanchez & Daniels 333 W Wacker Dr Chicago IL 60606-1220

DANIELS, JOHN HANCOCK, agricultural products company executive; b. St. Paul, Oct. 28, 1921; s. Thomas L. and Frances (Hancock) D.; m. Martha H. Williams, Dec. 23, 1942; children—Martha M., John Hancock, Jane P. Daniels Moffett, Christopher W. Student, St. Paul Acad., 1932-37; grad., Phillips Exeter Acad., 1939; B.A., Yale, 1943; grad., Advanced Mgmt. Program, Harvard, 1957. With Archer-Daniels-Midland Co., Mpls., 1946-96, successively mem. staff linseed oil div., prodn. mgr. alfalfa div., mgr. feed div., v.p., dir., 1946-53, pres., dir., 1958-67, chmn., 1967-72, dir., mem. exec. com., 1972-96; with Mulberry Resources Inc. Author: Nothing Could Be Finer, 1996, Affectionately H, 1999. With Bus. Council; trustee Com. Econ. Devel.; chmn. 1972 Decatur United Way Campaign; bd. dirs. Nat. Sporting Libr. Served from 2d lt. to capt. F.A., AUS, 1943-46. Decorated Bronze Star medal. Mem. Masters of Foxhounds Assn. Am., Yale Libr. Assocs. (trustee), Grolier Club, Elizabethan Club, Nat. Sporting Libr. (dir.). Republican. Episcopalian. Clubs: Links (N.Y.C.); Minneapolis; Woodhill (Minn.); Sprindale Hall (Camden, S.C.); Grolier. Home: Mulberry Plantation PO Box 549 Camden SC 29020-0549

DANIELS, JOHN PETER, lawyer; b. N.Y.C., Feb. 5, 1937; s. Jack Brainard and Isabelle (McConachie) D.; m. Lynn Eldridge, Aug. 28, 1978 (div. Jan. 1980); m. Susan Gurley, Apr. 1, 1983. AB, Dartmouth Coll., 1959; JD, U. So. Calif., Los Angeles, 1963. Bar: Calif. 1964; diplomate Am. Bd. Trial Advocates. Assoc. Bolton, Groff and Dunne, Los Angeles, 1964-67, Jones and Daniels, Los Angeles, 1967-70, Acret and Perrochet, Los Angeles, 1971-81; ptnr. Daniels, Baratta and Fine, Los Angeles, 1982—. Mem. Assn. So. Calif. Def. Counsel (bd. dirs. 1975-80), Fedn. Ins and Corp. Counsel. Club: Wilshire Country (Los Angeles). Avocations: scuba diving, golf, hunting. Office: Daniels Baratta & Fine 1801 Century Park E 9th Floor Los Angeles CA 90067

DANIELS, JONATHAN PAUL, web developer; b. Davenport, Iowa, Sept. 30, 1964; s. John Paul and Francine Roberta (Piperata) D.; children: Reece, Chase. BS in Computer Sci., Lehigh U., 1986, BS in Applied Math., 1986. Front office mgr. Westin Hotel Vail, Vail, Colo., 1987-90; cons. PC Info. Ctr., Allentown, Pa., 1991-92; analyst Rodale Press, Emmaus, Pa., 1992-94; messaging engr. Rodale Press, Emmaus, 1994-98, web engr., 1998—; cons. Rodale Inst. Exptl. Farm, Maxatawny, Pa., 1991-93; adv. East Penn Sch. Dist., Emmaus, 1995—. Democrat. Roman Catholic. Avocations: skiing, golfing, softball, dancing, Grateful Dead. Office: Rodale Press 33 E Minor St Emmaus PA 18098-0099

DANIELS, JOSEPH, neuropsychiatrist; b. Linden, N.J., Mar. 18, 1931; s. Bennie and Dora (Chese) D.; m. Shirley Perkins, July 20, 1996; children: Joan Marie, Jean Dorene. BA cum laude, Lincoln U., Oxford, Pa., 1953; MD, Howard U., 1957. Rotating enter Med. Ctr. Jersey City, 1957-58; resident in internal medicine Worcester (Mass.) City Hosp., 1958-59; resident in psychiatry Ancora (N.J.) Hisp., 1962-65; dir. outpatient clinic Christian Health Care Ctr., Wyckoff, N.J., 1966-70; dir. outpatient dept. Community Mental Health Ctr., N.J. Coll. Medicine, Newark, 1970-79; med. dir., pres. Ctr. for Growth and Reconciliation, East Orange, N.J., 1979-87; sr. staff psychiatrist Pine Rest Christian Hosp., Grand Rapids, Mich., 1987-96; cons. Kent County Cmty. Mental Health Ctr., Grand Rapids, 1996—; mem. Healthy Kent 2000 Health Com., 1993-94; cons. psychiatrist Newark Bd. Edn., 1976-84, East Orange Bd. Edn., Victory House, Newark, 1976-82, Project Rehab, Grand Rapids, 1990-91. Author: The Urban Mission, 1974. Founder, pres., chmn. bd. Ministry Reconciliation Fellowship, 1980-87; bd. dirs. Grand Rapids Reach Inc., pres., 1991-93; selected mem. Leadership Grand Rapids, 1993-94. Capt. M.C., U.S. Army, 1959-62. Fulbright Sr. scholarship fellow U. Zimbabwe Sch. of Medicine, 1998-99. Mem. Beta Kappa Chi. Baptist. Avocations: sports, writing, reeading, volunteering. Office: Kent County Cmty Mental Health Ctr Lakeside Dr Grand Rapids MI 49501-0165

DANIELS, KEITH ALLEN, materials engineering manager; b. Rantoul, Ill., June 4, 1956; s. Harcourt Albert Jr. and Alice Patricia Daniels. BS in Chemistry, U. Rochester, 1978; MS in Materials Sci. and Engring., U. Fla., 1988. Chemist Chem-tronics, Inc., El Cajon, Calif., 1982-85; rsch. engr. Dow Chem. Co., Freeport, Tex., 1988-91; rsch. assoc. LipoMatrix, Inc., Palo Alto, Calif., 1992-94; devel. engr. Cygnus, Inc., Redwood City, Calif., 1995-97; materials engrng. mgr. Duke Sci. Corp., Palo Alto, 1997—. Author: (poetry) What Rough Book, 1992 (Fallot Lit. award), Loopy is the Inner Ear, 1993, Dyscrasias: Selected Poems, 1997, Notes from the Antipodes, 1997, Satan is a Mathematician, 1998 (Rhysling award); editor: With All of Love: Selected Poems by James Blish, 1995, Arthur C. Clarke and Lord Dunsany: A Correspondence, 1998. Lt. USN, 1978-82. Mem. Am. Chem. Soc., Soc. Plastics Engrs. Avocations: hiking, camping, canoeing, rockhounding, writing. E-mail: anamnesis@compuserv.com. Office: Anamnesis Press PO Box 51115 Palo Alto CA 94303

DANIELS, KURT R., speech and language pathologist; b. Chgo., Oct. 22, 1954; s. Donald R. and Phyllis D. (Lenz) D.; m. Renee Perry, July 5, 1980. BS, Ea. Ill. U., 1976, MS, 1977. Cert. clin. competence speech/lang. pathology; lic. speech/lang. pathologist, nursing home adminstr; tchr's. cert. spl. K-12th grades. Hearing and speech specialist Shapiro Devel. Ctr., Kankakee, Ill., 1977-80; dysphagia specialist lead prof. W.A. Howe Devel. Ctr., Tinley Pk., Ill., 1980—; mem. adv. bd. program in comm. disorders Govs. State U., clin. adj. prof.; cons. in field; presenter in field of dysphagia and developmental disabilities. Recipient Editor's Choice award Nat. Libr. Poetry, 1994, 95. Mem. Am. Speech, Lang. and Hearing Assn., Ill. Speech, Lang. and Hearing Assn., Ill. Network for Augmentative and Alternative Comm., Internat. Soc. Poets, Chicagoland Dysphagia Forum (sec.). Office: Howe Clinics WA Howe Devel Ctr 7600 W 183d St Tinley Park IL 60477

DANIELS, LACY, microbiology educator; b. Mineral Wells, Tex., Mar. 2, 1950; s. Clay Clarence and Daisy Leota (Lacy) D.; m. Frances Marie Ufkes, May 23, 1984. B.A., U. Tex., 1972; M.S., U. Wis., 1974, Ph.D., 1978. Postdoctoral fellow U. Nijmegen, Netherlands, 1978; NIH fellow U. Wis., Madison, 1979-80, MIT, Cambridge, 1980-81; asst. prof. microbiology U. Iowa, Iowa City, 1981-86, assoc. prof., 1987-92, prof., 1993—; vis. scientist, World Bank project IX, U. Indonesia, Jakarta, 1985—; biotech. coordinator World Bank Project XVII, Indonesia, 1987-92. Contbr. articles to profl. jours. Fellow Am. Acad. Microbiology; mem. Am. Soc. Microbiology, Am. Chem. Soc., Am. Inst. Chem. Engrs., Phi Beta Kappa. Avocations: travel; camping. Office: U Iowa Dept Microbiology Iowa City IA 52242

DANIELS, LEGREE S., federal agency administrator. Student, Temple U.; LHD (hon.), Clark Atlanta U. Dep. sec. Commonwealth of Pa.; commr. election Pa. Dept. of State; asst. sec. civil Rights U.S. Dept. Edn.; bd. govs. U.S. Postal Svc., Washington, 1990—; past vice chmn. Nat. Electoral Coll. Past mem. Middle Atlanta Adv. Bd., U.S. Civil Rights Commn., Rep. Nat. Com., Pres.'s Commn. White House Fellows, Army Sci. Bd., Nat. Endowment for Democracy; bd. advisors Penn State, Harrisburg; bd. dirs. Ctr. Internat. Pvt. Enterprise, U.S. C. of C., John Heinz Harrisburg Sr. Ctr. Office: US Post Office 475 Lenfant Plz SW Washington DC 20260-0004*

DANIELS, MADELINE MARIE, psychotherapist, author; b. Newark, Oct. 14, 1948; d. William and Dorothy Barlow; m. Peter W. Daniels, Oct. 18, 1976 (div. July 27, 1988); children: Jonathan, Jedediah, Jeremiah. BA cum laude, CCNY, 1971; PhD, Union Grad. Sch., Yellow Springs, Ohio, 1975, Union Grad. Sch., Cin., 1988. Diplomate Am. Bd. Forensic Examiners. Lectr. Westchester C.C., 1973-74, Bronx (N.Y.) C.C., Purchase, 1973-74; mem. adj. faculty SUNY, Purchase, 1974-76; data processing coord. GTE Internat., 1976-78; lectr. divsn. continuing edn. U. N.H., 1979-87; exec. dir. Crossroads Ctr. Human Integration, East Kingston, N.H., 1979-88; adminstr. Spectrum Cross-Cultural Inst. Youth Inc., East Kingston, 1988-96; rsch./comm. cons. Metis Assocs., No. Calif., 1994-96; registered psychol. asst. with Dr. Harper Eureka, Calif., 1996—; lectr. Humboldt State U., 1998—; staff psychologist region III Parole Outpatient Clinic, Calif. Dept. Corrections, Eureka Station, 1998—; lectr., cons. in field. Cert. ind. biofeedback practitioner, clin. mental health counselor. Author: Realistic Leadership, 1983, Living Your Religion in the Real World, 1985, A Culturally Different Perspective on Psychology, 1989, (video) The Rainbow Classroom, 1991. Mem. APA, Am. Coll. Forensic Examiners, Internat. Coun. Psychologists (area chair 1988), Biofeedback Soc. Am., Soc. Psychol. Anthropology, N.H. Psychol. Orgn., Phi Beta Kappa. Office: Offices of Thomas Harper MD 350 E St Ste 301 Eureka CA 95501-0351

DANIELS, PRESTON A., mayor; b. Des Moines. B in Psychology, Drake U., MS in Health Sci. and Counseling. Probation officer 5th jud. dist. Dept. Corrections, tech. assistance to comty.-based programs; dir. ct. and comty. rels. Employee and Family Resources Iowa Managed Substance Abuse Care Plan; city councilman at large Des Moines, mayor; chmn. Des Moines Police Subcom. Mem. U. Iowa Adv. Bd. for Addiction Tech. Transfer Ctr.; mem. Tng. Adv. Bd. for Substance Abuse, State of Iowa; pres. Drake Neighborhood Assn.; active numerous neighborhood activities. Sgt. U.S. Army. Named Hon. Lt. Col. Ala. State Guard. Office: 400 E 1st St Des Moines IA 50309

DANIELS, RICHARD MARTIN, public relations executive; b. Delano, Calif., Feb. 24, 1942; s. Edward Martin and Philida Rose (Peterson) D.; m. Kathryn Ellen Knight, Feb. 28, 1976; children: Robert Martin, Michael Edward. A.A., Foothill Coll., 1965; B.A., San Jose State U., 1967; M.A., U. Mo., 1971. News reporter Imperial Valley Press, El Centro, Calif., summers 1963-66, San Diego (Calif.) Evening Tribune, 1967-68, Columbia Daily Tribune (Mo.), 1969-70; nat. news copy editor Los Angeles Times, 1966-67; staff writer San Diego Union, 1971-74, real estate editor, 1974-77; v.p. pub. relations Hubbert Advt. & Pub. Relations, Costa Mesa, Calif., 1977-78; ptnr. Berkman & Daniels, San Diego, 1979-91; prin. Nuffer, Smith, Tucker, Inc.,

1991-94; prin. RMD Comms., 1994-97; exec. dir. comms. San Diego City Schs., 1997—; lectr. various bus. groups and colls., Chmn. bd. dirs. March of Dimes San Diego County, 1984-87; bd. dirs. Nat. Coun. Vols., 1983-91. Served with USN, 1959-62. Mem. Pub. Rels. Soc. Am., Counselors Acad. (accredited). Republican. Office: 2261 Ritter Pl Escondido CA 92029-5608

DANIELS, ROBERT PAUL, special education administrator; b. Grand Junction, Colo., July 23, 1948; s. Paul R. and Joyce (Tew) D.; m. Gloria Linge, Sept. 24, 1968; children: Natalie, Kimberly, Emily, Robilyn. BS, Utah State U., 1970, MS, 1973; postgrad., U. Utah, 1975-78, U.S. Army War Coll., 1995. Cert. pub. adminstr., supr., tchr. Tchr. Viewmont High Sch., Bountiful, Utah, 1971-74; dir. Davis County Devel. Ctr., Farmington, Utah, 1974-81; exec. dir. Pioneer Adult Rehab. Ctr., Clearfield, Utah, 1981—; mem. adv. bd. Rehab. Tng. Project, Greeley, Colo., 1987-93; bd. mem. Nat. Industries for the Severely Handicapped, Vienna, Va., 1990—, chmn. bd. dirs. 1998—; Nat. Security fellow JFK Sch. Govt., Harvard U., 1994. Author: Integration of Special Education, 1989. Col. Utah Army Nat. Guard, 1970—. Recipient Golden Key, Utah Gov. Com., Salt Lake City, 1983, awards Utah Assn. Rehab. Facilities, Salt Lake City, 1986, Utah Rehab. Assn., Salt Lake City, 1989. Mem. Rotary (bd. mem. 1991). Mormon. Avocation: jogging. Office: Pioneer Adult Rehab Ctr 485 Parc Cir Clearfield UT 84015-1720

DANIELS, ROBERT SANFORD, psychiatrist, administrator; b. Indpls., Aug. 12, 1927; s. Harry H. and Mary (Bassett) D.; m. Vikki Ashley; children: Stephen, Allen, Lynn, Judith. BS, U. Cin., 1948, MD, 1951. Intern Cin. Gen. Hosp., 1951; resident U. Cin. Hosp., 1954-57; mem. faculty U. Chgo., 1957-71, dir. psychiat. cons. service, 1961-63, asso. prof. psychiatry, acting chmn. dept., 1963-66, clin. dir., 1966-68, asso. dean community and social medicine, 1968-71, prof. psychiatry and social medicine, 1970-71; dir. Center Health Adminstrn. Studies, Grad. Sch. Bus., 1970-71; dir. dept. psychiatry U. Cin., 1971-75; interim dean U. Cin. (Coll. Medicine), 1972-75; dean Coll. Medicine, U. Cin., 1975-86, also sr. v.p., 1982-86; dean La. State U. Sch. Medicine, New Orleans, 1986-95, exec. asst. to chancellor, 1995—; chief staff Cin. Gen. Hosp., 1972-86, Holmes Hosp., 1972-86; vis. prof. social medicine and clin. epidemiology St. Thomas' Hosp. Med. Coll., London, Eng.; sci. exchange visitor Ministry Health, Moscow, USSR; vis. scholar King Edward VII Hosp. Fund, London, 1977; cons. Cook County Hosp., Ill. State Psychiat. Inst.; spl. research community and group psychiatry, health planning, community health, 1967-69; Chmn. Ill. Mental Health Planning Bd.; mem., chmn. rev. com., psychiatry edn. br. Health Services and Mental Health Adminstrn., 1971-75; mem. nat. mental health adv. bd. NIMH, 1975-79; bd. dirs. Hamilton County Bd. Mental Health and Retardation, 1974-78. Asso. editor: Social Psychiatry. Bd. dirs. Central Ohio River Valley Planning Authority, 1979—. Served with AUS, 1946-47; Served with USAF, 1952-54. Recipient Stella Feis Hoffheimer award U. Cin., 1951. Mem. AMA, Am. Psychiat. Assn., Am. Group Psychotherapy Assn., Assn. Am. Med. Colls. (exec. coun. 1982-87, psychiatry residency rev. coun. 1990—, Daniel Drake medal 1988), Ill. Group Psychotherapy Soc. (pres. 1965-66), Ill. Psychiat. Soc. (pres. 1967), Phi Beta Kappa, Alpha Omega Alpha. Office: La State U Sch Medicine Office of the Chancellor 433 Bolivar St Rm 820 New Orleans LA 70112-2223*

DANIELS, ROBERT VINCENT, history educator, former state senator; b. Boston, Jan. 4, 1926; s. Robert Whiting and Helen Underwood (Hoyt) D.; m. Alice May Wendell, July 2, 1945; children: Robert H., Helen L. Turcotte, Irene L., Thomas L. AB, Harvard U., 1945, MA, 1947, PhD, 1951; LLD (hon.), U. Vt., 1994. Rsch. assoc. MIT, 1951-52; social sci. faculty Bennington Coll., 1952-53, 57-58; asst. prof. Slavic studies Ind. U., 1953-55; rsch. assoc. Columbia U., 1955-56; from asst. prof. history to prof. U. Vt., Burlington, 1956-88; prof. emeritus U. Vt., 1988—, chmn. dept., 1964-69, dir. exptl. program, 1969-71; mem. Vt. Senate, 1973-82, asst. minority leader, 1977-80, minority leader, 1981-82; chmn. Vt. Gov.'s Commn. Med. Care, 1974-75; mem. Vt. Health Policy Corp., 1977-80; mem. adv. com. on East Europe and USSR, Coun. on Internat. Exch. of Scholars, 1983-85; adv. coun. Ctr. for Internat. Polit. Studies, Rome, 1989—; adv. com. Vt.-Karelia, 1991—, co-dir. self-govt. tng. program, 1993-94; dir. U. Vt. Petrozavodsk U. partnership program, 1994-95. Author: The Conscience of the Revolution, 1960, Documentary History of Communism, 1960, rev. edit., 1993, The Nature of Communism, 1962, Studying History, 1966, Red October, 1967, The Russian Revolution, 1972, Fodor's Europe Talking, 1975, Russia-The Roots of Confrontation, 1985, Is Russia Reformable?, 1988, Year of the Heroic Guerrilla, 1989, Trotsky, Stalin and Socialism, 1992, The End of the Communist Revolution, 1993, Soviet Communism from Reform to Collapse, 1994, Russia's Transformation, 1997; editor: The University of Vermont: The First Two Hundred Years, 1991. Mem. Chittenden County (Vt.) Dem. Com., 1959—; mem. Burlington City Dem. Com., 1965—; chmn. policy and planning platform com. Vt. Dem. Party, 1962-66, 69-73, 76-80, mem. exec. com., 1981-85; alt. Dem. Nat. Conv., 1968; mem. Dem. Platform Com., 1980; bd. visitors USAF Acad., 1965-67. Ensign USNR, 1944-46. U.S.-Soviet Cultural Exchange scholar U. Moscow, 1966, USSR Acad. Scis. scholar, 1976, 84, 88; NEH fellow, 1971-72, Guggenheim fellow, 1980-81, Kennan Inst. fellow, 1985. Fellow Vt. Acad. Arts & Scis.; mem. Am. Hist. Assn. (pres. conf. Slavic and East European history 1976-77), Am. Assn. Advancement Slavic Studies (bd. dirs. 1968-71, v.p. 1991, pres. 1992, chmn. com. on govt. affairs 1993-94), Can. Assn. Slavists, Authors' Guild, Vt. Hist. Soc. (trustee 1968-71), Vt. Coun. World Affairs, Norwich Ctr./Bridges for Peace (bd. dirs. 1988-94), Harvard Club Vt. (pres. 1974-75). Home: 195 S Prospect St Burlington VT 05401-3519 Office: University of Vermont Dept of History Burlington VT 05405

DANIELS, RONALD DALE, conductor; b. San Mateo, Calif., Aug. 19, 1943; s. Worth W. and Margurite Pearl (Chandler) D.; m. Judith Monson, July 24, 1993; 1 child, Ryan Stark. BMus, San Francisco Conservatory, 1968. Conductor, music dir. Musical Arts of Contra Costa (Calif.) County, 1968-75, U. Calif., Berkeley, 1973-75, Contra Costa Symphony, 1976-79; conductor, music dir. Reno (Nev.) Philharm., 1979-98, conductor Laureate, 1998—; guest conductor various orchs.; grants rev. cons. in field. With USMC, 1966. Recipient Lucien Wulsin award Baldwin Piano Co., Tanglewood Festival, 1968, Gov.'s Art award State of Nev., 1981. Avocations: ice skating, skiing, sailing, hiking. Office: Reno Philharm Assn 300 S Wells Ave Ste 5 Reno NV 89502-1670

DANIELS, RONALD GEORGE, theater director; b. Niteroi, Rio de Janiero, Brazil, Oct. 15, 1942; came to U.S., 1991; s. Percy and Nellie (Chalmers) D.; m. Anjula Harman; children: Alexis, Eliena. Student, Fundacão Brasileira de Teatro, Rio de Janiero. Assoc. artistic dir. Am. Reperatory Theatre, Cambridge, Mass., 1991-96; head acting and directing programs Inst. for Advanced Theatre Tng. Harvard U., 1991-96; hon. assoc. dir. Royal Shakespeare Co., Stratford-upon-Avon, London; lectr. Shakespeare Inst., U. Birmingham, Friends Royal Shakespeare Co., others. Dir.: (stage prodns.) Coriolanus, Major Barbara, Who's Afraid of Virginia Wolf, Sweeney Todd, Ghosts, Hamlet, Drums in the Night, The Samaritan, Time Travelers, The Long and Short and the Tall, The Word, Measure for Measure, Fear and Miseries of the Third Reich, The Insect Play, Twelfth Night, A Midsummer Night's Dream, Pillars of the Community, Man is Man, The Children's Crusade, Female Transport, Sgt. Musgrave's Dance, Into the Mouth of Crabs, By Common Consent, The Motor Show, Made in Britain, Bang, Afore Night Come, Bingo, Puntila and His Servant Matti, Ivanov, Destiny, T'is Pity She's a Whore, The Lorenzaccio Story, The Sons of Light, Pericles, The Suicide, Timon of Athens, Hippolytus, Camille, Hansel and Gretel, Peer Gynt, Romeo and Juliet, Ashes, The Beastly Beatitudes of Balthazar B, Across from the Garden of Allah, Playing with Trains, The Tempest, Julius Cesar, Maydays, Breaking the Silence, The Danton Affair, The Women Pirates, Real Dreams, They Shoot Horses, Much Ado About Nothing, The Plain Dealer, The Clockwork Orange, Earwig, Richard II, The Seagull, As You Like It, The Dream of The Red Spider, Silence, Cunning, Exile, Cakewalk, Henry IV parts I and II, The Cherry Orchard, Henry V, The Threepenny Opera, The Tempest, Slaughter City, Long Day's Journey into Night, Blinded by the Sun, Anthony and Cleopatra, The Shepherd King, One Flea Spare, Madama Butterfly, Henry V and Richard II, Richard III, Macbeth, Remember This. Mem. Soc. Stage Dirs. and Choreographers, Dir.'s Guild Gt. Britain.

DANIELS, STEPHEN M., government official; b. Boston, Mar. 28, 1947; s. Everett Jerome and Helen Dorothy (Ettinger) D.; m. Maygene Louise Frost, June 25, 1972; children—Edward Frost, Leah Lillian. B.A., Yale U., 1968, J.D., 1972. Bar: Calif. 1972, D.C. 1973, U.S. Supreme Ct. 1980. Asst. to asst. sec. for legislation HEW, Washington, 1969-70; legislative analyst U.S. Office of Mgmt. and Budget, Washington, 1971; legislative asst. to Congressman U.S. Ho. Reps., Washington, 1972-73, with Com. on Govt. Ops., 1973-87, minority counsel Com. on Govt. Ops., 1980-87, minority staff dir. Com. on Govt. Ops., 1984-87; bd. contract appeals GSA, Washington, 1987—, chmn., 1992—. Commr. Congl. Softball League, Washington, 1977-81; pres. Capitol East Children's Ctr., Washington, 1982-83; trustee Capitol Hill Day Sch., Washington, 1988-92. Served to capt. USAR, 1970-71. Mem. ABA, Fed. Bar Assn., D.C. Bar Assn., Calif. Bar Assn. Avocations: baseball, home restoration, camping, bicycling. Home: 816 Massachusetts Ave NE Washington DC 20002-6016 Office: 1800 F St NW Washington DC 20405-0002

DANIELS, SUSAN M., commissioner. BA magna cum laude, Marquette U.; MS, Miss. State U.; PhD in Ednl. Psychology, U. N.C. Prof., head dept. Sch. Allied Health Professions, La. State U. Med. Ctr., New Orleans, 1978-88; assoc. commr. Rehab. Svcs. Adminstrn., Dept. Edn., Washington, 1988-91; assoc. commr. Adminstrn. on Devel. Disabilities, Dept. HHS, Washington, 1991-94; assoc. commr. Disability, Social Security Adminstrn., Washington, 1994, dep. commr. Disability and Income Security Programs,; spkr. in field. Avocations: reading, movies, playing cards, theater, travel. Office: Social Security Adminstrn Office Dep Commr 6401 Security Blvd Baltimore MD 21235-0001

DANIELS, WILLIAM ALBERT, food products executive; b. Westboro, Mass., Dec. 7, 1937; s. Roy Oliver and Florine (Francesco) D.; m. Anne Farrell Richardson, Apr. 15, 1967; children: Paul, Kimberly, David. Student, Boston U., 1959-61. Lic. real estate broker. Pres. W.A. Daniels Real Estate Co., Peabody, Mass., 1959-64; with sales Sears, Roebuck and Co., Saugus, Mass., 1964-67; pres. Antech Chem. Co., Middleton, Mass., 1968-78; treas., co-owner Richardson Farms Inc., Middleton, 1978—; corporator Danvers (Mass.) Sav. Bank, 1984—. Mem. New Eng. Ice Cream Retailers Assn., Nat. Trust for Hist. Preservation, Middleton Hist. Soc. Republican. Roman Catholic. Home: 105 Flint Farm Rd Middleton MA 01949-2491 Office: Richardson Farm Inc 156 S Main St Middleton MA 01949-2452

DANIELS, WILLIAM BURTON, physicist, educator; b. Buffalo, Dec. 21, 1930; s. William C. and Sophia (Penner) D.; m. Adriana A. Braakman, Sept. 2, 1958; children: Charlotte Mary, William Fredrik, Donald Christopher. BS in Physics, U. Buffalo, 1952; MS, Case Inst. Tech., 1955; PhD, Case Int. Tech., 1957. Instr. to asst. prof. Case Inst. Tech., 1957-59; rsch. scientist Union Carbide Corp., 1959-61; mem. faculty Princeton U., 1961-72, prof. solid state scis., 1967-72; Unidel prof. physics U. Del., Newark, 1972—; rsch. collaborator Brookhaven nat. Lab.; cons. U.S. Army Rsch. Lb.; guest scientist rsch. facility, Denmark, 1976; invité Coll. France, 1977; exch. prof. U. Paris, 1977; guest scientist IBM Zurich Lab., 1977; guest scientist Max Planck Inst. for Festkörperforschung. Recipient Alexander von Humboldt Sr. Scientist award, 1981, 92; John S. Guggenheim Meml. fellow, 1976-77. Fellow Am. Phys. Soc. Rsch. and publs. properties materials at high pressure, equation of state of solids, experimentation on solidified permanent gases, electronic structure of compressed solids, instrumentation high pressure rsch., non-linear optics. Office: U Del Dept of Physics Newark DE 19716

DANIELS, WORTH BAGLEY, JR., retired internist; b. N.Y.C., Jan. 3, 1925. MD, Johns Hopkins U., 1948. From asst. med. rschr. to rschr. Balt. City Hosp., 1954-57; physician, assoc. prof. Johns Hopkins U., 1958—; ret. Mem. AMA, ACP, Inst. Medicine-NAS, Am. Soc. Internal Medicine. Home: 210 Ridgewood Rd Baltimore MD 21210-2539*

DANIELSON, DAVID GORDON, health science facility administrator, general legal counsel; b. Minot, N.D., Dec. 18, 1954; s. Gordon Everett and Myla Eunice (Torgerson) D.; m. Lisbeth Annette Roehrich, June 9, 1979; children: Michael, Katherine, Laura, Anna, Emily. BSBA, U. N.D., 1977, JD, 1980; postdoctoral, U. Minn., 1980-82. Bar: N.D. 1980, U.S. Dist. Ct. N.D. 1983, U.S. Ct. Appeals (8th cir.) 1998; CPA, Minn., N.D. Tax specialist Deloitte, Haskins & Sells, Mpls., 1980-82, Eide Helmeke and Co., Fargo, N.D., 1982-84; exec. adminstr. Med. Arts Clinic, Minot, 1984-96; exec. dir. Phy Cor, Minot, 1996-98; chief adminstrv. officer Ctrl. Plains Clinic, Ltd., Sioux Falls, S.D., 1999—; exec. v.p. Teamcare, Inc., Minot, 1990-96, also bd. dirs.; gen. legal counsel Magic City Fin. Group, Inc., South Park Fin. Group, Inc.; gen. legal counsel Key Care Investment Co., also bd. dirs.; bd. dirs. Credit Bur. Minot; mem. electronic data interchange planning commn. State of N.D.; mem. dean's coun. Coll. Bus., Minot State U., mem. bd. regents, 1994-98. Bd. dirs. Domestic Violence Crisis Ctr., 1984-87, Minot Area C. of C., 1995-98, v.p.; mem. planning commn. City Minot, 1995-98; bd. dirs. Minot Pub. Libr., 1998. Mem. AICPA (area IV planning com. 1994-96), N.D. Soc. CPAs (chmn. legis. com. 1986-88, 94-97), N.D. Bar Assn. (CLE com. 1982-96), Am. Health Lawyers Assn., N.D. Med. Group Mgmt. Assn. (bd. dirs., legis. com., pres.-elect 1997-98), S.D. Med. Group Mgmt. Assn., Lambda Chi Alpha, Elks. Avocations: racquetball, reading, computers. Home: 719 E Inverness Dr Sioux Falls SD 57108

DANIELSON, GARY R., lawyer; b. Detroit, June 8, 1953; s. Ronald Gregory and Catherine (Gibson) D. BA in Psychology, Oakland U., Rochester, Mich., 1976; JD cum laude, Wayne State U., 1983. Bar: Mich. 1983, U.S. Dist. Ct. (ea. dist.) Mich., 1985, U.S. Supreme Ct. 1987. Sr. job placement counselor Ferndale (Mich.) Sch. Dist., 1976-79; employment and tng. adminstr. Oakland County Govt., Pontiac, Mich., 1979-82; sr. corp. labor rels. rep. Harper-Grace Hosps., Detroit, 1982-83; corp. labor rels. mgr. Vis. Nurse Assn., Detroit, 1983-85; atty., v.p., cons. Indsl. Rels., Inc., Detroit, 1985-90; pres. The Danielson Group, P.C., St. Clair Shores, 1990—. Pres., bd. dirs. St. Clair on Lake Condominium Assn., St. Clair Shores, Mich., 1987—. Mem. ABA, Mich. Bar Assn., Hosp. Pers. Adminstrs. Assn., Indsl. Rels. Rsch. Assn. Republican. Avocation: sailing. Office: Danielson Group PC 27735 Jefferson Ave Saint Clair Shores MI 48081-1309

DANIELSON, GORDON KENNETH, JR., cardiovascular surgeon, educator; b. Burlington, Iowa, Dec. 5, 1931; s. Gordon Kenneth and Helen H. (Hill) D.; m. Sondra Jean Bolich, Jan. 21, 1961; children: Gordon Kenneth III, Laura, Karen, Keith, Bruce, Susan, Jennifer. BA in Chemistry, U. Pa., 1953, M.D. (Pfizer, Senatorial, Clark scholar, Albert Einstein award 1956, Roche award 1956, Spencer Morris prize 1956), 1956, postgrad., 1960. Diplomate Am. Bd. Surgery, Am. Bd. Thoracic Surgery. Intern U. Mich. Hosp., Ann Arbor, 1956-57; asst. resident in surgery Hosp. of U. Pa., 1957-61, chief resident in surgery, 1961-62, gen. and thoracic surgeon, 1962-65, asst. chief surg. div. I, 1962-65; vis. fellow in thoracic surgery Thorax Kliniken, Stockholm, 1963-64; practice medicine specializing in thoracic and cardiovascular surgery Phila., 1963-65, Lexington, Ky., 1965-67, Rochester, Minn., 1967—; assoc. prof. surgery U. Ky. Med. Sch.; also chief cardiac surgery Univ. Hosp., 1965-67; mem. faculty Mayo Grad. Sch. Medicine, Rochester, Minn., 1967—, prof. surgery, 1975—, Joe M. and Ruth Roberts prof. surgery, 1987—; past chmn. divsn. thoracic and cardiovascular surgery, cons. cardiovascular and thoracic surgery Mayo Clinic/Mayo Found., 1967—, St. Mary's Hosp., Meth. Hosp., Rochester, 1967—; Am. Heart Assn. vis. tchr., Singapore, 1975, Amman, Jordan, 1981. Editor Cardiovascular Surgery, 1972-78; contbr. numerous articles to med. jours. Markle scholar in acad. medicine, 1962-67. Fellow ACS, Am. Coll. Cardiology; mem. Am. Assn. Thoracic Surgery, Am. Surg. Assn., Am. Heart Assn. (fellow coun. cardiovascular surgery), Soc. Thoracic Surgeons (a founder), Soc. Univ. Surgeons, Soc. Vascular Surgery, Mexican Soc. Cardiology (hon.), Assn. Thoracic and Cardiovascular Surgeons of Asia (hon.), India (hon.), Chile Soc. Cardiology and Cardiovascular Surgery (hon.), Colombian Soc. of Cardiology (hon.), Congenital Heart Surgeons Soc., Phi Beta Kappa, Alpha Omega Alpha. 1st fellow in congenital heart disease U.S.-USSR Health Exchange Program, 1973. Home: 6000 16th Ave NW Rochester MN 55901-2107 Office: Mayo Med Ctr 200 1st St SW Rochester MN 55905-0001

DANIELSON, JAMES WALTER, research microbiologist; b. Miller, S.D., June 6, 1940; s. Walter Henry and Florence Marie (Manning) D. BS, S.D. State U., 1968. Microbiologist FDA, Mpls., 1969-80, rsch. microbiologist, 1980—. Contbr. articles to profl. jours. including Jour. Parenteral Sci. Tech., Jour. Chromat. Sci., Jour. Assn. Official Analytical Chemists, Jour. Chromat. Recipient Pub. Health Svc. Spl. Recognition award, Washington, 1988. Mem. Assn. Official Analytical Chemists, Am. Soc. Microbiology. Democrat. Roman Catholic. Achievements include determination of effects of disinfectants on dialyzer membranes and development of methods for detecting ethylene oxide residuals in plastics and other materials; determining leached compounds from rubber and plastic in parenteral solutions; sporicidal testing of germicides and determination of glutaraldehyde and phenol in germicides. Avocations: dancing, tennis, volleyball. Home: 5925 Halifax Ave N Minneapolis MN 55429-2424 Office: FDA 240 Hennepin Ave Minneapolis MN 55401-1999

DANIELSON, URSEL REHDING, psychiatrist; b. Hamburg, Germany, Aug. 15, 1935; came to U.S., 1954; d. Martin George and Gerda Maria (Muller) Rehding; 1 child, Richard. BS, U. Vt., 1964, MD, 1967. Diplomate Am. Bd. Psychiatry and Neurology. Intern Robert Packer Hosp., Sayre, Pa., 1967-68; resident in psychiatry U. Vt., Burlington, 1968-71; chief resident McGill U. and Children's Hosp., Montreal, Quebec, Can., 1971-72; pvt. practice Burlington, 1972-86; med. dir. Vt. State Hosp., Waterbury, 1986-90; child psychiatrist Dept. Psychiatry U. Vt., Burlington, 1990-94, pvt. practice, Burlington, 1994—; cons. Franklin Grand Isle Mental Health Ctr., St. Albans, Vt., 1982-86, Essex Junction Sch. Sys., 1982-86, Chittenden Ctrl. Sch. Dist., 1972-86, Weeks Sch., Vergennes, 1972-80, Ogdensburg (N.Y.) State Hosp. Children's Svcs., 1980-84; asst. prof. dept. psychiatry U. Vt., Burlington, 1972-86, assoc. prof., 1986—, supr. psychiat. residents, 1972-98. Treas., dir. Providence Island Assocs., South Hero, Vt., 1988—; mem. Bd. Mental Health of State of Vt., 1992-98. Fellow APA; mem. Vt. Psychiat. Assn. (chair nominating com. 1984, 85, 88—, pres. 1985-86, rep. to APA assembly and area coun. 1978-84, 89-90). Avocations: boating, skiing, gardening, hiking, movies. Home: 29 Biscayne Hts Colchester VT 05446-1612

DANIELSON, WAYNE ALLEN, journalism and computer science educator; b. Burlington, Iowa, Dec. 6, 1929; s. Arthur Leroy and Bessie Ann (Bonar) D.; m. Beverly Grace Kinsell, Mar. 19, 1955 (dec. Oct. 1988); children: Matthew Henry, Benjamin Wayne, Grace Frances, Paul Arthur; m. LaVonne Walker Caffey, July 10, 1993; stepchildren: Kristin Marie, Bradley Neal. B.A., State U. Iowa, 1952; M.A., Stanford U., 1953, Ph.D., 1957. Reporter, research mgr. San Jose (Calif.) Mercury-News, 1953-54; acting asst. prof. Stanford U., 1956-57; asst. prof. journalism U. Wis., 1957-59; mem. faculty U. N.C., 1959-69, prof. journalism, 1963-69; research prof. Inst. Research Social Sci., 1963-69; dean Sch. Journalism, 1964-69; dean Sch. Communication, U. Tex. at Austin, 1969-79, prof. journalism and computer sci., 1969—, Jesse H. Jones prof. journalism, 1982-89; Dewitt C. Reddick chair, 1989; chmn. dept. journalism U. Tex. at Austin, 1991-93; mem. steering com. News Research Center, Am. Newspaper Pubs. Assn., 1964-73; mem. research com. AP Mng. Editors Assn., 1963-69. Author: (with G. C. Wilhoit, Jr.) A Computerized Bibliography of Mass Communication Research, 1944-64, (with Blanche Prejean) Programed News Style, 1977, 2d edit., 1988; contbr. articles to profl. jours.; founding editor: Journalism Abstracts, 1963-68, 71; mem. editorial bd. Journalism Quar, 1964-72; author, editor instructional computer program series. Mem. pub. rels. com. N.C. Heart Assn., 1963-67; chmn. faculty senate U. Tex., 1989-90. Mem. Assn. Edn. Journalism and Mass Comm. (chmn. publs. com. 1968-72, rsch. com. 1980-83, pres. 1970-71, Paul J. Deutschmann award 1993), Am. Assn. Schs. and Depts. Journalism (v.p. 1966-67, pres. 1967-68), Tex. Journalism Edn. Coun. (chmn. 1970-71), Phi Beta Kappa, Kappa Tau Alpha, Phi Kappa Phi. Office: U Tex Dept Journalism Austin TX 78712

DANIHER, JOHN M., retired engineer; b. LaJunta, Colo., Aug. 2, 1926; s. Gerald and Mary Isabelle (Manly) D.; m. Edna Erle Hoshall, Sept. 4, 1948; children: Lyn Mari, Suzanne Laurie, Patricia Gail, Jerome Matthew, Michael Kevin. AB, Western State Coll., Gunnison, Colo., 1948; postgrad. Idaho State U., 1957-74, U. Idaho, 1974-76. High sch. tchr., Grand Junction, Colo., 1948-52; salesman Century Metalcraft, Denver, 1952-53; chem. plant supr. U.S. Chem. Corps., Denver, 1953-56; sr. engr. instrument and controls Phillips Petroleum Co., Idaho Falls, 1956-76; project engr. E G & G Idaho, Idaho Falls, 1976-85, engrng. specialist, 1985-91; adv. Eastern Idaho Vocat. Tech. Sch., 1975-80. Cubmaster, Boy Scouts Am., 1970-75, asst. scoutmaster, 1975-80; v.p. Bonneville Unit Am. Cancer Soc., 1994, pres., v.p., 1995—. Recipient Cub Man of Yr., Boy Scouts Am., 1973. Mem. Am. Nuclear Soc. Roman Catholic. Club: K.C. (state dep. 1979-81, Supreme council 1979-84, 94) Home: 250 12th St Idaho Falls ID 83404-5370

DANILOFF, NICHOLAS, journalist, educator; b. Paris, Dec. 30, 1934; came to U.S., 1935; s. Serge Y. and Ellen Crosby (Burke) D.; m. Ruth Daniloff, June 21, 1961; children: Miranda, Caleb. AB cum laude, Harvard Coll., 1956, BA, Oxford U., 1959, MA, 1965. Copy boy Washington (DC) Post, 1956-57; sub editor, reporter UPI, 1959-80; bur. chief U.S. News and World Report, Moscow, 1981-86; from asst. prof. to prof. Northeastern U., Boston, 1989—; mem. adv. bd. Toda Inst. Peace, Cambridge/Tokyo, 1995—, New Eng. Press Assn., Boston, 1992—, Vorontsov Palace Meml. Trust, Vancouver, Can., 1994—. Author: The Kremlin and the Cosmos, 1972, Two Lives; One Russia, 1988. Avocations: jogging, rowing, marathon running. Office: Northeastern Univ 43 Greenleaf St Boston MA 02115-5003

DANILOV, VICTOR JOSEPH, museum management program director, consultant, writer, educator; b. Farrell, Pa., Dec. 30, 1924; s. Joseph M. and Ella (Tominovich) D.; m. Toni Dewey, Sept. 6, 1980; children: Thomas J., Duane P., Denise S. BA in Journalism, Pa. State U., 1945; MS in Journalism, Northwestern U., 1946; EdD in Higher Edn., U. Colo., 1964. With Sharon Herald, Pa., 1942, Youngstown Vindicator, 1945, Pitts. Sun-Telegraph, 1946-47, Chgo. Daily News, 1947-50; instr. journalism U. Colo., 1950-51; asst. prof. journalism U. Kans., 1951-53; with Kansas City Star, 1953; mgr. pub. relations Ill. Inst. Tech. and IIT Research Inst., 1953-57; dir. univ. relations and pub. info. U. Colo., 1957-60; pres. Profile Co., Boulder, Colo., 1960-62; exec. editor, exec. v.p. Indsl. Research Inc., Beverly Shores, Ind., 1962-69; pub., exec. v.p. Indsl. Research Inc., 1969-71; dir., v.p. Mus. Sci. and Industry, Chgo., 1971-77; pres., dir. Mus. Sci. and Industry, 1978-87, pres. emeritus, 1987—; dir. mus. mgmt. program, adj. prof. U. Colo., 1987—; mem. rural industrialization adv. group Dept. Agr., 1967; mem. panel internat. transfer tech. Dept. Commerce, 1968; mem. sci. info. coun. NSF, 1969-72; chmn. Conf. on Implications Metric Change, 1972, Nat. Conf. Indsl. Rsch., 1966-70; chmn. observance Nat. Indsl. Rsch. Week, 1967-70; chmn. Midwest White House Conf. on Indsl. World Ahead, 1972, Internat. Conf. Sci. and Tech. Museums, 1976, 82; mem. task force on fin. acctg. and reporting by non bus. orgns., others. Author: Public Affairs Reporting, 1955, Starting a Science Center, 1977, Science and Technology Centers, 1982, Science Center Planning Guide, 1985, Chicago's Museums, 1987, rev. edit., 1991, America's Science Museums, 1990, Corporate Museums, Galleries, and Visitor Centers: A Directory, 1991, A Planning Guide for Corporate Museums, Galleries, and Visitors Centers, 1992, Museum Careers and Training: A Professional Guide, 1994, University and College Museums, Galleries, and Related Facilities, 1996, Hall of Fame Museums: A Reference Guide, 1997; also articles; editor: Crucial Issues in Public Relations, 1960, Corporate Research and Profitability, 1966, Innovation and Profitability, 1967, Research Decision-Making in New Product Development, 1968, New Products--and Profits, 1969, Applying Emerging Technologies, 1970, Nuclear Power in the South, 1970, The Future of Science and Technology, 1975, Museum Accounting Guidelines, 1976, Traveling Exhibitions, 1978, Towards the Year 2000, 1981; editor profl. procs. Trustee Women of the West Mus., 1991—, v.p., 1991-99; trustee La Rabida Childrens Hosp. and Rsch. Ctr., 1973-83; mem. U. Chgo. Citizens Bd., 1978-87. Mem. Am. Assn. Mus. (exec. com. 1976-77, bd. dirs. 1985-88, chmn. mus. studies task force 1988-89), AAAS, Assn. Sci.-Tech. Ctrs. (bd. dirs. 1973-84, sec.-treas. 1973-74, pres. 1975-76), Internat. Coun. Mus. (com. on sci. and tech. mus. 1972—, vice chmn. 1977-87, chmn. 1982-83, bd. dirs. 1985-88), Chgo. Coun. on Fine Arts (chmn. 1976-84), Ill. Arts Alliance (bd. dirs. 1983-86), Sci. Mus. Exhibit Collaborative (pres. 1983-86), Mus. Film Network (pres. 1984-86). Home: 250 Bristlecone Way Boulder CO 80304-0413 Office: Univ Colo Mus Mus Mgmt Program Campus Box 218 Boulder CO 80309-0218

DANILOWICZ, DELORES ANN, pediatric cardiologist, pediatrics educator; b. Bradford, N.Y., Feb. 3, 1935; s. Kajetan Joseph and Bronislawa Anna (Luta) D.; m. Hugh Paul Gabriel, June 3, 1960. A.B., NYU, 1956, M.D., 1960. Diplomate Am. Bd. Pediat., Am. Bd. Pediat. Cardiology, Am.

Bd. Neonatology. Inter, resident pediatrics Jacobi Hosp., Bronx, 1960-63, cardiac fellow, 1963-65; postdoctoral fellow Johns Hopkins, Balt., 1965-66, Nat. Heart Inst., Bethesda, Md., 1966-68; asst. prof. NYU Med. Ctr., N.Y.C., 1968-72; assoc. prof. NYU Med. Ctr., N.Y.C., 1972-80; prof. pediatrics NYU Med. Ctr., N.Y.C., 1980—; dir. pediatric cardiac catheterization lab. U. Hosp., 1968—; admitting physician Univ. Hosp., Bellevue Hosp., Lenox Hill Hosp.; mem. Am. sub-bd. Pediatric Cardiology, 1985-89. Contbr. articles to profl. jours. NYU scholar, 1952-56; NYU Scholar, 1957-60; named Disting. Tchr. NYU Med. Sch., 1971, Disting. Tchr., 1976; NYU Pediatric House Staff, 1975. Fellow Am. Acad. Pediat, Am. Coll. Cardiology; mem. Am. Heart Assn.

DANISHEFSKY, SAMUEL J., chemistry educator; b. Bayonne, N.J., Mar. 10, 1936. BS, Yeshiva U., 1956; PhD in Chemistry, Harvard U., 1962. Fellow chemistry Columbia U., N.Y.C., 1961-63, now prof. chemistry, 1963—; asst. to prof. chemistry U. Pitts., 1963-79; prof. chemistry Yale U., New Haven, Conn., 1979-88, chmn. dept. chemistry, 1981-88; chair, dir. bio organic chemistry Sloan Kettering Inst., 1988—; cons. Merck Sharp & Dohme, 1973—, GE Co., 1977—, vis. prof. Iowa State U., 1974, U. Calif., 1977, Rice U., 1977, Tex. A&M, 1986; vis. lectr. Tex., 1979. Recipient Wolf Foundation (chemistry) award Wolf Foundation, 1995, Claude S. Hudson award in Carbohydrate Chemistry, 1997. Fellow AAAS, Am. Acad. Arts & Sci.; mem. NAS, Am. Chem. Soc. (Arthur C. Cope award 1998), Swiss Shem. Soc., Japanese Chem. Soc. Office: Sloan Kettering Inst 1275 York Ave New York NY 10021-6094*

DANISI, JOHN J., philosopher, educator; b. Bklyn., Mar. 19, 1948; s. Jack F. and Mary (Kelly) D.; m. Carolyn S. Swallum, Sept. 30, 1989; children: Mary, Jacqueline. BA cum laude, St. Louis U., 1969; MA, NYU, 1974, PhD, 1993. Cert. secondary sch. tchr., Mo. Jr. high sch. tchr. Annunciation Sch., St. Louis, 1969-71; instr. St. Louis U., 1970; adj. asst. prof. dept. philosophy. NYU, 1982—. Contbr. articles to profl. jours. Invited del. Citizen Amb. Program People to People Internat.; Philosophy Edn. Del. to China, 1993, Edn. Delegation to Berlin, 1994, Spokane, 1994. Fellowship Andrew W. Mellon fellow, NYU, 1981, NYU fellow, 1978-82, A. Ogden Butler fellowship NYU, 1987; recipient William James Prize Essay Am. Philos. Assn. Eastern div. 1986. Mem. Am. Philos. Assn., Soc. for the Advancement of Am. Philosphy, Leibniz Soc. Home: 4445 Post Rd Apt 8H Riverdale NY 10471-3449 Office: NYU Dept Philosophy 503 Main Bldg. New York NY 10003-6688

DANJCZEK, DAVID WILLIAM, manufacturing company executive; b. Phillipsburg, N.J., Sept. 29, 1951; s. William Emil and Erna (Lob) D. BSFS, Georgetown U., 1973; postgrad., Waseda U., 1973-74, Loyola U., L.A., 1977-78. Contract adminstr. Aero Products, Woodland Hills, Calif., 1974-76, sr. contract adminstr., 1976-78; dir. internat. ops. Litton Industries, Washington, 1978-90, v.p. internat. bus., 1990-93; v.p. govt. and internat. affairs Western Atlas Inc., 1993-97; staff v.p. Unova, Inc., 1997—; adj. prof. Georgetown U. Chair Industry sector adv. com. U.S. Dept. Commerce; bd. dirs. Exec. Coun. Diplomacy. Mem. Mfrs. Alliance Productivity and Innovation (chair global bus. coun.)), Am. Countertrade Assn. (sec.), Univ. Club, Internat. Aviation Club. Republican. Roman Catholic. Avocations: squash, bridge. Home: 1300 Crystal Dr Arlington VA 22202-3234 Office: UNOVA 1660 L St NW Washington DC 20036-5603

DANJCZEK, MICHAEL HARVEY, social service administrator; b. Phillipsburg, N.J., May 9, 1949; s. William Emil and Erna (Lob) D.; m. Cynthia Ann Johanson, June 9, 1973; children: William Emil II, Liesel J., Rachel L., Peter L. BA in Urban Studies, Lehigh U., Bethlehem, Pa., 1972, MEd in Social Restoration, 1974, EdD in Ednl. Adminstrn., 1985. Exec. dir. Lehigh Valley Opportunity Ctr., Bethlehem, Pa., 1972-74; pres., exec. dir. Children's Home, Easton, Pa., 1974—; adj. prof. Lehigh County C.C., 1987-91, Grad. Sch., Jersey City State Tchrs. Coll., 1989-92; treas. Pa. Coun. Children's Svcs., 1982-84; mem. Commn. on Accreditation, Nat. Assn. Homes for Children, 1982-87, chmn. bd. dirs., 1997-98; mem. authority bd. Northampton C.C., 1983—; v.p. Pa. Coun. Children's Svcs., 1985-87, bd. dirs., 1987-89; bd. dirs. Lehigh Valley Drug Treatment Program, 1986-88; mem. Ea. U.S. Svc. Coun. of Coun. on Accreditation Svcs. for Families and children, 1987-92; treas. Nat. Assn. Homes and Svcs. for Children, 1988-93, chmn. bd. dirs., 1997-98; bd. dirs. Twin Rivers Cmty. Bank, 1991—; bd. dirs. Coun. on Accreditation Svcs. for Family and Children, 1993—. Asst. wrestling coach Lafayette Coll., 1974-76; mem. exec. com. Rep. party of Northampton County, 1975-76; bd. advisors Jr. League Lehigh Valley, 1975-77; chmn. profl. adv. com. Family and Child Welfare of Lehigh Valley Cmty. Coun., 1976; mem. adv. bd. Cath. Social Svcs., Diocese of Allentown, 1976-81; mem. Wilson Boro Sch. Bd., 1980-83; bd. dirs. Pa. Coun. Vol. Child Care Agys., 1980-84; bd. dirs. Helen Beebe Speech and Hearing Ctr., 1980-89, pres. bd. dirs., 1987-89; bd. dirs. Parents Anonymous Pa., 1981—, pres. bd., 1981-85; gen. campaign chmn. United Way of Northampton and Warren Counties, 1982-83; bd. dirs. Great Valley Girl Scout Coun., 1983-89; chmn. Minsi Trail Drug Abuse Prevention Rally for Forks of Del., Boy Scouts Am., 1987; mem. St. Bernard's Ch. Parish Coun., 1991-93; chmn. elect, v.p. econ. devel. Two Rivers Area Commerce Coun., 1991-92; chmn. Northampton County Sports and Spl. Events Com., 1994—; mem. governing bd., CEO, chmn. BallYard, Inc., 1994—; mem. governing bd. St. Vincent's Home for Children, 1995—. Recipient Disting. Cmty. Svc. award Easton Area Jaycees, 1975, Disting. Svc. award Pa. Com. on Internat. Yr. of Child, 1979, Coll. Edn., Lehigh U., 1983, Disting. Alumni award Lehigh U., 1987, Gafney award Lehigh U. Assn. Ednl. Adminstrs., 1988, Pres. award for cmty. svc. Easton Area Sales and Mktg. Execs., 1990, Svc. to Mankind award Sertoma Club, 1991; inducted to Notre Dame H.S. Athletic Hall of Fame, 1990. Mem. Lehigh U. Alumni Assn. Home Club (bd. dirs. 1990—), Lehigh U. Alumni Assn. (bd. dirs. 1987-90), Northampton Country Club (bd. govs. 1985-94), Nat. Fellowship Child Care Execs. (exec. sec. 1993-98, pres. 1992-93), Two Rivers Area C. of C. (chmn. 1993-95), Rotary (past pres. Easton). Republican. Roman Catholic. Avocations: private pilot, golf, skiing, travel. Home and Office: Childrens Home Easton 25th St and Lehigh Dr Easton PA 18042

DANKANYIN, ROBERT JOHN, international business executive; b. Sharon, Pa., Sept. 4, 1934; s. John and Anna (Kohlesar) D.; m. Dorothy Jean Kuchel, Aug. 9, 1958 (div. June 1975); children: Douglas John, David Jay, Dana Jean; m. Georgia C. Oleson, Apr. 2, 1988 (dec. Sept. 1990); m. Charlene Marcella Bassett, May 16, 1998. BSCE, Pa. State U., 1956; MBA, U. So. Calif., 1961; MSEE, UCLA, 1963. Cert. level 2 Profl. Ski Instrs. Am. From mgr. mobile ICBM systems engring. dept. to mgr. space system lab. Hughes Aircraft Co., Culver City, Calif., 1956-68; program mgr. Litton Industries, Beverly Hills, Calif., 1968-70; v.p. program mgr. Litton Ship Systems, Culver City, 1970-71, Litton Ship Sys., Pascagola, Miss., 1971-73; asst. mgr. for U.S. Roland program, Canoga Pk., Calif. Hughes Aircraft Co., Culver City, Calif., 1975-77; asst. div. mgr. missile devel. div. Hughes Aircraft Co., Canoga Pk., Calif., 1977-84; div. mgr. land combat systems div. Hughes Aircraft Co., Culver City, Calif., 1984-86, group v.p. missile systems group, 1986-87; v.p., asst. group exec. missle systems group Canoga Park, Calif., 1987-88; v.p., asst. group exec. space and communication group, El Segundo, Calif. Hughes Aircraft Co., Culver City, Calif., 1988-89; corp. sr. v.p. diversification Hughes Aircraft Co., L.A., 1989-92, sr. v.p. bus. devel., 1992-93; sr. v.p., pres. Hughes Indsl. Electronics Co., L.A., 1993-95; group exec. Whittaker Corp., Westwood Village, Calif., 1973-75; pres., chmn. bd. Whittaker Community Devel. Corp., Englewood, Colo., Knoxville, Tenn., Westwood Village, San Juan, Calif., 1973-75; internat. bus. and mgmt. cons., pres., CEO ITI, Big Bear Lake, Calif., 1995—; chmn. Hughes Program Mgr. Devel. Course, L.A., 1976-88; chmn., bd. dirs. Light Valve Products, Inc., 1988-92, Hughes/Japan Victor Tech. Inc., 1992-95, Hughes Micro Electronics Ltd., Glenrothes, Scotland, Hughes Europa Ltd., Brussels, Belgium, 1993-95; bd. dirs. Hughes Environ. Sys., Inc., Long Beach, Calif.; Hughes España, Madrid, Spain, Aero Sys., Inc., Paris; dir. several wholly owned subs. including Direct TV, Spectrolab, Hughes Network Sys., RF Identification Sys.; lectr., guest spkr., author on tech. mgmt.; bus. ventures, fgn. mktg., def. conversion, diversifications and entrepreneurship. Editor Inter Fraternity/Sorority Newsletter Pa. State U., 1955-56. Chmn. indsl. and profl. adv. coun. Coll. Engring, Pa. State U.; ski instr. Bear Mountain Ski Resort, Big Bear Lake, Calif., 1990—; chmn. several indsl. task forces reporting to U.S. congl. coms. Voted Ordo Honorium by Kappa Delta Rho Fraternity, 1991, outstanding Engr. of the Yr. by Pa. State U., 1991; honored as outstanding engineering alumnus, 1992. Mem. Am. Def. Preparedness Assn. (bd. dirs. 1986-94, chmn. fin. com. 1990-94), Hughes Mgmt. Club, Aero Club So. Calif., Marina City Club, Riviera Country Club, Calif. Yacht Club. Republican. Roman Catholic. Avocations: skiing, scuba diving, sailing, hiking, fishing, golf. Home: 1 Catamaran St Marina Del Rey CA 90292

DANKER, MERVYN KENNETH, director of education; b. Cape Town, South Africa, Mar. 27, 1944; came to U.S., 1989; s. David Barry and Nina (Selbo) D.; m. Rochelle Gould, Dec. 16, 1969; children: Dionne Bonita, David Jonathan, Gareth Saul. BA, U. Cape Town, 1965, BEd, 1974. Cert. secondary edn. tchr., South Africa, Australia. Tchr. Camps Bay High Sch., Cape Town, 1967-76; vice prin. Herzlia High Sch., Cape Town, 1977; headmaster Theodor Herzl Sch., Port Elizabeth, Republic of South Africa, 1978-86, Carmel Sch., Perth, West Australia, 1986-89; dir. of edn. Solomon Schechter Day Sch., West Hartford, Conn., 1989-97; prin. Jewish Day Sch. of the North Peninsula, 1997—. Author: History of Theodor Herzl School, 1986. Jewish. Avocations: running, tennis, rugby, cycling, reading. E-mail: mrdanker@juno.com. Home: 22 Goldenridge Ct San Mateo CA 94402-3718 Office: Jewish Day Sch 525 42nd Ave San Mateo CA 94403-5032

DANKNER, JAY WARREN, lawyer; b. Bklyn., June 15, 1949; s. Morris and Frances Dankner; m. Iris Rose Terens, May 15, 1983; children: Danielle Renee, Nicole Beth. BA cum laude, Bklyn. Coll., 1970, JD cum laude, 1973. Bar: N.Y. 1974, Fla. 1974, U.S. Dist. Ct. (ea. and so. dists.) N.Y. 1974, U.S. Ct. Appeals (2d cir.) 1974, U.S. Supreme Ct. 1977, U.S. Dist. Ct. (no. dist.) N.Y. 1986. From assoc. to ptnr. Sullivan & Liapakis P.C., N.Y.C., 1974-94; ptnr. Dankner & Milstein, P.C., N.Y.C., 1994—; lectr. Practicing Law Inst., N.Y.C., 1983-87, N.Y. State Trial Lawyers Inst., 1985—, continuing legal edn. program Bklyn. Law Sch., 1986—, N.Y. State Bar Assn. CLE Programs, Nassau County Bar Assn., Queens Bar Assn.; mem. Bklyn. Law Rev., 1972-73; bd. dirs. Atty's Info. Exchange Group, Inc., 1981—. Author: Products Liability Practice Guide, 1988, Masters of Trial Practice, 1988, Deposing Corporate Defendants in Products Liability Actions, 1988, Trial Strategy - Plaintiffs View, 1988; contbr. articles to profl. jours. Named Best Trial Lawyers in the U.S., Town & Country, 1985. Mem. ABA, N.Y. State Bar Assn. (spl. com. on procedures for jud. discipline 1987-90), Assn. of Bar of City of N.Y. (mem. products liability com. 1993-94), Fla. Bar Assn., Assn. Trial Lawyers Am., N.Y. State Trial Lawyers Assn. (chair products liability com. 1991, 93-94), N.Y. County Lawyers Assn. Home: 524 E 72nd St New York NY 10021-9801 Office: Dankner & Milstein PC 41 E 57th St New York NY 10022-1908

DANKO, GEORGE, engineering educator; b. Budapest, Hungary, Apr. 3, 1944; came to U.S., 1986; s. Gyorgy and Ilona (Mihaly) D.; m. Eva Arvay, Dec. 14, 1976; 1 child, Reka. BSME, Tech. U. Budapest, 1968, PhD, 1976; MS in Applied Math., Eotovs U. of Scis., Budapest, 1975; PhD, Hungarian Acad. Scis., Budapest, 1985. Cert. Profl. Ski Instrs. Am. Assn. Asst. prof. Tech. U. Budapest, 1968-75, assoc. prof., 1979-86; fellow Hungarian Acad. Scis., Budapest, 1975-79; rsch. assoc. U. Nev., Reno, 1986-90, assoc. prof., 1990-95, prof. mining engring., 1995—; cons. Sierra Sci., Reno, 1990—; chmn. High-Level Radioactive Waste Mgmt. Conf., 1991, 92; portrait artist, Reno. Co-author: Methods for the Calculation of Pipeline Transients, 1976, Warming-up and Cooling of Electrical Machinery, 1982; contbr. articles to profl. jours. Com. rep. Truckee River Steering Com., Reno, 1993-94. Grantee U.S. Bur. Mines, 1986-97, U.S. Dept. Energy, 1991—, Clarkson Co., 1992—. Mem. ASME, ISES (internat. organizing com. 1993-94), IFAC (internat. program com. 1995—), Soc. Mining Engrs., Am. Nuclear Soc. Achievements include patents for methods and apparatus for the determination of the heat transfer coefficient, process and apparatus for the determination of thermophysical properties, underground cooling enhancement for nuclear waste repository, method and apparatus for underground nuclear waste repository, others. Office: U Nev Reno Mining Engring Dept/173 Reno NV 89557

DANKWORTH, CLEMENTINA DINAH See LAINE, CLEO

DANKWORTH, MARGARET ANNE, management consultant; b. Bellaire, Ohio, July 22, 1920; d. Charles Henry and Annie Harvey (Parks) D. BA, Ohio Wesleyan U., 1942; MA, NYU, 1949; postgrad., Mich. State U., 1960. Cert. assn. mgr. Bus. mgr. Nat. Recreation Assn., N.Y.C., 1948-50; dist. rep. Nat. Recreation Assn., Toledo, Ohio, 1950-58; asst. exec. dir. Am. Inst. of Pk. Execs., Ogle Bay Park, W.Va., 1958-66; advt. mgr., pub. rels. dir. Nat. Recreation and Pks. Assn., Washington, 1966-71; exec. dir. Am. Assn. Zool. Pks. and Aquariums, Wheeling, W.Va., 1958-75; cons. Am. Inst. for Leisure, Wheeling, W.Va., 1985—; owner Historic Morristown, Ohio, 1975—; founder Nat. Sch. for Zool. Adminstrn., 1975—; bd. dirs. Buckeye Savs. Bank; dir. Am. Mortgages, Am. Bankcorp., 1992—. Editor Parks and Recreation Mag., 1964-66; founder, editor AAZPA Newsletter, 1966-75. Bd. dirs. St Clairsville Pub. Libr., 1988—. Lt. USNR, 1943-46, ret., 1980. Mem. Historic Morristown Pres. Assn. (sr. bd. 1988—), Questers Nat. Trail (pres.), Ohio Historic Soc., Nat. Trust for Historic Preservation, Tues. Night Club, Delta Gamma (pres. 1988—). Republican. Methodist. Avocations: photography, historic preservation, travel, lecturing. Home: 145 Crisswill Rd Saint Clairsville OH 43950-1415 Office: Historic Morristown PO Box 335 Saint Clairsville OH 43950-0335

DANLEY, KERWIN, umpire; b. L.A., May 25, 1961. Former umpire Northwest League, Calif. League, Tex. League, Pacific Coast League, Internat. League; umpire maj. league baseball Nat. League, N.Y.C., 1998—. Office: Nat League 350 Park Ave New York NY 10022 also: Umpires Union 1735 Market St Philadelphia PA 19103

DANN, ALEXANDER WILLIAM, JR., lawyer; b. Pitts., Mar. 20, 1923; s. Alexander William and Ella (Berry) D.; m. Alexander William III, Thomas Semmes, Elise Dann Oschwald, Katherine Dann Pruett. BA, Cornell U., 1948, LLB, JD, 1951. Bar: Tenn. 1951, U.S. Tax Ct. 1962, U.S. Ct. Claims 1965, U.S. Dist. Ct. (we. dist.) Tenn. 1971, U.S. Supreme Ct. 1972, U.S. Ct. Appeals (5th cir.) 1972, U.S. Ct. Appeals (6th cir.) 1980, U.S. Dist. Ct. Ark. 1981. Assoc. Canada, Russell & Turner, Memphis, 1950-55; from assoc. to ptnr. Tual Younger & Dann, Memphis, 1956-58; ptnr. Younger & Dann, Memphis, 1958-60, Dann, Hills & Blackburn, Memphis, 1961-78, Dann, Davis, Davis & Blackburn, Memphis, 1978-86; pres., sr. atty. Dann & Associates, P.C., Memphis, 1986-95; ptnr., sr. atty. Dann, Allen & Murrell, Memphis, 1995—; legal counsel Miss. Valley Flood Control, Memphis, 1965—; cons. Western Dredging Assn., Seattle, 1988-97; cons., panelist Nat. Acad. Scis., Washington, 1987, 89. Contbr. articles to profl. jours. Commr. elections Shelby County, 1965-67, 67-69, 69-71; chmn. Shelby County Rep. Party, Memphis, 1970-72; mem. civic com. Shelby County Charter Commn., Memphis, 1968-69; chmn. bd. trustees Memphis Brooks Mus. of Art, 1965-85, Memphis Front Street Theatre, 1966. Lt. (j.g.) USNR, 1943-46. Mem. ABA, Am. Arbitration Assn. (panelist 1993—), Tenn. Bar Assn., Memphis Bar Assn., Memphis Country Club, Rotary, Alpha Delta Phi. Republican. Episcopalian. Avocations: waterfowl hunting, travel, oil painting, furniture woodworking, tennis. Home: 6246 Green Meadows Rd Memphis TN 38120-3101 Office: Dann Allen & Murrell 6263 Poplar Ave Ste 900 Memphis TN 38119-4724

DANN, FRANCIS JOSEPH, dermatologist, educator; b. N.Y.C., Aug. 26, 1946; s. Richard William and Helen (Brennan) D. BA, Columbia U., 1968, MD, 1972. Bd. cert. dermatologist Am. Bd. Dermatology. Pvt. practice specializing in dermatology, 1976-99; asst. clin. prof. dermatology UCLA, 1993—; recognized expert med. reviewer State of Calif., 1995; specialized tng. in leprosy USPHS Hosp., Carville, La., 1972, 95. Contbr. articles to profl. and med. jours. Recipient Cert. of Appreciation for charitable med. missions to The Philippines, 1986, 88, 92. Mem. AMA, Am. Acad. Dermatology, Philippine Med. Assn. Hawaii, L.A.-Metro Dermatology Soc., Pacific Dermatology Soc., L.A. Acad. Medicine (bd. dirs. 1995-99), Aloha Med. Mission. Roman Catholic. Avocations: sports, photography. Office: 100 UCLA Medical Plz Ste 545 Los Angeles CA 90024-6992

DANN, JOHN CHRISTIE, historian, library director; b. Wilmington, Del., May 3, 1944; s. C. Marshall and Catharine (Christie) D.; m. Orelia Sparrow, Jan. 24, 1970; children: Catharine Christie, Orelia Eliabeth. BA, Dickinson Coll., 1966; MA, Coll. William and Mary, 1970, PhD, 1975. Prof. history U. Mich., Ann Arbor, 1975—, curator of manuscripts William C. Clements Libr., 1971-77, dir. William C. Clements Libr., 1977—. Author: 101 Treasures, 1998; editor: The Revolution Remembered, 1980, The Nagle Journal, 1989; editor Am. Mag.; mem. various hist. and editl. bds. Mem. Dexter (Mich.) Village Coun., 1982-86. Mem. Cosmos Club (Washington), Azazels. Congregationalist. Avocations: fishing, golf. Home: 7580 4th St Dexter MI 48130-1424 Office: Clements Libr 909 S University Ave Ann Arbor MI 48109-1190

DANN, OLIVER TOWNSEND, psychoanalyst, psychiatrist, educator; b. Mansfield, Ohio, Aug. 10, 1935; s. Edward William and Mary Virginia (Townsend) D.; m. Linda Marie Schweers, July 15, 1961; children: Sara Katharine, Jonathan William Jenner, Luke Nathan Townsend, Jesse Charles. AB, Columbia U., 1958; MD, Yale U., 1962. Diplomate Am. Bd. Psychiatry and Neurology. Resident in psychiatry Yale U. Sch. Medicine, New Haven, 1963-67, asst., assoc. prof. psychiatry, 1967-79; clin. prof. psychiatry U. Miami (Fla.) Sch. Medicine, 1980—; dir. Fla. Psychoanalytic Inst., 1997—; pvt. practice, Miami, 1979—. Contbr. articles to profl. jours. Mem. Mayflower Soc., Jamestowne Soc., Huguenot Soc. Fellow (life) APA; mem. Am. Psychoanalytic Assn., Internat. Psychoanalytic Assn., Western New England Inst. Soc. Psychoanalysis, Balt.-Washington Inst. Soc. Psychoanalysis, Fla. Psychanalytic Inst. Soc. Found., Phi Beta Kappa, others. Avocations: sailing, canoeing, hiking. Home and Office: 4550 SW 74th St Miami FL 33143-6271

DANNELLY, WILLIAM DAVID, lawyer; b. Andalusia, Ala., 1951. SB, MIT, 1973; JD, U. N.C., 1977. Bar: N.C. 1977. Law clerk we. dist. U.S. Dist. Ct., N.C., 1977-78; ptnr. Hunton & Williams, Raleigh, N.C. Mem. N.C. Law Review, 1975-77; contbg. author: Toxic Tort and Hazardous Substance Litigation, 1995. Vice chmn. Environ. Concerns Ea. N.C. C. of C., 1990-95. Mem. Order of Coif. Office: Hunton & Williams One Hannover Square 14th Fl PO Box 109 Raleigh NC 27602-0109

DANNENBERG, ARTHUR MILTON, JR., experimental pathologist, immunologist, educator; b. Phila., Oct. 17, 1923; s. Arthur Mansbach and Marion (Loeb) D.; m. Aileen Rose Hart, Mar. 30, 1948; children: Arlene Jane, Andrew Loeb, Audrey Ann. A.B., Swarthmore Coll., 1944; M.D., Harvard U., 1947; M.A., U. Pa., 1951, Ph.D., 1952. Diplomate: Nat. Bd. Med. Examiners. Intern Albert Einstein Med. Ctr., Phila., 1947-48; research resident Children's Hosp., Phila., 1948-49; fellow Henry Phipps Inst. U. Pa., Phila., 1950-52, asst. prof., 1956-64; fellow U. Utah, 1952-54; assoc. prof. environ. health scis. Johns Hopkins U. Sch. Hygiene, Balt., 1964-73, prof., 1973—, prof. joint faculty Sch. Medicine, dept. pathology, 1976—. Assoc. editor: Am. Rev. Respiratory Diseases, 1979-84, mem. editorial bd., 1973-75; mem. editorial bd. Infection and Immunity jour., 1976-78; contbr. articles to profl. jours. and chpts. to books. Served as lt. comdr. Med. Research Unit 1, USN, 1954-56. Mem. Am. Soc. Investigative Pathology, Histochem. Soc., Am. Soc. Microbiology, Soc. for Leukocyte Biology (sec. 1975-76), Am. Assn. Immunologists, Am. Thoracic Soc., Soc. Investigative Dermatology. Home: 12 Lake Manor Ct Baltimore MD 21210-1017 Office: Johns Hopkins U Sch Hygiene Baltimore MD 21205-2179

DANNENBERG, KONRAD K., aeronautical engineer; b. Weissenfels, Germany, Aug. 5, 1912; came to U.S. 1945.; s. Hermann and Klara (Kittler) D.; m. Ingeborg M. Kamke, Apr. 8, 1944 (dec.); 1 child, Klaus Dieter; m. Jacquelyn E. Staiger, Mar. 31, 1990. MS Engring., Techn. U., Hannover, Ger., 1938. Asst. Tech. U., Hannover, 1938; engr. Tech. U., Frankfurt, Ger., 1939; rschr. HAP-Peenemuende, Germany, 1940-45; mgr. U.S. Army Ordnance, Ft. Bliss, Tex., 1945-50, ABMA, Huntsville, Ala., 1950-60, NASA/MSFC, Huntsville, 1960-73; assoc. prof. UTSI-U. Tenn., Tullahoma, 1973-78; cons. The Space & Rocket Ctr., Huntsville, 1978—. Author: In Memory of H. Oberth, 1990, Vahrenwald to Dresden, 1990; (with E. Stuhlinger) Rocket Center Peenemünde, 1993, Albert Püllenberg and the Gesellschaft für Raketenforschung, 1995, (with Donald Tarter) Mitchell R. Sharpe-Aerospace Historian, 1997. Lt. German Army, 1939-40. Recipient Meritorious Svc. award, U.S. Army, 1960, Exceptional Svc. award, NASA, 1969, Konrad K. Dannenberg scholarship, 1992. Fellow AIAA (chpt. chmn. 1967, Durand lectr. pub. svc. 1990), Holger N. Toftoy award, Hermann Oberth award 1996); mem. Hermann Oberth Soc. (hon., Golden Hermann Oberth medal 1994), Nat. Space Soc. (charter), Am. Rocket Soc. (chmn. 1962). Lutheran. Achievements include patents in rocket engine design. Home: 233 Cheswick Dr Madison AL 35757-8712

DANNENBERG, MARTIN ERNEST, retired insurance company executive; b. Balt., Nov. 5, 1915; s. Martin Ernest and Wilhelmina (Wilfson) D.; m. Esther Salzman, May 29, 1941 (dec. June 1989); children: Betsy, Richard; m. Margery Singer, Oct. 21, 1990; 1 child, Joan. Student, Johns Hopkins U., U. Balt. Law Sch. With Sun Life Ins. Co. Am., Balt., 1932—; v.p. adminstrn., then sr. v.p., sec. Sun Life Ins. Co. Am., 1966-76, dir., 1967—, vice chmn. bd., 1976-79, chmn. bd., 1979-87, chmn. emeritus, 1987—. Bd. dirs. Assoc. Placement and Guidance Bur., Balt. Urban Coalition, Balt. Goodwill Industries, Md. Life & Health Guaranty Assn., Balt. Choral Arts Soc., Sudden Infant Death Syndrome Inst., Levindale Geriat. Ctr. & Hosp.; mem. Mayor Balt. Adv. Com. Bus. Edn., Balt. County Phys. Fitness Commn., Md. Commn. Aging, Mayor Balt. Labor Market Adv. Commn.; assoc. gen. campaign chmn. United Way of Ctrl. Md.; exec. bd., v.p. Balt. coun. Boy Scouts Am.; v.p. Balt. City Coun. PTAs; exec. bd., v.p. N.W. Hosp. Ctr. With CIC, AUS, 1942-45, ETO. Decorated Bronze Star; named Disting. Citizen Md. Mem. Life Office Mgmt. Assn. (past chmn. combination co. com., systems and procedures council), Adminstrv. Mgmt. Soc. (past pres. Balt.), Life Insurers Conf., Nat. Assn. Life Cos., Am. Council Life Ins., Surburban Country Club, Center Club, Johns Hopkins Club.

DANNENBERG, ROGER BERRY, computer scientist; b. Houston, Mar. 9, 1955; s. Richard Martin and Isabel Drury (Holt) D.; m. Frances Lynn Krouse; 1 child, Richard Pierce. BSEE, Rice U., 1977; MSCE, Case Western Res. U., 1979; PhD, Carnegie Mellon U., 1982. Rsch. scientist Carnegie Mellon U., Pitts., 1982-89, sr. rsch. scientist, 1989—; artist-in-residence Am. Ctr., Paris, 1983; fellow Next, Inc., Palo Alto, Calif., 1988; ptnr. ESL at the Movies, LLC, Iowa City, 1998. Editor: Multimedia Design, 1994; patentee computer accompaniment, 1984; composer: In Transit, 1997. NSF grad. fellow, 1977-81. Mem. IEEE, Internat. Computer Music Assn. (bd. dirs. 1992-97), Assn. for Computing Machinery. Office: Carnegie Mellon U Sch Computer Sci Pittsburgh PA 15213

DANNER, BRYANT CRAIG, lawyer; b. Boston, Nov. 18, 1937; s. Nevin Earle and Marjorie (Harms) D.; m. Judith I. Baker, Aug. 23, 1958; 1 child Debra Irene. BA, Harvard U., 1960, LLB, 1963. Bar: Calif. 1963, U.S. Dist. Ct. (cen. dist.) Calif. 1963. Assoc. Latham & Watkins, L.A., 1963-70, ptnr., 1970-92; sr. v.p., gen. counsel So. Calif. Edison Co., Rosemead, Calif., 1992-95; exec. v.p., gen. counsel So. Calif. Edison Co., Rosemead, 1995—. Mem. L.A. County Bar Assn. (chmn. environ. sect. 1988-89). Avocations: fly fishing, photography. Office: So Calif Edison Co 2244 Walnut Grove Ave Rosemead CA 91770-3714

DANNER, KATHLEEN FRANCES STEELE, federal official; b. Kansas City, Mo., Oct. 28, 1960; m. Steve Danner, Jan. 18, 1996. Admissions counselor N.E. Mo. State U., Kirksville, 1980-83, assoc. dir. admissions, 1983-86, programming coord. dept. pub. svcs., 1986-87; Iowa, N.H. dir. Gephardt for Pres., St. Louis, 1987-88; mem. Mo. Ho. of Reps., Jefferson City, 1988-94; state dir. Clinton for Pres., 1991-92; regional dir. U.S. Dept. HHS, Kansas City, Mo., 1994—; acting dir. intergovtl. affairs U.S. Dept. HHS, Washington, 1998—; 1st v.p. Greater Kansas City Fed. Exec. Bd. Bd. dirs. Greater Mo. Found. Mem. Nat. Order Women Legislators, Women Legislators of Mo. (pres. 1989-92), Ctrl. Exch., Nat. Women's Polit. Caucus. Roman Catholic. Avocations: sports enthusiast, dancing, reading, politics. Home: 6 Nantucket Ct Smithville MO 64089-9605 Office: US Dept Health and Human Svcs 601 E 12th St Ste 210 Kansas City MO 64106-2808

DANNER, PATSY ANN (MRS. C. M. MEYER), congresswoman; b. Louisville, Ky., Jan. 13, 1934; d. Henry J. and Catherine M. (Shaheen) Berrer; m. Lavon Danner, Feb. 12, 1951 (div.); children: Stephen, Stephanie, Shane, Shavonne.; m. C.M. Meyer, Dec. 30, 1982. Student, Hannibal-LaGrange Coll., 1952; B.A. in Polit. Sci. cum laude, N.E. Mo. State U., 1972. Dist. asst. to Congressman Jerry Litton, Kansas City, Mo., 1973-76; fed. co-chmn. Ozarks Regional Commn., Washington, 1977-81; mem. Mo. State Senate, 1983-1992, 103rd-106th Congress from 6th Mo. dist., 1993—; mem. internat. rels. com., transp. and infrastructure com. Roman Catholic. Home: 6 Nantucket Ct Smithville MO 64089-9605 Office: US House of

Representatives Office of House Members 1207 Longworth Bldg Washington DC 20515-2506*

DANNER, PAUL KRUGER, III, telecommunications executive; b. Cin., Aug. 20, 1957; s. Paul Kruger Jr. and Phyllis Jean (Speak) D.; m. Cynthia Lee Hurst, May 5, 1984; children: Catherine Hurst, Elizabeth Speak, Caroline Tyree. BS, Colo. State U., 1979; MBA, Old Dominion U., 1986. Mktg. rep. Control Data Corp., Denver, 1985-86; dist. mgr. NEC Home Electronics (U.S.A.), Inc., Denver, 1987-88; regional mgr. NEC Home Electronics, Inc. subs. NEC Corp. (Tokyo), L.A., 1988-89, v.p. NEC Techs., Inc. subs., 1989-91; v.p. sales and mktg. Command Communications, Aurora, Colo., 1991-96; pres. Tech. Ventures, Inc., Denver, 1996-97; COO Zekko Corp., Ponte Vedra Bch., Fla., 1997-98, e.TV Commerce Inc., Jacksonville, Fla., 1998—. Lt. USN, 1979-85; comdr. USNR, 1985—. Mem. Navy League of U.S., U.S. Naval Inst., NRA, Ducks Unltd. Republican. Avocations: skiing, scuba diving, fly fishing, hunting, golf.

DANNER, RICHARD ALLEN, law educator, dean; b. Marshfield, Wis., Aug. 26, 1947; s. Reuben Mathias and Evelyn (Fischer) D.; m. Cheryl Clark Sanford, Jan. 27, 1973; children—Zachary Allen, Katherine Elizabeth. B.A., U. Wis., 1969, M.S., 1975, J.D., 1979; postgrad., MIT, 1973. Bar: Wis. 1979. Environ. law librarian U. Wis. Law Library, Madison, 1975-79; assoc. law librarian Duke U. Sch. Law, Durham, N.C., 1979-80, acting law librarian, instr., 1980-81, dir. law libr., 1981-93, asst. prof. law, 1981-82, assoc. prof., 1982-85, prof., 1985—, assoc. dean, 1993-98, sr. assoc. dean, 1998—; dir. Triangle Research Libraries Network, 1984-97. Author: Legal Research in Wisconsin, 1980, Strategic Planning: A Law Library Management Tool, 1991, 2d edit., 1996, Toward a Renaissance in Law Librarianship, 1997; editor Law Library Management Tool, 1991, Law Libr. Jour., 1984-94; co-editor: Introduction to Foreign Legal Systems, 1994; contbr. articles to profl. jours. With U.S. Army, 1969-71. Decorated Bronze Star. Mem. ABA, Am. Assn. Law Librs. (pres. 1989-90), ALA, State Bar Wis. Home: 2419 Tryon Rd Durham NC 27705-5511 Office: Duke U Sch Law Libr PO Box 90361 Durham NC 27708-0361

DANNHAUSER, STEPHEN J., lawyer; b. N.Y.C., May 23, 1950; s. Frank A. and Irene (Tinney) D.; m. Mary Elizabeth Robinson, July 1, 1973; children: Benjamin, Todd, Jess. BA with honors, SUNY, Stonybrook, 1972; JD with honors, Bklyn. Law Sch., 1975. Bar: N.Y. 1976. Atty. Weil Gotshal & Manges LLP, N.Y.C., 1975—, exec. ptnr., 1989—. Decisions editor Bklyn. Law Rev., 1974-75. Pres. N.Y. Police and Fire Windows and Children's Fund, N.Y.C., 1985—; chmn. corp. steering com. Nat. Minority Bus. Coun., N.Y.C., 1993; bd. dirs. Boys Harbor, Inc., E. Harlem, N.Y. Mem. ABA. Avocations: running, golf. Office: Weil Gotshal & Manges LLP 767 5th Ave New York NY 10153*

D'ANNIBALLE, PRISCILLA LUCILLE, contracting company executive; b. Martins Ferry, Ohio, Oct. 28, 1950; d. James Louis and Smyrna Isabell (Prieto) D'A; m. Terrence E. Holdren. BE, U. Toledo, 1973. Credit mgr. Kabat Distbg. Co., Toledo, 1973-80; comml. ops. officer Ohio Citizens Bank, Toledo, 1980-81, credit officer, 1981-82, mktg. officer, 1982-83, mortgage banking officer, 1983-85; owner, pres. D'Ann Enterprises, Inc. dba Paul Davis Systems, Holland, Ohio, 1985—; pres. district V Paul Davis Systems, Toledo, 1992-95, mem. nat. exec. com., 1992-95, treas. nat. exec. com., 1994-95; chmn. arbitration com. Paul Davis Systems, 1991. Mem. fund drive United Way, Toledo, 1982, Jr. Achievement, Toledo, 1983; bd. dirs. Voluntary Action Ctr., Toledo, 1981-82. Mem. Nat. Assn. Credit Mgmt. (bd. dirs. 1981-87, bd. dirs. Edinl. Forum 1976-82, pres. 1980, Credit Person of Yr. award 1982, Credit Exec. of Yr. award 1987), Holland-Springfield C. of C. (exec. bd. dirs. 1990-95, v.p. 1991-92, pres. 1993), Paul Davis Systems Franchisee Assn. (pres. 1991). Roman Catholic. Avocations: golf, swimming, gardening, antiques, traveling. Home: 704 Oak Park Dr Toledo OH 43617-2024 Office: D'Ann Enterprises Inc 1049 S Mccord Rd Holland OH 43528-9596

D'ANNOLFO, SUZANNE CORDIER, educational administrator, educator; b. Akron, Ohio, Oct. 20, 1946; d. Albert Tennyson and Luella Dorothy Cordier; m. Frank Joseph D'Annolfo, Feb. 12, 1982; children: Casey Cordier, Matthew Scott. BS, Boston U., 1970; student, Slippery Rock (Pa.) State U., 1964-67; MS, Cen. Conn. State U., 1973; EdD, Boston U., 1980. Tchr. West Hartford (Conn.) Pub. Schs., 1970-78, adminstr. health and phys. edn., dir. athletics, 1979-87; health coord. Farmington (Conn.) Pub. Schs., 1988-91; asst. prin. Farmington High Sch., 1991-93; prin. Litchfield (Conn.) High Sch., 1993-98, Nat. Sch. of Excellence; dir. curriculum and instrn. grades 9-12 Newington (Conn.) Pub. Schs., 1998—; coach U.S. Olympic Track and Field Team Learn-by-Doing Clinics, 1977-80; mem. Conn. Gov.'s Coun. on Phys. Fitness and Sport, 1978-87, 90—; drug cons. Nutmeg State Games; mem. edn. coun. U.S. Olympic Com.; dean U.S. Olympic Acad., First World-Scholar Athlete Games, Newport, R.I.; Ethics Fellow, Internat. Inst. of Sport, 1993. Author: Secondary Physical Education, Stress Management, Ideas II, Drugs and AIDS Education for Elementary Students. Bd. dirs. Spl. Olympics, West Hartford, 1979-87; cofounder Pvt. Victories health newsletter for high sch. students, 1991-98. Named to N.E. Women's Hall of Fame, 1994; recipient Nat. Educator award Milken Found., 1995. Mem. ASCD, NASSP, AAHPERD (com., spkr. nat. conv.), NEA, Conn. Assn. Health, Phys. Edn., Recreation and Dance (pres. 1981-82, Profl. Honor award 1986), Ctrl. Conn. Conf. (life, treas. 1984-87, Leadership award 1987), Nat. H.S. Coaches Assn. (track v.p. 1978-80, Conn. Cross Country Coach of Yr. award 1976, Track Coach of Yr. award), Conn. Prins. Acad., Blue Ribbon Human Resource Bank. Avocations: family, writing, swimming, biking, walking. Home: 30 Shadow Ln West Hartford CT 06110-1640 Office: Newington BOE 131 Cedar St Ste 2 Newington CT 06111-2698

DANOFF-KRAUS, PAMELA SUE, shopping center development executive; b. Gallup, N.Mex., Aug. 29, 1946; d. Isadore Harry and Armida Catherine (Ceccardi) Danoff; m. Milo Joseph Warner III, Dec. 28, 1968 (div. 1974); m. Robert Warren Kraus, Nov. 30, 1985; 1 child, Jillian Amaris. BA, U. N.Mex., 1968. Lic. in real estate, Calif. Real estate rep. Kaiser Aetna, Newport Beach, Calif., 1975-76; leasing agt. Alexander Haagen Co., Rolling Hills, Calif., 1976-77; dir. leasing Warren Kellogg & Assocs., Newport Beach, 1977-81, Center Devel. Co., Newport Beach, 1981-84; exec. v.p., ptnr. The Von Der Ahe Co., Newport Beach, 1984-86; ptnr. Marketplace Properties, Tustin, Calif., 1986-92; lectr. in field; panelist various convs., univs.; conductor seminars in field. Contbr. articles to profl. jours. Sponsor Californians Working Together to End Hunger and Homelessness, Los Angeles, 1988; mem. Orange County Performing Arts Ctr., 1983-85. Mem. Internat. Coun. Shopping Ctrs. (program chmn. 1987-89, small ctr. devel. com., state dir. pub. rels. and community affairs for Calif., 1989-92, chair pub. rels. and community svc. Western divsn. 1992-95), Calif. Bus. Properties Assn., Calif. Redevel. Assn., Women in Retail Real Estate, Chi Omega. Republican. Roman Catholic. Avocations: skiing, sailing, wine tasting, needlepoint, gardening. Home and Office: Danoff Kraus Enterprises 10182 Brier Ln Santa Ana CA 92705-1531

DANOS, HARRY JOHN, architect, educator, artist; b. Enfield, Conn., May 5, 1924; s. John Christopher and Alice (Panagiota) D.; m. Catherine Magiopoulos, Sept. 5, 1948; 1 child, Michael. Apprentice program, GE Co., 1943; USAF tng., Yale U., 1943-44; student, Springfield Jr. Coll., 1946-47; BArch, Syracuse U., 1952; MArch, Rice U., 1953; studied watercolors with Carlton Plummer, studied watercolors with Barbara Nechis; studied watercolors with Irving Shapiro, others. Registered arch., Conn., Vt., R.I. Arch., designer C.P. Kantianis, AIA, Springfield, Mass., 1952-55, Robert Carroll May (apprentice Frank Lloyd Wright), Hartford, 1955-57, Moore and Salsbury, U. Hartford, 1957-62, Charles DuBose Constn. Plz., 1952-55; prin., archtl. firm Harry Danos, AIA, Avon, 1955-80, Danos and Assocs., Archs., Hartford, 1962-80; staff arch., constrn. mgr. Associated Constrn. Co., Hartford, 1980-82; asst. dir. Bur. Pub. Works State of Conn., Hartford, 1982-84; profl. arch., devel. cons., 1984—; instr. art and arch. Syracuse U., Rice U., U. Hartford, Boston Archtl. Ctr., Guilford Handcrafts and Art Ctr., 1984—; dir. Aegean Art Workshops. Exhbns. include Peel Gallery, Danby, Vt., Leverett Gallery, Amherst, Mass., Hartford Nat. Bank, Waterford, Conn., E. Lyme Cmty. Ctr. Libr., Nat. Greek Am. Artists, Springfield, Mass.; represented in pvt. collections. Past chmn. E. Lyme Art League; exec. mem. E. Lyme Arts Coun.; mem. zoning and planning commn. Town of Avon, Conn., 1959-65; rep. Capitol Region Planning Agy., Avon, 1962-65. With USAF, 1944-46, WWII, PTO. Recipient Archtl. Award of Merit, Am. Assn. Sch. Adminstrs., 1965, Carl E. Shawyer award of merit Archtl. Precast Assn., 1975, Facilities Excellence award World Wide Volkswagen Corp.-Porsche-Audi Ea. Div., 1981, various achievement awards; named Winner, Chgo. Tribune Better Rooms Competition, 1950; fellowship grantee Rice U., 1952-53. Mem. AIA (corp., Medal 1952), Am. Arbitration Assn. (arbitrator), Conn. Watercolor Soc., Mystic Art Assn., Salmagundi Club, Avon Lions Club (past treas.). Avocation: watercolorist teacher. Home and Office: 148 Old Black Point Rd Niantic CT 06357

DANOS, PAUL, dean, finance educator. Chmn. acctg. dept. U. Mich., 1984-91, Arthur Andersen & Co. prof. acctg., 1985-95, dir. Paton Acctg. Ctr., 1988-91, sr. assoc. dean Sch. Bus. Adminstrn., -1992; dean, Laurence F. Whittemore prof. bus. adminstrn. Dartmouth Coll., Amos Tuck Sch. Bus. Adminstrn., Hanover, N.H., 1995—; chmn. MBA rev. team, chmn. comprehensive studies program exec. com., dir. acctg. PhD com., mem. exec. com., sch. bus. adminstrn., mem. doctoral studies com. Sch. Bus. Adminstrn., U. Mich. Author two text books; ah hoc editor The Acctg. Rev.; mem. editl. bd. Advances in Acctg.; consulting editor Rev. of Bus. and Econ. Rsch.; contbr. articles to profl. jours. Mem. audit com. City of Ann Arbor. Mem. Am. Acctg. Assn. (chair doctoral fellowship com., bd. govs. adminstrs. of acctg. programs exec. com. and database com.). Office: Amos Tuck Sch Bus 100 Tuck Hall Hanover NH 03755-9027*

DANOS, ROBERT MCCLURE, retired oil company executive; b. New Orleans, Dec. 9, 1929; s. Joseph A. and Muriel R. (McClure) D.; m. Barbara Umbach, Apr. 30, 1955; children: Robert M., Sally C., Susan M., Julie A., Richard F., Renee R. B.S. in Geology, Tulane U., 1950; M.S., La. State U., 1952. Geologist Texaco, Inc., New Orleans, 1955-67; staff geologist Texaco, Inc., Houston, 1967; div. geologist Texaco, Inc., Tulsa, 1968-70; exploration mgr. Texaco, Inc., Denver, 1970-80; sr. v.p. K N Energy, Inc., Lakewood, Colo., 1980-83; pres., chief exec. officer Midlands Energy Co., Lakewood, 1983-84; pres. McMoRan-Midlands Oil Co., New Orleans, 1984-86; pres., chief ops. officer McMoRan Oil & Gas Co., New Orleans, 1986-89; pres. Plains Petroleum Oper. Co., Lakewood, Colo., 1989-95; dir. Am. Exploration Co., Houston, 1996-97. 1st lt. U.S. Army, 1954. Mem. Am. Assn. Petroleum Geologists (del.), New Orleans Geolog. Soc. (v.p. 1965-67), Rocky Mountain Geolog. Assn., Bienville Club, Cherry Hills Country Club, Pickwick Club, Arlberg Club. Home: 124 High St Denver CO 80218-4018

DANOWSKI, JOHN, lacrosse coach; b. Mar. 12, 1954; m. Patricia; children: Kate, Matthew. BA, Rutgers U., 1976; MA, L.I. U., 1978. Asst. lacrosse coach L.I. U../C.W. Post, 1982; head coach L.I. U./C.W. Post, 1983-85; head lacrosse coach Hofstra U., Hempstead, N.Y., 1986—, dean univ. advisement, 1986-88, asst. dir. athletics, 1988-92; lectr. in field; T.V. instructional pieces ESPN, Fox TV Good Day N.Y.; served on U.S. Intercollegiate Lacrosse Assn. All American com., Top Twenty Coaches Poll; asst. coach North squad annual North-South Sr. All-Star game. Named F. Morris Touchstone Award winner U.S. Intercollegiate Lacrosse Assn., 1993, Nat. Lacrosse Coach of Yr., 1995, 96. Office: Hofstra U 120 Hofstra University Hempstead NY 11549-1200

DANS, PETER EMANUEL, medical educator; b. N.Y.C., June 17, 1937; s. Emanuel and Filomena (Lisanti) D.; m. Colette Lumina Lizotte, May 28, 1966; children: Maria Cristina, Paul Edouard, Thomas Emanuel, Suzanne Elise. BS in Chemistry, Manhattan Coll., 1957; MD, Columbia U., 1961. Intern, resident medicine Johns Hopkins Hosp., Balt., 1961-63; resident medicine Presbyn. Hosp., N.Y.C., 1963-64; fellow rsch. NIH, Bethesda, Md., 1964-67; infectious diseases fellow Harvard U., Boston, 1967-69; asst. prof. medicine U. Colo., Denver, 1969-74, assoc. prof., 1974-78; Robert Wood Johnson health policy fellow Inst. Medicine, Washington, 1976-77, sr. prof. assoc., 1977-78; assoc. prof. medicine Johns Hopkins U. Sch. Medicine and Health Policy and Mgmt., Balt., 1978—, Johns Hopkins U. Sch. Hygiene and Pub. Health, Balt.; clin. prof. Marshall U. Sch. Medicine, 1995—; mem. Md. Physician Bd. Quality Assurance, sec. 1988-92; ind. cons. disease mgmt., outcomes, ethics, 1996—; med. cons. Advanced Paradigm Inc., 1996—. Author: Boil the Water and Just Say Aah!, 1999, Physicians in the Movies, 1999; co-author: New Medical Market Place A Physician's Guide to the Health Care Revolution, 1988; dep. editor Annals of Internal Medicine, 1991-94; assoc. med. dir. GMIS, Inc., 1994-95; mem. editl. bd. Pharos, 1988—; contbr. articles to profl. jours., chpts. to books; film reviewer Physician at the Movies, Pharos. Pres. Falls Rd. Cmty. Assn., Cockeysville, Md., 1980-84, 87-90; mem. adv. com. on gifted talented program Baltimore County, 1981-90, mem. zoning adv. com., 1985-86, mem. commn. on aging, 1996-98; pres. parish coun. Shrine of Sacred Heart, Balt., 1981-83; bd. dirs. Ctr. Profl. Ethics U. Balt., 1999—; lector St. Francis Xavier, Balt., 1997—. Fellow ACP; mem. Epsilon Sigma Pi, Alpha Omega Alpha. Roman Catholic. Avocations: film, birdwatching. Home and Office: 11 Hickory Hill Rd Cockeysville Hunt Valley MD 21030-1624

DANSAK, DANIEL ALBERT, medical educator, consultant; b. McKeesport, Pa., Apr. 27, 1943; s. Henry Daniel and Mary (Francis) D.; m. Judith Lynn Rogers, May 9, 1981 (div. Apr. 1987); m. Melissa Ann Pickett, May 31, 1989. BS, Drexel U., 1966; MD, Georgetown U., 1970. Diplomate Am. Bd. Psychiatry and Neurology. Asst. chief psychiatry svc. VA, Washington, 1975-77; asst. prof. dept. psychiatry U. N.Mex., Albuquerque, 1977-84; assoc. prof. dept. psychiatry U. South Ala., Mobile, 1984—; cons. U.S. Dept. Labor, Albuquerque, 1981-84; cons. Ala. Dept. Edn., Mobile, 1986-90. Contbr. articles to profl. jours. Mem. bd. trustees Mobile Bay Area Partnership for Youth, 1989—. Lt. comdr. USNR, 1973-75. Fellow Am. Coll. Clin. Pharmacology; mem. AAAS, Am. Psychiat. Assn., Ala. Psychiat. Assn., Assn. Mil. Surgeons, Am. Soc. Addictive Medicine, Inst. Electronic Engrs. Republican. Roman Catholic. Avocation: fishing. Home: 4012 Dawson Dr Mobile AL 36619-9224 Office: U South Ala Dept Psychiatry 2451 Fillingim St Mobile AL 36617-2238

DANSBY, JOHN WALTER, retired oil company executive; b. Logan, W.Va., Dec. 29, 1944; s. Charles Eugene and Lillian (Maggard) D.; m. Karen Navarin, June 20, 1970; children: Andrew, David. B.S. in Econs, U. Pa., 1966; M.B.A., Emory U., 1967; Ph.D. in Econs, U. Ky., 1976. Fin. analyst Ashland (Ky.) Oil, Inc., 1970-71, staff economist, 1975-77, mgr. fed. energy programs, 1977-81, exec. asst., 1981, v.p. strategic planning, 1981-84, v.p. planning, 1984-92, adminstrv. v.p. and treas., 1992-98; vis. instr. Ohio U., 1980. Mem. U. Ky. Devel. Coun., U. Ky. Fellows.; vice chmn. Ky. Sci. and Tech. Coun. Mem. Nat. Assn. Bus. Economists, Internat. Assn. Energy Economists, N.Y. Penn Club. Home: 280 Bellefonte Cir Ashland KY 41101-2196 also: 106 Shadow Mountain Dr Sedona AZ 86336

DANSE, ILENE HOMNICK RAISFELD, physician, educator, toxicologist; b. Bklyn., June 24, 1940; d. Jack and Henrietta (Poverstein) Homnick; m. James Atherton Danse, Aug. 10, 1982; children: Arthur Raisfeld, Robin Raisfeld. BS, CUNY, 1960; MD, NYU, 1964; student, Pratt Inst., Art Students League, Bklyn. Mus. Art Sch. Diplomate Nat. Bd. Med. Examiners, Am. Bd. Internal Medicine, Am. Bd. Toxicology. Assoc. prof. internal medicine SUNY, Stony Brook, 1975-83, assoc. prof. pharmacology, 1977-83, dir. clin. pharmacology and toxicology Sch. Medicine, 1978-83; acting chairperson clin. pharmacology Northport VA Hosp., L.I., N.Y., 1978-83; sr. advisor Chevron Environ. Health Ctr., San Pablo, Calif., 1982-84; prin. ENVIROMED Health Svcs., Inc., Novato, Calif., 1985—; ind. med. examiner toxicology and internal medicine Dept. Indsl. Rels., State of Calif., 1985—; assoc. clin. prof. dept. medicine div. occupational and environ. medicine U. Calif., San Francisco, 1986—; assoc. clin. prof. dept. epidemiol. and preventive medicine U. Calif., Davis, 1991—; cons. in fields of toxicology, pharmacology, environ., occupational and internal medicine, 1984—; mem. bd. sci. advisors Am. Coun. Sci. and Health; mem. sci. rev. panel Hazardous Substances Data Base, Nat. Libr. Medicine. Author: Common Sense Toxics In the Workplace, 1991; contbr. articles to sci. pubs. Mem. bd. sci. advisors Am. Coun. on Sci. and Health; mem. sci. rev. panel Hazardous Substances Data Base, Nat. Libr. of Medicine. Fellow ACP, Am. Coll. Clin. Pharmacology; mem. AAAS, Am. Acad. Clin. Toxicology, Am. Chem. Soc. (environ. health and safety sect.), Am. Coll. Occupational Medicine, Am. Indsl. Hygiene Assn. (occupational medicine sect.), Am. Coll. Toxicology, Am. Soc. Pharmacology and Therapeutics, Soc. Toxicology, Western Occupational Med. Assn. Achievements include patent for epithelial cell growth-regulating composition containing polyamines, and method of its use. Office: ENVIROMED Health Svcs Inc # 346 448 Ignacio Blvd Novato CA 94949-6085

DANSEREAU, PIERRE, ecologist; b. Montreal, Can., Oct. 5, 1911; s. J.-Lucien and Marie (Archambault) D.; m. Françoise Masson, Aug. 29, 1935. BA, U. Montréal, 1932, BS Agr., 1936; DSc, U. Geneva, Switzerland, 1939; DSc (hon.), U. Sask., 1959, U. N.B., 1959, U. Strasbourg, France, 1970, U. Sherbrooke, 1971, Concordia U., 1971, U. Waterloo, 1972, U. Guelph, 1973, U. Western Ont., 1973, Meml. U. Nfld., 1974, McGill U., 1976, U. Ottawa, 1978, Royal Mil. Coll., 1990, Laurentian U, 1993, U. Laval, 1994. Mem. faculty U. Montréal, 1940-42, 45, 55-61, 68-71; with Service de Biogéographie, 1943-50; prof. botany U. Mich., 1950-55; asst. dir., prof. ecology N.Y. Bot. Garden, 1961-68; adj. prof. Columbia U., 1962-68; mem. staff U. Qué., Centre de Recherches Écologiques de Montréal, 1971-72; prof. ecology U. Qué., Montréal, 1972-76, prof. emeritus, 1976—; vice chmn. Can. Environ. Adv. Coun., 1972-76, Can. Fed. Task Force Housing and Urban Devel., 1968, Natural Scis. and Engring. Rsch. Coun., 1978-80; mem. Sci. Coun. Can., 1968-72, Can. Radio-TV Coun., 1968; v.p. Can. Commn. Internat. Biol. Programme, 1968; chmn. program urban devel. Sci. Coun. Can., 1970; pres. 1st Internat. Film Festival on Human Environ., 1973; sec. gen. Mich. Acad. Sci., Arts and Letters, 1953; 1st v.p. 9th Internat. Bot. Congress, 1959; chmn. bd. Gamma Inst., 1983-86; hon. chmn. Fondation de l'ACFAS, 1984; pres. Environment 2000, 1990, Festival Internat. du Film Scientifique de Qué., 1990; mem. internat. adv. com. rev. Ecodecision, 1992-94; bd. dirs. Biodome, Montréal, 1993-95. Author: Biogeography: An Ecological Perspective, 1957, Phytogeographia laurentiana II, 1959, Contradictions & Biculture, 1964; (with co-author) Studies on the Vegetation of Puerto Rico I and II, 1966; (with others) A Universal System for Recording Vegetation II, 1966, Dimensions of Environmental Quality, 1971, Inscape and Landscape, 1973, La terre des hommes et le paysage intérieur, 1973, Harmony and Disorder in the Canadian Environment, 1975, Ezaim: Écologie de la Zone de l'Aéroport International de Montréal, Le cadre d'une recherche écologique interdisciplinaire, 1976; co-author: Ecological Grading and Classification of Land-occupation and Land-use Mosaics, 1977; author: An Ecological Grading of Human Settlements, 1978, Harmonie et désordre dans l'environment canadien, 1980, Essai de classification et de cartographie écologique des espaces, 1985, Les dimensions écologiques de l'espace urbain, 1987, Interdisciplinary perspective on production-investment-control processes in the environment, 1990, L'envers et l'endroit: le désir, le besoin et la capacité, 1991, 2d edit., 1994; Biodiversity, Ecodiversity, Sociodiversity--trois aspects of diversity. Global biodiversity, 1997; editor: Challenge for Survival, 1970. Decorated Companion Order Can., 1969, Grand officer Ordre Nat. du Qué., 1992; recipient Pierre Fermat medal, 1960, Léo Pariseau medal, 1965, Pfizer prize, 1965, Prix David, Qué., 1959, Disting. Svc. award N.Y. Bot. Garden, 1969, Massey medal, 1973, Molson prize, 1974, Esdras-Minville prize, 1983, Marie-Victorin prize, 1983, Izaak Walton Killam prize, 1985, Knight of Ordre Nat. du Qué., 1985, Can. Bot. Assn. Lawson medal, 1986, Lifetime Achievement award Environ. Can., 1989, Premier's medal, Qué., 1989, Prix Interamerica, 1990, Qué. Youth Edn. Excellence prize, 1990, Grand Prix du Mérite forestier, 1990, Dawson medal, 1995; named Gt. Montrealer in Sci., 1978, Guggenheim fellow, 1949, Commonwealth Pres. fellow, 1961. Fellow Royal Soc. Can., Royal Soc. New Zealand (hon.); mem. Can. Mental Health Assn. (pres. Qué. 1972-74), Am. Teilhard de Chardin Assn. (pres. 1967), Ecol. Soc. Am. (v.p. 1968), Assn. Canadienne-Française pour l'Avancement des Scis. (sec. gen. 1945-46), Geog. Soc. Montreal (pres. 1957), Argentina Acad. Environ. Scis. (fgn. corr. mem. 1984), Acad. Scis. Lisbon (fgn. corr. mem. 1985), Ordre nat. du Qué. (pres. 1987-89), PEN Club Internat. (hon.). Office: U du Qué à Montréal, Case Postale 8888 Sta Ctr-ville, Montreal, PQ Canada H3C 3P8 *Teaching and research are parallel but complementary exercises. Contemplation and distillation in the ivory tower have to be fed by experience and exchange. My own experience has been mostly in the field: the sensorial witnessing of stones, plants, and animals, and men and cities, must be renewed all the time, in an endless addition to a personal treasury. But the translation into word-and-picture form needs interlocutors to test both the validity of perception and the communicability of rendering. This pulsation has varied in rhythm and content and has yielded both anxiety and happiness.*

DANTE, JOE, film director; b. Morristown, N.J.. Mng. editor Film Bulletin. Co-dir.: (films) Hollywood Boulevard, 1976, Twilight Zone:The Movie, 1983, Amazon Women on the Moon, 1987; dir. (films) Piranha, 1978, The Howling, 1980, Gremlins, 1984, Explorers, 1985, Innerspace, 1987, The Burbs, 1989, Gremlins II, The New Batch, 1990, Matinee, 1993, Runaway Daughters, 1994, The Second Civil War, 1997; co-screenwriter Rock 'n' Roll High School; editor (film) Grand Theft Auto, 1977. Mem. Dirs. Guild Am. Address: The Gersh Agy 232 N Canon Dr Beverly Hills CA 90210-5302

DANTINI, JULIE ANN, educational administrator, director, counselor; b. Susquehanna, Pa., Dec. 9, 1947; d. Guilio and Anna Louise (Pingeralli) D. BS, Mansfield (Pa.) U., 1969; MS, SUNY, Oneonta, 1972. Cert. elem. and spl. edn. tchr., guidance counselor, N.Y.. Educaotr Binghamton (N.Y.) City Sch. Dist., 1969-73, social worker, tchr. in charge visually impaired, 1973-79; vocat. rehab. counselor N.Y. State Edn. Dept., Binghamton, 1979-81, sr. vocat. rehab. couselor, 1981-85; dir. counseling Southern Tier, N.Y., 1985—; advisor, cons. Broome C.C., Binghamton, 1983-97; advisor N.Y. Assn. for Learning Disables, Albany, 1985-89, Peer Network NYU, N.Y.C., 1987, Cornell So. Tech. Assistance Ctr., 1993—; mem. steering com. psychology dept. SUNY-Binghamton, 1984-86; mgmt. team for rehab. svcs. adminstrn. grant Catskill Ind. Ctr., 1990-94; project adv. com. Internat. Ctr. for Disabled, 1991-96; liaison Tech. Assistance Ctr., Cornell U., 1992—. Cons. book Vocational Rehabilitation for Learning Disables Adults, 1984; guest editor Jour. Applied Rehab. Counseling, winter 1998; co-editor Manual for VES 1D Impartial Hearing Offices, 1997. Recipient Cert. of Merit, Gov. of N.Y., 1985, 91, Nat. Disting. Svc. Registry, 1989. Mem. Nat. Rehab. Assn., Nat. Rehab. Counseling Assn. Avocations: cross country skiing, sailing, golf. Home: 46 Moore Ave Binghamton NY 13903-3123 Office: NY State Edn Dept 44 Hawley St Binghamton NY 13901-4434

DANTO, ARTHUR COLEMAN, author, philosopher, art critic; b. Ann Arbor, Mich., Jan. 1, 1924; s. Samuel Budd and Sylvia (Gittleman) D.; m. Shirley Rovetch, Aug. 9, 1946 (dec. July 1978); children: Elizabeth, Jane; m. Barbara Westman, Feb. 15, 1980. BA, Wayne State U., 1948; MA, Columbia U., 1949, PhD, 1952; postgrad., U. Paris, 1949-50. Instr. U. Colo., 1950-51; mem. faculty Columbia U., 1952—, Johnsonian prof. philosophy, 1975-92, chmn. dept., 1979-87, co-dir. Ctr. for Study of Human Rights, 1978-92; prof. emeritus, 1992; Andrew W. Mellon Fine Arts lectr., 1995. Author: Analytical Philosophy of Knowledge, 1968, What Philosophy Is, 1968, Analytical Philosophy of History, 1965, Nietzsche as Philosopher, 1965, Analytical Philosophy of Action, 1973, Mysticism and Morality, 1972, Jean-Paul Sartre, 1975, The Transfiguration of the Commonplace, 1981 (Lionel Trilling Book prize 1982), Narration and Knowledge, 1985, The Philosophical Disenfranchisement of Art, 1986, The State of the Art, 1987, Connections to the World, 1989, Encounters and Reflections: Art in the Historical Present, 1990, Beyond the Brillo Box: Art in the Post Historical Period, 1992, Mark Tansey: Visions and Revisions, 1992, Robert Mapplethorpe, 1992, Embodied Meanings: Critical Essays and Aesthetic Meditations, 1994, Playing with the Edge: The Photographic Achievement of Robert Mapplethorpe, After the End of Art: Contemporary Art and the Pale of History, 1997 (Eugene Kayden prize 1997), The Body/Body Problem, 1999, Philosophizing Art, 1999; editor Jour. Philosophy, 1965—, pres., 1987—; art critic The Nation, 1984—; contbg. editor ARTFORUM. Bd. dirs. Amnesty Internat., 1970-75, gen. sec., 1973. Served with AUS, 1942-45. Recipient prize for disting. criticism Mfrs.-Hanover/Art World, 1985, George S. Polk award for criticism, 1985, Nat. Book Critics Circle prize for criticism, 1990, ICP Infinity prize for writing in photography, 1993; fellow Fulbright Found., 1949, Guggenheim Found., 1969, 82, Am. Coun. Learned Socs., 1961, 70; Fulbright disting. prof. Yugoslavia, 1976; Phi Beta Kappa prof. Arts and Scis.; mem. Am. Philos. Assn. (v.p. 1969, pres. 1983), Am. Soc. Aesthetics (v.p. 1987, pres. 1989). Fellow AAAS; mem. Am. Philos. Assn. (v.p. 1969, pres. 1983), Am. Soc. Aesthetics (v.p. 1987, pres. 1989), Coll. Art Assn. (Frank Jewett Mather prize for criticism). Office: 420 Riverside Dr New York NY 10025-7773

DANTON, JOSEPH PERIAM, librarian, educator; b. Palo Alto, Calif., July 5, 1908; s. George Henry and Annina (Periam) D.; m. Lois King, Dec. 25, 1948 (div.); children—Jennifer, Joseph Periam. Ed., U. Leipzig, Germany, 1925-26; A.B. magna cum laude, Oberlin Coll., 1928; B.S.,

Columbia, 1929; A.M., Williams Coll., 1930; Ph.D., U. Chgo., 1935, (Carnegie fellow, 1933-35). With N.Y. Pub. Libr., Williams Coll. Libr. and ALA, 1928-33; librarian, assoc. prof. bibliography Colby Coll., Waterville, Maine, 1935-36, Temple U., Phila., 1936-46; dean Sch. Librarianship, U. Calif.-Berkeley, 1946-61, assoc. prof., 1946-47, prof., 1947-76, prof. emeritus, 1976—; vis. prof. Grad. Library Sch., U. Chgo., 1942, Columbia, 1946; vis. lectr. U. Toronto, 1963, Univs. of Belgrade, Ljubljana, Novi Sad, Zagreb, 1965, U. B.C., 1968, 79, McGill U., 1969, U. P.R., 1970, U. Md., 1977, U. N.C., 1977, U. Tex., 1979, Hebrew U., Jerusalem, 1965, 85; Fulbright research scholar, Germany, 1960-61, Austria, 1964-65; surveyor and cons. numerous libraries; UNESCO Library Cons., Jamaica, 1968; del. Internat. Fedn. Library Assns. meeting, 1939-1972; Ford Found. cons. on libraries in SE Asia (with R. C. Swank), 1963; hon. research fellow U. London, 1974-75. Author: Education for Librarianship, 1946, Education for Librarianship, Paris, 1950, United States Influence on Norwegian Librarianship, 1890-1940, 1957, Book Selection and Collections: A Comparison of German and American University Libraries, 1963, Index to Festschriften in Librarianship, 1970, (with Jane F. Pulis) vol. 2, 1967-1975, 1979, Between M.L.S. and Ph.D, 1970, The Dimensions of Comparative Librarianship, 1973; editor: The Climate of Book Selection; Social Influences on Sch. and Pub. Libraries, 1959. Served as lt. USNR, 1942-45, PTO. Recipient Berkeley citation, 1976, Beta Phi Mu award, 1983; Guggenheim fellow, 1971. Mem. Assn. Am. Libr. Schs. (pres. 1949-50), Internat. Fedn. Libr. Assns. (chmn. com. libr. edn. 1967-72). Democrat. Home: 500 Vernon St Apt 402 Oakland CA 94610-5303 Office: U Calif Sch Info Mgmt & Sys Berkeley CA 94720

DANTONE, JOSEPH JOHN, JR., naval officer; b. Balt., Aug. 6, 1942; s. Joseph John and Miriam Edith (Moore) D.; m. Maria Elizabeth Szolnoky, May 4, 1968; children: Joseph John III, Marne Elizabeth. BS, U.S. Naval Acad., 1964; MS in Aero. Engring., Material Mgmt., Naval Postgrad. Sch., 1971; postgrad., Nuclear Power Sch., Orlando, Fla., 1982-83. Comd. ensign USN, 1964, advanced through grades to rear adm., 1991; pilot Fighter Squadron 84 USN, Oceana, Va., 1966-67; pilot Fighter Squadron 161 USN, San Diego, 1967-69, pilot/ops. Fighter Squadron 1, 1971-75; dep. for F-14 Program Naval Air Systems Command USN, Washington, 1975-77; comdg. officer Fighter Squadron 14 USN, Oceana, 1977-81; exec. officer USS Enterprise USN, Alameda, Calif., 1984-86, comdg. officer USS Wichita, 1986-87; comdg. officer USS Abraham Lincon Precom Unit, Newport News, Va., 1987-88; comdg. officer USS Dwight D. Eisenhower USN, Norfolk, Va., 1988-90; dir. program resource appraisal div. USN, Washington, 1990-92; comdr. Carrier Group Three, 1992-94; dep. dir. Nat. Reconnaissance Office (MS), Washington, 1994-96; dir. Def. Mapping Agy., Washington, 1996-97, Nat. Imagery and Mapping Agy., Reston, 1997-98; sr. v.p. Mid-Atlantic Region USAA, 1998—. Decorated meritorious svc. medal, def. superior svc. medal Legion of Merit, air medal, Navy commendation medal. Roman Catholic. Avocations: hunting, golf. Home: 1220 Misty Hollow Way Virginia Beach VA 23454

D'ANTONI, MIKE, professional basketball coach; b. Mullens, W.Va., May 8, 1951; m. Laurel D'Antoni; 1 child, Michael. Basketball player Kings NBA, 1973-1975, basketball player San Antonio Spurs, 1975-76; past basketball player Milan Italian League, winner 2 European Cups, 2 InterContinental Cups Milan, coach Milan, 1990-93, head coach Milan, 1996-97, winner Italian Cup, 1997; dir. player pers. Denver Nuggets NBA, 1997-98, profl. basketball coach Denver Nuggets, 1998—. Named to Marshall U. Hall of Fame, 1997. Office: care Denver Nuggets 1635 Clay St Denver CO 80204*

D'ANTONI, PHILIP, producer; b. Bronx, N.Y., Feb. 19, 1929; s. Peter and Josephine (Elici) D'A.; m. Ruth Ann Wiederecht, Sept. 12, 1953; children: Christopher, Jeanne, Carol, James, Robert. Student, Fordham U., 1948-50. Prodn. asst., asso. producer CBS-TV, 1949-53; v.p., dir. Mut. Broadcasting System, 1955-61; pres. D'Antoni/Weitz TV Prodns. Producer (weekly TV series) Movin' On, 1961-73, (films) Bullitt, 1968, The French Connection, 1971 (Acad. award), (spls.) Elizabeth Taylor in London, 1964, Sophia Loren in Rome, 1965, Melina Mercouri in Greece, 1966; producer, dir. (film) The Seven Ups, 1974, (TV movies) Strike Force, The Connection, Cabo, Inside-Outside, In Tandem, Rubber Gun Squad, 1974-77. Served with AUS, 1946-48. Mem. Dirs. Guild Am., Screenwriters Guild, Motion Picture Acad. Home: care of St Andrews G C 10 Old Jackson Ave Hastings On Hudson NY 10706

D'ANTONIO, JAMES JOSEPH, lawyer; b. Tucson, Jan. 13, 1959; s. Lawrence Patrick and Rosemary Catherine (Kane) D'A. Student, Tufts U., 1978-79; BA, U. Ariz., 1981, JD, 1984. Bar: Ariz. 1984, U.S. Dist. Ct. Ariz. 1984, U.S. Ct. Appeals (9th cir.) 1993. Assoc. Law Office of D'Antonio and D'Antonio, Tucson, 1984-93; pvt. practice law Law Offices of James J. D'Antonio, Tucson, 1993—. Chmn. bd. govs. U. Ariz. Coll. Law, 1983-84; mem. Pima County Teen Ct. Adv. Bd; mem. Health South Rehab. Inst., Tucson Cmty. Adv. Bd.; bd. dirs. Coyote Task Force. Named Outstanding Pro Bono Lawyer Pima County Vol. Lawyers Program, 1993. Fellow Ariz. Bar Found.; mem. ABA, Assn. Trial Lawyers Am., Ariz. Bar Assn., Ariz. Trial Lawyers Assn., Pima County Bar Assn. Office: 80 S Stone Ave Tucson AZ 85701-1713

D'ANTONIO, KAY BISHOP, special education educator; b. Sonora, Tex., July 26, 1953; d. Donald Kelley and Helen Joyce (Pope) B. BS in Edn., N.Mex. State U., 1979, MA in Instructional Psychology, 1989. Tchr. multiply impaired Las Cruces (N.Mex.) pub. schs., 1980-81, tchr. behavior disorders, 1981-87; master tchr. N.Mex. State U.-LCPS Exchange Prog., Las Cruces, 1987-88; facilitator/tchr. children with behavior disorders Las Cruces pub. schs., 1988-93; adminstr. spl. edn. Carlsbad (N.Mex.) Mcpl. Schs., 1993—, ednl. diagnostician, 1997—; adj. instr. N.Mex. State U., 1987-89; behavior cons., 1987-93. Mem. Coun. for Exceptional Children. Office: PO Box 1226 Carlsbad NM 88220-5897

D'ANTONIO, WILLIAM VINCENT, sociology educator; b. New Haven, Feb. 7, 1926; s. Albert and Marie (Nuzzo) D'A.; m. A. Lorraine Giorgio, June 15, 1950; children—JoAnne Marie, Albert C., Nancy L., Carla M., Raissa, Laura J. B.A., Yale U., 1948; M.A., U. Wis., 1953; Ph.D., Mich. State U., 1958. Master Spanish Loomis Sch., Windsor, Conn., 1949-54; instr. sociology Mich. State U., East Lansing, 1957-59; from asst. to prof. U. Notre Dame, South Bend, Ind., 1959-71; prof. sociology U. Conn., Storrs, 1971—. Author: (with others) Influentials in Two Border Cities, 1965, Female and Male Dimensions of Human Sexuality, 1974, Sociology: Human Society, 1971, 4th edit., 1984, American Catholic Laity in a Changing Church, 1989, Laity, American and Catholic, Transforming the Church, 1996; editor (with others) Power and Democracy in America, 1961, Religion, Revolution and Reform, New Forces for Change in Latin America, 1964, Families and Religions, 1983; contbr. articles to profl. jours. Pres. Arts of Tolland, 1972-78. Served with USN, 1944-46. Grantee Social Sci. Research Council, 1962, 64, Ethnic Heritage grant HEW, 1974, Lilly Endowment Three Yr. grant 1985-87, Louisville Inst. grant, 1999. Mem. Am. Sociol. Assn. (exec. officer 1982-91), Soc. for Sci. Study Religion (pres. 1977-79, exec. sec. 1970-76), AAUP (pres. Conn. U. chpt. 1979). Democrat. Roman Catholic. Club: Yale (Washington). Avocations: golf, tennis.

DANTZIG, GEORGE BERNARD, applied mathematics educator; b. Portland, Oreg., Nov. 8, 1914; s. Tobias and Anja (Ourisson) D.; m. Anne Shmuner, Aug. 23, 1936; children—David Franklin, Jessica Rose, Paul Michael. A.B. in Math. and Physics, U. Md., 1936; M.A. in Math., U. Mich., 1937; Ph.D. in Math., U. Calif.-Berkeley, 1946; hon. degree, Technion, Israel, Linkoping U., Sweden, U. Md., Yale U., Louvain U., Belgium, Columbia U., U. Zurich, Switzerland, Carnegie-Mellon U., U. Mich. Chief combat analysis br. Statis. Control Hdqrs. USAF, 1941-46, math. advisor, 1946-52; research mathematician Rand Corp., Santa Monica, Calif., 1952-60; prof., chmn. Ops. Research Ctr., U. Calif.-Berkeley, 1960-66; prof. ops. rsch. and computer sci. Stanford (Calif.) U., Calif., 1966—; chief methodology Internat. Inst. Applied System Analysis, Austria, 1973-74; cons. to industry. Author: Linear Programming and Extensions, 1963; co-author: Compact City, 1973, Linear Programming I Introduction, 1997; contbr. articles to profl. jours.; assoc. editor Math. Programming, Math. of Ops. Research, others. Recipient Exceptional Civilian Svc. medal War Dept, 1944, NAS award, 1971, in applied math. and numerical analysis, 1977, Nat medal of sci. for inventing linear programming and simplex algorithm, 1975, Von Neumann theory prize in ops. rsch., 1975, Harvey prize Technion, 1985, Silver medal Operational Rsch. Soc. Gt. Britain, 1986, Coors Am. Ingenuity award, 1989, Pender award U. Pa., 1995. Fellow Am. Acad. Arts and Scis., Econometric Soc., Inst. Math. Stats.; mem. AAAS, IEEE, Assn. Computing Machinery, Nat. Acad. Scis., Nat. Acad. Engring., Ops. Research Soc. Am., Am. Math. Soc., Math. Programming Soc. (chmn. 1973-74), Inst. Mgmt. Sci. (pres. 1966), Phi Beta Kappa, Sigma Xi, Phi Kappa Phi, Pi Mu Epsilon, Omega Rho Soc. E-mail: goerge-dantzig@worldnet.att.net. Home: 821 Tolman Dr Stanford CA 94305-1025 Office: Stanford Univ Dept Engring-Econ Systems and Ops Rsch Stanford CA 94305-4023

DANTZKER, DAVID ROY, health facility executive. MD, SUNY, Buffalo, 1967. Diplomate Am. Bd. Internal Medicine, Am. Bd. Pulmonary Medicine, Am. Bd. CCM. Intern Buffalo Gen. Hosp., 1967-68; resident in medicine SUNY Affiliated Hosp., Buffalo, 1968-70; fellow in pulmonary medicine U. Calif., San Diego, 1972-75; mem. med. staff N. Shore L.I. Jewish Health Sys., Great Neck, N.Y., 1990—; pres., CEO L.I. Jewish Med. Ctr., Great Neck, 1994-97; pres. N. Shore L.I. Jewish Health Sys., Great Neck, 1997—; prof. medicine Albert Einstein Coll. Medicine, 1990—. Author 7 books; contbr. 130 articles to profl. jours. Fellow ACP, Am. Coll. Chest Physicians. Office: N Shore L I Jewish Hlth Sys 145 Community Dr Great Neck NY 11021-5502

DANTZLER, DERYL DAUGHERTY, dean, law educator; b. Macon, Ga., Jan. 26, 1944; d. Marshall Harrison and Gertrude Earle (Baker) Daugherty; m. L. Keitt Dantzler, June, 1968 (div. 1975); 1 child, Kennon Otis. BA, Mercer U., 1964, JD, 1970. Bar: Ga. 1970, U.S. Dist. Ct. (mid. dist.) Ga. 1970, U.S. Ct. Appeals (5th and 11th cirs.) 1970, U.S. Supreme Ct. 1973. Assoc. Mincey, Kenmore & Bennett, Macon, 1970-73; ptnr. Bennett, Mobley & Dantzler, Macon, 1973-78; pvt. practice Macon, 1978-79; asst. prof. Law Sch., Mercer U., Macon, 1979-84, prof., 1984—, dir. trial practice, 1985—; dean Nat. Criminal Def. Coll., Inc., Macon, 1985—. Mem. Nat. Assn. Criminal Def. Lawyers (Presdl. Commendation 1985, 89, Lifetime Achievement award 1996), Assn. Continuing Legal Edn. Adminstrs., Ga. Bar Assn. Office: Mercer U Law Sch Macon GA 31207

DANTZMAN, GREGORY PETER, design engineer; b. Cudahay, Wis., Jan. 27, 1965; s. Thomas George and Charlotte Ruth (Ropicky) D.; m. Deanna Rose Nitkowski, Apr. 9, 1988; children: Rebecca, Zachary. BSEE, Milw. Sch. Engring., 1987, MSEM, 1993. Lic. engr.-in-tng., Wis. Product svc. engr. drives divsn. GE, Erie, Pa., 1987-89; control design engr., systems design engr. drives systems divsn. Allen-Bradley, Mequon, Wis., 1989-93; elec. engr. CH2M Hill, Milw., 1993-94; project engr. Bucyrus Internat., Inc., South Milwaukee, Wis., 1995-99; custom product devel. mgr. WAGO Corp., Brown Deer, Wis., 1999—. Mem. IEEE. Roman Catholic. Avocations: triathlons, softball, reading. Home: N60w23874 Butternut Ln Sussex WI 53089-3746

DANUATMODJO, CHERYL LYNN, home healthcare nurse; b. Kans., Mar. 23, 1962; d. Robert D. and Jo El Schlegel. Student, Wichita (Kans.) Practical Nursing Sch., 1983; AS, St. Mary of the Plains Coll., 1987, BSN, 1992. Nurses aide St. Joseph Med. Ctr., Wichita, 1981-82; staff nurse ARC, Wichita, 1984, Med. Pers. Pool, Wichita, 1984-87, St. Francis Regional Med. Ctr., Wichita, 1987-90; nurse Interim Healthcare, Wichita, 1990—. Mem. ARC Nurses Assn., Sedgwick County Assn. for Neonatal Nurses. Home: 501 E 63rd St N Wichita KS 67219-1211 Office: 333 S Broadway St Wichita KS 67202-4300

DANVERS, DAVID BELL, equity broker; b. Poughkeepsie, N.Y., Jan. 15, 1968; s. William David and Rachel (Bell) Rosenberg; m. Karen Minor, Sept. 24, 1994; children: Andrew Bennett, Erik Payson. BA in Econs, French, Union Coll., 1990. Cert. series 7 Nat. Assn. Securities Dealers. Asst. v.p. Salomon Smith Barney, N.Y.C., 1992—. Ptnr. in Edn., Bd. Edn., N.Y.C., 1995—; house capt. (repairs) Americares, New Canaan, Conn., 1996—. Mem. Nat. Assn. Securities Dealers, N.Y. Soc. Securities Analysts, Assn. for Investment Mgmt. and Rsch. Democrat. Methodist. Office fax: 212-723-8796. E-mail: dbellr@aol.com. Avocations: ice hockey, skiing, running. Home: 34 Woodchuck Lane Norwalk CT 06854

DANVERS, WILLIAM, consultant. BA with honors, Mich. State U., 1974; MA in Internat. Rels., George Washington U., 1980. Legis. asst. fgn. affairs U.S. Ho. of Reps., Washington, 1981-89; sr. advisor Strobe Talbot, 1993-94; legis. asst. for econ. affairs Sen. Joe Lieberman, 1989-92; acting sr. dir. for legis. affairs Nat. Security Coun., 1994-95, spl. asst. to pres., sr. dir. legis. affairs, 1995-97; Washington rep. Orgn. for Econ. Coop. and Devel., 1997-99; cons. Griffin, Johnson, Dover & Stewart, Washington, 1999—. Home: 110 S Buchanan St Arlington VA 22204-1346 Office: Griffin Johnson Dover & Stewart 1300 Connecticut Ave NW Washington DC 20036

DANVERS, WILLIAM C., federal official; b. Scranton, Pa., May 19, 1952; s. Harry Thomas and Martha Louise (McDonnell) D.; m. Gwendolyn Jose-Francoise Marié Sarni; children: Alexander, Camille. BA with highest hons., Mich. State U., 1974; MA in Spl. Studies, Geo. Washington U., 1980. Profl. staff mem. Subcom. Census and Population House Postal & Civil Svc. Com., Washington, 1981-86; legis. asst. fgn. affairs Ho. Reps., Washington, 1981-88; press sec. Rep. Robert Garcia (Dem. N.Y.), Washington, 1981-88, staff dir. subcom on internat. fin. and trade, 1987-89; staff dir. subcom. on policy rsch. Ho. Com. on Banking, Washington, 1989; legis. asst. Sen. Joseph Lieberman (Dem. Conn.) U.S. Senate, Washington, 1989-93; spl. adviser Strobe Talbott Ambassador at large new ind. states, Washington, 1989-93; dir. legis. affairs Nat. Security Coun., Washington, 1994-97; head Washington office Office Econ. Cooperation and Devel., 1997-99; cons. Griffin, Johnson, Dover and Stewart, Washington, 1999—. Contbr. articles to Jour. of Commerce, 1989—. Avocations: family, running, reading. Office: Griffin Johnson Dover & Stewart Ste 600 1300 Connecticut Ave Washington DC 20036

D'ANZA, LAWRENCE MARTIN, marketing educator; b. Hindsdale, Ill., June 20, 1953; s. Joseph James and Evelyn (Martinek) D'A.; m. Teresa D'Anza, June 14, 1980. BBEd, Eastern N.Mex. U., 1975; MA, U. N.Mex., 1984. Instr. cashiering Albuquerque Tech. Vocat. Inst., 1975-85; mktg. edn. tchr. coord. Eldorado High Sch., 1975-99; enrollment program coord. Del Norte High Sch., 1983-93; tchr. bus. mktg. Albuquerque Pub. Schs., 1984-85; bd. govs. N.Mex. DECA, 1988-90, 96-97, chmn., 1983-84, 89-91, conf. cons., 1978—, secondary adv. coun. Nat. DECA, 1992-93, 97-99, chairperson, 1998-99, nat. bd. dirs., 1993-96, conf. coord. western region, 1992, 96, 98, western region bd. dirs., 1993-98; bd. dirs. MarkEd, 1996-97; mem. N.Mex. Gov.'s Workforce Devel. Bd., 1996—; trustee Youth Opportunities in Retailing, 1996—. Recipient Nat. Educator award Milken Family Found., 1995. Mem. N.Mex. Mktg. Edn. Assn., Am. Vocat. Assn. (Region IV Mktg. Edn. Tchr. of Yr. 1994-95, Vocat. Tchr. of Yr. 1994-95), N.Mex. Vocat. Assn. (pres. 1995-96, N.Mex. Mktg. Tchr. of Yr. 1981-82, 87-88, 92-93, 93-94). Avocations: golf, softball, sports, traveling. Home: 8616 New Hampton NE Albuquerque NM 87111-1928 Office: Eldorado High Sch 11300 Montgomery Blvd NE Albuquerque NM 87111-2699

DANZA, TONY, actor; b. Bklyn., Apr. 21, 1951; married; children: Marc Anthony, Katherine Anne, Emily Lyn. Ed., U. Dubuque. Began career as profl. boxer; appeared in films Hollywood Knights, 1980, Going Ape, 1981, Cannonball Run II, 1984, She's Out of Control, 1989, Angels in the Outfield, 1994, Dear God, 1996, Illtown, 1996, A Brooklin State of Mind, 1997, Meet Wally Sparks, 1997; TV series include Taxi, ABC, 1978-83, Who's the Boss?, ABC, 1984-92 (also dir. episodes), Baby Talk, 1992, Hudson Street, 1995—; TV films include Doing Life, Wall of Tyranny, Single Bar, Single Women, Freedom Fighters (also exec. producer), Bob Hope: Laughing With the Presidents, 1996, 12 Angry Men, 1997; co-host TV spl. 99 Ways to Attract the Right Man; stage appearance Wrong Turn at Lungfish, 1993. Avocations: softball, running.

DANZBERGER, ALEXANDER HARRIS, chemical engineer, consultant; b. N.Y.C., Mar. 23, 1932; s. George Harris and Ruth P. (Alexander) D.; m. Jacqueline P. Pilcher, Mar. 12, 1954; children—Alison, Alexander, Diana, Robert; m. Anne Griggs Pierson, Apr. 23, 1977; stepchildren—Jennifer Pierson, Priscilla Pierson, Stephanie Pierson. BSChemE, MIT, 1953. Registered profl. engr., Mass., Colo. Mem. staff Arthur D. Little Inc., Cambridge, Mass., 1953-60; engring. mgr. Linde div. Union Carbide Corp., Tonawanda, N.Y., N.Y.C., 1961-70; chief engr. Booz, Allen & Hamilton, Florham Park, N.J., 1971-72, Marcom Cons., N.Y.C., 1973-75; v.p. Hydrotechnic Corp., N.Y.C., 1976-81; mgr. pollution control group Dames & Moore, Golden, Colo., 1982-83; pres. Danzberger and Assocs., Inc., Lakewood, Colo., 1983—. Served to 1st lt. U.S. Army, 1956-58. Recipient Kenneth B. Allen award N.Y. Water Pollution Control Assn., 1983. Fellow AICE; mem. ASME, Am. Acad. Environ. Engrs. (diplomate), Water Pollution Control Fedn., Colo. Mountain Club, Masons. Republican. Presbyterian. Home and Office: 737 S Youngfield Ct Lakewood CO 80228-2812

DANZIG, FREDERICK PAUL, newspaper editor; b. Springfield, Mass., Sept. 17, 1925; s. Phillip and Sylvia (Levin) D.; m. Edith Goret, Mar. 16, 1952; children: Steven, Ellen Kay. BA, Washington Sq. Coll., NYU, 1949. Copy boy AP, N.Y.C., 1943; reporter Herkimer (N.Y.) Evening Telegram, 1949, Port Chester (N.Y.) Daily Item, 1950-51; reporter, columnist UPI, N.Y.C., 1951-62; sr. editor Advt. Age, N.Y.C., 1962-68, exec. editor, 1969-84, editor, 1984-94; contbg. editor, 1995—; advt. newscaster Sta. wQXR, 1979-81, Sta. WMCA, 1982-86; adj. instr. New Sch. Social Rsch., N.Y.C.; pub. radio commentator, 1989-90; media cons. Comprehensive Cmty. Revitalization Program, N.Y.C, 1994-98; mem. adv. bd. Youth Law Ctr., Washington. Author: (with Ted Klein) How to be Heard, 1974, Publicity, 1985. Mem. adv. bd. Youth Law Ctr., Washington. Served with inf. AUS, 1943-46. Decorated Bronze Star, Purple Heart; recipient Alumni Achievement award NYU, 1983. Mem. 29th Inf. Divsn. Assn., Amagansett Hist. Assn., The Battle of Normandy Found., U.S. Holocaust Meml. Mus., Nature Conservancy, Internat. Mus. Cartoon Art (adv. adv. bd.), Sigma Delta Chi. Office: Advertising Age 220 E 42nd St Rm 920 New York NY 10017-0920

DANZIG, RICHARD JEFFREY, government official, lawyer; b. N.Y.C., Sept. 8, 1944; s. Aaron and Elinor (Moskowitz) D.; m. Andrea Auster, June 26, 1966; children: David, Lisa. B.A., Reed Coll., 1965; B.Phil., Magdalen Coll., Oxford U., 1967, D.Phil., 1968; J.D., Yale U., 1971. Bar: Calif. 1973, D.C. 1983. Asst. to pres. Rand Inst., N.Y.C., 1971; law clk. Justice White, U.S. Supreme Ct., Washington, 1971-72; fellow Harvard Soc. Fellows, 1975-77; asst. prof. Stanford Law Sch., 1972-75, assoc. prof., 1975-77; mem. faculty Harvard Program in the Law and Humanities, 1976; dep. asst. sec. of Def. for program devel. Dept. Def., Washington, 1977-79; acting prin. dep. asst. sec. of Def. for manpower, res. affairs and logistics Dept. Def., 1979, prin. dep. asst. sec., 1979-81; ptnr. Latham & Watkins, Washington, 1981-93; under sec. of the navy USN, Washington, 1993-97; sec of the navy USN, DC, 1998—; vis. prof. Georgetown U. Sch. Law, 1980-82; cons. Urban Affairs N.Y. Rand Inst., 1969-74; mem. NRC Com. Mil. Pers., 1983-91; cons. UN Ctr. Transnat. Corp., 1987-93; dir. Nat. Semiconductor Corp., 1987-93; dir. Internat. Human Rights Law Group, 1991-93, vice chmn., 1992-93; fellow Nat. Acad. Pub. Adminstrn., 1994—; adj. prof. Syracuse U. Maxwell Sch. Citizenship and Travelling Fellow Ctr. for Internat. Polit. Economy, 1997-98. Author: The Capability Problem in Contract Law, 1978; co-author: National Service: What Would It Mean?, 1986; contbr. articles to profl. jours. Trustee Reed Coll., 1984-88; pres., sec. USN, Washington, 1998—. Rockefeller Found. fellow, 1976-77; Rhodes scholar, 1965-68; recipient Herbert prize U. Oxford, 1967, Harlan Fiske Stone prize Yale Law Sch., 1970, Tony Friedrich Meml. award Internat. Human Rights Law Group, 1991. Mem. Calif. Bar Assn., Phi Beta Kappa. Home: 3670 Upton St NW Washington DC 20008-3125 Office: Sec of Navy 1000 Navy Pentagon Rm 4e686 Washington DC 20350-1000

DANZIG, SHEILA RING, marketing and direct mail executive; b. N.Y.C., Mar. 18, 1948; d. David and Yetta Ring; m. William Harold Danzig, Aug. 11, 1968; children: David Scott, Gregory Charles. BS, CUNY, 1968; PhD, Am. Coastline U., 1996. Tchr. N.Y.C. Bd. Edn., 1968-71; treas. Nat. Success Mktg. Inc., Sunrise, Fla., 1969—; pres. Innovative Comm. Market Cons., Plantation, Fla., 1984-87; cons. Crush Softball Team, Hollywood, Fla., 1986-87, The Eye Ctr., Sunrise, 1986-87, Bus. Expo., Plantation, 1987. Author: You Deserve to be Rich, 1972, A Free Press, 1990, A Better Medical Practice, 1986; author, pub.: Turn Your Computer Into A Money Machine, 1994; contbr. articles to profl. jours. Coord. Day Out program Mills Boys' Shelter, Ft. Lauderdale, Fla., 1985, 87, Put Seat Belts on Sch. Buses program Broward County Sch. Bd., 1986; vol. Miami Children's Hosp.; campaign dir. Help the Handicapped Keep Their Parking Spots, 1987. Mem. Mail Order Bus. Bd., Am. Med. Writers Assn., Plantation Bus. and Profl. Women's Assn., MADD, Speechcrafters. Office: Nat Success Mktg 2574 N University Dr Fort Lauderdale FL 33322-3045

DANZIG, WILLIAM HAROLD, marketing executive; b. Bklyn., Feb. 24, 1947; s. Sidney and Beatrice (Reiss) D.; m. Sheila Ring, Aug. 11, 1968; children: David Scott, Gregory Charles. BS in Acctg., Baruch Coll., 1969; MS in Edn., Long Island U., 1971; PhD, Am. Coastline U., 1996. Acct. JK Lasser, N.Y.C., 1972; tchr. N.Y.C. Bd. Edn., Queens, 1969-74; pres. Nat. Success Mktg. Inc., Ft. Lauderdale, Fla., 1969—; sponsor Coop. Bus. Edn., Broward County, Fla., 1986; participant Bus. Expo, Ft. Lauderdale, 1985; cons. Mail Market Monitor, Ft. Lauderdale, 1988—, Gulfstream Pub., Ft. Lauderdale, 1988—. Co-author: You Deserve to be Rich, 1975, Play to Win, 1982; publisher (computer program) Turn Your Computer Into A Money Machine, 1994. Mem. Mail Order Bus. Bd., Greater Ft. Lauderdale C. of C., B'nai Brith (chpt. bd. dirs. 1976). Republican. Jewish. Office: Nat Success Mktg Inc 2574 N University Dr Ste 201 Fort Lauderdale FL 33322-3045

DANZIGER, BRUCE EDWARD, structural engineer; b. N.Y.C., Feb. 14, 1964; s. Frederick Benjamin Danziger and Elise Lee (Saranow) Gold. BS in Archtl. Engring., Calif. Poly. U., 1988. Project engr. Ove Arup & Ptnrs., London, 1988-90, Sevilla, Spain, 1990-92, L.A., 1992-93, N.Y.C., 1993-97, San Francisco, 1997—. Recipient 1st prize MakMax Membrane Design Competition, 1993, Hon. Mention award, 1995, Hon. Mention award, 1996. Office: Ove Arup & Ptnrs 901 Market St Ste 260 San Francisco CA 94103-1735

DANZIGER, GERTRUDE SEELIG, metal fabricating executive; b. Chgo., Oct. 24, 1919; d. Isidor and Clara (Fuchs) Seelig; widowed; children: Robert, James. With Homak Mfg. Co., Inc., Chgo., 1966-79; pres. Homak Mfg. Co., Inc., 1979—. Patentee in field.

DANZIGER, GLENN NORMAN, chemical sales company executive; b. N.Y.C., Apr. 7, 1930; s. Victor and Freda (Lazar) D.; m. Florence Spielvogel, June 7, 1953; children: Jill Marla Danziger Hetson, Beth J. Danziger Keyes, Amy L. Tanenbaum. AB, Columbia U., 1952, BS in Chem. Engring., 1953. Chemist Breinig Bros., Hoboken, N.J., 1955-61; v.p., tech. dir. Flood and Conklin, Newark, 1961-65; tech. sales rep. Seaboard Chem. Corp., Lodi, N.J., 1965-75; pres. Seaboard Sales Corp., Paterson, N.J., 1975—. Author: Formulation of Organic Coatings, 1967. Lt. (j.g.) USNR, 1953-55. Mem. N.Y. Met. Soc. Coatings Technology, Nat. Paint and Coatings Assn. Democrat. Jewish. Avocations: travel, golf, skiing, reading. Office: Seaboard Sales Corp 881 Market St Paterson NJ 07513-1126

DANZIGER, JAMES NORRIS, political science educator; b. L.A., May 28, 1945; s. Edward and Beverly Jane Danziger; m. Lesley Robson, June 12, 1971; children: Nicholas James, Vanessa Margaret. BA, Occidental Coll., L.A., 1966; MA, Sussex U., Brighton, Eng., 1968; MA, PhD, Stanford U., 1974. Prof. polit. sci. U. Calif., Irvine, 1972—, chmn. dept. polit. sci., 1974-76, 81-83, 88-92, assoc. dean Sch. Social Scis., 1978-81, chmn. acad. senate, 1994-95; dean of undergrad. edn., 1995—; rsch. assoc. Ctr. Rsch. Info. Tech. & Orgns., Irvine, 1974—; scholar-in-residence LaVerne (Calif.) U., 1983-84; vis. prof. Univ. Pitts., 1996; vis. prof. Aarhus (Denmark) U., 1985. Author: Making Budgets, 1978, Understanding the Political World, 1991, 2nd edit., 1994, 3d edit., 1996, 4th edit., 1998; co-author: Computers and Politics, 1982, People and Computers, 1986; mem. editl. bd. local govt. studies, 1981—; assoc. editor Social Sci. Computer Rev. Bd. dirs. South Laguna Civic Assn., 1983-86, chair South Laguna Annexation Task Force, 1986, bd. dirs. Irvine Campus Housing Authority, 1996—. Recipient Disting. Teaching award U. Calif., 1979, Daniel Aldrich disting. svc. award, 1997; Marshall scholar Govt. of U.K., 1966-68; named Disting. Faculty Lectr. U. Calif. Acad. Senate, 1987; NSF grantee, 1973-79, 80-83, 1996-98. Mem. Am. Polit. Sci. Assn. (Leonard White award 1974), ASPA (Marshall Dimock award 1977), Phi Beta Kappa (pres. local chpt. 1988-89, sec.-treas. local chpt. 1996—), Pi Sigma Alpha (pres. local chpt. 1987—). Avocations: travel, basketball, tennis, cycling, literature. Office: U Calif Sch Social Scis Irvine CA 92697

DANZIGER, JEFF, political cartoonist, writer; b. N.Y.C., Nov. 14, 1943; s. Ralph and Marjorie (Mercer) D.; m. Jan Danziger, June 13, 1966; children: Matthew Mercer, Kim Chanthany. BA, U. Denver, 1966; MA, U. Vt., 1974; ArtsD (hon.), Coll. of Wooster, 1989, Middlebury Coll., 1992. Cartoonist Rutland (Vt.) Herald, 1975—, N.Y. Daily News, 1982-85, Christian Sci. Monitor, Boston, 1986-97, L.A. Times Syndicate, 1986—. Author: Rising Like The Tucson, 1991. Capt. U.S. Army, 1967-71, Vietnam. Finalist Pulitzer Prize in Editl. Cartooning, 1987, 93; recipient Overseas Press Club award for editl. cartooning, 1994. Mem. Salmagundi Club, St. Botolph's Club, Nat. Press Club. Avocation: painting. Home and Office: 420 W 47th St New York NY 10036-2312

DANZIGER, JERRY, broadcasting executive; b. N.Y.C., Jan. 23, 1924; s. Harry and Lillie (Lacher) D.; m. Zelda Bloom, Dec. 26, 1948; children: Sydney, Alan, Lee. Grad. high sch. With Sta. WTTV, Bloomington, Ind., 1950-53; ops. mgr. Sta. WTTV, Indpls., 1953-57; program mgr. Sta. WTSK-TV, Knoxville, Tenn., 1953; pres. Sta. KOB-TV, Albuquerque, 1957-88, v.p., 1983-88, pres., 1988-93, vice-chmn., 1993—; mem. Gov. N.Mex. Commn. for Film Entertainment, 1970-71. Bd. dirs. KIPC All Indian Pueblo Coun., 1975-88, Albuquerque Little Theatre, Albuquerque Pub. Broadcast, Albuquerque Jewish Welfare Fund, Albuquerque Econ. Devel. 1989-97, Albuquerque Conv. and Visitors Bur., 1990-93, Great Southwest Coun. Boy Scouts Am., 1994—; v.p. for TV AP Broadcasting, 1980-88, Goodwill Industries N.Mex., 1980, bd. dirs., 1991—; mem. Albuquerque Econ. Forum, 1997; adv. bd. AAA, 1995—. Recipient Compadre award Am. Women in Radio and TV, 1978, 80, Silver Medal award N.Mex. Advt. Fedn., 1990. Mem. N.Mex. Broadcasters Assn. (pres. 1972-73, Broadcaster of Yr. award, 1976, 78), Press Club, Advt. Club, Albuquerque Country Club. Office: Sta KOB-TV PO Box 1351 Albuquerque NM 87103-1351*

DANZIGER, LOUIS, graphic designer, educator; b. N.Y.C., 1923; m. Dorothy Patricia Smith, 1954. Student, Art Ctr. Sch., Los Angeles, 1946-47, New Sch., N.Y.C., 1947-48. Asst. art dir. War Assets Adminstrn., Los Angeles, 1946-47; designer Esquire mag., N.Y.C., 1948; freelance designer, cons. Los Angeles, 1949—; instr. graphic design Art Ctr. Coll. Design, Los Angeles, 1952-60, 86—, Chouinard Art Inst., Los Angeles, 1960-72; instr. Calif. Inst. Arts, 1972-88, head graphic design program, 1972-82; vis. prof. Harvard U., Cambridge, Mass., summers 1978-80, 83, 84, 86-88; instr. Art Ctr. Coll. Design; mem. graphic evaluation panel Fed. Design Program, Nat. Endowment Arts, 1975—; design cons. Los Angeles County Mus. Art, 1957—. Served with cav. U.S. Army, 1943-45; PTO. Recipient Disting. Achievement award Contemporary Art Coun., L.A. County Mus. Art, 1982, Disting. Designer award NEA, 1985, "Stars of Design" Lifetime Achievement award Pacific Design Ctr., 1997, numerous awards and medals in art design. Mem. Alliance Graphique Internationale, Am. Inst. Graphic Arts (medal 1998), Am. Ctr. for Design (hon.). Home: PO Box 660189 Arcadia CA 91066-0189

DANZIGER, PAULA, author; b. U.S., 1944. Tchr. jr. high sch. Author: The Cat Ate My Gymsuit, 1974 (N.J. Inst. of Tech. award 1976, Mass. Children's Book award Edn. Dept. of Salem State Coll. 1979, Nene award Hawaii Assn. of School Librs. and Hawaii Libr. Assn. 1980, Children's Choice award Internat. Reading Assn. and Children's Book Coun. 1980), The Pistachio Prescription, 1978 (Children's Book of Yr. citation Child Study Assn. 1978, Mass. Children's Book award Edn. Dept. of Salem State Coll. 1979, Children's Choice award Internat. Reading Assn. and Children's Book Coun. 1979, Nene award Hawaii Assn. of School Librs. and Hawaii Libr. Assn. 1980, Ariz. Young Reader award 1983), Can You Sue Your Parents for Malpractice?, 1979 (Children's Choice award Internat. Reading Assn. and Children's Book Coun. 1980, N.J. Inst. of Tech. award 1980, Land of Enchantment award N. Mex. Libr. Assn. 1982), There's a Bat in Bunk Five, 1980 (Children's Choice award Internat. Reading Assn. and Children's Book Coun. 1981, CRABbery award Prince George's County Meml. Librs. 1982, Young Reader's medal 1984), The Divorce Express, 1982 (Children's Choice award Internat. Reading Assn. and Children's Book Coun. 1983, Parents' Choice award for lit. Parents' Choice Found. 1982, Woodward Park School Annual Book award 1983, S.C. Young Adult Book award S.C. Assn. of School Librs. 1985), It's an Aardvark-Eat-Turtle World, 1985 (Parents' Choice award for lit. Parents' Choice Found. 1985, Children's Book of Yr. citation Child Study Assn. 1985), This Place Has No Atmosphere, 1986, Remember Me to Harold Square, 1987, Everyone Else's Parents Said Yes, 1989, Make Like a Tree and Leave, 1990, Not for a Billion Gazillion Dollars, 1992, Earth to Matthew, 1992, Thames Doesn't Rhyme with James, 1994, Amber Brown Is Not a Crayon, 1994, You Can't Eat Your Chicken Pox, Amber Brown Goes Fourth, 1995, Seguiremos Siendo Amigos, 1995, Amber Brown Wants Extra Credit, Amber Brown Sees Red, 1997. Address: Penguin Putnam Books for Young Readers 345 Hudson St Fl 14 New York NY 10014-4502*

DANZIGER, RAPHAEL, political scientist, researcher; b. Haifa, Israel, June 26, 1944; came to U.S., 1968; s. Norbert and Hanna Danziger; m. Carla Danziger, June 12, 1970; children: Elon, Tamar. BA in Polit. Sci. and History Islamic Countries, Hebrew U., Jerusalem, 1965; MA in Near Ea. Studies, U. Wash., 1970; MA in European and Near Ea. History, Princeton U., 1972, PhD in Near Ea. Studies, 1974. Rschr. Shiloah Ctr. for Mid. Ea. Studies Tel Aviv U., 1975-76; dep. dir. Inst. Mid. Ea. Studies U. Haifa, 1976-77; policy analyst commn. on internat. affairs Am. Jewish Congress, N.Y.C., 1981-86, asst. dir. commn. on internat. affairs, 1986-90; dir. rsch. and info. Am. Israel Pub. Affairs Com., Washington, 1990—; cons. Hudson Inst., Croton-on-Hudson, N.Y., 1974-75; vis. rsch. fellow dept. history U. Bergen, Norway, 1980; vis. fellow dept. Near Ea. studies Princeton (N.J.) U., 1981; lectr. dept. Mid. East history U. Haifa, 1975-81; vis. asst. prof. dept. history U. Wash., Seattle, 1980-81; lectr. in field. Author: Abd al-Qadir and the Algerians: Resistance to the French and Internal Consolidation, 1977; editor Near East Report, 1992—; contbr. articles to profl. jours. Lt. Israeli Army, 1965-68. Mem. Mid. East Studies Assn., Mid. East Inst. Office: Am Israel Pub Affairs Com 440 1st St NW Ste 600 Washington DC 20001-2017

DANZIGER, TERRY LEBLANG, public relations and marketing consultant; b. Jan. 20, 1933; d. Leon Leventhal and Dorothy Leblang; m. Arthur Lewis Danziger, Mar. 29, 1953; children: Robin Danziger-Ross, Stephen. Student, Syracuse U., 1950-52, C.W. Post Coll., 1962-66; BA in Psychology, Empire State Coll., 1974. Advt. copywriter, account exec. Grey Adv., Foote, Cone & Belding, Kaplan & Bruck, and others, N.Y.C., 1952-55; editorial writer Syosset (N.Y.) Tribune, 1956-62; pres. Mail Arts Co., Syosset, 1962-68; exec. dir. Nassau Easter Seal Soc., Crippled Children and Adults, Inc., Albertson, N.Y., 1968-74; pres. TLD Enterprises, Syosset, Bethpage, N.Y., 1974-77; regional dir. Telequin Ltd., N.Y.C., 1977-78; state pub. rels. dir., regional campaign dir. Arthritis Found. Fla., Miami, Ft. Lauderdale, 1978-79; pub. rels. dir. FPA Corp., Pompano Beach, Fla., 1979-81; pres. PR Mktg. Concepts, Boca Raton, Fla., 1980—. Adv. coun. NCCJ. Mem. Am. Mktg. Assn. (bd. dirs.), Pub. Rels. Soc. Am. (counselors acad.), Am. Bus. Women's Assn., Pub. Rels. Soc. Fla. (v.p.), Profl. Resource Network, Psi Chi. Office: PR Mktg Concepts 1280 S Powerline Rd Ste 120 Pompano Beach FL 33069-4339

DANZIS, ROSE MARIE, emeritus college president; b. Adrian, Pa.; d. Paul A. and Josephine (Bugala) Manger; m. James Gordon Channing, Jan. 24, 1954 (dec. 1973); children: Rose Marie Buhrman, Lorraine Genieczko; m. Sidney Danzis, June 1, 1986. Diploma, Jersey City Hosp. Sch. Nursing, 1949; B.S., N.Y. U., 1954; M.A., Columbia U., 1961, M.Ed., 1971, Ed.D., 1973. Staff nurse, asst. supr. Public Health Nursing Service, Jersey City, 1949-55; dir. health and recreation, clin. coordinator, asso. dir. nursing edn. Charles E. Gregory Sch. Nursing, Perth Amboy (N.J.) Gen. Hosp., 1958-66; chmn. dept. nurse edn., dir. health techs., dean div. health techs. Middlesex County Coll., Edison, N.J., 1966-78; pres. Middlesex County Coll., 1978-86; ret.; Mem. Middlesex County Comprehensive Health Planning Council, 1973-75, N.Y. Com. Regents External Degree in Nursing, 1972-80, Council on Continuing Edn. for Allied Health Personnel, N.J.; Regional Med. Program, 1968-71; chmn. N.J. Health Professions Edn. Adv. Council, N.J. Dept. Higher Edn., 1979-82, chmn. nursing subcom., 1975-78; mem. health careers com. J.F. Kennedy Hosp., 1972-75; chmn. Middlesex County Coll. Assembly, 1975-77; mem. Pres.'s Adv. Com. Sch. Allied Health, Coll. Medicine and Dentistry of N.J., 1976-79; commr. Middle States Assn. of Colls. and Schs.; chmn. Commn. High Edn., 1984-85; mem. liaison com. Am. Assn. Community and Jr. Colls. and Nat. League for Nursing, 1978-82; chmn. acad. affairs com. N.J. Council of Community Coll., pres., 1978-82; trustee Nat. Bank of N.J., 1979-81; exec. com. Acad. Pres.'s, Am. Assn. Community and Jr. Colls.; also exec. com. Internat./Intercultural Consortium. Contbr. articles to profl. jours. Recipient Torch of Liberty award Anti-Defamation League, 1981, Disting. Service award U. Medicine and Dentistry of N.J. Sch. Health Related Professions, 1983; named to Hall of Fame, Perth Amboy High Sch., 1985. Mem. Council of County Coll. Presidents, Am. Nurses Assn., Nat. League for Nursing, Am. Soc. Allied Health Professions, Am. Council on Edn., Am. Assn. Community and Jr. Colls. (bd. dirs. 1984-86), Coll. Consortium for Internat. Studies., Jersey City Sch. Nursing Alumni Assn., N.Y. U. Alumni Assn., Tchrs. Coll., Columbia Alumni Assn., Kappa Delta Pi. Home: 5055 Collins Ave Apt 8C Miami Beach FL 33140-2710 *An important principle, accepted early in my life, was that education is the key to a successful professional and personal life. I believe in goal-setting on a short term achievable basis, leading gradually to a higher long term goal. Upon making a decision regarding further study or accepting a position, total commitment is essential to success. I take my study and work seriously, but not myself. I truly enjoy all people and working with them.*

DANZL, DANIEL FRANK, emergency physician; b. Cin., Apr. 2, 1950; s. Frank Bernard and Mary Ellen (Doerger) D.; m. Joanna Colosimo Danzl, Nov. 25, 1978; children: Maggie, Julia. BS magna cum laude, U. Cin., 1972; MD, Ohio State U., 1976. Diplomate Am. Bd. Emergency Medicine. Intern St. Francis Med. Ctr., Peoria, Ill., 1976-77; resident in emergency medicine U. Louisville, 1977-79, asst. prof. emergency medicine, 1979-83, assoc. prof. emergency medicine, 1983-89, prof. emergency medicine, 1989-91, prof., chair, 1991—; bd. dirs., councilman-at-large Univ. Assn. for Emergency Medicine, 1988-89, indsl./govtl. rels. com., 1984-85, nominating com., 1987-88; bd. dirs. Soc. for Acad. Emergency Medicine, 1989, mem. annals of emergency meidcine task force, 1989; bd. dirs. Am. Bd. Emergency Medicine, sec.-treas., 1995-96, pres.-elect, 1996-97, pres. 1997—, mem. ad hoc com., oral examiner, 1982—; mem. Com. to Advise the Nat. ARC, 1984-87; reviewer for various med. jours. Author book chpts., monographs and textbooks including Airway Management in the Trauma Patient in the Clinical Practice of Emergency Medicine, 1991; editorial bd. Jour. Emergency Medicine, 1983—, Poisindex-Emergindex, 1982—, Jour. Wilderness Medicine, 1991—; contbr. more than 70 articles to Jour. Wilderness Medicine, Jpur. Emergency Medicine, Annals of Emergency Medicine, Am. Jour. Emergency Medicine, others. Mem. Water Safety Com. Nat. Safety Coun.-Pub. Safety Div., 1981-84; alternate med. dir. Jefferson Vocat. Edn.-Louisville EMS Paramedic Training Program, 1989-90, 90-91. Recipient Silver Tongue Orator award Soc. Tchrs. of Emergency Medicine, 1986, 88; grantee Office of Naval Resources, 1983-85, Key Pharmaceuticals, 1985, Hoffman-LaRoche, Inc., 1988, 89. Fellow Am. Coll. Emergency Physicians (nat. coun. mem. 1981-93, reference com. mem. 1981, 85, 89, rsch. com. mem. 1982-83, 83-84); mem. AMA (Physician's Recognition awards), NAS, Am. Soc. Circumpolar Health, Soc. for Academic Emergency Medicine (bd. dirs. 1989, task force 1989), Nat. Rsch. Coun., Undersea and Hyperbaric Oxygen Med. Soc., Ky. Chpt. Am. Coll. Emergency Physicians (councillor 1981-93, sec.-treas. 1983-84, pres.-elect 1984-85, pres. 1985-86), Wilderness Med. Soc., Phi Beta Kappa, Beta Theta Pi. Roman Catholic. Achievements include research on hypothermia. Home: 4804 Smith Rd Floyds Knobs IN 47119-9238 Office: U Louisville Dept Emergency Med 530 S Jackson St Louisville KY 40202-1675

DANZON, PATRICIA M., medical educator. BA, U. Oxford, 1968; MA, U. Chgo., 1969, PhD of Econs., 1973. Lectr. U. Chgo., 1972; rsch. economist, instr. Rand Corp., 1974-80; sr. rsch. fellow Hoover Inst. Stanford U., 1980-84; assoc. prof., adj. prof., lectr. Duke U., Durham, N.C., 1984-85; Celia Moh prof. Health Care Mgmt. Dept. Ins. & Risk Mgmt. U. Pa., Phila., 1985—; vis. asst. prof. Econ. Dept. U. Calif., 1978; vis. prof. Ctr. Study Economy and State U. Chgo., 1988-89. Office: U Pa Wharton Sch Health Care Sys Dept 3641 Locust Walk Philadelphia PA 19104-6218*

DAO, KHANH PHUONG THI, automotive executive, sales professional; b. Saigon, Vietnam, Apr. 3, 1970; came to the U.S., 1975; Student, Tex. Christian U., 1987-88, Tarrant County Jr. Coll., Ft. Worth, 1988, 89, Austin (Tex.) C.C., 1988-90, U. Tex., Arlington, 1991. Pres. Klaus Motors/Concours Detailing, Ft. Worth, 1990-92; fleet sales mgr. Toyota of Dallas, 1992-93; broker trainee, account exec. B.T.S.-Southwest Securities, Richardson, Tex., 1993-94; sales cons. Crest Infiniti/Autogroup, Plano, Tex., 1994-95; v.p. Edwards Petroleum/Devel. Inc., Dallas, 1995-96; pres., CEO, cons. Bang Entertainment/Devel. Inc., Dallas and Wilmington, Del., 1996—; prin. The Gotham City Club Ltd., Dallas, 1996—; sales cons. Park Place Porsche, Dallas, 1996—; ptnr. Voltaire Restaurant and Bar, Ltd., The Porsche Store, Dallas. Mem. Rep. Presdl. Task Force, Washington, 1989—. Mem. Porsche Cars N.A. (cert. Porsche specialist), Porsche Club N.A. Avocations: tennis, golf, traveling, collecting vintage timepieces, racing cars. Home: Ste 100B-LB207 3878 Oak Lawn Ave Dallas TX 75219-4460 Office: Voltaire 5150 Keller Springs Rd Dallas TX 75248

DAOUD, GEORGE JAMIL, hotel and motel consultant; b. Beirut, Oct. 20, 1948; came to U.S., 1958, naturalized, 1970; s. Jamil G. and Shafika E. Daoud; divorced; 5 children. BS, NYU, 1967; MPS, Cornell U., 1969. Gen. mgr. Holiday Inn, New London and Groton, Conn., 1974-75, Gentle Winds Beach Resort, St. Croix, V.I., 1975-78; pres., cons. Motor Inn Mgmt., Inc., Dayton, Ohio, 1973—; pres. Cen. Svcs. Group, Inc., First Group, Inc., Host Mgmt., Inc., Inn Group, Inc., 1981—, Metro Markets, Inc., Dayton, Triac Ventures, Inc., 1980-86. Mem Am. Hotel and Motel Assn. (cert. hotel adminstr., mem. Ednl. Inst.), Ohio Hotel and Motel Assn., Nat. Assn. Rev. Appraisers, Cert. Real Estate Rev. Appraisers, Masons. Republican. Roman Catholic. Office: Hotelvest Inc PO Box 730 Dayton OH 45402-0730

DAOUST, DONALD ROGER, pharmaceutical and toiletries company executive, microbiologist; b. Worcester, Mass., Aug. 13, 1935; s. G. Arthur and Alice Anne (Lavalee) D.; m. Johanna K. Kalinoski, May 30, 1959; children: Donna Jean, Stephen Michael, Sandra Marie. BA, U. Conn., 1957; MS, U. Mass., 1959, PhD, 1962. Sr. research microbiologist Merck Sharp & Dohme, Rahway, N.J., 1962-70, research fellow, 1970-72; mgr. biol. quality control Merck Sharp & Dohme, West Point, Pa., 1972-75; dir. quality control Armour Pharm. Co., Kankakee, Ill., 1975-76; v.p. quality assurance and regulatory compliance Armour Pharm. Co., Phoenix, 1976-78; v.p., quality control Carter-Wallace, Inc., Cranbury, N.J., 1978—. Contbr. articles to profl. jours., chpts. to books; patentee in field. Mem. Borough Council, South Plainfield, N.J., 1970-72; treas. George Washington council Boy Scouts Am., 1981-84, pres., 1984-87, area v.p., bd.dirs. NE region U.S., 1987—. Recipient Disting. Svc. award South Plainfield Jaycees, 1969, silver Beaver award Boy Scouts Am., 1988, Silver Antelope award N.E. region, 1992; named Outstanding Young Man, N.J. Jaycees, 1970. Mem. AAAS, Am. Soc. Microbiology, Am. Soc. for Quality Control, Pharm. Mfrs. Assn. (quality control adminstrn. 1979-82, adv. bd. 1982-94, rec. sec. 1986-88, vice chmn. 1988-90, chmn. 1990-92), Bedens Brook Club (Skillman, N.J.). Avocations: golf, jogging, reading, gardening. Home: 8 Fairway Dr Cranbury NJ 08512-1726 Office: Carter-Wallace Inc PO Box 1001 Cranbury NJ 08512-0181

DAPHNIS, NASSOS, artist; b. Krokeai, Greece, July 23, 1914; s. Panagiotes A. and Stamatico (Georgoulis) D.; m. Helen Avlonitis, Mar. 24, 1956 (div. 1987); children: Artemis, Demetrios. Student, Art Students League, N.Y.C., 1946-49, Acad. Frochot, Paris, 1950-51, Inst. Statale D'Arte, Florence, Italy, 1951-52. One-man shows Contemporary Arts Gallery, N.Y.C., 1938-47, Mint Mus., Charlotte, N.C., 1949, Collette Allendy Gallery, Paris, 1950, Leo Castelli Gallery, N.Y.C., 1959-61, 63, 65, 68, 71, 73, 75, 80, 83, 85, 86, 88, 90, 95, Toninelli Arte Moderna, Milan, Italy, 1961, Galerie Iris Clert, Paris, 1962, Franklin Siden Gallery, Detroit, 1967, Albright-Knox Mus., Buffalo, 1969, Everson Mus., Syracuse, N.Y., 1969, Brockton (Mass.) Art Center, 1970, Andre Zarre Gallery, N.Y.C., 1974, 76, 83, 85, 95, Printers Gallery, Ithaca, N.Y., 1975, Kingpitcher Gallery, Pitts., 1975, Phillips Gallery, Salt Lake City, 1980, Frank Fedele Fine Arts, N.Y.C., Eaton/Shoen Gallery, San Francisco, 1980, 85, Omega Gallery, Athens, 1983, Kouros Gallery, N.Y.C., 1985, Raynolds Gallery, Pitts., 1990, Iliana Tounta Comtemporary Art Ctr, Athens, Greece, 1990, Berta Walker Gallery, Provincetown, Mass., 1992; retrospective Boca Raton (Fla.) Mus., Butler Inst. Am. Art, 1993; exhibited in group shows, Pitts. Internat., 1958, 61, 70, Whitney Mus. Am. Art, N.Y.C., 1959, 61, 62, 64, 65, 67, Corcoran Gallery, Washington, 1959, 63, 69, Columbus (Ohio) Gallery Fine Art, 1960, Osaka (Japan) Mus. Fine Art, 1960, Guggenheim Mus., N.Y.C., 1961, Lever House, N.Y.C., 1961, Walker Art Center, Mpls., 1961, 62, Brandeis U., 1962, Washington Gallery Modern Art, 1963, Washington Sq. Galleries, N.Y.C., 1964, de Cordova Mus., Lincoln, Mass., 1965, Aldrich Mus., Ridgefield, Conn., 1969, Westbeth Ct. Gallery, N.Y.C., 1970, Tirca Karlis Gallery, Provincetown, Mass., 1972, Leo Castelli Gallery, N.Y.C., 1974, Birmingham (Ala.) Mus. Art, 1976, Albright Coll., Reading, Pa., 1976, Leo Castelli Gallery, N.Y., 1997, numerous others; represented permanent collections at, Mus. Modern Art, N.Y.C., Whitney Mus. Am. Art, N.Y.C., Albright-Knox Gallery, Buffalo, Albany (N.Y.) Mall, Guggenheim Mus., N.Y.C., Balt. Mus., Providence Mus., Chrysler Mus., Norfolk, Va., Tel Aviv Mus., Israel, Munson-Williams-Proctor Mus., Utica, N.Y., Akron (Ohio) Art Inst., Reading (Pa.) Mus., Ann Arbor (Mich.) Art Mus., Balt. Mus., Pitts. Mus. Art, Hirshhorn Mus., Washington, Aldrich Mus., Ridgefield, Conn., Everson Mus., Syracuse, N.Y., Utah Mus. Fine Art, Salt Lake City, Provincetown Art Assn. and Mus., Vorres Mus., Athens, Goulandris Mus., Andros, Greece, Butler Inst. of Am. Art, Youngstown, Ohio, Queens (N.Y.) Mus. Art, Grinnell (Iowa) Coll. Recipient Ford Found. award, 1972, Pitts. award, 1966, Nat. Found. Arts and Humanities award, 1966, Nat. Endowment on Arts/Boca Raton Mus. award, 1971, A.P. Saunders medal, 1973, Francis J. Greenburger Found. award, 1987, The Richard A. Florsheim Art Fund award, 1993; Guggenheim fellow, 1977; Pollock-Krasner Found. grant, 1987. Office: 362 W Broadway New York NY 10013-5303

D'APPOLONIA, ELIO, civil engineer, educator; b. Provence, Alta., Can., Apr. 14, 1918. BS, U. Alta., 1942, MS, 1946; PhD of Civil Engring., U. Ill., 1948; D of Engring., Carnegie-Mellon U., 1988, U. Genoa, 1988. Founder, owner D'Appolonia Consulting Engrs. Inc., 1965-84; cons. engring., vice chmn. STS Consultants, Pitts., 1984-88; cons. Pitts., 1988—. Mem. ASCE (Terzaghi lectr., Pickel award 1991), ASTM, Internat. Soc. Soil Mechanics, Engrs. Inst. Can., Nat. Soc. Profs. Engring. Home and Office: 1177 Mccully Dr Pittsburgh PA 15235-4714*

D'AQUINO, THOMAS, lawyer, business council chief executive; b. Trail, B.C., Can., Nov. 3, 1940; m. Susan Marion Peterson, 1965. BA, U. B.C., 1962, LLB, 1965; LhB, LLM, U. London, Ont., 1967; LLD (hon.), Queen't U., 1996. Adj. prof. law U. Ottawa, Ont., Can., 1975-83; chmn. Intercounsel Ltd.; pres., chief exec. Bus. Coun. on Nat. Issues, Ottawa, 1981—; former exec. asst. to Fed. Min., spl. asst. to Prime Min., Can., 1969-72; internat. cons. firm in London and Paris, 1972-75; frequent guest lectr.; mem. Chmn's Internat. Adv. Coun. of the Am.'s Soc.; adv. com. Can.-Japan Bus. Com.; founding mem. Pacific Coun. on Internat. Policy. Contbr. articles to profl. jours. Mem. World Econ. Forum Geneva, Inst. for Strategic Studies, London; assoc. Can. Corp. Higher Edn. Forum. Mem. Can. Bar Assn., Internat. Bar Assn., B.C. Law Soc. Office: Bus Coun on Nat Issues, 90 Sparks St Ste 806, Ottawa, ON Canada K1P 5B4

DAR, HUMA BASHIR, computer scientist, researcher, educator; b. Murree, Punjab, Pakistan, Oct. 22, 1963; came to the U.S., 1990; d. Bashir Uddin and Khalida Bashir Ahmad; children: Natasha Dar, Zavain Dar. BA in Math. and Computer Sci., U. Calif., Berkeley, 1995, MS in Computer Sci., 1999. Reader, tutor U. Calif., Berkeley, 1993-95, grad. student rschr., 1995—; rschr. Institut Nat. Polytechnique de Grenoble, France, 1997; presenter in field. Author of essays and poems. Mem. Women in Computer Sci. and Engring. (treas. 1995-96, v.p. 1996-97), Mensa Internat. (devel. officer 1980-81), Phi Beta Kappa. Avocations: writing, volunteering in schools, painting, reading, traveling.

DARABONT, FRANK, screenwriter, director. Screenwriter: (films) (with Wes Craven, Chuck Russell, and Bruce Wagner) A Nightmare on Elm Street 3: Dream Warriors, 1987, (with Russell) The Blob, 1988, (with Mick Garris, Jim Wheat, and Ken Wheat) The Fly II, 1989, (with Steph Lady) Mary Shelley's Frankenstein, 1994; dir.: (TV movies) Till Death Do Us Part, 1990, Buried Alive, 1990; screenwriter, dir.: (films) The Shawshank Redemption, 1994 (Academy award nomination best adapted screenplay 1994). Office: William Morris Agency 151 S El Camino Dr Beverly Hills CA 90212-2775*

DARAGAN, PATRICIA ANN, librarian; b. Ft. Worth, Mar. 3, 1953. BA with honors, Syracuse U., 1975, MLS, 1976. Libr. clk. Danbury (Conn.) Pub. Libr., 1969-74; grad. asst., libr. intern Canal Mus., Syracuse, N.Y., 1975-76, libr., registrar, 1976-78; fed. women's program mgr. USCG Acad. Libr., New London, Conn., 1979-80, cataloger, 1978-80, head tech. svcs., 1980-89, acting dir., 1989-90, libr. dir., 1990—; adj. faculty Mohegan C.C., Norwich, Conn., 1989—, mem. libr. tech. program regional adv. bd., 1989—; vice-chair Coun. Conn. Acad. Libr. Dirs., 1998-99. Bd. dirs. YWCA, Groton, Conn., 1981-83. Recipient Excellence in Equity award AAUW, 1992. Mem. ALA, Spl. Librs. Assn., Am. Soc. for Engring. Edn., Southeastern Conn. Libr. Assn. (bd. dirs. 1982-83), New Eng. Morgan Horse Assn. (membership chairperson 1983-90), Assn. Coll. Rsch. Librs. (com. bibliog. instrn. sect., planning com. 1994-96). Office: USCG Acad Libr 35 Mohegan Ave New London CT 06320-8100*

DARAIO, ROBERT REID, technical/video engineer; b. Bronx, N.Y., July 20, 1955; s. Vincent and Patricia (O'Neill) D.; m. Gayle Marie Palmieri, Nov. 26, 1983. BFA, SUNY, Purchase, 1977. Freelance video engr., 1978-99; staff master control tech. dir. WPIX Channel 11, 1999—. Clients include ABC, CBS, NBC, WNYW, WWOR, WPIX, WNET, CNN, TBS, AOB, MTV, VH-1, Fox Sports, ESPN, Universal Pictures, CTW, HBO, Showtime, USA Network. Mem. NATAS, Internat. Alliance Theatrical Stage Employees, Nat. Assn. Broadcast Engrs. and Technicians, Soc. Motion Picture and TV Engrs., Internat. Brotherhood Electrical Workers. Home: 20 N Broadway Apt D116 White Plains NY 10601-2106

D'ARBANVILLE-QUINN, PATTI, actress; b. N.Y.C., Mar. 4, 1951; m. Roger Mirmont (div.); m. Steve Curry; children: Jesse Wayne. Appeared in films Flesh, 1968, Bilitis, 1976, Big Wednesday, 1978, Time After Time, 1979, The Fifth Floor, 1980, Modern Problems, 1981, THe Boys Next Door, 1985, Call Me, 1988, Fresh Horses, 1988, Crossing the Mob, 1988, Wired, 1989, Snow Kill, 1990, The Fan, 1996, (tv episodes) Eddie Capra Mysteries, 1978, Barnaby Jones, 1980, Charlies Angels, 1980, Darkroom, 1982, Murder, She Wrote, 1984, Miami Vice, 1985, Crime Story, 1986, Midnight Caller, 1988, The Hitchhiker, 1989, Hallmark Hall of Fame, 1993, Father's Day, 1997, I Know What You Did Last Summer, 1997, Archibald the Rainbow Painter, 1998, Bad to the Bone, 1997, Celebrity, 1998. *

DARBELNET, ROBERT LOUIS, automobile association executive; b. Portland, Maine, Dec. 14, 1951; s. Jean Louis and Elizabeth (Matheson) D.; LL.B., Laval U., Quebec City, 1978; m. Mary Ann McCaughey, Aug. 27, 1977; children: John Kevin, Mary Jennifer. Dir. consumer protection dept. Que. (Can.) Automobile Club, Quebec City, 1973-76, dir. road and tech. services, 1976-78, dir. gen. ins. dept., 1978-79, dir. adminstrv. services, 1979-80, asst. gen. mgr., 1980-83, dir. gen., 1983-90; pres. 1990-94; tchr. bus. Coll. Ste. Foy (Que.), 1978-84, v.p., 1981-82, pres., 1982-86. Bd. govs. Coll. Sainte-Foy, 1980-86, bd. govs. alumni fund, 1980-88, v.p., 1982-88; trustee AAA Found for Traffic Safety, 1990—, sec., 1993-94; v.p. Internat. Tourism Commn., 1990-94, world training coun., 1995—, mgnt. com., 1995— Federation Internation. de l'Automobile (Paris), 1990-94; bd. dirs., Corp. de la Salle Albert Rousseau, 1990-94, pres. 1991-93; bd. dirs. Magnetothique, 1990-94, Quebec Safety League, 1989-94, Enfant Jesus Hosp., 1993-94, Union Canadienne Ins., 1993—, Industrielle Gen. Ins., 1993-94, Cooperants Ins. Gen., 1993-94, Am. Automobile Assn. (pres., CEO, 1994—, Products Forestiers, Montreal, Can., 1998—. Home: 1593 Rockdale Loop Heathrow FL 32746-5332 Office: 1000 Aaa Dr Heathrow FL 32746-5062

D'ARBELOFF, ALEXANDER V., electronics company executive. Co-founder, dir. Teradyne Corp., Boston, 1960—, pres., 1971-96, CEO, 1971-97, chmn. bd. dirs., 1977—; pres. MIT, Cambridge; bd. dirs. Stratus Computer, Inc., BTU Internat., Inc., PRI Automation, Inc., GeoTel Comm. Corp. Chmn. bd. trustees MIT, Cambridge, 1997—. Office: 77 Massachusetts Ave Cambridge MA 02139-4301*

DARBY, ANITA LOYCE, secondary school educator; b. Houston, May 16, 1964; d. Franklin Lile and Anita Florence (Carver) Keeling; m. Jim Steve Yarbray, June 20, 1987 (div. Nov. 1991); 1 child, Steven William; m. James

C. Darby, Apr. 26, 1997; stepchildren: Brian Keith, Dustin Blaine. BA in Polit. Sci./Pre-Law, U. Houston, 1986, MEd, 1988. Cert. tchr. secondary social studies; cert. driver safety edn. Retail clk. Five and Ten Shoe Store, Houston, 1980-81; clothing retail clk. Weiner's Dept. Store, Houston, 1981-82; poll worker, phone analyst polit. surveys Houston, 1982-84; cashier, clk. inventory Carmona's Festival, Houston, 1984-86; sec., computer clk. Houston C.C. System, 1986-88; social studies tchr. MacArthur H.S., Houston, 1988—; mem. textbook selection com. Aldine Ind. Sch. Dist., Houston, 1989-91. Clean-up vol./sponsor Houston Galveston Coun. Cmty. and Environ. Planning, 1993-94; poll worker, phone surveyor polit. candidates, Houston, 1982—, Austin, Tex., 1983-84; vol. Rep. Nat. Conv., Houston, 1991; cons./sponsor Teen Ct., Mock City Coun., Youth and Govt., Houston, 1990—; sponsor Class 1998, 99; judge Speech and Debate Tournament, 1997-99; mem. vertical team curriculum writing, 1997-99; coach Fed. Challenge, 1999; Olympic coach cert. level I Youth Alliance Bowling Assn., 1998; mem. Sunshine Com., 1998-99; facilitator Ch. Campus Improvement; mem. Houston Coun. on World Affairs; vol. Metro Go Texan Houston Livestock Show and Rodeo Scholarship com. Mem. Am. Fedn. Tchrs., Nat. Coun. for Social Studies, Adminstrn. and Supervision Assn., Tex. Coun. Social Studies, Aldine Coun. Social Studies, Internat. Order of Rainbow for Girls (past grand/state officer, Grand Cross), Order Ea. Star (past matron), Am. Polit. Sci. Assn., Tex. Coun. for Econ. Edn., Kappa Delta Pi. Avocations: singing, reading, swimming, political activism, public relations. Fax: 281-985-6338. Office: MacArthur High Sch 4400 Aldine Mail Rd Houston TX 77039-5999

DARBY, BARBARA ANN-LOFTHOUSE, chemical technician; b. Phila., Sept. 15, 1961; d. Robert William and Lina Evelyn (James) Lofthouse; m. Joseph Francis Darby, Dec. 23, 1988; children: Robert Lofthouse, Joseph. GED, Phila., 1982. Cert. biocides operator; indsl. firefighter. Chem. operator Rohm & Haas, Phila., 1992-95; chem. technician Rohm & Haas, La Porte, Tex., 1995—; tng. coord. Bayport Biocides. Active World Wildlife Fund, Washington, 1994—, Clear Lake Ind. Sch. Dist. PTA, 1995—, Nature Conservancy, Tex., 1995; vol. United Way Campaign, Rohm & Haas Plants, 1992—; mem. Habitat for Humanity, 1996—, Natural Resources Def. Coun., 1996—; bd. dirs. Bay Area Sharks/Sharkettes, Tex. Intercity Football, Inc. Football League. Lutheran. Avocations: wildlife defense, environmental activities, cars. Home: 1749 Hialeah Dr Seabrook TX 77586-2938 Office: Rohm & Haas Bay Port Biocides 13300 Bay Area Blvd La Porte TX 77572

DARBY, EDWIN WHEELER, retired newspaper financial columnist; b. Oakland, Md., Jan. 7, 1922; s. John Dade and Nell (Bosley) D.; children—Ann Wheeler, John Dade; m. Susan E. Kroening, Mar. 14, 1970; 1 son, George Kroening. B.S. in Journalism, Ohio U. White House corr. Time mag., 1948-55; midwest corr. Time and Fortune mags., 1956-58; financial editor, columnist Chgo. Sun-Times, 1958-95; ret., 1995. Author: The Fortune Builders, 1987. Recipient Marshall Field award, 1974, Loeb award, 1975. Mem. Tavern Club. Home: 2703 W Logan Blvd Chicago IL 60647-1831

DARBY, G(EORGE) HARRISON, lawyer; b. N.Y.C., Jan. 24, 1942; s. Stephen John and Madge B. (Lill) D. BA, Muhlenberg Coll., 1963; LLB, Bklyn. Law Sch., 1967. Bar: N.Y. 1967. Ptnr. Jackson Lewis Schnitzler & Krupman, L.A. and other offices, 1967—. Mem. child adv. group Internat. Inst. of L.A., 1989-96. Office: Jackson Lewis et al 1888 Century Park W Los Angeles CA 90067-6402

DARBY, JOSEPH BRANCH, JR., retired metallurgist, government official; b. Petersburg, Va., Dec. 12, 1925; s. Joseph Branch and Jessie Catherine (Frazier) D.; m. Eleanor Lee Daley, Mar. 25, 1951; children—Joseph III, John, Leslie, Peter. B.S., Coll. William and Mary, 1948, Va. Poly. Inst., 1951; M.S., U. Ill., 1955, Ph.D., 1958. Chemist Allied Chem. Corp., Hopewell, Va., 1948-49; devel. engr. Union Carbide Corp., Niagara Falls, N.Y., 1951-53; rsch. scientist Argonne (Ill.) Nat. Lab., 1958-86, assoc. dir. Fusion Energy Program, 1974-78, assoc. dir. ocean thermal energy conversion, 1978-84; program mgr. basic energy scis. Office Energy Rsch., Dept. Energy, Washington, 1986-94; adj. prof. U. Va. Sch. of Engring., Charlottesville, 1995-97; ret., 1997; vis. sr. rsch. fellow U. Birmingham, Eng., 1970-71. Co-editor: The Electronic Structure of the Actinides and Related Properties, 2 vols., 1974; mem. adv. bd. Jour. Less-Common Metals, 1971-82, Materials Letters, 1988-92; co-editor Jour. Nuclear Materials, 1971-84, chmn. bd. editors, 1984-90, mem. adv. bd., 1990-94; contbr. articles to profl. jours. Mem. Nominating Com. for Sch. Bd., Wheaton, Ill., 1961-63, for Coll. of DuPage Bd. Trustees, 1963-65. Served with A.C. USMC, 1944-46. Sci. Rsch. Coun. sr. fellow, 1970-71; recipient Loyalty award U. Ill., Disting. Editor award The Materials Soc., 1994. Fellow Am. Soc. for Metals (mem. energy council div., mem. nuclear metallurgy com.); mem. Metall. Soc. Am. Inst. Mining, Metall. and Petroleum Engrs., ASTM, AAAS, Fedn. Materials Socs. (bd. dirs. 1988-94), Cape Cod Geneal. Soc. (co-pres. 1996-98), Sigma Xi, Tau Beta Pi, Alpha Sigma Mu, Sigma Gamma Epsilon. Presbyterian (elder). Home: PO Box 655 25 Pine St Yarmouth Port MA 02675-1838

DARBY, KAREN SUE, legal education administrator; b. Columbus, Ohio, Sept. 15, 1947; d. Emerson Curtis and Kathryn Elizabeth (Bowers) Dum; m. R. Russell Darby, Dec. 21, 1974; children: David Randolph, Michael Emerson. BA magna cum laude, Capital U., Columbus, 1969; JD, Ohio State U., 1980. Bar: Ohio 1980, U.S. Dist. Ct. (so. dist.) Ohio 1981, Pa. 1998. High sch. English tchr. Columbus Pub. Schs., 1969-72; employee rels. specialist GE, Circleville, Ohio, 1972-74; mgr. EEO and manpower programs chem. met. div. GE, Worthington, Ohio, 1974-77; atty. Ohio Legal Rights Svc., Columbus, 1980-81; pvt. practice Columbus, 1981-90; assoc. dir. Ohio Continuing Legal Edn. Inst., Columbus, 1989-95; dir. Phila. Bar Edn. Ctr., 1995-97; assoc. dir. Pa. Bar Inst., Phila., 1997—; mem. rules adv. com. Supreme Ct. Ohio, Columbus, 1989-94. Author, editor: Civil Commitment in Ohio - A Manual for Respondents' Attorneys, 1980. Mem. divorce mediation panel Ohio State U. Commn. on Interprofl. Edn., Columbus, 1988-91; vol. Boy Scouts Am., Columbus, 1988-92, Columbus Pub. Schs., 1984-95. Mem. Pa. Bar Assn., Ohio State Bar Assn. (mem. family law com. 1991-95), Assn. Continuing Legal Edn., Phila. Bar Assn. Democrat. Lutheran. Avocations: organ, piano, gardening. Office: PBI-PBEC Edn Ctr 100 Penn Sq E Philadelphia PA 19107-3322

DARBY, MARIANNE TALLEY, elementary school educator; b. Adel, Ga., Nov. 8, 1937; d. William Giles and Mary (McGlamry) Talley; m. Roy Copeland Darby, Apr. 2, 1958; children: Susan, Leslie, Allison Darby Davis. Student, Emory U., 1955-57; BS in Early Childhood Edn., Valdosta (Ga.) State Coll., 1973. Cert. early childhood and elem. edn. tchr., Ga. Tchr. 2d grade Adel Elem. Sch., spring 1973, tchr. 1st grade, 1973-98, ret., 1998. Pres. Cook County Jaycettes, Adel, 1962. Teacher of Year, Cook Elem. Sch., 1998—. Mem. Internat. Reading Assn. (South Cen. Ga. coun.), Profl. Assn. Ga. Educators, Adel Garden Club, Alpha Epsilon Upsilon, Alpha Delta Kappa (sec. 1980-82), Sigma Alpha Chi, Alpha Chi, Kappa Alpha Theta. Republican. Methodist. Avocations: sewing, piano, reading, African violets. Home: 710 S Forrest Ave Adel GA 31620-3523

DARBY, MICHAEL RUCKER, economist, educator; b. Dallas, Nov. 24, 1945; s. Joseph Jasper and Frances Adah (Rucker) D.; children: Margaret Loutrel, David Michael; Lynne Ann Zucker-Darby, 1992; stepchildren: Joshua R. Zucker, Danielle T. Zucker. AB summa cum laude, Dartmouth Coll., 1967; MA, U. Chgo., 1968, PhD, 1970. Asst. prof. econ. Ohio State U., 1970-73; vis. asst. prof. econ. UCLA, 1972-73, assoc. prof., 1973-78, prof., 1978-87, 96—, prof. Anderson Grad. Sch. Mgmt., 1987-94, Warren C. Cordner prof. money and fin. mkts., 1995—, vice-chmn., 1992-93; dir. John M. Olin Ctr. for Policy, 1993—; assoc. dir. orgnl. rsch. program UCLA Inst. for Social Sci. Rsch., 1995—; assoc. dir. Ctr. for Internat. Sci., Tech., Cultural Policy Sch. Pub. Policy and Social Rsch., UCLA, 1996—; rsch. assoc. Nat. Bur. Econ. Rsch., 1976-86, 92—; asst. sec. for economic policy U.S. Dept. Treasury, Washington, 1986-89; mem. Nat. Commn. on Superconductivity, 1988-89; under sec. for econ. affairs U.S. Dept. Commerce, Washington, 1989-92; adminstr. Econs. and Stats. Adminstrn., 1990-92; v.p., dir. Paragon Industries, Inc., Dallas, 1964-83; mem. exec. com. Western Econ. Assn., 1987-90, v.p. 1998-99, pres.-elect 1999—; chmn. The Dumbarton Group, 1992—; adj. scholar Am. Ent. Inst. for Pub. Policy Rsch., 1992—; economist stats. income divsn. IRS, 1992-94; mem. Regulatory Coordination Adv. Com. of the Commodity Futures Trading Commn., 1992-96. Author: Macroeconomics, 1976, Have Controls Ever Worked: The Post-War Record, 1976, Intermediate Macroeconomics, 1979, 2d edit., 1986, The Effects of Social Security on Income and the Capital Stock, 1979, The International Transmission of Inflation, 1981, Labor Force, Employment, and Productivity in Historical Perspective, 1984, Reducing Poverty in America: Views and Approaches, 1996; editor Jour. Internat. Money and Fin., 1981-86, mem. editl. bd., 1986—; mem. editl. bd. Am. Econ. Rev., 1983-86, Contemporary Policy Issues, 1990-93, Contemporary Econ. Policy, 1994—, Internat. Reports, 1992-95. Bd. dirs. The Opera Assoc., 1992—; mem. acad. adv. bd. Ctr. Regulation and Econ. Growth of the Alexis de Tocqueville Instn., 1993-96. Recipient Alexander Hamilton award U.S. Treasury Dept., 1989; sr. fellow Dartmouth Coll., 1966-67, Woodrow Wilson fellow, 1967-68, NSF grad. fellow, 1967-69, FDIC grad. fellow, 1969-70, Harry Scherman rsch. fellow Nat. Bur. Econ. Research, 1974-75, vis. fellow Hoover Instn., Stanford U., 1977-78. Mem. Acad. Polit. Sci., Am. Econ. Assn., Am. Fin. Assn., Am. Statis. Assn., Nat. Assn. Bus. Economists, Mont Pelerin Soc., Royal Econ. Soc., So. Econ. Assn., Western Econ. Assn., Capitol Hill Club (D.C.). Episcopalian. Home: 18108 Meandering Way Dallas TX 75252-2763 Office: UCLA Anderson Grad Sch Mgmt Los Angeles CA 90095-1481

DARBY, WESLEY ANDREW, minister, educator; b. Glendale, Ariz., Sept. 19, 1928; s. Albert Leslie and Beulah E. (Lamb) D.; m. Donna Maye Bice, May 29, 1947; children: Carolyn Darby Eymann, Lorna Dale, Elizabeth Darby Larimer, Andrea Darby Perdue. Student, Bible Inst., L.A., 1946, No. Ariz. U., 1946-47, Rockmont Coll., Denver, 1948-50, Ariz. State U., 1965, St. Anne's Coll. Oxford U., Eng., 1978. Ordained to ministry Bapt. Ch., 1950. Pastor Sunnyside Bapt. Ch., Flagstaff, Ariz., 1947-48, First Bapt. Ch. of Clifton, Ariz., 1950-55, West High Bapt. Ch., Phoenix, 1955-90, 97-99; pastor emeritus West High Bapt. Ch., 1990—; dep. assessor Greenlee County, 1951-55; instr. English lit. and pastoral subjects Southwestern Conservative Bapt. Bible Coll., Phoenix, 1961-87. Contbr. articles to profl. jours. Chmn. bd. Conservative Bapt. Found. Ariz., 1974-83, Gospel Wings, 1960-88; v.p. Ariz. Bapt. Conf., 1976-83; pres. ariz. Alcohol-Narcotic Edn. Assn., 1968-90; dep. Maricopa County (Ariz.) Sheriff's Exec. Posse, 1993-97; chaplain Civil Air Patrol, 1951-55. Recipient God, Family and Country award Freeman Inst., 1981, Ronald Reagan Cert. of Excellence Maricopa County Rep. Com., 1996. Mem. Evang. Philos. Soc., Greater Phoenix Assn. Evangelicals (pres. 1960-63, 91-96), Ariz. Breakfast Club (chaplain 1969-96, pres. 1996—), Ariz. Militia (chaplain 1994—). Republican. Home: 5628 N 11th Dr Phoenix AZ 85013-1714 Office: 3301 N 19th Ave Phoenix AZ 85015-5761

D'ARCY, GERALD PAUL, engineering executive, consultant; b. Jackson, Mich., June 6, 1933; s. Merlin Wellington and Jessie Elizabeth (Sober) D.; m. Dorothy Lee Cordell, Nov. 27, 1953; children: Sherry, Janet, Nancy, Deborah, Helen. BS MechE, U. Tex., 1956; MS MechE, U. Colo., 1962; PhD, U. Tex., 1973. Registered profl. engr., Tex. Commd. 2d lt. USAF, 1956, advanced through grades to col., retired, 1986; asst. chief soil & rock mechanics group Air Force Weapons Lab., Kirtland AFB, N.Mex., 1962-67; research assoc. Lawrence Radiation Lab., Livermore, Calif., 1967-70; chief phys. & engring. scis. div. Air Force Systems Command, Andrews AFB, Md., 1973-74; chief guns, rockets & explosives div. Air Force Armament Lab., Eglin AFB, Fla., 1975-79; comdr. Air Force Geophysics, Hanscom AFB, Mass., 1979-84, Air Force Office of Sci. Research, Bolling AFB, Washington, 1984-86; v.p. Applied Research Assocs. Inc., Albuquerque, 1986-94; ret., 1994; mem. mech. engring. vis. com. U. Tex., Austin, 1976-79. Inventor soil stress gage, 1971; contbr. over 20 papers and articles to profl. publs. Decorated Legion of Merit, 1986; recipient Meritorious Svc. award (nuclear weapons devel.) U. Calif., Livermore, 1970; named Disting. Engring. Grad. U. Tex., Austin, 1985. Mem. Phi Kappa Phi. Democrat. Methodist. Avocation: woodworking. Home: 808 Plantation Way Panama City FL 32404-8603

DARCY, JOHN ARTHUR, artist; b. Apr. 24, 1950. BFA, Calif. Coll. Arts & Crafts, 1984. Office: PO Box 416 Albion CA 95410

D'ARCY, JOHN MICHAEL, bishop; b. Brighton, Mass., Aug. 18, 1932. Student, St. John's Sem., Brighton, 1949-57; ThD, Angelicum U., Rome, 1968. Ordained priest Roman Cath. Ch., 1957. Spiritual dir., prof. theology St. John's Sem., 1968-85; ordained titular bishop of Mediana and aux. bishop of Boston Archdiocese of Boston, 1975-85; bishop Diocese of Ft. Wayne-South Bend, Ind., 1985—. Office: Diocese of Ft Wayne-South Bend PO Box 390 1103 S Calhoun St Fort Wayne IN 46801*

DARCY, KEITH THOMAS, finance company executive, educator; b. N.Y.C., June 18, 1948; s. Donald and Geraldine (Kindermann) D.; m. Lynne Alison Cumming, June 17, 1972; children: Erin Lyn, Timothy James. BS in Econs., Fordham U., 1970; MBA, Iona Coll., New Rochelle, N.Y., 1974; postgrad., N.Y. Theol. Sem., 1988-89. With Bankers Trust Co., N.Y.C., 1970-77; v.p. Marine Midland Bank N.A., N.Y.C., 1977-82; CEO, IGM divsn. Gen. Reins. Corp., Stamford, Conn., 1982-83; dir. human resource divsn. Marine Midland Bank, N.Y.C., 1984-89; pres., CEO, The Leadership Group, Inc., N.Y.C., 1989-94; v.p., assoc. ethics officer Prudential Securities Inc., N.Y.C., 1994-96, sr. ethics advisor, 1996-97; assoc. dean, disting. prof. bus. Georgetown U., Washington, 1995-96; exec. v.p. office of the pres. IBJ Whitehall Bank and Trust Co., N.Y.C., 1997—; mem. adj. faculty Marymount Coll., 1978—, Mercy Coll., 1975-96; mem. faculty Am. Inst. CPCU at Wharton, U. Pa., 1994—; mem. faculty grad. mgmt. program Antioch U., Seattle, 1989-96; vis. prof. grad. program in human resources and orgnl. devel. and grad. program in orgnl. leadership Manhattanville Coll., Purchase, N.Y., mem. corp. adv. bd., 1989—; chmn. Leadership Inst., 1997—; exec. fellow Ctr. for Bus. Ethics, Bentley Coll., Waltham, Mass., 1993—; bd. dirs. Barat House, Purchase, N.Y., 1989—; dir. emeritus Ethics Officer Assn.; mem. steering com. Caux (Switzerland) Round Table, 1996—. *Darcy has combined a career in the financial services industry with his profession as an educator and his long term involvement promoting business ethics and values-based leadership. Darcy says "The real test is not what you say you believe, it's what you do with your beliefs. Unless you find ways to express them, they are an empty chalice."* Author: I Quit My Job Today, 1992; participating author Change Management, 1993, The Ethical Companion, 1998; co-author: The Ethics Companion, 1999; mem. editorial bd., contbr.: At Work: Stories of Tomorrow's Workplace, 1992—; featured in The Ethical Edge, The Portable Executive, Marchants of Vision, Career Crossroads. Treas. Westchester County Rep. Com., White Plains, N.Y., 1979-89; asst. treas. N.Y. State Friends for Jim Buckley, 1976; dir NCCJ, 1977-85; trustee Bedford Presbyn. Ch., N.Y., 1982-87; mem. Westchester Blue Ribbon Commn. to Formulate County Housing Policy, 1979; trustee March of Dimes, Westchester, 1978-84, chmn. Exec. Walkathon, 1978-81. Mem. Ethics Officers Assn. (dir. emeritus), Consumer Bankers Assn. at U. Va. (mem. faculty 1984-90), Caux (Switzerland) Round Table (affil.), Delta Mu Delta. Club: Soc. Friendly Sons of St. Patrick (pres. 1985). Home: Horseshoe Hl W Pound Ridge NY 10576 Office: IBJ Schroder Bank and Trust Co 1 State St New York NY 20004

D'ARCY, MICHAEL PATRICK, public relations professional; b. Pompton Plains, N.J., Aug. 31, 1970; s. John Martin and Konstanze C. (Muendlein) D'A. BA in Biol. Basis of Behavior, U. Pa., 1992. Tech. asst. N.Y. Acad. Medicine, N.Y.C., 1994-96; account exec. Ruder Finn, Inc., N.Y.C., 1997—; freelance film critic. Mem. Pub. Rels. Soc. Am., Met. Republic Club. Republican. Home: 427 Green Hill Rd Kinnelon NJ 07405-2143

D'ARCY, THOMAS P., real estate company executive; married; 4 children. BA, Bates Coll. Leasing, mgmt. and financing agt. office and retail offices, 1983-89; v.p. Bradley Real Estate, Northbrook, Ill., 1989-92, sr. v.p., 1992-95, exec. v.p., 1995-96, pres., CEO, 1996—, chmn., pres., CEO, 1998—. Office: Bradley Real Estate Inc 40 Skokie Blvd Ste 600 Northbrook IL 60062

DARDAI, SHAHID MOINUDDIN, computer science educator; b. India, May 11, 1940. Prof. computer sci. dept. Richard J. Daley Coll., Chgo., 1993—, data processing coord.; chairperson computer sci. dept. Richard J. Daley Coll., 1993—; adj. faculty math. and computer sci. dept. Chgo. State U., 1993—. Mem. Data Processing Mgmt. Assn., Phi Theta Kappa. Fax: (312) 838-7524. Office: Richard J Daley Coll 7500 S Pulaski Rd Chicago IL 60652-1242

DARDEN, BARBARA L., library director; b. Cleve., Apr. 6, 1947; d. Curley and Cora (Chambliss) Brown; m. Joseph S. Darden; children: Michelle, Crystal, Twilla. BS, Ohio State U., 1967; MS in Ednl. Media, Kent. State U. (Ohio), 1971, MLS, 1971. Adminstrv. supr. Cleve. pub. schs., 1968-72; libr. Cuyahoga C.C., Cleve., 1972-75, coord., 1975-77, interim dir., 1977-78, asst. dean, 1978-80, dir., 1980-84; dir. libr. Kean Coll., Union, N.J., 1984—; cons. Dembsy Assocs., Boston, 1967-81; editl. cons. Max Pub. Co., N.Y.C., 1967-81; cons. reader U.S. Office Edn., Washington, 1979-80; editl. cons. Jossey-Bass Pub. Co., 1979. Cons. editor Probe, 1975, Sch. Media Ctr., 1968, Booklist, 1969; contbr. articles to profl. jours. Bd. dirs. N.J. Adv. Bd. on the Status of Women, 1988, Africana Studies, 1988, N.J. State Libr. Adv. Bd., 1996; bd. dirs. N.J. Ednl. Activities Task Force Libr. Com. Recipient Phillips award Kent State U., 1970. Mem. ALA (chmn. pay equity com. 1996, chair LAMA-COLA 1999), Higher Edn. Reps., N.J. Acad. Libr. Network (chmn. 1987, bd. dirs. 1995—), Coun. N.J. Coll. Librs. (pres. 1987—), N.J. Libr. Assn., Oral History Soc., N.J. Hist. Soc., Libr. Adminstrn. Mgmt. Assn. (chair 1997-99, bd. dirs. 1999), Jr. League (Cleve. vice chmn. 1981, 83), Concerned Parents Club (pres. 1984), Women's City Club (adv. bd. 1997—). Avocations: music, reading. Office: Kean Univ Libr Morris Ave Union NJ 07083

DARDEN, CHRISTOPHER A., lawyer, actor, writer. BA in Criminal Justice, Calif. State U., San Jose; JD, U. Calif., San Francisco, 1980. Bar: Calif. 1980. Former atty. Nat. Labor Rels. Bd.; former asst. head dep. in spl. investigations divsn. L.A. County Dist. Attys. Office, former dep. dist. atty. in maj. crimes divsn.; actor, writer, 1996—; assoc. prof. law Sch. Law Southwestern U., L.A., 1996—. Author: (with Jeff Walter) In Contempt, 1996. Address: Brokaw Company 9255 W Sunset Blvd Ste 804 Los Angeles CA 90069-3305 Office: Southwestern U Sch Law 675 S Westmoreland Ave Los Angeles CA 90005*

DARDEN, CLAIBOURNE HENRY, JR., marketing research professional; b. Greensboro, N.C., June 26, 1943; s. Claibourne Henry and Gerry (Bonkemeyer); children: Claibourne III, Prentiss. BS, Washington & Lee U., 1966; MBA, Emory U., 1968. Pres. Darden Rsch. Corp., Atlanta, 1968—; TV commentator, spkr. in field. Bd. dirs. Nat. Wild Turkey Fedn., Edgefield, S.C., 1985—, Ga. Conservancy, Atlanta, 1985-91, Washington & Lee Alumni Assn., Atlanta, 1986-87. Mem. Am. Mktg. Assn. (bd. dirs. Atlanta chpt. 1970-75, Mktg. Profl. of Yr. 1976), Mktg. Rsch. Assn., N.Y. Yacht Club, Druid Hills Golf Club. Presbyterian. Avocations: hunting, sailing, fishing. Office: Darden Rsch Corporation 1534 N Decatur Rd NE Atlanta GA 30307-1000

DARDEN, DONNA BERNICE, special education educator; b. Portsmouth, Va., Sept. 15, 1956; d. Howard John and Joyce Bernice Jackson; m. John Holland Darden, June 20, 1975; children: Christopher John, Jamison Marie. AA, Piedmont Va. Community Coll., Charlottesville, Va., 1987; BA, U. Va., 1990, M of Teaching, 1990. Cert. tchr. spl. edn., learning disabilities, emotionally disturbed. Customer svc. rep. Landmark Communications, Inc., Norfolk, Va., 1976-79; computer operator Curtis Mathes Corp., Houston, 1979-80; chief fin. officer Darden, Inc./(div. ColorTyme TV), Charlottesville, 1980-87; learning disabilities tchr. Oakland Sch., Boyd Tavern, Va., 1990—; clin. instr. Curry Sch. of Edn. U. Va., 1995—. Mem. Albermarle County Rep. Com., Va., 1982—; area capt. Key West-Cedar Hills Community Assn., Albermarle County, 1985, 86, mem. chmn., 1987; swim meet assoc., Key West Swim Team, 1986-93; co-chmn. Rivanna Scenic River Adv. Bd., 1997—; active Cornerstone Cmty. Ch.; sec. Cornerstone Wesleyan Women, 1998-99, asst. dir. 1999—. Mem. Coun. Exceptional Children, Golden Key, Kappa Delta Pi. Avocations: music, tennis, gardening, nature. Home: 344 Key West Dr Charlottesvle VA 22911-8426 Office: Oakland Sch Boyd Tavern VA 22947

DARDEN, EDWIN SPEIGHT, SR., architect; b. Stantonsburg, N.C., Oct. 14, 1920; s. Edwin Speight and Sallie (Jordan) D.; m. s. Pauline K. Bartlett, Feb. 26, 1944; children: Edwin Speight III, Judith Ann, Diane Russell. BS in Archtl. Engring., Kans. State U., 1947. Registered architect, Calif. Assoc., Fred L. Swartz and William G. Hyberg, Fresno, Calif., 1949-59; ptnr. Nargis and Darden (Architects), Fresno, 1959-69; pres. Edwin S. Darden Assocs., Inc., Fresno, 1969-85, cons., 1985—; bd. dirs. Murphy Bank; mem. state adv. bd. Office of Architecture and Constrn., 1970-78; cons. ednl. facilities, 1975—. Prin. works include Clovis (Calif.) High Sch., 1969, Clovis W. High Sch., 1976, Ahwahnee Jr. High Sch., Fresno, 1966, Tehipite Jr. High Sch., Fresno, 1973, Fresno County Dept. Health, 1978, Floyd B. Buchanan Edn. Ctr., Clovis, 1990. Served to 1st lt. C.E., AUS, 1942-46. Fellow AIA; mem. Sigma Phi Epsilon, Alpha Kappa Psi. Presbyterian. Club: Fresno Rotary. Office: Edwin S Darden Assocs Inc 1177 W Shaw Ave Fresno CA 93711-3704

DARDEN, JOSEPH SAMUEL, JR., health educator; b. Pleasantville, N.J., July 25, 1925; s. Joseph Samuel and Blanche Catherine (Paige) D.; A.B., Lincoln U., 1948; M.A., N.Y.U., 1952, Ed.D. (Danforth Found. fellow), 1963; m. Barbara Cassandra Sellers, Dec. 30, 1955 (div. July 1979); 1 dau., Michele Irene. Instr. biol. scis. Clark Coll., Atlanta, 1952-55; asst. prof. Albany (Ga.) State Coll., 1955-58, prof., 1959-64; asst. prof. Kean U. of N.J., Union, 1964-67, prof. health edn., 1970—, coord. of health, 1977-79, chmn. dept. health and recreation, 1979-84, coord. of health, 1984—, dir. minority enrollment, 1988-94; adj. prof. health Wagner Coll., S.I., N.Y., 1965-88; cons. N.J. Dept. Edn., 1968-73, 76-88. Bd. advisors Marylawn of Oranges, 1971-73; bd. dirs. N.J. Council Family Relations, 1981-83; trustee Planned Parenthood of Essex County, N.J., 1985—. Served with AUS, 1944-46. Recipient Alumni Achievement award Lincoln U., 1993. Fellow Am. Assn. Health Edn. (charter); mem. Am. Alliance for Health, Phys. Edn., Recreation and Dance (Eastern dist. v.p. for health edn. 1971-72, dist. pres. 1974-75; Eastern dist. rep. 1979-82; honor award Eastern dist. 1976, nat. honor award 1985, Outstanding Tchr. award Eastern dist. 1983, Charles D. Henry award 1988, Edwin B. Henderson award 1991), Am. Sch. Health Assn. (governing council 1970-73, Disting. Service award 1971), Assn. Advancement Health Edn. (dir. 1975-78, Profl. Svc. award 1990, presdl. citation 1996), N.J. Health Edn. Council (founder 1967, honor award 1975), N.J. Assn. Health, Phys. Edn. and Recreation (v.p. health edn. 1967, Honor fellow award 1972, Disting. Leadership award 1975), Alpha Phi Alpha. Author: (with others) Growth Pattern and Sex Education, 1967, Updated Supplement to Growth Pattern and Sex Education, 1972, Toward a Healthier Sexuality: A Book of Readings, 1997. Home: 1416 Thelma Dr Union NJ 07083-6220 Office: Kean U NJ Union NJ 07083

DARDEN, WILLIAM HOWARD, JR., biology educator; b. Tuscaloosa, Ala., Apr. 25, 1937; s. William Howard and Jannie Belle (Herring) D.; m. Caroline Jackson, July 15, 1959; children: Leanne Carol, Michael Howard. B.S., U. Ala., Tuscaloosa, 1959, M.S., 1961; Ph.D., Ind. U., 1965. Asst. prof. biology U. Ala., Tuscaloosa, 1965-68, assoc. prof., 1969-73, prof., assoc. chmn. dept. biology, 1973-74, prof., chmn. dept. biology, 1974-96; prof. emeritus, 1996—. Contbr. articles to sci. jours. Bd. dirs. Springhill Lake Assn., 1980-85, So. Grass Tennis Club, 1979-81, Ala. Credit Union, 1987—. Predoctoral fellow NIH, 1963-65; grantee NSF, 1972, U. Ala., Tuscaloosa, 1965-71. Mem. Sigma Xi, Beta Beta Beta, Omicron Delta Kappa, Phi Kappa Phi. Am. Baptist. Home: 3628 Rainbow Dr Tuscaloosa AL 35405-5331 Office: U Ala PO Box 870344 Tuscaloosa AL 35487-0344

DAREHSHORI, NADER FARHANG, publishing sales executive; b. Shiraz, Iran, Dec. 15, 1936; came to U.S., 1961, naturalized, 1972; s. Zaki F. and Rokhsar (Farsimadan) D.; m. Anne C. Wagnild, Dec. 14, 1969 (dec.); m. Cynthia McGuffey, Aug. 3, 1991. BA in Econs., U. Wis., 1966, postgrad., 1966. Supt. village schs. Shiraz, 1959=61; from salesman to midwest sales mgr. Houghton Mifflin Co., Geneva, Ill., 1966-84; from v.p., gen. mgr. coll. divsn. midwest to chmn., CEO Houghton Mifflin Co., Geneva, 1984-91; chmn., pres., CEO Houghton Mifflin Co., Boston, 1991—. Democrat. Office: Houghton Mifflin Co 222 Berkeley St Fl 5 Boston MA 02116-3764

DARER, JOHN DAVID, insurance company executive; b. N.Y.C., July 2, 1961; s. Stanley P. and Susan H. (Silverstone) D. BS, Syracuse U., 1983. CLU; ChFC; cert. structured settlement cons. Spl. agt. Northwestern Mut. Life, N.Y.C., 1983—; exec. v.p. JJ Winston Inc., N.Y.C., 1988-94; prin. Internat. Settlement Design N.Y. Inc., N.Y.C., 1991-95; sr. v.p. Sheerin Corp., N.Y.C., 1995—. Mem. Nat. Assn. Life Underwriters (Nat. Quality award 1985—), Aviation Ins. Assn., N.Y. Self-Insured Assn., N.Y. Claim

Assn., Am. Soc. CLU and ChFC, Nat. Structured Settlement Trade Assn. (long range planning com. 1994-95, pub. rels. com. 1996—). Republican. Jewish. Avocations: scuba diving, golf, adventure travel, tennis. Home: 43 Harbor Dr Apt 309 Stamford CT 06902-7469 Office: Sheerin Corp 3 Park Ave Fl 29 New York NY 10016-5902

DARESTA, PAMELA BEAGLE, artist; b. Flint, Mich., Oct. 4, 1949; d. Harold Edward and Peggy Jean (Packer) Beagle; m. William Leroy Guest, Jan. 8, 1971 (div. Jan. 1979); m. Andrew Matteu Daresta, Feb. 14, 1982; 1 child, Christopher Kiel. Grad., Ringling Sch. of Art, Sarasota, Fla., 1970. Art instr. Hambrick Elem. Sch., Stone Mountain, Ga., 1986-90; artist instr. Chastain Art Ctr./City of Atlanta, 1975-90; mem. Fulton County Arts Coun., Atlanta, 1984-96, 97-99; artist-in-residence Ga. Coun. for the Arts, Atlanta, 1984-97, 98-99, St. Joseph Sch., Marietta, Ga., 1990-97, 98-99; mem. mus. adv. bd. Marietta Cobb Mus. of Art, 1995-97, 98, High Mus. of Art Family Workshops, 1995-97, High Mus. Picasso Workshops, 1997, Pop Art Workshop 98, Carlos Mus. Emory U. Children's Summer Workshop, 1998, 99. Artist: (hist. murals) McRae/Helena, Ga., 1995, Pineview, Ga., 1994, Dublin, Ga., 1995, Irwinton, Ga., 1996, Mural Talbotton, Ga., 1998, Lake Windward Sch. mural, 1999. Vol. YWCA Marietta, 1995, Atlanta Olympics, 1996; artists Art Papers Auction, Atlanta, 1993-95. Recipient Artist-Initiated Grant, Ga. Coun. for the Arts, Installation Fulton County Cen. Libr., 1984, Mural Grant Project, Fulton County Arts Coun. and Edn., 1996. Mem. Ga. Citizens for the Arts. Avocation: travel, mus. tours, reading. Home: 392 Mark AVe Marietta GA 30067-7254

DARGAN, JOHN HENRY, strategic planner; b. Dublin, Ireland, Dec. 16, 1965; s. Peter Anthony and Cecilia (Blake) D.; m. Janet Tsai Dargan, Aug. 31, 1997. B Engring., Trinity Coll., Dublin, 1987; MBA, U. Pa., 1993. Bus. analyst McKinsey & Co., London, 1987-89; assoc. GE Capital Corp., London, 1989-91; cons. Oliver, Wyman & Co., London, 1993-95; head of strategy London Stock Exchange, 1995-97; dir. spl. projects Warner Bros., L.A., 1997—; adviser Russian Privatization Inst., Moscow, 1992. Fulbright scholar, 1991, Palmer scholar, 1993. Roman Catholic. Home: 1264 Via Landeta Pls Vrds Est CA 90274-1969 Office: Warner Bros 4000 Warner Blvd Burbank CA 91522-0002

DARGAN, PAMELA ANN, systems and software engineer; b. Norfolk, Va.; d. Thomas J. and Stana E. (Verich) Piazza; m. W. Scott Dargan, Dec., 1990. BS in Math., Va. Poly. and State U., 1979; MS in Computer Sci., George Mason U., 1993. Programmer Control Data Corp., Rockville, Md., 1979-80; tech. staff BDM Corp., Mc Lean, Va., 1980-81, TRW Fed. Sys. Group, Mc Lean, Va., 1981-87; dep. program mgr. Mystech, Inc., Alexandria, Va., 1987-89; lead engr. MITRE Corp., Mc Lean, 1989-98; prin. Litton Tasc, Inc., Chantilly, Va., 1998—; program chair East Coast Artificial Intelligence Work Sta. Users Group, 1984-85; guest spkr., author on open sys. for internat. confs. and publs.; guest spkr. univs. and internat. confs. Contbr. chpts. to books and articles to profl. jours. Mem. IEEE, Assn. Computing Machinery, Internat. Coun. on Sys. Engring.

DARIAN, CRAIG CHARLES, executive film producer; b. Glendale, Calif., Mar. 18, 1955; s. Charles Ohan and Gloria (Berberian) D.; m. Kimberly Austin Brooke, Oct. 11, 1975; children: Jordan, Jessica, Kaitlin. Pres., gen. ptnr. Studio Systems Co., Beverly Hills, Calif., 1975-82; v.p., head of sales and bus. affairs Ryder Sound Svc., Inc., Hollywood, Calif., 1981-84; pres., chief exec. officer Glen Glenn Sound Studios, Inc., Hollywood, 1985-86; chmn., chief exec. officer Republic Studios, Inc., Hollywood, 1987-90; pres., chief exec. officer Matrix Studios, Inc., Hollywood, 1990-94; chmn., chief exec. officer Darian Group, Inc., San Marino, Calif., 1986—; co-chmn. Tricor Entertainment, Inc., San Marino, 1988—; mng. ptnr. ChinAmerica Ltd., San Marino, 1996—; exec. prodr., Carlo's Wake, 1998, exec. prodr., The Amati Girls, 1999, commr., co-founder Hollywood Entertainment Sports Assn., 1981-86; bd. suprs. Rep. Corp. Credit Union. Recipient Plaque Am. Cancer Soc., 1989, City of Hope, 1982. Mem. Am. Film Inst., Motion Picture and TV Coun. (chmn.), Acad. Motion Picture Arts and Scis. (Oscar nomination), Acad. of TV, Arts and Scis. (6 Emmy citations, Blue Ribbon panelist, judge Emmy Awards 1985-89), U. So. Calif. Cinema Circulus, Soc. Motion Picture and TV Engrs., Internat. Alliance Theatrical and Stage Employees, Hollywood C. of C. (bd. dirs., exec. com., trustee Hollywood Sign Trust, chmn. mgmt. com., Walk of Fame), Am. Heart Assn. (bd. dirs.), Senatorial Inner Circle, Prodrs. Guild Am. Home: San Marino CA Office: Tricor Entertainment Inc 1613 Chelsea Rd San Marino CA 91108-2419

DARIANO, JOSEPH, publishing company executive. Pres. govt. svcs. Reed Tech. & Info. Svcs., Fort Washington, Pa. Office: Reed Tech & Info Svcs 275 Gibraltar Rd Horsham PA 19044-2305*

DARIEN, STEVEN MARTIN, management consulting company executive; b. N.Y.C., Oct. 29, 1942; s. Leo and Laura Darien; m. Susan Ruth Kinsley, Nov. 29, 1942; children: Jodi Ellen, Andrew Todd. AB, Rutgers Coll., 1963; MBA, Columbia U., 1966. Claims settler Equitable Life, N.Y.C., 1963-64; mgmt. trainee Merck & Co., Inc., Rahway, N.J., 1966-69, mgr. coll. rels., 1969-74, exec. dir. pers. resources, 1974-79, exec. dir. U.S. Pers., 1979-85, v.p. employee rels., 1985-89, v.p. worldwide pres., 1989-90, v.p. human resources, 1990-96; pres. Darien Assocs., 1996-98; chmn., CEO The Cabot Adv. Group, Washington, 1998—; bd. dirs. Somerset Hosp. Chmn. Olin Inst. for Employment Practice and Policy; chmn. Olin Found. for Employment Policy and Practice. Mem. Columbia U. Bus. Sch. Alumni Assn. (v.p.).

DARIN, FRANK VICTOR JOHN, management consultant; b. Detroit, Feb. 16, 1930; s. Frank Peter and Marie D.; m. Barbara Nelson Lynn, July 13, 1957; children: Lynn A., Pamela L. BA in econs., Yale U., 1952; JD, U. Va., 1957. Bar: Mich. 1958. Labor rels. mgr. Ford Motor Co., Dearborn, Mich., 1957-64; dir. indsl. rels. office Ford Motor Co., Valencia, Venezuela, 1965-68; corp. pers. rels. mgr. Ford Motor Co., Dearborn, 1969-82, bus. ops. dir., 1983-87, v.p. Ford Fund, dir. corp. affairs staff, 1988-95; cons. sr. exec. mgmt. Darin Corp. Cons., Inc., Dearborn, Mich., 1995—. Bd. dirs. Henry Ford Health Sys., Dearborn, 1991—, New Detroit, Inc., 1991-95, Detroit Econ. Growth, 1993-97, Spoleto Festival U.S.A., Charleston, S.C., 1990-93, Van Patrick Found., Detroit, 1990—; CEO rep. bd. Detroit Renaissance, Inc., 1991-95, S.W. Detroit Bus. Assn., 1995—, Detroit Exec. Svc. Corps., 1996—, Mexicantown Devel. Corp., 1995—, Arab-Am. Caldean Coun., 1996—; bus. advisor Coun. Interlochen (Mich.) Acad. Arts, 1989-95, Wayne State U. Sch. Bus., 1993—. 1st lt. U.S. Army, 1952-54, Korea. Mem. Greater Detroit C. of C. (bd. dirs. 1991-95, vice chmn. 1994-95), Dearborn Country Club, Renaissance Club (Detroit). Episcopalian. Office: Darin Corp Cons Inc 429 N Beech Daly Rd Ste 200 Dearborn Heights MI 48127-3444*

DARION, JOE, librettist, lyricist; b. N.Y.C., Jan. 30, 1917; s. Isak and Rose (Nadelle) D.; m. Hellen Solomon, June 8, 1940. Student journalism, CCNY. Lyricist of popular songs including Ricochet, Changing Partners, Midnight Train, 1954-58; librettist opera, cantatas, song cycles including jazz opera Archy and Mehitabel; New Orleans Cantata, 1956-60; playwright, lyricist for Broadway prodns. Shinbone Alley, 1957; lyricist Broadway prodns. Man of La Mancha, 1965, Illya Darling, 1967; librettist for oratorio Galileo, 1967, cantata And David Wept, 1970, The Questions of Abraham, 1972, Christmas cantata A Handful of Souls, 1975, A Mass for Cain, 1978, opera Galileo Galilei, 1979; writer English sect. bilingual musical The Megilla, 1968; screenplay, lyrics Archy and Mehitabel, 1969; 72; writer play Better Than Wine, 1986, book and lyrics musical The Unicorn on Fashion Street, 1988, musical play Oswego, 1993. Served with USNR, World War II, PTO. Recipient Antoinette Perry award, 1965, 66, drama critics cir. award, 1965, 66, internat. broadcasting award, 1964, gold records award, Gabriel award, 1974, award Ohio State U. Telecomms. Ctr., 1975. Mem. ASCAP, Am. Guild Authors and Composers, Dramatists Guild, Nat. Acad. Rec. Arts and Scis. Jewish. Address: Pinnacle Rd PO Box 315 Lyme NH 03768-0315

DARIOTIS, TERRENCE THEODORE, lawyer; b. Chgo., Feb. 28, 1946; s. Theodore S. and Dorothy Mizzen (Thompson) D.; m. Jeanne Elizabeth Gibbons, Oct. 24, 1970; children: Sara Mizzen, Kristin Elizabeth, Jennifer Ann. BA in Philosophy, St. Joseph's Coll., Rensselaer, Ind., 1969; JD, Loyola U., Chgo., 1973. Bar: Ill. 1973, Fla. 1975, U.S. Tax Ct. 1993, U.S. Supreme Ct., 1978. Law clk. to presiding justice Appellate Ct. of Ill. (2d dist.), Waukegan, 1973-74; assoc. Keith Kinderman, Tallahassee, 1975-76; sole practitioner Tallahassee, 1976-82; ptnr. Kahn and Dariotis, P.A., Tallahassee, 1982-96, Warfel, Goldberg, Dariotis, Waldoch & Olive, P.A., Tallahassee, 1996—; adj. prof. Fla. State U. Coll. Bus., 1987-93. Roman Catholic. Office: Warfel Goldberg Dariotis Waldoch & Olive PA 2120 Killarney Way Tallahassee FL 32308-3402

DARIUS, FRANKLIN ALEXANDER, JR. (CHIP DARIUS), health administrator, educator, consultant; b. New Haven, Apr. 12, 1962; s. Frankln Alexander and Nancy (Fullerton) D.; m. Marla Joyce Borio, July 30, 1988. BS in Human Devel., U. Conn., 1985, MA in Communication, 1988. Cert. EMT, EMS instr., CPR instr. Account exec. Consultants & Designers, Inc., Hartford, Conn., 1988-89; dir. R&D Powerphone Inc., Madison, Conn., 1989-91; dir. training and devel. Holdsworth & Assocs., East Berlin, Conn., 1991-93, v.p., 1993—, COO, 1995—; adj. faculty U. Conn. Storrs, 1986—, Mattatuck C.C., Waterbury, Conn., 1989—; tng. cons. Bus. Svcs. Network, Waterbury, 1989—; cons. Nat. Emergency Number Assn., 1989—, office emergency med. svcs. State of Conn., 1993—, State of W.Va., 1993—, State of Minn., 1994—, State of N.D., 1994—, State of Colo., 1994—; mem. task force pub. info. and edn. Conn. Health Dept., 1992-97, chair, 1997-98, com. quality improvement emergency med. svcs. Am. Coll. Emergency Physicians, 1993—; officer Mid-State Regional Emergency Med. Svcs. Coun., 1992-94; bd. dirs. Conn. Soc. EMS Instrs., 1993-97. Editor: Dispatcher's Guide to Fires & Incidents, 1990; contbr. articles to profl. jours. Asst. scoutmaster Boy Scouts Am., Cheshire, Conn., 1980-86; trustee Multiple Sclerosis Soc., Hartford, 1984-86; pres. The Navigators, U. Conn., 1987; tng. officer Cromwell (Conn.) Fire Dept. Ambulance, 1990-91, v.p., 1992-98, dir., 1998—; co-founder Fellowship of Internat. Grad. Students, U. Conn., Storrs, 1985-88. Recipient Good Citizen award DAR, 1981, commendation Multiple Sclerosis Soc., 1984, 85, award Outstanding Young Men of Am., 1989. Mem. ASTM (com. F-30 on EMS), AAUP, ASTD, Conn. Soc. EMS-Instrs., Nat. Assn. EMTs, Alpha Phi Omega (1st v.p. 1984-85, Outstanding Brother of Yr. 1985), Hartford Christian Bus. and Profl. Assn., Promisekeepers. Baptist. Home: 58 South St Cromwell CT 06416-2240

DARKE, RICHARD FRANCIS, lawyer; b. Detroit, June 17, 1943; s. Francis Joseph and Irene Anne (Potts) D.; m. Alice Mary Renger, Feb. 14, 1968; children: Kimberly, Richard, Kelly, Sean, Colin. BBA, U. Notre Dame, 1965; JD, Detroit Coll. Law, 1969. Bar: Mich. 1969. Atty. AAA, Detroit, 1969-72; assoc. Oster & Mollett P.C., Mt. Clemens, Mich., 1972-73; ptnr. Small, Darke, Oakes P.C., Southfield, Mich., 1973-77; v.p., gen. counsel, sec. Fruehauf Corp., Detroit, 1977-92; ptnr. Darke & Wilson, Grosse Pointe Woods, Mich., 1993—. Mem. ABA, Mich. Bar Assn., Detroit Bar Assn., Machinery and Allied Products Inst. (counsel), Mich. Gen. Counsel Group, Essex Country Club, Lockmoor Club. Roman Catholic. Avocation: golfing. Home: 23173 Alger Ln Saint Clair Shores MI 48080-2624 Office: Darke & Wilson Ste 580 Pointe Plz 1925 1 Mack Ave Grosse Pointe Woods MI 48236*

DARKOVICH, SHARON MARIE, nurse administrator; b. Ft. Wayne, Ind., Dec. 10, 1949; d. Gerald Antone LaCanne and Ida Eileen (Bowman) LaCanne Cutler; m. Robert Eliot Ness, July 17, 1971 (dec. Aug. 1976); m. Paul Darkovitch, Jan. 23, 1981 (div. May 1994); 1 child, Amy Elizabeth. BSN, Case Western Res. U., 1973, BA in Psychology, 1978; cert. in advanced bioethics, Cleve. State U., 1990, MA in Philosophy and Bioethics, 1994. RN, Ohio. Staff nurse Univ. Hosps., Cleve., 1973, asst. head nurse, 1973-76; quality improvement coord. St. Luke's Med. Ctr., Cleve., 1976-83, 84-97, dir. nursing, 1983-84, quality improvement dir., 1997-98; dir. quality svcs. Lake Hosp. System, Inc., Painesville, Ohio, 1998—; cons. to long-term care facilities, 1986-92, pressure ulcer dressing devel. B.F. Goodrich Co., 1988-92; cons. to long term care facilities, 1989-93, cons. to ambulatory faculty for Joint Commn. for Accreditation of Health Care Orgns., Oakbrook, Ill., 1994, cons. to cmty. hosp. med. staff, bylaws, 1996; lectr. U. Akron, 1992-93, Northeast Ohio U. Coll. Medicine, 1993-95. Mem. ANA, Greater Cleve. Nurses Assn. (mem. dist. coun. on practice, 1982-84), Sigma Theta Tau. Avocations: reading, needlework, sewing, camping.

DARLING, GARY LYLE, carpet and furniture cleaning company executive; b. Passaic, N.J., Nov. 29, 1941; s. Earle Wallace and Lottie Anne (Shefcik) D.; B.A. in Bus. Adminstrn., Boston U., 1963; postgrad. Columbia U. Law Sch., 1963-64; m. Jane Constance Higgiston, Aug. 24, 1964; children—Susan Jane, Debra Ann, Eric Wallace. Data processing sales rep. Service Bur. Corp. subs. IBM, Boston, 1964-66; owner, pres. Renotex Corp., N.Y.C., 1966—. Mem. Assn. Interior Decor Specialists (pres. 1979-80), Carpet and Upholstery Cleaning Assn. (pres. 1974-76), Assn. Specialists in Cleaning and Restoration (treas. 1986—), N.Y. Rug Cleaners Inst. (dir. 1974—), Nat. Fedn. Ind. Bus., C. of C., Better Bus. Bur. Club: Englewood Field. Office: Renotex Corp 229 10th Ave New York NY 10011-4738

DARLING, GARY R., umpire; b. San Francisco, Oct. 9, 1957; m. Cheryl Hellmann, Dec. 19, 1987; children: Cameron, Courtney. Grad., Cosumnes River Jr. Coll. Baseball player Am. Legion; former umpire Northwest League, Calif. League, Ariz. Instrnl. League, Colombian Winter League, Puerto Rico Winter League, Pacific Coast League; umpire maj. league baseball Nat. League, N.Y.C., 1988—; with Umpires Union, Phila. Avocations: golf, basketball. Office: Nat League 350 Park Ave New York NY 10022 also: Umpires Union 1735 Market St Philadelphia PA 19103

DARLING, GEORGE CURTIS, minister, administrator; b. Xenia, Ohio, Nov. 23, 1928; s. Russell M. and Mary Elizabeth (Young) D.; m. Edna Pearlen Phillips, May 1, 1960; (div. Apr. 1973) 1 child, Curtis; m. Mary Elizabeth Miller, Oct. 24, 1952 (div. Aug. 1956), 1 child, Kirk; m. Evelyn Cornelia Woodfork, Apr. 10, 1976 (dec. Nov. 1998). Adrloma in Theology, Am. Bapt. Theol. Sem., Dayton, Ohio, 1970. Ordained to ministry Bapt. Ch., 1963. Pastor 2nd Bapt. Ch., Del., Ohio, 1966-71; supply pastor Tabernacle Bapt. Ch., Columbus, Ohio, 1974; pastor Flintridge Bapt. Ch., Columbus, 1980-91; v.p. Springfield (Ohio) Dist. Sunday Sch. and Bapt. Tng. Union. Author: (booklet) How to Find God, 1969. Bd. dirs., pres. Liberty Ctr., Delaware, Ohio, 1968-70; mem. Delaware County Community Action Orgn., 1967. With U.S. Army, 1950-52, Korea.; ret. USAF, 1988. Recipient Hon. Sci. award, Bausch & Lomb, 1946. Mem. Eastern Union Missionary Bapt. Assn. (statistical clk Ohio 1981-85, 3rd vice moderator 1985-87, 2nd vice moderator, 1987-91), Columbus Bapt. Ministers and Laity Bible League (instr. 1987-96). Home: 1927 Shadyt Ct Apt A Columbus OH 43229 *On cloudy days when the sun is hidden from view, flying above the clouds enables one to see the brightness of the sun. When things go wrong in my life, I take a spiritual trip beyond the darkness of the moment into the sunlight of hope.*

DARLING, JOHN ROTHBURN, JR., university president, business educator; b. Holton, Kans., Mar. 30, 1937; s. John Rothburn and Beatrice Noel (Deaver) D.; m. Melva Jean Fears, Aug. 20, 1958; children: Stephen, Cynthia, Gregory. BS, U. Ala., 1959, M.S., 1960; Ph.D., U. Ill., 1967; Ph.D. (hon.), Chung Yuan Christian U., Taiwan, 1998. Divisional mgr. J.C. Penney Co., 1960-63; grad. teaching asst. U. Ill., Urbana, 1965-66; asst. prof. mktg. U. Ala., Tuscaloosa, 1966-68; assoc. prof. mktg. U. Mo., Columbia, 1968-71; prof. adminstrn., coord. mktg. Wichita State U., 1971-76; dean, prof. mktg. Coll. Bus. and Adminstrn., So. Ill. U., Carbondale, 1976-81; v.p. acad. affairs and rsch., prof. internat. bus. Tex. Tech U., Lubbock, 1981-86; provost, v.p. acad. affairs, prof. mktg. and internat. bus. Miss. State U., Mississippi State, 1986-90; chancellor, disting. prof. internat. bus. La. State U., Shreveport, 1990-95; pres., prof. mktg. and internat. bus. Pittsburg (Kans.) State U., 1995—; mktg. rsch. cons. Southwestern Bell, 1970; sr. v.p. Boothe Advt. Wichita, 1972; pres. Bus. Rsch. Assocs., 1972-76; cons. Bus. Rsch. Assocs., 1976-82; spl. cons. FTC, Washington, 1972-75, U.S. Dept. Justice, 1973-74, Atty. Gen., State of Kans., 1972-76, Dist. Atty. 18th Jud. Dist., Wichita, 1972-76, Maya Internat. Inc., Houston, 1995—, Morrison and Assocs., Inc., Shreveport, 1995-97; vis. disting. prof. internat. mktg. Helsinki Sch. Econs. and Bus. Adminstrn., 1993—. Author: (with Harry A. Lipson) Marketing Fundamentals, Text and Cases, 1980, (with Raimo Nurmi) International Management Leadership: The Primary Competitive Advantage, 1997; mem. bd. cons. editors Jour. Advt., 1984—; mem. editl. rev. bd. Jour. Internat. Bus. Studies, 1991—, Jour. Entrepreneurship, 1997—; contbr. articles to profl. jours. Bd. dirs. Outreach Found., 1973-79, v.p., 1975-77; trustee Graceland Coll., Lamoni, Iowa, 1976-82; mem. mgmt. com. Park Coll., Kansas City, 1976-79. Dist. Eagle Scout Awd., Boy Scouts Amer., 1998. Mem. Am. Assn. Higher Edn., Am. Coun. on Edn., Am. Assn. State Colls. and Univs, Internat. Coun. Small Bus., Am. Mktg. Assn., Am. Mgmt. Assn., Acad. Internat. Bus., Am. Econs. Assn., Am. Arbitration Assn., (mem. nat. panel arbitrators and mediators 1993—), Nat. Assn. Intercollegiate Athletics (mem. governing bd. 1994-95), So. Bus. Adminstrn. Assn., So. Mktg. Assn., So. Econs. Assn., So. Assn. Colls. and Schs. (chair reaccreditation com. 1982-95, chair faculty qualifications criteria com. 1989-90, com. to rev. criteria for accreditation 1990-92, commr. 1992-95, Nat. Assn. State Univs. and Land-Grant Colls. (chair regional accreditation rev. com. 1989-90), Sales and Mktg. Execs. Internat., Beta Gamma Sigma, Phi Kappa Phi, Omicorn Delta Kappa, Phi Delta Kappa, Kappa Delta Phi, Mu Kappa Tau, Pi Sigma Epsilon, Alpha Kappa Psi, Chi Alpha Phi, Alpha Phi Omega, Phi Eta Sigma, Delta Mu Delta, Alpha Mu Gamma. Home: 515 E Ford St Pittsburg KS 66762-6311 Office: Office of the President Pittsburg State Univ 1701 S Broadway St Pittsburg KS 66762-5856

DARLING, JUANITA MARIE, correspondent; b. Columbus, Ohio, Apr. 7, 1954; d. Robert Lewis and Joanne Mae (Oiler) D. BA in L.Am. Studies, BA in Comms., Calif. State U., Fullerton, 1976; MA in Internat. Journalism, U. So. Calif., L.A., 1989; bur. chief, L.A. Times, Ctrl. America. Reporter Daily News Tribune, Fullerton; bus. editor The News, Mexico City; reporter Orange County Register, Santa Ana, Calif.; corr. L.A. Times, Mexico City, El Salvador; Cen. Am. bur. chief L.A. Times. Office: LA Times Times Mirror Sq Los Angeles CA 90053*

DARLING, LAWRENCE DEAN, engineering computing executive; b. Springfield, Ill., Dec. 20, 1936; s. John Darling and Virginia (Siltman) Vice; divorced; 1 child, Tena Louise. BSME, Northwestern U., 1960. Registered profl. engr., Ill. With Allis-Chalmers, Springfield, 1956-74; product engr. Fiat-Allis, Springfield, 1974-83; engring. computing mgr. Siebe Appliance Controls, Carol Stream, Ill., 1984-89, mgr. engring. computing., 1989-98; ret., 1998. Named Outstanding Dir., Springfield Jaycees, 1964; recipient Student Achievement award Wall St. Jour., 1960. Mem. ASME. Baptist. Avocations: bowling, reading, motorcycle and auto racing. Home: 545 Gundersen Dr Apt 102 Carol Stream IL 60188-2625

DARLING, PAMELA ANN WOOD, religious consultant, educator; b. Lake Forest, Ill., Aug. 31, 1943; d. Charles Edwards Jr. and Ann (Rayner) Wood. BA, Northwestern U., 1965; MS, Columbia U., 1971; MA, Gen. Theol. Sem., 1987, ThD, 1991. Cons. Episcopal Ch. Women's Program, 1985-96; adminstr. Episcopal Women's History Project, N.Y.C., 1985-91; fellow Gen. Theol. Sem., N.Y.C., 1987-91; spl. asst. to pres. House of Deps. Episcopal Ch. U.S.A., 1992—; adj. prof. ch. history Gen. Theol. Sem., 1991-93; mem. steering com. Nat. Network of Lay Profls., Episcopal Ch., 1987-90, mem. Gen. Bd. Examining Chaplains, 1991-97; bd. dirs. Episcopal Ch. Pub. Co., 1991-95; libr., cons. Preservation of Libr. Materials, 1971-90. Author: Preservation Planning Program, 1982, New Wine: The Story of Women Transforming Leadership and Power in the Episcopal Church, 1994, Stop Violence Against Women, 1994, Equally Applicable, 1994. Bd. dirs. Kirkridge, 1998—; adv. bd. Archives of Women in Theol. Scholarship Union Theol. Sem., 1998—. Recipient Esther J. Piercy award ALA, 1979. Mem. Episcopal Women's History Project (asst. treas. 1987-91), Episcopal Women's Caucus, Episcopal Communicators. Democrat. Home and Office: 501 Somerton Ave Philadelphia PA 19116-2026

DARLING, ROBERT EDWARD, designer, stage director; b. Oakland, Calif., Oct. 1, 1937; s. Irving Jackson and Helen Ellen (Hebel) D.; m. Ann Farris, Aug. 22, 1970. B.A., San Francisco State U., 1959; M.F.A., Yale U. Sch. Drama, 1963; student, Bayreuth Festspiel Meisterclasse, 1965. Creative problem solving, idea design/graphic facilatation and transition mgr. MG Taylor Corp., 1984—; with Darling Assoc. Garden Design, 1991—; former mem. opera-musical theatre policy panel Nat. Endowment for Arts; panelist Nat. Opera Inst., Nat. Inst. for Music Theater, OPERA Am., 1997—. Designer, dir. numerous opera, theatre and ballet prodns. throughout U.S. and Can., 1960—; N.Y.C. debut with Another Evening with Harry Stoones, 1962; San Francisco Opera debut with L'Elisir d'Amore, 1967; Santa Fe Opera debut with Anna Bolena, 1970, Chgo. Lyric Opera debut with Don Carlo, 1972; N.Y.C. Opera debut with Der Fliegende Hollander, 1976, Seattle Opera Tannhaüser, 1984; dir. and designer world premiers of Medea, 1972, Colonel Johnathan the Saint, 1972, The Infanta, 1975, The Last of the Mohicans, 1976, The Face, 1978, Soyazhe, 1979, Freddy the Leaf, 1987, 90-91 Williamstown Theatre Festival: Marat/Sade, 1990, Speed The Plow, 1991, Miami City Ballet, Pan Nuit Suite, Jewels, 1993, Recollections RLS, Wind in the Willows (musical premiere), debut Utah Festival Opera (Pagliacci, Gianni Schicchi), 1998; dramaturg-Coyote Tales, Kansas City Lyric Opera, 1998; artistic coord. Spring Opera Theatre, San Francisco, 1972, artistic adv. Kans. City (Mo.) Lyric Theatre, 1973; co-founder, prin. dir. Hidden Valley Opera Ensemble, Carmel, Calif., 1974-77; artistic dir. Central City Opera House Assn., Denver, 1977-82, Hidden Valley Opera, 1985-89; artistic prodr. Acorn Theatre, Washington, 1988—; site coord., founding mem. Alliance for New Music-Theater, 1994—; designs represented in collection Am. design Smithsomian Mus., Mus. of the City of N.Y., Prague Quadrennial Scenographic Design, 1987; contbr. articles to profl. jours. Mem. United Scenic Artists, Am. Guild Mus. Artists, Actors Equity-Can., OPERA Am., Logan Circle Assn., Washington Daffodil Soc. (past pres.). Democrat. Lutheran.

DARLING, SANDRA KAY, educational consultant, school administrator; b. St. Cloud, Minn., Sept. 22, 1946; d. Richard E. and Veronica K. (Lais) Mensa; m. Douglas John Darling, Nov. 19, 1970 (div. Feb. 1986); children: Scott Alan and David Douglas. BS, U. Minn., 1971, MEd, 1976; MEd, U. Minn., 1981, PhD, 1990. Tchr. Rockford (Minn.) Pub. Sch., Bloomington (Minn.) Pub. Sch.; dir. spl. edn., curriculum dir. Cook County Pub. Sch., Grand Marais, Minn., Lakevill (Minn.) Pub. Sch.; prin. Dist. 742 Schs., St. Cloud; sr. edn. cons. Nat. Computer Sys., Mesa, Ariz.; cons., pres. Human Dynamics, St. Cloud, 1984-97; assoc. prof. St. Cloud State U., 1988-94, Winona (Minn.) State U., 1992-94, St. Mary's U., 1994-97. Co-author: (book) Leadership for Special Education Administration, 1995; contbr. articles to profl. jours. Mem. state team Minn. Edn. Decision-Making Model Team, St. Cloud, 1993; mem. St. Cloud C. of C., 1994-96; examiner Minn. Quality Coun., Mpls., 1995, 96; bd dirs. ctrl. divsn. Minn. Telecom. Access Coun., St. Cloud, 1995-97; mem. state bd. Gov.'s Adv. Bd., Mpls., 1997. Recipient Instnl. Transformation Through Tech. award Minn. Dept. Children, Families and Learning, 1992-94, Acess to Application award Sci/Math Minn., 1995; Sch. Improvement Performance grantee Minn. Acad. Excellence Found., 1995-97. Mem. Assn. Supervision and Curriculum Devel. Avocations: boating, golf, gardening. Home: 743 W Nolan Way Chandler AZ 85248-6070 Office: Nat Computer Sys 827 W Grove Ave Mesa AZ 85210-4931

DARLING, SCOTT EDWARD, lawyer; b. Los Angeles, Dec. 31, 1949; s. Dick R. and Marjorie Helen (Otto) D.; m. Cynthia Diane Harrah, June 1970 (div.); 1 child, Smokie; m. Deborah Lee Cochran, Aug. 22, 1981; children: Ryan, Jacob. BA, U. Redlands, 1972; JD, U.S.C., 1975. Bar: Calif. 1976, U.S. Dist. Ct. (cen. dist.) Calif. 1976. Assoc. atty. Elver, Falsetti, Boone & Crafts, Riverside, 1976-78; ptnr. Falsetti, Crafts, Pritchard & Darling, Riverside, 1978-84; pres. Scott Edward Darling, A Profl. Corp., Riverside, 1984—; grant reviewer HHS, Washington, 1982-88; judge pro tem Riverside County Mcpl. Ct., 1980, Riverside County Superior Ct., 1987-88; bd. dirs. Tel Law Nat. Legal Pub. Info. System, Riverside, 1978-80. Author, editor: Small Law Office Computer Legal System, 1984. Bd. dirs. Youth Adv. Com. to Selective Svc., 1968-70, Am. Heart Assn. Riverside County, 1978-82, Survival Ministries, 1986-89; atty. panel Calif. Assn. Realtors, L.A., 1980—; pres. Calif. Young Reps., 1978-80; mem. GI Forum, Riverside, 1970-88; presdl. del. Nat. Rep. Party, 1980-84; asst. treas. Calif. Rep. Party, 1981-83; Rep. Congl. candidate, Riverside, 1982; treas. Riverside Sickle Cell Found., 1980-82, recipient Eddie D. Smith award; pres. Calif. Rep. Youth Caucus, 1980-82; v.p. Riverside County Red Cross, 1982-84; mem. Citizen's Univ. Com., Riverside, 1978-84, World Affairs Council, 1978-82, Urban League, Riverside, 1980-82. Calif. Scholarship Fedn. (life). Named one of Outstanding Young Men in Am., U.S. Jaycees, 1979-86. Mem. ABA, Riverside County Bar Assn., Speaker's Bur. Riverside County Bar Assn., Riverside Jaycees, Riverside C. of C. Lodge: Native Sons of Golden West. Avocations: skiing, swimming, reading. Office: 3697 Arlington Ave Riverside CA 92506-3938

DARLING, SHANNON FERGUSON, special education educator; b. Spokane, Wash., Feb. 25, 1968; d. Carl Frederick Jr. and Roberta Ernestine

(Phelps) Ferguson. BA in Elem. and Spl. Edn., La. State U., Shreveport, 1991. Cert. tchr., spl. edn. tchr., La., respite caregiver for handicapped foster children. Tchr. autistic spl. edn. Meadowview Elem. Sch., Bossier City, La., 1991—; spl. edn. com. to develop spl. edn. alternative program curriculum Bossier Parish, 1994-95, spl. edn. adv. coun., 1994-97, sec., 1994-97, coun. exceptional children, 1988-95. Vol. Com. for Spl. Arts Festival and Sports Day, 1993-94; vol. tutor Bossier Parish, 1992—; asst. dir. Camp Rainman: Autistic Camp, 1994—; vol. Alternat. Family Care Foster Svcs., 1985—, Caddo-Bossier Assn. Retarded Citizens, 1980-85; active Meadowview PTA, 1991—. Recipient Spl. Edn. Tchr. of Yr., Bossier Parish, 1994, PTA Educator of Distinction award, 1998; grantee Optimist Club, summer 1992, 93, 95, Isle of Capri Casino, summer 1994, 96, Nightmares: Charity Fundraising Com., fall 1995, Horseshoe Casino, summer 1996, Quota Club, winter 1996, PTA Educator of Distinction award, 1998, Bossier Dist. PTA, 1998, State PTA, 1998. Mem. Autism Soc. Am. (rep. to bd. dirs. mtgs. 1994—, mem. La. State Autism chpt. 1994—, sec. 1997—, mem. N.W. La. Autism chpt. 1994—, sec. 1994-96, pres. 1996—). Methodist. Home: 2704 Shed Rd Apt 186N Bossier City LA 71111-3311 Office: Meadowview Elem Sch 4315 Shed Rd Bossier City LA 71111-5299

DARLING, STEPHEN EDWARD, lawyer; b. Columbia, S.C., Apr. 12, 1949; s. Norman Rushton and Elizabeth (Clarkson) D.; m. Denise Howell, June 30, 1979; children: Julia Hanley, Edward McCrady, Elizabeth Rushton. BS in Banking, Fin., Real Estate, Ins., U. S.C., 1971, JD, 1974. Bar: S.C. 1974, U.S. Dist. Ct. S.C. 1975, U.S. Ct. Appeals (4th cir.) 1975, U.S. Ct. Appeals (5th cir.) 1976, U.S. Supreme Ct. 1982. From assoc. to ptnr. Sinkler, Gibbs & Simons, Charleston, S.C., 1974-87; ptnr. Sinkler & Boyd, Charleston, 1987—. Mem. ABA, S.C. Bar Assn., S.C. Def. Trial Attys. Assn. (exec. com. 1994—), Charleston County Bar Assn. (exec. com. 1989-90, 92-93), Internat. Assn. Def. Counsel, Southeastern Admiralty Law Inst., Met. Exch. Club (Charleston) (sec. 1980). Episcopalian. Home: 23 New St Charleston SC 29401-2546 Office: Sinkler & Boyd 160 E Bay St Charleston SC 29401-2120

DARLING, THOMAS, JR., retired rural electrification specialist; b. Wilkes-Barre, Pa., July 26, 1903; s. Thomas and Emma Childs (McClintock) D.; m. Dorothy Tuckerman Keyser, Oct. 27, 1962 (dec.). BA, Yale U., 1925; E.E., Internat. Corr. Sch., 1927. Rate engr. Pa. Power and Light, Allentown, Pa. and others, 1925-29, rural electrification engr., 1929-31; self-employed writer, lectr. world travels, 1931-33; rural electrical rep. Pa. Power & Light, 1933-41; valuation engr. Edison Light & Power Co., York, Pa., 1941-42; rate engr., power procurement engr., power planning engr. Rural Electrification Adminstrn., Dept. Agriculture, Washington, 1945-73; ret., 1973. Contbr. articles botanical jours.; serialized 18 installments travel story, 1939. Pres. Four Square Club, Allentown, 1940-41, Agriculture Amateur Movie Makers, Washington, 1960; mem. Bethlehem Bach Choir, Wilkes-Barre Concordia; violinist Allentown and Easton Symphony Orchs. With U.S. Army, 1942-45. Thomas Darling Nature Preserve, large tract glacial wetlands, source of Lehigh River and largest native spruce forest in State of Pa. named in his honor, Nature Conservancy, 1993. Mem. Yale Club (Washington), Am. Legion. Avocations: music, travel, photography, natural history. Home: 5008 Larno Dr Alexandria VA 22310-1238*

DARLINGTON, DAVID WILLIAM, management consultant; b. Boston, Oct. 3, 1945; s. Horace and Maude Beatrice (Pfalzgraf) D.; m. Stacey A. Mitchell, May 24, 1986; children: Elizabeth Joy, Christine Rebecca. BS, Babson Coll., 1974, MBA, 1976; postgrad. Northeastern U., 1977-80. Planning engr. Stone & Webster Engring. Corp., Boston, 1974-75; project adminstr. Northrop Corp., Norwood, Mass., 1975-80; mgr. program adminstrn. internat. systems div. Sanders Assos., Inc., Nashua, N.H., 1980-82; mgr. govt. bus. svcs.; cons., program mgr., contr. Arthur D. Little, Cambridge, Mass., 1982—. Served with USN, 1964-71. Mem. Am. Prodn. and Inventory Control Soc. (cert.), Inst. Cost Analysis (cert.), Performance Mgmt. Assoc., Nat. Contract Mgmt. Assn. (cert.), Inst. Mgmt. Accts., Appalachian Mountain Club, Beta Gamma. Home: 378 Charles Bancroft Hwy Litchfield NH 03052-8033

DARLINGTON, JUDITH MABEL, clinical social worker, Christian counselor; b. Deckerville, Mich., Nov. 29, 1942; d. Wallace and Mabel Lillian (Rich) Cole; m. Clare Robert Darlington, Dec. 15, 1962; children: Debra Lynn, Dawn Elizabeth. BA, Mich. State U., 1962; MSW, U. Mich., 1983. Tchr. Limestone (Maine) Presque Isle Schs., 1963-64; substitute tchr. Crestwood Sch. Dist., Dearborn Heights, Mich., 1971-74; monitor, tchr. Renewing Life Ministries, Annandale, Va., 1976-82; clin. social worker Westland (Mich.) Counseling Svc., 1983-84; family therapist, counselor Family Svc. of Detroit and Wayne County, Wyandotte, Mich., 1984-86; specialist substance abuse Plymouth (Mich.) Family Svc., 1986-87; exec. dir. Christian Conciliation Svc. of S.E. Mich., Detroit, 1987-90; pvt. practice clin. social worker/family therapist Brighton, Mich., 1990-97; founder, exec. dir. Christian Ctrs. for the Family, Inc., Brighton, 1997—; speaker in field. Mem. NASW (cert.), Am. Assn. Christian Counselors (charter), Christian Women's Club (chmn. Livonia chpt. 1981—), Inst. for Christian Conciliation, Kappa Delta Pi. Evangelical Presbyterian. Avocations: bicycling, skiing, reading. Home: 7911 Debora Dr Brighton MI 48114-9462 Office: 7015 Fieldcrest Dr Ste 150 Brighton MI 48116-8547

DARLINGTON, RICHARD BENJAMIN, psychology educator; b. Woodbury, N.J., Nov. 16, 1937; s. Charles Joseph and Eleanor (Collins) D.; m. Elizabeth Day, June 13, 1959; children: Jean Susan, Lois Heather. BA, Swarthmore Coll., 1959; PhD, U. Minn., 1963. Asst. prof. psychology Cornell U., Ithaca, N.Y., 1963-68, assoc. prof., 1968-80, prof., 1980—. Author: Radicals and Squares, 1975, (with others) Lasting Effects of Early Education, 1982, (with Patricia M. Carlson) Behavioral Statistics: Logic and Methods, 1987, Regression and Linear Models, 1990; contbr. articles to profl. jours.; contbr. chpts. to books. Project dir. Am. Friends Service Com., 1960, 61. Fellow NSF, 1959-60; fellow Woodrow Wilson Found., 1959-60; grantee HEW, 1977-81, Office of Edn., 1966-67, 70-71, Dept. of Labor, 1980-81. Fellow AAAS; mem. Phi Beta Kappa. Quaker. Home: 204 Fairmount Ave Ithaca NY 14850-4804 Office: Cornell Univ Dept Psychology Uris H Ithaca NY 14853

DARLINGTON, RONALD LAWRENCE, English language educator; b. Lethbridge, Alta., Can., Apr. 30, 1936; came to U.S. 1967; s. Joseph Lawrence and Lois Mary (Ashcroft) D.; m. Joanne Patricia Green, Sept. 26, 1959; children: Kimberley, Ronald II. BSc, Mont. State U., 1963, postgrad., 1966—. Tchr. Lethbridge Sch. Dist., 1963-64, Cranbrook (B.C.) Sch. Dist., 1965-66; tchr. English/writing Del Norte Unified Sch. Dist., Crescent City, Calif., 1967-95; co-developer field study course of history of Modoc War and geology of Lava Beds area; work with Hmong on learning basic English skills, 1997—. Author: 7th and 8th grade lang. program in speech, composition, mechanics, semantics, reference and grammar; co-author: Modoc - We Walk Through Time, 1990-91. Mem. NEA, Calif. Tchrs. Assn. Avocations: radio control boatracing. Home: 2934 Weston Way Rancho Cordova CA 95670

DARLOW, ANDREW J., photographer; b. Apr. 14, 1970. BS in Fin., Coll. of N.J., 1992. Dir. digital photography Regent Group, N.Y.C., 1993—; pres. Andy Darlow Artworks Ltd., N.J., 1997—. E-mail: andy@andydarlow.com.

DARLOW, GEORGE ANTHONY GRATTON, investor; b. Rochester, N.Y., June 16, 1938; s. Alfred Miltenberger and Lillian (Gratton) D.; divorced, Mar. 2, 1971; 1 child, Gillian. BA, Yale U., 1961; JD, Columbia U., 1971; LLD, Yale U., 1979, Columbia U., 1979, U. Rochester, 1979, Sweet Briar Coll., 1979. Trustee Am. Indian Archeol. Inst., Washington, Conn., 1973-93; chmn., trustee Inst. Am. Indian Studies, Washington, Conn., 1993—. With USN, 1961-64. Mem. Colony Found. (trustee 1995—), Ancient Free Accepted Masons (32nd Degree), Rotary Internat., Berzelius Soc., Beta Theta Pi, Lions Club. Republican. Episcopalian. Home: 35 Wykeham Rd Washington CT 06793 Office: PO Box 1102 Washington CT 06793

DARLOW, JULIA DONOVAN, lawyer; b. Detroit, Sept. 18, 1941; d. Frank William Donovan and Helen Adele Turner; m. George Anthony Gratton Darlow (div.); 1 child, Gillian; m. John Corbett O'Meara. AB, Vassar Coll., 1963; postgrad., Columbia U. Law Sch., 1964-65; J.D. cum laude, Wayne State U., 1971. Bar: Mich. 1971, U.S. Dist. Ct. (ea. dist.) Mich. 1971. Assoc. Dickinson, Wright, McKean, Cudlip & Moon, Detroit, 1971-78; ptnr. Dickinson, Wright, Moon, Van Dusen & Freeman, Detroit, 1978—; adj. prof. Wayne State U. Law Sch., 1974-75, 96; commr. State Bar Mich., 1977-87, mem. exec. com., 1979-83, 84-87, sec. 1980-81, v.p., 1984-85, pres.-elect 1985-86, pres. 1986-87, coun. corp. fin. and bus. law sect. 1980-86, coun. computer law sect. 1985-88; mem. State Officers Compensation Commn., 1994-96; chair Mich. Supreme Ct. Task Force on Gender Issues in the Cts., 1987-89. Reporter: Mich. Nonprofit Corp. Act, 1977-82. Bd. dirs. Hutzel Hosp., 1984—, Mich. Opera Theater, 1985—, Mich. Women's Found., 1986-91, Detroit Med. Ctr., 1990—, Marygrove Coll., 1996—; trustee Internat. Inst. Met. Detroit, 1986-92, Mich. Met. coun. Girl Scouts U.S., 1988-91, Detroit coun. Boy Scouts Am., 1988—; mem. exec. com. Mich. Coun. for Humanities 1988-92; mem. Blue Cross-Blue Shield Prospective Reimbursement Com., Detroit, 1979-81; v.p., mem. exec. com. United Found., 1988-95; mem. Mich. Gov.'s Bilateral Trade Team for Germany, 1992-98. Fellow Am. Bar Found. (Mich. State chairperson 1990-96; mem. state officers compensation commn., 1994-96); mem. Detroit Bar Assn. Found. (treas. 1984-85, trustee 1982-85), Mich. Bar Found. (trustee 1987-94), Am. Judicature Soc. (bd. dirs. 1985-88), Internat. Women's Forum (global affairs com. 1994—), Women Lawyers Assn. (pres. 1977-78), Mich. Women's Campaign Fund (charter), Detroit Athletic Club. Democrat. Office: Dickinson Wright Moon Van Dusen & Freeman 500 Woodward Ave Ste 4000 Detroit MI 48226-3416

DARMAN, RICHARD G., investor, educator, former government official, former investment banker; b. Charlotte, N.C., May 10, 1943; m. Kathleen Emmet, Sept. 1, 1967; children: William Temple Emmet, Jonathan Warren Emmet, Christopher Temple Emmet. BA cum laude, Harvard U., 1964, MBA, 1967, DSc (hon.). Dep. asst. sec. HEW, Washington, 1971-72; asst. to sec. Dept. Def., Washington, 1973; spl. asst. to atty. gen. Washington, 1973; fellow Woodrow Wilson Internat. Center for Scholars, Washington, 1974; prin., dir. ICF, Inc., Washington, 1975, 77-80; asst. sec. Dept. Commerce, 1976-77; lectr. public policy and mgmt. Harvard U., 1977-80; asst. to Pres. Reagan, The White House, Washington, 1981-85; dep. sec. Dept. Treasury, 1985-87; mng. dir. Shearson Lehman Hutton Inc., N.Y.C., 1987-88; dir. office mgmt. and budget, mem. Pres. Cabinet The White House, Washington, 1989-93; ptnr. The Carlyle Group, 1993—; prof. JFK Sch. Govt. Harvard U., 1998—. Editor: Harvard Ednl. Rev, 1970; contbg. editor U.S. News & World Report, 1987-88; author: Who's in Control?, 1996; contbr. articles to profl. jours. Trustee Bennington (Vt.) Coll., 1974-75, The Brookings Inst., 1987-88, Coun. for Excellence in Govt., 1995—, The New Eng. Funds, 1996—; mem. overseers com. to visit Kennedy Sch. Govt. Harvard U., 1988-98, Harvard Med. Sch., 1994-98. Office: The Carlyle Group 1001 Pennsylvania Ave NW Washington DC 20004-2505

D'ARMS, JOHN HAUGHTON, association executive, classics educator; b. Poughkeepsie, N.Y., Nov. 27, 1934; s. Edward Francis and H. Cristina (Coney) D'A.; m. Maria Teresa Waugh, June 3, 1961; children—Edward Justin, Helena Harriet. A.B., Princeton U., 1956; B.A., Oxford U., Eng., 1959; Ph.D., Harvard U., 1965; Doctorate (hon.), U. Montreal, 1998, Albright Coll., 1999. Asst. prof. Greek and Latin, U. Mich., Ann Arbor, 1965-67, assoc. prof., 1968-71, prof., chmn. dept. classical studies, 1972-75, 76-77, 80-85, prof. history, 1986-97, dean Rackham Sch. Grad. Studies, 1985-95, vice provost for acad. affairs, 1990-95; asst. prof. Intercoll. Center for Classics, Rome, 1967-68, prof. classics in residence Am. Acad. in Rome, 1971-72, prof. charge summer sch., 1971-73, dir., A.W. Mellon prof. classics, 1977-80, G.F. Else prof. classical studies, 1983-97; pres. Am. Coun. Learned Socs., N.Y.C., 1997—; mem. Sch. Hist. Studies, Inst. for Advanced Study, Princeton, N.J., 1975-76, Grad. Record Exams Bd., 1992—; bd. dirs. Rsch. Librs. Group, Inc., 1992-94; adj. prof. classics and history Columbia U., N.Y.C., 1997—. Author: Romans on the Bay of Naples, 1970; Commerce and Social Standing in Ancient Rome, 1981. Contbr. articles to profl. jours. Mem. Commn. of Ednl. and Cultural Exch. between Italy and U.S. (Fulbright Commn.), 1978-80; trustee Am. Acad. in Rome, 1973-76, 81-93 (Centennial medal 1995), Nat. Humanities Ctr., 1987—, MLA, 1998—; bd. dirs. Am. Coun. Learned Socs., 1973-77, 85-93; chmn. mng. com. Intercollegiate Ctr. for Classics in Rome, 1972-75; regional chmn. Mellon Nat. Grad. Fellowship Program in Humanities, 1982-83, 94-89, mem. nat. com., 1990—; term trustee Princeton U., 1970-74; chmn. overseer's com. to visit dept. classics Harvard U., 1992—; mem. com. Study rsch. doctorate programs in U.S., Nat. Rsch. Coun., Harvard U., 1992-95; apptd. Nat. Coun. Humanities, 1994-97; mem. adv. com. on spl. projects Ctr. for Advanced Study in Behavioral Scis., 1998—. Am. Council Learned Socs. fellow, 1971-72; John S. Guggenheim Found. fellow, 1975-76. Fellow Am. Acad. Arts and Scis.; mem. Am. Philol. Assn. (dir. 1977-80, com. Profl. Matters 1992-93), Archaeol. Inst. Am., Am. Hist. Assn., German Archaeol. Inst. (corr.), Soc. for Promotion Roman Studies (Britain), Am. Assn. Univs. (com. on grad. edn. 1988-90), Assn. Grad. Schs. (nat. com. 1989-91, pres. 1990), Am. Philos. Soc., Phi Beta Kappa. Club: Century Assn. (N.Y.C.). Home: 14 Sutton Pl S New York NY 10022-3071 Office: Am Coun Learned Socs 228 E 45th St New York NY 10017-3303

DARMSTANDLER, HARRY MAX, real estate executive, retired air force officer; b. Indpls., Aug. 9, 1922; s. Max M. and Nonna (Holden) D.; m. Donna L. Bender, Mar. 10, 1957; children: Paul William, Thomas Alan. B.S., U. Omaha, 1964; M.S., George Washington U., 1965; grad., Nat. War Coll., 1965. Commd. 2d lt. USAAF, 1943; advanced through grades to maj. gen. USAF, 1973; served with (15th Air Force), Europe, 1943, (5th Air Force), Korea, 1952; comdr.-in-chief Pacific, 1960-63, served with joint chiefs of staff, 1965-68; supreme comdr. (Allied Powers Europe), 1969-71; comdr. 12th Air Div. SAC, 1972, dep. chief of staff for plans, 1973; spl. asst. to chief of staff USAF, 1974-75; chmn. bd. and chief exec. officer Rancho Bernardo Savs. Bank, San Diego, 1983-90; ptnr. Allied Assocs., Colorado Springs, Colo., 1968—, D & H Inc., Woodland Park, Colo., 1979—; founding ptnr. Assocs. Group, San Diego, 1995—; cons. Mid East matters and bd. dirs. Palomar Pomerado Health Found. San Diego; bd. dirs. Clean Found., San Diego. Author numerous articles on nat. def. requirements. Elder, Rancho Bernardo Community Presbyn. Ch., San Diego. Decorated D.S.M. with oak leaf cluster, Legion of Merit with oak leaf cluster, D.F.C., Air medal with 3 oak leaf clusters; research fellow UCLA, 1969. Mem. AIAA, Order Daedalians, Soc. Strategic Air Command, Eagle Scout Alumni Assn., Bernardo Heights Country Club (San Diego, past pres.), Phi Tau Alpha. Home: 12193 Caminito Corriente San Diego CA 92128-4571

DARNALL, ROBERT J., steel company executive; married; 2 children. BA in Math., DePauw U., 1960; BSCE, Columbia U., 1962; MBA, U. Chgo., 1973. With Inland Steel Co., Chgo., 1962—; gen. mill foreman Inland Steel Co., East Chicago, Ind., 1967-68, asst. supt., 1969-1970, supt., 1971-75, asst. to v.p. steel mfg., 1975-77, asst. gen. mgr. flat product mills, 1977-79, gen. mgr., 1979, v.p. engring and corp. planning, 1981; exec. v.p. Inland Steel Co., Chgo., 1982, pres., 1984-86, chief oper. officer integrated steel segment, 1984-86; pres., chief oper. officer Inland Steel Industries, Inc., Chgo., 1986-94, chmn., pres., chief exec. officer, 1994-98, also bd. dirs.; chmn., pres., chief exec. officer Ispat N.Am. Inc., Chgo., 1998—; bd. dirs. Household Internat. Inc., Cummins Engring. Co. Inc. Bd. trustees U. Chgo., DePauw U.; dir. Argonne Nat. Lab.; chmn. bd. dirs. Jr. Achievement Chgo.; chmn. exec. com. Glenwood Sch. Boys; regional chmn. United Way/Crusade of Mercy. Mem. Internat. Iron and Steel Inst. (dir.), Am. Iron and Steel Inst. (dir.), Assn. Iron and Steel Engrs., Ill. Mfrs. Assn. (bd. dirs.). Office: 30 W Monroe St Chicago IL 60603-2493*

DARNALL, ROBERTA MORROW, association executive; b. Kemmerer, Wyo., May 18, 1949; d. C. Dale and Eugenia Stayner (Christmas) Morrow; m. Leslie A. Darnall, Sept. 3, 1977; children: Kimberly Gene, Leslie Nicole. BS, U. Wyo., Laramie, 1972. Tariff sec., ins. adminstr. Wyo Trucking Assn., Casper, 1973-75; asst. clerical supr. Wyo. Legislature, Cheyenne, 1972-77, congrl. campaign press aide, 1974; pub. rels. dir. Casper, Wyo., Wyo. Rep. Ctr. Com., 1976-77; asst. dir. alumni rels. U. Wyo., 1977-81; exec. dir. Alumni Assn., 1981—. Bd. dir. Ivison Meml. Hosp. Found. Mem. St. Matthews Altar Guild, Lector, and Acolyte (coord.), Higher Edn. Assn. Rockies, Am. Soc. Assn. Execs., Laramie C. of C. (past edn. com.), U. Wyo. Alumni Assn., Cowboy Joe Club, PEO (former courtesy com., officer), Zonta Internat. Republican. Episcopalian. Home: 15 Snowy View Ct Laramie WY 82070-5358 Office: PO Box 3137 Laramie WY 82071-3137

DARNELL, DORIS HASTINGS, storyteller, antique costume collector; b. Chgo., Sept. 14, 1916; d. Willard Seth and Faith Emily (Olmstead) Hastings; m. Howard Clayton Darnell, Aug. 27, 1938; children: Elizabeth Loyd, John Hastings, Eric Allen. BA in Latin, Bryn Mawr Coll., 1939. Head resident, asst. to dir. Pendle Hill Grad. Sch. Religious and Social Concerns, Wallingford, Pa., 1939-40; libr. Res. Room and sci. Bryn Mawr (Pa.) Coll., 1950-52; acting head of library Westtown (Pa.) Friends Sch., 1952-53; head of library Westtown (Pa.) Sch., 1954-55; libr. Res. Room Haverford (Pa.) Coll., 1953-54; exec. dir., editor Westtown Alumni Assn., 1955-64; coord. of recruitment, then assoc. exec. sec. for personnel Am. Friends Svc. Com., Phila., 1964-78; creator, owner A Century of Elegance in Costume and Story, State College, Pa., 1980—; former mem., gov. com. Pendle Hill, Westtown Sch., Friends Select Sch. (Pa.), 1948-78; mem. Rufus Jones Assocs., Haverford Coll.; founding trustee Allen Hilles Fund (Phila.), 1982-91, trustee emerita, 1991—. Mem. AAUW, Costume Soc. Am., Palmer Art Mus., Women in the Arts. Quaker. Home and Office: #C 36 500 Marylyn Ave State College PA 16801

DARNELL, JAMES EDWIN, JR., molecular biologist, educator; b. Columbus, Miss., Sept. 9, 1930; s. James Edwin and Helen (Hopkins) D.; m. Jane Roller, 1957; children: Christopher, Robert, Jonathan. BS, U. Miss., 1951; MD, Washington U., 1955, DSc, 1996. Intern Barnes Hosp., 1955-56; asst. to sr. surgeon USPHS, Bethesda, Md., 1957-60; asst. and assoc. prof. MIT, Cambridge, 1961-64; prof. Albert Einstein Coll. Medicine, N.Y.C., 1967; prof. Columbia U., 1968-74, chmn. dept. biol. scis., 1971-74; Vincent Astor prof. Rockefeller U., N.Y.C., 1974—, v.p. acad. affairs, 1990-91. Co-author: (textbooks) General Virology, 1967, 77, Molecular Cell Biology, 1986, rev. edits., 1990, 95. Recipient H.T. Rickets award U. Chgo., 1979, Internat. award Gairdner Found., Toronto, Ont., Can., 1986, Paul Janssen prize in Advanced Biotech. and Medicine, 1994, Bertner award in cancer rsch., 1996, Passano award, 1997, Milstein award, 1997, City of Medicine, 1998, E.B. Wilson award, 1998, Aurbach Lecture award, 1999, Lynen medal, 1999, Dickson Prize in Medicine, 1999, William B. Coley award, 1999, Gerald D. Aurbach lecture award, 1999. Mem. NAS, Am. Acad. Arts and Scis. (award 1973), Royal Soc. (fgn.), Japanese Biochem. Soc. (hon.). Office: Rockefeller U Molecular Cell Biology 1230 York Ave New York NY 10021-6399

DARNELL, RILEY CARLISLE, state government executive, lawyer; b. Clarksville, Tenn., May 13, 1940; s. Elliott Sinclair and Mary Anita (Whitefield) D., married, 5 children; BS, Austin Peay State U., 1962; JD, Vanderbilt U., 1965; m. Mary Penelope Crockarell, June 2, 1963; children: Neil Whitefield, Duncan Edward, Mary Eve, Penelope Joy, Dawson Riley. Bar: Tenn. 1965. Gen. practice, Clarksville, 1965-66, 69—; mem. Tenn. Ho. of Reps. from 67th Dist., 1971-80, treas. house-senate caucus, 1971-86, sec. house com. ways and means, chmn. joint house-senate fiscal rev. com., 1975-80; mem. Tenn. State Senate, 1980-92, chmn. transp. com., 1982-86, chmn. joint com. children and youth, 1987-89; senate majority leader, 1988-92; sec. of state of Tenn., Nashville, 1993—. Served to capt. JAGC, USAF, 1966-69. Democrat. Fellow Tenn. Bar Found.; mem. ABA, Montgomery County Bar Assn., Tenn. Trial Lawyers, Tenn. Bar Assn., Nat. Conf. State Legislators (jud. task force), So. Legis. Conf. (mem. fiscal affairs com.), Clarksville C. of C., Moose, Clarksville Downtown Civitan Club. Mem. Ch. of Christ. Home: 603 Waterloo Dr Clarksville TN 37043-6014 Office: State Capital Fl 1 Nashville TN 37243-0305

DARNELL, ROGER KENT, writer/producer; b. Greenville, Ill., May 5, 1966; s. James Kent and Lila Leona (Ridings) D.; m. Beth Ann Darnell, May 23, 1992. BA in Film, BA in Radio and TV, U. Ctrl. Fla., 1990, AA, 1989. Adminstrv. support specialist Analysis & Tech. Inc., Orlando, Fla., 1985-88; pres. U. Ctrl. Fla. Cinematography Assocs., Orlando, 1989-90; asst. to exec. prodr. Ivan Tors Entertainment, Orlando, 1991-92; prodr./cons. Gen. Video Inc., Altamonte Springs, Fla., 1992-93; writer World Trade Entertainment, Orlando, 1993; prin. Darnell Works, Inc., Orlando, 1988—; mktg. pub. rels. dir. Crest Nat. Hollywood Labs, 1998—; event co-prodr. Lisa Merlin House Celebrity Golf Tournament, Orlando, 1995; film festival judge Alamo Am. Film Festival for Students, L.A., 1995. Columnist, Observations, 1989-90; author poetry. With USAFR, 1985-90. Scripps Howard Found. fellow, 1990. Mem. Internat. TV Assn. (pub. chmn. 1994-95, video festival judge 1994-97). Avocations: photography, camping, rafting, snorkeling/diving, travel. Home: 211 E Esther St Orlando FL 32806-3018 Office: Darnell Works Inc 1327 Barrington Way #3 Glendale CA 91206

DARNTON, JOHN TOWNSEND, journalist; b. N.Y.C., Nov. 20, 1941; s. Byron and Eleanor Kate (Choate) D.; m. Nina Jane Lieberman, Aug. 21, 1966; children: Kyra, Liza, James. BS, U. Wis., 1966. Reporter N.Y. Times, N.Y.C., 1968-75; br. chief N.Y. Times, Lagos, Nigeria, 1975-76, Nairobi, Kenya, 1976-79, Warsaw, 1979-82, Madrid, 1982-84; met. editor N.Y. Times, N.Y.C., 1986-91, news editor, 1991-93; London corr. N.Y. Times, 1993-96, culture editor, 1996—; Ferris prof. Princeton (N.J.) U., 1991-92. Author: (novel) Neanderthal, 1996. Recipient Pulitzer prize, 1982, George Polk award L.I. U., 1979, 82. Mem. Century Club. Office: NY Times Culture News Dept 229 W 43rd St New York NY 10036-3959

DARNTON, ROBERT CHOATE, history educator; b. N.Y.C., May 10, 1939; s. Byron and Eleanor (Choate) D.; m. Susan Lee Glover, June 29, 1963; children: Nicholas Campbell, Catherine Choate, Margaret Townsend. BA, Harvard U., 1960; BPhil, Oxford U., Eng., 1962, DPhil, 1964. Reporter N.Y. Times, N.Y.C., 1964; jr. fellow Harvard U., 1964-68; asst. prof. history Princeton U., N.J., 1968-71, assoc. prof., 1971-72, prof., 1972—. Author: Mesmerism and the End of the Enlightenment in France, 1968, The Business of Enlightenment: A Publishing History of the Encyclopédie, 1775-1800, 1979 (Am. Hist. Assn. Leo Gershoy prize 1979), The Literary Underground of the Old Regime, 1982, The Great Cat Massacre and Other Episodes in French Cultural History, 1984 (L.A. Times book prize), The Kiss of Lamourette: Reflections in Cultural History, 1989, Edition et Sédition, L'univers de la littérature clandestine au XVIII e siècle, 1991 (Prix Chateaubriand), Berlin Journal, 1989-90, 1991, Gens de lettres, gens du livre, 1992, The Forbidden Best-Sellers of Pre-Revolutionary France, 1995 (Nat. Book Critics Circle award 1996), The Corpus of Clandestine Literature in France, 1995. Decorated officer Ordre des Arts et des Lettres; recipient Koren prize Soc. French Hist. Studies, 1973, MacArthur Found. prize, 1982. Fellow Am. Acad. Arts and Scis., Am. Philos. Soc.; mem. Am. Hist. Assn. (pres.-elect 1998, pres. 1999), Am. Soc. 18th-Dentury Studies (Clifford prize 1971, 73), Academia Europaea, Belgian Royal Acad. French Lang. and Lit. Office: Princeton U Dept History Princeton NJ 08540

DAROFF, ROBERT BARRY, neurologist; b. N.Y.C., Aug. 3, 1936; s. Charles and May (Wolin) D.; m. Jane L. Abrahams, Dec. 4, 1959; children: Charles II, Robert Barry, Jr., William Clayton. BA, U. Pa., 1957, MD, 1961. Intern Phila. Gen. Hosp., 1961-62; resident in neurology Yale-New Haven Med. Center, 1962-65; fellow in neuro-ophthalmology U. Calif. Med. Center, San Francisco, 1967-68; prof. neurology, assoc. prof. ophthalmology U. Miami (Fla.) Med. Sch.; also dir. ocular motor neurophysiology lab. Miami VA Med. Center, 1968-80; Gilbert W. Humphrey prof., chmn. dept. neurology Case Western Res. U. Med. Sch.; also dir. dept. neurology Univ. Hosps., Cleve., 1980-93; prof. neurology, assoc. dean Case Western U., 1994—; staff neurologist Cleve. VA Med. Ctr., 1980-93; chief of staff, sr. v.p. acad. affairs U. Hosp., Cleve., 1994—; med. adv. bd. chmn. sci. program com. Myasthenia Gravis Found., 1984-87, exec. com., 1992—, sec., 1995-96, vice chair, 1997—; med. adv. bd. Nat. Multiple Sclerosis Found., 1988-90, Soc. for Progressive Supranuclear Palsy, 1991-94; mem. nat. adv. eye coun. sensory and motor disorders vision panel NIH, 1980-83; mem. steering com. neurological disorders in comml. drivers U.S. Dept. Transp., chmn. task force, 1987; lectr. T.S. Srinivasan Endowment, Madras, India, 1994; Cumings lectr. Migraine Trust, London, 1994; lectr. Am. Coun. for Headache Edn., San Diego, 1996. Book rev. editor: Neuro-ophthalmology, 1981-86, mem. editl. bd., 1987—; assoc. editor Jour. Biomed. Systems, 1970-72; editor Neurol. Progress, Anns. of Neurology, 1981-84; editor-in-chief Neurology, 1987-96; co-editor World Neurology, 1991-98; mem. editl. bd. Annals of Neurology, 1977-86, Archives of Neurology, 1976, Nrology and Neurosurgery Update Series, 1978-93, Headache, 1980-86; mem. editl. coun. Neurologia Croatica, 1991—; mem. editl. bd. Contemporary Neurology Series, 1989-93; contbr. numerous articles to profl. jours. Chmn. Young Tae Kwon Do Acad., North Miami, 1977-80; bd. dirs. Benign Essential

Blepharospasm Rsch. Found., 1983—; trustee Fairhill Ctr. for Aging, 1988—, The Learning Corp., 1992—, Edison Bio Tech. Ctr., 1994—, Great Lakes Sci. Ctr., 1994—; mem. tech. adv. coun. BIOMEC, Inc., 1999—. Served with M.C. USAR, 1965-67. Recipient Ernst Jung-Medaille Für Medizin in Gold, 1993; Silver Jubilee Oration award Med. Coll. Trivandrum, India, 1994. Mem. AMA, Am. Neurol. Assn. (program adv. com. 1977-78, chmn. 1978, membership adv. com. 1980-83, chmn. 1981-83, nominating com. 1984, chmn. Annals of Neurology oversight com. 1984-86, councillor 1980-82, sec. 1985-89, pres.-elect 1989-90, pres. 1990-91, past pres. 1991-92, chair hon. membership com. 1994), Am. Acad. Neurology (chmn. sci. program com. 1973-75, exec. bd. 1987-96, pub. com. 1993—, Netter lectr. 1989), Rocky Mountain Neuro-ophthalmology Soc. (bd. dirs. 1980-86), N.Am. Neuro-ophthalmology Soc. (bd. dirs. 1986-94, chair cert. and accreditation com. 1997-98, publs. com. 1999—, Disting. Svc. award 1999), Barany Soc., Am. Assn. Study Headache (bd. dirs., sec., chmn. membership com. 1998—), Internat. Headache Soc., Clin. Eye Movement Soc. (founder), World Fedn. Neurology (fin. com. 1985—, chmn. 1990—, chmn. pubs. com. 1987—, exec. com. Rsch. Group on Neuro-Ophthalmology 1987-95), Coun. Biology Editors, Alliance for Brain Initiatives (founding mem.), Vietnam Vets. Inst. (bd. scholars 1998—), Assn. Columbiana de Neurologia (hon.), Acad. Med. Scis. Kazakhstan, Neuromuscular Disease Assn. Romania (internat. sci. com. 1991-93), Alpha Omega Alpha. Office: U Hosps Cleve 11100 Euclid Ave Cleveland OH 44106-1736

DAROFF, WILLIAM CLAYTON, lawyer; b. Miami Beach, Fla., Nov. 30, 1968; s. Robert Barry and Jane Linda (Abrahams) D.; m. Heidi Ilyse Krizer, Aug. 31, 1997. BA summa cum laude, Case Western Reserve U., 1995, JD, 1999, MA in Polit. Sci., 1999. Bar: Ohio 1999. Lead advanceman Kemp for Pres., Washington, 1986-88, Bush-Quayle '88, Washington, 1988; spl. asst. U.S. Dept. Energy, Washington, 1989-90; campaign mgr. Brachman for State Treas., Columbus, Ohio, 1990; spl. asst. to gov. State of Ohio, Columbus, 1990-92; dep. dir. Ohio Dept. Liquor Control, Columbus, 1992-93; pres. W. Daroff Consultants, Shaker Heights, Ohio, 1994-98; lead advanceman Dole-Kemp '96, Washington, 1996; assoc. Calfee, Halter & Griswold, LLP, Cleve., 1999—; summer assoc. Calfee, Halter & Griswold, LLP, Cleve., 1998. Sports editor East Side News, 1984-86; mem. editl. bd. Pub. Pers. Mgmt., 1991-92. Rep. nominee for Ohio State Rep., 11th Dist., 1994; mem. exec. com. Cuyahoga County Rep. Party, Cleve., 1987-88, 91—, mem. ctrl. com., 1987-88, 94—, exec. vice chmn. 1997—; alt. del. Rep. Nat. Conv., 1996; cochmn. candidate endorsement com. Cuyahoga County Rep. Party, 1997—; mem. edn. com. Young Leadership Divsn., Cleve. Jewish Cmty. Fedn., 1997—. Named to Honorable Order of Ky. Cols., 1992; recipient Meritorious Svc. award 4th Ward Rep. Club, 1989, 91, 93. Fellow Soc. for Am. Baseball Rsch.; mem. NRA (life), Cleve. Ripon Club, Columbus Athletic Club, Capital Club, Club at Key Ctr., Monday Thing Club (membership director 1989--), Case Western Res. U. Alumni Assn. (program com. 1998—). Republican. Jewish. Office: Calfee Halter & Griswold LLP 1400 McDonald Investment 800 Superior Ave Cleveland OH 44114

DA ROSA, ALISON, travel editor. Office: San Diego Union-Tribune 350 Camino De La Reina San Diego CA 92108-3003

DA ROZA, VICTORIA CECILIA, human resources administrator; b. East Orange, N.J., Aug. 30, 1945; d. Victor and Cynthia Helen (Krupa) Hawkins; m. Thomas Howard Kaminski, Aug. 28, 1971 (div. 1977); 1 child, Sarah Hawkins; m. Robert Anthony da Roza, Nov. 25, 1983. BA, U. Mich., 1967; MA, U. Mo., 1968. Contract compliance mgr. City of San Diego, 1972-75; v.p. personnel Bank of Calif., San Francisco, 1975-77; with human resources Lawrence Livermore (Calif.) Nat. Lab., 1978-86; pvt. cons. Victoria Kaminski-da Roza & Assocs., 1986—; lectr. in field; videotape workshop program on mid-career planning used by IEEE. Contbr. numerous articles to profl. jours. Mem. ASTD, Gerontol. Soc. Am., San Ramon Valley Gnealogy Soc. (pres. 1999-01), P.E.O. (officer chpt. RV 1989-01). Home and Office: 1835 Monte Sereno Dr Alamo CA 94507

DARR, ALAN PHIPPS, curator, historian; b. Kankakee, Ill., Sept. 30, 1948; s. Milton Freeman, Jr. and Margaret (Phipps) D.; m. Mollie Hayden Fletcher, June 28, 1980; children: Owen, Alexander. BA, Northwestern U., 1970; MA, Inst. Fine Arts, NYU, 1975, PhD in Art History, 1980; Cert., Mus. Tng., Met. Mus. Art, 1976, Mus. Mgmt. Inst., U. Calif. Berkeley, 1980. Grad. intern Met. Mus. Art, N.Y.C., 1976; instr. NYU, 1976; asst. curator Detroit Inst. Arts, 1978-80, assoc. curator, 1980-81, curator in charge European sculpture and decorative arts, 1981—, Walter B. Ford II Family curator European sculpture and decorative arts, 1997—; postdoctoral fellow Harvard U. Ctr. for Italian Renaissance Studies at Villa I Tatti, Florence, 1988-89; adj. prof. Wayne State U., Detroit, 1982—; Paul Mellon vis. sr. scholar Ctr. Advanced Study in Visual Arts, Nat. Gallery, Washington, 1994. Co-editor/co-author: Italian Renaissance Sculpture in the Time of Donatello, 1985-86, Donatello Studien, 1989, Verrocchio and Late Quattrocento Italian Sculpture, 1992, The Dodge Collection of Eighteenth Century French and English Art in the Detroit Institute of Arts, 1996, Woven Splendor: Five Centuries of European Tapestry in the Detroit Institute of Arts, 1996, others; contbr. articles to profl. jours. Nat. Endowment Arts Mus. Profls. Fellow, 1983; John J. McCloy fellow, 1980-81, Ford Found. fellow, 1975-78, Met. Mus. Art fellow, 1975. Office: Detroit Inst Arts 5200 Woodward Ave Detroit MI 48202-4094

DARR, CAROL C., lawyer; b. Apr. 24, 1951; d. Patt M. and Justine D.; m. Albert Louis May III Dec. 19, 1992. BA, U. Memphis, 1973, JD, 1976; M.Litt, Christ's Coll., Cambridge U., 1995. Bar: Tenn. 1977, D.C. 1981. Atty. Fed. Election Commn., 1976-77; asst. counsel U.S. Senate Com. on Rules & Adminstrn., 1977-79; dep. gen counsel Carter/Mondale Presidential Com., 1979-81; in house counsel Dem. Nat. Com., 1981-82; assoc. Skadden, Arps, Slate, Meagher & Flom, 1983-85; chief counsel Dukakis/Bentsen Com., Inc., 1987-91; gen. counsel Dem. Nat. Com., 1991-92; with Clinton/Gore Transition Com., 1992-93; actg. gen. counsel, dep. gen. counsel U.S. Dept. Commerce, 1993-94; assoc. Adminstrn. Nat. Telecom. and Info. Agy., Office Internat. Affairs, 1994-96; v.p. govt. affairs Info. Tech. Industry Coun., Washington, 1996-98; sr. v.p. bus. and pub. affairs Interactive Digital Software Assn., 1998—. Author: Political Parties, Presidential Campaigns, and National Party Conventions, 1992; Contributions and Expenditures by National, State, and Local Party Conventions, 1990; Active Corporate Participation, 1993; Candidates and Parties 1982, Registration and Reporting, 1981. Recipient U. Memphis Outstanding Young Alumnus award 1982. Mem. ABA, Fed. Bar Assn. (chair. com. on political campaigns and election laws 1983-85.

DARR, JOHN, insurance company executive; b. Balt., Oct. 9, 1951; s. Jack E. and Mary (Wurdack) D.; m. Sue Brezler, Jan. 5, 1980; children: Adrienne, Elena, Alex, Natalie. BS, Towson U., 1974; MBA, Loyola Coll., Balt., 1979. CPA, Md., Ill. Mgr. acctg. Md. Casualty Co., Balt., 1974-77; asst. to pres. First Federated Life Ins., Balt., 1977-80; mgr. fin. reporting RLI Ins. Co., Peoria, Ill., 1980-82; regional controller, v.p. Am. Internat. Underwriters, N.Y.C., 1982-83; asst. mgr. fin. reporting Royal Ins. Co., N.Y.C., 1983-84; v.p., treas. Seaboard Surety Co., N.Y.C., 1984-96; fin. acctg. and info. svcs. officer St. Paul Fire and Marine Ins. Co., St. Paul, 1996-98; bd. dirs. Seaboard Surety Co., N.Y.C., 1984-98. Advisor Jr. Achievement, Balt., 1975. Mem. Am. Inst. CPA's. Home: 9347 Wedgewood Dr Woodbury MN 55125-9303

DARR, MILTON FREEMAN, JR., banker; b. Oak Park, Ill., Oct. 30, 1921; s. Milton Freeman and Frances Anna (Kaiser) D.; m. Margaret Claire Phipps, Jan. 27, 1945; children: Alan Phipps, Bruce Milton. B.S., U. Ill., 1942. With LaSalle Nat. Bank, Chgo., 1946-80; asst. cashier LaSalle Nat. Bank, 1950-53, asst. v.p., 1953, v.p., 1954-62, exec. v.p., dir., 1962-64, pres., 1964-68, chmn. bd., chief exec. officer, 1968-73, pres., 1974-77, vice chmn. bd., 1977-80; organizer, founding dir. Buffalo Grove (Ill.) Nat. Bank, 1975. Mem. Bd. Edn. Dist. 88 Community High Sch., 1963-68, Nat. Bd. YMCA's, 1973-77; past chmn., mem. Ill. Gov.'s Adv. Bd. on Cancer Control; chmn. commerce and industry com., treas. Chgo. Com. for Project Hope; state crusade chmn. Ill. div. Am. Cancer Soc., 1967, 68, chmn. bd., 1973-75, nat. bd. dirs., 1975-78; chmn. bd. mgrs., v.p. bd. trustees YMCA Met. Chgo., 1970-72; chmn. bd. trustees Elmhurst Coll., 1982-87, hon. life trustee, 1998—; chmn. YMCA Retirement Fund, 1986-92, trustee emeritus, 1994; trustee Ill. Cancer Council, Better Govt. Assn.; life trustee Union League Boys and Girls Clubs; chmn. Armed Forces Week, 1987; bd. dirs. Chgo. Crime Commn., United Charities of Chgo., Mid-Am. chpt. ARC. Served to maj. USAAF, 1942-46. Recipient Distinguished Service award Am. Cancer Soc., 1976, Founders medal Elmhurst Coll., 1987; Citizen fellow Inst. Medicine of Chgo. Mem. Am. Inst. Banking (pres. Chgo. chpt. 1955-56, mem. exec. council 1956-59, nat. v.p. 1959-60, nat. pres. 1960-61), Am. Bankers Assn. (mem. adminstrv. com., exec. council 1960-61), Assn. Res. City Bankers (treas. 1969-72), Robert Morris Assos. (pres. Chgo. chpt. 1965-66), Chgo. Clearing House Assn. (past chmn.), Theta Chi. Presbyterian. Clubs: Rotarian (pres. 1973-74, Paul Harris fellow, Ches Perry fellow), Chicago, Bankers (pres. 1973), Economic, Executives, Union League (pres. 1968-69), Commerical (life, treas.) (Chgo.); Glen Oak Country; Eagle Ridge Golf. Home: Residence N206 5 Oakbrook Club Dr Oak Brook IL 60523-1348 Office: 135 S La Salle St Chicago IL 60603-4105

DARR, WALTER ROBERT, financial analyst; b. Phila., June 19, 1956; s. John Fluke Sr. and Lois Marilyn (Fry) D. BS in Commerce, Rider U., Lawrenceville, N.J., 1978; MBA, Rider U., 1991. Collateral analyst First Nat. Bank & Trust Co., Beverly, N.J., 1978-84; collateral analyst First Peoples Bank of N.J., Westmont, 1984-88, loan rev. analyst, 1988-92; loan acctg. tech. New Jersey Nat. Bank, Trenton, N.J., 1992-93; sr. credit analyst Carnegie Bank, N.A., Princeton, N.J., 1993-94, asst. cashier, sr. credit analyst, 1994-97; credit officer, credit dept. supv. Broad Nat. Bank, Newark, N.J., 1997—. Treas. Cinnaminson Bapt. Ch., 1983-87, deacon, 1988-89, 93-94; mem. Lewis Shearer Chorale/Garden State Chorale, 1982-94; chmn.-treas. Mercer County chpt. Child Evangelism Fellowship of N.J., 1996—. Recipient Sch. award Am. Legion Post, Medford, N.J., 1974. Republican. Baptist. Avocations: antique cars, bicycling, classical music, Victorian architecture. Home: 107 Manlove Ave Apt E-B Hightstown NJ 08520-3234 Office: Broad Nat Bank 905 Broad St Newark NJ 07102-2622

DARRABY, JESSICA L., lawyer, educator, writer; b. June 17. BA, UCLA, 1974; MA, U. Calif., 1976, JD, 1979. Bar: Calif. 1979. Gallery dir., owner Jessica Darraby Gallery, L.A., 1984-88; cons., expert witness, 1988—; adj. prof. Pepperdine Sch. Law, Malibu, Calif., 1988—; bd. dirs. Art Table, Inc., N.Y.C., 1993—, treas. So. Calif. exec. com., 1992-93, lawyer, 1993—. Author: Art, Artifact and Architecture Law, 1995—. Fellow Can. Council Fellowship Canadian Govt., 1975. Mem. ABA (copyright, sports and entertainment forum), Am. Soc. Appraisers (affiliate), Scribes, Contemporary Arts Coun., Mus. Modern Art (N.Y.C.), Exec. Women's Golf Assn., Whitney Circle, Whitney Mus. Am. Art. Office: Pepperdine Sch Law Malibu CA 90263

DARRAH, LARRY LYNN, plant breeder; b. Ithaca, N.Y., Oct. 9, 1943. BS with honors, Cornell U., 1965; PhD, Iowa State U., 1970. Maize geneticist USDA/U.S. AID, Kitale, Kenya, Africa, 1970-77; rsch. geneticist USDA, Columbia, Mo., 1977-91, rsch. leader, location coord., 1991—; assoc. prof., adj. prof. U. Mo., Columbia, 1979—. Contbr. over 100 articles to profl. jours. on corn breeding and quantitative genetics. Pres. Rock Bridge Elem. PTA, Columbia, 1983-84; sec. Cedar Lake Homeowners' Assn., Columbia, 1986-89. 1st lt. U.S. Army, 1965-67. Fellow Crop Sci. Soc. Am. (assoc. editor 1986-89), Am. Soc. Agronomy; mem. Coun. Agrl. Sci. Tech., Am. Soc. Agronomy, Crop Sci. Soc. Am., Phi Kappa Phi, Gamma Sigma Delta, Alpha Zeta, Sigma Xi. Achievements include research on corn breeding and quantitative genetics. E-mail: agrolld1@showme.missouri.edu. Office: USDA-ARS U Mo 110A Curtis Hall Columbia MO 65211-7020

DARRELL, NORRIS, JR., lawyer; b. Berlin, Germany, May 10, 1929; s. Norris and Doris Clare (Williams) D. (parents Am. citizens); m. Henriette Maria Haid, July 31, 1962; 1 child, Andrew. A.B., Harvard U., 1951, LL.B. cum laude, 1954. Bar: N.Y. 1955, U.S. Supreme Ct. 1965. Assoc. Sullivan & Cromwell, N.Y.C., 1956-65, ptnr., 1965-92; sr. ptnr. European office Sullivan & Cromwell, Paris, 1968-71, sr. counsel, 1993—; bd. dirs. IBJ Whitehall Bank & Trust Co., N.Y.C., USA Group, Inc., Fishers, Ind. Trustee Cold Spring Harbor Lab., Inc., 1974-81, United Student Aid Funds, Inc., Fishers, Ind., 1974-94, USA Group Inc., Fishers, Ind., 1993—, East Woods Sch., Oyster Bay, N.Y., 1974-79; hon. trustee Heckscher Mus., Huntington, N.Y. With U.S. Army, 1954-56. Fellow Am. Bar Found.; mem. Am. Law Inst., ABA, Assn. Bar City N.Y., Harvard Club N.Y., Pilgrims Club, River Club (bd. govs. 1978-98), Cold Spring Harbor Beach Club, Edgartown Yacht Club. Home: 44 Walnut Tree Ln Cold Spring Harbor New York NY 11724 Office: Sullivan & Cromwell 125 Broad St New York NY 10004-2498

DARRISON, CYNTHIA R., political consultant; b. Dec. 10, 1959. BA, Touro Coll.; MS in Indsl. & Labor Rels., Cornell U. Fin. dir. The Moynihan Com., N.Y.C., 1981-87; pres. Darrison & Assocs., LLC, Bklyn., 1989—; pvt. practice labor arbitration, 1989—. Office: 900 Ave H Ste 2H Brooklyn NY 11230-2832

DARROW, GEORGE F., natural resources company owner, consultant; b. Osage, Wyo., Aug. 13, 1924; s. George Washington and Marjorie (Ord) D.; m. Elna Tannehill, Oct. 23, 1976; children by previous marriage: Roy Stuart, Karen Josanne, Reed Crandall, John Robin. AB in Econs., U. Mich., 1945, BS in Geology, 1949. Geologist Amerada Petroleum Corp., Billings, Mont., 1949-50; v.p. Northwest Petroleum Co., 1951-58; prin. Resource Consultants, Billings, 1959-76; pres., CEO Crossbow Corp., Billings, 1962—; v.p. Kootenai Galleries, Bigfork, Mont., 1976—; sr. ptnr. Crossbow Assocs., resource mgrs., Bigfork, 1976—; chmn. Mont. Environ. Quality Coun., Helena, 1971-73; bd. dirs. Ord Ranch Corp., Lusk, Wyo.; apptd. faculty affil. U. Mont., 1995—. Contbr. articles on resource mgmt. and econs. to various publs. Elected mem. Mont. Ho. of Reps., 1967-69, 71-73, Mont. Senate, 1973-75; bd. dirs. Bigfork Ctr. Performing Arts, 1980—; apptd. mem. Mont. Ambs., 1994—. Lt. (j.g.) USNR, 1943-46, PTO. Fellow AAAS; mem. Internat. Soc. Ecol. Econs., Am. Assn. Petroleum Geologists (past pres. Rocky Mountain sect.), Am. Inst. Profl. Geologists (charter), Mont. Geol. Soc. (founder, charter), Billings Petroleum Club. Home and Office: Crossbow Corp 2014 Beverly Hill Blvd Billings MT 59102-2314 also: Paladin Farms 924 Chapman Hill Dr Bigfork MT 59911-6215

DARROW, JILL E(LLEN), lawyer; b. N.Y.C., Jan. 6, 1954; d. Milton and Elaine (Sklarin) D.; m. Michael V.P. Marks, May 14, 1987. AB in English, Barnard Coll., 1975; JD, U. Pa., 1978; LLM in Tax Law, NYU, 1983. Bar: Pa. 1978, N.Y. 1979, U.S. Tax Ct. 1982. Assoc. Shearman & Sterling, N.Y.C., 1978-79; assoc. Rosenman & Colin, N.Y.C., 1979-86, ptnr., 1987—. Mem. ABA, N.Y. State Bar Assn., Pa. Bar Assn., Phi Beta Kappa. Home: 860 5th Ave New York NY 10021-5856 Office: Rosenman & Colin LLP 575 Madison Ave Fl 26 New York NY 10022-2585

DARROW, STEVE, state legislator. BS, U. Vt. State rep. Vt. Ho. of Reps., 1993—. Supr. Nat. Resources Conservation Dist. Address: PO Box 880-e Putney VT 05346-0880

DARROW, WILLIAM RICHARD, pharmaceutical company executive, consultant; b. Middletown, Ohio, Sept. 7, 1939; s. Richard William and Nelda Virginia (Darling) D.; BA, Ohio Wesleyan U., 1960; MD, Western Res. U., 1964; PhD in Pharmacology, Case-Western Res. U., 1969; m. Janet Elizabeth Swan, June 20, 1964; children: James William, Susan Elizabeth, Margaret Ellen. Intern, Univ. Hosps., Cleve., 1964; sr. clin. rsch. assoc. CIBA Pharm. Co., 1969, asst. dir. clin. pharmacology, 1969-70; dir. clin. pharmacology CIBA-GEIGY Corp., 1970-75, exec. dir. clin. rsch., 1975-76; sr. v.p. rsch., med. dir. Wallace Labs. div. Carter Wallace, Inc., Cranbury, N.J., 1976-80; med. dir. Schering Labs. div. Schering-Plough Corp., Kenilworth, N.J., 1980, v.p. med. and regulatory affairs, 1981-82, sr. v.p. med. ops., 1982-94, sr. med. advisor, 1994—. Chmn. rsch. com. N.J. Health Scis. Group, 1973-76, mem. exec. com., 1973-74, 76-86, treas. 1977-80, v.p., 1980-86, Bernards Twp. Bd. Health, 1979-93, v.p., 1980, pres., 1981-85, 86-93; bd. dirs. N.J. Arthritis Found., 1990—, exec. com., 1991—, vice chmn., 1995-97, chmn. bd. dirs. 1997—; bd. dirs. Pharm. Rsch. Mfrs. Am. Ednl. and Rsch. Inst., 1993—, chmn. curriculum com., 1993-95; bd. dirs. Junior Achievement No. N.J., 1996; mem. sci. adv. bd. Clin. Rsch. Ctr. Robert Wood Johnson Med. Ctr., 1990—; mem. U.S. del. Internat. Conf. on Harmonization, 1991—. Recipient Roche award, 1962, Humanitarian of Yr. award Arthritis Found. N.J., 1994; USPHS postdoctoral fellow, 1965-69. Fellow Royal Soc. Medicine, Am. Acad. Pharm. Physicians, Acad. Medicine N.J.; mem. AMA, Am. Acad. Pharm. Physicians (life), Drug Info. Assn., N.J. Acad. Scis., Pharm. Rsch. Mfrs. Am. (mem. steering com. med. section 1984-96, program chmn. 1988-89, vice-chmn. 1989-90, chmn. 1990-92, past chmn. 1992-96), Pharm. Rsch. Mfrs. Am. Found. (sci. adv. bd. 1990—, chmn. 1994—, chief sci. advisor 1997—), Phi Gamma Delta, Phi Rho Sigma, Omicron Delta Kappa, Pi Delta Epsilon. Republican. Presbyterian. Home: 42 Palmerston Pl Basking Ridge NJ 07920-2524 also: 521 E Lake Rd Penn Yan NY 14527-9422

DARSCH, NANCY, professional basketball coach; b. Plymouth, Mass, 1958. BA, Springfield (Mass.) Coll., 1973. Coach Longmeadow (Mass.) H.S.; asst. coach U. Tenn., 1978-85; coach Ohio State U., 1985-97; head coach N.Y. Liberty, WNBA, 1997-98, Washington Mystics, WNBA, 98-; coach U.S.A. Olympic trials, 1980, 88, U.S.A. Pan Am. Games trials, 1979, 83; head coach U.S.A. Jr. Nat. basketball team, 1990; asst. coach U.S. Olympic team, 1984, 86. Office: Washington Mystics MCI Center 601 F St NW Washington DC 20004

DARSEY, JEROME ANTHONY, chemistry educator, consultant; b. Houma, La., Aug. 26, 1946; s. Elmer Joseph and Arline (Houghton) D.; m. Patricia Ann Bukowski, June 10, 1989; children: Brittany Angéle, Joseph Anthony, Mary Catherine. BS in Physics, La. State U., 1970, PhD in Chemistry, 1982. Asst. prof. chemistry and physics Gordon Coll. U. Ga. System, Barnsville, 1983-84; asst. prof. Tarleton State U./Tex. A&M U., Stephenville, Tex., 1984-88, assoc. prof., 1988-90; asst. prof. U. Ark., Little Rock, 1990-93, assoc. prof., 1993—; univ. scholar natural scis. Tarleton State U., Tex. A&M U., 1989-90; cons. Oak Ridge (Tenn.) Nat. Lab., 1990-95; cochmn. 1st workshop neural network applications to material scis. Dept. Energy, 1994; chmn. 1st APS Symposium on Applications of Artificial Neural Networks to Chemical Systems; invited lectr. 21st Australian Polymer Symposium, 1996. Sci. book reviewer Jour. Am. Chem. Soc.; contbr. articles to profl. jours. Grantee Am. Chem. Soc., 1986, 90, NSF, 1992, 96, NASA, 1994-96; named Outstanding Univ. Researcher, U. Ark., 1995. Fellow AAAS; mem. Am. Chem. Soc. (chmn. Ark. sect. 1993), Am. Phys. Soc., Ark. Acad. Sci., S.W. Theoretical Chemistry Conf. (chmn. 1986-87), Tex. Acad. Sci. (vice chmn. chemistry divsn. 1986-87, chmn. 1987-88). Home: 1514 Alberta Dr Little Rock AR 72227-5803 Office: U Ark Dept Chemistry 2801 S University Ave Dept Little Rock AR 72204-1099

DARSIN, JOSE A., transportation engineer; b. Buenos Aires, Oct. 18, 1965; came to U.S., 1992; s. Nicholas Darsin and Ana Maria Palazzolo; m. Marcela Calderace, July 7, 1991; children: Tomas, Sofia. Degree in civil engring., U. Buenos Aires, 1991; MS in Transp. Planning & Engring., Poly. U., N.Y.C., 1994, postgrad., 1994—. Registered profl. engr., Argentina. Tech. asst. Superctr. S.A., Buenos Aires, 1986-89, Impencco S.A., Buenos Aires, 1990-91; rsch. asst. Poly. U., N.Y.C., 1992-94; engr. Frederic R. Harris, Inc., N.Y.C., 1994, project mgr., 1995—; cons. World Bank, Washington, 1995. Scholar U. Buenos Aires, 1989, Poly. U., 1993. Mem. ASCE, ITE. Office: Frederic R Harris Inc 300 E 42nd St New York NY 10017-5947

DARST, BOBBY CHARLES, soil chemist, administrator; b. Atoka, Okla., Jan. 31, 1940; s. R.B. and Ellie (Sisson) D.; m. Patricia Ann Lane, Aug. 12, 1961; children: Bobby Charles Jr., Patricia Ann, Shanna Diane. BS, Okla. State U., 1962; MS, Auburn U., 1964, PhD, 1966. Staff agronomist Cities Svc. Co., Atlanta, 1966, dir. soil, plant testing, 1967-68, chief agronomist, 1969-70, regional sales mgr., 1971-72; s.w. dir. Potash & Phosphate Inst., Stillwater, Okla., 1973-86; v.p. Potash & Phosphate Inst., Atlanta, 1986-92, exec. v.p., 1992—; v.p. Found. for Agronomy Rsch., Atlanta, 1986-88, pres., 1988—; bd. dirs. Ark. Plant Food Edn. Soc., Little Rock, 1973-75, Coun. for Agrl. Sci. & Tech., Ames, Iowa, 1990-92, exec. com., 1993-96; adj. prof. Okla. State U., Stillwater, 1986. Author: Potash and Phosphate Institute Soil Fertility Manual, 1978; editor books, booklets and folders, 1986-91; Contbr. articles to profl. jours., chpts. to books. Vol. Wes Watkins for Congress campaign, Stillwater, Okla., 1982. Recipient award of Recognition, Nat. Fertilizer Solutions Assn., St. Louis, 1980, '81, Soil Fertility award, Okla. State U., 1986, Svc. award Tex. Forage and Grassland Coun., Georgetown, Tex., 1986. Fellow Am. Soc. Agronomy, Soil Sci. Soc. Am.; mem. Am. Forage and Grassland Coun. (v.p. 1986-87, pres. 1987-88, Merit cert. 1987, medallion 1990), Rivermont Country Club. Democrat. Baptist. Achievements include development of 1st high volume totally computerized soil testing laboratory in world equipped with then known technology; basic manual on soil testing now published in English, Spanish, Portugese, Chinese, French; led in standardization of soil testing procedures through sample exchange programs. Home: 9010 Nesbit Ferry Rd Lot 8 Alpharetta GA 30022-1603 Office: Potash & Phosphate Inst 655 Engineering Dr Ste 110 Norcross GA 30092-2837

DARST, DAVID MARTIN, investment banking company executive, writer, educator; b. Knoxville, Tenn., Nov. 14, 1949; s. Guy Bewley and Susan Mary (McGinnis) D.; m. Diane Wassman; children: Elizabeth Mathews, David Martin, Jr. BA, Yale U., 1969; MBA, Harvard U., 1971. Assoc. Goldman, Sachs & Co., N.Y.C., 1971-75, v.p., mgr., 1981—; v.p., resident mgr. Goldman, Sachs & Co., Zurich, Switzerland, 1975-81, CFO equities divsn., 1991-96; mng. dir. Morgan Stanley Dean Witter, N.Y.C., 1996—; vis. lectr. Coll. and Sch. Mgmt., Yale U., New Haven, 1981—, Bus. Sch., Harvard U., Boston, 1987—. Author: The Complete Bond Book, 1975, The Handbook of the Bond and Money Markets, 1981; contbr. articles to profl. jours. Bd. dirs. Deer Park Assn., 1985—, pres., 1989—; bd. dirs. Can.-U.S. Found. for Ednl. Exch., 1996—; bd. profl. advisors N.Y.C. Ballet, 1997—. William H. Donaldson Disting. Faculty fellow Sch. Mgmt. Yale U., 1986-87. Mem. The Money Marketeers, The Phelps Assn. (v.p., gov. 1974—), Assn. Internat. Bond Dealers (edn. com.), Yale Alumni Assn. of Greenwich (bd. dirs. 1996—), Yale Club of N.Y.C. (coun. 1987—, chmn. fin. com. 1987—). Office: Morgan Stanley Dean Witter 4th Fl 1221 Ave of the Americas New York NY 10020-1001

DARST, GUY B., JR., journalist; b. Spartanburg, S.C., Nov. 8, 1940; s. Guy B. and Susan Mary Darst; m. Caroline Carpenter Greve, Dec. 30, 1961. AB, Harvard U., 1963. Reporter Trentonian, Trenton, N.J., 1964-65; newsman UPI, Boston, 1965-69; staff writer Harvard U., Cambridge, Mass., 1969-73; newsman AP, Boston, 1973-77, Detroit, 1977-81, Washington, 1981-91; sr. writer Pasha Publ., Arlington, Va., 1991-94; chief editl. writer Boston Herald, 1994—. Office: Boston Herald 1 Herald Sq Boston MA 02106

DARST, MARY LOU, elementary education educator; b. Houston, Aug. 12, 1943; d. Carl Kennedy and Sara Catharine (Emmott) Hughes; m. William Maury Darst, Apr. 20, 1963 (wid. May 1990); children: Robert Maury, Catharine Fontaine Darst Knight. Student, Stephen F. Austin State Coll., 1961-63, Galveston Coll., 1970-72, 76-77, Galveston Coll., 1980, U. Tex. Med. Br., 1983-84; BA, U. Houston, 1989, MS, 1993; postgrad., U. St. Thomas, 1999. Cert. tchr. elem. edn., secondary English, ESL, Tex. Sec. William Temple Found., Galveston, 1979-80; with new accounts Tex. First Bank, Galveston, 1981-84; med. sec. U. Tex. Med. Br., Galveston, 1984-87; tchr. Galveston (Tex.) Ind. Sch. Dist., 1991—, Galveston Coll., 1995-96. Mem. Jr. League of Galveston, 1966-69; bd. dirs. YWCA, 1972-73. Title VII grantee U. Houston at Clear Lake, Webster, Tex., 1991-93. Mem. Assn. of Tex. Profl. Educators, Tex. Neurofibromatosis Found. (sec. 1987-89, pres. 1989-91), Rock Art, Galveston Art League, U. Tex. Med. Coll. Alumni Assn., Scenic Galveston, Phi Theta Kappa, Delta Kappa Gamma (vice-pres. Omicron chpt. 1995-96), Alpha Chi Omega. Democrat. Avocations: music, swimming, walking, writing, artist. Office: Galveston Ind Sch Dist Rosenberg Elem 721 10th St Galveston TX 77550-5115

DART, JOHN ROBERT, horticulturist; b. Montour, N.Y., July 25, 1925; s. Russel S. and Helen M. (Bristow) D.; m. Maryann Alexander, Aug. 20, 1951 (div. Jan. 1974); children: Ralph, Richard, Christopher. Student, U. Conn.; U.S. Mcht. Marine Acad., Kings Point, N.Y. Commd. ensign U.S. Mcht. Marines, 1944; advanced through grades to 1st engr. U.S. Mcht. Marines, $, $, 1957; ret., 1957; with Pratt & Whitney Aircraft Exptl., 1957-68; pres. Dart Tree Farm Corp., Middle Haddam, Conn., 1960—; with bldg. dept. Conn. Nat. Bank, Hartford, 1968—; with Justice Dept. U.S. Justice Dept., 1992-98; pres. Union Hill Cemetery, Middle Haddam, 1959—. Mem. Rotary (pres. 1983), Masons. Republican. Avocation: flying private aircraft. Home and Office: Easy St Middle Haddam CT 06456

DART, JOHN SEWARD, journalist, author; b. Peekskill, N.Y., Aug. 1, 1936; s. Seward Homer and Vella Marion (Haverstock) D.; m. Gloria Joan Walker, Aug. 31, 1957; children—Kim, John W., Randall, Christopher. BA, U. Colo., 1958. Staff writer UPI, Indpls. and L.A., 1961-65; sci. writer Calif. Inst. Tech., Pasadena, 1966-67; religion writer L.A. Times, 1967-98. Author: The Laughing Savior, 1976, The Jesus of Heresy and History, rev., expanded edit., 1988; co-author: Unearthing the Lost Words of Jesus, 1998; contbr. reports for Freedom Forum First Amendment Ctr., Vanderbilt U. Served with U.S. Army, 1958-61. Recipient Supple Meml. award Religion Newswriters Assn., 1980, Merrell Meml. award Jim Merrell Religion Liberty Found., 1980, William F. Leidt award Episcopal Ch., 1980, Angel award Religion in Media, 1985; NEH fellow Stanford U., 1973-74, First Amendment Ctr. fellow Vanderbilt U., 1992-93. Mem. Soc. Profl. Journalists (chpt. pres. 1976), Religion Newswriters Assn. (pres. 1990-92), Soc. Bibl. Lit. (mem.-at-large exec. com. Pacific Coast region 1990-95). Democrat. Home and Office: 12122 Bowmore Ave Northridge CA 91326-1002

DARTING, EDITH ANNE, pharmaceutical company coordinator; b. Hillsboro, Kans., Jan. 1, 1945; d. Sammuel E. and Carrie (Swehla) Jewett; m. John Ronald Darting, Aug. 11, 1978; children: Theresa Michelle, Lloyd L., Hope Marie. Grad., Emporia State Tchrs. Coll., 1963-65. Materials insp. Sterling Drug Inc., McPherson, Kans., 1977-78, auditor, 1978-82, coordinator, 1982-94; coord. Sanofi Winthrop, McPherson, 1994-97; quality asurance coord. Abbott Lab. Inc., 1997-98, mfg. quality assurance coord., 1998—. Mem. Am. Soc. for Quality. Republican. Methodist. Home: 320 N Birch St Hillsboro KS 67063-1135 Office: Abbott Lab Inc PO Box 1048 Mcpherson KS 67460

DARTON, ERIC, writer; b. N.Y.C., May 30, 1950; s. John Howard Darton and Beatrice Maria Kroll; m. Katie Kehrig, Nov. 21, 1980; 1 child, Gwendolyn Helena. BA with honors, Empire State Coll., 1990; MA, Hunter Coll., 1994. Art, dance and performance editor East Village Eye, N.Y.C., 1981-83; pres. Yomoma Arts, Inc., N.Y.C., 1985—; assoc. editor Conjunctions, N.Y.C., 1991-93; cons. Poets & Writers, Inc., N.Y.C., 1992-97; fiction editor Am. Letters and Commentary, N.Y.C., 1999—; lectr. Hunter Coll., N.Y.C., 1991—, Fordham U., N.Y.C., 1992-97, NYU, 1996—. Author: Free City, 1996, Divided We Stand, 1999. Franklin Furnance fellowship N.Y. State Council on the Arts, 1987, N.Y. Found. for the Arts fellowship N.Y. Found. for the Arts, 1991, fellowship in fiction Breadloaf Writers Conf., 1998. Mem. Pen Am. Ctr. E-mail: edarton@interport.net.

DARVAROVA, ELMIRA, violinist, concertmaster; came to U.S., 1986; MusB, State Conservatory, Sofia, Bulgaria, 1977, MusM, 1979; certificate, Guildhall Sch. Music, London, 1982; artist's diploma, Ind. U., 1987. Concertmaster Plovdiv (Bulgaria) Philharm. Orch., 1979-86, Owensboro (Ky.) Symphony Orch., 1986-88, Evansville (Ind.) Philharm., 1987-88; artistic dir., concertmaster Evansville Chamber Orch., 1987-88; assoc. instr. violin Ind. U. Sch. Music, Bloomington, 1986-88; acting concertmaster Rochester (N.Y.) Philharm., 1988; vis. lectr. Ind. U. Sch. Mus., 1988; guest concertmaster Columbus Symphony Orch., Columbus, Ohio; concermaster Met. Opera Orch., N.Y.C., 1989—, Chgo. Grant Park Symphony, 1990—; founding mem. New World Trio, 1991. Performer recitals and concerts throughout world. Recipient 1st medal internat. competition, Barcelona, Spain, 1979, hon. diploma, prize Tchaikovsky competition, Moscow, 1982, silver medal Viotti internat. competition, Vercelli, Italy, 1984, 3d prize internat. competition, Sion, Switzerland, 1985. Avocations: reading, studying foreign languages. First woman concertmaster in Met. Opera history. Office: Met Opera Orch Lincoln Ctr New York NY 10023

DARVAS, ENDRE PETER, artist; b. Kisvadra, Sz-Szatmar, Hungary, July 18, 1946; came to U.S., in 1957; s. Bela and Maria (Filtczer) Darvas. BFA, U. Tex., 1969. Pres. Studio Arts and Frames, Inc., South Lake Tahoe, Calif., 1974-78; owner Darvas Studio, South Lake Tahoe, 1969—. One-man shows include Dallas, 1963, Taos, N.Mex., 1971, Carmel, Calif., 1975, San Carlos, Mex., 1987, Galerias del Pacifico, Sonora, Mex., 1989, Studio Retrospective, Lake Tahoe, 1990, Sierra Galleries, Lake Tahoe, 1991-94, 98, Musco Costumbrista, Alamos Sonora, Mex., 1999; represented in permanent collections Sierra Galleries, Rosequist Gallery, Tucson, Galeria Bellas Artes, Bahia San Carlos, Sonora, James-Harold Gallery, Tahoe City, Calif., El Prado Gallery, Sedona, Ariz. Recipient numerous awards from art exhibits. Mem. Soc. Am. Impressionists, Southwestern Watercolor Soc. Avocations: sailing, tennis. Office: Darvas Studio PO Box 711 South Lake Tahoe CA 96156-0711

DARVILL, ALAN G., biochemist, botanist, educator; b. Redditch, Worchester, U.K., Jan. 27, 1952; came to U.S., 1976; s. Bryan Richard and Pamela Mary Darvill; m. Janet Elizabeth Jones, July 12, 1975; 1 child, Sarah Jayne. BS in Plant Biology, Wolverhampton Poly., U.K., 1973; PhD in Plant Physiology, Univ. Coll. Wales, Aberystwyth, 1976. Postdoctoral assoc. U. Colo., Boulder, 1976-78, sr. rsch. assoc., 1978-83, asst. prof. dept. molecular, cellular and devel. biology, 1983-84, assoc. prof., 1984-85; assoc. prof. dept. biochemistry and botany U. Ga., Athens, 1985-87, prof., 1988—, assoc. dir. Complex Carbohydrate Rsch. Ctr., 1985-87, dir., 1987—, co-dir. Ctr. for Plant & Microbial Complex Carbohydrates, 1987—. Contbr. more than 170 articles to profl. jours. Mem. AAAS, Am. Chem. Soc. (exec. com. divsn. carbohydrate chemistry 1993—, chmn. divsn. carbohydrate chemistry 1994-95), Soc. for Complex Carbohydrates. Office: U Ga Complex Carbohydrate Rsch Ctr 220 Riverbend Rd Athens GA 30602-1511

DARWIN, DAVID, civil engineering educator, researcher, consultant; b. N.Y.C., Apr. 17, 1946; s. Samuel David and Earle (Rives) D.; m. Diane Marie Mayer, June 29, 1968; children: Samuel David, Lorraine Marie. BS, Cornell U., 1967, MS, 1968; PhD, U. Ill., 1974. Registered profl. engr., Kans. Asst. prof. civil engring. U. Kans., Lawrence, 1974-77, assoc. prof., 1977-82, prof., 1982—, Deane E. Ackers disting. prof. civil engring., 1990—, dir. Structural Engring. and Materials Lab., 1982—; cons. David Darwin, Lawrence, 1976—. Author: Steel and Composite Beams with Web Openings, 1990; also numerous articles. Mem. Uniform Bldg. Code Bd. Appeals, Lawrence, 1978-84. Capt. U.S. Army, 1967-72, Vietnam. Grantee NSF, 1976—, Air Force Office Sci. Rsch., 1985-92, Civil Engring. Rsch. Found., 1991-95, Kans. Dept. Transp., 1980-82, 90—; recipient Miller award U. Kans., 1986, Irvin Youngberg Rsch. Achievement award, 1992. Fellow ASCE (editor Jour. Structural Engring. 1994—, Huber rsch. prize 1985, Moisseiff award 1991, state-of-the-art of civil engring. award 1996, Richard R. Torrens award 1997), Am. Concrete Inst. (pres. Kans. chpt. 1975, bd. dirs. 1988-91, Bloem Disting. Svc. award 1986, Arthur R. Anderson award for disting. rsch. 1992, Structural Rsch. award 1996); mem. AAAS, Am. Soc. Engring. Edn., ASTM, Am. Inst. Steel Constrn. (profl.), Prestressed Concrete Inst. (profl.), Post-Tensioning Inst. (profl.), Concrete Rsch. Coun. (chmn. 1990-96), Phi Kappa Phi (pres. U. Kans. chpt. 1976-78). Democrat. Unitarian. Avocations: swimming, walking. Office: U Kans Civil and Environ Engring Dept 2006 Learned Hall Lawrence KS 66044-7526

DARWOOD, JOHN JOSEPH, physician; b. Van Wert, Ohio, Feb. 6, 1956; s. Arthur Joseph and Marilyn Ruth Darwood. BS, U. Toledo (Ohio), 1978; MD, Wright State U., 1983, MS, 1989. Diplomate Am. Bd. Family Practice, Am. Bd. Preventive Medicine, Am. Bd. Occupl. Medicine, Am. Bd. Aerospace Medicine. Resident in family practice Good Samaritan Hosp., Dayton, Ohio, 1983-86; occupl. medicine physician Indsl. Med. Ctr., Dayton, 1986-90; physician Comprehensive Health Svcs. Kennedy Space Ctr. NASA, Fla., 1990—. Fellow Am. Acad. Family Physicians, Am. Coll. Occupl. and Environ. Medicine; mem. Nat. Mgmt. Assn. (chpt. pres. 1995-96, chpt. chmn. bd. dirs. 1997-99). E-mail: john.darwood-1@kmail.ksc.nasa.gov. Office: CHS-005 Kennedy Space Center FL 32899

DARY, DAVID ARCHIE, journalism educator, author; b. Manhattan, Kans., Aug. 21, 1934; s. Milton Russell and Ruth Engel (Long) D.; m. Carolyn Sue Russum, June 2, 1956; children: Catherine Lee, Carol Ann, Cynthia Kay, Cristina Sue. B.S. in Humanities, Kans. State U., 1956; M.S. in Journalism, Kans. U., 1970. Reporter, editor CBS News, Washington, 1960-63; mgr. local news NBC News, Washington, 1963-67; dir. pub. affairs Kans. Rep. State Com., Topeka, 1968; mem. faculty U. Kans., Lawrence, 1969-89, prof. journalism, 1970-89; dir. H.H. Herbert Sch. Journalism, U. Okla., Norman, 1989—; cons. broadcast journalism, 1967—. Author: Radio News Handbook, 1967, Manual De Noticias Radiofonicas, 1970, Television News Handbook, 1970, How to Write News for Broadcast and Print, 1973, The Buffalo Book, 1974, Comanche, 1976, True Tales of the Old-Time Plains, 1979, Cowboy Culture, 1981, Lawrence, Douglas County Kansas: An Informal History, 1982, True Tales of Old-Time Kansas., 1984, Entrepreneurs of the Old West, 1986, Kanzana 1854-1900: A Selected Bibliography, 1986, More True Tales of Old-Time Kansas, 1987, Picturial History of Lawrence, Douglas County, Kansas, 1993, Seeking Pleasure in the Old West, 1995, Red Blood & Black Ink: Journalism in the Old West, 1998; contbr. numerous articles to various mags. and newspapers. Mem. Okla. Hist. Soc. (bd. dirs. 1990-93), Kans. State Hist. Soc. (bd. dirs. 1972-91), Western History Assn., Westerners Internat. (pres. 1986-89), Western Writers Am. (pres. 1988-92), Masons, Kappa Tau Alpha. Office: U Okla Sch Journalism 860 Van Vleet Oval Norman OK 73019-2050

DAS, KALYAN, lawyer; b. Calcutta, India, June 23, 1956; s. Amulyaratan and Chaitaly (Mitra) D.; m. Pia Mukherjee, Feb. 18, 1986; children: Sabrina, Rahul. Barrister-at-Law, The Lincoln's Inn, London, 1979; Diploma, Assoc. of the Chartered Inst. of Arbitrators, London, 1980; LLM, NYU, 1989. Bar: Eng. 1979, Wales 1979, N.Y. 1983; advocate Supreme Ct. India, 1981; barrister and solicitor Melbourne, Australia, 1984. Barrister-at-law Fountain Ct. Temple, London, 1980-81; assoc. Malcolm A. Hoffmann, N.Y.C., 1981-82, White & Case, N.Y.C., 1983-88, Milbank, Tweed, Hadley & McCloy, N.Y.C., 1988-90; assoc. Seward & Kissel, N.Y.C., 1990-93, ptnr., 1993—. Editor: Company Law, 1980. Internat. v.p. Internat. Students' Trust, London, 1987—. Fellow Am. Coll. Investment Counsel (co-chair ann. meeting 1998); mem. ABA, N.Y. State Bar Assn., Assn. Bar City of N.Y., Am. Arbitration Assn. (panel mem.), Hon. Soc. Lincoln's Inn, Wine Soc. London, Met. Club (N.Y.C.). Avocations: sailing, tennis, travel. Home: 107 W 89th St Ph B New York NY 10024-1944 Office: Seward & Kissel 1 Battery Park Plz Fl 21 New York NY 10004-1485

DAS, KAMALENDU, chemist; b. Sylhet, Bangladesh, Feb. 2, 1944; came to U.S. 1971; s. Kailash and Prabhashini Das; m. Shyamali Chowdhury, Dec. 6, 1969; children: Mrinal Kanti, Sampa. BSc with honors, U. Dhaka, 1964, MSc, 1966; PhD, U. Houston, 1975. Asst. prof. Women's Coll. & Tolaram Coll., Bangladesh, 1966-71; instr. U. Houston, 1976-78; rsch. scientist, group leader Baker Sand Control, Houston, 1979-85; rsch. chemist, physical scientist, project mgr. U.S. Dept. Energy Fed. Energy Tech. Ctr., Morgantown, W.Va., 1985—. Contbr. articles to profl. jours. Fellow Am. Inst. Chemists; mem. Am. Chem. Soc., Soc. Petroleum Engrs., Internat. Union Pure and Applied Chemistry, Bangladesh Chem. and Biology Soc. N. Am. (treas. 1997-98, pres. 1999—), Mountaineer Toastmasters (pres. 1994-95, v.p. edn. 1995-96, TI dist. 13 area 3 gov. 1998-99, treas. 1998-99, divsn. A gov. 1999—). Home: 465 Lawnview Dr Morgantown WV 26505-2130 Office: US Dept of Energy Fed Energy Tech Ctr PO Box 880 Morgantown WV 26507-0880

DAS, SAJAL KUMAR, computer science educator, researcher; b. Dainhat, India, Jan. 3, 1960; came to U.S., 1985; s. Baidya Nath and Bimala (Dhani) D.; m. Nandini Dutta, Dec. 15, 1989; 1 child, Somak. BS in Physics with honors, Calcutta U., 1980, B in Tech., 1983; MS in Computer Sci., Indian Inst. Sci., 1984; PhD in Computer Sci., U. Ctrl. Fla., 1988. Teaching asst. computer sci. dept. Wash. State U., Pullman, 1985-86; rsch. asst. dept. computer sci. U. Ctrl. Fla., Orlando, 1986-88; asst. prof. dept. computer sci. U. North Tex., Denton, 1988-92, assoc. prof., 1993-98, dir. Ctr. for Rsch. in Parallel and Distributed Computing, 1990—, prof., 1998—; faculty advisor U. North Tex. Badminton Club, Denton, 1989-90; founding advisor India Student Assn. of U. North Tex., Denton, 1990-93; mem. steering com. Internat. Conf. on Computing and Info., Can., 1992; vis. prof. Bell No. Rsch., Dallas, 1993-94; mem. program coms. and adv. coms. several internat. confs.; speaker and presenter in field. Mem. editorial bd. Parallel Processing Letters, 1991—, Jour. Parallel Algorithms and Applications, 1992—; contbr. articles to profl. jours.; more than 70 refereed papers. Summer Rsch. fellow U. North Tex., 1990, Honor Prof. award U. North Tex., 1991; Rsch. grantee Higher Edn. Coordinating Bd., Tex., 1991, 93, 97, Travel grantee Goethe U., Germany, 1992, grantee Bell. No. Rsch., Dallas, 1993-94; Leonardo Fibinacci Inst. scholar, 1993. Mem. IEEE Computer Soc. (jour. reviewer, tech. sessions chair), Assn. for Computing Machinery (sponsoring faculty student chpt. U. North Tex.), N.Y. Acad. Scis., Sigma Xi. Office: Univ North Tex Dept Computer Sci PO Box 311366 Denton TX 76203-1366

DASBURG, JOHN HAROLD, airline executive; b. N.Y.C., Jan. 7, 1943; s. Jean Henry and Alice Etta Dasburg; m. Mary Lois Diaz, July 6, 1968; children: John Peter, Kathryn. AA, U. Miami, 1963; BS in Indsl. Engring., U. Fla., 1966, MBA, 1971, JD, 1973. Bar: Fla. 1974; CPA, Fla., Md. Mem. staff Peat Marwick Mitchell & Co., Jacksonville, Fla., 1973-78, tax ptnr. in charge, 1978-80; v.p. tax Marriott Corp., Washington, 1980-82, v.p. fin., 1982-84, sr. v.p., 1984-85, exec. v.p., CFO, chief real estate officer, 1985-88, pres. lodging group, 1988-89; pres., CEO Northwest Airlines, 1990—; bd. dirs. St. Paul Cos., Owens Corning. Author numerous published articles on tax law and tax acct. Lt. (j.g.) USN, 1966-69, Vietnam. Republican. Roman Catholic. *

DASCH, PAT (ANNE), society executive; b. Hampton Court, Surrey, Eng., Oct. 19, 1948; came to U.S., 1986; d. Arthur James and Eileen Dorothy (Adams) Kirk; m. Peter Malcolm Jones, Dec. 22, 1973 (div. 1981); m. Ernest Julius, Apr. 3, 1987. BA with honors, U. East Anglia, Norwich, Eng., 1975. Adminstrv. asst. Imperial Coll., London, 1968-72; adminstr. Wolfson Coll., Oxford, Eng., 1976-82; broadcaster, commentator Nat. Space Soc., Houston, 1984-88; planetary sci. rschr. Lunar Planetary Inst., Houston, 1986-88; planetary sci. analyst SAIC for NASA, Washington, 1988-94; editor in chief Ad Astra Mag., Nat. Space Soc., Washington, 1994-98; exec. dir. Nat. Space Soc., Washington, 1997—. Co-author: Images of Earth, 1984 (Best Remote Sensing Book of Yr.). Avocations: geology, hiking, travel, theater. Office: Nat Space Soc 600 Pennsylvania Ave SE Ste 201 Washington DC 20003-4344

DASCHER, PAUL EDWARD, university dean, accounting educator; b. Oct. 1, 1942; s. Albert Jacob abd Ruth (Mountney) D.; m. Nancy Patricia Byrne; children: Mitchell Paul, Heidi Beth. BS, Pa. State U., 1964, MS, 1966, PhD, 1969. Instr. acctg. Pa. State U., 1968-69; asst. prof. acctg. Va. Poly. Inst., Blacksburg, 1969-71, assoc. prof. acctg., 1971-73; prof. acctg. Drexel U., Phila., 1973-93, dept. head, 1974-77, dean coll. of Bus. and Adminstrn., 1977-93; dean Sch. Bus. Adminstrn. Stetson U., Deland, Fla., 1993—; prof. acctg. Stetson U., Fla., 1993—; vis. prof. Northeastern U., Boston, 1976; cons. Price Waterhouse and Co., N.Y.C., 1974-75; lectr. in field. Co-author: Financial Accounting, 1980, 4th edit., 1995, Accounting Readings, 1982, Managerial Accounting, 1985, 7th edit., 1997; contbr. numerous articles to profl. jours. Fellow Price Waterhouse & Co., Armstrong Cork Co.; recipient Nat. Assn. Accts. Socio-Econ. Disting. Service award, 1973, 75, 81, Drexel U. Faculty Appreciation award, 1977, Commendation Phila. chpt. Pa. Inst CPA's, 1977, Community Accts. Meritorious Service award, 1981; named one of Outstanding Young Men of Am., 1979. Mem. Am. Acctg. Assn., Fin. Execs. Inst., Inst. Mgmt. Accts. (nat. v.p. 1989-90), Accts. for Pub. Interest (pres. 1986-89), Alpha Kappa Psi, Beta Alpha Psi, Beta Gamma Sigma. Republican. Lutheran. Avocations: tennis, reading. Office: Stetson U Sch Bus Adm Deland FL 32720

DASCHLE, THOMAS ANDREW, senator; b. Aberdeen, S.D., Dec. 9, 1947; m. Linda Hall Daschle; children: Kelly, Nathan, Lindsay. B.A., S.D. State U., 1969. Fin. investment rep.; chief legis. aide, field coordinator Sen. James Abourzek, 1973-77; mem. 96th-97th Congresses from 1st S.D. Dist., 98th-99th Congresses at large, 1983-87; U.S. senator from S.D., 1987—, senate minority leader 104th Congress, 1995; Mem. Agrl. Nutrition & Forestry Com., Sen. Dem. Sterring & Coor. Com., Sen. Dem. Tech & Comm. Com., Chmn. Sen. Dem. Conf. Com., Chmn, Sen. Dem. Policy Com. Served to 1st lt. USAF, 1969-72. Recipient Nat. Commdr.'s award Disabled Am. Vets., 1980; named Outstanding Young Man of Yr., U.S. Jaycees, 1981. Democrat. Roman Catholic. Office: US Senate 509 Hart Senate Bldg Washington DC 20510*

DASGUPTA, AMITAVA, chemist, educator; b. Calcutta, India, May 6, 1958; came to U.S., 1980; naturalized U.S. citizen, 1996; s. Anil Kumar and Hasi Dasgupta. BS with honors, U. Calcutta, India, 1978; MS in Chemistry, U. Ga., 1981; PhD in Chemistry, Stanford U., 1986. Diplomate Am. Bd. Clin. Chemistry. Fellow in clin. chemistry U. Wash., Seattle, 1986-88; asst. dir. clin. chemistry U. Chgo., 1988-93; dir. clin. chemistry lab. U. N.Mex. Hosp., Albuquerque, 1993-97; assoc. prof. pathology and biochemistry U. N.Mex., Albuquerque, 1993-97; prof. pathology U. Tex.-Houston Med. Sch., 1998—; lectr in field. Reviewer jours. Clin. Chemistry, Nephron, Jour. Liquid Chromatography; contbr. articles to Clin. Chemistry, Am. Jour. Clin. Pathology, Jour. Am. Soc. Nephrology,. SYVA, 1990-91, Home Health Care, 1992-93. Fellow Nat. Acad. Clin. Biochemistry (Grannis award 1993); mem. Am. Assn. Clin. Chemistry, Acad. Clin. Labs. Physicians and Scientists. Hindu. Achievements include research in role of lipids and lipid peroxidation in the pathophysiology of disease; characterization of digoxin-like immunoreactive substance; drug-drug interaction and advantages of monitoring free drug concentrations. Home: 6431 Fannin St # Msb-2292 Houston TX 77030-1501 Office: U Texas Med School Dept Pathology 6431 Fannin St # Msb2292 Houston TX 77030-1501

DASGUPTA, GAUTAM, theater educator, journal editor and publisher; b. Calcutta, India, July 1, 1949; came to U.S., 1970; s. Medini Mohan and Jharna (Dutta-Roy) D.; m. Bonnie Marranca, Aug. 1, 1975. BSME, Jadavpur U., Calcutta, 1969; MFA in Theatre, U. Conn., 1971, MA in English, 1972. Founding pub. and editor PAJ Publs., N.Y.C., 1976—; editor Performing Arts Jour., N.Y.C., 1976—; prof. theater, chmn. dept. Skidmore Coll., Saratoga Springs, N.Y., 1990—; bd. dirs. Gale Gates et al, theater co., N.Y.C., 1995—. Co-author: American Playwrights: A Critical Survey, 1981; editor: Animations: A Trilogy for Mabou Mines, 1979, Interculturalism and Performance, 1991, Theatre of the Ridiculous, 1997, Conversations on Art and Performance, 1999; contbr. articles to profl. jours. Recipient Pierre Lecomte du Nouy Am. Found. award, 1980, 91, Obie award Village Voice, 1983, Stanislaw I. Witkiewicz prize, Poland, 1990; rsch. grantee Skidmore Coll., U.K. and Europe, 1993, 97; Berlin prize fellow Am. Acad. in Berlin, 1998-99. Avocations: reading, birdwatching, gardening, travel. Office: Skidmore Coll Theater Dept Saratoga Springs NY 12866

DAS GUPTA, SUBAL, physics educator, researcher; b. Calcutta, India, Aug. 11, 1939; emigrated to Can., 1960; s. Subodh Chandra and Pritilata (Sen) Das G.; m. Sanjukta Sen Gupta, Aug. 12, 1965; children: Monidipa, Nandini. MSc, Calcutta U., 1959; PhD, McMaster U., 1963. Nat. Scis. and Engring. Rsch. Coun. Can. post-doctoral fellow AECL, Chalk River, Ont., Can., 1963-64; rsch. sci. Tata Inst. for Fundamental Rsch., Bombay, India, 1964-65; postdoctoral fellow in physics McGill U., Montreal, Que., Can., 1965-66, asst. prof. physics, 1967-71; assoc. prof. McGill U., Montreal, Ont., Can., 1972-77, prof., 1978—, chair dept. physics, 1993-97, prof. physics, 1997—. Contbr. articles to profl. jours. Oper. grantee Nat. Sci. and Engring. Rsch. Coun., 1966—. Office: McGill U Dept Physics ERP 319, 3600 University St, Montreal, PQ Canada H3A 2T8*

DASH, ALEKHA K., pharmaceutical scientist, educator; b. Gobindapur, Orissa, India, Aug. 1, 1954; came to the U.S., 1984; s. Jagannath Dash and Flurence Panda; m. Kanchanbala Mohapatra, May 9, 1984; children: Debleena, Rohan Dipak. B in Pharmacy, Jadavpur U., Calcutta, 1981, M in Pharmacy, 1983; PhD, U. Minn., 1990. Registered pharmacist Orissa, India, 1975-77; pharmacy technician U. Minn. Med. Ctr., Mpls., 1984-90; tchg. and rsch. asst. U. Minn., Mpls., 1984-90; asst. prof. Creighton U., Omaha, 1990-95, assoc. prof., 1995—; adj. asst. prof. U. Nebr., Omaha, 1994—. Editor-in-chief Orissa Soc. of Ams., 1993-95; contbr. chpts. to books. Recipient John C. Kenific awards Health Future Found., Omaha, 1991, 93, Pharmaceutics award Pharm. Mfrs. Assn., Washington, 1993. Mem. AAAS, Am. Assn. Pharm. Scientists (award and publ. com. 1994—), Am. Assn. Colls. Pharmacy. Achievements include development of implantable delivery system for bone infections; use of microdialysis in implantable dosage form design; solid state characterization of tobramycin. Home: 13518 Sahler St Omaha NE 68164-6025 Office: Creighton Univ 2500 California Plz Omaha NE 68178-0001

DASH, J. GREGORY, physicist, educator; b. New York City, N.Y., June 28, 1923; s. Emanuel and Shirley Miriam (Nisinson) D.; m. Joan Ellen Zeiger, Jun. 23, 1945; children: Michael, Elizabeth, Anthony. BS, CCNY, 1944; PhD, Columbia, 1951; doct. hon. causa (hon.), U. D'Aix-Marseille, 1991. Physicist Los Alamos Scientific Lab., 1951-60; assc. prof. U. Wash., Seattle, Wash., 1960-64, prof., 1964-93; emeritus prof., 1993—; Advisor Natl. Sci. Found., Battelle Pacific NW Lab., RKK Ltd. Author Films on Solid Surfaces, 1975; editor Phase Transitions in Surface Films, 1980, Surface Physics, Cryogenics, Frozen Ground Rsch., Engring. Applications, Ice Physics in the Environment, 1999. With U.S.N., 1944-46. Fellow Guggenhiem Found., 1957. Fellow Am. Phys. Soc. (recipient Davisson-Germer prize, 1988). Office: U of Washington Physics Dept Seattle WA 98195

DASH, LEON DECOSTA, JR., journalist; b. New Bedford, Mass., Mar. 16, 1944; s. Leon DeCosta and Ruth Elizabeth (Kydd) D. BA, Howard U., 1968; DHD, Lincoln U., 1996. Reporter Washington Post, 1966-68, 71-79, African bur. chief, 1979-83, with investigations desk, 1984-98; prof. journalism & afro-Am. studies U. Ill., Champaign, 1998—; vis. prof. U. Calif.-San Diego, 1978. Author: (with Ben H. Bagdikian) The Shame of the Prisons, 1972, When Children Want Children: The Urban Crisis of Teenage Childbearing, 1989, Rosa Lee: A Mother and Her Family in Urban America, 1996 (Polit. Book award Washington Monthly Mag. 1997, 1st prize Harry Chapin Best Book award World Hunger Year Orgn. 1997). Peace Corps vol., Kenya, 1969-70. Recipient George Polk Meml. award Overseas Press Club, 1974, award for internat. news reporting Washington-Balt. Newspaper Guild, 1974, hon. mention Washington-Balt. Newspaper Guild, 1975, Internat. Reporting awards Africare, 1984, Capitol Press Club, 1984, 1st Place Journalism award Gen. News, Nat. Assn. Black Journalists, 1986, Investigative Reporters and Editors award, 1987, Editl. award for news series Chesapeake Associated Press (co-winner), 1987, 1st Prize award Washington-Balt. Newspaper Guild, 1987, Pres.'s award Washington Ind. Writers Assn., 1989, Editl. award Chesapeake Associated Press (co-winner), 1989, Martha Albrand Spl. Citation for Nonfiction PEN, 1990, Pulitzer Prize for explanatory journalism, 1995, 1st prize Robert F. Kennedy award for print journalism, 1995, Emmy award for pub. affairs NATAS, 1996, Polit. Book award The Washington Monthly Mag., 1997, Prevention for a Safer Soc. award Nat. Coun. on Crime and Delinquency for Rosa Lee book, 1997; fellow Henry J. Kaiser Family Found., 1995-96. Office: U Ill Dept Journalism 119 Gregory Hall Urbana IL 61801

DASH, STACEY, actress; b. Bronx, N.Y., Jan. 20, 1966. Appeared in films Moving, 1986, Tennessee Waltz, 1989, Mo' Money, 1992, Renaissance Man, 1994, Clueless, 1995, Illegal in Blue, 1995, Cold Heart, 1997; appeared in TV series Clueless, 1996. Office: Michael Slessinger & Assocs 8730 W Sunset Blvd Ste 220 Los Angeles CA 90069-2275*

DASHIELL, G. RONALD, marshal. U.S. marshal U.S. Dist. Ct. (ea. dist.) Wash., Spokane. Office: US Courthouse 920 W Riverside Ave Rm 888 Spokane WA 99201-1010*

DA SILVA, ERCIO MARIO, physician; b. Catajuczes, Mines, Brazil; s. Mario and Rosa (Pinto) da S.; m. Doris da Silva, Aug. 22, 1953; children: Robert, Suzanne. MD, U. Mines, Brazil, 1949. Diplomate Am. Bd. Colon Rectal Surgery. Pvt. practice. Mem. Am. Soc. Colon Rectal Surgery, Columbia Med. Soc. Home: 413 Brookshire Dr Columbia SC 29210-4203

DASKAL, PAUL LINN, psychiatric and mental health professional; b. Chgo., Jan. 19, 1955; s. Jordan and Jewel D.; m. Jenny E. Velarde, Aug. 3, 1986; children: Janelle M., Michelle N., Matthew J. Diploma, Luth. Gen. Hosp. Sch. Nursing, 1985; AA, Oakton Jr. Coll., 1986; BSN, No. Ill. U., 1991. Cert. psychiat. and mental health nurse. Staff nurse Hines (Ill.) VA Hosp., 1985-89; unit mgr. Macneal Hosp., Berwyn, Ill., 1989-90; staff nurse North Chgo. VA Hosp., North Chgo., Ill., 1990; psychiatric staff nurse Luth. Gen. Hosp., Park Ridge, Ill., 1990-96, USAF, 1996—. With USN, 1976-80. Home: 222A Jupiter Sheppard AFB TX 76311

DASKI, ROBERT STEVEN, federal civil servant; b. Altoona, Pa., Sept. 9, 1947; s. Steve and Margaret (Duey) D.; m. Maria Cañizares, Aug. 4, 1973; children: Robert Jr., William, John. BA, Clarion State Coll., 1969; MA, St. Francis Coll., 1970; diploma, U.S. Army War Coll., 1989. Labor economist, manpower analyst U.S. Dept. Labor, Washington, 1970-82; supervisory mgmt. analyst, program analyst Dept. Def., Washington, 1982—. Contbr. articles to profl. jours. Pres. PTA Cherry Run Elem. Sch., Burke, Va., 1984-

86; Springfield dist. chmn. Citizens Com. Sch. Bonds, Fairfax County, Va., 1986; scoutmaster troop 698 Boy Scouts Am., Burke, 1990-92, asst. scoutmaster, 1992—, mem. Order of Arrow, 1993—; mem. parent coun. Ferrum (Va.) Coll., 1995-99. Recipient Bronze Pelican award Arlington Diocese Cath. Com. on Scouting, 1995, Comdr.'s award for Civilian Svc., Dept. of Army, 1996. Mem. All Pa. Coll. Alumni Assn. Washington (exec. com. 1995-96). Avocations: reading, sports, community activities. Home: 9702 Velilla Rd Burke VA 22015-4159

DASKIN, MARK STEPHEN, civil engineering educator; b. Balt., Dec. 3, 1952; s. Walter and Betty Jane (Fax) D.; m. Babette Reva Levy, July 2, 1978; children: Tamar, Keren. BSCE, MIT, 1974; postgrad. study in Engring., Cambridge, England, 1975; PhD in Civil Engring., MIT, 1978. Tchg. asst. trans. sys. divsn. civil engring. MIT, Cambridge, 1976-77; asst. prof. civil engring. Univ. Tex., Austin, 1978-79; asst. prof. civil engring. Northwestern U., Evanston, Ill., 1980-83, assoc. prof. civil engring., 1983-89, prof., 1989—, chair dept. indsl. engring. and mgmt. scis., 1995—. Author: Network and Discrete Location: Models, Algorithms and Applications, 1995; editor-in-chief Transp. Sci., 1991-94; assoc. editor Location Sci., 1991—; contbr. articles to profl. jours. Bd. dirs. North Suburban Synagogue Beth El, Highland Park, Ill., 1991-94. Univ. Tex. Bur. Engring. Rsch. grant, 1978-79, Northwestern Univ. Transp. Ctr. grant, 1980, 81, NSF grant, 1980-82, 84-90, 93-97, 96-99, Urban Mass Transp. Adminstr. grant, 1982-84, 84-85, United Parcel Svc. grant, 1983-86, 91-92, Thermo-King Corp. grant, 1990-91, 92-94, Heartland Blood Ctr. grant, 1992, 96; recipient Fulbright Rsch. award, 1989-90, Burlington Northern Found. Faculty Achievement award, 1985, NSF Presdl. Young Investigator award, 1984, Scott Paper Leadership award, 1973-75. Mem. ASCE, Inst. Indsl. Engrs., INFORMS (v.p. publs. 1996—), Ops. Rsch. Soc. Am. (jour. editor 1991-94), Inst. Mgmt. Sci., Sigma Xi, Tau Beta Pi, Chi Epsilon. Avocations: swimming, photography. Office: Northwestern U Dept Indsl Engring Mgmt Sci Evanston IL 60208

DASMANN, RAYMOND FREDRIC, ecologist; b. San Francisco, May 27, 1919; s. William H. and Mary (McDonnell) D.; m. Elizabeth Sheldon, May 30, 1944; children—Sandra, Marlene, Lauren. A.B., U. Calif., Berkeley, 1948, M.A., 1951, Ph.D., 1954. Mem. faculty Humboldt State Coll., 1954-59, 62-66; research biologist Nat. Museums Rhodesia, 1959-61; lectr. zoology U. Calif., Berkeley, 1961-62; ecologist Conservation Found., Washington, 1966-70; sr. ecologist Internat. Union Conservation Nature, Morges, Switzerland, 1970-77; prof. U. Calif., Santa Cruz, 1977—. Author: Pacific Coastal Wildlife, 1957, Environmental Conservation, 1959, 84, African Game Ranching, 1963, Last Horizon, 1963, Wildlife Biology, 1964, 81, Destruction of California, 1965, A Different Kind of Country, 1968, No Further Retreat, 1971, Planet in Peril, 1972, Ecological Principles for Economic Development, 1973, The Conservation Alternative, 1975, California's Changing Environment, 1981; contbr. articles to profl. jours. Fellow AAAS (hon.), Calif. Acad. Scis. (hon.), World Conservation Union (hon.); mem. Am. Soc. Mammalogists, Wildlife Soc. (pres.), Soc. for Conservation Biology, Golden Gate Biosphere Res. Assn. (pres.). Home: 116 Meadow Rd Santa Cruz CA 95060-2014 Office: U Calif Dept Environ Studies Santa Cruz CA 95064

DASOVICH, E. MARTIN, accountant; b. Meadville, Pa., Oct. 7, 1967; s. Martin E. D. and Elaine C. (Johns) Horner. BS in Book Acctg., W. Va. U., 1990, MPA, 1991. CPA, Pa. Sr. mgr. KPMG Peat Marwick LLP, Pitts., 1991-99, Ernst & Young LLP, Walnut Creek, Calif., 1999—. Bd. dirs., treas. Pitts. area ISO 9000, 1993-99, users group; bd. dirs., sec. Best Friends, Inc., Beaver, Pa., 1995-99; mem. Pitts. Young Profls., Pitts., 1994-99, bd. dirs., pres. We. Pa. Cmty. Accts., Pitts., 1995-99. Named Vol. of Yr. We. Pa. Cmty. Accts., 1996, Named Most Valuable Vol., 1997. Mem. AICPA, Pa. Inst. CPAs, Healthcare Fin. Mgmt. Assn., Rivers Club. Republican. Avocations: tennis, racquetball, skiing, golfing. Home: 868 Morningside Way Pleasant Hill CA 94523-4708 Office: Ernst & Young LLP 1331 N California Blvd #200 Walnut Creek CA 94996

DASSANOWSKY, ROBERT VON, writer, editor, educator, producer; b. N.Y., Jan. 28, 1960; s. Elfi von Dassanowsky. Grad., Am. Acad. Dramatic Arts; BA with honors, UCLA, 1985, MA, 1988, PhD, 1992. Actor, 1975—; asst. prof. German, UCLA, 1992-93; asst. prof. German U. Colo., Colorado Springs, 1993-99, head German studies, 1993—, assoc. prof. German and film, dir. film studies, 1999—; councillor ProEuropa League Journalists and Scholars, 1998—. Author: (plays) The Brithday of Margot Beck, 1980, Briefly Noted, 1981, Vespers, 1982 (Beverly Hills Theatre Guild award 1984), Tristan in Winter, 1986, Songs of a Wayfarer, 1986, Coda, 1991, (criticism) Phantom Empires: The Novels of A. Lernet-Holenia and the Question of Postimperial Austrian Identity, 1996, Verses of a Marriage, Translation of Poetry Collection by Hans Raimund, 1996, Telegrams from the Metropole: Selected Poetry, 1999; founding editor Rohwedder: Internat. Jour. Lit. and Art, 1986-93; editor New German Rev., 1987-92, PEN CNT mag., 1992-98; contbg. editor Osiris: Internat. Jour. Lit. (Mass.), 1992—, Rampike (Can.), 1992—; contbg. author Encyclopedia of World Fiction of the 20th Century 1999-2000; bd. advisors Gale Encyclopedia of Multicultural America, 2d edit., 1999-2000; mng. editor Writers Forum, 1994-96; mem. editl. bd. Modern Austrian Lit., 1997—; mem. rsch. com. Almanach de Gotha, 1998—; author numerous poems; contbr. articles, revs., essays to jours. Mem. Pan Europa Union, Vienna, 1982—, Accademia Culturale d'Europa, Ital. City of L.A. cultural grantee, 1990, 91, 92, U. Colo. Pres. Fund for Humanities grantee, 1996; recipient Residency award Karolyi Found., France, 1979, Accademico Honoris Causa Diploma, Accademia Culturale d'Europa, Italy, 1989, Outstanding Letters Arts and Scis. Faculty award U. Colo., Colorado Springs, 1998. Mem. PEN (West bd. dirs. L.A. 1992-99, founder and pres. Colo. chpt. 1994-99), Internat. Lernet-Holenia Soc. (v.p. 1998—), Austrian Am. Film Assn. (v.p. 1997—), Soc. Cinema Studies, Poets and Writers, Modern Lang. Assn., Nat. Adv. Bd., Los Angeles Poetry Festival, SAG. Office: U Colo Dept Langs and Cultures Colorado Springs CO 80933

DASSARMA, BASUDEB, chemistry educator; b. Barisal, Bengal, India, Jan. 1, 1923; came to U.S., 1966; s. Ashutosh and Surabala (Sengupta) DasS.; m. Seba Sengupta, June 17, 1952; children: Urmi, Shiladitya. BSc, Brojo Mohan Coll., Barisal, 1944; MSc, Calcutta U., India, 1946, PhD, 1951. Rsch. assoc. U. Ill., Champaign-Urbana, 1953-55; lectr. in Chemistry Calcutta U., 1955-57; chemist in charge Geol. Survey of India, Calcutta, 1957-66, chmn., 1981-86; prof. of chemistry West Va. State Coll., Institute, 1966-91; prof. emeritus West Va. State Coll., 1992—; rsch. chemist Union Carbide, Charleston, W.Va., 1966; rsch. advisor Oak Ridge (Tenn.) Nat. Lab., 1971-72; project mgr. toxics U.S. Environ. Pollution Agy., Washington, 1986, Nat. Inst. for Chem. Studies, Charleston, 1988. Contbr. articles to profl. publs. Named Outstanding Educator, NSF, 1971, 73; travel fellow Internat. Conf. on Coordination Chemistry, 1980. Mem. Am. Chem. Soc. (sec. Kanawha Valley sect. 1993-97, symposia organizer 1998, Outstanding Sci. Achievement award 1971), K/P LEPC, Dunbar/Inst. CSA, W.Va. Acad. Sci. (life, pres. 1983-84), Air and Waste Mgmt. Assn., Lions. Home: 429 25th St Dunbar WV 25064-1613 Office: WVa State Coll Institute WV 25112

DASTGEER, GHULAM MOHAMMAD, surgeon; b. Kabul, Afghanistan, Apr. 27, 1939; came to U.S., 1979; s. Sofi Ghulam and Zubaida Majida (Tarin) D.; m. Nassrin Sadiqua Saidy, Sept. 1, 1960; children: Nazifa, Walid A., Afifa, Khalid A. MD, Kabul U., 1963. Cert. ACLS; lic. physician, Mass., N.Y.; ciplomate Am. Bd. Profl. Cons. Intern medicine/surgery Kabul U. Med. Sch., 1963-64; gen. surgeon Jalalabad, Afghanistan, 1965-68; resident sr. house officer orthopedics Singleton/Morriston Hosps., Swansea, Wales, 1970-73, resident (sr. house officer) oncology, 1973-74; chief resident, registrar gen. and thoracic surgery Wales and London, 1974-77; sr. resident surgery Leicester, Eng., 1973-74; chief resident gen. surgery Neath Gen. Hosp., Wales, 1974-77; chief resident thoracic surgery St. Helier/St. Thomas Hosps., Surrey and London, 1977-78; assoc. prof. gen. surgery, sr. registrar North Middlesex Hosp., London, 1978; staff physician ambulatory care/surgery VA Med. Ctr., Springfield/Northampton, Mass., 1987—; instr. gen. surgery Nangerhar (Afghanistan) Med. Sch., 1965-68; rsch. fellow U. Coll. Hosp. Med. Sch. Surg. Unit, London, 1969-70; hon. clin. instr. gen. surgery Neath. Gen. Hosp./Cardiff Med. Sch., Wales, 1975-79; lectr. gen. surgery Kabul U. Med. Sch., Afghanistan, 1978-79; instr. somatic medicine dept. psychiatry U. Mass. Med. Ctr., Northampton, 1980-83; asst. physician, asst. prof., chief somatic svcs. Harvard/McLean/Northampton Program, 1983-86; attending surgeon Mil. Hosp., Kabul, 1978-79; lectr. EMT pre-med program U. Mass., Amherst, 1985-90. Contbr. articles to profl. jours.; patentee in field. Recipient Honor award and letter VA, 1989, Spl. Contbn. award VA Med. Ctr., Northampton, 1988, Medallion Acad. Psychosomatics, 1985. Fellow Royal Coll. Surgeons (Scotland), Internat. Coll. Surgeons, Acad. Psychosomatic Medicine; mem. AMA (Physician's Recognition award 1983, 86, 89, 92, 95), Royal Coll. Physicians (London, licensiate), Islamic Med. Assn., Afghan Physicians Assn. Am. (pres.). Republican. Islam. Avocations: English and Arabic calligraphy, swimming, collecting inkwells. Office: Dept Vets Affairs Springfield Ambulatory Care 1550 Main St Rm 304 Springfield MA 01103-1427

D'ASTOLFO, FRANK JOSEPH, graphic designer, educator; b. Charleroi, Pa., July 19, 1943; s. Galderino Joseph and Gustina Evlyn (Petaccia) D'A. BA, Pa. State U., 1966; MA, U. Pitts., 1973. Graphic designer The United Fund, Pitts., 1968-69, Fisher Sci. Co., Pitts., 1969-73; instr. U. Pitts., 1972-76; graphic designer Pitt Studios, Pitts., 1973-74; design cons. Frank D'Astolfo Design, Pitts., 1974-77; instr. Tyler Sch. Art, Phila., 1977-80; design cons. Infield & D'Astolfo, N.Y.C., 1980-88; prof. Rutgers U., Newark, 1980—; design cons. Frank D'Astolfo Design, N.Y.C., 1988—; cons. in field; chmn. dept. art and design Rutgers U., Newark, 1989-92, dep. chmn. dept. visual and performing arts, 1992—; bd. dirs. Ringside Inc., N.Y.C., 1987—; mem. Newark Arts Coun., 1993-96. Graphic designer Print Mag., 1992, 93 (Fifty Best Ann. Reports 1984, 86, Best Logos and Symbols vol. II and III), Graphis Diagram I, 1988, Am. Corporate Identity 5-12, 15, 1989-96, 99 (awards of excellence), Metropolis The Architecture and Design Mag., New York, 1985. Design cons. Architects, Designers and Planners for Social Responsibility, N.Y.C., 1985, ICIS Internat. Ctr. for Integrating Studies, N.Y.C., 1983; dir. Com. for Cultural Awareness and Discussion, Pitts., 1977; cons. Shelly Friedman for Judge Com., Pitts., 1977. Recipient Gold award Art Dirs. Club Phila., 1981, Distinctive award Merit Soc. Pub. Designers N.Y., 1983, Cert. of Distinction Creativity, 19, 22 Art Direction mag., 1989, Silver award Case Coun. for Advancement and Support of Edn., 1985, Desi award Graphic Design U.S.A., 1982, 83, 85, 87, 88, 92, 94 (Am. Graphic Design award, 1994, 96), Typography 4 Print mag. Regional Design Ann., 1982, 84, 89, 92, 96, 98; Cert. of Merit Art Dirs. Club N.Y., 1978, 81, 85, 93, Cert. of Excellence Art Dirs. Club N.J., 1981, 82, 83, 85, 98, Inter Type Design 2 Award of Excellence, 1994, Graphis Letterhead 2 Award of Excellence, 1993, Cert. of Excellence Inter Logos and Trademarks II, 1992, Univ. and Coll. Designers Assn. award of Excellence, 1995), Warren I. Susman award for Excellence in Tchng., 1995, Am. Corp. Identity 2000 award, 1998, Cert. of Recognition for Logo Design, Graphic Logo Design 4 award of excellence, 1998.. Mem. Am. Inst. Graphic Arts (Cert. Excellence 1977, 83), Coll. Art Assn., Graphic Design Edn. Assn. Democrat. Roman Catholic. Home: 80 Warren St Apt 32 New York NY 10007-1038 Office: Rutgers U Dept Visual and Performing Arts Newark NJ 07102

DASTRUP-HAMILL, FAYE MYERS, city official; b. Sanford, Colo., Dec. 15; d. Earl Dixon and Kady Florence (Cornum) Faucett; m. Sherly K. Myers (dec.); children: Carla Pearce, Susan Kitley (dec.), Mary Jane James, Elizabeth Ireland; m. Merrill E. Dastrup, Sept. 22, 1972 (dec. July 1987); m. Wayne A. Hamill, Mar. 23, 1991. *Faye Myers Dastrup-Hamill grew up in Sanford, Colorado, a small farming community. Her Mormon Pioneer ancestors learned the value of hard work, also respect for government and its purpose. Her Uncle Bernard Bailey was a Colorado State Legislator, her Uncle George Irvin was an elected county official, and her mother, Florence Faucett, worked for the school district. Cousin Nile Brady was Assistant to US Secretary of Agriculture Benson, plus other positions. After college Faye worked for the Alamosa, Colorado City Attorney. These combined experiences, and others, helped Faye to become involved in Ontario, Calif. government, and she is grateful. Faye still enjoys her involvement.* Student, L.D.S. Bus. Coll., 1934-35; grad., Dale Carnegie Inst., 1953; degree in mcpl. works adminstrn., Mt. San Antonio Coll., 1960; student, Syracuse U. Inst., 1968; degree in tech. reporting, Chaffey Coll., 1970. Legal sec. W. W. Platt, City Atty., Alamosa, Colo., 1935-40; sec. pub. works dept. City of Ontario, Calif., 1957-60, dep. city clk., dep. city treas., 1960-64, city clk., 1964-73, city coun. mem., mayor and mayor pro tem, 1974-92; mem. part 150 implementation com. Ontario Airport, Calif., 1993—; chmn. noise adv. com., dept. trans. State of Calif. Ontario Airport, 1994—; sec. pers. dept. L.A. Housing Authority, 1948; mem. legis. subcom. So. Calif. Assn. Govts., chmn. hist. preservation and cultural arts com.; mem. revenue and taxation com. League of Calif. Cities, vice-chmn., chmn. Clks. Inst., gen. resolutions com., com. on environ. quality Inland Empire divsn.; chmn. San Bernardino County Planning Com., Criminal Justice; prese. So. Calif. City Clks. Assn., chmn. legis. com.; mem. exec. com. Valley Assn. of Cities; city coun. rep. Ontario Libr. Bd. Trustees. *Entrenched Ontario Government since 1957: Engineering Department, City Clerk, City Council, Mayor, Mayor pro Tempore (elected seven times), plus appointed positions. Faye Myers Dastrup has been called " A Woman Ahead Of Her Time"-" A True Pioneer Carving A Path For Women In The Field Of Politics". As an elected official, Faye represented Ontario on several regional and statwide organizations. Concerned for her City/People, Faye continues to assist many service organizations, receiving numerous prestigious honors and awards. Today Faye sits on Ontario's Library Board of Trustees, Airport Committees, Ontario Historical Society, and is Church Choir Director. She is a busy Wife, Mother and Grandmother.* Escort sch. classes through City Hall; judge sci. fairs and sch. and comty. events; life mem. Friends of Ontario Libr.; mem., donor Friends of Mus. of History and Art, Ontario; pres., treas., trustee Ontario (Calif.) City Libr., 1993—; choir dir., life mem. Ch. of Jesus. Recipient plaque with gold gavel So. Calif. City Clks. Assn., 1972, Women Helping Women award Soroptimist Internat. of Ontario, 1981, 1990 Woman of Yr. award State Legislature, State of Calif., 1990, Woman of Achievement award 90s Women's Conf., 1990, 1994 YWCA Woman of Achievement award West End YWCA, 1994, Elizabeth S. Genee Lifetime Achievement award, West End YWCA, 1994, Bryce Denton award Mus. of History and Art, 1996, Outstanding Effort with Calif. Water plaque San Bernardino County Waterworks Dist. #8, 1986, Outstanding Svc. plaque Ontario Air N.G., 1990, Leadership plaque San Bernardino County Sheriff's Dept., 1993, Founding, Support and Encouragement of Crime Stoppers Spl. Recognition plaque Ontario Police Dept., 1993, Outstanding Comty. Svc. plaque U.S. Congressman Jay Kim, 1994, Plaque and Spl. Cert. congratulating receipt of Elizabeth Genee Lifetime Achievement award, 1994, Pub. Svc. Award trophy Adrian Meewis, 1972, plaque for dedicated and meritorious svc. to Ontario, as mayor City Coun. and City Clk., 1986, Lifetime Achievement plaque San Bernardino County Supr. Larry Walker, 1994, Svc. plaque South Coast Air Quality Mgmt. Dist., 1987, decorated plaque Salvation Army, 1992, others. Mem. Calif. Assn. Libr. Trustees and Commrs., Comty. Concert Assn. Pomona Valley (donor), Ontario C. of C. (life, Svc. Award plaque 1992), Musicians Club of Pomona Valley. Mem. Ch. of Jesus Christ of LDS. Avocation: vocal soloist. Home: 761 W Hawthorne St Ontario CA 91762-1510

DATARS, WILLIAM ROSS, physicist, educator; b. Desboro, Ont., Can., June 14, 1932; s. Albert John and Leona Alberta (Fries) D.; m. Eleanor Wismer, Oct. 10, 1959; children—Timothy, Andrew, David. B.Sc., McMaster U., Hamilton, Ont., 1955; M.Sc., 1956; Ph.D., U. Wis., 1959. Physicist Def. Research Bd., 1959-62; mem. faculty McMaster U., 1962—, prof. physics, 1969-96, prof. emeritus, 1996—. E.W.R. Steacie fellow, 1968-70. Fellow Royal Soc. Can., Am. Phys. Soc.; mem. Can. Assn. Physics. Lutheran. Home: RR 2, Lynden, ON Canada L0R 1T0 Office: McMaster U, Dept Physics & Astronomy, Hamilton, ON Canada L8S 4M1

DATCU, IOANA, visual artist; b. Bucharest, Romania, Apr. 22, 1944; arrived in U.S., 1981; d. Marin and Niculina (Chitescu) D; m. Vasile Porcisanu, Aug. 5, 1967 (div. 1983); 1 child, Isabelle Ioana. BA, Pedagogical Inst., Bucharest, 1967; BFA summa cum laude, U. Minn., 1987, MFA, 1991. Tchr. biology high sch., Argova, Preasna, Romania, 1967-74; photography asst. U. Minn., St. Paul, 1985-86; photographer civil rights dept. City Hall, St. Paul, 1986-87; darkroom supervisor Film in the Cities, St. Paul, 1987-88; gallery asst., curator Paul Whitney Gallery, St. Paul, 1987-91; art instr. Minn. Mus. Am. Art, St. Paul, 1993-94; instr. drawing & painting U. Minn., Mpls., 1996-97. One-person exhbns. include Flanders Contemporary Art, Mpls., 1994, Winona (Minn.) State U., 1995, Mont. State U., Billings, 1996, Ea. Washington U., Cheney, 1996, Indpls. Art Ctr., 1996, Kansas City (Mo.) Artists Coalition, 1997, Grants Pass (Oreg.) Mus. Art, 1997, Trinity Presbyn. Ch., Denton, Tex., 1998, South Bend (Ind.) Mus. Art, 1998; juried group shows include North Park Coll., Chgo., 1991, Historic Trinity, Detroit, 1993, 95, 96, Barrett House Galleries, Poughkeepsie, N.Y., 1994, 96, Coll. St. Catherine, St. Paul, 1995, Minot State U., N.D., 1995, St. John's U., N.Y., 1995, Katherine E. Nash Gallery, Mpls., 1992, 95, 96, Focal Point Gallery, N.Y.C., 1996, SoHo Photo Gallery, N.Y.C., 1997, Greater Lafayette Mus. Art., 1997, Truman State U., Mo., 1998, McNeese State U., La., 1998, Attlboro Mus. Art, 1998, 99, New World Art Ctr., N.Y.C., 1999, Ctrl. Mo. State U., 1999, New American Paintings Exhibit in Print, Open Studio Press, 1995, Images of the Spirit Traveling Exhibit, 1995-97, CIVA CODEX III traveling exhibit, 1997—; works represented in CD-Rom collections of Art Comms. Internat., 1995, Artmax Internat., 1995, Ency. Internat. Women Artists, Alliance Women Artists, 1997, New Art Internat., Book Art Press, 1997. Grantee Pollock-Krasner Found., 1992, Minn. State Arts Bd., 1994; Jerome Found. Residency fellow, 1994; McKnight Photography fellow, 1992, fellow Arts Midwest NEA, 1994-95, Clowes Fund regional residency fellow, Indpls., 1997; Vt. Studio Ctr. Residency award, Johnson, Vt., 1997. Mem. Christians in the Visual Arts, Nat. Assn. Women Artists, Inc. Mem. Eastern Orthodox Ch. Avocations: classical music, movies, yoga, books, animals. Home and Studio: 9590 E Baby Creek Rd Bloomington IN 47408-9601

DATE, ELAINE SATOMI, physician; b. San Jose, Calif., Feb. 19, 1957. BS, Stanford U., 1978; MD, Med. Coll. Pa., 1982. Diplomate of Nat. Bd. Med. Examiners. Diplomate Am. Bd. Phys. Medicine and Rehab. Dir. phys. medicine and rehab. Stanford (Calif.) U. Sch. Medicine, 1985—, rehab. medicine sect. chief, 1988-90, head phys. medicine and rehab. div., 1990—, assoc. prof. dept. functional rehab., 1995—; rehab. medicine chief Palo Alto (Calif.) VA Med. Ctr., 1988—. Fellow Am. Acad. Phys. Medicine and Rehab., Am. Assn. Electromyography & Electrodiagnosis. Avocations: reading, jogging. Office: Stanford U Sch of Medicine 300 Pasteur Dr Palo Alto CA 94304-2203*

DATLOWE, DAYTON WOOD, space scientist, physicist; b. N.Y.C., Mar. 16, 1942; s. Samuel A. and Marghretta (Wood) D. m. Karen Janine Mc Caffrey, Aug. 3, 1974; children: Nicholas, Elizabeth, Peter. SB in Physics, MIT, 1964; PhD in Physics, U. Chgo., 1970. Scientist U. Calif., San Diego, 1970-76, Lockheed Martin Advanced Tech. Ctr., Palo Alto, Calif., 1976—. Contbr. articles to Jour. Geophys. Rsch., Astrophys. Jour., Solar Physics, Nuclear Instruments and Methods, Geophys. Rsch. Letters. Mem. IEEE, Am. Geophys. Union, Am. Astron. Soc. Achievements include research on X-rays and relativistic electrons from solar flares, electrons in the near-earth space environment, and X-rays from the earth's auroral zone. Office: Lockheed Martin ATC DL9-42 B255 3251 Hanover St Palo Alto CA 94304-1121

DATO, VIRGINIA MARIE, public health physician; b. Jersey City, Sept. 6, 1957; d. Steven C. and Virginia R. Dato; m. Michael Chancellor, May 17, 1986; children: David, Katherine. BA, Rutgers U., 1979; MD, U. Pitts., 1983; MPH, Columbia U., 1992. Diplomate Am. Bd. Pub. Health and Gen. Preventive Medicine; diplomate Am. Bd. Pediat. Pediatric resident Bellevue Hosp., NYU Med. Ctr., N.Y.C., 1983-86; Infectious disease fellow Children's Hosp. Mich., Detroit, 1986-88; sr. pub. health physician N.J. Dept. Health and Sr. Svcs., Trenton, 1988-97, co-dir. preventive medicine and pub. health residency, 1995-97; sr. pub. health physician Ctr. Pub. Health Practice U. Pitts., 1997—; chair topics in pub. health N.J. Dept. Health, Trenton, 1991-93; chair instnl. rev. bd. N.J. Dept. Health and Sr. Svcs., Trenton, 1995-97; co-dir. Pa. and N.E. Regional Pub. Health Tng. Project, 1998—; cons. Genesis Inc. Pa., 1998—. Mem. AMA, APHA, Am. Assn. Pub. Health Physicians (trustee 1997—, sec. 1998—), Am. Coll. Preventive medicine, Pa. Med. Soc. (mem. com. on pub. health 1998—). Office: Ctr Pub Health Practice 125 Parran Hall Pittsburgh PA 15261

DATTA, RATHIN, chemical engineer; b. Calcutta, India, Nov. 11, 1948; came to U.S., 1970; s. Amulya N. and Karuna Datta; m. Alicia Reyes, Sept. 14, 1974. BTech, Indian Inst. Tech., Kanpur, 1970; PhD, Princeton U., 1974. Engring. assoc. Merck & Co., Rahway, N.J., 1974-78; sr. engr. Exxon Rsch. & Engring. Co., Linden, N.J., 1978-82; rsch. scientist, sect. leader Corn Products/CPC Internat., Summit, Ill., 1982-87; v.p. rsch. Mich. Biotech. Inst., Lansing, Mich., 1987-92; tech. cons. Chgo., 1992—; advisor waste mgmt. and bioengring. Argonne Nat. Lab., 1992—; chief tech. officer NTEC EdSep Inc., Mt. Prospect, Ill., 1995—; mem. rsch. com. Nat. Corn Growners Assn., St. Louis, 1991-93. Mem. editl. bd. Jour. Indsl. Microbiology, Linden, N.J., 1985-90; contbr. articles to profl. jours., chpts. to books; patentee in field. Recipient Environ. Tech. of Yr. award Discover Mag., 1998, Presdl. Green Chemistry award U.S. EPA, 1998; grantee U.S. Dept. Energy, USDA, others. Mem. AAAS, AIChE (Ernest E. Thiele award 1996), Am. Chem. Soc., Soc. Indsl. Microbiology, Water Pollution Control Fedn., Inst. Food Technologists, Sierra Club. Avocations: tennis, squash, opera, sitar. Home and Office: 442 W Melrose St # 3 Chicago IL 60657-3834

DATTILO, NICHOLAS C., bishop; b. Mahoningtown, Pa., Mar. 8, 1932. Educated, St. Vincent Sem., Latrobe, Pa., St. Charles Borromeo Sem., Phila. Ordained priest Roman Cath. Ch., 1958, apptd. Eighth Bishop of Harrisburg, 1989, ordained Bishop of Harrisburg, 1990. Bishop Diocese of Harrisburg, Pa., 1990—. Home and Office: PO Box 2557 4800 Union Deposit Rd Harrisburg PA 17111-3710*

DATTNER, RICHARD, architect, educator; b. Bielsko, Poland, Sept. 12, 1937; came to U.S., 1946; s. David and Ella Dattner. Student, Archtl. Assn., London, 1957-58; BArch, MIT, 1960. Registered architect, N.Y., N.J., Fla., Pa., Conn., S.C.; cert. Nat. Coun. Archtl. Registration Bds. Pres., prin., architect Richard Dattner Archs. P.C., N.Y.C., 1964—; adj. prof. architecture Cooper Union, N.Y.C., 1962-69, CCNY, N.Y.C., 1970-80; disting. vis. prof. architecture U. Wis.-Milw., 1982; vis. design critic Columbia U., N.Y.C., Princeton (N.J.) U., Cornell U., Ithaca, N.Y., 1970-80. Author: Design for Play, 1969, Civil Architecture, 1994; inventor Streetscape modular shelters, 1972 (design award 1972), modular house constrn., Playcubes modular playground, Shelterscape modular canoples, 1996 (Design award 1996); prin. works include: Riverbank State Park, Estee Lauder Labs., 1992 Dem. Nat. Conv., Columbia U. Stadium, Asphalt Green, Aqua Ctr., N.Y.C. Prototype Intermediate Sch. Mem. adv. bd. Am. Revolution Bicentennial Commn., 1976; forum mem. White House Conf. on Children, 1970; mem. Bd. on Infrastructure and the Constructed Environment. Served with U.S. Army, 1960. Recipient Design award N.Y. State Assn. Architects, 1975, 87, 89, 93, Parks Coun. award, 1968, 72, 89, Design award Progressive Architecture Mag., 1975, Design award N.Y.C. Arts Commn., 1984, 86, 89. Fellow AIA (honor award 1971, Thomas Jefferson award 1994, Medal of Honor N.Y. chpt. 1992); mem. City Club of N.Y. (Bard award 1984, 89), Century Assn. Office: Richard Dattner Archs PC 154 W 57th St New York NY 10019-3321*

DATZ, ISRAEL MORTIMER, information systems specialist; b. N.Y.C., Feb. 11, 1928; s. A. Mark and Lillian (Barkin) D.; BS, CCNY, 1950; postgrad. U. Bergen (Norway), 1951-55; m. Gerd Elin Alme-Torkildsen, Apr. 30, 1956. Chief programming group Internat. Inst. Meteorology, Stockholm, Sweden, 1958-59; head support svcs. sect. NASA Goddard Space Flight Ctr., Greenbelt, Md., 1959-61; mathematician Army Strategy and Tactics Analysis Group, Bethesda, Md., 1961-63; acting chief div. ops. analysis Dept. Commerce Maritime Adminstrn. Washington, 1963-64; head computer div. marine engring lab. Annapolis (Md.) div. Naval Ship R & D Ctr., 1964-68, rsch. coord. math., 1968-72, tech. adv. ops. rsch. 1972-79; ind. cons., 1979-84; chief, studies and analysis, U.S. Army Engr. Sch., Ft. Leonard Wood, Mo., 1984-92; ind. cons., 1992—. Recipient summer stipend Woods Hole Oceanographic Instn., 1949, rsch. stipend The Geophysics Inst., Bergen, Norway, 1953. Fellow AAAS; mem. N.Y. Acad. Sci., Inst. Ops. Rsch. and Mgmt. Sci., Assn. Computing Machinery, Am. Def. Preparedness Assn., Am. Soc. Naval Engrs., Marine Tech. Soc., Soc. Naval Architects and Marine Engrs., U.S. Naval Inst. Author: Planning In A Military Context: An Army Perspective, Power Transmission and Automation for Ships and Submersibles; Planning Tools For Ocean Transportation. Contbr. articles to profl. jours. in U.S., Eng., Norway, Sweden, Germany. Home and Office: 1343 California Dr Rolla MO 65401-4529

DAUB, HAL, mayor of Omaha, former congressman; b. Fayetteville, N.C., Apr. 23, 1941; s. Harold John and Eleanor M. (Hickman) D.; m. Mary Mernin; children: Natalie Ann, John Clifford, Tammy Renee. BSBA, Washington U., St. Louis, 1963; JD, U. Nebr., 1966. Bar: Nebr. 1966, U.S.

Ct. Appeals (8th cir.), U.S. Ct. Customs and Patent Appeals, U.S. Supreme Ct. Assoc. Fitzgerald, Brown, Leahy, McGill & Strom, 1968-71; v.p., gen. counsel Standard Chem. Mfg. Co., 1971-80; mem. 97th-100th Congresses from 2nd Nebr. dist., 1981-1989, mem. ways and means com., subcoms. on health and social security; prin., nat. dir. fed. govt. affairs Deloitte & Touche Acctg. and Cons. Firm, 1981-94; mayor City of Omaha, 1994-97, Re-elected mayor, 1997-; pres. appointee to Nat. Adv. Coun. on Pub. Svc.; prin. Coun. for Excellence in Govt.; staff intern to U.S. Senator Roman Hruska from Nebr., 1966; elected pres. Republican Mayors and Local Elected Ofcls. of Nat. League of Cities, U.S. Conf. Mayors; chmn. pub. safety and crime prevention com. Nat. League of Cities, 1996-97, bd. dirs., 1997—. Mem. Congl. Regulatory Reform Task Force, 1981-83, Congl. Rep. Agrl. Task Force, 1981-88; co-founder Liability Ins. and Tort Reform Task Force, 1986; mem. exec. com. Rep. Nat. Congl. Com., 1981-88; co-founder, co-chmn. Budget Reform Task Force, 1981-84; jr. pres. Nebr. Founders' Day, 1971; jr. pres. Nebr. Founders' Day, 1971; mem. exec. com., bd. dirs. Combined Health Agys. Drive, 1976; pres. Douglas-Sarpy unit Nebr. Heart Assn.; bd. dirs. Metro Arts Coun., 1989-93; treas. Douglas County (Nebr.) Rep. Party, 1970-73, chmn., 1974-77; elder Presbyn. Ch. Capt. U.S. Army, 1963-68. Decorated Army Commendation medal with oak leaf cluster; named Outstanding Nebraskan, 1966; recipient Svc. award SAC, 1976, Outstanding Vol. of Yr. award Douglas-Sarpy unit Nebr. Heart Assn., 1976, Leadership awards (4) Coalition for Peace Through Strength, Guardian of Small Bus. awards (4), 1981-88, Omaha C. of C. award from minority bus., Watchdog of Treasury awards (5), 1981-88. Mem. Omaha Bar Assn., Nebr. Bar Assn., Nat. Assn. Credit Mgmt. (1st v.p. 1977), Res. Officers Assn., Am. Legion, 40 and 8, VFW, Urban League Nebr., Optimists, Masons (33d degree), Shriners, SAR, Kappa Sigma, Alpha Kappa Psi, Omicron Delta Kappa, Delta Theta Phi. Office: Office of the Mayor Omaha-Douglas Civic Ctr 1819 Farnam St Omaha NE 68183-1000

DAUB, PEGGY ELLEN, library administrator; b. Bluffton, Ohio, Oct. 15, 1949; d. Perry J. and Olive L. (Hoover) D.; m. Jeffrey H. Cooper, Dec. 13, 1975; 1 child, William P. Cooper-Daub. MusB summa cum laude, Miami U., 1972; MA, Cornell U., 1975; MSLS, U. Ill., 1980; PhD, Cornell U., 1985. Acting asst. music libr. Yale U., 1980-81, head of music tech. svcs., rare books libr. Music Libr., 1981-82; head Music Libr. U. Mich., Ann Arbor, 1982-89, head Spl. Collections & Arts Librs., 1989—; presenter Rare Books and Manuscript Sect. Pre-Conf., New Orleans, 1993, Bloomington, 1995 and others. Contbr. articles to profl. jours. Co-clk. Ann Arbor Friends Meeting, 1997—. Travel grantee Ctr. for Internat. Studies, Cornell U., 1977. Mem. ALA (Assn. Coll. and Rsch. Librs. rare books and manuscripts sect., mem. task force on interlibr. loan 1991-93, mem. preconf. program planning com. 1992-94), Music Libr. Assn. (bd. dirs. 1985-87, mem. resource sharing and collection devel. com. 1982-91), Rsch. Librs. Group (chairperson music program com. 1985-87, mem. steering com. 1982-87), Am. Musicol. Soc. (mem. coun. 1988-91, mem. coun. com. on minorities/diversity 1988-91), Phi Beta Kappa. Mem. Soc. of Friends. Office: U of Mich Spl Collections Libr 711 Graduate Libr Ann Arbor MI 48109-1205

DAUBE, PATRICIA BARRETT, health facility administrator; b. Pitts., July 12, 1943; d. James Patrick and Lena Gottlieba (Eyering) Barrett; m. Donald Gerard Daube, Apr. 17, 1971; children: Christa Ann, Donald Gerard, Jason Barrett, Jeremy Patrick. BA, LaRoche Coll., 1966; BSN, Carlow Coll., 1986. Cert. psychiat./mental health nurse. RN, psychiat. home health care Personal Touch, Pitts., 1987-89; RN, hosp. home health/mental health care Hosp. Home Health, Pitts., 1989-90; psychiat. nurse Nurses Inc., Monroeville, Pa., 1990—; staff RN Mayview State Hosp., Bridgeville, Pa., 1986-89; asst. mgr. clin. nursing Western Psychiat. Inst. and Clinic, U. Pitts. Med. Ctr., Pitts., 1989-93; nursing informatics coord. Office of Nursing Adminstrn. Western Psychiat. Inst. and Clinic, U. Pitts. Med. Ctr., 1993—; computer liaison nurse WPIC Info. Systems, 1992-93. Mem. Tri-State Computer Network. Home: 931 Lebanon Ave Pittsburgh PA 15234-2157

DAUBENAS, JEAN DOROTHY TENBRINCK, librarian, educator; b. N.Y.C.; d. Eduard J.A. and Margaret Dorothy (Schaffner) Tenbrinck; m. Joseph Anthony Daubenas, May 29, 1965. AB, Barnard Coll., 1962; grad. Am. Acad. Dramatic Arts, 1963; MA, N.Y. U., 1965; MLS, U. Ariz., 1972; PhD, U. Utah, 1986. Tchr., Beth Jacob Tchrs. Sem. Am., Bronx, 1965-66; caseworker, Dept. Social Services, N.Y.C., 1966-67; actress Boothbay (Maine) Playhouse, others, 1967-70; reference librarian Ariz. State U., Tempe, 1972-75; asst. librarian, asst. prof. library sci. Avila Coll., Kansas City, Mo., 1979-83; assoc. prof./librarian St. John's U., Jamaica, N.Y., 1983—; grad. asst. U. Utah, 1976-77. N.Y. State Regents scholar, 1958-62, U. Ariz. scholar, 1971-72. Mem. ALA, Actors Equity Assn., AAUP, Theatre Libr. Assn., Assn. Theatre in Higher Edn., Beta Phi Mu, Phi Kappa Phi. Roman Catholic. Office: St Johns U Library 8000 Utopia Pkwy Jamaica NY 11432-1343

DAUCH, RICHARD E., automobile manufacturing company executive; b. 1942. BS, Purdue U., 1964. With Gen. Motors Corp., 1964-75; group v.p. mfg. Volkswagen of Am., 1976-80; v.p. Chrysler Corp., 1980, exec. v.p. diversified ops., 1980-81, exec. v.p. stamping assembly diversified ops., 1981-84, exec. v.p. mfg., 1984-1994; pres., CEO American Axle & Mfg., 1994-97, chair, CEO, pres., 1997—. Recip. Eli Whitney Meml. Award, Soc. Mfg. Engrs., 1987; named industry leader of yr. Automotive Hall of Fame, 1997, mfr. of yr. Mich. Mfg. Assn., 1997, newsmaker of yr. Crain's Detroit Bus., 1998; recipient Ellis Island Medal of Honor, 1997. Office: American Axle & Mfg 1840 Holbrook St Detroit MI 48212-3442*

DAUENHAUER, RICHARD LEONARD, writer; b. Syracuse, N.Y., Apr. 10, 1942; s. Leonard George and Jane Grier D.; m. Nora Marks, Nov. 1973. BA in Russian, Syracuse U., 1964; MA in German, U. Tex., 1966; PhD in Comparative Lit., U. Wis., 1975. Asst. prof. comparative lit. Alaska Meth. U., Anchorage, 1969-75; staff assoc. Alaska Native Found., Anchorage, 1976-78; assoc. prof. humanities Alaska Pacific U., Anchorage, 1979-83; program dir. Sealaska Heritage Found., Juneau, 1983-97. Author: Glacier Bay Concerto, 1980, Frames of Reference, 1987; author, editor For Healing Our Spirit: Tlingit Oratory, 1990; contbr. articles to profl. jours. Recipient Govs. award Arts, State Alaska, 1989, Am. Book award Before Columbus Found., 1991; named Poet Laureate of Alaska, 1981-88; Fulbright fellow, 1966. E-mail: jfrld@uas.alaska.edu. Home: 3740 N Douglas Hwy Juneau AK 99801

DAUER, DONALD DEAN, investment executive; b. Fresno, Calif., June 1, 1936; s. Andrew and Erma Mae (Zigenman) D.; m. LaVerne DiBuduo, Jan. 23, 1971; children: Gina, Sarah. BS in Bus. Adminstrn.; postgrad., U. Wash., 1964. Loan officer First Savs. and Loan, Fresno, 1961-66, v.p., 1966-71, sr. v.p., 1971-81, exec. v.p., 1978-81; pres. Uniservice Corp., Fresno, 1976-81, Don Dauer Investments, Fresno, 1981—; pres., chief oper. officer Riverbend Internat. Corp., Sanger, Calif., 1985-89; chmn. bd. dirs. Univ. Savs. and Loan, 1991-92, acting pres., CEO, 1992; loan officer Norwest Mortgage, 1993-95; mgr. CMB Fin., 1995-96. Chmn. bd. dirs. City of Fresno Gen. Svcs. Retirement Bd., 1973-83, West Fresno Econ. and Bus. Devel. Program Bd., 1980-83; pres. bd. dirs. Cen. Calif. United Cerebral Palsy Assn., 1979-82; bd. dirs. Valley Children's Hosp. Found., Fresno, 1984-93; trustee, chmn. Valley Children's Hosp., 1987-93; bd. dirs. Youth for Christ USA, 1988-94; vice chmn. Riverbend Internat., 1985-91. Mem. Soc. Real Estate Appraisers (past pres.). Office: 2733 W Palo Alto Ave Fresno CA 93711-1110

DAUER, EDWARD ARNOLD, law educator; b. Providence, Sept. 28, 1944; s. Marshall and Shirly (Moverman) D.; m. Carol Jean Egglestone, June 18, 1966; children: E. Craig, Rachel P. AB, Brown U., 1966; LLB cum laude, Yale U., 1969. Bar: Conn. 1978, Colo. 1986. Asst. prof. law sch. U. Toledo, 1969-72; assoc. prof. law U. So. Calif., L.A., 1972-74; assoc. prof. law Yale U., New Haven, Conn., 1975-85, assoc. dean, 1978-83, dep. dean law sch., 1983-85; dean, prof. law U. Denver, 1985-90, dean emeritus, prof. law, 1991—; vis. scholar Harvard U. Sch. Pub. Health, 1996-97; of counsel Popham, Haik, Schnobrich and Kaufman, 1990-97; pres. CEJAD Aviation Corp. Author: Materials on a Nonadversarial Legal Process, 1978, Conflict Resolution Strategies in Health Care, 1993, Manual of Dispute Resolution: ADR Law and Practice, 1994 (CPr Book award 1994); contbr. articles to profl. jours. Bd. dirs. New Haven Cmty. Action Agy., 1978-81, Cerebral Palsy Found. Denver, 1989—, pres., 1992-95; founder, pres. Nat. Ctr. Preventive Law; mem. Colo. Commn. Higher Edn., 1987-91; commr. Colo. Advanced Tech. Inst., 1989-91. Recipient W. Quinn Jordan award Nat. Blood Found., 1994, Paella award Harvard Sch. Pub. Health, 1996, Sanbar award Am. Coll. Legal Medicine, 1999. Mem. Am. Law Inst., Order of Coif, U. Club, Greenwood Athletic Club. Republican. Jewish. Home: 5811 S Geneva St Greenwood Vlg CO 80111-3728 Office: U Denver Coll Law Denver CO 80220

DAUER, FRANCIS WATANABE, philosophy educator; b. Leipzig, Germany, Aug. 17, 1939; came to U.S., 1950, naturalized, 1954; s. Michael Satosi Watanabe and Dorothea W. Dauer; m. Margery Lilly Christensen, June 14, 1968 (div. Aug. 1982); children: Hilary Chisato Watahabe, Karen Aiko Watanabe; m. Teruko Motoo, Jan. 1, 1995. AB, Dartmouth Coll., 1960; MA, Harvard U., 1964, PhD, 1970; student, Oxford (Eng.) U., 1964-65. Lectr. philosophy U. Calif., Santa Barbara, 1967-69, asst. prof., 1969-75, assoc. prof., 1975-82, prof., 1982—, chmn., 1980-87, dir. edn. abroad in Japan, 1987-90; guest prof. Osaka U., Japan, 1990; vis. prof. Internat. Christian U., Japan, 1987-90. Author: Critical Thinking: Introduction to Reasoning, 1989; contbr. articles to profl. jours. Woodrow Wilson fellow, 1960; Harvard resident fellow, 1961, 62; Knox travelling fellow, 1964; U. Calif. summer faculty fellow, 1971. Mem. Am. Philos. Assn., Aesthetics Soc. Am., Hume Soc., Harvard Club So. Calif., Internat. House Japan. Office: U Calif Dept Philosophy Santa Barbara CA 93106

DAUGHENBAUGH, TERRY LEE, steel industry executive; b. Latrobe, Pa., July 20, 1939; s. Gladys Idella Hollobaugh; m. Cristine Zubaty, May 1, 1999; children: Thomas, Todd, Tracey; stepchildren: Leslie, Neil. BS, U. Pitts., 1968; postgrad., Columbia U., 1985. With Kennemetal Corp., Latrobe, Pa., 1957-58; with Latrobe (Pa.) Steel Co., 1958-92, project engr., 1968-70, melt shop supt., 1970-73, mgr. primary ops., 1973-85, gen. mgr. mfg., 1985-88, gen. mgr. primary ops. and engring., 1988-92; pres. Innovative Water Tech., Inc. divsn. Innovative Group, Latrobe, 1992; pres., owner Spl. D Co., Latrobe, 1992-96; pres., chmn. bd. dirs. Baker Pyromet, Inc., Greenville, Pa., 1994—; cons. to steel industry, 1992-96. Chmn. bd. Ea. Westmoreland Devel. Corp., Latrobe, 1995-98, chmn. transp. com., 1989—; mem. home rule commn. Borough of Latrobe, 1994-96; bd. dirs. Latrobe Area C. of C., 1995-98, Latrobe Area Devel. Coun., 1995—, Valley Players of Ligonier, 1997, Laurel Ballet, 1990-94, Westmoreland Blind Assn., 1987-89; coach, mgr., commr. Latrobe-Derry Area Teener League, 1974-84. Mem. Am. Iron and Steel Engrs., Iron & Steel Soc., Assn. Iron and Steel Engrs., Loyalhanna Watershed Assn., Latrobe Area Devel. Coun., Alumni Elec. Metal Makers Guild, Ingot Metallurgy Forum, SPRPC Citizens Adv. Panel, Touchdown Club, Teutonia Mannechor. Republican. Lutheran. Avocations: skiing, golf. Fax: (home) 724-539-0799; (office) 724-646-3104. Home: 1129 Lauralynn Dr Latrobe PA 15650-1145

DAUGHERTY, BILLY JOE, banker; b. Timpson, Tex., Jan. 31, 1923; s. David Albert and Kate (Smith) D.; m. Martha Carroum, May 14, 1942; children: Stephen Michael, Tony Fares, Kathryn Love. Grad., Tyler Comml. Coll., 1942; postgrad., So. State Coll., 1945-47; grad., So. Meth. U., 1969; student, Nat. Credit Lending Sch., U. Okla., 1969. Asst. v.p., asst. trust officer First Nat. Bank Magnolia (Ark.), 1947-52; plant acct. Republic Steel Corp., Magnolia, 1952-54; with Union Nat. Bank, Little Rock, 1954-70; v.p., cashier, sec. to bd. dirs. Union Nat. Bank, 1965-70, First State Bank & Trust Co., Conway, Ark., 1970-73; pres., dir. First State Bank & Trust Co., Conway, 1973-92; vice-chmn. bd., dir. Boatmen's Nat. Bank of Conway, 1992-96; adv. dir. Bank of Am., 1997—; bd. dirs. Conway Devel. Corp., pres., 1991-92, v.p. 1992-94; pres. adv. bd. Main Street Conway, 1988-91. Bd. dirs. Ark. Banking Sch.; mem. adv. bd. Salvation Army, 1967-70; bd. dirs. Met. YMCA, Little Rock, 1966-69; chmn. Columbia chpt. ARC, Magnolia, 1952-53; mem. budget com. United Fun Pulaski County (Ark.), 1962-65; treas. City Beautiful Com. Little Rock, 1965-67; treas. Ark. br. Am. Assn. UN, 1965-67; pres. Heart of Ark. Travel Assn., 1971-74; pres., dir. United Fund of Faulkner County, 1971-73; state treas. Radio Free Europe, 1960-72; chmn. Faulkner County Heart Fund Campaing, 1971; sec. to bd. dirs., trustee Union Nat. Found.; chmn. exec. com. conv. and vis. bur. Little Rock, 1964-66; chmn. bldg. com. Immanuel Bapt. Ch., Little Rock, 1964-66; treas. Downtown Little Rock Unltd., 1966-67, Faulkner County Centennial, Inc., 1973-74; bd. dirs. Ark. Heart Assn., 197-75, chmn. bd., 1972-73; trustee Ark. Bapt. Med. Ctr., sec.-treas., 1965-74; corp. mem. Bapt. Health Inc. (formerly Bapt. Med. Ctr.); bd. dirs. Am. Heart Assn., 1976-78, Goodwill Industries Ark., 1976-94; treas. Goodwill Industries Ark., 1984-89, 1st v.p., 1989-90, pres., 1991-92; supt. Sunday sch., chmn. bldg com. Bapt. ch., 1964-66; chmn. bd. deacons 1962-63; mem. fin. com., 1960-68, chmn. stewardship com. 1968). Served as sgt. USAAF, 1942-45, CBI. Mem. Faulkner County Fair Assn. (bd. dirs. 1972-94), Little Rock Clearing House Assn. (v.p. 1969, pres. 1965-66, sec.-treas. 1967-68), Ark. Bankers Assn. (pres. jr. bankers sect. 1950; bank dirs. adv. com. 1971-72, chmn. group II, 1977-78, bd. dirs. 1979-80), Conway C. of C. (pres. 1975), Vets. of the 68th Svc. Group China WWII (life), The Am. Legion Post #0001 Ark. (life), Little Rock Club, Conway Country Club, Western Hills Country Club (dir., sec. 1968-69), Sertoma (pres. 1961-62, gov. Ark. dist. 1962-63, bd. dirs. Midwest region 1963-64, treas. 1964-65), Lions (pres. Conway Club 1975). Home: 7 Kings Park Ln Conway AR 72032-3451

DAUGHERTY, CRAIG A., college financial aid director; b. Apr. 5, 1955. BBA, Ohio U., 1977. Asst. dir. fin. aid Ohio U., Athens, 1980-91; dir. fin. aid Kenyon Coll., Gambier, Ohio, 1991—. E-mail: daugherty@kenyon.edu. Office: Kenyon Coll Fin Aid Office Stephens Hall Gambier OH 43022

DAUGHERTY, FREDERICK ALVIN, federal judge; b. Oklahoma City, Aug. 18, 1914; s. Charles Lemuel and Felicia (Mitchell) D.; m. Marjorie E. Green, Mar. 15, 1947 (dec. Feb. 1964); m. Betsy F. Amis, Dec. 15, 1965. LL.B., Cumberland U., 1933; postgrad., Oklahoma City U., 1934-35, LL.B. (hon.), 1974; postgrad., Okla. U., 1936-37; HHD (hon.), Okla. Christian Coll., 1976. Bar: Okla. 1937. Practiced Oklahoma City, 1937-40; mem. firm Ames, Ames & Daugherty, Oklahoma City, 1946-50, Ames, Daugherty, Bynum & Black, Oklahoma City, 1952-55; judge 7th Jud. Dist. Ct., Oklahoma City, 1955-61; U.S. dist. judge Western, Eastern and No. Dists. Okla., Oklahoma City, 1961—; chief judge Western Dist. Okla., Oklahoma City, 1972-82; mem. Fgn. Intelligence Surveillance Ct., 1981-88, Temporary Emergency Ct. Appeals, 1983-93, Multi dist. Litigation panel, 1980-90; mem. codes of conduct com. U.S. Jud. Conf., 1980-87. Active local ARC, 1956—, chmn., 1958-60, nat. bd. govs., 1963-69, 3d nat. vice chmn., 1968-69; active United Fund Greater Oklahoma City, 1957—, pres., 1961, trustee, 1963—; pres. Community Coun. Oklahoma City and County, 1967-69; exec. com. Okla. Med. Rsch. Found., 1966-69. With AUS, 1940-45, 50-52. Decorated Legion of Merit with 2 oak leaf clusters, Bronze Star with oak leaf cluster, Combat Infantrymans badge; recipient award to mankind Okla. City Sertoma Club, 1962, Outstanding Citizen award Okla. City Jr. C. ofC., 1965, Disting. Alumni citation Samford U., 1974, Disting. Svc. citation Okla. U., 1973, Constn. award Rogers State Coll., 1988, Pathmakers award Oklahoma County Hist. Soc., 1991; named to Okla. Hall of Fame, 1969. Mem. Fed. Bar Assn., Okla. Bar Assn., Am. Bar Found., Sigma Alpha Epsilon, Phi Delta Phi, Men's Dinner Club (Oklahoma City) (pres. 1966-69), Kiwanis (pres. 1957, lt. gov. 1959), Masons (33 degree, sovereign grand insp. gen. in Okla. 1982-86), Shriners, Jesters. Episcopalian (sr. warden 1957).

DAUGHERTY, KENNETH EARL, research company executive, educator; b. Pitts., Dec. 27, 1938; s. Thomas Hill and Laura Elizabeth (Schuda) D.; B.S. in Chemistry, Carnegie-Mellon U., 1960; Ph.D. in Analytical Chemistry (DuPont, Shell Oil, Standard Oil, NSF fellow), U. Wash., 1964; M. Bus. Econs., Claremont Grad. Sch., 1971; m. Joan Kay Ogrosky, Dec. 22, 1961; children—Brian Earl, Kirsten Kay. Chemist, Marbon Chem.-Borg Warner, Washington, W.Va., 1960; research chemist Rohm and Haas Corp., Bristol, Pa., 1964; group leader, sr. staff Amcord, Riverside, Calif., 1966-71; assoc. prof. chemistry U. Pitts., 1971-73; dir. research and devel. Gen. Portland Inc., Dallas, 1973-77; dir. energy and materials sci. Inst. Applied Scis., North Tex. State U., Denton, 1977-79, prof. chemistry, 1979—, chmn. analytical div., 1980—, pres. KEDS Inc., KD Cons., 1977—; owner TRAC Labs., Denton, 1981—; adj. prof. chemistry U. Pitts., 1973—, N. Tex. State U., Denton, 1974—; adj. faculty Army Command and Gen. Staff Coll., 1983—; cons. in field. Served to col. AUS, 1964-66, Res., 1966—. Decorated Army Commendation medal, Army Achievement medal. Fellow Am. Inst. Chemists; mem. Research Soc. Am., ASTM, Rilem, Nat. (transp. research bd.), N.Y. acads. scis., Am. Ceramic Soc. (program chmn. 1986), Am. Chem. Soc. (chpt. pres. 1960, chmn. Dallas-Ft. Worth 1986), Applied Spectroscopy Soc., Soc. Petroleum Engrs., Soc. Plastics Engrs., Sr. Army Comdrs. Assn., Sigma Xi, Pi Kappa Alpha, Omicron Delta Epsilon, Phi Lambda Upsilon, Alpha Chi Sigma. Republican. Methodist. Clubs: Masons (32 deg.), Shriners, Rotary. Author numerous publs. in field. Patentee in field. Home: 1912 Hunskor Rd Oak Harbor WA 98277-8666

DAUGHERTY, LINDA HAGAMAN, private school executive; b. Denver, Jan. 25, 1940; d. Charles B. and Agnes May (Wall) Hagaman; m. Thomas Daniel Daugherty, Nov. 20, 1965; children: Patrick, Christina Marie. BS in Bus., U. Colo., 1961; postgrad., Tulane U., 1963-64, U. St. Thomas, 1990-91. Sr. systems analyst Lockheed Electronics NASA, Houston, 1966-73; sr. systems cons. TRW Systems Internat., Caracas, Venezuela, 1973-74; sy. systems cons. TRW Systems, L.A., 1974-75; sr. systems analyst Intercomp, Houston, 1979-80; cons. Daugherty Fin. Svcs., Inc., Katy, Tex., 1980-82, pres., 1979-91; mng. ptnr. Motivated Child Learning Ctrs., Katy, 1976—; pres. Williamsburg Country Day Sch., Katy, 1983—, Nottingham Country Day Sch., Katy, 1977—. Pres. Mason Creek Women Reps. Club, Katy, 1980; treas. Nottingham Country Civic Club, Katy, 1979; mem. adv. bd. Nottingham Country Club, 1982-85; co-founder Friends of Archaeology U. St. Thomas, pres., 1991-93; mem. Epiphany Ch. Social Works Commn.; asst. curator Archaeology Gallery, U. St. Thomas; mem. Friends of Boerne Pub. Libr., 1997—; San Antonio World Affair Coun. Mem. Houston Archeology Soc., Tex. Archeology Soc., Archaeology Inst. of Am., Boerne Women's Club. Roman Catholic. Avocations: archaeology, bridge. Office: Nottingham Country Day Sch PO Box 489 Boerne TX 78006-0489

DAUGHERTY, MARCUS VINCENT, mental health administrator; b. N.Y.C., Nov. 19, 1960; s. Fred Daugherty and Barbara (Blocker) Daugherty-Delegal; m. Linda Marie McKinzie, Nov. 23, 1990. BA, Hofstra U., 1983; MA, SUNY, New Paltz, 1991. Lic. tchr. elem. grades N.Y.C. Bd. Edn., 1997—. Rehab. counselor Vols. of Am., N.Y.C., 1988-90, coord. outreach case mgmt. svcs., 1990-91, asst. program dir., 1991-93; counselor Riverdale Mental Health Assn., Bronx, 1989—; coord. supervised residence Fedn. Employment and Guidance Svc., N.Y.C., 1993-96; clinician Montefiore Med. Ctr., Bronx, 1995-96; supr. BRC Human Svcs. Corp., N.Y.C., 1996—; mental health cons. Vols. of Am., 1993-94; com. mem. N.Y.C. Dept. Mental Health CSS Outreach Programs Com., N.Y.C., 1990-91; mentor Mentoring USA, Mount Vernon, N.Y., 1996—. Mem. ACA, Am. Mental Health Counselors Assn., Am. Psychol. Assn., Assn. Black Psychologists, N.Y. Assn. Black Psychologists, N.Y. State Psychol. Assn., Alpha Phi Alpha (exec. com. mem. Alpha Gamma Lambda chpt. 1997). Avocations: basketball, football, track, reading. Office: BRC Human Svcs Corp 91 Pitt St New York NY 10002-2512

DAUGHERTY, RICHARD ALLEN, musician, retired educator; b. Hillsdale, Ind., May 11, 1937; s. Clarence Albert and Hilda Helena (Watson) D.; m. Carolyn Kay Carpenter, May 12, 1956; children: Richard Allen Jr., Debbie Sue. MusB in Music Edn., DePaul U., 1970; MEd, Nat. Louis U., 1984; postgrad., various schs. Inter officer sales rep. Wabash Fibre Box, Chgo., 1956-63; band dir., acting dept. head Stagg H.S., Palos Heights, Ill., 1970-71; band dir. Palos Sch. Dist. 118, Palos Park, Ill., 1971-94; pvt. tchr., profl. musician, Chgo., 1994—; part-time musician, Chgo., 1956-70; guest clinician for high sch., grade schs. Woodwind performer throughout U.S. and Can., including for Henry Mancini, Tex Beneke, Andy Williams, The Osmonds, mus. shows including Hello Dolly, Mame, Fiddler on the Roof, also recs. Recipient recognition of dedication plaque Cardinal Band, Palos Park, 1979, svc. award Palos Dist. 118 Band Parents, 1994. Mem. Am. Fedn. Musicians. Avocations: golf, tennis, bicyclinb. Home and office: 390 Yorkfield Ave Elmhurst IL 60126-5318

DAUGHERTY, ROBERT MELVIN, JR., university dean, medical educator; b. Kansas City, Mo., May 2, 1934; s. Robert Melvin and Mildred Josephine (Johnson) D.; m. Sandra Allison Keller, Aug. 10, 1957; children—Robert Melvin III, Allison, Christopher. BS, Kans. U., 1956; MD, U. Kans., 1960; MS, U. Okla. Med. Ctr., 1964; PhD, U. Okla., 1965. Intern Jefferson Davis Hosp., Houston, 1960-61; resident U. Okla. Med. Ctr., Oklahoma City, 1961-63, asst. prof. physiology and medicine, 1965-66; assoc. prof. physiology and medicine Mich. State U. Coll. Human Medicine, East Lansing, 1969-71; prof., dir. Office Curriculum Implementation, 1969-76; prof. physiology and medicine U. Wyo. Coll. Human Medicine, Laramie, 1976-78; dean U. Wyo. Coll. Human Medicine, 1976-78; prof. physiology and medicine Ind. U. Sch. Medicine, Indpls., 1978-81; assoc. dean Ind. U. Sch. Medicine, 1978-81, dir. continuing med. edn., 1978-81; dean Sch. Medicine, U. Nev., 1981—; teaching scholar Am. Heart Assn., 1970-75. Mem. AMA (coun. med. edn. 1991—), LCME, Am. Physiol. Soc., Am. Heart Assn., Ctrl. Soc. for Clin. Investigation. Presbyterian. Home: 820 Marsh Ave Reno NV 89509-1945 Office: U Nev Sch Medicine Savitt Med Bldg 332 Reno NV 89557*

DAUGHERTY, TONDA LOU, special education educator; b. Aurora, Mo., Aug. 17, 1954; d. Wilbur E. McCuller and Gynith P. (Murphy) Frederick. BS in Edn., S.W. Mo. State U., Springfield, 1982; MA in Spl. Edn., U. Mo., Kansas City, 1986, EdS in Reading, 1988. Tchr. learning disabilities and behavior disorders Consolidated Sch. Dist. 4, Grandview, Mo., 1982—; ednl. cons. Perfection Form Pub. Co., Kansas City, 1990. Active PTA. Mem. ACA, Internat. Reading Assn., Coun. for Exceptional Children, Mo. State Tchrs. Assn., Phi Kappa Phi. Democrat. Roman Catholic. Avocations: swimming, reading, needlework, circuit training. Home: 9705 Oakley Ave Kansas City MO 64137-1349 Office: Conn-West Elem Sch 1100 High Grove Rd Grandview MO 64030-2473

DAUGHTON, DONALD, lawyer; b. Grand River, Iowa, Mar. 11, 1932; s. F.J. and Ethel (Edwards) D.; m. Sally Daughton; children by previous marriage: Erin, Thomas, Andrew, J.P. BSc, U. Iowa, 1953, JD, 1956. Bar: Iowa, 1956, Ariz., 1958. Asst. county atty. Polk County, Des Moines, Iowa, 1956, 1958-59; atty. Snell & Wilmer, Phoenix, 1959-64, Browder and Daughton, Phoenix, 1964-65; judge Superior Ct. of Ariz., Phoenix, 1965-67, 97—; atty. Browder Gillenwater and Daughton, Phoenix, 1967-72, Daughton Feinstein and Wilson, Phoenix, 1972-86, Daughton Hawkins and Bacon, Phoenix, 1986-88; resident mng. ptnr. Brian Cave, Phoenix, 1988-92; atty. Daughton Hawkins Brockelman Guinnan and Patterson, Phoenix, 1992-97; asst. county atty. Polk County, 1958-59 chmn. Phoenix Employees Relations Bd., 1976. Pres. Maricopa County Legal Aid Soc., 1971-73. 1st lt. JAG, USAF, 1956-58. Fellow Am. Bar Found., Ariz. Bar Found. (founder); mem. ABA (bd. govs. 1989-92, exec. com. 1991-92), State Bar Ariz. (chmn. pub. rels. com. 1980-84, jud. evaluation poll com. 1984-94), Iowa State Bar, Maricopa County Bar Assn. (bd. dirs. 1962-64), 9th Cir. Jud. Conf. (lawyer rep. 1981-84, 88), Nat. Acad. Arbitrators, Chartered Inst. Arbitrators, Univ. Club. Home: 6021 N 51st Pl Paradise Vly AZ 85253-5143 Office: Superior Ct of Ariz 201 W Jefferson St Phoenix AZ 85003-2205

DAUGHTREY, MARTHA CRAIG, federal judge; b. Covington, Ky., July 21, 1942; d. Spence E. Kerkow and Martha E. (Craig) Piatt; m. Larry G. Daughtrey, Dec. 28, 1962; 1 child, Carran. BA, Vanderbilt U., 1964, JD, 1968. Bar: Tenn. 1968. Pvt. practice Nashville, 1968, asst. U.S. atty., 1968-69, asst. dist. atty., 1969-72; asst. prof. law Vanderbilt U., Nashville, 1972-75; judge Tenn. Ct. Appeals, Nashville, 1975-90; assoc. justice Tenn. Supreme Ct., Nashville, 1990-93; circuit judge U.S. Ct. Appeals (6th cir.), Nashville, 1993—; lectr. law Vanderbilt Law Sch., Nashville, 1975-82, adj. prof., 1988-90; mem. faculty NYU Appellate Judges Seminar, N.Y.C., 1977-90, 94—. Mem. bd. editors ABA Jour., 1995—; contbr. articles to profl. jours. Pres. Women Judges Fund for Justice, 1984-85, 1986-87; active various civic orgns. Recipient Athena award Nat. Athena Program, 1991. Mem. ABA (chmn. appellate judges conf. 1985-86, chmn. jud. div. 1989-90, ho. of dels. 1988-91, standing com. on continuing edn. of bar 1992-94, commn. on women in the profession 1994-97, bd. editors ABA Jour. 1995—), Tenn. Bar Assn., Nashville Bar Assn. (bd. dirs. 1988-90), Am. Judicature Soc. (bd. dirs. 1988-92), Nat. Assn. Women Judges (pres. 1985-86), Lawyers Assn. for Women (pres. Nashville 1986-87). Office: US Ct Appeals US Customs House 701 Broadway Rm 304 Nashville TN 37203-3944*

DAUGHTREY, R. BRECKENRIDGE, city clerk. Degree in history, Old Dominion U., grad. degree in history, MPA. City clk. City of Norfolk, Va.,

1988—; overseer legis. dept. city govt., as well as divsn. archives and records mgmt.; exec. asst. mayor of Norfolk; past coord. cmty. outreach and involvement effort Nauticus, Norfolk; staff dir. commn. study of popular election of office of mayor, Norfolk. Past bd. mem. Tidewater Metro chpt. Am. Heart Assn.; past chair City of Norfolk United Way Campaign; alumnus, Leadership Hampton Rds.; vol. tutor Urban Discovery Ministry's Literacy Program; co-founder race rels. study circle, Norfolk. Mem. Internat. Inst. Mcpl. Clks., Nat. League Cities, Va. Mcpl. Clks. Assn. (past pres.), Va. Mcpl. League (past mem. policy com.), Norfolk Sister city Assn. (bd. mem., officer). Office: City Clerk 1006 City Hall 810 Union St Norfolk VA 23510-2717*

D'AUGUSTINE, ROBERT, university administrator, lawyer; b. Tacoma, Wash., Apr. 22, 1947; s. Anthony Patrick and Marie Colette; m. Marcia Morgan, June 6, 1970; children: Matthew, Allie. BA, U. Pa., 1968, MA, 1971; MBA, Rutgers U., 1982, JD, 1986. Exec. asst. to dean U. Medicine and Dentistry N.J., Newark, 1977-83, asst. v.p. acad. affairs, 1983-87, assoc. v.p. acad. adminstrn., 1987-98; assoc. v.p. faculty adminstrn. U. Medicine and Dentistry N.J., New Brunswick, 1998—. Contbr. articles to profl. jours. Co-founder, pres. Citizens for Quality Edn., Metuchen, N.J., 1988-93. With U.S. Army, 1968-70. Mem. Beta Gamma Sigma. E-mail: daugusti@umdnj.edu. Home: 7 Delmar Pl Metuchen NJ 08840

DAUKANTAS, GEORGE VYTAUTAS, counseling practitioner, educator; b. Stolzenau, Germany, Dec. 20, 1946; came to U.S., 1949; s. Ceslovas and Alexandra Daukantas. *Great-grand-uncle Simonas Daukantas (1793-1864), historian and prose writer, pioneer of Lithuanian Rennaissance, was born to a peasant family in the village of Kalvai, Samogitia. He was the first to write a history of Lithuania describing the language, people, their way of life, and religious beliefs. He wrote folk tales and proverbs and was a member of the honorable Flomat & Filaret Society. Great-uncle Theodoris Daukantas (1884-1960), was Minister of Defense of Lithuania, 1924-28. In 1991, a one-hundred Litas note was issued with his image and symbol.* AA magna cum laude, Lesley Coll., 1973; BA in Psychology, U. Mass., 1976; Cert. in Computer Opers., Control Date Inst., 1979; MA in Agy. Counseling, U. No. Colo., 1982; student, Cambridge Coll., 1998—. Cert. computer programming/ops.; nat. cert. counselor. Estate coord. St. Petersburgh, Fla., 1986-91; customer svc. rep., pc operator Applied Image Reprographics, Quincy, Mass., 1993-96; replacement tchr., substitute tchr. Boston Pub. Schs., 1997—. *Currently a graduate student candidate in counseling psychology program. Mr. Daukantas has an MA 1982 U. Northern Colorado, BA 1976 U. Massachusetts, Boston, magna cum laude 1974 Lesley College. He has a certificate from the Control Data Institute, computer programming/operations. He is pursuing national and state accreditation to become board certified as a licensed professional counselor. He has earned the National Defense Service Medal, the Army of Occupation medal (Berlin Brigade), the Army Reserve Component Achievement medal, and the Good Conduct medal. He is a member of ACA/ACES, MaHMCA, Amnesty International, 1999-2000 Who's Who in the East, life fellow and member of BAHBC.* Sgt. E-5 U.S. Army, 1964-67, USNG, 1975-82. Recipient Cert. Recognition During Cold War, U.S. Army, 1999. Mem. ACLU, Am. Counseling Assn./ACES, Am. Assn. Retired Persons, Assn. for Counselor Edn. and Supervision, Mass. Mental Health Counselor's Assn., Amnesty Internat. Democrat. Roman Catholic. E-mail: daukantas@hotmail.com. Home: 34 Mount Auburn St Apt 307 Cambridge MA 02138-6022

DAUKSHUS, A. JOSEPH, systems engineer; b. Tamaqua, Pa., Oct. 17, 1948; s. Anna N. Daukshus. BS in Aerospace Engring., Pa. State U., 1975. Devel. engr. Carl Zeiss Inc., Thornwood, N.Y., 1984-88; cons. Panasonic, Secaucus, N.J., 1988, Pratt & Whitney, E. Hartford, Conn., 1989; cons. AT&T, Largo, Fla., 1990, Somerset, N.J., 1990-91; cons. Torrington (Conn.) Co., 1990, Trecom Bus. Systems, Edison, N.J., 1990-91; systems engr. Canberra Industries, Meriden, Conn., 1991-93; sales assoc. Sears Roebuck and Co., Danbury, Conn., 1993-94; engr. EIS Internat., Stamford, Conn., 1995-96, Oxford Health Plans, Norwalk, Conn., 1996-98, Reuters, Stamford, 1998—; cons. Executone, Darien, Conn., 1994-95, NASDAQ Stock Market Inc., Trumbull, Conn., 1994-95. Mem. N.Y. Acad. Sci. Home: PO Box 8916 New Fairfield CT 06812-8916

DAUM, DAVID ERNEST, machinery manufacturing company executive; b. Pitts., July 31, 1939; s. Edward Charles and Esther (Horn) D.; m. Marilyn Nadeau, July 21, 1967; children—Anjeanette R., Matthew C. BSE, Princeton U., 1960; MBA, U. Calif., Long Beach, 1972. Sales engr. Joy Mfg. Co., Seattle and San Francisco, 1960-68; dist. mgr. Joy Mfg. Co., Mpls., 1968-70; pres. Sullair of So. Calif., Long Beach, 1970-75; v.p. Sullair Corp., Michigan City, Ind., 1975-85, Safway Steel Products, Milw., 1986-92; pres., owner Daum & Assocs., 1992—. Trustee, pres. Scaffolding, Shoring and Forming Inst. Am.; bd. dirs. Montessori Sch., Michigan City, 1970. Mem. Beta Gamma Sigma. Republican. Lutheran. Address: PO Box 4311 Roche Harbor WA 98250

DAUMAN, PHILIPPE P., telecommunications company executive. BA, Yale Coll., 1974; JD, Columbia Sch. Law, 1978. Ptnr. Shearman & Sterling, N.Y.C., 1978-93; sr. v.p., gen. counsel Viacom, N.Y.C., 1993-96, now exec. v.p., dep. chmn., also bd. dirs.; bd. dirs. Nat. Amusements, Inc., Lafarge Corp. Bd. trustees Mus. City of N.Y. Office: Viacom Inc 1515 Broadway New York NY 10036-8901

DAUPHINAIS, GEORGE ARTHUR, import company executive; b. Waterbury, Conn., Apr. 11, 1918; s. Arthur J. and Nell (Phillips) D.; m. Sarah McConnell, Dec. 27, 1942; children: Carol Joe, George William, Sarah Marie. B.S. in Mech. Engring., La. State U., 1942. Advanced engring. program Gen. Electric Co., Schenectady, 1942; engr. Gen. Electric Co., 1942-47; with H.K. Porter Co., Inc., Phila., 1947-59; successively plant engr., works mgr. H.K. Porter Co., Inc., 1947-52, v.p., gen. mgr., 1952-59; v.p. Electric Autolite Co., Toledo, 1960—; pres. Prestolite Internat. Co. div. Eltra Corp., 1964—; group v.p. Sangamo Electric Co., Springfield, 1965-76; pres. Dauphin Company. Mem. ASME, Tau Beta Pi, Sigma Alpha Epsilon. Home and Office: 218 Whitmoor Forest Ct Saint Charles MO 63304-0913

D'AURORA, JAMES JOSEPH, psychologist, consultant; b. Canton, Ohio, Feb. 10, 1949; s. James Joseph Sr. and Arsilia (Lombardi) D'A.; m. Denise Marie Linkenhoker, Dec. 28, 1974; children: Andrew David, Elizabeth Clare. BA, U. Notre Dame, 1971; MEd, Kent State U., 1974; PhD, U. Minn., 1984. Lic. psychologist, Minn., marriage and family therapist, Minn.; cert. Nat. Register Health Svc. Providers in Psychology. Pre-major adv. Coll. of Liberal Arts U. Minn., Mpls., 1974-75; intern Bach Inst., Mpls., 1975-77, staff psychologist, 1977-79; psychologist Loring Family Clinic, Mpls., 1979-81; pvt. practice Mpls., 1981-86; cons. psychologist Solstice: A Ctr. for Psychotherapy and Learning, St. Paul, 1986-89; pvt. practice St. Paul, 1989—; cons. in field, 1975—; researcher Family Renewal Ctr., Mpls., 1982-85, Golden Valley Health Ctr. Psychology Subsect., 1988-92. Lectr., lay homilist Christ the King Ch., mem. parish pastoral coun., 1991-96; interim sch. bd. Christ the King-St. Thomas the Apostle Sch., 1992, bd. dirs., 1992-96, mem. governance com., 1992. Mem. APA, Nat. Register Health Svcs. Providers in Psychology, Minn. Soc. Clin. Hypnosis, Minn Psychol. Assn. (chmn. ins. com. 1988-94), U. N.D. Alumni Assn. (candidate regional dir.), Notre Dame Club Minn. (bd. dirs. 1986-91, sec. 1987-88, v.p. 1988-89, pres. 1989-90), N.W. Athletic Club (adv. bd. club run 1997—, chairperson 1999—). Mem. Democratic Farm Labor Party. Roman Catholic. Qualifier, finisher 100th Boston marathon, 1996. Avocations: running, rock climbing, snorkeling. Home: 5536 Merritt Cir Edina MN 55436-2026 Office: 91 Snelling Ave N Ste 200 Saint Paul MN 55104-6753

DAUS, ARTHUR STEVEN, neurological surgeon; b. Louisville, Feb. 6, 1957; s. Arthur Theodore Daus Jr. and Marilyn Ann (McCord) Hanish; m. Victoria Lynn Schilla, July 10, 1982; children: Arthur S. Jr., Haley N. BS in Physics magna cum laude, Vanderbilt U., 1977; MD, St. Louis U., 1981. Diplomate Nat. Bd. Med. Examiners, Am. Bd. Neurol. Surgery; lic. physician, Ky., N.Mex., Ariz., Mo., Calif. Rotating intern in surgery U. Ky. Med. Ctr., Lexington, 1981-82, resident neurosurgeon, 1982-88; pvt. practice Midwest Neurosurgery Ctr., Joplin, Mo., 1988—; instr. cervical spine instrumentation A.M.E. Med. Co., Kansas City, Mo., 1992. Mem. Nat. Coalition of Physicians Against Family Violence, Chgo., 1994—. Named Ky. Col. State of Ky., 1985—. Mem. AMA (Physician's Recognition award 1990-94, 2 Physician's Recognition awards with spl. commendation 1993-96, 96—), So. Med. Assn., Jasper-Newton County Med. Soc., So. Neurosurg. Soc., Congress of Neurol. Surgeons, Am. Assn. Neurol. Surgeons (2 continuing edn. awards 1990-92, 93-95), Nat. Audubon Soc., Phi Beta Kappa. Republican. Roman Catholic. Avocations: chess, swimming, archery, riflery, horseback riding. Home: 5 Teal Dr Joplin MO 64804-5816 Office: Midwest Neurosurgery Ctr 1111 Mc Intosh Cir Ste 305 Joplin MO 64804-3693

DAUS, VICTORIA LYNN, nurse midwife; b. Cleve.; m. Arthur Steven Daus; 2 children. RN, Luth. Med. Ctr., Cleve., 1975; BSN, St. Louis U., 1982; MSN, U. Ky., 1987; D of Nursing, Case Western Res. U., 1996; postgrad. in nursing, Francis Payne Bolton Sch. Nursing. RN, Mo., Ohio, Ky., NSW, Australia. Nurse newborn nursery, neonatal intensive care nurse, pediatrics nurse Fairview Gen. Hosp., Cleve., 1975-78; neonatal intensive care nurse, neonatal transport nurse Royal Alexandria Hosp. for Children, Sydney, NSW, Australia, 1978-79; midwife Crown Street Women's Hosp., Sydney, 1979-80; labor and delivery nurse, postpartum nurse Deaconess Hosp., Cleve., 1980; neonatal intensive care nurse Cardinal Glennon Meml. Hosp. for Children, St. Louis, 1981-82; labor and delivery nurse Chandler Med. Ctr. U. Ky., Lexington, 1982-83; labor and delivery nurse, tchr. childbirth edn., labor and delivery charge nurse Humana Hosp., Lexington, 1983-85; coord. quality assurance Prince of Wales Hosp. for Children, Sydney, 1986; hosp. floater for coronary care, neurosurg., orthopedics and med., surg. nurse Good Samaritan Hosp., Lexington, 1985-87; clin. instr. obstetrics and pediatrics Lexington C.C., 1988. Mem. Am. Assn. Neurosci. Nurses, Am. Coll. Nurse-Midwives (cert.), Nat. Assn. Nurse Practitioners in Reproductive Health, N.Am. Nursing Diagnosis Assn., Assn. Reproductive Health Profls., Assn. Women's Health, Obstet. and Neonatal Nurses, Sigma Theta Tau. Republican. Roman Catholic.

DAUSER, KIMBERLY ANN, physician assistant; b. Detroit, Nov. 20, 1947; d. George Leonard and Jeanne (Austin) Wilkie; m. Steven Kent Dauser, Nov. 10, 1983; 1 child, Aaron Thomas. AA, Pensacola Jr. Coll., 1971; BS in Medicine, physician's asst. cert. in medicine, U. Ala., Birmingham, 1976; cert. in mgmt., Am. Mgmt. Assn., 1989; postgrad., U. West Fla., 1995—. Cert. physician's asst. Asst. mgr. Christo's, Gulf Breeze, Fla., 1966-67; teller, bookkeeper loan dept. Bank Gulf Breeze, 1967-72; med. tech. aide USN Hosp., Pensacola, 1972, physician's asst., 1972-73; physician's asst. John Kingsley, MD, Pensacola, 1976, Mountain Comprehensive Health Corp., Whitesburg, Ky., 1976-78; physician's asst. N.W. Fla. Nephrology, Pensacola, 1978-87, med. adminstr., 1987-95; med. adminstr. Nephrology Ctr. of Pensacola, Fla., 1987-95; COO Nephrology Ctr. Inc., Crestview, Pensacola, 1995—, Nephrology Ctr., Inc., Crestview, Pensacola, 1995-96, Nephrology Ctr. Assocs., Pensacola, 1995-96; regional COO, Renal Care Group Inc., Pensacola, Fla., 1996-98; COO Nephrology Ctr. Assoc. PA, 1998—. Fellow Am. Acad. Physician's Assts. (del. nat. mtg. 1978-95), Nat. Commn. on Cert. Physician's Assts., Fla. Acad. Physician's Assts. (mem. jud. com. 1979-80), Natural Wildlife Assn. Republican. Roman Catholic. Avocations: photography, antiques, reading, wildlife preservation. Office: Nephrology Ctr PA 1717 N E St Ste 403 Pensacola FL 32501-6334

DAUSSET, JEAN, immunologist; b. Toulouse, France, Oct. 19, 1916; s. Henri and Elizabeth D.; m. Rose Mayoral, Mar. 17, 1962. AB, Lycee Michelet, 1939; MD, U. Paris, 1945. Intern, then resident in internal medicine and hematology Paris Mcpl. Hosps., 1946-50; dir. lab. Nat. Transfusion Ctr., 1950-63; prof. immunohematology U. Paris, 1963-77; prof. exptl. medicine Coll. de France, Paris, 1977-87; dir. research unit on immunogenetics Hopital Saint-Louis, Paris, 1969-84; dir. Human Polymorphism Study Ctr., 1984—; researcher in field of man's histocompatibility system anbd human genome. Served to capt., World War II. Recipient Nobel prize in physiology or medicine, 1980, Honda prize Honda Found. Japan, 1987. Mem. Academie des Sciences de l'Institut de France, Am. Acad. Arts and Sci., NAS (Washington). Home: 9 rue Villersexel, 75007 Paris France Office: 27 Rue Juliette Dodu, 75010 Paris France

DAUSTER, WILLIAM GARY, lawyer, economist; b. Sacramento, Nov. 25, 1957; s. William Joe and Marianne Dauster; m. Ellen Lisa Weintraub, May 10, 1986; children: Matthew Isaac, Natanya Miriam, Emma Sophia. BA in Econs., Polit. Sci. and Internat. Rels., U. So. Calif., 1978, MA in Econs., 1981; JD, Columbia U., 1984. Bar: N.Y. 1985, U.S. Dist. Ct. (so. and ea. dists.) N.Y. 1985, D.C. 1986, U.S. Supreme Ct. 1997. Assoc. Cravath, Swaine & Moore, N.Y.C., 1984-86; chief counsel com. on budget U.S. Senate, Washington, 1986-94, acting staff dir., chief counsel, 1994, Dem. chief of staff, chief counsel, 1995-97, Dem. dep. staff dir., gen. coun. com. labor/human resources, 1997, Dem. chief of staff, chief counsel, 1997-98; counselor Wellstone Pres. Exploratory Com., 1998—. Author: Congressional Budget Act Annnotated, 1990, Budget Process Law Anntated, 1991, 1993; editor-in-chief Columbia Jour. Law and Social Problems, 1983-84; contbr. articles to profl. jours. Bd. visitors Columbia Law Sch., 1992—. Recipient Order of Palm, 1978; U. So. Calif. Trustee scholar, 1974, Harlan Fiske Stone scholar, 1982-84. Mem. ABA, D.C. Bar Assn., N.Y. Bar Assn., Skull and Dagger, Blue Key, Phi Beta Kappa, Phi Kappa Phi. Democrat. Jewish. Home: 9713 Connecticut Ave Kensington MD 20895-3528*

DAUTEL, CHARLES SHREVE, retired mining company executive; b. Cleve., Apr. 5, 1923; s. Robert Poe and Frances (Shreve) D.; m. Isabell Francis Brown, June 11, 1947; children: Charles Warren, Louis Craig. BSC, Ohio U., 1948; JD, U. Cin., 1952. Bar: Ohio 1952. With Nichols, Wood, Marx & Ginter, Cin., 1952-55, Eagle-Picher Industries, Inc., Cin., 1955-88; asst. sec., asst. gen. counsel Eagle-Picher Industries, Inc., 1958-70, sec., 1970-87, v.p., 1980-87. With AUS, 1942-46. Mem. Phi Delta Theta, Phi Delta Phi. Club: Hidden Valley Lake Country. Home: 1448 Brookridge Circle Dr Lawrenceburg IN 47025-9332

DAUTEN, DALE ALAN, newspaper columnist; b. Fairfield, Iowa, Sept. 30, 1950; s. Joel John and Jeri (Muck) D.; m. Sandy Kelley; children: Hilary, Trevor, Joel. BS, Ariz. State U., 1971, MS, 1972; postgrad., Stanford U., 1972-73. Rsch. analyst AMERCO, Phoenix, 1972-74; rsch. mgr. Armour-Dial Corp., Phoenix, 1974-75; v.p. Hollander Assn., Atlanta, 1975-80; owner, founder Rsch. Resources, Atlanta and L.A., 1980-88; columnist King Features, N.Y.C., 1992—; cons., Tempe, Ariz., 1988—; syndicated columnist The Corporate Curmudgeon, 1992—, Kate & Dale Talk Jobs, 1996—. Author: Quitting, 1980, Taking Chances, 1986, The Max Strategy, 1996, The Gifted Boss, 1999. Author: Quitting, 1980, Taking Chances, 1986, The Max Strategy, 1996. Mediator State Atty. Gen., Phoenix, 1992—; commr. Tempe Planning and Zoning Commn., 1993—; v.p., bd. dirs. Tactile Mus. for the Blind, Tempe, 1995—. E-mail: dale@dauten.com. Office: c/o King Features 235 E 45th St New York NY 10017-3305

DAVATZES, NICKOLAS, broadcast executive; married; 2 children. BA, St. John's U., M. Various exec. positions Xerox Corp., 1965-75, v.p. sales and mktg., 1975-77; pres. Intext Comm. Sys., 1978-80; pres., CEO A&E TV Networks, N.Y.C., 1983—; Mem. adv. bd. Colls. Bus. Adminstrn. St. John's U.; bd. govs. Banff TV Festival. Founder Conn. Found. Childhood Leukemia. Formerly with USMC. Recipient Hist. Found. Heritage award USMC, Chevalier des Arts et Lettres French Govt., 1992, Pres.'s award Cable TV Pub. Affairs Assn, 1996, Vanguard award Cable TV Adminstrn. and Mktg. Soc., 1996; co-recipient Salute to Freedom award USS Intrepid Found., 1995. Mem. Brit. Acad. Film and TV Arts (east coast, trustee), Nat. Cable TV Assn. (Vanguard award 1994), Nat. Acad. Cable Programming. *

D'AVELLA, BERNARD JOHNSON, JR., publishing company executive, lawyer; b. Orange, N.J., Jan. 6, 1945; s. Bernard Johnson and Aida Santa (Magliacane) D'A.; m. Elaine Anne Benucci, Aug. 11, 1973; children: Bernard J. III, Anthony N. Student, Princeton U., 1962-66; AB, Rutgers U., 1970; JD, U. Penn., 1973. Bar: N.J. 1973, U.S. Dist. Ct. N.J. 1973. Assoc. atty. Hannoch Weisman, Newark, 1973-78; ptnr., dir. Hannoch Weisman, Newark, Roseland, Trenton, N.J., 1978-98; mng. ptnr., dir. Hannoch Weisman, Newark, Roseland, Trenton, 1980-91; pres., COO Prudent Pub. Co. and The Gallery Collection, Ridgefield Park, N.J., 1998—. Class pres. Princeton U., mem. exec. com., 25th reunion com., former chmn. Maclean fellow sel. com.; treas., trustee The Joint Connection; chmn. emeritus bd. dirs. N.J. State Opera; chmn. ethics commn. Borough of Roseland, N.J.; chmn. Juvenile Conf. Com. Twp. of Essex Fells, N.J. Sgt. U.S. Army, 1967-69. Decorated Bronze Star, Bronze Star with oak leaf cluster, Air medal, Army Commendation medal. Mem. ABA, N.J. State Bar Assn., Assn. Fed. Bar, Essex County Bar Assn., Princeton Alumni Assn. Essex County (exec. com., alumni schs. com., past pres.), Essex Fells Country Club, Fellsbrook Paddle and Tennis Club, Mantoloking Yacht Club. Avocations: opera, house restoration and design, antiques and classic automobiles, tennis, golf. Home: 105 Rensselaer Rd Essex Fells NJ 07021-1400 Office: Prudent Pub Co Inc 65 Challenger Rd Ste 2 Ridgefield Park NJ 07660-2111

DAVENNY, WARD LESLIE, artist, educator; b. Hartford, Conn., July 27, 1951; s. Ward McConnell and Ena Grace (Nelson) D.; Sara L. Frankel, May 9, 1987; Maya Caitlin, Ivan. BFA in printmaking, San Francisco Art Inst., 1977; MFA in printmaking and painting, Yale U., 1982. Tchg. asst. Yale U., 1981-82, Yale Summer Sch. Music and Art, Norfolk, Conn.; asst. printer Prudential Press Old Lyme (conn.) Artworks, 1982-83; lectr. printmaking and drawing U. Conn., Storrs, 1985-87, asst. prof., 1988; asst. prof. U. Hawaii at Manoa, Honolulu, 1988-92; asst. prof. Dickinson Coll., Carlisle, Pa., 1992-94, assoc. prof., 1994—; instr. beginning and advanced Intaglio and Lithography, George Walter Vincent Smith Art Mus., Springfield, Mass., 1983-84, Northampton (Mass.) Printmaking Workshop, 1983-84, printmaking Assumption Coll., Worchester, Mass., 1985, Worchester Mus. Art, 1985, figure drawing, Intaglio, Wesleyan U. Grad. Studies Program, Middleton, Conn., 1987; guest lectr. U. N.H., 1984, R.I. Coll., 1986, Mt. Holyoke Coll. South Hadley, Mass, 1987, Hampshire Coll, Amherst, Mass., 1987, Yale U. Summer Program, 1988, Wright State, Dayton, Ohio, 1992, Pa. Sch. Art and Design, Lancaster, 1993, Gettysburg (Pa.) Coll, 1994, Pa. State U., Univ. Park, 1995. One-man shows include Thorne's Gallery, Northampton, Mass., 1980, Mary Ryan Gallery, N.Y.C., 1984, 86, 89, 93,. Ford Found Materials grantee, Yale U., 1980, Mass. Arts Lottery grantee, 1983, U. Conn. Rsch. Found. grantee, 1987, U. Hawaii Rsch. Coun. grantee, 1989, R&D grantee Dickinson Coll., 1993; fellow Nat. Endowment for Arts, 1985, 93-94. Mem. Honolulu Printmakers (v.p. 1989),. Office: Dickinson Coll Weiss Ctr Carlisle PA 17013

DAVENPORT, ALAN GARNETT, civil engineer, educator; b. Madras, India, Sept. 19, 1932; came to Can., naturalized; s. Tom and May Davenport; m. Sheila Rand Smith, Apr. 13, 1957; children—Thomas Sidney, Anna Margaret, Andrew Hope, Clare Rand. BA, Cambridge U., Eng., 1954, MA, 1958; MASc, U. Toronto, Ont., Can., 1957, DEng (hon.), 1989; PhD, U. Bristol, Eng., 1960; D. in Applied Sci. (hon.), U. Louvain, Belgium, 1979; D. in Tech. (hon.), Tech. U. Denmark, 1982; DSc (hon.), McGill U., Montreal, Que., Can., 1983, U. Toronto, Ont., 1989; DEng (hon.), Waterloo (Ont., Can.) U., 1986; DSc (hon.), U. Guelph, Ont., 1993, U. La Plata, Argentina, 1993; DEng, Carlton U., 1996, U. Bristol, 1998. Lectr. U. Toronto, Ont., Can., 1955-57; research officer Nat. Research Council, Ottawa, Ont., Can., 1957-58; asst. prof., then prof. U. Western Ont., London, Can., 1960—, dir. Boundary Layer Wind Tunnel Lab., 1960—; dir. Ctr. for Studies in Constrn., 1990—; cons. on numerous bldgs., bridges and towers, including World Trade Ctr., N.Y.C., CN Tower, Toronto, Sears Bldg., Chgo., Sunshine Skyway Bridge, Fla., Hong Kong and Shanghai Bank Bldg., Hong Kong, Bank of China Bldg., Hong Kong, Great Belt Bridge, Denmark, Normandy Bridge, France. Editor: Can Jour. Civil Engring., 1974-79, mem. editorial bd., 1979-81. Chmn. Can. nat. com. UN-Internat. Decade for Natural Disaster Reduction, 1993—. Recipient Nobel prize, 1963, Cancam medal Cancam 83, Saskatoon, Sask., Can., 1983, Queen Elizabeth medal, 1952-77, gold medal Inst. Structural Engrs., 1987, Oleg A. Kerensky medal, 1988, Ernest C. Manning award of distinction, 1990, Can. Confedn. medal, 1967-92, Killam prize, 1993, Can. gold medal for sci. and engring. Natural Sci. and Engring. Rsch. Coun. Can., 1994, Gold ribbon d'Or award French Autoroute Authority for contbns. to design of Normand bridge and Irois bridge, Hellmuth prize for rsch. U. Western Ont. Fellow Can. Soc. Civil Engring. (A.B. Sanderson award 1985), Engring. Inst. Can. (Duggan medal 1960, Gzowski medal 1963, 78, Julian C. Smith medal), Royal Soc. Can. (Rutherford lectr. 1988); mem. Am. Meteorol. Soc., Can. Meteorol. Soc. (prize in Applied Meterology 1965), ASCE (State of Art Civil Engring. award 1973, Can-Am Civil Engring. award 1977), Assn. Profl. Engrs. Ont. (Silver medal 1977, Bell Canada Forum award, 1992), Internat. Assn. Bridge and Structural Engring. (Award of Merit), Internat. Assn. Shell Structures (Tsubai prize 1997), Nat. Acad. Engring. (fgn. assoc.), Can. Acad. of Engring. (elected founding mem., pres.), Royal Acad. of Engring. (fgn. mem.). Avocations: sailing; squash; tennis. Home: 412 Lawson Rd, London, ON Canada N6G 1X8 Office: U Western Ont Boundary Layer, Wind Tunnel Lab Engring Sci, London, ON Canada N6A 5B9

DAVENPORT, ALFRED LARUE, JR., manufacturing company executive; b. Upland, Calif., May 6, 1921; s. Alfred Larue and Nettie (Blocker) D.; m. Darrow Ormsbee Beazlie, May 16, 1950 (div. 1953); m. Jean Ann Given, June 21, 1957 (wid. Apr. 1990); children: Lawrence, Terisa, Lisa, Nancy; m. Inez Bothwell, Aug. 8, 1993. Student, Chaffey Jr. Coll., Ontario, Calif., 1940; BE in Indsl. Engring., U. So. Calif., 1943. Weight engring. Lockheed Aircraft, Burbank, Calif., 1940-41; ptnr. Pacific Traders, L.A., 1946-48; founder, pres. Pactra Industries, Inc., L.A., 1947-79; owner Davenport Internat., Ltd., Encino, Calif., 1979—; pres., founder Trans Container, Inc., Upland, Calif., 1970-79; pres., owner Pactra Hobby, Inc., Encino, Calif., 1983—, Davenport Export-Import, Inc., Encino, Calif., 1982-93; cons. Plasti-Kote, Inc., Medina, Ohio, 1985-87; pres. Pactra Coatings Inc., Hobby Div., Upland, 1985-89; mgr. craft div. Plasti-Kote Inc., Medina, Ohio, 1989-92; bd. dirs. R.C. Dudek, Inc., Oxnard, Calif.; stockholder, v.p., mktg. dir. Enviroman Inc., 1994-97; dir. mktg. Therap Ease Products, 1996—. Lt. USN, 1943-46. Recipient Blue Key, U. So. Calif., L.A., 1942. Mem. So. Calif. Hobby Industry Assn. (sec. 1959-62), Hobby Industry Assn. Am. (dir. 1961-64), Young Pres. Orgn. (L.A. chpt.), World Bus. Coun. (bd. dirs. 1980-84), Woodland Hills Country Club (treas. 1981-83), Balboa Basin Yacht Club, Travelers Century Club, Sigma Phi Epsilon (v.p. 1954-81, alumni bd. dirs. 1955-75, alumni house bd. dirs. 1997—, Alumni of Yr. award 1975, Disting. Bro. award 1979, Alumni Hall of Fame 1997). Republican. Congregationalist. Avocations: tennis, golf, power yachting. Home: 5330 Dubois Ave Woodland Hills CA 91367-6017 Office: Davenport Internat-Pactra Hobby Prod Inc Therap-Ease Prod 18075 Ventura Blvd Encino CA 91316-3517

DAVENPORT, ANN ADELE MAYFIELD, home care agency administrator; b. New Orleans, Nov. 12, 1941; d. Henry Louis and Myrtie Iola (Cason) Mayfield; m. John Wayne Davenport, June 18, 1966; children: Steven Lyle, Daniel Ryan, Elaine Adele. BA, Southeastern La. Coll., 1963; MA in Edn., George Peabody C., 1965; MA in Sociology, Tex. Tech. U., 1971. Tchr. various schs., 1963-70; instr. of sociology Tex. Tech. U., Lubbock, 1970-74, James Madison U., Harrisonburg, Va., 1981-82, Ga. So. Coll., Statesboro, 1982-84; 5th grade tchr. Bulloch county Schs., Statesboro, Ga., 1985-87; gerontology project coord. Dept. of Nursing Ga. So. Coll., 1987-88; project dir. Sr. Companion Program Ctr. for Rural Health and Rsch., Ga. So. U., Statesboro, 1988-93; instr. dept. health sci. edn. Ga. So. Coll., Statesboro, 1993-95; exec. dir. Ogeechee Home Health Agy., Statesboro, 1995—. Editor various newsletters, 1987—. Bd. dirs. Citizens Against Violence, Statesboro, 1987-88, Habitat for Humanity, 1990—; pres. Coun. on Children and Parents, Statesboro, 1988-89, 93-94; mem. steering com. Bulloch County Commn. on Human Svcs., 1989—; mem. adminstrv. bd. dirs., coun. on ministries, nominating com. Pittman Park United Meth. Ch.; pres. Ogeechee Wellness Coun., 1992—; bd. dirs. Ogeechee Home Health Agy., 1989-93. Mem. Ga. Rural Health Assn. (sec. 1988-89, editor state newsletter 1989—), So. Sociol. Soc., Ga. Gerontol. Assn., Ga. Sociol. Assn., AAUW (newsletter editor Statesboro 1987-89), Am. Soc. on Aging, Nat. Coun. on the Aging, Am. Rural Health Assn. Avocations: tennis, reading. Home: 1 Greenwood Ave Statesboro GA 30458-5032 Office: Homebound Svcs Inc PO Box 2473 Statesboro GA 30459-2473

DAVENPORT, BETTY, special education educator; b. Birmingham, Ala., Feb. 15, 1953; d. William Harry and Edna Earl (Staggs) Davenport; children: David, Daniel. Dental technician, Carrer Acad., Atlanta, 1973; BS in Spl. Edn. with honors, Auburn U., Montgomery, 1992, M in Mild Learning Handicapped, 1994. Cert. spl. edn. tchr., Ala. Dental technician Clanton (Ala.) Dental Lab., 1973-86; tchr. asst. Clanton Elem. Sch., 1988—, tchr. spl. edn., 1992—; tchr. emotionally conflicted Children's Harbor (Ala.) Sch.; edn. coord. Cmty. Intensive Treatment for Youth, Clanton, Ala., 1994—. Sec. Thorsby (Ala.) Band Boosters, 1989-91; parade organizer Thorsby Swedish Heritage Com., 1992-93. Mem. NEA, Ala. Edn. Assn., Coun. for Exceptional Children, Kappa Delta Phi, Phi Kappa Phi. Baptist. Avocations:

crafts, playing piano, singing, special olympics. Home: 1801 9th St N Clanton AL 35045-2478

DAVENPORT, BILL, sculptor; b. Greenfield, Mass., 1962. BFA in Sculpture, R.I. Sch. Design, 1986; MFA in Sculpture, U. Mass., 1990. One-man shows include Student Uniion Gallery, U. Mass., Amherst, 1990, Wierzbowski Gallery, Houston, 1993, Inman Gallery Viewing Room, Houston, 1994, 95, 99, Cristinerose Gallery, N.Y.C., 1997, Good/Bad Art Collective, Denton, Tex., 1997, Sala Diaz, San Antonio, 1998, Angstrom Gallery, Dallas, 1999; group shows include Wheeler Gallery, Providence, R.I., 1984, Helme House Gallery, Kingston, R.I., 1985, Bristol (R.I.) Art Mus., 1986, Hampden Gallery, U. Mass., Amherst, 1988, 89, Art league Houston, 1991, Robinson Gallery, Houston, 1991, Cullen Ctr. Gallery, Houston, 1992, 94, Graham Gallery, Albuquerque, 1992, Allen Ctr. Gallery, Houston, 1992, Hillwood Art Mus., L.I. Univ., 1993, Inman Gallery, Houston, 1993, 94, 96, 98, Whitney Mus. Am. Art, 1993, Conduit Gallery, Dallas, 1994, Lambert Hall, Houston, 1994, Ctr. Gallery, Bucknell U., Lewisburg, Pa., 1995, Lawndale Art Performance Ctr., Houston, 1995, U. Tex., San Antonio, 1995, San Antonio Mus. Art, 1995, Spanish Kitchen Gallery, L.A., 1996, Barry Whistler Gallery, Dallas, 1996, Cristinerose Gallery, N.Y.C., 1997, Arlington (Tex.) Mus. Art, 1997, Angstrom Gallery, Dallas, 1997, Austin (Tex.) Mus. Art, 1998, Smart Mus. Art, U. Chgo., 1998, City Gallery Chastain, Atlanta, 1998, Galveston (Tex.) Arts Ctr., 1998, Kohler Arts Ctr., 1999, Weatherspoon Art Gallery, U. N.C., 1999, Contemporary Art Collective, Las Vegas, 1999. Core fellow Mus. Fine Arts, Houston, 1990-92; Individual Artist grantee Cultural Arts Coun. Houston Harris County, 1996, Louis Comfort Tiffany grantee, 1997. Office: c/o Inman Gallery 1114 Barkdull Houston TX 77006

DAVENPORT, C. W., historic site director; b. Seguin, Tex., Sept. 3, 1940. Chief warrant officer USCG, 1959-87; numerous positions Battleship Texas State Hist. Site, Laporte, Tex., 1987-93, ship's mgr., 1993—. Office: Battleship Texas State Hist Site 3527 Battleground Rd La Porte TX 77571-9773*

DAVENPORT, DAVID, university president, lawyer; b. Sheboygan, Wis., Oct. 24, 1950; s. E. Guy and Beverly J. (Snoddy) D.; m. Sally Nelson, Aug. 13, 1977; children—Katherine, Charles, Scott. B.A., Stanford U., 1972; J.D., U. Kans., Lawrence, 1977. Bar: Calif. 1977, U.S. Dist. Ct. (so. dist.) Calif., 1977. Assoc. Gray, Cary, Ames & Frye, San Diego, 1977-78; min. Ch. of Christ, San Diego, 1979; law prof. Pepperdine U., Malibu, Calif., 1980—, gen. counsel, 1981-83, exec. v.p., 1983-85, pres., 1985—. Contbr. articles to profl. jours.; contbr. to Fed. Antitrust Law, 1985. Mem. Adminstrv. Conf. of U.S., Washington, 1984-86; bd. overseers Hoover Inst., Stanford U.; bd. dirs. L.A. World Affairs Coun., Nat. Legal Ctr. for Pub. Interest, Washington. Mem. Mchts. and Mfrs. Assn. Calif. (bd. dirs. 1985—), Am. Assn. Pres. of Ind. Colls. and Univs. (bd. dirs. 1985—, pres.), Young Pres. Orgn., Calif. C. of C. (bd. dirs.), Order of Coif. Republican. Office: Pepperdine U Office of President 24255 Pacific Coast Hwy Malibu CA 90263-0002*

DAVENPORT, DOROTHY DEAN, retired nurse; b. Grandview, Idaho, Sept. 29, 1924; d. William Christian and Frances Beatrice (Campbell) Forcher; m. Richard Ellis Davenport, May 26, 1946 (dec. May 1982); children: Robert Ray, William Lee, Gary Edward, James Ellis. Student, Walla Walla Coll., 1942-44; ADN, Loma Linda U., 1946, 49-50. RN, W.Va. Office nurse Corona, Calif., 1946-49; nursing educator Jengre (Nigeria) Hosp., 1956-58; home health nurse Appalachian OH-9, Bluefield, W.Va., 1984-86, clinic charge nurse, 1986-89, health edn. tchr., 1989-91, nutrition counselor WIC program, 1995-98; ret. Appalachian OH-9, Bluefield; tchr. courses in field, 1998-99. Author: Who Found Klippy and Other Stories, 1960, His Guiding Hand, 1993. Trustee, mem. conf. com., mem. fin. com. Mountain View Conf. of Seventh-day Adventists, Parkersburg, W.Va., 1993—; bd. dirs. Valley View Seventh-day Adventist Ch., Bluefield, 1977—. Avocations: walking, nature crafts, bird watching, gardening, music, landscaping. Home: RR 2 Box 383-bb Bluefield WV 24701-9676 Office: Appalachian OH-9 RR 2 Box 382 Bluefield WV 24701-9648

DAVENPORT, GERALD BRUCE, lawyer; b. Adrian, Mich., May 17, 1949; s. Bruce Nelson and Mildred Louise (Avis) D.; m. RoxAnn Ferguson, Dec. 27, 1975; children: Jonathan Gerald, Christopher Bruce, Timothy Charles. AB, U. Mich., 1971; JD, U. Tex., 1975. Bar: Tex. 1975, Okla. 1993. Pvt. practice Law Office of Gerald B. Davenport, Cedar Park, Tex., 1975-77; atty. Milchem Inc., Houston, 1977-81, Baker Hughes Prodn. Tools Inc., Houston, 1981-87; sr. atty. Baker Hughes Inc., Houston, 1987-88; gen. atty. environ. law Tex. Ea. Corp., Houston, 1988; atty. Browning-Ferris Industries, Houston, 1988-89, mgr. environ. law sect., 1989-92; asst. gen. counsel environ. law Mapco Inc., Tulsa, 1992-94; of counsel McKinney, Stringer & Webster, P.C., Tulsa, 1994-95; dir. Davenport & Williams, P.C., Tulsa, 1995-96; shareholder Hall, Estill, Hardwick, Gable, Golden & Nelson, P.C., Tulsa, 1996—. Contbr. articles to profl. jours. Mem. ABA, State Bar Tex. (environ. law sect.), Okla. Bar Assn. (environ. law sect.), Houston Bar Assn. (chmn. environ. law sect. 1992). Republican. Office: Hall Estill Hardwick Gable Golden & Nelson PC 320 S Boston Ave Ste 400 Tulsa OK 74103-3704

DAVENPORT, GWEN (MRS. JOHN DAVENPORT), author; b. Colon, C.Z., Oct. 3, 1910; d. James Farquharson and Gwen (Wigley) Leys; m. John Davenport, Feb. 5, 1937; children: Christopher, John Farquharson, Juliet Rathbone. AB, Vassar Coll., 1931. Author: A Stranger and Afraid, 1943, Return Engagement, 1945, Belvedere; motion picture prodn. Sitting Pretty, 1947, Family Fortunes, 1949, Candy for Breakfast, 1950, The Bachelor's Baby, 1957, The Wax Foundation, 1961, Great Loves in Legend and Life, 1964, Time and Chance, 1993; Contbr. short stories to nat. mags. Home: 308 Penruth Ave Louisville KY 40207-1833 *Every solution creates a new problem.*

DAVENPORT, HORACE WILLARD, physiologist; b. Phila., Oct. 20, 1912; s. Horace Willard and Elizabeth (Langendorf) D.; m. Virginia Dickerson, Feb. 1, 1945 (dec. Mar. 1968); 2 sons; m. Ingeborg L. Epstein, Aug. 15, 1969. B.S., Calif. Inst. Tech., 1935, Ph.D., 1939; B.A., U. Oxford, Eng.; B.A. (Rhodes scholar 1935-38), 1937, B.Sc., 1938, D.Sc., 1961. Instr. physiology U. Pa. Med. Sch., Phila., 1941-1943; instr. physiology Harvard Med. Sch., 1943- 45; prof., head dept. physiology U. Utah Med. Sch., 1945-56; prof. dept. physiology U. Mich., Ann Arbor, 1956—; chmn. dept. U. Mich., 1956-78, William Beaumont prof., 1978-83, prof. emeritus, 1983—; vis. prof. Mayo Found., 1962-63. Contbr. to articles on med. history to profl. jours. Recipient Friedenwald medal Am. Gastroent. Assn., 1980. Mem. NAS, Am. Physiol. Soc. (pres. 1961-62), Brit. Soc. Gastroenterology (hon.). Home: 3850 Galleria Woods Dr Birmingham AL 35244-1098

DAVENPORT, JAMES GUYTHON, minister; b. Columbia, N.C., Sept. 15, 1932; s. Llewellyn Harrison and Lillian Mae (Brickhouse) D.; m. Bethany Lavinia Sawyer, Nov. 23, 1956 (div. July 1983); 1 child, Kathleen Nina Davenport Ingram; m. Jacqueline Ann Wilson, Aug. 5, 1983; children: Daniel, Jeffrey, Jack, Jerry. AA, Chowan Coll., 1963; BA, Miss. Coll., 1965; MDiv, Southeastern Bapt. Theol. Sem., 1968; Clin. Pastoral Edn. Cert., Cen. State Hosp., Milledgeville, Ga., 1971; DD, Bethany Theol. Sem., 1991. Ordained to ministry So. Bapt. Conv., 1963; cert. hosp., instnl., mil. chaplain. Pastor Holy Grove Bapt. Ch., Powellsville, N.C., 1963, Siloam Bapt. Ch., Windsor, N.C., 1965-68, Fellowship Bapt. Ch., Ettrick, Va., 1968-70, 71-83, Dinwiddie (Va.) Bapt. Ch., 1983-85, McKenney (Va.) Bapt. Ch., 1983-95; ret.; substitute tchr. Dinwiddie County Sch. Bd., 1985-95; chaplain CAP, Hopewell, Va., 1969-83, Ettrick-Matoaca rescue Squad, 1973-74, Petersburg (Va.) Correctional Ctr., 1974-83; staff counselor Southside Area Counseling Svc., Petersburg, 1968-91. Vol. fireman St. Brides Fire Dept., Chesapeake, Va., 1959-61; mem. Ettrick-Matoaca Rescue Squad, 1968-74, Planning Commn., McKenney, 1989-94; election ofcl. Dinwiddie County, 1985-95; chaplain Petersburg FOP, 1975-80 (Outstanding Svc. plaque 1977); election official Buckingham County, 1996. Mem. Petersburg Bapt. Assn. (sec. 1974). Home: RR 1 Box 5160 Dillwyn VA 23936-8752 *I have found that all too often when people want to change their life for the better they depend only on their own will power and never realize that God has given us the power of the Holy Spirit to work with ours in our transformation.*

DAVENPORT, JAMES ROBERT, retired city official, retired utility executive; b. Roanoke, Va., Jan. 8, 1930; s. Henry Ashby and Mary Bruce (Doss) D.; m. Catherine Lee Wright, July 14, 1956; children: James Robert Jr., Catherine D. BA in Econs., Roanoke Coll., Salem, Va., 1952; MBA, U. N.C., 1955. Adminstrv. asst. Appalachian Power Co. (now Am. Elec. Power), Roanoke, 1955-63, area devel. cons., 1963-69; area mgr. Appalachian Power Co. (now Am. Elec. Power), Martinsville, Va., 1969-77; divsn. mgr. Appalachian Power Co. (now Am. Elec. Power), Lynchburg, Va., 1977-91; ret. Mem. City Coun., Lynchburg, 1993-98, vice mayor, 1995-98, chmn. fin. and planning com., 1995-98; bd. dirs. Region 2000, Lynchburg, 1994-98; dir. CentraHealth, Inc., Lynchburg, 1987—, chmn. bd. trustees 1990-93; dir. Va. Bapt. Hosp., Lynchburg, 1982-87, treas., 1985-86; mem. Indsl. Devel. Authority, City of Lynchburg, 1982-93, 98—, chmn., 1985-93; dir. Lynchburg Area Devel. Corp., 1977—, Ctrl. Va. Industries, Lynchburg, 1979-83, chmn. bd., 1980; dir. Presbyn. Home, Inc., Lynchburg, 1980-83, vice chmn. bd., 1983; mem. Lynchburg Rep. City Com., 1993—; bd. dirs. United Way of Ctrl. Va., Lynchburg, 1980-83, Daily Bread, Lynchburg, 1988-92, Ctrl. Lynchburg, Inc., 1980-82, Jr. Achievement, Lynchburg, 1980-83; mem. econ. and tech. devel. adv. com. Ctrl. Va. C.C., Lynchburg, 1988; chmn. Downtown Action Commn., Lynchburg, 1979-82; pres. Southeastern Cmty. Devel. assn., Roanoke, 1976; chmn. United Way of Martinsville and Henry County, Va., 1976. 1st Lt. U.S. Army, 1952-55. Recipient Outstanding Citizen award NCCJ, 1990. Mem. Greater Lynchburg C. of C. (pres. 1980-81, econ. devel. dept. head 1979-80, exec. adv. coun. 1982-86, Team 2000 1985-88, named Pro-Opera Civica 1988), Rotary Club of Lynchburg (v.p. 1983-84), Boonsboro Country Club. Presbyterian (elder). Avocations: tennis, church activities, travel. Home: 2131 Burnt Bridge Rd Lynchburg VA 24503-2215

DAVENPORT, JANET LEE, real estate saleswomen, small business owner; b. Napa, Calif., Dec. 10, 1938; d. George Perry and Stella Dolores (Ramalho) Gomez; m. Bingo George Wesner, Aug. 4, 1957 (July 1978); children: Bing George, Diane Estelle; m. Marvin Eugene Davenport, Jan. 13, 1979. Student, U. Calif., Davis, 1956-57, Nat. Jud. Coll., 1975-79. Co-owner, operator Bar JB Ranch, Benicia, Calif., 1960-71, Lovelock, Nev., 1971-78; owner, mgr. Wesner Bookkeeping Svc., Lovelock, 1973-78; chief tribal judge Ct. Indian Offenses, Lovelock, 1975-79; justice of peace, coroner County of Pershing, Lovelock, 1975-79; paralegal, legal sec. Samuel S. Wardle, Carson City, Nev., 1979; dep. ct. adminstr. Reno Mcpl. Ct., Reno, 1979-81; co-owner horse farm Reno, 1979—, freelance real estate investor, 1979—; real estate saleswoman Merrill Lynch Realtors, Sparks, Nev., 1981-82; realtor, farm and ranch div. mgr. Copple and Assocs., Realtors, Sparks, 1982-91; real estate saleswoman Vail and Assocs. Realty, Reno, Nev., 1991—; co-owner, operator Lovelock (Nev.) Merc. Co., 1988—; sec. Nev. Judges Assn., 1977-78. Dir. Pershing County Drug and Alcohol Abuse Council, Lovelock, 1976-78. Mem. Reno/Sparks Bd. Realtors, Nat. Assn. Realtors, Nev. Assn. Realtors, Am. Quarter Horse Assn. Republican. Roman Catholic. Home: 4805 Sinelio Dr Reno NV 89502-9510 Office: Vail and Assocs Realty 1700 S Virginia St Reno NV 89502-2811

DAVENPORT, LAWRENCE FRANKLIN, school system administrator; b. Lansing, Mich., Oct. 13, 1944; s. Theodore and Bernice (Alexander) D.; m. Cecelia Jackson, Sept. 24, 1966; children—Laurence, Anita, Anthony. B.A., Mich. State U., 1966, M.A., 1968; Ed.D., Fairleigh Dickinson U., 1975. Vice pres. devel. Tuskegee Inst., Ala., 1972-74; pres. edn1. complex San Diego C.C., 1974-79, provost, 1979-81; assoc. dir. ACTION, Washington, 1981-82; asst. sec. U.S. Dept. Edn., Washington, 1982-87; asst. sec. mgmt. and adminstrn. U.S. Dept. Energy, Washington, 1987-89; assoc. vice chancellor U. Calif., San Francisco, 1989-92; pres. Lawrence Davenport & Assocs., Mercer Island, Wash., 1989—; CFO, Seattle Pub. Schs., 1992-94; v.p. fin. and ops., CFO, Milton Hershey (Pa.) Sch., 1994—. Co-author (with Petty): Career Education and Minorities, 1973. Presbyterian.

DAVENPORT, LEE LOSEE, physicist; b. Schenectady, N.Y., Dec. 31, 1915; m. Anne S. Davenport, 1944; children: Jeanne Treder, Carol Davenport. BS, Union Coll., 1937; MS, U. Pitts., 1940, PhD in Physics, 1946. Rsch. assoc. radar MIT, Cambridge, Mass., 1941-46; rsch. fellow constrn. cyclotron Harvard U., Cambridge, Mass., 1946-50; exec. v.p. Perkin-Elmer Corp., Norwalk, Conn., 1950-57; pres. Sylvania Corning Nuclear Corp., Bayside L.I., N.Y., 1957-60; v.p. planning Sylvania Elec. Prodn., Inc., N.Y.C., 1960-62; pres. GTE Labs. Inc., Stamford, Conn., 1962-77; v.p., chief scientist GTE, 1977-80, cons. telecomm., 1980—; asst. dir. Electronics Rsch. Lab., U. Pitts, 1946, corp. dir., 1980-92. Fellow IEEE, Am. Phys. Soc. (life); mem. Nat. Acad. Engring., Sci. Rsch. Soc. Am. Home: 61 Winding Ln Greenwich CT 06831-3704

DAVENPORT, LINDSAY, professional tennis player; b. Palos Verdes, Calif., June 8, 1976. Profl. tennis player, 1993—. Ranked 3d Doubles (with Chanda Rubin), 1993; recipient 3 career pro singles titles (1) Lucerne, 1993, (2) Brisbane, Lucerne, 1994, 95; winner singles & doubles (with Jana Novotna) Bausch & Lomb Champioships, 1997; named to Olympic Team 1996; gold medalist singles, 1996; ranked #1 1998, # 2, 1999; winner Bank of the West, 1998, Toshiba Classic, 1998, Acura Invitational, 1998, U.S. Open, 1998, European Championships, 1998, Toray Pan Pacific (doubles) 1999, Sydney Internat., 1999; Wimbledon, 1999. Office: US Tennis Assn 70 W Red Oak Ln White Plains NY 10604-3602*

DAVENPORT, MANUEL MANSON, philosophy educator; b. Colorado Springs, Colo., June 14, 1929; s. Ernest Alfred and Anna (Brauer) D.; divorced; children: Marian, Mark, Mitchel, David, Brian, Linda. AB, Bethany Nazarene Coll., 1950; MA, Colo. Coll., 1954; PhD, U. Ill., 1957. Elem. sch. tchr., 1950-52; instr. Colo. Coll., 1956-57; asst., assoc. prof. Colo. State U., 1957-67; prof. philosophy Tex. A&M U., College Station, 1967—, head dept., 1967-76; disting. vis. prof. USAF Acad., 1980-81, 94-95. Served with U.S. Army, 1952. Recipient Faculty Achievement awards, 1959, 60, 69, 78, 80, 82, 89; Rockefeller Found. grantee, 1962-63. Mem. AAUP (past chpt. pres.), Southwestern Philos. Soc. (past pres.), Am. Philos. Assn., Am. Soc. for Aesthetics (Rocky Mountain divsn. pres.), Mountain Plains Philos. Assn. (past chmn.), Phi Kappa Phi, Omicron Delta Kappa. Home: 4009 Shawnee Cir Bryan TX 77802-3629 Office: Tex A&M U Dept Philosophy College Station TX 77843-4237

DAVENPORT, PAMELA BEAVER, rancher, small business owner; b. Big Spring, Tex., Nov. 18, 1948; d. Frank Jones and Doris Glynn (Wills) Beaver; m. Robert Sampson Davenport, Feb. 2, 1982; 1 child, Danielle. BS in Mktg. and Textiles, Tex. Tech U., 1969, MS, 1970; cert. in spinal orthotics, Northwestern U., 1976. Adminstrv. asst. Tex-Togs, Inc., El Paso, Tex., 1971-75; dir. edn. Camp Internat., Jackson, Mich., 1975-79; realtor Tom Carpenter, Realtor, San Angelo, Tex., 1979-83; retailer Davenport Barber & Beauty, San Angelo, 1985-95; owner, mgr. The Little Gym, San Antonio, 1995-97; rancher, 1968-. Contbr. articles to profl. jours. Vice chmn. adv. bd. San Angelo Recreation Dept., 1987-88; chmn. adv. bd. Recreation Dept., River Stage, 1990; chmn. Tom Green County Adult Literacy Coun., 1989-90; publicity chmn. San Angelo Cultural Affairs Coun., 1986; treas. San Angelo Commun. Hosp. Aux., 1980-82; publicity chmn. Christmas at Old Fort Concho, 1986; mem. Leadership San Angelo. Mem. AAUW (cultural chmn. Tex. bd. 1988-89, pres. 1986-88, chmn. conv. 1984-86). Methodist. Avocations: reading, painting, traveling. Home and Office: 107 Longsford San Antonio TX 78209-1822

DAVENPORT, PAUL, university administrator, economics educator. BA in Econs. with gt. distinction/honors, Stanford U., 1969; MA, U. Toronto, 1970, PhD, 1976. Prof. econs. McGill U., Montreal, Que., Can., 1972-89, assoc. dean grad. studies, 1982-86, vice prin. planning and computer svcs., 1986-89; pres., vice chancellor U. Alta., Edmonton, Alta., Can., 1989-94, U. Western Ont., London, Can., 1994—; chair Assn. Univs. and Colls. Can., 1997-99, Coun. Ont. Univs., 1999—. Editor: (with Richard H. Leach) Reshaping Confederation: The 1982 Reform of the Canadian Constitution, 1984. Mem. exec. com. Corp. Higher Edn. Forum; mem. policy program adv. com. on econ. growth Can. Inst. for Advanced Rsch.; mem. bd. govs. London Health Scis. Ctr., Loncon Econ. Devel. Corp. Mem. Can. Assn. Economists, Am. Econ. Assn., Phi Beta Kappa. Office: U Western Ont-Off of President, Stevenson-Lawson Bldg, London, ON Canada N6A 5B8

DAVENPORT, RICHARD W., academic administrator; b. Marysville, Mo., June 24, 1945; s. Bud W. and Marcella (Vestrem) D.; m. Sharlene F. Midalski, Aug. 1, 1963; children: Natalie, Ryan. BA, U. Nebr., Kearney, 1967; MS, Colo. State U., 1969; PhD, Iowa State U., 1977. Speech pathologist, hearing specialist Delaware County Spl. Edn., Manchester, Iowa, 1969-70; tenure track instr. dept. speech Iowa State U., Ames, 1970-77; asst. prof. St. Cloud (Minn.) State U., 1977-80; chair, prof. Winona (Minn.) Consortium, 1980-86; assoc. dean acad. affairs We. State Coll., Gunnison, Colo., 1986-90; interim dean, acting provost, v.p. acad. affairs Ctrl. Mich. U., Mt. Pleasant, 1990-94, provost, v.p. acad. affairs, 1994—; presenter in field. Contbr. articles to profl. jours. Recipient Outstanding Tchr. award Tri-Coll. U. Program, 1985, Internat. Leadership award Acad. Bus. Adminstrn., 1997. Mem. AAUP, Am. Assn. Higher Edn., Am. Assn. State Colls. and Univs., Am. Assn. Colls., Am. Coun. Edn., Phi Delta Kappa (hon.). Avocations: writing, reading, carpentry, furniture refinishing. Home: 263 Four Square Dr Mount Pleasant MI 48858-9084 Office: Ctrl Mich U 112 S Washington St Mount Pleasant MI 48858-2513

DAVENPORT, ROBERT RALSEY, writer; b. Brookline, Mass., Apr. 30, 1950; s. Harry Augustus and Jean Ann (Yeager) D. BA, Middlebury Coll., 1972; JD, St. John's U., N.Y.C., 1979; MBA, Harvard U., 1984; MFA, UCLA, 1999. Bar: N.Y. 1980, Calif. 1988. Atty. U.S. Dept. Justice, Washington, 1979-81, Office Gen. Counsel Dept. Navy, Washington, 1981-82; creative exec. Twentieth Century-Fox Film Corp., L.A., Calif., 1983, Columbia Broadcasting System, L.A., 1984-85, Viacom Prodns., L.A., 1986-87; dir. bus. affairs New World TV, L.A., 1987-88; exec. v.p. Soaring Eagle Prodns., L.A., 1988-89; pres. The Historic Trust, L.A., 1992—. Author: The Davenport Genealogy, 1982, Hereditary Society Blue Book, 1992, 94, 95, 96, 97, 98, 99, Rich and Famous Baby Name Book, 1994, Pet Names of The Rich and Famous, 1995, The Celebrity Almanac, 1995, The Celebrity Birthday Book, 1996, Roots of the Rich and Famous, 1998. Lt. col. JAGC, U.S. Army; lt. USN. Mem. Soc. of Cincinnati (past pres. Calif. chpt.), DAV (life), Order of Indian Wars of U.S., Aztec Club of 1847, VFW (life), Mil. Order of the Purple Heart (life). Office: The Historic Trust PO Box 1989 Beverly Hills CA 90213-1989

DAVENPORT, RONALD, lawyer; b. New Haven, May 23, 1963. Bachelors, Yale U., 1985; degree in law, Harvard U., 1988. Bar: Pa., D.C. Atty. Bd. Gov. Fed. Res., Washington, 1988—. Mem. Loft Bd., N.Y.C., Wibur Force U., Coun. Econ. Priority, Louise Wise Svcs. Inc. Office: 24th Fl 655 3rd New York NY 10017*

DAVENPORT, THOMAS HERBERT, small business owner; b. Sandusky, Ohio, Mar. 15, 1933; s. Orme and Elva Mae (Bragg) D.; m. Annetta Henman, June 22, 1963; children: Deborah Ann, Mark Thomas, Brenda Kay. Grad., Coyne Electronic Sch., 1954-55. Lic. FCC gen. radio telephone. Clk. Nickel Plate R.R., Bellevue, Ohio, 1951-52, 53-54; electronic technician various firms, Sandusky, 1955-56; prin. Bellevue Radio and TV, 1955—. Numerous inventions in field. Cpl. U.S. Army, 1952-53, 2d. lt USAF Aux., 1980-84. Mem. Am. Legion. Republican. Avocations: inventing, cartooning, gardening, poetry, reflexology. Home: 111 Seneca Dr Bellevue OH 44811-1635 Office: Bellevue Radio & TV 109 W Center St Bellevue OH 44811-1351

DAVENPORT, WILBUR BAYLEY, JR., electrical engineering educator; b. Phila., July 27, 1920; s. Wilbur Bayley and Cora (Reifsnyder) D.; m. Joan Purington, Nov. 3, 1945; children: Mark Wilbur, Sally Davenport. B. Elec. Engring., Ala. Poly. Inst., 1941; M.S. in Elec. Engring, M.I.T., 1943, D.Sc., 1950. Mem. faculty M.I.T., 1949-82, prof. elec. engring., 1960-82, assoc. head dept. elec. engring., 1971-72, head dept. elec. engring. and computer sci., 1974-78; vis. prof. elec. engring. U. Hawaii, Manoa, 1982-87, 89-93; adj. research prof. elec. engring. Naval Postgrad. Sch., 1982-83; asst. dir. Lincoln Lab., 1963-65, assoc. dir. research lab. electronics, 1961-63; dir. Center for Advanced Engring. Study, 1972-74, Gen Rad, Inc., Concord, Mass., 1974-82; mem. sci. year editorial adv. bd. Field Enterprises Ednl. Corp., 1974-76; mem. Carnegie Commn. on Future Pub. Broadcasting, 1977-79; cons. to govt. and industry, 1961—. Author: (with William L. Root) An Introduction to the Theory of Random Signals and Noise, 1958, Probability and Random Processes, An Introduction for Applied Scientists and Engineers, 1970. Served to lt. (j.g.) USNR, 1943-46. Recipient certification of commendation Navy Dept., 1960. Fellow IEEE, AAAS, Am. Acad. Arts and Scis.; mem. Nat. Acad. Engring., Sigma Xi, Tau Beta Pi, Phi Kappa Phi, Eta Kappa Nu, Spiked Shoe. Home: 1120 Skyline Dr Medford OR 97504-8585

DAVENPORT, WILLIAM HAROLD, mathematics educator; b. Jackson, Tenn., Dec. 21, 1935; s. John Heron and Mary (Troutt) D.; m. Mary Janice Johnson, Mar. 18, 1960; children—Mark Edson, Amber Yvette; m. Sandra Elaine Holloway, July 30, 1973; children—William Harold II, David Carleton, Bennett John Joseph. B.S., U. Tenn., 1962; M.S., Tex. A&M U., 1966; Ph.D. in Math., U. Ala., 1971. Aerospace technologist NASA Manned Spacecraft Ctr., Houston, 1962-64; research mathematician Brown Engring. Co., Huntsville, Ala., 1966-67; teaching fellow, instr. math. U. Ala., University, 1967-71; mathematician U.S. Army Missile Command, Huntsville, 1971-72; asst. prof. math. U. Petroleum and Minerals, Dhahran, Saudi Arabia, 1972-77, Columbus Coll., Ga., 1977-81; assoc. prof. U. Ark., Little Rock, 1981-87, Northwestern State U., Natchitoches, La., 1987-88, Mesa State Coll., Grand Junction, Colo., 1988—. Served with USN, 1954-58. Mem. Am. Math. Soc., Math. Assn. Am., Sigma Pi Sigma, Phi Kappa Phi, Pi Mu Epsilon, Kappa Mu Epsilon, Sigma Xi. Roman Catholic. Avocation: tennis.

DAVEREDE, HEIDI MARIANNE, government official; b. Bridgeton, N.J., Jan. 1, 1962; d. Ferdinand Leokadia and Marianne Lina (Nolte) Merk; m. Alex Joseph Daverede, May 24, 1984. BS in Marine Engring., U.S. Naval Acad., 1984; MBA, Fla. Inst. Tech., 1997. Logistics mgmt. specialist Naval Supply Sys. Command, Arlington, Va., 1989-92, program mgr., 1992-95; transp. specialist Def. Logistics Agy., Ft. Belvoir, Va., 1995—; mem. profl. enhancement program Office of Sec. of Def., Washington, 1997-98; program mgr. reengring. Dept. of Def. transp., 1999—. Lt. (j.g.) USN, 1984-89. Mem. Nat. Def. Transp. Assn. Republican. Lutheran. Avocations: needlework, gardening, bicycling, computers, reading. Home: 7116 Lois Ln Lanham Seabrook MD 20706-1106 Office: Defense Logistics Support Command 8725 John Kingman Rd Fort Belvoir VA 22060

DAVES, DON MICHAEL, minister; b. Wichita Falls, Tex., Mar. 4, 1938; s. Floyd Lee and Johnnie Majorie (Dunn) D.; m. Patricia N. McLean, Aug. 29, 1958; children: Paul Lee, Donna Michelle. BA, Midwestern U., 1959; ThM, So. Meth. U., 1963; D. Humanities (hon.), Southwestern Coll., 1971. Ordained to ministry Meth. Ch., 1963. Pastor 1st Meth. Ch., Holliday, Tex., 1963-66, Prarie Heights Meth. Ch., Grand Prairie, Tex., 1966-72; minister to soc. North Tex. Conf. United Meth. Ch., 1972-77; pastor Meml. United Meth. Ch., Dallas, 1977-78; assoc. pastor Preston Hollow United Meth. Ch., Dallas, 1978-81, 1st United Meth. Ch., Duncanville, Tex., 1981-85; pastor 1st United Meth. Ch., Cedar Hill, Tex., 1985-91; assoc. pastor Walnut Hill United Meth. Ch., Dallas, 1992-95; pastor First United Meth. Ch., VanAlstyne, Tex., 1995-99; ret., 1999; former mem. North Tex. Conf.; mem. United Meth. Ch.; trustee Charlton Meth. Hosp., Dallas, 1986-95; mentor pastor Perkins Sch. Theology Intern Program, 1996-97; registrar Sherman-McKinney Bd. Ministry, 1996—. Author: Devotional Talks for Children, 1961, Famous Hymns & Their Writers, 1962, Sermon Outlines on Romans, 1962, Meditations on Early Christian Symbols, 1963, Come with Faith, 1964, Young Readers Book of Christian Symbolism, 1967, Advent: A Calendar of Devotions, 1971, Joy is Now, 1988. Named for Best Children's Book by Tex. Author, Tex. Inst. Letters, 1968. Mem. Am. Assn. Pastoral Counselors, Rotary, Order of St. Luke. Home: 5200 Keller Springs Rd 231 Dallas TX 75244 Office: PO Box 125 Van Alstyne TX 75495-0125

DAVES, DONALD RAE, entertainment industry executive; b. L.A., Dec. 6, 1930; s. Lester Brent and Edwina (Tothill) D.; m. Eleana Farrell, Jan. 26, 1957; children: Victoria Daves Bennett, Antoinette Daves Johnson. BA, U. So. Calif., 1955. Asst. dir. Dirs. Guild Am., L.A., 1957-65; asst. gen. mgr. Samuel Goldwyn Studios, L.A., 1973-80; v.p. Warner Bros. Hollywood Studios, West Hollywood, Calif., 1980-96; pres. Hill-Daves Prodns., 1996—. Dir., prodn. mgr. (TV) Bonanza, 1965-70; assoc. producer (film) Key West, 1972. V.p. West Hollywood Community Alliance, 1988-90; bd. dirs. Warner Bros. Hollywood Studio Fed. Credit Union, 1995—. Sgt. USAF, 1951-52. Mem. Phi Delta Theta. Republican. Episcopalian. Avocations: collecting paper weights, sports, antique smoking pipes.

DAVES, GLENN DOYLE, JR., science educator, chemist, researcher; b. Clayton, N.Mex., Feb. 12, 1936; s. Glenn Doyle and Billye (Parker) D.; m. Pamela Gannarelli, Sept. 5, 1959; children: Laura Lee Daves Schantz, Anne Kathryn, Glenn Graham. BS, Ariz. State U., 1959; PhD, MIT, 1964; PharmD (hon.), U. Uppsala, Sweden, 1987. Rsch. chemist Midwest Rsch. Inst., Kansas City, Mo., 1959-61, Stanford Rsch. Inst., Palo Alto, Calif., 1964-67; asst. prof. chemistry Oreg. Grad. Ctr., Beaverton, 1967-72, assoc. prof., 1972-74, prof., 1974-81, chmn. dept., 1972-79; prof., chmn. dept. chemistry Lehigh U., Bethlehem, Pa., 1981-88; prof. chemistry, dean sci. Rensselaer Poly. Inst., Troy, N.Y., 1989—; vis. scientist NIH, Bethesda, Md., 1988. Co-editor: Advances in Polyamine Research, Vols. 1-2, 1978, Biologically Active Principals of Natural Products, 1984; contbr. numerous articles to profl. jours. Recipient numerous grants NIH, Am. Cancer Soc., U.S. Forest Svc., 1971—. Mem. Am. Chem. Soc., Internat. Soc. Heterocyclic Chemistry, Coun. for Chem. Rsch. (governing bd. 1985-86, chair manpower and resource com. 1984-87, mem. membership com. 1991). Democrat. Office: Rensselaer Poly Inst Sch Sci 110 8th St Troy NY 12180-3522

DAVEY, CLARK WILLIAM, newspaper publisher; b. Chatham, Ont., Can., Mar. 3, 1928; s. William and Marguerite (Clark) D.; m. Joyce Gordon, Sept. 13, 1952; children: Richard Gordon, Kevin William, Clark Michael. BA in Journalism, U. Western Ont., 1948, LLD (hon.), 1986. With Chatham Daily News, 1948-51; mng. editor No. Daily News, Kirkland Lake, Can., 1951; hydro. seaway corr. Globe and Mail, 1951-55; mem. Parliamentary Press Gallery, Ottawa, 1956-60; fgn. editor Globe and Mail, 1960-63, mng. editor, 1963-78; pub. Vancouver (B.C., Can.) Sun, 1978-83, Montreal Gazette, 1983-89; pres., chmn. The Canadian Press, 1981-83; pub. Ottawa Citizen, 1989-92; v.p. Southam Inc., 1983-92; dir. Am. Press Inst., 1988-94; commr. Ottawa Hydro, 1999—; pres. Michener Awards Found., 1993-98. Named to Can. News Hall of Fame, 1992. Office: 29 Madawaska Dr, Ottawa, ON Canada K1S 3G5

DAVEY, KENNETH GEORGE, biologist, university official; b. Chatham, Ont., Can., Apr. 20, 1932; s. William and Marguerite (Clark) D.; m. Jeannette Isabel Evans, Nov. 28, 1959 (separated); children: Christopher Graham, Megan Jeannette, Katherine Alison. BSc, U. Western Ont., 1954, MSc, 1955; PhD, Cambridge (Eng.) U., 1958. NRC Can. fellow U. Toronto, Ont., 1958-59; Drosier fellow Gonville and Caius Coll., Cambridge U., 1959-63; asso. prof. parasitology McGill U., Montreal, Que., Can., 1963-67; prof. parasitology and biology McGill U., 1967-74, dir. Inst. Parasitology, 1964-74; prof., chmn. dept. biology York U., Downsview, Ont., 1974-81; dean of sci. York U., 1982-85, disting. research prof., 1984—, v.p. acad. affairs, 1986-91; past pres. Huntsman Marine Lab.; pres. Biol. Coun. Can., 1979-81; mem. animal biology grant selection com. Natural Scis. and Engring. Rsch. Coun. Can., 1980-83, group chmn. life scis., 1983-86, mem. com. grants and scholarships, 1983-86; mem. panel on tropical health NIH, 1978-82; pres. World Exec. Coun., Inst. de la Vie; coun. Royal Can. Inst., 1996—, v.p., 1998—; mem. Nat. Coun. on Ethics in Human Rsch., 1998—. Author: Reproduction in the Insects, 1965; editor Internat. Jour. Invertebrate Reprodn., 1978-86; mem. editl. bd. Internat. Jour. Parasitology, 1973-80, Exptl. Parasitology, 1970-76, Can. Jour. Zoology, 1966-76, editor, 1994—; assoc. editor Ency. Reprodn.; contbr. articles to profl. jours. Decorated officer Order of Can., 1997; recipient Queen's Jubilee medal Govt. Can., 1977, Hitschfeld award, Can. Assn. Rsch. Adminstrs., 1997. Fellow Royal Soc. Can. (sec. Acad. Sci. 1979-85), Entomol. Soc. Can. (Gold medal 1985); mem. Soc. Exptl. Biology, Internat. Union Biol. Scis. (Can. nat. com. 1977-82), Can. Soc. Zoologists (pres. 1981-82, Fry medal 1987), Can. Com. Univ. Biology Chmn. (chmn. 1975-77, Disting. Biologist medal 1992), Biol. Coun. Can. (Gold medal 1987). Office: York Univ, Dept Biology, North York, ON Canada M3J 1P3

DAVEY, LYCURGUS MICHAEL, neurosurgeon; b. N.Y.C., Feb. 20, 1918; s. Michael Marco and Elizabeth (Delaveris) D.; m. Artemis Diana Pappas, June 7, 1942; children: Michael Dean, Elaine Anne, Elizabeth. BA, Yale U., 1939, MD, 1943. Diplomate Am. Bd. Neurol. Surgery, 1954. Surg. intern New Haven Hosp., 1943-44, asst. resident in surgery, 1946-50, William Harvey Cushing fellow, 1947-48, resident neurosurgeon, 1951-52; asst. resident in neurosurgery Hartford Hosp., 1950-51; clin. clk. Nat. Hosp., London, summer 1954; clin. instr. neurosurgery Yale U., 1952-60, asst. clin. prof., 1960-68, asso. clin. prof., 1968-77, clin. prof., 1977—; assoc. fellow Trumbull Coll. Yale U., 1959—; cons. practice in neurosurgery New Haven, 1952—; attending neurosurgeon Vets. Meml. Med. Ctr. (formerly Meriden-Wallingford Hosp.); emeritus Hosp. St. Raphael; assoc. sect. chief emeritus Yale-New Haven Med. Ctr.; bd. dirs. MD Health Plan, Tex. Citrus Found. Served to comdr. USNR, 1942-46, 52-54; capt. Res. ret. 1973. Fellow ACS, Internat. Coll. Surgeons; mem. AMA, Naval War Coll. Found., Inc. (life), U.S. Naval Inst. (life), Naval Res. Assn. (life), Navy League of U.S. (life), Conn. Med. Soc. (chmn. sect. on neurosurgery 1971-72), Conn. Soc. Neurol. Surgeons, New Haven County Med. Soc. (pres. 1987), New Haven Med. Assn. (pres. 1972), Am. Assn. Neurol. Surgeons, New Eng. Neurosurg. Soc., Congress Neurol. Surgeons (Disting. Svc. award 1966), Assn. Rsch. in Nervous and Mental Diseases, Soc. Med. Cons. to Armed Forces, Internat. Platform Assn., Assn. Yale Alumni in Medicine (pres. 1995-97). Home: 1010 Hartford Tpke North Haven CT 06473-3038 Office: 60 Temple St New Haven CT 06510-2716 also: 2 Church St S New Haven CT 06519-1717 *My life has been enriched by treating tasks as a challenge to my resourcefulness, knowledge, originality, inventiveness and faith. The task becomes a game rather than a chore.*

DAVID, BARBARA MARIE, medical, surgical nurse; b. Wisconsin Rapids, Wis., Mar. 3, 1935; d. Stanley Spencer and Olga Agatha (Bissig) Stark; m. Russell Paul David, Jan. 19, 1957; children: Dennis James, John Paul. Diploma, St. Joseph's Hosp. Sch. Nursing, Marshfield, Wis., 1956. Cert. med./surg. nurse, clin. nurse 3. Asst. to dir. nursing rsch. St. Joseph's Hosp., Marshfield, Wis., 1968-70, head nurse, ICU, 1964-67, 70-71, staff nurse, 1983—. Mem. ANA, Wis. Nurses Assn. (treas. dist. 18), Acad. Med.-Surg. Nurses, Nat. League Nurses. Home: 2007 S Maple Ave Marshfield WI 54449-4957 Office: St Joseph's Hosp 611 Saint Joseph Ave Marshfield WI 54449-1832

DAVID, CHRISTOPHER MARK, lawyer; b. Buffalo, Nov. 19, 1965; s. Thomas Leonard and Anne (Nickodemus) D.; m. Elizabeth Martina Wilson, Aug. 31, 1991; 1 child, Taylor Dawn. AA, Miami Dade C.C., 1989; BA, U. Fla., 1990; JD, U. Miami, 1993. Bar: Fla. 1993, U.S. Dist. Ct. (so. dist.) Fla. 1995. Ptnr. Hall, David and Joseph, P.A., Miami, Fla., 1993—, Hall, David and Joseph, PA, Miami, Fla., 1999—. Sgt. U.S. Army, 1983-87. Mem. ATLA, ABA, Acad. Fla. Trial Lawyers, Dade County Bar Assn. Office: Hall David and Joseph P A 1428 Brickell Ave Fl 8 Miami FL 33131-3438

DAVID, CLIVE, event planning executive; b. Manchester, Eng., June 6, 1934; came to U.S., 1957, naturalized, 1962; s. Marcus Wiener and Claire Rose (Levy) Wiener Kattenburg. Student, Blackpool Tech. Coll., 1951-52, Royal Coll. Art, 1955-57. Designer Chippendale's, London, 1955-57; asst. to pres. pub. relations Maybruck Assocs., N.Y.C., 1959; Ea. regional dir. City of Hope, Phila., 1960-62; pres. Clive David Assocs., N.Y.C., Clive David Enterprises div. Party Enterprises Ltd., Beverly Hills, Calif., Party Enterprises, Ltd., Beverly Hills, 1962—; lectr. Party Planning par excellence, 1966—. Arranger major parties including Miss Universe Coronation Ball, Miami Beach, 1965, State visit of Queen Elizabeth and Prince Philip, Duke of Edinburgh, Bahamas, 1966, An Evening at the Ritz-Carlton, Boston, 1967, 69, Un Ballo in Maschera, Venice, 1967, An Evening over Boston, 1968, M.G.M. Cavalcade of Style, L.A., 1970, Symposium on Fund Raising through Parties, L.A., 1970, Great Midwest Limestone Cave Party, Kansas City, 1972, Une Soiree de Gala, Phila., 1972, 11th Anniv. of the Mike Douglas Show, Phila., 1972, The Mayor's Salute to Volunteers, Los Angeles, 1972, Twenty Fifth Anniv. Salute to Israel, Jerusalem, 1973, The Bicentenary, 1976, The World Affairs Council Silver Ball, Boston, 1977, The Ohio Theatre Jubilee, Columbus, 1978, Mayor's Salute to Vols., 1978, Dedication and Gala Performance, Northwestern U. Performing Arts Ctr., 1980, Metromedia Gala, Los Angeles Bicentennial, 1981, The Albemarle Weekend, Charlottesville, 1985, The La Costa Weekend, Carlsbad, 1987, The Embassy Ball, N.Y.C., 1987, The Lagoon Cycle Premiere, Los Angeles, 1987, State Visit Gala for Her Majesty Queen Elizabeth, Miami, 1991, The Grand Brazilian Clambake, Southampton, 1995, The Democratic Senatorial Campaign Committee Gala, Charlottesville, 1996, DSCC reception for Hillary Rodham Clinton, 1996, Rep. Nat. Conv. Team 100 Reception, San Diego, 1996; mem. Pres.' Summit for Am.'s Future Leadership Roundtable, Phila., 1997; contbr. articles to profl. jours. Served with Royal Arty. Brit. Army, 1953-55. Recipient Freedom Found. award Valley Forge, Pa., 1961, City of Hope award Phila., 1962, Mayor's medal for vol. services Los Angeles, 1972, Shalom award State of Israel, 1974, Mayor's medal City of Columbus; named hon. citizen City of Columbus. Mem. AFTRA. Jewish. Office: 282 S Reeves Dr Beverly Hills CA 90212-4005 *I consider myself so fortunate to participate in events that bring joy, employment and funds to diversified causes, and maybe leave a miniscule contribution to history.*

DAVID, EDWARD EMIL, JR., electrical engineer, business executive; b. Wilmington, N.C., Jan. 25, 1925; s. Edward Emil and Beatrice (Liebman) D.; m. Ann Hirshberg, Dec. 23, 1950; 1 dau., Nancy. B.S., Ga. Inst. Tech., 1945; M.S., MIT, 1947, Sc.D., 1950; D.Engring. (hon.), Stevens Inst. Tech., 1971, Poly. Inst. Bklyn., 1971, U. Mich., 1971, Carnegie-Mellon, 1972, Lehigh U., 1973, U. Ill.-Chgo., 1973, Rose-Hulman Inst. Tech., 1978, U. Fla., 1982, Rensselaer Poly. Inst., 1982, Rutgers U., 1984, N.J. Inst. Tech., 1985, U. Pa., 1985. Exec. dir. research Bell Telephone Labs., Murray Hill, N.J., 1950-70; sci. adviser to Pres. Nixon; dir. Office Sci. and Tech., Washington, 1970-73; exec. v.p. Gould, Inc., 1973-77; ind. cons., 1977, 86—; v.p. Exxon Corp., N.Y.C., 1978-80; pres. Exxon Research and Engring. Co., Florham Park, N.J., 1977-86, EED, Inc., Bedminster, N.J., 1986—; bd. dirs. Lord Corp., Erie, Pa., Intermagnetics Gen. Corp., Guilderland, N.Y., Calif. Microwave, Inc., Redwood City, Inter-VU, Inc., San Diego, Internat. Media Rsch. Found., Tokyo, On-Line Computer Libr. Ctr., Inc., Dublin, Ohio, Space Hab, Inc., Arlington, Va., Protein Polymer Techs., Inc., San Diego; cons. NSC, 1974-77; mem. def. sci. bd. U.S. Dept. Def., 1974-75; mem. tech. adv. bd. Chrysler Corp., 1985-93; chmn. Nat. Task Force on Tech. and Soc.; U.S. rep. to NATO Sci. Com., 1979-95; mem. adv. bd. AMP, Inc., Harrisburg, Pa., Bellcore, Livingston, N.J., Electric Power Rsch. Inst., Palo Alto, Calif., Inst. Def. Analyses, Alexandria, Va., 1993-95, Poly Ventures, Farmingdale, N.Y., Rowan Coll. N.J., Glassboro; active White House Sci. Coun., 1980-88, N.J. Commn. on Sci. and Tech. Mem. Bicentennial adv. com. Chgo. Mus. Sci. and Industry, 1974-75; mem. adv. bd. Office of Phys. Scis., NRC, 1976-81; mem. Pres.'s Commn. on Nat. Medal of Sci., 1975-78; mem. vis. com. to div. phys. scis. U. Chgo., 1976—; mem. adv. coun. Humanities Inst., 1976—; trustee Aerospace Corp., 1974-81, chmn. bd. trustees, 1975-81; life mem. corp. MIT, 1974—, also mem. exec. com., energy adv. bd.; bd. dirs. Summit (N.J.) Speech Sch., 1967-70; mem. Marshall Scholarships Adv. Council.; mem. adv. and resource coun. Princeton U.; mem. cons. sci. com. Chateaubriand Scholarships; trustee Carnegie Instn. of Washington, 20th Century Fund, John Simon Guggenheim Meml. Found. Served with USNR, 1943-46. Recipient Outstanding Young Engr. award Eta Kappa Nu, 1954, George W. McCarty award Ga. Inst. Tech., 1958, award Summit Jr. C. of C., 1959, award of merit ASME, 1971, Harold Pender award Moore Sch., U. Pa., 1972, N.C. award, 1972, award for disting. contbn. Soc. Rsch. Adminstrs., 1980, N.J. Sci. and Tech. medal, 1982, medal Indsl. Rsch. Inst., 1983, Scientist of Yr. award R & D mag., 1984, Fahrney medal Franklin Inst., 1985, Pub. Svc. award Conf. Bd. Math. Csic., 1985, Silver Stein award MIT, 1991; named to Hall of Fame, Ga. Inst. Tech., 1994. Fellow IEEE, AAAS (bd. dirs. 1974-75, 77-82, pres. 1977-78, chmn. bd. dirs. 1979-80), Acoustical Soc. Am., Am. Acad. Arts and Scis., Audio Engring. Soc.; mem. NAS (coun. 1995), NAE (Bueche award 1984), Am. Philos. Soc., Assn. Computing Machinery, Am. Soc. for Engring. Edn. (Hall of Fame 1993), Engring. Soc. Detroit, Nat. Acad. Pub. Adminstrn. Patentee in field. Office: EED Inc PO Box 435 Bedminster NJ 07921-0435*

DAVID, GEORGE, psychiatrist, economic theory lecturer; b. N.Y.C., Feb. 19, 1940; s. Norman and Jennie (Danziger) D. BA, Yale U., 1961; MD, NYU, 1965. Intern Children's Hosp., San Francisco, 1965; resident in psychiatry Colo. Psychiat. Hosp., Denver, 1965-66; practice medicine specializing in psychiatry San Francisco; staff Calif. Pacific Med. Ctr., San Francisco, 1966-67, San Mateo County (Calif.) Mental Health Svcs., 1968-71; lectr. on application of econ. theory to personal decision making. Mem. San Francisco Clin. Hypnosis (v.p. 1973-74). Libertarian. Office: 399 Laurel St San Francisco CA 94118-1951

DAVID, GEORGE ALFRED LAWRENCE, industrial company executive; b. Bryn Mawr, Pa., Apr. 7, 1942; s. Charles Wendell and Margaret (Simpson) D.; m. Barbara Osborn, Sept. 4, 1965; children: Eliza Pell, Hannah Lawrence, Henry Gibb. BA, Harvard U., 1965; MBA, U. Va., 1967. Asst. prof. fin. and acctg. U. Va., Charlottesville, 1967-68; v.p. The Boston Cons. Group, 1968-75; sr. v.p. corp. planning and devel. Otis Elevator Co., N.Y.C., 1975-77, sr. v.p., gen. mgr. Latin Am. ops., West Palm Beach, Fla., 1977-81, pres. N.Am. ops., Farmington, Conn., 1981-85, pres., CEO Otis Elevator Co., 1985-89, chmn., 1989-97; sr. v.p. (parent company) United Techs. Corp., 1988-89, exec. v.p. and pres. comml./indsl., 1989-92, pres., COO, 1992—, CEO, 1994—, chmn., 1997—. Chmn. Greater Hartford chpt. ARC, 1985-87, US-ASEAN Coun. Bus. and Tech., 1995—, Nat. Minority Supplier Devel. Coun., 1998—; trustee Wadsworth Atheneum, Hartford, 1984—; bd. dirs. Inst. Internat. Econs., Washington, 1996—. Republican. Episcopalian. Office: United Techs Corp 1 Financial Plz Ste 22 Hartford CT 06103-2607 also: Otis Elevator Co 10 Farm Springs Rd Farmington CT 06032-2526*

DAVID, HAL, lyricist; m. Eunice Forester; children: Jim, Craig. MusD (hon.), Lincoln Coll., 1991. Books: What the World Needs Now and Other Love Lyrics, (with Burt Bacharach) Bacharach and David Songbook; Songs include Raindrops Keep Fallin' On My Head (Acad. award), The Look of Love (Acad. award nomination), What's New Pussycat? (Acad. award nomination), Alfie (Acad. award nomination), Wives and Lovers, Casino Royale, It Was Almost Like a Song (all Grammy award nomination), What the World Needs Now is Love, To Love a Child (written for Foster Grandparents' Program), To All the Girls I've Loved Before (recorded by Julio Iglesias and Willie Nelson), America Is (official song of Liberty Centennial campaign for restoration of Statue of Liberty and Ellis Island); chief collaborator: Burt Bacharach; other collaborators include Henry Mancini, Joe Raposo; Broadway show Promises, Promises (Grammy award, Tony award nomination); films include April Fools; record producer for Dionne Warwick. Elected Songwriters Hall Fame, Nashville Songwriters Hall Fame Internat.; recipient Presdl. award National Association Recording Merchandisers, Creative Achievement award B'nai B'rith, Entertainer of Yr. award Cue Mag. Mem. ASCAP (pres. 1980—), Songwriters Guild Am., Lyricists Guild Am., Dramatist Guild, Authors League. Address: 15 W 53rd St New York NY 10019-5401 *How do you create a hit? I don't know. When I sit down to work, I write what I feel. What happens afterwards is out of my hands. The only thing I'm sure of is you can't write a hit if you don't write a song. Of course, the act of creation, itself, is only one part of being a professional songwriter. To succeed and sustain, you have to have a knowledge of the other parts of the music business. You have to recognize that you are in business for yourself, and as president of your own company, you must be on top of all its aspects.*

DAVID, HERBERT ARON, statistics educator; b. Berlin, Dec. 19, 1925; came to U.S., 1957, naturalized, 1964; s. Max and Betty (Goldmann) D.; m. Vera Reiss, May 13, 1950 (dec.); 1 child, Alexander John; m. Ruth Finch, Dec. 1, 1992. B.Sc., Sydney U.(Australia), 1947; Ph.D., Univ. Coll. London U., 1953. Rsch. officer Commonwealth Sci. and Indsl. Rsch. Orgn., Sydney, 1953-55; sr. lectr. dept. stats. U. Melbourne, Australia, 1955-57; prof. stats. Va. Poly. Inst., 1957-64; prof. U. N.C., Chapel Hill, 1964-72; dir. stat. lab., head dept. stats. Iowa State U., Ames, 1972-84, prof. stats., 1972-96, Disting. prof. liberal arts and scis., 1980-96, disting. prof. emeritus, 1996—. Author: The Method of Paired Comparisons, 1963, 2d edit., 1988, Order Statistics, 1970, 2d edit., 1981; co-editor: Advances in Biometry, 1996. Recipient J. Shelton Horsley award Va. Acad. Scis., 1963, Wilks award in Army Rsch., 1983. Fellow AAAS, Am. Statis. Assn., Inst. Math. Stats.; mem. Biometric Soc. (editor Biometrics 1967-72, pres. 1982-83), Internat. Statis. Inst. Jewish. Home: 460 Westwood Dr Ames IA 50014-3570

DAVID, IVO A., real estate broker, artist; b. St. Leucio Sannio, Italy, Nov. 22, 1934; came to U.S., 1961; s. Arduino and Clarice-Olga (Lepore) D.; m. Nancy Pugliese, Sept. 26, 1962 (dec. Nov. 1997). Grad., Lyceum of Sci., Italy; MFA, Acad. Fine Arts, Naples, Italy, 1958; grad., Acad. Fine Arts Paestum Acad., Italy, 1975, Internat. Acad. Micenei, Reggio, Italy, 1976. Lic. real estate broker, N.J. Planning designer Candeub/Fleissig Assoc., Newark, 1963-66; chief architect Design Fed. Warehouses, Newark, 1966-74; archtl. designer Raritan Ctr., Edison, N.J., 1970-75; pres., broker, developer Union (N.J.) Ctr. Realty Corp., 1972—, art advt. cons., 1975—. Illustrator: Divine Comedy, 1970 (Gold medal Acad. Art/Micenei Reggio Cal 1997); exhibited in numerous one man shows in U.S. and Europe, 1960—; author: Manifesto of Fusionism, 1956. Mem. Greater Union County Assn. Realtors. Avocation: tennis. Home: 1950 Haines Ave Fl 1 Union NJ 07083-3711 Office: Union Ctr Realty Corp 1238 Stuyvesant Ave Union NJ 07083-3822

DAVID, JAMES, information officer; b. Jan. 24, 1966. Dep. press dir. to Senator John Ashcroft U.S. Senate, 1995—. Office: 316 Senate Hart Office Bldg Washington DC 20510-2504

DAVID, JOHN DEWOOD, biology educator; b. Alton, Ill., Dec. 1, 1942; s. Wade Dewood and Mary (Kemper) D.; m. Nancy M. Rock, Feb. 6, 1972; children: Henry Wade, Katherine Leslie. BA in Chemistry and Biology, Wabash Coll., 1964; PhD in Molecular Biology, Vanderbilt U., 1969. Postdoctoral fellow U. Calif., San Francisco, 1969-72; asst. prof. U. Mo., Columbia, 1972-78, assoc. prof., 1978—, chair divsn. biol. scis., 1989—; mem. task force on tchg. of sci. and math. in secondary schs. U. Mo.-Columbia and Mo. State Dept. Edn., 1983-85; mem. task force on restructuring tchg. preparation U. Mo.-Columbia, 1994—, mem. sci., math., engring. and tech. task force, 1997—. Contbr. articles to profl. jours. Bd. dirs. Columbia Soccer Club, 1989-92. Med. rsch. fellow Giannini Found., 1970-72; grantee Howard Hughes Med. Inst., 1989-99; recipient recognition award for integration of rsch. and edn. NSF, 1997—. Mem. AAAS, Soc. for Developmental Biology, Soc. for Cell Biology., Beta Beta Beta (hon.). Democrat. Presbyterian. Avocations: soccer refereeing, gardening. Office: U Mo 105 Tucker Hall Columbia MO 65211-7400

DAVID, JOHN R., internist, educator; b. Eng., Feb. 15, 1930; married; 2 children. BA, U. Chgo., 1951, BS, 1955, MD, 1955; D (hon.), U. F. Ceara, 1991. Diplomate Am. Bd. Internal Medicine. From intern to asst. resident Mass. Gen. Hosp., 1955-57; clin. assoc. Nat. Inst. Arthritis and Metab Dis., 1957-59; trainee Rheumatism Rsch. Unit, Eng., 1959-60; resident med. Mass. Gen. Hosp., 1960-61; fellow NYU, 1961-64, asst. prof. medicine, 1964-66; asst. physician-in-chief Robert B. Brigham Hosp., 1966-82; prof., chair dept. tropical pub. health Harvard Sch. Pub. Health, Boston, 1981-97, prof. immunology and infectious diseases, 1997—; prof. medicine NYU, 1973—; sr. assoc. med. Brigham & Women's Hosp., 1980-82, asst. chief Dept. Rheumatol-immunol., 1982—, sr. physician Dept. Medicine, 1982—, sci. adv. bd. Internal Lab. Rsch. Animal Disease, 1980—, Burroughs Wellcome vis. prof. Johns Hopkins U., Balt., 1983, Royal Soc. Medicine, Eng., 1984; cons. sci. working group Dir. Cmty. Disease, 1981—. Mem. steering com. Cmty. Immunology Tuberclosis, 1984—; mem. sci. adv. com. New Eng. Biolabs, 1982—; ad hoc cons. Bd. Sci. Coun. Rev. Lab. Parasitic Diseases, NIH, 1984—. Mem. Inst. Medicine Nat. Acad. sci., Am. Soc. Tropical Medicine and Hygiene (pres. 1989), Am. Soc. Clin. Investigation, Am. Assn. Immunologists, Am. Fedn. Clin. Rsch., Am. Rheumatism Assn., Infcctious Disease Soc. Am., Soc. Exptl. Biology and Medicine, Am. Assn. Physicians, Am. Acad. Arts and Sci. Rsch. Office: Harvard Sch Pub Health Dept Immunology/Inf Disease 665 Huntington Ave Boston MA 02115-6021*

DAVID, JOSEPH RAYMOND, JR., writer, periodical editor; b. Chgo., July 9, 1936; s. Joseph R. Sr. and Elsie (Sarakhan) D. BA, Lake Forest Coll., 1957. Freelance writer various pubs., 1970—; editor Education in Focus, Alexandria, Va., 1990; cons. Annenberg CPB Math & Sci. Project, 1993. Author: The Fire Within, 1981, Glad You Asked!, 1986, Teacher of the Year, 1996. Mem. Washington Press Club. Home: PO Box 2 Alexandria VA 22313-0002

DAVID, MARILYN HATTIE, lawyer, retired military officer; b. Biloxi, Miss., May 22, 1953; d. Walter Edward and Irma Lee (Shattles) D. BS in Psychology cum laude, Duke U., 1975; MA in Criminal Justice, Webster Coll., 1979; JD with honors, Tulane U., 1982; LLM Govt. Contracts and Procurement Law, George Washington U., 1996. Bar: Miss. 1982. Commd. 2d lt. USAF, 1975, advanced through grades to lt. col., 1991; base dir. telecom. USAF Security Svc., San Antonio, 1976-77, chief presentations prodn. br., 1977-79; asst. staff judge adv. civil and labor law USAF Air Tng. Command, Biloxi, Miss., 1982-83; asst. staff judge adv. criminal law USAF Air Tng. Command, Biloxi, 1983-84; chief of claims, civilian pers. and fiscal law USAF Pacific Air Force, Kunsan Air Base, Republic of Korea, 1984; area def. counsel USAF Judiciary, Kunsan Air Base, Republic of Korea, 1984-85; staff atty. telecom. law and policy Office of the Chief Regulatory Counsel, Def. Comm. Agy., Washington, 1985-87; trial atty. civilian pers. Air Force Gen. Litigation Divsn., Washington, 1987-90; team leader constant quality improvement tng. USAF Judge Adv. Gen.'s Dept., Washington, 1991-92; trial atty. fed. contract litigation USAF Contract Law Divsn., Washington, 1992-94; dep. dir. acquisition law USAF Devel. and Test Ctr., Fort Walton Beach, Fla., 1994-96; ret., 1996. Decorated Meritorious Svc. medal, Air Force Meritorious Svc. medal with four oak leaf clusters, Air Force Commendation medal, Nat. Def. Svc. medal, Air Force Overseas Ribbon, Air Force Longevity Svc. ribbon with four oak leaf clusters, Air Force Small Arms Expert Marksmanship ribbon, Air Force Tng. ribbon. Mem. NAFE, AAUW, Miss. Bar Assn., Ret. Officers Assn.

DAVID, MICHEL LOUIS, geostatistician, consultant; b. Agon, Manche, France, Sept. 17, 1945; arrived in Can., 1967; s. Rene Joseph David and Leonie Jeanne Bottey; m. Ellen Bondurant, July 4, 1997; children: Kaitlin Dakota Bondurant-David, Justin M. Nevada Bondurant-David. Ingénieur civil des mines, École des Mines, Nancy, France, 1967; MSc, U. Montreal, Que., Can., 1969, PhD, 1973. Prof. École Polytechnique, Montreal, Can., 1967-87; pres. Gamma Geostat Internat. Inc., 1977—; pres. Geostat Systems Internat. Inc., Montreal, 1981-91, Denver, 1981-92. Author: Geostatistical Ore Reserve Estimation, 1977, Handbook of Applied Advanced Geostatistical Ore Reserve Estimation, 1988; editor: Advanced Geostatistics in the Mining Industry, 1976, Geostatistics for Natural Resources Characterization, 1984. Fellow Royal Can. Soc.; mem. Order of Engrs, Internat. Assn. Math. Geology (W.C. Krumbein medal, 1988), Soc. Mining Engrs., Can. Inst. Mining and Metallurgy (Selwyn G. Blaylock medal, 1989). Avocation: minerals. Office: Geostat Sys Internat Inc, 800 Blvd Chomedey Twr C Ste 500, Laval, PQ Canada H7V 3Y4

DAVID, MILES, association and marketing executive; b. Newark, Mar. 29, 1926; s. Samuel Harry and Estelle Rachel (Sklower) Ginsberg; m. Florence Cotton, Dec. 7, 1952; children: Steven, Amelia, Heidi. BA, NYU, 1946; postgrad., Columbia U., 1946. Assoc. editor Sci. Illustrated mag. McGraw-Hill Co., N.Y.C., 1946-48; editor Sponsor mag., N.Y.C., 1948-58; with Radio Advt. Bur., N.Y.C., 1958-86; formerly v.p. and dir. promotion, exec. v.p., pres., vice chmn., chief exec. officer, bd. dir. Radio Advt. Bur., adv. bd. dirs.; pres. Am. Values: The Community Action Network; pres. nat. mktg. strategy nat. advertisers Mkt. Soundings subs. TradeOne Mktg. Inc., New York, 1986-88; vice chmn. TradeOne Mktg. Inc., New York, 1988—; Lectr. Tobe-Coburn Sch. for Fashion Careers; speaker in field to nat., internat. groups.; formerly bd. dirs. Brand Names Found.; bd. dirs. Advt. Coun., Nat. Assn. Promotional and Advt. Allowances. Editor: Sponsor mag. (George W. Polk award). Former chmn. Scarsdale Adv. Coun. on Cable TV; mem. nominating com. Scarsdale Village Trustees; mem. procedure com. Non-Partisan Elections, Scarsdale; mem. exec. com. bd. dirs. Am. Values Cmty. Action Network. With AUS, 1943-45, ETO. Recipient Morris Meister award; named Outstanding Alumnus Bronx High Sch., Sci. Man of Yr. Radio Trade Assn., 1975, 76; named to Hall of Fame of Co-op Advt., 1997. Mem. Internat. Radio, TV Soc., Broadcast Pioneers, Perstare et Praestare, Scarsdale Club (N.Y.), Town Club (com. pub. rels. 1970-74). Jewish. Adminstr. Higbee Study, use of radio for dept. stores, and All-Radio Methodology Study, how to measure radio. Home: 235 Fox Meadow Rd Scarsdale NY 10583-1641 Office: TradeOne Mktg 440 9th Ave New York NY 10001-1620

DAVID, REUBEN, lawyer; b. Baghdad, Iraq, June 12, 1928; came to U.S., 1951; s. Isaac Solomon David and Tefaha (Nisan) Solomon D.; m. Nesta Paley David; 1 child, Aram. License in Law, Iraq Law Coll., Baghdad, 1951; BA, NYU, 1958, JD, 1962. Bar: Iraq 1951, N.Y. 1969. Asst. corp. counsel City of N.Y., 1970-76, chief legal unit dept. personnel, 1976-78; dep. dir. for legal affairs N.Y.C. Employees' Retirement System, 1978—. Mem. ABA, N.Y. State Bar Assn. Home: 30 5th Ave New York NY 10011-8859 Office: 220 Church St Rm 1607 New York NY 10013-6301

DAVID, RONALD BRIAN, child neurologist; b. Richmond, Va., Aug. 3, 1937; m. Candace M. Heiderich; children: Ronald Bryan, Susan D. Soueidan, Elizabeth D. Kurtz, Thomas Edwin, Whitney Pund, Jennifer Pund. BS, Eastern Mennonite Coll., 1960; MD, Med. Coll. Va. Sch. Medicine, 1964. Diplomate Am. Bd. Psychiatry & Neurology, Am. Bd. Pediatrics, Nat. Bd. Med. Examiners, Am. Bd. Child Neurology. Fellow in pediatrics Mayo Grad. Sch. Medicine, Rochester, Minn., 1965-67, fellow in child neurology, 1967-70; from asst. prof. to assoc. prof. Med. Coll. Va., Richmond, 1970—; vis. prof. Coll. William & Mary. Editor: Pediatric Neurology for the Clinician, 1992; series editor: Mosby Neurology-Psychiatry Access Series, 1996; editor: Child and Adolescent Neurology, 1996; contbr. articles to profl. jours., chpts. to books. Fellow Am. Acad. Neurology, Am. Acad. Cerebral Palsy & Child Devel., Am. Acad. Pediatrics; mem. Am. Neurol. Assn., Child Neurology Soc., Internat. Neuropsychol. Soc., Learning Disabilities Coun., Am. Epilepsy Found., Va. Neurol. Soc., Va. Pediat. Soc., Orton Soc. Office: Children's Hosp Svcs 1825 Monument Ave Richmond VA 23220-2801

DAVID, THEOHARIS LAMBROS, architect, educator; b. Farmingdale, N.Y., June 9, 1938; s. Lambros L. and Thalia (Joaniddes) D.; m. Margarita T. Leptos, July 29, 1967; children: Melissa T., Alexis L. BArch, Pratt Inst., 1961; MArch, Yale U., 1964; studied with Serge Chermayeff and Paul Rudolph. Registered arch., N.Y., N.J., Republic of Cyprus; cert. Nat. Coun. Archtl. Registration Bd. Draftsman Harry M. Prince FAIA, N.Y.C., 1960-64; designer Whittlesy & Conklin Archs./Planners, N.Y.C., 1964-65, William F. Pedersen Assocs., N.Y.C., 1965-66, K. Vafeades, Arch., Nicosia, Cyprus, 1965-66; asst. arch. J & A Philippou, Archs., Nicosia, 1966-67, 72; sr. designer Max O. Urbahn Assocs., N.Y.C., 1968-72; ptnr. David & Dikaios Assocs., Architecture/Planning, Nicosia, N.Y.C., Bahrain, 1973-87; prin. Theo David & Assocs., N.Y.C., 1987—, Theo David Cons. Arch./Planner, Nicosia, 1992—; founding dir. CAEC Architecture/Engring. Cons., Ltd., Cyprus, 1975; mem. faculty Pratt Inst., Bklyn., 1968-69, asst. prof. arch., 1969-79, assoc. prof., 1979-83, prof. arch., 1983—; nominator Aga Khan Award for Arch., 1984—; disting. juror 1st Presdl. Arch. Awards, Cyprus, 1992; guest lectr. U. Thessaloniki, Greece, 1972, Hellenic Conf. on Tall Bldgs., Athens, Greece, 1975, U. So. Calif., L.A., Archtl. Assn., London, 1982, Cyprus Archs. Assn. and Am. Ctr., Nicosia, 1982, 92, Tex. A&M U., 1984, Cyprus Popular Bank Cultural Ctr., Nicosia, 1987, 91, Hellenic Bank Cultural Ctr., Limassol, Cyprus, 1993, many others; guest critic CCNY, N.Y.C., Archtl. Assn., London, Temple U., Phila., Columbia U., N.Y.C., Yale U., New Haven, U. So. Calif., L.A., others. Author: Housing of a Culture/Cyprus, 1982; exhbns. include Pratt Manhattan Ctr., N.Y.C., 1971, 83, Pratt Inst. Gallery, Bklyn., 1978, Urban Ctr., N.Y.C., 1981, Cyprus House, N.Y.C., 1984, 92, Shafler Gallery Pratt Inst., Bklyn., 1987, Mcpl. Arts Soc., N.Y.C., 1987, Disting. Drawing Gallery, N.Y.C./AIA, 1988, Parson Sch. Design, N.Y.C., 1991, Higgins Hall Gallery, Pratt Inst., 1994; contbr. articles to profl. jours. Mem. design adv. com. Pub. Devel. Corp., N.Y.C., 1986; 1st v.p. Am. Cyprus Congress, N.Y.C., 1990-94; appointed mem. adv. com. for New Cultural Ctr., Cyprus Govt., 1992. Served U.S. Army, 1962-63. Grantee N.Y. State Coun. on Arts, 1982, Pratt Rsch. Coun., 1983; recipient Design award Nat. Inst. Archtl. Edn., 1961, Bard Honor award City Club, N.Y., 1992, 1st prize G.S.P. Stadium Competition, Cyprus, 1993. Fellow AIA (N.Y. chpt., mem. overseas practice com. 1980-82, mem. disting. arch. awards com. 1984-93, chmn. design awards program 1989-90, Interior Design award AIA Jour. 1988, Design Excellence citation 1993, Design citation 1993, Archs. Designers & Planners for Social Responsibility Project award 1994), Am. Planning Assn. (chmn. com. on N.Y. Waterfront 1984-86, mem. urban task force for N.Y.C. 1990-93). Greek Orthodox. Office: Theo David & Assocs 200 Varick St New York NY 10014-4810 also: PO Box 310, Nicosia Cyprus also: Pratt Inst Sch Arch Brooklyn NY 11205

DAVID, WARD STANTON, bank officer, retired federal agency executive; b. Bertrand, Nebr., Nov. 29, 1934; s. Stanton S. and Helen M. (Gifford) D.; married Aug. 12, 1956; children: Kimberly, Teri, Mickey, Stanley, Rod. BS in Agriculture, U. Nebr., 1956. Conservationist USDA, North Platte, Nebr., 1957-59; work unit conservationist USDA, Holdrege, Nebr., 1959-68; dist. conservationist USDA, Alma, Nebr., 1968-75; area conservationist USDA, Tucumcari, N.Mex., 1975-83, Escondido, Calif., 1983-86; divsn. ops. mgr. USDA, Washington, 1986-93, ret., 1993; ops. mgr. Bank of Am., Fallbrook, Calif., 1994—. Author: Ask Not for Victory, 1991; contbr. articles to various publs. Mem. sch. bd. Alma, 1971-75. With USAFR, 1956-57. Mem. Soc. Conservation Soc. Am. (charter, pres. 1967-69), Am. Assn. Ret. Persons (officer). Republican. Methodist. Avocations: sports, writing, reading, jogging, movies. Home: 2321 Morro Rd Fallbrook CA 92028-4410 Office: Bank of Am 1125 S Main St Fallbrook CA 92028-3326

DAVIDGE, ROBERT CUNNINGHAME, JR., hospital administrator; b. Schenectady, Jan. 1, 1942; s. Robert Cunninghame and Jean (Humphrey) D.; m. Margie Ann Green, May 20, 1961; children: Robert Cunninghame, III, Donna Marie, Christopher Hayne, Michael Rayburn. B.S., Fla. State U., 1965; M.B.A., U. Fla., 1967. Asst. adminstr. Tallahassee Meml. Hosp., 1967-69; adminstr. Cathedral Health and Rehab. Center, Jacksonville, Fla., 1969-73; exec. v.p. Tallahassee Meml. Regional Med. Center, 1973-79; pres., chief exec. officer Our Lady of Lake Regional Med. Center, Baton Rouge, 1979—; mem. Fla. Bd. Examiners Nursing Home Adminstrs., 1970-75; bd. dirs. Big Bend Med. Edn. Found., 1974-79, Neighborhood Health Center, Inc., Tallahassee, 1974-79, Big Bend Health Plan, 1974-79, Easter Seals N. Fla., 1971-73; mem. White House Health and Mental Health Task Force, 1971, Fla. Conf. Aging, 1971; mem. devel. bd. Fla. State Bank, 1973-79; Bd. dirs. Jacksonville Art Mus., 1972-73, Safety Council Greater Baton Rouge, 1981. Chmn. Southeast Hosp. Conf., 1985-86; vol. bd. dirs. Baton Rouge, Inc., 1987—; bd. dirs. Sta. WRKF pub. radio, 1987—, adv. bd. La. State U. Grad. Sch. Social Work; bd. dirs. La. Sr. Olympics, 1990—, chmn. Greater Baton Rouge United Way, 1992, bd. dirs. La. Assn. of bus. and industry, 1992, Greater Baton Rouge Healthcare Alliance, 1992, La. Pan Am. Commn., 1990—, chmn. medical com. With USAF, 1959-63. Grantee HEW, 1974. Fellow Am. Coll. Healthcare Execs. (regent for La. 1984-90); mem. Am. Hosp. Assn. (sect. on aging and long-term care services 1987-90), La. Hosp. Assn. (sec.-treas. 1982-83, chmn. 1983-84), Southeastern Hosp. Conf. (chmn. 1985-86), Res. Officers Assn., Soc. Air Force Res. Med. Svc. Corps Officers (pres. 1989-90), Beta Gamma Sigma. Republican. Roman Catholic. Clubs: Rotary (past dir. Tallahassee, bd. dirs. Baton Rouge club 1988-91), KC. Home: 9205 Hilltrace Ave Baton Rouge LA 70809-2614 Office: Our Lady Lake Regional Med Ctr 5000 Hennessy Blvd Ste 6002 Baton Rouge LA 70808-4350

DAVIDORF, JONATHAN MICHAEL, ophthalmologist; b. Skokie, Ill., Nov. 16, 1965; s. Bernard Sherwin and Eleanor Joyce (Michaelson) D.; m. Jaime Lynn Ching, Sept. 30, 1995; 1 child, Carolena Malia. BA with honors magna cum laude, U. Calif., Berkeley, 1987; MD, U. Calif., San Diego, 1992; postgrad., Instituto Internat., Madrid, Spain, 1987. Diplomate Am. Bd. Ophthalmology. Intern UCLA Sch. of Medicine, Torrance, 1992-93; resident in ophthalmology Ohio State U., Columbus, 1993-96; fellow in refractive surgery Instituto Zaldivar, Mendoza, Argentina, 1996-97; pvt. practice West Hills, Calif., 1997—, Maloney Vision Inst., L.A., 1998—; clin. instr. ophthalmology Jules Stein Eye Inst., UCLA Sch. of Medicine, 1998—; prin. investigator Refractec, Laguna Hills, Calif., 1998—. Author: LASIK: Principles and Practice, 1997; contbr. articles to profl. jours. Fellow Am. Acad. of Ophthalmology; mem. Internat. Soc. of Refractive Surgery, Am. Soc. of Cataract and Refractive Surgery, Calif. Assn. of Ophthalmology, Calif. Med. Assn. Avocations: surfing, skiing deep powder and big moguls, playing piano, tennis, basketball. Office: Ste 201 7230 Medical Ctr Dr West Hills CA 91307 Office: Maloney Vision Inst 10921 Wilshire Blvd Ste 900 Los Angeles CA 90024

DAVIDOVICH, LOLITA, actress; b. Toronto, Ont., Can., July 15, 1961. Actress: (films) Class, 1983, Adventures in Babysitting, 1987, The Big Town, 1987, Blaze, 1989, The Object of Beauty, 1991, JFK, 1991, The Inner Circle, 1991, Raising Cain, 1992, Leap of Faith, 1992, Boiling Point, 1993, Intersection, 1994, Cobb, 1994, Harvest of Fire, 1996, For Better or Worse, 1996, Jungle2Jungle, 1997, Sante Fe, 1997, Touch, 1997, Mystery Alaska, 1998, Gods and Monsters, 1998, (TV) Two Fathers' Justice, 1985, Uncut Gem, 1990, Prison Stories: Women on the Inside, HBO, 1991 (ACE award nomination best actress in a movie or mini-series 1991), Keep the Change, 1992, Indictment, HBO, 1995, Dead Silence, 1997, No Vacancy, 1999, Four Days, 1999. Office: Internat Creative Mgmt 8942 Wilshire Blvd Beverly Hills CA 90211-1934*

DAVIDOVSKY, MARIO, composer; b. Medanos, Buenos Aires, Argentina, Mar. 4, 1934; came to U.S., 1960; s. Natalio and Perla (Bulanska) D.; m. Elaine Blaustein, Nov. 19, 1961; children: Matias Gabriel, Adriana. Dir. Electronic Music Center, Princeton and Columbia univs., 1964-94; vis. lectr. Sch. Music, U. Mich., 1964; guest prof. Inst. di Tella, Buenos Aires, 1965; prof. music CCNY, 1968-80; prof. music Columbia U., 1981-94, McDowell prof. music, 1989-94; Fanny Peabody Mason prof. music Harvard U., 1994—; dir. Composer's Conf. Wellesley (Mass.) Coll. Composer chamber music, orchestral works, also works for electronic music.; recs. on, Columbia, Sonnova, C.I.R. Nonesuch, Turnabout, New World, Wergo, Bridge records. Bd. dirs. The Koussevitsky Music Found. in Libr. Congress, Fromm Found., Harvard U.; founder, bd. dirs. Robert Miller Fund for Music. Recipient award Koussevitzky Found., 1964, award Libr. of Congress, 1964, Nat. Inst. Arts and Letters, 1965, Creative Arts award Brandeis U., 1965, Aaron Copeland award Tanglewood, 1966, Naumburg award, 1971, Pulitzer prize in music, 1971, Seamus Nat. award, 1994, Cristoph & Stephan Kaske music prize, Munich, 1997; Guggenheim fellow, 1961-62, 62-63; Rockefeller fellow, 1964, 65. Mem. Am. Acad. Arts and Letters.

DAVIDOW, JEFFREY, ambassador to Mexico; b. Boston, Jan. 26, 1944; m. Joan Labuzoski; 2 children. BA, U. Mass., 1965; MA, U. Minn., 1967; postgrad., Osmania U., Hyderabad, India, 1968-69. Joined Fgn. Svc., Dept. State, 1969; polit. officer Santiago, Chile, 1974-76, Capetown/Pretoria, Republic of South Africa, 1976-78; desk officer Office So. African Affairs, Dept. State, 1978-79; Congl. fellow, 1979-82; head U.S. Liaison Office Am. Embassy, Harare, Zimbabwe, 1982-83; fellow Ctr. for Internat. Affairs, Harvard U., 1983-85; dir. Office Regional Affairs and Office So. African Affairs, Dept. State, 1985-86; dep. chief of mission Am. Embassy, Caracas, Venezuela, 1986-88; U.S. amb. to Republic of Zambia, Lusaka, Republic of Zambia, 1988-90; dep. asst. secy. for African affairs Dept. State, Washington, D.C., 1990-93; U.S. amb. to Venezuela Dept. State, Caracas, 1993-96; asst. sec. state for inter-Am. affairs Dept. State, Washington, 1996-98; amb. to Mex., 1998—. Fellow Ctr. Internat. Affairs, Harvard U., 1982. Fellow Am. Polit. Sci. Assn. (congrl. staff aide). Office: Am Embassy, Paseo de Ta Reforma 305, 06500 Mexico City DF, Mexico also: Am Embassy, PO Box 31617, Lusaka Zambia

DAVIDOW, JENNY JEAN, counselor, writer; b. Santa Monica, Calif., Mar. 25, 1953; d. Ray M. Davidow and Caroline D. (Kos) Lackmann; m. Bret S. Lyon, June 10, 1988. BA, UCLA, 1974; MA, Internat. Coll., Santa Monica, 1981; D Clin. Hypnotherapy, Am. Inst. Hypnotherapy, Irvine, Calif., 1994. Cert. clin. hypnotherapist. Pvt. practice L.A., 1981-92, Santa Cruz, Calif., 1992—; seminar leader, L.A., 1981-92, Santa Cruz, 1992—; bd. dirs. Tidal Wave Press, Santa Cruz; featured guest various TV and radio shows, L.A., 1983-88; spkr. Whole Life Expo, L.A., 1983-87; mem. Am. Bd. Hypnotherapy, 1989—. Author: Dream Therapy Workbook, 1983, Embracing Your Subconscious, 1996, Corners of the Soul, 1998; contbr. articles to various publs.; creator, presenter audiotape collection Comfortable and Capable, 1994. Mem. Assn. for Humanistic Psychology, Found. for Shamanic Studies, Focusing Inst., World Wildlife Fund (ptnr. in conservation 1995), Sierra Club (life). Democrat. Avocations: photography, gardening.

DAVIDOW, JOEL, lawyer; b. N.J., July 24, 1938; s. Isadore Davidow; m. Katherine Davidow-Lucas (div.); children: Elizabeth, Judith; m. Debra Lynn Miller; children: Abigail, Molly. AB, Princeton U., 1960; LLB, Columbia U., 1963; postdoctoral, U. London, Stanford U. Bar: D.C. 1965, N.Y. 1981. Legal asst. to commr. U.S. Fed. Trade Commn., Washington, 1964-65; assoc. Freeman & Hanley, Chgo., 1969-70; trial atty. Antitrust divsn. U.S. Dept. Justice, Washington, 1966-69, evaluation atty. Antitrust divsn., 1970-73, chief fgn. commerce sect. Antitrust divsn., 1973-77, dir. policy planning antitrust div., 1978-81; ptnr. Mudge, Rose, Guthrie, Alexander & Ferdon, N.Y.C., 1981-87; ptnr., head internat. sect. Dickstein, Shapiro & Morin, Washington, 1987-93; ptnr., vice chmn. Ablondi, Foster, Sobin & Davidow, Washington, 1993—; del. UN Conf. Restrictive Practice, Geneva, 1974-80; adj. prof. law Columbia U., N.Y.C., 1982-87, Am. U. 1987-91, George Mason U. 1992-99; arbitrator U.S.-Can. Free Trade Agreement, Washington, Ottowa, 1991-94. Author: Antitrust Rules for International Business (Bur. Nat. Affairs 1995); fgn. antitrust editor Antitrust Bulletin, 1981; adv. bd. Bur. Nat. Affairs Antitrust Bulletin, 1981; ocntbr. articles to profl. jours. Mem. ABA. Democrat. Avocation, tennis. Home: 3658 Upton St NW Washington DC 20008-3125 Office: Ablondi Foster Sobin & Davidow 1150 18th St NW # 9 Washington DC 20036-3816

DAVIDOW, LAWRENCE ERIC, lawyer; b. East Patchogue, N.Y., Sept. 6, 1961; s. Wallace F. and Norma F. (Findelstein) D.; m. Debra Ann Bardugon, Apr. 10, 1988; children: Nicholas, Ryan, Rebecca. BA, Tulane U., 1983, JD, 1986. Bar: N.Y. Assoc. atty. Davidow & Davidow, Patchogue, N.Y., 1987-92; pres. Davidow & Davidow, Islandia, N.Y., 1992-97, mng. ptnr., 1997-98; mng. ptnr. Davidow, Davidow, Siegel & Stern LLP, Islandia, 1998—. Mem. legal adv. com. L.I. Alzheimers Assn.; bd. dirs. L.I. Cmty. Found., Jericho, N.Y., 1996—; founder, past pres. Suffolk chpt. Am. Parkinson's Disease Assn. Mem. Nat. Acad. Elder Lay Attys. (bd. dirs.), Assn. Profl. Fin. Cons., Suffolk County Estate Planning Coun. (pres. 1999), Advancement Commerce and Industry (bd. dirs.). Avocations: racquetball, golf, fine cigars. Office: Davidow Davidow Et Al 1 Suffolk Sq Ste 330 Islandia NY 11722-1543

DAVIDOW, MALCOLM HARTLEY, management consultant; b. Jacksonville, Fla., May 13, 1963; s. Stanley and Joan Phyllis (Carlin) D. Student, Hebrew U., Jerusalem, Israel, 1983-84; BA, Tulane U., 1985; MBA, George Washington U., 1990. Asst. issues dir. Friends of Bob Graham Com., Campaign for U.S. Senate, Washington, 1986; import-export mgr. Four Seasons div. Standard Motor Products, Inc., Grapevine, Tex., 1986-88; sr. internat. cons. Strategic Resources Corp., Washington, 1989; cons. Andersen Cons., Washington, 1990—. Asst. scoutmaster Boy Scouts Am., Dallas, 1987-88, Washington, 1990-91. Mem. Pi Sigma Alpha. Avocations: photography, backpacking, water and snow skiing, autos. Office: Andersen Cons 1666 K St NW Washington DC 20006-2803

DAVIDS, NORMAN, engineering science and mechanics educator, researcher; b. N.Y.C., Mar. 17, 1918; s. Max and Sarah (Flint) Davidowitz; m. Frances White, Mar. 17, 1945; children: Gerald, Laura, Stuart. B.S., CCNY, 1937; M.S., NYU, 1938, Ph.D., 1940. Instr. CCNY, 1941; physicist C.E., Cin., 1942; mathematician Carnegie Inst. Tech., Washington, 1943-45; instr. Johns Hopkins U., Balt., 1945-47; assoc. prof. engring. mechanics Pa. State U., University Park, 1947-53; prof. Pa. State U., 1953-78, prof. emeritus, 1978—; mem. Inst. Advanced Study, Princeton, N.Y., 1941-42; project dir. NIH, Bethesda, Md., 1968-78, Ballistics Research Labs., Aberdeen, Md., 1961-66; sr. sci. adviser Army Research Office, Durham, N.C., 1961. Editor: International Symposium on Stress Waves, 1960; contbr. articles to profl. jours. Recipient Naval Ordnance Devel. award Carnegie Inst., 1945; Fulbright scholar Israel Inst. Tech., 1959. Fellow Am. Acad. Mechanics (past treas., dir.); mem. ASME, Soc. Engring. Sci., Phi Beta Kappa, Sigma Xi. Democrat. Jewish. Home: 236 E Irvin Ave State College PA 16801-6103 Office: Pa State U Engring Sci and Mechs Dept University Park PA 16802

DAVIDSEN, DONALD R., state legislator. Assemblyman dist. 127 N.Y. State Assembly. Address: 103 Gansevoort St Bath NY 14810-1305

DAVIDSON, ABRAHAM ABA, art historian, educator, photographer; b. Dorchester, Mass., June 27, 1935; s. Isaac and Ruth (Feinsilver) D. AB in Archtl. Scis. cum laude, Harvard U., 1957; postgrad., Hebrew U., Jerusalem, 1957-58; AM in Art History, Boston U., 1960; B in Jewish Edn., Hebrew Tchrs. Coll., Boston, 1960; PhD in Art History, Columbia U., 1965. Vis. lectr. art history U. Iowa, 1963-64; instr. Wayne State U., Detroit, 1964-65; asst. prof. Oakland U., Rochester, Mich., 1965-68; mem. faculty Tyler Sch. Art, Temple U., Phila., 1968—, prof. art history, 1975—; vis. asst. prof. U. Mass., Amherst, summers 1965-67, U. Colo., summer 1968; Thomas P. Johnson disting. vis. scholar Rollins Coll., Winter Park, Fla., 1997; cons. Burlington County C.C., Pemberton, N.J., 1976-77. Author: The Story of American Painting, 1974, 79, Japanese transl., 1976, The Eccentrics and Other American Visionary Painters, 1978, Early American Modernist Painting, 1910-1935, 1981, 3d edit., 1990, Ben Solowey, 1988, Ralph Albert Blakelock, 1996, also articles; one-man exhbns. of photographs Temple U., 1972, 82, Painted Bride Gallery, Phila., 1974, Burlington County C.C., 1978, Gloucester County (N.J.) Coll., 1979, 92, Villanova U., 1982, Pavilion Galleries Burlington County Hosp., Mt. Holly, N.J., 1987, 1521 Café Gallery, 1997; represented in permanent collections Bank Leumi, Cigna Corp., Lehigh U., Sch. Pharmacy, Temple U., Villanova U., Sheldon Meml. Art Gallery, U. Nebr., Free Libr. Phila., Newark Pub. Libr.; numerous TV appearances. Recipient Group 17 prize photography Detroit Inst. Arts, 1969, NEH grantee, 1985. Office: Tyler Sch Art Beech and Penrose Aves Elkins Park PA 19126

DAVIDSON, ANNE STOWELL, lawyer; b. Rye, N.Y., Feb. 24, 1949; d. Robert Harold and Anne (Breeding) D. BA magna cum laude, Smith Coll., 1971; JD cum laude, George Washington U., 1974. Bar: D.C. 1975, U.S. Dist. Ct. D.C. 1975, U.S. Ct. Appeals (D.C. cir.) 1975, U.S. Supreme Ct. 1980. Asst. chief counsel drug enforcement FDA, Rockville, Md., 1974-78; counsel Abbott Labs., North Chicago, Ill., 1978-79, U.S. Pharm. Ops. Schering-Plough Corp., Kenilworth, N.J., 1979-83; sr. counsel Sandoz Pharms. Corp., Inc., East Hanover, N.J., 1983-86; v.p., assoc. gen. counsel Sandoz Pharms. Corp., Inc., East Hanover, 1987-96; assoc. gen. counsel Novartis Pharms. Corp., East Hanover, 1997—. Contbr. articles to profl. jours. Trustee N.J. Pops Orch. Recipient Dawes prize Smith Coll., 1971. Mem. ABA, Pharm. Mfrs. Assn., Food and Drug Law Inst., Non-prescription Drug Mfrs. Assn. (govt. affairs com.), Smith Coll. Club (pres. 1981-82). Republican. Presbyterian. Office: Novartis Pharms Corp 59 State Route 10 East Hanover NJ 07936-1005

DAVIDSON, BILL (WILLIAM JOHN DAVIDSON), entertainment journalist, author; b. Jersey City, Mar. 4, 1918; s. Louis J. and Gertrude (Platt) D.; m. Muriel Roberts, May 21, 1960 (dec. Sept. 1983); 1 child, Carol; m. Maralynne Beth Nitz, July 27, 1986. BA, NYU, 1939. Assoc. editor Collier's mag., N.Y.C., 1946-56; contbg. editor Look mag., N.Y.C., 1956-61; editor-at-large Saturday Evening Post, N.Y.C., 1961-69; radio commentator NBC, N.Y.C., 1968-71; TV writer Universal Studios, Universal City, Calif., 1971-76; contbg. editor TV Guide, Radnor, Pa., 1971-90, L.A. Mag., 1992-95; chmn. alumni communications com. NYU, 1959-64; freelance writer, 1992—. Author: The Real and the Unreal, Six Brave Presidents, 1962, Indict and Convict, 1971, (with Sid Caesar) Where Have I Been?, 1982, Spencer Tracy: Tragic Idol, 1988, Jane Fonda: An Intimate Biography, 1990, (with Danny Thomas) Make Room for Daddy, 1991. Mem. N.Y. County Dem. com., N.Y.C., 1948-50. Served as sgt. U.S. Army, 1941-45, ETO. Recipient Disting. Reporting award Sigma Delta Chi, 1951, 53, Albert Lasker Med. Journalism award, 1953, Disting. Journalism award Family Service Assn. Am., 1963. Mem. Writers Guild Am. West. Democrat. Home: 13225 Morrison St Sherman Oaks CA 91423-2156

DAVIDSON, BONNIE JEAN, gymnastics educator, sports management consultant; b. Rockford, Ill., Nov. 19, 1941; d. Edward V. and Pauline Mae (Dubbs) Welliver; m. Glenn Duane Davidson, June 4, 1960 (dec. Oct. 1993); children: Lori Davidson Aamodt, Wendy Davidson Seerup. Student, Rockford Coll., 1965, Rock Valley Coll., Rockford, 1969-77. Founder, owner, dir. Gymnastic Acad. Rockford, 1977-95; pres., dir., owner Springbrook, Ltd., swim and tennis club, Rockford, 1986-95; rep. trampoline and tumbling com. AAU, 1989—; coach nat. and world champion athletes; mgr., judge, head del. U.S.A. gymnastics teams, 1980—; speaker, lectr., clinician in field.; mem. organizing coms. world championships, also others, 1982—. Contbr. World Book Ency. Bd. dirs. U.S. Olympic Com., 1995—, U.S.A. Gymnastics, 1991—; instr. ARC. Named one of Most Interesting People, Rockford mag., 1987; recipient YWCA Janet Lynn Sports award, 1996. Mem. Internat. Fedn. Trampoline and Tumbling (internat. judge, mem. tech. com. 1986—, del. to congress 1976-86, hon. lifetime mem. 1998), Internat. Fedn. Sports Acrobats (internat. judge), U.S.A. Trampoline and Tumbling Assn. (hon. life; nat. tumbling chairperson 1980-88, advisor 1988—, Coach of Yr. award 1980, Outstanding Contbn. to the Sport award 1987, 96, Master of Sport award 1989), U.S. Sports Acrobatics Fedn. (hon. life; v.p. 1984-95), Nat. Judges Assn. (exec. dir.). Republican. Avocations: travel, skiing, golf, bicycling, tennis.

DAVIDSON, CARL B., retired oil company executive; b. Trenton, N.J., Apr. 17, 1933; s. Jack O. and Pearl (Watkins) D.; m. Lois Greenwald, June 28, 1959; children: Andrew William, Jane Hope Shelton. A.B., Rutgers U., 1954, LL.B., 1957. Bar: D.C. 1957, N.Y. 1960. Asst. to gen. mgr. Koret Inc., N.Y.C., 1957-58; field atty. NLRB, N.Y.C., 1958-65; with Texaco Inc., N.Y.C. and Westchester, N.Y., 1965—; asst. to v.p., then asst. sec. Texaco Inc., 1971-74, corp. sec., 1974-87, v.p., corp. sec., 1987-98; ret., 1998. Pres. Texaco Found., 1990-97. Home: 608C Heritage Hills Somers NY 10589

DAVIDSON, CHANDLER, sociologist, educator; b. May 13, 1936; m. Sharon Lavonne Plummer, Nov. 1, 1986. BA, U. Tex., 1961; PhD, Princeton U., 1969. Prof. sociology Rice U., Houston, 1966—, prof. polit. sci., 1997—, chair dept. sociology, 1979-83, 86-89, 1995—; co-prin. investigator NSF, 1988-92, Rockefeller Found., 1990. Author: Biracial Politics, 1972, Race and Class in Texas Politics, 1990; editor: Minority Vote Dilution, 1984, (with Bernard Grofman) Controversies in Minority Voting, 1992, (with Grofman) Quiet Revolution in the South, 1994. Fulbright scholar, 1961-62; Woodrow Wilson fellow, 1963-64, rsch. fellow Nat. Endowment for Humanities, 1976-77; recipient Gustavus Myers Ctr. Human Rights award for outstanding book on human rights, 1993, Ally award Ctr. for the Healing of Racism, 1996, Brown award for superior tchg., Rice U., 1997, 99, Brown award for excellence in tchg. Rice U., 1998. Mem. Am. Sociol. Assn., Am. Polit. Sci. Assn. (Fenno prize 1995), Philos. Soc. Tex., Phi Beta Kappa. Office: Rice U Dept Sociology 6100 S Main St Houston TX 77005-1892

DAVIDSON, CHARLES SPRECHER, physician; b. Berkeley, Calif., Dec. 7, 1910; s. Charles Sprecher and Mary (Blossom) D. A.B., U. Calif. at Berkeley, 1934; M.D., C.M., McGill U., 1939; M.A. (hon.), Harvard, 1953. Intern, house officer medicine San Francisco Hosp., 1939-41; research fellow medicine Harvard Med. Sch. and asst. resident physician Thorndike Meml. Lab., Boston City Hosp., 1941-42; various appointments, 1942-44; asso. dir. of II and IV Harvard Med. Services, Boston City Hosp. and asso. physician (Thorndike Meml. Lab.), 1948-63, asso. dir., 1964-70, acting dir., 1970-74; vis. physician (Boston City Hosp.), 1965, acting head dept. medicine, 1970-74; asso. prof. medicine Harvard Med. Sch., 1953-68, prof., 1969-73, William Bosworth Castle prof. medicine, 1974-77, prof. emeritus, 1977—; vis. prof. medicine MIT, 1974-77, sr. lectr. health scis. and tech., 1977—, program dir. Clin. Rsch. Ctr., 1974-77; assoc. dir. Harvard U. med. unit, Boston City Hosp., 1972-73; cons. Mt. Auburn Hosp., Cambridge, Cambridge Hosp.; hon. dir. Med. Found., Inc.; scholar-in-residence Fogarty Internat. Ctr., NIH, 1972-73; bd. dirs. Theobald Smith Rsch. Inst., 1984-96; chair Truro (Mass.) Conservation Commn., 1976-93; trustee Truro Conservation Trust. Contbr. to profl. jours. Recipient Alexander D. Stewart Meml. prize, 1939, E.V. McCollum award Am. Soc. Clin. Nutrition, 1966, Joseph Goldberger award AMA, 1991, Environ. Excellence award Ctr. for Coastal Studies, 1993. Master ACP; mem. Am. Gastroent. Soc., Am. Acad. Arts and Scis., Assn. Am. Physicians. Home: 15 Union Field Rd Truro MA 02666 Office: 100 Memorial Dr Cambridge MA 02142-1314

DAVIDSON, COLIN HENRY, architect, educator; b. Exeter, Eng., Mar. 4, 1928; emigrated to Can., 1968, naturalized, 1975; s. Douglas Nangle and Dulcie Rose (Winter) D.; m. Lucienne Fiant, Jan. 18, 1956; children: Dominique, Philip. Diploma architecture, Brussels Royal Acad., 1951; M.Arch., M.I.T., 1955. Archtl. asst. Luccichenti/Monaco, Rome, 1951-54; asst. architect Architects' Collaborative, Cambridge, Mass., 1954-55, London County Council, 1956-60; pres. C.H. Davidson Cons., London, 1960-68; prof. architecture U. Montreal, 1968—; dean Faculty Environ. Design, 1976-85, ACSA disting. prof., 1997—; founder Indsl. Forum Rsch. Group, 1969; founder, pres. IF Rsch. Corp.; exec. dir. Cibat-Montreal Internat. Bldg. Ctr., Inc.; sec. Can. Bldg. Sys. Network; co-prin. CeVeC Bldg. Industry Strategic Opportunities Watch Ctr. Prin. works include Cosmos and SB2 industrialized bldg. sys.; housing, Basildon, Essex, Eng., 1967; co-author: Industrialized Building and the Architect, 1961; author numerous works in field of info. sci. in bldg. including 4 thesauri in bldg. sci. and tech., bldg. procurement and tech. transfer. Mem. Internat. Coun. Rsch. and Innovation in Bldg. and Constrn. (mem. program com., coord. commn. W102), Internat. Union of Bldg. Ctrs. (v.p.), Order of Archs. Que. Office: U Montreal, PO Box 6128, Montreal, PQ Canada H3C 3J7 *I have constantly been torn by the dilemma of the Architect: man-of-the-arts or man-of-science. Having opted for the latter (perhaps out of fear of the former), I find I must work in a* *scientific near-vacuum. For this reason, I dedicate my life to problems of research and its application, to the transfer of information in the building process.*

DAVIDSON, CYNTHIA ANN, English language educator, poet; b. San Diego, June 13, 1960; d. Donald Alan and Rosemary Lorraine (Drehobl) Poe. BA in English, Northeastern Ill. U., 1983, MA in Lit., 1989; PhD in English, U. Ill., Chgo., 1997. Libr. tech. asst. Northeastern Ill. U., Chgo., 1983-87, univ. tchg. asst., 1987-89; adj. English faculty Triton Coll., River Forest, Ill., 1989-90; coll. prep. instr. Harold Washington Coll., Chgo., 1990-91; univ. tchg. asst. U. Ill., Chgo., 1991-97, lectr. English, 1997-98; lectr. writing program SUNY, Stony Brook, 1998—; mem. young scholars' com. Ill. Humanities Coun., Chgo., 1994; participant poetry readings Café Voltaire Emerging Artists Project, Chgo., 1995, Caffé Trevi for Voices of Italian Am., Chgo., 1995. Author: (book) Athena's Mother; contbr. essays and articles to sci. fiction and poetry collections; editor, pub.: (electronic jour.) Rio: A Jour. of the Arts, 1997—; contbr. Contemporary Women Poets, 1998. Talent scholar in creative writing Northeastern U., 1979-81; Presdl. grantee for innovative tchg., 1999—. Mem. MLA, Associated Writing Programs, Acad. Am. Poets. Home: 104 Hoyt Ln Port Jefferson NY 11777 Office: SUNY 202 Humanities Stony Brook NY 11194

DAVIDSON, DANIEL IRA, lawyer; b. Bklyn., Sept. 19, 1936; s. Mitchell and Minnie (Needleman) D.; m. Susan Bettina Thomas, Mar. 13, 1966; 1 child, Jill. *Wife Susan B. Davidson is arts editor and theater reviewer, Washingtonian Magazine, and has contributed to the New York Times, Washington Post, L.A. Times, and other publications. Daughter Jill Davidson, BA, Columbia College, summa cum laude, Phi Beta Kappa, is attending Harvard Law School.* AB, Columbia Coll., 1957; JD, Columbia U., 1959. Bar: N.Y. 1959, U.S. Ct.Appeals (2d cir.), 1960, U.S. Ct. Appeals (D.C. cir.), 1970, D.C., 1972, U.S. Ct. Appeals (9th cir.), 1975, U.S. Ct. Appeals (5th cir.), 1980, U.S. Ct. Appeals (10th and 11th cirs.), 1981, U.S. Supreme Ct., 1982. Editor Columbia Law Rev., 1958-59; law clk. to Judge Harold R. Medina U.S. Ct. Appeals 2d Cir., 1960; assoc. Cravath, Swaine & Moore, N.Y.C., 1961-65; spl. asst. to asst. sec. state East Asia and Pacific Affairs, Washington, 1965-67; spl. asst. to ambassador U.S. Dept. State, Washington, 1967-68; U.S. del. to Paris Peace Talks on Vietnam Paris, 1968-69; mem. staff Nat. Security Coun., Washington, 1969; assoc. Wilmer, Cutler & Pickering, Washington, 1969-70; exec. asst. to W. Averell Harriman Washington, 1971-72; assoc. Prather, Levenberg, Seeger, Doolittle, Farmer & Ewing, Washington, 1972-73; assoc. Spiegel & McDiarmid, Washington, 1973-74, ptnr., 1974—; mem. Com. on Internat. Affairs Dem. Policy Coun., Washington, 1971-72; cons. U.S. Dept. State, Washington, 1978-79, pub. mem. fgn. svc. selection bd., 1995; mem. Coun. on Fgn. Rels.; lectr. in polit. sci. CUNY, 1960. Editor: Columbia Law Review; Contbr. articles and book revs to The Economist, NY Times, LA Times, Wash. Post, London Fin. Times, The Atlantic, others. 1st lt. USAR, 1960-66. Fellow Salzburg Seminary in Am. Studies, 1959. Mem. Phi Beta Kappa. Jewish. Home: 2900 Brandywine St NW Washington DC 20008-2138 Office: Spiegel & McDiarmid 1350 New York Ave NW Ste 1100 Washington DC 20005-4798*

DAVIDSON, DANIEL MORTON, lawyer; b. Lynbrook, N.Y., July 9, 1950. BA summa cum laude, Williams Coll., 1972; JD magna cum laude, Harvard U., 1975. Bar: D.C. 1975, Calif. 1977, U.S. Tax Ct. 1979, U.S. Supreme Ct. 1992. Law clk. Mass. Supreme Ct., 1975-76; ptnr. Sidley & Austin, Washington, 1985-98, Hogan & Hartson, L.L.P., Washington, 1998—. Contbr. articles to profl. jours. Mem. ABA, D.C. Bar Assn., State Bar Calif., Phi Beta Kappa. Office: Hogan & Hartson LLP 555 13th St NW Ste 900W Washington DC 20004-1161

DAVIDSON, DAVID SCOTT, architect; b. Great Falls, Mont., Dec. 17, 1925; s. David Adams and Florence Mae (Scott) D.; m. Marjorie Luella Huffman, Sept. 10, 1949; children: Carol M., Marilyn S., Scott L., Bruce F., Craig S. Student, U. Utah, 1943, Pasadena City Coll., 1944; B.S. in Architecture, Mont. State U., 1950. Registered architect, Mont. Architect in tng. Shanley & Shanley Architects, Great Falls, 1950-52; architect van Teylingen, Knight, van Teylingen, Great Falls, 1952-54; prin. David S. Davidson, Architect, Great Falls, 1954-56; ptnr. Davidson & Kuhr Architects, Great Falls, 1956-75; pres. Davidson & Kuhr Architects, P.C., Great Falls, 1975—; dir., pres. Great Falls Arts Assn., 1980-83; dir., pres. Mont. Inst. Arts, 1981—; mem. state constrn. adv. council State of Mont., 1983-84; dir., v.p. Paris Gibson Square, Great Falls, 1982—. Mem. Great Falls Zoning Bd., 1972-75; mem. rehab. com. Great Falls Housing Task Force, 1975-78; chmn. architecture div. United Way, 1975-78; dir. Great Falls Symphony Assn., 1992-93. Served with U.S. Army, 1943-46. Recipient 1st honor Mont. chpt. AIA, 1973, 75; recipient honor award in architecture Mont. chpt. AIA, 1973, 74, 78, 83, merit in architecture Mont. chpt. AIA, 1965, 2 awards U.S. Dept. Energy, 1986, Interior Design award Arch. Record, 1976, Internat. Union Bricklayers and Allied Crafts award, 1986, 87, 92. Fellow AIA (chpt. pres. 1965-66, dir. 1962-66), Great Falls Soc. Architects (pres. 1958-59), Jr. C. of C. (dir. 1956-60). Home: 1212 Buena Dr Great Falls MT 59404-3750 Office: Davidson and Kuhr Archs PC 401 Division Rd Great Falls MT 59404-1409

DAVIDSON, (MARIE) DIANE, publisher; b. L.A., Mar. 6, 1924; d. Charles Casper and Stella Ruth (Bateman) Winnia; divorced, 1953; children: David William, Ronald Mark. AB, U. Calif., Berkeley, 1943; MA, Calif. State U., Sacramento, 1959. cert. secondary tchr., 1944. Tchr. Campbell (Calif.) High Sch., 1944-45; actress Pasadena (Calif.) Playhouse, 1945, U.S.O. Camp Shows, N.Y.C., 1946-47; tchr. El Camino H.S., Sacramento, 1954-85; illustrator, publisher, editor Swan Books, Fair Oaks, Calif., 1979-99. Author: Feversham, 1969; editor: History of Trinity Episcopal Church, Folsom, California, 1856-1994, 1996; contbr. articles to Shakespeare mag. Mem. NEA, PEN, Authors Guild, Calif. Writers Club, Calif. Tchrs. Assn., Phi Beta Kappa, Pi Lambda Theta. Democrat. Episcopalian. Avocations: gardening, writing. Home: 8146 Toyon Ave Fair Oaks CA 95628-7633

DAVIDSON, DONALD HERBERT, philosophy educator; b. Springfield, Mass., Mar. 6, 1917; s. Clarence Herbert and Grace (Anthony) D.; m. Nancy Hirschberg, Apr. 4, 1975 (dec. 1979); 1 child, by previous marriage, Elizabeth Ann; m. Marcia Cavell, July 3, 1984. B.A., Harvard U., 1939, M.A., 1941, Ph.D., 1949; DDL honoris causa, Oxford U., 1995, LittD (hon.), 1995. Instr. philosophy Queen's (N.Y.) Coll., 1947-50; from asst. prof. to prof. Stanford (Calif.) U., 1951-67; prof. Princeton (N.J.) U., 1967-70, chmn. dept. philosophy, 1968-70, lectr. with rank of prof., 1970-76; prof. Rockefeller U., N.Y.C., 1970-76, U. Chgo., 1976-81, U. Calif., Berkeley, 1981—; apptd. Willis S. and Marion Slusser prof., vis. prof. Tokyo U., 1955; Gavin David Young lectr. U. Adelaide, 1968; John Locke lectr. Oxford (Eng.) U., 1970; vis. prof. U. Sydney, 1968, U. Pitts., 1972, U. Capetown, 1980, U. Venice, 1991, U. Rome, 1993, law & philosophy NYU, 1993; John Dewey lectr. U. Minn., 1975; Matchette Found. lectr. U. Wis., 1976; Carus lectr., 1980; Hägerstrom lectr., 1980; Josè Gaos vis. lectr. U. Mex., 1980; George Eastman vis. prof. Balliol Coll., Oxford, 1984-85; Kant lectr. Stanford U., 1986; S.J. Keeling Meml. lectr. Greek philosophy Univ. Coll., U. London, 1986; Fulbright Disting. lectr., India, 1985-86; Selfridge lectr. Lehigh U., 1986; Thalheimer lectr. Johns Hopkins U., Balt., 1987, David Ross Boyd lectr. U. Okla., 1988, John Dewey lectr. Columbia U., 1989, Alfred North Whitehead lectr. Harvard U., 1990, Heisenberg lectr., Munich, 1981; Kant lectr. U. Munich, 1993, Spinoza lectr. Jerusalem U., 1993, Grambieh and Orr lectr. Dartmouth Coll., 1993, Alan Donagan meml. lectr. Notre Dame, 1994, Josep Ferrater Mora lectr., Girona Spain, 1994; Franquini chair lectr. U. Leuven, Belgium, 1994; Jean Nicod lectr. Caen & Paris, 1995; Shearman Meml. lectr. Univ. Coll., London, 1995; Hill vis. prof. U. Minn., 1997. Co-Author: (with Patrick Suppes) Decision Making: An Experimental Approach, 1957; author: Essays on Actions and Events, 1980, Inquiries into Truth and Interpretation, 1983; co-editor: (with J. Hintikka) Words and Objections, 1969, (with Gilbert Harman) Semantics for Natural Language, 1970, The Logic of Grammar, 1975; mem. editorial bd. Philosophia, 1970—, Theoretical Linguistics, 1973—, Theory and Decision, 1974—, Erkenntnis, 1974—, Current Commentary in the Behavioral and Brain Sciences, 1976—. Served to lt. (s.g.) USNR, 1942-45, MTO. Recipient Hegel prize City of Stuttgart, Fed. Republic Germany, 1991; Teschemacher fellow in classics and philosophy, 1939-41; Rockefeller fellowship in humanities, 1945-46; Rockefeller fellowship for research, 1948; Ford Faculty fellowship, 1953-54; Am. Council Learned Socs. fellowship, 1958-59; NSF research grants, 1964-65, 68; fellow Center Advanced Study Behavioral Scis., 1969-70; Guggenheim fellow, 1973-74; fellow All Souls Coll. Oxford U., 1973-74; vis. fellow Research Sch. Social Scis., Australian Nat. U., 1977; hon. research fellow Univ. Coll., London, 1978; Sherman Fairchild Disting. scholar Calif. Inst. Tech., 1989. Fellow Am. Acad. Arts and Scis., AAAS, Brit. Acad. (corr.); mem. Am. Philos Assn. (sec. Pacific Coast div. 1956-59, v.p. 1961, pres. Eastern div. 1973-74, pres. Pacific div. 1985-86), Am. Philos Soc., Institute Internacional de Philosophie, Norwegian Acad. Sci. and Letters, AAUP. Office: U Calif Philosophy Dept Berkeley CA 94720

DAVIDSON, DONALD WILLIAM, advertising executive; b. Toronto, Ont., Can., May 18, 1938; s. John Harvie and Harriet Gertrude D.; m. Olive Margaret Somerville, July 28, 1962; children: Scott, Susan. Student U. Toronto, York U. Account exec. E.L. Ruddy, Toronto, 1957-68, Foster & Kleiser, Detroit, 1968-70; v.p. Outdoor Advt. Sales, 1971-72; v.p. Montreal, 1972-73, v.p. mktg. group, 1973-75, v.p. nat. sales Claude Neon Ltd., Toronto, 1975-77, exec. v.p., 1977-79; pres. Mediacom Inc., Toronto, 1979-80, chmn., pres., 1980-84; exec. v.p., chief operating officer Gannett Outdoor, N.Y.C., 1984-86, pres., chief exec. officer, 1986-96; pres. Trading Bay Media, 1996—; past vice chmn. Traffic Audit Bur. Trustee Madison Sq. Boys and Girls Club. Mem. Can. Outdoor Measurement Bur. (past vice chmn.), The Advt. Council (bd. dirs.), Lambton Golf and Country Club. Home: 641 5th Ave # 34D2 New York NY 10022-5908 Office: 237 Park Ave New York NY 10017-3140

DAVIDSON, DONETTA, state government official. County clk. and recorder Bent County, Colo., 1978-86; dir. of elections State of Colo., 1986-94; county clerk and recorder Arapahoe County, Colo., 1994-99; sec. of state State of Colo., 1999—. Office: 1600 Broadway Ste 200 Denver CO 80202*

DAVIDSON, ED, tour operator; b. Buffalo, N.Y., July 9, 1940. BS, Rensselaer Polytech. Inst., 1962, postgrad., 1963. Jet fighter pilot U.S. Navy, 1963-70; charter boat capt., environ. activist Fla. Keys, 1970-83; eco-tour concessionaire Biscayne Nat. Park, Nat. Park Svc., Homestead, Fla., 1984-93; chmn. Fla. Audubon Soc., 1995-98; internat. eco-tourism Dobbin Internat., 1995—; pres. Tropical Everglades Visitors Assn., 1989-92; cons. Nat. Marine Sanctuary Program, 1980—. Asst. producer Marine Eco-Video Land & Sea Trust Project, 1994. Pres. Fla. Keys Land & Sea Trust, 1992-94; chmn. Zoning Bd. and Planning Coun., 1976-78. Lt. cmdr. USN, 1963-70, Vietnam. Decorated 24 Combat medal U.S. Navy, 1965-67, Commendation award South Fla. Eco-system Restoration Task Force Asst. Sec. Interior, 1996. Office: 10800 Overseas Hwy Marathon FL 33050-3499

DAVIDSON, ERIC HARRIS, molecular and developmental biologist, educator; b. N.Y.C., Apr. 13, 1937; s. Morris and Anne D. B.A., U. Pa., 1958; Ph.D., Rockefeller U., 1963. Research asso. Rockefeller U., 1963-65, asst. prof., 1965-71; asso. prof. devel. molecular biology Calif. Inst. Tech., Pasadena, 1971-74; prof. Calif. Inst. Tech., 1974—, Norman Chandler prof. cell biology, 1981—. Author: Gene Activity in Early Development, 3d edit, 1986. NIH grantee, 1965—; NSF grantee, 1972—. Mem. Nat. Acad. Scis. Research, numerous publs. on DNA sequence orgn., gene expression during embryonic devel., gene regulation. Office: Calif Inst Tech Div Biology Mail Code 156 29 Pasadena CA 91125

DAVIDSON, ERNEST ROY, chemist, educator; b. Terre Haute, Ind., Oct. 12, 1936; s. Roy Emmette and Opal Ruth (Hugunin) D.; m. Reba Faye Minnich, Jan. 27, 1956; children: Michael Collins, John Philip, Mark Ernest, Martha Ruth. B.Sc. (Union Carbide fellow), Rose-Hulman Inst., 1958; Ph.D. (NSF fellow), Ind. U., 1961. NSF Postdoctoral fellow U. Wis.-Madison, 1961-62; asst. prof. chemistry U. Wash., 1962-65, assoc. prof., 1965-68, prof., 1968-84; prof. Ind. U., Bloomington, 1984-86, disting. prof., 1986—; disting. vis. prof. Ohio State U., 1974-75; vis. prof. IMS, Japan, 1984, Technion, Israel, 1985; cons. Lawrence Livermore Labs. Editor: Jour. Computational Physics, 1975—, Internat. Jour. Quantum Chemistry, 1975—, Jour. Chem. Physics, 1976-78, Chem. Physics Letters, 1977-84, Jour. Am. Chem. Soc., 1978-83, Jour. Phys. Chemistry, 1982-90, Accounts of Chem. Rsch., 1984-92, Theoretica Chimica Acta, 1985—, Chem. Revs., 1986—; contbr. numerous articles on density matrices and quantum theory of molecular structure to profl. jours. Battelle Meml. Inst. Sloan fellow, 1967-68; Guggenheim fellow, 1974-75; laureate l'Academie Internationale des Sciences Moleculaires Quantiques, 1971. Mem. Internat. Acad. Quantum Molecular Scis. (Hirschfelder prize in theoretical chemistry 1997-98), NAS, Am. Chem. Soc. (Computers in Chemistry award 1992), Am. Acad. Arts and Scis., Am. Phys. Soc., Sigma Xi, Phi Lambda Upsion, Tau Beta Pi. Home: 1013 Woodbine Ct Bloomington IN 47401-5445 Office: Ind U Chemistry Dept 800 E Kirkwood Ave Bloomington IN 47405*

DAVIDSON, EUGENE ABRAHAM, biochemist, university administrator; b. N.Y.C., May 27, 1930; s. Jack and Sophie Miriam (Deutsch) D. B.S., UCLA, 1950; Ph.D., Columbia U., 1955. Postdoctoral fellow, instr. U. Mich., 1955-58; asst. prof. biochemistry Duke U., 1958-62, assoc. prof., 1962-65, prof., 1965-67; prof., chmn. dept. biol. chemistry M.S. Hershey Med. Center, Pa. State U., 1967-87, assoc. dean for edn., 1975-87; prof., chmn. dept. biochemistry and molecular biology Georgetown U., Washington, 1988—; mem. Nat. Bd. Med. Examiners, Part I; cons. in field. Author: Carbohydrate Chemistry, 1967; contbr. numerous articles to profl. publs.; Editorial reviewer for numerous jours. Guggenheim fellow, 1965-66; NIH grantee, 1958—. Mem. AAAS, Am. Soc. Biol. Chemists, Assn. Med. Sch. Depts. Biochemistry, Biochem. Soc., Am. Assn. Cancer Research, Soc. Complex Carbohydrates, Glycoconjugate Soc. (pres. 1985-87), Sigma Xi. Home: 5506 Nebraska Ave NW Washington DC 20015-1256 Office: Georgetown U Dept Biochem/Molecular Biology Washington DC 20007

DAVIDSON, EUGENE ARTHUR, author; b. N.Y.C., Sept. 22, 1902; s. William and Bertha (Passarge) D.; m. Louise Keil, Apr. 6, 1928 (div.); children: Eugene Passarge, Lisa; m. Suzette Morton Zurcher, Nov. 1968 (dec. May 1996). A.B., Yale, 1927, postgrad., 1927-28; Litt.D. (hon.), Park Coll., 1977. Mem. editorial dept. Yale Univ. Press, 1929-59, editor, 1931-59, dir., 1938-59, chmn. com. on publs.; editor Modern Age, 1960-70. Author: The Death and Life of Germany, 1959, The Trial of the Germans, 1967, The Nuremberg Fallacy, 1973, The Making of Adolf Hitler, 1977, The Unmaking of Adolf Hitler, 1996; contbr. articles, book revs. and poetry to mags. including The Progressive. Pres. Found. Fgn. Affairs, Washington, 1957-70; Chmn. Conf. European Problems, hon. pres. 1986. Clubs: P.E.N. (N.Y.C.); Arts (Chgo.); Elizabethan (New Haven); Birnam Wood (Santa Barbara, Calif.). Address: 780 Riven Rock Rd Santa Barbara CA 93108-1123

DAVIDSON, EZRA C., JR., physician, educator; b. Water Valley, Miss., Oct. 21, 1933; s. Ezra Cap and Theresa Hattie (Woods) D.; children: Pamela, Gwendolyn, Marc, Ezra K. BS cum laude, Morehouse Coll., 1954; MD, Meharry Med. Coll., 1958. Diplomate: Am. Bd. Ob-Gyn. (examiner 1973—). Intern San Diego County Gen. Hosp., 1958-59; resident in ob-gyn. Harlem Hosp., N.Y.C., 1963-66, asst. attending ob-gyn, obstet. coordinator maternal and infant care clinics, 1967-68; dir. departmental research, assoc. attending, acting chmn. ob-gyn, co-dir. coagulation research lab. Roosevelt Hosp., N.Y.C., 1968-70; fellow blood coagulation, asst. ob-gyn Columbia U. Coll. Physicians and Surgeons, N.Y.C., 1966-67, instr. dept. ob-gyn, 1967-69, asst. clin. prof., 1970; cons. ob-gyn Office Health Affairs, OEO, Washington, 1970-72; prof. Charles R. Drew U. of Medicine and Sci., L.A., 1971—, acad. v.p., 1982-87, chmn. dept. ob.-gyn., 1971-96, assoc. dean primary care, 1997—; prof. U. So. Calif., Los Angeles, 1971-80, UCLA, 1980—; chief svc. dept. ob-gyn. King/Drew Med. Ctr., L.A., 1971-96; attending physician dept. ob-gyn. L.A. County-U. So. Calif. Med. Ctr., 1971-80; mem. nat. med. adv. com. Nat. Found. March of Dimes, 1972-76; bd. cons. Internat. Childbirth Edn. Assn., 1973-81; mem. sec.'s adv. com. population affairs HEW, 1974-77, chmn. svcs. task force, 1975-77; chmn. bd. dirs. L.A. Regional Family Planning Coun., 1975-77; bd. dirs. Nat. Alliance Sch. Age parents, 1975-79; mem. corp. bd. Blue Shield, Calif., 1989—; chmn. fertility and maternal health drugs adv. com. FDA, 1992-96, active, 1990-96; mem. adv. com. to the dir. NIH, 1995, mem. dirs. adv. panel on clin. rsch., 1995—; mem. roundtable on health care quality Inst. of Medicine, 1995-98; mem. coun. grad. med. edn. HHS, 1997—; bd. dirs. Blue Shield of Calif. Bd. dirs. The Calif. Wellness Found., 1995—, chmn., 1996-98; bd. dirs. Children's Bur. So. Calif., 1999—, v.p., 1995-99; bd. dirs. Jacobs Inst. of Womens Health, 1999—. Served with USAF, 1959-63. Johnson Found. Health Policy fellow Inst. Medicine, Nat. Acad. Scis., 1979-80. Fellow ACS, Am. Coll. Ob-Gyn. (nat. sec. 1983-89, pres.-elect 1989—, pres. 1990-91), Royal Coll. Ob-Gyn., L.A. Ob-Gyn. Soc. (pres. 1982-83); mem. Am. Gyn.-Ob Soc., N.Am. Soc. Pediatric and Adolescent Gynecology (pres.-elect 1993-94, pres. 1994-95), Pacific Coast Ob-Gyn. Soc., Ob-Gyn. Assembly So. Calif. (chmn. 1989-90), Nat. Med. Assn. (chmn. nat. sect. ob-gyn. 1975-77, mem. sci. coun. 1979-88, trustee 1989-95, chmn. bd. trustees 1992-95), Golden State Med. Assn. (pres. 1989-90), Assn. Profs. Ob-Gyn. (pres. 1989-90). Office: 12021 Wilmington Ave Los Angeles CA 90059-3019

DAVIDSON, FRANCES, film and video producer; b. L.A., June 26, 1941; d. Daniel Bemis and Frances Godwin Williams; m. John Melvin Davidson, May 27, 1972; children: Emily, Jean. BA, Pomona Coll., 1963; MA, Stanford U., 1964. Vol. Peace Corps, Ethiopia, 1965-68; dir. Rodeo (Calif.) Child Devel., 1969-75; psychologist Centro de Integracion Juvenil, Tijuana, Mex., 1975-78; pres. Davidson Films, Inc., San Luis Obispo, Calif., 1979—. Prodr. (film) Piaget's Devel. Theory: An Overview, 1989 (Awards 1990-91), Erik H. Erikson: A Life's Work, 1991 (Awards 1992), (video) Aging Successfully: Psychol. Aspects of Growing Old, 1998 (CINDY Competition Silver award 1998); writer, prodr. (video) How Children Learn, 1997 (CINDY Competition Gold award 1998). Pres. bd. dirs. PTA, San Luis Obispo, 1990-96; bd. dirs. Black and Gold Booster H.S. orgn., San Luis Obispo, 1996—. Democrat. Avocation: gardening. Fax: 805-543-6253. E-mail: dfi@davidsonfilms.com. Office: Davidson Films Inc 668 Marsh St San Luis Obispo CA 93401

DAVIDSON, FRANK PAUL, retired macroengineer, lawyer; b. N.Y.C., May 20, 1918; s. Maurice Philip and Blanche (Reinheimer) D.; m. Izaline Marguerite Doll, May 19, 1951; children: Roger Conrad, Nicholas Henry, Charles Geoffrey. BS, Harvard U., 1939, JD, 1948; DHL (hon.), Hawthorne Coll., 1987. Bar: N.Y. 1953, U.S. Dist. Ct. (so. dist.) N.Y. 1953. Dir. mil. affairs, gen. counsel Houston C. of C., 1948-50; contract analyst Am. Embassy, Paris, 1950-53; assoc. Carb, Luria, Glassner & Cook, N.Y.C., 1953-54; pvt. practice law N.Y.C., 1955-70; founding pres., counsel, bd. dirs. The Inst. for the Future, 1967-70; rsch. assoc. MIT, Cambridge, Mass., 1970-96; also chmn. system dynamics steering com. Sloan Sch. Mgmt., coord. macro-engrng. Sch. Engring., MIT; semi-ret., 1984; pres. Tch. Studies Inc., N.Y.C., 1957-96, vice chmn. Inst. for Ednl. Svcs., Bedford, Mass., 1980-84, spl. lectr. Société des Ingénieurs et Scientifiques de France, 1991, NAS del. to Renewable Resources Workshop, Katmandu, Nepal, 1981, governing bd. Channel Tunnel Study Group, 1957-85, co-founder Channel Tunnel Study Group, London, Paris, 1957, apptd. to NASA Exploration Task Force, Washington, 1989, mem. internat. sci. and tech. com. Ocean Cities Symposium, Monaco, 1995. Author: Macro: A Clear Vision of How Science and Technology Will Shape Our Future, 1983, Macro: Big is Beautiful, 1986; editor: series of AAAS books on macroengring., Tunneling and Underground Transport, 1987; co-editor: Macro-Engineering, Global Infrastructure Solutions, 1992, Solar Power Satellites, 1993, 2nd edit., 1998, Macro-Engineering and The Earth: World Projects for the Year 2000 and Beyond, 1998; mem. editorial bd. Interdisciplinary Sci. Revs., 1985—; mem. adv. bd. Tech. in Soc., 1979—, Mountain R&D, 1981—, Project Appraisal, 1986-98. Bd. dirs. Internat. Mountain Soc., Boulder, Colo., 1981—, Assn. Prospective 2100, Paris, 1997; trustee Norwich (Vt.) Ctr., 1980-83, mem. steering com. Am. Trails Network, 1986-88, bd. dirs. Am. Trails Washington, 1988-90. RCAC, 1941-46, ETO; Troop Leader 10th Cdn., Armed Rgt. (Fort Garry Horse), Intelligence Officer and Squadron Leader, GSO III (Intelligence) Second Armoured Brigade Group, maj. Tex. State Guard; apptd. to Senate Ft. Garry Horse, 1995. Recipient Key to City Osaka, Japan, 1987; elected Mem. Honoraire, Pres. d'Honneur Assn. Louis Armand, Paris, 1996-99; Lewis Mumford Fellow Rensselaerville Inst., 1982. MEM ABA, Internat. Assn. Macro-Engring. Socs. (bd. dirs. 1987—, hon.chmn. 1997—), Am. Soc. Macro-Engrng. (bd. dirs. 1982—, vice chancellor 1983-97, pres. 1997—, chmn. 1998), Assn. Bar of City of N.Y. (internat. law com. 1959-62), Major Projects Assn. (mem. overseas adv. com. U.K. 1995—), Knickerbocker (N.Y.C.) Club, St. Botolph (Boston) Club, MIT Quarter Century Club. Home: 26A Parker St Lexington MA 02421-4907

DAVIDSON, GEORGE A., JR., utility company executive; b. Pitts., July 28, 1938. BS, U. of Pitts., 1960. Chmn., chief exec. officer, dir. Consol. Natural Gas Co., Pitts. Office: Consol Natural Gas Co CNG Tower 625 Liberty Ave 22nd Fl Pittsburgh PA 15222-3199*

DAVIDSON, GEORGE ALLAN, lawyer; b. N.Y.C., Apr. 6, 1942; s. George Roger and Jean Allan (McKaig) D.; m. Annette L. Richter, Sept. 4, 1965; children: Emily, Charlotte. AB, Brown U., 1964; LLB, Columbia U., 1967. Bar: N.Y. 1967, U.S. Dist. Ct. (so. and ea. dists.) N.Y. 1969, U.S. Ct. Appeals (2d cir.) 1970, U.S. Supreme Ct. 1974, U.S. Tax Ct. 1974, U.S. Ct. Appeals (D.C. cir.) 1976, U.S. Dist. Ct. (no. dist.) Calif. 1980, U.S. Ct. Appeals (9th cir.) 1981, U.S. Ct. Appeals (5th cir.) 1982, U.S. Dist. Ct. (no. dist.) N.Y. 1982, U.S. Ct. Appeals (11th cir.) 1983, U.S. Ct. Appeals (1st cir.) 1986, U.S. Ct. Appeals (7th cir.) 1992. Law clk., 1967-68; assoc. Hughes Hubbard & Reed, N.Y.C., 1968-74, ptnr., 1974—; dir. P.R. Legal Def. and Edn. Fund, Inc., 1980-84, Legal Aid Soc., 1979-92, pres. 1987-89, N.Y. Lawyers for Pub. Interest, Inc., 1984-86, Columbia Law Sch. Alumni Assn., 1987-91, Practicing Attys. for Law Students, 1989—, VIP Cmty. Svcs., 1994—. Fellow Am. Coll. Trial Lawyers; mem. ABA, Internat. Bar Assn., Fed. Bar Council, Am. Law Inst., N.Y. Sci. Policy Assn., N.Y. State Bar Assn., Assn. Bar City N.Y., Nat. Assn. Coll. and Univ. Attys., Union Internationale des Avocats, Century Assn. Contbr. writings to legal publs. Office: Hughes Hubbard & Reed LLP 1 Battery Park Plz Fl 12 New York NY 10004-1482

DAVIDSON, GEORGE THOMAS, JR., minister, educator; b. Winchester, Mass., Dec. 4, 1916; s. George Thomas and Allie Elizabeth (Patterson) D.; BS, Bowdoin Coll., 1938; DEd (hon.), 1976; postgrad. Columbia U., 1938-39; MA, Boston U., 1954, postgrad., 1959-61; m. Frances Ray, Sept. 30, 1944; children: Richard G., Raylene Alice Newbury. Tchr., coach Kennett High Sch., Conway, N.H., 1939-42, vice-prin., 1946-47, prin., 1947-57, tchr.-coach, 1957-59, sch. counselor, 1959-61, dir. guidance services, 1961-76; cons. admissions testing program Regional Office of Coll. Bd., 1976-80; interim lay preacher Congl. Chs., Bartlett, Jackson, Fryeburg, Chocorua, Tamworth, Conway, Ossipee, N.H., 1951-53; lay minister First Christian Ch., Freedom, N.H., 1953-70; ordained to ministry Christian Ch., 1970; minister 2d Congl. Ch., Ossipee, N.H., 1969-89, pastor emeritus, 1994—, First Christian Ch., Freedom, N.H., 1970-89, pastor-emeritus, 1989—; Protestant chaplain N.H. State Police, 1973—; vis. instr. U. N.H., 1964-67, 71-72, Gorham State Coll., 1967-70, N.H. Dept. Edn., 1970-72. Mem. Carroll County YMCA Com., State YMCA Youth Com.; mem. Gov's. Adv. Bd. Tech. Services in Health Field; mem. N.H. Interscholastic Athletic Assn.; pres. N.H. Assn. Secondary Sch. Prins., 1953-54; owner, dir. Camp Wakuta for Boys, 1951-67; mem. county com. Gov's. Com. on Crime and Juvenile Delinquency; bd. dirs. Carroll County Mental Health Services; co-founder, exec. sec. Mount Washington Citizens Scholarship Found.; dir. Conway Adult Basic Edn. Program; moderator 2d Congl. Ch., Conway, N.H.; coach North Conway Am. Legion Baseball; vice-chmn. N.H. State Adv. Council Vocat.-Tech. Edn.; tour guide N.H. Coll. and Univ. Council; sports announcer Sta. WBNC, Conway, N.H.; test center supr. Coll. Bd., Fryeburg, Maine; trustee Fryeburg Acad., 1985-89, trustee emeritus, 1989—; chaplain Carroll County Sheriff's Dept., 1985—, Conway Fire Dept., 1985—. Served to capt. USAAF, 1942-46. Named Carroll County Educator of Year, 1954; recipient First Achievement award N.H. Personnel and Guidance Assn., 1966, Disting. Bowdoin Educator award Bowdoin Coll. Alumni Assn., 1967, Carl Lundholm award State N.H., 1972, Granite State award U. N.H., 1976, Disting. Service award New Eng. Assn. Coll. Admissions Counselors, 1976, Gov's. Commendation for Service to Youth, 1976, Community Service award Freedom Old Home Week Sunday Service, 1979, Service to Community award Conway Grange, 1979, citation, Col. Presby of N.H. State Police, 1993; Disting. Service award Mt. Washington Valley Kiwanis Club, 1983, White Mts. Treas. award Mt. Washington Valley C. of C., 1994; Scholarships named in his honor 1st Christian Ch. and Ossipee 2d Congrl. Ch., 1982, Fellowship Room named in his honor Freedom 1st Christian Ch., 1987, Baseball Field named in his honor Kennett H.S., 1984; Charter mem. Kennett High Eagle Sports Hall of Fame, 1991. Mem. Nat. Assn. Coll. Admissions Counselors (assembly del. 1967-69), New Eng. Assn. Coll. Admissions Counselors (dir. 1970-74), N.H. Vocat. Assn. (pres.), N.H. Sch. Counselors Assn. (pres. 1969-70), Rotary (Paul Harris Fellow North Conway chpt. 1988). Home: RR 1 Box 1695 Freedom NH 03836-9729

DAVIDSON, GERARD H., JR., lawyer; b. San Diego, Oct. 7, 1943. BA cum laude, Wake Forest U., 1965, JD, 1968. Bar: N.C. 1968. Ptnr. Smith, Helms, Mulliss & Moore, Greensboro, N.C. Capt. JAGC, U.S. Army, 1968-73. Hankins scholar. Mem. ABA, DRI, Phi Delta Phi. Office: Smith Helms Mulliss & Moore First Union Tower 300 N Greene St Ste 1400 Greensboro NC 27420-1927*

DAVIDSON, GLEN HARRIS, federal judge; b. Pontotoc, Miss., Nov. 20, 1941; s. M. Glen and Lora (Harris) D.; m. Bonnie Payne, Apr. 25, 1973; children: Glen III, Gregory P. B.A., U. Miss, 1962, J.D., 1965. Bar: Miss. 1965, U.S. Ct. Appeals (5th cir.) 1965, U.S. Supreme Ct. 1971. Asst. dist. atty. First Jud. Dist., Tupelo, Miss., 1969-74; dist. atty. First Jud. Dist., 1975; U.S. atty. U.S. Dist. Ct. (no. dist.) Miss., Oxford, 1981-85; U.S. district judge U.S. Ct. House, Aberdeen, Miss., 1985—; atty. Lee County Sch. Bd., Miss., 1974-81. Bd. dirs. Community Devel. Found., Tupelo, 1976-81; mem. exec. bd. Yocona Council Boy Scouts Am., 1972—. Served to maj. USAF, 1966-69. Mem. Fed. Bar Assn. (v.p. 1984), Miss. Bar Found., Lee County Bar Assn. (pres. 1974), Assn. Trial Lawyers Am., Miss. Prosecutors Assn. Presbyterian. Lodge: Kiwanis (pres. Tupelo 1978). Office: US Dist Ct PO Box 767 Aberdeen MS 39730-0767*

DAVIDSON, GORDON BYRON, lawyer; b. Louisville, June 24, 1926; s. Paul Byron and Elizabeth (Franz) D.; m. Geraldine B. Geiger, Dec. 21, 1948; children: Sally Burgess, Stuart Gordon. A.B., Centre Coll., 1949; J.D., U. Louisville, 1951; LL.M., Yale U., 1952. Law clk. Supreme Ct. U.S., 1954; of counsel Wyatt, Tarrant & Combs, Louisville, 1955-92, mng. ptnr., 1978-92; bd. dirs. Duff & Phelps Utilities Income, Inc., Warner A. Jones Farm, Inc., Norton Healthcare, Inc., Warben, Inc.; dir. BellSouth Corp., 1986-95. Pres. Louisville Ctrl. Area, Inc., 1971-73; chmn. River City Mall Com., 1973-74, Louisville Devel. Com., Ky. Ctr. for Arts, 1980-95, Louisville Area C. of C., 1986, trustee; bd. dirs., chmn. Norton Childrens Hosps., 1973-75, Louisville Fund for Arts, 1987-93; trustee emeritus Centre Coll. Recipient Louisville Citizen of Yr. award, 1973-74, Mayor's Fleur de Lis award, 1974, Louisville Man of Yr. award, 1981, Outstanding Lawyer of Ky. award, 1984, Disting. Alumnus award U. Louisville Law Sch., 1982, Disting. Citizen award City of Louisville, 1987, Man of Vision award, 1991, Ky. Commonwealth award, 1995, Caritas Found. award, 1998; named to Louisville Male High Sch. Hall of Fame, 1989. Mem. Harmony Club, Landing Country Club, Jefferson Louisville Country Club, Denbarn Club, Lawyers Club, Gulf Stream Bath and Tennis Club (Fla.), Gulf Stream Golf Club (Fla.). Democrat. Presbyterian. Home: 435 Lightfoot Rd Louisville KY 40207-1853 also: 1102 N Vista Del Mar Delray Beach FL 33483 Office: Wyatt Tarrant & Combs Citizens Plz Louisville KY 40202-2815

DAVIDSON, HERBERT ALAN, Near Eastern languages and cultures educator; b. Boston, May 25, 1932; s. Louis Nathan and Ettabelle (Baker) D.; m. Kinneret Bernstein; children: Rachel and Jessica. BA, Harvard U., 1953, MA, 1955, PhD, 1959. Lectr. Harvard U., Cambridge, Mass., 1960-61; asst. prof. UCLA, 1961-66, assoc. prof., 1966-72, prof., 1972-94, prof. emeritus, 1994—, chmn. dept. near eastern langs. and cultures, 1984-91. Author: The Philosophy of Abraham Shalom, 1964, medieval Hebrew transls. of Averroes' Middle Commentary on the Isagoge and Categories, 1969, English transl., 1969, Proofs for Eternity, Creation, and the Existence of God in Medieval Islamic and Jewish Philosophy, 1987, Alfarabi, Avicenna, and Averroes on Intellect, 1992; contbr. articles and book revs. to profl. jours. Office: UCLA Dept Near Ea Langs and Cultures 405 Hilgard Ave Los Angeles CA 90095-9000*

DAVIDSON, HERBERT M. (TIPPEN), JR., newspaper owner; b. Chgo., Aug. 10, 1925; s. Herbert Marc and Liliane (Refregier) D.; m. Josephine Field, Dec. 27, 1947 (dec. July 1995); children: Marc, Julia. Student, Juilliard Sch., 1942-43, 45-46; Mus.D. (hon.), Stetson U., 1975. Reporter Chgo. Daily News, 1949-50; city editor Daytona Beach (Fla.) News-Jour., 1951-53, mng. editor, 1953-56, gen. mgr., 1957-85, pub., co-editor, 1998, pres., CEO, 1998—. Pres. Ctrl. Fla. Cultural Endeavors, Inc., Daytona Beach, 1963—; chmn. Fine Arts Coun. of Fla., 1970-75, 81-82, Fla. Alliance for Arts, 1998—; prodr., artistic dir. Seaside Music Theater, Daytona Beach, 1976—, mem., 1999—. Cpl. U.S. Army, 1942-44, PTO. Named Ambassador of the Arts, State of Fla., Tallahassee, 1982, Hon. mem. London Symphony Orch., 1989, honoree Daytona Beach Community Coll.'s Tippen and Josephine Field Davidson Endowment for the Arts, 1992; hon. officer civil divsn. Order of the Brit. Empire, 1998. Mem. Am. Soc. Newspaper Editors. Avocations: music; theater; handicraft; philately. Home: 1608 N Oleander Ave Daytona Beach FL 32118-3415 Office: Daytona Beach News-Jour 901 6th St Daytona Beach FL 32117-3352

DAVIDSON, HUBERT JAMES, JR., lawyer, educator; b. Kosciusko, Miss., Jan. 14, 1949; s. Hubert James and Ida Mae (Hill) D.; m. Jamie Jill Alexander, May 20, 1978; children: Michael Alexander, Benjamin Hill, Elizabeth Kate. BA, U. Miss., 1971, JD, 1974. Bar: Miss. 1974. Ptnr. Carter & Davidson, Columbus, Miss., 1974—; instr. Miss. U. for Women, Columbus, 1975-86, asst. prof., 1986-90, assoc. prof., 1990-96, prof., 1996—, dir. Emergency Physicians Svcs., Columbus, 1986-95. Pres. Lowndes Cmty. Found., Columbus, 1994—; dir., v.p. Miss. Sch. for Math. and Sci. Found., Columbus, 1996—; bd. dirs. Salvation Army, Columbus, 1988—. Named Boss of the Yr., Lowndes County Legal Secs. Assn., 1978. Mem. Miss. Bar Assn. (chmn. com. on complaints 1987, co-chmn. paralegal study and cert. com. 1994), Exchange Club of Columbus (pres. 1981, dir. 1982), Columbus Lowndes C. of C. (chmn. 1992). Methodist. Avocations: tennis, reading, travel. Home: 1020 7th St N Columbus MS 39701-3408 Office: Carter & Davidson 407 7th St N # Columbus MS 39701-4679

DAVIDSON, HUGH MACCULLOUGH, French language and literature educator; b. West Point, Ga., Jan. 21, 1918; s. Robert Calvin Davidson Sr. and Anne Della Stripling; m. Loretta Jane Miller, June 15, 1951; 1 child, Anne Stripling Davidson. AB in Romance Langs., U. Chgo., 1938, PhD in Romance Langs., 1946; MA (hon.), Yale U., 1967. Instr. French U. Chgo., 1946-48, asst. prof. French, 1948-53, asst. dean coll., 1951-53; asst. prof. romance langs. Dartmouth Coll., 1953-56, prof. romance langs., 1956-62, chmn. dept. romance langs., 1957-59; prof. romance langs. Ohio State U., 1962-67, 68-73; prof. French lit. U. Va., 1973-78, commonwealth prof. French lit., 1978, 1978-90, commonwealth prof. French lit. emeritus, 1990—; vis. prof. French U. Mich., 1967; univ. examiner French and gen. linguistics, humanities U. Chgo., 1946-48; chmn. Coll. French staff U. Chgo., 1948-53; Thomas Jefferson fellow Downing Coll., Cambridge U., Eng., 1979-80; vis. prof. U. Paris Sorbonne, 1982-83; vis. com. humanities and arts Case We. Res. U., 1967; cons. div. edn. programs NEH, 1977; conducts seminars in field. Author: Audience, Words, and Art, 1965, The Origins of Certainty: Means and Meanings in Pascal's Pensées, 1979, Blaise Pascal, 1983, Pascal and the Arts of the Mind, 1993; co-author: A Concordance to the Pensées of Pascal, 1975, A Concordance to Pascal's Les Provinciales, 1980; asst. editor: The Idea and Practice of General Education, 1948; mem. editl. bd. Continuum: Problems in French Literature from the Late Renaissance to the Early Enlightenment, EMF: Studies in Early Modern France; contbr. articles to profl. jours. Capt. U.S. Air Corps. Gen. Edn. fellow Carnegie Found., 1948-49; Fulbright Sr. fellow for rsch. in France, 1959-60; Sr. Rsch. fellow Nat. Found. Arts and Humanities, 1967-68. Mem. MLA (mem. editl. com. publs. 1968-73), Am. Assn. Tchrs. French, Am. Soc. Eighteenth-Century Studies, N. Am. Soc. Seventeenth-Century French Lit., Assn. internat. des études françaises, Soc. internat. d'étude du XVIIe siècle, Soc. internat. d'étude du XVIIIe siècle, Soc. des amis de l'Inst. de littérature française de l'Univ. de Paris Sorbonne, Soc. des amis de Port-Royal, Phi Beta Kappa (mem. nat. Senate 1982-88). Episcopalian. Avocations: history of painting, sculpture, and architecture, history of the liberal arts of grammar, rhetoric, logic, dialectic and their applications in art, science, and philosophy, music. Address: Apt 456 590 Isaac Prugh Way Kettering OH 45429-7405 Office: U Va Dept French Lit 302 Cabell Hall Charlottesville VA 22908

DAVIDSON, JACK LEROY, academic administrator; b. Indpls., July 14, 1927; s. Lawrence L. and Emma (Jones) D.; m. Ina Stanfill, June 20, 1948; children: William (dec.), Nancy, Evan. BA, Franklin Coll., 1949; MA, Ind. U., 1955, Ed. Adminstrn., 1961, PhD, 1967. Tchr., guidance counselor, coach Mitchell (Ind.) Pub. Schs., 1949-57; elem. prin., supervising prin. Vincennes (Ind.) Pub. Schs., 1957-59; supt. Worthington (Ind.) Pub. Schs., 1959-61, Salem (Ind.) Pub. Schs., 1961-65, Oak Ridge (Tenn.) Pub. Schs., 1965-68, Manatee County (Fla.) Pub. Schs., 1968-70, Austin (Tex.) Pub. Schs., 1970-80, Tyler (Tex.) Public Schs., 1980-91; spl. asst. to pres. U. Tex., Tyler, 1991-96; vis. prof. U. Tex.; chmn. Tex. Adv. Com. on Ednl. Improvement. Schs.; cons. Tex. Edn. Agy. Author: Effective School Board Meetings, 1970, The Superintendency & Leadership for Effective Schools, 1987; Contbr. articles to ednl. jours. Bd. dirs., pres. Southwest Ednl. Devel. Lab.; charter mem. Tex. Commn. on Inter-Govtl. Rels.; bd. dirs. Austin Jr. Achievement; pres. bd. dirs. Salvation Army. With USNR, 1945-47. Recipient Super Supt. award Tex. PTA, 1982, award of honor Nat. Sch. Pub. Rels. Assn., 1990, Disting. Svc. award AASA, 1992; named one of 100 Top Exec. Educators Exec. Educator mag., 1984, 89. Mem. Am. Assn. Suprs. Curriculum Devel., Am. Assn. Sch. Adminstrs., Tex. Assn. Sch. Adminstrs., Rotary (pres. Tyler club), Phi Delta kappa (outstanding educator award 1992). Methodist (deacon, dir.). Home: 1807 Piccadilly Pl Tyler TX 75703-2409 *The only real profit in life comes from the satisfaction gained in service to others.*

DAVIDSON, JAMES JOSEPH, III, lawyer; b. Lafayette, La., July 27, 1940; s. James Joseph and Virginia Lee (Dunham) D.; m. Kay Cecile Holloway, Aug. 7, 1962; children—Kimberly Kay, James Joseph IV, Lynda Leigh, Virginia Holland. B.A., U. S.W. La., 1963; J.D., Tulane U., 1964. Bar: La. 1964, U.S. Dist. Ct. (we. dist.) La. 1965, U.S. Dist. Ct. (ea. dist.) La. 1979, U.S. Dist. Ct. (mid. dist.) 1986, U.S. Ct. Appeals (5th cir.) 1972, U.S. Supreme Ct. 1975, U.S. Ct. Appeals (11th cir.) 1981. Ptnr. Davidson, Meaux, Sonnier, McElligott & Swift, Lafayette, La., 1964—. Mem. exec. bd. Evangeline Area council Boy Scouts Am., 1969-80; trustee U. S.W. La. Found., 1981—, pres., 1988-91. Fellow Am. Bar Found. (life); mem. La. State Bar Assn. (del. 1970-96), La. Bar Found., Am. Judicature Soc., La. Assn. Def. Counsel (dir. 1975-77), Nat. Assn. R.R. Trial Counsel, Am. Bd. Trial Advocates (adv.), Am. Counsel Assn., Internat. Assn. Def. Counsel, Assn. Def. Trial Attys., Assn. Transp. Practitioners. Republican. Baptist. Home: 539 Girard Park Dr Lafayette LA 70503-2601 Office: PO Box 2908 Lafayette LA 70502-2908

DAVIDSON, JAMES MELVIN, academic administrator, researcher, educator; b. The Dalles, Oreg., Apr. 16, 1934; s. Melvin Archie and Kathryn Naomie (Crooks) D.; m. Margaret May Tewinkel, June 29, 1957; children: Deborah Joy, Jodi May, Michelle Anne. BS, Oreg. State U., 1956, MS, 1958; PhD, U. Calif., Davis, 1965. Asst. prof. to assoc. prof. Okla. State U., Stillwater, 1965-72, prof., 1973-74; vis. assoc. prof. U. Fla., Gainesville, 1972-73, prof., 1974-79, asst. dean for rsch., 1979-86, dean for rsch., 1986-92, v.p. agrl. nat. resources, 1992-98; sci. adv. com. Nat. Ctr. for Groundwater Res., Ada., Okla., 1979-86; groundwater res. rev. com. EPA Sci. Adv. Bd., Washington, 1984-86; water sci. and tech. bd. Nat. Acad. Sci., Washington, 1982-86. Co-editor: Virus Aspects of Applying Municipal Waste to Land, 1976, Environmental Impact of Non-point Source Pollution, 1980, Sludge-Health Risks of Land Application, 1980, Effects of Conservation Tillage on Groundwater Quality, 1987. Grantee EPA. Fellow Am. Soc. of Agronomy (chair environ. quality 1978), Soil Sci. Soc. Am. (chair soil physics 1984); mem. Alpha Zeta, Sigma Xi. Achievements include research in movement and sorption of pesticides and other organic solutes in soil systems in order to develop, test, and modify existing conceptual mathematical models for simulating the movement of water and solutes in homogeneous and nonhomogeneous soils.

DAVIDSON, JAMES WILSON, clinical psychologist; b. Muncie, Ind., Apr. 22, 1950; s. James Wayne and Mary Marguerite (Sanford) D.; m. Nancy Lee Hendershott, Aug. 30, 1969; children: Melissa Ann, Amanda Corynne, Kevin Patrick. BS, Mich. State U., 1972; PhD, Kent State U., 1975; postgrad., Ashland (Ohio) Theol. Sem., 1980-82. Ordained to ministry Assemblies of God, 1988. Coord. Ctr. on Rsch. and Evaluation, Ashtabula, Ohio, 1974-77; pres. The Children's Ctr., Ashtabula, 1978-80, Computech Data Systems, Ashtabula, 1978-82; v.p. Davidson Assocs., Ashtabula, 1977-86; assoc. pastor First Assembly of God, Ashtabula, 1986-88; sr. pastor Metro Ch., Cleve., 1988-94; CEO Heart and Hand Found., Cleve., 1988—, LifeLine Counseling Ctr., 1994—; dir. Ohio Dist. Coun. Urban Missions Ministries, Columbus, 1990—. Recipient 414th Point of Light award White House, 1991, Health award UNICEF, 1992, 93, Ptnr. Agy. Excellence award CMHA, 1992, 93; Kent State U. fellow, 1973-74. Mem. APA, Am. Assn. Christian Counselors. Republican. Avocations: flying, writing, travel, snorkeling. Home: 2627 Courtland Blvd Cleveland OH 44118-4737 Office: Heart and Hand Found PO Box 93813 2570 Woodhill Rd Cleveland OH 44104-2404

DAVIDSON, JANINE ANNE, military officer; b. Oxnard, Calif., Apr. 24, 1966; d. James Patrick and Joanne (Extale) D.; m. David Jerome Golan, May 4, 1996. BS in Archtl. Engring., U. Colo., 1988; postgrad., U. S.C., 1999—. Commd. 2nd lt. USAF, 1988, advanced through grades to capt., 1992; student pilot Williams AFB, Ariz., 1989-90; C-130 cargo pilot, exec. officer, scheduler 345 Airlift Squadron, Yokola AB, Japan, 1990-93; instr. pilot, flight comdr., acad. instr. 557 Flying Tng. Squadron, USAF Acad., Colorado Springs, 1993-96; pioneer C-17 pilot 14th Airlift Squadron, Charleston AFB, S.C., 1996-98. Vol. case worker disaster preparedness ARC, S.C., 1999—. ROTC scholar USAF, U. Colo., 1984-88. Mem. Women Mil. Aviators. Avocations: skiing, rock climbing, flying, travel. Home: 1413 Franklin St Columbia SC 29201

DAVIDSON, JOAN GATHER, psychologist; b. Long Branch, N.J., Jan. 26, 1934; d. Ralph Paul and Hilde (Bresser) Gather; m. Harry Gene Davidson, Sept. 14, 1957; children: Guy, Marc, Kelly. BA, Shorter Coll., 1956; BA cum laude, U. South Fla., 1982; MS, Fla. Inst. Tech., 1986, PsyD, 1987. Lic. psychologist, Fla., RN, Ga. Clin. instr. Ga. Bapt. Sch. Nursing, Atlanta, 1956-59; dir. nurses Aidmore Hosp., Atlanta, 1959-60; dir. insvc. edn., asst. dir. nurses Bayfront Med. Ctr., St. Petersburg, Fla., 1960; instr. St. Petersburg Jr. Coll., 1971-76; pvt. practice St. Petersburg-Clearwater, 1987—. Mem. Am. Psychol. Assn., Fla. Psychol. Assn., Nat. Register Health Svc. Providers in Psychology, Assn. for Advancement Psychology, Am. Assn. Christian Counselors, Psi Chi, Phi Kappa Phi. Republican. Baptist. Home: 11600 87th Ave Largo FL 33772-3613 Office: 2430 Estancia Blvd Ste 101 Clearwater FL 33761-2631

DAVIDSON, JOEL, surgeon; b. Pitts., June 23, 1939; s. Jack and Clara (Locker) D.; m. Linda Lee, Sept. 2, 1984; children: Amy Kubas, Shana, Sharon. BS, Washington & Jefferson U., 1960; MD, U. Pitts., 1964. Intern Washington (Pa.) Hosp., 1964-65; resident West Penn Hosp., Pitts., 1965-69; surgeon Davidson/Rosen Chartered, Las Vegas, Nev., 1970—; vice chief of surgery Sunrise Hosp., Las Vegas, 1979-82; pres. Nev. Peer Rev. Orgn., Las Vegas, 1985. Bd. dirs. Am. Cancer Soc., Las Vegas, 1988-90. Capt. USAFR, 1969-73. Fellow ACS, AMA, Am. Bd. Surgeons, Am. Soc. for Laser Medicine and Surgery, Nev. State Med. Soc., Clark County Med. Soc. (bd. trustees 1973-84, pres. 1982-83). Jewish. Avocations: traveling, gardening. Office: Davidson/Rosen Chartered 3196 S Maryland Pkwy Ste 204 Las Vegas NV 89109-2313

DAVIDSON, JOHN HUNTER, agriculturist; b. Wilmette, Ill., May 16, 1914; s. Joseph and Ruth Louise (Moody) D.; m. Elizabeth Marie Boynton, June 16, 1943; children: Joanne Davidson Hildebrand, Kathryn Davidson Bouwens, Patricia. BS in Horticulture, Mich. State U., 1937, MS in Plant Biochemistry, 1940. Field rschr. agrl. chems. Dow Chem. Co., Midland, Mich., 1936-42; with R&D agrl. products Dow Chem. Co., Midland, 1946-72, tech. adviser R&D agrl. products, 1972-80, tech. adviser govt. rels., 1980-84, cons., 1984—. Contbr. articles on plant pathology, horticulture and weed control to profl. jours. Lt. USNR, 1945. Mem. Am. Chem. Soc., Am. Soc. Hort. Sci., Weed Sci. Soc., Am. Pathol. Soc., Exch. Club of Midland, Phi Kappa Phi, Alpha Zeta. Republican. Home: 4319 Andre St Midland MI 48642-3779

DAVIDSON, JOHN ROBERT, dentist; b. Peru, Ind., Apr. 28, 1947; s. John Howard and Kathryn (Loughran) D.; m. Jean-Marie Dobler, Jan. 23, 1965 (div. Oct. 1972); children: James Michael, Jennifer Renee; m. Linda Mary Seasock, Oct. 22, 1977 (dec. Aug. 1997); children: Kathryn Cherise, John Richard. BS, Purdue U., 1969; DDS, UCLA, 1972. Diplomate Am. Bd. Forensic Dentistry, Am. Bd. Forensic Examiners. Gen. practice dentistry Granada Hills, Calif., 1972-74; prof. clin. and community dentistry, dir. of clinics Ferris State Coll., Big Rapids, Mich., 1974-75; pvt. practice dentistry specializing in oral implantology Peru, Ind., 1975—; dental staff mem. Dukes Meml. Hosp., Peru, 1975—; dep. coroner Miami County, 1987—. Drive chmn. United Way of Miami County, Peru, 1977, 78, bd. dirs., 1977-84; mem. Utility Service Bd., Peru, 1984-86, chmn., 1986; trustee 1st Bapt. Ch., Peru, 1979-82, 84-86, chmn. bd. trustees, 1986. Recipient Citizen of Yr. award, Peru, 1978, Pride award, Grissom AFB Community Council, Peru, 1980. Fellow Internat. Congress of Oral Implantologists, Am. Coll. Oral Implantologists (assoc.); mem. ADA, Am. Coll. Forensic Examiners, Ind. Dental Assn., Wabash Valley Dental Soc., Peru Area C. of C. (bd. dirs. 1976-83, Outstanding Service award 1979), Mensa, Masons, Elks, Rotary (chmn. scholarship com. Peru, 1975—). Fax: 765 473-5804. Home and Office: 27 N Park Ave Peru IN 46970-1718

DAVIDSON, JOHN ROBERT (JAY), banking executive; b. L.A., Mar. 30, 1950; s. John Robert Davidson and Carolyn Rose Monson; m. Kristina Maria Jonson, Dec. 29, 1978; children: Joshua Kingseley, Michelle Maria. BSME, U. N.D., 1972; postgrad., AMP Corp. Leadership Coll., 1990. Engr. Dow Chem. Co., Pauls Valley, Okla., 1972-74; investor Mpls., 1974-77; account exec. AMP Inc., Boulder, Colo., 1977-83; mkt. mgr. AMP Inc., Harrisburg, Pa., 1983-86; dist. mgr. AMP Inc., Denver, 1986-90, nat. mgr., 1990-95; chmn. of bd., CEO 1st Am. State Bank of Denver, 1995—; dir./cons. Am. State Bank, Williston, N.D., 1988—, dir. funds mgmt. com., 1994—, dir. exec. com., 1996—; mem. exec. com., chmn. bd. dirs. First Am. State Bank, Denver, 1995—. Supporter Am. Heart Assn., Colo., Kempe Children's Found., Arapahoe Home, Colo. Easter Seals, F.A.C.E.S., Colo. Symphony Orch., Vols. of Am., Boy Scouts Am., Children's Hosp., Arthritis Found.; bd. dirs. Kempe Children's Found., treas., exec. com., 1999—, mem. fin. com. and funds mgmt. com.; mem. Rep. Nat. Com.; mem. devel. bd. Am. Heart Assn.; bd. dirs. Easter Seals Colo.; event co-chairperson Arapahoe House, Easter Seals Colo., bd. dirs.; apptd. to Bd. Colo. Housing & Fin. Auth., 1999—. Recipient Presdl. Legion of Merit, Colo. Rep. Party. Mem. Masons, Presdl. Legion of Merit. Avocations: snow skiing, mountain biking, photography, computers, music. Home: 5780 S Goldsmith Pl Englewood CO 80111 Office: 1st Am State Bank 8390 E Crescent Pkwy Greenwood Village CO 80111

DAVIDSON, JOY ELAINE, mezzo-soprano; b. Ft. Collins, Colo., Aug. 18, 1940; d. Clarence Wayne and Jessie Ellen (Bogue) Ferguson; m. Robert Scott Davidson, Aug. 9, 1959; children: Lisa Beth, Robert Scott II, Jeremy Fergus, Bonnie Kathleen, Jordan Christian. B.A., Occidental Coll., Los Angeles, 1959; postgrad., Fla. State U., 1961-64. Robert A. Carrie Mastronardi endowed prof., 1995—; dir. vocal/opera dept. New World Sch. of Arts Coll./Conservatory Divsn., Miami, Fla. 1992—. Debut 1965 with Miami Opera; has performed with Met. Opera, opera cos. throughout U.S. and Can., La Scala, Vienna State Opera, Bayerische State Opera, Lyons (France) Opera, Welsh Opera, Florence (Italy) Opera, Torino (Italy) Opera. (recipient Gold medal Internat. Competition Young Opera Singers, Sofia, Bulgaria 1969), Rio de Janeiro; performed with numerous orchs. including N.Y. Philharm., Los Angeles Philharm., Boston Orch., Pitts. Orch., Columbus (Ohio) Orch.; rec. artist. Named Outstanding Miami Artist at Orange Bowl; recipient Mastronardi endowed chair, 1995, NISOD award for tchg. excellence, 1996, Roberta Rymer Balfe award Fla. Grand Opera. Mem. PEO, United Meth. Women, Sigma Alpha Iota, Zeta Tau Zeta. Methodist. Avocations: swimming, camping, cycling, church activities. Home: 5751 SW 74th Ave Miami FL 33143-1735 Office: Vocal Opera Dept New World Sch Coll Conservatory Divsn 300 NE 2nd Ave Miami FL 33132-2204 *Success awaits those who dare to dream big enough. The success achiever is the possibility thinker.*

DAVIDSON, JULI, creativity consultant; b. Houston, Aug. 23, 1960; d. Martin J. Davidson and Ruth Marder. Diploma, Park Sch., Brooklandville, Md., 1978; Cert., Richmond Coll., Surrey, Eng., 1978; student, Austin Coll., U. N.Mex, others, 1978-84, Hollywood Film Inst., 1996. Cert. med. terminology and transcription, 1981. Pres. mail order co. Surrenderings, Inc., Albuquerque, 1989-93; owner, artist Juli Davidson Studio Gallery, Albuquerque, 1987-89; freelance writer, editor, photographer Albuquerque, 1985-86; pres., paper artist, writer SI: A Paperworks Gallery, Sante Fe, 1993; exec. adminstr. Albuquerque Art Bus. Assn., 1989; bd. sec. Albuquerque United Artists, 1988; media, entertainment, and multimedia creativity cons. Author: Organic Plant Care: Root Division, 1998; editor, pub. 2C3P ZN, 1995; contbr. to various publs. and subject of various art revs.; writer, pub. mail-order publs., 1995; pub. creativity products for The Creative Process; screenplay and teleplay contest critic Southwest Writers Workshop, 1996; mkt. rsch. theatrical film reviewer, Audience Response, 1995; sitcom bible and pilot writer Think Tank Ink Prods, 1995; author screenplay Rockinghorse (shown at N.Y. Internat. Ind. Film and Video Festival 1998). Recipient 2d and 3d place photography awards Churches in New Mexico Exhibit, 1985, 4th place Colorfest Human Interest Category, Colo., 1986; recipient writing award Garden Writers Assn. of Am., 1993, for publishing handmade booklet on dividing and multiplying potted plants. Studio: PO Box 21669-WW Albuquerque NM 87154-1669

DAVIDSON, KAREN SUE, computer software designer; b. Chgo., July 24, 1950; d. Woodrow Wilson and Velma Louise (Dickinson) D. BS in Comm., U. Ill., 1972; MBA, De Paul U., 1977. Microsoft cert. profl. News prodr. Sta. WIND, Westinghouse Broadcasting Co., Chgo., 1973-75; mktg. rep. divsn. data processing IBM, Chgo., 1977-80, process industry specialist, 1980; industry applications specialist IBM, White Plains, N.Y., 1981-83; sr. sales rep. Wang Labs., Chgo., 1983-84; ptnr. KDA-K Davidson & Assocs., Centralia, Ill., 1984-88; pres. KDA Software Inc., Centralia, 1988—; instr. Belleville (Ill.) Area Coll., 1992, mem. office and tech. adv. bd., 1998—, chair, 1999—; vis. lectr. So. Ill. U., Carbondale, 1994; mem. rev. bd. State of Ill. Pvt. Enterprise. Author/designer software programs; contbr. articles to profl. pubs. State of Ill. Small Bus. Adv. Bd., Internat. Trade/Export Rep., 1990-93; WordPerfect cert. resource instr. WordPerfect Corp., 1991—; apptd. to State of Ill. Small Bus. 100, 1996. Named Outstanding Working Woman of Ill. Fedn. Bus. & Profl. Women's Clubs, 1990. Mem. Soc. Profl. Journalists, Ind. Computer Cons. Assn. (pres. St. Louis chpt. 1998-99), Ill. Software Assn., Chgo. High Tech. Assn. Assn. St. Louis Info. Sys. Trainers (v.p. 1988), Centralia Cultural Soc., Inventors' Assn. St. Louis, Greater Centralia C. of C. (bd. dirs. 1990-93, good will amb. 1990), Rotary, Zeta Tau Alpha. Presbyterian. Office: KDA Software Inc PO Box 1163 315 E 3rd St Centralia IL 62801-3919

DAVIDSON, KENNETH LAWRENCE, lawyer, educator; b. Tulsa, Feb. 4, 1945; s. Joe and Elsie (Hutchens) D.; m. Anne Devine; children: Rebecca Marie, Deborah Shannon. BSBA, U. Tulsa, 1968, JD, 1970; LLM, Georgetown U., 1975. Bar: Okla. 1970, U.S. Dist. Ct. (no. dist.) Okla. 1970, U.S. Ct. Mil. Appeals 1971, D.C. Ct. Appeals 1975, U.S. Supreme Ct. 1977, Ill. 1990. Assoc. CEO, assoc. legal counsel Bd. Regents Okla. State U. and A&M Colls., Stillwater, 1976-90; gen. counsel Regency Univs. System Ill. Bd. Regents, Springfield, 1990-96; parliamentarian, univ. counsel, bd. trustees No. Ill. U., DeKalb, 1995-97, counsel for governance, risk mgmt., equity svcs., 1997—; adj. assoc. prof. Coll. Edn. Okla. State U., 1986-90; adminstrv. law judge Okla. Dept. Edn., Oklahoma City, 1978-90. Bd. dirs. YMCA Aquatic Club, Stillwater, 1985-86, Judith Karman Hospice, Stillwater, 1987. Capt. JAGC, USAF, 1970-76. Decorated Meritorious Svc. medal, Commendation medal. Mem. Ill. Bar Assn., DeKalb County Bar Assn., Okla. Bar Assn., D.C. Bar Assn., Nat. Assn. Coll. and Univ. Attys., Kappa Sigma. Democrat. Office: No Ill U 302 Lowden Hall Dekalb IL 60115

DAVIDSON, LAURA JANETTE, nurse practitioner, educator; b. Fulton, Mo., Mar. 11, 1949; d. James C. and Audrey (Clyman) Yates; m. Douglas Davidson, 1972 (div. 1980). Diploma, Mercy Sch. Nursing, Ft. Scott, Kans., 1970; BSN, S.W. Mo. State U., 1983; MSN, U. Tex., Houston, 1990. RN, Kans.; CEN, FNP, ACLS; cert. advanced RN practitioner. Staff nurse med.-surg. Mercy Hosp., Ft. Scott, 1970; nurse corp Wilford Hall USAF Med. Ctr., 1970-74; staff nurse med.-surg. Audie Murphy VA Hosp., San Antonio, 1974-75, Bethania Hosp., Wichita Falls, Tex., 1975-79; staff nurse, supr. emergency dept. Cox Med. Ctr., Springfield, Mo., 1979-87; grad. asst. U. Tex. Health Sci. Ctr., Houston, 1988-90; clin. asst. prof. U. Kans. Sch. Nursing, Kansas City, 1990—; staff nurse emergency dept. Shawnee Mission (Kans.) Med. Ctr., 1991-97; clin. instr. St. John's Sch. Nursing, Springfield, 1983-85. Mem. Am. Acad. Nurse Practitioners, Emergency Nurses Assn. (sec.-treas. local chpt. 1983-97), Sigma Theta Tau (sec. local chpt. 1986—). Office: Univ Kans Sch Nursing 3901 Rainbow Blvd Kansas City KS 66160-7502

DAVIDSON, LEE DAVID, insurance executive; b. Worcester, Mass., Sept. 1, 1959; s. Charles and Edith (Dwyer) D.; m. Tracy Eileen Stephenson; children: Adam, Ashley, Amanda. Student, Wachusett C. C., Gardner, Mass., 1991. Mgr. Black and White Restaurant, Spencer, Mass., 1982-84; asst. mgr. Valle's Steak House, Worcester, Mass., 1984; with Worcester Police Dept., 1985; facilities profl. State Mut. Ins., Worcester, 1985-86, self acctg., 1986-88, compliance analyst, 1988-92, mgr. compliance, 1992-94, asst. v.p., 1994—; dir. Allmerica Benefit Agy. Inc., 1996—; v.p. Sterling Risk Mgmt., Inc., 1996—; asst. v.p. Allmerica Fin. Life and Annuity Co., 1996—; treas. Fellowship Club, Worcester, 1994-95; v.p., bd. dirs. Allmerica Benefits, Inc., 1997—. Trustee South Athol United Meth. Ch., 1994—, treas., 1999—. With USN, 1977-81. Mem. Elks, Am. Legion. Republican. Avocations: woodworking, golf, swimming. Home: 420 Templeton Rd Athol MA 01331-9769 Office: First Allmerica Fin Life Ins Co 440 Lincoln St Worcester MA 01653-0002

DAVIDSON, MARK EDWARD, lawyer; b. Niskayuna, N.Y., Aug. 18, 1952; s. Robert E. and Mary E. (Morton) D.; m. Mary Helen Woods, June 4, 1977; children: Michael S., Jeffrey P., Kara M. BA, SUNY, Stony Brook, 1974; JD, Georgetown U., 1977. Bar: N.Y. 1978, U.S. Dist. Ct. (so. and ea. dists.) N.Y., U.S. Ct. Appeals (2d and 11th cirs.). Assoc. Shea & Gould, N.Y.C., 1977-85, ptnr., 1986-92; sr. counsel Proskauer Rose LLP, N.Y., 1992—. Author: (with others) Handbook of Auditing and Accounting, 1989, 90; editor jour. Am. Criminal Law Rev., 1976-77. Panelist N.Y. State Surrogate Decision Making Panel, Albany, 1988—; spl. master N.Y. State Supreme Ct., N.Y.C., 1988—. Mem. ABA. Avocations: reading, hiking, canoeing, wine collecting, computers. Office: Proskauer Rose Goetz & Mendelsohn 1585 Broadway New York NY 10036-8200*

DAVIDSON, MAYER B., medical educator, researcher; b. Balt., Apr. 11, 1935; s. David and Esther (Crockin) D.; m. Naomi Berger, Nov. 25, 1961 (div. 1977); children: Elke W., Seth J.; m. Roseann Herman, Aug. 31, 1980. AB, Swarthmore Coll., 1957; MD, Harvard U., 1961. Diplomate Am. Bd. Internal Medicine, Am. Bd. Endocrinology and Metabolism. Intern Bellevue Hosp., N.Y.C., 1961-62, jr. asst. resident, 1962-63; sr. asst. resident U. Wash. Affiliated Hosps., Seattle, 1963-64; rsch. fellow dept. endocrinology and metabolism King County Hosp., U. Wash., Seattle, 1964-66; asst. prof. medicine UCLA Sch. Medicine, 1969-74, from assoc. prof. to prof., 1974-95, clin. prof., 1996—, acting chief div. endocrinology and metabolism, 1973-74; dir. diabetes program Cedars-Sinai Med. Ctr., L.A., 1979-95; assoc. dir. clin. diabetes City of Hope Nat. Med. Ctr., 1995-98; dir. clin. trials unit Charles R. Drew U.; nat. advisor Diabetes Ctr. Humana Hosp., Phoenix, 1985-91; attending physician diabetic clinic Boston City Hosp., 1966-68; clin. asst. Harvard Med. Sch., 1968-69; cons. AMA Dept. Drugs. Author: Diabetus Mellitus: Diagnosis and Treatment, 4th edit., 1998; contbr. 23 chpts. to books, numerous revs., editls., articles and abstracts; presenter 133 sci. papers; mem. editl. bd. Jour. Clin. Endocrinology and Metabolism, 1981-84, 93-95, Jour. Diabetes Care, 1984-87, Geriatrics, 1986—, Diabetes Reports, 1987-89, Today in Medicine,1987-88, Clin. Diabetes, 1989-92, Diabetes Spectrum, 1989-92, Diabetes Rsch. & Clin. Practice, 1992-95. Co-founder, bd. dirs. free med. facility Venice (Calif.) Family Clinic, 1970. Maj. Med. Svc. Corps U.S . Army, 1966-69. USPHS rsch. fellow Nat. Inst. Arthritis and Metabolic Diseases, 1965-66; recipient Upjohn award for Outstanding Diabetes Educator, 1990, Robert H. Williams/Rachmiel Levine award for sci. contbns. and humanism in tng. young rschrs., 1995, Banting medal for Disting. Svc., 1998; named to Best Doctors in Am., 1992-93, 95-96, 96-97. Fellow ACP; mem. AAAS, Am. Diabetes Assn. (rsch. prizes 1965, 66, R&D award 1974-75, rsch. 1978-81, bd. dirs. 1986-89, 93—, v.p. 1995-96, pres.-elect 1996-97, pres. 1997-98), Am. Fedn. Clin. Rsch., Western Soc. Clin. Rsch., Endocrine Soc., Am. Soc. Clin. Investigation, Western Assn. Physicians, Am. Assn. Diabetes Educators (editl. bd. jour. 1980-83), Boylston Med. Soc., Am. Diabetes Assn. (pres. 1997-98), Sigma Xi. Democrat. Jewish.

DAVIDSON, MICHAEL W., psychologist; b. Lafayette, Ind., June 12, 1959; s. Forster and Nadya Davidson; m. Gretchen G. Gabriel, May 18, 1985; children: Victoria, Annaliese, Zachary. MBA, U. Kans., 1988; MA, U. Mo., Kansas City, 1993; PhD, U. So. Miss., 1996. Lic. psychologist, Ark., Tenn. Pvt. practice, Blytheville and Jonesboro, Ark., 1996—. Mem. APA, ACA, Tenn. Psychol. Assn., Memphis Area Psychol. Assn., Mensa. Avocations: writing, reading, cooking, travel. Office: 415 Chickawasba Blytheville AR 70000

DAVIDSON, NANCY BRACHMAN, artist, educator; b. Chgo., Nov. 3, 1943; d. Philip and Jane (Blanch) Brachman; m. Donald Davidson, July 15, 1961 (div. 1977); 1 child, Lance A.; m. Greg Drasler, June 15, 1985. BEd, Northeastern Ill. U., 1965; BA, U. Ill., Chgo., 1972; MFA, Sch. Art Inst., Chgo., 1975. Vis. asst. prof. U. Ill., Champaign, 1977-79, Williams Coll., Williamstown, Mass., 1980-84; vis. artist, assoc. prof. SUNY, Purchase, 1984—. One woman shows include Berkshire Mus., Pittsfield, Mass., 1982, Marianne Deson Gallery, Chgo., 1978, 81, 83, 88, Richard Anderson Gallery, 1991, 93, 95, Shoshana Wayne Gallery, Santa Monica, Calif., 1997, Nova Sin Gallery, Prague, Czech Republic, 1998, Neuberger Mus., Purchase, N.Y., 1998, Inst. Contemporary Art, U. Pa., Phila., 1999; exhibited in group shows at Albright-Knox Gallery, Buffalo, 1980, Mus. Contemporary Art Chgo., 1984, Art Inst. Chgo., 1974, 78, 79, Bad Girls West-UCLA, 1994. Fellow NEA, 1978, Mass. Coun. Arts, 1981, Ford Found., 1978; Mass. Coun. Arts grantee, 1984, Anonymous Was a Woman grantee, 1997. Home: 137 Duane St Apt 4W New York NY 10013-3892

DAVIDSON, NOREEN HANNA, financial services company executive; b. Hartford, Conn., Sept. 13, 1950; d. Morris A. and Allene Sullivan (Gotis) Bezzini; m. Herbert L. Davidson, May 27, 1983 (div. 1991); 1 child, Stephanie Wells. BA, Stephens Coll., 1972. Senate intern U.S. Senator Thomas Dodd, Washington, 1970; legis. aide Mo. State Senate, Jefferson City, 1972; liaison econ. stabilization and White House Exec. Office of Pres., Washington, 1972-74; senate staff U.S. Senator Jacob Javitts, Washington, 1974; dir. legislation Nat. Assn. Plumbing, Heating and Cooling Contractors, Washington, 1975-77, Am. Aviation Found., Washington, 1977-81; mgr. nat. sales Nat. Standards, Bethesda, Md., 1981-84; v.p. Great Lakes Investment, Reston, Va., 1984-91; dir., v.p., br. mgr. Meyers, Pollack, Robbins, Inc., McLean, 1991-97; v.p. Wheat First Union, 1998—; mem. adv. bd. Heritage Fin. Corp., McLean, 1988-90. Author, editor Fixed Income newsletter Fin. Mgmt. Group, 1990, 91, Legislative News newsletter Nat. Assn. Plumbing, Heating and Cooling Contractors, 1976. Mem. exec. staff Presdl. Inaugral for Reagan, Washington, 1984, mem. staff, 1980, Presdl. Inaugral for Nixon, Washington, 1972; mem. PTA. Recipient cert. of appreciation Presdl. Inaugral Com., 1984. Mem. Nat. Assn. Security Dealers (cert. series 7, 63, 24), Hunt Club Assn. (fin. advisor), Stephens Coll. Alumni, Hunt Club Girls Club (pres. 1988-89), Rotary Internat. Republican. Roman Catholic. Avocations: contract bridge, golf, sailing, travel, skiing. Office: Wheat First Union 20 S King St Leesburg VA 20175-3007

DAVIDSON, NORMAN RALPH, biochemistry educator; b. Chgo., Apr. 5, 1916; s. Bernard Ralph and Rose (Lefstein) D.; m. Annemarie Behrendt, July 11, 1942; children: Terence Mark, Laureen Davidson Reitman Agee, Jeffrey Norman, Brian Lee. BS, U. Chgo., 1937, PhD in Chemistry, 1941; BS, Oxford (Eng.) U., 1939; DSc (hon.), U. Chgo., 1992, Scripps Rsch. Inst., 1999. Research scientist Manhattan Project U. Chgo., 1942-46; instr. chemistry Calif. Inst. Tech., Pasadena, 1946-49, asst. prof., 1949-52, assoc. prof., 1952-57, prof., 1957-82, Chandler prof. chem. biology, 1982-86, prof. emeritus, 1986—, acting chair div. biology, 1989, exec. officer div. biology, 1990; sr. cons. Am Gen., Thousand Oaks, Calif., 1992—; mem., chmn. biophysics and biophys. chemistry study sect. NIH, Bethesda, Md., 1964-88, mem. nat. adv. coun. human genome rsch., 1989-93. Author: Statistical Mechanics, 1962. Rhodes scholar, 1938-39; recipient Calif. sect. award Am. Chem. Soc., 1954, Peter Debye award in phys. chemistry, 1971; named Calif. Scientist of Yr., Calif. Mus. Sci. and History, 1980, Nat. Medal of Sci., 1996. Mem. NAS (Dickson prize sci. 1985, Robert A. Welch award in chemistry 1989). Office: Calif Inst Tech Div Biology 156 # 29 Pasadena CA 91125

DAVIDSON, PHILLIP THOMAS, retail company executive; b. Hartford, Conn., Aug. 12, 1925; s. Samuel M. and Rachel (Levine) D.; m. Barbara Jarmon, Nov. 27, 1970; children: Merry Davidson Bush, Thomas H., Anthony H., Wendy E., Phillip T. Jr. BS, Trinity Coll., 1948. Co-chmn., co-CEO, D&L Venture Corp., New Britain, Conn., 1948-97, Weathervane Retail Corp., New Britain, 1948-97; former v.p. Conn. Banc Fedn.; former trustee 1st Bank Corp., New Haven, New Britain Bank & Trust Co.; former mem. exec. com. and bd. dirs. Frederick Atkins, Inc., N.Y.C.; former lectr. on industry issues and econs. U. Hartford, U. Conn., Syracuse U., New Eng. Newspaper Guild, N.H. C. of C.; mem. adv. bd. Conn. Nat. Bank. Author books and articles on retail industry and real estate and leasing. Chmn., corporator, bd. dirs., chmn., exec. com., chmn. planning com. and fin. com. New Britain Gen. Hosp.; bd. dirs. D&L Found., Inc.; past bd. dirs. Inst. of Living, Hartford Conv. Bur., New Britain Found. for Pub. Giving, Conn. Pub. Expenditure Coun., Family Svcs. in New Britain, numerous health and welfare agys.; trustee Berkshire Sch., 1983-89; chmn. United Cmty. Svcs. Greater New Britain, 1960-62, 82-84, bd. dirs., 1982-92; chmn. parent's fund St. Lawrence U., numerous others. Officer USNR, WWII, PTO. Recipient nat. award for ind. retailer of yr. Nat. Retail Mchts. Assn., 1979, Citizen of Yr. award Elks Club, New Britain, 1987. Mem. Nat. Retail Fedn. (bd. dirs., exec. com., fin. com.), Internat. Coun. Shopping Ctrs., Conn. Bus. and Industry Assn. (past bd. dirs.), New Britain C. of C. (past pres.), Hartford Club, New Britain Club, Hop Meadow Country Club. Home: 4 Eastview Dr Simsbury CT 06070-3010 Office: D&L Venture Corp/ Weathervane Retail Corp 300 John Downey Dr New Britain CT 06051-2908

DAVIDSON, REX L., association executive; b. Amarillo, Tex., May 2, 1949; s. Harold and Shirley (Turk) D.; m. Joyce Dawson, May 23, 1970; children: Adam, Anne. BA, Tex. Tech. U., 1971, MA, 1973. V.p. Goodwill Industries of Houston, Inc., 1975-77; exec. dir. Goodwill Industries of Lubbock, Inc., Tex., 1977-79; pres. Goodwill Industries of N.J., Inc., Harrison, N.J., 1979-82; exec. dir. Goodwill Industries of Greater N.Y., Inc., Astoria, 1982—; pres. Nat. Rehab. Facilities Coalition, 1997—. Pres. N.Y. State Rehab. Assn., Albany, N.Y., 1990-92, N.Y. State Industries for the Disabled, 1996; chmn. bd. dirs. The Lamb's Ctr., N.Y.C., 1989-94; ptnr. N.Y.City Partnership, 1988—. Recipient Leadership award Life Svcs. for Handicapped, Inc., N.Y.C., 1994, Kenneth K. King Outstanding Mgmt. award, 1996, Goodwill Industries Indsl. Watkins award. Mem. Goodwill Industries Internat. Found. (bd. dirs. 1994-96), David Rockefeller Fellows Adv. Com., Goodwill Global Inc. (bd. dirs. 1998), BBB Edn. and Rsch. Found. (bd. dirs. 1996). Home: 150 E 57th St New York NY 10022-2700 Office: Goodwill Industries NY 4-21 27th Ave Astoria NY 11102

DAVIDSON, RICHARD ALAN, data communications company executive; b. Chgo., June 25, 1946; s. Jacob Aaron and Belle Rina (Feldman) D.; m. Sharyn Gail Ellman, Aug. 19, 1973; children: Kevin Scott, Caryl Elise. BSEE, U. Mich., 1970; MBA, Northwestern U., 1975. Project engr. Motorola, Inc., Schaumburg, Ill., 1967-74; ptnr. Feature Film Svcs., Skokie, Ill., 1974-77; mgr. planning Motorola, Inc., Schaumburg, Ill., 1977-78, mgr. mktg., 1978-79; tech. dir. Voice & Data Systems, Chgo., 1979-82; engring. mgr. Infolink Corp., Northbrook, Ill., 1982-84; pres. Davidson Data Communications, Lake Forest, Ill., 1984—; v.p. engring. Feature Film Svcs., Skokie, 1976—. Inventor pay TV system; contbr. articles to profl. jours. Unit commr. Boy Scouts Am., Lake County, Ill., 1989—; comms. officer USAF Aux. CAP, 1991—. Recipient Cert. of Appreciation Boy Scouts Am., 1990. MEm. IEEE, Assn. for Computing Machinery, Assn. for MBA Execs., North Shore Radio Club (tech. dir.), Tau Delta Phi. Republican. Jewish. Avocations: amateur radio, electronics, photography. Home and Office: 1900 S Millburne Rd Lake Forest IL 60045-4112

DAVIDSON, RICHARD J., medical association administrator. Pres. Am. Hosp. Assn., Washington. Office: American Hospital Association 325 7th St NW Ste 700 Washington DC 20004-2809

DAVIDSON, RICHARD K., railroad company executive; b. Allen, Kans., Jan. 9, 1942; s. Richard B. and Thelma (Rees) D.; m. Trish Davidson; children: Richard Byron, Elizabeth Ann. BA in History, Washburn U., 1965, D of Commerce (hon.), 1984. Brakeman, conductor Mo. Pacific R.R., St. Louis, 1960-66, transp. tng. program, 1966, asst. trainmaster, trainmaster, 1966-75, asst. supt. to asst. v.p. ops., 1975-76; v.p. ops. Mo. Pacific Railroad, St. Louis, 1976-85; v.p. ops. Union Pacific R.R., Omaha, 1985-89, exec. v.p. ops., 1989-91, chmn., CEO, 1991—; pres. Union Pacific Corp., Omaha, 1994—, COO, 1995-97, chmn., pres., COO, 1997—. Mem. Happy Hollow Club. Office: Union Pacific RR 1416 Dodge St Omaha NE 68179-5966

DAVIDSON, RICHARD LAURENCE, geneticist, educator; b. Cleve., Feb. 22, 1941. B.A., Case Western Res. U., 1963, Ph.D., 1967. Asst. prof. Harvard Med. Sch., Boston, 1970-73, assoc. prof. microbiology and molecular genetics, 1973-81; research assoc. human genetics Children's Hosp. Med. Ctr., Boston, 1970-81; head dept. molecular genetics U. Ill. Med. Ctr., Chgo., 1981—, Benjamin Goldberg prof. genetics, 1981—; co-dir. Cell Cult Ctr., MIT, Boston, 1975-81; mem. mammalian genetics study sect. NIH, 1975-81; mem. human cell biology adv. panel NSF, 1973-75. Editor-in-chief: Somatic Cell Genetics. U.S. Air Force Office Research-NRC fellow, 1967-68, Ctr. Molecular Genetics, Paris, 1967-70. Mem. AAAS, Tissue Culture Assn., Cell Biology Assn. Office: U Ill at Chicago Head Dept Mol Gen (M/7 669) 900 S Ashland Ave # 669 Chicago IL 60607-4004*

DAVIDSON, ROBERT ALLAN, umpire; b. Chgo., Aug. 3, 1952; m. Denise Nesheim, Sept. 27, 1980; children: Amber Adelle, Andrea Lynn. Student, U. Minn. Umpire Midwest League, Fla. State League, So. League, Dominican Republic Winter League, Am. Assn., Nat. League, 1983—. Office: Nat League 350 Park Ave New York NY 10022 Office: Umpires Union 1735 Market St Philadelphia PA 19103

DAVIDSON, ROBERT BRUCE, lawyer; b. N.Y.C., May 6, 1945. BS in Econs. cum laude, U. Pa., 1967; JD, Columbia U., 1972. Bar: N.Y. 1973, U.S. Dist. Ct. (so. and ea. dists.) N.Y. 1973, U.S. Ct. Appeals (2d cir.) 1975, U.S. Ct. Appeals (D.C. cir.) 1981, U.S. Supreme Ct. 1979, U.S. Tax Ct. 1984, U.S. Ct. Appeals (fed. cir.) 1989, U.S. Ct. Appeals (3d cir.) 1990. Assoc. Baker & McKenzie, N.Y.C., 1972-79, ptnr., 1979—; mem. adv. bd. World Arbitration Inst., N.Y.C., 1984—. Author: (with others) Voting Laws and Procedures, 1973; also articles. Vol. U.S. Peace Corps, Philippines, 1968-70. Mem. ABA, Assn. of Bar of City of N.Y. (chair 1982-85, com. on internat. law 1986-89, com. on arbitration 1999—), Am. Fgn. Law Assn. (bd. dirs.), Maritime Law Assn. U.S., Fed. Bar Coun., Am. Arbitration Assn. (mem. internat. panel, 1997—, panel for large complex cases 1997—). Office: Baker & McKenzie 805 3rd Ave New York NY 10022-7513

DAVIDSON, ROBERT C., JR., manufacturing executive; b. Memphis, Oct. 3, 1945; s. Robert C. Sr. and Thelma (Culp) D.; m. Alice Faye Berkley, Jan. 5, 1978; children: Robert III, John Roderick, Julian. BA, Morehouse Coll., 1967; MBA, U. Chgo., 1969. V.p. Urban Nat. Corp., Boston, 1972-74, Avant Garde Enterprises, Los Angeles, 1974-76; pres. Surface Protection Industries, Los Angeles, 1976—, now CEO. Bd. dirs. Pasadena Art Workshop, 1986—; planning commr. City of Pasadena, 1986—. Mem. Young Pres. Orgn. Club: 100 Black Men (Los Angeles). Avocations: tennis, skiing. Office: Surface Protection Industries Inc 3411 E 14th St Los Angeles CA 90023-3803*

DAVIDSON, ROBERT DONALD, civilian military employee; b. Palmyra, Tenn., Oct. 11, 1942; s. Lonnie Howard and Carrie Estell (Jackson) D.; m. Sandra Gail Temple, June 30, 1961 (div. July 1968); m. Mary Patricia Baker, May 30, 1969; children: William Robert, Donald Jeffrey, Patrick Jason, Michael Shawn, Nathan Scott. BS, Austin Peay State U., 1976. Date processor, 1960-70; office mgr. Cumberland Milling Co., Clarksville, Tenn., 1970-73; electronic acctg. machine operator Dept. of Def., U.S. Army, Ft. Campbell, Ky., 1973-74; acct. Dept. of Def., U.S. Army, Ft. Campbell, 1974-76, internal auditor, 1976-80, mgmt. analyst, 1980-83, supr. oper. acct., 1983-84, program analyst, 1984, mgmt. analyst, 1985—. Pub. Duck's Old Time Jour., 1987—, Palmyra-Then to Now, 1997, Southside-Then to Now, 1998. With USMC, 1966-69, USCG Res., 1974—. Republican. Avocations: geneology, history. Home: 3351 Oakridge Rd Palmyra TN 37142-2339

DAVIDSON, ROBERT WILLIAM, merchant banker; b. Colfax, Wash., Sept. 18, 1949; s. William Martin and Lena (Soli) D.; m. Molly Evoy, Apr. 16, 1977; children: Ford Patrick, Matthew Harpur, Marshall Andrew. AB, Harvard U., 1971. Exec. dir. Sabre Found., Cambridge, Mass., 1971-72; adminstrv. asst. Congressman Joel Pritchard, Washington, 1973-79; asst. sec. state State of Wash., Olympia, 1979-80; pres. Frayn Fin. Printing, Seattle, 1982-87, Frayn Printing Co., Seattle, 1985-87; exec. dir. Woodland Park Zool. Soc., Seattle, 1987-93, pres., 1993-94; prin. Alistar Capital Group, Bellevue, Wash., 1994—; mem. adv. com. Wash. State Software Ind. Devel. Bd., 1984-85. Chmn. pub. funding com. Mayor's Zoo Commn., Seattle, 1984-85; dir. Discovery Inst., 1992—, Internat. Snow Leopard Trust, 1994-96; mem. sch. bd. Cath. Archdiocese of Seattle, 1995-98; mem. Seattle U. Exec. Masters in Not-for-Profit Mgmt. vis. com., 1995-96; mem. King County Bond Oversight Com., 1986-93. Mem. N.W. Devel. Officers Assn. (pres. 1994), Downtown Rotary Club (v.p. found. 1997-98), Wash. Athletic Club. Republican. Roman Catholic. Avocations: tennis, photography. Office: Alistar Capital Group 600 108th Ave NE Ste 1014 Bellevue WA 98004-5129

DAVIDSON, ROGER H(ARRY), political scientist, educator; b. Washington, July 31, 1936; s. Ross Wallace and Mildred (Younger) D.; m. Nancy Elizabeth Dixon, Sept. 29, 1961; children: Douglas Ross, Christopher Reed. AB magna cum laude, U. Colo., 1958; PhD, Columbia U., 1963. Asst. prof. govt. Dartmouth Coll., Hanover, N.H., 1962-68; assoc. prof. polit. sci. U. Calif., Santa Barbara, 1968-71, prof., 1971-83, assoc. dean letters and sci., 1978-80; sr. specialist Congl. Rsch. Svc., Washington, 1980-88; prof. govt., politics U. Md., College Pk., 1981-99; profl. staff mem. U.S. Ho. of Reps., Washington, 1973-74; rsch. dir. U.S. Senate, Washington, 1976-77; cons. White House, 1970-71, U.S. Com. on Violence, Washington, 1968-69; vis. prof. U. Calif., Santa Barbara, 1994, 99—; Leon Sachs vis. scholar Johns Hopkins U., 1997. Author: The Role of the Congressman, 1969; co-author: A More Perfect Union, 4th edit., 1989; editor: The Postreform Congress, 1992, Remaking Congress, 1995, Understanding the Presidency, 2d edit., 1999; co-editor: Ency. of the U.S. Congress, 1995, Remaking Congress, 1995, Masters of the House, 1998; contbr. articles to profl. jours. Co-chmn. Upper Valley Human Rights Coun., Hanover, N.H., 1966-68; chmn. Goleta Valley Citizens Planning Group, Santa Barbara, 1974-76; bd. dirs. Dirksen Congl. Ctr., Governance Inst.; rsch. com. of legis. specialists Internat. Polit. Sci. Assn.; mem. adv. commn. on records of Congress Nat. Archives and Records Adminstrn., 1995—. Woodrow Wilson Nat. Found. fellow, 1958, Gilder fellow Columbia U., 1960, Faculty fellow Dartmouth Coll., 1965-66. Mem. Nat. Capital Area Polit. Sci. Assn. (pres. 1985-86), Legis. Studies Group (charter, nat. chmn. 1980-81), Am. Polit. Sci. Assn. (joint com. mem. Project 87-Am. Hist. Assn./Am. Polit. Sci. Assn., chmn. congl. fellowship com. 1990, 93, endowed programs com. 1994-95, chmn. 1995-96, co-chmn. exec. com. Centennial Campaign 1997—), Western Polit. Sci. Assn. (bd. editors 1977-78), Nat. Acad. Pub. Adminstrn. Baptist. Avocations: music, history. Home: 400 E Pedregosa St # L Santa Barbara CA 93103 Office: Dept Polit Sci U Calif Santa Barbara CA 93106

DAVIDSON, RONALD CROSBY, physicist, educator; b. Norwich, Ont., Can., July 3, 1941; s. William Crosby and Annie Beatrice (Caley) D.; m. Jean Farncombe, May 18, 1963; children: Cynthia Christine, Ronald Crosby Jr. BSc, McMaster U., 1963; PhD, Princeton U., 1966. Faculty dept. physics U. Md., 1968-78; prof. physics MIT, 1978-91; prof. astrophys. scis. Princeton U., 1991—; vis. scientist Los Alamos Sci. Lab., 1974-75; asst. dir. for applied plasma physics Office of Fusion Energy Dept. Energy, Washington, 1976-78; dir. Plasma Fusion Center MIT, Cambridge, Mass., 1978-88; chmn. magnetic fusion adv. com., 1982-86; dir. Princeton Plasma Physics Lab., 1991-96. Author: Methods in Nonlinear Plasma Theory, 1972, Theory of Nonneutral Plasmas, 1974, 2d edit., 89, Physics of Nonneutral Plasmas, 1991. Recipient Disting. Assoc. award Dept. Energy, 1986, Leadership award Fusion Power Assocs., 1986, Kaul Found. Excellence award, 1993; Ford Found. fellow, 1963-64, Imperial Oil fellow, 1963-66, Sloan Rsch. Found. fellow, 1970-72. Fellow AAAS, Am. Phys. Soc. (chmn. div. plasma physics, 1983-84). Office: Princeton U Plasma Physics Lab PO Box 451 Princeton NJ 08543-0451

DAVIDSON, SHEILA KEARNEY, lawyer; b. Paterson, N.J., Dec. 16, 1961; d. John James and Rita Barbara (Burke) Kearney; m. Anthony H. Davidson, Oct. 5, 1996; 1 child, Andrew John. BA cum laude, Fairfield U., 1983; JD, George Washington U., 1986. Bar: N.Y. 1987, U.S. Dist. Ct. (so. dist.) N.Y. 1987, D.C. 1989. Assoc. Shearson Lehman Bros., Inc., N.Y.C., 1986-87; staff atty. Nat. Assn. Securities Dealers, N.Y.C., 1987-89, regional atty., 1989-90, sr. regional atty., 1990-91; regional counsel N.Y. Life Ins. Co., N.Y.C., 1991-93, assoc. counsel, 1993-94, asst. gen. counsel, 1994-95, v.p., assoc. gen. counsel, 1995-97, sr. v.p. in charge of corp. compliance dept., 1998—. Mem. ABA, Securities Industry Assn., D.C. Bar Assn., Fairfield U. Alumni Club N.Y. (pres. 1988-90), Phi Delta Phi. Republican. Roman Catholic. Office: NY Life Ins Co 51 Madison Ave New York NY 10010-1603

DAVIDSON, SHIRLEY JEAN, elementary and secondary educator; b. DuQuoin, Ill., June 2, 1946; d. Richard Haley and Doris Jean Gaddis; m. Philip H. Davidson, Aug. 30, 1969; children: Susan Elizabeth, Matthew Philip. BS in Elem. Edn., So. Ill. U., Carbondale, 1969; MAT in Learning Disabilities and Reading, Rockford Coll., 1982; MA in Sch. Adminstrn., Concordia U., River Forest, Ill., 1997. Cert. in sch. adminstrn., learning disabilities, soocial emotion disorders, educable mentally handicapped, elem. edn., reading, Ill. Thcr. 4th grade Coulterville (Ill.) Elem. Sch., 1968-70; tchr. 2d grade Gifford (Ill.) Grade Sch., 1970-73, Rockton (Ill.) Grade Sch., 1973-85; reading/learning disabilities specialist Rockford (Ill.) Area Literacy Coun., 1988-93; spl. edn. tchr. Byron (Ill.) Sch. Dist., 1995-96, Dist. 47, Crystal Lake, Ill., 1993-95, 96—; ind. reading cons. Elco Industries, Rockford, 1991-92; mem. peacemaking com. Indian Prairie Sch., Crystal Lake, 1998-99, mem. tech. com., 1997-99, mem. social com., 1996-97. Active First Presbyn. Ch., Rockford, 1975—. Mem. ASCD, Crystal Lake Elem. Tchrs. Assn., Pi Lambda Theta, Phi Kappa Phi. Avocations: tennis, reading, cross stitch. Office: Indian Prairie Sch 651 Village Rd Crystal Lake IL 60014

DAVIDSON, STANLEY J., lawyer; b. Chgo., Oct. 22, 1946. BA with honors, U. Ill., 1968; JD, Loyola U., 1971. Bar: Ill. 1971, U.S. Dist. Ct. (no. dist.) Ill. 1973, U.S. Ct. Appeals (7th cir.) 1982, U.S. Supreme Ct. 1982. Law clk. to Hon. Thomas J. Moran Ill. Appellate Ct. (2nd dist.), 1971-73; ptnr. Hinshaw & Culbertson, Chgo. Mem. ABA, Am. Soc. Hosp. Attys., Ill. State Bar Assn., Chgo. Bar Assn., Appellate Lawyers Assn. (bd. dirs. 1978-80, treas. 1982-83, sec. 1983-84, v.p. 1984-85, pres. 1985-86), Soc. Trial Lawyers, Am. Bd. Trial Advocates, Def. Rsch. Inst., Decalogue Soc. Lawyers. Office: Hinshaw & Culbertson 222 N La Salle St Ste 300 Chicago IL 60601-1081

DAVIDSON, STEVEN J., emergency physician; b. Phila., Mar. 9, 1950; s. Jay Howard and Claire Beverly (Silverman) D.; m. Simone F. Mogul, June 21, 1987; children: Zoey Samuel, Masha Kalinkina. AB in Chemistry, Temple U., 1971, MD, 1975; MBA, U. Pa., 1989. Diplomate Am. Bd. Emergency Medicine. Intern in acute care Med. Coll. Pa., 1975-76, resident in emergency medicine, 1976-78; instr., asst. prof., assoc. prof. surgery Med. Coll. Pa., Phila., 1978-84, assoc. prof. emergency medicine, 1984-89, prof. emergency medicine, 1989-97, vis. prof., 1997—, head divsn. emergency med. svc., 1988-96; chmn. emergency medicine Maimonides Med. Ctr., Bklyn., 1995—; med. dir. Phila. Emergency Med. Svc., 1983-94; oral examiner Am. Bd. Emergency Medicine, 1980—, bd. dirs., 1986-95. Assoc. editor Yearbook of Emergency Medicine, 1981-99; guest reviewer Annals of Emergency Medicine, 1983-99, Prehosp. and Disaster Medicine, 1992-97, Acad. Emergency Medicine, 1993-99; mem. editl. bd. Preshosp. Emergency Care, 1997—. Fellow Am. Coll. Emergency Physicians (bd. dirs. Pa. chpt. 1979-85, Emergency Svc. award 1992), Soc. Acad. Emergency Medicine (pres. 1985-86), Nat. Assn. Emergency Med. Svc. Physicians. Office: Maimonides Med Ctr Dept Emergency Medicine 4802 10th Ave Brooklyn NY 11219-2916

DAVIDSON, STUART WEST, lawyer; b. Natick, Mass., June 21, 1957; s. Edward William and Sonya (Westleman) D.; m. Ann Cohen, Oct. 8, 1988; 1 child, Anita Rose. BA in Polit. Sci., Johns Hopkins U., 1979; JD cum laude, Harvard U., 1982. Bar: Pa. 1982, D.C. 1983. Ptnr. Willig, Williams & Davidson, Phila., 1982—; trustee Johns Hopkins U., 1979-84; adv. coun. environ. and occupl. health Johns Hopkins U. Sch. Hygiene and Pub. Health, 1983-93; adv. coun. labor studies Pa. State U., 1985—; nat. labor adv. bd. State of Israel Bonds, 1996—; mem. lawyers coord. com. AFL-CIO; bd. dirs. Devel. Corp. of Israel. Contbr. articles to profl. jours.; speaker at various nat. conf. Mem. adv. bd. Pa. State Labor Bd.; mem. Golden Slipper

Found., 1999—. Mem. ABA, Pa. Bar Assn., Phila. Bar, Am. Arbitration Assn., Indsl. Rels. Rsch. Assn., Internat. Found. Employee Benefit Funds, SHOMRIM, Omicron Delta Kappa, Phi Beta Kappa. Home: 7501 Fowler St Philadelphia PA 19128-4149 Office: Willig Williams Davidson 1845 Walnut St 24th Fl Philadelphia PA 19103-4708

DAVIDSON, THOMAS FERGUSON, chemical engineer; b. N.Y.C., N.Y., Jan. 5, 1930; s. Lorimer Arthur and Elizabeth (Valentine) D.; m. Nancy Lee Selecman, Nov. 10, 1951; children: Thomas Ferguson, Richard Alan, Gwyn Ann. BS in Engring., U. Md., 1951; HHD (hon.), Weber State U., 1998. Sr. project engr. Wright Air Devel. Ctr., Dayton, Ohio, 1951-58; dep. dir. Solid Sys. Divsn., Edwards, Calif., 1959-60; mgr. govt. ops. Thiokol Chem. Corp., Ogden, Utah, 1960-64; dir. aerospace mktg. Thiokol Chem. Corp., Bristol, Pa., 1965-67; dir. tech. mgmt. Thiokol Chem. Corp., Ogden, 1968-82; v.p. tech. Morton Thiokol Inc., Chgo., 1983-88, Thiokol Corp., Ogden, 1989-90; cons. Ogden, 1990—; subcom. lubrications and wear NACA, Washington, 1955-57; chmn. Joint Army, Navy, NASA, Air Force exec. com., 1959-60. Editor: National Rocket Strategic Plan, 1990; contbr. articles to profl. jours. Chmn. bd. dirs. Wesley Acad., Ogden, 1990-94; trustee Family Counseling Svc., Ogden, 1991-98; bd. dirs. Habitat for Humanity Internat., 1991-93, Weber State Wildcat Club, 1996—, Utah Musical Theatre, 1997—, ARC No. Utah, 1998—, Weber State Alumni Assn., 1998—; chmn. bd. dirs. ARC No. Utah, 1999—; trustee Weber State U., 1999—;. Fellow AIAA (assoc., sect. chmn. 1979-80, chmn. AIA rocket propulsion com. 1987-90, mem. AIA aerospace tech. com. 1987-90, Wyld Propulsion award 1991); mem. Am. Newcomen Soc., Smithsonian Instn., Exch. Club, Ogden Golf and Country Club, Weber State Wildcat Club. Republican. Methodist. Home: 4755 Banbury Ln Ogden UT 84403-4484

DAVIDSON, THOMAS MAXWELL, international management company executive; b. N.Y.C., Dec. 14, 1937; s. Alfred Edward and Claire Helen (Dreyfus) D.; m. Ruth Elizabeth Bovenkerk, Dec. 8, 1962; children: Douglas Edward, Anne Elizabeth. BA, Vanderbilt U., 1959; MBA, Columbia U., 1961. Mgr. Ford Motor Co., Dearborn, Mich., 1963-72; dir. credit ops. White Motor Corp., Eastlake, Ohio, 1972-73, v.p., treas., 1976-77; sr. v.p., chief ops. officer White Motor Credit Corp., Cleve., 1973-75, pres., chief exec. officer, 1975-77, also bd. dirs.; sr. v.p. fin., chief fin. officer, dir. Tex. Gas Transmission Corp., Owensboro, Ky., 1977-81; exec. v.p., chief fin. officer Arrow Electronics, Inc., N.Y.C., 1981-87; exec. v.p. Greenwich, Conn., 1987-89, also bd. dirs., 1981-94; pres., chief exec. officer Doctors Capital Corp., Greenwich, 1989-90, also bd. dirs.; pres., CEO San Francisco/Moscow Teleport, Inc., 1990-93, also bd. dirs., 1990-93; pres., CEO Internat. Techs., Inc., Greenwich, Conn., 1993—; Med. Info. Internat., 1995—; bd. dirs. SOVAM Teleport, Russia, Sovintel, Russia, Baltic Comms., Ltd., Russia, 1990-93; bd. dirs., chair, CEO XXI Century Hotel Network Ltd., 1998—. Served with U.S. Army, 1959. Mem. Athletic Club. Home: 131 Doubling Rd Greenwich CT 06830-4040 Office: Internat Techs Inc 35 Mason St Greenwich CT 06830-5433

DAVIDSON, THOMAS NOEL, business executive; b. Evansville, Ind., Oct. 4, 1939; s. Harry R. and Helen E. Davidson; m. Sally Anne Fries, 1958; children: Thomas N. Jr., John C., James R., Jennifer J. BSc with honors, Mich. State U., 1961. Chmn. bd. dirs. Quarry Hill Group, Nutech Precision Metals Inc., Quarry Hill Ptnrs.; past prin. owner and dir. Am. Brass Co., Ansonia Brass, Atco Controls, Inc., Buffalo Brass Co., Carborundum Abrasives, Inc., Cramco, Inc., Hanson Inc., Jensen Fitting Mfg., Ltd., Jensen Fittings Corp., PCL Industries Ltd., Sandbright & Co., Sklar-Peppler Furniture Inc., Stephenson's Rent-all Inc., Union Drawn Steel Ltd., Volstatic, Inc.; bd. dirs. Can. Pub. Corp., Derlan Industries Ltd., MDC Corp., Nutech Precision Metals L.P., The Am. Mus. Flyfishing, Pennekamp Rsch. Inst., Nat. Marine Sanctuary adv. bd., Varity Corp., Lucas Varity, Nations Bank So. Fla., Clemmer Industries, Ocean Reef Club, Ocean Reef Cmty. Assoc., Ocean Reef Historical Soc.; past chmn. Gen. Trust Corp. Past chmn. Hugh MacMillan Children's Found., Ocean Reef Cmty. Assn., Ocean Reef Club, Inc., Can. CPGA Golf Championship, Metro Toronto Conv. Ctr.; past bd. dirs. Con. Smythe Rsch. Found., Westhem Corp., USF&G (Can.), Nat. Club, Can. Club, Silcorp Ltd., others; bd. dirs. Ocean Reef Cmty. Found.; chmn. Ocean Reef Cultural Ctr. Recipient Fin. Post Can. award 1979; named Entrepreneur of Yr. by Fin. Post. Mem. Soc. Plastics Engrs. (past dir.), Soc. Plastics Industry (past chmn., Man of Yr. award 1985), Variety Ability Systems Inc. (past dir.), Variety Village (past dir.), Young Pres. Orgn. (internat. pres. 1988-89), World Pres. Orgn. (bd. dirs., internat. pres. 1997), Can. Club (past bd. dirs., N.Y. and Toronto), Nat. Club Toronto (past bd. dir.), Rosedale Golf Club (Toronto), Bayview Country Club (past bd. dirs.), Card Sound Golf Club (bd. dirs.), English Turn Golf & Country lub (New Orleans), Griffith Island Club (Wiarton, Ont., past chmn.), Ocean Reef Club (past chmn.), The Caledon Mountain Trout Club (Inglewood, Ont.), Tau Beta Pi, Pi Tau Sigma. Home: Ocean Reef Club 7 Sunrise Cay Rd Key Largo FL 33037-5301 Office: Quarry Hill Group PO Box 83 Key Largo FL 33037-0083

DAVIDSON, TOM WILLIAM, lawyer; b. Madison, Wis., Oct. 10, 1952; s. Alvin William and Louise Elizabeth (Zeratsky) D.; m. Linda Mary Greiber, July 27, 1974; children—Jessica, Heather, Thomas. B.A., U. Wis.-Madison, 1977, J.D., 1974. Bar: U.S. Dist. Ct. (we. dist.) Wis. 1977, Wis. 1977, U.S. Supreme Ct. 1986, U.S. Ct. Appeals (D.C. cir.) 1986, D.C. Ct. Appeals 1991. Gen. atty. FCC, Washington, 1977-79, trial atty., 1979; assoc. Sidley & Austin, Washington, 1980-84, ptnr., 1985-91; ptnr. Akin, Gump, Strauss, Hauer & Feld, LLP, Washington, 1992—; dir. Marlin Broadcasting, Inc., 1996. Active Burke Centre Community Assn., Burke, Va., 1977-79, chmn. Bass Pond Cluster Bd., 1977-78. Mem. ABA, FBA, Fed. Comm. Bar Assn., Lowe's Island Club, Tournament Players Club at Avenal, Phi Beta Kappa, Phi Eta Sigma, Phi Kappa Phi. Avocations: golf, softball, soccer, basketball, racquetball. Office: Akin Gump Strauss Hauer & Feld LLP Ste 400 1333 New Hampshire Ave NW Washington DC 20036-1564

DAVIDSON, VALERIE LAVERGNE, institute administrator; b. Chgo., Nov. 23, 1949; d. Richard W. and Jeraldine (Schliephake) D.; m. David Townsend Mason III, Aug. 16; children: Yuri R. Mason, Tatiana D. Mason. BA, Calif. State U., Northridge, 1985; MS in Health Adminstrn., Calif. State U., L.A., 1994; cert. in human performance, U. So. Calif., 1996. Supr. support svcs. St. John's Hosp., Santa Monica, Calif., 1976-81; administrator Western Ctr. on Law & Poverty, Inc., Los Angeles, Calif., 1983—; cons. in field. Contbr. articles to profl. jours. Pres. Sch. Bus. Alumni Calif. State U., 1995-98, adv. mem. health care mgmt. program., 1995—. Mem. So. Calif. Assn. for Healthcare Development, Healthcare Execs. of So. Calif., , Phi Kappa Phi. Home and Office: 11260 Overland Ave Apt 20F Culver City CA 90230-5542

DAVIDSON, WILLIAM A., career officer; m. Peg Bell; children: Dawn, Michael. BS in Law Enforcement and Corrections, Fla. State U., 1968; grad., Squadron Officer Sch., 1974; MS in Criminal Justice, George Washington U., 1978; grad., Armed Forces Staff Coll., 1981, Air War Coll., 1984, Fed. Exec. Inst., 1991. Commd. 2d lt. USAFR, 1968, advanced through grades to comdr., 1972; with Air Force Office Spl. Investigations, Offutt AFB, Nebr., 1969-71, Tan Son Nhul Air Base, Vietnam, 1971-72; detachment comdr. Air Force Office Spl. Investigations, Robins AFB, Ga., 1972-74; chief air force polygraph program Air Force Office Spl. Investigations, Bolling AFB, Washington DC, 1974-80; dep. comdr. ops. dist. 45 Air Force Office Spl. Investigations, Rep. S. Korea, 1981-83; plans and programs asst., adminstrv. asst. office sec. air force Pentagon, Washington, 1983-86, mil. asst., adminstrv. asst. office sec. air force, 1986-88, dir. security & investigative programs office sec., Air Forc, 1988-90, dep. adminstrv. asst., 1990-94, adminstrv. asst. to sec. air force, 1994—. Mem. Nat. Def. Indsl. Assn. (bd. dirs. Washington chpt.), Am. Soc. Indsl. Security, Am. Polygraph Assn., Internat. Assn. Chiefs Police, Sr. Exec. Svc. Office: Office Adminstrv Asst 1720 Air Force Pentagon Washington DC 20330-1720

DAVIDSON, WILLIAM M., diversified company executive, professional basketball executive; b. 1921; divorced. LL.B., Wayne State U.; B.B.A., U. Mich.; JD, Wayne State U. Pres. chief exec. officer Guardian Glass Co., Northville, Mich., 1957-68; pres., chief exec. officer, dir. Guardian Industries Corp., Northville, Mich., 1968—; majority owner Detroit Pistons, NBA, 1974—, mng. ptnr. Served with USN. Office: Guardian Industries Corp 2300 Harmon Rd Auburn Hills MI 48326-1714 also: care Detroit Pistons 2 Championship Dr Auburn Hills MI 48326-1753*

DAVIDSON-SHEPARD, GAY, secondary education educator; b. Long Beach, Calif., Dec. 15, 1951; d. Leyton Paul and Ruth Leona (Gritzmaker) Davidson; m. Daniel A. Shepard, June 24, 1983. BA, U. Calif., Irvine, 1972; MA, Columbia Pacific U., 1986. Cert. elem. and secondary edn. tchr. Tchr. mid. sch. Ocean View Sch. Dist., Huntington Beach, Calif., 1973—; team mem. Calif. learning assessment system State Dept. of Edn., Sacramento, 1987—; chief reader Orange County pentathlon and decathlon Orange County Dept. Edn., Costa Mesa, Calif., 1980—; sr. reader new standards State Dept. Edn., Sacramento, 1995—; lang. arts cons. various sch. dists., Calif., 1976—; chief reader Calif. Learning Assessment System, Sacramento, 1993—; sr. reader New Stds., 1995—; table reader Golden State Exams, 1997—. Author/cons.: Teacher's Guide for Direct Assessment Writing, 1990; test writer Acad. Pentathlon Test, 1984—, Dist. Lang. Art Proficiency Test, 1980—. Mem. NEA, AAUS, AAUW, Nat. Assn. Tchrs. of English, Calif. Reading Assn., Mensa, Calif. Tchrs. Assn., Ocean View Tchrs. Assn. Democrat. Avocations: reading, camping, travel, cooking. Home: 6782 Rook Dr Huntington Beach CA 92647-5641 Office: Mesa View Sch 17601 Avilla Ln Huntington Beach CA 92647-6612

DAVID-WEILL, MICHEL ALEXANDRE, investment banker; b. France, Nov. 23, 1932; came to U.S., 1977; s. Pierre Sylvain and Berthe Marie (Haardt) David-W.; m. Helene Lehideux, July 20, 1956; children: Beatrice David-Weill Stern, Cecile David-Weill de la Baume, Natalie Merveilleux du Vignaud, Agathe. Ed., Inst. Scis. Politiques, 1953. Ptnr. Lazard Freres & Co., 1961-65; ptnr. Lazard Freres & Cie, 1965—, sr. ptnr., 1975—; dir., dep. chmn. Lazard Bros. & Co., Ltd., 1965—; sr. ptnr. Lazard Freres & Co., N.Y.C., 1977-95; chmn. Lazard Freres & Co. LLC, N.Y.C., 1995—; chmn. bd., dir. Eurafrance, 1972—; vice chmn. BSN-Gervais-Danone, 1970—, Groupe Danone, 1970—; bd. dirs. ITT Industries, Dannon Co. Inc., N.Y. Stock Exch., 1995—. Bd. govs. Soc. of N.Y. Hosp.; trustee Met. Mus. Art, 1985—. Mem. Academie des Beaux-Arts (mem. inst.). Clubs: Brook (N.Y.C.), Knickerbocker (N.Y.C.). Office: Lazard Freres & Co LLC 30 Rockefeller Plz Fl 59 New York NY 10112-5900

DAVIE, JOSEPH MYRTEN, physician, pathology and immunology educator, science administrator; b. La Porte, Ind., Oct. 14, 1939; s. John James and Dorothy Elizabeth (Hash) D.; m. Janet Sue Whorwell, Dec. 17, 1960; children: Shelley, Jennifer, Melissa. A.B., Ind. U., 1962, M.A., 1964, Ph.D., 1966; M.D., Washington U., St. Louis, 1968. Intern Washington U., 1968-69; staff assoc. NIH, 1969-71; resident Nat. Cancer Inst., 1971-72; assoc. prof. pathology Washington U. Sch. Medicine, 1972-75, asst. prof. microbiology, 1972-73, assoc. prof. microbiology, 1973-75, prof., head microbiology and immunology, prof. pathology, 1975-87; sr. v.p. research G.D. Searle and Co., Skokie, Ill., 1987, pres. research and devel., 1987-92, corp. sr. v.p. sci. and tech., 1993; v.p. rsch. Biogen, Inc., Cambridge, Mass., 1993-98; sr. v.p. rsch. Biogen, Inc., Cambridge, 1999—. Assoc. editor: Jour. of Immunology, 1975-78; sect. editor, 1978-82. Served with USPHS, 1969-71. Mem. Am. Soc. Microbiology, Am. Assn. Immunologists, Am. Assn. Pathologists, Inst. Medicine, Royal Soc. Medicine. Office: Biogen Inc 14 Cambridge Ctr Cambridge MA 02142-1481

DAVIES, ALFRED ROBERT, physician, educator; b. Troy, Ohio, May 20, 1933; s. Alfred Willis and Lois Prugh (Shilling) D.; m. Shirley Gray Culp, June 23, 1956; children: Ann D. Moyer, Robert Lane. A.B., Ohio Wesleyan U., 1955; M.D., U. Cin., 1959. Resident in internal medicine U. Cin., 1959-63; practice medicine specializing in internal medicine Troy, Ohio, 1965-76; clin. prof. medicine Wright State U., 1977—, chmn. dept. medicine, 1977-81; clin. prof. medicine Ohio State U. Coll. Medicine; v.p., chief med. dir. Nationwide Ins. Co. Columbus, Ohio 1990-98. Pres. Miami Valley (Ohio) Heart Assn., 1972-73; mem. First Meth. Ch., Troy, 1965; trustee Stouder Meml. Hosp., 1977-85, Shepherd Hill Hosp., Newark, Ohio, 1990-93, Harding Hosp., Columbus, 1994—; mem. Ohio Pub. Health Coun., 1981-91, chmn., 1987-88. Served with M.C. USNR, 1963-65. Named One of Ohio's Outstanding Young Men, 1968; recipient Troy Community Service award, 1981. Fellow ACP; mem. AMA, Am. Acad. Ins. Medicine (exec. coun. 1993-96), Health Ins. Assn. Am. (health edn. com.), Am. Coll. Physicians Execs. (chmn. ins. soc. 1988-90), Ohio Med. Assn., Ohio Soc. Internal Medicine (pres. 1989-90), Franklin County Acad. Medicine, Columbus Wellness Coun., Omicron Delta Kappa. Republican. Home: 1401 Peters Rd Troy OH 45373-3820

DAVIES, BRIAN EWART, environmental sciences educator; b. Newport, Wales, Aug. 7, 1937; s. Arthur Ewart and Charlotte (Bennett) D.; m. Gillian Jones, Dec. 29, 1964; children: Ffion C.W., Melissa G.W. BSc, Wales U., Bangor, 1959, PhD, 1963. Head lab. W.J. Chafer Ltd., Doncaster, Eng., 1962-64; lectr. Univ. Coll. Wales, 1965-76; sr. lectr. Dyfed-Wales, 1976-85; prof. dept. environ. sci. Bradford (Eng.) U., Yorkshire, 1985-96, also pro-vice-chancellor; adj. prof. earth sci. Clemson (S.C.) U., 1993-96, prof. geol. scis., 1996—. Author more than 140 published works. Home: Boscobel Country Club 203 Leslie Ln Pendleton SC 29670-8812 Office: Clemson U Dept Geol Scis 340 Brackett Hall Clemson SC 29634-1908

DAVIES, CHARLES R., lawyer. BS, Duquesne U., 1964; JD, Georgetown U., 1967. Bar: D.C. 1968. Asst. v.p., asst. gen. counsel Geico Corp., Washington, 1978, v.p., gen. counsel, 1992—. Office: Geico Corp Gelco Plz Washington DC 20076

DAVIES, DAVID GEORGE, lawyer; b. Waukesha, Wis., July 19, 1928; s. David Evan and Ella Hilda (Degler) D.; m. Elaine Kowalchik, May 12, 1962; children: Thea Kay, Bryn Ann, Degler Evan. B.S., U. Wis., 1950, J.D., 1953. Bar: Wis. 1953, Ariz. 1959. Trust rep. First Nat. Bank of Ariz., Phoenix, 1957-58; asst. trust officer First Nat. Bank of Ariz., 1958-62, trust officer, head bus. devel. in trust dept., 1962-66, v.p., trust officer, 1966; practice in Phoenix, 1967—; assoc. Wales & Collins, 1967-68; ptnr. Wales, Collins & Davies, 1968-75, Collins, Davies & Cronkhite, Ltd., 1975-85, David G. Davies, Ltd., 1986—; Instr. bus. law local chpt. C.L.U.s, 1965; instr. estate and gift taxation, 1973—; instr. estate planning Phoenix Coll., 1968—; past instr. Maricopa County Jr. Coll. Pres. Central Ariz. Estate Planning Council; pres., bd. dirs. Vis. Nurse Service, United Fund Agy.; chmn. bd. Beatitudes Campus of Care; bd. dirs. Phoenix chpt. Nat. Hemophilia Found.; bd. dirs., treas. trusteeship St. Luke's Hosp. Med. Ctr., Phoenix, 1982—; mem. adv. bd. planned giving com. Salvation Army, 1997—. Served to capt. JAGC, AUS, 1953-57. Mem. Central Assn. Life Underwriters (asso.), ABA, Wis. Bar Assn., State Bar Ariz., Am. Assn. Homes for Aged (legal affairs com., future com.). Congregationalist (chmn. bd. trustees, moderator). Office: 5110 N 40th St Ste 236 Phoenix AZ 85018-2151

DAVIES, DENNIS RUSSELL, conductor, music director, pianist; b. Toledo, Ohio, Apr. 16, 1944. BA, Juilliard Sch. Music, 1966, MA, 1968, DMA, 1972. Music dir. Norwalk (Conn.) Symphony Orch., 1968-72, St. Paul Chamber Orch., 1972-80, Cabrillo Music Fest, 1974-92, White Mountain Festival Arts, 1975-77; condr. Juilliard Ensemble, 1968-74, Flying Dutchman Bayreuth Festival, 1978-80; prin. condr. Bklyn. Philharm., 1991-95; now music dir. Am. Composers Orch., 1995—; regular guest condr. Netherlands Opera, 1973-82, Berlin Philharm., Vienna Radio Orch., Chgo. Lyric Opera; guest condr. Stuttgart (Germany) Opera, 1976-80, music dir., 1980-87; gen. music dir., Bonn, 1987-95; chief condr. Stuttgart Chamber Orch., 1995—, Vienna Radio Symphony Orch., 1996. Office: American Composers Orchestra 1775 Broadway Ste 525 New York NY 10019-1903*

DAVIES, DON, education educator; b. Mpls., Dec. 28, 1926; s. Clifford Goetz and Gladys (Herr) D.; m. Mary Joyce Davies; children: Druanne, Donna. BA in Journalism, Stanford U., 1948, MA in Ednl. Adminstrn., 1949; EdD in Curriculum and Tchr. Edn., Columbia U., 1956. Tchr. Beverly Hills (Calif.) H.S., 1949-53; edn. instr. Adelphi Coll., 1953-56; asst. prof. edn. San Francisco State Coll., 1956-57; asst. prof. edn., dir. student teaching U. Minn., 1957-61; exec. sec. Nat. Commn. on Tchr. Edn. and Profl. Stds. NEA, 1961-67; assoc. commr. Dept. Edn., 1968-73; fellow in social sci. Yale U., 1973-74; pres. Boston U. Inst. for Responsive Edn., 1973-94; prof. edn. Boston U., 1974-96, prof. emeritus, 1996—, co-dir. Nat. Rsch. and Devel. Ctr. on Families, Communities, 1990-96; vis. prof. Northeastern U.; adv. bd. Equity and Choice; presenter in field. Author: Low Income Parents and the Schools, 1989, Resource Guide on Parent and Citizen Parcipation in Education, 1988, Parents Make a Difference: An Evaluation of New York City's 1987-88 Parent Involvement Program, 1988, Portrait of Schools Reaching Out, 1992, Communities and Their Schools, 1981, Leading the Way, 1980, Schools Where Parents Make a Difference, 1976, Partnerships for Student Success, 1996; editor Jour. of Tchr. Edn., 1961-67; contbr. articles to profl. jours. Trustee Cambridge Coll.; v.p. Gores' planning com. Ann. Family Reunion Conf. With USN, 1945-46. Recipient Disting. Svc. medal Dept. Edn., 1971, Internat. Achievement award Nat. Coalition for Parent Involvement in Edn., 1994; grantee John D. and Catherine T. MacArthur Found., Pew Charitable Trusts, Leon Lowenstein Found., Aaron Diamond Found., Charles Stewart Mott Found., J.M. Found., Boston Globe Found., Nat. Inst., Edn., 1976-79. Mem. AAUP, Am. Edn. Rsch. Assn., Nat. Coalition of Community Edn. Leaders, Families as Educators Spl. Interest Group, Politics of Edn. Spl. Interest Group, Nat. Soc. for Study Edn., Phi Delta Kappa. Democrat. Avocations: travel, reading. Office: Northeastern Univ Inst for Responsive Edn 50 Nightingale Hall Boston MA 02115

DAVIES, GARETH JOHN, lawyer, trade executive; b. Neath, Wales, Jan. 30, 1944; s. Gwyn and Molly (Blann) D.; m. Maureen Martin, Sept. 1, 1973; children: Trudy, Allison. Solicitor and Notary, Coll. Law, London, 1969. Pros. solicitor South Wales Police Authority, 1969-70; asst. co. sec. Beecham Rsch. Internat., London, 1970-71; ptnr. Scott Jenkins and Davies, Swansea, Wales, 1972-76; chief adminstr. Ont. Travel Industry Conf., Toronto, 1977-78; exec. dir. Alliance Can. Travel Assns., Ottawa, Ont., 1978-89; sec. gen. Universal Fedn. Travel Agts.' Assn., Monaco, 1989-95; pres. Travel Consulting Group, Ottawa, 1995—, Universal Fedn. Travel Agts.' Assn.; rep. more than 90 countries Nat. Travel Agts. Assns. Mem. Yacht Club of Monaco, Royal Ocean Racing Club, Bristol Channel Yacht Club. Office: Travel Consulting Group, 331 Kintyre Pvt, Ottawa, ON Canada K2C 3M6

DAVIES, GARRY, biology educator; b. Blackpool, Eng., Jan. 12, 1943; came to U.S., 1954; s. John Verdon and Nellie (Rowley) D.; m. Rebecca Sue Truesdell, May 13, 1973. B of Forestry, Stephen F. Austin State Coll., 1967; MSc in Forestry, Stephen F. Austin State U., 1973; PhD in Forestry, Tex. A&M U., 1981. Seasonal naturalist Nat. Pk. Svc., Yellowstone Nat. Pk., Wyo., summers 1972-85; curator of collections Nat. Pk. Svc., Anchorage, 1987-90; asst. prof. biology U. Alaska, Anchorage, 1990—. Vol. sci. tchr. Anchorage Elem. Schs., 1990—; comty. advisor Toshiba-Nat. Sci. Tchrs. Assn. Explora Vision Awards, 1996. With USN, 1967-71. Herbarium grantee Alaska Native Plant Soc., 1996. Avocations: cross country skiing, canoeing, rafting. Home: 8800 Tempest Cir Anchorage AK 99507-3969 Office: U Alaska 3211 Providence Dr Anchorage AK 99508-4614

DAVIES, GEORGE PATRICK, city official; b. Newark, Aug. 2, 1966; s. George Patrick and Frances M. (Kaminski) D.; m. Virginia Annette Cutchins, Apr. 1, 1995. Cert. in Internat. Bus. Studies, Copenhagen U., 1987; BS in Mgmt. Sci., Kean Coll. of N.J., 1989; M.Urban and Reg. Planning, Va. Commonwealth U., 1991. Planning intern Richmond (Va.) Reg. Planning Dist. Commn., 1990; tchg. asst. Va. Commonwealth U., Richmond, 1991; cmty. planner Va. Dept. Housing & Cmty. Devel., Richmond, 1991-92; coord. housing and grant devel. Cmty. Alternatives Mgmt. Group, Virginia beach, 1992-96; housing specialist City of Portsmouth, Va., 1996-98; real estate devel. specialist Norfolk (Va.) Redevel. and Housing Authority, 1998—. Mem. Hampton Roads Reg. Consortium, Chesapeake, 1997—. Mem. Am. Planning Assn., Nat. Assn. Housing and Redevel. Ofcls., Nat. Trust for Hist. Preservation, Phi Kappa Phi. Office: Norfolk Redevel & Housing Authority 10th Fl 201 Granby St Norfolk VA 23510

DAVIES, HUGH MARLAIS, museum director; b. Grahamstown, South Africa, Feb. 12, 1948; came to U.S., 1956; s. Horton Marlais and Brenda M. (Deakin) D.; children: Alexandra, Dorian; m. Lynda Forsha; 1 stepdaughter, Mackenzie Forsha Fuller. AB summa cum laude, Princeton U., 1970, M.F.A., 1972, PhD, 1976. Dir., Univ. Gallery, U. Mass., Amherst, 1975-83, Mus. of Contemporary Art, San Diego (formerly La Jolla Mus. Contemporary Art,) Calif., 1983—; vis. prof. fine arts Amherst Coll., 1980-83; mem. mus. com. Rose Art Mus., Brandeis U., 1981-83; mem. adv. coun. dept. art and archeology Princeton U., 1989, panel mem. fed. adv. com. internat. exhbns., 1990-94; panel mem. Mass. Bay Transit Authority, Artist Selection Panel, 1990. Author: Francis Bacon: The Early and Middle Years: 1928-58; co-author: Sacred Art in a Secular Century: 20th Century Religious Art, 1978, Francis Bacon (Abbeville), 1986. Nat. Endowment Arts fellow, 1982. Mem. Am. Assn. Mus., Coll. Art Assn., Assn. Art Mus. Dirs. (trustee), Am. Fedn. Arts. Office: Mus Contemporary Art San Diego 700 Prospect St La Jolla CA 92037-4228*

DAVIES, JOHN ARTHUR, physics and engineering educator, scientist; b. Prestatyn, North Wales, Mar. 28, 1927; emigrated to Can., 1940; s. Francis James and Doris Annie (Edkins) D.; m. Florence Smithson, July 29, 1950; children: Susan, Chris, Cathy, Paul, Jim, Anne. B.A. with honors in Chemistry, St. Michael's Coll., Toronto, 1947; M.A. in Phys. Chemistry, U. Toronto, 1948, Ph.D. in Phys. Chemistry, 1950; D.Sc. (hon.), Royal Roads Mil. Coll., 1984, Salford U., Eng., 1993. With Atomic Energy of Canada, Chalk River, Ont., 1950-85; prof. engring. and physics McMaster U., Hamilton, 1969-92, prof. emeritus, 1992—; vis. prof. physics U. Aarhus, Denmark, 1964-65, 69-70; vis. physicist Nobel Inst. Physics, Stockholm, Sweden, 1962, Calif. Inst. Tech., 1969, Osaka U., Japan, 1972. Author: (with J.W. Mayer, L. Eriksson) Ion Implantation, 1970; contbr. over 200 articles to prof. jours. Can. Ramsay Meml. fellow, 1954-56; recipient Noranda medal Chem. Inst. Can., 1965, Callinan award Am. Electrochem. Soc., 1968, W.B. Lewis medal Can. Nuclear Soc., 1998. Fellow Royal Soc. Can., Bohmische Phys. Soc.; mem. Chem. Inst. Can., Can. Assn. Physics, Danish Royal Soc. Roman Catholic. Home and Office: Box 224, 7 Wolfe Ave, Deep River, ON Canada K0J 1P0

DAVIES, KELVIN JAMES ANTHONY, research scientist, educator, consultant, author; b. London, Oct. 15, 1951; came to U.S., 1975, dual citizenship, 1993; s. Alfred B. and Phyllis (Garcia) D.; m. Joanna Davies, Sept. 14, 1980; children: Sebastian, Alexander. BEd, Liverpool/Lancaster (Eng.) U., 1974; BS summa cum laude, MS, U. Wis., 1976, 77; CPhil, U. Calif., Berkeley, 1979, PhD, 1981; DSc (hon.), U. Moscow, Russia, 1993; MD (hon.), U. Gdansk, Poland, 1995; D of Univ. (hon.), U. Buenos Aires, 1998. Instr. Beal Sch. for Boys, London, 1974-75; rsch. asst. U. Wis., Madison, 1975-77; rsch. asst. U. Calif., Berkeley, 1977-80, lectr. physiology dept. physiology and anatomy, 1980-81; rsch. assoc. dept. biochemistry, inst. toxicology U. So. Calif., L.A., 1981-82, asst. prof. biochemistry, toxicology, 1983-86, assoc. prof. biochemistry, toxicology, 1986-90, prof. biochemistry, toxicology, 1990; inst., sr. rsch. assoc. dept. physiology and biophysics med. sch. Harvard U., 1982-83; prof. biochemistry and molecular biology Albany (N.Y.) Med. Coll., 1991-96, John A. Muntz Univ. prof., 1991-96, chmn. dept. biochemistry and molecular biology, 1991-96, prof. molecular medicine dept. medicine, 1993-96; prof., assoc. dean rsch. Andrus Gerontology Ctr. U. So. Calif., L.A., 1996—; James E. Birren chair gerontology, dir. Andrus Rsch. Inst., 1996—; dir. Nat. Parkinson's Found. Lab., 1996—; founder, dir. STAR program U. So. Calif./L.A. County Schs. Dist., 1984-90; dir. grad. studies inst. toxicology U. So. Calif., 1985-90, mem. cell biology program, 1986-91, fellow inst. molecular medicine, 1988-91; hon. dist. prof. Russian State Med. U., Moscow, 1989; coun. mem. Gordon Rsch. Confs. Frontiers of Sci., 1995-96. Author: Oxidative Damage and Repair: Chemical, Biological and Medical Aspects, 1992, Oxygen '93, 1994, The Oxygen Paradox, 1995; editor in chief: (jour.) Free Radical Biology and Medicine, 1981—, Biochemistry and Molecular Biology Internat., 1999, IUBMB-LIFE, 1999; mem. editl. bd. Advances in Free Radical Biology and Medicine, 1985-87, The Biochem. Jour., 1989-95, Amino Acids, 1991—, Methods in Enzymology, 1991—, Molecular Aspects of Medicine, 1993—; assoc. editor: Jours. Gerontology, 1996—, Cell and Molecular Life Scis., 1996—; contbr. over 200 articles to profl. jours. and books. Active Arts Coun., Pasadena, Calif., 1988-90; pres. Calif. Philharm. Orch. Found., 1996—; bd. govs. The Albany Acad. for Boys, 1994-96. Recipient Chancellors award for Rsch., U. Calif., Berkeley, 1981, Young Investigator award NIH, 1984, 50th Anniversary medal U. Gdansk, 1995; rsch., program project grantee NIH, 1983—; fellow Hoffman-La Roche, 1981, Arco, 1981, Am. Heart Assn., 1982, NIH, 1983. Fellow AAAS, CNR (Italy), Russian Acad. Scis., Gerontol. Soc. Am.; mem. Am. Coll. Sports Medicine, Am. Physiol. Soc. (Harwood S. Belding award 1982), Am. Soc. for Biochemistry and Molecular Biology, Internat. Union Biochemistry and Molecular Biology (coun. mem. 1995—), Biochem. Soc., Biophys. Soc., European Soc. Free Radical Rsch., Internat. Soc. Free Radical Rsch. (coun. 1988—), Internat. Cell rsch. Orgn., N.Y. Acad. Sci.,

Rsch. Coun. New Zealand, The Oxygen Soc. (fellow, sec. gen. 1987-90, pres. 1992-95, Disting. Achievement award 1997), Sigma Xi, Phi Beta Kappa, Kappa Delta Pi. Avocations: opera, symphony, cricket, soccer, food and wines. Office: Univ So Calif Andrus Gerontology Ctr 3715 Mcclintock Ave Rm 306 Los Angeles CA 90007-4013

DAVIES, KIMBERLY ANN, sociology educator; b. Columbus, Ohio, June 14, 1965; d. Richard Thomas Jr. and Marcia Ann (McNerney) D. BA in Women's Studies cum laude, Ohio State U., 1988, BA in Sociology cum laude, 1988, MA in Sociology, 1990, PhD in Sociology, 1996. Asst. prof. Augusta (Ga.) State U., 1996—; founder, mem. Moral Maximalists, Augusta, 1997—; presenter in field. Contbr. articles to profl. jours. Mem. Acad. of Criminal Justice Scis., Am. Soc. of Criminology, Am. Sociol. Assn. (sect. on undergrad. edn.), Ga. Sociol. Soc. (rsch. bd.), Mid South Sociol. Assn. (mem. women's caucus), Nat. Women's Studies Assn., Southern Criminal Justice Assn. Office: Augusta State U Sociology 2500 Walton Way Augusta GA 30904

DAVIES, LAURA, golfer; b. Coventry, Eng., Oct. 5, 1963. Profl. golfer, 1987—. 15 career victories; named Mem. Brit. Empire, Queen Elizabeth II, 1988. Office: care LPGA 100 International Golf Dr Daytona Beach FL 32124-1082*

DAVIES, MARY ELIZABETH, principal; b. Jersey City, N.J., Aug. 4, 1935; d. Daniel Joseph and Lillian Gertrude (Metzler) D. BS, Coll. of St. Elizabeth, 1962; postgrad., Boston Coll., 1991—. Cert. elem. tchr., N.J.; mem. Sisters of Charity of St. Elizabeth, Roman Cath. Ch., 1953. Tchr. St. Mary Sch., Waterbury, Conn., 1956-60, St. Augustine Sch., Union City, N.J., 1960-71, Our Lady of Mt. Carmel Sch., Ridgewood, N.J., 1971-75, St. Joseph Sch., West Milford, N.J., 1975-82, St. Francis Sch., Ridgefield Park, N.J., 1982-84, Our Lady of Victory Sch., Harrington Park, N.J., 1984-85, St. Matthew Sch., Ridgefield, 1985-86, St. Paul Sch., Clifton, N.J., 1986-89, St. Mary Sch., Wharton, N.J., 1989-91; tchr., vice prin. St. Therese Sch., Succasunna, N.J., 1991-92, acting prin., 1992-93, prin., 1993—, 1993—; reading coord. Mt. Carmel Sch., Ridgewood, 1971-75; coord. computer club for primary grades St. Mary's, Wharton, N.J., 1990-91; edn. adv. bd. Sister of Charity Schs., 1990-98; area prin. coord. Paterson Diocese, 1995-97. Mem. Nat. Cath. Edn. Assn. (coord.), ASCD, Learnig Resource Ctr./No. Satellite, Instr. Book Club, Tchr. Book Club. Democrat. Roman Catholic. Avocations: sewing, latch hooking, reading, walking, photography, tutoring. Home: 35 Rockaway Ave Rockaway NJ 07866-3904 Office: St Therese Sch 135 Main St Succasunna NJ 07876-1315

DAVIES, MERTON EDWARD, planetary scientist; b. St. Paul, Sept. 13, 1917; s. Albert Daniel and Lucile (McCabe) D.; AB, Stanford, 1938, postgrad., 1938-39; m. Margaret Louise Darling, Feb. 10, 1946; children: Deidra Louise Stauff, Albert Karl, Merton Randel. Instr. math. U. Nev., 1939-40; group leader Math. Lofting, Douglas Aircraft Co., El Segundo, Calif., 1940-48; sr. staff Rand Corp., Santa Monica, Calif., 1948-59, 62—, liaison USAF, Washington, 1959-62. U.S. observer inspected stas. under terms Antarctic Treaty, 1967; TV co-investigator Mariner Mars, 1969, 71, Mariner Venus/Mercury 1973 Mission, Voyager Mission, Galileo Mission, Magellan Mission, Mars Observer Mission, Clementine Mission, Mars Global Surveyor Mission. Fellow AIAA (assoc.); mem. AAAS, Am. Soc. Photogrammetry. Author: (with Bruce Murray) The View from Space, 1971; (with others) Atlas of Mercury, 1978. Patentee in field. Home: 1414 San Remo Dr Pacific Palisades CA 90272-2737 Office: Rand Corp 1700 Main St Santa Monica CA 90401-3297

DAVIES, MICHAEL NORMAN ARDEN, lawyer, business executive; b. Prestatyn, Wales, Dec. 20, 1932; arrived in Can., 1940; s. Francis James and Doris Annie (Edkins) D.; m. Lida Diana Sartori, July 1, 1959; children: Alexandra, Douglas, Julie. BA, U. Toronto, 1955; LLB, Osgoode Hall Law Sch., 1959. Law clk. to chief justice Supreme Ct. Ont., Toronto, Can., 1959-60; solicitor Zimmerman, Haywood & Turville, Toronto, 1960-61; gen. counsel Found. Group Cos., Toronto, 1962-69, Metro Ctr. Devel. Ltd., Toronto, 1969-74; v.p., gen. counsel Can. Realties Ltd., Toronto, 1974-77; assoc. gen. counsel Can. GE Co. Ltd., Toronto, 1977-87; v.p., sec., gen. counsel GE Can. Inc., Mississauga, Ont., 1987—; bd. dirs. GE Capital Can., Inc., GE Can. Inc., GE Capital Mortgage Ins. Co., Can. Matthew Wilson Meml. scholar Osgoode Hall, 1959. Mem. Can. Bar Assn., Albany Club, Lambton Golf and Country Club. Avocations: golf, skiing, tennis, scuba diving. Home: 2 Colchester Ct, Etobicoke, ON Canada M9A 4S5 Office: GE Can Inc, 2300 Meadowvale Blvd, Mississauga, ON Canada L5N 5P9*

DAVIES, MICHAEL S., security analyst; b. East Orange, N.J., Feb. 11, 1955; s. Robert John and Eillen D.; m. Mary Lou Donnelly, June 17, 1987; children: Marissa Michelle, Michael Anthony, Raymond James, Brigette Danielle. BA in Econs., Columbia U., 1982; MBA, UCLA, 1991. CFA. Bus. mgr. Yankee Book Pub., Contoocock, N.H., 1983; dir. vertical markets First Software Corp., Lawrence, Mass., 1983-85; sr. analyst, chief exec. officer Mktg. Strategies Internat., Inc., Mission Viejo, Calif., 1985-89; exec. v.p., dir. rsch. Fairmont Fin. Group, Inc., Newport Beach, Calif., 1989-90; v.p. corp. mktg. Am. Savs. Bank, Irvine, Calif., 1990-91; v.p. cons. BEI Golembe Inc., Washington, 1992-93; dir. equity rsch. Utendahl Capital Ptnrs., N.Y.C., 1993-98; v.p., sr. tech. analyst Punk Ziegel & Co., N.Y.C., 1998—; cons. Apple Computer, Cupertino, Calif., 1986-88, Compaq Computer, Houston, 1988. Mem. Assn. for Investment Mgmt. and Rsch., N.Y. Soc. Security Analysts.

DAVIES, PAUL LEWIS, JR., retired lawyer; b. San Jose, Calif., July 21, 1930; s. Paul Lewis and Faith (Crummey) D.; m. Barbara Bechtel, Dec. 22, 1955; children: Laura (Mrs. Segundo Mateo), Paul Lewis III. AB, Stanford U., 1952; JD, Harvard U., 1957. Bar: Calif. 1957. Assoc. Pillsbury, Madison & Sutro, San Francisco, 1957-63, ptnr., 1963-89; gen. counsel Chevron Corp., 1984-89; bd. dirs. FMC Corp. Hon. trustee Calif. Acad. Scis., trustee, 1970-83, chmn., 1973-80; pres. Herbert Hoover Found.; bd. overseers Hoover Instn., chmn., 1976-82, 91-93; hon. regent U. of Pacific, regent, 1959-90. Lt. U.S. Army, 1952-54. Mem. Bohemian Club, Pacific-Union Club, Villa Taverna, World Trade Club (San Francisco), Claremont Country Club, Lakeview (Oakland, Calif.), Cypress Point (Pebble Beach, Calif.), Sainte Claire (San Jose, Calif.), Collectors, Explorers, Links (N.Y.C.), Met. Club, Chgo. Club, Phi Beta Kappa, Pi Sigma Alpha. Republican. Office: 50 Fremont St Ste 3520 San Francisco CA 94105-2239

DAVIES, PETER HO, writer, educator; b. Coventry, Eng., Aug. 30, 1966; came to the U.S., 1992; s. Thomas Enion Davies and Sook Ying Ho; m. Lynne Anne Raughley, Dec. 18, 1994. BS in Physics, U. Manchester, Eng., 1987; BA in English, Cambridge (Eng.) U., 1989; MA in Creative Writing, Boston U., 1993. Lectr. Emory U., Atlanta, 1996-97; asst. prof. U. Oreg., Eugene, 1997-99, U. Mich., Ann Arbor, 1999—; bd. mem. Varsity Publs. Ltd., Cambridge, 1990-93; trustee Varsity Trust, Cambridge, 1991—; mem. writing com. Fine Arts Work Ctr., Provincetown, Mass., 1996—. Author: The Ugliest House in the World: Stories, 1997 (H.L. Davis Oregon Book award 1998); author of short stories. Fellow fine Arts Work Ctr., Provincetown, 1994, Nat. Endowment for the Arts, 1998.

DAVIES, PETER JOHN, plant physiology educator, researcher; b. Sudbury, Middlesex, Eng., Mar. 7, 1940; came to U.S., 1966; s. William Bertram and Ivy Doreen (Parmentier) D.; m. Linda Kay DeNoyer, Aug. 2, 1976; children: Kenneth DeNoyer, Caryn Parmentier. BSc with honors, U. Reading, Eng., 1962; MS, U. Calif., Davis, 1964; PhD, U. Reading, 1966. Instr. Yale U., New Haven, 1966-69; asst. prof. plant physiology Cornell U., Ithaca, N.Y., 1969-75, assoc. prof., 1975-83, prof., 1983—, chmn. sect. plant biology, 1992-96; vis. prof. Cambridge (Eng.) U., 1976-77, Univ. Coll. of Wales, Aberystwyth, 1983-84, U. Minn., 1984, U. Tasmania, Australia, 1996-97. Author: (with others) The Life of the Green Plant, 1980, Control Mechanisms in Plant Development, 1970; editor: Plant Hormones and Their Role in Plant Growth and Redevelopment, 1987, Plant Hormones: Physiology, Biochemistry and Molecular Biology, 1995; editor-in-chief Plant Growth Regulation, 1987-92. Mem. Am. Soc. Plant Physiology, Internat. Plant Growth Substance Assn. (coun. 1991-98). Office: Cornell U Plant Biology Ithaca NY 14853

DAVIES, RICHARD JOHN, oncologist; b. Trowbridge, Wiltshire, England, May 16, 1950; s. Thomas John and Gladys Maureen (Turner) D.; m. Mary Kathleen Brumfield, Sept. 2, 1980; children: Keely, Courtney, Spencer. MBBS, U. London, 1973. Surg. house officer Whipps Cross Hosp., London, 1974; med. house officer The London Hosp., 1974-76; resident in surgery Tulane U., New Orleans, 1976-80; chief resident in surgery Tulane U./Charity Hosp., New Orleans, 1980; rsch. fellow Yale U. Med. Coll., New Haven, 1980-81; fellow in surg. oncology Sloan Kettering Cancer Ctr., N.Y.C., 1981-83, chief surg. fellow, 1983; from asst. to assoc. prof. surgery U. Calif., San Diego, 1983-93; prof. surgery U. Med. & Dental N.J., 1993—. Fellow Am. Cancer Soc., 1982-83; grantee NIH, 1984—. Mem. AAAS, Alton Oschner Surg. Soc., Am. Coll. Surgeons, Assn. Acad. Surgery, Soc. Surg. Oncology, Soc. Univ. Surgeons, Soc. Surgery Alimentary Tract, Nat. Adjuvant Breast & Bowel Project, Pacific Coast Surg. Soc., Internat. Coll. Surgeons, European Soc. Mastology, N.J. Med. Soc., N.Y. Surg. Soc., Bergen County Med. Soc. Avocations: sailing, skiing, theater, reading, travel. Office: Hackensack U Med Ctr 30 Prospect Ave Hackensack NJ 07601*

DAVIES, ROGER, geoscience educator; b. London, Aug. 29, 1948; came to U.S., 1972, naturalized, 1985; s. Trevor Rhys and Gracie Rhys (Beaton) D.; m. Corinne Marie Scofield, Oct. 29, 1977 (div. 1999); children: Colin, Gavin. BS with honors, Victoria U., Wellington, N.Z., 1970; PhD, U. Wis., 1976. Meteorologist New Zealand Meteorol. Svc., Wellington, 1971-77; scientist U. Wis., Madison, 1977-80; from asst. prof. to assoc. prof. atmospheric sci. Purdue U., West Lafayette, Ind., 1980-87; assoc. prof. McGill U., Montreal, Que., Can., 1987-95; from assoc. prof. to prof. U. Ariz., Tucson, 1995—; mem. Earth Radiation Budget Expt. Sci. Team, 1980-92, First Internat. Satellite Cloud Climatology Project, Regional Exptl. Sci. Team, 1984-87, Internat. Radiation Commn., 1993—. Assoc. editor: Jour. Geophys. Rsch., 1987-92; contbr. articles and book revs. to profl. publs. Rsch. grantee NASA. Mem. Am. Meteorol. Soc., Am. Geophys. Union. Avocations: sailing, tennis. Office: U Ariz Inst Atmospheric Physics PAS Bldg 81 Tucson AZ 85721

DAVIES, TIM, online information company executive. COO NEXIS, a divsn. of Lexis-Nexis, Miamisburg, Ohio, 1997—. Office: Lexis-Nexis 9443 Springboro Pike Miamisburg OH 45342-4425*

DAVIES, WILLIAM RALPH, service executive; b. Santa Barbara, Calif., Aug. 17, 1955; s. Ralph Emmett and Georgann Marie (Cordingly) D.; m. Karen L. Blake, May 12, 1984 (div. 1999). AA in Real Estate, Am. River Coll., 1978; BS in Fin., Ins. and Real Estate, Calif. State U., Sacramento, 1980; postgrad. in Internat. Bus., Golden Gate U., 1982-84. Real estate assoc. Kiernan Realtors, Sacramento, 1975-77; co-owner real estate firm Sacramento, 1977, pvt. practice real estate cons., property mgr., 1978-80; broker assoc. MBA Bus. Brokers, Sacramento, 1980-85, pres., 1985—; pres. WRD Cons. Group, Sacramento, 1984—; bd. dirs. WRD, Inc., Sacramento. Mem. Assisted Living Fedn., Calif. Assisted Living Facilities Assn. (bd. dirs.). Republican. Avocations: history, bridge, golf. Office: 895 Embarcadero Dr Ste 203 El Dorado Hills CA 95762

DAVIES-MCNAIR, JANE, retired educational consultant; b. Topeka, May 21, 1922; m. K. Robert Davies, Aug. 27, 1949; m. John D. McNair June 4, 1989. BE, Nat. Louis U. (formerly Nat. Coll. Edn.), Evanston, Ill., 1944, ME, 1958; postgrad., Columbia U., Ill. State U., Nat. Coll. Edn. Tchr. various schs., Oak Park, Ill., Hillside, N.J., Elmont, N.Y., 1944-58; tchr. Sch. Dist., Dwight, Ill., 1959-67, Streater, Ill., 1968; asst. county supt. Livingston County, Pontiac, Ill., 1969-72; project cons., supr., trainer early prevention of sch. failure K W Curriculum Svc. Office, Peotone, Ill., 1972-77; freelance cons., speaker early childhood edn. Ill., 1977-80; ret., 1980. Author: Resource Guide for Developing Pre-Academic, Learning Skills and Other guides for the Early Prevention of School Failure, The Gifted and the Biligual and Migrant Programs. Mem. AAUW, DAR, State Evaluation Team, Nat. Assn. Edn. Young Children, Assn. Childhood Edn. (early childhood), Nat. Soc. Sons and Daus. of Pilgrims, Am. Assn. Ret. Persons, Ill. Ret. Tchrs. Assn. (dir. Region II), Ill. Edn. Assn. (life and ret. life com.), Internat. Platform Assn., Gen. Fedn. Women's Club, Delta Kappa Gamma.

DAVIES SILCOTT, LOMA GEYER, freelance writer, English educator; b. Chgo., July 14, 1934; d. Fred Harry and May Belle (Perry) Geyer; m. Robert Eugene Davies, Sept. 5, 1954; (dec. Nov., 1982); children: Kathleen, Daniel, Joel, John; m. Ralph R. Silcott, Jan. 8, 1994. BS, Valparaiso U., 1970; MS, Purdue U., 1975. Legal sec. Gavit and Richardson, Gary, Ind., 1954-58; tchr. Hobart (Ind.) H.S., 1970-87; freelance writer, 1975—; assoc. prof. Oglala Lakota Indian Coll., Rapid City & Kyle, S.D., 1995—. Author: (books) The Nuts and Bolts Writer's Manual, 1991, 201 Happy Hints, 1991, Cook's Corner Recipe Collection, 1991, Senior Sense, 1995. Mem. Nat. Writers Assn., Rapid Valley Faith Bapt. Ch. Republican. Avocations: sewing, knitting, quilting, reading, piano and organ. Home: 1777 Zinnia St Rapid City SD 57703-6280 Office: Oglala Lakota Indian College PO Box 490 Kyle SD 57752-0490

DAVIGNON, CHARLES PHILIAS, priest; b. Albany, Vt., Nov. 5, 1930; s. Nellie Mae Pudvah. STL, U. Montreal, Que., Can., 1956; MA, Cath. U. Am., 1960, PhD, 1973. Ordained priest Roman Cath. Ch., 1956. Assoc. pastor St. Augustine's Parish, Montpelier, Vt., 1960-66; prin. St. Michael's High Sch., Montpelier, 1960-66; assoc. mem. Maryknoll Fathers, dir. lang. dept. Sch. Spl. Studies, San Marcos Nat. U., Lima, Peru, 1967-69; dir. Communication Ctr., Puno, Peru, 1969-72, Diocesan Office Communications, Burlington, Vt., 1972-74, 88—; v.p. devel., dir. Ctr. for Mission Studies Maryknoll (N.Y.) Sch. Theology, 1974-79; pastor St. Mary Star of Sea Ch., Newport, Vt., 1980-88, St. John Vianney Ch., South Burlington, Vt., 1988-94, Blessed Sacrament Ch., Stowe, Vt., 1994-96; coord. Office of Justice and Peace, Maryknoll, N.Y./L.Am. Desk-Office of Internat. Justice and Peace, U.S. Cath. Conf., Washington, 1974-79. Address: 4 Prospect St Essex Junction VT 05452-3614 *Once a person is called, gifted and graced, one mission remains—to seek ways and means of sharing who and what you are with others.*

DAVILA, JANET PATRICIA, women's health nurse, educator; b. Orange, Calif., Nov. 20, 1950; d. Andrew Leo and Catherine Frances (Heinz) Holtz; m. Jose Luis Davila, Oct. 27, 1973; children: Janelle Catherine, Jill Christine, Jolynn Marie. BSN, U. San Francisco, 1972; student, UCLA, 1986. Cert. childbirth educator; cert. lactation cons.; cert. parenting educator. Staff nurse med.-surg. St. Joseph's Hosp., Orange, Calif., 1972-73; staff nurse in ob-gyn., surgery, orthopedics USAF Hosp., Wiesbaden, West Germany, 1974-77; ob-gyn. and labor and delivery staff nurse Marian Med. Ctr., Santa Maria, Calif., 1978—, women's health coord., 1989, perinatal in-svc. coord., 1992—. Vol. facilitator, trainer Am. Cancer Soc., 1991, bd. dirs. Calif. divsn., 1996—. Mem. AWHONN, Am. Soc. for Psychoprophylaxis in Obstetrics, Internat. Childbirth Edn. Assn., LaLeche League Internat., Internat. Lactation Cons. Assn., U. San Francisco Alumni Assn., Sigma Theta Tau. Office: Marian Med Ctr 1400 E Church St Santa Maria CA 93454-5906

DAVILA, NORMA, developmental psychologist and program evaluator; b. Rio Piedras, P.R., Dec. 17, 1962; d. Fernando and Ana (Maldonado) D. BA in Psychology, Yale U., 1985; MA in Behavioral Sci., U. Chgo., 1988, PhD in Psychology, 1991. Asst. edn. coord. Head Start, New Haven, 1984-85; rsch. asst. Disengagement of Talent Project, Chgo., 1985-86; rsch. asst. Chgo. Stress Project, 1986-87, project coord., 1987; sr. pro-analyst Rsch. Pros, Chgo., 1988-89; instr. dept. psychology St. Xavier Coll., Chgo., 1988-89, 90, Roosevelt U., Chgo., 1990-91; asst. prof. dept. psychology U. P.R., Rio Piedras, 1991-96, assoc. prof. dept. psychology, 1997—; dir. evaln. and assessment PR-SSI Project, Rio Piedras, 1996—, dir. evaln., 1993-95, dir. evaln. and assessment, 1996—; co-prin. investigator, PR-SSI project dir. PR/N.Y.C. Ednl. Linkages Demonstration Project; career counselor and career devel. instr. Women Employed, Chgo., 1991. Recipient Trustee's Fellowship U. Chgo., 1985-86, Minority Grad. Incentive Program Fellowship, State of Ill., 1986-89, Dissertation of Yr. Fellowship, Dorothy Danforth Compton Found., 1990-91; NISE fellow, 1998-99. Mem. APA, Psychol. Assn. of P.R., Am. Ednl. Rsch. Assn., Am. Evaluators Assn. Avocations: cooking, reading, watching fgn. films. Office: Dept Psychology U Puerto Rico Rio Piedras PR 00936

DAVILA, REBECCA TOBER, health and physical education educator; b. Dallas, Apr. 10, 1942; d. Antonio M. and Aurora Tober (Benavides) D. BS, Tex. Woman's U., 1964, MA, 1969; Cert. in Mgmt. and Adminstrn., North Tex. State U., 1983. Cert. health edn. specialist. Camp counselor Heart O the Hills, Kerrville, Tex., 1962-67; tchr. San Antonio Ind. Sch. Dist., 1964-67; grad. asst. Tex. Woman's U., Denton, 1967-68; tchr., dept. chair Lewisville (Tex.) Ind. Sch. Dist., 1968—. Vol. Am. Heart Assn., Lewisville, 1980s, 90s, Kidney Found., Lewisville, 1980s, Christian Comty. Action, Lewisville, 1980s, 90s. Mem. Tex. Assn. for Health, Phys. Edn., Recreation and Dance (v.p. health divsn. 1994, workshop dir. region XI 1990, 91, 92, membership chair 1992-93, pres. 1999, Health Tchr. of Yr. 1991), Tex. State Tchrs. Assn. (pres. local chpt. 1984-85), Delta Kappa Gamma (pres. local chpt. 1988-90, Achievement award 1989). Democrat. Roman Catholic. Avocations: gardening, reading, fishing, golf, refinishing antique furnisher.

DAVILA, RODOLFO G., pharmaceutical company executive; b. Mar. 27, 1934. BS, U. Tex., 1955. Pres. Davila Pharmacy Inc., San Antonio, 1955—. Office: Davila Pharmacy Inc 1423 Guadalupe San Antonio TX 78207

DAVION, ETHEL JOHNSON, school system administrator, curriculum specialist; b. Raleigh, N.C., July 21, 1948; d. John Arthur and Ethel Mae (Morgan) Johnson; 1 child, Laura Christal. BA, Livingstone Coll., 1971; MA, Glassboro (N.J.) State U., 1983. Cert. tchr., prin., supr., N.J. Sr. English tchr. Camden (N.J.) Bd. Edn., 1977-81; tchr. of English Westfield (N.J.) Bd. Edn., 1982-85, Union County Regional Dist. 1, Berkeley Heights, N.J., 1981-82, Hillside (N.J.) Bd. Edn., 1985-87; supr. English, lang. arts Irvington (N.J.) Bd. Edn., 1987-92; vice prin. Frank H. Morrell H.S., Irvington, N.J., 1992-95; prin. Frank H. Morrell H.S., Irvington, 1996—; writer, researcher Collegiate Rsch. Systems, Camden, 1976-77; participant profl. devel. programs Harvard U., 1989, Notre Dame U., 1990. Author: A Tutorial Approach to Teaching English, 1983; Teachers' Resource Manual, 1987; contbr. articles to jours. Bd. dirs., sec. Emmanuel Tabernacle, Linden, N.J., 1988. Recipient Resolution Town Coun. Irvington, 1992. Fellow N.J. Edn. Assn., Nat. Coun. Tchrs. English; mem. Linden Scholarship Guild (sec. 1985—), Assn. for Supervision and Curriculum Devel., Prin. and Suprs. Assn., Irvington Adminstrs. Assn. (treas.), Internat. Platform Assn., Good Samaritans Club, Obsidian Civic Club (Westfield, historian 1985—), Diversity 2000 Coun. (sec. 1997—). Democrat. Pentecostal.

DAVIS, A. DANO, grocery store chain executive; b. 1945. Student, Stetson U. With Winn-Dixie Stores Inc., Jacksonville, Fla., 1968—, corp. v.p., mgr. Jacksonville div., 1978-80, sr. v.p. and regional dir. Jacksonville and Orlando (Fla.) and Atlanta divs., 1980-82, pres., 1982-88, chmn., CEO, also bd. dirs., 1988—. Office: Winn-Dixie Stores Inc PO Box B Jacksonville FL 32203-0297*

DAVIS, ADAM BROOKE, English educator; b. St. Louis, Apr. 14, 1961; s. Paul Douglas-Bozzell and Joan (Wollbrinck) D.; m. Andrea Wiedermann, Aug. 26, 1983; children: Naomi, Clement, Paul, August. BA in English, U. Mich., 1983, MA in English, 1984; PhD in English, U. Mo., 1991. Asst. prof. Truman State U., Kirksville, Mo., 1991-97; assoc. prof. Truman State U., Kinksville, Mo., 1997—; guest prof. Albert-Ludwigs U., Freiburg, Germany, 1991-92. Contbr. articles, essays, poetry, fiction to profl. jours. Huggins fellow U. Mo., 1984-87, Cowden fellow U. Mich., 1984. Fellow Alexander von Humboldt Found.; mem. Mo. Folklore Soc. (bd. govs. 1996—), AAUP, Nat. Coun. Tchrs. English, Conf. Coll. Composition and Comm., Internat. Soc. Anglo Saxonists, Medieval Acad. Am., KC. Home: 804 E Illinois St Kirksville MO 63501-5206

DAVIS, ALAN JAY, lawyer; b. Phila., Feb. 4, 1937; s. Rudolph Alan and Adele (Saver) D.; m. Roslyn Kutcher, Oct. 4, 1939; children: Jennifer C., Michael R. BA, U. Pa., 1957; JSD, Harvard U., 1960. Bar: Pa. 1961, U.S. Dist. Ct. (ea. dist.) Pa. 1961, U.S. Ct. Appeals (3d cir.) 1961, U.S. Supreme Ct. 1979. Law clk. to chief judge U.S. Ct. Appeals (3d cir.), Phila., 1960-61; assoc. Wolf, Block, Schorr & Solis-Cohen, Phila., 1961-66; chief asst. dist. atty. Office Dist. Atty., Phila., 1966-68; ptnr. Wolf, Block, Schorr & Solis-Cohen, Phila., 1968-91, chmn. litigation dept., 1987-91; sr. litigation ptnr. Ballard Spahr Andrews & Ingersoll, Phila., 1991—; spl. master to investigate prison system and sheriff's dept. Ct. of Common Pleas, Phila., 1968-70; lectr. law U. Pa. Sch. Law, Phila., 1973-77; City Solicitor Phila., 1980-82; chief labor negotiator Southeastern Pa. Transp. Authority, Phila., 1982, Sch. Dist. Phila., 1984, 96, City of Phila., 1991-93. Chmn. met. adv. bd. Anti-Defamation League of B'nai B'rith, Phila., 1986-88; mem. sch. com. Germantown Friends Sch., Phila., 1986-88; trustee Free Libr. of Phila., 1995-98; pres. U. Pa. Law Sch. Am. Inns of Ct., 1998—. Fellow Am. Coll. Trial Lawyers; mem. ABA, Pa. Bar Assn., Phila. Bar Assn., Am. Law Inst., Pyramid Club. Democrat. Jewish. Office: Ballard Spahr Andrews & Ingersoll 1735 Market St Fl 51 Philadelphia PA 19103-7501

DAVIS, ALBERT RAYMOND, secondary education educator; b. Kansas City, Aug. 30, 1943; s. John Henry and Marsoleat E. (Minuette) D.; m. Rachel E., Feb. 14, 1971; children: Angelique Marie, Aaron Lee. BA in English/German, U. Mo., 1970; MA in Edn., Pacific Luth. U., 1972. Tchr. English, Tacoma Pub. Schs., 1970—; tchr. curriculum devel. Evergreen Coll., Tacoma, 1994-98; tchr., mentor Mesa, Tacoma, 1982-83; television instr. Tacoma Pub. Schs., 1984-91. Co-author: (test accreditation manual) Helping Students Achieve, 1986. With U.S. Army, 1962-65. Recipient Mesa Instr. award, 1984. Avocations: gardening, exercising, reading, volunteering. Office: Wilson HS 1202 N Orchard St Tacoma WA 98406-3299

DAVIS, ALISON B., company executive. BA, Douglas Coll. Pres. Davis-Hays & Co. Inc., 1984—. Office: 80 Grand Ave River Edge NJ 07661

DAVIS, ALLEN, professional football team executive; b. Brockton, Mass., July 4, 1929; s. Louis and Rose (Kirschenbaum) D.; m. Carol Segall, July 11, 1954; 1 son, Mark. Student, Wittenberg Coll., 1947; A.B., Syracuse U., 1950. Asst. football coach Adelphi Coll., 1950-51; head football coach Ft. Belvoir, Va., 1952-53; player-personnel scout Baltimore Colts, 1954; line coach The Citadel, 1955-56, U. So. Calif., 1957-59; asst. coach San Diego Chargers, 1960-62; gen. mgr., head coach Oakland Raiders (now Los Angeles Raiders), 1963-66, owner, mng. gen. ptnr., 1966—, now pres., gen. ptnr.; former mem. mgmt. council and competition com. Nat. Football League. Served with AUS, 1952-53. Named Profl. Coach of Year A.P., Profl. Coach of Year U.P.I., Profl. Coach of Year Sporting News, Profl. Coach of Year Pro-Football Illustrated, 1963; Young Man of Yr. Oakland, 1963; only individual in history to be an asst. coach, head coach, gen. mgr., league commr. and owner. Mem. Am. Football Coaches Assn. Office: Oakland Raiders 1220 Harbor Bay Pkwy Alameda CA 94502-6570

DAVIS, ALLEN FREEMAN, history educator, author; b. Hardwick, Vt., Jan. 9, 1931; s. Harold Freeman and Bernice Susan (Allen) D.; m. Roberta Hazel Green, June 16, 1956 (div.); children: Gregory Freeman, Paul Studley. A.B., Dartmouth Coll., 1953; M.A., U. Rochester, 1954; Ph.D., U. Wis., 1959. Instr. history Wayne State U., Detroit, 1959-60; asst. prof. history U. Mo., Columbia, 1960-63; assoc. prof. U. Mo., 1963-68; prof. Temple U., Phila., 1968—; vis. prof. U. Tex., Austin, 1983, U. Amsterdam, 1986-87, John Adams chair. Co-author: March of American Democracy, Vol. V, 1966, Spearheads for Reform, 1967, 84, American Heroine, 1973, (with others) The American People, 1986, 4th edit., 1998, (with Jim Watts) Generations, 1974, 78, 83, (with Fredric Miller and Morris Vogel) Still Philadelphia, 1983, Philadelphia Stories, 1988, also numerous articles; editor: (with Harold D. Woodman) Conflict and Consensus in American History, 1966, 9th edit., 1997, (with Mary Lynn McCree) Eighty Years at Hull House, 1969, (with Mark Haller) The Peoples of Philadelphia, 1973, 98, Jane Addams on Peace, War and International Understanding, 1974, For Better or Worse, 1980, (with Mary Lynn Bryan) 100 Years at Hull House, 1990. Served with AUS, 1954-56. Danforth Grad. fellow, 1953-59, Am. Council Learned Socs. sr. fellow, 1971-72, NEH fellow, 1975-76, Fulbright fellow, 1986-87, Am. Philos. Soc. grantee, 1962, 65. Mem. Am. Hist. Assn., Orgn. Am. Historians, Am. Studies Assn. (treas. 1971-72, exec. sec. 1972-77, pres. 1989-90, Bode-Pearson award 1996), Soc. Am. Historians. Home: 2032 Waverly St Philadelphia PA 19146-1343 Office: Temple U History Dept Philadelphia PA 19122

DAVIS, ALTON THOMAS, judge, lawyer; b. Petoskey, Mich., July 23, 1947; s. Alton Thomas Davis and Helen Marie (Waldron) Tull; m. Sandra Kay Shellfish; children: Brion Colleen, Colby Galen. AA, North Ctrl. Mich. Coll., 1967; BS, We. Mich. U., 1969; JD, Detroit Coll. Law, 1974. Bar: Mich., 1974. Ptnr. Kent & Davis PC, Grayling, Mich., 1975-80; pros. atty. Crawford County, Grayling, Mich., 1979-80; pvt. practice Grayling, Mich., 1980-84; judge 46th jud. cir. State of Mich., 1985—; trustee Mich. Bldg. Authority, 1984. Chmn. Crawford County Dem. Com., Grayling, 1980-84, Crawford County Fair Bd., 1990-95; area coord. for Gov. Blanchard, no. Mich., 1983-84. Mem. Rotary Club (pres. 1990-92, Paul Harris fellow), Mich. Jud. Inst. (faculty 1994—), Mich. Judges Assn. (exec. com. 1995—), Mich. State Bar Assn. (chmn. Criminal Jury Instructions com. 1995—). Episcopal. Avocations: reading, writing, fishing, travel. Office: 46th Circuit COurt 200 Michigan Ave Grayling MI 49738-1743 Home: 216 Misty Way Grayling MI 49738-8642

DAVIS, ALVIN G., company executive; b. Post, Tex., Nov. 12, 1927; m. Barbara Ann Hext, July 28, 1955; children: Glen Robert Davis, Debra Ann Garland, Jay Todd. Student, Tex. A&M, 1944; BS in Agr., Tex. Tech. Coll., 1951; postgrad., South Plains Coll., 1980; grad., Tex. Tech. U., 1983-84. Agrl. advisor, asst. cashier, asst. v.p. Brownfield (Tex.) State Bank and Trust Co., 1952-64; owner, mgr. Hub Specialty Co., Post and Brownfield, 1952-59, The Cowboy Stores, Tex., 1959-79; exec. v.p., dir. First Nat. Bank, Clovis and Melrose, N.Mex., 1964-65; exec. v.p., gen. mgr. Ranching Heritage Assn. and Endowment Fund Nat. Ranching Heritage Ctr., Tex. Tech. U., Lubbock, Tex., 1981-93; ret., 1994; owner, operator livestock farm; responsible for breeding, raising, showing, mktg. Quarter, Paint and Appaloosa horses, 1956-81; spkr. in field. Pub., writer numerous poems. Active Monterey Ch. of Christ, Lubbock, 1981—, elder, 1988-90; mem. Lubbock Heritage Soc., W. Tex. Hist. Assn., Tex. Mus. Assn.; mem. numerous 4-H Clubs; participant numerous livestock shows. With U.S. Army, 1946-47. Recipient Appreciation award Hockley County, Tex. Soil Conservation Dist., 1994, Appreciation award San Juan Spring Roundup, 1995, Peter McCue award Petersburg, Ill., 1998, numerous outstanding svc. awards. Mem. Am. Cowboy Culture Assn., Inc. (pres., founder), Am. Jr. Rodeo Assn. (adminstr., founder), Nat. Intercollegiate Rodeo Assn. (adminstr., life mem.), Nat. We. Artists Assn. (adminstr., founder), Former Tex. Ranger Assn. (life mem.), Old Trl. Drivers Assn. Tex. (hon. lifetime pres.), Ranching Heritage Assn. (chmn., adminstr., life mem.), Tex. Cowboy Reunion Old Timer's Assn. (life mem.), Tex. Tech. Animal Sci. Alumni Assn. (pres.), We./English Retailers Am. (chmn., founder, life mem.), We. Music Assn. (pres., Bill Wiley award 1995), Tex. Cowboy Poets Assn. (chmn., founder), Youth Rodeo Found. Am. (chmn., founder), Post C. of C. (mgr.), Brownfield C. of C. (pres.), Levelland C. of C. (pres.), Nat. Cowboy Symposium & Celebration (pres., chmn.), Am. Chuckwagon Assn. (pres.), Am. Legion. Fax: 806-795-4749. Home: 4124-62d Dr Lubbock TX 79413

DAVIS, ANDRE MAURICE, judge, educator; b. Balt., Feb. 11, 1949; m. Chanda B. Hudson, May 1, 1971 (div. Oct. 1974); 1 child, Ahmed Jamal; m. Margaret Olevia Roberts, Aug. 15, 1987. BA, U. Pa., 1971; JD, U. Md., 1978. Asst. housing mgr. Housing Authority Balt., 1972-74, equal employment opportunity specialist, 1974-75; law clk. Hon. Frank A. Kaufman U.S. Dist. Ct., Balt., 1978-79; law clk. to Hon. Francis D. Murnaghan, Jr., U.S. Ct. Appeals for 4th Cir., Balt., 1979-80; appellate atty. Civil Rights Divsn. Dept. Justice, Washington, 1980-81; asst. U.S. atty. Office of U.S. Atty., Balt., 1981-83; assoc. atty., litigation Frank, Bernstein, Conaway and Goldman, Balt., 1983-84; from instr. to asst. prof. Sch. Law U. Md., Balt., 1984—; assoc. judge Dist. Ct. Md. for Balt. City, 1987-90, Cir. Ct. for Balt. City, Balt., 1990-95; judge U.S. Dist. Ct., Balt., 1995—. Bd. dirs., instr. Jud. Inst. Md.; mem. Dist. Ct. Commr. Edn.; pres., bd. dirs. Legal Aid Bur., Inc.; v.p., bd. dirs. Big Bros. and Big Sisters of Ctrl. Md., Ind.; trustee Goucher Coll., Park Heights Acad., Balt. Urban League, Inc.; mem. Gov.'s Task Force on Black and Minority Mental Health. Mem. ABA, Md. Bar Assn., Balt. City Bar Assn., Monumental City Bar Assn., U. Md. Sch. Law Alumni Assn., Serjeants' Inn Law Club, Lawyers Round Table, Rule Day Law Club, Wranglers Law Club, Inns of Ct., Phi Alpha Delta. Office: US Courthouse 101 W Lombard St Baltimore MD 21201-2626

DAVIS, ANDREW, film director, screenwriter; b. Chgo.. BS Comm., U. Ill., 1964. Film industry experience includes asst. cameraman: Medium Cool, 1969; cinematographer: Lepke, 1975, Over the Edge, 1979, Angel, 1984; dir., prodr., co-screenwriter: Stony Island; dir. The Final Terror, 1983, Code of Silence, 1985, The Package, 1989, Under Siege, 1992, The Fugitive, 1993, Steal Big, Steal Little, 1995, A Perfect Murder, 1998; dir., co-prodr., co-story: Above the Law, 1988; co-screenwriter: Beat Street, 1984; dir., prodr. Chain Reaction, 1996. Office: Creative Artists Agy 9830 Wilshire Blvd Beverly Hills CA 90212-1825*

DAVIS, ANN CALDWELL, history educator; b. Alliance, Ohio, June 3, 1925; d. Arthur Trescott and Jane Caldwell D. BA, Western Reserve U., 1947; MA, Columbia U., 1955; PhD, Columbia Pacific U., 1987. Cert. tchr., Ill., Ohio. Pres. The Clio Found. Inc., St. Petersburg, Fla., 1955—; tchr. Supr. Child Enterprise, Evanston, Ill., 1956-60; human rels. coun. U. Chgo., 1957-58, asst., 1961; tchr., dept. chair Evanston Pub. Schs., 1961-85; project English Northwestern U., Evanston, 1963-64; cons. Dist. #65 Sch., Evanston, 1985-90. Presenter, author: (speech) Do-it-Yourself Help For The Top 10%, 1964, The Non-Graded School, 1976, Social Studies Reading & Reference Skills, 1979; author: (video) U.S. & Ill. Constn., 1986. Vol. Meals ON Wheels, Treasure Island, Fla., 1990-94, Pinellas County Schs., Fla., 1991, steering com. St. Petersburg, Fla., 1995, health care chair Older Women's League, St. Petersburg, 1995. Mem. Am. Assn. of U. Women, Orgn. of Am. Historians, Ill. & Nat. Edn. Assn. Office: The Clio Found Inc PO Box 5110 Gulfport FL 33737-5110

DAVIS, ANNA JANE RIPLEY, elementary education educator; b. Uhrichsville, Ohio, Sept. 7, 1931; d. Emmet Frank and Lillie Hazel (Kinsey) Ripley; m. H. Joe Davis, Mar. 16, 1951; children: Alan Joe, Kendal Jay. Assoc., Asbury Coll., 1953; BS with honors, Kent State U., 1962, MEd with honors, 1978, postgrad., 1980-94; student, Richmond Coll., London U., St. Andrews U., Dundee U., Cambridge U., U. Paris, Rome, U. Amsterdam. Cert. tchr., Ohio. Tchr. Kenston Schs., Chagrin Falls, Ohio, 1953-55, 58-62, Firestone's Rubber Plantation, Harbel, Liberia, West Africa, 1962-64, Newbury (Ohio) Schs., 1964-65, Orange Schs., Pepper Pike, Ohio, 1965-98; chaperone, counselor Am. Inst. for Fgn. Study, summers 1968-81. Author children's books. Active Chagrin Falls and Pepper Pike PTA, Am. Field Svc., Chagrin Falls, Pepper Pike Garfield Meml. United Meth. Ch.; mem. edn. commn. and libr. com. Geauga County Personal Growth Com. for Workshops; bd. mem. Geauga County Pub. Libr. Friends, libr. com., Sunday sch. com., Care Bears com., membership com.; book project vol. Geauga County Libr. for Amish Schs., ARC, 1955-99, elem. sch. tutor, 1998—. Mem. NEA, ASCD, Ohio Edn. Assn., N.E. Ohio Tchr. Assn., Orange Tchrs. Assn. Avocations: family, travel, cycling, hiking, reading, writing.

DAVIS, ANNALEE RUTH CONYERS, clinical social worker; b. Bentonville, Ark., July 8, 1944; d. Lloyd Milton and Jessie Alberta (Robe) Conyers; m. Rushton Eric Davis, Aug. 26, 1967 (div. Apr. 1980); children: Michelle Leigh, Rushton Kendrick. BA, Hendrix Coll., 1966; MSW, U. Okla., 1982. Internat. cert. alcohol and drug counselor; diplomate Internat. Acad. Behavioral Medicine, Counseling and Psychotherapy; lic. marriage and family therapist, Okla.; lic. clin. social worker, Okla.; diplomate in clin. social work; cert. critical incident debriefer; bd. cert. expert in traumatic stress. Psychiat. intern Tulsa Psychiat. Ctr., 1980-82, postgrad. intern, 1982-83; clin. social worker New Choice, Inc., Tulsa, 1983-85; pvt. practice Tulsa, 1985—; bd. dirs. Associated Ctrs. for Therapy; chairperson Quality Assurance and Program Devel. Coms. Head edn. com. Sunbelt Alliance, Tulsa, 1978-80; mem. Fgn. Policy Study Group, Tulsa, 1980-88, LWV, Tulsa, 1978—; mem., tchr. Meth. Ch., Tulsa, 1967-90; bd. dirs. Ctr. Christian Counseling, 1978-88. Mem. NASW (diplomate), Am. Acad. Experts in Traumatic Stress (diplomate, clin. mem.), Acad. Cert. Social Workers, Okla. Assn. Social Workers, Okla. Assn. Profl. Alcohol/Drug Counselors, Okla. Assn. Alcohol and Drug Abuse, Internat. Acad. Behavioral Medicine, Counseling and Psychotherapy. Democrat. Methodist. Home: 6714 E 76th St Tulsa OK 74133-3422

DAVIS, ANTHONY, composer, pianist, educator; b. Paterson, N.J., Feb. 20, 1951; m. Cynthia Aaronson-Davis; 1 child: Jonah. BA in Music, Yale U., 1975; student, Wesleyan U. Lectr., music and Afro-Am. studies Yale U., New Haven, 1981-82; resident fellow Berkeley Coll. of Mus., Yale U., 1981-82; sr. fellow, Soc. of the Humanities Cornell U., Ithaca, N.Y., 1987; prof. Yale U Sch. Music, 1990-98; prof. music U. Calif., San Diego, 1998—; vis. composer Yale Sch. Music, 1990, 93, 96; vis. lectr. Afro-Am. studies Harvard U., 1992-96; composer-in-residence Detroit Symphony Orch., Miss. Symphony Orch., 1995. Composer: film scores for A Man around the House, Steve Hannock, 1981, Miraj, 1983; compositions include Middle Passage, Hemispheres, (operas) X: The Life and Times of Malcolm X, 1986, Wayang No. 5, 1984, Wayang No. 6, 1985, song was sweeter even so, 1987, violin concerto 1988, Notes from the Underground, 1988, Under the Double Moon, 1989, Tania, 1992, (incidental music) Angels in Ameria: Millennium Approaches-Part One, 1993, Part Two-Perestroika, 1993, Esu Variations, 1995, Jacob's Ladder, 1997, Amistad, 1997; violin sonata, 1991; performer: Wayang No. 5, 1984, 87, Still Waters, 1984; solo performer Carnegie Hall, 1983, Berklee Theater, 1984, Joyce Theater (N.Y.C.), 1984, Exploratorium (San Francisco), 1984, Nippon Theater (Seattle), 1984, Portland Ctr. for Visual Arts, 1984, Erie Art Museum, 1987; recs. include Of Blues and Dreams, 1978, Lady of the Mirrors, 1979, Variations in Dreamtime, 1981, Episteme, 1981, I've Known Rivers, 1982, Hemispheres, 1983, Middle Passage, 1984, Undine, 1987; mem. ensemble, Episteme. Recipient Bessie award, 1984, Esquire Registry award. 1984, award AAAL, 1996, Nat. Endowment of the Arts, N.Y. Found. of Arts, Mass. Arts Coun., Chamber Music Am., Lila Wallace Fund/Meet the Composer Fund for Jazz and Opera Am.; Grammy nominee 1992. Bd. dirs. Parabola Arts Found. Inc.; mem. NYSCA (panelist 1983-85), ASCAP. *

DAVIS, BARBARA JOYCE WIENER, accountant, investment manager, financial consultant, educator; b. Berkeley, Calif., Aug. 28, 1947; d. Milton and Kathryn Gertrude (Weiss) Wiener; 1 child, Scott Evan. BA in Psychology, U. Calif., Davis, 1970; MA in Psychology, San Jose State U., 1986; lifetime tchg. credential, U. Calif., Riverside, 1971; MS in Psychology, Pacific Grad. Sch. Psychology, Palo Alto, Calif., 1998; PhD in Clin. Devel.-Orgnl. Psychology, Ctr. for Psychol. Studies, Albany, Calif. Cert. tchr., Calif. Investment mgr. Cupertino, Calif., 1968—; tchr. elem. edn. Santa Clara (Calif.) Unified Sch. Dist., 1971-83; acct., pres. Owl Land Co., Inc., San Leandro, Calif., 1981—, pres.; rsch. and stats. cons. Cupertino, 1984—; tchr. stats. Chabot Coll., Hayward, Calif., 1990-91; tutor stats. San Jose (Calif.) State U., 1984-86; reading tutor to target students Lincoln Elem. Sch., Cupertino (Calif.) Unified Sch. Dist., 1996-97. Vol. Congregation Beth David, 1997-98, Contact Crisis Lines, 1998—. Mem. APA, AAUW, NAFE, NOW, Women's Am. Overseas Rehab. Tng., B'nai B'rith, Calif. Psychol. Assn., Santa Clara Psychol. Assn., Mensa, Parents Without Ptnrs. Avocations: gardening, interior design, dancing, antiques, teaching. Office: 7608 Erin Way Cupertino CA 95014-4343

DAVIS, BARBARA LANGFORD, financial advisor; b. Newberry, S.C., Jan. 2, 1957; d. Ella Mae (Harp) Langford; m. G. Bernard Davis, Aug. 8, 1981; children: Bryant Mckenzie, Brandan Langford. BA in Sociology, Newberry Coll., 1979. CFP. Customer svc. mgr. Riegel Textile Co., Johnston, S.C., 1979-80; knitwear dept. mgr. Riegel Textile Co., Johnston, 1980-82; fin. advisor Am. Express Fin. Advisors Inc., Columbia, S.C., 1982—. Past bd. dirs. Family Shelter, Columbia Forum, Greater Columbia C of C, Leadership Columbia; bd. dirs. Leadership S.C., Midlands Tech. Coll. Found., Jr. Achievement, Columbia Conv. and Visitors Bur., Congaree Swamp. Mem. Internat. Assn. Fin. Planners, Newberry Coll. Lettermen's Club (bd. dirs.), Newberry Coll. Indian Club (bd. dirs.), Inst. Cert. Fin. Planners, S.C. Soc. Cert. Fin. Planners. Avocations: basketball, bowling, reading, writing, gospel music. Home: 2 Cardigan Ct Columbia SC 29210-6112 Office: Am Express Fin Advisors Inc 140 Stoneridge Dr Ste 650 Columbia SC 29210-8257

DAVIS, BARBARA M(AE), librarian; b. Cranston, R.I., Dec. 23, 1926; d. Harrie S. and Marguerite M. (Cameron) D.; SB in Chemistry, Brown U., 1948; MS in Library Sci., Simmons Coll., 1956. Asst. rsch. libr. R & D dept. Cabot Corp., Cambridge, Mass., 1948-57, rsch. libr., 1957-61, rsch. libr. Billerica (Mass.) Rsch. Ctr., 1961-68, head tech. info. svcs., 1968-81, mgr. tech. info. center, 1981-87 . Dir. Cabot Boston Credit Union, 1956-59, 61-64, 72-78, clk., 1961-64, 72-77, v.p., 1977-78. Vol., Lexington Coun. on Aging, 1990—, Lexington Hist. Soc., 1991-97; chmn. research com. Greater Boston Young Rep. Club, 1959-61; treas. Women's Rep. Club Lexington, 1988— ; committeeperson Lexington Republican Town Com., 1993—; del. Mass. Rep. Conv., 1994, 98. Mem. Am. Chem. Soc. (sec. div. chem. lit. 1961-65), Spl. Libraries Assn. (chmn. Boston chpt. 1965-66, chmn. chemistry div. 1971-72), Simmons Coll. Library Sch. Alumni (v.p. 1965-66). Home: 37 Drummer Boy Way Lexington MA 02420-1222

DAVIS, BARBARA SNELL, college educator; b. Painesville, Ohio, Feb. 21, 1929; d. Roy Addison and Mabelle Irene (Denning) Snell; children: Beth Ann Davis Schnorf, James L., Polly Denning Davis Spaeth. BS, Kent State U., 1951; MA, Lake Erie Coll., 1981; postgrad. Cleve. State U., 1982-83. Cert. reading specialist, elem. prin., Ohio. Dir. publicity Lake Erie Coll., Painesville, 1954-59; tchr. Mentor (Ohio) Exempted Village Sch. Dist., 1972-86, prin., 1986—97; educator Lake Erie Coll., 1997—. Bd. Trustees Mentor United Meth. Mem. Delta Kappa Gamma (pres. 1982-84), Phi Delta Kappa (pres. 1992-93), Theta Sigma Phi (charter). Contbr. articles to profl. jours. Home: 7293 Beechwood Dr Mentor OH 44060-6305 Office: College Hall Lake Erie Coll Painesville OH 44077

DAVIS, BENJAMIN GEORGE, theologian, educator; b. Honesdale, Pa., July 6, 1941; s. Benjamin George and Laura Teneyck (Swingle) D.; m. Janet Marie Gorden, June 21, 1980; children: Leslie Anne, John Nathan. AB, U. Mich., 1967, AM, 1969; M.Th., U. Nottingham, England, 1982; D. Min., St. Mary's Sem. & Univ., Balt., 1985. Draftsman, designer Munson Mill Machinery Co., Utica, N.Y., 1961-62; design engr. Gen. Motors Corp., Warren, Mich., 1963-66; devel. coord. City of Ann Arbor, Mich., 1967; research economist Exec. Office of the Pres., Washington, 1970; sr. assoc. RMC Research Corp., Bethesda, Md., 1971-75; dir. Research Svcs., Inc., Clinton, Md., 1975-80; regional dir. World Relief, Landover, Md., 1981-86; dir. Evangelicals for Social Action, Washington, 1987-89; pastor St. John United Ch., Columbia, Md., 1989-90; prof. St. Mary's Sem. and U., Balt., 1986—; assoc. dean Balt. Internat. Coll., 1988-95; exec. dir. The Religious Coalition, Frederick, Md., 1995-98; acad. dean Potomac Coll., Washington, 1998—. Author: A Modern Interpretation of Revelation, 1982, Understanding World Cultures: The United States and Canada, 1990, Economics: An Integrated Approach, 1997; editor: The Dictionary of Essential English, 1987. Pres. Fgn.-born Info. and Referral Network, Columbia, 1986-92; chmn. Coalition fo r Refugee Resettlement, Washington, 1985-86; chairperson Md. Refugee Adv. Coun., Balt., 1985-86. Recipient Gov.'s Citation State of Md., 1985, 86; NDEA fellow in economics U. Md., 1969-71, Rickard's fellow in theology U. Nottingham, 1980-81. Mem. Assn. for Psychol. Type, Assn. Overseas Educators, Mensa, Omicron Delta Epsilon. Avocations: jazz, photography, motorcycling. Home: 6580 Madrigal Ter Columbia MD 21045-4628 *The search for certainty in life leads only up blind alleys. Accepting the ambiguity and moving forward in faith is all.*

DAVIS, BERTHA L., dean women, Bible educator; b. Canton, Miss., Sept. 21, 1937; d. Leon Otho and Lucille Oscar Williams; m. Archie Lee Davis, Sept. 11, 1960 (dec. Aug. 1984); 1 child, Rickie Allen. B Religion, Ch. of Christ Bible Inst., N.Y.C., 1981, B Theology, 1994; MA in Bible, Columbia (S.C.) Internat. U., 1996; D Theology, Internat. Outreach Sch., Columbia, 1998. Cert. tchr., S.C.; cert. missionary, N.Y. Sec. 3M Co., Wayne, Mich., 1969-74, Cath. Guardian Soc., Bklyn., 1974-75; pres., instr. Ch. of Christ Bible Inst., Detroit, 1976-87; word processing specialist, typist Mich. Bell Telephone, Detroit and Livonia, Mich., 1977-82, AT&T, Southfield, Mich., 1982-87; group home mgr. State of Miss., Jackson, 1987-89; dean women, prof. W.L. Bonner Bible Coll., Columbia, S.C., 1995—. Pentecostal. Avocations: sewing, reading Biblical literature. Home: 100 Amsterdam Dr Apt E Columbia SC 29210-5836

DAVIS, BERTRAM HYLTON, retired English educator; b. Ozone Park, N.Y., Nov. 30, 1918; s. Hubert Edwin and Gladys (Greenidge) D.; m. Ruth Austin Benedict, Jan. 11, 1946; children: Ralph Paul, Kathryn Davis Kohler, Richard Austin. Grad., Phillips Acad., Andover, Mass., 1933-37; student, Hamilton Coll., Clinton, N.Y., 1937-39; A.B., Columbia, 1941, M.A., 1948, Ph.D., 1956; LL.D., Dickinson Coll., 1974. Lectr. English Hunter Coll., 1947-48; instr., then asst. prof. English Dickinson Coll., 1948-57; staff assoc. AAUP, 1957-63, dep. gen. sec., 1963-67, gen. sec., 1967-74; prof. English Fla. State U., Tallahassee, 1974-85, svc. prof., 1985-90, prof. emeritus, 1991—. Author: Johnson Before Boswell, 1960, A Proof of Eminence, 1973, Thomas Percy, 1981, Thomas Percy: A Scholar-Cleric in the Age of Johnson, 1989; editor (Sir John Hawkins): Life of Samuel Johnson LL.D, 1961; editor bull., AAUP, 1960-65; field editor Twayne's English Authors Series, 1977-93; mem. editorial com. Yale Edition of Works of Samuel Johnson, 1979—. Served to capt. AUS, 1941-46. Guggenheim fellow, 1974. Mem. ACLU, MLA, Johnsonians, South Atlantic Modern Lang. Assn., Cosmos Club, Am. Soc. for 18th Century Studies. Home: 2309 Domingo Dr Tallahassee FL 32304-1310

DAVIS, BILLIE JOHNSTON, school counselor; b. Charleston, W.Va., Sept. 24, 1933; d. William Andrew Jr. and Garnet Macil (Johnston) D. BS, Morris Harvey Coll., 1954; MA, W.Va. U., 1959. Nat. bd. cert. counselor; W.Va. lic. profl. counselor. Tchr. math. Kanawha County Schs., Charleston, 1954-59, counselor, 1959-98; mem. public edn. study commn. W.Va. Legislature, 1980. Mem. W.Va. Commn. on Juvenile Law, 1982-97; bd. dirs. W.Va. Com. for Prevention Child Abuse, W.Va. Sch. Health Adv. Com.; appointed W.Va. rep. at Tchr.'s Inaugural Experience for Inauguration of Pres. George Bush by Gov. of W.Va., 1989; mem. subcom. W.Va. Health Care Task Force, 1992; bd. trustees W.Va. Youth Advocate Program, 1993-95, Nat. Youth Adv. Program, 1994-95; mem. oversite com. W.Va. Juvenile Predisposition Plan, 1993-97. Recipient Anne Maynard award W.Va. Sch. Counselor Assn., 1986; named Am. mid./jr. high Sch. Counselor of Yr. Am. Sch. Counselors Assn., 1987, Citizen of Yr., Dunbar Lions Club, 1987. Mem. Am. Assn. Counseling and Devel. (Spl. Recognition award 1991), W.Va. Assn. Counseling and Devel. (pres. 1964-66, legis. chmn. 1974-98, spl. award legis. svcs. 1981), W.Va. Edn. Assn. (past legis. chmn.), Kanawha County Sch. Counselors Assn. (pres., legis. chmn. 1974-98), W.Va. Sch. Counselors Assn. (chmn. gov. rels., parliamentarian), Alpha Delta Kappa (past chpt. pres.), Phi Delta Kappa. Democrat. Baptist. Home: 12 Warren Pl Charleston WV 25302-3613

DAVIS, BLONDELL GILLIAM, business manager, evangelist, artist, author; b. Ft. Pierce, Fla., Dec. 21, 1942; d. Fred Douglas and Mary Louise Gilliam; m. Levoid Davis, July 15, 1962; 1 child, Sherry Yvonne. AA, Lincoln Jr. Coll. Ordained to ministry Apostolic (Holiness) House of Prayer. Dist. evangelist House of Prayer, Tampa, Fla., 1980—, mgr. bakery, 1987—. Author: Miracles on the Mind, 1993, Miracles Never Cease; editor Ho. of Prayer Gospel Press. Avocations: writing, cooking, drawing, painting, sewing. Home: 3210 E Lambright St Tampa FL 33610-3609 Office: The House of Prayer 3006 E Ellicott St Tampa FL 33610-2136

DAVIS, BOBBY EUGENE, business owner; b. Cleve., May 21, 1960; 1 child, Channing R. Student, Cuyahoga C.C., 1991-93. Owner Eagles Wings Limousine Svc., South Euclid, Ohio, 1994—; case mgr. State Dept. MRDD, Cleve., 1982-84; meter reader Cleve. Water Dept., 1984-86; pipe repairman City of Cleve., 1986—. Author: Where Went the Love, 1998. Drama dir. local ch.; spkr. at chs. Avocations: basketball, bowling, swimming, golf.

DAVIS, BONNIE CHRISTELL, judge; b. Petersburg, Va., July 13, 1949; d. Robert Madison and Margaret Elizabeth (Collier) D. BA, Longwood Coll., 1971; JD, U. Richmond, 1980. Bar: Va. 1980, U.S. DDist. Ct. (ea. dist.) Va. 1980, U.S. Ct. Appeals (4th cxir.) 1982. Tchr. Chesterfield County Schs., Chesterfield, Va., 1971-77; pvt. practice, Chesterfield, 1980-83; asst. commonwealth atty. Chesterfield County, 1983-93; judge Juvenile and Domestic Rels. Ct. for 12th Jud. Dist. Va., 1993—; adviser Youth Svcs. Commn., Chesterfield, 1983-93; cons. Task Force on Child Abuse, 1983-93, Met. Richmond Multi-Discipline Team on Spouse Abuse, 1983-93, Va. Dept. of Children for handbook "Step by Step Through the Juvenile Justice System in Virginia, 1988; mem. nat. adv. com. for prodn. on missing and runaway children Theatre IV; mem. adv. group to set stds. and tng. for Guardians Ad Litem, Supreme Ct. Va., 1994; chmn. jud. adminstrn. com. Jud. Conf. Va. for Dist. Cts., 1995-97; mem. state adv. com. for CASA and children's Justice Act, 1998—. Co-author: Juvenile Law and Practice in Virginia, 1994. Mem. Chesterfield County Pub. Schs. Task Force on Core Values, 1999. Mem. Va. State Bar (bd. govs. family law sect. 1997—), Va. Bar Assn., Va. Trial Lawyers Assn., Met. Richmond Women's Bar Assn., Chesterfield-Colonial Heights Bar Assn., Quota Club. Baptist. Home: 415 Lyons Ave Colonial Heights VA 23834-3154 Office: Chesterfield Juvenile and Domestic Rels Dist Ct 9600 Krause Rd Chesterfield VA 23832-6717

DAVIS, BRENDA D., journalist; b. Oct. 8, 1950. Student, U. Tex. Computer operator Mobil Oil Corp., Dallas, 1975-86; reporter The Short Horn, Arlington, Tex., 1996-98. Address: 4830 Diamond Creek Dr Midlothian TX 76065-6433

DAVIS, BRIAN ADAM, physician; b. Chgo., Jan. 21, 1966; s. Paul Michael and Arlene Carol (Feinman) D.; m. Edith Carpio Bautista, May 23, 1992. BS magna cum laude, No. Ill. U., 1986; MD, Meharry Med. Coll., 1992. Intern Hosp. of U. Pa./Presbyn. Med. Ctr., Phila., 1992-93; resident U. Medicine and Dentistry N.J., Newark, 1993-96; assoc. attending Runnells Specialized Hosp., Berkeley Heights, N.J., 1994-97; clin. asst. prof. dept. phys. medicine and rehab. U. Utah, Salt Lake City, 1997—; staff physiatrist dept. phys. medicine and rehab. Salt Lake Regional Med. Ctr., Salt Lake City, 1997—; cons. dept. phys. medicine and rehab. Primary Children's Med. Ctr., Salt Lake City, 1997—; fellow Kessler Sports Inst., West Orange, N.J., 1996-97; cons. dept. phys. medicine and rehab. svcs. Vets. Affairs/N.J. Health System, Lyons, 1996-97; instr. dept. phys. medicine and rehab. U. Medicine and Dentistry N.J., Newark, 1997; med. advisor Utah State Boxing Commn., 1998—; mem. Salt Lake organizing com. Paralympics Med. Svcs. Com., 1998—, mem. aux. faculty divsn. phys. therapy. Contbr. articles to profl. jours. Student asst. I Have a Future, Nashville, 1991; med. dir. Paralympic Polyclinic U. Utah 2002 Paralympics, med. adv. paralympic br. Salt Lake Orgn. Com. Mem. AMA (AMA/Glaxo Leadership award), Am. Coll. Sports Medicine, Am. Acad. Phys. Med. & Rehab., Assn. Acad. Physiatrists, Utah Med. Assn., Salt Lake County Med. Assn., U.S. Amateur Boxing Assn., KC (participant, fundraiser 1985-86), Phi Kappa Delta (participant health screening 1990-92), Sigma Alpha Mu (participant, fundraiser 1985-86), Alpha Omega Alpha. Independent. Avocations: singing, collecting rare record albums, martial arts. Home: 2625 Stringham Ave Apt 119B Salt Lake City UT 84109-3912 Office: U Utah Hosp Dept Phys Med and Rehab 50 N Medical Dr # Ir15 Salt Lake City UT 84132-0001

DAVIS, BRITTON ANTHONY, retired lawyer; b. Highland Park, Ill., Jan. 2, 1936; s. James Archie and Anita (Blanke) D.; m. Lynn Marriott Wegner, 1958 (dec. 1975); children: Hilary, Shepard; m. Peggy M. Swint, 1986; children: Stephen Swint, Thomas Swint. Student, Denison U., 1954-57; B.S. in Law, Northwestern U., 1959, LL.B., 1960. Bar: Ill. 1960. Assoc. Haight & Hofeldt, Chgo., 1959-89; pvt. practice law Winnetka, Ill., 1989-96. Vol. Children's Spl. Edn. Programs, Winnetka. Mem. ABA, Bar Assn. 7th Fed. Cir., Patent Law Assn. Chgo. Club: Indian Hill (Winnetka, Ill.); Chgo. Curling; Pioneer Hose Co. No. 1 (Robesonia, Pa.). Home: 285 Linden St Winnetka IL 60093-3826

DAVIS, BRUCE, cultural organization administrator. Exec. dir. Acad. Motion Picture Arts Sci., Beverly Hills, Calif. Office: Acad Motion Picture Arts Assn 8949 Wilshire Blvd Beverly Hills CA 90211-1972*

DAVIS, BRUCE GORDON, retired principal; b. Fulton, Tex., Sept. 2, 1922; s. Arthur Lee and Clara Katherine (Rouquette) D.; B.A., U. Tex., 1950; M.Ed., U. Houston, 1965; m. Mary Virginia Jackson, Aug. 31, 1946; children—Ford Rouquette, Barton Bolling, Katherine Norvell Davis McLendon. Tchr., Edison Jr. High Sch., Houston, 1951; tchr. Sidney Lanier Jr. High Sch., Houston, 1957-60, asst. prin., 1966-74, prin., 1974-83; tchr. Johnston Jr. High Sch., Houston, 1960-66; prin. Sidney Lanier Vanguard Sch., Houston, 1974-82; ret., 1983. Served with USMC, 1942-45; with U.S. Army, 1951-57. Mem. Nat. Assn. Secondary Sch. Prins., Tex. Assn. Secondary Sch. Prins., Houston Profl. Adminstrs., U.S. Army Officers Res. Assn., Houston Congress Tchrs., Am. Legion. Republican. Presbyterian. Club: Masons. Home: 6614 Sharpview Dr Houston TX 77074-6338

DAVIS, C. VANLEER, III, lawyer; b. Camden, N.J., 1942. AB summa cum laude, Princeton U., 1964; LLB magna cum laude, Harvard U., 1967.

Bar: Pa. 1969. Law clk. to Hon. Abraham L. Freedman U.S. Ct. Appeals (3d cir.), 1967-68; ptnr. Dechert Price & Rhoads, Phila.; lectr. Pa. State U. Tax Conf., 1980, mem. planning com., 1986—, chair, 1991-92; lectr. grad. tax program Temple U., 1988-89. Author: (with Jay Zagoren) Pennsylvania Limited Liability Company Forms and Practice Manual, 1996. Mem. Phi Beta Kappa. Office: Dechert Price & Rhoads 4000 Bell Atlantic Tower 1717 Arch St Ste 3 Philadelphia PA 19103-2793*

DAVIS, CALVIN DE ARMOND, historian, educator; b. Westport, Ind., Dec. 3, 1927; s. Harry Russell and Abbie Jane (Moncrief) D. A.B., Franklin Coll., Ind., 1949; M.A., Ind. U., 1956, Ph.D., 1961. Tchr. Wilson Sch., Columbus, Ind., 1949-51, 53-54; asst. prof. history Ind. Central Coll., Indpls., 1956-57; teaching assoc. Ind. U., 1958-59; asst. prof. history U. Denver, 1959-62; asst. prof. history Duke U., Durham, N.C., 1962-64, assoc. prof., 1964-76, prof., 1976-96, prof. emeritus, 1996—; cons. NEH, 1974. Author: The United States and the First Hague Peace Conference, 1962 (Albert J. Beveridge award 1961), The United States and the Second Hague Peace Conference, 1976. Served to cpl. U.S. Army, 1951-53. Mem. Am. Hist. Assn., Orgn. Am. Historians, Soc. Historians Am. Fgn. Relations, Conf. Peace Research in History (council 1979-81). Mem. Christian Ch. Home: 907 Monmouth Ave Durham NC 27701-1707 Office: Duke U Dept History Durham NC 27708

DAVIS, CAROL LYN, research consultant; b. West Palm Beach, Fla., Oct. 22, 1953; d. Robert Lee and Barbara Jean (Collett) D. BFA in Studio Arts, Tex. Christian U., Ft. Worth, 1975; MA in Am. Studies, Tex. Christian U., 1977. R&D product line designer Am. Handicrafts/Merribee Needlearts, Ft. Worth, 1977-81; ceramics/china sales cons. Dillard's, Ft. Worth, 1981-82; dept. mgr. Stripling-Cox, Ft. Worth, 1982-83; freelance ceramic ans string art designer, 1982-83; with phase III, IV, V hist. sites inventory Tarrant County (Tex.) for Hist Preservation Coun., 1983-86, Page, Anderson & Turnbull, Inc., San Francisco, 1983-86; rep. Tarrant County Greater Ft. Worth Housing Starts Tex. Update, Inc., 1987-94; with M/PF Rsch., Inc., Dallas, 1989-94; sales adminstrv. asst. Hulen Bend subdivsn. Perry Homes, Inc., A Joint Venture, Ft. Worth, 1994—. Author pamphlets in field. Mem. mgmt. adv. panel Chem. Week, 1981; mem. alternative precinct election judge Dem. Party, 1994—. Mem. Royal Over-Seas League (London). Democrat. Episcopalian. Home: 7800 Garza Ave Fort Worth TX 76116-7717

DAVIS, CAROLE CARRERA, watercolor artist; b. Washington, July 18, 1942; d. Felix Laurence and Martha Caroline (Schnautz) C.; m. Charles Young Davis, June 30, 1962; children: Sylvia Lynn, Cynthia D. May. Student in art and art history, Mary Washington Coll., 1960-62; BA in Art, Va. Poly. Inst. and State U., 1978. Instr. watercolor painting Reynolds Homestead, Critz, Va., 1985, 86; instr. watercolor painting Degas program Montgomery County Schs., Christiansburg, Va., 1990-91; instr. watercolor painting Visual and Performing Arts Inst., Blacksburg, Va., 1993; instr. watercolor I and II Va. Poly. Inst. and State U., Blacksburg, 1996; artist-in-residence for watercolor Margaret Beeks Elem. Sch., Blacksburg, 1997; watercolor instr. Summer Arts Inst. for Talented and Gifted, Radford, Va., 1986. One- and 2-person exhbns. include Block Prints Gallery, Blacksburg, Va., 1982, Nat. Bank Blacksburg, 1983, 91, Exec. Offices V.P.I. and S.U., 1985, Reynolds Homestead, 1986, Miller and Main St. Galleries, Blacksburg, 1986, William King Art Ctr., Abingdon, Va., 1989, Fine Arts Ctr. New River Valley, Pulaski, Va., 1989, Montgomery Mus., Christiansburg, Va., 1991, Shenandoah Valley Arts Ctr., Waynesboro, Va., 1991, YMCA, Roanoke, Va., 1992, Mill Mountain Coffee and Tea, Blacksburg, 1992, Perspective Gallery, Va. Tech. and Living Gallery, North Cross Sch., Roanoke, 1993, Piedmont Art Assn., Martinsville, Va., 1992, U. Va. Health Scis. Ctr., Charlottesville, 1993, Wallace Hall Gallery, Va. Tech., 1993, Ctr. Behavioral Medicine, Radford, Va., 1994, Dean Witter, Blacksburg, 1994, Waste Policy Inst., Blacksburg, 1996, IMPAXX, Ltd., Blacksburg, 1996, 1st Nat. Bank, Christiansburg, 1997, The Arts Depot Gallery, Abingdon, 1998, Alleghany Highlands Arts Crafts Ctr., Clifton Forge, Va., 1998, Southwest Va. C.C., 1999; numerous group exhbns., 1982—; represented in pub. and corp. permanent collections Carilion New River Valley Med. Ctr., Radford, Va., Cmty. Hosp., Roanoke, Shenandoah Club, Roanoke, Roanoke County Courthouse, Salem, Va., Bank of Va., Roanoke, Dominion Bank, Roanoke, Neurology Clinic Blacksburg, Surg. Assocs., Blacksburg, Snyder and Assocs., Blacksburg, Northside Presbyn. Ch., Blacksburg, United Meth. Ch., Blacksburg, Urology Assocs. New River Valley, Blacksburg, others; contbr.: The Best of Watercolor: Painting Composition, 1997, The Best of Watercolor: Painting Color, 1997, Artimis XII, 1989. Bd. dirs. Newport (Va.) Village Studio, treas., 1996—; bd. mem. Arbor Day com., Blacksburg, 1995-97; mem. art benefit com. Free Clinic for New River Valley, 1995-97. Recipient Bowles award Bath County Ann. Art Show, 1996, Intertape Systems, Inc. Purchase award, 1994, New River Art '91 Original Frameworks award, 1991, Highlands Art Festival award of merit, 1988, 89, 91, VWS XII Nancy & Carson Moore award 1991, Highlands Art Festival award of distinction, 1990, Best Bot. Painting award Showcase of the Arts, 1990, Blacksburg Juried Art Show awards 1989, 90, 97, AAUW award 1989, Franklin Square Gallery 9th Ann. Exhbn. Best-in-Show Purchase award, 1989, Adirondacks (N.Y.) Nat. Exhbn. Am. Watercolors N.Y. Watercolor Soc. award 1989, Lynchburg Arts Festival C & P Telephone Co. award, 1989, Showcase of the Arts Best-in-Show award 1989, Roanoke Festival in the Park award for body of work, 1988, Bath County Ann. Art Show Best-in-Show award, 1988, Judge's Choice award, 1988, Showcase of Arts award of merit, 1988, Nat. Works on Paper Competition award of excellence, 1988. Mem. Va. Watercolor Soc. (artist mem.; sec. 1986-87, hospitality chmn. 1993-94), Blacksburg Regional Art Assn. exhbns. co-chair 1994-98, v.p. 1995-97, sch. art liaison, 1982-94), Phi Kappa Phi. Avocations: gardening (master gardener), tennis, skiing, bicycling. Home and Studio: 567 Hickory Hill Cir Blacksburg VA 24060-9239

DAVIS, CAROLE JOAN, psychologist; b. Norristown, Pa., Aug. 15, 1942; d. John Morgan and Eva (Pierson) D.; children: Kevin Jae, Kara Megan. AB in English Lit., U. Pa., 1964; MA in Psychology, Temple U., 1967; PhD in Child Devel. and Clin. Evaluation, Bryn Mawr (Pa.) Coll., 1973. Lic. psychologist Pa. Sr. clin. psychologist Camden County Psychiat. Hosp., Lakeland, N.J., 1967-76; psychologist counselling ctr. staff Chestnut Hill Coll., Phila., 1976-89; psychologist hearing impaired programs Phila. (Pa.) Sch. Dist., 1984-85; pvt. practice Phila., 1974-89, New Britain, Pa., 1989-98; cons. psychologist Pa. Sch. for Deaf, Phila., 1970-84, Luth. Children & Family Svc., Phila., 1974-80, Willis & Elizabeth Martin Sch., Phila., 1975-84, Overbrook Sch. for Blind, 1978-94; psychologist Colonial Sch. Dist. 1994-95; adj. prof. psychology Chestnut Hill Coll. Grad. Divsn., Phila., 1980-98; psychologist APOGEE MHM, 1995-98; adj. faculty Coll. Notre Dame, Balt., 1999—. Mem. Am. Psychol. Assn., Pa. Psychol. Assn., Phila. Soc. Clin. Psychologists (exec. bd. 1981-83), Nat. Register of Health Svc. Providers in Psychology, Psychologists for the Ethical Treatment Animals. Home: 28 Heavrin Ct Baltimore MD 21236-2981

DAVIS, CAROLYNE KAHLE, health care consultant; b. Penn Yan, N.Y., Jan. 31, 1932; d. Paul Frederick Kahle and Alice Edgerton (Kahle) Cargill; m. Ott Howard Davis, June 28, 1953; 1 son, Richard Ott. BS in Nursing, Johns Hopkins U., 1954; MS in Nursing, Syracuse U., 1965, PhD in Higher Edn. Adminstrn., 1972; LittD (hon.), Georgetown U., 1982; DSc (hon.), U. Evansville, 1982, U. Medicine & Dentistry N.J., 1984; LLD (hon.), Adelphi U., 1985; LHD (hon.), Med. U. S.C., 1986; DSc (hon.), Eastern Mich. U., 1989; DHL (hon.), Med. Coll. of N.Y., 1992. Chmn. baccalaureate nursing program Syracuse U., 1969-73; dean sch. nursing U. Mich., Ann Arbor, 1973-75, prof. nursing and edn., 1973-81, assoc. v.p. acad. affairs, 1975-81; adminstr. Health Care Fin. Adminstrn. HHS, Washington, 1981-85; cons. Ernst & Whinney, Washington, 1985-89, Ernst & Young, Washington, 1989-97; bd. dirs. Beckman Inst., Irvine, Calif., Prudential Ins. Co. of Am., Newark, Merck, Rahway, N.J., Beverly Enterprises, Fort Smith, Ark., Minimed. Sylmar, Calif. Mem. editorial bd. Nursing Economics, Pitman, N.J.; contbr. more than 100 articles to profl. jours. Bd. dirs. ARC, 1988-94; trustee U. Pa. Med. Ctr., Phila., 1987—; vice chmn. bd. trustees Nat. Rehab. Hosp., 1993-97; mem. health adv. com. GAO, 1990-97; vis. com. Med. U. S.C., U. Mich. Med. Ctr. Recipient Disting. Alumnus award Johns Hopkins U., 1981, Alumni award Syracuse U. Sch. Edn., 1983, Alumni award U. Mich., 1984, Spl. Recognition award Assn. Am. Med. Colls., 1986; named one of the Top Young Leaders in Am. Acad. Mag., 1978. Mem. NAS Inst. Medicine, Nat. League for Nursing (bd. dirs. 1979-81, chmn. Cmty. Health Accreditation Program 1987-92, Presdl. award 1993). Sigma Theta Tau, Phi Delta Kappa. Republican. Avocation: gardening.

DAVIS, CHARLES CARROLL, aquatic biologist, educator; b. Azusa, Calif., Nov. 24, 1911; s. William Allen and Maude (Snyder) D.; m. Sally May Jacobsen, June 11, 1936; children: Peter Thomas, Betsy Ann. A.B., Oberlin Coll., 1933; M.S., U. Wash., 1935, Ph.D., 1940. Biologist II State of Md., 1942-43; instr. sci. Jacksonville Jr. Coll., 1944-46; asst. prof. zoology U. Miami, Coral Gables, Fla., 1946-48; asst. prof. biology Western Res. U., Cleve., 1948-52; assoc. prof. Case Western Res U., 1953-63, prof., 1964-68; prof. biology Meml. U. Nfld., St. John's, Can., 1968-78; ret. Meml. U. Nfld., 1978, prof. emeritus, 1984—, prof. (part-time), 1978-84; guest prof. aquatic biology U. Tromsø, Norway, 1975-76, Addis Ababa U., Ethiopia, 1986-87; adj. prof. biology U. Waterloo, Ont., Can., 1986-87; cons. for zoology terms New World Dictionary, 1965-69, 82-88. Author: The Pelagic Copepoda of the Northeastern Pacific Ocean, 1949, The Marine and Fresh-water Plankton, 1955, The Snouters Revisited: a Sequel, 1995; adv. editor Internat. Revue der gesamten Hydrobiologie, 1974-92; contbr. numerous articles on plankton, eutrophication of Lake Erie, hatching mechanisms of invertebrate eggs, biol. prodn. to profl. jours. Fellow AAAS, Ohio Acad. Sci.; mem. Ecol. Soc. Am., Am. Soc. Limnology and Oceanography, Plankton Soc. Japan, Internat. Soc. Limnology, Freshwater Biol. Assn. U.K., Can. Soc. Zoologists. Home: 12 Blackmarsh Rd Apt 310, Saint John's, NF Canada A1E 1S3 Office: Meml Univ of Nfld, Dept Biology, Saint John's, NF Canada A1B 3X9 *In all things, within the limits of my capabilities, to do what seems directly or indirectly of greatest value to humanity, regardless of its current popularity or unpopularity, and without aiming particularly at financial gain, honors or recognition, or especially at excelling over others. To trust all humans until they prove themselves untrustworthy, and to work towards a society in which no one will have occasion to be untrustworthy.*

DAVIS, CHARLES HARGIS, information scientist, educator; b. Tell City, Ind., Sept. 23, 1938; s. Charles Alban and Ruth Elizabeth (Hargis) D. BS, Ind. U., 1960, AM, 1966, PhD, 1969; postgrad., U. Munich, 1960-61. Asst. editor Chem. Abstracts Svc., Columbus, Ohio, 1962-65; chem. info. specialist Aerospace Rsch. Applications Ctr., Ind. U., 1965-66; dir. systems ERIC Clearing House on Reading Ind. U., 1967-69; asst. prof. libr. sci. Drexel U., 1969-71; assoc. prof. U. Mich., 1971-76; prof., dean faculty of libr. sci. U. Alta., Edmonton, Can., 1976-79; prof. U. Ill. Grad. Sch. Libr. and Info. Sci., Champaign-Urbana, 1979-93; dean U. Ill., Champaign-Urbana, 1979-86, prof. emeritus, 1993—; adj. prof., vis. scholar Ind. U. Sch. Libr. and Info. Sci., Bloomington, 1988-97, sr. fellow, 1997—; spkr., condr. workshops and seminars, cons. in field. Author: Illustrative Computer Programming for Libraries: Selected Examples for Information Specialists, 1974, co-author (with Gerald W. Lundeen) 2d edit., 1981; (with James E. Rush) Information Retrieval and Documentation in Chemistry, 1974, Guide to Information Science, 1979; (with Gerald W. Lundeen and Debora Shaw) Pascal Programming for Libraries, 1988; (with Andrew Bullen) Database Techniques for Librarians 1993; cons. editor Greenwood Press, Westport, Conn., 1974-79; contbr. numerous articles, rev., bibliographies and columns to profl. publs. Recipient Louise Maxwell award Alumni Assn. Ind. U. Sch. Libr. and Info Sci., 1982; Republic West Germany fellow, 1960-61; NSF rsch. grantee, 1959-60. Mem. AAAS, ALA (chmn. libr. rsch. round table 1978-79), Am. Chem. Soc., Am. Soc. Info. Sci. (chmn. student chpt. Ind. U. 1967-68, chmn. Ind. state chpt. 1968-69, treas. Delaware Valley chpt. 1971, chmn. Mich. chpt. 1974-75, chmn. Western Can. chpt. 1978-79, nat. pres. 1982-83, Watson Davis award 1978), Assn. Computing Machinery, Assn. Am. Libr. Schs. (chmn. rsch. com. 1976-78), N.Y. Acad. Scis., Phi Lambda Upsilon, Beta Phi Mu, Sigma Xi. Office: Ind U Sch Libr & Info Sci Bloomington IN 47405

DAVIS, CHARLES LEE, fire marshal; b. Anchorage, July 24, 1940; s. Edward V. and De Ette C. (Scholberg) D.; m. Mary Margaret Walker, Aug. 24, 1963; 1 child, Edward Charles. LLB, U. Idaho, 1966; grad. 28th Recruit Acad., Alaska Dept. Pub. Safety, 1977. Bar: Alaska 1967; cert. firefighter, Alaska, fire svc. instr., Alaska; uniform fire code cert., cert. mech. inspector, cert. plans examiner Internat. Conf. Bldg. Ofcls.; Nat. Fire Acad. fire/arson investigation, fire prevention specialist II; World Safety Orgn. cert. safety specialist, safety mgr., safety and security dir., level II fire extinguisher permit, Alaska. Law clk., atty. Hughes, Thorsness, Lowe, Gantz & Clark, Anchorage, 1966-68; adjustor, appraiser Gen. Adjustment Bur., Alaska, 1968-73; adjuster, damage appraiser Alaska Adjusting Co., Fairbanks, 1974-75; dep. fire marshal State of Alaska, Fairbanks, 1975-99. Contbr. posters, cards and photographs to numerous publs. Mem., past vestry mem., jr. warden St. Matthew's Episcopal Ch., Fairbanks, chmn. endowment bd., 1991—. Recipient prize Joint Pubs. of Am. Jurisprudence-Bancroft Whitney Co., 1966; scholar Rocky Mountain Mineral Law Inst., 1966. Mem. NRA, Alaska Bar Assn., Pioneers of Alaska (life, igloo #4), Moose (life lodge 1392), Alaska No.Ch. ICBO (founder, dir., v.p., pres.). Episcopalian. Avocations: photography, farming, bowling, skiing, home construction, physical fitness. Home: 1359 Great View Ln Fairbanks AK 99712-2136 Office: Alaska Dept Pub Safety Divsn Fire Prevention 1979 Peger Rd Fairbanks AK 99709-5257

DAVIS, CHARLES RAYMOND, political scientist, educator; b. Hampton, Va., Jan. 16, 1945; s. Cecil Raymond and Fronda Gail (Bradshaw) D.; m. Terry Lorraine Barr, Oct. 1, 1963 (div. July 1979); children: Kimberly Dawn Ingram, Charles Robert; m. Raymonda Carolyn Mays, Feb. 12, 1982. BA in Polit. Sci., U. Louisville, 1974; MA in Polit. Sci., U. Ky., 1975, PhD of Polit. Sci., 1985. Instr. Jefferson Community Coll., Louisville, 1976; claims rep. Aetna Casualty, Madisonville, Ky., 1977-78; rsch. asst. U. Louisville, 1979-80; rsch. analyst Ky. Health Svcs., Frankfort, 1981-85; asst. prof., masters degree program coord. U. So. Miss., Long Beach, 1986-89; asst. prof. U. So. Miss., Hattiesburg, 1989, assoc. prof., 1991-99, prof., 1999—; policy analyst Ky. Gov.'s Coalition on Health Costs, Frankfort, 1982; acting dir. grad. studies, U. So. Miss., Hattiesburg, 1990. Author: Organization Theories and Public Administration, 1996; editl. bd. Internat. Jour. Orgn. Theory & Behavior, 1997; contbr. numerous articles to profl. jours. Mem. AAUP, ASPA, Am. Polit. Sci. Assn., So. Polit. Sci. Assn., Northeastern Polit. Sci. Assn., Miss. Polit. Sci. Assn., Miss. chpt. ASPA. Mem. Ch. of Christ. Avocations: photography, travel, reading, music, history of old West. Home: 417 Browns Bridge Rd Hattiesburg MS 39401-8703 Office: U So Miss Dept Polit Sci Southern Sta # 5108 Hattiesburg MS 39406

DAVIS, CHARLES THEODORE, baseball player; b. Kingston, Jamaica, Jan. 17, 1960. Grad. H.S., Dorsey H.S., L.A. With San Francisco Giants, 1987, Minn. Twins, 1991; designated hitter Calif. Angels, 1993-96; with Kansas City Royals, 1997—, N.Y. Yankees, 1997—. Named to All-Star Team, 1984, 86, 94. Office: New York Yankees Yankee Stadium E 161st & River Ave Bronx NY 10451*

DAVIS, CHERYL SUZANNE, critical care nurse; b. Ft. Worth, Aug. 9, 1946; d. James Theodore and Christine Lenora (Wells) Harper; m. Charles F. Davis, June 29, 1969; children: James, Michael, Chris. AD, Nicholls State U., 1984, BSN, 1996. RN, La.; CCRN; ACLS, PALS. Staff nurse ICU Leonard Chabert Med. Ctr., Houma; home health and pool nurse Med. Team, New Orleans; primary care and charge nurse emergency rm. Terrebonne Gen. Med. Ctr., Houma; primary care nurse Med Force Internat., New Orleans. Mem. AACN, Sigma Theta Tau, Phi Eta Sigma. Home: 200 Midland Dr Houma LA 70360-6232

DAVIS, CHRIS, aerospace company executive; b. 1951. BS, U. Fla., M in Fin. and Stats. Fin. mngr. GE, 1976-84; mngr. fin. analysis military and data sys. ops. GE Aerospace, 1984-86, mngr. fin. planning and analysis military and data sys. ops., 1986-88, v.p. fin., govt. svcs. divsn. GE Comm. and Svcs., 1988-90, CFO GE Elec. Sys. divsn., 1990-93; exec. v.p., CFO, adminstrv. officer Gulfstream Aerospace Corp., 1993—. Office: Gulfstream Aerospace Corp PO Box 2206 Savannah GA 31402-2206*

DAVIS, CHRISTINA, artist; b. Garden City, N.Y.; d. Henry de Villiers and Emma Christina (Mann) Williams; m. Scott Livingston Davis, June 7, 1968; children: Peter, Cornelia, Scott. BA, L.I. U., 1968; Cert. of Bot. Illustration, N.Y. Bot. Gardens, Bronx, 1995. Drawing instr. Cmty. Club of Hempstead and Garden city, 1984-94. Exhibited in one-woman shows at Garden City Libr., 1988, Shelter Rock Libr., Albertson, N.Y., 1989; exhibited in group shows at Skidmore Coll., Saratoga Springs, N.Y., Brigham Young U., Provo, Utah, Berkeley (Calif.) Art Ctr., Guild Hall Art Show, Easthampton, N.Y., Nassau County Mus. Art, N.Y. Bot. Gardens, S.W. Tex. U., San Marcos, Corbin Art Ctr., Spokane, New Eng. Wildflower Soc., Framingham, Mass., N.Y. State Mus., Albany, Fine Arts Mus. L.I., N.Y. State Biennial, 1998, numerous others; contbr. articles to jours. and newsletters. Pres. Cathedral Women, Cathedral of Incarnation, Garden City, 1985-88; pres. Cathedral Svc. League Episcopal Cathedral of L.I., Garden City, 1982-84; mem. bd. TWIGS, Winthorp U. Hosp., Mineola, N.Y., 1981-85. Recipient Chelsea Ctr. Showcase award, 1993, Smithtown Twp. Art Ctr. award, 1992, Honorable Mention award Eastern Orchid Congress, 1996, 97, 2nd place, 1998. Mem. Art League of L.I., Nassau County Art League, Am. Soc. Bot. Artists, Guild of Natural Sci. Illustrators (steering com. N.Y. chpt. 1995-98), Nat. Assn. Women Artists. Avocation: skiing, golf, lap-swimming.

DAVIS, CHRISTOPHER, writer, retired writing educator; b. Phila., Oct. 23, 1928; s. Edward and Josephine Blitzstein Davis; (div.); children: Kirby, Katherine, Emily, Sarah, S.O. Sally Warner. BA, U. Pa., 1955. Writing tchr. U. Pa., Phila., 1958-69, Bryn Mawr (Pa.) Coll., 1977-95. Author: Lost Summer, 1958, First Family, 1959, A Kind of Darkness, 1962, Belmarch, 1964, The Shamir of Dachau, 1966, Sad Adam-Glad Adam, 1966, Ishmael, 1967, A Peep Into the 20th Century, 1971 (Nat. Book award nominee 1971), The Producer, 1972, The Sun in Mid-Career, 1975, Suicide Note, 1977, Waiting For It, 1980, Dog Horse Rat, 1990, (play) A Peep Into The 20th Century, 1988. Recipient Career award Am. Acad. and Inst. Arts and Letters, N.Y.C., 1991. Mem. Authors Guild. Avocation: sculpture. Home: 2284 Norwic Pl Altadena CA 91001

DAVIS, CHRISTOPHER KEVIN, equipment company executive; b. Ogden, Utah, Apr. 8, 1959; s. James LaVerne and Margaret Mary (Brewer) D.; m. Christine Marie Davis, Oct. 27, 1984; children: Jennifer Lee, Christopher Kevin, Kelly Anne. A in Liberal Arts, Meremac Coll., St. Louis, 1979; B of Gen. Studies, U. Mo., St. Louis, 1988. Lic. in real estate sales. Prodn. supr. Survival Tech., St. Louis, 1982-84; salesman Cardinal Properties Real Estate Co., St. Louis, 1981-84; packaging supr. Sigma Aldrich Chem., St. Louis, 1984-85; sales mgr. Gen. Turf and Grounds Equipment Co., St. Louis, 1985-86; sales mgr. TNT Golf Car & Equipment Co., St. Peters, Mo., 1986-91, gen. mgr., 1991-93; pres., CEO Gateway Power Equipment, St. Louis, 1993—; v.p. Eco-Green Techs., Inc., St. Louis, 1996—. Mem. Missouri Valley Turfgrass Assn., Missouri Valley Golf Course Supts., Profl. Grounds Maintenance Assn., So. Ill. Golf Course Supts., Ozark Golf Course Supts. Roman Catholic. Avocations: hunting, fishing, golf. Office: Gateway Power Equipment Inc 11565 Page Service Dr Saint Louis MO 63146-3530

DAVIS, CHRISTOPHER LEE, lawyer; b. Washington, Dec. 1, 1950; s. Martin Thomas and Margaret (Babcock) D.; divorced; children: Finn Christian, Ian Dunmore. BA with honors, Middlebury Coll., 1972; JD cum laude, Union U., 1975. Bar: Vt. 1975, U.S. Dist. Ct. Vt. 1975, U.S. Ct. Appeals (2d cir.) 1975. Assoc. Gear & Kittell, Burlington, Vt., 1975-78; ptnr. Gear, Kittell & Davis, Burlington, 1979-81, Gear & Davis, Inc., Burlington, 1981-90, Gear, Davis & Kehoe, Inc., 1991-92, Langrock, Sperry & Wool, Burlington, 1992—; bd. dirs. Vt. Legal Aid, Burlington, 1983-88; mem. Vt. Profl. Conduct Bd., 1984-93, adv. com. Vt. Civil Rules, 1985-96, mem. Vt. Jud. Conduct Bd., 1998—. Chief notes editor Albany Law Rev. Bd. dirs. Children's Legal Services, Burlington, 1981-83. Mem. ABA, Vt. Bar Assn. (bd. mgrs. 1980-84), Chittenden County Bar Assn. Club: Burlington Rugby Football (pres. 1978-83, 86-88). Office: Langrock Sperry & Wool PO Box 721 275 College St Burlington VT 05401-8320

DAVIS, CHRISTOPHER LYTH, professional association executive; b. Buffalo, N.Y., May 28, 1949; s. Paul Benning and Eunice Carolyn (Lyth) D. BA, U. N.C., 1971; JD, SUNY, Buffalo, 1975. Bar: N.Y. 1975, D.C. 1980. Adminstr. aide Mayor, Buffalo, 1972-74; legis. counsel City of Buffalo, N.Y., 1974-76; mgmt. assoc., Office of Mgmt. and Budget Exec. Office of the Pres., Washington, 1977-78; spl. asst. to the Pres. The White House, Washington, 1979-81; assoc. Surrey & Morse, Washington, 1981-85; CEO Investment Program Assn., Washington, 1986—; exec. dir. The Money Mgmt. Inst., Washington, 1997—; cons., advisor Cen. European Inst., Washington, 1990—. Mem. Nat. Skeet Shooting Assn. (dir. 1984—), Va. Skeet Shooting Assn. (pres. 1990—), Phi Beta Kappa. Office: Investment Program Assn 1101 17th St NW Ste 703 Washington DC 20036-4721

DAVIS, CLARENCE, state legislator; b. Danburg, Ga., Sept. 25, 1942; m. Barbara Jean Theresa Holder. BA, Morgan State U., MS. Assoc. prof.; del. Dist. 45 Md. State Delegation, 1983—. Author: Teen Pregnancy: Thief of Life, 1986. Adminstr. Human Svcs.; mem. Groove Phi Groove Social Fellowship G.G. Hon. col. Md. N.G. Mem. VFW, Vietnam Vets. Am., Buffalo Soldiers Assn., Am. Legion, Assn. Black Social Workers, Elks, Masons (regional action com.). Address: 323 Lowe House Off Bldg 6 Gov Bladen Blvd Annapolis MD 21401

DAVIS, CLARICE MCDONALD, lawyer; b. New Orleans, Jan. 20, 1941; d. James A. and Helen J. (Ross) McDonald. BA, U. Tex., 1962, MA, 1964; JD, So. Meth. U., 1968. Bar: Tex. 1969, U.S. Dist. Ct. (no. dist.) Tex. 1970, U.S. Ct. Appeals (5th cir.) 1971, U.S. Supreme Ct. 1973. Law clk. to presiding justice U.S. Ct. Appeals (5th cir.), Dallas, 1969-71; ptnr. Akin, Gump, Strauss, Hauer & Feld, Dallas, 1971—; comments editor Southwestern Law Jour., 1967-68; instr. Southern Methodist Univ. Sch. of Law, 1968-69. Bd. visitors So. Meth. U., Dallas, 1979-82, v.p. Law Sch. Alumni Adv. Coun., 1992, pres. 1993-94, mem. bd. govs., 1995-98. Avocations: photography, swimming, running, golf. Home: 6317 Churchill Way Dallas TX 75230-1807 Office: Akin Gump Strauss Hauer & Feld 1700 Pacific Ave Ste 4100 Dallas TX 75201-4675

DAVIS, CLAYTON, writer, pilot; b. Portersville, Ala., Feb. 27, 1931; s. Horace Milton Davis and Agnes Zama Meadows; m. Irene Alice Brink, Apr. 8, 1952; children: Lynne, Keith Harold. AA in Math. and History, San Antonio Coll., 1966; BA in Russian and Russian Studies, Syracuse U., 1967; postgrad., U. Md., 1971-75. Cert. comml. pilot and airline transport pilot, Md. Enlisted USAF, 1947, advanced through grades to master sgt., 1966, ret., 1970; math. tchr. Anne Arundel County Schs., Annapolis, Md., 1970-77; pilot Met. Air Charter, Balt., 1977-89, dir. ops., 1981-87; freelance writer Severna Park, Md., 1989—; flight instr., Md. Author: Flying Secrets, 1992, Flying Stories, 1992, So, You Want to Be a Pilot, 1999; contbr. to Redfield (S.D.) Press, New Bay Times, Deale, Md., Severna Park Voice, Md. Founding mem. Md. Aviation Hist. Task Force. Mem. Nat. Writers Assn. (founder, pres. Balt.-Washington chpt. 1993). Republican. Lutheran. Avocations: photography, flying, gardening. Home: 2 Brenda Ct Severna Park MD 21146-3604

DAVIS, CLIVE JAY, record company executive; b. Bklyn., Apr. 4, 1933; s. Herman and Florence (Brooks) D.; children: Fred, Lauren, Mitchell, Douglas. BA magna cum laude, N.Y. U., 1953; LLB cum laude, Harvard U., 1956. Bar: N.Y. bar 1957. Assoc. firm Rosenman Colin Freund Lewis & Cohen, N.Y.C., 1958-60; gen. atty. Columbia Records, 1960-65, pres., 1966-73; pres. Arista Records, Inc., N.Y.C., 1974—, pres., CEO. Author: Clive: Inside the Record Business, 1975. Recipient Humanitarian award Anti-Defamation League, 1970; named Man of Yr. Am. Parkinson Disease, 1972, Record Co. Exec. of Yr. Nat. Assn. TV and Radio Announcers, 1973, Nat. Pop Music Survey, 1974, 78, 80, 84, 87, 90-93, Pres. of Yr., Man of Yr. City of Hope, 1978, Man of Yr. Martell Found. for Cancer, Leukemia and AIDS Rsch., 1980, 85, Humanitarian of Yr. Am. Cancer Soc., 1985, Martin Luther King Humanitarian of Yr. award Congress Racial Equality, 1991, Man of Yr., Friars, 1992. Mem. Record Industry Assn. Am. (pres., chmn. bd. 1972-73, now dir.). Office: Arista Records Inc 6 W 57th St New York NY 10019-3901 *Experience has taught me to speak out again and again and, with right on one's side, the voice is eventually heard. Cheers for the reasoned vigilantes in society who prevent those in power from overwhelming the rights of the individual who otherwise cannot surface.*

DAVIS, CONCELOR DOMINQUEZ, mental health therapist, counselor; b. July 17, 1957; s. Lafayette Will and Stella Pearl (Dunning) D.; m. Rasute Jankeviciute, Jan 31, 1997. BBA in Mktg., St. Mary's U., San Antonio, 1991; MA in Counseling, Ministerial Tng. Inst., L.A., 1996; PhD in Bibl. Counseling, Friends Internat. Christian U., 1999. Ordained lic. min. Ch. of God Pentecostal, 1996. Owner Davis Industries, San Antonio, 1985-91, Eva's Crystal Place, San Antonio, 1988-91; counselor Borgess Hosp., Kalamazoo, Mich., 1991-93; fiscal officer Passages Alternative Living, Chgo., 1994; resident coord. Hallmark, Chgo., 1994-96; mental health counselor Columbia Woodland Hosp., Hoffman Estates, Ill., 1996-97; clin. therapist

Columbia Osteo. Family Health Ctr., Chgo., 1997-98, dir. child and adolescent counseling, 1998—, dir. family roots child and adolescent counseling, dir. mental health program; counselor Kalamazoo Probation Enhancement Program; cons. Taylor Crawford Group, Chgo. Author: (booklets) Live for Christ, 1995, First Love Then Marriage, It's Time to Wake Up, 1995; prodr. TV show Ch. of God, Kalamazoo, editor PBS program; developer Eyroy method for cognitive-behavioral approach to psychotherapy, 1997. With USMC, 1976-79. Recipient cert. of achievement Cable Access Ctr., Kalamqzoo. Mem. Am. Assn. Christian Counselors, Am. Assn. Christian Counseling, Ill. Counseling Assn., Charles Menninger Soc., Delta Sigma Phi. Avocations: sailing, travel, rafting. Home: 5820 N Kenmore Ave Apt 802 Chicago IL 60660-3763

DAVIS, CRYSTAL MICHELLE, oil company administrator; b. Havre de Grace, Md., Dec. 7, 1967; d. William Edward and Thelma LaBeatrix (Patterson) D. BA in Polit. Sci., U. Mass., 1989; postgrad., George Washington U., 1995—. Exec. asst. Matshushita Electric Corp. of Am., Washington, 1989-94; adminstrv. asst. Ernst & Young LLP, Washington, 1991-94; staff asst. BP Amoco, Washington, 1995-99; health educator NOVAM, 1999. Vol. Clinton Presdl. Campaign, Washington, 1992; vol. emergency rm. Children's Nat. Med. Ctr., Washington, 1993—; vol. enrollment/logistics teams The Experience Inc., Balt., 1993-94; vol. firefighter Arlington County Fire Dept., 1997—. Recipient W.E.B. DuBois scholarship U. Mass., 1985-89. Mem. Women in Govt. Rels. Avocations: horseback riding (dressage), reading, aviculture.

DAVIS, DAISY SIDNEY, history educator; b. Bay City, Tex., Nov. 7, 1944; d. Alex C. and Alice M. (Edison) Sidney; m. John Dee Davis, Apr. 17, 1968; children: Anaca Michelle, Lowell Kent. BS, Bishop Coll., 1966; MS, East Tex. State U., 1971; MEd, Prairie View A&M, 1980; postgrad., Tex. A&M U. Cert. profl. lifetime secondary tchr., Tex.; mid-mgmt. adminstr. Tchr. Dallas pub. schs., 1966—; instr. Am. History El Centro Coll., 1991—; adv. Am. history telecourse Dallas Cournty C.C. dist. Coord. Get Out the Vote campaign , Dallas, 1972, 80, 84, 88, 92, 94, 96, 98; pres., sec., bd. trustees The Amazons, St. John Bapt. Ch., 1995-98. Recipient Outstanding Tchr. award Dallas pub. schs., 1980, Jack Lowe award for ednl. excellence, 1982; Free Enterprise scholar So. Meth. U., 1987; Constl. fellow U. Dallas, 1988; named to Hall of Fame, Holmes Acad., 1979. Mem. NEA, Tex. State Tchrs. Assn., Classroom Tchrs. Dallas (faculty rep. 1971-77), Dallas County History Tchrs. (faculty rep. 1997—), Afro-Am. Daus. Republic of Tex. (founder), Zeta Phi Beta. Democrat. Baptist. Club: Jack & Jill, (Dallas) (rec. sec., v.p., chair Beautillion Ball, pres., Disting. Mother award). Home: 1302 Mill Stream Dr Dallas TX 75232-4604 Office: 3000 Martin Luther King Jr Blv Dallas TX 75215-2412

DAVIS, DANNY (GEORGE JOSEPH NOWLAN), musician; b. Dorchester, Mass., May 29, 1925; s. Francis Parker and Elizabeth (Halpin) N.; m. Barbara Ann Bernier, Apr. 28, 1951; children: Kerry, Gavin, Kim, Tara. Attended pub. high sch. owner, mng. dir. Daydan Music Inc., Nashville, Acoustic Music Inc., Lawday Music Inc., Nashville. Trumpetist several orchs., including: Gene Krupa, 1944-45, Art Mooney, 1946, Sammy Kaye, 1950, Freddy Martin, 1951-52; producer, MGM Corp., N.Y.C., 1960-66, RCA, 1968-71, founder, leader, Nashville Brass, 1968—, composer; albums include: The Danny Davis Singers, Dream Country, Latest and Greatest, Orange Blossom Special, Texas, The Best of Danny Davis & The Nashville Brass, Christmas with Danny Davis and The Nashville Brass, Down Home Favorites. Recipient Grammy awards for best instrumental group 1969-74. Mem. Nashville C. of C. (dir.), Country Music Assn. (best instrumental group year award 1969, 70, 71, 72, 73, 74), Am. Fedn. Musicians, Nat. Acad. Rec. Arts and Scis. (past pres.), AFTRA. Roman Catholic.

DAVIS, DANNY K., congressman; b. Parkdale, Ark., Sept. 6, 1941; m. Vera Davis; children: Jonathon, Stacey. BA, Ark. A. M. & N. Coll., 1961; MA, Chgo. State U., 1968; PhD, Union Inst., 1977. Mem. Congress from 7th Ill. dist., 1997—; mem. com. on govt. reform and oversight, com. on small bus. Chgo. alderman, 1979-90; commr. Cook. County, 1990-96; candidate Chgo. mayor, 1991; founder, pres. Westside Assn. for Community Action; pres. Nat. Assn. Community Health Ctrs.; co-chmn. Clinton/Gore/Moseley-Braun Ill. campaigns, 1992; bd. dirs. Nat. Housing Partnership. Office: 3333 W Arthington St Ste 130 Chicago IL 60624-4102*

DAVIS, DARRELL L., automotive executive; b. Sharon, Pa., Aug. 8, 1939; s. Paul Darrell and Dorothy Jane (Snyder) D.; m. Jacqueline Donna Pain, July 18, 1986; children: Paul Darrell II, Robert Tod. BS, Youngstown State U., 1963; cert. Stanford Exec. Program, Stanford U., 1987; cert. Global Leadership Program, U. Mich., 1993. Svc. rep., warranty mgr., dist. mgr., asst. zone mgr. Chrysler Motors Corp., Orlando, Fla., 1966-77; zone mgr. Chrysler Motors Corp., Omaha, 1977-78, Troy, Mich., 1978-79; nat. distbn. mgr., regional mgr., gen. mgr. import export ops., gen. sales mgr. Chrysler Motors Corp., Detroit, 1979-88; pres., chief exec. officer Alfa Romeo Distbrs. N. Am., Orlando, 1988-91; gen. sales mgr. Chrysler Corp., Orange, Calif., 1991-93; v.p. Chrysler Internat. Corp., Detroit, 1993-95; gen. mgr. Europe Chrysler Corp., Detroit, 1993-95; pres., COO Chrysler Fin. Corp., Southfield, Mich., 1995-97, chmn., CEO, 1997—; v.p. Chrysler Corp., 1997-99; bd. mgmt. Daimler Chrysler Svcs. AG, 1999—; pres., CEO Daimler Chrysler Fin. Svcs. N.Am., LLC, 1999—. Bd. dirs. Boys and Girls Clubs of S.E. Mich., 1998—. Lt. U.S. Army, 1963-65. Republican. Avocations: auto collecting, American history.

DAVIS, DAVID AARON, journalist; b. San Diego, Feb. 8, 1959; m. M. Caroline Berry, Sept. 5, 1987; children: Anne Elizabeth, Caroline Camille, Aaron Edward. BA, Colo. Coll., 1983; MSJ, Columbia U., 1985. Reporter The Gazette, Charleston, W.Va., 1986, The Dayton (Ohio) Daily News, 1987-90, The Plain Dealer, Cleve., 1990—; Paul Miller Journalism lectr. Okla. State U., 1996. Recipient Best Consumer Journalism award Nat. Press Club, Washington, 1987, Sigma Delta Chi award for investigative reporting Soc. Profl. Journalists, Greencastle, Ind., 1993, Freedom of Info. award AP Mng. Editors Assn., 1993, Max Karant award excellence in aviation reporting Aircraft Owners & Pilots Assn., 1993, 94, George Polk award L.I. U., 1995, Heywood Brown award Comms. Workers of Am., 1998. Mem. Investigative Reporters & Editors Inc. (IRE medal 1993), Soc. Environ. Journalists. Office: The Cleveland Plain Dealer 1801 Superior Ave E Cleveland OH 44114-2198*

DAVIS, DAVID BRION, historian, educator; b. Denver, Feb. 16, 1927; s. Clyde Brion and Martha (Wirt) D.; m. Toni Lisa Hahn, Sept. 9, 1971; children: Adam Jeffrey, Noah Benjamin; children by previous marriage: Jeremiah Jonathan, Martha Elizabeth, Sarah Brion. A.B. summa cum laude, Dartmouth Coll., 1950, Litt.D., 1977; A.M., Harvard, 1953, Ph.D., 1956; M.A., Oxford U., 1969; L.H.D., U. New Haven, 1986; Litt.D., Columbia U., 1999. Scheduler Cessna Aircraft Co., Wichita, Kan., 1950-51; instr. history Dartmouth, 1953-54; mem. faculty Cornell U., 1955-69, prof. history, 1963-69, Ernest I. White prof. history, 1964-69; prof. history Yale U., 1969—, Farnam prof. history, 1972-78, Sterling prof. history, 1978—, assoc. dir. Nat. Humanities Inst., 1975, dir. Gilder Lehrman Ctr. Study Slavery Resistance Abolition, 1998—; Fulbright lectr., Hyderabad, India, 1967, univs. Guyana and W.I., 1974; Walter Lynwood Fleming lectr. So. history La. State U., 1969; Harmsworth prof. Oxford (Eng.) U., 1969-70; fellow Center Advanced Study Behavioral Scis., 1972-73, Henry E. Huntington Library, 1976; Benjamin Rush lectr. Am. Psychiat. Assn., 1976; French-Am. Found. chair in Am. civilization Ecole des Hautes Etudes en Sciences Sociales, Paris, 1980-81; Fulbright lectr., Israel, Holland, Italy, 1981; Patten lectr. Ind U., 1981; Hanes lectr. U. N.C., 1982; Thompson lectr. Vassar Coll., 1983; Robert Fortenbaugh Meml. lectr. Gettysburg Coll., 1983; disting. scholar in residence Ky. State U., 1984; mem. Internat. Conf. on Capitalism and Slavery, Bellagio, Italy, 1984; Phi Beta Kappa vis. lectr., 1984-85; disting. resident Westminster Coll., Salt Lake City, 1985; project dir. research grants NEH, 1980, 81; Gilbert Osofsky lectr. U. Ill., Chgo., 1986; Arnold Shankman lectr. Winthrop Coll., Rock Hill, S.C., 1987, William W. Cook lectr. U. Mich. Sch. Law, 1988; Elijah Lovejoy lectr. Colby Coll., 1989; James Neal Primm lectr. U. Mo.-St. Louis, 1989; Goltz lectr. Bowdoin Coll., 1989; William E. Massey Sr. lectr. Harvard U., 1989; Athearn lectr. U. Colo., 1990; Scofield lectr. U. Mo., Kansas City, 1991; lectr. Soc. Fellows NYU, 1991, U. Houston, 1991; participant conf. Hamilton Coll., 1992; tchr. summer course Gilder-Lehrman Inst., 1994, 95, 96, 97; John Hope Franklin lectr. Adelphi Coll., 1995; Paley lectr. Hebrew U., Jerusalem, 1995; lectr. Black History Month Coll. Charleston, 1995, Worcester State Coll., 1995; Taft lectr., U. Cin., 1996, lectr. Vanderbilt U., 1996, Conf. on Slave Trade U. Chgo., 1997, Ohio Hist. Soc., 1997, Coll. of Charleston, 1997, 98, Conf. on New World Slavery Rutgers U., 1997, N.J. Con. Hist. Edn., 1997, Cornell U., 1998, N.Y. Bar Assn., 1998, Omohundro Inst. Early Am. Hist. and Culture, Williamsburg, 1998, Villanova U., 1999, Inst. Hist. Rsch., London, 1999. Author: Homicide in American Fiction, 1790-1860, A Study in Social Values, 1957, The Problem of Slavery in Western Culture, 1966, rev. edit., 1988 (Italian,trans.), The Slave Power Conspiracy and the Paranoid Style, 1969, The Problem of Slavery in the Age of Revolution, 1770-1823, 1975, rev. edit. 1999, Slavery and Human Progress, 1984, From Homicide to Slavery: Studies in American Culture, 1986, Revolutions: Reflections on American Equality and Foreign Liberations, 1990 (German trans.); co-author: The Great Republic, 1977, 4th edit., 1992, The Antislavery Debate, 1992; editor: Ante-Bellum Reform, 1967, The Fear of Conspiracy, 1971, Ante-Bellum American Culture: An Interpretive Anthology, 1979, 97; co-editor: The Boisterous Sea of Liberty: A Documentary History of America From Discovery Throught the Civil War, 1998; contbr. N.Y. Review of Books. Mem. Subcom. internal security Dem. Nat. Policy Coun., Pulitzer Prize Com., 1968, Bancroft Prize Com., 1989; co-chair adv. bd. Gilder-Lehrman Inst. Am. History, 1995—, tchr. summer sem., 1994-99. With AUS, 1945-46. Recipient Anisfield Wolf award in race relations, 1967, Pulitzer prize for nonfiction, 1967, Mass Media award NCCJ, 1967, Bancroft prize, 1976, Nat. Book award for history and biography, 1976, Presdl. medal Dartmouth Coll., 1991; Guggenheim fellow, 1958-59; Fulbright grantee, 1980; NEH fellow, 1983-84, Gilder-Lehram Inaugural fellow, 1996-97. Fellow Am. Acad. Arts and Scis., Brit. Acad. (corr.); mem. Am. Philos. Soc. (adminstrv. bd. Benjamin Franklin papers), Mass. Hist Soc., Am. Hist. Assn. (Albert J. Beveridge award 1975), Inst. Early Am. History and Culture (coun. 1976-79), Am. Antiquarian Soc., Soc. Am. Historians, Orgn. Am. Historians (pres. 1988-89, chair Frederick Jackson Turner award com. 1989, Lincoln prize com. 1992), Milan Group in Early U.S. Hist. Jewish. Home: 733 Lambert Rd Orange CT 06477-1806

DAVIS, DAVID OLIVER, radiologist, educator; b. Danville, Ill., June 25, 1933; s. Oliver and Anna Marie (Collignon) D.; m. Agnes Layden, Dec. 26, 1955; children: Karen, Kathy, Diane, Janet, Nancy. BS, U. Ill., 1954; MD, St. Louis U., 1958. Diplomate Am. Bd. Radiology. Intern Starkloff Meml. Hosp., St. Louis, 1958-59; resident USPHS Hosp., S.I., N.Y., 1959-61, Columbia Presbyn. Med. Center, N.Y.C., 1962-63; asst. prof. radiology Washington U., St. Louis, 1966-68; assoc. prof. Washington U., 1968-70; prof. U. Utah, 1970-72; prof. George Washington U., 1972—, prof. neurology, 1977—, chmn. dept. radiology, 1978-82, 91-96, prof. neurosurgery, 1985—; vis. prof. U. Calif., San Francisco, 1985; cons. UCLA, 1995-96, UNS; sec.-gen. 12th Internat. Symposium on Neuroradiology. Editor: Principles of Diagnostic Radiology, 1971, Reconstruction Tomography in Diagnostic Radiology and Nuclear Medicine, 1977; mem. editl. bd. Jour. Computer Assisted Tomography, 1977-88, Am. Jour. Neuroradiology, 1979-90, Neuroradiology, 1971-80; mem. editl. exec com. Jour. Investigative Radiology, 1971-80. Served with USPHS, 1959-64. NIH spl. fellow, 1964-66. Fellow Am. Coll. Radiology (mem. coun. steering com. 1992-94, mem. bd. chancellors 1994-99), Am. Heart Assn. (stroke coun.); mem. AMA, Am. Soc. Neuroradiology (sec. 1971-74, pres. 1979-80, chmn. publs. com. 1988-92, alt. counselor 1991-92, counsellor 1992-94), D.C. Med. Soc., D.C. Radiol. Soc. (pres. 1983-84, alt. counselor 1982-85, counsellor 1985-91), Assn. Univ. Radiologists, Soc. Chmn. Acad. Radiology Depts. (sec.-treas. 1981-83), Acad. Radiology Rsch. (bd. dirs. 1994-99), Internat. Microcirculation Soc., Blue Grass Radiology Soc. (hon.), Radiol. Soc. N.Am., Am. Roentgen Ray Soc. (mem. exec. coun. 1992-95, alt. del. to AMA 1995—), North Pacific Soc. Neurology and Psychiatry (hon.), Am. Head and Neck Radiology, Phila. Roentgen Soc. (hon.), Western Neuroradiology Soc., Am. Assn. Neurol. Surgeons, Am. Soc. Spine Radiology Splty. and Svcs. Soc. Office: George Washington U Med Ctr Dept Radiology 901 23rd St NW Washington DC 20037-2327

DAVIS, DAVID WILLIAM, transportation consultant; b. Belden, Nebr., June 2, 1932; s. Abner Paul Gries and Juanita (Jarvis) D.; m. Albie Muldavin, May 20, 1956 (div. 1972); children: Michele, Matthew, Benjamin, Carol; m. Andronike E. Janus, Feb. 22, 1976. B.A., U. Calif.-Berkeley, 1954. With State of Calif., Sacramento, Calif., 1957-66; staff assoc. President's Task Force, Washington, 1966-67; research assoc. Brookings Instn., Washington, 1967-68; exec. dir. Econ. Devel. and Indsl. Connm., dir. Office Pub. Service, dept., adminstrv. services for fiscal affairs City of Boston, 1968-71; dir. Office of Budgets Harvard U., Cambridge, Mass., 1971-75; exec. dir. Mass. Port Authority, Boston, 1975-91, N.J. Hwy. Authority, Woodbridge, 1991-94; transp. cons. Boston, 1994—; bd. dirs. Greater Boston Conv. and Tourist Bur., 1976-88, Internat. Bus. Ctr. New Eng., Boston, 1977-91, Fgn. Bus. Coun., Boston, 1978-91. Author: (with others) Making Federalism Work, 1969 (Brownlow 1970). Chmn. Boston Indsl. and Fin. Authority, 1971-80; bd. dirs. Ford Hall Forum, 1981-94, Boston Harbor Assocs., Inc., 1977-82, World Affairs Council, 1986-91; mem., chmn. Marshall selection com. Brit. Consulate, Boston, 1982-88. Fellow Nat. Acad. Pub. Adminstrn. Democrat. Home: 16 Acorn St Boston MA 02108-3501

DAVIS, DEBORAH CECILIA, auditor; b. Mt. Pleasant, Mich., Aug. 7, 1952; d. Arthur Francis Schaefer and Ninamae Ellen Reber. BBA summa cum laude, Western Mich. U., 1974. CPA. Acct. Phoenix Optical, Bay City, Mich., 1968-70; analyst 2nd Nat. Bank, Saginaw, Mich., 1970-72; acct. Deloitte & Touche, Saginaw, Mich., 1975-77; cost acct. AC Sparkplug div. GM, Flint, Mich., 1977-78; corp. auditor GMC, Detroit, 1980; sr. statistician Detroit Diesel Allison divsn. GM, 1980-83; sr. budget, forecast analyst Cen. Foundry divsn. GM, Saginaw, 1983-91; fin. dir. City of Bay City, Mich., 1991-94; corp. supplier auditor GM, 1994-97; sr. internal auditor Standard Products Co., Dearborn, Mich., 1997—. Avocations: gemology, reading.

DAVIS, DEBORAH LYNN, lawyer; b. N.Y.C., Apr. 23, 1948; d. Melvin Jerome and Beatrice (Greenapple) D. BS, Case Western Res. U., 1970, JD, 1973. Bar: N.Y. 1974, U.S. Dist. Ct. (ea. and so. dists.) N.Y. 1974. Staff atty., dir. litigation Community Action for Legal Svcs., Inc., Bklyn., 1974-77, 78-81; atty. BLS Legal Svcs., N.Y.C., 1977-78; assoc. Gallet & Dreyer, N.Y.C., 1981-86; ptnr. Wagner, Davis & Gold, P.C., N.Y.C., 1986—. Contbg. author chpts. in book. Incorporator, officer, bd. dirs. N.Y. Svc. Program for Older People, Inc., 1978-91; mem. Family Ct. Panel Screening and Oversight com. 1st Jud. Dept., 1985-88, vice-chair screening applicants, 1985-87. Mem. N.Y. State Bar Assn., N.Y. County Lawyers Assn., N.Y. Women's Bar Assn. Office: Wagner Davis & Gold PC 99 Madison Ave New York NY 10016-7419

DAVIS, DEBRA GREER, music educator, pianist; b. Crocker, Mo., Mar. 4, 1956; d. Clifford Eugene and Emogene Telitha (Bullock) Greer; m. Rodney Neal Davis, July 1, 1978; children: Neal Stephen, Kimberly Reneé, Paul Andrew. B of Music Edn., S.E. Mo. State U., 1978. Cert. vocal music educator, K-12; cert. tchr., Mo., Iowa. Pvt. piano instr. Cape Girardeau, Mo., 1980-96; ch. pianist First Bapt. Ch., Cape Girardeau, Mo., 1987-90; music educator Cape Girardeau (Mo.) Pub. Sch., 1987-91, St. Augustine Sch., Kelso, Mo., 1991-93, Altenburg (Mo.) Pub. Sch., 1991-96; nursing libr. St. Francis Med. Ctr., Cape Girardeau, 1992-96; music educator Spickard (Mo.) R-2 Sch., 1996-97, Harrison R-IV Sch., Gilman City, Mo., 1997—; instr. Music Preparatory Program, S.E. Mo. State U., Cape Girardeau, 1990-92; dist. music try-out judge S.E. Mo. Dist. Music Educators, Cape Girardeau, 1992; sr. grant coord. disease prevention com. St. Francis Med. Ctr., Cape Girardeau, 1995-96, mem. healing environment, 1994-96. Accompanist: (cassette tape) Open Your Hear's Door-Charlene Peyton, 1994; editor: (booklet) Ann. Nursing Report-St. Francis Med. Ctr., 1995. Accompanist L.J. Schultz Mid. Sch. Choir, Cape Girardeau, 1992-93, Cape Girardeau H.S. Chamber Choir, 1993, Charles Clippard Elem. Sch. Choir, Cape Girardeau, 1996, Mo. Bapt. Conv., Cape Girardeau, 1994. Mem. Mo. Educators Assn., Music Educators Nat. Conf. Avocations: counted cross stitch, music.

DAVIS, DEFOREST P., architectural engineer. From staff cons. to chmn., CEO Lester B. Knight & Assocs., Inc., Chgo., 1966-91, pres., CEO, 1987-91, chmn., CEO, 1991—. Trustee Knight Charitable Trust, Chgo., 1989—, Lake Forest (Ill.) Coll., 1992—, St. George's Sch., Newport, R.I., 1988-97, Grant Hosp. and Healthcare Ctr. Found., Chgo., 1992—; mem. adv. bd. dirs. Code, Hennessy & Simons, Chgo., Fiduciary Mgmt. Assocs., Chgo., Constrn. Bus. Rev., McLean, Va.; bd. dirs. Surgipath Med. Industries, Inc., Richmond, Ill. Mem. Chgo. Club (pres.), Econ. Club Chgo. (membership com.), Exec.'s Club Chgo. Office: Lester B Knight & Assocs 549 W Randolph St Ste 420 Chicago IL 60661-2291

DAVIS, (SHELTON) DELANE, petroleum engineer; b. Waynesboro, Miss., Nov. 10, 1953; s. Frank and Katherine (Giles) D.; m. Teresa Blackledge, Aug. 27, 1977; children: Julia, Justin, John. BS PTE, Miss. State U., Starkville, 1979. Ops. engr. Mobil Oil Corp., Morgan City, La., 1979-83; reservoir engr. Mobil Oil Corp., New Orleans, Midland, Tex., 1983-87; reservoir engr., advisor Mobil Oil Corp., New Orleans, 1987-92; v.p. ops. Smith Prodn. Co., Jackson, Miss., 1992-95; v.p. bus. devel., bd. dirs. Hogan Exploration Inc., Columbia, La., 1996—. Mem. Soc. Petroleum Engrs. (chmn. Miss. sect. 1995-96, bd. dirs. 1996—). Republican. Baptist. Achievements include U.S. patent for puzzle; research confirming timko-fertl shale resistivity ratio correlation. Home: 425 Main St PO Box 1586 Columbia LA 71418-1586 Office: Hogan Exploration Inc PO Box 1149 Columbia LA 71418-1149

DAVIS, DEMPSIE AUGUSTUS, former air force officer, educator; b. Roebuck, S.C., Oct. 11, 1929; s. Dempsie Augustus and Hontas (Frey) D.; m. Sally Frey, Mar. 5, 1956; children: Elizabeth, Peggy, Dempsie. BS, U.S. Mil. Acad., 1955; Edn. with Industry, A.F. Inst. Tech., 1961; MS in Bus. Econ., Clairmont Coll., 1969; diploma in nat. security mgmt., Indsl. Coll., 1973. Commd. 2d lt. USAF, 1955, advanced through grades to col., 1978; served as maintenance officer and test support pilot USAF Spl. Weapons Detachment, Nev., 1967-69; project officer Sci. Advisors Office, Mil. Assistance Command Vietnam, Saigon, Vietnam, 1969-70; systems mgr. USAF Air Logistics Ctr., Warner Robins AFB, Ga., 1970-72; chief F-15 logistics evaluation USAF, Edwards AFB, Calif., 1972-75, dir. flight test evaluation, 1975-77; dir. Joint Acquisition Logistics, Eglin AFB, Fla., 1977-79; ret. USAF, 1979; sr. engring. mgr. Westinghouse, Balt., 1981-82; fin. cons., prof. U. S.C., Spartanburg, S.C., 1982-90; tchr., video prodr. Spartanburg, 1990-99, sports shooting, 1999—. Decorated Legion of Merit, Bronze Star, Meritorious Service medal, Air medal, Joint Svcs. Commendation medal, Air Force Commendation medal; recipient Leading Skeet award Nat. Skeet Shooting Assn., San Antonio, 1958. Mem. Nat. Sporting Clays Assn. (life), NRA (life, Disting. Expert 1964), Quail Unltd. (charter), Ducks Unltd., Masons (32 degree). Avocations: upland hunting, clay shooting, reading, handball, travel.

DAVIS, DOLLY, religious organization administrator. Dir. Ladies Auxiliary of the Pentecostal Free Will Baptist Ch., Dunn, N.C. Office: The Pentecostal Baptist Ch PO Box 1568 Dunn NC 28335-1568*

DAVIS, DON CLARENCE, university president; b. Ardmore, Okla., June 7, 1943; s. Clarence L. and Wilma (Henson) D.; m. Beverly Gearheard, Aug. 30, 1969; children: Casey, Joshua. BJ, U. Okla., 1965, JD, 1969. Journalist Okla. Jour., 1966-69; sole practice Lawton, Okla.; gen. counsel Northrop Worldwide Aircraft Corp., Lawton; mem. Okla. Legislature, Lawton, 1970-80; pres. Cameron U., Lawton, 1980—; mem. profl. standards bd. Okla. State Dept. Edn.; bd. dirs., sec. Home Savs. Bank, Lawton. Chmn. United Way, Lawton, 1986. Recipient Mental Health Assn. award, 1978, Legis. Leadership award Am. Legion, 1977; named one of Ten Best Legislators, 1976, Five Best Legislators, 1977 Okla. Monthly, Top Ten Legislators Okla. Pub. Co., 1980, Outstanding Young Men Lawton Jaycees, 1979. Mem. AMA, Okla. Bar Assn., Comanche Bar Assn., Okla. Trial Lawyers Assn. (Legislator of Yr. award 1977), Comanche Cattlemen's Assn., Okla. Edn. Assn. (Friend of Edn. award 1974), NEA, Lawton C. of C., YMCA, Cameron U. Assn., March of Dimes Found. Democrat. Baptist. Club: Saddle and Sirloin. Lodges: Elks, Rotary. Avocation: outdoorsman. Office: Cameron U 2800 W Gore Blvd Lawton OK 73505-6377*

DAVIS, DON D., III, author, lawyer; b. Hollywood, Calif., Aug. 14, 1970; s. Donald D. and Miriam S. D. Ba, U. Calif., Santa Barbara, 1992; MA, San Francisco State U., 1995; JD, Tulane U., 1998. Bar: Calif. Author: There Is No Magic, 1995. Avocations: travel, skiing, literature, theater, film. E-mail: threediii@aol.com.

DAVIS, DON H., electronics executive. Engring. sales trainee Allen-Bradley (aquired by Rockwell 1985), 1963-66; dist. mgr. Allen-Bradley (aquired by Rockwell 1985), Birmingham, Ala., 1966-79; gen. mgr. programmable contr. divsn. Allen-Bradley (aquired by Rockwell 1985), 1979-80, v.p. programmable contr. divsn., 1980-82, v.p., gen. mgr. indsl. control divsn., 1982-85, sr. v.p., 1985-86, head indsl. control group, 1986-87, sr. v.p., gen. mgr. indsl. computer and comm. group, 1987-89, pres., 1989-93, corp. sr. v.p., pres. automation, 1993-95, pres., COO, 1995-97, pres., CEO, 1997-98; chmn., CEO Rockwell Internat. Corp., 1998—; bd. dirs. Sybron Internat., Ingram Micro, Inc. Nat. trustee Boys and Girls Clubs Am.; chmn. bd. L.A. Mfg. Learning Ctr.; regent Milw. Sch. Engring. Mem. Internat. Soc. for Measurement and Control (hon. chmn.), Nat. Elec. Mfrs. Assn. (past chmn. bd. govs.), Bus. Roundtable, The Conf. Bd. (sr.). Office: Rockwell Internat Corp PO Box 5090 Costa Mesa CA 92628-5090

DAVIS, DONALD ALAN, author, news correspondent, lecturer; b. Savannah, Ga., Oct. 5, 1939; s. Oden Harry and Irma Artice (Gay) D.; m. Robin Murphy, Mar. 17, 1983; children by previous marriage—Russell Glenn, Randall Scott. B.A. in Journalism, U. Ga., 1962. Reporter Athens (Ga.) Banner-Herald, 1961-62, Savannah Morning News, 1962; with UPI, 1963-65; reporter, editor St. Petersburg (Fla.) Times, 1965-66; with UPI, 1967-83, Vietnam corr., 1971-73, New Eng. editor, 1977-80, White House corr., 1981-83; polit. reporter, columnist San Diego Union, 1983-91; pub. Pacific Rim Report newsletter, 1985-88; instr. journalism Boston U., 1979; instr. writing U. Colo., 1998—; lectr. U.S. Naval War Coll., 1983, Queen Elizabeth 2, 1991, Vistafjord, 1992; bd. dirs. Fgn. Corr. Club, Hong Kong, 1974. Author: The Milwaukee Murders, 1991, The Nanny Murder Trial, 1992, Bad Blood, 1994, Death of An Angel, 1994, Fallen Hero, 1994, Appointment with the Squire, 1995, Death Cruise, 1996, A Father's Rage, 1996, The Gris-Gris Man, 1997, Hush, Little Babies, 1997, The Last Man on the Moon, 1999. Fellow Keizai Koho Ctr., Tokyo, 1985. Presbyterian. Office: 6350 Modena Ln Longmont CO 80503-8770

DAVIS, DONALD EUGENE, real estate management executive; b. Huntington, W.Va., July 18, 1931; s. James and Madge Elizabeth (Queen) D.; m. Elba Natalia Philippi, Sept. 3, 1955; children: Jeannette Natalia, James Edward. Student, Marshall U., 1949-51, Cameron U., 1979. Cert. Supervisory Air Traffic Control Specialist. Sales rep. Nabisco, Parkersburg, W.Va., 1955-56; with air trafficc control FAA, San Juan, P.R., 1956-64, Miami, Fla., 1964-68, Huntington, W.Va., 1968-82; co-owner Davis & Philippi, Inc., Hato Rey, P.R., 1982-94; pres. CAA Caribe Fed. Credit Union, San Juan, 1961-63. Inventor USN adopted wheelhouse damage control plotting chart. Instn. rep. Cub Scouts of Am., Miami, 1965-66; vol. VA Med. Ctr., Huntington, 1986-88. With USN, 1951-55, Korea. Mem. Internat. Platform Assn., Am. Legion, Masons, Rotary. Democrat. Avocations: boating, fishing, golf, rare coin collecting, fgn. travel. Home: 907 9th Ave Apt 2 Huntington WV 25701-2841 Office: Woodwinds Corp 1108 11th Ave Ste 2 Huntington WV 25701-3568

DAVIS, DONALD GORDON, JR., librarian, educator; b. San Marcos, Tex., Aug. 15, 1939; s. Donald Gordon and Ethel Dorothy (Henning) D.; m. Avis Jane Higdon, Dec. 6, 1969; children: Lucinda Ellen, Samuel Higdon, Caroline Louise. BA, UCLA, 1961; MA, U. Calif., Berkeley, 1963, MLS, 1964; PhD, U. Ill., 1972; MA, Austin Presbyn. Theol. Sem., 1996. Adminstrv. asst. Biola Coll. Library, La Mirada, Calif., 1961-62; sr. library asst. U. Calif., Berkeley, 1961-64; sr. reference librarian Fresno State Coll. Library, 1964-68, head dept. spl. collections, 1966-68; asst. prof. library sci. U. Tex., Austin, 1971-77, assoc. prof., 1977-86, prof., 1986—; bd. dirs., v.p. Logos Bookstore, Austin, 1974-80; vis. prin. lectr. Birmingham (Eng.) Poly., 1980-81; coord. Libr. History Seminars VI, Austin, 1980, VII, Chapel Hill, N.C., 1985, VIII, Bloomington, Ind., 1990; coord. Ann. Tex. Libr. History Colloquium, 1982—, Tex. Group for the Study of Books and Print Culture, 1995—; mem. planning com. Libr. History Seminar IX, 1995. Author: The Association of American Library Schools, 1915-68, 1974, Reference Books in the Social Sciences and Humanities, 1977, American Library History: A Bibliography, 1978, ARBA Guide to Library Science Literature, 1970-83, 1987, American Library History: A Comprehensive Guide to the Literature,

1989, Encyclopedia of Library History, 1994, Librarianship and Library Science in India: An Outline of Historical Perspectives, 1994; editor: Librararies and Culture: Proc. of Library History Seminar VI, 1981, Libraries, Books and Culture: Proc. of Library History Seminar VII, 1986, History of Library an Information Science Education: Library Trends, 1986, Reading and Libraries, proc. of Library History Seminar VIII, 1991, Libraries and Philanthropy, proc. of Libr. History Seminar IX, 1996, Libraries and Culture jour., 1976—; mem. editl. bd. America: History and Life, 1979—, Annual Bibliography of the History of the Printed Book and Libraries, 1994—, Library History (UK), 1998—. Pres. PTA Robert E. Lee Sch., Austin, 1979-80; mem. adv. bd. Am. History and Life, 1979—, Heritage Soc. Austin, 1987-92; v.p. Hyde Park Neighborhood Assn., 1983-84; asst. scoutmaster local troop Boy Scouts Am., 1987-91; active USA-USSR Citizens Dialogue, Austin, 1985-93. Recipient Tex. Excellence Tchg. award, 1991-92; Am. Inst. Indian Studies fellow, 1988, Newberry Libr. fellow, 1974, John P. Commons Tchg. fellow, 1986-87, 95, 998-99, 99—. Mem. Am. Hist. Assn., ALA (chmn. libr. history round table 1978-79, internat. rels. com. 1988-92, exec. com. internat. rels. roundtable 1990-92), Internat. Fedn. Libr. Assns., Roundtable of Editors of Libr. Jours. (exec. com. 1987—), Round Table on Library History (exec. com. 1978—), Am. Printing History Assn., Assn. Libr. Info. and Sci. Edn., Assn. Bibliography History (exec. bd. 1982-85), Fellowship Christian Librs. and Info. Specialists (exec. com. 1978-87, 97—), Tex. Ctr. for Book (adv. coun. 1987—), Am. Antiquarian Soc. (adv. bd. program in history of book 1987-93), Conf. Faith and History, Hymn Soc. (U.S. and Can.), Libr. Assn. U.K., Tex. Libr. Assn. (mem. program com. archives and local history round table 1997—), Orgn. Am. Historians, InterVarsity Christian Fellowship (nat. faculty and grad. student adv. bds. 1990—), Librarians Christian Fellowship (U.K., v.p. 1990—), Book Club Tex., Soc. promoting Christian Knowledge, Presbyn. Hist. Soc., Presbyn. Hist. Soc. S.W., Tex. State Hist. Assn. (program com. for 1992), World History Assn., Beta Phi Mu (Golden Ann. Disting. award 1999), Phi Kappa Phi. Presbyterian. Home: 3900 Avenue C Austin TX 78751-4519 Office: U Tex Grad Sch Libr and Info Sci Austin TX 78712-1276

DAVIS, DONALD RAY, entomologist; b. Oklahoma City, Mar. 28, 1934; s. Esker Arnold and Mildred Louise (Fortson) D.; m. Mignon Marie Bush, Sept. 29, 1972; children: Marisa Marie, Steven Ray. BA, U. Kans., 1956; PhD, Cornell U., 1962. With Smithsonian Instn., Washington, 1961—, assoc. curator, then curator entomology, 1961-76, chmn. dept., 1976-81, curator entomology, 1981—. Contbr. articles to profl. jours. Recipient Smithsonian Instn. Rsch. Found. award, 1966-67, 73-74, Scholarly Studies grantee, 1990-92, Am. Philos. Soc. grantee, 1963. Mem. Biol. Soc. Washington (pres. 1984-85), Lepidopterists Soc. (Jordan medal 1977, pres. 1985), Assn. Tropical Biology, Entomol. Soc. Am., Hennig Soc., Nat. Speleological Soc., Soc. Systematic Zoology, Entomol. Soc. Washington (pres. 1979), Washington Biologists Field Club. Office: Smithsonian Instn Stop 127 Washington DC 20560 *I believe that life's major goal should be to contribute something of lasting value to earth's diverse heritage. Perhaps the most permanent heritage anyone can bequeath lies in the discovery of new knowledge. By thus enriching our common heritage, I feel that I can partially repay, in my own humble way, for the enormous privilege of having once lived on this fascinating planet.*

DAVIS, DONALD ROBERT, nutritionist, researcher, consultant; b. La Jara, Colo., Mar. 19, 1941; s. Robert Cristopher and Ida Mary (Blissard) D.; m. Vera Elaine Wilson, June 27, 1980 (div. Aug. 15, 1989). Grad., Calif. Inst. Tech., 1962; PhD, UCLA, 1965; post-doctoral fellow, Calif. Inst. Tech., 1965-67. Instr. Calif. Inst. Tech., Pasadena, 1965-67; asst. prof. U. Calif., Irvine, 1967-74; rsch. scientist assoc. U. Tex., Austin, 1974-86, rsch. assoc., 1986—; mem. bd. trustees Internat. Acad. Nutrition and Preventive Medicine, 1983-85, The Wacker Found., 1987—; dir. Roger J. Williams Nutrition Inst., 1987-90; sr. rsch. cons. Ctr. for Improvement of Human Functioning, Wichita, Kans., 1989—. Editor-in-chief Jour. Applied Nutrition, 1986-91; mem. editl. bds. Jour. Applied Nutrition, 1978—, Jour. Internat. Acad. Preventive Medicine, 1983-85, Jour. Advancement in Medicine, 1997—; contbr. over 40 articles to profl. jours; co-developer nutrient content software, Nutricircles, 1985—. Instr. Lifetime Learning, Austin, 1978—. Recipient Rsch. fellowship NSF, Washington, 1965-67; grantee Found. for Nutritional Advancement, Washington, 1986. Mem. AAAS, Am. Coll. Nutrition, Internat. Am. Assn. Clin. Nutritionists, Acad. Orthomolecular Medicine. Office: Biochem Inst Univ Tex Austin TX 78712

DAVIS, DOROTHY SALISBURY, author; b. Chgo., Apr. 26, 1916; d. Alfred Joseph and Margaret Jane (Greer) Salisbury; m. Harry Davis, Apr. 25, 1946 (dec.). AB, Barat Coll., Lake Forest, Ill., 1938. Mystery and hist. novelist, short story writer. Author: A Gentle Murderer, 1951, A Town of Masks, 1952, Men of No Property, 1956, Death of an Old Sinner, 1957, A Gentleman Called, 1958, The Evening of the Good Samaritan, 1961, Black Sheep, White Lamb, 1963, The Pale Betrayer, 1965, Enemy and Brother, 1967, God Speed The Night, 1968, Where the Dark Streets Go, 1969, Shock Wave, 1972, The Little Brothers, 1973, A Death in the Life, 1976, Scarlet Night, 1980, A Lullaby of Murder, 1984, Tales for a Stormy Night, 1985, The Habit of Fear, 1987. Recipient Life Achievement award Boucheroon, 1989. Mem. Authors Guild, Mystery Writers of Am. (former pres., recipient Grand Master award 1985), Adams Roundtable. Home: PO Box 595 Palisades NY 10964-0595

DAVIS, DOUGLAS MATTHEW, artist, educator, author; b. Washington, Apr. 11, 1933; s. Douglas Matthew and Pauline Elizabeth (Burton) D. B.A., Am. U., 1956; M.A., Rutgers U., 1958. Art critic Newsweek mag., 1969-77, gen. editor, 1977-80, sr. writer architecture, photography, contemporary ideas, 1980-88; artist-in-residence TV Lab. Sta. WNET-TV, N.Y.C., 1972; lectr. Cooper Union, UCLA, Osaka (Japan) U. of Arts; Fulbright lectr., Russia, 1994—, Chgo. Art Inst., 1994; dir. Internat. Network for Arts, 1976—; dir. ind. project Solomon R. Guggenheim Mus., Russian-Am. Co.; advisor architecture and design U.S. Dept. State Art in Embassies Program, 1986—; vis. prof. Art Ctr. Coll., Pasadena, 1989-90, UCLA, 1990-91; adj. prof. Columbia U., N.Y.C., 1990, adj. prof. Fine Art U. So. Calif., L.A., 1992-93; cons. in media Rockefeller Found., N.Y.C., 1990-91; cons. in Web site design P.S.I. Inst. for Art and Urban Resources; fulbright scholar Moscow State U., 1995; disting. vis. artist Ramapo Coll., 1996; lectr. Parsons Sch. of Design, 1998; cons. in digital media The Cornell Theory Ctr., N.Y.C., 1997. Exhibited videotapes, films, drawings, prints, objects in one-man shows, including, San Francisco Mus. Modern Art, 1975, Everson Mus., Syracuse, N.Y., Whitney Museum Am. Art, N.Y.C., 1977, 81, Neue Galerie, Aachen, W. Ger., 1978, Neuer Berliner Kunstverein, Berlin, 1978, Folkwang Mus., Essen, W. Ger., 1979, Galerie Stampa, Basel, Switzerland, 1979, P.S.I. Gallery, N.Y.C., 1980, Mus. Sztuki, Lodz, Poland, 1982, 95, Wadsworth Atheneum, Hartford, Conn., 1983, Guggenheim Mus., 1988, Lehman Coll. Art Gallery, 1994-95; exhibited in group shows, including, Whitney Mus. Am. Art, 1971, 75, 85, Mus. Contemporary Art, Chgo., 1975, Cracow (Poland) Bienale, 1976, Venice (Italy) Biennale, 1976, 78, Kassel (W. Ger.) Documenta 6, 1977, Met. Mus., N.Y.C., 1982, Mus. Modern Art, 1984, Kolnischer Kunstverein, 1989, Kwangiu Biennale, 1995, Gov.'s Conf. on Art & Tech., N.Y.C., 1998, Ruebling Hall, Williamsburg, N.Y.C., 1999, Whitney Mus. Am. Art, N.Y.C., 1999, Nene Galerie, Graz, Austria, 1999, Zentrum fuer Kunstund Media, Karlsruhe, Germany, 1999; represented in permanent collections, Hirschorn Mus., Washington, Ludwig Mus., Cologne, Victoria and Albert Mus., London, Met. Mus. Art, N.Y.C., Wadsworth Atheneum, Hartford, Conn., Dahlem Mus., W. Berlin, Guggenheim Mus., N.Y.C., Los Angeles; appeared in various telecasts and radio performances, U.S. and Europe, 1969—; author: Art and the Future, 1973, Artculture: Essays on the Post-Modern, 1977, Photography as a Fine Art, 1983, The Museum Transformed, 1990, The Five Myths of Television Power, 1993. Nat. Endowment for Arts fellow, 1971, 75, 80; Deutscher Akademischer Austauschdients artists fellow Berlin, 1977; fellow Graham Found., 1988, Trust for Mut. Understanding, 1989, 91. Mem. Artist's Equity, Coll. Art Assn. Address: 80 Wooster St New York NY 10012-4393

DAVIS, DUANE LEE, marketing educator; b. Aurora, Ill., July 10, 1950; s. Loren Gene and Gladys Lillian (Vandeveer) D. BS cum laude, No. Ill. U., 1972; MBA, So. Ill. U., 1975; D. Bus. Adminstrn., U. Ky., 1978. Nat. accounts mgr. Century Drill & Tool, Chgo., 1972-74; asst. prof. No. Ill. U., DeKalb, 1977-78; assoc. prof. U. Cen. Fla., Orlando, 1978-91, prof., 1991—; lectr. U. Md., Heidelberg, Fed. Republic Germany, 1984-85; acting chair U. Cen. Fla., Orlando, 1989-91; Fulbright scholar Univ. do Algarve, Faro, Portugal, 1991-92, Univ. do Porto, Portugal, 1991-92; vis. prof. Pepperdine U., Malibu, Calif., 1987, Univ. do Porto, Portugal, 1999; cons. numerous clients, 1985—. Author: Business Research for Decision Making, 1985, rev. edit., 1996, 99; contbr. articles to profl. jours. Named one of Outstanding Young Men in Am., U.S. Jaycees, 1980. Mem. Am. Mktg. Assn. (Hugh G. Wales Faculty Advisor 1981-82), So. Mktg. Assn., Am. Assn. for Advances in Health Care Rsch. Avocations: offshore fishing, reading, traveling. Office: U Cen Fla PO Box 25000 Orlando FL 32816-0001

DAVIS, DWIGHT, cardiologist, educator; b. Winston-Salem, N.C., Apr. 11, 1948; s. James C. Davis; m. Lorna Jean Enck, July 30, 1988; 1 child, Nathan James. BS, N.C. A&T State U., 1970; MD, U. Rochester, 1975. Rsch. asst. U. Rochester, N.Y., 1970-71; intern in medicine Boston U. Hosp., 1975-76, resident in medicine, 1976-78; cardiology fellow Duke U. Med. Ctr., Durham, N.C., 1978-81; asst. prof. medicine, cardiology divsn. Pa. State U., Hershey, 1981-87, assoc. prof., 1987-92, disting. lectr., 1986, prof. medicine, 1992—, cardiology dir. heart transplantation, artificial organs and preclinical tchg. program, dir. cardiology preclinical tng. program, 1984—, dir., cardiology fellow tng. program, 1984-87, dir. cardiac catheterization lab., 1987—, med. dir. cardiac rehab. program, 1988—, dir. clin. cardiology program, 1991—, asst. dean for admissions, 1994-99, assoc. dean admissions and student affairs, 1999—; vice chmn. faculty affairs faculty senate Pa. State U., University Park, 1988—; mem. med. alumni coun. U. Rochester Sch. Medicine and Dentistry, 1992—; various disting. lectureships. Contbr. numerous articles to profl. jours.; editorial reviewer Annals Internal Medicine, 1983—; editorial adv. bd. Primary Cardiology, 1985—. Mem. Pa. Coun. on Aging, Harrisburg, 1989—. Recipient Outstanding Physician award Pa. State U. Sch. Medicine, 1984, Disting. Tchg. awards, 1988-89, Tchr. of Yr. award, 1991, Disting. Prof. award for tchg., 1991, Outstanding Tchr. of Yr. award med. sch. class of 1995, 93, Outstanding Tchr. of Yr. award med. sch. class of 1997, 1995, Alumni Excellence award N.C. A&T State U., 1986, Disting. Alumni award Nat. Assn. Equal Opportunity in Higher Edn., 1987. Fellow Am. Coll. Cardiology, Am. Coll. Angiology; mem. AAAS, Am. Heart Assn. (fellow coun. on clin. cardiology, rsch. com. Pa. affiliate 1992—, pres. elect Pa. affiliate 1997, pres. elect Pa./Del affiliate 1998), Am. Fedn. Clin. Rsch., Am. Assn. Med. Colls. (pres. elect North East group on student affairs 1998), Am. Assn. Cardiovasc. and Pulmonary Rehab. (expert panel cardiac rehab. guidelines project 1992—, chair cardiac rehab. criteria devel. panel 1995—), N.Y. Acad. Scis., Alpha Omega Alpha. Mem. United Ch. of Christ. Achievements include discovery that abnormalities of the sympathetic nervous system in patients with heart failure is due to an increase in norepinephrine spillover and a decrease in norepinephrine clearance from the circulation. Avocations: chess, drama, reading. Office: Pa State U Coll Medicine Divsn Cardiology PO Box 850 Hershey PA 17033-0850

DAVIS, EARL JAMES, chemical engineering educator; b. St. Paul, July 22, 1934; s. Leo Ernest and Mary (Steiner) D.; children: Molly Kathleen, David Leo. BS cum laude, Gonzaga U., 1956; PhD, U. Wash., 1960. Design engr. Union Carbide Chems. Co., South Charleston, W.Va., 1956; from asst. prof. chem. engrng. to assoc. prof. Gonzaga U., Spokane, Wash., 1960-68, dir. computing ctr., 1967-68; rsch. fellow Imperial Coll., London U., 1964-65; assoc. prof. chem. engrng. Clarkson U., 1968-73, head socio-environ. program, 1972-74, prof., 1973-78, chmn. chem. engrng. dept., 1973-74, assoc. dir. Inst. Colloid and Surface Sci., 1974-78; prof., chmn. chem. and nuclear engrng. dept. U. N.Mex., 1978-80; dir. engrng. divsn., prof. Inst. Paper Chemistry, Appleton, Wis., 1980-83; rsch. fellow in chem. engrng. U. Wash., Seattle, 1957-60, prof., 1983—; sr. scientist, cons. Unilever Rsch. Lab., Port Sunlight, Eng., 1974-75; vis. scholar NAS/Chinese Acad. Scis., China, 1989. Assoc. editor Aerosol Sci. and Tech., 1993-97; mem. editl. bd. Jour. Colloid and Interface Sci., 1984-86, Jour. Aerosol Sci., 1992—; regional editor (N.Am. and S.Am.) Colloid and Polymer Sci., 1994—; editor-in-chief Jour. Aerosol Sci., 1999—; contbr. articles to sci. publs. NSF fellow, 1964-65, grantee, 1963-89, 92—; recipient Burlington No. award for rsch., 1988; Leeds and Northrup fellow U. Wash., 1960. Fellow AAAS, mem. AIChE (adminstr. Design Inst. Multiphase Processing 1979-87), Am. Chem. Soc., Am. Assn. Aerosol Rsch. (treas. 1990-92, David Sinclair award 1991, v.p. 1996-97, pres. 1997-98), Soc. Applied Spectroscopy, Sigma Xi, Phi Lambda Upsilon. Achievements include rsch. on air pollution control, chem. waste disposal, aerosol phys. chemistry and colloid sci. Office: U Wash Dept Chem Engrng PO Box 351750 Seattle WA 98195-1750

DAVIS, EDGAR GLENN, science and health policy executive; b. Indpls., May 12, 1931; s. Thomas Carroll and Florence Isabelle (Watson) D. m. Margaret Louise Alandt, June 20, 1953; children: Anne-Elizabeth Davis Polestra, Amy Alandt, Edgar Glenn Jr. AB, Kenyon Coll., 1953; MBA, Harvard U., 1955. With Eli Lilly & Co., Indpls., 1958-91, mgr. budgeting and profit planning, 1963-66, mgr. econ. studies, 1966-67, mgr. Atlanta sales dist., 1967-68, dir. market research and sales manpower planning, 1968-69, dir. mktg. plans, 1969-74, exec. dir. pharm. mktg. planning, 1974-75, exec. dir. corp. affairs, 1975-76, v.p. corp. affairs, 1976-90, v.p. health care policy, 1990; pres., chmn. bd. dirs. Centre for Health Sci. Info., Boston, 1990—; fellow Ctr. for Bus. and Govt. Kennedy Sch. of Govt. Harvard U., 1991—; adj. prof. Butler U., Indpls.; exec. in residence Coll. of Bus., Butler U.; pres. Eli Lilly and Co. Found., 1976-88; mem. Inst. Ednl. Mgmt., Harvard U. Grad. Sch. Edn., 1987; mem. Inst. Medicine NAS, 1981—; chmn. staff Bus. Roundtable Task Force on Health, 1981-85; U.S. rep. UN Indsl. Devel. Orgn. Conf., Lisbon, 1980; participant UNIDO meeting of experts on pharms., 1981; rep. to UN Commn. on Narcotic Drugs, Vienna, 1981, UN Econ. and Social Coun., N.Y.C., 1981, UN Indsl. Devel. Orgn. Conf. Casablanca, 1981, Budapest, 1983, Madrid, 1987; trustee Boston Biomed. Rsch. Inst., 1991—; fellow Ctr. for Bus. and Govt., Kennedy Sch. Govt., Harvard U.; co-chmn. Harvard Conf. on Govt. Role in Civilian Tech., 1992, Harvard Conf. Pharmaceutical Rsch., Innovation and Pub. Policy, 1993; co-chmn. Harvard Biotech. Roundtable, 1991—; vis. scholar and advisor Health and Welfare Unit, Inst. for Econ. Affairs, London, vis. scholar Green Coll. Oxford (Eng.) U., 1994—; chmn. Nat. Fund for Med. Edn., 1994—, San Francisco; lectr. in field.; dir. English Speaking Union, Indpls. Contbr. articles to profl. jours. Pres., chmn. bd. Indpls. Health Inst., 1988-91; trustee Kenyon Coll., Gambier, Ohio, Eiteljorg Mus. Am. Indian and Western Art; pres. bd. trustees Boston Biomed. Rsch. Inst.; chmn. Nat. Fund for Med. Edn., 1996—; bd. dirs. Carnegie Coun. on Ethics and Internat. Affairs and accredited nongovtl. observer rep. to UN, Goodwill Found. Ind. Inc., 1987-95, Sta. WFYI Pub. TV, Indpls., 1983-91, Indpls. Mus. Art, Am. Symphony Orch. League, 1987-92, Nat. Health Coun., 1984-91, Pub. Affairs Coun., Washington, Nat. Fund for Med. Edn.; bd. advisors Christian Theol. Sem., N.C. Schl Arts, Bishops Sch., LaJolla, Calif.; chmn. bd. dirs. Ind. Repertory Theatre, 1979-85; vice chmn., exec. com., bd. dirs. Indpls. Symphony Orch. and Ind. State Symphony Soc., 1977-91; chmn. task force on fine arts Commn. for Future of Butler U.; chmn. exec. com. Pan Am. Econ. Leadership Conf., 10th Pan Am. Games, Indpls.; mem. Chgo. Coun. on Fgn. Rels. Fellow The Hudson Inst. (sr. adj. Indpls.); mem. NAM (bd. dirs., vice-chmn. health policy com. 1987-91), Met. Club (Washington), Edgartown Yacht Club, Naples (Fla.) Yacht Club, Woodstock Club, Royal Poinciana Golf Club (Fla.), Contemporary Club, Lambs Club, Crooked Stick Golf Club, Chappaquiddick Beach Club, Edgartown Golf Club, N.Y. Yacht Club, Traders Point Hunt Club, Reform Club London. Fax: (317) 940-9455. Office: Butler U Coll Bus Adminstrn 4600 Sunset Ave Indianapolis IN 46208-3487

DAVIS, EDMOND RAY, lawyer; b. Glendale, Calif., Sept. 4, 1928; s. Archie Allen and Eve Mae (Hoover) D.; m. Ruby Evelyn Davis, Oct. 17, 1954; children: Phillip A., Sandra A. Ed., Pepperdine Coll.; JD, U. Calif., San Francisco, 1952. Bar: Calif. 1952, U.S. Dist. Ct. (cen. dist.) Calif. 1952. Assoc. Bailie, Turner & Sprague, 1955-60; trust counsel Security Pacific Nat. Bank, 1960-67; ptnr. Overton, Lyman & Prince, Los Angeles, 1967-87, Brobeck, Phleger & Harrison, Los Angeles, 1987—; chmn. legal adv. com. San Marino Unified Sch. Dist., 1981—; mem. legal com. Music Ctr. Found., Performing Arts Council, Los Angeles County, 1980—. Chmn., pub. adminstr. Pub. Guardian Adv. Commns., Los County Bd. Suprs., 1974-76; bd. dirs. Braille Inst. Am., Inc., 1974—, Children's Bur. Los Angeles, Children's Bur. Found.; pres. Calif. Jaycees, 1962. With U.S. Army, 1952-54. Recipient Alumni award Pepperdine Coll., 1962. Fellow Am. Coll. Trust and Estate Counsel (chmn. Calif. chpt. 1981-86); mem. Internat. Acad. Estate and Trust Law (academician), State Bar of Calif. (chmn. estate planning, trust and probate law sect. 1977-78), L.A. County Bar Assn. (exec. com., probate and trust law sect. 1986-89, Arthur K. Marshall award Probate and Trust Law sect. 1991), Order of Coif, Calif. Club, Chancery Club, Breakfast Club. Office: Brobeck Phleger & Harrison 550 S Hope St Los Angeles CA 90071-2627 also: Brobeck Phleger & Harrison Spear St Tower 1 Market Pla San Francisco CA 94105

DAVIS, EDWARD BERTRAND, federal judge; b. W. Palm Beach, Fla., Feb. 10, 1933; s. Edward Bertrand and Mattie Mae (Walker) D.; m. Patricia Lee Klein, Apr. 5, 1958; children: Diana Lee Davis, Traci Russell, Edward Bertrand, III. JD, U. Fla., 1960; LLM in Taxation, N.Y. U., 1961. Bar: Fla. 1960. Pvt. practice Miami, 1961-79; counsel High, Stack, Lazenby & Bender, 1978-79; U.S. dist. judge So. Dist. Fla., 1979—. Served with AUS, 1953-55. Mem. Fla. Bar Assn., Dade County Bar Assn. Office: US Dist Ct 301 N Miami Ave Miami FL 33128-7702

DAVIS, EDWARD WILSON, business administration educator; b. Thomaston, Ga., Aug. 4, 1935; s. James Royland, Jr. and Hazel (Bass) D.; m. Patricia Gail Forrest, Oct. 20, 1962; children: Matthew Wilson, Edward Royland. BS in Mech. Engrng, Ga. Inst. Tech., 1957, MS in Indsl. Engrng, 1959; postgrad., Swiss Fed. Inst. Tech., 1957-58; MPhil, Yale U., 1967, Ph.D., 1968. Project leader Ops. Research, Inc., Washington, 1960-64; asst. prof. Harvard Bus. Sch., Cambridge, Mass., 1968-73; vis. asso. prof. Sloan Sch. Mgmt., M.I.T., Cambridge, 1973-74; assoc. prof., then prof. U. N.C., Chapel Hill, 1974-78; prof. Grad. Sch. Bus. Adminstrn., U. Va., Charlottesville, 1978—, Oliver Wight prof. bus. adminstrn., 1984-91, Isidore Horween rsch. prof., 1991-96; cons. various pvt. and public cos., U.S. and Europe. Author: Case Studies in Material Requirements Planning, 1978; co-author: Project Management with PERT & CPM, 3d edit., 1983; editor: Project Management, 1974, 2d edit., 1982. Council mem. Pilgrim Congregation Ch., 1972-74; cub scout and boy scout leader Occoneechee council Boy Scouts Am., 1974-77. IBM faculty fellow in internat. bus., 1976. Mem. Am. Mgmt. Assn., Inst. Mgmt. Scis., Am. Inst. Indsl. Engrs., Project Mgmt. Inst., Am. Inst. Decision Scis., Am. Prodn. and Inventory Control Soc. (dir. Ednl. and Research Found., presdl. award 1974, 89), Raven Soc. Presbyterian. Office: PO Box 6550 Charlottesville VA 22906-6550

DAVIS, EGBERT LAWRENCE, III, lawyer; b. Winston-Salem, N.C., Dec. 30, 1937; s. Egbert Lawrence Jr. and Eleanor (Layfield) D.; m. Alexandra Holderness, Aug. 25, 1962; children: Alexandra Davis Hipps, Egbert L. IV, Lucinda Davis McCarroll, Pamela L. AB, Princeton U., 1960; LLB, Duke U., 1963; MBA, George Washington U., 1966. Bar: N.C. 1963. Assoc. Womble, Carlyle, Sandridge & Rice, Winston-Salem, N.C., 1965-70, ptnr., 1970-82; ptnr. Womble, Carlyle, Sandridge & Rice, Raleigh, N.C., 1982-97; of counsel Womble, Carlyle, Sandridge & Rice, Raleigh, 1997—. Mem. editl. bd. Duke U. Law Jour., 1963. Sec. Wachovia Realty Investments, Winston-Salem, 1969-82; rep. N.C. Ho. of Reps., Raleigh, 1970-74; sen. N.C. Senate, Raleigh, 1974-78; chmn. N.W. Environ. Preservation Com., Inc., Winston-Salem, 1980; chmn. trustees N.C. Bapt. Hosp., Winston-Salem, 1981-82; chmn. N.C. Dem. Party, Raleigh, 1989-91, N.C. Family Bus. Forum, 1993—; N.C. Prison Fellowship State coun., 1994-97; exec. com. N.C. Coun. for Econ. Edn., 1996—, Ea. Ctr. for Regional Devel., 1996-97; bd. dirs. N.C. chpt. Coastal Conservation Assn. Named Citizen of Yr. Winston-Salem Mayor's Com. on Employment of the Handicapped, 1971, Young Man. of Yr. Winston-Salem Jaycees, 1972; recipient Freedom Guard award N.C. Jaycees, 1973, U.S. Jaycees, 1973. Mem. Am. Judicature Soc., N.C. Bar Assn. (bd. govs. 1979-82), Wake County Bar Assn., Raleigh Rotary Club (pres. 1986-87). Democrat. Presbyterian. Avocations: jogging, water sports, tennis, biking. Office: Womble Carlyle Sandridge PO Box 831 Raleigh NC 27602-0831

DAVIS, ELEANOR KAY, museum administrator; b. Rome, Nov. 10, 1935; d. Fred H. and Hazel (Turner) D.; children: Victoria Elaine Davis Reich, Gregory Brian. BA, Berry Coll., 1957; MA, Western Md. Coll., 1962; PhD, Ga. State U., 1975. Tchr. biology and physics Jonesboro High Sch., Clayton, Ga., 1957-58; tchr. physics and biology S.W. DeKalb High Sch., Decatur, Ga., 1958-59; tchr. biology, physics and phys. sci. Taneytown High Sch., Carroll County, Md., 1959-61; chmn. physics and biology Coosa High Sch., Rome, Ga., 1961-62, tchr. biology and physics, 1962-65; tchr. physics Briarcliff High Sch., Decatur, 1966-72; adminstrv. coord. Fernbank Sci. Ctr., Atlanta, 1972-84; exec. dir. Fernbank Mus. Natural History, Atlanta, 1984—, 1992—. Named Outstanding Mus. Profl., Ga. Assn. Mus. and Galleries, 1983, Woman of Achievement, Atlanta Bus. Women's Assn., 1984; mem. Acad. of Women Achievers, Atlanta YWCA, 1987. Mem. AAAS, AAUW, Ga. Assn. Mus. and Galleries, Am. Assn. Mus., Southeastern Mus. Conf. Office: Fernbank Mus Natural History 767 Clifton Rd NE Atlanta GA 30307-1221*

DAVIS, ELENA DENISE, accountant; b. Rome, N.Y., June 24, 1953; d. Robert Frederick and Arlene Ruth (Fravor) Vrooman; m. Joseph E. Davis, Dec. 24, 1975 (div. Nov. 1988); children: JoAnna Lynn, Robert George, Crystal Leigh. AS, Jefferson C.C., Watertown, N.Y., 1975; BSBA, Orlando Coll., 1995, BS in Acctg., 1995; postgrad., Fla. Met. U., 1999—. Staff acct., asst. mgr. Vrooman's Tire & Rd. Svc. Inc., Adams, N.Y., 1975-89; claim assoc. Hartford Ins., Maitland, Fla., 1989-97; acct. Raybob Plumbing Co. Inc., Orlando, 1997-98, Ctrl. Sweeping Svc., Inc., Winter Garden, Fla., 1998-99. Active Boy Scouts Am., Girl Scouts Am., PTA; Sunday sch. tchr. Methodist Ch., 1984-89. Home: PO Box 721 Ocoee FL 34761-0721

DAVIS, ELISE MILLER (MRS. LEO M. DAVIS), writer; b. Corsicana, Tex., Oct. 12, 1915; d. Moses Myre and Rachelle (Daniels) Miller; student U. Tex., 1930-31; m. Jay Albert Davis, June 27, 1937 (dec. June 1973); 1 dau., Rayna Miller (Mrs. Michael Edwin Loeb); m. 2d, Leo M. Davis, Aug. 23, 1974. Freelance writer, 1945—; merchandiser and dir. Jay Davis, Inc., Amarillo, Tex., 1956-73; instr. mag. writing U. Tex., Dallas, 1978; lectr. creative writing Baylor U., Waco, Tex., 1980, 81, 83. Mem. Am. Soc. Journalists and Authors (bd. dirs. 1985-91). Author: The Answer Is God: The Personal Story of Dale Evans and Roy Rogers, 1955; articles to periodicals including Reader's Digest, Woman's Day, Nation's Business, others. Home: 7838 Caruth Ct Dallas TX 75225-8123

DAVIS, ELIZABETH HAWK, English language educator; b. Ft. Smith, Ark., Sept. 6, 1945; d. Arthur Carlton and Lolitta (Poe) Hawk; m. Leo Carson Davis, Aug. 31, 1968. BA, U. Ark., 1967, BM, 1967, MA, 1969; EdD, East Tex. State U., 1989. Classroom tchr. Springdale (Ark.) Pub. Schs., 1967-68; lectr. U. Md., Heidelberg, Fed. Republic Germany, 1978-79; from instr. to asst. prof. performing arts So. Ark. U., Magnolia, 1981-92, assoc. prof., 1992-96, chair English and fgn. langs. dept., 1993—, prof., 1996—. Contbr. articles to profl. jours. Organist First Presbyn. Ch., Magnolia, 1984—. Mem. MLA, Nat. Coun. of Tchrs. of English, Ark. Tchrs. of Coll. English, Ark. Philol. Assn., Phi Beta Kappa. Office: So Ark U PO Box 9356 Magnolia AR 71753

DAVIS, EMERY STEPHEN, wholesale food company executive; b. Kansas City, Mo., Dec. 31, 1940; s. Vernon Albert and Berneice Marie (Brenner) D.; m. Hildegarde Retzer; children: Angelica, Matthew, Nicholas. Student, Met. Coll., Kansas City, Mo., 1958-59; cert., Stanford U., 1981. Mgr. distbn. Fleming Cos., Kansas City, Mo., 1960-71; mgr. distbn. Fleming Cos., Fremont, Calif., 1972-75, dir. warehousing Topeka, 1975-77, dir. distbn. Ea. region, Phila., 1977-79, v.p. distbn., Oklahoma City, 1979-82, sr. v.p. distbn., 1982-85, exec. v.p. distbn., 1985—; exec. v.p. Scrivner Group Fleming Cos., Inc., Oklahoma City, 1994-95, exec. v.p. ops., 1996-97; exec. v.p. food distbn. Fleming Cos., Inc., Okla., 1998—; coun. mem. for Continuing Edn. and Pub. Svc. Coun., U. Okla., 1996. Mem. adv. bd. coun. continuing edn. U. Okla., 1996. Served with U.S. Army, 1962-63. Recipient profl. achievement award Traffic Mgmt. Publ., 1980. Mem. Nat. Am. Wholesale Grocers' Assn. (chmn. productivity com., bd. govs. 1995), Nat. Assn. Wholesaler/Distbrs. (bd. dels.), Nat. Coun. Phys. Distbn. Mgmt. Home: 6208 Waterford Blvd Apt 80 Oklahoma City OK 73118-1112 Office: Fleming Cos Inc PO Box 26647 Oklahoma City OK 73126-0647*

DAVIS, ERIC KEITH, professional baseball player; b. L.A., May 29, 1962; m. Erica D. Baseball player Cin. Reds, 1980-91, 96, L.A. Dodgers, 1991-93, Detroit Tigers, 1993-94, Balt. Orioles, 1997-98, St Louis Cardinals, 98-. Mem. Nat. League All-Star Team, 1987, 89, Nat. League Silver Slugger team, 1987,89, NL Gold Glove 1987-89; named to Sporting News Nat. League. All-Star team, 1987, 89; named Nat. League Comeback Player of Yr., 1996. Player in World Series, 1990. Office: St Louis Cardinals 250 Stadium Plaza Saint Louis MO 63102*

DAVIS, ERIC WAYNE, professional football player; b. Anniston, Ala., Jan. 26, 1968. Student, Jacksonville State U. Cornerback San Francisco 49ers, 1990-96, Carolina Panthers, 1996—. Selected to Pro Bowl, 1995, 96; named Super Bowl Champion, 1994. Office: Carolina Panthers 800 S Mint St Charlotte NC 28202-1502*

DAVIS, ERNESTINE BADY, nurse educator, administrator; b. Atlanta, Apr. 8, 1943; d. Henry Benjamin and Martha (Shropshire) Bady; m. Luther Davis Jr., Aug. 14, 1965 (dec.); children: Luther III, Ella Michelle. BSN, Tuskegee U., 1965; MSN, Med. Coll. Ga., 1973; EdD, U. Ala., 1979. Instr. Tuskegee (Ala.) U., 1971-77; asst. prof. U. Ala. Weekend Coll., Tuscaloosa, Ala., 1977-80, Capstone Coll. Nursing, Tuscaloosa, Ala.; prof. U. North Ala., Florence; asst. to pres. minority affairs; cultural diversity cons. Ala. Early Intervention Sys. Contbr. articles to profl. jours. Named Outstanding Young Women of Am., Zeta Woman of Yr., Zeta Phi Beta Soc.; recipient Lillian Harvey award, 2000 Notable Am. Women award. Mem. Am. Cancer Soc., Delta Sigma Theta, Phi Kappa Phi. Home: 110 Colonial Dr Florence AL 35633-1456

DAVIS, ERROLL BROWN, JR., utility executive; b. Pitts., Aug. 5, 1944; s. Erroll Brown and Eleanor Margaret (Boykin) D.; m. Elaine E. Casey, July 13, 1968; children: Christopher, Whitney. Diploma in elec. engring., Carnegie-Mellon U., 1965; MBA in Fin., U. Chgo., 1967. Corp. fin. staff Ford Motor Co., Detroit, 1969-73, Xerox Corp., Rochester, N.Y., 1973-78; v.p. fin. Wis. Power and Light Co., Madison, 1978-82, v.p. fin and pub. affairs, 1982-84, exec. v.p., 1984-87, pres., 1987, pres., CEO, 1988-98; pres., CEO Alliant Energy, Madison, 1998—; also bd. dirs.; pres. WPH Holdings, 1990-98; bd. dirs. BP Amoco Inc., PPG Industries. Active Selective Svc. Bd., Madison, 1982—; mem. bd. regents U. Wis., 1987-94; bd. dirs. United Way Dane County, 1984-89, chmn. bd. dirs., 1987; life trustee Carnegie Mellon U.; bd. dirs. Competitive Wis., 1989—, Ednl. Comm. Bd., 1992-94; chmn. Start Smart of Dane County. Mem. Am. Soc. Corp. Execs., Wis. Mfg. and Commerce (bd. dirs. 1986—, chmn. 1994-95), Am. Gas Assn. (bd. dirs. 1990-95), Electric Power Rsch. Inst. (vice-chmn., acting chmn., bd. dirs. 1990-98), Assn. Edison Illuminating Cos. (bd. dirs. 1993-99), Edison Electric Inst. (bd. dirs. 1995—), Iowa Bus. Coun., Nuclear Energy Inst. Avocations: tennis, golf. Home: PO Box 1347 Madison WI 53701-1347 Office: Alliant Energy 222 W Washington Ave Madison WI 53703-2719

DAVIS, EVAN ANDERSON, lawyer; b. N.Y.C., Jan. 18, 1944; s. Richard T. and Charlotte (Upham) D.; m. Mary Carroll Rothwell; 1 child, Sara Mei-Ping. BA, Harvard U., 1966; JD, Columbia U., 1969. Bar: N.Y. 1970, U.S. Dist. Ct. (so. dist.) N.Y. 1973, U.S. Ct. Appeals (2d cir.) 1973, U.S. Dist. Ct. (ea. dist.) N.Y., 1978, U.S. Supreme Ct. 1979. Law clk. to judge U.S. Ct. Appeals (D.C. cir.), 1969-70; law clk. to Justice Potter Stewart U.S. Supreme Ct., 1970-71; gen. counsel N.Y.C. Budget Bur., 1971-72; chief consumer protection div. N.Y.C. Law Dept., 1972-74; task force leader, impeachment inquiry staff U.S. Ho. of Reps., 1974; assoc. Cleary, Gottlieb, Steen & Hamilton, N.Y.C., 1975-78; ptnr. Cleary, Gottlieb, Steen & Hamilton, 1979-85, 91—; counsel to gov. of N.Y., 1985-90; vice chmn., bd. dirs. Fund for N.Y.C., 1982-85; trustee Columbia U., 1993—, mem. exec. com., 1994—, chair fin. com. Editor-in-chief Columbia Law Rev., 1968-69. Treas. Sch. for Field Studies, 1991-95; dir. Franklin and Eleanor Roosevelt Inst., 1993—, mem. exec. com., 1994—; dir. Mus. of Hudson Highlands, 1991—, Storm King Sch., 1991-98; bd. visitors Helen Hayes Hosp., 1992-98, mem. coun. fgn. rels.; chairperson N.Y. Fair Election Project, 1998—. Recipient Hopkins medal St. David's Soc., N.Y., 1988, Bruckner medal Fed. Bar Coun., 1990, Aquarium Environ. award Wildlife Conservation Soc., 1995. Mem. ABA (ho. of dels. 1983-85, 91-93, chmn. spl. com. youth edn. for citizenship 1986-88, chmn. standing com. pub. edn.), Assn. Bar City N.Y. (chmn. exec. com. 1982-83, v.p. 1983-84), Legal Aid Soc. (v.p. 1983-85, 97—, exec. com. 1992—), Am. Law Inst., N.Y. State Bar Assn. (com. to revise ethics rules 1992—, commn. on middle income access to legal svc. 1995—). Home: 6 Eagle Head Cornwall On Hudson NY 12520-1720 Office: Cleary Gottlieb Steen & Hamilton 1 Liberty Plz Fl 38 New York NY 10006-1470

DAVIS, EVELYN Y., editor, writer, publisher, investor; b. Aug. 16; d. Herman H. and Marian (Witteboom) DeJong; m. William Henry Davis, 1957 (div. 1958); m. Marvin Knudsen, 1969 (div. 1970); m. Walter O. Froh Jr., 1991 (div. 1994). Student, Western Md. Coll., George Washington U., N.Y. Inst. Fin. Editor, pub., Highlights and Lowlights, 1964—. Trustee Evelyn Y. Davis Found., 1989—; mem. adv. bd. George Washington U. Med. Ctr.; hon. bd. govs. Art Inst. of Chgo. Fellow JFK Ctr. for Performing Arts. Mem. Luther Rice Soc. (life), Capitol Hill Club (life), Smithsonian Benefactors Cir., Andrew Carnegie Soc. (life). Home: Watergate East 2510 Virginia Ave NW Washington DC 20037-1904 Office: Highlights and Lowlights Watergate Office Bldg 2600 Virginia Ave NW Ste 215 Washington DC 20037-1905 *To me power is greater than love, and I did not get where I am by standing in line, nor by being shy.*

DAVIS, FLORENCE ANN, lawyer; b. Pitts., Feb. 22, 1955; d. Richard Davis and Charlotte (Saul) McGhee; m. Kevin J. O'Brien, May 28, 1978; children: Rebecca Davis, Sarah Davis. AB, Wellesley U., 1976; JD, NYU, 1979. Bar: N.Y. 1980, U.S. Dist. Ct. (ea. and so. dists.) N.Y., N.Y. Ct. Appeals (2d cir.), U.S. Tax Ct., U.S. Supreme Ct. Assoc. atty. Sullivan & Cromwell, N.Y.C., 1979-86; litigation counsel Morgan Stanley & Co., N.Y.C., 1986-88, v.p., 1988-90, dir. compliance, 1989-90, prin., 1990-95; v.p., gen. counsel Am. Internat. Group, N.Y.C., 1995—. Root-Tilden scholar NYU Law Sch., 1976-79. Mem. Securities Industry Assn. (v.p. edn. Compliance and Legal div. 1992, exec. com. Compliance and Legal div. 1990-92). Office: American International Group Inc 70 Pine St New York NY 10270-0002*

DAVIS, FLOYD ASHER, neurologist; b. Chester, Pa., June 10, 1934; s. Jacob J. Davis and Sarah Pomerantz; m. Joan Esme Rylander, June 3, 1962; children: Stephanie, Jacalyn. BS in Biology, Franklin and Marshall Coll., 1956; MD, U. Pa., 1960. Diplomate Am. Bd. Neurology and Psychiatry. Vis. scholar in neurochemistry and neurophysiology Coll. Physician and Surgeons, Columbia U., N.Y.C., 1960-63; resident in neurology Mt. Sinai Hosp., N.Y.C., 1963-66; prof. neurology Rush Med. Sch., Chgo., 1968—; sr. attending neurologist Rush-Presbyn.-St. Luke's Med. Ctr., Chgo., 1968—, dir. Multiple Sclerosis Ctr., 1972—; Robert Borwell Endowed prof. Rush-Presbyn.-St. Luke's Med. Ctr., 1974. Contbr. over 100 articles to profl. jours. Capt. Med. Corp U.S. Army, 1966-68. Mem. Am. Neurol. Assn., am. Acad. Neurology (dir. continuing edn. courses), Nat. Multiple Sclerosis Soc. (numerous positions). Avocations: golf, fishing, music. Office: Rush Multiple Sclerosis Ctr 1735 W Harrison St Chicago IL 60612

DAVIS, FRANCES KAY, lawyer; b. Phila., Apr. 1, 1952; d. Francis Kaye and Ida May (Lamplugh) D. BA, Mount Holyoke Coll., 1974; MA, Duke U., 1976; JD, Villanova U., 1983-86. Legal asst. Cozen, Begier & O'Connor, Phila., 1982-83; summer assoc. Montgomery, McCracken, Walker & Roads, Phila., 1985, assoc., 1986-89; assoc. Cozen & O'Connor, Phila., 1989-95, Jackson/LeGros, 1996; ptnr., shareholder LeGros Law Ptnrs., Berwyn, PA and Princeton, N.J., 1996—; gen. ptnr. April Racing Stables, 1991-95, Steel Fist Video Co., 1994-97, April Racehorses Mgmt., Inc., 1997—. Contbr. articles to profl. jours. Capt. USAF, 1977-82. Mem. ABA, ATLA (Trial Advocacy award Phila. chpt. 1986), Phila. Bar Assn., Welsh Soc. Phila. (bd. stewards 1990-93, scholar 1984-85, chmn. scholarship com. 1990-92, counselor 1992-94, chmn. women's com. 1992-94), InterAm. Bar Assn. Avocations: reading, horseback riding, martial arts.

DAVIS, FRANCIS RAYMOND, priest; b. Washington, Feb. 10, 1920; s. Frank Raymond and Ruth Madeline (Donovan) D.; B.A., St. Bernard's Sem., Rochester, N.Y., 1941; M.L.S., Cath. U. Am., 1953. Ordained priest Roman Cath. Ch., 1945; asst. pastor St. Ambrose Ch., Rochester, 1945-50; prof. lit. St. Bernard's Sem., 1950-51, librarian, 1950-69, prof. speech., 1958-67; pastor Our Lady Lourdes Ch., Elmira, N.Y., 1969-78; pastor St. Mary's Ch., Dansville, N.Y., 1978-80, St. Patrick's Ch., Corning, N.Y., 1980-90. Mem. Chemung county gen. edn. bd. Diocese of Rochester, 1971-78; mem. exec. com. Chemung County (N.Y.) Council Aging, 1972-76; mem. adv. com. Chemung County Office for Aging, 1973-78; mem. exec. com. Ecumenical Preaching Mission, 1977-78; bd. dirs. All Saints' Acad., Corning, 1986-90, founder. Fellow Internat. Biog. Assn.; mem. ALA, Cath. Library Assn. (officer sem. sect. 1958-61), Ch. and Synagogue Library Assn. (nominating com. 1979), Elmira Vicinity Ministerial Assn. (officer 1972-73). Author articles and book revs. Address: 155 State St Corning NY 14830-2534

DAVIS, FRANK DANIEL, retired journalist; b. Brookville, Pa., Dec. 30, 1925; s. Frank and Essie (Martz) D.; m. Beverley Anne Smith, Feb. 25, 1950; children: Blake M., Mark J., Sally A., Lynn E., Timothy T., Wendy B., Quentin M. BA in Journalism, Pa. State U., 1947; MA in Journalism, Northwestern U., 1948. Dir. publicity and info. Pa. Human Rels. Commn., Harrisburg, 1957-86; reporter The Tribune-Democrat, Johnstown, Pa., 1948-57; ret. Pres. Friendship Force Grtr. Harrisburg, 1995. Named to Pa. Voter Hall of Fame, Commonwealth Pa. Dept. State, 1998. Mem. NAACP (sec. Grtr. Harrisburg chpt. 1993-94), Soc. Profl. Journalists (membership chmn. Ctrl. Pa chpt. 1975-80). Avocations: slide photography, gardening, travel. Home: 200 Gettysburg Pike Mechanicsburg PA 17055

DAVIS, FRANK TRADEWELL, JR., lawyer; b. Atlanta, Feb. 2, 1938; s. Frank T. and Sue (Burnett) D.; m. Winifred Storey, June 23, 1961; children: Frank, Frederick, Gordon. AB, Princeton U., 1960; JD, George Washington U., 1963; LLM, Harvard U., 1964. Bar: Ga. 1963, D.C. 1966, U.S. Ct. Appeals (5th cir.) 1963, U.S. Ct. Appeals (11th cir.) 1982, U.S. Supreme Ct. 1968. Assoc. Hansell, Post Brandon & Dorsey, Atlanta, 1964-67; ptnr. Hansell & Post, Atlanta, 1968-77, 79-86, Long, Aldridge & Norman, Atlanta, 1986—; ptnr., gen. counsel Pres.'s Reorgn. Project Office of Pres., 1977-79; vis. instr. U. Ga. Law Sch., 1964-66, Ga. State U. Law Sch., 1988-90; vis. prof. Emory U. Law Sch., 1992—. Author: Business Acquisitions, 1977, (2d edit.), 1982; contbr. articles to legal jours. Bd. dirs. Nat. Inst. Justice, 1980-81, Westminster Schs., 1969—, chmn. bd. dirs., 1984-89; sr. warden All Saints' Episcopal Ch., 1982; bd. dirs. Va. Sem., 1980-94, exec. com., 1985-89; mem. Atlanta Charter Commn.; chmn. Atlanta Crime Commn., 1977; mem. bd. councilors Carter Presdl. Ctr., 1988—; chmn. Rotary Ednl. Found. Atlanta. Lt. USNR, 1960-62. Mem. Am. Law Inst., Atlanta C. of C. (bd. dirs. 1975-77), Piedmont Driving Club (Atlanta), Chevy Chase Club (Md.), Rotary (pres. Atlanta chpt. 1990-91, bd. dirs., sec. 1988-89, chmn. bd., 1991-92, chmn. Ednl. Found. 1997—). Home: 9 Nacoochee Pl NW Atlanta GA 30305-4164 Office: 303 Peachtree St NE Ste 5300 Atlanta GA 30308-3264

DAVIS, FRED, journalist, educator; b. Columbia, S.C., Feb. 14, 1947; s. Nathaniel Lewis Sr. and Arneatha Pearl (Robinson) D.; m. Joan Sineta Walker, Jan. 14, 1967; children: Alex LaMar, Kevin Alexander. BS in English Edn., N.C. A&T State U., 1969. City/coun. reporter WFMY-TV/CBS, Greensboro, N.C., 1969-70; govtl. reporter WJRT-TV/ABC, 1970-74, dir. documentaries and pub. affairs, 1974-75; anchor-reporter WMAL-TV (WJLA-TV/ABC), Washington, 1975; various positions in field to reporter, news editor WRC-TV/NBC News, Washington, 1975; gen. assignment, news program svc. reporter KNBC-TV/NBC News, Burbank, Calif., 1976; writer/reporter KHJ-TV/Ind., Hollywood, Calif., 1976-78; anchor/editor WIS-TV/NBC, Columbia, S.C., 1978-80; asst. news dir., sr. producer WJXT-TV/CBS, Jacksonville, Fla., 1980-81; staff writer Jacksonville Jour./Fla. Pub. Co., 1981; news dir. ABC Direction Radio Network/ABC News, N.Y.C., 1981-88; weekly commentator CBS-owned radio stas., 1992; self-syndicated columnist S.C. newspapers, 1992—; Disting. prof. mass media mgmt. Wash. State U., Pullman, 1995-97; columnist The Seattle Times, The Spokesman-Rev., 1996—; adj. prof. Edward R. Murrow Sch. of Comm., Wash. State U., Pullman, 1997—; cons./host Sta. KWSU-TV (PBS), 1997—; owner media svcs./broadcast news consultancy, 1989—; vis. lectr. Benedict Coll., Columbia, 1979-80, 90, Coll. of Journalism U. S.C., 1987, Coll. Journalism & Mass Comm., U. Nebr., Lincoln, 1997—; mem. Journalism and Mass Comm. del. to China, Citizens Ambassador Program, 1996, Italy, Switzerland, Austria, 1997, S. Africa, 1999; expert media witness Libel Def. Resource Ctr., San Diego, 1997; del. People to People Internat., Russia, Finland, 1998; cons., host KWSU-TV, KUON-TV, 1997—; cons., writer The Gallup Org., Lincoln, Nebr., 1999—; del. News World conf., Barcelona, Spain, 1999; lectr. Coll. Journalism & Mass. Comm., U. Nebr., Lincoln, 1997-99, U. Nebr., 1999—. Contbr. articles to USA Today; provider news commentaries for CBS-owned radio stas. in N.Y., L.A., Chgo., Phila., San Francisco, Detroit, Mpls.; columnist The Seattle Times, The Royal Gazette, Bermuda, The Spokesman-Rev., 1996—. Bd. visitors, N.C. A&T State U., Greensboro, 1988—; del. Russia and Finland People to People Internat., 1998. Recipient awards Leadership Flint (Mich.), 1973, Internat. Radio Festival of N.Y., 1983-88, Ohio State award ABC Radio, 1986, Nat. Press Club award, 1984, 85, Comm. Excellence to Black Audiences award of distinction ABC Dir./Radio Network, 1987, b'nai b'rith Edward R. Murrow Brotherhood award, 1986, Disting. Alumni award Nat. Assn. for Equal Opportunity in Higher Edn., 1988. Mem. PGA Ptnrs. (charter mem.), Internat. Platform Assn., Radio-TV News Dirs. Assn., Am. Fedn. TV and Radio Artists, Acad. TV Arts and Scis., Nat. Assn. Black Journalists, Soc. Profl. Journalists, Nat. Geog. Soc., U.S. Golf Assn., S.C. Press Assn., Assn. for Edn. in Journalism and Mass Comm., Broadcast Edn. Assn., Planetary Soc., The Folio Soc., Alpha Phi Alpha. Baptist. Avocations: gourmet cooking, racquetball, golf, tennis, barbecue judging. Office: U Nebr Coll Journalism & Mass Comm PO Box 85543 Lincoln NE 68501-5543

DAVIS, FRED DONALD, JR., optometrist; b. Greenville, S.C., Oct. 16, 1959; s. Barbara Ann (Poteet) D.; m. Barbara Carol Howell, Dec. 20, 1979; children: Julie Marie, Daniel Jesse. Student, Columbia (Tenn.) State Coll., 1980; BS, David Lipscomb U., 1984; OD, So. Coll. Optometry, 1988. Optician Bob Petty Optical, Nashville, 1978-84; lab. asst. Donelson Hosp., Nashville, 1977-84; optometrist Eye Specs Unltd., Old Hickory, Tenn., 1988—. Mem. Gideon, Wilson County, Tenn, 1990—. Recipient Low Vision award Noir Technologies, 1988. Mem. Am. Optometric Assn. (low vision sect., contact lens sect.), Tenn. Optometric Assn., Middle Tenn. Optometric Soc., Tenn. Soc. to Prevent Blindness, Lions. Mem. Ch. of Christ. Avocation: softball. Home and Office: Eye Specs Unltd 4961 Lebanon Rd Old Hickory TN 37138-4103

DAVIS, G. REUBEN, lawyer; b. Muskogee, Okla., Nov. 5, 1943; s. Glenn Reuben and Margaret Elizabeth (Linebaugh) D.; m. D. Candace Jensen, June 17, 1967; children: Clay Reuben, Hayden Jensen. BA, Westminster Coll., 1966; JD, U. Okla., 1973. Bar: Okla. 1973, U.S. Dist. Ct. (no. dist.) Okla. 1973, U.S. Ct. Appeals (10th cir.) 1973, U.S. Supreme Ct. 1988. Assoc. Boone, Smith, Davis, Hurst & Dickman, Tulsa, 1973-78, ptnr., 1978—. Past pres. Tulsa Cystic Fibrosis Found., bd. dirs., 1976—; trustee Hillcrest Med. Ctr., Inc., Tulsa, 1979, Alexander Trust, Tulsa Found.; v.p., bd. dirs. Indian Nations coun. Boy Scouts Am., 1987—. Mem. ABA, Am. Inns Ct., Okla. Bar Assn., Tulsa County Bar Assn. (v.p. 1986-87, pres. 1988-89), Order of Coif. Republican. Methodist. Avocations: running, tennis, golf. Office: Boone Smith Davis Hurst & Dickman 100 W 5th St Ste 500 Tulsa OK 74103-4215

DAVIS, GAY RUTH, psychotherapist, social welfare educator, author, researcher, consultant; b. Bellingham, Wash., Sept. 19, 1935; d. Lee Laverne Wickersham and Altha (Lund) Wickersham Knight; m. Paul Cushing Davis, Dec. 20, 1956; children: Jeffrey Richards, Jennifer Lynn. Student, Brigham Young U., 1953-55; BA summa cum laude, Western Wash. U., 1976; MSW, U. Wash., 1978, PhD, 1985. Diplomate in clin. social work. Dir. Social Svcs. Sound Health Assn., Tacoma, 1977-78; social work profl. Harborview Med. Ctr., Seattle, 1979-81; instr. Sch. Social Work U. Wash., Seattle, 1984-85; pvt. practice cons. social work and psychotherapy Seattle, 1985-98; prin. investigator NINCDS Rsch., 1980-81; coord. Adult Svcs. Tng. Project, U. Wash., 1983-84. Contbr. articles to profl. jours. Mem. adv. bd. LDS Social Svcs., 1990-91. Grantee Wash. Dept. Health and Human Services, 1981-82. Mem. NASW (diplomate, qualified clin. social worker), Nat. Registry Clin. Social Work, Wash. Assn. Social Workers (cert.), Assn. Mormon Counselors and Psychotherapists. Democrat. Mormon. Avocations: genealogy, writing.

DAVIS, GEENA (VIRGINIA DAVIS), actress; b. Wareham, Mass., Jan. 21, 1957; m. Richard Emmolo, 1981 (div. 1983); m. Jeff Goldblum, 1987 (div. 1990); m. Renny Harlin, 1993. BFA, Boston U., 1979; attended, New England Coll., Henniker, N.H. Founder Genial Pictures; mem. My. Washington (N.H.) Repertory Theatre Co. Motion picture appearances include Tootsie, 1982, Fletch, 1985, Transylvania 6-5000, 1985, The Fly, 1986, Beetlejuice, 1988, The Accidental Tourist, 1988 (Academy award Best Supporting Actress, 1989), Earth Girls Are Easy, 1989, Quick Change, 1990, Thelma and Louise, 1991 (Acad. award nominee Best Actress 1991, British Acad Film and TV Arts award Best Actress in leading role 1991, Golden Globe award nominee Best Actress 1991), A League of Their Own, 1992, Hero, 1992, Angie, 1994, Speechless, 1994, Cutthroat Island, 1995, The Long Kiss Goodnight, 1996; TV series: Buffalo Bill, 1983-84, Sara, 1985; appeared in TV film Secret Weapons, 1985, episodes series Family Ties, 1984. Address: ICM 8942 Wilshire Blvd Beverly Hills CA 90211-1934 also: ICM 40 West 57th St New York NY 10019

DAVIS, GENE, civil engineer; b. Lower Peach Tree, Ala., Apr. 21, 1935; s. Edgar Thomas and Una (Smith) D.; m. Betty Marie Davidson; children: Jean Marie Davis, Jenifer Davis Cerny, Joanna Davis Haran, James Andrew Davis. BSCE, U. Ala., 1958; MS in Mgmt., Naval Postgrad. Sch., 1969; cert., Armed Forces Staff Coll., 1974. Commd. ensign USN, 1958, advanced through grades to Capt., 1980; resident engr. Navy Project Office, Cape Canaveral, Fla., 1960-63, Dir. of Constrn. in South East Asia, Bangkok, Thailand, 1963-65; program mgr. Pacific divsn., Naval Civil Engring., Honolulu, 1965-68; exec. officer Naval Constrn. Bat. 121, Gulfport, Miss., 1968-70; dir. constrn. planning Hdqrs., Naval Civil Engring., Washington, 1974-76; comdg. officer Naval Constrn. Bat. 133, Gulfport, 1976-78; chief of staff Naval Constrn. Regiment, Port Hueneme, Calif., 1978-81; comdr. officer Pub. Works Ctr., Great Lake, Ill., 1981-83; vice comdr. Pacific divsn., 1983-86, dir. constrn. Diego Garcia, 1986-87; retired USN, 1987; sr. group engr. Martin Marietta, Orlando, 1987-92; ops. mgr. Brown & Root Inc., Houston, 1992—; civil engr. cons., 1997-98; v.p. RSI, Inc., 1997-98. Author: Analysis of the Imperial Iranian Navy Construction Program, 1974. Mem. ASCE, SPE, Soc. Am. Mil. Engrs. (pres. Diego Garcia post 1992), USN Inst. Republican. Roman Catholic. Home: PO Box 535 Thomasville AL 36784-0535

DAVIS, GEORGE A., pharmacologist, medical researcher. Pharmacy intern Kroger Pharmacy, Little Rock, 1990-93; pharmaceutics lab asst. Clin. Pharmacokinetics Lab. U. Ark., 1991-93; clin. staff pharmacist Med. Ctr. U. Ky., Lexington, 1993-97, lectr., 1995—, asst. prof. dept. pharm. practice and sci., 1997—; mem. resident recruitment com., resident survey com. U. Ky. Med. Ctr., 1993-95; presenter in field. Jour. referee Pharmacotherapy, Annals of Pharmacotherapy, Am. Jour. Health Sys. Pharmacy; contbr. articles to profl. jours. Psychiat. Drug Therapy fellow Am. Soc. Hosp. Pharmacists, 1995, Geriatric Drug Therapy fellow, 1996. Mem. Am. Soc. Health Sys. Pharmacists, Am. Coll. Clin. Pharmacy, Kappa Psi. Office: U Ky Coll Pharmacy 800 Rose St Rm 117 Lexington KY 40536-0001

DAVIS, GEORGE CULLOM, historian; b. Aurora, Ill., May 2, 1935; s. George Cullom and Mary Elizabeth (Scripps) D.; m. Marilyn Louise Whittaker, June 22, 1957 (div. Mar. 1974); children: Catherine, Lesa, Charles; m. Ann Elizabeth Chapman, May 27, 1976. AB, Princeton U., 1957; MA, U. Ill., Urbana, 1961, PhD, 1968. Instr. Punahou Sch., Honolulu, 1957-59, U. Ill., Urbana, 1962-64; asst. prof. Ind. U., Bloomington, 1964-70, assoc. dean, 1967-70; assoc. prof. Sangamon State U., Springfield, Ill., 1970-74, prof., 1974-95; prof. emeritus, 1995—; prof. history U. Ill.-Springfield, 1974—; dir., sr. editor Lincoln Legal Papers Documentary Edit., 1988—; bd. dirs. Bank One, Springfield; cons. John Nuveen & Co., Chgo., 1989—, Meml. Med. Ctr., Springfield, 1991—. Author: History With a Tape Recorder: An Oral History Handbook, 1972, 4th edit., 1985; co-author: Oral History: From Tape to Tape, 1977, Bench and Bar on the Illinoir Frontier, 1979, The Prairie Bondman, 1996, Memorial Days, 1997; editor: Bicentennial Studies in Sangamon History, 1973-78; co-editor: The Public and the Private Lincoln: Contemporary Perspectives, 1979, Abraham Lincoln Association Papers, 1981-86; contbr. numerous articles to profl. jours.; editl. advisor Scholar Book Revs. on CD-ROM, 1991-93. Del. Dem. Nat. Conv., 1972; pres. Springfield Pub. Schs. Found., 1987-88. Recipient Pelzer award Orgn. Am. Historians, 1962, award of Merit Ill. State Hist. Soc., 1975, Writer of Yr. award Friends of Lincoln Libr., 1989; Fulbright Rsch. scholar, 1987-88; fellow Newberry Libr., 1977, NEH/Woodrow Wilson Found. Inst., 1980, NEH Summer Inst. on Pub. History, 1984; grantee Ill. Bicentennial Commn., 1974-75, Ill. State Libr., 1975, 79-81, Ill. Legis. Coun., 1979-87, Ill. Humanities Coun., 1980-82, NEH, 1990-92, 94—, Nat. Hist. Publs. and Records Commn., 1990—, Ill. Bar Found., 1990-91, Ency. Britannica, 1991, Shelby C. Davis Found., 1991—, William Nelson Cromwell Found., 1992—. Mem. Manuscript Soc., Assn. for Documentary Editing (chmn. constitution com. 1990-94, pres. 1997-98), Ill. Coalition of Libr. Advocates (bd. dirs. 1982-84), Ill. Humanities Coun. (bd. dirs. 1983-89, vice chair 1985-87, chair 1987-89), Ill. Assn. for Advancement of History, Ill. State Hist. Soc. (v.p. 1974-75, 82-83, bd. dirs. 1979-82, exec. com. 1979-82, adv. bd. 1994—), Sangamon County Hist. Soc. (bd. dirs. 1971-74, 79-82, v.p. 1981-82, 90-91, pres. 1991-92), Orgn. Am. Historians (treas. 1984-93), Oral History Assn. (nominating com. 1978-79, 85-87, colloquium program com. 1978, chmn. nat. workshop 1979, nat. coun. 1980-85, v.p. 1982-83, pres. 1983-84), Abraham Lincoln Assn. (bd. dirs. 1977—, chmn. publs. com. 1981-87, v.p. 1984-86, pres. 1995-96). Democrat. Home: 2624 E Lake Shore Dr Springfield IL 62707-5533 Office: Lincoln Legal Papers Old State Capitol Springfield IL 62701

DAVIS, GEORGE DONALD, executive land use policy consultant; b. Oneida, N.Y., Nov. 19, 1942; s. Pearl Floyd and Kathrine Virginia (Connolly) D.; m. Anita Face Riner, June 26, 1976; children: Maria Lisa, Brett Hollis, Sarah Bessie, Lara Emily; stepchildren: Andrea G. Riner, Joel S. Riner. BS in Forestry, SUNY, 1964; postgrad., Cornell U., 1968, 70. Forester, pub. land adminstr. U.S. Forest Svc. Dept. Agr., Colo., 1964-68; ecologist Gov. N.Y. State Temp. Study Commn. on Future of Adirondacks, 1969-71; pvt. land use and natural resources cons. Ithaca, N.Y., 1971; dir. planning Adirondack Park Agy., Ray Brook, N.Y., 1971-76; exec. dir. Wilderness Soc., Washington, 1976-77; spl. asst. U.S. Forest Svc., Washington, 1977-79; dep. forest supr. Idaho Panhandle Nat. Forests, Coeur d'Alene, 1979-82; land use, natural resource cons. Wadhams, N.Y., 1982-94; program dir. Adirondack Coun., 1983-88; exec. dir. Adirondack Land Trust, 1984-88; prin. Davis Assocs., 1988—; pres. Ecol. Sustainable Devel., Inc., 1994-97; coord. Global Assocs. in Sustainable Develop., 1997—; project dir. Land Use Policy and Allocation Program for Lake Baikal Watershed in Russia, 1991-93, Lake Hovsgol/Selenge River Watershed in Mongolia, 1992-94, Ussuri River Watershed in Russian Far East and China, 1993-97, Altai Rep. Russia, 1994—, Atlantic Regions Nicaragua, 1994—; exec. dir. Gov. Commn. on Adirondacks in the 21st Century, 1989-90; mem. environ. task force Rockefeller Bros. Fund; mem. Hudson Basin project task force Rockefeller Found. Co-author: The Unfinished Agenda, 1977, Developing a Land Conservation Strategy, 1987, Ecosystem Representative as a Criterion for World Wilderness Designation, 1987, 2020 Vision: Fulfilling the Promise of the Adirondack Park, 1988, Completing the Adirondack Wilderness System, 1990, The Lake Baikal Region in the Twenty-First Century: A Model of Sustainable Development or Continued Degradation?, 1993, A Comprehensive National Program of Sustainable Land Use Policies for the Lake Hovsgol-Selenge River Watershed, 1994, A Sustainable Land Use and Allocation Program for the Ussuri/Wusuli River Watershed and Adjacent Territories, 1996; contbr. to profl. pubs. Active Gov. N.Y. State Forest Industry Task Force, 1987-89, N.Y.-New Eng. Gov. Task Force on No. Forest Lands, 1988-90. MacArthur fellow, 1989—. Roman Catholic. Home and Office: 2482 N 32d St Springfield OR 97477-7900 *The basic goal of my life has been to promote land and natural resource stewardship, through direct action and example, to help insure that our planet's resources are more equitably distributed among members of the present generation and are sufficient for future generations.*

DAVIS, GEORGE EDWARD, industrial designer; b. Hugo, Okla., July 3, 1928; s. Silas William and Florence Elva (White) D.; m. Betty Sue Walker, July 21, 1951; children: Susan Elizabeth, Laura Ellen. student U. Tex., 1946-49; BA, Art Ctr. Coll. of Design, L.A., 1956. Registered interior designer, Tex. Staff designer Friedrich Refrigeration Co., San Antonio, 1957; design dir. comml. div. Woodarts Co., Houston, 1958-59; staff designer Brede, Inc., Houston, 1960-61; designer, co-founder Concept Planners and Designers, Houston, 1962-64; mgr. archtl. dept. Lockheed-Calif. Co., NASA Manned Spacecraft Ctr., Clear Lake, Tex., 1965-66; staff designer Litton Industries, office products div., Austin, San Antonio, 1967-68; staff designer Clegg Design Group, San Antonio, 1969-76; ind. design cons., San Antonio, 1977—; interior designer for USAA, San Antonio, 1991—; dir. Systemics, Inc., San Antonio, Christian Bookmark, Inc., San Antonio, 1972-88. Trustee, San Antonio Christian Sch., 1973-82, chmn. bd., 1979-80; bd. elders Christ Presbyterian Ch., San Antonio, 1982-85; mem. Zoning Commn., City of Castle Hills, 1983-93, councilman City Coun., 1993-94, Architectural Rev. Com., 1995—. Served with USAF, 1950-54. Decorated D.F.C., Air medal with 3 oak leaf clusters. Mem. AIA (profl. affiliate), Tex. Soc. Architects (profl. affiliate, award of merit 1968). Home: 205 Wisteria Dr Castle Hills TX 78213-2109 Office: PO Box 13385 San Antonio TX 78213-0385

DAVIS, GEORGE KELSO, nutrition biochemist, educator; b. Pitts., July 2, 1910; s. Ross Irwin and Jennie (Kelso) D.; m. Ruthanna Wood, Jan. 25, 1936; children—Dorothy Jeanne (Mrs. Arthur C. Aikin, Jr.), Mary Ellen (Mrs. W. Edgar Benedict), Ruthanna Marie (Mrs. Donald W. Davidson), Virginia Kay (Mrs. John M. Fedison), Robert Wyatt, George William. B.S., Pa. State U., 1932; Ph.D., Cornell U., 1937. Research asst. Cornell U., 1932-37; research asst. prof. chemistry Mich. State U., 1937-42; prof. nutrition, animal nutritionist U. Fla., Gainesville, 1942-79; prof. emeritus U. Fla., 1979—, dir. nuclear scis., 1960-65, dir. biol. scis., 1965-70; dir. research U. Fla., Gainesville, 1970-75; prof. human nutrition U. Hawaii, 1985; Mem. Fla. Nuclear Commn.; chmn. Internat. Biol. Program Sect. Use and Mgmt. Biol. Resources, U. Fla. Council Oak Ridge Asso. Univs.; cons. minister agr., Costa Rica, univs. Costa Rica, Buenos Aires, San Marco, Peru, U. Agraria, Peru, Sao Paulo, Brazil, FAO, Dept. Agr., OEA-INTA, Argentina, Dept. Health, Edn. and Welfare, Nutrition Found., Fla. Dept. Agr.; mem. food and nutrition bd., com. animal nutrition, internat. biol. program com. Nat. Acad. Sci.-NRC, also chmn. bd. agr. and renewable resources, 1980-82; dir. human nutrition research grants program U.S. Dept. Agr., 1977-79; rev. bds. NSF, Nat. Acad. Scis., NIH; U. Fla. Faculty lectr., 1960; hon. prof. U. Chile, 1961—; Wellcome vis. prof. U. Ill., 1978; pres. Nat. Nutritional Consortium, 1977-78. Editor: (with A.E. Harper) Nutrition in Health and Disease and International Development. Mem. editorial bd. Jour. Animal Sci.; contbr. articles to profl. jours., chpts. books. Recipient Faculty award Fla. Blue Key, 1958, Disting. Faculty award U. Fla., 1960, Scientist of Yr. award Mus. Sci. and Industry Fla. 1981, Disting. Alumnus award Pa. State U., 1982, Disting. Achievement award U. Fla., 1996, George F. Hixson award 1997. Fellow Am. Inst. Nutrition (chmn. com. nutrition and trace elements 1961-64, nat. exec. com. jour. 1961, Borden award 1964, C.A. Elvehjem award 1985, mem. council 1971-74, pres. 1975-76, chmn. fellows com. 1984-92); mem. NAS, AAAS, Am. Inst. Biol. Scis. (chmn. S.E. regional coun. biol. satellite programs 1965-72), Am. Chem. Soc. (sec.-treas. Fla. 1955, chmn. 1958, Fla. award 1956, Kenneth A. Spencer award 1980, chmn. Frasch awards com. 1980-91), Am. Soc. Animal Sci. (nat. v.p. 1961-62, sec. So. sect. 1960-61), Am. Soc. Biol. Chemists, Soc. Exptl. Biology and Medicine, Am. Dairy Assn., Am. Nuclear Soc., Soc. for Environ. Geochemistry and Health (pres. 1976-77), Fedn. Am. Socs. Exptl. Biology (chmn. pub. affairs com. 1975-77), Internat. Union Nutrition Scis. (chmn. U.S. nat. com., pres. XII Internat. Nutrition Congress), Sao Paulo Vet. Soc. (hon.), Peruvian Vet. Assn. (hon.), Kiwanis, Sigma Xi (pres. Fla. 1956-57), Alpha Zeta, Phi Lambda Upsilon, Gamma Sigma Delta, Phi Eta Sigma, Phi Sigma, Gamma Sigma Epsilon, Phi Kappa Phi, Blue Key. Home: 2903 SW 2nd Ct Gainesville FL 32601-9057

DAVIS, GEORGE LINN, banker; b. Des Moines, July 9, 1934; s. James Cox and Elizabeth (Linn) D.; m. Anne Roberts, May 1955 (div. Jan. 1967); children: James, Elliott, George Linn; m. Mary Elizabeth Graham, Apr. 27, 1968; children: Stephen, Thomas. B.A., Yale U., 1956; M.B.A., Harvard U., 1958. Sr. v.p. Citibank NA, N.Y.C., 1958-81; exec. v.p. First Chgo. Corp., Chgo., 1981-87; Citicorp/Citibank group exec. N.Am. Fin. Group, N.Y.C., 1987-90; chmn. Scarborough Ptnrs., Inc., N.Y.C., 1990—; pres., CEO, bd. dirs. 1st Am. Bankshares Inc., Washington, 1990-91; bd. dirs. Sealy Inc.; CEO Banco de Venezuela Internat., Syscon Inc.; mem. adv. bd. Charterhouse Internat., Inc. Trustee Central Park Conservancy, Nat. Stroke Assn. Mem. Robert Morris Assocs., Assn. Equipment Lessors (bd. dirs. 1974-76), Chgo. Club, Glenview Club, Sleepy Hollow Country Club. Republican. Office: Scarborough Partners Inc 450 Park Ave Fl 6 New York NY 10022-2605

DAVIS, GEORGE OSMOND, communications executive; b. Seattle, July 30, 1957; s. George Osmond Sr. and Delores Lillian (Smith) D.; m. Jan Perkins; children: Felecia, Michele, Mark. Student, Portland State U., 1981-83; BS in Bus. Adminstrn. and Mgmt., U. Redlands, Calif., 1993; MBA, U. So. Calif., 1996. Technician Sta. KYYX, Seattle, 1976-77; technician, announcer Sta. KYAC, Seattle, 1977-78; radio announcer Sta. KORD, Tri-Cities, Wash., 1979-80; master control operator Sta. KNDU-TV, Tri-Cities, 1979-80; assign editor Sta. KGW-TV, Portland, Oreg., 1980-83; remote supr. Sta. KOMO-TV, Seattle, 1983-84; transmission supr. ABC-TV, L.A., 1984-87; video ops. mgr. IDB Communications, Culver City, Calif., 1987—, dir. west coast ops., 1990, gen. mgr. west coast ops., 1991-95; v.p. western region ops. Keystone Comms., Culver City, 1995-96; v.p. worldwide satellite ops. Sony Pictures Entertainment, Culver City, 1996—; v.p. internat. channels ops. Columbia Tri-Star Internat. TV (Sony Pictures); bd. dirs. L.A. Pub. Access Channel. Bd. dirs. Calif. African Am. Mus. Mem. Black Journalists Assn. (chmn. bd. L.A. chpt. 1986-88, dir. Western region). Dem. Catholic. Avocations: running, reading, golf. Office: Sony Pictures Ent 10202 Washington Blvd Culver City CA 90232-3119

DAVIS, GERALD, umpire; b. St. Louis, Feb. 22, 1953; m. Lynn Mentzel, Oct. 9, 1980; 1 child, Jeremy Joseph. Profl. baseball player St. Louis; umpire Midwest League, Ea. League, Am. Assn., Fla. Instrnl. League, P.R. Winter League, Nat. League, 1985—; basketball coach U. Wis.-Fox Valley Jr. Coll. Avocation: golf. Office: Nat League 350 Park Ave New York NY 10022 Office: Umpires Union 1735 Market St Philadelphia PA 19103

DAVIS, GLENN, communications company executive. Chief tech. officer Project Cool Inc., Palo Alto, Calif., 1996—. Office: Project Cool Inc 450 Kipling St Palo Alto CA 94301-1529*

DAVIS, GLORIA JEAN, gerontology clinical specialist; b. Victoria, Va., Oct. 27, 1949; d. James and Hattie (Ruffin) Davis; m. Babafemi Elufiede, 1980; 5 children. AA, Morris Harvey Coll., Charleston, W.Va., 1971; BA in Sociology and Psychology, U. Charleston, 1979; MA in Gerontology and Sociology, Fisk U., Nashville, 1985. Cert. Reiki master. Charge nurse Kanawha Valley Hosp., Charleston, W.Va., 1971-72; community nurse ACTION/V.I.S.T.A., Washington, 1972-74; geriatric nurse Riverside Nursing & Convalescent Home, St. Albans, W.Va., 1977-78; nurse mgr. St. Francis Hosp., Charleston, 1974-81; mem. Crossroads Africa, Kenya, East Africa, 1980-81; substance abuse specialist, nurse/counselor Shawnee Hills Treatment Ctr., St. Albans, 1981-83; nurse therapist Psychogeriatric unit Parkview Med. Ctr., Nashville, 1984-85; gerontology clin. specialist West Paces Ferry Hosp., Atlanta, 1987-88; asst. dir. nursing, clin. specialist Glenwood Manor Nursing Home, Decatur, Ga., 1988-89; dir. nursing, asst. adminstr. Glenwood Manor Nursing Home, 1989-92; gerontology clin. specialist Providence Convalescence, 1992-94; healthcare cord. Adult Care & Share, 1994-99; wellness dir. Sunrise Eastover, 1999—; dir. rehab. svcs. Providence Convalescence; gerontology clin. specialist cons.; long-term care specialist; instr. C.P. C.C., Charlotte, N.C., 1995—. Recipient award of nursing excellence N.C. Inst. Nursing, 1997. Mem. ARC, Gerontol. Soc. Am., Am. Soc. of Aging, Holistic Nurses Soc., Adult Day Care Assn., So. Gerontol. Assn.

DAVIS, GORDON RICHARD FUERST, retired biologist, translator; b. Prince Albert, Sask., Can., Apr. 5, 1925; s. Louis James Davis and Nora Sylvia Fuerst; m. Marie Bérengère Pauline Bérubé, May 25, 1949; children: Joseph Richard Kevin, Marie Mélanie Élise, Marie Raymonde Joceline, Marie-Thérèse Danielle. B.Sc. in Zoology with honors, McGill U., 1948, M.Sc., 1949, Ph.D., 1952. Agrl. scientist biol. control unit Can. Dept. Agr., Que., 1948-52; research officer research br. Can. Dept. Agr., Saskatoon, Sask., 1952-65, research scientist research br., 1965-85; translator Co-Operators Fin. Svcs. Ltd., Regina, Sask., Can., 1987-90; pres., mng. dir. Triple-D Translation Svcs., Regina, Sask., 1990-95; mem. Div. III sci. curriculum com. Sask. Dept. Edn., 1974-80. Contbr. articles to profl. jours. Bd. trustees Saskatoon Catholic Bd. Edn., 1974-77; mem. Sask German Council, Inc., rep to Concordia German Language Sch., 1986-87, v.p., 1986-87. Served with Royal Can. Navy Vol. Res., 1944-45. Carpenter Teaching fellow, 1950-51. Mem. Nutrition Soc. Can. (sec. 1973-77, v.p. 1979-80, pres. 1980-81), Can. Fedn. Biol. Socs. (dir. 1973-77, 80-81, hon. sec.-treas. 1980-84), Life Ins. Inst. Can. (linguistic services sect. 1987-92), Assn. Translators and Interpreters Sask. (assoc.). Roman Catholic. Home: 2345 Broad St Apt 507, Regina, SK Canada S4P 1Z1 *A knowledge of as many areas of learning as possible and a general understanding of related and unrelated fields help to push back the limitations of our horizons; a dedication to one goal at a time; a desire to improve the environment for the general good and acknowledgement by future inquirers of the value of the contributions that one has made: all provide their own opportunities in a hostile world.*

DAVIS, GRAY, governor; b. N.Y.C., Dec. 26, 1942; m. Sharon Ryer, Feb. 20, 1983. BA cum laude, Stanford U., 1964; JD, Columbia U., 1967. Chief of staff to Gov. Jerry Brown State of Calif., Sacramento, 1974-81, mem. Calif. State Assembly, 1982-86, state contr., 1986-94, lt. gov., 1995-99, gov., 1999—; chmn. Housing and Community Devel. Com., Calif. Coun. on Criminal Justice, Franchise Tax Bd., State Lands Commn.; mem. Bd. Equalization, State Tchrs. Retirement System, Pub. Employees Retirement System, Nat. Coun. Institutional Investors. Founder Calif. Found. for the Protection of Children. Office: Office of Governor State Capitol Sacramento CA 95814-4906*

DAVIS, GREGORY T., radio station executive. Gen. mgr. WRR-FM, Dallas. Office: WRR-FM PO Box 159001 Dallas TX 75315-9001*

DAVIS, H. ALAN, retired airline captain, consultant; b. Knoxville, Tenn., Apr. 24, 1932; s. Fred Edwin Davis and Rose Lee (Perrin) Davis Williams; m. Betty Jean Carter, June 11, 1951; children: Cynthia Lynn Davis Roper, Linda Susan Davis Williamson, Scott Alan. BS, Jackson Coll., Honolulu, 1965; disting. grad., Indsl. Coll. of Armed Forces, 1970; M of Arts in Teaching, Rollins Coll., 1972; EdD, Nova U., 1980. Cert. FAA in airline transport. Commd. 1st sgt. USAF, 1951, advanced through grades to maj., 1972; dir. ops., chief pilot Sky Safari Air Travel Club, Orlando, Fla., 1972-73; co. check airman, capt. Rich Internat. Airways, Miami, Fla., 1979-85; dept. chmn., tchr. Maynard Evans High Sch., Orlando, 1973-85; co. check airman, line capt. Trans Air Link Corp., Miami, 1985-92; with ops. dept. Walt Disney World, Orlando, Fla., 1992-94; chief pilot Hemisphere Internat. Airlines, Miami, 1994-96; ret., 1996; entertainment ops. staff Walt Disney World, 1996—; Air Santo Domingo line capt. APA Internat., 1992-93. Recipient Nat. Achievement award, Am. Soc. Aerospace Edn., 1980. Mem. DAV (life), Aircraft Owners and Pilots Assn., Retired Officers Assn., Shriners, Masons, Quiet Birdmen. Republican. Avocations: golfing, hunting, fishing. Home: 8208 Banyan Blvd Orlando FL 32819-4145

DAVIS, HARLEY CLEO, retired military officer; b. Van Buren, Ark., May 7, 1941; s. Aleta (Johnson) D.; m. Patricia Ann White, Mar. 9, 1985. BS, Ark. Tech. U., 1963; MA, Ea. Ky. U., 1972; exec. devel. program, U. N.H., 1987. Commd. 2d lt. U.S. Army, 1963, advanced through grades to maj. gen., 1993; platoon leader 1st Bn., 50th inf., 2d Armored Div., 1963; various assignments, 1963-80; comdr. 3d Bn., 5th Spl. Forces Group, Ft. Bragg, N.C., 1980-82; chief leadership br. Hdqrs. Dept. of the Army, Washington, 1982-84; chief of staff JFK Spl. Warfare Ctr. and Sch., Ft. Bragg, 1985-86; comdr. 5th Spl. Forces Group, Ft. Campbell, Ky., 1987-89; asst. comdt. JFK Spl. Warfare Ctr. and Sch., Ft. Bragg, 1989-91; dep. commdg. gen. U.S. Army Sp. Ops. Command, Ft. Bragg, 1991-92; comdg. gen. U.S. Army Spl. Forces Command (Airborne), Ft. Bragg, 1992-95; dep. commdg. gen. Fifth U.S. Army (west), Ft. Lewis, Wash., 1995-97. Decorated DSM with oak leaf cluster, Legion of Merit, Soldier's Medal, Bronze Star with two oak leaf clusters, Air medal with with oak leaf cluster. Office: Internatl Charter Inc of Oregon 1860 Hawthorne Ave NE Ste 390 Salem OR 97303

DAVIS, HARRY REX, political science educator; b. Ozona, Tex., Nov. 9, 1921; s. Rex Oris and Mima (Gowin) D.; m. Ruth Elizabeth Greenlee, Sept. 6, 1947; children: Peter Gowin, Scott Andrew, Martha Greenlee. BA summa cum laude, Tex. Christian U., 1942; AM, U. Chgo., 1949, PhD, 1951; postdoctorate, Union Theol. Sem., 1952-53. Teaching fellow Tex. Christian U., 1945-46; mem. faculty dept. govt. Beloit (Wis.) Coll., 1948-90, assoc. prof., 1956-59, prof., 1959-90, chmn. dept., 1959-84, prof. emeritus, 1990—; Cons. ch. and soc. dept. World Council Chs., 1969. Author: (with others) Small City Government, 1962, Colleges and Commitments, 1971; Editor: (with others) Reinhold Niebuhr on Politics, 1960. Mem. Beloit City Coun., 1959-60; chmn. Beloit Dem. Com., 1956, 61-63; mgr. campaigns congl. candidates; mem. Beloit Bd. Ethics, 1975-81, Wis. Gov.'s Coun. on Jud. Selection, 1983-86; mem. Beloit Bd. Health, 1996—, chmn., 1996-98. With USAAF, 1942-45. Ford faculty fellow, 1952-53; Social Sci. Research Council grantee; Rockefeller Found. grantee. Mem. Midwest Polit. Sci. Assn. (sec.-treas. 1959-65, mem. exec. coun. 1966-68), Am. Polit. Sci. Assn. (chmn. Burdette award com. 1979), Am. Soc. Polit. and Legal Philosophy, Soc. Christian Ethics. Democrat. Presbyterian (elder, coun. on ch. and society 1965-72, Gen. Assembly commr. 1991). Home: 735 Harrison Ave Beloit WI 53511-5529 Office: Beloit Coll Dept Government Beloit WI 53511

DAVIS, HARVEY, commercial photographer, videographer; b. Poughkeepsie, N.Y., July 19, 1946; s. Harvey and Louise (Rowe) D.; m. Jeanette Cuchelo, Feb. 7, 1997; 1 child, Debra Bova. Student, Dutchess C.C., Poughkeepsie, N.Y., 1965-67. Profl. photographer N.Y., 1975—. Mem. YMCA, Poughkeepsie, 1975—. Mem. Dutchess County Profl. Photographers Assn., Profl. Photographers of Am. Avocations: camping, fishing, jogging. E-mail: www.pojonews.com/dpv. Office: 111 College Ave Poughkeepsie NY 12603-2804

DAVIS, HELEN GORDON, former state senator; b. N.Y.C., Dec. 25; m. Gene Davis; children: Stephanie, Karen, Gordon. BA, Bklyn. Coll.; postgrad., U. South Fla., 1967-70. Tchr., High Sch. Commerce, N.Y.C., Hillsborough High Sch., Tampa, Fla.; grad. asst. U. South Fla., 1968; mem. Fla. Ho. of Reps. (1st woman to be elected in 1974 from Hills Co., 1st woman to chair the legis. delegation), 1974-88, state senator, 1988-92; mem. Fla Supreme Ct. Commn. on Gender Bias in the Cts., 1988-90; mem. Fla. Supreme Ct. Commn. on Mediation and Arbitration, 1987—. chmn. senate appropriations subcom. human svcs., mem. rules com., internat. trade and econ. devel. com., health and rehab. svcs. com. Jud. chmn. Local Govt. Study Commn. Hillsborough County (Fla.), 1964; mem. Tampa Commn. on Juvenile Delinquency, 1966-69, Mayor's Citizens Adv. Com., 1966-69, Quality Edn. Commn., 1966-68, Gov.'s Citizen Com. for Ct. Reform, 1972, Hillsborough County Planning Commn., 1973-74; mem. Gov.'s Commn. on Jud. Reform, 1976; mem. employment com. Commn. Community Relations, 1966-69; by-laws chmn. Arts Coun. Tampa, 1971-74; 1st v.p. Tampa Symphony Guild, 1974; bd. dirs. U. South Fla. Found., 1968-74, Stop Rape, 1973-74; founder Ctr. for Women, Tampa, 1978; past pres. PTA; active adv. commn. Nat. Child Care Action Campaign, Nat. Ctr. for Crime and Delinquency; chair Hillsborough Dem. Exec. Com., also pres. Recipient U. South Fla. Young Democrats Humanitarian award, 1974, Diana award NOW, 1975, Woman of Achievement in Arts award Tampa, 1975, Tampa Human Rels. award, 1976, Hannah G. Solomon Citizen of Yr. award, 1980, St. Petersburg Times/Fla. Civil Liberties award, 1980, Friend of Edn. award, 1981, Fla. Alliance for Responsible Parenting award, 1981, Humanitarian award Judeo-Christian Clinic, 1984, Fla. Network of Runaway Youth award, 1985, Ctr. for Women Leader-advocate Friend award, 1985, Nat. Assn. Juvenile Ct. Judges Appreciation award 1986, Legis. Leadership appreciation Centre for Women, 1986, Children's Crisis Ctr. Leadership award, 1987, AAUW leadership award, 1987, Hillsborough County Halfway House appreciation, 1988, Martin Luther King award City of Tampa, 1988, Nat. Fedn. Dem. Women appreciation, 1989, Dept. Legal Affairs appreciation, 1990, Superwoman award Mus. Sci. and Industry, 1990, Nat. Childcare Merit award Nat. Assn. Sch. Psychologists, 1992, Am. Judicature award Am. Judicature Assn., 1993; named. Fla. Motion Picture and TV Outstanding Legislator, 1990, others; elected to Fla. Women's Hall of Fame, 1999. Mem. LWV (pres. Hillsborough County 1966-69, lobbyist, Fla. adminstrn. of justice chmn. 1969-74), Temple Guild Sisterhood (past pres.), Am. Arbitration Assn., Hills County Expy. Authority, Fla. Supreme Ct. Commn. Arbitration. Home: 45 Adalia Ave Tampa FL 33606-3301*

DAVIS, HENRY ARNOLD, healthcare company executive; b. Memphis, Mar. 3, 1964; s. James Arthur and Eddie Lee Davis; 1 child, Tamala R. BSEE, Yale U., 1986; MBA, Stanford U., 1992. Ops. analyst Allied Signal Aerospace, Torrance, Calif., 1992-93, sr. ops. analyst, 1993; engagement mgr. Allied Signal, Inc., Morristown, N.J., 1994; mgr. new bus. devel. Allied Signal Comml. Avionics sys., Olathe, Kans., 1995, distbn. mgr., 1995-96; dir. procurement Rockwell Automotive, Troy, Mich., 1996-97; plant mgr. Meritor Automotive, Canal Fulton, Ohio, 1997-99; v.p. Materials Aultman Health Found., Canton, Ohio, 1999—. Vol. coach East Palo Alto Mid. Sch., Palo Alto, Calif., 1992. Mem. Nat. Black MBA Assn., C. of C. (bd. trustees 1997). Avocations: golf, tennis, skiing, reading, chess. Home: 6964 Queensgate St NW Canton OH 44718-3804 Office: Aultman Health Found 2600 6th St SW Canton OH 44710

DAVIS, HENRY BARNARD, JR., lawyer; b. East Grand Rapids, Mich., June 3, 1923; s. Henry Barnard and Ethel Margaret (Turnbull) D.; m. Margaret Lees Wilson, Aug. 27, 1946; children: Caroline Dellenbusch, Laura Davis, George B. BA, Yale U., 1945; JD, U. Mich., 1950; LLD, Olivet Coll., 1983. Bar: Mich. 1951; U.S. Dist. Ct. (we. dist.) Mich. 1956, U.S. Ct. Apls. (6th cir.) 1971, U.S. Supreme Ct. 1978. Assoc. Allaben, Wiarda, Hayes & Hewitt, 1951-52; ptnr. Hayes, Davis & Dellenbusch PLC, Grand Rapids, 1952—. Mem. Kent County Bd. Commrs., 1968-72, Community Mental Health Bd., 1970-94, past chmn.; trustee, sec. bd. Olivet Coll., 1965-91, chmn. law com., gen. counsel, 1975-91, trustee emeritus 1991—; bd. dirs. Jr. Achievement Grand Rapids, 1960-65; chair Grand Rapids Historic Preservation Com., 1977-79. Republican. Trustee, East Congregational Ch., 1979-81. Served with USAAF, 1943-46; Philippines. ABA, Mich. Bar Assn., Grand Rapids Round Table (pres. 1969). Lodge: Masons. Home: 30 Mayfair Dr NE Grand Rapids MI 49503-3831 Office: 535 Fountain St NE Grand Rapids MI 49503-3421

DAVIS, HENRY JEFFERSON, JR., former naval officer; b. Quincy, Fla., May 6, 1929; s. Henry and Sara Jewell (Davis) D.; m. Ernestine Hunt Tully, June 8, 1955; children: Frances Cornelia Davis Wallington, Jessica Leigh Davis Coughlin, H.J. Davis V, George Walton Davis II. Student, U. Fla., 1947-48; B.S., Fla. State U., 1952; postgrad., U.S. Naval Acad., 1949-51; M.S., U.S. Naval Postgrad. Sch., 1962. Commd. ensign U.S. Navy, 1952, advanced through grades to rear adm., 1977; comdg. officer Naval Security Group Activity, Winter Harbor, Maine, 1968-70; asst. chief of staff to comdr. in chief U.S. Pacific Fleet, dir. Naval Security Group Pacific, 1973-76; chief Nat. Security Agy., Pacific, cryptologic adv. to comdr. in chief Pacific, 1976-77; asst. dir. plans and resources Nat. Security Agy., 1977-79, dep. dir. ops., 1979-82; ret., 1982; mgmt. cons. State of Fla. Info. Resource Commn., 1984-92. Mem. Gadsden County (Fla.) Sch. Bd., 1984-94, chmn., 1988-91, 93-94; bd. dirs. Fla. Sch. Bd. Assn., 1990-92; mem. Quincy-Gadsden Airport Authority, 1994—; trustee Fla. Bapt. Theol. Coll., 1995—; dir., treas. Gadsden Arts Inc., 1996—. Decorated Def. Superior Service medal, Bronze star, Def. Meritorious Service medal, others. Baptist.

DAVIS, HERBERT OWEN, lawyer; b. D.C., June 11, 1935; s. Owen Steir and Claudie Lea (Pointer) D.; children: Herbert O. Jr., Ann P., Paul B. BA, U. N.C., 1957; JD, Duke U., 1960. Bar: N.C. 1960, U.S. Dist. Ct. (mid. dist.) N.C. 1960. Assoc. Smith Moore Smith Schell & Hunter, Greensboro, N.C., 1960-66, ptnr., 1966-86; ptnr. Smith Helms Mulliss & Moore, Greensboro, 1986—; bd. dirs. Custom Industries, Inc., Greensboro. Editor in chief Duke Law Jour., 1959-60. Mem. ABA, N.C. Bar Assn., Greensboro Country Club, Greensboro City Club (bd. dirs.), The Carolina Club, Phi Beta Kappa. Home: 2303 Danbury Rd Greensboro NC 27408-5123 Office: Smith Helms Mulliss & Moore 300 N Greene St Ste 1400 Greensboro NC 27401-2171

DAVIS, HOWARD JEFFREY, lawyer; b. Phila., Oct. 2, 1955; s. Herbert U. and Elma G. Davis; m. Barbara Salter, Aug. 10, 1980; children: Sara, Amanda, Eliza. BA, Princeton (N.J.) U., 1977; JD, U. Chgo., 1980. Assoc. Schnader, Harrison, Segal & Lewis, Phila., 1980-83; assoc. Kleinbard, Bell & Brecker, Phila., 1984-85, ptnr., 1986-98, mng. ptnr., 1999—; bd. dirs. The Robert Filter Group, Darby, Pa., 1990—, GDG Internat., Inc., Pa., 1986, JJB Group, Phila., 1994—; guest lectr. Pa. Bar Ins., Phila., 1994—. Bd. dirs. Phila. Geriatric Ctr., 1996—; bd. trustees Fed. of Jewish Agencies, Phila., 1993—, exec. com., 1996—. Recipient Young Leadership award Fedn. of Jewish Agencies, 1992. Mem. ABA (corp. sect.), Pa. Bar Assn., Phila. Bar Assn. Avocations: golf, tennis, reading. Home: 2 Wayne Cir Lower Gwynedd PA 19002-1931 Office: Kleinbard Bell & Brecker 1900 Market St Ste 700 Philadelphia PA 19103-3573

DAVIS, HOWARD TED, engineering educator; b. Hendersonville, N.C., Aug. 2, 1937; s. William Howard and Gladys Isabel (Rhodes) D.; m. Eugenia Asimakopoulos, Sept. 15, 1960 (dec. July 1996); children: William Howard II, Maria Katherine. BS in Chemistry, Furman U., 1959; PhD in Chem. Physics, U. Chgo., 1962. Postdoctoral fellow Free U. of Brussels, 1962-63; asst. prof. U. Minn., Mpls., 1963-66, assoc. prof., 1966-69, prof., 1969-80, prof., head chem. engring. and materials sci., 1980-95, dean Inst. Tech., 1995—, Regent's prof., 1997—. Editor: Springs of Creativity, 1981; author: Statistical Mechanics of Phases, Interfaces and Thin Films, 1995; contbr. over 400 articles to sci. and engring. jours. Fellow Sloan Found., 1967-69, Guggenheim Found., 1969-70. Mem. AAAS, AIChE (Walker award for excellence in publs. 1990), NAE, Am. Chem. Soc., Soc. Petroleum Engrs., Minn. Fedn. Engring. Socs. (Disting. Engr. 1998). Democrat. Methodist. Avocations: tennis, golf, reading, movies. Home: 1822 Mount Curve Ave Minneapolis MN 55403-1018 Office: U Minn 421 Washington Ave SE Minneapolis MN 55455-0373

DAVIS, H(UMPHREY) DENNY, publisher; b. Fayette, Mo., May 8, 1927; s. Lionel Winchester and Sarah Elizabeth (Denny) D.; m. Barbara Ellen Hartsgrove, June 6, 1954; 1 child, Thomas Shackelford. Student, Central Meth. Coll., Fayette, 1944-45, 46-47; BJ, U. Mo., 1949. Reporter, wire editor S.E. Missourian, Cape Girardeau, 1949-54; corr. UPI, Oklahoma City, Tulsa, Denver, 1954-55; exec. UPI, Albuquerque, 1955-56; bur. mgr. UPI, Lima, Peru, 1955-58; mgr. for Brazil UPI, Rio de Janeiro, 1958-68; mgr. no. div. Latin Am. Mexico City, 1968-75; regional exec. Charlotte, N.C., 1975-78; founder, owner pub. Wood Creek Corp., Fayette, 1978—; editor Fayette Advertiser and Democrat-Leader, Fayette, 1984—. Author profl. manual; contbr. articles to mags. and newspapers. Chmn. Fayette Planning and Zoning Commn., 1980-87; chmn. Howard County Rep. Cen. Com., Fayette, 1982-98; pres. Franklin or Bust, Inc., Fayette, 1988—; mem. Santa Fe Trail Nat. Hist. Trail Nat. Adv. Coun., 1991-97. With USN, 1945-46, 50-51. Mem. NRA, Santa Fe Trail Assn., Fayette Round Table Club (pres. 1989-90), Fayette Area C. of C. (pres. 1979), Fayette Area Heritage Assn. (v.p. 1989-91), Am. Legion. Republican. Episcopalian. Avocation: local history. Home: 400 N Church St Fayette MO 65248-1125 Office: Wood Creek Corp 202 E Morrison St Fayette MO 65248-1306

DAVIS, IRVIN, advertising, public relations, broadcast executive; b. St. Louis, Dec. 18, 1926; s. Julius and Anna (Rosen) D.; m. Adrienne Bronstein, Apr. 25, 1968; 1 child, Jennifer Alison. BSBA, Washington U., 1950; postgrad., St. Louis U., 1952; D Humanities (hon.), Nat. Coll., 1981. Pres. Clayton-Davis & Assoc., Inc., St. Louis, 1953—, Admiral Broadcasting Corp., St. Louis, 1983—; c.p., bd. dirs. Nat. Acad. TV Arts and Scis., 1982—; bd. dirs. Truman Bank; pres. Galtex Broadcasting. Author: (books) Room for Three, Comprehensive Tng. in Advt. and Pub. Relations; producer (film) Family Album, 1974, Use It in Good Health, Charlie, 1975. V.p. Boys Town Mo., St. James, 1976-99, Make Today Count, 1985-86; bd. dirs. Crusade Against Crime, St. Louis, 1984-99; bd. dirs. Jackie Joyner Kersee Found., 1997-99. Capt. USAF, 1945-47, PTO. Recipient Freedom Found. award, 1975, Internat. Film and TV Festival award, 1973-75, Internat. Broadcasting award Hollywood Advt. Club, 1965, 77, 82, 83, Cinegolden Eagle award Coun. on Internat. Non-Theatrical Events, 1975, Nat. Emmy award, 1991. Mem. Pub. Relations Soc. Am. (accredited), Advt. Club, Press Club, Am. Med. Writers Assn. Office: Clayton-Davis & Assoc Inc 8229 Maryland Ave Saint Louis MO 63105-3697

DAVIS, J. B., furniture manufacturing executive. CEO Klaussner Furniture Group. Office: Klaussner Corp PO Box 220 Asheboro NC 27204-0220*

DAVIS, J. BRATTON, federal judge. Bar: S.C. Chief bankruptcy judge for S.C., U.S. Bankruptcy Ct., Columbia, 1969—. Office: US Bankruptcy Ct 1100 Laurel St Columbia SC 29201-2423

DAVIS, J. STEVE, advertising agency executive; b. Alliance, Nebr., Feb. 26, 1945; s. John P. and Ruth M. (Annen) D.; m. Courtney Boyd Crowder, June 28, 1973; children: Cullen Boyd, J. Scott, Robert Charles. BA, U. Nebr., 1967. Asst. account exec. Benton & Bowles Inc., N.Y.C., 1972-73, account exec., 1973-76, v.p., account supr., 1976-79, sr. v.p., mgmt. supr., 1978-79, 81-85; sr. v.p., account dir. Benton & Bowles Inc., Brussels, 1979-81, N.Y.C., 1985-90; pres. Altschiller Reitzfeld Davis Tracy-Locke, Inc., N.Y.C.; exec. v.p., gen. mgr. J. Walter Thompson, Chgo., 1990-96; dir.

worldwide bd. J. Walter Thompson, 1991; pres., CEO, dir. Young & Rubicam, N.Y.C., 1996-97; chmn., CEO Wells BDDP, New York, NY, 1998—; pres., COO Qorvis Media Group, Inc., San Francisco, 1997-98; pres. Qorvis Media Group, San Francisco, 1998—; bd. dirs. Qorris Media Group, San Francisco. Bd. dirs. Steppenwolf Theatre Co., Chgo., 1993, Off The Street Club, 1993, pres., 1995. Named Exec. of Yr. Midwest Advt. Agy., 1992. Mem. Chgo. Econs. Club (chmn. advt. & mass media membership com. 1995), Westmoreland Club, Sigma Chi (publs. bd. 1998—). Office: Qorvis Media Group 201 3rd St Ste 700 San Francisco CA 94103-3143

DAVIS, JACK WAYNE, JR., internet publisher; b. Toledo, Ohio, May 21, 1947; s. Jack Wayne and Virginia (Moore) D.; m. Amélie Claiborne Matthews, June 24, 1977; 1 child, Claiborne Levering. Grad., Harvard Coll., 1969. Mng. editor Figaro, New Orleans, 1972-73; reporter, columnist, asst. city editor, city editor Item, New Orleans, 1973-80; metro editor The Times - Picayune, New Orleans, 1980-83; assoc. metro editor, night metro editor, metro editor The Chgo. Tribune, 1983-87; editor, v.p. Daily Press, Newport News, Va., 1987-94; pres., pub., CEO Daily Press, Newport News, 1994-98; pres. Tribune Interactive Inc., 1998—. Frank Knox fellow U. Rajasthan, India, 1971, Profl. Journalism fellow Stanford U., 1977-78. Mem. Am. Soc. Newspaper Editors. Avocations: sculling, reading. Office: Tribune Interactive Inc 435 N Michigan Ave Chicago IL 60611-4066

DAVIS, JAMES ALLAN, gerontologist, educator; b. Portland, Oreg., May 20, 1953; s. Alfred Jack and Anne (Dickson) D.; m. Lois Carol Lindsay, Dec. 17, 1978; children: Sarah Elizabeth, Matthew Simon. BS, U. Oreg., 1975, MS, 1976, EdD, 1980. State mental health gerontologist Oreg. Mental Health Div., Salem, 1978-80; project dir. Oreg. Long Term Care Tng. Project, Salem, 1979-80; tng. specialist Nat. Assn. Area Agys. on Aging., Washington, 1981; asst. dir. for internships and vol. svc. exptl. learning programs U. Md., 1981-86, mem. rsch. and instructional faculty, 1982-86; com. adminstr. Oreg. State Human Resources Com., Salem, 1987; exec. dir. Oreg. State Coun. Sr. Citizens, Salem, 1987-90; program coord. for sr. mental health care Oreg. Sr. and Disabled Svcs. Div., Salem, 1989—; pres. James A. Davis and Assocs. Inc., Portland, 1991—; state project dir. Oreg. Assn. RSVPs; vis. asst. prof. Ctr. for Gerontology, U. Oreg., 1990-92; co-chair Audio-Visual Program, Internat. Congress Gerontology, 1985; nat. gerontology acad. adv. panel, Nat. Hosp. Satellite Network, 1983-85; presenter nat. confs. on aging, health care, exptl. edn., age stereotyping; lobbyist United Srs. Oreg., Oreg. State Coun. Sr. Citizens, 1987—, Oreg. State Denturist Assn., Oreg. State Pharmacist Assn., Oreg. Soc. Physician Assts., Oreg. Legal Techs. Assn., Oreg. Dental Lab. Assn., Wash. Denturist Assn., Nat. Denturist Assn. Co-author: TV's Image of the Elderly, 1985; contbg. editor Retirement Life News, 1988-92; sr. issues editor Sr. News, 1989-96; contbr. articles to profl. jours.; producer, host approximately 400 TV and radio programs. Founding pres. Oreg. Alliance for Progressive Policy, 1988-89; co-chair mental health com., vice chair legis. com., Gov.'s Commn. on Sr. Svcs., 1988-89; exec. coun., media chair Human Svcs. Coalition Oreg., 1988-89; bd. dirs. Oreg. Health Action Campaign, 1988-92; 2d v.p., bd. dirs. Oreg. State Coun. for Sr. Citizens, 1977-80, 90-92, Oreg. Medicaid Com., 1996—; co-chair Oreg. Medicare/Medicaid Coalition, 1995—, Oreg. Long Term Care Campaign, 1996—; mem. Gov's Task Force for Volunteerism, State of Md., 1983-84, State Legis. Income Tax Task Force, 1990; vice chair Oreg. State Bd. Denture Technology, 1991-96; mem. com. for assessment on needs for volunteerism, Gov.'s Vol. Coun., State of Md., 1984-86; project dir. Oreg. Assn. Ret. and Sr. Vol. Programs, 1995—; mem. exec. bd. dirs. Oreg. Advocacy Coalition of Srs. and People with Disabilities, 1997—; chmn., bd. dirs. Oreg. Campaign for Patient Rights, 1997—. Recipient Disting. Svc. award City of Salem, 1980, Spl. Human Rights award, 1981, Svc. award U. Md., 1984, Hometown U.S.A. award Community Cable TV Producers, 1988, Disting. Svc. award Oreg. State Coun. Sr. Citizens, 1991. Mem. Nat. Assn. State Mental Health Dirs. (nat. exec. com. 1978-80, vice chmn. 1979-80, mem. aging div., spl. cons. 1981-82), Gerontol. Soc. Am. (mental health task force 1982-84, co-chmn. 1983-84), Nat. Gray Panthers (nat. bd. dirs. 1984-92, nat. exec. com. 1984-87, co-chmn. nat. program com. 1984-87, nat. media chair 1985-92, program co-chmn. nat. biennial conv. 1986, nat. health task force 1981—, co-chmn. 1983-84, chmn. mental health subcom. 1981-86, editor Health Watch, 1982-84, state program developer Oreg. chpt. 1979-80, 89, lobbyist 1987—), Nat. Denturist Assn. (exec. dir. 1992-98). Democrat. Office: James A Davis and Assocs Inc 1020 SW Taylor St Ste 610 Portland OR 97205-2511

DAVIS, JAMES E., professional association executive. BS in Civil Engring., N.C. State U., 1970, M in Civil Engring., 1972; M in Regional Planning, U. N.C., 1972; postgrad., U. Md., 1974-76. Registered profl. engr., N.J., D.C. Mgmt. trainee So. Rlwy. Co., Atlanta, 1970-72; assoc. Barton-Aschman Assocs., Washington, 1972-73; mem. tech. staff The MITRE Corp., McLean, Va., 1973-74; chief pre-award rev. br. U.S. Dept. Transp., Urban Mass Transp. Adminstrn., Washington, 1974-75, sr. program analyst, 1976-77, divsn. chief N.Y. and Seattle fed. regions, 1977-78, dir. office of grants assistance, 1978-82, dep. assoc. adminstr. for grants mgmt., 1982-83; asst. dir. rail transp. Port Authority of N.Y. and N.J., N.Y.C., 1983-84; dir. ops. rsch. Sea-land Svcs., Inc., Elizabeth, N.J., 1985-89; asst. exec. dir. ASCE, N.Y.C., 1989-94, exec. dir., CEO, 1994—. Ford Found. fellow, 1972. Fellow ASCE; mem. Am. Mgmt. Assn., Am. Soc. Assn. Execs., Greater Washington Soc. Assn. Execs., Coun. Engring. and Sci. Soc. Execs. Office: ASCE 1801 Alexander Bell Dr Reston VA 20191-4344*

DAVIS, JAMES HENRY, retired psychology educator; b. Effingham, Ill., Aug. 6, 1932; s. Kenneth E. and Forest (Naylor) D.; m. Elisabeth Bachman, June 27, 1954; children—Stephen J., Kristin E., Leah E. B.S., U. Ill., 1954; M.A., Mich. State U., 1958, Ph.D., 1961. Asst. instr. psychology Mich. State U., East Lansing, 1959-60; instr. psychology Miami U., Oxford, Ohio, 1960-61, asst. prof. psychology, 1961-65, assoc. prof. psychology, 1965-66; vis. assoc. prof. psychology Yale U., New Haven, 1966-67; vis. assoc. prof. psychology U. Ill., Champaign, 1967-68, assoc. prof., 1968-70, prof. psychology, 1970-97, prof. emeritus psychology, 1997; fellow Ctr. for Advanced Study in Behavioral Scis., 1987-88. Author: Group Performance, 1969; editor: (with W. Brandstatter and H.C. Schuler) Dynamics of Group Decisions, 1978, (with W. Brandstatter and G. Stocker-Kreichgauer) Group Decision Making, 1982, (with G.M. Stephenson) Progress in Applied Social Psychology, Vol. I, 1981, Vol. II, 1984, (with Erich Witte) Understanding Group Behavior, Vol. 1 and Vol. 2, 1996; contbr. articles to profl. jours. Served with U.S. Army, 1954-56. Fellow Am. Psychol. Soc.; mem. Psychonomic Soc., Midwestern Psychol. Assn., Soc. Exptl. Social Psychologists, AAAS, Soc. for Judgment and Decision Making, Soc. Math. Psychology, Sigma Xi. Home: 10 Lake Park Rd Champaign IL 61822-7101

DAVIS, JAMES HORNOR, III, lawyer; b. Clarksburg, W.Va., Oct. 9, 1928; s. James Hornor II and Martha (Maxwell) D.; m. Ouida Caldwell, July 1, 1950; children—James Hornor IV, Lewis Caldwell. A.B., Princeton U., 1950; LL.B., U. Va., 1953. Bar: W.Va. 1953. Ptnr. firm Preston & Davis, Charleston, 1953-65, Spilman, Thomas, Battle & Klostermeyer, Charleston, 1965-86; of counsel Campbell, Woods, Bagley, Emerson McNeer & Herndon, Charleston, 1987—; Mem. W.Va. Ho. of Dels., 1961-62, W.Va. Senate, 1963-66; pres. Dingess-Rum Properties, Inc.; bd. dirs. Bank One W.Va., N.A. Trustee Ea. Mineral Law Found. Served with USAF, 1953-55. Fellow ABA (life); mem. Am. Law Inst., Am. Judicature Soc. (dir. 1978-81), W.Va. Jud. Coun. (chmn. 1973-81), W.Va. Bar Assn. (pres. 1985-86), Kanawha County Bar Assn., Nat. Coun. Coal Lessors (chmn. 1980—), W.Va. Mfrs. Assn. (chmn. 1973-75, hon. dir.). Democrat. Episcopalian. Office: Campbell Woods Bagley et al PO Box 2393 Charleston WV 25328-2393

DAVIS, JAMES LEE, lawyer; b. High Point, N.C., May 2, 1940. AB with high honors, Guilford Coll., 1968; JD with honors, U. N.C., 1971. Bar: N.C. 1971. With Ward and Smith P.A., New Bern, N.C. Charles A. Dana scholar. Mem. N.C. State Bar, N.C. Bar Assn. (chmn. real property sect. coun. 1981-82), Craven County Bar Assn. (pres. 1978-79), Order of Coif. Office: Ward and Smith PA PO Box 867 1001 College Ct New Bern NC 28562-4972

DAVIS, JAMES LUTHER, retired utilities executive, lawyer; b. Memphis, May 8, 1924; s. Luther and Sarah (Carter) D.; m. Natalie Young, Jan. 26, 1947; children: James Luther, Fred C., Peggy E. BBA, U. Ariz., 1946, LLB, 1949. Bar: Ariz. 1949. Sole practice Tucson, 1949-52, asst. city atty., 1952-53, city mgr., 1953-55; with Tucson Gas & Electric Co. (now Tucson Electric Power Co.), 1955-96, exec. v.p., 1958-59, pres., 1959-76, also bd. dirs., 1961-89, emeritus, 1989-96, chmn. bd., 1967-88; bd. dirs. El Paso br. Fed. Res. Bd., Dallas, 1974-77, chmn. 1976-77. Mem. charter rev. com. City of Tucson, 1965-71; bd. dirs. Tucson Airport Authority, 1957-62, 64-70, pres., 1965; bd. dirs. Tucson Med. Ctr., 1955-58, 59-65, pres., 1957-58; mem. Tucson Indsl. Devel. Bd., 1959-64; bd. dirs. Ariz. Town Hall, 1962-74, 78-82, Health Planning Coun. Tucson, 1964-71, Tucson Regional Plan, 1966-89, United Way, 1985-88; bd. dirs. Green Fields Sch., 1964-69, chmn. bd., 1964-66; bd. dirs. U. Ariz. Found., 1985-92, dir. emeritus, 1992-96. Mem. Nat. Assn. Mfrs. (bd. dirs. 1960-62), Pacific Coast Gas Assn. (bd. dirs. 1958-60), Pacific Coast Elec. Assn. (bd. dirs. 1972-86, pres. 1978-79), Western Energy and Supply Assn. (bd. dirs. 1964-76), Tucson C. of C. (bd. dirs. 1958-60, 64-66, 80-90, chmn. 1987-88), So. Ariz. Water Resources Assn. (bd. dirs. 1982-88, pres. 1987), Blue Key, Tucson Country Club, Phi Gamma Delta, Alpha Kappa Psi, Phi Delta Phi. Home: 6781 N Altos Primero Tucson AZ 85718-2054

DAVIS, JAMES MCCOY, real estate executive; b. Columbus, Ohio, Oct. 19, 1914; s. James McCoy and Laura Victoria (Smith) D.; m. Phyllis Ruth Rowe, Jan. 24, 1948; children: Perine Davis Ceperley, Linda Davis Bryson, Carol, Paul, Jamie Davis Micalizzi. BBA, Ohio State U., 1937; postgrad., Union Theol. Sem., N.Y.C., 1937-39; BD, Oberlin Grad. Sch. Theol., 1942; MA, Columbia U., 1947, EdD, 1952; MDiv (hon.), Vanderbilt U., 1973. Minister First Congl. Ch., Ravenna, Ohio, 1939-42; field exec. Congl. Christian Com. War Victims and Services, N.Y.C., 1942-43; counselor for internat. services U. Wash., Seattle, 1948-54; dir., assoc. prof. U. Mich., Ann Arbor, 1954-64; v.p. Inst. Internat. Edn., N.Y.C., 1964-67; provost U.S. Internat. U., San Diego, 1967-70; pres. Northwestern Mich. Coll., Traverse City, 1970-73; realtor James M. Davis, San Diego, 1974-77; pres. James M. Davis Inc. & Assocs., San Diego, 1977—. Contbr. articles to profl. jours. Pres. World Affairs Coun., San Diego, 1981-83; chmn. bd. Consumer Credit Counselors, San Diego, 1988-89; mem. San Diego County Grand Jury, 1990-91; v.p. Baja Presbyn. Missions, 1994—. Capt. U.S. Army, 1943-46. Decorated Bronze Star with oak leaf cluster. Mem. Nat. Assn. Fgn. Student Affairs: Assn. Internat. Educators (life, pres. 1959-60), Calif. Assn. Realtors (bd. dirs. 1978-79, 88), San Diego Assn. Realtors (com. chmn. 1978-79, 88), Soc. Mayflower Descs., Rotary. Republican. Presbyterian. Avocations: community service, travel. Home: 4906 Pacifica Dr San Diego CA 92109-2311

DAVIS, JAMES NORMAN, neurologist, neurobiology researcher; b. Dallas, Oct. 24, 1939; s. Moses and Ruth (Grossman) D.; m. Frances Isabel Cantor, May 1, 1965; children—Amanda, Adam, Joanna. B.A., Cornell U., 1961, M.D., 1965. Diplomate Am. Bd. Neurology and Psychiatry. Intern Bellevue Hosp., N.Y.C., 1965-66; rsch. assoc. Lab. Chem. Pharmacology Nat. Heart Inst.-NIH, Bethesda, Md, 1966-68; resident Duke U., 1968-69, asst. prof., 1972-77, assoc. prof. medicine and pharmacology, 1977-80, prof. medicine, 1980-92, prof. pharmacology, 1987-92, prof. neurobiology, 1989-92; prof., chmn. dept. neurology SUNY, Stony Brook, 1992—; resident in neurology Cornell U.-N.Y. Hosp., 1969-72, North Shore Hosp., 1971; instr. neurology Cornell U., 1969-71; Fulbright fellow U. Goteborg, Sweden, 1972. Contbr. articles to profl. jours. Served with USPHS, 1966-68. Mem. Am. Neurol. Assn., Soc. Neurosci., Am. Soc. Pharmacology and Exptl. Therapeutics, Am. Acad. Neurology, N.C. Soc. Neurosci. (pres. local chpt. 1981-82). Democrat. Jewish. Home: 45 Southgate Rd Setauket NY 11733-1540 Office: SUNY Neurology Dept HSC T12-020 Stony Brook NY 11794-8121

DAVIS, JAMES O(THELLO), physician, educator; b. Tahlequah, Okla., July 12, 1916; s. Zemry and Villa (Hunter) D.; m. Florrilla Louise Sides, Dec. 27, 1941; children: Janet Ruth, James Lawrence. M.A. in Zoology, U. Mo., 1939, Ph.D., 1942, B.S. in Medicine, 1943; M.D., Washington U., 1945. Intern Barnes Hosp., St. Louis, 1945-46; investigator Lab. Kidney and Electrolyte Metabolism, Nat. Heart Inst., Bethesda, Md., 1949-57; chief sect. on exptl. cardiovascular disease Lab. Kidney and Electrolyte Metabolism, Nat. Heart Inst., 1957-66; asso. prof. physiology Temple U. Sch. Medicine, Phila., 1955-56; vis. asso. prof. physiology Johns Hopkins Sch. Medicine, 1961-64; vis. prof. physiology U. Va. Sch. Medicine, 1964; prof., chmn. dept. physiology U. Mo. Sch. Medicine, Columbia, 1966-82; prof. emeritus U. Mo. Sch. Medicine, 1982—. Mem. editorial bd. Am. Jour. Physiology, 1961-63, 66-69, Endocrinology, 1962-65, Circulation Research, 1962-66, 71-76, 78-81, Hypertension, 1979-80. Served with AUS, 1943-45; Served with USPHS, 1946-66. Recipient AMA Golden Apple award for teaching U. Mo., 1968, Sigma Xi Rsch. award U. Mo., 1971, Modern Medicine Disting. Achievement award, 1973, Alumni gold medal U. Mo., 1973, Volhard award, 1974, CIBA award for hypertension rsch., 1975, Carl J. Wiggers award, 1976, citation of merit U. Mo. Sch. Medicine, 1981, Disting. Alumnus award Coll. Arts & Scis. U. Mo., 1993; James O. Davis Disting. Professorship in Cardiovascular Rsch. established in his honor, U. Mo. Sch. Medicine, 1987; James O. Davis Disting. Lectureship in Cardiovascular Sci. established in his honor, U. Mo. Sch. Medicine, 1995; named Hon. Sesquicentennial Prof. U. Mo., 1989. Mem. Am. Heart Assn. (mem. med. adv. council, vice chmn. council for high blood pressure research 1970-72, chmn. council 1972-74), Am. Physiology Soc. (council 1974-78, steering com. circulation group 1978-81, pres. circulation sect. 1981), Endocrine Soc., Soc. Exptl. Biology and Medicine, Nat. Inst. Health Extramural Program, Assn. Physiology Dept. Chairmen (council 1971-74), Inter-Am. Soc. Hypertension (council 1978-80), Internat. Soc. Hypertension (pres. 1980-82), Nat. Acad. Scis., Sigma Xi, Alpha Omega Alpha. Home: 612 Maplewood Dr Columbia MO 65203-1764

DAVIS, JAMES ROBERT, cartoonist; b. Marion, Ind., July 28, 1945; s. James William and Anna Catherine (Carter) D.; 1 son, James Alexander. B.S., Ball State U., Muncie, Ind., 1967. Artist, Groves & Assocs., advt., Muncie, 1968-69; asst. to cartoonist: Tumbleweeds comic strip, 1969-78; cartoonist: Garfield comic strip, 1978—; TV script Here Comes Garfield, 1982, Garfield on the Town, 1983 (Emmy award 1984), Garfield in the Rough, 1984 (Emmy award 1985), Garfield's Halloween Adventure, 1985 (Emmy award 1986), Garfield in Paradise, 1986, Garfield Goes Hollywood, 1987, The Garfield Christmas Special, 1987; author: Garfield at Large, 1980, Garfield Gains Weight, 1981, Garfield Bigger Than Life, 1981, Garfield Weighs In, 1982, Garfield Takes the Cake, 1982, Garfield Treasury, 1982, Here Comes Garfield, 1982, Garfield Sits Around the House, 1983, Garfield Second Treasury, 1983, Garfield Eats His Heart Out, 1983, Garfield Tips the Scale, 1984, Garfield Loses his Feet, 1984, Garfield: His Nine Lives, 1984, Garfield Makes It Big, 1985, Garfield Rolls On, 1985, Third Garfield Treasury, 1985, Garfield Out to Lunch, 1986, The Unabridged, Uncensored, Unbelieveable Garfield Book, 1986, Garfield Food for Thought, 1987, The 4th Garfield Treasury, 1987, The Garfield Cat Naming Book, 1988, Garfield Chews the Fat, 1989, The 5th Garfield Treasury, 1989, Happy Birthday, Garfield, 1989, Garfield, Tiens Bon La Rampe, 1989, Garfield's Longest Catnap, 1989, Garfield The Big Star, 1989, Garfield in the Park, 1989, Garfield and the Tiger, 1989, Mini-Mysteries featuring Garfield, 1990, Garfield: The Me Book: A Guide to Superiority, How to Get It, Use It, and Keep It, 1990, Garfield's Judgement Day, 1990, Garfield's Feline Fantasies, 1990, Garfield Stories, 1990, Garfield on the Farm, 1990, Garfield Hangs Out, 1990, Garfield Goes to Waist, 1990, The Sixth Garfield Trasury, 1991, Garfield: The Truth About Cats, 1991, Garfield: Seasons Greetings, 1991, Garfield Thanksgiving Special, 1991, Garfield Takes Up Space, 1991, Garfield Says a Mouthful, 1991, Garfield Gets a Life, 1991, Garfield's Ghost Stories, 1992, Garfield Vacation Greetings, 1992, Garfield Learns About Thoughtfulness: Don't Be Late!, 1992, Garfield Learns About Planning: Surprize Party, 1992, Garfield Learns About Money: Money Madness!, 1992, Garfield Learns About Fire Safety: Where's the Fire?, 1992, Garfield Learns About Cooking: Any Cat Can Cook, 1992, Garfield Learns about Conservation: Endangered Odie?, 1992, Garfield Keeps His Chin Up, 1992, Garfield By the Pound, 1992, Garfield Birthday Greetings, 1992, The Seventh Garfield Treasury, 1993, Garfield's Big Fat Hairy Joke Book, 1993, Garfield Takes His Licks, 1993, Garfield Hits the Big Time: His 25th Book, 1993, Garfield's Tales of Mystery, 1994, Garfield's Night Before Christmas, 1994, Garfield's Insults, 1994, Garfield's Haunted House: And Other Spooky Tales, 1994, Garfield's Furry Tales, 1994, Garfield's Big Fat Scary Joke Book, 1994, Garfield's Big Fat Holiday Joke Book, 1994, Garfield Insults, Put-Downs, 1994, Garfield Fat Cat, 1994, Garfield Discovers America, 1994, Garfield's Son of Big, Fat Hairy Jokes, 1994, Big Hairy Garfield, 1994, Garfield, The Easter Bunny?, 1995, Garfield's Stupid Cupid: And Other Silly Stories, 1995, Garfield Fat Cat 3 Pack, 1995, Garfield Dishes It Out, 1995. Mktg. Hall of Fame award Am. Mktg. Assn., 1982; recipient Disting. Alumnus award Am. Assn. State Colls. Univs. Mem. Nat. Cartoonists Soc. (Best Humor Strip of 1981, 86, Segar award 1985, Cartoonist of Yr. 1990), Newspaper Comics Council. Protestant. Republican. Office: Universal Press Syndicate 4520 Main St Ste 700 Kansas City MO 64111-7701

DAVIS, JAMES VERLIN, insurance brokerage executive; b. DeKalb, Ill., Dec. 14, 1935; s. Verl J. and Esther (Thomas) D.; m. Anita Taylor, June 10, 1961; children: Elizabeth Lee Parsons, Jonathan J., Amy L. Hardman. BA, Wabash Coll., 1957; MA, Vanderbilt U., 1963; PhD, Cornell U., 1967. Sports editor Crawfordsville (Ind.) Jour.-Rev., 1953-56; claims and methods analyst Prudential Ins. Co., Chgo., 1957-58, 60-61; fin. analyst Ford Motor Co., Dearborn, Mich., 1963-64; prof. Owen Grad. Sch. Mgmt., Vanderbilt U., Nashville, 1967-78, acting dean, 1973-76; with Willis Corroon Corp., 1976—; v.p. Willis Corroon Corp., Nashville, 1979—; dir. Willis Corroon Ams., Nashville, 1981—; divsnl. v.p. Willis Corroon Corp., Nashville, 1989—, chmn., chief exec. officer advanced risk mgmt. services, 1981-90, chmn., chief exec. officer nat. resource div., 1990-91; chmn., CEO Advanced Risk Mgmt. Svcs., Nashville, 1992—; bd. dirs. Meridian Ins. Co. Ltd., Hamilton, Bermuda. Author: The Adjustment of Stock Prices to New Information, 1967, (with Dennis Rondinelli) Local Management of Federal Grants-in-Aid, 1973; contbr. over 30 articles to profl. jours. Bd. dirs. Spencer Edn. Found., N.Y.C., 1984—. Served with U.S. Army, 1958-60. Ford Found. fellow Cornell U., 1964-66; Ayres fellow Stonier Grad. Sch. Banking, 1974. Mem. Am. Econ. Assn. Am. Fin. Assn., Fin. Mgmt. Assn., Am. Risk and Ins. Assn., Cornell Club (N.Y.C.). Republican. Presbyterian. Avocations: running, scuba diving, travel, tennis. Home: 815 Foster Hl Nashville TN 37215-2454 Office: Willis Corroon Corp Adv Risk Mgmt Svcs Divsn 26 Century Blvd Nashville TN 37214-3695

DAVIS, JAMES WESLEY, university program administrator, artist, writer, composer; b. L.A., Oct. 9, 1940; s. Charles Wesley and Hazel Virginia (Porter) D.; m. Linnea Sharsmith, Mar. 31, 1962 (div. 1978); children: Marc Jerome, Timothy Andrew; m. Ellen Alva Hales, Oct. 6, 1990. BA in Edn., Calif. Coll. Arts & Crafts, Oakland, 1964; BFA, Calif. Coll. Arts & Crafts, 1965; MFA, U. Colo., 1967, MA, 1970. Lectr. art dept. U. Ark., Fayetteville, 1967-96; prof. art dept. Western Ill. U., Macomb, 1969-81; instr. art dept. U. Colo., Denver, 1981; dir. performance art prodns. Denver, 1981-83; head art dept. East Tex. State U., Commerce, 1983-88; chair art dept. Ind. State U., Terre Haute, 1988-89; dir. inter-arts ctr. San Francisco State U., 1989—; bd. dirs. Paul Dresher Ensemble, San Francisco, 1994—. Exhibited in over 100 mus. exhbns. worldwide, 1984—; represented in permanent collections over 20 museums; contbr. to profl. jours.; composer over 50 musical works; performer in field. Recipient purchase awards 8 museums worldwide, 1970—, award Swarovski Internat., Belgium, 1968, award Phelan Commn., Oakland, 1975. Office: San Francisco State U Inter-Arts Ctr 1600 Holloway Ave San Francisco CA 94132-1722

DAVIS, JANE G., corporate lawyer; b. N.Y.C., May 3, 1949. BA in French, Elmira (N.Y.) Coll., 1971; MA in French, U. Pitts., 1973; JD, Duquesne U., 1978. V.p., gen. counsel and sec. Joy Technologies, Inc., 1988-95, York Internat. Corp., York, Pa., 1995—. Mem. ABA, Pa. Bar Assn. Office: York Internat Corp 631 S Richland Ave York PA 17403-3445*

DAVIS, JANE STRAUSS, business owner; b. Chgo., July 3, 1944; d. Joseph Loeb and Leanore (Purvin) Strauss; m. Muller Davis, Dec. 28, 1963; children: Melissa Davis Smith, Muller Jr., Joseph; m. Robert B. Holzkamp, Oct. 17, 1998. BA with honors in Am. Culture, Northwestern U., 1980, postgrad. studies in Am. History, 1980-81. With residential sales Kenneth Friend Realty, Winnetka, Ill., 1971-74, J.H. Kahn Realty, Glencoe, Ill., 1974-77; v.p. personal trust dept. Harris Trust & Savs. Bank, Chgo., 1983-89; v.p. Bankers Trust Co. Pvt. Bank, Chgo., 1989-90; founder Jane Davis Connections, Chgo., 1991—, Connections Next Step, 1993—, Young Chgo. Authors, 1992-95, Charlotte.Com, Inc., Chgo., 1996—; founder Charlotte Com, Inc.; dir. Met. Family Svcs. Mem. woman's bd. Rush-Presbyn.-St. Luke's Med. Ctr., Chgo., 1978—; co-chmn. med. rsch. campaign Michael Reese Med. Ctr., Chgo., 1982-96; mem. costume com. Chgo. Hist. Soc., 1980-90; mem. campaign for gt. tchrs. Northwestern U., Evanston, Ill., 1988-90, mem. vis. com., 1989—, mem. coun. of 100; mem. Chgo. Symphony Orch. Woman's Assn., 1990-98; mem. coun. Children's Meml. Hosp. Med. Rsch. Inst., 1991-98; mem. Coun. of 100, The Chgo. Bd.; chmn. 50th anniversary day celebration Roosevelt U., Chgo., 1995, co-chmn. Itzhak Pearlman concert, 1996; mem. Tree of Life Min. Mission, 1996—, Leadership Broward Found. Class XVIII. Address: Flying Fox Farm PO Box 171 Argyle WI 53504

DAVIS, JANET MARIE GORDEN, secondary education educator; b. Springfield, Mo., Jan. 6, 1938; d. Ura Arlond and Evelyn Ruby (Nickols) Gorden; m. Benjamin George Davis, June 21, 1980; children: Leslie Anne, John Nathan. BS, S.W. Mo. U., 1960, MA, 1969; PhD, U. Md., 1992. Tchr. Springfield Schs., 1960-64; instr. USAFE-U. Md., Germany, 1965-67, S.W. Mo. U., Springfield, 1969-70; tchr., dept. chair Baltimore County, 1977—; cons. in internat. edn. World Relief Corp., Wheaton, Ill., 1984; asst. prof. Balt. Internat. Coll., 1993-95. Author: For the Love of Literature: A Survey of Fiction, 1989, For the Love of Literature: Reading and Writing Nonfiction, 1989. Fulbright fellow, Eng., 1980-81. Mem. Dickens Fellowship, Fulbright Assn., Phi Kappa Phi. Baptist. Avocations: piano, animal rights, Victorian poetry. Home: 6580 Madrigal Ter Columbia MD 21045-4628

DAVIS, JEREMY MATTHEW, chemist; b. Bakersfield, Calif., Aug. 5, 1953; s. Joseph Hyman and Mary (Pavetto) D.; m. Bernadette Sobkiewicz, Aug. 28, 1976 (div.); children: Andrew Jeremy, Christopher Peter. BS in Biol. Scis., U. Calif., Irvine, 1974; M in Pub. Adminstrn., Calif. State U., Long Beach, 1983. Chemist I, II, Orange County Water Dist., Fountain Valley, Calif., 1977-84, chemist supr., 1984—. Papers in field. Lay eucharistic minister St. Margaret of Scotland Episcopal Ch., San Juan Capistrano, Calif. Named Lab. Person of Yr., Calif. Water Environment Assn., Santa Ana River Basin, 1984. Mem. Am. Water Works Assn., Toastmasters Internat. (pres. Watermeisters club 1996, 99, gov. C-5 founder's dist. area 1999—). Office: Orange County Water Dist PO Box 8300 Fountain Valley CA 92728-8300

DAVIS, JERRY ALBERT, architect; b. Austin, Feb. 18, 1947; s. Albert Wesley and Jean (Sprinkle) D.; m. Nancy Ann Davis, June, 1966 (div. June 1971); children Davis Lee, Kelley Jean; m. Mary Ann Overly, Oct. 20, 1984. BS with honors, U. Tex., 1970, BArch, 1971. Designer H.K. Smith Architects, Dallas, 1971-74, Hesson & May Assocs., San Antonio, 1974-75; assoc. project mgr. 3D/I, Austin, 1975-77, N.Y.C., 1978-79; project mgr. Skidmore, Owings & Merrill, N.Y.C., 1979; sr. prin. Hellmuth, Obata & Kassabaum, N.Y.C., 1979—. Mem. AIA. Club: University. Avocations: sailing, sports, travel. Office: Hellmuth Obata & Kassabaum 630 Avenue Of The Americas Fl 6 New York NY 10011-2007*

DAVIS, JERRY ARNOLD, judge; b. Waukegan, Ill., July 1, 1946; s. Bobbie and Mary Alice (Trammel) Davis; m. Barbara Purse Beach, June 17, 1972 (div. Sept. 1978); m. Deborah Selph Davis, Dec. 12, 1980; children: Michael Scott, Stuart Sheffield. BA, Miss. State U., Starkville, 1968; JD, U. Va., 1971. Bar: Miss. 1971. Atty.-adviser Dept. of Justice, Washington, 1975-80; asst. U.S. atty. Dept. of Justice, Jackson, Miss., 1980-84; U.S. magistrate judge U.S. Cts., Aberdeen, Miss., 1984—; criminal investigator USAF, Topeka, 1971-72. Capt. U.S. Army, 1972-75. Mem. ABA, Fed. Bar Assn. (chpt. v.p. 1986-90), Am. Judicature Soc., Miss. Bar Assn. Democrat. Episcopalian. Avocations: reading, baseball, fishing, basketball. Office: US Magistrate Judge PO Box 726 Aberdeen MS 39730-0726

DAVIS, JERRY RAY, retired railroad company executive; b. Sylvan Grove, Kans., June 30, 1938; s. Ralph Jacob and Clara Willamine (Jennsen) D.; m. Patricia L. Stauffer, Sept. 12, 1958; children: Richard, Roger, Anthony, Randall. MS in Mgmt., MIT, 1976. Telegrapher Union Pacific R.R., Salina, Kans., 1957-59; telegrapher, dispatcher Kans. Colo., 1959-65; asst. supt. safety and courtesy Union Pacific R.R., Kansas City, 1968; trainmaster Utah div. Union Pacific R.R., Salt Lake City, 1969-71; trainmaster Idaho div. Union Pacific R.R., Idaho Falls, 1971-73; asst. to gen. supt. transp. Union Pacific R.R., Omaha, 1973; asst. supt. Oreg. div. Union Pacific R.R., Portland, 1973-74; supt. Utah div. Union Pacific R.R., Salt Lake City, 1974-75; asst. gen. supt. transp. Union Pacific R.R., Omaha, 1976-78, gen. supt. eastern dist., 1978, asst. v.p. ops., 1979-81, v.p. ops., 1981-86, exec. v.p. ops.,

1986-89; pres. CSX Rail Transport, Jacksonville, Fla., 1989-91, exec. v.p. ops., 1991-92, exec. v.p. ops., COO, 1992—. Mem. adv. coun. USO; active Luth. Social Svcs. Mem. Am. Assn. R.R. Supts., Ry. Fuel and Oper. Officers Assn., First Coast Mfrs. Assn., Nat. Freight Transp. Assn., TPC, River Club, San Jose Country Club. Republican. Lutheran. Home: 10077 Fieldcrest Dr Omaha NE 68114-4938*

DAVIS, JIM, congressman, lawyer; m. Peggy Bessent; children: Peter, William. BA, Washington and Lee U.; JD, U. Fla. Pvt. practice law Tampa, Fla., 1982-88; ptnr. Bush, Ross, Gardner, Warren and Rudy, Tampa, Fla., 1988; mem. Fla. Ho. of Reps., 1988-97, majority leader; mem. 105th Congress from 11th Fla. dist., 1997—; class pres. 105th Congress. Office: 418 Cannon HOB Washington DC 20515

DAVIS, JIM, university basketball coach; b. Englewood, Tenn.; m. Bobbie Henderson; 1 child, Todd. BS in Health and Phys. Edn., Tenn. Wesleyan Coll., 1970; postgrad., East Tenn. State U.; MS in Supervision and Adminstrn., Tenn. Tech. U., 1975. Coach McMinn County (Tenn.) H.S., Charleston (Tenn.) H.S., Madisonville (Tenn.) H.S., Englewood (Tenn.) Jr. H.S., Roane State C.C., Harriman, Tenn., 1978-85; asst. coach Fla. Lady Gators Basketball Team; coach Mid. Tenn. State U., 1986-87; head coach women's basketball Clemson (S.C.) U., 1987—. Inducted into Tenn. Jr. and C.C. Athletic Assn. Hall of Fame, 1996; named Coach of Yr., ACC, 1989, 94. Mem. Tiger Brotherhood. Office: Clemson U care Athletic Dept Women's Basketball Office Clemson SC 29634*

DAVIS, JIMMY FRANK, assistant attorney general; b. Lubbock, Tex., June 14, 1945; s. Jack and Fern Lisemby D.; M. Joyce Zelma Hart, Nov. 6, 1976; children: Jayme Leigh, Julee Ellen. BS in Edn., Tex. Tech. U., 1968; JD, U. Tex., 1972. Bar: Tex. 1972, U.S. Supreme Ct. 1975, U.S. Dist. (no dist.) Tex. 1976, U.S. Ct. Appeals (5th cir.) 1976, U.S. Ct. Appeals (11cir.) 1981. Asst. criminal dist. atty. Lubbock County, 1973-74, adminstrv. asst., 1976-77; county and dist. atty. Castro County, Tex., 1977-92; asst. atty. gen. Tex., 1993—. Mem. State Bar of Tex. (com. admissions dist. 16 1974-78, dist. 13 1983-92, govt. lawyers sect., coun. mem. 1991-92), Tex. Dist. and County Attys. Assn., Lubbock County Jr. Bar Assn. (pres. 1977), Tex. Tech. Ex Students Assn. (dist. rep. 1981-84, bd. dirs. 1985-90), Coll. of State Bar of Tex. (continuing legal edn. 1984-93), Kiwanis of Lubbock (pres. 1977), Kiwanis of Dimmitt (pres. 1981), Delta Theta Pi. Office: PO Box 5280 401 50th St PO Box 5280 Lubbock TX 79408

DAVIS, JOAN, English language educator; b. N.Y.C., June 7, 1948; d. John Patrick and Marian McInerney; m. William George Davis, July 24, 1971. BA, Coll. St. Rose, 1970; M, Binghamton U., 1976. English tchr. Owego (N.Y.) Free Acad., 1970—, chair English dept., 1991—; adj. instr. English Syracuse (N.Y.) Univ., 1987—; chair curriculum com. Mid. States Assn. Evaluation Vis. Team, 1993. Mem. Tioga County (N.Y.) Planning Bd., 1982-88. Mem. N.Y. State English Coun. (Tchr. Excellence award 1991, regional co-dir. 1997-99), Nat. Coun. Tchrs. English, Delta Kappa Gamma Soc. Internat. Avocations: reading, gardening, skiing. Office: Owego Free Acad 1 Sheldon Guile Blvd Owego NY 13827-1095

DAVIS, JOAN CARROLL, museum director; b. Binghamton, N.Y., Sept. 20, 1931; s. Homer Leslie and Ruby Isabelle (Stone) G.; m. Frederic E. Davis, Aug. 22, 1953; children—Timothy, Terri, Tami, Traci, Todd, Tricia. Student Bob Jones U., 1949-52. Supr. Day Care Ctr. Bob Jones U., Greenville, 1953-63; docent Univ. Art Gallery, Greenville, 1964-73, dir., 1974—. Republican. Baptist. Office: Bob Jones Univ 1700 Wade Hampton Blvd Greenville SC 29614-1000

DAVIS, JOANNE FATSE, lawyer; b. Bridgeport, Conn., June 8, 1956; m. Thomas J. Davis, Jr. BS, Boston U., 1977; JD, U. Bridgeport, 1982. Bar: Conn. 1982, N.Y. 1983. Motions law clk. U.S. Ct. Appeals (2d cir.), N.Y.C., 1982-83; assoc. Debevoise & Plimpton, N.Y.C., 1983-89; sr. corp. counsel Uniroyal Chem. Co., Middlebury, Conn., 1989—; bd. dirs. Legal Ctr. Conn. Nonprofit Orgns. Inc.; sec. The Corp. Bar Fund. Mem. Am. Corp. Counsel Assn., Conn. Bar Assn., The Corporate Bar, Assn. Bar City of N.Y., Soc. Farsarotul. Eastern Orthodox. Office: Uniroyal Chem Co Inc World Hdqrs Middlebury CT 06749

DAVIS, JOE DAVID, broadcast executive; b. Charleston, W.Va., Mar. 25, 1944; s. Maynard R. and Mary Jane (Entsminger) D.; m. Paulette Groves, July 2, 1966 (div. Jan. 1973); m. Carolyn Bradley, Apr. 19, 1975; children: Katherine Peterson, Jeff Davis, Sarah Dunn, Webb. BS, Wheaton (Ill.) Coll., 1966; MS in Edn., U. So. Calif., 1969. Faculty assoc. Ariz. State U., Tempe, 1971-75; pres. Davis Eaton, Inc., Phoenix, 1975-85, Practice Resources, Inc., Scottsdale, Ariz., 1983-85; v.p. JAF Ministries, Agoura, Calif., 1985-89, Salem Media Corp., N.Y.C., 1992—, Salem Comm. Corp., N.Y.C., 1994—; gen. mgr. Sta. WMCA, N.Y.C., 1989—, Sta. WWDJ, Hackensack, N.J., 1994—. Mem. Manhattan adv. bd. Salvation Army, N.Y.C., 1993—, chmn. comm. com., 1992—; mem. organizing bd. N.Y. Urban Partnership, N.Y.C., 1992-93. With U.S. Armed Forces Radio and TV Svc., Athens, Greece. Fellow Am. Acad. Human Svcs.; mem. Nat. Assn. Broadcasters, Nat. Religious Broadcasters (contbr. articles to mag.), N.Y. Market Radio, Am. Broadcast Pioneer, Broadcast Found. Republican. Avocations: golf, gourmet cooking, computers. Office: Salem Media Inc 201 Route 17 Ste 601 Rutherford NJ 07070-2574

DAVIS, JOEL, publisher; b. Chgo., Apr. 5, 1934; s. Bernard George and Sylvia (Friedman) D.; m. Carol Sue Barnett, Aug. 3, 1958; children: Charles Michael, Andrew Barnett, Jonathan William. B.A., Brown U., 1957; student, Columbia U., summer 1953. With Davis Publs., Inc., N.Y.C., 1957-92; exec. v.p. Davis Publs., Inc., 1959-68, pres., 1969-92; pres. Sylvia Porter's Personal Fin. Mag. Co., 1982-89, Woodworker, Inc., Westport, Conn., 1993-95; ptnr. Davis/Herschbein & Assocs., L.L.C., Westport, 1996—; pres. Archtl. Designs, Inc., Westport, 1996—; bd. dirs. Mut. N.Y., Money Series Fund Inc. Mem. exec. com. gen. devel. coun. Brown U., 1962-77, Young Pres. Orgn., 1971-83; vice chmn. Brown Devel. Coun., 1968-69; nat. chmn. univ. fund Brown U., 1965-68; regional dir. Assoc. Alumni Brown U., 1965-67, trustee, mem. corp., 1968-73; mem. adv. and exec. com. Brown U., 1971-73, chmn. budget and fin. com., 1971-73, chmn. nat. alumni schs. program, 1982-85; bd. dirs. Brit. Am. Ednl. Found., 1977-80; trustee Westport Pub. Libr., 1992—, v.p., 1994-97, pres. 1997-99; trustee Brookfield Craft Ctr., 1992-94. Mem. Am. Arbitration Assn. (nat. panel), Mag. Pubs. Am. (bd. dirs. 1969-94, sec. 1979-81, vice chmn. mktg. com. 1969-73, exec com. 1971-88, fin. com. 1974-88, chmn. membership com. 1975-91), Brown Club (N.Y.C. bd. govs. 1963-69), Weston Field Club. Home: 15 Crooked Mile Rd Westport CT 06880-1124 Office: Archtl Designs Inc 274 Riverside Ave Westport CT 06880-4808

DAVIS, JOHN ADAMS, JR., electrical engineer, roboticist, corporate research executive; b. Winston-Salem, N.C., May 26, 1944; s. John Adams and Jean Elizabeth (Bowles) D.; m. Sharon Kay Hammons, Dec. 19, 1965; 1 child, Heather Noelle. BSEE with honors, N.C. State U., 1971; MS in Engring., Fla. Tech. U., 1976; MBA, Loyola Coll., Balt., 1980. Design engr. Martin Marietta Corp., Orlando, Fla., 1971-76; sr. program mgr. Martin Marietta Corp., Glen Burnie, Md., 1988-89; sr. engr., project mgr. Gould, Inc., Glen Burnie, Md., 1976-79, program mgr., 1984-88; mgr. data systems Bendix Corp., Columbia, Md., 1979-81; corp. ops. mgr. Vector Automation, Inc., Balt., 1981-82; dir., div. mgr. Ill. Inst. Tech. Rsch. Inst., Chgo., 1982-83; gen. mgr. Marine Systems div., dir. corp. bus. area Eastport Internat., Inc., Upper Marlboro, Md., 1989-93; pres. JADE Rsch. Corp., Severna Park, Md., 1993—; pres., cons. Bustech Co., Severna Park, 1982-84; leading expert on U.S. Govt.'s Small Bus. Innovative Rsch. Program; speaker profl. confs. Contbr. articles to profl. jours. Bd. dirs. Cape Arthur Community Improvement Assn., Severna Park, 1981-82, 89-90; mem. Md. Gov.'s Com. to Elect Sch. Bd., 1982. Sgt. USAF, 1965-68, Vietnam. Recipient USAF Commendation medal. Mem. AIAA, IEEE (bd. dirs. 1978-79), Am. Def. Preparedness Assn., Assn. U.S. Army, Assn. Proposal Mgmt. Profls., Hazardous Materials Controls Rsch. Inst., Am. Nuclear Soc., Marine Tech. Soc. (remotely operated vehicle com.), Assn. Unmanned Vehicle Systems (bd. trustees 1993-96, Mem. of Yr. 1991, tech. co-chmn. nat. conf. and exhbn. 1991, 92, 93, v.p. Capitol chpt.), Tau Beta Pi, Eta Kappa Nu. Republican. Presbyterian. Avocations: snow and water skiing, boating, swimming, ch. choir, chess. Office: JADE Rsch Corp 5 Linda Ln Severna Park MD 21146-3234

DAVIS, JOHN ALBERT, lawyer; b. Seattle, July 29, 1940; s. Carl Lee and Helen Irene (Corner) D.; m. Judith Ann colvin, June 21, 1959 (div. 1978); children: John Albert, James Colvin, Jennifer Lynn. Student, U. Calif., Berkeley, 1957-58; postgrad., Diablo Valley Coll., 1962; JD, Golden Gate U., 1970. Bar: Calif. 1971, U.S. Dist. Ct. (no. dist.) Calif. 1971, U.S. Ct. Appeals (9th cir.) 1971, U.S. Supreme Ct. 1986. Pres. Cal-State Distbrs., Oakland, Calif., 1959-78; pvt. practice Oakland, 1978-81, San Ramon, 1985—; v.p., chief operating officer Madre Mining, Ltd., Sacramento, 1981-85; pres., bd. dirs. O'Hara Resources, Ltd., Vancouver, B.C., Can., 1989—; bd. dirs. Troy Gold Industries, Ltd., Calgary, Alta., Can. Mem. Calif. Bar Asns., Commwealth Club Calif., Sequoia Woods Country Club. Republican. Presbyterian. Office: PO Box 2096 San Ramon CA 94583-7096

DAVIS, JOHN ALLEN, JR. (JEFF DAVIS), financial planner; b. Canton, Ohio, Apr. 9, 1952; s. John Allen and Esther Marie (Falcone) D.; m. Donna Z. Davis, Dec. 5, 1981; children: John III, NIcholas, Rachel. BSJM, U. Fla., 1975. CFP, 1990. Asst. wrestling coach U. Fla. Athletic Assn., Gainesville, 1975-79; assoc. gen. agt, unit mgr. Ky. Cen. Life, Gainesville, 1979-83; assoc. Jack McGriff & Assocs., Gainesville, 1983-88; ptnr. Bowling, Whitaker & Davis, Gainesville, 1988-90; pvt. practice Gainesville, 1990—; guest speaker on fringe benefits U. Fla., 1991; pres. and chief investment officer Falcon Fin. Mgmt., Inc; co-host radio show Dollars and Sense with Jeff and Donna Davis. Columnist Gainesville Sun. Commr. Gainesville Sport Organizing Com., 1990-94; event dir. USA Wrestling, Gainesville, 1990-93, Nat. Espoir Wrestling Championships, 1991, 92; staff wrestling, athlete escort, tng. site supr. Centennial Olympic Games; mem. Holy Faith Cath. Ch. Mem. Inst. of CFP's, Registry Fin. Planners, Estate Planning Coun. Gainsville, Gainesville C. of C., Pres.'s Coun. U. Fla., UAA Letterman's Club, Kiwanis (com. chmn., bd. dirs. Gainesville). Avocations: sports, reading, music. Office: Falcon Fin Mgmt Inc 2631 NW 41st St Gainesville FL 32606-7470

DAVIS, JOHN CHARLES, lawyer; b. Kansas City, Mo., Mar. 4, 1943; s. Ralph B. Jr. and Helen M. (Schneider) D.; m. C. Jane Reusser, June 18, 1966; children: Tracy A., Matthew S. BA, U. Kans., 1965; JD, U. Mich., 1968. Bar: Mo. 1968, Kans. 1983. Stockholder Stinson, Mag & Fizzell, P.C., Kansas City, 1968—; chmn. Fed. Estate Tax Symposium, 1986-87. Chmn. Bacchus Found., Kansas City, 1974; bd. dirs. Crittenten, Kansas City, 1988-94, vice chmn., 1990-92; trustee Schutte Found., Kansas City, 1986—, U. Kansas City, 1989—, treas., 1994—, counsel, 1996—; trustee Village Presbyn. Ch. Found., chmn., 1991-93; elder Village Presbyn. Ch., 1994-97; bd. dirs. Gamma O Edn. Found., 1991—, Heart of Am. Counsel, Boy Scouts Am., 1995—, exec. com., 1996—. Fellow Am. Coll. Trust and Estate Counsel (by-laws com. 1987-96, chmn. 1996-99, program com. 1993-96); mem. ABA, Mo. Bar Assn., Kans. Bar Assn., Estate Planning Soc. Kansas City (pres. 1990-91), Nelson-Atkins Mus. Soc. Fellows, Univ. Club (Kansas City, Mo. v.p. 1989-90), Gamma Omicron (pres., bd. dirs. 1979-85). Presbyterian. Avocations: squash, Hopi art, Marklin trains, travel, photography. Home: 6421 High Dr Shawnee Mission KS 66208-1935 Office: Stinson Mag & Fizzell PC 1201 Walnut St PO Box 419251 Kansas City MO 64141-6251

DAVIS, JOHN CHRISTOPHER, zoologist, aquatic toxicologist; b. Bristol, Eng., Oct. 21, 1944; came to Can., 1948; m. Theresa Colleen Davis; children: Pamela, Paul. BS, U. Victoria, B.C., Can., 1966; MS, U. B.C., 1968, PhD, 1971. Rsch. scientist Fisheries Rsch. Bd. Can., West Vancouver, B.C., 1971-78, assoc. dir., 1978-80; dir. gen. Ont. region Can. Dept. Fisheries and Oceans, Ottawa, 1980-82; dir. gen. Pacific and Feshwater Fisheries Pacific/Freshwater Fisheries, Can. Dept. Fisheries/Oceans, Ottawa, Ont., 1982-86; regional dir. sci. Pacific region Fisheries and Oceans of Can., Sidney, B.C., 1986-99; asst. dep. min. rsch. Sci. Dept. Fisheries and Oceans of Can., Ottawa, 1999—; advisor sci. adv. bd. Internat. Joint Commn., 1981-83; negotiator Can-USA Yukon Salmon Treaty, 1985-88, High Seas Driftnet Negotiations, North Pacific, 1987-91; del. North Pacific Marine Sci. Orgn. Treaty, 1989-91. Contbr. articles to profl. jours. Del. N. Pacific Marine Sci. Orgn., 1992—. Achievements include research on sublethal effects of pollutants on aquatic organisms and on oxygen criteria developed for aquatic life. Office: Can Dept Fisheries and Oceans, 200 Kent St, Ottawa, ON Canada KIA 0E6*

DAVIS, JOHN EUGENE, restaurant owner, disc jockey; b. Buffalo, Aug. 27, 1948; s. Stanley and Dorothy (Svennson) D.; m. Carolyn Elizabeth Cummings, June 14, 1969; children: John, Jady. AA, Niagara County C.C., 1968; BA, Oneonta State U., 1970; MS, Russell Sage Coll., 1974. Tchr. Schenectady (N.Y.) City Sch. Dist., 1970-92; pres. PJ's Bar-B-Q, Inc., Saratoga Springs, N.Y., 1986—, Sarasoda, Inc., Saratoga Springs, 1998—. Active Rep. Chairman's Club, Saratoga Springs. Mem. Nat. Restaurant Assn., N.Y. State United Tchrs., Schenectady Fedn. Tchrs., Greater Saratoga C. of C., United Restaurant Hotel Tavern Assn. of N.Y. State, Nat. Rifle Assn., N.Y. State Restaurant Assn., Lions (Lion of the Yr. 1984-85). Methodist. Avocations: physical fitness, boating, fishing, football. Home: 1 Kaydeross Ave Saratoga Springs NY 12866-8736 Office: PJ's Bar-B-Q Inc RR 9 Saratoga Springs NY 12866-9809

DAVIS, JOHN HERSCHEL, surgeon, educator; b. Coraopolis, Pa., May 11, 1924; s. John Herschel and Fern (Pew) D.; m. Peggy Lou Seyler, Sept. 7, 1946; children: Karen LaRue, Wendy Sue, Halle Rive'. Student, Allegheny Coll., 1942-43; M.D., Western Res. U., 1948. Diplomate: Am. Bd. Surgery. Intern Univ. Hosps., Cleve., 1948-49, resident, 1955-56; asst. prof. surgery Western Res. U., Cleve., 1956-59, assoc. prof. surgery, 1959-64, prof., 1964-69; dir. surgery Cleve. Met. Hosp., 1966-69; prof. dept. surgery U. Vt., Burlington, 1969—; dir. Am. Bd. Surgery, Phila., Am. Bd. Emergency Medicine, East Lansing, Mich., Am. Trauma Soc., Chgo., 1978—; chmn. surgery sect. NIH, Washington, 1982—. Editor: Current Concepts of Surgery, 1965, Jour. of Trauma, 1974, Clinical Surgery, 1987, Essentials of Clinical Surgery, 1991; Am. editor: Brit. Jour. Injury; editorial bd.: Medfact; corr. editor: Journal de Traumatologie, Jour. Injury. Mem. Bar. Rev. Com. Vt. Supreme Ct., 1982. Served to capt. U.S. Army, 1950-53. Recipient William Peck Rsch. award Western Res. U., 1961; recipient Surgeon of Year award Nat. Safety Coun., N.Y.C., 1979. Fellow ACS (Scudder Oration award 1979, Disting. Svc. award 1991); mem. AAAS, Am. Assn. for History of Medicine, Am. Surg. Assn., Am. Assn. Surgery Trauma, Am. Burn Assn., Am. Fedn. Clin. Rsch., Am. Heart Assn., Am. Trauma Soc., Central Soc. Clin. Rsch., Central Surg. Soc., Chittenden County Med. Soc., Collegium Internationale Chirurgiae Digestivae, Digestive Disease Found., Eastern Surg. Soc., Halsted Soc., Internat. Soc. for Burn Injuries, Italian Surg. Rsch. Soc., Nat. Rsch. Coun. of Nat. Acad. Scis., New Eng. Soc. for Vascular Surgery, New Eng. Surg. Soc. (Nathan Smith award 1997), N.Y. Acad. Scis., Soc. Internationale de Chirurgie, Soc. Exptl. Biology and Medicine, Soc. Med. Cons. to Armed Forces, Soc. Surgery Alimentary Tract, Soc. Surg. Chairmen, Soc. for Vascular Surgery, Surg. Biology Club II, Thirty-eighth Parallel Med. Soc., Vt. State Med. Soc. (Disting. Svc. award 1990), Allen O. Whipple Med. Soc., Sigma Xi, Alpha Omega Alpha. Republican. Club: Ethan Allen (Burlington). Home: 21 Ridgewood Dr Burlington VT 05401-2625 Office: U Vt Coll Medicine Given Bldg Burlington VT 05405

DAVIS, JOHN JAMES, religion educator; b. Phila., Oct. 13, 1936; s. John James and Cathryn Ann (Nichols) D.; m. Carolyn Ann. BA, Trinity Coll., Dunedin, Fla., 1959, DD (hon.), 1968; MDiv, Grace Coll. & Grace Theol. Sem., Winona Lake, Ind., 1962, ThM, 1964, ThD, 1967. Instr. Grace Coll. & Grace Theol. Sem., 1963-65, prof. of Old Testament, 1965—, exec. v.p., 1976-82, pres., 1986-93; exec. dean Near East Sch. Archaeology, Jerusalem, 1970-71; area supr. Tekoa Archeol. Expdn., Jordan, 1968, 70, Raddana Expdn., Jordan, 1974, Heshbon Expdn., Jordan, 1976, Abila Archeol. Expdn., Jordan, 1982, 84. Author: Paradise to Prison, 1975 (Book of Yr.), The Perfect Shepherd, 1979 (Book of Yr.) 14 other books. Chmn., bd. dirs. Kosciusko Comty. Hosp., 1994-95. Recipient Gold award United Way, 1980, Conservation award Barbee Property Owners Assn., 1983; named Outdoor Writer of Yr., Ind. Dept. Natural Resources, 1986, to the Koscivsko County Rep. Hall of Fame, 1992. Mem. Am. Schs. of Oriental Research, Near East Archeol. Soc., Outdoor Writers Assn., Hoosier Outdoor Writers Assn. (pres. 1984-86). Avocations: fishing, hunting, photography. Home: PO Box 557 Winona Lake IN 46590-0557 Office: Grace Theol Sem 200 Seminary Dr Winona Lake IN 46590-1224*

DAVIS, JOHN MACDOUGALL, lawyer; b. Seattle, Feb. 20, 1914; s. David Lyle and Georgina (MacDougall) D.; m. Ruth Anne Van Arsdale, July 1, 1939; children: Jean, John, Bruce, Ann, Margaret, Elizabeth. B.A., U. Wash., 1936, LLB, JD, 1940. Bar: Wash. 1940. Assoc. Poe, Falknor, Emory & Howe, Seattle, 1940-45; pvt. practice Seattle, 1945-46; ptnr. Davis & Riese, Seattle, 1946-48, Emory, Howe, Davis & Riese, Seattle, 1948-50, Howe, Davis & Riese, Seattle, 1951-53, Howe, Davis, Riese & Aiken, Seattle, 1953-58, Howe, Davis, Riese & Jones, Seattle, 1958-68, Davis, Wright, Todd, Riese & Jones, Seattle, 1969-85; of counsel Davis, Wright & Jones, Seattle, 1985-89, Davis Wright Tremaine, Seattle, 1990—; lectr. U. Wash. Law Sch., 1947-52. Bd. dirs. Virginia Mason Hosp., Seattle, 1952-79, pres., 1970-72; bd. dirs. Pacific Sci. Ctr., 1971-90, dir. emeritus, 1991—, past pres., past chmn.; trustee Whitman Coll., 1971-86, chmn., 1983-86; bd. dirs. Blue Cross Wash. and Alaska, 1982-89, Diabetic Trust Fund, 1954—, Wash. Student Loan Guaranty Assn., 1978-83; mem. adv. bd. Chief Seattle council Boy Scouts Am.; mem. Mercer Island Sch. Bd., 1956-66. Served with USNG, 1931-34. Recipient Disting. Eagle Scout award, 1982. Mem. ABA, Wash. State Bar Assn. (merit award 1965), Seattle-King County Bar Assn. (pres. 1960-61), Order of Coif, Rainier Club (Seattle), The Mountaineers Club, Phi Delta Phi, Alpha Delta Phi. Presbyterian. Clubs: Rainier (Seattle). Avocation: mountain climbing. Home: 9104 Fortuna Dr #3305 Mercer Island WA 98040-3166 Office: Davis Wright Tremaine 2600 Century Sq 1501 4th Ave Ste 2600 Seattle WA 98101-1688

DAVIS, JOHN P., career officer; b. Birmingham, May 15, 1946; m. Nancy Huttemeyer; children: Kathryn, Tricia. BS, U.S. Naval Acad., 1968; MS in Elec. Engring., Naval Postgrad. Sch., 1969. Commd. ensign USN, 1969, advanced through grades to rear admiral, 1991; served on USS Pogy, 1970-74; engring. officer USS Daniel Webster, 1974-78; dept. head, post dept. head detailer Bur. Naval Pers., 1978-81; exec. officer USS Memphis, 1981-84; commdg. officer USS Jacksonville, 1984-87, USS Glenard P. Lipscomb, 1988; dep. commdr. Submarine Squadron 6, 1988-89; head Undersea & Artic Warfare Br. Office Chief Naval Ops., 1989-91, dir. Advanced Submarine R&D, 1991-92, program mgr. Advanced Capability Torpedo Program, 1992-96, program mgr. Undersea Weapons Program Office, 1996; dir. Office Submarine Tech. Naval Sea Sys. Command, 1996-97, program exec. officer Submarines, 1997—. Office: USN 2531 Jefferson Davis Hwy Arlington VA 22242-0001*

DAVIS, JOHN PHILLIPS, JR., lawyer; b. Pitts., June 1, 1925; s. John Phillips and Jean Stout (Miller) D.; m. Mary McCreery Oates, Sept. 13, 1952; children: George B., John P. III, Elizabeth Davis Bennett, Mary O. Student, Williams Coll.; AB, Harvard U., 1947, JD, 1950. Bar: Pa. 1951. Pvt. practice Pitts.; ptnr. Reed Smith Shaw & McClay, 1961-87, counsel, 1988—; dir. Firth Sterling, Inc., Pitts. Gage and Supply Co., Bloom Engring., Co., Inc. Bd. dirs. Pitts. Child Guidance Ctr., 1960-63, Staunton Farm Found., 1964-91, pres., 1968-85, Vis. Nurse Assn., Allegheny County, 1955-68, pres., 1962-64, Snyder Found., 1979-87, Met. Pitts. Pub. Broadcasting, Inc. Sta. WQED, 1984-90, Hist. Soc. Western Pa., 1986-97, v.p., 1991-94; trustee Shady Side Acad., Pitts., 1959-95, chmn., 1971-74, Ellis Sch., Pitts., 1969-74, Robert S. Waters Charitable Trust, 1971—, Carnegie Inst., 1985-91, Carnegie Mus. Art, 1985—. With AUS, 1943-45, ETO. Decorated Bronze Star, Purple Heart. Mem. Am. Law Inst., ABA, Pa. Bar Assn. (chmn. jr. bar conf. 1957), Allegheny County Bar Assn. (pres. jr. bar sect. 1955). Republican. Episcopalian. Clubs: Duquesne, Fox Chapel Golf (bd. dirs., sec. 1985-92). Home: 144 North Dr Pittsburgh PA 15238-2310 Office: PO Box 2009 435 6th ave Pittsburgh PA 15230

DAVIS, JOHN ROWLAND, university administrator; b. Mpls., Dec. 19, 1927; s. Roland Owen and Dorothy (Norman) D.; m. Lois Marie Falk, Sept. 4, 1947; children—Joel C., Jacque L., Michele M., Robin E. B.S., U. Minn., 1949, M.S., 1951; postgrad., Purdue U., 1955-57; Ph.D., Mich. State U., 1959. Hydraulic engr. U.S. Geol. Survey, Lincoln, Nebr., 1950-51; instr. Mich. State U., 1951-55; asst. prof. Purdue U., 1955-57; lectr. U. Calif., Davis, 1957-62; hydraulic engr. Stanford Research Inst., South Pasadena, Calif., 1962-64; prof. U. Nebr., Lincoln, 1964-65, dean coll. engring. and architecture, 1965-71; faculty rep. intercollegiate athletics U. Nebr.; prof., head dept. agrl. engring. Oreg. State U., Corvallis, 1971-75; instl. athletic rep. Oreg. State U., 1972-87, dir. Agrl. Expt. Sta., assoc. dean Sch. Agr., 1975-85, dir. spl. programs Office of Academic Affairs, assoc. dir. athletics, 1987-89, prof. emeritus, assoc. dir. athletics, 1989—; mem. governing bd. Water Resources Research Inst., 1975-85; dir. Western Rural Devel. Center, 1975-85, Agrl. Research Found., Jackman Inst.; cons. Stanford Research Inst., Dept. Agr., Consortium for Internat. Devel.; dir. Engrs. Council Profl. Devel., 1966-72; pres. Pacific-10 Conf., 1978-79. Contbr. articles to profl. jours. Served with USNR, 1945-46. Fellow Am. Soc. Agrl. Engrs. (dir. 1971-73, agrl. engr. of year award Pacific N.W. region 1974), NCAA (v.p. 1979-83, sec.-treas. 1983-85, pres. 1985-87). Home: 2940 NW Aspen St Corvallis OR 97330-3307 Office: Oreg State U Gill Coliseum Corvallis OR 97331

DAVIS, JOHN WARREN, program integrator; b. York, Pa., Feb. 14, 1946; s. Frank Asbury Jr. and Lillian Margaret (Billings) D. BA in Polit. Sci., Drake U., 1968; AA in Real Estate, San Diego City Coll., 1976; MS in Acquisition and Contract Mgmt., West Coast U., 1987; postgrad., Walden U., 1992—. Real estate sales staff, 1972-79; clk. GS 3 Naval Ocean Sys. Ctr., 1979-80; contract intern, contract adminstr. Office of Naval Rsch., 1980-84; contract specialist, warranted ordering officer Gen. Svc. 1102-11 Naval Weapons Sta., 1984-86; contract specialist Gen Svc. 1102-12 Navy Space Sys. Activity, 1986-88; procurement analyst Gen Svc. 102-12 COMNAVAIRPAC, 1988-98; def. contract mgr. Def. Contract Mgmt. Command, 1998—; del. San Diego State U. to the Nat. Acad. Conf. for Contract Mgmt. Educators, 1991, 92, 93; profl. cons. Computer Applications, Inc., 1992; mem. tech. program com., chairperson for electronic data interchange Soc. of Logistics Engrs., 1995; mem. Golden Hill planning com. City of San Diego; adj. instr. San Diego State U., chmn. curriculum rev. com. for acquisitiion. Author, Paperless Contracting, The EDI Revolution, 1995, contbr. articles to profl. publs. With U.S. Army, Vietnam, 1968-72. Fellow Nat. Contract Mgmt. Assn. (cert. profl. contract mgr.); mem. ABA (mem. sub-com. pub. law sector, sub-com. on intellectual property), SAR (nat., Calif. and San Diego chpts.), Am. Arbitration Assn. (nat. panel mem.), Soc. Govt. Meeting Planners (v.p. San Diego chpt.), Soc. Logistics Engrs., San Diego Athletic Club, San Diego Writers and Editors Guild, Author's Guild (past pres.). Episcopalian. Avocations: swimming, traveling. Home: PO Box 620657 San Diego CA 92162-0657 Office: DCMC (GSOC) 7675 Dagget St Ste 200 San Diego CA 92111-2256

DAVIS, JOHN WILLIAM, government science and engineering executive. BSME, U. Tex., 1957; MSME, So. Meth. U., 1962; PhD in Aerospace Engring., Okla. State U., 1972. Aerodynamics design engr., sr. and lead wind tunnel engr. Chance Vought Corp., Grand Prairie, Tex., 1957-61; chief gas dynamics sect. Marshall Space Flight Ctr. NASA, Huntsville, Ala., 1961-75, exptl. investigations br. chief Ames Rsch. Ctr., 1975-80; dir. Propulsion Wind Tunnel Facility Calspan Corp./Arnold Engring. Devel. Ctr. Ops., Arnold AFB, Tenn., 1980-87, v.p., gen. mgr., 1987-1994; vice pres., gen. mgr. Micro Craft Tech./Arnold Engring. Devel. Ctr.Ops., Arnold AFB, Tenn., 1994, chief engr. micro crafttech., 1994-95, AEDC chief scientist, 1995—; exec. dir. U. Tenn./Calspan Ctr. Aerospace Rsch.; bd. dirs. U. Tenn./Calspan Ctr. Space Transp. and Applied Rsch. Contbr. 38 articles to profl. jours. Bd. dirs. Tenn. Valley Aerospace Region, Hands-On Sci. Ctr., trustee, chmn. fin. com. Recipient Ground Testing award Am. Inst. of Aeronautics and Astronautics, 1994. Fellow AIAA (Ground Testing award 1994, mem. ground testing and simulation tech. com., mem. honors and awards subcom., 1992, liaison officer to thermophysics tech. com.), Arnold Engring. Devel. Ctr., Internat. Test and Evaluation Assn., Air Force Assn., Nat. Mgmt. Assn., Supersonic Tunnel Assn. (past pres., sec., mem.-at-large, exec. bd. dirs.). Office: Arnold Engring Devel Ctr-CN 1099 Avenue C Ste 106 Arnold AFB TN 37389-9010

DAVIS, JOLENE BRYANT, magazine publishing executive consultant; b. Lehigh, Iowa, Dec. 11, 1942; d. Joseph Albert and Joyce (Olson) Bryant; m. Richard Alan Alper, Feb. 12, 1967 (dec. July 1975); m. Steven Andrew Davis, Apr. 16, 1979; children: Bryant David, Suzanne Joyce. BA, U. Iowa, 1964; MA, Calif. State U., San Jose, 1972. Registered dietitian, Ind. Home economist The Oregonian, newspaper, Portland, 1965-67; dietitian Ind. U. Sch. Medicine, Indpls., 1973-74; clin. dietitian U. Calif. Hosps. and Clins.,

San Francisco, 1974-75, chief clin. dietitian, 1975-78, chief rsch. dietitian Clin. Study Ctr., 1979-83; pub., chief exec. officer Our Kids mag. Branford Pub., Inc., San Antonio, 1984-99, v.p., 1988-98; ptnr. Serendipity Video Prodns., 1996—; also bd. dirs., v.p. Branford Pub., Inc., San Antonio, 1983-99; sports nutritionist San Antonio Spurs, 1993—; sec., bd. govs. Parenting Publs. Am., San Antonio, 1988-89; v.p., bd. dirs. The Magik Theatre, 1995—. Mem. San Antonio Conservation Soc., 1985—; bd. dirs. Jewish Family Svc. Assn., San Antonio, 1986-88, Family Resource Ctr., San Antonio, Children's Bereavement Ctr. South Tex., 1997—; chmn. cultural arts PTA, San Antonio, 1988-94; vol. McNay Art Mus., 1996-98; pres. Alamo Heights Schs. Choir Boosters Club, 1999—. Recipient Life Mem. award PTA, 1994, Supt.'s award N.E. Ind. Sch. Dist., 1995-96. Mem. Women in Comms. (editor Best Mag. Column and Mag. award of Merit 1988, 90), Am. Dietetic Assn., Soc. Nutrition Edn., San Antonio Dist. Dietetic Assn., Soc. Profl. Journalists, Pi Beta Phi. Avocations: volunteer elementary school art history teaching, antiques, rare book collecting, genealogy, travel. Home: 178 Country Ln San Antonio TX 78209-2228 Office: Branford Pub Inc 8400 Blanco Rd Ste 201 San Antonio TX 78216-3055

DAVIS, JOSEPH LLOYD, educational administrator, consultant; b. Crawfordsville, Iowa, May 4, 1927; s. Whitfield and Jane (Lloyd) D.; m. Margaret Florence Cooper, Dec. 28, 1949; children: Stephen Joseph, Thomas Whitfield, Jane Ellen. BSc, Ohio State U., 1949, MA, 1955, PhD, 1967. Reporter Ohio State Jour., 1943-49, 52-53; tchr. Morey Jr. H.S., Denver, 1949-52, Central H.S., Columbus, Ohio, 1953-54; asst. dir. adminstrv. research Columbus Public Schs., 1954-56, dir. publs. and public info., 1956-60, exec. asst. to supt., 1960-64, asst. supt. spl. services, 1964-77, supt. of schs., 1977-82; exec. dir. Ohio Coun. Vocat. Edn., 1985-96; trustee Ctr. of Sci. and Industry; past pres. Columbus Rotary; adj. prof. Ohio State U., 1983—; founder, dir. emeritus Ohio State U. Nat. Acad. for Supt.; mem. sch.-to-work com. Gov.'s Workforce Devel. Bd.; cons. and author in field. Active Interprofl. Commn. Ohio, 1999—. With USN, 1945-46, 50-51. Recipient award for civic leadership Columbus Area C. of C., 1980, Liberty Bell award Columbus Bar Assn., 1980; named to Pub. Schs. Hall of Fame, Columbus, Ohio, 1993. Mem. Am. Assn. Sch. Adminstrs. (disting. svc. award 1989). Nat. Sch. Pub. Rels. Assn. (pres.'s award 1980), Assn. for Career and Tech. Edn., Ohio Vocat. Assn., Buckeye Assn. Sch. Adminstrs., Nat. Soc. Study Edn., Horace Mann League, Rotary (Rotarian of Yr. award 1994), Torch Club Columbus, Phi Delta Kappa, Epsilon Pi Tau (laureate), Kappa Delta Pi, Omicron Tau Theta. Presbyterian.

DAVIS, JOSHUA MALCOLM, lawyer; b. Worcester, Mass., May 11, 1965; s. William Merritt and Jessica Ann (Hoffmann) D.; m. Susan Marysol Flink, Aug. 11, 1991; children: Emerson Jacob, Malcolm Christopher. BA, Swarthmore Coll., 1987; JD, U. Chgo., 1991. Bar: Mass. 1992; U.S. Ct. Appeals (10th cir.), 1992; U.S. Dist. Ct. (Mass.), 1993; U.S. Ct of Appeals (1st Cir.), 1993; U.S. Supreme Ct., 1995; U.S. Ct. of Appeals (2nd Cir.), 1997. English tchr. St. Paul's Sch., Concord, N.H., 1987-88; law clerk Hon. Stephanie K. Seymour U.S. Ct. Appeals (10th cir.), Tulsa, 1991-92; assoc. Hill & Barlow, Boston, 1992-99, mem., 1999—; tchg. asst. torts Harvard Law Sch., Cambridge, Mass., 1997, part-time lectr. law, Northeastern U. Sch. of Law, 1998. Contbr. Mass. Lawyers Weekly, 1994, 98. Mem. ABA, Mass. Bar Assn., Boston Bar Assn. Democrat. Avocations: golf, reading. Office: Hill & Barlow 1 International Pl Boston MA 02110-2602

DAVIS, JUDY, actress; b. Perth, Australia, Apr. 23, 1955; m. Colin Friels, 1984; children: Jack, Charlotte. Student, Nat. Inst. Dramatic Art, Sydney, Australia. Appearences include: (film) High Rolling, 1976, My Brilliant Career, 1979 (Best Actress Sammy award Australian Film and TV Awards 1979, Best Actress award Brit. Acad. Film and TV Arts 1981, Best Newcomer Brit. Acad. Film and TV Arts 1981), Hoodwink, 1981 (Best Supporting Actress Sammy award Australian Film and TV Awards 1981), Winter of Our Dreams, 1981 (Best Actress Sammy award Australia Film and TV Awards 1981), Heatwave, 1982, The Final Option, 1983, A Passage to India, 1984 (Acad. award nominee for best actress 1984), Kangaroo, 1986, High Tide, 1987, Georgia, 1988, Alice, 1990, Impromptu, 1991, Barton Fink, 1991, Naked Lunch, 1991 (Best Supporting Actress award N.Y. Critics Cir. 1991), Where Angels Fear to Tread, 1991, Husbands and Wives, 1992 (Acad. award nominee for best supporting actress 1992), The Ref, 1994, The New Age, 1994, Children of the Revolution, 1996, Absolute Power, 1996, Blood and Wine, 1996, Deconstructing Harry, 1996, Celebrity, 1997, The Echo of Thunder, 1998; (TV movies) A Woman Called Golda, 1982 (Emmy award nominee 1982), The Merry Wives of Windsor, 1982, Rocket to the Moon, 1986, One Against the Wind, 1991, Serving in Silence: The Margarethe Cammermeyer Story, 1995 (Emmy award); (TV miniseries) Water Under the Bridge, 1982; (stage) Lulu (Frank Wedekind), Piaf (Pam Gem), Insignificance (Terry Johnson), 1982, Echo of Thunder (Emmy nomination), 1997, (TV prodn.) Dash & Lily, 1997 (Emmy nomination). Office: care Shanahan Mgmt, PO Box 478, Kings Cross NSW 2011, Australia

DAVIS, JULIA MCBROOM, college dean, speech pathology and audiology educator; b. Alexandria, La., Sept. 29, 1930; d. Guy Clarence and Addie (McElroy) McBroom; m. Cecil Ponder Davis, Aug. 25, 1951 (div. 1981); children: Mark Holden, Paul Houston, Anne Hamilton; m. David G. Reynolds, Aug. 26, 1987. BA, Northwestern State U., Natchitoches, La., 1951; MS, U. So. Miss., 1965, PhD, 1966. Cert. in clin. competence in audiology Am. Speech-Lang.-Hearing Asn. Asst. prof. U. So. Miss., Hattiesburg, 1966-69, assoc., 1969-71; assoc. prof. Southwestern State U., Hammond, 1971; faculty U. Iowa, Iowa City, 1971-87; prof., chmn. dept. speech pathology and audiology U. Iowa, 1980-85, assoc. dean Coll. Liberal Arts, 1985-87, dir. Speech and Hearing Ctr., 1979-80; dean Coll. Social and Behavioral Scis. U. South Fla., Tampa, 1987-90, assoc. provost, 1990-91; dean Coll. Liberal Arts, U. Minn., Mpls., 1991-96, prof., 1991-97. Author: (with Edward J. Hardick) Rehabilitative Audiology for Children and Adults, 1981; editor: Our Forgotten Children, 1977; assoc. editor Jour. Speech Hearing Research, 1975-77, Jour. Speech Hearing Disorders, 1982-83. Pres., bd. of trustees Minn. Foun. for Better Hearing & Speech, bd. of trustees Mpls. Found., Ballet Arts of Minn., Iowa City Crisis Ctr.; bd. dirs. Crisis Intervention Ctr. Fellow Am. Speech-Hearing-Lang. Assn. (chmn. program com. 1980-81), Iowa Speech and Hearing Assn. (v.p.-liaison 1972-73, honors 1985); mem. Acad. Rehabilitative Audiology (pres. 1979-80), Iowa Conf. for Hearing Impaired (pres. 1975-76), Sigma Xi. Democrat. Methodist. Home: 55 Rita Lyn Ct Iowa City IA 52245-3504

DAVIS, JULIAN MASON, JR., lawyer; b. Birmingham, Ala., July 30, 1935; s. Julian Mason Sr. and Madeline (Harris) D.; m. June Carolyn Fox, Aug. 11, 1957; children: Karen Madeline, Julian Mason III. BA, Talladega (Ala.) Coll., 1956; JD, SUNY, Buffalo, 1959. Bar: Ala. 1960, U.S. Dist. Ct. (no. dist.) Ala. 1961, U.S. Ct. Appeals (5th cret.) 1961, U.S. Tax Ct. 1979, U.S. Ct. Appeals (11th cret.) 1981, U.S. Dist. Ct. (mid. dist.) Ala. 1989, U.S. Supreme Ct. 1993. With Sirote & Permutt P.C., Birmingham; bd. dirs. Protective Indsl. Ins. Co., Birmingham, chmn. bd., 1988—; bd. dirs. Energen Corp., So. Rsch., all Birmingham. Mem. pres.'s cabinet U. Ala. Mem. ABA, Nat. Bar Assn., Ala. Bar Assn. (bar commr. 1987-96), Birmingham Bar Assn. (sec., treas. 1978-79, pres. 1984-85). Democrat. Avocations: golf, reading. Office: Sirote & Permutt PC 2222 Arlington Ave S Birmingham AL 35205-4004

DAVIS, JULIE KRAMER, communications executive; b. N.Y.C., Apr. 20, 1957; d. Jerome Kramer and Roberta Luttrell; m. Steven Curt Davis, Aug. 24, 1980; 1 child, Benjamin Herman. BA in English, Binghamton U., 1979; MS in Corp. Comm., Ithaca Coll., 1990; MA in Edn. and Human Devel., The George Washington U., 1996. Reporter Stas. WENE-AM-FM and WMRV-AM-FM, Endicott, N.Y., 1979; news dir. Sta. WINR-AM-FM, Binghamton, N.Y., 1979-81; prodr., reporter and personality Sta. WSKG-TV, Binghamton, 1981-89; multimedia specialist Westinghouse Savannah River Co., Aiken, S.C., 1990-96; corp. comm. dir. Cracker Barrel Old Country Store, Lebanon, Tenn., 1996—; instr. Broome C.C., Binghamton, 1988-90; presenter at various confs., 1992, 95-96. project mgr. and designer (CD-ROM) VOCs in Non-Arid Soil, 1995 (Gold prize Georgia VidFest 1995). Recipient Outstanding Achievement award The SIGCAT Found., 1996, Parthenon awardPub. Rels. Soc. Am., 1998, The Communicator award Print Media Competition, 1999. Mem. Internat. Assn. Bus. Communicators, Internat. Soc. Performance Improvement, Coun. Comm. Mgmt., Phi Kappa Phi. Office: Cracker Barrel Old Country Store 307 Hartman Dr Lebanon TN 37087-2519

DAVIS, KAREN, fund executive; b. Blackwell, Okla., Nov. 14, 1942; d. Walter Dwight and Thelma Louise (Kohler) Padgett; 1 child, Kelly Denise Collins. BA, Rice U., 1965, PhD, 1969. Asst. prof. econs. Rice U., 1969-70; econ. policy fellow Social Security Adminstrn. Brookings Instn., Washington, 1970-71, rsch. assoc., 1971-74, sr. fellow, 1974-77; dep. asst. sec. for planning and evaluation, health HEW, Washington, 1977-80; adminstr. health resources adminstrn. USPHS, Washington, 1980-81; prof. Johns Hopkins U., Balt., 1981-92; chmn., 1983-92; exec. v.p. Commonwealth Fund, N.Y.C., 1992-94, pres., 1995—; bd. dirs. Mt. Sinai Med. Ctr., 1995—; mem. Physican Payment Rev. Commn., 1986-94; dir. Commonwealth Fund Commn. on Elderly People Living Alone, 1985-91; vis. lectr. Harvard U., 1974-75. Author: National Health Insurance: Benefits, Costs and Consequences, 1975, Health and the War on Poverty, 1978, Medicare Policy: New Directions for Health and Long-Term Care, 1986, Health Care Cost Containment, 1990. Mem. Inst. Medicine, Am. Econs. Assn., Phi Beta Kappa. Democrat. Methodist. Home: 176 E 77th St New York NY 10021-1908 Office: The Commonwealth Fund The Harkness House 1 E 75th St New York NY 10021-2692*

DAVIS, KATHRYN WARD, fundraising executive; b. Florence, S.C., Oct. 11, 1949; d. Richard Dixon Ward and Kathryn (McFarland) Duncan; m. Michael R. Bumgardner, Feb. 16, 1974 (div. Nov. 1982); children: Carolyn E., Christopher G.; m. David Addison Davis, May 28, 1983. BA in English, U. N.C., 1971. Dir. devel. WFAE Radio, U. N.C., Charlotte, 1980-82, WUNC Radio, U. N.C., Chapel Hill, 1982-84, U. N.C. Hosps. Med. Found., Chapel Hill, 1984-87, St. Joseph Med. Found., Balt., 1987-88; exec. dir. MCG Found., Mt. Clemens, Mich., 1989-95; dir. devel. Leader Dogs for the Blind, Rochester, Mich., 1995-98; chief devel. officer Southeast Mich. chpt. ARC, Detroit, 1998—; fundraising coun. Macomb County Lit. Coun., Mt. Clemens, 1991. Tutor Macomb County Reading Ptnrs., 1992. Recipient Outstanding Vol. award Macomb County, 1996. Mem. Nat. Soc. Fundraising Execs. (bd. dirs. Greater Detroit chpt. 1998—), Kiwanis of Sterling Heights (bd. dirs. 1994-98, pres. 1996-97), Women's Econ. Club. Republican. Epsicopalian. Avocations: music, reading, family, swimming, travel. Office: SE Mich Chpt Am Red Cross 100 Mack Ave Box 33351 Detroit MI 48232-5351

DAVIS, KATHRYN WASSERMAN, foundation executive, writer, lecturer; b. Phila., Feb. 25, 1907; d. Joseph and Edith (Stix) Wasserman; m. Shelby Cullom Davis, Jan. 4, 1932; children: Shelby M. Cullom, Diana Davis Spencer, Priscella Alden (dec.). BA, Wellesley Coll., 1928; MA, Columbia U., 1931; D of Polit. Sci., U. Geneva, 1934; law degree (hon.), Columbia U., 1997. Researcher Coun. on Fgn. Rels., N.Y.C., 1934-36, State of Pa., Phila., 1936-37; writer and lectr. on fgn. affairs N.Y., 1937—; ptnr. Shelby Cullom Davis & Co., N.Y.C., 1985—; pres. The Shelby Cullom Davis Found., N.Y.C., 1985—; lectr. on fgn. affairs. Author: Soviets at Geneva, 1934. Trustee Wellesley Coll., 1983—; v.p. Women's Nat. Rep. Club, 1976—, chmn. internat. affairs com.; bd. govs. Harvard U., mem. vis. com. Russian studies, 1986—; past pres. LWV. Recipient life achievement award Women's Nat. Rep. Club, 1990, gold medal for disting. svc. to humanity Nat. Inst. Social Scis., 1990, Claire Booth Luce medal Heritage Found., 1991, Plymouth Com. award Mayflower Soc., 1992, Life Accomplishment award Internat. House, 1995. Mem. Cosmopolitan Club (N.Y.C., com. fgn. visitors), Sleepy Hollow Club (Scarborough N.Y.), N.Y. Harbor Club, Seal Harbor Club (Maine), Jupiter Island Club (Hobe Sound, Fla.), The Everglades Club, Inc. (Palm Beach, Fla.). Avocations: skiing, tennis, swimming, travel. Home: PO Box 689 Hobe Sound FL 33475-0689 Office: Shelby Cullom Davis & Co LP 609 5th Ave New York NY 10017-1021*

DAVIS, KATHY, critical care nurse; b. Dayton, Ohio, June 8, 1957; d. Jonas S. and Freeda Mae (Workman) Brewer; m. Terry Davis, July 1, 1972; children: Terry, Jason, Kevin. BSN, Wright State U., 1988. Critical care intern Miami Valley Hosp., Dayton, primary nurse ICU, 1992; staff nurse CCU VA Med. Ctr. (stationed at Wright Patterson AFB Medical Ctr.), 1992-97, cardiology nurse specialist, 1997—. Home: 706 Kauffman Ave Fairborn OH 45324-3812

DAVIS, KEIGH LEIGH, aerospace engineer; b. Mitchell, S.D., Oct. 6, 1954; d. Clarence Ralph and Katherine Lee Schilling; m. Glenn Nickerson Davis, Nov. 24, 1992. BS in Aerospace Engring. & Mechanics, U. Minn., 1976; MS in Aerospace Engring., U. Dayton, 1983. Stability and control project engr. Flight Stability and Control Br., USAF, Wright Patterson AFB, Ohio, 1976-85, E-3/Joint Stars Program Office, Wright Patterson AFB, 1985-86; lead stability, control & flying qualities project engr. Advanced Tactical Fighter Program, Wright Patterson AFB, 1986-88, Advanced Tactical Fighter Sys. Program Office, Wright Patterson AFB, 1988-90; stability and control project engr. Joint Tactical Autonomous Weapon Sys. Program Office, Wright Patterson AFB, 1990-91; lead br. engr. Flight Stability and Control Br., Wright Patterson AFB, 1991-94; stability and control tech. specialist Flight Mechanics Br., Wright Patterson AFB, 1993—; chmn. MIL-STD-1797 pilot-in-the-loop oscillation update team ASC/ENFT, Wright Patterson AFB, 1992-95, responsible engr. for flying qualities of piloted aircraft mil. std., 1992—, co-chmn. USAF flying qualities devel. process team, 1995—. Mem. AIAA (sr.), Soc. Women Engrs. (life), Order of Ea. Star (pres.).

DAVIS, KEITH EUGENE, psychologist, educator, consultant; b. Clifton, N.C., May 15, 1936; s. Ted Eugene and Mary Flossie (Rol) D.; m. Dorothy Ann Reeves, Feb. 23, 1968; 1 child, Kristin Lee; children from previous marriage: Rachel, Rebecca, Jessica. BA, Duke U., 1958, PhD, 1963. Instr. psychology Princeton U., 1961-62; asst. prof. U. Colo., Boulder, 1962-67, assoc. prof., 1967-70; prof., chmn. dept. psychology Livington Coll., Rutgers U., New Brunswick, N.J., 1970-73; prof. U.S.C., Columbia, 1973—; adj. prof. health adminstrn., health promotion/edn. U. S.C., Columbia, 1991—, univ. provost, 1974-78; chair dept. psychology U.S.C., Columbia, 1994-96; founder The Paradigm Group, mgmt. cons.; mgmt. cons., mem. population study sect. Nat. Inst. Child Health and Human Devel., 1973-76; mem. mental health rsch. edn. rev. com. NIMH, 1979—, chmn., 1980-83; chmn. State Plan Adv. Com., S.C. State Dept. Mental Health, 1976-78; pres. past participants Greater Columbia Forum, 1975-76. Author: Advances in Experimental Social Psychology, 1963; author, editor: Advanced in Descriptive Psychology, 1981; editor: The Social Construction of the Person, 1985; contbr. to Thoretical Perspectives on Personal Relationships, 1993; assoc. editor: Personal Relationships, 1993-97; contbr. 85 articles to profl. jours. Bd. dirs. Columbia Area Mental Health Ctr., 1976-82, chmn. bd. dirs., 1981. Woodrow Wilson fellow, 1958-59, So. Fellowships Fund fellow, 1958-61. Fellow Am. Psychol. Soc.; mem. APA, Am. Sociol. Assn., Internat. Soc. for Study of Personal Relationships (program chair 1992), Mind Assn., Nat. Coun. Family Rels., Soc. Descriptive Psychology (1st pres. 1979-81), Phi Beta Kappa, Omicron Delta Kappa. Home: 1808 Catawba St Columbia SC 29205-3010 Office: U SC Dept Psychology Columbia SC 29208

DAVIS, KENNETH LEON, psychiatrist, pharmacologist, medical educator; b. N.Y.C., Sept. 10, 1947; married, 1972; 2 children. BA, Yale U., 1969; MD, Mt. Sinai Med. Sch., 1973. Diplomate Am. Bd. Psychiatry and Neurology. Intern Stanford U., 1973-74, resident, 1973-76, life sci. rsch. assoc., 1975-76; clin. psychiat. cons. Santa Clara Valley Med. Ctr., 1976-79; chief dept. psychiat. VA Med. Ctr., 1979-87; asst. dir. Stanford Psych. Clin. Rsch. Ctr., VA Med. Ctr., 1975-79; rsch. assoc. Stanford Psych. Clin., 1974-79; assoc. prof. psychiatry and pharmacology Mt. Sinai Sch. Medicine, 1979-84; dir. schizophrenia biol. rsch. ctr., 1981-91; prof. Mt. Sinai Sch. Medicine, 1984—, chair dept. psychiatry, 1987—, Esther and Joseph Klingenstein prof., 1994—. *In 1979, spearheaded Mount Sinai's research program in the biology of schizophrenia and was the first director of the Schizophrenia Biological Research Center at the Bronx VA Hospital. Currently directs Mount Sinai's National Institute of Mental Health-funded center in schizophrenia, a project dedicated to understanding the neurobiology of schizophrenia, and particularly its cognitive deficits. Also directs Mount Sinai's National Institute of Aging (NIA) supported Alzheimer's Disease Research Center. Work has focused on all aspects of experimental therapeutics. Coordinated and completed the multicenter NIA-funded trial of Tacrine, and is currently conducting studies with antiinflammatory compounds to slow the course of Alzheimer's disease.* Editor Alzheimer's Disease and Associated Disorders, Biol. Psychiatry, Clin. Neuropharmacology, Harvard Review of Psychiatry, Internat. Jour. Geriatric Psychiatry, Internat. Jour. Geriatric Psychopharmacology, Jour. Geriatric Psychiatry & Neurology, Jour. Psychiatric Rsch., Jour. Am. Geriatrics Soc., Schizophrenia Rsch., Neuropsychopharmacology, Jour. Exptl. Cognitive and Behavioral Neurosci., Molecular Psychiatry, Sociedade de Psiquiatria Do Rio Grande Do Sul; author, co-author over 400 sci. articles. Recipient A. E. Bennett Clin. Sci. Rsch. award, 1977, Saul Horowitz Jr. Meml. award, 1977-78, Solomon Silver award, 1981, Joel Elkes Internat. award ACNP, 1986, Daniel H. Efron Excellence in Rsch. award, 1990, Rita Hayworth award Alzheimer's Assn., 1991, Lifetime Sci. award Inst. Advanced Sci. in Immunology and Aging, 1992. Mem. Am. Coll. Neuropsychopharmacology, Am. Psychiat. Assn. (APA/KEMPF award 1999), Soc. Biol. Psychiatry (Gold medal award 1999). Achievements include research in the biological basis of senile dementia of the Alzheimers' type, and schizophrenia. Office: Mount Sinai School of Medicine Dept Psychiatry 1 Gustave L Levy Pl New York NY 10029-6500

DAVIS, KENNETH SIDNEY, writer; b. Salina, Kans., Sept. 29, 1912; s. Charles DeForest and Lydia (Ericson) D.; m. Florence Marie Olenhouse, Feb. 19, 1937 (dec. Mar. 1987); m. Jean Stafford Dormer, July 21, 1990. B.S., Kans. State U., 1934; M.S., U. Wis.-Madison, 1935; Litt.D. (hon.), Assumption Coll., 1968. Reporter Daily Capital, Topeka, 1934; info. specialist Soil Conservation Service, USDA, Upper Miss. Valley region, 1935-40; editor plant newspaper Hercules Powder Co., 1942-43; war corrs. attached to SHAEF Doubleday and Co., N.Y.C., 1944; instr. journalism NYU, N.Y.C., 1945-47; spl. asst. to Milton S. Eisenhower, pres. Kans. State U. and chmn. U.S. Commn. for UNESCO, 1947-49; editor Newberry Library Bull., Newberry Library, Chgo., 1955-59; mem. personal staff Adlai E. Stevenson, Chgo., 1955-56. Author: (novels) In the Forests of the Night, 1942 (Friends of Am. Writers award 1943), The Years of the Pilgrimage, 1948, Morning in Kansas, 1952, (non-fiction) Soldier of Democracy, A Biography of Dwight Eisenhower, 1945, River on the Rampage, 1953, A Prophet in His Own Country: The Triumphs and Defeats of Adlai E. Stevenson, 1957, The Hero: Charles A. Lindbergh and the American Dream, 1959, (with John A. Day) Water, The Mirror of Science, 1961, Experience of War: The U.S. in World War II, 1965, The Cautionary Scientists: Priestley, Lavoisier, and the Founding of Modern Chemistry, 1966, The Politics of Honor: A Biography of Adlai E. Stevenson, 1967, Eisenhower: American Hero, 1969, FDR: The Beckoning of Destiny, 1882-1928, 1972 (Soc. Am. Historians Francis Parkman prize 1973), Invincible Summer, An Intimate Portrait of the Roosevelts (based on the recollections of Marion Dickerman), 1974, Kansas: A Bicentennial History, 1976, FDR: The New York Years 1928-1933, 1985, FDR: The New Deal Years 1933-1937, 1986; FDR: Into the Storm 1937-40, 1993, FDR: The War President, 1940-1943, 1999; editor: The Paradox of Poverty in America, 1969, Arms, Industry, and America, 1971. Recipient Centennial award Kans. State U., 1963; Guggenheim fellow, 1974, 76. Fellow Soc. Am. Historians. Club: Century (N.Y.C.). Avocations: gardening; hiking. Home: 3330 Arrowhead Dr Manhattan KS 66503-9172

DAVIS, KENNETH WAYNE, English language educator, business communication consultant; b. Chariton, Iowa, June 22, 1945; s. Wayne Pitman and Jeanne Frances (West) D.; m. Bette Hargrove, Nov. 28, 1970; Cassandra Alice, Evan Thomas. BA, Drake U., 1967; MA, Columbia U., 1968; PhD, U. Mich., 1975. From asst. prof. English to assoc. prof. U. Ky., Lexington, 1975-88; assoc. prof. to prof. Ind. U.-Purdue U., Indpls., 1988—, dept. chair, 1998—; bus. cons., Lexington, 1977-88; pres. Komei, Inc., 1994—. Author: Better Business Writing, 1983, (with others) Business Communication for the Information Age, 1988, Rehearsing the Audience, 1988, (with others) Writing: Process, Product, and Power, 1993; prodr.: 2001: Lessons in Leadership videoconf., 1991; numerous other books and articles. Bd. dirs. Shepherd's House, Inc., Lexington, 1986-88, Waycross Camp and Conf. Ctr., 1995—, World Trade Club Ind., 1998—. Sgt. U.S. Army, 1968-71. Woodrow Wilson fellow, 1967; recipient Faculty Service award Nat. Univ. Continuing Edn. Assn., 1987. Mem. ASTD, Nat. Coun. Tchrs. English, Assn. Bus. Comm., Assn. Profl. Comm. Cons., Amnesty Internat. Episcopalian. Avocations: theater, travel. Office: Ind U-Purdue U Dept English 425 University Blvd Indianapolis IN 46202

DAVIS, KIM MCALISTER, real estate sales executive, real estate broker; b. Woodruff, S.C., Dec. 30, 1958; d. James Calhoun and Nancy (Caldwell) McAlister; m. Robert James Godfrey (div.); 1 child, Lindsey Paige; m. Don Brigham Davis. BA in Elem. Edn., U. S.C., 1982, MBA, 1983—, postgrad., 1998—. Cert. tchr., S.C.; lic. real estate, Fla.; lic. CAM. Adminstrv. asst. to pvt. physician, Woodruff, 1977-78; sales rep. Reimer's Dept. Store, Woodruff, 1978-80; tchr. Spartanburg County Sch. Dist., Woodruff, 1982-83; pres., owner Godfrey Carpets, Inc., Woodruff, 1983-88; pharm. sales rep. Parke-Davis Pharm. Co., Ponte Vedra Beach, Fla., 1989-90; co-owner, ptnr. Ponte Vedra Realty, Inc., Ponte Vedra Beach, 1996—; real estate salesperson, 1993—; ptnr., co-owner Ponte Vedra Beach Realty, 1996—. Mem. decorating com. 1st Bapt. Ch., Woodruff, 1984-87; chmn. bd. dirs. Small Towns Program, Woodruff, 1987-88; Rep. candidate for Spartanburg County Coun., 1987; mem. S.C. Rep. Com.; sustaining mem. S.C. Rep. Party; bd. dirs. pres. 1991-93, Ponte Vedra-Palm Valley Elem. Sch. Parent Tchr. Student Orgn.; sustaining mem. Fla. Rep. Party; bd. dirs. St. Johns Pub. Edn. Found., St. Johns County Edn. Found.; mem. human resources strategic planning com. St. Johns County Pub. Schs.; Rep. candidate St. Johns County Sch. Bd., 1994. Named Young Careerist of the Yr., Bus. and Profl. Women, 1984. Mem. Nat. Fedn. Ind. Bus., Greater Woodruff Area C. of C. (pub. spkr., bd. dirs. 1985-87, pres. 1986), Bus. and Profl. Women (v.p. 1985), Woodruff Jr. Women's Club, Ponte Vedra Assn. Realtors, Disting. Million Dollar Club, St. John's County C. of C. (Ponte Vedra coun., exec. bd.), Ponte Vedra Beach C. of C. (inaugural bd. dirs. 1995-98). Avocations: golf, tennis, running, swimming, reading, fishing. Home: 8160 Seven Mile Dr Ponte Vedra FL 32082-3109

DAVIS, KIMBERLY BROOKE, art gallery director; b. L.A., 1953. BFA, Pratt Inst., N.Y.C., 1975; postgrad., Hunter Coll., N.Y.C. Dir. Bernard Jacobson, L.A., 1979-84, N.Y.C., 1983; dir. L.A. Louver, Venice, Calif., 1985—. Office: L A Louver 45 N Venice Blvd Venice CA 90291-4127

DAVIS, KRISTIN W., periodical editor; m. Michael A. Davis, Oct. 1, 1988. BA, Am. U., 1987. Copy editor Changing Times mag., Washington, 1987-89; assoc. editor Kiplinger's Personal Fin. Mag., Washington, 1989-93, sr. assoc. editor, 1993—. Author: Financing College, 1996. Mem. Nat. Press Club (Consumer Journalism award 1999), Soc. Am. Bus. Editors and Writers.

DAVIS, LANCE ALAN, research and development executive, metallurgical engineer; b. Ridley Park, Pa., Nov. 19, 1939; s. Earl W. and Ruth Naomi (Lentz) D.; m. Susan Ruth Kroesser, July 28, 1962; children: Susan, Virginia, Lance Jr. BS in Metall. Engring., Lafayette Coll., 1961; M in Engring., Yale U., 1963, PhD, 1966. Applied scientist research staff Yale U., New Haven, Conn., 1966-68; staff physicist Allied Chem. Corp., Morristown, N.J., 1968-74, mgr. strength physics, 1974-78, mgr. Metglas Devel. sect., 1978-80; dir. materials lab. Allied Corp., Morristown, 1980-84; v.p. R&D, Allied-Signal, Inc., Morristown, 1984-94; dir. Office of Tech. Transition Dept. Defense, 1994-99; exec. dir. NAE, Washington, 1999—. Contbr. numerous articles to profl. jours., chpts. to books; co-inventor 6 patents. Mem. AIME, NAE, Am. Soc. for Metals, Am. Phys. Soc., Materials Research Soc., Sigma Xi, Phi Beta Kappa, Tau Beta Pi. Home: 4006 Ellicott St Alexandria VA 22304-1012 Office: Nat Acad Engring 2101 Constitution Ave NW Washington DC 20418

DAVIS, LANCE EDWIN, economics educator; b. Seattle, Nov. 3, 1928; s. Maurice L. and Marjorie Dee (Seibert) D.; m. Susan Elizabeth Gray, Dec. 2, 1977; 1 child, Maili. BA, U. Wash., Seattle, 1950; PhD (Ford Found. dissertation fellow summer 1956), Johns Hopkins U., 1956. Teaching asst. U. Wash., 1950-51, 52-53; teaching asst., then instr. Johns Hopkins U., 1953-55; from instr. to prof. econs. Purdue U., 1955-62; mem. faculty Calif. Inst. Tech., Pasadena, prof. econs., 1968—, Mary Stillman Harkness prof., 1980—; rsch. assoc. Nat. Bur. Econ. Rsch., 1979—. Author: The Growth of Industrial Enterprise, 1964; co-author: The Savings Bank of Baltimore, 1956, American Economic History: The Development of a National Economy, 2d rev. edit, 1968, Institutional Change and American Economic Growth, 1971,

Mammon and the Pursuit of Empire: The Political Economy of British Imperialism, 1860-1912, 1987, Internat. Capital Markets and Economic Growth 1820-1914, 1994, In Pursuit of Leviathan: Technology, Institutions, Productivity and Profits in American Whaling, 1816-1906, 1997, Evolving Financial Markets and Foreign Capital Flows: Britain, the Americas, and Australia, 1870-1914, 1999; co-editor: American Economic Growth: An Economist's History of the United States, 1971; mem. bd. editors Jour. Econ. History, 1965-73, Explorations in Economic History, 1984-88, THESIS, Theory, and History of Econ. and Social Instns. and Structures, with Soviet and Western Scholars, 1991—. With USNR, 1945-48, 51-52. Recipient Arthur Cole prize Econ. History Assn., 1966, Alica Hanson Jones prize, 1998; Ford Found. Faculty fellow, 1959-60; Guggenheim fellow, 1964-65; fellow Ctr. for Advanced Study in Behavioral Scis., 1985-86. Fellow Am. Acad. Arts and Scis.; mem. Coun. 1 Rsch. Econ. History (chmn. 1973-74, 75-76), Econ. History Assn. (pres. 1978-79, trustee 1980-82, Alice Hanson Jones prize 1998), Anglo-Am. Hist. Assn. (gov. 1978-80), Econs. Inst. (policy and adv. bd. 1984-87), Cliometric Soc. (trustee 1993-97). Home: 1746 Grevelia St South Pasadena CA 91030-2753 Office: Calif Inst Tech Humanities and Social Scis Div Pasadena CA 91125

DAVIS, LARRY, park director; b. Price, Utah, Sept. 24, 1937. BA, Brigham Young U., 1968, M in Anthropology, 1975. Asst. Anasazi State Park, Boulder, park mgr., 1970—. Mem. Am. Assn. Mus. Office: Anasazi State Park PO Box 1429 Boulder UT 84716-1429*

DAVIS, LARRY MICHAEL, military officer, health-care manager, consultant; b. Lodi, Ark., Mar. 30, 1947; s. Harmon Odell and Jeanice (White) D.; m. Linda Ruth Blanchard, Mar. 22, 1969; children: Elizabeth Blanchard, Brooke Alison. BS, U. Ark., 1969; MA, Pepperdine U., 1978; postgrad., USAF Air U., 1975, 83-84. Commd. 2nd lt. USAF, 1969, advanced through grades to col., 1985; navigator, instr. navigator 596th Bombardment Squadron; radar navigator 62d Bombardment Squadron, 1971-75; instr. navigator, asst. curriculum mgr. 450th Flying Tng. Squadron, Mather AFB, Calif., 1975-76; asst. navigator sect. chief Standardization and Evaluation divsn. 323rd Flying Tng. Wing, Mather AFB, Calif., 1976-78; air ops. staff officer Tng. Analysis div. HQ Air Tng. Command, Randolph AFB, Tex., 1978-79; chief navigation tng. HQ Air Tng. Command, Randolph AFB, Tex., 1979-81; air ops. officer 99th Strategic Reconnaissance Squadron Beale AFB, Calif., 1982-83, wing chief of inspection 9th Strategic Reconnaissance Wing, 1983-84; reconnaissance ops. staff officer, reconnaissance emergency war order plans officer, chief reconnaissance plans divsn. HQ Strategic Air Command, Offutt AFB, Nebr., 1984-87; comdr. 3550th USAF Recruiting Squadron, Indpls., 1987-89; comdr. 3555th USAF Recruiting Squadron Milw., 1988; dep. comdr. 3501st USAF Recruiting Group, Hanscom AFB, Mass., 1989-91; health-care cons., customer svc. mgr. Electronic Data Systems, Indpls., 1991-96; mgr. provider rels. Unisys Corp., Frankfort, Ky., 1996-97; mgr. client svcs. Unisys Corp., Tallahassee, Fla., 1997; dir. network devel. and provider rels. Healthplan Southeast, Tallahassee, 1997—. Decorated D.F.C., Air medal with three oak leaf clusters. Mem. Ret. Officers Assn., Air Force Assn., Rotary (mem. health sharing com. 1989-90), Blue Key, Alpha Zeta, Alpha Gamma Rho. Baptist. Avocations: golf, tennis. Home: 3485 Welwyn Way Tallahassee FL 32308-8204

DAVIS, LAURA ARLENE, retired foundation administrator; b. Battle Creek, Mich., Apr. 14, 1935; d. Paul Bennett and Daisy E. (Coston) Borgard; m. John R. Davis, Aug. 7, 1955; children: Scott Judson, Cynthia Ann Davis Welker. BS, Ctrl. Mich. U., 1986. Sec. Mich. Loan Co., Battle Creek, 1952-56; legal sec. Ryan, Sullivan & Hamilton, Battle Creek, 1957-64; exec. sec. W.K. Kellogg Found., Battle Creek, 1965-76, adminstrn./program asst., 1976, fellowship dir., 1977, asst. v.p. adminstrn., asst. corp. sec., 1978-84, v.p. corp. affairs, corp. sec., 1984-95, spl. asst. to pres., CEO, 1996-97; cons. Mich. State U., 1998—. Pres. bd. dirs. Charitable Union, Battle Creek, 1983-85; mem. allocations panel United Way of Battle Creek, 1983, v.p. cmty. rels., 1990-91, 1st v.p., 1994, pres. of bd., 1995-97; bd. dirs. Battle Creek Gas Co., 1988—, Riding for the Handicapped Cheff Ctr., 1991-96, sec., 1992; trustee Binder Park Zoo; mem. adv. coun. Argubright Bus. Coll., 1989-90; mem. Visionquest 5000, 1989; mem. selection com. Cmty. Leadership Acad.; bd. dirs. Coun. Mich. Founds., 1994-97; mem. membership com. Recipient Athena award C. of C., Cmty. Svc. award J.C. Penney. Mem. Adminstrv. Mgmt. Soc. (pres. chpt. 1982-83), Am. Mgmt. Assn., Nat. Touring Network (bd. mem. 1997—, sec. 1998—), Battle Creek C. of C. Home: 101 Brighton Park Battle Creek MI 49015-9615

DAVIS, LAWRENCE A., academic administrator. Chancellor U. Ark., Pine Bluff, 1991—. Office: U Ark Office of Chancellor PO Box 4982 Pine Bluff AR 71611-4982*

DAVIS, LAWRENCE EDWARD, church official; b. Louisville, Aug. 14, 1939; s. George Edward and Isabel (Gerow) D.; m. Joan Cynthia Rhodes, June 20, 1959 (dec. Mar. 1984); children: Terri L., Todd E., Cynthia Davis Kennedy, Wendy J.; m. Barbara Irene Oldford, Mar., 1985. BS, Nyack Coll., 1961; MDiv, New Brunswick Theol. Sem., 1968; DDiv (hon.), King Coll., 1991. Pastor Christian Missionary Alliance, Detroit; exec. pastor World Presbyn., Livonia, Mich., 1974-82; stated clk. Evang. Presbyn. Ch., Livonia, 1981—; adj. prof. Reformed Theol. Sem., Jackson, Miss., 1988—. Mem. Nat. Assn. Evangelicals (bd. adminstrn. 1983—). Home: 38646 Silken Glen Dr Northville MI 48167-8960 Office: Evang Presbyn Ch 29140 Buckingham Ste # 5 Livonia MI 48154-4586*

DAVIS, LAWRENCE O., federal judge. LLB, U. Mo., 1958. Atty. Jenny, Cole & Davis, Union, Mo., 1963-71; pros. atty., 1967-70; magistrate judge Franklin County, 1971-74; jdudge Mo. Cir. Ct., 20th Jud. Cir. Mo., 1975-92; magistrate judge U.S. Dist. Ct. (ea. dist.) Mo., St. Louis, 1992—. Served with USAF, 1959-62, USAFR, 1962-65. Office: 1114 Market St Rm 838 Saint Louis MO 63101-2090

DAVIS, LAWRENCE WILLIAM, radiation oncologist; b. N. Braddock, Pa., Sept. 5, 1935; s. William Paul Davis and Julia Helen Zukas; children: James G., Karen E. BS, Juniata Coll., Huntington, Pa., 1957; MA, U. Pa., 1969; MBA, Temple U., 1984; MD, Georgetown U., 1961. Diploamte Am. Bd. Radiology (trustee 1981-95, asst. exec. dir. radiation oncology 1994—); lic. physician Pa., Md., N.Y., Ga. Asst. instr. radiology U. Pa., Phila., 1962-66, instr. radiology, 1966, 68-69, asst. prof. radiology, 1969-72, assoc. prof. radiology, 1972-75; prof. radiation therapy Thomas Jefferson Sch. Medicine, 1975-84; prof. and chmn. radiation oncology Albert Einstein Coll. Medicine, Bronx, 1984-91, Emory U., Atlanta, 1991—; cons. Armed Forces Radiobiology Rsch. Inst., Bethesda, 1968-70; exec. com. of med. staff Montefiore Med. Ctr., 1984-87, 1990-91, div. coun., 1988-89; prof. svc. com. Phila. div. Am. Cancer Soc., 1970-75. Contbr. numerous articles to profl. jours.; assoc. editor Internat. Jour. Radiation Oncology, 1986—; editorial bd. Neuro Oncology, 1989—, assoc. editor, 1991—; editorial bd Am. Jour. Clin. Oncology, 1991—. Capt. USAF, 1966-68. Fellow Am. Cancer Soc., Phila., 1963-64, NIH, 1964-66, Am. Cancer Soc. traineeship, 1968-71. Fellow Am. Coll. Radiology; mem. AMA, AAAS, Am. Assn. Cancer Rsch., Am. Coll. Radiology (commn. on radiation oncology 1981-90, bd. chancellors 1993—), Am. Soc. Therapeutic Radiology and Oncology (chmn. bd. 1988-89, pres. 1987-88), Am. Coll. Hosp. Adminstrs., Am. Mgmt. Assn., Am. Radium Soc. (pres. 1992-93), Am. Soc. Clin. Oncology, Med. Assn. Atlanta, N.Y. Acad. Scis., Ga. State Med. Soc., Ga. State Radiol. Soc., Radiation Rsch. Soc., Radiol. Soc. N.Am., Alpha Omega Alpha. E-mail: davis@radonc.emory.org. Office: Emory Clinic 1365 Clifton Rd NE Atlanta GA 30322-1013

DAVIS, LEONARD, violist; b. Willimantic, Conn., May 19, 1919; s. Maurice and Clara (Klemer) D.; m. Frieda Reisberg, Dec. 7, 1946. Diploma, Juilliard Grad. Sch., 1941. Violist, prin. violist N.Y. Philharm. Orch., N.Y.C., 1949-91; mem. faculty Manhattan Sch. Music, N.Y.C., 1985—; editor Internat. Music Co.; concert artist in U.S., Europe, and the Orient; tchr., clinician various conservatories worldwide, 1970—; recs. include complete J.S. Bach solo Suites for Viola. Contbr. articles to profl. jours. Juilliard Grad. Sch. fellow, 1937-41. Mem. Am. Viola Soc., Am. String Tchr. Assn. Jewish. Avocations: poetry writing, painting, chamber music. Home: 185 West End Ave Apt 7C New York NY 10023-5542

DAVIS, LEONARD MCCUTCHAN, speech educator; b. Duffy, W.Va., July 14, 1919; s. Arch Goff and Ressie (McCutchan) D.; m. Mary Abrilla Bateman, Aug. 28, 1948; children: Leonard McCutchan, Anne Edmondson, James Mansfield. AB, W.Va. U., 1948, MA, 1950; PhD, Northwestern U., 1958. Dir. forensics Montevallo U., 1950-54; teaching fellow Northwestern U., 1953-54; instr. Nat. High Sch. Speech Inst., 1954; prof. W.Va. U., Morgantown, 1954-89, emeritus prof., 1989—; chmn. dept. speech W.Va. U., 1966-72; vis. prof. speech U. Calif., Santa Barbara, 1965-66, 67-68, U. Ariz, summer 1966; faculty Va. Sch. Bank Mgmt., 1961-91; prof. W.Va. Wesleyan Coll., Buckhannon, 1990-93; lectr. bus. and profl. communications UCLA; lectr. mgmt. communications U. Calif., Berkeley; cons. in mgmt. communications for industry and hosps. Hist. preservation officer State of W.Va., 1973-78; chmn. Gov.'s Bd. of Rev. for Hist. Preservation, 1975-78; mem. W.Va. Archives and History Commn., 1978-80; chmn. W.Va. Capitol Bldg. Commn.; mem. Hist. W.Va. Capitol Commn. Author: Mr. Lincoln Goes to Gettysburg, 1960, Night of Assassins (Death and Funeral of Abraham Lincoln), 1959, General Nathan Goff, Orator and Statesman, 1951, Communications in High-Risk Occupations, 1970, Perceived Power as a Mediator of Management Communication Style, 1980, Individual Differences Among Employees, 1982, Power in Organizations: Communications Techniques and Strategies, 1984; Relationship of Supervisor Use of Power and Affinity-Seeking Strategies with Subordinate Satisfaction, 1986. Editor: Official Statements and Papers of Governor Arch A. Moore, Jr., 3 vols. Contbr. monthly article Banking News; Author: A History of the Story of Oral Communication at West Virginia University, 1997. Served with AUS, 1941-45. Recipient Order of Vandalia award W.Va. U. Mem. Internat. Communication Assn., Eastern Communication Assn., World Communication Assn., Speech Communication Assn., Beta Theta Pi, Delta Sigma Rho. Methodist. Lodges: Masons, Rotary. Home: 401 Rotary St Morgantown WV 26505-2227

DAVIS, LINDA JACOBS, municipal official; b. Miami, July 10, 1955; d. Martin Jacque and Doris Harriet (Stucker) Jacobs; m. John Joseph Mantos, Jan. 1, 1984 (dec. 1988); m. Perry Davis, June 4, 1989; children: Aaron, Jacob. Student, U. South Fla., 1977. Mgr. Werner Erhard & Assocs., San Francisco, 1978-82, program leader, 1979-90; asst. exec. dir. The Breakthrough Found., San Francisco, 1982-88; owner Mantagaris Galleries, San Francisco, 1988-92; dir. mktg. devel. Marin Child Care Coun., San Rafael, Calif., 1992-94; dir. devel. and pub. affairs Planned Parenthood of Marin, Sonoma and Menodcino, Calif., 1994-96; ptnr. Women's Initiative for Leadership Devel., 1994-96; pres., CEO Mill Valley C. of C., 1996—; profl. fund-raiser. Vol. The Hunger Project, Fla., 1977-78; bd. dirs. Marin Child Care Coun.; appointed commr. Marin Commn. on Women, 1994-97; vol. Leadership Team, Novato Unified Sch. Dist., 1994—. Recipient Outstanding Young Women Am. Mem. NOW (pres. local chpt.), Marin Women's Coalition. Democrat. Jewish. Avocations: exercise, gardening, writing, public speaking, politics. Home: 419 Karla Ct Novato CA 94949-5478 Office: Mill Valley C of C 85 Throckmorton Mill Valley CA 94941

DAVIS, LINWOOD LAYFIELD, lawyer; b. Winston-Salem, N.C., Jan. 24, 1940; s. Egbert Lawrence Jr. and Eleanor (Layfield) D.; m. Martha Hannah Hatch, June 23, 1963; children: Hannah Anne, Jane Elizabeth, Linwood Jr., Susannah. AB cum laude, Princeton U., 1962; JD, Duke U., 1967. Bar: N.C. 1967, N.C. Supreme Ct., 1967, U.S. Tax Ct., 1973, U.S. Dist Ct. (mid. dist.) N.C., 1975, U.S. Ct. Appeals (4th cir.) N.C., 1975, U.S. Claims Ct., 1980. Assoc. Womble Carlyle Sandridge & Rice PLLC, Winston-Salem, N.C., 1967-74, mem., 1974—; revenue laws study com. N.C. Legis. Rsch. Commn., 1979-81. Active Leadership Winston-Salem, 1990; vice-chmn. campaign United Way Forsyth County, 1976, campaign chmn., 1977, bd. dirs., 1976-78; chmn. new dimensions campaign Arts Coun., Inc., 1979-80, bd. trustees, 1979-84; bd. dirs. Forsyth Health Planning Coun., 1970-76, chmn., 1973-75, Amos Cottage, 1969-78, pres., 1971-73; bd. dirs. Children's Ctr. Physically Handicapped, 1967-78, v.p., 1969-71; bd. dirs. Crisis Control Ministry, Inc., 1975-78, N.C. Outward Bound Sch., 1982-88, N.C. Citizens for Bus. and Industry, 1987-94, 96—; deacon First Bapt. Ch., 1973—, mem. children's ctr. com., 1973, long range planning com., 1973-74, mem. stewardship chmn., 1976, bd. trustees, 1980-82, 86-88, chmn., 1981-82, mem. charter and bylaw com., 1990—; adv. com. Reynolds Health Ctr., 1975-78; bd. trustees N.C. Bapt. Hosp., 1985-88, 91-94, 96—, bldg. com., investment com., exec. com., chmn. trustees, 1999—; trustee N.C. Bapt. Hosp. Sch. Pastoral Care Found., Inc., 1978-82; bd. dirs. Med. Ctr. Wake Forest Univ. Baptist, 1990-93, 96—, vice-chmn., 1992, chmn., 1993, 97; trustee N.C. Sch. Arts, 1977-85; adv. coun. Wake Forest U. Planned Giving, 1988-90, chmn., 1988-89; chmn. capital campaign for new bldg. N.C. Bapt. Found., 1988-89; nat. chmn. Duke U. Law Sch. Ann. Fund, 1991-92; bd. vis. Wake Forest U. Divinity Sch., 1997—. 1st lt. USAR, 1962-64. Recipient Disting. Svc. award Winston-Salem Jaycees, 1973, Forsyth Duke U. Alumni Assn., 1984. Fellow Am. Coll. Trust and Estate Coun.; mem. ABA (bus. law sect., sect. taxation, com. exempt orgns., real property, probate and trust law sect.), N.C. State Bar Assn., Forsyth County Bar Assn. (pres. 1997-98), Winston-Salem Rotary Club, Greater Winston-Salem C. of C. (bd. dirs. 1983-87), Princeton U. Alumni Assn. Winston-Salem (pres., past chmn. local ann. giving and schs. com., class of 62 agt. 1992-97, exec. com. alumni coun. 1993-95, alumni assn.). Home: 930 Arbor Rd Winston Salem NC 27104-1026 Office: Womble Carlyle Sandridge & Rice PLLC PO Box 84 Winston Salem NC 27102-0084

DAVIS, LISA CORINNE, artist; b. Balt., Jan. 22, 1958; d. Robert Clarke and Elaine C. (Carsley) D.; m. Colin Murray Cathcart, Oct. 25, 1986; children: G. Davis Cathcart, Corinne Davis Cathcart. BFA, Pratt Inst., 1980; MFA, CUNY, 1983. One-man shows include June Kelly Gallery, N.Y.C., Print Club, Phila., 1993, 2d St. Gallery, Charlottesville, Va., 1994, Mcpl. Gallery, Atlanta, 1994, Halsey Gallery, Charleston, S.C., 1994, Dell Pryor Galleries, Detroit, 1994, Project Room Bronx Coun. on the Arts, N.Y., 1996; group shows include Inroads Gallery, N.Y.C., 1984, U.S. Capitol Bldg., Washington, 1986, The Schenectady Mus., N.Y., 1986, Ridge St. Gallery, N.Y.C., 1987, 88, Christie's, N.Y.C., 1989, 90, Artist's Space, N.Y.C., 1990, 91, Okeanos Gallery, Berkeley, Calif., 1992, Pyramid Atlantic Workshop, Washington, 1992, Print Club, Phila., 1992, Granary Books, N.Y.C., 1993, Kenkeleba Gallery, N.Y.C., 1993, Orgn. Ind. Artists, N.Y.C., 1993, Art in General, N.Y.C., 1993, 94, The Bronx Mus. Arts, 1993, 96, Butters Gallery, Portland, Oreg., 1993, Barrett House Galleries, Poughkeepsie, N.Y., 1994, Gallery Annext, N.Y.C., 1994, City Without Walls, Newark, 1994, Papermill, N.Y.C., 1995, Ctr. Contemporary Art, Newark, 1996. Regional fellow Mid-Atlantic Arts Found., 1992, fellow NEA, 1995-96, artists' feow N.Y. Found. for Arts, 1997. Studio: 321 Greenwich St Ste 4 New York NY 10013-3340

DAVIS, LORRAINE JENSEN, writer, editor; b. Omaha, Apr. 2, 1924; d. Theron R. and L. Mildred (Henkel) Jensen; m. Richard Morris Davis, Apr. 4, 1959 (dec.); 1 child, Laura Jensen. B.A., U. Denver, 1946. Copywriter Glamour mag., N.Y.C., 1946-54, prodn. editor, 1954-61; prodn. editor Vogue Children mag., N.Y.C., 1963-66. Writer, assoc. features editor, Vogue mag., N.Y.C., 1966-77; mng. editor, writer women's news column, 1977-88; editorial dir. Condé Nast Books, 1988-91; editor: Vogue Living and Food Guide, 1975; editorial cons.: Vogue Beauty and Health Guide, 1979-82; editor: Cooking with Colette (by Colette Rossant), 1975, Fairchild Dictionary of Fashion (by Charlotte Calasibetta), 1975, English translation Paul Bocuse's French Cooking, 1977. Recipient Disting. Citizen award Alpha Gamma Delta, 1981. Mem. NOW. Democrat. Episcopalian. Club: Cosmopolitan. Home: 425 E 63rd St Apt W3J New York NY 10021-7822

DAVIS, LOUIS POISSON, JR., lawyer, consultant; b. Washington, July 17, 1919; s. Louis Poisson and Edna (Shethar) D.; m. Emily Elizabeth Carl, Feb. 7, 1943; 1 child, Cynthia. BSc, U.S. Naval Acad., 1941; postgrad., Princeton U., 1947-48; JD, Rutgers U., 1953. Bar: N.Y. 1954, Ill. 1963, U.S. Dist. Ct. (so. dist.) N.Y. 1956, U.S. Dist. Ct. (no. dist.) Ill. 1965, U.S. Supreme Ct. 1964. Mgr. engring. Esso Std. Oil, Linden, N.J., 1946-57; sr. economist, head econs. and market rsch. dept. Internat. Petroleum Co., Lima, Peru, 1957-60; asst. overseas ops. AMF Internat. Abbott Labs., North Chicago, Ill., 1962-65; gen. mgr. Far East ops. Ralston Purina Co.; pres. Ralston Purina Eastern, Hong Kong, 1966-71; dir. internat. devel. Archer Daniels Midland Internat., Decatur, Ill., 1972-74; lectr., rschr. internat. law and mgmt., N.Y.C., 1974-76; corp. rep. Europe, Mid East, Africa, Alexander & Baldwin Agribus, Inc., Abidjan, Ivory Coast, 1976, Madrid, Spain, 1977; internat. atty., cons., Sarasota, Fla., 1978-98; cons. Sarasota County Office of Sci. Advisor, 1985-86, Office of Gen. Counsel, 1989-91; vol. income tax assistance program IRS, 1983-98; cons., seminar leader Chipsoft, Inc., 1989-90; vol. atty. Gulfcoast Legal Svcs., 1987-91; instr. Sarasota Tech. Inst., 1990-98; cert. cons. Capsoft Devel. Corp. Legal Automation Software, 1991; gen. counsel Manasota Industry Coun., Inc., 1984-89; bd. dirs. Siesta Key Assn., v.p., 1993-94, 98—. Lt. comdr. USN, 1937-46. Mem. ABA, Hong Kong Country Club, Oaks Club (Sarasota). Republican. Episcopalian. Home and Office: 620 Mangrove Point Rd Sarasota FL 34242-1230

DAVIS, LOUISE MINNIE, writer; b. Chattanooga, Tenn., Sept. 5, 1935; d. Moses McKelton and Lillie Mae (Glover) Smith; m. Robert Lee Martin, 1952 (div. 1964); children: Bobby Lee, Loretta, Enrico, Alexander, Jacqueline; m. Will Davis Jr., Dec. 18, 1979. BS, Va. State U., 1979. Lic. cosmetologist, Ohio, Va. owner Potpourri Palace, Petersburg, Va., 1998; cosmetologist, Ohio. Author: (books) Brittini in ABC Land, 1994, A Mother Pray, 1998. Mem., tchr. Meml. Chapel, Ft. Lee, 1980—. Mem. Disabled Am. Vets., NCO Wives Club (v.p. 1997-98), Sigma Gamma Rho. Home: 1616 N Valor Dr Petersburg VA 23803-4641

DAVIS, LOURIE IRENE BELL, computer education and information systems specialist; b. Las Vegas, N.Mex., Apr. 8, 1930; d. Currie Oscar and Minnie I. (Rodgers) Bell; m. Robert Eugene Davis, Aug. 21, 1950; children: Judith Anne, Robert Patrick, (adopted) Jaime Alleyn, (adopted) Flint Christopher. BS, West Tex. U., 1959; student Ea. N.Mex. U., 1947-49, U. Tulsa, 1980-81. Cert. elem. tchr., lang. arts, soc. studies, music, grades 4-6, Okla., 1949-51, Texas, 1959-65, Okla., 1966-73; programmer/analyst Blue Cross/Blue Shield Okla., Tulsa, 1972-75, mgr. systems, 1977-81, dir. info. systems, 1981-82, mgr. project control, 1982-83, mgr. info. ctr., 1984-85, mgr. profl. cons. and tng., 1985-87; computer sci. instr. Tulsa Jr. Coll., 1975-76; faculty devel. coord. CAID Okla. State U., Okmulgee, 1987-90; computer bus. and edn. cons. Davis Cons., 1991—; adminstrv. officer Intertel, Inc., 1991-95, pres., CEO, 1995—; systems curriculum coord.; mem. computer sci. adv. bd. Tulsa Jr. Coll., 1976-83, adj. instr., 1977-83, 1993-94; mem. steering com. U.S. Senate bus. adv. bd., 1981-88; ind. cons., Tulsa, 1987; lectr. computer assisted instruction success League of Innovation Conf., St. Louis, 1989, Music Users Group Conf., U. Tenn., Chattanooga, 1989, Pres's. Day Des Moines Area C.C., 1990. Mem. budget panel United Way Tulsa, 1981-87, Allocations Exec. Com. Appreciation award, 1987; mem. U.S. Rep. Presdl. Task Force, 1982-93; mem. Holy Family Sch. Bd., 1991-95, nominating com. chair, 1993, sec., 1993-95. Winner League of Innovation for C.C.s. Competition, IBM, 1989. Mem. Assn. Systems Mgmt. (regional dir. 1985-86, chpt. membership chair 1982-84; internat. awards 1980, 84), NAFE, AAUW, Tulsa Area Systems Edn. Assn. (recorder 1980-81), Higher Edn. Acad. Coun. of Okla., Sierra Club, Habitat for Humanity, Alpha Chi, Mensa, Intertel (nat. acceptance com. chair 1978, dir. region VIII 1987-91, membership officer 1991-95, chmn. bd. 1995—, pub. Integra, Jour. Interel 1992—, awarded lifetime mem. and appreciation award, 1997). Republican. Mem. Unity Ch. of Christianity. Home and Office: Davis Cons 2403 W Oklahoma St Tulsa OK 74127-3027

DAVIS, LOWELL LIVINGSTON, cardiovascular surgeon; b. Urbanna, Va.. BS in Biology, Morehouse Coll., 1949; MS in Biology, Atlanta U., 1950; MD, Howard U., 1955; postgrad., U. Pa., 1959-60. Diplomate Am. Bd. Surgery, Am. Bd. Thoracic Surgery. Intern Jersey City (N.J.) Med. Ctr., 1955-56; resident Margaret Hague Maternity Hosp., Jersey City, 1956-57; resident ob-gyn. Elmhurst (N.Y.) Gen. Hosp., 1957-58, chief resident ob-gyn., 1958-59; resident in gen. surgery U.S. VA Hosp., Tuskegee, Ala., 1960-61; resident to chief resident in gen. surgery Nassau County Med. Ctr., Hempstead, N.Y., 1961-64; resident in cardiothoracic surgery Cook County Hosp., Chgo., 1967-68, sr. resident, 1968-69; pvt. practice N.Y.C., 1964-65, pvt. practice thoracic and cardiovascular surgery, 1975—; clin. assoc. prof. surgery L.A. County Gen. Hosp., U. So. Calif. Med. Sch., 1988—; fellow U. Oreg., Portland, 1972, St. Vincent Hosp., Portland, 1972, Med. Coll. Wis., Milw., 1973, Pacific Med. Ctr. Inst. of Med. Scis., San Francisco, 1974, Allen-Bradley Med. Scis. Rsch. Lab. Med. Coll. Wis., 1975, Hosp. for Sick Children, London, 1977-78, Tex. Heart Inst., Houston, 1983, Cardiac Surgery Rsch. Lab., Hadassah Med. Sch. and U. Hosp., Jerusalem, 1987; vis. surgeon NYU Med. Sch., 1991, Mayo Clinic, Rochester, Minn., 1991, U. Dusseldorf, Germany, 1991, Deutsches Herzzentrum, Berlin, 1991, Deutsches Herzzentrum, Munich, 1991, Klinik für Thorat-Herz-Und Gefab Chirurgie, Hanover, Germany, 1991, U. Vienna, Austria, 1992. Contbr. articles to profl. jours. With USN, 1943-46, USNR, 1965-71, comdr., 1965-67, capt. USNR, 1970. Recipient Asiatic Pacific Campaign medal with one Gold Star, Presdl. Unit citation. Fellow ACS, Internat. Coll. Angiology, Am. Coll. Angiology, Internat. Coll. Surgeons, N.Y. Acad. Medicine, Am. Coll. Chest Physicians, Am. Coll. Cardiology; mem. AAAS, Assn. Mil. Surgeons U.S., Am. Assn. for Thoracic Surgery, Soc. Thoracic Surgeons, Albert Starr Cardiac Surg. Soc. (founding), Am. Coll. Emergency Physicians, Lyman Brewer III Internat. Surg. Soc., Royal Soc. Medicine, Denton A. Cooley Cardiovasc. Surgery Soc., L.A. Surg. Soc. Home: 4518 186th St # 202 Redondo Beach CA 90278

DAVIS, LUANE RUTH, theatrical director, performer; b. Binghamton, N.Y., Sept. 10, 1960; d. Paul Joseph and Ruth Hardin (Wheeler) D., m. Jonathan Allen Fluck, (div. Dec. 1994). BA, Hunter Coll., 1983; MA, Goddard Coll., 1992; stage interpretation in ASL cert., The Juilliard Sch., 1994. Performer Broadway, regional, stock prodns., 1979—, Delta Queen Steamboat Co.; dir., choreographer showcase, cruise lines, children's shows, 1986—; adminstr. Maverick Theatre, N.Y.C., 1986-88; artistic dir. Interborough Repertory Theatre, N.Y.C., 1986—; writer self help, children's musicals, 1990—; pub. edn. specialist Dept. Mental Retardation Devel. Disabilities, N.Y.C., 1990-95; program coord. for deaf svcs. St. Vincent's Hosp., N.Y.C., 1997-98; mem. faculty Nt. Tech. Inst. for the Deaf Rochester (N.Y.) Inst. Tech., 1998—; Am. Sign Lang. interpreter; creator Del-Sign acting technique, Interborough Repertory Theatre, N.Y.C., 1992—, spkr. in field; presenter Nat. Inst. Trial Lawyers. Author: (self-help) Taking Stage, 1995; (musical) Women of the American Revolution, 1991, The World in Her Hands: The Story of Helen Keller, 1993; author, prodr.: (musical) The Little Matchgirl, 1995. Active many accessibility issues for the disabled, N.Y.C. Recipient Women of Achievement award Gov. Pataki's Women Run N.Y.C., 1998. Mem. AFTRA, DAR, Actor's Equity Assn., League of Prof. Theatre Women, Registry of Interpreters of the Deaf, Deaf Entertainment Guild. Episcopalian. Avocations: sports, refinish furniture, teach children literacy. Home: 25 Mayapple Ln West Henrietta NY 14586 Office: Interborough Theatre 154 Christopher St Ste 3B New York NY 10014-2840

DAVIS, LUTHER, writer, producer; b. N.Y.C., Aug. 29, 1921; s. Charles Thomas and Henriette (Roesler) D.; m. Dorothy deMilhau, Nov. 3, 1943 (div. 1961); children: Noelle, Laura Duval. BA, Yale U., 1938. Author: (play) Kiss Them for Me, 1945, (libretto with Charles Lederer) Kismet (Tony award 1953); prodr. Timbuktu, 1978 (Tony nomination 1979), (libretto) Grand Hotel, 1989 (Tony nomination 1990), 15 solo screenplays including The Hucksters, 1946, A Lion Is in the Street, 1950, Across 110th Street, 1972; author, prodr. Lady in a Cage, 1964; numerous TV series, pilots and episodes. Served to maj. USAAF, 1942-45, CBI, ETO. Recipient Tony award, 1953. Mem. Dramatists Guild Am., Writers Guild Am.-West, League Am. Theaters and Prodrs., Acad. Motion Picture Arts and Scis., PEN.

DAVIS, LYNN ETHERIDGE, political scientist; b. Miami, Fla., Sept. 6, 1943; d. Earl DeWitt and Louise (Featherston) Etheridge. BA, Duke U., 1965; MA, Columbia U., 1967, PhD, 1971. Lectr. Miles Coll., Birmingham, Ala., 1966-67; asst. prof. polit. sci. Bernard Coll., Columbia U., N.Y.C., 1970-74; rsch. assoc. Internat. Inst. for Strategic Studies, London, 1973; program analysis staff Nat. Security Council, 1974; asst. prof., lectr. dept. polit. sci. Columbia U., 1974-76; prof., staff mem. Senate Select Com. on Intelligence, 1975-76; dep. asst. sec. of def. for policy plans and nat. security affairs Office of the Under Sec. for Policy, Dept. Def., Washington, 1977-79, asst. dep. under sec. for policy planning, 1979-81; rsch. Internat. Inst. Strategic Studies, London, 1981-82; prof. national security affairs National War Coll., Washington, 1982-85; dir. studies Internat. Inst. Strategic Studies, London, 1985-87; hon. sr. rsch. fellow, dept. war studies Kings Coll., London, 1988-90; rsch. fellow John Hopkins Fgn. Policy Inst, Paul H. Nitze Sch. Advanced Internat. Studies, 1988-91; v.p. army rsch. divsn., dir. Arroyo Ctr. RAND, Santa Monica, Calif, 1991-93; sr. fellow RAND, Washington, 1997—; under sec. for arms control and internat. security affairs Dept. State, Washington, 1993-97. Author: The Cold War Begins, Soviet American

Conflict Over Eastern Europe, 1974. Woodrow Wilson fellow, 1965-66, 69-70, 81-82; Columbia U. fellow, 1965-66, 68-69; recipient David D. Lloyd prize Harry S. Truman Library, 1976. Mem. Coun. on Fgn. Rels., Phi Beta Kappa. Home: 827 S Lee St Alexandria VA 22314-4333 Office: RAND 1333 H St NW Washington DC 20005-4707

DAVIS, LYNN HAMBRIGHT, culinary arts educator; b. Gaffney, S.C., Aug. 7, 1950; d. Samuel Anderson and Elizabeth (Nolen) Hambright; m. Ronnie Dale Davis, Aug. 10, 1969; children: Marty, Jennifer. BS in Home Econs. Edn., Winthrop Coll., 1972, MS in Home Econs. Edn., 1982, EDS, 1996. Cert. secondary home econs. edn. tchr., early childhood edn., N.C., S.C. Tchr. Crest Sr. High, Shelby, N.C., 1975-76; dietitian Cleveland Meml. Hosp., Shelby, 1977-78; tchr. culinary arts and food sci. tech. Cherokee Tech. Ctr., Gaffney, 1978—; chairperson Staff Devel. Com. and Culinary Arts Craft Coun., Gaffney, 1978—; advisor Future Homemakers Am., Gaffney, 1978—. Mem. NEA, Am. Vocat. Assn. (region II policy com. 1992-95, state rep. region II 1992-95), S.C. Edn. Assn., S.C. Vocat. Assn. (v.p. 1991-92, Tchr. of the Yr. 1997), Nat. Assn. Tchrs. Family & Consumer Sci., S.C. Assn. Tchrs. Family & Consumer Sci. (pres. 1991-92, advisor 1992-93, Tchr. of Yr. 1995, 97), Am. Home Econs. Assn., S.C. Assn. Family & Consumer Sci. (sec. food svc. adminstrs. com. 1991-92, Tchr. of Yr. 1993), Home Econs. Edn. Assn., Kappa Delta Phi. Democrat. Baptist. Avocations: reading, computers. Home: 2100 Albert Blanton Rd Shelby NC 28152-8151 Office: Cherokee Tech Ctr 3206 Cherokee Ave Gaffney SC 29340-3500

DAVIS, LYNN HARRY, secondary education educator; b. Jamestown, N.Y., Mar. 6, 1949; s. Harry Lynn and Marjorie Ellen (Greenwood) D.; m. Patricia Ann Carapella; 1 child, Matthew Michael. BS, SUNY, Fredonia, 1971. Cert. tchr., N.Y. Sci. tchr. West Genesee Sch. Dist., Camillus, N.Y., 1972—; adult edn. computer tchr. West Genesee Sch. Dist., 1985-91, Syracuse U. Teaching Ctr., 1984-86; tech. support specialist Teaching Ctr. Syracuse U., 1991—; chmn. Sci. Bldg., West Genessee Sch. Dist., 1983-88, coord. sci. curriculum, 1988—. Contbr. numerous articles to profl. jours. Strategic planning com. mem. West Genesee Cen. Schs.; fundraiser United Way, Syracuse, 1978-81, YMCA, Syracuse, 1981; mem. Friends of Zoo, 1987-98. Mem. ASCD, N.Y. State United Tchrs. (del. 1980-85), Am. Fed. of Tchrs., Nat. Sci. Tchrs. Assn., West Genesee Tchrs. Assn. (v.p. for negotiations 1979-85, sec. 1986—, newsletter editor 1986—, webmaster 1997—). Avocations: golf, photography, computers. Home: 14 Blackwood Dr Liverpool NY 13090-3764 Office: West Genesee Cen Sch Dist Ike Dixon Rd Camillus NY 13031-9619

DAVIS, LYNN KAREN, health facility administrator; b. New Haven, Conn., Jan. 11, 1951; d. Benny and Loretta (Haroskiewicz) D. BSN, Boston U., 1972, MSN, 1977; CAGS, Simmons Coll., 1997. Cert. nursing adminstr. ANA; lic. nursing home adminstr. Staff nurse to charge nurse to head nurse to asst. dir. nursing Boston City Hosp., 1973-82; dir. women's health and med.-surg. nursing Charlton Meml. Hosp., Southcoast Hosps. Group, Fall River, Mass., 1983-98. Past pres. Fall River chpt. Big Bros./Big Sisters. Mem. Am. Orgn. Nurse Execs., Mass. Orgn. Nurse Execs. (bd. dirs., chair membership com.), S.E. Mass. Orgn. Nurse Execs. (past pres.), Sigma Theta Tau. Home: 35 Pilgrim Village Rd Taunton MA 02780-6937

DAVIS, M. G., lawyer; b. Concho County, Tex., Nov. 11, 1930; s. Zack and Olive (Clifton) D.; m. Jeanne Focke, Feb. 7, 1959; children: Linda Jeanne, Lisbeth Dianne. BBA, Tex. Tech. U., 1952; JD, U. Tex., 1958. Bar: Tex., 1957, U.S. Supreme Ct., 1964; atty. Gen. Land Office, Austin, Tex., 1959-60, firm Smith, Porter & Caston, Longview, Tex., 1960-61; v.p. Am. Title Co. Dallas, 1961-67; owner, operator Security Land Title Co., Amarillo, Tex., 1967-69; pres. Dallas Title Co., Houston, 1969-70, Guardian Title, Houston, 1970-72, Collin County Title Co., Plano, Tex., 1972-87; pvt. practice, Plano, 1972-82; ptnr. firm Davis & Davis, Dallas, 1982-93, Davis & Sallinger, L.L.P., Dallas, 1993-98, Davis & Davis, Richardson, Tex., 1999—; guest lectr. U. Houston, Richland Jr. Coll. Chmn. Selective Service Bd. 46, 1982-92; mem. legis. task force, employer support for guard and reserve affairs TNGA. 1st lt. USAF, 1952-54; Korea. Recipient Involved Citizen award Dallas Morning News, 1980. Mem. State Bar Tex., Dallas Bar Assn., Coll. State Bar of Tex., Sons Republic Tex., Tex. Land Title Assn. (v.p. 1970-71), Tex. Tech. Ex-Students Assn. (dir. 1961-63), Collin County Title Assn. (pres. 1977), Dallas Mortgage Bankers Assn., Collin County U. Tex. Ex-Students Assn. (pres. 1980), U. Tex. Ex-Students (exec. council 1983-86), Alpha Tau Omega. Democrat. Episcopalian. Home: 3708 Canoncita Ln Plano TX 75023-6001 Office: Davis & Davis Ste 1701 N Greenville Ave Richardson TX 75081-6271

DAVIS, MARC, astrophysics educator; b. Canton, Ohio, Sept. 8, 1947; s. Herman and Jennie (Finer) D.; m. Paula Finegold, Aug. 24, 1969 (div. 1977); m. Nancy Ruth Turak, Aug. 10, 1980; children: Jeremy, Adam. SB, MIT, 1969; MA, Princeton U., 1971, PhD, 1973. Instr. Princeton (N.J.) U., 1973-74; asst. prof. Harvard U., Cambridge, Mass., 1974-79, assoc. prof., 1979-81; prof. astrophysics and astronomy U. Calif., Berkeley, 1981—, chmn. dept. astronomy, 1989. Contbr. numerous articles to sci. jours. Fellow AAAS, Am. Phys. Soc.; mem. NAS, Am. Astron. Soc., Internat. Astron. Union. Office: U Calif Dept Astronomy 601 Campbell Hall Berkeley CA 94720-3411*

DAVIS, MARGARET BRYAN, paleoecology researcher, educator; b. Boston, Oct. 23, 1931. AB, Radcliffe Coll., 1953; PhD in Biology, Harvard U., 1957. NSF fellow dept. biology Harvard U., Cambridge, Mass., 1957-58, dept. geosci. Calif. Inst. Tech., Pasadena, 1959-60; research fellow dept. zoology Yale U., New Haven, 1960-61, prof. biology, 1973-76; research assoc. dept. botany U. Mich., Ann Arbor, 1961-64, assoc. research biologist Great Lakes Research div., 1964-70, research biologist, assoc. prof. dept. zoology, 1966-70, research biologist, prof. zoology, 1970-73; head dept. ecology and behavioral biology U. Minn., Mpls., 1976-81, prof. dept. ecology, evolution and behavior, 1976-82, Regents prof. ecology, 1982—; vis. prof. Quaternary Research Ctr., U. Wash., 1973; vis. investigator environ. studies program U. Calif., Santa Barbara, 1981-82; mem. adv. panel for ecology NSF, 1976-79, mem. sci. adv. com. for biology, behavior and social scis., 1989-91, mem. adv. panel for geol. record of global change, 1991-92; mem. planetary biology com. NRC, 1981-82, mem. global change com., 1987-90, mem. screening com. in plant scis., internat. exch. of persons com. 1972-75, mem. sci. and tech. edn. com., 1984-86; vis. rsch. scientist scholarly exch. com. NAS/Nat. Rsch. Coun., People's Republic of China; mem. U.S. nat. com. Internat. Union Quaternary Rsch., 1966-74. Mem. editorial bd. Quaternary Research, 1969-82, Trends in Ecology and Evolution, 1986-92. Recipient Sci. Achievement award Sci. Mus. Minn., 1988, Alumnae Recognition award Radcliffe Coll., 1988, Nevada medal, 1993, Merit award Botanical Soc. Am., 1998. Fellow AAAS, Am. Acad. Arts and Scis, Geol. Soc. Am.; mem. NAS (nominations com. 1988), Ecol. Soc. Am. (pres. 1987-88, Eminent Ecologist award 1993), Am. Quaternary Assn. (councillor 1969-70, 72-76, pres. 1978-80), Internat. Assn. Vegetation Sci., Internat. Assn. for Great Lakes Research (bd. dirs. 1970-73), Nature Conservancy (bd. dirs. Minn. chpt. 1979-85), Brit. Ecol. Soc. (hon.), Phi Beta Kappa, Sigma Xi. Office: U Minn Dept Ecology 100 Ecology Bldg 1987 Upper Buford Cir Saint Paul MN 55108-6097

DAVIS, MARGARET THACKER, critical care, medical and surgical nurse; b. Greensboro, N.C., June 7, 1925; d. Tiller Foltz and Lucy Wright (Spencer) Thacker; m. Joe Southard Davis, Feb. 4, 1961; 1 child, Dana Lee. Diploma in nursing, Baylor U., Dallas, 1947; student, Ea. N.Mex. U., Roswell, 1978. RN, N.Mex., Tex., Fla. Office nurse Drs. Britt & Cafaro, St. Augustine, Fla., 1947-50, Dr. Robert J. Rowe, Dallas, 1950-61, Dr. F.A. English, Roswell, 1964-74; charge nurse post anesthesia care unit Ea. N.Mex. Med. Ctr., Roswell, 1990-91, ret., 1991. Named Employee of Month, Ea. N.Mex. Med. Ctr., 1985. Mem. ANA, Am. Soc. Post Anesthesia Nurses (charter), Post Anesthesia Nurses Assn. N.Mex. (bd. dirs. 1980-86, sec. 1986-87, legis. com. 1989-90), N.Mex. Nurses Assn. (dist. 5 sec. 1983-85, 91-93, pres. 1986-88, bd. dirs. 1988-90, 92-94, 96-98, membership chmn. 1988-90, chmn. nominating com. 1990, Nurse of Yr. award 1989, search for excellence award 1990, dist. 5 honored nurse 1995), Baylor U. Sch. Nursing Alumni Assn.

DAVIS, MARIA TERESA, architect; b. Galveston, Tex., May 3, 1961; d. John Thomas and Mary Frances D. B of Environ. Design, Tex. A&M U., 1982, MArch, 1984. Registered architect, Tex. Grad. asst. Tex. A&M U., College Station, 1984; interior architect Group 4 Architects, Bryan, Tex., 1984-85; v.p. HKS, Inc., Dallas, 1984—. Mem. AIA, Tex. Soc. of Architects. Office: HKS Inc 1111 Plaza of the Americas N 1919 McKinney Ave Dallas TX 75201

DAVIS, MARJORIE ALICE, former city official; b. Newton, Mass., July 1, 1917; d. Herbert Francis and Harriet Cole (Dodge) Parmenter; AB, Wellesley Coll., 1939; spl. grad. student Radcliffe Coll., 1941; cert. Harvard U., 1940; spl. courses in social work Boston U., 1961-62; m. Charles William Davis, Aug. 31, 1940 (dec.); children: Harriet Parmenter, Charles Edwin II. Exec. dir. Mid-Essex Area coun. Girl Scouts U.S.A., South Hamilton, Mass., 1952-59, Greater Lynn coun., 1959-63, Merrimack River coun., Andover, Mass., 1963-80; mem. Wenham Bd. Selectmen, 1972-89, chmn., 1977-87. Mem. Met. Area Planning Coun., Boston, 1975—, sec., 1984—, v.p., 1990-92, pres., 1992-93, mem. Mass. Com. Criminal Justice, 1974; v.p. Mass. Assn. Reg. Planning Agys.; exec. dir. Essex County Greenbelt Assn., 1980; mem. Lynn (Mass.) Area Pvt. Industry Coun., 1972-92, bd. dirs. Healthquarters, 1981, treas., 1982-83; v.p., 1983-86, pres., 1986-89; mem. ct./Cmty. Rels. Com. for Essex County, 1975; pres. Hamilton-Wenham Cmty. Svc., 1970-80, bd. dirs., 1983-87; sec. United Fund of Central North Shore, (v.p. United Way of Mass, 1982-88) 1969-84; mem. exec. com. Essex County Adv. Bd., 1983-89, sec., 1984-89; pres. Bay Area Vis. Nurses Assn., 1963-73, Bay area dir., 1983—; v.p. Mass. chpt. Children Am. Revolution, 1944; mem., chmn. Republican Town Com.; corporator North Shore Music Theater, Beverly, Mass., 1992—. Mem. Mass. Selectmen's Assn., Essex County Selectmen's Assn. (pres. 1984-85, bd. dirs.), Women Elected Mcpl. Ofcls., Mass. Mcpl. Assn. (bd. dirs.), Halibut Point State Park (Mass. chmn. adv. com. 1981—), Mass. Assn. Regional Planning Agys. (v.p. 1995-97), Christ Ch. Women (pres. 1987-92), Singing Beach club (Manchester, Mass.), Myopia Hunt Club (Hamilton). Home: 143 Grapevine Rd Wenham MA 01984-1801

DAVIS, MARK E., chemical engineering educator. Prof. dept. chemistry Calif. Inst. Tech., prof. chem. engrng. Recipient Alan T. Waterman award Nat. Sci. Found., 1990, Ipatieff prize Am. Chemical Soc., 1992. Office: Calif Inst Tech Dept Chemistry 210-41 1200 E California Blvd Pasadena CA 91125-0001*

DAVIS, MARK M., microbiologist, educator; b. Paris, Nov. 27, 1952. BA in Molecular Biology, Johns Hopkins U., 1974; PhD in Molecular Biology, Calif. Inst. Tech., 1981. Fellow lab. of immunology NIH, Bethesda, Md., 1980-82, staff fellow lab. of immunology, 1982-83; asst. prof. med. microbiology Stanford (Calif.) U. Sch. Medicine, 1983-86, assoc. prof. microbiology and immunology, 1986-91, prof. microbiology and immunology, 1991—, dir. predoctoral program in immunology, 1994—; assoc. investigator Howard Hughes Med. Inst., Stanford U., 1987-91, faculty coord., 1989—, investigator, 1991—; instr. Cold Spring Harbor (N.Y.) Lab., 1983; mem. sci. adv. bd. Damon Runyon-Walter Cancer Found., 1985-88; co-organizer UCLA Symposium, 1987; mem. allergy and immunology study sect. divsn. rsch. grants NIH, 1988-92. Recipient Intra-Sci. Rsch. Found. award 1980, Youth Scientist award Passano Found., 1985, Eli Lilly award 1986, Kayden award N.Y. Acad. Scis., 1986, Howard Taylor Ricketts award U. Chgo., 1988, Gairdner Found. award, 1989, King Faisal Internat. prize 1995, Sloan prize Gen. Motors Rsch. Found., 1996; scholar PEW Found. 1985-89. Mem. Nat. Acad. Scis. Office: Stanford U Sch Medicine Howard Hughes Med Inst Beckman Bldg Stanford CA 94305-9991

DAVIS, MARTIN CLAY, lawyer, professor; b. Tulsa, Okla., Dec. 12, 1947; s. James William and Vera Ruby (Hatcher) D.; m. Rebecca Jo Strong, Aug. 22, 1970; children: Christopher James, Jennifer Alice. BA, U. Ark., 1970; JD, Vanderbilt U., 1973. Bar: Tex. 1973, U.S. Tax Ct. 1985, cert. specialist estate planning, probate law State Bar Tex. Assoc. atty. Gary, Thomasson, Hall & Marks, Corpus Christi, Tex., 1973-77, partner, 1977-94; partner Davis, Hutchinson & Wilkerson, LLP, Corpus Christi, Tex., 1994—; adj. prof. Corpus Christi (Tex.) State U., 1980-83, 87, Tex. A&M U.-C.C., 1993; bd. dirs. Corpus Christi Estate Planning Coun. (pres. 1985-86); pres. Am. Assn. Individual Investors, Corpus Christi subchpt., 1995-96; lectr. various profl. assns. Assoc. Editor: Vanderbilt Law Rev., 1972-73. Pres. Family Counseling Svc., Corpus Christi, 1984; trustee, chmn. United Meth. Ch., 1998. Recipient Leadership award, Corpus Christi C. of C., 1980. Fellow, Tex. Bar Found., Am. Coll. Trust & Estate Counsel; mem. ABA (subcom. chmn. taxation sect., 1975-80), State Bar Tex. (estate planning and probate law adv. commn., taxation sect.); planning com. advanced estate planning and probate course, 1982, 85, 91, planning com. wills and probate inst. 1985, 87, 88, com. to revise the Tex. Trust Act), Order of the Coif. Avocations: tennis, basketball, teaching. Office: Davis Hutchinson & Wilkerson LLP Frost Bank Plz Ste 1270 Corpus Christi TX 78470

DAVIS, MARTIN S., investment company executive; b. N.Y.C.. Student, CUNY, NYU. With Samuel Goldwyn Prodns., N.Y.C., 1947-55, Allied Artists Corp., N.Y.C., 1955-58; with Paramount Pictures Corp., N.Y.C., 1958-69, COO, 1966-69; sr. v.p. Paramount Communications Inc. (formerly Gulf & Western Inc.), N.Y.C., 1969-74, exec. v.p., 1974-83, chmn. exec. com., chief exec. officer, 1983-94; mng. ptnr. Wellspring Capital Mgmt. L.L.C., N.Y.C., 1995—; bd. dirs. Nat. Amusements, Inc., parent co. Viacom, Inc. Chmn. N.Y. chpt. Nat. Multiple Sclerosis Soc., Montefiore Med. Ctr.; trustee Carnegie Hall, Thomas Jefferson Meml. Found., Inc. Office: Wellspring Capital Mgmt LLC 620 5th Ave New York NY 10020-2402*

DAVIS, MARVIN, petroleum company executive, entrepreneur; b. Newark, Aug. 28, 1925; s. Jack Davis; m. Barbara Davis; 5 children. BSCE, NYU, 1947. Gen. ptnr., owner Davis Oil Co., Denver; co-owner 20th Century-Fox, 1981-85. Office: Davis Cos 2121 Ave Of Stars Ste 2800 Los Angeles CA 90067-5010

DAVIS, MARVIN ARNOLD, manufacturing company executive; b. St. Louis, Nov. 16, 1937; s. Sam and Pauline (Neuman) D.; m. Trudy Brenda Rein, Aug. 11, 1968; children: Julie, Jeffrey. BS in Chem. Engring., Washington U., St. Louis, 1959; MBA in Fin.and Mktg., Washington U., 1966. Lead engr. Standard Oil Calif., San Francisco, 1962-64; product mgr. Shell Chem. Co., N.Y.C., 1966-69; group controller Pfizer, Inc., N.Y.C., 1969-75; exec. v.p. Good Hope Industries, New Orleans, 1975-77; pres., chief exec. officer Reed Industries, Inc., Stone Mountain, Ga., 1978-79; pres. Sentrex Ltd., Atlanta, 1977-82; v.p. Sentry Ins., 1982-84; cons., pres. Grisanti Galef Goldress, 1984-97; chmn., CEO Petrowax PA Inc., 1991-93, Datamax Corp., 1996—; chmn., CEO Petrowax PA, Inc., 1992-94, Signal Apparel Corp., 1993-94; chmn. Folger Adams Corp., Simplicity Pattern Co., Pandick Press; instr. Farleigh Dickinson U., 1968-71; lectr. Washington U., 1966, 77; cons. in field; bd. dirs. Wherehouse Enterntainment Corp., Fairlanes Bowling Corp., Celluland Corp., Northwest Pipe and Casing Co., Z Axis Corp., Crown Crafts Corp., Turn Around Mgmt. Assn., Cherokee Corp.; pres. AMA Fund, Inc. Author: The Profit Prescription, 1985, Turnaround, 1987. Active Seville Recreation Assn. Served to lt. USNR, 1959-62. Recipient scholarship Washington U., 1959, fellow, 1968. Mem. DeKalb C. of C., Citrus Club, Beta Gamma Sigma, Alpha Chi Sigma. Jewish. SD. Office: Datamax Corp 4501 Parkway Commerce Blvd Orlando FL 32808-1089

DAVIS, MARY BYRD, conservationist, researcher; b. Cardiff, Wales; came to U.S., 1947; d. John Dymond and Joanna Inger (Falconer) Byrd; m. Robert Minard Davis; children: Carol, John. BA, Agnes Scott Coll., 1958; MA, U. Wis., 1968, PhD, 1972; MLS, Simmons Coll., 1974. Acquisitions libr. No. Mich. U., Marquette, 1974-75; asst. libr. Georgetown (Ky.) Coll., 1975-78; libr. U. Ky., Lexington, 1978-83; freelance writer and editor Georgetown, 1983-90, 93—; staff writer, office mgr. Earth First Jour., Canton, N.Y., 1990; co-founder and pub. Wild Earth, Canton, N.Y., 1991-92; assoc. editor Wild Earth, Richmond, Vt., 1993—; dir. Yggdrasil Inst., Georgetown, Ky., 1994—. Author: The Military Civilian Nuclear Link, 1988, Guide de L'Industrie Nucleaire Francaise, 1988, The Green Guide to France, 1990, Going Off the Beaten Path: An Untraditional Travel Guide to the U.S., 1991, Old Growth in the East: A Survey, 1993, La France nucléaire: matières et sites, 1997; co-author: Les Déchets nucléaires militaires Français, 1994; editor: Eastern Old-Growth Forests: Prospects for Rediscovery and Recovery, 1996, Eastern Old-Growth Notes, 1997—. Bd. dirs. Centre de Documentation et de Recherche sur la Paix et les Conflits, Lyon, France, 1989—, Wildlands Ctr. for Preventing Roads, Missoula, Mont., 1996—. Mem. Nat. Writers Union, Sierra Club (editor energy report 1986-87, exec. com. Cumberland chpt. 1982-84), Phi Beta Kappa.

DAVIS, MARY CHRISTINE, artist, art educator; b. May 23, 1951; d. James Richard and Gilda Marie (Tomasso) Joyce; m. J. Ronnie Davis. BS, U. South Ala., Mobile, 1986; MFA, U. New Orleans, 1998. Tchr. elem. sch. Mobile Pub. County Schs., 1985-89; teaching asst. U. New Orelans, Mobile, 1998; tchr. Maryvale Elem. Sch., Mobile, 1986-88, Meadowlake Elem. Sch., Mobile, 1988-89; tchg. asst. U. New Orleans, 1998—. One-woman show U. New Orleans, 1998; group shows U. So. Ala., 1985, include St. Tammany, New Orelans, 1993, 94, 95, World Trade Ctr., New Orleans, 1994, U. New Orleans, 1996, 97, Lino, 1998. Paul Harris fellow Rotary Internat., 1988-89; recipient 6th pl. award USTF Southeastern Championships Marathon Event, 1979. Mem. Omicron Delta Kappa, Alpha Theta Epsilon, Kappa Delta Pi.

DAVIS, MARY DUESTERBERG (MIMI), librarian, publisher; b. Houston, June 27, 1934; d. Leonard A. Duesterberg and Lillian Palmire (Walter) Van Pelt; m. James Watson Davis, June 3, 1953 (dec.); children: James Watson Jr., John Van Pelt (dec.), Mary Lynn (dec.), Kenneth Walter (dec.). BS in Psychology, U. Houston, 1980; postgrad., Rice U., 1981-82; M in Theol. Studies, So. Meth. U., 1986; MS, U. North Tex., 1990. Lay adv. bd. mem. Southern Meth. U., Dallas, 1985-86; reference libr. Southern Meth. U., Bridwell Theol. Libr., Dallas, 1986-89, Plano Pub. Libr. System, Tex., 1989-93; assoc. dir. Waco-McLennan County Library, 1993-95, 1996—; owner All Things Press Pub. Co., 1993-95; libr. sys. analyst Ameritech Libr. Svcs., Provo, Utah, 1995-96; assoc. dir. Waco-McLennan County Libr., 1996—; summer faculty Perkins Sch. Theology, So. Meth. U., Dallas, 1988-95. Sunday sch. tchr. 1st Meth. Ch., Houston, 1980-83, retreat leader, 1980—. Bd. dirs. Habitat for Humanity, Salt Lake City, 1996, Abundant Life I Am Ministries, Dallas, 1992—; mem. spkrs. bur. Utah AIDS Found., 1994-95. Mem. ALA, Tex. Libr. Assn. Home: 2905 Lake Shore Dr Apt 204 Waco TX 76708-1003 *My religious beliefs are my rules and guide for living—sometimes that means keeping things and pondering them in my heart and sometimes it means speaking openly to the world, at great risk—such is the paradox.*

DAVIS, MARY ELIZABETH, speech pathologist, educator, counselor; b. Larned, Kans., July 1, 1930; d. LeRoy D. and Katheryn (Herndon) Harris; m. W.G. Davis, Apr. 3, 1969; children: Pamela Koch, Michelle Dalton; 1 stepchild, Wendy Garton. BA, Calif. State U., Fresno, 1959, MA, 1982. Cert. resource specialist, speech pathologist tchr., deaf tchr., counselor, Calif. Dir. recreation and occupl. therapy Wyo. State Hosp., Evanston, 1956-58; tchr. Fresno Unified Sch. Dist., 1960-80, Barton County C.C., Great Bend, Kans., 1990—. Mem. Am. Counseling Assn., Nat. Bd. Cert. Counselors. Home: 534 W 4th St Larned KS 67550-3410

DAVIS, MARY LOU, secondary education educator; b. Lansford, Pa., Aug. 25, 1943; d. Lester Earl and Susan (Depuy) Snyder; m. David Hugh Davis, June 29, 1968; children: Scott David, Sean Geoffrey. BA in Math., Susquehanna U., 1965; MEd in Math., West Chester Coll., 1969. Cert. tchr. N.Y., Pa. Math. tchr. Marple Newton Sch. Dist., Broomall, Pa., 1965-68, Arlington Ctrl.Sch. Dist., Poughkeepsie, N.Y., 1968-73, 77-79; math. tchr. Spackenkill Union Free Sch. Dist., Poughkeepsie, 1979—, dept. chmn., 1988-91, ctrl. treas., 1994—; adj. math. tchr. Dutchess C.C., Poughkeepsie, 1973-77, Marist Coll., Poughkeepsie, 1983, 1992-93. With Jr. League of Poughkeepsie, 1979—; v.p. Arlington Sch. Bd., Poughkeepsie, 1993-94; budget com., past program chmn. Dutchess County Sch. Bd., Poughkeepsie, 1988-94; active Mid-Hudson Alumnae Panhellenic, 1988—; mem. pub. rels. com. Habitat for Humanity, 1995—; auditing chmn., past treas., past trustee Poughkeepsie United Meth. Ch. Recipient Vision award IBM-Semiconductor Rsch. Corp. Competitiveness Found. Edn. Alliance, 1991. Mem. AAUW (v.p. for membership 1999), ASCD, Am. Fedn. Tchrs., Nat. Coun. Tchrs. of Math., N.Y. State Tchrs. Union (retirement del., chmn. pub. rels. and polit. action com. 1995—), Assn. Math. Tchrs. of N.Y. State, Dutchess County Math. Tchrs. Assn., Advocacy for Gifted and Talented Edn. in N.Y. State, Dutchess-Ulster-Sullivan-Orange Math. League (pres. 1984-98), Dutchess County Pub. Rels. Com. Republican. Avocations: reading, skiing, travel. Home: 369 Andrews Rd Lagrangeville NY 12540-6124 Office: Spackenkill High Sch 112 Spackenkill Rd Poughkeepsie NY 12603-5099

DAVIS, MAXINE MOLLIE, nurse; b. Salem, Oreg., July 19, 1932; d. Maxwell C. and Audrey M. (Pratt) O'Brien; m. Harold Robert Davis, July 18, 1954; children: Jackie, Julie. Cert., Good Samaritan Sch. Nursing, 1953. RN, Oreg. Supr. operating room Blue Mountain Gen. Hosp., Prairie City, Oreg., 1953-54; staff nurse Eugene (Oreg.) Hosp. and Clinic, 1955-56; office nurse pvt. practice, Brookings, Oreg., 1956-57; operating room staff nurse So. Oreg. Gen. Hosp., Grants Pass, 1964-67, supr. operating room, 1969-86, dir. surgical services, 1986-94. Bd. mem. Coalition for Kids, Citizens' Rev. Bd. Mem. Assn. Operating Rm. Nurses (past pres.), N.W. Med. Teams, OES. Episcopalian. Home: 1312 NW B St Grants Pass OR 97526-1120 Office: So Oreg Med Ctr 1505 NW Washington Blvd Grants Pass OR 97526-1088

DAVIS, MAYNARD KIRK, accountant; b. Montreal, Que., Can., Aug. 31, 1949; s. Holbrook Reineman and Sarah DeForest (Maynard) D.; m. Joanne Margaret Daugherty, Aug. 5, 1972; children: Tamara Anne, Eric Maynard, Ian Holbrook. BA, U. Pa., 1973; MS, U. Mass., Amherst, 1977; MS in Indsl. Adminstrn., Carnegie Mellon U., 1979. Fin. analyst Corning Inc., Corning, N.Y., 1979-80; plant contr. Corning Inc., Solon, Ohio and Danville, Va., 1980-83; ops. analyst Corning Inc., Corning, 1983-84, bus. contr., 1984-87, govt. contract adminstrn. mgr., 1987-92, project planner/contr., 1992-95, contr. Corning Glass Ctr., 1995-96; dir. fin. conservation sci. divsn. The Nature Conservancy, Arlington, Va., 1997—. Trustee youth programs Chemung County YMCA, Elmira, N.Y., 1985-94, , bd. dirs., 1986-89; trustee Arthur Vining Davis Founds., Jacksonville, Fla., 1989-98; class D soccer coach USSF. Mem. Inst. Mgmt. Accts., Nat. Contract Mgmt. Assn. E-mail: davismk@erols.com. Home: 2400 Beekay Ct Vienna VA 22181-3001 Office: The Nature Conservancy 4245 N Fairfax Dr Ste 100 Arlington VA 22203-1606

DAVIS, MELODIE MILLER, writer, editor; b. Sarasota, Fla., Dec. 2, 1951; d. Vernon U. and Bertha Mae (Stauffer) Miller; m. Stuart Perry Davis, May 29, 1976; children: Michelle Dawn, Tanya Ruth, Doreen Estella. Student, U. Barcelona, 1973-74; BA, Eastern Mennonite Coll., 1975. Sec., rschr., writer Mennonite Broadcasts, Inc., Harrisonburg, Va., 1975-77; prodr. Mennonite Media, Harrisonburg, Va., 1977-79, exec. prodr., 1979-81, print prodr., 1981-97, columnist (syndicated by Globe Syndicate 1997—), 1987—; editor Shalom Found., Grottoes, Va., 1995—. Author: Becoming a Better Friend, 1988, Working, Mothering, and Other Minor Dilemmas, 1983, Departure, 1991, Why Didn't I Just Raise Radishes?, 1994 (Angel award 1995). Big Sister Big Bros./Big Sisters, Harrisonburg, 1977-80; editor Music Boosters/Broadway (Va.) H.S., 1996—. Recipient Woman of Distinction award Girl Scouts USA, 1995, Media award Skyline Literacy Coun., 1996. Mem. Va. Press women (treas. 1993-95), Nat. Fedn. Press Women (Va. Communicator of Achievement award 1993), Internat. Women's Media Found., Coun. on Ch. and Media, Newspaper Features Coun., Inc. Presbyterian. Avocations: travel, gardening, flowers, hiking. Office: Mennonite Media 1251 Virginia Ave Harrisonburg VA 22802-2434

DAVIS, MICHAEL, medical educator; b. Bronxville, N.Y., Nov. 14, 1942; s. Pearce and Lucia (Bates) D.; children: Nathaniel, Alexander. BA, Northwestern U., 1965; PhD, Yale U., 1969. Rsch. assoc. Yale U. Sch. Medicine, New Haven, 1969-70, asst. prof., 1970-75, assoc. prof., 1975-84, prof., 1984-98; Robert W. Woodruff prof. psychiatry Emory U. Sch. Medicine, Atlanta, 1998—. Contbr. over 150 articles to profl. jours.; author 25 book chpts. USPHS Rsch. Scientist award NIMH, 1975-79, 80-85, 85-90, 90-95, 95—; Sterling fellow Yale U., 1969. Fellow Am. Psychol. Assn., Am. Psychol. Soc., AAAS; mem. Soc. for Neurosci., Am. Coll. Neuropsychopharmacology, Soc. for Psychophysiology, Phi Beta Kappa. Office: Emory U Sch Medicine Dept Psychiatry 1639 Pierce Dr Rm 4311 Atlanta GA 30322

DAVIS, MICHAEL CHASE, aerospace industry executive, consultant, retired naval officer; b. Fullerton, Calif., Oct. 12, 1931; s. Arthur Elling Davis and Mary Stafford (O'Brien) Greene; m. Edna Elisabeth Ann Gulick, Apr. 9, 1983 (dec. May 1998); children: Michael Chase Jr., Mark Stafford. BS, U.S. Naval Acad., 1953; SM, MIT, 1961, ScD, 1961. Commd. ensign USN, 1953, advanced through grades to capt., 1971; design supt. Mare Island Naval Shipyard, Calif., 1966-68; sys. analyst Office Asst. Sec. Def., Washington, 1968-70; ship design dir. Trident Submarine and Aegis Warships, Naval Sea

Sys. Command, Arlington, Va., 1970-75; comdg. officer David Taylor Naval Ship Rsch. and Devel. Ctr., Bethesda, Md., 1975-77; ret., 1977; program mgr. Sci. Applications, Inc., Arlington, 1977-79; program mgr., dir. Sea Shadow Stealth Ship and other marine programs, Lockheed Martin Missiles and Space Co., Sunnyvale, Calif., 1979-96; pub. Ovarian Cancer Internet Website, 1996-99. Decorated Legion of Merit, 1977; recipient DAR award for seamanship, 1953, D.W. Taylor award for sci. achievement, 1963, award for sci. achievement Bur. Ships, 1963, Joint Svc. commendation Sec. Def., 1970. Mem. IEEE, Am. Soc. Naval Engrs. (coun. mem. 1971-73), U.S. Naval Inst. Republican. Address: 816 Klee Mill Rd Westminster MD 21157

DAVIS, MICHAEL J., judge; b. 1947. BA, Macalester Coll., 1969; JD, U. Minn., 1972. Law clk. Legal Rights Ctr., 1971-73, atty., 1975-78; with Office Gen. Counsel Dept. Health, Edn. and Welfare, Social Security Adminstrn., Balt., 1973; criminal def. atty. Neighborhood Justice Ctr., 1974; atty., commr. Mpls. Civil Rights Commn., 1977-82; pub. defender Hennepin County, 1978-83; judge Hennepin County Mcpl. Ct., 1983-84, Hennepin County Dist. Ct. (4th jud. dist.), 1984-94, U.S. Dist. Ct. Minn., St. Paul, 1994—; constnl. law instr. Antioch Mpls. C.C., 1974; criminal def. trial practice instr. Nat. Lawyer's Guild, 1977; trial practice instr. William Mitchell Coll. Law, 1977-81, Bemidji Trial Advocacy Course, 1992, 93; adj. prof. U. Minn. Law Sch., 1982—, Hubert H. Humphrey Sch. Pub. Affairs, 1990; instr. Minn. Inst. Legal Edn., 1990—, lectr. Civil Trial Practice Inst., 1991-92; lectr. FBI Acad., 1991, 92. Recipient Outstanding Alumni award Macalester Coll., 1989, Good Neighbor award Sta. WCCO Radio, 1989. Mem. ABA, Nat. Bar Assn., Minn. Minority Lawyers Assn., Am. Inns. of Ct., Fed. Bar Assn., Fed. Judges Assn., Hennepin County Bar Assn., Minn. State Bar Assn., Minn. Lawyers Internat. Human Rights Com. (past mem. bd. dirs.), Internat. Acad. Trial Judges, Nat. Assn. for Pub. Interest Law Fellowships for Equal Justice (bd. dirs.), 8th Cir. Jury Instruction Com., U.S. Assn. Constitutional Law. Office: US Dist Ct Minn 300 S 4th St Ste 14E Minneapolis MN 55415-2251

DAVIS, MICHAEL JORDAN, civil engineer, natural gas company executive; b. Hudson, N.Y., Aug. 30, 1957; s. Ronald James and Virginia Ann (Jordan) D.; m. Camellia Jane Poland, Dec. 24, 1984; children: Kelly Dewayne, Elizabeth Ann. BSCE, Syracuse U., 1980. Field engr. Tenn. Gas Pipeline, Lafayette, La., 1980-85; divsn. engr. supr. Tenn. Gas Pipeline, Enfield, Conn., 1989-91; engr. Tenneco Gas, Houston, 1985-86, pipeline engr., 1986-89, mgr. drafting, 1991-94; dist. supt. Tenn. Gas Pipeline, Houma, La., 1994-97; mgr. codes, stds. and records Tenn. Gas Pipeline, Houston, 1997-98, mgr. pipeline design and codes, 1998—. Mem. Am. Gas Assn. (mem. gas piping tech. com.), So. Gas Assn., Coast Conservation Assn., League Am. Bicyclists, Rails-to-Trails Conservancy. Republican. Methodist. Avocations: bicycling, salt water fishing, swimming. Home: 3135 Mossy Elm Ct Houston TX 77059-3227 Office: Tenn Gas Pipeline 1001 Louisiana St Houston TX 77002-5089

DAVIS, MICHAEL S., lawyer; b. Brookline, Mass., Aug. 1, 1947; s. Ralph and Beatrice (Levy) D.; m. Madelyn O. Davis, Aug. 16, 1970; children: Gregory, Adam, Bethany. AB, U. Rochester, 1969; JD cum laude, Boston U., 1972. Bar: N.Y. 1973, U.S. Dist. Ct. (so. and ea. dists.) N.Y. 1974, U.S. Ct. Appeals (2d cir.) 1974, U.S. Supreme Ct. 1979, U.S. Ct. Claims, 1980. Assoc. Chadbourne & Parke, N.Y.C., 1972-82; sr. counsel corp. litigation Am. Internat. Group, N.Y.C., 1982-88; ptnr. Zeichner, Ellman & Krause, LLP, N.Y.C., 1999—; asst. adj. prof. C.W. Post Ctr., L.I. U., Glen Cove, N.Y., 1975-79. Editor Boston U. Law Rev., 1970-72. Mem. Citizens Ctr. for Children of N.Y., Inc., 1978-87; pres. Pelham (N.Y.) Jewish Ctr., 1986-88. Mem. ABA, Assn. Bar City of N.Y., Am. Arbitration Assn., Huguenot Bridge Club. Democrat. Office: Zeichner Ellman & Krause 575 Lexington Ave New York NY 10022

DAVIS, MICHAEL W., lawyer; b. N.Y.C., Nov. 12, 1950. BA magna cum laude, SUNY, Binghamton, 1972; JD cum laude, Northwestern U., 1975. Bar: Ill. 1975, U.S. Supreme Ct. 1981. Ptnr. Sidley & Austin, Chgo.; prof. products liability law Chgo. Kent Coll. Law, 1984-88. Mem. drug and med. device steering com. Def. Rsch. Inst. Mem. Internat. Assn. Defense Coun., Legal Club Chgo. Office: Sidley & Austin 1 First Natl Plz Chicago IL 60603-2003

DAVIS, MORAINE TAYLOR, non-profit organization administrator; b. Grand Island, Nebr.; d. Darrel Austin and Myrna Jeanne (Richards) D. BA in Philosophy, U. Nebr., 1990, BA in English, 1991, M of Cmty. and Regional Planning, 1993. Exec. dir. Lincoln County Cmty. Devel. Corp., North Platte, Nebr., 1996—; mem. North Platte Area Devel. Task Force. Co-author: History of Grand Island Senior High, 1935-65, 1986. Bd. dirs. North Platte Area Habitat for Humanity, 1997—; bd. dirs. Gt. Plains HIV/AIDS Regional Cmty. Planning Bd., 1996—; mem. Lincoln County Sioux Lookout Com., North Platte, 1996-97; bd. dirs., pres. North Platte chpt. U. Nebr.-Lincoln Alumni Assn., 1998—. Mem. Nat. Fedn. Bus. and Profl. Women., Nebr. Assn. Cmty. Housing Devel. Orgn. (sec. 1997-98), Old West Coun. (sec. 1997—). Avocations: hiking, reading, puzzles, crocheting, music. Home: 1216 W 4th St North Platte NE 69101 Office: Lincoln County Cmty Devel Corp PO Box 1263 North Platte NE 69103-1263

DAVIS, MORRIS SCHUYLER, astronomer; b. Bklyn., Dec. 14, 1919; s. Nathan Samuel and Helen (Gross) D.; m. Dorothy Irene Hall, May 26, 1945; children: Glenn Craig, Elizabeth Davis Nyblade, Cynthia Louise Davis, Deborah Susan Davis, Katherine Davis Stalberg, Martha Holly Davis Werlen. B.A., Bklyn. Coll., 1946; M.A., U. Mo., 1947; Ph.D., Yale U., 1950. Dir. Computer Ctr., Yale U., New Haven, 1956-66, also research assoc. astronomy; pres. dir. Triangle Univs. Computation Ctr., Research Triangle Park, N.C., 1966-70; Morehead prof. astronomy U. N.C., Chapel Hill, 1970-85, Morehead prof. astronomy emeritus, 1985—. Fellow AAAS; mem. Univ. Research Assn. (trustee 1977-83, exec. editor Celestial Mechanics 1985-89), Am. Astronom. Soc., Internat. Astron. Union. Unitarian. E-mail: msdavis@physics.unc.edu. Home: 404 N Estes Dr Chapel Hill NC 27514-7629 Office: U NC CB#3255 Dept Physics and Astronomy Phillips Hall 039A Chapel Hill NC 27599-3255

DAVIS, MULLER, lawyer; b. Chgo., Apr. 23, 1935; s. Benjamin B. and Janice (Muller) D.; m. Jane Lynn Strauss, Dec. 28, 1963 (div. July 1998); children: Melissa Davis Smith, Muller, Joseph Jeffrey; m. Lynn Atraus, Jan. 23, 1999. Grad. with honors, Phillips Exeter (N.H.) Acad., 1953; BA magna cum laude, Yale U., 1957; JD, Harvard U., 1960. Bar: Ill. 1960, U.S. Dist. Ct. (no. dist.) Ill. 1961. Practice law Chgo., 1960—; assoc. Jenner & Block, 1960-67; ptnr. Davis, Friedman, Zavett, Kane & MacRae, 1967—; lectr. continuing legal edn., matrimonial law and litigation; legal adviser Michael Reese Med. Research Inst. Council, 1967-82. Author: (with Sherman C. Feinstein) The Parental Couple in a Successful Divorce, Illinois Practice of Family Law, 1995, 97, 98-99; mem. editl. bd. Equitable Distbn. Jour., 1984—; contbr. articles to law jours. Bd. dirs. Infant Welfare Soc., 1975-96, hon. bd. dirs., 1996—, pres., 1978-82; co-chmn. gen. gifts 40th and 45th reunions Phillips Exeter Acad., chair class capital giving, 1994-98. Capt. U.S. Army, Ill. N.G., 1960-67. Fellow Am. Acad. Matrimonial Lawyers (bd. mgrs. Ill. chpt. 1996—), Am. Bar Found.; mem. ABA, SCRIBES, Fed. Bar Assn., Ill. Bar Assn., Chgo. Bar Assn. (matrimonial com. 1968-83, sec. civil practice com. 1979-80, vice chmn. 1980-81, chmn. 1981-82), Am. Soc. Writers on Legal Subjects, Chgo. Estate Planning Coun., Legal Aid Soc. (vice chmn. matrimonial bar 1991-95, vice chmn. 1995-97, chmn. 1997—), Law Club Chgo., Tavern Club, Lake Shore Country Club, Chgo. Club. Republican. Jewish. Home: 2110 N Fremont St Chicago IL 60614-4306 Office: 140 S Dearborn St Chicago IL 60603-5202

DAVIS, NATHAN, actor; b. Chgo., May 22, 1917; s. Fred and Rose (Marcus) D.; m. Metta Talmy, July 12, 1941; children: Jo Ellen Friedman, Andrew, Richard. Appeared in films Thief, Risky Business, Burglar, Tough Guys, Poltergeist III, Flowers in the Attic, Chain Reaction, others; appeared on TV in Jack's Place, Wise Guy, Cheers, Untouchables, Missing Persons, Frasier, ER, others; appeared on Broadway in Grapes of Wrath, Cort Theatre; appeared in regional theatre including Steppenwolf Theatre, Nat. Jewish Theatre, Goodman Theatre, Pheasant Run Theatre, Court Theatre, Wisdom Bridge Theatre, others. Recordist, Blind Svc., Chgo. Sgt. U.S. Army, 1943-45, ETO. Mem. SAG, AFTRA, Actors Equity (emeritus bd. dirs.).

DAVIS, NATHAN CHILTON, federal agency administrator; b. St. Albans, N.Y., May 2, 1954; s. Nathan Chilton Davis and Ferne Irene Snyder; m. Deborah Laurie Nygaard, Apr. 15, 1973; children: Nathan Chilton III and Richard Randall (twins), Jaime Rae, Evan Michael. AS, U. Calif., San Diego, 1979; BS, Kensington U., 1994. Cert. emergency paramedic, arson investigator, auditor. Fire chief, paramedic Salton City Svcs., Salton Sea, Calif., 1975-78; emergency paramedic City of San Bernardino/Riverside, Calif., 1978-79; detention officer U.S. Immigration, El Centro, Calif., 1981-83, physician asst., 1983-85; tng. administrator U.S. Immigration, Laguna Niguel, Calif., 1985-87, dep. asst. regional commr., 1987-88; officer in charge U.S. Immigration, El Centro, 1988-95; asst. chief enforcement officer U.S. Immigration, Washington, 1995—; instr. Fed. Law Enforcement Tng. Ctr., U.S. Dept. Justice, 1985; course developer U.S. Immigration Svc., 1986; arson investigator Riverside (Calif.) County FireDept., 1975; pres. Fed. Exec. Bd., 1991-95; chair Career Opportunity Program Adv. Coun., 1993. Author: Executive Protection, 1984, revised, 1994, Detention Operations, 1985, Corporate Violence, 1993, Leader's Guide to Office Management, 1994; numerous tng. programs. Capt. U.S. Army, 1980-88. Recipient Life Saving medal Salton Cmty. Svcs., 1980, Army Commendation award Dept. Def., 1987, Performance award, 1994 (v.p. Al Gore), commendation, 1995; nominated Innovation in Am. Govt. award JFK Sch. of Bus., Harvard U., 1994, Ins. Commrs. award for excellence, 1994. Mem. Am. Correctional Assn. (gold), Am. Assn. Correctional Psychology. Avocations: flying, writing, travel, scuba diving, teaching. Home: 9594 Basilwood Dr Manassas VA 20110-7926 Office: US Immigration 425 I St NW Washington DC 20536-0001

DAVIS, NATHANIEL, humanities educator; b. Boston, Apr. 12, 1925; s. Harvey Nathaniel and Alice Marion (Rohde) D.; m. Elizabeth Kirkbride Creese, Nov. 24, 1956; children: Margaret Morton Davis Mainardi, Helen Miller Davis Presley, James Creese, Thomas Rohde. Grad., Phillips Exeter Acad., 1942; AB, Brown U., 1944, LLD, 1970; MA, Fletcher Sch. Law and Diplomacy, 1947, PhD, 1960; postgrad. Russian lang. and area, Columbia, Cornell U., Middlebury Coll., 1953-54, U. Central de Venezuela, 1961-62; Norwich U., 1989. Asst. history Tufts Coll., 1947; joined U.S. Fgn. Service, 1947; 3d sec. Prague, Czechoslovakia, 1947-49; vice consul Florence, Italy, 1949-52; 2d sec. Rome, Italy, 1952-53, Moscow, USSR, 1954-56; Soviet desk officer State Dept., 1956-60; 1st sec. Caracas, Venezuela, 1960-62; acting Peace Corps dir. Chile, 1962; spl. asst. to dir. Peace Corps, 1962-63, dept. asso. dir., 1963-65; U.S. minister to Bulgaria, 1965-66; sr. staff Nat. Security Council (White House), 1966-68; U.S. ambassador to Guatemala, 1968-71; to Chile, 1971-73; dir. gen. Fgn. Service, 1973-75, asst. sec. of state for African affairs, 1975; U.S. ambassador to Switzerland, 1975-77; State Dept advisor and Chester Nimitz prof. Naval War Coll., 1977-83; lectr. Naval War Coll., San Diego, 1991—; Alexander and Adelaide Hixon prof. humanities Harvey Mudd Coll., Claremont, Calif., 1983—; faculty exec. com. Harvey Mudd Coll., 1986-89, acting dean of faculty, 1990; mem. Mellon Found. Grant Inter-coll. Steering Com. for the Six Claremont Colls., establishing a Summer Lang. Inst. and coordinated lang. program; mem. Consortiumn, Task Force on the Future of the Clairmont Colleges, 1996, Fulbright scholarship, Moscow, Russia, 1996-97; lectr. U.S. history Centro Venezolano-Americano, 1961; lectr. Russian and Soviet history Howard U., 1962-65, 66-68; lectr. constnl. law and social problems Salve Regina Coll., 1981-83; vis. prof. Russian State U. Humanities, 1996-97; mem. governing bd. European Union Ctr. Calif., 1998—. Author: The Last Two Years of Salvador Allende, 1985, Equality and Equal Security in Soviet Foreign Policy, 1986, A Long Walk to Church: A Contemporary History of Russian Orthodoxy, 1995. Mem. ctrl. com. Calif. Dem. Party, 1987-90, 91—, mem. exec. bd., 1993—, mem. exec. com., bus. and profl. caucus, 1992-96; mem. L.A. County Dem. Ctrl. Com., 1988-90, 92—, regional vice chmn., 1994-96; del. Dem. Nat. Conv., 1988, 92, 96; del. So. Calif. conf. United Ch. of Christ, 1986-87. Lt. (j.g.) USNR, 1944-46. Recipient Cinco Aguilas Blancas Alpinism award Venezuelan Andean Club, 1962, Disting. Pub. Svc. award U.S. Navy, 1983, Elvira Roberti award for outstanding leadership Los Angeles County Dem. Party, 1995, Spl. Merit award (as author) So. Calif. Motion Picture Coun. Mem. AAUP (pres. Claremont Coll. chpt. 1992-96, rep. so. Calif. pvt. colls., Calif. coun.), Am. Fgn. Svc. Assn. (bd. dirs., vice chmn. 1964), Coun. on Fgn. Rels., Am. Acad. Diplomacy, Nat. Book Critics Cir., Cosmos Club, Phi Beta Kappa. Home: 1783 Longwood Ave Claremont CA 91711-3129 Office: Harvey Mudd Coll 301 E 12th St Claremont CA 91711-5901

DAVIS, NICHOLAS HOMANS CLARK, finance company executive; b. N.Y.C., Dec. 1, 1938; s. Feltz Cleveland and Loraine Vanderpool (Homans) D.; children from previous marriage: Loraine, Helen, Alexandra, Eleanor; m. Brenda Jean Molen, Dec. 18, 1982; children: Nicholas, Elizabeth. BA in Geology with honors, Princeton U., 1961; MBA in Fin., Stanford U., 1963. Chartered fin. analyst; cert. NYSE supervisory analyst. Research analyst Fahnestock & Co., N.Y.C., 1963-67; mgr. research Andresen & Co., N.Y.C., 1967-71; dir. research Boettcher & Co., Denver, 1971-75; v.p. corp. fin. White Weld & Co., Denver, 1975-78; v.p. asset mgmt. Paine Webber Co., Denver, 1978-92; chmn., pres. Mont. Investment Advisors, Inc., Bozeman, 1991—; Trustee, investment officer Thenen Found., Montclair, N.J., 1966—. Chmn. Jr. Achievement Gallatin County. Mem. Venture Capital Assn. Colo. (founder, bd. dirs., treas. 1982—), Denver Soc. Security Analysts (chmn., pres. 1972—), Riverside Country Club, Rotary. Avocations: skiing, flyfishing, deepwater voyaging, writing, backpacking. Home: 2302 Springcreek Dr Bozeman MT 59715-6035 Office: Mont Investment Advisors Inc 104 E Main St # 416 PO Box 7090 Bozeman MT 59771-7090

DAVIS, OTTO ANDERSON, economics educator; b. Florence, S.C., Apr. 4, 1934; s. Otto and Pauline (Anderson) D.; m. Carolyn Quinn, Dec. 26, 1962; children—Craig, Wendy, Ross. A.B., Wofford Coll., 1956; M.A., U. Va., 1957, Ph.D., 1960. Asst. prof. econs. Grad Sch. Indsl. Adminstrn., Carnegie-Mellon U., Pitts., 1960-65; assoc. prof. Grad Sch. Indsl. Adminstrn. Carnegie-Mellon U., 1965-67, prof., 1967-68, prof. polit. economy Sch. Urban and Public Affairs, 1968-81, W.W. Cooper univ. prof. econs. and pub. policy, 1981—, assoc. dean, 1968-75, dean, 1975-81; rsch. dir. Pa. Tax Commn., 1979-82; bd. visitors Air U., Maxwell AFB, 1980-83. Contbr. book revs. and articles to profl. jours. Fellow Econometric Soc.; mem. Public Choice Soc. (pres. 1970-72), Assn. Public Policy Analysis and Mgmt. (policy council, pres. 1982-83), Am. Econ. Assn., Am. Polit. Sci. Assn., Am. Soc. Public Administrn. Office: Carnegie-Mellon U Dept Social Decision Scis Porter Hall # 223F Pittsburgh PA 15213-3890

DAVIS, PAMELA BOWES, pediatric pulmonologist; b. Jamaica, N.Y., July 20, 1949; d. Elmer George and Florence (Welsch) Bowes; m. Glenn C. Davis, June 28, 1970 (div. Mar. 1987); children: Jason, Galen. AB, Smith Coll., 1968; PhD, Duke U., 1973, MD, 1974. Internal medicine intern Duke Hosp., 1973-74, resident in internal medicine, 1974-75; sr. investigator NIAMD/NIH, Bethesda, Md., 1977-79; asst. prof. U. Tenn. Coll. Medicine, Memphis, 1979-81; asst. prof. Case Western Res. U. Sch. Medicine, Cleve., 1981-85, assoc. prof., 1985-89, prof., 1989—, chief pediat. pulmonary divsn., 1985—, vice chmn. rsch. dept., 1994-96; pres. Am. Fedn. for Clin. Rsch., Thorofare, N.J., 1989-90; trustee Rsch. Am., Arlington, Va., 1989-90; mem. adv. coun. Nat. Inst. Diabetes, Digestive and Kidney Diseases, 1992-96. Contbr. articles to profl. jours. Chmn., med. adv. coun. Cystic Fibrosis Found., Bethesda, 1988-90. Recipient Samuel Rosenthal award in acad. pediat., 1996, Maurice Saltzman award Mt. Sinai Health Care Found., 1998. Fellow ACP; mem. Am. Pediatric Soc., Am. Acad. Pediatrics, Am. Physiol. Soc., Am. Thoracic Soc., Soc. for Pediatric Rsch., Phi Beta Kappa, Sigma Xi. Office: Rainbow Babies/Child Hosp 2101 Adelbert Rd Cleveland OH 44106-2624

DAVIS, PATRICIA M., literacy educator; b. Lloydminster, Alberta, Can., Nov. 16, 1932; d. George E. and Edith May (Kent) McKerihan; m. Harold M. Davis, Dec. 17, 1958 (dec. Dec. 24, 1971); children: Harold Neal, Rosemary Anne. BA, Dallas Bapt. Coll., 1981; MA, U. Tex., Rustin, 1988, PhD, 1994. From grass roots worker to materials cons., tchr. trainer Summer Inst. Linguistics/Min. Edn., Peruvian Amazon region, 1963-84; literacy trainer Summer Inst. Linguistics, England, 1979, 88, U. Oreg., 1985-88; internat. literacy and edn. cons. Summer Inst. Linguistics, Dallas, 1995—; literacy trainer, Ethiopia, 1992, Kenya, 1994, 97, U. N.D., 1995, 98, 99, Singapore, 1995, Asia, 1997, Peru, 1997-98, The Philippines, 1999. Author: Cognition and Learning, 1991, La enseñanza del castellano como segunda lengua entre los grupos etnolingüísticos de la Amazonia, 1997; co-author: Bilingual Education: An Experience in Peruvian Amazonia, Spanish edit., 1979, English edit., 1981. Mem. Internat. Reading Assn., Comparative and Internat. Edn. Soc., Alpha Chi, Kappa Delta Pi, Phi Kappa Phi. Avocations: sewing, entertaining, reading anthropology. Office: Summer Inst Linguistics 7500 W Camp Wisdom Rd Dallas TX 75236-5628

DAVIS, PAUL B., mechanical engineer, civil engineer, retired; b. N.Y.C., Jan. 20, 1909; s. Samuel and Esther (Schwartz) D.; m. Sally Vogel (dec.), Nov. 24, 1932; children: Gerald Joseph, Audrey Thea Coll. Student, Poly. U. N.Y., 1928. Engring. draftsman Mcpl. Pub. Works, N.Y.C., 1929-41; asst. engr. Bd. Water Supply, N.Y.C., 1941-42; sr. designer to asst. supt. design nuclear/fossil fuel stas. Ebasco Svcs., Inc., N.Y.C., 1942-66; mgr. Spanish projects Ebasco Overseas Corp., Madrid, 1966-72; project engring. mgr. Burns & Roe, Hempstead, N.Y., 1973-76; ednl. coord. Argonne Nat. Lab., Argonne, Ill., 1977. Dir. Poinciana Condominium Assn., Lake Worth, Fla., 1979-86. Mem. NSPE (life), N.Y. State Soc. Profl. Engrs., Sierra Club, Zionist Orgn. Am., World Jewish Congress, B'nai B'rith, Nat. Wildlife Fedn., The Nature Conservancy, Poinciana Country Club. Avocations: Spanish culture, golf, oil painting, bridge, swimming. Home: 3520 Whitehall Dr Apt 303 West Palm Beach FL 33401-1072

DAVIS, PAUL BRYAN, political science educator; b. L.A., June 13, 1947; s. Michael and Rebecca (Badner) D. AA in Polit. Sci., Santa Monica Coll., 1967; BA, Calif. State U., Long Beach, 1969; MA, San Diego State U., 1971; PhD, U. Utah, 1978. Instr. polit. sci. San Diego State U., 1971-73; lectr. polit. sci. U. Utah, Salt Lake City, 1974-76; prof. polit. sci. Truckee Meadows C.C., Reno, Nev., 1976—, Sierra Nevada Coll., Incline Village, Nev., 1977-79, U. Nev., Reno, 1980-93, U. Md. European divsn., 1984-85, U. Pitts., 1995; adminstrv. analyst City of San Diego, 1972; mem. nat. adv. bd. Dushkin Pub., Conn., 1990-94; lectr., rschr. in field. Co-author: Introduction to Political Terrorism, 1989; contbr. revs., articles to profl. publs.; TV and radio analyst ABC, CBS, NBC, 1981—. Campaign coord. Utah State Presl. Campaign for Senator Frank Church, 19767, Nev. State Presdl. Campaign for Senator Eugene McCarthy, 1976, Nev. State Presdl. Campaign for Congressman John Anderson, 1980; mem. Washoe County Nev. Rep. Ctrl. Com., Reno, 1996—; mem. state ctrl. com. Nev. State Rep. Party, Reno, 1996—; rschr. for Rep. Nat. Conv., San Diego, 1996; co-developer internat. seminar Nev. World Trade Coun., Reno, 1996. Recipient cert. of appreciation City of San Diego, 1972, Bd. Regents Tchr. award for prof. of yr. State of Nev., 1999; named Outstanding Prof. of Yr., Phi Theta Kappa, 1996; grantee NEH, 1990, U.S. Inst. Peace, 1995; Fulbright fellow, India, 1990, Israel, 1982, Egypt, 1986, NEH rsch. fellow, 1983. Mem. Am. Fedn. Tchrs., Am. Polit. Sci. Assn., Policy Studies Orgn., Internat. Polit. Sci. Assn., Western Gerontol. Soc., Presdl. Studies Assn., Animal Protection Inst. Am., Fulbright Alumni Assn., Phi Sigma Alpha. Avocations: travel, lecturing. Home: PO Box 50666 Sparks NV 89435-0666 Office: Truckee Meadows CC 7000 Dandini Blvd Reno NV 89512-3901

DAVIS, PAUL JOSEPH, endocrinologist; b. Chgo., Oct. 28, 1937; s. Paul Albert and Maxine Lydia (Mason) D.; m. Faith Ainsworth Baker, Dec. 8, 1962; children: Matthew, John, Sarah. BA magna cum laude, Westminster Coll., 1959; MD cum laude, Harvard U., 1963. Intern Bronx Municipal Hosp. Center, 1963-64, resident in medicine, 1964-67; clin. assoc. NIH, Bethesda, Md., 1967-69; sr. staff assoc. NIH, 1969-70; head endocrinology div. Balt. City Hosps., 1970-75; prof. medicine, head endocrinology div. SUNY, Buffalo Med. Sch., 1975-90, also vice chmn. dept. medicine; prof., chmn. dept. medicine, assoc. dean for clin. rsch. Albany Med. Coll., Albany Med. Ctr., N.Y., 1990—; chief med. svc. VA Med. Ctr., Buffalo, 1980-90; mem. merit rev. bd. endocrinology VA; bd. dirs. Am. Bd. Internal Medicine. Fellow ACP (gov. Upstate N.Y. region), Gerontol. Soc.; mem. Am. Fedn. Clin. Rsch., Am. Soc. Biochemistry and Molecular Biology, Am. Thyroid Assn. (bd. dirs., pres. 1997—), Endocrine Soc., Bd. Sci. Counselors, Nat. Inst. Aging. Research and publs. on mechanisms of action of thyroid hormone, effects of aging on endocrine function. Home: 35 Old South Rd West Sand Lake NY 12196-2104 Office: Clin Rsch Initaitive Mailcode 54 47 New Scotland Ave Albany NY 12208*

DAVIS, PAUL MICHAEL, sales executive, transportation company executive; b. Burlington, N.C., Apr. 18, 1940; s. Paul P. and Margaret (Mebane) D.; m. Sarah Gillon, Aug. 11, 1963; children: Paul Michael Jr., Jennifer Lynn. BSBA, U. N.C., 1962. Terminal mgr. McLean Trucking Co., various locations, 1964-86; asst. to v.p. McLean Trucking Co., Indpls., 1971-72, dist. mgr., 1972-79; v.p. McLean Trucking Co., Kearny, N.J., 1979-81, Memphis, 1981-86; sr. v.p. sales, mktg. Builders Transport, Inc., Camden, S.C., 1986-98, v.p. dedicated fleet div., 1989-98; v.p. dedicated svcs. Landair Transport, Inc., Greenville, Tenn., 1998—. Mem. Sertoma. Republican. Lutheran. Fax: 803-427-8420. Office: 2943 W Dekalb St Ste 3 Camden SC 29020

DAVIS, PAUL MILTON, communications administrator; b. Effingham, Ill., Dec. 21, 1938; s. Plaford Milton and Zona Matilda (Buchholz) D.; m. Marilynne Bohne, Aug. 26, 1961; children: Paul Mark, Glenn Stokes, Marinell Kathryn. Student, Georgetown (Ky.) Coll., 1956-58, Baylor U., 1958-60; BA, U. Ill., 1963. Anchor-reporter news dept. WCIA-TV, Champaign, Ill., 1960-67, news dir., 1967-80; news dir. WGN-AM and TV, Chgo., 1980-83, WGN-TV, Chgo., 1983-93; pres. Tribune Broadcasting News Network, Inc., Chgo., 1990-91, cons., 1993—; news dir. WLVI-TV, Boston, 1994-96; pres. The Paul Davis Co., 1994-98; sr. v.p. Found. for Am. Comms., L.A., 1998—; v.p. First Amendment Congress, 1979-87; mem. World Press Freedom Com.; chmn. UPI Broadcast Adv. Bd., 1983-88, mem. editorial rev. com., 1987; mem. nat. adv. com. Ctr. for Info. Law, John Marshall Law Sch.; mem. nat. adv. bd. Wharton Sch. Broadcast Mgmt. Programs, U. Pa., 1978-81; underwriter RTND Found. Directory of Minority Resources, 1996. Co-author Jane Pauley Task Force Report on State of Broadcast Journalism Edn., 1996; contbr. articles to profl. jours. Founding bd. mem., pres. Boys Club, Champaign/Urbana, 1968-71; pres. bd. Family Svc. Champaign County, 1969-72; nat. treas. Family Svc. Assn. Am., N.Y.C., 1975-77; chmn. Ill. Dept. Pub. Aid Title XX Adv. Coun., Springfield, Ill., 1977-79; v.p., founder United Way Ill., 1975-79; mem. adv. bd. Ill. Dept. Children and Family Svcs., 1968-70. Named Citizen of Yr., NASW, Champaign County, 1969; recipient award Nat. Ctr. Freedom of Info. Studies, Loyola U., Columbia-Dupont Citation, numerous reporting awards from wire svc. and profl. assns. Mem. NATAS (bd. govs., Gov.'s award Chgo. chpt. TV Acad. 1993), Radio-TV News Dirs. Assn. (pres. 1979, chmn. EEO com., disting. svc. award), Soc. Profl. Journalists (pres. 1989), Ill. News Broadcasters Assn. (pres. 1966, Illinoisan of Yr. 1993), Ill. State Bar Assn. (past chmn. media law com., mem. subcom. on cameras in the ct.), ABA (mem. media-law com. 1992—), Headline Club Chgo. (mem. bd. 1982-87, mem. long range planning com.), Ill. Freedom of Info. Coun. Avocations: fgn. travel, journalist assessment. Home: 17241 Boswell Pl Granada Hills CA 91344-1021 Office: Found Am Comms 3800 Barham Blvd Ste 409 Los Angeles CA 90068-1042

DAVIS, PAUL RICK, military career officer; b. Houston, Sept. 15, 1943; s. Paul Allen and Dorothy Mae (Meadows) D.; m. Gail Elaine Myers, Dec. 12, 1977; children: Brent, Sandra, Heidi, Jesse. BA, Ariz. State U., 1967. Commd. 2d lt. USAF, 1967, advanced through grades to col., 1992; comdr. USAF spl. ops. forces USAF, Turkey, 1993-94; rancher. Assoc. advisor Creation Evidences Mus.; mem. U.S. Team Roping Championship. Decorated Legion of Merit, three Meritorious Svc. medal, three Air Force Commendation medal, seven Air medals USAF; recipient Helicopter Heroism award Avco-Lycoming, Las Vegas, Nev., 1984. Mem. Vietnam Helicopter Pilot Assn., Res. Officers Assn., Am. Quarter Horse Assn., Christian Cowboys Assn. Republican. Avocations: rodeo cowboy, fly fishing, scuba diving, golfing, hunting. Home: RR 1 Box 115 Dublin TX 76446-9796

DAVIS, PAUL ROBERT, investment manager, portfolio manager; b. Lynn, Mass., Mar. 17, 1964; s. Harold S. and Diane Aida Davis; m. Liane D'Alessandro, Oct. 12, 1991. AB, Dartmouth Coll., 1986; MBA, Harvard U., 1991. Assoc. cons. Monitor Co., Cambridge, Mass., 1985-86, cons., 1986-88, project mgr., 1988-89; v.p., prin. Yeager Wood & Marshall, N.Y.C., 1990-96, CFO, 1991-94; sr. v.p. Hagler, Mastrovita & Hewitt, Boston, 1996-98; v.p. David L. Babson & Co., Cambridge, 1998—. Mem. Harvard Club N.Y., Assn. Investment Mgmt. and Rsch. (CFA, Chartered Investment Counselor), Dartmouth Alumni Assn. (leadership agt. 1988—). Avocations: offshore ocean yacht racing, animation art collecting, reading, Tonkinese cats. Office: David L Babson & Co One Memorial Dr Cambridge MA 02142

DAVIS, PEGGY HAMLETTE, banking executive; b. Prince Edward County, Va., June 28, 1940; d. Ellis Edward and Ruth Elizabeth Hamlette; m. Lewis James Davis, Dec. 23, 1956; children: Timothy Lewis, Melissa Jane. Cone winder Drakes Branch, Va., 1958-59; burling and mender Brookneal, Va., 1959-64, data processor, 1964-66, office clk., 1973-76; head teller Bank of Charlotte County, Phenix, Va., 1976—, from exec. sec. to asst. v.p., 1977—. Sunday sch. tchr. So. Bapt. Ch., Phenix; treas. Bethel Bapt. Ch., Phenix, 1988—; pres. Homemakers Club, Phenix, 1973-77. Avocations: singing, playing guitar, sewing, art, crossword puzzles. Home: Highway 746 # 54 Phenix VA 23959 Office: Bank of Charlotte County Charlotte & Berkley Sts PO Box 336 Phenix VA 23959-0336

DAVIS, PETER (PETER PATHFINDER DAVIS), priest; b. Jersey City, Mar. 22, 1937; s. Joseph Anthony and Adele Elizabeth (Claveloux) D.; m. Catharine Buenz, 1958 (div. 1979); children: Richard, Robert; m. Wende Elizabeth Young, Dec. 31, 1994. Student, Rutgers U., 1973, U. Okla., 1979, Pacific Luth. U., 1980. Founder, archpriest Aquarian Tabernacle Ch. (Wicca), Seattle, 1979—; pub. info. officer Covenant of the Goddess, Berkeley, Calif., 1985-86; founding bd. dirs. Wiccan Info. Network, Vancouver, Can.; mem. religious adv. commn. Wash. Dept. Corrections; organizer Pagan Ch. Conf., 1990, other ann. confs. Contbg. author: Witchcraft Today, 1991; editor Panegyria, 1984-97. Councilman, then mayor Andover Twp., N.J., 1960-76; mem. Selective Svc. Bd., Newton, 1971-76; commr. Sussex County Election Commn., 1973-74; trustee Ctr. for Non-Traditional Religion, Seattle, 1980—, past pres. With N.J.A.R.N.G., 1956-62. Mem. Interfaith Coun. Wash. (sr. del. 1990—, pres. 1995-97), Am. Soc. for Indsl. Security (cert. protection profl.), Fellowship of Isis. Democrat. Office: Aquarian Tabernacle Ch PO Box 409 Index WA 98256-0409 *Our whole society is in disarray and our children, in confusion. What is desperately needed is the re-establishment of clear limits of societally acceptable behavior, for both ourselves and our youngsters. Ecology should be considered a sacramental duty. Only by abandonment of today's "maybe" limits in favor of clear, firm, unequivocal yet equitable behavioral limits can we hope to restore moral stability. Personal responsibility starts at home with each of us, where "no" once again needs to mean, simply, "no", and not "maybe."*

DAVIS, PETER FRANK, filmmaker, author; b. Santa Monica, Calif., Jan. 2, 1937; s. Frank and Tess (Slesinger) D.; m. Johanna Mankiewicz, Sept. 13, 1959 (dec. July 1974); children—Timothy, Nicholas; m. Karen Zehring, June 10, 1979 (div. Dec., 1995); children: Jesse, Antonia. AB magna cum laude, Harvard U., 1957. Editorial asst. N.Y. Times, N.Y.C., 1958-59; writer, interviewer Sextant Film Prodns., N.Y.C., 1961-64; writer, assoc. producer NBC News, N.Y.C., 1964; writer, producer CBS News, N.Y.C., 1965-72; freelance filmmaker N.Y.C., 1972-82, freelance writer, 1976—; vis. lectr. various univs., 1974-75. Documentary cons. Pumping Iron, 1978, Gilda Live, 1980; writer, prodr.: (TV documentaries) The Heritage of Slavery, 1968, The Battle of East St. Louis, 1969, The Selling of the Pentagon, 1971 (Emmy award 1971, Peabody award 1971, Writers Guild Am. award 1971, George Polk award 1971); prodr. The Best Hotel on Skid Row, 1990; writer Age 7 in America, 1991; prodr., writer JACK, 1993; assoc. prodr., writer (documentary) Hunger in America, 1968 (Writers Guild Am. award 1968); dir., prodr.: (films) Hearts and Minds, 1974 (Oscar award 1975); Middletown, 1982; co-writer (TV film) Haywire, 1980; contbg. editor Esquire Mag., 1985-92; author: Hometown, 1982, Where is Nicaragua?, 1987, If You Came This Way, 1995; also articles in The Nation, Esquire, New York Woman, TV Guide, New York Times mag. Served with AUS, 1959-60. Recipient Saturday Rev. award, 1970, 71; Poynter fellow Yale U., 1971, assoc. fellow, 1972—. Mem. Writers Guild Am., Authors Guild Am. Democrat. Home and Office: PO Box 357 Castine ME 04421-0357

DAVIS, PETER GRAFFAM, music critic; b. Concord, Mass.; s. Edmund and Susan (Graffam) D. BA, Harvard U., 1958; MA, Columbia U., 1962. Music critic, editor N.Y. Times, 1967-81, N.Y. Mag., 1981—; music editor High Fidelity Mag., N.Y.C., 1967-74. Author: The American Opera Singer, 1825 to the Present, 1997. Office: NY Mag 444 Madison Ave New York NY 10022-6903

DAVIS, PHILIP J., mathematician; b. Lawrence, Mass., Jan. 2, 1923; s. Frank and Annie (Shrager) D.; m. Hadassah Finkelstein, Jan. 2, 1944; children: Abigail, Frank, Ernest, Joseph. BS, Harvard U., 1943, PhD, 1950; PhD honoris causa, Roskilde U., Denmark, 1997. Chief numerical analysis sect. Nat. Bur. Standards, Washington, 1958-63; prof. applied math. Brown U., Providence, 1963-92; prof. emeritus, 1993—. Author: Lore of Large Numbers, 1961, Interpolation and Approximation, 1963, Numerical Integration, 1967, 3.1416 and All That, 1969, The Schwarz Function, 1974, Circulant Matrices, 1979, The Mathematical Experience, 1981 (Am. Book award 1983), The Thread, 1981, Descartes' Dream, 1986, No Way, 1987, Thomas Gray, Philosopher Cat, 1988, The Spiral of Theodorus, 1993, Thomas Gray in Copenhagen, 1995, Mathematical Encounters of the Second Kind, 1996. Recipient Math. award Washington Acad. Scis., 1960, Chauvenet prize Math. Assn. Am., 1963, Lester R. Ford award, 1983, George Polya award, 1987, Math. Comm. award, 1997. Mem. Math. Assn. Am., Am. Math. Soc. Home: 175 Freeman Pky Providence RI 02906-4620 Office: Brown Univ Math Dept Providence RI 02912

DAVIS, PRESTON AUGUSTUS, management consultant; b. Norfolk, Va., Jan. 1; s. Charles Adam and Mattie (Johnson) D.; m. Helen G. Davis, Sept. 7, 1946 (div. June 1970); children: Gwendolyn E., Preston A. Jr., Juan McGill, Karen L., June; m. Mary E. Pierson, Aug. 22, 1971. BSBA, W.Va. State Coll., 1949; MS in Adminstrn., George Washington U., 1974; MS in Exec. Mgmt., Command and Gen. Staff Coll., 1965. V.p. Morgan State U., 1970; bd. dirs. USDA Fed. Credit Union, Washington, 1972—. Author: Fire Power of a Chinese Communist Army, 1965, Signatures of Soviet Nuclear Missile Systems, 1966, Communist Firepower Threat to the Free World, 1966. Recipient Award of Excellence SBA, 1984; named Alumnus of Yr., W.Va. State Coll., 1990. Mem. Am. Soc. Pub. Adminstrn., Washington C. of C., Kiwanis Internat. (disting. gov. 1988-89, trustee 1998—), Masons, Tuskegee Airmen Assn., Phi Delta Kappa, Omega Psi Phi. Avocations: photography, traveling. Address: PO Box 1342 Washington DC 20024

DAVIS, RANDY LEE, soil scientist; b. L.A., Nov. 23, 1950; s. Willie Vernon and Joyce Christine (Manes) D. AA, Yuba Community Coll., 1972; BS in Soils and Plant Nutrition, U. Calif., Berkeley, 1976. Vol. soil scientist U.S. Peace Corps, Maseru, Lesotho, 1976-79; soil scientist Hiawatha Nat. Forest, Sault Saint Marie, Mich., 1979-86; project soil scientist Bridger-Teton Nat. Forest, Jackson, Wyo., 1986-91, forest soil scientist, 1991-97, soil and water program leader, 1997—; detailed soil scientist Boise (Idaho) Nat. Forest, 1989, 92, Mendocino (Calif.) Nat. Forest, 1996. Editor Soil Classifiers newsletter; contbr. articles to profl. jours. Pres. Sault Community Theater, Sault Saint Marie, 1984-86. Mem. Am. Chem. Soc., Soil Sci. Soc. Am., Soil and Water Conservation Soc. (bd. dirs. 1991-92, chpt. pres. 1993-97), Am. Water Resources Assn., Internat. Soc. Soil Sci., Soc. for Range Mgmt. Methodist. Home: PO Box 7795 Jackson WY 83002-7795 Office: Bridger-Teton Nat Forest PO Box 1888 Jackson WY 83001-1888

DAVIS, RAYMOND, JR., physical chemistry researcher; b. Washington, Oct. 14, 1914; s. Raymond D. and Ida Rogers (Younger) D.; m. Anna Marsh Torrey, Dec. 4, 1948; children: Andrew Morgan, Martha Safford Davis Kumler, Nancy Elizabeth Davis Klemm, Roger Warren, Alan Paul. BS, U. Md., 1937, MS, 1939; PhD, Yale U., 1942; DSc, U. Pa., 1990, Laurentian U., 1997. Chemist Dow Chem. Co., Midland, Mich., 1937-38, Monsanto Chem. Co., Dayton, Ohio, 1946-48; sr. chemist Brookhaven Nat. Lab., Upton, N.Y., 1948-84; rsch. prof. dept. physics and astronomy U. Pa., Phila., 1984—. Contbr. articles to profl. jours. Served with USAAF, 1942-46. Recipient Boris Prejel prize N.Y. Acad. Scis., 1955, award for nuc. applications in chemistry Am. Chem. Soc., 1979. Mem. AAAS, NAS (Comstock prize 1978), Am. Phys. Soc. (Tom W. Bonner prize 1988, W.K.H. Panofsky prize 1992), Am. Geophys. Union, Am. Astron. Soc. (Beatrice M. Tinsley prize 1994, George Ellory Hale prize 1996). Home: 28 Bergen Ln Blue Point NY 11715-2111 Office: U PA Dept Physics and Astronomy Philadelphia PA 19104

DAVIS, RAYMOND GILBERT, retired career officer, real estate developer; b. Fitzgerald, Ga., Jan. 13, 1915; s. Raymond Roy and Zelma Miranda (Tribby) D.; m. Willa Knox Heafner, Apr. 25, 1942; children: Raymond Gilbert, Jr., Gordon Miles, Willa Kay Kerr. BS in Chem. Engring. with honors, Ga. Sch. of Tech., 1938; postgrad., Marine Basic Sch., Phila., 1954, Marine Corps Sch., Quantico, Va., 1954-55, Nat. War Coll., Washington, 1959-60. Commd. 2d lt. USMC, 1938, advanced through grades to gen., 1971, served in USS Portland, 1939, exec. officer, battery comdr., 1941-42, exec. officer, 1942-43, commdg. officer, 1943-44; tactical insp. Marine Corps Schs. USMC, Quantico, Va., 1944-45, chief inf. sect. Marine Air-Inf. Sch., 1945-47; asst. chief of staff USMC, Guam, 1947-49; insp.-instr. USMC, Chgo., 1949-50; commdg. officer USMC, Korea, 1950-51; action officer USMC, Washington, 1951-53; asst. dir. Marine Sch. USMC, Quantico, 1955-57; asst. G-2 USMC, Washington, 1957-59; chief analysis br., mem. staff comdr. in chief U.S. Forces, Paris, 1960-63; asst. divsn. comdr. USMC, Okinawa, 1963-64; commdg. gen. USMC, Philippines, 1963-64; asst. dir. pers. USMC, Washington, 1964-65, asst. chief of staff, 1965-68; dep. commdg., then commdg. gen. USMC, Vietnam, 1968-69; dep. edn. dir. Marine Corps Devel. and Edn. Command USMC, Quantico, 1969-70, commdg. gen., 1970-71; asst. comdt. USMC, 1971-72, ret., 1972; exec. v.p. Ga. C. of C., 1972-74; pres. RGMW, Inc., Stockbridge, Ga., 1975—; apptd. by Pres. Bush as chmn. Korean War Vets. Meml. Adv. Bd.; chmn. Greater Atlanta Marine Corps Coordination Coun. Trustee, mem. bd. visitors Valley Forge Mil. Acad., Wayne, Pa., Marine Mil. Acad., Harlington, Tex., chmn. bd. trustees, 1991; bd. visitors Berry Coll., Mount Berry, Va., 1973—. Decorated Medal of Honor, Navy Cross, Silver Star with 1 gold star, Legion of Merit with 1 gold star, Bronze Star, Purple Heart; Nat. Order of Vietnam, 4th and 5th class, Vietnamese Cross of Gallantry with 3 palms. Mem. Retired Officers Assn. (past pres., hon. pres. for life, past pres., life bd. dirs. First marine Divsn. Assn., life mem., bd. dirs. Third Marine Divsn. Assn.), Am. Legion (life), Vets of Fgn. Wars (life), Marine Corps League (life), Disabled Am. Vets, (life), Korean War Vets. Assn. (pres. North Ga. chpt.). Office: 2530 Overlake Ln Stockbridge GA 30281-5240

DAVIS, RECE, anchor, reporter; b. Muscle Shoals, Ala., Dec. 14, 1965. BA in Broadcast News and Pub. Affairs, U. Ala., 1988. Radio announcer in select media outlets Ala., 1983-93; gen. assignment reporter Sta. WCFT-TV, Tuscaloosa, Ala., 1987-88; sports reporter, weekend sports anchor, sports dir. Sta. WRBL-TV, Columbus, Ga., 1988-93; sports anchor/reporter Sta. WJRT-TV, Flint, Mich., 1993-95; anchor/reporter SportsCenter ESPN, 1995—; anchor/reporter SportSmash ESPN2, 1995—; anchor RPM 2Night, 1997—, NBA 2Night, 1996-97. Office: care ESPN 605 3rd Ave New York NY 10158-0180

DAVIS, REGINA CATHERINE (GINA DAVIS), advocate; b. Miami, Apr. 7, 1951; d. Leonard William and Elizabeth (Sirback) Bartish; m. James P. Davis, Jr., Feb. 1, 1974 (div. 1984); 1 child, Jesse Lee; m. Reginald W. Morris, June 7, 1997. Student, U. Md., 1993—. V.p. Davis Prodns., N.Y.C., 1974-84; exec. recruiter Cornell Comp Corp., N.Y.C., 1984-90; recruitment cons. Washington, 1990-91; v.p. MainFrame Applications, Inc., Washington, 1991-92; pres. Assn. Rape & Assault Prevention, Silver Spring, Md., 1993—; founder Morristar Prodns., LLC, 1998; pres. Round Robin Records, Chicadog Pub.; founder GD Assocs. Profl. Recruitment Firm; expert witness before Ho. of Reps. and State Sen.; mgr. blues musician Reggie Wayne Morris. Active PTA, N.Y.C., 1976-83; vol. Beth Israel Hosp., N.Y.C., 1976; den. leader Cub Scouts Am., N.Y.C., 1979-83; mem. steering com. Md. Commn. Women Legis. Agenda, 1994; active Legis. Agenda for Md. Women, 1994-95; outreach vol. Montgomery County Sexual Assault Program, 1995; mem. Md. Coalition Against Sexual Assault. Mem. Women's Leadership Conf. Va. Democrat. Office: Assn Rape & Assault Prevention PO Box 3307 Silver Spring MD 20918-3307

DAVIS, REX DARWIN, business consultant; b. Skiatook, Okla., June 11, 1924; s. Ivan Francis and Ruth Mae (Nabors) D.; m. Amelia Roberts Fry, Apr. 14, 1979; children by previous marriage: Deborah Ruth, Kathleen Marie. LLB, U. Okla., 1949; postgrad., Princeton U., 1966. Exec. asst. to asst. regional commr. Bur. Alcohol Tobacco and Firearms, Cin., 1962-66, asst. regional commr., 1966-70; dir. Bur. Alcohol Tobacco and Firearms, Washington, 1970-78; pres. Nat. Assn. Beverage Importers, Inc., Washington, 1978-85, Delta Cons., Inc., Washington, 1985-95; pres., chief exec. officer New Europe Wines, Inc., 1991-95; exec. dir. Pres.'s Forum of Beverage Alcohol Industry, 1990—; chmn. Lic. Beverage Info. Coun., Washington, 1981-85, Internat. Fedn. Wine & Spirits, Paris, 1982-85. Author: Federal Searches and Seizures, 1964. Vice chmn. Sky Ranch Found., Washington, 1983-85; pres. Treas. Hist. Assn., 1978-79. 1st lt. USAAF, 1943-45. Decorated Purple Heart, Air medal; recipient Chevalier de Merite Agricole French Gov., 1983, award for exceptional svc. Dept. Treasury, 1978, Meritorious svc. award 1977; named Fed. Employee of Yr. Cin. chpt. Fed. Bus. Assn., 1965; Meritorious award William A. Jump Found., 1959. Mem. Am. Soc. Assn. Execs., Okla. Bar Assn., Pi Kappa Alpha, Internat. Club, Princeton Club. Avocations: golf, tennis, snorkeling, stamp collecting. Home and Office: Delta Cons Inc 311 10th St SE Washington DC 20003-2130

DAVIS, REX LLOYD, insurance company executive; b. Des Moines, Dec. 29, 1929; s. Leon Mack and Mercedes Johanna (Lamar) D.; m. Sally JoAnne Richard, Apr. 14, 1952; children: Kristine Lynn, Craig Thomas. JD, Drake U., 1952. Bar: Iowa, U.S. Dist. Ct. Iowa, U.S. Supreme Ct.; C.P.C.U., C.L.U. With Employers Mut. Casualty Co., Des Moines, 1954-66; regional v.p. Employers Mut. Casualty Co., Phila., 1966-72; exec. v.p. Ranger Ins. Co., Houston, 1972-75; pres. Ranger Ins. Co., 1975-84; pres., chief operating officer Ranger Ins. Mgrs., Ranger Internat. Ins. Ltd., Ranger County Mut.; atty.-in-fact Ranger Lloyds, Houston, 1975-84; pres., chief operating officer Rex L. Davis & Assocs., Inc., 1984—; chmn. United Republic Reins. Co., 1986-92, also bd. dirs.; v.p. Old Republic Standard Ins. Co., 1988—; bd. dirs. Standard Holding Corp. Bd. dirs. Salvation Army. Mem. Houston Bar Assn., Soc. CPCUs, Soc. CLUs, Lakeside Country Club (Houston), Petroleum Club (Houston), Delta Theta Phi. Office: Rex L Davis & Assocs 2450 Fondren Rd Ste 102 Houston TX 77063-2320

DAVIS, RICHARD, musician, music educator; b. Chgo., Apr. 15, 1930; s. Robert and Elenora (King) Johnson; children: Persia, Joshua. MusB in Edn., Vandercook Coll. Music, 1952; postgrad., Manhattan Sch. Music, 1964-66; MusD, Vandercook Coll., 1992; doctorate (hon.), Vandercook Coll. Music, 1993. From assoc. prof. to prof. music U. Wis., Madison, 1976—; cons. numerous orgns. including Williams Coll. in Search of Black Faculty, Tex. Tech. U. of Jazz Notation, John Simon Guggenheim Meml. Found., Wis. Union Theater Directorate; lectr. on jazz and religion numerous colls. and workshops; advisor and adjudicator for university, profl. and civic orgns.; mem. Wis. Arts Bd. (grantee 1980-81), Mount Horeb Arts Council; owner Sympatico Music Pubs. Inc. String bass player numerous nat. appearances, 1980—, including Berkeley Jazz Festival, Fletcher Henderson Meml. Concert, Jazz Showcase, Chgo., Sweet Basil Club, N.Y.C., New Orleans Jazz Heritage Festival, Richard Davis Quartet in Concert, N.Y., Chgo. Jazz Workshop; internat. tours including Japan with Elvin Jones, Israel Philharm. with Lalo Schrifrin, London, France and Spain with Elvin Jones and McCoy Turner, Paris with Sun Ra, Archie Shepp, Don Cherry; also numerous TV and radio appearances; author: The Bass Tradition, 1984-85, (with M.C. Gridley) Jazz Styles, 1985; contbg. editor Yugolsavian Jazz mag., Jazz Spotlite mag.; contbr. articles and revs. to profl. and ednl. mags.; rec. artist numerous albums, 1979—, including Muses, Way Out West, Josh, Rip Off, To Dance (Nikki Cole), I'm Wired (Stormy Rice), Cauldron (Larry Levy), Very Rare (Elvin Jones), Live at the Village Vanguard with Mingus Dynasty, Vocalese (Manhattan Transfer), Richard Davis & Friends Live at Sweet Basil, 1994. Recipient Critics Poll award Down Beat mag., 1967-74, Reader's Poll award, 1967-72, Arts Midwest Jazz Master award, 1993; U. Wis. Grad. Sch. grantee, 1979, 80-81. Mem. Internat. Composers Soc., Internat. Soc. Bassists, Internat. Platform Assn., ASCAP (Spl. Popular award 1979-83, 84-85), Nat. Assn. Jazz Educators, Nat. Acad. Rec. Arts and Scis., Nat. Endowment of the Arts (grantee 1982-83, 83-84), Nat. String Artists, Screen Actors Guild, Am. Jazz Found., Kappa Kappa Psi. Avocation: horsemanship. Home: 902 W Shore Dr Madison WI 53715-1818 Office: U Wis 4415 Humanities Bldg Madison WI 53706 also: Muse Records 106 W 71st St New York NY 10023-4060 *My high school teacher instilled in me the idea that it's not what you want to be in life, but what you do every day to attain that goal. That's the discipline I applied to achieve my success.*

DAVIS, RICHARD BRADLEY, internal medicine, pathology educator, physician; b. Iowa City, Iowa, Nov. 6, 1926; s. Bradley Nelson and Gladys Mae (Fairbanks) D.; m. Jean Nixeen Anderson, June 22, 1957; children—Janet, Stephen, Catharine. B.S., Yale U., 1949; M.D., State U. Iowa, 1953; Ph.D., U. Minn., 1964. Intern Mary Fletcher Hosp., Burlington, Vt., 1953-54; resident Mary Fletcher Hosp., 1954-56; instr. U. Minn., Mpls., 1959-64; asst. prof. medicine U. Minn., 1964-69; vis. investigator Sir William Dunn Sch. Pathology, Oxford, Eng., 1964-65, MRC Blood Coagulation Research Unit, Churchill Hosp., Oxford, 1965; asso. prof. medicine U. Nebr., Omaha, 1969-73; prof. medicine U. Nebr., 1973-94, acting dir. div. hematology, 1974-76, prof. pathology, 1976-94, dir. hematology div., 1976-79, emeritus prof. internal medicine, 1994—. Contbr. articles to sci. publs. Served with U.S. Army, 1945-46. Borden Undergrad. Med. Research grantee, 1953; USPHS career devel. awardee, 1961-69. Fellow A.C.P., Central Soc. Clin. Research, Am. Fedn. Clin. Research, Am. Soc. Exptl. Pathology, N.Y. Acad. Scis., Am. Assn. History of Medicine Soc. Exptl. Biology and Medicine, Am. Soc. Hematology, Royal Micros. Soc., Internat. Soc. Haemostasis and Thrombosis, Omaha Mid-West Clin. Soc., Sigma Xi, Alpha Omega Alpha, Phi Beta Pi, Theta Kappa Psi. Home: 103 Woodhall Spa Williamsburg VA 23188-9138

DAVIS, RICHARD CALHOUN, dentist; b. Manhattan, Kans., Jan. 4, 1945; s. William Calhoun and Alison Rae (Wyland) D.; Danna Ruth Ritchel, June 13, 1968; 1 child, Darin Calhoun. Student, Ariz. State U., 1963-65, BA, 1978; BA, U. Ariz., 1966; DDS, U. of Pacific, 1981. Retail dept. head Walgreens, Tucson, 1965-66; mgmt. trainee Walgreens, Tucson, San Antonio, 1967-70; asst. store mgr. Walgreens, Baton Rouge, 1970-72; field rep. Am. Cancer Soc., Phoenix, 1972-74; dept. head Lucky Stores, Inc., Tempe, Ariz., 1976-78; practice dentistry specializing in gen. dentistry Tucson, 1981—; bd. dirs. Home Again, Inc. Chmn. bd. Capilla Del Sol Christian Ch., Tucson, 1984. Fellow Internat. Congress Oral Implantologists, Am. Coll. Oral Implantology, Am. Soc. Osseointegration; mem. ADA, Acad. Gen. Dentists, Am. Straight Wire Orthodontic Assn., Am. Assn. Functional Orthodontics, Sleep Disorders Dental Soc., So. Ariz. Bus. Assn. (treas. 1998), N.W. Dental Study Club, Optimists (past pres. N.W. club, preceptorship in dental implantology), Elks. Republican. Mem. Disciples of Christ Ch. Avocation: golf, skiing, watersports, fishing, camping. Office: 2777 N Campbell Ave Tucson AZ 85719-3101

DAVIS, RICHARD CARLTON, state agency administrator; b. Salem, Mass., June 10, 1948; s. William Montgomery and Ruth Wiley (Durkee) D.; m. Patricia Lynn Paquette, Apr. 6, 1974; children: Susannah, Amanda, Adam. BA, Concord Coll., 1969; postgrad., U. Iowa. Orientation tchr. Iowa Dept. for the Blind, Des Moines, 1971-73, rehab. tchr., 1973-77, rehab. counselor, 1977-80, sr. svc. specialist, 1980-86; so. area supr. N.Mex. Commn. for the Blind, Alamogordo, 1987-91, orientation ctr. adminstr., 1987-92; asst. commr. State Svcs. for the Blind, Minn. Dept. of Econ. Security, St. Paul, 1992—; cons. Nebr. Svcs. for the Visually Impaired, Lincoln, 1980, Am. Printing House for the Blind, Louisville, 1992. coord./vol. field svc. rep. Job Opportunities for the Blind, Balt., 1979-86; chair, vice chair Mayor's com. for the Handicapped, Alamogordo, 1990-92; bd. dirs. White Sands Press Club, Alamogordo, 1988-92. Recipient Silver award United Way, 1991, over 100% Goal award, 1990, Founders award N.Mex. Commn. for the Blind, 1992, Wayne E. Bonnell award Nat. Fedn. of the Blind, 1982, Gov.'s commendation, 1998. Mem. Nat. Coun. of State Agencies for the Blind (bd. dirs. 1992-98, treas. 1999—), Coun. of State Adminstrs. of Vocat. Rehab., Nat. Fedn. of the Blind (Des Moines Chpt. award 1983), Alamogordo Rotary Club. Avocations: camping, fishing, bicycling, canoeing, snowshoeing. Home: 136 Canterbury Rd Circle Pines MN 55014-1777 Office: Dept of Econ Security State Svcs for the Blind 2200 University Ave W Ste 240 Saint Paul MN 55114

DAVIS, RICHARD EARL, lawyer; b. Jackson, Mich., Aug. 13, 1951; s. Richard Allen and Velva Elizabeth (England) D.; m. Paula Hurst, Dec. 9, 1972; children: Richard Seth, Tessa Rebecca. BA, U. So. Fla., 1973, MA, 1975; JD cum laude, Stetson U., 1977. Bar: Fla. 1978, U.S. Ct. Appeals (11th cir.), U.S. Dist. Ct. (mid. dist.) Fla.; bd. cert. city, county and local govt. law Fla. Bar. Asst. county atty. Hillsborough County, Fla., 1978-85; assoc. Holland & Knight, Tampa, Fla., 1985-88, ptnr., 1988-96; ptnr. Mechanik & Davis, Tampa, Fla., 1996-97, Richard E. Davis, P.A., Tampa, Fla., 1997—; lectr. in land use in field. Mem. ABA, Hillsborough County Bar Assn., Fla. Bar Assn., Am. Planning Assn., Fla. Outdoor Advertisers Assn., Outdoor Advertisers of Am. Assn., Stetson Lawyers Assn., Tampa Downtown Partnership, Tampa Bay Soc. Club, Greater Tampa C. of C., Bay Area Mfrs. Assn. Office: 400 N Tampa St Ste 1050 Tampa FL 33602-4707

DAVIS, RICHARD EDMUND, facial plastic surgeon; b. Washington, Apr. 7, 1958. BS, U. Ga., 1981, MS, 1983; MD, Med. Coll. Ga., 1987. Diplomate Am. Bd. Otolaryngology, Am. Bd. Facial Plastic and Reconstructive Surgery. Intern U. N.C., Chapel Hill, 1987-88, resident in otolaryngology, 1988-92; fellow, instr. Oreg. Health Sci. U., Portland, 1992-93; asst. prof. facial plastic and reconstructive surgery U. Miami (Fla.) Sch. Medicine, 1993—; mem. staff VA Med. Ctr., Portland, Oreg., 1992-93, Jackson Meml. Hosp., Miami, 1993—, VA Med. Ctr., Miami, 1993—. Mem. AMA, Am. Acad. Otolaryngology Head and Neck Surgery, Am. Acad. Facial Plastic and Reconstructive Surgery (Sir Harold Gilies award 1993), Fla. Soc. Facial Plastic and Reconstructive Surgery. Office: U Miami Hosp and Clinic 1475 NW 12th Ave Ste 4027 Miami FL 33136-1002

DAVIS, RICHARD FRANCIS, city government official; b. Providence, Aug. 18, 1936; s. Walter Francis and Mary Elizabeth (Gearin) D.; m. Virginia Catherine Oates, Aug. 27, 1960; children: Walter Douglas, John Richard, Theresa Catherine. BS, U. Ark., Little Rock, 1964; student city and regional planning, MIT, summer, 1964; postgrad., Carnegie Mellon U., 1973. Planner Met. Area Planning Commn., Little Rock, 1964-66; mem. Met. Planning Commn. Kansas City, Mo., 1966-67; dir. econs. Met. Planning Commn. Kansas City, 1967-69, dir. ops., 1969-71; exec. dir. Mid-Am. Regional Council, Kansas City, 1972-77; gen. mgr. Kansas City Area Transp. Authority, 1977—; instr. city planning U. Mo., Kansas City, 1973-74; Planning commr. City of Gladstone, Mo., 1967-69, 81-90, city councilman, 1969-71, mayor, 1971-72, chmn. park bd., 1972-76, mem. bd. zoning adjustment, 1993—; mem. Clay County (Mo.) Indsl. Devel. Commn., 1972-77, Council on Edn., Kansas City, 1974-82, treas., chmn. interdist. rels. com.; bd. dirs. Mo. Pub. Transit Assn., 1979—, pres., 1987-89; bd. dirs. Kans. Pub. Transit Assn., 1979—; trustee Black Econ. Union, 1984-88; bd. dirs., treas. Heart of Am. United Way Vol. Ctr., 1985-87. V.p. Brooktree Homeowners Assn., 1979-80. Served with USAF, 1955-59. Recipient Transp. Svc. award Kansas City chpt. Conf. of Minority Transit Officials, 1987. Mem. Am. Soc. Pub. Adminstrn. (pres. Kansas City chpt. 1980, Pub. Adminstr. of Yr. award 1973, L.P. Cookingham award 1991), Am. Planning Assn., Am. Pub. Transit Assn. (bd. dirs. 1980-93, 94—, mem. govtl. affairs and legis. steering com., v.p. mgmt. and fin. com. 1984-86, v.p. govt. affairs com. 1991-93). Home: 3612 NE Brooktree Cir Kansas City MO 64119-2229 Office: 1200 E 18th St Kansas City MO 64108-1606

DAVIS, RICHARD FRANK, state legislator; b. Ann Arbor, Mich., Sept. 9, 1945; s. Paul E. and Irmagene (Blair) D.; m. Constance Ann Meeker, 1966; children: Robert, Joanna, Stephen. BS, Case Inst. Tech., 1967; postgrad., U. Wis., 1967-69; PhD, Yale U., 1972. Rsch. assoc. EI DuPont, Wilmington, Del., 1972—; rschr. agr. products dept. DuPont, 1972—; mem. Dist. 26 Del. State Ho. of Reps., 1983-98, chmn. corrections com., 1984-92, mem. pub. safety com., 1984-92, mem. judiciary com., 1984-92, mem. appropriations com., 1984-92, chmn. appropriations com., 1993-98, co-chmn. joint fin. com., 1993-98; former chmn. bd. CONTACT, Wilmington. Post-doctoral fellow Ohio State U., 1972. Mem. Am. Chem. Soc., Am. Legis. Exch. Coun. (Outstanding State Legislator), Nat. Conf. of State Legislatures (chmn. fiscal, oversight, and intergovtl. affairs com.), Nat. Right to Life, Tri Woods Civic Assn. Address: 200 Stewards Ct Bear DE 19701

DAVIS, RICHARD JOEL, lawyer, former government official; b. N.Y.C., Mar. 27, 1946; s. Herbert H. and Sylvia (Ginesin) D.; m. Nancy R. Davis. B.A., U. Rochester, 1966; J.D., Columbia U., 1969. Bar: N.Y. 1970. Law clk. to Judge Jack B. Weinstein, U.S. Dist. Ct. for Eastern Dist. N.Y., 1969-70; asst. U.S. atty. So. Dist. N.Y., 1970-73; task force leader Watergate Spl. Prosecution Force, Washington, 1973-75; assoc. Weil, Gotshal and Manges, N.Y.C., 1976-77; partner Weil, Gotshal and Manges, 1981—; asst. sec. of the treasury for enforcement and ops. Dept. Treasury, Washington, 1977-81; instr. in trial advocacy Harvard U.; instr. Nat. Inst. Trial Advocacy. Co-author: American Hostages in Iran, 1988. Mem. Task Force on Ops. of Phila. Police Force, 1986, Task Force on Use and Security of Central Park, 1989; mem. Mayor's Commn. on Police Corruption, 1995—, chmn. 1996—; chmn. Randall's Island Sports Found. Mem. ABA, Legal Aid Soc. N.Y.C. (v.p. 1987-91, bd. dirs. 1987-92), Citizens Union (bd. dirs. 1991-97, vice chmn. 1993-97), Boys Harbor (bd. dirs. 1993—, co-chmn. lawyers com. on violence 1994-98, bd. dirs. parks coun. 1994—). Office: Weil Gotshal & Manges 767 5th Ave Fl Concl New York NY 10153-0119*

DAVIS, RICHARD MALONE, economics educator; b. Hamilton, N.Y., June 2, 1918; s. Malone Crowell and Grace Edith (McQuade) D. AB, Colgate U., 1939; MA, Cornell U., 1941, PhD, 1949. From instr. to assoc. prof. econs. Lehigh U., Bethlehem, Pa., 1941-54; assoc. prof. econs. U. Oreg., Eugene, 1954-62, prof., 1962-83; prof. emeritus U. Oreg., 1983—. Contbr. articles to profl. jours. Served with U.S. Army, 1942-45, CBI. Mem. Phi Beta Kappa. Republican. Home: 1040 Ferry St Apt 503 Eugene OR 97401-3332 Office: Univ Oreg Dept Econs Eugene OR 97403

DAVIS, RICHARD SHERMER, JR., aerospace company operations manager; b. Raleigh, N.C., May 14, 1942; s. Richard Shermer Sr. and Martha Hayes (Myers) D.; m. Paula Kay Harwell, Jan. 15, 1972; children: Melissa Michelle, Richard Shermer III, Stephen Scott. BS, N.C. State U., 1965; MS, Troy State U., 1981. Commd. 2d lt. USAF, 1966, advanced through grades to col., 1988, retired, 1992; aerospace defense cons. Royal Saudi Air Force, Taif, Saudi Arabia, 1993-97; site ops. mgr. Alsalam Aircraft Co., Ltd., Khamis Mushayt, Saudi Arabia, 1997—. Author: Instructor Pilot Instructional Manual, 1995. Decorated Legion of Merit, Disting. Flying Cross (3), Meritorious Svc. medal (4), Air medal (15); Paul Harris fellow Rotary Internat. Mem. Air Force Assn., St. Albans Lodge, Daedalians. Republican. Avocations: hunting, fishing, skiing, scuba diving. Home: 650 Allegheny Dr Colorado Springs CO 80919-1114*

DAVIS, ROBERT BARRY, technician, religious studies educator; b. Greenville, S.C., June 30, 1953; s. Robert Berry and Alda Lowe (Wilson) D.; m. Terry Denise Merritt Hippensteel (div.); children: David Barry, Terry Lee; m. Barbara Anne Scott (div.); m. Tracey Lynn Simpson, Apr. 18, 1999. B in Biblical Studies, Logos Christian Coll., Jacksonville, Fla., 1996; postgrad., Logos Christian Coll., 1997-99. Technician Delta Mills, Piedmont, S.C., 1979-89, 94-95, Fabri-Kal, Greenville, 1989-93; asst. tchr. Child Devel. Ctr. New Life Christian Fellowship, Greenville, 1996-98; acad. dean, instr. Logos Bible Coll., 1996-98; technician Constar Internat., Greenville, summer 1997; minister Ind. Ministry, 1978-99; radio minister, Simpsonville, S.C., 1997. Author: Hebraic Perspectives of the Gospel, 1995, Little Nut to a Tree of Life, 1997, Post Graduate Bible College Course: The Feasts of Israel, 1998. Republican. Avocations: hiking, camping. Home and Office: 200 Sleepy Hollow Rd Piedmont SC 29673-7614

DAVIS, ROBERT EDWARD, state supreme court justice; b. Topeka, Aug. 28, 1939; s. Thomas Homer and Emma Claire (Hund) D.; m. Jana Jones; children: Edward, Rachel, Patrick, Carolyn, Brian. BA in Polit. Sci., Creighton U., 1961; JD, Georgetown U., 1964. Bar: Kans. 1964, U.S. Dist. Ct. Kans. 1964, U.S. Tax Ct. 1974, U.S. Ct. Mil. Appeals 1965, U.S. Ct. Mil. Review, 1970, U.S. Ct. Appeals (10th cir.) 1974, U.S. Supreme Ct. 1982. Pvt. practice Leavenworth, Kans., 1967-84; magistrate judge Leavenworth County, 1969-76, county atty., 1980-84, judge dist. ct., 1984-86; judge Kans. Ct. Appeals Jud. Br. Govt., Topeka, 1986-93; justice Kans. Supreme Ct., Topeka, 1993—; lectr. U. Kans. Law Sch., Lawrence, 1986-95. Capt. JAGC, U.S. Army, 1964-67, Korea. Mem. Am. Judges Assn., Kans. Bar Assn., Leavenworth County Bar Assn. (pres. 1977), Judge Hugh Means Am. Inn of Ct. Charter Orgn. Lawrence. Roman Catholic. Office: Justice Robert E Davis 301 W 10th Ave Topeka KS 66612

DAVIS, ROBERT EDWARD, retired communication educator; b. Wichita, Kans., Apr. 2, 1931; s. Edward Lorenzo and Dorrinda Belle (Packer) D.; m. Jacqueline Peggy Baas, Aug. 22, 1955 (div. 1979); children: Robert J., Sarah J., James E.; m. Martha Toni Merrill, Jan. 8, 1983. BA, U. No. Iowa, 1953; MA, U. Iowa, 1956, PhD, 1965. Instr. Grundy Ctr. (Iowa) High Sch., 1953-54; asst. to dir. radio and TV U. No. Iowa, Cedar Falls, 1954-58; lectr., instr. dept. speech and theatre Hunter Coll., N.Y.C., 1961-63, 65-66; asst. prof. dept. speech U. Mich., Ann Arbor, 1966-69; from assoc. prof. to prof. and chmn. dept. cinema and photography So. Ill. U., Carbondale, 1969-74; prof. and chmn. Dept. Radio-TV-Film, U. Tex., Austin, 1974-87, John T. Jones Jr. Centennial prof. in communication, 1987-89, now emeritus, 1989—; mem. Pacific Grove Planning Commn., 1999—. Author: Response to Innovation, 1976; co-producer, dir. (film) Maple Sugar Farmer, 1973 (7 nat. and internat. awards); writer, performer, dir., producer over 1000 ednl. radio and tv programs; contbr. articles to profl. jours. Mem. Pacific Grove City Coun., 1990-98; mayor pro-tem Pacific Grove, 1994-98. Republican. Methodist. Avocations: travel, photography. Home: 1212 Del Monte Blvd Pacific Grove CA 93950-2029

DAVIS, ROBERT H., financial executive, arbitrator, mediator, educator; b. Phila., Mar. 26, 1943; 1 child, Michelle R. Student, L.A. Valley Coll., 1965-67, Alexander Hamilton Inst., 1965-68; grad., Stanford U., 1980, Pepperdine U., 1981. Cert. arbitrator, mediator, counselor Am. Arbitration Assn., Singapore Arbitration Ctr. and Inst. Internat. Negotiation and Conflict Mgmt. Contr., credit mgr. Wyo. Machinery Co., Casper, 1978-83; contr., sec.-treas., dir. John E. Burns Drilling Co., Casper, 1979-82; comptroller, v.p. Philip Crosby Assocs., Inc., Winter Park, Fla., 1982-84, 84—; v.p., treas. Crosby Assocs. Internat., Inc., Winter Park, Fla.; pres., CEO Davis, Keller & Davis, New Orleans, Oreg., Wash., 1989-98; dir. credit, arbitration and legal affairs JBS, Inc., Stafford, Tex., 1998—; mgmt. cons., internat. arbitrator/mediator, author, lectr. Am. Arbitration Assn., Singapore Arbitration Ctr., fin. cons. Western Energy Co., Huey's Smoked Meats, Nashville, Trans-Equip, Casper, Three Percent, Inc., Riverton, Wyo., 1979-80; mem. subcom. U.S.A.-NAFTA, Washington; apptd. mem. by sec. commerce and U.S. Trade Rep. Wash. Export coun.; mem. customs com. Dept. Commerce Industry Consultation Program; cons. U.S.A./NAFTA nat. com. Alliance for GATT Pres.'s Export Coun.; asst., sr. internat. arbitrator Korean Comml. Arbitration Commn., 1996; bd. dirs. NACM, Houston. Author: Charting Your Business Practices-U.S. Small Business Adminstrn., Transnational Arbitration as a Means of Managing Corporate Risks, International Risk Management for U.S. Small Businesses, Leasing as a Secondary Source of Financing in the Heavy Equipment Industry. Arbitrator, mediator BBB of Oreg.; mem. adv. bd. dirs. Highland Park Cmty. Ch., 1980—. With USNR, 1961-63. Mem. Nat. Assn. Credit Mgmt. (state rep. 1979-82, founder, chmn. Casper Credit Group), Soc. Profls. in Dispute Resolution, Am. Soc. Internat. Law, Credit Mgrs. Assn. So. Calif. (dir. bus. re-orgn. and bankruptcy 1973-74), Credit Rsch. Found., Am. Mgmt. Assn., Practicing Law Inst. (assoc.), Stanford U. Alumni Assn., Internat. Platform Assn., Internat. Inst. Negotiation and Conflict Mgmt. (Australia), Order of Demolay (sr. award 1960).

DAVIS, ROBERT HARRY, physiology educator; b. Wilkes Barre, Pa., July 16, 1927; s. Cyril Davis and Clara Umhla; m. Irene Kasper, June 12, 1953; children: Sally Ann Mediche, Susn Ann Newcomer. BS in Biology, Kings Coll., 1950; MS in Biology, Newark Coll., 1955; PhD in Encocrinology, Rutgers U., 1958; postgrad. in Pharmacology, Cin. Coll. Medicine, 1959. Rsch. scientist Warner Inst., Morristown, N.J., 1950-55; teaching fellow Rutgers U., New Brunswick, N.J., 1955-58; rsch. sect. head Richardson-Merell Co., Cin., 1958-59; chief endocrinology Willow Brook State Hosp., N.Y.C., 1959-63; assoc. prof. biology Villanova (Pa.) U., 1963-66; chief endocrinology Fitzgerald Hosp., Lansdowne, Pa., 1966-68; assoc. prof. physiology Hahnemann Med. Coll., Phila., 1966-75; prof. biology St. Joseph's U., Phila., 1966-77; prof. physiology Pa. Coll. Podiatric Medicine, Phila., 1975-94; cons. Fla. Food Products, Eustis, 1987-89, Terry Corp., Melbourne, Fla., 1984-87. Contbr. numerous articles to profl. jours.; editor Jour. Am. Podiatric Med. Soc., 1975—. With USN, 1945-46. Recipient 19 awards for rsch. in podiatric medicine, 1975—, 1 found. award in ob-gyn, 1969. Mem. APA, Am. Phys. Soc., Christian Businessmen's Com., Christian Fellowship, Pa. Coll. Podiatric Medicine. Republican. Avocations: sports, church work. Home: 307 Abrams Mill Rd Kng Of Prussa PA 19406-1703 Office: Pa Coll Podiatric Medicine 8th & Race Sts Philadelphia PA 19107

DAVIS, ROBERT LEACH, retired government official, consultant; b. Torrington, Conn., July 20, 1924; s. Clarence Adelbert and Ruth Mabel (Leach) D.; m. Lorraine Lillian Szabla, Sept. 16, 1950; children: Russell, Cynthia, Vicki, Scott, Gregg. B.A. in Psychology, U. Mich., 1949. Claims examiner Social Security Adminstrn., Chgo., 1950-52; investigator and personnel specialist U.S. CSC, Chgo., 1952-67; personnel dir. U.S. Post Office Region, Chgo., 1967-71; div. chief, asst. bur. dir. U.S. CSC, Washington, 1971-78; dep. asst. sec. for adminstrn. and mgmt. Dept. Labor, Washington, 1978-82. Served with AUS, 1943-46. Decorated Purple Heart. Democrat. Unitarian-Universalist. Home: 1025 Fox Meadow Way Concord CA 94518-2906

DAVIS, ROBERT NORMAN, hospital administrator; b. Plainfield, N.J., July 30, 1938; s. Norman DuBois and Geraldine Elizabeth (Sliker) D.; B.S. civil engring., Pa. State U., 1960; M.S. in Mgmt., Rensselaer Poly. Inst., 1970; m. Elizabeth Ann Paine, June 15, 1985; children—Keith Robert, Kathryn Beth, Karl Thomas. Dir. plant ops. Am. Hosp. Assn., Chgo., 1964-68; dir. mgmt. engring. Hosp. Assn. of N.Y., Albany, 1968-72; assoc. exec. dir. United Hosp., Portchester, N.Y., 1973-75; regional mgr. Arthur Young & Co., N.Y.C., 1975, Medicus Systems Corp., Nashville, 1976-79; pres. Resource Devel. Assos., Hendersonville, Tenn., 1979-96; assoc. adminstr. Vanderbilt U. Hosp., Nashville, 1979-81; adminstr. Meml. div. Charleston (W.Va.) Area Med. Ctr., 1981-83; pres. Resource Devel. Assocs., 1983-86; prin. Ernst & Young Health Care, 1996—. Bd. dirs., treas. Middle Tenn. Youth Soccer Inc., 1979-82. Served with M.S.C., USAF, 1960-63. Fellow Am. Coll. Healthcare Execs., Hosp. Info. Mgmt. Systems Soc. (dir. 1972-75, hon. fellow 1985). Baptist. Contbr. articles to profl. jours. Home: 116 Hidden Pt Hendersonville TN 37075-5541

DAVIS, ROBERT PAUL, physician, educator; b. Malden, Mass., July 3, 1926; s. Samuel and Sarah (Lemberg) D.; m. Ruby Black, Sept. 5, 1953; children—Edward L., John R., Elizabeth A. A.B. cum laude, Harvard U., 1947, M.D. magna cum laude, 1951, A.M., 1955; A.M. (ad eundem), Brown U., 1967. Diplomate: Am. Bd. Internal Medicine, subsplty. bd. nephrology. Intern Peter Bent Brigham Hosp., Boston, 1951-52; asst. medicine Peter Bent Brigham Hosp., 1952-55, sr. asst. resident physician, 1955-56, chief resident physician, 1956-57; jr. fellow Soc. of Fellows Harvard, 1952-55; asst. medicine Harvard Med. Sch., 1956-57; asst. prof. medicine U. N.C., 1957-59; asst. prof. medicine Albert Einstein Coll. Medicine, 1959-66, assoc. prof., 1967; career scientist Health Research Council, N.Y.C., 1962-67; asst. vis. physician Bronx Mcpl. Hosp. Center, 1959-65, assoc. vis. physician, 1966-67; physician in chief Miriam Hosp., Providence, 1967-74; dir. renal and metabolic diseases Miriam Hosp., 1974-79; prof. med. sci. Brown U., 1967-84, prof. emeritus, 1984—, chmn. sect. in medicine div. biol. and med. scis., 1971-74; vis. scientist Ins. Biol. Chemistry of U. Copenhagen, 1965-66; past mem. corp. Butler Hosp., Jewish Family and Children's Service; mem. sci. adv. council N.E. Regional Kidney Program; vice chmn. R.I. Advisory Commn. Med. Care and Edn. Found.; chmn. med. adv. bd. R.I. Kidney Found.; past bd. dirs. Associated Alumni Brown U.; mem. med. adv. bd. New Eng. sect. Am. Liver Found., 1986—; trustee New Eng. Organ Bank, Boston, 1969—, treas., 1970—; pres. End-Stage Renal Disease Coordinating Council Network 28, New Eng., 1978-79. Assoc. editor: R.I. Med. Jour, 1971-80; contbr. articles to profl. jours. Served as ensign USNR, 1944-46; as lt. (j.g.) M.C. 1951. Traveling fellow Commonwealth Fund, 1965-66; Willard O. Thompson Meml. traveling scholar A.C.P., 1965. Fellow AAAS, ACP; mem. Am. Fedn. Clin. Research, Am. Soc. Transplant Physicians, Harvey Soc., Biophys. Soc., N.Y. Acad. Medicine, Am. Heart Assn., N.Y. Acad. Sci., Am. Soc. Cell Biology, Soc. Gen. Physiologists, Am. Physiol. Soc., Am. Soc. Artificial Internal Organs, Internat. Soc. Nephrology, Clin. Diabetes Assn. R.I. (pres. 1970-71), Providence, R.I. med. socs., Am. Soc. Nephrology, Am. Soc. Pediatric Nephrology, Soc. for Health and Human Values, Am. Philos. Assn., Phi Beta Kappa, Sigma Xi. Home: 75 Prospect St Providence RI 02906-1330 Office: Brown U Ste 400B 245 Waterman St Providence RI 02906-5215

DAVIS, ROBERT SCOTT, criminal justice educator; b. Piqua, Ohio, Sept. 24, 1942; s. Robert Walter and Dorothy Belle D.; m. Joyce Louise Davis, Dec. 16, 1967; 1 child, Amanda Louise. AA in Edn., Miami-Dade C.C., Fla., 1968; BS in Acctg., Fla. Atlantic U., 1970; MS in Criminal Justice, Fla. Internat. U., 1987. Sr. auditor Holtz & Co. CPA's, Miami, 1970-74; budget analyst World Jai-Alai, Inc., Miami, 1974-80; prisoner counselor Dade County Dept. Corrections, Miami, 1980; jud. asst. Adminstrn. Office Cts. (11th jud. cir.), Miami, 1982; dep. dir. Adv. Program, Inc., Miami, 1985; asst. prof. Miami-Dade C.C., Miami, 1987-95; program mgr. criminal justice N.Mex. State U., Grants, 1996—. With USN, 1961-65. Presbyterian.

DAVIS, ROBIN REED, lobbyist, feminist advocate; b. Jacksonville, Fla., Oct. 4, 1946; d. William Woodworth and Anne Calloway (Robertson) Reed; m. William Robert Davis, May 11, 1970; 1 child, Eric Reed Davis. BA, N.C. State U., 1969, MA, 1973; PhD, Duke U., 1982. Pres. N.C. NOW, Raleigh, 1986-88, 95—, registered lobbyist, 1986—, pres. polit. action com., 1986-88; dir. NOW, Washington, 1988-90, regional dir., 1996—; founder N.C. Women's Lobby, Raleigh, 1986. Editor: We Are You, 1984. Mem. state exec. com. N.C. Dem., Raleigh, 1990—. Grantee Fund So. Cmtys., 1984. Democrat. Methodist. Avocations: photography, gardening. Fax: 919-834-4073. E-mail: robindavis@aol.com. Home: 2012 Glenwood Ave Raleigh NC 27608-1440 Office: NC NOW 206 Morson St Raleigh NC 27601

DAVIS, ROGER EDWIN, lawyer, retired discount chain executive; b. Lakewood, Ohio, Dec. 29, 1928; s. Russell G. and Irma (Aboline) D.; m. Eva Grace Keeler, July 25, 1953 (div. Feb. 1980); children: Susan Lee, Lisa Ann, Steven Russell; m. Yvonne L. Berich, June 1, 1980. A.B., Harvard U., 1950; LL.B., U. Mich., 1953. Bar: Mich. 1953. Pvt. practice Detroit, 1955-60; assoc. Langs, Molyneaux & Armstrong, 1955-60; counsel Avis Enterprises, 1961-62; with legal dept. S.S. Kresge Co. (now Kmart Corp.), 1963-70, v.p., gen. counsel, sec., 1970-85, sr. v.p., gen. counsel, sec., 1985-91, ret., 1991. Served with AUS, 1953-55. Mem. State Bar Mich., Fla. Bar, Pine Lake Country Club (pres. 1991), Bonita Bay Club.

DAVIS, ROGER LEWIS, lawyer; b. New Orleans, Jan. 27, 1946; s. Leon and Anada A. (Russ) D.; m. Annette Vucinich; 1 child, Alexandra. BA, Tulane U., 1967; MA, UCLA, 1969; PhD, UCLA, 1971; JD, Harvard U., 1974. Bar: Calif. 1974. Assoc. Orrick, Herrington & Sutcliffe, L.L.P., San Francisco, 1974-79, ptnr., 1980—, chmn. pub. fin. dept., 1981—. Mem. Bay Area Coun., San Francisco, 1988-90. Fellow Am. Coll. of Bond Counsel; mem. ABA (tax sect., mem. com. tax exempt financing), Nat. Assn. Bond Lawyers (mem. com. profl. responsibility and securities law and disclosure), Calif. Pub. Securities Assn. (dir. 1998—). Office: Orrick Herrington & Sutcliffe LLP 400 Sansome St San Francisco CA 94111-3143

DAVIS, RON LEE, clergyman, author; b. Carroll, Iowa, Oct. 17, 1947; s. David Clarence and Elizabeth Regina (Thompson) D.; m. Shirley Louise O'Connor, Aug. 31, 1973; children: Rachael LeeAnn, Nathan Paul. BA cum laude, Tarkio (Mo.) Coll., 1969; MDiv cum laude, Dubuque (Iowa) Theol. Sem., 1971; DDiv, Bethel Theol. Sem., St. Paul, 1977. Ordained to ministry Presbyn. Ch., 1971. Chaplain Minn. Vikings, Mpls., 1975-80; assoc. pastor Hope Presbyn. Ch., Mpls., 1971-80; sr. pastor First Presbyn. Ch., Fresno, Calif., 1981-86, Community Presbyn. Ch., Danville, Calif., 1986-91; tchr. Bible Oakland (Calif.) A's, 1990-91; writer, 1983—; invited speaker at gen. sessions and confs. and on TV. Author: Gold in the Making, 1983, A Forgiving God in an Unforgiving World, 1984, Healing Life's Hurts, 1986, A Time for Compassion, 1986, Courage to Begin Again, 1988, Mistreated, 1989, Becoming a Whole Person in a Broken World, 1990, Mentoring, 1990. Mem. pres.'s adv. coun. Fellowship of Christian Athletes; bd. dirs. Youth for Christ, cen. Calf., 1982-85, Fresno Pacific Coll., 1983-84. Recipient award for outstanding leadership State Bar; named to Outstanding Young Men of Am. Avocation: running. Home: 3950 Stoneridge Dr Apt 7 Pleasanton CA 94588-8342

DAVIS, RONALD, artist, printmaker; b. Santa Monica, Calif., June 29, 1937. Student, U. Wyo., 1955-56, San Francisco Art Inst., 1960-64. Announcer, Sta. KVWO, Cheyenne, Wyo., 1958-59; instr. U. Calif., Irvine, 1966. Represented in permanent collections: Albright-Knox Gallery, Buffalo, Los Angeles County Mus., Mus. Modern Art, N.Y.C., Mus. Contemporary Art, Los Angeles, TateGallery, London, San Antonio Mus. Art, San Francisco Mus. Art, Whitney Mus., N.Y.C., Va. Mus., Richmond, Walker Art Ctr., Minn. and other internat. pub. collections; 57 one-man shows include Leo Castelli, N.Y.C., Nicholas Wilder Gallery, Los Angeles, BlumHelman Los Angeles, Asher/Faure, Los Angeles, John Berggruen, San Francisco, Kasmin Gallery, London, Mirvish Gallery, Toronto, N.Y. Acad. Scis., N.Y.C., Sedona Arts Ctr., Ariz., Oakland (Calif.) Mus., retrospective, 1976, numerous others; also numerous nat. and internat. group shows. Yale-Norfolk Summer Sch. Music and Art grantee, 1962, Nat. Endowment Arts grantee, 1968. Studio: PO Box 293 Arroyo Hondo NM 87513-0293 Address: care Gemini Gel 8365 Melrose Ave Los Angeles CA 90069-5419

DAVIS, RONALD P., secondary school educator; b. McKees Rocks, Pa., Dec. 15, 1970; s. Paul H. and Loretta M. (Crenshaw) D.; m. Gabrielle D. Teich, Feb. 14, 1998. BS in Edn., Slippery Rock U., 1992, MA in Student Personnel, 1994; postgrad., Nova Southeastern U. Head camp counselor Boys and Girls Club, Pitts., 1989-93; resident advisor dept. residence edn. Slippery Rock (Pa.) U., 1991-94, grad. asst. Office Student Life, 1993-94; tchr. Stranahan H.S., Ft. Lauderdale, Fla., 1994—, athletic dir., 1995—; pres. Visions in Edn., Plantation, Fla., 1995—; speaker in field. Contbr. articles to profl. jours. Democrat. Lutheran. Avocations: baseball, football, animals, dancing, travel. Home: 1074 SW 42d Ter Deerfield Beach FL 33442

DAVIS, RONALD WAYNE, genetics researcher, biochemistry educator; b. Moroa, Ill., July 17, 1941; s. Lester and Gerzella Mary (Brown) D.; m. Janet L. Dafoe, May 2, 1949; children: Whitney Allen, Ashley Halcyon. BS, Ea. Ill. U., 1964; PhD, Calif. Inst. Tech., 1970. Postdoctoral fellow Harvard U., Cambridge, Mass., 1970-71; asst. prof. biochemistry Stanford (Calif.) U., 1972-77, assoc. prof., 1977-80, prof., 1980—; mem. sci. adv. bd. Collaborative Rsch., Bedford, Mass., 1978—. Author: Manual for Genetic Engineering, 1980. Recipient Eli Lilly award in microbiology, 1976, U.S. Steel award in molecular biology, 1981, Louis S. Rosensthiel award Brandeis U., 1992. Mem. NAS. Avocation: backpacking. Office: Stanford U Sch Medicine Dept Biochemistry Stanford CA 94305*

DAVIS, ROY KIM, otolaryngologist, health facility administrator; b. Logan, Utah, Jan. 20, 1947; m. JoNell Davis; children: Kimberly, Roy Neal, Tamralyn, Cynthia Joy, Mindy Anne, Ricks Eric. BS magna cum laude, Utah State U., 1972; MD, U. Utah, 1975. Diplomate Am. Bd. Otolaryngolgoy. Resident in prespecialty surgery Madigan Army Med. Ctr., 1975-76, resident in otolaryngology, 1976-79; fellow Boston U., 1979-80; instr. surgery Uniformed Svcs. U. Health Scis., Bethesda, Md., 1980-81, asst. prof. surgery, 1981-83; asst. chief otolaryngology svc. Walter Reed Army Med. Ctr., 1980-83; from asst prof. to assoc. prof. U. Utah, Salt Lake City, 1983-85; chief otolaryngology head and neck surgery S.L. VA Med. Ctr., Salt Lake City, 1986-93; dir. John A. Dixon Laser Inst. U. Utah, 1993-98; adj. prof. comm. disorders U. Utah, 1993—, prof. surgery, 1993; course instr. Am. Acad. Otolaryngology; scientific dir. Rocky Mountain Cancer Data System, 1985-96; mem. head and neck com. S.W. Oncology Group, 1985—; vis. prof. Madigan Army Medical Ctr., 1980, Brooke Army Medical Ctr., 1981, Tripler Army Medical Ctr., 1982, U. N.C., 1986, U. Tex., 1988, Szent-Gyorgyi Albert Univ., Szeged, Hungary, 1989, First Pavlov Medical Inst., Leningrad, USSR, 1990, Univ. Keil, Germany, 1990, Georg-August U., Gottingen, Germany, 1990, 96, Wilhelm-Pieck Univ. Rostock, Germany, 1990, U. Indonesia, Jakarta, 1995, Bowman-Gray Med. Sch.-Wake Forest U., 1996; guest examiner Am. Bd. Otolaryngology, 1994-95, 99. Co-author numerous books and book chpts.; contbr. articles to profl. jours. Mem. Jon A. Huntsman Cancer Inst. Fellow Am. Acad. Otolaryngology, Am. Laryngological Assn., Am. Soc. Laser Medicine and Surgery, Am. Coll. Surgeons, Am. Soc. Head and Neck Surgery; Soc. Univ. Otolaryngolgoists, Utah Soc. Otolaryngology, Am. Laryngo., Rhinol. & Otol. Soc., Am. Bronchoesophagol. Soc., Soc. Univ. Otolaryngologists, Alpha Epsilon Delta, Am. Laryngo. Assn. Office: Otolaryngology Head & Neck Surgery 3C134a U Utah Hlth Scis Ctr Salt Lake City UT 84132

DAVIS, RUSS ERIK, oceanographer, educator; b. San Francisco, Mar. 8, 1941; s. Henry Fairfax Davis and Enid L. (Kuchel) Davis Wood; m. Sandra Powell, June 21, 1963 (div. 1972); 1 child, Erik Russ; m. Linda D. Welzig, Nov. 6, 1995. B.S. in Chem. Engring., U. Calif.-Berkeley, 1963; M.S., Stanford U., 1967, Ph.D., 1967. Asst. research geophysicist Scripps Instn. of Oceanography, La Jolla, Calif., 1967-69, chmn. ocean research div., 1979-83, prof. oceanography, 1969—. Contbr. over 50 articles to profl. jours. Patentee. Recipient A.G. Huntsman award, 1997. Fellow Am. Geophys. Union, Am. Meteorology Soc.; mem. Nat. Acad Sci. Office: Scripps Instn Oceanography La Jolla CA 92093

DAVIS, RUSSELL C., career officer. Student pilot tng., Graham Air Base, Fla., Vance AFB, Okla., 1958-60; BA in Gen. Edn., U. Nebr., Omaha, 1963; JD, Drake U., 1969; student, Air Command and Staff Coll., 1973, Indsl. Coll. Armed Forces, 1979, Harvard U., 1989. Commd. 2d lt. USAF, 1960, advanced through grades to lt. gen., 1998; strategic bombardment pilot 4347th Combat Crew Tng. Wing, McConnell AFB, Kans., 1960; various pilot assignments USAF, 1960-68; flight comdr. 124th Tactical Fighter Squadron Iowa NG, Des Moines, 1968-70; air ops. officer 132d Tactical Fighter Group Iowa Air NG, Des Moines, 1970-77, officer in charge Command Post, 132d Tactical Fighter Wing, 1977-78; dep. comdr. ops. Hdqs. Iowa Air NG, Des Moines, 1978-79; dep. chief manpower and personnel Air NG Support Ctr., Andrews AFB, Md., 1979-80; exec. to chief NG bur., Pentagon, Washington, 1980-82, vice chief, 1995-98; chief NG bur., Pentagon, Arlington, Va., 1998—; wing comdr. 113th Tactical Fighter Wing D.C. Air NG, Andrews AFB, 1982-90; Air NG asst. to comdr. Tactical Air Command, Langley AFB, 1990-91; comdg. gen. D.C. NG, Washington, 1991-95. Former mem. bd. trustees Drake U. Decorated D.S.M., Legion of Merit with oak leaf cluster, Small Arms Expert Marksmanship Ribbon. Recipient Roy Wilkins Achievement award NAACP, 1984, Air Force Assn. Svc. award Air Force Assn. Hdqs., 1985; scholar Tuskegee U., 1956-58; Ira Eaker fellow Tony Anthony chpt. Air Force Assn., 1988. Office: NGB/CV 2500 Army Pentagon Washington DC 20310-2500

DAVIS, RUSSELL HADEN, pastoral psychotherapist; b. Washington, Nov. 26, 1940; s. Walter Haden Davis and Virginia (Russell) Edge; m. Iva Lee Crocker, 1964; children: Brandon Denise, Haden Arnold. BA, U. Va., 1962; MDiv, Union Theol. Sem., N.Y.C., 1965; ThM, So. Bapt. Theol. Sem., Louisville, 1966; STM, Union Theol. Sem., N.Y.C., 1978, PhD, 1986. Ordained to ministry So. Bapt. Ch., 1961. Clin. chaplain Ky. State Reformatory, LaGrange, 1966-71, Ctrl. State Hosp., Milledgeville, Ga., 1971-77; assoc. minister The Riverside Ch., N.Y.C., 1977-86; asst. prof. psychiatry and religion Union Theol. Sem., N.Y.C., 1986-91; mem. faculty Blanton-Peale Gard. Inst. Pastoral Psychotherapy, N.Y.C., 1989-91; dir. Psy-Law, N.Y.C., 1989-91; asst. prof. U. Va., 1994, assoc. prof., 1994-95; pvt. practice pastoral psychotherapy, 1974—; exec. dir. Assn. for Clin. Pastoral Edn., Inc., Decatur, Ga., 1995-98; pres. Legacy Group Internat., 1998—. Author: Freud's Concept of Passivity, 1993; also articles. Bd. dirs. Inst. for Relationship Therapy, N.Y., 1981-88, Counseling Ctr., Riverside Ch., 1978-82. Named Ky. Col., State of Ky., 1970; fellow Union Theol. Sem., 1979-81, rsch. grantee, 1987-90; fellow Oaklawn Found., 1980. Fellow soll. Chaplains (bd. cert.),sCommonwealth Ctr. Lit. and Cultural Change (assoc.); mem. Assn. Clin. Pastoral Edn. (cert. supr.), Am. Assn. Pastoral Counselors.

DAVIS, RUTH A., ambassador; b. Phoenix, May 28, 1943. BA, Spelman Coll., 1966; MSW, U. Calif., Berkeley, 1968. Consular officer Kinshasa, Zaire, 1969-71, Nairobi, Kenya, 1971-73, Tokyo, 1973-76, Naples, Italy, 1976-80; spl. asst. internat. affairs Mayor of Washington, 1980-82; sr. watch officer ops. ctr. Dept. State, 1982-84, chief tng. and liaison, bur. pers., 1984-86; consul gen. Barcelona, Spain, 1987-91; amb. to Benin, 1992-96; prin. dept. asst. sec. State for Consular Affairs Dept State, Washington, 1995-97, dir. nat. fgn. affairs tng. ctr., 1997—; mem. sr. seminar Fgn. Svc. Inst., 1992. Office: Fgn Svc Inst 4000 Arlington Blvd Arlington VA 22204*

DAVIS, RUTH CAROL, pharmacy educator; b. Wilkes-Barre, Pa., Oct. 27, 1943; d. Morris David Davis and Helen Jane Gillis. BS, Phila. Coll. Pharmacy and Sci., 1967; AA in Elec. Engring., ITT Tech. Inst., 1999. Cert. pharmacist, Pa., Md. Mgr. pharmacist Fairview Pharmacy, Etters, Pa.; mgr., pharmacist Neighborcare Pharmacy, Balt.; dir. ambulatory svcs. Rombro Health Svcs., Balt.; tchr., pharmacist Boothwyn Pharmacy, Phila.; pharm. cons. Nat. Rx Svcs. of Pa.; Eagle Managed Care, 1996; pharmacist Pharmastat Inc., 1996—. Republican. Baptist. Avocations: training and raising American quarter horses, music, reading. Home and Office: 75 Lion Dr Hanover PA 17331-3849

DAVIS, RUTH LOUISE-WEINGARTNER, video company administrator, former military officer; b. Phila., July 27, 1947; d. Russell Warren and Mono Francis (Marshall) Weingartner; m. Louis Robbert Davis, Oct. 25, 1974; children: Adam Andrew, Meredith Louise. BA in German, Rutgers U., 1969; MBPA in Bus. & Govt. Rels., Southeastern U., 1981, MBPA in Pers. Mgmt./Labor Rels., 1983. Sales assoc. Maison Blanche, Lafayette, La., 1994-95; subs. tchr. Lafayette Parish Sch., 1995-97.; prodn. coord. Creative Video Svc. Inc., 1997—. With U.S. Army, 1970-75, USAR, 1969-98. Home: 403 River Woods Lafayette LA 70508

DAVIS, RUTH MARGARET (MRS. BENJAMIN FRANKLIN LOHR), technology management executive; b. Sharpsville, Pa., Oct. 19, 1928; d. W. George and Mary Anna (Ackermann) D.; m. Benjamin F. Lohr, Apr. 29, 1961. BA, Am. U., 1950; MA, U. Md., 1952, PhD, 1955. Statistician FAO, UN, Washington, 1946-49; mathematician Nat. Bur. Standards, 1950-51; head ops. rsch. div. David Taylor Model Basin, 1955-61; staff asst. Office Dir. Def. Rsch. and Engring. Dept. Def., 1961-67; asso. dir. rsch. and devel. Nat. Libr. Medicine, 1967-68; dir. Lister Hill Nat. Center for Biomed. Communications, 1968-70; dir. Inst. for Computer Scis. and Tech. Nat. Bur. Standards, 1970-77; dep. undersec. def. for rsch. and engring., 1977-79; asst. sec. resource applications U.S. Dept. Energy, 1979-81; pres., CEO Pymatuning Group Inc., 1981—; chmn. Aerospace Corp.; bd. dirs. Ceridian Inc., Varian Assocs., BTG, Inc., SSDS, Inc., Premark Internat., Inc., Prin. Fin. Group, Inc., Tupperware Inc.; trustee Consol. Edison Co. of N.Y.; lectr. U. Md., 1955-57, Am. U., 1957-58; vis. prof. computer sci. U. Pa., 1969-72; adj. prof. U. Pitts.; cons. Office Naval Rsch., Washington, 1957-58; mem. Md. Gov.'s Sci. Adv. Coun., 1971-77; chmn. nat. adv. coun. Elec. Power Rsch. Inst., 1975-76. Contbr. articles to profl. jours. Trustee Inst. Def. Analysis; bd. visitors Cath. U. Am. Recipient Rockefeller Tech. Mgmt. award 1973, Fed. Woman of the Yr. award, 1973, Systems Profl. of Yr. award, 1979, Disting. Svc. medal U.S. Dept. Def., 1979, Disting. Svc. medal U.S. Dept. Energy, 1981, Gold medal, 1981, Ada A. Lovelace award, 1984, Disting. Alumnus award U. Md., 1993; inducted into Computer News Hall of Fame, 1988. Fellow AIAA, Soc. for Info. Display; mem. AAAS, Am. Math. Soc., Math. Assn. Am., Nat. Acad. Engring., Nat. Acad. Pub. Adminstrn., Nat. Acad. Arts and Scis., Washington Philos. Soc., Phi Kappa Phi, Sigma Pi Sigma, Tau Beta Pi. Office: Pymatuning Group Inc 4900 Seminary Rd Ste 570 Alexandria VA 22311-1811 *The rapid rate of change in our lives due principally to technology and changing personal values makes adaptability and flexibility key ingredients to success. The one essential invariant of success is integrity, accompanied by compassion.*

DAVIS, RYAN WESLEY, military officer, navigator; b. Colombra, Mo., Nov. 17, 1973; s. Donald Wesley and Carol Grace (Bachmeyer) D. BS in Polit. Sci., USAF Acad., Colorado Springs, Colo., 1996. Commd. 2d lt. USAF, 1996; asst. to clin. prof. nat. security studies dept. polit. sci. USAF Acad., Colorado Springs, 1996; student navigator Tng. Wing 6, Pensacola, Fla., 1997-98; dep. comdr. 325 Fighter Wing, 1999—. Mem. Acad. Polit. Sci., USAF Acad. Assn. of Grads. Home: 10040 Centre St Pensacola FL 32506-9554

DAVIS, SAMUEL, hospital administrator, educator, consultant; b. N.Y.C., Sept. 30, 1931; s. Morris and Ethel (Levowitz) D.; m. Ellen Darce Kalker, June 16, 1957; children: Joseph Evan, Thomas Adam, Jonathan Edward, Jessica Ann. B.A., CCNY, 1952; M.S., Columbia U., 1957. Acct. Roosevelt Hosp., N.Y.C., 1954-55; relief adminstr. Meml. Center Cancer and Allied Diseases, N.Y.C., 1955-56; adminstrv. resident, then adminstrv. asst. to dir. and dir. ambulatory care services Roosevelt Hosp., 1956-59; mem. adminstrv. staff Hillside Hosp., Glen Oaks, N.Y.C., 1959-72, exec. v.p., 1970-72; exec. cons. L.I. Jewish-Hillside Med. Center, New Hyde Park, N.Y., 1972; exec. pres. Mt. Sinai Hosp., Mpls., 1972-75; dir. Mt. Sinai Hosp., N.Y.C., 1975-81, pres., 1981-85; sr. v.p. Mt. Sinai Med. Center, N.Y.C., 1975-77, exec. v.p., 1978-84; pres. EcuMed, N.Y.C., 1984-85; prin. Sam Davis & Assocs., Rye, N.Y., 1986—; sr. dir. Delta Cons. Group, N.Y.C., 1990-98; assoc. prof. adminstrv. medicine Mt. Sinai Med. Sch., 1975-79, acting chmn., 1977-79, Edmond A. Guggenheim prof. health care mgmt., chmn. health care mgmt., 1979-84, disting. service prof. health care mgmt., 1984—; adj. prof. health care adminstrn. Baruch Coll., CUNY, 1978-87; prof. mgmt., clin. prof. Sch. Pub. Health Columbia U., 1988—; cons. health care strategy and orgnl. change, 1976—; dir. health care research, The Ctr. for Mgmt., CUNY; vice chmn. bd. dirs. Hennepin County (Minn.) Health Coalition, 1973-75; mem. health adv. com. Minn. Met. Health Bd., 1974-75; mem. Hennepin County Health and Social Services Adv. Bd., 1974-75. Author: Decision Analysis in Hospital Administration, 1974; contbr. articles to profl. jours. Trustee Mpls. Fedn. Jewish Service, 1973-75; chmn. health and welfare div. N.Y.C. Fedn. Jewish Philanthropies, 1975-76; trustee, mem. exec. com. Montefiore Med. Ctr., Bronx, N.Y., 1985—. Served with AUS, 1952-54. Recipient Humanitarian award NCCJ, 1984; fellow social studies and humanities CCNY, 1952; WHO fellow, 1970; sr. fellow Wharton Sch. U. Pa., 1986—. Fellow Am. Coll. Hosp. Adminstrs., Am. Pub. Health Assn.; mem. Am. Assn. Hosp. Planning, Am., N.Y. State hosp. assns., Am. Mgmt. Assn., Herman Biggs Soc. Office: Sam Davis & Assocs 74 Greenhaven Rd Rye NY 10580-2210

DAVIS, SARAH IRWIN, retired English language educator; b. Louisburg, N.C., Nov. 17, 1923; d. M. Stuart and May Amanda (Holmes) D.; m. Charles B. Goodrich, Nov. 18, 1949 (div. 1953). AB, U. N.C., 1944, AM, 1945; PhD, NYU, 1953. Teaching asst. English dept. NYU, 1948-51; tchr. English Elizabeth Irwin High Sch., N.Y.C., 1951-53; editor coll. texts Henry Holt, N.Y.C., 1953-55; editor coll. texts, enclopedias McGraw-Hill, N.Y.C., Rome, 1953-60; asst. prof. English Louisburg (N.C.) Coll., 1960-63; asst. prof. English Randolph-Macon Woman's Coll., Lynchburg, Va., 1963-70, assoc. prof. English, 1970-75, chairperson Am. studies, 1971-87, prof. English and Am. studies, 1975-87, ret., 1987. Contbr. articles to profl. jours. Mem. MLA, Am. Studies Assn., N.C.-Va. Coll. English Assn. (various coms.), Franklin County Hist. Soc. (pres. 1989-94). Home: PO Box 246 Louisburg NC 27549-0246 also: PO Box 998 Chapel Hill NC 27514-0998

DAVIS, SCOTT JONATHAN, lawyer; b. Chgo., Jan. 8, 1952; s. Oscar and Doris (Koller) D.; m. Anne Megan, Jan. 4, 1981; children: William, James, Peter. BA, Yale U., 1972; JD, Harvard U., 1976. Bar: Ill. 1976, U.S. Dist. Ct. (no. dist.) Ill. 1976, U.S. Ct. Appeals (7th cir.) 1977, U.S. Ct. Appeals (8th cir.) 1986. Law clk. to judge U.S. Ct. Appeals (7th cir.), Chgo., 1976-77; assoc. Mayer, Brown & Platt, Chgo., 1977-82, ptnr., 1983—. Bd. editors Harvard Law Rev., 1974-76; contbr. articles to profl. jours. V.p. Chgo. Police Bd. Home: 838 W Belden Ave Chicago IL 60614-3236 Office: Mayer Brown & Platt 190 S La Salle St Ste 3100 Chicago IL 60603-3441

DAVIS, SHELBY MOORE CULLOM, investment executive, consultant; b. Phila., Mar. 20, 1937; s. Shelby Cullom and Kathryn (Wasserman) D.; m. Wendy Ann Adams, June 20, 1959 (div. 1975); children: Andrew, Christopher, Victoria; m. Gale Abbie Lansing, Apr. 17, 1976; children: Lansing, Alida, Edith. AB with honors, Princeton U., 1958. V.p. in charge rsch. Bank of N.Y., N.Y.C., 1958-66; founding ptnr. Davis, Palmer & Biggs, N.Y.C., 1966-78; sr. v.p. Fiduciary Trust Co., N.Y.C., 1978-83, cons., 1983—; pres. various mut. funds Davis Selected Advisers, Santa Fe, 1983—; also dir. all mut. funds Davis Selected Advisers, 1969-78, 83—. Contbr. articles to Fin. Analysts Jour. Bd. dirs., trustee Beekman Downtown Hosp., N.Y.C., early 1960s; bd. dirs. Am. Cancer Soc., N.Y.C., early 1970s. Mem. N.Y. Soc. Security Analysts (bd. dirs. 1965), Univ. Club, River Club (N.Y.C.), Harbor Club (Seal Harbor, Maine), Tuxedo Club (Tuxedo Park, N.Y.), Jupiter Island Club. Republican. Avocations: skiing; mountain climbing; travel; swimming; tennis. Home: PO Box 25185 Jackson WY 83001-7000 Office: Davis Selected Advisers PO Box 1688 Santa Fe NM 87504-1688

DAVIS, SHIRLEY HARRIET, social worker, editor; b. Brookline, Mass., June 27, 1922; d. Jacob and Matilda (Goldberg) Freedman; m. Edward H. Davis, Nov. 11, 1943; children: Anita Maureen Davis Winn, Lawrence Paul. AB, Calvin Coolidge Coll., 1944; postgrad., Simmons Sch. of Social Work, 1944-45. Social worker Travelers Aid of N.Y., N.Y.C., 1944-48; dir. Community Svc. Workshop of Woodmere (N.Y.) Acad., 1966-70; v.p. for program and membership West End Ave. Peninsula Hosp. Ctr., Edgemere, N.Y., 1973-80; dir. Family Practice Playroom Coll. Medicine, Downstate Med. Ctr., Bklyn., 1977-83; officer mgr. Edward H. Davis, M.D., Loxahatchee, Fla., 1983-93; dir. publicity and pub. rels. Fla. Atlantic Region of Hadassah, 1994—; publ. com. Am. Jewish Congress Genetics of Breast Conf., 1997; publ. chair Walk for Better Health Fla. Atlantic Region Hadassah, 1998—, ann. spring conf. Fla Atlantic Region of Hadassah, 1995—. Editor: Hadassah of Wellington Fla., 1990-93. V.p. membership Hadassah of Wellington, 1992-94, bulletin bus. mgr.; dir. publicity and pub. rels., bd. dirs. Fla. Atlantic Region of Hadassah, 1994—; chair Fla. Atlantic Region of Hadassah Women's Health Symposium, 1996, 97, 98, 99. Wellington chpt. honoree Fla. Atlantic Region of Hadassah ann. Woman of Valor awards, 1996, honoree Fla. Atlantic Region of Hadassah 13th Ann. Spring Conf. for Excellence in Publicity and Pub. Rels., 1998; recipient Nat. Hadassah Love of a Lifetime award, 1996. Republican. Jewish. Avocation: amateur radio. Home: 13604 Firewood Ct West Palm Beach FL 33414-8522

DAVIS, SHIRLEY ROSS See SULLIVAN, SHIRLEY ROSS

DAVIS, SIDNEY FANT, lawyer, author; b. Louisville, May 14, 1934; s. Sidney Fant and Harriet Virginia (Price) D.; m. Sylvia Sue Hussey, Feb. 15, 1958; children: Susan, Kathleen, Sydney. BS, U.S. Naval Acad., 1956; JD, U. Fla., 1963. Bar: Fla. 1963, Ga. 1968, S.C. 1980, Tenn. 1986. Asso., then partner firm Jennings, Watts, Clarke & Hamilton, Jacksonville, Fla., 1963-67; from atty. to v.p., asst. gen. counsel Delta Air Lines, Inc., Atlanta, 1967-79; v.p., gen. counsel Springs Industries, Inc., Ft. Mill, S.C., 1979-85; sec. Springs Industries, Inc., 1980-85; mng. ptnr. Heiskell, Donelson, Bearman, Adams, Williams & Kirsch, Knoxville, Tenn., 1985; pres. S.F. Davis & Co., Atlanta, 1986-87; v.p., gen. counsel Intercredit Corp., Atlanta, 1987-89; pres., chief exec. officer AVLEASE, Ltd., Atlanta, 1989-93; pvt. law practice, 1993-97; of counsel Kelly, Price, Passidomo & Siket, Naples, Fla., 1997-98; pvt. practice Naples, 1998—; guest lectr. Vandervilt U. Coll. Law. Author: Delta Air Lines: Debunking the Myth, 1989; exec. editor: U. Fla. Law Rev., 1962-63. Served as aviator USN, 1956-60. Mem. ABA (1st prize article sect. corp., banking and bus. law 1969), Am. Soc. Corp. Secs. (pres. S.E. region 1974-75, nat. dir. 1981-85, chmn.-elect 1983-84, chmn. 1984-85). Republican. Clubs: Capital City (Atlanta), University (N.Y.C.), Commerce Club (Atlanta). Home: 191 Via Perignon Naples FL 34119-4727

DAVIS, STANLEY NELSON, hydrologist, educator; b. Rio de Janeiro, Brazil, Aug. 6, 1924; s. Nelson Caryl and Mary Faye (Caulkins) D.; m. Barbara Jean Wickham, Apr. 14, 1949 (div.); children: Gerald Nelson, Ruth Ann, Darlene Grace, Randall Wayne, Betty Jean, Nancy Faye.; m. Augusta G. Felty, Feb. 12, 1982; children—Tara Devi, Locana Kamala. B.S. in Geology, U. Nev., 1949; M.S., U. Kans., 1951; Ph.D., Yale, 1955. Geologist U.S. Bur. Reclamation, 1949, Mo. Geol. Survey, 1952, 53, 55; instr. U. Rochester, 1953-54; mem. faculty Stanford, 1954-67, prof. geology, 1965-67; prof. geology U. Mo., 1967-73, chmn. dept., 1969-72; asso. dean Coll. Arts and Scis., 1972-73; prof. geology Ind. U., Bloomington, 1973-75; prof. hydrology U. Ariz., Tucson, 1975—; head dept. hydrology and water resources U. Ariz., 1975-79; Vis. prof. U. Chile, Santiago, 1960-61; tchr. Bowling Green U., summer 1963, Princeton, summer 1965, U. Hawaii, fall 1966; instr. U. Oriente in Venezuela, summer 1967-68, 72; lectr. Am. Geol. Inst.; mem. East Greenland Expdn., Arctic Inst. N. Am., summer 1959; cons. to govt. and industry, 1955—. Author: Hidrogeologia, 1961, (with R.M. DeWiest) Hydrogeology, 1966, (with P. Reitan and R. Pestrong) Geology, Our Physical Environment, 1976, (with D.J. Campbell, H.W. Bentley, T.J. Flynn) Ground Water Tracers, 1984; also articles. Served with AUS, 1943-46, PTO. Fellow AAAS, Geol. Soc. Am. (O.E. Meinzer award 1989), Am. Geophys. Union; mem. Assn. Ground Water Scientists and Engrs., Soc. Econ. Paleontologists and Mineralogists, Sigma Xi. Home: 6540 W Box Canyon Dr Tucson AZ 85745-9681 Office: U Ariz Dept Hydrology & Water Resources Tucson AZ 85721

DAVIS, STEPHEN ARNOLD, artist, educator; b. Ft. Worth, Apr. 24, 1945; s. Leo M. and Bernice J. (Rosenwasser) D.; 1 child, Asa. Student, U. Madrid, 1966; BA in Polit. Sci., Claremont (Calif.) Men's Coll., 1967; postgrad., U. Tex., Austin, 1967-68; MFA, Claremont Grad. Sch., 1971. Tchr. San Francisco Art Inst., 1972, U. Calif., Santa Barbara, 1978, SUNY, Purchase, 1982, Hunter Coll., 1987-93, Stanford U., 1994-95; NEA artist-in-residence The Hudson River Mus., Yonkers, N.Y., 1978; curator Hansen Fuller Gallery, San Francisco, 1970; artist-in-residence U. Santa Clara, 1975-77, Wright State U., 1977, Sarah Lawrence Coll., 1979-80; vis. artist U. Victoria, 1975, 80; Lansdowne lectr. U. Victoria, Can., 1991. One-man shows at Hansen-Fuller Gallery, San Francisco, 1972, 74, 76, Malinda Wyatt Gallery, N.Y.C., 1981, 85, 80 Langton St. Gallery, San Francisco, 1982, Wanda Hansen, San Francisco, 1982, The Banff (Can.) Centre, 1983, Washington Project for the Arts, 1986, Gallery Paule Anglim, San Francisco, 1987, Mattress Factory, Pitts., 1990, The Addison Gallery of Am. Art, Andover, Mass., 1990, Jernigan Wicker Gallery, San Francisco, 1992, 95; exhibited in group shows at Oakland (Calif.) Mus., 1972, Univ. Art Mus., Berkeley, Calif., 1972, 75, San Francisco Art Inst., 1973, Whitney Mus., N.Y.C., 1973, 77, Krannert Art Mus., Champagne, Ill., 1974, Ft. Worth Art Mus.-San Francisco Art Mus., 1975-76, Fla. State U.-Phoenix Art Mus., 1982, Yale U., New Haven, 1983, Malinda Wyatt Gallery, N.Y.C., 1984, 85, Pino Molica Gallery, N.Y.C., 1990, 91, Addison Gallery Am. Art, Andover, Mass., 1991, Hunter Coll., 1993; represented in permanent collections at San Francisco Mus. Art, Oakland Mus., Univ. Art Mus., Berkeley, Addison Gallery Am. Art, Andover, Mus. Contemporary Art, L.A., also pvt. and corp. collections; editor: (with Geoffrey Young) Work Mag., 1975. Grantee SECA, San Francisco Mus. Art, 1972, Nat. Endowment for Arts, 1975-76, 78-79, 87-88, Tiffany Found., 1983, Pollock-Krasner Found., 1991-92, Gottlieb Found., 1993-94, Joan Mitchell Found., 1995-96. Home: 70 Thomas St New York NY 10013-3820

DAVIS, STEPHEN EDWARD FOLWELL, banker; b. Auckland, N.Z., July 12, 1964; s. George Folwell and Elizabeth Ann (Strother) D. BA, Harvard Coll., 1987. Rsch. intern The Brookings Instn., Washington, 1984; sales intern Lotus Devel. Corp., Cambridge, Mass., 1986-87; fin. analyst Salomon Bros. Inc., N.Y.C., 1987-89; interest rate swap trader Kidder Peabody & Co., N.Y.C., 1989-90; derivatives trader Deutsche Bank AG, N.Y.C., 1990-95; proprietary trader Dai-Ichi Kangyo Bank, Ltd., 1995-96; head derivatives trading Hypo Bank AG, N.Y.C., 1996-97; pres. Davis Equities, N.Y.C., 1997—. Researcher book: The Ultimate Insiders, 1989. Homesteading coord., dir. Crimson Impact Inc., N.Y.C., 1991—; treas. The Quadrille Soc., N.Y.C., 1991—. JFK Sch. Govt. grantee, 1984; Lindsay Exeter Meml. scholar, 1983. Mem. Fgn. Policy Assn., Harvard Club of N.Y., Japan Soc. Avocations: foreign policy, golf, running. Home: 54 W 74th St Apt 608 New York NY 10023-2420

DAVIS, STEPHEN HOWARD, applied mathematics educator; b. N.Y.C., Sept. 7, 1939; s. Harry Carl and Eva Leah (Axelrod) D.; m. Suellen Lewis, Jan. 15, 1966. BEE, Rensselaer Poly. Inst., 1960, MS in Math, 1962, PhD in Math., 1964. Research mathematician Rand Corp., Santa Monica, Calif., 1964-66; lectr. in math. Imperial Coll., London U., 1966-68; asst. prof. mechanics and materials sci. Johns Hopkins U., 1968-70, assoc. prof., 1970-75, prof., 1975-78; prof. engring. sci. and applied math. Northwestern U., 1979—, Walter P. Murphy prof., 1987—; dir. Ctr. for Multiphase Fluid Flow and Transport, 1986-88; cons. in field; vis. prof. math. Monash U., Australia, 1973; vis. prof. chem. engring. U. Ariz., 1977; vis. prof. aerospace and mech. engring., 1981; vis. scientist Institut für Aerodynamik-ETH, Zurich, Switzerland, 1971; vis. scientist Dept. Math. Ecole Polytechnique Federale, Lausanne, Switzerland, 1984, 85, vis. prof. 1987, 88, 91; mem. U.S. Nat. Com. for Theoretical and Applied Mechanics, 1978-87. Asst. editor Jour. Fluid Mechanics, 1969-75, assoc. editor, 1975-89; contbr. articles to profl. jours. Recipient Alexander von Humboldt award, 1994, Fluid Dynamics prize, Am. Physical Soc., 1994. Fellow Am. Phys. Soc. (chmn. divsn. fluid dynamics 1978-79, 87-88, councillor divsn. fluid dynamics 1980-82); mem. NAE, Am. Acad. Arts and Scis., Soc. Indsl. and Applied Math. (coun. 1983-87), Sigma Xi, Pi Mu Epsilon. Home: 1199 Edgewood Rd Lake Forest IL 60045-1308 Office: Northwestern U McCormick Sch Engring/Applied Scis Sheridan Rd Evanston IL 60208

DAVIS, STERLING EVAN, television executive; b. Mpls., Feb. 10, 1941; s. Lyman Eugene and Ruby Elizabeth (Larson) D.; m. Bonnie S. Taylor, Jan. 15, 1977; children: Evan, Emily, Robin. BA, Taylor U., 1963; postgrad., U. So. Calif., L.A., 1968-70. Chief engr. Metrotape, Hollywood, Calif., 1974-78; v.p. ops. The Vidtronics Co., Hollywood, 1978; chief engr. Telemation Prodns., Seattle, 1978-82; dir. ops. Sta. KTVU, Inc., Oakland, Calif., 1982-98; v.p. engring. Cox Broadcasting, Atlanta, 1998—. Bd. dirs. Easter Seal Soc. Lt. USN, 1963-67, Vietnam. Mem. IEEE, Soc. Motion Picture & TV Engrs., Audio Engring. Soc., Soc. Broadcast Engrs. Office: Cox Broadcasting PO Box 105357 Atlanta GA 30348-5357

DAVIS, STEVEN ANDREW, dermatologist; b. San Antonio, May 28, 1947; s. Herbert and Phyllis D.; m. Jolene Bryant; children: Bryant, Suzanne. BA in Econs., Yale U., 1969; MD, U. Tex., 1973. Diplomate Am. Bd. Dermatology. Intern U. N.Mex. Hosp., Albuquerque, 1973-74; resident in dermatology U. Calif.-San Francisco Med. Ctr., 1974-77; pvt. practice, San Antonio, 1977—. Author: How To Stay Healthy in an Unhealthy World, 1983; columnist Syndicated King Features, Speaking of Your Health, 1984-86; featured on CBS radio network show Speaking of Health, 1976— (Am. Heart Assn., Am. Acad. Family Physicians and Am. Assn. Blood Banks awards). Fellow Am. Acad. Dermatology; mem. AMA, Tex. Med. Assn., Bexar County Med. Assn. Office: 8038 Wurzbach Rd Ste 450 San Antonio TX 78229-3814

DAVIS, STEVEN MICHAEL, air force officer, test pilot; b. Everett, Wash., Nov. 6, 1961; s. Raymond A. and Leila E. Davis; m. Margaret Louise Cleaver, Sept. 2, 1992. BS in Physics, USAF Acad., 1984; MS in Aerospace Engring., U. So. Calif., 1991, MS in Systems Mgmt., 1996. Commd. 2nd lt. USAF, 1980, advanced through grades to maj., 1996; KC-10A aircraft comdr. 6th Air Refueling Squadron, March AFB, Calif., 1990-91, KC-10A instr. pilot, 1991; wing tactics officer 22d Air Refueling Wing, March AFB, Calif., 1991-92; student test pilot USAF Test Pilot Sch., Edwards AFB, Calif., 1992-93; chief test pilot 418th Flight Test Squadron, Edwards AFB, Calif., 1993-95; ops. officer Detachment 1, 46th Ops. Group, Hurlburt Field, Fla., 1995-98; chief test pilot Air Mobility, Warfare Ctr., Ft. Dix, N.J., 1998—; dir. BBD Liquidation Corp., Redlands, Calif., 1994-99. Sec. Inland Empire Space Group, Riverside, Calif., 1991-93. Decorated Air medal, 1991, Lt. Gen. Bobby Bond Memorial Aviator Awd., 1997, NDIA Air Force Tester of the Year, 1997, Meritorious Svc. Medal, 1998. Mem. AIAA, Soc. Exptl. Test Pilots, Nat. Space Soc. Avocations: rebuilding automobiles, remodeling houses, hockey, scuba diving, bicycling. Office: USAF 33 Flight Test Sq 5656 Texas Ave Fort Dix NJ 08640-5403

DAVIS, SUSANNE MARIE, writer, educator; b. Norwich, Conn., Mar. 3, 1960; d. Andrew Davis and Marguarite (Prevett) Hogan; m. Peter Ralph Kochenlarger, Aug. 16, 1986; two children. BA, U. Conn., 1982; MFA, U. Iowa, 1990. Assoc. news dir. Harvard Law Sch., Cambridge, Mass., 1985-88; English educator Iowa State U., Ames, 1990-92; instr. Wesleyan U., Middletown, Conn., 1993—; instr. U. Hartford, Conn., 1994-96, U. Conn., Storrs, 1997—. Author: Lay Me Down to Sleep, 1995.

DAVIS, TAMMIE LYNETTE, music educator, director; b. Kingsport, Tenn., Jan. 17, 1961; d. James T. and Gertrude (Bridges) D. BS in Music Edn., Tenn. Technol. U., 1983; MEd in Ednl. Leadership, East Tenn. State U., 1992. Cert. tchr., Tenn. Chorus and orchestra director John Sevier Mid. Sch., Kingsport, 1983—; chmn. dept. fine arts John Sevier Mid. Sch., 1987, 91-93, chmn. adv. bd., 1991-93; participant Music Educators Nat. Conf., 1981—, Tenn. Arts Acad., 1993. Violist Kingsport Symphony Orch., 1979-89, 92-94, bd. dirs., 1987-89; violist Johnson City Symphony Orch., 1995—; mem. (hammered dulcimer folk group) Wire Kwire, Kingsport, 1986—. Designated Career Ladder Tchr. II, State of Tenn., 1992; named one of Outstanding Music Educators, Gov.'s Sch. for Arts, Tenn., 1990. Mem. NEA, ASCD, Tenn. Edn. Assn., Nat. Sch. Orch. Assn., Am. Choral Dirs. Assn., Am. String Tchrs. Assn., East Tenn. Vocal Assn., East Tenn. Sch. Band and Orch. Assn. (orch. chmn. 1992-94), Kingsport Edn. Assn. (treas. 1992-94, pres.-elect 1994-95, pres. 1995-96), Nat. Assn. for Preservation and Perpetuation of Storytelling, Tenn. Assn. for Preservation and Perpetuation of Storytelling, Bays Mountain Dulcimer Soc. (pres. 1988-90). Avocations: collecting figurines, reading, writing, performing folk music, flea marketing. Home: 2021 Pendragon Rd Kingsport TN 37660-3432 Office: John Sevier Mid Sch 1200 Wateree St Kingsport TN 37660-4550

DAVIS, TERESA AGNES, school psychologist, educator; b. New Bedford, Mass., July 28, 1933; d. Robert George and Theresa Agnes (Gurl) McMillan; m. William J. Davis, June 29, 1957; children: Theresa, William, James, Kathleen, Robert, John, Jacqueline. AB, Marquette U., 1955; MEd, Boston Coll., 1958; EdD, Boston U., 1978. Cert. sch. psychologist, Mass.; lic. ednl. psychologist, Mass. Tchr. English Westwood (Mass.) Pub. Schs., 1955-58; sch. psychologist Walpole (Mass.) Pub. Schs., 1978-85, Natick (Mass.) Pub. Schs., 1985—; rsch. asst. prof. Boston U., 1978-85; clin. asst. prof. Northeastern U., Boston, 1994—; mem. Ctr. Sch. Integrated Svcs. Harvard U., Cambridge, Mass.; mem. adv. bd. Comprehensive Health Grants, Natick. Contbr. articles to profl. jours. Mem. Nat. Assn. Sch. Psychologists (Mass. del. 1993—, co-chair child and profession com.), Mass. Sch. Psychologist Assn. (pres. 1992-94, Cert. Appreciation 1994, Sch. Psychologist Yr. 1995). Democrat. Roman Catholic. Home: 9 Drake Cir Apt 3 Walpole MA 02081-4316 Office: Natick High Sch 15 West St Natick MA 01760-4396

DAVIS, TERRELL, football player; b. San Diego, Oct. 28, 1972. Student, Long Beach State U., U. Ga. Running back Denver Broncos; player AFC Championship Game, 1997, Super Bowl, 1997, Pro Bowl, 1996, 97. Named Sprotng News NFL-Pro Team Running Back, 1996, 97. Office: Denver Broncos 13655 Broncos Pkwy Englewood CO 80112-4150*

DAVIS, TERRY L., historical association executive; b. Kokomo, Ind., Mar. 28, 1953. BA, Ind. Wesleyan U., 1990, MBA, 1992. Cert. Nat. Soc. Fundraising Execs. Dir. bus. and institutional advancement Ind. Humanities Coun., 1994; exec. dir., CEO, Am. Assn. State and Local History, Nashville, 1994—; presenter in field; mem. faculty Seminar for Hist. Adminstrn., Colonia Williamsburg. Bd. dirs. Habitat for Humanity, mem. nom. com.; active Shipp's Bend United Meth. Ch. Avocations: auto racing, motorcycle riding, hunting, fishing. Fax: 615-255-2979. Office: AASLH 1717 Church St Nashville TN 37203-2921*

DAVIS, THOMAS EDWARD, prosecutor; b. Canton, Ill., Nov. 7, 1954; s. Roger Verne and Marilyn Joann (Dabney) D.; m. Noreen O'Brien, July 14, 1984; children: Dylan, Connor, Owen. BA in Philosophy, U. Tenn., 1976; JD, Rutgers U., 1979. Bar: Ill. 1979. Asst. state's atty. McLean County State's Atty., Bloomington, Ill., 1979-84; enforcement atty. Ill. EPA, Springfield, 1984-88; asst. atty. gen. Ill. Atty. Gen., Springfield, 1988-90, bur. chief, 1990—. Active McLean County Crimestoppers, Bloomington, Ill., 1984. Mem. Midwest Environ. Enforcement Assn. (chairperson 1997). Avocation: soccer. Home: 711 W Fayette Ave Springfield IL 62704-2709 Office: Ill Atty Gen 500 S 2nd St Springfield IL 62701-1705

DAVIS, THOMAS HENRY, airline executive; b. Winston-Salem, N.C., Mar. 15, 1918; s. Egbert L. and Annie (Shore) D.; m. Nancy Carolyn Teague, Oct. 28, 1944; children: Thomas Henry, Winifred (Mrs. Blackwell Bennett Pierce), George Franklin, Nancy (Mrs. Nancy McGloughlin), Juliana Davis (Mrs. Steven West). Student, U. Ariz., 1935-39; LL.D. (hon.), Wake Forest U., 1984. Aircraft salesman Piedmont Aviation, Inc., Winston-Salem, 1940; v.p., treas. Piedmont Aviation, Inc., 1941-43, pres., treas., 1943-81, chmn. bd., chief exec. officer, treas., 1981-83, chmn. exec. com., 1983-88; bd. dirs. Brendles, Inc.; dir. emeritus Wachovia Corp., Duke Power Co., ALLTEL Corp., USAir, Inc. ;mem. Winston-Salem Redevel. Commn., Utilities Commn., 1955-75. Trustee Wake Forest U. Recipient Winston-Salem-Forsyth County. of C. Disting. Service award, 1954, Frank Dawson trophy for outstanding service to aviation in N.C., 1949; U. Ariz. Alumni Achievement award, 1976; Tony Jannus award for service to air transp. industry, 1980; William R. Ong Meml. award for meritorious svc. to gen. aviation industry Nat. Air Transportation Assn., 1993; named to Va. Aviation Hall of Fame, 1980; Disting. Service award N.C. Citizens Assn., 1983; Daniel Guggenheim medal, 1984, Achievement award Aero Club Washington, 1983, Aviation Trail Blazer award Dayton, Ohio C. of C., 1983; Thomas H. Davis fellowship in pulmonary medicine established by Am. Lung Assn., 1985; named to N.C. Bus. Hall of Fame, 1988; named Citizen of the Carolinas. Mem. Soaring Soc. Am., Newcomen Soc., Winston-Salem C. of C. (past pres., Disting. Community Service award 1986), Pi Kappa Alpha (Order of West Range). Democrat. Baptist. Clubs: Rotary, Forsyth Country, Old Town (Winston-Salem); Wings (N.Y.C., Disting. Achievement award 1989); Skyline Country (Tucson). Home: 1190 Arbor Rd Winston Salem NC 27104-1104 Office: Smith Reynolds Airport PO Box 2720 Winston Salem NC 27102-2720 *Never depend on someone else to do for you what you can and should do for yourself.*

DAVIS, THOMAS HILL, JR., lawyer; b. Raleigh, N.C., June 11, 1951; s. Thomas Hill and Margie Wayne (Perry) D.; m. Julia Dee Wilson, May 31, 1980; children: Thomas Hill III, Alexander Erwin, Julia Hadley, Hunter McDowell. BA, N.C. State U., 1973; JD, Wake Forest U., 1976. Bar: N.C. 1976, U.S. Dist. Ct. (ea. and middle dist.) N.C. 1976, U.S. Ct. Appeals (11th cir.) 1982, U.S. Ct. Appeals (4th cir.) 1986, U.S. Supreme Ct. 1979. Reporter Winston-Salem (N.C.) Jour., 1974-76; asst. atty. N.C. Dept. Justice, Raleigh, 1976-88; gen. ptnr. Poyner & Spruill, Raleigh, 1988—; arbitrator Am. Arbitration Assn., Charlotte, N.C., 1990—; lectr. Campbell U. Sch. Law, Buies Creek, N.C., 1992. Supplement editor: Construction Litigation, 1992; contbg. author: Public & Private Contracting in North Carolina, 1985, North Carolina Adminstrative Law, 1996; contbr. articles to profl. jours. Mem. N.C. R.R. Legis. Study Commn., Raleigh, 1985-87; legal counsel N.C. Aeronautics Coun., Raleigh, 1981-88. Capt. N.C. State Def. Militia, 1993—. Mem. N.C. Bar Assn. (Appreciation award 1989), Wake County Bar Assn. (VLP award 1995), North Hills Club, Lions. Democrat. Presbyterian. Avocations: fly fishing, wing shooting, photography, tennis. Home: 608 Blenheim Pl Raleigh NC 27612-4943 Office: Poyner & Spruill 3600 Glenwood Ave Raleigh NC 27612-4945

DAVIS, THOMAS M., III, congressman; b. Minot, N.D., Jan. 5, 1949; m. Peggy Davis; 3 children. BA in Polit. Sci., Amherst Coll., 1971; JD, U. Va., 1975. Page U.S. Senate, 1964-67; pvt. practice, 1975-79; v.p., gen. counsel Advanced Techs., 1979-90; mem. Mason Dist., 1979-91; chmn. Fairfax County Bd. Suprs., 1992-94; gen. counsel PRC, Inc., 1990-94; mem. 104th-106th Congress from 11th Va. dist., 1995—; mem. govt. reform and oversight com., govt. mgmt. com. Republican. Office: US House Reps 224 Cannon Washington DC 20515-4311

DAVIS, THOMAS PHILIP, investment banker; b. Sussex, N.J., Mar. 23, 1953; s. Thomas Hobart and Josephine (Gurka) D. BS, Villanova U., 1975; MPA, Columbia U., 1985. Asst. project mgr. N.Y. State Divsn. Housing, N.Y.C., 1984-88; pub. fin. investment banker Monarch Fin. Corp., N.Y.C., 1988-95, J.B. Hanauer & Co., Parsippany, N.J., 1995-97; mgmt. cons., CEO Euest Enterprises, Sussex, N.J., 1997—. Author rsch. papers in field. Mem. staff Garrett for Congress, Newton, N.J., 1998; hering officer Keogh-Dwyer Correctional Facility, Newton, 1998. Rsch. fellow U. Va., 1983. Mem. ASPA, Sierra Club. Roman Catholic. Avocations: long distance running, hiking, contemporary jazz, landscaping, writing. E-mail: aries@garden.net. Home and Office: 63 Walnut St Sussex NJ 07461

DAVIS, THOMAS PINKNEY, secondary school educator; b. Seminole, Okla., Oct. 10, 1956; s. George Pinkney and Flora Elizabeth (Bollinger) D.; m. Leslie Anne Workman, Jan. 26, 1990; children: Brianna Elizabeth, Mary Katherine, James Pinkney, Robert McKenzie; stepchildren: Christopher Lee, Jennifer Dawn, Matthew Joseph, Daniel Jacob, Joshua Issiac Beene. BS with Honors, East Cen. U., Ada, Okla., 1979, BA with Honors, 1979. Dir. math. lab. East Cen. U., 1991-92; tchr., chair math. dept. Roosevelt (Okla.) High Sch., 1992-93; tchr. math., chair math. dept. Keota (Okla.) High Sch., 1993—; book reviewer Jour. Assn. of Lunar and Planetary Observers/The Strolling Astronomer; adj. instr. Connors State Coll., 1998—. Reviewer Sci. Books and Films, 1986—. Fellow Brit. Interplanetary Soc., Soc. Antiquaries of Scotland; mem. AIAA, Am. Astronautical Soc., Assn. Lunar and Planetary Observers, Nat. Coun. Tchrs. Math., Okla. Coun. Tchrs. Math., Okla. Acad. Sci., Alpha Chi, Pi Gamma Mu. Republican. Episcopalian. Home: RR 2 Box 4117 Stigler OK 74462-9633 Office: Keota High Sch PO Box 160 Keota OK 74941-0160

DAVIS, THOMAS WILLIAM, computer company executive; b. Belvidere, Ill., Mar. 14, 1946; s. Thomas William and Charlotte Ann (Schildgen) D.; m. Lyndel Etta Schuettpelz, Apr. 3, 1971; 1 child, Bryan William. BSEE, Milw. Sch. Engring., 1968; MSEE, U. Wis., Milw., 1971. Registered profl. engr., Wis. From asst. prof. to assoc. prof. elec. engring. Milw. Sch. Engring., 1971-75, head computer engring. tech., 1975-77, prof. 1976-94, chmn. dept. elec. engring., 1977-84, dean rsch., 1981-84, dean acads. and rsch., 1984-87, v.p. academics, dean faculty, 1987-89, sr. v.p. 1989-94; exec. v.p. Super Steel Products Corp., Milw., 1994-96, sr. v.p., 1996-98; pres. Milw. Rehab. Ctr., 1997—; pres. Prophet Tech. LLC, 1998—; lectr. U. Wis., Milw., 1973-76. Author: Problems in Measurements, 1968, (textbooks) Computer Aided Analysis, 1973, Introduction to Interactive Programs, 1978, Experimentation with Microprocessor Applications, 1981; patentee in field. Warning and communications officer Ozaukee County Emergency Govt., Wis., 1981-82; sgt. reserves Grafton Police Dept., Wis., 1976—; corp. mem. svcs. Curative Rehab. Ctr, Gov.'s Quality Improvement Task Force, Gov.'s Sci. and Tech. Coun.; bd. dirs. Jordan Controls, Inc., Jagemann Stamping, Mechanical Industries Inc., Amalga Composites Co, Curative Rehab. Svcs., Inc., Resolute Sys., Inc.; past pres. Milw. Coun. Engring. and Sci. Socs., MSOE Alumni Assn., Inc. Mem. IEEE (sr., student activity dir. 1972-73), Engrs. and Scis. Milw. (past pres.), Robotics Internat., Soc. Mfg. Engrs. (sr.), Am. Soc. Engring. Edn. (membership policies com.), Milw. Sch. Engring. Alumni Assn. (achievement award 1968, 25th ann. Outstanding Alumnus award 1993, pres. 1997-98), UWM Alumni Assn. (outstanding alumnus award 1995), Wis. Soc. Profl. Engrs. (past pres. Milw. chpt.), Phi Kappa Phi, Tau Alpha Pi, Eta Kappa Nu. Avocation: flying, amateur radio. Home: 5590 Gray Log Ct Grafton WI 53024-9622 Office: Prophet Technologies 1550 N Prospect Ave Milwaukee WI 53202-6501

DAVIS, THURMAN M., federal agency administrator. BArch, Hampton U.; grad., Army Engr. Sch., Fed. Exec. Inst. Intern U.S. Gen. Svcs. Adminstrn., 1963, asst. regional adminstr. Mid-Atlantic region; acting regional adminstr. Mid-Atlantic region U.S. Gen. Svcs. Adminstrn., Phila.; regional adminstr. Nat. Capital region U.S. Gen. Svcs. Adminstrn., dep. adminstr., 1995—; participant Pres. Exec. Exch. Program, 1973; with Dalton, Dalton, Little, Newport. Recipient Richard Allen award Bethel African Meth. Episcopal Ch., Bryn Mawr, Pa. Mem. ASPA, Sr. Execs. Assn., Conf. Minority Pub. Adminstrs., Nat. Forum Black Pub. Adminstrs., Federally Employed Women and Blacks in Govt., 100 Black Men Greater Washington, Alpha Phi Alpha (life). Office: US Gen Svcs Adminstrn 18th & F Sts NW Washington DC 20405

DAVIS, TROY ARNOL, reflexologist, hypnotherapist; b. Quitman, Tex., Apr. 5, 1921. Student, Am. Inst. Reflexology, Am. Inst. Med. Hypnoanalysts. Cert. reflexologist; cert. hypnotherapist. Practice reflexology and hypnotherapy, Karnes City, Tex. Contbr. articles to profl. publs.; songwriter, poet. Served with USN, WWII. Recipient Presdl. medal of merit, Presdl. Task Force. Mem. Internat. Soc. Poets. Home: PO Box 295 Karnes City TX 78118-0295

DAVIS, VALERIE JEANNE, physical education educator; b. Killeen, Tex., June 2, 1959; d. Larry M. and Phyllis Ann (Etzler) D. BA, Coll. of Mt. St. Joseph, 1981; MA, No. Ky. U., 1986. Program organizer Van Wert (Ohio) City Parks, 1977; phys. edn. instr. Our Lady of Lourdes Sch., Cin., 1981-83; activities coord. Cin. Recreation Commn., 1983; phys. edn./computer edn. instr., varsity volleyball coach Clermont Northeastern Local, Batavia, Ohio, 1983—, tech. dir. primary sch., 1995—; self employed entertainer Sneakers the Clown; IRS tax examiner. Developer/author: (curriculum) Physical Management, 1989. Fundraiser March of Dimes, Cin., 1988-89, Am. Cancer Soc., Cin., 1987, 90; clown of yr. Children's Hosp. Named Top Tax Editor in Nation, IRS, 1980, Clown of Yr., Children's Hosp., 1992. Mem. AAHPERD, Ohio Assn. Health, Phys. Edn., Recreation and Dance, Ohio High Sch. Volleyball Coach's Assn. (state poll voter 1987-91), S.W. High Sch. Volleyball Coach's Assn., Nat. Fedn. Interscholastic Coach's Assn., Funnie Company Clown Assn. Lutheran. Avocations: reading, traveling, boating, sports, clowning. Home: 300 Miami Valley Dr Loveland OH 45140-7541 Office: Clermont Northeastern South Broadway Owensville OH 45160

DAVIS, VENITA PAULA, elementary school educator; b. New Castle, Pa., July 14, 1940; d. Curtis B. and Mable M. (Hughes) D. BA, Spelman Coll., 1972; MS in Edn., Ind. U., Gary, 1981; postgrad., Purdue U., Valparaiso U. Tchr. art Gary Community Sch. Corp., 1972—. Named Outstanding Tchr. of Yr., Aetna Elem. Sch. PTA, 1989; recipient poetry awards. Mem. Am. Fedn. Tchrs. Home: 2570 Jackson St Gary IN 46407-4043 Office: Aetna Elem Sch 1327 Arizona St Rm 111 Gary IN 46403-3642

DAVIS, VERA, elementary school educator; b. Cornish, N.H., Sept. 16, 1940; d. Francis Edward and Alice Cone (Parkhurst) Williams; m. John T. Davis, July 3, 1968; 1 child, William Guy. BS, Castleton (Vt.) State Coll., 1962; M in Reading, Coll. St. Joseph, Rutland, Vt., 1992. Cert. tchr. Tchr. 2d grade Town of Cavendish, Proctorsville, Vt., Title I tchr., 1996—. Mem. NEA, Vt. Edn. Assn. Home: 66 Main St Ludlow VT 05149-1113

DAVIS, VINCENT, political science educator; b. Chattanooga, May 3, 1930; married; 3 children. B.A., Vanderbilt U., 1952; M.P.A., Woodrow Wilson Sch., Princeton U., 1959, M.A., 1960, Ph.D., 1961. Mem. faculty dept. politics, research asst. Center Internat. Studies, Princeton U., 1959-61, vis. research prof., 1969-70; mem. faculty Dartmouth Coll., 1961-62; mem. faculty Grad. Sch. Internat. Studies, research asso. Social Sci. Found. U. Denver, 1962-71; Patterson prof. internat. studies U. Ky., Lexington, 1971-98, dir. Patterson Sch. Diplomacy and Internat. Commerce, 1971-93; Nimitz prof. polit. sci. U.S. Naval War Coll., 1970-71; prof. emeritus U. Ky., Lexington, 1998—; exec. coun. Inter-Univ. Seminar Armed Forces and Soc., U. Chgo., 1972-79; chmn. civilian adv. panel Sec. Def. Com. Excellence in Mil. Edn., 1974-76; cons., lectr. in field; mem. internat. affairs fellowships com. Coun. on Fgn. Rels., N.Y.C., 1980—; adj. fellow Ctr. Strategic and Internat. Studies, Washington, 1992—; speaker NATO Conf. on Post-Soviet States of Eastern and Cen. Europe, Oslo, 1992; mem. Sec. State's Adv. Bd. on Hist. Archives and Documentation; bd. dirs. UN Assn. U.S.A., Rep. Nat. Policy Forum. Author: Postwar Defense Policy and the U.S. Navy, 1943-46, 1966, The Admirals Lobby, 1967, The Politics of Innovation, 1967, The Analysis of International Politics, 1971, Henry Kissinger and Bureaucratic Politics: A Personal Appraisal, 1979, The Post-Imperial Presidency, 1980; co-author, co-editor: Reorganizing America's Defense, 1985; also monographs, spl. reports; editor: Sage Papers in Internat. Studies, 1971-77; contbr. to profl. jours., encys. Served with USN, 1952-56; capt. Res. ret. Mem. Internat. Studies Assn. (exec. dir. 1964-71, chmn. intensive panels 1972-74, pres. 1976-77), Am. Polit. Sci. Assn., Internat. Inst. Strategic Studies. Home: 3533 Gloucester Dr Westmorland Lexington KY 40510-9758 Office: U Ky Patterson Sch Diplomacy and Intl Commerce 455 Patterson Office Tower Lexington KY 40506-0027 *Young people coming of age in the 1990's are entering adulthood in a nation and world with rapidly shifting political-economic relationships dramatically different from anything we have known before. Trying to help students figure out the exact meaning of these shifts, and how to cope with them in their own professional and personal lives, is the central challenge to me for the remainder of my career as we enter the new millennium.*

DAVIS, W. JEREMY, dean, law educator, lawyer; b. Pitts., Apr. 13, 1942; s. Winthrop Neuffer and Eleanor (Power) D.; m. Jacqueline Dvoracek, June 11, 1966; children: Jeremy Michael, Sarah Elizabeth. BSBA, U. Denver, 1964, JD, 1970; LLM, Yale U., 1980. Bar: Colo. 1970, N.D. 1973. Pvt. practice law Denver, 1970-71; asst. prof. U. N.D., Grand Forks, 1971-74, assoc. prof., 1975-82, dean, prof. law, 1983—, gen. counsel, 1993—. With U.S. Army, 1965-68. Fellow Bush Found., 1979-80. Mem. State Bar Assn. N.D. (bd. govs. 1982—), N.D. Trial Lawyers Assn. (bd. govs. 1986—). Home: 131 Conklin Ave Grand Forks ND 58203-1622 Office: U ND Sch Law PO Box 9003 Grand Forks ND 58202-9003

DAVIS, WALTER BARRY, quality assurance professional; b. New London, Conn., July 10, 1942; s. Luna Alonzo and Mary Elizabeth (Shell) D.; children: Alexandria Elizabeth, Cody Ashton Samuel; m. Carol Michael Fairchild, Nov. 24, 1984. Student, U. Utah, 1959-60; BS in Physics, U.S. Naval Acad., 1964; MA in Bus., Cen. Mich. U., 1978. Cert. nuclear plant operator, nuclear weapons mgr., quality auditor. Commd. ensign USN, 1964, advanced through grades to comdr., 1978; exec. officer Nuclear Submarine Repair Ship, Kings Bay, Ga., 1981-83; dep. head missile br. Strategic Systems Program Office, Washington, 1983-85; ret., 1985; program mgr. missile chaff Tracor Aerospace, Austin, Tex., 1985-86, dir. mfg. strategic Counter Measures, 1986-89, program mgr. indsl. modernization, 1989-92, mgr. employee programs, 1991-92; program mgr. supplier quality Intertek Svcs., Fairfax, Va., 1992-95; divsn. mgr. supplier quality Harris Farinon, San Antonio, Tex., 1995-98; presenter in field. Examiner Am. Radio Relay League, Austin, 1990-92. Mem. AIAA, Am. Soc. Quality Control, Assn. for Mfg. Excellence, Soc. for Mfg. Engrs. Home: 401 Meadow Creek Dr Pflugerville TX 78660-2844 Office: Harris Farinon 5727 Farinon Dr San Antonio TX 78249-3410 *Died Aug. 21, 1998.*

DAVIS, WALTER STEWART, lawyer; b. Evanston, Ill., Mar. 31, 1924; s. Walter Stewart Sr. and Nina Louise (Nixon) D.; m. Betty May Grede, Apr. 19, 1947; children: Walter Stewart III, Susan L. Davis Daigneau, Thomas W., Judith A., Davis Pequet, Robert J. BS, Northwestern U., Evanston, 1947; JD, Northwestern U., Chgo., 1950. Bar: Ill. 1950, Wis. 1953, U.S. Ct. Appeals (2nd, 6th, 7th and D.C. cirs.), U.S. Supreme Ct. 1964. Gen. atty. Butler Bros., Chgo., 1950-51; sr. ptnr. Davis & Kuelthau, Milw., 1952—; gen. counsel Grede Foundries, Inc., Milw., 1962—; chmn. bd. dirs. Thomas Industries, Louisville, 1987-95; bd. dirs. Grede Foundries, Milw., Grucon Corp., Milw. Trustee Village of Elm Grove, Wis., 1958-64, George Williams Coll., Downers Grove, 1980-92; bd. dirs. YMCA Met. Milw., 1964-92, Congl. Home, Brookfield, Wis., 1970-80, 87-89. Served to 1st lt. USAF, 1942-45, 51-52, ETO. Decorated Air medal with 2 oak leaf clusters. Mem. Milw. Bar Assn., Wis. Bar Assn., Internat. Bar Assn., Acad. Basic Edn. (bd. dirs. 1962-89), The Milw. Club, Blue Mound Golf and Country Club (bd. dirs., pres. 1974-80). Republican. Congregationalist. Avocations: golf, reading. Office: Davis & Kuelthau 111 E Kilbourn Ave Ste 1400 Milwaukee WI 53202-6613

DAVIS, WAYNE ALTON, computer science educator; b. Ft. Macleod, Alta., Can., Nov. 16, 1931; s. Frederick and Anna Mary (Barr) D.; m. Audrey M. Zorolow, July 17, 1959 (div. 1989); children: Fredrick M., Peter W., Timothy M.; m. Patricia Ruth Syme, Mar. 24, 1990. BSE, George Washington U., 1960; MSc, U. Ottawa, 1963, PhD, 1967. Sci. officer Def. Research Bd., Ottawa, Ont., 1960-68; research scientist Dept. Communications, Ottawa, 1968-69; vis. scientist NRC, Ottawa, 1975-76; assoc. prof. U. Alta., Edmonton, 1969-77, prof. computing sci., 1977-91, prof. emeritus, 1991—, acting chmn. computing sci., 1982-83; acting dir. Alta. Centre for Machine Intelligence and Robotics, 1988-89; lectr. U. Ottawa, 1965-69; sessional lectr. Carleton U., 1967; cons. Editor: The Barrs of Ardenville, 1978; editor Procs. Graphics Interface, 1994, 95, 96, 97, 98. Grantee NRC, 1970-78; research grantee Natural Scis. and Engring. Research Council, 1978-92; strategic grantee Natural Scis. and Engring. Research Council, 1981-83; grantee Def. Research Bd., 1974-76; hon. prof. Harbin Shipbldg. Engring. Inst., People's Republic of China, 1985. Mem. Can. Info. Processing Soc. (pres. 1978-79), Can. Human Computer Comms. Soc. (pres. 1981-96), Can. Soc. Computational Study of Intelligence (treas. 1976-86), IEEE, ACM. Anglican. Clubs: Faculty, Canadian Legion, Rotary. Home: Box 817 605-21st St, Fort Macleod, AB Canada T0L 0Z0 Office: U Alta, Dept Computing Sci, Edmonton, AB Canada T6G 2H1

DAVIS, WAYNE KAY, university dean, educator; b. Findlay, Ohio, Mar. 23, 1946; s. Albert Wayne and Freida Evelyn (Winkle) D.; m. Patricia Ann Krimmer, May 26, 1967; 1 child, J Brandon. B.A., Central Bible Coll., 1967; M.A., U. Mich., 1969, Ph.D., 1971. Research scientist Ctr. Research Learning and Teaching, Ann Arbor, Mich., 1971-73; asst. prof. U. Mich. Med. Sch., Ann Arbor, 1973-77, assoc. dir. edn. resources and research, 1976-78, assoc. prof., 1977-82, dir. edn. resources and rsch., 1978-98, prof., 1982—, asst. dean, 1982-86, assoc. dean, 1991-98; adv. mem. ad hoc study sect. Nat. Heart, Lung and Blood Inst., NIH, Bethesda, Md., mem. site visit team Nat. Inst. Arthritis, Metabolic and Digestive Diseases, NIH, Bethesda, 1978-91; cons. Multipurpose Arthritis Ctr., NIH, Bethesda, 1981-83; vis. scholar U. Calif. Med. Sch., San Diego, 1984-85. Author: A Guide to MTS and Remote Terminal Operation, 1972; mem. edit. bd. Diabetes Care, 1983-86; assoc. editor Acad. Medicine, 1988-89; contbr. chpts. and articles to med. jours. Bd. dirs. Washtenaw County unit Mich. Heart Assn., 1977-79. Recipient Best Article 1982 award Assn. Diabetes Educators. Mem. Am. Ednl. Research Assn. (program chmn. div. I, v.p. 1985-87), Assn. Am. Med. Colls. (nat. chair group on ednl. affairs 1994-95), Am. Diabetes Assn., Soc. Dirs. Rsch. in Med. Edn. (pres. 1990-91, 93-94), Phi Delta Kappa, Gt. Lakes Cruising Club, Seven Seas Cruising Assn. Office: U Mich Dept Med End G1215 Towsley Centre 1515 Hospital Dr Ann Arbor MI 48109-0624*

DAVIS, WENDELL, JR., lawyer; b. N.Y.C., June 22, 1933; m. Penelope Case, May 17, 1969; children: Jennifer C., Virginia W., Peter T. A.B. cum laude, Harvard U., 1954, LL.B. cum laude, 1961. Bar: Conn. 1961, N.Y. 1963, U.S. Dist. Ct. (so. and ea. dist.) N.Y. 1964, U.S. Dist. Ct. Conn. 1966, U.S. Ct. Appeals (2d cir.) 1966, U.S Ct. Appeals (5th cir.) 1972, U.S. Supreme Ct. 1973. Law sec. to Justice Charles D. Breitel, N.Y.C., 1964-65; ptnr. Scheuermann & Davis and predecessor firms, N.Y.C., 1975-78, 92—, Emmet, Marvin & Martin, N.Y.C., 1978-91; Pres. Carnegie Hill-90th St. Inc., 1977-80. Bd. dirs. United Way Larchmont, 1984-91, chmn. 1989. Lt. USNR, 1957. Mem. Am. Law Inst., Assn. Bar City N.Y., Harvard Club, Univ. Club Larchmont (gov. 1991-94, pres. 1993-94). Home: 28 Huguenot Dr Larchmont NY 10538-1935 Office: Scheuermann and Davis Ste 500 One State St Pla New York NY 10004

DAVIS, WILLIAM ALBERT, theme park director; b. New Haven, Sept. 10, 1946; s. Arthur Wilson Davis and Dorothy May (Hellyer) Jordan; m. Rebecca Marsden Haile, Apr. 8, 1965; children: William Albert Jr., Anna Catherine. BA in Profl. Arts, Brooks Inst. Photography, 1971; BSBA, San Diego State U., 1980. Photographer, owner Davis-Hixon Photography, Santa Ana, Calif., 1971-73; photographer Sea World, Inc., San Diego, 1973, sales rep., 1974-76, sales mgr., 1976-78, mktg. mgr. fast food subs., 1978-80, corp. planning assoc., 1980-81; dir. mktg. Sea World Ohio, Aurora, 1981-85, v.p. mktg., 1985-86, pres., 1986-88; pres. Sea World Fla., Orlando, 1988-97; exec. v.p., gen. mgr. Sea World of Calif., 1997—; bd. dirs. Hubbs-Sea World Rsch. Inst., San Diego, Marine Rsch. Ctr., Sea World, Orlando, Calif. Travel and Tourism Commn. Bd. dirs., exec. com. Conv. and Visitors Bur. Orange County, Orlando, 1988-97, pres.-elect, 1990, pres., 1991, chmn., 1992-93; mem. bd. Efficient Transp. for Community Orlando, 1988-97; mem. adv. coun. Dick Pope Sr. Inst. Tourism Studies, Orlando, 1989-97; commr. Fla. Tourism Commn., 1991—; trustee United Arts of Ctrl. Fla., 1992—; mem. U. Ctrl. Fla. Found., 1994-97; mem. White House Com. on Tourism, 1995, mem. exec. com. San Diego Conv. and Visitors Bur., 1997—, Super Bowl XXXII Host com. Staff sgt. USAF, 1965-69, Vietnam. Fellow Am. Assn. Zool. Parks and Aquariums; mem. San Diego C. of C. Roundtable, Brooks Inst. Alumni Assn., Kiwanis (bd. dirs. Aurora club 1985-87, 1st v.p. 1987—). Avocations: golf, photography, family. Office: Sea World Calif 500 Seaworld Dr San Diego CA 92109*

DAVIS, WILLIAM ALLISON, II, lawyer; b. High Point, N.C., May 2, 1942; s. Robert Dorsey and Frances Elizabeth (Taylor) D.; m. Elizabeth Gray Heefner, June 18, 1966; children: Sarah Scott, Elizabeth Taylor. AB in Econs., U. N.C., 1964; LLB, Duke U., 1967; LLM in Taxation, NYU, 1968. Bar: N.C. 1967. Assoc. Womble Carlyle Sandridge & Rice, Winston-Salem, N.C., 1968-72, ptnr., 1972—. Trustee N.C. Sch. Arts, Winston-Salem, vice chmn., 1990, chmn., 1992-96; chmn. N.C. Film Coun., 1994-96; chmn. Winston-Salem Piedmont Triad Film Commn., 1993-96; trustee The Penland (N.C.) Sch., 1998—. Mem. Winston-Salem C. of C. (chmn. 1991). Democrat. Presbyterian. Avocations: hiking, skiing, traveling, fishing. Office: Womble Carlyle Sandridge & Rice PO Drawer 84 1600 One Triad Park Winston Salem NC 27101-3828*

DAVIS, WILLIAM ARTHUR, writer, editor; b. Boston, Dec. 13, 1932; s. Martin Patrick and Elizabeth Agnes (McMahon) D.; m. Christina Marie Tree, Sept. 2, 1972; children: Liam Christopher, Timothy Alfred, Christopher John. BS in Journalism, Boston U., 1995. Reporter Biddeford (Maine)-Saco Jour., 1958-59, Gardner (Mass.) News, 1960-62; reporter, feature writer Worcester (Mass.) Telegram, 1962-66, Boston Herald, 1966-67; reporter Salem (Mass.) Evening News, 1967; writer Boston Globe, 1967-70, travel editor, travel writer, 1970-90, lifestyle and travel writer, 1990—. Author: Berlitz Guide to Helsinki, 1980; co-author: The Kennedy Library, 1981, Massachusetts: An Explorer's Guide, 1998. With U.S. Army, 1953-56. Recipient Econ. Impact award Travel Industry Am., 1983, La Pluma DePlata, Govt. of Mex., 1985, 90. Mem. Soc. Am. Travel Writers (bd. dirs. 1973-77, chmn. editor's coun. 1984-86, Lowell Thomas award 1988, 90), Harvard Travellers Club. Democrat. Roman Catholic. Avocations: snow shoeing, walking, book collecting. Home: 15 Whittier St Cambridge MA 02140-2611 Office: Boston Globe 135 Morrissey Blvd Boston MA 02107-2378

DAVIS, WILLIAM E., utility executive. With Niagara Mohawk, chmn., CEO, 1993—. Office: Niagara Mohawk 300 Erie Blvd W Syracuse NY 13202-4250

DAVIS, WILLIAM EUGENE, federal judge; b. Winfield, Ala., Aug. 18, 1936; s. A.L. and Addie Lee (Lenahan) D.; m. Celia Chalaron, Oct. 3, 1963. J.D., Tulane U., 1960. Bar: La. 1960. Assoc. Phelps Dunbar Marks Claverie & Sims, New Orleans, 1960-64; ptnr. Caffery Duhe & Davis, New Iberia, La., 1964-76; judge U.S. Dist. Ct., Lafayette, La., 1976-83, U.S. Ct. Appeals (5th Cir.), Lafayette, 1983—. Mem. ABA, La. Bar Assn., Maritime Assn. U.S. Republican. Office: US Ct Appeals Ste 500 800 lafayette St Lafayette LA 70501-6945

DAVIS, WILLIAM GRENVILLE, lawyer, former Canadian government official; b. Brampton, Ont., Can., July 30, 1929; s. Albert Grenville and Vera M. (Hewetson) D.; m. Helen MacPhee, 1953 (dec. 1962); children—Neil, Nancy, Catherine, Ian; m. Kathleen Mackay, 1963; 1 dau., Meg. BA, U. Toronto, 1951; grad., Osgoode Hall Law Sch., 1954; LLD (hon.), Waterloo Luth. U., 1963, Western Ont. U., 1965, U. Toronto, 1967, McMaster U., 1968, Queen's U., 1968, Windsor U., 1969; DU (hon.), Ottawa U., 1980; LHD (hon.), Yeshiva U., N.Y., Nat. U. of Ireland, U. Tel Aviv. Bar: Ont. 1955. Ptnr. Davis, Webb and Hollinrake, Brampton, 1955-59; mem. Provincial Parliament Ont. from Peel Riding, 1959, 63; mem. Peel North Riding, 1967, 71, Brampton Riding, 1975; 2d vice-chmn. Hydro-Electric Power Commn. of Ont., 1961-62; minister of edn. Province of Ont., 1962-71, also minister of univ. affairs, 1964-71, premier, 1971-85; apptd. spl. envoy on acid rain by prime minister of Can., 1985-86; of counsel Tory Tory DesLauriers & Binnington, Toronto, 1986—; apptd. mem. Privy Coun. Queen Elizabeth II, 1982—; adv. com. Ford Motor Co. Can. Ltd.; bd. dirs. Corel Corp., Algoma Steel Corp., First Am. Title Ins. Co., Internat. Comfort Products Corp., Magna Internat., Inc., NIKE Can. Ltd., Power Corp. Can., Seagram Co. Ltd., Can. Imperial Bank Commerce, Magellan Aerospace Corp., St. Lawrence Cement, First Am. Title Co., Dylex Ltd. Author: Education in Ontario, 1965, Building an Educated Society, 1816-1966, 1966, other publs. Leader Progressive Conservative Party, 1975-81. Recipient Order of Ont. award; named Companion, Order of Can. Mem. Can. Bar Assn., Ont. Bar Assn., Albany Club (Toronto), Kiwanis, Masons. Mem. United Ch. Office: Tory Tory DesLauriers Binnington, PO Box 270 Aetna Tower Ste 3000, Toronto, ON Canada M5K 1N2*

DAVIS, WILLIAM HOWARD, lawyer; b. Monmouth, Ill., May 24, 1951; s. Orville Francis and Alice Gertrude (Hennenfent) D.; m. Susan Claire Parris, April 11, 1981; children: Benjamin Patrick, Jackson Mitchell, Claire Marie. BA with honors, U. South Fla., 1974; JD with high honors, Fla. State U., 1977. Bar: Fla. 1977, U.S. Dist. Ct. (no. dist.) Fla. 1977, U.S. Dist. Ct. (mid. dist.) Fla. 1986, U.S. Ct. Appeals (11th cir.) 1986, U.S. Supreme Ct. 1993. Assoc. Thompson, Wadsworth, Messer & Rhodes, Tallahassee, 1977-80; ptnr. Wadsworth & Davis, P.A., Tallahassee, 1980—; instr. law Fla. State U., 1976-77. Editor notes and comments Fla. State U. Law Rev., 1976-77. Bd. dirs. Legal Aid Found., Inc., 1980-81, Fla. Legal Svcs., Inc., 1988-96, pres., 1993; pres. student govt., chmn., state coun. student body pres. State U. Sys. Fla., 1973-74. Mem. Acad. Fla. Trial Lawyers, Fla. Bar Assn. (2d cir. judge nominations commn. 1986-90, chmn. 2d cir. jud. grievance com. 1988-90), Fla. Bar Found. (bd. dirs. 1993-94, 97—, legal assistance to poor grant com. 1993—, exec. com. 1998—), Tallahassee Bar Assn. (bd. dirs. 1982-88, pres. 1986-87), Fla. Assn. Criminal Def. Lawyers, Am. Inns of Ct. (master of bench emeritus, exec. com. Tallahassee 1994—), Cath. Charities (bd. dirs. Tallahassee region 1995—, pres. 1999), Gulf Winds Track Club, Capital Tiger Bay Club, Omicron Delta Kappa, Phi Sigma Alpha. Democrat. Home: 914 Mimosa Dr Tallahassee FL 32312-3012 Office: Wadsworth & Davis PA 203 N Gadsden St Ste 1 Tallahassee FL 32301-7633

DAVIS, WILLIAM MAXIE, JR., lawyer; b. Elizabethtown, N.C., June 7, 1932; s. Willie Maxie and Lucy Victoria (Dowless) D.; m. Shirley Jane Smith, Mar. 24, 1987. B. Gen. Edn., U. Nebr., 1965; MA, U. So. Calif., 1970; JD, N.C. Cen. U., 1986. Bar: N.C. 1986, U.S. Dist. Ct. (we., ea. and mid. dists.)

N.C., U.S. Ct. Appeals (4th cir.), U.S. Supreme Ct. 1989. Commd. 2d lt. U.S. Air Force, 1958, advanced through grades to lt. col, 1974, ret., 1975; asst. county mgr., personnel officer, dir. of planning, dir. of emergency mgmt. Bladen County, Elizabethtown, 1976-83; asst. pub. defender N.C. 26th Jud. Dist., Charlotte, 1986—; dir. plans, programs U.K. Comm. Region, Eng., 1967-71; chief systems implementations br. USAF, Hdqrs. SAC, 1971-73; chief career devel., assignments for communications-electronics officers USAF, 1973-75. Pres. Help Every Loving Parent, 1988—; county dir. Boy Scouts Am., Bladen County, N.C., 1976; pres. bd. dirs. Vistana SPA Condo Homeowners Assn., 1992—. Profiled in Champion mag., 1992. Mem. N.C. Bar, N.C. Acad. Trial Lawyers, Elizabethtown-White Lake C. of C. (bd. dirs. 1975-77), Nat. Bd. Trial Advocacy (cert. criminal trial advocacy 1993), Am. Legion, VFW, DAV. Home: PO Box 35006 Charlotte NC 28235-5006 Office: Office Pub Defender 720 E 4th St Charlotte NC 28202-2823

DAVIS, WILLIAM WALTER, recruiter, trainer; b. Pewee Valley, Ky., Jan. 5, 1946; s. B.E. Garvey and Clara Virginia (Gordon) D. BA, U. Louisville, 1967. Vol. cmty. devel. U.S. Peace Corps, Colombia, 1967-69; sr. clk. Man. Rent Rev. Commn., Winnipeg, 1976-78; coord. Man. region Can. Univ. Svcs. Overseas, Winnipeg, 1978-79, nat. bd. dirs., 1979; devel. educator Sask. Cross-Cultural Centre, Inc., Saskatoon, Can., 1979-88; trainer So. Empowerment Project, Inc., Maryville, Tenn., 1988—; mem. Can. Union Pub. Employees, Winnipeg, 1976-78, local 3012, Sask., 1984-85, pres. dist. coun., 1986-87; founding mem. Nat. Organizers Alliance, Washington, 1992. Mem. editl. com. NOA's Ark, 1994-97; columnist Appalachian Reader, 1998—; contbr. articles to profl. jours. Mem. adv. bd. Nat. Coalition Bldg. Inst. East Tenn., 1996-98. Named Ky. Col., 1967; Windcall resident Common Counsel Found., 1998. Avocations: genealogy, gardening. Home: 1525 Barbra Estates Dr Seymour TN 37865-3637 Office: So Empowerment Project Inc 343 Ellis Ave Maryville TN 37804-5824

DAVIS, WYLIE HERMAN, lawyer, educator; b. Macon, Ga., May 26, 1919; s. Wylie Herman and Florine (Burdick) D.; m. June Marie Patterson, Nov. 9, 1957; children: Ann Marie, Neil, John, Alan; children by previous marriage: Louise, June Elizabeth. A.B., Mercer U., 1940, LL.B. magna cum laude, 1947, J.D., 1947; LL.M., Harvard U., 1948. Bar: Ark. 1953, Ill. 1958, Ga. 1968, U.S. Supreme Ct. 1958, U.S. Ct. Mil. Appeals 1958. Instr. English, Mercer U., 1946; asst. prof. law U. Ark., Fayetteville, 1948-50, assoc. prof., 1950-52, prof., 1952-55, 70-72, disting. prof. law, 1972-89, disting. prof. emeritus, 1989—; dean Law Sch. U. Ark., 1973-78, C.W. Oxford lectr., spring 1985; prof. law U. Tex., 1955-56, U. Ill., 1956-67, U. Ga., 1967-70; of counsel Davis, Cox and Wright, Fayetteville, 1976-88; pvt. practice cons. comml., ins., maritime law and labor arbitration, 1948—; summer research fellow U. Wis., 1962; chmn. drafting com. on contracts multistate bar exam Nat. Conf. Bar Examiners, 1971-96; Earl F. Nelson vis. prof. law U. Mo., Columbia, 1979-80; vis. summer prof. George Washington U., 1952, 64, U. Mich., 1958, U. Utah, 1960, 90, U. N.C., 1968, U. S.C., 1974, U. Ala., 1982, Tex. Tech U., 1983; vis. prof. law McGeorge Sch. Law, U. Pacific, 1988-93, U. N.C., spring 1990; disting. vis. prof. Tex. Wesleyan U. Sch. Law 1993—; faculty mem. Nat. Jud. Coll., Reno, 1989. Contbr. articles to legal jours. Bd. govs. Antaeus Inst., 1973-88. Lt. comdr. USNR, 1940-45, PTO; commd. admiral Tex. Navy, 1995. Recipient cert. of recognition Ark. Bar Assn., 1979. Mem. Ret. Officers Assn., Am. Law Inst., Maritime Law Assn. U.S., Order of Barristers (emeritus), Rotary (pres. 1978-79, Paul Harris fellow 1983—), Order of Coif, Phi Alpha Delta. Home and Office: 580 Crest Dr Fayetteville AR 72701-3716 *Living and working successfully with other people often depends on good guesswork - an acquired ability to intuit the unknowable and unscrew the inscrutable.*

DAVIS, YOLETTE MARIE TOUSSAINT, home nursing administrator, parish nurse, camp nurse; b. Port-au-Prince, Haiti, May 8, 1956; d. Edner Casimir and Ursule (Lamour) Toussaint; children: Jacques Edner, Noelle Lorraine. BSN, Incarnate Word Coll., San Antonio, 1985; cert. flight nurse, Sch. Aerospace Medicine, San Antonio, 1988; cert. in basic critical care, U. Tex., San Antonio, 1989; cert. in battlefield nursing, Sch. Aerospace Medicine, San Antonio, 1989; postgrad., Incarnate Word Coll. RN, N.Y., Calif., Ohio, Fla., Tex.; cert. ACLS, cert. parish nurse, prog. grad., Univ. of The Incarnate Word, 1997, cert. Gerontology Nursing, dir., Nursing Administration in Long Term Care. Staff nurse pediatrics unit Humana Hosp. San Antonio; staff-charge nurse surg. ICU, Humana Hosp. Met., San Antonio; pvt. practice nurse San Antonio; staff nurse Wilford Hall Med. Ctr.; capt. USAFR, 1991; asst. DON Avalon Pl., Alamo Height Health and Rehab. Ctr., San Antonio; DON Pearsall (Tex.) Manor Health & Rehab. Ctr., 1995; asst. dir. nursing, wound care mgr. Silver Creek Manor, San Antonio, Tex., 1995—. Capt. USAF Reserve 433d Contingency Hosp., Wilford Med. Ctr., Tex., vol., Parish Nurse Intern., St. Matthews Catholic Church, 1998, Santa Rosa Hlth. Care Pool, 1998—, Morningside Pvt. Pay Home Health, 1996—, vol. African Amer. Educating for a Cure, and Amer. Cancer Soc. Mem. NAFE, Nat. Assn. Orthopedic Nursing, Women in Bus., Wound Ostomy and Continence Nurses Soc. Home and Office: 6102 Prince Charles San Antonio TX 78240-4990

DAVISH, WILLIAM MARTIN, priest, educator; b. Phila., Feb. 1, 1913; s. William Gilbert and Helen Marie (Kirwan) D. AB, Georgetown U., 1939; PhL, Woodstock (Md.) Coll., 1940, STL, 1947; MLS, Cath. U., 1948; DD (hon.), Loyola Coll., Balt., 1983. Ordained priest Roman Catholic Ch. Asst. prof., libr. Loyola Coll., 1949-52, assoc. dean, 1952-57, 76-83, assoc. prof., head libr., 1957-64, prof., 1964-76, prof. emeritus, libr., 1983-94, copy editor, tutor, 1994—; asst. to pres. Loyola Coll., 1967-76; editl. cons. Fordham U. Quar., N.Y.C., 1980-92. Co-editor: Theology of Creation, 1997; contbr. articles to profl. publs. Recipient Outstanding Tchr. award Nat. Forum Religious Educators, 1976. Mem. ALA, KC. Democrat. Avocations: poetry, playwriting, contract bridge. Office: Loyola Coll 4501 N Charles St Baltimore MD 21210-2601

DAVIS-HARTENSTEIN, SHARON LYNNE, juvenile parole officer, human services program consultant; b. Bowling Green, Ohio, Oct. 20, 1964; d. Keith and Edna Gail (Keeran) Davis; m. Allen Dale Hartenstein, May 6, 1989; children: Kendra and Morgan (twins). AS in Juvenile Advocacy and Intervention, Terra C.C., 1985, AS in Law Enforcement, 1986; cert. in Ohio Peace Officer tng., Owens C.C., Police Acad., 1986. Aux. police officer Elmore (Ohio) Police Dept., 1984-86; juvenile probation officer Ottawa County Juvenile Ct., Port Clinton, Ohio, 1985; childcare worker Parmadale, Parma, Ohio, 1986-87; juvenile parole officer State of Ohio, Dept. Youth Svcs., Toledo, 1987—, edn. and employment cons., 1994—; mem. adv. bd. Toledo Pub. Schs., 1994—, Lucas County Edn. Svc. Ctr., Toledo, 1994—; chmn. Lucas County Local Interagy. Transition Team, Toledo, 1994—; spkr. Northwest Ohio schs., orgns.; creator, coord. Operation Tighten-Up, Toledo, 1999; grantwriter, 1994—. Vol. United Way, Toledo, 1995-97, United Health Svcs., Toledo, 1997; tchr. Bible sch., Bethel United Bretheren Ch., 1983-90; tchr. Bible sch., mem. youth growth-enrichment team, Oak Harbor United Bretheren Ch., 1996-97, St. John's U.C.C., 1998—; leader Girl Scouts of Am., 1998—; vol. Trinity U.C.C., Fostoria United Bretheren Ch., 1998—; mem. Gang Task Force, 1993—, Neighborhood, 1995-97. Mem. Mothers of Twins. Avocations: camping, singing, writing, crafts, reading. Office: State Ohio Dept Youth Svcs 1 Govt Ctr Rm 1016 Toledo OH 43604

DAVIS-JEROME, EILEEN GEORGE, principal; b. N.Y.C., Nov. 10, 1946; d. Rennie and Flora May (Compton) George; m. Bruce Davis, Aug. 8, 1970 (div. 1978); m. Frantz Jerome, Sept. 7, 1982; 1 child, Thais Davis. BFA, Pratt Inst., 1968; MA, CUNY, 1971, PD, 1990; EdD, Nova Southeastern U., 1998. Lic. ednl. adminstr., prin., instrn. specialist, N.Y. Tchr. fine arts Herbert Lehman High Sch., Bronx, N.Y., 1971-75; tchr. English/fine arts Jr. High Sch. 131, Bronx, 1975-76; tchr. English Jr. High Sch. 22, Bronx, 1976-79; tchr. fine arts Andrew Jackson High Sch., Cambria Heights, N.Y., 1979-83, coord. art dept., 1986-92; admissions counselor Fashion Inst. Tech., SUNY, N.Y.C., 1983-85; coord. Queensborough Coll. Project Prize, Bayside, N.Y., 1991-92; project dir. Andrew Jackson Magnet High Sch., Cambria Heights, N.Y., 1993—, project dir. humanities and the arts, 1994—; ednl. adminstr. Queens High Sch. Office, N.Y.C. Pub. High Schs., Corona, N.Y., 1993-94; prin. humanities and the arts Magnet H.S., Cambria Heights, N.Y., 1994—; coord. internat. studies Friends of Jackson High Sch., Cambria Heights, 1986-93, equal opportunity coord., 1989-92; exam asst. N.Y. C. Bd. Edn., Bd. Examiners, Bklyn., 1983-87; curriculum/career cons. Fashion Inst., SUNY, Detroit, Washington, Phila., 1983-86. Curriculum writer N.Y. State Project ot Implement Career Edn., 1975, N.Y. State Futuring, 1984; proposal writer Magnet Sch. Funding, 1993; author: Resource Book, 1989. Mem., speaker Cambria Heights Civic Assn., 1983; mem. N.Y. Urban League, N.Y.C.; vol. Mayor's Vol. Action/Alpha Sr. Cr., Cambria Heights, 1984; vol. Black Spectrum Theatre Co., 1983-86; mem. coord. coun. h.s. divsn. N.Y.C. Bd. Edn., 1997—. Recipient Recognition award Black Spectrum Theatre Co., 1983, Speakers award N.Y.C. Bd. Edn. Open Doors, 1983-84, Black Exec. Exch. Program Nat. Urban League, N.Y.C., 1984, Developer Grant award Impact II Grant, N.Y.C., 1989, Laurelton Club Prol. award, 1996; named Educator of Yr. NAACP/ACT-50, N.Y.C., 1992. Mem. ASCD, N.Y. State Art Tchrs. Assn., N.Y.C. Art Tchrs. Assn. (v.p., sec. 1983-85, cert. 1983-86), Cultural Heritage Alliance (assoc., Recognition award 1986), Delta Sigma Theta (chair arts and letters 1991-97, Golden Life award 1991), Phi Delta Kappa (Disting. Cert. 1994). Democrat. Episcopalian. Avocations: painting, travel, dance, writing, theater. Office: Magnet HS Humanities and the Arts 20701 116th Ave Combria Heights NY 11411-2211

DAVIS LASH, CYNTHIA, public health nurse; b. Torrance, Calif., Nov. 21, 1954; d. Glenn Earl and Evelyn Kathryne (Sawyer) Davis; children: Kathryne Jewell Stockwell, Robin Allan Stockwell; m. Tom B. Lash, Dec. 24, 1995. BSN cum laude, U. So. Calif., 1986; MSN in Home Health Adminstrn., Calif. State U., L.A., 1991; postgrad., Oreg. Health Scis. U., 1995—. RN, Calif., Oreg., Wash.; cert. pub. health nurse, AIDS educator, BCLS instr. Nursing educator Kaiser Permanente Med. Ctr., Anaheim, Calif., 1988, staff nurse labor and delivery room, 1986, staff nurse med.-surg. unit, 1987, pub. health nurse, 1988-93; DON Pulse Health Svcs., 1993; hospice case mgr. Cmty. Hospice Care, Orange County, Calif., 1993-94; after hours patient care coord. Legacy Vis. Nurse Assn., Portland, Oreg., 1995; dir. Cmty. Home Health and Hospice, Vancouver, Wash., 1996-97; home infusion nurse Permanente N.W. Region, Portland, 1997—; clin. instr. Biola U., La Mirada, Calif., 1993; clin. instr. sch. nursing Walla Walla Coll., Portland, 1994-95; presenter in field. Edwin M. Goethe Meml. scholar; Nat. Inst. Nursing Rsch. fellow, 1995. Mem. Gold Key, Sigma Theta Tau. Home: 1615 SW Walters Rd Gresham OR 97080-5375

DAVISON, BRUCE, actor; b. Phila., June 28, 1946; s. Marian E. and Clair W. D. BFA, Pa. State U., NYU. Stage appearances include Oh Dad, Poor Dad, Mama's Locked You in the Closet and I'm Fellin' So Bad, 1966; Broadway debut Tiger at the Gate, 1967, King Lear, 1968, A Home Away From Home, 1969, Streamers, L.A., 1978, A Life in the Theatre, 1980, The Elephant Man, 1980, Sorrows of Stephen, 1981, The Front Page, 1982, Richard III, 1984, The Glass Menagerie, 1984, Caine Mutiny Court Martial, 1984, The Normal Heart, 1986, The Cocktail Hour, 1989-90; TV appearances (series) Hunter, 1984-86, Harry and the Hendersons, 1991-92; (TV movie) Deadman's Curve, 1978, Summer of My German Soldier, 1979, The Lathe of Heaven, 1980, Mind Over Murder, 1980, Tomorrows Child, 1982, The Gathering, 1982, Incident at Crestridge, 1982, Ghost Dancing, 1983, Poor Little Rich Girl: The Barbara Hutton Story, 1987, Lady in a Corner, 1989, Stolen: One Husband, 1990, Live! From Death Row, 1992, Down Out and Dangerous, 1995, Hidden in America, 1996, After Jimmy, 1996, Color of Justice, 1997, Little Girl Fly Away, 1998; film appearances Last Summer, 1969, Strawberry Statement, 1970, Willard, 1971, Jerusalem File, 1972, Peege, 1972, Ulzana's Raid, 1973, Mame, 1974, Mother, Jugs and Speed, 1975, Short Eyes, 1978, Brass Target, 1978, High Risk, 1981, A Texas Legend, 1982, Lies, 1983, Crimes of Passion, 1984, Spies Like Us, 1985, The Ladies Club, 1986, Misfit Brigade, 1988, Longtime Companion, 1990, Steel and Lace, 1990, Short Cuts, 1993, 6 Degrees of Separation, 1993, Homage, 1994, Far From Home: The Adventures of Yellow Dog, 1995, The Skateboard Kid II, 1995, The Cure, 1995, The Baby-Sitters Club, 1995, Grace of My Heart, 1996, The Crucible, 1996, Lovelife, 1997, Apt Pupil, 1998, Paulie, 1998. Office: William Morris Agy care Brian Dubin 1325 Ave of the Americas New York NY 10019*

DAVISON, C. HAMILTON, greeting card executive; b. Providence, June 23, 1959; s. Charles Hamilton and Lessie Hall Lang (Busbee) D.; m. Dorothy Donovan Schneeberger, June 10, 1989; children: C. Carter, William Lang, Laura. BSBA, Vanderbilt U., 1982; MS, U. Tex., 1984. Prin. Tecton Energy of La., Shreveport, 1983-84; internat. sales rep. Paramount Cards Inc., Pawtucket, R.I., 1984-85, internat. sales mgr., 1985-86, v.p. internat., 1986-87, v.p. internat. and mktg., 1987-88, pres., 1988—, CEO, 1995—, also bd. dirs.; econ. policy coun. UN Assn. of U.S.A., N.Y.C., 1990-93; bd. dirs. Food Scv., Inc., Tufco Techs., Valley Resources, audit com. Bd. dirs. Westminster Sr. Ctr., Providence, 1989-92. Mem. No. R.I. C. of C. (bd. dirs. 1994-97), Young Pres. Orgn. (New Eng. exec. com. 1994-95), Greeting Card Assn. (exec. com. 1992-97, pres. 1996, bd. dirs.), Am. Assn. of Petroleum Geologists, Agawam Hunt Club, Dunes Club, ToKolan Club. Office: Paramount Cards Inc 400 Pine St Pawtucket RI 02860-1833

DAVISON, CALVIN, retired lawyer; b. Norwood, Ohio, Jan. 9, 1932; s. Emberson and Hazel Hildreth (Jenz) D.; m. Carole Ann Sawyer, Apr. 3, 1971; 1 child, Douglas Sawyer. AB cum laude, Miami U., Oxford, Ohio, 1953; JD cum laude, Harvard U., 1959. Bar: D.C. 1959, U.S. Dist. Ct. D.C. 1959, U.S. Ct. Appeals (D.C. cir.) 1959, U.S. Ct. Appeals (6th cir.) 1973, U.S. Ct. Appeals (2d cir.) 1979, U.S. Ct. Appeals (4th cir.) 1991, U.S. Supreme Ct. 1964. Assoc. Pogue & Neal, Washington, 1959-65, ptnr., 1965-67; ptnr. Jones, Day, Reavis & Pogue, Washington, 1967-79, Crowell & Moring, Washington, 1979-97. Contbr. articles to profl. jours. Lt. j.g. USN, 1953-56. Mem. ABA, D.C. Bar Assn., Univ. Club, City Tavern Club (Washington). Avocations: swimming, tennis. Home: 4950 Quebec St NW Washington DC 20016-3231

DAVISON, CHARLES HAMILTON, financial executive; b. Providence, Dec. 20, 1926; s. Ernest H. and Margery C. (Crowell) D.; m. Lessie Hall Lang Busbee, Aug. 16, 1958; children: Charles Hamilton, James Lang, Andrew Burwell. A.B., Dartmouth Coll., 1950; M.B.A., N.Y. U., 1953. C.P.A. Accountant Hurdman & Cranstoun, N.Y.C., 1950-55; partner firm Comery, Davison & Co., Providence, 1955-64; mng. partner Peat, Marwick, Mitchell & Co., Providence, 1964-65; mng. partner New Eng. Area Peat, Marwick, Mitchell & Co., 1965-67, mng. partner Chgo. office, mem. exec. com. Midwest Area, 1967-77; dep. chmn. Peat, Marwick, Mitchell & Co., N.Y.C., 1977-80; vice chmn., chmn. fin. com., mem. exec. com. Smith Barney, Harris Upham & Co., N.Y.C., 1980-82; chmn., chief exec. officer Paramount Cards Inc., 1983-95. Pres., bd. dirs. United Charities Chgo.; bd. dirs. Community Fund Chgo., Inc., R.I. Philharmonic; trustee Roosevelt U., Inst. on Man and Sci.; chmn. fin. com., mem. exec. com. Kenyon Coll.; mem. adv. council Northwestern U. Grad. Sch. Mgmt.; bd. overseers Amos Tuck Sch., Dartmouth Coll., NYU Grad. Sch. Bus.; mem. vis. com. Grad. Sch. Bus., U. Chgo. Serve with USAAF, 1944-46. Mem. Am. Inst. C.P.A.'s, Ill., N.Y. socs. C.P.A.'s, Chgo. Assn. Commerce and Industry (dir., v.p., policy com.). Republican. Congregationalist. Clubs: Commercial of Chgo; Round Hill (Greenwich, Conn.); Indian Hill, Belle Haven; Racquet and Tennis (N.Y.C.); To Kalon (Pawtucket, R.I.); Agawam Hunt, University, Hope (Providence); Chicago (Chgo.); Johns Island (Vero Beach, Fla.). Home: 551 Indian Harbor Rd Vero Beach FL 32963-3514 Office: Paramount Cards Inc 400 Pine St Pawtucket RI 02860-1833

DAVISON, DANIEL P., retired banking executive; b. N.Y.C., Jan. 30, 1925; s. F. Trubee and Dorothy (Peabody) D.; m. Catherine Cheremeteff, June 27, 1953; children: Daniel P. Jr., George P., Henry P. BA, Yale U., 1949; JD, Harvard U., 1952. Assoc. White & Case, N.Y.C., 1952-55; exec. v.p. Morgan Bank, N.Y.C., 1955-79; chmn., CEO U.S. Trust, N.Y.C., 1979-90; chmn. Christie's, N.Y.C., 1990-94, Burlington No. Sante Fe R.R., Fort Worth, 1996-97. Treas. Florence Gould Found., N.Y.C., 1983—. Recipient Legion of Honor, France. Mem. Piping Rock Yacht Club, Seawanhaka Yacht Club, N.Y. Yacht Club. Republican. Episcopalian. Avocations: sailing, fishing, hunting. Home: 90 Peacock Ln Locust Valley NY 11560-1019 Office: c/o US Trust 114 W 47th St New York NY 10036-1510

DAVISON, EDWARD JOSEPH, electrical engineering educator; b. Toronto, Ont., Can., Sept. 12, 1938; s. Maurice and Agnes (Quinlan) D. Assoc., Royal Conservatory of Music, Toronto, 1957; B.A., U. Toronto, 1960, M.A., 1961; Ph.D., Cambridge U., 1964, Sc.D., 1977. Asst. prof. dept. elec. engring. U. Toronto, 1964-66, assoc. prof., 1968-74, prof. dept. elec. engring. and computers, 1974—; asst. prof. dept. elec. engring. and computer scis. U. Calif., Berkeley, 1966-67; dir. Elec. Engring. Consociates Ltd., Toronto, 1977—; elected Hon. prof. of Beijing Inst. of Aeronautics and Astronautics, 1986; pres. Elec. Engring. Consociates, Ltd., Toronto, 1997—. Assoc. editor: Jour. Automatica, 1974-87, Jour. Large Scale Systems: Theory and Applications, 1979-90, Jour. Optimal Control and Methods, 1983—; cons. editor IEEE Transactions on Automatic Control, 1985. Contbr. numerous articles infield to profl. jours. Athlone fellow, 1961-63; E.W.R. Steacie Meml. fellow, 1974-77; Killam Research fellow, 1979-80, 81-83. Fellow Royal Soc. Can., IEEE (v.p. Control Systems Soc. 1979-80, mem. adminstrv. com. 1977-83, dir. Soc. mag. 1980-82, assoc. editor jour. Trans. on Automatic Control 1974-76, editl. adv. bd. IEEE Procs. 1980-81, Centennial medal 1984, elected disting. mem. 1984); mem. IEEE Control Systems Soc. (pres.-elect 1982-83, pres. 1983-84, Hendrik W. Bode Lectr. prize 1997), Profl. Engrs. Ont. (cons. engr. 1979—), Internat. Fedn. Automatic Control (vice chmn. theory com. 1978-87, chmn. 87-90, Quazza medal 1993, vice chmn. tech. bd. 1990-93, coun. mem. 1990-96, vice chmn. IFAC policy com. 1996—), Russian Acad. Nonlinear Scis. Office: Univ Toronto, Dept Elec Engring & Computer, Toronto, ON Canada M5S 1A4

DAVISON, FREDERICK CORBET, foundation executive; b. Atlanta, Sept. 3, 1929; s. Frederick Collins and Gladys (Carsley) D.; m. Dianne Castle, Sept. 3, 1952; children—Frederick Corbet, William Castle, Anne Harper. D.V.M., U. Ga., 1952; Ph.D., Iowa State U., 1963; H.H.D. (hon.), Presbyn. Coll., 1977; LL.D. (hon.), Mercer U., 1979; hon. degree, U. N.B., Can., 1985. Pvt. practice veterinary medicine Marietta, Ga., 1952-58; rsch. assoc. Iowa State U., Ames, 1958-60, asst. prof., 1960-63; assoc. Inst. Atomic Research, Ames, 1960-63; asst. dir. dept. sci. activities AVMA, Chgo., 1963-64; dean sch. vet. medicine U. Ga., Athens, 1964-66; vice chancellor Univ. System Ga., 1966-67, pres., 1967-86; pres. U. Ga., Athens, 1967-86, prof. vet. medicine, Fred C. Davison chair Sch. Vet. Medicine, 1986-88; pres., chief exec. officer Nat. Sci. Ctr. Found., Inc., Augusta, Ga., 1988—; bd. dirs. EduTrek, Southeastern Tech. Ctr.; trustee Presbyn. Coll. Contbr. articles to profl. jours. Mem. NE Ga. commn. Boy Scouts Am., past pres. Area 5; hon. mem. bd. counselors Oxford Coll. Recipient Disting. Achievement award Iowa State U., 1979, Disting. Svc. award Univ. Ga., 1975, Appreciation award, 1976, Silver Beaver award and Silver Antelope award Boy Scouts Am.; named Georgian of Yr. Ga. Assn. Broadcasters, 1980. Mem. Am., Ga. vet. med. assns., Sigma Xi, Phi Kappa Phi, Sigma Alpha Epsilon, Omega Tau Sigma, Alpha Zeta, Phi Zeta, Gamma Sigma Delta. Office: Nat Sci Ctr Found Inc PO Box 15577 Augusta GA 30919-1577

DAVISON, KENNETH EDWIN, American studies educator; b. East Cleveland, Ohio, May 4, 1924; s. Gordon Edwin and Mildred K. (Smith) D.; m. Virginia Nell Rentz, June 14, 1959; children: Robert Edwin, Richard Allen. A.B., Heidelberg Coll., 1946; A.M., Western Res. U., 1951, Ph.D., 1953. Asst. prof. history, polit. sci. Heidelberg Coll., Tiffin, Ohio, 1952-56, assoc. prof. polit. sci., 1956-59, prof., 1959-64, prof. history, dir. Gen. Edn. Program, 1964-67, prof., chmn. Am. studies dept., 1967-83, prof., chmn. history and Am. studies dept., 1983-89, emeritus prof. history and Am. studies, 1989—; vis. prof. Am. studies Bowling Green State U., 1972, 73, 74, 75, 89, 93; cons. Tiffin Hist. Trust, 1976-89; pub. hist. and cons. in field, 1992—. Author: Cleveland and the Civil War, 1962, The Presidency of Rutherford B. Hayes, 1972, The American Presidency: A Guide to Bibliographical Sources, 1983, (with others) Ohio's Heritage, 1984, rev. edit., 1989, 92, 95; editor: (with others) Ohio History Resource Guide, 1991; guest editor: Ohio History, 1968; editor Hayes Hist. Jour., 1976-82; book rev. editor Presdl. Studies Quar., 1978-86, book rev. counselor, 1986-88; contbg. author Collier's Ency., 1964, 68, Am. Educator's Ency., 1965, also articles and revs. to profl. jours. Chmn. Heidelberg Cmty. Lecture and Concert Series, 1956-63; mem. Ohio com. for pub. programs in humanities, 1973-80, mem. exec. com., 1977-80; chmn. Tiffin-Seneca Bicentennial Commn., 1974-77, 87-89; bd. dirs. Seneca County Mus., 1976-90, Seneca County Mus. Found., 1990-98, Heritage Village Bd., 1992-93; mem. lay bd. Mercy Hosp., 1983-86; trustee Ohio Preservation Alliance, 1992-96; historian Roadtrek Internat., 1996-98. Recipient Ohioana Library Book award, 1973; grantee Am. Philos. Soc., 1963-64, Nat. Endowment Humanities summer seminar, 1978, 81, 87, Can. Embassy Faculty Enrichment, 1979, 80, 81, Gerald R. Ford Found., 1983. Mem. Orgn. Am. Historians, Ohio-Ind. Am. Studies Assn. (pres. 1965, 66), Am. Assn. State and Local History (cert. of commendation 1993), So. Hist. Assn., Ohio Acad. History (editor newsletter 1971-74, pres. 1986-87, Disting. Svc. award 1989), Am. Studies Assn. (nat. exec. coun. 1968-78, nat. treas. 1973-78), Ohio Hist. Soc. (rsch. adviser 1968-75, bd. trustees ex officio 1986-87), Ctr. for Study of Presidency (bd. editors 1974-98), Presidency Rsch. Group, Ohio Assn. Hist. Socs. and Mus. (trustee at-large 1986-92, exec. com. 1991-92), Tiffin Hist. Trust (Preservation award 1998), Pi Kappa Delta, Phi Alpha Theta. Presbyterian (elder 1991-93). Home: 125 Hampden Park Tiffin OH 44883-3344

DAVISON, MICHAEL S., JR., military officer. BS, U.S. Mil. Acad.; MS in Fgn. Affairs, Georgetown U.; grad., U.S. Army Command/Gen. Staff, Brit. Army Staff Coll., Nat. War Coll. Commd. 2d lt. U.S. Army, 1964, advanced through grades to lt. gen., 1997; comdr. Co. C, 5th bn., 7th cavalry U.S. Army, Vietnam, 1967-68; bn. sr. advisor airborne divsn. adv. detachment U.S. Mil. Assistance Command, Vietnam, 1971-72; exec. officer 3d bn. 64th armor 3d infantry divsn. U.S. Army Europe, Germany, 1977-79; dep. dir. deep attack program Office of Dep. Chief of Staff for Ops. and Plans, U.S. Army, Washington, 1984-85; asst. dep. chief of staff for ops. and plans U.S. Army Europe and 7th Army, Germany, 1987-88; dir. requirements and integration Office of Dep. Chief of Staff for Ops. and Plans, U.S. Army, Washington, 1988-89; asst. divsn. comdr. 5th infantry divsn. Ft. Polk, La., 1989-91; dep. comdg. gen. U.S. Army Combined Arms Command for Tng., Ft. Leavenworth, Kans., 1991-92; chief Office of Mil. Coop., Egypt, 1992-94; comdg. gen. U.S. Army Security Assistance Command, Alexandria, Va., 1994-97. Decorated Def. Disting. Svc. medal, Disting. Svc. medal, Silver Star, Legion of Merit, Bronze Star medal with V device and oak leaf cluster, Bronze Star with 3 oak leaf clusters, Purple Heart with oak leaf cluster, Def. Meritorious Svc. medal. Office: Def Security Corp Crystal Gateway N Ste 303 1111 Jefferson Davis Hwy Arlington VA 22202

DAVISON, PETER HUBERT, editor, poet; b. N.Y.C., June 27, 1928; s. Edward and Natalie (Weiner) D.; m. Jane Auchincloss Truslow, Mar. 7, 1959 (dec. July 1981); children: Edward Angus, Lesley Truslow; m. Joan Edelman Goody, Aug. 11, 1984. A.B. magna cum laude, Harvard U., 1949; Fulbright scholar, St. John's Coll., Cambridge (Eng.) U., 1949-50. Page U.S. Senate, 1944; asst. editor Harcourt, Brace & Co., 1950-51, 53-55; asst. to dir. Harvard U. Press, 1955-56; assoc. editor Atlantic Monthly Press, 1956-59, exec. editor, 1959-64, dir., 1964-79, sr. editor, 1979-85; poetry editor Atlantic Monthly, 1972—; editor Peter Davison Books Houghton Mifflin Co., Boston, 1985-98, poetry editor, 1985-98; mem. adv. bd. Nat. Transl. Ctr., 1965-68; policy panelist in lit. Nat. Endowment for Arts, 1980-83; Phi Beta Kappa Vis. Scholar, 1989-90. Author: (poems) The Breaking of the Day, 1964, The City and the Island, 1966, Pretending to Be Asleep, 1970, Dark Houses, 1971, Walking the Boundaries, 1974, A Voice in the Mountain, 1977, Barn Fever and Other Poems, 1981, Praying Wrong: New and Selected Poems, 1957-1984, 1984, The Great Ledge, 1989, The Poems of Peter Davison 1957-1995, 1995, (prose) One of the Dangerous Trades: Essays on the Work and Workings of Poetry, 1991; autobiography Half Remembered, 1973, rev. edit., 1991, The Fading Smile, Poets in Boston From Robert Frost to Robert Lowell to Sylvia Plath, 1955-60, 1994; editor: Hello, Darkness: The Collected Poems of L.E. Sissman, 1978, The World of Farley Mowat, 1980; contbr. poems, articles to numerous mags., anthologies. Trustee Fountain Valley Sch., 1967-75; mem. corp. Yaddo, 1978—. Served with AUS, 1951-53. Winner competition Yale Series Younger Poets, 1963; recipient Poetry award Nat. Inst. Arts and Letters, 1972, James Michener award Acad. Am. Poets, 1981, New Eng. Book award for Lit. Excellence New Eng. Booksellers Assn., 1995. Mem. Phi Beta Kappa. Clubs: Examiner, St Botolph (Boston); Harvard (N.Y.C.). Office: The Atlantic Monthly 77 N Washington St Ste 500 Boston MA 02114-1916

DAVISON, RICHARD, physician, educator; b. Buenos Aires, Nov. 7, 1937; came to U.S., 1966; s. Charles Edward and Matilde (Muller) D.; m. Lisette Glusberg, July 1, 1965; 1 child, Sebastian. MD, U. Buenos Aires, 1963. Diplomate Am. Bd. Internal Medicine, Am. Bd. Cardiovascular Diseases, Am. Bd. Critical Care Medicine. Intern Inst. Med. Rsch., Buenos Aires, 1964; resident Passavant Meml. Hosp., Chgo., 1966-68, chief resident, 1968-69; cardiology fellowship VA Hosp., Chgo., 1969-71; asst. prof. Northwestern U. Sch. Medicine, Chgo., 1973-81, assoc. prof., 1981—, chief sect.

critical care medicine, 1982—, chief sect. cardiology, 1988-92; dir. med. intensive care area Northwestern Meml. Hosp., Chgo., 1973—. Contbr. articles to profl. jours. Recipient Thrombolysis in Myocardial Infarction award NIH. Fellow Am. Coll. Cardiology, Am. Coll. Physicians, Council of Clin. Cardiology (Am. Heart. Assn.), Soc. Critical Care Medicine; mem. Am. Heart Assn., Alpha Omega Alpha. Office: Northwestern Meml Hosp Sect Critical Care 251 E Chicago Ave Ste 726 Chicago IL 60611-2646

DAVISON, RUTH HILTON, elementary education educator; b. Waterville, Maine, Mar. 12, 1938; d. David Russell and Anna Carolyn (Trimble) Hilton; m. A. Howard Davison, Sept. 9, 1958.; children: Howard H., Beth A., Heather R. BS in Edn., U. Maine, Farmington, 1968; MS in Edn., U. Southern Maine, 1982. Cert. Literacy Specialist K-12. Tchr. Union 48, Maine, 1968-69, 70-71, Union 51, Maine, 1971-79; reading coord. Boothbay (Maine) Region Elem. Sch., 1979—; lead tchr. Elem. Literacy New Standards Maine Dept. Edn., Augusta, 1989—. Mem. Maine Reading Assn. (pres. 1988-90, exec. bd. 1986—, IRA Literacy award 1994), New England Reading Assn. (exec. bd. 1990-97, Spl. Recognition award 1998), Maine Coun. English Lang. Arts, Internat. Reading Assn. (coord. 1991-94, 96-98), Nat. Coun. Tchrs. of English. Home: 188 Boothbay Rd Edgecomb ME 04556-3020 Office: Boothbay Region Elem Sch 238 Townsend Ave Boothbay Harbor ME 04538-1839

DAVISON, VICTORIA DILLON, real estate executive; b. Ada, Okla., Jan. 11, 1949; d. Wiliam Jackson Jr. and Helen Lucille (Cate) Dillon; m. Charles Alton Jewett, July 7, 1973 (div.); m. Denver Norris Davison, May 31 1985; stepchildren: Shaun, Malia, Denver II. BFA, Tulane U., 1970. Exec. sec. ITT Corp., Washington, 1970-71; adminstrv. asst. Berens Associated, Washington, 1972-73; real estate trainee Equitable Life Assurance Soc. Comml. Real Estate, Washington, 1974-75, real estate analyst, sr. appraiser, 1976-82; v.p. Am. Security Corp., Washington, 1983-85; exec. v.p. Ada Shopping Ctr., Inc., 1985—; pres. Victoria Properties, Ltd., Ada, 1989—; bd. dirs. W.J. Dillon Co., Inc., Ada, Ada Shopping Ctr. Inc. Jr. warden and vestry St. Luke's Episcopal Ch., Ada, 1990-91. Mem. Ada Area C. of C. (bd. dirs. 1990, co-chmn. area retail 1990-92), Appraisal Inst. (MAI), Edn. for Ministry (award 1992), Ada Music Club, Tanti, Leadership Ada. Republican. Avocations: writing music, bridge, antiques, dance club. Home: 825 W Kings Rd Ada OK 74820-8045 Office: Victoria Properties Ltd 902 Arlington Ctr Ste 196 Ada OK 74820-2883

DAVIT, FRANK TORINO, accountant; b. Rockford, Ill., June 20, 1961; s. Torino and Ernestina (Mazzoli) D. BS in Accountancy, No. Ill. U., 1983. CPA. Managerial acct. Ingersoll Engrs., Inc., Rockford, 1984-88, ptnr.-in-charge acct. and fin. svcs., 1988-92, CFO, 1992—; CFO, 1993—. Mem. Inst. Mgmt. Accts. (Rockford chpt.). Republican. Roman Catholic. Avocations: collecting sports memorabilia, golf. Home: 6594 Rolling Hedge Ln Rockford IL 61108 Office: Bourton Group 5100 E State St Rockford IL 61108-2398

DAVITT, F. GEORGE, lawyer; b. Buffalo, Dec. 24, 1956; s. J. Alan and Mary Helen (George) D.; m. Lynda A. Ceremsak, Jan. 2, 1988; children: Caroline, Samuel. LLB, U. Toronto, 1980; BCL, Oxford (Eng.) U., 1982. Bar: Ontario 1983, N.Y. 1984, Mass. 1995. Assoc. Davis, Polk & Wardwell, N.Y.C., 1984-93; assoc. Testa, Hurwitz & Thibeault, Boston, 1993-94, ptnr., 1995—. Roman Catholic. Avocations: tennis, wine. Office: Testa Hurwitz & Thibeault LLP 125 High St Boston MA 02110

DAVOE, DAVID, communications executive. CFO News Am. Corp., N.Y.C. Office: News Am Corp 1211 Avenue Of The Americas New York NY 10036-8701*

DAW, HAROLD JOHN, lawyer; b. N.Y.C., July 6, 1926; s. Joseph and Dorothy (Dannenberg) D.; m. Meryl Kann, Sept. 25, 1960. A.B., Union Coll., 1950; LL.B., Columbia U., 1954. Bar: N.Y. 1955. Assoc. Shearman & Sterling, N.Y.C., 1954-62, ptnr., 1962-89. Served with USN, 1944-46, ETO. Mem. ABA, N.Y. State Bar Assn., Bar Assn. City N.Y., Phi Beta Kappa. Club: University. Home: 15 Buena Vista Dr Westport CT 06880-6602

DAW, MAUREEN BRIDGETTE, special education educator, administrator; b. Chgo., Nov. 24, 1952; d. James Edward Sr. and Margaret Constance (McNulty) D. BA in Spl. Edn. and Elem. Edn., Northeastern Ill. U., 1974; MS in Sch. Guidance and Counseling, Chgo. State U., 1983; PhD in Edn., U. Ill., Chgo., 1996. Cert. tchr. elem. K-12, EMH K-12, LD/SED K-12, adminstrv. K-12, sch. guidance and counseling, Ill. Tchr. S.W. Cook County Coop. for Spl. Edn., Oak Forest, Ill., 1974-90; tchr. North Palos Sch. Dist. # 117, Hickory Hills, Ill., 1990-98, dept. chair spl. edn. dept., 1997—; dir. Spl. Children's Ctr., Chgo., 1973-88; vis. prof. U. Ill., Chgo., 1995-98; presenter Am. Assn. of Colls. for Tchr. Edn., 1996; mem. Sch. Dist. # 117 Inclusion Com., 1995—. Author: (book) Celebrate the Struggle: Teacher Decision Making and Collaborative Consultation, 1996. Mem. CEC (presenter 1995-96), Am. Edn. Rsch. Assn., Phi Delta Kappa. Avocation: golf. Home: 10207 S Sawyer Ave Evergreen Park IL 60805-3757

DAWALT, KENNETH FRANCIS, former army officer, former aerospace company executive; b. Salem, Ind., Aug. 18, 1911; s. Dan and Nelle (Whitson) D.; m. Kathryn Marie King, June 9, 1940; children: Karen King Gould, Karie Whitson Dawalt Nicholson. BS, U.S. Mil. Acad., 1936; grad., Command and Gen. Staff Coll., 1943, Army War Coll., 1954. Commd. 2d. lt. U.S. Army, 1936, advanced through grades to brig. gen., 1961, instr., then asst. prof. physics U.S. Mil. Acad., 1941-45, assigned to 442d Arty. Group, 1945, comdr. 999th F.A. Bn., also 1st Republic Korea Div. Arty., 1950-51, assigned research and devel. Dept. Army, 1951-53, mem. faculty Command and Gen. Staff Coll., 1954-57, U.S. del. to NATO, 1957-60, comdr. 2d U.S. Army Missile Command, 1960-61, comdr. 30th Arty. Brigade, 1961-63, dep. dir. Def. Atomic Support Agy., 1963-66, dep. dir. army research and devel. (internat. programs), 1966-70, mem. mil. liaison com. AEC, 1966-70; mem. NATO Army Armaments Group Brussels, 1966-70; ret., 1970; exec. v.p. European Aerospace Corp., N.Y.C., 1970-76; cons. in field, 1976—. Decorated D.S.M., Silver Star, Legion of Merit with oak leaf cluster; Chungmu Disting. Mil. Service medal (Korea). Mem. Assn. U.S. Army, Assn. Grads. U.S. Mil. Acad., Army Navy Country Club, Masons, Beta Theta Pi. Methodist. Home: 9229 Arlington Blvd Apt 545 Fairfax VA 22031-2517

DAWBER, PAM, actress; b. Detroit; d. Gene and Thelma D.; m. Mark Harmon, Mar. 21, 1987; 2 children. Ed., Oakland Community Coll. Worked as model and appeared in commls.; appearances inclued (TV series) ABC-TV's Mork and Mindy, 1978-82, CBS-TV's My Sister Sam, 1986-88, Life and Stuff, 1996—, (TV movies) The Girl the Gold Watch and Everything, Remembrance of Love, NBC, 1982, Last of the Great Survivors, 1983, Through Naked Eyes, 1983, The Wife for Hire, 1985, Wild Horses, 1985, American Geisha, 1986, Quiet Victory: The Charles Wedemeyer Story, 1988, Do You Know the Muffin Man?, 1989, Face of Fear, 1990, The Man Who Had Three Wives, 1993, Web of Deception, 1994, A Child's Cry for Help, 1994, Trail of Tears, 1995, Journey Home, 1996, (films) The Wedding, Stay Tuned, (Broadway play) My Fair Lady; Joe Papp's L.A. prodn. Pirates of Penzance, L.A. prodn. Love Letters, 1991. Worked as model and appeared in commls.; appearances include (TV series) ABC-TV's Mork and Mindy, 1978-82, CBS-TV My Sister Sam, 1986-88, 101 Dalmations, (TV movies) The Girl the Gold Watch and Everything, Remembrance of Love, NBC, 1982, Last of the Great Survivors, 1983, Through Naked Eyes, 1983, This Wife for Hire, 1985, Wild Horses, 1985, American Geisha, 1986, Quiet Victory: The Charlie Wedemeyer Story, 1988, Do You Know the Muffin Man?, 1989, Face of Fear, 1990, Stay Tuned, 1992, The Man Who Had Three Wives, 1993, Web of Deception, 1994, A Child's Cry for Help, 1994, Trail of Tears, 1995, A Stranger to Love, 1996, Cameras Rolling: 20 Days on Set, 1999, Don't Look Behind You, 1999, Journey Home, 1996, (films) The Wedding, Stay Tuned, (Broadway play) My Fair Lady: Joe Papp's L.A. prodn. Pirates of Penzance, L.A. prodn. Love Letters, 1991; prodr. Life...and Stuff, 1997; TV guest appearances The Twilight Zone, 1985, Dream On, 1990. Nat. spokeswoman Big Bros., Big Sisters of Am. Office: care Mimi Weber 9738 Arby Dr Beverly Hills CA 90210-1203*

DAWES, DOMINIQUE, gymnast, Olympic athlete; b. Silver Spring, Md., Nov. 20, 1976. Student, U. Md., 1995—. Mem. U.S. Olympic Team, Barcelona, Spain, 1992, Atlanta, 1996. Recipient Arch McDonald award Touchdown Club Washington, 1995, McDonald's Balancing It All award, 1995, Henry P. Iba Citizen Athlete award, 1995, Gold medal team competition Olympic Games, Atlanta, 1996, Bronze medal floor exercise Olympic Games, Atlanta, 1996; named USA Gymnastics' Athlete of Yr., 1993, Sportsperson of Yr. USA Gymnastics, 1994; placed 3rd for team Olympic Games, Barcelona, Spain, 1992, 2d in all around and floor exercise, 1st in vault and balance beam, 3rd uneven bars Coca-Cola Nat. Championships, Salt Lake City, 1993, 2d in uneven bars and balance beam World Gymnastics Championships, Birmingham, Eng., 1993, 1st in all around, vault, balance beam and floor exercise McDonald's Am. Cup, Orlando, 1994, 1st in all around, vault, uneven bars, balance beam and floor exercise Coca-Cola Nat. Championships, Nashville, 1994, 1st in all around NationsBank World Team Trials, Richmond, Va., 1994, 2d for team World Championships, Dortmund, Germany, 1994, 1st in uneven bars and floor exercise, 3rd in balance beam Coca-Cola Nat. Championships, New Orleans, 1995. Avocations: reading books, dancing, acting. Office: care USA Gymnastics Pan Am Plz 201 S Capitol Ave Ste 300 Indianapolis IN 46225-1058*

DAWES, DOUGLAS CHARLES, retired career officer; b. Detroit, Nov. 24, 1952; s. Carl Joseph and Margaret Elisabeth D.; m. Theresa Neel, June 9, 1990. BBA in Mgmt., Loyola U., New Orleans, 1974; grad. with honors, Command and Gen. Staff Coll., 1987; MA in Procurement and Acquisition Mgmt., Webster U., St. Louis, 1990. Field artillery officer U.S. Army, various locations, 1974-80; asst. fin. officer U.S. Army, Ft. Sill, Okla., 1980-82; deputy fin. and acctg. officer U.S. Army, Fed. Republic of Germany, 1982-86, Ft. Carson, Colo., 1986-87; comdr. and fin. officer U.S. Army, Ft. Carson, 1987-88, budget officer, asst. div. comptr., 1988-90, div. comptr., 1990-91; chief joint pay operation Joint Svc. Software, Def. Fin. and Acctg. Svc., Denver, 1991-94; ret., 1994; payroll mgr. Neodata Svcs., Inc., Louisville, Colo., 1995-98; corp. payroll mgr. Corp. Express, Inc., Broomfield, Colo., 1998—. Vol., water safety instr. trainer ARC. Mem. Disabled Am. Vets. (life), Delta Sigma Pi (life, chancellor Delta Nu chpt. 1973, 1st v.p. 1974), Am. Legion, Am. Payroll Assn. Republican. Avocations: skiing, scuba, softball, volleyball, antique car restoration. Home: 17523 E Caspian Pl Aurora CO 80013-4172

DAWES, LYELL CLARK, publishing company executive; b. Balt., Apr. 10, 1931; s. Lyell Clark and Anne (Mehorter) D.; m. Patricia Clarke Clinton, Nov. 1955; children: William, Elizabeth; m. Jessie Scott Pollock, Dec. 27, 198l; step-children: Sterling, Clement. AB, U. N.C., 1953. With McGraw Hill Pub. Co., 1956-65; pub. mgr. RCA Instrnl. Systems, Palo Alto, Calif., 1965-67; v.p., dir. Macmillan Info., N.Y.C., 1967-69; group v.p., dir. Westinghouse Learning Corp., N.Y.C., 1969-76; dir. ISI Press, Phila., 1978-80; founder, pres. University City Info. Co., Phila., 1982; chmn., CEO Cobblestone Pub., Inc., Peterborough, N.H., 1982-96; pvt. practice pub., media cons. Peterborough, N.H., 1996—. Bd. dirs. N.H. Assn. for Blind, Concord, 1985-87, Monadnock Hospice, Peterborough, N.H., 1989-90; edn. com. Ridgewood (N.J.) Sch. Dist., 1973; mem. Econ. Devel. Authority, Peterborough, 1997-99. 1st lt. USMC, 1954-55, Korea. Mem. IEEE, Woods Hole Oceanographic Inst. Assn., Rotary, Univ. Club, Naval War Coll. Found. Home: 579 E Mountain Rd Peterborough NH 03458-2309

DAWES, ROBERT LEO, research company executive; b. Big Spring, Tex., Mar. 5, 1945; s. William Robert and Josephine Melloo (Duflot) D.; m. Rosemary Mae Nelson, Oct. 10, 1970; children: Sara Michelle, Karen Melissa. BS in Math., Tex. Tech U., 1966, MS in Math., 1968; PhD in Math., U. Tex., 1977. Mem. tech. staff Tex. Instruments, Inc., Dallas, 1975-81; sr. specialist E-Systems, Inc., Garland, Tex., 1981-85; pres. Martingale Rsch. Corp., Allen, Tex., 1985-94, QED Corp., Parker, Tex., 1995—; founder, chair Metroplex Inst. Neural Dynamics, Dallas, 1986-90. Mem. city coun. City of Parker (Tex.), 1988—. Lt. USNR, 1968-71. Mem. IEEE (chmn. Dallas chpt., Acoustics, Speech and Signal Processing Soc. 1988), Internat. Neural Network (chair math. and theory spl. interest group 1990-92). Avocation: ham radio. Home: 4308 Sycamore Ln Parker TX 75002-5908 Office: QED Corp 4308 Sycamore Ln Parker TX 75002-5908

DAWES, ROBYN MASON, psychology educator; b. Pitts., July 23, 1936; s. Norman H. and Zita (Hill) D.; children by previous marriage: Jennifer, Molly. BA in Philosophy, Harvard U., 1958; MA in Clin. Psychology, U. Mich., 1960, PhD in Math. Psychology, 1963; PhD (hon.), U. Goteborg, Sweden, 1999. Rschr. Ann Arbor (Mich.) VA Hosp., 1962-67; lectr. U. Mich., Ann Arbor, 1963-66, asst. prof., 1966-67; assoc. prof. psychology U. Oreg., Eugene, 1967-71, prof., 1971-85, co-head dept. psychology, 1972-73, acting head, 1979-80, head, 1981-85; prof. psychology Carnegie Mellon U., 1985—, head dept. social and decision scis., 1985-90, 95-96, univ. prof., 1992—, Charles J. Queenan Jr. univ. prof., 1997—; rsch. scientist Oreg. Rsch. Inst., Eugene, 1967-76, v.p., 1973-74; NATO lectr., The Hague, The Netherlands, 1968; vis. prof. U. Calif., Santa Barbara, 1975-75; cons. numerous insts. and orgns.; Olof Palme vis. prof. U. Stockholm and U. Goteborg, 1999. Author: Fundamentals of Attitude Measurement, 1972, Rational Choice in an Uncertain World, 1988 (William James book award div. gen. psychology Am. Psychol. Assn.), House of Cards: Psychology and Psychotherapy Built on Myth, 1994, paperback edit., 1996; co-author: (with C.H. Coombs and A. Tversky) Mathematical Psychology: An Elementary Introduction, 1970; contbr. articles to profl. jours; mem. editl. bds., cons numerous profl. jours. and publs. Rackham Summer fellow, 1961, James McKean Cattell Sabbatical fellow, 1978-79; del. NAS, USA-USSR Acad. Scis. Seminar Decision Making, Moscow-Tblisi, USSR, 1979; fellow Ctr. Advanced Study in Behavioral Scis., 1980-81, Ctr. for Rationality and Interactive Decision Making The Hebrew U. of Jerusalem, 1994. Fellow AAAS, Am. Psychol. Soc., Am. Assn. Applied and Preventative Psychology (mem. exec. bd. 1991—); mem. Oreg. Psychol. Assn. (pres. 1984-85), Am. Statis. Assn., Pub. Choice Soc., Psychometric Soc., West Coast Small Group Rsch. Soc. (pres. 1977-78), Judgement and Decision Making Rsch. Soc. (chmn. exec. bd. 1988, exec. bd. 1994-95), Soc. Advancement of Socio-Econs. (exec. bd. 1991—), Sigma Xi. Office: Carnegie Mellon U Dept Social & Decision Scis Pittsburgh PA 15213 *It took a while to understand the wisdom of Herodotus to "take good counsel with (ourselves): for even if the event turns out contrary to one's hopes, still one's decision was right"--always drawing support from the knowledge that the future is uncertain.*

DAWIS, RENÉ V., psychology educator, research consultant; b. Manila, Philippines, Dec. 29, 1928; came to U.S., 1953; s. Vicente Mercado and Dolores (Villanueva) D.; m. Lydia A. Villareal; children: Stevan, Myriam, Dolores, Vicente, Eugenio, Joaquin, David. BA, U. Philippines, 1951; MA, U. Minn., 1955, PhD, 1956. Instr. U. of Philippines, Quezon City, 1951-56, asst. prof., 1956-57; research assoc. U. Minn., Mpls., 1957-62, assoc. prof. indsl. relations, 1962-65, prof. indsl. relations, 1965-70, prof. psychology, 1968-97, prof. emeritus psychology, 1997—; sr. rsch. fellow Ball Found., 1998—. Author: (with L. Lofquist) Adjustment to Work, 1969, A Psychological Theory of Work Adjustment, 1984, Essentials of Person-Environment-Correspondence Counseling, 1991, (with R. Fruehling, N. Oldham) Psychology: Human Relations and Work Adjustment, 1989, (with R. Fruehling) Psychology: Realizing Human Potential, 1996, (with D. Lubinski) Assessing Individual Differences in Human Behavior, 1995; also numerous jour. articles, monographs, book chpts. Recipient Ann. Research awards Div. Rehab. Counseling, Am. Personnel and Guidance Assn., 1960, Am. Rehab. Counseling Assn., 1965, Am. Personnel and Guidance Assn., 1967; H.G. Heneman Teaching award Indsl. Relations Ctr., U. Minn., 1970, Research award Am. Rehab. Counseling Assn., 1974. Fellow Am. Psychol. Assn.; mem. Am. Psychol. Soc. Roman Catholic. Avocations: music appreciation, reading, TV, travel. Office: U Minn Dept Psychology 75 E River Rd Dept Minneapolis MN 55455-0344

DAWKINS, JIMMIE ANGELA, art educator; b. Ft. Oglethorpe, Ga., Sept. 24, 1942; d. James Harold and Neva Valeria (Dauley) Dawkins; m. Melville Madden Drake, Feb. 14, 1964 (div. Feb. 1967); 1 child, John Michael. B.Visual Art, Auburn (Ala.) U., 1964; MFA, Pratt Inst., Bklyn., 1968. Graphic designer Obata Studio, Tokyo, 1965-67; studio asst. Richard Rogers Inc., N.Y.C., 1970-71; tchg. asst. Art Students League, N.Y.C., 1972-73; instr. U. Ala., Huntsville, 1974-75, adj., 1975—; assoc. prof. art Ala. A&M U., Normal, 1975—. One-woman shows Artist's Workshop and Gallery, Huntsville, 1976, Meridian (Miss.) Mus. Art, 1977, Ala. A&M U., 1977, 79, 86, 94, Stillman Coll., Tuscaloosa, Ala., 1978, Athens Coll., 1979, U. North Ala., 1982, U. Ala., Huntsville, 1986, The Gallery at Nativity, 1989, 92, also others; 3-person show Huntsville Hilton, 1994; exhibited in numerous group shows, including Ala. A&M U., 1976-80, 82, 85, 86, 87, 89, 95, 96, Anniston (Ala.) Mus. Natural History, 1983, Jacksonville (Ala.) State U., 1984, Auburn (Ala.) U., 1985, U. North Ala., 1986, U. Ala., Birmingham, 1986, U. Ala., Huntsville, 1989, North Ala. Coll., 1989, Huntsville Art League, 1994, Connie Ulrich's Gallery, 1994, Huntsville Mus. Art, 1995, Holland Smith Gallery, 1996; represented in permanent collections Pratt Inst., Bklyn., Hunsville Mus. Art, also numerous pvt. collections. Named to Outstanding Young Women of Am., 1978; John Carroll Meml. scholar Art Students League, 1967; Grad Art Fellowship Fund award Pratt Inst., 1970; NEH fellow, 1977, Fulbright-Hays fellow, 1981, 93. Episcopalian. Avocations: early music, performing on recorders, harpsichord and viola da gamba. Office: Alabama A&M Univ Dept Art Normal AL 35762

DAWKINS, MARVA PHYLLIS, psychologist; b. Jacksonville, Fla., Apr. 12, 1948; d. Ralph and Altamese (Padgett) D.; student U. Freiburg, Germany, 1969-70; BS, Stetson U., 1971; MS, Fla. State U., 1972, PhD, 1975. Rsch. asst. Fla. State U., Tallahassee, 1970-72; clin. intern, psychology dept. Presbyn.-St. Luke's Med. Ctr. and mental health dept. Mile Square Health Ctr., Chgo., 1973-74; staff psychologist, dir. aftercare treatment program, mental health dept. Mile Square Health Ctr., Chgo., 1974-75, staff psychologist, coordinator devel. disabilities program, 1976-79; asst. prof. psychology U. North Fla., Jacksonville, 1975-76, Rush U.-Presbyn. St. Luke's Med. Ctr., Chgo., 1976—; pvt. practice clin. psychology, 1977—; exec. dir. Inst. for Community Mental Health, 1979—; cons. safety evaluation program Isaac Ray Ctr., 1986-91; dir. Ctr. for Applied Psychology and Forensic Studies, 1991—; psychology cons. Disability Policy Br. Social Security Adminstrn., Chgo, 1980—. Registered psychologist, Ill. Mem. Am. Psychol. Assn., Assn. Black Psychologists.

DAWN, CLARENCE ERNEST, history educator; b. Chattanooga, Dec. 6, 1918; s. Fred Hartman and Hettie Lou (Gibson) D.; m. Pansie Mozelle Dooley, July 8, 1944; children: Julia Anne, Carolyn Louise. B.A., U. Chattanooga, 1941; M.A., Princeton U., 1947, Ph.D., 1948. Instr. history U. Ill., Urbana, 1949-52, asst. prof., 1952-55, assoc. prof., 1955-60, prof., 1960—, prof. emeritus, 1989—; dir. U. Ill. Tehran Research Unit, Iran, 1972-74; fellow Inst. Advanced Studies, Hebrew U., Jerusalem, 1981-82. Author: From Ottomanism to Arabism, 1973; Contbr. articles to profl. jours. Served with AUS, 1942-46; Served with U.S. Army, 1951-52. Social Sci. Research Council World Area fellow, 1948-49; fellow joint com. on Near and Middle East Social Sci. Research Council and Am. Council Learned Socs., 1966-67; Fulbright-Hays fellow, 1966-67. Mem. Middle East Studies Assn., Middle East Inst. Home: 1504 S Grove St Urbana IL 61801-5117

DAWOOD, MOHAMED YUSOFF, obstetrician, gynecologist; b. Singapore, Singapore, Sept. 13, 1943; came to U.S., 1974; s. Sheikh and Fatimah (Hussein) D.; m. Firyal Sultana Khan, July 14, 1978; children: Fatimah Sultana, Fauzia Sultana, Firdaus Sultana, Hassan Yusoff. MB, ChB, U. Sheffield, Yorkshire, Eng., 1968, MD with gold medal, 1974; M of Medicine, U. Singapore, 1972. Diplomate Am. Bd. Obstetrics and Gynecology, Am. Bd. Reproductive Endocrinology. First asst. in ob-gyn. U. Melbourne, 1974; from instr. to assoc. prof. ob-gyn. Cornell U. Med. Coll., N.Y.C., 1974-79; prof. ob-gyn. U. Ill., Chgo., 1979-90; Berel Held prof. ob-gyn. and reproductive scis. U. Tex. Med. Sch., Houston, 1990—; lectr. U. Singapore, 1973-74; cons., editorial cons., reviewer in field. Author: Green's Gynecology, 1990, Dysmenorrhea, 1981, Premenstrual Syndrome and Dysmenorrhea, 1985, Oxytocin, vol. 2, 1984, Prostaglandin Inhibition in Obstetrics and Gynecology, 1983; contbr. articles to profl. jours. Recipient Gold medal Jaycee Jr. C. of C. Singapore, 1973. Fellow ACS, ACOG, Am. Gynecol. & Obstet. Soc., Royal Coll. Ob-Gyn. (Edgar Gentilli prize 1974, Gold medal 1973); mem. Endocrine Soc. Achievements include research in prostaglandins in the causation of menstrual cramps and relief by blocking prostaglandins; role of oxytocin in human parturition, bone-depleting effect of GnRH agonists during treatment of endometriosis; presence of neurohypophyseal peptides in primate and human ovaries; regulation of primate corpus luteum. Office: Univ Texas Medical School 6431 Fannin St Ste 3204 Houston TX 77030-1501

DAWSON, ADAM, private investigator, former newspaper editor; b. N.Y.C., May 4, 1950; s. Martin and Renee D.; m. Constance Jo Stewart, Oct. 21, 1950. BA, Syracuse Univ., N.Y., 1972. Lic. private investigator, Calif. Press sec. U.S. Congressman M. Blouin, Washington, 1977-78; reporter Evening News, Annapolis, Md., 1978-79, Daily News, L.A., 1979-84; L.A. bureau chief Orange County Register, Santa Ana, Calif., 1984-88; city editor Journal Tribune, Biddeford, Maine, 1988-89; owner Dawson Ryan Assocs., L.A., 1989—; sr. instr. UCLA Extension, L.A., 1981-91. Mem. sports advisory coun. City Santa Monica, Calif., 1996—. Named Best Investigative Reporting Valley Press Club, L.A., 1982, named Best Investigative Series Orange County Press Club, 1986. Office: Dawson Ryan Assocs 12021 Wilshire Blvd # 846 Los Angeles CA 90025-1200

DAWSON, ARMETTA K., mental health and geriatric nurse; b. Sheldon, Iowa, Sept. 13, 1938; d. Charles Milton and Tillie Klazina (Visser) Miller; m. C. Richard Dawson, Sept. 3, 1983; children: Randall Dale Schiernbeck, Richard Lee Schiernbeck, Robert Allen Schiernbeck; stepchildren: Joy Matusiewicz, Craig Dawson. Diploma, Meth. Sch. Nursing, Sioux City, Iowa, 1959; AS with highest honors, North Iowa Community Coll., Mason City, 1979; AA in Nursing Home Adminstrn., Des Moines Community Coll., 1980; BSN, Grand View Coll., Des Moines, 1988. Cert. in psychiat. nursing. Provisional adminstr. Park Manor, Ft. Dodge, Iowa; charge nurse psychiat. unit Iowa Luth. Hosp., Des Moines; staff nurse Nursefinders, Des Moines; supr. Iowa Jewish Sr. Life Ctr., Des Moines; surg. nurse Planned Parenthood, Des Moines. Mem. First Christian Ch.; supporter Am. Indian Coll. Found, So. Poverty Law Ctr., Am. Mus. Natural History, Nat. Mus. Women in the Arts, Habitat for Humanity Internat., Nat. Mus. Am. Indian, Ams. Helping Ams. Mem. AAUW, Am. Assn. Ret. Persons, Sigma Theta Tau. Democrat. Home: 941 37th St Des Moines IA 50312-3115

DAWSON, CHANDLER ROBERT, ophthalmologist, educator; b. Denver, Aug. 24, 1930; married; 3 children. AB, Princeton U., 1952; MD, Yale U., 1956. USPHS epidemiologist Communicable Disease Ctr., 1957-60; resident dept. ophthalmology Sch. Medicine U. Calif., San Francisco, 1960-63; asst. clin. prof. U. Calif., San Francisco, 1963-66, asst. prof. in residence, 1966-69, assoc. prof. opthalmology, 1969-75, prof. ophthalmology, 1975-97, prof. emeritus, assoc. dir. Francis I. Proctor Found., 1970-84, dir., 1984-95; fellow Middlesex Hosp. Med. Sch., London, 1963-64; co-dir. WHO Collaborating Ctr. for Reference and Rsch. on Trachoma and other Chlamydial Infections, 1970-79, dir. Collaborating Ctr. for Prevention of Blindness and Trachoma, 1979—. Recipient Knapp award AMA, 1967, 69, Medaille Trachome, 1978. Mem. Am. Soc. Microbiology, Am. Acad. Ophthalmology, Assn. Rsch. Vision & Ophthalmology. Achievements include rsch. in epidemiology of infectious eye diseases and cataracts; prevention of blindness; pathogenesis of virus diseases of the eyes; electron microscopy of eye diseases; clinical trials of treatment for trachoma and for herpes simplex eye infections. Office: U Calif San Francisco Francis I Proctor Found Rsch Ophthalmology San Francisco CA 94143-0412*

DAWSON, DAVID M., neurologist; b. Dec. 12, 1930. AB, Harvard Coll., 1952; MD, U. Mich., 1956. Prof. neurology Harvard Med. Sch., Boston. Address: 100 Keyes Rd Concord MA 01742

DAWSON, DAVID SMITH, television executive; b. Chgo., Apr. 25, 1945; s. Thomas H. and Norma (Smith) D.; m. Heidi Caye Henderson; children: Cory Andrew, Ashley Kathleen. AA, San Diego Mesa Coll., 1965; BA, San Diego State U., 1967, MA, 1968. Producer, dir. Sta. KFMB-TV, San Diego, 1963-68; prodn. supr. live ops. CBS-TV, Hollywood, Calif., 1968-72; producer, dir. Sta. KHJ-TV, Hollywood, 1972-75, Sta. KCOP-TV, Hollywood, 1975-81; mgr. broadcast ops. and engring. ABC-TV, Hollywood, 1981-85; v.p. post prodn. ops. Premore, Inc., North Hollywood, 1985-98; broadcast cons., 1998—; asst. prof. Los Angeles City Coll., 1981-85. contbr. Los Angeles Childrens Outreach, 1985—. Mem. Acad. TV Arts and Scis. (Emmy award 1969, 71), Soc. Motion Picture and TV Engrs., Nat. Assn. Broadcasters, Dirs. Guild Am., Am. Film Inst. Republican. Avocations: golf, computers. Home: 25263 Via Tanara Santa Clarita CA 91355-3236 Office: Ste 345 14431 Ventura Blvd Sherman Oaks CA 91423

DAWSON, DENNIS RAY, lawyer, manufacturing company executive; b. Alma, Mich., June 19, 1948; s. Maurice L. and Virginia (Baker) D.; m. Marilynn S. Gordon, Nov. 26, 1971; children: Emily Lynn, Brett Thomas. AA, Gulf Coast Coll., 1968; AB, Duke U., 1970; JD, Wayne State U., 1973. Bar: Mich. 1973, U.S. Dist. Ct. (ea. dist.) Mich. 1973, U.S. Dist. Ct. (we. dist.) Mich. 1975. Assoc., Watson, Wunsch & Keidan, Detroit, 1973-75; mem., Coupe, Ophoff & Dawson, Holland, Mich., 1975-77; staff atty. Amway Corp., Ada, Mich., 1977-79; corp. counsel Meijer, Inc., Grand Rapids, Mich., 1979-82; sec., corp. counsel Tecumseh Products Co., 1982-92; corp. counsel, asst. sec. Holnam Inc., Dundee, Mich., 1992-93; v.p., gen. counsel, sec. Denso Internat. Am. Inc., 1993—; exec. com. Bank of Lenawee, Adrian, Mich., 1984-93, also bd. dirs.; adj. prof. Aquinas Coll., Grand Rapids, 1978-82; govt. regulation and litigation com. Outdoor Power Equipment Inst. Inc., Washington, 1982-92. Trustee Herrick Meml. Hosp., 1988-91, Tecumseh Civic Auditorium, 1986-89; mem. adv. coun. Montessori Children's House and Acad., Adrian, 1987-93. Mem. ABA, Mich. State Bar Assn., Am. Soc. Corp. Secs., Am. Corp. Counsel Assn., Mich. Mfrs. Assn. (lawyers com. 1987-92), Lenawee C. of C. (bd. dirs. 1988-92). Office: Denso Internat America Inc PO Box 5133 24777 Denso Dr Southfield MI 48034-5244

DAWSON, DERMONTTI FARRA, professional football player; b. Lexington, Ky., June 17, 1965. Degree in edn., U. Ky., 1988. Center Pitts. Steelers, 1988—. Selected to Pro Bowl, 1992-94, 96; named to Sporting News NFL All-Pro Team, 1994. Office: 300 Stadium Cir Pittsburgh PA 15212-5721*

DAWSON, DONALD ANDREW, mathematics educator, researcher; b. Montreal, Que., Can., June 4, 1937; s. William Norman Cecil and Frances Malcolm (Andrew) D.; m. Elizabeth Jean Hilton, May 9, 1964; children: Michael, Suzanne. BSc, McGill U., Montreal, 1958, MSc, 1959; PhD, MIT, 1963. Sr. engr. Raytheon Corp., Bedford, Mass., 1962-63; assoc. prof. McGill U., 1963-70; prof. Carleton U., Ottawa, Ont., Can., 1970-99; dir. The Fields Inst. for Rsch. in Math. Scis., Toronto, Can.; prof. emeritus Carleton U., 1999—. Assoc. editor: Electronic Jour. of Probability, 1998; contbr. articles to profl. jours. Fellow Inst. Math Stats. (assoc. editor Annals of Probability jour. 1987-90), Internat. Stats. Inst., Royal Soc. Can.; mem. Can. Math. Soc. (co-editor in chief jour. 1988-93), Can. Statis. Soc., Am. Math. Soc., Bernoulli Soc. (adv. bd. stochastic processes application 1982—). Avocations: cross-country skiing, walking, music appreciation. Office: The Fields Inst, 222 College St, Toronto, ON Canada M5 T3J1

DAWSON, EARL BLISS, obstetrics and gynecology educator; b. Perry, Fla., Feb. 1, 1930; s. Bliss and Linnie (Calliham) D.; BA, U. Kans., 1955; student Bowman Gray Sch. Medicine, 1955-57; MA, U. Mo., 1960; PhD, Tex. A&M U., 1964; m. Winnie Ruth Isbell, Apr. 10, 1951; children: Barbara Gail, Patricia Ann, Robert Earl, Diana Lynn. Rsch. instr. dept. ob-gyn. U. Tex. Med. br., Galveston, 1963-65, rsch. asst. prof., 1965-68, rsch. assoc. prof., 1968-89, assoc. prof. dept. ob-gyn., 1989—; cons. Interdeptl. Com. on Nutrition for Nat. Def., 1965-68; cons. Nat. Nutrition Survey, 1968-69. Scoutmaster Boy Scouts Am., 1969—. With USNR, 1947-52. Nutrition Rsch. fellow, 1960-61; NSF scholar, 1961-62; NIH Rsch. fellow, 1962-63. Mem. Tex., N.Y. Acads. Scis., Am. Fert. Soc. Am. Inst. Nutrition, Am. Soc. Clin. Nutrition, Am. Coll. Nutrition, Am. Fertility Soc., Soc. Exptl. Biology and Medicine, Soc. Environ. Geochemistry and Health, Sigma Xi, Phi Rho Sigma. Baptist. Mason. Club: Mic-O-Say (Kansas City, Mo.). Author: Effect of Water Borne Nitrites on the Environment of Man; contbr. numerous articles to profl. jours., chpts. to books. Achievements include research on prenatal nutrition, male fertility, epidemiology of lithium in Tex., biochemical changes associated with pre-menstrual syndrome. Home: 3431 S Peach Hollow Cir # 8 Pearland TX 77584-8006 Office: U Tex Med Br Dept Ob-Gyn Galveston TX 77550

DAWSON, EDWARD JOSEPH, merger and acquisition executive; b. Rochester, Pa., Apr. 1, 1944; s. Ralph Edward and Evelyn May (Riggle) D.; m. Lynda Sue Weir, 1975; 5 children. BS in Indsl. Mgmt., Carnegie Mellon U., 1966; MBA in Fin., U. Chgo., 1968. Computer systems analyst, corp. fin. analyst, Tex. Instruments Corp., Dallas, 1968-70, product planning mgr. digital systems div., 1970-72, mgr. comml. equipment bus. objective, 1972-74, mgr. mktg. electronic watch div., 1975-76, mgr. mktg. home video systems, 1976-77; sr. v.p. ops. and mktg. Capital Alliance Corp., Dallas, 1977-80, exec. v.p. merger ops., 1980-81, chmn. bd., CEO, pres., 1981— ; sec. M&A Internat., 1988, v.p. 1989, 96, pres. 1990, 97. Pres. Marina del Rey Homeowners Assn., 1982-84. Lic. security broker/dealer, real estate broker. Mem. Omicron Delta Kappa, Beta Theta Pi. Mem. Church of Christ. Home: 818 Stratford Dr Southlake TX 76092-7109 Office: Capital Alliance Corp 2777 N Stemmons Fwy Ste 1220 Dallas TX 75207-2293

DAWSON, EUGENE ELLSWORTH, university president emeritus; b. Kansas City, Kans., Jan. 23, 1917; s. Harold Lambert and Betty Ross Dawson; m. Arlene Wilburma Clark, May 7, 1935; children: Eugene Jr., Clark (dec.), LoLita, Edward, Brent, Deborah. BA, Pittsburg (Kans.) State U., 1940; STB, Harvard U., 1944; PhD, Boston U., 1949; postgrad., U. Chgo., 1953; DHL (hon.), U. Colo., 1967; HHD (hon.), Regis U., Denver, 1967; DLitt (hon.), Keuka Coll., Keuka Pk., N.Y., 1968; DD (hon.), U. Redlands, Calif., 1978; postgrad., St. Elizabeth's Hosp., Washington, 1978-79. Asst. prof. psychology Pittsburg State U., 1946-48, dean of adminstrn., prof. psychology, 1949-57; pres. Colo. Woman's Coll., Denver, 1957-70; pres. U. Redlands, 1970-78, pres. emeritus, 1978—; instr. summer sessions U. Chgo, Kent State U., U. Houston, Western Oreg. U., Iliff Sch. Theology; cons. higher edn. and human svcs., 1980—; evaluator grants to univs. and ednl. instns., 1990—. Contbr. articles to profl. jours., chpts. to books. Bd. dirs. Estes Pk. Ch. of the Air, 1980—, Qualife Wellness Cmty., Denver, 1982—, Samaritan Counseling Ctr., Denver, 1985—; sec. bd. trustees Temple Hoyne Buell Found., Englewood, Colo., 1990—; sec. bd. dirs. Buell Devel. Corp., Englewood, 1990—. Recipient Outstanding Alumni award Pittsburg State U., 1957, Meritorious Svc. award, 1977, Talmud Torah award Congregation Hebrew Edn. Alliance, Denver, 1969. Mem. Colo. Harvard Club, Nebr. PTA (life), Rotary Internat. (Paul Harris fellow So. Calif. divsn. 1972, pres. Denver chpt. 1964-65, dist. gov. 1967-68, Denver Rotary Found., 1985—), Phi Delta Kappa, Omicron Delta Kappa. Baptist. Avocations: tennis, hiking, reading, travel. Home: Longs Pk Rt 1361 Willow Ln Estes Park CO 80517-7324 Office: TH Buell Found 2700 E Hampden Ave Englewood CO 80110-7614

DAWSON, FRANCES EMILY, poet, nurse; b. Augsburg, Germany, Dec. 7, 1952; d. Emmett C. Jr. and B. Louise (Boddie) D. BS in Nursing, Pa. State U., 1974. RN, D.C. Staff nurse Howard U. Med. Ctr., Washington, 1974-75, charge nurse, 1975-77. Author: Live for Today, 1986, With You in Mind, 1987, Reflections, 1988, (poetry cassette rec.) Soul Connection, 1992. Active Disabled Resource Ctr., Lupus Found. Am., Calif. Assn. Physically Handicapped; model Operation Confidence Program for the Disabled, 1985-86, head cheerleader drill team, 1985-86; mem. Long Beach Task Force for the Ams. with Disabilities Act, 1994—; active Christ 2d Baptist Ch., 1985—. Recipient Golden Poetry award, 1985-92, excellence in lit. award Pinewood Poetry, 1987-89. Mem. BMI, Walt Whitman Guild, Internat. Soc. Poets (hon. charter), Pa. State U. Alumni Assn., Detroit Black Poets Guild. Democrat. Baptist. Avocations: needlepoint, sewing. Home: 250 Pacific Ave Long Beach CA 90802-3000

DAWSON, GERALD LEE, engineering company executive; b. Santa Ana, Calif., July 6, 1933; s. Harold Guy and Violet Jean (Swanson) D.; m. Shirley Jean Webb, Dec. 28, 1966; children: Debbi Lynn, John Guy. Grad. high sch., Santa Ana. Technician Beckman Instruments, Costa Mesa, Calif., 1954-55, mgr. quality control, 1955-57; mgr. Nat. Theaters, Santa Ana, 1958-59; customer engr. IBM Corp., Santa Monica, Calif., 1959-63; engring. specialist IBM Corp., Lexington, Ky., 1963-65, engr., 1965-70, engring. mgr., 1970-75, prodn. engr., 1975-82, sr. engr., 1982-89; pres. MAS-HAMILTON Group/MAS-HAMILTON Security Internat., Lexington, 1990—, chief tech. officer, 1994—. Patentee electronic keyboard, 11 electronic combination locks, access control systems. Bus. chmn. United Way, Calif., 1958; chmn. Rep. campaign, Calif., 1957. Mem. Robotics Internat., Soc. Mfg. Engrs., Elks, Moose (prelate 1969-70). Avocations: flying, golf, fishing, travel.

DAWSON, HORACE GREELEY, JR., former diplomat, government official; b. Augusta, Ga., Jan. 30, 1926; s. Horace Greeley Dawson; m. Lula M. Cole, Aug. 30, 1953; children: Horace Greeley III, Horace Gregory. AB, Lincoln (Pa.) Coll., 1949, LLD (hon.), 1990; AM, Columbia U., 1950; PhD, Iowa State U., 1960. Instr. English So. U., Baton Rouge, 1950-53; assoc. prof., dir. pub. rels. N.C. Cen. U., Durham, 1953-62; joined U.S. Fgn. Svc., 1962; svc. in Uganda, Nigeria, Liberia, Manila; mem. sr. seminar in fgn. policy Fgn. Svc. Inst., 1970-71; amb. to Botswana, 1979-83; dep. examiner Dept. State, U.S. Fgn. Svc., 1982-84; dir. equal opportunity and civil rights USIA, 1985-89; program dir. Sch. Comm. Howard U., Washington, 1989-90, dir. Patricia Roberts Harris program in pub. affairs, 1990-94, asst. to pres. for pub. affairs and comms., 1994-95; dir. Ralph J. Bunche Internat. Affairs Ctr., 1996—; vis. prof. U. Lagos, Nigeria, 1966-67, U. Md., 1971-79; bd. dirs. Ctr. for the Pub. Policy and Diplomacy Lincoln U. Author: Handbook for High School Newspaper Advisors, 1961, The Relationship Between Business and Government in Japan, 1980; contbr. chpt. to: Exporting America, Essays on American Studies Abroad; contbr. articles to profl. publs.; co-editor: New Dimensions in Higher Education, 1961; mng. editor Coll. Lang. Assn. Jour., 1957-60. Chmn. pro tem, sr. bd. stewards Met. AME Ch., 1988-98. With AUS, 1944-46. Mem. NAACP, Am. Fgn. Svc. Assn., Coun. Fgn. Rels., Fgn. Student Svc. Coun. (bd. dirs.), World Affairs Coun. (bd. dirs.), Assn. Black Am. Ambs. (former pres., chmn.), Alpha Phi Alpha World Policy Coun.

DAWSON, HOWARD ATHALONE, JR., federal judge; b. Okolona, Ark., Oct. 23, 1922; s. Howard Athalone and Mamie (Watson) D.; m. Marianne Atherholt, Feb. 2, 1946; children—Amy, Suzanne. B.S. in Commerce, U. N.C., 1946; J.D., George Washington U., 1949. Bar: D.C. 1949, Ga. 1958. Pvt. practice Washington, 1949-50; atty. civil div. Office Chief Counsel, IRS, 1950-53, asst. regional counsel Atlanta region, 1953-56, regional counsel, 1957; asst. chief counsel adminstrn. Office Chief Counsel, IRS, Washington, 1958-62; judge U.S. Tax Ct., Washington, 1962—; chief judge U.S. Tax Ct., 1973-77, 83-85, sr. judge, 1985—; prof. law, dir. grad. tax program U. Balt. Sch. Law, 1986-89; David Brennan Disting. prof. law U. Akron Sch. Law, spring 1986; Disting. adj. prof. law U. San Diego Sch. Law, spring 1991. Served with AUS, 1943-45, ETO; capt. Res. Mem. ABA, D.C. Bar Assn., Fed. Bar Assn., Chi Psi, Delta Theta Phi. Office: US Tax Court 400 2nd St NW Washington DC 20217-0002

DAWSON, JAMES RICHARD, fire and safety engineer; b. Fond du Lac, Wis., July 1, 1936; s. Cecil V. and Helen (Greider) D.; m. Martha Bromley, June 10, 1959; children: Heather Joy Dawson Cudworth, Jamie Dawson Strebing. Cert. safety profl., master fire fighter. With Mut. Fire Inspection Bur. New Eng., Salem, Mass., 1959-61, Home Ins. Co., Milw., 1961-65; safety dir. Amron Corp. divsn. Gulf and Western Co., Waukesha, Wis., 1965-69; fire and safety engr. Ind. U., Bloomington, 1969—. CEO, trustee Bloomington Twp., 1979-98. Mem. Am. Soc. Safety Engrs., Nat. Fire Protection Assn., Vets. of Safety, Ind. Twp. Trustees Assn. (Twp. Trustee of Yr. 1985), Ind. Vol. Fireman's Assn., Fraternal Order Police. Republican. Methodist. Home: 3899 E Bethel Ln Bloomington IN 47408-9509 Office: Ind U Poplars Rm 705 400 E 7th St Bloomington IN 47405-3024

DAWSON, JOHN FREDERICK, retired architect; b. Stambaugh, Mich., Sept. 4, 1930; s. Frederick John and Myrtle (Olson) D.; m. Ruth Jennette Opland, May 8, 1954; children—Craig Frederick, Cindy Paulette. BArch, U. Mich., 1953. Registered arch., Mich., Md., D.C. Instr. U. Mich., 1956-60, asst. prof. architecture, 1960-63; dir. govtl. affairs AIA, Washington, 1963-65; v.p. Louis C. Kingscott & Assos. Inc., Washington and Kalamazoo, 1965-70; pres. Development Services, Inc., Kalamazoo, 1970-72; exec. v.p. Spanpark Corp., Kalamazoo, 1972-75; mgmt. cons. to architects, 1975-76; dir. adminstrn. Bus. and Instl. Furniture Mfrs. Assn., 1976-77; owner Solar Unltd., 1977-82; pres. Solar Solutions, Inc., 1980-84; v.p. tech. svcs. Maxam Tech., Inc., 1984-87; sr. architect David Volkert & Assoc., 1988-89; v.p. adminstrn. Edmunds & Kidd, Inc., 1989; architect/preservation officer facilities mgmt. divsn., dir. Exec. Office of the Pres., Washington, 1990-95; hist. pres. cons. Turner Constrn. Co., 1997—; preservation inspection cons. Turner Constrn. Co., 1997—; vice chmn. Kalamazoo Energy Policy Adv. Com., 1980-82. Pres. Whitley Park Condo. Assn., 1997-98, bd. dirs., 1997—. With AUS, 1953-55. Home: 5828 Mira Serena El Paso TX 79912

DAWSON, JOHN MYRICK, plasma physics educator; b. Champaign, Ill., Sept. 30, 1930; s. Walker Myrick and Wilhelmina Emily (Stephan) D.; m. Nancy Louise Wildes, Dec. 28, 1957 (dec. May 1994); children: Arthur Walker, Margaret Louise. B.S., U. Md., 1952, M.S., 1954, Ph.D., 1957. Fulbright scholar Inst. Plasma Physics, Nagoya, Japan, 1964-65; research physicist Plasma Physics Lab. Princeton U., 1956-73, head theoretical group, 1965-73; prof. plasma physics UCLA, 1973—, assoc. head Inst. for Plasma Physics & Fusion Engring., 1976-88; cons. in field; John Danz lectr. U. Wash., 1974; guest Russian Acad. Scis., 1971; invited lectr. Inst. Plasma Physics, Nagoya, Japan, 1972; Kerst lectr. U. Wis., 1994. Contbr. articles in field to profl. jours. Recipient Exceptional Sci. Achievement award TRW Sys., 1977, James Clerk Maxwell prize in plasma physics, 1977; named Calif. Scientist of Yr., 1978. Aneesur Rahman Prize, Am. Physical Soc., 1994. Fellow AAAS, Am. Phys. Soc. (chmn. plasma div. 1970-71, Aneesun Rahmah prize 1994); mem. NAS, N.Y. Acad. Scis., N.J. Acad. Scis., Sigma Xi, Sigma Pi Sigma, Phi Kappa Phi. Unitarian. Patentee in field. Home: 359 Arno Way Pacific Palisades CA 90272-3348 Office: Univ Calif 405 Hilgard Ave Los Angeles CA 90095-9000

DAWSON, KAREN OLTMANNS, school health nurse, womens health nurse, educator; b. El Centro, Calif., Mar. 14, 1947; d. Victor Roy and Lois Louise Oltmanns; m. Arthur B. Dawson, Sept. 13, 1970; children: David, Jonathan, Stephen, Matthew, Anna-Lisa. BSN, UCLA, 1969; postgrad., U. Calif., Irvine, 1980; MA, U. Colo., Denver, 1992. Cert. vocat. nurse, Colo., instr. nursing Calif., Colo., pub. health nurse, early childhood spl. edn. instr. Staff nurse, maternal-child Swedish Med. Ctr., Englewood, Colo., 1986-92, parent educator, 1983—; nurse, spl. edn. tchr. Cherry Creek Acad., 1995-97—; adminstr. early intervention ctr. for children with spl. needs, 1997-98; dir., v.p. A. Dawson Tutoring, Inc., 1998—; clin. instr. C.C. of Denver, Arapahoe C.C., Littleton, Colo.; spl. edn. tchr. Hope Ctr., Denver, 1992-93. Spl. edn. tchr. United Cerebral Palsy Assn., Denver, 1993-95. Mem. Neonatal ICU Connections Task Force, Swedish Med. Ctr. Colo. Consortium for Preterm Infant Devel.

DAWSON, LEWIS EDWARD, minister, retired military officer; b. Louisville, Oct. 26, 1933; s. Lewis Harper and Zelma Ruth (Hocutt) D.; m. Margaret Ellen Poor, July 29, 1956; children: Edward Rhodes, David Harper, Deborah Louise, Virginia Ruth. BA, Baylor U., 1954; MDiv, So. Bapt. Sem., 1960; postgrad., Presbyn. Sch. Christian Edn., 1977—. Ordained to ministry So. Bapt. Conv., 1960. Pastor Finecastle (Va.) Bapt. Ch. and Zion Hill Bapt. Ch., 1960-63, First So. Bapt. Ch., Great Falls, Mont., 1963-67; commd. capt. USAF, 1967, advanced through grades to col., 1983; chaplain McCoy AFB, 1967-69, Vietnam, 1969-70, Sheppard AFB, 1971-73, RAF, Chicksands, Eng., 1973-76, Keesler AFB, 1977-79; sr. chaplain Ankara (Turkey) Air Sta., 1979-81; mem. USAF Chaplain Res. Bd. Maxwell AFB, 1981-84; sr. chaplain Wright-Patterson AFB, 1984-87; sr. chaplain Elmendorf AFB, Alaska, 1987-89, ret., 1989; assoc. dir. mil. chaplaincy Home Mission Bd., Atlanta, Ga., 1989-93; assoc. to dir. chaplaincy divsn. Home Mission Bd., So. Bapt. Conv., Alpharetta, Ga., 1994-97; pastoral ministries assoc. First Bapt. Ch., Jonesboro, 1997-99; ret., 1999; clk. Triangle Bapt. Assn., 1965-66; chmn. Mont. Indian mission com. Mont. So. Bapt. Fellowship, 1965-66, treas., 1965-66. Mem. exec. coun. Save the Children Fund, Shefford, Eng., 1973-76. Decorated Bronze Star, Meritorious Svc. medal with 4 oak leaf cluster, Legion of Merit, Air Force Commendation medal. Home: 1926 Coventry Way Jonesboro GA 30236-2688 *When the weapons of war are exploding all around you as well as when you are secure at home with family, God is with you. God is in the logistics business, supplying all that people need as we make ourselves available to God.*

DAWSON, MARY E., government official; b. Halifax, N.S., Can., June 23, 1942; d. Thomas Paul and Florence Margaret (Thurston) McMillan; m. Peter Dawson, Aug. 30, 1969; children: David, Emily. BA with honors in Philosophy, McGill U., 1963, BCL, 1966; DESD, U. Ottawa, 1968; LLB, Dalhousie U., 1970. Tax rschr. Revenue Can., Ottawa, 1967-68, legal counsel, 1968-69; tchg. fellow Dalhousie U., 1969-70; legis. drafter Dept. Justice, 1970-79, assoc. chief legis. counsel, 1980-86, asst. dep. minister pub. law, 1986-88, assoc. dep. minister, 1988—. Active mem. Parkdale United Ch.; mem. adv. bd. Ctr. for Rsch. and Edn. on Women and Work, Sch. Bus., Carleton U. McGill U. scholar, 1960, Lyon William Jacobs Q.C. award, 1965, 78. Mem. Internat. Bar Assn. (chmn. govt. law com.), N.S. Bar, Que. Bar, Ont. Bar. Avocations: Nordic skiing, swimming, theatre, reading. Home: 97 Reid Ave, Ottawa, ON Canada K1H 1T1 Office: Dept Justice, Rm SAT-5081, Ottawa, ON Canada K1A 0H8

DAWSON, MARY RUTH, curator; b. Highland Park, Mich., Feb. 27, 1931; d. John Elson and Olga Josephine (Down) D. B.S., Mich. State Coll., 1952; postgrad., U. Edinburgh, 1952-53; Ph.D., U. Kans., 1957. Instr. zoology Smith Coll., 1958-61; asst. program dir. NSF, Washington, 1961-62; mem. staff Carnegie Mus., Pitts., 1962—, curator, 1971—, chmn. earth sci. div., 1973-97, acting dir., 1982-83; adj. prof. earth scis. U. Pitts., 1971—. Recipient Arnold Guyot award Nat. Geog. Soc., 1981, Woman in Sci. award Chatham Coll., 1983; named Disting. Dau. Pa., 1987; Dr. Hum, Chatham Coll., 1999, Fulbright scholar, 1952-53; fellow AAUW, 1958-59; research grantee NSF, 1961-62, 65—. Fellow Geol. Soc. Am., Arctic Inst. N.Am.; mem. Soc. Vertebrate Paleontology (v.p. 1972-73, pres. 1973-74), Paleontol. Soc., Paläontologische Gesellschaft, Bernese Mountain Dog Club Am., Am. Soc. Mammalogists, Phi Beta Kappa. Research, publs. on Tertiary Lagomorpha, 1957—, early Tertiary Holarctic rodents, 1960—, Arctic paleontology, 1975—. Office: Carnegie Mus 4400 Forbes Ave Pittsburgh PA 15213-4080

DAWSON, MIMI WEYFORTH, government affairs consultant; b. St. Louis, Aug. 31, 1944; d. Francis Griffin and Jeanne (Gething) Weyforth; m. Rhett Brewer Dawson, Jan. 15, 1976; 2 children: Elizabeth Stuart, Andrew Brewer. AB, Washington U., St. Louis, 1966. Press sec., legis. asst. to Rep. James Symington, Mo. Dist., 1973; pres. sec., chief staff Sen. Bob Packwood, Oreg., 1973-81; commr. FCC, Washington, 1981-87; dep. Sec. U.S. Dept. of Transportation, Washington, DC, 1987-89; govt. affairs cons. Wiley, Rein and Fielding, Washington, 1989—; apptd. U.S. Holocaust Meml. Coun., 1992-98; adj. fellow Ctr. for Strategic and Internat. Studies. Mem. Atlantic Coun. U.S. (bd. dirs. 1995—). Republican. Roman Catholic. Office: Wiley Rein and Fielding 1776 K St NW Washington DC 20006-2304

DAWSON, NANCY ANN, hematologist, oncologist; b. San Francisco, Nov. 21, 1953; d. Malcolm Bryon and Helen Dorothy (Jones) D.; m. Neal Thomas Baron, Aug. 22, 1981; children: Blake Bryon Baron, Drew Randall Baron. AB, U. Calif., Berkeley, 1975; MD, Georgetown U., 1979. Diplomate Am. Bd. Internal Medicine, Am. Bd. Internal Medicine-Hematology, Am. Bd. Internal Medicine-Oncology, Nat. Bd. Med. Examiners; lic. MD, Md., Va. Commd. 2nd lt. U.S. Army, 1976, advanced through grades to col., 1997; intern in internal medicine Walter Reed Army Med. Ctr., Washington, 1979-80, residency internal medicine, 1980-82, fellowship hematology-oncology, 1982-85; tchg. fellow, instr. dept. medicine Uniformed Svcs. U. of Health Scis., Bethesda, Md., 1980-82, 83-85, asst. prof. dept. medicine, 1985-92, assoc. prof. dept. medicine, 1992-98, prof. dept. medicine, 1998-99; staff physician hematology-oncology svcs., asst. chief Walter Reed Army Med. Ctr., Washington, 1985-99, 88-90, asst. dir. intern tng. and transitional year program, 1990-91, dir. intern tng. and transitional year program, 1991-94, transitional program advsor to chief grad. med. edn., 1992-94, chief hematology-oncology, 1994-95, dir. clin. rsch., 1995-99; hematology-oncology cons. to Surgeon Gen. of U.S. Army, 1998, chief, hematology-oncology svc., 1999; dir., Genito-urinary med. oncology, Greenbaum Cancer Ctr., U. Maryland; prof. of med., U. of Maryland. Editor: Prostate Cancer, 1994; contbr. chpts. to books and articles to profl. jours. Recipient Am. Med. Women's Assn. Disting. Student citation, 1979. Fellow Am. Coll. Physicians; mem. AMA, Am. Soc. Clin. Oncology, Assn. Mil. Surgeons of U.S., Am. Soc. Hematology, Women in Cancer Rsch., Am. Urol. Assn. Democrat. Roman Catholic. Home: 7721 Curtis St Chevy Chase MD 20815-4913 Office: Walter Reed Army Med Ctr Hematology Oncology Cl Washington DC 20307

DAWSON, PATRICIA LUCILLE, surgeon; b. Kingston, Jamaica, W.I., Sept. 30, 1949; came to U.S. 1950.; d. Percival Gordon and Edna Claire (Overton) D.; m. Stanley James Hiserman, Sept. 6, 1980; children: Alexandria Zoe, Wesley Gordon. BA in Sociology, Allegheny Coll., 1971; MD, N.J. Med. Sch., Newark, 1977; MA in Human and Orgn. Devel., The Fielding Inst., 1996, PhD in Human and Orgnl. Sys., 1998. Membership dir. N.J. ACLU, Newark, 1972; resident in surgery U. Medicine and Dentistry N.J. N.J. Med Sch., 1977-79; Virginia Mason Med. Ctr., Seattle, 1979-82; pvt. practice specializing in surgery Arlington, Wash., 1982-83; dir. med. staff diversity Group Health Coop., Seattle, 1993-98; staff surgeon Group Health Coop., 1983-98; pvt. practice Seattle, 1998—. Fellow ACS, Seattle Surg. Soc.; mem. Am. Med. Women's Assn., Physicians for Social Responsibility, Assn. Women Surgeons, Wash. Black Profls. in Health Care, NOW. Avocations: fiction, walking, cooking. Office: Providence Comp Breast Ctr Jefferson Twr 1600 E Jefferson St Ste 300 Seattle WA 98122-5645

DAWSON, PAULA DAYL, oncological nurse; b. Mount Airy, N.C., Apr. 30, 1956; d. Walter Samuel Dawson and Sybil Ann (Adkins) Anderson. AAS in Nursing, Surry C.C., Dobson, N.C., 1992. RN, N.C. Instr. Miller-Motte Bus. Coll., Winston-Salem, N.C., 1992-93; hematology-oncology staff nurse Wake Forest U. Bapt. Med. Ctr. Comprehensive Cancer Ctr., Winston Salem, N.C., 1992-98; asst. clin. nurse mgr. Wake Forest U. Bapt. Med. Ctr. Comprehensive Cancer Ctr., Winston Salem, 1998—; mem. Shared Governance Steering Com., Wake Forest U. Bapt. Med. Ctr., Winston-Salem, 1996-97. Vol. instr. first aid, saftety and disaster svcs., Surry Count chpt ARC, Mt. Airy, N.C.. 1992—, bd. mem., co-chair disaster svcs., 1997-98; basic cardiac life support instr. Am. Heart Assn., Winston-Salem, 1994—. Mem. Oncology Nursing Soc. (cert. oncol. nurse), Piedmont Triad Oncology Nursing Soc., Nat. League of Nursing, N.C. Nurses Assn. Democrat. Avocations: flower gardening, reading, photography, walking, needlework. Office: Wake Forest U Bapt Med Ctr Medical Center Blvd Winston Salem NC 27103

DAWSON, PHILIP, history educator; b. Ann Arbor, Mich., Nov. 28, 1928; s. John Philip and Emma Van Nostrand (McDonald) D.; m. Ellen Greene, Feb. 6, 1954 (div. Oct. 1980); children: John, Elizabeth; m. Evelyn Raskin, Jan. 23, 1981 (dec. Sept. 1995); m. Kathryn Callaghan, Jan. 18, 1997. BA, U. Mich., 1950, MA, 1951; PhD, Harvard U., 1961. Reporter The Washington Post, 1953-55; tchg. fellow in history Harvard U., Cambridge, Mass., 1957-59, 60-61; instr. history Harvard U., Cambridge, 1961-64; asst. prof. history Stanford (Calif.) U., 1964-70, assoc. prof. history, 1970-73; prof. history Bklyn. Coll. CUNY, 1973-98; Author: Provincial Magistrates and Revolutionary Politics in France, 1789-1795, 1972; co-editor: The French Revolution and the Meaning of Citizenship, 1993; contbr. articles to profl. jours. Fellow NEH, 1987-88. Mem. Soc. des Etudes Robespierristes, Soc. de l'Histoire de Paris et de l'Ile-de-France, Soc. for French Hist. Studies. Home and Office: 56 7th Ave New York NY 10011-6672

DAWSON, ROBERT A., physician assistant; b. Mpls., July 22, 1956; s. Wesley James and Ruth (Johnson) D.; m. Meridith Ford, June 16, 1979; children: Joel, Meolody, Bethany. BS in Med. Sci., Anderson-Broaddus Coll., 1986; BA in Criminology, Indiana U. of Pa., 1979; MPAS, U. Nebr., 1998. Cert. NCCPA. Physician asst. in internal medicine So. West Virginia CUME, Beckley, W.Va., 1986-87; advanced to capt. to USAF, 1987—; physician asst. in family practice USAF, Barksdale AFB, La., 1987-94; orthopedic residency USAF, Andrews AFB, Md., 1994-95; staff orthopaedic physician asst. USAF, Langley AFB, Va., 1995—; staff credentials officer, 2nd Med. Group, Barksdale AFB, 1989-94, founder, dir. health/wellness, 1993-94, disaster team chief, 1993-94; officer-in-charge orthopaedic clin. 1st. Med. Group, Langley AFB, 1994—. Lay minister United Meth. Ch., Nestorville, W.Va., 1984-86; prison minister Cappo Peterson Ctr., Shreveport, La., 1990-94; active children's ministry Christian Ctr. of Shreveport, 1990-94, adult Sunday Sch. tchr., 1990-94. Mem. Am. Acad. Physician Assts., Soc. of Air Force Physician Assts. Republican. Office: 1st Med Group SGOSO Pine St Langely AFB VA 23665

DAWSON, ROBERT EARLE, utilities executive; b. Canton, Ill., Mar. 18, 1923; s. Harry Earle Lamont and Inez Goldie (Brewer) D.; m. Nancy Jane Hill, Aug. 5, 1950; children: Jeffery Owen, David Bruce, William Scott, Sue Ann. BSEE, U. Ill., 1949. Registered profl. engr., Ohio. Jr. engr. Ohio Pub. Service Co., Sandusky, 1949-50; distribution fieldman Ohio Edison Co., Lorain, 1950-52; indsl.sales rep. Ohio Edison Co., Warren, 1952-61; sr. indsl. sales rep. Ohio Edison Co., Akron, 1961-63; indsl. sales supr. Ohio Edison

Co., Elyria, 1963-67; supt. electric and steam sales Ohio Edison Co., Youngstown, 1967-68; div. mgr. Ohio Edison Co., Massillon, 1968-88, ret., 1988. Pres. Massillon Mus. Found., Inc., 1987, 87-91, Massillon Devel. Found., 1972-76, United Way of Western Stark County, Massillon, 1980-81, Massillon Area C. of C., 1979 (award of merit 1986). Named Humanitarian of the Yr., KC Massillon Coun. #554, 1988. Republican. Presbyterian. Lodges: Rotary, Masons. Avocations: woodworking, gardening, golf. Home: 1714 11th St NE Massillon OH 44646-4140

DAWSON, ROBERT KENT, government relations expert; b. Scottsboro, Ala., Jan. 22, 1946; s. C. Paul and Lallie F. (Cook) D.; m. Susan Bernice Lee, Jan. 25, 1969; children: Amy Johanna, Stephen Paul. BS, Tulane U., 1968; JD, Samford U., 1971. Bar: Ala. 1971. Legis. asst. U.S. Rep. Jack Edwards, Washington, 1972-74; adminstr. com. pub. works and transp. U.S. Ho. of Reps., Washington, 1974-81; dep. asst. sec. civil works U.S. Dept. Army, Washington, 1981-84, asst. sec. civil works, 1984-87, assoc. dir. Office Mgmt. and Budget, 1987-89; vice chmn. Cassidy and Assocs., Washington, 1989-97; pres. Dawson & Assocs., Washington, 1998—. Served to lt. U.S. Army, 1971. Recipient award Nat. Legal Aid and Defender Assn., 1971, Disting. Achievement in Art and Sci. Advocacy award Internat. Acad. Trial Lawyers, 1971, Silver Key award ABA, 1971; named Water Statesman of Yr., Nat. Water Research Assn., 1986. Mem. Ala. State Bar Assn., Songwriter's Assn. of Washington. Republican. Avocation: singer/songwriter of country music. Home: 1214 Key Dr Alexandria VA 22302-3408 Office: Dawson and Assocs 1225 I St NW Ste 500 Washington DC 20005-3914

DAWSON, STEPHANIE ELAINE, city manager; b. Norwalk, Conn., Nov. 12, 1956. BA, Cornell U., 1979; MPA, Marist Coll., 1994. Cert. Project Mgmt. Inst., Inst. for Cert. Computing. Ops. analyst Irving Trust Co., N.Y.C., 1981-82, ops. mgr., 1982-85; sys. analyst Dept. Gen. Svcs., N.Y.C., 1986-88, sr. project mgr., 1988-91, dir., 1991-95; project mgr., cons. Port Authority N.Y. and N.J., N.Y.C., 1995-98, mgr. capital programs, 1998—; dir. projects, chpt. liaison PMI/ISSIG, Darbury, Pa. Panel leader emerging tech. ASPA, 1993; mem. adv. group Emerging Tech. Adv. Group AIIM, 1995-99; internat. del. to South Africa, People to People Mission, 1997. Maj. Army Nat. Guard, 1979—. Recipient Women in Law and Govt. recognition Nat. Assn. Negro Bus. and Profl. Women's Clubs, N.Y., 1999. Mem. Alpha Kappa Alpha. E-mail: STPDawson@aol.com. and SD@PANYNJ.Gov. Fax: 212-435-4537. Office: Port Authority NY and NJ One World Trade Ctr New York NY 11375

DAWSON, STEPHEN EVERETTE, lawyer; b. Detroit, May 14, 1946; s. Everette Ivan and Irene (Dresser) D.; m. Consiglia J. Bellisario, Sept. 20, 1974; children: Stephen Everette Jr., Gina C., Joseph J. BA, Mich. State U., 1968; MA, U. Mich., 1969, JD, 1972. Bar: Mich. 1972, U.S. Dist. Ct. (ea. dist.) Mich. 1972, U.S. Supreme Ct. 1978, U.S. Ct. Appeals (6th cir.) 1980. Assoc. Dickinson, Wright, Moon, Van Dusen & Freeman, Detroit, 1972-79; ptnr. Dickinson, Wright, PLLC, Bloomfield Hills, Mich., 1979—; adj. prof. law U. Detroit, 1986-88. Mem. ABA, Am. Coll. Real Estate Lawyers, Mich. State Bar Assn. (mem. coun. real property law sect. 1986—, chairperson 1992-93), Phi Beta Kappa. Republican. Avocations: jogging, reading. Office: Dickinson Wright PLLC 525 N Woodward Ave Ste 2000 Bloomfield Hills MI 48304-2970

DAWSON, STUART OWEN, landscape architect, urban designer; b. Urbana, Ill., Apr. 27, 1935; s. Alva Owen and Mildred (Kemp) D.; m. Virginia Wilson (div. July 1968); children: Julie Dawson Orsatti, Emilie Sue, Mark Owen; m. Ellen Washington, Oct. 24, 1970. BFA in Landscape Architecture, U. Ill., 1957; MFA in Landscape Architecture, Harvard U., 1958. Registered landscape architect in 30 states. Draftsman U. Ill., Urbana, 1955-56; draftsman, designer Sasaki, Walker, Assocs., Watertown, Mass., 1957-58, assoc., 1959-62; prin. Sasaki, Dawson, DeMay and Assocs., Watertown, 1962-70; v.p. Sasaki & Assocs., Watertown, 1970—; advisor The Waterfront Ctr., Washington; resident Am. Acad. Rome; instr. Harvard Grad. Sch. Design, 1990-93, U. Ill., Urbana, 1997-98; spkr. and tchr. in field. Prin. works include Deere and Co. Corp. Hdqs., Moline, Ill., TRW Corp. Hdqs., Lindhurst, Ohio, McDonalds Corp. Hdqs., Oak Brook, Ill., Downtown and Waterfront, Newburyport, Mass., Arts Dist., Dallas, Rice U., Houston, Enid Haupt Garden, The Smithsonian Inst., The Kennedy Ctr., Washington, Fountain Plaza, Buffalo, Boston Waterfront Pk. and Long Wharf, Christian Sci. Ctr., Boston, Detroit Riverpark, Charleston (S.C.) Waterfront Pk., Maritime Ctr., Boulder (Colo.) Mall, Betty Marcus Pk., Dallas, Frito-Lay Corp. Hdqs., Plano, Tex., Capitol City Landing and Riverfront and COSI, Indpls., Scioto Riverfront, Columbus, Ohio, Fed. Campus, Oklahoma City, Doosan Meml. Pk., Seoul, Korea. Trustee Hurricane Island Outward Bound, Rockland, Maine; founding commr. Boston Landmarks, 1972-76; juror Salem Witch Trial Tercentenary Mem. Competition. 1st lt. U.S. Army, 1957-60; peer profl., Design Excellence Program, U.S. G.S.A. Pub. Bldgs. DSvcs., 1996-98; mem. alumni coun. Harvard Grad. Sch. Design, 1990-96. Fellow Am. Soc. Landscape Architects (mem. design awards jury 1985, chmn. 1986-87, juror coun. of fellows 1989-91, chmn. student awards jury 1990); mem. Boston Soc. Landscape Architects, Reading Rm. (York Harbor, Maine), York Golf and Tennis Club, Harvard Faculty Club. Avocations: sailing, drawing, dog sledding, fly fishing, skiing. Home: Big Pine Island PO Box 1113 York Harbor ME 03911-1113 Office: Sasaki Assocs Inc 64 Pleasant St Watertown MA 02472-2316

DAWSON, SUZANNE STOCKUS, lawyer; b. Chgo., Dec. 29, 1941; d. John Charles and Josephine (Zolpe) Stockus; m. Daniel P. Dawson Sr., Sept. 1, 1962; children: Daniel P. Jr., John Charles, Michael Sean. BA, Marquette U., 1963; JD cum laude, Loyola U., Chgo., 1965. Bar: Ill. 1965, U.S. Dist. Ct. (no. dist.) Ill. 1965. Assoc. Kirkland & Ellis, Chgo., 1965-71, ptnr., 1971-82; ptnr. Arnstein & Lehr, Chgo., 1982-89, Foley & Lardner, Chgo., 1989-94; spl. counsel publicly held corps. Glenview, Ill., 1995-97; corp. counsel Baxter Healthcare Corp., Deerfield, Ill., 1997-98, sr. counsel, 1998—. Mem. various coms. United Way Chgo.; corp. adv. bd. Sec. State of Ill., 1973; past mem. bd. advisors Loyola of Chgo. Law Sch.; trustee Lawrence Hall Youth Svcs., Chgo., 1983-98, pres., 1991-93, chair 1993-96; mem. adv. bd. Cath. Charities Chgo., 1985—; mem. exec. com., bd. governance Notre Dame High Sch., Niles, Ill., 1990-97. Recipient Founder's Day award Loyola U., 1980, St. Thomas More award Loyola of Chgo. Law Sch., 1983. Mem. ABA, Am. Arbitration Assn. (appointed mem. nat. panel of comml. arbitrators 1996—), Ill. Bar Assn. Roman Catholic. Avocations: piano, choir singing, gardening, skiing, gourmet cooking. Home: 2113 Valley Lo Ln Glenview IL 60025-1724 Office: Baxter Healthcare Corp One Baxter Pkwy Deerfield IL 60015-4633

DAWSON, THOMAS CLELAND, II, financial executive; b. Washington, Mar. 9, 1948; s. Allan D. and Barbara Jane (Dodge) D.; m. Moira Jane Haley, June 1, 1974; children: Thomas III, Andrew, Catherine. B.A. with honors in Econs., Stanford U., 1970, M.B.A. with honors, 1978; postgrad., Princeton U., 1970-71. Fgn. service officer U.S. Dept. State, Washington, 1971-76, economist, 1971-72, asst. to under sec. for econ. affairs, 1972-74; consul., econ. officer Am. Consulate Gen., Rio de Janeiro, Brazil, 1974-76; cons. McKinsey & Co., Washington, 1978-81; dep. asst. sec. U.S. Dept. Treasury, Washington, 1981-84; asst. sec. U.S. Dept. Treasury, 1984-85; dep. asst. to Pres., exec. asst. to chief of staff The White House, Washington, 1985-87; exec. v.p. Regdon Assoc., Alexandria, Va., 1987-89; U.S. exec. dir. Internat. Monetary Fund, Washington, 1989-93; 1st v.p. Merrill Lynch and Co., N.Y.C., 1993-94, dir., 1995—. Mem. Reagan-Bush Planning Task Force, Alexandria, Va., 1980; assoc. dir. Taft for Senate campaign, Cin., 1970. Woodrow Wilson fellow, 1970. Mem. Army and Navy Club (Washington), Kenwood Country Club (Bethesda, Md.), Beacon Hill Club (Summit, N.J.). Republican. Episcopalian. Home: 50 Portland Rd Summit NJ 07901-3045 Office: World Fin Ctr North Tower New York NY 10281-1325

DAWSON, VIRGINIA SUE, newspaper editor; b. Concordia, Kans., June 6, 1940; d. John Edward and Wilma Aileen (Thompson) Morgan; m. Neil S. Dawson, Nov. 28, 1964; children: Shelley Diane Dawson Sedwick, Lori Ann, Christy Lynn. BS in Home Econs. and Journalism, Kans. State U., 1962. Cert. Am. Assn. Family and Consumer Scis. Asst. publs. editor Ohio State U. Coop. Extension Svc., Columbus, 1962-64; home editor Ohio Farmer mag., Columbus, 1964-78; food editor Columbus Dispatch, 1978—. Recipient Commn. award Ohio Poultry Assn., 1980. Mem. Assn. Food Journalists, Ohio Newspaper Women's Assn. (several writing and newspaper design awards 1985-94). Avocations: biking, running, reading, cooking. Office: Columbus Dispatch 34 S 3rd St Columbus OH 43215-4241

DAWSON, WALLACE DOUGLAS, JR., geneticist; b. Louisville, Mar. 15, 1931; s. Wallace Douglas and Ida Belle (Hieatt) D.; m. Victoria Hollowell; 3 children. B.S., Western Ky. U., 1954; M.S., U. Ky., 1959; Ph.D. (NSF Coop. fellow), Ohio State U., 1962. Asst. prof. biology U. S.C., 1962-66, asso. prof., 1966-71, prof., 1971—, chmn. dept. biology, 1974-77, George Bunch prof. biology, 1977-81; vis. scientist div. mammals Smithsonian Instn., 1979. Served to 1st lt. USAF, 1955-57. Recipient Disting. Teaching award S.C. Honors Program, 1977, 85; NIH grantee, 1964, 71, 99; NSF grantee, 1985, 90, 93, 97. Mem. AAAS, Am. Genetic Assn., Am. Soc. Mammalogists, Assn. Southeastern Biologists, Genetics Soc. Am., Soc. Study Evolution, S.C. Acad. Sci., Soc. Molecular Biology and Evolution, Mammalian Genome Soc., Sigma Xi. Rsch. and publs. in field. Office: U SC Dept Biol Scis Columbia SC 29208

DAWSON, WILLIAM RYAN, zoology educator; b. Los Angeles, Aug. 24, 1927; s. William Eldon and Mary (Ryan) D.; m. Virginia Louise Berwick, Sept. 9, 1950; children: Deborah, Denise, William. Student, Stanford, 1945-46; BA, UCLA, 1949, MA, 1950, PhD, 1953; DSc, U. Western Australia, 1971. Faculty zoology U. Mich., Ann Arbor, 1953-94, prof., 1962-94, D.E.S. Brown prof. biol. scis., 1981-94, chmn. div. biol. scis., 1974-82, dir. Mus. Zoology, 1982-93, D.E.S. Brown prof. emeritus, 1994—; lectr. Summer Inst. Desert Biology, Ariz. State U., 1960-71, Maytag prof., 1982; rschr. Australian-Am. Edn. Found., U. Western Australia, 1969-70; Carpenter lectr. San Diego State U., 1996; mem. Speakers Bur., Am. Inst. Biol. Sci., 1960-62; mem. adv. panel NSF environ. biology program, 1967-69; mem. adv. com. for rsch. NSF, 1973-77; adv. panel NSF regulatory biology program, 1979-82; mem. R/V Alpha Helix New Guinea Expdn., 1969; chief scientist R/V Dolphin Gulf of Calif. Expdn., 1976; mem. R/V Alpha Helix Galapagos Expdn., 1978. Editorial bd.: Condor, 1960-63, Auk, 1964-68, Ecology, 1968-70, Ann. Rev. Physiology, 1973-79, Physiol. Zoology, 1976-86; co-editor: Springer-Verlag Zoophysiology and Ecology series, 1968-72; assoc. editor: Biology of the Reptilia, 1972, Birds of N.Am., 1997—. Served with USNR, 1945-46. USPHS Postdoctoral Research fellow, 1953; Guggenheim fellow, 1962-63; Recipient Russell award U. Mich., 1959, Distinguished Faculty Achievement award, 1976; Wheeler Lectr. U. N.D., 1986. Fellow AAAS (council del. 1984-86), Am. Ornithol. Union (Brewster medal 1979); mem. Am. Soc. Zoologists (pres. 1986), Am. Physiol. Soc., Ecol. Soc. Am., Cooper Ornithol. Soc. (hon., Painton award 1963, Miller Rsch. award 1996), Phi Beta Kappa, Sigma Xi, Kappa Sigma. Home: 1376 Bird Rd Ann Arbor MI 48103-2351

DAWSON-AUGUST, ANNIE LEE, state official; b. Sumter, S.C., Sept. 29, 1953; d. Wallace Roland Dawson and Nettie Dorothy (Baldwin) Kinsey; m. Algie Winslow Cuffee, Nov. 25, 1972 (div. 1984), Henry August Jr., Aug. 27, 1988. AS, Pierce Jr. Coll., 1973; BS, LaSalle U., 1988; cert., Urban League Leadership Inst., 1991. Billing clk. Atlantic Richfield Co., Phila., 1969-71; stockbroker's aide Sade & Co., Phila., 1971-72; data entry supr. U.S. Computers, Inc., Tacoma, 1972-74; claims adjuster Equitable Life Assurance Soc., Phila., 1975-77; auditor marine payroll Keystone Shipping Co., Phila., 1980-82; maintenance acctg. technician Dept. Army, Edgemont, Pa., 1982-85; intern automotive maintenance mgmt. Southeastern Pa. Transp. Authority, Phila., 1985-86, quality assurance adminstr., 1985-91, mgr. program devel., 1990-92, cmty. rels. coord., 1992-96, supr. field svc., 1996-97; dir. ops. Santee Wateree Regional Transp. Authority, Sumter, S.C., 1997—. Editor Comto Mag., 1992—. Pres. block com., North Phila., 1985—; tchr., instr. Phila. Mayor's Literacy Program, 1985—. Mem. Nat. Assn. Black Accts. (Outstanding Mem. award 1983, sec. 1986-87), NAFE, Conf. Minority Transp. Ofcls. (pres. 1987-89, regional pres. 1990-92, editor newsletter-mag. 1994-99), Am. Passenger Transport Assn. (subcom. 1986—), Progressive Network Inc. Club (treas. Phila. chpt. 1985—). Democrat. Avocations: bowling, sewing, cooking, rug hooking, photography. Office: Santee Wateree Regional Transp Authority 21 Holmes Gardner Rd Sumter SC 29151

DAXON, TOM, state agency administrator. Dir., sec. fin. and revenue Okla. State Fin. Office, Oklahoma City. Office: Okla State Fin Office 2300 N Lincoln Blvd Rm 122 Oklahoma City OK 73105-4801

DAY, ADRIENNE CAROL, artist, art educator; b. Jackson, Miss., Dec. 13, 1955; d. Robert Maxwell and Phyllis Mary (Roberts) D. BFA, U. Okla., 1986; MFA, Ariz. State U., 1990. Adj. instr. Mesa (Ariz.) C.C., 1990; artist-in-residence Arts Coun. Okla., Okla. City, 1991—; vis. lectr. dept. art U. Ctrl. Okla., Edmond, 1993-98; adj. prof. art Okla. City U., 1996—; adj. asst. prof. U. Okla. Coll. Liberal Studies, Norman, 1997—; coord., organizer Suite Okla. exchange portfolio, 1997. One-woman shows include Ariz. State U., Tempe, 1990, Individual Artists of Okla. exhbn., Okla. City, 1993, ARC Gallery, Chgo., 1995, Leslie Powell Gallery, Lawton, Okla., 1996, U. Southeastern Okla., Durant, 1998; exhibited in group shows at Ariz. State U., Tempe, 1989 (purchase award), Guadalupe Cultural Arts, Ctr., San Antonio, 1989 (cash award), Greenville (N.C.) Mus. Art, 1989, Ind. U., 1989, Shemer Art Ctr. and Mus., Phoenix, 1990, Kirkpatric Ctr. Gallery, Okla. City, 1991, Okla. City Art Mus., 1992, Fla. State U. Mus., Tallahassee, 1993, Corcoran Sch. Art, Washington, 1994-97, U. Ctrl. Okla. Faculty Exhibit, Edmond, 1994-97, Austin Peay U., Clarksville, Tenn., 1994, I.A.O/M.A.R.S. Exchange Exhibit, Phoenix, 1995, Alexander Hogue Gallery, U. Tulsa, Okla., 1997, Truman State U., 1998, Columbia (Mo.) Coll., 1998; represented in permanent collections Haarmann and Reimer Corp., Germany, Corcoran Mus., Washington, U. Ctrl. Okla., Fred Jones Mus., Carol Reese Mus., East Tenn. State, U. Tenn., Knoxville, Miss. State U., U. Texas, Tyler, Fellers & Co., Okla. City, U. Fla., Gainsville, Bradley U., Peoria, Ariz. State U., Ohio U., Athens, Brigham Young U., U. Utah, U. Alberta. Recipient Letzeiser Gold medal U. Okla. Sch. Art, Norman, 1987, Abraham and Bessie Lehrer Meml. award Ariz. State U., 1989, faculty purchase award Presdl. Ptrns. U. Ctrl. Olka., Edmond, 1995; first alt. Fourth Annual Nathan Cummings Travel fellow Ariz. State U., 1989; Artist Project grantee Ariz. Commn. on the Arts, 1991, Sudden Opportunity grantee Okla. Visual Arts Coalition, Okla. City, 1992. Democrat. Home and Office: PO Box 6354 Norman OK 73070-6354

DAY, ANGELA RIDDLE, occupational health nurse, educator; b. Greenville, S.C., Oct. 23, 1963; d. Earl C. and Sandra (Grooms) Riddle; m. Herbert Day, May 26, 1984; 2 children. BSN, Clemson U., 1985. RN, S.C.; cert. occupational health nurse; cert. occupational hearing conservationist, pulmonary function technician, CPR, first aid instr. Staff nurse St. Francis Hosp., Greenville, 1985-86; dir. occupational health nursing, ednl. coord. North Hills Med. Ctr., Greenville, 1986-94; occupational health nrse BMW Mfg. Corp., Greer, S.C., 1994-96; cons. in field, 1996—. Mem. Am. Assn. Occupational Health Nurses, S.C. State Assn. Occupational Health Nurses (com. chmn.). E-mail: Aabonz@aol.com. Office: 215 Covington Rd Greenville SC 29617-2007

DAY, ANTHONY, newspaper writer; b. Miami, Fla., May 12, 1933; s. Price and Alice (Alexander) D.; m. Lynn Ward, June 25, 1960; children—John, Julia (dec.). A.B. cum laude, Harvard U., 1955, postgrad. (Nieman fellow), 1966-67; L.H.D. (hon.), Pepperdine U., 1974. Reporter Phila. Bull., 1957-60, Washington, 1960-69; chief Washington bur. Phila. Bull., 1969; chief editorial writer L.A. Times, 1969-71, editor editorial pages, 1971-89, sr. corr., 1989-95; contbg. writer L.A. Times Book Review, 1995—. Mem. Signet Soc. Harvard, Asia Soc., Inst. Current World Affairs.

DAY, BURNIS C., artist, educator; b. Hepzibah, W.Va.; s. Jeff Monroe and Willie Etta (Porter) D. Student, Art and Design Coll., Detroit, 1964-66, Famous Artists Sch., 1965-67; AA, Oakland C.C., Farmington Hills, Mich., 1969. Keyliner and photostat operator Freuhauf Corp., Detroit, 1970-71; art dir. Urban Screen Process, Detroit, 1971-73; instr. art Pittman's Galleries, Inc., Detroit, 1973-74; art assoc. Cal Summers House of Art, Detroit, 1971-77; with 21st Century Video, Detroit; free-lance advt. and painting, Detroit, 1977—; instr. art Wayne County C.C., 1985—, St. Scholastica Summer Day Camp, Detroit, 1995-98; juror Mich. State Fair, Detroit, 1992, Arts for Parks, Jackson Hole, Wyo., 1994; fiedl videographer Inst. for Survey Rsch., Temple U., Phila., 1992-93; instr. painting on TV satellite UAW-Chrysler Nat. Tng. Ctr., Detroit, 1995-99. One-man shows include Pittman Galleries, Detroit, 1981; exhibited in group shows The Gallery Tanner, L.A., 1984, The Laramie Art Guild, Wyo., 1979, The N.Mex. Art League, 1979, Nat. Theatre, Lagos, Nigeria, 1977; represented in permanent collections Detroit Inst. Arts, City of N.Y., U. Utah Mus. Fine Arts, Mus. No. Ariz., Mus. Art, Ponce, P.R., Las Vegas Art Mus., Kauai Regional Libr., Lihue, Hawaii, The White House, U. Mo. Mus. Art and Archaeology, Columbia, Washington County Mus. Fine Arts Md., U. Mont. Mus. Fine Arts, N.Mex. Highlands U., Ft. Smith (Ark.) Art Ctr., Fish U. Art Galleries, Tenn., Mus. City N.Y.; author: Burnis C. Day's Neogeometric Paintings (His Travels, Art and Artist), 1999. Vol. svc. camera operator pub. access program Comcast Cable TV, 1988. Recipient various awards for art, including 1st place award for mural People's Art and Detroit Recreation Dept., 1976, 2d place, 1977, cert. of recognition U.S. Zone Com., Lagos, Nigeria, 1977. Avocations: nature, outdoors, reading. Office: PO Box 255 Detroit MI 48231-0255

DAY, CHARLOTTE ELLEN, education administrator; b. Milw., Nov. 5, 1946; d. Paul Christopher and Mary Bridget (McGinn) Brust; m. Peter Leonard Day, Sept. 15, 1973 (div. Feb. 1983); 1 child, Steven. BS in Polit. Sci., Santa Clara U., 1968; MS in Ednl. Leadership, Calif. State U., Hayward, 1992. Elem. tchr. Lincoln Elem., Richmond (Calif.) Unified Sch. Dist., Calif., 1969-89; vice prin. Bayview Elem. Unified Sch. Dist., San Pablo, Calif., 1989-91; project asst. Richmond (Calif.) Unified Sch. Dist., 1991-94; prin. Mira Vista Elem. West Contra Costa Unified Sch. Dist., Richmond, 1994-95, bilingual LEP monitor, 1995-97; reform coord. Washington Elem., Point Richmond, Calif., 1997—; mentor tchr. Richmond (Calif.) Unified Sch. Dist., 1984-85, 85-86, 87-88; new tchr. coach St. Mary's Coll., Moraga, Calif., 1993-94; ELIC facilitator, 1997—. mem. ASCD, Calif. Sch. Leadership Assn., Santa Clara Alumni Assn.

DAY, CHON, cartoonist; b. Chatham, N.J., Apr. 6, 1907; s. Lawrence and Nell Hunter (Van Orden) D.; m. Irene Townley, June 2, 1934; children—Clinton, Robert, Stephen. Student, Lehigh U., 1926, Art Students League, N.Y.C., 1929. Cartoons appearing in New Yorker, Saturday Evening Post, numerous other mags.; author, illustrator: I Could Be Dreaming, 1945, What Price Dory, 1955, Brother Sebastian, 1957, Brother Sebastian Carries On, 1959, Brother Sebastian at Large, 1961 (Recipient Best gag cartoonist award Nat. Cartoonists Soc. 1956, 62, 70, Best Spl. Features award 1969, named to R.I. Heritage Hall of Fame 1972). Named to R.I. Journalism Hall of Fame, 1989. Mem. Nat. Cartoonists Soc. Baptist. Clubs: Lions (past pres.), Westerly Yacht. Address: 22 Cross St Westerly RI 02891-2330

DAY, COLIN LESLIE, publisher; b. St. Albans, Eng., July 19, 1944; came to U.S., 1978; s. Archibald William Dagless and José (Greenfield) D.; m. Jennifer Ann Jones, July 30, 1966; children: Matthew, Gudrun. B.A., Oxford U., 1966, M.A., 1968; Ph.D., U. Stirling, 1973. Research officer N.I.E.S.R., London, 1966-68; research fellow Stirling U., Scotland, 1968-71, lectr. in econs., 1971-75; sr. econs. editor Cambridge Univ. Press, U.K.; sr. econs. editor Cambridge Univ. Press, N.Y.C., 1976-81, editor-in-chief, 1981-82; editorial dir. Cambridge Univ. Press, 1982-87; dir. U. Mich. Press, 1988—; bd. dirs. Assn. Am. Univ. Presses, 1986-89, 92-95, pres., 1993-94. Co-author: Company Financing in United Kingdom, 1974; contbr. articles to prof. jours. Justice of peace County of Perthshire, Scotland, 1970-75; chmn. West Perthshire Labour Party, 1972-75. Home: 276 Sumac Ln Ann Arbor MI 48105-3013 Office: U Mich Press PO Box 1104 839 Greene St Ann Arbor MI 48104-3209

DAY, DAVID OWEN, lawyer; b. Long Beach, Calif., Apr. 3, 1958; s. Robert Owen and Linda Sue (Weaver) D.; m. Vicki Temple Butler, Sept. 24, 1980; children: Candi, Chad, Charles, Chase, Catelyn. BA magna cum laude, E. Tenn. State U., 1980; JD with high honors, U. Tenn., 1984. Bar: Tenn. 1984, U.S. Dist. Ct. (mid. dist.) Tenn. 1984, U.S. Ct. Appeals (6th cir.) 1990, U.S. Supreme Ct. 1990; cert. civil trial specialist, Nat. Bd. Trial Advocacy and Tenn. Commn. on Continuing Legal Edn. and Specialization. Assoc. Law Office of Donald G. Dickerson, Cookeville, Tenn., 1984-87; ptnr. Dickerson and Day Attys. at Law, Cookeville, 1987-90; pvt. practice Cookeville, Tenn., 1990-96; ptnr. Day & Birdwell, P.C., Cookeville, 1997—; lectr. Bank Adminstrv. Inst., 1990, Tenn. Bankers Assn., 1993, Tenn. Consol. Ret. Sys., 1996, Am. Inst. Banking, 1996. Asst. editor Tennessee Law Review, 1982-83. Frederick T. Bonham scholar U. Tenn., 1981, Harold C. Warner scholar U. Tenn., 1982, Carl W. Miller scholar U. Tenn., 1983. Mem. ABA, ATLA, Tenn. Trial Lawyers Assn., Putnam County Bar Assn., Tenn. Bar Assn., Phi Kappa Phi, Alpha Lambda Delta. Ch. of Jesus Christ of Latter-day Saints. Avocations: song writing, singing, playing basketball, pub. speaking, traveling. Home: PO Box 704 Cookeville TN 38503-0704 Office: 19 S Jefferson Ave Cookeville TN 38501-5911

DAY, DONALD SHELDON, lawyer; b. Boston, Nov. 3, 1924; s. Israel and Frances (Goldberg) D.; m. Edythe Greenberg, July 8, 1945; children—Clifford L., Richard J., Halee Beth. BA, Bates Coll., 1946; LLB, Cornell U., 1948. Bar: N.Y. 1948. Past chmn. bd. Saperston and Day P.C., Buffalo, 1979-96; pres. World Union for Progressive Judaism, 1988-95; bd. dirs. various corps. Gen. chmn. United Jewish Fund Campaign, Buffalo, 1971-73, 75; past co-chmn. Western N.Y. chpt. NCCJ; past pres. United Jewish Fedn. Buffalo; past chmn. bd. Childrens Hosp. Buffalo, Union Am. Hebrew Congregations; trustee Forest Lawn Cemetery and Crematory, Hebrew-Union Coll. With AUS, 1942-45. Mem. Am., N.Y. State, Erie County bar assns., Order of Coif, Phi Kappa Phi. Jewish (past pres. temple). Office: Saperston & Day PC 3 Fountain Plz Buffalo NY 14203-1486

DAY, DORIS (DORIS VON KAPPELHOFF), singer, actress; b. Cin., Apr. 3, 1924; d. Frederick Wilhelm and Alma Sophia von Kappelhoff; m. Al Jorden, Mar. 1941 (div. 1943); 1 son, Terry; m. George Weilder, 1946 (div. 1949); m. Marty Melcher, Apr. 3, 1951 (dec. 1968). Student pub. schs., Cin. Made profl. dancing appearance with Doherty & Kappelhoff, Glendale, Calif.; singer Karlin's Karnival, Sta. WCPO-Radio, with bands Barney Rapp, Bob Crosby, Fred Waring, Les Brown; singer, leading lady, Bob Hope NBC radio show, 1948-50, Doris Day CBS show, 1952-53; singer Columbia Records, 1950—, Hooray for Hollywood col.1, 1988, A Day At The Movies, 1989, The Essence of Doris Day, 1993, Duet with The Andre Previn Trio, 1996; star Warner Bros. Studio; motion pictures include Romance on the High Seas, 1948, My Dream is Yours, 1949, Young Man With a Horn, 1950, Tea For Two, 1950, West Point Story, 1950, Lullaby of Broadway, 1951, On Moonlight Bay, 1951, I'll See You in My Dreams, 1951, April in Paris, 1952, By the Light of the Silvery Moon, 1953, Lucky Me, Yankee Doodle Girl, 1954, Love Me or Leave Me, 1955 (selected as 1 of 10 best films by N.Y. Herald Tribune), Pajama Game, 1957, Teacher's Pet, 1958, Tunnel of Love, 1958, It Happened to Jane, 1959, Pillow Talk, 1959, Midnight Lace, 1960, Jumbo, 1962, That Touch of Mink, 1962, The Thrill of It All, 1963, Please Don't Eat the Daisies, 1960, Lover Come Back, 1962, Send Me No Flowers, 1964, Do Not Disturb, 1965, The Glass Bottom Boat, 1966, Caprice, 1967, The Ballad of Josie, 1968, Where Were You When The Lights Went Out, 1968, With Six You Get Eggrolls, 1968, Sleeping Dogs, Hearts and Souls, 1993, That's Entertainment III, 1994; TV series The Doris Day Show, 1970-73, Doris Day & Friends, 1985-86, Doris Day's Best, 1985-86; appeared on TV spl. The Pet Set, 1972. Founder Doris Day Animal League, Washington, 1987. Winner 1st prize (with Jerry Doherty) as best dance team in Cin.; recipient Laurel award as leading new female persoanlity in motion picture industry, 1950; named top audience attractor, 1962; recipient Am. Comedy Lifetime Achievement award, 1991. Christian Scientist. Office: care Doris Day Animal League 227 Massachusetts Ave NE Washington DC 20002-4963 also: Columbia Records 550 Madison Ave New York NY 10022-3211

DAY, DOUGLAS EUGENE, public information officer; b. Granite Falls, Minn., Sept. 22, 1956; s. Donald Day and Marilyn (Antonson) Cusick; children: Derek, Chad. Program dir. KBRL Radio, McCook, Nebr., 1976-77, KCOW Radio, Alliance, Nebr., 1977-78, 80; asst. programming dir. WQTC Radio, Two Rivers, Wis., 1978-80; program dir. WZRK Radio, Houghton, Mich., 1980-81; program dir., reporter WOMT/WQTC Radio, Manitowoc, Wis., 1981-89; nuclear comms. supr. Wis. Pub. Svc., Green Bay, 1989—. Active Two Rivers City Coun., 1995-99, pres., 1997-99. Home: 4504 Parkway Blvd Two Rivers WI 54241-1046 Office: Wis Pub Svc 600 N Adams St Green Bay WI 54301-5146

DAY, ELIZABETH A., press secretary; b. Pensacola, Fla., May 25, 1967; m. Dennis Scott Day; 1 child. BS in Commn. cum laude, Fla. State U., 1989. Asst. to dirs. congl. rels. The Heritage Found., 1990-92; personal asst. to chief of staff Office of Senator Thad Cochran, Washington, 1992-94, press asst., 1994-96, press sec., 1997—. Office: 326 Senate Russell Office Washington DC 20510-2402

DAY, EMERSON, physician; b. Hanover, N.H., May 2, 1913; s. Edmund Ezra and Emily Sophia (Emerson) D.; m. Ruth Fairfield, Aug. 7, 1937; children: Edmund Perry, Robert Fairfield, Nancy, Bonnie, Sheryl. B.A., Dartmouth Coll., 1934; M.D., Harvard U., 1938. Intern Presbyn. Hosp., N.Y.C., 1938- 40; fellow in cardiology Johns Hopkins U., 1940-42; asst. resident medicine N.Y. Hosp., 1942; med. dir. internat. div. Trans World Airline, N.Y.C., 1945-47; asst. prof. preventive medicine and pub. health Cornell U. Med. Coll., 1947-50, assoc. prof. clin. preventive medicine and pub. health, 1950-54, prof. preventive medicine Sloan Kettering div., 1954-64; chmn. dept. preventive medicine Meml. Hosp., N.Y.C., 1954-63; dir. Strang Cancer Prevention Clinic, 1950-63; mem., chief div. preventive medicine Sloan-Kettering Inst., N.Y.C., 1954-64; cons. in geriatrics Cold Spring Inst., Cold Spring-on-Hudson, N.Y., 1952-57; dir. N.Y.C. Dept. Health Cancer Detection Center, 1947-50, Strang Clinic, Inc., 1963-66, PMI-Strang Clinic, 1966-69; pres. Preventive Medicine Inst., 1963-69, hon. pres., mem. bd. trustees, 1969—; v.p., med. dir. Medequip Corp., 1969-76, sr. med. cons., 1976-82; med. v.p. Health Mgmt. Internat., Inc., 1982-84; med. dir. Physicians for Med. Cost Containment, Inc., 1984-94; prof. medicine Northwestern U. Med. Sch., 1976-81, prof. emeritus, 1981—; assoc. dir. Northwestern U. Cancer Center, 1976-81; med. dir. Portes Cancer Prevention Center, 1978-79; attending physician Northwestern Meml. Hosp., 1976-81, vis. physician, 1981—; lectr. Cook County Grad. Sch. Med., 1977-90; mem. Northwestern U. Med. Assocs., 1980-81; med. dir., chmn. dept. internal medicine Chgo. Splty. Hosp. and Med. Center, 1981-84; hon. staff physician Evanston, Glenbrook hosps., 1976—; attending physician, mem. med. bd. James Ewing Hosp., Meml. Hosp., N.Y.C., 1950-64; founder, sr. mem. PMX Med. Group, N.Y.C., 1956—70; adj. prof. biology N.Y. U., 1965-70; mem. cancer detection com. Internat. Union Against Cancer, 1954-70; pres. N.Y.C. div. Am. Cancer Soc., 1963-64; med. cons. Medidata Health Services, Inc., 1985-90. Contbr. numerous articles to profl. jours. Served as flight surgeon ATC USAAF, 1942-45. Recipient Bronze medal Am. Cancer Soc., 1956, professorship in early detection Ill. div., 1976-79. Fellow ACP, N.Y. Acad. Medicine, N.Y. Acad. Scis. (pres. 1965), APHA, Am. Occupl. Med. Assn., Am. Geriatrics Soc., Internat. Acad. Cytology (hon.); mem. AMA, Am. Soc. Cytopathology (founding mem., pres. 1958, now hon. mem., Papanicolaou award 1978), Am. Soc. Preventive Oncology, Internat. Health Evaluation Assn., Soc. for Advanced Med. Sys. (founding dir. 1969-81), Am. Assn. Med. Sys. and Informatics (founding dir. 1981-84), Harvey Soc., Chgo. Clin. Ethics Program (charter mem.), Century Assn. (N.Y.C.), Ill. Med. Soc., Chgo. Med. Soc., Med. Cons. Svcs. Assn., Phi Beta Kappa, Alpha Omega Alpha, Zeta Psi. Club: Century Assn. (N.Y.C.). Home and Office: 320 Pebblebrook Rd Northbrook IL 60062-5624

DAY, GEORGE EVERETTE, lawyer, retired military officer; b. Sioux City, Iowa, Feb. 24, 1925; m. Doris Merlene Sorensen; 4 children. BS, Morningside Coll., 1950, DHL, 1974, MA, St. Louis U., 1964; JD, U. S.D., 1949; LLD, Troy State U., 1991. Bar: S.D. 1949, Fla. 1977. Commd. 2d lt. USAF, 1951, advanced through grades to col., fighter pilot Korean Conflict, 1951-52; mem. 31 tac fighter wing USAF, Tuy Hoa Air Base, Vietnam, 1967; prisoner of war Vietnam, 1967-73; ret.; pvt. practice Day & Meade, Ft. Walton Beach, Fla.; tchr. world politics, internat. law, polit. geography St. Louis U., Parks Coll. Aero. Tech.; tchr. law Troy State U.; vis. lectr. Freedom's Found. program St. Francis Coll., U. Scranton; lectr. in field. Author: Return with Honor, 1989; contbr. articles to mags. Nat. chmn. Vets. for Reagan, 1984; nat. campaign vol. Pres. Bush Campaign, 1992; past sec. Fla. VA Commn.; mem. Def. Adv. Com.; bd. dirs. Air Force Armament Mus.; former advisor Air Force Assn., Washington. Decorated Medal of Honor, Air Force Cross, DSM, Silver Star, Legion of Merit, DFC, Air medal with nine oak leaf clusters, Bronze Star with two oak leaf clusters, Bronze Star, Purple Heart with three clusters, two Vietnamese Gallantry Crosses, Vietnamese Wings; recipient Bus. Assoc. of Yr. award Am. Bus. Women's Assn., 1988. Mem. ATLA, Medal of Honor Soc., Acad. Trial Lawyers, Okaloosa/Walton Bar Assn., Fla. Trial Lawyers Am., Acad. Fla. Trial Lawyers. Home: 4105 Collingswood Rd Pensacola FL 32514-6410 Office: Day and Meade 32 Beal Pkwy SW Fort Walton Beach FL 32548-5391*

DAY, GERALD W., wholesale grocery company executive. With Albertson's, Heber City, Utah, 1945-72; CEO Days Markets; chmn., bd. dirs. Associated Food Stores Inc. Office: Day's Market 890 S Main St Heber City UT 84032-2463

DAY, GILES WILLIAM, JR. (BILL DAY), religious studies educator; b. Goffstown, N.H., June 21, 1954; s. Giles William and Iris Noreen (Bond) D.; m. Geraldine Fay, June 11, 1977; children: Giles W. IV, Marie Elaine, Marsha Ellen, Michael Kenneth. B in Religious Edn., Glen Cove Bible Coll., Rockland, Maine, 1977. Ordained to ministry Bapt. Ch., 1981; cert. Am. Assn. Christian Schs. Pastor Bapt. Ch., Amity, Maine, 1977-78; tchr. secondary Calvary Christian Acad., Patten, Maine, 1978-81; tchr. Limestone (Maine) Christian Acad., 1983-84, Cherryfield (Maine) Christian Acad., 1984-85, Maranatha Christian Acad., Addison, Maine, 1985-87, Calvary Family Sch., Warren, Maine, 1992-97, Coastal Christian Sch., Waldaboro, Maine, 1997—. Chmn. Rep. Com., Cushing, Maine, 1994-96. Avocations: chess, fishing, camping. Home: RR 1 Box 1140 Cushing ME 04563-9600

DAY, HARRY GILBERT, nutritional biochemist, consultant; b. Lovilia, Iowa, Oct. 8, 1906; s. John Freeman and Minta Emma (Spencer) D.; m. W. Marie Miller, July 10, 1933 (dec. 1968); children: Margaret Day Pruden, Barbara Day Baumann, Robert M.; m. Gertrude Elizabeth Parr, Aug. 14, 1969 (dec. 1991). AB, Cornell Coll., 1930; ScD, Johns Hopkins U., 1933; ScD (hon.), Cornell Coll., 1967. Postdoctoral fellow Nat. Rsch. Coun., Johns Hopkins U., Balt., 1933-34; fellow gen. edn. bd., Rockefeller Found., Yale U., New Haven, 1934-36; assoc. biochemistry Johns Hopkins U., 1936-40; from asst. prof. to prof. chemistry Ind. U., Bloomington, 1940-50, prof. chemistry, 1950-76, retired, 1976, chmn. dept. chemistry, 1951-62, assoc. dean rsch. and advanced studies, 1967-72; mem. select com. GRAS Substances, Fedn. Am. Soc. Exptl. Biology, Bethesda, Md., 1973-82. Co-developer first successful fluoridized dentifrice; author books; contbr. numerous articles to profl. jours. Mem. Bloomington City Coun., 1963-71. Grantee AMA, 1940-41, others; named Outstanding Alumnus in Pub. Health Johns Hopkins U., 1988; Harry G. Day Lectureship named in his honor Ind. U., 1987, Harry G. Day Lecture Hall named in his honor, 1990; named to Monroe County (Ind.) Hall of Fame, 1995. Fellow AAAS, AIN, Ind. Acad. Sci. (pres. 1962-63), Am. Inst. Nutrition (pres. 1971-72); mem. Am. Chem. Soc. (exam. com. 1959-85), Am. Soc. Biol. Chemists, Kiwanis (pres. 1957-58). Republican. Methodist. Home: 1154 Linden Dr Bloomington IN 47408-1204 Office: Ind U Dept Chemistry Bloomington IN 47405

DAY, HOWARD WILMAN, geology educator; b. Burlington, Vt., Nov. 17, 1942; s. Wilman Forrest and Virginia Louise (Morton) D.; m. Johanna Smith, June 11, 1966; children: Kristina, Sarah, Susan. AB, Dartmouth Coll., 1964; MS, Brown U., 1968, PhD, 1971. Asst. prof., then assoc. prof. geology U. Okla., Norman, 1970-76; from asst. prof. to prof. geology U. Calif., Davis, 1976—, chmn. dept., 1990-96. Co-editor Jour. Metamorphic Geology, 1985-92; contbr. articles to profl. jours. Fulbright fellow, Norway, 1964, Alexander von Humboldt fellow, Fed. Republic Germany, 1977. Fellow Geol. Soc. Am., Mineral Soc. Am.; mem. Am. Geophys. Union. Office: U Calif Dept Geology Davis CA 95616

DAY, JACQUELINE FRANCES, museum director. BA in English, Antioch Coll.; MA in Folklore, Ind. U.; student, Tulane U., Wash. State U. Instr. N.D. State U., Fargo, 1973-75; Curator Idaho State Historical Soc., Boise, 1975-77; program officer Assn. Humanities Idaho, Boise, 1977-84; field rschr. Mont. Historical Soc., Helena, 1984; dir. Beall Park Art Ctr., Bozeman, Mont., 1984-86; exec. dir. Regional Council of Historical Agencies, Syracuse, N.Y., 1986-90, Gallery Assn. of N.Y. State, Hamilton, 1990-92; dir. Adirondack Mus., Blue Mountain Lake, N.Y., 1992—; Mem. State Historical Records Advisory Bd., N.Y., 1996—. Bd. dirs. Adirondack Architectural Heritage Consortium, 1993-95, Friends and Visitors Interpretive Ctr., 1993—. Mem. Am. Assn. State Local History, Museum Assn. N.Y. (bd. dirs.). Office: Adirondack Museum Rt 28 N & 30 Box 99 Blue Mountain Lake NY 12812*

DAY, JAMES, television executive; b. Alameda, Calif., Dec. 22, 1918; s. James Magee and June (Reeve) D.; m. Beverley Anne Hare, Apr. 12, 1943; children: Meredith Johnson, Douglas Craig, Alan Kent, James Ross. BA, U. Calif., Berkeley, 1941; postgrad., Stanford U., 1951; LHD (hon.), Newark State Coll., Newark, N.J., 1972. Dir. pub. svc. NBC, San Francisco, 1946-49; radio specialist Civil Info. & Edn. Sect./Supreme Commdr. Allies/ Pacific, Tokyo, 1949-51; dep. dir. Radio Free Asia, San Francisco, 1951-53; pres., gen. mgr. KQED (TV-FM), San Francisco, 1953-69; pres. Nat. Ednl. TV, N.Y.C., 1969-71, WNET-TV, N.Y.C., 1971-73; prof. radio, TV Bklyn. Coll., CUNY, N.Y.C., 1976-89, prof. emeritus, 1989—; pres. Publivision Inc., N.Y.C., 1973—; pres. Timely Prodns. for TV, N.Y.C., 1989—; founding dir. Children's TV Workshop, Pub. Broadcasting Svc., Internat. Pub. TV Screening Conf., Comm. Improvement, Inc. Author: The Vanishing Vision: The Inside Story of Public Television, 1995, interviewer: (TV) Kaleidoscope, 1954-69, Day at Night, 1973-74, Conversations with Eric Hoffer, 1967, Conversations with Arnold Toynbee, 1968. Capt. U.S. Army, 1941-46. Recipient Robert C. Kirkwood award, San Francisco Found., 1966, Golden Plate award, Am. Acad. Achievement, Dallas, 1968, 50th Anniversary Dirs. award, Ohio State U., Columbus, 1986; resident scholar Rockefeller Study Ctr., Bellagio, Italy, 1978. Mem. Internat. Inst. Comm., Soc. Profl. Journalists. Avocations: photography, swimming. Home: 115 E 86th St New York NY 10028-1057 Office: Publivision Inc One Lincoln Pla New York NY 10023

DAY, JOHN ARTHUR, lawyer; b. Madison, Wis., Sept. 21, 1956; s. John Donald and Elinor Roletta (Heath) D. BS, U. Wis., Platteville, 1978; JD, U. N.C., 1981. Bar: Tenn. 1981, U.S. Dist. Ct. (mid. dist.) Tenn. 1981, U.S. Ct. Appeals (6th cir.) 1982; civil cert. Nat. Bd. Trial Advocacy 1991. Assoc. Boult Cummings Conners & Berry, Nashville, 1981-86, ptnr., 1987-92; shareholder Branham & Day, P.C., 1993—; mem. Civil Justice Reform Act adv. group U.S. Dist. Ct. (mid. dist.) Tenn., 1991-95; bd. dirs. Nat. Bd. Trial Advocacy. Co-author: Tennessee Law of Comparative Fault, 1997; founder, editor Tenn. Tort Law Letter, 1995—; contbr. articles to profl. jours. Com. mem. Cohn Roundtable, Nashville, 1988; assoc. Harry Phillips Inn of Ct., 1990-92. Mem. Tenn. Trial Lawyers Assn. (bd. govs. 1984-85, treas. 1985-89, v.p. 1989-93, pres. 1993-94, immediate past pres. 1994-95, legal edn. com. chairperson 1985-86, legis. com. chairperson 1987-90, CLE com. 1984-97, pub. rels. com. 1986-88, long range planning com. 1991-93), Assn. Trial Lawyers Am. (Tenn. pub. rels. rep. 1986-87, people's law sch. com. co-chairperson 1986-88, pub. rels. com. 1986-91, chairperson 1988-89, edn. com. 1987-88, pub. affairs com. 1987-89, publs. com. 1990-93, vice chmn. 1991-93, co-chairperson 1992-93, key person com. 1987-89, nursing home litigation group 1985-89, chmn. 1987-89, mem. exec. com. 1994-95, chair pres.'s coun. 1994-95), Nashville Bar Assn. (bd. dirs. 1998—, circuit and chancery ct. com. vice-chairperson 1988, chairperson 1989, fee disputes com. 1984-85, 87, vice chmn. 1988, chmn. 1989, bd. dirs. 1998—), Lawyers Involved for Tenn. (trustee 1988—), Tenn. Bar Assn. (local rules com. 1986-87, mem. litigation sect. coun. 1989-90, nat. bd. trial advocacy, bd. dirs. 1998—, stds. com. 1998—). Democrat. Home: 18107 Crowne Brook Cir Franklin TN 37067 Office: Branham & Day PC Ste 1950 150 4th Ave N Nashville TN 37219-2415

DAY, JOHN CHARLES, chemical company executive; b. Richhill, Pa., Apr. 21, 1941; s. John albert and Margaret May (Mooney) D.; m. Ann Kathryn Chester, Aug. 27, 1961; children: Johanna Leigh Day, John Michael Day. BS in Chem. Engring., W. Va. U., 1963. Prodn. supt. E.I. DuPont, Cleve., 1972-75; bus. mgr. E.I. DuPont, Wilmington, Del., 1975-79; asst. plant mgr. E.I. DuPont, Memphis, 1979-81, plant mgr., 1981-83; dir. mfg. DuPont de Brasil, Sao Paulo, 1983-87, E.I. DuPont, Wilmington, 1987-91; v.p., engring. tech. Rollins Envrion. Svc., Wilmington, 1991-95, group v.p., ops., 1995-97; v.p. safety, health environ. Millennium Chems., Inc., Hunt Valley, Md., 1997—. Bd. dirs. United Way of Memphis, 1981-83, Escola Graduada, Sao Paulo, 1983-87, Jr. Achievement, Memphis, 1981-83; twp. supr. Franklin Twp., Kemblesville, pa., 1989-97. Republican. Methodist. Avocations: diving, woodworking. Home: 135 Versailles Cir Apt B Towson MD 21204-6928 Office: Millenium Chems 200 Internal Cir Ste 5000 Towson MD 21030

DAY, JOHN DENTON, retired company executive, cattle and horse rancher, trainer, wrangler, actor, educator; b. Salt Lake City, Jan. 20, 1942; s. George W. and Grace (Denton) Jenkins; m. Susan Hansen, June 20, 1971; children: Tammy Denton Wadsworth, Jeanett B, Lloyd. Student, U. Utah, 1964-65; BA in Econs. and Bus. Adminstrn. with high honors, Westminster Coll., 1971. Riding instr., wrangler Uinta wilderness area U-Ranch, Neola, Utah, 1955-58; stock handler, driver, ruffstock rider Earl Hutchinson Rodeo Contractor, Idaho, 1959; wrangler, riding instr. YMCA Camp Rodger, Kamas, Utah; with Mil. Data Cons., Inc., L.A., 1961-62, Carlseon Credit Corp., Salt Lake City, 1962-65; sales mgr. sporting goods Western Enterprises, Salt Lake City, 1965-69; founder Rockin d Ranch, Millcreek, Utah, 1969; ski instr. Brighton (Utah) Ski Sch., 1969-71; Western rep. PBR Co., Cleve., 1969-71; dist. sales rep. Crown Zellerbach Corp., Seattle and L.A., 1971-73; pres., founder Dapco paper, chem., instl. food and janitorial supplies, Salt Lake City, 1973-79, John D Day Greeting Cards, 1990—; owner, founder, pres. John D. Day, mfrs. reps., 1972—; dist. sales mgr. Surfonics Engrs., Inc., Woods Cross, Utah, 1976-78, Garland Co., Cleve., 1978-81; rancher Heber, Utah, 1976-90, horse tng. facility, horsemanship sch. and ranch, Temecula, Calif., 1984-90, St. George, Utah, 1989—; sec. bd. Acquadyne, 1974, 75. Actor, dir., prodr. (movies) The Big Sky, 1952, Rebel Without a Cause, 1955, Devils Brigade, 1967, Coyote Summer, 1995, (videos) Someday Soon, 1993, A Tour of Snows Canyon, 1993, All For the Love of Horse, 1982-83, Stallion Management, 1985, others; tv commls., Chev., Palmer, others; contbr. articles to jours., including Western Artist. Group chmn. Tele-Dex fund raising project Westminster Coll.; founder, supr. vol. group Day's Rangers, 1990—; vol. Dixie Nat. Forest, 1989-94, USDA Forest Svc.; 1st U.S. wilderness ranger USDA, US Forest Svc., Dixie Nat. Forest, Pine Valley Ranger Dist., Pine Valley Mountain Wilderness, So. Utah, 1994—. With AUS, 1963-64. Recipient grand nat. award Internat. Customer Car Show, San Diego, 1962, Key to City, Louisville, 1964, Champion Bareback Riding award, 1957, Vol. award USDA Forest Svc., 1991, 92, 93, nominated U.S. Vol. award, Safety award Dixie Nat. Forest, P.V.B.D., 1992-98; recipient Outstanding Performance award USDA, 1995, 98, Cert. Appreciation, 1997, DNF Outstanding Svc. award, 1997, Pine Valley Mountain Wilderness; Dally team roping heading and heeling champion, 1982. Mem. Internat. Show Car Assn. (co-chmn. 1978-79), Am. Quarter Horse Assn. (life, high point reining champion 1981, qualified for world championship, Dodge, Toyota Fall Futurite Circuit Champion Working Cowhorse 1994-95, World Championship Show qualifier and participant Oklahoma City Sr. Cutting 1994), Intermountain Quarter Horse Assn. (sr. reining champion 1981, champion AMAT reining 1979-81), Utah Quarter Horse Assn. (state champion AMAT reining 1979, 80, AMAT barrel racing 1980, working cowhorse champion 1982, trained working cowhorse and rider champion 1992, 98, trained amateur reining horse and rider champion 1996, open cutting res. champion 1993-95, 97, open cutting champion 1994, Menlove Dodge Toyota Fall Futurity circuit champion working cowhorse, 1994-95, open working cowhorse champion & broadmare halter champion 1995, Rose cir. working cowhorse champion 1995, 98, Rose Cir. Open working cowhorse champion, showed cir. champion Brodmare at Halter Rose cir. open cutting champion 1996, 97, bd. dirs. 1992-94, trained amateur barrel racing and amateur pole bending horse and rider 1998, State Reserve Champion amateur cutting horse and rider), Profl. Horseman's Assn., Nat. Cutting Horse Assn. (affiliate), Profl. Cowhorseman's Assn. (world champion team roping, heeling 1986, 88, high point rider 1985, world champion stock horse rider 1985-86, 88, world champion working cowhorse 1985, PCA finals open cutting champion, 1985-88, PCA finals 1500 novice champion 1987, PCA finals all-around champion 1985-88, inducted into Hall of Fame 1988, first on record registered Tex. longhorn cutting contest, open champion, PCA founder, editor newsletter 1985-89, pres. 1984-88), World Rodeo Assn. Profls. (v.p. Western territory 1989-98, judge nat. high sch. rodeo, cutting horse and rodeo queen contest, 1990—, hon. v.p. Western Terr. U.S. 1998—). Home and Office: PO Box 55 Saint George UT 84771-0055 also: 2323 S 1800 E Saint George UT 84790-6206

DAY, JOHN FRANCIS, city official, former savings and loan executive, former mayor; b. Cleve., Mar. 14, 1920; s. Frank S. and Susan Josephine (O'Brien) D.; m. Gertrude Jane Schmitt, Dec. 29, 1941 (dec.); children: Susan, Mary, Timothy, Gertrude, Kathryn, Patrick, Fanchon, Josephine; m. Charlene Ann Thee, Nov. 8, 1986. Ed., Western Res. U., Staunton (Va.) Mil. Acad. Formerly with Cosgrove & Co., Seaboard Fin.; former v.p. Calif. Fed. Savs. & Loan, Los Angeles; mayor Glendale, Calif., 1981-82, mem. city council, 1977-89. Mem. Small Wilderness Area Preservation. Served with AUS, 1941-45. Decorated knight Equestrian Order of Holy Sepulchre of Jerusalem. Mem. Am. Legion. Democrat. Roman Catholic. Club: K.C. Home: 4977 Lake Dr Florence OR 97439-8404

DAY, JOHN G., lawyer. BA, Oberlin Coll., 1958; JD, Case Western Reserve U., 1961. Bar: Ohio 1962, D.C. 1965, Conn. 1986. Chief counsel Conn. Gen. Life Ins. Co., Conn. Gen. Corp., 1982; sr. v.p., chief counsel CIGNA Cos., 1986; lectr. Law Sch. U. Conn., 1991; spl. counsel U.S. sec. trans., 1968; deputy supt. ins., N.Y., 1973-75; commr. ins., Va., 1975-78. Bd. dirs. Child Coun., Hartford Actions. Mem. Greater Hartford C. of C. (bd. dirs.). Office: CT General Life Ins Co 900 Cottage Grove Rd Bloomfield CT 06002-2920*

DAY, JOHN ROBERT, lawyer; b. Brighton, Iowa, Sept. 8, 1919; s. Wilbur Brinton and Isabelle (Kilgore) D.; m. Cornelia Prentiss Shrauger, July 28, 1940; children: Dennis Dean, Edward Gordon. BA, U. Iowa, 1940, JD, 1942. Bar: Iowa 1942, U.S. Supreme Ct. 1946. Mem. legal staff OPA-USA, Washington, 1942-43; ptnr. Livingston & Day, Washington, Iowa, 1946—. Author: War Letters, 1945. Sec. bd. dirs. Lake Darling Youth Ctr., Brighton, Iowa, 1951—; chmn. bd. Halcyon House Retirement Home, Washington, Iowa, 1955-70. Lt. USN, 1943-46. Presbyterian. Avocations: college football, college basketball. Home: 1005 S Iowa Ave Washington IA 52353-1126 Office: Day Meeker Lamping & Schlegel 112 S Ave B Washington IA 52353-1705

DAY, JOHN SIDNEY, management sciences educator; b. Newton, Mass., Oct. 13, 1917; s. Franklin Everett and Marion (Guild) D.; m. Barbara Jane Felch, Nov. 20, 1940; children: John Sidney, Stephen L. Student, Tufts U., 1935-37, Oxford Sch. Bus. Adminstrn., 1939; M.B.A. with distinction, Harvard U., 1950, D.C.S., 1956; D. in Mgmt. (hon.), Purdue U., 1993. Asst. to pres. C. Carlson Co., Boston, 1939-40, 45-46; instr. Oxford Sch. Bus. Adminstrn., Cambridge, Mass., 1946-48; research asst. Harvard Grad. Sch. Bus. Adminstrn., Cambridge, Mass., 1950-51; research asso. Harvard Grad. Sch. Bus. Adminstrn., 1951-53, asst. prof., 1953-56; assoc. prof. Purdue U., Lafayette, Ind., 1956-59; prof. indsl. mgmt. Purdue U., 1959-83, dean Krannert Grad. Sch. Mgmt., 1969-78, v.p. for devel., 1978-83, Krannert prof. mgmt., 1983-86, v.p. emeritus, 1986—. Author: (with L. Bollinger) Management of New Enterprises, 1952, Subcontracting Policy in the Airframe Industry, 1956, (with P. Donham) New Enterprise and Small Business Management, 1960. Bd. dirs. Purdue Research Found., 1980-83; mem. Tippecanoe County (Ind.) chpt. ARC, 1968-74, chmn., 1974; treas. Tippecanoe County Easter Seal Soc., 1977-82, 27-78; mem. West Lafayette Econ. Devel. Commn., chmn., 1975-83; mem. nat. adv. council SBA, 1976-78; trustee Joint Council on Econ. Edn., 1976-78; pres. Oak Point Community Assn., Inc., 1980-86; bd. dirs. Home Hosp., 1972-78, pres., 1977; bd. dirs. Am. Assemblies Collegiate Schs. Bus., 1974-78, pres., 1977-78. Served to col. USMCR. Decorated Bronze Star (2); Ford Found. fellow, 1959-60; named Hon. Sec. of State Ind.; receipent Sagamore of the Wabash. Mem. 1st Marine Div. Assn., Dataw Island Club, Retirees Assn. (Beaufort City pres. 1991-92), Masons, Rotary. Home and Office: 808 Hamilton St Beaufort SC 29902-4710

DAY, JOHN W., international corporation executive; b. Chgo., Feb. 25, 1933; s. John W. and Gay (Potters) D.; m. Barbara Cline, 1955; children: Lisa, Karen. BS in Bus., Northwestern U., 1955. Mgr. acctg. missile div. tech. applications USAF, 1957-61, mgr. fin. tech. applications, 1961-63; successively mgr. acctg. and audit, dir. fin., mng. dir., group dir., v.p. European div., pres. French div., group v.p. diversified ops. Chrysler Corp., 1963-79, v.p., controller, 1979-81; exec. v.p. Internat. Chrysler Corp., 1981-84; pres. Bendix group Allied-Signal Corp., 1984-88; pres. automotive div. Allied Signal, Southfield, Mich., 1989-91; pres. Allied-Signal Internat. Inc., Morristown, N.J., 1991-93; bd. dirs. NBD Bancorp and the Budd Co. Capt. USMC, 1955-57. Mem. Soc. Automotive Engrs., Detroit Athletic Club, Bloomfield Hills Country Club. Office: 319 E 50th St Apt 7E New York NY 10022-7938*

DAY, KATHLEEN PATRICIA, financial planner; b. West Palm Beach, Fla., Nov. 16, 1947; d. John I. and Lorraine A. (Risavy) Simmons; m. Bryan Patrick Day, Sept. 20, 1969; children: Kevin Kristopher, Amy Teresa. BS in Med. Tech., U. Fla., 1969; MBA, Fla. Internat. U., 1980. Cert. Fin. Planner; Chartered Fin. Analyst. Credit analyst corp. lending Southeast Bank NA, Miami, Fla., 1981-83; fin. cons. in pvt. practice Miami, 1983-87; pres. Integrated Asset Mgmt. Inc., Miami, 1987-88; fin. planner Raymond James & Assocs., Miami, 1988; pres. Kathleen Day & Assoc. Inc., Miami, 1989—; guest lectr. Miami Dade Community Coll., Miami, 1988-89, Barry U., 1989. Controller, bd. dirs. Delphi Found., Miami, 1985-88. Mem. Inst. Cert. Fin. Planners, Assn. Investment Mgmt. & Rsch., Internat. Assn. Fin. Planners. Avocations: sailing, Snow skiing. Office: Kathleen Day and Assocs 7355 SW 87th Ave Ste 300 Miami FL 33173-3565

DAY, KEVIN THOMAS, banker, community services director; b. London, Aug. 24, 1937; came to U.S., 1957; s. William Stanley and Mary Ann (Hook) D.; m. Mary Violet Scheuber, Aug., 1960. BA, Brisbane Tech. Coll., Queensland, Australia, 1957. Pres. Americana Investments, San Francisco, 1960-63; stockbroker Sutro and Co., San Francisco, 1963-66; regional v.p. Am. Express Investment Co., San Francisco, 1966-70; dir. mktg. ITT Fin. Svcs., N.Y.C., 1970-78; pres. Exec. Assocs., Reno, Nev., 1978-83, First Interstate Bank Found., Reno, 1983-1991; exec. dir. Cath. Community Svcs., Reno, 1991—; chmn. Nev. Fgn. Trade Zone, Reno, 1986-91, Desert Rsch. Inst., Reno. Pres. Econ. Devel. Authority, Reno, 1985, Nev. Mus. Art, 1989-91; mem. exec. com. Western Indsl. Nev., Reno, 1985-90; commr. Nev. Commn. on Econ. Devel., Carson City, 1987-90. Named Man of Yr., Reno mag., 1988, Torch of Liberty award, 1989; named to Nev. Order of Silver Spur, 1990. Republican. Roman Catholic. Avocations: sailing, wilderness camping, art collecting. Home: 4835 Pinesprings Dr Reno NV 89509-6504 Office: Cath Community Svcs 500 E 4th St Reno NV 89512

DAY, KRISTEN VALADE, legislative staff member; b. Detroit, Apr. 29, 1969. BA, Mich. State U., 1991. Staff asst./LC Congressman Bill Ford, Washington, 1991-94; legis. asst. Rep. James Barcia, Washington, 1994-98, legis. dir., 1999—. Office: Office US Rep James Barcia 2419 Rayburn House Office Washington DC 20515-2205*

DAY, L. B., management consultant; b. Walla Walla, Wash., Sept. 16, 1944; s. Frank Edmond and Geraldine Eloise (Binning) D. BS, Portland State Coll., 1966; MBA, George Washington U., 1971. Design mktg. cons. Leadership Resources Inc., Washington, 1970-71; faculty mem. USDA Grad. Sch. of Spl. Programs, Washington, 1971-74; dir. Office of Employee Devel. Oreg. Dept. Transp., Salem, 1972-75; prin. Day-Henry Assoc. Inc., Portland, Oreg., 1975-78, Day-Floren Assocs. Inc., Portland, Oreg., 1978-95, LB Day & Co., Portland, Oreg., 1996—; cons. Allergan, Arthur Andersen & Co., AMD, Egghead.com, Intel Corp., Fujitsu, Peek, Exabyte, Sequent Computer Sys., VLSI Tech., Inc., Pharmacia & Upjohn, also others; mem. faculty Am. Bankers Assn., Bank trainers Sch., 1981-84; adj. prof. Willamette U. Grad. Sch. Adminstrn., Salem, 1978, Oreg. Grad. Inst., 1994; bd. dirs. Microchip Tech., Inc., CFI Pro Svcs. Author: The Supervisory Training Program, 1977, Performance Management, 1981, Team-Oriented Management, 1989; contbr. articles to profl. jours. With U.S. Army, 1967-70. Scottish Rite fellow George Washington U., 1970. Mem. ASTD. Avocations: marathon runner, horseback riding. Office: L B Day & Co Inc 806 SW Broadway Fl 11 Portland OR 97205-3333

DAY, LUCILLE LANG, health facility administrator, educator, author; b. Oakland, Calif., Dec. 5, 1947; d. Richard Allen and Evelyn Marietta (Hazard) Lang; m. Frank Lawrence Day, Nov. 6, 1965 (div. 1970); 1 child, Liana Sherrine; m. 2nd, Theodore Herman Fleischman, June 23, 1974 (div. 1985); 1 child, Tamarind Channah. AB, U. Calif., Berkeley, 1971, MA, 1973, PhD, 1979. Teaching asst. U. Calif., Berkeley, 1971-72, 75-76, research asst., 1975, 77-78; tchr. sci. Magic Mountain Sch., Berkeley, 1977; specialist math. and sci. Novato (Calif.) Unified Sch. Dist., 1979-81; instr. sci. Project Bridge, Laney Coll., Oakland, Calif., 1984-86; sci. writer and mgr. precollege edn. programs, Lawrence Berkeley (Calif.) Nat. Lab., 1986-90, life scis. staff coord., 1990-92; mgr. Hall of Health, Berkeley, Calif., 1992—; lectr. St. Mary's Coll. of Calif., Moraga, 1997—. Author numerous poems, articles and book reviews; author: (with Joan Skolnick and Carol Langbort) How to Encourage Girls in Math and Science: Strategies for Parents and Educators, 1982, Self-Portrait with Hand Microscope (poetry collection), 1982, Fire in the Garden (poetry collection), 1997. NSF Grad. fellow, 1972-75; recipient Joseph Henry Jackson award in lit. San Francisco Found., 1982. Mem. No. Calif. Sci. Writers Assn., Nat. Assn. Sci. Writers, Math/Sci. Network, Soc. for Pub. Health Edn. (No. Calif. chpt.), Phi Beta Kappa, Iota Sigma Pi. Home: 1057 Walker Ave Oakland CA 94610-1511 Office: Hall of Health 2230 Shattuck Ave Berkeley CA 94704-1416

DAY, MARY, artistic director, ballet company executive; b. Washington; trained by Lisa Gardinier. ArtsD (hon.) Shenandoah Conservatory, DHL (hon.) Mount Vernon Coll. Co-founder Washington Sch. of Ballet, 1944—; founder Washington Ballet, 1976—. Recipient Mayor's award, Woman of Achievement award WETA-TV, Met. Dance award, Founders award Cultural Alliance, Excellence in Teaching Chautauqua Dance award, sr. Svcs. Disting. award IONA.; named Washingtonian of Yr. Washingtonian mag. Office: Washington Ballet 3515 Wisconsin Ave NW Washington DC 20016-3085*

DAY, MARYLOUISE MULDOON (MRS. RICHARD DAYTON DAY), appraiser; b. St. Louis; d. Joseph A. and Dorothy (Lang) Muldoon; A.B., Washington U., St. Louis, 1940; postgrad. Air U., 1958, George Washington U., 1963-64; grad. Real Estate Inst. Md., 1972; m. Richard Dayton Day, Aug. 15, 1959. Intelligence specialist U.S. Air Force, Washington, 1947-60; program officer, spl. asst. to dir. project devel. VISTA, OEO, 1965-67; with Joint Intelligence Bur., London, Eng., 1953; appraiser, cons. on antiques, fine arts, 1969—; pres. Agts. For Sales Ltd., 1974—, Marylouise M. Day, Inc., 1978—. Recipient citation U.S. Air Force, 1960. Fellow Inc. Soc. Valuers and Auctioneers (London), Am. Soc. Appraisers (chpt. 1st v.p. 1977-78, pres. 1978-79, chmn. fine arts forum 1976-78, gov. Region 3 1980-82, internat. sec. 1982-84, treas. ednl. found. 1986-91); mem. Appraisers Assn. Am., Irish Georgian Soc., Winterthur Guild, Assn. Former Intelligence Officers, Decorative Arts Trust, Delta Gamma. Club: Kenwood Golf and Country (Bethesda, Md.). Home: 4928 Sentinel Dr Bethesda MD 20816-3591

DAY, MAURICE JEROME, automobile parts distributing company executive; b. Saginaw, Mich., Jan. 3, 1913; s. Thomas and Margaret (Cavanaugh) D.; m. Mary Fitzgerald, Aug. 12, 1944 (dec. 1989); children: Mary Joann, Jeanne Ellen, Paul Maurice, Barbara Claire. B.S., Mich. State U., 1934, M.S., 1935, Ph.D., 1937. Metallurgist Carnegie-Ill. Steel Corp., Gary, Ind., 1937-38; tech. trade rep. Carnegie-Ill. Steel Corp., Chgo., 1941-45; mgr. alloy div. Carnegie-Ill. Steel Corp., 1945-47; phys. chemist U.S. Steel Research Lab., Kearny, N.J., 1938-41; metall. engr. U.S. Steel Corp., Pitts., 1947-52; mgr. materials and processes div. Armour Research Found., Chgo., 1952-53; asst. dir. Armour Research Found., 1953-54; v.p. research and devel. Crucible Steel Co. Am., Pitts., 1955-57; v.p. tech. Crucible Steel Co. Am., 1957-59, v.p. comml., 1959-63, sr. v.p., 1963-65; indsl. cons., 1965-68; pres., dir. Hawley Mfg. Co., San Francisco, 1966-76; chmn. bd. Argus, Inc., 1969-75; pres. Argus, Inc, 1970-75; chmn. bd., chief exec. officer, dir. Seaport Corp., Sacramento, 1975—; pres., chief exec. officer, dir. Noma Worldwide, Inc., 1979-84; dir. Brown Co. N.Y.C., Crucible Steel Co. Can., Oxford Electric Corp., Argus, Inc., Interphoto Corp., Crucible Steel Internat. (S.A.), Trent Tube Co.; Chmn. manganese panel, minerals and metals adv. bd., mem. panel guided missiles Nat. Acad. Scis.; Trustee Packaging Found., chmn. bd., 1963-65. Mem. Am. Ordnance Assn., Navy League U.S., Am. Soc. Metals, Def. Orientation Conf. Assn., A.I.S.I., Pa. Soc. Club: Duquesne (Pitts.). Home and Office: 5750 Ridgetown Cir Dallas TX 75230-2658

DAY, NEIL MCPHERSON, trade association executive; b. Springfield, Mass., June 4, 1935; s. William Roland and Helen (McPherson) D.; m. Vivian Shirley Smith, July 25, 1964; children: Neil Jr., Alfred. BA in English, Trinity Coll., Hartford, Conn., 1957; LLB, Cornell U., 1963. Bar: Mass. 1963, Conn. 1971. Assoc. Bulkley, Richardson, Ryan, Burbank, Springfield, 1963-71; asst. gen. counsel MIB, Inc., Greenwich, Conn., 1971-76, exec. dir., 1976-77; gen. counsel MIB, Inc., Westwood, Mass., 1976-98, pres., CEO, 1977-98. Active in fund raising Cornell U., Trinity Coll., bd. fellows, 1994-96. Mem. ABA, Mass. Bar Assn., Conn. Bar Assn., Appalachian Mountain Club (bd. dirs. 1983-88, fin. com. 1983—, audit com. 1992—, pres.'s soc. 1994—, fundraiser). Avocations: expert skier, mountaineer, sailor.

DAY, PETER RODNEY, geneticist, educator; b. Chingford, Essex, Eng., Dec. 27, 1928; came to U.S., 1963; m. Lois Elizabeth Rhodes, May 26, 1951; children: Susan Catherine, Rupert Peter, William Rodney. BS in Botany, Birbeck Coll., Eng., 1950; PhD, U. London, 1954. Sr. scientific officer John Innes Inst., Hertford, Eng., 1957-63; assoc. prof. Ohio State U., Columbus, 1963-64; chief, genetics dept. Conn. Agrl. Expt. Sta., New Haven, 1964-79; dir. Plant Breeding Inst., Cambridge, Eng., 1979-87; prof. genetics, dir. Rutgers U., New Brunswick, N.J., 1987—; sec. Internat. Genetics Fedn., 1984-93; trustee Internat. Ctr. for Maize and Wheat Improvement, Mexico City, 1986-92; chmn. Mng. Global Genetic Resources Bd. on Agrl., NAS, Washington, 1986-93. Author: Fungal Genetics, 1963, Genetics of Host-Parasite Interaction, 1974. Commonwealth Fund fellow U. Wis., 1954-56; Guggenheim Meml. fellow U. Queensland, 1972. Home: 394 Franklin Rd New Brunswick NJ 08902-2718 Office: Biotech Ctr 59 Dudley Rd New Brunswick NJ 08901-8520

DAY, RICHARD, museum administrator; b. Buffalo, June 8, 1951. Pres. Nat. Warplane Mus., Horseheads, N.Y.; dep. Erie County Sheriff's Dept. Mem. N.Y. Bar Assn. Office: Saperston & Day 3 Fountain Plz 1100 M&T Ctr Buffalo NY 14203*

DAY, RICHARD EARL, lawyer, educator; b. St. Joseph, Mo., Nov. 2, 1929; s. William E. and Geneva C. (Miller) D.; m. Melissa W. Blair, Feb. 2, 1951; children: William E., Thomas E. BS, U. Pa., 1951; JD with distinction, U. Mich., 1957. Bar: Ill. 1957, D.C. 1959, S.C. 1980. Assoc. Kirkland & Ellis, Chgo., 1957-58, Howrey Simon Baker & Murchison, Washington, 1958-61; asst. prof. law U. N.C., Chapel Hill, 1961-64; assoc. prof. Ohio State U., Columbus, 1964-66, prof., 1966-75; prof. U. S.C., Columbia, 1975-76, 80-86, dean, 1977-80, John William Thurmond chair disting. prof. law, 1986-99, disting. prof. law emeritus, 1999—; cons. U.S. Office Edn., 1964-66; course dir. Ohio Legal Ctr. Inst. Columbus, 1970-75; vis. prof. law U. Southampton (Eng.), fall 1988. Author: The Intensified Course in Antitrust Law, 1972, rev. edit., 1974; book rev. editor Antitrust Bull., 1968-71, adv. bd., 1971—; adv. bd. Antitrust and Trade Regulation Report, 1973-76, Jour. Reprints for Antitrust Law and Econs., 1974—. Ohio commr. Nat. Conf. on Uniform State Laws, 1967-75, S.C. commr., 1977-80; mem. Ohio Gov.'s Adv. Coun. Internat. Trade, 1972-74, S.C. Jud. Coun., 1977-80; chmn. S.C. Appellate Def. Coun., 1977-80, S.C. Com. Intellectual Property and Unfair Trade Practices Law, 1981-87. Lt. USNR, 1952-55. Named John William Thurmond Disting. Prof. Law. Mem. ABA, S.C. Bar Assn. (bd. govs. 1977-80), Am. Law Inst. Methodist. Home: 204 Saint James St Columbia SC 29205-3074 Office: U SC Law Ctr Main and Green Sts Columbia SC 29208

DAY, RICHARD PUTNAM, marketing, strategic planning and employee benefits consultant, arbitrator; b. Hartford, Conn., Feb. 13, 1930; s. Godfrey Malbone and Sheila (Wilson) D.; m. Patricia Ann Brady, Jan. 26, 1957; children: Richard Jr., Stephen, Thomas, Gregory, Katharine, Martha, Ward, Emily. Student, The Choate Sch., 1948; AB, Middlebury Coll., 1952. With group field sales Conn. Gen. Life Ins. Co., Hartford, Detroit, Toledo, Phoenix, 1952-61; dir. sales group Bankers Life Nebr. (name changed to Ameritas Life Ins. Corp.), Lincoln, 1961-73, v.p. group, 1973-87, exec. v.p. group, 1987-91, exec. v.p. bus. devel., 1991-93; prin. R.P. Day Consulting, Paradise Valley, Ariz., 1993—; dir. Nat. Health Care Svcs., Jacksonville, Fla., 1988-95. Trustee, pres. bd. Madonna Profl. Care Ctr., Lincoln, 1970-80, trustee Lincoln Gen. Hosp., 1980. Lt. USN, 1952-56. Mem. VFW, Internat. Soc. Cert. Employee Benefit Specialists (bd. dirs. pres. governing coun., chmn. bd. 1986), Am. Soc. CLUs, Internat. Found. Employee Benefit Plans, Profl. Ins. Mass-Mktg. Assn., Mass-Mktg. Ins. Inst., Nat. Assn. Dental Plans, Am. Legion, Retired Officers Assn., Country Club of Lincoln, Scottsdale Country Club, Blue Key Honor Soc., Phi Kappa Tau. Republican. Episcopalian. Avocation: golf. Home: 6530 N 61st St Paradise Valley AZ 85253-4235

DAY, RICHARD SOMERS, author, editorial consultant; b. Chgo., June 14, 1928; s. Milo Frank and Ethel Mae (Somers) D.; m. Lois Patricia Beggs, July 8, 1950; children: Russell Frank, Douglas Matthew, Gail Lesllie. Student, Ill. Inst. Tech., 1946, U. Miami, 1947. Promotion writer, editor Portland Cement Assn., 1958-62, promotion writer, 1963-66; editor Am. Inst. Laundering, Joliet, Ill., 1962-63; free-lance writer Monee, Ill., 1966-69, Palomar Mountain, Calif., 1969-87. Cons. editor home and shop Popular Sci. mag., N.Y.C., 1966-89; editorial cons. St. Remy Multimedia, Montreal, Que., Can., 1987—; pres., exec. prodr. Vi-Day-O Prodns. Inc., Palomar Mountain, 1991-98; author numerous home imiprovement and repair books including: Patios and Decks, 1976, Automechanics, 1982, Do-It-Yourself Plumbing--It's Easy with Genova, 1987, Building Decks, Patios, and Fences, 1992 (Nat. Assn. Home and Workshop Writers Stanley Tools Do-It-Yourself Writing award 1992); editor: (newspaper) Powderlines, 1958; (mag.) Concrete Hwys. and Pub. Improvements, 1958-62; (mag.) Soil-Cement News, 1960-62, Fabric Care, 1962-63; prodr. videos: How to Cure Toilet Troubles, 1994, Mountain Man Horse packing, 1994; contbr. chpts. to books. Bd. dirs. Palomar Mountain Planning Orgn., 1984-91. Mem. Nat. Assh. Home and Workshop Writers (mng. editor newsletter 1982-96, bd. dirs. 1974—, pres. 1984-85). Home: PO Box 10 Palomar Mountain CA 92060

DAY, ROBERT ANDROUS, English language educator, former library director, editor, publisher; b. Belvidere, Ill., Jan. 18, 1924; s. Floyd Androus and Mabel May (Dorn) D.; m. Betty Lucy Johnson, Aug. 27, 1949; children—Nancy, Barton, Robin. BA, U. Ill., 1949; MS, Columbia U., 1951. Librarian, Sci. and Tech. div. Newark Pub. Library, 1951-53; librarian, editor Inst. Microbiology Rutgers U., 1953-60, dir. Coll. of South Jersey Library, 1960-61; mng. editor Am. Soc. Microbiology, Washington, 1961-80; dir. ISI Press, Phila., 1980-86; v.p. Inst. for Sci. Info., Phila., 1984-86; prof. English U. Del., Newark, 1986—; tchr. sci. writing; pub. cons. NSF, NIH, others. Author: How to Write and Publish a Scientific Paper, 1979, 5th edit., 1998, Scientific English: A Guide for Scientists and Other Professionals, 1992, 2d edit., 1995. With USAAF, 1943-46. Mem. AAAS, Coun. Biology Editors (chmn. 1977-78), Soc. Scholarly Pub. (pres. 1982-84), Am. Med. Writers Assn., Soc. Tech. Comm., European Assn. Sci. Editors, Assn. Tchrs. Tech. Writing. Home: 77 Ritter Ln Newark DE 19711-5174 Office: U Del Dept English Newark DE 19716

DAY, ROBERT DWAIN, JR., foundation executive, lawyer; b. Stockton, Calif., Dec. 14, 1950; s. Robert Dwain and June Rita (Kartcher) D.; m. Carol Robin Tyler; children: Leslie Carroll, Ryan Tyler. BS, Va. Poly. Inst., 1974; JD, U. S.C., 1977. Bar: S.C. 1977, D.C. 1978. Forester USDA Forest Svc., Washington and Columbia, S.C., 1973-77; dir. resource policy Soc. Am. Foresters, Bethesda, Md., 1977-81; resident fellow Resources for the Future, Washington, 1981-82; exec. dir. Renewable Natural Resources Found., Bethesda, 1982—; corp. sec. RNRF Title Holding Corp., 1997—; cons. Office of Tech. Assessment U.S. Congress, Washington, 1981-82; mem. nat. task force Soc. Am. Foresters, Bethesda, 1982-83; advisor The Conservation Found., Washington, 1978-79; mem. adv. coun. Coll. Natural Resources, Utah State U., 1992-96; mem. nat. awards coun. for environtl. sustainability Renew Am. Inc., 1997-98. Author policy analysis column Jour. of Forestry, 1977-81; editor: Renewable Resources Jour., 1982—. Mem. AAAS, D.C. Bar Assn., S.C. Bar Assn., Soil and Water Conservation Soc., Environ. Law Inst., Coun. Engring. and Sci. Soc. Execs., Montgomery County Soc. for Assns. (exec. com. 1992-94, 98—). Home: 2191 Canterbury Way Potomac MD 20854-6105 Office: Renewable Natural Resources 5430 Grosvenor Ln Ste 220 Bethesda MD 20814-2193

DAY, ROBERT EDGAR, retired artist, educator; b. Clinton Falls, Minn., Dec. 27, 1919; s. Judson LeRoy and Blanche Leone (Finch) D.; m. Helen Marie Hanson, Aug. 13, 1944 (dec.); children: Marion Eve, Cynthia Lynn, Brian Louis; m. Kathryn Jean Griswold, June 7, 1969. Student, U. Minn., 1937-39; BA magna cum laude, St. Olaf Coll., 1943; MA, U. Iowa, 1946, PhD, 1958. Instr. art and English, art supr. pub. schs. Owatonna, Minn., 1943-45, Winona, Minn., 1946-49; instr., asst. prof. art edn. and appreciation Kent State U., 1949-56; assoc. prof. art history and sculpture No. Ill. U., 1958-60; prof., chmn. dept. art La. State U., 1960-65; prof. U. Colo., Boulder, 1965-88, prof. emeritus fine arts, 1988—; chmn. dept. fine arts U. Colo., 1965-68; high sch. wrestling coach, 1943-49; chmn. adv. com. Anglo-Am. Art Mus., 1961-63, dir. art history program in Italy, 1971, 73, 74, 76, 77, 78, 81, 82, 84, 87. Exhibited The Harvester, Regional Sculpture Invitational, Beaumont (Tex.) Art Mus., 1963. Danforth Found. tchr. grantee, 1957; Recipient Purchase award Ohio Printmakers Assn., Purchase award Dayton (Ohio) Mus., 1951. Home: 940 Cypress Ln Louisville CO 80027-9428 *During my career in art and its history, I have come to realize in an ever deeper sense that people are more important than artifacts, and that underlying all values and meaningful human relationships is the working of an infinite and personal God. The great possibilities in any human creative effort can only be understood in this light.*

DAY, ROBERT MICHAEL, oil company executive; b. Winnfield, La., Jan. 28, 1950; s. Robert Neal and Virginia Ruth (Franklin) D.; m. Noelie Barron, Dec. 20, 1975; children: Robert Michael Jr., Brionne. BS, La. State U., 1976; MBA, U. Houston-Clear Lake, 1989. Roustabout, floorman Global Marine Drilling Co., Houston, 1976-77; sales engr. NL Baroid Petroleum Svcs., Houston, 1977-78; drilling technician East Tex. div. Exxon Co., USA, Houston, 1978-79; sr. drilling technician Southeastern div. Exxon Co., USA, New Orleans, 1979-81, drilling supt., 1981-84; drilling supt. hdqrs. Exxon Co., USA, Houston, 1984-89; drilling supt. Offshore div. Exxon Co., USA, New Orleans, 1989-91; ops. supr. hdqrs. drilling Exxon Co., Internat., Houston, 1991—. Contbr. articles to profl. jours. Ruling elder Clear Lake Presbyn. Ch., Houston, 1987-88. With U.S. Army, 1969-73. Mem. Soc. Petroleum Engrs., Soc. of the 1st Inf. Divsn., Masons, Sigma Pi. Republican. Home: 20730 Chappell Knoll Dr Cypress TX 77429-5510

DAY, ROBERT WINSOR, cancer researcher; b. Framingham, Mass., Oct. 22, 1930; s. Raymond Albert and Mildred (Doty) D.; m. Jane Alice Boynton, Sept. 6, 1957 (div. Sept. 1977); m. Cynthia Taylor, Dec. 16, 1977; children: Christopher, Nathalia, Natalia, Julia. Student, Harvard U., 1949-51; MD, U. Chgo., 1956; MPH, U. Calif., Berkeley, 1958, PhD, 1962. With USPHS, 1956-57; resident U. Calif., Berkeley, 1958-60; research specialist Calif. Dept. Mental Hygiene, 1960-64; asst. prof. sch. medicine UCLA, 1962-64; dep. dir. Calif. Dept. Pub. Health, Berkeley, 1965-67; prof., chmn. dept. health services Sch. Pub. Health and Community Medicine, U. Wash., Seattle, 1968-72, dean, 1972-82, prof., 1982—; pres., dir. Fred Hutchinson Cancer Rsch. Ctr., Seattle, 1981-97, pres., dir. emeritus, 1997—, mem. pub. health scis., 1997—; mem. Nat. Cancer Adv. Bd., 1992-98, Nat. Cancer Policy Bd., 1996—; cons. in field. Fellow AAAS, Am. Pub. Health Assn., Am. Coll. Preventive Medicine; mem. Am. Soc. Clin. Oncology, Soc. Preventive Oncology, Am. Assn. Cancer Rsch., Assn. Schs. Pub. Health (pres. 1981-82), Am. Assn. Cancer Insts. (bd. dirs. 1983-88, v.p. 1984-85, pres. 1985-86, chmn. bd. dirs., 1986-87). Office: Fred Hutchinson Cancer Rsch Ctr PO Box 19024 LM-120 Seattle WA 98109-1024

DAY, ROLAND BERNARD, retired chief justice state supreme court; b. Oshkosh, Wis., June 11, 1919; s. Peter Oliver and Joanna King (Wescott) D.; m. Mary Jane Purcell, Dec. 18, 1948; 1 dau., Sarah Jane. B.A., U. Wis., 1942, J.D., 1947. Bar: Wis. 1947. Trainee Office Wis. Atty. Gen., 1947; assoc. mem. firm Maloney & Wheeler, Madison, Wis., 1947-49; 1st asst. dist. atty. Dane County, Wis., 1949-52; partner firm Day, Goodman, Madison, 1953-57; firm Wheeler, Van Sickle, Day & Anderson, Madison, 1959-74; legal counsel mem. staff Sen. William Proxmire, Washington, 1957-58; justice Wis. Supreme Ct., Madison, 1974-95, chief justice, 1995-96; Mem. Madison Housing Authority, 1960-64, chmn., 1961-63; regent U. Wis. System, 1972-74. Served with AUS, 1943-46. Mem. ABA, State Bar Wis., Am. Trial Lawyers Assn., Ygdrasil Lit. Soc. (pres. 1968), Madison Torske Klubben, Masons (33rd degree). Mem. United Ch. of Christ. Clubs: Madison, Madison Lit.

DAY, RONALD ELWIN, consulting executive; b. Randolph, Vt., Dec. 15, 1933; s. John Ellis and Esther Murle (Tabor) D.; A.A., Pasadena City Coll., 1958, student, 1958-59; B.A., U. Calif., Santa Barbara, 1961; M.B.A., UCLA, 1962; m. Elizabeth Jean McKeage, June 26, 1955; children—Gary Alan, Kathi Ellen, Judy Anne, Jeffrey Evan. Internal auditor North Am. Aviation, Downey, Calif., 1962-64; systems and procedures mgr. Proto Tool Co., Los Angeles, 1964-65; computer programmer First Nat. Bank, Boston, 1966-67; project mgr., 1967-73, systems analyst 1974-77, system planning com. chmn., trust div., 1977-89, trust info. mgmt. system adminstr., 1977-89; pres. Edge System Projects, Inc., North Reading, Mass., 1990—. With USAF, 1952-56. Mem. Soc. Advancement of Mgmt., U.S. Ski Assn., Nat. Geog. Soc., Boston Computer Soc., Assn. Systems Mgmt., Alpha Gamma Sigma. Republican. Home and Office: 2 Bigham Rd North Reading MA 01864-2904

DAY, RONALD RICHARD, financial executive; b. York, Pa., Nov. 14, 1934; s. Russell Aldinger and Rosa Ellenora (Reever) D.; m. Patricia Glee Duncan, Nov. 24, 1956. BS in Econs., Lebanon Valley Coll., Annville, Pa., 1956; postgrad. U.S. Army Fin. Sch., Indpls., 1957, Lehigh U., 1961. Mgr. cost control and systems Mack Trucks, Inc., Allentown, Pa., 1963-67; mgr. cost acctg. Am. Chain div. Acco Babcock Co., York, 1967-70; div. controller, 1970-82, v.p. fin. and acctg., Chain & Forged Prods. Group, 1982-89; pres., sr. v.p., contr., chief fin. officer AAA So. Pa., 1990—; committeeman York County Republican party, 1972-74; sec. Optimist Internat., York, 1973; bus., chmn. York County chpt. Am. Heart Assn., 1987-89. Served to 1st lt. U.S. Army, 1957-59. Mem. York Area C. of C., Internat. Platform Assn., Lafayette Club, Outdoor Country (York) Club, Masons, Shriners, Order of De Molay (mem. adv. bd. 1975-89), Rotary (sec. West York club, 1988-92), (pres. 1993-94). Lutheran. Avocations: golf, hunting, fishing, boating, travel. Home: 2430 Ramblewood Rd York PA 17404-3941 Office: AAA So Pa 116 E Market St York PA 17401-1219

DAY, ROSALEE P., probation officer; b. Norwood, Ga., Nov. 2, 1943; d. John Kendrick and Louise (Woods) Porter; m. Emanuel and Rosalee Day; 1 child, Kimberly Ann Hopewell. BSW, Temple U., 1976, MSW, 1977. Lic. social worker. Title supervising U.S. probation officer U.S. Probation Office, Phila.; ret., 1997; social work cons., 1997—. Mem. Delta Sigma Theta.

DAY, RUSSELL CLOVER, state agency administrator; b. Concord, N.H., June 29, 1943; s. Alan C. and Lois M. (Huntington) D.; m. Carol Ann Tasker, July 9, 1965; children: Jennifer Marie, Jeffrey Russell. BA, New England Coll., 1965; postgrad., Fairfield U., 1965, U. N.H., 1965-67; M in Human Svcs. Adminstrn., Antioch U., Keene, N.H., 1978. Examiner Soc. Security Disability Determination Svc., Concord, 1969-73, supr., 1973-81, dep. dir., 1981-85, adminstr., 1985—. Trustee New England Coll., 1987-89; mem. supervisory com. N.H. Fed. Credit Union, chairperson, 1995-97, bd. dirs., 1997—. Mem. Nat. Coun. Disability Determination Dirs. (exec. com. 1991-94), Masons, Lions Club (pres. 1983-84, chmn. region 1, dist. 44-N 1995-96), New Eng. Coll. Alumni Assn. (chmn. 1987-89). Republican. Congregationalist. Avocations: fishing, boating, stamp collecting, photography. Home: 73 Wallace Rd Goffstown NH 03045-1823 Office: Social Security Disability Determination Svc PO Box 452 Concord NH 03302-0452

DAY, STACEY BISWAS, physician, educator; b. London, Dec. 31, 1927; came to U.S. 1955, naturalized 1977.; s. Satis B. and Emma L. (Camp) D.; m. Ivana Podvalova, Oct. 18, 1973; 2 children. MD, Royal Coll. Surgeons, Dublin, Ireland, 1955; PhD, McGill U., 1964; DSc, Cin. U., 1971. Intern King's County Hosp., SUNY Downstate Ctr., 1955-56; resident fellow in surgery U. Minn. Hosp., 1956-60; hon. registrar St. George's Hosp., London, Eng., 1960-61; lectr. exptl. surgery McGill U., Montreal, Que., Can., 1964; asst. prof. exptl. surgery U. Cin. Med. Sch., 1968-70; assoc. dir. basic med. research Shriner's Burn Inst., Cin., 1969-71; from asst. to assoc. prof. pathology, head Bell Mus. Pathobiology U. Minn., Mpls., 1970-74; dir. biomed. communications and med. edn. Sloan-Kettering Inst., N.Y.C., 1974-80; mem. Sloan-Kettering Inst. for Cancer Research, 1974-80; mem. adminstrv. council, field coordinator, 1974-75; prof. biology Sloan Kettering div. Grad. Sch. Med. Sci. Cornell U., 1974-80, ret., 1980; clin. prof. medicine div. behavioral medicine N.Y. Med. Coll., 1980-92; prof. biopsychosocial medicine, chmn. dept. community health U. Calabar (Nigeria) Sch. Medicine, 1982-85; prof. internat. health, dir. Internat. Ctr. for Health Scis. Meharry Med. Coll., Nashville, 1985-89, dir. WHO Collaborating Ctr. ICHS, 1987-89; founding dir. WHO Collaborating Ctr., Nashville, 1987-89, emeritus dir., 1989; adj. prof. family and community medicine U. Ariz. Coll. Med. Scis., Tucson, 1985-89; univ. prof. internat. health U. Calabar, Nigeria, 1989—; permanent vis. prof. med. edn. Oita Med. Univ., Japan, 1992—; Arris and Gale Lectr., Royal Coll. Surgeons, Eng., 1972; vis. lectr., Ireland, 1972; vis. prof. U. Bologna, 1977, Kyushu, Japan, 1990, U. Mauritius, 1991, Bratislava U., 1991, Japan, 1992, 1993, Beijing, China, 1993; vis. prof. health comm. U. Santiago, Chile, 1979-80, Colombo, Sri Lanka, 1996, South India, 1996, U. S.F. De Quito, Ecuador, 1996; vis. prof. Oncologic Rsch. Inst., Tallinn, Estonia, 1976, All India Insts. Health, 1976, U. Maiduguri, 1982, Kyushu, Japan, 1990; vis. acad. Oxford (Eng.) U., 1993-95; moderator med. cartography and computer health Harvard U., 1978, Acad. Scis., Czechoslovakia, 1987, Australia, 1988; Fulbright prof. Charles U., Czechoslovakia, 1989, hon. prof. Coll. of Health Sciences, Universad San Francisco De Quito (Ecuador) 1996; cons. Pan Am. Health Assn., 1974-90, U.S.-USSR Agreement for Health Cooperation, 1976, WHO Collaborating Centre Meharry Med. Coll., Nashville, 1985, NAFEO/AID, 1986-89; mem. expert com. for health, manpower devel., WHO, 1986-90; cons. Div. Strengthening Health Care Resources WHO, Geneva, 1987-90, UN-FSSTD, 1987, AID/Joint Memorandum of Understanding, W. Africa, Kenya, Sudan, So. Africa, 1985-89, to dean med. coll. faculty Med. and Health Scis., ABHA, Province of Asir, Saudi Arabia, 1981, to dir. High Tatras symposia Post Grad. Med. Inst., Bratislava, 1990—, to rector Universidad Autonoma Agraria Antonio Narro, Saltillo, Mexico, 1987-89; pres., chmn., Pub. Cultural and Ednl. Prodns., Montreal, U.S., 1966-85; bd. dirs. Internat. Health, African Health Consultancy Svc., Nigeria, Ekologia & Zivot, Slovakia; bd. dirs., v.p. Am. Sci. Activities Mario Negri Rsch. Found., 1975-80; hon. founding chmn., bd. dirs. Lambo Found. U.S.; v.p., trustee Cancer Relief Found., Calabar; pres., exec. dir. Internat. Found. for Biosocial Devel. and Human Health, 1978-86, chmn., 1986—; mem. Medzinárodny Poradny Vybor Nadácie Ekológia Zivot, Re. Slovakia, 1995—; cons. Inst. Health, Lyfford Cay, Bahamas, 1981, Govt. Cross River State, Nigeria, Itreto State and H.H. Obong of Calabar, Nat. Bd. Advs., Am. Biog. Inst., 1982—; cons. cmty. health and health comms. Navaho Nation, Sage Meml. Hosp., Ganado, Ariz., 1984; founder, cons. Primary Self-Health Clinics, Oban, Ikot Oku Okono, and Ikot Imo, Nigeria, 1982-84; cons. High Tatras Internat. Health Symposia, Slovakia, 1990—; apptd. ambassador Gov. State of Tenn., 1986—; adj. clin. prof. medicine N.Y. Med. Coll.; hon. prof. Coll. Scis. Salud U. San Francisco, Quito, Ecuador, 1996; researcher in field. Writer, 1965—; author: (verse) Collected Lines, 1966, (play) By the Waters of Babylon, 1966, (verse) American Lines, 1967, (play) The Music Box, 1967, Three Folk Songs Set to Music, 1967, Poems and Etudes, 1968, (novel) Rosalita, 1968, The Idle Thoughts of a Surgical Fellow, 1968, Edward Stevens-Gastric Physiologist, Physician and American Statesman, 1969, (novella) Bellechasse, 1970, A Leaf of the Chaatim, 1970, Ten Poems and a Letter from America for Mr. Sinha, 1971, Curling's Ulcer: An Experiment of Nature, 1972, Tuluak and Amaulik: Dialogues on Death and Mourning with the Innuit Eskimo of Point Barrow and Wainwright, Alaska, 1974, East of the Navel and Afterbirth: Reflections from Rapa Nui, 1976, Health Communications, 1979, The Biopsychosocial Imperative, 1981, What Is Survival: The Physician's Way and the Biologos, 1981, Developing Health in the West African Bush, 1995, Moudrost Samuraju (in Czech), 1998, Selected Poems and Embers of a Medical Life, 1999; editor: Death and Attitudes Toward Death, 1972, Membranes, Viruses and Immune Mechanisms in Experimental and Clinical Disease, 1972, Ethics in Medicine in a Changing Society, 1973, Communication of Scientific Information, 1975, Trauma: Clinical and Biological Aspects, 1975, Molecular Pathology, 1975, (with Robert A. Good) series Comprehensive Immunology, 9 vols., 1976-80, Cancer Invasion and Metastasis-Biologic Mechanisms and Therapy, 1977, Some Systems of Biological Communication, 1977, Image of Science and Society, 1977, What Is a Scientist, 1978, Sloan Kettering Inst. Cancer Series, 1974-80, (with K. Inokouchi) Selections From The Chronicle of The Hagakure as Wisdom Literature: The Way of The Samurai of Saga Domain, 1993; editor-in-chief, mem. editl. bd.: Health Communications and Informatics, 1974-80; editor in chief: The American Biomedical Network: Health Care System in America Present and Past, 1978, A Companion to the Life Sciences, Vol. 1, 1979, A Companion to the Life Sciences, Vol. 2, Integrated Medicine, 1980, A Companion to the Life Sciences, Vol. 3: Life Stress, 1981, Advance to Biopsychosocial Health, 1984; editor in chief, mem. editorial bd. Health Communications and Biopsychosocial Health; editor: (with others) Cancer, Stress and Death, 1979, 2d edit., 1986, Computers for Medical Office and Patient Management, 1981, Readings in Oncology, 1980, Biopsychosocial Health, 1981; editor: Primary Health Care Guidelines: A

Training Manual for Community Health, 2d edit., 1986, (with T.A. Lambo) Contemporary Issues in International Health, 1989; sr. editor (with Salat and others): Health and Quality of Life in Changing Europe in the Year 2000, 1992, Hagakure-Spirit of Bushido, (with H. Koga), 1993, (with K. Inokuchi) Selections from the Chronicles of the Hagakure as Wisdom Literature: The Way of the Samurai of Saga Domain, 1993, (with Salát) Health Management, Organization, and Planning in Changing Eastern Europe, 1993, The Medical Student and the Mission of Medicine in the Twenty First Century, (in Japanese, with M. Kobayashi and K. Inokuchi), 1995, The Wisdom of Hagakure, 1996, Developing Health in the West African Bush (2 parts), 1995, Letters of Owen Wagensteen to a Surgical Fellow: with a memoir, 1996, Man and Mu: The Cradle of Becoming and Unbecoming, 1997, Czech Caesura: Golden Prague and the Black Years (Notes from Diaries 1970-1990), 1998, Moudrost Samuraju Trigon, 1998 (in Czech), Selected Poems and Embers of a Medical Life, 1998; mem. editl. bd.: Annual Reviews on Stress, Jour. Stress; cons. editl. bd. Comprehensive Medicine (Japan); also co-editor various publs.; contbr. articles to profl. lit.; producer TV and radio health edn. programs, Nigeria, TV film River Blindness (Onchocerciasis) in Africa, 1988. Served with Brit. Army, 1946-49. Recipient Moynihan medal Assn. Surgeons Gt. Britain and Ireland, 1960, Reuben Harvey triennial prize Royal Coll. Physicians, Ireland, 1957, Arris and Gale award Royal Coll. Surgeons, Eng., 1972, disting. scholar award Internat. Communication Assn., 1980, Sama Found. medal, 1982, disting. citation Hagakure Soc., 1992, Nat. Svc. medal Royal Brit. Legion, 1993; named to Hon. Order Ky. Cols., 1968; named Chieftan Ntufam Ajan of Oban Ejagham People, Cross River State, Nigeria, 1983; hon. prof. Del Colegio De Ciencas De La Salud De La Universidad San Francisco De Quito, 1996; recipient Chieftan Obong Nsong Idem Ibibio Nigeria, 1983, Mgbe (Ekpe) honor Nigeria, commendation WHO address Fed. Govt. Nigeria, Calabar, 1983, Leadership in Internat. Med. Health citation Pres. U.S., 1987, WHO medal, 1987, Agromedicine citation Commr. of Agr., State of Tenn., 1987, Assembly citation State of N.Y., 1987, Citation Congl. Record., 1987; Maestro Honorifo, U. Autonoma Agraria, Coahuila, Mex., 1987; presented Key to the City of Nashville, 1987; recipient Vice-Chancellor's Citation and Presentation for Primary Health Care Teaching in Nigeria, U. Calabar, 1988; Pamětni medal Postgrad. Med. Coll., Prague, 1991, Gold medal U. of Bratislava, 1991, Disting. Citation Hagakure Rsch. Soc., Japan, 1992, Nat. Svc. medal Royal Brit. Legion, 1993, Citation Commendation from Pres. Kyoto Prefectural U. Medicine, Japan, 1993, Citation Commendation on Contbn. to Med. Edn. from Pres. Oita Med. U., Japan, 1997; addresses presented by people of Ikot Imo, Nsit Anyang, Oban, 1982-84, Commendation from King of Calabar, 1984; Ciba fellow Can., 1965; Stacey Day Ward named in his honor by Fed. Min. and Gov. of Cross River State, Calabar Med. Ctr., Nigeria, 1986; charter mem. U.S. Normandy Com., 1988; 1st fgn. hon. mem. Hagakure Res. Soc. (Samurai), Kyushu, Japan, 1991. Fellow Zool. Soc. London Royal Micros. Soc., Royal Soc. Health, World Acad. Arts and Scis., Japanese Found. for Biopsychosocial Health (internat. hon. fellow and most disting. mem.), African Acad. Sci., African Acad. Med. Scis. (founder); mem. AAS, AMA, APHA, Am. Burn Assn., Internat. Burn Assn., Can. Authors Assn., N.Y. Acad. Scis., Am. Assn. History Medicine, Am. Inst. Stress (bd. dirs.), Am. Anthrop. Assn., Am. Rural Health Assn. (v.p. internat. sci. affairs, bd. dirs.), Soc. Med. Geographers USSR. Home: 6 Lomond Ave Chestnut Ridge NY 10977-6901 *I have tried to assimilate all that is good in many cultures and to bring about a synthesis of these expressions in my own life and writings. It is as if I must find a third eye that can see what is best in all men, to integrate them newly into a changing world, and to be as much a releasing force as to be an absorbing force. This direction, I believe, commits one to an unceasing philosophy to unlearn and to relearn.*

DAY, STEVEN M., accounting educator, accountant; b. Cedar City, Utah, July 19, 1960; s. Wilford Higbee and Raeona (Mackelprang) D.; m. Laurana Wittwer, June 1, 1984; children: Steven Michael, Scott Erle, Ryan. AA in Acctg., Utah Valley Community Coll., Orem, 1980; BS in Acctg., So. Utah State Coll., 1982; MACC, So. Utah U., 1992. CPA, Utah. Staff acct. Claude Slack, CPA, Cedar City, 1980-82; audit mgr. Arthur Young & Co., CPAs, Reno, Nev., 1982-83; asst. controller Frontier Enterprises, Inc., Carson City, Nev., 1983-85; owner Steven M. Day, CPA, St. George, Utah, 1985—; prof. acctg. Dixie Coll., St. George, 1985—; pres. R&D Devel., Inc., St. George, Utah, 1995—; advisor Distbg. Edn. Clubs of Am., St. George, 1987-89, Future Bus. Leaders of Am., St. George, 1990—. Mem. AICPAs, Utah Assn. CPAs (pres. So. chpt. 1988-89). Republican. LDS. Avocations: camping, hunting, antiques. Home: 1001 S Joe Cir Saint George UT 84790-4024 Office: Dixie Coll Business Dept Saint George UT 84770

DAY, STOCKWELL BURT, government official; b. Barrie, Ont., Can., Aug. 16, 1950; s. Stockwell and Gwendolyn (Gilbert) D.; m. Valorie Martin Day, Oct. 2, 1971; children: Logan, Luke, Ben. Auctioneer Alta., Can., 1972-74; dir. Teen Challenge Outreach Ministries, Edmonton, Alta., 1974-75; contractor Comml. Interiors, Alta., 1976-78; sch. adminstr./asst. pastor Bentley (Alta) Christian Centre, 1978-85; mem. Legis. Assembly Alta. Legis., Edmonton, 1986—, govt. caucus whip, 1989-92, govt. house leader, 1994-97, min. of labor, 1992-96, min. of family and social svcs., 1996-97, provincial treas., acting premier, 1997—; chmn. Alta. Tourism Edn. Coun., Edmonton, 1987-89, Premier's Coun. on Family, Edmonton, 1990-92. Mem. Red Deer Rotary, Red Deer Legion (assoc.). Avocations: tennis, roller blading, backpacking, reading. Office: Government of Alberta, 224 Legislature Bldg, Edmonton, AB Canada T5K 2B6

DAY, STUART REID, lawyer; b. Laramie, Wyo., July 2, 1959; s. Richard Erwin and Evelyn (Reid) D.; m. TimAnn Day, Jan. 18, 1980; children: Shelby Rochelle, Erica Rachel. BS, Ariz. State U., 1981; JD, U. Wyo., 1984. Assoc. Williams, Porter, Day & Neville, Casper, Wyo., 1984-87, ptnr., 1987—; mem. unauthorized practice of law com. Wyo. State Bar. Mem. ABA, ATLA, Wyo. Bar Assn. (bd. dirs., vice chmn., bd. CLE 1992-93, chmn. bd. CLE 1994-95), Colo. Bar Assn., Def. Rsch. Inst., Natrona County Bar Assn. (treas. 1989, v.p. 1990, pres. 1991), Casper C. of C. (bd. dirs. 1989-91, 97—). Office: PO Box 10700 Casper WY 82602-3902

DAY, WILLIAM HUDSON, mechanical engineer, turbomachinery company executive; b. Lynn, Mass., Feb. 4, 1937; s. Hudson Smith and Annie (Reynolds) D.; m. Susan Phelps, July 22, 1961; children: Andrew, Carolyn. BME, Cornell U., 1960; MSMechE, Poly. Inst. N.Y., 1966, PhD, 1970. Mgr. high temp. turbine project Gen. Electric Gas Turbine Div., Schenectady, 1967-71, mgr. systems engring., 1971-73, mgr. advanced product planning, 1973-77, mgr. advanced programs, 1977-79; v.p. advanced programs United Technologies, Hartford, conn., 1979-81; exec. v.p. Elliott Co., Jeanette, Pa., 1981-83, dir. strategic planning, 1983-85; dir. gas turbine engring. and new product devel. Turbo Power & Marine Systems, United Techs. Turbo Power, Middletown, Conn., 1985-95; mgr. advanced indsl. programs United Tech. Pratt & Whitney, East Hartford, Conn., 1995—. Inventor in field; contbr. articles to profl. jours. Pres. Woodhaven Homeowners Assn., Scotia, N.Y., 1973-75; scoutmaster Boy Scouts Am., 1977-79; bd. dirs. Boy Scouts, Greensburg, Pa., 1983-85. Served to 2d lt. U.S. Army, 1960-61. Mem. ASME. Republican. Home: 25 Longview Rd Avon CT 06001-2935 Office: Untied Techs Pratt & Whitney 400 Main St # 165 22 East Hartford CT 06108-0968

DAYA, JACKIE, publishing company executive. Sr. v.p., CFO Cahners Pub. Co., Newton, Mass., to 1999; exec. v.p. Robert Barghaus, 1999—. Office: Cahners Pub Co 492 Beacon St Apt 74 Boston MA 02115*

DAYE, CHARLES EDWARD, law educator; b. Durham, N.C., May 14, 1944; s. Ecclesiastes and Addie Lula (Roberts) D.; m. Norma Lowery, Dec. 19, 1976; stepchildren: Clarence L. Hill, III, Tammy H. Roundtree, N.C. Central U., 1966; JD, Columbia U., 1969. Bar: N.Y. 1970, D.C. 1971, N.C. 1975, U.S. Supreme Ct. 1979. Assoc. Dewey, Ballantine, Bushby, Palmer & Wood, N.Y.C., 1969; law clk. U.S. Ct. Appeals (6th cir.) 1969-70; assoc. Covington & Burling, Washington, 1970-72; prof. law Sch. Law, U. N.C., Chapel Hill, 1972-81, 85—, Henry Brandis Prof. Law, 1991—; dean, prof. law Sch. Law, N.C. Central U., Durham, 1981-85; cons. N.C. Dept. Adminstrn., 1975; mem. Triangle Housing Devel. Corp., 1973—, chmn. 1977-93; chair N.C. Poverty Project, 1990—. Mem. ABA (mem. commn. on minorities in the profn., 1990-95, pres. law sch. admission coun., 1991-93), N.C. Assn. Black Lawyers (Lawyer of Yr. 1980, pres. 1976-78, exec. sec. 1979—), N.C. Bar Assn. Democrat. Baptist. Author: (with Mandelker et al) Housing and Community Development, 1981, 2d edit. 1989 (with Morris) N.C. Law of Torts; contbr. articles to profl. jours. Home: 3400 Cambridge Rd Durham NC 27707-4508 Office: Univ NC Law Sch Chapel Hill NC 27599-3380*

DAYER-BERENSON, LINDA, adult and critical care nurse, educator; b. Trevose, Pa., Aug. 29, 1960; d. Robert E. and Mary Ellen (Hunt) Dayer; m. Richard P. Berenson, Jan. 22, 1984; children: Justin, Jarret. Diploma, Frankford Hosp. Sch. Nursing, Phila., 1988; AA, Pa. State U., Abington, 1988; BSN, U. of the State of N.Y., Albany, 1989; MSN, Widener U., Chester, Pa., 1992, postgrad; postgrad., U. Medicine & Dentistry. RNCS clin. specialist med.-surg. nursing, adult nurse practitioner. Staff nurse ICCU and med. surg. Frankford Hosp-Torresdale, Phila., 1989-93; instr. nursing Frankford Hosp. Sch. Nursing, 1989-93, 94-97; staff nurse intensive care unit West Jersey-Voorhees, 1993; advanced practice nurse, clin. asst. prof. U. Medicine and Dentistry, Sch. Nursing, Stratford, N.J., 1998—; nurse instr. Burlington County Coll., 1993-94. Pub. RN Mag., ANNA Jour., Nursing Spectrum. Roth Found. scholar, 1986-88. Mem. ANA, AANP, Acad. Med./Surg. Nurses, Golden Key Nat. Honor Soc., Sigma Theta Tau, Alpha Sigma Lambda. Office: UMDNJ Sch Nursing Camden Campus 221-223 S 6th St Camden NJ 08103

DAY-GOWDER, PATRICIA JOAN, retired association executive, consultant; b. Lansing, Mich., Apr. 9, 1936; d. Louis A. and Johanna (Feringa) Whipple; m. Duane Lee Day, Jan. 7, 1961 (div.); children: Kevin Duane, Patricia Kimberley; m. William A. Gowder, Nov. 30, 1986. BA, Mich. State U., 1958; MA, Lindenwood (Mo.) Coll., 1979; postgrad., U. So. Calif., 1982-83. Cert. secondary tchr., Calif. Calif. health edn. asst. YWCA, Rochester, N.Y., 1958-59; tchr. jr. high schs. Flint, Mich., 1959-61; tchr. Brookside Acad., Montclair, N.J., 1963-68; adult program dir. YMCA, Long Beach, Calif., 1968-73; cmty. edn. dir. Paramount (Calif.) Unified Sch. Dist., 1973-78; exec. dir. counseling ctr. Arcadia, Calif., 1978-80; sr. citizens program dir. City of Burbank, Calif., 1981-83; div. dir. Am. Heart Assn., L.A., 1983-87; exec. dir. Campfire Orgn., Pasadena, 1987-89; exec. dir. greater L.A. chpt. Nat. Found. Ileitis and Colitis, 1989-90; mgr. sr. citizens, mktg. dept. Meth. Hosp. So. Calif., 1989-98, ret., 1998; cons. mktg., planning and special events 50 Mktg., Inc., Glendora, Calif., 1998—; cons. community edn. State Dept. Edn., Fed. Office Community Edn., L.A. County Office Edn. Bd. dirs., v.p. Children's Creative Ctr., Long Beach, Calif., 1969-73, Traveler's Aid Soc., 1969-72; vice-chmn. Cerritos YMCA, 1968-73. Mott Found. fellow, 1977-78. Mem. AAUW, Western Gerontology Assn., NAFE, Calif. Cmty. Edn. Assn. (sec.-treas. 1974-77), LWV. Democrat. Congregationalist. Avocations: tennis, hiking, bicycling, painting, reading. E-mail: p54year@aol.com. Home and Office: 170 Oak Forest Cir Glendora CA 91741-3718

DAY-LEWIS, DANIEL (DANIEL MICHAEL BLAKE DAY-LEWIS), actor; b. London, England, Apr. 29, 1957; s. Cecil and Jill (Balcon) D.-L.Children: son Gabriel Kane. Student, Bedales and Bristol Old Vic Theatre Sch. Appeared in plays Class Enemy, Funny Peculiar, Bristol, Eng., Look Back in Anger, Dracula, Bristol and London, Another Country, London, Futurists, Romeo, Thisbe, R.S.C., Hamlet, 1989; appeared in TV show Insurance Man; films include: Sunday Bloody Sunday, 1971, Ghandi, 1982, The Bounty, 1984, A Room with a View, 1986, My Beautiful Laundrette, 1986, Nanou, 1986, The Unbearable Lightness of Being, 1988, Stars and Bars, 1988, Eversmile, New Jersey, 1989, My Left Foot, 1989 (Academy Award best actor 1989), The Last of the Mohicans, 1992, The Age of Innocence, 1993, In the Name of the Father, 1993 (Academy Award nomination best actor 1993), The Crucible, 1996, The Boxer, 1997. Office: William MorrisAgy 151 S El Camino Dr Beverly Hills CA 90212-2775*

DAYMENT, DAVID, airport executive; b. Toronto, Oct. 4, 1959. BBA, Seneca Coll., Toronto, 1982. Pvt. pilot Buttonville Airport, 1980-83, airport supr., 1983-88, mgr. airport ops., 1988—. Office: Buttonville Airport, Box 100 2833 16th Ave, Markham, ON Canada L3R 0P8*

DAYNARD, RICHARD ALAN, law educator; b. N.Y.C., July 19, 1943; s. David M. and Sarah (Weidenbaum) D.; m. Carol S. Iskols, Aug. 9, 1975; children: David J., Gabriela C. BA, Columbia U., 1964, MA in Sociology, 1970; JD, Harvard U., 1967; PhD in Urban Studies and Planning, MIT, 1980. Bar: N.Y. 1967, U.S. Ct. Appeals (6th cir.) 1986, U.S. Supreme Ct. 1986, U.S. Ct. Appeals (11th cir.) 1987, U.S. Ct. Appeals (5th cir.) 1996. Law clk. 2d cir. U.S. Ct. Appeals, N.Y.C., 1967-68; teaching fellow Columbia U., N.Y.C., 1968-69; asst. prof. law Northeastern U., Boston, 1969-71, assoc. prof. law, 1971-73, prof. law, 1973—; lectr. Tufts Med. Sch., Boston, 1975-89; internat. lectr. and cons. Editor-in-chief Tobacco Products Litigation Reporter, 1985—; assoc. editor: Tobacco Control: An Internat. Jour., 1998—; contbr. articles in field to profl. jours. Chmn. Tobacco Products Liability Project, Boston, 1984—; pres. Group Against Smoking Pollution of Mass., Boston, 1983—, Clean Indoor Air Ednl. Found., Boston, 1983-92, Tobacco Control Resource Ctr., Inc., Boston, 1993—; pres. Stop Teenage Addiction to Tobacco, 1996-98. Mem. ABA, Am. Pub. Health Assn., Law and Soc. Assn., Phi Beta Kappa. Home: 90 Commonwealth Ave Boston MA 02116-3040 Office: Northeastern U Sch Law 400 Huntington Ave Boston MA 02115-5005

DAYS, DREW S., III, lawyer, law educator; b. 1941; m. Ann Ramsay Langdon, 1966; children: Alison, Elizabeth. Degree in Eng. Lit. with honors, Hamilton Coll., 1963; LLB, Yale U., 1966. Bar: Ill. 1966, N.Y. 1970. Assoc. Cotton, Watt, Jones & King, Chgo., 1966-67; vol. Peace Corps., Honduras, 1967-69; assoc. counsel NAACP Legal Def. Fund, N.Y.C., 1969-73, 75-77; assoc. prof. Temple U., 1973-75; asst. atty. gen. Dept. of Justice, Washington, 1977-81; assoc. prof. Yale U., New Haven, 1981-86, prof., 1986-93, Alfred M. Rankin chair Law Sch., 1991-93; solicitor gen. Dept. Justice, Washington, 1993-96; dir. Schell Ctr. for Internat. Human Rights Yale U. Law Sch., 1988-93. Bd. dirs. John D. and Catherine T. MacArthur Found., Petra Found., Hamilton Coll. Mem. Am. Law Inst., Am. Bar Found., Am. Acad. Arts and Scis., Coun. on Fgn. Rels., Inter-Am. Dialogue. Office: Yale Law Sch PO Box 208215 New Haven CT 06520-8215

DAY-SALVATORE, DEBRA LYNN, medical geneticist; b. Hoboken, N.J., Oct. 23, 1953; m. Francis P. Salvatore, Sr., Dec. 24, 1988. BA in Biology, Harvard U., 1975; MS in Pharmacology, NYU, 1979, PhD in Pharmacology, 1982; MD, Case Western Res. U., 1986. Diplomate Am. Bd. Med. Genetics, Am. Bd. Pediats. Grad. fellow dept. pharmacology NYU Med. Ctr., 1978-79; sr. rsch. asst. dept. medicine Case Western Res. U., Cleve., 1979-82, rsch. assoc. dept. molecular biology and microbiology, 1982-84; pediatric and adolescent medicine resident Cleve. Clinic Found., 1986-89; med. genetics fellow Robert Wood Johnson Med. Sch., New Brunswick, N.J., 1990-91, asst. prof. pediatrics, 1990—, coord. perinatal genetics dept. ob-gyn., 1991-92, dir. divsn. reproductive and perinatal genetics dept. ob-gyn., 1992—, asst. prof. ob-gyn. and reproductive scis. and pediatrics, 1992—, acting chief divsn. clin. genetics, dept. ob-gyn. and reproductive scis., 1993—; physician Robert Wood Johnson Univ. Hosp., New Brunswick, 1990—; physician St. Peter's Med. Ctr., 1992—, chief divsn. clin. genetics, 1996—; mem. genetic adv. bd. N.J. State Dept. Health's Parental and Child Adv. Com.; mem. med. adv. bd. Cryo-Cell Internat. Genetics editor Jour. of Perinatology, 1993—; contbr. articles, abstracts to profl. jours. Cons. N.J. Interagency Adoption Coun. Mem. AAAS, AMA, Am. Acad. Pediatrics (mem. N.J. chpt.), Am. Soc. Cell Biology, Am. Soc. Human Genetics, Human Genetics Assn. N.J. (mem. legis. com.), N.Y. Acad. Sci. Office: Saint Peter's Med Ctr 254 Easton Ave # 4410 New Brunswick NJ 08901-1766

DAYSON, DIANE HARRIS, superintendent, park ranger; b. N.Y.C., Feb. 14, 1953; d. Robert Gene and Dessie Lee (Osborne) Harris; m. Kevin Maurice Dayson, Sept. 15, 1978; children: Dayna Renee, Kyle Ryan. BA in Early Secondary Edn. & Am. History, SUNY, Cortland, 1975; postgrad., NYU, 1998—. With Nat. Pk. Svc. U.S. Dept. Interior, 1975—, law enforcement ranger, 1977-79, concessions specialist, 1979-81; site mgr. Nat. Pk. Svc. U.S. Dept. Interior, N.Y.C., 1984-87; supt. Nat. Pk. Svc. U.S. Dept. Interior, Oyster Bay, N.Y., 1987-90, Morristown, N.J., 1990-93, Hyde Park, N.Y., 1993-95; supt. Statue of Liberty Ellis Island, N.Y.C., 1996—; ambassador to Amsterdam, 1998. Active United Way, Dutchess County; exch. steward, Manchester, Eng., 1994; bd. dirs. Christian Ministry in Nat. Parks, 1997—. Mem. NAFE, Oyster Bay C. of C. Republican. Roman Catholic. Avocations: travel, knitting, reading. Office: Statue of Liberty Ellis Island Liberty Is New York NY 10004-1467

DAYTON, NANCY CHERYL, English educator; b. Marion, Ind., Feb. 12, 1963; d. William Russell and Joanne Lois (Clement) Klinger; m. Stephen Bruce Dayton, Aug. 17, 1991. BA, Ind. Wesleyan U., 1985; MA, Ind. U., 1987; PhD, Miami U., Oxford, Ohio, 1996. Instr. English Ball State U., Muncie, Ind., 1987-88, Taylor U., Upland, Ind., 1988-92; asst. prof. English Taylor U., Upland, 1992-97, assoc. prof. English, 1997—. Choir mem. Lake View Wesleyan Ch., Marion, Ind., 1988—, Sunday sch. tchr., 1994—. Mem. MLA, Ind. Coll. English Assn. (reporter), Popular Culture Assn., Willa Cather Meml. Found. Avocations: collecting antiques and political memorabilia. Office: Taylor Univ Dept English 500 W Reade Ave Dept English Upland IN 46989-1002

DAYTON, SKY, communications company executive. Grad., Delphi Acad., 1988. Mgr. computer graphics dept. Mednick & Assocs., 1988-90; founder Cafe Mocha, L.A., 1990-92; co-founder Dayton Walker Design, 1992-94; founder, chmn. Earthlink Network, Pasadena, Calif., 1994—. Mem. Assn. Online Profls. (bd. dirs.), Internet Access Coalition. Office: Earthlink Network 3100 New York Dr Pasadena CA 91107-1500

DAZE, ERIC, professional hockey player; b. Montreal, Can., July 2, 1975. Selected 4th found NHL entry draft Chgo. Blackhawks, 1993; left wing Beauport QMJ Hockey League, 1992-95, Chgo. Blackhawks, 1995—; named to QMJ Hockey League All-Star first team, 1993-94, 94-95. Recipient Can. Hockey League Most Sportsmanlike Player of Yr. award, 1994-95, Frank J. Selke Trophy, 1994-95; named Sporting News Rookie of Yr., 1996. Office: c/o Chicago Blackhawks 1901 W Madison St Chicago IL 60612-2459*

DAZEY, WILLIAM BOYD, retired lawyer; b. Chgo., Sept. 23, 1915; s. Alva William and Emma Mayo (Boyd) D.; m. Dolores Ann Melton, July 20, 1959; children: Barbara Ann Dazey Lantos, William Melton, Thomas Sumner, Daniel Putnam, Johnathan Mayo. Student, U. Ill., 1933; LL.B., Cumberland U., 1935. Bar: Tex. 1940. Ptnr. firm Godard & Dazey, Texas City, 1940-58; cons. Japan UN Assn., Tokyo, 1958-60; legal advisor Japan Consul Gen., Houston, 1960-86; ptnr. Dazey & Newey, Houston, 1970-80. Served to 2d lt. U.S. Army, 1942-46. Decorated Bronze Star with oak leaf cluster, Purple Heart; Third Order Sacred Treasure (Japan). Mem. ABA, State Bar Tex., Nat. Order Battlefield Commns., Japan-Am. Soc. Houston (founder, past pres.), Am. Inst. for Internat. Steel (emeritus), Torch Club, Phi Delta Theta. Democrat. Unitarian. Home: 419 E Hathaway Dr San Antonio TX 78209-6416

D'AZZO, JOHN JOACHIM, electrical engineer, educator; b. N.Y.C., Nov. 30, 1919; s. Domenick and Jacqueline (Cappello) D'A.; m. Betty G. McBride, June 13, 1953; 1 child, Dennis. BEE, CCNY, 1941; MSEE, Ohio State U., 1950; PhD, Salford U., Eng., 1978. Registered profl. engr., Ohio. Quality control engr. Western Electric Co., Kearney, N.J., 1941-42; devel. engr. Air Materiel Command, Wright Patterson AFB, Ohio, 1942-46; prof. elec. engring. Air Force Inst. Tech., Wright Patterson AFB, Ohio, 1947-98, prof. emeritus, 1998—; head dept. elec. engring. Air Force Inst. Tech., Wright Patterson AFB, 1984-95. Author: Feedback Control System Analysis and Synthesis, 1960, 2d edit., 1966, Linear Control System Analysis and Design, 1975, 4th edit., 1995. Served to 2d lt. U.S. Army, 1945-46. Named Outstanding Engr. Affiliate Socs. Ohio, 1962, 86. Fellow IEEE, AIAA (assoc.); mem. Am. Soc. for Engring. Edn., Sigma Xi, Tau Beta Pi, Eta Kappa Nu. Roman Catholic. Home: 3923 Winthrop Dr Beavercreek OH 45431-3148 Office: Air Force Inst Tech 2950 P St Wright Patterson AFB OH 45433-7765 *The spread of fundamental knowledge to new generations is a necessary task. Assisting individuals in developing approaches for applying theoretical results to practical applications is very rewarding. This must be done with understanding for the individual as a person.*

DAZZO, NICHOLAS JOHN, economist; b. Dec. 15, 1963. MA, NYU, 1992. Sales assoc. Donaldson, Lufkin & Jenrette, N.Y.C., 1986-88; columnist Am. Banker, N.Y.C., 1988-89; v.p. J.P. Morgan, N.Y.C., 1989—. Home: 1207 Woodside Rd Scotch Plains NJ 07076

DCAMP, CHARLES BARTON, educator, musician; b. Fairfield, Iowa, Feb. 16, 1932; s. Glenn Franklin and Nina Clarice (Larson) DC.; m. Ruth Joyce MacDonald, June 27, 1953; children: James Charles, Douglas Kevin, David Michael, Richard Manley, Paul Frederick, Jon Barton. *Son James Charles, BA, MA, band director, Uvalde, Texas; married Karen Wernett; children: Byron, Nathan, Jocelyn. Son Douglas Kevin, BS, program analyst, Buffalo, Minnesota; married Ronda McNally; children: Scott, Jarod. Son DavidMichael, BA, MA, computer service, Cavy, Illinois; married Sheila Erickson; children: Tim, Melissa. Son Richard Manley, BA, MA, PhD, German teacher, Davenport, Indiana; married Michelle Lafrenz; children: Hannah, Stephen. SonPaul Frederick, BA, computer analyst, Bettendorf, Iowa; married Deborah Taylor; children: Amy, Joel, Robert. Son Jon Barton, BS, MS, engineer, Eagan, Minnesota;married Kristine Reich; children: Andrew, Heidi* Student Bradley U., 1950-51; B.S., U. Ill., 1956, M.S., 1957; Ph.D., U. Iowa, 1980. Tchr., Watervliet (Mich.) Pub. Sch., 1958-61; tchr. music United Twp. High Sch., East Moline, Ill., 1961-63; band dir. Pleasant Valley (Iowa) Schs., 1963-74; prof. music St. Ambrose U., Davenport, Iowa, 1974—, also dir. bands, chmn. div. fine arts and chmn. dept. music; guest dir., adjudicator festivals, music contests Iowa, Ill., Minn.; producer Quad-City Music Guild, 1973-77, music dir.,1967—; chmn. Iowa All-State Band, 1971-74; instr. woodwinds Bemidji State U. Band Camp, 1967-92. Mem. Riverdale Vol. Fire Co., 1966-75, pres., 1971-73; founder, first conductor Quad-City Wind Ensemble, 1987—; choirmaster Bettendorf Presbyn. Ch. Choir, 1982-94. Served with AUS, 1952-55. Recipient Karl King Disting. Svc. award Iowa Bandmasters, 1987, Disting. Svc. to Music Edn. award Iowa Music Educators Assn., 1995; named to Quad City Music Guild Hall of Fame, 1997. Mem. NEA (life), Iowa Bandmasters Assn. (past pres., Karl King Disting. Service award 1987), Nat. Cath. Bandmasters Assns., Coll. Band Dirs. Nat. Assn., Music Educators Nat. Conf., Iowa Music Educators (pres.), Am. Fedn. Musicians, Am. Philatelic Soc., Am. Sch. Band Dirs. Assn., Nat. Band Assn. (Iowa state chmn.), Quad City Stamp Club (editor newsletter 1993—), Masons, Hi-12 (Davenport chpt.), Shriners (Kaaba shrine), Davenport York Rite, Phi Mu Alpha Sinfonia, Phi Delta Kappa, Tau Kappa Epsilon. Republican. Methodist. Editor, Iowa Music Educator mag., 1978-80 ; publisher arrangements for concert band; contbr. articles to profl. jours. Home: 803 W Rusholme St Davenport IA 52804-1927 Office: Saint Ambrose U Music Dept Davenport IA 52803

DCAMP, RICHARD MANLEY, secondary education educator; b. Watervliet, Mich., July 28, 1959; s. Charles Barton and Ruth Joyce (MacDonald) D; m. Michelle Ann Lafrenz, June 18, 1994; children: Hannah Marie, Stephen Richard. BA, St. Ambrose U., 1982; MA, U. Iowa, 1991, DPhil, 1995. Tchr. elem. art Pleasant Valley (Iowa) Cmty. Schs., 1982-83; tchr. English, Fed. Upper Level H.S., Linz, Austria, 1983-84; tchr. art, music and German, Assumption H.S., Davenport, Iowa, 1984-88; tchr. art and English, Pleasant Valley H.S., 1988-89; instr. music history Scott C.C., Bettendorf, Iowa, 1986-88; instr. German, U. Iowa, Iowa City, 1989-95, U. Wis., Oshkosh, 1995-98; tchr. Davenport Cmty. Schs., 1998—. Mem. MLA, Am. Coun. Tchrs. Fgn. Langs., Am. Assn. Tchrs. German, Internat. Assn. Learning Labs., Orff Schulwerk Assn. Roman Catholic. Avocations: painting, calligraphy, gardening, music. Office: Davenport North HS 626 3 53d St Davenport IA 52806

DEA, DONALD DON, business executive; b. May 12, 1954; s. Kim Fun and Moy (Sleu) D.; m. Catherine L. Dea, Oct. 20, 1984; children: Erin Jennifer, Alexander Gregory. BA, Western Md. Coll., 1976; MBA, Duke U., 1978; postgrad., MIT, 1988. With Xerox Corp., 1978—; mgr. fin. and adminstrn. real estate ops. Xerox Corp., Rochester, N.Y., 1986-87, mgr. planning adn disposition real estate ops., 1987-89, mgr. market channel devel., 1989-90, gen. mgr. channel ops. (OEM/VAR) and devel., 1990—, gen. mgr. U.S. ops., 1991; gen. mgr. channel strategic ptnr. devel., 1992—; spl. asst. to atty. gen. dept. justice Pres.'s Exec. Exch. program, Washington, 1982-83; gen. mgr. Channel Strategic Ptnr. Devel., 1992; co-founder Alaris Corp., AvN COD, 1996—. Mem. bd. alumni advisors Duke U. Fuqua Sch. Bus., Durham, N.C., 1988—; pres., v.p., controller Assn. for Blind and Visually Impaired, Rochester, 1986—; bd. dirs. Salvation Army, Rochester, 1985—. Recipient John Seaman award Balt. Poly. Inst., 1968, Alumni Citizenship award Western Md. Coll., 1976, MBA award Pensions & Investment, 1988. Mem. Western Md. Coll. Alumni Assn. (pres. 1987—).

Home: 12 Saint Ebbas Dr Penfield NY 14526-9786 Office: AVN 46 North Ave Webster NY 14580-3008

DEACON, DAVID EMMERSON, advertising executive; b. Toronto, Ont., Can., July 22, 1949; s. Donald Mac Kay and Florence (Campbell) D.; m. Kathryn Robinson (divorced); m. Mary Cecilia Eberle, July 23, 1982 (divorced). Student, Brock U., St. Catherines, Ont., 1968-70, Casa Sch. Fine Arts, Paris, 1970-71. Chmn. election orgn. Liberal Party Ont., Toronto, 1973-75; chmn., editor polit. alerts F.H. Deacon, Hodgson Inc., Toronto, 1975-79, v.p. retail sales, 1979-84; gen. mgr. Porsche div. VW Can., Toronto, 1984-87; pres. Deacon Day Advt., Toronto, 1988-94; chmn. Lowe SMS, Toronto, 1994-96; mng. dir., COO, CFO Padulo Integrated, Toronto, 1996—. Illustrator: (poetry) Sun Street, 1970; records include Over the Line, 1994, The Iron Clock, 1996. Chmn. campaign tng. Fed. Liberty Party, 1977-79; pres. Ont. Liberal Party, 1983-85; chmn. Ont. campaign John Turner Leadership, 1984. Winner Can. Endurance Racing championship Can. Automobile Sport Club, 1980. Mem. Toronto Club. Avocations: skiing, tennis, windsurfing, sailing, riding.

DEACON, JOHN STANLEY RAYMOND, physician; b. Oct. 25, 1939. BSc, U. Toronto, Can., 1966; MD, U. Rochester, 1970. Dir. neonatal ICU Foothills Hosp., Calgary, Can., 1975-80; asst. prof. pediat. U. Calgary, 1975-80; pediatrician, neonatologist St. Joseph's Hosp., Milw., 1980—. Office: 5000 W Chambers St Milwaukee WI 53210-1650

DE ACOSTA, ALEJANDRO DANIEL, mathematician, educator; b. Buenos Aires, Feb. 1, 1941; came to U.S., 1981; s. Wladimiro and Telma (Reca) de A.; m. Martha Callejo, Aug. 19, 1966; children: Alejandro Elias, Diego Andrés. Lic. in math. scis., U. Buenos Aires, 1965; PhD, U. Calif., Berkeley, 1969. Instr. math. MIT, Cambridge, 1970-71; asst. prof. U. La Plata, Argentina, 1972-75; assoc. prof. U. Buenos Aires, 1975; rschr. Venezuelan Inst. Sci. Investigation, Caracas, 1976-82; vis. prof. U. Wis., Madison, 1981-82; vis. prof. dept. math. and stats. Case Western Res. U., Cleve., 1983, prof., 1984—. Assoc. editor Annals Probability, 1985-90; mem. editl. bd. Jour. Theoretical Probability, 1987—; contbr. articles to math. jours. Recipient prize in math. Nat. Rsch. Coun. Venezuela, 1978. Fellow Inst. Math. Stats.; mem. Am. Math. Soc. Office: Case Western Res U Dept Maths Cleveland OH 44106

DEACY, THOMAS EDWARD, JR., lawyer; b. Kansas City, Mo., Oct. 14, 1918; s. Thomas Edward and Grace (Scales) D.; m. Jean Freeman, July 10, 1943 (div. 1988); children: Bennette Kay Deacy Kramer, Carolyn G., Margaret Deacy Vickrey, Thomas, Ann Deacy Krause; m. Jean Holmes McDonald, 1988. J.D., U. Mo., 1940; M.B.A., U. Chgo., 1949. Bar: Mo. 1940, Ill. 1946. Practice law Kansas City, 1940-42; ptnr. Taylor, Miller, Busch & Magner, Chgo., 1946-55, Deacy & Deacy, Kansas City, 1955—; lectr. Northwestern U., 1949-55, U. Chgo., 1950-55; dir., mem. exec. com. St. L.-S.F. Ry., 1962-80; dir. Burlington No. Inc., 1980-86; mem. U.S. team Anglo-Am. Legal Exchange, 1973, 77. Mem. Juv. Protective Assn. Chgo., 1947-55, pres., bd. dirs., 1950-53; mem. exec. bd. Chgo. coun. Boy Scouts Am., 1952-55; pres. Kansas City Philharmonic Orch., 1961-63, chmn. bd. trustees, 1963-65; trustee Sunset Hill Sch., 1963-73; trustee, mem. exec. com. u. Kansas City, 1963—; trustee Mo. Law Sch. Found., pres., 1973-77, Kans. chpt. The Nature Conservancy, 1994—. Capt. AUS, 1942-45. Fellow Am. Coll. Trial Lawyers (regent 1968—, treas. 1973-74, pres. 1975-76), Am. Bar Found; mem. Am. Law Inst., Jud. Conf. U.S. (implementation com. on admission of attys. to fed. practice 1979-86), ABA (commn. standards jud. adminstrn. 1972-74, standing com. fed. judiciary 1974-80), Ill. Bar Assn., Chgo. Bar Assn., Mo. Bar, Kansas City Bar Assn., Lawyers Assn. Kansas City, Chgo. Club, La Jolla (Calif.) Country Club, La Jolla Beach and Tennis Club, Kansas City Club, Kansas City Country Club, River Club, Quod Erat Bonus Homo Honor Soc., Beta Gamma Sigma, Sigma Chi. Home: 2724 Verona Cir Shawnee Mission KS 66208-1265 Office: 920 Main St Ste 1900 Kansas City MO 64105-2010

DEAHL, WILLIAM EVANS, JR., minister; b. Twin Falls, Idaho, Apr. 21, 1945; s. William Evans Deahl Sr. and Cora Elizabeth Hardberger; m. Diane Elizabeth Davis, June 4, 1967. BS, Nebr. Wesleyan U., Lincoln, 1966; MA, No. Ill. U., DeKalb, 1968; MDiv., MST, Iliff Sch. Theology, Denver, 1970, 81; PhD, So. Ill. U., Carbondale, 1974. Ordained to ministry United Meth. Ch., 1969. Instr. speech and theatre Nebr. Wesleyan U., Lincoln, 1970-71, 82-84; chmn. speech and theatre Va. Intermont Coll., Bristol, 1972-74; instr. speech and theatre Ea. Mont. Coll., Billings, 1974-76; chmn. speech and theatre Midland Luth. Coll., Fremont, Nebr., 1976-82; min. Nebr. Wesleyan U., Lincoln, 1984-92; instr. speech S.E. C.C., 1993-95; min. 1st United Meth. Ch., Kearney, Nebr., 1995-98, Calvary United Meth. Ch., Fremont, 1998—; minister United Meth. Ch., Ryegate, Mont., 1975-76, Rising City, Nebr., 1976-82, First United Meth. Ch., Springfield, Nebr., 1982-83, Grace United Meth. Ch., Lincoln, 1983-95. Co-author: Speech Liberal Arts Context, 1981; contbr. articles to profl. jours. Recipient Bishop Baker Grad. award United Meth. Ch., 1989. Mem. Am. Acad. Religion, Assn. for Religion and Intelligent Life, Assn. Coll. and Univ. Chaplains, Order of St. Luke, Levinas Soc. Nebr., Abraham Heschel Soc., Order of DeMolay. Office: Calvary United Meth Ch 2438 E 12th St Fremont NE 68025 *The unceasing quest for excellence and beauty in life, especially in relationship to the divine, community, and friendship, is necessary to escape the constant lure of conformity and mediocrity so rampant in our culture.*

DEAK, CHARLES KAROL, chemist; b. Budapest, Hungary, Sept. 26, 1928; s. Karoly and Ida (Benes) D.; came to U.S., 1955, naturalized, 1961; BS, Eotvos Coll., Budapest, 1948; student Sorbonne, Paris, 1949; postgrad. Wayne State U., 1957-61; bd. cert. forensic examiner; m. Jenny Bocinski, Apr. 9, 1958; children: James, Christine. With Frankel Co., Inc., Detroit, 1957-73, quality control mgr., 1968-71, mgr. tech. svcs., 1971-73; pres. Analytical Assocs., Inc., Detroit, 1973-92; pres. C.K. Deak Tech. Svcs., Inc., 1992—. Cert. profl. chemist. Fellow Am. Inst. Chemists; mem. Am. Chem. Soc., ASTM, Am. Soc. Metals, Assn. Analytical Chemists, Photog. Soc. Am. Roman Catholic. Patentee in chem. firefighting agts. and dense metal separation. Club: Internat. Brotherhood Magicians. Home: 29844 Wagner Dr Warren MI 48093-8635

DEAK, ISTVAN, historian, educator; b. Szekesfehervar, Hungary, May 11, 1926; came to U.S., 1956, naturalized, 1962; s. Istvan and Anna (Timar) D.; m. Gloria Gilda Alfano, July 4, 1959; 1 dau., Eva. U. Budapest, 1945-48; Student, Sorbonne, 1950-51, U. Md., Munich, W. Ger., 1953-55; M.A., Columbia U., 1958, Ph.D., 1964. Journalist, librarian and bookseller Budapest, Paris and Munich, 1945-56; instr. history Smith Coll., 1962-63; mem. faculty Columbia U., 1963—, prof. history, 1973-93; Seth Low prof. History Columbia U., N.Y.C., 1993—; mem. Inst. Advanced Study, Princeton, N.J., fall 1981; pres. Conf. on Slavic and East European History, 1985. Author: Weimar Germany's Left-Wing Intellectuals: A Political History of the Weltbühne and Its Circle, 1968, The Lawful Revolution: Louis Kossuth and the Hungarians, 1848-1849, 1979, Hungarian edit., 1983, 2d edit., 1994, German edit., 1989, Beyond Nationalism: A Social and Political History of the Hapsburg Officer Corps, 1848-1918, 1990, German edit., 1991, 2d edit., 1995, Hungarian edit., 1993, Italian edit., 1994; co-editor: Eastern Europe in the 1970's, 1972, Everyman in Europe: Essays in Social History, 2 vols., 2d edit., 1981, 3d edit., 1989. Recipient Lionel Trilling Book award Columbia U., 1979; German Acad. exchange fellow, 1960-61; Guggenheim fellow, 1970-71; Fulbright-Hays travel fellow, 1973, 84-85; fellow Woodrow Wilson Ctr. for Scholars, Washington, 1985. Mem. Hungarian Acad. Scis., Am. Hist. Assn., Am. Assn. Advancement Slavic Studies (Wayne S. Vuchinich Book prize). Home: 410 Riverside Dr New York NY 10025-7974 Office: Columbia U 1229 Internat Affairs Bldg New York NY 10027

DEAKIN, JAMES, writer, former newspaperman; b. St. Louis, Dec. 3, 1929; s. Rogers and Dorothy (Jeffrey) D.; m. Doris Marie Kanter, Apr. 14, 1956; 1 son, David Andrew. AB, Washington U., St. Louis, 1951. Mem. staff St. Louis Post-Dispatch, 1951-81, Washington corr., 1953-80, White House corr., 1955-80; adj. assoc. prof. journalism George Washington U., 1981-87; fellow Woodrow Wilson Internat. Ctr. for Scholars, 1980-81. Author: The Lobbyists, 1966, Lyndon Johnson's Credibility Gap, 1968, Straight Stuff, 1984, A Grave for Bobby, 1990; co-author: Smiling Through the Apocalypse, 1971, The Presidency and The Press, 1976, The American Presidency, Principles and Problems, vol. II, 1983, The White House Press on the Presidency, 1983; contbr. numerous articles to mags. Recipient Disting. Alumnus citation Washington U., 1973, Merriman Smith award for White House reporting, 1977; Markle Found. grantee, 1981. Mem. White House Corrs. Assn. (pres. 1974-75). Home and Office: 4 Burr Ave Barrington RI 02806-4205

DEAKTOR, DARRYL BARNETT, lawyer; b. Pitts., Feb. 2, 1942; s. Harry and Edith (Barnett) D.; children: Rachael Alexandra, Hallie Sarah. BA, Brandeis U., 1963; LLB, U. Pa., 1966; MBA, Columbia U., 1968. Bar: Pa. 1966, Fla. 1980, N.Y. 1980. Assoc. firm Goodis, Greenfield & Mann, Phila., 1968-70, ptnr., 1971; gen. counsel Life of Pa. Fin. Corp., Phila., 1972; asst. prof. U. Fla. Coll. Law, Gainesville, 1972-74, assoc. prof., 1974-80; assoc. firm Mershon, Sawyer, Johnston, Dunwody & Cole, Miami, Fla., 1980-81, ptnr., 1981-84; ptnr. Walker Ellis Gragg & Deaktor, Miami, 1984-86, White & Case, Miami, 1987-95, Johannesburg, South Africa, 1995—. Mem. Dist. III (Fla.) Human Rights Advocacy Com. for Mentally Retarded Citizens, 1974-78, chmn., 1978-80; mem. adv. bd. Childbirth Edn. Assn. Alachua County, Fla., 1974-80; mem. Resource Devel. Bd., Mailman Ctr. for Child Devel., 1981-88. Mem. Fla. Bar, Downtown Athletic Club (Miami). Office: White & Case 200 S Biscayne Blvd Ste 4900 Miami FL 33131-2352 also: White & Case, Forum Bldg, 2 Maude St, Sandton Johannesburg 2196, South Africa

DEAKYNE, WILLIAM JOHN, library director, musician; b. Harrisburg, Pa., June 25, 1936; s. William John and Hazel (Brown) D.; 1 child, Linda Tang Deakyne. MusB, U. Hartford, 1961; MLS, Villanova U., 1962; Diploma in French, Berlitz Sch., Phila., Stamford, Conn., 1967, 69. Cert. libr., N.J., Mass., N.Y., Wash. Dir. Meuser Meml. Libr., Easton, Pa., 1962-64; dir. Coyle Free Libr., Chambersburg, Pa., 1964-65, Free Libr. Springfield Twp., Phila., 1965-68, Darien (Conn.) Libr., 1968-78, East Lyme (Conn.) Libr., 1979—. Organist (composed Jeu de Clochette, 1964); contbr. articles to profl. jours. V.p. East Lyme C. of C., Niantic, Conn., 1985. Mem. Am. Cathedral of the Holy Trinity, Paris, 1998—. Mem. ALA (del. to Internat. Fedn. Libr. Assn. meetings Chgo., Copenhagen 1969), Les Amis de Vielles Maisons. Democrat. Avocation: promoting English pipe organs in the U.S., restoration of pipe organs in France. Home: Westchester Dr East Lyme CT 06333 Office: East Lyme Pub Libr 39 Society Rd Niantic CT 06357-1100

DEAL, BRUCE ELMER, physical chemist, educator; b. Lincoln, Nebr., Sept. 20, 1927; s. Roy Walter and Edith Alice (Fiddock) D.; m. Rachel Vera Birmingham, Sept. 3, 1950; children: Donald Bruce, Michael David, Diane Marie. AB in Chemistry, Nebr. Wesleyan U., 1950; MS in Phys. Chemistry, Iowa State U., 1953, PhD in Phys. Chemistry, 1955. Rsch. chemist Kaiser Aluminum & Chem. Corp., Spokane, Wash., 1955-59; rsch. engr. Rheem Semicondr./Raytheon Corp., Mountain View, Calif., 1959-63; mgr. R&D Fairchild Camera & Instrument Corp., Palo Alto, Calif., 1963-88; prin. technologist Nat. Semicondr., Santa Clara, Calif., 1988-89; v.p. Advantage Prodn. Tech., Sunnyvale, Calif., 1989-92; cons. prof. elec. engring. Stanford (Calif.) U., 1976—; instr. Continuing Edn. Inst.-Europe, Finspang, Sweden, 1982-91; adj. prof. elec. engring. Santa Clara U., 1988—. Author or co-author numerous tech. publs., 1953—; holder 9 patents in field. Com. chmn. Boy Scouts Am., Palo Alto, 1965-70. Recipient Lifetime Achievement award Semiconductor Equipment and Materials, Inc., 1998. Fellow IEEE (Tech. Achievement award 1973), AAAS, Franklin Inst. (life, cert. of merit 1975), Electrochem. Soc. (v.p. 1985-88, pres. 1988-89, Tech. award Electronics Divsn. 1974, Callinan Tech. award 1982, Solid State Sci. and Tech. award 1993); mem. Materials Rsch. Soc., Cornwall Family Hist. Soc., Sigma Xi. Republican. Presbyterian. Avocations: philately, genealogy, playing French Horn. Home: 638 Towle Pl Palo Alto CA 94306-2535 Office: Stanford U Elec Engring Dept Stanford CA 94305

DEAL, ERNEST LINWOOD, JR., banker; b. Florence, Ala., Jan. 5, 1929; s. Ernest Linwood and Nell W. (Willingham) D.; m. Mary Cooper, Dec. 27, 1952; children: Theresa Lynn, Sarah Street, Matthew Cooper, Jennifer Willingham. Student, Florence State Coll., 1947-49; BS, U. Ala., 1952; postgrad., Southwestern Grad. Sch. Banking, So. Meth. U., 1961. V.p. Tex. Commerce Bank, Houston, 1956-65; sr. v.p. Capital Nat. Bank, Houston, 1965-71; pres., CEO Fannin Bank, Houston, 1971-82, chmn., CEO, 1982; chmn., chief exec. officer InterFirst Bank, Houston, 1983, First City Nat. Bank (name changed to First City Tex.), Houston, 1984-88; sr. chmn. First City Tex., Dallas, 1988-91; chmn. bd. dirs., pres., CEO First City Tex., Austin, 1991-92; chmn. adv. bd. Frost Nat. Bank-Austin, 1993—; bd. dirs. Houston Trust Co. Bd. visitors M.D. Anderson Hosp., Houston, 1971—; bd. dirs. Phi Gamma Delta Ednl. Found., 1996—; past chmn. Houston Pks. Bd., Houston Aviation Com.; chmn. local organizing com. U.S. Olympic Festival, 1986; Tex. state chmn. U.S. Olympic Com., 1989-93, S.W. regional chmn., 1993—, nat. fin. com.; past chmn. bd. trustees, life trustee Kinkaid Sch.; trustee Southwestern Grad. Sch. Banking. Lt. USNR, 1952-55. Mem. U. Ala. Alumni Assn., Houston C. of C. (bd. dirs., exec. com.), Am. Bankers Assn. (governing coun., state v.p., govt. rels. coun. 1977-82, v.p. 1978-79), Tex. Bankers Assn. (bd. dirs.), Assn. Res. City Bankers (chmn. golf com.), Houston Country Club, Preston Trail Golf Club (Dallas), Austin Country Club, Phi Gamma Delta (bd. trustees 1990-96), Delta Sigma Pi, Omicron Delta Kappa. Republican. Presbyterian. Office: Frost Nat Bank-Austin PO Box 1727 816 Congress Ave Austin TX 78701-2442

DEAL, JOSEPH MAURICE, university dean, art educator, photographer; b. Topeka, Aug. 12, 1947; s. Percy Harold and Laura Jean (Close) D.; m. Christine Adkin Bertelson, Aug. 8, 1981 (div. 1987); 1 child, Meredith Ivy; m. Betsy Sara Ruppa, July 20, 1991. BFA, Kansas City Art Inst., 1970; MA, U. N.Mex., 1975; MFA, U. N. Mex., 1978. Dir. exhbns. Internat. Mus. Photography at George Eastman House, Rochester, N.Y., 1975-76; prof. art U. Calif., Riverside, 1976-89, assoc. dean, 1986-89; dean Sch. Art Washington U., St. Louis, 1989—; mem. overview panel visual arts program Nat. Endowment for Arts, Washington, 1990-93, panel chair, 1992-93. Subject of book: Joe Deal: Southern California Photographs 1976-86, 1992. Fellow Nat. Endowment for the Arts, 1977, 80, John Simon Guggenheim Found., 1983. Mem. Coll. Art Assn. (bd. dirs. 1997—). Office: Washington U 1 Brookings Dr # 1031 Saint Louis MO 63130-4899

DEAL, NATHAN J., congressman, lawyer; b. Aug. 25, 1942; m. Sandra Dunagan; children: Jason, Mary Emily, Carrie, Katie. BA, Mercer U., 1964, JD, 1966. Atty., 1968—; asst. dist. atty. N.E. cir. Hall County, Ga., 1970-71, judge, juvenile court, 1971-72; mem. Ga. State Senate, 1980-93; pres. Pro Tempore, 1991-92; mem. 103d Congress from 9th Ga. Dist., 1993—; mem. 105th Congress from 9th Ga. Dist., 1996—, mem. commerce com., edn. and the workforce com.; mem. com. on commerce, subcoms. on energy and power, telecomm. and fin., commerce, trade and hazardous materials. Capt. JAGC, U.S. Army, 1966-68. Republican. Office: US Ho Reps 2437 Rayburn HOB Washington DC 20515-1009*

DEAL, THERRY NASH, college dean; b. Iredell County, N.C., Apr. 21, 1935; d. Stephen W. and Betty (Sherrill) Nash; m. J.B. Deal, July 10, 1954 (dec. 1990); children: Melaney Dawne, J. Bradley. BS in Home Econs., U. N.C., 1957, MS, 1961, PhD in Child Devel., 1965; postgrad., Harvard U., 1984, 87. Instr. pub. schs. Iredell County, N.C., 1959-61; instr. U. N.C., Greensboro, 1961-65; prof. U. Ga., Athens, 1965-72; dept. chair Ga. Coll., Milledgeville, 1972-82, dir. continuing edn. and pub. svcs., 1982-84, dean continuing edn. and pub. svcs., 1984-95, dean emeritus, 1996—; bd. dirs. Pvt. Industry Coun., Baldwin Co.; vis. prof. Lanzhou Comml. Coll., China, 1993; participant World Conf. on Women, Beijing, 1995; appointed mem. Ga. Child Coun. Author numerous poems; contbr. articles to profl. jours. Mem. Am. Home Econs. Assn., Nat. Coun. Adminstrs. of Home Econs., Nat. Assn. Edn. of Young Children, Milledgeville/Baldwin County C. of C., DAR., Phi Kappa Phi, Omicron Nu, Delta Kappa Gamma. Democrat. Methodist. Office: Ga Coll Clark St Milledgeville GA 31061

DEAL, TIMOTHY, government executive; b. St. Louis, Sept. 17, 1940; s. Edward F. and Loretta (Fuemulier) D.; m. Jill Brady, Sept. 5, 1964; children: Christopher, Bart. BA, U. Calif., Berkeley, 1962; postgrad., San Francisco State Coll., 1964-65, Am. U., 1972-73. With U.S. Embassy, Tegucigalpa, Honduras, 1966-68, Warsaw, Poland, 1969-72; econ. counselor U.S. Embassy, London, 1981-85; various fgn. svcs. assignments Dept. State, Washington, 1972-76; sr. staff mem. Nat. Security Coun., The White House, Washington, 1976-81; dep. U.S. Rep. U.S. Mission to OECD, Paris, 1985-88; dir. office Ea. European/Yugoslav affairs Dept. State, 1988-89; spl. asst. to pres. for nat. security affairs Nat. Security Coun., The White House, 1989-92; minister, dept. chief of missions U.S. Embassy, London, 1992-96; ret., 1996; sr. v.p. U.S. Coun. for Interat. Bus., Washington, 1996—. Capt. U.S. Army, 1963-65. Avocations: theater, cinema, sports. Home: 5721 Macarthur Blvd NW Washington DC 20016-5304 Office: 1015 15th St NW Ste 975 Washington DC 20005-2605

DEAL, WILLIAM THOMAS, school psychologist; b. Canton, Ohio, Dec. 18, 1949; s. Richard Lee and Rheta Lucille (Gerber) D.; m. Paula Nespeca, Aug. 5, 1972. BS, Bowling Green State U., 1972; MA, John Carroll U., 1977; postgrad. Kent State U., 1979—. Sci. tchr. Westlake Schs., 1972-76, head bldg. sci. dept., 1974-76; intern sch. psychologist Garfield Heights Schs., 1976-77, sch. psychologist, 1977—; pvt. practice psychology, Parma Heights, Ohio, 1982-84. Alternate mem. adv. council Cuyahoga County Spl. Edn. Service Ctr., 1977—. Recipient Cert. of Recognition, Garfield Heights Bd. Edn., 1980; Outstanding Achievement award Cleve. Assn. for Children with Learning Disabilities, Inc., 1980; named Psychologist of Yr. Cleveland Sch., 1990. Mem. Nat. Assn. Sch. Psychologists, United Teaching Profession, Ohio Sch. Psychology Assn., Cleve. Assn. Sch. Psychologists, Phi Delta Kappa. Republican. Mem. Reformed Ch. Home: 5290 Kings Hwy Cleveland OH 44126-3059 Office: 4900 Turney Rd Cleveland OH 44125-2501

DEALE, ROBERT ELMER, JR., state official; b. Balt., Apr. 14, 1944; s. Robert Elmer and Wilhelmina Catherine (Erhardt) D.; m. Carole Sue Self, Oct. 5, 1969; 1 child, Rebekah Erin. AA in Police Adminstrn., Catonsville C.C., 1976; BA in History, U. Balt., 1983; MA in Hist. Studies, U. Md., 1988. Police officer Baltimore County Police Dept., Towson, Md., 1964-95, background investigator, 1996; coord. traffic safety program MDOT-Office Traffic & Safety, Frederick, Md., 1997—; historian, curator Baltimore County Police Dept., 1988—. Scoutmaster Boy Scouts Am., Balt., 1969-80, dist. chmn., 1978; bd. dirs. Glenmount Sch. PTA, Balt., 1994-95, pres., 1995-97. Recipient Silver Beaver award, 1979. Mem. Md. Hist. Soc., Anne Arundel County Genealogical Soc., FOP. Office: Frederick County Hwy Safety Task Force 5111 Buckeystown Pike Frederick MD 21704-8305

DE ALESSI, ROSS ALAN, lighting designer; b. San Francisco, Apr. 16, 1955; s. August Eugene De Alessi and Angela Maria (Caredio) Leonard; m. Susan Tracey Stearns, Aug. 11, 1990; 1 child, Chase Arthur. BFA, Stephens Coll., 1978. In-house lighting designer GUMP'S, San Francisco, 1981-84; prin. Ross De Alessi & Assoc., San Francisco, 1984-87, Luminae Lighting Design, San Francisco, 1987-93; prin., co-founder Ross De Alessi Lighting Design, Seattle, 1993—. Works include GUMP'S Christmas Windows, San Francisco (Award of Distinction Gen. Electric, 1986, Spl. Citation 1989, Edwin F. Guth Award of Merit Illuminating Engring. Soc. 1989, 90), TAB Products Showroom, L.A. (Award of Distinction Gen. Electric 1987), St. Augustine's Ch., Pleasanton, Calif. (Sect. award Illuminating Engring. Soc. 1988), L.A. Quinta (Calif.) Resort Plz. Fountains (Award of Excellence Gen. Electric 1988, Paul Waterbury Award of Excellence Illuminating Engring. Soc. 1989), McKesson Bldg. Lobby, San Francisco (Award of Excellence Gen. Electric 1988, Edwin F. Guth Award of Merit Illuminating Engring. Soc. 1989), Brown & Bain, Phoenix (Award of Merit Gen. Electric 1989), Saxe Gallery, San Francisco (Edwin F. Guth Award of Merit Illuminating Engring. Soc. 1989), Plz. Pk., San Jose, Calif. (Paul Waterbury Spl. Citation Illuminating Engring. Soc. 1990), The Palace of Fine Arts, San Francisco (Edison Award Gen. Electric 1990, Paul Waterbury Award of Excellence Illuminating Engring. Soc. 1991, Award of Excellence Internat. Assn. Lighting Designers 1991), Le Touessrok, Island of Mauritius (Award of Merit Gen. Electric 1993, Sect. Award Illuminating Engring. Soc. 1994, Paul Waterbury Award of Excellence 1994), St. Patrick's Sem., Menlo Park, Calif. (Edison award Gen. Electric 1993, Edwin F. Guth Award of Excellence Illuminating Engring. Soc. 1994, Citation Internat. Assn. Lighting Designers 1994), Palace of the Lost City, Republic of Boputhatswana (Award of Merit Gen. Electric 1992, Paul Waterbury Award of Excellence 1993, Award of Excellence Internat. Assn. Lighting Designers 1993), Wells Fargo Bank-Flagship Bank, San Francisco (Award of Excellence Gen. Electric 1992, Award of Merit Illuminating Engring. Soc. 1993, Citation Internat. Assn. Lighting Designers 1993), Santa Barbara County Courthouse, Santa Barbara (Paul Waterbury Award of Merit Illuminating Engring. Soc. 1995, Award of Excellence Internat. Assn. Lighting Designers 1995), City of Bridges, Cleve. (Edison award 1995, Paul Waterbry award Illuminating Engring. Soc. 1997), MGM Grand Gateway of Entertainment, Las Vegas (award of excellence Gen. Elec. 1998, Edwin F. Guth award of excellence Illuminating Engring. Soc. 1999, award of merit Internat. Assn. Lighting Designers 1999). Mem. Internat. Assn. Lighting Designers (lighting cert.), Nat. Coun. on the Certification Lighting Profls., Illuminating Engring. Soc., Washington Athletic Club. Avocations: scuba diving, traveling. Office: Ross De Alessi Lighting Design 2815 2nd Ave Ste 280 Seattle WA 98121-1261

DEALY, JANETTE DIANE, marketing consultant; b. Phoenix, Jan. 5, 1950; d. Henry Melvin Clatterbuck and Dorothy (Eakin) Newman. Student World Campus Afloat, Chapman Coll., 1967-68; BA in Anthropology and Archeology, Ariz. State U., 1972. Owner, mgr., buyer Walls Galore and Bath Decor, Corvallis, Oreg., 1977-84; mgr., trainer, buyer Bloomingdales, Dallas, 1984-85; mgr. Frederick and Nelson, Seattle, 1986-87; buyer The Bon Marché, Seattle, 1987-89; mktg. cons. Kinder-Harris, 1989-93; lectr., cons. merchandising and display, 1993—; intern trainer Oreg. State U., 1981-83. Writer light fiction and mag. articles; painter portraits. Mem. Downtown Mchts. Assn., Corvallis, 1977-84, Oreg. Homebuilders Assn., Corvallis, 1977-84; vol. Make-A-Wish Found., Bailey-Boushay Hospice. Mem. Am. Business Woman's Assn. (Corvallis chpt.). Republican.

DEALY, JOHN MICHAEL, chemical engineer, educator; b. Waterloo, Iowa, Mar. 23, 1937; s. Milton David and Ruth Marion (Dorton) D.; m. Jacqueline Dery, Aug. 22, 1964; 1 child, Pamela. B.S., U. Kans., 1958; M.S., U. Mich., 1959; Ph.D., 1963, postdoctoral fellow, 1964. Asst. prof. chem. engring. McGill U., Montreal, Que., Can., 1964-67; assoc. prof. McGill U., 1967-72, prof., 1972—, chmn. dept., 1993-94; dean engring., 1994-99; cons. indsl. rheology and polymer processing. Author 3 books on melt rheology and plastics processing; contbr. numerous articles to profl. jours. Fellow Soc. Plastics Engrs.; mem. Can. Acad. Engring., Soc. Rheology (pres. 1987-89), Sigma Xi, Tau Beta Pi. Home: 315 Roslyn Ave, Montreal, PQ Canada H3Z 2L7 Office: McGill U Chem Engring Dept, 3610 University St, Montreal, PQ Canada H3A 2B2

DEAM, CONNIE MARIE, school nurse; b. Des Moines, Iowa, May 23, 1952; d. Abbie and Mary Alice (Lee) Polito; m. Rich Deam, Jan. 1, 1974; children: Seth, Maria, Ira. ADN, NIA Community Coll., Mason City, Iowa, 1974; BSN cum laude, Upper Iowa U., 1981. Rn, Iowa; cert. health occupations instr. School nurse Sheffield Chapin Consolidated Sch. Dist., Sheffield, Iowa, 1984—; dir. client svcs. Caring Pregnancy Ctr., Mason City, Iowa, 1997—; health occupations instr., 1995—. Grantee AASHA, Substance Abuse Prevention, Community. Mem. Nat. Sch. Nurses Assn., Iowa Sch. Nurses Assn. (sec., treas. Area II).

DEAN, ANDREW GRISWOLD, epidemiologist; b. Rochester, N.Y., Apr. 4, 1938; m. Consuelo Beck-Sagué; 1 child, Jeffrey A. Student, Wesleyan U., Middletown, Conn., 1956-58; AB summa cum laude, Oberlin Coll., 1960; MD cum laude, Harvard U., 1964, MPH, 1972. Diplomate Am. Bd. Preventive Medicine; lic. Ga. Intern King County Hosp., Seattle, 1964-65; SA surgeon and surgeon USPHS (Peace Corps), Hargeisa, Somali Republic, 1965-67; staff Pacific Rsch. Sect. Nat. Inst. Allergy and Infectious Diseases, Honolulu, Hawaii, 1967-71; resident in preventive medicine U. Hawaii, Honolulu, 1968-70; epidemiologist WHO, Arua, Uganda, 1972-73; asst. prof. tropical pub. health Sch. Pub. Health Harvard U., Cambridge, Mass., 1973-74; epidemic intelligence svc. officer Ark. State Dept. Health Bur. Disease Control, Atlanta, Ga., 1974-76; project dir. Pacific Ctr. for Geog. Disease Rsch., Honolulu, 1976-78; state epidemiologist and dir. communicable disease control Minn. Dept. Health, Mpls., 1978-79, dir. divsn. disease prevention and control, 1979-84; med. epidemiologist Ctr. for Disease Control, Atlanta, 1984-90; chief sys. devel. and support br. divsn. surveillance and epidemiology Ctrs. for Disease Control and Prevention, Atlanta, 1991-96, chief Epi-Info. Devel. Team, 1996—; asst. clin. prof. tropical medicine and microbiology, Sch. Medicine U. Hawaii, 1968-72, clin. assoc. prof., 1977-78; assoc. prof. biometry U. Ark., 1974-76; adj. assoc. prof. epidemiology U. Minn. Sch. Pub. Health, 1978-84; human subjects coord. Epidemiology Program Office, 1986-95; mem. med. adv. com. Ctrs. for Disease Control, 1986-92;

adj. assoc prof. Internat. Health, Rollins Sch. of Pub. Health, Emory U., 1994—. Contbr. numerous articles to profl. jours; author users manuals for med. computer use; contbr. chpts. to books in pub. health field. Vol. Waikiki Drug Clinic, Honolulu, Cambridge Med. Clinic, 1971-72; bd. mem. Internat. Health Vols., Minn., 1979-83. With USPHS, 1965-71, 74-76, 1984—. Recipient Nat. Applied Epidemiology award Coun. State and Territorial Epidemiologists, 1996. Fellow Am. Coll. Epidemiology; mem. APHA, Phi Beta Kappa, Sigma Xi, Alpha Omega Alpha. Avocations: jogging, photography, Spanish. Home: 2877 Mcclave Dr Doraville GA 30340-1941 Office: Ctrs for Disease Control Mailstop C08 1600 Clifton Rd NE Atlanta GA 30329-4018

DEAN, BEALE, lawyer; b. Ft. Worth, Feb. 26, 1922; s. Ben J. and Helen (Beale) D.; m. Margaret Ann Webster, Sept. 3, 1948; children: Webster Beale, Giselle Liseanne. BA, U. Tex., Austin, 1943, LLB, 1947. Bar: Tex. 1946. Asst. dist. atty. Dallas, 1947-48; assoc. Martin, Moore & Brewster, Ft. Worth, 1948-50; mem. Martin, Moore, Brewster & Dean, 1950-51, Pannell, Dean, Pannell & Kerry (and predecessor firms), 1951-65; ptnr. Brown, Herman, Scott, Young & Dean, Ft. Worth, 1965-71, Brown, Herman, Scott, Dean & Miles, Ft. Worth, 1971-98, Brown, Herman, Dean, Wiseman, Liser & Hart, LLP, Ft. Worth, 1998—; spl. asst. Atty. Gen. Tex., 1959-61. Regent Nat. Coll. Dist. Attys., 1985—. With AUS, 1942-45, ETO. Mem. ABA, Bar Assn. Fifth Fed. Cir., Ft. Worth-Tarrant County Bar Assn. (past pres. 1971-72, Blackstone award 1991), Am. Coll. Trial Lawyers, State Bar Tex. (dir. 1973-75), Am. Bar Found., Tex. Bar Found. (charter mem.), Ft. Worth Boat Club, Ridglea Country Club, Ft. Worth Club. Presbyterian. Office: 200 Ft Worth Club Bldg Fort Worth TX 76102-4905

DEAN, BILL VERLIN, JR., lawyer; b. Oklahoma City, Jan. 11, 1957; s. Bill V. and Mary Lou (Dorman) D.; m. Christine Potter; children: Bill V. III, Mary Megan. BS, Cen. State U., 1978; JD, Oklahoma City U., 1981. Bar: Okla. 1982, U.S. Dist. Ct. (we. dist.) Okla. 1983, (no. dist.) Okla. 1986, (ea. dist.) Okla. 1987, Tex. 1990, N.Y. 1992, U.S. Ct. Appeals (10th cir.) 1986; lic. real estate broker and ins. agt. Second dep. assessor Okla. County Assessor, Oklahoma City, 1978-80; atty. Struthers Oil and Gas Corp., Oklahoma City, 1980-82; cons. Bill Dean & Co., Jones, Okla., 1978—; ptnr. Dean & Assocs. P.C., Jones, Okla., 1982—; pres. Dean Ins. Agy. Ltd., 1986—, Casualty Corp. Am., Inc., 1999—; dir. Union Mutual Ins. Co.; dir. Union Mutual Ins. Co.; CEO Casualty Corp. of Am., Inc. Mem. Okla. County Bar Assn., Okla. Bar Assn., Tex. Bar Assn., N.Y. Bar Assn., Shriners. Methodist. Home: 200 Cherokee St Jones OK 73049-7709 Office: Dean & Assocs P C PO Box 1060 110 E Main St Jones OK 73049-7706

DEAN, CHERYL ANN, urban planner; b. Moline, Ill., Sept. 28, 1964; d. Daniel and Donna (Manning) Tworek; m. Stephen Samuel Dean, Sept. 18, 1993; 1 child, Jamie Mcayla. BA, U. Iowa, 1987, MA, 1989. From staff planner to sr. planner Indian River County, Vero Beach, Fla., 1989-92; sr. planner City of Altamonte Springs, Fla., 1992-94; from asst. planning dir. to acting planning dir. Douglas County, Douglasville, Ga., 1995-96; sr. cmty. & regional planner Appalachian Coun. Govts., Greenville, S.C., 1997—. Mem. Am. Inst. Cert. Planners, Am. Planning Assn., S.C. Iowa Club, S.C. chpt. Am. Planning Assn. E-mail: dean@scacog.org. Home: 112 Raintree Dr Taylors SC 29687-4516

DEAN, DEAREST (LORENE GLOSUP), songwriter; b. Volin, S.D., Oct. 4, 1911; d. John Henry and Bessie Marie Donnelly Peterson; m. Eddie Dean, Sept. 11, 1931; children: Donna Lee Knorr, Edgar Glosup II. Grad. high sch., Yankton, S.D. Bd. dirs. Acad. Country Music, Hollywood, 1960-62. Composer songs including: One Has My Name, 1948, The Lonely Hours, 1970, 1501 Miles of Heaven, 1970, Walk Beside Me, 1980. Sec. ARC, Burbank, Calif., 1943. Mem. ASCAP. Republican. Roman Catholic. Avocation: golf.

DEAN, DIANE D., youth service agency executive, fund development consultant; b. Detroit, Aug. 26, 1949; d. Edward Lesley and Ada V. (Spann) D. Student, Mich. State U., 1966-68; BS, N.C. Argl. and Tech. State U., 1971; MS, Ind. U., 1973; postgrad., Stanford U. Summer Inst., 1981, UCLA, 1982-83; cert. in non-profit mgmt., Case Western Res. U., 1991; student, Harvard Grad. Sch. of Edn., summer 1995; grad., Ind. U. Fund Raising Sch., 1995. Area coord. U. Miami, Coral Gables, 1973-75; dir. housing Occidental Coll., L.A., 1975-78; asst. dir. admissions assistance and sch. rels. U. So. Calif., L.A., 1978-80; from asst. dir. to assoc. dir. admissions, dir. ops. LEAD program UCLA, 1980-85; dir. incentive grants and scholarship programs Nat. Action Coun. Minorities in Engring., N.Y.C., 1985-90; mgmt. cons. Girl Scouts U.S.A., N.Y.C., 1990-95, fund devel. cons., 1995—; appointed rep. Grad. Mgmt. Admissions Coun., Santa Monica, Calif., 1981-85. Author and editor: Directory of Minority Pers. Associated with Admissions, 1979-85. Named to J & B Winners Circle, Paddington Corp., N.Y.C., 1984. Mem. ASTD, NAFE, Nat. Assn. Fund Raising Execs., Nat. Assn. Student Pers. Adminstrn. (regional co-chair 1985), Corp. Women's Network, Assn. Coll. and Univ. Housing Officers (chair regional membership com.), Assn. Girl Scout Exec. Staff (bd. dirs.), N.Y. Women's Agenda, N.Y. Coalition of 100 Black Women, Trans Africa, Black Women's Forum, Girl Scouts U.S.A. (life), Schomberg Soc. for Preservation of Black Culture, Nat. Urban League, Women in Fin. Devel., UCLA Alumni Assn. (life), N.C. Agrl. and Tech. State U. Alumni Assn., Cass Tech H.S. Alumni Assn. (life), Alpha Kappa Alpha (v.p. 1969-71). Avocations: spectator sports, collecting African Am. art and dolls, collecting basketball trading cards, reading, travel. Office: Girl Scouts USA 420 5th Ave Fl 9 New York NY 10018-2798

DEAN, EDWIN BECTON, business owner; b. Danville, Va., Feb. 7, 1940; s. Edwin Becton and Lois (Campbell) D.; m. Deirdre Anne Jacovides, Aug. 16, 1964; children: Jennifer E., Kristin R., Brian N. BS in Physics, Va. Poly. Inst. and State U., 1963, MS in Math., 1965; postgrad. George Washington U., 1974-77; cert. profl. study engring. mgmt., Old Dominion U., 1998. Technician, assoc. engr. Johns Hopkins U. Applied Physics Lab., Laurel, Md., 1959-64; physicist, mathematician, electronic engr., and ops. rsch. analyst Naval Surface Warfare Ctr., Silver Spring, Md., 1964-79; owner, mgr. Gen. Bus. Svcs. and Beta Systems, Virginia Beach, Gen. Bus. Services and Beta Systems, 1979-84, Virginia Beach (Va.) Communique Inc., Virginia Beach, Va., 1980-81; registered rep. First Investors Corp., Arlington, Va., 1971-85; dir. Tips Club of Virginia Beach, Inc., 1980-82; computer specialist Naval Supply Systems Command, Norfolk, Va., 1982-83; head cost estimating office NASA Langley Rsch. Ctr., Hampton, Va., 1983-90; tech. resource mgr. Space Exploration Initiative Office NASA Langley Rsch. Ctr., 1990-94, sr. rsch. engr. multidisciplinary optimization br., 1994-98; owner The DFV Group, Virginia Beach, Va., 1996-98; pres. The DFV Group, Virginia Beach, 1999—; chmn. ops. and support subgroup Space Sys. Cost Analysis Group, 1998—; presenter in field. Mem. editl. bd. Internat. Jour. Agile Mfg., Internat. Jour. Advanced Mfg. Sys., 1999—; contbr. articles to profl. jours. NASA fellow, 1963-65. Mem. IEEE, AIAA (space ops. and support tech. com. 1997—), Assn. for Computing Machinery, Internat. Soc. Parametric Analysts (past chmn. bd. dirs.), Inst. for Ops. Rsch. and Mgmt. Scis., Am. Statis. Assn., Am. Soc. for Quality Control, Am. Assn. Cost Engrs., Internat. Neural Network Soc., Internat. Coun. Sys. Engrs., Soc. for Indsl. and Applied Math., Am. Math. Soc., Soc. Am. Value Engrs., Inst. Mgmt. Accts., Soc. for Cost Estimating and Analysis, Am. Soc. for Engring. Mgmt., N.Y. Acad. Scis., QFD Inst., Am. Soc. Engring. Mgmt., Sigma Pi Sigma, Pi Mu Epsilon, Phi Kappa Phi. Office: The DFV Group 2412 Whaler Ct Virginia Beach VA 23451

DEAN, EDWIN ROBINSON, government official, economist; b. South Bend, Ind., July 25, 1933; s. William Stover and Eleanor (Hatcher) D.; m. Emily Rebecca Finlay, Feb. 2, 1963; children: Gabrielle N., Natalie R. BA in Philosophy magna cum laude, Yale U., 1955; postgrad., Gokhale Inst. Politics-Econs., Poona, India, 1955-56; PhD in Econs., Columbia U., 1963. Instr., then asst. prof. econs. Columbia U., N.Y.C., 1960-68; assoc. prof. Queens Coll., CUNY, 1968-72; program dir. Am. Friends Svc. Com., N.Y.C., 1970-73; supervisory equal opportunity specialist in econs. U.S. Commn. on Civil Rights, 1973-80; sr. assoc. Nat. Inst. Edn., Washington, 1980-83, acting asst. dir., 1983; supervisory economist Bur. Labor Stats., Washington, 1983-85, chief div. productivity rsch., 1985-89, assoc. commr. Office Productivity and Tech., 1989—. Author: The Supply Responses of African Farmers: Theory and Measurement in Malawi, 1966, Plan Implementation in Nigeria, 1962-66, 1972; contbg. author: The Challenge Ahead: Equal Opportunity in Referral Unions, 1976, Non-referral Unions and Equal Employment Opportunity, 1982; editor: The Controversy over the Quantity Theory of Money, 1965, Education and Economic Productivity, 1984; contbr. articles and book revs. to profl. jours. Scholar Yale U., 1951-55; Howland travel fellow Yale U., 1955, Seager fellow in econs., 1956, 57, William Bayard Cutting travel fellow Columbia U., 1958, fellow NSF, summers 1961-62; rsch. grantee Columbia U. Coun. for Rsch. in Social Scis., 1964, Rockefeller Found., Ibadan, Nigeria, U.S., 1965-67. Mem. Am. Econ. Assn. (mem. exec. com. conf. rsch. income and wealth 1994—, chair OECD working party industry stats. 1998—). Unitarian. Office: Bur of Labor Stats 2 Massachusetts Ave NE Washington DC 20212-0022

DEAN, ERIC ARTHUR, auditor, accountant; b. Dayton, Ohio, Oct. 26, 1964; s. Mose Arthur and Betty Jane (Graham) D. BS in Liberal Studies, West Chester U. Pa., 1987; postgrad., Kutztown U. CPA, Pa.; cert. govt. fin. mgr., fraud auditor, internal auditor. Various positions Pa. Dept. Auditor Gen., Harrisburg, 1987-96, audit specialist II, audit mgr., 1996—; spl. asst. to office mgr., tax preparer Jackson-Hewitt Tax Svc., Harrisburg, 1995—; fitness instr., cons. Workout Plus at Strawberry Square, Harrisburg, 1995—; freight handler, forklift operator Roadway Express, Carlisle, 1995—. Vol. Big Brothers Mentoring program, Camp Hill Correctional Facility; mem. audit com. St. Paul's Bapt. Ch. 2d lt. Pa. Army N.G., 1987-95; with USMC Res., 1982-88. Mem. AICPA, Assn. Cert. Fraud Examiners (assoc.), Pa. Inst. CPAs, Assn. Govt. Accts., Internat. Fraud Tng. Inst., Inst. Internal Auditors, Dauphin County Young Reps., Nat. Assn. Black Accts., Am. Aerobic Assn. Internat., Internat. Fraud Tng. Inst., Internat. Sports Medicine Assn. (cert.). Avocations: physical fitness, nutrition, current affairs, computers, mentoring. Home: 1338 N 6th St Harrisburg PA 17102-1408 Office: Auditor Gen Performance Audits 303 Finance Building Harrisburg PA 17120-0018

DEAN, FRANCIS HILL, landscape architect, educator; b. San Francisco, Oct. 1, 1922; s. John Samuel and Ethel (Hill) D.; m. Myrtle Oda Enoltt, Sept. 1, 1944 (dec. 1969); children: Gary Dean, Tamara Dean; m. Carolyn Anderson Bower, Aug. 12, 1971; stepchildren: Deborah Friou, Linda Friou, Sally Friou, George Friou. BS, U. Calif., Berkeley, 1948; M in Liberal Arts, U. So. Calif., 1984. Lic. landscape architect, Calif. Designer Eckbo, Royston & Williams, Los Angeles and San Francisco, 1948-58; prin. Eckbo, Dean & Williams, Los Angeles, San Francisco and Seattle, 1958-64; prin., v.p. Eckbo, Dean, Austin & Williams, Pasadena, San Francisco, 1964-73, EDAW Inc., Newport Beach and San Francisco, 1973-79; lectr. Calif. State Poly. U., Pomona, Calif., 1976-87; prof. Calif. State Poly. U., Pomona, 1987-89, ret., 1992; landscape cons. U. Calif.-Santa Barbara, 1972-76; mem. adv. council U. Calif. Ext. Landscape Arch. program, Irvine, 1979-87; landscape archtl. works include Riverside Mall, Calif., Santa Ana-Santiago Creek Study, 1966, Huntington Beach Cen. Pk., 1970-73, San Marcos Creek Study, 1991; vis. lectr. U. Guelph, Ont., Can., 1981, La. State U., 1980, Osaka (Japan) U., 1973, Internat. Urban Ecosystem Symposium, Osaka, 1990. Mem. Fire Protection Task Force, Orange County, Calif., 1976-77, South Laguna Civic Assn., 1974-92, Save Elysian Park Com., L.A., 1963-67. Served to capt. USAAF, 1942-45, ETO. Recipient Profl. awards Concrete Industry, 1971, Am. Inst. Planners, 1971, Calif. Parks and Recreation Soc., 1973. Fellow Am. Soc. Landscape Architects (jury mem., local chpt., L.A., 1984, San Francisco, 1983, Seattle, 1993, Portland, 1994, L.A. Chpt. AIA, 1983, Profl. award 1972), Calif. Coun. Landscape Arcitects (honor award 1991 Richard J. Newtra award for profl. excellence 1995), Sigma Lambda Alpha (disting.).

DEAN, GEOFFREY, book publisher; b. Newcastle-upon-Tyne, Eng., Sept. 18, 1940; s. Thomas Craig and Mildred Catherine (Hoggard) D.; m. Philma Marina Patterson, Aug. 10, 1963; children: Andrea Samantha, Christopher Michael. B.A., U. Toronto, 1961. With McGraw-Hill Co. Can. Ltd., 1961-66; coll. editor McGraw-Hill Co. Can. Ltd., Scarborough, Ont., 1962-66; sales mgr. Methuen Publs., Toronto, 1966-70; mktg. mgr., then v.p. mktg. Van Nostrand Reinhold Ltd., Scarborough, 1970-76; pres., dir. John Wiley & Sons. Can. Ltd., Rexdale, Ont., 1976-86; cons. Geoffrey Dean Enterprises, 1986—; pres. Tech. Instrnl. Products Inc., 1987-88, Scriptographic Communications Ltd., Willowdale, Ont., 1989-91; dir. Youth Employment Svc., Toronto, 1995—; mem. adv. bd. on sci. pub. Nat. Rsch. Coun. Can., 1982-84; chmn. Book and Periodical Coun., 1988-89; mem. project assessment com. Book Pub. Industry Devel. Program, Govt. Can., 1987-91. Bd. dirs. Can. Diabetes Assn., 1987-89. Mem. Can. Book Pubs. Coun. (pres. 1983), Ont. Bus. Edn. Assn. (hon. pres. 1982-84), Granite Club (Toronto), Rotary. Home and Office: 33 Deepglade Cres, Willowdale, ON Canada M2J 1B3

DEAN, GEORGE ALDEN, advertising executive; b. Chgo., June 2, 1929; s. George Abiathar and Velma Clio (Shields) D.; children: George Alden, Diane Flach; m. Jane Kentnor Pratt, Apr. 12, 1975. BA, Princeton U., 1952; MBA, Harvard U., 1956. With DFS, Dorland Worldwide Inc., N.Y.C., 1956—; mgmt. supr. DFS, Dorland Worldwide Inc., 1970—, exec. v.p., 1968-88; exec. v.p. Mktg. Sounding Bd., Fairfield, Conn.; co-chair Women's Campaign Sch., Yale U. Sch. Law. Bd. dirs. United Home Care, Women's Campaign Fund, 1993—, Shubert Theatre; fin. chmn. Mauwehu coun. Boy Scouts Am., 1968-73; bd. visitors Babcock Sch. Wake Forest U.; founder 50/50 by 2000; trustee YWCA, Bridgeport; co-chmn. bd. dirs. Women's Campaign Sch., Yale U. 1st lt. arty. AUS, 1952-54, Korea. Decorated Bronze Star. Episcopalian. Home: 944 Pequot Ave Southport CT 06490-1420 Office: PO Box 34 Fairfield CT 06430-0034

DEAN, GEORGE ARTHUR, physician, art educator; b. Detroit, Sept. 19, 1931; s. Sam and Mary (Iskowitz) D.; m. Vivian Lipsitz, June 15, 1952; children: Keith, Stephen, Laurie, Randy. BA in history, Wayne State U., 1953, MD, 1956. Diplomate Am. Bd. Family Practice. Assoc. prof. dept. family medicine Wayne State U., Detroit; pvt. practice Family Physician of Am., 1985-86. Contbr. articles to chess collector publs.; lectr. in field. Patron Detroit Inst. Art, Mary Hill Mus., Golden Dale, Wash., Royal Acad., London. Lt. U.S. Navy, 1956-58. Mem. Chess Collectors Internat. (founder, pres., adminstr. Victoria & Albert Mus., London 1986—, Bavarian State Mus., Munich 1988—. Avocations: golf, swimming. Home: 1135 Charrington Rd Bloomfield Hills MI 48301-2114

DEAN, HOWARD, governor; b. N.Y.C., N.Y., Nov. 17, 1948; s. Howard Brush and Andrea (Maitland) D.; m. Judith Steinberg; children: Anne, Paul. BA, Yale U., 1971; MD, Albert Einstein Coll. Medicine, 1978. Intern, then resident in internal medicine Med. Ctr. Hosp. Vt., 1978-82; practice medicine specializing in internal medicine Shelburne, Vt.; mem., house edn. com., mcpl. corps. and elections com., rules com. Vt. House of Reps., Montpelier, 1983-86, asst. minority leader, 1985-86; lt. gov. State of Vt., Montpelier, 1986-91; gov. State of Vt., 1991—; asst. clin. prof. medicine U. Vt. Coll. Medicine. Bd. dirs. Vt. Developmental Capabilities Council, U. Vt. Council, Vt. Adv. Commn. Intergovtl. Affairs, Vt. State Bd. Nat. Forests; founder Vt. Youth Conservation Corps; sponsor Long Trail Preservation Fund. Home: 325 S Cove Rd Burlington VT 05401-5447 Office: Office of Governor Pavilion Office Bldg 109 State St Montpelier VT 05609-0001*

DEAN, HOWARD M., JR., food company executive; b. 1937; married. BBA, So. Meth. U., 1960; MBA, Northwestern U., 1961. With Dean Foods Co., Inc., Franklin Park, Ill., 1955—, internal auditor, 1965-68, asst. to v.p. fin., 1968-70, pres., 1970-89, CEO, 1987—, chmn., 1989—. Served to lt. (j.g.) USN, 1962-65. Office: Dean Foods Co 3600 River Rd Franklin Park IL 60131-2185*

DEAN, JACK, protective services official; b. Denton, Tex., June 16, 1937. AA, Tyler (Tex.) Jr. Coll.; ed. hwy. patrol program, Tex. Dept. Pub. Safety, 1960. With Tex. Hwy Patrol, Pecos, Tex., 1961-64, Tyler, Tex., 1964-70; with Tex. Rangers, McAllen, 1970-74; sgt. Tex. Rangers, Waco, 1974-78; capt. Tex. Rangers, San Antonio, 1978-93; U.S. marshal U.S. Cts., Western dist. Tex., 5th cir., San Antonio, 1994—. Mem. Tex. Ranger Found., Tex. Sheriffs Assn., Masons. Office: Office of US Marshal John H Woods US Courthouse 655 E Durango Blvd San Antonio TX 78206-1102

DEAN, JACK PEARCE, retired insurance company executive; b. Shreveport, La., Aug. 26, 1931; s. James Albert and Nina (Smith) D.; m. Elizabeth Anne Tillman, June 5, 1952; children—Linda Susan Dean Ratchford, Cynthia Anne Dean Thomas, James David. B.S. in Bus. Adminstrn., Acctg., La. Tech. U., Ruston, 1951. C.P.A. Audit supr. Peat, Marwick, Mitchell & Co., C.P.A.s, New Orleans and Jackson, Miss., 1958-63; treas. Lamar Life Ins. Co., Jackson, 1963-64, v.p., treas., 1964-68, sr. v.p., treas., 1968-73, pres., 1973-89, also dir.; v.p. Lamar Life Corp., 1972-73, pres., 1973-83, chmn. bd. dirs., 1983-88; dir. Am. Council of Life Ins., Washington, 1978-81. Pres. United Way of Capital Area, Jackson, 1975, v.p., 1974, campaign chmn., 1973; pres. Goodwill Industries of Miss., Jackson, 1972; chmn. Life Ins. Polit. Action Com., 1981-84. Named Outstanding Alumnus of Yr., Coll. of Adminstrn. and Bus., La. Tech. U., 1974; recipient Service to Humanity award Miss. Coll., 1978, Vol. Activist award D.H. Holmes/Germaine Monteil, 1987. Mem. Am. Inst. CPA's, Soc. La. CPA's, Miss. Soc. CPA's, Jackson C. of C. (pres. 1986, bd. dirs. 1974-76, 1981-87), Health Ins. Assn. Am. (bd. dirs. 1985-88), Miss. Life & Health Ins. Guaranty Assn. (chmn. 1985-88). Baptist. Lodge: Rotary (Jackson). Avocations: genealogy, personal computer, swing era recorded music collection. Home: 110 Country Club Dr Madison MS 39110-8809

DEAN, JAMES BENWELL, lawyer; b. Dodge City, Kans., May 23, 1941; s. James Harvey and Bess (Benwell) D.; m. Sharon Ann Carver, Sept. 1, 1962 (div. 1991); m. Patricia A. Bostick, Aug. 23, 1993 (div. 1999); children: Cynthia G. Dean Vosburgh, James M. Student, Southwestern Coll., 1959-60, U. Colo., 1961; BA, Kans. State U., 1962; JD, Harvard U., 1965. Bar: Colo. 1965, U.S. Dist. Ct. Colo. 1965, U.S. Tax Ct. 1966, Nebr. 1971, U.S. Ct. Appeals (10th cir.) 1971. From assoc. to ptnr. Tweedy & Mosley, Denver, 1965-71, Kutak Rock Cohen Campbell Garfinkle & Woodward, Omaha, 1971-73; ptnr. Mosley, Wells & Dean, Denver, 1973-77, Kutak Rock & Huie, Denver, 1977-81, James B. Dean, P.C., Denver, 1981-91, Dean, McClure, Eggleston & Husney, Denver, 1991-95; James B. Dean, PC, Denver, 1995—; spl. asst. atty. gen. State of Colo., Denver, 1989—; lectr. U. Ark. Law Sch., Fayetteville, 1982-86, C.C. Aurora, Colo., 1996-97. Co-editor Agricultural Law Jour., 1979-84; contbr. articles to profl. jours. Mem. ABA (advisor bd. forum com. on rural lawyers and agrl. bus. 1983-89), Nebr. Bar Assn., Colo. Bar Assn. (sec. agrl. law sect. 1991-94, bd. dirs. 1989—), Denver Bar Assn., Am. Agrl. Law Assn. (pres. elect 1985-86, pres. 1986-87, bd. dirs. 1981-83, Disting. Svc. award 1989). Republican. Avocations: photography, woodworking, hiking, piano. Office: 4155 E Jewell Ave Ste 703 Denver CO 80222-4511

DEAN, JAMES M., investment adviser; b. Atlanta, Oct. 14, 1951. BA, Am. U., 1976; JD, U. Chgo. Law Sch., 1979. Bar: Utah, 1979. Pvt. practice law Salt Lake City, 1980-85; first v.p. Am. Fin. Assurance Corp., Kansas City, Mo., 1986-91; investment adviser Paine Webber, Atlanta, 1991-96; judge pro tem Sm. Claims Ct., Salt Lake City, 1983-85. Contbr. articles to various publs. Lawyers com. The Atlanta Opera, 1996-98; sr. advisor Mayor's Office, Atlanta, 1997-98. Roman Catholic. Avocations: jazz, running, gospel music. Office: Milliken and Michaels 1126 Blowing Rock Rd Boone NC 28607

DEAN, JEAN BEVERLY, artist; b. South Paris, Maine, Aug. 23, 1928; d. Henry Dyer and Doris Filena (Judd) Small; m. Samuel Lester Dean. AS, Becker Coll., Worcester, Mass., 1948; AA, Edison Coll., Ft. Myers, Fla., 1980. Artist Ft. Myers, 1963—. One person shows include Edison C.C. Gallery, Ft. Myers, Joan Ling Gallery, Gainesville, Fla., Berry Coll., Mt. Berry, Ga., Gallery 10, Asheville, N.C., Sanibel (Fla.) Gallery, 1993, Barrier Island Group for the Arts, Sanibel, 1994, 96, Sanibel Gallery, 1995, Gallery Mido, Belleview Mido Resort, Belleair, Fla., 1996, No. Trust Bank, Ft. Myers, 1996, Lee County Alliance of the Arts, Ft. Myers, 1996, Art League of Manatee County, Fla., 1996, Naples (Fla.) Libr., 1997, Sy Zy Gy Gallery, Ft. Myers, 1998, Barnes and Noble, Ft. Myers, 1999; exhibited in group shows at S.E. Painting and Sculpture Exhbn., Jacksonville, Fla., Southeastern Ctr. for Contemporary Art, Ybor City, S.W. Fla. Internat. Airport, 1991, 95, Ctr. Art Show, St. Petersburg, Fla., 1991, Ridge Juried Art Show, Winter Haven, Fla., 1992, Fla. Artists Group, Sarasota, 1992, Women's Caucus for Art, Sarasota, 1993, Polk Mus., Lakeland, Fla., 1993, Daytona (Fla.) Mus., 1994, Women's Caucus Art Nat. Show, San Antonio, 1995, Capitol Gallery, Tallahassee, 1995, Women's Caucus Art State Show, Sarasota, 1995, Women's Caucus for Art, Miami, 1996, 98, Fla. Artist Group, Winter Haven, 1996, Jacksonville Art Mus., 1998, Edison Coll., 1999, Ft. Myers, Fla. So. Coll., Lakeland, 1999; represented in permanent collections Am. Embassy, Madrid, Edison Coll., First Fed. Savs. and Loan, Ft. Myers and Naples, Fla., NCNB Bank, Tampa, HealthPark, Ft. Myers, Clara Barton House, Washington, Hirshhorn Collection. Mem. Lee County Alliance for Arts, 1994, 95, 96, 97, 98, 99; chair invitational com. Barrier Island Group for Arts, Sanibel, 1994, 95, 96, 97, 98, 99; founder Open Doors Lee County Alliance of the Arts, Fla., 1990—. Recipient more than 100 awards. Mem. Nat. Mus. Women in the Arts (charter mem.), Maine Coast Artists, Women's Caucus for Art, Fla. Artists Group. Democrat. Unitarian. Home: 17643 Captiva Island Ln Fort Myers FL 33908-6115

DEAN, JIMMY, meat processing company executive, entertainer; b. Plainview, Tex., Aug. 10, 1928; s. G. O. and Ruth (Taylor) D.; m. Donna L. Meade, Oct. 1991; children from previous marriage: Garry, Connie, Robert. Student public schs., Plainview. Pres. Jimmy Dean Meat Co., Plainview, Tex., 1969-72; chmn. bd. Jimmy Dean Meat Co., Dallas, 1972-91, Jimmy Dean Foods, Cordova, Tenn., 1991—. Entertainer, Washington area, 1948-57; host: Morning Show, CBS-TV, Washington, 1957, Jimmy Dean Show, N.Y.C., 1958-59, Jimmy Dean Show, ABC-TV, 1963-65; appeared on: radio and TV show Town & Country Jamboree, 1950's; entertained, U.S. Armed Forces, Caribbean, 1952, Europe, 1953, rec. artist, 1953—; records include Big Bad John, 1961 (Gold Record); I.O.U, 1976 (Gold Record). Served with USAAF, 1946-48. Recipient Georgie award as outstanding performer in field of live entertainment for country music AGVA, 1972, Timmie award Touchdown Club, Washington, 1987; named to Hall of Fame Washington Area Music Assn., 1986. Mem. Actors' Equity Assn., AFTRA, Screen Actors Guild. Office: Jimmy Dean Foods Ste 400 8000 Centerview Pkwy Cordova TN 38018-4255*

DEAN, JOHN AURIE, chemist, author, chemistry educator emeritus; b. Sault Ste. Marie, Mich., May 9, 1921; s. Aurie Jerome and Gertrude (Saw) D.; m. Elizabeth Louise Cousins, June 20, 1943 (div. 1981); children: Nancy Elizabeth, Thomas Alfred, John Randolph, Laurie Alice, Clarissa Elaine; m. Peggy DeHart Beeler, Oct. 23, 1981; stepchildren: Diane Barbara, Lisa Lynn, James Edward, Jonathan Curtis. BS in Chemistry, U. Mich., 1942, MS in Chemistry, 1944, PhD, 1949. Tchg. fellow in chemistry U. Mich., Ann Arbor, 1942-44, 45-46, lectr. in chemistry, 1946-48; chemist X-100 Phase Manhattan Project Chrysler Corp., Detroit, 1944-45; assoc. prof. chemistry U. Ala., Tuscaloosa, 1948-50; asst. prof. chemistry U. Tenn., Knoxville, 1950-53, assoc. prof., 1953-58, prof. chemistry, 1958-81, prof. emeritus, 1981—; cons. Union Car Nuclear Div., Oak Ridge, 1953-74, Stewart Labs., Knoxville, 1968-81; vis. lectr. Peoples Republic of China, 1985. Author: Instrumental Methods of Analysis, 1948, 7th edit., 1988, Flame Photometry, 1960, Chemical Separation Methods, 1969, Flame Emission and Atomic Absorption Spectrometry, Vol. 1, 1969, Vol. 2, 1971, Vol. 3, 1975, Lange's Handbook of Chemistry, 15th edit., 1998, Handbook of Organic Chemistry, 1986, Solutions Manual for Instrumental Methods of Analysis, 7th edit., 1988, The Chemist's Ready Reference Handbook, 1990, Analytical Chemistry Handbook, 1995; contbr. articles to profl. jours., chpts. to books. Mem. Am. Chem. Soc. (Charles H. Stone award Carolina-Piedmont sect. 1974), Soc. Applied Spectroscopy (hon., chmn. S.E. sect. 1971-73, editor newsletter 1984-95, Disting. Svc. award 1991, Outstanding Svc. award 1995), Archaeol. Inst. Am., East Tenn. Soc. (pres. 1980-81), U.S. Naval Inst. (life), Sigma Xi, Phi Kappa Phi. Presbyterian. Address: 715 Garden Villa Way Knoxville TN 37909

DEAN, JOHN GUNTHER, diplomat; b. Germany, Feb. 24, 1926; came to U.S., 1939, naturalized, 1944; s. Joseph and Lucy (Askenaczy) D.; m. Martine Duphenieux, Dec. 26, 1952; children: Catherine Dean Curtis, Paul, Joseph. B.S. magna cum laude, Harvard U., 1947, M.A., 1950; Doctorate, U. Paris, 1949. With ECA, Am. embassy, Paris, 1950-51, Am. embassy, Brussels, 1951-53; asst. econ. commr. Am. embassy, Saigon, 1953-56; polit. officer Am. embassy, Laos, 1956-58; consul Am. consulate, Togo, 1959-60; chargé d'affaires Am. Embassy, Mali, 1960-61; with Dept. State, Washington, 1961-65; polit. officer Am. embassy, Paris, 1965-69; regional dir. CORDS in Central Vietnam, 1970-72; dep. chief mission Am. embassy, Laos, 1972-74; ambassador to Cambodia, 1974-75, to Denmark, 1975-78, to Lebanon, 1978-81, to Thailand, 1981-85, to India, 1985-88; adv. U.S. delegation to UN, 1963; now mem. adv. bds. several nat. and internat. cos. and instns. Served to 2d lt. AUS, 1944-46. Fellow Center for Internat. Affairs

Harvard, 1969-70. Clubs: Harvard (N.Y.C.); Kenwood Golf and Country (Washington). Office: 29 Blvd Jules Sandeau, Paris 16, France

DEAN, JOHN WILSON, JR., business consultant, retired army officer; b. Evanston, Wyo., Mar. 8, 1918; s. John Wilson and Reta (Murdock) D.; m. Lucille Lorraine Forster, July 3, 1942 (dec.); children—Patricia Ann (Mrs. William J. Staffa), John Wilson III. Student, Brigham Young U., 1935-37, 39-41; grad., Armed Forces Staff Coll., 1954, Nat. War Coll., 1959. Enlisted U.S. Army, 1941, commd. 2d lt. F.A., 1941, advanced through grades to brig. gen., 1967; ret., 1971; sec.-treas. Dean Bros. Cattle Co. Decorated D.S.M., Legion of Merit with 2 oak leaf clusters, Bronze Star with 2 oak leaf clusters, Army Commendation medal with 4 oak leaf clusters; also decorated by France, Belgium, Italy, Netherlands. Mem. Assn. U.S. Army, Ret. Officers Assn. Home and Office: care Patricia D Staffa 8705 Nanlee Dr Springfield VA 22152

DEAN, JURRIEN, biomedical researcher, physician; b. N.Y.C., Mar. 22, 1947; s. Joel Partridge and Phyllis Jane (van Dyk) D.; m. Ann Dean; children: Jeremy, Benjamin, Laura, William. BA, Columbia U., 1969, MD, 1973. Diplomate Am. Bd. Internal Medicine. Resident Presbyn. Hosp., N.Y.C., 1973-75; postdoctoral fellow Lab. Chem. Biology NIAMDD, NIH, Bethesda, Md., 1975-81; genetics fellow Johns Hopkins Hosp., Balt., 1977-78; sr. investigator Lab. Cellular and Devel. Biology NIDDK, NIH, Bethesda, 1981-91, sect. chief Lab. Cellular and Devel. Biology, 1991—, lab. chief, 1994—. Capt., sr. surgeon USPHS, 1975—. Recipient Commendation award USPHS, 1990, Outstanding Svc. medal USPHS, 1993. Mem. Am. Soc. Clin. Investigation, Am. Soc. for Biochemistry and Molecular Biology, Am. Soc. Cell Biology, Am. Soc. Devel. Biology. Office: NIDDK/NIH Bldg 6/Rm B1-0606 Lab Cellular & Devel Biol 9000 Rockville Pike Bethesda MD 20892-0001*

DEAN, KARL, public defender; b. Sioux Falls, S.D., Sept. 20, 1955. BA, Columbia U., 1978; JD, Vanderbilt U., 1981. Asst. pub. defender Govt. Nashville, Davidson (Tenn.) County, 1983-90, pub. defender, 1990—. Office: Office of the Public Defender 1202 Stahlman Bldg 211 Union St Nashville TN 37201-1502*

DEAN, LEE, protective services executive; b. Ardmore, Okla., 1950. BA, Calif. State U., Sacramento; JD, Lincoln U., Sacramento, 1984. Pastrolman L.A. Police Dept., 1972-73; patrolman to chief dep. Sacramento Sheriff's Dept., 1974-91; chief of police Vacaville (Calif.) Police Dept., 1991-95, San Bernardino (Calif.) Police Dept., 1996—. Co-author: Target: Excellence. Office: San Bernardino Police Dept PO Box 1559 San Bernardino CA 92402-1559*

DEAN, LEESA JANE, musician; b. N.Y.C., Aug. 26, 1961; d. Jesse and Diana (Jaffe) D. BFA magna cum laude, Leonard Davis Ctr., N.Y.C., 1983; student, Wesleyan U., Middletown, Conn., 1978-80. Group mem., co-founder Candela-Arista Recording Group, N.Y.C., 1983; freelance musician Chuck Berry, Paul Young, Oliver Lake, Brook Benton, N.Y.C., 1983-91; freelance interactive media prodr./composer Polygram, Time-Warner, GE, N.Y.C., 1992-94; pres., CEO Soundz in Action Inc., N.Y.C., 1993—; interactive media/computer cons. N.Y.C., 1992—. Author, creator, prodr.: Flipside, 1995, Chilltown, 1997; composer: Montage of a Dream Deferred, 1984, Smashing the Treadmill; author: Hocus Pocus!, 1997, Shock, Rock & Roll, 1995; creator, programmer, prodr.: Chilltown Online, 1998; creator, writer Chilltown Comix, 1998; exec. prodr., creator, writer Chilltown (TV series), 1999; composer, prodr. TV and radio comml., 1994. Recipient Winner Xeric Found. grant for comics. Mem. Am. Soc. Composers, Authors and Publishers, Am. Fedn. TV and Radio Artists, Am. Fedn. Musicians.

DEAN, LESLIE ALAN (CAP DEAN), economic and social development consultant; b. Indpls., June 18, 1940; s. Henry Lloyd and Margaret Ann (Pfafman) D.; m. Jeanne Louise Lambert, Apr. 14, 1962; children: David Richard, Laura Elizabeth. BA, U. Ill., 1963, MA, 1966; postgrad., U. Pitts., 1968-69. Internat. loan analyst Bank of Calif., San Francisco, 1970; joined Fgn. Svc., 1970; devel. officer U.S. AID, Washington, 1970, 77-79, Vientiane, Laos, 1971-75, Kathmandu, Nepal, 1975-77, Islamabad, Pakistan, 1979-83, Dar Es Salaam, Tanzania, 1983-85; asst. mission dir. U.S. AID, Lusaka, Zambia, 1985-87, mission dir. sr. fgn. svc., 1988-90; office dir. U.S. AID, Washington, 1990-92; mission dir. U.S. AID, Pretoria, South Africa, 1992-96; dep. asst. adminstr. Africa Bur. U.S. AID, Washington, 1996-98; program specialist Internat. Found. Edn. & Self Help, Phoenix, 1999. Capt. USAF, 1964-68. Recipient Sr. Fgn. Svc. Performance award U.S. AID, 1988, 89, 90, 92, 97, Adminstr's. Disting. Career award, 1998. Mem. Phi Eta Sigma. Presbyterian. Avocations: swimming, reading, travel.

DEAN, LYDIA MARGARET CARTER (MRS. HALSEY ALBERT DEAN), nutrition coordinator, author, consultant; b. Bedford, Va., July 11, 1919; d. Christopher C. and Hettie (Gross) Carter; m. Halsey Albert Dean; children: Halsey Albert Jr., John Carter, Lydia Margerae. Grad., Averett Coll.; BS, Madison Coll., 1941; MS, Va. Poly. Inst. and State U., 1951; postgrad., U. Va., Mich. State U.; PhD, D Nutrition Sci., UCLA, 1985. Cert. nutrition specialist Am. Coll. Nutrition, 1993-99. Dietetic intern, clin. dietitian St. Vincent de Paul Hosp., Norfolk, Va., 1942; jr. physicist U.S. Naval Op. Base, Norfolk, 1943-45; clin. dietitian Roanoke Meml. Hosps., 1946-51; assoc. prof. Va. Poly. Inst. and State U., 1946-53; community nutritionist Roanoke, Va., 1953-60; dir. dept. nutrition and dietetics Southwestern Va. Med. Ctr., Roanoke, 1960-67; food and nutrition cons. Nat. Hdqs. ARC, Washington, 1967—; staff and vol. Nat. Hdqs. ARC, 1973—; nutrition scientist, cons. Dept. Army, Washington, 1973—, Dept. Agr., 1973—; pres. Dean Assocs.; cons., assoc. dir. Am. Dietetic Assn., 1975—; coord. new degree program U. Hawaii, 1974-75; dir., nutrition coord. pub. health HHS, Washington, 1973-95, vol., 1996; pres., rschr. Dean and Assocs., Washington, 1995—; mem. task force White House Conf. Food and Nutrition, 1969—; chmn. fed. com. Interagy. Com. on Nutrition Edn., 1970-71; tech. rep. to AID and State Dept.; chmn. Crusade for Nutrition Edn., Washington, 1970—; participant, cons. Nat. Nutrition Policy Conf., 1974. Author: (with Virginia McMasters) Community Emergency Feeding, 1972, Help My Child How to Eat Right, 1963, rev. edit., 1978, The Complete Gourmet Nutrition Cookbook: The Joy of Eating Well and Right, 1978, rev. edit., 1982, The Stress Foodbook, 1980; contbr. articles to profl. jours. Trustee World U., 1987—; apptd. rsch. bd. advisors Am. Biog. Inst., 1990. Named Women's Inner Cir. of Achievement N.Am., 1990. Fellow APHA, Internat. Inst. Cmty. Svc.; mem. AAUW (Hall of Fame 1992), Am. Dietetic Assn., Bus. and Profl. Women's Club (cons. 1970—, pres. 1981-82), Am. Home Econs. Assn. (rep. and treas. joint congl. com.), Inst. Food Technologists (blue ribbon spkr. 1972). Home: 7816 Birnam Wood Dr Mc Lean VA 22102-2709 *In very early years of my life with the freedom to think and the background of family influence I realized that my life had a purpose and that I must work to fulfill that purpose. This belief has been my most motivating factor. Each day I have kept in mind the long-range goals for my life and on a daily basis I have set daily goals to be accomplished. In order to attain these goals I have used planning, self-discipline, willingness to sacrifice, hard work, a faith in and love for God, country, and individual people. A good and loving husband and children have served as a strong support system.*

DEAN, MARILYN FERWERDA, nursing consultant and administrator; b. Oak Park, Ill., Oct. 5, 1938; m. Frank Dean; children by previous marriage: Cathy Cree Denisco, Cliff Cree; stepchildren: Derek, Jeff Dean. BSN, U. Miami (Fla.), 1960; MPH, U. Mich., 1963. With Broward County Health Dept., Fort Lauderdale, Fla., 1960-65, supr., 1963-65; with Med. Pers. Pool, Fort Lauderdale, 1971-78; dir. nursing svc. North Beach Med. Ctr., Ft. Lauderdale, 1978-79, regional dir. Med. Pers. Pool, 1979-82, nat. dir. profl. and consumer affairs, 1982-85, nat. dir., health care svcs., 1985-92; Interim Health Care Nat. Dir. Health Care Svcs., 1992-98; instr. Broward Community Coll., 1975-78. Mem. editl. bd. Home Health Care Nurse mag., 1996—. Bd. dirs. Luth. High Sch., 1980-83. Mem. ANA (bd. dirs.), Nat. League Nursing, Am. Assn. Continuity of Care, Inservice Educators S. Fla. (pres. 1977-78), Assn. Care of Children's Health, Nat. Hospice Orgn. Lutheran. Home: 5500 NE 26th Ave Fort Lauderdale FL 33308-3314 Office: 2050 Spectrum Blvd Fort Lauderdale FL 33309-3008

DEAN, MICHAEL M., lawyer; b. Phila., Jan. 7, 1933. B.A., Antioch Coll., 1954; J.D. cum laude, U. Pa., 1957. Bar: Pa. 1957. Fulbright fellow U. London, 1962-63; ptnr. Wolf, Block, Schorr & Solis-Cohen, Phila., 1966—; dir., mem. exec. com. University City Sci. Ctr., Phila., 1974-86, 89—, counsel, 1974—, vice chair, 1998—; counsel Ave. of the Arts, Inc., Phila., 1992—, University City Dist., 1998—. Bd. dirs., exec. com. Ctrl. Phila. Devel. Corp., 1974—, pres., 1987-90, chmn., 1990-95; counsel, bd. dirs., exec. com., chmn. endowment trust Diagnostic and Rehab. Ctr., Phila., 1980—; exec. com., bd. dirs., sec. Ctr. City Dist., 1990, counsel, 1991—.

DEAN, MICHAEL P., dean; b. Mar. 1, 1946. BA, Emory U., 1968; MA, Miss. State U., 1972; PhD, U. S.C., 1977. Asst. prof. U. Miss., University, 1978-92, assoc. dean coll. liberal arts, 1992—. E-mail: mdean@olemiss.edu. Home: 439 County Rd 251 Thaxton MS 38871-9756

DEAN, PAUL JOHN, magazine editor; b. Pitts., May 11, 1941; s. John Aloysius and Perle Elizabeth (Thompson) D.; m. Jo-ann Tillman, Aug. 19, 1972 (div. Mar. 1981); children: Jennifer Ann, Michael Paul. Student engring., Pa. State U., 1959-60. Gen. mgr. Civic Ctr. Honda Co., Pitts., 1965-68, Washington-Pitts. Cycle Co., Canonsburg, Pa., 1968-70; nat. svc. mgr. Yankee Motor Co., Schenectady, 1970-73; competition congressman Am. Motorcyclist Assn., 1971, 72, trustee, sec. bd., 1988-91, chmn., 1991-97; bd. dirs. AMA ProRacing, 1997—; adv. bd., guest speaker L.A. Trade Tech. Coll., 1974-90; trustee Am. Motorcyclist Heritage Found., 1990-91. Engring. editor Cycle Guide mag., Compton, Calif., 1973-74, editor-in-chief, 1974-80, editorial dir., 1980-84; editor-in-chief Cycle World mag., Newport Beach, Calif., 1984-88, editorial dir. Cycle and Cycle World mags., 1988-92; v.p., editorial dir. Cycle World Mag. Group, 1992—; author manuals. Served with AUS, 1964-65. Home: 5915 Arabella St Lakewood CA 90713-1203 Office: Hachette Filipacchi Mags 1499 Monrovia Ave Newport Beach CA 92663-2752

DEAN, PAUL REGIS, law educator; b. Leetonia, Ohio, July 12, 1918; s. Edward Joseph and Catherine (Sheets) D.; m. Delores M. Fitch, July 14, 1945 (dec. 1987); children—Mary E., Lawrence E. (dec.), Patricia, John, Paul, William, Delores, Teresa, Brian. Student, DeSales Coll., Toledo, 1936-38; B.A., Youngstown State U., 1940; LL.B., Georgetown U., 1946, LL.M., 1952, LL.D., 1969. Bar: D.C. 1946, Va. 1954. Law clk. to presiding judge D.C. Ct. of Appeals, 1946-47; prof. law Georgetown U., 1947-54, 69-88; dean U. Law Ctr., Georgetown U., 1954-69, dean emeritus and prof. emeritus, 1988—; legal adviser to Pres.'s Com. Govt. Contract Compliance, 1952-53; neutral trustee United Mine Workers Am. Health and Retirment Funds, 1971-94; mem. Pres.'s Commn. Pension Policy, 1979-81, D.C. adv. com. U.S. Civil Rights Commn., 1961-63; trustee, v.p. Loyola Found. Inc., 1957—. Served to lt. USNR, 1942-46. Fellow Am. Coll. Trust and Estate Counsel; mem. Am. Arbitration Assn., Va. Bar Assn., Bar Assn. D.C. (Lawyer of Yr. award 1971), Delta Theta Phi. Home: 3313 Garland Dr Falls Church VA 22041-2510 Office: 600 New Jersey Ave NW Washington DC 20001-2022

DEAN, RICHARD ANTHONY, mechanical engineer, engineering executive; b. Bklyn., Dec. 22, 1935; s. Anthony David and Anne Mylod Dean; m. Sheila Elizabeth Grady, Oct. 5, 1957; children: Carolyn Anne, Julie Marie, Richard Drews. BSME, Ga. Inst. Tech., 1957; MSME, U. Pitts., 1963, PhDME, 1970. Registered profl. engr., Calif. From jr. engr. to mgr. thermal and hydraulic engring. Westinghouse Nuclear Energy Sys., 1959-70; v.p., tech. dir. water reactor fuels General Atomics, San Diego, 1970-74, v.p. uranium and light water reactor fuel, 1974-80, sr. v.p., 1980-92; pres. Leading Edge Engring., San Diego, 1993—; cons. U.S. Congress Office Tech. Assessment. 1st lt. U.S. Army, 1957-59. Mem. AAAS, ASME (former chmn. nuclear fuels tech. com.), Am. Nuclear Soc. (gen. chmn. annual meeting 1993), Global Found. (bd. advisors), Internat. Thermonuclear Experimental Reactor. Achievements include the develpoment of commercial nuclear power stations; advanced the understanding of boiling heat transfer phenomena; invention of advanced nuclear fuel assembly. Home: 6699 Via Estrada La Jolla CA 92037-6432 Office: Leading Edge Engring 13100 Kirkham Way Ste 210 Poway CA 92064-7128

DEAN, RICHARD HENRY, surgeon, educator; b. Radford, Va., June 16, 1942; s. Howard Lee and Minnie Yates (Crowder) D.; children: Richard Lancaster, Harrison Blaylock, Howard Lee Alexander, Williams Cabler. BA, Va. Mil. Inst., 1964; MD, Med. Coll. Va., 1968. Diplomate Am. Bd. Surgery (bd. dirs. 1993—), Am. Bd. Gen. Vascular Surgery, Am. Bd. Plastic Surgery. Surg. intern Vanderbilt U. Hosp., 1968-69, surg. asst. resident, 1969-73, chief. surg. resident, 1973-74, asst. prof. surgery sch. medicine, 1975-77, assoc. prof. surgery, 1977-81, prof. surgery, 1981-86, head divsn. vascular surgery sch. medicine, 1978-86; vascular rsch. fellow, instr. surgery Northwestern U. Hosp, 1974-75; Richard T. Meyers prof. and chmn. surgery Bowman Gray Sch. Medicine Wake Forest U., Winston-Salem, N.C., 1987-89, dir. divsn. surg. scis., chmn. dept. gen. surgery Bowman Gray Sch. Medicine, 1989-97, sr. v.p. health affairs, 1997—; dir. Wake Forest U. Baptist Med. Ctr., Winston-Salem, N.C., 1997—; vis. prof. U. Vienna, Austria, 1980, U. NSW, Sydney, Australia, 1982, U. Queensland, Brisbane, Australia, 1984, U. Rochester (N.Y.) Med. Ctr., 1986, 2nd Internat. Symposium on Ischemia, Madrid, 1986, U. Health Scis., Bethesda, Md., 1987, East Carolina U., Greenville, N.C., 1987, Ga. Bapt. Med. Ctr., Atlanta, 1988, Roanoke (Va.) Meml. Hosp., 1988, Ea. Va. Med. Sch., Norfolk, 1988 (two lectures), Mayo Clinic, Rochester, Minn., 1989, Med. Coll. Va., Richmond, 1990, W.Va. U. Health Sci. Ctr., Charleston, 1990, Va. Vascular Soc., Hot Spring, 1990, First All-Union Congress Cardiovascular Surgery, Moscow, 1990, Carolinas Heart Inst., Charlotte, 1991, U. Miami Sch. Medicine, 1991, Allegheny Gen. Hosp., Pitts., 1992, Northwestern U. Med. Sch., Chgo., 1992, U. Minn., Mpls., 1992, Nat. Naval Med. Ctr., Bethesda, 1992, Emory U. Sch. Medicine/Emory Hosp., Atlanta, 1992, Internat. Symposium Hosp. Universitario, Madrid, 1993, Ruprect-Karls-Universitat Heidelberg, Germany, 1993, La. State U. Med. Ctr., Shreveport, 1993, U. N.C., Chapel Hill, 1993, U. Man., Winnipeg, Can., 1993, U. Cin. Med. Ctr., 1993; Paul Dudley White vis. prof. U. Sao Paulo and Campinas, Brazil, 1982; Deryl Hart lectr. Duke U. Med. Sch., 1991; mem. Coun. on Cardio-Thoracic and Vascular Surgery, 1990-91; dir. Am. Bd. Plastic Surgery, 1995—; guest lectr. in field. Editor: (with J.A. O'Neill Jr.) Vascular Disorders of Childhood, 1983, (with W.P. Ritchie and G. Strele Sr.) General Surgery, 1994, (with J.S.T. Jao and D.C. Brewster) Current Diagnosis and Treatment in Vascular Surgery, 1995; mem. editl. bd. Jour. Vascular Surgery, Annals of Vascular Surgery; contbr. numerous chpts. to books and articles to sci. and profl. jours. Recipient Superior Performance award, 1997. Fellow ACS (N.C. chpt., cardiovascular com. 1987), Am. Heart Assn. (stroke coun., coun. high blood pressure rsch.); mem. AMA, Am. Bd. Surgery (cons. com. on vascular surgery 1986-92, dir. 1993—), Am. Surg. Assn. (adv. membership com. 1991—), Internat. Soc. Cardiovascular Surgery (vis. prof. First Sci. Congress 1992), Internat. Soc. for Surgery, Soc. Univ. Surgeons, Soc. for Vascular Surgery (recorder, publs. com. 1992—), Assn. for Acad. Surgery (exec. coun. 1978-80, nominating com. 1980), So. Assn. Vascular Surgery (program com. 1982-85, exec. coun. 1985-88, pres.-elect 1988-89, pres. 1990-91), Forsyth-Stokes-Davie County Med. Assn., So. Calif. Vascular Surgery Soc. (hon.), So. Med. Assn., So. Surg. Assn. (v.p. 1997-98), S.E. Surg. Congress, Va. Surg. Assn. (hon.), H. William Scott, Jr. Soc. (sec. 1982-87, pres. 1988-89). Home: 268 S Pine Valley Rd Winston Salem NC 27104 Office: Wake Forest U Sch Medicine Medical Center Blvd Winston Salem NC 27157-1003*

DEAN, ROBERT BRUCE, architect; b. Brockton, Mass., Jan. 15, 1949; s. Robert George and Marjorie Gertrude (O'Donnell) D.; m. Mary Hood Hoskinson, June 18, 1977; children: Robert Maxwell, Anne, Claire. BA, U. Pa., 1971; MArch, Columbia U., 1976. Registered architect, N.Y., Conn. Staff architect Skidmore, Owings & Merrill, Architects, N.Y.C., 1976-77; job capt. Stephen Jacobs & Assn., N.Y.C., 1977-78; staff architect Johnson-Burgee Architects, N.Y.C., 1978-79; pvt. practice architecture N.Y.C. and Syracuse, 1979-85; project architect Robert A.M. Stern Architects, N.Y.C., 1985-86; pres. Dean Design, Inc., New Canaan, Conn., 1986—; adj. assoc. prof. Columbia U., N.Y.C., 1978-83; asst. prof. Syracuse U., 1980-84. Contbr. articles to profl. jours. Bd. dirs. Redding Hist. Soc.; mem. Planning Commn. Town of Redding, Dem. Town com. Grantee Syracuse U., 1982, grantee Nat. Endowment Arts, 1983-84; William Kinne Fellow, 1976. Mem. AIA, Conn. Soc. Architects. Democrat. Congregationalist. Avocations: American cultural and commercial history. Office: Dean Design Inc 111 Cherry St New Canaan CT 06840-5530

DEAN, ROBERT CHARLES, JR., mechanical engineer, entrepreneur, innovator; b. Atlanta, Apr. 13, 1928; s. Robert C. and Ruth (Andrew) D.; m. E. Nancy Hayes, Sept. 22, 1951; children: Margaret S., James C., Elizabeth S., Martha A., Charles E. BS, MS, MIT, 1949, ScD, 1954. Project engr. Ultrasonic Corp., 1949-51; head advanced engring. dept. Ingersoll-Rand Co., 1956-60; dir. research Thermal Dynamics Cor., 1960-61; dir. Ecol. Sci. Corp., 1968-70; co-founder, pres. Creare Inc., 1961-75, Ecol. Research Corp., 1968-70, Hypertherm, Inc., 1968-69; co-founder, chmn. bd., prin. engr. Creare Innovations Co., 1976-79; founder Verax Corp., Hanover, N.H., 1979, pres., 1979-83, chmn. bd., dir. sci. and tech., 1983-87; founder, chmn. Synosys Corp. (now PerSeptive Biosystems), 1987-89; pres. Synergy Rsch. Corp., Hanover, 1989-96, chmn., 1994-96; pres. Synergy Innovations, Inc., Hanover, 1996—; asst. prof. mech. engring. MIT, 1951-56; prof., then adj. prof. Thayer Sch. Engring. Dartmouth Coll., 1960—; adj. prof. engring. Northeastern U., 1988-93, IBM Disting. scholar, 1989; mem. turbine and compressor subcom. NACA, 1954-55. Author numerous articles and patentee in field; editor: Jour. Fluid Engring., 1973-79. Trustee Phillips Acad., Andover, Mass., 1978-81. Recipient Gold medal Pi Tau Sigma, 1953, Master Designer award Product Engring. mag., 1967, Tibbett's Pioneer award, 1996. Fellow ASME (chmn. hydraulics divsn. 1962-63, dir. Turbomachinery Inst. 1968-73, Thurston lectr. 1977, chmn. bioprocess engring. program 1987-89, Fluids Engring. award 1979, medal 1996); mem. NAE (edn. adv. com. 1987-90, steering com. on commercialization of tech. 1987-90, biotech. peer com. 1987-93, chmn. 1989, bioprocess engring. com. 1990-92, Draper prize com. 1993). Home: 5 Penny Ln Norwich VT 05055 Office: Synergy Innovations Inc PO Box 5488 Hanover NH 03755-5488*

DEAN, ROBERT FRANKLIN, insurance company executive; b. Houston, Nov. 1, 1942; s. Claude Nathan and Nellie Gladis (Davis) D.; m. Kathy Copeland, Aug. 16, 1963 (div. Jan. 1970); 1 child, Robert Franklin Jr.; m. Betsy Ellen Kniehl, Sept. 20, 1975 (dec. Jan. 1994); children: James, Kyle, Courtney Elizabeth; m. Charlene Harmon Sailors, Feb. 25, 1995. BBA in Bus. Mgmt., U. Houston, 1968. Cert. safety profl. Safety engr. Gulf Ins. Group, Houston, 1968-69, Indsl. Indemnity Ins., Houston, 1969-75; loss control mgr. Crum & Forester Ins. Group, Houston, 1975-78; sr. mktg. cons. Aetna Ins. Co., Houston, 1978-80; v.p. mktg. div. Stanley Ins., Houston, 1980-81; pres., chief exec. officer Dean & Draper Ins. Agy. Inc., Houston, 1981—. Head football coach Alief Youth Assn., Houston, 1975-81; mem. steering com. Rep. Party, Houston, 1988; bd. trustees Harris County Impact Political Action Com., 1991-96. Recipient Cert. of Appreciation, Spring Br. Sch. Dist., 1985, Outstanding Svc. award Tex. Automotive Assn., 1985; named Agt. of the Yr., Travelers Ins. Co., 1999. Mem. Am. Soc. Safety Engrs. (cert. com. on edn. Houston chpt. 1975-76), Houston Gemini Automation Group (bd. dirs. Houston chpt. 1989-90, pres. 1990-92), Ind. Ins. Agts. of Am. (bd. dirs. Houston chpt. 1991-96), Houston Assn. of Ins. Agts. (legis. com. 1993-94, mem. recreation com., charitable events bd. liaison, bd. dirs. charitable found.), Gemini User of Am. Republican. Episcopalian. Avocations: golf, health, motorcycling, choir, swimming. Office: Dean & Draper Ins Agy 11011 Richmond Ave Ste 333 Houston TX 77042-6707

DEAN, RONALD GLENN, lawyer; b. Milw., Feb. 18, 1944; m. Mary Blumberg, Jan. 25, 1969; children: Elizabeth Lucile, Joshua Henry. BA, Antioch Coll., 1967; JD, U. Wis. 1970. Bar: Wis. 1970, Calif. 1971; assoc. Mink & Neiman, L.A., 1971; pvt. practice, L.A., 1971-74; ptnr. Margolis, McTernan, Scope & Sacks, L.A., 1974-77; pvt. practice, Pacific Palisades, 1977—; mem. judge pro-tem program L.A. County Bar, 1978-91; judge pro tem Beverly Hills Mcpl. Ct., 1980-90; arbitrator L.A. Superior Ct., 1980—, L.A. County Fee Dispute Panel, 1979-86, 94—, Santa Monica Mcpl. Ct., 1980—; referee for disciplinary matters State Bar Ct., 1980-88, supervising referee, 1984-88, rev. dept. 1988-90, judge pro tem 1990-94. Bd. dirs. Pacific Palisades Residents Assn., 1983—, pres., 1985-88; counsel to Pacific Palisades Cmty. Coun., 1983-92; C. of C. rep. to Cmty. Coun., 1995—; mem. Councilman's Citizen Adv. Com. to Develop Palisades Specific Plan, 1983-85; bd. govs. Pacific Palisades Civic League, 1987-89; exec. bd. Pacific Palisades Dem. Club, 1990—, pres., 1991, 96; mem. Palisades P.R.I.D.E., 1996—, pres., 1997-98, bd. dirs. Fellow Coll. Labor & Employment Lawyers; mem. Am. Arbitration Assn. (panel 1974-95), ABA (co-chmn. employee benefits com, labor sect., bd. sr. editors Employee Benefits Law 1995-98, plaintiff co-chair, nat. insts. subcom.), BNA Pension and Benefits Reporter (adv. bd. 1995—), Wis. Bar Assn., Calif. Bar Assn., Calif. State Bar (chmn. pension and trust benefits com. of labor sect. 1984), L.A. County Bar Assn. Antioch Alumni Assn. (dir. 1982-88), Pacific Palisades (Calif.) C. of C. (bd. dirs. 1995—). Office: 15135 W Sunset Blvd Ste 280 Pacific Palisades CA 90272-3735

DEAN, SHERVIN CHRISTOPHER, emergency medicine physician; b. Teheran, Iran, June 21, 1967; came to U.S., 1975; s. Ru Steven and Parvin (Mohyeddin) D.; m. Wendy Katherine Brown, Sept. 24, 1994. BA in English and Biology cum laude, Cornell U., 1989; MD, U. Tex., Houston, 1993. Resident in neurosurgery Dartmouth-Hitchcock Med. ctr., Lebanon, N.H., 1993-95; emergency room physician Franklin (N.H.) Regional Hosp., 1995—; cons. Norwich (Vt.) Tech. Cons., 1994—. Author: (novel) Paolo and Francesca, 1996. Avocation: medical applications of virtual reality technology. Office: Franklin Regional Hosp 15 Aiken Ave Ste 6 Franklin NH 03235-1299

DEAN, STANLEY ROCHELLE, psychiatrist; b. Stamford, Conn., Feb. 13, 1908; s. Jacob and Gerta (Rochelle) D.; m. Belle Katzman, July 11, 1934; children: Lori Dean Schonfeld, Michael Louis; m. Marion Jamieson, Nov. 8, 1967. B.S., U. Mich., 1930, M.D. cum laude, 1934. Diplomate Am. Bd. Psychiatry and Neurology. Intern Hurley (Mich.) Hosp., 1934-35; resident in psychiatry Taunton (Mass.) State Hosp., Boston Psychopathic Hosp., 1935-37; sr. physician Fairfield State Hosp., Newtown, Conn., 1937-40; practice medicine specializing in psychiatry Stamford, 1940-64; practice psychiatry specializing in schizophrenia, family and marriage counseling Miami, Fla., 1964—; clin. prof. psychiatry U. Fla., U. Miami, Fla.; founder Research in Schizophrenia Endowment, 1958-62. Author-editor: Schizophrenia: the First Ten Dean Award Lectures, 1973, Psychiatry and Mysticism, 1975; (with Robert Cancro) Research in the Schizophrenic Disorders: The Stanley R. Dean Award Lectures, 2 vols., 1984; contbr. articles to profl. jours. Recipient prize for rsch. New Eng. Psychiat. Assn., 1942, Silvano Arieti award Am. Acad. Psychoanalysis, 1987, Pioneer in Rsch. award Nat. Alliance for Mentally Ill., 1987, Stanley R. Dean award named in honor Fund Behavioral Scis. and Am. Coll. Psychiatrists. Fellow Am. Psychiat. Assn. (joint commn. pub. affairs), Am. Coll. Psychiatrists (Bowis Gold medal 1991); mem. Am. Assn. Social Psychiatry (pres. 1980-82), Alpha Omega Alpha, Phi Kappa Phi. Address: 1800 NE 114th St Miami FL 33181-3438 *Thought is a form of energy.*

DEAN, THOMAS A., research laboratory executive. Dir. R&D So. Testing & Rsch. Labs., Wilson, N.C. Office: Southern Testing & Rsch Lab 3809 Airport Dr Wilson NC 27896-8653*

DEAN, WALTER JERYL JERRY, newswriter; b. Little Rock, Oct. 12, 1945; s. Joseph Edward and Nola Fay (Beard) D.; m. Regina Newby Dean, Apr. 30,1983; children: David, Daniel, Megan, Mandy. BA in English, Hendrix Coll., 1967. Writer Conway (Ark.) Log Cabin Dem., 1966-67; writer Ark. Dem., Little Rock, 1965-66, polit. editl. writer, 1972-80; feature, news writer Ark. Gazette, Little Rock, 1980-91; feature writer, politics Ark. Dem.-Gazette, Little Rock, 1992-95; bus. writer Knoxville (Tenn.) News-Sentinel, 1995—. Capt. U.S. Air Force, 1970-72. Recipient Best News Story award Associated Press Mng. Editors, 1986, Best Health Related Feature, 1995. Mem. Newspaper Guild. Methodist.

DEAN, WARREN MICHAEL, construction company executive; b. Great Falls, Mont., Apr. 27, 1944; s. Warren Earl and Mary Amelia (Sankovich) D.; m. Pamela Carol House, June 18, 1977; children: Marc, Drew, Molly, Anna. BArch, Mont. State U., 1969; MArch in Urban Design, U. Colo., Denver, 1973; MBA, U. Denver, 1982. Registered architect, Colo. Architect Davis Partnership, Denver, 1973-74; project mgr. CRS Constructors/Mgrs., Denver, 1974-78, v.p., 1978-82, group v.p., 1982-83; pres. CRSS Constructors Inc., Denver, 1983-88; exec. v.p. CRSS Commercial Group, Inc., Denver, 1988-90; v.p. CRSS, Inc., Greenville, S.C., 1990-92; chmn., CEO CRSS Constructors, Inc. (subs. Jacobs Engring. Group), Houston, 1993—; group v.p., corp. officer Jacobs Engring. Group, Inc., Houston, 1997—. Contbr. articles to profl. jours.; speaker in field. Mem. Denver Concert Chorale, 1974-77; bd. dirs. Jr. Achievement Metro Denver, 1985-88, chmn., 1987-88; bd. dirs. Jr. Achievement Southeast Tex., Inc., 1998—; bd. dirs.

Denver Opera Co., 1976-77. Served to lt. USNR, 1969-72. Advanced Acad. scholar Mont. St. U., 1967-69. Mem. AIA (com. architecture for edn. 1982—), Soc. Am. Milit. Engrs., Constrn. Industry Inst., Planning Execs. Inst., Denver C. of C. (chmn. com. econ. devel.), Colo. Soc. Architects, Rotary. Roman Catholic. Office: Jacobs Engring Group Inc 4848 Loop Central Dr Ste 270 Houston TX 77081-2211

DEAN, WILLIAM EVANS, aerospace industry executive; b. Greenville, Miss., July 6, 1930; s. George Thomas Dean and Martha Myrtle (Evans) Carlton; m. Dorothy Sue Hamilton, Oct. 14, 1953; children: Janet Lea, Jody Anne, Justin H. B in Aero. Engring., Ga. Inst. Tech., 1952; MBA, Pepperdine U., 1970; PhD in Aero Engring., Columbia State U., 1997. FAA cert. airplane and instrument flight instr. Commd. officer USAF, 1952, advanced through grades to maj., 1962; divsn. mgr., dir. Rockwell Internat. Corp., L.A., 1962-67, v.p., divsn. gen. mgr., 1967-80; exec. v.p. Acurex Corp., Mountain View, Calif., 1981-82; pres., COO Acurex Corp., Mountain View, 1982-83, pres., CEO, 1983-90, chmn., 1990-91; assoc. dir. Ames Rsch. Ctr. NASA, Moffett Field, Calif., 1991-93, dep. ctr. dir., 1994-97; dir. Univs. Space Rsch. Assn., Columbia, Md., 1997—; lectr. Calif. State U., Chico, 1988, Santa Clara U., 1993-98. Contbr. articles on gen. mgmt. and aero. engring. to profl. jours. Bd. dirs. NCCJ, San Jose, Calif., 1984-97, co-chmn., 1988-91; bd. dirs. Santa Clara County Mfg. Group, San Jose, 1984-91, vice-chmn., 1988-91; bd. dirs. Saddleback Community Coll., Mission Viejo, Calif., 1976-77, United Fund, Orange County, Calif., 1971; United Way, Santa Clara County, San Jose, 1985-91; vice-chmn., bd. advisors Leavey Sch. Bus., Santa Clara U., 1987-97, vice chmn., 1989-91; tech. com. Orange County bus. Coun., 1998—. Maj. USAF, 1952-62. Decorated Air Force Commendation medal with oak leaf cluster; named Disting. Engring. alumnus Ga. Inst. Tech., 1995; recipient Spl. Svc. award United Way, 1986, Astronaut Personal Achievement award NASA Astronaut Corps, 1972, 84, Outstanding Contbn. to Manned Exploration of the Moon award NASA, 1972, Medal for Outstanding Leadership, 1995, Group Achievement awards, 1995, Disting. Svc. medal, 1997, Silver Knight of Mgmt. award Nat. Mgmt. Assn., 1978, Commendation Cert. Calif. State Assembly, 1986, Pres.' award Santa Clara U., 1993; inducted to Engring. Hall of Fame, Ga. Inst. Tech., 1997. Fellow AIAA (bd. dirs. 1979-86, 91-95, Space Shuttle award 1984), Am. Astron. Soc.; mem. Am. Electronics Assn. (edn. found. 1982-88), Aircraft Owners and Pilots Assn., Air Force Assn., Armed Forces Comm. and Electronics Assn. Republican. Baptist. Office: Universities Space Rsch Assn Orange county Site 13422 Laurinda Way Santa Ana CA 92705-1926

DEAN, WILLIAM GEORGE, geography educator; b. Toronto, Ont., Can., Nov. 29, 1921; s. William Ashton and Alice Mary (Firstbrook) D.; m. Elizabeth Efreda Johnston, Sept. 18, 1948 (div.); children: Peter Hugh, Robin Elizabeth; m. Wendy Jean Muerkoester, Dec. 5, 1989. BA with honors, U. Toronto, 1949, MA, 1950; PhD, McGill U., 1959; LLD (hon.), U Toronto, 1997. Research geographer Dept. Lands, B.C., 1951-53; asst. prof. United Coll. U., Winnipeg, Man., Can., 1953-56; lectr. geography U. Toronto, 1956-58, assoc. prof., 1958-69, prof., 1969-87, prof. emeritus, 1987—; research geographer Mines and Tech. Surveys, Ottawa, Ont., 1956-57; Arctic research cons. Rand Corp., Santa Monica, Calif., 1954-56; cons. Ont. Dept. Hwys., 1961-64; dir., editor Econ. Atlas of Ont., 1961-69; dir. Hist. Atlas of Can., 1975-93. Editor: Canadian Geographer, 1960-67. Lt. Royal Can. Arty., 1941-45. Arctic Rsch. fellow Carnegie Found., 1950-52, NSF fellow, 1963, Can. Coun. fellow, 1969-70, 77-78; recipient prize Trinity Coll., 1949, W.W. Atwood Gold medal Pan Am. Inst. Geography and History, 1973, Can. Assn. Geographers award for profl. svc., 1984, Gold medal Royal Can. Geog. Soc., 1988, spl. citation Assn. Am. Geographers, 1990, Centenary medal Royal Soc. Can., 1994, Spl. Cert. merit Can. Hist. Assn., 1994, Distinction award Can. Cartographic Assn., 1994. Mem. Nat. Yacht Club, Royal Can. Curling Club, Bayview Country Club, Prince Edward Cruising Club, Kappa Alpha, Sigma Xi (Scientific rsch. award). Office: U Toronto Dept Geography, 100 Saint George St, Toronto, ON Canada M5S 1A1

DEANE, DEBBE, psychologist, journalist, editor, consultant; b. Coatesville, Pa., July 30, 1950; d. George Edward and Dorothea Alice (Martin) Mays; widowed; children: Theo, Vonisha, Lorise, Voniece. AA in Psychology, Mesa Coll., 1989; BA Psychology, San Diego State U., 1993; MA in Psychology, Nat. U., 1995; postgrad., U.S. Internat. U., 1995—. News dir. Sta. KLDR, Denver, 1976-78; host, reporter Sta. KMGH-TV, Denver, 1978-81; news anchor, editor Sta. KHOW, Denver, 1978-79; news & pub. affairs dir. Sta. KLZ, Denver, 1979-80, Sta. KCBQ, San Diego, 1980-82; news anchor Sta. KOGO, San Diego, 1983-84; news anchor, reporter Sta. KCST-TV, San Diego, 1984-87; dir. comm. Omni Corp., San Diego, 1987—; news anchor Sta. KFI, L.A., 1990-91; sr. psychiat. therapist Behavioral Health Group, San Diego, 1993—; media liaison United Negro Coll. Fund, San Diego, 1990-92; dir. comm. United Chs. of Christ, San Diego, 1989-92; cons. San Diego Assn. Black Journalists, 1985-92, San Diego Coalition Black Journalists, 1985-92; broadcast media cons., 1995—. *Ms. Deane was the 1st African American licensed in the United States to teach radio and television production (broadcasting). She was licensed by the State of Colorado Board of Accreditation for Community Colleges; Occupational Education was issued April 5, 1978. She has appeared in the national publication "Essence Magazine" as Career Woman of the Year, 1974. She is a highly sought-after motivational speaker, and is a guest lecturer at various state colleges and universities.* Campaign fin. analyst San Diego County Registrar of Voters, San Diego, 1990; cons. San Diego County Office Disaster Preparedness, 1990-91, Nu Way Youth Ctr. & Neighborhood House, Inc., San Diego, 1991-92; counselor Project STARRT, San Diego, 1991-92; cons. United Way Home Start, Inc. Family Self-Sufficiency Program, 1996—; cons. and program coord. San Diego Healthy Start, Inc., 1997—, Samuel L. Gompers Secondary Inst. Math., Sci. & computer Tech., 1997—. Recipient San Diego Black Achievement award Urban League, 1989, Best News Show & Spot News award San Diego Press Club, 1985, Golden Mike award So. Calif. Broadcast Assn., L.A., 1986; named one of Top 25 Businesswomen Essence Mag., 1978, Outstanding Humanitarian Worldvision, 1993, Outstanding Humanities Alumna Mesa Coll., 1993, Woman of the Year, 1996 American Biographical Inst. Mem. AFTRA, APA, Am. Women in Radio & TV, Women in Comm., Black Students Sci. Orgn. (sec. 1989-91), Africana Psychol. Soc. (media coord. 1990-92), Psi Chi. Democrat. Avocations: photography, fashion design, travel, volunteering, skiing. Home: 3545 Valley Rd #1 Bonita CA 91902-4164

DEANE, JAMES GARNER, magazine editor, conservationist; b. Hartford, Conn., Apr. 5, 1923; s. Julian Lowrie and Miriam (Grover) D. B.A., Swarthmore Coll., 1943. Mem. editorial staff Washington Star, 1944-60; edn. editor Washington Star, 1952-57, classical recs. critic, 1952-60; ind. researcher, vol. in conservation activity, 1961-68; assoc. editor Nat. Parks Mag., 1968-69, editor, 1969; asst. editor The Living Wilderness, Washington, 1969-71, exec. editor, 1971-75, editor, 1975-81; now editor Defenders mag., Washington, 1981—; v.p. Defenders of Wildlife, Washington, 1997—; Washington corr. Mus. Courier, 1945-55; contbg. editor High Fidelity mag., 1953-55; mem. com. transp. environ. rev. process Transp. Research Bd. NRC, 1974-77; Am. co-chmn. Can. U.S. Environ. Council, 1975—. Bd. dirs. Arctic Internat. Wildlife Range Soc., 1979—; trustee Com. of 100 on Federal City, 1967-90, 1st vice chmn., 1967-69; chmn. Potomac Valley Conservation and Recreation Council, 1967. Served with AUS, 1946-47. Recipient award Edn. Writers Assn., 1956, Public Service award Washington Newspaper Guild, 1956, Charles Carroll Glover award Nat. Park Service, 1967. Club: City Tavern. Home: 4200 Cathedral Ave NW Apt 114 Washington DC 20016-4900 Office: 1101 14th St NW Ste 1400 Washington DC 20005-5601 *Protection of as many as possible of the remaining wild places and, with them, of the marvelous diversity of living species on our crowding planet is one of the imperatives of our time. This need can be met only by developing worldwide understanding of its crucial importance. That is the challenging task of the nature-conservation movement. I find it exhilarating to be making some contribution, however modest, to the accomplishment of that task through the techniques of journalism.*

DEANE, LELAND MARC, plastic surgeon; b. N.Y.C., June 18, 1952; s. Maurice Allen and Barbara Elaine (Ushkow) D.; m. Danielle Anne Sheft, Nov. 21, 1993. BS, Union Coll., 1974; MD, SUNY, Bklyn., 1978. Diplomate Am. Bd. Surgery, Am. Bd. Plastic Surgery. Intern, then resident in surgery New Eng. Med. Ctr., 1978-83; resident in plastic surgery Ea. Va. Grad. Sch. Medicine, 1983-85; fellow in hand surgery Jefferson Med. Coll., 1986; pvt. practice L.I. Plastic Surg. Group P.C., Garden City, N.Y., 1986—; mem. surg. rev. com. Winthrop U. Hosp., Mineola, N.Y., 1986—, mem. resident edn. com., 1992—; instr. surgery Cornell Med. Coll., 1989—. Contbr. articles to profl. jours. Advisor Mothers of Super Twins, L.I., 1995—. Grantee So. Med. Assn., 1984. Fellow ACS, Am. Acad. Pediat.; mem. Am. Soc. Plastic and Reconstructive Surgeons, Northea. Soc. Plastic Surgeons, N.Y. Regional Soc. Plastic and Reconstructive Surgery, Seawanhaka Corinthian Club, N.Y. Yacht Club. Avocations: sailing, photography. Office: LI Plastic Surg Group PC 999 Franklin Ave Garden City NY 11530-2913

DEANE, RICHARD H., JR., federal judge; b. 1952. BA, U. Ga., 1974, JD, 1977; LLM, U. Mich., 1979. Asst. U.S. atty. No. Dist. Ga.; magistrate judge U.S. Dist. Ct. (no. dist.) Ga., Atlanta, 1994-98; U.S. atty. No. Dist. Ga., Atlanta, 1998—. Office: 1800 US Courthouse 75 Spring St SW Atlanta GA 30335

DEANE, SALLY JAN, health services administrator, consultant; b. Downey, Calif., Sept. 24, 1948; d. Virgil Eldred and Pearl Jan (Kettell) D. BA, Whittier Coll., 1970; MEd, Boston U., 1971, MPH, 1988. Mgr. community health Peter Bent Brigham Hosp., Boston, 1974-76; coord. WIC program Martha Eliot Health Ctr., 1976-78; dir. S.W. Boston WIC program Shattuck Hosp. Corp., 1978-80; exec. dir. Fenway Community Health Ctr., 1980-84; exec. asst. commr. Boston Dept. Health & Hosps., 1984-86; assoc. dir. spl. projects Health Policy Inst. Boston U., 1986-87; dir. ambulatory reimbursement Mass. Medicaid, 1987-88; assoc. Cambridge (Mass.) Mgmt. Group, 1989; ptnr. Integrated Health Strategies Inc., Cambridge, Mass., 1990-96; adj. asst. clin. prof. Pub. Health Boston U., 1994—; v.p. Chadwick Martin Bailey, Boston, 1996-98; mng. ptnr. Strategic Healthcare Innovations LLC; cons. Mass. Dept. Pub. Health, Boston, 1978-80, Citicorp Corp. Hdqrs., N.Y.C., 1986. Mem. Mayor's Task Force on AIDS, Boston, 1983-86; v.p. Trustees Charitable Donations, Boston, 1984-88. Mem. Mass. Pub. Health Assn., Am. Pub. Health Assn., Women in Health Care Mgmt. Presbyterian. Home: 94 Charles St Boston MA 02114-4643 Office: Strategic Healthcare Innovations LLC 94 Charles St Boston MA 02114-4643

DEANGELIS, CATHERINE D., pediatrics educator; b. Scranton, Pa., Jan. 2, 1940; m. James C. Harris. BA, Wilkes Coll., 1965; MD, U. Pitts., 1969; MPH, Harvard U., 1973. RN, Pa., N.Y.; diplomate Nat. Bd. Med. Examiners, Am. Bd. Pediatrics. Intern in pediatrics Children's Hosp., Pitts., 1969-70; resident in pediatrics Johns Hopkins Hosp., Balt., 1970-72, teaching fellow pediatrics dept. internat. health Sch. Pub. Health, 1972; pediatrician Roxbury Comprehensive Health Clinic, Boston, 1972-73; asst. prof. pediatrics Coll. Physicians and Surgeons, asst. prof. health svc. adminstrn. Sch. Pub. Health Columbia U., 1973-75; mem. staff divsn. pediatric ambulatory care, dir. med. edn. Child Care Project Columbia Presbyn. Med. Ctr., 1973-75; asst. prof. pediatrics Sch. Medicine U. Wis., 1975-77, assoc. prof. pediatrics Sch. Medicine, 1977-78; dir. ambulatory pediatric svcs. U. Wis. Hosps., 1975-78; assoc. prof. pediatrics Johns Hopkins Sch. Medicine, 1978-85; dir. pediatric primary care and adolescent medicine Johns Hopkins Hosp., 1978-84, co-dir. adolescent pregnancy program, 1979-82; with dept. health svcs. adminstrn. and dept. internat. health Johns Hopkins Sch. Hygiene and Pub. Health, 1980-90; dir. residency tng. dept. pediatrics Johns Hopkins Hosp., 1983-90, dir. divsn. gen. pediatrics and adolescent medicine, 1984-90; deputy chmn. dept. pediatrics Johns Hopkins Sch. Medicine, 1983-90, prof. pediatrics, 1986—, assoc. dean acad. affairs, 1990-93, sr. assoc. dean acad. affairs and faculty, 1993-94; vice dean acad. affairs and faculty, 1994—; mem. Gov.'s Task Force to Evaluate Health Care in Wis. State Prisons, 1975-78; chmn. ambulatory care com. U. Wis. Hosp., 1976-78; mem. med. sch. admissions com. U. Wis. Sch. Medicine, 1976-78, chmn., 1977-78; mem. exec. coun. dept. pediatrics and Children's Ctr., Johns Hopkins U. Sch. Medicine, 1982-90, chmn. fin. com. dept. pediatrics, 1984-85, chmn. assoc. prof.'s promotion com., 1985-88; chmn. com. developing Women's Health Ctr. at Johns Hopkins Med. Instns., 1993—; mem. Gov.'s Task Force on Women's Health, Md., 1993—, chair 1994—; mem. search com. U. Wis., 1976, Johns Hopkins Sch. Medicine, 1984, 88, 92, 93; mem. nat. review com. for accreditation of nurse practitioners Am. Nurses' Assn., 1975-79, co-chmn., 1977; mem. peer review com. nurse practitioner programs divsn. nursing Health Resources Agy., Dept. Health, Edn. and Welfare, 1979-81; mem. Nat. Commn. on Nursing, 1985-86, Physician Consortium on Substance Abuse Edn., 1989—; mem. clin. scholar's adv. com. Robert Wood Johnson Found., 1992-94, Assn. Acad. Health Ctrs., 1993—; mem. Assn. Health Svcs. Rsch., 1993—; with immunization team, Nicaragua, 1969; subintern Harbel Hosp., Liberia, West Africa, 1969; organizer immunization program Peru, 1972, West Indies Sch. Nursing, 1977; mem. editorial bd. The Hosp. Med. Staff, 1982—, Pediatrician, 1984—, Jour. of Pediatrics, 1986—, Pediatric Annals, 1990—, Pediatrics in Review, 1990—, Archives of Pediatrics and Adolescent Medicine, 1993—; reviewer Acad. Medicine, Am. Jour. Diseases of Children, Am. Jour. Medicine, Clin. Pediatrics, Jour. Pediatrics, Med. Care, Pediatrics; writer weekly column Balt. Sun, 1987-90. Author: Basic Pediatrics for the Primary Care, 1984; editor: An Introduction to Clinical Research, 1990; editor: (with others) Principles and Practice of PEdiatrics, 1990, 2d edit., 1994; assoc. editor Pediatric Annals, 1990—; editor Archives of Pediatrics and Adolscent Medicine, 1993—. Mem. steering com. Rural Health Planning, Wis.; cons. Robert Wood Johnson Found., 1973—; mem. adv. group on improving outcomes for children Pew Charitable Trusts, 1991-92; mem. adv. panel medicine Pew Health Profession's Commn.; mem. nat. adv. com. Robert Wood Johnson Clin. Scholars Program, 1992—. NIH fellow, 1973; recipient George Armstrong award Ambulatory Pedicatric Assn., Acad. Adminstrn. and Health Policy scholarship Assn. Acad. Health Ctrs., 1993. Fellow APHA, Am. Acad. Pediatrics (govt. affairs com. 1984-88, chpt. III youth com. N.Y. chpt. 1974-75, chmn. adolscent com. Md. chpt. 1981-84); mem. Am. Pediatr. Soc. (sec., treas. 1989—), Am. Bd. Pediatrics (examiner 1986—, long range planning com. 1990-91, chmn. ling range planning com. 1992—, bd. dirs. 1990—, fin. com. 1991—, sec., treas. 1993-95, chair-elect 1995-96, chair 1996, search com. 1990), Soc. Adolscent Medicine, Alpha Omega Alpha. Office: Johns Hopkins Sch Medicine 720 Rutland Ave Ste 106 Baltimore MD 21205-2196*

DE ANGELIS, JUDY, anchorwoman; b. Passaic, N.J., Oct. 1, 1949; d. Fredrick and Patricia (Zollo) De An.; m. Barry Sheffield, Aug. 28, 1977; children: Alexader, Katelin, Corrine. Student, Hartt Sch. Music, Hartford, Conn., 1968-69; BA in Speech and Drama, U Hartford, 1971; MA in Edn., Montclair State U., 1973. Lic. 3d class operator FCC. Anchor Sta. WALK-AM-FM, Patchogue, N.Y., 1978-79, Sta. WGBB-FM, Freeport, N.Y., 1979-80, Sta. WKJY-FM, Hempstead, N.Y., 1980, Sta. WHLI, Hempstead, 1980, Sta. WCBS-FM, N.Y.C., 1980-81; reporter, anchor Sta. WNBC, N.Y.C., 1981-88; morning anchor Sta. WINS, N.Y.C., 1988—; co-owner Sheffield Studios, Mahwah, N.J.; freelance anchor The Source, 1982-88; freelance anchor NBC Radio Network, 1982-888, host talk-net, 1989-90; news anchor HBO Entertainment, 1988; indsl. voice-over Odyssey Prodns., N.Y.C., 1981-88; comml. voice-over DWJ, Ridgewood, N.J., 1994—, Gourvitz Comm., N.Y.C., 1995—; cons. Media Placement Svcs., Glen Rock, N.J., 1994—. Author: (documentary) Child Abuse: The Darker Side of Growing Up, 1982 (Olive awrd N.Y.C. Coun. of Chs., 1983; appeared on Broadway in Rockabye Hamlet, 1976. Lectr. on broadcasting all ednl. levels, 1985—; dir. religious edn. Christ Episcopal Ch., Ridgewood, 1995—; troop leader Girl Scouts U.S.A., 1994—. Recipient award for pub. svc. N.Y. Deadline Club,, 1982, spl. citation Office N.Y.C. Comptr., 1983. Mem. AFTRA, Actors Equity, Ramapo-Bergen Animal Refuge. Democrat. Avocations: carpentry, swmming, gardening, crossword puzzles. Office: 1010 WINS Radio 888 7th Ave New York NY 10106-0001

DEANGELIS, MICHELE F., school system administrator; b. Boston; d. Carmine and Maria C. Parziale; m. Arthur DeAngelis, Feb. 27, 1971 (dec. Sept. 1987). BS in Edn., U. Mass., Boston, 1960; MEd, Boston U., 1964; cert. advanced grad. study edn. adminstrn., Northeastern U., 1976, EdD in Ednl. Adminstrn., 1986; cert. nat. superintendent's acad., George Washington U., Am. Assn. Sch. Adminstrs., 1992; postgrad., Harvard U., 1993—. Cert. supt. schs., asst. supt. schs., adminstr. spl. edn., reading supr. and specialist, prin. Classroom tchr. Somerville (Mass.) Pub. Schs., 1960-64; reading specialist Dept. Def. Schs., Germany, 1964-67; reading supr. Prince George's County Schs., Bowie, Md., 1967-69; sch. adminstr. cen. office Tewksbury (Mass.) Pub. Schs., 1969—; owner, operator Candelabra Restaurant, Malden, Mass., 1970-72; chief exec. officer Mish Art Diamond Tool Co., Inc., Woburn, Mass., Paterson, N.J., 1973-84; cons., trainer Ednl. Enhancement Assn., Inc., Woburn, 1986—; adv. bd. mem. Merrimack Edn. Collaborative, Chelmsford, Mass., 1979—, Camp Paul for Handicapped Children, Chelmsford, 1988-90, Harvard U. Prins. Ctr., Cambridge, Mass., 1991—; mem. Mass. Bar Assn. Juvenile Justice Conf. Task Force, 1991—, Blue Ribbon Sch. Task Force, 1991—, high sch. accreditation team New Eng. Assn. Schs. and Colls., 1991, 93, 97; bd. dirs. Juvenile Justice Task Force, Greater Lowell Area, Mass., 1990—; steering com. mem. Merrimack Valley Coalition for Children, Lawrence, Mass., 1990—; ctrl. office rep. Harvard U. Prins. Ctr., 1991-93; mem. Harvard Supts. Round Table, 1998—. Cand. Sch. Com., Somerville, 1969; mem. Ward 2 Civic Assn., Somerville, 1969-80; campaign worker Reelect Mary Tomeo Campaign, Somerville, 1971-75, Elect George Spartichino Campaign, Cambridge, 1990; friends Sturbridge Village, 1987—; mem. community svc. com. Mass. Bar Assn., 1992—. Recipient commendation Mass. State Dept. Edn., 1985, cert. Appreciation Lowell Task Force Recognition Support Attendant Day Care Program, 1990, cert. Appreciation Mass. Commr. Office Children., letter Appreciation Mass. Bar Assn., 1991, cert. Appreciation, Tewksbury Pub. Schs., 1991, 92, 93. Mem. ASCD, Internat. Reading Assn., Coun. Exceptional Children, N.E. Coalition of Ednl. Leaders, Mass. Adminstrs. for Spl. Edn., Am. Assn. Sch. Adminstrs., Hamilton Reservoir Assn, Kappa Delta Pi, Pi Lambda Theta. Avocations: pianist, drama prodn., travel. Fax: (978) 640-7844. Home: 255 Lexington St Woburn MA 01801-5925 Office: Tewksbury Pub Schs 320 Pleasant St Tewksbury MA 01876-2789

DEANGELO, ANTHONY JAMES, media specialist, architect, writer, communication specialist; b. Des Moines, Oct. 24, 1956; s. Jimmie Robert and Mary Rose (Carpino) DeA.; m. Amy Katherine Petted, June 26, 1991; children: Nicholas. BArch, U. Ark., 1980; postgrad., NYU, 1985-86, Inst. Design & Constrn., Bklyn., 1982, Poly. of Cen. London, 1980. Registered architect N.Y., Mass., Ill., Iowa; registered contractor, Iowa. Designer Robert Rodin, Architect, N.Y.C., 1981; project engr. Richard Balser Assocs., Engrs., N.Y.C., 1982; design assoc. Stephen Lepp, P.C., Architect and Planner, N.Y.C., 1983; asst. project mgr. Rafael Vinoly Architects, P.C., N.Y.C., 1984; owner Architectura N.Y., N.Y.C., 1985-88; project mgr. David Leibowitz, Architects/Planners, N.Y.C., 1989-90; owner de Angelo Architecture & Devel., LC, N.Y.C., L.A., Des Moines, 1990-98; CEO Interactive Resources, Inc., Des Moines, 1996; pres., CEO Media Prodns.,Inc., Des Moines, 1996; sys. mgr. IT bus. and contract mgmt. Equitable Life Ins. Co. Iowa, 1998—; tchr. archtl. photography U. Ark., 1979. Designer assoc. wks. pub. in Archtl. Record, Progressive Arch., Interiors, N.Y. Times. Mem. AIA (com. for long range planning 1990, pub. affairs com. for internat. rels. 1990, scholastic award in field of arch. 1979), N.Y. Assn. Architects, Nat. Coun. Archtl. Registration Bds. (cert.), Tau Sigma Delta, Omicron Delta Kappa. Home: 5813 Waterbury Cir Des Moines IA 50312-1321 Office: Equitable Iowa Co 909 Locust St Des Moines IA 50309-2899

DEANO, EDWARD JOSEPH, JR., lawyer, state legislator; b. New Orleans, Jan. 17, 1952; s. Edward Joseph and Alice Evelyn (Lanusse) D.; m. Susan Kathleen Bailey, Mar. 17, 1990. BS, U. Southwestern La., 1973; JD, La. State U., 1976. Formerly city atty. City of Mandeville, La.; formerly prosecutor Mandeville Misdemeanor Ct.; now ptnr. Deano & Deano, Mandeville; state rep. La. Ho. of Reps., Baton Rouge, 1984-96; town atty. Town of Abita Springs, 1996—; mem. civil law com., 1984-88, mcpl. and parochial affairs com., 1984-88, commerce com., 1988-92, ways and means com., 1992—, ins. com., 1992-96; chmn. house sub-com. on recreation, 1984-88, subcom. econ. devel., 1988-92. Past pres. St. Tammany Humane Soc., St. Tammany Taxpayer's Assn., Mandeville Horizons; charter mem. Habitat for Humanity; past mem. Mandeville Vol. Fire Dept.; past coord. asst. St. Tammany dist. Boy Scouts Am.; mem. Mandeville City Charter Commn. Named Conservationist of Yr. St. Tammany Sportsmen's League, 1985, La. Wildlife Fedn., 1995, Legislator of Yr. La. Preservation Alliance, 1988, Alliance for Good Govt., 1988, 89, La. Alliance for Mentally Ill, 1989, La. Assn. Justices of the Peace and Constables, 1989, 93; recipient Gov.'s award. Mem. La. Bar Assn., Covington Bar Assn. Democrat. Roman Catholic. Avocations: outdoors, historical research, travel. Office: Deano & Deano 895 Park Ave Mandeville LA 70448-4920

DE ANTONI, EDWARD PAUL, cancer control research scientist; b. San Francisco, Mar. 7, 1941; s. Attilio Mario and Zita Elizabeth (Lolich) DeA.; m. Karen Dolores Thode, Jan. 22, 1966; children: Marc Edward, Christopher Earl. A.B., U. San Francisco, 1962; Ph.D., Cornell U., 1971. Vol. Peace Corps, Turkey, 1964-66; sr. analyst Planning Bur. State of S.D., Pierre, 1973-76; dir. health planning Dept. Health, 1976-81; asst. dir. Assoc. Sch. Bds. S.D., 1981-84; dir. cancer control program Colo. Dept. Health, 1986-90; rsch. dir. Cancer Ctr., Porter Meml. Hosp., Denver, 1991-92; chair genitourinary cancer control Southwest Oncology Group, 1991-97; rsch. dir. Prostate Cancer Edn. Coun., 1991-97; asst. prof. urology Health Sci. Ctr., U. Colo., Denver, 1992—. Woodrow Wilson fellow, 1962-63; ESEA fellow, 1966-69. *The life of the mind, inspired by a classic liberal education and by a faith in truth, has been a major force in my life. I realize, however, that such learning enriches most when it is embedded in a life of practical affairs, when it enlivens my relationships with others, and when it is used to seek a good beyond myself.*

DEAR, DANA LOVORN, critical care nurse; b. Columbus, Miss., July 4, 1958; d. Ralph Edward and Elizabeth Lou (Callaway) Lovorn; m. Thomas Talmadge Dear, Apr. 21, 1978; children: Billy, Ben. ADN, Meridian (Miss.) C.C., 1992; BSN, U. Miss., 1993; MSN, Miss. U. for Women, 1995. RN, Miss., BLS, ACLS, CCRN, CFNP. Nurse practioner emer. rm. Riley Meml. Hosp., Meridian, Miss., 1992—. Dir. adult choir Fellowship Bapt. Ch., Enterprise, Miss., 1992—, BP screening chmn., youth coun. mem. Mem. ANA, AACN (cert.), Miss. Nurses Assn., Miss. Bapt. Nursing Fellowship, Sigma Theta Tau, Theta Beta chpt. Avocations: music, aerobics, swimming. Home: 3488 CR 24 Hickory MS 39332-9602 Office: Riley Meml Hosp 1102 Constitution Ave Meridian MS 39301-4096

DEAR, RONALD BRUCE, social work educator; b. Phila., Sept. 23, 1933; s. John David and Margaret (McDade) D.; 1 child, Bruce. BA, Bucknell U., 1955; honors cert., U. Aberdeen, Scotland, 1955; MSW, U. Pitts., 1957; PhD in Social Work, Columbia U., 1972. Cert. social worker, N.Y., Wash. Chief social worker Mental Hygiene Cons. Svc., Aberdeen Proving Ground, Md., 1958-60; chief Neuropsychiat. Clinic, 7th Inf. Divsn., Korea, 1960-61; residence dir. Horizon House, Inc., Phila., 1961-64; prof. U. Wash., Seattle, 1970—; vis. prof. U. Bergen, Norway, 1984, U. Trondheim, Norway, 1996; faculty lobbyist U. Wash., 1983-85, 88-91, faculty pres., 1993-95; master tchr. Coun. on Social Work Edn., 1991, 93, 94, 97; mem. adv. bd. Internat. Population and Family Assocs., 1994—; bd. dirs. Wash. Future, 1994—. Editor: Poverty in Perspective, 1973; contbr. articles to profl. jours. and encys. Apptd. by gov. to income assistance adv. com., 1987-93, to adv. com. for Dept. S ocial and Health Svcs., 1980-83, Human Svcs. Policy Ctr., 1996—, adv. com. Wash. State Econ. Svcs., 1996—; mem. nat. adv. bd. Educating Students to Influence State Policy and Legislation, 1997—; appeared in centennial program of Columbia U. Sch. of Social Work, 1998. 1st lt. U.S. Army, 1957-61. Mem. NASW (Social Worker of Yr. Wash. chpt. 1981, mem. staff legis. N.Y.C. chpt. 1968-69), Acad. Cert. Social Workers, Coun. on Social Work Edn. Avocations: travel in over 45 countries, photography, hiking. Home: 7328 16th Ave NE Seattle WA 98115-5737 Office: U Wash Sch Social Work 4101 15th Ave NE Seattle WA 98105-6250

DEARDEN, ROBERT JAMES, retired pharmacist; b. Phila., Sept. 25, 1932; s. Raymond Francis and Genevieve (Hendershot) D.; m. Marie Elizabeth Harrell, Aug. 21, 1954; children: Cherylanne, James, Jeanette, Denise. BS in Pharmacy, Temple U., 1955. Registered community pharmacist, Fla., N.J., Pa. Pharmacist, mgr. Merck Sharp and Dohme, Phila., 1955-57, Roman Pharmacy, Phila., 1957-63; pharmacist Phila. Polio Immunization Drive, 1963; pharmacist, pres. Barclay Pharm. Surg. Corp., Cherry Hill, N.J., 1964-83; pharmacist, mgr. Eckerd Drug Corp., Clearwater, Fla., 1983-95; ret., 1995; preceptor Fla. State Bd. Intern Program, Sarasota, 1986-95. V.p., treas. Wedgewood Lakes Condo. Assn. Mem. Am. Pharm. Assn., Fla. Pharm. Assn., Nat. Audubon Soc., Kappa Psi. Republican. Roman Catholic. Avocations: attending major league baseball spring training, travel, swimming, bicycling. Home: 5202 Wedgewood Ln Sarasota FL 34235-7020

DEARDOFF, R. BRUCE, automotive executive. CEO Island Lincoln-Mercury Group, 1985—. Office: Island Lincoln-Mercury 1850 E Merritt Island Cswy Merritt Island FL 32952-2665*

DEARDORFF, KATHLEEN UMBECK, nursing educator, researcher; b. Chgo., June 26, 1944; d. Paul Frederick and Lois Margaret (Deiters) Umbeck; m. Bruce Phillip Deardorff, Dec. 23, 1979; children: Sarah Louise, Philip Paul. Diploma, Evangelical Sch. Nursing, Oaklawn, Ill., 1965; BSN, U. Pa. Sch. Nursing, Phila., 1969, MSN, 1974. RN Ill., Pa., Tex.; ACCE ASPO Lamaze. Staff nurse obstetrics Christ Communty Hosp., Oaklawn, Ill., 1965-66; staff nurse obstetrics Hosp. of the U. Pa., Phila., 1966-68, asst. instr. obstetrics, 1968-72; obstetrics practitioner tchr., unit leader Rush U., Chgo., 1974-77; asst. prof. maternity Elmhurst Coll., Ill., 1977-78, 80-82; lectr. maternity Trinity Christian Coll., Palos Heights, Ill., 1984; obstetrics intake liaison Hinsdale Family Medicine Ctr., Hinsdale, Ill., 1988-91; facilitator of post partum depression group Good Samaritan Hosp., Downer Grove, Ill., 1989-91; instr. maternity U. Tex., Tyler, 1992—, rsch. asst., 1994—; cons. Burnham & Hammond, Inc., Chgo., 1979-80, Trinity Christian Coll., Palos Heights, Ill., 1983-84; mem. nat. bd. Depression after Delivery, 1991-94. Contbr. to profl. jours. Advisor Naperville YMCA, Ill., 1987-88; vol. nat. hotline Depression after Delivery, 1989-94; communty rels. com. United Way, Tyler, 1993-94. Mem. Am. Soc. Psychoprophylaxis in Obstetrics (exec. com. 1986-87, chair 1987-89), Ill. Region Depression After Delivery (coord. 1989-91), Tex. Region Depression After Delivery (coord. 1991-94), Assn. Women's Health Obstet. and Neonatal Nurses, Post Partum Support Internat., Sigma Theta Tau. Presbyterian. Avocations: gardening, horseback riding, skiing, camping, hiking. Office: U Tex 3900 University Blvd Tyler TX 75701-6622

DEARDOURFF, JOHN D., political consultant; b. Greenville, Ohio, Mar. 11, 1933; s. David J. and Ella S. (McGreevey) D.; m. Mary Jane McFerran, Feb. 1, 1958 (div. Nov. 1969); children: Anne, Katherine; m. Elisabeth A. Griffith, Apr. 10, 1970; children—Megan, John. A.B., Wabash Coll., 1955; M.A., Fletcher Sch. Law and Diplomacy, 1956. Polit. cons. Deardourff/The Media Co., McLean, Va. Nat. co-chmn. Voters for Choice; chmn. Pub. Voice, Washington; trustee Children's Def. Fund, Washington, League of Conservation Voters, Washington, Nat. Environ. Trust, Washington. Inst. of Politics fellow Kennedy Sch. of Govt., Harvard U., 1977; Conroy fellow St. Paul's Sch., Concord, N.H., 1978. Roman Catholic. Clubs: Chevy Chase (Md.). Avocations: art; tennis; golf; roller coasters. Home: 8300 Georgetown Pike Mc Lean VA 22102-1203 Office: Deardourff/The Media Co 8328 Georgetown Pike Mc Lean VA 22102-1203

DEARIE, RAYMOND JOSEPH, federal judge; b. 1944. AB, Fairfield U., 1966; JD, St. John's U., 1969. Pvt. practice law Shearman & Sterling, N.Y.C., 1969-71, Surrey & Morse, N.Y.C., 1977-80; chief Appeals div. U.S. Dept. Justice, 1971-74, chief gen. crimes sect., 1974-76, chief Criminal div., 1976-77; exec. asst. U.S. Atty.'s Office, 1977; asst. U.S. atty. U.S. Dist. Ct. (ea. dist.) N.Y., 1971-77, chief asst. U.S. atty., 1980-82, U.S. atty., 1982-86; judge U.S. Dist. Ct. (ea. dist.) N.Y., Bklyn., 1986—. Contbr. articles to profl. jours. Bd. dirs. Daytop Village, L.I. Coll. Hosp. Mem. ABA, N.Y. State Bar Assn., Assn. of Bar of City of N.Y., Fed. Bar Coun. Office: US Dist Ct 225 Cadman Plz E Brooklyn NY 11201-1818*

DEARING, DAVID RICHARD, secondary education educator; b. Pitts., Sept. 10, 1943; s. George Duff and Madelyn Alice (Teeters) D.; m. Sally Anne Case, July 6, 1963 (div. July 1975); 1 child, Juliet Elizabeth; m. Susan Hoffman, May 28, 1977; children: Brent Edward, Caitlin Elizabeth. BS, Edinboro (Pa.) U., 1969. Cert. permanent tchr., N.Y. Tchr. English, Wattsburg (Pa.) Sch., 1969-71, dept. chmn., 1970-71; tchr. English, Henley Sch., N.Y.C., 1971-72; tchr. English, Windham (N.Y.)-Ashland-Jewett Ctrl. Sch., 1972—, dept. chmn., 1990—; Fulbright exch. tchr., London, 1983-84; supr. ski sch. Actor Greenroom Players, Windham, 1993—. Tchr. scholar Albany (N.Y.) Times Union, 1997. Democrat. Avocations: skiing, boating, motorcycling, climbing, cycling. Home: HC01 Box 22 Susquehanna Turnpike Durham NY 12422

DEARING, REINHARD JOSEF, city official; b. Bamberg, Fed. Republic of Germany, May 1, 1947; came to U.S., 1960; m. Michele Jack, Feb. 14, 1967 (div. Oct. 1980); 1 child, Lauren; m. Patricia Lee Pollack, Jan. 2, 1982; 1 child, Bradford. AA, La. State U., Baton Rouge, 1968, BA, 1975, MA, 1977, ABD, 1979. CPM, Tulane U., 1989. Adminstrv. officer La. Nat. Bank, Baton Rouge, 1972-75; teaching asst. La. State U., 1975-79; adj. asst. prof. U. So. Miss., Natchez, 1977-79; chief of staff, chief adminstrv. officer City of Slidell, La., 1979—; cons. La. Mcpl. Assn., Baton Rouge, 1985-87. Author: The Waffen-SS: A Representative Study, 1977; contbr. articles to profl. jours. Mem. Gov.'s Mcpl. Policy Task Force, PJPHS sch. bd. Officer U.S. Army, 1968-72. Decorated Silver Star; named Hon. State Senator, La. Mem. La. Mcpl. Assn., Nat. League Cities, St. Tammany Mcpl. Assn., Am. Pub. Works Assn., La. State Alumni Assn. (dir. 1985-87), Assn. U.S. Army, Am. Legion, Internat. City Mgrs. Assn., Mil. Order of the Stars and Bars, Sons of Confederate Vets., Lions. Republican. Avocations: historic research, fencing, racquetball, jogging. Office: City of Slidell PO Box 828 Slidell LA 70459-0828

DE ARMAS, FREDERICK ALFRED, foreign language educator; b. Havana, Cuba, Feb. 9, 1945; came to U.S., 1959, naturalized, 1968; s. Alfredo and Ana Maria (Galdos) De A. B.A. magna cum laude, Stetson U., DeLand, Fla., 1965; Ph.D. (Carnegie fellow 1965-68), U. N.C., 1968. Mem. faculty La. State U., Baton Rouge, 1968-88, prof. Spanish, 1978-88, acting chmn. dept., 1979-80, dir. grad. studies, 1980-85; prof. Spanish and comparative lit. Pa. State U., 1988-91, Disting. prof. Spanish and comparative lit., 1991—, fellow Inst. for Arts and Humanities, 1989—; vis. assoc. prof. U. Mo., Columbia, summer 1977, vis. prof., fall 1986; vis. prof. Duke U., spring 1994. Author: The Four Interpolated Stories in the Roman Comique, 1971, Paul Scarron, 1972, The Invisible Mistress, 1976, The Return of Astraea, 1986, The Prince in the Tower, 1993, Heavenly Bodies, 1996, A Star-Crossed Golden Age, 1998, Cervantes, Raphael and the Classics, 1998, also articles; editor: Pa. State U. Studies in Romance Literatures, 1991—; mem. editorial adv. bd. Bull. Comediantes, 1981—, Hispanófila, 1981-88, PMLA, 1985-89, Hispania, 1993-95, Jour. Interdisciplinary Lit. Studies, 1993—; assoc. editor South Central Rev., 1987-89, Comparative Literature Studies, 1989—; coeditor Critical Perspectives on Calderón de la Barca, 1981. NEH grantee, summer 1979; NEH fellow, 1985, 95, summer inst., 1989, dir. summer isnt., 1994. Mem. MLA, Comparative Lit. Assn., Renaissance Soc. Am., Am. Assn. Tchrs. Spanish and Portuguese, Assn. Internat. Hispanistas, Hispanic Soc. Am. (Corr.). Office: Pa State Univ Dept Spanish Italian Portuguese University Park PA 16802

DEARMON, THOMAS ALFRED, automotive industry and life insurance executive; b. Montgomery, Ala., Dec. 28, 1937; s. Thomas A. and Rose (Giardina) D.; m. Leigh Caroline Smith, Dec. 28, 1963 (dec. May 1989); children: Jacob Thomas, Joshua Carter; m. Betty Marie Anderson, June 22, 1991. BBA, U. Okla., 1961; JD, Oklahoma City U., 1968. Bar: Okla. 1968; CPA, Okla. Audit mgr. Arthur Andersen & Co., Oklahoma City, 1961-68; account exec. F.I. DuPont, Oklahoma City, 1968-73; sr. v.p., CFO, dir. Fred Jones Auto Group Inc., and Fred Jones Cos., 1973-98; CFO, v.p., sec.-treas. Ford Retail Network of Tulsa, LLC, 1998—; pres., dir. Century Holdings, Inc. and subs., Century Life Assurance, Century Property and Casulaty Ins., Century Mgmt. Co., 1983-98; sec., dir. emeritus Hist. Preservation Inc., Oklahoma City. Bd. dirs. Oklahoma City Philharm. Orch., 1989-96, pres., 1994-95; mem. bd. mgmt. Downtown YMCA, 1992—. With U.S. Army, 1963. Mem. Okla. Bar Assn., Okla. Soc. CPAs, Fin. Execs. Inst., Downtown Lions of Oklahoma City (pres. 1985-86), Oklahoma City Econs. Club (bd. dirs.), Men's Dinner Club (bd. dirs.). Democrat. Methodist. Office: 10810 E 45th St Tulsa OK 74146

DEASON, EDWARD JOSEPH, lawyer; b. Pasadena, Calif., July 5, 1955; s. Edward Patrick Deason and Marye Annette (Erramouspe) Kennedy; m. Charlotte Thunberg, Aug. 1, 1987; children: Keelin Marie, Erin Michelle. BA, Loyola Marymount U., 1977, JD, 1982. Bar: Calif. 1983, U.S. Dist. Ct. (ctrl. dist.) Calif. 1983, U.S. Dist. Ct. (ea. dist.) Calif. 1987, U.S. Ct. Appeals (9th cir.) 1993, U.S. Supreme Ct. 1994. Assoc. Law Offices Edwin C. Martin, L.A., 1983-86; ptnr. Martin & Deason, L.A., 1986-94; pvt. practice L.A., 1994—. Mem. ATLA, Consumer Attys. of Calif., Trial Lawyers for Pub. Justice, L.A. Lawyers Club, Loyola Scott Moot Ct. Democrat. Roman Catholic. Office: 21515 Hawthorne Blvd Ste 1000 Torrance CA 90503-6505

DEASON, JONATHAN PIERCE, environmental engineer, federal agency administrator; b. Charleston, S.C., Feb. 8, 1948; married; 3 children. BS in Civil Engring., U.S. Mil. Acad., 1970; MBA in Mgmt., Golden Gate U., 1975; MS in Environ. Engring., Johns Hopkins U., 1978; PhD in Environ. Systems, U. Va., 1984. Registered profl. engr., Va. Commd. U.S. Army, 1970, advanced through grades to capt.; engr. officer U.S. Army Corps of Engrs., 1970-75, civil engr. North Atlantic Divsn., 1975-78; chief water resources program U.S. Bur. Indian Affairs, 1978-82; sr. policy advisor office of water policy U.S. Dept. Interior, 1982-83; spl. asst. Office Asst. Sec. of Army, 1983-86; mgr. Nat. Irrigation Water Quality Program U.S. Dept. of Interior, Washington, 1986-89, dir. Office of Environ. Policy and Compliance, 1989-94; v.p. environ. affairs Am. Rd. and Transp. Builders Assn., Washington, 1994-96; prof. environ. and energy mgmt. program George Washington U., Washington, 1994—; adj. prof. environ. and energy mgmt. George Wash. U., 1984-94; chmn. fed. liaison group Bd. Environ. Studies and Toxicology Nat. Rsch. Coun./NAS, 1990-91; mem. nat. panel of experts U.S. Com. Irrigation and Drainage, 1987; chmn. Pres.'s Task Force Indian Water Resources Devel., 1978-80. Author: (with others) Risk Based Decision Making in Water Resources, 1989; contbr. over 50 articles to profl. jours. Col. USAR. Recipient Engring. Achievement award Va. Engring. Found., 1993, Founder's medal and Fed. Engr. of Yr. award Nat. Soc. Profl. Engrs., 1992, Arthur S. Flemming award Jr. C. of C., 1984. Mem. Am. Soc. Civil Engrs. (bd. trustees scholarship trust 1992-93, pres. nat. capital sect. 1990-91, Meritorious Svc. award 1988), Am. Water Resources Assn. (dir. Chesapeake region 1989-91). Home: 7001 Petunia St Springfield VA 22152-3428 Office: Policy and Compliance Environ Policy and Compliance George Washington U Washington DC 20052

DEASY, CORNELIUS MICHAEL, architect; b. Mineral Wells, Tex., July 19, 1918; s. Cornelius and Monetta (Palmo) D.; m. Lucille Laney, Sept. 14, 1941; children—Diana, Carol, Ann. B. Arch., U. So. Calif., 1941. Practice architecture, Los Angeles, 1946-76, partner, Robert D. Bolling, 1960-76; Prin. works include prin. offices student union, Calif. State U., Los Angeles.; Author: Design for Human Affairs, 1974, Designing Places for People, 1985. Vice pres. Los Angeles Beautiful; dir. Regional Plan Assn. Commr., Los Angeles Bd. Zoning Appeals, 1973—. Recipient numerous design awards, Nat. Endowment Arts award, 1983. Fellow AIA (past pres., dir. So. Calif. chpt., chmn. com. research). Home and Office: Davenport Creek Farm 4979 Davenport Creek Rd San Luis Obispo CA 93401-8109

DEASY, JACQUELINE HILDEGARD, insurance consultant; b. Rotterdam, The Netherlands, Oct. 17, 1959; came to U.S., 1960; d. Fred and Joyce (Snell) Lamsfus; m. Thomas W. Deasy, Sept. 27, 1980; 1 child, Sara Y. AAS in Bus. Adminstrn., Niagara County C.C., Sanborn, N.Y., 1993; BS in Commerce, Niagara U., 1995; diploma in Ins. Regulatory Compliance, 1998, cert. in Underwriting Life and Health I., 1998. Lic. ins. agt., N.Y.; Assoc., Customer Svc., 1992, Assoc., Ins. Agy. Adminstrn., 1996; fellow Life Mgmt. Inst. Svc. analyst Specific Solutions, Inc., Williamsville, N.Y., 1982-84; cons. Comml. Union Life Ins. Co. N.Y., Buffalo, 1984-98—, Leadership Niagara, Buffalo, 1995; policyowner svcs. supr. Comml. Union Life Ins. Co. N.Y., Buffalo, 1999—. Cert. tutor Literacy Vols. Am., North Tonawanda, N.Y., 1995; vol. speakers bur. Ronald McDonald House, Buffalo, 1995—; tchr. religious edn. St. Francis of Assisi, Tonawanda, 1995; mem. Leadership Niagara, Niagara Falls, N.Y., 1995, bd. dirs., 1997—. Fellow Life Mgmt. Inst. Soc. Upstate NY; mem. AAUW, Am. Soc. CLU and ChFC, Greater Niagara Assn. Life Underwriters, Buffalo Life Underwriters Assn. (pub. rels. media mgr. 1995), Niagara County C.C. Alumni Assn. (exec. officer, treas. 1994—), Greater Niagara Assn. Life Underwriters, Phi Theta Kappa, Delta Epsilon Sigma, Alpha Beta Gamma, Sigma Alpha Sigma. Democrat. Roman Catholic. Avocations: aerobics, reading, traveling. Home: 1058 Thomas Fox Dr E North Tonawanda NY 14120-2957 Office: CU Life Ins Co NY 100 Corporate Pkwy Ste 300 Buffalo NY 14226-1280

DEASY, WILLIAM JOHN, construction, marine dredging, engineering and mining company executive; b. N.Y.C., June 22, 1937; s. Jeremiah and Margaret (Quinn) D.; m. Carol Ellyn Lemons, Feb. 1, 1963; children: Cameron, Kimberly. BS in Civil Engring, Cooper Union, 1958; LLB, U. Wash., 1963. With Morrison Knudsen Corp., Boise, Idaho, 1964-88, v.p. N.W. region, 1972-75, v.p. mining, 1975-78, group v.p. mining, 1978-83, exec. v.p. mining, shipbuilding and mfg., 1983-84, pres., chief operating officer, 1984-85, pres., chief exec. officer, bd. dirs., 1985-88; vice chair, pres., CEO, bd. dirs. T.L. James & Co., New Orleans, 1991-99; chmn. bd. T.L. James & Co., Inc., 1999—; bd. dirs. World Trade Ctr. of New Orleans, C.of C. of New Orleans & The River Region; bd. trustees Loyola U., New Orleans; mem. exec. com. C. of C. of New Orleans & The River Region, East Jefferson Coun. Mem. La. Com. of 100. Mem. Jefferson Bus. Coun., Constrn. Industry Round Table, Moles, Beavers. Home: 2427 Camp St Apt C New Orleans LA 70130-5645 Office: T L James & Co Inc PO Box 20115 New Orleans LA 70141-0115

DEATERLA, MICHAEL FRANKLIN, journalist, publicity specialist; b. Columbus, Ohio, Dec. 26, 1952; s. Suzanne Rita (Deaterla) Storms; children: Catherine Rene, Christopher Michael; m. Sara Jane Robbins Moore, Mar. 27, 1999. BS in Journalism, Ohio U., 1975. Reporter Portsmouth (Ohio) Daily Times, Portsmouth, 1976-78, entertainment editor, 1978-90, lifestyle editor, 1990; owner MFD Publicity, Portsmouth, 1991-95; city editor The Cmty. Common, Portsmouth, 1991—, audio text dir., 1994-96; tech. advisor Ohio Valley Film Bur., Portsmouth, 1990; pub. rels. agt. Portsmouth River Days Festival. Public rels. com. United Way, Portsmouth, 1984, 1991-93; founder-pres. Scioto Valley chpt. Nat. Ry. Hist. Soc., 1983-88. Recipient Governer's award media category Ohio Arts Coun., 1982, Series-Cable TV regulation AP Soc. Ohio, 1982. Roman Catholic. Avocations: history-genealogy, photography, cooking, carpentry, football. Home: 314 Pearl St Jackson OH 45640 Office: PO Box 1191 Portsmouth OH 45662-1191

DEATHERAGE, WILLIAM VERNON, lawyer; b. Drumright, Okla., Apr. 17, 1927; s. William Johnson and Pearl Mae (Watson) D.; m. Priscilla Ann Campbell, Sept. 16, 1932; children: Thomas William, Andrea Susan. BS, U. Oreg., 1952, LLB with honors, 1954. Bar: Oreg. 1954, U.S. Dist. Ct. Oreg. 1956. Ptnr. Frohnmayer, Deatherage, Pratt, Jamieson & Clarke & Moore, Medford, Oreg., 1954—; bd. dirs. Oreg. Law Inst., U. Oreg. Found. Served with USN, 1945-48. Mem. Am. Coll. Trial Lawyers, Internat. Acad. Trial Lawyers, Delta Theta Phi, Rogue Valley Country Club (pres. 1988), Rogue River Valley Univ. Club. Democrat. Episcopalian. Address: 2592 E Barnett Rd Medford OR 97504-8345

DEATLEY, JAMES HARRY, prosecutor. BBA cum laude, Baylor U., 1972, JD, 1974. Bar: Fla., Tex., U.S. Dist. Ct. (no. dist.) Fla, U.S. Dist. Ct. (ea., we. and so. dists.) Tex., U.S. Ct. Appeals (5th and 11th cirs.). Asst. staff judge advocate Brooks AFB, 1975-76; area def. counsel Torrejon AFB, Madrid, Spain, 1976-78; cir. def. counsel Maxwell AFB, Montgomery, Ala., 1978-82; asst. fed. pub. defender No. Dist. Fla., 1979-80; pvt. practice, 1980-82; exec. asst. U.S. atty. Ea. Dist. Tex., 1982-85; asst. U.S. atty., chief Austin-Waco divsns. West Dist. Tex., 1985-89, 1st asst.-criminal, 1990-93, U.S. atty., 1993-96, sr. litigation counsel, 1996-97; U.S. atty. So. Dist. Tex., 1997—; speaker in field. Contbr. articles to profl. jours. Recipient Atty. Gen.'s award for disting. svc., 1996. Office: US Attys Office PO Box 61129 Houston TX 77208-1129

DEATON, BEVERLY JEAN, nursing administrator, educator; b. Plainview, Ill., Oct. 15, 1942; d. Charles Byron Kirby and Wilma Irene Crocker Kirby Novy; m. John H. Deaton, May 18, 1963; children: Mary Kathryn Deaton Lovejoy, Amy Christine Deaton Williams. Diploma, St John's Hosp. Sch. Nursing, Springfield, Ill., 1963; BSN, So. Ill. U., Edwardsville, 1986, MSN, 1994. RN, Ill.; cert. inpatient obstet. nursing, ACLS instr. Maternity staff nurse St. Francis Hosp., Litchfield, Ill., 1971-76, maternity supr., 1976-81, dir. maternity, 1981—; childbirth educator, 1975—; presenter at cmty. and profl. orgn. confs. Named Nurse of Yr., March of Dimes, Chgo., 1994. Fellow Am. Coll. Cert. Childbirth Educators; mem. AWHONN (vice chair Ill. sect. 1995-96, dist. VI 1997, nat. bd. dirs. 1999—), Sigma Theta Tau. Christian. Avocations: travel, photography. Home: PO Box 374 Litchfield IL 62056-0374 Office: St Francis Hosp PO Box 1215 Litchfield IL 62056-0999

DEATON, WILLIAM W., JR., federal judge; b. 1930. BA, U. N.Mex., 1957; JD, Georgetown U., 1966. Bar: N.Mex. 1966. Ptnr. Smith, Ransom & Deaton, Albuquerque, 1966-71, Deaton & Twohig, Albuquerque, 1981-85; asst. fed. pub. defender Office Pub. Defender, Albuquerque, 1972-75, fed. pub. defender, 1975-81; judge. N.Mex. Dist. Ct. for 2d Jud. Dist., Albuquerque, 1985-89; magistrate judge U.S. Magistrate Ct., Albuquerque, 1989—. With U.S. Army, 1951-53. Mem. Albuquerque Bar Assn. (pres. 1983). Office: US Magistrate Ct US Courthouse 500 Gold Ave SW Albuquerque NM 87102-3118

DEAVENPORT, EARNEST W., JR., chemical executive; b. Macon, Miss.. BS chem. engring., Mississippi State U.; MA in Mgmt., MIT. Chem. engr. Eastman Chem. Co., 1960; pres. Carolina divsn. Eastman Chem. Co., S.C., 1982; asst. gen. mgr. Eastman Chem. Co., 1985; v.p. Kodak, 1985, pres. and group v.p., 1993; chmn., CEO Eastman Chem., Kingsport, Tenn., 1994—; chmn. Am. Plastics Coun.; bd. dir. First Am. Corp. Alfred P. Sloan fellow MIT; recipient Exec. Excellence award Chem. Mgmt. and Resources Assn., 1995. Mem. Chem. Mfg. Assn. (bd. dir. 1994—), Soc. Chem. Industry (exec. com. Am. section). Office: Eastman Chem Co PO Box 511 Kingsport TN 37662-5000*

DEAVER, DARWIN HOLLOWAY, former utility executive; b. Topeka, Oct. 6, 1914; s. Glenn Harry and Mabel (Holloway) D.; m. Jane Harriet Miller, Apr. 26, 1941; children: James Miller, Robert Holloway, Henry Crandon. Ph.B., Washburn Coll., 1935; M.B.A., Harvard, 1937. Investment analyst Delafield & Delafield, N.Y.C., 1937-39, Continental Casualty Co., Chgo., 1939-41, Harris Hall & Co., Chgo., 1946-49; asst. to pres. Automatic Electric Sales Corp., Chgo., 1949-50; supply sales mgr. Automatic Electric Sales Corp., 1953-55, pres., 1955-62; exec. v.p., dir. Automatic Electric Co., 1962-64, pres., dir., 1964-67; exec. v.p. mfg. United Telecommunications, Inc., Kansas City, Mo., 1967-75; exec. v.p. fin. United Telecommunications, Inc., 1975-79, also dir., 1968-79. Lt. USNR, 1941-45, lt. comdr. 1950-52. Mem. Kansas City Country Club, Mountain Lake Club. Republican. Episcopalian. Home: Mountain Lake PO Box 832 Lake Wales FL 33859-0832

DEAVER, PETE EUGENE, civil and aeronautical engineer; b. Ft. Worth, Mar. 8, 1936; s. Elmer Jack and Mattie Alline (Kelley) D.; m. Birdie Jo Foster, Apr. 30, 1954; children: Pete Eugene, Jr., Stephen Lewis, Mickey Jo, Robert. BS in Civil Engring., Cramwell Inst., 1957, BS in Geology, 1964; student, U. Tex., Arlington, 1954-61; MS in Engring. Mgmt., Pacific Western U., 1992, PhD in Mgmt., 1994. Aircraft engr. Gen. Dynamics Corp., Ft. Worth, 1957-61; project engr. ejection seat studies Kirk Engring. Co., Bethpage, N.Y., 1961-64; sr. engr. Ling Tempco Vought Aeros., Dallas, 1964-65; stress engr. Boeing Aircraft Co., Seattle, 1965-66; sr. aero. engr. Gen. Dynamics Corp., Albuquerque, 1966-74; owner, operator Deaver Engring. Co., Midland, Tex., 1974-84; cons. constrn. and petroleum industry. Served with USNR, 1952-54. Registered profl. engr., N.Mex., Tex. Mem. NSPE, Nat. Resource Conservation Commn., Soc. Exploration Geophysicists, Tex. Soc. Profl. Engrs., Masons (32 deg.). Baptist. Author: Basic Stress Analysis for Engineers and Draftsmen, 1967; Drilling Manual for Rotary Drilling, 1981, Rock Bit Design and Evaluation, 1992, Factors Affecting Rock Bit Penetration Rate, 1992, Solids Control in Drilling Muds, 1992, Drilling Management, 1994. Home: 2200 Sharpshire Ln Arlington TX 76014-3526

DEAVER, PHILLIP LESTER, lawyer; b. Long Beach, Calif., July 21, 1952; s. Albert Lester and Eva Lucille (Welton) D. Student, USCG Acad., 1970-72; BA, UCLA, 1974; JD, U. So. Calif., 1977. Bar: Hawaii 1977, U.S. Dist. Ct. Hawaii 1977, U.S. Ct. Appeals (9th cir.) 1978, U.S. Supreme Ct. 1981. Assoc. Carlsmith, Wichman, Case, Mukai & Ichiki, Honolulu, 1977-83, ptnr., 1983-86; ptnr. Bays, Deaver, Hiatt, Lung & Rose, Honolulu, 1986, mng. ptnr., 1986-95. Contbr. articles to profl. jours. Dir. Parents and Children Together. Mem. ABA (forum com. on the Constrn. Industry), AIA (affiliate Hawaii chpt.), Am. Arbitration Assn. (arbitrator). Home: 2471 Pacific Heights Rd Honolulu HI 96813-1029 Office: Bays Deaver Hiatt Lung & Rose PO Box 1760 Honolulu HI 96806-1760

DEAVER, SHARON MAE, special education educator; b. Sacramento, Calif., Oct. 14, 1937; d. Lloyd C. and Beryl Goldie (Wilimzig) Estes; m. John Morris Coon, Nov. 4, 1955 (dec. Apr. 1991); children: Debra Leigh, Robert Allen, Linda Michelle, Janis Gayle; m. Roscoe Ferrell Deaver, July 30, 1994. AA, Mt. San Antonio Coll., 1971; BA with honors, Calif. State U., L.A., 1974, MA, 1981. Cert. elem. tchr., spl. educator of learning handicapped, severely handicapped, resource specialist, Calif. Classroom music specialist Pasadena (Calif.) Christian Sch., 1974-76; spl. educator East Whittier (Calif.) City Sch. Dist., 1976-81, West Covina (Calif.) Unified Sch. Dist., 1981-82; resource specialist Bassett High Sch., La Puente, Calif., 1982-83; resource specialist Light & Life Christian Schs., Duarte, Calif., 1983-87, tchr. third grade, 1986-87; resource specialist Walnut (Calif.) Valley Unified Sch. Dist., 1987-89; spl. educator El Monte (Calif.) City Sch. Dist., 1989—. Recipient Grant Calif. State, 1978-81. Mem. Coun. for Exceptional Children, Sigma Alpha Iota (chmn. scholarship com. 1970-80), Kappa Alpha Phi. Presbyterian. Avocations: music, needlework, sewing, church work. Home: Space 82 1245 W Cienega Ave San Dimas CA 91773 Office: Cherrylee Sch 5025 Buffington Rd El Monte CA 91732-1499

DEAVERS, JAMES FREDERICK, optometrist; b. St. Augustine, Fla., Apr. 23, 1947; s. James Lonnie and Gwen Eula (Fields) D.; m. Janet Allen, Jan. 1, 1995; children: Samuel, Chris, Marie, Robin, Shea, Christy. BS, So. Coll. of Optometry, Memphis, 1979, OD, 1978. Optometrist Berkeley Eyecare, 1980-95, Cmty. Eyecare Specialists, Moncks Corner, S.C., 1995—, Eyeplus, Lexington, S.C., 1997-99. Staff sgt. USAF, 1965-69. Mem. Am. Optometric Assn., Rotary Internat. Republican. Avocations: travel, running. Office: Community Eyecare 118 B Cumbie Plz Moncks Corner SC 29461

DEB, SOMNATH, software company executive; b. Silchar, India, July 20, 1965; came to U.S., 1987; s. Sudhirendra Kumar and Namita (Dev) D.; m. Susmita Bose, Oct. 12, 1992. BTech with honors, Indian Inst. Tech., Kharagpur, 1987; MS, U. Conn., 1990, PhD, 1994. Chief scientist Qualtech Sys. Inc., Storrs, Conn., 1995—. Contbr. articles to profl. jours. Mem. IEEE (sr.), Eta Kappa Nu. Avocations: internet, computers, table tennis, long drives. Office: Qualtech Sys Inc 66 Davis Rd Storrs Mansfield CT 06268-2524

DEBAKEY, ERNEST GEORGE, physician, surgeon; b. Lake Charles, La., Feb. 17, 1912; s. Shaker and Raheega DeB.; m. Marsha Lauder, Apr. 8, 1999; 1 child, Elizabeth. BS Pharmacy, Tulane U., 1931, MD, 1939. Diplomate Am. Coll. Surgeons. Intern Charity Hosp., New Orleans, 1939-40, resident, 1941-42, 45-48; resident thoracic surgery Washington U., St. Louis, 1940-41; pvt. practice Mobile, Ala., 1948-93; prof. emeritus surgery Tulane U., 1949—, U. South Ala., Mobile, 1973—; staff dept. surgery Mobile Infirmary Med. Ctr., Providence Hosp., Springhill Meml. Hosp., USA-Doctors. Chmn. DeBakey Fund Drug Edn. Program, Mobile, 1992-93, DeBakey Fund Perioperative Nursing Continuing edn., 1989-93, DeBakey awards excellence perioperative nursing. Major USAF, 1942-45, CBI. Recipient award excellence Mobile Infirmary Med. Ctr., 1993; named Physician of Yr. Mobile County Med. Auxiliary, 1993; dept. surgery Mobile Infirmary Med. Ctr. named DeBakey Surg. Ste. in his honor, 1988, Ernest G. DeBakey Charitable Found., 1997. Fellow Am. Coll. Surgeons; mem. Ala. Thoracic Soc. Republican. Episcopalian. Office: 1729 Springhill Ave Mobile AL 36604-1411

DEBAKEY, LOIS, science communications educator, writer, editor; b. Lake Charles, La.; d. S. M. and Raheega (Zorba) DeBakey. BA in Math., Tulane U., MA in Lit. and Linguistics, 1959, PhD in Lit. and Linguistics, 1963. Asst. prof. English Tulane U., 1963-64; asst. prof. sci. communication Tulane U. Med. Sch., 1963-65, assoc. prof. sci. communication, 1965-67, prof. sci. comm., 1967-68, lectr., 1968-80, adj. prof., 1981-92; prof. sci. comm. Baylor Coll. Medicine, Houston, 1968—; mem. biomed. libr. rev. com. Nat. Libr. Medicine, Bethesda, Md., 1973-77, bd. regents, 1981-86, cons., 1986—, co-chmn. permanent paper task force, 1987—, lit. selection tech. rev. com., 1988-93, chmn., 1992-93, outreach planning panel, 1988-89; dir. courses in med. comm. ACS and other orgns.; bd. trustees DeBakey Med. Found.; exec. coun. Commn. on Colls. So. Assn. Colls. and Schs., 1975-80; mem. nat. adv. coun. U. Soc. Calif. Ctr. Continuing Med. Edn., 1981, steering com. Plain English Forum, 1984, founding bd. dirs. Friends Nat. Libr. Medicine,

1985—, chmn. med. media award of excellence com. FNLM, 1992—, adv. com. Soc. for Preservation English Lang. Literature, 1986, Nat. Adv. Bd. John Muir Med. Film Festival, 1990-92, The Internat. Health and Med. Film Festival, Acad. of Judges, 1992-93; mem. adv. coun. U. Tex. at Austin Sch. Nursing Found., 1993—; cons. legal writing com. cons. ABA, 1983—; former cons. Nat. Assn. Std. Med. Vocabulary; pioneered instruction in sci. communication in meds. schs. Sr. author: The Scientific Journal: Editorial Policies and Practices, 1976; co-author: Medicine: Preserving the Passion, 1987; mem editorial bd.: Tulane Studies in English, 1966-68, Cardiovascular Research Center Bull., 1971-83, Health Communications and Informatics, 1975-80, Forum on Medicine, 1977-80, Grants Mag, 1978-81, Internat. Jour. Cardiology, 1981-86, Excerpta Medica's Core Jours. in Cardiology, 1981—, Health Comm. and Biopsychosocial Health, 1981-82, Internat. Angiology, 1985—, Jour. AMA, 1988—; mem. usage panel: Am. Heritage Dictionary, 1980—; cons. Webster's Medical Desk Dictionary, 1986, editl. adv. Encyclopedia Britannica; contbr. articles on biomed. communication and sci. writing, literacy, also other subjects to profl. jours., books, encys., and pub. press. Active Found. for Advanced Edn. in Sci., 1977—; trustee DeBakey Med. Found., 1995—. Recipient Disting. Svc. award Am. Med. Writers Assn., 1970, Bausch & Lomb Sci. award, 1st John P. McGovern award Med. Libr. Assn., 1983, Outstanding Alumna award Newcomb Coll., 1994; fellow Am. Coll. Med. Informatics, 1990, Royal Soc. for Encouragement of Arts Mfrs. and Commerce, 1991. Fellow Am. Coll. Med. Informatics; mem. Internat. Soc. Gen. Semantics, Med. Libr. Assn. (hon.), Coun. Biology Editors (dir. 1973-77, chmn. com. on editl. policy 1971-75), Coun. Basic Edn. (spl. com. writing 1977-79), Assn. Tchrs. Tech. Writing, Dictionary Soc. N.Am., Nat. Assn. Sci. Writers, Soc. for Health and Human Values, Com. of Thousand for Better Health Regulations, Golden Key, Phi Beta Kappa. Office: Baylor Coll Medicine 1 Baylor Plz Houston TX 77030-3411

DEBAKEY, MICHAEL ELLIS, cardiovascular surgeon, educator, scientist; b. Lake Charles, La., Sept. 7, 1908; s. Shaker Morris and Raheeja (Zorba) DeB.; m. Diana Cooper, Oct. 15, 1936; children: Michael Maurice, Ernest Ochsner, Barry Edward, Denis Alton, Olga Katerina; m. Katrin Fehlhaber, July 1975. BS, Tulane U., 1930, MD, 1932, MS, 1935, LLD (hon.), 1965; Docteur Honoris Causa, U. Lyon, France, 1961, U. Brussels, 1962, U. Ghent, Belgium, 1964, U. Athens, 1964; DHC, U. Turin, Italy, 1965, U. Belgrade, Yugoslavia, 1967; LLD, Lafayette Coll., 1965; MD (hon.), Aristotelean U. of Thessaloniki, Greece, 1972; DSc, Hahnemann Med. Coll., 1973; D honoris causa, U. Buenos Aires, 1982; Docteur honoris causa, U. Louis Pasteur, Paris, 1991; D Mil. Medicine & Surgery honoris causa, Uniformed Svc. U. Health Scis., 1996; D Letters in Medicine (hon.), Baylor Coll. Medicine, 1996; D (hon.), Russian Mil. Med. Acad., 1996; D in Medicine (hon.), Karolinska Inst., 1997; DSc (hon.), Pa. State U., 1998. Diplomate Nat. Bd. Med. Examiners, Am. Bd. Surgery, Am. Bd. Thoracic Surgery. Intern Charity Hosp., New Orleans, 1932-33, asst. surgery, 1933-35; asst. surgery U. Strasbourg, France, 1935-36, U. Heidelberg, Fed. Republic of Germany, 1936; instr. surgery Tulane U., New Orleans, 1937-40, asst. prof., 1940-46, assoc. prof., 1946-48; prof., chmn. dept. surgery Baylor Coll. Medicine, 1948-93, Disting. svc. prof., 1968—, v.p. med. affairs, 1968-69, CEO, 1968-69, pres., 1969-79, Olga Keith Wiess prof. of surgery, 1981—, chancellor, 1978-96, chancellor emeritus, 1996—; pres. The DeBakey Med. Found., 1961—; dir. Nat. Heart Blood Vessel Rsch. Demonstration Ctr. Baylor Coll. Medicine, Tex., 1975-85; dir. DeBakey Heart Ctr., Baylor Coll. Medicine, 1985—; chancellor emeritus Baylor Coll. Medicine, 1996—; surgeon-in-chief Ben Taub Gen. Hosp., 1963-93; sr. attending surgeon Meth. Hosp.; clin. prof. surgery U. Tex. Dental Br., Houston; cons. surgery VA Hosp., St. Elizabeth's Hosp., U. Tex., M.D. Anderson Hosp., St. Luke's Hosp., Tex. Children's Hosp., Tex. Inst. Rehab. and Rsch. Brooke Gen. Hosp., Brooke Army Med. Ctr., Ft. Sam Houston, Tex., Walter Reed Army Hosp., Washington, D.C.; mem. med. adv. com. Office Sec. Def., 1984-50, Ams. for Substance Abuse Prevention, 1984; mem. med. adv. bd. Internat. Brotherhood Teamsters, 1985—; chmn. com. surgery NRC, 1953, mem. exec. com. 1953; mem. com. med. svcs. Hoover Commn.; founding bd. dirs.Friends of Nat. Libr. of Medicine, 1985—, mem. bd. regents Nat. Libr. Medicine, 1956-60, 94-98, chmn., 1959, 98; past mem. nat. adv. heart coun. NIH; mem. Nat. Adv. Health Coun., 1961-65, Nat. Adv. Coun. Regional Med. Programs, 1965—, Nat. Adv. Gen. Med. Scis. Coun., 1965, Program Planning Com., Com. Tng., Nat. Heart Inst., 1961—; mem. civilian health and med. adv. coun. Office Asst. Sec. Def.; chmn. Pres.'s Commn. Heart Disease, Cancer and Stroke, 1964; mem. adv. coun. Nat. Heart Lung and Blood Inst., 1982-87; mem. Tex. Sci. and Tech. Coun., 1984-86; chmn. Found. Biomed. Rsch., 1988—, Physicians for Health in the Middle East, 1991—; trustee, v.p. Baylor Med. Found.; chmn., med. adv. bd. The DeBakey Heart Ctr. Health Letter; adv. bd. Family Cir.; internat. sci. coun. Fondation Cardiologique Princesse Liliane; adv. Dag Hammarskjöld Med. Sci. Prize Com.; mem. bd. visitors Uniformed Svcs. U. Health Scis., U. Calif.-Davis Sch. Medicine; mem. Baylor Coll. Med. Bd. Trustees, 1996; foreign adj. prof. Karolinska Inst., 1997. Author: (with Robert A. Kilduffe) Blood Transfusion, 1942; (with Gilbert W. Beebe) Battle Casualties, 1952; (with Alton Ochsner) Textbook of Minor Surgery, 1955; (with T. Whayne) Cold Injury, Ground Type, 1958, A Surgeon's Visit to China, 1974, The Living Heart, 1977, The Living Heart Diet, 1985, The Living Heart Brand Name Shopper's Guide, 1992, The Living Heart Guide to Eating Out, 1993, The New Living Heart Diet, 1996, The New Living Heart, 1997; editor: Yearbook of Surgery, 1958-70; chmn. adv. editl. bd. Medical History of World War II; founding editor Jour. Vascular Surgery, 1984-88; contbr. over 1500 articles to med. jours. Mem. Tex. Constl. Revision Commn., 1973. Col. Office Surgeon Gen., AUS, 1942-46; now Col. Res.; cons. to Surgeon Gen., 1946—; disting. mem. U.S. Army Med. Dept. Rgt., 1989. Decorated Legion of Merit, 1946, Independence of Jordan medal 1st Class, Merit order of Republic 1st Class Egypt, comdr. Cross of Merit Pro Utiliate Hominum Sovereign Order Knights of Hosp. of St. John of Jerusalem in Denmark; recipient Rudolph Matas award, 1954, Internat. Soc. Surgery Disting. Svc. award, 1958, Modern Medicine award, 1957, Leriche award Internat. Soc. Surgery, 1959, Great medallion U. Ghent, 1961, Grand Cross, Order Leopold Belgium, 1962, Albert Lasker award for clin. research, 1963, Order of Merit Chile, 1964, St. Vincent prize med. scis. U. Turin, 1965, Orden del Libertador Gen. San Martin Argentina, 1965, Centennial medal Albert Einstein Med. Ctr., 1966, Gold Scalpel award Internat. Cardiology Found., 1966, Eleanor Roosevelt Humanities award, 1969, Meritorious Civilian Service medal Office Sec. Def., 1970, USSR Acad. Sci. 50th Anniversary Jubilee medal, 1973, Britannica Achievement in Life award, 1979, Medal of Freedom with Distinction Presdl. award, 1969, Disting. Svc. award Internat. Soc. Atherosclerosis, 1979, Centennial award ASME, 1980, Marian Health Care award St. Mary's U., 1981, Inst. Med. Nat. Acad. Sci., 1981, Soc. Biomaterials award for clin. rsch. in biomaterials Clemson U. and Soc. Biomaterials, 1983, Humana Heart Inst. award, 1985, Theodore E. Cummings award, 1987, Nat. Med. of Sci. award 1987, Presdl. Medal Sci., 1987, first issue Michael DeBakey medal ASME, 1989, Inaugural award Scripps Clinic and Rsch. Found., 1989, DeBakey-Bard Chair in Surgery, Baylor Coll. of Medicine, 1990, Disting. Svc. award Am. Legion, 1990, Lifetime Achievement award Found. for Biomed. Rsch., 1991, Jacobs award Am. Task Force for Lebanon, 1991, Maxwell Finland award Nat. Found. for Infectious Diseases, 1992, Lifetime Achievement award Acad. Med. Films, 1992, Order of Independence First Class medal United Arab Emirates, 1992, Academy of Athens award, 1992, Cmdrs. Cross Order of Merit (Fed. Germany), 1992, Pres. Disting. Svc. award Baylor Coll. Medicine, 1992, Gibbon award Am. Soc. Extracorporeal Tech., 1993, named in his honor Michael E. DeBakey Libr., Svc. Outreach award Friends of the Nat. Libr. Medicine, 1993, Alton Ochsner award relating smoking to health, 1993, Thomas Jefferson award AIA, 1993, Ellis Island Medal of Honor, 1993, Lifetime Achievement award Am. Heart Assn., 1994, Caring Spirit award Inst. Religion Tex. Med. Ctr., 1994, Samaritan Living Legend award Women's Internat. Ctr., 1994, Giovanni Lorenzini Med. Fedn. prize for basic biomed. rsch., 1994, Disting. Svc. award Tex. Soc. Biomedical Rsch., 1994, Heart Saver award Save A Heart Found., Cedars-Sinai Med. Ctr., 1994, Honor award United Meth. Assn. Health & Welfare Ministries, 1995, Michael E. DeBakey chair in Pharm. Baylor Coll. Med., 1995, Nat. Order of Vasco Nunez de Balboa (Panama), 1995, Health Care Hall of Fame Modern Healthcare, 1996, Sci. Rschr. of XX Century award govt. of Argentine Republic, 1996, Am. Inst. Aeronautics and Astronautics Pub. Svc. award, 1997, Boris Petrovsky Internat. Surgeons award, Inaugural honor for disting. physicians and scientists Med. Ctr. La. Found., 1997, Premio Giuseppe Corradi award, Bevagna, Italy, 1997, Rotary Nat. award, 1997, Tulane Coll. Sequicentennial medal, 1997, Fire of Genius award So. Utah U., 1997, Commonwealth Trust award for invention and sci., 1997; Michael E. DeBakey Heart Inst. Wis. named in his honor Kenosha Hosp. and Med. Ctr., 1992; Michael E. DeBakey, M.D. award for Excellence in Visual Edn. named in his honor, 1993; DeBakey Scholar in Cardiovasc. Scis. MD-PhD Program named in his honor Baylor Coll. Medicine, 1994; Michael E. DeBakey, MD Excellence in Rsch. award named in his honor Baylor Coll. Medicine, 1994, Michael E. DeBakey H.S. Health Professions named in his honor, dedication of Northwestern U. Med. Sch. book, 1995; named One of 200 Most Influential People in Telemedicine Telemedicine 200 Ctr. Pub. Svc. Comm., 1996, One of Top Ten Heroes, Millenium Soc., 1996, First Laureate of Boris Petrovsky Gold medal Russian Mil. Med. Acad., 1997, Legends of Tex. Bridge honoree, 1997, Barney Clark award Artificial Heart Lab. and Medforte Rsch. Found. U. Utah, 1998, Legends of Cardiology award Assn. Black Cardiologists, 1998, John P. McGovern Lecture award Cosmos Club Found., 1998, Spirit Charity award Med. Ctr. La. Found., 1998, Lifetime Achievement award Rsch. Am., 1998, Am. Legends award Nat. Ethnic Coalition Orgns. Found., Inc., 1998, Lighting the Path to Success award Young Profls. Houston, 1998, Great Cross of Order St. James and Sword Govt. Portugal, 1998, others. Fellow ACS (Ann. award Southwestern Pa. chpt. 1973), Inst. of Medicine Chgo. (hon.), Royal Coll. Physicians and Surgeons of U.S. (hon., disting. fellow 1992), Am. Inst. Med. and Biol. Engring. (founding fellow 1993), Biomaterials Sci. and Engr., Soc. Biomaterials, Am. Coll. Cardiology (hon.), Am. Coll. Health Care Execs. (hon.); mem. AAAS, Royal Soc. Medicine, Halsted Soc., Am. Heart Assn., So. Soc. Clin. Rsch., Southwestern Surg. Congress (pres. 1952), Soc. Vascular Surgery (pres. 1954), Soc. Vascular Surg. Lifeline Found. (pres. 1989), AMA (Disting. Svc. award 1959, Hektoen Gold medal 1954, 70), Am. Surg. Assn. (Disting. Svc. award 1981, pres. 1989), So. Surg. Assn. (pres. 1989-90, chmn. coun. 1995—), Western Surg. Assn., Am. Assn. Thoracic Surgery (pres. 1959), Internat. Cardiovascular Soc. (pres. 1958, pres. N.Am. chpt. 1964), Assn. Internat. Vascular Surgeons (pres. 1983), Mex. Acad. Surgery (hon.), Soc. Clin. Surgery, Nat. Acads. Practice Medicine, Internat. Coll. Angiology (hon. fellow), Soc. Univ. Surgeons, Internat. Soc. Surgery, Soc. Exptl. Biology and Medicine, Hellenic Surg. Soc. (hon.), Bio-med. Engring. Soc. (bd. dirs. 1968), Uniformed Svc. Alumni Assn. (life hon.), Houston Heart Assn. (mem. adv. coun. 1968-69), Soc. Nacional de Cirugia (hon., Cuba), Japanese Assn. Thoracic Surgery (first fgn. hon. mem. 1989), Med. Lib. Assn. (hon.), Assn. Française de Chirurgie (hon.), University Club (Washington), Houston Club (hon.), Acad. of Athens, Sigma Xi (William Procter prize for scientific achievement 1995), Michael E. DeBakey H.S. for Health Professions, 1996, Telemedicine 200 Ctr. for Pub. Svcs., Alpha Omega Alpha. Episcopalian. Achievements include development of roller pump universally used in the heart-lung machine, of Dacron artificial arteries and Dacron-velour arteries as surgical replacement of diseased arteries now used throughout the world, of first successful patch-graft angioplasty, of fundamental concept of therapy in arterial disease, of left ventricular bypass pump for cardiac assistance and first successful clinical application; first successful resection and graft replacement of fusiform aneurysm of descending thoracic aorta; first successful carotid endarterectomy for cerebrovascular insufficiency; first successful resection and graft replacement of aneurysm of distal aortic arch; first successful resection of dissecting aneurysm of thoracic aorta; first successful resection of aneurysm of thoracoabdominal aorta with replacement by graft including celiac, superior mesenteric and both renal arteries; first successful resection and graft replacement of aneurysm of ascending aorta; others. Office: Baylor Coll Medicine 1 Baylor Plz Houston TX 77030-3411 also: Tex Med Ctr 6535 Fannin St Houston TX 77030-2705

DEBAKEY, SELMA, science communications educator, writer, editor, lecturer; b. Lake Charles, La.. BA, Newcomb Coll., Tulane U., New Orleans, postgrad. Dir. dept. med. communication Ochsner Clinic and Alton Ochsner Med. Found., New Orleans, 1942-68; prof. sci. communication Baylor Coll. Medicine, Houston, 1968—; editor Cardiovascular Research Ctr. Bull., 1970-84; mem. panel judges Internat. Health and Med. Film Festival, 1992. Author: (with A. Segaloff and K. Meyer) Current Concepts in Breast Cancer, 1967; past editor Ochsner Clinic Reports, Selected Writings from the Ochsner Clinic; contbr. numerous articles to sci. jours., chpts. to books. Named to Tex. Hall of Fame. Mem. AAAS, Soc. Tech. Communication, Assn. Tchrs. Tech. Writing, Am. Med. Writers Assn. (past bd. dirs.; publ., nominating, fellowship, constn., bylaws, awards, and edn. coms.), Council Biol. Editors (past mem. trn. in sci. writing com.), Soc. Health and Human Values, Modern Med. Monograph Awards Com., Nat. Assn. Standard Med. Vocabulary (former cons.). Office: Baylor Coll Medicine 1 Baylor Plz Houston TX 77030-3411

DEBARBADILLO, JOHN JOSEPH, metallurgist, management executive; b. York, Pa., Jan. 27, 1942; s. John Joseph and Esta Dorothy (Knaub) deB.; m. Marianne Kathryn Kissane, Aug. 28, 1965; children: Christine, Elena. BS in Metallurgy, Lehigh U., 1963, MS in Metallurgy, 1965, PhD in Metallurgy and Materials Scis., 1967. Rsch. metallurgist Paul D. Merica rsch. lab. Inco Ltd., Suffern, N.Y., 1967-70, sect. mgr., 1970-82, dept. mgr., 1982-84; asst. to v.p. tech. Inco Alloys Internat., Huntington, W.V., 1984, mgr. R & D, 1984-88, dir. R&D planning, 1989-93; mgr. process improvement, 1993-96; mgr. aerospace materials devel. Inco Alloys Internat., Huntington, W.Va., 1996—; mem. tech. rev. bd. Generic Rsch. Ctr., U.S. Bur. Mines, Washington, 1985-93; mem. materials engring. tech. adv. com. W.Va. U., Morgantown, 1989—; chmn. W.Va. adv. bd. exptl. program to stimulate competitive rsch., 1994-98; mem. W.Va. Sci. and Technology Adv. Coun., 1996—. Editor: Sulfide Inclusions in Steel, 1974, Solid State Powder Processing, 1990, Structural Applications of Mechanical Alloying, 1990, 2d edit., 1993; contbr. articles to profl. jours.; patentee in field. V.p. Jaycees, Warwick, N.Y., 1972-78. Fellow Am. Soc. for Metals; mem. AIME (Hunt award 1977), Sigma Xi. Democrat. Roman Catholic. Avocations: competitive swimming, gardening. E-mail: jdebarba@inco.net. Fax: 304-526-5973. Office: Spl Metals Corp PO Box 1958 Huntington WV 25720-1958

DE BARBIERI, MARY ANN, nonprofit management consultant; b. Winston-Salem, N.C., May 1, 1945; d. Robert Carroll and Annie Louise (Neal) Hutcherson; m. Alfredo Emanuelle De B.; children: Maria Luisa, Riccardo Roberto. BA in Theatre Arts, Mary Washington Coll., 1967; student, Herbert Berghof Studio, 1967-69. With J. Walter Thompson, N.Y.C., 1967-68; asst. to producer Norman Twain Prodns., N.Y.C., 1968-69, Contemporary Theatre Co., N.Y.C., 1971-74; co. mgr. Folger Theatre Group, Washington, 1974-77, bus. mgr., 1977-80; mng. dir. Shakespeare Theatre at the Folger, Washington, 1980-90; performing arts cons. Alexandria, Va., 1990-92; dir. The Found. Ctr., Washington, 1992-94; pres. De Barbieri and Assocs., 1994—; adj. prof. arts mgmt. grad. program Am. U., 1994—; treas. League of Washington Theatres, 1983-86; chair selection com. The Washington Post/Washington Coun. Agys. Award for Excellence in Nonprofit Mgmt., 1997, 98, 99. Bd. dirs. Washington Area Lawyers for Arts, 1984-94, Cultural Alliance Greater Washington, 1986-96, Nat. Soc. Fundraising Execs., 1993-96, v.p. edn., 1995, treas., 1996; chair Performing Arts Coun., Alexandria, Va., 1981-84; founder, first chair Alexandria Commn. for Arts, 1984-88, theatre commr., 1984-94; contbr. to study of downtown stages for new theatre in Washington, 1985; v.p., bd. dirs. Cultural Alliance Greater Washington, 1990-96; mem. panel Va. Commn. for the Arts, 1990-96. Recipient Outstanding Svc. to Theatre Community award League of Washington Theatres, 1990. Home and Office: 3812 Ft Worth Ave Alexandria VA 22304-1709

DEBARD, ROGER, investment executive; b. Cleve., Nov. 10, 1941; d. Victor and Margaret Ann (Henderson) DeB.; m. Janet Marie Schulz, July 3, 1965; children: Eila Burns, Ryan Alexander. BS, Bowling Green State U., 1963; MBA, Case Western Res. U., 1968; MA, Claremont Grad. Sch., 1978, PhD, 1981. Asst. v.p. A.G. Becker & Co., L.A., 1972-76; sr. portfolio mgr. Scudder Stevens & Clark, L.A., 1976-81; v.p. Crocker Investment Mgmt., L.A., 1981-85; exec. v.p. Hotchkis and Wiley Funds, L.A., 1985—; prin., 1992-94; gen. ptnr. Hotchkis and Wiley, L.A., 1994-95; mng. dir., mem., 1995—; mng. dir. Merrill Lynch Mercury, London, 1997—; adj. prof. fin. Pepperdine U., L.A., 1981-85. Mem. The Founders-Music Ctr. L.A., L.A. World Affairs Coun., 1988—, L.A. Libr. Assn., 1976—, pres. 1980-81. Recipient First Pl. Pub. award Investment Dealers Digest, 1971, Outstanding Svc. award City of L.A., 1980; grad. fellow Rand Grad. Inst., 1974-76. Mem. L.A. Bd. Bond Club (sec./dir. 1986-89), L.A. Soc. Fin. Analysts, Newcomer Soc., Yosemite Assoc., Calif. Club, Bel-Air Bay Club, L.A. Country Club, Sigma Chi. Republican. Episcopalian. Avocations: rare books, golf, tennis. Home: 48 Haldeman Dr Santa Monica CA 90402-1004 also: PO Box 6926 230 Gaduate Ln Ketchum ID 83353 Office: Hotchkis and Wiley 725 S Figueroa St Ste 4000 Los Angeles CA 90017-5400

DEBARDELEBEN, JOHN THOMAS, JR., retired insurance company executive; b. Ft. Benning, Ga., Aug. 28, 1926; s. John Thomas and Erin Gautier (Howard) DeB.; m. Martha Evelyn Graves, Sept. 24, 1946 (div. Mar. 1989); children: John T. III, Charles G., Eve Lamar; m. Florence Barbara Kaiser, Oct. 7, 1989. B.A., Vanderbilt U., 1947. C.L.U., Am. Coll., 1963. Agt., asst. mgr. N.Y. Life Ins. Co., Nashville and Chattanooga, 1951-56; gen. mgr. N.Y. Life Ins. Co., Knoxville, Tenn., Savannah, Ga. and Montgomery, Ala., 1957-70; regional v.p. N.Y. Life Ins. Co., Chgo., 1971-76; v.p. N.Y. Life Ins. Co., N.Y.C., 1976-78, sr. v.p., 1978-82, exec. v.p., 1982-89. Mem. Rep. County Com., Montgomery, Ala., 1963-64; active Crusade of Mercy, Chgo., 1972-75, United Way of Tri-State, N.Y.C., 1979-81. Recipient First Founder's award Health Ins. Assn. Am., 1988. Mem. Nat. Assn. Life Underwriters, Am. Soc. C.L.U.s, Gen. Agts. and Mgts. Conf., Health Ins. Assn. Am. (mem. fed. programs com. 1985-89, chmn. 1987-88, Founder's award 1988), Rotary Club, Montgomery, Chgo. C. of C. Home: 1628 Balihai Ct Gulf Breeze FL 32561-2787

DEBARI, VINCENT ANTHONY, medical researcher, educator; b. Jersey City, Feb. 1, 1946; s. Vincent and Josephine C. (Buzzanco) DeB.; m. Margaret A. Danning, Feb. 28, 1970; children: Michele, Christopher V., Jillanne. BS, Fordham U., Bronx, N.Y., 1967; MS, Newark Coll. Engring., 1970; PhD, Rutgers U., 1981. Rsch. and devel. chemist Witco Chem. Corp., Oakland, N.J., 1967-73; rsch. chemist St. Joseph's Hosp. & Med. Ctr., Paterson, N.J., 1973-81, dir. renal lab., 1981-89, dir. rheumatol lab., 1989—, dir. rsch., 1988-95; assoc. prof. medicine Seton Hall U. Sch. Grad. Med. Edn., South Orange, N.J., 1988-95, prof., 1995—, dir. rsch. internal medicine, 1989—; cons. Rutgers U., 1981, Biomed. Clin. Labs., Wayne, N.J., 1985, Micro-Membranes Inc., Newark, 1986-89, GenCare Biomed. Rsch. Corp., Mountainside, N.J., 1989—; med. staff affiliate St. Joseph's Hosp. & Med. Ctr., St. Michael's Med. Ctr., Newark. Contbr. over 50 articles to profl. jours. Bd. dirs. Lupus Erythematosus Found. N.J., Elmwood Park, 1983-91; trustee Paquannock Twp. (N.J.) Bd. Edn., 1986-91, Bay Head Shores Club, Point Pleasant, N.J., 1993. Grantee Lupus Found., Elmwood Park, N.J., 1978—, Lions Found., 1981-85; recipient Boston Biomedica award Clin. Ligand Assay Soc., 1989. Fellow Nat. Acad. Clin. Biochemistry, Am. Inst. Chemists; mem. Am. Assn. Clin. Chemistry (chmn. N.J. 1990-92, chair clin. and diagnostic immunology div. 1991-93, Disting. Svc. award 1989, Clin. Chem. Recognition award 1984, 87, 90, 92, Bernard F. Gerulat award 1990), Nat. Coun. Univ. Rsch. Adminstrn., Am. Fedn. Clin. Rsch., Am. Coll. Rheumatology. Roman Catholic. Achievements include recognition of neutrophil defects in chronic hemodialysis patients, studies of autoantibodies in systemic autoimmune diseases and in AIDS, investigation of pathophysiologic effects of endotoxins, studies of relationship between surface electrochemistry and phagocytosis; rsch. on electrophoretic methods to study clonotype restrictions; developed first international standards for antibodies to beta-2-glycoprotein I for patients with antiphospholipid syndrome; developed first standards for antibodies to B2glycoproteinI. Office: St Josephs Hosp & Med Ctr 703 Main St Paterson NJ 07503-2621

DEBARTOLO, EDWARD JOHN, JR., professional football team owner, real estate developer; b. Youngstown, Ohio, Nov. 6, 1946; s. Edward J. and Marie Patricia (Montani) DeB.; m. Cynthia Ruth Papalia, Nov. 27, 1968; children: Lisa Marie, Tiffanie Lynne, Nicole Anne. Student, U. Notre Dame, 1964-68. With Edward J. DeBartolo Corp., Youngstown, Ohio, 1960—, v.p., 1971-76, exec. v.p., 1976-79, chief adminstrv. officer, 1979-94; pres., CEO, 1995—; owner San Francisco 49ers, 1977-97; chmn. bd. DeBartolo Realty Corp., 1994—; chmn., CEO DeBartolo Entertainment, Inc. Trustee Youngstown State U., 1974-77; nat. adv. coun. St. Jude Children's Rsch. Hosp., 1978—, local chmn., 1979-80; chmn. local fund drive Am. Cancer Soc., 1975—; mem. Nat. Cambodia Crisis Com., 1980—; chmn. 19th Ann. Victor Warner award, 1985, City of Hope's Spirit of Life Banquet, 1986; apptd. adv. coun. Coll. Bus. Adminstrn. U. Notre Dame, 1988; adv. coun. Nat. Assn. People with AIDS, 1992; bd. dirs. Cleve. Clinic Found., 1991; lifetime mem. Italian Scholarship League. With U.S. Army, 1969. Recipient Man of Yr. award St. Jude Children's Hosp., 1979, Boy's Town of Italy in San Francisco, 1985, Sportsman of Yr. award Nat. Italian Am. Sports Hall of Fame, 1991, Cert. of Merit, Salvation Army, 1982, Warner award, 1986, Silver Cable Car award San Francisco Conv. and Visitors Bur., 1988, Nat. Football League Man of Yr. award Football News, 1989, Svc. to Youth award Cath. Youth Orgn., 1990, Hall of Fame award Cardinal Mooney High Sch., 1993. Mem. Internat. Coun. Shopping Ctrs., Italian Scholarship League (life), Tippecanoe Country Club, Fonderlac Country Club, Dapper Dan Club (dir. 1980—). Office: Edward J DeBartolo Corp PO Box 9128 Youngstown OH 44513-0128 also: care San Francisco 49ers 4949 Centennial Blvd Santa Clara CA 95054-1229 *Personal philosophy: Success in business and sporting competition relies on the same basic ingredients--hire the best qualified people and then provide them with the leadership and best resources to accomplish the task.**

DEBARTOLO, JACK, JR., architect; b. Youngstown, Ohio, May 6, 1938; s. Jack and Virginia (Sassinelli) DeB.; m. Patsy McLamore, Aug. 15, 1958; children: Ava, Gina, Jack III. B.Arch., U. Houston, 1962; M.Arch., Columbia U., 1964. Sr. v.p., dir. design Caudill Rowell Scott, 1964-73; sr. v.p. William Wilde & Assocs., Tucson, 1973-75; pres. Anderson DeBartolo Pan Inc., Phoenix, 1975-85; dir. design, founding prin. Anderson DeBartolo Pan Inc., Tucson, 1973-95; prin. DeBartolo Archs. Ltd., Phoenix, 1995—; Fellow Am. Inst. of Archs., bd. dirs., U. of Ariz. Found., mem. of exec. comm. of AIA Col. of Fellows, chancellor, 1997. Notable works include: (award winning project), CRS Office Bldg., Houston, Joilet Jr. Coll., Ill., Pima Cmty. Coll., Tucson, West Campus & Life Sci. Bldg of Ariz. State U. Deacon Phoenix First Assembly Ch. Fellow AIA (past pres. Ariz., So. Ariz. chpt., chmn. jury of fellows 1987-90, chancellor Coll. of Fellows 1997); mem. Tuscon Tomorrow, City of Tuscon Pres.'s Club, U. Ariz. Found. Bd., Ariz. State U. Coll. Architecture Coun. of Design Excellence. Republican. Club: Tucson Breakfast. Office: DeBartolo Archs Ltd 4450 N 12th St Ste 268 Phoenix AZ 85014-6010*

DEBAS, HAILE T., gastrointestinal surgeon, physiologist, educator; b. Asmara, Eritrea, Feb. 25, 1937; came to U.S., 1981; s. Tesfaye and Keddes (Gabre) D.; m. Ignacia Kim Assing, May 23, 1969. BS in Biology, U. Coll., Addis Ababa, Ethiopia, 1958; MD, CM, McGill U., Montreal, Que., Can., 1963. Intern Ottawa (Ont.) Civic Hosp., Can., 1963-64; resident in surgery U. B.C., Vancouver, Can., 1964-69, asst. prof. surgery, 1971-75, assoc. prof., 1976-80; fellow in gastrointestinal physiology UCLA, 1972-74, prof. of surgery, 1981-85; chief gastrointestinal surgery U. Wash., Seattle, 1985-87; prof., chmn. dept. surgery U. Calif., San Francisco, 1987-93; dean U. Calif. Sch. Medicine, San Francisco, 1993—, chancellor, 1997-98, vice chancellor med. affairs, 1998—; key investigator Ctr. for Ulcer Rsch. and Edn., UCLA, 1980-90; cons. Bd. Med. Quality Assurance, Calif., 1981—; bd. dirs. Am. Bd. Surgery, 1990. Mem. editorial bd. Am. Jour. Physiology, Am. Jour. Surgery, Jour. Surg. Rsch., Western Jour. Medicine, Gastroenterology; contbr. articles to profl. jours. and chpts. to books. Fellow Med. Rsch. Coun. of Can., 1972-74; rsch. grantee NIH, 1976—. Fellow ACS, Royal Coll. Physicians and Surgeons Can.; mem. Am. Surg. Assn., Am. Gastroent. Assn. (bd. govs. 1995—), Am. Assn. Endocrine Surgeons, Collequium Internat. Chirugiae Digestivae, Soc. Univ. Surgeons, Soc. Surgeons Alimentary Tract (trustee 1984-89), Soc. Black Acad. Surgeons (pres. 1998-99), Inst. Medicine, Am. Acad. Arts and Scis., Internat. Hepato-Biliary Pancreatic Assn. (pres. 1991-92), Assn. Minority Acad. Physicians (pres. 1992-93). Office: U Calif Sch Medicine Office of the Dean 513 Parnassus Ave # S224 San Francisco CA 94143-0410

DEBAT, DONALD JOSEPH, media consultant, columnist; b. Chgo., Sept. 29, 1944; s. Chester Louis and Marie Dorothy (Mehok) DeB.; m. Heidi Loretta Meinhardt, Sept. 3, 1966 (div. Aug. 1984); children: Aimee Lisa, Erik Andreas; m. Sara Elizabeth Benson, Aug. 20, 1994; children: Donald Edward, Herbert Lankford. AA, Wright Jr. Coll., 1963; BJ, U. Mo., 1966, MA, 1968. Editorial asst. Ency. Brittanica, Chgo., summer 1965; reporter, Sunday editor Columbia Missourian, 1966-67; fin. reporter Chgo. Daily News, 1968-73, sports copy editor, 1974-75, real estate editor, 1976-78; real estate editor Chgo. Sun-Times, 1978-88, asst. mng. editor, real estate, 1988-94; real estate columnist Crain News Svc., Chgo., 1995—; pres. Donald J. DeBat & Assocs., Inc., Chgo., 1995—. Author: The Mortgage Manual, 1986, 2d edit., 1989, Home Refinancing, 1986; author, editor: Living in Greater Chicago, 1988-94. Recipient numerous awards for articles in real estate field. Mem. Nat. Assn. Real Estate Editors (bd. dirs., editor of best real estate sect. award 1978, 83, 84, 92), Nat. Trust for Hist. Preservation. Avocations: 16-inch slow pitch softball, handball, real estate renovation, travel, skiing. Fax: (312) 944-8877. Office: Crane Comm Inc 740 N Rush St Chicago IL 60611-2546 also: Donald J DeBat & Assocs Inc 1838 N Lincoln Park W Chicago IL 60614-5308

DEBAUCHE, JACQUELINE JEAN, wildlife rehabilitator; b. Milw., Apr. 15, 1964; d. John and Mary (Baker) Quesnell; m. David J. DeB., Mar. 3, 1990; stepchildren: Theresa, Angela, Ronald, Alisha. BA in Biology, Coll. St. Teresa, 1986. Lic. wildlife rehabilitator. Dir. rehab. Northwoods Wildlife Ctr., Minocqua, Wis., 1989-97, Feathered Friends, Arbor Vitae, Wis., 1997—. Editor (newsletter) Hoots and Howls, 1993—. Mem. Internat. Wildlife Rehab. Coun., Nat. Wildlife Rehab. Assn., Wis. Wildlife Rehabilitators (bd. dirs. 1989—). Avocations: birding, hiking, cross-country skiing. Home: PO Box 751 Woodruff WI 54568-0751

DEBEAR, RICHARD STEPHEN, library planning consultant; b. N.Y.C., Jan. 18, 1933; s. Arthur A. and Sarah (Morrison) deB.; m. Estelle Carmel Grandon, Apr. 27, 1951; children: Richard, Jr., Diana deBear Fortson, Patricia deBear Talkington, Robert, Christopher, Nancy deBear Naski. BS, Queens Coll. CUNY, 1953. Sales rep. Sperry Rand Corp., Blue Bell, Pa., 1954-76; pres. Libr. Design Assocs., Plymouth, Mich., 1976-97, Am. Libr. Ctr., Plymouth, 1981—; bldg. cons. to numerous librs., 1965—. Mem. ALA, Mich. Libr. Assn. (oversight com. Leadership Acad. 1990—). Office: Am Libr Ctr Inc 1149 S Main St Plymouth MI 48170-2213

DE BEIXEDON, S(USAN) YVETTE, psychologist; b. Pasadena, Calif., Jan. 2, 1965; d. Edward Kingsland Framaux and Margaret Pauline (Rinderknecht) de B.; m. Jacques E. Mitrani, Dec. 21, 1985 (div. Oct. 22, 1992); m. Richard E. Bresnahan, May 14, 1994; children: Paul, Taylor, Hannah, Dane. BA, U. Calif., San Diego, 1985; MA, PhD, Northwestern U., 1990. Lic. psychologist, Calif., Ga., Tenn. Pvt. practice, Monarch Beach, Calif., 1995—; founder Profl. Alliance for Total Health. Author: Lovers & Survivors, 1995. Mem. APA, South Orange County C. of C. Episcopalian. Avocations: travel, gourmet cooking, health and fitness. Office: 28 Monarch Bay Plz Ste L Monarch Beach CA 92629-3455

DEBELLO, MARGUERITE CATHERINE, oncological nurse; b. Detroit, Nov. 25, 1964; d. Frank J. Jr. and Gail C. (Hahn) Fisher; m. David DeBello, Aug. 10, 1985; children: Anthony, Daniel, Matthew. Diploma, Hurley Med. Ctr. Sch. Nursing, Flint, Mich., 1985; BSN, U. Mich., Flint, 1990; MSN, Oakland U., 1997. Cert. oncology nursing. Clin. nurse Harper Hosp., Detroit, 1985-92, case mgr. extender, 1992-98; adj. nursing faculty Oakland C.C., Rochester, Mich., 1998—. Mem. Oncology Nursing Soc., Sigma Theta Tau (Theta Psi chpt.).

DEBENEDETTI, PABLO GASTON, chemical engineering educator; b. Buenos Aires, Mar. 30, 1953; came to the U.S., 1980; U.S. citizen; s. Sergio Isaias and Francine Fanny (Lehmann) D.; m. Silvia Irene Strauss, July 11, 1987; children: Gabriel Alejandro, Dina Sonia. BS in Chem. Engring., Buenos Aires U., 1978; MS, MIT, 1981, PhD, 1985. Rsch. engr. O de Nora Impianti Elettrochimici, Milan, Italy, 1978-80; asst. prof. dept. chem. engring. Princeton (N.J.) U., 1985-90, assoc. prof., 1990-94, prof. chem. engring., 1994—, dept. chair, 1996—, class of 1950 prof., 1998—; Vaughan lectr. Calif. Inst. Tech., 1992; Katz meml. lectr. City Coll. CUNY, 1997; Wohl meml. lectr. U. Del., 1997; Cary lectr. Ga. Inst. Tech., 1998. Author: Metastable Liquids Concepts and Principles, 1996; mem. editl. bd. Jour. Supercritical Fluids, 1988—, Supercritical Fluid Sci. and Tech., 1995—, Jour. Chem. Engring. Data, 1996—; contbr. articles to profl. jours. including Jour. Chem. Physics, Jour. Phys. Chemistry, Nature, Phys. Rev. Letters, Molecular Physics, Am. Inst. Chem. Engr. Jour., others. Named NSF Presdl. Young Investigator, 1987; European Econ. Cmty. fellow, 1978, Camille and Henry Dreyfus Tchr. scholar, 1989, Guggenheim fellow, 1991. Mem. AAAS, N.Y. Acad. Scis., Am. Inst. Chemical Engrs. (Profl. Progress award 1997), Am. Chemical Soc., Am. Physical Soc., Sigma Xi. Achievements include research in protein processing and separations with supercritical fluids; thermodynamics of supercritical fluids and mixtures; thermodynamics of supercooled and glassy water; thermodynamics and statistical mechanics of metastable systems; thermodynamics of polyamorphic phase transitions. Office: Princeton U Dept Chem Engring Princeton NJ 08544

DE BENEDICTIS, DARIO, arbitrator, mediator; b. Providence, Aug. 22, 1918; s. Anthony and Efra (Bassani) DeB.; m. Leanna May Carlson, July 22, 1950; Marc, Don, Gail. AB, U. Calif., Berkeley, 1946; JD, Harvard U., 1949. Bar: Calif., 1949, U.S. Supreme Ct., 1962. Draftsman, title examiner Calif. Pacific Title Co., Redwood City, 1936-38, 39-46; law sec. to Judge Clifton Mathews U.S. Circuit Ct., San Francisco, 1949-50; ptnr. Thelen, Marrin, Johnson and Bridges, San Francisco, 1950-88, of counsel, 1989-93; instr. San Francisco Law Sch., 1949-53, lectr. U. Calif. Bus. Sch. Extension, 1965-72, Golden Gate U., San Francisco, 1973-75; lectr., author Fed. Publs., Washington, 1978-89; judge pro tem Mcpl. Ct., San Francisco, 1980-97; chmn. 14 dispute review bds. Caltrans, 1996—; mem. Dispute Rev. Bd. Found. Contbg. author to handbooks on constrn. practices. Bd. dirs. Legal Aid Soc., San Francisco, 1952-88, Camron-Stanford House Preservation Assn., 1992-94; mem. Calif. Pub. Works Contract Arbitration Com., panel of arbitrators. Capt. U.S. Army, 1942-46, PTO, lt. col. USAR, 1946-62; ret. Mem. ABA, FBA, Calif. Bar Assn., San Francisco Bar Assn., Am. Arbitration Assn. (nat. panel arbitrators, nat. panel mediators, panel Large Complex Case Program-Constrn., Disting. Svc. award for outstanding contbn. in area of comml. disputes 1990), Soc. Profls. in Dispute Resolution, Calif. Dispute Resolution Coun., Assoc. Gen. Contractors Calif. (Assocs. Achievement award 1992). Fax: 925-280-0601. Home and Office: 1200 Rockledge Ln Apt 3 Walnut Creek CA 94595-2877

DE BERARDINIS, CHARLES ANTHONY JOSEPH, physician; b. Passaic, N.J., July 1, 1961; m. Karen Ann Brooks, Nov. 13, 1993; children: Matthew, Sarah. BA in Biology, Ithaca Coll., 1983; DO, U. Medicine and Dentistry N.J., 1989. Diplomate Nat. Bd. Osteo. Med. Examiners. Resident in internal medicine Kennedy Meml. Hosp., Stratford, N.J., 1990-92; fellow in cardiology Deborah Heart & Lung Ctr., Browns Mills, N.J., 1992-96; attending cardiologist cardiac catheterization lab. Deborah Heart and Lung Ctr., Brownsmills, N.J., 1996—. Fellow Am. Coll. Cardiology; mem. Am. Osteo. Assn., Am. Coll. Osteo. Internists (diplomate, bd. cert. internal medicine and cardiology). Office: Deborah Heart & Lung Ctr Trenton Rd Browns Mills NJ 08015

DEBERRY, FISHER, college football coach; b. Cheraw, S.C., June 9, 1938; m. LuAnn DeBerry; children: Joe, Michelle. BA, Wofford Coll., 1960. Coach, tchr. high schs., S.C., 6 yrs.; asst. football coach Wofford Coll., Spartanburg, S.C., 2 yrs., Appalachian State Coll., Boone, N.C., 9 yrs.; quarterbacks coach Air Force Acad., USAF Acad., Colo., 1980-81, offensive coord., 1981-83, head football coach, 1984—; led teams in Ind. Bowl, 1984, Blue Bonnnet Bowl, 1985, Freedom Bowl, 1987, Liberty Bowl, 1989-92, Copper Bowl, 1995, Las Vegas Bowl, 1997. Motivational spkr. to religious and corp. groups; fund raiser Easter Seals, March of Dimes, Salvation Army; chmn. Am. Heart Assn. Named Western Athletic Conf. Coach of Yr., 1985, 95, Nat. Coach of Yr., 1985. Mem. Fellowship Christian Athletes. Office: Hdqs USAF Acad 2304 Cadet Dr Ste 200 USAF Academy CO 80840*

DE BETHMANN, HEIDI ELIZABETH, architect; b. Mineola, N.Y.; d. Daniel René and Carol Ann (King) Luthringshauser; m. Alexandre J. de Bethmann, Oct. 29, 1988; children: Elodie Elizabeth, Elise Anne. BA, Wellesley Coll., 1984; MArch, MIT, 1988. Registered architect, N.Y. Architect Ellerbe Beckett, N.Y.C., 1988-89; assoc., sr. designer Butler Rogers Baskett, N.Y.C., 1989—. Home: 131 E 81st St New York NY 10028-1450 Office: Butler Rogers Baskett 475 Tenth Ave New York NY 10018

DEBEVOISE, A. CLAY, artist; b. Morristown, N.J., May 4, 1954; s. Thomas M. and Ann (Taylor) D.; m. Linda J. Derick, Oct. 13, 1979 (div. Jan. 1987); 1 child, Nell M. Derick Debevoise. BA, Trinity Coll., Hartford, Conn., 1975; MFA, Sch. Visual Arts, N.Y.C., 1993. Adj. faculty Sch. Visual Arts, N.Y.C., 1994-96, Internat. Ctr. Photography, N.Y.C., 1996, San Francisco Art Inst., 1999—. Exhibited in solo shows at Trinity Coll., Artworks Gallery, Pulse Art, N.Y.C., Brecht Forum, N.Y.C., others; exhibited in group shows at Cooper Union, N.Y.C., Ctrl. Arts Collective, Tucson, Bannister Gallery/R.I. Coll., Providence, Wadsworth Atheneum, Hartford, Real Art Ways, Hartford, Austin State U., Nacogdoches, Tex., So. Exposure, San Francisco, Neuberger Mus., Purchase, N.Y., Fuller Mus., Brockton, Mass., 1999; represented in collections N.Y. Bklyn Mus. Art, Columbus (Ohio) Mus. Art., Fogg Art Mus., Harvard U. Art Mus., Cambridge, Mass., N.Y. Pub. Libr., Cin. Art Mus., Wadsworth Atheneum, Hartford, Conn., others; contbr. articles to profl. jours. Mem. Am. Assn. Museums, Coll. Art Assn. E-mail: info@clayd.com.

DEBEVOISE, DICKINSON RICHARDS, federal judge; b. Orange, N.J., Apr. 23, 1924; s. Elliott and Josephine (Richards) D.; m. Katrina Stephenson Leeb, Feb. 24, 1951; children: Kate, Josephine Debevoise Davies, Mary Debevoise Rennie, Abigail D. Byrne. BA, Williams Coll., 1948; LLB, Columbia U., 1951. Bar: N.J. 1953, U.S. Supreme Ct. 1956. Law clk. to Hon. Phillip Forman, chief judge U.S. Dist. Ct. for Dist. N.J., 1952-53; assoc. firm Riker, Emery & Danzig, Newark, 1953-56; partner firm Riker, Danzig, Scherer, Debevoise & Hyland, Newark, 1957-79; judge U.S. Dist. Ct. for N.J., 1979—; adj. prof. constitutional law Seton Hall U., 1992-94; pres. Newark Legal Services Project, 1965-70; chmn. N.J. Gov.'s Workmen's Compensation Study Commn., 1972-73; mem. N.J. Supreme Ct. Adv. Com. on Jud. Conduct, 1974-78; chmn. N.J. Disciplinary Rev. Bd., 1978-79; mem. Lawyers Adv. Com. for 3d Circuit, 1975-79, chmn., 1979; chmn. N.J. Legal Services Adv. Council, 1976-78. Asso. editor: N.J. Law Jour, 1959-79. Trustee Ramapo Coll., N.J., 1969-73, chmn. bd., 1971-73; trustee Williams Coll., 1969-74, Fund for N.J., 1985—; trustee Hosp. Ctr. at Orange, N.J., v.p., 1975-79; pres. Democrats for Good Govt., 1956-60, active various presdl., senatorial, gubernatorial campaigns; active St. Stephens Episcopal Ch. Sgt. U.S. Army, WWII, 1st lt. Korean War. Decorated Bronze Star. Fellow Am. Bar Found.; mem. ABA, N.J. Bar Assn., Fed. Bar Assn. (v.p. 1976), Assn. Fed. Bar State N.J. (v.p. 1977-79), Essex County Bar Assn. (treas. 1960-64, trustee 1968-71), Am. Law Inst., Judicature Soc., Columbia Law Sch. Assn. (bd. dirs., pres. 1992-94). Office: US Dist Ct PO Box 999 Newark NJ 07101-0999

DE BEVOISE, LEE RAYMOND, editor, nurse, writer, photographer, webmaster; b. Paterson, N.J., Aug. 24, 1948; m. Sharon De Bevoise; children: Suzanne, Richard (dec.). Student, Glassboro State Coll., 1968; ASN, Cumberland C.C., Vineland, N.J., 1974; student, Stockton State Coll., 1981; MS in Comm. summa cum laude, La Salle U., 1996. RN, N.J., Pa. Editor The Artery Millville (N.J.) Hosp., 1970-73; staff instr. ARC, Phila., 1981-94; v.p. De Bevoise & Assocs., Friend, Nebr., 1993—; adj. prof. La Salle U., 1996—; editor, webmaster www.fishdreams.com, 1997—; RN computer specialist Bryan Home Health Care Svc., Lincoln, 1998—. Columnist The Daily Jour., Millville, N.J., 1990-97; field editor Disabled Outdoors mag., Grand Marais, Minn., 1994-97; editor The South Jersey Angler Mag., Vineland, N.J., 1996-97. Asst. advisor Med. Explorer Post, Millville, 1971-72; trustee Millville Day Care Ctr., 1974-77; co-chmn. adv. com. State Assemblyman Salmon, Millville, 1986-89; trustee, deacon, treas. Open Bible Bapt. Ch., Millville, 1986-95; dir. pub. rels. Meadowwood Environ. Sanctuary, Millville, 1990-97, S.J. Sportsmen's Jamboree, Maurice River Twp., N.J., 1990-96. With USN, 1969-70. Recipient 1st place award Bi-cenntenial Photography, 1976. Mem. Boat Writers Internat., Boating Writers Internat., Outdoor Writers Assn. Am., Kodak Profl. Network, Internat. Freelance Photographers Orgn., Mason-Dixon Outdoor Writers Assn. (Gatco Best Mag. column award, Pete Greer Meml. award 1st runner up for best black and white photography). Avocations: personal computers, fishing, shooting sports, environmental concerns, boating. Home: 607 S Pine St Friend NE 68359-1534 Office: De Bevoise & Assocs 607 S Pine St Friend NE 68359-1534

DEBEY, MARY, educator; b. Hull, Iowa, June 2, 1950; d. Tony and Jeanette DeBey; m. Ron Hoffman, Aug. 20, 1971 (div.); m. Roy Kanwit, Oct. 9, 1981; 1 child, Ariana. BA, Bklyn. Coll., 1974; MA, U. Vt., 1977; PhD, SUNY, Albany, 1994. Tchr. Grace Presch., Bklyn., 1970-76; dir. ARSU Early Child, Fair Haven, Vt., 1977-84, Renss. Head Start, Troy, N.Y., 1984-85; prof. Hudson Valley C.C., Troy, 1985-98; dir., prof. Bennington (Vt.) Coll., 1998—. Home: PO Box 153 Spencertown NY 12165-0153 Office: Bennington Coll Bennington VT 05201

DEBEYSSEY, MARK SAMMER, molecular and cellular biologist; b. Putnam, Conn., Mar. 24, 1966; s. Ghaleb and Widad Debeyssey. BS cum laude, U. Conn., 1988, MS in Moleduclar and Cell Biology, 1992. Sr. toxicologist Ciba-Geigy, Farmington, Conn., 1988-89; rsch. scientist U. Conn. Health Ctr., Farmington, 1989-90; molecular and cellular biologist VA Med. Ctr., West Haven, Conn., 1990-94, Albert Einstein Sch. Medicine, Bronx, N.Y., 1994—; sr. lead analyst Bayer Pharm.-Wang Global, West Haven, Conn., 1998—. Contbr. articles to profl. jours. Chmn. Am. Druze Soc., Conn., 1990-91. Recipient Superior Performance award Dept Vets. Affairs, 1991. Mem. AAAS, Am. Chem. Soc., Planetary Soc. (assoc.), Am. Mus. Natural History, Archaeol. Inst. Am. (assoc.), Smithsonian Nat. Assocs. Office: Bayer Corp Wang Global 400 Morgan Ln West Haven CT 06516-4175

DEBICKI, ANDREW PETER, foreign language educator; b. Warsaw, Poland, June 28, 1934; came to U.S., 1948, naturalized, 1955; s. Roman and Jadwiga (Dunin) D.; m. Mary Jo Tidmarsh, Dec. 29, 1959 (dec. 1975); children: Mary Beth, Margaret; m. Mary Elizabeth Gwin, May 16, 1987. BA, Yale U., 1955, PhD, 1960. Instr. Trinity Coll., Hartford, Conn., 1957-60; asst. prof. Grinnell (Iowa) Coll., 1960-62, asso. prof., 1962-66, prof., 1966-68; prof. Spanish U. Kans., Lawrence, 1968-76; Univ. Disting. prof. Univ. Kans., 1976—; dir. Hall Ctr., 1989-93; dean Grad. Sch. and Internat. Programs; mem. Test of English as a Fgn. Lang. Policy Coun.; mem. Grad. Record Exam. Bd. Author: La poesia de Jose Gorostiza, 1962, Estudios sobre poesia espanola contemporanea, 1968, 81, Damaso Alonso, 1970, 74, La poesia de Jorge Guillen, 1973, Poetas hispanoamericanos contemporaneos: Punto de vista, perspectiva, experiencia, 1976, Poetry of Discovery, 1982, 87, Angel Gonzalez, 1989, Spanish Poetry of the Twentieth Century, 1994, 97; contbr. articles to various publs. Guggenheim fellow, 1970-71, 80, Nat. Humanities Ctr. fellow, 1980, 92-93, Am. Coun. Learned Socs. fellow, 1966-67, NEH sr. rsch. fellow, 1992-93. Mem. MLA (exec. coun. 1989-93), Am. Assn. Tchrs. Spanish and Portuguese. Home: 1445 Applegate Ct Lawrence KS 66049-2937 Office: U Kans Grad Studies/Internat Prgms Lawrence KS 66045

DE BLASI, TONY (ANTHONY ARMANDO DE BLASI), artist; b. Alcamo, Italy, Jan. 1, 1933; came to U.S., 1938, naturalized, 1959; s. Frank and Josephine (Frisella) De B.; m. Eva Machauf; children from previous marriage: Keith, Eric. Student, Art Students League, N.Y.C., 1957-59; BA, U. R.I., 1961; MFA, Ind. U., 1963; student of William Leete, Kingston, R.I., 1959-61; student of James McGarrell, Bloomington, Ind., 1961-63; student of William Bailey, Bloomington, 1961-63, student of Rudy Pozzatti, 1961-63; student of others. Chmn., instr. dept. of art Washington and Jefferson Coll., Washington, Pa., 1963-66; prof. painting and drawing Mich. State U., East Lansing, 1966-86; instr. Sch. Visual Arts, N.Y.C., 1988-90. One-man shows of paintings 1963—, including Kresge Art Mus., Mich. State U., East Lansing, 1969, 72, 76, Spectrum Gallery, N.Y.C., 1969, 69, 71, 73, Detroit Art Inst., 1972, Razor Gallery, N.Y.C., 1975, 77, Western Mich. U., Kalamazoo, 1979, Wake Forest U., Winston-Salem, N.C., 1980, Urban Inst. Contemporary Art, Grand Rapids, Mich., 1981, Andrews U., Berrien Springs, Mich., 1983, Louis K. Meisel Gallery, N.Y.C., 1985, 87, 88, 89, 91, 93, 95, Hokin Kaufman Gallery, Chgo., 1988, Hokin Gallery, Bay Harbor Island, Fla., 1990, 92, SUNY Fine Arts Gallery, Oneonta, N.Y., 1998; numerous group shows 1963— including Penthouse Gallery Mus. of Modern Art, N.Y.C., 1968, Henri Gallery, Washington, 1968, 70, Riverside Mus., N.Y.C., 1970, Spectrum Gallery, 1970, 71, Eastern Mich. U., Ypsilanti, 1972, Corcoran Gallery, Washington, 1973, Razor Gallery, N.Y.C., 1975, 77, 78, 79, Grand Rapids Art Mus., 1980, Neill Gallery, N.Y.C., 1980, Detroit Inst. Arts, 1969, 70, 82, Ball State U. Gallery, Muncie, Ind., 1983, Louis K. Meisel Gallery, N.Y.C., ann. 1984-90, Summit Art Show, N.J., 1985, 69th Regement Armory, N.Y.C., 1988, Islip Art Mus., N.Y., 1993; represented in permanent collections Detroit Art Inst., Ind. U. Mus. Fine Arts, Bloomington, Ulrich Mus. Art, Wichita, Kans., Rose Art Mus., Brandeis U., Waltham, Mass., City Nat. Bank, Detroit, Greenfield Energy Corp., L.A., Best Products Co. Inc., Richmond, Kresge Art Mus., East Lansing, Mich., also numerous pvt. collections; represented by Louis K. Meisel Gallery, N.Y.C., 1984-96, Dorothy Blau Gallery, Bay Harbor Island, Fla., 1997—. Served with USN, 1951-55. Recipient Albert Kahn Assoc. Architects and Engrs. prize, 1969, Founders Purchase prize (1st prize) Detroit Art Inst., 1970, Mich. Fine Arts Competition award of excellence Birmingham-Bloomfield Art Assn., 1982; Tiffany Found. grantee, 1966, Mich. Coun. for Arts Individual Artist grantee, 1983.

DE BLASIS, JAMES MICHAEL, artistic director, producer, stage director; b. N.Y.C., Apr. 12, 1931; s. James and Sarah (de Felice) de B.; m. Ruth Hofreuter, Aug. 25, 1957; 1 child, Blythe. BFA, Carnegie Mellon U., 1959, MFA, 1960. Mem. drama faculty Carnegie Mellon U., 1960-62; head drama dept. Onondaga C.C., Syracuse, N.Y., 1963-72; head Opera Workshop, Syracuse, 1969-70; adv. of opera Corbett Found., Cin., 1971-76; gen. dir. Cin. Opera Assn., 1973-87, artistic dir., 1988-96; internat. ind. stage dir. of opera, 1962—. Artistic advisor, Pitts. Opera, Inc., 1979-83. With U.S. Army, 1951-53. Recipient award Omicron Delta Kappa, 1959, Alumni award Bellaire High Sch., 1974, award in arts adminstrn. Gov. Ohio, 1989, Post/Corbett award for performing artist Corbett Found./Cin. Post, 1989. Mem. Actors Equity, Am. Guild Mus. Artists, Drama Alumni Carnegie Mellon U., Beta Theta Pi, Omicron Delta Kappa. Republican. Episcopalian.

DE BLIJ, HARM JAN, geography educator, editor; b. Schiedam, The Netherlands, Oct. 9, 1935; s. Hendrik and Nelly (Erwich) de B.; m. Katherine Ruth Powers, Dec. 27, 1964 (div. 1972); children: Tanya Powers, Hugh James; m. Bonnie Helen Doughty, Dec. 15, 1977. BS, U. Witwatersrand, Johannesburg, Republic South Africa, 1955; MA, Northwestern U., 1957, PhD, 1959; DSc (hon.), Marshall U., 1991; HHD (hon.), R.I. Coll., 1995. Lectr. U. Natal Pietermaritzburg, Republic South Africa, 1959-60; asst. prof. Northwestern U., Evanston, Ill., 1960-61; from asst. prof. to prof. and assoc. dir. African Studies Ctr. Mich. State U., East Lansing, 1961-68; prof., chmn. dept. geography U. Miami, Coral Gables, Fla., 1968, prof., 1968-95, assoc. dean Coll. Arts and Scis., 1976-78; editor Nat. Geographic Rsch. mag. Nat. Geographic Soc., 1984-90; Disting. prof. Sch. Fgn. Svc., Georgetown U., 1990-95; scholar, scientist U. South Fla., St. Petersburg, 1995-97; John Deaver Drinko Disting. Prof. Marshall U., Huntington, W.Va., 1998—; geography editor Good Morning Am., ABC-TV, 1990-96; geography analyst NBC News, 1996-98; cons. pubs., govt. agys. Author: Africa South, 1962, Dar es Salaam: a Study in Urban Geography, 1963, A Geography of Subsaharan Africa, 1964, Systematic Political Geography, 1967, Mombasa: an African City, 1968, Geography: Regions and Concepts, 1971, Essentials of Geography, 1973, Man Shapes the Earth, 1974, Human Geography, 1976, African Survey, 1977, Wine: A Geographic Appreciation, 1983, Wine Regions of the Southern Hemisphere, 1985, Earth '88: Changing Geographic Perspectives, 1988, Physical Geography of the Global Environment, 1992, Viticulture in Geographic Perspective, 1992, Nature on the Rampage, 1994, Harm de Blij's Geography Book, 1995; editor: Jour. Geography, 1970-75, National Geographic Research, 1984-90; writer TV series on Africa, 1962-67. Fellow Northwestern U. African Studies program, 1958-59. Fellow African Studies Assn., Am. Geog. Soc. (hon.); mem. Orgn. for Tropical Studies (bd.dirs. 1971-74), Assn. Am. Geographers (councillor 1970-72, sec. 1972-75, steering com. Southeastern div. 1971-73), Phi Beta Kappa, Sigma Xi, Phi Kappa Phi.

DEBO, VINCENT JOSEPH, lawyer, manufacturing company executive; b. Bklyn., Feb. 14, 1940; s. George and Letitia (Ruggiero) D.; m. Linda Mellucci, June 25, 1966; 1 dau., Jennifer Lynn. BS, Fordham U., 1961, JD, 1964. Bar: N.Y. 1965, U.S. Dist. Ct. (so. and ea. dists.) N.Y. 1967, U.S. Tax Ct. 1969, U.S. Ct. Appeals (2d cir.) 1967, U.S. Supreme Ct. 1969. Assoc. various law firms, N.Y.C., 1964-70; corp. counsel Bangor Punta Corp., Greenwich, Conn., 1970-73; from asst. gen. counsel, asst. sec. to v.p., gen. counsel internat. Rheem Mfg. Co., N.Y.C., 1973—, dir., officer various corp. subs. and joint ventures. Mem. ABA (subcoms.). Home: 4 Greenlea Ct Westport CT 06883-3016 Office: Rheem Mfg Co 405 Lexington Ave Fl 22D New York NY 10174-0307

DEBOCK, RONALD GENE, real estate company executive; b. Buckley, Wash., Sept. 12, 1928; m. Donna J. DeBock, Sept. 24, 1949; children: Beverly J. DeBock Satter, Gary, Janice. BA, N.W. Coll., Kirkland, Wash., 1953; MDiv., Western Evangelical Sem., Portland, Oreg., 1960; AA, Tacoma (Wash.) C.C., 1979; PhD, Calif. Grad. Sch. Theology, Glendale, 1979. Ordained minister Assemblies of God Ch., 1953-96. Commd. ensign USNR, 1957, advanced through grades to lt. comdr., 1971, chaplain, 1958-71; founder, owner Rainier Rentals, Puyallup, Wash., 1975—, Fireball Publs., Puyallup, 1993—; instr. Am. sign lang. Cmty. Ednl. Opportunity, Orting, Wash., 1995-96. Author: Practice What You Preached, 1993. Active Aloha Hotel Chapels Ministry, Honolulu, 1988-96; bd. dirs. Romanian Renewal Internat., 1993-96, v.p., 1995-96; del. Pierce County Rep. Conv.; charter mem. Rep. Presdl. Task Force. Decorated Vietnam Cross of Gallantry with palm; recipient Delta Epsilon Chi award, 1975, Paul Harris award Rotary, 1992. Mem. Wash. Assn Realtors, Inc., Puyallup C. of C., Mil. Chaplains Assn. USA, VFW, DAV. Avocations: deep sea fishing, oriental languages. Office: Fireball Pubs 422 W Main Ave Ste P Puyallup WA 98371-5324

DEBOER, DAVID JAMES, transportation executive; b. Kalamazoo, Apr. 11, 1938; s. James Frederick and Marion Elaine (Teal) DeB.; m. Sandra Lou Ogden, Aug. 29, 1959; children: Kathleen, James, Christopher. AB, U. Mich., 1960, MBA, 1963. Asst. dir. market rsch. N.Y. Cen. R.R., N.Y.C., 1963-69; mgr. cargo mktg. Trans World Airlines, N.Y.C., 1969-71; dir. office of policy U.S. Dept. Transp.-Fed. R.R. Adminstrn., Washington, 1971-77; office of policy Interstate Commerce Com., Washington, 1977-78; asst. v.p. So. Pacific R.R., San Francisco, 1978-84; pres. Greenbrier Intermodal, Walnut Creek, Calif., 1984—. Author: Piggyback and Containers, 1992; contbr. articles to profl. jours. Vice chair citizens adv. com. Met. Transport Com., Bay Area, 1996. Mem. Intermodal Assn. N.Am. (bd. dirs. 1991-97, chmn. 1997, Silver Kingpin award 1997), Nat. Rail Intermodal Assn. (bd. dirs. 1982-91), Univ. Club San Francisco. Office: Greenbrier Intermodal 100 Pringle Ave Ste 450 Walnut Creek CA 94596-7151

DE BOER, PIETER CORNELIS TOBIAS, mechanical and aerospace engineering educator; b. Leiden, Netherlands, May 21, 1930; s. Pieter and Willemina (Zuydam) deB.; m. Joan Lieshout, June 7, 1956; children: Maarten P., Claire E., Yvette E. MechE degree, Delft U. Tech., 1955; PhD in Physics, U. Md., 1962. Rsch. asst., assoc. Tech. U. Delft, 1954-55; rsch. assoc. U. Md., 1957-62, rsch. asst. prof., 1962-64; asst. prof. Cornell U., 1964-68, assoc. prof., 1968-74; prof. Sibley Sch. Mech. and Aerospace Engring., Cornell U., 1974—, assoc. dir., 1982-91; mem. tech. staff Aerospace Corp., summer 1963, 65, 67, 95, 97, 99; vis. prof. von Karman Inst. for Fluid Dynamics, Belgium, 1968, Cornell Aero. Lab., Buffalo, 1969, Tech. U. Delft, 1985-86; mem. tech. staff Ford Motor Co., 1971-73, gas turbine div. GE Co., 1978-78; cons. Conelec, Elmira, N.Y., Allied Chem., Inc., Mt. Clemens, Mich., Inst. for Def. Analyses, Arlington, Va., others. Assoc. editor N.Am. Applied Scientific Rsch., 1987-98; contbr. articles to profl. jours. With Dutch Army, 1955-57. NATO fellow, 1968. Fellow AIAA (assoc.); mem. ASME, AAUP, Am. Phys. Soc., Am. Soc. Engring. Edn., Internat. Assn. Hydrogen Energy, Royal Inst. Ingenieurs (The Netherlands), Royal Netherlands Acad. Scis. (corr.), N.Y. State Ski Racing Assn./Nordic (pres.), Golden Key, Rsch. Club Cornell U., Finger Lakes Cycling Club, Finger Lakes Runners Club, Cayuga Nordic Ski Club (pres.), Sigma Xi, Pi Tau Sigma, Sigma Pi Sigma. Office: Cornell U Sibley Sch Mech Aerospace Upson Hall Ithaca NY 14853

DE BOLD, ADOLFO J., pathology and physiology educator, research scientist; b. Paraná, Argentina, Feb. 14, 1942; arrived in Can., 1968; s. Adolfo E.G. and Ana (Patriarca) deB.; m. Mercedes L. Kuroski; children: Adolfo A., Alejandro J., Cecilia I., Gustavo A., Pablo G. B.Sc. (hon.), Faculty Chem. Sci., Cordoba, Argentina, 1968; M.Sc. in Pathology, Queen's U., Kingston, Ont., 1971, PhD in Pathology, 1973. Cert. clin. chemist. Demonstrator in physics Nat. U. Cordoba, 1961-62, demonstrator normal and path. histology, 1964-67; resident, chief resident Nat. Hosp., Clinicas, Cordoba, 1966-68; asst. prof., lab. scientist Queen's U. and Hotel-Dieu Hosp., Kingston, 1974-82, assoc. prof., 1982-85, prof., 1985-86; prof. pathology and physiology U. Ottawa, Ont., Can., 1986—; bd. dirs. research U. Ottawa Heart Inst. at Ottawa Civic Hosp., 1986—. Discovered Atrial Natriuretic Hormone, 1981, patented, 1986; contbr. over 100 sci. articles and chpts. to books in field. Bd. dirs. Heart Inst., Ottawa, 1986-93. Decorated officer Order of Can.; recipient Gairdner Internat. award Gairdner Found.,

Toronto, 1986, Manning Prin. award Manning Found., Alta., Can., 1986, Sci. Achievement award Am. Soc. Hypertension, 1986, rsch. achievement award Can. Cardiovasc. Soc., 1986, CIBA award Am. Heart Assn., 1994; Disting. Rsch. Prof. award Ont. Heart and Stroke Found. Fellow Royal Soc. Can.(McLaughin medal of excellence in rsch. 1988), Royal Coll. Physicians and Surgeons (Can.), AAAS; mem. Can. Hypertension Soc., Am. Soc. for Hypertension, Internat. Soc. Hypertension (Rsch. Achievement award), Internat. Soc. Heart Rsch., Am. Sect. Can. Fedn. Biol. Socs., Histochem. Soc., U.S. Acad. Pathology, Can. Acad. Pathology, Am. Soc. Cell Biology, Can. Soc. Cell Biology, Internat. Acad. Pathology, Am. Assn. Pathology, Fedn. Am. Soc. Exptl. Biology, Microscopial Soc. Can., Soc. Exptl. Biology and Medicine, Can. Soc. Anatomy, N.Y. Acad. Sci. Roman Catholic. Avocation: classical guitar. Office: U Ottawa Heart Inst. 40 Ruskin St, Ottawa, ON Canada K1Y 4W7

DEBOLD, JOSEPH FRANCIS, psychology educator; b. Boston, Nov. 3, 1947; s. Joseph Francis and Patricia (Miltimore) DeB.; m. Carol Lynn Hook, Dec. 20, 1969. AB, UCLA, 1969; PhD, U. Calif., Irvine, 1976. Trainee U. Calif. NICHD Devel. & Reproductive Biology, Irvine, 1971-75; instr., rsch. assoc. Mich. State U., East Lansing, 1975-77; asst. prof. Carnegie-Mellon U., Pitts., 1977-79; asst. prof. Tufts U., Medford, Mass., 1979-83, assoc. prof., 1983-91, chmn. dept. psychology, 1990-93, prof., 1991—; vis. rsch. assoc. Children's Hosp. Med. Ctr., Boston, 1981-85; advisor NSF, Washington, 1989-92. Mem. editorial bd. Hormones and Behavior, 1987-92; contbr. articles to profl. jours., chpts. to books. Grantee NSF, 1986-99, Nat. Inst. Alcoholism and Alcohol Abuse, 1980—, Biomed Rsch. Support Program, 1990-91. Mem. AAAS, Soc. for Neurosci., Nat. Assn. Advisors for Health Professions, N.Y. Acad. Scis., Rsch. Soc. on Alcholism, Sigma Xi, Psi Chi. Avocations: motorcycling, tennis, volleyball. Office: Tufts U Dept Psychology Paige Hall Medford MA 02155

DE BOOR, CARL, mathematician; b. Stolp, Germany, Dec. 3, 1937; m. Matilda C. Friedrich, Feb. 6, 1960 (div. Sept. 12, 1984); children—C. Thomas, Elisabeth, Peter, Adam; m. Helen L. Bee, Jan. 2, 1991. Student, Universitaet Hamburg, 1956-59, Harvard U., 1959-60; Ph.D., U. Mich., 1966. Rsch. mathematician Gen. Motors Research Labs., 1960-64; asst. prof. math., computer sci. Purdue U., 1966-68, assoc. prof., 1968-72; prof. math., computer sci. U. Wis.-Madison, 1972—; vis. staff mem. Los Alamos Sci. Labs., 1970—. Author: (with S. Conte) Elementary Numerical Analysis, 1972, 1980, A Practical Guide to Splines, 1978, (with J.B. Rosser) Pocket Calculator Supplement for Calculus, 1979, (with K. Höllig and S. Riemenschneider) Box Splines, 1993. Named John Von Neumann lectr. Soc. Indsl. and Applied Math., 1996. Fellow Am. Acad. Arts and Scis.; mem. Nat. Acad. Engring., NAS, Soc. Indsl. and Applied Math., Leopoldina, Phi Beta Kappa. Office: U Wis Depts Computer Scis Math Madison WI 53706

DE BORCHGRAVE, ARNAUD, editor, writer, lecturer; b. Brussels, Oct. 26, 1926; s. Count Baudouin and Audrey (Townshend) de B.; m. Dorothy Solon, Apr. 1950; 1 child, Arnaud; m. Eileen Ritschel, Mar. 31, 1959; 1 child, Trisha; m. Alexandra D. Villard, May 10, 1969. Student, Maredsous, Belgium, 1936-39, King's Sch., Canterbury, Eng., 1940-42. Free-lance writer Eastern Europe, 1946-47; staff United Press, Western Europe, 1947-51; mgr. Benelux Countries, 1949-51; European Corr. Newsweek, Paris, North Africa, Middle East, Indo-China, 1951-54; fgn. editor, sr. editor Newsweek, 1955-59, chief fgn. corr., 1959-62, mng. editor internat. edits., 1962-63, chief Newsweek Corr., 1964-80; columnist, TV host; sr. assoc. Ctr. for Strategic and Internat. Studies, 1981-85; editor in chief The Washington Times and Insight Mag., 1985-91; dir. Global Organized Crime Project, sr. advisor Ctr. for Strategic and Internat. Studies, Washington, 1991—; pres., CEO UPI, 1999—. Served with Brit. Royal Navy, 1942-46. Decorated commandeur de l'Ordre de Leopold II, Medaille Maritime Belge; recipient Medal of Honor Def. Council, 1980, Medal of Honor World Bus. Council, 1981, Washington Dateline award Soc. Profl. Journalists, also numerous awards for fgn. reporting. Mem. Am. Soc. Newspaper Editors, Internat. Press Inst., Inter-Am. Press Assn., Coun. on Fgn. Rels., Racquet and Tennis Club, Met. Club, Econ. Club of Washington, Nat. Press Club. Home: 2801 New Mexico Ave NW Washington DC 20007-3921 Office: Ctr for Strategic and Internat Studies 1800 K St NW Washington DC 20006-2202

DEBOW, JAY HOWARD CAMDEN, public relations executive; b. Flushing, N.Y., Sept. 21, 1932; s. Thomas Howard and Dorothea (Camden) DeB.; m. audrey Ellison, May 4, 1957 (div. 1985); children: Stacy, Carolyn, Jennifer, Hollis; m. Suzanne Hayat, Nov. 12, 1986. AB, U. Ga., 1955. Reporter Athens (Ga.) Banner Herald, 1954; news writer UPI, N.Y.C., 1955; v.p. pub. rels. Merrill Anderson Co., N.Y.C., 1956-60; founder, pres. Jay DeBow & Ptnrs., Inc., N.Y.C., 1960-89; pres. Jay DeBow & Ptnrs. Omnicom Pub. Rels. Network, N.Y.C., 1990-92; founder, mng. prin. The Energy Team, 1993—; bd. dirs. Pub. Rels. Coun., 1997—; chmn. bd. advisors Salvation Army Manhattan. Recipient Ad Week Nat. Mktg. Program award, 1990, Cipra award Inside PR Mag., 1991. Mem. Nat. Investor Rels. Inst. (former chmn. govt. affairs com., ethics com., mem. steering com., sr. Investor Rels. Roundtable), Pub. Rels. Soc. Am. (Silver Anvil award 1991), Internat. Inst. Comms., Counselors Acad., Internat. Pub. Rels. Assn., N.Y. Soc. Security Analysts, Assn. Investment Mgrs., Soc. Profl. Journalists, Nat. Press Club (Washington), Met. Club (N.Y.C.; bd. govs., chmn., mem. com.). Home: 530 Park Ave Apt 6J New York NY 10021-8015

DEBOW, THOMAS JOSEPH, JR., advertising executive; b. N.Y.C., May 18, 1936; s. Thomas Joseph DeBow and Evelyn Francis (Brooks) Menck; m. Rosalinda Angelini, Sept. 9, 1961; children: Yvette, Thomas J III, Walter Brooks. V.p. McCann Ericson, N.Y.C., 1965-69; dir. Young and Rubicam, N.Y.C., 1969-71; pres. Curry DeBow, N.Y.C., 1971-74; v.p. BBDO, N.Y.C., 1974-76; chmn. DeBow Comm. Ltd., N.Y.C., 1976-95, DeBow Comm., Ltd., 1995—. Mem. Cystic Fibrosis Found., dir., 1988—; vice chmn. Len Caricu Entreprolebrity Golf Tournament, 1990; vice chmn. children's legacy com. Franciscan Sisters of the Poor Found., 1996—. Mem. Friar's Sunshine Com. (chmn. 1987—, Friar of Yr. 1990), Knollwood Country Club, N.Y. Athletic Club. Home: 55 E 86th St New York NY 10028-1059 Office: DeBow Comm Ltd 350 W 31st St New York NY 10001-2726

DE BRANGES DE BOURCIA, LOUIS, mathematics educator; b. Paris, Aug. 21, 1932; s. Louis and Diane (McDonald) deB.; m. Tatiana Jakimow, Dec. 17, 1980; 1 child, Konstantin. BS, MIT, 1953; PhD, Cornell U., 1957. Prof. Purdue U., Lafayette, Ind., 1962-88, disting. prof. of math., 1989—. Fellow Sloan Found., 1963-66, Guggenheim Found., 1967-68; recipient Humboldt prize Alexander Humboldt Found., 1986-88, Ostrowski prize Alexander Ostrowski Found., 1989. Home: Hameau de l'Yvette, Batiment D Chemin des Graviers, F-91190 Gif Sur Yvette France Office: Purdue U Dept Math Lafayette IN 47907-1395

DEBRECZENY, PAUL, Slavic language educator, author; b. Budapest, Hungary, Feb. 16, 1932; came to U.S., 1960; s. Zsigmond and Margit Ibolya (Csanady) D.; m. Gillian Marjorie Butterworth, Oct. 30, 1959; children: Louise, Martin. BA in Russian Studies, Eotvos U., Budapest, 1953, BA in Hungarian Studies, 1955; PhD in Russian Lit., U. London, 1960. Research assoc. Inst. Lit. Studies, Hungarian Acad. Scis., Budapest, 1955-56; trans. editor Pergamon Press, Oxford, Eng., 1959-60; from asst. to assoc. prof., dept. chmn. Tulane U., New Orleans, 1960-67; assoc. prof. U. N.C., Chapel Hill, 1967-74, prof., chmn., 1974-79, prof. Slavic langs., 1979-83, Alumni disting. prof. Russian and comparative lit., 1983—, chmn. humanities div., 1984-86; dir. Ctr. for Slavic, Eurasian and East European Studies U. N.C.-Duke U., Chapel Hill, 1991-94. Author: Nickolay Gogol and His Contemporary Critics, 1966, Temptations of the Past, 1982, The Other Pushkin, 1983, 2d rev. edit. in Russian, 1996, Social Functions of Literature: Alexander Pushkin and Russian Culture, 1997; translator: The Captain's Daughter and Other Stories by Alexander Pushkin, 1992; translator, editor: Literature and National Identity, 1970, Alexander Pushkin's Complete Prose Fiction, 1983; editor: Chekhov's Art of Writing: A Collection of Critical Essays, 1977, American Contributions to the Ninth International Congress of Slavists, Vol. 2: Literature, 1983; editor: Russian Visual and Narrative Art: Varieties of Seeing, 1994; mng. editor: The Pushkin Journal, 1993-96, the Pushkin rev., 1997-98; mem. adv. bd. Slavic and East European Jour., 1978—, Slavonica, U.K., 1984—, Studies in Short Fiction, 1990—. Awarded Golden Key City of New Orleans, 1967. Mem. AAUP, MLA, Am. Assn. Tchrs. Slavic and East European Langs. (v.p. 1978-79), Am. Assn. for Advancement of Slavic Studies, So. Conf. on Slavic Studies (v.p. 1979, pres. 1980, Sr. Scholar award 1987), N.Am. Pushkin Soc. (pres. 1993). Democrat. E-mail: pdebrecz@email.unc.edu. Home: 304 Hoot Owl Ln Chapel Hill NC 27514-2743 Office: U NC Dept Slavic Langs Chapel Hill NC 27599-3165

DEBREU, GERARD, economics and mathematics educator; b. Calais, France, July 4, 1921; came to U.S., 1950, naturalized, 1975; s. Camille and Fernande (Decharne) D.; m. Françoise Bled, June 14, 1945; children: Chantal, Florence. Student, Ecole Normale Supérieure, Paris, 1941-44, Agrégé de l'Université, France, 1946; DSc, U. Paris, 1956; Dr. Rerum Politicarum honoris causa, U. Bonn, 1977; D. Scis. Economiques (hon.), U. Lausanne, 1980; DSc (hon.), Northwestern U., 1981; Dr. honoris causa, U. des Scis. Sociales de Toulouse, 1983, Yale U., 1987, U. Bordeaux I, 1988. Rsch. assoc. Centre Nat. De La Recherche Sci., Paris, 1946-48; Rockefeller fellow U.S., Sweden and Norway, 1948-50; rsch. assoc. Cowles Commn., U. Chgo., 1950-55; assoc. prof. econs. Cowles Found., Yale, 1955-61; fellow Ctr. Advanced Study Behavioral Scis., Stanford U., 1960-61; vis. prof. econs. Yale U., fall 1961; prof. emeritus U. Calif., Berkeley, 1962—, prof. Miller Inst. Basic Rsch. in Sci., 1973-74, prof. math., 1975—, univ. prof., 1985—; Guggenheim fellow, vis. prof. Ctr. Ops. Rsch. and Econometrics, U. Louvain, 1968-69, vis. prof., 1971, 72, 88; Erskine fellow U. Canterbury, Christchurch, New Zealand, 1969, 87, vis. prof., 1973; Overseas fellow Churchill Coll., Cambridge, Eng., 1972; Plenary address Internat. Congress Mathematicians, Vancouver, 1974; vis. prof. Cowles Found. for Rsch. in Econs., Yale U., 1976; vis. prof. U. Bonn, 1977; rsch. assoc. Cepremap, Paris, 1980; faculty rsch. lectr. U. Calif., Berkeley, 1984-85, univ. prof., 1985—, Class of 1958 Chair, 1986—; vis. prof. U. Sydney, Australia, 1987; lectr. in field. Author: Theory of Value, 1959, Mathematical Economics: Twenty Papers of Gerard Debreu, 1983; assoc. editor Internat. Econ. Rev., 1959-69; mem. editorial bd. Jours. Econ. Theory, 1972—, SIAM Jours. on Applied Math., 1976-79, Jours. of Complexity, 1985—, Games and Econ. Behavior, 1989—, Econ. Theory, 1991; mem. adv. bd. Jours. Math. Econs., 1974—; correspondent Math. Intelligencer, 1983-84. Served with French Army, 1944-45. Decorated Chevalier de la Légion d'Honneur, Commandeur de l'Ordre National du Mérite, Officier Le Légion d'Honneur; recipient Nobel Prize in Econ. Scis., 1983, Berkeley Citation, 1991; sr. U.S. Sci. awardee Alexander von Humboldt Found., 1977. Fellow AAAS, Econometric Soc. (mem. coun. 1964-72, 78-85, Fisher-Schultz lectr. 1969, exec. com. 1969-72, 80-82, pres. 1971), Am. Econ. Assn. (disting. fellow 1982, pres.-elect 1989, pres. 1990); mem. NAS (chmn. sect. econ. scis. 1982-85, com. human rights 1984-90, chair class V behavioral and social scis. 1989-92, mem. Coun. of NAS of USA 1993—), Am. Philos. Soc., French Acad. Scis. (fgn. assoc.), Berkeley Fellows.

DE BRIER, DONALD PAUL, lawyer; b. Atlantic City, Mar. 20, 1940; s. Daniel and Ethel de B.; m. Nancy Lee McElroy, Aug. 1, 1964; children: Lesley Anne, Rachel Wynne, Danielle Verne. B.A. in History, Princeton U., 1962; LL.B. with honors, U. Pa., 1967. Bar: N.Y. 1967, Tex. 1977, Utah 1983, Ohio 1987. Assoc. firm Sullivan & Cromwell, N.Y.C., 1967-70, Patterson, Belknap, Webb & Tyler, N.Y.C., 1970-76; v.p., gen. counsel, dir. Gulf Resources & Chem. Corp., Houston, 1976-82; v.p. law Kennecott Corp. (former subs. BP America Inc.), Salt Lake City, 1983-89; assoc. gen. counsel BP America Inc., Cleve., 1987-89; gen. counsel BP Exploration Co. Ltd., London, 1989-93; exec. v.p., gen. counsel Occidental Petroleum Corp., L.A., 1993—. Bd. dirs. L.A. Philharm., 1995—. Served to lt. USNR, 1962-64. Mem. Calif. Club, Riviera Tennis Club. Home: 699 Amalfi Dr Pacific Palisades CA 90272-4507 Office: Occidental Petroleum Corp 10889 Wilshire Blvd Los Angeles CA 90024-4201

DE BRIGARD, EMILIE, anthropologist, consultant; b. N.Y.C., Dec. 11, 1943; d. A. Lincoln and Ruth Emilie (Jaeger) Rahman; m. Raul de Brigard, June 11, 1966; 1 child, George. BA, Harvard Coll., 1963; MA, U. Calif., 1972. Guest curator dept. of film Mus. of Modern Art, N.Y.C., 1972-73; asst. to dir. human studies film archives Smithsonian Instn., Washington, 1975-77; prin. programmer Margaret Mead Film Festival Am. Mus. Natural History, N.Y.C., 1977-78; faculty Harvard Summer Sch., Cambridge, Mass., 1980-86; pres. Internat. Film Seminars, Inc., N.Y.C., 1981-83; vis. lectr. dept. anthropology Yale U., New Haven, Conn., 1989-91; pres. Soc. for Visual Anthropology, Washington, 1995-97, FilmResearch, Higganum, Conn., 1970—; cons. Choreometrics Project, N.Y.C., 1970-73; mem. Comité Internat. des Films de l'Homme, Paris, 1977—. Author: (books) The History of Ethnographic Film, 1971, Anthropological Cinema, 1973, Cine Antropológico, 1978; producer (film) Margaret Mead: A Portrait by a Friend, 1978. Elector Wadsworth Atheneum, Hartford, Conn., 1985-94, 1996—; corporator Conn. Inst. for the Blind-Oak Hill, Hartford, Conn., 1996—. Recipient scholarship Harvard U., Cambridge, Mass., 1963-64, fellowship, Yale U., New Haven, Conn., 1987-88; grantee: Wenner-Gren Found., N.Y.C., 1970-72, Tinker Found., N.Y.C., 1976. Fellow Am. Anthrop. Assn., Royal Anthrop. Inst.; mem. Soc. Woman Geographers, Town and County Club, Quinnipiack Club, Harvard Club of So. Conn. (v.p. 1995—), Saturday Morning Club. Avocations: costume and textiles. Home: 285 Riverside Dr Apt 7E New York NY 10025-5266 Office: FilmResearch 8 Christian Hill Rd Higganum CT 06441-4030

DEBRINCAT, SUSAN JEANNE, nutritionist; b. Detroit, Oct. 7, 1943; d. Lloyd Brode and Florence Claire (Majewski) Greenleaf; m. Raymond Frank DeBrincat, June 19, 1965; children: David Lloyd, Mark Joseph. BS magna cum laude, Mich. State U., 1965. Cert. med. technologist, Am. Soc. Clin. Pathologists. Med. technologist Harper Hosp., Detroit, 1965-66, South Macomb Hosp., Warren, Mich., 1966; art teacher YWCA, Berkley, Mich., 1969-80; master coord. Shaklee Corp., West Bloomfield, Mich., 1977—; lifetime master Shaklee Corp., West Bloomfield, 1990—, sr. master coord., facilitator for pacific inst., 1997—; nutritional counselor, fashion, color, image, makeup counselor, mgmt. and leadership trainer, motivational speaker, pres. club & found. club for Shaklee Corp.; interior designer. Painter oil, acrylic, watercolors. Mem. Rep. Nat. Com. Pres.'s Club, Found. Club, Phi Kappa Phi, Delta Zeta. Roman Catholic. Avocations: painting, art and antiques, reading, travel. Office: DeBrincat Assocs 30475 Birchway Dr Franklin MI 48025-1503

DEBRO, JULIUS, university dean, sociology educator; b. Jackson, Miss., Sept. 25, 1931; s. Joseph and Seleana (Gaylor) D.; m. Darlene Conley; children—Renee Denys, Blair. B.A. in Polit. Sci., U. San Francisco, 1953; M.A. in Sociology, San Jose State U., 1967; Ph.D., U. Calif.-Berkeley, 1975. Research asst. U. Calif. Sch. Criminology, Berkeley, 1964-68; instr. dept. sociology Laney Coll., Alameda, Calif., 1968-69, Alameda Coll., Oakland, Calif., 1971, U. Md., College Park, 1971-72; asst. prof. Inst. for Criminal Justice and Criminology U. Md., 1972-79; mem. faculty Atlanta U., 1979-91, prof. criminal justice, 1979-91, chmn. dept. pub. adminstrn., 1979-80, chmn. dept. Criminal Justice Inst., 1979-89, chmn. dept. sociology, 1985-86; assoc. dean Grad. Sch., acting asst. provost U. Wash., Seattle, 1991—, affiliate prof. society and justice program, 1991—; mem. adv. bd. dirs. Criminal Justice Rev., 1977-87; prin. investigator Joint Commn. on Criminology and Criminal Justice Edn. and Standards, 1978-79; v.p. Atlanta Met. Crime Commn., 1986, pres., 1987; mem. investigative bd. Ga. Bar Assn., 1987; editor Blacks in Criminal Justice quar. news mag., 1987—. Assoc. editor Criminal Justice Quar., 1989—. Chmn. program evaluation com. Boys and Girls Home, Montgomery County, Md., 1979; bd. dirs. YMCA, Bethesda, Md., 1979, Totem Coun. Girl Scouts. Served to col. USAR, 1953-84. NIMH fellow, 1969-70; Ford fellow, 1971; grantee NIMH, 1974, Law Enforcement Assistance Adminstrn., 1979-81; postdoctoral rsch. assoc. Narcotic and Drug Rsch. Inc., N.Y.C., 1989-90; Inter-Univ. Seminar on Armed Forces and Soc. fellow, 1989; Western Soc. Criminology fellow, 1989; recipient Herbert Bloch award for Outstanding Svcs. to Criminal Justice Criminology, svc. to Am. Soc. Criminology. Fellow Narcotic Drug Rsch.; mem. NAACP, Nat. Assn. Blacks in Criminal Justice (editor quar. news mag. 1987—), Nat. Assn. Black Sociologists, Am. Sociol. Assn., Acad. Criminal Justice Sci., Urban League, Rotary, Alpha Phi Alpha, Sigma Pi Phi (boule Alpha Omicron chpt.). Democrat. Home: 11531 36th Ave NE Seattle WA 98125-5632 Office: U Wash 201 Adminstrn Bldg AG-10 Seattle WA 98195

DE BROUX, PEGGY C., English educator, French educator, publisher; b. Skidmore, Tex., Jan. 14, 1935; d. Robert Willis and Evelyn Laura (Wooten) King; m. Bob Cole, June 4, 1954 (div. July 1964); children: Heather Kay, Michael Harold; m. Jay de Broux, July 14, 1970 (dec.). BA in Comparative Lit., U. Wash., 1967, MA in Comparative Lit., 1968; MA in French, U. B.C., 1976. Instr. comparative lit. Hiram Scott Coll., Scottsbluff, Nebr., 1970-71; instr. English and French Flagler Coll., St. Augustine, Fla., 1972-74; legal sec. Atty. Gen.'s Office, Seattle, 1989-93; instr. English and French Peninsula Coll., Port Angeles, Wash., 1993—; owner, operator Strait Pub., Port Angeles, 1994—; co-chair grad. fgn. lang. seminars 35th Fgn. Lang. Conf., U. Ky., Lexington, 1982; facilitator 5-week creative writing workshops Strait Pub. Pres. Olympic Unitarian-Universalist Fellowship, Port Angeles, 1995-97. Naomi Clark scholar Port Townsend (Wash.) Writers' Conf., 1995. Mem. AAUW, MLA, Macintosh Users Group (sec. Port Angeles chpt.). Democrat. Avocations: reading, piano, walking. Home: 240 W 3rd St Port Angeles WA 98362-2827

DE BRUHL, MARSHALL, writer, editor, publishing consultant; b. Woodfin, N.C., Nov. 3, 1935; s. Arthur Marvin and Janie Myra (Wright) De B. AB, Duke U., 1958. Editor U. Pa. Press, 1963-64; mem. editorial staff Crowell-Collier Macmillan, 1964-67; with Charles Scribner's Sons, N.Y.C., 1967-85; mng. editor Dictionary Sci. Biography, Dictionary of Middle Ages Charles Scribner's Sons, v.p., dir. Reference Book div.; then sr. v.p. Scribner Book Cos., Inc.; with Doubleday Pub. Co., N.Y.C., 1986-88; exec. editor Anchor Press; cons. editor HarperCollins, 1988-91, Henry Holt, 1992-94. Author: Sword of San Jacinto: A Life of Sam Houston, 1993; co-editor: International Thesaurus of Quotations, 1996. Lt. (j.g.) USNR, 1959-62. Mem. PEN. Club: Century Assn. Home: 8 Outlook Ave East Hampton NY 11937-1238 also: 148 Elk Mount Rd Asheville NC 28804

DEBS, BARBARA KNOWLES, former college president, consultant; b. Eastham, Mass., Dec. 24, 1931; d. Stanley F. and Arline (Eugley) Knowles; m. Richard A. Debs, July 19, 1958; children: Elizabeth, Nicholas. BA, Vassar Coll., 1953; PhD, Harvard U., 1967; LLD, N.Y. Law Sch., 1979; LHD, Manhattanville Coll., 1985. Freelance translation editor Ency. of World Art divsn. McGraw-Hill Pub., N.Y.C., 1959-62; from asst. prof. to prof. Manhattanville Coll., Purchase, N.Y., 1968-86, pres., 1975-85; trustee, chmn. collections com. N.Y. Hist. Soc., 1985-87, pres., CEO, 1988-92; cons. non-profit orgns. pvt. practice, 1992—. Contbr. articles on Renaissance and contemporary art to profl. publs. Mem. N.Y. Council Humanities, 1978-85; mem. Westchester Med. Ctr. Hosp. Implementation Bd., 1978-84; mem. Westchester County Bd. Ethics, 1979-84; trustee N.Y. Law Sch., 1979-89; trustee Geraldine R. Dodge Found., 1985—; bd. dirs. Internat. Found. for Art Rsch., 1985-92; trustee Com. Econ. Devel., 1985-94, Bklyn. Mus. Art, 1996—; ; mem. Coun. Fgn. Rels., 1983—; mem. Commn. Ind. Colls. and Univs. of N.Y., 1977-79; mem. com. on higher edn., adv. council to Dems. N.Y. State Senate, 1979-85; mem. exec. bd. Bard Ctr. for Decorative Arts, 1995—; mem. adv. bd. Greenwich Hist. Soc., 1995—; bd. govs. Fgn. Policy Assn., 1996—; hon. trustee Manhattanville Coll., 1996—, Midori Found., 1998—. AAUW Nat. fellow and Ann Radcliffe fellow, 1958-59; Am. Council Learned Socs. grantee, 1973; Fulbright fellow Scuola Normale, Pisa, Italy, 1953, U. Rome, 1954. Mem. Am. Coun. on Edn. (chmn. commn. acad. affairs 1977-79), Young Audiences (nat. dir. 1977-80), Renaissance Soc. Am., Coll. Art Assn., Phi Beta Kappa. Club: Cosmpolitan, Century Assn.

DEBS, RICHARD A., investment banker; b. Providence, Oct. 7, 1930; s. Abraham George and Madge (Fatool) D.; m. Barbara Knowles, July 19, 1958; children: Elizabeth Anderson, Nicholas. BA summa cum laude, Colgate U., 1952; postgrad. (Fulbright scholar), Cairo U., 1952-53; MA, Princeton U., 1956, PhD, 1963; LLB, Harvard U., 1958, grad. Advanced Mgmt. Program, 1973. Bar: N.Y. 1960. Researcher joint project Harvard-Princeton, 1958-59; with Fed. Res. Bank of N.Y., N.Y.C., 1960-76; legal dept. Fed. Res. Bank of N.Y., 1960-64, asst. counsel, 1964-69, sec. of bank, 1965-69, v.p. govt. bonds and securities, 1969-72, v.p. loans and credits, 1969-72, v.p. open market ops., 1972, sr. v.p., 1973, 1st v.p., chief adminstrv. officer, 1973-76; alt. mem. Fed. Open Market Com., 1973-76; mng. dir. Morgan Stanley & Co., Inc., 1976-87; pres. Morgan Stanley Internat. Inc., 1976-87; chmn. R.A. Debs & Co., 1987—; adv. dir. Morgan Stanley Group, 1987—; chmn. The Malaysia Fund Inc., 1987—; bd. dirs. IBJ Schroder Bank & Trust Co., Aubrey G. Lanston & Co., Saudi Internat. Bank, London; advisor Bank Julius Baer, 1987—, United Gulf Group (Kuwait), 1987—, Dai-Ichi Mut. Life, Tokyo, 1988—, Nissho Iwai Corp., Tokyo, 1990—; chmn. com. fiscal agy. ops. Fed. Res. System, 1969-76; mem. Fed. Res. Steering Com. on Payments Mechanism, 1973-76, Fed. Res. Steering Com. on Internat. Banking, 1973-76; allied mem. N.Y. Stock Exchange, also chmn. adv. com. internat. capital markets; mem. com. multinat. enterprises U.S. coun. Internat. Bus.; mem. internat. capital markets adv. com. Fed. Res. Bank of N.Y.; mem. Nat. Commn. on Pub. Svc. (The Volcker Commn.); mem. Overseas Devel. Coun.; mem. U.S. Office Pers. Mgmt. Task Force on Pay Reform; mem. World Bank Adv. Group on Pvt. Sector Devel.; mem. bus. adv. coun. European Bank for Reconstrn. and Devel., Russian-Am. Banking Forum; mem. Take Stock in Am. Com., 1973-76; mem. Egypt-U.S. Bus. Coun.; mem. adv. coun. Near Eastern program Princeton U.; mem. N.Y. State Savs. Bond Com., 1973-76; adv. coun. Am. Inst. Banking, 1973-76. Contbr. articles on internat. banking to profl. publs. Chmn. emeritus, trustee Carnegie Hall; bd. dirs. Fedn. Protestant Welfare Agys.; trustee Carnegie Endowment for Internat. Peace, Am. Univs. Field Staff; trustee Am. U., Beirut, vice chmn., 1981-94, chmn., 1994—; bd. dirs. Am. Council on Germany; mem. vis. com. Middle East Center Harvard U., 1976-82, mem. vis. com. Ctr. for Internat. Affairs; mem. Group of 30; also mem. exec. com. Bretton Woods Com.; U.S. chmn. U.S.-Saudi Arabia Bus. Coun. Mem. ABA (com. Middle Eastern law), Assn. Bar City N.Y., Coun. Fgn. Rels., C. of C. U.S. (internat. policy com., chmn. subcom. on internat. econ. devel. 1979-87), Egyptian Am. C. of C. (chmn.), N.Y. C. of C. and Industry, Japan Soc., Asia Soc., Fgn. Policy Assn. (bd. govs.), Econs. Club, Century Assn. (N.Y.C.), Larchmont Yacht (N.Y.), River Club, Phi Beta Kappa Assocs. Office: Morgan Stanley & Co 1221 Ave of Americas New York NY 10020-1001

DEBUNDA, SALVATORE MICHAEL, lawyer; b. Phila., June 17, 1943; s. Salvatore and Marie Ann (Carilli) DeB.; children: Lauren, David. BS in Econs., U. Pa., 1965, JD, 1968. Bar: Pa. 1968, U.S. Supreme Ct. 1977. Law clk. to justice Phila. Ct. of Common Pleas, 1968-69; asst. gen. counsel ARA Services, Inc., Phila., 1969-74; sr. assoc. Cohen, Verlin, Sherzer & Porter, Phila., 1974-75; v.p., sec., gen. counsel AEL Industries, Inc., Montgomeryville, Pa., 1975-80; v.p., gen. counsel Cooper Assocs., Inc., Marlton, N.J., 1980-81; v.p. cable TV devel. Greater Media, Inc., East Brunswick, N.J., 1981-85; ptnr., chmn. media/entertainment law group Fox, Rothschild, O'Brien & Frankel, Phila., 1985-91; shareholder, dir. Pelino & Lentz, PC, Phila., 1991—. Mem. ABA, Pa. Bar Assn., Phila. Bar Assn., Fed. Comm. Bar Assn. Avocations: sports, owning thoroughbred horses. Office: Pelino & Lentz PC One Liberty Pl 32d Fl Philadelphia PA 19103-7393

DEBUONO, BARBARA ANN, physician, state official; b. N.Y.C., Apr. 13, 1955; d. Richard Francis and Catherine (Brutto) DeB.; m. David Lavington Farren, June 1, 1980; children: Adam, Douglas. BS, U. Rochester, 1976, MD, 1980; MPH, Harvard U., 1984. Diplomate Am. Bd. Internal Medicine, Nat. Bd. Med. Examiners. Intern in internal medicine New Eng. Deaconess Hosp., Boston, 1980-81, jr. med. resident, 1981-82, sr. med. resident, 1982-83; clin. fellow Brown U., Providence, 1984-86, clin. instr. dept. medicine, 1987-90, clin. asst. prof. medicine, 1990—; med. epidemiologist R.I. Dept. Health, Providence, 1986, state epidemiologist, med. dir. Office Disease Control, 1986-91; dir. dept. health State of R.I., 1991-94; commr. NY State Dept. Health, Albany, 1994—; lectr. in field. Contbr. articles to profl. jours. Apptd. commr. of health by Gov. George E. Pataki, State of N.Y., 1995—. Robert Wood Johnson Found. Ednl. scholar U. Rochester Sch. Med., 1976-80; recipient James L. Tulis Disting. Study Lectureship award New Eng. Deaconess Hosp., 1992; named Women of Yr. by Bus. and Profl. Women's Club Providence, 1989, Person of Yr. by The Women's Youth League R.I., 1990, Woman of Yr. by R.I. Fedn. Bus. and Profl. Women's Clubs, 1991. Fellow ACIP, Am. Coll. Physicians (mem. CDC cancer project adv. panel 1992—); mem. AMA, APHA, Am. Soc. Microbiology, Assn. State and Territorial Health Officials (sec.-treas., mem. HIV com. 1989—, mem. breast and cervical cancer com. 1991—, mem. immunizations task force 1991—), Coun. State and Territorial Epidemiologists (mem. HIV com. 1989-91, mem. exec. com. 1991), Infectious Disease Soc. Am., Providence Med. Assn., R.I. Med. Soc. (mem. AIDS exec. com. 1988—), R.I. Med. Women's Assn. (R.I. Women Physician of Yr. 1988), R.I. Environ. Health Assn., Hosp. Assn. R.I. (mem. AIDS task force 1988—), Am. Coll. Physicians (mem. R.I. chpt., mem. exec. coun.), Women Execs. in Govt. Avocations: swimming, tennis, gardening. Office: NY State Dept of Health Corning Tower Empire State Plaza Albany NY 12237*

DE BURLO, COMEGYS RUSSELL, JR., investment advisor, educator; b. Phila.; s. Comegys Russell and Margaret (Whitehurst) de B.; m. Edith Power Thatcher; children: Jane Thatcher, Charles Russell, John Todd. BS, Swarthmore Coll.; MBA, U. Pa.; DBA, Harvard U. Past CFO Tufts U., v.p., prof., treas., hon. treas.; v.p. Ednl. Testing Svc., Princeton, N.J.; dir. UST Corp., NIH, Nat. Cancer Inst., Cancer Program Adv. Com., Cancer Rsch. Ctrs. Rev. Com., Am. Coun. on Edn., Com. on Taxation; pres., prin. The de Burlo Group Inc., 1987—. Past adv. com. No. Calif. Cancer Program; past mem. sci. adv. com. U. N.Mex. Cancer Treatment Ctr., Ohio State U. Comprehensive Cancer Ctr., 1983-97; pres. Mass. Assn. Schs. and Colls.; trustee Cambridge Friends Sch., Belmont Hill Sch., Moses Brown Sch., Lincoln Sch., BB&N Sch.; bd. mgrs. New Eng. Yearly Meeting; commr. pub. trust funds. With USNR. Fellow Royal Hort. Soc.; mem. Nat. Coun. Univ. Rsch. Adminstrs., Nat. Assn. Coll. and Univ. Bus. Officers, Assn. for Investment, Mgmt. and Rsch., Boston Security Analysts Soc., Internat. Assn. for Comparative Rsch. on Leukemia and Related Diseases (treas.), Am. Rhododendron Soc. (treas. Mass. chpt.), Swarthmore Coll. Alumni Coun., Harvard Club, Green Mountain Club, Appalachian Mountain Club, Am. Rhododendron Soc. (treas. Mass. chpt.), Tau Beta Pi. Office: 50 Federal St Boston MA 02110-2500

DEBUS, ALLEN GEORGE, history educator; b. Chgo., Aug. 16, 1926; s. George Walter William and Edna Pauline (Schwenneke) D.; m. Brunilda Lopez-Rodriguez, Aug. 25, 1951; children: Allen Anthony George, Richard William, Karl Edward. B.S., Northwestern U., 1947; A.M., Ind. U., 1949; Ph.D., Harvard U., 1961; postgrad., U. Coll. London, 1959-60; D.Sc. h.c., Cath. U. Louvain, 1985. Research chemist Abbott Labs., North Chicago, Ill., 1951-56; asst. prof. U. Chgo., 1961-65, assoc. prof. history, 1965-68, prof., 1968-78, Morris Fishbein prof. history sci. and medicine, 1978-96, Morris Fishbein prof. emeritus, 1996—; dir. Morris Fishbein Ctr. for Study History Sci. and Medicine, 1971-77; Disting. vis. prof. Ariz. ctr. for medieval and renaissance studies Ariz. State U., 1984; vis. prof. Inst. Chemistry, U. São Paulo, Brazil, 1990; mem. internat. adv. com. Tel-Aviv U. The Cohn Inst. History and Philosophy of Sci. and Ideas, Ctr. for History and Philosophy of Sci. of Hebrew U. of Jerusalem; mem. internat. adv. bd. Annali dell'Istituto e Museo di Storia della Scienza di Firenze; cons. lit. and sci. curriculum Ga. Inst. Tech. Author: The English Paracelsians, 1965, 66, (with Robert P. Multhauf) Alchemy and Chemistry in the 17th Century, 1966, The Chemical Dream of the Renaissance, 1968, 2d edit., 1972, Science and Education in the 17th Century, 1970, (with Brian Rust) The Complete Entertainment Discography, 1973, 2d rev. edit., 1989, The Chemical Philosophy, 2 vols., 1977, Man and Nature in the Renaissance, 1978, 15th rev. edit., 1995, Italian transl., 1982, Spanish transl., 1985, 86, 2d edit., 1995, Japanese transl., 1986, Chinese transl., 1988, Greek transl., 1997, Robert Fludd and His Philosophical Key, 1979; Science and History: A Chemist's Appraisal, 1984, Chemistry, Alchemy and the New Philosophy, 1550-1700, 1987, The French Paracelsians: The Chemical Challenge to Medical and Scientific Tradition in Early Modern France, 1991, Paracelso e la Tradizione Paracelsiana, 1996; editor: World Who's Who in Science from Antiquity to the Present, 1968, Science, Medicine and Society in the Renaissance, 2 vols, 1972, Medicine in Seventeenth-Century England, 1974; editor reprint: Theatrum Chemicum Britannicum (1652), 1967, John Dee's Mathematicall Praeface (1570), 1975; editor: (with Ingrid Merkel) Hermeticism and the Renaissance: Intellectual History and the Occult in Early Modern Europe, 1988, (with Michael T. Walton) Reading the Book of Nature: The Other Side of the Scientific Revolution, 1998; mem. bd. adv. editors Physis Rivista internazionale de storia della scienza, Nuncius, The 16th Century Jour.; adv. editor: History of Science; hon. bd. editors Incognita; programmed 3 records released by Smithsonian Instn. Music of Victor Herbert, 1979; contbr. articles to profl. jours. Social Sci. Rsch. Coun. fellow, 1959-60; Fulbright fellow, 1959-60; Fels Found. fellow, 1960-61; Guggenheim fellow, 1966-67; overseas fellow Churchill Coll. Cambridge (Eng.) U., 1966-67, 69; mem. Inst. Advanced Study Princeton, N.J., 1972-73; NEH fellow Newberry Libr., Chgo., 1975-76; fellow Inst. for Rsch. in Humanities U. Wis., Madison, 1981-82, NEH, 1987, Folger Shakespeare Libr., Washington; rsch. grantee Am. Philos. Soc., 1961-62, Wellcome Trust, 1962, NIH, 1962-70, 74-75, 77-78, 92-97, NSF, 1961-63, 71-74, 80-83, Am. Coun. Learned Socs., 1966, 70, 71. Fellow AAAS (mem. electorate nominating com., sect. L 1974-77, chmn. com. 1974); mem. History of Sci. Soc. (council 1962-65, 87-90, program chmn. 1972, Pfizer award 1978, Sarton medal 1994, Disting. lectr. 1996), Soc. Study Alchemy and Early Chemistry (mem. council 1967—), Am. Assn. for History Medicine (program com. 1975), Brit. Soc. for History Sci., Internationale Paracelsus Gesellschaft, Am. Chem. Soc. (asso. mem. history of chemistry div., exec. com. 1969-72, Dexter award 1987), Soc. Med. History of Chgo. (sec.-treas. 1971-72, v.p. 1972-74, pres. 1974-76, mem. council), Académie Internat. d'Histoire de la Medecine, Société Internationale d'Histoire de la Medecine, Academie Internat. d'Histoire des Scis. (corr. 1971, membre effectif 1991), Am. Inst. History of Pharmacy (Edward Kremers award 1978, adv. panel hist. activity 1979-81, awards com. 1981—), Am. Soc. Reformation Research, Assn. Recorded Sound Collections, Midwest Junto for History of Sci. (pres. 1983-84), Academia das Ciencias de Lisboa. Patentee in field. Office: U Chgo Dept History Chicago IL 60637

DEBUS, ELEANOR VIOLA, retired business management company executive; b. Buffalo, May 19, 1920; d. Arthur Adam and Viola Charlotte (Pohl) D.; student Chown Bus. Sch., 1939. Sec., Buffalo Wire Works, 1939-45; home talent producer Empire Producing Co., Kansas City, Mo., sec. Owens Cornig Fiberglass, Buffalo; pub. rels. and publicity Niagara Falls Theatre, Ont., Can.; pub. rels. dir. Woman's Internat. Bowling Congress, Columbus, Ohio, 1957-59; publicist, sec. Ice Capades, Hollywood, Calif., 1961-63; sec. to contr. Rexall Drug Co., L.A., 1963-67; bus. mgmt. acct. Samuel Berke & Co., Beverly Hills, Calif., 1967-75; Gadbois Mgmt. Co., Beverly Hills, 1975-76; sec., treas. Sasha Corp., L.A., 1976-92; former bus. mgr. Dean Martin, Debbie Reynolds, Shirley MacLaine. Mem. Am. Film Inst. Republican. Contbr. articles to various mags.

DEBUSK, F. AMANDA, export administration executive. BA, U. Richmond; JD, Harvard U. Ptnr. internat. trade dept. O'Melveny & Myers, LLP; asst. sec. export enforcement Dept. of Commerce, Washington. Office: Dept of Commerce Bur Export Adminstrn 14th and Constitution NW Washington DC 20230

DEBUSK, MANUEL CONRAD, lawyer, business executive; b. Grosvenor, Tex., June 13, 1914; s. Elias C. and Ollie (Lewis) DeB.; m. Jean Shelley Henry, Jan. 18, 1992. B.A., Tex. Technol. Coll., 1933; LL.B., So. Meth. U., 1941. Bar: Tex. 1942. Adminstrv. asst. FHA, Washington, Dallas, 1934-41; spl. agt. FBI, 1941-46; partner DeBusk & DeBusk, Dallas, 1946—. Mem., chmn. coordinating bd. Tex. Colls. and Univs., 1969-70; Chmn. Dallas County Dem. Party, 1967-71; bd. dirs., chmn. bd. regents Tex. Technol. Coll., 1959-65; pres. DeBusk Found., Assn. Small Founds.; mem. Coun. on Founds. Mem. Tex. Bar Assn., Tex., Nat. mortgage bankers assns., Nat. Lefthanded Golf Assn. (past pres.), Cosmopolitan Internat. (past internat. pres.). Home: 7365 Elmridge Dr Dallas TX 75240-3623 Office: 2089 N Collins Blvd Richardson TX 75080-2664 *One's yardstick, whether business or avocation, must be to leave the world a better place that it was before you touched it.*

DEBUSSCHERE, DAVID ALBERT, brokerage executive, retired professional basketball player and team executive; b. Detroit, Oct. 16, 1949; s. Marcel D. and Dorothy D. DeB.; m. Gerri Warnock, 1968; children: Michelle, Peter, Dennis. Grad., Detroit U., 1962. Baseball player, pitcher Chgo. White Sox, Am. League, 1962-63; basketball player, coach Detroit Pistons, NBA, 1962-68; basketball player N.Y. Knickerbockers, 1968-74, mem. world champion team, 1970, 73, former exec. v.p., dir. basketball ops.; v.p., gen. mgr. N.Y. Nets, Am. Basketball Assn., 1974-75; commr. Am. Basketball Assn., 1975-76; v.p. Williamson, Picket & Gross Inc., N.Y.C. Author: The Open Man, 1970. Player NBA All-Star Team, 1966-68, 70-73. Office: Williamson Picket & Gross Inc 85 John St 8th Fl New York NY 10038*

DECAMINADA, JOSEPH PIO, insurance company executive, educator; b. Gebo, Wyo., Oct. 17, 1935; s. Pio and Ida (Franch) D.; m. Genevieve Caputo, Aug. 30, 1958; 1 child, Joseph. BA magna cum laude, St. Francis Coll., 1956; JD, St. John's U., 1959; postgrad., Harvard U., 1978-79. CPCU, CLU; chartered fin. cons. From corp. sec. to sr. v.p., sec. Atlantic Mut. Ins. Co., Centennial Ins. Co., N.Y.C., 1971-86, exec. v.p., sec., 1986-96; past chmn. bd. dirs. CPCU-Harry J. Loman Found., Motor Vehicle Accident Indemnification Corp., N.Y. Property Ins. Underwriting Assn., Ind. Fedn. N.Y. Contbr. articles to profl. jours. Chmn. bd. dirs. Coll. Mt. St. Vincent, Riverdale, N.Y. Decorated Knight of Malta; recipient Brotherhood award NCCJ, 1991; named Ins. Man of Yr. Recovery Forum, 1978; Anglo-Am. fellow B.D. Cooke & Ptnrs., Ltd., London, 1966. Mem. Soc. CPCU (nat. pres. 1984-85, Disting. Svc. award 1989, Eugene A. Toale Meml. award N.Y. chpt. 1974), Soc. CLU, World Trade Club. Home: 3 Ridgecrest N Scarsdale NY 10583-2013

DECAMP, GRAYDON, journalist; b. Cin., Feb. 6, 1934; s. James Milton and Anne Hetherington (Graydon) DeC.; m. Diane Johnson, Aug. 18, 1956 (div. Sept. 6, 1988); 1 child, James Douglass; m. Sherrill Snooks, Apr. 20, 1991. A.B., Williams Coll., 1956. Tchr. English Eaglebrook Sch., Deerfield, Mass., 1956-57; reporter, columnist Cin. Post, 1960-68, city editor, 1969-70; politics editor Cin. Enquirer, 1970-74, asst. city editor, 1975; editor Enquirer mag., Cin., 1976-81; freelance writer.; sr. editor Traverse mag., Prism Publs., Traverse City, Mich., 1989-94; pub., editor Bayshore Books, Elk Rapids, 1994—; adj. faculty Coll. Mount St. Joseph, Cin., 1983-89. Author: Blue and Gold: The Annapolis Story, 1975, The Grand Old Lady of Vine Street: A History of the Cincinnati Enquirer, 1991; editor: 100 Years at Mackinac, 1995, (with Sherill DeCamp) The Connoisseur Up North, A Food-Lover's Guide to Northern Michigan, 1996. Mem. adv. bd. Hoxworth Blood Ctr., Cin., 1981-88, chmn., 1986-88; bd. dirs. Better Housing League, Cin., 1983-86, Joy Outdoor Edn. Ctr., Cin., 1984-89; co-chmn. Cin. Housing Partnership, 1983-85; trustee Asgard/Goodwill, Traverse City, 1990-92; mem. bd. dirs. Traverse Symphony Orch., Traverse City, Mich., 1991—, pres., 1994-95. Mem. Soc. Profl. Journalists (pres. chpt. 1974, dir. 1975). *

DE CANI, JOHN STAPLEY, statistician, educator; b. Canton, Ohio, May 8, 1924; s. John Mustin and Ada Louise (Stapley) deC.; m. Jessie Montrose Farr, Dec. 17, 1955 (dec. Sept. 1969). B.S., U. Wis., 1948; M.B.A., U. Pa., 1951, Ph.D., 1958. Mem. faculty U. Pa., Phila., 1948—; assoc. prof. stats. U. Pa., 1963-72, prof., 1972-95; prof. emeritus, 1995—; chmn. dept. stats. U. Pa., 1972-78; cons. to cos., agys., including USN, 1957—, NAACP., 1967—, EEOC, 1976—. Author: (with R. C. Clelland) Basic Statistics, 1973; contbr. articles to profl. jours. Served with USAAF, 1943-45. Recipient Distinguished Teaching award Lindbach Found., 1964; recipient Wharton disting. teaching award, 1978, 95, 97; Fulbright grantee Norway, 1959-60. Fellow Am. Statis. Assn., Royal Statis. Soc.; mem. Inst. Math. Statistics, Biometric Soc. Clubs: Royal Norwegian Yacht (Oslo); Sailing of Chesapeake. Home: 226 W Rittenhouse Sq Apt 1715 Philadelphia PA 19103-5709

DECARLO, DEENA M., mortgage company executive; b. Greenwich, Conn., Aug. 26, 1967; d. James Vito and Grace Joyce (Chiappetta) DeC. BA, Fordham U., 1989. Closing coord. Lomas Mortgage USA, Stamford, Conn., 1989; closing coord. Fleet Mortgage Svcs., Stamford, 1990, corp. svcs. coord., 1990-91, mgr. ops., tng. mgr., 1991-92; sr. loan processor, asst. sec. Prudential Real Estate Fin. Svcs., Trumbull, Conn., 1992-94; mgr. ops., asst. sec. Prudential Real Estate Fin. Svcs., Trumbull, 1994; mgr. ops., asst. sec. Conn. Home Mortgage, Trumbull, 1994—, v.p. ops.; co-developed Prudential Real Estate Fin. Svcs. and Conn. Home Mortgage; notary public, Conn., 1989—. Author: Processing Manual, 1992. Sponsor Christian Children's Fund, Va., 1989—. Roman Catholic. Avocations: reading, painting, exercising. Home: 224 Berkley Rd Fairfield CT 06432-4420

DECARLO, WILLIAM S., lawyer; b. Bayonne, N.J., Apr. 11, 1950. BS, U. Pa., 1971, MA, 1976; JD, Georgetown U., 1976. Bar: N.J. 1977, N.Y. 1977, Ill. 1986. Ptnr. Sidley & Austin, Chgo. Office: Sidley & Austin 1 First Natl Plz Chicago IL 60603-2003

DÉCARY, ROBERT, judge; b. Montreal, Que., Can., May 26, 1944; s. Jacques M. Décary and Madeleine Toupin. BA, Coll. Brebeuf, Montreal, 1963; LLL, U. Montreal, 1966; LLM, U. London, 1968. Bar: Quebec 1967. Polit. asst. Sec. State External Affairs, Ottawa, Ont., Can., 1970-73; lawyer Deschênes, de Grandpré, Montreal, 1973-80, Noël, Décary & Assocs., Hull, Que., 1980-90; judge Fed. Ct. Appeal, Ottawa, Ont., Can., 1990—. Contbr. essays to publs. Mem. Can. Bar Assn. (coun.). Office: Fed Ct Appeal, Supreme Ct Bldg, Ottawa, ON Canada K1A 0H9

DECASTRO, FERNANDO JOSE, pediatrics educator; b. Havana, Cuba, Nov. 11, 1937; s. Fernando R. and Maria A. (Freyre) deC.; m. Catalina, June 9, 1962; children: Maria, Ana, Fernando, Ramon, Teresa, Pablo, Jose Manuel. MD, Tulane U., 1962; MPH, U. Mich., 1966. Intern, resident, fellow U. Mich., 1962-66; clin. prof. pediatrics St. Louis U., 1976—; dir. toxicology Arcadia Valley Hosp., Pilot Kove, Mo., 1992—. Contbr. articles to profl. jours. Fellow APHA, Am. Acad. Pediatrics, Am. Coll. Emergency Physicians, Am. Coll. Med. Toxicology, Am. Acad. Clin. Toxicology, Am. Fedn. Clin. Rsch. Office: Arcadia Valley Hosp Hwy 21 Pilot Kove MO 63663

DE CASTRO, HUGO DANIEL, lawyer; b. Panama City, Panama, Sept. 12, 1935; came to U.S., 1947; s. Mauricio Fidanque and Armida Rebecca (Salas) de C.; m. Isabel Shapiro, July 25, 1958; children: Susan M., Teresa A., Andrea L., Michele L. BSBA in Econs. cum laude, UCLA, 1957, JD summa cum laude, 1960. Bar: Calif. 1961; CPA, Calif. Prin. de Castro, West & Chodorow Inc., L.A., 1961—; lectr. UCLA, 1962-67, 68, counsel to dean Law Sch., 1963—; commr. tax adv. com. State Bar Calif. Editor UCLA Law Rev., 1959-60, Taxation for Lawyers, 1971-88; contbr. articles to profl. jours. Trustee Stephen S. Wise Temple; trustee, bd. dirs., sec. UCLA Found.; bd. dirs., sec. Western L.A. Found. Mem. ABA 9chmn. taxation subcom.), ACLU, L.A. County Bar Assn., Beverly Hills Bar Assn. (bd. dirs. Law Found.), L.A. C. of C. (former chmn., dir.), L.A. World Affairs coun., Am. Jewish Com., Del Rey Yacht Club (Calif., former dir., officer), Founders of Music Ctr., Las Hadas Country Club (Mex.), Pi Lambda Phi. Office: de Castro West & Chodorow 10960 Wilshire Blvd Ste 1400 Los Angeles CA 90024-3702

DE CASTRO, JIMMY, radio station executive. Pres. KTRH-AM, Houston. Office: KTRH-AM PO Box 1520 Houston TX 77251-1520*

DECELL, HAL C., federal agency administrator; m. Jane DeCell; children: Caroline, Clayton, Charles. BA, Tulane U., 1971; JD, George Mason U., 1981. Bar: D.C. 1981. Past legis. dir. Washington, past press sec., past spl. projects dir.; past chief staff, adminstrv. asst. to congressman Jamie L. Whitten, mem. house appropriations com. Ho. of Rep.; asst. sec. congl. and intergovtl. rels. Dept. HUD, Washington, 1995—. Office: U.S. Dept HUD Congl and Intergovtl Rels 451 7th St SW Washington DC 20410-0001*

DECERCHIO, JOHN, advertising company executive. With W.B. Doner & Co., Southfield, Mich., 1974—, mem. creative dept., 1978-82, v.p., assoc. creative dir., 1982-84, sr. v.p., creative dir., 1984-90, vice chmn., exec. creative dir., 1990—. Recipient Cannes Gold Lion, Andy, Clio, Effie, Bessie-Canada, Caddy-Best of Show, numerous others. Office: W B Doner & Company 25900 North Western Hwy Southfield MI 48034*

DECESARE, DONALD E., broadcasting executive; b. Jersey City, Mar. 6, 1947; s. Emilio D. and Anita T. DeCesare; m. Catherine M. Fahey, June 20, 1970; 1 child, Elizabeth Ann. BA, U. Pitts., 1967; MA, U. Conn., 1969. News dir. Sta. WGCH-AM, Greenwich, Conn., 1972-74; reporter Westinghouse Broadcasting Corp., N.Y.C., 1974-76; writer CBS News div. CBS Inc., N.Y.C., 1976-78, news editor, 1978-80, fgn. producer, 1980-83, sr. fgn. producer, 1983-85, mgr. N.Y./New England bur., 1985-87, fgn. editor, 1987-89, v.p. news coverage, 1989-90, v.p. ops., 1990-96; pres. Crossroads Comm. LLC, Norwalk, Conn., 1996—; owner/operator WMRD-AM, Middletown, Conn., 1996—, WLIS-AM, Old Saybrook, Conn., 1996—. Bd. dirs. Conn. Broadcasters Assn., Conn. Pub. Access Network, Middlesex County United Way, Old Saybrook C. of C. Recipient Columbia DuPont award Columbia U., 1989; Overseas Press Club award, 1990. Mem. Conn. Broadcasters Assn. (bd. dirs.), Old Saybrook C. of C. (bd. dirs.). Avocations: Latin American art, furniture making, computers. Office: Crossroads Comm LLC 157 N Seir Hill Rd Norwalk CT 06850-1333 also: PO Box 1150 777 River Rd Middletown CT 06457-3922 also: PO Drawer W 77 Springbrook Rd Old Saybrook CT 06475-1225

DECHANT, VIRGIL C., fraternal organization administrator; b. Antonino, Kans., Sept. 24, 1930; s. Cornel J. and Ursula (Legleiter) D.; m. Ann Schafer, Aug. 20, 1951; children: Thomas, Daniel, Karen, Robert. Hon. degree, Pontifical Coll. Josephinum, Columbus, Ohio, St. Anselm's Coll., Manchester, N.H., St. Leo's Coll., Fla., Mt. St. Mary's Coll., Emmitsburg, Md., St. John's U., S.I., N.Y., Providence Coll., Sacred Heart U., Bridgeport, Conn., Pontifical U. Santo Tomas, Manila, Assumption Coll., Worcester, Mass., Albertus Magnus Coll., New Haven; hon. degree, St. Thomas U., St. Paul, Kans. Newman Coll., Wichita, Franciscan U., Steubenville, Ohio. With KC, 1948—, dir., asst. supreme sec., supreme master 4th degree, 1963, supreme sec., 1967-77; supreme knight, CEO KC, New Haven, 1977—; appointee Pontifical Coun. for the Family, 1982—; consultor Pontifical Coun. for Social Comm., 1990—; hon. cnosultor of Vatican City State, 1988; mem. Coun. of Supreindency, Inst. for Works of Religion (Vatican Bank), 1990—. Bd. dirs. Nat. Shrine Immaculate Conception, Washington, Pontifical Coll. Josephinum, Columbus; trustee Cath. U. Am.; commr. Christopher Columbus Quincentenary Commn. for founding of Ams., 1992; apptd. auditor Snyod Am., 1997. Decorated Knight St. Gregory the Great promoted to comdr. with Star elevated to Knight Grand Cross, Knight Grand Cross Equestrian Order Holy Sepulchre, Holy Land Pilgrim Shell, Knight Grand Cross Order Pius IX, Knight Sovereign Mil. Order of Malta; named one of Gentleman of His Holiness, Pope John Paul II, 1987; appointed to Extraordinary Synod of Bishops in Vatican, 1985, Synod of Bishops on Laity, 1987; recipient Cross of Merit with Golden Star of Holy Sepulchre of Jerusalem, 1990. Office: Knights of Columbus 1 Columbus Plz Ste Ll New Haven CT 06510-3326

DECHAR, PETER HENRY, artist; b. N.Y.C., Apr. 19, 1942; s. Edouard and Diane D.; m. Natasha Gratcheva, Apr. 23, 1999. Prin. Peter Dechar Inc. Archtl. Furniture. Exhibited one-man shows, Cordier & Ekstrom Gallery, N.Y.C., 1967, 69, 75, Twentieth Century Art from the Rockefeller Collection, N.Y.C., 1969, Mus. Modern Art, N.Y.C., 1969, group shows, Larry Aldrich Mus., Ridgefield, Conn., 1967, Krannert Art Mus., 1967, Whitney Mus. Art, N.Y.C., 1967, 69; represented in permanent collections, Mus. Modern Art, N.Y.C., Whitney Mus. Art, N.Y.C., Larry Aldrich Mus., Ridgefield, Conn., Walker Art Ctr., Fiberglass Tower Art Collection, Julien Levy Collection, Chase Manhatten Collection, Rockefeller Collection.

DE CHASTELAIN, A(LFRED) JOHN G(ARDYNE) D(RUMMOND), Canadian army officer, diplomat; b. Bucharest, Rumania, July 30, 1937; emigrated to Can., 1955, naturalized, 1962; s. Alfred George G. and Marion Elizabeth (Walsh) de C.; m. MaryAnn Laverty, Sept. 9, 1961; children: Duncan John, Amanda Jane. Student, Fettes Coll., Edinburgh, Scotland, 1950-55, Mt. Royal Coll. Calgary, Can., 1956; BA with honors in History, Royal Mil. Coll., Can., 1960; grad., Brit. Army Staff Coll., 1966; D in Mil. Sci. (hon.), Royal Mil. Coll. Can., 1996. Commd. 2d lt. Can. Army, 1960, advanced through grades to gen., 1989; comdg. officer 2d Bn. Princess Patricia's Can. Light Inf., 1970-72; comdr. Can. Forces Base, Montreal, Que., 1974-76; comdr. Can. Contingent UN Force in Cyprus, 1976-77; comdt. Royal Mil. Coll. Can., Kingston, Ont., 1977-80; comdr. 4th Can. Mechanized Brigade Group, Lahr, Fed. Republic Germany, 1980-82; dir. Gen. Land Doctrine Nat. Def. Hdqrs., Ottawa, 1982-83; dep. comdr. Mobile Command, St. Hubert, Que., 1983-86; asst. dep. min. pers. Nat. Def. Hdqrs., Ottawa, Ont., Can., 1986-88; vice chief of Def. Staff Nat. Def. Hdqrs., 1988-89, chief of Def. Staff, 1989-93; Can. amb. to U.S. Washington, 1993. Past v.p. Scouts Can.; chief Defence Staff, 1994-95; mem. Internat. Body on Decommissioning of Arms in No. Ireland, 1995-96; mem. ind. chmn. No. Ireland Peace Talks, 1996-98; chmn. Ind. Internat. Commn. on Decommissioning of Arms in No. Ireland, 1997—. Decorated comdr. Order Mil. Merit (Can.), officer Order of Can., comdr. Order St. John of Jerusalem, Hellenic Commendation medal of Merit and Honor (Greece), Vimy award, 1992, comdr. Legion of Merit (U.S.), Companion of Honour (U.K.). Mem. Dominion of Can. Rifle Assn. (past pres.), Royal Scottish Country Dance Soc., St. Andrew's Soc., Royal Mil. Coll. Club, Royal Can. Legion, Royal Can. Mil. Inst. Home: 170 Acacia Ave, Ottawa, ON Canada K1M 0R3

DECHELLIS, GIACOMO JOHN, controller, accountant; b. Detroit, Oct. 30, 1965; s. Remo and Flora Teresa (Cianferra) DeC. BA in Bus. Adminstrn. and Acctg., Wayne State U., 1989, MBA, 1993. CPA, Mich. Trust analyst II instnl. trust acctg. Comerica Bank, Detroit, 1989-91, trust analyst III, 1991-93; tax cons. Deloitte & Touche LLP, Detroit, 1993-95, sr. tax cons., 1995-97, contrl. Mich. audit and enterprise risk svcs. groups, 1997—. Mem. AICPA, Mich. Assn. CPA's, Golden Key. Avocations: travel, foreign languages. Home: 21903 Elizabeth St Saint Clair Shores MI 48080-2003 Office: Deloitte & Touche LLP 600 Renaissance Ctr Ste 900 Detroit MI 48243-1807

DECHER, RUDOLF, physicist; b. Wuerzburg, Ger., Aug. 22, 1927; came to U.S., 1960, naturalized, 1967; s. Hermann Alexander and Karola (Krenig) D.; m. Christa Anna Frick, Jan. 7, 1956; children—Peter H., Marianne C. M. in Physics, U. Wuerzburg, W. Ger., 1950, Ph.D. in Physics, 1954. Research scientist Dynamit AG, Troisdorf, W. Ger., 1955-60; with NASA Marshall Space Flight Ctr., Huntsville, Ala., 1960-94; retired NASA, 1994; chief astrophysics div., space sci. lab. NASA Marshall Space Flight Ctr., 1970-86, asst. dir. space sci. lab., 1986-89, chief astrophysics div., space sci. lab., 1989-93, asst. dir. space sci. lab., 1993-94; prin. rsch. scientist Ctr. for Space Plasma & Aeronomic Rsch Inst. for Space Physics, Astrophysics & Edn., U. Ala., Huntsville, 1995—. Recipient Exceptional Service medal NASA, 1977. Mem. Am. Phys. Soc., AIAA. Roman Catholic. Home: 718 Owens Dr SE Huntsville AL 35801-2034

DECHERD, ROBERT WILLIAM, newspaper and broadcasting executive; b. Dallas, Apr. 9, 1951; s. Henry Benjamin Jr. and Isabelle Lee (Thomason) D.; m. Maureen Healy, Jan. 25, 1975; children: William Benjamin, Audrey Maureen. AB cum laude, Harvard U., 1973. Exec. v.p. Dallas Morning News, 1980-83; exec. v.p. A.H. Belo Corp., Dallas, 1981-84, pres., chief operating officer, 1985-86, chmn., chief exec. officer, 1987-94, chmn., pres. and CEO, 1994—, also bd. dirs.; dir. Kimberly-Clark Corp., 1996—. Pres. Dallas Symphony Assn., 1979-80, Dallas Symphony Found., 1984-86, St. Mark's Sch., Tex., 1988-91; chmn. Dallas Parks Found., 1985-87, Dallas Soc. Profl. Journalists, 1978; trustee Tomas Rivera Policy Inst., 1992—; incorporator, pres. Freedom. of Info. Found. Tex., 1978. Recipient Disting. Svc. award Dallas Jaycees, 1985, Am. Newspaper Exec. of Yr. award Adweek mag., 1985, citation of honor AIA, 1988, Seymour Preston award Nat. Assn. Ind. Schs. Coun. Advancement and Support Edn., 1989, James Madison award Freedom of Info. Found. Tex., 1989, Henry Cohn Humanitarian award Anti-Defamation League, 1992, Freedom of Speech award The Media Inst., 1998; named to the Tex. Bus. Hall of Fame, 1995; recipient St. Mark's Disting. Alumnus award, 1998. Mem. Tex. Soc. Architects (hon.), Newspaper Assn. Am. (mem. exec. bd. 1992-96). Office: A H Belo Corp PO Box 655237 Dallas TX 75265-5237

DE CHERNEY, ALAN HERSH, obstetrics and gynecology educator; b. Phila., Feb. 13, 1942; s. William Aaron and Ruth (Hersh) DeC.; m. Deanna Faith Saver, June 26, 1966; children: Peter, Alexander, Nicholas. BS in Natural Scis., Muhlenberg Coll., 1963; MD, Temple U., 1967; MA (hon.), Yale U., 1985. Diplomate Am. Bd. Ob.-Gyn. (examiner 1984—, bd. dirs. 1995—), Am.Bd. Reproductive Endocrinology (bd. dirs. 1988-94), Nat. Bd. Med. Examiners (examiner 1987-90). Intern in gen. medicine U. Pitts., 1967-68; resident in ob-gyn. U. Pa., Phila., 1968-72, instr. dept. ob-gyn, 1970-72; asst. prof. ob-gyn. Yale U. Sch. Medicine, New Haven, 1974-78, assoc. prof., 1979-84, prof., 1984-91, John Slade Ely prof. ob-gyn, 1987-92, dir. div. reproductive endocrinology, dept. ob-gyn, 1982-92, lectr. dept. biology, 1985-92; Louis E. Phaneuf prof., chmn. dept. ob-gyn. Tufts U. Sch. Medicine, 1992-96; prof., chmn. dept. ob-gyn. UCLA, 1996—. Maj. U.S. Army, 1972-74. Recipient Disting. Alumni award Temple U., 1989, Muhlenberg Coll., 1994. Fellow ACOG, Am. Fertility Soc. (pres. 1994-95), Am. Assn. History of Medicine, Soc. for Assisted Reproductive Tech. (pres. 1987-88), Soc. Reproductive Endocrinologists (pres. 1988), Soc. Reproductive Surgeons (charter, pres. 1991), Endocrine Soc., European Soc. Human Reproductions and Embryology, Soc. Gynecologic Surgeons, Soc. for Study of Reproduction, Soc. Gynecologic Investigation (pres. 1994-95). Office: UCLA Sch Medicine Dept Ob/Gyn 27-117 CHS Mail Code 174017 10833 Le Conte Ave Los Angeles CA 90095-3075

DECHERNEY, GEORGE STEPHEN, research scientist, research facility administrator; b. Wilmington, Del., June 16, 1952; s. Herman George and Grace Antoinette (Lewis) DeC.; m. Cleonice Anne DiSabatino, June 9, 1992; children: Elizabeth, Constance, Sarah, Elliot. BA, Columbia U., 1974; MD, Temple U., 1978; MPH, Columbia U., 1998. Instr. Vanderbilt U., Nashville, 1983-84; asst. prof. Uniformed Svcs. U., Bethesda, Md., 1985-89; dir. Diabetes and Metabolic Ctr., Wilmington, 1989—; clin. assoc. prof. Thomas Jefferson Univ., Phila., 1989—; chief clin. pharmacology, endocrinology Christiana Care Health Sys., Newark, 1990—, dir., 1990—; assoc. prof. biology U. Del., 1991—; invited internat. speaker 50th anniversary Greenslopes Hosp., Brisbane, Australia; bd. dirs. Wilmington Charter Sch. Math. and Sci., 1996. Editor-in-chief: Del. Med. Jour., 1998—. Trustee Christiana Care HealthSystem, 1998—. Maj. USAF, 1986-89. Mem. AMA, Am. Diabetes Assn. (pres. Del. affiliate 1990-95), N.Y. Acad. Scis., Endocrine Soc., Am. Soc. Quality (regional councilor 1998—). Achievements include research in endocrinology, in diabetes mellitus, in aerospace medicine. Office: Clin Pharmacology Rsch Ctr Ste 419 4755 Ogletown-Stanton Rd Newark DE 19718

DECHERT, PETER, photographer, writer, foundation administrator; b. Phila., Dec. 17, 1924; s. Robert and Helen Hope (Wilson) D.; m. Phoebe Jane Booth; children: Sandra, Robin Booth, Caroline. BA, U. Pa., 1948, MA, 1950, PhD, 1955. Owner, Peter Dechert Assocs., Bryn Mawr, Pa., 1956-68; asst. dir. Sch. of Am. Rsch., Santa Fe, 1968-71; pres. Indian Arts Fund, Santa Fe, 1971-72; pres. S.W. Found. for Audio-Visual Resources, Santa Fe, 1973-77; self-employed writer, photographer, Santa Fe; tchr., cons. photog. comm., 1964—. Author: Canon Rangefinder Cameras, 1933-68, 1985, The Contax Connection, 1990, Olympus Pen SLR Cameras, 1989, Canon SLR Cameras, 1959-91, 1992, The Contax S Camera Family, 1991, Los Alamos Ranch Book of Rosters, 1991; former contbg. editor Shutterbug mag., other photographic periodicals; contbr. articles on history and design of miniature cameras and other photog. topics to profl. publs. Bd. dirs. St. Vincent Hosp. Found. (pres. 1981-83, v.p. 1983-84); vestry Ch. of the Holy Faith, 1994-97; mem. St. Anthony Hall. With AUS, 1943-46. Mem. N.Mex. Poetry Soc. (pres. 1969-74), Am. Soc. Media Photographers, S.W. Assn. Indian Arts, Pa. Soc. SAR, N.Mex. Jazz Workshop, Don Quixotes of Santa Fe, Phi Beta Kappa. Address: PO Box 636 Santa Fe NM 87504-0636

DE CHINO, KAREN LINNIA, engineering business analyst; b. Hartford, Conn., Dec. 31, 1955; d. George Arthur and Carol Ann (Nelson) Holmelund; m. Frank Louis De Chino, Mar. 22, 1979; 1 child, Brittanie Francis. BA in Psychology, Montclair State Coll., 1978; MS in Applied Psychology, Stevens Inst. Tech., 1992. Counselor Livingston (N.J.) Youth Svcs. Bur., 1974-77; adminstrv. asst. Bamberger's, Newark, N.J., 1978-80; nursing scheduler St. Barnabas Med. Ctr., Livingston, 1981-83; tng. adminstr. Singer-Kearfott, Little Falls, N.J., 1983-86; human resources rep. Kearfott Guidance & Navigation Corp., Little Falls, N.J., 1986-89; mgr. bus. & adminstrn. IEEE Stds., Piscataway, N.J., 1989-92, dir. tech. programs, 1992-96; sr. prin. analyst ARINC, Shrewsbury, N.J., 1996—. Office: ARINC 179 Avenue Of The Cmn Shrewsbury NJ 07702-4804

DECHTER, BRADLEY GRAHAM, music arranger, orchestrator; b. Hollywood, Calif., Nov. 6, 1956; s. Ted and Nancy Louise (Graham) D.; m. Maureen Joy Smith, Aug. 1, 1982; 1 child, Graham Ingler. BA in Music, Yale Coll., 1978; MusM, Yale U., 1979. Freelance saxophonist L.A., 1980—, music copyist, 1981-85, arranger, orchestrator, 1981—, composer, 1981—; instr. jazz and saxophone Western Mich. U., Kalamazoo, 1979-80, Santa Monica (Calif.) Coll., 1981-82; producer "Concerts for a Sunday Afternoon", Manhattan Beach, Calif., 1989. Arranger including (TV show) Moonlighting, 1987-89 (Emmy Nominations 1988, 89); composer/arranger (motion picture) Tap, 1986; orchestrator (motion picture) Pretty Woman, 1990, Flatliners, 1990, The Package, 1989, Three Men and A Little Lady, 1990, King Ralph, 1991, Prince of Tides, 1991, City Slickers, 1991, Grand Canyon, 1991, Glengarry Glenross, 1992, The Last of the Mohicans, 1992, Year of the Comet, 1992, Dave, 1993, The Fugitive, 1993, Outbreak, 1995, Restoration, 1995, Sneakers, 1994, Wyatt Earp, 1994, French Kiss, 1994, Waterworld, 1995, The Juror, 1995, The Mirror Has Two Faces, 1996, One Fine Day, 1996, The First Wives' Club, 1996, Dante's Peak, 1997, Liar, Liar, 1997, Father's Day, 1997, Space Jam, 1996, Alien Resurrection, 1998, Devil's Advocate, 1998, Elmo in Grouchland, 1998, Jane Austen's Mafia, 1998, Paulie, 1998, A Perfect Murder, 1998, The Postman, 1998, Mumford, 1999, My Favorite Martian, 1999, Snow Falling on Cedars, 1999; arranger including (record album) Elton John Live in Australia, 1987 (Gold Album 1988), Johnny Mathis Sings Ellington, 1990, Protosynthesis, 1990, Goya: A Life in Song with Placido Domingo, 1989, The Majesty of Christmas, 1987, Symphonic Lloyd Webber, 1990, The King and I Concert Album, 1993, McCoy Tyner Plays Bacharach, 1997, Superbowl XXV, 1991, 1996 Olympics Telecast, Jack Jones Sings Gershwin, 1991. Mem. ASCAP, NARAS, Am. Fedn. Musicians. Democrat. Avocations: cooking, gardening, fatherhood, jazz saxophone, travel. Home: 995 Iva Ct Cambria CA 93428-2913 Office: care DIGS Music Ste 880 11777 San Vicente Blvd Los Angeles CA 90049

DECI, EDWARD LEWIS, psychologist, educator; b. Clifton Springs, N.Y., Oct. 14, 1942; s. Charles Henry and Janice Margaret (Upchurch) D. AB, Hamilton Coll., 1964; postgrad., London Sch. Econs., 1965; MBA, U. Pa., 1967; PhD, Carnegie-Mellon U., 1970. Postdoctoral fellow Stanford U., 1973-74; mem. faculty U. Rochester, N.Y., 1970—; chair dept. psychology U. Rochester, 1993-94, prof. psychology, 1978—; pvt. practice psychotherapy, 1975—; pres. Inst. for Rsch. and Reform in Edn., 1995-97, chmn., 1997—; orgnl. cons., 1970—; lectr., cons. in Bulgaria, Can., Germany, Israel, Japan, Norway, Italy, Poland, Sweden, U.K., Jordan, Thailand, Australia. Author: The Psychology of Self-Determination, 1980, Intrinsic Motovation, 1975; co-author: Industrial and Organizational Psychology, 1977, Intrinsic Motivation and Self-Determination in Human Beahvior, 1985, Why We Do What We Do, 1995. Trustee Monhegan (Maine) Conservation Assocs., 1982-89, 92-95; pres. Monhegan Mus. Assn., 1984—. NIMH grantee, 1977-78, 89-94, NSF grantee, 1981-83, Nat. Inst. Child Health and Human Devel. grantee, 1986-89, 90-96. Fellow APA, Am. Psychol. Soc. Office: U Rochester Psychology Dept Rochester NY 14627

DECIO, ARTHUR JULIUS, manufacturing company executive; b. Elkhart, Ind., Oct. 19, 1930; s. Julius A. and Lena (Alesia) D.; m. Patricia George, Jan. 6, 1951; children: Terrence, Jamee, Linda, Jay, Leigh Allison. Student, DePaul U., 1949-50; DBA (hon.), Salem Coll., W.Va., 1973; LLD, U. Notre Dame, 1975, Ind. State U., Terre Haute, 1978; LLD (hon.), St. Mary's Coll., Notre Dame, Ind., 1996; D. Bus. (hon.), Vincennes U., 1991; D Humanitarian Svc. (hon.), Hillsdale Coll., 1993; LittD (hon.), Purdue U., 1999. Pres. Skyline Corp., Elkhart, 1956-72; chmn. bd., chief exec. officer Skyline Corp., 1959-98, chmn. bd., 1998—; bd. dirs. Schwarz, Morton Grove, Ill., NiSource (formerly NIPSCO Industries, Inc.), Hammond, Ind.; past dir. adv. council Coll. Commerce DePaul U.; past mem. adv. coun. Coll. Engring., U. Notre Dame, also Coll. Bus. Adminstrn.; past bd. govs. NFL Alumni; founding dir. Elkhart (Ind.) Community Found.; dir. Ara Parseghian Med. Rsch. Found., Quality Dining, Mishawaka, Ind. Past dir. Spl. Olympics Internat., Washington; fellow, trustee U. Notre Dame; trustee, past chmn. Holy Cross Coll., Notre Dame, Ind., trustee Hillsdale Coll., Mich.; past mem. adv. bd. Goshen (Ind.) Coll., Ind. U., South Bend; past mem. coun. advisors Ctr. for the Homeless, South Bend; past mem., pres. coun. Ind. U.; past mem. Logan Cmty. Adv. Coun., South Bend; past chmn. Elkhart Urban League Membership Drive, Elkhart Gen. Hosp. Major Capital Campaign, Bicentennial Commn. Elkhart County, Salvation Army New Hdqrs. Bldg. Drive, 1975; hon. chmn. Salvation Army Christmas Fund Drive, 1972-98; past mem. Commn. on Presdl. Scholars, Presdl. appointment, 1978; pres. Elkhart Gen. Hosp. Found.; past dir. Nat. Italian-Am. Found., Washington; past chmn. adv. coun. United Way, Elkhart, past dir., campaign chmn., 1966; past dir. Cath. Diocese of Ft. Wayne-South Bend, bd. dirs. diocesan fin. coun.; past dir. Banc One Ind. Corp., Indpls., Bank One., Indpls., Midwest Commerce Banking Co., Elkhart, Ind., Fed. Reserve Bank Chgo.; founding mem., trustee Aux Chandelles Trust for Mentally Retarded, Elkhart; past chmn., trustee Holy Cross Coll., Notre Dame, Ind.; trustee Hillsdale (Mich.) Coll.; life mem., past chmn., chmn. exec. com. nat. adv. bd. Salvation Army, Washington; conf. chmn. Salvation Army Adv. Orgns. Conf., London, 1989; life mem. NAACP, exec. bd. Elkhart County chpt., 1980-82; chmn. for special gifts/bldg. campaign St. Thomas the Apostle Ch., Elkhart, Ind., 1963; co-chmn. capital campaign Elkhart Conf. Superblock, 1976, Goshen Coll. Uncommon Cause Campaign, 1983, hon. co-chmn. capital campaign Marmion Acad., Aurora, Ill., 1998-99; chmn. Salvation Army capital campaign, 1990; co-chmn. capital campaign Sta. WNIT-TV Pub. TV, 1991; chmn. Living Faith Campaign, Congregation Holy Cross, Ind. Province; chmn. Sign of Hope campaign Congregation Holy Cross, Ind. Province; life trustee. Marmion Acad., Aurora, Ill.; past mem., bd. advisors Mundelein (Ill.) Sem. of U. St. Mary of the Lake; past dir. Elkhart Urban League, Elkhart Gen. Hosp., No. Ctrl. Ind. Med. Edn. Found., South Bend, Nat. Jr. Achievement, Greencroft Found., Elkhart; past dir. Jr. Achievement Elkhart, pres. 1965-66; past trustee Stanley Clark Sch., South Bend, LaLumiere Sch., Laporte, Ind.; mem. Coun. on Devel. Choices for the 80's, Urban Land Inst.; Presdl. appointment Low Income Housing task force, 1970; past Presdl. appointee as commr. Christopher Columbus Quincentenary Jubilee Commn., Washington; mem. Internat. Summer Spl. Olympics Com., Inc., 1987; co-chmn. capital campaign Assn. for Disabled of Elkhart County, 1985; hon. chmn. capital campaign for Elkhart Cmty. Day Care Ctr., 1987; bd. govs. Ind. Colls. of Ind.; 1st chmn. annual bishop's appeal fund drive Diocese of Ft. Wayne-South Bend, 1987; bd. dirs., past chmn. Regional Approach for Progress, South Bend; past pres. Elkhart Park Found., Elkhart; founding dir., charter bd. dirs. Michiana Pub. Broadcasting Corp., Elkhart. Recipient U. Portland (Oreg.) medal, 1972, Golden Plate award Acad. Achievement Dallas, 1967, Others award Salvation Army, 1972, William Booth award Salvation Army, 1987, Alexis de Tocqueville Soc. award United Way Am., 1987, Sagamore of the Wabash award State of Ind., 1977, 85, Community Service award Elkhart County br. NAACP, 1980, Marmion Centurion award Marmion Mil. Acad., 1979, Achievement award Jr. Achievement, 1974, Humanitarian award Elkhart Urban League, 1981, Community Service award Elkhart Urban League, 1977 Disting. Am. award Moose Krause chpt. NFL Found. and Hall of Fame, 1984, Book of Golden Deeds award Elkhart Noon Exchange Club, 1984, E. M. Morris award Div. Bus. and Econs., Ind. U.-South Bend, 1985, Alumni Leadership award Marmion Mil. Acad., 1964, Wall of Fame award Assn. for the Disabled, 1985; Salvation Army Hon. Adv. Bd. Mem. award, 1971, Columbus Day award for outstanding Italian-Am., 1973, Elkhart Bar Assn. Liberty Bell award, 1976, Aux Chandelles Village Found. OK award, 1976, Life Hon. Membership award Elkhart Urban League, 1980, Outstanding Contbn. award Elkhart Urban League, 1982, Nat. Italian-Am. Found. Career Achievement award, Washington, 1984, Disting. Citizen of Yr. award No. Ind. council Boy Scouts Am., 1988, Ind. Individual Philanthropist of Yr. award, 1984, Mobile Home Hall of Fame, 1975, Industry Man of Yr. award Iowa Manufactured Housing Assn., 1976, Calif. Manufactured Housing Assn., 1977, N.J. Manufactured Housing Assn., 1977. Arthur J. Decio Vol. of Yr. award established by Elkhart United Way, 1984, Journi Industrialist of Yr. award The Exec. Jour. Bd. Dirs., 1989, Howard J. Kenna, C.S.C. award Congregation of Holy Cross, Ind. Province U. Notre Dame, 1989, John J. Cavanaugh award U. Notre Dame Alumni Assn., 1989, James R. Price/Automated Builder Achievement in Housing award Automated Builder mag., 1990, Man of Yr. award Notre Dame Club of St. Joseph Valley, 1990, Ind. Spl. Cause award Ind. Assn. Rehab. Facilities, 1991, Helping Hands award Hospice St. Joseph County, Inc., 1991, Labor Humanitarian award United Labor Agy., Elkhart, Ind., 1991, Alumni of Yr. award St. Vincent's Parish, Elkhart, 1993, John W. Meaney Founders award Michiana Pub. Broadcasting Corp., 1993, Disting. Aux. Svc. Cross Salvation Army Internat. Hdqrs., London, 1995, Cross of Hope award Bros. of Holy Cross and Holy Cross Coll., Notre Dame, 1996, outstanding kindness award ADEC, 1997, special internat. olympics award, 1997. Past mem. and past chmn. Manufactured Housing Inst. Washington, Ind. Acad. (apptd. 1978), Chgo. Pres. Assn., Chief Execs. Orgn., World Bus. Coun., Marmion Benedictine Abbey (life affiliate, Aurora, Ill.), Knights of Malta; hon. mem. Elkhart Rotary Club. Roman Catholic. Clubs: Chicago; Country of Fla. (Village of Golf); Delray Beach Yacht (Fla.); Ocean of Fla. (Ocean Ridge); Signal Point Country (Niles, Mich.); Casino (Chgo.). Home: 3215 Greenleaf Blvd Elkhart IN 46514-4357 Office: Skyline Corp 2520 Bypass Rd Elkhart IN 46514-1584

DECIUTIIS, ALFRED CHARLES MARIA, medical oncologist, television producer; b. N.Y.C., Oct. 16, 1945; s. Alfred Ralph and Theresa Elizabeth (Manko) de C.; m. Catherine L. Gohn. *Family originated in Aquila. Key dates in family history include: 893, first ranked among the nobles of Italy; In 1140, at the assizes of Ariano, merged by Rogger II with the Campaneschi; 1527, merger of Italian and Spanish branches; 1629, created "Princes of the Holy Roman Empire"; 1711, ancestor Giovanni Nocerino. discovered remains of Herculaneum; 1860, numbered among Garibaldi's 1000; 1901, Count Salvatore de Ciutiis, translated work leading to Concordate of 1929; 1920s, Count Vincenzo de Ciutiis appointed ambassador to Spain; 1930s, Count Vincente de Ciutiis, Count of Madrid, assassinated in Spanish Civil War.* B.S. summa cum laude, Fordham U., 1967; M.D., Columbia U., 1971. Diplomate Am. Bd. Internal Medicine, Am. Bd. Med. Oncology. Intern N.Y. Hosp.-Cornell Med. Ctr., N.Y.C., 1971-72, resident, 1972-74; fellow in clin. immunology Meml. Hosp.-Sloan Kettering Cancer Ctr., N.Y.C., 1974-75, fellow in clin. oncology, 1975-76, spl. fellow in immunology, 1974-76; guest investigator, asst. physician exptl. hematology Rockefeller U., N.Y.C., 1975-76; practice medicine, specializing in med. oncology Los Angeles, 1977—; host cable TV shows, 1981—; med. editor Cable Health Network, 1983—, Lifetime Network, 1984—; mem. med. adv. com. 1984 Olympics; co-founder Meditrina Med. Ctr., free out-patient surg. ctr., Torrance, Calif., physician asst. supr., 1984; mem. fgn. policy leadership project Ctr. for Internat. Affairs, Harvard, Ill. Syndicated columnist Coast Media News, 1980's; producer numerous med. TV shows; contbr. articles to profl. jours.; author first comprehensive clin. description of chronic fatique syndrome as a neuro-immunologic acquired disorder. Founder Italian-Am. Med. Assn., 1982; co-founder Italian-Am. Legal Alliance, L.A., 1982—; mem. gov. bd. med. coun. Italian-Am. Found.; mem. Italian-Am. Civic Com., L.A., 1983, UCLA Chancellor's Assocs., Cath. League for Civil and Rel. Liberty, World Affairs Coun., L.A., Boston Mus. Fine Arts, Met. Mus. Served to capt. M.C., U.S. Army, 1972-74. Leukemia Soc. Am. fellow, 1974-76. Fellow ACP, Internat. Coll. Physicians and Surgeons; mem. AMA (Physician's Recognition award 1978-80, 82-85, 86-89, 89-91, 91-94, 94-96, 96—), Am. Soc. Clin. Oncology, N.Y. Acad. Sci. (life), Calif. Med. Assn., Los Angeles County Med. Assn., AAAS, Am. Union Physicians and Dentists, Internat. Health Soc., Am. Pub. Health Assn., Am. Geriatrics Soc., Chinese Med. Assn., Drug Info. Assn., Nat. Geographic Soc. (life), Internat. Platform Assn., Am. Soc. Hematology (emeritus), N.Y. Acad. Scis. (life), Fondazione Giovanni Agnelli, Smithsonian Instn., Nature Conservancy, Nat. Wildlife Fedn., Mensa, Phi Beta Kappa, Alpha Omega Alpha, Sigma Xi. Achievements include first comprehensive clinical description of chronic fatigue syndrome as a neuro-immunologic disorder probably caused by a retrovirus with multi-system complications. Avocations: collecting, reading, hunting, fishing, astronomy. The deCiutiis family was first ranked among the nobles of Italy in 893, designated a princely family and given the title of "Princes of the Holy Roman Empire" in 1629. Office: PO Box 384 Agoura Hills CA 91376-0384

DECK, JUDITH Z., adult nurse practitioner; b. Washington, Dec. 22, 1941. Student, Yale U., 1968-69; BS, SUNY, Buffalo, 1965, MS, 1990. Staff nurse Alaska Psychiat. Inst., Anchorage, 1966; nurse in burn unit Emergency Hosp., Buffalo, 1969-70; nurse Gateway, Williamsville, N.Y., 1971, 82-88; nurse practitioner Buffalo VA Med. Ctr., 1990-91, Millard Fillmore Hosp., Buffalo, 1992-97, Ob/Gyn. Assocs. of Western N.Y., 1993, Buffalo Gen. Hosp., 1993-95, Bros. of Mercy Nursing and Rehab. Ctr., Clarence, N.Y., 1995—. Mem. alumni adv. bd. Sch. of Nursing SUNY, Buffalo. Recipient S. Mouchly Small award, 1965, Panhellenic award, 1959. Mem. N.Y. State Coalition Nurse Practitioners, Am. Acad. Nurse Practitioners, Sigma Theta Tau.

DECK, PAUL WAYNE, JR., federal judge; b. Sioux City, Iowa, Aug. 20, 1946; s. Paul W. and Marie I. (Larrabee) D.; m. Prudy J. Anthony, Aug. 9, 1969; children: Paul, Kathryn, Jonathan, Benjamin, Christopher, Patrick, Andrew. BA in Polit. Sci. and History, U. Nebr., 1968, JD, 1971. Asst. county atty. Woodbury County Attys. Office, Sioux City, Iowa, 1972-76; assoc. Paul W. Deck Law Offices, Sioux City, Iowa, 1972-76; prin. Deck & Deck, Sioux City, Iowa, 1976—; U.S. Magistrate judge U.S. Dist. Ct., Sioux City, Iowa, 1976-98. Cubmaster Boy Scouts of Am.; coach Boys Club, Little League, YMCA. Capt. USAR, 1970-76. Mem. Nebr. Bar Assn., Iowa Bar Assn., Woodbury County Bar Assn., Iowa Def. Coun. Assn., Iowa Assn. Workers Compensation Attys. (chmn. rules rev. com. 1982-86, mem. adv. com. Iowa Workers Compensation), Rotary. Methodist. Office: Deck & Deck 635 Frances Bldg 505 5th St Sioux City IA 51101-1500*

DECKARD, STEVE WAYNE, science educator, academic administrator; b. Lawrenceville, Ill., Apr. 9, 1953; m. Mary E. Chester, May 5, 1982; 1 child, Daniel. BS, McKendree Coll., 1975; MS, U. Ill., 1980; EdD, U. Sarasota, 1986; PhD in Christian Edn., Vision Internat. U., 1995. Cert. secondary and cmty. coll. tchr., Calif. Prof. The King's Coll., Briarcliff, N.Y., 1989-92; asst. prof. Inst. Creation Rsch., Santee, Calif., 1991-97; v.p. acad. affairs Trinity Bible Coll., 1997—. Author: Homeschooling Laws All Fifty States, (9 edits., 1985—. Office: Inst Creation Rsch 10946 Woodside Ave N Santee CA 92071-2833

DECKELBAUM, NELSON, lawyer; b. Washington, Apr. 1, 1928; s. Fred and Rose (Egber) D.; m. Louann Jacobs, Oct. 19, 1952; children: David Alan, Todd Stuart. B.S., Georgetown U., 1950, J.D., 1952. Bar: D.C. 1952, Md. 1957, U.S. Supreme Ct. 1966. Practice law Washington, 1952—; sr. partner Deckelbaum Ogens Reiser & Shedlock, Chartered, 1974—; Staff mem. Commn. on Govt. Security, 1956. Chmn. Democratic precinct, Montgomery County, Md., 1958. Served with USAF, 1952-54. Named in Best Lawyers in Am. Fellow Am. Coll. of Bankruptcy; mem. Am., Md., D.C. bar assns., Am. Judicature Soc., Georgetown Univ. Alumni Assn., Woodmont Country Club, Univ. Club (pres. 1994-95), D.C. Real Estate Commn. Home: 5104 52nd Ct NW Washington DC 20016-4374 Office: Deckelbaum Ogens Reiser & Shedlock Chartered 1140 Connecticut Ave NW Ste 703 Washington DC 20036-4089 also: 6701 Democracy Blvd Bethesda MD 20817-1572

DECKER, CATHERINE HELEN, English language educator; b. Lower Merion, Pa., June 1, 1965; d. Leonard Edward and Harriet Anne D.; m. Roland Curt Burgess, May 25, 1991. BA, LaSalle U., 1987; MA, U. Rochester, 1989, PhD, 1994. Instr. English U. Rochester, N.Y., 1989-92; lectr. English SUNY, Geneseo, 1990-91; instr. English Auburn (Ala.) U., 1993, San Bernardino (Calif.) Valley Coll., 1995, 97; instr. arts and humanties Chaffey Coll., Rancho Cucamonga, Calif., 1995—; instr. English Calif. State U., San Bernardino, 1995-97; rschr. psychology U. Calif., Riverside, 1992—; rschr. ESTC, Riverside, Calif., 1993. Contbr. book rev. to Wordworth Cir., 1995; editl. asst.: (electronic jour.) Electric Dreams, 1994-95; webmistress: (web sites) The Regency Fashion Page, The Regency Page, Neurosci. Program UCR Homepage. Competitive scholar La Salle U., 1983-87; Sproull fellow U. Rochester, 1987-89, fellow, 1989-90, NEH summer seminar fellow, 1995. Mem. Am. Soc. 18th-Century Studies, Aphra Behn Soc. (comm. chair 1994-95, editor newsletter 1995), Cat Lovers of Am., Freedom Valley Girl Scout Alumnae. Democrat. Unitarian Universalist. Avocations: fashion research, bargello, Cornhusker football fan. Office: U Calif Riverside Dept Psychology 1419 Life Scis Riverside CA 92521-0426

DECKER, CHARLES RICHARD, investment executive; b. Murphysboro, Ill., Mar. 13, 1937; s. Ernest George and Joyce Ellen (Gibson) D.; m. Jeanine Ann Cowell, June 6, 1959; children: Ann Marie Britt, Lynn Rochelle Lake, Charles Ernest. BBA, U. Miss., 1959; MBA, Ind. U., 1962, EdD, 1968; cert., Harvard U., 1981. Cert. fin. planner, 1990. Asst. prof. Ill. State U., Normal, 1968-70, chmn. dept. bus. adminstrn., 1970-74; dean sch. bus. Millikin U., Decatur, Ill., 1974-80; provost, v.p. Millikin U., Decatur, 1980-86, Grover M. Hermann prof. bus. policy, 1986-98; investment mgr., bd. dirs. John Warner Fin. Svcs. Inc., 1996—. Contbr. articles to profl. jours. Bd. dirs. Decatur Civic Ctr., 1984-92, vice chmn., 1986-87, chmn., 1987-92; bd. dirs. United Way of Decatur and Macon County, 1984-87, Boys Club, Decatur, 1980-82; mem. exec. bd. Lincoln Trails Coun. Boy Scouts Am., 1988-93, SME chair, 1989-91, v.p., 1990-93. Mem. North Cent. Assn. Acad. Deans (pres. 1984-85), C. of C. (bd. dirs. 1976-79, v.p. 1979), Alpha Lambda Delta, Phi Delta Kappa, Phi Kappa Phi, Omicron Delta Kappa, Sigma Chi. Avocations: photography, tennis, biking, golf. Home: 1740 Illini Dr Decatur IL 62521-9169

DECKER, CHRISTINE MARIE, healthcare administrator; b. Morristown, N.J., Feb. 4, 1947; d. George and Jenneke (Van Dyken) Laufenberg; m. James J. Decker, Oct. 5, 1968; children: James, Johanna. BSN, Villanova U., 1968; postgrad., Rider Coll., 1984—. RN, N.J., Pa. Supr. residential and profl. svcs. State of N.J., Skillman, 1981-82; mgr. quality assurance Managed Care System, Mt. Holly, N.J., 1987-88; program dir. health care accreditation programs N.J. Hosp. Assn., Princeton, 1982-87; asst. v.p. corp. quality assessment U.S. Healthcare, Blue Bell, Pa., 1988-95; quality mgmt. cons., northeast health svcs. team AETNA, Wayne, Pa., 1995-96; dir. PricewaterhouseCoopers, Phila., 1996—. Mem. Nat. Assn. Healthcare Quality, N.J. Assn. Quality Assurance Profls. (sec. bd. dirs.). Home: 6 Charred Oak Ln Hightstown NJ 08520-1804

DECKER, CYNTHIA J. SCHAFER, community and occupational health nurse; b. Easton, N.Y., July 4, 1950; d. Frederick Phillip III and Mary Louise (Whelden) Schafer; m. Charles Robert Decker, Jr., Feb. 23, 1974. Diploma, Samaritan Hosp. Sch. Nursing, Troy, N.Y., 1972; BS in Health Care Mgmt., Empire State Coll., 1995. RN, N.Y.; cert. QMRP. Head nurse, medication nurse Samaritan Hosp., 1972-73; nurse operating and recovery rooms, med.-surg. floor Community Hosp. Schoharie County, Cobleskill, N.Y., 1973-78; coord., field nurse Upjohn HealthCare Svcs., Albany, N.Y., 1978-84; program nurse sheltered workshop Schoharie County Assn. Retarded Children, Schoharie, N.Y., 1984-93; health svcs. adminstr. Schoharie County Assn. Retarded Children, Schoharie, 1993—. Sec. Schoharie County Sheriff's Tactical Search and Rescue Force, 1995. Mem. N.Y. State Mental Retardation-Devel. Disabled Nurses Assn. (rec. sec. 1987-88, 90-92, seminar com., past mem. newsletter com.), Samaritan Hosp. Sch. Nursing Alumni Assn. Office: Schoharie Co Chpt NYS ARC PO Box 307 Schoharie NY 12157-0307

DECKER, DAVID ALFRED, lawyer; b. Waukegan, Ill., Nov. 30, 1937; s. Alfred D. and Marian (Bellows) D.; m. Mary Louise Kirby, Apr. 1, 1967; children: Kathleen, David Jr., Michael. Grad. in Liberal Arts, Lake Forest Coll., 1960; JD, Northwestern U., 1963. Bar: Ill. 1964. Atty. Pretzel & Stouffer, Chgo., 1964-65, Phillip E. Howard, Chgo., 1965-67, Howard & Decker, Chgo., 1967-79, David Decker & Assoc., Waukegan, Ill., 1969-87, Decker and Linn, Ltd., Waukegan, Ill., 1987—. Cpl. U.S. Army, 1956-58. Fellow Internat. Acad. Trial Lawyers, Am. Coll. Trial Lawyers; mem. Am. Trial Lawyers Assn. (bd. govs. 1980—), Ill. State Bar Assn. (pres. 1994-95), Ill. Trial Lawyers Assn. (pres. 1985-86). Democrat. Roman Catholic. Avocations: golf, literature, jazz. Office: Decker and Linn Ltd 215 N Utica St Waukegan IL 60085-4235

DECKER, DENNIS DALE, industrial designer; b. Stuttgart, Germany, July 23, 1954; came to U.S., 1955; s. Gregory Royce and Violet Louise (Keniston) D. BS in Agriculture, U. Ariz., 1977. Draftsman Maricopa County Assessor, Phoenix, Ariz., 1972-73; sr. landscape designer Del Webb, Sun City, Ariz., 1974-76; regional rschr. Sunset Mag., Tucson, 1977; pvt. practice landscape designer Tucson, 1977-79; flight attendant Pan Am. Airways, Honolulu and N.Y.C., 1979-86; sr. indsl. designer Handler, N.Y.C., 1988-93; indsl. designer Decker Design, N.Y.C., 1993-96; design product mgr. Polo Ralph Lauren, N.Y.C., 1996-98; design dir. Prescriptives, 1998—; commr. publs. Phoenix Coll., 1972-73; guest instr. Parsons Sch. Design, N.Y.C., 1992-93. Illustrator, artist Growing Fields, El Independiente, Tucson, 1976-77; editorial cartoonist Sepia Mag., Ft. Worth, 1979-81; design represented in permanent collection Cooper Hewitt Mus., N.Y.C., Mus. Modern Art, N.Y.C. Recipient Consumer Products Design award Indsl. Design mag., 1991, 94, First Place award Mcpl. Art Soc., 1993. Mem. Indsl. Designers Soc. Am. (Bronze Design award 1992), Phi Theta Kappa, Alpha Zeta. Democrat. Avocation: restoring historic buildings. Fax no. 212-944-2273; email: dd230@aol.com. Home: 29 W 37th St Studio 1 New York NY 10018-6232

DECKER, FRANZ PAUL, symphony conductor, educator; b. Cologne, Germany; s. Caspar and Elisabeth (Scholz) D.; m. Christa Terka, May 26, 1969; children: Arabella, Ariadne. Grad. high sch.; student, State Inst. for Mus. Edn., Cologne; M.Conducting, U. Cologne; Dr. honoris causa, Concordia U., Montreal, Que., Can. Choir dir., asst. condr., Municipal Theater, Giessen, 1945, condr. opera, Cologne, 1945, municipal dir. music, Krefeld, from 1946, prin condr., State Opera house, Wiesbaden, 1950-53, permanent dir., Municipal Symphony Orch., Wiesbaden, 1953-56, general music director, Bochum, 1956-64, chief condr., artistical dir., Rotterdam Philharmonic Orch., 1962-68, permanent condr., mus. dir., Montreal Symphony Orch., 1967-76, guest condr. opera and concerts worldwide; prin.

guest condr. New Zealand Symphony, 1981-89, music dir., 1990-94; chief condr. and artistical dir. Orquestra Sinfonica de Barcelona, 1986—; prin. guest condr. Nat. Arts Ctr. Orch., Ottawa, 1991—; composer symphonies, opera, oratories, chamber music. Decorated Edgar Roquette Pinto medal Brazil, 1963, Herscheppend Schep Ik medal Netherlands, 1968; Order of Merit 1st class Fed. Republic of Germany; Jubilee medal Queen Elizabeth II. Club:, (). Address: 2 Kronenburgerstrasse, 50935 Koeln 41, Germany also: National Arts Centre Orchestra, P.O. Box 1534, Stn B, Ottawa, ON Canada K1P 5W1*

DECKER, GILBERT FELTON, manufacturing company executive; b. Marietta, Ga., June 23, 1937; s. Felton Ambrose and Mary Irene (Pettyjohn) D.; children: Carlyle F., Donna L., Michael T. BSEE, Johns Hopkins U., 1958; MS, Stanford U., 1966. Systems engr. Sylvania Electronics Products, Mountain View, Calif., 1964-66; program mgr. ESL, Inc., Sunnyvale, Calif., 1966-69; v.p. engring. ESL, Inc., 1969-75, v.p. ops., 1975-77, pres., 1978-82; v.p. new ventures TRW Inc., 1982-85; pres. Penn Central Fed. Systems Co., 1985-90; pres., chief exec. officer Acurex Corp., Mountain View, Calif., 1990-93; asst. sec. rsch. devel. and acquisition Dept. Army, Washington, 1994-97; pvt. cons., 1997—. Chmn. fund-raising com. Jobs for Progress, Inc., fund-raising div. United Way, Army Sci. Bd., 1987-89; mem. engring. adv. bd. Johns Hopkins U. Served with U.S. Army, 1958-64. Mem. Am. Electronics Assn. (mem. exec. com.), Santa Clara County Mfrs. Group (dir.), Res. Officers Assn., Assn. U.S. Army, Air Force Assn., Assn. Old Crows, Army Sci. Bd. (chmn.), Am. Def. Preparedness Assn., Tau Beta Pi, Eta Kappa Nu, Pi Tau Sigma. *

DECKER, JAMES LUDLOW, management consultant; b. Batavia, N.Y., Nov. 5, 1923; s. James Ludlow and Ruth Adeline (Peard) D.; B.Aero.Engring., Rensselaer Poly. Inst., 1944; postgrad. Textron Advanced Mgmt. Program, Harvard U., 1974; m. Bette Wilson Botzler, Jan. 31, 1997. Registered profl. engr., Md. With The Martin Co., Balt., 1944-67; dep. mgr. Lunar Module, Apollo Office, NASA, Houston, 1963; program mgr. surface effect ship program U.S. Navy, Washington, 1967-72; v.p., gen. mgr. Bell Aerospace Can., Grand Bend, Ont., 1972-74; prin. J.L. Decker, Cons., Potomac, Md., 1974—; guest lectr. AIAA, 1972-79, Can. Aeros. and Space Inst., 1973-79, George Washington U., 1974, Royal Aero. Soc., 1972, Aero. Engring. Rensselaer Poly. Inst., 1990—; cons. USN, Maritime Adminstrn., USCG, NRC Can., Can. Coast Guard, various corps., 1972—. Pres., Greenbrier Community Assn., 1956-57; regional chmn. Rensselaer Fund, 1982; mem. Congl. Subcom. to Rev. NASA Adv. Com. Utilization, 1987; mem. pres.'s adv. coun. Meredith Coll., 1999. Buffalo Alumni scholar, 1941-44, N.Y. State Regents scholar, 1941-44, Rensselaer Alumni fellow, 1991. Mem. AIAA (assoc. fellow), Soc. Naval Architects and Marine Engrs., Am. Soc. Naval Engrs., Rensselaer Soc. Engrs., N.Y. Acad. Sci., Patroons of Rensselaer, Cosmos Club, Washington, Sigma Xi, Tau Beta Pi. Republican. Baptist. Club: Towson Golf and Country. Contbr. articles to profl. jours.; patentee in field. Address: 1 Shawnery Ct Baldwin MD 21013-9657

DECKER, JOHN LAWS, physician; b. Bklyn., June 27, 1921; s. John William and Margaret (Laws) D.; m. Lucille Macbeth, Nov. 13, 1954; children: Virginia Elliott, David Laws, Margaret Cauthorn, Susan Curtis. BA, U. Richmond, 1942; MD, Columbia U., 1951. Intern, asst. resident, chief resident medicine Presbyn. Hosp., N.Y.C., 1951-55; research fellow medicine Mass. Gen. Hosp., 1955-58; instr. medicine Columbia Coll. Physicians and Surgeons, 1954- 55; tutor med. scis. Harvard Med. Sch., 1957-58; from instr. to assoc. prof. medicine U. Wash. Med. Sch., 1958-65; chief arthritis and rheumatism br. Nat. Inst. Arthritis, Diabetes and Digestive and Kidney Diseases, NIH, Bethesda, Md., 1965-83; assoc. dir. clin. care, dir. Clin. Ctr. NIH, Bethesda, Md., 1983-90, scientist emeritus, 1990—. Contbr. articles to profl. jours. Served to lt. USNR, 1942-46. Decorated Purple Heart. Master ACP (bd. govs. 1982-86), Am. Coll. Rheumatology (pres. 1972-73, gold medal 1989); mem. Phi Beta Kappa, Alpha Omega Alpha, Omicron Delta Kappa, Phi Gamma Delta, Nu Sigma Nu. Home: 10201 Grosvenor Pl Apt 801 Rockville MD 20852-4614

DECKER, JOHN WILLIAM, steel company executive; b. Cleve., July 15, 1948; s. James William and Betty Erdmann (Smith) D.; m. Elaine Marie Metz, Aug. 30, 1971; children: Amanda Elaine, Gregory John. BS, Lincoln Meml. U., 1966-70; MEd, Kent (Ohio) State U., 1970-72. Cert. tchr., adminstr., Ohio. Elem. tchr. Parma (Ohio) City Schs., 1970-78; corp. sec., treas. Decker Steel & Supply, Inc. (formerly Decker Reichert Steel & Supply, Inc.), Cleve., 1978-83, v.p., 1983-85, pres., chmn., chief exec. officer, 1985—. Ruling elder Parma South Presbyn. Ch., Parma Heights, Ohio, 1979-81, 83-92, 96—, clk. of session, 1983-94, chmn. fin. com. , 1995-96, chmn. properties coun., 1997—; mem. Am. Theater Orgn. Soc., Playhouse Square Vol. Group; co-chmn. cmty. fin. com. Parma City Schs., 1994-97; apptd. Parma Bd. Edn., 1997, elected, 1998—, v.p., 1999—. Mem. Greater Cleve. Growth Assn. Republican. Lodge: Masons. Avocations: choral group singing, pipe organ playing, repair and building, collecting antique telephones. Home: 9634 Greenbriar Dr Cleveland OH 44130-4756 Office: 4500 Train Ave Cleveland OH 44102-4515

DECKER, JOSEPHINE I., health clinic official; b. Barling, Ark., May 24, 1933; d. Ralph and Ada A. (Claborn) Snider; m. William Arlen Decker, Feb. 4, 1952; 1 child, Peter A. BS in Health Mgmt., Kennedy Western U., 1986, MS in Bus. Adminstrn., 1987. With Southwestern Bell Tel. Co., Ft. Smith, Ark., 1951-52; with Holt Crock Clinic, Ft. Smith, 1952—, bus. adminstr., 1970—. Bd. dirs. Sparks Credit Union; mem. adv. coun. Northside H.S., Southside H.S., Ft. Smith, Ft. Worth Girls Shelter, Ft. Worth Credit Bur. Mem. Credit Women Internat., Soc. Cert. Consumer Credit Execs. Office: Holt Krock Clinic 1500 Dodson Ave Fort Smith AR 72901-5128

DECKER, JUDITH ANN, computer science educator; b. LeMars, Iowa, Sept. 14, 1943; d. Lyle Adolph and Viola Helen (Stratmann) Rachuy; m. John F. Decker, Aug. 3, 1967. BA, U. Dubuque, 1965; MS, U. Iowa, 1967, U. Ill., 1980. Instr. math. U. Nebr., Omaha, 1967-70; programmer, statistician Met. Life Ins. Co., N.Y.C., 1970-72; instr. data processing McHenry County Coll., Crystal Lake, Ill., 1972-75, Rock Valley Coll., Rockford, Ill., 1976-78, Highland Community Coll., Freeport, Ill., 1978-79; assoc prof. computer sci. Clarke Coll., Dubuque, Iowa, 1982—; cons. Stockton (Ill.) Data Svcs., 1976-80. Mem. Assn. for Computing Machinery, Upsilon Pi Upsilon, Kappa Delta Pi, Phi Kappa Delta, Delta Kappa Gamma. Home: 5186 S Schuller Rd Stockton IL 61085-9359 Office: Clarke Coll 1550 Clarke Dr Dubuque IA 52001-3117

DECKER, KATE DELANO CONDAX See CONDAX, KATE DELANO

DECKER, KURT HANS, lawyer, educator, author; b. Sept. 23, 1946; s. Hans Emil and Gertrude Elsa (Nestler) D.; m. Hilary McAllister, Aug. 13, 1973; children: Kurt Christian, Allison McAllister. BA in History, Thiel Coll., 1968; MPA, Pa. State U., 1973; JD, Vanderbilt U., 1976; LLM in Labor, Temple U., 1980. Bar: Pa. 1976, U.S. Tax Ct. 1977, U.S. Ct. Internat. Trade 1977, U.S. Ct. Claims 1979, U.S. Dist. Ct. (mid. dist.) Pa. 1976, U.S. Dist. Ct. (ea. dist.) Pa. 1980, U.S. Ct. Appeals (3d cir.) 1980, U.S. Supreme Ct. 1980. Asst. atty. gen. Gov.'s Office Pa. Bur. Labor Rels., Harrisburg, 1976-79; ptnr. Stevens & Lee, Reading, Pa., 1979—; adj. prof. indsl. rels. St. Francis Coll., Pa., 1985—, Widener Sch. Law, Harrisburg, Pa., 1993—; seminar spkr.; rschr. in field. Author: Employee Privacy: Law and Practice, 1987, Employee Privacy Forms and Procedures, 1988, A Manager's Guide to Employment Privacy: Law, Procedures and Policies, 1989, The Individual Employment Rights Primer, 1991, Covenants Not to Compete, 1993, Drafting and Revising Employment Policies and Handbooks, 1994, Privacy in the Workplace: Rights, Procedures and Policies, 1994, Hiring Legally: A Guide for Employees and Employers, 1999; co-author: Drafting and Revising Employment Contracts, 1991, Drafting and Revising Employment Handbooks, 1991, Individual Employee Rights in a Nutshell, 1995; editor: Jour. Individual Employment Rights, 1992—; adminstrv. editor Vanderbilt Jour. Transnat. Law; bd. editors Jour. Collective Negotiations in Pub. Sector, 1982—; contbr. chpts. to books, articles to profl. jours. With U.S. Army, 1968-72. Decorated Army Commendation medal. Mem. ABA (sect. labor and employment law), Pa. Bar Assn. (sect. labor and employment law), Phila. Bar Assn. (News Media award 1985), Berks County Bar Assn., Soc. for Human Resource Mgmt., Sigma Phi Epsilon, Phi Alpha Delta. Lutheran. Office: Stevens & Lee 111 N 6th St Reading PA 19601-3501

DECKER, MALCOLM DOYLE, insurance executive; b. Springfield, Mo., Sept. 10, 1946; s. Doyle Vancle and M. Evelyn (Barton) D.; m. Janis Kay Mount, June 1, 1968; children: Matthew William, Carrie Elizabeth. BS in Edn., S.W. Mo. State U., 1969. CLU, ChFC. Tchr., coach Camdenton (Mo.) Sch. Sys., 1971-75; agt. State Farm Ins. Cos., Lebanon, Mo., 1975-78, agy. mgr., 1978-95, agy. field cons., 1995-98; agy. adminstrv. asst. State Farm Ins. Cos., Columbia, Mo., 1999—; agt. State Farm Ins. Cos., Camdenton, Mo., 1999—. Pres. Laclede County Sheltered Workshop, Lebanon, 1978-81; mem. Lebanon Park Bd., 1982-83, pres., 1983; mem. Lebanon R-3 Sch. Bd., 1983-89; mem. Lebanon Babe Ruth Baseball World Series, 1985-95, exec. dir., 1991-94. 1st lt. U.S. Army, 1969-71, Vietnam. Mem. South West Mo. State Univ. Alumni (alumni bd., pres. 1996), Optimist Club (pres. 1975—), Masons (honor master 1983), Scottish Rite, Shriners. Southern Baptist. Avocations: flying, golf. Office: PO Box 650 Camdenton MO 65020

DECKER, MARK RICHARD, lawyer; b. Plainfield, N.J., Feb. 29, 1952; s. Mark and Margaret Mary (Flynn) D.; m. Erin Ann, Brian Richard, Raymond Mark. BA, Wesleyan U., Middletown, Conn., 1974; JD, Rutgers U., 1979. Asst. dean admissions Wesleyan U., Middletown, Conn., 1974-76; law sec. Superior Ct. N.J., Elizabeth, 1979-80; assoc. Ravin, Sarasohn, Cook, Baumgarten & Fisch, West Orange, N.J., 1980-85; v.p., gen. counsel Beneficial Comml. Corp., Peapack, N.J., 1985-88; counsel Stryker Tamms & Dill, Newark, 1988-89; v.p., gen. counsel Connell Fin. Co., Inc., Westfield, N.J., 1990—, The Connell Co., Westfield, 1993—. Bd. counsel Maplewood Twp. Rent Leveling Bd., Maplewood, N.J., 1983-89; cubmaster pack 4 Cub Scouts, Maplewood, 1991-93; chmn. pastoral counsel Our Lady of Sorrows Ch., South Orange, N.J., 1992-93. Mem. Am. Corp. Counsel Assn., Equipment Leasing Assn. (mem. legal com. 1995—), N.J. State Bar Assn. Avocations: hiking, canoeing, reading, family. Office: Connell Co 45 Cardinal Dr Westfield NJ 07090-1019*

DECKER, MICHAEL LYNN, lawyer, judge; b. Oklahoma City, May 5, 1953; s. Leroy Melvin and Yvonne (Baird) D.; m. Robin Strom, July 25, 1987. BA, Oklahoma City U., 1975, JD, 1978; grad., Nat. Jud. Coll., U. Nev., Reno, 1990. Bar: Okla. 1978, U.S. Ct. Appeals (10th cir.) 1979, U.S. Dist. Ct. (we. dist.) Okla. 1985, U.S. Supreme Ct. 1994. Assoc. Bay, Hamilton, Lees, Spears, and Verity, Oklahoma City, 1978-80; assoc. dir. devel. Oklahoma City U., 1980-81, asst. dean, Sch. of Law, 1981-82; sr. oil and gas adminstrv. law judge Okla. Corp. Commn., Oklahoma City, 1982-92, sr. asst. gen. counsel oil and gas conservation, 1992-95, deputy gen. counsel oil and gas conservation, 1995—; campaign staff intern U.S. Senator Henry Bellmon's Re-election Campaign, 1974; mem. Civil Arbitration Panel, U.S. Dist. Ct. (we. dist.) Okla., 1985—; seminar spkr. Am. Inst. Profl. Geologists (Okla. sect.), 1985; mem. dean's adv. com. Oklahoma City U. Law Sch., 1986; mem. sys. rev. bd. Okla. Corp. Commn., 1990-93, mem. process mgmt. rev. team, 1995-96; lectr. adminstrv. law Vanderbilt U. Sch. Law, 1993. Trustee Oklahoma City U., 1989-91, mem. alumni bd. dirs., 1988-95, also mem. devel. com., long range planning com. and adminstrv. liaison com.; mem. com. of twenty Oklahoma City Art Mus., 1987-95, co-chair omelette party, 1990; vol. Contact Teleminster, Oklahoma City, 1986-91, bd. dirs., 1987-90; mem. rev. bd. Okla. Corp. Commn., 1990; mem. adminstrv. bd. St. Luke's United Meth. Ch., 1988-92, chair missions com., 1993-94; bd. dirs. March of Dimes, Western Okla., 1990-93; mem. Class XI Leadership Oklahoma City, 1993; area rep. Okla. Mozart Fest., Bartlesville, 1988—. Mem. Okla. Bar Assn. (mineral law sect., environ. law sect.), Okla. County Bar Assn. (exec. com. young lawyers sect. 1978-82, mem. law day com. 1979-88, chmn. law day luncheon spkr. com. 1985-88), Oklahoma City Mineral Lawyers Soc., Lions, Phi Alpha Delta, Lambda Chi Alpha (treas. bldg. corp. 1984-89, pres. 1989-91, Outstanding Alumnus award 1983), Oklahoma City Dinner Club, Lester Raymer Soc. (Lindsborg, Kans.). Republican. Home: 2008 NW 44th St Oklahoma City OK 73118-1902 Office: Okla Corp Commn State Capitol Complex Jim Thorpe Bldg PO Box 52000-2000 Oklahoma City OK 73152-2000

DECKER, OSCAR CONRAD, JR., retired army officer; b. Moorefield, Nebr., Oct. 10, 1924; s. Oscar Conrad and June L. (Brunner) D.; m. Ella Mae Tillson, Nov. 8, 1944; children: Kathleen, Linda, David. B.S. in Bus. Adminstrn., U. Nebr., 1951; M.S. in Internat. Affairs, George Washington U., 1969; student, Command and Gen. Staff Coll., 1959-60, Armed Forces Staff Coll., 1964, Navy War Coll., 1968-69; D.Engring. (hon.), Mich. Technol. U., 1983. Served as enlisted man U.S. Army, 1943-46, commd. 2d lt., 1951, advanced through grades to maj. gen., 1976; mem. staff Dept. Army, Pentagon Washington, 1964-67; comdr. bn. Vietnam, 1967; exec. to Asst. Sec. of Army for installations and logistics, Pentagon, 1972-73; project mgr. U.S. Army Tank Automotive Command, Warren, Mich., 1969-72; dir. procurement and prodn. U.S. Army Tank Automotive Command, 1973-75, dep. comdg. gen., 1975-76, comdg. gen., 1976-83; ret., 1983. Decorated Legion of Merit with 3 oak leaf clusters, D.S.M., Army Commendation medal; named to Army Ordnance Hall of Fame, 1985. Mem. VFW, Am. Legion, Assn. U.S. Army, U.S. Armor Assn., Nat. Def. Indsl. Assn. Lutheran. *

DECKER, PETER RANDOLPH, rancher, former state official; b. N.Y.C., Oct. 1, 1934; s. Frank Randolph and Marjorie (Marony) D.; m. Dorothy Morss, Sept. 24, 1972; children: Karen, Christopher, Hilary. BA, Middlebury Coll., Vt., 1957; MA, Syracuse U., 1961; PhD, Columbia U., 1974. Tchr. Cate Sch., Carpinteria, Calif., 1961-63; sr. writer Congl. Quar., Washington, 1963-64; asst. to pres. Middlebury (Vt.) Coll., 1964-67; staff asst. Sen. Robert Kennedy, Washington, 1967-68; corr. AP, Laos, 1970; instr./lectr. Columbia U., N.Y.C., 1972-74; asst. prof. Duke U., Durham, N.C., 1974-80; owner, operator Double D Ranches, Ridgway, Colo., 1980—, Lewellen, Nebr., 1993—; commr. agr. State of Colo., Denver, 1987-89; pres. Decker & Assocs., Denver, Colo., 1989—; dir. Inst. Am. West, Nat. Western Stock Show, Denver; bd. dirs. Fed. Res. Bd. Kansas City, Denver, Western Colo. Bank, Montrose; pres. Telluride Bancorp, Inc., 1990-97. Author: Fortunes and Failures, 1978, old Fences, New Neighbors, 1998; contbr. articles to profl. jours. and mags. Overseer Middlebury Coll., 1988—, Colo. Commn. on Higher Edn., 1985-93; chmn. Ouray County Dem. Party, 1982-85; chmn. Ouray County Planning Commn., 1981-85; chmn. Colo. Endowment Humanities, 1982-85. Lt. U.S. Army, 1957-60, capt. Res., 1960-67. English Speaking Union scholar, 1952-53; Nat. Endowment for Humanities fellow Yale U., 1977-78, Rockefeller Found. fellow, 1979-80. Mem. Nat. Cattlemen's Assn., Nebr. Cattlemen's Assn., Colo. Livestock Assn., Denver Athletic Club, Elks. Democrat. Home: Double D Ranch 395 Race St Denver CO 80206-4118

DECKER, PETER WILLIAM, academic administrator; b. Grand Rapids, Mich., Mar. 20, 1919; s. Charles B. and Ruth E. (Thorndill) D.; m. Margaret I. Stainthorpe, June 10, 1944; children: Peter, Marilyn, Christine, Charles. BS, Wheaton Coll., 1941; postgrad. Northwestern U., 1942-43, U. Mich., 1958-60; DSc, London Inst. Applied Rsch., 1973, LLD, 1975, DSTh, Midwestern Baptist Bible Sem., 1995. With advt. dept. Hotels Windermere, Chgo., 1942, Princess Pat Cosmetics, Chgo., 1943; market rsch. investigator A.C. Nielson Co., Chgo., 1944-48; pres. Peter Decker Constrn. Co., Detroit, 1948-60; sales mgr. Century Chem. Products Co., Detroit, 1961-62, v.p., 1962-63, pres., 1963-75; sr. ptnr. G & D Advt. Assocs., 1967-78; v.p., treas., exec. dir. Christian Edn. Advancement, Inc., 1975-95; registrar, instr. N.T. Greek, Missions and Theology Birmingham (Mich.) Bible Inst., 1973-86; prof. Midwestern Baptist Coll., 1984—, dir. student fin. aid, 1984—, trustee, 1985—, mem. exec. com., 1986—, asst. to pres., 1985-90, treas., 1991-95; bd. dirs., prof., trustee Midwestern Bapt. Bible Seminary, 1995—, v.p. Midwestern Bapt. Bible Seminary Grad. Sch., 1998—. Author: Getting to Know New Testament Greek, Christology, The Pauline Epistles. Scout master, Boy Scouts of Am., 1956-61, neighborhood commr., 1961-66, scout master, 1956-61, merit badge counselor, emeritus, 1979—; mem. Bd. Rev., Beverly Hills, Mich., 1957-63; chmn. Bd. Rev. Southfield Twp., Mich., 1964-67; past pres., Beverly Hills Civic Assn., 1956, bd. dirs. 1953-57; trustee, deacon, Birmingham Mich. Bible Inst., instr. Bible Inst.; bd. dirs. Mich. Epilepsy Ctr. and Assn., 1957-71, exec. com., 1962-67. Recipient Arrowhead Honor award Boy Scouts Am., 1965. Mem. AAAS, ASTM, Mich. Edn. Assocs., Inc. (exec. com. 1994—, treas. 1994-95), Detroit Soc. Model Engrs. (pres. 1958, 62, bd. dir. 1955-71), Chem. Splty. Mfg. Assn., Nat. Geog. Soc., Internat. Platform Assn., The Heritage Found., Smithsonian Instn. Assocs., Archaeol. Inst. Am., Bibl. Archaeol. Soc., Bible-Sci. Assn., Creation Rsch. Soc., Mich. Student Fin. Aid Assn., Midwest Assn. Student Fin. Aid Adminstrs. Republican. Avocations: biographies, writings of great Christians. Home: 32210 Rosevear St Beverly Hills MI 48025-3921 Office: Midwestern Baptist Coll 825 Golf Dr Pontiac MI 48341-2379

DECKER, RAYMOND FRANK, scientist, technology transfer executive; b. Afton, N.Y., July 20, 1930; s. Bernett Hurd and Mildred (Bisbee) D.; m. Mary Birdsall, Dec. 27, 1951; children: Susan, Elizabeth, Catherine, Laura. BS, U. Mich., 1952, MS, 1955, PhD, 1958. With Inco Ltd., 1958-82, v.p. corp. tech. and diversification ventures, 1978-82; v.p. rsch. and corp. rels. Mich. Technol. U., Houghton, 1982-86; pres., CEO Univ. Sci. Ptnrs., Inc., 1986-98; pres. ASM Internat., 1986-87; founding chmn. Thixomat, Inc., 1988—, also bd. dirs.; founding chmn. Wavemat, Inc., 1987-88; bd. dirs. Lindberg Corp., Spl. Metals Corp.; adj. prof. Poly. Inst. Bklyn., 1962-66, NYU, 1968, U. Mich., 1997—; cons. KMS Fusion, Inc., Howmet Turbine Components, Alcoa, GE, GM, 1985—; Van Horn disting. lectr. Case-Western Res. U., 1975; mem. materials adv. bd. NASA, 1969, Nat. Bur. Standards, 1973, NSF, 1985-86; mem. Nat. Materials Adv. Bd., 1982-88; mem. exec. com. Strategic Hwy. Rsch. Program, 1986-93, long-range planning com. The Metall. Soc., 1985-87, State rsch. Fund Panel Mich., 1983-86; chmn. Rsch. & Tech. Coordinating Com. of Fed. Hwy. Adminstrsn., 1995-98; trustee Foundry Ednl. Found., 1975-77, Welding Rsch. Coun., 1975-80; chmn. bd. trustees Mich. Energy and Resource Rsch. Assn., 1985-86; keynote spkr. on superalloys Seven Springs Conf., 1980, NAE, 1980—. Author: Strengthening Mechanisms in Nickel-base Superalloys; editor: Maraging Steels. Chmn. alumni com. Material Sci. & Engring. Dept., U. Mich., Ann Arbor, 1995—, mem. Nat. Materials Com., 1995; vice chmn. coun. Congregational Ch., Ann Arbor, Mich. Recipient IR-100 award, 1964, Sesquicentennial award U. Mich., 1967, Disting. Grad. award U. Mich., 1994. Fellow Am. Soc. Metals Internat. (chmn. materials systems and design divsn. 1971-73, trustee 1976-79, chmn. organizing com. World Materials Congress 1988, Campbell Meml. lectr. 1985, Gold medal 1981, chmn. diamond decade com. 1980-81, hon. mem. 1991); mem. AIME (lectr. Inst. Metals divsn. 1973, R.F. Mehl medal 1973), AAAS. Congregationalist. Co-inventor maraging steels, Thixomolding machine. Home: 3065 Provincial Dr Ann Arbor MI 48104-4117

DECKER, RICHARD KNORE, lawyer; b. Lincoln, Nebr., Sept. 15, 1913; s. Fred William and Georgia (Kilmer) D.; m. Fern Iona Steinbaugh, June 12, 1938. AB, U. Nebr., 1935, JD, 1938. Bar: Nebr. 1938, U.S. Supreme Ct. 1941, D.C. 1948, Ill. 1952. Trial atty. antitrust div. Dept. Justice, 1938-52; ptnr. Lord, Bissell & Brook, Chgo., 1953-84, of counsel, 1984—. Trustee Village of Clarendon Hills (Ill.), 1960-64; chmn. bd. elders Community Presbyn. Ch., Clarendon Hills, 1963-66; mem. Christ Ch. of Oak Brook; chmn. bd. Community House, Hinsdale, Ill., 1976, Robert Crown Center Health Edn., Hinsdale, Ill., 1981-83, also bd. dirs. With USNR, 1942-45, lt. comdr. ret. Mem. ABA (chmn. antitrust sect. 1971-72), Ill. Bar Assn. (gov. 1969-73, chmn. antitrust sect. 1964-66), Chgo. Bar Assn. (chmn. antitrust law com. 1956-59), Law Club Chgo. Republican. Clubs: Met., Hinsdale Golf (pres. 1968). Home: 196 Pheasant Hollow Dr Burr Ridge IL 60521-5051 Office: 115 S La Salle St Ste 2900 Chicago IL 60603-3801

DECKER, ROBERT OWEN, history educator, clergyman; b. Lafayette, Ind., Nov. 6, 1927; s. Samuel Owen and Helen Dale (Noble) D.; m. Margaret Ann Harris, May 30, 1948; 1 child, Terry Lynn Decker DeIulis. AB, Butler U., 1953; AM, Ind. U., 1958; PhD, U. Conn., 1970. Ordained to ministry Congregational Ch., 1990. Instr. City of LaPorte (Ind.) Schs., 11956-59; instr. Ctrl. Conn. State U., New Britain, 1959-63, asst. prof., 1963-73, assoc. prof., 1973-77, prof. history, 1977-89, prof. emeritus, 1989—; editor manuscripts Wesleyan U. Press, 1977-89; advisor NEH, 1977-89, Connecticut River Found. Author: Whaling Industry of New London, 1973, The Whaling City: A History of New London, 1976, A Student Guidebook to American History, 1983, Hartford Immigrants, 1987, The New London Merchants, 1986, Cromwell, Connecticut 1650-1990: The History of A River Port Town, 1991; contbr. articles and book revs. to profl. jours. Mem. Christian Activities Coun., Hartford, 1965—, pres., 1972-74, 76-78, historian, 1983—, life mem., 1996—; bd. dirs. Hartford Inner City Exch., 1971-81, chmn. bd., 1977-80; chmn. state legis. adv. com. Conn. Devel. Disabilities Coun., 1973-75; evaluator programs Conn. Humanities Coun.; historian Rocky Hill (Conn.) Congl. Ch., 1985-89, Conn. 350th Com., 1985-89; justice of peace, Rocky Hill, 1985—, constable, 1986-89, apptd. town historian, 1988—; mem. Assn. Conn. Mcpl. Historians, 1988—, membership sec., 1994—, pres., 1996-97; pastor Eagle Rock Congl. Ch., 1989-93, Bozrah Centre Congl. Ch., 1994-95, supply pastor, 1995—; mem. exec. bd. Conn. Congl. Christian Chs., 1995—; mem. UCC Hist. Com., 1989-92; dir. Old Towne Tourism Dist. Conn., 1989-90. Served with U.S. Army, 1946-48, 50-51. Asian Studies grantee, 1959; Am. Studies grantee, 1959; Danforth grantee, 1962; Munson Maritime grantee, 1961; Smithsonian Inst. grantee, 1963. Mem. Orgn. Am. Historians, Am. Hist. Assn., New Eng. Hist. Assn., Conn. Hist. Assn., Assn. for Study of Conn. History, AAUP, New London County Hist. Soc., Am. Waldensian Aid Soc. (pres. Hartford chpt. 1986-89), Masons, (Master Stepney Lodge 1990, 92, Master's award 1992, Arthur E. Warner award 1996, Grand Chaplain 1997—, High Priest Delta chpt. 1998-99, Knight Mason 1998—), Phi Alpha Depta. Republican. Congregationalist (life deacon). Home: 2623 Main St Rocky Hill CT 06067-2507 Office: Fellowship Conn Congl Chs 277 Main St Hartford CT 06106-1818

DECKER, SHARYN LYNN, newspaper reporter; b. Santa Rosa, Calif., Nov. 6, 1960; d. Richard Lee and Vicki Catherine (Whearty) D. AA with honors, Shoreline C.C., Seattle, 1989; BA in Bus. Administrn. and Comm. magna cum laude, U. Wash., 1994. Groundskeeper Evergreen Washelli, Seattle, 1980-98; reporter news svcs. U. Wash., Seattle, 1994; freelance writer, 1994—; intern reporter The Herald, Everett, Wash., 1995-96; bus. reporter Valley Daily News, Kent, Wash., 1996, The Herald, Everett, Wash., 1998; contbg. writer The Herald Bus. Jour., Everett, 1998; reporter The Enterprise Newspapers, Lynnwood, Wash., 1999; reporter, The Enterprise Newspapers, Wash., 1999. contbrg. writer, The Herald Bus. Jour., Everett, Wash., 1998. Recipient Hon. Mention, Wash. Press Assn. Communicator Excellence Contest, 1998. Mem. Nat. Soc. Profl. Journalists (sec. Western Wash. profl. chpt. 1995-98, honorable mention Pacific Northwest Excellence Journalism comp. 1995), U. Wash. Comm. Alumni Assn., Golden Key Nat. Honor Soc., Beta Gamma Sigma, Phi Beta Kappa. Avocations: photography, travel. E-mail: sharyn1000@aol.com. Home: 9626 234th St SW Edmonds WA 98020-5036

DECKER, SUSAN CAROL, elementary education educator; b. Syracuse, N.Y., Sept. 24, 1951; d. Jerome Herbert and Eleanor May (DeRoo) Fuchs; m. John M. Decker, Feb. 13, 1971; children: Steven, Jennifer. BS in Elem. Edn., SUNY, Oneonta, 1989, MS in Elem. Edn., 1994. Cert. elem. tchr., N.Y. Tchr. Johnson City (N.Y.) Schs., 1990-92, Windsor (N.Y.) Ctrl. Schs., 1992—. Illustrator (book) Advanced Manufacturing Methods, 1988. 4H human devel. com. Cornell-Coop. Ext., Binghamton, N.Y., 1987-89; leader Girl Scouts Am., Windsor, 1990-94. Mem. N.Y. State United Tchrs. (union rep. 1996—, bldg. rep. 1996). Avocation: travel. Home: 87 Baker Rd Windsor NY 13865-1538

DECKER, WALTER JOHNS, toxicologist; b. Tannersville, N.Y., June 13, 1933; s. H. Russell and Leola May (Coons) D.; m. Barbara Allen Hart, Aug. 19, 1961; children: Karl Hart, Reid Johns, Sam Travis. BA, SUNY, Albany, 1954, MA, 1955; PhD, George Washington U., 1966. Commd. 2d lt. U.S. Army, 1955, advanced through grades to lt. col., 1970, ret., 1975; assoc. prof. U. Tex. Med. Br., Galveston, 1976-83; pres. Toxicology Cons. Svcs., El Paso, Tex., 1984-97; adj. clin. prof. Tex. Tech. U., El Paso, 1991—. Contbr. articles to jours. Clin. Toxicology, Vet. and Human Toxicology, Toxicology and Applied Pharmacology, others. Mem. sci. rev. panel Nat. Libr. Medicine's Hazardous Substance Data Bank, Bethesda, Md., 1985—; chair steering com. West Tex. Poison Ctr., El Paso, 1994-96. Recipient Aesculapius award Tex. Med. Assn., 1977. Fellow Am. Acad. Clin. Toxicology; mem. Soc. Toxicology. Episcopalian. Achievements include research in toxicology.

DECKER, WAYNE LEROY, meteorologist, educator; b. Patterson, Iowa, Jan. 24, 1922; s. Albert Henry and Effie (Holmes) D.; m. Martha Jane Livingston, Dec. 29, 1943; 1 dau., Susan Jane. B.S., Central Coll., Pella, Iowa, 1943; postgrad., UCLA, 1943-44; M.S., Iowa State U., 1947, Ph.D., 1955. Meteorologist U.S. Weather Bur., Washington and Des Moines, 1947-49; mem. faculty U. Mo. at Columbia, 1949—, prof. atmospheric sci., 1958-67, prof., chmn. dept. atmospheric sci., 1967-91; prof. emeritus U. Mo.,

Columbia, 1992—; dir. coop. inst. applied meteorology U. Mo. at Columbia, 1985-92; cons. climatologist, 1992—; chmn. com. climatic fluctuations and agrl. prodn. NRC, 1975-76; bd. dirs. Council for Agrl. Sci. and Tech., 1978-85, mem. exec. com., 1981-85. Fellow Am. Meteorol. Soc.; mem. Internat. Soc. Biometeorology (treas.), Am. Geophys. Union, Am. Agronomy Soc., Sigma Xi, Gamma Sigma Delta. Home: 1007 Hulen Dr Columbia MO 65203-1414 Office: U Mo 116 Gentry Hall Columbia MO 65211

DECKER, WILLIAM ALEXANDER, editor; b. Williamsport, Pa., Feb. 20, 1952; s. John Christian and Elizabeth (Tally) D.; m. Cynthia Morris, Aug. 8, 1981; children: Kurtis William, Laura Elizabeth. BA, Bucknell U., 1974; MA, Wheaton Grad. Sch., 1979, Luth. Northwestern Theol. Sem., 1987. News reporter Grit Newspaper, Williamsport, Pa., summers 1970-73; mgr., editor publicity dept. Wycliffe Bible Translators and Summer Inst. of Linguistics, Republic of Philippines, 1974-76, Ukarumpa, Papua New Guinea, 1983-85; editor Town and Country Newspaper, Seneca, Ill., 1979-82; asst. editor Am. Luth. Ch., Mpls., 1986-87; asst. to editor Luth. Partners Evang. Luth. Ch. in Am., Chgo., 1988-94; mng. editor Luth. Partners Evangelical Luth. Ch. in Am., Chgo., 1994—; mem. Associated Ch. Press, Washington, 1988—; assoc. in ministry Evang. Luth. Ch. in Am., Chgo., 1988—. Organizer, fundraiser, walker CROP (hunger) Walk, Des Plaines, 1990—; mem. Arthritis Found., Chgo., 1992—; adult religious edn. tchr. Luth. Congregations, 1979—. Mem. Bread for the World, Concord Coalition, Religious Pub. Rels. Coun., Common Cause. Avocations: piano, bicycling, singing, swimming. Home: 619 Yale Ct Des Plaines IL 60016

DECKERS, PETER JOHN, dean; b. Boston, Feb. 13, 1941; married, 1964; 7 children. BA cum laude, Coll. of the Holy Cross, 1962; MD cum laude, Boston U., 1966. Diplomate Nat. Bd. Med. Examiners, Am. Bd. Surgery. Med. intern Boston City Hosp., 1966-67; jr. asst. resident gen. surgery Boston U. Med. Ctr., Univ. Hosp., 1967-68; clin. assoc. surgery br. Nat. Cancer Inst., NIH, Bethesda, 1968-70; resident gen. surgery Boston U. Med. Ctr., U. Hosp., 1971, UPSHS trainee in acad. surgyer, 1971-72, resident in gen. surgery, 1972-73, chief resident in gen. surgery, 1973-74; staff surgeon Boston City Hosp., 1974-84; asst. prof. surgery Boston U. Sch. Medicine, 1974-78; dean U. Conn. Sch. of Medicine, 1995—; cons., attending staff gen. surgery John Dempsey Hosp./U. Conn. Health Ctr., 1984—, VA Med. Ctr., 1984-89; sr. staff dept. surgery Hartford Hosp., 1984—; program dir. Hartford Hosp.-U. Conn. Integrated Surg. Residency Program, 1984-94; dir. divsn. of gen. surgery Hartford Hosp., 1984-87; adj. prof. surgery Dartmouth Coll., Hanover, N.H., 1984-95; interim chief divsn. of gen. surgery U. Conn. Sch. of Medicine, 1985-86, interim chmn., 1985-86; sr. staff dept. surgery New Britain Gen. Hosp., 1989—, Dept. Surgery, Mt. Sinai Hosp., 1989—, St. Francis Hosp. and Med. Ctr., 1988—; chmn. dept. surgery Hartford Hosp., 1987-94, chmn. dept. surgery, 1987-94; Murray-Heilig prof., chmn. dept. surgery U. Conn. Sch. of Medicine, 1987-95; surgeon-in-chief John Dempsey Hosp., 1990-94; program dir. U. of Conn. Integrated Gen. Surg. Residency Tng. Program, 1990-94; interim divsn. chief, divsn. of gen. surgery U. Conn. Sch. Medicine, 1991-92, interim dean, 1992-94; exec. v.p. for clin. affairs U. Conn. Health System, 1994-95; exec. v.p. for physician practice orgn. U. Conn. Health System, 1995—. Editl. bd. Breast Surgery: Index and Reviews, 1993—, Surg. Oncology, 1991—; contbr. numerous articles to profl. jours. Recipient First Prize James Ewing Resident Rsch. award, 1971; recipient numerous grants. Mem. Transplantation Soc., Am. Assn. for Cancer Rsch., Eastern Coop. Oncology Group, Assn. for Acad. Surgery, Am. Assn. for Cancer Edn., Am. Fedn. for Clin. Rsch., Mass. Med. Soc., Am. Radium Soc. (exec. com. 1989-91), Am. Soc. of Clin. Oncology, Soc. of Surg. Oncology (mem. coms.), Soc. of Univ. Surgeons, New England Cancer Soc. (pres. 1993, pres.-elect, 1992, exec. coun. 1991-94), Boston Surg. Soc., N.H. Med. Soc., Societe Internationale de Chirurgie, Bay State Health Care, Soc. for the Surgery of the Alimentary Tract, New England Surg. Soc. (treas. 199—), Pilgrim Ind. Practice Assn., Internat. Acad. of Oncology, Assn. for Surg. Edn. (bd. dirs. Assn. for Surg. Edn. Found. 1993), Assn. of Program Dirs. in Surgeons (pres.-elect 1990-91, pres. 1991-92), Conn. State Med. Soc. (mem. cancer coordinating com. 1990-91), Capital Area Individual Practice Assn., Am. Cancer Soc. (Hartford chpt.), Connecticare, Hartford County Med. Assn., Soc. of Surg. Chmn. Home: 134 Clifton Ave West Hartford CT 06107-1720 Office: Univ of Conn Health Ctr 263 Farmington Ave Farmington CT 06030-0001

DECKER SLANEY, MARY TERESA, Olympic athlete; b. Bunnvale, N.J., Aug. 4, 1958; d. John and Jacqueline Decker; m. Ron Tabb (div. 1983); m. Richard Slaney, June 1, 1985; 1 child, Ashley Lynn. Student, U. Colo., 1977-78. Amateur runner, 1969—, holder several world track and field records, 1980—; winner 2 gold medals at 1500 and 3000 meters World Track and Field Championship, Helsinki, Finland, 1983; mem. U.S. Olympic teams, 1980, 84; cons. to CBS Records, Timex, Eastman Kodak. Recipient Jesse Owens Internat. Amateur Athlete award, 1982, Sullivan award AAU, 1982; named Amateur Sportswoman of the Yr., Women's Sports Found., 1982, 83, Top Sportswoman A.P. Europe, 1985. Address: USATF 1 Rca Dome Ste 140 Indianapolis IN 46225

DECKERT, CLINTON ALLEN, artist; b. Chicopee, Mass., May 17, 1959. Supr. Har-Conn Chrome Co., West Hartford, Conn., 1981—; pres. In Home Art Svc., New Britain, Conn., 1996-98; programming chmn. Artworks Gallery, Inc., Hartford, Conn., 1990—, pres., 1992, 99, v.p., 1993-98; lectr. Naugatuck Valley C.C., Waterbury, 1996, Meriden (Conn.) Art Assn., 1995. One man shows include Pierce Steel Gallery at Nutmeg TV, Plainville, Conn., 1998, Artworks Gallery, Hartford, Conn., 1997, 94, 91, Eclipse Salon Gallery, Boston, 1997, 92, Naugatuck Valley C.C., Waterbury, Conn., 1996, Zuzu's Cafe Gallery, Hartford, 1995, West Hartford Libr., 1988, Small Walls Gallery, Hartford, 1998, Exposure LTD., Manchester, Conn., 1998, Senator Lieberman's Office of the U.S. Senate, Conn., New Space Gallery, Manchester, 1999; exhibited in two-person shows at Pump House Gallery, Hartford, 1995, Promenade Gallery at Bushnell Hall, Hartford, 1993; exhibited in group shows at New Britain Mus. Am. Art, 1997, 96, 95, 91, 90, 89, Conn. Acad. Fine Arts, New Britain, 1997, Kougeas Gallery, East Boston, 1996-97, Jorgensen Hall U. Conn., 1996, Colt Bldg., Hartford, 1997, 96, Conn. Artist Showcase, Hartford, 1996, Art Guild, Farmington, Conn., 1998, 92, Canton (Conn.) Gallery on the Green, 1995, Stamford Art Assn. Nat. Faber Birren Color Award Show, 1992, Art/Place, Southport, Conn., 1991. Individual Artist fellow The Greater Hartford Arts Coun., 1999. Home and Office: 346 Commonwealth Ave New Britain CT 06053-2409

DECKERT, FRANK, park administrator; m. Gloria Quick; children: Christopher, Jason, Alisa. BS in Forest Mgmt., Humboldt State Coll. With U.S. Forest Svc., Calif., 1963-66; ranger, dist. naturalist Shenandoah Nat. Park Nat. Park Svc., Va., 1967-71; dist. ranger Isle Royale Nat. Park Nat. Park Svc., Mich., 1971-73; interpretive specialist Lake Mead Nat. Recreation Area Nat. Park Svc., Ariz., Nev., 1973-75; chief park naturalist Big Bend Nat. Park Nat. Park Svc., Tex., 1975-80; regional chief of interpretation Alaska Regional Office Nat. Park Svc., Anchorage, 1980-86; supt. Petersburg Nat. Battlefield Nat. Park Svc., 1986-92, supt. Carlsbad (N.Mex.) Caverns Nat. Park, 1992—. Trustee San Vicente Common Sch. Dist. Recipient Silver Beaver award Boy Scouts of Am., 1992. Mem. Carlsbad Rotary Club (v.p./pres. elect 1997—). Office: 3225 National Parks Hwy Carlsbad NM 88220-5354*

DECKERT, HARLAN KENNEDY, JR., manufacturing company official; b. Evanston, Ill., May 22, 1923; s. Harlan Kennedy Sr. and Lady Otey (Hutton) D.; BS, U. Calif., Berkeley, 1949; MBA, U. So. Calif., 1962; m. Mary Emma Eldredge, Nov. 27, 1971; children: Mary Adrienne, Christine Ann, Daniel Gregory, Deborah Alice. Systems analyst Northrop Corp., Hawthorne, Calif., 1949-53, supr. engring. adminstrv. svcs., 1953-57, adminstrv. systems engr., 1957-59; with AiResearch Indsl. div. Garrett Corp., Torrance, Calif., 1959-88, systems svc. adminstr., 1962-72, mgr. adminstrv. svcs., 1972-75, adminstr. internat. ops., 1975-80, sr. staff advisor Garrett Automotive Group Allied-Signal, Inc., 1980-88, ret., 1988. Active mem. L.A. County Mus. Art, Wild Beast Soc., docent: Greater L.A. Zoo Assn.; mem. L.A. County Mus. Natural History, San Luis Obispo Zool. Soc., Exotic Feline Breeding Compound, African Wildlife Found., Friends Cabrillo Marine Aquarium, Assn. Zoo & Aquarium Docents; supporting mem. Living Desert. With USAAF, 1943-46, CBI, capt. USAFR, 1946-57. Mem. Am. Assn. Zoo Keepers, Am. Zoo and Aquarium Assn., Nat. Wildlife Fedn., San Diego Zool. Soc. (Keeper's Club), World Wildlife Fund, Nature Conservancy, Wildlife Waystation, Sierra Club, Jane Goodall Inst., Santa Monica Mus. Flying. Home: 2433 33rd St Santa Monica CA 90405-2103

DECKERT, MYRNA JEAN, youth organization executive; b. McPherson, Kans., Nov. 4, 1936; d. Francis J. and Grace (Killion) George; m. Ray A. Deckert, Sept. 29, 1957; children: Rachelle, Kimberly, Charles, Michael. AA, Coll. of Sequoias, 1956; BBA, U. Beverly Hills, 1983, MBA, 1984. Youth dir. Asbury Meth. Ch., El Paso, Tex., 1960-63; teen program dir. YWCA, El Paso, 1963-69, assoc. exec. dir., 1969-70, CEO, 1970—; chair strategic planning com. Tex. Dept. Pub. and Regulatory Svcs., 1994-97. pres. Exec. Forum, 1991-92; bd. dirs. Chase Bank of Tex., El Paso; chmn. Tex. State Title XX DayCare Providers, 1987-89; commr. Housing Authority City of El Paso, 1989-92; former chair bd. trustees Columbia Med. Ctr. East, 1992-97, deans adv. com. Tex. Tech. Med. Ctr.; past trustee Dues/High Tower Found.; chair Leadership EP, 1994-95; trustee Unite El Paso; mem. Tex. Challenge Adv. Com., 1998. Recipient Hannah Soloman Cmty. Svc. award Nat. Coun. Jewish Women, Sertoma Club award Svc. to Mankind, 1974, Cmty. Svc. award League United L.Am. Citizens, 1980, Humanitarian award, 1994, Vol. Svc. award Vol. Bur., 1984, Merit award Adalante Mujer, 1986, Social Svc. award KVIA/Sunturians, 1986, Excellence award Nat. Assn. YWCA Execs., 1990, Racial Justice award YWCA of the U.S.A., 1991, Disting. Svc. award Rotary of El Paso, 1997, Citizen of Yr. award Greater El Paso Assn. Realtors, 1998; named Woman of Yr., AAUW, 1975, Dir. of Yr., United Way El Paso County, 1985, First Lady of El Paso, Beta Sigma Phi, 1991, One of 10 Most Influential Women, El Paso Times, 1995, Citizen of Yr., Mil. Order of World Wars, 1996; inducted into El Paso Women's Hall of Fame, 1990, El Paso Hist. Soc. Hall of Honor, 1995, Hall of Fame/Coll. of Sequoias, 1995, Hall of Honor, 1996, Jr. Achievement Bus. Hall of Honor, 1998, Bravo award LWV, 1999; named Citizen of Yr., El Paso Bd. Realtors, 1999. Mem. Coun. of Agy. Execs., Rotary (Club of El Paso, v.p. 1990-93, Disting. Svc. award 1997). Methodist. Home: 4276 Canterbury Dr El Paso TX 79902-1352

DECKO, KENNETH OWEN, trade association administrator; b. New Haven, Aug. 7, 1944; s. Charles C. and Frances D.; m. Marilyn Seaver, Oct. 21, 1972; children: Kurt, Amy. Student, Duke U.; J.D., U. Conn., 1969. With Conn. Bus. and Industry Assn., Hartford, 1970—; pres. Conn. Bus. and Industry Assn., 1981—. Served with USAR, 1969-70. Office: 370 Asylum St Hartford CT 06103-2025*

DECKROSH, HAZEN DOUGLAS, retired state agency educator and administrator; b. Defiance, Ohio, Apr. 13, 1936; s. Lawrence L. and Martha L. Deckrosh; m. Carol Ann Everett, Nov. 25, 1970; children: Stephanie, Todd, Douglas, Nadia Nicole. BS, Ohio No. U., 1959; MEd, U. Toledo, 1980. Cert. tchr., Ohio. Phys. edn. and history tchr., coach Waynesfield (Ohio)-Goshen Jr. High Sch., 1959-61; coach, history, phys. edn. tchr. Coshocton (Ohio) Sacred Heart High Sch., 1961-63; health-phys. edn. tchr., coach West Holmes Jr. High Sch., Millersburg, Ohio, 1965-70; tchr. history and govt., coach Elida High Sch., 1973-77; occupational work experience tchr.-coord., coach Spencerville (Ohio) High Sch., 1973-77; occupational work edn. tchr., coord. Four County Vocat. Sch., Archbold, Ohio, 1977-82; vocat. supr. Jefferson County Vocat. Sch., Steubenville, Ohio, 1986-87; occupational work experience tchr., coord. Ohio Dept. of Youth Svcs., Columbus, 1987-94; ret., 1994; pres. DYS Coordinators, Columbus, 1990-94; ski instr. Swiss Valley, Mich., 1995—; GED instr. Correction Ctr. Northwest Ohio. Editor: Threaded Fasteners, 1987; contbr. articles to profl. publs. Mem. Am. Youth Hostels, Lima, 1972—. Mem. NEA, Ohio Edn. Assn., Am. Vocat. Assn., Ohio Vocat. Assn., Occupl. Work Experience Coords. Assn. (state adv. coun., Lima rep. 1977-80, Columbus rep. 1991-94), Full Gospel Bus. Men's Fellowship Internat., Gideons Internat. (treas., then sec.), 5th Dist. Ofcls. Assn. (v.p., rules interpreter), Capitol West Umpires Assn. (rules interpreter 1991-93), Lima Umpires Assn. (sec.-treas. 1973-77), Ret. Tchrs. Assn. (pres.), Alpha Sigma Phi. Republican. Avocations: sports officiating, high school and college sports, teaching skiing. Home: 12265 County Road 150 Montpelier OH 43543-9613

DECOEN, MARY T. OZEREKO See **OZEREKO-DECOEN, MARY T.**

DE COLOMBÍ-MONGUIÓ, ALICIA, poet, foreign language educator; b. Buenos Aires; came to the U.S., 1967; d. Carlos and Rosa de Colombí; m. Luis Monguió, Aug. 8, 1979. BA in History, U. Santa Clara, 1969; MA in Spanish and Portuguese, Stanford U., 1971, PhD in Spanish and Humanities, 1973. Asst. prof. Spanish Mills Coll., Oakland, Calif., 1973-79; faculty mem. Bennington (Vt.) Coll., 1979-82; prof. Spanish SUNY, Albany, 1982-84, 86—, chair dept. Hispanic and Italian studies, 1986-90, rsch. prof. Hispanic and humanities studies, 1998—; prof. Spanish U. Ariz., 1984-86; chair divsn. letters Mills Coll., Oakland, 1975-79; chair fgn. langs. and lits. Bennington Coll., 1979-82; head dept. Spanish and Portuguese U. Ariz., Tucson, 1984-86; chair dept. Hispanic and Italian studies SUNY, Albany, 1986-90, rsch. prof. Hispanic and humanities studies, 1998—. Author: De amor y poesia en la Espana Medieval, 1976, Petrarquismo Peruano, 1985; author 3 books poetry; contbr. over 80 articles and monographs on medieval and renaissance poetry and poetics to profl. publs. Recipient Diploma de Honor, U. P.R., Mayagüez, 1981; Guggenheim fellow, 1978-79. Mem. MLA, Assn. Internat. Hispanistas, Renaissance Soc. Am. Avocations: gardening, traveling. Home: 24 Berkshire Dr E Clifton Park NY 12065

DECONCINI, BARBARA, association executive, religious studies educator; b. Phila., Feb. 15, 1944; d. Edwin Francis and Anne Marie (Farrell) DeC.; m. Walter James Lowe, June 30, 1979. AB in English, Rosemont Coll., 1968; MA in English, Bryn Mawr Coll., 1973; PhD in Humanities, Emory U., 1980. Assoc. dean Rosemont (Pa.) Coll., 1971-74; from lectr. to prof. Atlanta Coll. of Art, 1975-91, interim pres., 1985, acad. dean, 1986-91; prof. religion and culture Emory U., Atlanta, 1991—; exec. dir., treas. Am. Acad. Religion, Atlanta, 1991—; coord. long-range instnl. and ednl. planning Soc. of the Holy Child, 1973-75; treas. Southeastern Commn. for Study of Religion, 1989-91; chair various acad. sessions in field. Author: Narrative Remembering, 1990; contbr. numerous articles to profl. publs. Bd. dirs. Art Papers, Atlanta, 1988-91, Rosemont Coll., 1992—, chmn. acad. com.; trustee Scholars Press, Atlanta, 1991—, chmn. bd. trustees, 1994-97; bd. dirs. Ga. Artists Internat. Exhibit Fund, 1988-92. Alliance of Ind. Colls. of Art grantee. Mem. Am. Coun. Learned Socs. (chmn. exec. com. coun. adminstrv. officers 1995-97, bd. dirs. 1996-98), Am. Acad. Religion (bd. dirs. 1989—, cons. for reorgn. arts, lit. and religion sect. 1990, mem. program com. 1986-89, pres. S.E. sect. 1984-85, program chair 1983-84, 84-85, exec. com. 1980-83), So. Assn. Colls. and Schs. (accreditation evaluator), Mid. States Assn. Colls. and Schs. (accreditation evaluator), Phi Beta Kappa, Omicron Delta Kappa. Office: Am Acad Religion 825 Houston Mill Rd NE Ste 300 Atlanta GA 30329-4246

DE CONCINI, DENNIS, lawyer, former United States senator, consultant; b. Tucson, May 8, 1937; s. Evo and Ora (Webster) DeC.; children: Denise, Christina, Patrick Evo. BA, U. Ariz., 1959, LLB, 1963. Bar: Ariz. 1963, D.C. 1963. Mem. firm Evo DeConcini; ptnr. DeConcini & McDonald, Tucson, 1968-73; dep. Pima County atty. Sch. Dist. 1, 1971-72, county atty., 1972-76; U.S. Senator from Ariz., 1977-95; atty. Perry-Romani Assocs., Washington, 1995—, De Concini, McDonald, Yetwin & Lacy, Tuscon, 1995—; mem. appropriations com., U.S. Senate, chmn. subcom. on Treasury, Postal Svc. and Gen. Govt.; mem. subcom. on Def., subcom. on Energy and Water Devel., subcom. on Fgn. Ops., subcom. on Interior Related Agys.; mem. Jud. com.; chmn. subcom. on Patents, Copyrights and Trademarks; mem. subcom. on Antitrust, Monopolies and Bus. Rights, subcom. on the Constitution, com. on Rules and Adminstrn., com. on Vets. Affairs; chmn. select com. on Intelligence; chmn. Commn. on Security and Cooperation in Europe; select com. Indian Affairs; mem. Internat. Narcotics Control Caucus, West Coalition of Senators; former pres., bd. dirs. Shopping Ctrs., Inc.; bd. dirs. Fed. Home Mortgage Corp., Schuff Steel. Chmn. legis. com. Tucson Dem. Cmty. Coun., 1966-67; mem. major gifts com., devel. fund drive St. Joseph's Hosp., 1970, mem. devel. coun., 1971-73; bd. dirs. Nat. Ctr. for Missing and Exploited Children, 1995—; mem. major gifts com. Tucson Mus. and Art Ctr. Bldg. Fund, 1971; adminstr. Ariz. Drug Control Dist., 1975-76; precinct committeeman Ariz. Dem. Ctrl. Com., 1958—; mem. Pima County Dem. Ctrl. Com., 1958-67, Dem. State Exec. Com., 1958-68; state vice chmn. Ariz. Dem. Com., 1964-66, 70-72; vice chmn. Pima County Dem. Com., 1970-73. Served to 2d lt. JAG U.S. Army, 1959-60. Named Outstanding Ariz. County Atty., 1975. Mem. ABA, NAACP, Nat. Dist. Attys. Assn., Am. Judicature Soc., Ariz. Bar Assn., D.C. Bar Assn., Ariz. Sheriffs and County Attys. Assn., Ariz. Pioneer Hist. Soc., Pima County Bar Assn., U. Ariz. Alumni Assn., Pres.'s Club, Tucson Fraternal Order Police, Phi Delta Theta, Delta Sigma Rho, Phi Alpha Delta. Roman Catholic.

DECONINCK, ISABELLE F., marketing and promotion specialist, writer; b. Brussels, Belgium, Nov. 6, 1961; came to U.S., 1985; d. Paul and Francoise (Fages) D. BA in French Lit., Sorbonne, 1984; MA in Music, U. Okla., 1989; MA in Comparative Lit., U. Minn., 1992. Asst. editor EAR Mag., N.Y.C., 1990; editor, pub. rels. specialist Am. Internat. Artists, N.Y.C., 1993-97; dir. prodn. and artist promotion Ocean Records, N.Y.C., 1996-97; dir. promotions and miktg. The Kitchen Ctr. for Music, Dance, Performance, N.Y.C., 1997—; freelance writer. Author articles on poets and writers The Villager, 1997—; editor The Integrated Arts People Newsletter, 1994-97. Mem. Nat. Fedn. of Press Women (profl. mem.), Nat. Writers Union.

DECONTI, ROBERT W., plastic surgeon; b. Dec. 8, 1961; m. Karen Deconti; children: Ashley, Christopher. BS in Marine Scis. magna cum laude, U. So. Calif., 1983; MD, U. Va., 1987. Diplomate Am. Bd. Surgery, Am. Bd. Plastic Surgery; BCLS; cert. undersea and hyperbaric medicine; flt. medicine. Jr. surg. resident Alton Ochsner Med. Foun., New Orleans, 1987-89, sr. surg. resident, 1989-91, extracorporeal membrane oxygenation fellow, 1989, chief surg. resident, 1991-92; plastic surgery fellow U. Va., Charlottesville, 1992-93, chief plastic surgery fellow, 1993-94; asst. clin. prof. dept. surgery and plastic surgery Med. Coll. Va.; active staff various hosps. including Med. Coll. Va. Hosps., St. Mary's Hosp., Henrico Doctors' Hosp. Richmond Meml. Hosp., Capital Med. Ctr., Va., others; rschr. in field, including Children's Hosp. Nat. Med. Ctr., Washington, U. So. Calif.'s Marine Sci. Lab., Santa Catalina Island, Calif., U. Va. Med. Ctr.; presenter in field. Contbr. articles to profl. jours. Recipient scholarships U. So. Calif., Carnation Industry, others; named to Outstanding Young Americans. Fellow Am. Coll. Surgeons; mem. AMA, Med. Soc. Va., Am. Soc. Plastic and Reconstructive Surgeons, Am. Soc. Aesthetic Plastic Surgery, Richmond Acad. Medicine, others. Avocations: running, cycling, snow skiing, tennis, golf.

DE CORDOVA, FREDERICK TIMMINS, television producer, director; b. N.Y.C., Oct. 27, 1910; s. George and Margaret (Timmins) de C.; m. Janet Thomas, Nov. 27, 1963. B.S., Northwestern U., 1931. Author: (autobiography) Johnny Came Lately, 1988; prodr.-dir. Warner Bros. Pictures, 1943-48, Universal Internat. Pictures, 1948-53, CBS and NBC, 1953; prodns. include Tonight Show, 1970-97 (Emmy award NATAS 1963, 68, 76, 79, 92), prodr.-dir. Burns and Allen Show, Jack Benny Program, My Three Sons. Mem. Bel Air Country Club (L.A.). Home: 1875 Carla Rdg Beverly Hills CA 90210-1936 Office: NBC Burbank CA 91523

DECOSTA, BENJAMIN, airport administrator. Airport mgr. Hatsfield Internat. Airport, Atlanta, 1998—. Office: Hatsfield Internat Airport Airport Adminstrn Atlanta GA 30320*

DECOSTA, FRANK, artist; b. Nov. 19, 1943; m. Imogene Sharp; children: Micheal, Selena. Student, Newark Sch. Fine & Indsl. Arts, 1961-64, Art Student's League, 1964-66; AS, Allegany Coll.; studied with Steven Asseal, N.Y. Acad. Art, 1998. One-man shows include Pacific Grove (Calif.) Art Ctr., 1986, Frostburg (Md.) State U., 1990, Gallery Next, Frostburg, 1991, Thompson Park Art Gallery, Lyncroft, N.J., 1992, Cardinal Gallery, Annapolis, Md., 1992, Meteorol. Charles St., Balt., 1995, Washington County Mus., Hagerstown, Md., 1996, Cumberland Creative Arts Ctr., Md., 1997, Allegany Coll., Md., 1998, (with sculptor) Del. State U., Dover, 1991, Creative Arts Ctr., Cumberland, 1992, Ridge St. Gallery, N.Y.C., 1992; exhibited in group shows at Fiji Nat. Mus., Suva, 1978, Monterey (Calif.) County Ann., 1980, 82, Pacific Grove Art Ctr., 1988, 85, 87, Monterey (Calif.) Mus., 1981, 89, Pascal Art Gallery, Md., 1990, Howard County Art Ctr., Ellicott City, Md., 1990, Reston (Va.) Art Ctr., 1991, BAUhouse, Baot., 1990, 91, Frederick Arts Found., 1992, Messiah Coll., Harrisburg, Pa., 1993, Huntington (W.Va.) Mus. Art, 1992, 94, Meyerhoff Gallery, Balt., 1994, Mattawoman Art Ctr., La Plata, Md., 1995, Galleria Communiale, 1995, Washington County Mus. Find Arts, 1991, 93, 94, 95, 96, Anton Gallery, Washington, 1996, Daniel Perez Gallery, N.Y.C., 1997, La Mama La Galleria, N.Y.C., 1997, John A. Cade Ctr. for Fine Arts Gallery, 1998; represented in permanent collections at So. Alleghenies Mus. Art, Loretto, Pa., Washington County Mus. Fine Arts, Christ Luth. Ch., La Vale, Md., Cannery Row, Monterey, St. Jude's Roman Cath. Ch., Monterey Peninsula, Calif. Home: 505 Cumberland St Cumberland MD 21502

DECOSTA, PETER F., chemical engineer; b. New Bedford, Mass.; s. Anthony and Deolinda (DeSouza) DeC. BS with distinction, U. Mass., 1962; MA, U. Conn., 1966; cert., U. R.I., 1968; MS, MIT, 1970; cert., Boston U., 1979, Northeastern U., 1980; profl. engring. degree, U. Wis., 1981. Chemist Portsmouth Naval Shipyard, N.H., 1962-64; quality assurance engr. U.S. FDA, Boston, 1966-71; systems analyst U.S. EPA, Washington, 1971-75; ops. rsch. analyst U.S. Army Natick (Mass.) Rsch., Devel. and Engring. Ctr., 1976-83, phys. scientist, 1983-86, gen. engr., 1986—; part-time instr. Northeastern U., Boston, 1987—, Worcester (Mass.) Poly. Inst., 1984-90, Mass. Bay Community Coll., Wellesley, 1983—. Contbr. articles to profl. jours. Planner, Planning Bd. City of New Bedford, Mass., 1975; mem. ch. activities, charities; mem. Leadership Cir. WGBH-TV (PBS), Boston, 1992, WBUR-AM/FM (NPR), Boston, 1997; charter mem. U.S.S. Constn. Mus., 1992; mem. John F. Kennedy Presdl. Libr. Found., Nat. Trust for Hist. Preservation. Commonwealth scholar U. Mass., 1958-62, City of New Bedford scholar, 1958-62, Allied Chem. Co. scholar, 1960-62; U. Conn. teaching fellow, 1964-65, NSF fellow Boston Coll., 1965, Advanced Engring. fellow MIT, 1969-70, NSF/AAAS fellow MIT, 1984; recipient Natick Comdr.'s award U.S Army Natick Rsch., Devel. and Engring. Ctr., 1981, 86. Fellow Am. Inst. Chemists; mem. AIChE (cert.), AAUP, AAAS, Future Techs. Inst., Am. Chem. Soc., Geol. Soc. Am., Planetary Soc., Mus. Sci., John F. Kennedy Presdl. Libr. Found., Libr. of Congress Assocs. (charter mem.), Smithsonian Nat. Assocs., Old Dartmouth Hist. Soc. (New Bedford Whaling Mus.), Children's Mus., MIT Faculty Club, MIT Club Southeastern Mass., Nature Conservancy, Sigma Xi, Alpha Chi Sigma, Phi Lambda Upsilon. Avocations: gemology, coin and stamp collecting. Office: US Army Natick Rsch Devel and Engring Ctr Kansas St Natick MA 01760-5056

DECOSTA, STEVEN C., municipal official; b. Bklyn., July 6, 1949. BA, Queens Coll., 1971; JD, Hoffstra U., 1974. Trial examiner N.Y.C. Office Collective Bargaining, 1980-82, assoc. gen. counsel, 1982-88, gen. counsel, 1988-95, chmn., 1995—. Office: NYC of Collective Bargaining 40 Rector St Fl 7 New York NY 10006-1705*

DECRANE, ALFRED CHARLES, JR., petroleum company executive; b. Cleve., June 11, 1931; s. Alfred Charles and Verona (Marquard) DeC.; m. Joan Elizabeth Hoffman, July 3, 1954; children: David, Lisa, Stacie, Stephanie, Sarah, Jennifer. BA, U. Notre Dame, 1953; JD, Georgetown U., 1959; LHD (hon.), Manhattanville Coll., 1990. Bar: Va. bar 1959, D.C. bar 1959, Tex. bar 1961, N.Y. bar 1966. Legal dept. Texaco, Inc., Houston, 1959-64, N.Y.C., 1964-66; asst. to vice chmn. bd. Texaco, Inc., 1965-67, asst. to chmn. bd., 1967-68, gen. mgr. producing dept. Eastern hemisphere, 1968-70, v.p., 1970-76, sr. v.p., gen. counsel, 1976-77, sr. v.p., dir., 1977-78, exec. v.p., 1978-83, pres., 1983-86, chmn. bd. dirs., 1987-96, chmn., chief exec. officer, 1993-96; bd. dirs. Birmingham Steel Corp., CIGNA Corp., Bestfoods Corp, Harris Corp., Corn Products Internat., U.S. Global Leaders Growth Fund, Ltd. Trustee U. Notre Dame. 1st lt. USMCR, 1954-55. Mem. ABA (sect. sec. 1964-67, co-founder Natural Resources Law Jour. mineral law sect.). Office: PO Box 1247 Greenwich CT 06836-1247

DECRISTOFARO, JOHN GEORGE, artist, designer; b. Greenport, N.Y., Dec. 20, 1959; s. Rudolf Zaninetti and Dyan DeCristofaro. Design cons. Lexington (N.C.) Furniture, 1991-97; pres. DeCristofaro Designs, Miami, Fla., 1997—; pres. Love Paintings website, 1998. Avocations: art, gardening, tennis, graphic design, internet. E-mail: john@lovepaintings.com. Office: DeCristofaro Designs 4308 NE 2d Ave Miami FL 33137

DECROCE, ALEX, state legislator; b. Morristown, N.J., June 10, 1936; m. Betty Lou Bisson, 1994; 3 children. Student, Seton Hall U. Chmn. Morris

County (N.J.) Rep. Com., 1971-72, freeholder, 1984-89, dir., 1986—; mem. Morris County Bd. Elections, 1973-82, chmn., 1977-81; assemblyman N.J. State Assembly, 1989—, dep. spkr., 1994—; chmn. transp., labor N.J. RR & Transp. Mus. Commn., 1994—; ptnr. Gallo-DeCroce, Inc., Parsippany-Troy Hills; pres. Gal-Lex & Tedesco. Recipient Legislator of Yr. award Transp. Am. Legis. Exch. Coun., 1992, Appreciation award Coun. Spl. Transp., 1993, Legis. award Utility-Transp. Contractors, 1993. Mem. Morris, West Essex and Parsippany C. of C., Rotary (Outstanding Citizen of Parsippany 1991). Address: 101 Gibraltar Dr Ste 2-d Morris Plains NJ 07950-1287*

DECROSTA, SUSAN ELYSE, graphic designer; b. Cambridge, Mass., Aug. 28, 1956; d. Joseph Mario and Gertrude Ermelinda (Galligani) DeC. BFA, Mass. Coll. Art, 1980. certified art tchr., supr. Graphic artist Nixdorf Computer Corp., Burlington, Mass., 1981-86; lead artist, illustrator Raytheon Co., Andover, Mass., 1986-94; graphic designer Raytheon Svc. Co., Burlington, Mass., 1994—; artist, illustrator Rivers, Trainor, Doyle, Providence, 1987; freelance graphic artist, 1980—; guest speaker to design and illustration students Northeastern U., 1992. Vol. AIDS Action Com., Boston. Recipient Excellence award Soc. Tech. Communications & Art Direction, 1986. Mem. Art Alumni Assn. Avocation: dancing, painting. Office: Raytheon Svc Co 2 Wayside Rd Burlington MA 01803-4607

DECROW, KAREN, lawyer, author, lecturer; b. Chgo., Dec. 18, 1937; d. Samuel Meyer and Juliette (Abt) Lipschultz; m. Alexander Allen Kolben, 1960 (div. 1965); m. Roger DeCrow, 1965 (div. 1972, dec. 1989). BS, Northwestern U., 1959; JD, Syracuse U., 1972; DHL (hon.), SUNY, Oswego, 1994. Bar: N.Y., U.S. Dist. Ct. (no. dist.) N.Y. Resorts editor Golf Digest mag., Evanston, Ill., 1959-60; editor Am. Soc. Planning Ofcls., Chgo., 1960-61; writer Ctr. for Study Liberal Edn. for Adults., Chgo., 1961-64; editor Holt, Rinehart, Winston, Inc., N.Y.C., 1965; textbook editor L.W. Singer, Syracuse, N.Y., 1965-66; writer Ea. Regional Inst. for Edn., Syracuse, 1967-69, Pub. Broadcasting System, 1977; tchr. women and law, 1972-74; nat. bd. mem. NOW, 1968-77, nat. pres., 1974-77, also nat. politics task force chair; cons. affirmative action; pvt. practice, Jamesville, N.Y.; lectr. topics including law, gender, internat. feminism to corps., polit. groups, colls. and univs., U.S., Can., Mex., Finland, China, Greece, former USSR; nat. coord. Women's Strike for Equality, 1970; N.Y. State del. Internat. Women's Yr., 1977; originator Schs. for Candidates; participant DeCrow-Schlafly ERA Debates, from 1975; founder (with Robert Seidenberg) World Woman Watch, 1988; gender issues advisor Nat. Congress for Men; mem. Task Force on Gender Bias. Author: (with Roger DeCrow) University Adult Education: A Selected Bibliography, 1967, American Council on Education, 1967, The Young Woman's Guide to Liberation, 1971, Sexist Justice, 1974, First Women's State of the Union Message, 1977, (with Robert Seidenberg) Women Who Marry Houses: Panic and Protest in Agoraphobia, 1983, Turkish edit., 1988, 2d Turkish edit., 1989, United States of America vs. Sex: How the Meese Commission Lied About Pornography, 1988, (with Jack Kammer) Good Will Toward Men: Women Talk Candidly About the Balance of Power Between the Sexes, 1994; editor: The Pregnant Teenager (Howard Osofsky), 1968, Corporate Wives, Corporate Casualties (Robert Seidenberg), 1973; contbr. articles to USA Today, N.Y. Times, L.A. Times, Chgo. Tribune, Nat. Law Jour., Women Boston Globe, Vogue, Mademoiselle, Ingenue, Newsday, Chgo. Sun Times, Penthouse, Washington Post, L.A. Times Mag., Policy Review, Miami Herald, Internat. Herald Tribune, Social Problems, Houston Chronicle, Pitts. Press, Nat. NOW Times, Syracuse U. Mag., San Francisco Chronicle, Civil Rights Quar., Women Lawyers Jour., other newspapers, mags.; regular columnist: Syracuse New Times; columnist N.Y. Times Spl. Features; recording: Opening Up Marriage, 1980. Hon. trustee Elizabeth Cady Stanton Found.; active Hon. Com. to Save Alice Paul's Birthplace; Liberal candidate for Mayor of Syracuse, 1969. Recipient Profl. Recognition award for best newspaper column Syracuse Press Club, 1990, Best Column award, 1994-95, Best Column award N.Y. Press Assn., 1991-92, 95, award Barnard Coll., Vet. Feminists of Am. and the Barnard Ctr. for Rsch. on Women, Woman of Achievement/Distinction award Gov. George E. Pataki, 1998. Mem. NOW, Onondaga County Bar Assn.(profl. ethics com.), N.Y. Women's Bar Assn. (ctrl. N.Y. chpt. pres. 1989-90, jud. screening com.), N.Y. Bar Assn., ACLU (Ralph E. Kharas Disting. Svc. in Civil Liberties award 1985), Elizabeth Cady Stanton Found. (bd. trustees), Working Women's Inst. (bd. advisors), Syracuse Friends Chamber Music, Atlantic States Legal Found., Yale Polit. Union (hon. life), Nat. Congress Men (gender issues advisor), Mariposa Edn. & Rsch. Found., Nat. Coun. Children's Rights (adv. panel), Wilderness Soc., Northwestern U. Alumni Assn., Women's Inst. Freedom Press, Art Inst. Chgo., Nat. Women's Polit. Caucus, Theta Sigma Phi. Address: 7599 Brown Gulf Rd Jamesville NY 13078-9636 *I feel especially lucky to be able to participate, as Holmes said, in the passion of our times. The movement to create equality between women and men is the most interesting and exciting during this period in history. My goal is a world where the gender of a baby will have little or no relevance to future pursuits or pleasures - personal, political, economic, social, or professional. It is exhilarating to watch society change in that direction.*

DE CUSATIS, CASIMER MAURICE, fiber optics engineer; b. Hazleton, Pa., Dec. 23, 1964; s. Casimer Maurice and Helen (Paytas) De C.; m. Carolyn Jean Sher, Aug. 5, 1992; children: Anne Shirley, Rebecca Lynn. BS magna cum laude, Pa. State U., 1986; MS, Rensselaer Poly Inst., 1988; PhD, 1990. Rsch. asst. Rensselaer Poly. Inst., Troy, N.Y., 1986-90; staff engr. IBM, Kingston, N.Y., 1990-93; adv. engr. IBM, Poughkeepsie, N.Y., 1993-99, sr. engr., 1999—; rsch. assoc. Apollo Lightcraft Program NASA-Univ. Space Rsch. Assn., 1988-90; spkr. Internat. Conf. on Acousto-Optics, Leningrad, USSR, 1990, invited spkr. Internat. Conf. on Acousto-Optics and Applications, Gdansk, Poland, 1992; v.p. R & D S3 Optical Software, 1995. Co-author: Acousto-Optics: Fundamentals and Applications, 1991, Optoelectronics for Data Communication, 1995; editor: Handbook of Applied Photometry, 1997, Handbook of Fiber Optic Data Communication, 1998; guest editor: Optical Engineering/Spl. Issue on Optical Data Communication, 1998; contbr. articles to Applied Optics, Jour. Selected Areas in Comm., Ultrasonics Symposium, Optics News, Optical Engring., Encyclopedia of Electrical and Electronics Engineering, SPIE procs.; guest editor Optical Engring., 1998. Recipient Internat. Man of Yr. award Men of Achievement, 1993, IBM Intranet Spotlight Profile, 1998, IBM Engring. Excellence award, 1998, Photonics Spectra Circle of Excellence award IBM 9729, Optical Wavelength Divsn. Multiplexer, 1996, Data Comms. Mag. Hot Product award IBM 9729, 1997, Product Design and Devel. Mag. Top 30 Products award for automated fiber optic cable tester, 1996, 5000 Personalities of the World, 1998, Millenium Medal, 1998, Internat. Cultural Diploma of Honor Am. Biographical Inst., 1997, Man of Yr. award, 1998, Blue Ribbon award Optical Soc. Am., 1998; named 10DC Industry Champion fiber optic datacom protocols, 1995—, one of Outstanding People of 20th Century, 1998. Mem. IEEE (IBM visions in edn. program, 1996, spokesman Nat. Engring. Week, 1999), NSF (program com.), Soc. of Photo-optical Instrumentation Engrs., Coun. Optical Radiation Measurement, Optical Soc. Am. (book pub. com. 1993-96, re-engring. com. 1995-96, liaison to AIP book pub. com. 1995, publ. tech. com. 1996—, editor OSA photonics tech. home page 1996—, organizer and spkr. tech. group meeting on optical datacom 1996, 98, Blue Ribbon award 1998), Conf. on Lasers and Electro-Optics (program com. on optoelectronic interconnect and processing 1998, emerging techs. com. 1998), Inst. for Optical Data Comm. (spkr. ann. meeting 1995, pres. 1996—), Mensa, Golden Key Nat. Honor Soc., Chimes Nat. Honor Soc., Golden Key Honor Soc., Sigma Xi, Tau Beta Pi, Eta Kappa Nu, Omicron Delta Kappa, Sigma Pi Sigma, Pi Mu Epsilon, Alpha Lambda Delta, Phi Eta Sigma. Achievements include 16 patents, 20 patents pending on fiber optic and electrical transmission line interface to multichip modules, fiber optic test equipment optical disk storage and service tools for fiberoptic links. Office: IBM Dept HHLA MS P343 522 South Rd Poughkeepsie NY 12601-5400

DE DATTA, SURAJIT KUMAR, soil scientist, agronomist, educator; b. Shwebo, Upper Burma, Burma, Aug. 1, 1936; s. Dinanath and Birahini De Datta; m. Vijayalakshmi L., April 20, 1967; 1 child Raj Kumar De Datta. BS in Agrl., Banaras Hindu U., 1956; MS Soil Sci. and Agrl. Chem., Indian Agrl. Rsch. Inst., New Delhi, India, 1958; PhD Soil Sci., U. Hawaii, 1962. Postdoctoral agrl. experiment station Ohio State U., Columbus, 1962-63; prof. agronomy and soil sci. U. Philippines, Los Banos, Philippines, 1964-91; assoc. agronomist Internat. Rice Rsch. Inst., Manila, Philippines, 1964-69, agronomist, 1969-85, radiological health and safety officer, 1967-78, acting head dept. soil chem., 1975-76, dept. head, agronomy, 1967-89, principle scientist, 1986-91, program leader, 1990-91; assoc. dean internat. agrl. Va. Tech., Blacksburg, Va., 1993, dir., office internat. rsch. and devel., 1991, prof. crop and soil environ. sciences, 1991—, chair, 1996-97; bd. dirs. S.E. Consrotium for Internat. Devel., Washington; prin. investigator IPM CRSP Project (USAID), Va. Tech., 1993; vis. prof. Purdue U., 1971-72, Kasetsart U., Thailand, 1984-91, Ctrl. Luzon State U., Nueva Ecija, Philippines, 1983-91; vis. scientist U. Calif., Davis, 1978-79; hon. prof. Dniepropetrovsk State Agrarian U., Ukraine, USSR, 1998. Author: Principles and Practices of Rice Production, 1981; consulting editor: Fertilizer Rsch. Jour. 1978-96; contbr. over 350 articles to profl. jours. Recipient Internat. Soil Sci. award Soil Sci. Soc. Am., 1986, Best Paper award Weed Sci. Pest Control Coun. Philippines, 1986, Eminence award Bureau of Plant Industry, Philippines, 1987, Best Paper award Asian-Pacific Weed Sci. Soc., Taiwan, 1987, Second Best Paper award Asian-Pacific Weed Sci. Soc., Korea, 1989, Agronomic Rsch. award Am. Soc. Agronomy, 1990, Norman Borlaug award, New Delhi, India, 1992, Outstanding Alumnus award Coll. Tropical Agr. Human Resources, U. Hawaii, 1998. Fellow Am. Soc. Agronomy (chmn. internat. agronmomy divsn. 1982-83), Soil Sci. Soc. Am. and Indian Soc. Soil Sci., Internat. Svc. in Agronomy, Nat. Acad. Agrl. Scis. (India); mem. Crop Sci. Soc. Am., Internat. Soil Sci. Soc., Asian-Pacific Weed Sci. Soc., Internat. Weed Sci. Soc. Hindu. Home: 512 Floyd St Blacksburg VA 24060-5071 Office: Office Internat Rsch & Devel Virginia Tech 1060 Litton Reaves Hall Blacksburg VA 24061-0334

DEDDENS, ALAN EUGENE, otolaryngologist, head and neck surgeon; b. Louisville, Aug. 17, 1959; s. Eugene H. and Patricia A. (Silliman) D.; m. Ann Marie Gwynn, May 22, 1987; children: Kelci M., Marissa A. BS in Biomed. Engring., Tulane U., 1981; MD, U. Louisville, 1987. Field design biomed. engr. Med. Sys. divsn. GE Co., 1981-83; intern Barnes-Jewish Hosp., St. Louis, 1987-88; resident in otolaryngology Barnes Hosp.-Wash. U., St. Louis, 1988-93, fellow, 1993-94. Recipient Resident Tchg. award Dept. Otolaryngology, HNS, Continuing Med. Edn. Achievement award AAO-HNS, 1997—, AMA Physician's Recognition award, 1997—. Fellow ACS, Am. Acad. Otolaryngology-Head and Neck Surgery, Am. Acad. Otolaryngologic Allergy (examiner oral bd., 1995, 96, 97), Am. Acad. Facial Plastic and Reconstructive Surgery, Tau Beta Pi, Alpha Eta Mu Beta. Achievements include research in design of implantable stimulator; influence of an environment on the developing vestibular system; implantable middle ear hearing aid project. Office: Piedmont Health Care Oto-Head Neck Surgery 707 Bryant St Statesville NC 28677-4142

DEDEAUX, PAUL J., orthodontist; b. Pass Christian, Miss., Feb. 22, 1937; s. Mack and Harriet D.; m. Janet Louise Harter, June 29, 1971; children: Michele, Kristen, Kelly. BA, Dillard U., 1959; DDS, Howard U., 1963; MS, Fairleigh Dickinson U., 1975. Pvt. practice, Washington, 1976-93, Santa Ana, Calif., 1976-93; instr. Howard U., Washington, 1967-69; dental dir. Dr. Martin Luther King Health Ctr., Bronx, N.Y., 1969-70, dentist, 1970-76; chief dentist Calipatria State Prison, Calif., 1993-96, Calif. Med. Facility, Vacaville, 1996—; instr. Howard U., Washington, 1967-69; cons. Hostos C.C., Bronx, 1971-76; mem. adv. panel Dental Econs. mag., 1976; adj. assoc. prof. Columbia U., N.Y.C., 1970-72. Contbr. articles to profl. jours. Capt. U.S. Army, 1963-67, USAR, 1975—, col., 1985—, comdr., 1994—. Mem. Am. Assn. Orthodontists, Pacific Coast Soc. Orthodontists, ADA, Calif. Dental Assn., Assn. Mil. Surgeons of U.S. Democrat. Methodist. Avocations: photography, fishing. Home: 940 Celestine Cir Vacaville CA 95687-7853 Office: Calif Med Facility PO Box 2000 1600 California Dr Vacaville CA 95687

DEDERER, MICHAEL EUGENE, public relations company executive; b. Seattle, Apr. 30, 1932; s. Michael and Clare (Collon) D.; separated; children—David M., Claire M. B.A. in Journalism, U. Wash., 1953. Account exec. Hugh A. Smith Mktg. & Pub. Relations Co., Seattle, 1956-59; account exec. Kraft, Smith & Ehrig, Inc., Seattle, 1959-63; account exec. Jay Rockey Pub. Relations and The Rockey Co., Inc., Seattle, 1963, v.p., 1970-78, exec. v.p., 1978-86, pres., 1986-94; vice chmn. The Rockey Co., Inc., Seattle, 1994-98, sr. cons., 1998—. Served to 1st lt. U.S. Army, 1953-55. Mem. Pub. Rels. Soc. Am. (pres. Wash. chpt. 1970). Roman Catholic. Avocations: Alpine skiing; fly fishing. Office: Rockey Co Inc 2121 5th Ave Seattle WA 98121-2596*

DEDERER, WILLIAM BOWNE, music educator, administrator; b. Poughkeepsie, N.Y., July 15, 1945; s. William Morgan and Marion (Bowne) D.; m. Julia Yvonne Ary; 1 child, William Rockwell. BS in Music Edn., SUNY, Fredonia, 1967; MusM in Edn., U. Mich., 1968, D Mus. Arts in Performance, 1975. Prof. trumpet SUNY, Fredonia, 1969-82; dean Boston Conservatory, 1982-96, v.p. for acad. affairs, 1996-98; dean conservatory of music Capital U., 1998—; choir dir. 1st United Meth. Ch., Fredonia, 1976-82, 1st Presbyn. Ch., Fredonia, 1969-73, dir. of music, 1st Presbyn. Ch., Haverhill, Mass., 1983-87. Mem. Nashua Symphony, 1986-98. Mem. Internat. Trumpet Guild, Pi Kappa Lambda, Phi Mu Alpha (nat. exec. com. 1979-88, nat. pres. 1985-88). Office: Conservatory of Music Capital U Columbus OH 43209

DEDERICK, ROBERT GOGAN, economist; b. Keene, N.H., Nov. 18, 1929; s. Frederic Van Dyck and Margaret (Gogan) D.; m. Margarida N. Magalhaes, Aug. 24, 1957; children: Frederic, Laura, Peter. AB, Harvard U., 1951, AM, 1953, PhD, 1958; postgrad., Cornell U., 1953-54. Econ. research mgr. New Eng. Mut. Life Ins. Co., Boston, 1957-64; assoc. economist No. Trust Co., Chgo., 1964; v.p., assoc. economist No. Trust Co., 1965-69, v.p., economist, 1969-70, sr. v.p., chief economist, 1970-81, exec. v.p., chief economist, 1983-94, econ. cons., 1994—; mem. panel of econ. advisers Congl. Budget Office; mem. econ. adv. bd. U.S. Commerce Dept., 1968-70, 75-76, 83-85, asst. sec. commerce for econ. affairs, 1981-82, under sec. commerce for econ. affairs, 1982-83; prin. RGD Econs., Hinsdale, 1994—. Fellow Nat. Assn. Bus. Economists (pres. 1973-74, governing coun. 1969-75); mem. Tech. Cons. Bus. Coun., Conf. Bus. Economists (chmn. 1984-85), Harvard Discussion Group Indsl. Economists, Am. Bankers Assn. (alumni coun.), Am. Fin. Assn., Am. Econ. Assn., Econ. Club, Execs. Club (Chgo.), Harvard Club (Chgo.), Hinsdale Golf Club, Capital Hill Club (Washington). Home: 113 S County Line Rd Hinsdale IL 60521-4722 Office: RGD Economics 113 S County Line Rd Hinsdale IL 60521-4722 also: Northern Trust Company 505 Lasalle St Chicago IL 60610-4298

DEDERICK, RONALD OSBURN, lawyer; b. Chgo., Aug. 26, 1935; s. Clint Goddard and Isabel Lucille (Osburn) D.; m. Dorothy Hope Spence; children: Cynthia Rae Dederick Stroili, Kenneth Scott. BA, U. Va., 1957, JD, 1962. Bar: N.Y. 1962, U.S. Dist. Ct. (so. dist.) N.Y. 1964, Conn. 1969, U.S. Dist. Conn. 1970, U.S. Supreme Ct. 1990. Assoc. Sullivan & Cromwell, N.Y.C., 1962-69; ptnr. Durey & Pierson, Stamford, Conn., 1969-79, Day, Berry & Howard, Stamford, 1979—. Bd. dirs. Vol. Action Coun., Stamford, 1972-79, Guardianship Advocacy Resource Program, Inc., Stamford, 1984—; trustee, sec. West Conn. Multiple Sclerosis Soc., 1985—; chair Greenwich (Conn.) Arts Coun., 1990-94. Capt. USNR, ret. Fellow Am. Bar Found., Am. Coll. Trust and Estates; mem. ABA (chair multistate com. 1984-87), Conn. Bar Assn. (chair probate sect. 1988-90), Conn. Bar Found. (James W. Cooper fellow), Stamford Regional Bar Assn. (bd. dirs. 1982-88), Internat. Bar Assn., Internat. Acad. Estate and Trust Law, Rotary (pres. Stamford 1980-81, Paul Harris fellow 1984), Milbrook Club (pres. 1980-81). Republican. Presbyterian. Avocations: golf, fishing. Office: Day Berry & Howard 1 Canterbury Grn Ste 7 Stamford CT 06901-2047

DEDERT, STEVEN RAY, marketing professional, consultant; b. Franklin, Ind., Feb. 17, 1953; s. Ralph Edward and Martha Elizabeth (Weisman) D.; children: Eric Allen, Tammi Michelle. AA, St. John's Coll., Winfield, Kans., 1973; BSBA, U. Denver, 1975. CPA, Ind. Audit sr. Coopers & Lybrand, Indpls., 1975-78; controller Am. Med. Mgmt., Inc., Indpls., 1978-82, Moorfeed Corp., Indpls., 1982-84; chief fin. officer, controller Midwest Energy Mgmt., Indpls., 1984-86; pres. Cleaning Solution, Inc., Indpls., 1986-89; chief fin. officer, dir. ops. Corinthian Pharm. Systems, Inc., Indpls., 1990-93; ptnr. Hometown Living Ctrs., Inc., Indpls., 1991-97; cons. CPA and software installer, 1997—; cons. acct., 1980—. Treas. bd. dirs. Greater Indpls. Assn. for Luth. Secondary Edn., 1978-82; mgr. Franklin Twp. Little League, 1985-87. Mem. Ind. CPA Soc., AICPA. Avocations: family activities, participant sports. Home and Office: 201 Dixie Dr # 103 Indianapolis IN 46227-2825

DEDMAN, BILL, journalist; b. Chattanooga, Tenn., Oct. 14, 1960; s. Harold C. and Bobbye (Griswold) D.; m. Pamela J. Belluck, Sept. 5, 1993; 1 child, Justin. Student, Wash. U., St. Louis, 1978-81. Reporter Warrensburg (Mo.) Star-Journal, 1981, Blue Springs (Mo.) Examiner, 1981-82, Chattanooga Free Press, 1983, Chattanooga Times, 1984-86, Knoxville News-Sentinel, 1986-87, Atlanta Journal-Constitution, 1987-89, Washington Post, 1989-91; fellow Freedom Forum Media Studies Ctr. Columbia U., N.Y.C., 1992-93; contbg. writer Mother Jones Mag., 1993-94; writer N.Y. Times, 1997—; Hearst vis. fellow U. Md. Coll. Journalism, 1993-94; dir. computer-assisted reporting AP, 1994-97; reporter N.Y. Times, 1997—; adj. lectr. Northwestern U. Author: The Color of Money: Home Mortgage Lending Practices Discriminate Against Blacks, 1988; contbr. articles to profl. jours. Recipient Pulitzer prize for investigative reporting, 1989, Robert F. Kennedy Journalism award grand prize, 1989, Worth Bingham prize, 1989, numerous others. Mem. Investigative Reporters and Editors (bd. dirs. 1990-96, award 1989). *

DEDMAN, ROBERT HENRY, sales executive; b. Rison, Ark., Feb. 15, 1926; s. Robert Henry and Cornelia D.; m. Nancy McMillan, Dec. 6, 1952; children: Robert H. Jr., Patricia Dedman Dietz. BA, U. Tex., 1946, BS, 1948, LLB, 1948; LLM, So. Meth. U., 1953. Foun., chmn. Club Corp. Internat., Dallas, 1957—; mem. State Hwy. Commn., Austin, Tex., 1981-85, 87-91; adv. dir. Stewart Info. Svcs., 1989—. Chmn. bd. trustees, So. Meth. U., Dallas, 1993-96, active, 1976—. Named to Tex. Bus. Hall of Fame, 1987, Entrepreneur of Yr., Dallas, 1980, Marketer of Yr., Dallas, 1986; recipient Horatio Alger award, Washington, 1989. Republican. Methodist. Avocations: tennis, golf. Office: ClubCorp Internat Ste 700 3030 Lyndon B Johnson Fwy Dallas TX 75234-7763*

DEDOMINIC, PATTY (LEE DEDOMINIC), personnel executive; b. Glendale, Calif., Mar. 5, 1951; d. Harold and Eleanor Timm; m. Gene Sinser, Apr. 19, 1986; children: Eric, Christopher, Nicholas. Student, UCLA, 1975-79. Mgr. Task Force Temp Services, Los Angeles, 1972-75; dist. mgr., trainer Avon Products, Pasadena, Calif., 1975-78; pres., CEO, founder PDQ Personnel Services Inc., Los Angeles, 1979—; mem. SBA Adv. Council, Los Angeles, 1985-86; mem. Am. Arbitration Assn.; mem. adv. bd. Los Angeles Ort. Tech. Inst., 1986-87, Los Angeles City Coll., 1987; lectr. in field. Author: Management Savvy and Career Corner; contbr. numerous articles on career devel., job search, recruitment and entrepreneurship to profl. jours. Treas. Los Angeles Women's Campaign Fund, 1985-86; advisor Sen. Garamendi's Long Range Planning Task Force, State of Calif., 1985-86. Mem. Am. Bus. Women's Assn. (Boss of Yr. 1986), Nat. Assn. Women Bus. Owners (chmn., v.p., pres. 1983-84, advisor 1985-86), Women in Mgmt. (chmn., v.p., pres. 1979-82, Woman of Yr. award 1984), West Los Angeles Execs. Assn. Avocations: real estate, antiques. Office: PDQ Personnel Services Inc 5900 Wilshire Blvd Ste 400 Los Angeles CA 90036-5013

DEDONATO, DONALD MICHAEL, obstetrician/gynecologist; b. Bridgeport, Conn., Apr. 25, 1952; s. Michael Anthony and Mary Jane (Zawadski) DeD.; m. Susan Mary Naulty, June 15, 1974; children: Mark Dominic, David Nicholas. BA in Chemistry cum laude, Coll. Holy Cross, 1974; MD, Loyola U., Maywood, Ill., 1977. Intern Loyola Foster McGaw Hosp., Maywood, Ill., 1977-78; resident Ohio State U. Hosp., Columbus, Ohio, 1978-81; ob-gyn. Ob-Gyn. Assocs., Arlington Heights, Ill., 1981-87, DeDonato, Goodnough and Geittmann, Ob-Gyn., Arlington Heights, 1987-92; pres., CEO N.W. Women's Cons., Arlington Heights, 1993—; clin. instr. Northwestern U. Med. Ctr., Chgo., 1981—; chmn. dept. ob-gyn. Northwest Cmty. Healthcare, 1998—. Recipient CIBA award. Mem. AMA, Am. Assn. Med. Colls. (Loyola rep.), Chgo. Med. Soc., Ill. State Med. Soc., Am. Bd. Ob-Gyn., Am. Assn. Gyn. Laparoscopists, Garden Camera (pres. 1985-86, 92-93), Phi Beta Kappa, Alpha Sigma Nu. Avocation: photography. Office: NW Womens Cons 1630 W Central Rd Arlington Heights IL 60005-2407

DEDRICK, KENT GENTRY, retired physicist, researcher; b. Watsonville, Calif., Aug. 9, 1923; s. Frederick David and Matilda (Redman) D.: 1 child, Susan Marie. BS in Chemistry and Physics, San Jose (Calif.) State U., 1946; MS in Phys. Scis., Stanford U., 1949, PhD in Theoretical Physics, 1955. Rsch. assoc. U. Mich., Ann Arbor, 1954-55, Stanford U., 1955-62; math. physicist Stanford Rsch. Inst., Menlo Park, Calif., 1962-75; cons. scientist Atty. Gen.'s Office State of Calif., Sacramento, 1976-80; with marine tech. safety dept. State Lands Commn., Sacramento, 1980-81, rsch. specialist, 1981-92; cons. scientist phys. and environ. scis., 1992—. Contbr. articles to profl. jours.; composer instrumental and vocal works, 1978—. Pres. Com. for Green Foothills, Palo Alto, Calif., 1972-74; founding co-chmn. So. Crossing Action Team, San Francisco Bay area, 1970-72, chmn. Bayfront com. Sierra Club, Palo Alto, 1967-72. Mem. Am. Phys. Soc., Am. Geophys. Union, Soc. Wetland Scientists, Sigma Xi. Achievements include co-discovery of mathematical theorem on Lagrange and Taylor series. Home: 1360 Vallejo Way Sacramento CA 95818-3450

DE DUVE, CHRISTIAN RENÉ, chemist, educator; b. Thames-Ditton, Eng., Oct. 2, 1917; s. Alphonse and Madeleine (Pungs) de D.; m. Janine Herman, Sept. 30, 1943; children: Thierry, Anne, Françoise, Alain. M.D., U. Louvain, Belgium, 1941, Ph.D., 1945, M.Sc., 1946; D honoris causa, U. Turin, 1969, U. Leiden, 1970, U. Sherbrooke, 1970, U. Lille, 1973, Cath. U. Santiago, Chile, 1974, U. René Descartes, Paris, 1974, State U. Liege, 1975, State U. Ghent, 1975, Gustavus Adolphus Coll., St. Peter, Minn., 1975, U. Rosario, Argentina, 1975, U. Aix-Marseille II, 1979, U. Keele, 1982, Katholieke U. Leuven, 1984, Karolinska Inst., Stockholm, 1986, U. Montreal, 1992, Rockefeller U., 1997. Lectr. physiol. chemistry faculty medicine Cath. U. Louvain, 1947-51, prof., head dept. physiol. chemistry, 1951-85, emeritus prof., 1985—; prof. biochem. cytology Rockefeller U., N.Y.C., 1962-74, Andrew W. Mellon prof., 1974-88, prof. emeritus, 1988—; vis. prof. Albert Einstein Coll. Medicine, Bronx, N.Y., 1961-62, Chaire Francqui State U. Ghent, 1962-63, Free U. Brussels, 1963-64, State U. Liège, 1972-73, Facultés Universitaires Notre-Dame de la Paix, Namur, 1990-91; Mayne guest prof. U. Queensland, Brisbane, Australia, 1972; pres. Internat. Inst. Cellular and Molecular Pathology, Brussels, 1974-91. Mem. editorial bd. Subcellular Biochemistry, 1971-87, Preparative Biochemistry, 1971-80, Molecular and Cellular Biochemistry, 1973-80. Mem. Conseil d'Administrn. du Fonds Nat. de la Recherche Scientifique, 1958-61; mem. Conseil de Gestion du Fonds de la Recherche Scientifique Médicale, 1959-61; mem. Commn. Scientifique du Fonds de la Recherche Scientifique Médicale, 1958-61; mem. Comité des Experts du Conseil Nat. de la Politique Scientifique, 1958-61; mem. adv. bd. Ciba Found., 1960-85; mem. adult devel. and aging research and tng. rev. com. Nat. Inst. Child Health and Devel., NIH, 1970-73; mem. adv. com. for med. research WHO, 1974-79; mem. sci. adv. com. Max Planck-Inst. für Immunbiologie, 1975-78, Ludwig Inst. Cancer Research, 1985-91, Mary Imogene Bassett Research Inst., 1986-90, Clin. Research Inst. Montreal, 1986—; mem. biology adv. com. N.Y. Hall of Sci., 1986—; adv. sci. com. Basel Inst. for Immunology, 1989-93. Recipient Prix des Alumni, 1949, Prix Pfizer, 1957, Prix Francqui, 1960, Prix Quinquennal Belge des Sciences Médicales, 1967 (Belgium); Gairdner Found. Internat. award merit (Can.), 1967; Dr. H.P. Heineken prize (The Netherlands), 1973; Nobel prize for physiology or medicine, 1974; Harden award Biochem. Soc. (Gt. Britain), 1978; Theobald Smith award Albany Med. Coll., 1981; Jimenez Diaz award, 1985. Fellow AAAS; mem. NAS, Royal Acad. Medicine, Royal Acad. Belgium, Am. Chem. Soc., Biochem. Soc., Am. Philos. Soc., Am. Soc. Biol. Chemists, Pontifical Acad. Sci., Am. Soc. Cell Biology (coun. 1966-69, E.B. Wilson award 1989), Soc. Chimie Biologique, Soc. Belge Biochim. (pres. 1962-64), Deutsche Akademie der Naturforscher Leopoldina, Koninklyke Akademie voor Geneeskunde (Belgium), European Assn. Study Diabetes, European Molecular Biology Orgn., European Cell Biology Orgn., Internat. Soc. Cell Biology, N.Y. Acad. Scis., Soc. Belge de Physiologie, Sigma Xi; fgn. assoc. Am. Acad. Arts and Scis., Royal Soc. London, Royal Soc. Can., Académie des Sciences de Paris, Académie des Sciences d'Athénes, Academia Europaea, Deutsche Gesellschaft für Zellbiologie; numerous hon. memberships. Office: Rockefeller U 1230 York Ave New York NY 10021-6399 also: ICP, 75 Ave Hippocrate, B-1200 Brussels Belgium

DEE, FRANCIS X., lawyer; b. N.Y.C., July 13, 1944. BA, Manhattan Coll., 1966; JD, Cath. U. Am., 1969; LLM in Labor Law, NYU, 1975. Bar: N.Y. 1970, N.J. 1972, U.S. Supreme Ct. 1981. Atty. NLRB, 1969-72; labor counsel Litton Industries, 1972-76; sr. ptnr. Carpenter, Bennett & Morrissey, Newark, 1976—. Fellow Am. Coll. Trial Lawyers, Coll. Labor and Employment Lawyers; mem. ABA (litigation sect., com. on devel. law under nat. labor rels. act labor and employment law sect. 1975—), N.Y. State Bar Assn. (litig., labor and employment law sects.), N.J. State Bar Assn. (litig. sect., del. to gen. coun. 1985-92, exec. bd. 1983-92, mgmt. co-chair com. on practice and procedure under nat. labor rels. act 1980-83, sec. labor employment law sect. 1987-89, vice chmn. 1989-91, chmn. 1991-92), Essex County Bar Assn. Office: Carpenter Bennett & Morrissey Three Gateway Ctr 100 Mulberry St Fl 17 Newark NJ 07102-4004

DEE, JON FACUNDO, financial services executive; b. Borongan, The Philippines, July 6, 1949; arrived in U.S., 1976; s. Facundo Dee and Guadalupe Abordo; m. Tess de Ungria Calma, Oct. 10, 1976; children: Bernadette, Paolo Angelo, Kristina. BSBA in Acctg., Mapua Inst. Tech., The Philippines, 1968; MBA, Ateneo de Manila U., 1983. CPA, The Philippines. Corp. bookkeeper Nat. Irrigation Adminstrn., Quezon City, The Philippines, 1968-70; treas. fgn. exch. Philippine Nat. Bank, Manila, 1970-86; owner Century Fin. Svcs., Daly City, Calif., 1988—. Bd. dirs. Westlake Subdivsn. Improvement Assn., Daly City, 1995—; mem. Dem. Nat. Com., San Mateo County Dem. Com., 1996—. Mem. Nat. Assn. Realtors, Calif. Assn. Realtors, Golden Gate Rose Soc. of San Francisco, Mission Merchants Assn., San Francisco Assn. Realtors, San Francisco C. of C., Commonwealth Club, Sierra Club. Roman Catholic. Avocations: writing, gardening, photography. Home: 9 Lake Vista Ave Daly City CA 94015-1013 Office: Century Fin Svcs 86 88th St Daly City CA 94015-1603

DEE, PAULINE MARIE, artist; b. Concord, N.H., Jan. 9, 1933; d. Arthur Joseph and Anna Marie (Marquis) Champagne; m. Edmond Francis Dee, July 2, 1955; children: James Francis, Diane Mary. Bus. Cert., Burdett Coll., Lynn, Mass. Membership chmn. Danvers (Mass.) Art Assn., 1986-92, v.p., 1990-92; founder Pauline Dee Studio for Oil Painting, 1989; v.p. Lynnfield (Mass.) Art Guild, 1991-93, pres., 1994-96; v.p. Saltbox Gallery, Topsfield, Mass., 1995—; demonstrator in field; cons. Kohinor Accent Program, Bloomsbury, N.J., 1995—; founder Pauline Dee Studio, 1989; instituted Lynnfield Art Guild Scholarship Fund, 1993. Exhibited in solo shows at Woman's Club of Boston, 1980, Naval Officers Club, Pearl Harbor, Hawaii, 1994; represented in numerous pvt. collections. Cons. Peabody (Mass.) Internat. Festival, 1995; bd. dirs. North Shore Art Assn., Gloucester, Mass., 1996. Recipient achievement awards, 1985-95; Lynnfield Arts Lottery grantee, 1996. Mem. Our Lady Guadalupe Sodality (prefect 1966-68). Roman Catholic. Avocations: art, golf, swimming, photography, walking. Home: 16 Samoset Rd Peabody MA 01960-3504

DEE, ROBERT FORREST, retired pharmaceutical company executive; b. Cin., July 8, 1924; s. Raymond H. and Mary (Owen) D.; m. Virginia Winston Verner, Sept. 10, 1948 (div. 1979); children: Jacqueline, Robert R., John, Catherine, Thomas; m. 2d Jean T. Tanney, Jan. 2, 1980; 1 child, Patrick. A.B., Harvard U., 1946; LL.D. (hon.), Phila. Coll. Pharmacy and Sci., 1978; L.H.D. (hon.), Med. Coll. Pa., 1979. With SmithKline Corp., Phila., 1948-87; successively market research analyst, asst. to adminstrv. v.p., dir. Animal Health div., dir. consumer, animal and instrument products, v.p., dir. consumer, animal and instrument products, exec. v.p., pres., chief exec. officer, chmn.; bd. dirs. United Techs. Corp., Air Products and Chems. Inc.; mem. adv. bd. Volvo Internat. Bd. dirs. U.S. Council for Internat. Bus., Com. Econ. Devel.; trustee Heritage Found. Served with AUS. Mem. Nat. Assn. Mfrs. (chmn. exec. com.), Bus. Council, Conf. Bd., Council Fgn. Relations, Mgmt. Execs. Soc. Episcopalian. Office: PO Box 1539 709 Swedeland Rd Kng Of Prussa PA 19406-2711*

DEE, SCOTT ALLEN, veterinarian; b. Rochester, Minn., Sept. 27, 1958; s. Richard Walter and Pauline Kay (Anderson) D.; m. Lisa Ann Bell, Oct. 9, 1993. BA in Biology, Gustavus Adolphus Coll., 1981; MS in Veterinary Microbiology, U. Minn., 1985, DVM, 1987, PhD in Vet. Medicine, 1996. Diplomate Am. Coll. Vet. Microbiologists. Vet., ptnr. Swine Health Ctr., Morris, Minn., 1987-99; assoc. prof. in swine medicine U. Minn. Coll. of Vet. Medicine, 1999—; mem. adv. bd. Swine Health and Prodn., St. Paul, 1991—, NOBL Labs., Sioux Ctr., Iowa, 1992—, Pfizer Animal Health, Lee Summit, Mo., 1994—; spkr. Internat. Porcine Reproductive and Respiratory System Conf., Copenhagen, 1995, St. Paul, 1992; del. Conf. Rsch. Workers in Animal Disease, 1995; assoc. prof. dept. clin. and population scis. Coll. Vet. Medicine, U. Minn. Author: Veterinary Clinics of North America: Swine Reproduction, 1992, Current Veterinary Therapy III, 1993, Diseases of Swine, 8th edit., 1997, Merck Veterinary Manual, 8th edit., 1997, Current Veterinary Therapy IV, 1998; splty. editor Compendium Continuing Edn., 1995; contbr. articles to profl. jours. Recipient First Decade award Gustavus Adolphus Coll., 1991, Allen D. Leman Sci. in Practice award, 1996, Disting. Alumni Cert., U. Minn. Coll. Vet. Medicine, 1996, Dist. Alumni Lect., U. Minn. CVM, 1997. Mem. AVMA (Practitioner Rsch. award 1998), Am. Assn. Swine Practitioners (Swine Practitioner of Yr. 1996), Minn. Vet. Med. Assn., Minn. Acad. Vet. Practice. Office: U Minn Coll Vet Medicine 385 Animal Sci/Vet Medicine Bldg 1988 Fitch Ave Saint Paul MN 55108

DEEB, MARY-JANE, editor, educator; b. Alexandria, Egypt, Aug. 27, 1946; came to U.S., 1973; d. Alix and Stephanie (Klanscek) Anhoury; m. Marius K. Deeb, Sept. 27, 1969; 1 child, Hadi K. BA in Sociology, Am. U., Cairo, 1967, MA in Sociology, 1972; PhD in Internat. Rels., Johns Hopkins U., 1987. Rsch. assoc. Ford Found., Beirut, Lebanon, 1972-73; cons. UN Econ. Commn. for Western Asia, Beirut, 1980, UNICEF, Beirut, 1980-81; project dir. U.S. AID, Beirut, 1982-83; asst. professorial lectr. George Washington U., Washington, 1988-89, 93, 97, Georgetown U., Washington, 1991, 94; asst. prof. Am. U., Washington, 1989-94, adj. assoc. prof., 1994-98; editor Mid. East Jour., Washington, 1995-98; Arab world area specialist Libr. of Congress, Washington, 1998—; external reviewer for grant proposals U.S. Inst. Peace, Washington, 1991, 92, 97; testified on subcom. on Africa fgn. rels. com. U.S. Ho. of Reps., 1991, 92, 98; testified before the select com. on intelligence, U.S. Senate, 1996; testified on fgn. rels. com. U.S. Senate, 1997, UN Monitor of Algerian legislative elections, 1997; dir. Algeria program Corp. Coun. on Africa; Arab world area specialist Libr. Congress, 1998—. Author: Libya Since the Revolution, 1982, Libya's Foreign Policy, 1991; co-editor: Hasib Sabbagh from Palestinian Refugee to Citizen of the World, 1996; book rev. editor Internat. Jour. Mid.-East Studies, 1989-94; contbr. articles, revs. to profl. jours. and encys., and chpts. to books; interviewed on numerous TV programs, including CBS Evening News, ABC News, NBC Nightly News, CNN Headline News, Fox Morning News, PBS, and in news publs., including N.Y. Times, Washington Post, Time mag., L.A. Times, The Christian Sci. Monitor, U.S.A. Today, Boston Globe, Tokyo Shimbum, Yomouri, others. Mem. UN Assn., Am. Polit. Sci. Assn., Internat. Studies Assn., Mid. East Studies Assn. N.Am., Women's Caucus for Polit. Sci., Am.-Tunisian Assn. (exec. bd. 1989—), World Affairs Coun., Women in Fgn. Policy. Roman Catholic. Office: Libr Congress African and Middle Ea Divsn Jefferson Bldg 101 Independence Ave Washington DC 20540-4820

DEEG, EMIL WOLFGANG, manufacturing company executive, physicist; b. Selb, Germany, Sept. 20, 1926; came to U.S., 1967, naturalized, 1975; s. Fritz and Trina (Poehlmann) D.; m. Hedwig M.S. Kempf, Aug. 25, 1953; children: Wolfgang, Martin, Bernhard, Renate. Dipl. Physiker, U. Wuerzburg, 1954, Dr. rer. nat., 1956. Rsch. asst. Max Planck Inst., Wuerzburg, 1954-59; mem. tech. staff Bell Telephone Labs., Allentown, Pa., 1959-60; rsch. assoc. Jenaer Glaswerk Schott U. Gen., Mainz, Germany, 1960, dir. rsch., 1960-65; assoc. prof. physics and solid state sci. Am. U., Cairo, 1965-67; mgr. ceramic rsch. Am. Optical Corp., Southbridge, Mass., 1967-71, mgr. materials rsch., 1971-73, dir. process and materials rsch., 1973-75, dir. inorganic materials R&D, 1975-77, tech. adviser, 1977-78; sr. scientist Anchor Hocking Corp., Lancaster, Ohio, 1978-79, mgr. materials R&D, 1979-80; mgr. glass tech. Bausch & Lomb, Rochester, N.Y., 1980-82; mgr. glass and fiber devel. Mead Office Sys., Richardson, Tex., 1982-84; project mgr. AMP, Inc., Harrisburg, Pa., 1984-92; cons., Lemoyne, Pa., 1992—; mem. Internat. Commn. on Glass, 1963-81, Internat. Commn. for Optics, 1964-66; cons. NASA Spacelab Program, 1971-78; expert witness on glass product patent litigation German Patent Office, 1978-81. Author: (with H. Richter) Glas im Laboratorium, 1966; editor AMP Jour. Tech., 1993-98; patentee in field; contbr. chpts. to books, articles to profl. jours. Pres. PTA, Woodstock, Conn., 1970-71; committeeman Mohegan coun. Boy Scouts Am., 1967-73; trustee Woodstock Acad., 1971-78; overseer Old Sturbridge Village, Inc., 1972-81; chmn. Optical Info. Ctr., Southbridge, 1976-77. With German Army, 1944-45. Fellow Am. Ceramic Soc. (emeritus); mem. Optical Soc. Am. (emeritus), Nat. Inst. Ceramic Engrs., Internat. Tech. Inst. (inductee Hall of Fame for Engring., Sci. and Tech. 1988), ASM Internat., Engrs. Soc. Pa. (dir. 1996-98), Lions (pres. Woodstock chpt. 1975, zone chmn. dist. 23 C, Lions Internat. 1976-78). Home and Office: 501 Ohio Ave Lemoyne PA 17043-1525

DEEGAN, JOHN, JR., academic administrator, researcher; b. Elizabeth, N.J., Nov. 18, 1944; s. John and Margaret (Pignataro) D.; m. Anita Hope Rochelle, Dec. 19, 1964; children: Michael J., Matthew B. Student, Monmouth Coll., West Long Branch, N.J., 1962-64; BS, Evangel Coll., Springfield, Mo., 1967; MA, U. Mich., 1969, PhD, 1972. Asst. prof. Rice U., Houston, 1972-75, U. Rochester, N.Y., 1975-80; assoc. prof. U. Rochester, 1980; spl. asst. to dep. adminstr. EPA, Washington, 1980; dir. Love Canal Project, 1980-82; assoc. dean Sch. Pub. Health U. Ill., Chgo., 1982-86, acting dean, 1983-85; prof. U. No. Iowa, Cedar Falls, 1986-89, dean Coll. Social and Behavioral Scis., 1986-89; provost, v.p. acad. affairs, prof. U. So. Maine, Portland, 1989-94; dean coll., v.p. acad. affairs, prof. Westminster Coll., New Wilmington, Pa., 1994—; cons. EPA, 1983-86; trustee Ill. Cancer Coun., 1983-86; bd. dirs. Leopold Ctr. for Sustainable Agr. State of Iowa, 1987-89. Contbr. articles to sci. jours. Recipient EPA Bronze medal award, 1982; U. Rochester fellow in preventive medicine, 1979, Acad. Adminstrn. fellow Am. Coun. on Edn., 1986-87. Mem. AAAS, APHA, Am. Chem. Soc., Sigma Xi, Delta Omega. Democrat. Presbyterian. Avocations: fishing, golfing. Office: Westminster Coll Office Acad Affairs New Wilmington PA 16172

DEEGAN, MARY JO, sociology educator; b. Chgo., Nov. 27, 1946; d. William James and Ida May (Scott) Deegan; life ptnr. Michael Ray Hill. AS, Lake Mich. Coll., 1966; BS, Western Mich. U., 1969, MA, 1973; PhD, U. Chgo., 1975. Asst. prof. U. Nebr., Lincoln, 1975-80, assoc. prof., 1980-89, prof., 1989—; med. trainee U. Chgo. Ctr. for Health Adminstrn., 1972-75; grad. asst. Western Mich. U., 1969-71.; del. Conf. on Directions in Health Econs., New Orleans, 1972. Author: Jane Addams and Men of the Chicago School, 1892-1918, 1988 (Choice award, 1989-90), American Ritual Dramas, 1989; editor: Women in Sociology, 1991, American Ritual Tapestry, 1998; co-editor: Women and Disability, 1985, Women and Symbolic Interaction, 1987, Feminist Ethics in Social Research, 1989, With Her in Ourland (by C.P. Gilman), 1997, Play, School and Society, 1999; contbr. 80 articles to profl. jours., chpts. to books. Mem. Am. Sociol. Assn., Internat. Sociol. Assn., Harriet Martineau Sociol. Soc. Office: Dept Sociology 711 Oldfather Hall U Nebraska Lincoln NE 68588-0324

DEEGAN, MICHAEL WARREN, volunteer overseas organization administrator; b. Tenn., 1947. BS, U. Ala., 1969; MBA, Calif. State U., 1976. With Teledyne, U.S. Ind. Coalition; pres. Agrl. Coop. Devel. Internat./Vol & Overseas Coop. Assistance, Washington. Home: 1524 Victoria Farms Ln Vienna VA 22182 Office: Agrl Coop Devel Internat Vol & Overseas Coop Asst 50 F St NW Ste 1075 Washington DC 20001-1532

DEEGEN, UWE FREDERICK, marine biologist; b. Freising, Germany, Mar. 27, 1948; came to U.S., 1953; s. Friedrich Rudolf and Maria Magdalena (Dyrda) D.; m. Barbara Lynn Cannon, Aug. 7, 1982; 1 child, Jennifer Marie. BS, U. So. Miss., 1970, MS, 1972; PhD, U. Tex., 1979. Cert. fed. grants adminstr. Dept. Commerce, shellfish sanitarian FDA. Grad. rsch. assoc. U. So. Miss., Hattiesburg, 1970-72; instr. biology Biloxi (Miss.) Sr. High Sch., 1972-73; instr. biology Pensacola (Fla.) Jr. Coll., 1973-74; grad. fellow U. Tex., Austin, 1974-76; staff scientist Miss. Marine Resources Coun., Long Beach, 1976-80; chief saltwater fisheries Miss. Bur. Marine Resources, Long Beach, 1980-89; sr. systems analyst Miss. Dept. Wildlife, Fisheries, and Parks, Biloxi, 1989-95; chief marine fisheries Miss. Dept. Marine Resources, Biloxi, 1995-96, dep. dir. Dept., 1995—; mem. Gulf Mex. Fishery Mgmt. Coun., Tampa, Fla., 1980-89; mem. tech. rev. com. U.S./Israel Binat. Agrl. R&D Fund, 1980-86; vice chmn. statis. subcom., chmn. rec. fisheries com. Gulf States Fisheries Commn., Ocean Springs, 1983-87; mem. freshwater inflow adv. com. EPA/Gulf Mex. Program, 1990—. Author: Mathematical Modeling of Oxygen Distribution in Streams, 1972; columnist Coastal Fishing, 1983—; contbr. articles to profl. jours. Tournament weightmaster Miss. Trout Invitational Tournament, Pass Christian, 1985—, Long Beach Jaycees Fishing Tournament, 1989—. Recipient King Neptune award Miss. Deep Sea Fishing Rodeo Bd. Dirs., Gulfport, Miss., 1991. Mem. Am. Fisheries Soc. (cert., mem. estuarine and marine resources com. 1993—), Estuarine Rsch. Fedn., Internat. Gamefish Assn., Kappa Mu Epsilon, Beta Beta Beta, EPA Gulf of Mex. Program Habitat Focus Team, Gulf of Mex. Fishery Mgmt. Coun. Essential Fish Habitat Com. Lutheran. Avocations: fishing, backpacking, raquet sports, landscape gardening, nature photography. Home: 121 E 4th St Long Beach MS 39560-6107 Office: Miss Dept Marine Resources 1141 Bayview Ave Ste 101 Biloxi MS 39530-1613

DEEKENS, ELIZABETH TUPMAN, writer; b. Washington, Aug. 25, 1926; d. William Spencer Tupman and Isabelle McNeil Roberts; m. William Carter Deekens, July 30, 1955 (dec. 1988); children: Arthur Carter, Christine Deekens Old, Catherine Deekens Ward. Student, George Washington U., 1945-49. parish sec. All Souls Episcopal Ch., Washington, 1951-52; Washington corres. The Living Ch., Mpls., 1951-52; woman's editor Episcopal Churchnews, Richmond, Va., 1952-57; mem. Episcopal Churchwomen Bd., Diocese of Va., Richmond, 1968; mem. Bishop's Liturgical Commn., Diocese of Va., 1975; newsletter editor Vestry, Ch. of Epiphany, Richmond, 1974-82; editor, layreader St. Martin's Ch., Richmond, 1983—. Contbr. articles to mags. including Seventeen, Good Housekeeping, features to various newspapers. Mem. publicity staff First Mills Godwin Gubernatorial Campaign, 1965; v.p. corp. comms. Va. Hosp. Assn., 1968-88. Recipient numerous state and nat. writing awards. Fellow Am. Soc. Hosp. Mktg. and Pub. Rels.; mem. Va. Hosp. Mktg. and Pub. Rels. (a founder, bd. dirs. 1969-88, treas. 1975-85), Richmond Pub. Rels. Assn. (pres. 1983-84), Va. Press. Women, Internat. Order of St. Luke the Physicians (sec.-treas. 1989-91, convener Richmond chpt. 1996-98), Stephen Minister Lay Pastoral Care Ministry. Home: 9711 Royerton Dr Richmond VA 23228-1217

DEEKLE, PETER VAN, library director; b. N.Y.C., May 30, 1946; s. William Cleveland and Marian Elizabeth (Maynard) D.; m. Barbara Eugenia Maier, Aug. 8, 1970; children: Lee Christina, Glenna. BA in English, U. Pa., 1968; MS in Libr. and Info. Sci., Drexel U., 1973; DEd, Temple U., 1987. Asst. extension svcs. libr. Montgomery County/Norristown (Pa.) Pub. Libr., 1971-73; assoc. dir. libr. Allegany Community Coll., Cumberland, Md., 1973-77; head nonprint media svcs. U. Md. Librs., College Park, 1977-81; asst. dean acad. affairs, chmn. instrl. resources div. Harrisburg Area Community Coll., 1981-88; libr., dir. honors program Susquehanna U., Selinsgrove, Pa., 1988-93; dir. Madeleine Clark Wallace Libr., Wheaton Coll., Norton, Mass., 1993—; chair com. interlibr. cooperation-comprehensive planning coun. State Libr. Pa., 1982-83. Vol., English tchr. Peace Corps, Iran, 1968-70. Mem. ALA, Assn. Coll. and Rsch. Librs., Mid. State Assn. Colls. and Schs. (cons. commn. higher edn. accreditation team visits), New Eng. Assn. Schs. and Colls. (cons. accreditation team visits), Pa. Libr. Assn. (pres. 1990-91), Md. Assn. Cmty. and Jr. Colls. (chair learning resources divsn. 1977, mem. Mass. master plan for libraries 1993-95, chair Southeast Mass. coop. libraries 1995-97, co-chair LAMA fund raising/fund fare exch. com. 1997-99). Office: Madeleine Clark Wallace Lib Wheaton Coll Norton MA 02766

DEEL, FRANCES QUINN, retired librarian; b. Pottsville, Pa., Mar. 9, 1939; d. Charles Joseph and Carrie Miriam (Ketner) Q.; m. Ronald Eugene Deel, Feb. 5, 1983. B.S., Millersville State Coll., 1960; M.L.S., Rutgers U., 1964; M.P.A., U. West Fla., 1981. Post librarian U.S. Army Armor (Desert Tng. Ctr.), Ft. Irwin, Calif., 1964-66; staff librarian Mil. Dist. of Washington, 1966-67; supervisory librarian 1st Logistical Command, APO San Francisco, 1967-68; tech. process specialist Naval Edn. and Tng. Supervisory Command, Washington, 1968-77, Pensacola, Fla., 1968-77; chief tech. library USAF Armament Lab., Eglin AFB, Fla., 1977-81; dir. command libraries Air Force Systems Command (Andrews AFB), Washington, 1981-92; mem. exec. adv. council Fed. Library and Info. Network, Washington, 1983-86; libr. Air Force Dist. of Washington (Bolling AFB), Washington, 1992-94; dir. Navy Dept. Libr., Washington, 1994; ret., 1994. Mem. ALA (dir.-at-large armed forces libraries sect. Chgo. 1983-86), Spl. Libraries Assn., D.C. Library Assn. Roman Catholic. Home: 9225 Forest Haven Dr Alexandria VA 22309-3216

DEEL, GEORGE MOSES, elementary school educator; b. Haysi, Va., Apr. 9, 1938; s. Emory Floyd and Nancy Jane Deel. BS, Emory (Va.) & Henry Coll., 1961; MEd, Radford (Va.) U., 1965. Cert. tchr. Tchr. math. and gen. sci. Grundy (Va.) Jr. High Sch., 1961-79; resource tchr. gifted and academically talented Vansant (Va.) Elem. Sch., 1979-91; ret., 1991; cons. on gifted and talented Vansant (Va.) Elem. Sch., 1991—. Mem. NEA, Assn. Supervision and Curriculum Devel., Va. Edn. Assn., Buchanan Edn. Assn. Avocations: reading, working with computers, listening to music, football spectator. Home and Office: RR 2 Box 168 Haysi VA 24256-9503

DEELY, MAUREEN CECELIA, community health nurse; b. Washington, Feb. 8, 1960; d. Thomas Michael and Felice R. (Alvarez) D. AA, Montgomery Coll., 1984. Staff RN Phi Szabo PG Count/Detention Ctr., Upper Marlboro, Md., 1984-85, Sands Nursing Svcs. Inc., Silver Spring, Md., 1985-86, Windsor HomeCare Inc./Alliance Against AIDS, Washington, 1988-89; community health nurse Montgomery County Health Dept., Silver Spring, 1989—; mem. adv. bd. for cmty. programs for clin. rsch. on AIDS Washington Regional AIDS Program, 1990—; mem. AIDS adv. com. Montgomery Hospice Soc., 1993; panelist, field reviewer to develop treatment improvement protocol Ctr. Substance Abuse Treatment, 1993; mem. cmty. adv. bd. Nat. Women's Interagy. HIV Study, 1993; Washington Area Consortium alt. rep. Nat. Cmty. Adv. Bd. for Nat. WIHS, 1994, rep., cmty. adv. bd.; spkrs. bur. NAPWA-Nat. Assn. people with AIDS; nat. rep. Washington Area Consortium for Nat. WIHS; mem. Met. Washington Regional HIV Health Svcs. Planning Coun., 1995; mem. cmty. adv. bd. Md. AIDS Adminstrn., 1996; bd. dirs. HIV Cmty. Coalition, 1996, PWA Com. Md., Inc., 1997; chair Women's Interagy. HIV Study, Nat. Cmty. Adv. Bd., 1997; spkr., presenter in field. V.p. Suburban Md. HIV/AIDS Alliance, 1996, sec., 1996, pres., 1997-98; mem. Nat. AIDS Health Fraud Task Force FDA, 1997; mem. Cmty. Adv. Bd. Food and Friends, 1997; mem. Suburban Md. HIV Prevention Regional Work Group, 1997; mem. nat. adv. bd. for rev. and synthesis of HIV/AIDS related consumer/client level evaluations Health Resources Svcs. Adminstrn.; recuperative care coord. for homeless, 1998; co-chair Suburban Md. HIV Care Consortium, 1998; mem. helth care and corrections task force and panel Met. Washington Coun. Govts. Recipient Cheryl D. Friedman award Montgomery County Dept. Health and Human Svcs., 1995, Outstanding Svc. award Montgomery County Dept. Correction and Rehab., 1996.

DEEM, GEORGE, artist; b. Vincennes, Ind., Aug. 18, 1932; s. George C. and Laura (Bobe) D. Student, Vincennes U., 1951-52; BFA, Sch. Art Inst. Chgo., 1958. Tchr. painting Sch. Visual Arts N.Y.C., 1965-66, Leicester (Eng.) Coll. Art and Design, 1966-67, U. Pa., 1968; artist in residence Evansville Mus. Arts and Scis., 1979; vis. artist Ill. State U., Normal, 1982, The Branson Sch., Ross, Calif., 1995; sec. exec. com. MacDowell Colony Fellows, 1982-87. One man shows Allan Stone Gallery, N.Y.C., 1963, 64, 65, 66, 68, 69, 75, 77, Sneed Gallery, Rockford, Ill., 1968, 69, 72, 76, 80, Merida Gallery, Louisville, 1966, 68, 69, 78, 83, Indpls. Mus. Art, 1974, Witte Meml. Mus., San Antonio, 1975, Evansville (Ind.) Mus. Arts and Scis., 1979, Greenberg Gallery, St. Louis, 1979, On View Downtown Gallery, Indpls., 1986, Evansville (Ind.) Mus. Arts and Scis., 1993, Harn Mus. Art, U. Fla., Gainesville, 1993, Mitchell Mus. Art, Mt. Vernon, Ill., 1993, Polk Mus. Art, Lakeland, Fla., 1994, Ind. State Mus., Indpls., 1994, Eckert Fine Art Gallery, Indpls., 1994, Capricorn Gallery, Bethesda, Md., 1994, Wichita (Kans.) Ctr. for Arts, 1994; group shows include Whitney Mus. Am. Art, N.Y.C., 1978, Pa. Acad. Fine Arts, 1981, Allentown (Pa.) Art Mus., 1983, Ft. Wayne (Ind.) Mus. Art, 1984, Nancy Hoffman Gallery, N.Y.C., 1985, 86, 87, 88, 89, 90, 91, 94, 98, Flint (Mich.) Inst. Arts, 1993, Nassau County Mus. of Art, N.Y., 1994; Museum of Art, U. of Oregon, Eugene, 1996, Pavel Zoubok/Mary Delahoyd Gallery, N.Y.C., 1998; represented in permanent collections Indpls. Mus. Art, Evansville Mus. Arts and Sci., Stiftung Ludwig, Aachen, Germany, Vassar Coll. Art Gallery, Mus. Fine Arts, Houston, Miami U. Art Mus., Oxford, Ohio, Weatherspoon Art Gallery U. N.C., Greensboro, Chase Manhattan Bank, N.Y.C., Cleary Gottlieb Steen & Hamilton, N.Y.C., 1st Nat. Bank Boston, Ariz. State U. Art Mus., Tempe, Tony Bilson & Co., Sydney, Australia, Hallmark Cards, Inc., Kansas City, Mo., Mirage Resorts, Inc., Las Vegas, State Russian Mus., St. Petersburg, Mus. of Modern Art, San Francisco; commns. Nutter, McLennen & Fish, Boston, 1988, Paul, Weiss, Rifkind, N.Y., 1989; subject of video profile, 1993; Art School: An Homage To The Masters, paintings by George Deem, introduction by Irene McManus, Thames and Hudson, LTD., London, 1993, Chronicle Books, San Francisco, 1993; contbr. articles to profl. jours. Served with U.S. Army, 1953-55. Home and Office: 10 W 18th St New York NY 10011-4617

DEEMS, NYAL DAVID, lawyer, mayor; b. Cleve., Jan. 24, 1948; s. Nyal Wilbert and Octavia C. (Roush) D.; children: Brooke Elizabeth, Nyal Christopher, Holly Jean, Eric Wellington, Georgia Octavia. BA in Internat. Studies, Miami U., 1969; JD, U. Ga., 1976. Bar: Ga. 1976, Mich. 1976, U.S. Dist. Ct. (we. dist.) Mich., U.S. Dist. Ct. (no. dist.) Ga. Assoc. then ptnr. Varnum, Riddering, Wierengo & Christenson now Varnum, Riddering, Schmidt & Howlett, Grand Rapids, Mich., 1976—. Co-author: Michigan Real Estate Sales Transactions, 1983, Real Estate Development, 4 vols., 1988, A Practical Guide to Winning Land Use Approvals and Permits, 1989, Michigan Real Estate Practice and Forms, 1989, Michigan Business Formbook, 1989, Michigan Basic Practice Handbook, 1989. Commr. City of East Grand Rapids, Mich., 1982-85, mayor, 1985-95; chmn. Grand Rapids Met. Coun., 1990-95. Lt. USN, 1969-73. Mem. ABA, Ga. Bar Assn., Mich. Bar Assn. (chmn. water law com. 1984-86, real property coun. 1984—, chairperson 1989), Grand Rapids Bar Assn., Am. Coll. Real Estate Lawyers, Am. Coll. Mortgage Attys. Home: 431 Cambridge Blvd SE Grand Rapids MI 49506-2806 Office: Varnum Riddering Schmidt Howlett 333 Bridge St NW Ste 1700 Grand Rapids MI 49504-5356

DEEN, THOMAS BLACKBURN, retired transportation research executive; b. Lexington, Ky., Apr. 4, 1928; s. Encil and Utha Leola (Blackburn) D.; m. Bettie Marie Taylor, Nov. 28, 1954; children—Robin Elaine, Tomi Clair, Rebecca Lea, Samuel Encil. B.S.C.E., U. Ky., 1951; postgrad., U. Chgo., 1951-52; transp. cert., Yale U., 1956. Asst. city traffic engr. Nashville, 1956-57; dir. Nashville Met. Area Transp. Study, 1957-59; applied sci. rep. IBM, Nashville, 1959-60; dir. planning Nat. Capital Transp. Agy., Washington, 1960-64; sr. v.p. Alan M. Voorhees & Assos., McLean, Va., 1964-78; chmn., pres. PRC Voorhees, McLean, 1978-80; exec. dir. Transp. Research Bd., Nat. Acad. Scis., Washington, 1980-94; vice chmn. bd. PADCO, Inc., Washington, 1973—; mem. adv. bd. Civil Engring. Rsch. Found., Washington, HITECH exec. com. ex-officio, 1993-94; mem. civil engring. dept. vis. com. U. Tex., Austin, 1993-95. Editl. bd.: Traffic Engring. and Control mag, London, 1981-95, Transp. Planning and Tech. Loughborough, U.K., 1978-95; mem. publs. bd. Public Roads, 1993-94. Mem. transp. adv. com. MIT, 1983-94; adv. bd. Rice U., Houston, 1983-89; vice chmn. bd. dirs. Family Savs. and Loan Assn., 1982-85; bd. cons. ENO Found. for Hwy. Traffic, Saugatuck, Conn., 1981-83, 90-93; trustee Matson Meml. Fund, Washington, 1977-80, Am. Pub. Works Research Found., 1986-89; chmn. bd. Voorhees and Partners, Melbourne, Australia, 1975-78; mem. exec. com. Strategic Hwy. Rsch. Program, 1989-93; bd. dirs. Nat. Ctr. for Asphalt Tech., 1991-96, Internat. Road Federation, Washington, 1992-94; mem. bd. regents ENO Ctr. for Transp. Edn., 1991-95; adv. bd. Nat. Transit Inst., Rutgers U., New Brunswick, N.J., 1992-94. 1st lt. USAF, 1951-55. Recipient Outstanding ROTC Grad. medal U. Ky., 1951, George S. Bartlett award AASHTO, 1993, Ronald D. Kenyon Rsch. and Edn. award, 1993, Transp. Sci. and Ethic award, 1994, Pike Johnson award for outstanding rsch. Transp. Rsch. Bd. Nat. Acad. Scis., 1976, William Carey Svc. award Transp. Rsch. Bd., 1995, P.D. McLean award, 1995; named to Hall of Distinction U. Ky., 1998. Mem. Inst. Trans. Engrs. (Matson Meml. award 1995), Nat. Acad. Engring., Intelligent Transp. Soc. Am. (chair strategic com. 1991-92, chair planning com. 1991-96), Tau Beta Pi, Sigma Pi Sigma. Baptist. Home: 416 Butlers Lndg Stevensville MD 21666-3050

DEENY, ROBERT JOSEPH, lawyer; b. Cedar Rapids, Iowa, Jan. 8, 1941; s. Myles C. and Betty S. (Schissel) D. BA, Ariz. State U., 1963; JD, Cath. U., Washington, 1970. Bar: Ariz. 1971, U.S. Dist. Ct. (D.C. cir.) 1971, D.C. 1978, U.S. Supreme Ct. 1978, U.S. Ct. Appeals (9th cir) 1980. Field examiner NLRB, Phoenix, 1964-67; exec. asst. to chief adminstrv. judge NLRB, Washington, 1967-70; field atty. NLRB, Phoenix, 1970-72; with Shimmel Hill, Phoenix, 1972-79, Snell & Wilmer, Phoenix, 1979—. With USMCR, 1960-63. Mem. ABA, Ariz. State Bar, S.C. Bar Assn., Maricopa

County Bar, Phoenix Country Club. Office: Snell & Wilmer 1 Arizona Ctr Phoenix AZ 85004*

DEEPAK, ADARSH, meteorologist, aerospace engineer, atmospheric scientist; b. Sialkot, India, Nov. 13, 1936. BS, Delhi U., 1956, MS, 1959; PhD in Aerospace Engr., U. Fla., 1969. Lectr. physics DB & KM Cols., Delhi U., 1959-63; instr. phys. sci. U. Fla., 1965-68, rsch. assoc. aerospace engring., 1970-71; fellow Nat. Rsch. Coun. Marshall Space Flight Ctr., NASA, 1972-74; rsch. assoc. prof. physics & geophys. sci. Old Dominion U., 1974-77; pres. Inst. Atmospheric Optics & Remote Sensing, Hampton, Va., 1977-84, 93—, Sci. & Tech. Corp., Hampton, Va., 1979—; rsch. assoc. U. Fla. and Wayne State U., 1970-72; mem. panel remote sensing & data acquisition NASA/OAST Technol. Workshop, 1975; NSF travel grant to visit Indian insts., 1976; adj. prof. physics Coll. William & Mary, 1979-80; leader U.S. Del. Internat. Workshop Appln. Remote Sensing Rice Prod., India, 1981. Recipient U.S. SBA Minority Small Businessperson of Yr. award Richmond Dist., 1990. Mem. Am. Assn. for Aerosol Rsch., AAAS, Optical Soc. Am., Am. Meteorol. Soc., Am. Chem. Soc., Am. Geophys. Union. Achievements include research in remote sensing of atmospheric particulate and gaseous pollutants and motions, using laser doppler, optical scattering and photographic techniques from space airborne and ground platforms, theory of radiative transfer in scattering atmospheres, fogs and clouds, inversion methods for remotely sensed data. Office: Sci & Tech Corp PO Box 7390 Hampton VA 23666-0390

DEER, PHILIP JAMES, JR., ophthalmologist; b. El Dorado, Ark., Sept. 27, 1933; s. Philip James and Polly Pearl (Dial) D.; m. Florence Elizabeth Ross, June 2, 1955; children: Philip James III, Ashley Ross, Sloan Deer Powell. Student, Hendrix Coll., 1951-53; MD, U. Tenn., Memphis, 1957; postgrad., Harvard U., Boston, 1961. Diplomate Am. Bd. Ophthalmology. Resident in ophthalmology U. Tenn., 1961-64; pvt. practice, Little Rock, 1964—; med. cons. Ark. Rehab. for Blind, Little Rock, 1967—. Bd. dirs. Hendrix Coll., Conway, Ark., 1972-89. Lt. M.C., USN, 1958-60. Mem. Ark. Med. Soc., Pulaski County Med. Soc., Little Rock Country Club. Democrat. Methodist. Avocations: tennis, reading. Home: 16 Longfellow Ln Little Rock AR 72207-3750 Office: 8500 W Markham St Ste 133 Little Rock AR 72205-2454

DEER, RICHARD ELLIOTT, lawyer; b. Indpls., Sept. 8, 1932; s. Leon Leslie and Mary Jane (Ostheimer) D.; m. Lee Todd, Feb. 22, 1958; children: William K., Laura A., Susannah T., Thomas E. A.B., DePauw U., 1954; LL.B. magna cum laude, Harvard U., 1957. Bar: Ind. 1957, U.S. Dist. Ct. (no. and so. dists.) Ind. 1957, U.S. Ct. Appeals (7th cir.) 1957, U.S. Ct. Appeals (9th cir.) 1990, U.S. Supreme Ct. 1962. Assoc. firm Barnes & Thornburg and predecessor firm, Indpls., 1957-65, ptnr., 1965—, chmn. mgmt. com., 1990-93; dir. Flagship Capital Corp., Indpls. Author: Indiana Corporation Law and Practice, 1990, Supplement, 1994; co-author: Indiana Limited Liability Company Forms and Practice Manual, 1996, Supplement, 1997; bd. editors Harvard Law Rev., 1956-57; contbr. articles to legal jours.; chief reporter: The Lawyer's Basic Corporate Practice Manual, 3d edit., 1984. Mem. Indpls. Coun. Fgn. Relations, Ind. Corps. Survey Commn., 1983—. Fellow Am. Bar Found., Ind. Bar Found.; mem. Indpls. Bar Assn., Ind. State Bar Assn. (past chmn. corp., banking and bus. law sect.), ABA (drafting com., exec. planning group of legal opinion project sect. bus. law, 3d party legal opinion report 1991), Am. Law Inst. Clubs: Hillcrest Country, Players, Columbia. Home: 6629 Marmont Cir Indianapolis IN 46220-4230 Office: Barnes & Thornburg 11 S Meridian St Indianapolis IN 46204-3506

DEERE, CYRIL THOMAS, retired computer company executive; b. Rockville, Conn., Apr. 28, 1924; s. Albert Bertram and Belle Murdie (King) D.; m. Shirley Ann Scheiner, June 2, 1945; children: Sandra Deere Leinz, Kathryn Deere Lloyd. B.S., Yale U., 1948. With Lee Paper Co., Vicksburg, Mich., 1949-50, Addressograph-Multigraph Corp., Hartford, Conn. and Cleve., 1950-69; founder Data Card Corp., Minnetonka, Minn., 1969-81; v.p. mktg. Data Card Corp., 1969-75, sr. v.p., 1975-77, exec. v.p., 1977-80, pres., 1980-82, dir. plastics div., 1974-81; pres., dir. Can. Data Card Ltd., Toronto, Ont., 1974-81; chmn. bd. Data Card Internat., 1977-78;; founder, dir. Data Card Japan, 1980-81; founder, pres. Card Tech. Corp., Saddlebrook, N.J., 1983-85; chmn. bd. dirs. Columbine Bus Inc., Arvada, Colo., 1997-98. Served with USMC, 1943-44. Decorated Purple Heart. Mem. Am. Nat. Stds. Inst. (1st chmn. credit card stds. com. 1968-73), Input/Output Systems Assn. (pres. 1975), Univ. Club Denver, Oak Creek Country Club (Sedona, Ariz.), Mt. Vernon Country Club (Genesee, Colo.). Clubs: Univ. (Denver), Oak Creek Country (Sedona, Ariz.). Home: 6863 Westwoods Cir Arvada CO 80007-7687 also: Sundance # 47 55 Cathedral Rock Dr Sedona AZ 86351-8630

DEERE, DON U., civil engineer; b. Corning, IA, Mar. 17, 1922; m., 1944; two children. BS, Iowa State Col., 1943; MS, U. Colo., 1949; PhD in Civil Engring., U. Ill., 1955. Jr. mine engr. Phelps Dodge Corp., Ariz., 1943-44; mine engr., explorations dept. Potash Co. Am., N.M., 1944-47; from asst. prof. to assoc. prof. Civil Engring. Col. A & M U. P.R., 1946-50, head dept., 1950-51; partner Found. Engring. Co., P.R., 1951-55; from assoc. prof. to prof. Civil Engring. and Geology U. Ill., Urbana, 1955-76; affiliate prof. Dept. Geology and Civil Engring. U. Fla., 1972—; cons. Nat. Acad. Scis.; pres. Internat. Soc. Rock Mechanics, 1968-73; chmn. U.S. Nat. Com. on Tunneling Tech., 1972; internat. cons. hydroelectric engring., 1972—; cons. Geologic Soc. Am., 1976-79. Mem. Nat. Acad. Scis., AAAS, Nat. Acad. Engring., Geological Soc. Am., ASCE, Assn. Profl. Geological Scis., Soc. Mining Engrs. *

DEERING, ALLAN BROOKS, soft drink company executive; b. Chappaqua, N.Y., Apr. 1, 1934; s. Clarence and Muriel (Lee) D.; m. Carol Ann Werle, Apr. 14, 1957; children: Peter Brooks, Andrew Werle. BA, Columbia U., 1956. Systems analyst IBM Corp., White Plains, N.Y., 1956-58; EDP mgr. R. H. Donnelly Corp. N.Y.C., 1958-68; dir. systems and data processing W. R. Grace & Co., N.Y.C., 1968-76, asst. v.p., 1975, dir. info. systems SCM Corp., N.Y.C., 1976-81; dir. mgmt. info. services Pepsi Co., 1981-86, v.p. mgmt. info. services, 1986—. Mem. Mayor's Industry Adv. Bd. for Data Processing, N.Y.C., 1978, adv. bd. Pace U. Sch. Computer Sci., Omicron. Mem. Data Processing Mgmt. Assn., Soc. Mgmt. Info. Systems (bd. dirs.), N.Y. Computer Execs. Roundtable, Grocery Mfrs. Am. (chmn. systems com.), Rocky Point Club, Old Greenwich Yacht Club, Milbrook Club. Home: 3 Perkley Ln Riverside CT 06878-2309 Office: Pepsico Inc Anderson Hill Rd Purchase NY 10577

DEERING, ANNE-LISE, artist, real estate salesperson; b. Oslo, June 20, 1935; d. Reidar Ingolf Dahlsrud and Dagny Elfrida (Grönneberg) Nilsen; m. Reginald Atwell Deering, Oct. 20, 1956 (div. July 1992); children: Eric, Mark, Linda, Norman. BA in Art, Pa. State U., 1977, postgrad., 1990-91. Lic. real estate salesperson, Pa. Rsch. asst. Yale U., New Haven, 1955-57; ceramic artist/potter State College, Pa., 1977-98; real estate agt. Coldwell Banker Univ. Realty, State College, 1992-93, Century 21 Corman Assocs., State College, 1993-99; artist mem. Art Alliance Ctrl. Pa., 1977—. Editor Ctrl. Pa. Guild of Craftsmen newsletter, 1994. mem. visual arts adv. com. Ctrl. Pa. Festival of Arts, 1989-93, co-chair, 1991-93, jury and rules co-chmn. for sidewalk sales com., 1993-97. Mem. Nat. Assn. Realtors, Pa. Assn. Realtors, Centre County Assn. Realtors, Pa. Guild Craftsmen (bd. dirs. 1980-83, 85-98), Ctrl. Pa. Guild Craftsmen (pres. 1986-87, 93-94, v.p. 1985, 91, 92, coord., chair ann. Christmas sale), Am. Mus. Women in the Arts (charter), Am. Medallic Sculpture Assn., Art Alliance Ctrl. Pa. (chair mems. juried exhibit 1978, bd. dirs. 1978-79, Gallery Shop participant 1989-99, steering com. 1994-97), Washington Potters Assn., Seattle Metals Guild. Avocations: photography, music, dance. Home: 24229 92nd Ave W Edmonds WA 98020

DEERING, FRED ARTHUR, retired insurance company executive; b. Winfield, Kans., Jan. 12, 1928; s. Frederick A. and Lucile (Phillips) D.; m. Isabell Staufenberg, June 14, 1949; m. Elizabeth Kimball MacMillan, Apr. 12, 1979; children: Anne Deering Buchanan, Kate. BS, U. Colo., 1951, LLD, 1951; LHD (hon.), Loretto Heights Coll., 1984. Bar: Colo. 1951. Assoc. firm Gorsuch, Kingis, Campbell, Walker & Grover, Denver, Denver, 1951-54; ptnr. Gorsuch, Kingis, Campbell, Walker & Grover, Denver, 1954-62; v.p., gen. counsel Security Life of Denver, 1962-66, pres., CEO, 1966-82, chmn., CEO, 1982-91, chmn., 1991-93; chmn. exec. com., 1994-95; bd. dirs. ING Am. Ins. Holdings, Inc.; chmn., CEO, dir. Midwestern United Life Ins. Co., 1983-89, Halifax Life Ins. Co., Toronto, 1985-88; vice-chmn. bd. Invesco Funds Group, chmn., 1968-90; instr. Am. Inst. Banking, 1953-57; guest lectr. Colo. Sch. Law, 1958-59. Editor-in-chief Rocky Mountain Law Rev. Trustee Loretto Heights Coll., 1968-88, chmn. bd. dirs., 1968-84, chmn. emeritus, 1984-88; bd. dirs. Wallace Village for Children, 1968-78, Met. United Fund, 1969-71, Porter Hosp., 1970-79, U. Colo. Found., 1972-75; mem. adv. com. Met. Assn. for Retarded Children, Denver, 1970-71, Denver Rsch. Inst., 1972-76; trustee Huebner Found., 1980-85, St. Mary's Acad., Denver, 1989-95, 97—; bd. dirs. Inst. Internat. Edn., Denver, 1986-92, Nat. Western Stock Show, 1990-96, Invesco, Global Health Scis. Fund, Ptnrs. for Health, Fin. Designs Ltd. With U.S. Army, 1946-47. Named Colo. Businessman of Yr. Alpha Kappa Psi, 1977, Disting. Law Alumnus, U. Colo., 1982. Mem. ABA, Colo. Bar Assn., Denver Bar Assn., Am. Judicature Soc., Colo. Life Conf., Life Office Mgmt. Assn. (bd. dirs. 1977-81, 82-85, chmn. 1983-84), Denver C. of C., Met. Denver Execs. Club (pres. 1970-71), Old Baldy Club, Cherry Hills Country Club (bd. dirs. 1973-76, pres. 1975-76), Wigwam Club, Bang-a-Way Club, The Oaks Country Club, Univ. Club, Order of Coif, Sigma Alpha Epsilon. *My life has been influenced more by a handful of people than by events or any other factors. Therefore, I am inclined to think that the lives of others may be more important than anything else in shaping our own careers and destinies.*

DEERING, RONALD FRANKLIN, librarian, minister; b. Paxton, Ill., Oct. 6, 1929; s. Minor Franklin and Grace Gilmour (Perkins) D.; m. Geraldine Gibbons, June 27, 1953 (dec. Jan. 1965); m. Edith Ann Proctor, June 12, 1966; children: Mark David, Daniel Timothy. BA summa cum laude, Georgetown (Ky.) Coll., 1951; MDiv, So. Bapt. Theol. Sem., 1955, PhD, 1962; MLS, Columbia U., 1967. Ordained to ministry So. Bapt. Conv., 1950. Pastor 1st Hilltop Bapt. Ch., North College Hill, Ohio, 1949-50; instr. in Bible Georgeton (Ky.) Coll., 1950-51; pastor Blue River Bapt. Ch., Salem, Ind., 1954-59; instr. Greek, N.T. So. Bapt. Theol. Sem., Louisville, 1958-61, theol. libr., 1962-95, assoc. v.p. for acad. resources, 1995—; chmn. So. Bapt. Hist. Commn., Nashville, 1987-90; interim pastor 31 chs. in Ind., Ky., 1961-90; del. Bapt. World Alliance, Miami, Fla., Toronto, Ont., Can., L.A., 1965, 80, 85. Contbr. articles to profl. jours. Eli Lilly Theol. Librarianship grantee, 1967. Mem. AAUP, ALA, Southeastern Libr. Assn., Am. Theol. Libr. Assn. (nat. pres. 1984-85), Ky. Libr. Assn., Phi Alpha Theta, Beta Phi Mu, Sigma Tau Delta. Democrat. Home: 3111 Dunlieth Ct Louisville KY 40241-2937 Office: So Bapt Theol Sem 2825 Lexington Rd Louisville KY 40280-0001

DEERING, THOMAS PHILLIPS, lawyer; b. Winfield, Kans., Feb. 15, 1929; s. Frederick Arthur and Lucile (Phillips) D.; m. Marilyn Marie Anderson, Sept. 6, 1952; children: Thomas P. Jr., Robert E., Paul A. BS, U. Colo., 1951, LLB, 1956. Bar: Oreg. 1956, Colo. 1956, U.S. Dist. Ct. Oreg. 1956. Assoc. Hart Spencer McCulloch Rockwood & Davies (now Stoel Rives), Portland, Oreg., 1956-62; ptnr. Stoel Rives LLP, Portland, 1962—; active Western Pension & Benefits Conf., 1989—; mem. faculty Am. Law Inst.-ABA, 1985-96. Co-author: Tax Reform Act of 1986, 1987. Bd. dirs. Girl Scouts Columbia River Coun., Portland, 1961-70; trustee, moderator First Unitarian Ch., Portland, 1967-70; trustee, pres. Catlin Gabel Sch., Portland, 1970-76; bd. dirs., v.p. ACLU, Portland, 1966-71, 73-80; chmn. Multnomah County Task Force on Edgefield Manor, Portland, 1972-75; bd. dirs., treas. Portland Art Mus., Contemporary Arts Coun., 1986-88; mem. City County Task Force on Svc. Evaluation, Portland, 1982-85, Citizen's Adv. Com. West Side Corridor Project, Portland, 1988-93; bd. govs. Pacific N.W. Coll. Art, 1991—, chair, 1996—; mem. collections com. Portland Art Mus., 1992-96; trustee Oreg. Coll. Art and Craft Endowment, Portland, 1991-97. With U.S. Army, 1952-54. Recipient Disting. Mem. award Western Pension & Benefits Conf., 1999. Fellow Am. Coll. Tax Coun.; mem. ABA (tax sect., EB com. 1989—), Portland City Club. Democrat. Avocations: hiking, skiing, sailing, reading. Home: 5235 SW Burton Dr Portland OR 97221-2517 Office: Stoel Rives LLP 900 SW 5th Ave Ste 2600 Portland OR 97204-1268

DEERMAN, RUTH GILLETT, sales professional, flying instructor; b. El Paso, Tex., June 17, 1915; d. Otis Theodore and Katie Yvette (Textor) Gillett; m. Charlie Luther Deerman, Nov. 25, 1933 (dec. June 1992). Student, U. Tex., El Paso, 1966. Ccert. pvt. pilot, comml. instrument pilot, helicopter pilot, advanced ground sch. instr., flight instr. Flight instr. Border Aviation, El Paso, 1944; flight and ground instr. S.W. Air Rangers, El Paso, 1968; beauty cons. Mary Kay Cosmetics, El Paso, 1969-70, ind. sales dir., 1970-75, ind. sr. sales dir., 1975—; tchr. flying and ground sch., 1945—; accident prevention coucncilor FAA, 1972-80. Bd. dirs. Am. CCancer Soc.c, 1957-67; pres. Providence Meml. Hosp. Aux., 1960-61; past treas. Womans Coub El Paso; past bd. dirs. YWCA, El Paso; past pres. Women's Missionary Union, 1st Bapt. Ch. Named Tex. Flying Farmers State Queen, 1955; winner All Woman Transcontinental Air Race, 1954; inducted into El Paso Aviation Hall of Fame, 1983; honored with granite plaque Internat. Forest of Friendship, 1977; recipient Jimmie Kolp award for contbg. to aviation and 99s, 1975. Mem. NAFE, Nat. Assn. Flight Instr., 99s (lic. women pilots, past internat. pres.), Whirly Girls (Whirly Girl # 78), Silver Wings, El Paso Aviation Assn. (v.p. 1947), 66s (founder), Clowns of Am. Internat., El Paso C. of C. (coms. woman's dept.), PEO, Ladies Oriental Shrine Am. (FAA accident prevention councilor 1972-80), Daus. of Nile (queen 1951-52), Order Ea. Star (worthy matron 1945). Republican. Avocations: bowling, golf. Home and Office: 405 Camino Real Ave El Paso TX 79922-2003

DEERNOSE, KITTY, museum curator; b. Crow Agency, Mont., Apr. 14, 1956. AA in Mus. Studies, Inst. Am. Indian Arts, Santa Fe, 1985. Mus. intern Heard Mus. Anthropology and Primitive Art, Phoenix, 1984; interpreter Little Bighorn Battlefield Nat. Monument, Crow Agency, Mont., 1985-90, mus. curator, 1990-99; mus. intern in Crow studies Smithsonian Instn., Washington, 1988. Recipient White Glove award Nat. Park Svc., 1995. Mem. Am. Assn. Muss., Am. Assn. State and Local History, Mountain Plains Mus. Assn. Office: Little Bighorn Battlefield Nat Monument PO Box 39 Crow Agency MT 59022-0039*

DEES, C. STANLEY, lawyer; b. Tulsa, June 24, 1938. AB, Princeton U., 1960; LLB, U. Va., 1963. Bar: Va. 1963, D.C. 1964. Ptnr. McKenna & Cuneo, LLP, Washington; lectr. U. Va. Law Sch. Contbr. articles to profl. jours. Trustee Legal Aid Soc. D.C., 1970-83, pres., 1978-80. Fellow Am. Bar Found.; mem. ABA (chmn. fed. cts. com. 1977-78, jud. remedies com. 1978-80, program com. 1980-81, coun. mem. 1981-84, sec. 1984-85, vice-chmn. pub. contract law sect. 1985-86, chmn. pub. contract law sect. 1987-88), U.S. Ct. Fed. Claims Bar, D.C. Bar (vice-chmn. 1974-75, chmn. 1975-77, steering com., govt. contracts and litigation divsn.), Va. State Bar, Coun. Def. and Space Indsl. Assns. (chmn. 1991-93), Nat. Security Indsl. Assn. (v.p. 1983-90, trustee 1990—), D.C. Bar Found. (adv. com.), Order of Coif. Office: McKenna & Cuneo LLP 1900 K St NW Washington DC 20006-4004*

DEES, HARRY C., JR., federal judge; b. 1945. BA, DePauw U., 1967; JD, Ind. U., 1974. Bar: Ind. Atty. Hertwig & Decker, Terre Haute, Ind., 1974-75; sole practitioner, 1975-78; atty. Tabor & Dees, 1978-86; bankruptcy judge U.S. Dist. Ct. (no. dist.) Ind., South Bend, 1986—; dep. pub. defender Vigo County, Terre Haute, 1976-78, dep. prosecutor, 1979-83; judge Juvenile Ct. of Vigo County, 1979-83; asst. prof. Ind. State U., 1983-85; adj. assoc. prof. Sch. Law, U. Notre Dame, 1988—. Elder, Sunnyside Presbyn. Ch. Capt. USAF, 1967-71; lt. col. Ind. Air N.G., 1976-92. Decorated Bronze Star medal. Mem. Ind. State Bar, St. Joseph County Bar Assn., Terre Haute Bar Assn., Nat. Conf. Bankruptcy Judges, Am. Bankruptcy Inst., N.G. Assn. U.S., Rotary Internat. Office: 234 Rodibaugh US Courthouse 401 S Michigan St South Bend IN 46601-2365

DEES, JULIAN WORTH, retired academic/research administrator; b. Henderson, N.C., Feb. 20, 1933; s. Charles Andrew and Gertrude Elizabeth (Lancaster) D.; m. Bernita June Funk, Aug. 29, 1954; children: Sandra Eileen Dees Anthony, Mark Alan, Gregory Linn. BS in Radio Engring., Tri-State U., Angola, Ind., 1953, BS in Adminstrv. Engring., 1954; MSEE, U. Cin., 1955. Registered profl. engr., Ga. Microwave engr. IT&T Labs., Ft. Wayne, Ind., 1955-60; project mgr., sr. engr. Martin Marietta Corp., Orlando, Fla., 1960-71; dir. electromagnetic lab. Ga. Inst. Tech., Atlanta, 1971-80, assoc. v.p. rsch., dir. office contract adminstrn., prin. rsch. engr., 1980-98; asst. sec., asst. treas Ga. Tech. Rsch. Corp., Atlanta, 1980-98; bd. dir. Coun. on Rsch. & Tech., Washington. Contbr. articles to jours. in field; patentee in field. Named Author of Yr., Martin Marietta Corp., 1965. Fellow IEEE (Engr. of Yr. Orlando chpt. 1968); mem. Soc. Rsch. Adminstrs. (sr.), Coun. on Govtl. Rels., Nat. Coun. Univ. Rsch. Adminstrs. Avocations: woodworking, judging barbeque cook-offs. Home: 2128 Rosser Pl Stone Mountain GA 30087-1517

DEES, SANDRA KAY MARTIN, psychologist, research scientist; b. Omaha, Apr. 18, 1944; d. Leslie B. and Ruth Lillian (May) Martin; m. Doyce B. Dees. BA magna cum laude, Tex. Christian U., 1965, MA, 1972, PhD, 1989. Cert. Montessori Soc., 1977. Adminstrv. asst., rsch. coord. Hosp. Improvement Project, Wichita Falls (Tex.) State Hosp., 1968-69; caseworker adoptions Edna Gladney Home, Ft. Worth, 1970-71; psychologist Mexia (Tex.) State Sch., 1971-72; sch. psychologist Ft. Worth Ind. Sch. Dist., 1971-78, program evaluator, 1978-86; pvt. counselor, 1986-88; rsch. scientist Tex. Christian U., Ft. Worth, 1989—, mem. adj. faculty, 1991-92, mem. grad. faculty, 1994—; bd. dirs Because We Care, Ft. Worth, 1988-97, Hill Sch., 1994—. Contbr. articles to profl. jours. Dallas TCU Women's Club creative writing scholar, 1962-64, Virginia Alpha scholar, 1963; NASA rsch. asst., 1965-67; USPHS trainee, 1967-68. Mem. APA, Am. Ednl. Rsch. Assn., Mental Health Assn., Mortar Board, Mensa, Sigma Xi, Alpha Chi, Phi Alpha Theta, Psi Chi, Phi Delta Kappa. E-mail: S.DEES@tcu.edu. Home: 29 Bounty Rd W Fort Worth TX 76132-1003 Office: Tex Christian U Dept Psychology Fort Worth TX 76129

DEES, STEPHEN PHILLIP, agricultural finance executive, lawyer; b. Tulsa, Feb. 21, 1943; s. Jesse Raymond and Mary Adelia (Ledbetter) D.; m. Mary Louise Porter, June 26, 1966 (div. Oct. 1986); children: Emily Ann, Daniel Ledbetter, Matthew Louis; m. Kristine Ann Odenwald, Oct. 10, 1987 (div. Apr. 1992); 1 child, Charles Jesse; m. Linda Petsch, Sept. 3, 1995. BA, Washington U., 1965, JD, 1967. Bar: Mo. 1967. Assoc. Stinson, Mag, Thomson, McEvers & Fizzell, Kansas City, Mo., 1967-71; ptnr. Stinson, Mag & Fizzell, Kansas City, 1971-84; v.p., gen. counsel Farmland Industries Inc., Kansas City, 1984-87, sec., 1986-91, v.p. law and adminstrn., 1987-93, now exec. v.p. bus. development & internat. mktg., dir. gen., 1993-98; dir. gen. Farmland Industries, S.A. de C.V. of Mex., 1993-95; ptnr. Rochdale Prins., 1998—. Officer, bd. dirs. Gt. Am. Basketball League, Shawnee Mission, Kans., 1979-86, commr., 1983-86; mem. Sister Cities Commn., Kansas City, 1982-90. Served with USAF, 1967, then with Res. Mem. ABA, Mo. Bar (vice chmn. labor law com. 1977-80, chmn. 1980-81), Lawyers Assn. Kansas City (bd. dirs. 1983-86, treas. 1989-91), Kansas City Met. Bar Assn., Order of Coif. Republican. Jewish. Avocations: stamp collecting, racquetball, travel. Home: 4511 N Mulberry Dr Kansas City MO 64116-4652

DEES, SUSAN COONS, physician, educator; b. Hancock, Mich., May 26, 1909; d. George Herbert and Myrta Amanda (Vogel) Coons; m. John Essary Dees, Jan. 7, 1935; children—Elizabeth, John Essary, Nancy, Susan. B.A., Goucher Coll., 1930; M.D., Johns Hopkins U., 1934; M.S., U. Minn., 1938. Diplomate Am. Bd. Pediatrics, Am. Bd. Allery and Immunology. Intern Johns Hopkins Hosp., Balt., 1934-35; asst. resident in medicine U. Rochester, N.Y., 1935-36; fellow in allergy and pediatrics U. Minn., Mpls., 1936-37; from assoc. prof. to prof. Duke U., Durham, N.C., 1939-79, prof. emeritus, allergy cons. Duke U. Med. Ctr., 1979—; chief div. pediatric allergy Duke U. Med. Ctr., 1940-79. Contbr. articles to profl. jours. Recipient Von Pirquet award Georgetown U., 1977. Fellow Am. Acad. Allergy (v.p. 1973, B. Ratner award 1971, Disting. Clinician award 1990), Am. Coll. Allergists (2nd v.p. 1978, Bela Schick award 1972); mem. N.C. Pediatric Soc. (pres. 1960). Democrat. Episcopalian. Office: Duke U Med Ctr Dept Pediatrics PO Box 2923 Durham NC 27715-2923

DEES, TOM MOORE, II, internist; b. Dallas, Mar. 4, 1931; s. Tom Hawkins and Maida Elizabeth (Board) D.; m. Suzanne Settle, Feb. 20, 1971; children: Tom Moore III, David Walsh. BA, Johns Hopkins U., 1952; MD, Southwestern Med. Sch., 1956. Intern Bellevue Hosp., N.Y.C., 1957, resident, 1958-59; rsch. fellow in cardiology Southwestern Med. Sch., Dallas, 1961; internist, ptnr. pvt. practice medicine MedProvider, Dallas, 1962—; dir. and mng. ptnr. Swiss Ave. Med. Bldg., Dallas, 1984—; clin. asst. prof. medicine Southwestern Med. Sch., Dallas, 1962—; assoc. attending physician Baylor Med. Ctr., Dallas, 1962—. Mem. dist. commn. Boy Scouts Am., Dallas, 1963-72; mem. ofcl. bd. Highland Park Meth. Ch., Dallas, 1963-72. Capt. USAF, 1959-61. Mem. ACP (life), AMA, Am. Soc. Internal Medicine, Johns Hopkins U. Alumni Assn. (pres. North Tex. chpt 1964-68), Tex. Club of Internists (pres. 1992-93). Republican. Avocations: hunting, fishing, gardening. Home: 3649 Strafford Ave Dallas TX 75205-2810 Office: 3434 Swiss Ave Ste 420 Dallas TX 75204-6240

DEETS, DWAIN AARON, aerospace technology executive; b. Bell, Calif., Apr. 16, 1939; s. Kenneth Robert and Mildred Evelyn (Bergman) D.; m. Catherine Elizabeth Meister, June 18, 1961; children: Dennis Allen, Danelle Alaine. AB, Occidental Coll., 1961; MS in Physics, San Diego State U., 1964; ME, UCLA, 1978. Rsch. engr. Dryden Flight Rsch. Ctr., NASA, Edwards, Calif., 62-78, 79-85; hdqrs. liaison engr. NASA, Washington, 1978-79; mgr. NASA, Edwards, 1979-85; dir. rsch. engring. Dryden Flight Rsch. Ctr., Edwards, 1990-96, dir. aerospace projects, 1996-97, dir. flight rsch. R&T, 1997—; hdqrs. mgr. flight rsch. NASA, Washington, 1988-89; chmn. Reusable Launch Vehicles Non-Advocate Rev., 1995-96. Contbr. articles to tech. publs. Recipient Exceptional Svc. medal NASA, 1988, Pres. Rank award SES, 1998. Fellow AIAA (assoc., Wright Bros. lectr. aeros. 1987); mem. Soc. Automotive Engrs. (chmn. aerospace control and guidance systems com. 1988-90). Democrat. Office: NASA Dryden PO Box 273 Edwards CA 93523-0273

DEETS, HORACE, association executive; b. Charleston, S.C., 1938. MA, Cath. U. Dir. outreach Washington Hosp. Ctr.'s Project for Alkoholism and Drug Abuse, Equal Employment Opportunity Commn.; various mgmt. positions, dir. Exec. Staff Office, Am. Assn. of Ret. Persons, Washington, until 1988, exec. dir., COO, 1988—; mem. bd. councilors Andrus Gerontology Ctr., U. So. Calif.; bd. advisors Emory Ctr. for Leadership and Career Studies, Emory Bus. Sch., Leadership Coun. of Aging Orgns., Conf. Bd., Internat. Fedn. on Aging.; mem. individual investors adv. com. N.Y. Stock Exch. Bd. dirs. Office: AARP 601 E St NW Washington DC 20049-0003*

DEFALCO, FRANK DAMIAN, civil engineering educator; b. Worcester, Mass., Apr. 25, 1934; s. Vincent Peter and Rose Marian DeFalco; 1 child, Lisa Ann. B.S., Worcester Poly. Inst., 1958, M.S., 1960; Ph.D., U. Conn., 1974. Geodetic engr. Western Electric Co., N.Y.C., 1960-61; prof. civil engring. Worcester Poly. Inst., 1961-99, prof. emeritus, 1999—; Fulbright prof. Baghdad, Iraq, 1965-67; pres. DeFalco Engring., Inc., 1974—; cons. engr. Contbr. articles to profl. jours. Chmn. Worcester Planning Bd., 1990-91. Recipient Fulbright lecturing award, 1965-67, Trustees' teaching award Worcester Poly. Inst., 1977. Fellow ASCE; mem. Am. Soc. Engring. Edn., Am. Concrete Inst., Am. Congress Surveying and Mapping, Am. Inst. Steel Constrn., Nat. Soc. Profl. Engrs., Skull, Order of Omega, Sigma Xi, Chi Epsilon. Home: PO Box 1001 Worcester MA 01613-1001 Office: Worcester Poly Inst Dept Civil Engring Worcester MA 01609

DEFAZIO, JOHN LORENZO, retired manufacturing executive; b. Pitts., Aug. 10, 1923; s. Pasquale A. and Marianne (Angotti) D.; student Carnegie Inst. Tech., 1941-42, 1945-46, U. Fla., 1942-43, U. Pitts., 1947-48, Air U.; m. Marian C. Scarpino, June 29, 1946; children: Patricia Marie, John Lorenzo, Therese Marie, Joann Marie, Rosemarie, Anthony Amedeo, Richard Michael. With Nuttall div. Westinghouse Electric Corp., Pitts., 1941-55; advt. staff rep., 1955-59, mgr. advt. and sales promotion, Youngwood, Pa., 1960-64, mktg. communications rep., electronic components, splty. products group, Pitts., 1964-68, components and materials group, 1968-70, mktg. services mgr. semicondr. div., Youngwood, Pa., 1970-73, mktg. communications mgr. components and materials group (now Industry Products Co.), 1973-83, ret., 1983 Chmn. inquiry com. Mktg. Communications Research Inst. Program chmn. Morningside Football Team. Major Air Force Res. Mem. Pitts. Advt. Club, Assn. Indsl. Advt., Air Force Assn., Res. Officers Assn., Air Force Hist. Soc., Bus./Profl. Advertisers Assn., Italian Execs. Am. Home: 3833 Logans Ferry Rd Pittsburgh PA 15239-2944 Office: PO Box 463 Oakmont PA 15139-0463

DEFAZIO, LYNETTE STEVENS, dancer, choreographer, educator, chiropractor, author, actress, musician; b. Berkeley, Calif., Sept. 29; d. Honore and Mabel J. (Estavan) Stevens; children: J.H. Panganiban, Joanna Pang. student U. Calif., Berkeley, 1950-55, San Francisco State Coll., 1950-51; studied classical dance teaching techniques and vocab. with Gisella Caccialanza and Harold and Lew Christensen, San Francisco Ballet, 1952-56; D. Chiropractic, Life-West Chiropractic Coll., San Lorenzo, Calif., 1983, cert. Techniques of Teaching U. Calif., 1985, BA in Humanities, New Coll. Calif., 1986; Lic. Chiropracter, Mich. Diplomate Nat. Sci. Bd.; eminence in dance edn., Calif. Community Colls. dance specialist, standard services, childrens ctrs. credentials Calif. Dept. Edn., 1986. Contract child dancer Monogram Movie Studio, Hollywood, Calif., 1938-40; dance instr. San Francisco Ballet, 1953-65; performer San Francisco Opera Ring, 1960-67; performer, choreographer Oakland (Calif.) Civic Light Opera, 1963-70; dir. Ballet Arts Studio, Oakland, Calif., 1960; teaching specialist Oakland Unified Sch. Dist., 1965-80; fgn. exchange dance dir. Academie de Danses-Salle Pleyel, Paris, France, 1966; instr. Peralta Community Coll. Dist., Oakland, 1971—, chmn. dance dept., 1985—; cons., instr. extension courses UCLA, Dirs. and Suprs. Assn., Pittsburg Unified Sch. Dist., 1971-73, Tulare (Calif.) Sch. Dist., 1971-73; researcher Ednl. Testing Services, HEW, Berkeley, 1974; resident choreographer San Francisco Childrens Opera, 1970—, Oakland Civic Theater; ballet mistress Dimensions Dance Theater, Oakland, 1977-80; cons. Gianchetta Sch. Dance, San Francisco, Robicheau Boston Ballet, TV series Patchwork Family, CBS, N.Y.C.; choreographer Ravel's Valses Nobles et Sentimentales, 1976. Recipient Foremost Women of 20th Century, 1985, Merit award San Francisco Children's Opera, 1985, 90. Author: Basic Music Outlines for Dance Classes, 1960, rev., 1968, Teaching Techniques and Choreography for Advanced Dancers, 1965, Basic Music Outlines for Dance Classes, 1965, Goals and Objectives in Improving Physical Capabilities, 1970, A Teacher's Guide for Ballet Techniques, 1970, Principle Procedures in Basic Curriculum, 1974, Objectives and Standards of Performance for Physical Development, 1975, Techniques of the Ballet School, 1970, rev., 1974, The Opera Ballets: A Choreographic Manual Vols. I-V, 1986. Assoc. music arranger Le Ballet du Cirque, 1964; assoc. composer, lyricist The Ballet of Mother Goose, 1968; choreographer: Valses Nobles Et Sentimentales (Ravel), Transitions (Kashevaroff), 1991, The New Wizard of Oz, 1991, San Francisco Children's Opera (Gingold); Canon in D for Strings and Continuo (Pachelbel), 1979; appeared in Flower Drum Song, 1993, Gigi, 1994, Fiddler on the Roof, 1996, The Music Man, 1996, Sayonara, 1997, Sayonara, 1997; violinist Oakland Cmty. Concert Orch., 1995—. Mem. Calif. State Teacher Assn., Bay Area Chiropractic Research Soc., Profl. Dance Teacher Assn. Home and Office: 4923 Harbord Dr Oakland CA 94618-2506

DEFAZIO, PETER A., congressman; b. Needham, Mass., May 27, 1947; m. Myrnie Daut. BA in Econs. and Polit. Sci., Tufts U., 1969; postgrad., U. Oreg., 1969-71, MS in Pub. Adminstrn./Gerontology, 1977. Aide to U.S. Rep. Jim Weaver, 1977-82; sr. issues specialist, caseworker, dist. field office U.S. rep. Jim Weaver, 1977-78, legis. asst. Washington office, 1978-80, dir. constituent services, 1980-82; mem. commn. representing Springfield Lane County (Oreg.) Commn., 1982-86; mem. 100-103rd Congresses (now 106th Congress) from 4th Oreg. dist., Washington, D.C., 1987—; ranking minority mem. resources com., mem. transp. and infrastructure com. Mem. Lane County Econ. Devel. com., Ingergovtl. Relations com.; bd. dirs. Eugene-Springfield Met. Partnership; Lane County Dem. precinct person, 1982—. Served with USAFR. Mem. Assn. of Oreg. Counties (legis. com.), Nat. Assn. of Counties (tax and fin. com.). Office: US Ho of Reps 2134 Rayburn Bldg Washington DC 20515-3704

DEFEE, VICKI JEAN, elementary education educator; b. Pasadena, Tex., Jan. 22, 1960; d. Freddie Joe and Evelyn Sue Grounds; m. George Edward Defee, Aug. 15, 1985; children: Dustin Allen, Kristin Michelle. BS, U. Houston, 1983, MEd, 1998. Cert. reading recovery, early childhood edn., ednl. adminstrn. Tchr. pub. schs., Pasadena, 1983-87; early childhood dir. pvt. schs., Pasadena, 1989-93; tchr. pub. schs., LaPorte, Tex., 1995—. Pres. PTO, LaPorte, 1991-94. Mem. ASCD, Nat. Assn. Elem. Prins., Reading Recovery Tchrs. N.Am., Phi Delta Kappa. Republican. Baptist. Avocations: softball, reading, shopping. E-mail: VDefee@aol.com. Home: 5237 Ridgecrest LaPorte TX 77571 Office: LaPorte Ind Sch Dist 301 E Fairmont LaPorte TX 77571-6418

DEFEIS, ELIZABETH FRANCES, law educator, lawyer; b. N.Y.C.; d. Francis Paul and Lena (Amendola) D. BA, St. John's U., 1956, JD, 1958, JSD (hon.), 1984; LLM, NYU, 1971; postgrad., U. Milan, Italy, 1963-64, Inst. Internat. Human Rights, 1991. Bar: N.Y. 1959, U.S. Dist. Ct. (fed. dist.) 1960, U.S. Dist. Ct. (so. dist.) N.Y. 1961, U.S. Supreme Ct. 1965, U.S. Dist. Ct. (ea. dist.) N.Y. 1978, N.J. 1983. Asst. U. S. atty. So. Dist. N.Y., Dept. Justice, 1961-62; atty. RCA Corp., 1962-63; assoc. Carter, Ledyard & Milburn, N.Y.C., 1963-69; atty. Bedford Stuyvesant Legal Svcs. Corp., 1969-70; prof. law Seton Hall U., Newark, 1971—, dean Sch. Law, 1983-88; vis. prof. St. Louis U. Sch. Law, 1988, St. John's U. Sch. Law, 1990, U. Milan, Italy, 1996; Fulbright-Hays lectr., Iran, India, 1977-79; lectr. Orgn. Security and Cooperation in Europe, Russia, Turkmenistan, Tajikistan, Azerbaijan; vis. scholar Ctr. Study of Human Rights, Columbia U., 1989; project dir. TV series Women and Law, 1974-80; narrator TV series Alternatives to Violence, 1981—; mem. com. women and cts. N.J. Supreme Ct., 1982-95; trustee Legal Svcs. N.J., 1983-88; mem. 3rd Cir. Task Force on Equality in the Cts., 1995—; tech. cons. on Constitution of Armenia, 1992-95; project dir. T.V. series Pub. Internat. Law.; legal expert Armenia election OSCE, 1998. Chair Albert Einstein Inst., Boston, 1995—. Fulbright-Hays scholar Milan, Italy, 1963-64, Fulbright-Hays, Orgn. for Security and Cooperation in Europe scholar, Armenia, Russia, Italy, 1996; Ford Found. fellow, 1970-71. Mem. ABA, Nat. Italian Am. Bar Assn. (dir.), Columbian Lawyers Assn., Assn. of Bar of City of N.Y. (chair internat. law com., coun. internat. affairs), N.J. Bar Assn., Nat. Italian Am. Found. Office: Seton Hall U Law Sch One Newark Ctr Newark NJ 07102

DEFELICE, EUGENE ANTHONY, physician, medical educator, consultant, magician; b. Beacon, N.Y., Dec. 24, 1927; s. Domenick and Louise (Grippo) DeF. BS, Columbia U., 1951; MD, Boston U., 1956. Ciba fellow, lectr. pharmacology Boston U. Sch. Medicine, 1954-57; intern Newton (Mass.) Wellesley Hosp., 1957; practice medicine specializing in internal medicine North Miami, Fla., 1958-61; asst. dir. clin. rsch. Warner Lambert Rsch. Inst., Morris Plains, N.J., 1961-64; dir. clin. rsch. Bristol Labs. (now Bristol Meyers Squibb), Syracuse, N.Y., 1965-66; dir. clin. rsch. Sandoz Inc. (now Novartis Inc.), East Hanover, N.J., 1967-68, exec. dir. clin. research, 1969-70, dir. sci. affairs and comml. devel., 1970-74, dir. corp. sci. devel., 1974, v.p. corp. sci. devel., 1974-77, v.p. internat. med. rsch., med. advisor, 1977-83; prof. biochemistry, microbiology and pub. health, dir. rsch. New Eng. Coll. Pharmacy, 1956-58; practice in medicine, cons. in medicine and med. rsch., Morristown, N.J., 1961-87, East Schodack and Albany, N.Y., 1988—; clin. assoc. prof. medicine Coll. Medicine and Dentistry N.J.-Rutgers Med. Sch., 1977-84; clin. prof. medicine UMD-Robert Wood Johnson Med. Sch., 1985—; clin. prof. anesthesiology UCLA, 1978-83. Contbr. numerous articles to profl. jours. cons. to editor; mem. internat. editl. com.: Triangle, Sandorama, 1977-81. Served with U.S. Army, World War II. Named hon. citizen of Italy; named to Notable Italian-Am. Hall of Fame. Fellow Am. Geriat. Soc., Acad. Psychosomatic Medicine; mem. Soc. Am. Magicians, Internat. Brotherhood Magicians; emeritus mem. numerous profl. socs. Home and Office: PO Box 9160 Albany NY 12209-0160 *Success in life comes from constancy of purpose, diligent work, living according to sound moral and religious principles, and having faith and hope in the future. Helping to make the world a better place to live in, autographing one's work in excellence, and doing good by others are the rewards which bring happiness.*

DE FELITTA, FRANK PAUL, producer, writer, director; b. N.Y.C.; s. Pat and Genevieve (Sibilio) De F.; m. Dorothy Gilbert; children: Eileen Raymond. Student, U. N.C., New Sch. Social Research, 1948. Dir.-writer, CBS, 1950-57, dir. programming, Nat. Telefilms Assos., 1959-61, producer, writer, dir., NBC, from 1962, producer, dir., writer, Universal Studios, 1968-69; film documentaries include Music of the South, 1955; sci. series Conquest, 1957; natural sci. series Adventure, 1953-55; hist. series Odyssey, 1958, The Chosen Child, 1962 (Writers Guild award), Emergency Ward, 1962 (Emmy award), Experiment in Excellence, 1963 (Sch. Bell award), Battle of the Bulge, 1964, The Stately Ghosts of England, 1964, The World of the Teenager, 1966 (Robert J. Flaherty award), Pearl Harbor, 1966 Golden Eagle award; dir., author: films Trapped, 1973, The Two Worlds of Jennie Logan, 1979 (Silver Halo award), Killer in the Mirror, 1986, Scissors, 1990; dir.: film Dark Night of the Scarecrow, 1981; (Brotherhood award of Nat. Conf. Christians and Jews for film Mississippi- A Self Portrait, George Washington Honor medal of Freedoms Found. for film The American Image.); Author: films The First of January, 1970, The Savage Is Loose, 1971, Audrey Rose, 1977, The Entity, 1981; novels Oktoberfest, 1972, Audrey Rose, 1975, The Entity, 1978, Sea Trial, 1980, For Love of Audrey Rose, 1982, Golgotha Falls, 1984, Funeral March of the Marionettes, 1990. Recipient Peabody award, 1954, 63, Thomas Alva Edison award, 1958, 2 Gold Eagle awards Coun. on Internat. Non-Theatrical Events. Mem. Writers Guild Am., Dirs. Guild Am.

DEFENDI, VITTORIO, medical research administrator, pathologist; b. Treviglio, Italy, Nov. 16, 1928; married, 1955; 3 children. MD, U. Pavia, 1951. Instr. pathology dept. U. Pavia, 1951-52; pathologist virus sect. Lederle Labs., N.Y.C., 1956-58; assoc. pathologist Med. Sch., U. Pa., 1958-64, assoc. prof., 1964-68, Wistar prof., 1968-74; prof. pathology, chmn. dept. pathology Sch. NYU Sch. Medicine, N.Y.C., 1974—; Brit. Coun. scholar Postgrad. Med. Sch., U. London, 1952-53; Fulbright fellow Med. Sch., U. Vt., 1953-54; rsch. fellow Detroit Inst. Cancer Rsch., 1954-56; assoc. mem. Wistar Inst., 1958-64, mem. staff, 1964-74; rsch. prof. Am. Cancer soc., 1973—. Leukemia Soc. scholar, 1962-66. Mem. Am. Soc. Cell Biology, Am. Soc. Exptl. Pathology, Histochem. Soc., Am. Assn. Immunology, Am. Assn. Cancer Rsch. Achievements include research in viral oncology; tumor biology; mechanism of immunological defense. Office: NYU Sch Medicine Dept Pathology 550 1st Ave New York NY 10016-6481

DE FERRARI, GABRIELLA, curator, writer; b. Tacna, Peru, June 3, 1941; came to U.S., 1959, naturalized, 1964; d. Armando and Delia De Ferrari; children: Nathaniel, Gabriella, Jeppson. BA, St. Louis U., 1962; MS, Tufts U., 1965; MA, Harvard U., 1981. Dir. Inst. Contemporary Art, Boston, 1975-77; acting curator Busch Reisinger Mus., Harvard U., Cambridge, Mass., 1978-79; asst. dir. for curatorial affairs and program Fogg Art Mus., 1979-82; cons. editor Travel Leisure. Author: A Cloud on Sand, 1990, Gringa Latina A Woman of Two Worlds, 1995. Trustee New Sch. U., N.Y.C. Office: 10 Jay St New York NY 10013-2861

DEFFENBAUGH, RALSTON H., JR., immigration agency executive, lawyer; b. Oakland, Calif., Apr. 12, 1952; s. Ralston H. and Marion F. (Funda) D.; m. Miriam Ruth Boraas, Oct. 24, 1976; children: Natalie, Carl. BA, U. Colo., 1973; JD, Harvard U., 1977. Bar: Colo. 1977. Atty. Ireland, Stapleton & Pryor, Denver, 1977-80; asst. to gen. sec. Lutheran World Fedn., Geneva, 1981-85; dir. Luth. Office for World Community, N.Y.C., 1985-90; exec. dir. Luth. Immigration & Refugee Svc., N.Y.C., 1991—; legal advisor Luth. Bishops and Coun. of Chs., Namibia, 1989-90. Recipient Arnold E. Carlson award Gustavus Adolphus Coll., St. Peter, Minn., 1991, Graven award Wartburg Coll., 1994, Sylvester Michelfelder award Trinity Luth. Sem., 1995. Office: Luth Immigration & Refugee Svc 700 Light St Baltimore MD 21230

DE FIGUEIREDO, MARIO PACHECO, food scientist; came to U.S., 1951; s. Joao Manuel Pacheco and Maria Alcina de Figueiredo; m. Maria Mildred Tellis; 1 child, Mark Anthony. SB, MIT, 1955, SM, 1958, PhD, 1963; MBA, U. Chgo., 1968. V.p. Sara Lee, Chgo., 1963-73; tech. dir. Farmland Foods, Chgo., 1976-78, Ralston Purina, St. Louis, 1978-85; v.p. Hershey Foods, Chgo., 1973-76, Allied Lyons, St. Louis, 1985-93; prin. Mario de Figueiredo Consulting, Chesterfield, Mo., 1993—. Author: Food Microbiology, 1976; editor Jour. Food Quality, 1978-88. MEm. APHA, Am. Inst. Chemists; mem. Inst. Food Technologists, N.Y. Acad. Scis. Office: Mario de Figueiredo Consulting PO Box 341 Chesterfield MO 63006-0341

DEFILIPPI, GEORGE, career military officer; b. Mobile, Ala., Sept. 6, 1947; s. George and Margaret Josephine (Lazzari) DeF.; m. Patricia Naismith McAdam, July 21, 1969; children: Jocelyn, Gwendolyn, Geoffrey, James. BS, USAF Acad., Colorado Springs, 1969; MS, Air Force Inst. Technology, Dayton, Ohio, 1977. Enlisted USAF, 1969, advanced through ranks to col.; exec. sec., program mgr. Scientific Adv. Bd. USAF, HQ USAF, Washington, 1984-86; chief tng. divsn. 602d Tactical Air Control Wing USAF, Davis Mountain AFB, Ariz., 1986-88; cmdr. 22d Tactical Air Support Tng. Squadron USAF, Davis Mountain AFB, 1988-89, cmdr. 23d Tactical Air Support Squadron, 1989-90; cmdr. Air Liaison Office XVIII Airborne Corps USAF, Ft. Bragg, N.C., 1991-93; cmdr. Air Liaison Office to 3d Rep. Korea Army USAF, Uijongbu, Korea, 1992-93; mil. staff specialist Undersec. Def. Acquisition & Tech. USAF, Washington, 1993-96, mil. asst. to dir. strategic tactical systems, 1996—. Vol. Arlington (Va.) Emergency Winter Shelter, 1993—; mem. Arlington Com. of 100, 1994—; vestry mem. St. George's Episcopal Ch., 1996—. Mem. Assn. Unmanned Vehicle Sys. (bd. dirs. capitol chpt. 1993—). Episcopal. Avocations: jogging, swimming. Office: Office of Undersec Def 3090 Defense Pentagon Rm 3e130 Washington DC 20301-3090

DEFILIPPO, DOMINIC JOSEPH, special effects inventor; b. N.Y.C., Oct. 12, 1929; s. Raphaelle and Lucia DeF.; m. Undine Michaelle Dressler, Dec. 1, 1995. Pres. DeFilippo Studio Inc., N.Y.C., 1962—. Dir., set designer (TV comml.) Levolor Four Seasons, 1985 (Clio award 1985). Home: PO Box 699 Roscoe NY 12776-0699

DEFLEUR, LOIS B., university president, sociology educator; b. Aurora, Ill., June 25, 1936; d. Ralph Edward and Isabel Anna (Cornils) Begitske; m. Melvin L. DeFleur (div.). AB, Blackburn Coll., 1958; MA, Ind. U., 1961; PhD in Sociology, U. Ill., 1965; HHD (hon.), U. Alaska, 1999. Asst. prof. sociology Transylvania Coll., Lexington, Ky., 1963-67; assoc. prof. Wash. State U., Pullman, 1967-74, prof., 1975-86, dean Coll. Liberal Arts, 1981-86; provost U. Mo., Columbia, 1986-90; pres. Binghamton U., SUNY, 1990—; disting. vis. prof. USAF Acad., 1976-77; vis. prof. U. Chgo., 1980-81; bd. dirs. N.Y. State Electric and Gas. Author: Delinquency in Argentina, 1965; (with others) Sociology: Human Society, 3d edit. 1981, 4th edit., 1984, The Integration of Women into All Male Air Force Units, 1982, The Edward R. Murrow Heritage: A Challenge for the Future, 1986; contbr. articles to profl. jours. Mem. Wash. State Bd. on Correctional Svcs. and Edn., 1974-77, State of N.Y. Edn. Dept. Curriculum and Assessment Coun., 1991-94, Trilateral Task for N.Am. Ednl. Collaboration, USIA, 1993-95. Recipient Disting. Alumni award Blackburn Coll., 1991; grantee NIMH, 1969-79, NSF, 1972-75, Air Force Office, 1978-81. Mem. NCAA (pres. commn. 1996, exec. com. 1997-98), Am. Sociol. Assn. (publs. com. 1979-82, nominations com. 1984-86, coun. mem. 1987-90), Pacific Sociol. Assn. (pres. 1980-82), Coun. Colls. of Arts and Scis. (bd. dirs. 1982-84, pres. 1985-87), Aircraft Owners and Pilots Assn., Internat. Comanche Soc., Nat. Assn. State U. and Land-grant Colls. (exec. com. 1990-93, chair coun. of pres. 1994-95, chmn. bd. dirs. 1996-97), Am. Coun. Edn. (bd. dirs. 1994—, v.p. chair-elect 1997-98, chair bd. dirs. 1998-99), Consortium Social Sci. Assns. (bd. dirs. 1993-96). Office: Binghamton U Office of Pres PO Box 6000 Binghamton NY 13902-6000

DEFLEUR, MARGARET H., communications educator; b. Toledo, Nov. 29, 1949; d. Bart Anthony and Elizabeth Paula (Poch) Hanus; m. Melvin Lawrence DeFleur, Dec. 29, 1978. BA, U. Miami, Coral Gables, Fla., 1984, MBA, 1987; PhD, Syracuse U., 1994. Adj. prof. Syracuse U., 1992; asst. prof. Boston U., 1994—; vis. scholar Harvard U., 1996-98; dir. Health Comm. Program, Boston U., 1997—. Author: Computer-Assisted Investigative Reporting: Development and Methodology, 1997; contbr. articles to profl. jours. Mem. Assn. for Edn. in Mass Comm. and Journalism, Nat. Comm. Assn. Home: 20 Burnett Rd Southborough MA 01772-1467 Office: Boston U Coll Comm 640 Commonwealth Ave Boston MA 02215-2422

DEFLORIO, MARY LUCY, physician, psychiatrist; b. Chgo.; d. Anthony Ralph adn Bernice B. (Bounell) DeF.; m. Robert Y. Shapiro, Dec. 27, 1986. BA with distinction, U. Wis.; MD, MPH, U. Ill., Chgo., 1984; cert. writing program, Columbia U., 1988-91. Cert. emergency med. technician. Adjudicator Fed. Disability Program, Ill. and Mass.; vocat. counselor U. Ill., Chgo.; resident internal medicine Mercy Hosp., Chgo., 1984-85; med. examiner Dept. Pub. Aid State of Ill., Chgo., 1985-87; resident psychiatrist St. Vincent's Hosp., N.Y.C., 1987-90; fellow cons. liaison psychiatry Meml. Sloan Kettering/Cornell Med. Ctr., N.Y.C., 1991-93; chief fellow Meml. Sloan Kettering, N.Y.C., 1992-93; attending physician Div. Psychiatry/Dept. Neurology Meml. Sloan Kettering and Cornell Med. Coll., N.Y.C., 1993-95; pvt. practice N.Y., 1996—. Recipient Med. Econs. Writing award, 1987; James scholar U. Ill., Gen. Assembly scholar. Mem. AMA (Nutritional scholar 1983-84), Am. Women's Assn., Nat. Rehab. Assn., Assn. Acad. Psychiatrists (Mead-Johnson fellow 1990), Am. Psychiat. Assn. (Br. Rsch. award 1990), Am. Psychiat. Arts Assn. (black and white photography award 1993, 96, poetry award 1993). Roman Catholic. Avocations: writing, photography.

DEFOOR, J. ALLISON, II, state agency officer, lawyer; b. Coral Gables, Fla., Dec. 6, 1953; s. James Allison Sr. and Marjorie (Keen) DeF.; m. Terry Ann White, June 24, 1977; children: Melissa Anne, Mary Katherine, James Allison III. BA, U. So. Fla., 1976; JD, Stetson U., 1979; MA, U. So. Fla., 1979; postgrad., Harvard U., 1989; MDiv Candidate, So. Fla. Ctr. Theol. Studies, 1994—. Bar: Fla. 1979, U.S. Dist. Ct. (so. dist.) Fla. 1980, U.S. Ct. Appeals (5th cir.) 1981, U.S. Ct. Appeals (11th cir.) 1982. Asst. pub. defender, 1979-80; asst. state's atty. 16th Cir., Key West, Fla., 1980-83, dir. narcotics task force, 1981-83; judge Monroe County, Plantation Key, Fla., 1983-87; assoc. Cunningham, Albritton, Lenzi, Warner, Bragg & Miller, Plantation Key, 1987-89; sheriff Monroe County, Fla., 1989-90; sr. v.p. CEO Wackenut Monitoring Systems Inc., Coral Gables, Fla., 1991-92; gen. counsel, sec. HEM Pharm. Corp., Phila. and Key Largo, 1992-93; ptnr. Hershoff, Lupino DeFoor & Gregg, Tavernier, Fla., 1993-99; environ. policy coord. State of Fla., Office of Gov., Tallahassee, 1999—; environ. policy coord., exec. Everglades Nat., State of Fla., Office of Gov.; adj. faculty St. Leo Coll., Key West, 1980-81, U. So. Fla., Ft. Myers, 1981-82, Fla. Internat. U., Miami, 1985, U. Miami Law Sch., 1985-99 ; faculty Nat. Jud. Coll., Reno, Nev., 1985-86; trustee So. Fla. Ctr. for Theol. Studies, 1992-99, chair, 1996-99; So. Fla. Jail Ministries, 1996-99, Fla. Audubon Soc., 1996-99. Editor U. Miami Law Rev., 1985; author: (books) DeFoor & Schultz, Fla. Civil Procedure Forms with Practice Commentary, 1989, Odet Philippe, Peninsular Pioneer, 1997 (Safety Harbor Mus., Fla.). Chmn. Monroe County Rep. Exec. Com., 1987-88, 94, state committeeman, 1994-99; mem . Fla. Rep. Exec. Com., 1995-96, 97-99; del. Rep. Nat. Conv., 1992; Rep. nominee for Lt. Gov. of Fla., 1990. Named one of Five Outstanding Young Men in Fla., Jaycees, 1984, Ten Outstanding Young Men in Am., Jaycees, 1985; recipient Merit award Fla. Crime Prevention Commn., 1982, Leadership Fla. Class V. Mem. ABA, Fla. Bar (bd. govs. 1995-97), Monroe County Bar Assn., Mensa, Fla. Keys Bar Assn., Ocean Reef Club (Key Largo, Fla.), Islamorada Fishing Club, Key West Yacht Club, Explorer's Club (New York), Upper Keys Rotary (pres. 1987-88). Republican. Episcopalian. Avocations: scuba diving, sailing, golf. Home: 19 Snapper Ave Key Largo FL 33037-4719 Office: Office of the Gov Tallahassee FL 32301 Office: State of Fla Office of Gov 1501 The Capitol Tallahassee FL 32099-6001

DE FORD, DOUGLAS ATMETLLA, biochemical, biomechanical and industrial engineer; b. San Jose, Costa Rica, Nov. 26, 1945; s. Douglas N. and Enriqueta (Atmetlla) De F.; m. Maria Felicia Zamora, July 9, 1972 (div.); children: Fabiola de Prada, Dougie, Christopher, Steve. Degree in mech. engring., Monterrey Inst. Tech., 1970; MS in Biotechnology, Teesside U., England, 1985, PhD in Biochem. Engring., 1988; postgrad., Nat. U., 1990. Chief engr. CCSS Health Svcs., San Jose, Costa Rica, 1975-78; prodn. mgr. Blue Ribbon Meat Processing, Alajuela, Costa Rica, 1978-80; indsl. cons. CCSS Health Svcs., 1980-83; biotech. rschr. North East Biotech. Ctr., Middlesbrough, England, 1983-88; internat. cons. UNIDO, Vienna, Austria, 1988-96; gen. mgr. Pharma Ancla Labs., San Jose, 1988-90; chmn., founder British C. of C., San Jose, 1991-93; dir. rsch. & devel. CCSS Health Svcs., 1990-94; pres. BioBellessa Tropical Biotech., San Jose, 1988—. Author: Industrial Park for Health, 1982, The Concept of Bioreactor Number Applied to Fermentation Scale-Up, ACHEMA, 1985, Frankfurt am Main, Germany, Scale-up of Bioreactors: Physiological Effects on Microorganisms, BIOTECH Asia, Singapore, 1985, Scale-up-down Biotech Operations and Processes, 1988. British Coun. grantee, 1983-88, CCSS Health Svcs. grantee, 1983-87. Mem. Inst. Chem. Engring., Coll. Engrs. and Architects, CIEME, Biotech. Nat. Coun. Achievements include auto-sledge vehicle for bamboo transportation in bamboo farms; tropical biopharmaceutical active principles from Costa Rica BioDiversity; Anti-Colitis: Juanilamine; Anti-Hypertension and Anti-Hyperglycaemia Agent: Courarine, 1990-95; cibernetic simulation for bioreactor full scale-up-down; novel design multipurpose continuous high retention time algal pond for effluents degradation; novel design/development of a photolysis pretreatment reactor for agricultural and industrial wastewater affluents, 1993. Avocations: nature photography, country hicking, camping, soccer. Home: PO Box 5097 Oakland CA 94605-0097

DEFORD, FRANK, sportswriter, television and radio commentator, author; b. Balt., Dec. 16, 1938; s. Benjamin F. Jr. and Louise (McAdams) D.; m. Carol Penner, Aug. 28, 1965; children: Christian McAdams, Scarlet Faith. BA, Princeton U., 1962. Writer Sports Illustrated mag., N.Y.C., 1964-89, 98—; editor, pub. The Nat. Sports Daily, N.Y.C., 1989-91; contbg. editor Newsweek, 1991-93, 96-98, Vanity Fair, 1993-96; commentator Nat. Pub. Radio, Washington, 1980—, Cable News Network, N.Y.C., 1980-86, NBC Sports, N.Y.C., 1986-89, ESPN Radio, N.Y.C., 1991-98, HBO, N.Y.C., 1994—. Author: Five Strides on the Banked Track, 1971, There She Is, 1971, Cut 'n' Run, 1972, The Owner, 1976, Big Bill Tilden: The Triumphs and the Tragedy, 1976, Everybody's All-American, 1982, Alex: The Life of a Child (Christopher award), 1983, The Spy in the Deuce Court, 1986, The World's Tallest Midget, 1987, Casey on the Loose, 1989, Love and Infamy, 1993, (screenplay) Trading Hearts, 1988. Trustee Cystic Fibrosis Found., Washington, 1973—, chmn., 1984—. First winner award for excellence in sport journalism Ctr. for Study of Sport in Soc., Northeastern U., 1985, award for disting. svc. to journalism U. Mo., 1987, Emmy award for TV writing and commentary, 1988, Cable Ace award for TV writing, 1995; named Sportswriter of Yr. Nat. Assn. Sportswriters and Sportscasters, 1982, 84, 85, 86, 87, 88; named to Sportswriter Hall of Fame, 1998; voted Nat. Mag. Writer of Yr. Wash. Journalism Rev., 1987, 88, Best U.S. Sportswriter Am. Journalism Rev., 1992. Democrat. Episcopalian. Home and Office: PO Box 1109 Greens Farms CT 06436-1109

DEFOREEST, JOANNE MARIE, educator; b. Seattle, May 28, 1961; d. Robert Gregory and Millicent (Barnes) DeF.; m. Frederick Andrew McCandless, Dec. 21, 1996; 1 stepchild, Aaron David. BA, Gonzaga U., 1985; MEd, Seattle Pacific U., 1993. Cert. tchr., Wash. Tchr. Spokane (Wash.) Diocese, 1986-89; ednl. cons. pvt. practice, Wash., 1989—; tchr. Seattle Archdiocese, 1989-94, Achieve Prep, Edmonds, Wash., 1994-95; reading specialist/tchr. Shoreline (Wash.) Sch. Dist., 1995—; adj. prof. Seattle Pacific U., Western Washington U., 1995—. Inventor in field. Mem. ASCD, Wash. Orgn. Reading Devel., Internat. Reading Assn., Holy Names Alumnae Assn. (pres. Alumnae Assn. bd. 1993-96). Democrat. Roman Catholic. Avocations: gardening, hiking, fishing, arts and crafts, reading. Home and Office: 9624 242d Pl SW Edmonds WA 98020

DE FOREST, ROY DEAN, artist, sculptor; b. North Platte, Nebr., Feb. 11, 1930. Student, Yakima Jr. Coll., 1949-50, Calif. Sch. Fine Arts, 1950-52; BA, San Francisco State Coll., 1953, MA, 1958. Dir. Larsen Gallery, Yakima Jr. Coll., 1958-60; instr. Calif. Coll. Arts & Crafts, Oakland, 1964-65; from asst. prof. to assoc. prof. U. Calif., Davis, 1965-82, prof., 1985—. One-person shows include Calif. Palace Legion of Honor, San Francisco, 1971, Inst. Contemporary Art, Boston, 1977, 78, Marilyn Butler Gallery, Santa Fe, 1989, Frumkin/Adams Gallery, N.Y., 1990, 93, Fuller Groass Gallery, San Francisco, 1990, Stanford Mus. Art, Calif., 1990, John Berggruen Gallery, San Francisco, 1992, Whitney Mus. Am. Art, N.Y., 1973, San Francisco Mus. Modern Art, 1974, George Adams Gallery, N.Y.C., 1997, Paris Gibson Square Museum, Gt. Falls, Mont., 1998—, others; exhibited works at San Francisco Mus. Art, 1957, Calif. Palace Legion of Honor, San Francisco, 1962, 63, 64, Art Inst. Chgo., 1964, Walker Art Ctr., Mpls., 1965, Oakland (Calif.) Mus., 1966, Ark. Arts Ctr., Little Rock, 1998, John Berggruen Gallery, San Francisoc, 1998, Museum of Modern Art, N.Y.c., 1997, Sawhill Gallery, James Madison U., Harrisonburg, Va., 1997, others; represented in permanent collections San Francisco Mus. Art, Art Inst. Chgo., Joslyn Art Mus., Omaha, Phila. Mus. Art, Whitney Mus. Am. Art, N.Y., others. Recipient Nealie Sullivan award San Francisco Art Assn., 1964, Purchase prize La Jolla Art Mus., 1965; grantee Nat. Endowment Arts, 1972. Mem. San Francisco Art Assn. Office: George Adams Gallery 41 W 57th St Fl 7 New York NY 10019-3409

DEFOREST, WALTER PATTISON, III, lawyer; b. Ft. Sill, Okla., Dec. 4, 1944; s. Walter P. Jr. and Mary E. (Miller) DeF.; m. Anna Thun. BA, U. Pitts., 1966; JD, Harvard U., 1969. Bar: U.S. Ct. Appeals (2d and 3d cirs.) 1973, U.S. Ct. Appeals (4th, 5th and D.C. cirs.) 1978, U.S. Ct. Appeals (10th cir.) 1981, U.S. Ct. Appeals (11th cir.), U.S. Ct. Appeals (7th cir.) 1986, U.S. Ct. Appeals (fed. cir.) 1995, U.S. Supreme Ct. 1974. Assoc. Reed, Smith, Shaw & McClay, Pitts., 1969-77, ptnr., 1978-93; ptnr. DeForest & Koscelnik, Pitts., 1994—; instr. Grad. Sch. Indsl. Adminstrn. Carnegie Mellon U., Pitts., 1974-75. Mem. adv. com. Big Bros. and Big Sisters Western Pa., Pitts., 1984—; bd. dirs. Pa. Small Bus. Advocacy Coun., Harrisburg, 1984-89, 92. Mem. ABA (litigation, labor sects.), Pa. Bar Assn. (litigation, labor sects.), Allegheny County Bar Assn. (litigation sect., fed. ct. sect.). Office: DeForest & Koscelnik 3000 Koppers Bldg 436 7th Ave Pittsburgh PA 15219-1826

DEFORGE, KATHERINE ANN, secondary education educator; b. Syracuse, N.Y., Nov. 2, 1950; d. Edward Carroll and Genevieve (Pretko) Miles; m. Timothy Edward DeForge, June 26, 1976; 1 child, Tanya Emily. AA, Maria Regina Coll., Syracuse, 1969; BA, LeMoyne Coll., Syracuse, 1972; MS in Edn., SUNY, Cortland, 1978. Tchr., supr. social studies Assumption Cath. Acad., Syracuse, 1972-81, Bishop Grimes H.S., East Syracuse, N.Y., 1981-88, Marcellus (N.Y.) Ctrl. Schs., 1988—; test cons. N.Y. State Edn. Dept., Albany, 1984—; mem. testing and assessment com. N.Y. State Edn. Dept.; social studies cons. Onondaga-Cortland-Madison BOCES. NEH grantee, 1986, 94. Mem. ASCD, Nat. Coun. for Social Studies, N.Y. State Coun. for Social Studies, N.Y. State Social Studies Suprs. Assn. (sec. 1997-99, v.p. 1999—), Ctrl. N.Y. Coun. for Social Studies (sec. 1986-88, treas. 1989-91, v.p. 1993-95, pres. 1995-97, Outstanding Social Studies Educator award 1992). Republican. Roman Catholic. Avocations: travel, reading, theatre, crafts. Home: 230 Malverne Dr Syracuse NY 13208-1841 Office: Marcellus Ctrl Schs Reed Pky Marcellus NY 13108

DEFORREST, MATTHEW MCCOY, educator, freelance writer; b. Boston, Jan. 21, 1968; s. Daniel John III and Sandra Ann (Murphy) DeF. BA in English, Boston U., 1990; MA in Anglo-Irish Lit., U. Coll., Dublin, 1991; PhD in Irish Lit. and Mythology, Boston U., 1996. Tchg. asst. Boston U., 1995-96; adj. prof. English, adj. prof. comms. Wingate (N.C.) U., 1997—; adj. prof. English U. N.C., Charlotte, 1997—; respondent liaison Seventh Ann. Grad. Irish Studies conf., Boston, 1992-93. Author: Yeats and the Stylistic Arrangements of Experience, 1999; contbr. articles to profl. jours. Mem. MLA, Am. Conf. for Irish Studies, Assn. Lit. Scholars and Critics, Internat. Assn. for the Study Irish Lit., Boston Yeats Soc. (exec. com. 1992-97). Roman Catholic. E-mail: mmdeforest@worldnet.att.net. Office: U NC at Charlotte Dept English Charlotte NC 28223

DE FRANCESCO, JOHN BLAZE, JR., public relations company executive; b. Stamford, Conn., May 22, 1936; s. John Blaze and Mae (Matyscyk) DeF.; m. Louise C. Terlizzo, Nov. 1, 1958 (div. 1983); children: Daryl, Jay, Dana, Dorian; m. Diana Picchietti, Oct. 20, 1990. B.S., U. Conn., 1958. Sr. v.p. Daniel J. Edelman, Inc., Chgo., 1967-77; exec. v.p. Ruder Finn & Rotman, Inc., Chgo., 1977-85; prin., CEO DeFrancesco/Goodfriend Pub. Relations, 1985—. Bd. dirs. Ill. Divsn. Vocat. Rehab., 1976-78; mem. pub. rels. adv. bd. Gov.'s State U., 1994—. Comdr. USN, 1958-67; comdr. USNR; ret. 1979. Recipient 3 Silver Anvil awards Pub. Rels. Soc. Am., 5 Golden Trumpet awards Publicity Club, Chgo. Mem. Pub. Rels. Soc. Am., Am. Mktg. Assn., Sales and Mktg. Execs. of Chgo., Chgo. Assn. Dir. Mktg., Navy League U.S., Naval Res. Assn. Naval Order of U.S. Roman Catholic. Home: 18785 Saint Andrews Dr Monument CO 80132-8824 Office: De Francesco/Goodfriend Pub Rels 444 N Michigan Ave Chicago IL 60611-3903

DEFRANCISCO, JOSEPH E., military officer. BS, U.S. Mil. Acad.; MA in History, Rice U.; grad., U.S. Army Command/Gen. Staff, U.S. Army War Coll. Commd. 2d lt. U.S. Army, 1965, advanced through grades to lt. gen., 1996; ret., 1998; exec. officer 1st bn. 18th field arty. regiment VII Corps U.S. Army Europe, Germany, 1978-80, officer in charge ops. element VII Corps Arty., 1980-81; spl. asst. to asst. divsn. comdr. 9th infantry divsn. Ft. Lewis, Wash., 1981-82; chief tng. divsn. Office of Asst. Chief of Staff for Ops. and Plans, I Corps, Ft. Lewis, Wash., 1984-85; comdr. 7th infantry divsn. (light) arty. Ft. Ord, Calif., 1988-90; exec. to sec. of Army Office of Sec. of Army, Washington, 1990-92; asst. divsn. comdr. 24th infantry divsn. Ft. Stewart, Ga., 1992-93; asst. chief of staff C-3/J-3/G-3 UN Command/Combined Forces, U.S. Forces Korea, 1993-94; comdg. gen. 24th infantry divsn. Ft. Stewart, 1994-96; dep. comdr. in chief, chief of staff U.S. Pacific Command, Camp H.M. Smith, Hawaii, 1996-98; from instr. to asst. prof. dept. history, assoc. dir. instr. support br., exec. officer directorate of automated data processing audio-visual support U.S. Mil. Acad., West Point, N.Y., 1974-78. Decorated Def. Disting. Svc. medal, Disting. Svc. medal with oak leaf cluster, Silver Star, Legion of Merit with 4 oak leaf clusters, Bronze Star with V device (with oak leaf cluster), Bronze Star with 2 oak leaf clusters, Purple Heart, Def. Meritorious Svc. medal.

DEFRANTZ, ANITA, physical education educator. Recipient William G. Anderson award, 1992. Office: AAHPERD c/o Taba Iffland Dir Membership 1900 Association Dr Reston VA 20191-1598

DE FRIES, JOHN CLARENCE, behavioral genetics educator, institute administrator; b. Delrey, Ill., Nov. 26, 1934; s. Walter C. and Irene Mary (Lyon) De F.; m. Marjorie Jacobs, Aug. 18, 1956; children: Craig Brian, Catherine Ann. BS, U. Ill., 1956, MS, 1958, PhD, 1961. Asst. prof. U. Ill., Urbana, 1961-66, assoc. prof., 1966-67; rsch. fellow U. Calif., Berkeley, 1963-64; assoc. prof. behavioral genetics and psychology U. Colo., Boulder, 1967-70, prof., 1970—, dir. Inst. for Behavioral Genetics, 1981—. Author: (with G.E. McClearn) Introduction to Behavioral Genetics, 1973, (with Plomin and McClearn) Behavioral Genetics: A Primer, 1980, 3rd edit., 1997, (with R. Plomin) Origins of Individual Differences in Infancy, 1985; (with R. Plomin and D.W. Fulker) Nature and Nurture During Infancy and Early Childhood, 1988, Nature and Nurture During Middle Childhood, 1994; co-founder Behavior Genetics jour., 1970, mem. editl. adv. bd.; cons. editor Jour. Learning Disabilities. 1st lt. U.S. Army, 1957-65. Grantee in field. Fellow AAAS (sect. J), Internat. Acad. for Rsch. in Learning Disabilities; mem. Am. Psychol. Soc., Am. Soc. Human Genetics, Behavior Genetics Assn. (sec. 1974-77, pres. 1982-83, Th. Dobzhansky award for outstanding rsch. in field 1992), Internat. Soc. for Study of Ind. Differences, Internat. Dyslexia Assn., Rodin Remediation Acad. and Found. Office: U Colo Inst Behavioral Genetics CB447 Boulder CO 80309-0447

DE FRIESE, GORDON H., health services researcher; b. Trion, Ga., Apr. 25, 1942. BS, Middle Tenn. State U., 1963; MA, U. Ky., 1966, PhD, 1967. Instr. dept. behavioral sci. U. Ky. Med. Ctr., Lexington, 1966-67; asst. prof. sociology and social psychology Cornell U., Ithaca, N.Y., 1969-71; rsch. assoc. Cecil G. Sheps Ctr. for Health Svcs. Rsch. U. N.C., Chapel Hill, 1971—, asst. prof. sociology, 1971-77, asst. prof. family medicine Sch. Medicine, 1973-75, clin. assoc. prof. dept. epidemiology Sch. Pub. Health, 1978-82, assoc. prof. Sch. Medicine, 1976-82, prof. Sch. Medicine, 1982—, prof. Sch. Pub. Health, 1982—, prof. dept. dental ecology Sch. Dentistry, 1986—, co-dir. Robert Wood Johnson Found. Clin. Scholars Program, 1986—; dir. Cecil G. Sheps Ctr. Health Svcs. Rsch., Chapel Hill; adj. asst. prof. Sloan Inst. Hosp. Adminstrn.; dir. U.S. Army Armor Sch. Electives Divsn., Fort Knox, Ky., 1967-69; co-dir. Comprehensive Health Planning Tng. Program of the Dept. of Sociology and City and Regional Planning and the Sloan Inst. Hosp. Adminstrn., Cornell U., Ithaca, 1969-71; co-dir. grad. program in med. sociology Dept. Sociology, U. N.C., Chapel Hill, 1971-76; dir. Cecil G. Sheps Ctr. for Health Svcs. Rsch., U. N.C., Chapel Hill, 1973; dir. N.C. Coop. Health Info. Sys., N.C. Dept. Human Resources, 1974-78; staff cons. Joint Com. on Health, N.C. Gen. Assembly, 1973-74; chmn. Ad Hoc Com. to Plan for the Devel. of a N.C. Ctr. for Health Stats., 1973-74; cons. dept. human resources State N.C.; cons. N.C. Med. Peer Rev. Found., Inc., 1974, Internat. Assn. Bds. of Examiners in Optometry, 1974-82, N.C. Regional Med. Program, 1974, Rsch. Triangle Inst., Ctr. for Health Studies, 1974, others; mem. adv. com. Robert Wood Johnson Found. Program for Demonstration and Rsch. on Health Care Costs, 1986-91; mem. nat. adv. bd. Ctr. for Rural health Svcs., Policy and Rsch., U. N.C., 1987-89; mem. global adv. com. on health sys. rsch. WHO, Geneva, 1987—; v.p. for rsch. and evaluation Nat. Ctr. for Health Edn., 1987-89; chmn. adv. panel on preventive health svcs. for the elderly under medicare Office of Tech. Assessment, Congress of the U.S., 1988-89; bd. dirs. Profl. Examination Svc., Inc., N.Y.C., exec. com., 1989—; pres., CEO N.C. Inst. Medicine; cons. and presenter in field; numerous other career related activities. Author: (with B.D. Barker) Assessing Dental Manpower Requirements: Alternative Approaches for State and Local Planning, 1982; editor: (with J.W. Bawden) Planning for Dental Care on a Statewide Basis: The North Carolina Dental Manpower Project, 1981, (with T.C. Ricketts, J.S. Stein) Methodological Advances in Health Services Research, 1989; editor Health Svcs. Rsch., 1983—; co-editor (spl. issue) Jour. Family and Cmty. Health, 1982; assoc. editor Social Forces, 1971-76, Drugs in Health Care, 1974-76, Jour. Health and Social Behavior, 1985-87, Am. Jour. Health Promotion, 1986-92; mem. editl. bd. Health Care Mgmt. Rev., 1977-93, Med. Care, 1980-83, Internat. Jour. Health Scis., 1989—, Jour. Gerontology: Med. Scis., 1989-91, Comparative Health Policy: Nations, States, Cmtys., 1993—; book rev. editor Health Svcs. Rsch., 1979-84; contbr. chpts. to books and articles to profl. jours. Fellow N.Y. Acad. Medicine; mem. APHA (med. care sect.), NAS, Am. Sociol. Assn. (sect. on med. sociology), Inst. Medicine, Nat. Rural Health Assn., Assn. for Health Svcs. Rsch. (bd. dirs. 1982-90, pres.-elect 1983-85, pres. 1985-86), Found. for Health Svcs. Rsch. (bd. dirs. 1982—, pres. 1986-87), Soc. for Gen. Internal Medicine, Soc. for Pub. Health Policy, N.C. Pub. Health Assn. (sect. on epidemiology and stats.), Sigma Xi. Office: U NC Cecil G Sheps Ctr Health Svcs Rsch 725 Airport Rd # 7590 Chapel Hill NC 27514-5714*

DE FRONZO, JOSEPH MICHAEL, village manager; b. Dec. 10, 1948. M in Internat. Law and Bus., Columbia U., N.Y.C., 1978. CEO Importing and Distbg. of Wines, N.Y.C., 1992-97; exec. dir. to Senator Maltese N.Y. State Senate, Albany, 1989-97; dir. internat. divsn. Empire State Devel. Corp., N.Y.C., 1997-98; mgr. Village of Port Chester, N.Y., 1998—.

DEGANN, SONA IRENE, obstetrician-gynecologist, educator; b. Homs, Syria, 1952; d. Papken Stephan and Helen Irene (Wadsworth) Mugrditchian; m. A. David Degann, May 11, 1983; children: Alexander, Seta. BSc, Am. U. Beirut, Lebanon, 1975; MS, U. Mich., 1976; MD, Johns Hopkins U., 1983. Diplomate Am. Bd. Ob-Gyn. Resident in ob-gyn N.Y. Hosp., N.Y.C., 1983-87, staff; clin. instr. Cornell U. Sch. Medicine, N.Y.C., attending Ob-Gyn New York Hosp., N.Y.C. Fellow Am. Coll. Ob-Gyn.; mem. AMA, Med. Soc. State N.Y., N.Y. County Med. Soc.

DE GARCIA, LUCIA, marketing professional; b. Medellin, Colombia, June 26, 1942; came to the U.S., 1962; d. Enrique Giraldo Botero and Carolina (Vega) Estrada; m. Alvaro Garcia Osorio, July 30, 1962; children: Carolina Alexandra, Claudia Maria. BS, Nat. U., 1962. Engring. arch. designer Vorhees, Trindle & Nelson, Newport Beach, Calif., 1974-78; pres., CEO Elan Internat., Newport Beach, 1984—; speaker, lectr. on success, protocol in bus. with Latin Am., free trade agreement between U.S. and Mexico. Editor: Elan mag., 1988-90. Trustee Nat. U., Calif., 1989-93; area campaign mgr. Bush for Pres., Orange County, Calif., 1988, Christopher Cox for Congress, 1988, Pete Wilson for Gov., 1990, People to Watch, 1994; bd. dirs. ARC, 1985-90, Am. Cancer Rsch. Ctr., 1986—; active South Coast Repertory Theater, 1982—. Named Dama de Distincion U.S./Mexico Found., 1991, Hispanic Woman of Yr. LULAC, 1986, One on the 10 Most Influential Women in Orange County, Orange County Metropolitan, 1994, One of the Hispanic 100 Most Influential in the U.S., Hispanics Bus. Mag., 1994; recipient Internat. award U.S. Hispanic C. of C., 1992. Mem. U.S./Mexico Found. (trustee 1990—), Latin Bus. Assn. (bd. dirs. 1992-93), World Trade Ctr. Assn. Republican. Roman Catholic. Avocations: travel, arts, hiking, walking on the beach. Home: 17532 Wayne Ave Irvine CA 92614-6658 Office: Elan Internat 620 Newport Center Dr Fl 11 Newport Beach CA 92660-6420

DEGARIS, ANNESLEY HODGES, lawyer, educator; b. Birmingham, Ala., June 23, 1963; s. John A. Jr. and Lena Kate (Hodges) DeG.; m. Ashley H. DeGaris, July 1, 1995. BS in Pub. Adminstrn. magna cum laude, Samford U., 1985; JD magna cum laude, Cumberland Sch. Law, 1988; LLM, U. Melbourne, Australia, 1992. Bar: Ala. 1989, U.S. Dist. Ct. (no. dist.) Ala. 1989, U.S. Ct. Appeals (11th cir.) 1992, U.S. Dist. Ct. (mid. dist.) Ala. 1995, U.S. Dist. Ct. (so. dist.) Ala. 1996, U.S. Supreme Ct. 1995. Jud. law clk. U.S. Dist. Ct., Huntsville, Ala., 1988-89; staff atty. U.S. Ct. Appeals 11th Cir., Atlanta, 1991-93; assoc. Johnson & Cory, Birmingham, 1993-95; ptnr. Cory, Watson, Crowder & DeGaris, Birmingham, 1995—; adj. prof. Emory U. Sch. Law, Atlanta, 1992-93; prof. constnl. law Birmingham Sch. Law, 1993—. Casenote editor Cumberland Law Rev.; contbr. articles to profl. jours. Rotary Found. scholar Rotary Internat., Australia, 1990. Mem. ATLA, ABA, Ala. Trial Lawyers Assn., Vestavia Hills Rotary. Avocations: backpacking, travel. Office: Cory Watson Crowder & DeGaris Pc 2131 Magnolia Ave S Birmingham AL 35205-2808

DE GASPER, EDGAR EUGENE, food services consultant; b. Buffalo, N.Y., Oct. 16, 1922; s. James Joseph and Marie-Theresa (Vidan) De G.; married, 1951, divorced, 1972; m. Beatrice Louise Herskin, Dec. 22, 1976; children: Michael, Kathleen, Lisa, Mary Jo, Colleen, Rosemary. BS, Cornell U., 1942; MS, Canisius Coll., Buffalo, 1947; Doctorate (hon.), Nat. Assn. Food Equipment Mfr. Cert. Food Exec., Internat. Food Svc. Execs. Assn., Fla., 1973. Owner, mgr. Riviera Restaurant, Niagara Falls, N.Y., 1948-51; mgr. Brookfield Country Club, Clarence, N.Y., 1951-53, Bethlehem Steel Suprs. Club, Lackawanna, N.Y., 1953-54, Howard Johnson's Restaurants, Buffalo, 1955-56; dir. food svcs. City of Buffalo Bd. Edn., 1957-90; ret., 1990; food svc. cons., Western N.Y., 1991—. Capt., USMC, 1942-47, U.S. and Pacific. Named Hon. Rear Admiral, USN, Washington, 1986, Hon. Brigadier Gen., U.S. Army, Ft. Lee, Va., 1991, Hon. Brigadier Gen., USMC, Washington, 1992. Mem. Internat. Food Svc. Execs. Assn. (internat. pres. 1972-74, 86), N.Y. State Sch. Food Svc. Assn. (pres. 1968), Cornell Soc. Hotelmen (pres. 1971-72), Can. Food Svc. Execs. Assn. (dir. 1988—). Roman Catholic. Avocation: recreational flying. Home and Office: 348 Mill St Williamsville NY 14221-5118

DEGATANO, ANTHONY THOMAS, educational association administrator; b. Elizabeth, N.J., Apr. 2, 1950; s. Anthony James and Leonora (Malta) D.; m. Jeanne Marie Stevens, Apr. 15, 1972; 1 child, David. BA, Rider Coll., 1971; MA, Kean Coll., 1975. Cert. tchr., supr., prin., chief sch. adminstr. Elem. tchr. Elizabeth Bd. Edn., 1971-77, adult edn. instr., 1972-74, cons., 1977-81; dir. Union County Edn. Svc. Commn., Westfield, N.J., 1981-86, Ind. Child Study Teams, Inc., Jersey City, 1986—; bd. dirs. Ednl. In-Roads, Jersey City, 1997—; regional v.p. Sylvan Learning Systems, Inc., 1988—. Author: (curriculum guide) Alternate Math Program, 1980, (guide books) Teacher Handbook, 1982, Teacher Resource Book, 1983; editor: Mathematics Series, 1992. 1st pres., founder Union County Commn. Adminstrs. Assn., 1983-86; pres. Herbert Hoover PTO, 1991-92; chmn. edn.-budget subcom. Citizen Adv. Com., Edison, N.J.,m 1992; mem. N.J. Edn. Commr.'s Adv. Com., Trenton, 1988—, PTA/PTO Adv. Coun., Edison, 1991-92; chmn. local edn. agy. Data Rev. Collection and Approval Com., 1992—. Named Outstanding Young Man of Am., U.S. Jaycees, 1983; recipient Recognition for Svc., N.J. Commr. of Edn., 1990, Union County Edn. Svc. Commn. Adminstrs. Assn., 1986. Mem. N.J. Assn. Fed. Program Adminstrs., ASCD, N.J. Coun. Am. Pvt. Edn. Avocations: reading, fishing, scuba diving, gardening, skiing. Home: 148 Howard Ave Edison NJ 08837-3030 Office: ICST Inc 377 Danforth Ave Jersey City NJ 07305-1904

DEGEEST, ELAINE BECK, artist; b. Burlington, Iowa, Dec. 2, 1960; d. Donald Louis and Virginia Clara (Taeger) Beck; m. Randy Scott DeGeest, Mar. 22, 1989; children: Hannah, Jonathan. BA, U. No. Iowa, 1983. Cert. social studies, art tchr., Iowa. Social studies tchr. Twin Cedars H.S., Bussey, Iowa, 1983-86; Knoxville (Iowa) Jr.H.S., 1987-90; artist self-employed Oskaloosa, Iowa, 1990—. Commd. numerous portraits. Bd. dirs. YWCA, Oskaloosa, 1991-93; mem. Main St. Oskaloosa Design Com., 1991-93; sec. Ctrl. United Meth. Ch. Adminstrv. Coun., Oskaloosa, 1996-98. Recipient 1st Pl. Art on the Square, Main St. Oskaloosa, 1996, Pella ARts Coun., 1997, 1st Pl. Family Art Festival, Indian Hills C.C., Ottumwa, Iowa, 1997. Paintings include It's a Race between Education of Catastrophe, 1993, Htel Lobby, 1994, Girl Missing, 1995, Kids, 1991. Avocations: reading, bicycling, cooking.

DEGENER, CAROL MARIE-LAURE, lawyer; b. N.Y.C., Sept. 4, 1961; d. John Michael and Marie-Laure Murat (Frank) D. BA, Columbia U., 1983, MA, 1984; JD, Harvard U., 1987. Bar: Mass. 1988, N.Y. 1990. Assoc. corp. fin. Goldman Sachs & Co., N.Y.C., 1987-89; assoc. corp. dept. Donovan Leisure Newton & Irvine, N.Y.C., 1989-95, Seward & Kissel, N.Y.C., 1996—. Mem. N.Y. State Bar Assn. (com. on securities regulation 1993—), Bar Assn. City N.Y. (com. on corp. law 1991—), New York County Lawyers' Assn. (com. on securities and exchs. 1991—), Harvard Law Sch. Assn. N.Y. Office: Seward & Kissel 1 Battery Park Plz Fl 20 New York NY 10004-1485

DEGENFORD, JAMES EDWARD, electrical engineer, educator; b. Bloomington, Ill., June 11, 1938; s. Fred Eldon and Edna D.; m. Sharon Lee Sloop, Mar. 14, 1959; children: James Todd, Rebecca Lynn, Connie Marie, Robert Scott, Sarah Anne, Amy Elizabeth. BSEE, U. Ill., 1960, MSEE, 1961, PhD, 1964. Registered profl. engr., Md. Rsch. assoc. U. Ill., Urbana, 1964-65; sr. engr. Westinghouse Electric Corp., Balt., 1965-70, fellow engr., 1970-76, advisory engr., 1976-83, mgr., 1984-96; elec. engr. Northrop Grumman Corp., Balt., 1996—; lectr. U. Md., College Park, 1965-70. Contbr. numerous articles, papers to profl. jours.; 6 patents in field. Sloan Found. fellow, 1960, Ford Found. fellow, 1961, U. Ill. Fellow IEEE; mem. Microwave Theory and Techniques Soc. (sec.-treas. adminstrv. com. 1975-76, fin. chmn. 1976-85). Republican. Presbyterian. Avocations: music, electronics, woodworking. Office: Northrop Grumman Corp PO Box 1521 Baltimore MD 21203

DEGENHARDT, ROBERT ALLAN, architectural and engineering firm executive; b. Kearney, Nebr., May 29, 1943; s. Robert Franklin and Florence Elizabeth (Spohnheimer) D.; children: Barry, Christopher, Kathleen. BSME, U. Nebr., 1965, MSME, 1968. Registered profl. engr., D.C. and all states except Alaska and Hawaii. Project engr. Davis & Wilson Architects and Engrs., Lincoln, Nebr., 1964-68, White Sands (N.Mex.) Missile Range, 1968-70, Sundstrand Aviation, Rockford, Ill., 1970-74; dir. engring. Davis, Fenton, Stange, Darling, Architects and Engrs., Lincoln, 1974-77; v.p. mech. engring. Durrant Engrs. Inc., Madison, Wis., 1977-1980; dir. mech. engring . Ellerbe Assocs. Inc., Mpls., 1980-82, dir. archtl./engring. svcs., 1982-83, v.p., dir. ops., 1983-85; sr. v.p., dir. Ellerbe Becket Inc., Washington, 1985-89; exec. v.p., COO Ellerbe Becket Co., Mpls., 1989-93, pres., COO, 1993-94, pres., CEO, 1994-98, CEO, 1998—. Mem. Minn. Ctr. for Corp. Responsibility, 1993—. 1st lt. U.S. Army, 1968-70. Mem. AIA Large Firm Roundtable, Am. Cons. Engrs. Coun. Design Profls. Coalition (officer 1992-98), Constrn. Industry Roundtable, U.S. C. of C. (internat. polic com.), Sigma Xi, Pi Tau Sigma. Republican. Lutheran. Avocations: backpacking, fly-fishing. Office: Ellerbe Becket Co 800 Lasalle Ave Minneapolis MN 55402-2014

DE GENNARO, RICHARD, retired library director, library advisor; b. New Haven, Mar. 2, 1926; s. Ralph and Acquilina (Pedicini) De G.; m. Birgit M. Erikson, June 12, 1953; children: Ralph, George, Christina. BA, Wesleyan U., 1951, MA, 1960; MS in LS, Columbia U., 1956; postgrad., Univs. Paris, Madrid and Perugia, 1951-55; grad. Advanced Mgmt. Program, Harvard U., 1971; DHL (hon.), Wabash Coll., 1991. Jr. acct. Atlas Constructors, Morocco, 1952-53; reference librarian N.Y. Pub. Libr., 1956-58, dir., 1987-90; successively reference librarian, asst. dir., assoc. univ. librarian systems devel., sr. assoc. univ. librarian Harvard U. Libr., 1958-70; dir. librs. U. Pa., 1970-86, adj. prof. English, 1979-86; libr. Harvard Coll., 1990-96; vis. prof. Grad. Libr. Sch., U. So. Calif., 1968-69; cons. libr. bldgs., tech. and mgmt.; mem. overseers com. to visit libr., Harvard U.; cons. MIT, Johns Hopkins U.; mem. adv. bd. Chem. Abstracts Svc., 1967-70; mem. Palinet bd. Union Libr. Catalogue, 1970—; mem. com. internat. sci. and tech. info. programs NAS-NRC, 1977-79; mem. Mellon Found. JSTOR Bd., 1995—; sr. libr. advisor JSTOR; mem. governing bd. Rsch. Librs. Group, 1979-89, sr. vis. fellow, 1980-81, chmn., 1984-95; Bowker lectr., 1979; Lazerow lectr., 1984. Author: Shifting Gears, Information Technology and the Academic Library, 1984, Libraries, Technology, and the Information Marketplace, Selected Papers, 1987; contbr. articles to profl. jours. Bd. dirs. Ctr. for Rsch. Librs., 1977-81; trustee U. Pa. Press, 1978-82. With USN, 1942-46. Recipient Disting. Alumnus award Wesleyan U., 1991; Hugh Atkinson award, 1993; named Acad. Rsch. Libr. of Yr., 1991; Coun. Libr. Resources fellow, 1971; Rockefeller Found. Ctr. fellow, Bellagio, Italy, 1981; info. tech. fellow U. Edinburgh, 1984. Mem. Assn. Rsch. Librs. (pres. 1975, dir. 1973-76), ALA (pres. info. sci. and automation div. 1975), Am. Soc. Info. Soc. (Melvil Dewey medal 1986), Century Assn. Club, Grolier Club, Harvard Club. Home: 70 Turtle Bay Dr Branford CT 06405-4977

DE GENNES, PIERRE-GILLES, physicist, educator; b. Paris, Oct. 24, 1932. Ed, Ecole Normale Superieure, PhD. Rsch. scientist Centre d'Etudes Nucleaires de Saclay, 1955-59; prof. solid state physics U. Paris, Orsay, 1961-71; prof. Coll. de France, Paris, 1971—; dir. Ecole de Physique et Chimie, Paris, 1976—; sci. adv. for chem. physics Rhone Poulenc, France, 1988—. Author: Superconductivity of Metals and Alloys, 1965, The Physics of Liquid Crystals, 1973, Scaling Concepts in Polymer Physics, 1979, Simple Views on Condensed Matter, 1992-97, Les Objets Fragiles, 1994. Ensign French Navy, 1959-61. Recipient Nobel prize in physics, 1991. Mem. AAAS, Académie des Sciences, Dutch Acad. Scis., Royal Soc., Ukrainian Acad. Scis., Brazilian Acad. Scis. Nat. Acad. Scis. Avocations: skiing, drawing, hiking, windsurfing. Office: Ecole de Physique et Chimie, 10 rue Vauquelin, 75005 Paris France

DEGENSHEIN, JAN, architect, planner; b. Bklyn., Sept. 15, 1946; s. Harry and Beverly (Oppenheimer) D.; m. Lynne Sheren, Sept. 1, 1968 (div. Mar. 1978); 1 child, Britta; m. Nadja Hoyer-Booth, June 1, 1980; children: Oleg, Anya. BS Archtl. Scis., Washington U., 1967; BArch, MS in Planning, Pratt Inst., 1970; postgrad., CUNY, 1979-84. Registered architect, N.Y., N.J., Conn., Pa., Vt.; cert. NCARB. Associate architect R.C. Weinberg & Assocs., N.Y.C., 1968-70, Seiler Nakrosis Kerner, Liberty, N.Y., 1970-72; v.p. Degan Enterprises Inc., New City, N.Y., 1973-78; pres., prin. Jan Degenshein Architect-Planner, New City, 1975-83; pres. Degenshein Denker Assocs. P.C., Nyack, N.Y., 1983-88, Degenshein Denker Bodnar P.C., Nyack, 1988-91; prin., pres. Jan Degenshein Architects-Planners, Nyack, N.Y., 1991—; guest critic Pratt Inst. Sch. Architecture, 1982, CCNY Sch. Architecture, 1990. Author: Atlantic-Schermehorn Corridor, 1970. Chmn., com. mem. Rockland County (N.Y.) Art in Pub. Places, 1987—; v.p., trustee Blue Rock Sch., West Nyack, 1989-95; mem. bd. advisors Martin Luther King Multi-Purpose Ctr., Spring Valley, N.Y., 1991—; vol., mem. bd. advisors, bd. dirs. Vol. Counseling Svcs., New City, 1994—; mem. environ. adv. coun. U.S. Rep. Benjamin Gilman, 1993-96; mem. campaign cabinet Arts Fund for Rockland, Rockland County, 1990-92; mem. N.Y. State Bldg Ofcls. Conf., 1994—, Interfaith Forum on Religious Art and Architecture, 1983—, Arts Coun. of Rockland, 1986—; nominating com. Rockland County coun. Girl Scouts U.S., 1991-94; coord. Leadership Rockland Econ. Devel. Day, 1995—, bd. dirs., 1995—, sec., 1999—, mem. selections com., fin. com.; mem. Rockland Mcpl. Planning Fedn., 1990—, assoc. dir., 1997—, mem. bd. dirs. Housing Action Coun., 1998—; mem. retention and expansion com. Rockland Econ. Devel. Corp., 1996—. Recipient archtl. excellence award Orange County Bd. Realtors, 1988, 89, Rockland County Execs. Arts award, 1995, nominee, 1994. Mem. AIA (honor award for archtl. excellence Westchester/Mid-Hudson 1987, 88, 92, 94, 96, cmty., design awards Westchester-Mid-Hudson chpt. 1987, 88, 94, 96, Rockland County Beatification award 1992, 94), Am. Inst. Cert. Planners, Am. Planning Assn., Rockland County Builders Assn. (Assoc. of Yr. 1978, Builder of Yr. 1980), Leadership Rockland (dir. 1994—, pres. alumni assn. 1994-96), Rockland Bus. Exchange (v.p. , pres. membership com. 1993-97), Rockland Coalition for Democracy and Freedom (dir. 1995), Am. Forum for Global Edn. (advisor 1995-97), Hist. Soc. Rockland, Computer and Telecom. Initiative Rockland (chairperson nominating com. 1996, bd. dirs. 1997—), Rockland Bus. Assn. (mem. svcs. com. 1996, chair amb.'s com. 1996-98, comms. and advocacy com. 1997—, bd. dirs. 1997—), Nyacks C. of C. (v.p. 1988-89). Avocations: graphic arts, cooking, gardening, golf, tennis. Office: 205 S Broadway Nyack NY 10960-4425

DE GEORGE, LAWRENCE JOSEPH, diversified company executive; b. N.Y.C., May 6, 1916; s. Frank Phillip and Frances (Cavallo) DeG.; m. Florence A. Efel, Dec. 18, 1943; children: Lawrence F., Peter R. BSEE, Princeton U., 1936; MS, MIT, 1938. Assoc. prof. elec. engring. Columbia U., 1938-39; field engr. Radio Engring. Lab., N.Y.C., 1939-41; pres. Times Wire and Cable Co., Inc., div. Internat. Silver Co., Wallingford, Conn., 1946; also v.p., dir. Times Wire and Cable div., 1958-64, pres., 1964-68; v.p., dir.

Insilco Corp., Meridan, Conn., 1968-72; exec. v.p. Insilco Corp., 1972-77, vice chmn., 1976-77; chmn., pres. Times Fiber Communications, Inc., Meriden, 1977-84, chmn., chief exec. officer, 1985-92; chmn., chief exec. officer LPL Techs. Inc., Wallingford, Conn., 1985-97, Amphenol Corp., Wallingford, Conn., 1987-97; chmn., CEO DeG Capital Ptnrs. Ltd., Wallingford; dir. Travelers Equities Fund, Inc., Hartford, Conn. Lt. comdr. USNR, 1941-46. Republican. Clubs: Princeton (N.Y.C.); Farms Country, Wallingford. Home: 176 Spyglass Ln Jupiter FL 33477-4037 Office: DeG Capital Ptnrs Ltd Ste 410 140 Intracoastal Pointe Dr Jupiter FL 33477-5094

DE GERENDAY, LACI ANTHONY, sculptor, educator; b. Budapest, Hungary, Aug. 17, 1911; came to U.S., 1912; s. László and Ilona (Jiraszek) de G.; m. Mary Ellen Lord, 1939 (dec. 1976); 1 child, Lynn; m. Elisabeth Gordon Chandler, May 12, 1979. Student, S.D. State Sch. Mines, Rapid City, 1929-30, Ursinus Coll., Collegeville, Pa., 1931-32, Nat. Acad. Design, N.Y.C., 1932-34, Beaux Arts Inst., N.Y.C., 1934-35. Prof. Lyme (Conn.) Acad. Fine Arts, 1979—; sculptor, 1936—. Exhbns. include Nat. Acad. Design, Pa. Acad., Boston Mus., Pa. Mus., Mus. San Francisco, Mus. Ariz., Cin. Mus., Mus. Rhode Island, Mus. Modern Art, Grand Ctrl. Galleries, Schonemann Gallery, Ferargil Gallery, Nat. Sculpture Soc., Arch. League, Corning Glass, N.J. Art Mus., N.Y. Coliseum, Salmagundi Club, Rockefeller Ctr., Loeb Ctr. NYU, Acad. Arts Letters, Lever House, Allied Artists, French Gallery, Smithsonian Inst., Nat. Arts Club, Sculpture Ctr., Am. Bible Soc., Hudson Valley Arts Assn., Nat. Collection Fine Arts, Washington, Mus. Fine Arts, Springfield, Mass., Foothills Art Ctr., Golden Colo., Florence Griswold Mus., Old Lyme, Conn., Madison (Conn.) Gallery, Old State House, Hartford, Conn., Cathedral St. John Divine, N.Y.C., Fedn. Medaille, British Mus., London, Am.'s Tower, N.Y.C., Brookfield Zoo, Chgo., Newington-Cropsey Found. Gallery, Hasting-on-Hudson, N.Y., Slater Mus., Nat. Acad. Mus., N.Y., 1998, Pub. Sculpture by Nat. Academicians, 1998; two man shows include Art Ctr, Old Lyme, Wall Focus Gallery, Chester, Conn.; prin. works include wood carving Courthouse, Aberdeen, S.D., bronze medal Hall of Fame Great Ams., NYU, bronze relief Torrington, Conn., sculpture Nat. Gallery Art, Washington, Gold medal Soc. Elec. Engrs., wood relief Post Office, Tell City, Ind., bronze relief Chgo., bronze equestrian relief Mus. Algiers, Algeria, mermaid fountain N.Y.C. Garden, bronze relief portrait Bklyn. C.C., N.Y.C., bronze archl. relief Modern Art Foundry, N.Y.C., silver coin Nat. Commemorative Soc., bronze medal Soc. Medallists, others. With U.S. Mil., 1943-46. Recipient Citation, City of N.Y., First prize N.J. Art Assn., Radding award Mus. Fine Arts, Springfield, 1977, Silver medal Allied Artists Am., 1977, Wendel Clinedinst award, 1982, 4 Battle Stars, Bronze Arrowhead U.S. Mil. Fellow Nat. Sculpture Soc. (mem. coun., Lindsey Morris Meml. award 1955, 81, 91, Bennett prize 1963, Roman Bronze Foundry award 1980, John Spring Art Founder award 1992); mem. Nat. Acad. Design (academician, Ellen Speyer prize 1947, 63, 91, Daniel Chester French Gold medal 1995), Nat. Arts Club (Salzman award 1994), Hudson Valley Arts Assn. (Mrs. John Newington award 1979, Elliot Liskin Meml. award 1995), Nat. Soc. Lit. Arts, Am. Medallic Soc., Fedn. Internat. Medaille. Republican. Avocations: golf, walking, hiking, horseback riding. Home & Studio: 2 Mill Pond Ln Old Lyme CT 06371-1118

DEGERSTROM, JAMES MARVIN, retired engineering executive; b. Owosso, Mich., Aug. 9, 1933; s. John Marcellus and Emma Judith (Folkadahl) D.; m. Ann Blandford, July 3, 1964. BSME, Mich. State U., 1955; MBA, DePaul U., 1966. Cert. plant engr., 1991. Adminstrv. asst. Sunbeam Corp., Chgo., 1955-61; mfg. supt. Internat. Register Co., Inc., Chgo., 1961-65; sr. engr. Kitchens of Sara Lee, Inc., Deerfield, Ill., 1965-71; pres. Edmanson Bock Caterers, Chgo., 1972; mgr. bldg. ops. Jewel Cos., Inc., Barrington, Ill., 1972-81; dir. plant ops. Copley Meml. Hosp., Aurora, Ill., 1981-86, Little Co. Mary Hosp., Evergreen Park, Ill., 1986-88; dir. facilities Oak Park Hosp., 1988-89; mgr. plant engring. Honeywell, Inc., Joliet, Ill., 1989-90; dir. facilities mgmt. South Suburban Hosp., Hazel Crest, Ill., 1990-98; ret., 1998; bd. dirs., treas. Credit Union, Kitchens of Sara Lee, 1966-70. With USAF, 1957-65. Mem. Am. Inst. Indsl. Engrs., Am. Inst. Plant Engrs. (sec. 1977-79, pres. chpt. 5 1991, cert. of recognition Am. Inst. Plant Engrs. Conf. 1977), Toastmasters (dis. officer 1982-86, pres. 1981, area gov. 1982, lt. gov. 1983-84, dist. gov. 1984-85). Home: 102 Knollwood Ct Oak Brook IL 60523-1518

DE GETTE, DIANA LOUISE, lawyer, congresswoman; b. Tachikawa, Japan, July 29, 1957; came to U.S., 1957; d. Richard Louis and Patricia Anne (Rose) De G.; m. Lino Sigismondo Lipinsky de Orlov, Sept. 15, 1984; children: Raphaela Anne, Francesca Louise. BA magna cum laude, The Colo. Coll., 1979; JD, NYU, 1982. Bar: Colo. 1982, U.S. Dist. Ct. Colo. 1982, U.S. Ct. Appeals (10th cir.) 1984, U.S. Supreme Ct. 1989. Dep. state pub. defender Colo. State Pub. Defender, Denver, 1982-84; assoc. Coghill & Goodspeed, P.C., Denver, 1984-86; sole practice Denver, 1986-93; of counsel McDermott & Hansen, Denver, 1993-96; mem. Colo. Ho. of Reps., 1992-96, asst. minority leader, 1995-96; mem. U.S. Ho. of Reps. (Colo.), 1997—. Editor: (mag.) Trial Talk, 1989-92. Mem. Mayor's Mgmt. Rev. Com., Denver, 1983-84; resolutions chair Denver Dem. Party, 1986; bd. dirs. Root-Tilden Program, NYU Sch. Law, N.Y.C., 1986-92; bd. trustees, alumni trustee Colo. Coll., Colorado Springs, 1988-94. Recipient Root-Tilden scholar NYU Sch. Law, N.Y.C., 1979, Vanderbilt medal, 1982. Mem. Colo. Bar Assn. (bd. govs. 1989-91), Colo. Trial Lawyers Assn. (bd. dirs., exec. com. 1986-92), Colo. Women's Bar Assn., Denver Bar Assn., Phi Beta Kappa, Pi Gamma Mu. Avocations: reading, backpacking, gardening. Office: McDermott & Hansen 1890 Gaylord St Denver CO 80206-1211

DEGHETT, STEPHANIE COYNE, writer, educator; b. Saranac Lake, N.Y., Aug. 31, 1951; d. Ward Robert and Alice Mae (Marshall) C.; m. Victor John DeGhett, Aug. 2, 1980; 1 child, Torie Rose. BA magna cum laude, SUNY, Potsdam, 1976; MA, U. Vt., 1981. Asst. coord. Sch.-within-a-Sch. Potsdam Coll., 1977; manuscript reviewer ABT Assocs., Cambridge, Mass., 1978; cons. Grad. Studies Office/SUNY, Potsdam, 1978; ednl. coord. CETA Title VI Projects, Potsdam, 1978; grad. tchg. fellow U. Vt., Burlington, 1979-81; prof., writing program SUNY, Potsdam, 1981—. Poetry editor Blueline mag., Potsdam, 1987—; contbr. poetry to River of Dreams: American Poems, 1990, New Eng. Rev., 1994; showed photographs at Del Bello Gallery, Toronto, 1991. Reading vol. Lawrence Ave. Elem. Sch., Potsdam, 1995—; bd. dirs. Environ. Mgmt. Coun., Canton, N.Y., 1984-86. Mem. Nat. Coun. Tchrs. English, Assn. Tchrs. Advanced Composition, SUNY Writers Coun. Democrat. Episcopalian. Avocations: skiing, gardening, photography, birding. Home: 25 Wheeler Rd Potsdam NY 13676-3404 Office: SUNY at Potsdam Pierrepont Ave Potsdam NY 13676

DEGHETTO, KENNETH ANSELM, engineering and construction company executive; b. Clifton, N.J., Apr. 1, 1924; s. Anselm and Linda (Zanetti) DeG.; m. Helen Zschack, Nov. 5, 1944; children: Donna, Glenn. B.S., U.S. Mcht. Marine Acad., 1943; B.Mech. Engring., Rensselaer Poly. Inst., 1950. Registered profl. engr., N.Y., N.J., Wash., Fla., Alaska. With Foster Wheeler Corp., Livingston, N.J., 1951-96, dir., 1972-96, v.p., 1973-76, exec. v.p., 1976-84, chmn. bd., 1983-87; chmn. bd. Foster Wheeler Internat. Corp., Livingston, N.J., 1975-85, also bd. dirs.; brd. dirs. adv. brd., Mack-Cali Realty Corp. Mem. Rensselaer Sch. of Engring. adv bd., nat. chmn. U.S. Mcht. Marine Acad. Kings Point Challenge; chmn. Am. Found. for U. of the W.I.; vice-chmn. Bus. Coun. for Internat. Understanding. Lt. USNR, 1943-46. Fellow ASME, Brit. Inst. Mech. Engrs.; mem. Nat. Assn. Corrosion Engrs., Sigma Xi, Tau Beta Pi, Tau Pi Sigma. Lutheran. Clubs: Royal and Ancient Golf (St. Andrews, Scotland); Montclair (N.J.) Country, Brit. Engring. Golfing Soc. (capt. 1990). Home: 42 Cornell Dr Livingston NJ 07039-5518 Office: Foster Wheeler Corp Perryville Corp Park Clinton NJ 08809

DEGIACOMO, ROBERT J., federal judge. Former judge and chief judge, 1st jud. dist. N.Mex. dist. Ct.; magistrate judge U.S. Dist. Ct. N.Mex., Albuquerque. Address: PO Box 1549 Albuquerque NM 87103-1549

DEGIOVANNI-DONNELLY, ROSALIE FRANCES, biology researcher, educator; b. Bklyn., Nov. 22, 1926; d. Frank and Rose (Quartuccio) DeGiovanni; m. Edward Francis Donnelly, Sept. 23, 1961; children: Edward F. Jr., Francis M. BA, Bklyn. Coll., 1947, MA, 1953; PhD, Columbia U., 1961. Adj. prof. microbiology and genetics George Washington U., Washington, 1968—; research biologist FDA, Washington, 1968-88. Contbr. articles to profl. jours. Recipient Merit award FDA, 1970. Mem. AAAS, AAUW, Italian Cultural Soc., Environ. Mutagen Soc., N.Y. Acad. Scis., Am. Soc. Microbiology, Sigma Xi, Sigma Delta Epsilon. Democrat. Roman Catholic. Clubs: McLean Indoor. Avocations: theater, swimming, tennis, travel, photography. Home: 1712 Strine Dr Mc Lean VA 22101-4744 Office: George Washington U Microbiology Dept Washington DC 20052

DEGIUSTI, DOMINIC LAWRENCE, medical science educator, academic administrator; b. Treviso, Italy, Mar. 30, 1911; came to U.S., 1916, naturalized, 1925; s. Angelo L. and Angela (DeNegri) DeG.; m. Dianna Dobrzechowski, June 28, 1974; children—Lenore (Mrs. Antoine Noujaim), Angelo, Peter. B.S., Coll. of St. Thomas, St. Paul, 1936; M.S., U. Mich., 1938; Ph.D. (DuPont fellow), U. Wis., 1943. Instr. Coll. of St. Thomas, 1936-38, asst. prof., 1942-43, 46-47; asst. in helminthology U. Mich. Biol. Sta., 1939-41, 46-51; instr., asst. prof. NYU Coll. Medicine, N.Y.C., 1943-46; research assoc. U. Minn. Coll. Medicine, 1946-47; asst. prof. Catholic U. Am., Washington, 1947-49; assoc. prof. dept. biology Wayne State U., Detroit, 1949-57; prof. dept. biology and Sch. Medicine dept. comparative medicine Wayne State U., 1957-81, prof. emeritus, 1981—, chmn. dept. biology, 1967-72, chmn. dept. comparative medicine, 1978-79; mem. staff dept. pathology Detroit Gen. Hosp. Hutzel Hosp. Markle Found. fellow to Central Am., 1945; Fulbright Research fellow to Naples, Italy Zool. Sta., 1952; La. State U. fellow to Caribbean, 1957. Fellow N.Y. Acad. Scis., AAAS, Am. Inst. Fishery Research Biologists; mem. Am. Soc. Parasitologist (mem. council 1964-67), Am. Soc. Tropical Medicine and Hygiene, Am. Soc. Zoology, Am. Soc. Protozoology, Am. Micros. Soc. (mem. council 1963-69, v.p. 1965, pres. 1966), Helminthology Soc. Washington, Mich. Acad. Sci., Arts and Letters, Mich. Entomol. Soc. (pres. 1954), Sigma Xi. Home: 20440 Balfour St Apt 1 Harper Woods MI 48225-1543

DEGNAN, AMY MARIE, journalist; b. Mpls., Dec. 27, 1974; d. John and Maureen (McCanna) D. Grad., U. St. Thomas, 1997. Rschr. 48 Hours CBS News, Washington, 1997; reporter Sta. KDLH-TV, 1998—. Mem. Soc. Profl. Journalists. Avocations: running, singing, guitar, karate, youth leadership. Home: 9946 Balmoral Ln Eden Prairie MN 55347-3126

DEGNAN, JOHN JAMES, III, physicist; b. Phila., Dec. 10, 1945; s. John James Jr. and Ruth Dolores (Vece); m. Adele Susan Henry, June 27, 1969; children: Adam John, Andrew Paul. BS in Physics, Drexel U., 1968; MS in Physics, U. Md., 1970, PhD in Physics, 1979. Student trainee NASA Goddard Space Flight Ctr., Greenbelt, Md., 1964-67, physicist, 1968-72, sr. physicist, 1972-79, sect. head, 1979-89, dep. mgr. crustal dynamics project, 1989-93, head office space geodesy and altimetry projects, 1993-96, head office geosci. tech., 1996—; instr. Drexel U., Phila., 1967-68; assoc. mem. Adv. Group on Electron Devices, 1980-85, dep. mem. 1985-89; adj. prof. physics Am. U., Washington, 1988—; chmn. CSTG SLR/LLR Subcommn., 1992-98, Internat. Laser Ranging Svc., 1998— (and governing bd. 1998—); tech. bd. Wegener, 1992—, Am. Geog. Union Steering Com. for Geodesy, 1998—. Contbr. articles to profl. jours. Mem. Common Cause, Annapolis, Md., 1970—; v.p., treas. Pasadena Theatre Co., Md., 1982—. Drexel Bd. Trustees scholar, 1963; recipient Marple-Newtown Sch. Dist. Hall of Fame award, Disting. Alumnus, 1989, Moe I. Schneebaum Meml. award for engring. NASA/GSFC, 1987. Mem. IEEE (sr.), Optical Soc. Am., Am. Phys. Soc., Am. Geophys. Union (steering com. geodesy 1998—), Planetary Soc., Laser Comm. Soc. (charter), Nat. Space Club, Sierra Club, Sigma Pi Sigma, Sigma Pi. Roman Catholic. Home: 928 Barracuda Cove Ct Annapolis MD 21401-4719 Office: NASA Goddard Space Flight Ctr Greenbelt MD 20771

DEGNAN, JOHN MICHAEL, lawyer; b. Mpls., Apr. 2, 1948; s. John F. and Lorraine A. D.; m. Barbara B. Degnan; children: John Patrick, Amy Marie, David Charles. BA, U. Minn., 1970; JD, William Mitchell Coll. Law, 1976. Bar: Minn. 1976, U.S. Dist. Ct. Minn. 1976, U.S. Ct. Appeals (8th cir.) Minn. 1976, U.S. Supreme Ct. 1976. Ins. underwriter Marsh & McLennan, Mpls., 1973-76; lawyer, pres. Bassford, Heckt, Lockhart, Tresdell, Briggs & Mullin, P.A., Mpls., 1976—; lectr. in field. Bd. dirs. Hennepin County Pub. Libraries, 1980-84, Storefront Youth Action, 1981-83, Mediation Ctr., 1991—. 1st lt. U.S. Army, 1971-72, Vietnam. Mem. ABA, Minn. State Bar Assn. (ins. com., lectr. convs. 1984-85, civil trial cert. governing coun., cert. trial specialist), Hennepin County Bar Assn. (mem. professionalism com.), Nat. Bd. Trial Advocacy (cert. civil trial specialist), Am. Bd. Trial Advocates, Minn. Def. Lawyers Assn (bd. dirs. 1986—, pres. 1990-91), Minn. Soc. Hosp. Attys., Def. Rsch. Inst., Am. Soc. Law and Medicine, Richfield Jaycees (past pres.). Avocations: running, tennis, golf, boating, sports. Office: Bassford Lockhart Tresdell & Briggs 3550 Multifoods Tower Minneapolis MN 55402

DEGNAN, MARTIN J., rubber products corporation executive, lawyer. BA, U. Toledo, 1970, JD, 1974. Bar: Ohio 1974. Assoc. counsel Toledo Trust Co., 1974-78; assoc. counsel Rubbermaid Inc., Wooster, Ohio, 1978-88, assoc. gen. counsel, asst. sec., 1988-89, v.p., assoc. gen. counsel, asst. sec., 1989—. Office: Rubbermaid Inc 1147 Akron Rd Wooster OH 44691-2596

DEGNITZ, DOROTHY ELSIE, nurse; b. Wis., Aug. 13, 1936; d. Fredrick William and Elsie Emily (Lawrenz) D. BSN, Northwestern U., 1959; cert., Frontier Sch. Nursing, 1968; diploma in nursing edn., Armidale (Australia) Coll., 1981; MA in Social Sci., Azusa (Calif.) Pacific U., 1986. RN, Wis. Instr. psychiat. nursing Sch. Nursing, Evanston (Ill.) Hosp., 1960-66; missionary nurse tchr. Bd. for Mission Svcs., St. Louis, 1966-67, 68-70, Papua New Guinea, 1971-87; nursing supr. infirmary and nights Bethesda Luth. Home and Svcs., Watertown, Wis., 1987-94, part-time staff nurse, 1994—. Mem. Nat. League for Nursing, Wis. Nurse's Assn. (membership com.). Home: 1202 S 9th St Watertown WI 53094-6604

DE GOFF, VICTORIA JOAN, lawyer; b. San Francisco, Mar. 2, 1945; d. Sidney Francis and Jean Frances (Alexander) De G.; m. Peter D. Coppelman, May 2, 1971 (div. Dec. 1978); m. Richard Sherman, June 16, 1980. BA in Math. with great distinction, U. Calif., Berkeley, 1967, JD, 1972. Bar: Calif. 1972, U.S. Dist. Ct. (no. dist.) Calif. 1972, U.S. Ct. Appeals 1972, U.S. Supreme Ct. 1989; cert. appellate law specialist, 1996. Rsch. atty. Calif. Ct. Appeal, San Francisco, 1972-73; Reginald Heber Smith Found. fellow San Francisco Neighborhood Legal Assistance Found., 1973-74; assoc. Field, De Goff, Huppert & McGowan, San Francisco, 1974-77; pvt. practice Berkeley, Calif., 1977-80; ptnr. De Goff and Sherman, Berkeley, 1980—; lectr. continuing edn. of bar, Calif., 1987, 90-92, U. Calif. Boalt Hall Sch. Law, Berkeley, 1981-85, dir. appellate advocacy, 1992; cons. Calif. Civil Practice Procedure, Bancroft Whitney, 1992; mem. Appellate Law Adv. Commn., 1995; apptd. applicant evaluation and nomination com. for State Bar Ct. by Calif. Supreme Ct., 1995; pvt. atty., clk. ct. com. Calif. Ct. Appeals, 1997-99; mem. com. on appellate practice ABA, 1997. Author: (with others) Matthew Bender's Treatise on California Torts, 1985. Apptd. to adv. com. Calif. Jud. Coun. on Implementing Proposition 32, 1984-85; mem. adv. bd. Hastings Coll. Trial and Appellate Adv., 1984-91; expert 20/20 vision project, commn. on future cts. Jud. Coun. Calif., 1993, apptd. to appellate standing adv. com., 1993-95; apptd. to Appellate Indigent Def. Oversight Adv. Com., State of Calif., 1995—; com. on appellate stds. of ABA Appellate Judges Conf., 1995-96; com. on appellate practice ABA, 1997; adv. bd. Witkin Legal Inst., Bancroft Whitney, 1996—; bd. dirs. Calif. Supreme Ct. Hist. Soc. (sec. 1999—), State Bar Calif., Appellate Law Cons. Group, 1994-95; appointee 9th Jud. Cir. Hist. Soc. Hon. Cecil Poole Biography Project, 1998. Fellow Woodrow Wilson Found., 1967-68. Mem. Calif. Trial Lawyers Assn. (bd. govs. 1980-88, amicus-curiae com. 1981-87, editor-in-chief assn. mag. 1980-81, Presdl. award of merit 1980, 81), Calif. Acad. Appellate Lawyers (sec.-treas. 1989-90, 2d v.p. 1990-91, 1st v.p. 1991-92, pres. 1992-93), Am. Acad. Appellate Lawyers, Edward J. McFetridge Am. Inn of Cts. (counsellor 1990-91, edn. chmn. 1991-92, social chmn. 1992-93, v.p. 1993-94, pres. 1994-95), Boalt Hall Sch. Law U. Calif. Alumni Assn. (bd. dirs. 1989-91), Order of Coif. Jewish. Office: 1916 Los Angeles Ave Berkeley CA 94707-2419

DEGOS, LAURENT, hematologist, educator; b. Paris, July 9, 1945; s. Robert Degos and Monique Lortat-Jacob; m. Françoise Fouchard, Dec. 22, 1971; children: Juliette, Cécile, Vincent. MD, U. Paris, 1972, PhD, 1973. Intern Hosp. de Paris, 1967; asst. prof. hematology U. Paris VII, 1979-86, prof., 1986—, dir. Inst. Universitaire d'Hematologie, 1993—; dir. transplantation immunity unit Nat. Inst. Health and Med. Rsch. (INSERM), Paris, 1985—; chief svc. Hosp. St. Louis, France, 1990—; pres. sci. bd. GENSET, France, 1989—, Inst. Etudes Politique de la Santé, 1993—. Author: ABCD de HLA, 1988, Le Don Recu (award Acad. des Sci. 1992), Greffes d'organes, 1994, Textbook on Malignant Hematology, 1998, Kouvelles Aventures de Candide, 1999,. Decorated officier Ordre du Merite, 1984; named Dr. of Yr., Impact Medicin, 1991; recipient Svan Killman award Leukemia Jour., 1992, Ligue Contre. de Cancer Comt Savoie, 1993, Kettering award GM, 1994, Inst. Curie Loubaresse award, 1996, Perrine Tennis Cup, 1996, Charles-Rodolphe Brupbacher award, 1997. Mem. Coll. des Hematologistes (sec. gen. 1986), Am. Soc. Hematology, Am. Assn. Cancer Rsch., French Acad. Scis. Avocations: violin, tennis. Home: 52 rue de Clichy, 75009 Paris France Office: Inst d'Hematologie-Hopital, Ave C Vellefaux, 75010 Paris France

DE GRAF, WILLIAM BRADFORD, career officer; b. San Francisco, Jan. 10, 1926; s. Gerald and Margaret Graham (Sharp) De G.; m. Robin Wilde, June 10, 1950; children; Gwyneth Margaret, Bradford Rankin, Scot Wilde, Leslie Adele. BS, USMA, 1950; MS, Purdue Univ., 1954. Inf. platoon leader Co. F143rd Inf., Germany, 1945; inf. platoon leader Korea Co. M21st Inf., Korea, 1950-51; instr. USMA, West Point, N.Y., 1954-57; staff officer systems analysis OSD Pentagon, Washington, 1967-69; cmdr. 1st bde divsn. 1st Inf., 1969-70; staff Nat. War Coll., Ft. McNair, D.C., 1970-72; staff nat. security coun. White House, Washington, 1972-74; divsn. mgr. SAIC, McLean, Va., 1974-87. Decorated Combat Infantryman's badge (3), Leion of Merit (3). Mem. USMA Class of 1950 (chmn. 1970—, pres.), West Point Soc. DC (treas. 1991—), Army Retirement Residence Found.,(1995—, pres.), Phi Kappa Phi. Avocations: duplicate bridge, stamp collecting, raquetball. Home: 5903 Mount Eagle Dr Apt 1618 Alexandria VA 22303-2533

DEGRAFF, DAVID CHARLES, purchasing executive; b. Rochester, N.Y., Mar. 17, 1954; s. Gerald Stuart and Elizabeth T. (DiLiddo) D.; m. Margaret M. Degraff. Machine designer Davenport Machine Tool, Rochester, N.Y., 1973-75; tool designer Jasco Tools Inc., Rochester, N.Y., 1976-80, Morgood Tool Corp., Rochester, N.Y., 1981-84; sr. engr. Jasco Precision Co., Rochester, N.Y., 1985-97; mgr. re-engring. outsourcing LSI Inc., Rochester, N.Y., 1998—. Founder Med/Event Inc., Rochester, 1974; bd. dirs. N.Y. State Emergency Health Svcs. Coun., 1982-85, Empire Nine Regional Health Svcs., Upstate N.Y., 1980-85, Chili (N.Y.0 Pub. Libr., 1973-75, Nat. Kidney Found. of Upstate N.Y., 1989, pres. 1996—. Recipient Cert. of Merit Kodak Internat. Photo Competition, 1982, Cmty. Svc. award Empire Nine, Upstate N.Y., 1983, 84, Vol. Excellence award Nat. Kidney Found., 1994, Gift of Life award, 1998. Avocations: photography, community service. Home: 4 Camden Ct Fairport NY 14450-9603 Office: 750 Saint Paul St Rochester NY 14605-1737

DEGRANDI, JOSEPH ANTHONY, lawyer; b. Hartford, Conn., 1927; m. Yolanda Salica; children: Terese, Lisa, Donna. BS, Trinity Coll., Hartford, 1949; MS, George Washington U., 1950, LLB, 1952. Bar: D.C. 1952, U.S. Supreme Ct. 1956. Ptnr. Beveridge, DeGrandi, Weilacher & Young, Washington, 1962—; mem. adv. bd. Marymount Sch., Arlington, Va., pres., 1969-72; mem. Pres.'s Adv. Com. on Indsl. Innovation, 1978-79; legal advisor U.S. delegation Diplomatic Conf. for Revision of Paris Conv., Nairobi, Kenya, 1981, Treaty on Harmonization of Patent Laws, The Hague, 1991. Recipient Disting. Alumnus award George Washington U., 1982. Fellow Am. Bar Found.; mem. FBA, IBA, ABA (chmn. sect. patent, trademark and copyright law 1981-82, dep. del. 1986-89, del. to ho. of dels. 1989—, nominating com. 1989-92, 98—), Inter-Am. Bar Assn., Nat. Coun. Patent Law Assns. (sec. 1971-75, adv. panel 1975-79), The Fed. Cir. Bar Assn., Bar Assn. D.C. (bd. dirs. 1968-69, chmn. patent, trademark and copyright law sect. 1967-68), D.C. Bar Assn. (chmn. divsn. patent, trademark and copyright law 1978-79), N.Y. Intellectual Property Law Assn., Patent Lawyers Club Washington (pres. 1959), Nat. Lawyers Club (bd. govs. 1984-92, v.p. 1989-92, acting pres. 1991-92), Am. Judicature Soc., Am. Intellectual Property Law Assn. (bd. mgrs. 1976-79, 2d v.p. 1984-85, 1st v.p. 1985-86, pres.-elect 1986-87, pres. 1987-88), Giles S. Rich Am. Inn of Ct. (master emeritus), Patent and Trademark Inst. Can., Internat. Assn. for Protection Indsl. Property (treas.-gen. 1989—), Chartered Inst. Patent Agts. (Gt. Britain), Internat. Patent and Trademark Assn. (exec. com. 1978-83, 89—, v.p. 1983-89), Licensing Execs. Soc., Inter-Am. Assn. Indsl. Property, Internat. Intellectual Property Assn. (exec. com. 1989—), Federation Internationale des Conseils en Propriete Industrielle, Thomas Moore Soc. Am., Internat. Club Washington (bd. govs. 1991-95), Rotary, Nu Beta Epsilon. Lodge: Rotary. Office: Smith Gambrell & Russell LLP Intellectual Property Gr 1850 M St NW Ste 800 Washington DC 20036-5809

DEGRANDPRE, CHARLES ALLYSON, lawyer; b. Manchester, N.H., July 7, 1936; s. Arthur Vital and Andrea Amanda (L'Etoile) DeG.; m. Patricia Rahn DeGrandpre, Oct. 9, 1982. AB, Clark U., 1958; JD, U. Mich., 1961. Bar: N.H. 1961, U.S. Dist. Ct. N.H. 1964, U.S. Supreme Ct. 1969. Dir. McLane, Graf, Raulerson & Middleton, P.A., Portsmouth, N.H., 1968—; trustee, chair Smith Found., Manchester, 1986—; bd. dirs. Piscataqua Cmty. Found., 1990-97. Author: Probate Law and Procedure, 1990, 2d edit., 1996, Wills, Trusts and Gifts, 1992, 3d edit., 1997. Chair bd. trustees Canterbury Shaker Village, 1992-97; trustee Strawbery Banke Mus., 1996—; chmn. bd. dirs. N.H. Bar Found., 1997—. Recipient N.H. Vol. of Yr. award Office of Gov., Concord, N.H., 1982. Fellow Am. Coll. Trust and Estate Counsel; mem. N.H. Bar Assn. (Pres.'s award 1983). Avocations: hiking, reading, wine. Home: 60 Pleasant Point Dr Portsmouth NH 03801-5265 Office: McLane Graf Raulerson & Middleton PO Box 4316 30 Penhallow St Portsmouth NH 03801-3816

DE GRASSI DI SANTA CRISTINA, LEONARDO, art historian, educator; b. East Orange, N.J., Mar. 2, 1928; s. Romulus-William and Anna Sophia (Sannicolo) DeG.; m. Dolores Marie Welgoss, June 24, 1961; children: Maria Christina, Paul. BA, U. So. Calif., 1950, BFA, 1951, MA, 1956; postgrad., Harvard U., 1953, Istituto Centrale del Restauro di Roma, 1959-60, U. Rome, 1959-60, UCLA, 1970-73. Tchr. art Redlands (Calif.) Jr. High Sch., 1951-53, Toll Jr. High Sch., Glendale, Calif., 1953-61, Wilson Jr. High Sch., Glendale, 1961; mem. faculty Glendale Coll., 1962—, prof. art history, 1974-92, chmn. dept., 1972, 89, prof. emeritus, 1992—. Prin. works include: (paintings) high altar at Ch. St. Mary, Cook, Minn., altar screen at Ch. St. Andrew, El Segundo, Calif., 1965-71, 14 Stas. of the Cross Ch. St. Mary, Cook, Minn., altar screen at Ch. of the Descent of the Holy Spirit, Glendale, 14 Stas. of the Cross at Ch. of St. Benedict, Duluth, Minn; also research, artwork and dramatic work for Spaceship Earth exhbn. at Disney World, Orlando, Fla., 1980. Decorated Knight Grand Cross Holy Sepluchre, 1974, knight St. John of Jerusalem, 1976, knight Order of Merit of Republic of Italy, 1973 Cross of Merit, 1984, 89; named First Disting. Faculty, 1987, Outstanding Educator of Am., 1971. Mem. Art Educators Assn., Am. Rsch. Ct. Egypt, Tau Kappa Alpha, Kappa Pi, Delta Sigma Rho. Office: 1500 N Verdugo Rd Glendale CA 91208-2809

DE GRAZIA, ALFRED, philosopher, behavioral scientist; b. Chgo., Dec. 29, 1919; s. Alfred J. and Katherine (Lupo) de G.; m. Jill B.L. Oppenheim, May 11, 1942 (dec.); children: Catherine de Grazia Vanderpool, Victoria F. de Grazia Paggi, Jessica M. de Grazia Jeans, Paul R., John S., Carl M., Christopher; m. Nina Mavridis, Dec. 21, 1972 (div.); m. Anne-Marie Hueber, Apr. 23, 1982. *Practically all two score descendants of Alfred J. de Grazia, Sr., bandmaster settled in Chicago at the turn of the century, became intellectuals and musicians. Many studied and lived by The University of Chicago. Son Alfred, 20, was scholar, musician and athlete there, lecturing on comparative election systems. Pearl Harbor halted work. Returning from Africa and Europe, where he had taken the surrender of many places, liberated many prisoners and slave workers, and became commander of 7A combat propaganda operations against enemy communications and morale, he met two year old daughter Cathy, heavy player in parents' uniquely literary million word, war-front /home-front correspondence.* A.B., U. Chgo., 1939, Ph.D., 1948; student, Columbia Law Sch., 1940-41. Mem. faculty Northwestern U., 1948, U. Minn., 1948-50, Brown U., 1950-52, Stanford U., 1952-57; research prof. social theory NYU, 1959-83; vis. lectr. U. Istanbul, Turkey, U. Rome, U. Gothenburg, Sweden, U. Bombay, India; rector (pro tem) U. New World, Switzerland, 1971; cons. in field, 1948—; chmn. bd. Princeton Info. Tech., Inc., 1967-70; adv. bd. Simulmatics Corp., 1967. *Founded journal ABS to advance Chicago School's world leadership of political science. Turning to World Union for "What is to be Done with Our World?" he set up HQ in India, and instituted l'Universite du noveau monde (Switzerland) for educational reconstruction. Restrained, resumed study of catastrophes, culminating in ten volumes of integrated quantavolu-*

tions, assigning human origins to schizoid traumas of ancient disasters, associated with solar system binary evolution, restating the earth sciences, and advancing a supra-real poly-theist universe. Warning against glorifying past, assessing resources the nation might commit to new millenium, he published on the Web an American historical epic. Author: Public and Republic, 1949, Elements of Political Science, 1952, World Politics, 1949, The Western Public, 1954, The American Way of Government, 1957, Grass Roots Private Welfare, 1958, American Welfare, 1960, Science and Values in Administration, 1961, Political Behavior and Organization, 2 vols, 1962, Apportionment and Representative Government, 1963, Republic in Crisis, Congress Against the Executive Force, 1965, The Velikovsky Affair, 1966, Congress and the Presidency, 1965; (poetry) Passage of the Year, 1967; Kalos: What Is to be Done with Our World, 1973, Politics for Better or Worse, 1973, 8 Bads-8 Goods: The American Contradictions, 1975, Art and Culture: 1001 Questions on Policy, 1979, Chaos and Creation: Quantavolution in Human and Natural History, 1981, Homo Schizo II: Human Nature and Behavior, 1983; Home Schizo I: Human and Cultural Hologensis, 1984, God's Fire: Moses and the Management of Exodus, 1984, The Disastrous Love Affair of Moon and Mars, 1984, The Lately Tortured Earth, 1984, The Burning of Troy, 1984, The Divine Succession: A Science of Gods Old and New, 1984, Cosmic Heretics, 1984, (with Earl R. Milton) Solaria Binaria, 1985, The Student, 1991, The Taste of War, 1992, The Babe, 1992, The End of Spydom, 1992, Strengthening the UN, 1997, (with Earl R. Milton) A Cloud over Bhopal, 1985; editor: Congress: First Branch of Government, 1966; founder, editor jour.: Am. Behavioral Scientist, 1957-66; author, prodr. (CD-Rom) Quantavolution and Catastrophes', 1997. Mem. U.S. del. to UNESCO, 1960; first pres. Found. Vol. Welfare, 1957-59; chmn. research com. N.Y.C. Republican party, 1961; cons. Rep. Nat. Com., 1964; organizer Ind. Voters, Ill., 1946-48, Calif., 1953-56. Served to capt. AUS, 1942-46, ETO; adv., Korea, 1951-52, Vietnam, 1967-68. Decorated Bronze Star, others. Designer computerized reference retrieval system in social scis., Universal Reference System, 1962-67. E-mail: Aldegrazia@aol.com. Office: care Metron Publs PO Box 1213 Princeton NJ 08542-1213

DE GRAZIA, SEBASTIAN, political philosopher, author; b. Chgo., Aug. 11, 1917; s. Alfred Joseph and Catherine Cardinale Lupo de G.; m. Miriam Lund Carlson; children: Alfred Joseph III, Margreta, Sebastian; m. Anna Maria d'Annunzio di Montenevoso; children: Marc, Tancredi; m. Lucia Heffelfinger. AB, U. Chgo., 1939, PhD, 1947. With FCC, 1941-43, OSS, 1943-45; mem. faculty U. Chgo., 1945-50; cons. bus. firms, state and U.S. Govt., 1947—; dir. research study time, work and leisure Twentieth Century Fund, 1957-61; prof. polit. philosophy Rutgers U., 1962-88; vis. prof. U. Florence, Italy, 1950-52, Princeton U., 1957, 91-92, U. Madrid, 1963, John Jay Coll. Criminal Justice, 1967-71, Inst. Advanced Study Princeton, 1983. Author: The Political Community, 1948, Errors of Psychotherapy, 1953, Of Time, Work and Leisure, 1962, Masters of Chinese Political Thought, 1973, Machiavelli in Hell, 1989 (Pulitzer Prize for biography 1990), A Country with No Name, 1997. Grantee Am. Philos. Soc., Social Sci. Research Council, Am. Council Learned Socs.; Fulbright prof. Mem. Am. Polit. Sci. Assn., Am. Soc. Polit. and Legal Philosophy, Institut Internat. de Philosophie Politique. Clubs: Cosmos (Washington); Nassau, Prettybrook (Princeton); Century (N.Y.C.).

DE GREGORIO, ANTHONY, advertising executive. Pres., chief creative officer Publicis/Bloom, Inc., N.Y.C. Office: Publicis/Bloom Inc 304 E 45th St New York NY 10017-3425*

DEGROAT, JAMES STEPHEN, financial services executive; b. El Paso, Mar. 6, 1951; s. James Dayton and Mary Carolyn (Steadman) DeG.; m. Martha Davis Crowson, Feb. 11, 1972; children: James Stephen Jr., Janet Dayton. BBA, U. Tex., El Paso, 1972, MBA, 1975; grad. diploma in banking, So. Meth. U., 1981. CFP, ChFC, CLU, Tex. Banking officer First City Nat. Bank, El Paso, 1972-77; chmn., CEO InterFirst Bank, N.A., El Paso, 1978-86; pres., CEO Surety Savings Assn., El Paso, 1986-89; agent Lincoln Fin. Advisors, El Paso, 1989-91, sales mgr., 1991-95, gen. agent, owner, 1995—; dir. Sierra Med. Ctr., El Paso, 1986-89. Sun Bowl Assn. pres. El Paso Sun Bowl, 1992; pres. Keep El Paso Beautiful, 1991, Sunturians, El Paso, 1983, 84, U. Tex. Alumni Assn., El Paso, 1985; dir., past pres. Ronald McDonald House, El Paso. Recipient Outstanding Young Man award Jaycess, El Paso, 1983, Golden Nugget Outstanding Grad. award U Tex. El Paso, 1986. Mem. Internat. Assn. Fin. Planners, El Paso Assn. Life Underwriters, Rotary Club (co-chair membership 1995-97), Soc. for Fin. Svcs. Profls. (v.p. El Paso chpt.). Episcopalian. Avocations: jogging, golf, mountain climbing, skiing, water skiing. Office: Lincoln Fin Advisors Ste A-100 413 Rio Bravo El Paso TX 79902

DEGROAT, WILLIAM CHESNEY, pharmacology educator; b. Trenton, N.J., May 18, 1938; s. William Chesney and Margaret (Welch) deG.; m. Dorothy Marion Albertson, June 13, 1959; children: Allyson L., Cynthia L., Jennifer L. BSc, Phila. Coll. Pharmacy and Sci., 1960, MSc, 1962; PhD, U. Pa., 1965, postgrad., 1965-66; postgrad., Australian Nat. U., Canberra, 1966-67. Vis. research fellow John Curtin Sch. Med. Research, Canberra, 1967-68; asst. prof. U. Pitts. Med. Sch., 1968-72, assoc. prof., 1972-77, prof. pharmacology, 1977—, acting chmn. dept. pharmacology, 1978-80, adj. prof. pharmacy, 1978-88, prof. psychology, 1982-86, mem. ctr. of neurosci., 1984—, prof. dept. behavioral neurosci., 1986-94, prof. dept. neurosci., 1995-96; vis. prof. U. Coll., London, 1998; mem. neurobiology study sect. NIH, 1983-88; vis. scientist NIAAA-NIH, 1989-90. Mem. editl. bd. Jour. Pharmacology and Exptl. Therapeutics, 1975—, Jour. Autonomic Nervous Sys., 1979—, assoc. editor, 1985-94, Neurology and Urodynamics, 1982—, Am. Jour. Physiology, 1983—, Life Scis., 1993—, Urology, 1996—; editl. cons. profl. jours.; contbr. articles to profl. jours., chpts. in books. NSF fellow, 1962-63; pharmacology fellow Riker Pharm. Co., 1966-67; NSF fellow, 1966-67; recipient research Career Devel. award NIH, 1972-77. Mem. AAAS, N.Y. Acad. Scis., Am. Soc. Pharmacology and Exptl. Therapeutics, Soc. for Neurosci. (treas., 1994-95), Internat. Brain Rsch. Orgn., Am. Gastroent. Assn., Urodynamics Soc. (Lifetime Achievement award 1995), Internat. Med. Soc. of Paraplegia, Soc. for Basic Urologic Rsch., Am. Motility Soc., Am. Autonomic Soc., Internat. Soc. for Autonomic Neurosci., Sigma Xi, Rho Chi. Republican. Methodist. Home: 6357 Burchfield Ave Pittsburgh PA 15217-2732 Office: U Pitts Med Sch W-1352 Biomed Sci Tower Terrace St Pittsburgh PA 15213

DEGROODT, JESSE, municipal official, sports writer; b. Hudson, N.Y., Feb. 28, 1958; s. Jesse Jay and Vera Mae (Wilder) DeG.; m. Leslie Rebecca Rueckheim, May 7, 1988; children: Zachary, Elijah. BA, Syracuse U., 1984. Asst. editor Chatham (N.Y.) Courier, 1992-95. Avocations: sports, computers. E-mail: Jdegroodt@aol.com. Home: 134 Highland Rd Chatham NY 12037-3604

DEGROOT, LESLIE JACOB, medical educator; b. Ft. Edward, N.Y., Sept. 20, 1928. B.S., Union Coll., 1948; M.D., Columbia U., 1952. Intern, asst. resident in medicine Presbyn. Hosp., N.Y.C., 1952-54; health physician Nat. Cancer Inst., 1954-55; physician U.S. Mission, Afghanistan, 1955-56; clin. and research fellow medicine Mass. Gen. Hosp., Boston, 1956, 58-60, resident, 1957-58, asst., 1960-64, asst. physician, 1964-66; assoc. prof. exptl. medicine MIT, 1966-68, assoc. dir. dept. nutrition and food sci. Clin. Research Ctr., 1966-68; prof. endocrinology Pritzker Sch. Medicine, U. Chgo., 1968—, chief thyroid study unit, 1968—, chief endocrinology sect., 1980-87. Nat. Cancer Inst. clin. fellow, 1954-55. Mem. Assn. Am. Physicians, Am. Thyroid Assn., Endocrine Soc., Am. Soc. Clin. Investigation, Am. Fedn. Clin. Research. Office: Univ Chgo Med Ctr MC3090 5841 S Maryland Ave Chicago IL 60637-1463

DE GROOTE, ROBERT DAVID, general and vascular surgeon; b. Hackensack, N.J., Aug. 30, 1951; s. Emiel and Filomena Lillian (Candio) De G. BS in Biology, Fordham U., 1973; MD, Autonomous U. Guadalajara, Jalisco, Mex., 1978. Diplomate Am. Bd. of Surgery. Resident gen. surgery U. Medicine and Dentistry N.J. Med. Sch., Newark, 1979-84, fellow critical care medicine, 1981-82, fellow vascular surgery, 1984-86; fifth pathway St. Joseph's Hosp., Paterson, N.J., 1978-79; attending surgeon Hackensack (N.J.) Med. Ctr., 1986—. Contbr. articles to Surgery, Stroke, Archives of Surgery, Annals of Vascular Surgery. Named Man of Yr., Lyndhurst, N.J. chpt. Italian-Am. Nat. Svc. Orgn., 1993. Fellow ACS; mem. AMA, Internat. Soc. for Cardiovascular Surgery, Soc. for Critical Care Medicine, Ea. Vascular Soc. Roman Catholic. Office: 83 Summit Ave Hackensack NJ 07601-1262

DEGUATEMALA, JOYCE, sculptor; b. Feb. 25, 1938; d. Cassius Albert and Martha (Prado Solares) Bush; m. Jason Leander Vourvoulias, Oct. 13, 1956; children: Albert Leander, Sabrina Marie, William Craig. Student in fine arts, U. Autonoma de Mex., 1958, U. Wis., 1959, Silpakorn U., Bangkok, 1960-62; Cert. in Physics, U. San Carlos, Guatemala, 1969. artist-in-residence Brandywine Workshop, Phila., 1993, past bd. dirs.; resident Djerassi Found., Woodside, Calif., 1994; invitational cultural specialist, lectr. workshops, juror Biannual, Honduras, 1999. One-woman shows include Mus. Contemporary Latin Am. Art OAS, Washington, 1977, Marian Locks Gallery, Phila., 1979, 84, 85, 90, Barbara Gillman Gallery, Miami, Fla., 1982, 92, 93, 94, Northwood Inst., West Palm Beach, Fla., 1982, 14 Sculptors Gallery, N.Y.C., 1987, 88, 90, 92, Estela Shapiro Gallery, Mexico City, 1988, 90, 92, Djerassi Found., Woodside, 1994; exhibited in group shows Bienal Internat. do Sao Paulo, Brazil, 1975, 83, Marian Locks Gallery, Phila., 1979, 85, Macondo Gallery, Guatemala City, 1979, William Pa. Meml. Mus., Harrisburg, Pa., 1982, Mus. Latin Am. Contemporary Art, OAS, Washington, 1983, 90, Noyes Mus., Oceanville, N.J., 1983, Outdoor Sculpture/Fairmount Park, Phila., 1986, 14 Sculptors Gallery, 1987, 88, 89, 90, 91, 2d Internat. Ephemeral Sculpture Exhbn., Fortaleza, Brazil, 1989, Olympiad of Art, Seoul Olympic com. and the Guggenheim Mus., Seoul, Korea, 1988, Temple Gallery, Phila., 1987, Pub. Art on the Plaza, Phila., 1987, Inst. Contemporary Art U. Pa., Phila., 1991, Art Alliance, Phila., 1991, Lehigh U., Bethlehem, Pa., 1991, Exhbn. Fortaleza, Brazil, 1991, Kingsborough C.C., Bklyn., 1992, Abington Art Ctr., Jenkintown, Pa., 1992, 94, Phila. Coll. Textiles and Sci., Phila., 1992, Cen. Conn. State U., New Britain, 1992, Metro-Dade Art in Pub. Places, Miami, 1993, Barbara Gilman Gallery, Miami, 1993, 95, 96, 99, Brandywine Workshop, Phila., 1994, Internat. Art Exhbn., Miami Beach, 1995, Museo Am. Madrid, 1997, State Mus. of Pa., 1999, Open Space Gallery, Allentown, Pa., 1999, Barbara Gillman Gallery, 1999, numerous others; represented in permanent collections Nat. Mus. History and Fine Arts of Guatemala City, Mus. Contemporary Latin Am. Art, Washington, OAS, Ringling Bros. Mus. Art, Sarasota, Fla., Noyes Mus., Oceanville, N.J., Washington, Lehigh U., Bethlehem, Pa., Hershey Foods Corp. Tech. Ctr. (Pa.), Cedar Crest Coll., Allentown, Pa., Pan Am. Bank, Miami, Mus. Modern Art, Chapultepec, Mexico City, Hansen Properties, Ambler, Pa., Fed. Res. Bank, Phila., Please Touch Mus., Phila., Exmibal, El Estor, Guatemala, Olympiad Art, Art Pk., Seoul, Korea, Fla. Internat. U., Miami, others, and numerous private collections; sculpture commd. for Elkins Park Free Libr., Pa., 1985, AnnMarie Sculpture Garden, Prince Frederick, Md., 1998, State Mus. Pa., Harrisburg, 1998. Mem. adv. bd. Latin Am. and Caribbean Ctr., Fla. Internat. U., Miami. Address: 320 Fairview Rd Glenmoore PA 19343-1402

DEGUILIO, JON E., lawyer; b. Hammond, Ind., June 15, 1955; s. Ernest Michael and Jeanne (Hochis) D.; m. Barbara Jo Wieser, Oct. 3, 1981; 1 child, Suzanne Jeanne. BA, U. Notre Dame, 1977; JD, Valparaiso U., 1981. Bar: Ind. 1981, U.S. Dist. Ct. (so. dist.) Ind. 1981, U.S. Dist. Ct. (no. dist.) Ind. 1981. Pub. defender Lake County Ct., Crown Point, Ind., 1984-87; dep. prosecutor Lake County Prosecutor's Office, Crown Point, 1981-84; 87-94; assoc. James Wieser Law Offices, Highland, Ind., 1981-94; U.S. atty. Northern Dist. Dept. Justice, Dyer, Ind.; atty. Highland Police Commn., Highland, Ind., 1987— and Highland Water Bd., 1987—; legal advisor, Lake County Sheriff, Crown Point, Ind., 1986-87; atty. Hammond and East Chgo. Fedn. of Tchrs., 1986—. Councilman Hammond City Council, 1984-87; mem. Lake County Med. Ctr. Devel. Agy., 1988—, Greater Hammond Community Services, 1987—; treas. Little Calumet River Basin Com., 1986. Mem. Lake County Bar Assn. (bd. dirs. 1988-90), Justinian Soc. Democrat. Avocations: basketball, bolf, reading. Home: 8944 Liable Rd Hammond IN 46322-2248 Office: 1001 Main St Ste A Dyer IN 46311-1234*

DE HAAN-PULS, JOYCE ELAINE, sales account representative; b. Grand Rapids, Mich., Dec. 22, 1941; d. Harry Herman and Dorothy Elaine (Kikstra) DeHaan; student Calvin Coll., 1960-61; BS with honors, Grand Valley State Colls., 1978; postgrad. U. Sarajevo, Yugoslavia, 1978, Grad. Inst., Siedman Grad. Coll., 1979—; M in Communications Wayne State U., 1986 ; children: Bruce Todd, Daniel Lane, Cristy-Ann Sara Elizabeth Puls. Owner, operator Joyce Elaine's Beauty Parlor, Grandville, Mich., 1960-64; asst. assessor City of Hudsonville, Mich., 1978; dir. displaced homemaker program Women's Resource Ctr., Grand Rapids, 1979-81; visual products rep. 3M Corp., Grand Rapids, 1982-85, sr. account rep., Detroit, 1985-89, regional sales mgr. S.E. Mich., 1989-93; v.p. mktg. TransContinental Traders, Ltd., Detroit, 1993—; mem. Ottawa County (Mich.) CETA Adv. Bd. Bd. dirs. Downtown Day Care Ctr., Grand Rapids, 1972. Recipient Cert. of Appreciation Bishop of Saigon, Vietnam, 1969; Top Sales rep. 3M/US, 1983, VIP, 1983, 84, 85, 86, 87, 88, 89; Phillip Morris scholar, 1975. Mem. Preservation Wayne, Detroit Internat. Vis. Coun. Mem. NAFE, Internat. Visitors Coun., Nat. Assn. Fgn. Students, Grand Rapids Coun. on World Affairs, Am. Soc. Pub. Adminstrn, Hist. Indian Village Assn. Republican. Home: 1060 Parker St Detroit MI 48214-2613 Office: Transcontinental Traders Ltd 1060 Parker St Ste 100 Detroit MI 48214-2613

DE HAAS, DAVID DANA, emergency physician; b. Hollywood, Calif., May 31, 1956; S. Martin and Norma (Deutsch) De H.; m. Mary Danuta Przybylowski, June 27, 1982; children: Lindsay Alexandra, Heather Brittany, Lance Austin. BS in Biochemistry, UCLA, Westwood, Calif., 1979; MD, Chgo. Med. Sch., 1983. Diplomate Am. Bd. Internal Medicine, Am. Bd. Emergency Medicine, Nat. Bd. Med. Examiners; cert. provider advanced trauma life support, ACLS, Pediatric Advanced Life Support, BCLS, Med. Disaster Response, instr. ACLS, Pediatric Advanced Life Support, Med. Disaster Response. Resident emergency medicine/internal medicine Kern Med. Ctr., Bakersfield, Calif., 1983-87; assoc. med. dir. Family Care Med. Assocs., Huntington Beach, Calif., 1987—; emergency physician Anaheim (Calif.) Meml. Hosp., 1988—; asst. clin. prof. medicine dept. internal medicine U. Calif.-Irvine Med. Ctr., Orange, 1989—; emergency physician St. Bernardine Med. Ctr., San Bernardino, Calif., 1991—; ptnr. Calif. Emergency Physicians Med. Group, San Bernardino, 1991—; expert reviewer Med. Bd. Calif.; affiliate faculty ACLS, Pediatric Advanced Life Support, Am. Heart Assn.; vice chmn. dept. emergency medicine St. Bernardine Med. Ctr., ACLS dir., dir. quality assurance/continuous quality improvement dept. emergency medicine; mem. edn. com. Med. Disaster Response; ptnr.Calif. Emergency Physician Med. Group. Fellow ACP, Am. Coll. Emergency Physicians; mem. AMA, Calif. Med. Assn., Orange County Med. Soc., Soc. Orange County Emergency Physicians (bd. dirs.), Assn. Clin. Faculty U. Calif., Irvine Coll. Medicine. Avocations: pin collecting, gardening, reading, 1st edit. book collecting, western Americana. Home: 26882 Via La Mirada San Juan Capistrano CA 92675-4935 Office: St Bernardine Med Ctr 2101 N Waterman Ave San Bernardino CA 92404-4836

DEHAAS, JOHN NEFF, JR., retired architecture educator; b. Phila., July 4, 1926; s. John Neff and Sadie Lavinia (Hagel) DeH.; m. C. Bernice Wallace, Dec. 27, 1950; children: Kenneth Eric, Jocelyn Hilda. BArch, Tex. A&M U., 1948, MEd, 1950. Registered architect, Mont. Instr. Tex. A&M U., College Station, 1948-50, U. Tex., Austin, 1950-51; successively instr. to prof. Mont. State U., Bozeman, 1951-80; supervisory architect Historic Am. Bldgs. Survey, summers San Francisco, 1962, Bozeman, 1963, 65, Wilm., 1969; cons. Mont. Historic Preservation Office, Helena, 1977-78, mem. rev. bd., 1968-79. Author: Montana's Historic Structures, Vol. 1, 1864, Vol. 2, 1969, Historic Uptown Butte, 1977; editor quar. newsletter Mont. Ghost Town Preservation Soc., 1972—. Bd. dirs. Mont. Assn. for Blind, Butte, 1984-95. Recipient Centennial Preservation award Mont. Historic Preservation Office, 1989, Dorothy Bridgman award for Outstanding Svc. to the Blind Montana Assn. for the Blind, 1990. Fellow AIA (com. on historic resources 1974—); mem. Mont. Hist. Soc. (trustee's award 1989). Republican. Methodist. Home: 1021 S Tracy Ave Bozeman MT 59715-5329

DEHAINAUT, RAYMOND KIRK, international studies educator; b. South Charleston, W.Va., May 19, 1930; s. Oscar DeHainaut and Edith (Kirk) Cochrum; m. Claudiene Delaine Munday, June 7, 1953; 1 child, Raymond Marc. BS cum laude, W.Va. U., 1952; MDiv, Vanderbilt U. Divinity Sch., 1954; PhD, Drew U., 1970. Campus minister La. State U., Baton Rouge, 1954-58, Rutgers U., New Brunswick, N.J., 1959-62; ednl. missionary Student Christian Movement, Cordoba, Argentina, 1964-68; campus minister U. South Fla., Tampa, 1969-72; ednl. missionary, dir. NCC Com. Intercultural Dialogue, Bogota, Colombia, 1972-76; campus minister U. South Fla., 1976-85; ednl. missionary United Meth. Gen. Bd. Global Missions, N.Y., 1985-95; adj. prof. internat. studies U. South Fla., 1995—; exchange dir. student work Soochow U., China, 1979-80. Author: Faith and Ideology in Latin American Perspective, 1972; contbr. articles to profl. pubs. Pres. Meth. Fedn. Social Action, 1977-78; dist. supt., dir. Sch. Barahona, Dominican Republic, 1990-93. Recipient MSM Ball award for peace with jusctice work in El Salvador, 1980, Lee and Mae Ball award MFSA, 1982. Mem. Amnesty Internat., Phi Beta Kappa. Home: 9707 Woodland Ridge Dr Temple Terrace FL 33637-4956

DE HARTOG, JAN, writer; b. Haarlem, Holland, Apr. 22, 1914; s. Arnold Hendrik and Lucretia (Meyjes) de H.; m. Angela Priestley, 1946; children: Arnold, Sylvia, Nicholas, Catherine; m. Marjorie Mein, 1961; children: Eva, Julia. Student, Amsterdam Naval Coll., 1930. Staff mem. Amsterdam Municipal Theatre, 1932-37; writer-in-residence, lectr. creative playwriting U. Houston, 1962. Author: (plays) Mist, 1938, De Ondergang van de Vrijheid, 1939 (Gt. Nat. Drama prize 1939), Skipper Next to God, 1946, This Time Tomorrow, 1947, The Fourposter, 1951 (Tony award 1952), Death of a Rat, 1956, William and Mary, 1964, (novels) The Lost Sea, 1951, Mary, 1951, The Distant Shore, 1952, The Little Ark, 1954, A Sailor's Life, 1956, The Spiral Road, 1957, The Inspector, 1960, Waters of the New World, 1961, The Artist, 1963, The Hospital, 1964, The Call of the Sea, 1966, The Captain, 1966, The Children, 1968, The Peaceable Kingdom, 1971, The Lamb's War, 1979, The Trail of the Serpent, 1983, Star of Peace, 1984, The Peculiar People, 1992, The Outer Buoy, 1994, (mus.) I Do, I Do, 1966. Captain, Netherlands Merchant Marine. Recipient Netherlands Cross of Merit; named Officier de l'Academie, France, 1952, Commandeur of Netherlands Lion by Queen Beatrix of the Netherlands, 1996. Mem. Coun. of Am. Master Mariners. Mem. Soc. of Friends. Office: care The Lantz Office 888 7th Ave Ste 3001 New York NY 10106*

DE HAVILLAND, OLIVIA MARY, actress; b. Tokyo, July 1, 1916; naturalized, 1941; d. Walter Augustus and Lilian Augusta (Ruse) de H. (parents British subjects); m. Marcus Goodrich, Aug. 26, 1946 (div.); 1 child, Benjamin Briggs Goodrich (dec.); m. Pierre Galante, Apr. 2, 1955 (div.); 1 child, Gisele. Student schs. and convent in, Calif.; doctorate (hon.), Am. U., Paris, 1994. Made stage debut as Hermia in: Midsummer Night's Dream (Max Reinhardt prodn.), Hollywood Bowl, 1934; 1st motion picture in same role, 1935; actress: (films) including Captain Blood, Anthony Adverse, Robin Hood, Gone With the Wind (nominated for Acad. award 1939), Strawberry Blonde, Hold Back The Dawn (nominated for Acad. award 1941), Princess O'Rourke, To Each His Own (Acad. award for best actress 1946), Dark Mirror, The Snakepit (nominated for Acad. award 1948, N.Y. Critics Award 1948, Laurel Award for best performance 1948-53), The Heiress (Acad. award for best actress 1949, N.Y. critics award), My Cousin Rachel 1952, Not As A Stranger, 1954, Ambassador's Daughter, 1955 (Belgian Critics Prix Femina), Proud Rebel, 1957, Light in the Piazza, 1961, Lady in a Cage, 1963 (British films and filming award), Hush, Hush Sweet Charlotte, 1964, Airport '77, 1976, The Swarm, 1978; TV appearances include Noon Wine, 1966, The Screaming Woman, 1972, Roots: The Next Generations, 1979, Murder is Easy, 1981, Charles and Diana: A Royal Romance, 1982, North and South, II, 1986, Anastasia: The Mystery of Anna, 1986 (Golden Globe award, Emmy nomination), The Woman He Loved, 1988; theatre includes (on Broadway) Romeo and Juliet, 1951, Candida, 1952, A Gift of Time, 1962, (summer stock) What Every Woman Knows, Westport, Conn., Easthampton, Long Island, 1946, Candida, same plus 9 other summer theatres, 1951; (legitimate) Transcontinental Tour Candida 1951-52, (245 Performances); lecture tours, U.S., 1971-80; toured Army and Navy hosps. in U.S., Alaska, Aleutians, South Pacific, 1943-44, Europe, 1957-61; pres. jury Cannes Film Festival, 1965; participant: narration of France's Bicentennial gift to U.S. Son et Lumiere, 1976, Bicentennial Service, Am. Cathedral in Paris, 1976; author: Every Frenchman Has One, 1962. Trustee Am. Coll. in Paris, 1970-71, Am. Libr. in Paris, 1974-81. Recipient Women's Nat. Press Club award for outstanding accomplishment in theater presented by Pres. Truman, 1950; Am. Legion Humanitarian award, 1967; Hon. degree of Doctor of Humane Letters from The Am. U. of Paris, 1994. Mem. Screen Actors Guild, Acad. of Motion Picture Arts and Scis. Democrat. Address: BP 156, 75764 Paris Cedex 16, France*

DEHAYES, DANIEL WESLEY, management executive, educator; b. Columbus, Ohio, Sept. 23, 1941; s. Daniel Wesley and June Rosiland (Page) DeH.; married Lisa A. Gregoline; children: Sarah Baxter, Benjamin Wesley. BA in Math. and Computer Sci., Ohio State U., 1963, MBA, 1964, PhD in Bus. Adminstrn., 1968. Asst. prof. systems analysis Naval Postgrad. Sch., Monterey, Calif., 1967-69; asst. prof. sch. bus. Ind. U., Bloomington, Ind., 1969-72, assoc. prof.sch. bus., 1972-79, prof. sch. bus., 1979—, dean of acad. computing, 1981-86, asst. v.p. info. tech., 1987-88; dir. Ctr. For Entrepreneurship and Innovation, Ind. U., Bloomington, 1989-98; exec. dir. Inst. Rsch. on the MIS, 1989-92, chmn. exec. edn., 1992-93; cons. in field. Textbook author; contbr. articles to profl. jours. Served to capt. U.S. Army, 1967-69. Recipient fellowships and grants. Mem. Decision Scis. Inst., Acad. Mgmt. Republican. Methodist. Office: Indiana University School of Business Bloomington IN 47405

DE HERRERA, JUAN ABRAN, United States marshal; b. Costilla, N.Mex., Jan. 2, 1942; s. Gilbert and Maria (Arellano) De H.; m. Roberta Jo Vogel, June 22, 1959; 5 children. Grad., Nat. Crime Prevention Inst. Acad., 1975, Nat. FBI Acad., 1976; grad. in adminstrn. of jail facilities, U. Colo., 1977; BA in Edn., U. Wyo., 1993. Patrol officer Rawlins (Wyo.) Police Force, 1965-67, sgt. patrol divsn., 1968-71, lt. patrol divsn., 1972-76, chief of police, 1977-82, ret., 1986; U.S. marshal dist. of Wyo. apptd. by Pres. Clinton Dept. Justice, Cheyenne, 1996; boxing coach Am. Athletic Union, 1963-82. Mem. city counsel, 1987-92, Wyo. State Libr. Bd., 1988-91. Hearst Minority scholar U. Wyo., 1988, 89, 90, 91, Sundin scholar, 1988, 89, 90, 91, SEO scholar, 1990, Nat. Hispanic scholar, 1990, 91, 92; state and regional nat. Golden Gloves champion. Mem. Nat. FBI Acad. Assocs., Wyo. Peace Officers Assn., Rawlins Police Protective Assn., Pershing Elem. Sch. Parent Tchr. Assn. (life), K of C. Roman Catholic. Avocations: family camping, cross country skiing, boating, hunting, walking.

DEHMELT, HANS GEORG, physicist; b. Germany, Sept. 9, 1922; came to U.S., 1952, naturalized, 1962; s. Georg Karl and Asta Ella (Klemmt) D.; 1 child from previous marriage, Gerd; m. Diana Elaine Dundore, Nov. 18, 1989. Grad., Graues Kloster, Berlin, Abitur, 1940; D Rerum Naturalium, U. Goettingen, 1950; D Rerum Naturalium (hon.), Ruprecht Karl-Universitat, Heidelberg, 1986; DSc (hon.), U. Chgo., 1987. Postdoctoral fellow U. Goettingen, Germany, 1950-52, Duke U., Durham, N.C., 1952-55; vis. asst. prof. U. Wash., Seattle, 1955; asst. prof. physics U. Wash., 1956, asso. prof., 1957-61, prof., rsch. physicist, 1961—; cons. Varian Assocs., Palo Alto, Calif., 1956-76. Contbr. articles to profl. jours. Recipient Humboldt prize, 1974, award in basic research Internat. Soc. Magnetic Resonance, 1980, Rumford prize Am. Acad. Arts and Scis., 1985, Nobel prize in Physics, 1989, Nat. Medal of Science, 1995; NSF grantee, 1958—. Fellow Am. Phys. Soc. (Davisson-Germer prize 1970); mem. Am. Acad. Arts and Scis., Am. Optical Soc., Nat. Acad. Scis., Sigma Xi. Co-discoverer (with Hubert Krüger) nuclear quadrupole resonance, 1949; inventor schemes using single trapped atomic particles as million-fold quantum amplifier, employed them as a leader of groups in for the first time permanently isolating and identifying at rest in vacuum an individual electron, a subatomic particle, a charged atom, ion Astrid, an antimatter particle, positron Priscilla, and in demonstrating spontaneous quantum jumps and measuring magnetism and size on single electron and positron with precisions 1,000 times higher than previously attained on millions of them. Home: 1600 43rd Ave E Seattle WA 98112-3205 Office: U Wash Physics Dept Box 35-1560 Seattle WA 98195-1560

DEHN, JOSEPH WILLIAM, JR., chemist; b. Bklyn., Feb. 18, 1928; s. Joseph William and Anna Jane (McMahon) D.; m. Mary Baxevanis, June 28, 1953; children—Joseph W. III, George John. B.A., Columbia Coll., N.Y.C., 1949; M.S., Stevens Inst. Tech., 1953; Ph.D, Poly. Inst. Bklyn., 1964. Sr. chemist Interchem. Corp., N.Y.C., 1949-63, Clifton, N.J., 1963-64; group leader chemist Wallace & Tiernan Inc., Belleville, N.J., 1964-67; sr. scientist Shulton Inc., Clifton, 1967-70; sr. chemist Process Chem. div. Diamond Shamrock Corp., Morristown, N.J., 1971-87; sr. chemist Atlantic Industries div. Jepson Corp., Nutley, N.J., 1988-90; sr. rsch. chemist Pall Corp., Glen

Cove, N.Y., 1990—. Patentee in field; contbr. articles to sci. jours. Mem. AAAS, Am. Chem. Soc., Am. Inst. Chemists, N.Y. Acad. Sci., Am. Assn. Textile Chemists and Colorists, N.Y. Pigment Club, Sigma Xi, Phi Lambda Upsilon. Home: 52 Berkshire Rd Great Neck NY 11023-1416 Office: Pall Corp 30 Sea Cliff Ave Glen Cove NY 11542-3690

DEHNER, JOSEPH JULNES, lawyer; b. Cin., Nov. 28, 1948; s. Walter Joseph and Bess (Humphries) D.; m. Noel Julnes, Nov. 19, 1983; children: Holly Julnes, Sara Julnes. AB, Princeton U., 1970; JD, Harvard Law Sch., Cambridge, Mass., 1973. Bar: Ohio 1973, U.S. Dist. Ct. (no. and so. dists.) Ohio 1975, Fla. 1986, U.S. Dist. Ct. (ea. dist.) Ky. 1988, U.S. Ct. Internat. Trade 1992. Law clk. to judge U.S. Court Appeals, Cleve., 1973-75; assoc. Kyte, Conlan, Wulsin & Vogeler, Cin., 1975-78, Frost & Jacobs, Cin., 1978—; chmn. Universal Transactions Inc., 1991-95; co-mgr. Ukraine Investments Ltd. Author: Structured Settlements and Periodic Payment Judgments, 1986, A Guide to Soviet Businesspeople on American Business Law, 1991, Doing Business in Russia, 1992, Dispute Resolution and China, 1994, A Foreign Investors Guide to Ukraine, 1995; contbr. articles to profl. publs. Sec., v.p. Cin. Preservation Assn., 1978-86; mem. Cin. Planning Commn., 1984-85; pres. Charter Com. Greater Cin., 1982-86; chmn. Cin.-Kharkiv Sister City Project, 1988-91; trustee Princeton U., 1970-74, Ohio Hist. Soc., 1974-78; chancellor Episcopal Diocese of So. Ohio, 1997—. Mem. ABA, Internat. Bar Assn., Pub. Investors Arbitration Bar Assn., Ohio State Bar Assn. (chmn. internat. law com. 1989-91), Cin. Bar Assn., Sixth Cir. Jud. Conf. Episcopal. Avocations: tennis, family, reading. Home: 822 Yale Ave Terrace Park OH 45174-1258 Office: Frost & Jacobs 2500 PNC Ctr 201 E 5th St Ste 2500 Cincinnati OH 45202-4182

DE HOFF, JOHN BURLING, physician, consultant; b. Balt., May 28, 1913; s. George William and Pearle Ann (Burling) De H.; m. Mabelle Audrey Dunn, July 9, 1938; children: Susan De Hoff Montgomery, John Howard. MD, Johns Hopkin's U., 1939, MPH, 1967. Diplomate Am. Bd. Preventive Medicine, Am. Bd. Pub. Health. Med. intern Mt. Sinai Hosp., N.Y.C., 1939-41; asst. resident in psychiatry N.Y. Hosp., 1946; pvt. practice internal medicine Balt., 1947-65; asst. commr. Balt. City Health Dept., 1965-69, resident in pub. health, 1966-68, dep. commr., 1969-75, commr., 1975-84; advisor to mayor City of Balt., 1984-87; med. cons. Bd. Phys. Quality Assurance, State of Md., Balt., 1987-97; med. cons. Social Security Adminstrn., 1986-89. Contbr. articles to profl. jours. and community health publs. Col. USAR, 1935-65, ETO. Commonwealth fellow N.Y. Hosp., 1946; Jacobi medalist Mt. Sinai Med. Ctr., N.Y.C., 1983. Fellow APHA (mem. governing coun.); mem. Am. Assn. Pub. Health Physicians (pres. 1977), U.S. Conf. Local Health Officers (pres. 1979), Md. Med. Soc. (councillor, del.), Balt. City Med. Soc. (pres. 1974). Democrat. Presbyterian. Home and Office: 13801 York Rd Apt N7 Cockeysville MD 21030-1855

DEHORATIUS, EDMUND FRANCIS, secondary education educator; b. Phila., July 7, 1973; s. Francis Joseph and Mary Louise (Angentieri) DeH. AB, Duke U., 1995. Upper sch. tchr. Latin, Bancroft Sch., Worcester, Mass., 1995—. Fargo-Gauthier grantee Bancorf Sch., 1996. Mem. Am. Classics League, Renaissance Soc. Am., Medieval Acad., Am. Inst. Archaeology, Classical Assn. New Eng., Mass. Fgn. Lang. Assn. Avocations: soccer, writing, reading. Office: Bancroft Sch 110 Shore Dr Worcester MA 01605-3198

DEHORATIUS, RAPHAEL JOSEPH, rheumatologist; b. Phila., Sept. 16, 1942; s. Pasquale P. and Edith R. DeH.; m. Kathleen M. Carson, Aug. 21, 1965; children: Nicole, Danielle. BS, St. Joseph's U., Phila., 1964; MD, Jefferson Med. Coll., 1968. Med. intern Jefferson Med. Coll., Phila., 1968-69, asst. prof. medicine, 1976-78, assoc. prof. medicine, 1978-82; med. resident U. N.Mex., Albuquerque, 1969-70, rheumatology fellow, 1972-74, asst. prof. medicine, 1974-76; prof. medicine Hahnemann U., Phila., 1982-92, Jefferson Med. Coll./Thomas Jefferson U., Phila., 1992—; chmn. profl. meetings Am. Coll. Rheumatology, Atlanta, 1988-91, edn. coun., 1988-91. Contbr. articles to profl. jours./publs. Maj. USAF, 1970-72. Recipient Lupus Rsch. grant Commonwealth of Pa., Arthritis Rsch. grant. Fellow Am. Coll. Physicians, Am. Coll. Rheumatology; mem. Assn. Am. Immunologists, Am. Fedn. Clin. Rsch. Home: 667 Sproul Rd Villanova PA 19085-1216 Office: Thomas Jefferson Univ 613 Curtis Bldg 1015 Walnut St Philadelphia PA 19107-5005

DEHORITY, EDWARD HAVENS, JR., retired accountant, lawyer; b. Elwood, Ind., Aug. 5, 1930; s. Edward Havens and Gladys Magdaline (Vermillion) D.; m. Jeanne Wilson Davies, Jan. 31, 1953 (dec. 1983); children: Edward Havens III, John Davies; m. Miriam Frances Arnold, Jan. 1, 1984; stepchildren: David Arnold Newman, William Truslow Newman. BS, Ind. U., 1952; JD, Georgetown U., 1956. Bar: Va. 1956; CPA, Ohio 1962. Atty. FTC, Washington, 1956, Cleve., 1957-58; tax acct. Ernst & Young, Cleve., 1958-63; tax mgr. Ernst & Young, Atlanta, 1963-66, ptnr.-in-charge, tax, 1966-70, adminstrv. ptnr., regional ptnr.-in-charge, tax., 1970-72; client relations ptnr. Ernst & Young, Cleve., 1972-78; mng. ptnr. Ernst & Young, Stamford, Conn., 1978-88; trustee, treas. Southern Fed. Tax Inst., Atlanta, 1963-72; lectr. tax subjects, 1964-72; bd. dirs. UST, Inc., 1991—. Contbr. articles to profl. jours. Capt. Cancer Crusade, Atlanta, 1968, Rep. Roundtable, Greenwich, Conn., 1979-88; campaign chmn. United Way, Greenwich, 1984-85, pres. 1986-88. 1st lt. USAF, 1952-54. Mem. U.S. Golf Assn. (sr. amateur com.), Am. Srs. Golf Assn., World Srs. Golf Assn., So. Srs. Golf Assn., Internat. Sr. Golf Soc., 200 Club, Biltmore Forest Golf Club, Blind Brook Club, Chattooga Club, Everglades Club, Loblolly Bay Club, Loblolly Pines Golf Club, Medalist Golf Club, Piedmont Driving Club, Peachtree Golf Club, Wade Hampton Golf Club, Beta Theta Pi. Republican. Presbyterian. Home (winter): 7783 SE Golfhouse Dr Hobe Sound FL 33455-8011

DE HOSTOS, EUGENIO LUIS, cell biologist; b. San Juan, P.R., Nov. 15, 1961; s. Eugenio Maria and Carolina (Anca) de H. BS, Yale U., 1983; PhD, Stanford U., 1989. Postdoctoral fellow Max Planck Inst., Munich, 1989-92, U. Calif., San Francisco, 1992-95; asst. prof. Rice U., Houston, 1995-98; asst. rsch. scientist U. Calif., San Francisco, 1998—. Recipient Career Devel. award Am. Heart Assn., 1993—; postdoctoral fellow A. von Humboldt Found., 1989-91, NIH, 1992-93. Mem. Am. Soc. for Cell Biology. Avocations: travel, reading, the outdoors. Office: VAMC 113B U Calif 4150 Clement St San Francisco CA 94121

DE HOYOS, DEBORA M., lawyer; b. Monticello, N.Y., Aug. 10, 1953; d. Luis and Marion (Kinney) de H.; m. Walter C. Carlson, June 20, 1981; children: Amanda, Greta, Linnea. BA, Wellesley Coll., 1975; JD, Harvard U., 1978. Bar: Ill. 1978, U.S. Dist. Ct. (no. dist.) Ill. 1980. Assoc. Mayer, Brown & Platt, Chgo., 1978-84, ptnr., 1985—, mng. ptnr., 1991—; bd. dirs. Northwestern Healthcare; bd. trustees Providence St. Mel. Sch. Contbr. chpt. to Securitization of Financial Assets, 1991. Chmn. strategic issues com. Econ. Devel. Commn., Chgo., 1992; trustee Chgo. Symphony Orch. Bd. dirs. Chicagoland C. of C. Office: Mayer Brown & Platt 190 S La Salle St Ste 3100 Chicago IL 60603-3441

DEICKEN, RAYMOND FRIEDRICH, neuropsychiatrist, clinical neuroscientist; b. Honolulu, June 28, 1957; s. Raymond T. and Miriam (Ogata) D. AB, Stanford U., 1980, MS, 1980; MD, U. Calif., San Francisco, 1984. Diplomate Nat. Bd. Med. Examiners, Am. Bd. Psychiatry and Neurology. Resident physician U. Calif., San Francisco, 1984-88, rsch. fellow, 1988-91, asst. prof. psychiatry, 1991-97, assoc. prof., 1997—; staff physician VA Med. Ctr., San Francisco, 1991—; invited lectr. World Congress of Biol. Psychiatry Symposium on Brain Imaging, Nice, France, 1997, Soc. Biol. Psychiatry Symposium on Magnetic Resonance Spectroscopy, San Francisco, 1993, Internat. Symposium on Schizophrenia, Sao Paulo, Brazil, 1998. Reviewer manuscripts Biol. Psychiatry, 1987—, Psychiatry Rsch., 1992—; contbr. articles to profl. jours. Alumni mentor Stanford U. Student Alumni Mentor Program, 1993—. Recipient Young Investigator award Nat. Alliance for Rsch. on Schizophrenia and Depression, 1992, 94, Stanley Found. rsch. award Nat. Alliance for Mentally Ill, 1997, 98, VA Physician Rsch. Assoc. Career Devel. award, 1991-95; Dista fellow Soc. Biol. Psychiatry, 1991. Mem. AMA, Soc. Biol. Psychiatry, Internat. Soc. Magnetic Resonance in Medicine, Am. Psychiat. Assn., Internat. Soc. Neuroimaging in Psychiatry, N.Y. Acad. Scis. Episcopalian. Home: 197 Carnelian Way San Francisco CA 94131-1780 Office: Dept Veterans Affairs Med Ctr 4150 Clement St San Francisco CA 94121-1545

DEIGHTON, LEN, author; b. London, Feb. 18, 1929. Author: The Ipcress File, 1962 (motion picture U.S., 1963), Horse Under Water, 1963, U.S. edit. 1968, Funeral in Berlin, 1964 (motion picture U.S., 1965), Ou Est le Garlic/Basic French Cooking, 1965, 2d edit., 1979, U.S. edit., 1977, Action Cook Book, 1965, Cookstrip Cook Book, 1966, Billion Dollar Brain, 1966 (motion picture U.S., 1966), An Expensive Place to Die, 1967, Len Deighton's Dossier, 1967, Only When I Larf, 1968 (motion picture U.S., 1968), Bomber, 1970 (radio drama U.S., 1970), U.S. Edit. of Declarations of War, 1971, Close-Up, 1972, Spy Story, 1974 (motion picture U.S., 1974), Eleven Declarations of War, 1975, Yesterday's Spy, 1975, Twinkle, Twinkle, Little Spy, 1976, Catch a Falling Spy, 1976, Fighter, 1977, U.S. edit., 1978, SS-GB, 1978, U.S. edit., 1979, Blitzkreig, 1979, U.S. edit., 1980, XPD, 1981, Goodbye Mickey Mouse, 1982, Berlin Game, 1983, Mexico Set, 1984, London Match, 1985, Winter: A Berlin Family 1899-1945, 1987, U.S. edit., 1988, Spy Hook, 1988, Spy Line, 1989, Spy Sinker, 1990, Basic French Cookery Course, 1990, ABC of French Food, 1989, U.S. edit., 1990, MAMista, 1991, City of Gold, 1992, Violent Ward, 1993, Blood, Tears & Folly, 1993, Faith, 1994, U.S. edit., 1995, Hope, 1995, U.S. edit., 1996, Charity, 1996; co-author: The Assassination of President Kennedy, 1967, Airshipwreck, 1978, U.S. edit., 1979, Battle of Britain, 1980, 2d edit., 1990, U.S. edit., 1980; (13-part TV series) Game, Set & Match, 1985. Office: care Jonathan Clowes Ltd, 10 Iron Bridge House, Bridge Approach London NW1 8BD, England

DEIHL, MICHAEL ALLEN, federal agency administrator; b. Bluffton, Ind., Apr. 22, 1952; s. Robert W. and Betty J. (Miller) D.; m. Deborah Ann Crabb, June 16, 1973; 1 child, Samantha Lynn. BSEE, Colo. State U., 1974. East slope area mgr. ECPO Bur. Reclamation, Loveland, Colo., 1981-85, chief com. and control divsn., ECPO, 1985-87; chief maintenance divsn. Hoover Dam Bur. Reclamation, Boulder City, Nev., 1987-90; project mgr. Alaska Power Adminstrn., Dept. Energy, Juneau, 1990-92, dir. power divsn., 1992, adminstr., 1992-95; adminstr. Dept. Energy Southwestern Power Adminstrn., Tulsa, 1995—. Office: Southwestern Power Admin One W 3d St PO Box 1619 Tulsa OK 74101-1619

DEININGER, DAVID GEORGE, judge; b. Monroe, Wis., July 9, 1947; s. Wilbur Emerson and Anna Emilie (Karlen) D.; m. Mary Carol Nussbaum, June 4, 1969; children: Jonathan David, Christopher Jacob, Emilie Joanne. BS, U.S. Naval Acad., 1969; JD, U. Wis., 1978. Bar: Wis. 1978, Ill. 1978, U.S. Dist. Ct. (we. dist.) Wis. 1978. Ptnr. Benkert, Spielman, Asmus & Deininger, Monroe, 1978-87; legislator Wis. State Assembly, Madison, 1987-94; of counsel Brennan, Steil, Basting & MacDougall, S.C., Monroe, 1988-94; cir. ct. judge Green County, 1994-96. Active Monroe Sch. Bd., 1986-89, Monroe Theatre Guild, 1980—; chmn. Green County Rep. Cen. Com., Monroe, 1982-84. Lt. USN, 1969-75. Mem. Green County Bar Assn. (pres. 1982-83), Wis. State Bar Assn., Am. Legion, VFW, Optimists (pres. Monroe chpt. 1984-85). Avocations: bridge, cross country skiing, boating. Home: 814 19th Ave Monroe WI 53566-1661 Office: Ct Appeals Dist IV Madison WI 53703-3330

DEISENHOFER, JOHANN, biochemistry educator, researcher; b. Zusamaltheim, Bavaria, Germany, Sept. 30, 1943; came to U.S., 1988; s. Johann and Thekla (Magg) D.: m. Kirsten Fischer-Lindahl, June 19, 1989. Diploma in Physics, Technische U., Munich, 1971, PhD, 1974, Doctor habilis, 1987. Postdoctoral fellow Max-Planck Inst. Biochemie, Martinsried, Fed. Republic of Germany, 1974-76, staff scientist, 1976-88; investigator Howard Hughes Med. Inst., Dallas, 1988—; prof. biochemistry U. Tex., Dallas, 1988—. Contbr. over 75 sci. papers to profl. publs. Recipient Nobel prize for chemistry, 1988; co-recipient Biol. Physics prize Am. Phys. Soc., 1986, Otto Bayer prize, 1988; decorated The Knight Commader's Cross (Badge and Star) Of the Order of Merit of Germany, 1990, Bavarian Order of Merit, 1992. Mem. AAAS, Nat. Acad. Scis. U.S.A., Am. Crystallographic Assn., German Biophys. Soc., The Protein Soc., Biophys. Soc., Academia Europaea.

DEISENROTH, CLINTON WILBUR, electrical engineer; b. Louisville, Aug. 9, 1941; s. Clifton Earl and Nell (Pierce) D.; m. Lisbeth D. Isaacs, May 10, 1974; 1 dau., Susan Michelle. BEE, Ga. Inst. Tech., 1965. With Raytheon Co., 1966-81, div. mgr. Addington Labs., Inc., solid state products div., Santa Clara, Calif., 1975-77, program mgr. electromagnetic systems div., Goleta, Calif., 1977-79, dir. surface navy electronic warfare systems, 1979-81; sr. v.p. systems div. Teledyne-MEC, 1981-84; pres. Teledyne CME, 1984-90; exec. v.p., gen. mgr. Aerospace Products div. G&H Tech., Inc., 1990-92; v.p. bus. devel. Whittaker Electronic Systems, 1992-94, v.p., gen. mgr., 1994-96, pres., 1996; pres. CWD and Assocs. Mem. IEEE. Home: 2052 Hartwick Circle Thousand Oaks CA 91360-1905

DEISLER, PAUL FREDERICK, JR., retired oil company executive; b. El Paso, Tex., Jan. 20, 1926; s. Paul Frederick and Jeanie Donnelly (Monroe) D.: m. Ellen Louise Bardwell, June 15, 1950; children: Jane Ellen, Paul Conrad, Julia Monroe. BS in Chem. Engring, Tex. A&M U., 1948; MS, Princeton U., 1949, PhD, 1952. With Shell Oil Co., various locations, 1952—, v.p. transp. and supplies, 1969-71; dir. supply and refining Compañia Shell de Venezuela, 1971-73; v.p. Chem. Co., Houston, 1973-74; v.p. research and engring. products Shell Oil Co., Houston, 1974-76; v.p. health, safety and environment Shell Oil Co., 1976-86; dir. Chem. Industry Inst. Toxicology, 1975-86; bd. dirs. Am. Indsl. Health Council, 1977-81, 84-85; chmn. adv. coun. dept. chem. engring. Princeton U., 1978-81; vis. exec. prof. Sch. Bus., U. Houston, 1986-90, mem. curriculum adv. bd. Inst. Corp. Environ. Mgmt., 1992-93; mem. exec. com. Sci. Adv. Bd., EPA, 1986-94, cons., 1994—; mem. environ. adv. coun. Rohm and Haas Co., 1989-93; adj. prof. environ. risk assessment U. Tex. Sch. Pub. Health, 1990-94; mem. policy com. Ctr. for Global Studies, Houston Advanced Rsch. Ctr., The Woodlands, Tex., 1992-98; chair policy com. Houston Advanced Rsch. Ctr., The Woodlands, 1995-96. Editor: Reducing the Carcinogenic Risk in Industry, 1984; area editor for health and environ. risk analysis Risk Analysis: An Internat. Jour., 1997, 98; author articles on environ. health risk assessment and mgmt. Bd. dirs. ARC, Houston, 1975-80; chmn. fin. com. Houston Sci. Fair, 1974-76; alumni councilor Tex. A&M Research Found., 1977—, trustee, 1986—; bd. dirs. Tex. Inst. for Advancement of Chem. Tech., 1988—; mem. governing coun. Inst. for Bus., Ethics and Pub. Issues, U. Houston, 1987-90. Served with USN, 1944-46, PTO. Fellow Soc. Risk Analysis (pres. 1986-87); mem. AAAS, AIChE, N.Y. Acad. Scis., U.S. Naval Inst., Assn. Princeton Grad. Alumni (bd. dirs. 1976-79), Am. Petroleum Inst. (chmn. health, environ. and safety gen. com. 1983-84), Am. Chem. Soc., Soc. for Regulatory Toxicology and Pharmacology, Sigma Xi, Tau Beta Pi, Phi Kappa Phi. Address: PO Box 5819 Austin TX 78763-5819

DEISSLER, MARY ALICE, foundation executive; b. Oneanta, N.Y., Dec. 30, 1955; d. George W. and Carol (Zorda) Baker; m. James N. Deissler, Nov. 24, 1987; children: Benjamin, Eliza. BA, U. Mass., 1978; MBA, Babson Coll., 1982. Fin. analyst Digital Equipment Corporation, Maynard, Mass., 1978-82; devel. dir. Handel & Haydn Soc., Boston, 1984-89, gen. mgr., 1984-89, exec. dir., 1990—; pres., bd. dirs. Studebaker Movement Theatre Co., Boston, 1986-88. Bd. dirs. Early Music Am., N.Y.C., 1989—, v.p., 1991—, pres., 1994; bd. dirs. Babson Coll., 1990-94, Chorus Am., 1991—, v.p., 1992, pres.-elect, 1996, pres., 1997, pres. bd. dirs., 1997; mem. bd. Arts/Boston, 1994—, bd. dirs.; bd. dirs. Boston Ptnrs. in Edn.; treas. Handel House of Am. Found. Mem. Am. Symphony Orch. League. Office: Handel & Haydn Soc 300 Massachusetts Ave Boston MA 02115-4544

DEISSLER, ROBERT GEORGE, fluid dynamicist, researcher; b. Greenville, Pa., Aug. 1, 1921; s. Victor Girard and Helen Stella (Fisher) D.; m. June Marie Gallagher, Oct. 7, 1950; children—Robert Joseph, Mary Beth, Ellen Ann, Anne Marie. BS, Carnegie Inst. Tech., 1943; MS, Case Inst. Tech., 1948; PHD, Case Western Res. U., 1989. Researcher Goodyear Aircraft Corp., Akron, OH, 1943-44; aero. rsch. scientist NASA Lewis Rsch. Ctr., Cleve., 1947-52, chief fundamental heat transfer br., 1952-70, staff scientist, sci. cons. fluid physics, 1970-94, disting. rsch. assoc., 1994—; fellow Lewis Rsch. Acad., 1983—; staff scientist sr. level emeritus, 1994. Author: Turbulent Fluid Motion, Taylor and Francis, 1998; contbr. articles to profl. jours.; areas of rsch. fluid turbulence, turbulent heat transfer, turbulent solutions of equations of fluid motion, nonlinear dynamics and chaos, meteorol. and astrophysical flows, radiative heat transfer in gases, heat transfer in powders. Served as lt. (j.g.) USNR, 1944-46. Recipient Max Jacob Meml. award ASME/Am. Inst. Chem. Engrs., 1975; NACA/NASA Exceptional Svc. award, 1957, Outstanding Publ. award, 1978; Lewis Rsch. Acad. fellow, 1983—. Fellow AIAA (Best Paper award 1975, Tech. Achievement award 1981), ASME (Heat Transfer Meml. award 1964); mem. Am. Phys. Soc., Sigma Xi. Roman Catholic. Avocations: violin, reading, walking. Home: 4540 W 213th St Fairview Park OH 44126-2106 Office: NASA Lewis Rsch Ctr 21000 Brookpark Rd Cleveland OH 44135-3191 *It is desirable that research be fundamentally based, even when it is undertaken with a view toward an application. Then the research will likely be worthwhile, regardless of whether or not the application materializes.*

DEITER, NEWTON ELLIOTT, clinical psychologist; b. N.Y.C., Dec. 12, 1931; s. Benjamin and Anna (Leibowitz) D. BS, UCLA, 1957; MS, Leland Stanford, 1960; PhD in Clin. Psychology, U. Chgo., 1965. Cert. in clin. psychology. Pvt. practice clin. psychology L.A., 1965-90; exec. dir. Nat. Family Planning Coun., L.A., 1965-76, Gay Media Task Force, L.A., 1976-86; staff cons. Aaron Spelling Prodns., L.A., 1980-90, spl. cons. NBC, L.A., 1970-79, cons. broadcast stds. dept. CBS, L.A., 1968-82, cons. City Coun., City of L.A., 1975-85. Columnist Bottomline Mag., 1992—, Palm Springs Presents Mag., 1996—. Mem. Dem. Ctrl. Com., L.A., 1972-76; bd. dirs. Gay Cmty. Svcs. Ctr., L.A., 1970-75, Am. Cancer Soc., L.A., 1972-77, Palm Springs Gay Tourism Coun., 1993-95, Desert Gay Tourism Guild, 1996-99; commr. L.A. Probation Commn., 1977-85; mem. bd. advisors San Francisco Sheriffs Dept., 1969-79; vice chmn. recreation and pks. commr. City of Rancho Mirage, 1997—. Lt. col. USAFR, 1950-75. Inductee, Internat. Gay Travel Assn. Hall of Fame, 1994. Mem. NATAS, Press Club L.A., Internat. Gay Travel Assn. (bd. dirs. 1986-93, pres. 1991-92), Desert Bus. Assn. (v.p. 1993, bd. dirs. 1992), Internat. Food, Wine and Travel Writers Assn. (bd. dirs., v.p./treas. 1995-97, pres. 1997-99, treas. 1999—), Air Force Assn., Am. Mensa, Masons. Avocations: photography, wine making, travel writing. Home: 71426 Estellita Dr Rancho Mirage CA 92270-4215 Office: Rancho Mirage Travel 71-428 US Highway 111 Rancho Mirage CA 92270-4130

DEITERS, SISTER JOAN ADELE, psychotherapist, nun, chemistry educator; b. Cin., Apr. 28, 1934; d. Alfred Harry and Rose Catherine (Rusche) D. BA, Coll. Mt. St. Joseph, Cin., 1963; M Christian Spirituality, Creighton U., Omaha, 1985; PhD, U. Cin., 1967. Joined Sisters of Charity, Roman Cath. Ch., 1952; prof. chemistry Coll. Mt. St. Joseph, Cin., 1968-78; prof. chemistry Matthew Vassar Jr. chair, Vassar Coll., Poughkeepsie, N.Y., 1978-96. Contbr. articles to profl. jours. Mem. Am. Chem. Soc., Sisters of Charity, Sigma Xi. Democrat. Home and Office: 397 Hooker Ave # 1 Poughkeepsie NY 12603-3626

DEITRICH, RICHARD ADAM, pharmacology educator; b. Monte Vista, Colo., Apr. 22, 1931; s. Robert Adam and Freda Leona (Scott) D.; m. Mary Margaret Burkholder, Jan. 29, 1954; children: Vivian Gay, Leslie Lynn, Lori Christine. BS, U. Colo., 1953, MS, 1954, PhD, 1959. Postdoctoral fellow, then instr. Johns Hopkins U., Balt., 1959-63; asst. prof., then assoc. prof. U. Colo., Denver, 1963-76, prof. pharmacology, 1976—, sci. dir. Alcohol Rsch. Ctr., 1977—; vis. prof. U. Berne, Switzerland, 1973-74. Editor: Development of Animal Models, 1981, Initial Sensitivity to Alcohol, 1990; contbr. over 100 articles to sci. publs. Pres. Mile High Coun. on Alcoholism, Denver, 1972-73; moderator 1st Universalist Ch., Denver, 1979. With U.S. Army, 1954-56. Grantee Nat. Inst. Alcoholism, 1977—, Nat. Inst. Communicative Disease and Stroke, 1963, numerous others. Mem. Rsch. Soc. on Alcoholism (pres. 1981-83), Internat. Soc. Biomed. Rsch. on Alcoholism (treas. 1986-94), Am. Soc. Pharmacology, Am. Soc. Biol. Chemistry. Avocations: photography, fishing, camping. Office: Univ Colo 4200 E 9th Ave Denver CO 80220-3700

DEITRICK, WILLIAM EDGAR, lawyer; b. N.Y.C., July 30, 1944; s. John English and Dorothy Alice (Geib) D.; m. Emily Jane Posey, June 22, 1968; children: William Jr., Elizabeth, Peter. BA, Johns Hopkins U., 1967; JD, Cornell U., 1971. Bar: Ill. 1972, U.S. Dist. Ct. (no. dist.) Ill. 1972, U.S. Ct. Appeals (7th cir.) 1976, D.C. 1981. Ptnr. Gardner, Carton and Douglas, Chgo., 1972-85; sr. v.p., dep. gen. counsel, mgr. litigation div. Continental Bank N.A., 1985-91; ptnr. Mayer, Brown & Platt, Chgo., 1991—. Contbr. articles to profl. jours. Trustee North Shore Country Day Sch., 1992-97; gov. mem. Shedd Aquarium; With U.S. Army, 1968-70. Mem. ABA, Ill. Bar Assn., Chgo. Bar Assn., Johns Hopkins U. Alumni Assn. (class agt. 1967-95), Cornell Law Sch. Chgo. Alumni Assn. (chmn. 1985-87). Clubs: Legal, Univ. (Chgo.); Indian Hill (Winnetka, Ill.). Home: 365 Greenwood Ave Glencoe IL 60022-2045 Office: Mayer Brown & Platt 190 S La Salle St Ste 3100 Chicago IL 60603-3441

DEITZ, PAULA, magazine editor; b. Trenton, N.J., Apr. 26, 1938; d. David and Rosalie (Nathanson) D.; m. (George) Frederick Morgan, Nov. 30, 1969. BA, Smith Coll., 1959; MA, Columbia U., 1969. Asst. editor Bollingen series Bollingen Found., N.Y.C., 1962-67; assoc. editor The Hudson Rev., N.Y.C., 1967-75, co-editor, 1975-98, editor, pres., 1998—; rsch. asst. Pakistan Mission to UN, N.Y.C., 1961; lectr. Columbia U., N.Y.C., 1962. Contbr. articles on art, architecture, landscape design to newspapers and mags. Bd. counselors Smith Coll., 1992-96. Mem. Cosmopolitan Club, Colony Club. Avocation: swimming. Office: The Hudson Rev 684 Park Ave New York NY 10021-5043*

DEITZ, SUSAN ROSE, newspaper advice columnist; b. Far Rockaway, N.Y., Mar. 21, 1934; d. Emanuel and Florence Jean (Goodstein) Davis; m. Morris J. Mandelker, Nov. 29, 1975; 1 son, Scott Richard; m. Richard Alan Deitz, Dec. 22, 1958 (dec. 1967). Student Smith Coll., Barnard Coll., N.Y.C., Art Students League, N.Y.C., Stella Adler Theater Studio. Syndicated advice columnist L.A. Times Syndicate, 1975—; mem. faculty New Sch., N.Y.C., 1977-79; radio personality, 1979; columnist Prodigy Svcs., White Plains, N.Y., 1987-93; spkr. satellite conf. NAFE, 1990; lectr. L.A. Times Syndicate Spkrs. Bur. Author: (novel) Valency Girl, 1976, Single File, 1989, paperback edit., 1990. Mem. Women in Communications (Outstanding Mem. award 1984), Authors Guild, Newspaper Features Assn., Overseas Press Club (elect), Smith Coll. Club. E-mail: sumor123@aol.com.

DEJAMMET, ALAIN, diplomat. Perm. rep. of France to UN N.Y.C., 1995—. Office: Perm Mission of France to UN 1 Dag Hammarskjöld Plz 245 E 47th St Fl 44 New York NY 10017-2201

DE JANOSI, PETER ENGEL, research manager; b. Pecs, Hungary, June 26, 1928; came to U.S., 1947; s. Paul E. and Kitty de Janosi; m. Monica Reis, Nov. 30, 1963; children: Paul, Nicholas, Alexander. BA, Conn. Wesleyan U., 1950; MA, U. Mich., 1951, PhD, 1956; PhD (hon.), Budapest U. Econs., 1997. Economist Standard Oil Co. of N.J., N.Y.C., 1956-62; program officer in charge Ford Found., N.Y.C., 1962-80; v.p. Russell Sage Found., N.Y.C., 1980-90; dir. Internat. Inst. Applied Systems Analysis, Laxenburg, Austria, 1990-96; sr. advisor Lead Internat., N.Y.C., 1998—; mem. adv. coun. Cornell U. Coll. of Human Ecology, Ithaca, N.Y., 1985-90; mem. goven. coun. Internat. Inst. for Applied Systems Analysis, Laxenburg, Austria, 1987-90; mem. exec. com. The Internat. Fedn. of Insts. of Advanced Studies, 1993-96; governing bd. Inst. Internatl. Global Environ. Strategies, Japan, 1997—. Recipient Cross of Honor first class Republic of Austria, golden decoration Province and City of Vienna. Mem. Am. Econ. Assn., Coun. on Fgn. Rels., Century Assn. Home: 5 Leroy Pl Chappaqua NY 10514

DEJARNETTE, FRED ROARK, aerospace engineer; b. Rustburg, Va., Oct. 21, 1933; married, 1951; 2 children. BS, Ga. Inst. Tech., 1957, MS, 1958; PhD in Aerospace Engring., Va. Polytech. Inst., 1965. Aerodynamic engr. Douglas Aircraft Co., Inc., 1958-61; aerospace engr. Langley Rsch. Ctr. NASA, 1963-65; assoc. prof. aerospace engring. Va. Polytech. Inst., 1965-70; assoc. prof. N.C. State U., 1970-71, prof., 1971-93, grad. adminstr., 1973-83, assoc. head, 1980-83, dept. head, prof. mechanical & aerospace engring., 1993—; cons. Rsch. Triangle Inst., 1979-89. Fellow AIAA (Thermophysics award 1995), Soc. Automotive Engring. Achievements include research in aerodynamics and computational fluid dynamics. Office: NC State U Dept Mech & Aerospace Engring Box 7910 Raleigh NC 27695-7910*

DEJARNETTE, SHIRLEY SHEA, treasurer; b. Bradford, Pa., Feb. 21, 1943; d. James H. and Jean L. (Dennis) Shea; m. Jaquelin Harrison DeJarnette, Mar. 21, 1978; 1 child, Shea Ann. AA, Stephens Coll., Columbia, 1963; BS in Bus. Adminstrn., U. Mo., 1966; Program for Mgmt.

Devel. Cert., Harvard U., 1982. CFA. Asst. trust officer Boatmen's Nat. Bank St. Louis, 1966-74; mgr. investor rels. Kraft, Inc., Glenview, Ill., 1974-77; dir. investment rsch. Cummins Engine Co., Columbus, Ind., 1977-78; asst. treas. Mead Corp., Dayton, Ohio, 1978-86; v.p., exec. Chase Manhattan Bank, N.Y.C., 1986-89; mng. dir. DeJarnette Inv Adv, Wintergreen, Va., 1989-90; asst. v.p. investment and banking U. Mo., Columbia, 1990—; mem. adv. bd. TR Assocs. Realty, Boston, 1995. Mem. Leadership Dayton, 1983—; bd. trustees Stephens Coll., Columbia, Mo., 1992-96; bd. dirs. Mead Corp Found., Dayton, Ohio, 1986. Mem. Assn. Investment Mgmt. and Rsch. (mem. disciplinary review com.), St. Louis Soc. Fin. Analysts, Fin. Mgmt. Assn. Home: 2616 Johnson Dr Columbia MO 65203-1520 Office: U Mo Sys 215 University Hall Columbia MO 65211

DEJESUS-KELLOGG, SARA E., federal judge; b. 1947. JD, U. P.R., 1975; LLM, U. Miami, 1978. Bar: P.R. Law clk. to Hon. Jose V. Toledo and Gilberto Gierbolini U.S. Dist. Ct. for Dist. P.R., 1974-76; assoc. Jimenez & Fuste, San Juan, Brown, Newsome & Cordova, San Juan; bankruptcy judge for P.R., U.S. Bankruptcy Ct., Hato Rey, 1986—; former adminstrv. law judge Social Security Adminstrn. Office: US Bankruptcy Ct Federico Degetau Fed Bldg 150 Carlos Chardon Ave 495 Hato Rey PR 00918

DE JONG, ARTHUR JAY, education consultant, former university president; b. Paterson, N.J., Feb. 24, 1934; s. Peter A. and Anna (Vander Schaaf) De J.; m. Joyce Van Doorn, Dec. 21, 1957; children: Mark, Beth, Paul, Ruth and Richard (twins). B.A., Central Coll., Pella, Iowa, 1956; B.D., Western Theol. Sem., 1959; M.Th., Princeton Theol. Sem., 1962; S.T.D., San Francisco Theol. Sem., 1971. Chaplain Central Coll., 1960-66, dir. counseling, 1966-69, assoc. acad. dean, 1969-71, acting acad. dean, 1971-72, asst. to pres., 1972-78, instr. in religion, 1960-62, asst. prof. religion, 1962-68, assoc. prof., 1968-72, prof., 1972-78; pres. Muskingum Coll., 1978-87, Whitworth Coll., Spokane, Wash, 1988-92; cons. on ch.-related higher edn., 1992—; bd. dirs. council Ind. Colls., 1976-78. Author: Making It To Adulthood: The Emerging Self, 1972, Reclaiming A Mission: New Directions for the Church Related College, 1990; contbr. chpt. to book. Mem. Asheville Choral Soc. *

DE JONG, DAVID SAMUEL, lawyer, educator; b. Washington, Jan. 8, 1951; s. Samuel and Dorothy (Thomas) De J.; m. Tracy Ann Barger, Sept. 23, 1995; 1 child, Jacob Samuel. BA, U. Md., 1972; JD, Washington and Lee U., 1975; LLM in Taxation, Georgetown U., 1979. Bar: Md. 1975, U.S. Dist. Ct. Md. 1977, U.S. Tax Ct. 1977, U.S. Ct. Appeals (4th cir.) 1978, U.S. Supreme Ct. 1979, D.C. 1980, U.S. Dist. Ct. D.C. 1983, U.S. Ct. Claims, U.S. Ct. Appeals (fed. cir.) 1983; CPA, Md.; cert. valuation analyst. Atty. Gen. Bus. Svcs., Inc., Rockville, Md., 1975-80; ptnr. Stein, Sperling, Bennett, De Jong, Driscoll, Greenfeig & Metro P.A., Rockville, 1980—; adj. prof. Southea. U., Washington, 1979-85, Am. U., Washington, 1983—; instr. U. Md., College Park, 1986-87, Montgomery Coll., Rockville, 1983. Co-author: (ann. book) J.K. Lasser's Year-Round Tax Strategies, 1989—; editor Notes and Comments, Washington and Lee U. Law Rev., 1974-75. V.p. Seneca Whetstone Homeowners Assn., Gaithersburg, Md., 1981-82, pres. 1982-83. Mem. ABA, AICPA, Am. Assn. Atty.-CPAs (bd. dirs. 1997—, sec. 1998-99, treas. 1999—), Md. Bar Assn., Montgomery County Bar Assn. (chmn. tax sect. 1991-92, treas. 1996-97), D.C. Bar Assn., Md. Assn. CPAs, D.C. Inst. CPAs, Nat. Assn. Cert. Valuation Analysts, Inst. Bus. Appraisers, Phi Alpha Delta. Office: 25 W Middle Ln Rockville MD 20850-2214

DE KANTER, ELLEN ANN, English language professional, educator; b. Spokane, Wash., Mar. 10, 1926; d. George L. and Alison P. (Christy) Tharp; m. Scipio de Kanter, Feb. 2, 1949 (dec.); children: Scipio, Georgette, Robert, Adriana. BA, Mexico City Coll.-U. of Ams., 1947; MEd, U. Houston, 1972, MA in Spanish, 1974, EdD, 1979. Dir. bilingual edn., prof. U. St. Thomas, Houston, dir. bilingual edn., 1979—. Contbr. articles to profl. jours. Title VII grantee, 1986-89, 88-91, 89-92, 92-93, 92-95, 94-97, 95-98, 97-99, 98—. Mem. Nat. Assn. Bilingual Edn. (chmn. 1989 conf., program chair 1993 conf.), Houston Area Assn. Bilingual Edn. (pres. 1987-88), Inst. Hispanic Culture (bd. dirs. 1989-90). Home: 3015 Meadowview Dr Missouri City TX 77459-3308 Office: U St Thomas 3800 Montrose Blvd Houston TX 77006-4626

DEKAY, BARBARA ANN, social worker; b. Louisville, Mar. 29, 1955; d. William Richard and Mildred Anita (Chapin) DeK.; div. 1989; 1 child, Jonathan Richard; m. Jonathon P. Hubbert, 1994. BA, U. Louisville, 1976, MSSW, 1979. Lic. clin. social worker, Ky. Residential aide Lynwood Treatment Ctr., Louisville, 1976-77; house mgr. Phoenix House Louisville Dept. Human Svcs., 1977-79; Ohio County coord. Green River Comprehensive Care Ctr., Owensboro, Ky., 1980-82; psychiat. social worker VA Med. Ctr., North Chicago, Ill., 1982; psychiat. social worker VA Med. Ctr., Louisville, 1982-83, 84-86, med.-surg. social worker, 1983-84, outpatient therapist, 1986-93, outpatient coord. post-traumatic stress disorder unit, 1993-94; asst. dir. emergency psychiatry svc., dept. psychiatry and behavioral scis., sch. medicine U. Louisville, 1994-95; team leader Ctr. for Supported Living, Seven. Counties Svc., 1995-97; cons., therapist Naval Ordnance Sta., Louisville, 1989-93; cons. U.S. Post Office, Louisville, 1990, Flair T. Cons., Inc., 1994—, Bingham Child Guidance Clin., 1998—. Mem. Nat. Assn. Social Workers, ARC Disater Svcs., AAUW. Republican. Episcopalian. Avocations: counted cross-stitch, bicycling, golf, pool, photography. Home: 10409 Cady Cove Ct Louisville KY 40223-3404 Office: Bingham Child Guidance Clin 200 E Chestnut St Louisville KY 40202-1822

DEKEL, EDDIE, economics educator; b. N.Y.C., Sept. 28, 1958; s. Johanan and Arza (Landau) D.; m. Ayelet Tabak, Aug. 15, 1982; children: Elior, Maáyan. Ba, Tel Aviv U., 1981; PhD, Harvard U., 1986. Miller rsch. fellow U. Calif., Berkeley, 1986-88, assoc. prof. econs., 1988—. Contbr. articles to profl. jours., 1986—. 1st sgt. Israel Def. Forces, 1977-80. Sloan dissertation fellow Sloan Found., 1985-86, Sloan rsch. fellow, 1990—; NSF rsch. grantee, 1988—. Mem. Am. Econ. Assn., Econometric Soc. Office: Univ Calif Dept Econs Berkeley CA 94720

DEKKER, EUGENE EARL, biochemistry educator; b. Highland, Ind., July 23, 1927; s. Peter and Anne (Hendrikse) D.; m. Harriet Ella Holwerda, July 5, 1958; children: Gwen E., Paul D., Tom R. A.B., Calvin Coll., 1949; M.S., U. Ill., 1951, Ph.D., 1954. Instr. U. Louisville Med. Sch., 1954-56; instr. biol. chemistry U. Mich. Med. Sch., Ann Arbor, 1956-58, asst. prof., 1958-65, assoc. prof., 1965-70, prof., 1970-94, assoc. chmn. dept., 1975-88, emeritus prof., 1994—. Served with USN, 1945-46. Mem. AAAS, Am. Chem. Soc., Am. Soc. Biol. Chemists, Am. Soc. Plant Physiologists, Oxygen Soc., Protein Soc., Sigma Xi, Phi Lambda Upsilon. Mem. Christian Reformed Ch. Home: 2612 Manchester Rd Ann Arbor MI 48104-6500 Office: U Mich Med Sch Dept Biol Chemistry Ann Arbor MI 48109-0606

DEKKER, GEORGE GILBERT, literature educator, literary scholar, writer; b. Long Beach, Calif., Sept. 8, 1934; s. Gilbert J. and Laura (Barnes) D.; m. Linda Jo Bartholomew, Aug. 31, 1973; children by previous marriage: Anna Allegra, Clara Joy, Ruth Siobhan, Laura Daye. B.A. in English, U. Calif.-Santa Barbara, 1955; M.A. in English, 1958; M.Litt., Cambridge U. (Eng.), 1961; Ph.D. in English, U. Essex (Eng.), 1967. Lectr. U. Wales, Swansea, 1962-64; lectr. in lit. U. Essex, 1964-69, reader in lit., 1969-72, dean Sch. Comparative Studies, 1969-71; assoc. prof. English Stanford (Calif.) U., 1972-74, prof., 1974—, chmn. dept., 1978-81, 84-85, Joseph S. Atha prof. humanities, 1988—, dir. program in Am. Studies, 1988-91, assoc. dean grad. policy, 1993-96. Author: Sailing After Knowledge, 1963, James Fenimore Cooper the Novelist, 1967; Coleridge and the Literature of Sensibility, 1978, The American Historical Romance, 1987; editor: Donald Davie: The Responsibilities of Literature, 1983. Nat. Endowment Humanities fellow, 1977; Inst. Advanced Studies in Humanities fellow U. Edinburgh (Scotland), 1982; hon. fellow, Clare Hall Cambridge, 1997, Stanford Humanities Ctr., 1997. Mem. MLA. Democrat. Office: Stanford U Dept English Stanford CA 94305 *Over the past forty years I have divided my personal and professional life between the U.S. and Britain—not England alone, but Ireland, Scotland and Wales, too. This experience has given the distinctive stamp to my work as a teacher and writer, making me as much at home with Scott as with Hawthorne, with a British as well as an American university. I think I might write a good book on Henry James some day.*

DEKKER, MARCEL, publishing company executive; b. Amsterdam, The Netherlands, Feb. 12, 1931; came to U.S., 1939, naturalized, 1945; s. Maurits and Rozetta S. (Roos) D.; m. Harriett Gromb, July 21, 1967; children—Russell Maurits, David Robert, Jacqueline. B.S., N.Y. U., 1957. Advt. and import mgr. Intersci. Pub. Co., N.Y.C., 1958-62; pres., chief exec. officer Marcel Dekker, Inc., N.Y.C., 1963—; mng. dir. Marcel Dekker, AG, Basel, Switzerland, 1968—. Served with USAF, 1951-55. Club: Burning Tree Country (Greenwich, Conn.). Office: Marcel Dekker Inc 270 Madison Ave Fl 4 New York NY 10016-0671*

DEKMEJIAN, RICHARD HRAIR, political science educator; b. Aleppo, Syria, Aug. 3, 1933; came to U.S., 1950, naturalized, 1955; s. Hrant H. and Vahede V. (Matossian) D.; m. Anoush Hagopian, Sept. 19, 1954; children: Gregory, Armen, Haig. B.A., U. Conn., 1959; M.A., Boston U., 1960; Middle East Inst. cert., Columbia U., 1964, Ph.D., 1966. Mem. faculty SUNY, Binghamton, 1964-86; prof., chmn. dept. polit. sci. U. So. Calif., Los Angeles, 1986-90, prof. internat. bus. Marshall Sch. Bus.; also master Hinman Coll., 1971-72; lectr. Fgn. Svc. Inst., Dep. State, 1976-87; vis. prof. Columbia U., U. Pa., 1977-78; cons. Dept. State, AID, USIA, UN. Author: Egypt Under Nasir, 1971, Patterns of Political Leadership, 1975; Islam in Revolution, 1985, 2nd edit., 1995, Ethnic Lobbies in U.S. Foreign Policy, 1997; contbr. articles to profl. jours. Pres. So. Tier Civic Ballet Co., 1973-76. Served with AUS, 1955-57. Mem. Am. Polit. Sci. Assn., Middle East Inst., Middle East Studies Assn., Internat. Inst. Strategic Studies, Internat. Polit. Sci. Assn., Skull & Dagger, Pi Sigma Alpha, Phi Alpha Theta. Home: 1644 Oakengate Dr Glendale CA 91207-1552 Office: U So Calif Dept Polit Sci Los Angeles CA 90089-0044

DEKOK, DAVID, writer, reporter; b. Holland, Mich., July 17, 1953; s. Paul W. and Olga (Kilian) DeK.; m. Lisa W. Brittingham, Oct. 1, 1988; children: Elizabeth B., Lydia B. BA, Hope Coll., Holland, 1975. Reporter The News-Item, Shamokin, Pa., 1975-87, The Patriot-News, Harrisburg, Pa., 1987—; cons. PBS documentary Centralia Fire, 1982-83; guest lectr. Bucknell U., Lewisburg, Pa., 1988-97. Author: Unseen Danger: A Tragedy of People, Government and Centralia Mine Fire, 1986. Del. Mich. Dem. Conv., 1972; mem. St. Stephen's Episcopal Sch. Bd., 1999—. Recipient Keystone Press award Pa. Newspaper Pubs. Assn., 1979, 86, 87, 90, 99, Pub. Svc. award AP Mng. Editors of Pa., 1981, Janus award Mortgage Bankers Am., 1992. Mem. Investigative Reporters and Editors, Nat. Press Club (Freedom of the Press award 1995), Soc. Profl. Journalists (pres. ctrl. Pa. chpt. 1989-91, Spotlight award 1995), Newspaper Guild, St. Stephen's Episcopal Sch. Bd., 1999—. Episcopalian. Home: 113 Conoy St Harrisburg PA 17104-1608

DEKOK, ROGER GREGORY, air force officer; b. Kenosha, Wis., Jan. 10, 1947; s. Roger Gerritt Dekok and Hazel Deloris (Wilkinson) Busche; m. Carolyn Susan Flinkow, June 15, 1968; children: Kristen Laura, Ryan Matthew. BA in Math., U. Wis., 1968; MS in Sys. Mgmt., Air Force Inst. Tech., 1979, postgrad., 1978-79; attended, Air War Coll., 1983-84. Commd. 2d lt. USAF, 1968, advanced through grades to maj. gen., 1995; space sys. staff officer HQ, Pentagon USAF, Washington, 1979-83; dir. space plans HQ Air Force Space Command USAF, Maxwell AFB, Ala., 1983-84; dir. space programs Nat. Security Coun., White House USAF, Washington, 1987-88, spl. asst. to Pres., Nat. Security Coun., White House, 1988; comdr. 1st Space Wing USAF, Peterson AFB, 1989-90; comdr. 50th Space Wing USAF, Falcon AFB, Colo., 1990-93; dir. plans HQ Air Force Space Command USAF, Peterson AFB, 1993-95; dir. ops. U.S. Space Command, Peterson AFB, 1995-96; comdr. Space and Missle Systems Ctr., L.A., 1996-98; dep. chief of staff for plans and programs USAF-Pentagon, Washington, 98—. Recipient Nat. Space Achievement award Nat. Rotary Club, 1987, James V. Hartinger award for career space achievement NSIA, 1995. Mem. Air Force Assn., Nat. Space Club (bd. govs. 1988-89, 96—). Lutheran. Avocations: golf, skiing, tennis, personal computing. Office: USAF/XP 1070 Air Force-Pentagon Washington DC 20330-1070*

DEKOSKY, STEVEN TRENT, neurologist; b. Camden, N.J., Mar. 23, 1947; s. Aaron and Evelyn (Gorlen) DeK.; divorced; children: Allison, Lauren. AB in Psychology, Bucknell U., 1968; MD, U. Fla., 1974. Post-doctoral fellow, instr. neurology U. Va. Sch. Medicine, Charlottesville, 1978-79; asst. prof. neurology, anatomy U. Ky. Coll. Medicine, Lexington, 1979-85; grad. faculty U. Ky. Grad. Sch., Lexington, 1981-90; assoc. prof. anatomy and neurology U. Ky. Coll. Medicine, Lexington, 1985-90, interim chmn. dept. neurology, 1985-87; prof. psychiatry U. Pitts. Sch. Medicine, 1990—, prof. neurology, neurobiology, 1990—, grad. faculty, 1991—; vis. prof. psychology U. Calif., Irvine, 1983; co-dir. Alzheimer's disease rsch. ctr. U. Pitts. Med. Ctr., 1990-94, dir., 1994—, U. Ky. Med. Ctr., 1985-90; task force on Alzheimer's disease State of Ohio, Columbus, 1986-92; med. sci. adv. bd. Alzheimer's Assn., 1992—; dir. behavioral neurology of aging tng. program U. Pitts., 1990—. Mem. Am. Neurol. Assn. (Presd. award 1988), Am. Acad. Neurology, Am. Soc. Neurochemistry, Am. Heart Assn. (stroke coun.), N.Y. Acad. Scis., Soc. Neurosci., Soc. Exptl. Neuropathology (councillor 1990-92), Behavioral Neurology Soc. Office: U Pitts 3811 Ohara St Pittsburgh PA 15213-2593

DEKU, AFRIKADZATA, Afrikan-scholar, researcher, writer, educator; b. Kadjebi, Ghana, Dec. 13, 1949; m. Yayra Deku; children: Mawunyo, Aku Sika, Mawulolo. BA with honors, U. Cape Coast, Ghana, 1977; MSc, U. Ife, Nigeria, 1981; diploma, Inst. Internat. D'Adminstrn. Pub., Paris, 1983; MPhil, U. Paris XI, Sorbonne, 1983, PhD, 1985. Lic. mediator, arbitrator, negotiator. Ind. post-doctoral rsch. scholar U. Denver, 1986-87; founder, chief exec., prof. pan-Afrikan studies Afrikan Culture Inst., 1987—; vis. assoc. prof. Afrikan history Clark Atlanta U., 1990-91; vis. assoc. prof. Africana studies Morris Brown Coll., Atlanta, 1990; vis. assoc. prof. Afrikan culture, continuing edn. dept. Ga. State U., 1990; pub. The Afrikan Truth, 1994—, Continental Afrikan Pubs., 1990—; vis. prof. French and Afrikan lit. Wofford Coll., Spartanburg, S.C., 1988-89, Converse Coll., Spartanburg, 1989; trainer, guest speaker Clemson U. 4-H Operation Pride, 1994—; resident guest artist Kennedy Middle Sch., Aiken, S.C., 1997, Jackson (S.C.) Mid. Sch., 1998, S.C. Writers Ann. Workshop Conf. Faculty, Manuscript Evaluator; poetry judge Pan-African Poetry Recitals, Myrtle Beach, 1998; lectr., spkr. and cons. in field. Author: (poetry) We Are All Continental Afrikans, 1991, Sacred Verses For My Afrikan Queen, 1992, Sacred Afrikan Spiritual Power From Within, 1993, Agbenoxevie Menye, Ablodesafui, Agbedefu (Ewe poetry), Courage, Mere Afrique, Cris de Tonnerre, Coups de Marteau, A Toi le Paradis de Ma Langue (Afrikan Poetry in French); (plays) No Where is Heaven, Breaking the Bloody Sword of Apartheid, (rsch. books) L'Union Continentale Africaine, vols. 1-3, 1986, Continental Afrikan Power Now, 1987, The Afrikan-Centric Perspective of the Afrikan World Crisis, 1988, Continental Afrikan Manifesto, 1999, Continental Afrikan Power in Figures, 1989, The Afrikan Gospel of Total Happiness Now and Always, 1991, The Power of Afrikan-Centricity, 1992, AFRIKAMAWUNYA or the Holy Afrikan Bible, 1997, Continental Afrika: From Two Hundred Million Seasons to the Present, 1994, The Power and Benefits of Continental Afrikan Culture, 1994, How to Be a Continental Afrikan Again, 1994, Positive Self-Knowledge Technology, 1994, Positive Goal Achievement Technology, 1994, Positive Problem-Solving Technology, 1996, Positive Decision-Making Technology, 1999, Positive Financial Security Technology, 1999, I Want To Tell You Why, 1995, From Eagle to Chicken and Back, 1995, Socialist/Communist Practices by USA Governments Past and Present, 1999, Continental Afrikan Constitution of the Continental Afrikan Republic, 1998—. Founder Afrikan-Centricity Movement, Continental Afrikan Govt. Orgn., Continental Afrikan Found., Continental Afrikan Devel. Authority. Grantee S.C. Arts Commn., 1990-91; scholar Ghana Govt., 1970-72, 73-77, Commonwealth, 1975, 77, 78, French Govt., 1982-85; recipient OYO State Bursary award, 1980-81, Spartanburg, S.C. Arts Coun. award, 1989-90, S.C. Arts Commn. grant, 1990-91. Mem. ABA, Am. Arbitration Assn., S.C. Coun. for Mediation and Alternative Dispute Resolution, Internat. Biog. Assn., Internat. Platform Assn., French PhD Holders Assn., African Studies Assn., African Heritage Studies Assn., Am. Polit. Sci. Assn. E-mail: afrikalion@aol.com. Home: 182 Stribling Cir Spartanburg SC 29301-1651 also: Box 209, Dansoman Accra Ghana

DEKUYPER, MARY HUNDLEY, non-profit consultant; b. Syracuse, N.Y., Feb. 23, 1939; d. Edwin Graves and Edna Thompson (Smith) Hundley; m. Frederick Timothy DeKuyper, June 17, 1961; children: Gordon, Sarah. AB, Wellesley Coll., 1960. Adminstr. Calvert Sch., Balt., 1960-65; cons., 1981—; cons. Assn. Governing Bds., Washington, 1992—, Nat. Ctr. Nonprofit Bd., Washington, 1992—, Venetian Group, 1996—; presenter Girls Inc., Vols. Am., ARC, Nat. Ctr. Non-profit Bds., numerous others, 1981-98. Mem exec. com. Planned Parenthood Md., 1989-98, chair nominating com., 1989-90, chair devel. com., 1990-92, chair strategic planning com., 1992-94, vice chair bd. 1990-96, chair com. bd. devel., 1994-96, vice chair, 1997—; chair bd. dirs. ARC Greater Chesapeake and Potomac Blood Region, 1992-94, chair bd. devel. com., 1994-96, ex-officio, 1997— (Mary H. DeKuyper award, 1994); exec. com. ARC Ctrl. Md. chpt., 1989-92, chair blood svcs. com., 1988-92, vice chair bd., 1990-92, chair transition com., 1991, vice chair bd., 1996, chair bd., 1996-98 (William J. Casey award 1989); pub. support com. ARC Nat. Bd. Govs., 1993—, vice chair biomedical svcs. bd., 1994-96, vice chair audit com., 1996—, history and edn. ctr. adv. bd., 1996—, exec. com., 1996—; pres. nat. bd. Girls Inc., 1986-90, chair nat. adv. com. trustee edn. project, 1992-95, trustee educator, 1995—; mem. fin. commn. Episcopal Diocese Md., 1993-97, chair program and budget com., 1995-98; bd. dirs. United Way of Ctrl. Md., 1996—, mem. exec. com. Recipient Mary H. DeKuyper Trustee Svc. award Bryn Mawr Sch., 1989, Exemplary Cmty. Svc. award Health and Welfare Coun., 1990; named Md.'s Top 100 Women, 1996. Mem. Jr. League Balt. (pres. 1975-77, Sustainer award 1988), Hamilton St. Club (treas. 1991-95), Wellesley Coll. Club. Democrat. Episcopalian. Home and Office: 4422 Underwood Rd Baltimore MD 21218-1150

DE LA CADENA, RAUL ALVAREZ, physician, physiology and thrombosis educator; b. Mexico City, Dec. 31, 1959; came to U.S., 1985; s. Raul A. and Florencia (Garnica) De La C; m. Donna Lynn Schlam, Aug. 18, 1985; 1 child, Philippe Alexander. BS in Biology, Centro Universitario Mexico, 1979; MD, LaSalle U., Mexico City, Mex., 1984. Med. intern Nutrition Nat. Inst., Mexico City, 1983-84, rsch. assoc., 1984-85; rsch. tng. Temple U. Sch. Medicine, Phila., 1985-86, postdoctoral trainee, 1986-89, asst. prof., 1989-98, assoc. prof., 1998—, minority mentor program, 1988—, asst. dean, 1998—, dir. recruitment, admissions and retention minority program, 1998—; invited lectr. in field. Contbr. articles to Jour. Lab. Clin. Med., Blood, Am. Jour. Physiology., Jour. Clin. Invest., Am. Jour. Pathology; contbr. chpt. to book. Recipient Sol Sherry award Temple U., 1988, Young Scientists Travel award Internat. Soc. Thrombosis and Haemostasis, 1989, Rsch. Svc. award NIH, 1986-89, Clin Investigator award, 1991-96, award Am. Cancer Soc., 1997—; AHA grantee, 1991-92, 93-95. Fellow ACP; mem. N.Y. Acad. Scis., Am. Fedn. Clin. Rsch., Am. Soc. Hematology, Am. Soc. Investigative Pathology. Jewish. Office: Temple U Sch Medicine OMS-403 3400 N Broad St Philadelphia PA 19140-5104

DE LA CANCELA, VICTOR, psychologist; b. Bronx, N.Y., Dec. 18, 1952; s. Luis Fernandez and Guillermina (Ortiz) De La C. BA cum laude, CCNY, 1974, MPhil, 1979, MPH, 1995, PhD, 1981. Lic. marriage, family and child counselor, Calif.; lic. psychologist, Calif., Mass., N.Y.; cert. health svcs. provider, Mass.; cert. HIV counselor, N.Y. Intern, clin. fellow Med. Sch. Harvard U., 1977-79; supervising psychologist Boston City Hosp., 1979-81; dir. outpatient svcs. San Fernando Valley Cmty. Mental Health Ctr., Van Nuys, Calif., 1982-83; dir. Latino mental health Cambridge (Mass.) Hosp., 1983-85; dir. family svcs. Brookside Cmty. Health Ctr., Boston, 1985-88; dir. cmty. programs Dr. S.C. Fuller Cmty. Mental Health, Boston, 1988-89; sr. v.p. N.Y.C. Health and Hosps. Corp., 1990-95; asst. clin. prof. Coll. Physicians and Surgeons Columbia U., N.Y.C., 1990-92, 93—; asst. in psychology Beth Israel Hosp., Boston, 1979-81; network supr. Boston City Hosp., 1983-89; assoc. psychologist Brigham and Women's Hosp., Boston, 1985-88; asst. prof., psychologist Columbia-Presbyn. Med. Ctr., N.Y.C., 1990-96; instr. Harvard Med. Sch., Boston, 1979-81, lectr., 1983-88; lectr. U. Mass., Boston, 1985-89; cons. Puerto Rican Youth Devel. Leadership, Boston, 1983-86, Concilio Hispano Cambridge, Inc., 1988-90, Martha Eliot Health Ctr., Boston, 1989-90, Boriken Health Ctr., N.Y., 1995, Bronx Ctr. Cmty Svcs., 1995, Ctr. for Substance Abuse Prevention, SAMHSA, 1995—, Ctr. for Substance Abuse Treatment, 1996, Tremont-Crotona Family Day Care Ctrs., 1998—; pres., CEO Salud Mgmt. Assocs., Riverdale, N.Y., 1995—; psychologist Comprehensive Habilitation Svcs., N.Y., 1995—; clin. adminstr. Gateway Counseling Ctr., Bronx, N.Y., 1996—. Contbr. numerous articles to profl. jours. Recipient Pres. Svc. award N.Y. Assn. Black Psychologists, 1990, Outstanding Contbn. award, 1991, U.S. Surgeon Gen.'s cert. of appreciation, 1993. Fellow APA (commr. 1994-96, pres. clin. psychology of ethnic minorities sect. 1999, 5th ann. achievement award, cert. HIV/AIDS trainer), Am. Orthopsychiat. Assn., Acad. Clin. Psychology, Soc. Pub. Health Edn., Prescribing Psychologists Register (diplomate, regional dir., outstanding PIONEER leadership award), Network for Multicultural Tng. in Psychology, Am. Bd. Profl. Psychology (diplomate in clin. psychology); mem. Nat. Hispanic Psychol. Assn. (pres. 1986-90, Outstanding Contbn. award 1989, Exemplary Leadership and Svc. 1990), Nat. Puerto Rican Policy Network, Assn. Hispanic Mental Health Profls., Latino Behavioral Health Network. Home: 2727 Palisade Ave Riverdale NY 10463-1020 Office: Salud Management Assocs Highpoint-on-the-Hudson Riverdale NY 10463-1020

DELACATO, CARL HENRY, education educator; b. Pottstown, Pa., Sept. 10, 1923; s. Ercole S. and Julia (de Bartolomeo) D.; m. Janice E. Fernstrom, June 20, 1951; children—Elizabeth F., Carl Henry, David F. B.S. in Edn, West Chester State Coll., 1945; M.S. in Edn, U. Pa., 1948, Ed.D., 1952. Asst. headmaster Chestnut Hill Acad., Phila., 1945-64; founder, dir. Chestnut Hill Reading Clinic, 1948; prof. Avery Postgrad. Inst., Phila., 1963-73; prof., chmn. dept. devel. edn. U. Plano, Tex., 1965-70; asso. dir. inst. Para Le Orgn. Neurologica, Buenos Aires, 1967-70, Insts. Achievement Human Potential, Phila., 1953-73; dir. Inst. Rehab. of Brain Injured, Morton, Pa., 1974-89, Centrao de Rahabilitacao NS de Gloria, Sao Paulo, Brazil, 1976—; pres. Delacato & Delacato Consultants in Learning, Plymouth Meeting, Pa., 1970—; cons. Asociacion Para Ayuda Lesionados Cerebales, Barcelona, Spain, 1970-89 ; hon. dir. of The Delacato Center, Holon, Israel, 1974—; dir. of Delacato project at Padagogische Hochschule Rheinland Abteilung fur Heilpadaggogik, Koln, W. Ger., 1975—, Delacato project TIKVA, Haifa, Israel, 1976—; bd. dirs. Delacato and Delacato, Naples, Italy, Delacato Consultation Ctr., Benelux; others. Author: The Treatment and Prevention of Reading Problems, 1959, Diagnosis and Treatment of Speech and Reading Problems, 1963, Elementary School of the Future, 1964, Neurological Organization and Reading, 1966, A New Start for the Child with Reading Problems, 1970, The Ultimate Stranger. The Autistic Child, 1974, contbr. numerous articles on rehab. and edn. to profl. jours.; editor: Am. Lectures in Edn. and Learning, 1969—. Vice pres. U.S. World Orgn. Human Potential, 1968-73; mem. Pa. Commn. Human Potential, 1969-70, Gov. Sergipe (Brazil) Commn. Human Potential, 1968-70; bd. dirs. Centre for Neurol. Rehab., Morton, Pa., 1974—. Recipient Disting. Alumnus award West Chester Coll., 1978, award Greater Long Beach (Calif.) Soc. for Autistic Children, 1977, Diploma Socio-Benmento Porto Allegra, Brazil, 1965, Diploma de Honra Ho Merito Piracioba, Brazil, 1965, Diploma de Reconheciemen, to Sao Paulo, 1965, Diploma e Medalha Comemorative de APAE Rio de Janeiro, 1965, Gold Medal Honor Brazil, 1960, Statuette with Pedestal award Internat. Rehab. Forum, 1966, 1st. Trailblazer award U. Plano, 1966. Mem. NSF. Address: Thomas Rd Philadelphia PA 19118

DELACATO, JANICE ELAINE, learning consultant, educator; b. Bklyn., June 6, 1926; d. Frode Siegfried and Vilma (Riis) Fernstrom; m. Carl Henry Delacato, June 20, 1951; children: Elizabeth Delacato Putnam, Carl Henry, David Fernstrom. AB, Bryn Mawr Coll., 1948. Tchr., Rydal Hall, Ogontz Sch., Pa., 1948-49, The Spence Sch., N.Y.C., 1949-50, Chestnut Hill Acad., Phila., 1950-52; co-dir. The Chestnut Hill Reading Clinic, Phila., 1951-65, Delacato & Delacato, Cons. in Learning, Phila., 1972-88; mgr. Morton (Pa.) Book Store, 1972-88; co-dir. The Delacato & Delacato Conf. on Autism and Learning Disabilities, 1979-82. Chmn. fund-raising com. Springside Sch., 1969-71; treas. Main St. Fair Antiques Booth, Chestnut Hill Hosp., 1965-77. Recipient Main St. Fair award Chestnut Hill Hosp., 1972. Mem. AAUW. Republican. Unitarian. Club: Phila. Cricket. Editor newsletter Temple U. Med. Center Women's Aux., Phila., 1953-65; class editor Bryn Mawr Coll. Alumnae Bull., 1966-79. Home: The Glen 700 Thomas Rd Philadelphia PA 19118-4601 Office: Delacato and Delacato Plymouth Plz Ste 107 Plymouth Meeting PA 19462-1305

DE LA CHAPELLE, ALBERT, education educator. Prof., chair dept. of med. genetics U. Helsinki; dir. Human Cancer Genetics Program Comp Cancer Ctr. Arthur G James Cancer Hosp. and Rsch. Inst., Ohio State U., Columbus, 1998—; prof., chair divsn. human cancer genetics d dept. med. microbiology/immunology Ohio State U., Columbus, 1998—. Office: Ohio State Univ, Dept Microbiology/Immunolog, Columbus 00014, Finland

DELACOTE, GOERY, museum director. Exec. dir. The Exploratorium, San Francisco. Office: The Exploratorium 3601 Lyon St San Francisco CA 94123-1099*

DELA CRUZ, JOSE SANTOS, retired state supreme court chief justice; b. Saipan, Commonwealth No. Mariana Islands, July 18, 1948; s. Thomas Castro and Remedio Sablan (Santos) Dela C.; m. Rita Tenorio Sablan, Nov. 12, 1977; children: Roxanne, Renee, Rica Ann. BA, U. Guam, 1971; JD, U. Calif., Berkeley, 1974; cert., Nat. Jud. Coll., Reno, 1985. Bar: No. Mariana Islands, 1974, U.S. Dist. Ct. No. Mariana Islands 1978. Staff atty. Micro. Legal Svcs. Corp., Saipan, 1974-79; gen. counsel Marianas Pub. Land Corp., Saipan, 1979-81; liaison atty. CNMI Fed. Laws Commn., Saipan, 1981-83; ptnr. Borja & Dela Cruz, Saipan, 1983-85; assoc. judge Commonwealth Trial Ct., Saipan, 1985-89; chief justice Supreme Ct. No. Mariana Islands, 1989-95; retired, 1995; mem. Conf. of Chief Justices, 1989-95, Adv. Commn. on Judiciary, Saipan, 1980-82; chmn. Criminal Justice Planning Agy., Saipan, 1985-95. Mem. Coun. for Arts, Saipan, 1982-83; chmn. Bd. of Elections, Saipan, 1977-82; pres. Cath. Social Svcs., Saipan, 1982-85. Mem. No. Marianas Bar Assn. (pres. 1984-85). Roman Catholic. Avocations: golf, reading, walking. Office: Commonwealth Supreme Ct Civic Ctr Saipan MP 96950 *There is an inherent goodness in every person, no matter how bad that person may appear. Recognizing that goodness in each gives us hope that the future of mankind will not be destructive.*

DELA CRUZ, PABLITO SULIT, pediatrician, neurologist; b. Pulilan, The Philippines, June 29, 1961; came to U.S., 1991; s. Eustaquio and Catalina Dela Cruz; m. Maria Lily Dela Cruz, Jan. 18, 1989; children: Jose Miguel, Jacinta Marie, Jean Bernadette, Anne Catherine. BS cum laude in Biology, U. of The Philippines, 1980, MD, 1985. Diplomate Am. Bd. Neurology and Psychiatry, Am. Bd. Pediatrics. Resident in pediatrics Sinai Hosp., Balt., 1991-93; resident in neurology Johns Hopkins Hosp., Balt., 1993-96; pediatrician, pediatric neurologist Rome (N.Y.) Med. Group, 1996—. Fellow Am. Acad. Pediatrics. Office: Rome Med Group 1801 Black River Blvd Rome NY 13440

DELAFUENTE, CHARLES, lawyer, educator, journalist; b. N.Y.C., Oct. 6, 1945; s. Maurice and Rose (Schulder) De La F.; m. Jill Rosenfeld, Apr. 8, 1979; children: Marc, Carla. Student, Queens Coll., Flushing, N.Y., 1962-66; BA, SUNY, Albany, 1979; JD cum laude, Yeshiva U., N.Y.C., 1981. Bar: N.Y. 1982, D.C. 1985. Night city editor N.Y. Post, N.Y.C., 1969-78; assoc. Herzfield & Rusin, N.Y.C., 1981-83; atty. Fed. Jud. Ctr., Washington, 1984-85; fgn. desk editor UPI, Washington, 1985-87; asst. city editor Daily News, N.Y.C., 1987-90; asst. mng. editor Times Union, Albany, N.Y., 1990-94; dep. met. editor Daily News, N.Y.C., 1949-95; editor Record, Troy, N.Y., 1995-96; ptnr. Forman & De La Fuente, Latham, N.Y., 1997-98; staff editor N.Y. Times, 1998—; del. N.Y. State Fair Trial/Free Press Com., Albany, 1994-96; adj. prof. George Washington Coll. Law, Washington, 1985-87, Cardozo Law Sch. Yeshiva U., 1989-90. Mem. ABA, N.Y. State Bar Assn., Order of Barristers.

DE LA FUENTE RAMIREZ, JUAN RAMON, Mexican government official; b. Mexico City, Sept. 5, 1951; married; 3 children. MSc, U. Minn. Prof. Nat. Nutrition Inst.; rschr. Mex. Inst. Psychiatry; dir. health rsch. program U.N.A.M., dir. med. faculty, 1991—; sec. health Govt. of Mex., Washington, 1995—; vis. prof. several fgn. univs. Author books on health rsch. Vol. internat. health orgns. Office: Deleg Cuauht moc, Lieja 7-1 er Piso Col Juarez, Mexico City 06696, Mexico*

DE LA GARZA, KIKA (ELIGIO DE LA GARZA), former congressman; b. Mercedes, Tex., Sept. 22, 1927; s. Dario and Elisa (Villarreal) de la G.; m. Lucille Alamia, May 29, 1953; children: Jorge Luis, Michael Alberto, Angela Dolores. Student, Pan Am. Coll., Edinburg, Tex., 1947-48; LLB, St. Mary's U., San Antonio, 1951; LLD (hon.), Lincoln U. of Mo., 1982, U. Md., 1985, Hanyang U., Seoul. Bar: Tex. 1951. Mem. from Hidalgo County Tex. Ho. of Reps., 1953-64; mem. 89th-104th Congresses from 15th Tex. dist., Washington, 1965-96. With USNR, World War II; with AUS, Korea. Democrat. *

DE LA GARZA, LEONARDO, university administrator. AA, Bee County Coll.; BBA in Mgmt. and Fin. summa cum laude, St. Edward's U.; PhD in Ednl. Adminstrn., U. Tex.; postgrad., Harvard U. Dean of instrn. Austin (Tex.) C.C., 1974-78, v.p. for acad. affairs, 1978-84; exec. v.p. Bee County Coll., Beeville, Tex., 1984-91; pres. El Paso (Tex.) County C.C., 1991-93, Santa Fe (N.Mex.) C.C., 1993-97; chancellor Tarrant County Jr. Coll. Dist., Ft. Worth, 1997—; guest lectr. doctoral program C.C. Leadership, U. Tex., Austin; guest lectr. Coll. Edn. Program in Higher Edn., U. North Tex., 1997; adj. prof. C.C. Leadership Program, U. Tex., Austin, 1998, Higher Edn. Program, U. North Tex., Denton, 1998; bd. trustees The Coll. Bd., N.Y.C., 1993—; mem. Commn. on Internat. Programs of the Am. Coun. on Edn., 1996, North Tex. Edn. Coun. on Advanced Tech., 1997, The Chair Acad.'s Internat. Adv. Bd., 1997; mem. pres.'s network Internat. Edn. of Am. Coun. on Edn., 1996; mem. higher edn. c.c. pres.'s adv. panel W.K. Kellogg Found., 1996; mem. nat. adv. com. of c.c. rsch. ctr. Tchrs. Coll., Columbia U., N.Y.C., 1997; presenter in field. Mem. editl. bd.: C.C. Jour. of Rsch. and Practice, 1997—. Mem. Santa Fe Econ. Devel. Commn.; bd. trustees Providence Meml. Hosp. El Paso; pres. sch. bd. Our Lady of Victory Parish Sch.; bd. dirs. Bee County pub. Libr., Am. Heart Assn. Harvard U. fellow U. Tex. at Austin C.C. Leadership Program, 1992; Student Assn. acad. scholar St. Edward's U., Acad. Merit scholar. Mem. Am. Assn. C.C. (bd. dirs. 1995—, bd. dirs. Nat. C.C. Hispanic Coun. 1996-98, chmn. audit and fin. com. 1997-98, internat./intercultural svcs. 1998—), Tex. Assn. Pub. C.C. (mem. exec. com.), N.Mex. Assn. C.C. (chmn. legis. affairs com. 1996-97, pres.-elect 1997-98), Assn. C.C. Trustees (adv. com. of pres.), Santa Fe C. of C., Santa Fe Del Sur Rotary Club, El Paso Rotary Club, Greater El Paso C. of C., El Paso Hispanic C. of C., Beeville Rotary Club, South Austin Rotary Club, Phi Kappa Phi, Alpha Chi, Phi Theta Kappa. Fax: (817) 515-5450. E-mail: ldlgarza@tcjc.cc.tx.us. Office: Tarrant County Jr Coll Dist 1500 Houston St Fort Worth TX 76102

DELAGI, EDWARD FRANCIS, physician, retired educator; b. N.Y.C., Nov. 4, 1911; s. Michael Nicholas and Angela (Ciani) D.; m. Westa Vespa, Feb. 16, 1941; children—West Ann (Mrs. Richard Hanafin), Edwina (Mrs. Donald Askew). B.S., Fordham U., 1934; M.D., Hahnemann Med. Coll., 1938. Intern Fordham Hosp., Bronx, N.Y., 1938-40; resident Bronx VA Hosp., 1951-54, chief ward sect. phys. medicine and rehab., 1954-56; dir. phys. medicine and rehab. Misericordia Hosp., Bronx, 1958-65; attending physician Bronx Municipal Hosp. Ctr., 1956-85; cons. phys. med. and rehabilitation No. Westchester Hosp., Misericordia Hosp., Bronx, St. Joseph's Hosp., Yonkers, N.Y.; asst. prof. dept. rehab. medicine Albert Einstein Coll. Med., Bronx, 1950-55, assoc. prof., 1959, 64, prof., 1964-85, prof. emeritus, 1985—. Served with AUS, 1941-45. Decorated Bronze Star. Fellow ACP, Am. Acad. Phys. Medicine and Rehab., N.Y. Acad. Medicine; mem. AAAS, Am. Congress Phys. Medicine. Home: 6178 SE Riverboat Dr Stuart FL 34997-1527

DE LA GUARDIA, MARIO FRANCISCO, electrical engineer; b. Havana, Cuba, Dec. 4, 1936; came to U.S., 1979; s. Mario D. and Catalina (Bascon-cillos) de la G.; m. Nery Esther Agudo, Aug. 23, 1970; 1 child, Mario Felix. BS in Elec. Engring., U. Havana, 1963; M of Applied Sci., U. Waterloo, Ont., Can., 1976. Registered profl. engr., Fla. Assoc. prof. U. Havana, 1964-67; researcher Acad. Scis. Cuba, Havana, 1967-71; design engr. Braun S.A., Madrid, 1971-73, Nat. Cash Register Can. Ltd., Waterloo, 1976-79; sr. engr. Coulter Electronics, Inc., Hialeah, Fla., 1979-80; programmer project systems Burroughs Corp., Coral Springs, Fla., 1980-81; prin. engr. Racal Milgo, Inc., Sunrise, Fla., 1981-90; sr. software engr. Coulter Corp., Miami, Fla., 1991—. Patentee in field. Active Foster Parents, 1976—. Mem. IEEE. Republican. Roman Catholic. Avocations: personal computers, swimming, bicycling. Home: 13211 SW 39th Ter Miami FL 33175-3235 Office: Beckman Coulter Inc 11800 SW 147th Ave Miami FL 33196-2500

DE LA GUARDIA, PABLO ANTONIO, marketing administrator; b. July 31, 1971. MBA, Nova South Eastern U., 1997; postgrad., Georgetown U., 1998—. Dir. mktg. City of Knowledge, Republic of Panama, 1996—. Email: delguap@gunet.georgetown.edu. Office: 4545 MacArthur Blvd NW #104 Washington DC 20007

DE LAGUNA, FREDERICA, anthropology educator emeritus, author, consultant; b. Ann Arbor, Mich., Oct. 3, 1906; d. Theodore and Grace Mead (Andrus) de L. AB, Bryn Mawr Coll., 1927; PhD, Columbia U., 1933; LHD (hon.), U. Alaska, 1982. Asst., field dir. U. Pa. Mus., Phila., 1931-35; assoc. soil conservationist U.S. Soil Conservation Svc., 1936; lectr. anthropology Bryn Mawr (Pa.) Coll., 1938-41, asst. prof., 1941-42, 46-49, assoc. prof., 1949-55, prof. anthropology, 1955-75, William R. Kenan, Jr. prof. emeritus, 1975—; vis. lectr., vis. prof. U. Pa., U. Calif., Berkeley, Bryn Mawr Coll. Author: The Thousand March: Adventures of an American Boy with Garibaldi, 1930, The Archaeology of Cook Inlet, Alaska, 1934, reprinted, 1975, The Arrow Points to Murder, 1937, Fog on the Mountain, 1938, reprinted 1995; (with Kaj Birket-Smith) The Eyak Indians of the Copper River Delta, Alaska, 1938, Prehistory of Northern America as Seen From the Yukon, 1947, Chugach Prehistory: The Archaeology of Prince William Sound, 1956, reprinted 1967, The Story of a Tlingit Community, 1960; (with others) The Archeology of the Yakutat Bay Area, Alaska, 1964, Under Mount Saint Elias, 3 vols., 1972, Voyage to Greenland: A Personal Initiation into Anthropology, 1977, reprinted, 1995, Tales from the Dena, 1995; editor: Selected Papers from the American Anthropologist 1888-1920, 1960, reprinted 1976, The Tlingit Indians (George Thornton Emmons), 1991; advisor, participant documentary film More than Words, 1994; subject of documentary film Reunion Under Mt. St. Elios, 1996. Lt. comdr. USNR, 1942-45. Recipient Lindback award for Disting. Teaching, Bryn Mawr Coll., 1975, Rochester Mus. award and fellow, 1941; fellow Columbia U., 1930-31, NRC, 1936-37, Rockefeller Found., 1945-46, Wenner-Gren Found., 1949-50, Social Sci. Research Council, 1962-63; grantee Am. Philos. Soc., Arctic Inst. of N.Am., Bryn Mawr Coll., NEH, NSF, U. Pa. Mus., Wenner-Gren Found. for Anthrop. Rsch. Fellow AAAS; mem. Am. Anthrop. Assn. (pres. 1966-67, Disting. Svc. award 1986), Arctic Inst. N.Am. (hon. life), NAS, Soc. for Am. Archaeology (1st v.p. 1949-50, 50th Ann. award 1986), No. Studies Assn. (internat. secretariat, hon. pres. 1991—), Phila. Anthropology Soc. (pres. 1939-40), Alaska Anthrop. Assn. (hon. life, award for lifetime contbn. to Alaskan anthropology 1993), Homer (Alaska) Natural History Soc. (hon. life, Silver Trowel award), Before Columbus Found. (Am. Lifetime Book award 1995). Democrat. E-mail: delaguna@netaxs.com. Home and Office: 3300 Darby Rd # 1310 Haverford PA 19041-1067

DELAHANTY, EDWARD LAWRENCE, management consultant; b. South Bend, Ind., Feb. 17, 1942; s. Edward Lawrence and Rosemary Margaret (DeVreese) D.; m. Rebecca A. Paczesny, June 22, 1963; children: David Edward, Debra Ann. BS in Math., U. Notre Dame, 1963. Enrolled actuary. Asst. actuary Aetna Life & Casualty Co., Hartford, Conn., 1963-70; mng. ptnr. Hewitt Assocs., Mpls., 1971-85, mem. exec. com., 1981-87, 90-95; southeast region mng. prin., Hewitt Assocs., L.L.C., Atlanta, 1986—; v.p., sec.-treas., bd. dirs. CMI Stores Inc., 1983-85; bd. dirs. Brandt Barringmann Inc., 1981-84; bd. dirs. United Telco, Inc., 1992-95; Fellow Soc. Actuaries; mem. Am. Acad. Actuaries, Enrolled Actuary, Am. Compensation Assn., Atlanta Area Compensation Assn., So. Employee Benefits Conf., Atlanta Nat. Golf Club, Musgrove Mill Golf Club, Peachtree Club, Ravinia Club, Buckhead Club, 191 Club, Wexford Golf Club. Home: 86 Blackland Ct NW Atlanta GA 30342-4434 Office: 3350 Riverwood Pkwy SE Ste 80 Atlanta GA 30339-6401

DELAHANTY, REBECCA ANN, school system administrator; b. South Bend, Ind., Oct. 18, 1941; d. Raymond F. and Ann Marie (Batsleer) Paczesny; m. Edward Delahanty, June 22, 1963; children: David, Debbie. BA, Coll. of St. Catherine, Minn., 1977; MA, Coll. St. Thomas, Minn., 1983; PhD, Ga. State U., 1994. Cert. in adminstrn. and supervision, Ga. Initiator, tchr. gifted kindergarten Dist. 284 Sch., Wayzata, Minn., 1977-83; gifted kindergarten coord. St. Barts Sch., Wayzata, 1983-85; prin. Dabbs Loomis Sch., Dunwoody, Ga., 1987-91; asst. to supt. Buford (Ga.) City Schs., 1993-98, supt., 1998—; mem. staff devel. adv. coun. Ga. *As an educator, Dr. Rebecca Delahanty began her career as a paraprofessional and succeeded to become the superintendent of a school system. She has dedicated her life to education and believes that all students can achieve high standards. Through grant writing, including Pay for Performance and School Improvement Grants totaling $100,000, $83,000, and $150,000 during the years 1996, 1997, and 1998, the system showed a 12% increase in test scores, an expansion of parental and community involvement, a lower drop out rate, and widened the use of intructional technology.* Contbr. article to profl. publ. Mem. ASCD, Am. Ednl. Rsch. Assn., Nat. Assn. Gifted Children, Minn. Coun. Gifted and Talented, Phi Delta Kappa, Omicron Gamma.

DELAHAYE, ALFRED NEWTON, retired journalism educator; b. West Baton Rouge Parish, La., June 4, 1929; s. Alfred and Lillian (Hebert) D. BA in Journalism, La. State U., 1949, MA in Journalism, 1951; PhD in Journalism, U. Mo., 1970. Mng. editor Houma (La.) Courier, Terrebonne Press, 1953-57; dir. pub. info. Nicholls State U., Thibodaux, La., 1957-67, 83-90, disting. prof. journalism, 1984-90, prof. emeritus journalism, 1990—; instr. journalism U. Mo., Columbia, 1967-69. Contbr. news stories, editls. to profl. publs. Mem. Soc. Profl. Journalists, Assn. for Edn. in Journalism and Mass Comm., La. State U. Journalism Alumni Assn. (founding pres. 1954), Phi Kappa Phi (founding pres. Nicholls chpt. 1974). Democrat. Roman Catholic. Avocations: reading, travel. Home: 610 Fairway Dr Thibodaux LA 70301-3726 Office: Nicholls State U Dept Mass Comm Thibodaux LA 70310

DE LA HOYA, OSCAR, Olympic athlete, professional boxer; b. Montabello, Calif., Feb. 4, 1973. Olympic boxer, lightweight divsn. Barcelona, Spain, 1992; champion jr. lightweight divsn. World Boxing Orgn., 1994, champion lightweight divsn., 1994—; champion lightweight divsn. Internat. Boxing Fedn., 1995—; champion lightweight divsn World Boxing Council, 1996—. Recipient Gold medal lightweight boxing divsn. Olympics, Barcelona, 1992. Office: care Top Rank Boxing 3980 Howard Hughes Pkwy Ste 580 Las Vegas NV 89109-0995*

DELAHUNT, WILLIAM D., congressman; s. Bill Sr. and Ruth Delahunt; children: Kirstin, Kara. BA, Middlebury Coll., 1963; JD, Boston Coll., 1967. Asst. clk. Norfolk Superior Ct.; legal counsel Quincy Police Dept.; pvt. practice law, 1971-75; dist. atty. State of Mass.; mem. 105th Congress from 10th Mass. dist., 1997—, mem. judiciary resources com. mem. Quincy City Coun., 1971; mem. Mass. Ho. of Reps., 1973-75, asst. majority leader. With USCGR, 1963-71. Office: 1517 Longworth House Office Bldg Washington DC 20515*

DELAHUNTY, JOSEPH LAWRENCE, state senator, business investor; b. Portland, Maine, June 5, 1935; s. Joseph Edward and Jane (Faulkner) D.; m. Gail Ruth Ruppert, Sept. 2, 1961; children: Deborah Baker, Joseph Jr., Devin, Brian, William. Student, Bryant Coll., 1955-57. Store mgr. W.T. Grant Co., Wethersfield, Conn., 1957-75; dist. mgr. W.T. Grant Co., N.H., Vt., Mass.; regional mgr. W.T. Grant Co., N.E. U.S.; owner, pres. Windham Nurseries & Florist Inc., 1975-83; pres. Car-Del Property Mgmt. Co., 1983—; owner, pres. Fireside Inn motel, Salem, N.H., 1985-87, Delahuntys Auto-Wash, Salem, 1988—; mem. N.H. State Senate, Concord, 1986—, pres., 1995-98; owner Delahunty's Nursery, Wyndham, N.H.; senate majority leader N.H. State Senate. Mem. Salem Bd. Selectmen. Served with U.S. Army, 1958-60. Republican. Roman Catholic. Home: 14 Old Farm Rd Salem NH 03079-1278 Office: Delahuntys Nursery 41 Range Rd Rt 111 Wyndham NH 03087*

DE LA IGLESIA, FELIX ALBERTO, pathologist, toxicologist; b. Cordoba, Argentina, Nov. 27, 1939; s. Andres Avelino and Rosalia (Figueroa) De La I.; m. Graciela Moreno, May 19, 1964; children: Felix Andres, Jose Vicente, Alberto Victor. MD, U. Cordoba, 1964. Dir. Warner-Lambert Rsch. Inst., Toronto, Ont., 1972-79; dir. toxicology Warner-Lambert/Parke-Davis, Ann Arbor, Mich., 1979-83, v.p. pathology and exptl. toxicology Parke-Davis Pharm. Rsch.; prof. pathology U. Toronto Sch. Medicine, 1981—; adj. prof. toxicology and pathology U. Mich. Med. Sch. of Pub. Health, 1982—. Author: Molecular Biochemistry of Human Disease, 1985, Drug Toxicokinetics, 1993, Drug-Induced Hepatotoxicity, 1996. Served to 1st lt. Argentine Army Inf., 1954-56. Fellow Acad. Toxicological Scis. Avocations: collecting antique microscopes, vintage sports cars. Home: 2307 Hill St Ann Arbor MI 48104-2651 Office: Parke-Davis Pharmaceutical Res 2800 Plymouth Rd Ann Arbor MI 48105-2495

DELAKAS, DANIEL LIUDVIKO, retired foreign language educator; b. Springfield, Mass., Aug. 25, 1921; s. Alexander and Eva (Poska) D.; m. Mimi Cordich, July 22, 1945; 1 son, David Mark. Student, Smith Coll., 1936-40, U. Rochester, 1940-42; AB, Bklyn. Coll., 1946; postgrad., Columbia, 1946, U. Paris, 1948; diploma, U. Firenze, Italy, 1957; postgrad., Sophia U., Tokyo, 1974, Ill. State U., 1974, Harvard Alumni Coll., 1977, 79, 81, Harvard Inst. for Learning in Retirement, 1983, 84, 87, 88, summers 89, 90, 91. From lectr. to asst. prof. Northwestern U., 1948-56; prof. Romance langs. Ripon (Wis.) Coll., 1956-83, chmn. dept., 1956-69, 74-83; English as Second Lang. instr. U. Autonoma Benito Juárez de Oaxaca (Mex.), 1983-86; co-dir. course Inst. in Learning in Retirement Harvard U., 1991; fellow Harvard U., 1954, 73; vis. scholar Harvard Alumni Coll., 1975-79, vis. fellow, 1977, 78; fellow E. Asian Summer Inst. in Japanese, U. Ill., Urbana, 1972, Japanese Studies in Liberal Arts Coll., Monmouth Coll., 1974, Earlham Coll., 1975; vis. summer prof. U. Wash., 1960, U. Maine, 1961, U. Besançon, France, 1962, 63, Stillman Coll., Tuscaloosa, Ala., 1964, Tufts U. (also assoc. dir. NDEA Inst.), 1965, U. Toulouse, France, 1966, 68, U. Alaska, 1967; fgn. lang. orientation officer NBBS-Holland-Am. Lines, summers 1950-56; reader French advanced placement Ednl. Testing Svc., Princeton, N.J., 1958-63; cons., fgn. lang. editor Sci. Rsch. Assocs., Chgo., 1963-65; academic dir. Academic Yr. Abroad, Inc., Paris, 1969-70; cons., conf. participant UNESCO, Paris, 1970; Mem. charter com., constn. writer, regional pres. N.E. Wis. Fgn. Lang. Orgn. (New-Flo), 1968-69; exec. com. Insts. Coll. Tchg. as a Career, Marquette U.-U. Wis. at Madison, 1960-63; mem. exec. steering com. Inst. Humanities for Mid-west Coll. Faculty Mems., U. Chgo., 1971-73; participant Mid-West faculty seminars U. Chgo. Ctr. for Continuing Edn., 1974-75, 77-78, 80-83; participant English as fgn lang. seminar Harvard U., summer 1983; vis. cons. in English as fgn. lang. U. Oaxaca (Mex.), 1983-86, tchr. English as a second lang., Centro de Idiomas, U. Benito Juárez de Oaxaca, 1984-85; mem. violin sect. Belles Artes Orquestra de Camara, ann. 1984-94, mem. 2d violin sec. Cape Ann Symphony, 1988-93, Gordon Coll. Symphony, 1994-97, Republic of China, Hong Kong, Singapore and Bangkok, 1986, Pakistan, India, Nepal, 1987, Egypt, Israel, 1989, Turkey, 1993, Vienna, Budapest, Prague, Bratislavia, Berlin, 1994, Austria, Czech Republic, Slovakia, Germany, 1994, Belgium, Holland, France, 1995, Morocco, 1996, London, Wales, Scotland, York, 1998; participant Harvard Inst. Learning in Retirement, 1988-90. Contbr. to yearbooks, encys. With USAAF, 1942-43, 104th Inf. Div., 1944-45. Decorated Bronze Star, chevalier de l'Ordre des Palmes Académiques (France), 1967; recipient Presdl. citation. Mem. AAUP, MLA (co-editor ann. French 17th Century Studies 1952-83), Am. Assn. Tchrs. French, Am. Assn. Tchrs. Italian, Internat. Comparative Lit. Assn., Assn. Internat. des études françaises, Assn. Internat. des. Docteurs de l'Univ. de Paris, Assn. des Membres de l'Ordre des Palmes Acads., Phi Sigma Iota (nat. exec. sec. 1964-74). Home: 70 Pigeon Hill St Rockport MA 01966-1255 also: Rancho San Felipe Aptdo 376, 68000 Oaxaca de Juárez Oaxaca Mexico *There is great joy in the very process of learning, no matter what the age, no matter what the field.*

DELAMARTER, THELDA JEAN HARVEY, secondary education educator; b. Stafford, Kans., June 15, 1924; d. Guy Wright and Versa Jane (Reece) Harvey; m. Floyd Lourain Delamarter, Dec. 13, 1944 (dec. May 1996); children: Linda Lee, Donna Harris, Janie Steljes. BA, Friends U., Wichita, Kans., 1945; teaching cert., Northwestern State Tchrs. Coll., 1958; MA in English, Wichita State U., 1965, postgrad., 1965-92. Cert. tchr. speech, theatre arts, English, psychology, music, social studies, Kans. Tchr. music Jet (Okla.) Pub. Schs., 1951-54, 57-59; tchr. lang. arts Unified Sch. Dist. 260, Derby, Kans., 1959-95, chmn. dept., 1972-84; ret. Unified Sch. Dist. 260, Derby, 1995; pvt. tchr. piano and organ; lectr. Weight Watchers, 1972—. Organist Woodlawn United Meth. Ch., Derby, 1959-98. Nominated Kans. Tchr. of Yr. 1990. Mem. Derby Edn. Assn. (sec. 1962-63, various comms. 1963-70, Derby's Master Tchr. 1994-95). E-mail: theldade-lamarter@prodigy.net. Home: PO Box 10 775 N Woodlawn Blvd Derby KS 67037-0010 Office: Derby HS 920 N Rock Rd Derby KS 67037-3552

DELAND, MICHAEL REEVES, energy executive; b. Boston, Dec. 13, 1941; s. Frank Stanton and Susan Robertson (Reeves) D.; m. Jane Slocum, Aug. 18, 1973; children: Stanton, Melissa, Holly. AB, Harvard U., 1963; JD, Boston Coll., Newton, Mass., 1969. Bar: Mass. 1970. Mgr. U.S. Congl. campaign, Concord, Mass., 1970; staff asst. to pres. U. Mass., Boston, 1971; chief enforcement br. EPA, Boston, 1971-76, regional adminstr., 1983-89; environ. counsel Environ. Rsch. Tech., Concord, 1976-83; chmn. Pres. Coun. on Environ. Quality, Washington, 1989-93; vice chmn. Am. Flywheel Systems Inc., Washington, 1993—; bd. adv. HYDRO Que., 1993-96. Chmn. bd. Nat. Orgn. on Disability; mem. World Com. on Disability, 1996—; dir. Mgmt. Inst. Environ and Bus., 1990-96, World Resources Inst., 1997—, Globe Newspaper Co., 1998—; mem. corp. Woods Hole Oceanographic Instn., 1993—; trustee Noble and Greenough Sch., Dedham, Mass., 1976-82; vestryman Trinity Episcopal Ch., Boston, 1976-78, St. John's Ch. Lafayette Sq., Washington, 1998—; bd. dirs. Assoc. Harvard Alumni, 1977-79. Lt. (j.g.) USN, 1963-65. Recipient award Mass. Audubon Soc., 1986, Spl. Achievement award Nat. Wildlife Fedn., 1989. Mem. The Country Club (Brookline, Mass.), Beverly Yacht Club, Met. Club, Chevy Chase Club, Phi Beta Kappa (hon.). Republican. Avocation: sailing. Home: 498 Point Rd Marion MA 02738-1922 Office: Am Flywheel Systems Inc 1350 I St NW Ste 700 Washington DC 20005-7202*

DE LANEROLLE, NIMAL GERARD, process engineer; b. Colombo, Sri Lanka, Nov. 26, 1945; came to U.S., 1980; s. Eustace Joseph and Pearl Norberta (Jayasundera) de L.; m. Suranganee Mary Amarasingha, Sept. 8, 1973. BSc in Engring., U. Sri Lanka, Peradeniya, 1970; M.Tech., Brunel U., Uxbridge, Eng., 1977; PhD, SUNY, Stony Brook, 1987. Cert. mfg. engr.; chartered engr., U.K.; registered profl. engr. Instr. U. Moratuwa, Sri Lanka, 1970-71; engr. Sri Lanka Transp. Bd., Werahera, 1971-73; lectr. U. Moratuwa, 1976-79; teaching and rsch. asst. SUNY, Stony Brook, 1980-85; assoc. prin. engr. Standard Microsystems Corp., Hauppauge, N.Y., 1985—; with Std. Mems Inc., Hauppauge; cons. Samuel Sons Ltd., Colombo, Sri Lanka, 1978-79, Brookhaven Nat. Lab., Upton, N.Y., 1991; rsch. adv. materials sci. dept. SUNY, 1987-90; editorial advisor Jour. of Metals, 1988—; adj. prof. dept. mech. engring. SUNY, 1992—, vis. prof. Editor: Microstructural Science for Thin Film Metallizations in Electronic Applications; contbr. articles to profl. jours. Fulbright scholar, 1979; recipient rsch. award Nat. Sci. Coun., Sri Lanka, 1978, rsch. assistantship SUNY, 1983-85. Mem. Metall. Soc. (mem. com. electronic and photonic device materials 1979), Instn. Mech. Engrs. (U.K.), Sigma Xi. Achievements include patent for Method for Fabricating Reliable Semiconductor Devices; mechanism for the degradation of titanium silicide thin films. Home: 104 Van Brunt Manor Rd East Setauket NY 11733-3901 Office: Standard Microsystems Corp PO Box 18047 Hauppauge NY 11788-8847

DE LANEY, ALLEN YOUNG, retired surgeon; b. Arrington, Tenn., 1917; s. Joseph Peter and Mary Williams (Glover) D.; m. Margaret Duncan, May 30, 1947 (div. Jan. 1978); children: Allen G., Philip Andrew, Bruce Duncan, Mary Elizabeth Johnston; m. Thelma Lou House, Apr. 7, 1979; children: Stewart B. White, Joseph S. White. BS, U. Ark., 1937; MD, Tulane U., 1940. Diplomate Am. Bd. Surgery. Intern Grady Hosp., Atlanta, 1940-41; resident in pathology New Eng. Deaconess Hosp., Boston, 1941; resident in surgery New Orleans VA Hosp., 1948-52; fellow in surgery Tulane U., New Orleans, 1947-50; asst. chief surgeon USS Haven UASA Naval Hosp. Shop Inchon, Pusan, Korea, 1950-51; chief surgeon U.S. VA Hosp., Poplar Bluff, Mo., 1952-53; chief of staff Alachua Gen. Hosp., Fla., 1976-78; courtesy staff Alachua Gen. Hosp., 1987—; courtesy staff, trustee North Fla. Regional Hosp., Gainesville, 1969-76; ret., 1988; chmn. Alachua County Emergency Medicine Coun., Gainesville, 1975-80. Pres. bd. dirs. Boys Club, Gainesville, 1955, Alachua County Thoracic Soc., Gainesville, 1956; bd. dirs. ARC, United Fund; mem. bus. coun. LWV, 1967-69; mem. Gainesville City Planning Cb., 1961-69; comdr. cons. Gainesville chpt. U.S. Power Squadron, 1985; Disting. mem. pres.'s coun. U. Fla. Comdr. MC USNR, ret. Fellow ACS; mem. AMA, Fla. Thoracic Soc. (prs. 1961-62), Fla. Soc. Gen. Surgeons, Fla. Sheriffs Assn. (hon. life), Sigma Chi.

DELANEY, BRIAN, communication executive, educator; b. Boston, Aug. 3, 1946; s. Charles Joseph and Margaret Eleanor (Hagen) D.; m. Christine Shannon, June 25, 1973 (div. Mar. 1994); children: Shannon, Brendan; m. Sallie Magagh, June 8, 1996; 1 child, Sophia. BA, U. Mass., 1974; JD, New England Sch. Law, 1977. Legal asst., press sec. Sen. Edward M. Kennedy, Washington, 1971-85; exec. v.p., dir. Clarke & Co., Boston, 1985—; dir., lectr. seminars, Clarke Crisis Ctr., Boston, 1990—, adj. prof., Boston U., 1992—. Com. mem. United Way Mass., Boston, 1994—. With USN Spl. Forces, 1966-70, Vietnam. Decorated Bronze Star, 2 Purple Hearts. Mem. Eastward Ho Country Club. Avocations: sailing, skiing, golf. Office: Clarke & Co 535 Boylston St Boston MA 02116-3720

DELANEY, CALDWELL, museum director. Dir. Mus. City of Mobile, Ala. Office: Mus of City of Mobile 355 Government St Mobile AL 36602-2315 Home: 8 South Ann Street Mobile AL 36604

DELANEY, CORNELIUS FRANCIS, philosophy educator; b. Waterbury, Conn., June 30, 1938; s. Patrick Francis and Margaret (Gavigan) D.; 1 child, Cornelius Francis Jr. MA, Boston Coll., 1961; PhD, St. Louis U., 1967. Prof. philosophy U. Notre Dame, Notre Dame, Ind., 1967—, chmn. philosophy dept., 1972-82, dir. honors program, 1989—. Author: Mind and Nature, 1969m The Synoptic Vision, 1977, Science, Knowledge and Mind, 1993, The Liberalism-Communitarianism Debate, 1994, New Essays on the Philosophy of C.S. Pierce, 1998. Recipient Madden award U. Notre Dame, 1974, Bicentennial award Boston Coll., 1976, Pres.'s award U. Notre Dame, 1984, Sheedy award U. Notre Dame,1987. Mem. Am. Cath. Philos. Assn. (pres. 1985), C.S. Peirce Soc. (pres. 1986), Am. Philos. Assn. (exec. com. 1983-85). Office: U Notre Dame Dept Philosophy 336 O'Shaughnessy Hall Notre Dame IN 46556-5639*

DELANEY, GARY LOUIS, retired military officer, management consultant; b. Burlington, Vt., Feb. 10, 1945; s. William Maurice and Madeline Helen (Chicoine) D.; m. Jeanie Elizabeth Humphrey Rickerson, June 25, 1966 (div. Aug. 1978); children: Teresa, Jeffrey; m. Julia Ann Roman Roberts, Nov. 18, 1978; children: Deborah, Marie, David, Michael. BS, Fla. State U., 1970, MBA, 1971. Cert. profl. contracts mgr. Commd. 2d lt. USAF, 1970; advanced through grades to col., 1987, ret., 1996; air staff tng. officer USAF Hdqtrs./Pentagon, Washington, 1977-78; acquisition staff officer USAF Hdqtrs. Sys. Command, Andrews AFB, Md., 1978-81; asst. prof. and dir. Grad. Contracting Program Air Force Inst. Technology, Wright-Patterson AFB, Ohio, 1984-88; dir. of contracting F15 Sys. Program Office, Wright-Patterson AFB, Ohio, 1988-89, Robins AFB, Ga., 1990-93; comdr. 11th Contracting Squadron, Bolling AFB, D.C., 1993-96; mgmt. cons., educator Delaney & Assocs., Wake Forest, N.C., 1996—. Contbg. editor: Air Force Inst. of Technology/Jour. of Logistics, Dayton, 1986-88. Com. mem. Boy Scouts of Am., Bowie, Md., 1995-96. Decorated Legion of Merit (2); rsch. grantee Nat. Assn. of Purchasing Mgrs., Oradell, N.J., 1983, others. Fellow Nat. Contract Mgmt. Assn. (v.p. 1993—); mem. Am. Legion, Retired Officers' Assn., Air Force Assn., Fla. State U. Alumni Assn. (chpt. v.p. 1991—). Roman Catholic. Avocations: tennis, softball, reading, chess, music. Home: 1022 Oxwich Dr Wake Forest NC 27587-7469 Office: Delaney & Assocs 1022 Oxwich Dr Wake Forest NC 27587-7469

DELANEY, HERBERT WADE, JR., lawyer; b. Leadville, Colo., Mar. 30, 1925; s. Herbert Wade and Marie Ann (Garbarino) DeL.; m. Ramona Rae Ortiz, Aug. 6, 1953; children: Herbert Wade III, Paula Rae, Bonnie Marie. BSBA, U. Denver, 1949, LLB, 1951. Bar: Colo. 1951, U.S. Supreme Ct. 1959. Pvt. practice, Denver, 1953-64, 1965-91, 94—; mem. firm DeLaney and Sandven, P.C., 1992-94; faculty U. Denver, Colo., 1960-61, 89; ptnr. DeLaney & West, Denver, 1964-65. Capt. JAG's Dept., USAF, 1951-53. Mem. Colo. Bar Assn., Denver Bar Assn., Am. Legion, Masons, Elks, Phi Alpha Delta. Office: 50 S Steele St Ste 660 Denver CO 80209-2811

DELANEY, JOHN ADRIAN, mayor; b. Lansing, Mich., June 29, 1956; s. James Edward and Mary Anne (Langius) D.; m. Gena Barrett, Sept. 6, 1980; children: William Langius, Adrian Anne, Marye Margaret, James Barrett. BA in History, U. Fla., 1977, JD, 1981. Bar: Fla. 1981. With State Atty.'s Office, Jacksonville, Fla., 1981-91; chief asst. state atty. 4th cir. State Atty.'s Office, Jacksonville, Fla., 1986-91; gen. counsel City of Jacksonville, 1991-92, 94-95, chief of staf, mayor, 1992-94, mayor, 1995—. Mem. Leadership Jacksonville, 1986, Leadership Fla.-13; chmn. St. Paul's Episcopal Sch. Bd. Mem. Inn. of Ct., Blue Key (pres. 1980), Rotary, Delta Upsilon. Roman Catholic. Avocation: camping. Home: 110 Bowles St Jacksonville FL 32266-4917 Office: Office of the Mayor 220 E Bay St Jacksonville FL 32202-3429

DELANEY, JOHN WHITE, lawyer; b. Springfield, Mass., Feb. 28, 1943; s. Frank T. and Emily (White) D.; m. Betsey Secor; children: Erin, Elizabeth. AB, Harvard U., 1964, JD, 1967. Bar: Mass. 1967, U.S. Dist. Ct. Mass. 1968. Staff asst. to U.S. senator Leverett Saltonstall Washington, 1966; law clk. Mass. Superior Ct., Boston, 1967-68; asst. atty. gen. Atty. Gen.'s Office, Boston, 1968-69; legis. asst. Gov. Commonwealth of Mass., Boston, 1969-73; asst. sec. consumer affairs and bus. regulation Commonwealth of Mass., 1973-76; exec. dir. Boston Mcpl. Rsch. Bur., 1976-80; dir. govt. and community affairs Bank of Boston, 1980-89; sr. ptnr. Hale and Dorr, Boston, 1989—; dir. New England Legal Found., Boston, 1986—. Dir. Robert F. Kennedy Action Corps, Boston, 1973-92; sec. Coordinating Com., Boston, 1984-87; trustee, mem. exec. com. Mass. Taxpayers Found., Boston, 1986—; trustee Boston Mcpl. Rsch. Bur., 1991—; mem. standing com. The Trustees of Reservations, 1993—; dir. Greater Boston C. of C., 1992—; pres. Friends of RFK Children's Action Corp. Inc., 1996—. Office: Hale and Dorr LLP 60 State St Ste 25 Boston MA 02109-1816

DELANEY, JOSEPH P., bishop; b. Fall River, Mass., Aug. 29, 1934. Student, Cardinal O'Connell Sem., Mass., Theol. Coll., Washington, N.Am. Coll., Rome, R.I. Coll. Ordained priest Roman Catholic Ch., 1960; ordained bishop of Fort Worth, 1981—. Office: 800 W Loop 820 S Fort Worth TX 76108-2936*

DELANEY, KEVIN FRANCIS, retired naval officer; b. Wolcott, Conn., Sept. 23, 1946; s. John Delaney; m. Patricia Delaney, June 8, 1968; children: Kelly, Diana, Seana. BS in Engring., U.S. Naval Acad., Annapolis, Md., 1968; M in Bus., George Washington U., 1977; postgrad., MIT, 1984, Harvard U., 1993. With. USN, advanced through grades to rear admiral, 1991, ret., 1998; commdg. officer Heli Anti-Sub Squadron 32, Norfolk, Va., 1980-82, 82-84; air ops. officer USS Guadal Canal, 1984-86; commdg. officer HSL-31 Helo Sea Control Wing 3, Mayport, 1987; commdg. officer Naval Air Sta., Jacksonville, Fla., 1989-91; dir. shore activities readiness U.S. Atlantic Fleet, Norfolk, Va., 1993-94; dir. shore installation mgmt. Chief Naval Ops., Washington, 1994-95; comdr. Naval Base Jacksonville, 1995-98; exec. v.p. Coggin Automotive Group, Jacksonville, Fla., 1999—. Bd. mem. 12 Who Care Selection Com., Jacksonville, 1995-96, Vol. Jax, Inc., Jacksonville, 1995-96, Childrens Haven, Orange Park, Fla., 1995-96; chmn. Navy/Marine Corp. Relief Soc., Jacksonville, 1995-96; bd. mem. Salvation Army, United Way, USO, YMCA, Jr. Achievement. Mem. C. of C. (bd. mem.), Rotary (pres.). Home: 4551 Swilcan Bridge Ln N Jacksonville FL 32224-5618 Office: Coggin Automotive Group 4306 Pablo Oaks Ct Jacksonville FL 32224-9631

DELANEY, KIM, actress; b. Phila., Nov. 29, 1961; 1 child, Jack. Appeared in (TV series) All My Children, 1981-84, 94, Tour of Duty, 1987, The Fifth Corner, 1992, NYPD Blue, 1995— (Emmy award 1997), (TV movies) First Affair, 1983, Perry Mason: The Case of the Sinister Spirit, 1987, Cracked Up, 1987, Christmas Comes to Willow Creek, 1987, All My Darling Daughters, Please Take My Daughters, 1988, Something Is Out There, 1988, The Broken Cord, 1992, Lady Boss, 1992, Closer and Closer, The Disappearance of Christina, 1993, Tall, Dark, and Deadly, 1995, Tall Dark and Deadly, 1995, All Lies End in Murder, 1997, The Devil's Child, 1997, (films) That Was Then...This Is Now, 1985, The Delta Force, 1986, Hunter's Blood, 1987, Campus Man, 1987, The Drifter, 1988, Hangfire, 1991, Body Parts, 1991, The Force, 1994, Inferno, Darkman II: The Return of Durant, 1994, Dark Goddess, 1994, Serial Killer, 1995, Project: Metalbeast, 1995, Closer and Closer, 1995. Avocations: biking, swimming, working out, watching films. Office: care The Gersh Agy 232 N Canon Dr Beverly Hills CA 90210-5302*

DELANEY, MARY ANNE, pastoral educator; b. Waltham, Mass., Feb. 15, 1926; d. Thomas Joseph and Mary Teresa (Berry) D. BA, Regis Coll., 1953; MEd, U. Mass., Boston, 1973; MDiv, Andover Newton Theol. Sch., Newton Ctr., Mass., 1978. Tchr. various schs., Mass., 1953-73; pastoral counselor Boston City Hosp., 1974-76; dir. pastoral care Cape Breton Hosp., Sydney River, N.S., Can., 1978-81, Nova Scotia Hosp., Dartmouth, 1981-86, Misericordia Hosp., Edmonton, Alta., Can., 1986-91; pastoral counselor Assn. Pastoral Edn., Waltham, Mass., 1992-96, Emmanuel Coll., Boston, 1996—; supr. pastoral edn. Leland Retirement Home, Waltham, Mass., 1992—; vice chair bioethics consultative svc. Misericordia Hosp., Edmonton, 1987-91; vis. scholar Andover Newton Theol. Sch., 1991-92. Trustee Inst. Pastoral Tng., Halifax, N.S., Can., 1981-86; mem. commn. on ecumenism Archdiocese of Halifax, 1982-86; mem. of the Congregation of Sisters of St. Joseph, Boston, 1945—. Mem. Can. Assn. Pastoral Edn. (cert. com. 1987-91), Assn. for Clin. Pastoral Edn. (cert. supr., accreditation com. 1993-98, cert. com. 1998—). Roman Catholic. Avocations: international travel, classical music, art, reading. Home and Office: 16 Cutter St Waltham MA 02453-5911

DELANEY, MATTHEW MICHAEL, school administrator, fine arts educator; b. Boston, Mar. 13, 1948; s. Matthew Michael and Julia Agnes (Perry) D.; m. Patricia Louise Tirrell, Mar. 22, 1970; children: Sara Linde, Elizabeth Kerrin. BS in Art Edn., Mass. Coll. Art, 1970; MEd, Bridgewater State Coll., 1974; MA, Boston Coll., 1981. Nat. bd. cert. in art; cert. fine arts tchr. PK-12, fine arts supervisor/ dir. PK-12, secondary tchr. history, social studies, prin., asst. prin. Instr. fine arts Brockton Pub. Schs., Mass., 1970-74; from instr. fine arts to PK-12 regional curriculum coord., elective curriculum coord. Whitman-Hanson Regional Sch. Dist., Mass., 1974—; adj. faculty mem. Mass. Coll. Art, Curriculum in the Visual Arts; facilitator for NBCT candidate support program, U. Mass. at Dartmouth; photographer Brockton Daily Enterprise, 1972-76, Patriot Ledger, 1976-82; instr. fine arts Brockton Art Ctr., 1973-74; cmty. sch. coord. Brockton Pub. Schs., 1971-74; facility Tech. Study Com., Whitman, 1993-94; mem. supt. search com., Abington, Mass., 1991-92; mem. Effective Schs. Com., Whitman-Hanson, 1982-84, instrnl. adv. coun., 1989—, faculty adv. coun., selected for field study Nat. Bd. Cert.. Art; art and music curriculum rep. North River Collaborative; presenter workshops in U.S. and France; peer assessor U.S. Dept. Edn., 1999; scorer Nat. Bd. Profl. Tchg. Standards, 1999. Photographic works in collection Internat. Ctr. for Photography/George Eastman House, Rochester, N.Y.; contbr. art and design to Kiwanis, Spl. Olympics, Shriners, and others; articles to profl. jours. NEH grantee, 1992, Horace Mann grantee, 1988, 89; recipient U.S. Presdl. Recognition, 1997, citation by Mass. State Legislature, 1998, Mass. Senate 1999; cert. of honor Commonwealth of Mass., 1999. Mem. NEA, ASCD, Mass. Tchrs. Assn. (disting. svc. award 1988, recognition achievement award 1997, Whitman-Hanson Regional Sch. Dist. Outstanding Leadership award 1997), Nat. Art Edn. Assn., Abington Cultural Coun., Abington Music Parents Assn., Mass. Art Edn. Assn., Boston Coll. Alumni Assn., Mass. Coll. Art Alumni Assn. Democrat. Episcopalian. Avocations: skiing, sailing, cycling, travel, playing guitar. Office: Whitman-Hanson Regional Sch Dist 600 Franklin St Whitman MA 02382-2599

DELANEY, PAUL WILLIAM, English language educator; b. Lexington, Ky., Aug. 25, 1948; s. Hugh Emery and Cumie Lee (Olliff) D.; m. Dianne Elaine Mitten, June 9, 1968; children: Elizabeth Suzanne, Arthur David. BA, Asbury Coll., 1968; MA, Emory U., 1969, PhD, 1972. Prof. English, Westmont Coll., Santa Barbara, Calif., 1972—. Author: Tom Stoppard: The Moral Vision of the Major Plays, 1990; editor: Tom Stoppard in Conversation, 1994. Mem. Conf. on Christianity and Lit. (bd. dirs. 1993—). Episcopalian. Home: 2530 Selrose Ln Santa Barbara CA 93109-1863 Office: Westmont Coll 955 La Paz Rd Santa Barbara CA 93108-1023

DELANEY, ROBERT PATRICK, librarian, writer; b. Miles City, Mont., Mar. 16, 1961; s. Alfred John and Ann Lois (D'Ambrosia) D. AAS in Broadcast Comm., Suffolk County C.C., 1982; BA in English magna cum laude, Dowling Coll., 1985; MSLS, L.I. U., 1987. Grad. asst. Southampton (N.Y.) Campus Libr., L.I. U., 1986-87, libr., 1987—; libr. Babylon (N.Y.) Pub. Libr., 1987-88; librarian Farmingdale (N.Y.) Campus Libr., Poly. U., 1988, C.W. Post Campus Libr., L.I. U., Brookville, N.Y., 1989—. Author: Dreamfinder, 1986, Nightfawn and the Gleam, 1989, Brightblossom and the Gleam, 1990, The Sinking Star, 1990, Sex and the Single Elf, 1993, The Quiet and Fertile Plain, 1995, There Goes the Neighborhood, 1997. Mem. Suffolk County Libr. Assn., Soc. for Preservation of Film Music, Internat. Arthurian Soc. Avocations: Shakespeare, poetry, filmscores, Arthurian legends, mythology. E-mail: www.geocities.com/broadway/1906. Home: 34 University Dr Lake Ronkonkoma NY 11779-1905

DELANEY, ROBERT VERNON, logistics and transportation executive; b. Passaic, N.J., Mar. 16, 1936; s. Edward Aloysius and Helen Margaret (Gauthier) D.; m. Elissa Ornato, June 15, 1963; children: Edward, James. BBA, NYU, 1963, MBA, 1966; postgrad., St. Louis U., 1967-69, Am. U., 1971-72. Registered practitioner Surface Transp. Bd. formerly ICC. Transp. mgr. Nabisco, N.Y.C., 1958-62; distbn. mgr. Monsanto Co., St. Louis, 1963-70; dir. phys. distbn. Md. Cup Corp., Owings Mills, 1970-74; mgr. internal cons. Pet Inc., St. Louis, 1974-78; mgr. distbn. planning Internat. Paper Co., N.Y.C., 1978-83; sr. v.p. Leaseway Transp. Co., Cleve., 1983-87; practice leader for transp. Arthur D. Little, Inc., Cambridge, Mass., 1988-89; exec. v.p. Cass Info. Sys., St. Louis, 1990—; founder Warehousing Edn. and Rsch. Coun., Oak Brook, Ill., 1977; bd. dirs. Pvt. Carrier Conf., Inc.; faculty Acad. Advanced Traffic, 1966; guest lectr., frequent spkr. ednl. and profl. orgns. Co-author Transportation Strategies for the Eighties, 1982, The Distribution Handbook, 1984; mem. editl. rev. bd. Transportation Quar., Internat. Jour. Phys. Distbn. and Materials Mgmt.; contbr. articles to newspapers and bus. pubs. Mem. transp. com. The New England Coun., Boston, 1978-82. St. Louis Regional Commerce & Growth Assn., 1975-78; bus. advisor Norman Thomas H.S., N.Y.C., 1979-82. Staff sgt. U.S. Army, 1953-56. Recipient Salzberg Medallion award for transp., Syracuse U., 1988. Mem. Am. Soc. Transp. and Logistics (cert., Joseph Scheleen award for excellence 1992), Coun. Logistics Mgmt. (exec. com. 1976-84, sec. 1983-84, Disting. Svc. award 1981), Nat. Coun. Phys. Distbn. Mgmt. (John Drury Sheahan Disting. Svc. award 1981), Nat. Press Club (Washington, author ann. State of Logistics report). Republican. Avocations: education. Office: Cass Info Systems 13001 Hollenberg Dr Bridgeton MO 63044-2410

DELANEY, ROBERT VINCENT, former gas company executive, economic development consultant; b. N.Y.C., Oct. 1, 1934; s. Charles Peter and Alice Mary (O'Rorke) D.; m. Marie Josephine Monaco, Oct. 13, 1956; children: Robert Vincent, Richard Clement, Charles John, Christopher Raymond, Elizabeth Marie. BS in Acctg., Fordham U., 1956; grad. advanced mgmt. program, Harvard U., 1979. Tax mgr. Bklyn. Union Gas Co., 1965-66, personnel mgr., 1966-71, asst. v.p. human resources, 1971-75, v.p. engring., 1975-81, sr. v.p. customer ops., 1981-88, group sr. v.p., chief adminstrv. officer, 1988-90; prin. CPS Cons., N.Y.C., 1990—; chmn. bd. Greater Jamaica Devel. Corp., N.Y.C.; bd. dirs. Queens Overall Econ. Devel. Corp., N.Y.C.; faculty advisor N.Y.C. Tech. Coll., 1968-92. Bd. dirs. Jr. Achievement N.Y., 1972-78, Coop. Edn. Commn. N.Y.C., 1977-82, N.Y. Hall Sci., N.Y.C., 1983-92, Queens Symphony Orch., 1981-91; pres. Harvard AMP Class of 1979, Cambridge; pub. mem. Bd. Cert. for Profl. Engrs. and Land Surveyors State of N.Y., Albany, 1977-87. Capt. arty., U.S. Army, 1957. Recipient Outstanding Svc. award Jr. Achievement, 1980, Disting. Citizen award Queens Symphony Orch., 1980, Bus. Friends of Arts award Borough of Queens, 1984, merit award Am. Legion, 1985, leadership award Greater Jamaica Devel. Corp., 1997. Mem. Am. Gas Assn. (taxation com. 1962-64, customer acctg. com. 1965-67, chmn. pers. com. 1970-73, chmn. fin. and adminstrv. sect. 1982-83, award of merit 1979), Harvard Bus. Sch. Club of N.Y. (bd. dirs.), Harvard U. Club, Bklyn. Club, Beta Gamma Sigma. Republican. Roman Catholic. Avocations: tennis, stickball (three sewer hitter). Home and Office: 1025 Fifth Ave New York NY 10028-0134

DELANEY, THOMAS CALDWELL, JR., city official; b. Danville, Va., Jan. 1, 1918; s. Thomas Caldwell and Ethel Bernard (Loving) D.; m. Lois Jean Fitzsimmons, July 20, 1960. B.S., Spring Hill Coll., 1941; M.A., U. Ala., 1952. Dean, head dept. history Univ. Mil. Sch., Mobile, Ala., 1941-56; headmaster Wright Sch., Mobile, 1956-65; mus. dir., head dept. mus. City of Mobile, 1965-92, dir. emeritus, 1992; mem. Nat. Hist. Records Adv. Bd., 1978-81; historian Mobile C.W. Centennial Commn., Mobile 250th Anniversary Celebration, 1961. Author: Deep South, 1942, 80, Remember Mobile, 1948, 69, 80, Story of Mobile, 1953, 61, 80, Phoenix Volunteer Fire Company of Mobile, 1838-1888, 1967, The First Hundred Years, 1968, Craigheed's Mobile, 1968, Confederate Mobile, 1971, Raphael Semmes, 1978, Mobile Sextet, 1981; author articles. Bd. dirs. Ala. First Capital Commn., 1961-65. Mem. Ala. Mus. Assn. (dir. 1978—), Southeastern Mus. Conf., Am. Assn. Museums, Ala. Hist. Assn. (pres. 1962), Hist. Mobile Preservation Soc. (dir. 1950-60), Smithsonian Assos., Nat. Archives, Fenollosa Soc. Japan (hon. charter). Presbyterian. Club: Rotary. Home: 8 S Ann St Mobile AL 36604-2145

DELANEY, WILLIAM FRANCIS, JR., reinsurance broker; s. William F. and Viola (Kelly) D.; m. Virginia Beers; children: Marcia, Gayle. Student, Ecole Albert de Mun, Nogent sur Marne, France, Douai Sch., Eng.; Oxford and Cambridge Sch. Cert.; AB, Princeton U.; LLB, Harvard U.; student, NYU, Practising Law Inst., Ins. Soc. N.Y.; Studied law, Paris. Bar: N.Y., U.S. Supreme Ct. Atty. Irving Trust Co., N.Y.C.; gen. counsel Am. Internat. Underwriters Group; N.Y. reins. mgr. Fairfield & Ellis; pres. Delaney Offices, Inc., N.Y., 1954—; founding mem., broker, N.Y. Ins. Exchange; reins. intermediary and cons. for U.S. and world wide; reins. lectr. Ins. Soc. N.Y. Author: Reinsurance Laws of South America and Mexico; contbr. articles to ins. publs. Mem. Ins. Soc. N.Y. Roman Catholic. Clubs: Princeton, Deal Golf. Office: 4365 Bridle Way Reno NV 89509-2904

DELANEY-LAWRENCE, AVA PATRICE, secondary school educator; b. Knoxville, Tenn., Apr. 12, 1960; d. William J. and Lena (Guilford) Delaney; 1 child, Brian. BS, U. Tenn., 1982; MA, Clark Atlanta U., 1994. Cert. English tchr. grades 7-12, Ga., Tenn. Substitute tchr. Knoxville City Schs., 1982; English tchr. Chattanooga (Tenn.) City Schs., 1982-85, Atlanta Pub. Schs., Therrell H.S., 1985—; testing cons. R&R Evaluations, Decatur, Ga., 1985-87; ednl. cons. Harris Learning Sys., Atlanta, 1988—. Mem. Nat. Assn. Educators, Nat. Coun. Tchrs. English, Zeta Phi Beta. Home: PO Box 724373 Atlanta GA 31139-1373

DELANO, LESTER ALMY, JR., advertising executive; b. New Bedford, Mass., Nov. 28, 1928; s. Lester A. and Beatrice (Thomas) D.; m. Margaret Dent (div.); 1 child, Leslie Ann; m. Helaine Shipper; children: Oliver Evan, Peter Franklin. Student, Amherst Coll., Brown U.; MA, U. Chgo. Mktg. cons. Chgo., 1950-54; v.p. North Advt., Inc., Chgo., 1955-60; pres. Dodge & Delano, Inc., N.Y.C., 1961-71, Tinker, Dodge & Delano, Inc., 1971-76; chmn., chief exec. officer Tinker, Campbell-Ewald Inc., N.Y.C., 1976-77; pres. Campbell-Ewald Internat., London, Eng., 1977-80, Marschalk Campbell-Ewald Worldwide, N.Y.C., 1980-85; chmn. exec. com. Lowe Marschalk Worldwide, 1986-87; exec. dir. The Lowe Group PLC, N.Y.C., 1987—; bd. dirs. Octagon Worldwide, N.Y.C. Author: Creative Advertising Planning. Served with USN, 1945-48. Home: 115 Central Park W New York NY 10023-4153 Office: The Lowe Group PLC 1114 Avenue Of The Americas New York NY 10036-7703 also: Octagon Wolrdwide Ltd, 6 Eaton Gate, London SW1W 9BJ, England

DELANO, VICTOR, retired naval officer; b. Washington, Dec. 20, 1919; s. Harvey and Marcia (Murdock) D.; m. Jacqueline Stinson (dec. 1990); children: Katherine Delano Jahnig, Harvey II. BSEE with distinction, U.S. Naval Acad., 1941; MS in Physics, MIT, 1949; postgrad., Indsl. Coll. Armed Forces, 1961-62. Ensign USN, 1941, advanced through grades to capt., 1959; staff comdr. 2d Fleet, 1956-58, Atlantic Fleet, 1963-65; chief of staff Atlantic Amphibious Force, 1966-67; mem. Office Chief of Naval Ops., 1967-69; ret., 1969; pres. Wichita Eagle-Beacon Pub., 1970-71. V.p., treas. Naval Hist. Found., Washington, 1980—; trustee Naval Acad. Found.; trustee, bd. dirs. Avon (Conn.) Old Farms Sch., 1980-92, 95—; bd. dirs. Friends Nat. Zoo, Washington, 1971-80, Episc. Ctr. for Children, Washington, 1975-84, 88-94, Kingsbury Ctr., Washington, 1986-95. Decorated Legion of Merit (2), Bronze Star, Purple Heart, Chevalier du Tastevin. Mem. Naval Inst., Naval Acad. Alumni Assn., Mil. Order Carabao, Pearl Harbor Survivors Assn., Chevy Chase Club, Metropolitan Club (Washington), Army-Navy Club, Princess Anne Country Club (Virginia Beach, Va.), Las Campanas Club (Santa Fe), Eagle Creek Golf and Country Club (Naples, Fla.). Clubs: Chevy Chase (Md.); Metropolitan (Washington), Army-Navy; Princess Anne Country (Virginia Beach, Va.); Las Campanas (Santa Fe). Avocation: golf. Home: 5610 Wisconsin Ave Apt 1409 Chevy Chase MD 20815-4439 Home (Winter): 760 Waterford Dr Apt 201 Naples FL 34113-8013

DELANY, DANA, actress; b. N.Y.C., Mar. 13, 1956. Student, Wesleyan U. Appeared in TV series Love of Life, 1979-80, As the World Turns, 1981, Magnum PI, 1986-88, Sweet Surrender, 1987, China Beach, 1988-91 (Emmy award for best actress in a drama series 1989, 92), Good Housekeeping, 1995, Wing Commander Academy, 1996, Superman, 1996, The Rescuers, 1998; (TV movie) Threesome, 1984, Liberty, 1986, A Winner Never Quits, 1986, A Promise to Keep, 1990, The Enemy Within, 1994, Choices of the Heart: The Margaret Sanger Story, 1995, For Hope, 1996, The Patron Saint of Liars, 1998; (miniseries) Wild Palms, 1993, True Woman, 1997, resurrection, 1999; (films) The Fan, 1981, Almost You, 1984, Where the River Runs Black, 1986, Masquerade, 1988, Patty Hearst, 1988, Moon over Parador, 1988, Housesitter, 1992, Light Sleeper, 1992, Tombstone, 1993, Exit to Eden, 1994, Live Nude Girls, 1995, Fly Away Home, 1996, Wide Awake, 1997; on Broadway, A Life, 1980-81, in Translations, 1995. Office: Internat Creative Mgmt 8942 Wilshire Blvd Beverly Hills CA 90211-1934

DELAP, JOE GENE, educator; b. Vinita, Okla., Oct. 4, 1959; s. Jimmy Dodson and Kathryn Fairchild D.; m. Melanie Esry, Aug. 20, 1988; childre: Shelby Joseph, Kennedy Christine. MA in Polit. Sci., U. Ark., 1985; MA in Gemran Studies, Ind. U., 1987, PhD, 1992; hon. degree, U. Ark., 1982. Teaching asst. Wilhelm-Bracke Gesamtschule, Braunschweig, Germany, 1983-84, U. Ark., Fayetteville, 1984-85; assoc. instr. Ind. U., Bloomington, 1985-93; asst. prof. langs. Kans. Wesleyan U., Salina, 1993-94, chair dept. langs., 1994—; pruefungsbeauftragter Goethe-Inst., N.Y.C., 1998—. Author: Beginning Dutch Workbook, 1993, Key to Beginning Dutch Workbook, 1993. Team mem. Kans. State Bd. Edn., Topeka, 1994-95; mem. tech. com. Unified Sch. Dist. 305 Sch. Dist., Salina, 1995-96. Rsch. grantee Dutch Govt., 1990; Fulbright scholar, 1983, 98, Nikenrode scholar, 1988. Mem. Am. Assn. Tchrs. German (past pres. Kans. chpt.), Kans. Fgn. Lang. Assn. (conf. chair 1994-96), Kans. Assn. Tchrs. German (pres. 1997-98), Civitan Club Salina (sec. 1997—). Office: Kans Wesleyan U 100 E Claflin Salina KS 67401-6196

DELAP, TONY, artist; b. Oakland, Calif., Nov. 4, 1927; s. Truman Henry and Catherine (Yontz) D.; m. Kathleen Rose Campbell, Dec. 27, 1964; children—Kelly Rose, Jack Henry. A.A., Menlo Jr. Coll., 1947; student, Claremont Grad. Sch., 1947-49. Prof. U. Calif. at Irvine, 1965-91. Exhibited group shows, San Francisco Mus., Oakland Mus., Whitney Mus., U. Ill., Mus. Modern Art N.Y., L.A. County Mus., Pasadena Mus., one man shows, Dilexi Gallery, San Francisco, 1963, 67, Robert Elkon Gallery, N.Y.C., Felix Landau Gallery, L.A., 1966, 68, U. Calif. at Irvine, Nicholas Wilder Gallery, L.A., 1972, 74, 76, Calif. Inst. Tech., 1974, Calif. State U., Long Beach, 1974, John Berggruen Gallery, San Francisco, 1972, 76, Jan Turner Gallery, L.A., 1987, 89, 91, Modernism Gallery, San Francisco, 1986, 89, 92, 96, Klein Gallery, Chgo., 1985, Beatrix Wilhelm Gallery, Stuttgart, Germany, 1992, Gudrun Spiel Vogel Gallery, Munich, 1993, Works Gallery, Santa Ana, Calif., 1992, Allene Lapides Gallery, Santa Fe, N.Mex., 1992, Mark Moore Gallery, Santa Monica, Calif., 1994-95, 98, Calif. State U., Fullerton, 1994; represented in permanent collections: Whitney Mus., Mus. Modern Art N.Y.C., Walker Art Inst., Tate Gallery, London, Long Beach Mus. Art, Los Angeles County Mus. Art, Santa Barbara (Calif.) Mus. Art, Newport Harbor Art Mus., Newport Beach, Calif., Guggenheim Mus., N.Y.C. Address: 225 Jasmine St Corona Del Mar CA 92625-3035

DELAPA, JUDITH ANNE, business owner; b. Bad Axe, Mich., Feb. 1, 1938; d. John Vincent and Ellen Agatha (Peters) McCormick; m. James Patrick DeLapa, Jan. 10, 1959; children: Joseph Anthony, James P. II, John M., Gina M. BS, Mich. State U., 1959, MA, 1985. Tchr. various schs., Mich., 1959-64; co-founder Saluto Foods Corp., Benton Harbor, Mich., 1963-76; founder Earthtone Interiors, St. Joseph, Mich., 1977-82, High Impact Mktg. Svcs., Grand Rapids, Mich., 1987—; mktg. rsch. and mgt. cons., writer various clients; nationwide. Author: High-Impact Business Strategies, 1993, The McCormick-DeLapa Family Cookbook, 1997. Bd. dirs. Econ. Club Grand Rapids, Grand Rapids Symphony Orch.; ofcl. del., life mem. Nat. Tax Summit, 1998; mem. exec. com. Rep. Presdl. Roundtable; exec. com., pres. The Samaraitan found.; mem. The Senatorial Trust. Judith A. DeLapa Perennial Garden named in her honor Michigan State U. Avocations: reading, travel, theater. Office: High Impact Mktg Svcs 2505 E Paris Ave SE Grand Rapids MI 49546-6100

DE LA PIEDRA, JORGE, orthopedic surgeon; b. Peru, Feb. 11, 1923; came to U.S., 1960; naturalized, 1963; s. Luis G. and Rosa M. (Quinones) de la P.; m. June M. Daugherty, May 1, 1955; children: Ana Maria, Jorge Antonio, James Michael. grad. Facultad de Ciencias, Universidad de San Marcos, Lima, Peru, 1942, Facultad de Medicina, MD, 1950. Diplomate Am. Bd. Orthopedic Surgery, Am. Bd. Profl. Disability Cons. Intern, Army Hosp., Lima, 1951-52; rotating intern Augustana Hosp., Chgo., 1952-53; resident in orthopedic surgery St. Francis Hosp., Peoria, Ill., 1953-54, Charlotte (N.C.) Meml. Hosp., 1954-57; fellow in orthop. divsn. Duke U. Hosp., 1956-57; acting chief orthopedic dept. Social Security Adminstrn. Hosp. #1, Lima, 1958-59; orthopedic Surgeon Mullens (W.Va.) Hosp., 1960-66; practice medicine specializing in orthopedic surgery, Princeton, W.Va., 1966—; mem. staff Princeton Community Hosp., 1966—, dir., 1974—. Served with Peruvian Army, 1951-52. Recipient award Disting. Physicians of Am. Fellow Internat. Coll. Surgeons, Am. Acad. Disability Evaluating Physicians; mem. AMA (physician's award 1969, 72-74, 77, 80, 84), W.Va. State Med. Assn., Mercer County Med. Soc., Am. Fracture Assn., So. Med. Soc., Latin Am. Soc. Orthopedic Surgeons, Orthopedic Rsch. and Edn. Found. (life), Peruvian Acad. of Surgery. So. Orthopedic Soc., W.Va. Orthopedic Soc., Peruvian Am. Med. Soc., Nat. Assn. Disability Evaluating Physicians (charter). Roman Catholic. Lodge: K.C.

DELAPLAINE, GEORGE BIRELY, JR., newspaper editor, cable television executive; b. Frederick, Md., Dec. 9, 1926; s. George B. and Ruth (Carty) D.; m. Elizabeth Barker, Aug. 12, 1955; children: George III, James, Edward, John. BBA, Johns Hopkins U., 1948. From reporter to publisher Frederick News-Post, 1949—; v.p. Frederick Brick Works, Inc., 1989—; pres. Frederick Cablevision Inc., GS Communications, C/R TV Cable. Named Honorary Am. Farmer Nat. Future Farmers Am., 1987; recipient Disting. Eagle Scout award, 1997. Mem. Kiwanis, Eagles, Jaycees, Masons. Republican. Episcopalian. Office: Frederick News-Post 200 E Patrick St Frederick MD 21701-5632

DE LAPPE, GEMZE, dancer, educator, choreographer; b. Portsmouth, Va., Feb. 28, 1922; d. Birch Wood and Maureen (McDonough) de L.; m. John Carisi, 1959; children—Peter, Jonathan. Student H.S. Music and Art, N.Y.C., 1935-39; student Michael Fokine Ballet, 1930-39, Irma Duncan, Isadora Duncan Sch., 1929-31; DFA (hon.) Niagara U., 1989. Artist-in-residence Smith Coll., Northampton, Mass., 1979-92, prof. emeritus, 1992—; leading mem. Agnes de Mille Dance Theatre Co., N.Y.C., 1954—; premier dancer Broadway prodns. including Oklahoma!, Carousel, Brigadoon, Paint Your Wagon (Donaldson award), The King and I; mem. Am. Ballet Theatre, N.Y.C. 1953-54; appeared in Fall River Legend, Gala Performance, Billy, The Kid and Fancy Free; staged recent prodns. of Oklahoma! in London and Australia; dir. restages of several Rogers and Hammerstein musicals internationally including Takarazuka Co., Japan and Antwerp and Munich Volksoper; choreographer revivals of Finians Rainbow, South Pacific, Unsinkable Molly Brown; (films) Justine, Credo, 1968; appeared with Robert Joffrey Co.'s TV prodn. of Agnes de Mille's Conversations About the Dance; appeared in Sylvia Fine's muscial comedy Tonight; Booth Theatre (highest critical acclaim), The Gorey Stories. Restaged original choreography of Agnes de Mille with additional choreography of Ms. de Lappe for Carousel Houston Opera Co. and Omaha Opera Co., 1990; choreographer Abe Lincoln in Ill. at Vivian Beaumont Theatre, 1996, dances of Brigadoon for N.Y.C. Opera, 1996. Mem. Soc. Stage Dirs. and Choreographers, Actors Equity Assn., SAG, Am. Guild Mus. Artists, AFTRA. Home: 251 W 92d St Apt 7D New York NY 10025-7335

DE LA RENTA, OSCAR, fashion designer; b. Santo Domingo, Dominican Republic, July 22, 1932; s. Oscar and Maria Antonia (deFiallo) de LaR.; m. Francoise de Langlade, Oct. 31, 1967 (dec. 1983); 1 adopted child, Moises; m. Anne E. de la Renta, Dec. 26, 1989. Student, Santo Domingo U., Academia de San Fernando, Madrid. Mem. staff Balenciaga's AISA, Madrid; asst. to Antonio Castillo at Lanvin, Paris, 1961-63; chief designer Elizabeth Arden, N.Y.C., 1963-65; chief designer, chmn. bd. dirs. Oscar de la Renta, Ltd., N.Y.C., 1973—; designer Pierre Balmain, Paris, 1993—. Bd. dirs. La Casa del Nino Orphanage and Sch., Santo Domingo, Met. Opera, Carnegie Hall, Thirteen/WNET, Hispanic Designers, Spanish Inst. Decorated Order Juan Pablo Duarte, Order Cristobal Colon (Dominican Republic); recipient Coty awards, 1967, 68, Golden Tiberius award, 1968, Received Lifetime of Achievement award The Coun. of Fashion Designers of Am., 1990; Neiman-Marcus award, 1968; Fragrance Found. award 1978; Living Legend award Am. Soc. Perfumers, 1995; named to Coty Hall of Fame, 1973. Mem. Coun. Fashion Designers Am. (bd. dirs.). Office: Oscar de la Renta Ltd 550 7th Ave Fl 8 New York NY 10018-3203*

DELARM, JOAN SHARON, social worker, psychotherapist; b. Ticonderoga, N.Y., Dec. 16, 1946; d. Cecil William and Bertha Dorothy (Gordon) DeL. BS in Edn., Coll. St. Joseph the Provider, 1972; MEd, St. Rose Coll., 1976; MSW, Adelphi U., 1985. Cert. social worker, N.Y., tchr., N.Y.; cert. diplomate in advanced social work. Tchr. various schs., 1968-80; family life educator Warren County Community Maternity Svcs., Albany, 1980-84; clin. social worker Dept. Social Svcs., Granville, N.Y., 1984-85, Saratoga (N.Y.) Mental Health Agy., 1984-85; social worker, client coord. Wilton (N.Y.) Devel. Ctr., 1985-86; psychiat. social worker admissions inpatient St. Lawrence Psychiat. Ctr., Ogdensburg, N.Y., 1986-88; psychotherapist St. Lawrence Psychiat. Ctr., Massena, N.Y., 1988-92; pvt. practice Massena, 1992—; trained facilitator of multiple family groups concerned with alcohol and sexual abuse; cons. St. Lawrence County Hospice, Potsdam, 1989-92; program developer Warr en County, Washington County, 1980-84; part time tchr. St. Regis Mohawk Indian Reservation; part time coll. instr. alcohol, chem. dependency program Mater-Dei-Coll.; EAP cons., counselor Alcoa Corp. Svc. Provider for N.Y. Power Authority, 1991. Author: (handbook) Nourishing Ourselves and Others, 1980. Dem. del. for State of Vt., Washington, 1967. Recipient Quality Assurance award St. Lawrence Psychiat. Ctr., Ogdensburg, 1989. Fellow N.Y. State Soc. Clin. Social Work Psychotherapists; mem. NASW (cert.), Acad. Clin. Social Workers. Democrat. Roman Catholic. Avocations: cross country, poetry, walking, biking, tennis. Office: 74 Andrews St Massena NY 13662-1858

DE LA ROCHA, CARLOS A., retired physician; b. Santo Domingo, Dominican Republic, Aug. 12, 1934; s. Carlos A. and Germania (Contin) de la R.; m. Penelope Lynn Lansing, May 20, 1961; children: C. Andrew, Maria L., Michael J., David L., Alicia M., Juan A. MD, Univ. de Santo Domingo, 1958. Diplomate Am. Bd. Surgery. Rotating intern City Hosp. at Elmhurst, Queens, N.Y., 1958-59; asst. resident surgery Albert Einstein Med. Ctr., Phila., 1959-60; asst. resident surgery Ellis Hosp., Schenectady, N.Y., 1960-62, chief resident surgery, 1962-63; tchg. fellow surgery St. Clares Hosp., Schenectady, 1963-65; asst. attending surgeon St. Clares and Ellis Hosp., 1965-69, attending surgeon, 1969-98; ret., 1998; chmn. tissue unit Ellis Hosp., 1985-90; mem. Ellis Hosp. Found. Bd., 1988-94. Fellow Am. Coll. Surgeons; mem. Am. Soc. Gen. Surgeons, N.Y. State Soc. Surgeons, N.Y. State and County Med. Soc. Republican. Roman Catholic. Avocations: travel, classical music. Office: C A de la Rocha MD PC 1310 Union St Schenectady NY 12308

DE LA ROZA, GUSTAVO LUIS, pathologist; b. N.Y.C., Jan. 28, 1962; s. Gustavo Alberto and Carmen Alicia (Romera) de la R. MD, U. Buenos Aires, 1987. Diplomat Am. Bd. Pathology. Pathologist MD Anderson Cancer Ctr., Houston, 1993-94; assoc. Pathology Pvt. Practice, Buenos Aires, 1994-95; pathologist, asst. prof. U. Medicine and Dentistry N.J., Newark, 1995-98; dir. cytopathology sect. The Permanente Med. Group, Inc., Santa Clara, Calif., 1998—; dir. cytopathology sect. U. Hosp., Newark, 1996-98. Fellow Coll. Am. Pathologists; mem. Am. Clin. Pathologists, Am. Soc. Cytopathology, Am. Acad. Pathology, Can. Acad. Pathology, Calif. Med. Assn., Santa Clara County Med. Soc. Office: Kaiser Permanente Med Ctr Dept Pathology 900 Kiely Blvd Rm 40C Santa Clara CA 95051

DE LARROCHA, ALICIA, concert pianist; b. Barcelona, Spain, May 23, 1923; d. Eduardo and Teresa (De La Calle) de L.; m. Juan Torra, June 21, 1950; children: Juan, Alicia. Grad. (prize extraordinary, Gold medal), Acad. Marshall, Barcelona; MusD (hon.), U. Ann Arbor, 1979, Middlebury Coll., 1981, Carnegie-Mellon, 1985. Debut, Barcelona, 1929, solo recitalist, concert pianist maj. orchs. in, Europe, U.S., Can., Cen. and S.Am., South Africa, New Zealand, Australia, Japan; dir. Acad. Marshall, 1959—; rec. artist: Hispavox, CBS, Decca-London; records: (Grammy awards 1974, 75, 88, 91, nominations 1967, 75, 77, 82, 84, 90, 91, 92, 93, 1st Gold medal Merito a la Vocacion 1973), Spanish Encores, Spanish Fireworks, Spanish Music (I-IV). Recipient Harriet Cohen Internat. Music award, 1956, Franz Liszt award, 1989, Principe de Asturias award 1994, UNESCO award 1995; Paderewski Meml. medal, 1961; Grand prix du Disque Acad. Charles Cros, 1960, 74; Edison award, 1968, 78, 89; decorated Order Civil Merit Order, 1962, Isabel la Catolica, Spain, 1972; hon. academician Bayerische Akademie der Schönen Künste, Munich; real academia Bellas Artes San Fernando, Madrid, R.A.B.B.A.A., Granada; comdr. dans l'Ordre des Arts et des lettres, Paris. Mem. Musica en Compostela (dir.), Hispanic Soc. Am. (corr.), Internat. Piano Archives (hon. pres.). Office: Farmaceutic Carbonell, 46-48 Atic, Barcelona 34, Spain also: Columbia Artists Mgmt Inc care Wilford Div 165 W 57th St New York NY 10019-2201

DE LASA, JOSÉ M., lawyer; b. Havana, Cuba, Nov. 28, 1941; came to U.S., 1961; s. Miguel and Conchita de Lasa; m. Maria Teresa Figueroa, Nov. 23, 1963; children: Maria Teresa, José, Andrés, Carlos. BA, Yale U., 1968, JD, 1971. Bar: N.Y. 1973. Assoc. Cleary, Gottlieb, Steen & Hamilton, N.Y.C., 1971-76; legal dept. Bristol-Myers Squibb Co., N.Y.C., 1976-94; sr. v.p., sec. and gen. counsel Abbott Labs., 1994—; lectr. internat. law, various locations. Bd. dirs. Chgo. Children's Mus., 1995—, The Resource Found., 1989—, Internat. Inst. Rural Reconstrn., 1989—. Mem. ABA, N.Y. County Bar Assn., Assn. of Bar of City of N.Y. Roman Catholic. Office: Abbott Laboratories D-364 AP6D-2 100 Abbott Park Rd North Chicago IL 60064*

DELATEUR, BARBARA JANE, medical educator; b. Hoquiam, Wash., Nov. 17, 1936. Student, Marylhurst (Oreg.) Coll., 1954-56; BS in Philosophy, St. Louis U., 1959; MD, U. Wash., 1963, MSc, 1968. Cert. Am. Bd. Phys. Medicine and Rehab.; lic. physiatrist, Wash., Md. Rotating intern U. Hosp., U. Wash., 1963-64; resident dept. phys. medicine and rehab. U. Hosp., 1964-67; instr. dept. phys. medicine and rehab. U. Wash. Sch. Medicine, 1967-68, asst. prof., 1968-71, assoc. prof., 1971-76, prof. dept. rehab. medicine, 1976-93; prof., dir. dept. phys. medicine and rehab. Johns Hopkins U. Sch. Medicine, Balt., 1993—; Lawrence Cardinal Shehan chair phys. medicine and rehab., 1993—, joint prof. health policy & mgmt. Sch. Hygiene & Pub. Health, 1994—; acting physiatrist-in-chief Rehab. Medicine Svc. Harborview Med. Ctr., Seattle, 1970-72, physiatrist-in-chief, 1972-93; dir. Muscular Dystrophy Clinic Meml. Hosp., Yakima, Wash., 1979-88; dir. dept. phys. medicine and rehab. Johns Hopkins Hosp., Balt., 1993—; med. dir. dept. rehab. medicine Good Samaritan Hosp., Balt., 1993—; vis. prof. dept. rehab. medicine and dept. internal medicine SUNY, Syracuse, 1988; cons. physiatrist Johns Hopkins Geriatrics Ctr., Johns Hopkins Bayview Med. Ctr., Balt., 1994—; vis. lectr. dept. phys. medicine Coll. Medicine, Ohio State U., 1985; Arthur Grant lectr. U. Tex., San Antonio, 1992; Marquette lectr. Jefferson Med. Coll., Phila., 1993; spkr. various univs. and orgns.; pres. Phys.Medicine and Rehab./Edn. and Rsch. Found., 1990-94; mem. governing coun. sect. rehab. hosps. and programs Am. Hosp. Assn., 1993—; mem. adv. bd. Wash. State Divsn. Vocat. Rehab., 1979-84. Contbr. articles to profl. jours.; mem. editl. bd. Archives Phys. Medicine and Rehab., 1978-84, Health After 50, Johns Hopkins Hosp., 1994—; reviewer Jour. Am. Geriatrics Soc., 1994—. Recipient Elizabeth and Sidney Licht award for sci. writing, 1990, Excellence in Tchg. award N.J. Med. Sch., 1992, Excellence in Rsch. Writing award Assn. Acad. Physiatrists and Am. Jour. Phys. Medicine and Rehab., 1992, Golden Goniometer award Phys. Medicine and Rehab. Residents, 1995, Labe Scheinberg award, Meeting of Consortium of MS Ctrs., Portland, Oreg., 1995. Fellow Am. Acad. Phys. Medicine; mem. AMA, Am. Acad. Phys. Medicine and Rehab. (bd. govs. 1983-90, v.p. 1986-887, pres-elect 1987-88, pres. 1988-89, past-pres. 1989-90, Disting. Clinician award 1998), NAS, Am. Burn Assn., Am. Congress Rehab. Medicine, Assn. Acad. Physiatrists (Disting. Academician award 1998), Internnt. Assn. for Study of Pain, King County Med. Assn., Northwest Assn. Phys. Medicine and Rehab. (pres. 1974-76), Gerontol. Soc. Am. (clin. medicine sect.), Wash. State Med. Assn. Office: Good Samaritan Profl Bldg 5601 Loch Raven Blvd Rm 403/406 Baltimore MD 21239-2905*

DE LA TORRE FALZON, ALICIA MARIA, Spanish language educator; b. Jan. 26, 1952. PhD, George Washington U., 1988. Assoc. prof. Spanish, adj. prof. Am. U., Washington, 1983-91; prof. Spanish, asst. divsn. chair fgn. lang. dept. No. Va. C.C., Annandale, 1997—; fgn. lang. peer group chair Va. C.C. Sys., Williamsburg, 1998. E-mail: nvfalza@nv.cc.va.us.

DE LAUDER, ROY ALLEN, business administrator; b. Washington, Oct. 4, 1950; s. Roy Allen Sr. and Sarah Travis (Ward) De L.; m. Christine Ann Narbut, Feb. 28, 1976; children: Nicole, Matthew. BA in History, Clemson U., 1972; MS in Sys. Mgmt., U. So. Calif., overseas campus, 1984. Commd. ensign USN, 1972, advanced through grades to lt. comdr., 1980; ret. USN, Washington, 1993; document rschr. Potomac Personnel Temp. Agy., McLean, Va., 1993, currency reporting asst., 1993; adminstrv. asst. PRC Inc., McLean, 1994-95, govt. property coord., procurement coord., 1995—. Editor newsletter Va. chpt., Palatines to Am., 1993; active PTA Green Acres Elem. Sch., 1987—; cub master Boy Scouts Am., 1997—. Mem. Nat. Property Mgmt. Assn. (cert., v.p. Va. chpt. 1998), Nat. Eagle Scout Assn. Avocation: genealogy. Office: Litton/PRC 1500 Prc Dr Mc Lean VA 22102-5002

DELAUDER, WILLIAM B., academic administrator. Dean arts and scis. N.C. Agrl. and Tech. State U., Greensboro, until 1987; pres. Del. State U., Dover, 1987—. Office: Del State U Office of Pres 1200 N Dupont Hwy Dover DE 19901-2202*

DELAURA, DAVID JOSEPH, English language educator; b. Worcester, Mass., Nov. 19, 1930; s. Louis and Helen Adeline (Austin) DeL.; m. Ann Beloate, Aug. 19, 1961; children: Michael Louis, Catherine, William Beloate. A.B., Boston Coll., 1955, A.M., 1958; Ph.D., U. Wis., 1960. Mem. faculty U. Tex. at Austin, 1960-74, prof. English, 1968-74; Avalon Found. prof. humanities, prof. English U. Pa., Phila., 1974-99, chmn. dept., 1985-90, univ. ombudsman, 1993-97. Author: Hebrew and Hellene in Victorian England: Newman, Arnold, and Pater, 1969; editor: Victorian Prose: A Guide to Research, 1973; contbr. chpts. to books, articles and revs. to profl. publs. Mem. Modern Lang. Assn. (ann. award for outstanding article 1964), AAUP. Home: 31 Orchard Ln Villanova PA 19085-1133 Office: U Pa Dept English Philadelphia PA 19104-6273

DELAURO, ROSA L., congresswoman. Student, London Sch. Econs. & Polit. Sci., 1962-63; BA in History and Polit Sci. cum laude, Marymount Coll., 1964; MA in Internat. Politics, Columbia U., 1966. Tng. assoc. Community Progress Inc., New Haven, Conn., 1967-69; instr. in internat. rels. Albertus Magnus Coll., 1967-68; adminstrv. asst. Nat. Urban Fellows, 1969-72, asst. dir., dir., 1972-75; city coord. Carter-Mondale Presdl. Campaign, New Haven, 1976; exec. asst. Mayor Frank Logue, New Haven, 1976-77, campaign mgr., 1977; exec. asst., devel. adminstr. City of New Haven, 1977-79; campaign mgr. Chris Dodd for U.S. Senate, 1979-80, 86; adminstrv. asst. U.S. Senator Christopher J. Dodd, Washington, 1981-87; state dir. Mondale-Ferraro Presdl. Campaign, N.J., 1986; ptnr. DeLauro-Geller, 1987-88; regional dir. Dukakis for Pres. Campaign, N.Y., N.J., Con.., 1988; exec. dir. EMILY's List, 1989; first elected to U.S. Ho. of Reps., 1990; mem. 102nd-105th Congresses 3rd Conn. dist., 1991—; mem. House Appropriations com. 105th Congress, chief dep. minority whip; del. to Dem. Nat. Conv., 1984; bd. dirs. Pax Ams. Past pres. New Haven Arts Coun. Assoc. fellow Timothy Dwight Coll., Yale U.; recipient Leadership award Am. Com. on Italian Migration. Mem. Nat. Italian-Am. Found., Dem. Women for Progress. Office: US House of Reps 436 Cannon Bldg Washington DC 20515-0703*

DELAWIE, HOMER TORRENCE, architect; b. Santa Barbara, Calif., Sept. 24, 1927; s. Fred Ely and Gertrude (Torrence) D.; m. Billie Carol Sparlin (div. 1969); m. Ethel Ann Mallinger, Sept. 3, 1973; children: Gregory, Claire, Shandell, Tracy, Stephanie, Scott. BS in Archtl. Engring., Calif. Poly. State U., San Luis Obispo, 1951. Registered architect, Calif. Pvt. practice architecture San Diego, 1958-61; founder, chief exec. officer Delawie Wilkes Rodrigues Barker & Bretton Assocs., San Diego, 1961—. Mem. Planning Commn., City of San Diego, 1969-82; adv. bd. KPBS Pub. TV. Recipient Award of Merit Calif. chpt. Am. Inst. Planners, Lay Citizens award Phi Delta Kappa, 1975, award Calif chpt. Am. Planning Assn., 1982; named Disting. Alumnus, Calif. Poly. State U., 1972. Fellow AIA (over 60 design awards 1973—, Architects Svc. award Calif. coun. 1973, spl. award San Diego chpt. 1978, Pub. Svc. award Calif. coun. 1981, Outstanding Firm award San Diego chpt. 1986). Democrat. Home: 2749 Azalea Dr San Diego CA 92106-1132 Office: Delawie Wilkes Rodriques Barker & Bretton Assocs 2827 Presidio Dr San Diego CA 92110-2722

DELAY, DOROTHY (MRS. EDWARD NEWHOUSE), violinist, educator; b. Medicine Lodge, Kans., Mar. 31, 1917; d. Glenn Adney and Cecile (Osborn) DeLay; m. Edward Newhouse, Mar. 5, 1941; children: Jeffrey H., Alison Dinsmore. Student, Oberlin Coll., 1933-34, MusD (hon.), 1981; BA, Mich. State U., 1937; Artists diploma, Juilliard Grad. Sch. Music, 1941; DFA (hon.), Mich. State U., 1991; LHD (hon.), U. Colo., 1991; DMusic (hon.), Columbia U., 1994, Duquesne U., 1998. Prof. violin The Juilliard Sch., N.Y.C., 1947—, Starling prof. violin, 1987—; mem. faculty Sarah Lawrence Coll., 1948-87, Meadowmount Summer Sch. Music, Westport, N.Y., 1948-70; Dorothy DeLay prof. Aspen Summer Music Sch., 1971—; Starling prof. violin U. Cin., 1974—; vis. prof. violin Phila. Coll. Performing Arts, 1977-83, New Eng. Conservatory, 1978-87, Royal Coll. Music, Eng., 1987—; condr. Master classes univs. and conservatories in U.S., Europe, Asia, Africa, Near East.; dir. DeLay Int. of the Starling Found., Juilliard Sch. Music, 1996—. Solo, chamber music performances in, U.S., Can., S.Am., 1937-46, violinist, founder, Stuyvesant Trio, 1940-42; Contbr. articles on violins, violinists to various encys. Decorated Order of the Sacred Treasure (Japan); recipient Outstanding Artist-Tchr. award Am. String Tchrs. Assn., 1975, Highest Honor citation Fedn. of Music Clubs, 1983, Gov.'s award State of Kans., 1982, Alumni Accomplishment award Mich. State U., 1984, King Solomon award Am.-Israel Cultural Found., 1985, Disting. Svc. award Ministry of Culture, Republic of Korea, 1991, Nat. Medal of the Arts with Presdl. Citation, 1994, Am. Eagle award Nat. Music Coun., 1995; Sanford fellow Yale U. Fellow Royal Coll. Music, Gt. Brit.; mem. Mu Phi Epsilon (award of merit 1989). Home: 349 N Broadway Upper Nyack NY 10960-1522 Office: Juilliard Sch 60 Lincoln Center Plz New York NY 10023-6588

DELAY, SUSAN LYNE, software trainer; b. Miami, Okla., July 8, 1950; d. Libert H. and Helen J. (Kelley) Burnett; m. Ron Medonic, Dec. 2, 1970 (div. Sept. 1979); children: Keith, Terri; m. Richard D. Delay, Nov. 30, 1985. AS, Pitts. State Coll., 1970; BS, U. San Diego, 1974; MEd, St. Mary Coll., 1994. Instr. Nat. Coll., Kansas City, Mo., 1985-89; chair computer sci. dept. Donnelly Coll., Kansas City, Kans., 1984-94; instr. Longview C.C., Kansas City, Mo., 1994—; trainer EPI, Kansas City, Kans., 1995—. Vol. HAbitat for Humanity, Kansas City, 1992. UCSD scholar, 1970-71. Fellow Horse Aid. Democrat. Roman Catholic. Avocation: cross country horse racing. Home: 6721 Bell Rd Shawnee KS 66217-9510

DELAY, THOMAS D. (TOM DELAY), congressman; b. Laredo, Tex., Apr. 8, 1947; s. Charles Ray and Maxine (Wimbish) DeL.; m. Christine Furrh, Aug. 26, 1967; 1 child, Danielle. BS, U. Houston, 1970. Gen mgr. Redwood Chem., Houston, 1970-73; owner, operator Albo Pest Control, Stafford, Tex., 1973-84, pres., 1984—; mem., appropriations com. vice chmn. adminstrn. com., chmn. budget and oversight of transp. com. Tex. Ho. of Reps., Austin, 1979-84; mem. 99th-105th Congresses from 22d Tex. dist., 1985—, mem. HUD com., mem. appropriations com., majority whip; mem. appropriations and pub. health coms. Tex. Ho. of Reps.; mem. Grace Caucus, Washington, 1985—; mem. U.S.-Mexico Interparliamentary Del., Washington, 1985-86; mem. Republican study com. Sci. and Tech. Task Force, 1985-86; mem. Rep. research com. Regulatory Reform Caucus, 1985-86. Bd. dirs. Youth Opportunities Unltd., Houston; precinct chmn. Republican Party, Simonton, Tex., 1974-78; Gala chmn. Ft. Bend County "War on Drugs" Coalition, 1987; adv. bd. CloseUp Found.; active drug abuse and rehab. ctr. Odyssey House, Tex; adv. bd. Joint Ctr. for Urban Mobility Research, Houston; mem. Ft. Bend Arts Adv. Council. Recipient Legislator of Yr. award Tex. Assn. to Improve Distbn., 1983; ABC's Outstanding Legislator for the 67th Session Leadership award Young Conservatives of Tex., 1984; Nat. Security Leadership award Coalition Peace Through Strength, Washington, 1985-90; Freshman Class Rep., U.S. House GOP Com. on Coms., Washington, 1985-86; Golden Bulldog award Watchdog of the Treasury , 1985-90. Mem. Congl. Leaders for a Balanced Budget, Greater Houston Pest Control Assn. (former pres.), Tex. Pest Control Assn. (bd. dirs.), Southwest Energy Council, Am. Legis. Exchange Council, Nat. Conf. State Legislators, Fort Bend County Fair Assn. (life). Baptist. Clubs: Sweetwater Country (Sugar Land, Tex.); Fort Bend 100. Lodge: Rotary. Avocations: hunting; skiing; golf. Office: US Ho of Reps 341 Cannon House Office Bldg Washington DC 20515-4322*

DELBANCO, NICHOLAS FRANKLIN, English educator, writer; b. London, Aug. 27, 1942; came to U.S., 1948; s. Kurt and Barbara Gabriele Delbanco; m. Ela Greenhouse, Oct. 12, 1970; children: Francesca Barbara, Andrea Katherine. AB, Harvard U., 1963; MA, Columbia U., 1966. Mem. faculty Bennington (Vt.) Coll., 1966-85; prof. English Williams Coll., Williamstown, Mass., 1983, Skidmore Coll., Saratoga Springs, N.Y., 1984; Robert Frost Collegiate prof. English U. Mich., Ann Arbor, 1985—; dir. MFA in writing program U. Mich., 1985-96; vis. prof. Iowa U. Writer's Workshop, Iowa City, 1980; vis. adj. prof. Columbia U., N.Y.C., 1981, 96-98; founding dir. Bennington Writing Workshops, 1978-85; chair fiction panel Nat. Book Awards, N.Y.C., 1997; vis. fellow Woodrow Wilson Nat. Found., Princeton, N.J., 1981—. Author: Group Portrait: Conrad, Crane, Ford, James & Wells, 1983, The Writer's Trade, 1990, Running in Place: Scenes from the South of France, 1991, In the Name of Mercy, 1995, Old Scores, 1997, others; editor: Stillness and Shadows, 1985, Speaking of Writing, 1990, Bernard Malamud on Life and Art, 1996, others. Mem. nat. adv. bd. Share Our Strength, Writers Harvest, Washington, 1994—; hon. co-chair Mintekko, Bennington, 1996; mem. Arts Am., USIA, Washington, 1992; mem. governing bd. Mich. Journalism Fellows Program, 1990—. Fellow Nat. Endowment for Arts, 1973, 82, J.S. Guggenheim Meml. Found., 1980. Fellow Internat. Am. Studies and Lang. Faculty Salzburg; mem. Authors Guild, Authors League, PEN, Century Assn., Signet Soc., Phi Beta Kappa. Home: 428 Concord St Ann Arbor MI 48104 Office: U Mich Hopwood Rm Angell Hall Ann Arbor MI 48109

DELBANCO, THOMAS LEWIS, medical educator, researcher; b. London, Dec. 7, 1939; came to U.S., 1948; s. Kurt and Barbara Gabriele (Bernstein) D.; m. Jill Martin Behrens, Dec. 13, 1964; children: Steven, Suzanne, Jennifer. BA, Harvard U., 1961; MD, Columbia U., 1965. Diplomate Am. Bd. Internal Medicine. Intern in medicine Bellevue Hosp., N.Y.C., 1965-66, resident, 1967-68; resident Presbyn. Hosp., N.Y.C., 1966-67; chief resident Harlem Hosp. Ctr., N.Y.C., 1968-69; prof. medicine Harvard Med. Sch., Boston, 1971—; mem. staff, dir. div. gen. medicine and primary care Beth Israel Hosp., Boston, 1971—; dir. Picker/Commonwealth Program Patient-Centered Care, 1987—; chmn. Picker Inst., 1994—; mem. coun. APHA, 1983-85; mem. program com. Inst. Medicine, NAS, 1991—. Editor: 4 books; contbr. numerous articles to profl. jours. Vice chmn. United Way Mass. Bay, Boston, 1987-91; co-dir. Learning Through Drama Program, Lexington, Mass., 1982-90; bd. dirs. Health Commons Inst., 1994—. Maj. U.S. Army, 1969-71. Robert Wood Johnson Health Policy fellow Inst. Medicine, 1977-78. Fellow ACP; mem. Am. Fedn. Clin. Rsch., Soc. Gen. Internal Medicine (pres. 1986-87, councillor), Nat. Pub. Health and Hosps. Inst. (bd. dris.), Inst. of Medicine (program com), Nat. Acad. Scis. Jewish. Avocation: violin. Office: Beth Israel Deaconess Med Ctr 330 Brookline Ave Boston MA 02215-5400*

DELBOURGO, JOËLLE LILY, publishing executive; b. Alexandria, Egypt, Sept. 10, 1953; came to U.S., 1960; d. Edward Daniel and J. Andrée (Domergue) D.; m. Lewis Foster Patton, May 16, 1976 (div. May 1996); children: Caroline Emily, Andrew David. Student, Vassar Coll., 1970-72; BA, Williams Coll., 1974; MA, Columbia U., 1975. Editorial asst. Bantam Books, N.Y.C., 1975-76, asst. editor, 1976-78, assoc. editor, 1978-80; sr. editor Ballantine Del Rey Fawcett Ivy Books div. Random House Inc., N.Y.C., 1980-81, exec. editor, 1981-83, editor-in-chief, 1983-86, v.p., editor-in-chief trade books, 1986-89, editor-in-chief hard cover books and trade paperback, 1990-95; v.p., editl. dir. HarperCollins, N.Y.C., 1996, sr. v.p., assoc. publ., editor-in-chief, 1997—. Columbia faculty fellowship, 1974-75. Mem. Phi Beta Kappa. Office: HarperCollins Div of Random House Inc 10 E 53rd St Fl Cellar1 New York NY 10022-5299

DEL CAMPO, C. ALICIA, theater scholar; b. Aug. 14, 1956. MA in Anthropology, U. Chile, Santiago, 1984; MA in Spanish Lit., U. Minn.,

1987; PhD in Spanish, U. Calif., Irvine, 1998. Tchg. assoc. U. Calif., Irvine, 1993-97; lectr. Calif. State U., Long Beach, 1997—; conf. coor. Nat. Women's Studies Assn., 1988; cons. Inst. on Las Mujeres, U. Minn., 1989. E-mail: cdelcamp@csulb.edu. Home: 13625 Almond St Tustin CA 92782

DEL CAMPO, MARTIN BERNARDELLI, architect; b. Guadalajara, Mexico, Nov. 27, 1922; came to U.S., 1949; s. Salvador and Margarita (Bernardelli) Del C.; BA, Colegio Frances Morelos, Mexico City, 1941; Archtl. degree Escuela Nacional de Arquitectura, Mexico City, 1948; m. Laura Zaikowska, May 25, 1945; children: Felicia (dec.), Margarita, Mario. Ptnr., Del Campo & Fruiht, architects, Santa Rosa, Cal., 1955-56, Del Campo & Clark, San Francisco, 1957-63; mgr. Hotel Victoria, Oaxaca, Mexico, 1964-67; pres. Gulli-Del Campo, architects, San Francisco, 1968-70; ptnr. Del Campo Assocs., San Francisco, 1977-81. Lectr. archtl. design Coll. Environmental Design, U. Calif., Berkeley, 1973-74. Mem. AIA. Archtl. works include: Calif. Med. Facility South, Vacaville, Phillip Burton Fed. Bldg. remodeling, San Francisco, Hall of Justice, San Francisco, San Francisco Airport Internat. Terminal, Mex. Heritage Gardens, San Jose, Four Seasons Tower, San Francisco. Address: Del Campo & Maru Architects Inc 45 Lansing St San Francisco CA 94105-2611

DEL CAMPO, ROBERT A., federal judge, lawyer; b. 1937. BA, L.A. State Coll., 1960; JD, Southwestern U., L.A., 1970. Bar: Calif. 1970. Dep. dist. atty., 1970-72; pvt. practice, Arroyo Grande, Calif., 1972—; part-time magistrate judge for ctrl. Calif., U.S. Magistrate Ct., A, 1987—. With USMC, 1960-64. Office: 415 El Camino Real Arroyo Grande CA 93420-2647

DEL CHIARO, MARIO ALDO, art historian, archeologist, etruscologist, educator; b. San Francisco, Apr. 22, 1925; s. Casimiro and Elisa (Bianchi) A.; m. Christina Falkman, Sept. 13, 1958; children: Kari Louise, Marco Claudio, Paola Christina. A.B., U. Calif.-Berkeley, 1950, M.A., 1951, Ph.D., 1956. Teaching asst. art history U. Calif. at Berkeley, 1950-51, 55, Univ. fellow in art, 1951-52; John Wesley Britton traveling fellow in classics, 1952-53; Met. Mus. Art fellow N.Y.C., 1953-54, grantee Am. Numismatic Soc. Seminar, 1954; faculty U. Calif., Santa Barbara, 1956—, prof. art history, 1966-94, prof. emeritus, 1994; chmn. dept. U. Calif.-Santa Barbara, 1969-72; Mem. archeol. staff for excavations in Turkey, Yugoslavia, Egypt, Sicily and Italy; dir. U. Calif.-Santa Barbara archeol. expdns. to, Tuscany, Italy. Author: The Genucilia Group: A Class of Etruscan Red-Figured Plates, 1957, Etruscan Red-Figured Vase-Painting at Caere, 1974, The Etruscan Funnel Group: A Tarquinian Red-Figured Fabric, 1974; exhbn. catalogues Greek Art in Private Collections of Southern California, 1963, Etruscan Art from West Coast Collections, 1967, Roman Art in West Collections, 1973, Etruscan Ghiaccio Forte, 1976, Re-exhumed Etruscan Bronzes, 1981; Classical Art, Sculpture in the Santa Barbara Mus. Art, 1984; editor: Corinthiaca, Studies in Honor of Darrell A. Amyx, 1986; contbr. book revs. and articles to profl. jours. Decorated cavaliere ufficiale Order of Merit (Italy), 1992; recipient Internat. award in archaeology Tutto Maremma, Italy, 1990; Am. Philos. Soc. grantee, 1957, 75, NEH grantee, 1977; Prix de Rome fellow Am. Acad. in Rome, 1958-60; Sr. Faculty fellow Humanities Inst. U. Calif. at Berkeley, 1967-68. Mem. Archeol. Inst. Am., Explorers Club, Istituto Studi Etruschi ed Italici, Florence, Deutsches Archäologisches Inst., Istituto Archeologico Rome, European Acad. Scis. and Art, Salzburg, Phi Beta Kappa. Home: Hope Ranch 1376 Estrella Dr Santa Barbara CA 93110-2418

DEL COLLE, PAUL LAWRENCE, communications administrator, educator; b. Lynn, Mass., Dec. 16, 1950; s. Alfiero Luigi and Doris Claire (Rich) D.; m. Ellen Mary Ambrose, May 26, 1979. BA, Holy Cross Coll., 1972; MS, Boston U., 1975; PhD, NYU, 1990. News dir. Sta. WGNG, Providence, 1972-73; writer, assoc. prodr. Boston U. Prodns., 1974-76; instr. comms. Iona Coll., New Rochelle, N.Y., 1976-80; asst. prof. comms. William Paterson Coll., Wayne, N.J., 1980-83, Marist Coll., Poughkeepsie, N.Y., 1983-90; pres., owner D.C. Media Cons., 1981-93; asst. prof. comms. Coll. of Mt. St. Vincent, Riverdale, N.Y., 1991-95; journalism lectr. NYU, 1995; sr. media analyst Forbes for Pres., Inc., 1995-96; media analyst John McLaughlin and Assocs., 1996-97; pres. sec. Yonkers (N.Y.) Pub. Schs., 1997-98; comm. project mgr. Integrated Supply Chain, IBM, 1998—; judge news/documentary divsn. Emmy awards NATAS, 1988—; cons. in field. Writer TV show The Pennant Chase, 1988; writer, announcer (radio spots) Thanks to You, 1986, (video news releases) Positalker/Grand Union, 1982; writer (book review) Review of Broadcasting: An Introduction, 1981, Review of Writing News for Broadcast, 1981, (mag. article) Bicentennial Burger Boutique, 1975; contbg. book reviewer Bookscapes, 1994-96. Cons. United Way of Dutchess County, Poughkeepsie, 1984-92; vol. Mental Health Assn., 1983-97, Am. Heart Assn., Poughkeepsie, 1989—, Am. Diabetes Assn., 1998—. Recipient Scholarship Internat. Radio/TV Found., 1988, 90, 94, Grad. Assistantship Boston U., 1973-74; named Outstanding Young Men in Am., 1981; tchg. fellow Poynter Inst. for Media Studies, St. Petersburg, Fla., 1993. Roman Catholic. Avocations: gardening, baseball memorabilia. Home: 20 Copley Ct Briarcliff Manor NY 10510-1463

DEL COLLIANO, GERARD ANTHONY, publisher; b. Hoboken, NJ, July 20, 1946; s. Gerard Victor and Adele (Visconti) Del Colliano; m. Judy Gallagher, Mar. 28, 1970 (div. June 1978); 1 child, Gerard R.; m. Laura Loro, Feb. 14, 1983; 1 child, Daria Rose; m. Cheryl Baker, Sept. 12, 1998. BS in Communications, Temple U., 1968. Announcer Sta. WDVR, Phila., 1965-66; announcer, personality Sta. WFIL-TV, AM/FM, Phila., 1966-68; personality Sta. WIBG Radio, Phila., 1968-69, program dir., 1972-74; announcer Sta. WIP Radio, Phila., 1969-71; program dir. Sta. WIFI Radio, Phila., 1971-72; publisher Inside Radio Inc., Cherry Hill, N.J., 1974—. Democrat. Roman Catholic. Avocations: Dale Carnegie instr. Office: Inside Radio Inc 1930 Marlton Pike E Ste S93 Cherry Hill NJ 08003-4210

DEL COLLO, MARY ANNE DEMETRIS, school administrator; b. Norristown, Pa., May 10, 1949; d. John and Julia (Chale) Demetris; m. William Paul Del Collo, July 1, 1973; children: Margaux, Julia, Nicole. BS, West Chester State U., 1971; MEd, Rosemont Coll. Tech., 1995, Widener U., 1997. Cert. elem. tchr. and sch. adminstr., Pa. Tchr. Phoenixville (Pa.) Area Sch. Dist., 1971-97, adminstr., 1997-98; adminstr. Methacton Sch. Dist., Norristown, Pa., 1998—. Mem. AAUW, Pa. Assn. Elem. and Secondary Sch. Prins., Hellenic Univ. Club, Nat. Middle Sch. Assn., vice pres., Chi Gamma Chapt., 1998—, Kappa Delta Pi. Avocations: technology, walking, reading, antiquing, traveling. Office: Methacton Sch Dist Eagleville Rd Norristown PA 19403

DEL CONDE, TERESA, museum director, art historian, researcher; b. Mexico City, Mexico, Jan. 12, 1939; m. Corona Uhink, Dec. 16, 1961 (dec.); children: Carmen, Tessa, Guillermo, Laura. Student, U. Nacional Autonoma de Mex., 1958-62, 70-77, PhD in Philosophy, 1984; attended, Universita degli Studi, Rome, 1962-64, Warburg Inst., 1982. Dir. Artes Plasticas INBA, Mexico City, 1982-87; dir. Mus. Modern Art, Mexico City, 1990—. Author: Francisco Toledo, 1980, Las Ideas Estéticas de Freud, 1987, Jose Clemente Orozco, 1981, Frida Khalo, la pintora y el Mito, 1992, Historia mínima del Arte Mexicano en el Siglo XX, 1994, Reedición del libro Las Ideas Estéticas de Freud, 1994, Agregar estos ultimos dos libros, Tres generaciones: Rodolfo Morales, Francisco Toledo y Julio Galan, 1997, Tres maestros: Reflexiones: Francis Bacon, Robert Motherwell y Rufino Tamayo, 1997; contbr. essays, art criticisms jours., mags., profl. books. Recipient John Simmon Guggenheim Meml. Found. award, 1982; Ital. Govt. scholar, 1962. Avocations: music, cinema writing, fiction, producing TV programs. Office: Museo de Arte Moderno, Paseo Reforma & Gandhi, Mexico City 11560, Mexico

DEL DUCA, BETTY SPAHR, association executive; b. Warren, Ohio, Nov. 12, 1930; d. Sullivan and Elizabeth (St. Clair) Spahr; children: Gretchen, Carolyn. BS, Case Western Res. U., 1952, MS, 1954, PhD, 1957, MBA, 1973. Sr. rsch. scientist Nat. Aeronautics & Space Adminstrn., Clevel., 1956-71; mgr. internat. ops., mgr. spl. projects The Standard Oil Co., Clevel., 1973-86; v.p. strategic planning Ameritrust Corp., Clevel., 1987-92; dir. fin. & adminstrn. AAUW, Washington, 1993-98; CEO Technol. Exec. Inst., 1998—; pres. AcromaTech Group, Inc., 1999—; dir. supply emergency team Internat. Energy Agy., Paris, 1984-86; chair fed. women's program Fed. Exec. Bd., Cleve., 1969-71. trustee Case Western Res. U., Cleve., 1988-92, chair ann. fund, 1989-93; pres. bd. dirs. Cuyahoga City Hosp. Found., Cleve., 1983-85. Grantee USPHS, 1952-56. Mem. AAUW, Am. Soc. Assn. Execs. Office: Tech Exec Inst 1700 N Moore St Ste 1650 Arlington VA 22209

DEL DUCA, RITA, educator; b. N.Y.C., Apr. 1, 1933; d. Joseph and Ermelinda (Buonaguro) Ferraro; m. Joseph Anthony Del Duca, Oct. 29, 1955; children: Lynn, Susan, Paul, Andrea. BA, CUNY, 1955. Elem. tchr. Yonkers (N.Y.) Pub. Schs., 1955-57; tchr. kindergarten Sacred Heart Sch., Yonkers, 1962-64; tchr. piano, Scarsdale, N.Y., 1973-79; asst. office mgr. Foot Clinic, Hartsdale, N.Y., 1977-85; tchr. ESL, Linguarama Exec. Sch., White Plains, N.Y., 1985-89; ESL tutor, Scarsdale, 1989—. Dist. leader Greenburgh (N.Y.) Rep. Com., 1991-92. Mem. ASCAP. Avocations: oil painting, piano teaching, tennis, theatre arts. Home and Office: 6 Paradise Dr Scarsdale NY 10583-1522

DELEHANT, RAYMOND LEONARD, botanist, educator; b. New Haven, June 30, 1937; s. John Patrick and Dorothy Barbara (Luft) D. BS, So. Conn. State U., 1959, MS, 1964; postgrad., U. Colo., 1965, U. Calif., Berkeley, 1966, U. Vt., 1967. Permanent cert. tchr., Conn. Instr. botany So. Conn. State U., New Haven, part-time 1964-71; sci. tchr. jr. high sch. Bd. Edn., North Haven, Conn., 1959-95, emeritus, 1995—; cons. textbook program Rand McNally Co., 1974; sci. fameworks curriculum com. Conn. State Dept. Edn., 1995—; fellow Conn. Acad. Math., Sci. and Tech., 1996; project com. cons. Conn. Acad. Math., Sci. and Tech., Conn. Sci. Assessment Project. Camp dir. nature section Boy Scouts Am., summers 1953, 57, 64, merit badge counselor Quinnipiac Council New Haven, 1964-70; asst. ranger West Rock Nature Ctr., New Haven, 1956, 58; rep. Citizens Pk. Council, New Haven, 1974-75; chmn. bd. trustees Park Oaks Sr. Commr. Assn., New Haven, 1964—. NSF fellow 1966, 67; recipient Eagle Scout award Boy Scouts Am. 1955. Mem. Nat. Sci. Tchrs. Assn. (mem. program com. 1999 convention), Conn. Sci. Tchrs. Assn. (life, pres., 1979-83, 95—, chmn. handbook com., John Prymack award 1975, spl. recognition 1990), Conn. Sci. Suprs. Assn., Sequassen Alumni Assn. (sec. 1970-72), Ecol. Soc. Am., Park Oaks Sr. Commr. Assn. (chmn. bd. trustees, treas.), Conn. Acad. Math. Sci. and Tech. (mem. pres.'s coun. 1995—). Roman Catholic. Avocations: photography, hiking, camping, wood carving, home repairs. Home: 122 Dorrance St Hamden CT 06518-3342

DELEÖN, JOHN JOSEPH, city agency executive; b. San Antonio, May 6, 1944; s. Charles and Mary R. (Gonzales) DeL.; m. Irene Guerrero, June 16, 1995; 1 child: André; stepchildren, Andrea Parks, Roland Herrera, David and Francesca Herrera (twins). BSPA, Century U., 1991. Staff cons. to sec. U.S. Dept. HUD, Washington; acting dir. EEO Def. Mapping Agy.; advisor to sec. U.S. Treasury; dir. manpower Cabinet Com. on Opportunities for Spanish-Speaking People; recruiter, intern U.S. Dept. Labor; officer deLeön Enterprises, Inc., San Antonio, 1981-85; pvt. practive mgmt./polit. cons. San Antonio, 1981-86; accts. exec. S.W. Bell, San Antonio, 1986-87; sr. compliance officer U.S. Dept. Labor, Albuquerque, 1987-91; asst. dist. dir. U.S. Dept. Labor, Houston, 1991-98; dir. minority women bus. enterprise City of Houston, 1998—; bd. dirs. SER Corp., Houston. Co-author: Handbook for Dept. of the Treasury Program for Spanish-Speaking People, 1973. Bd. dirs. Tejano Democrats, Harris County, Tex., 1997—. With U.S. Army, 1964-67, Vietnam. Recipient Spl. award Nat. Ednl. Svc. Bd., 1980, Appreciation award Nat. Image Inc., 1981, Pub. Svc. award Houston Exec. Bd., 1993, 95, Hammer award V.P. Al Gore, 1996, Achievement award U.S. Dept. of Labor 1994. Mem. Nat. Assn. Hispanic Fed. Execs., Inc., Houston Hispanic C. of C. Roman Catholic. Avocations: travel, cycling, photography, walking. Home: 1022 E T C Jester Blvd Houston TX 77008-6358

DE LEON, JOHN LOUIS, public defender; b. North Miami, Fla., Feb. 14, 1962; s. Leon Juan and Lydia (Diaz Cruz) de L. AB cum laude, U. Miami, 1983; JD, Georgetown U., 1986; M in Internat. Affairs, Columbia U., 1992. Bar: Fla. 1987, U.S. Supreme Ct. 1993. V.p. Bristol Investment Group, Coral Gables, Fla., 1982-85; jud. intern to Judge Francis Bason Fed. Bankruptcy Ct., Washington, 1986; asst. pub. defender Office Pub. Defender for 11th Jud. Cir., Miami, 1987—; law clk. Geiger, Riggs & Freud, P.A., Miami, Fla., 1986-87; mem. bd. arbitrators Nat. Assn. Security Dealers, N.Y.C., 1989; press officer, intern. Delegation of the Commn. of the European Communities, UN, N.Y.C., 1990; mem. steering com. Georgetown Criminal Justice Clinic, Georgetown U. Law Ctr. Bd. dirs. Citykids, Inc., Miami, 1986; mem. adv. bd. Douglas MacArthur Sr. H.S., Miami; mem. audience devel. commn. Mus. Contemporary Arts, North Miami, Fla.; bd. dirs. Urban Environment League, Miami. Mem. ABA, Cuban Am. Bar Assn., Nat. Assn. Criminal Def. Lawyers, Am. Civil Liberties Union, Fla. Assn. Pub. Defenders, ACLU (bd. mem. Dade County chpt., pres.), Amnesty Internat., Golden Key, Phi Delta Phi, Phi Kappa Phi, Pi Sigma Alpha. Roman Catholic. Avocations: reading, politics, arts. Home: 1805 Ixora Rd Miami FL 33181-2309 Office: Pub Defender Svc 1320 NW 14th St Miami FL 33125-1609

DE LEON, LIDIA MARIA, magazine editor; b. Havana, Cuba, Sept. 10, 1957; d. Leon J. and Lydia (Diaz Cruz) de L. B.A. in Communications cum laude, U. Miami, Coral Gables, Fla., 1979. Staff writer Miami Herald, Fla., 1978-79; editorial asst. Halsey Pub. Co., Miami, 1980-81, assoc. editor, 1981, editor, 1981—, editor Delta Sky mag., 1983-95. Mem. Am. Soc. Mag. Editors, Am. Assn. Travel Editors, Golden Key, Sigma Delta Chi. Democrat. Roman Catholic. Avocation: tennis.

DE LEON, RUDY, government official. BA in History, Loyola U., L.A., 1974; grad. exec. program, Harvard U., 1984; grad. seminar XXI program in fgn. politics, MIT, 1987. Legis. asst. U.S. Senate, Washington, 1975-77; legis. asst. U.S. Ho. of Reps., Washington, 1977-80, legis. asst., adminstrv. asst., 1980-85, profl. staff mem., Com. on Armed Svcs., 1985-89, staff dir., Com. on Armed Svcs., 1989-93; spl. asst. to sec. and dep. sec. of def. Dept. Def., Washington, 1993-94; under sec. of Air Force Dept. of Air Force, Washington, 1994-97; under sec. def. & readiness Dept. of Air Force, 1997—. Decorated D.S.M. Office: Dept of Defense Personnel & Readiness 4000 Defense Pentagon Washington DC 20301-4000

DE LEON, SYLVIA A., lawyer; b. Corpus Christi, Tex., Mar. 2, 1950. BA, Briarcliff Coll., 1972; JD, U. Tex., 1976. Bar: Tex. 1976, D.C. 1977. Ptnr. Akin, Gump, Strauss, Hauer & Feld LLP, Washington; adj. prof. law Georgetown U. law ctr., 1988-90; bd. dirs. Amtrak, Nat. Railroad Passenger Corp., 1994-98, chair corp. strategy com. Bd. dirs. U. Tex. Law Assn., 1985-89, 92—, U. Tex. Devel. Bd., 1996—; coord. issues transp. cluster group Clinton-Gore Presdl. Transition Team, 1992; commr. Nat. Commn. Ensure Strong Competitive Airline Industry, 1993. Mem. Bar Assn. D.C., State Bar Tex. (chmn. fed. law and regulations com. 1984-87). Office: Akin Gump Strauss Hauer & Feld Ste 400 1333 New Hampshire Ave NW Washington DC 20036-1564

DE LEONARDIS, NICHOLAS JOHN, bank executive, financial lecturer, educator; b. Chgo., Nov. 13, 1929; s. John and Marie (Janik) De L.; m. Mary Ellen Kloss, Aug. 17, 1957; children: Deborah Marie, Valerie Ann, Nicolette Mary, Regina Ellen, John Paul. BS, De Paul U., 1951, MA, 1968. Salesman Asher J. Goldfine & Co., Chgo., 1953-55. Mem. trust dept. staff First Nat. Bank Chgo., 1955-63, with mcpl. sales dept., 1963-65, v.p. money mkt. ctr., 1965-80, v.p., chmn. money mgmt. com., 1980-85; sr. v.p., treas. La Salle Nat. Bank, subs. Algemene Bank Nederland, N.V., 1985-90; sr. v.p., chmn. asset and liability com. La Salle Nat. Corp.; exec. in residence dept. fin. De Paul U., Chgo., 1990—, lectr., 1968-78, dir. DePaul-People's Republic China Project, 1990-95; lectr. MBA program De Paul, Hong Kong, 1997—; guest lectr. bankers' seminars, Poland, 1992—; grad. sch. banking U. Wis., Madison, 1980-87; mem. Dixon Assn. for Retarded Citizens, 1984, Gov.'s task force on Future of Mental Health in Ill., 1986-87; cons Polish Bankers, Warsaw, 1997; mem. com. specialist assignment and evaluation Chgo. Stock Exchange, 1993—; commn. review the state's mental health code, 1988; mem. adv. com. devel. disabilities Ill. Dept. Mental Health and Devel. Disabilities, 1993—. Contbr. articles to profl. publs. Trustee, past chmn. Found. Hearing and Speech Rehab., Chgo., 1968-92; pres. Dixon (Ill.) Assn. Retarded Citizens, 1984—. Mem. Union League Chgo., Heidelberg Club Internat., Delta Mu Delta, Beta Gamma Sigma. Office: De Paul U Dept Fin 1 E Jackson Blvd Ste 6126 Chicago IL 60604-2287

DELEVORYAS, THEODORE, botanist, educator; b. Chicopee Falls, Mass., July 22, 1929; s. Basil John and Sophie John (Dulchinos) D.; m. Nancy Lou Foster, June 23, 1956 (div. 1978); children: Matthew Torrey, Christopher Theodore; m. Cecilia Ann Dean, Aug. 14, 1981. BS, U. Mass., 1950; MS, U. Ill., 1951, PhD, 1954; MA (hon.), Yale U., 1968. Asst. prof. botany Mich. State U., East Lansing, 1955-56; instr. botany Yale U., New Haven, 1956-58, asst. prof., 1958-60, assoc. prof. biology, 1962-68, prof. biology, 1968-72; assoc. prof. botany U. Ill., Urbana, 1960-62; prof. botany U. Tex., Austin, 1972-94; prof. emeritus, 1995—; chmn. dept. botany, U. Tex., Austin, 1974-80, div. biol. scis., 1982-89. Author: Morphology and Evolution of Fossil Plants, 1962, Plant Diversification, 1966, rev. edit., 1977; co-author: Morphology of Plants and Fungi, 5th rev. edit., 1987; editor in chief Am. Jour. Botany, 1985-89. Fellow NRC, 1954-55, Guggenheim Found., 1964-65. Mem. Bot. Soc. Am. (treas. 1968-72, v.p. 1973, pres. 1974), Internat. Orgn. Palaeobotany (pres. 1978-81). Office: U Tex Dept Botany Austin TX 78713-7640*

DELFINO, JOSEPH JOHN, environmental engineering sciences educator; b. Port Chester, N.Y., Oct. 6, 1941; s. John J. and Frances C. (Santoro) D.; m. Dorothy Delfino; children: Janelle, Justin. BS in Chemistry, Holy Cross Coll., 1963; MS in Chemistry, U. Idaho, 1965; PhD in Civil and Environ. Engring. & Water Chemistry, U. Wis., 1968. From instr. to assoc. prof. chemistry USAF Acad., Colorado Springs, Colo., 1968-72; sect. head, tech. mgr. IBT & Nalco Environ. Sci., Northbrook, Ill., 1972-74; sect. head environ. scis. Wis. State Lab. Hygiene, Madison, 1974-82; from asst. prof. to assoc. prof. U. Wis., Madison, 1974-80; assoc. dir. water resources ctr. U. Wis., 1977-78, prof. civil and environ. engring., 1980-82; prof. environ. engring. sci. U. Fla., Gainesville, 1982—, affiliate prof. chemistry, 1990—, chmn. dept. environ. engring. sci., 1990-99; affiliate prof. natural resources and environment U. Fla., 1994—; interim dir. Ctr. for Wetlands and Water Resources U. Fla., Gainesville, 1995; mem. adv. bds. Fla. State U. Sys. Ctr. for Solid and Hazardous Waste Mgmt., 1996-99, Ctr. Environ. Studies, 1996-99; mem. adj. faculty U. Colo., Colorado Springs, 1969-71, Ill. Inst. Tech., Chgo., 1973. Writer, co-originator, chief tech. advisor documentary Fla. Water Story, Sta. WEDU-TV, Tampa, Fla.; contbr. articles on water chemistry and environ. scis. to profl. publs. Mem. Citizens Environ. Quality Coun., Northbrook, 1972-74; mem. Mercury Tech. Adv. Com., State of Fla., 1991-93. Capt. USAF, 1968-72; mem. Alachua County Air Quality Commn., Fla., 1999. Recipient Pub. Svc. award Univs. Coun. on Water Resources, 1990. Fellow AAAS; mem. Am. Chem. Soc. (mem. exec. com. environ. chem. divsn. 1973-76, editor Envirofacs environ. chem. divsn. 1973-76, student awards com. environ. chem. divsn. 1995-97, com. on environ. improvement 1998—, Cert. of Merit environ. chem. divsn. 1991), Assn. Environ. Engring. and Sci. Profs., Am. Soc. Engring. Edn. (mem. awards policy com. 1997—). Office: U Fla Dept Environ Engring and Scis PO Box 116450 310 Black Hall Gainesville FL 32611-6450

DEL FOSSE, CLAUDE MARIE, aerospace software executive; b. Paris, June 27, 1940; came to the U.S., 1963; s. Guy and Gabrielle (Bouyges) D.F.; m. Genevieve Juliette Des Devises, Dec. 23, 1971; children: Laurent Fabrice, Olivier Andre, Oriane Gabrielle. Diploma in Engring. Ecole Nat. Supérieure, d'Arts et Métiers, Paris, 1963; MS, Calif. Inst. Tech., 1964; MBA, U. Paris, 1966. Software engr. Soc. d'Info. Appliquée, Paris, 1964-67, Control Data Corp., L.A., 1968-69; sr. tech. staff CACI, Inc., L.A., Washington, 1969-78; v.p., div. mgr. CACI, Inc., Washington, 1979-84; cons., chief scientist Bite, Inc., Washington, 1984-86; mgr. program devel. Software Productivity Consortium, Reston, Va., 1986-89; v.p. tech. transfer Software Productivity Consortium, Herndon, Va., 1989—; bd. dirs. Winter Simulation Conf., 1979-82, gen. chmn., 1981. Bd. dirs. Lincolnia Park Recreational Club, Alexandria, Va., 1981, 82, 88. NATO fellow, 1964, Fulbright fellow, 1964. Mem. AFCEA, AIAA, Tech. Transfer Soc. Avocations: tennis, skiing. Home: 5229 Chippewa Pl Alexandria VA 22312-2023

DELFS, ANDREAS, performing company executive; b. Flensburg, Germany. Grad., Hamburg Conservatory, 1981; MA, Juilliard Sch., 1984. Staff conductor Lüneburg Stadttheater; music dir. Hamburg U. Orch.; musical asst. Hamburg State Opera; guest conductor Bremen State Theater, 1981; dir. Pitts. Youth Symphony; resident conductor Pitts. Symphony, 1986-90; music dir. Orch. Suisse Jeunes, 1984-95, Bern Opera, 1991-94; conductor N.Y. City Opera, 1995-96; music dir. Milw. Symphony Orch., 1997—; gen. music dir. Hannover State Opera and Orch.; guest conductor Phila. Orchestra at Carnegie Hall, 1998, London Philharmonic, 1997, Dallas Symphony Orch., 1997, Houston Symphony, 1996-98, Junge Deutsche Philharmoni, Germany, 1995-98, others; guest conductor Bern Symphony Orch., Minn. Orch., Detroit Symphony, Rochester Philharmonic, others. Bruno Walter scholar Juilliard Sch.; Steinburg fellow Pitts. Symphony. Office: Milw Symph Orch 330 E Kilbourn Ave Ste 900 Milwaukee WI 53202-3141

DELGADO, GEORGE ERNEST, financial consultant; b. Paterson, N.J., Apr. 27, 1948; s. Manuel and Mary Alice (O'Brien) D.; m. Elaine Marie Egan, Oct. 13, 1990; children: Lisa, Michael. CBI. Flight instr. Gen. Aviation, Teterboro, N.J., 1969-70; acct. exec. R.J. Berlow & Co., Teterboro, 1970-73; mgr. Aero Ins. Agy., Washington, 1973-77; asst. v.p. Alexander & Alexander, Phila., 1977-78; v.p. Frank B. Hall & Co., N.Y.C., 1978-91, Willis Corroon Aerospace, N.Y.C., 1991-96; pres. Castle Consultants, N.Y.C., 1995—. *Founder and President of Castle Consultants, and a renowned specialist in business sales, valuations, mergers, and aquisitions. Mr. Delgado earned the Certified Business Intermediary (CBI) designation in 1996. He is a member of the International Business Brokers Association Education Committee, Director of the New York Association of Business Brokers, a Senior Business Analyst with Business Evaluation Systems and affiliate of the Business Brokers Network. Before founding his own firm, Mr. Delgado was Vice President of Willis Corroon, an insurance firm headquarters in London, where he handled multi-million dollar transactions. He is a Marine Corp Vietnam Veteran.* Cpl. USMC, 1966-69, Vietnam. Mem. Americas Soc., Soc. CPCU, Internat. Bus. Brokers Assn. (cert. bus. intermediary; edn. com.), N.Y. Assn. Bus. Brokers (chair membership com.), Ctrl. Park Conservancy, Wildlife Conservation Soc. Roman Catholic. Avocations: tennis, skiing. Office: Castle Consultants 237 Park Ave Fl 21 New York NY 10017-3140

DELGADO, GLORIA ENEIDA, medical nurse; d. Francisca Benitez; children: Daniel, Othoniel. AAS in Nursing, Bronx Community Coll., 1977; BS in Behavioral Sci., Mercy Coll., 1983. Staff nurse Montifiori Hosp. Ctr., N.Y.C.; case mgr., health practitioner, RN Multi-Purpose Sr. Svcs. Program, L.A.; staff nurse U. Community Hosp., Tampa, Fla.; RN specialist State of Fla., Tampa.

DELGADO, JANE, health executive, writer; b. Havana, Cuba, June 17, 1953; d. Juan Lorenzo Delgado Borges and Lucila Aurora Navarro Delgado. BA, SUNY, New Paltz, 1973; MA, NYU, 1975; MS, W. Averell Harrimann Sch., 1981; PhD in Clin. Psychology, SUNY, Stony Brook, 1981. Children's talent coord. Children's TV Workshop, 1973-75; rsch. asst. SUNY, Stony Brook, 1975-79; social sci. analyst U.S. Dept. Health and Human Svcs., 1979-83, health policy advisor, 1983-85; pres., CEO COSSMHO, 1985—; pvt. practice in psychology, 1979—; bd. dirs. Nat. Health Coun., 1986—, Carter Ctr. Mental Health Taskforce, 1991—, Vestar, Inc., 1993-95; trustee The Kresge Found., Found. Child Devel., 1989—. Author: Salud! A Latina's Guide to Total Health: Body, Mind, and Spirit, 1997. W.K. Kellogg Found. Nat. fellow, 1988, NIMH fellow, 1975-79; recipient Surgeon Gen.'s award, 1992; recipient Health & Sci. Latina Excellence award, 1995; named SUNY Alumna of Yr., 1993. Mem. Hispanics in Philanthropy (bd. dirs. 1997—). Office: COSSMHO 1501 16th St NW Washington DC 20036-1499*

DELGADO, RAMON LOUIS, educator, author, director, playwright, lyricist; b. Tampa, Fla., Dec. 16, 1937; s. Eloy Vincent and Hildegard (Chapman) D. BA, Stetson U., 1959; MA, Baylor U., 1960; MFA, Yale U., 1967; PhD, So. Ill. U., 1976. Tchr., Lyman H.S., Longwood, Fla., 1960-62; mem. faculty Chipola Jr. Coll., Marianna, Fla., 1962-64, Ky. Wesleyan U., 1967-72, Hardin-Simmons U., 1972-74, So. Ill. U., 1974-76, St. Cloud (Minn.) State U., 1976-78; prof. speech and theatre Montclair State U., Upper Montclair, N.J., 1978—. Evaluator N.J. Teen Arts Festival, 1980, 81; judge Am. Theatre Assn. Coll. Theater Festival, 1980, 82, 83, 84, 85, N.J. Teen Galaxy Competition, 1984; sec. Forest St. Manor Condo Assn., 1997—.

Recipient Samuel French Play award, 1966; U. Mo. Play award, 1971, 75; playwriting awards Am. Coll. Theatre Festival, 1976, 77, 78; playwright-in-residence INTAR, 1980; Grand prize Music City Song Festival contest, 1988, 7 Hon. mentions, 1989; Midwest Profl. Playwrights fellow, 1978; Ford Found. grantee, 1961. Mem. Dramatists Guild, Assn. For Theatre in Higher Edn., Nashville Songwriters Assn. Internat., Nat. Theatre Conf., Theta Alpha Phi, Phi Kappa Phi. Democrat. Plays include: Waiting for the Bus, 1968, Once Below A Lighthouse, 1972, The Jerusalem Thorn, 1979; A Little Holy Water, 1983; Stones, 1983 The Flight of the Dodo, 1990, Remembering Booth, 1997; editor: The Best Short Plays, 1981-89; author: Acting with Both Sides of Your Brain, 1986; contbr. articles to profl. jours. Home: 16 Forest St Apt 107 Montclair NJ 07042-3519 Office: Montclair State U Dept Theatre and Dance Upper Montclair NJ 07043

DELGADO, ROGER R., surgeon, educator; b. El Paso, Jan. 11, 1946; s. Roger R. and Eva (West) D.; m. Linda Susan Ferguson, Dec. 27, 1968; children: Jessica Lorraine, Nathan Roger. BA, U. Tex. El Paso, 1966; MD, U. Tex. Galveston, 1970. Diplomate Am. Bd. Surgery. Intern R.E. Thomason Horst, El Paso, 1970-71; resident surgery Naval Regional Med. Ctr., Portsmouth, Va., 1971-75; staff surgeon Naval Regional Med. Ctr., Camp Pendleton, Calif., 1975-78; pvt. practice surgeon Sebastopol, Santa Rosa, Calif., 1978—; assoc. clin. prof. U. Cal. San Francisco, 1978—; chief staff Palm Dr. Hosp., Sebastopol, 1980-81, bd. trustees, 1980-83, 90-94, dir. surg. svcs., 1996—. Contbr. articles to profl. jours. Fellow ACS; mem. Soc. Clin. Vascular Surgery, Soc. Am. Gastrointestinal Endoscopic Surgeons, Beta Beta Beta. Roman Catholic. Avocations: skiing, biking. Office: Santa Rosa Sebastopol Hosp 6800 Palm Ave Ste C-1 Sebastopol CA 95472-4251

DELGADO-COLON, AIDA M., federal judge; b. 1955. BA, U. P.R., 1977; JD, Cath. U. P.R., 1980. Bar: P.R. 1980. Dir. investigations P.R. Gov.'s Adv. Bd. on Labor; 1st asst. fed. pub. defender; magistrate judge for P.R. U.S. Magistrate Ct., San Juan, 1994—; mem. Fed. Bar Exam. Com., 1986—; mem. local rules com. Fed. Dist. Ct., 1991—; chmn. interpreters and ct. reports com. U.S. Dist. Ct. for P.R., 1994—, mem. criminal justice act com., 1994—, EEO coord., 1995—. Mem. Fed. Magistrate Judges Assn., Women Judges Assn., P.R. Bar Assn., Cath. U. P.R. Law Sch. Alumni Assn. Office: Ruiz-Nazario Fed Bldg 150 Carlos Chardon Ave 181 San Juan PR 00918

DELGADO-RODRIGUEZ, MANUEL, secondary school educator; b. Caguas, P.R., Dec. 15, 1932; s. Manuel Delgado-Planas and Angelina Rodriguez-Andaluz. MA in Edn. and History, U. P.R., 1969. Tchr. English Juncos (P.R.) H.S., 1962; social studies/Spanish tchr. Ponce de Leon Jr. H.S., Humacao, P.R., 1962; tchr. history Univ. H.S., Rio Piedras, P.R., 1963-65, 67—; mem. curriculum com. Univ. H.S., Rio Piedras, coord. presdl. classroom for young Ams., 1970—, personnel com. Mem. ASCD, P.R. Assn. Historians, Nat. Coun. for Social Studies. Home: PO Box 461 Humacao PR 00792-0461

DEL GIUDICE, VINCENT ALBERT, reporter; b. Paterson, N.J., Feb. 13, 1958; s. Vincent J. and Alba B. (Strobino) Del G.; m. Pamela Porter, Dec. 29, 1985; children: Sam, Caroline. BA in Sociology, Wittenberg U., 1980; MA in Journalism, Ohio State U., 1981. Spl. writer Dayton (Ohio) Daily News, 1978-81; reporter, editor UPI, Washington, 1982-90; reporter Bloomberg News, Washington, 1990—. EMT Cherrydale Vol. Fire Dept., Arlington, Va., 1985-92. Recipient Life Saving award Am. Heart Assn., 1989, Vol. Svc. award Arlington County, 1989, Reporting award Am. Soc. Bus. Writers, 1996. Avocation: amateur radio operator. Office: Bloomberg News 228 National Press Bldg Washington DC 20045

DEL GUERCIO, LOUIS RICHARD MAURICE, surgeon, educator, company executive; b. N.Y.C., Jan. 15, 1929; s. Louis and Hortense (Ardengo) Del G.; m. Paula Marie Helene de Vautibault, May 18, 1957; children: Louis, Francsca, Paul, Catherine, Maria, Michelle, Christopher, Anthony. BS, Fordham U., 1949; MD, Yale U., 1953. Diplomate: Am. Bd. Surgery, Am. Bd. Thoracic Surgery. Intern Columbia-Presbyn. Med. Center, N.Y.C., 1953-54; resident St Vincent's Hosp., N.Y.C., 1954-58, Cleve. City Hosp., 1958-60; practice medicine specializing in thoracic surgery, 1960—; mem. faculty Albert Einstein Coll. Medicine, N.Y.C., 1960-71; assoc. prof. Albert Einstein Coll. Medicine, 1966-70, prof. surgery, 1970-71, dir. Clin. Research Center-Acute, 1967-71; dir., clin. prof. surgery N.J. Coll. Medicine, Newark, 1971-76; prof. surgery N.Y. Med. Coll., N.Y.C., 1976—; chmn. dept. N.Y. Med. Coll., 1976—; chief surgery Westchester County Med. Center, 1976—; cons. surgeon other hosps.; mem. surg. study sect. NIH, 1970-74; mem. com. on shock NRC-Nat. Acad. Scis., 1969-71; mem. merit rev. bd. VA, 1971-74; mem. health care tech. study sect. Dept. HHS, 1980-84; cons. Nat. Ctr. Health Services Research, 1980-84; chmn. bd. dirs. Daltex Med. Scis., Inc. Author: (with B.G. Clarke) Urology, 1956, The Multilingual Manual for Medical History Taking, 1972, (with S.G. Hershey, R. McConn) Septic Shock in Man, 1971; editor-in-chief Critical Care Monitor, 1980-85, Complications in Surgery, 1990—; contbr. articles to med. jours.; patentee in field. With Mcht. Marine, 1946-47; with AUS, 1949-51; col. med. dept. USAR, 1990—. Recipient award in medicine Fordham U. Alumni Assn., 1974, Gold award Am. Acad. Pediats., 1973, Humanitarian award Boys' Towns of Italy, 1994; Am. Thoracic Soc. fellow, 1959-60; grantee Health Rsch. Coun. N.Y., 1965-71, NIH, 1962-71. Fellow ACS, Coll. of Critical Care Medicine; mem. Am. Trauma Soc. (founding mem.), Soc. Critical Care Medicine (founding mem., pres. 1976), Am. Surg. Assn., Am. Physiol. Soc., Soc. Univ. Surgeons, Equestrian Order of HOly Sepulchre of Jerusalem. Home: 14 Pryor Ln Larchmont NY 10538-4021 Office: NY Med Coll Dept Surgery Valhalla NY 10595 *Adaptability and the determination of what is possible are the keys to personal success and contentment.*

DELI, ANNE TYNION, financial services executive; b. Milw., Apr. 18, 1956; m. Steven F. Deli. BA in History and French, Georgetown U., 1978. Acct. exec. Dancer Fitzgerald Sample, N.Y.C., 1978-80; acct. supr. Grey Advt., N.Y.C., 1980-82; v.p. Wells Rich Greene, N.Y.C., 1982-84; sr. v.p. Lawrence Charles Free, N.Y.C., 1984-86; prin. Anspach Grossman Portugal, N.Y.C., 1986-88; sr. v.p. Siegel & Gale, N.Y.C., 1988-93; v.p., global mktg. Harley-Davidson, Inc., Milw., 1993-95; pres., founder North River Strategies, Milw./Chgo., 1995-97; pres., CEO, co-founder Unicorn Fin. Svcs., Chgo., 1997—. Republican. Avocations: world travel, early 19th century furniture, tennis, golf. Office: Unicorn Fin Svcs Inc 150 S Wacker Dr Ste 2520 Chicago IL 60606-4202

DELI, STEVEN FRANK, financial services executive; married; 1 child. BA in Econs., Northwestern U., 1973; MBA, Harvard U., 1977. Staff mem. comml. and real estate banking dept. Continental Ill. Nat. Bank, Chgo., 1973-75; investment banker Warburg Paribas Becker Inc., Chgo., 1977-84; mng. dir., head corp. fin. Dean Witter Reynolds, Inc., Chgo., 1984-92; founder, chmn., CEO Eaglemark Fin. Svcs., Inc., 1992-99; founder, chmn. Unicorn Fin. Svcs., Inc., 1997—. Mem. fin. com. and gov. mem. Chgo. Symphony Orch.; mem. Chgo. Com. of the Chgo. Coun. on Fgn. Rels. and Mid-Am. Com.; past sr. warden, vestryman Christ Ch., Winnetka, Ill. Mem. Chgo. Club (past bd. dirs.), Econ. Club Chgo., Indian Hill Club, Commonwealth Club.

D'ELIA, CHRISTOPHER FRANCIS, marine biologist; b. Bridgeport, Conn., Aug. 7, 1946; s. Francis G. and Marian Frances (Wakeman) D'E.; m. Jennifer Anne Hunnicutt, June 10, 1973; 1 child, Tallmadge Wakeman. AB, Middlebury Coll., 1968; PhD, U. Ga., 1974. Postdoctoral scholar UCLA, 1974; vis. asst. prof. U. So. Calif., Los Angeles, 1975; Noyes postdoctoral fellow Woods Hole Oceanographic Inst., Mass., 1975-77; asst. prof. Chesapeake Biol. Lab., U. Md., Solomons, Md., 1977-83, assoc. prof., 1983-88, prof., 1988-99; biol. oceanography program dir. Nat. Sci. Found., Washington, 1987-89; dir. Md. Sea Grant Coll., 1989-98, v.p. rsch. U. Albany, SUNY, 1999—; mem. rsch. planning adv. group, rsch. priorities workgroup Chesapeake Bay Program, 1989-91, sci. and tech. adv. com., 1993-98; cons. govt. and industry, 1976—; regional rep. Coastal Resources Adv. Com. Md., 1982-83; mem. adv. panel ocean scis. div. NSF, Washington, 1982-84; mem. adv. com. Md. Sea Grant Program, 1980-86; chmn. Mid-Altantic Regional Marine Rsch. Bd., 1991-96; mem. science adv. bd. ecol. processes and effects com. marine monitoring com. U.S. EPA, 1991; mem. Leadership Md., 1997. Mem. editorial bd. Limnology and Oceanography, 1983-86; contbr. articles to profl. jours. Disting. Patrick scholar Acad. Nat. Scis., Phila., 1982-83; NSF grantee, 1978-81, 85-87, 89-98); grantee EPA, 1978-82, ERDA, 1976, Dept. Energy, 1979, NOAA, 1989-98. Fellow AAAS; mem. Am. Soc. Limnology and Oceanography, Ecol. Soc. Am. (chmn. pub. affairs com. 1989-91, vice chair 1991-92), Estuarine Rsch. Fedn. (v.p. 1989-91, pres. 1991-93, past pres. 1993-95), Internat. Soc. Reef Studies, Nat. Assn. Environ. Profs (bd. dirs. Md. 1985-86), Nat. Assn. State Univs. and Land Grant Colls. (bd. on oceans and atmosphere, exec. com., chair edn. com., chair spl. task force on reorganization, co-chair bd. 1994-95), Sea Grant Assn. (pres. 1991-92, 99, chair fed. rels. com. 1992-93), Coun. Sea Grant Dirs. (chair-elect, chair budget com. 1994), Coun. Sci. Soc. Pres. (sec. 1993-96, treas. 1997, chair-elect 1998, chair 1999), Sigma Xi, Cosmos Club. Avocations: sailing, skiing, private pilot. Office: U Albany Office VP for Rsch Adminstrn 227 1400 Washington Ave Albany NY 12222

DELIBERO, MARY SMELLIE, insurance company professional, pianist, soprano; b. Hartford, Conn., Nov. 6, 1950; d. Robert Henderson and Dorothy Lee (Jones) Smellie; m. Philip Lee DeLibero, Dec. 18, 1976 (div. 1987); children: Anthony Philip, Mark Edward. MusB, Queens Coll., Charlotte, N.C., 1972; MusM, Hartt Coll. of Mus., West Hartford, Conn., 1975; student, Inst. European Studies, Vienna, Austria, 1971. Instr. piano Westfield (Mass.) State Coll., 1974-83, Hartt Sch. of Mus., West Hartford, 1974-78; underwriter CIGNA Corp., Retirement and Investment Svcs., Hartford, Conn., 1984-88; trainer/tech. writer, 1988-91; strategic devel. specialist CIGNA Corp., Group Pension Div., Hartford, Conn., 1991, mgr. tax reporting and processing, 1992-96, transition mgr., 1996-99; mem. diversity coun. CIGNA, Hartford, Conn., 1995—, asst. dir., 1999—; solo and chamber recitalist, Conn., Mass., N.Y. 1974—. Events Coord. United Way (CIGNA Campaign), Hartford, 1986 (solicitor 1988), com. mem. CARE SHARE, Hartford, 1987; chair music com. First Ch. Christ Congl., W. Hartford, 1993-94, deacon, 1994-97; vol. Capitol Region Conf. Chs. Nursing Home Chaplaincy, 1997—. Presser Found Mus. scholar, Charlotte, N.C. 1970; recipient Charlotte Mus. Club Award, 1971, 76. Mem. Cert. Instr. Soc. for Profl. Adminstrs. and Record Keepers (Spark), Delta Omicron (pres. 1971-72). Congregational. Home: 14 Randal Ave West Hartford CT 06110-1743

DELIENNE, JACQUELYN E., e-commerce developer and publisher, management consultant, electronic comme; b. Little Rock, Ark., Aug. 3, 1947; d. John Henry and Blanche Evon (Green) E.; m. Dennery Delienne; 1 child, Christopher Malik. Student, Harvard U., 1964-66; BSBA, SUNY, Albany, 1980; postgrad., Golden Gate U. and Columbia Pacific U. CPA, Calif., S.C. Assoc. acct. Deloitte Haskins & Sells CPAs, San Francisco, 1979-82, Friedlander & Daiker CPAs, San Francisco, 1982-83; pvt. practice acctg. San Francisco, 1983-84; contr. Sheriar Press Inc., Myrtle Beach, S.C., 1984-86; pvt. practice acctg. North Myrtle Beach, S.C., 1987-91; pub. Windy Hill Publs., North Myrtle Beach, 1987-93; CFO Health Care Ptnrs., Inc., Conway, S.C., 1993-96; bus. process and strategy cons., mgr. Qualcomm., Inc., San Diego, 1997—; pub. Renaissance 9, 1998—; pvt. practice therapeutic edn. and performance enhancement, Myrtle Beach, 1988-91; bd. dirs. Internat. Coun. on Sys. Engring., San Diego. Mem. Company of Friends, Incose, San Diego Software Industry Coun., Stellcommunicators Toastmasters (pres. 1998—). Avocations: biking, vol. work. Office: Health Care Ptnrs 3584 Windthrift Way Ste 293 Oceanside CA 92056-2100

DELIFORD, MYLAH EAGAN, mathematics educator; b. Chgo., Nov. 7, 1948; d. Charles L.G. Eagan and Shirley R. (Bennett) Lewis; m. Albert Deliford Jr., Nov. 27, 1971 (div. Dec. 1984). BS in Edn., Chgo. State U., 1969; MA in Math., Northea. U., 1977. Tchr. Chgo. Bd. Edn., 1969—. Mem. Math. Assn. Am., Nat. Coun. Tchrs. Math., NABSE, Chgo. Elem. Tchrs. Math. Club, Met. Math. Club Chgo., Ill. Coun. Tchrs. Math., Benjamin Banneker Assn. Democrat. Roman Catholic. Home: 7467 N Ridge Blvd Chicago IL 60645-1902 Office: Dunbar Vocat Career Acad 3000 S King Dr Chicago IL 60616-3452

DELIGIORGIS, STAVROS G., retired literature educator; b. Sulina, Romania, Sept. 14, 1933; s. Alexander and Maria (Calligas) D.; children—Maria, Katerina. B.A., Nat. U., Athens, 1960; M.A., Yale U., 1958; Ph.D., U. Calif., Berkeley, 1966. Asst. prof. U. Iowa, Iowa City, 1965, prof., 1972-96, co-dir., corroboree Gallery of New Concepts, 1975-85, dir. M.F.A. program in transl., 1980-81; vis. assoc. prof. U. Ill., Champaign-Urbana, 1969-70; vis. prof. comparative lit. U. Mass., Amherst, 1974-75; vis. prof. English and Am. poetry Scuola Superiore Traduttori-Interpreti U. Trieste, 1988. Author: Narrative Intellection in Boccaccio's Decameron, 1975; translator Romanian poetry of N. Stanescu, Miron Georgescu, Cezar Baltag, M. Sorescu to English, 1976-86, Halo: Translation of Romanian Poems of Paul Celan, 1991, At the Gates of Morn: Four Contemporary Romanian Poets, 1998; contbr. articles to profl. jours. U. Ill. Ctr. for Advanced Study fellow, 1968-70; Fulbright grantee, researcher, 1977-78, sr. lectr. in Am. lit. U. Bucharest, 1978-79. Mem. MLA, Am. Comparative Lit. Assn., Medieval Acad. Am.

DELIGNE, PIERRE RENÉ, mathematician; b. Brussels, Oct. 3, 1944; s. Albert and Renée (Bodart) D.; m. Elena Vladimirovna Alexeeva, Sept. 9, 1980; children: Natalia, Alexis. Licence en mathématiques, ULB (Université Libre de Bruxelles), Brussel, 1966, PhD in Mathematics, 1968. Jr. scientist Fond National de la Recherche Scientifique Belgium, Brussel, 1967-68; vis. mem. Institut des Hautes Etudes Scientifiques, Bures sur Yvette, France, 1968-70; permanent mem. Inst. des Hautes Etudes Scientifiques, Bures sur Yvette, France, 1970-84; prof. Inst. for Advanced Study, Princeton, N.J., 1984. Editor Pub. Math. Institut des Hautes Etudes Scientifiques, 1970; contbr. articles to profl. jours. Recipient Fields medal Internat. Math. Union, 1978; Crafoord prize, 1988. Mem. Associé Etranger Academie des Sciences, AAAS (fgn. hon.), Royal Belgian Acad. Office: Inst for Advanced Study Sch Mathematics Olden Ln Princeton NJ 08540

DE LIMANTOUR, CLARICE BARR, food scientist; b. Allentown, Pa., Dec. 24, 1918; d. Joseph Robert and Laura (Wirthlin) Barr; m. Julio Edwardo Iturbide Limantour, Sept. 13, 1940 (dec. 1972); children: Jose' Ignacio, Julio Edwardo. BS, Rutgers U., 1938, MS, 1940; postgrad., U. Mexico, 1946-49, Rutgers U., 1949-50. Advisor Nat. Sch. Feeding Program, Mexico City, 1947-49; pres. Factory Feeding Corp., Mexico City, 1950-58; advisor Nat. Factory Feeding Program, Mexico City, 1958-60; developer New Food Product-Gen. Foods, White Plains, N.Y., 1960-61, New Food Product-Gen. Mills, Reynolds, 1961-63, New Food Product-Miles Labs., 1963-64; cons. New Food Products-various cos., 1964-78; pres., researcher Limantour Devel. Corp., Pa., 1966-91, chmn. of bd., 1988—; developer Cliffdale Farms, Quakertown, Pa., 1988—; pvt. practice cons. Durham, Pa. Inventor in field of freezing of all classes of emulsions. Mem. Bucks County Conservancy Assn., Doylestown, Pa., 1989-91, Fine Arts Club, N.Y.C., 1984-88, Republican Club, Pa., 1982-89, Citizens Against Govt. Waste, Washington, 1988-91. Republican. Episcopalian. Avocations: reading, music, traveling, sailing, bird watching. Home: 905 Durham Rd Durham PA 18039 Office: Cliffdale Farms 181 Kelly Rd Quakertown PA 18951-4209

DE LIO, ANTHONY PETER, lawyer; b. Bklyn., June 29, 1928; s. David V. and Margaret M. De L.; m. Marie DiTrani, July 19, 1952; children: Anthony P., Donna Marie Maistros, Lois Anne Cromwell; m. Margit Kaye, May 2, 1992. BS in Physics, Poly Inst. Bklyn., 1953; JD with honors, George Washington U., 1957. Bar: D.C. 1957, Conn. 1958, U.S. Dist. Ct. Conn. 1958. With patent dept. Bendix Corp., Washington, 1954-56; patent advisor U.S. Navy Dept., Washington, 1957; assoc. Blair & Spencer, Stamford, Conn., 1957-60; ptnr. Spencer, Rockwell & Bartholow, Stamford, 1960-62, Rockwell & De Lio, New Haven, 1962-64, De Lio and Libert, New Haven, 1981-84, De Lio & Assocs., New Haven, 1984-91, De Lio & Peterson, New Haven, 1991—; lectr. in field. Contbr. articles to legal jours. Chmn. Hamden Planning and Zoning Commn., 1969-81; alt. commr. Hamden Zoning Bd. Appeals, 1981-85. Served with USMC, 1946-48. Mem. ABA, Am. Intellectual Property Law Assn., Conn. Intellectual Property Law Assn., Internat. Intellectual Property Law Assn., Quinnipiack Club (New Haven), New Haven Country Club, Amity Club (New Haven), Alpha Phi Delta. Democrat. Roman Catholic. Office: 121 Whitney Ave New Haven CT 06510-1242

DE LISA, JOEL ALAN, rehabilitation physician, rehabilitation facility executive; b. Seattle, Mar. 18, 1942; s. Joseph Phillip and Alice Georgia (Jensen) DeL.; m. Janet Hopper, July 25, 1971. BS in Zoology, Wash. State U., 1964; MD, U. Wash., 1968, MS, 1976. Diplomate Am. Bd. Phys. Medicine and Rehab. (chmn. 1993-98). Intern St. Josephs Hosp., Phoenix, 1968-69; resident in phys. medicine and rehab. U. Wash., Seattle, 1972-75; med. dir., chief med. officer Kessler Inst. Rehab., West Orange, N.J., 1987-93; sr. v.p., chief med. officer Kessler Rehab. Corp., West Orange, 1994—; pres. Kessler Med. Rehab. Rsch. and Edn. Corp., West Orange, 1998—; prof., chmn. dept. phys. medicine and rehab. Univ. Medicine and Dentistry N.J., Newark, 1987—; chmn. dept. phys. medicine and rehab. St. Barnabas Med. Ctr., Livingston, N.J., 1990-98; spkr. Taiwan Nat. U. Hosp., 1995, 23d ann. meeting Korea Acad. Rehab. Medicine, 1995. Author: Manual of Nerve Conduction Velocity and Clinical Neurophysiology, 1994, Principles and Practice of Rehabilitation Medicine, 1998. Mem. AMA, Assn. Acad. Physiatrists, Am. Acad. Phys. Medicine and Rehab., Am. Congress Rehab. Medicine, Am. Paraplegic Soc. (hon., pres. Jackson Heights chpt. 1989-91, Excellence award 1995). Office: Kessler Med Rehab Rsch and Edn Corp 1199 Pleasant Valley Way West Orange NJ 07052-1424

DE LISI, JOANNE, communications executive, educator; b. Bklyn.; d. Louis Anthony and Maria Anna De Lisi. BA, Hunter Coll., 1972, MA, 1977; postgrad., N.Y.U. Cert. tchr., N.Y. Asst. instr. Hunter Coll., N.Y.C., 1974-75; instr. N.Y.U., 1974-78; instr. Bklyn. Coll., 1978-82, dir. forensics, 1981-82, asst. dir. acad. prep. program, 1980-82; adjunct lctr. City U. System, N.Y.C., 1983-91; cons. communication N.Y.C., 1976—; Faculty advisor Alpha Tau Omega, Blkyn. Coll., 1980-82. Profl. entertainer, 1953-75; contbr. articles to profl. jours. Judge Am. Legion Forensics Tournament, 1995-99; pub. rels. officer Queens County Am. Legion Aux., 1991-93, v.p., girls state chmn., 1993-94, pres. 1994-95, delegation chmn. for N.Y. state Dept. Conv., 1995, leadership chmn., parliamentarian, 1997-98; pub. rels. officer, newsletter editor Leonard Unit Am. Legion Aux., 1993-94, sec. 1993-94; nat. security chmn., jr. activity chmn., pub. rels. dir. Glendale Unit Am. Legion Aux., 1995—, pres., 1996-98; nat. del. Am. Legion Aux., 1996. Recipient nat. award of excellence POW/MIA, Am. Legion Aux., 1995, nat. awards U.S.O. and Savings Bonds Jr. Activities Am. Legion Aux., 1996-98, Vets. Affairs Nat. award, 1998. Mem. NAFE, Speech Communication Assn. (conf. chair info. com. 1980), Kappa Delta Pi. Roman Catholic. Clubs: Hunter Alumni Orgn., Fencers Am. Avocations: antique collector, travel, jewelry making, fencing dir. Office: Wyckoff Heights Sta PO Box 370029 Brooklyn NY 11237-0029

DE LISIO, STEPHEN SCOTT, lawyer; b. San Diego, Dec. 30, 1937; s. Anthony J. and Emma Irving (Cheney) DeL.; m. Margaret Irene Winter, June 26, 1964; children: Anthony W., Stephen Scott, Heather E. Student, Am. U., 1958-59; BA, Emory U., 1959; LLB, Albany Law Sch., 1962; LLM, Georgetown U., 1963. Bar: N.Y. 1963, D.C. 1963, Alaska 1964. Practice law Fairbanks, 1963-71, Anchorage, 1972-96; asst. dist. atty. Fairbanks, 1963-65; assoc. McNealy & Merdes, 1965-66; lectr. U. Alaska, 1965-67; ptnr. Staley, DeLisio & Cook, 1966-93, DeLisio, Moran, Geraghty & Zobel, Inc., 1994—; bd. dirs. Woodstock Property Co., Inc., Pasit Inc., Challenger Films Inc.; vice chmn. Crosstown CBMC, 1986-87, chmn., 1987-88, 90-91, area coord., 1987-92; city atty., Fairbanks, 1967-70, Barrow, 1969-72, Ft. Yukon and North Pole, 1970-72; past sec. U. Alaska Heating Corp., Inc.; past sec.-treas. Trans-Alaska Electronics, Inc., Baker Aviation, Inc.; arbitrator, mem. Alaska regional coun. Am. Arbitration Assn. Author: (with others) Law and Tactics in Federal Criminal Cases, 1964. Rep. precinct committeeman, 1970-76; chmn. Alaska Rep. Rules Com., Anchorage Rep. Com., 1973; v.p. We The People, 1977-79; vice-chmn. Alaska Libertarian party, 1983-84; mem. nat. com. Libertarian party, 1982-85; past pres. Tanana Valley State Fair Assn.; past v.p. Fairbanks Mental Health Assn., Fairbanks United Good Neighbors Fund; deacon Anchorage Bible Fellowship, 1986-90, elder, 1990—; bd. dirs. Anchorage Community Chorus, 1975-77, Commonsense for Alaska, 1987-94, Alaska chpt. Lupus Found., 1989-96; chmn. bd. Alaska Voluntary Health Assn., 1993-96; former bd. dirs. Greater Fairbanks Community Hosp. Found.; met. dir. Christian Businessmen's Outreach, 1993-94, bd. dirs. Anchorage, 1985—; Alaska coord. Crown Ministries, 1991-93; met. dir. Anchorage Christian Businessmen's Com. U.S.A., 1994—. Recipient Jaycee Disting. Service award, 1968. Mem. Am. Trial Lawyers Assn., Am. Judicature Soc., Alaska Bar Assn., D.C. Bar Assn., Anchorage Bar Assn., Spenard Bar Assn. (pres. 1975-77), U.S. Jaycees (past dir.), Alaska Jaycees (past pres.), Fairbanks Jaycees (past pres.), Chi Phi, Pi Sigma Phi, Woodstock Golf Inc. Club (pres. 1984—). Home: 5102 Shorecrest Dr Anchorage AK 99515-1029 Office: DeLisio Moran et al 943 W 6th Ave Anchorage AK 99501-2023 *A well-defined sense of values and the courage and determination to adhere to it is as essential to a life of purpose and fulfillment, as the rising of the sun is to life on this planet. The challenge is to develop values that are as relevant to the changes of tomorrow as to the reality of the now and the past. The "situation ethics" approach is as disastrous as a smashed rudder on a storm tossed vessel. The Truth and Life is found in Christ Jesus.*

DELISLE, ALAN H., city commissioner; m. Kim DeLisle: children: Alexa, Alaina. BA in Comm. and Journalism, St. John Fisher Coll., Rochester, N.Y.; MS in Polit. Sci., SUNY, Albany, 1985. Senate fellow State of N.Y., Albany, 1986; legis. dir. Office of Sen. Anthony M. Masiello, Albany; confidential aide for intergovtl. affairs and policy Mayor Masiello, Buffalo, N.Y.; commr. cmty. devel. City of Buffalo, 1996-97; pres. Buffalo Econ. Renaissance Corp., 1997—. Avocations: jazz, sports, Colonial history. Office: Buffalo Econ Renaissance Corp 925 City Hall 617 Main St Buffalo NY 14203*

DELJUNCO, TIRSO, federal agency administrator. Bd. govs. U.S. Postal Svc., Washington, 1984-96, chmn., 1996-97, mem. bd. govs., 1997—. Office: US Postal Service Board of Governors 475 Lenfant Plz SW Washington DC 20260-1531*

DELL, ERNEST ROBERT, lawyer; b. Vandergrift, Pa., Feb. 6, 1928; m. Karen D. Reed, May 8, 1965; children: Robert W., John D., Jane C. B.S., U. Pitts., 1949, M.Litt., 1953; J.D., Harvard U., 1956. Bar: Pa. 1957, U.S. Supreme Ct. 1961; C.P.A., Pa. Ptnr. firm Reed Smith Shaw & McClay, Pitts., 1956—; adj. prof. law Duquesne U. Law Sch., Pitts., 1960-86; bd. dirs. Atty's. Liability Assurance Soc., Inc., Chgo., Atty's. Liability Assurance Soc. (Bermuda) Ltd. Mem. ABA, Fed. Bar Assn., Pa. Bar Assn., Allegheny County Bar Assn., AICPAs, Pa. Inst. CPAs. Home: 119 Riding Trail Ln Pittsburgh PA 15215-1521 Office: Reed Smith Shaw & McClay Mellon Sq 435 6th Ave Ste 2 Pittsburgh PA 15219-1886*

DELL, LINDA TREESE, gifted and talented education educator; b. Altoona, Pa., Apr. 3, 1943; d. Elliott Milton and Virginia May (Allen) Treese; m. David Guy Brickley, Feb. 19, 1966 (div. Apr. 1981); children: Terri Michelle, David Guy Jr.; m. Jay Arthur Dell, July 16, 1983. BS in Elem. Edn., Pa. State U., 1965; MED in Math., Ind. U. Pa., 1988. Tchr. Hollidaysburg (Pa.) Sch. Dist., 1965-66, 68-69, Am. Dependent Schs., Adana, Turkey, 1966-67, Va. Christian Acad., Woodbridge, 1972-73; dir., owner Cloverdale Kindergarten, Woodbridge, 1973-80; tchr. of gifted Appalachian Intermediate Unit, Ebensburg, Pa., 1980-91; tchr. instructional support, gifted support Spring Cove Sch. Dist., Roaring Spring, 1991—; cons. John's Hopkins U., Balt.,. Recipient Project Excel award NSF Ind. U. Pa., 1988. Mem. NEA, Nat. Assn. Female Execs., Assn. Curriculum and Supervision, Pa. Edn. Assn., Pa. Middle Sch. Assn. (bd. dirs.), Spring Cove Edn. Assn. Republican. Avocations: music, cross stitching, walking, patio gardening, antique collection. Home: 316 Allegheny St Hollidaysburg PA 16648-2013 Office: Spring Cove Sch Dist Roaring Spring PA 16673

DELL, MICHAEL S., manufacturing executive; b. Houston, 1965; s. Alexander and Lorraine D.; m. Susan Lieberman, Oct. 23, 1989. Student, U. Tex., 1983-84. Founder Dell Computer Corp. (formerly PC's Ltd.), Austin, 1984—, now chmn., CEO. Recipient Entrepreneur of Yr. award Inc. Mag., 1990, Customer Satisfaction award JD Power, 1991, 93; named CEO of Yr. Fin. World Mag., 1993. Office: Dell Computer Corp 1 Dell Way Round Rock TX 78682-0001*

DELL, RALPH BISHOP, pediatrician, researcher; b. Mt. Village, Alaska, July 31, 1935; s. Elwin B. and Elizabeth B. (Bishop) D.; m. Kathryn M. Bownass, June 17, 1957 (div. Dec. 1982); children: Laura, Kenneth; m. Karen K. Hein, Aug. 28, 1983; stepchildren: Ethan Hein, Molly Hein. BA, Pomona Coll., 1957; MD, U. Pa., 1961. Diplomate Am. Bd. Pediatrics. Intern and resident Children's Hosp. Med. Ctr., Boston, 1961-63; NIH postdoctoral fellow Coll. Physicians and Surgeons, Columbia U., N.Y.C., 1963-66, assoc., 1966-67, asst. prof. pediatrics, 1967-72, assoc. prof., 1972-78, prof., 1978-97; Dir. Inst. for Lab. Animal Rsch., NRC, Washington, 1997—.

Author 3 books, 100 research papers; co-inventor amino acid solution. Recipient Research Career Devel award NIH, 1966-71, Career Scientist award Health Research Council N.Y., 1972-75; Fogarty Sr. Internat. fellow NIH, 1975-76. Mem. Am. Pediat. Soc., Am. Physiologic Soc., Am. Soc. Clin. Investigation, Soc. for Pediat. Rsch., Assn. for Computing Machinery, Am. Assn. Accreditation Lab. Animal Care (coun. on accreditation). Democrat. Home: 3905 Huntington St NW Washington DC 20015-1913 Office: NRC Inst for Lab Animal Rsch 2101 Constitution Ave NW Washington DC 20418-0007

DELL, ROBERT CHRISTOPHER, geothermal sculptor, scenic artist; b. Nyack, N.Y., Feb. 22, 1950; s. Edward John and Laurel Jean (McGrath) D.; children: Robert Carroll, Malcolm Vincent, Terrence Edwardl; m. Siena Gillan Porta, May 30, 1986. BS in Edn., SUNY, Oneonta, 1972; MFA in Sculpture, SUNY, New Paltz, 1975. mem. arch. and cmty. appearance bd. rev. Orangetown, N.Y., 1979—, vice-chmn., 1987—; dir. visual arts Vriesland W. Hudson Art Ctr., Pearl River, N.Y., 1978-80, artist-in-residence, 1980; guest spkr. Cooper Union, N.Y.C., 1994, MIT, 1994, 97, Harvard U., 1995, Nassau C. C., 1999; rsch. fellow Ctr. Advanced Visual Studies MIT, 1993-95, rsch. affil., 1995-97. Solo shows include Vorpal Gallery, Chgo., 1978, N.Y.C., 1981, 88, San Francisco, 1985, New Acquisitions Gallery, Syracuse, 1983, Blue Hill Cultural Ctr., Pearl River, N.Y., 1987, 98-99, Am. Cultural Ctr., Reykjavik, Iceland, 1988, geothermal sculpture installation, Krisuvik, Iceland, 1988, Mid-Hudson Arts and Sci. Ctr., Poughkeepsie, N.Y., 1992, Castle and Old Faithful, Grotto Geyser Groups Yellowstone Nat. Park, Wyo., 1996, Kresge Oval MIT, 1997 group shows include Meyeroff Gallery, Md. Inst. Art, Balt., 1980, Thronja Gallery, Springfield, Mass., 1984-93, 14 Sculptors Gallery, N.Y.C., 1985, 94, New Acquisitions Gallery, 1982-87, SUNY, New Paltz, 1987, MIT Mus., Cambridge, Mass., 1990-91, Siegel Gallery, Lehigh U., Bethlehem, Pa., 1991-92, Barbara Gibson Gallery, Nyack, N.Y., 1992, Perlan, Reykjavic, (permanent geothermal sculpture installation), 1991—, Galleri Ofeigur, Reykjavik, 1993-94, MIT Mus./Ctr. Advanced Visual Studies MIT, 1994, Tisch Gallery Tufts U., Mass., 1995, Carpenter Ctr. Visual Arts Harvard U., Cambridge, Mass., 1995, ArtSpace Gallery, New Jersey City (N.J.) U., 1998-99, Firehouse Art Gallery Nassau C. C., Garden City, N.Y., 1999, Galleri Fold, Reykjavik, 1998-99; permanent collections include Fulbright Commn., Reykjavik, Syracuse U., Mus. Fine Art, Springfield, Mass., MacDowell Colony, Peterborough, N.H., SUNY, Town of Orangetown (N.Y.); subject of video Hitavaetur MIT, Circumstantial Prodns., 1991, News Story, Frettir, geothermal sculpture State TV Iceland, 1993-96; scenic artist motion pictures, TV shows; master scenic artist One Life to Live ABC, 1988— (Daytime Emmy award 1995). Fellow MacDowell Colony, 1980, Am. Scandinavian Found., 1999—; Collaboration Art, Sci. and Tech. grantee Syracuse U., 1978, NYSCA grantee, 1986, Fulbright rsch. grantee, 1988, Ptnrs. of Ams. grantee, 1993, grantee Robert E. Brennan Found., 1993, Waterloo Found. Arts, 1994, Coun. Arts at MIT, 1997. Home: 421 Washington St Tappan NY 10983-2703

DELL, ROBERT MICHAEL, lawyer; b. Chgo., Oct. 4, 1952; s. Michael A. and Bertha Dell; m. Ruth Celia Schiffman, May 29, 1976; children: David, Michael, Jessica. BGS, U. Mich., 1974; JD, U. Ill., 1977. Bar: U.S. Dist. Ct. (no. dist.) Ill. 1977, U.S. Ct. Appeals (7th cir.) 1977, U.S. Dist. Ct. (no. dist.) Calif. 1990. Law clk. to justice U.S. Ct. Appeals (7th cir.), Chgo., 1977-79; assoc. Latham & Watkins, Chgo., 1982-85, ptnr., 1985—, mng. ptnr. San Francisco office, 1990-94, firm chmn. and mng. ptnr., 1995—. Home: 19 Tamal Vista Ln Kentfield CA 94904-1005 Office: Latham & Watkins 505 Montgomery St Ste 1900 San Francisco CA 94111-2552*

DELL, THOMAS CHARLES, nurse anesthetist; b. Port Huron, Mich., May 28, 1959; s. John W. and Lois M. (Bell) D.; m. Peggy L. Reynolds, July 2, 1983; children: Adam, Aubree, Andrea. AS, St. Clair County Community Coll., Port Huron, Mich., 1979; BSN, No. Mich. U., 1981; BS, Mercy Coll. Detroit, 1985; MS, Gooding Inst. Nurse Anethesia, Panama City, Fla., 1998. RN, Mich.; cert. nurse anesthetist. Nurse Marquette (Mich.) Gen., 1981-83; nurse Mercy Hosp., Port Huron, 1983-85, nurse anesthetist, insvc. coord., 1985-88; nurse anesthetist Saber Salisbury and Assoc., Southfield, Mich., 1988-89; chief nurse anesthetist McKenzie Meml. Hosp., Sandusky, Mich., 1989-98; clin. and didactic instr. U. Mich./Hurley Med. Ctr. Sch. Nurse Anesthesia, Flint, 1998—. Mem. Am. Assn. Nurse Anesthetists, Mich. Assn. Nurse Anesthetists. Avocations: table tennis, bicycling, trumpet playing.

DELL, WARREN FRANK, II, management consultant; b. Louisville, Aug. 8, 1945; s. George Justus and Opal Lee (Roberts) D.; m. Theresa LoParco, July 11, 1970; child, Stacy Lee. BS, Northeastern U., 1968; MBA, Iona Coll., 1973. Cert. mgmt. cons. Systems analyst Am. Can Co., Greenwich, Conn., 1968-69; cons. Info. Techniques, Inc., Norwalk, Conn., 1969-70; systems analyst Colgate Palmolive, N.Y.C., 1970-72, supr. mktg. stats., 1972-73, mgr. forecast and adminstrn., 1973-77; cons. Case and Co., Stamford, Conn., 1977-80, prin., 1980-83, sr. ptnr., dir., 1983-85; prin. Cresap, a Towers Perrin Co., N.Y.C., 1985-86, v.p., 1986-90; pres. Dellmart & Co., Stamford, Conn., 1989—. Contbr. articles to profl. jours. Mem. Coun. Logistics Mgmt., Warehouse Edn. Rsch. Coun., Food Distbn. Rsch. Soc., Am. Philatelic Soc., Inst. Mgmt. Cons. Strategic Leadership Forum, Comite Internat. Des Entreprises A Succursates. Republican. Avocations: stamp collecting, golf, travel. Office: Dellmart & Co 125 Hardesty Rd Stamford CT 06903-4327

DELLACORTE, CHRISTOPHER, engineer, tribologist; b. Port Jefferson, N.Y., Dec. 10, 1963; s. Franklin Alfred and Suzanne DellaCorte; m. Patricia DellaCorte. BS, Case Western Res. U., 1986, MS, 1987, PhD, 1987. Rsch. engr. Case Western Res. U., Cleve., 1986-87, NASA, Cleve., 1987—. Contbr. over 50 articles to profl. jours. Bd. dirs. Medina (Ohio) County Bd. Mental Retardation and Devel. Disabilities, 1992-96. Mem. ASME (Burt L. Newkirk award 1996, conf. planning com. 1995—), Soc. Tribologists and Lubrication (assoc. editor, solid lubricants com. chair 1989-92). Avocations: mechanical devices, technical history, natural history. Office: NASA Glenn Rsch Ctr 21000 Brookpark Rd Cleveland OH 44135-3191*

DELLA-GIUSTINA, JO-ANN SUBOTIN, lawyer; b. Springfield, Mass., Sept. 6, 1951; d. Joseph Augustus and Jennie Delores (Subotin) Della-G. BA, Clark U., 1972; MA, Columbia Coll., Chgo., 1983; JD, Chgo.-Kent Coll. Law, 1987; postgrad., CUNY, 1998—. Bar: Ill. 1987, Mass. 1996, N.Y. 1998, U.S. Dist. Ct. (no. dist.) Ill. 1987, N.Y. 1998. Tchr. S.W. Ind. Sch. Dist., San Antonio, 1976-78, Malcolm X Coll., Chgo., 1978-80; dir. pub. rels. H&R Block, Chgo., 1983-85; asst. corp. counsel City of Chgo., 1987-89; sr. atty. Office of Cook County Pub. Defender, Chgo., 1989-90; judicial law clk. to Justice David Cerda Ill. Appellate Ct., Chgo., 1990-98; cons. Am. Planning Assn., Chgo., 1990-98; bd. dirs. loan repayment and assistance program IIT Chgo., 1995-97; presenter in field. Author: Blossom of the Flower, 1990; author (legal jour.) Land Use Law and Zoning Digest, 1990-98; contbr. articles to profl. jours. Pres. Greenwood Ct. Condominium Assn., Chgo., 1989-98. Mem. Justinian Soc. Lawyers, Nat. Assn. Women Lawyers (named Outstanding Law Grad. 1987), Women in Film (programs com. 1992-94), Acad. Criminal Justice, Nat. Women's Studies Assn., Am. Soc. Criminology, Nat. Italian-Am. Bar Assn., Order of Coif. Avocations: travel, reading. Home: 322 W 57th St #33J New York NY 10019

DELLAPA, GARY J., airport terminal executive. Aviation dir. Miami Internat. Airport, Miami, FL, 1994-. Office: Miami Intl Airport PO Box 59-2075 AMF Miami FL 33159-2075*

DELLAPORTAS, GEORGE, physician, medical facility administrator; b. Greece, Feb. 3, 1932; came to U.S., 1967; s. John and Alexandra Dellaportas; m. Teresa Kritikos, Jan. 4, 1962; children: Alexander, John. MD, U. Athens, 1957; MPH, Johns Hopkins U., 1968, PhD, 1971. Asst. prof. Athens Sch. Medicine, 1959-61; physician Greek Ministry Pub. Health, 1961-65; assoc. prof. Sch. Pub. Health, Ethiopia, 1965-67; resident Grtr. Balt. Med. Ctr., 1968-70; assoc. prof. Sch. Medicine U. Sherbrooke, Can., 1970-71; dir., chief. med. examiner Ingham County, Lansing, Micyh., 1971-75; prof., chmn. Sch. Medicine U. Ill., 1976-82; dir. Health Dist. 6-Tex. Dept. Health, Temple, 1976-76, Okal. City County Health Dept., 1982-85; adminstr. health programs Whitley Ctr., Clinton, S.C., 1985—. Contbr. articles to profl. jours. Lt. Greek Armed Forces, 1957-59. Avocations: statistics, economics, history.

DELLA ROCCO, KENNETH ANTHONY, lawyer; b. Bridgeport, Conn., Sept. 5, 1952. BA, Sacred Heart U., Fairfield, Conn., 1974; JD, U. Bridgeport, 1982. Bar: Conn. 1983, U.S. Dist. Ct. Conn. 1985, N.Y. 1988, U.S. Supreme Ct. 1991. Assoc. Cummings & Lockwood, Stamford, Conn., 1982-88; asst. gen. counsel Melville Corp., Rye, N.Y., 1988-90, dir. legal affairs, counsel, 1990-94, asst. corp. sec., 1990-95, v.p. legal affairs, gen. counsel, 1994-95; counsel Cacace, Tusch & Santagata, Stamford, 1996—. Mem. ABA, Conn. Regional Bar Assn., N.Y. State Bar Assn. Office: Cacace Tusch and Santagata 777 Summer St Stamford CT 06901-1022

DELLAS, ROBERT DENNIS, investment banker; b. Detroit, July 4, 1944; s. Eugene D. and Maxine (Rudell) D.; m. Shila L. Clement, Mar. 27, 1976; children—Emily Allison, Lindsay Michelle. B.A. in Econs., U. Mich., Ann Arbor, 1966; M.B.A., Harvard U., Cambridge, 1970. Analyst Burroughs Corp., Detroit, 1966-67, Pasadena, Calif., 1967-68; mgr. U.S. Leasing, San Francisco, 1970-76; pres., dir. Energetics Mktg. & Mgmt. Assn., San Francisco, 1978-80; sr. v.p. E.F. Hutton & Co., San Francisco, 1981-85; prin. founder Capital Exchange Internat., San Francisco, 1976—; gen. ptnr. Kanland Assocs., Tex., 1982, Claremont Assocs., Calif., 1983, Lakeland Assocs., Ga., 1983, Americal Assocs., Calif., 1983, Chatsworth Assocs., Calif., 1983, Walnut Grove Assocs., Calif., 1983, Somerset Assocs., N.J., 1983, One San Diego Assocs., Calif., 1984, Big Top Prodns., L.P., Calif., 1994. Bd. dirs., treas. Found. San Francisco's Archtl. Heritage. Mem. U.S. Trotting Assn., Calif. Harness Horse Breeders Assn. (Breeders award for Filly of Yr. 1986, Aged Pacing Mare, 1987, 88, Colt of Yr. 1990), Calif. Golf Club San Francisco. Office: Capital Exch Internat 1911 Sacramento St San Francisco CA 94109-3419

DELLA SANTA, LAURA, principal. Prin. Mater Christi Sch., Burlington, Vt. Recipient Elem. Sch. Recognition award U.S. Dept. Edn., 1989-90. Office: Mater Christi Sch 50 Mansfield Ave Burlington VT 05401-3389*

DELLERE, DIANA MARIE, school psychologist; b. Colby, Kans., Apr. 2, 1968; d. Alvin Dale and Lois Marie (Towns) D. AA, Colby (Kans.) C.C., 1988; BS, Ft. Hays State U., 1990, MS, 1992; EdS, 1994. Cert. sch. psychologist, Kans. Sch. psychologist Wichita (Kans.) Pub. Schs., 1993—. Big sister Big bros./Big Sisters, Wichita, 1997. Mem. Nat. Assn. Sch. Psychologists, Kans. Assn. Sch. Psychologists (editor 1995-97, 99—, assoc. editor 1998-99), Wichita Sch. Psychology Assn. (sec., pres. 1999—). Republican. Roman Catholic. Avocations: reading, crafts, quilting, sewing, children.

DELLEUR, JACQUES WILLIAM, civil engineering educator; b. Paris, Dec. 30, 1924; came to U.S., 1952, naturalized, 1957; s. Georges Leon and Simone (Rossum) D.; m. DeLores Ann Horne, June 18, 1957; children: James Robert, Ann Marie. Civil and Mining Engr., Nat. U. Colombia, 1949; M.S. in Civil Engring., Rensselaer Poly. Inst., 1950; D.Engring. Sci., Columbia U., 1955. Civil engr. R.J. Tipton and Assocs., 1950-52; from research asst. to instr. civil engring. and engring. mechanics Columbia U., 1952-55; mem. faculty Purdue U., 1955-95, prof. hydraulic engring. and hydrology, 1963-95, prof. emeritus hydraulic engring., 1995—, head hydromechanics and water resources area, 1965-76, head hydraulic and systems engring. area, 1988-90, 91-92; assoc. dir. Purdue U. Water Resources Rsch. Ctr., 1971-89, acting dir., 1983; researcher fluid mechanics U. Grenoble, Fance, 1961-62, hydrology and environ. fluid mechanics French Nat. Hydraulics Lab., Chatou, France, 1968-69, 76-77, statis. hydrology U. Brussels, Belgium, 1991; NSF sr. exch. scientist U. Grenoble, France, 1983-84; vis. prof. U. Quebec, Canada, 1996—, Vrije U., Brussels, 1995—; scientific coun. Revue des Sciences de L'eau Water Scis. Scientific Interest Group/Nat. Inst. Scientific Rsch., Quebec, 1988—; vis. lectr. Ecole Polytechnique Federale de Lausanne, Switzerland, 1991, 93, 95, 97. Author and co-author 2 books on statis. hydrology; co-author book on urban hydorlogy; editor: Handbook of Groundwater Engineering, 1998; assoc. editor: Handbook of Civil Engineering, 1995; also articles, reports in field. Fellow Ind. Acad. Sci.; mem. ASCE (Freeman fellow 1961-62, chmn. fluid dynamics com. 1964-66, task com. mechanics of turbulence 1964-69, task com. hydraulics of bridges 1963-68, task com. on rehab. urban drainage infrastructure 1988-90, cochmn. task com. on urban drainage rehab. & techniques 1990-94, chmn. com. urban water resources 1994-95, internat. bd. advisors Jour. Hydrologic Engring. 1996—), Am. Geophys. Union (chmn. urban hydrology com. 1978-83), Am. Water Resources Assn., Am. Soc. Engring. Edn., Internat. Assn. Hydraulic Rsch. (U.S. del. joint com. on urban storm drainage with Internat. Assn. Water Quality 1987-93), Internat. Assn. Sci. Hydrology, Ind. Water Resources Assn. (Charles Harold Bechert award 1992). Home: 124 Mohican Pl West Lafayette IN 47906-2159 Office: Purdue U Sch Civil Engring West Lafayette IN 47907-1284*

DELLINGER, WALTER ESTES, III, lawyer, educator; b. Charlotte, N.C., May 15, 1941; s. Walter Estes and Grace Phelan (Lawing) D.; m. Anne Elizabeth Maxwell, June 12, 1965; children—Hampton, Andrew. AB with honors, U. N.C., 1963; LLB, Yale U., 1966. Bar: N.C. 1970. Assoc. prof. law U. Miss., 1966-68; law clk. to Justice Hugo L. Black, U.S. Supreme Ct., 1968-69; assoc. prof. law Duke U., 1969-72, prof. law, 1972-93, 98—; assoc. dean Duke U. Law Sch., 1974-76, acting dean, 1976-78; vis. prof. U. So. Calif. Law Ctr., 1973-74, U. Mich. Law Sch., 1977, Cath. U. Leuven, Belgium, 1985; prof. in residence U.S. Dept. Justice, Washington, 1980-81; asst. atty. gen. for legal counsel U.S. Justice Dept., Washington, 1993-96; acting Solicitor Gen. of the U.S., 1996-97; cons., draftsman N.C. Criminal Code Commn., 1970-78. Mem. bd. editors Yale Law Jour., 1965-66. Rockefeller Found. Humanities fellow, 1981-82. Mem. Am. Bar Assn., N.C. State Bar. Democrat. Home: 4714 Taproot Ln Durham NC 27705-8100 Office: Duke U Sch Law Box 90389 Science Dr & Towerview Rd Durham NC 27708*

DELLIS, FRÉDY MICHEL, travel exchange company executive; b. Frasnes-lez-Gosselies, Hainaut, Belgium, Aug. 11, 1945; s. Ernest and Josee (Bailly) D.; m. Agnes A. Parms, Aug. 20, 1984; children: Jennifer Sarah, Nelson Charles, Spencer Jack. Student, Sorbonne, Paris, 1968-69; grad. advanced mgmt. program, Harvard U., 1985. Chief acct. Hertz Luxembourg, Brussels, 1969-70; sales mgr. Hertz Belgium, Brussels, 1971-74, regional mgr., 1975; gen. mgr. Hertz Scandinavia, Stockholm, 1976-77, Europcar France, Paris, 1977-78; asst. v.p. ops. Hertz Corp., Dallas, 1978; gen. mgr. Hertz Benelux, Amsterdam, The Netherlands, 1979-80; v.p. ops. Hertz Europe, London, 1980-82; pres. Hertz Europe, Middle East, Africa, London, 1982-89; exec. v.p. Hertz Corp., N.Y.C., 1987-89; pres. Hertz Internat., London, 1987-90; chmn. Axus S.A., Brussels, 1989-90; pres. Burger King Internat., Miami, Fla., 1990-91; CEO, Europcar Internat. S.A., Paris, 1991-95; group mng. dir. Europe, Middle East, Africa RCI Europe Ltd., Eng., 1995—. Roman Catholic. *

DELLO JOIO, NORMAN, olympic athlete, equestrian; children: Daniela, Norman Nicholas. Olympic equestrian jumper Barcelona, Spain, 1992. Recipient Equestrian Individual Jumping Bronze medal Olympics, Barcelona, 1992, Gold medal Pan Am. Games, 1979, World Cup, Vienna, Austria, 1983. Mem. Olympic Team, 1980. Office: care US Olympic Com One Olympic Plz Colorado Springs CO 80904-5760 also Office: Nat Grand Prix League 1309 Manor House Dr Tallahassee FL 32312-9025*

DELLO JOIO, NORMAN, composer; b. N.Y.C., Jan. 24, 1913; s. Casimir and Antoinette (Garramone) Dello J.; m. Barbara Bolton, 1974; children: Victoria, Justin, Norman. Student, All Hallows Inst., 1926-30, Coll. City N.Y., 1932-34, Inst. Mus. Art, 1936, Juilliard Grad. Sch., 1939-41, Yale Sch. Music, 1941; Mus.D. (hon.), Colby Coll., Lawrence Coll., U. Cin., 1967, St. Mary's Coll., 1969, Susquehanna U., 1980. Tchr. composition Sarah Lawrence Coll., 1945-50, Mannes Coll. Music, 1952—; commentator Met. Opera broadcasts; dean Sch. for the Arts, Boston U., 1972-78; Mem. research adv. council U.S. Office Edn.; adv. council State U. N.Y., Potsdam; chmn. policy com. contemporary music Ford Found. Composer: Ballet On Stage, 1944, Ricercari; for piano and orch., 1946, Variations- Chaccone- Finale, 1947, Diversion of Angeles; dance, 1948, Concertante for Clarinet and Orch, 1949, New York Profiles; for orch., 1949, The Triumph of St. Joan; opera, 1950, Psalm of David: chorus and orch., 1950, Song of Affirmation; soprano, chorus, narrator, orch., 1950, The Tall Kentuckian; score for musical play, 1952, Song of the Open Road; chorus, 1952, (opera) The Ruby, 1953, The Lamentation of Saul, 1954, The Trial at Rouen, 1955, Mediations on Ecclesiates, 1956, Air Power, symphonic suite, 1956, Ballad of the 7 Lively Arts, 1957, To St. Cecilia, 1958, (opera) Blood Moon; also: Variations and Fantasy for Piano and Orchestra, 1961; score Songs of Adieu, The Louvre, NBC TV, 1965 (Emmy award), Beyond Every Horizon; for Symphonic band Antiphonal Fantasy; organ, brass, strings, 1965, Songs of Walt Whitman for Orch. and Chorus, 1966, Capriccio; for piano, 1968, Fantasies on Theme of Haydn, 1968, Time of Snow; ballet, 1968, Proud Music of the Storm; chorus, brass, organ, 1967, Days of the Modern; chorus, brass, percussion, 1968, Evocations; chorus, orch., 1970, Psalm of Peace; chorus, organ, french horn, trumpet, 1971, Mass; chorus, organ, brass Concertante for Wind Instruments, 1972, Of Crows and Clusters; chorus and piano, 1972, Suite for Flute and Piano, 1973, Suite for Clarinet and Piano, 1973, Suite for Organ, 1973, Folio for Piano, 1973, Lyric Fantasies for Viola and Strings, 1973, The Poet's Song, 1973, Leisure, 1973, Mass to the Blessed Virgin; organ and chorus, 1974, Satiric Dances; band, 1974, Stage Parodies; piano 4 hands, 1974, Mass of the Eucharist in honour of Pope John XXIII; organ, brass, strings and chorus, 1975, Notes from Tom Paine; chorus and piano, 1975, Colonial Variants; orch., 1976, Southern Echoes, 1976, Colonial Ballads; band, 1977, As of a Dream; orch., soloists, chorus, narrator and dancers, 1978, Sonata for Trumpet and Piano, 1978, Songs of Remembrance; voice solo and orch., 1978, Salute to Scarlatti; piano, 1978, The Psalmist's Meditation; chorus and piano, 1978, Variations; piano, 1980, Hymns Without Words; chorus and piano, 1979, Ballabili; dances for orch., 1981; chorus and piano Love Songs at Parting, 1982; string orch. East Hampton Sketches, 1983; piano and 4 hands Song at Springtide, 1984; concert band Aria and Roulade, 1983; chorus and concert band Let Us Sing a New Song, 1984, concert band Metaphrase, 1985, orch. Variants on a Bach Chorale, 1985, piano Introduction and Fantasies, 1985, Short Intervallic Etudes for Piano, 1986, Sing a Song Universal for chorus and piano, 1987, Nativity for chorus, soloists and orch., 1987, The Quest, 1990, mixed chorus and piano, A Memory: Men's Chorus and Piano, 1991, Songs of Memory, 1991, Variants on a Medieval Tune, 1993, Reflections on an Ancient Hymn for chamber orch., 1996, Salute to the Orch. Chamber Orch. Player, 1997, chamber orchestra Divertimento, 1997, Reflections on an Ancient Tune, 1997, piano 2 Songs Without Words, 1997, String Quartet, "Lyrical Interludes," 1998, concert band Fantasies, The Vigil for Mixed Chorus and Brass Instruments, band arrangement Jubilant Song, (music for TV series) Air Power, Directimento for Chamber Orch., 1997; Lyrical Movement for string orch., 1995. Chmn. planning com. Ford Found.; Bd. dirs. Am. Music Center. Recipient Elizabeth Sprague Coolidge award, 1937; recipient Town Hall Composition award, 1941, N.Y. Music Critics Circle award, 1949, 58, Pulitzer prize for music, 1957, Emmy award for TV Score; Guggenheim fellow, 1943-44; Am. Acad. Arts and Letters grantee, 1945. Mem. Nat. Acad. Arts and Letters (coun.), Broadcast Music, Devon Yacht Club. Home: PO Box 154 East Hampton NY 11937-0154 *Whatever recognition I have received for my creative work, I owe for the most part, to an understanding mother and disciplinarian father. In this, my 70th year, I give thanks for a loving wife, a composer son whose music I feel will be an extension of myself into the future, and a son who is an Olympic equestrian of whom I am proud.*

DELL'OSSO, LOUIS FRANK, neuroscience educator; b. Bklyn., Mar. 16, 1941; s. Frank and Rose (Perrone) Dell'O.; m. Aquilina Marie Ferlo, May 22, 1965 (div. 1976); single ptnr. Charlene Hale Morse, Sept. 30, 1977. B.E.E., Bklyn. Poly. Inst., 1961, postgrad., 1961-63; Ph.D., U. Wyo., 1968. Co-dir. Ocular Motor Neurophysiology Lab. VA. Med. Ctr., Miami, Fla., 1972-80; asst. prof. biomed. engring. and surgery U. Miami, 1970-72, asst. prof. neurology, 1972-75, assoc. prof. neurology, 1975-79, prof. neurology, 1979-80; dir. Ocular Motor Neurophysiology Lab. VA Med. Ctr., Cleve., 1980—; prof. neurology and biomed. engring. Case Western Res. U., Cleve., 1980—; cons. Westinghouse Research Lab, Pitts, 1966-67, 70-71, Mt. Sinai Hosp., Miami, FL, 1972-75. Bd. dirs. Vineland Galloway Civic Assn., Miami, 1973-76. Grantee NIH, 1971-77; grantee VA Med. Ctr., 1972—, NSF, 1970. Fellow N.Am. NeuroOphthalmology Soc.; mem. IEEE, Engring. in Medicine and Biology Soc. (sr., chpt. chmn. 1977-78), Assn. Rsch. in Vision and Ophthalmology, Soc. Neurosci., AAAS, Train Collectors Assn. Democrat. E-mail: /fd@po.cwru.edu. Home: 2356 Tudor Dr Cleveland OH 44106-3212

DELLOSSO, ROY J., sales executive; b. Newark, Oct. 13, 1953; m. Joanne Mateer, May 13, 1978; children: Kathryn, Michael, Daniel. BA in Psychology, Jersey City (N.J.) State Coll., 1977. Sales rep. Ind. Ins. Broker, Atlantic Highlands, N.J.; dist. sales rep. Indsl. Appraisal, Atlantic Highlands. Mem. sch. bd. Atlantic Highlands Elem. Sch., 1993—; past pres. Sandy Hook Little League, Atlantic Highlands, 1995. Polit. Orgns. Atlantic Highlands, 1995-96; pres., CEO Jersey Shore Sch. Ins., 1998—. Mem. Lions Club. Democrat. Roman Catholic. Home: 75 Asbury Ave Atlantic Highlands NJ 07716-1431

DELLUMS, RONALD V., former congressman, health facility administrator; b. Oakland, Calif., Nov. 24, 1935; m. Leola Roscoe Higgs; 3 children. A.A., Oakland City Coll., 1958; B.A., San Francisco State Coll., 1960; M.S.W., U. Calif., 1962. Psychiat. social worker Calif. Dept. Mental Hygiene, 1962-64; program dir. Bayview Community Ctr., San Francisco, 1964-65; from assoc. dir. to dir. Hunters Point Youth Opportunity Ctr., 1965-66; planning cons. Bay Area Social Planning Coun., 1966-67; dir. concentrated employment program San Francisco Econ. Opportunity Coun., 1967-68; sr. cons. Social Dynamics, Inc., 1968-70; mem. 92nd-104th Congresses from 9th Calif. Dist., 1971-98; former chmn. house com. on D.C., former mem. permanent select com. on intelligence, chmn. house armed svcs. com., 1993; pres. Healthcare Internat. Mgmt., Washington, 1998—; lectr. San Francisco State Coll., U. Calif., Berkeley; mem. U.S. del. North Atlantic Assembly, ranking minority mem. Nat. Security Com.; former chmn. Congl. Black Caucus, Calif. Dem. Congl. Del. Author: Defense Sense: The Search For A Rational Military Policy, 1983. Mem. Berkeley City Coun., 1967-71. With USMCR, 1954-56. Democrat. Office: Healthcare Internat Mgmt 1825 I St NW Ste 400 Washington DC 20006-5415 also: 1301 Clay St Ste 1000N Oakland CA 94612-5233*

DELMAN, MICHAEL ROBERT, physician; b. N.Y.C., Oct. 28, 1942; s. Alex and Dorothy (Scher) D.; m. Joan Ellen Dubin, July 9, 1967; children: Keith Andrew, Danna Lee. BA, Alfred U., 1963; MD, N.Y. Med. Coll., 1968. Diplomate Am. Bd. Gastroenterology, Am. Bd. Quality Assurance and Utilization Rev. Physicians, Am. Bd. Internal Medicine. Intern N.Y. Med. Coll.-Met. Hosp. Ctr., 1968-69, resident in internal medicine, 1969-70, chief resident in internal medicine, 1970-71; resident in gastroenterology, 1971-72; fellow gastroenterology N.Y. Med. Coll.-Met. Hosp. Ctr., 1972-73; asst. clin. prof. medicine SUNY, Stony Brook, 1974—; chief chem. dependency svcs. Southside Hosp., Bay Shore, N.Y., 1989—, chmn. med. staff quality assurance, 1992-97, pres. med. staff, 1997-98, sr. v.p. for med. affairs, 1999—, chief dept. medicine, 1999—. Surgeon, vol. fireman East Islip (N.Y.) Fire Dept., 1978—. Recipient McAulay award East Islip Soccer Club, 1984, citation Town of Islip, 1992. Fellow ACP, Am. Coll. Gastroenterology; mem. Am. Gastroenterology Assn., Am. Soc. Addiction Medicine (cert.), Am. Soc. Gastrointestinal Endoscopy, N.Y. Acad. Gastroenterology, N.Y. State Med. Soc. Avocations: golf, fishing, reading, guitar, music. Office: East Islip Med Assocs 45 E Main St East Islip NY 11730-2502

DELMAR, EUGENE ANTHONY, architect; b. Gallitzin, Pa., June 8, 1928; s. Frank and Viola (Bocci) DiMaria; m. Bettie Hardin, Apr. 7, 1951; children: Diana, Daniel, David. B.Arch., Columbia U., 1954; M.Arch. in Urban Design, Catholic U. Am., 1971. Architect Ronald S. Senseman, FAIA, Washington, 1954-59; pres. Eugene A. Delmar, Silver Spring, Md., 1959-93, Delmar Architects, P.A., Olney, Md., 1993—; mem. vis. com. Sch. Architecture U. Md., 1975. Important works include Electrophysics Lab., Columbia, Md., Montgomery County Jud. Ctr., Natatorium, Washington, Charlotte Hall Vets. Retirement Home, Denton Courthouse/Multi-Svc. Ctr., Brooke Grove Elem. Sch., F. Douglass H.S., Springbrook H.S., Rocky Hill Mid. Sch., Blake H.S., Francis Scott Key Elem. Sch., Rockville Nursing Home, Treatment and Learning Ctr. Mem. code enforcement bd. Dept. Econ. and Community Devel. Md., 1973-76; mem. Montgomery County Beautification Com., 1965, Montgomery County Sign Rev. Bd., 1968-71; bd. dirs. Rockville Nursing Home. Served to 2d lt. C.E., U.S. Army, 1946-48. Recipient Disting. Service award U.S. Jaycees, 1964, E.B. Morris Disting. Service award, 1976. Fellow AIA (First award design 1966, award of merit for design Potomac Valley chpt. 1966, bd. dirs. Potomac Valley chpt. 1992-97; mem. Md. Soc. Architects (pres. 1972-73), Sigma Chi. Clubs: Silver Spring Lions (pres. 1978-79), Columbia University. Office: Delmar Architects PA 3411 Olandwood Ct Ste 205 Olney MD 20832-1488

DELMAR, MARIO, cardiac physiology educator; b. Mexico City, Feb. 26, 1958; came to U.S., 1983; s. Mario Raul and Maria Mercedes (Junco) D.; m. Susana Senties, Mar. 26, 1982; children: David, Andrea. MD, U. A. Metropolitana, Mexico City, 1980; PhD, CINVESTAV-IPN, Mexico City, 1986. Rsch. assoc. Inst. Nacional de Cardiologia, Mexico City, 1982-84; rsch. assoc. SUNY Health Sci. Ctr., Syracuse, 1983-86, rsch. asst. prof., 1986-88, asst. prof. pharmacology, 1988-93, assoc. prof., 1993-98, dir. pharmacology grad. program, 1991—; prof., 1998—. Contbr. articles to profl. jours., 10 pub. book chpts. Named finalist Young Investigator's award Interamerican Soc. Cardiology, 1985; recipient K.M. Rosen fellowship North Am. Soc. Pacing and Electrophysiology, 1987; finalist Louis N. Katz Basic Sci. Rsch. Prize for Young Investigator Am. Heart Assn., 1988, Pres.'s Rsch. award SUNY/Health Sci. Ctr., 1990. Mem. AAAS, Biophysical Soc., Am. Heart Assn. Achievements include determination of importance of membrane potassium channels in the modulation of cell excitability of cardiac cells; characterization of celular mechanisms responsible for cyclic activation failure of the heart (Wenckebach periodicity); research in role of cell-to-cell communication in the synchronization of electrical activity in the heart, molecular basis of intercellular communication in heart. Home: 4611 Dartmouth Cir Manlius NY 13104-2524 Office: SUNY Health Sci Ctr 766 Irving Ave Syracuse NY 13210-1602

DELMORO, RONALD ANTHONY, elementary school principal; b. N.Y.C., June 14, 1948; s. Alfred and Ann Delmoro; m. Denna Loeb Delmoro, Dec. 27, 1987; children: Nicole, Ronald, Daniel, Stephen. BA in History, Iona Coll., 1970; MS in Edn., New Paltz State U., 1972; profl. diploma, Fordham U., 1975. Elem. sch. tchr. Yorktown Sch., Yorktown Heights, N.Y., 1970-75, 76-80, secondary sch. tchr., 1975-76, pub. sch. adminstr., 1980—; adj. prof. Mercy Coll., Dobbs Ferry, N.Y., 1997—. Author: Handbook for Site Based Decision Making in Elementary Schools, 1990. Religion instr. St. Patrick's Ch., Yorktown, 1970-80; dir. teen ctr. Parks and Recreation, Yorktown, 1972-80, dir. men's football, 1982—. Mem. ASCD, Yorktown Adminstrs. and Supervisors (pres. 1989—), Nat. Assn. of Elem. and Secondary Sch. Prins. Roman Catholic. Avocations: research, sports, photography. Home: 2377 Rela Ln Yorktown Heights NY 10598 Office: Brookside Sch 2285 Broad St Yorktown Heights NY 10598

DELO, ELLEN SANDERSON, lawyer; b. Nassawadox, Va., Nov. 29, 1944; d. Robert G. and Daisy B. (Hitchens) Sanderson; m. Arthur C. Delo Jr., Mar. 20, 1971; 1 child, Marjorie Cotton Delo. BA, U. Richmond, 1966; JD, Rutgers U., 1977; LLM, NYU, 1985. Bar: N.J., 1977, U.S. Dist. Ct. N.J., 1977, U.S. Tax Ct., 1987, U.S. Ct. Appeals (2nd cir.) 1997, D.C. 1999. Law clk. to Hon. John J. Geronimo N.J. Superior Ct., 1977-78; assoc. Lamb Hutchinson Chappell Ryan & Hartung, Jersey City, 1978-80, Chasan Leyner Holland & Tarrant, Jersey City, 1980-84; assoc. Stryker Tams & Dill, Newark, 1985-92, ptnr., 1993-98; exec. compensation assoc. Bachelder Law Offices, N.Y.C., 1998—; lectr. on tax issues. Contbr. articles to profl. jours. Lay reader Summit Ridge Nursing and Rehab. Ctr., West Orange, N.J., Inglemoor Care Ctr., Livingston, N.J. Mem. ABA (tax sect., employee benefits com.). Democrat. Episcopalian. Avocation: animal welfare organizations and activities. Home: 340 Montrose Ave South Orange NJ 07079-2439

DE LOACH, BERNARD COLLINS, JR., retired physicist; b. Birmingham, Ala., Feb. 19, 1930; s. Bernard Collins and Ada Blanche (Moore) De L.; m. Annie Ruth Wilson, Aug. 24, 1951; children: Linda Louise, Bernard Collins III. BS in Physics, Auburn U., 1951, MS in Physics, 1952; PhD in Physics, Ohio State U., 1956. Mem. tech. staff AT&T Bell Labs., Holmdel, N.J., 1956-63; supr. AT&T Bell Labs., Murray Hill, N.J., 1963-66, dept. head, 1966-89, ret., 1989; courtesy prof. engrng. sci. U. Ctrl. Fla., Orlando, 1993—. Author tech. papers and lectures; patentee in field. Recipient Stuart Ballantine medal Franklin Soc., 1975. Fellow IEEE (David Sarnoff medal 1975, co-recipient Engrng. Excellence medal, 1993). Avocations: camping, jogging, guitar playing.

DELOACH, DANIEL, city clerk; b. Savannah, Ga., Aug. 20, 1948. BA, David Lipscomb Coll., Nashville, 1970; MA, U. So. Fla., 1972. Instr. Miami-Dade Cmty. Coll., Miami, Fla., 1973-74; adminstr. Atlantic Christian Schs., Miami, Fla., 1974-79; adminstrv. asst. to Mayor City of Hialeah, Fla., 1980, deputy city clerk, city clerk, 1987—. Mem. Dade City Municipal Clerks Assn. Office: City of Hialeah Office of the City Clerk 501 Palm Ave Rm 310 Hialeah FL 33010-4719*

DELOACH, (ELISE) DEBRA, critical care nurse, administrator; b. Miami, Fla., July 18, 1961; d. Hugh Frank and Elise Lind (Gardner) DeL.; m. Bruce Charles Fisher, Aug. 8, 1981 (div. 1985); children: Bruce Charles Jr., Taylor Elise; m. David Gray, Sept. 23, 1990; 1 child, Taylor Elise. BSN, Fla. Internat. U., North Miami, 1984. Cert. ACLS. Charge nurse surg. unit North Miami Med. Ctr., 1985-86, ICU-CCU nurse, 1987-89, nurse mgr. telemetry unit, 1989-90; nurse mgr. progressive care unit Parkway Regional Med. Ctr., Miami, 1990-91, mem. staff cardiac catherization lab., 1991-92, staff nurse oper. room and post anesthesia care unit, 1992-98; staff RN ICU Indian River Meml., Vero Beach, Fla., 1998—.

DELOACH, ROBERT EARL, II, civil and environmental engineer, consultant; b. Jacksonville, Fla., Nov. 18, 1937; s. Robert Earl Sr. and Wyolen Lavina (Sweat) DeL.; m. Patricia Ann Baird, Apr. 9, 1960 (div. Feb. 1974); 1 child, Alison Jeanne; m Charlene Elizabeth Kinney, Oct. 21, 1978; children: Kenneth Jefferson Wiggins, Christine Elizabeth. AA, U. Fla., 1962, B in Civil Engrng., 1965; M in Sanitary Engrng., Ga. Inst. Tech., 1968. mgmt. cons. City of Warner Robins (Ga.), 1986—.; lic. profl. land surveyor, Fla., Ga.; lic. profl. engr., Fla., Ga., Ala., Tenn. Pub. health engr. Ga. Water Quality Control Bd., Atlanta, 1965-66, water quality control engr., 1966-68, chief ops. sect., 1968-69; assoc. Flood & Assocs., Inc., Jacksonville, Fla., 1969-77; presdl. exch. exec. The White House, Washington, 1977-79; v.p. Flood Engrs. Architects Planners, Inc., Atlanta, 1979-80, sr. v.p., 1980-82; sr. v.p. Flood Engrs. Architects Planners, Inc., Macon, Ga., 1982-91, Flood Engrs., Inc., Macon, 1991-93; pres. DeLoach Engrng. Cons., Macon, 1993—; cons. City of Warner Robins, Ga., 1986-93. Officer Jacksonville Jaycees, 1969-77. Inducted in U. Fla. Hall of Fame, 1964. Mem. Am. Cons. Engrs. Coun., Fla. Blue Key, Delta SigmPhi (pres. Gainesville chpt. 1957-58). Democrat. Baptist. Home: 719 Forest Ridge Dr W Macon GA 31204-1511 Office: DeLoach Engrng Cons 148 State St PO Box 6116 Macon GA 31208-6116

DELOACH, ROBERT EDGAR, corporate executive; b. Daytona Beach, Fla., Jan. 6, 1939; s. Ollie Newman and Sally Gertrude (Schrowder) DeL. Student U. Alaska-Anchorage, 1967-69, Alaska Meth. U., 1970, Pacific Luth. U., 1972. Lic. elec. engr. and adminstr., Alaska, 1979; lic. pvt. pilot, real estate broker, ins. agt. Former chmn. bd. Alaska Stagecraft, Inc., Anchorage; pres. BG Systems Co., BG Tax & Acctg., Inc., The Electric Doctor, Inc., Apollo Travel, Inc.; former pres. Coastal Electronics, Inc.; former owner-mgr. Bargain Towne, Anchorage. Active Anchorage Community Theatre, Anchorage Theater Guild. Mem. Assn. Ind. Accts., Internat. Assn. Theatrical Stage Employees and Moving Picture Machine Operators U.S. (past pres. local 770), Ind. Elec. Contractors Assn., Internat. Assn. Elec. Insps. Home: 1207 W 47th Ave Anchorage AK 99503-6917

DELOACHE, WILLIAM REDDING, pediatrician; b. Camden, S.C., Mar. 27, 1920; s. William Redding and Louise Blakeney (Zemp) DeL.; m. Bond Davis, Sept. 7, 1943; children: Frances D., William Redding Jr. Student, Furman U., Greenville, S.C., 1937-38; BA, Vanderbilt U., 1941, MD, 1943. Diplomate Am. Bd. Pediatrics; lic. Tenn. Healing Arts.; cert. med. examiner, S.C. Intern pediatrics Vanderbilt Hosp., Nashville, 1944, resident pediatrics, 1947-48; resident pediatrics N.C. Bapt. Hosp., Bowman Gray, Winston-Salem, 1948-49; pvt. practice Greenville, S.C., 1949-53; ptnr. Christie Pediatric Group, Greenville, 1953-72; dir. nurseries Greenville Hosp. Sys., 1972-77, dir. med. edn., 1977-82; assoc. exec. dir. Am. Bd. Pediatrics, Chapel Hill, N.C., 1982-87; ofcl. examiner Am. Bd. Pediatrics, Chapel Hill, 1976-90; assoc.,sr. assoc. Greenville Meml. Hosp., Greenville Hosp. Sys., 1994-92; mem. pediatric staff St. Francis Hosp., Greenville, 1949-92; assoc. prof. pediatrics Med. U. S.C., 1973-87; mem. bd. Vanderbilt U. Med. Ctr., Nashville, 1985-91, mem. adv. bd., 1991—. Contbr. articles to profl. jours. Elder Fourth Presbyn. Ch., Greenville. Capt. U.S. Army, 1944-46. Mem. AMA, Am. Acad. Pediatrics (career achievement award S.C. chpt. 1987), Greenville County Med. Soc. (pres. 1971), S.C. Med. Assn., So. Soc. Pediatric Rsch., So. Perinatal Assn., Greenville C. of C. (bd. mem.), Rotary Club (mem. bd. 1976—), Greenville Country Club, Poinsett Club. Avocations: woodworking, gardening, travel, tennis. Home: 72 Round Pond Rd Greenville SC 29607-3717

DEL OLMO, FRANK, newspaper editor; b. L.A., May 18, 1948; s. Francisco and Margaret Rosalie (Mosqueda) D.; m. Karen Margaret King, Feb. 6, 1970 (div. Sept. 1982); 1 child, Valentina Marisol; m. Magdalena Beltran-Hernandez, Nov. 10, 1991; 1 child, Francisco Manuel. Student, UCLA, 1966-68; BS magna cum laude in Journalism, Calif. State U., Northridge, 1970. Reporter-intern L.A. Times, 1970-71, gen. assignment reporter, 1971-80, columnist, editorial bd., 1980-90, deputy editor, 1990-98, assoc. editor, 1998—; instr. Chicano Studies, Calif. State U., 1970-71; contbg. editor Race Relations Reporter, Nashville, 1973-75; on-air host, writer "Ahora" Sta. KCET-TV, L.A., 1974; chief writer, rschr. KNBC, 1975; bd. contbrs., freelance reporter Nuestro Mag., 1976-81; program co-dir. Summer Program Minority Journalists, 1990, faculty mem. 1979, vis. faculty mem. 1978, 80-83, 85, 89; vis. profl. Dow-Jones Newspaper Fund U. So. Calif. Sch. Journalism, 1975, bd. dirs. Numerous lectrs., presentations at colls., univs. Named Senior Faculty of Summer Program Minority Journalists Inst. Journalism Edn.; recipient Emmy award, 1976, Sigma Delta Chi Achievement award, 1982, Profl. Achievement award UCLA Alumni, 1990, Pulitzer Prize, 1984; Neiman fellowship Harvard U., 1987-88. Office: Los Angeles Times 202 W 1st St Los Angeles CA 90012-4105

DELONG, DAVID G., architect, urgan planner, educator. Bachelors, U. Kans.; M in Architecture, U. Pa., 1963; PhD in Arch. History, Columbia U., 1976. With Conklin & Rossant, N.Y.C.; restoration arch. Harvard-Cornell Archeol. Expedition, Sardis, Turkey, 1967-68; sr. designer, then assoc. John Carl Warnecke & Assocs., N.Y.C., 1969-74; prof., chair grad. program hist. preservation Columbia U., N.Y.C., U. Pa., Philadelphia, 1984—; bd. dirs. Frank Lloyd Wright Bldg. Conservancy, Phila. Hist. Preservation Corp., Nat. Coun. Preservation Edn.; dir. Preservation Alliance Greater Phila.; cons. in field. Author: Bruce Goff: Toward Absolute Architecture, Historic American Buildings: Texas, 2 vols., Calif., 4 vols., New York, 8 vols., The Architecture of Bruce Goff: Buildings and Projects, 1916-74; co-author: Frank Lloyd Wright: Designs for an American Landscape, Louis I. Kahn: In the Realm of Architecture (AIA Internat. Book award); editor: Working with Mr. Wright: What It Was Like, Wright in Hollywood: Visions of a New Architecture; co-editor: American Architecture: Innovation and Tradition. Fulbright fellow, 1967-68, Chettle Vis. fellow U. Sydney, 1992; vis. scholar Getty Ctr. History Art and Humanities, 1989. Mem. Soc. Arch. Historians (dir.). Office: U Pa Grad Program Hist Pres 115 Meyerson Hall Philadelphia PA 19104-6311

DELONG, DEBORAH, lawyer; b. Louisville, Sept. 5, 1950; d. Henry F. and Lois Jean (Stepp) D.; m. Michael A. Marrero, Jan. 12, 1981; children: Amelie DeLong, Samuel Prentice. B.A., Vanderbilt U., 1972; J.D., U. Cin., 1975. Bar: Ohio 1975, U.S. Dist. Ct. (so. dist.) Ohio 1975, U.S. Ct. Appeals (Fed. cir.) 1990, (11th cir.), 1995, U.S. Supreme Ct. 1982. Assoc. Paxton & Seasongood, Cin., 1975-82, ptnr., 1982-88; ptnr. Thompson, Hine & Flory, 1989—. Contbr. articles to profl. jours. Bd. dirs. Cin. Opera, People Working Cooperatively, Inc. Mem. ABA, Ohio State Bar Assn., Cin. Bar Assn., Arbitration Tribunal U.S. Dist. Ct., Ohio, 1984. Republican. Episcopalian. Office: Thompson Hine & Flory 312 Walnut St Ste 1400 Cincinnati OH 45202-4089*

DELONG, DONALD R., accountant; b. Muskegon, Mich., Sept. 3, 1946; m. Susan K. Jourden; children: Kristy, Andrew. BS in Acctg., Ferris State U., Big Rapids, Mich., 1968. CPA, Mich. Staff acct. Alexander Grant & Co., Muskegon, 1970-75; co-founder Brickley Delong, P.C., Muskegon, 1975—, mng. ptnr., pres., 1985—; co-owner, officer Raydon Lumber Co., Inc., Shoreline Group, Inc., Shoreline Land Co.; ptnr. KIMA Properties, Van Mill Square, Bluffton Bay Estates; mem. adv. bd. dirs. No. Boiler and Mech. Contractors, Inc., 1978—, J. Mollema & Sons, Inc., 1980—; mem. acctg. com. Mich. Dept. Edn., 1986—. Co-author: State of Michigan School Accounting Manual, 1989. Bd. dirs., pres. YMCA, Muskegon, 1991, bd. dirs. Camp Pendaleuan, 1993—; chmn. bd. trustees McGraft Ch., Muskegon, 1988-90. Mem. Mich. Assn. CPAs (state acctg. com. 1982-94). Avocations: boating, tennis, land investments, hunting. Office: Brickley Delong PC PO Box 999 500 Terrace Plz Muskegon MI 49443

DE LONG, JACOB EDWARD, real estate broker; b. Syracuse, N.Y., Oct. 5, 1939; s. Jacob Edward and Eva Ann (Sposato) D.; children: Edward Andrew, Michael Anthony, Sean Michael (dec.). Grad. high sch., Fayetteville, N.Y. Sales rep. Ill. Shade Div., Slick Airways, Chgo., 1963-67; dir. mktg. Bean Bros. Inc., Walton, N.Y., 1967-71; real estate sales Longley Jones Assoc., Syracuse, 1971-73, Radclif Real Estate, Syracuse, 1973-76; comml. real estate J. Edward De Long Real Estate, Syracuse, 1976-80, Eagan Real Estate Inc., Syracuse, 1980—; pres. bd. dir. The Andrew Nelson Self Help Ctr., Syracuse. Fund raiser, Friends of the Burnet Park 200, Syracuse, 1986. Sgt. USAF, 1957-62. Mem. N.Y. State Bd. Realtors, Onandaga Bd. Realtors, Onondaga Ski Club, Am. Legion, Rotary. Republican. Roman Catholic. Office: Eagan Real Estate Inc 1200 Mony Plz Tower 1 Syracuse NY 13202-2720

DELONG, JAMES CLIFFORD, air transportation executive; b. N.Y.C., Jan. 29, 1940; s. Mary (Oles) DeL.; m. Nancy L. Hill; children: Andrew Hill, Theodore James. BS, Colgate U.; MA, U. Calif. Asst. mgr. Wichita Midcontinent Airport, 1970, airport mgr., 1971-74; asst. mgr. Houston Inter-Continent Airport, 1975-77, airport mgr., 1980-85; airport mgr. Houston Hobby Airport, 1978-79; dep. dir. dept. aviation Houston Dept. Aviation, 1986-87; dir. aviation Phila. Divsn. Aviation, 1987-93, Denver Divsn. Aviation, 1993-98; gen. mgr. Reg. Airport Authority of Louisville and Jefferson County, Ky., 1998—. Bd. dirs. Phila. Conv. and Vis. Bur., 1992-93. Pilot, USAF, 1963-70. Mem. Am. Assn. Airport Execs. (bd. dirs. 1989), Internat. Civil Aviation Orgn. (helicopters panel 1985—), Airport Operators Internat. (bd. dirs. 1990, info. sys. com. 1988, chmn. tech. com. 1979), Airport Coun. Internat. (bd. dirs., chmn. 1996), Nat. Transp. Rsch. Bd. (exec. bd. dirs. 1992-95), Variety Club Internat. (bd. dirs. 1992-93). Avocations: classical guitar, restoration antique autos, motorcycling. Office: Louisville Intl Airport Regional Airport Authority PO Box 9129 Louisville KY 40209-0129*

DELONG, JANICE AYERS, education educator; b. Bedford, Va., May 8, 1943; d. Lloyd Edward and Minnie Hilda (Updike) Ayers; m. Elmer Mason Nance, Aug. 22, 1964 (dec. May 16, 1968); m. Robert Edward DeLong, Dec. 3, 1970; children: Michael Anthony, Tonya Lynne, Kara Susanne; 1 stepchild, Kimberly Beth. BA, Lynchburg Coll., 1965, MEd, 1970; MEd, Lynchburg Coll., 1987; postgrad., Shenandoah U., 1994. Tchr. Bedford (Va.) County Sch. System, 1965-68; social worker Dept. Social Svcs., Bedford, 1969-70; tchr. Longwood Ave. Christian Sch., Bedford, 1976-80, Timberlake Christian Sch., Lynchburg, Va., 1980-85; instr. Liberty U., Lynchburg, Va., 1985—; presentor at numerous reading and children's lit. workshops. Coauthor: Core Collection for Small Libraries, 1997. Mem. choir, nursery worker Lakewood Bapt. Ch., Lynchburg, 1990—. Mem. Internat. Reading Assn., Nat. Coun. Tchrs. English, Appalachian Tchrs. Network, Kappa Delta Pi (Golden Apple award 1990). Republican. Baptist.

DE LONG, KATHARINE, retired secondary education educator; b. Germantown, Pa., Aug. 31, 1927; d. Melvin Clinton and Katherine Frances (Brunner) Barr; m. Alfred Alvin De Long, June 21, 1947; children: Renée, Claudia, Jane. AA, Mesa Jr. Coll., Grand Junction, Colo., 1962; BA, Western State Coll., Gunnison, Colo., 1964; MA, Colo. State U., 1972. Camp dir. Kannah Creek Girl Scout Camp, 1960-64; tchr. Mesa County Valley Sch. Dist. #51, Grand Junction, 1964-84, dept. chmn., 1970-79; ret., 1984; tour coord., escort Mesa Travel, 1990—; substitute instr. Mesa State Coll., 1986-90; student council sponsor Mesa County Valley Sch., 1976-80; bd. dirs. Am. Red Cross, mem. disaster team, 1996—. Bd. dirs. Chipeta Girl Scout Coun., Grand Junction, 1960-66; pct. committeewoman Mesa County Dem. Party; mem., vice-chmn. Profl. Rights and Responsibilities Commn. for Dist. #51 Schs., Grand Junction, 1978-84; trustee Western Colo. Ctr. for the Arts, Grand Junction, 1987-88; mem. Mesa County Hist. Soc. Mem. AAUW (pres. local chpt. 1979-81, chmn. state cultural interest), AARP (Colo. legis. com. area I, asst. state dir., transp. task force, dist. dir. dist. 1, del. to nat. conv., dir. state conv. 1991), LWV (Grand Junction Area, sec. bd. dirs. 1995—), Pub. Employees Retirement Assn. (legis. adv. com. 1990-91), Colo. Ret. Sch. Employees Assn. (v.p.), Phi Theta Kappa. Congregationalist. Avocations: music, theatre, swimming, hiking, travel.

DELONG, LANCE ERIC, physics educator, researcher; b. Denver, Nov. 12, 1946; s. Robert Earl and Svea Virginia (Selander) DeL.; m. Michele Denise Arranaga, Dec. 30, 1977 (div. Mar. 1983); m. Mary Jane Gorham, Sept. 1983; children: Kristin Ann, Rebecca Jane, Eric Zachary, Tyler Gorham. BA, U. Colo., 1968; MS, U. Calif., San Diego, 1969, PhD, 1977. Asst. prof. physics U. Va., Charlottesville, 1977-79; asst. prof. U. Ky., Lexington, 1979-83, assoc. prof., 1983—; scientist-in-residence materials sci. and tech. div. Argonne (Ill.) Nat. Lab., 1985-86, faculty rsch. participant, 1986-89; mem. user group high-flux isotope reactor Oak Ridge (Tenn.) Nat. Lab., 1983—; rsch. assoc. Ames (Iowa) Lab., 1984—; expert div. materials rsch. NSF, Washington, 1988, program dir. low temperature physics, 1989. Co-editor procs. of Rare Earth Rsch. Confs., 1986, 88, 93, 96; contbr. over 95 articles to profl. jours. Recipient rsch. opportunity award Rsch. Corp., 1988; Cottrell rsch. grantee, 1983, rsch. grantee U.S. Dept. Energy, 1981-84, 88-89, 96—, NSF, 1991—. Mem. Am. Phys. Soc., Am. Assn. Physics Tchrs. Avocations: physical conditioning, soccer, rugby. Office: Physics and Astronomy Univ of Kentucky Lexington KY 40506-0055

DELONG, MARY ANN, educational administrator; b. Chester, Pa., July 11, 1944; d. Ann (Anthony) Fiduk; m. J. Thomas DeLong, Feb. 13, 1965. BS, West Chester U., 1966; MS, Kutztown U., 1970. Lic. mental health counselor, elem. tchr., adminstr., Fla. Tchr. Exeter Sch. Dist., Pa., 1966-68, Gov. Mifflin Sch. Dist., Shillington, Pa., 1968-71; guidance counselor Wilson Sch. Dist., West Lawn, Pa., 1971-73; guidance counselor Marion County Sch. Bd., Ocala, Fla., 1973-75, coordinator, testing, 1975-79, supr., guidance, testing and research, 1979—. Bd. dirs. Marion Citrus Mental Health Ctr., Ocala, 1982-88, pres. 1987; treas. Marion County Child Advocacy Coalition, 1996-97; chairperson Fla. Statewide Assessment Adv. Com., 1984-85; mem. Fla. Writing Assessment Adv. Com., 1990-93; active Fla. Task Force Counselor Supervision, 1981-83; pres. Beta Phi chpt. Epsilon Sigma Alpha, Ocala, 1981-82, 91-92. Named Educator of Yr., Mental Health Assn. Marion County 1984, Adminstr. of Yr., hon. mention award Fla. Sch. Counselors Assn. 1984. Mem. Fla. Assn. Counselor Educators and Suprs., Fla. Assn. Test Adminstrs. (bd. dirs.), Fla. Ednl. Research Assn. (bd. dirs., membership chmn.), Am. Assn. Suprs. and Adminstrs, Altrusa Internat. Avocations: waterskiing; boating; reading; cats. Home: 311 SE 54th Ct Ocala FL 34471-3464 Office: Marion County Sch Bd PO Box 670 Ocala FL 34478-0670

DE LOOPER, WILLEM JOHAN, artist, museum curator; b. The Hague, Netherlands, Oct. 30, 1932; came to U.S., 1950; s. Henri Bastiaan and Wilhelmina Johanna (Huizinga) De L.; m. Frauke Weber, Feb. 14, 1969. B.A., Am. U., 1957. Mem. staff Phillips Collection, Washington, 1959-72; asst. curator Phillips Collection, 1972-74, assoc. curator, 1974—, curator, 1982-87, cons. curator, 1987-95. Represented in permanent collections Nat. Gallery of Art, Hirshhorn Collection and Sculpture Garden, Fed. Res. Bank, Richmond, Va., NSF, Phillips Collection, Corcoran Gallery Art; one-man shows include Jefferson Place Gallery, 1966-74, Phillips Collection, Washington, 1975, 95-96, Protech-McIntosh Gallery, 1975-80, R.R. Kornblatt Gallery, Washington, 1983, 85, 87, 89; group exhbns. include Group Seven, Washington Gallery Modern Art, 1968, Washington 20 Years, Balt. Mus. Art, 1970, Art Now, Kennedy Ctr., Washington, 1974, Golden Door—Artists Immigrants of Am. 1987-1976, Hirshhorn Mus. and Sculpture Garden, 1977, NAS, 1997, Galerie L., Hamburg, West Germany, 1979, retrospective, No. Va. C.C., 1975, Fed. Res. Bd., Washington, 1978, Tilghman Gallery, Boca Raton, Fla., 1986; Shippee Gallery, N.Y.C., 1988, Jones-Troyer-Fitzpatrick Gallery, Washington, 1989-90, 92, 95, Atrium Gallery, Washington, 1989-90, 92, 95, Atrium Gallery, St. Louis, 1990, 92, 95, 98, A Retrospective Exhbn. 1966-1996, U.Md., College Park, 1996. Panelist D.C. Commn. on Arts and Humanities, Washington, 1986-87. Served with U.S. Army, 1957-59.

DE LORCA, LUIS E., educational administrator, educator, speaker; b. L.A., Oct. 18, 1959; s. Patricia Jean Clougher Harvey. AA, Rio Hondo Jr. Coll., Whittier, Calif., 1983; BA, Calif. State Poly. U., 1989; MA in Humanities, Calif. State U., Dominguez Hills, 1997; tchg. credential, Nat. U., 1997; adminstrv. credential, U. So. Calif., 1998. Football coach various high schs., So. Calif., 1980; pub. rels. dir. Calif. Poly Pomona Music Dept., 1987-89; pres. Exclusive Concepts, L.A., 1987-89; lifeguard L.A. City Recreation Dept., 1980-87; tchr. English Cathedral H.S., L.A., 1989-90; tchr., rsch. specialist Whittier (Calif.) Union H.S., 1990; founder, dir. The Learning Advantage Ctr., Whittier, 1991—; elem. tchr. St. Paul of the Cross Sch., La Mirada, Calif., 1993-95; CEO New Ednl. Wave Inc., Whittier, 1994—; tchr. L.A. County Office Edn., 1995-98; asst. prin. Bassett Unified Sch. Dist., 1998—. Active Big Bros. of Am., Fair Housing, Greenpeace. Mem. Whittier C. of C., Cousteau Soc. Democrat. Avocations: scuba, martial arts, swimming, handball, skiing. Home: # 102 16040 Leffingwell Rd Apt 102 Whittier CA 90603-3139

DELORENZO, DAVID A., food products executive; b. 1947. Colgate U.; MBA, U. Pa. With Dole Food Co., Inc., Thousand Oaks, Calif., 1970—, exec. v.p., 1990-91, 93—, pres., 1991-93; pres. Dole Food Co., Internat., 1993—. Office: Dole Food Co Inc 31365 Oak Crest Dr Westlake Village CA 91361-4633

DELORENZO, DAVID JOSEPH, retired public relations executive; b. Auburn, N.Y., Nov. 25, 1932; s. Joseph Robert and Marie (Hahn) DeL.; m. Margaret Mae Pinckney, July 21, 1956; children: David William, Mary Beth DeLorenzo Waldo. Student public schs., Auburn. With lab. Gen. Electric Co., Auburn, 1951, 54-57; asst. bur. chief Elmira Star Gazette, 1957-58; bur. chief Syracuse (N.Y.) Post Standard, 1958-66; polit. writer, city hall reporter Auburn Citizen-Advertiser, 1966-71, asst. sports editor, 1971-77; editor Bowling mag. Am. Bowling Congress, Greendale, Wis., 1977-81; asst. mgr. pub. relations dept. Bowling mag. Am. Bowling Congress, 1981-82, mgr. pub. relations dept., 1982-96; ret. Sports chmn. Cayuga County (N.Y.) March of Dimes, 1965-77. Served with USCG, 1951-54. Recipient writing awards including 5 1st place awards Cayuga County Fire-Police Assn., 1960-65; Journalism award Auburn Police Benevolent Assn., 1974; First place writing award Profl. Bowlers Assn., 1982; Bowling Mag. writing awards. Mem. Bowling Writers Assn. Am. (pres. 1974-75, meritorious service award 1976, exec. dir. 1997-98), Mid-Am. Bowling Writers (pres. 1986-88), Nat. Sportscasters and Sportswriters Assn. Democrat. Roman Catholic. Home: 175 55th Ave #205 Saint Pete Beach FL 33706 *Fortunate most aptly describes my life. With little background, I first was accepted as a newspaperman which led to being editor of a national publication and eventually to my former position of public relations manager of the world's largest sports membership organization. I sincerely appreciate the confidence so many others had in me through the years.*

DELORENZO, DAVID W. J., human resources manager, health consultant; b. Auburn, N.Y., Jan. 15, 1957; s. David J. and Margaret M. (Pinckney) DeL.; m. Lori DeLorenzo, June 5, 1981 (div. Mar. 1996); 1 child, David C. AAS, Cayuga County C.C., Auburn, 1978; student, Niagara U.; diploma in environ. health/battlefield, flight nurse, Brooks AFB Sch. Aerospace Med., San Antonio. Cert. occupl. hearing conservationist, EMT-D, ACLS, BLS and first aid instr.; cert. hazardous material tech., spirometry NIOSH; bd. cert. occupl. health nurse specialist Am. Bd. Occupl. Health Nurses; FAA lic. pvt. pilot. RN, trauma ICU S.U.H. Upstate Med. Ctr., Syracuse, N.Y.; RN ICU Niagara Falls (N.Y.) Meml. Med. Ctr.; RN, surgical ICU VA Med. Ctr., Buffalo, N.Y.; mgr. human resources, Worldwide Midrange Engrg. health cons. Cummins Engrng. Co., Inc., Columbus, Ind. Active Jamestown Area Safety Coun., Chautauqua County Health Coalition. Maj. USAFR. Decorated Meritorious Svc. medal, Air Force Commendation medal for nursing mgmt., 1st Oak Leaf Cluster, Nat. Def. medal, Armed Forces Res. medal, USAF Suggestion award, Armed Forces Volunteerism medal; Andrew Murphy Meml. scholar, Flight Nurse Honor Grad. scholar. Mem. Soc. Human Resource Mgmt., Am. Occupl. Health Nurses, N.Y. State Assn. Occupl. Health Nurses, Northeastern Assn.

Occupl. Health Nurses, Res. Officers Assn. (life mem.). Home: 3597 Cardinal Ln Columbus IN 47203-4506

DE LORENZO, WILLIAM E., foreign language educator. BA in Spanish and Speech, Montclair State U., MA in Speech and Drama; PhD in Fgn. Lang. Edn. and Tchr. Edn., Ohio State U. Tchr. Spanish various locations, N.J.; asst. prof. Spanish, Montclair State Coll.; assoc. prof., coord. fgn. lang./2d lang. edn. U. Md., College Park; organizer, co-dir. symposium for fgn. lang. tchr. candidates. Mem. Am. Coun. on Tchg. Fgn. Langs. (charter, Florence Steiner award 1992). Office: U Md Dept Curriculum-Instrn Rm 2311 Harold Benjamin Bldg College Park MD 20742*

DELOREY, JOHN ALFRED, printing company executive; b. Malden, Mass., July 13, 1924; s. John Alfred and Alice Gertrude (Collins) D.; m. Ann M. Abbott, Dec. 27, 1952; children—Debra Ann, Michael John, David Abbott. BS in Econs., Boston Coll., 1950; MBA, Harvard U., 1953. Plant mgr. Container Corp. Am., Renton, Wash., 1965-69; mgf. mgr. Container Corp. Am., Carol Stream, Ill., 1969-73; gen. mgr. Container Corp. Am., St. Louis, 1973-77, Carol Stream, 1977-81; v.p., divsn. gen. mgr. Container Corp. Am., St. Louis, 1981-82; exec. v.p. W.F. Hall Printing Co., Chgo., 1982-87; v.p. Container Corp. Am., 1987-93; pres. DeLorey & Assocs., Oak Brook, Ill., 1993—; dir. Container Corp. Am. Polit. Action Com., Chgo., 1981-86. Author: (with others) Consumer Packaging, 1953. Served to maj. USAF, 1942-53, ETO. Decorated DFC, Air medal with 3 oak leaf clusters, European Theater medal with 3 battle stars. Mem. Paperboard Packaging Assn. (dir. midwest region 1977-81). Republican. Roman Catholic. Clubs: Butterfield Country, Harvard Bus. Avocations: golf; swimming; skiing; bridge; reading. Home and Office: DeLorey & Assocs 194 Briarwood Loop Oak Brook IL 60523-8714

DELOUISE, TIA CAPUTI, university executive; b. Jersey City, Sept. 13, 1949; d. Lawrence and Mildred (De Riso) Caputi; m. Patrick Anthony DeLouise, Nov. 5, 1983. BA, Montclair State U., 1971; MA, NYU, 1983. Tchr. bus. edn. Berkeley Sch., White Plains, N.Y., 1976-81; dept. chair bus. edn. Berkeley Sch., West Paterson, N.J., 1981-86; acad. dean Berkeley Sch., Woodbridge, N.J., 1986-87; v.p., dean Berkeley Coll., N.Y.C., 1987-93; v.p. acad. support svcs. Berkeley Coll., West Paterson, 1993-94, sr. v.p. academics, 1994-98, v.p., registrar, 1998—. Recipient Outstanding Tchr. award Assn. Ind. Colls., 1985. Mem. Am. Assn. Collegiate Registrars and Admissions Officers, Nat. Bus. Edn. Assn., N.J. Bus. Edn. Assn. (exec. bd. 1985-86), Ea. Bus. Edn. Assn., Am. Mgmt. Assn., Phi Delta Kappa. Home: 154 Eagle St North Arlington NJ 07031-5819 Office: Berkeley Coll 44 Rifle Camp Rd West Paterson NJ 07424-3353

DELOYHT-ARENDT, MARY I., artist; b. Independence, Mo., Mar. 10, 1927; d. Frank Howard and Edith Isobel Strickland; m. William Joseph Arendt; children: Tracey McKee, Tammy Strnatka. AA, Columbia Coll., 1946; BA in Fine Arts, U. Mo., 1949. Group exhibits include Brea Art Ctr., Conejo Valley Mus., San Bernardino County Mus., West Bend Gallery, Western Colo. Ctr., Grady Gammage Auditorium, Ariz. State U., Tex. U., San Antonio, Goddard Art Ctr., Ardmore, Okla., Waldorf Astoria, N.Y.C., Utah State U., Gonzaga U., Ad Gallery, Spokane, The Casino, Avalon, Calif.; represented in pvt. collections Valley Nat. Bank, Empire Machinery, Giant Industries, First Interstate Bank, Thunderbird Bank, Ariz. Biltmore, Marriott Camelback Inn, GalleyA., Taos, N.Mex., S.R. Brennen, Carmel, Calif. and Scottsdale, Ariz., Scotchmist Gallery, Tucson, Courtyard Gallery, New Buffalo, Mich. Mem. Nat. Watercolor Soc. (signature), Ariz. Watercolor Soc. (Royal mem.), Ariz. Artists Guild, Plein Air Painters Am., 22x30 Profl. Critique Group.

DELOZIER, MAYNARD WAYNE, marketing educator; b. Newport News, Va., Apr. 21, 1945; s. Raymond Leo and Jean (Burton) D. PhD, U. N.C., 1971. Lectr., U. N.C.-Greensboro, 1969-70; asst. prof. Va. Poly. Inst. and State U., 1970-71; asst. prof. Wright State U., 1971-73; assoc. prof. U. S.C., Columbia, 1976-87; disting prof. mktg. Nicholls State U., 1987—. Mem. Am. Mktg. Assn., Acad. Mktg. Sci. (gov.), Am. Acad. Advt., So. Mktg. Assn., Southwestern Mktg. Assn. Author: The Marketing Communications Process, 1976, Consumer Behavior Dynamics, 1977, Experimental Learning Exercises in Marketing, 1977, Marketing Management, 1978, Retailing, 1982, Retailing Casebook, 1982, Retailing Workbook, 1982, Promotion Management and Marketing Communications, 1986, Retailing: Principles and Practices, 1986, Retailing: Principles and Practices (with instructors textbank and discussion question manual), 1986, Study Guide to Retailing: Principles and Practices, 1986, Retailing Principles and Practices 3rd edit. (instructors textbank and discussion question manual), 1989, Study Guide to Retailing: Principles and Practices, 1989. Home: 302 Marcello Blvd Thibodaux LA 70301-6922 Office: Coll Bus Adminstrn Nicholls State U Thibodaux LA 70310

DELP, R. LEE, meat packing company executive. CEO Moyer Packing, Souderton, Pa. Office: Moyer Packing PO Box 395 Souderton PA 18964-0395*

DELP, WILBUR CHARLES, JR., lawyer; b. Cedar Rapids, Iowa, Oct. 26, 1934; s. Wilbur Charles and Irene Frances (Flynn) D.; m. Patricia Lynn Vesely, June 22, 1963; children: Marci Lynn, Melissa Kathryn, Derek Charles. B.A., Coe Coll., 1956; LL.B., NYU, 1959. Bar: Ill. 1960, U.S. Supreme Ct. 1962. Assoc. Sidley & Austin, Chgo., 1959-68, ptnr., 1968—; lectr. securities law seminars. With USAF, 1959-65. Mem. ABA (securities com.), Chgo. Bar Assn., Law Club (Chgo.), Legal Club (Chgo.), Mid-Day Club (Chgo.), Phi Beta Kappa, Phi Kappa Phi. Home: PO Box 97 Wayne IL 60184-0097 Office: Sidley & Austin 1 First Natl Plz Chicago IL 60603-2003

DEL PAPA, FRANKIE SUE, state attorney general; b. 1949. BA, U. Nev.; JD, George Washington U., 1974. Bar: Nev. 1974. Staff asst. U.S. Senator Alan Bible, Washington, 1971-74; assoc. Law Office of Leslie B. Grey, Reno, Nev., 1975-78; legis. asst. to U.S. Senator Howard Cannon, Washington, 1978-79; ptnr. Thornton & Del Papa, 1979-84; pvt. practice Reno, 1984-87; sec. of state State of Nev., Carson City, 1987-91; atty. gen. State of Nev., 1991—. Mem. Sierra Arts Found. (bd. dirs.), Trust for Pub. Land (adv. com.), Nev. Women's Fund. Democrat. Office: Office of Atty Gen Capitol Complex 100 N Carson St Carson City NV 89701-4717*

DELPASSAND, EBRAHIM SEYED, pathologist, nuclear medicine physician; b. Ghasvin, Iran, Feb. 4, 1957; s. Ahmad Seyed Delpassand and Soghra U. Akbari; m. Azar Imani, Feb. 12, 1978; children: Nahal, Ayda, Alia. MD, Tehran (Iran) U., 1982. Diplomate Am. Bd. Nuclear Medicine. Intern Tehran U. Hosp., 1981-82; resident in anatomical and clin. pathology Baylor Coll. Medicine, 1986-88, 90-91, resident in nuclear medicine, 1988-90; physician-in-chrage Vahdati AFB, Iran, 1983-85; clin. instr. in radiology Baylor Coll. Medicine, 1990, asst. prof. pathology, 1991-98; asst. prof. nuclear medicine and pathology U. Tex. M.D. Anderson Cancer Ctr., Houston, 1992—, assoc. prof. nuclear medicine, 1998—; mem. radiation safety com. Ben Taub Gen. Hosp., Houston, 1990. Contbr. articles to profl. jours. Grantee Moran Found., Houston, 1989-90. Fellow Am. Coll. Nuclear Medicine; mem. AMA, Am. Assn. Nuc. Cardiology, Am. Coll. Nuc. Medicine (nuc. medicine instrumentation com. 1989), Am. Coll. Nuc. Physicians, Coll. Am. Pathologists, Soc. Nuc. Medicine (cardiovasc. and brain coun. 1989), Soc. of Iranian-Am. Health Care Profls. Tex. (pres. 1998—), Harris County Med. Soc. Office: U Tex MD Anderson Cancer Ctr 1515 Holcombe Blvd Houston TX 77030-4009

DEL PESCO, SUSAN MARIE CARR, state judge; b. Long Beach, Calif., May 20, 1946; d. Clarence Monroe and Leona (Goings) Carr; m. Thomas W. Del Pesco, Aug. 28, 1965; children: Joseph Thomas, Nicholas Paul. Student, UCLA, 1963-65; BA, U. Calif., Santa Barbara, 1967; JD, Widener U., 1975. Bar: Del. 1975, U.S. Dist. Ct. Del. 1975, U.S. Ct. Appeals (3d cir.) 1982. Assoc. Schnee & Castle, Wilmington, Del., 1976-81; dir. Prickett, Jones, Elliott, Kristol & Schnee, Wilmington, 1981-88; assoc. judge Del. Superior Ct., Wilmington, 1988—; mem. Del. Supreme Ct. Bd. on Profl. Responsibility, 1979-86, Permanent Lawyers Adv. Com. for U.S. Dist. Ct. Del., 1985-88. Bd. dirs. Del. Theatre Co., 1987-92, pres., 1990; co-chair Del. Gender Fairness Task Force, 1993-95. Recipient Outstanding Alumnae award Del. Law Sch., 1987, She Knows Where She's Going Girls' Clubs award, 1989. Mem. Del. State Bar Assn. (treas. 1978-79, v.p. New Castle 1984-85, v.p. at large 1985-86, pres.-elect 1986-87, pres. 1987-88, exec. com. jud. mem. 1997-98, Women's Leadership award 1996), Phi Delta Phi. Republican. Office: Daniel L Herrmann Courthouse 1020 N King St Wilmington DE 19801-3349

DELPESCO THORNTON, NANCY ROSE, artist, educator; b. Bklyn., May 2, 1939; d. Alphone Joseph and Margery Dora (Thompson) Bolduc; m. Andrew Del Pesco, Aug. 8, 1959 (div. July 1966); children: Belinda, Robin, Todd (dec.), Nancy, James; m. Stephen Wayne Thornton, Mar. 16, 1990. Owner, operator Lindenmuth Gallery, Rockport, 1973-76, DelPesco Needlepoint Design, Rockport, Mass., 1975-76, Workingman's Gallery, Santa Barbara, Calif., 1977-79, retail lingerie store and women's home party bus., Santa Barbara, 1980-83, Women's Painting Co., Santa Barbara, 1983-89; owner, operator DelPesco Fine Arts, Santa Barbara, Wash., California, 1989-97, Fernandina Beach, Fla., 1997—; demonstrating artist Ritz Carlton Hotel, Amelia Island, Fla., 1998—; owner AdLib Greetings/art cards storefront, Fernandina Beach, 1997—. Author: (children's books) Over the Garden Wall, 1997, It's OK to be Different, 1997, Best Buddies, 1998; contbr. art to Best of Acrylics by the Rockport Publishers, 1996. Tchr. art mental hosp., Essex, Mass., 1974-75, city jail, Essex, 1974-75; counselor Battered Women's Ctr., Santa Barbara, 1979-80. Mem. Valley Artists Guild (treas. 1994-95, pres. 1995-96, Gold medal 1994, Best of Show 1995), Valley Watercolor Soc. (exhibit chmn. 1995-96, sec. 1996-97, Best of Show 1996). Avocations: dancing, walking, reading, helping others. E-mail: nancy@art-cardsplus.com. Home: 1416 S 14th St Fernandina Beach FL 32034-3047 Studio: DelPesco Fine Arts 1241 S 8th St Fernandina Beach FL 32034

DELPH, DONNA JEAN (MAROC), education educator, consultant, university administrator; b. Hammond, Ind., Mar. 7, 1931; d. Edward Joseph and Beatrice Catherine (Ethier) Maroc; m. Billy Keith Delph, May 30, 1953 (div. 1967); 1 child, James Eric. BS, Ball State U., 1953, MA, 1963, EdD, 1970. Cert. in ednl. adminstrn./supervision, reading specialist, Ind.; cert. elem. sch. tchr., Ind., Calif. Elem. tchr. Long Beach (Calif.) Community Schs., 1953-54; elem. tchr., reading specialist, asst. dir. elem. edn. Hammond Pub. Schs., 1954-70; prof. edn. Purdue U. Calumet, Hammond, 1970-84, 88-90, prof. emeritus, 1990—, head dept. edn., dir. tchr. edn., 1984-88; cons. pub. schs., Highland, Ind., 1970-88, Gary, Ind., 1983-88, East Chicago, Ind., 1987-88, Hammond, 1970-88; speaker/workshop presenter numerous profl. orgns., Hammond, 1964—; mem. exec. coun. Nat. Coun. Accreditation Tchr. Edn., 1991-97. Author: (with others) Individualized Reading, 1967; contbr. articles, monographs to profl. jours. Bd. dirs. Bethany Child Care and Devel. Ctr., Hammond, 1972-77. Recipient Outstanding Teaching award Purdue U. Calumet, 1981. Mem. Assn. Tchr. Educators, Assn. for Supervision and Curriculum Devel. (rev. coun. 1987-91, bd. dirs. 1974-85), Internat. Reading Assn., Ind. Reading Profs. (pres. 1985-86), Pi Lambda Theta. Office: Purdue Univ Calumet Dept Education Hammond IN 46323

DEL PRADO, SERGIO, professional soccer team executive; b. Havana, Cuba; came to U.S., 1962; m. Leslie; children: Monica, Eric. BS in Bus. Adminstrn., Calif. State U., Long Beach. Formerly with L.A. Kings/Nat. Hockey League, dir. mktg., corp. acct. mgr., 1997-92, Hispanic broadcast mgr., 1992-94, corp. account mgr., dir. mktg.; gen. mgr. L.A. Galaxy, 1999—. Office: care LA Galaxy 1010 Rose Bowl Dr Pasadena CA 90025*

DEL RASO, JOSEPH VINCENT, lawyer; b. Phila., Dec. 21, 1952; s. Vincent and Dolores Ann (D'Adamo) Del R.; m. Anne Marie McGloin, Apr. 17, 1982; children: Joseph Vincent Jr., Katherine Anne, Marianna. BS in Acctg., Villanova U., 1974, JD, 1983. Bar: Pa., 1983, Fla. 1988. Exec. v.p. Belgrade Constrn., Inc., Wayne, Pa., 1974-80; atty. SEC, Washington, 1983-85; assoc. Dechert, Price & Rhoads, Washington, 1986-88; ptnr. Holland & Knight, Ft. Lauderdale, Fla., 1988-92, Stradley, Ronon, Stevens & Young, Phila., 1992-98, Pepper Hamilton LLP, Phila., 1998—; bd. dirs. Nat. Italian-Am. Found., Belgrade Constrn., Inc., Telespectrum Worldwide, Inc. Co-editor-in-chief Villanova Jour. Law and Investment Mgmt. Bd. consultors Villanova U. Sch. Law. Mem. Broward County Bar Assn., ABA, Villanova U. Alumni Assn. (class agt. 1974—), Union League Phila., Aronimink Golf Club. Republican. Roman Catholic. Office: Pepper Hamilton LLP 18th & Arch Sts 3000 Two Logan Sq Philadelphia PA 19103

DEL ROSARIO, MARIANO BORAS, JR., artist; b. Naga, The Philippines, Nov. 20, 1955; came to U.S., 1981; s. Mariano Platon Sr. and Rosita (Boras) Del R.; m. Amy Meredith Solomon, Oct. 18, 1991. BFA, U. The Philippines, 1978; MFA, Md. Inst. Coll. of Art, 1983. Instr. Art Students League of N.Y. One-person shows include The Cultural Ctr. of Philippines, 1981, Soho Ctr. Visua Artists, N.Y.C., 1988, OK Harris Gallery, N.Y.C., 1988, 91, 93, 96, 98, West Galle ry, Metro-Manila, The Philippines, 1996; exhibited in mus. shows at Mus. Philippine Art, Manila, 1980, Balt. Mus. Art, 1983, Queens Mus. Art, N.Y., 1987, 89, Bronx Mus. Arts, N.Y., 1989, Butler Inst. Am. Art, Youngstown, Ohio, 1995, Cultural Ctr. Philippines, Manila, 1997; exhibited in group shows at Asian Pacific Am. Studies Inst. Gallery, NYU, 1999, Rotunda Gallery, Bklyn., 1999. Fellow Glassell Sch. Art, 1983-84, Asian Cultural Coun., 1996-97; grantee Pollock-Krasner Meml. Found., 1989-90; recipient Thirteen Artists award Cultural Ctr. The Philippines, 1978, BCAT/Rotunda GAllery Artist Residency, Bklyn., 1999. Home: 175 Willoughby St Apt 12L Brooklyn NY 11201

DEL ROSARIO, REMEDIOS K., commissioner water department Atlanta. BS in Chemistry, Far Eastern U., Manila, The Philippines; MPA, U. Mich. Coll. instr. Far Eastern U., Manila, The Philippines, 1964-74; jr. asst. water systems chemist Detroit Water and Sewage Dept., 1974-77, sr. chemist, 1977-78, asst. sewage plant lab. supr., 1978-81, supr. sewage plant lab., 1981-86, asst. chief wastewater treatment plant, 1986-89, asst. dir. water supply ops., 1989-93; commr. dept. water City of Atlanta, 1993—. Mem. LWV, Nat. Assn. Environ. Profls., Inst. Hazardous Materials Mgmt., Philippine Tech. Soc. Mich. (immediate past pres., bd. dirs.), Ga. Water and Pollution Control Soc., Leadership Detroit Alumni Assn. Office: City of Atlanta Water Dept Ste 5700 55 Trinity Ave SW Atlanta GA 30335*

DEL ROSARIO, ROSE MARIE, clinical sociologist, educator, consultant; b. Manila, July 20, 1946; d. Vernon Roger and Justina (Lopez) Lemme; married (div. 1989); children: Marjorie Lou Iannella, Tina Marie Bidney. BS in Sociology, Ariz. State U., 1974, MA, 1978, PhD, 1987. Info. specialist U.S. Women's Army Corps, Anniston, Ala., 1966-68; edn. counselor U.S. Armed Forces Edn. Ctr., Clayton, Panama Canal Zone, 1971-73; rsch. codir. cmty. needs assessment projects Mesa City Coun., Ariz., 1976-77; instr. U. Phoenix, 1977-78, 81-82; dir. comprehensive manpower ctr. Phoenix Urban League, 1978-82; field underwriter N.Y. Life Inst. Co., Scottsdale, Ariz., 1983-84; instr., grad. assoc. dept. sociology Ariz. State U., Tempe, 1984-87; program assoc., nat. coord. The Nat. Conf. of Christians and Jews, Inc., 1987-91; dir. office of coop. edn. Our Lady of the Lake U., San Antonio, 1991-94; sr. edn. cons. Advanced Edn. Models and Assocs., San Antonio, 1991-94; pres. Genesis Network, Inc., 1994-99; ednl. specialist Appalachia Edn. Lab., Inc., Arlington, Va., 1999—; instr. dept. sociology Palo Alto Coll. and San Antonio Coll., 1992-94; adj. asst. prof. Dental Diagnostic Ctr., U. Tex. Health Sci. Ctr., San Antonio, 1992-95; mem. resource devel. com. Internat. Folk Culture Ctr., 1992-94; mentor undergrad. and grad. students Sociologists' AIDS Network, Am. Sociol. Assn., 1992—; adj. asst. prof. sociology dept. U. Miami, Fla., Coral Gables, 1995—; vis. scholar Postdoctoral Programs in Geriatrics, Washington, 1993; rschr. HIV/AIDS, U. Mich., Ann Arbor, 1994. Contbr. numerous reports and articles to profl. publs. Mem. Pres.'s Coun. of the Filipino Club of Ariz., 1982-89; alumna Valley Leadership Program for Phoenix Met. Area, 1981—; dir., choreographer Philippine Performing Arts of Ariz., 1976-84; pres. Filipino club of Ariz., 1982, 84; asst. dir. Southeastern Desegregation Assistance Ctr., Miami, 1996-97. Fellow Am. Sociol. Assn., Doctoral Minority Fellowship Program, 1986-87, Presdl. Svc. award Filipino Club of Ariz., 1982, 84, Humanitarian award Ariz. Affiliate of the League of United Latin Am. Countries, 1982, Spl. Svc. Recognition award Filipino Club of Ariz., 1981; grantee in field. Mem. AAUP, Am. Sociol. Assn., Coop. Edn. Assn., Nat. Assn. for Asian & Pacific Am. Educators, Soc. for Women in Sociology, Sociologists' AIDS Network, Tex. Coop. Edn. Assn., Alpha Kappa Delta, Phi Kappa Phi. Democrat. Avocations: profl. Philippine folk dancing.

DEL RUSSO, ALESSANDRA LUINI, law educator; b. Milan, Italy, Jan. 2, 1916; d. Avvocato Umberto and Candita (Recio) Luini; m. Carl R. del Russo, Apr. 12, 1947; children: Carl Luini, Alexander David. PhD in History with honors, Royal U., Milan, 1939; SJD summa cum laude, Royal U., Pavia, Italy, 1943; LLM in Comparative Law, George Washington U., Washington, 1949. Bar: Md. 1956, Md. Ct. Appeals, Ct. of Appeals (Milano) 1947, U.S. Ct. Appeals (D.C. cir.) 1950, U.S. Supreme Ct. 1955. Legal adviser Allied Mil. Govt. and Ct., Milan, 1945-46, U.S. Consulate Gen., Milan, 1946-47; pvt. practice Washington, Bethesda, Md., 1950-58; atty. adviser Legis. Ref. Libr. of Congress, Washington, 1958-59; atty. U.S. Commn. on Civil Rights, Washington, 1959-61; prof. Howard U. Sch. Law, Washington, 1961-81, dir. grad. program, 1972-74; prof. emerita Howard U. Sch. Law, 1981—; adj. prof. Stetson U. Coll. Law, St. Petersburg, Fla., 1980-95, adj. prof. emerita, 1995—; professorial lectr. George Washington U. Law Ctr., 1970-80; mem. legal cons. com. U.S. Commn. on Status of P.R., Washington, 1965-66; lectr. in field. Author: International Protection of Human Rights, 1971; editor and chmn. of symposium on International Law of Human Rights, Howard U. Sch. of Law, Washington, 1965; contbr. numerous articles to internat. and Am. profl. jours. Rsch. grant Howard U., 1963. Mem. ABA, Brit. Inst. Internat. and Comparative Law, Am. Soc. Internat. Law. Republican. Roman Catholic. Achievements include 1st woman to receive LLM in Comparative Law from George Washington U. Avocations: travels, foreign languages, collecting antique books, genealogy. Home: 400 Ocean Trail Way Apt 908 Jupiter FL 33477-5527

DEL SESTO, JANICE MANCINI, opera company executive. Gen. dir. Boston Lyric Opera Co., Boston, Mass. Office: Boston Lyric Opera Co 45 Franklin St Boston MA 02110-1300

DELSON, SIDNEY LEON, architect; b. Chgo., Apr. 10, 1932; s. Robert and Evelyn (Fistel) D.; m. Elizabeth Pfannmuller, Sept. 10, 1955; children: Karen Lee, Sara Jeanne, Matthew Robert. BArch, Pratt Inst., 1959. Registered architect, N.Y. Archtl. draftsman Irving G. Kay, N.Y.C., 1957-59; project architect William B. Tabler Assocs., N.Y.C., 1959-62; architect-designer Union Carbide Corp., Tarrytown, N.Y., 1962-64; archtl. dept. head Metcalf and Eddy Engrs., N.Y.C., 1965-66; devel. adminstr. N.Y. State Facilities Devel. Corp., N.Y.C., 1966-80, dir. design, 1980-91; pvt. practice architecture Bklyn., 1991-99, East Hampton, N.Y., 1999—. Editor: Design Procedure Manual, 1986, 2d edit., 1988, 3d edit., 1991. Mem. Community Planning Bd. Bklyn., 1968-71, vice chmn., 1971; chmn. adv. com. Bklyn. Mus. Community Gallery, 1970-73. Served as sgt. U.S. Army, 1951-53. Fellow AIA; mem. N.Y. State Assn. Architects (bd. dirs. 1982-85, 89, sec.-treas. 1988, Matthew W. DelGaudio award 1992), Am. Cons. Engrs. Coun. (peer rev. 1987—), Am. Arbitration Assn. (panelist 1971—).

DEL TORO, BENICIO, actor; b. Santurce, P.R., Feb. 19, 1967. Appeared in films Licence To Kill, 1989, China Moon, 1994, The Usual Suspects, 1995, The Funeral, 1996, The Fan, 1996, Joy Ride, 1996, Cannes Man, 1996, Basquiat, 1996, Excess Baggage, 1997, Fear and Loathing in Las Vegas, 1998. Office: IFA Talent Agy 8730 W Sunset Blvd Ste 490 Los Angeles CA 90069-2277*

DEL TORO, ILIA, retired education educator; b. Ponce, P.R., July 17, 1918; d. Gerardo Gabriel and Angela (Robledo) del T.; m. Claudino Santiago. BA, U. P.R., Rio Piedras, 1940; MA in Edn., NYU, Rio Piedras, 1958. Elem. tchr. State Dept. Instrn., 1941-44, tchr. high sch. social studies, 1944-57; instr. high sch. social studies Coll. Edn. U. P.R., Rio Piedras, 1957-59, officer external resources, 1975-76, assoc. prof., 1979-86, coord. student teaching, 1979-86, supr. student teaching, methods in high sch. social studies, edn. sociology, elem. edn. in social studies, curriculum and teaching dept., 1959-71, coord. Inst. Family Fin., 1962-69; coord. EPDA/U.S. Project, 1970-75. Author: The Acts of the Cabildo of Ponce, Puerto Rico: 1812-23, 1993; author papers in field. Puerto Rican del. to Edith Macy Girl Scout Camp, 1947; v.p. Liceo Ponceño North Zone Ex Alumnae and Friends Chpt.; mem. lady aux. Salvation Army, 1990-91, v.p. P.R. chpt.; bd. dirs. ex alumnae Ponce High Sch. '36. Mem. NEA, Assn. Supervision and Curriculum Devel. (nat. bd.), Assn. Tchr. Educators., Nat. Coun. Social Studies, P.R. Tchr. Assn., Assn. Ret. Profs. (bd. dirs.), Assn. Tchr. Educators (pres. Puerto Rican chpt.), Future World Soc., Smithsonian Instn., Phi Delta Kappa (pres. of ceremonials, 1978, 84-85, Outstanding Educator, San Juan chpt. Diamond Jubilee, 1981), Friends of Ponce, AARP, Delta Kappa Gamma (state founder, 1976, chpt. pres., 1978-80, state pres. 1983-85, Golden Gift Fund scholar Leadership/Mgmt. seminar Exec. Devel. Ctr. U. Ill. 1983-85, mem. internat. exec. com., mem. state bd. 1987—, bd. dirs. state and Alpha chpt. P.R. internat. soc.), Soc. Puerto Rican Genealogy. Roman Catholic. Home: 506 Parque De Las Fuentes San Juan PR 00918

DEL TUFO, ROBERT J., lawyer, former US attorney, former state attorney general; b. Newark, Nov. 18, 1933; s. Raymond and Mary (Pellecchia) Del T.; m. Katherine Nouri Hughes; children: Barbara, Ann, Robert, David. B.A. cum laude in English, Princeton U., 1955; J.D., Yale U., 1958. Bar: N.J. 1959. Law sec. to chief justice N.J. Supreme Ct., 1958-60; assoc. firm Dillon, Bitar & Luther, Morristown, N.J., 1960-62, ptnr., 1962-74; asst. prosecutor Morris County, N.J., 1963-65; 1st asst. prosecutor, 1965-67; 1st asst. atty. gen. State of N.J., 1974-77; dir. criminal justice, 1976-77; U.S. atty. Dist. of N.J., Newark, 1977-80; prof. Rutgers U. Sch. Criminal Justice, 1979-81; ptnr. firm Stryker, Tams & Dill, 1980-86, Hannoch Weisman, 1986-90; atty. gen. State of N.J., 1990-93; ptnr. Skadden, Arps, Slate, Meagher & Flom, N.Y.C. and Newark, 1993—; commr. N.J. State Commn. of Investigation, 1981-84; instr. bus. law Fairleigh-Dickinson U., 1964; mem. N.J. State Bd. Bar Examiners, 1967-74; mem. criminal law drafting com. Nat. Conf. Bar Examiners, 1972—; bd. dirs. Nat. Victim Ctr., 1995—; Nat. Italian Am. Found., 1995—, Integrity Inc., 1995—, John Cabot U. in Rome, 1997—, N.J. Pub. Interest Law Ctr., 1996—, Daytop Village Found., 1998—, Planned Parenthood, 1999—; mem. com. on character N.J. Supreme Ct., 1982-84; spl. master, fed. jail overcrowding litigation, Essex County, 1989-90. Bd. editors Yale U Law Jour; contbr. articles to profl. jours. Mem. law enforcement adv. com. County Coll. of Morris, 1970-85; mem. Morris County Ethics Com., 1968-71, Morris County Jud. Selection Com., 1970-72, Essex County Jud. Selection Com., 1982-84; v.p., mem. exec. com. United Fund of Morris County, 1966-70; chmn. Morris Twp. Juvenile Conf. Com., 1963-74; bd. dirs. Nat. Found. March of Dimes, 1966-68, Vis. Nurse Assn. Morris County, 1963-70, Morristown YMCA, 1970-74; trustee Newark Acad., 1976-95, 97—, pres. bd. dirs. 1983-87; bd. regents St. Peter's Coll., 1979-85. Fellow Am. Bar Found.; mem. Am., N.J., Morris County bar assns., Nat. Dist. Attys. Assn., Yale Law Sch. Assn. (exec. com. 1978-84), Order of Coif. Home: 13 Ober Rd Princeton NJ 08540-4917 Office: Skadden Arts Slate Meagher & Flom One Newark Ctr Newark NJ 07102 also: 919 3rd Ave New York NY 10022-3902

DELUCA, ANNETTE, professional golfer; b. North Bergen, N.J., May 13, 1968. Golfer LPGA, 1989—; mem. Asian Tour, 1993, mem. Gold Coast Tour, 1994, 95, 3 Gold Coast victories, 1995; qualifier U.S. Women's Open, 1994, 95. Avocations: fishing, water sports, Harley Davidson motorcycles, movies, working out. Office: c/o LPGA 100 International Golf Dr Daytona Beach FL 32124-1082*

DELUCA, ANTHONY J., director small and minority business program in United State Air Force; b. N.Y.C., Apr. 29, 1946; s. Joseph Anthony and Jean (Trentalange) DeL.; m. Mary Alaimo, June 18, 1967; children: Renee, Joseph, Regina. B in Econs., Fordham U., 1967; M in Pub. Adminstrn., Troy State U., 1976. Cert. Acquisition Profl. Level III. USAF procurement officer Eglin AFB, Fla., 1967-72, civil svc. various positions with the deputy for procurement and mfg., 1972-78; procurement analyst, USAF mem. Fed. Acquistion Regulation Project Office, 1978-79; supervisory procurement analyst Hdqs. Air Force Syss. Command, Andrews AFB, Md., 1979-82; advanced from first command competition advocateto deputy Air Force competition advocate gen. Hdqs. Air Force Syss. Command, Andrews AFB, 1984-87; first civilian competition advocate gen. Office of the Asst. Sec. of the Air Force (Acquistion), Washington, 1987; dir. Air Force Office Small and Disadvantaged Bus. Utilization, Washington, 1990—. Air Force Assn. Ira Eaker fellow; Meritorious Civilian Svc. award, Exceptional Civilian Svc. award, Presidential Meritorious Rank award, Minority Participation Program award Latin Am. Mgmt. Assn., Fed. Advocate award SBA. Mem. Sr. Exec. Assn., Air Force Assn., Air Force Contract Adjustment Bd.; chairperson Air Force Women-Owned Bus. Coun. and Air Force Historically Black Coll. and U. and Minority Instn. Adv. Bd. Roman Catholic. Avocations: biking, music. Office: Dept of Air Force Small Disadvantaged Bus Utilization 1060 Air Force Pentagon Washington DC 20330-1060*

DE LUCA, CARLO JOHN, biomedical engineer; b. Bagnoli del Trigno, Italy, Oct. 12, 1943; came to the U.S., 1973; s. John and Josephine (De Blasio) DeL.; m. Christine M. Rafferty. B in Applied Sci., U. B.C., Can., 1966; MS, U. N.B., Can., 1968; PhD, Queen's U., 1972. Lectr. U. N.B. Computing Ctr., Fredericton, 1968; lectr. biomed. engring. unit Queen's U., Kingston, Ont., Can., 1969-70, lab. instr. dept. anatomy, 1970-71, lectr. dept. anatomy, 1971-72, asst. prof. dept. anatomy, 1972-73; lectr. MIT, Cambridge, Mass., 1973—; rsch. assoc. in orthopaedic surgery Children's Hosp. Med. Ctr., Harvard U. Med. Sch., Boston, 1973-79, prin. rsch. assoc. in orthopaedic surgery, 1979-84, dir. Neuromusclar Rsch. Lab., 1980-84; adj. assoc. prof. biomed. engring. Boston U., 1977-84, prof. biomed. engring., 1984—, rsch. prof. neurology, 1985—, dir. NeuroMuscular Rsch. Ctr., 1984—, chmn. dept. biomed. engring., 1986; dean Coll. Engring., Boston U., 1986-89; founder, pres. DelSys, Inc., 1993—; cons. Liberty Mut. Rsch. Ctr., Hopkinton, Mass., 1973-94; rsch. mem. Harvard-MIT divsn. health sci. and tech., 1978-84; affiliated scientist New Eng. Regional Primate Ctr., 1977-87; mem. nat. and internat. coms. Founding editor-in-chief Jour. Electromyography and Kinesiology, 1990; mem. editl. bds. sci. jours.; co-author: Muscles Alive; contbr. articles on biomed. engring. and neurophysiology to sci. publs. Founder, pres. Neuromuscular Rsch. Found., 1985—. Recipient Volvo award Internat. Soc. for Study of Lumbar Spine, 1989, Wartenweiler Lecture award Internat. Soc. Biomechanics, 1993, Stuart Reiner Meml. Lectr. award Am. Assn. Electrodiagnostic Medicine, 1994, United Cerebral Palsy Found. Tech. award, 1999; named to Italian Cultural Ctr. Hall of Fame, Vancouver, Can., 1991; Ont. Govt. fellow, 1969-70; grantee RSA, VA, NIH, NASA, U.S. Army, USAF. Fellow IEEE, Am. Inst. Med. and Biol. Engring. (founding fellow 1993, Basmajian Lectr. award 1998); mem. AAAS, Biomed. Engring. Soc., Internat. Soc. Electrophysiol. Kinesiology (sec. gen. 1976-80, sec. 1980-84, v.p. 1985-88, pres. 1988-92), Can. Med. and Biol. Engring. Soc., Soc. Neuro-Sci., Orthopaedics Rsch. Soc., Dante Alighieri Soc. (bd. govs. 1986-88), Mass. Tech. Park Corp. (bd. govs. 1987-90), Harvard Club Boston, Sigma Xi. Home: 107 Livingston Rd Wellesley MA 02482-7308 Office: Boston U NeuroMuscular Rsch Ctr 19 Deerfield Boston MA 02215-2407

DELUCA, DOMINICK, medical educator, researcher. BA in Bacteriology, UCLA, 1969, PhD in Microbiology, 1974. Predoctoral fellow NIH dept. bacteriology UCLA, 1970-74, rsch. asst. dept. bacteriology, 1974; postdoctoral fellow Leukemia Soc. Am., Walter and Eliza Hall Inst., Parkville, Australia, 1974-77; scientist cancer biology program Frederick (Md.) Cancer Rsch. Ctr., 1977-80; asst. prof. biochemistry Med. U. S.C., Charleston, 1980-85, assoc. prof. biochemistry, 1985-90; assoc. prof. microbiology and immunology U. Ariz., 1990—; mem. pub. policy com. Ariz. Diabetes Control Coun., 1997—; mem. AIDS rsch. program basic scis. rev. panel U. Calif., 1996—. Mem. editl. adv. bd. Devel. and Comparative Immunology, 1995—; contbr. articles to profl. jours., chpt. to books. Recipient Developing Scholar award Health Scis. Found. Med. U. S.C., 1987, Rsch. award NIH, 1983, 86, 89, Rsch. award Juvenile Diabetes Found., 1988, 98, Ariz. Disease Control Rsch. Commn., 1992, 96, 98, Am. Diabetes Assn., 1995. Mem. Am. Assn. Immunologists, Southeastern Immunology Conf. (pres. elect 1982-83, pres. 1983-84, bd. dirs. 1985), Ariz. Cancer Ctr. Office: U Ariz Dept Micro Immuno PO Box 245049 Tucson AZ 85724-5049

DELUCA, JOHN RICHARD, II, city planning administrator, geography educator; b. Kansas City, Mo., Oct. 10, 1966; s. John Richard and Trudy Clara (Leavey) DeL.; m. Jennifer Ann Gibson, June 29, 1991; children: John, Julie. BS, Cen. Mo. State U., 1989; MS, Okla. State U., 1993. Cartographer Jackson County, Kansas City, Mo., 1994-95; geography instr. Cen. Mo. State U., Warrensburg, 1995—; planning and zoning adminstr. City of Raymore, Mo., 1996—. Mem. A-Plus adv. com. Raymore-Peculiar Sch. Dist., Peculiar, Mo., 1997—. Mem. Am. Planning Assn. Roman Catholic. Avocations: photography, hiking, fishing. Home: 1605 Cooper Dr Raymore MO 64083-8114 Office: City of Raymore 104 N Madison St Raymore MO 64083-9147

DELUCA, KRISTIN LEIGH, graphic designer; b. Oct. 16, 1974. BA, Tex. A&M U., 1996. News editor Bryan-College Station Eagle, Bryan, Tex., 1996-97; graphic artist Tops Printing, College Station, Tex., 1997-98; desktop pub. Kelly Svcs./CTB McGraw-Hill, Monterey, Calif., 1998—. E-mail: luka@redshift.com.

DELUCA, MARY, telecommunications engineer; b. Bronx, N.Y., Dec. 11, 1960; d. Dante and Julia (Ruotolo) DeL. BEE, Manhattan Coll., 1983. Traffic engr. MCI Internat., Rye Brook, N.Y., 1983-84; ops. supr. MCI Internat., Stamford, Conn., 1984; pvt. line engr. MCI Internat., Rye Brook, 1984-85; switch engr. MCI Telecommunications, Washington, 1985-89; sr. engr. network systems planning MCI Telecommunications, Richardson, Tex., 1989-91; sr. engr. FCC, Washington, 1991-96; designated fed. officer, alt. and tech. advisor N.Am. Numbering Coun., 1996; sr. mgr. carrier industry devel. MCI Telecomm., Washington, 1996-98. Mem. IEEE, Communications Soc. IEEE. Office: MCI 1801 Penn Ave NW Washington DC 20002

DELUCA, MICHAEL, film company executive. Pres. prodn. and devel. New Line Cinema, L.A. Office: New Line Cinema 2d flr 116 N Robertson Blvd Los Angeles CA 90048 also: New Line Cinema 888 Seventh Ave 20th Flr New York NY 10106*

DELUCA, PATRICK PHILLIP, pharmaceutical scientist, educator, administrator; b. Scranton, Pa., Sept. 7, 1935; m. Judy Beitzel, June 16, 1956; children: Paul, Thomas, Patrick, Donald, Michelle, Michael. BS in Pharmacy, Temple U., 1957, MS in Pharmacy, 1960, PhD in Pharmacy (SKF W.G. Karr fellow), 1963. Analytical chemist SKF Co., 1957-59; instr., research asso. Temple U., 1959-62; sr. research pharmacist CIBA Co., Summit, N.J., 1963-66; plant mgr. CIBA Co., 1966-69, dir., 1969-70; dir. Cormedics Corp., Somerville, N.J.; mem. faculty U. Ky., 1970—; prof., asso. dean U. Ky. (Coll. Pharmacy), 1972-87, dir. ctr. for pharmaceutical sci. and tech., 1987-88, chair faculty pharm. scis., 1998—; cons. to pharm. industry and FDA. Editor-in-chief Jour. Pharm. Devel. and Tech., 1995; contbr. numerous articles and sci. papers to profl. jours. Mem., pres. parish pastoral coun. Christ the King Cathedral, 1996—. Recipient Leo G. Penn award Temple U., 1957, Lunsford-Richardson Pharmacy Rsch. award Richardson Merrell Co., 1960, 62, Best Paper Toward Advancement Indsl. Pharmacy award N.J. Pharmacy Discussion Group, 1965, Disting. Alumni award Temple U., 1989, Outstanding Educator award in U.S., 1974, Sturgill Rsch. award U. Ky., 1995; also numerous grants. Fellow Am. Assn. Pharm. Scientists (bd. dirs. 1986-88, Rsch. Achievement award 1988, Outstanding Manuscript award in pharm. devel. and technology 1998), Acad. Pharm. Sci. (pres. 1979-80), Inst. for Advanced Biotech. (sr.); mem. Am. Pharm. Assn., Parenteral Drug Assn. (Rsch. Achievement award 1975), Am. Soc. Hosp. Pharmacists (Rsch. award 1975), Am. Assn. Indian Pharm. Scientists, N.Y. Acad. Sci., Am. Soc. Enteral and Parenteral Nutrition, Sigma Xi, Rho Chi. Research, publs. in pharm. tech., novel drug delivery. Home: 3292 Nantucket Rd Lexington KY 40502-3269 Office: U Ky Coll Pharmacy Rose St Lexington KY 40536-0082

DELUCA, PETER, state agency administrator, lawyer; b. Binghamton, N.Y., Apr. 7, 1946; s. Frank Emelio and Harriet Eloise (Munson) DeL.; m. Susan Lorraine Thompson, June 8, 1968 (div. Jan. 1972); m. Jean Francine Szymanski, May 8, 1982; 1 child, Mario Frank. BA, Coll. of Idaho, Caldwell, 1968; JD, Willamette U., 1975. Bar: Oreg. 1975, U.S. Dist. Ct. (Oreg. dist.) 1979. Emplyee rep. Oreg. Pub. Employees Union, Salem, 1975-76; legal counsel Oreg. Pub. Employees Union, 1976-83; project analyst Oreg. Exec. Dept., Salem, 1983-84; asst. atty. gen. Oreg. Dept. Justice, Salem, 1984-87; chief labor lawyer, asst. atty. gen. Oreg. Dept. Justice, 1987-92, trial atty., asst. atty. gen., 1992-94; adminstr. labor rels. State of Oreg., Salem, 1994-96; adminstr. Oreg. OSHA, Salem, 1996—. Scoutmaster Candalaria Cub Scouts, Salem, 1990-93; area rep. South Salem Neighborhood Assn., 1994—; chair task force on employee bargaining, Gov. Oreg., Salem, 1996. Democrat. Avocations: snow skiing, hiking, fishing, camping, travel. Office: Oreg OSHA 350 Winter St NE Rm 430 Salem OR 97310-1321

DELUCA, RONALD, former advertising agency executive, consultant; b. Reading, Pa., Oct. 28, 1924; s. Nicola and Grace (Carabello) DeL.; m. Lois Ann Hall, Nov. 27, 1952; children: Christine, Diane, Patricia, Maria, Lisa, Nicholas. Certificate comml. art, Pratt Inst., 1949; B.F.A., Syracuse U., 1951; B.A., New Sch. Social Research, 1966. Artist J.C. Penney, N.Y.C., 1951-52; designer Remington Rand, N.Y.C., 1952-53; art dir. Roy S. Durstine (advt.), N.Y.C., 1954-56, Kenyon & Eckhardt (advt.), N.Y.C., 1956-66; head creative group Grey Advt., N.Y.C., 1966-67; with Kenyon & Eckhardt Advt., N.Y.C., 1967-85; exec. v.p., vice chmn. Kenyon & Eckhardt Advt., 1976-85; pres. Bozell Jacobs, Kenyon & Eckhardt, N.Y.C., 1986-89, vice chmn., 1989-91; cons., 1991—. Home and Office: PO Box 551 Hancock NY 13783-0551

DELUCCA, LEOPOLDO ELOY, otolaryngologist, head and neck surgeon; b. Santurce, P.R., Nov. 1, 1952; s. Leopoldo Claudio and Laura Iris (Juncos) DeL.; m. Judith Lynn McClellan, June 11, 1977; children: Lauren Denise, Gina Fay. Pre-med. degree, U. P.R., 1973; MD, Jefferson Med. Coll., Phila., 1977. Diplomate Am. Bd. Otolaryngology. Otolaryngologist Ft. Dodge (Iowa) Med. Ctr., 1981-86; practice medicine specializing in otolaryngology Ft. Dodge, 1986—; active med. staff Trinity Regional Hosp., Ft. Dodge, 1981—, chief of surgery, 1985—, pres. med. staff, 1991—; vol. faculty Coll. Osteo. Medicine and Surgery, Des Moines, 1981-82. Bd. dirs. Trinity Regional Hosp., 1993—; tenor Trinity Singers. Fellow ACS, Am. Acad. Otolaryngology-Head and Neck Surgery, Am. Acad. Facial Plastic and Reconstructive Surgery. Republican. Roman Catholic. Avocation: guitar. Home: 2626 Woodland Dr Fort Dodge IA 50501-7130 Office: Physicians Office Bldg 200 Kenyon Rd Ste 200 Fort Dodge IA 50501-5762

DELUCCA, ROBERT KENNETH, adult education educator, writer, translator; b. Pitts., Oct. 14, 1957; s. Michael and Catherine Delucca; m. Roberta Ricci, May 11, 1998. BA, Columbia U., 1982; MA, Johns Hopkins U., 1995, PhD, 1998. Freelance writer, translator, 1984—; vis. lectr. Johns Hopkins U., Balt., 1991-95, Duke U., Durham, N.C., 1997-99. Contbr. articles to profl. jours. Fullbright fellow, 1997; Mellon fellow, 1997. Mem. MLA, Am. Assn. Italian Studies. Avocation: writing. E-mail: r.delucca@duke.edu. Office: Duke U Romance Studies 205 Languages Box 90257 Durham NC 27708

DELUCCHI, GEORGE PAUL, accountant; b. Richmond, Calif., Apr. 20, 1938; s. George Carl and Rose Caroline (Golino) D. BA, San Jose State U., 1959. CPA, Calif. Ptnr. Delucchi, Swanson & Co., Santa Clara, Calif., 1968-74, Delucchi, Swanson & Sandival, Santa Clara, 1974-76, Delucchi, Sandoval & Co., Santa Clara, 1976-77, Wolf & Co., San Jose, Calif., 1977-78; v.p. Lautze & Lautze, San Jose, 1978-82, also bd. dirs.; sr. ptnr. G.P. Delucchi & Assocs. (name changed to Delucchi, Robinson, Streit & Co., San Jose, 1982-95, Delucci, Hawn & Co., LLP, San Jose, 1996—. Treas. Crippled Children's Soc., San Jose, 1967-71, San Jose Catholic Charities, 1984-96, F. Schmidt Found. for Youth; bd. dirs. Serra Med. Found., Mission City Cmty. Fund, Bill Wilson Marriage and Family Counseling Ctr.; pres. Santa Clara Police Activity League, 1977-78; mem. bd. fellows Santa Clara U., 1975-94; chmn. pioneer dist. Santa Clara coun. Boy Scouts Am., 1992-94. Lt. U.S. Army, 1959-62. Mem. AICPA, Calif. Soc. CPAs (bd. dirs. 1993-95, treas. 1995-96, sec. 1996-97, pres., 1998—), Silicon Valley Capital Club, Serra Club, Elks (Santa Clara exalted ruler 1969-70), Rotary (pres. 1993-94, bd. dirs. 1986-89), Knights of Malta (invested, Knight of Magistral Grace). Republican. Roman Catholic. Avocations: model railroad, scuba diving, sailing, woodworking. Home: 774 Circle Dr Santa Clara CA 95050-5927 Office: 1871 The Alameda Ste 400 San Jose CA 95126-1753

DELUCE, RICHARD DAVID, lawyer; b. Nanaimo, B.C., Can., Oct. 3, 1928; came to U.S., 1929; s. Robert and Myrtle (Hickey) DeL; m. Joanne Strang, Sept. 10, 1955; children: David S., Amy Jane Eigner, Daniel R. AB, UCLA, 1950; JD, Stanford U., Palo Alto, Calif., 1955. Bar: Calif., 1955, U.S. Dist. Ct. (no. dist.) Calif. 1955, U.S. Ct. Appeals (9th cir.) 1955, U.S. Dist. Ct. (cen. dist.) Calif. 1956, U.S. Supreme Ct. 1963, U.S. Dist. Ct. (so. dist.) Calif. 1972. Rsch. atty. Calif. Supreme Ct., San Francisco, 1955-56; assoc. Lawler, Felix & Hall, L.A., 1956-62, ptnr., 1962-90; prtnr. Arter, Hadden, Lawler, Felix & Hall, L.A., 1990—. Co-author: California Civil Writ Practice, 2d edit., 1987. Capt. U.S. Army, 1951-53, Korea. Fellow Am. Coll. Trial Lawyers, Am. Bar Found.; mem. Calif. Club. Home: 3617 Paseo Del Campo Palos Verdes Peninsula CA 90274-1161 Office: Arter Hadden Lawler Felix 725 S Figueroa St Ste 3400 Los Angeles CA 90017-5434

DE LUCIA, FRANK CHARLES, physicist, educator; b. St. Paul, June 21, 1943; s. Frank Charles and Muriel Ruth (Rinehart) D.; m. Shirley Ann Wood, June 25, 1966; children: Frank Charles, Elizabeth Ann. BS, Iowa Wesleyan Coll., 1964; PhD, Duke U., 1969. Instr, research assoc. Duke U., Durham, N.C., asst. prof., assoc. prof.; program mgr. Army Research Office, Research Triangle Park, N.C.; prof. Duke U., Durham, chmn. physics dept.; prof., chmn. dept. physics Ohio State U., Columbus, 1990-98, prof., 1998—. Mem. Am. Phys. Soc., IEEE, Optical Soc. Am., Phi Beta Kappa. Office: Ohio State U Dept Of Physics Columbus OH 43210

DELUCIA, GENE ANTHONY, government administrator, computer company executive; b. Methuen, Mass., Feb. 20, 1952; s. Antonio Gitano and Carmen Theresa (Carpenito) DeL. BS, Boston Coll., 1973; MBA, Northeastern U., 1980. Project mgr. Delphi div. Arthur D. Little Inc., Lowell, Mass., 1975-78; gen. mgr. eastern region Arthur D. Little Inc., 1978-80; systems devel. mgr. Wang Labs. Inc., Lowell, 1980-83; pres., CEO Computer Innovations Inc., Lowell, 1983-86; pres. Corp. Investment Bus. Brokers, North Andover, Mass., 1986-88; v.p. Maximus Inc., Falls Church, Va., 1988-90, div. pres., 1990-96; pres. Strategic Visions Inc., Amesbury, Mass., 1996-97; mng. ptnr. Renaissance Govt. Solutions, Exeter, N.H., 1997—. Mem. AOPA. Avocations: skiing, racquetball, electronics, flying, golf. Home: 129 N End Blvd Salisbury MA 01952-2209 Office: Renaissance Govt Solutions Ste 306 One Hampton Rd Exeter NH 03833

DELUGACH, ALBERT LAWRENCE, journalist; b. Memphis, Oct. 27, 1925; s. Gilbert and Edna (Short) D.; m. Bernice Goldstein, June 11, 1950; children: Joy, David, Daniel, Sharon. B.J., U. Mo., 1951. Reporter Kansas City (Mo.) Star, 1951-60, St. Louis Globe Democrat, 1960-69, St. Louis Post Dispatch, 1969-70; investigative reporter Los Angeles Times, 1970-89. Served with USNR, 1943-46. Recipient Pultizer prize for spl. local reporting, 1969, Gerald Loeb award for disting. bus. and fin. journalism, 1984. Home: 4313 Price St Los Angeles CA 90027-2815

DELUGO, ERNEST MARIO, JR., electrical engineer; b. N.Y.C., Sept. 25, 1950; s. Ernest M. and Irma (Maisonett) DeL.; m. Yolanda Garcia, Oct. 17, 1991; children: Jessica, Lisa, David. BSEE, Polytech. Inst. N.Y., 1971; MBA fin., U. Conn., 1995. Cert. cogeneration engr., project mgr. Field engr. General Elec. Co., N.Y.C., 1971-75; elec. engr. General Elec. Co., Schenectady, N.Y., 1975-81; constrn. engr. Burns & Roe, Oradell, N.J., 1977; sr. control sys. engr. Bechtel Power, Ann Arbor, Mich., 1981-84; sr. elec. engr. General Elec. Co., Schenectady, 1984-86, prin. engr., 1986-88; v.p. General Elec. Co., Stamford, Conn., 1988-92; sr. v.p. Ridgewood (N.J.) Power Corp., 1992-94; pres., sr. ptnr. DeLugo Tech. LLC, Bethel, Conn., 1994—. Author: Project Management: Managing the Investors' Perspective, 1995; contbr. articles to profl. jours. Recipient Project Mgmt. award Gov. of South Korea, 1979. Mem. IEEE, Project Mgmt. Inst., Am. Mgmt. Assn., Assn. Energy Engrs. Avocation: model railroading. Home: 18 Payne Rd Bethel CT 06801-1239 Office: Delugo Techs LLC 18 Payne Rd Bethel CT 06801-1239

DELUHERY, PATRICK JOHN, state senator; b. Birmingham, Ala., Jan. 31, 1942; s. Frank B. and Lucille (Donovan) D.; B.A. with honors, U. Notre Dame, 1964; B.Sc. (Econ.) with honors, London Sch. Econs., 1967; m. Margaret Morris, 1973; children: Allison, Norah, Rose. Legis. asst. U.S. Senator Harold Hughes, Washington, 1969-74; legis. asst. U.S. Senator John Culver, Washington, 1975; asst. prof. econs. and bus. adminstrn. St. Ambrose U., Davenport, Iowa, 1975—; mem. Iowa State Senate, 1979—; ins. agt., 1989—. Democrat. Roman Catholic. Home: 11839 110th Ave Davenport IA 52804-9110 Office: Iowa Senate Statehouse Des Moines IA 50319

DELUISE, DAVID, actor; b. Nov. 11. T.V. and movie actor. Appeared in films Hot Stuff, 1979, The Liars' Club, 1993, Robin Hood: Men in Tights, 1993, The Silence of the Hams, 1994, Kicking and Screaming, 1995, Dracula: Dead and Loving It, 1995, Where Truth Lies, 1996, Hairshirt, 1998, Between the Sheets, 1998; T.V. series include 3d Rock From the Sun, 1996, Jesse, 1998—; also T.V. guest appearances 21 Jump St., 1987, Home Improvement, 1991, SeaQuest DSV, 1993, Lois & Clark: The New Adventures of Superman, 1993, Ellen, 1994, The Single Guy, 1995. Office: c/o Bright-Kaufmann-Crane Prodns Bldg 140 Rm 130 300 S Lorimar Burbank CA 91522

DELUNA, D.N., literary educator; b. L.A., Dec. 16, 1959. Student, Santa Monica Coll., 1978; BA summa cum laude, U. So. Calif., 1980, MA in English, 1984; PhD in English, Johns Hopkins U., 1993. Tchg. asst. U. So. Calif., 1981, writing tutor, 1983; tchg. asst. in contemporary Am. Letters Johns Hopkins U., Balt., 1992, lectr. in New Asian Am. and Latino writing, 1993, lectr. in intro. to fiction and poetry writing, 1993—, lectr. in contemporary Asian Am. fiction, 1994—; part-time instr. bilingual Spanish-English elem. sch., 1978. Contbr. revs., articles, conf. papers to profl. publs. Mem. MLA, Am. Soc. for Eighteenth-Century Studies, Milton Soc. Am., Am. Journalism Historians Assn., Bibliographical Soc. Am. Home: Colonnade Condos 3801 Canterbury Rd Baltimore MD 21218-2370 Office: Johns Hopkins U Writing Seminars Baltimore MD 21218

DE LUNG, JANE SOLBERGER, independent sector executive; b. Anniston, Ala., July 9, 1944; d. Samuel and Margaret Polk (Oldham) S.; m. Harry Leonard De Lung, Apr. 23, 1965 (div. 1972); m. Charles F. Westoff, May 2, 1997. BA in History, Emory U., 1966; MA in Urban Planning, Roosevelt U., Chgo., 1972. Exec. asst. Cook County Legal Assistance, Chgo., 1967-69; asst. dir. family planning Am. Coll. Ob-Gyn, Chgo., 1969-71; v.p. Ill. Family Planning Coun., Chgo., 1971-80; asst. commr. Chgo. Dept. Pub. Health, 1981-82; pres. Pub. Solutions, Princeton, N.J., 1982-88, Population Resource Ctr., N.Y.C., 1988—. Bd. dirs. Princeton Area Cmty. Planning, 1983-85, Planned Parenthood Mercer County, Trenton, N.J., 1986-96, UN Assn. U.S.A.; mem. adv. bd. dept. sociology Princeton U., 1991—. Mem. APHA, AAUW, LWV, Population Assn. Am. Democrat. Episcopalian. Office: Population Resource Ctr 15 Roszel Rd Princeton NJ 08540-6248

DELUSTRO, FRANK ANTHONY, biomedical company executive, research immunologist; b. N.Y.C., May 8, 1948; s. Frank and Yolanda (Lombardi) DeL.; m. Barbara Mary Cervini, May 4, 1974; 1 child, Laura Marie. BS, Fordham U., 1970; PhD, SUNY, Syracuse, 1976. Rsch. assoc. dept. immunology Med. U. S.C., Charleston, 1976-78, instr. dept. medicine, 1978-80, asst. prof. dept. medicine, 1980-83; mgr. immunology R & D Collagen Corp., Palo Alto, Calif., 1983-85, mgr. clin. sci., 1985-86, dir. med. affairs, 1986-88, program dir., 1988-90, v.p., 1990-91, sr. v.p., 1991-96; pres., CEO Cohesion Corp., Palo Alto, 1996-98; pres. Cohesion Technologies, Inc., Palo Alto, 1998—. Contbr. articles to profl. jours. Mem. Am. Assn. Immunology, Am. Urol. Assn., Soc. Biomaterials, Soc. Investigative Dermatology. Office: Cohesion Technologies Inc 2500 Faber Pl Palo Alto CA 94303-3329

DELUSTRO, FRANK JOSEPH, financial executive, consultant; b. N.Y.C., June 30, 1947; s. Nicholas and Mary (Garafola) DeL.; m. Maria Palma, July 16, 1972. BS, L.I. U., 1970. Various mgmt. acct. and fin. positions, 1970-81, pvt. practice acct., tax cons., 1981-88; contr. VEP, West Caldwell, N.J., 1988-90; chief fin. officer Xaverian High Sch., Bklyn., 1990-94; founder FDL Assocs., A Capital Search and Secure Group, Bklyn., 1994—; cons. various engring. firms, N.Y.C., 1979—, income tax cons. Trustee Xaverian H.S., 1990-94; chmn. adv. bd. Salvation Army, Bklyn.; treas. Civil Ct. Judgeship Campaign, 1991; chmn. ARC Bklyn. chpt.; trustee Adelphi Acad., L.I. Univ. Alumni Bd. Mem. Inst. Mgmt. Accts. (v.p., contrs. coun., bd. dirs. N.Y. chpt.), Bayfort Benevolent Assn. (pres.), Cathedral Club (bd. dirs.). Avocations: boating, fishing, viniculture. Home: 4117 Avenue S Brooklyn NY 11234-5009 Office: FDL Assocs PO Box 340462 Brooklyn NY 11234-0462

DE LUTIS, DONALD CONSE, investment manager, consultant; b. Rome, N.Y., Apr. 25, 1934; s. Conse R. and Mary D.; m. Ruth L.; 1 child, Dante. BS in Econs., Niagara U., 1956; MBA, Boston Coll., 1962. V.p. John Nuveen & Co., Inc., San Francisco, 1968-74; acct. exec. Dean Witter & Co., London, 1975-77; sr. investment officer Buffalo Savs. Bank, N.Y., 1978-80; exec. v.p. Robert Brown & Co., Inc., San Francisco, 1980-89, Capitol Corp. Asset mgmt., 1989-91; exec. v.p., dir. Pacific Securities, Inc., San Francisco, 1989-91; chmn. Orrell & Co., Inc., 1991-98; mng. dir. Coast Ptnrs. Securities, Inc., 1998—; Commr. San Francisco Bay Conservation and Devel. Commn., 1983-93, State of Calif. Commn. Housing and Community Devel., 1974-77. Served with USAF, 1957-58. Mem. Nat. Assn. Bus. Economists, San Francisco Bond Club. Republican. Roman Catholic. Office: 601 California St Ste 1400 San Francisco CA 94108

DEL VALLE, CEZAR JOSE, artist, writer, theatre historian; b. Washington, Apr. 14, 1945; s. Cezar and Ida Marie (MacIntosh) Del V.; m. Irene Dorthea DuVal, Sept. 1963 (div. Aug. 1968); m. Darleen Jeanette Travers, Sept. 21, 1968; 1 child, Corinne. Grad. high sch., Suitland, Md., 1963. Co-owner Talking of Michaelangelo Gallery, Washington, 1973; concert promoter MacIntosh Prodns., Alexandria, Va., 1976-78; performers agt., Alexandria and N.Y.C., 1976-82; lectr. Smithsonian Instn., Washington, 1973, North Va. Community Coll., 1973; curator 11th Ann. Invitational Art Show, Annapolis, Md., 1973; lectr. Mus. of Holography, N.Y.C., 1988-91; bd. dirs. Nebreuko Theatre Co., 1984; artist-in-residence Pawtucket, R.I., 1994; lectr., walking tours for librs. and hist. socs.; cons. in theatre history. Exhibited in over 17 solo exhbns., 115 group shows, including L.I. U., Bklyn., 1974, 89, Cameravision, L.A., 1981, Wolfe St. Gallery, Alexandria, Va., 1973-75, Belanthi Gallery, Bklyn., 1982; group shows include Cleve. Photographic Workshop, 1981, 89, Mus. of Hudson Highlands, Cornwall-on-Hudson, N.Y., 1983, Transamerica's Celebrate the Athlete, L.A., 1984, Photospiva '91, Joplin, Mo., 1991, OIA Artists Salon, N.Y.C., 1991, Newark Mus., 1992, Monmouth Mus., Lincroft, N.J., 1993, Barron Arts Ctr., Woodbridge, N.J., 1993, William's Art Ctr., Rutherford, N.J., 1993, Gallery 450, N.Y.C., 1993, Printmaking Coun. N.J., Somerville, 1994, Galleri 8, Portland, Oreg., 1994, Rotunda Gallery, NYC, 1998, Salon Exhbn., NYC, 1998, Gallery 128, NYC, 1999; represented in permanent collections Kinsey Inst., Ind. U., Word Craft, Redwood City, Calif., Tampa (Fla.) Mus. of Art, numerous pvt. collections; work pub. in photographic annual; contbr. articles to profl. jours. Columnist Alexandria Port Packet, 1976; bd. dirs. Tuesday Evening Hour, 1996—; bd. trustees Old Stone House Hist. Interpretive Ctr. Mem. Internat. Platform Assn., Bklyn. Hist. Soc., Theatre Hist. Soc. Am., Bklyn. Coord. Coun. for Preservatio of Neighborhood History. Avocations: cooking, travel, theatre. Home and Studio: 433 16th St Brooklyn NY 11215-5820

DEL VALLE, IRMA, protective services official, poet; b. Mayaguez, P.R., Feb. 7, 1937; came to the U.S., 1956; d. Francisco Del Valle and Felicita Feliciano; m. Martinez, July 11, 1966; 1 child. D in Criminal Justice magna cum laude, Mercy Coll., 1977; MLitt, CUNY, 1980; postgrad., NYU. Cmty. info. coord. Met. Mus. Art, N.Y.C., 1969-70; pub. rels. asst. Model Cities Adminstrn., N.Y.C., 1970-75; case worker Human Resources Adminstrn., N.Y.C., 1980-86; investigator N.Y. State Dept. Social Svc., N.Y.C., 1986—. Author: Versos Para Ti, 1967, Enonasion, 1970, Senderos, 1974, Polvo Poetico, 1989. Mem. Am. Poets Orgn. Roman Catholic. Avocation: reading poetry.

DELWICHE, PATRICIA ELLEN, family nurse practitioner; b. Green Bay, Wis., June 22, 1952; d. Arthur W. and Armella E. (Reininger) Schmidt; m. Edmond Michael Delwiche, June 6, 1975; children: Emily Elizabeth, Danielle Patricia. Diploma in nursing, Holy Family Hosp. Sch. Nursing, 1973; BSN, U. Wis., Green Bay, 1984; MSN, U. Wis., Oshkosh, 1994. Staff nurse med./surg. unit St. Vincent Hosp., Green Bay; staff nurse blood program ARC, Green Bay; staff nurse hospice, pediatrics and med./surg. units Bellin Meml. Hosp., Green Bay, behavioral health educator, 1988-90; patient educator Shawano (Wis.) Community Hosp., 1991; diabetes nurse educator Clintonville (Wis.) Community Hosp., 1991-92; diabetes/health nurse educator Family Practice Clin., Clintonville, Wis., 1992-94; family nurse practitioner Waupaca (Wis.) Family Medicine, 1995—. Mem. ANA (cert. family nurse practitioner, advanced practice nurse prescriber), Am. Acad. Nurse

Practitioners, Am. Diabetes Assn., Am. Assn. Diabetes Educators (cert.), Fox Valley Health Profls.

DELY, STEVEN, aerospace company executive; b. N.Y.C., July 16, 1943; m. Kristine Jon Kolbe, June 7, 1975; 1 child, Jonathan Laurence. BBA, CCNY, 1966; JD, Bklyn. Law Sch., 1968; postgrad. program mgmt. devel., Harvard U., 1979. Bar: N.Y. 1972, U.S. Supreme Ct. 1983. Corp. counsel, dir. personnel services Grumman Allied Industries Inc., Garden City, N.Y., 1971-75, gen. counsel, sec., 1976-78; v.p. human resources Melville, N.Y., 1979-82; dir. human resources Grumman Corp., Bethpage, N.Y., 1982-85; v.p. resources and adminstrn. Grumman Electronics Systems div., Bethpage, 1985-86; v.p., asst. to chmn. bd. Grumman Corp., Bethpage, 1986-91, v.p. exec. staff, 1991-92, sr. v.p. exec. staff, corp. sec., 1993-94; co-founder Dispute Resolutions Inc., Jericho, N.Y., 1998—. Capt. U.S. Army, 1969-71.

DEMA-ALA, RELIE L., medical/surgical nurse; b. Dumangas, Iloilo, Philippines, May 30, 1951; d. Ireneo and Ceferina (Lobaton) D. Diploma, St. Paul's Sch. Nursing, Iloilo, 1972; BSN, St. Paul Coll., Manila, 1974. Cert. med.-surg. nurse. Staff nurse in orthopedics Meml. Med. Ctr., Savannah, Ga.; charge nurse surg. unit Hollywood Presbyn. Med. Ctr., L.A.; staff nurse surg. unit Glendale (Calif.) Meml. Hosp. Mem. Calif. Nurses Assn., St. Paul Nurses Assn.

DEMAIN, ARNOLD LESTER, microbiologist, educator; b. N.Y.C., Apr. 26, 1927; s. Henry and Gussie (Katz) D.; m. Joanna Kaye, Aug. 2, 1952; children: Pamela Robin Demain McCloskey, Jeffrey Brian. BS, Mich. State U., 1949, MS, 1950; PhD, U. Calif., Berkeley, 1954; hon. doctorate, U. Leon, Spain, 1997. Rsch. asst. U. Calif., Davis, 1952-54; rsch. microbiologist Merck & Co., Inc., Danville, Pa., 1954-56, Rahway, N.J., 1956-65; founder, head of dept. ferm. microbiology Merck & Co., Inc., Rahway, 1965-69; prof. of ind. microbiology MIT, Cambridge, 1969—. Editor 7 books; contbr. more than 425 articles to profl. jours. With U.S. Navy, 1945-47. Recipient Hotpack award Can. Soc. Microbiology, 1978, Rubro award Australian Soc. Microbiology, 1978, Indsl. Microbiology award Italian Pharm. Assn., 1989, Hans Knoll meml. award, Germany, 1990, G. Mendel award Czech Acad. Sci., 1998. Mem. NAS, Soc. Indsl. Microbiology (pres. 1990, Charles Thom award 1978, Waksman Tchg. award 1995), Am. Soc. Microbiology (Waksman award N.J. br. 1975, Biotech. award 1990, Disting. Svc. award 1994, Alice C. Evans award 1998), Am. Chem. Soc. (Marvin Johnson biotech. award), Mex. Acad. Sci., French Soc. Microbiology (hon.), Soc. Actinomycetes Japan (hon.). Achievements include 16 patents; elucidation of biosynthetic pathway to penicillins and cephalosprins; recognition of phenomenon of biochemical regulation of secondary metabolism; discovery of role of lysine and amino adipic acid in penicillin biosynthesis. Office: MIT Biology Dept 68-223 77 Massachusetts Ave Cambridge MA 02139-4307

DEMAIO, DOROTHY WALTERS, tutorial school administrator, consultant; b. Durham, N.C., Sept. 24, 1944; d. Rudolph Breece and Dorothy L. (Davis) Walters; divorced; 1 child, Mary Margaret Urquhart. BA in Elem. Edn., U. N.C., 1966. Asst. dir. media ctr. Atlanta Speech Sch., 1974-78; dir. nursery St. Patrick's Epis. Ch., 1982-84; adminstr. tutorial sch. for ESOL and spl. edn., 1984-93, educable mentally handicapped mid. sch. tchr., 1993-94; tchr. math. and sci. Dodds Sch., Sicily, Italy, 1994—; Japanese/Am. ESOL cons. Atlanta, 1983-93. Chmn. Lone Troop com. Mem. DAR, Ga. Assn. for Children with Learning Disabilities, Tomadichi Soc., Colonial Dames, Phi Delta Kappa. Avocations: painting, choral music, dance. Office: 78 Saratoga Dr Ceiba PR 00735-2513

DEMARCHI, ERNEST NICHOLAS, aerospace engineering administrator; b. Lafferty, Ohio, May 31, 1939; s. Ernest Costante and Lena Marie (Cireddu) D.; m. Sharon Titherley; B.M.E., Ohio State U., 1962; M.S. in Engring., UCLA, 1969; children—Daniel Ernest, John David, Deborah Marie. Registered profl. cert. mgr. With Space div. Rockwell Internat., Downey, Calif., 1962—, mem. Apollo, Skylab and Apollo-Soyuz missions design team in electronic and elec. systems, mem. mission support team for all Apollo and Skylab manned missions, 1962-74, mem. Space Shuttle design team charge elec. systems equipment, 1974-77, in charge Orbiter Data Processing System, 1977-81, in charge Orbiter Ku Band Communication and Radar System, 1981-85, in charge orbitor elec. power distbr., displays, controls, data processing, 1984-87, in charge space based interceptor flt. exper., 1987-88, kinetic energy systems, 1988-90, ground based interceptor program, 1990-97, dep. program mgr. Nat. Missile Def. Program, 1997—. Recipient Apollo Achievement award NASA, 1969, Apollo 13 Sustained Excellent Performance award, 1970, Astronaut Personal Achievement Snoopy award, 1971; Exceptional Service award Rockwell Internat., 1972, Outstanding Contbn. award, 1976; NASA ALT award, 1979; Shuttle Astronaut Snoopy award, 1982; Pub. Service Group Achievement award NASA, 1982; Rockwell Pres.'s award, 1983, 87; registered profl. engr., Ohio. Mem. AIAA, ASME, Nat. Mgmt. Assn., Varsity O Alumni Assn. Home: 8227 E Hillsdale Dr Orange CA 92869-2440 Office: 12214 Lakewood Blvd Downey CA 90242-2655

DEMARCO, ANNEMARIE BRIDGEMAN, telecommunications company manager; b. Long Beach, N.Y., July 27, 1960; d. Benet Eugene and Rosemarie Anne Bridgeman; m. James Thomas DeMarco, Feb. 22, 1987; 1 child, Katherine Deborah. BS, Cornell U., 1982. Writer Am. Re-Ins. Co., N.Y.C., 1983-85; systems analyst AT&T, East Brunswick, N.J., 1986-87, project mgr., 1987-89; product mgr. AT&T, Bridgewater, N.J., 1989-90; billing mgr. AT&T, Basking Ridge, N.J., 1990-92; comm. mgr. AT&T, Warren, N.J., 1992—; mktg. mgr. AT&T, Bridgewater, N.J., 1993-94; new bus. devel. coach AT&T Growth Svcs., Bridgewater, 1995—, dist. mgr. strategic planning, 1997—; freelance writer, speaker, 1991—; presenter philanthropic, mgmt. and career devel. workshops, 1991-95; participant AT&T Insight Program, 1993, leadership advisor, 1995. Mng. editor: (newsletter) BSM Today, 1991 (HARP award), BAISline (3 Effie awards 1994); author: (textbooks) Assessing and Improving Not for Profit Performance, 1991, First Step Career Development Workbook, 1991; columnist Westfield (N.J.) Leader newspaper. Ch. sch. dir. Cornell Cath. Ch., Ithaca, N.Y., 1981-82; capt./campaign AT&T United Way 1991-92, Somerset/Basking Ridge/East Brunswick, 1991; facilitator AT&T Adopt an Angel Program, Bridgewater, 1989; cons. trainer Good Counsel, Hoboken, N.J., 1990-92, bd. dirs., 1992-93, Support Ctr. of N.J., Newark, 1990, chairperson; mem. Westfield Rep. Women's Club, 1991. Recipient Comm. award United Way, 1992; named Alt. finalist for Ideal Am. Couple Contest, Family Circle Mag./Am. Greeting Cards, N.Y.C., 1989, Young Career Woman of Westfield, Bus. and Profl. Women's Club, 1990. Mem. Cornell Alumni Assn. (alumni admissions amb. 1990-93), Cornell Alumni Assn. no. N.J. Roman Catholic. Home: 354 W Dudley Ave Westfield NJ 07090-4021

DEMARCO, DAVID G., registered nurse, pharmaceuticals researcher; b. Oradell, N.J., Dec. 1, 1966; s. Arthur F. and Mary E. (Beck) DeM. BS, LaSalle U., Phila., 1989; MS, Villanova U., 1991; BSN, Thomas Jefferson U., 1994. RN, Pa., N.J. Health care cons. Shotz, Miller, Glusman P.C., Phila., 1988-89; staff RN Magee Rehab. Hosp., Phila., 1994-95; clin. rsch. asst. Corning Besselaar, Inc., Princeton, N.J., 1995; clin. rsch. assoc. Corning Besselaar, Inc., Princeton, 1996; project assoc. Covance Inc., Princeton, 1996-97; clin. rsch. assoc. II PharmaNet, Inc., Princeton, 1997-98; sr. clin. rsch. assoc. Pharmanet, Inc., Princeton, 1999—; guest spkr. Thomas Jefferson U. Alumni Assn., Phila., 1997—. Mem. Assocs. Clin. Rsch. Profls., Drug Info. Assn., Toastmasters. Republican. Roman Catholic. Avocations: ocean water sports, biking, skiing. Home: 262 Birch Hollow Dr Bordentown NJ 08505-4261 Office: PharmaNet Inc 504 Carnegie Ctr Princeton NJ 08540-6242

DEMARCO, ROLAND R., foundation executive; b. Mt. Morris, N.Y., July 21, 1910; s. Marion and Mary (Scalzette) DeM.; m. Lydia Hees, June 23, 1934; children—Richard, Ronald, Lynn. Diploma, Geneseo State Tchrs. Coll., 1930; BS, N.Y. State Coll. Tchrs., 1934; AM, Columbia U., 1937, PhD, 1942; student, U. Munich, Germany, 1937, Shrivenham Am. U., Eng., 1945; postgrad., Officers Candidate Sch., 1944, Air Intelligence Sch., 1944; LLD, Chungang U., Seoul, Korea, 1959; DLitt, Sung Kyun Kwan U., Seoul, 1969; D.Litt., Hanyang U., Seoul, 1974. Instr. Gowanda Pub. Schs., 1930-34; dir. social studies East Islip H.S., N.Y., 1934-38; instr. social scis. Coll. Charleston, 1939, Columbia U., 1939-40; staff mem. Air Intelligence Sch., 1944-45; vis. prof. Columbia U., 1946-47; prof. history, head dept. social scis. Ala. State Tchrs. Coll., 1940-46, pres. dept., dean, 1949, from adminstrv. head to pres., 1949-52; pres. Finch Coll., 1952-70, pres. emeritus, cons., 1970-75; chmn., CEO Internat. Human Assistance Programs, Inc., N.Y.C., 1973-82, hon. chmn., 1982-84, 85-96, pres., CEO, 1984-85; head history dept. Finch Jr. Coll., 1947-49; curriculum cons. Jackson County Schs., Ala., 1940-43; mem. Nat. Adv. Coun. Edn. Disadvantaged Children, 1971-73; exec. vice chmn., chmn. ednl. adv. com. Am.-Korea Found., 1953-64, pres., 1964-68, 71-73, hon. chmn., 1968-71, chmn., chief exec. officer, 1973-75. Author: The Italianization of African Natives, 1943, The Comeback Country, Vol. I: Light of the East, an Insight into Korea, 1972. Contbr. articles to profl. jours. Founder Fathers of Am.-Korean Found., 1952; trustee Allen Stevenson Sch. Boys, pres., 1956-58; bd. dirs., treas. Council Higher Ednl. Instns., N.Y.C.; pres. All Am. Open Karate Championships, 1965-80, Karate Championships North Am., 1967-80; v.p. World Taekwan Do Fedn., 1973-82; trustee Universidad Politecnica de P.R., San Juan, 1974-85; bd. dirs. Am. Behavioral Scis., 1967-80; color commentator ABC-TV Wide World of Sports for Billiard Championship Match, 1962. Served to 1st lt. USAAF, 1943-46. Decorated Order Cultural Merit Nat. medal (Korea); named hon. citizen of Seoul, 1964; knight officer Order of Merit (Italy); recipient Disting. Alumni award SUNY, 1969, Disting. Alumni award Coll. Arts and Sci. at Geneseo, 1971. Home: 1400 East Ave Rochester NY 14610-1611

DE MARCO, THOMAS JOSEPH, periodontist, educator; b. Farmingdale, N.Y., Feb. 12, 1942; s. Joseph Louis and Mildred Nora (Cifarelli) De M.; children: Todd Gordon, Kristin Alice, Lisa Anne. B.S., U. Pitts., 1962; D.D.S., 1965; Ph.D., certificate in Periodontology, Boston U., 1968; cert. in fin. planning, Coll. Fin. Planning, Denver, 1976. Certificate in clin. hypnosis. Practice dentistry specializing in periodontics and implants Cleve., 1968—; mem. staff Met. Gen. Hosp., Cleve., Univ. Hosp., Cleve., VA Hosp., Cleve.; asst. prof. periodontics and pharmacology Case-Western Res. U., 1968-70, assoc. prof., 1970-73, prof., 1973-84; asso. dean Case-Western Res. U. (Sch. Dentistry), 1972-76, dean, 1976-84; pvt. practice periodontia, 1984—. Author review books in dentistry, book on fin. planning, also articles on periodontology, pharmacology, fin. planning. Grantee Air Force Office Sci. Research, 1969; grantee Upjohn Co., 1970; grantee Columbus Dental Mfg. Co., 1971. Mem. Am. Acad. Periodontology, Internat. Assn. Dental Research, Am. Soc. for Preventive Dentistry (past pres. Ohio chpt.). Home: 12208 Fox Run Trl Chesterland OH 44026-2044 Office: 26900 Cedar Rd Cleveland OH 44122-1148*

DEMARCO-DENNIS, ELEANOR (POPPY DEMARCO-DENNIS), elementary education educator, community activist; b. Boston, Nov. 28, 1937; d. Alvin Randolph Sweeney and Eleanor Beatrice (Marcy) Lee; m. John R. DeMarco, Dec. 30, 1966 (div. 1974); 1 child, Cambria; m. Richard Dennis, Jan. 15, 1980 (dec.); 1 child, Eric. BA in Psychology, Biology, Math., San Francisco State U., 1960; MA in Psychology and Counseling, San Diego State U., 1970. Caseworker San Diego County Welfare Dept., 1962-64; tchr., resource specialist La Mesa (Calif.) and Spring Valley Schs., 1964-97; owner Bea Sweeney Tech. Resource Ctr., Solana Beach, Calif., 1990—. Mem. San Dieguito (Calif.) Citizen Planning Bd., 1972-84; legis. asst. environ. San Diego County Supr., 1974-84; mem. exec. bd., exec. dir. Cmty. Coalition Network, 1991—, Calif. Dem. Exec. Bd., 1992—; bd. dirs. Unitarian Svc. Com., 1976-82; mem. Nat. Jewish Dem. Com. Recipient Ted Bass Tchr. in Politics award Calif. Tchrs. Assn., 1992. Mem. AAUW, LWV, Nat. Women's Polit. Caucus, Calif. Elected Women's Assn. Edn. and Rsch. Home: 4690 North Ln Del Mar CA 92014-4134 Office: # 421 991C Lomas Sante Fe Dr Solana Beach CA 92075-2125

DEMAREST, CHRIS LYNN, writer, illustrator; b. Hartford, Conn., Apr. 18, 1951; s. Robert and Shirley Mavis (Johnston) D.; m. Anne Larkin Dorsey Upson, Feb. 2, 1982 (div. Sept. 1986); m. Laura Langdon Gillespie, Oct. 26, 1992; 1 child, Ethan Barnes. BFA in Painting, U. Mass., 1976. Freelance illustrator ad agys., mags., newspapers, children's books, Boston, 1977-80; freelance author, illustrator N.Y. Times, Reader's Digest, IBM, AT&T, Yankee mag., others, Boston, 1980—. Author, illustrator: Lindberg, 1993 (Sch. Libr. Jour. Best Book award 1993), My Little Red Car, 1992 (Parent's Choice award 1992), Plane Ship Bus Train, 1996 (1st Place N.Y. Book Show). Mem. Meriden Vol. Fire Dept. Recipient Ky. Bluegrass award Children of Ky., 1991, 94. Mem. Soc. Children's Books Authors and Illustrators (tchr. creative writing and illustrating 1993—). Avocations: mountain biking, canoeing, guitar. Home and Office: PO Box 397 102 Main St Meriden NH 03770 also: DK Ink 95 Madison Ave New York NY 10016

DEMAREST, DANIEL ANTHONY, retired lawyer; b. Plainfield, N.J., June 13, 1924; s. William Gustavus and Rosemary Anne (MacElhinny) D. A.B., Harvard U., 1948, LL.B., 1951. Bar: N.Y. 1951. Assoc. Simpson Thacher & Bartlett, N.Y.C., 1951-61; ptnr. Gaston Snow Beekman & Bogue and predecessor firm, N.Y.C., 1961-86; ret. Dir. Bay Found., 1986—, Josephing Bay Paul and C. Michael Paul Found., 1986—. Served with M.I., U.S. Army, 1943-46. Mem. Assn. Bar City N.Y., Phi Beta Kappa. Democrat. Episcopalian. Clubs: Knickerbocker (N.Y.C.). Home: 510 E 85th St New York NY 10028-7430

DEMAREST, DAVID FRANKLIN, JR., banker, former government official; b. Glen Ridge, N.J., Oct. 8, 1951; s. David Franklin Demarest and Alison (Clark) Fahrer; m. Leigh Ann Wisniewski, Feb. 5, 1977 (div. 1981); m. Sarah Tinsley, July 16, 1983; 2 children. BA, Upsala Coll., 1973. Dep. dir. local elections Republican Nat. Com., Washington, 1977-80; dir. pub. and intergovtl. affairs U.S. Trade Rep., Washington, 1981-84; asst. U.S. Trade Rep. Exec. Office of Pres., Washington, 1984; dep. undersec. U.S. Labor Dept., Washington, 1985-87, asst. sec. labor, 1987-88; dir. comm. George Bush for Pres. Com., 1988; dir. pub. affairs Presdl. Transition Office, 1988-89; asst. to pres. for comm. White House, Washington, 1989-92; sr. cons. Internat. Mgmt. and Devel. Group, Ltd., Alexandria, Va., 1993; dir. corp. comms., exec. v.p. Bank of Am., San Francisco, 1993-99; exec. v.p. corp. rels. Visa Internat., San Francisco, 1999—. Presbyterian. Home: 28 Cypress Pl Sausalito CA 94965 Office: Visa Internat PO Box 8999 San Francisco CA 94128-8999*

DEMAREST, SYLVIA M., lawyer; b. Lake Charles, La., Aug. 16, 1944; d. Edmand and Emily D.; m. James A. Johnston, Jr., Oct. 31, 1975 (div. Dec. 1979). Student U. S.W. La., 1963-66; J.D., U. Tex., 1969. Bar: Tex. 1969, U.S. Supreme Ct. 1973, U.S. Ct. Appeals (5th cir.) 1970, U.S. Ct. Appeals (7th cir.) 1979, U.S. Ct. Appeals (11th cir.) 1980, U.S. Dist. Ct. (no. dist.) Tex. 1970, U.S. Dist. Ct. (ea. dist.) Tex. 1970, U.S. Dist. Ct. (so. dist.) Tex. 1972. Reginald H. Smith Community Lawyer fellow, Corpus Christi and Dallas, 1969-71; house counsel Tex. Inst. Ednl. Devel., San Antonio, 1972-73; staff atty. Dallas Legal Services Found., Inc., 1973, exec. dir., 1973-76; sole practice, Dallas, 1977-78; mgr. product litigation, dir. Windle Turley, P.C., Dallas, 1978-83; sole practice, 1983-85; ptnr. Demarest & Smith, 1985—; mem. faculty trial advocacy program So. Meth. U. Law Sch., 1984; lectr. Contbr. articles to profl. jours. Mem. ABA, State Bar Tex., Assn. Trial Lawyers Am., Dallas Bar Assn., Dallas Trial Lawyers Assn. (past pres.), Dallas Inn of Ct. (master of the bar 1989—). Democrat. Home: 1812 Atlantic St Dallas TX 75208-3002 Office: 2305 Cedar Springs Rd Ste 350 Dallas TX 75201-7807

DE MARGITAY, GEDEON, acquisitions and management consultant; b. Budapest, Hungary, Mar. 6, 1924; s. Joseph and Anne (de Bessenyei) de M.; came to U.S., 1953, naturalized, 1958; student U. Budapest Grad. Sch. Econs., 1941-44, Ecole des Scis. Politiques, Paris, 1946-48; m. Virginia Varet Martin, Dec. 30, 1963. With N.Y. Times, 1947-50, European info. div. Mut. Security Agy., 1950-53; with N.Y. Times, 1954-61; chief exec. Magnum Photos, Inc., N.Y.C., 1961-63; with Time Inc., 1964-75, dir. mktg. services Time/Life TV, 1975; dir. broadcast and corp. planning NBC, 1975-78; acquistions and mgmt. cons., N.Y.C., 1978—. Mem. Assn. for Systems Mgmt., Internat. Radio-TV Soc., World Future Soc., Am. Acad. Polit. and Social Sci. Republican. Presbyterian. Co-author: Broadcasting: The Next Ten Years, 1977. Address: 65 E 96th St New York NY 10128-0730

DE MARIA, ANTHONY JOHN, electrical engineer; b. Santa Croce, Italy, Oct. 30, 1931; came to U.S., 1935; s. Joseph and Nicolina (Daddona) De M.; m. Katherine M. Waybright, Aug. 29, 1953; 1 dau., Karla Kay. BS in Elec. Engring., U. Conn., 1956, PhD in Elec. Engring., 1965; MS, Rensselaer Poly. Inst., 1960. Acoustic research engr. Andersen Lab., West Hartford, Conn., 1956-57; magnetic research engr. Hamilton Standard Div. United Techs. Corp., Windsor Locks, Conn., 1957-58; asst. dir. rsch. electronics and photonics United Techs. Rsch. Ctr., East Hartford, Conn., 1958-94; founder, chmn., CEO DeMaria ElectroOptics Sys., Inc., Bloomfield, Conn., 1994—; rsch. prof. Photonics Rsch. Ctr. U. Conn., Storrs, 1994-98; instr. electronics U. Hartford, 1957-60; adj. prof. physics Rensselaer Poly. Inst. Grad. Ctr., Hartford, 1970-77; lectr. in lasers UCLA, 1974-82; mem. adv. group on electronic devices Dept. Def., 1977-86, chmn., 1980-85; mem. evaluation com. on electromagnetic tech. Nat. Bur. Standards, 1977-79; mem. Ctr. Elec. and Electronic Engring., 1979-83; mem. LANL Adv. Com. for Chemistry and Laser Sci., 1985-92. Author: Lasers, Vol. III, 1972, Vol. IV, 1976; Contbr. articles to profl. jours. Mem. Air Force Sci. Adv. Bd., 1981-86. Recipient Disting. Alumnus award U. Conn., 1978, Disting. Engring. award, U. Conn., 1983, Davies medal and award Rensselaer Poly. Inst., 1980, Air Force Meritorious medal for civilian svc., 1986. Fellow IEEE (editor Jour. Quantum Electronics, Morris N. Liebman meml. award 1980), SPIE (bd. dirs. 1995-99), Optical Soc. Am. (v.p. 1979, pres. 1981, chmn. bd. editors 1986-89, Frederic Ives medal 1988), Am. Phys. Soc.; mem. NAE (Farichild Disting. scholar 1982-83, Calif. Inst. Tech.), NAS, Conn. Acad. Scis. and Engring. (pres. 1994-99). Address: DeMaria ElectroOptics Sys 1280 Blue Hills Ave Bloomfield CT 06002-1301

DEMARIA, ANTHONY NICHOLAS, cardiologist, educator; b. Elizabeth, N.J., Jan. 12, 1943; s. Anthony and Charlotte DeMaria; m. Delores Horn; children: Christine, Anthony, Jonathon. BA, Coll. Holy Cross, 1964; MD, N.J. Coll. Medicine, 1968. Diplomate Am. Bd. Internal Medicine, Am. Bd. Cardiovascular Disease, Am. Bd. Cardiovascular Medicine. Intern St. Vincent Hosp., Worcester, Mass., 1968-69; resident USPHS Hosp., Staten Island, N.Y., 1969-71; fellow cardiology U. Calif., Davis, 1969-73, asst. prof. medicine, 1972-77, assoc. prof. medicine, 1977-81, prof. medicine, 1977-81; prof. medicine, chief cardiology div. U. Ky., Lexington, 1981-92; dir. Ky. Heart Inst., Lexington, 1989—; prof. medicine, chief cardiology U. Calif. Sch. Medicine, San Diego, 1992—, vice chmn. internal medicine, 1998—; mem. rev. bds. Vets. Adminstrn. Med. Research Merit in Cardiovascular Studies, Nat. Inst. Health, NSF, NIH, NHLBI, U. Calif., U.S. Food and Drug Adminstrn.; chmn. Diagnostic Radiology Study Sect. NIH; vice-chmn. dept. medicine U. Calif., San Diego, 1998—. Mem. editl. bd. Am. Heart Jour., Am. Jour. Cardiac Imaging, Circulation, Am. Jour. Cardiology, Jour. Am. Coll. Cardiology, Health News from New Eng. Jour. Medicine; assoc. editor Jour. Club, Cardiology, Jour. Am. Coll. Cardiology; editl. cons. Am. Jour. Physiology, Annals Internal Medicine, Archives Phys. Medicine and Rehab., Catheterization and Cardiovascular Diagnosis, Jour. Clin. Investigation, New Eng. Jour. Medicine; contbr. numerous articles to profl. jours. ; host Cardiology Update, Lifetime Med. TV. Recipient Humanitarian award Theodore and Susan Cummings, 1978, Disting. Alumnus award Coll. Medicine and Dentistry of N.J., 1988, Echocardiography award Tufts U., 1988, award of excellence Am. Acad. Med. Adminstrs., 1994, William Hawry award Am. Med. Writers Assn., 1996; named one of Best Doctors in Am., Best Heart Specialist in U.S. Good Housekeeping mag., 1996; Golden Empire Heart Assn. grantee, Am. Heart Assn. grantee, Ky. Heart Assn. grantee, Vet. Adminstrn. grantee, Nat. Heart, Lung and Blood Inst. grantee; teaching scholar Am. Heart Assn. Fellow Am. Coll. Cardiology (chmn. 27th ann. scientific session 1978, cardiovascular procedures com., govt. rels. com., v.p. elect 1986, pres. elect 1987-88, pres. 1988—, active various coms., Young Investigator award 1976), Am. Coll. Physicians, Am. Coll. Chest Physicians; mem. Am. Heart Assn. (bd. dirs. work evaluation unit Yolo Sierra chpt., Ky. chapter, active various coms., Teaching scholar 1979-82), Am. Fedn. Clin. Rsch., Yolo County Med. Socs., Am. Inst. Ultrasound in Medicine (bd. dirs.), Am. Soc. Echocardiography (bd. dirs. 1975-87, v.p. 1983-85, pres. 1985-87, assoc. editor), N.Am. Soc. for Cardiac Radiology, Assn. U. Cardiologists. Roman Catholic. Office: U Calif Med Ctr 225 Dickinson St Ste 360 San Diego CA 92103-1910

DEMARIA, MICHAEL BRANT, psychologist; b. Norwalk, Conn., Apr. 23, 1962; s. Francesco and Jacqueline (Campbell) DeM.; m. Kathleen Jean Kies, July 4, 1982; 1 child, Danielle. BA in Psychology magna cum laude, U. West Fla., 1982, BA in Philosophy magna cum laude, 1982; MA in Psychology, Duquesne U., Pitts., 1983, PhD in Clin. Psychology, 1987. Lic. clin. psychologist, Fla.; registered play therapist; diplomate in expressive therapy. Doctoral intern Bapt. Hosp. and Lakeview Ctr., Pensacola, Fla., 1985-86; resident Clin. Psychology Assn., Pensacola, 1986-88, clin. psychologist, 1988-89; founder, clin. psychologist, pres., clin. dir. DeMaria and Assoc., Pensacola, 1989—; therapist Counseling Ctr. Point Park Coll., Pitts., 1983-84, Ctr. Tng. and Rsch. in Psychology Duquesne U., 1983-86, instr. Psychology Dept., 1983-85, rsch. asst., 1983-85; faculty assoc. U. West Fla., 1985—; cons. Adolescent Stress Ctr. Bapt. Hosp., Pensacola, 1985-89, IMPACT Program, 1986-88, Child Protection Team, 1986-89; cons./expert witness State Atty. Office, Pensacola, Renascence Recovery Ctr., Anchorage Counseling Svcs., Community Drug & Alcohol Commn., Rivendale Hosp.; speaker in field. Author: Horns and Halos: Towards the Blessing of Darkness, 1992; contbr. articles to The Humanistic Psychologist, Internat. Journey of Play Therapy, Art and Psychotherapy: An International Jour. Mem. Fla. Legis. Task Force on Child Abuse and Neglect Reports, 1988—. Recipient Merit scholarship Dept. Psychology, Dept. Philosophy U. West Fla., Alumni Found. scholarship. Mem. APA, Soc. for Personality Assessment, Assn. for Play Therapy, Southeastern Psychol. Assn., Fla. Psychol. Assn. (treas. 1989—), Psi Chi, Phi Kappa Phi. Avocations: music, film, writing, video art, skiing. Office: 512 E Zarragossa St Pensacola FL 32501-6155

DEMARIA, ROBERT, JR., English language educator; b. N.Y.C., Nov. 30, 1948; s. Robert and Maddalena (Buzzeo) DeM.; m. Joanne Thielen Long, Aug. 21, 1977; children: Alexander Thielen, David MacDonald. AB, Amherst Coll., 1970; PhD, Rutgers U., 1975. Asst. prof. Vassar Coll., Poughkeepsie, N.Y., 1975-82, assoc. prof., 1982-87, Henry Noble MacCracken prof. english, 1987—. Author: Johnson's dictionary..., 1986, Life of Samuel Johnson, 1993, Johnson and the Life of Reading, 1997; editor: British Literature 1640-1789, 1996; editl. bd. Yale Edit. of Johnson's Works, 1996—. Guggenheim fellow, 1992-93, Ctr. for Advanced Study in Behavioral Scis. fellow Stanford, Calif., 1992-93. Mem. MLA, Samuel Johnson Soc. Office: Vassar College Box 140 124 Raymond Ave Poughkeepsie NY 12604-0002

DEMARIA, WALTER, sculptor; b. Albany, Calif., Oct. 1, 1933. BA in History, U. Calif., Berkeley, 1957, MA in Art, 1959. Organized happenings U. Calif., Berkeley, Calif. Sch. Art, San Francisco, 1959-60. One-man shows include 9 Great Jones St., N.Y.C., 1963, Paula Cooper Gallery, N.Y.C., 1965, Cordier & Ekstrom Gallery, N.Y.C., 1966, Nicholas Wilder Gallery, L.A., 1968, Galerie Heiner Friedrich, Munich, 1968, Dwan Gallery, N.Y.C., 1969, Kunstmuseum, Basel, Switzerland, 1972, Hessisches Landesmuseum, Darmstadt, 1974, Heiner Friedrich, N.Y.C., 1977, 79, 19 Waverly Place, N.Y.C., 1977, Dia Art Found., N.Y.C., 1979, 80, 88, Ctr. Georges Pompidou, Paris, 1981, 83, Mus. Boymans-van Beuningen, Rotterdam, 1984-85, Arthur M. Sackler Mus., Cambridge, Mass., 1986, Xavier Fourcade, Inc., N.Y.C., 1986, Staatsgalerie, Stuttgart, Germany, 1987-88, Moderna Museet, Stockholm, 1989, Daimler-Benz, Mohringen, 1989, Gagosian Gallery, N.Y.C., 1989, 92, 65 Thompson St., N.Y.C., 1989, Kunsthaus Zurich, 1992, others; exhibited in group shows at The Jewish Mus., N.Y.C., 1966, Whitney Mus., N.Y.C., 1966, 67, 68, 69, 76, 80, 84, Dwan Gallery, N.Y.C., 1967, 68, 69, Phila. Mus. Art, 1967, L.A. Mus. Art, 1967, Richard Feigen Gallery, N.Y.C., 1967, Kunsthalle Dusseldorf, Germany, 1968, Kunsthalle Hamburg, Germany, 1968, Bellamy-Goldowsky Gallery, N.Y.C., 1968, Pinakothek, Munich, 1968, Nat. Galerie, Berlin, 1968, Kunsthalle Bern, Switzerland, 1968, 69, Stedelijk Mus., Amsterdam, The Netherlands, 1969, 86, 90, Mus. Modern Art, N.Y.C., 1970, 79, The Solomon R. Guggenheim Mus., N.Y.C., 1971, 75, 78, 82, 85, 87, 88, 89, Stadt Mus., Leverkusen, 1973, Paula Cooper Gallery, N.Y.C., 1974, Hayward Gallery, London, 1980, Vassar coll. Art Gallery, Poughkeepsie, N.Y., 1982, Mus. Contemporary Art, L.A., 1983, Wadsworth Atheneum, Hartford, Conn., 1984, Galeries nationales du Grand Palais, Paris, 1984, Brooke Alexander, Inc., N.Y.C., 1985, Modern Art Ctr. Calouste Gulbenkian Found., Lisbon, Portugal, 1985, Mus. Modern Art, Ft. Lauderdale, Fla., 1986, Xavier Fourcade, Inc., N.Y.C., 1986, Kunsthalle Bremen, Germany, 1986, Inst. Contemporary Art U. Pa., Phila., 1987, Kunstmuseum Bern, Switzerland, 1987, Deste Found. for Contemporary Art, Greece, 1990, Nippon Conventional Ctr., Tokyo, 1990, Musee Cantonal des Beaux-Arts, Lausanne, 1990, Indpls. Mus. Art, 1991, Mus. fur Moderne Kunst, Frankfurt am Main, Germany, 1991, Va. Mus. Fine Arts, Richmond, 1992, Susan Sheehan Gallery, N.Y.C., 1993, others: represented in permanent collections, Mus. Modern Art, Dia Art Found., Whitney Mus.

Am. Art, N.Y.C., Solomon R. Guggenheim Mus., Basel (Switzerland) Kunstmuseum; pioneer in earthworks. Recipient Mather Sculpture prize Art Inst. Chgo. 1976. Recipient Internat. prize for fine arts, State of Baden-Wür Hemberg, Fed. Republic Germany, 1986; Guggenheim fellow, 1969-70. Mem. Royal Acad. Fine Arts (Stockholm, fgn. mem. 1989—). Office: care Gagosian Gallery 980 Madison Ave New York NY 10021-1848*

DE MARIA Y CAMPOS, MAURICIO, United Nations official. Head planning & policy unit Mex. Nat. Sci & Tech. Coun., 1971-72; dep. dir. evaluation dept. tech transfer Ministry Trade & Industry, 1973-74, dir. gen. fgn. investment, 1974-77, vice-min. indsl. devel., 1982-88; dir.-gen. tax incentives & fiscal promotion Ministry Fin., 1977-82; exec. v.p. Banco Mexicano SOMEX, Mexico City, 1989-92; dir.-gen. UN Indsl. Devel. Orgn., Vienna, Austria, 1993-97; amb.-at-large, adv. to UN Africa and Mid. East. Office: Ministry of Fgn Affairs, Tlaltelolco, Mexico City Mexico

DEMARINIS, BERNARD DANIEL, engineering management consultant; b. N.Y.C., Aug. 7, 1946; s. Frank Bernard and Rose (Marchese) DeM.; m. Nancy Camille Iafrate; children: Leonard, Leo, Frank Daniel. BEE, CUNY, 1968; MSEE, Poly. Inst. Bklyn., 1971; MBA, Fairleigh Dickinson U., 1980. Engr. microwave Wheeler Labs./Hazeltine Corp., Smithtown, N.Y., 1968-71; sr. engr. ITT, Nutley, N.J., 1971-76; sr. mng. assoc. Booz Allen & Hamilton, Tinton Falls, N.J., 1976—; course organizer, instr., cons. in field; tech. chmn. com. internat./regional confs., Assn. U.S. Army, Am. Def. Preparedness Assn., Armed Forces Communications Assn. Editor (proceedings) IEEE Conf., AFCEA Conf., 1976-89; contbr. articles to profl. jours. Mem. IEEE (chmn. Princeton chpt. 1974-75, sr.), AFCEA (regional v.p. 1985—, pres. Ft. Monmouth chpt. 1982-83, INGLES award 1983, Pinnacle of Excellence, 1988, Disting. Young AFCEAN, 1980, Meritorious Svc. award, 1984), Assn. U.S. Army (v.p. Ft. Monmouth chpt. 1987-89, Best Chpt. award 1989, Cert. Commendation 1988), Nat. Security Indsl. Assn. (bd. dirs. 1989—), Lions (v.p. Monroe, N.J. 1988—), KC. Roman Catholic. Office: Booz Allen & Hamilton Inc 151 Industrial Way E Ste 1 Eatontown NJ 07724-3399

DE MARINO, DONALD NICHOLSON, international business executive, former federal agency administrator; b. Greensburg, Pa., Sept. 28, 1945; s. Thomas C. and Sue Eleanor (Nicholson) De M.; m. Caroline Mack, Dec. 27, 1967 (div. 1981); children: Christopher Tyson, Benjamin Nicholson; m. Betsy Reiver, July 18, 1981; children: Alexander Reiver, William McCurdy. BA, U. Pa., 1967. Dir. Mack & Nicholson, West Chester, Pa., 1972-76; bus. cons. The Nicholson Group, Inc., N.Y.C., 1976-81; sr. project officer U.S.-Saudi Arabian Joint Commn. on Econ. Cooperation, Riyadh, Saudi Arabia, 1981-84, dir., 1985-87; mgr. Litton Industries Offset Investment Programs, Riyadh, 1984-85; sr. project adviser The Arab Investment Co., Riyadh, 1985; internat. bus. cons., prin. De Marino Assocs., Coatesville, Pa., 1987-88; dep. asst. sec. Africa, Near East and South Asia U.S. Dept. Commerce, Washington, 1989-90; U.S. advisor Tata Group of India, 1991—; chmn. Nat. U.S.-Arab C. of C., 1991—; pres. De Marino Assocs., Inc., 1992—; lectr. Wharton Sch. Advanced Mgmt. Program, 1994-96; nat. adv. com. Mid. East Policy Coun.; chmn. Arab-Fgn. C. of C., 1999—. Mem. nat. adv. bd. Mid. East Policy Coun. Decorated Chevalier, Sovereign Mil. Order of Temple of Jerusalem; recipient Disting. Svc. award Govt. of Saudi Arabia, 1987. Mem. Sovereign Mil. Order Temple Jerusalem (chevalier templars), Arab-Fgn. C. of C. (chmn. 1999—), Racquet Club, Mask and Wig Club. Republican. Presbyterian. Home: 43 Longview Rd Coatesville PA 19320-4311 Office: PO Box 791 Unionville PA 19375-0791

DE MARNEFFE, BARBARA ROWE, volunteer; b. Boston, June 2, 1929; d. H.S. Payson and Florence Van Arnhem (Cassard) Rowe; m. James Hopkins, Oct. 9, 1954 (div. 1969); m. Francis de Marneffe; stepchildren: Peter, Daphne, Colette. *Early New England ancestors include: Preacher John Eliot who, in 1663, translated the first Bible printed in America in the language of the Algonquin Indians; Orator James Otis urged Bostonians to oppose the British and start the Revolution; Captain John Hussey discovered the sperm whale, leading to Nantucket's prosperity. Father's cousin, Peter Trimble Rowe, was the first Episcopal Bishop of Alaska and first to use an airplane to visit his diocese. Father, Henry Stuart Payson Rowe, Harvard '22, was President of the Associated Harvard Clubs in 1956. Sister, Pamela Otis Rowe Peabody, is documentary filmmaker living in Washington, DC.* BA, Vassar Coll., 1952; postgrad., Boston U., 1959. Tchr. Chapin Sch., N.Y.C., 1952-54; adminstrv. asst. to dean Sch. of Indsl. Mgmt. MIT, Cambridge, Mass., 1959-60; asst. pub. rels. dir. Peter Bent Brigham Hosp., Boston, 1960-61, pub. rels. dir., 1961-63; pub. rels. cons. Diabetes Found. and Joslin Clinic, Boston, 1963-64; pub. rels. dir. McLean Hosp., Belmont, Mass., 1964-68; mgr. pub. affairs Cambridge (Mass.) C. of C., 1975-78; pres. de Marneffe Selections, Cambridge, 1978-90. Contbr. articles to profl. jours. Trustee Archives of Am. Art of the Smithsonian Inst., Washington, D.C., 1983—; com. mem. Ellis Meml. Settlement House Antiques Show, 1968-89; bd. dirs. Friends of McLean Hosp., Belmont, Mass., 1967-89; officer, bd. dirs. Family Counseling Svc. of Cambridge, 1969-78; Mass. Rep. State Committeewoman, 1977-80; exec. sec. Cambridge Rep. City Com., 1956-57; pub. rels. dir. Peabody for Congress Campaign, Newton, Mass., 1968; bd. dirs. Nat. Com. on the Treatment of Intractable Pain, Washington, 1980-90; trustee Peterborough Players, N.H., 1983-89; docent N.C. Mus. of Art, Raleigh, 1992-93; chair Friends of the Pain Ctr. Mass. Gen. Hosp., Boston, 1995-99; corporator Brookline (Mass.) Savings Bank, 1995—; mem. adv. coun. Farnsworth Art Mus., Rockland, Maine; vestry Emmanuel Episcopal Ch., Dublin, N.H, 1995—. Mem. Jewelers of Am., Inc., Vassar Club (pres. Boston chpt. 1989). Avocations: medicine, business, politics, historical preservation, decorative arts, tennis. Home: 126 Coolidge Hl Cambridge MA 02138-5522

DE MARNEFFE, FRANCIS, psychiatrist, hospital administrator; b. Brussels, May 7, 1924; arrived in England, 1940; came to U.S., 1950; s. Armand Gustave and Esther Magdalen (Loveday) de M.; m. Nancy Marie Edmonds, Aug. 5, 1955 (div. Sept. 1967); children: Peter Loveday, Daphne Elizabeth, Colette; m. Barbara Cassard Rowe, Dec. 5, 1969. *Earliest Belgian ancestor was on the Second Crusade in 1103. Great Great Grandfather Sir Hilgrove Turner captured the Rosetta Stone from the French and escorted it back to London in 1802. At sixteen, Francis bicycled to France on government order to escape German invasion; later sailing to England when France surrendered. Son Peter, Ph.D. in Philosphy from Harvard University, is married to Katrin Borland. Daughter Daphne, Ph.D. in Psychology from University California Berkeley, is married to Terrence Becker, and has three children. Daughter Colette, Ph.D. in Psychology from George Washington University, is married to Martin Trimble, and has three children.* MB, BS, U. London, 1950. Diplomate Am. Bd. Psychiatry and Neurology. Intern Muhlenberg Hosp., Plainfield, N.J., 1950-51; asst. resident in psychiatry Mass. Gen. Hosp., Boston, 1952; teaching fellow in psychiatry Med. Sch. Harvard U., Boston, 1955-56, rsch. fellow, 1955-56; resident in psychiatry McLean Hosp., Belmont, Mass., 1953-54, staff psychiatrist, 1955-90, cons. psychiatrist, 1990—; gen. dir. McLean Hosp., Belmont, 1962-87, gen. dir. emeritus, 1987—, pres., CEO McLean Health Svcs., Inc., 1986-89; med. dir. Holly Hill Mental Health Svcs., Raleigh, N.C., 1990-93; instr. psychiatry Med. Sch. Harvard U., 1961-66, lectr. 1966—; mem. accreditation coun. psychiat. facilities Joint Commn. on Accreditation of Hosps., Chgo, 1979-84, mem. tech. adv. com., 1979-84, chmn. accreditation, 1970-72, mem. coun., 1970-79; adminstr. McLean divsn. Hall-Mercer Hosp., Phila., 1969-87; v.p. Hall-Mercer Hosp., 1980-87; exec. v.p. Belmont programs Mass. Gen. Hosp., Boston, 1986-87; clin. prof. psychiatry U. N.C., Chapel Hill, 1991-93; assoc. cons. prof. psychiatry Duke U. Med. Sch., 1991-93, v.p. Wake County Mental Health Assn., 1992-93, med. staff Rex Hosp., Raleigh, N.C., 1993; mem. Corp. Ptnrs. Health Care Inc., Boston, 1994—; trustee working group McLean Hosp., 1996, co chair on com. on expanding svcs. and revs.; cons. Exec. Svcs. Corps., Boston, 1996—. Author: Introduction to Adolescent Patients in Transition, 1974, contbg. author: The Changing Mental Health Scene, 1976; mem. editl. bd. McLean (Hosp.) Jour., 1976-90. Trustee Guidance Camps, Inc., Boston, 1968-90, Preschool, Inc., Cambridge, Mass., 1961-62, Concord Acad. Mass., 1975-78, Nat. Assn. Pvt. Psychiat. Hosps., Washington, 1982-85, 93-94, McLean Hosp. Corp., Belmont, 1985-87; mem. Corp. of Family Svc. Assn. Greater Boston, 1978-81; hon. trustee Concord Acad., 1978—; bd. dirs. Mass. chpt. Nat. Com. for Prevention of Child Abuse, Boston, 1979-81, Health Planning Coun. Greater Boston, 1972-76; chmn. med. divsn. United Way, 1986; mem. Mass. Gen. Hosp. Corp., 1988-94, coll. Des Conseillers of French Libr. & Cultural Ctr., Boston, 1995—; bd. dirs. Friends of McLean, 1995—, 1st v.p., 1997-99, pres., 1999—. Served as flying officer RAF, 1943-46. Recipient Presdl. award Nat. Assn. Pvt. Psychiat. Hosps., 1991. Licentiate Royal Coll. Physicians; fellow Am. Psychiat. Assn. (life), Am. Coll. Psychiatrists (hon. fellowship com.), Royal Coll. Psychiatrists, Mass. Med. Soc., Am. Coll. Mental Health Adminstrn.; mem. Royal Coll. Surgeons, Eng. Ctrl. Neuropsychiat. Hosp. Assn. (pres. 1986-87), The Country Club (Brookline), Somerset (Boston) Club, Harvard of Boston, Leander (Henley-on-Thames, England), Cambridge Boat, Thames Rowing (London), Lake (Dublin, N.H.) Club. Home: 126 Coolidge Hl Cambridge MA 02138-5522 Office: McLean Hosp 115 Mill St Belmont MA 02478-1048

DE MARR, MARY JEAN, English language educator; b. Champaign, Ill., Sept. 20, 1932; d. William Fleming and Laura Alice (Shauman) Bailey. B.A., Lawrence Coll., 1954; M.A., U. Ill., 1957, Ph.D., 1963; postgrad., Universitaet Tuebingen, 1954-55, Moscow State U., 1961-62. Asst. prof. English Willamette U., 1964-65; asst. prof. English Ind. State U., 1965-70, asso. prof., 1970-75, prof., 1975-95, prof. emerita English and women's studies, 1996—. Author: Colleen McCullough: A Critical Companion, 1996; co-author: Adolescent Female Portraits in the American Novel, 1961-81: An Annotated Bibliography, 1983, The Adolescent in The American Novel Since 1960, 1986; Am. editor: Annual Bibliography of English Language and Literature, 1979-90; editor, contbr. In the Beginning: First Novels in Mystery Series, 1995. Recipient Fulbright assistantship, 1954-55. Mem. MLA, Modern Humanities Research Assn., AAUP, Nat. Council Tchrs. English, ACLU, Phi Beta Kappa, Phi Kappa Phi. Home: 594 Woodbine Terre Haute IN 47803-1760 Office: Ind State U Dept English Terre Haute IN 47809

DEMAR-SALAD, GERALDINE, real estate sales and development executive, management consultant; b. Schenectady, N.Y., June 19, 1929; d. Matthew Peter and Mary Theresa (Sullivan) Relihan; m. Neil Joseph Demar, Aug. 5, 1950 (dec.); 1 child, Maureen Ann Demar-Hall; m. Bernard Salad, June 27, 1987 (dec.); stepchildren: Andrew, Jane Salad-Bingham. BS, SUNY, Albany, 1979; MS, Russell Sage Coll., 1982. Cert. real estate broker, appraiser, cons.; cert. residential specialist. Real estate sales, 1964-69; dir. Mcpl. Leased Housing Program, Schenectady, 1969-71; pres. Geraldine M. Demar Realty & Devel., Schenectady, 1971—; pres Demar-Salad & Assocs., Mgmt. Consultants, Schenectady, 1988—; panel mem. Housing for Elderly, Housing for Low Income Families, Housing and Devel. Capitol Dist Region, N.Y. Active Fla. West Coast Symphony League, Fla. Ballet Ambassadors, Selby (Fla.) Bot. Gardens League, Friends of Schenectady Mus., League Schenectady Symphony Orch., Saratoga (N.Y.) Performing Arts Ctr.; mem. Gov.'s Panel for Housing for the Elderly and Low Income Families in N.Y. State; mem. com. for Housing and Devel. for the Capitol Dist. Region of N.Y. State. Mem. AAUW, Nat. Assn. Realtors (grad. realtors inst. 1973, cert. residential specialist 1980), Soc. Real Estate Appraisers, N.Y. State Assn. Realtors, N.Y. State Assn. Real Estate Appraisers, Grad. Realtors' Inst., Nat. Trust for Historic Preservation, Schenectady Bd. Realtors, Albany Inst. History and Art, New Coll. Libr. Assn., Nat. Mus. Racing, Mohawk Golf and Country Club, Country Club Sarasota. Unitarian. Avocations: creative writing, poetry, antiques, travel, the arts. Home: 1149 Ruffner Rd Schenectady NY 12309-4612 Home (winter): 4021 Via Mirada Sarasota FL 34238-2750

DEMARTIN, CHARLES PETER, lawyer; b. N.Y.C., Aug. 21, 1952; s. Samuel Peter and Rose Marie (Parisi) DeM.; m. Frances Gloria Vitrano, Apr. 4, 1981; children: Stephen, Charles, Joseph. BS, SUNY, Binghamton, 1974; JD, St. John's U., Jamaica, N.Y., 1977. Bar: N.Y. 1978, D.C. 1978, U.S. Dist. Ct. (ea. and so. dists.) N.Y. 1978, U.S. Ct. Appeals (2d cir.) 1983; U.S. Dist. Ct. Ariz., 1993. Assoc. Hartman & Lerner, Mineola, N.Y., 1978-80; pvt. practice law Garden City, N.Y., 1980, 85-87; counsel Curtis, Zaklukiewicz, Vasile & Devine, Merrick, N.Y., 1980-82, 85-87; ptnr. DeMartin, Kranz, Davis & Hersh, Hauppauge, N.Y., 1981-85, Damadeo & DeMartin, Hicksville, N.Y., 1987-88; pvt. practice law Huntington, N.Y., 1989-92; ptnr. McCarthy, McCarthy & DeMartin, Huntington, 1992-94; pvt. practice law Huntington, N.Y., 1994—. Mem. N.Y. State Bar Assn., Nassau County Bar Assn., D.C. Bar Assn., Brookville Country Club. Republican. Roman Catholic. Avocations: golf, sports, photography. Home: 2 Bluebird Ln Huntington NY 11743-6502 Office: 870 W Jericho Tpke Huntington NY 11743-6037

DEMARTINI, FRANK THOMAS, film company executive, lawyer; b. Oyster Bay, N.Y., Feb. 23, 1962; s. Frank Anthony and Grace Marie (Lombardi) DeM. AB, Syracuse U., 1983; JD cum laude, Touro Coll., Huntington, N.Y., 1986. Bar: Calif. 1986. Atty. Edwin J. Richards & Assocs., Santa Anna, Calif., 1986-88; prin. v.p. Pentalpha Film Group, Hollywood, Calif., 1987-89; atty. Lewis & Co., Santa Monica, Calif., 1988; owner Martin and DeMartini Law Firm, L.A., 1988-92; ptnr. Anderson & DeMartini, 1992-98; owner Palladin Film Group, 1994-98; ptnr. Barab, Anderson, Barton, DeMartini, Kline and Coate LLP, Beverly Hills, 1996-97; owner, CEO DeMartini/Anderson Prodns., L.A., 1998—; cons. Dianne Bridget Beatty, L.A., 1987-89, Ashton Nolley, 1987-90, Dy Sharr Music Pub., 1988-92, Beholder Film corp., 1989-92, ALB Prodns., Inc., 1989—. Prodr. Motel Blue, 1997, The Replacement, 1999; assoc. prodn. Crystal Lake, 1990, Loving Deadly, 1994; asst. producer TV show The Laughter Co., 1986. Asst. committeeman Nassau County Rep. Com., Salisbury, N.Y., 1985-86. Mem. ABA (tax entertainment com.). Roman Catholic. Avocations: music, theater. Office: Anderson & DeMartini 3765 Motor Ave # 710 Los Angeles CA 90034-6403

DEMARTINI, ROBERT JOHN, textile company executive; b. N.Y.C., Apr. 4, 1919; s. Andrew John and Regina Louise (Bosetti) D.; m. Carol Elaine Bauer, Feb. 5, 1945; children: Nancy Demartini Warner, David, Regina Demartini Carter. BS, MIT, 1941. Registered profl. engr., Mass. Textile engr. Russell Mfg. Co., Middletown, Conn., 1941-43; textile application engr. Gen. Electric Co., Schenectady, 1943-51; with Huyck Corp., 1951-79; exec. v.p. internat. ops. Huyck Corp., Wake Forest, N.C., 1973-79; dir. King Fifth Wheel Corp., 1977-82; pres. Demartini Devel. Industries, 1979—; gen. ptnr. REICO Ltd., 1980-86; adj. prof. N.C. State U., 1980-87. Contbr. articles to profl. jours. Bd. dirs. N.C. World Trade Coun., 1976-79, Ctr. for New Bus. Devel., 1979-82; exec. adviser U. N.C. Sch. Bus. Adminstrn., 1985-87; chmn. Flat Rock Inc. Project, 1993-95. Mem. Kenmure Golf Club, Seabrook Island Club. Patentee in field. Office: 208 Pineholt Ln Flat Rock NC 28731-9767

DEMARTINI, RODNEY J., executive director religious organization, priest; b. San Francisco, May 16, 1947; s. Eugene Louis DeMartini and Dina Inez Fabbri. BA in Philosophy/Theology, Chaminade U., 1969; MTh, U. Notre Dame, 1974, MAin Liturgical Studies (Rsch.), 1974; MA in Counseling Psychology, Santa Clara U., 1987. Dept. chairperson religious studies Archbishop Riordan H.S., San Francisco, 1970-72; dir. campus ministry ArchbishopMitty H.S., San Jose, Calif., 1976-78, prin., 1978-85. Author: Be With Me, Lord, 1982; contbr. articles on ministry to persons with HIV/AIDS and ednl. challenges facing the Church and soc. Outstanding Alumnus award Santa Clara U., Calif., 1989. Bd. dirs. AIDS Svc. Providers Assn. of the Bay Area (pres. 1989-93), Aris Project in Santa Clara County (pres. 1986-91), Nat. Cath. AIDS Network in San Francisco; dir. AIDS Edn. for the Archdiocese of San Francisco, 1988-93; mem. Secondary Schs. Exec. Com. of the Nat. Cath. Ednl. Assn. (sec. 1982-88), Washington. Successfully lobbying the Nat. Cath. Ednl. Assn. to place resources for AIDS edn. on the nat. agenda for elem. and secondary schs.; helped to found Western State Cath. AIDS Coalition and Nat. Cath. AIDS Network. Address: 12500 Dupont Rd Sebastopol CA 95472-9777

DEMARTINO, ANTHONY GABRIEL, cardiologist, internist; b. Bronx, Oct. 7, 1931; s. Agostino and Vincenzina (Clarizia) DeM.; BS cum laude, Iona Coll., 1953; MD, SUNY, 1957; m. Marlene Mignone, Aug. 8, 1964; children: Anthony Augustin, Laura Jean. Intern, Univ. div. Kings County Med. Center, Bklyn., 1957-58, med. resident, 1960-62; fellow cardiopulmonary Cornell U., N.Y. Hosp., 1962-64; acting chief medicine Fordham div. Misericordia Fordham Affiliation, Bronx, 1964-65; physician in charge cardiac lab. Misericordia-Fordham Affiliation, 1965-69; attending physician dept. medicine and cardiology Our Lady of Mercy Med. Ctr., Bronx, 1967—, sr. physician, 1995—, mem. med. bd., 1985-93; attending physician dept. medicine and cardiology Lawrence Hosp., Bronxville, N.Y., 1977—, mem. med. bd., 1989-94, sec., treas. Med. Bd. Lawrence Hosp., 1996-97, assoc. dir. Dept. Medicine, Lawrence Hosp., Bronxville, N.Y., 1993-97; practice medicine, specializing in cardiology and internal medicine, Bronx and Bronxville, 1964—; v.p. med. bd. Misericordia Hosp. Med. Center, Bronx, 1973-75, pres., 1975-77; clin. asst. prof. medicine N.Y. Med. Coll., 1971—; hon. police surgeon N.Y.C.; asst. physician Presbyn. Hosp., N.Y., 1996—; asst. in medicine Columbia U., N.Y.C., 1996—. Trustee, Misericordia Hosp., 1977-83; sec., treas. med. bd. Lawrence Hosp., 1996-97. Served to capt., M.C., U.S. Army, 1958-60. Nat. Heart Inst. fellow, 1962-64. Diplomate Nat. Bd. Med. Examiners, Am. Bd. Internal Medicine (cardiovascular disease). Fellow ACP/Am. Soc. Internal Medicine, Am. Coll. Cardiology, Council Clin. Cardiology of Am. Heart Assn., Am. Coll. Chest Physicians, N.Y. Cardiol. Assn.; mem. AMA, Westchester County, N.Y. County Med. Soc., Amer. Coll. of Med. Roman Catholic. Contbr. articles to profl. jours; editorial bd. N.Y. Med. Quar., 1980-84. Office: 4350 Van Cortlandt Park E Bronx NY 10470-1875 also: 77 Pondfield Rd Bronxville NY 10708-3809

DE MASSA, JESSIE G., media specialist. BJ, Temple U.; MLS, San Jose State U., 1967; postgrad., U. Okla., U. So. Calif. Tchr. Palo Alto (Calif.) Unified Sch. Dist., 1966; librarian Antelope Valley Joint Union High Sch. Dist., Lancaster, Calif., 1966-68, ABC Unified Sch. Dist., Artesia, Calif., 1968-72; dist. librarian Tehachapi (Calif.) Unified Sch. Dist., 1972-81; media specialist, free lance writer, 1981—; assoc. Chris DeMassa & Assocs., 1988—. Contbr. articles to profl. jours. Mem. Statue of Liberty Ellis Island Found., Inc.; charter supporter U.S. Holocaust Meml. Mus., Washington; supporting mem. U.S. Holocaust Meml. Coun., Washington. Named to Nat. Women's Hall of Fame, 1995. Fellow Internat. Biog. Assn.; mem. Calif. Media and Libr. Educators Assn., Calif. Assn. Sch. Librs. (exec. coun.), AAUW (bull. editor chpt., assoc. editor state bull., chmn. publicity, 1955-68), Nat. Mus. Women in Arts (charter), Hon Fellows John F. Kennedy Libr. (founding mem.), Women's Roundtable of Orange County, Nat. Writer's Assn. (so. Calif. chpt.), Calif. Retired Tchrs. Assn. (Harbor Beach divsn. 77), The Heritage Found., Claremont Inst., Libr. of Congress (nat. charter mem.), Cato Inst. Home: 9951 Garrett Cir Huntington Beach CA 92646-3604

DEMATTEIS, CLAIRE, state director. BA in Comm. and Polit. Sci., U. Del.; JD, Widener U., 1991. Assignment editor, writer WHYY-TVIZ, Wilmington, Del., 1987-88; legis/gen. assignment reporter WBOC-TV, Salisbury, Mo., 1988-92, Dover, Del., 1988-92; weekend anchor WBOC-TV, Salisbury, Dover, 1989-90; dep. campaign mgr. Castle for Congress '92, 1992; legal asst. Office of Gov. Michael N. Castle, Wilmington, 1992-94; press spokesperson, legis. asst. Office of Rep. Michael N. Castle, Washington, 1993-94; campaign mgr. Castle for Congress '94, Washington, 1994; legal counsel U.S. Senate jud. com. Office of Senator Joseph Biden, Washington, 1995, state dir., 1995—. Bd. dirs. Del. Spl. Olympics. Recipient Best Pub. Affairs Show, AP Awards, Sch. Bell Media award Del. State Edn. Assn. Mem. ABA, Del. State Bar Assn. (chairperson women and the law sect., exec. com. mem.), Pa. Bar Assn., Dem. Women's Club Del., Univ. Del. Alumni Assn. (sec., bd. dirs.). Office: J Calea Boggs Fed Bldg 844 King St Rm 6021 Wilmington DE 19801

DEMATTEO, GLORIA JEAN, insurance saleswoman; b. Perth Amboy, N.J., May 23, 1943; d. John J. and Helena (Elias) Kancz; m. Ronald D. DeMatteo, Feb. 20, 1965 (div. Nov. 1987); children: Douglas J., Keith G. Student, Berkeley Sch., 1961. CLU. Exec. sec. Rhodia Inc., New Brunswick, N.J., 1961-65; real estate saleswomen Mid-Jersey Realty, East Brunswick, N.J., 1974-79; ptnr. Realty World Garden of Homes, East Brunswick, 1979-81; spl. agt. Prudential Ins. Co. Am., Iselin, N.J., 1981—. V.p. Belcourt Condo Assn., North Brunswick, N.J., 1987-88. Mem. Nat. Assn. Life Underwriters (nat. sales achievement award, nat. quality award), Soc. Fin. Svc. Profls., Prudential Leaders Club. Avocations: bridge, hiking, dancing, theater. Home: 463 Andover Pl East Brunswick NJ 08816-5121 Office: Prudential Ins Co 100 Metro Park S Lawrence Harbor NJ 08878-2001

DE MAURET, KEVIN JOHN, geologist; b. Bayonne, N.J., Feb. 21, 1957; s. Ferdinand and Mary (Kyprious) de M. BA in Geoscis., Jersey City State Coll., 1978; MS in Geology, Rutgers U., 1984. Cert. profl. geologist, Del., Ind., Tenn., Wyo., Pa. Rsch. asst. Lamont-Doherty Geol. Observatory, Palisades, N.Y., 1982-84, Ocean Drilling Program, College Station, Tex., 1984-86; project supr. IT Corp., Edison, N.J., 1986-88; project mgr. EFP Assocs., Inc., Matawan, N.J., 1988-90; pres., chief exec. officer Innovative Environ. Cons., Inc., Morristown, N.J., 1990—. Mem. Union and Middlesex County Hazardous Materials Adv. Coun. Mem. Am. Assn. Petroleum Geologists, Am. Geophys. Union, Am. Inst. Profl. Geologists, Am. Water Resources Assn., N.J. Water Pollution Control Assn., N.Y. Acad. Scis., Soc. Econ. Paleontologists and Minerologists, Assn. Ground Water Scientists and Engrs., Water Pollution Control Fedn., Assn. Environ. Health of Soils. Office: Innovative Environ Cons Inc PO Box 9210 Morristown NJ 07963-9210

DEMAUSE, LLOYD, psychohistorian; b. Detroit, Sept. 19, 1931; s. Leon and Martha (Koren) DeM.; m. Susan Hein; children: Neil, Jennifer, Jonathan. Student, GM Inst., 1948-52; AB, Columbia U., 1957, postgrad., 1957-61; postgrad., Nat. Psychol. Assn. for Psychoanalysis, 1959-60. Founder Atcom Inc. (pub.), 1959; chmn. bd., dir. Inst. for Psychohistory; pub. Psychohistory Press; mem. faculty N.Y. Center for Psychoanalytic Tng. Editor, author: Jimmy Carter and American Fantasy, The History of Childhood, The New Psychohistory, A Bibliography of Psychohistory, Foundations of Psychohistory, Reagan's America; editor: Jour. Psychohistory. With AUS, 1952-54. Mem. Internat. Psychohist. Assn. (pres.). E-mail: psychhste@tlac.net. Home and Office: Inst for Psychohistory 140 Riverside Dr New York NY 10024-2605

DEMAY, PATRICIA ANN, elementary educator, education educator; b. Jackson, Mich.; d. C.E. and Myrtle (Bleicher) DeM. BA, Siena Heights Coll., 1956, MA in Sch. Adminstrn., 1965; EdS, U. Tenn., 1973, EdD, 1980. Tchr. grades 1-6 various schs. Mich., Fla., Ill., 1948-65; prin. St. Jude, Flint, Mich., 1965-68; tchr., prin. St. Joseph, Adrian, Mich., 1968-71; prof. Barry Coll., Miami, 1971-72; grade 1-2 tchr. Bailey Sch., Hillsdale, Mich., 1972-80; libr. dir. Hillsdale Cmty Sch., 1978-80; prof. edn. U. West Ala., Livingston, 1980—. Reviewer children's books; contbr. articles to profl. jours. Past pres. Livingston Interfaith Coun., 1988—; spkr. local orgns., 1987-97; mem. People to People reps. to Russia, Hungary. Mem. Internat. Reading Assn., Reading and Children, Alpha Delta Kappa (past pres. 1982-87), Nat. Coun. Tchrs. English, Internat. Bd. on Books for Young People, Children's Literature Assn. Avocations: photography, quilting, knitting, travel. Office: U of West Ala Station 32 Livingston AL 35470

DEMBER, WILLIAM NORTON, psychologist, educator; b. Waterbury, Conn., Aug. 8, 1928; s. David and Henrietta (Siegel) D.; m. Cynthia Fox, Dec. 21, 1958; children: Joanna, Laura, Gregory. AB, Yale U., 1950; MA, U. Mich., 1951, PhD, 1955. Instr. dept. psychology U. Mich., 1954-56; asst. prof. Yale U., 1956-59; mem. faculty U. Cin., 1959-98, prof. psychology, 1965-98, asst. dean, grad. sch., 1965-67, head dept. psychology, 1968-76, 79-81, dean Coll. Arts and Scis., 1981-86, disting. rsch. prof., 1989, prof. and dean emeritus, 1998. Author: Psychology of Perception, 1960, 2d edit., 1979, Visual Perception, 1964, General Psychology, 1970, 2d edit., 1984, Exploring Behavior and Experience, 1971, Spontaneous Alternation Behavior, 1989; contbr. articles to profl. jours. Fellow APA, Am. Psychol. Soc.; mem. Midwest Psychol. Assn. (pres. 1976), Ea. Psychol. Assn. Developed and tested theory of motivation applying to behavior of human beings and animals. Research contributions to visual metacontrast, optimism/pessimism, and sustained attention. Home: 920 Oregon Trl Cincinnati OH 45215-2536 Office: U Cin Dept Psychology Cincinnati OH 45221-0376

DEMBLING, PAUL GERALD, lawyer, former government official; b. Rahway, N.J., Jan. 11, 1920; s. Simon and Fannie (Ellenbogen) D.; m. Florence Brotman, Nov. 22, 1947; children: Ross Wayne, Douglas Evan, Donna Stacy. B.A., Rutgers U., 1940, M.A., 1942; J.D., George Washington U., 1951. Bar: D.C. 1952. Grad. asst., teaching fellow Rutgers U., 1940-42; economist Office Chief Transp., Dept. Army, 1942-45; since practiced in Washington; indsl. relations NACA, 1945-51, spl. counsel, legal adviser, gen. counsel, 1951-58; asst. gen. counsel NASA, 1958-61, dir. legis. affairs, 1961-63, dep. gen. counsel, 1963-67, gen. counsel, 1967-69, chmn. bd. contract appeals, 1958-61, vice chmn. inventions and contbns. bd., 1959-67; mem. and alt. rep. U.S. del. UN Legal Subcom. Com. on Outer Space, 1964-69; gen. counsel GAO, 1969-78; partner Schnader, Harrison, Segal & Lewis,

Washington, 1978-93, sr. counsel, 1994—; prin. author NASA Act, 1958; professorial lectr. George Washington U. Law Sch., 1965-86. Co-author: Federal Contract Management, 1988, Essentials of Grant Law Practice, 1991; editor in chief Fed. Bar Jour., 1962-69; contbr. articles to profl. jours. Recipient Meritorious Civilian Service award War Dept., 1945; Disting. Service medal NASA, 1968; Nat. Civil Service League award, 1973. Fellow AIAA (chmn. com. law and sociology 1969-71), Nat. Contract Mgmt. Assn. (bd. advisers 1973—), Nat. Acad. Pub. Adminstrn., Am. Bar Found. (life); mem. ABA (coun., public contract law sec. 1983-84, vice chmn. 1984-85, chmn. elect 1985-86, chmn. 1986-87), FBA (nat. coun. 1963—, pres. Capitol Hill chpt. 1977-78, nat. sec. 1978-79, pres.-elect 1981-82, nat. pres. 1983-84, bd. dirs. bldg. corp. 1989—), D.C. Bar (mem. steering com. govt. contracts and litigation sect. 1989-95), Procurement Roundtable (bd. dirs. 1984—, vice chmn. 1988—), Internat. Inst. Space Law (pres. Am. assn. 1970-72, Internat. Astronaut. Fedn. award 1992), Cosmos Club, Nat. Lawyers Club, Phi Delta Phi. Home: 10524 Kipling Way Lake Worth FL 33467-8615 Office: Schnader Harrison Segal & Lewis 1300 I St NW Washington DC 20005-3314

DEMBO, LAWRENCE SANFORD, English educator; b. Troy, N.Y., Dec. 3, 1929; s. Irving and Mildred (Spiwak) D.; m. Royce Benderson, Mar. 15, 1953. B.A., Syracuse U., 1951; M.A., Columbia, 1952; Ph.D., Cornell U., 1955. Instr. English Cornell U., 1959-60; asst. prof. UCLA, 1960-65; Fulbright lectr. Montpellier, France, 1963-64; prof. English U. Wis., Madison, 1965-90, prof. emeritus, 1990—. Author: Hart Crane's Sanskrit Charge, A Study of the Bridge, 1960, The Confucian Odes of Ezra Pound, A Critical Appraisal, 1963, Conceptions of Reality in Modern American Poetry, 1966, The Monological Jew, A Literary Study, 1988, Detotalized Totalities: Synthesis and Disintegration in Naturalist, Existential, and Socialist Fiction, 1989; editor: Nabokov, The Man and His Work, 1967, Criticism, Speculative and Analytical Essays, 1968; co-editor: The Contemporary Writer: Interviews with Sixteen Novelists and Poets, 1972, Doris Lessing, Critical Studies, 1974, Directions for Criticism, 1977, Interviews with Contemporary Writers, Second Series, 1972-82, 83; editor in chief: Contemporary Literature, 1966-90; mem. editorial bd. Am. Lit., 1973-76; author poetry/contbr. regional jours. Served to lt. USNR, 1955-65. Guggenheim fellow, 1968-69; Am. Council Learned Socs. fellow, 1977-78. Home: 3434 Valley Creek Cir Middleton WI 53562-1990 Office: U Wis Madison 7164 Helen White Hall Madison WI 53706-1416

DEMBOWSKI, PETER FLORIAN, foreign language educator; b. Warsaw, Poland, Dec. 23, 1925; came to U.S., 1966, naturalized, 1974; s. Wlodzimierz and Henryka (Sokolowski) D.; m. Yolande Jessop, June 29, 1954; children: Anne, Eve, Paul. B.A. with honors, U. B.C., 1952; Doctorat d'Universite, U. Paris, France, 1954; Ph.D., U. Calif. at Berkeley, 1960. Instr. French U. B.C., 1954-56; asst. prof. French U. Toronto, 1960-63, assoc. prof., 1963-66; mem. faculty U. Chgo., 1966-95, prof. French, 1970-95, Disting. Svc. prof., 1989-95, prof. emeritus, 1995—, dean students div. humanities, 1968-70, chmn. dept. Romance langs. and lits., 1976-83, resident master Snell-Hitchcock halls, 1973-79; vis. mem. Sch. Hist. Studies, Inst. Advanced Study, Princeton, N.J., 1979-80. Author: La Chronique de Robert de Clari, 1963, Jourdain de Blaye, 1969, Ami et Amile, 1969, La Vie de sainte Marie l'Egyptienne, 1977, Jean Froissart and his Meliador, 1983, Jean Froissart, Le Paradis d'Amour et l'Orloge Amoureus, 1986, Erec et Enide, 1994. Served with Polish Army, 1944-46. Decorated Cross of Valor, Cross of Service with swords (Poland), Chevalier des Palmes Academiques (France); Guggenheim fellow, 1970-71; Danforth Found. assoc., 1976-84. Fellow Am. Acad. Arts and Scis.; mem. Société de Linguistique Romane (councillor 1995—), Medieval Acad. Am. (councillor 1980-82). Office: U Chgo Dept Romance Langs and Lit 1050 E 59th St Chicago IL 60637-1559

DEMBROW, DANA LEE, lawyer; b. Washington, Sept. 29, 1953; parents: Daniel William and Catherine Louise (Carder) D. BA, Duke U., 1975; JD, George Washington U., 1980. Bar: D.C., Md., W.Va. Law clk. D.C. Superior Ct., Washington, 1979-80; assoc. Smink & Scheuermann, Washington, 1980-81, Reback & Parsons, Washington, 1981-82, Howard M. Rensin, Hyattsville, Md., 1984-86; mem. com. on constitutional and adminstrv. law Md. Ho. of Dels., 1986-92; mem. jud. com. Md. State Legis., 1993—; chair county affairs com., Montgomery Del., 1994—; can. for congress, Md.'s 4th Congl. Dist., 1992; chair subcom. on civil law and procedure House Judiciary Com., 1994—. Chair Colesville Strawberry Festival, 1998, 99. Office: 220-A Lhob Annapolis MD 21401

DEMBSKI, STEPHEN MICHAEL, composer, university music composition professor; b. Boston, Dec. 13, 1949; s. Theodore Arthur and Minna Morris (Baldauf) D.; m. Sonja Sullivan, July 9, 1988; children: Melissa Leonora, Rachel Michalena. BA, Antioch Coll., 1973; MA, SUNY, Stony Brook, 1975; MFA, Princeton U., 1977, PhD, 1980. Dir. advanced composition program U. Wis., Madison, 1982—; prof., 1982—; bd. dirs. Composers' Recordings, Inc., N.Y.C., Internat. Soc. Contemporary Music, N.Y.C., N.Y. New Music Ensemble, Phantom Arts, Boston; vis. asst. prof. Dartmouth Coll., Hanover, N.H., 1978-81, Bates Coll., Lewiston, Maine, 1982. Composer musical scores including Trio, 1977, Alba, 1980, Alta, 1981, At Baia, 1984, Spectra, 1985, The Show, 1986, Sonata for Violin and Piano, 1987-88, Digit, 1978, Stacked Deck, 1979, Altamira, 1983, On Ondine, 1991, Two Scenes from Elsaveta, 1992, So Fine, 1993, For Five, 1994, Hornbill, 1994, Memory's Minefield, 1994, Needles & Pins, 1994, Out of My System, 1995, Sonotropism, 1996, Brass Attacks, 1998, Le Monde Merengue, 1998; composer recordings including CRI, 1988, 90, Vienna Modern Masters, 1990, Music and Arts, 1997; condr. recordings include Scott Fields' 48 Motives, Cadence, 1996; editor: (with others) Milton Babbitt-Words About Music, 1987. Fellow Howard Found., Providence, 1986-87, Nat. Endowment for the Arts, Washington, 1979, 81, 86; recipient Goddard Lieberson award Am. Acad. and Inst. of Arts and Letters, 1982, Segnalazione: Premio Musicale award Citta di Trieste, 1990. Mem. ASCAP, Soc. for Music Theory, Am. Music Ctr. Home: 96 Perry St Apt 22B New York NY 10014-5501 Office: U Wis Sch of Music 455 N Park St Madison WI 53706-1405

DEMEGRET, A. JEAN HUGHES, secondary education educator, artist; b. Hancock County, Ind., Oct. 22, 1927; d. Harlin E. and Melva L. Hughes. BAE, Butler U., 1949; student, John Herron Art Inst., Indpls.; MA, Columbia U., 1965; postgrad., No. Ill. U., Europe, 1966. Tchr. art Indpls. Pub. Schs., 1949-51; tchr. art and English Fortville (Ind.) Sch. Sys., 1951-62; supr. art dept. Greenfield (Ind.) Ctrl. H.S., 1962-84; tchr. adult art high schs., Indpls. and Greenfield. Exhibited paintings in Hoosier Art Show, 1960s and 70s, Ind. State Fair, 1960s and 70s, Columbia U. Art Gallery, 1963-66, others. Mem. Indpls. Mus. Art. Mem. Hancock County Ret. Tchrs., Bus. and Profl. Women (past pres.), Order Eastern Star, Ind. Sch. Women's Club, Nat. Art Educators Assn., Nat. Women in Art, Internat. Soc. Educators in Art, Delta Kappa Gamma (past pres.). Methodist. Avocations: painting portraits and horses, music, travel. Home: 411 S Main St Fortville IN 46040-1610

DEMELLO, AUSTIN EASTWOOD, astrophysicist, concert artist, poet, writer; b. New Bedford, Mass., Oct. 15, 1939; s. Manuel and Dora (Eastwood) De M; children: Adragon Eastwood De Mello, Brad Steven. BA in English, UCLA, 1974; MSc in Physics and Astronomy, Met. Coll. Inst., London, 1977, DSc in Theoretical Astrophysics, 1981. Engring. writer Raytheon Co., Santa Barbara, Calif., 1982; dir. research and sci. publs. Cosmosci. Research Inst., Sunnyvale, Calif., 1983—; sr. engring. writer, cons. Lockheed Martin, Sunnyvale, 1997. Author: Black Night Poetry, 1960, Tengu, 1962, (record) El Duende Flamenco, 1965, The Metagalactic System, 1969, The Four States of Man, 1971, Early Development of the Scientific Mind, 1981, Theory of Cosmodynamics, 1983, The Cosmotorsion Effect, 1984, James Bay Missionaries, 1986, The Origin and Influence of Flamenco Music on the Classics, 1992, Offenbach and the Can-Can Dance, 1993, Adragon: The Youngest Scholar, 1993, Legacy of Poetry and Philosophy, 1993, The Magic Formula, 1993, Views of Chaos, 1993, Haiku of the Sea Poet, 1997, Beware the Dragon of the Id, 1997, Evolution of an Assassin, 1997, The Scholar and the University, 1997, The Violent Life, 1997, (staged screen play) Petenera, 1997, The Ollave, 1998, Count Quentin, 1998. Acad. Merit scholar UCLA, 1972-74. Mem. AIAA, AAAS, N.Y. Acad. Sci., Am. Astronautical Soc., Mensa Internat. Home: PO Box 461 Moss Landing CA 95039-0461 Office: CSR Inst 663 S Bernardo Ave Sunnyvale CA 94087-1020

DE MELLO, F. PAUL, electrical engineer; b. Goa, India, July 20, 1927. BS, MIT, 1947, MS, 1948. Sr. engr. GE, 1955-69, prin. engr. dynamics and control, sec., treas., 1969-73, v.p., sec., 1973-87; prin. cons. Power Technologies, Inc., Schenectady, N.Y., 1987—. Contbr. articles to numerous tech. publs. Fellow IEEE (mem. Sys. Controls Subcom. & Joint Working Group Plant Response), Instrument Soc. Am.; mem. Nat. Acad. Engring., Computer Inst. Application Sci. & Engring. Office: Power Technologies Inc PO Box 1058 Schenectady NY 12301-1058*

DEMENCHONOK, EDWARD VASILEVICH, philosopher, linguist, researcher, educator; b. Vitebesk, Belarus, Jan. 1, 1942; came to U.S., 1992; s. Vasiliy Ivanovich Demenchonok and Olga Stanislavovna Plovinskaya; m. Sondra Marisa Franceil, July 1, 1993; children: Anna, Leonid. *Mother, Olga Stanislavovna Plovinskaya, despite the harsh conditions of repression, preserved the cultural heritage and substantially contributed to her children's education. Brother, Leonid Petrovich Yakovlev, received an M.S. from the Polytechnic Institute, Minsk, in 1962, and is a civil engineer and architect. He constructed the Memorial Complex Khatyn for victims of the Nazi occupation near Minsk and, also, the Institute of Physics of the Belarus Academy of Sciences, among others. Wife, Sondra Marisa Franceil, received an ED.S. from the University of Georgia, and is an educator and fiber artist. She is currently doing research on the handspinning and weaving techniques and fibers of the ancient eastern Mediterranean cultures.* BA in Music, Mus. Coll., Minsk, Belarus, 1961; MA in Russian and Spanish, Moscow State U. Lomonosov, 1969; PhD, Russian Acad. Scis., Moscow, 1977. Rschr., then sr. rschr. Inst. Philosophy Russian Acad. Scis., 1970-95; assoc. prof. Moscow State U. Lomonosov, 1982-84; prof. Moscow State Pedagogic U., 1991-92; prof. Spanish Am. dept. Acad. Slavic Culture, Moscow, 1991-92; assoc. prof. Spanish Brewton-Parker Coll., Mt. Vernon, Ga., 1994-95; assoc. prof. fgn. langs. Ft. Valley (Ga.) State U., 1995—; vis. rschr. Acad. Scis. Cuba, 1978, 79, 83; vis. prof. U. INCCA Colombia, Bogota, 1988-90; vis. prof. Spanish U. Ga., Athens, 1992-93; lectr. literature Spanish Am. thought and philosophy at various instns., including U. Cordoba, Argentina, 1987, Inst. Missionary Theology, Bogota, 1990, Nat. Inst. Sci. Rsch. Coord. Colombia, Bogota, 1989, 90, Inst. Faith and Secularity, Madrid, Spain, 1992, U. Complutense Madrid, 1992, others; participant profl. confs., most recently Internat. Congress of L.Am. Philosophy: Ethics in L.Am., Bogota, 1990, Internat. Congress: East and West, Dialogue of Cultures in Contemporary World, Moscow, 1992, 9th Internat. Congress in Galicia: Philosophy and Nation, Pontevedra, Spain, 1992, 2nd Internat. Congress L.Am. Philosophy, San Juan, P.R., 1993, 93rd Ann. Meeting Am. Philos. Assn., Chgo., 1995, 94th Ann. Meeting, Phila., 1997, Americas Coun. First Ann. Conf., Savannah, Ga., 1997, An Interdisciplinary Conf.: Hispanics: Cultural Locations, San Francisco, 1997, 45th Ann. Conf. of Southeastern Coun. on Latin Am. Studies, Savannah, Ga., 1998, 20th World Congress of Philosophy: Philosophy Educating Humanity, Boston, 1998, 3d World Congress Internat. Soc. Universalism, Wellesley, Mass., 1998, 13th Ann. Internat. Conf. in Lit., Visual Arts, and Cinema, Atlanta, 1998, Fulbright Seminar on Tradition and Transformation in Singapore and Malaysia, 1998, 38th Ann. S.E. Conf. of Assn. for Asian Studies, Athens, Ga., 1999, 14th Inter-Am. Congress of Philosophy, Puebla, Mex., 1999. *Edward Demenchonok participated in educational reforms in Russia and in founding the Academy of Slavic Culture. He has more than 25 years of research work in the Russian Academy of Sciences. He specializes in contemporary Western philosophy and was the first person in Russia to publish works about Latin American philosophy and theology of liberation. His publications furthered the Russian people's knowledge of Western philosophical thought and the concepts of human individuality, freedom, and democracy. He contributed to the democratic transformation in Russia. His fields of research work include: philosophical anthropology, philosophy of culture, social philosophy and ethics. He critically analyzed behaviorist and technocratic theories. He promotes the humanistic concept of man and culture.* Author: Contemporary Technocratic Thought in the U.S.A., 1984; (in Spanish) América Latina en la Época de la Revolución Científico-Téchnica, 1990, Filosofía en el Mundo Contemporaneo, 1990, Filosofía Latinoamericana: Problemas y Tendencias, 1990; editor: Problems of Philosophy and Culture in Latin America, 1983, Contemporary Catholic Philosophy, 1985, New Tendencies in Western Social Philosophy, 1988; contbr. articles to profl. jours., chpts. to books. Mem. MLA (participant convs. 1992, 93), L.Am. Studies Assn. (participant XVIII congress 1994), Am. Philos. Assn., Internat. Soc. Universalism, Russian Philosophical Soc., Assn. Cultural Rschrs. Russia, Assn. for Philosophy and Liberation, Southeastern Coun. Latin Am. Studies, Soc. for Iberian and L.Am. Thought. Russian Orthodox. Avocation: music.

DE MENIL, LOIS PATTISON, historian, philanthropist; b. N.Y.C., May 15, 1938; d. Charles Krone and Julia Anne (Hasson) Pattison; m. Georges Francois Conrad de Menil, Aug. 3, 1968; children: John-Charles, Joy-Alexandra, Benjamin, Victoria. AB, Wellesley Coll., 1960; diploma, Inst. d'Etudes Politiques, Paris, 1962; Lic. in Law, U. Paris, 1962; PhD, Harvard U., 1972. Pres. D. M. Found., N.Y.C., 1986—; counsellor to Ministry of Culture, Romania, 1997—; mem. Coun. Fgn. Rels., 1976—, Inst. for Strategic Studies, London, 1978—, French Inst. Internat. Rels., Paris, 1980—, U.S. Coun. on Germany, N.Y.C., 1978—, Festival d'Automne, Paris, 1997—. Author: Who Speaks for Europe?, 1978; editor, translator: The African Unity Movement, 1965, French Foreign Policy under De Gaulle, 1967. Mem. internat. coun. Mus. Modern Art, N.Y.C., 1975—; mem. vis. com. to art mus. Harvard U., Cambridge, Mass., 1977—; vice-chair bd. dirs. Dia Ctr. for Arts, N.Y.C., 1985-96; vice-chair trustees coun. Nat. Gallery Art, Washington, 1988-97, Centre d'Art Contemporain, Geneva, 1995—; bd. dirs. World Monuments Fund, N.Y.C., 1990—, Groton Sch., 1991—. Fulbright scholar, France, 1960-62; Ford Found. fellow, 1966-68. Mem. Century Assn., Univ. Club, River Club, Harvard Club, Fishers Island Country Club, Phi Beta Kappa. Episcopalian. Avocations: art, skiing, tennis, adventure travel. Home: 120 E 70th St New York NY 10021-5007 Office: D M Found 149 E 63rd St New York NY 10021-7405

DE MENT, IRA, judge; b. Birmingham, Ala., Dec. 21, 1931; s. Ira Jr. and Helen (Sparks) DeM.; m. Ruth Lester Posey; 1 child, Charles Posey. AS, Marion Mil. Inst., 1951; AB, U. Ala., 1953, LLB, 1958, JD, 1969. Bar: Ala. 1958, U.S. Dist. Ct. (mid. dist.) Ala. 1958, U.S. Ct. Appeals (5th cir.) 1958, U.S. Supreme Ct. 1966, U.S. Dist. Ct. (so. dist.) Ala. 1967, U.S. Dist. Ct. D.C. 1972, U.S. Ct. Appeals (D.C.) 1972, U.S. Tax Ct. 1972, U.S. Customs and Patents Appeals 1976, U.S. Dist. Ct. (no. dist.) Ala. 1977, U.S. Ct. Appeals (11th cir.), 1981, U.S. Ct. Mil. Appeal 1972. Law clk. Sup. Ct. Ala., 1958-59; asst. atty. gen. State of Ala., 1959, spl. asst. atty. gen., 1966-69, 81-92; asst. U.S. atty., Montgomery, Ala., 1959-61; pvt. practice Montgomery, 1961-69, 77-92; U.S. dist. judge (mid. dist.) Ala., 1992—;acting U.S. atty. Mid. Dist. Ala. 1969, U.S. atty., 1969-77; asst. atty., legal advisor to police and fire depts. City of Montgomery, 1965-69; instr. Jones Law Sch., 1962-64; instr. Montgomery Police Acad. 1964-77; lectr. constl. law Ala. Police Acad., 1971-75; instr. law enforcement U. Ala., 1967, mem. adj. faculty New Coll., 1974-75, adj. prof. psychology, 1975-92; spl. counsel to Gov. State Ala., 1980-88, gen. counsel Commn. on Aging, 1980-82. Lt. col. USAR, 1953-74; maj. gen. USAFR ret. Recipient Disting. Service award Internat. Assn. Firefighters, 1975; Rockefeller Pub. Service award, Woodrow Wilson Sch. Pub. and Internat. Affairs Princeton U., 1976; named Alumnus of Yr. Marion Mil. Inst., 1988, Significant Sig award Sigma Chi Fraternity, 1998, Judicial Award of Merit Ala. State Bar., 1998. Mem. ABA, Fed. Bar Assn., D.C. Bar Assn., Ala. Bar Assn. (mem. editorial adv. bd. The Alabama Lawyer 1966-72), Am. Judicature Soc.,Nat. Assn. Former U.S. Attys., Phi Alpha Delta. Republican. United Methodist. Clubs: Masons, Shriners. Address: PO Box 2149 Montgomery AL 36102-2149

DEMENT, JAMES ALDERSON, JR., lawyer; b. Clinton, Okla., Sept. 11, 1947; s. James Alderson and Ruby (Weaver) DeM.; m. Sally Anne Wylder, June 6, 1970; children: Stephen, Suzanne, Jonathan. BA summa cum laude, Tex. Christian U., 1969; JD in Internat. Affairs, Cornell U., 1972. Bar: N.Y. 1973, Tex. 1974. Assoc. Alexander & Green, N.Y.C., 1972-73; assoc. Baker & Botts, Houston, 1977-85, ptnr., 1998—; ptnr., chmn. corp. tax and internat. sect. Butler & Binion, LLP, Houston, 1985-97; adj. prof. U. Houston, 1987-88. Mem. edtl. rev. bd. The Internat. Lawyer, 1987-94. Trustee Houston Ballet Found., 1989-96, Brazos Presbyn. Homes, Inc., 1990-96. Capt. USAF, 1973-77. Fellow Tex. Bar Found.; mem. State Bar Tex. (internat. law sect., chmn. 1989-90), Internat. and Comparative Law Ctr. Southwestern Legal Found. (adv. coun. 1986—), Houston Bar Assn. (internat. law sect., pres. 1989-90). Presbyterian. Office: Baker & Botts LLP 1 Shell Plz 910 Louisiana St Houston TX 77002-4991*

DEMENT, WILLIAM CHARLES, sleep researcher, medical educator; b. Wenatchee, Wash., July 29, 1928; s. Charles Frederick and Kathryn (Severyns) D.; m. Eleanor Weber, Mar. 23, 1956; children: Catherine Lynn, Elizabeth Anne, John Nicholas. B.S., U. Wash., 1951; M.D., U. Chgo., 1955, Ph.D., 1957. Bd. cert. in clin. polysomography. Intern Mt. Sinai Hosp., N.Y.C., 1957-58, research fellow dept. psychiatry, 1958-63; assoc. prof. dept. psychiatry and behavioral scis. Stanford U., 1963-67, prof., 1967—; dir. Stanford Sleep Disorders Clinic and Lab., 1970—, Sleep Research Lab., Stanford, Calif., 1963—; chmn. U.S. Surgeon Gen.'s Joint Coord. Coun., Project Sleep, 1979—, Nat. Commn. on Sleep Disorders Rsch., 1990-92. Author: Some Must Watch While Some Must Sleep, 1972, The Sleep Watchers, 1992; editor-in-chief: Sleep, 1977—; mem. editorial bd. Neurobiology of Aging, 1982—. Recipient medal Intra-Sci. Research Found., 1981; recipient Disting. Service award U. Chgo. Med. Alumni Assn., 1978. Mem. Sleep Research Soc. (founder), Assn. Sleep Disorders Ctrs. (pres. 1982 Nathaniel Kleitman prize), Inst. Medicine of Nat. Acad. Scis., Psychiat. Research Found., Soc. Neurosci., Western EEG Soc., Am. EEG Soc., Am. Physiol. Soc. Office: Stanford Sleep Disorders Ctr 701 Welch Rd Ste 2226 Palo Alto CA 94304-1711*

DEMERATH, NICHOLAS JAY, III, sociology educator; b. Boston, Nov. 10, 1936; s. Nicholas J. and Helen Louise (Titus) D.; m. Judith Wood Richie, June 25, 1960; children: Loren Roberts, Peter Wells, Benjamin Burroughs. AB magna cum laude, Harvard U., 1958; MA, U. Calif., Berkeley, 1962, PhD, 1964. Instr. to prof. sociology U. Wis., 1962-72; exec. officer Am. Sociol. Assn., Washington, 1970-72; prof., chmn. sociology U. Mass., Amherst, 1972—; vis. prof. Yale U., 1992, Harvard U., 1993. Author: Social Class in American Protestantism, 1965 (with R.A. Peterson) System, Change and Conflict, 1967, (with P.E. Hammond) Religion in Social Context, 1968, (with M.T. Aiken and G. Marwell) Dynamics of Idealism, 1971, A Tottering Transcendence, 1973, (with K.F. Schuessler and O.N. Larsen) Social Policy and Sociology, 1974, (with G. Marwell) Sociology: Perspectives and Applications, 1976, (with Rhys H. Williams) A Bridging of Faiths, 1992, (with P.D. Hall, T. Schmitt, R.H. Williams) Sacred Companies. 1997; book rev. editor: Am. Sociol. Rev., 1965-68. Rsch. fellow, grantee Danforth Found., 1965, NIMH, 1960-62, New World Found., 1966; Lilly Endowment grantee for church-state rsch., 1983—; Fulbright Indo-Am. fellowship to India, 1993. Mem. Am. Sociol. Assn. (chmn. publs. com. 1975-77, chmn. endowment com. Am. Sociol Found. 1984-88), Eastern Sociol. Soc. (v.p. 1975, pres. 2000—), Soc. for Sci. Study Religion (pres. 1997—), Amherst Nickwits (fixtures sec.). Democrat. Home: 30 Harris Mountain Rd Amherst MA 01002-3521

DEMERDASH, NABEEL ALY OMAR, electrical engineer; b. Cairo, Apr. 26, 1943; came to U.S., 1966; s. Aly Omar and Aziza D.; m. Esther Adel Feher, Feb. 22, 1969; children: Yvonne, Omar, Nancy. BScEE with 1st class honors, Cairo U., 1964; MSEE, U. Pitts., 1967, PhD, 1971. Tchg. asst. in elec. engring. Cairo U., 1964-66, U. Pitts., 1966-68; engr. Westinghouse Electric Corp., Pitts., 1968-72; asst. prof. elec. engring. Va. Poly. Tech. Inst. and State U., Blacksburg, 1972-77, assoc. prof. elec. engring., 1977-81, prof., 1981-83; prof. dept. elec. and computer engring. Clarkson U., Potsdam, N.Y., 1983-94; prof., chmn. dept. elec. and computer engring. Marquette U., Milw., 1994-97, prof. dept. elec. and computer engring., 1994—; cons. Sundstrand Corp., Rockford, Ill., 1985—. Contbr. articles to profl. jours. Recipient cert. recognition NASA, 1979, cert. of teaching excellence Va. Poly. Inst. and State U., 1980. Fellow IEEE (subcom. chmn. 1988-92, 94-97, Nikola Tesla award 1999); mem. IEEE Power Engring. Soc. (disting. lectr. 1987—, Elec. Machinery Com. prize paper award 1993, working group award 1994, PES prize paper award 1993, working group award 1994), Indsl. Electronics Soc. (Disting. Spkr. award 1990—), Electromagnetics Acad. Achievements include development of three dimensional finite element vector potential and coupled 3D vector potential-scalar potential methods of solution of electromagnetic fields in electric devices; time-stepping coupled finite element-state space computer simulation models and design of electronically operated/controlled AC and DC motor drive.s. Office: Marquette Univ Elec Computer Engring Dept PO Box 1881 Milwaukee WI 53201-1881

DE MERE-DWYER, LEONA, medical artist; b. Memphis, May 1, 1928; d. Clifton and Leona (McCarthy) De M. BA, Rhodes Coll., Memphis, 1949; MSc, U. Memphis, 1984; PhD, Kennedy-Western U., 1990. Lic. embalmer, funeral dir.; m. John Thomas Dwyer, May 10, 1952; children: John, DeMere, Patrice, Brian, Anne-Clifton DeMere Dwyer, McCarthy-DeMere Dwyer. Med. artist for McCarthy DeMere, Memphis, 1950-80; pres. Aesthetic Med. & Forensic Art, 1984—; speech therapist, Memphis, 1950-82; lectr. on med. art univs., conf., assns.; cons. in prostheses Vocat. Rehab. Svcs.; elected expert witness in funeralization Nat. Forensic Ctr. Author: AIDS: Care of Health Care Workers in the Workplace. Bereavement counselor, organizer Ladies of St. Jude, Memphis, 1960; active Brooks Art Gallery League of Memphis; mem. God's Unfinished Bus. com. Temple Israel; vice dir. Tellico Hist. Found., 1980-80; mem. exec. bd. Chickasaw council Boy Scouts Am.; active Rep. campaign coms. Recipient Disting. Svc. award Gupton-Jones Coll. Mortuary Sci., 1981, Silver medal Sons of the Am. Revolution medal, 1985, Martha Washington medal. Mem. Nat. Foresic Ctr. (expert witness funeralization 1991—), Fedn. Internat. de'Automobile (internat. car racing 1972, lic.), Assn. Med. Illustrators, Am. Assn. Med. Assts., Emergency Dept. Nurses Assn., Am. Physicians Nurses Assn., Am. Soc. Plastic and Reconstructive Surgeons Found. (guest mem., cons.), Women in Law (chmn. assocs.), Exec. Women Am., Brandeis U. Women, DAR (1st v.p. regent 1980), UDC (pres. Nathan Bedford Forrest chpt.), Cotton Carnival Assn. (chairperson children's ct. 1968-70), Pi Sigma Eta, Kappa Delta (adv.), Kappa Delta Pi. Clubs: Tenn., Royal Matron Amaranth (Faith Ct.), Sertoma (1st female mem. Memphis, elected pres. 1989-90) (Memphis). Contbr. articles to profl. jours. Home: 1000 Murray Hill Ln Apt 304 Memphis TN 38120-2668

DEMERJIAN, KENNETH LEO, atmospheric science educator, research center director; b. Cambridge, Mass., Sept. 10, 1945; married; 2 children. BA in Chemistry, Northeastern U., 1968; MS in Phys. Chemistry, Ohio State U., 1970, PhD in Phys. Chemistry, 1973. Grad. teaching asst. Ohio State U., 1968-71, rsch. asst., 1972-73; rsch. assoc. Calspan Corp., 1973-74; phys. scientist, acting chief Model Devel. Br. EPA, 1974-75, supervisory phys. scientist, chief Atmospheric Modeling and Assessment Br., 1976-81, dir. meteorology divsn. ARL, 1981-85; prof. dept. environ. health and toxicology, environ. chemistry Sch. Pub. Health SUNY, N.Y. State Dept. Health, Albany, 1988—; assoc. divsn. applied scis. Harvard U., 1986—; dir. Atmospheric Scis. Rsch. Ctr. SUNY, Albany, 1986—, prof. dept. atmospheric sci., 1988—, chmn. dept. atmospheric sci., 1988-90; vis. scientist environ. sci. and physiology Sch. Pub. Health, rsch. fellow Energy and Environ. Policy Ctr. J.F. Kennedy Sch. Govt. Harvard U., 1984-85; adj. prof. chemistry SUNY, Albany, 1986—; lectr. in field. Contbr. articles to profl. jours. Mem. AAAS, Am. Chem. Soc., Am. Meteorol. Soc., Am. Geophys. Union, Air and Waste Mgmt. Assn. Achievements include research in chemical kinetics and mechanistic pathways of elementary atmospheric reactions and the development of reaction mechanisms of polluted and clean atmospheres, instrumentation development and measurement of atmospheric trace gas constituents, diagnostic analysis of atmospheric processes and air quality simulation modeling, experimental and theoretical studies of actinic solar flux and photolytic rate constants of atmospheric species, sources and evaluation of uncertainty in theoretical models of atmospheric processes, air quality and pollutant exposures, the articulation and effective use of scientific uncertainty in the decision making process. Office: SUNY Atmospheric Scis Rsch Ctr 251 Fuller Rd Albany NY 12203-3698

DEMERS, JUDY LEE, state legislator, university dean; b. Grand Forks, N.D., June 27, 1944; d. Robert L. and V. Margaret (Harming) Prosser; m. Donald E. DeMers, Oct. 3, 1964 (div. Oct. 1971); 1 child, Robert M.; m. Joseph M. Murphy, Mar. 5, 1977 (div. Oct. 1983). BS in Nursing, U. N.D., 1966; MEd, U. Wash., 1973, postgrad., 1973-76. Pub. health nurse Govt. D.C., 1966-68, Combined Nursing Service, Mpls., 1968-69; instr. pub. health nursing U. N.D., Grand Forks, 1969-71, assoc. dir. Medex program, 1970-72, dir., family nurse practitioner program, 1977-82, assoc. dir. rural health, 1982-85, dir. undergrad. med. edn., 1982-83, assoc. dean, 1983—; rsch. assoc. U. Wash., Seattle, 1973-76; mem. N.D. Ho. of Reps., 1982-92; mem. N.D. Senate, 1992—; cons. Health Manpower Devel. Staff, Honolulu, 1975-81, Assn. Physician Asst. Programs, Washington, 1979-82; site visitor, cons. AMA-Com. Allied Health Edn. Accreditation, Chgo., 1979-81. Author:

Educating New Health Practitioners, 1976; mem. editorial bd.: P.A. Jour., 1976-78; contbr. articles to profl. jours. Sec., bd. dirs. Valley Family Health, Grand Forks, N.D., 1982—; exec. com., bd. dirs. Agassiz Health Systems Agy., Grand Forks, 1982-86; mem. N.D. State Daycare Adv. Com., 1983-93, Mayor's Adv. Com. on Police Policy, Grand Forks, 1983-85, N.D. State Foster Care Adv. Com., 1985-87, N.D. State Hypertension Adv. Com., 1983-85, Gov.'s Com. on DUI and Traffic Safety, 1985-91, Statewide Adv. Com. on AIDS, 1985-90; bd. dirs. Casey Found. Families First Initiative, 1988-97, Comprehensive Health Assn. N.D., 1993-95, United Health Found. 1990-97, Northern Valley Mental Health Assn., 1994—; mem. adv. bd. Mountainbrooke (formerly Friendship Place), 1992-96; adv. com. Ruth Meiers Adolescent Ctr., Grand Forks, 1988—, Altru Health Sys. Corp. Bd., 1997—; mem. Commn. on Future Structure of VA Health Care, 1990-91; bd. dirs. Red River Valley Cmty. Action Progam, 1991—; mem. Resource and Referral Bd. Dirs., 1990—; mem. caring coun. N.D. Blue Cross and Blue Shield Caring Program for Children, 1995—; coun. mem. N.D. Health Task Force, 1992-94; mem. healthcare subcom. Northern Gt. Plains Econ. Devel. Commn., 1995-96; mem. FCC's Adv. Commn. on Telecomms. and Healthcare, 1996. Recipient Alpha Lambda Delta award, 1963, Pub. Citizen of Yr. award N.D. chpt. Nat. Assn. Social Workers, 1986, Golden Grain award N.D. Dietitics Assn., 1988, Person of Yr. award U. N.D. Law Women Caucus, 1990, Legislator of Yr. award Northern Valley Labor Coun., 1990, N.D. Martin Luther King Jr. award, 1990, Legislator of Yr. award N.D. Mental Health Assn., 1993, Dick Shea award for contbn. to high edn. AAUP, 1995, Voices award N.D. Children's Caucus, 1995; U. Wash. regional med. program service fellow, 1972-73; Toll fellow, 1989, U. Wash. Kellogg Allied Health fellow, 1972. Mem. AAUW, NOW, ACLU, LWV, Am. Nurses Assn., N.D. Nurses Assn. (mem. cabinet on edn. and practice 1982-86, Nurse of Yr. 1983), Am. Pub. Health Assn., Am. Ednl. Research Assn., N.D. Pub. Health Assn., N.D. Mental Health Assn., The ARC (Assn. for Retarded Citizens), Pi Lambda Theta, Sigma Theta Tau. Democrat. Home: 901 University Ave Apt 508 Grand Forks ND 58203-3611 Office: U ND Sch Medicine 501 N Columbia Rd Grand Forks ND 58203-2817

DEMERS, LAURENCE MAURICE, science educator, consultant, editor; b. Lawrence, Mass., May 9, 1938; s. Laurence Onezime and Doris Corrine (Goulet) D.; m. Susan Ruth Bernard, Sept. 29, 1962; children: Laurence H., Michele L., Marc B., Christopher J., Andrew J. AB, Merrimack Coll., 1960; PhD, SUNY Upstate Med. Ctr., Syracuse, 1970. Postdoctoral fellow Med. Sch., Harvard U., Boston, 1970-72, instr., 1972-73; asst. prof. M.S. Hershey Med. Ctr., Pa. State U., Hershey, Pa., 1973-76, assoc. prof., 1976-80, prof., 1980—, disting. prof., 1997—; cons. Robert Wood Johnson Pharm Rsch. Inst., Raritan, N.J., 1978—; bd. dirs. dBi Labs. Inc., Harrisburg, Pa.; vis. prof. U. Oxford, Eng., 1981-82. Editor: Liver Function Testing, 1978, Premenstrual Syndrome, 1985, Premenstrual Syndrome and Menopausal Mood Disorders, 1989; editl. editor Clin. Chemistry Jour., 1990—. Eucharistic min. St. Joan of Arc Cath. Ch., Hershey, 1981—, mem. Knights of Malta, 1990—. Capt. Med. Svc. Corps, U.S. Army, 1961-65. Recipient Lalor award Lalor Found., 1973, Fogarty Internat. award Fogarty Ctr., NIH, 1981, Pharm. Mfrs. Assn. award, 1974. Fellow Nat. Acad. Clin. Biochemistry (pres. 1984-85 Dubin award 1991); mem. Endocrine Soc., Am. Assn. Clin. Chemistry (pres. 1997, Ames award 1986), Am. Soc. Clin. Pathology, N.Y. Acad. Scis., Assn. Clin. Scientists, Acad. Clin. Lab. Physicians and Scientists, Hershey Country Club. Avocations: golf; tennis. Home: 1175 Stonegate Rd Hummelstown PA 17036-9776 Office: Pa State U MS Hershey Med Ctr University Dr Hershey PA 17033

DEMERS, NORA EGAN, immunologist, biologist, educator; b. Richmond Heights, Mo., May 8, 1962; d. Paul Burdette and Catherine Eleanor W.; m. Roy R. Demers, July 7, 1982; 3 stepchildren. BS, U. Mo., Rolla, 1989; MS, Oreg. State U., 1993, PhD, 1996. Tech. asst. Woodward-Clyde Cons., Portland, 1995-96; grad. teaching & rsch. asst. Oreg. State U., 1990-96, Hatfield Marine Sci. Ctr., Dept. Zoology, Dept. Fisheries, 1990-96; asst. prof., coord. biology program Fla. Gulf Coast U., 1997—; vis. prof. Evergreen State Coll., 1996-97. Contbr. articles to profl. jours. Mem. AAAS, Nat. Biology Tchrs. Assn., Internat. Soc. Devel. & Comparative Immunologists, Assn. Women in Sci. Avocations: reading, biking, jigsaw puzzles. E-mail: ndemers@fgcu.edu. Office: Fla Gulf Coast U Coll Arts & Scis Fort Myers FL 33965

DEMERY, DOROTHY JEAN, secondary school educator; b. Houston, Sept. 5, 1941; d. Floyd Hicks and Irene Elaine Burns Clay; m. Leroy W. Demery, Jan. 16, 1979; children: Steven Bradley, Rodney Bradley, Craig Bradley, Kimberly Bradley. AA, West L.A. Coll., Culver City, Calif., 1976; AS, Harbor Coll., Wilmington, Calif., 1983; BS in Pub. Adminstrn., Calif. State U., Carson, 1985; MS in Instructional Leadership, Nat. U., San Diego, 1991. Cert. real estate broker, tchr. math. and bus. edn., bilingual tchr., crosscultural lang. and acad. devel.; lang. devel. specialist. Eligibility social worker Dept. Pub. Social Svcs., L.A., 1967-74; real estate broker Dee Bradley & Assocs., Riverside, Calif., 1976—; tchr. math L.A. Unified Sch. Dist., 1985-91; math/computer sci. tchr. Pomona (Calif.) Unified Sch. Dist., 1991—; adj. lectr. Riverside C.C., 1992-93; mem. Dist. Curriculum Coun./Report Card Task Force, Pomona, 1994—; bd. dirs. Associated Pomona Tchrs. Chairperson Human Rights Com., Pomona, 1992—, sec. steering com., 1993—, adv. bd., 1993—; mem. polit. action com. Assoc. Pomona Tchrs., 1993-94. Recipient Outstanding Svc. award Baldwin Hills Little League Assn., L.A., 1972. Mem. Nat. Bus. Assn., Nat. Coun. Tchrs. Math., Aux. Nat. Med. Assn., Alpha Kappa Alpha. Avocations: hiking, tennis, walking. Home: PO Box 2796 Riverside CA 92516-2796 Office: Simons Middle School 900 E Franklin Ave Pomona CA 91766-5362

DEMES, DENNIS THOMAS, religious studies educator; b. Jersey City, N.J., Apr. 10, 1949; s. Thomas Joseph and Lillian (Harabedian) D. BA, St. John's Coll., Brighton, Mass., 1974; MS in Edn., Princeton U., 1979, ThM, 1979. Cert. advanced religious educator. Religious Educator Archdiocese of Boston, 1974-79; dir. religious edn. St. John's the Evangelist Parish, Winthrop, Mass., 1976-81, Holy Rosary Parish, Lawrence, Mass., 1981-83; Prior Soc. St. Benedict of Nursia, Boston, 1984—; adj. prof. St. Thomas U., Miami, Fla., tchr. history of Christian thought/Western civilization Pope John Paul II H.S., Boca Raton, Fla. Pastoral min. Ascension Cath. Ch., Boca Raton, 1990—, dir. adult edn. Recipient Cath. Campaign for Am. award, 1994. Mem. Nat. Cath. Educators Assn., Soc. St. Benedict. Office: Ascension Cath Ch 7250 N Federal Hwy Boca Raton FL 33487-1606 *As the first stage of life in the womb prepares and nourishes us for the stage after birth, so too does earthly life nourish and prepare us for ultimate life with God.*

DEMETER, STEVEN, neurologist, publishing company executive; b. Budapest, Hungary, Jan. 12, 1947; came to U.S., 1957; s. Arpad and Ilona (Wiesner) D.; m. Diane Simkin, Jan. 8, 1984; children: Sara, Nikki. BS, CUNY, 1969; MD, N.Y. Med. Coll., 1973. Diplomate Am. Bd. Psychiatry and Neurology. Intern Beth Israel Med. Ctr., N.Y.C., 1973-74; neurology resident Albert Einstein Coll. Medicine, Bronx, N.Y., 1974-77; inst. neurology N.Y. Med. Coll., N.Y.C., 1977-79; fellow in behavioral neurology U. Iowa Coll. Medicine, Iowa City, 1979-81; fellow Ctr. for Brain Rsch., U. Rochester (N.Y.) Sch. Medicine, 1981-84, instr. neurology, 1982-84, asst. prof. Ctr. for Brain Rsch., 1984-87, asst. prof. neurology, 1987-89, clin. asst. prof., 1989-91, clin. assoc. prof., 1991-93; pres. electronic pub. Arbor Pub. Corp., San Diego, 1990—; assoc. clin. prof. neurosci. U. Calif., San Diego, 1995—; neurology cons. Rochester Psychiat. Ctr., 1985-91. Contbr. numerous articles to med. jours. Grantee Scottish Rite Schizophrenia Rsch. Found., 1987-90, Whitehall Found., 1990-93, NIH, 1991-94. Fellow Am. Acad. Neurology, Royal Soc. Medicine (London); mem. AAAS, Soc. for Neurosci., Tourette Syndrome Assn. (med. com. 1985-93, bd. dirs. 1987-93). Office: Arbor Pub Corp Ste 120 10393 San Diego Mission Rd San Diego CA 92108-2134

DEMETREON, DAIBOUNE ELAYNE, minister; b. Brunswick, Maine, Aug. 5, 1945; d. James Demetreon and Grace Lewis; m. James Allison Devine, Mar. 3, 1986; children from previous marriage: William Anthony Decker, James Steven Decker; 6 grandchildren. Degree, Unity Sch. Practical Christianity & Ordination, 1975; postgrad., Rio Salado Coll., 1992; BA in Psychology, Ottawa U., 1994, M in Profl. Counseling, 1999. Ordained min. Unity Ch., 1975; cert. practitioner Neuro-Linguistic Program. Sr. min. Unity of Ann Arbor, Mich., 1975-77, Unity of Boulder, Colo., 1977-78, Unity of Colorado Springs, 1980-86, Unity of Scottsdale, Ariz., 1989-95; chmn. World of One Fellowship, Colorado Springs, 1986—, pastoral counselor, Scottsdale, 1989—; adv. bd. dirs. Boulder (Colo.) Psychiat. Inst., 1977-78; campus min. U. Mich., Ypsilanti, 1975-77; conductor workshops chaplains program U.S. Army, Ft. Carson; vol. Am. Fgn. Svcs., 1996—. Author, narrator audio tape Transformations, 1985; host talk show God and You, 1983; contbr. articles to profl. publs. Chem. dependency counselor St. Luke's Hosp., 1993-96; Am. Fgn. Svc. vol., 1996—; counselor/advocate for children at risk, Scottsdale, Ariz., 1999—. Avocations: gardening, sewing, hiking, camping, sculpture. Office: World of One Fellowship 269 SW Winterpark Cir Lee's Summit MO 64081

DEMETRESCU, MIHAI CONSTANTIN, research scientist, educator, computer company executive; b. Bucharest, Romania, May 23, 1929; s. Dan and Alina (Dragosescu) D.; M.E.E., Poly. Inst. of U. Bucharest, 1954; Ph.D., Romanian Acad. Sci., 1957; m. Agnes Halas, May 25, 1969; 1 child, Stefan. Came to U.S., 1966. Prin. investigator Research Inst. Endocrinology Romanian Acad. Sci., Bucharest, 1958-66; research fellow dept. anatomy UCLA, 1966-67; faculty U. Calif.-Irvine, 1967-83, asst. prof. dept. physiology, 1971-78, assoc. researcher, 1978-79, assoc. clin. prof., 1979-83; v.p. Resonance Motors, Inc., Monrovia, Calif., 1972-85; pres. Neurometrics, Inc., Irvine, Calif., 1978-82; pres. Lasergraphics Inc., Irvine, 1982-84, chmn., chief exec. officer, 1984—. Mem. com. on hon. degrees U. Calif.-Irvine, 1970-72. Postdoctoral fellow UCLA, 1966. Mem. Internat. Platform Assn., Am. Physiol. Soc., IEEE (sr.). Republican. Contbr. articles to profl. jours. Patentee in field. Home: 8 Sunset Hbr Newport Coast CA 92657-1706 Office: 20 Ada Irvine CA 92618-2303

DEMETRION, JAMES THOMAS, art museum director; b. Middletown, Ohio, July 10, 1930; s. Tom and Susie (Tsifiklis) D.; m. Barbara Parrish, 1954; 1 child, Elaine. BS in Edn., Miami U., 1952; hon. doctorate, Simpson Coll., 1984. Curator Pasadena Art Mus., Calif., 1964-66; dir. Pasadena Art Mus., 1966-69, Des Moines Art Ctr., 1969-84, Hirshhorn Mus. & Sculpture Garden, Washington, 1984—; mem. Mus. adv. panel Nat. Endowment for Arts, 1973-76, co-chmn., 1974-76; mem. IRS Art Adv. Panel, 1983-86. Mem. Assn. Art Mus. Dirs. (treas. 1976-77, pres. 1979-80). Office: Hirshhorn Mus-Sculpture Garden Independence Ave at 8th St SW Washington DC 20560

DE METZ, DELLA CHRISTINE, executive, writer, social consultant, food worker; b. Elkhart, Ind., Jan. 14, 1959; 1 child, Nathan Allen Flores. Student, Purdue U., 1977-78, Ivy Tech. Vocat. Coll., 1994—. Retail sales Pepsico Franchise, Elkhart, Ind., 1980; bus. mgmt. McGrory Corp., Elkhart, Ind., 1990-91, bus. fin., 1990-91; entrepreneur Elkhart, Ind., 1990—; with meat dept. Kroger Co., 1997—; with retail food, comml. industry, 1997—; mem. safety com./meat dept. Kroger and Co.; mem. UFCW Union Local 700. Author of poems. Vol. Homeless Shelter, Elkhert, 1993, Greenpeace, The Wilderness Soc., Washington, 1993, World Wildlife Fund, Sierra Club, Washington, 1993. Recipient Silver Poet award, The World of Poetry, Calif., 1990. Mem. Am. Mgmt. Assn. (mgmt. assoc. 1993), Nat. Wildlife Fedn., Internat. Soc. Poets, Nat. Libr. Poetry, Ind. Food and Comml. Workers (local 700). Avocations: auto repair, writing, motorcycles, reading, antique cars.

DEMICHELE, MARK ANTHONY, stage director, educator, actor; b. Syracuse, N.Y., Aug. 18, 1958; s. Onofrio Mark and Faye Ann (Venturin) DeM.; m. Amy Ellen (Friedman), Apr. 5, 1986; children: Zachary Mark, Olivia Rose. BA with honors, SUNY, Stony Brook, 1980; MFA, U. Ariz., 1985. Dir., writer Telemation Prodns., Phoenix, 1986-88; dir. edn. Ariz. Theatre Co., Tucson, 1988-89; guest dir. Ark. Repertory Theatre, Little Rock, 1989, 90, 97, Am. Southwest Theatre Co., Las Cruces, N.Mex., 1994-96; assoc. artist Phoenix Theatre, 1990-92; prof. theatre arts Phoenix Coll., 1990-95; asst. dir. Manitoba Theatre Centre, 1993; res. dir., prodr. New Work's Festival, 1998—; asst. dir. Bainsville Prodns., Studio City, Calif., 1985-86; dir. artist roster Ariz. Commn. on Arts, Phoenix, 1988-91; chair Arizona Coll. Theatre Festival, 1992-94; faculty assoc. Ariz. State U. West, 1994-96. Dir. (play) Cowboy Mouth, 1983 (nominated Best Show 1983), Embroidered: Yarns, 1989, The Mystery of Irma Vep, 1990, The Absent Voice, 1992 (nominated Best Show Am. Coll. Theatre Festival 1992-94), One Man's Dance (ariz. award Best Prodn. New Play 1995); dir., writer (TV show) MGI Wafer Transfer System, 1987 (Merit award 1987), Safemove, Safetrip, Safestor, 1989; dir., adaptor (play) Theatrix, 1990; actor: (play) Word of Mouth, 1989, The Wrath of Kali, 1995, Laughter on the 23rd Floor, 1997, White Picket Fence, 1998, (films) The Vagrant, 1992, Four Eyes and Six Guns, 1992, Suture, 1993, A Stranger to Love, 1996, My Son is Innocent, 1996, No One Would Tell, 1996, A Stranger in My Home, 1996, Jerome, 1997, Lethal Invasion, 1997. Miller fellow U. Ariz., 1981, Haldeman scholar U. Ariz., 1984; Ariz. Commn. on the Arts grantee, 1990. Mem. SAG, Actors Equity Assn., Soc. Stage Dirs. and Choreographers. Democrat. Roman Catholic. Avocations: numismatics, philately. Home: 1327 W Mackenzie Dr Phoenix AZ 85013-3018 Office: MDM Prodns 1327 W Mackenzie Dr Phoenix AZ 85013-3018

DE MICHELE, O. MARK, utility company executive; b. Syracuse, N.Y., Mar. 23, 1934; s. Aldo and Dora (Carno) De M.; m. Faye Ann Venturin, Nov. 8, 1957; children: Mark A., Christopher C., Michele M., Julianne; m. Barbara Joan Stanley, May 22, 1982; 1 child, Angela Marie. BS, Syracuse U., 1955; hon. doctorate, No. Ariz. U., 1997. Mgr. Seal Right Co., Inc., Fulton, N.Y., 1955-58; v.p., gen. mgr. L.M. Harvey Co. Inc., Syracuse, 1958-62; v.p. Niagara Mohawk Power, Syracuse, 1962-78; v.p. Ariz. Pub. Svc., Phoenix, 1978-81, exec. v.p., 1981-82, pres., CEO, 1982-97, also bd. dirs.; pres., CEO Greater Phoenix Econ. Coun., 1997-98; chmn., CEO Urban Realty Ptnrs. LLC, 1998—; bd. dirs. Ariz. Pub. Svc. Co. Pres. Jr. Achievement, Syracuse, 1974-75, Phoenix, 1982-83, United Way Ctrl. N.Y., Syracuse, 1978, Ariz. Opera Co., Phoenix, 1981-83, Phoenix Symphony, 1984-86, United Way Phoenix, 1985-86, Ariz. Mus. Sci. and Tech., 1988-90; pres. Childrens Action Alliance, 1989-92; chmn. Valley Sun United Way, 1984-86, Phoenix Econ. Coun., 1991-94; chmn. Morrison Inst. Pub. Policy at Ariz. State U.; chmn. Ariz. Cities in Schs., 1994-97, Nat. Environ. Edn. Found., 1997—. Named Outstanding Young Man of Yr., Syracuse Jaycees, 1968, Phoenix Man of Yr., Phoenix Ad Club, 1992; recipient Humanitarian award Nat. Conf., 1995. Mem. Phoenix C. of C. (chmn. bd. 1986-87). Republican. Clubs: Phoenix Country, Ariz. (Phoenix). Home: 5309 N 24th Pl Phoenix AZ 85016-3648 Office: Urban Realty Ptnrs LLC 2415 E Camelback Rd Ste 700 Phoenix AZ 85016-4245

DEMIERI, JOSEPH L., bank executive; b. N.Y.C., Aug. 31, 1940; s. Leo A. and Frances (Garone) DeM.; m. Anne Patricia McCue, May 15, 1965. B.B.A., Tex. A&M U., 1962. C.P.A., N.Y. With Peat, Marwick, Mitchell & Co., N.Y.C., 1962-68; v.p., controller City Investing Co., N.Y.C. and Beverly Hills, Calif., 1968-82; exec. v.p. Motown Industries, Los Angeles, 1982-84; chmn., CEO Calif. Millworks Corp., Valencia, 1985-95; sr. v.p., CFO Western Security Bank, Burbank, Calif., 1995—. Home: 6259 Ebbtide Way Malibu CA 90265-3608 Office: 4100 W Alameda Ave Burbank CA 91505-4153

DEMILES, EDWARD, agent; b. Indpls., Sept. 22, 1962; s. Lee Henry and Gearldine (Woolridge) DeM. BA in Bus., U.S. Army Sch. Adminstrn., 1982. Lic. agt. Am. Fedn. Musicians. V.p. Festival City Prodns., Indpls., 1978-81; founder, chief exec. officer Sahara Records & Filmworks Co., Chgo., 1981—, The Edward DeMiles Co., Chgo., Dallas, Indpls., 1984—; pub. rels/promotions dir. The Edward DeMiles Co., Dallas, 1984—, entertainment agt., 1987—; tv producer Black Knight Prodns., Indpls., 1980-81; prodn. coord. USO Presents Suzanne Somers Show, Karlsrule, West Germany, 1982; concert promoter In Clubhouse Promotions, Oklahoma City, 1984-85. Mem. Am. Fedn. Musicians. Office: The Edward DeMiles Co 117 W Harrison Bldg #S627 Chicago IL 60605-1709

DE MILLE, BARBARA MUNN, writer, former English literature educator; b. Buffalo, Feb. 24, 1932; d. Carl Alfred Munn and Helen Shelden Stout; m. William De Mille, Sept. 11, 1952. BA magna cum laude, SUNY, Buffalo, 1970, MA, 1975, PhD, 1978. Adj. prof. SUNY, Albany, 1978-80; prof. Jinan U., Guangzhou, China, 1980-81; asst. prof. Coll. William and Mary, Williamsburg, Va., 1981-85; weekly commendator N.E. Pub. Radio, Albany, 1993-95. Contbr. essays and articles to various publs., including N.Y. Times, Newsday, Christian Sci. Monitor, Chronicle Higher Edn., Jour. Family Life, South Atlantic Rev., Studies English Lit., Hartford courant, Downeast, Conradiana. NEH fellow Cornell U., 1986; grantee Vogelstein Found., 1987. Mem. Phi Beta Kappa.

DEMILLE-CAMACHO, DIANNE LYNNE, mathematics educator, administrator; b. Dundas, Ontario, Can., Mar. 21, 1948; d. Leslie Benjamin and Helen Isobel (Don) DeMille; m. Tate Stanley Casey, June 16, 1971 (div. June, 1975); 1 child, Marie Anne; m. Thomas John Camacho, Aug. 30, 1980 (div. June, 1999); children: Patricia Suzanne, Tara Lynne. BA in Math., Whittier Coll., 1970, secondary tchg. credential, 1972; postgrad., Walden U. Math. tchr. Mater Dei H.S., Santa Ana, Calif., 1972-79, Santa Ana (Calif.) H.S., 1979; instr. math. Coast C.C., Costa Mesa, Calif., 1979-81; math. tchr., mentor tchr. Downey (Calif.) Unified, 1979-93; specialist So. Calif. Regional Algebra Project Orange County Dept. Edn., Costa Mesa, 1993-98, coord. assessmt/Golden State exams. devel. algebra/geometry, 1996—; mem. math. adv bd. Downey Unified Sch. Dist., 1983—; cons., presenter confs., Orange County Dept. Edn., Costa Mesa, 1986—, Calif. State Dept. of Edn., Sacramento, 1989—; chief math devel. team Calif. Learning Assessment Sys.; chief reader, table leader Stds. Adv. Golden State Math. Exam.; mem. devel. team, chief reader Calif. State Regional Lead Assessment, coord. devel. team, 1996—; reviewer Am. Coll. Testing. Author: (book) Batch Basic, 1973; author and project specialist (series of books and workbooks) So. Calif. Regional Algebra Project Focus on Algebra, Focus on Geometry, 1989—, (units in book) Math A, Investigating Mathematics, 1989. Recipient Wright Bros. Innovative Tchrs. award, Rockwell Co., L.A., 1991; grantee Rockwell Co., 1992. Mem. ASCD, Nat. Coun. Tchrs. of Math., Calif. Math. Coun. (Nominee Presidential award 1986). Home: 5243 Hersholt Ave Lakewood CA 90712-2732 Office: Orange County Dept Edn 200 Kalmus Dr Costa Mesa CA 92626-5922

DEMILLION, JULIANNE, health and fitness specialist and personal trainer, rehabilitation consultant; b. Monessen, Pa., Dec. 20, 1955; d. William Vincent and Enise Mary (Tocci) DeM. BA, BS, U. Pitts., 1977; cert. massage therapist Phoenix Therapeutic Massage Coll., 1985. Mgr. program devel. Exclusively Women Spas, Scottsdale, 1977-81; pvt. exercise therapist, Scottsdale, 1981-83, ; cons. City of Phoenix, 1981-88; cons., pvt. personal trainer, Scottsdale, 1983—; instr. advanced techniques Phoenix Therapeutic Massage Coll., 1986-90. Mem. NAFE, Am. Massage Therapy Assn. (State Meritorious award 1989), Ariz. Massage Therapy Assn. (sec.-treas. 1986-90, Svc. award 1991), Internat. Dance and Exercise Assn., Circulo-Systems Ltd., Am. Coll. Sports Medicine.

DEMING, DAVID LAWSON, art educator; b. Cleve., May 26, 1943; s. Lawson Joseph and Mary Rita (Basile) D.; m. Ann Elizabeth Haldeman, Sept. 4, 1965; children: Matthew Lawson, Lisa Ann, Michael David. BFA, Cleve. Inst. Art, 1967; MFA, Cranbrook Acad. Art, Bloomfield Hills, Mich., 1970. Instr. Boston U., 1967-68, U. Tex., El Paso, 1970-72; asst. prof., assoc. prof. art U. Tex., Austin, 1972, prof., 1985, chmn. art dept., Marguerite Fairchild prof. art, 1991-96; interim dean Coll. of Fine Arts U. Tex., Austin, 1996-97, dean, 1997-98; pres. Cleve. Inst. Art, 1998—. Sculptures represented in permanent collection Columbus (Ohio) Mus. Art, Ark. Art Ctr., Little Rock, U. Tex. Southwestern Regional Med. Ctr. Dallas; included in White House Garden Exhbn. of Am. Sculptors, 1995. Recipient award of honor Austin chpt. AIA, 1983. Mem. Internat. Sculpture Assn. Roman Catholic. Office: Cleveland Inst of Art 11114 E Blvd Cleveland OH 44106*

DEMING, FRANK STOUT, lawyer; b. Oswego, Kans., Aug. 12, 1927; s. Robert Orin Jr. and Helen Josephine (Stout) D.; m. Carolyn Ruth Kauffman, June 24, 1950; children: Frank S. Jr., Christianna Deming Jacobsen, David M., Robert W. BS in Econs., U. Pa., 1949, LLB, 1952. Bar: Pa. 1953, U.S. Dist. Ct. (ea. dist.) Pa. 1953, U.S. Ct. Appeals (3d cir.) 1953, U.S. Ct. Appeals (9th cir.) 1965. Assoc., then ptnr., now of counsel Montgomery, McCracken, Walker & Rhoads, Phila., 1952—; bd. dirs. New Covenant Trust co. Contbr. articles to profl. jours. Trustee Bricker Found., Phila., 1980—, Presbyn. Ch. (U.S.A.) Found., Jeffersonville, Ind., 1989-94, chmn., 1993, mem. gen. assembly coun., Louisville, 1990-91; dir. Presbyn. Children's Village, 1992-94. Sgt. U.S. Army, 1946-47. Fellow Am. Coll. Trust and Estate Counsel; mem. ABA, Pa. Bar Assn., Phila. Bar Assn., Mil. Figure Collectors Am., Phi Delta Theta, Beta Alpha Psi, Beta Gamma Sigma. Republican. Avocations: travel. Home: Riddle Village 410 Hampton Media PA 19063-6009 Office: Montgomery McCracken Walker & Rhoads 123 S Broad St Fl 25 Philadelphia PA 19109-1029

DEMING, FREDERICK LEWIS, banker; b. Des Moines, Sept. 12, 1912; s. Fred Kemp and Erva Pearl (Smyres) D.; m. Corinne Inez Wilson, Feb. 4, 1935; children: Frederick Wilson, Richard Louis. A.B., Washington U., St. Louis, 1934, M.A., 1935, Ph.D., 1941. Mgr. research dept to 1st v.p. Fed. Res. Bank, St. Louis, 1941-57; pres. Fed. Res. Bank, Mpls., 1957-65; undersec. for monetary affairs U.S. Dept. Treasury, Washington, 1965-69; gen. ptnr. Lazard Freres & Co., N.Y.C., 1969-71; pres. Nat. City Bancorp., Mpls., 1971-82. Trustee Washington U., 1966—; trustee Macalester Coll., 1959—, Endowment Fund, ARC, Washington, 1965-86. Democrat. Clubs: Minneapolis, Met, Cosmos. Home: 4235 E Lake Harriet Blvd Minneapolis MN 55409-1724

DEMING, WILLIS RILEY, lawyer; b. Ada, Ohio, Nov. 28, 1914; s. Cliffe and Okla (Riley) D.; m. Dorothy Arline Hill, 1950 (div. 1971); children: Susan Elizabeth, Deborah Anne Gunst, David Riley; m. Constance S. Mori, 1971 (div. 1986); m. Olive Plunkett Rose, 1994 (dec. 1999). BA, Ohio State U., 1935, JD, 1938. Bar: Ohio 1938, Calif. 1947, D.C. 1957. Pvt. practice Columbus, Ohio, 1938-39; casualty claim examiner Am. Surety Co., N.Y.C., 1939-41; chief bds. and claims rev. br. San Francisco Port of Embarkation, 1946-47; mem. Treadwell and Laughlin, San Francisco, 1947-54; mem. Brobeck, Phleger & Harrison, San Francisco, 1954-56, Washington, 1956-60; pvt. practice Washington, 1961-62; with Matson Nav. Co., San Francisco, 1962-71, 74-92, sec., 1962-73, gen. counsel, 1967-71, 74-92, sr. v.p., 1982-92; ret.; v.p., sec., gen. counsel Alexander & Baldwin, Inc., Honolulu, 1968-74. Served to lt. col. AUS, 1941-46; col. U.S. Army, ret. Mem. ABA, State Bar Calif., Soc. for Asian Art (pres. 1995-97), World Trade Club (San Francisco), Claremont Country Club (Oakland). Methodist. Home: 5649 Country Club Dr Oakland CA 94618-1715

DEMINT, JAMES WARREN, congressman, marketing executive; b. Greenville, S.C., Sept. 2, 1951; s. Thomas Eugene and Betty (Rawlings) Batson; m. Deborah Henderson, Nov. 6, 1951; children: Jake, Ginger, Timothy, Donna. BS Communications, U. Tenn., 1973; MBA, Clemson (S.C.) U., 1979. Sr. sales rep. Scott Paper Co., Greensboro, N.C., 1973-75; writer Henderson Advt., Greenville, 1975-81; v.p. Leslie Advt., Greenville, 1981-83; chief exec. officer, pres. The Demint Mktg. Group, Greenville, 1983—; mem. 106th Congress from 4th S.C. dist., 1999—; speaker, workshop leader, Success 88 Small Bus. Admin. and So. Bell 1988. Chmn. bd. Greensville Vocat. Rehab. Ctr. 1986, Christian Bus. Men's Com., 1983, Mitchel Rd. Christian Acad., 1988, 1st v.p. Speech, Hear and Learning Ctr., 1986. Mem. Greenville C. of C., S.C. C. of C., Rotary. Republican. Presbyterian. Avocations: sailing, running, biking, tennis, music. *

DEMISSIE, YEMANE I., filmmaker. Student, UCLA. Dir. acquisitions Prodr. Svcs. Group, Inc., L.A. and London, 1987-92. Exhbns. include Internat. Festival Visual Arts, Hungary, 1997, Vues d'Afrique, Montreal, 1997, Seattle Internat. Film Festival, 1997, Fribourg Film Festival, Switzerland, 1997, Internat. Film Festival Rotterdam, The Netherlands, 1997, Hamptons Internat. Film Festival, N.Y.C., 1997, M-NET All Africa Film Awards, South Africa, 1997 (Paulin Vieyra Merit award for outstanding work in cinema), Pitts. Film Festival, 1998, Third Internat. Film Festival, Kerala, India, 1998, Midnight Sun Film Festival, Finland, 1998, Urban World Film Festival, N.Y.C., 1998, L.A. Pan African Film Festival, 1999; filmmaker Axed at the Rectory, 1986, History of the Cave, Part I, 1986, Kentu, 1987, Uncle Vanya, 1986, Three Kinds of Light, 1987, Testify!, 1988, Bicycle Encounter, 1988, African Artists Series, 1993. Recipient Federico DeLaurentis award L.A., Cert. of award for outstanding achievement in African film U. Calif. San Diego, Hon. Mention, Urban World Film Festival, Nantes Mayor's award Nantes Festival des 3 Continents, European Union Spl. Mention, Pan African Film and TV Festival, Burkina Faso, Spl. Jury prize and COE prize So. African Film Festival, Zimbabwe, First Pl. award Nat. Black Programming Consortium; John Simon Guggenheim Meml. Found. fellow, 1999; Nat. Resources fellow; grantee Nat. Black Programming Consortium Prodn.; Calif. Arts Coun. Artists fellow; ind. film and videomaker grantee Am. Film Inst.

DE MITA, FRANCIS ANTHONY, mathematics educator; b. N.Y.C., Oct. 13, 1927; s. Michael Joseph and Rachel Catherine (Prudente) DeM.; m. Lois Marie Smith, Mar. 22, 1934; children: Francis Anthony Jr., Michael Spencer. BS, NYU, 1950, MA, 1951; diploma in mgmt., Cornell U., 1988. Tchr. math. Bedford Park Acad., N.Y.C., 1951-53, Valley Stream (N.Y.) Cen. High Sch., 1953-90; chmn. dept. math. Valley Stream (N.Y.) Central High Sch., 1981-90, ret., 1990; asst. prof. math. Queensborough Community Coll., N.Y.C., 1964-96; pres., chmn. bd. Nassau Educators Fed. Credit Union, Valley Stream, 1967—. Contbr. articles to mags. Founder, pres. East Central Civic Assn., Valley Stream, 1967-69, 79-89; bd. dirs. Friends of Arts, V.S. C. of C.; Nat. Assn. Fed. Credit Unions; adv. coun. WLIW21-PBS TV, L.I.; bus. adv. com. B.O.C.E.S., L.I. Cpl. U.S. Army, 1946-48. NSF grantee, 1958-65; named Vol. of Yr., Nat. Assn. Fed. Credit Unions, Denver, 1981, Dir. of Yr. Credit Union Execs. Soc., Honolulu, 1989; recipient Congl. citation U.S. Congress, 1982, Businessman of Yr., Valley Stream C. of C., 1998. Mem. Nat. Assn. Credit Union Pres., Elks, Lions (pres. 1973-74), Nat. Italian-Am. Found. Republican. Roman Catholic. Avocations: photography, golf, opera, computers, travel. Home: 108 E Euclid St Valley Stream NY 11580-4145 also: 55 Forest Dr Lake Monticello VA 22963-2116

DEMITCHELL, TERRI ANN, law educator; b. San Diego, Apr. 10, 1953; d. William Edward and Rose Annette (Carreras) Wheeler; m. Todd Allan DeMitchell, Aug. 14, 1982. AB in English with honors, San Diego State U., 1975; JD, U. San Diego, 1984; MA in Edn., U. Calif., Davis, 1990; EdM, Harvard U., 1997. Bar: Calif. 1985, U.S. Dist. Ct. (so. dist.) Calif. 1985; cert. elem. tchr., Calif. Tchr. Fallbrook (Calif.) Union Elem. Sch. Dist., 1976-86; adminstrv. asst. gen. counsel San Diego Unified Sch. Dist., 1984; assoc. Biddle and Hamilton, Sacramento, 1986-88; instr. U. N.H., 1990-93; teaching asst. U. Calif., Davis, 1987. Author: The California Teacher and the Law, 1985, The Law in Relation to Teacher, Out of School Behavior, 1990, Censorship and the Public School Library: A Bicoastal View, 1991; contbr. chpt. to book: The Limits of Law-Based School Reform, 1997. Ava. Calif. Bar Assn., Internat. Reading Assn.

DEMITCHELL, TODD ALLAN, education educator; b. Portsmouth, Va., Aug. 9, 1947; s. Wilfred E. and Mary Anna (Hughes) DeM.; m. Terri A. Wheeler, Aug. 14, 1982. BA, U. La Verne, 1969, MA, 1973; EdD, U. So. Calif., 1979; MA, U. Calif., Davis, 1990. Tchr. Pomona (Calif.) Unified Sch. Dist., 1969-71; tchr. South Bay Union Elem. Sch. Dist., Imperial Beach, Calif., 1974-75, lead tchr., 1975-78; asst. prin. Fallbrook (Calif.) Union Elem. Sch. Dist., 1978-80, prin., 1980-83; supt., prin. Pauma (Calif.) Sch. Dist., 1983-86; dir. pers. and labor rels. Travis (Calif.) Unified Sch. Dist., 1986-89; postdoctoral vis. scholar, rsch. asst. Nat. Ctr. Ednl. Leadership Harvard U., Cambridge, Mass., 1989-90; asst. prof. U. N.H., Durham, 1990-96, coord. grad. studies, 1993-95, assoc. chair dept. edn., 1995-98, assoc. prof., 1996—, chair acad. affairs com., faculty senate, coord. adminstrn. and supervision program, 1998—; design team Sch. Leaders Acad., N.H., 1991-93. Co-author: Teacher Unions and TQE: Building Quality Labor Relations, 1994, The Limits of Law-Based School Reform: Vain Hopes and False Promises, 1996; mem. authors com. Education Law Reporter; contbr. more than 60 articles to profl. jours. Mem. AASPA, Am. Ednl. Rsch. Assn., Edn. Law Assn. Office: U NH Morrill Hall Durham NH 03824

DEMITRA, PAVOL, professional hockey player; b. Dubnica, Slovakia, Nov. 29, 1974. Drafted left wing/ctr. Ottawa (Can.), 1993-96; traded left wing/ctr. St. Louis Blues, 1996—; represented Slovia in 1998 Winter Olympics, Nagano, Japan. Office: c/o St Louis Blues 1401 Clark St Louis MO 63103*

DEMKO, GEORGE JOSEPH, geographer; b. Catasauqua, Pa., Apr. 10, 1933; s. George and Anna (Scarba) D.; m. Jeanette Edwina Small, Aug. 29, 1959; children: Megan, Kerstin. BS, West Chester U., 1958; MS, So. Ill. U., 1959; PhD, Pa. State U., 1964; postgrad., Moscow State U., USSR; DSc (hon.), Shawnee State U. of Ohio, 1995. Instr. Pa. State U, State College, 1963-64; asst. prof. Ind. U., Bloomington, 1964-65; prof. Ohio State U., Columbus, 1965-83; program dir. Geography and Regional Sci., NSF, Washington, 1983-84; The Geographer, dir. Office of The Geographer, State Dept., Washington, 1984-89; dir. Rockefeller Ctr. for Social Scis., Dartmouth Coll., Hanover, N.H., 1989-95, prof. geography, 1989—; cons. Internat. Research and Exchanges Bd., Princeton, N.J., 1970-95, NASA, 1979-80, Microsoft Corp., 1992—; head subcommn. on geography, US/USSR, Princeton, 1980-91. Author: The Russian Colonization of Kazakhstan, 1966, Kazakh transl., 1998, Discovery in Geography, 1980, Regional Development in East and West Europe, 1986, Perspectives on Soviet Geography, 1980, Geography in the USSR and U.S.: A Spectrum of Views, 1992, Why In The World: Adventures in Geography, 1993, Populations at Risk in America, 1995, Reordering the World: Geopolitical Perspectives on the 21st Century, 1995; contbr. numerous articles to profl. jours. Sgt. USMC, 1951-54, Korea. Named Outstanding Alumnus, W. Chester (Pa.) U., 1980, University Fellow, Pa. State U., State College, 1986; recipient numerous grants and awards for research and teaching from the Nat. Sci. Found., Rockefeller Found., Gold Medal award for scholarly contbns. Charles U., Parague, Czech Republic, 1998, others. Mem. Assn. Am. Geographers (pres. 1986-88), Am. Assn. for Advancement of Slavic Studies (exec. dir. 1969-74), Kennan Inst. for Advanced Russian Studies (acad. advisor 1982-86), Russian Geog. Soc. (hon.). Avocations: sailing, squash, piano. Home: 2 Wintercroft Cir Grantham NH 03753-0744 Office: Dartmouth Coll Dept Geography Hanover NH 03755*

DEMLER, MARVIN CHRISTIAN, air force officer; b. North Tonawanda, N.Y., Oct. 23, 1909; s. Ernest Frederick and Bertha Wilhelmina (Krull) D.; m. Willena Mayverette Brown; children: James Carl, Roger Lee. BSME, NYU, 1931, Aero. Engr., 1934; student, Air Corps Flying Sch., 1931-32; MS in Aero. Engring., U. Mich., 1941; ScD (hon.), NYU, 1967. 2d lt. U.S. Army Air Res., 1932-34; sales and svc. engr. Lycoming div. Avco, Williamsport, Pa., 1934-38; commd. 2nd lt. U.S. Army Air Corps., 1938; advanced through grades to maj. gen. USAF, 1958, ret. 1971. Decorated D.S.M. with oak leaf cluster, Legion of Merit with 2 oak leaf clusters, Bronze Star medal, others. Fellow AIAA; mem. Planetary Soc., Order of Daedalians, Internat. Club, Mil. Order of the World Wars, Sigma Xi. Republican. Avocations: sports, walking, travel. Address: 7309 River Crescent Dr Annapolis MD 21401-7728

DEMLOW, DANIEL J., lawyer; b. Ludington, Mich., Oct. 16, 1944; s. Richard M. and Nan (Jager) D.; m. Catherine M. Jerzak, Aug. 7, 1982; children: Sara Beth, Michelle Catherine. BA, Mich. State U., 1966; JD, U. Mich., 1969. Atty. Fraser Trebilock Davis & Foster, Lansing, Mich., 1969-70, Securities Bur., Lansing, State of Mich., 1970-71; dep. dir. Mich. Dept. Commerce, Lansing, 1971-73; commr. ins. Ins. Bur., Lansing, 1973-75; chmn. Mich. Pub. Svc. Commn., Lansing, 1975-81; assoc. Honigman Miller Schwartz & Cohn, Lansing, 1985—. Fellow Mich. State Bar Found. Republican. Presbyterian. Avocations: tennis, boating, grouse hunting. Home: 3773 Yosemite Dr Okemos MI 48864-3838 Office: Honigman Miller Schwartz & Cohn 222 N Washington Sq Lansing MI 48933-1325

DEMME, JONATHAN, director, producer, writer; b. Baldwin, L.I., N.Y., Feb. 22, 1944; m. Joanne Howard; children: Ramona, Brooklyn. Ed., U. Fla. With Avco Embassy Films, 1966, Pathe Films, 1966-67; with publicity dept. United Artists, 1968-69; writer Film Daily, 1966-68. Film work includes co-screenwriter, dir.: Hot Box; story developer: Black Mama White Mama, 1975; screenwriter, dir. Caged Heat, 1974, Crazy Mama, 1975, Fighting Mad, 1976; dir.: Citizen's Band, 1977, Last Embrace, 1979, Melvin and Howard, 1980 (Best Dir. award), Swing Shift, 1983, Stop Making Sense, 1984, Swimming to Cambodia, 1987, Married to the Mob, 1988, The Silence of the Lambs, 1991 (Best Dir. Acad. award 1991), Cousin Bobby, 1992, Philadelphia, 1993, Mandela, 1996, Beloved, 1998, Storefront Hitchcock, 1998; dir., co-prodr.: Something Wild, 1986; prodr.: Miami Blues, 1990; exec. prodr.: Devil in a Blue Dress, 1995; dir., actor That Thing You Do!, 1996; dir.: (TV movie) Who Am I This Time?, 1982, (documentary film) Accumulation with Talking Plus Water Motor; (music videos) UB40, Chrissie Hynde, Sun City Video of Artists United Against Apartheid, Suzanne Vega; (PBS series) A Family Tree; prodr.: Haiti: Dreams of Democracy, Women & Men 2 (A Domestic Dilemma). Mem. Dirs. Guild Am. Office: care Bob Bookman Creative Artists Agy 9830 Wilshire Blvd Beverly Hills CA 90212-1804 also: Clinica Estetico 127 W 24th St # 7 New York NY 10011-1914*

DEMMER, RICHARD JAMES, biologist; b. Madison, Wis., Mar. 19, 1949; s. Lawrence Frederick and Caroline Laura (Erdman) D.; m. Gay Louise Zerwer, Sept. 4, 1981. BS in Biology, U. Ctrl. Fla., 1976, MS in Biology, 1981; MS in Forest and Range Mgmt., Wash. State U., 1984. Dist. naturalist Fla. Dept. Natural Resources, Orlando, 1978-80; tech. illustrator Advanced Rsch. and Devel., Miami, Fla., 1981-82; interpretive naturalist Jewel Cave Nat. Monument Nat. Park Svc., 1982; drafter Tech. Staff Inc., Seattle, 1984-88; biologist Dept. Interior Bur. Land Mgmt., Prineville, Oreg., 1988—. Author: (poetry) Desert Light, 1995, National Library of Poetry, 1996. With U.S. Army, 1969-71. Mem. Soc. NW Vertebrate Biology, Pacific NW Amphibian and Reptile Consortium, Oreg. Natural Desert Assn., Xi Sigma Pi. Avocations: writing poetry, watercolor painting, backpacking, bird watching. Home: PO Box 51 Prineville OR 97754 Office: Bur Land Mgmt Dept Interior PO Box 550 Prineville OR 97754-0550

DEMMLER, ALBERT WILLIAM, JR., retired editor, metallurgical engineer; b. Pitts., Feb. 21, 1929; Albert William and Hester Louisa (Dye) D.; m. Donna Lou Frederick, Feb. 16, 1957; children: Richard Frederick, Keith Alan (dec.), Diane Leslie, Debra Lynn. PhB in Liberal Arts, U. Chgo., 1948; BS in Metall. Engring., U. Mich., 1951, MS in Metall. Engring., 1952, PhD, 1955. Rsch. engr. Alcoa Rsch. Labs., New Kensington, Pa., 1955-68; registered rep. Butcher & Singer, Pitts., 1968-74; exec. searcher Reese Assoc., Pitts., 1974-76; assoc. editor Soc. Automotive Engrs. Inc. Mags., Warrendale, Pa., 1976-90, sr. editor, 1990-99; ret., 1999. Patentee in field. Mem. NRA, Soc. Automotive Engrs., Am. Soc. Metals Internat., Automotive Press Assn., Hypnotism Soc. Pa., Tarentum Dist. Sportsmens Club, Pa. Rifle and Pistol Assn., Pa. Gun Collectors Assn., Crowfoot Rod & Gun Club, Mensa, Tau Beta Pi, Phi Lambda Upsilon, Sigma Xi. Democrat. Presbyterian. Avocations: competitive rifle, pistol, hypnosis. Home: 132 Glenview Dr New Kensington PA 15068-4900

DEMMLER, JOHN HENRY, lawyer; b. Pitts., June 20, 1932; s. Ralph Henry and Catherine (Hollinger) D.; m. Janet Rice, July 20, 1957; children: Richard H., Ralph W., Carol L. BA, Princeton U., 1954; LLB cum laude, Harvard U., 1959. Bar: Pa. 1960, U.S. Dist. Ct. (we. dist.) Pa. 1960. Assoc. Reed Smith Shaw & McClay, Pitts., 1959-65, ptnr., 1966-93, of counsel, 1994—; dir. Duquesne Light Co., Pitts., 1977-90. Trustee Shady Side Acad., Pitts., 1969-75, 77—, vice chmn., 1980-84, chmn., 1984-87; chmn. Fox Chapel Borough Zoning Hearing Bd., 1993—. Mem. Pa. Bar Assn. (pub. utility law sect. 1976—), Duquesne Club, Fox Chapel Golf Club, HYP Pittsburgh Club. Republican. Episcopalian. Home: 102 Foxtop Dr Pittsburgh PA 15238-2202 Office: Reed Smith Shaw & McClay 435 6th Ave Pittsburgh PA 15219-1886

DEMOLA, JAMES, SR., church administrator. Asst. gen. overseer, dist. overseer Christian Ch. of N. Am., 1986—; sr. pastor Springs of LIfe Christian Ctr., Mullica Hill, N.J., 1963—; appears, prodr. cable TV program The Word is Alive. Office: Springs of Life Christian Ctr Rt 77 Mullica Hill NJ 08062

DEMOND, JEFFREY STUART, cable television and telecommunications executive; b. Morristown, N.J., June 27, 1955; s. Marvin Harry DeMond and Lois Ann (Worrell) Kramer; m. Helene Regina Sullivan, Dec. 24, 1987; children: Brendan, Christopher. BS, U. Ala., 1978. CPA, N.Y. Sr. mgr. Peat, Marwick, Mitchell & Co., N.Y.C., 1978-85; exec. v.p., CFO Bresnan Comm. Co., White Plains, N.Y., 1985—; lectr., adj. prof. Hunter Coll., N.Y., 1984-85. Composer various popular music, 1974—; performer Sailcat record album Cathouse, 1976. Named an Outstanding Musician, Nat. Assn. Jazz Educators, 1978, Outstanding Jazz Soloist, Stan Kenton Coll. All-Star Orch., 1978. Mem. AICPA, Nat. Cable TV Assn. (mem. acctg. com.), Cable TV Tax Profls. Inst., N.Y. State Soc. CPA's, Beta Gamma Sigma. Avocations: guitar, performing, composing music. Office: Bresnan Comm Co 709 Westchester Ave White Plains NY 10604-3023

DEMONE, ROBERT STEPHEN, hotel company executive; b. June 13, 1932; s. Urban Roy and Effie Elfreda (Meisner) DeM.; m. Jean Valerie Snedden, June 26, 1954 (dec. June 1984); children: Susan Liane, Jill Carol; m. Joanna Stefania Tchorek, Mar. 22, 1985. B Com, Dalhousie U., Halifax, N.S., 1952; dipl. bus. mgmt., U. We. Ont., London, Can., 1970. Chartered acct., 1954. Corp. tax assessor Revenue Can., Halifax, 1955-56; works acct. Can. Rock Salt Co. Ltd., Pugwash, N.S., 1956-62; comptr. Ben's Ltd., Halifax, 1962-67; various sr. fin. and acctg. positions Can. Pacific Ltd., Montreal, 1967-77, Toronto, Ont., 1977-79; v.p. fin. and acctg. Can. Pacific Enterprises Ltd., Toronto, 1979-81; pres., COO, bd. dirs. Maple Leafe Mills Ltd., Toronto, 1981-83, pres., CEO, bd. dirs., 1984-85, pres., CEO, chmn. bd., 1985-87; chmn., pres., CEO, dir. Can. Pacific Hotels Corp., Toronto, 1987-97; vice chmn. Can. Tourism Commn., Toronto, 1994—; asst. v.p. fin. and acctg., dir. acctg.; chmn., CEO, dir. Can. Pacific Securities Ltd., Toronto, 1977-81; bd. dirs. The Sumitomo Bank of Can. Mem. Can. Inst. Chartered Accts., Que. Order Chartered Accts., Ont. Inst. Chartered Accts. Anglican. Office: Can Pacific Hotels Corp, 123 Front St W, Toronto, ON Canada M5J 2M2

DEMONSABERT, WINSTON RUSSEL, chemist, consultant; b. New Orleans, June 12, 1915; s. Joseph Francis and Davida Elizabeth (Gullett) deM.; m. Eleanor Ray Ranson, Aug. 8, 1955; 1 child, Winston Russel. BS in Chemistry, Loyola U., New Orleans, 1937; MA in Edn., Tulane U., 1945, PhD in Chemistry, 1952. Asst. prof. Loyola U., New Orleans, 1948-49, assoc. prof., 1949-55, prof., 1955-66; chief chemist Nat. Center for Disease Control, Dept. Health and Human Services, Atlanta, 1966-69, chief contract liaison br. Nat. Center for Health Services Research, 1969-73, chief extramural programs Bur. Drugs, FDA, Rockville, Md., 1973-79, scientist adminstr. office of interagy sci. coordination, office of commr. FDA, after 1979; now cons., govt. liaison environ. chemistry and toxicology; assoc. prof. Tulane U., 1957-58; research chemist Am. Cyanamid Co., 1957-58; vice-chmn. Interagy. Testing Com., 1982. Committeeman Boy Scouts Am., New Orleans and Atlanta; mem. curriculum coms. New Orleans Pub. Sch. Bd., 1965. Fellow AAAS, Am. Inst. Chemists (chmn. La. chpt. 1958-60, chmn. Ga. chpt. 1968-69, pres. D.C. chpt. 1982-83); mem. Am. Chem. Soc. (past chmn. La. sect.). Roman Catholic. Contbr. to Ency. Americana, Ency. Chemistry, also profl. jours. Achievements include research in environmental effects (detection, prevention and treatment) of toxic wastes, pesticides and air pollution, and zirconium chemistry. Home and Office: 4317 Lake Trail Dr Kenner LA 70065-1541

DEMONTE, CLAUDIA ANN, artist, educator; b. Astoria, N.Y., Aug. 25, 1947; d. Joseph James and Ammeda Ellen (Heiss) DeM.; m. William Edward McGowin, May 28, 1977. BA, Coll. Notre Dame, 1969; MFA, Cath. U., 1971. Instr. Bowie State Coll., Md., 1971-72, Prince Georges C.C., Largo, Md., 1972; prof. dept. art U. Md., College Park, 1972—; dir. Art Workshops, New Sch. Social Rsch., N.Y.C., 1980-94; USIA artist in residene (Sofia) Bulgaria, 1982; mem. art bd. Queens Coll., N.Y. Selected exhbns.: Corcoran Gallery of Art, 1976, Contemporary Arts Center, New Orleans, Cranbrook Acad., 1978, Marianne-Deson Gallery, 1979, Miss. Mus., Fort Worth Mus., Washington Project for the Arts, 1980, Marion Locks Gallery, Miami Dade Gallery, Xochipilli, 1981, 86, 95, New Sch. Social Research, Swope Gallery, 1982, Queens Mus., N.Y., Stamford Mus., Conn., Gallery 121, Antwerp, Belgium, 1985, Gracie Mansion Gallery, N.Y., 1987, Brentwood Art Gallery, St. Louis, 1987, Nina Freunenheim Gallery, Buffalo, N.Y., 1987, Internat. Rev. of the Arts Arsenal, Amalfi, Italy, 1987, Esbo Mus., Helsinki, Finland, 1988, Jones Troyer Fitzpatrick Gallery, Washington, 1988, 93, Evanston (Ill.) Art Ctr., 1989, Gracie Mansion Gallery, N.Y., Barbara Gillman Gallery, Miami, 1991, 92, 94, Gallery 86, Lodz, Poland, Slow Art , Painting in N.Y. Now, P.S. 1 Mus., N.Y., 1991, Internat. Biennial of Paper Art, Duren, Germany, 1992, Haggerty Mus., Wis., 1993, Nina Freudenheim Gallery, Buffalo, 1994, Leedy Voulkos Gallery, Kansas City, Mo., 1996, Panaroma Gallery, Barcelona, Spain, Silpakorn U., Bangkok, 1997, Retrospective, Choklafabuken, Malmo, Sweden, 1998, Liesbeth Lip Gallery, Rotterdam, The Netherlands, 1999; pub. collections include Indpls. Mus., Stamford Mus., Miss. Mus., Prudential Life Ins., Hyatt-Regency, Chem. Bank, Best Products, U. Md., Mus. Modern Art, New Orleans Mus., Minn. Mus., Grand Rapids Mus., Mich., UCLA, Corcoran Gallery of Art, Bklyn. Mus., Indpls. Mus., Bass Mus., Tucson Mus., Boca Raton Mus.; commns. Kingdom of Saudi Arabia, 1993; author: (with Judy Bachrach) The Height Report, 1983. Mem. art bd. Queens (N.Y.) Coll. Recipient award Am.-Italian Assn., 1971, Head Balt. Bus., 1972, Creative award Me., 1974, 77, 83, 87; N.Y. Found. for the Arts fellow, 1989—, N.Y.C. Dept. Cultural Affairs Art in Pub. Places Sculpture Commn., 1991, N.Y.C. Dept. Cultural Affairs Mural Commn. fellow 1993, sculpture commn. N.Y.C. Dept. Cultural Affairs, 1997, N.Mex. State Art Commn., Sculpture Commn., Socorro, 1998. Democrat. Home: 96 Grand St New York NY 10013-2633 Office: U Md Art Dept College Park MD 20742

DE MONTEBELLO, PHILIPPE LANNES, museum administrator; b. Paris, May 16, 1936; came to U.S., 1951, naturalized, 1955; s. Roger L. and Germaine (de Croisset) de M.; m. Edith Bradford Myles, June 24, 1961; children: Marc, Laure, Charles. B.A. magna cum laude, Harvard U., 1961; M.A., NYU Inst. Fine Arts, 1963; LL.D. (hon.), Lafayette Coll., 1979; D.H.L. (hon.), Bard Coll., 1981; D.F.A. (hon.), Iona Coll., 1982. Assoc. curator European paintings Met. Mus. Art, N.Y.C., 1963-69; dir. Mus. Fine Arts, Houston, 1974-77; vice dir. for curatorial and ednl. affairs Met. Mus. Art, 1974-77, acting dir., 1977-78, dir., 1978—; mem. adv. coun. depts. art and archaeology Columbia U.; mem. Fogg, Fellow, Fogg Mus., Harvard U. Author: Peter Paul Rubens, 1969; mem. editorial bd. Internat. Jour. of Mus. Mgmt. and Curatorship. Trustee, NYU Inst. Fine Arts. Served to 2d lt. AUS, 1956-58. Decorated chevalier Legion d'Honneur (France), Encomienda de Numero de la Orden Isabel la Catholica (Spain), officier Ordre de Leopold (Belgium), Knight Commdr. Pontifical Order of St. Gregory the Great; recipient NYU Grad. Sch. Alumni Achievement award, 1978, gold medal Nat. Inst. Soc. Sci., 1989, The Spanish Inst., 1992, Rebekah Kohut award Nat. Coun. Jewish Women, 1993, NYU Alumni Assn. Disting. Alumni award, 1998; Woodrow Wilson fellow, 1961-62; Gallatin fellow, 1981. Mem. Assn. Art Mus. Dirs. (works of art com.), Mus. Coun. N.Y.C., Am. Fedn. of the Arts (trustee, exec. com.), Am. Assn. Mus. Avocations: collecting Old Master drawings, chess, tennis. Home: 1150 5th Ave New York NY 10128-0724 Office: The Met Mus of Art 1000 5th Ave New York NY 10028-0113

DEMONTIGNEY, JAMES MORGAN, health services administrator; b. Wilkes-Barre, Pa., Aug. 2, 1947; s. James DeMontigney and Elizabeth Morgan-deMontigney; m. Sharon Ann Frake-DeMontigney, Dec. 11, 1971; children: Rachelle Ann, Marc James. BA in Polit. Sci., U. Tenn., 1969, MSW, 1975. Caseworker Burlington County Welfare, Mt. Holly, N.J., 1969-71; parole officer N.J. Bur. Parole, Trenton, 1971; social worker N.J. Divsn. Pub. Welfare, Hamilton Township, 1971-73, N.J. Divsn. Youth and Family Svcs., Trenton, 1973, 75-78; casework supr. N.J. Divsn. Youth and Family Svcs., Camden, 1981-83; rsch. assoc. Bur. Rsch. N.J. Divsn. Youth and Family Svcs., Trenton, 1983-85, stds. and procedures technician, 1986-87; social worker N.J. Divsn. Med. Assistance and Health Svcs., Trenton, 1978-79, social work supr., 1979-81; field svc. supr. N.J. Divsn. Med. Assistance and Health Svcs., Woodbury, 1987; program devel. specialist office of home care programs N.J. Divsn. Med. Assistance and Health Svcs., Trenton, 1987—. Mem. Mt. Holly (N.J.) Twp. Rep. Com., 1983—, chmn., 1985—; mcpl. coord. Reagan for Pres. Campaign, Mt. Holly, 1984, Bush for Pres. Campaign, Mt. Holly, 1988, 92, Saxton for Congress Campaign, Mt. Holly, 1988, 90, 92, 94, 96, Allen, Faulkner, Williams Campaign, Mt. Holly, 1997; phonebank coord. Kean for Gov. Campgn, Burlington County, N.J., 1985; mcpl. coord. Whitman for Gov. Campaign, 1993, 97; mem. Mt. Holly Twpl. Planning Bd., 1986-93, chmn. 1990-96; mem. Mt. Holly Bd. Ethics, 1986-92; bd. dirs. Strength to Love, Inc., Mt. Holly, 1992-97; mem. adv. com. Burlington County Cmty. Devel. Block Gratn, 1998-99; mem. Mt. Holly Holly, 1998—, Citizens Concerned for Mt. Holly, 1998—. Mem. Comm. Workers Am., Mt. Holly Twp. Rep. Club (charter mem. 1983—, pres. 1984, 89, 90, 91). Avocations: antiques, collectables, coins, stamps, sports. Home: 305 Ridgway St Mount Holly NJ 08060-1443 Office: NJ Divsn Med Assistance Cn 712 Trenton NJ 08060

DEMOREST, MARK STUART, lawyer; b. Chambley, France, Mar. 14, 1957; came to U.S., 1960; s. Raymond Phillip and Maud Jane (Dahle) D.; m. Patricia Louise Button, July 28, 1979; children: Melissa, Matthew, Kristin, Kevin, Ryan. AB magna cum laude, Harvard U., 1979; JD magna cum laude, U. Mich., 1983. Bar: Mich. 1983, U.S Dist. Ct. (ea. dist.) Mich. 1983, U.S. Ct. Appeals (6th cir.) 1984, U.S. Ct. Appeals (7th cir.) 1986, U.S. Supreme Ct. 1993, U.S. Dist. Ct. (cen. dist.) Ill. 1995, U.S. Ct. Appeals (4th cir.) 1995, U.S. Dist. Ct. (we. dist.) Mich. 1996. Assoc. Dykema Gossett, Detroit, 1983-85, Simpson & Moran, Birmingham, Mich., 1985-87; ptnr. The Robert P. Ufer Partnership, Bloomfield Hills, Mich., 1987-92, Hainer, Demorest & Berman, P.C., Troy, Mich., 1993-98; pvt. practice Law Offices of Mark S. Demorest, 1998—. Mem. ABA, State Bar Mich., Def. Rsch. Inst., Oakland County Bar Assn., Harvard Club of Ea. Mich. (schs. com.), Order of Coif. Methodist. Avocation: sports. Office: Law Offices of Mark S Demorest 19853 W Outer Dr Ste 300 Dearborn MI 48124

DE MORI, RENATO, computer science educator, researcher; b. Milan, Aug. 5, 1941. PhD, Poly. U., Turin, Italy, 1967. Prof., chmn. U. Turin, 1977-79, prof., 1979-84; prof., chmn. Concordia U., Montreal, Que., Can., 1984-85; dir. Sch. Computer Sci. McGill U., Montreal, Que., Can., 1986-95; prof. Sch. Computer Sci. McGill U., Montreal, Que., 1995-96; v.p. rsch. Centre Recherche Informatique Montreal, 1987-94; prof. U. Avignon, France, 1997—; mem. Nat. Scis. and Engring. Council Can., 1983-89; assoc. Can. Inst. Advanced Rsch. Author: Computer Models of Speech, 1983; editor: Computer Perceptions, 1982, Spoken Dialogs with Computers, 1998; contbr. over 100 articles to profl. jours. Fellow IEEE Computing Soc.; mem. Assn. Computing Machinery, Can. Artificial Intelligence Soc. (v.p. 1986-88), Am. Assn. Artificial Intelligence. Office: U d'Avignon Lab Info BP1228, 339 Chemin Menajeries, 84911 Avignon CEDEX 9, France

DE MORNAY, REBECCA, actress; b. Santa Rosa, Calif., Aug. 29, 1962. Student, Lee Strasberg Theatre Inst., Los Angeles; also studied with Kristin Linklater. Apprentice with Francis Coppola's Zoetrope Studio, 1981. Actress: (films) Risky Business, 1983, Testament, 1983, The Slugger's Wife, 1985, The Trip to Bountiful, 1985, Runaway Train, 1985, Beauty and the Beast, 1986, And God Created Woman, 1987, Feds, 1988, Dealers, 1989, Backdraft, 1991, The Hand That Rocks the Cradle, 1992, guilty as Sin, 1993, The three Musketeers, 1993, Never Talk to Strangers, 1995, The Winner, 1997; (plays) Born Yesterday, 1988, Marat/Sade, 1990; (TV) The Murders in the Rue Morge, 1986, By Dawn's Early Light, 1990, An Inconvenient Woman, 1992, Blind Side, 1993, Getting Out, 1994, The Shining, 1997.

DEMOS, DAVE, marketing executive. V.p. sales, mktg. Am. Axle & Mfg., Detroit, v.p. sales and bus. devel., 1997-99, v.p. procurement, 1999—. Office: Am Axle & Mfg 1840 Holbrook St Detroit MI 48212-3442*

DEMOS, JOHN PUTNAM, history educator, writer, consultant; b. Cambridge, Mass., May 2, 1937; s. Raphel D. and Jean Pauline (Demos) McMorran; m. Elaine Virginia Damis, July 27, 1963; children: Alison Virginia, Moira McMorran. B.A., Harvard U., 1959, postgrad., 1963-68; postgrad., Oxford U., Eng., 1959-60; M.A., U. Calif.-Berkeley, 1961. Teaching fellow Harvard U., Cambridge, Mass., 1966-68; from asst. prof. to prof. history Brandeis U., Waltham, Mass., 1968-86; Samuel Knight prof. history Yale U., New Haven, 1986—. Author: A Little Commonwealth, 1970, Remarkable Providences, 1972, Entertaining Satan, 1982 (Frederick Bancroft prize 1983), Past, Present, and Personal, 1986, The Unredeemed Captive, 1994. Mem. council Carnegie Council on Children Carnegie Corp. N.Y., N.Y.C., 1972-77; mem. com. on child research and pub. policy Nat. Acad. Scis., Washington, 1978-81; vol. Peace Corps, Ghana, 1961-63. Recipient Horace Kidger award New Eng. History Tchrs. Assn., 1980, Francis Parkman prize, 1995, Ray Allen Billington prize, 1995.; finalist Nat. Book award (non-fiction), 1994. Mem. Am. Hist. Assn. Democrat. Office: Yale U History Dept 320 York St PO Box 208324 New Haven CT 06520-8324*

DEMOS, NICHOLAS JOHN, physician, surgeon, researcher; b. Tripolis, Greece, Apr. 5, 1930; came to U.S., 1949; s. John Nicholas and Vakoula (Haritopoulos) D.; chilcren: Victoria N., Stephanie N. BS, Northwestern U., 1952, MS in Pathology, 1954, MD, 1955. Cert. Gen. Surgery, thoracic Surgery, Gen. Vascular Surgery. Resident in surgery Northwestern U. Med.

Sch., Chgo., 1955-58, 60-63; lt. commdr. USN, 1958-60; resident in thoracic surgery Seton Hall U. Med. Sch., Jersey City, N.J., 1960-63; NIH fellow surgical cardiology Seton Hall U. Med. Sch., 1963-64; chief cardiovascular surgery Christ Hosp., Jersey City, N.J., 1977—; chief dept. surgery St. Francis Hosp., Jersey City, N.J., 1979-84; chief thoracic surgery Meadowlands Hosp., Secaucus, N.J., 1994—; clin. prof. surgery Newark Med. Sch., 1998—; past pres. Med. Staff Christ Hosp., Jersey City, N.J., 1980, N.J. Soc. Thoracic Surgeons, 1980, N.J. Soc. Vascular Surgery, 1980; liaison officer ACS, 1980—. Author: Stapled Gastroplasty, 1974, Surgery of Esophogus (movies), 1970—, Thorascopic Surgery of Esophogus; patentee of surgical instrument, 1987. Fellow Am. Coll. Cardiology, ACS; mem. Soc. Thoracic Surgeons, N.J. Soc. Vascular Surgery, Am. Gastroenterological Assn. Greek Orthodox. Avocations: photography, painting. Office: 142 Palisade Ave Jersey City NJ 07306-1108

DEMOSS, HAROLD RAYMOND, JR., federal judge; b. Houston, Tex., Dec. 30, 1930; s. Harold R. and Jessy May (Cox) DeM.; m. Judith Phelps; children: Harold R. III, Louise Holland. BA, Rice U., 1952; LLB, U. Tex., 1955. Assoc. Bracewell & Patterson, Houston, 1957-61, ptnr., 1961-91; judge U.S. Ct. of Appeals (5th cir.), HOUSTON, 1991—. Area chmn. Bush Congl. Campaign, Houston, 1968; Harris County vice chmn. Tower Senate Campaign, Houston, 1972, Ford/Dale Campaign, 1976; Harris County chmn. Loeffler for Gov. Primary, 1986; Harris County co-chmn. Reagan/Bush Campaign, 1980, 84; Tex. State chmn. Bush for Pres. Primary, 1979-80, Tex. vice chmn., 1988; mem. platform group Bush for Pres., Washington, 1988; rsch. analyst Bush/Quayle Campaign, 1988; del. Rep. State Conv., Houston, 1968; dist. del. at large Rep. Nat. Conv., Houston, 1980, alternate del. at large, 1984, 88; vestryman St. Martin's Episcopal Ch., Houston, 1968-72; mem. exec. bd. Episcopal Diocese Tex., 1983-86, chmn. planning com., 1985-88, del. Diocesan Conv., 1976-88; chmn. bd. Tex. Bill Rights Found., Houston, 1969-70; bd. dirs. Amigos de las Americas, 1974-76; pres. Tanglewood Homeowners Assn., 1987. Sgt. U.S. Army, 1955-57. Fellow Tex. Bar Assn. (life); mem. ABA, Internat. Bar Assn., Am. Judicature Soc., Maritime Law Assn. U.S., Houston Bar Assn. (bd. dirs. 1969-71, 1st v.p. 1972-73), Tex. Assn. Def. Counsel (bd. dirs. 1972-74), The Houston Club, The Houstonian Club. Avocations: fishing, waterskiing. Office: US Courthouse 515 Rusk St Rm 12015 Houston TX 77002-2605*

DEMOSS, JON W., insurance company executive, lawyer; b. Kewanee, Ill., Aug. 9, 1947; s. Wendell and Virginia Beth DeMoss; m. Eleanor T. Thornley, Aug. 9, 1969; 1 child, Marc Alain. BS, U. Ill., 1969, JD, 1972. Bar: Ill. 1972, U.S. Dist. Ct. (cen. dist.) Ill. 1977, U.S. Supreme Ct. 1978, U.S. dist. Ct. (no. dist., trial bar) Ill. 1983. In house counsel Assn. Ill. Electric Coop., Springfield, 1972-74; registered lobbyist Ill. Gen. Assembly, Springfield, 1972-74; asst. dir. Ill. Inst. for CLE, Springfield, 1974-85; exec. dir. Ill. State Bar Assn., 1986-94; pres., CEO ISBA Mut. Ins. Co., Chgo., 1994—. Bd. dirs. Springfield Symphony Orch., 1982-87, Ill. Inst. for CLE, 1986-89, Nat. Assn. of Bar Related Ins. Cos., 1989, pres., elect., 1998-99; bd. dirs. Lawyers Reins. Co., 1997—; bd. visitors John Marshall Law Sch., 1990—. Capt. U.S. Army, 1972. Fellow Am. Bar Found. (life, co-chmn. projects to prepare Appellate Handbook 1978, 90), Ill. Bar Found. (bd. dirs. 1983-85); mem. ABA (mem. ho. of dels. 1979-85, 89, 91, 93-94), Nat. Conf. Bar Pres., Ill. State Bar Assn. (pres. 1984-85, bd. govs. 1975-85, chmn. com. on scope and correlation of work 1982-83, chmn. budget com. 1983-85, chmn. legis. com. 1983-84, 85, chmn. com. on merit selection of judges 1977, del. long-range planning conf. 1972, 78, liaison to numerous coms. and sects.), Chgo. Bar Assn., Lake County Bar Assn., U. Ill. Coll. Dean's Club, La Chaine des Rotisseurs (Chgo.), Ordre Mondial des Gourmet Degustateurs (Chgo.), Les Gourmets (Chgo.). Home: 180 Norwich Ct Lake Bluff IL 60044-1914 Office: ISBA Mutual Ins Co First National Plaza 20 S Clark St Ste 910 Chicago IL 60603-1803

DE MOSS, LLOYD G., community service executive; b. Polk County, Iowa, Nov. 4, 1939; s. Lloyd Harvey De Moss and Marian Helen (Kirkindahl) Carstens; m. Helen K. Snider, Feb. 26, 1972; children: Todd, Kirby. BS, Morningside Coll., 1962; MS, U. Iowa, 1972. Tchr., coach Ctrl. City (Iowa) H.S., 1962-71; exec. dir. United Action For Youth, Iowa City, 1971-72; pvt. stock broker, sales rep. Des Moines, 1972-81; correctional counselor Iowa State Corrections, Clarinda, 1981-83; exec. dir. Area XII Alcohol & Drug, Carroll, Iowa, 1993-95, Cmty. Opportunities, Carroll, Iowa, 1995—. Mem. staff/parish rels. Meth. ch., 1996—. Mem. Masonic Lodge (officer 1992—), Nat. Assn. of Cmty. Action Agencies. Dem. Avocations: gardening, landscaping, hunting, fishing, pets. Office: Cmty Opportunities Inc 603 W 8th St Carroll IA 51401-2209

DEMOSS, NANCY, foundation administrator; b. N.C., 1938. Chmn., CEO Arthur S. DeMoss Found., W. Palm Beach, Fla. Office: Arthur S DeMoss Found 777 S Flagler Dr Ste 1600 W Palm Beach FL 33401*

DE MOSS, ROBERT GEORGE, religious foundation executive; b. Albany, N.Y., Mar. 8, 1928; s. Stephen Efthin and Ann (Simon) De M.; m. Dora Sterious, Sept. 16, 1950; children: Rebecca Ann, Robert G. Jr., Stephen Mark, John Christopher, Timothy Paul. BS, Syracuse U., 1950; BA, Westminster Sem., Phila., 1953, MA, 1954; PhD, Temple U., 1959. Math. tchr. Ea. Christian High Sch., Patterson, N.J., 1956-62; prof. philsophy Covenant Coll., Lookout Mountain, Tenn., 1965-67; tchr. philosophy Pa. State U., King of Prussia, 1963; v.p. Arthur De Moss Found., St. Davids, Pa., 1970-79, pres., 1980—; tchr. philosophy Messiah Coll., Phila, 1970-77; prof. philosophy Geneva Coll., Phila, 1978, 79. Elder Presbyn. Ch., Hatboro, Pa., 1963-73; lay minister Presbyn. Ch., Glenside, Pa., 1980—. Pfc. U.S. Army, 1945-46. Author book revs. Westminster Jour., 1962-70, Presbyn. Guardian, 1965-70. Republican. Avocations: tennis, ping pong, playing guitar and piano, jogging. *

DEMOTS, HENRY, cardiologist; b. Delavan, Wis., June 1, 1940; s. Henry and Bertha (Vanderpol) DeM.; m. Myrna Joyce Slotemaker, July 12, 1963; children: David Henry, Daniel Alan, Sharon Lynn. BS, Calvin Coll., 1962; MD, Northwestern U., 1966. From instr. medicine to prof. medicine, chief cardiology Oreg. Health Sci. U., Portland, 1971—. Fellow Am. Coll. Cardiology (bd. govs.), Coun. Clin. Cardiology, Am. Coll. Physicians; mem. Assn. Profl. Cardiologists. Avocation: hiking. Home: 3040 NW 153rd Ave Beaverton OR 97006-5310 Office: Oreg Health Scis U 3181 SW Sam Jackson Pk Rd Portland OR 97201

DEMOULAS, TELEMACHUS A., retail grocery company executive; b. 1923; married. With DeMoulas Supermarkets, Inc., Tewksbury, Mass., 1954—, now pres., treas., CEO. Office: DeMoulas Supermarkets Inc 875 East St Tewksbury MA 01876-1495*

DEMOUTH, ROBIN MADISON, lawyer, corporate executive; b. Warwick, N.Y., Apr. 2, 1939; s. Claude Cornelius and Mary Louise (Shaw) D.; m. Mary Eileen Burns, April 25, 1992. BA, U. Va., 1961; postgrad., U. Ill., 1962; JD, John Marshall Law Sch., 1965; LLM, Lawyer's Inst., 1970; MBA, U. Chgo., 1976. Bar: Ill. 1966, U.S. Supreme Ct. 1970. Assoc. Madsen & Friese, Chgo., 1965-67; atty. Stewart-Warner Corp., Chgo., 1965-70, sr. atty., 1970-78, sec., chief legal officer, 1978-81, sec., gen. counsel, 1981-83, v.p., sec., gen. counsel, 1983-88; sec., gen. counsel Sandoz Corp., Des Plaines, Ill., 1989-98; v.p., gen. counsel, sec. Valent U.S.A. Corp., Walnut Creek, Calif., 1998—; mem. Gt. Lakes Commn., 1975-78; mem. internat. trade and port promotional adv. com. State of Ill., 1975-78. Bd. dirs., v.p., counsel Easter Seal Soc. of Met. Chgo. Inc., 1983-87. Mem. ABA, Am. Soc. Corp. Secs., Am. Assn. Corp. Counsel, Chgo. Bar Assn., Nat. Agrl. Chem. Assn. (vice chmn. law com. 1993, chmn. law com. 1995-96), Chgo. Yacht Club (bd. dirs. 1987, vice commodore 1992, commodore 1995-96, bd. dirs. 1995—), Mackinaw Island Yacht Club, Judd Gold Adaptive Sailing Found. (dir., 1990—), Econ. Club Chgo. Republican. Episcopalian. Avocation: sailing. Home: 6170 Mazuela Dr Oakland CA 94611 Address: Sandoz 1000 Tower Ln Ste 245 Bensenville IL 60106-1042

DEMPSEY, CECELIA See BYRNE-DEMPSEY, CECELIA

DEMPSEY, CEDRIC W., sports association administrator; b. Apr. 14, 1932; m. June Dempsey, Aug. 22, 1953; children: Linda, David, Marcia. BA in Phys. Edn. and History, Albion Coll., MA in Edn.; PhD in Phys. Edn., U. Ill.; LLD (hon.), Albion Coll. Grad. asst., asst. football and basketball coach, head tennis coach Albion (Mich.) Coll., 1954-56, head basketball & cross country coach, phys. edn. instr., 1959-62, dean of men, 1962-63; grad. asst., counselor profl. students, dir. placement svc. U. Ill., Urbana, 1956-59; asst. basketball coach, supr. undergrad. health, phys. edn. & recreation, asst. prof. U. Ariz., Tucson, 1963-65, asst. dir. health, phys. edn., recreation & athletics, assoc. prof., 1965-67, dir. athletics, 1982-93; dir. athletics, chair phys. edn. & recreation U. of the Pacific, Stockton, Calif., 1967-79; dir. athletics San Diego State U., 1979, U. Houston, 1979-82; pres. NCAA, Overland Park, Kans., 1993—; sec.- treas. exec. com. NCAA, adminstrn. com., coun. and joint policy bd., chair budget subcom., mem. numerous other coms. Recipient Kathy Miller Courage award Phoenix Press Box Assn., 1988, Disting. Alumni award Albion Coll., 1993; named to Albion Coll. Inaugural Hall of Fame, 1989, U. Pacific Sports Hall of Fame, 1991. Office: NCAA 6201 College Blvd Overland Park KS 66211-2422*

DEMPSEY, DAVID ALLAN, company official, small business owner; b. Eglin AFB, Fla., Sept. 5, 1957; s. David Leroy and Marguerite (Thomas) D.; m. Debra Kay Gross, Jan. 22, 1982; children: Nakia, Elisabeth, David. AS in Restaurant Mgmt., C.C. of Air Force, Maxwell AFB, Ala., 1987, AS in Contracts Mgmt., 1989; BS in Logistics Sys. Mgmt., Colo. Tech. U., 1995. Cert. lay spkr. United Meth. Ch. Postal asst. U.S. Postal Svc., Wilmington, Del., 1974-75; enlisted man USAF, 1975, advanced through grades to master sgt., 1991; ret., 1995; sr. subcontract adminstr. TRW, Inc., Colorado Springs, Colo., 1995-98; contract mgr. Harris Tech. Svcs. Corp., Colorado Springs, Colo., 1998—; v.p. TRW Colorado Springs Employee Assn., 1998. Pres. bldg. accountability com. Evans Elem. Sch., Colorado Springs, 1993—; coord. D-Day, Share Colo., Ctrl. United Meth. Ch., Colorado Springs, 1993—, also Sunday sch. tchr.; candidate for sch. bd. dirs. Falcon Sch. Dist. 49, Colorado Springs, 1995, 96, mem. long range planning com., 1996—, chmn. citizen's facility study com.; mem. planning and design com. Sand Creek H.S., Colorado Springs, 1995—; mem. sch. fee adv. com. El Paso County Bd. Commrs., Colorado Springs, 1996—; precinct capt. El Paso County Dem. Com., 1996-97; mem. El Paso County (Colo.) Park Adv. Bd., liaison park fee adv. com.; chmn. Commitment for Kids com., Colorado Springs; mem. Mt. Olive Coll. Alumni Assn., Mt. Olive, N.C., Pikes Peak Urban League, Colorado Springs; vol. dist. 39 sch.-bus. alliance Jr. Achievement, 1999—; sec. El Paso County Dem. Com., 1999—. Mem. Nat. Contract Mgmt. Assn. (publicity chmn. 1996-98, chpt. pres. 1998-99, employment chmn. 1996-98), Noncommd. Officers Assn. (chmn. 1995), Ret. Enlisted Assn., Toastmasters (v.p. 1994-95, pres. 1995), So. Colo. Bus. Links. Avocations: reading, watching movies, volunteering.

DEMPSEY, EDWARD JOSEPH, lawyer; b. Lynn, Mass., Mar. 13, 1943; s. Timothy Finbar and Christine Margaret (Callahan) D.; m. Eileen Margaret McManus, Apr. 15, 1967; children: Kristen A. Stofi, Katherine B. Aydin, Shelagh E., James P. *Grandparents James and Catherine (Naegle) Dempsey having emigrated from Rosscarerry, Ireland and grandparents Matthew and Catherine Callahan having emigrated from Cork, Ireland, Edward Dempsey honored their memory by registering his Iris citizenship* AB, Boston Coll., 1964; JD, Cath. U. Am., 1970. Bar: D.C. 1970, Conn. 1982. Assoc., Arent, Fox, Kintner, Plotkin & Kahn, Washington, 1970-72, Akin, Gump, Strauss, Hauer & Feld, Washington, 1972-75; supervisory trial atty. EEOC, Washington, 1975-79; assoc. Whitman & Ransom, Washington, 1979-81, Farmer, Wells, McGuinn & Sibal, Washington, 1981-82; ptnr. Farmer, Wells, Sibal & Dempsey, Washington and Hartford, Conn., 1983-84; dir. indsl. relations and labor counsel United Technologies Corp., Hartford, 1985—. Capt. USNR (ret.). Mem. ABA. *Edward Dempsey was editor-in-chief of the Catholic University Law Review from 1969-1970. He represented Sikorsky Aircraft Corporation before the Connecticut Supreme Court in the cases Parsons v. Sikorsky Aircraft and Cotto v. Sikorsky Aircraft. Before retiring from the U.S. Naval Reserve in 1991, he had served as Commanding Officer-Reserve Crew (SELRPS Coordinator) U.S.S. Steinaker (DD-863) and at the Naval War College, Newport, R.I.* Office: United Techs Bldg Hartford CT 06101

DEMPSEY, HOWARD STANLEY, lawyer, mining executive, investment banker; b. LaPorte, Ind., Aug. 12, 1939; s. Howard Taft and Katheryn Alice (Prichard) D.; m. Judith Rose Enyart, Aug. 20, 1960; children: Howard Stanley, Whitney Owen, Bradford Evan, Matthew Charles. Student, Colo. Sch. Mines, 1956-57; BA, U. Colo., 1960, JD, 1964; cert., Harvard Sch. Bus., 1969. Bar: Colo. 1964. Ind. mine operator Colo. and Wyo., 1958-60; indsl. engr. Climax Molybdenum Co., Golden, Colo., 1960-61, asst. resident atty., 1964-65, resident atty., 1965-68, div. atty. western ops., 1968-72; gen. atty. law dept. western area, dir. environ. affairs AMAX Inc., Denver, 1972-76, v.p., 1977-83; ptnr. Arnold & Porter, Denver, 1983-87; pres. Denver Mining Fin. Co., 1987—; chmn., chief exec. officer Royal Gold, Inc., Denver, 1987—, also bd. dirs.; pres. Environ. Strategies, Inc., 1991—; chmn. AMAX Australia Ltd., 1980-83; chmn., exec. com. AMAX Iron Ore, 1980-83; bd. dirs., dep. chmn. Australian Consol. Mines Ltd., 1980-83; bd. dirs. Hazen Rsch., Inc., Golden, Colo., Dakota Mining Corp., Denver, Behre Dolbear, Denver. Author: Mining the Summit, 1978; contbr. articles to profl. jours. Trustee Rocky Mountain Mineral Law Found., pres., 1980-81. Mem. Nat. Mining Assn. (mem. public lands com. 1967—, chmn. 1994—),Mining History Hall of Fame Mus. (bd. govs. 1998—, Am. Bar Assn. (chmn. hard minerals com. 1975-76), Colo. Bar Assn. (council mem. mineral law sect. 1971-73), Colo. Natural Resources Law Ctr. (bd. dirs. 1998—), Colo. Mining Assn. (pres. 1980-81), Continental Divide Bar Assn. (sec.-treas. 1969-73), Colo. Hist. Soc. (bd. dirs., chmn. 1991-93), Soc. Mining Law Antiquarians (pres. 1979-81), Mining and Metall. Soc. Am., Mining History Assn. (pres. 1992-94), Mountain States Employers Coun. (bd. dirs. 1990—), Masons, Rotary. Presbyterian. Clubs: Rollings Hills Country (Golden); Am. Alpine, Univ., Colo. Mountain (Denver); Harvard (N.Y.C.), Am. Nat. (Sydney, Australia). Lodges: Masons, Rotary. Office: Royal Gold Inc 1660 Wynkoop St Ste 1000 Denver CO 80202-1132

DEMPSEY, JACQUELINE LEE, special education director; b. Pitts., Jan. 4, 1951; d. Alexander and Catherine (Rankin) D. BS, Edinboro (Pa.) State Coll., 1972, MEd, 1974; PhD, U. Pitts., 1983. Tchr. Allegheny Intermediate Unit, Pitts., 1975-77, master tchr., 1977-78, instructional advisor, 1978-81, project dir., 1981-86, program adminstr., 1985-86; exec. dir. The Early Learning Inst., Pitts., 1986-95; pres. Early Childhood Internat., Pitts., 1995—; guest field reviewer Exceptional Children, 1989-95. Chair Pa. Early Intervention Interagy. Coord. Coun., 1992-93; mem. Gov.'s Commn. on Children and Families, 1992-93. Mem. Coun. for Exceptional Children, Early Intervention Providers Assn. Pa. (vice chair 1986-88), Pitts. Area Coun. Adminstrv. Women in Edn. (pres. 1985-86), Phi Delta Kappa. Office: Early Childhood Internat 46 Walnut St Pittsburgh PA 15205-3117

DEMPSEY, JAMES RAYMON, industrial executive; b. Red Bay, Ala., Oct. 4, 1921; s. Newman W. and Maude (Berry) D.; m. Dolores Barnes, Jan. 19, 1943 (dec. Sept. 1997); children: Susan, David Barnes, Anne. Student, U. Ala., 1937-39; BS, U.S. Mil. Acad., 1943; MS, U. Mich., 1947, D of Engring. (hon.), 1964. Commd. 2d lt. U.S. Army, 1943; advanced through grades to lt. col. USAF, 1951; with photo reconnaissance squadron Eng., France, World War II; squadron comdr., 1945; guided missiles project officer, then chief guided missile projects (Research and Devel. Directorate, Air Force Hdqrs.), 1948- 49; exec. officer to (Dep. Chief Staff for Devel.), 1950-51; chief project sect. (Air Force Missile Test Center), Patrick AFB, Fla.; then operations officer missile test range (Air Force Missile Test Center), 1951-53, resigned, 1953; asst. to v.p. planning Convair div. Gen. Dynamics Corp., 1953-54; dir. Gen. Dynamics Corp. (Atlas program), 1954-57; mgr. Gen. Dynamics Corp. (Convair-Astronautics div.), 1957-58; v.p. Gen. Dynamics Corp. (Convair div.), 1958-61; sr. v.p. Gen. Dynamics Corp.; pres. Gen. Dynamics Astronautics, 1961-65, Gen. Dynamics Convair, 1965-66; v.p. missiles, space and electronics group Avco Corp., 1966-68, v.p., group exec. govt. products group, 1968-75; pres. Digital Broadcasting Corp., 1978-79; mng. partner J.J. Finnigan Industries, Duluth, Ga., 1978-85; pres. Southeastern Rail Car Co., 1986-89; pvt. investor, 1990—; trustee Phoenix Series Fund, 1968-91, Big Edge Series Fund, 1985-91, Phoenix Multi-Portfolio Fund, 1989-91, Precious Metal Holdings, 1980-93, Keystone Internat., 1987-93; chmn. bd. Transatlantic Capital Corp., Transatlantic Investment Corp., 1984-86; mem. spl. com. on space tech. NASA. Decorated Air Medal with clusters, D.F.C. U.S.; Croix de Guerre France). Fellow AIAA, Am. Astronaut. Soc.; mem. Air Force Assn. (bd. dirs. 1958-59), Burning Tree Club, Congl. Country Club. Home and Office: 4081 Ridgeview Cir Mc Lean VA 22101-5809

DEMPSEY, JENNIFER CAMILLE, art educator, artist; b. Erie, Pa., Mar. 3, 1973; d. Jack Leroy Dempsey and Sherri Lucille Baxter-Dempsey. BFA, U. Pa., 1995; cert. fine arts, Pa. Acad. Fine Arts, 1995; MA in Art and Art Edn., Columbia U., 1999. Cert. art edn. tchr., N.Y.C. Substitute art instr. Sch. Dist. City of Erie, Pa., 1995-96; sec., asst. Erie Hist. Mus., 1996-97; art edn. program project asst. Columbia U. Tchrs. Coll., N.Y.C., 1997-98; artist-in-residence Lake Erie Brig Niagara History Course, Ctrl. H.S., Erie, 1996; adj. faculty visual art H.S. for the Performing and Visual Arts, Erie, 1995-97; student art tchr. LaGuardia H.S. for Music and Art and the Performing Arts, N.Y.C., 1998, Midtown West Sch., N.Y.C., 1999. One-person shows include Potscape Gallery, Erie, Pa., 1997; exhibited in group shows Pa. Acad. of Fine Arts, Phila., 1994, Mus. Am. Art, Phila., 1995, State of the Art Gallery, Ithaca, N.Y., 1996, Erie Art Mus., 1996, Potscape Gallery, Erie, 1997, LaGuardia H.S. for Music and Art, 1998, Nat. Art Edn. Assn., Chgo., 1998, Macy Gallery, Tchrs. Coll., Columbia U., N.Y.C., 1998. Recipient Amelia Earhart Leadership award Zonta II Orgn., Erie, 1990; scholar Bus. and Profl. Women's Orgn., Erie, 1991, Pa. Acad. Fine Arts, Phila., 1992-93, Columbia U. Tchrs. Coll., N.Y.C., 1998-99. Mem. Nat. Art Edn. Assn., Am. Assn. Mus., Coll. Art Assn. Avocations: printmaking, painting, mixed media art, music, public mural projects. E-mail: jcd37@columbia.edu. Home: PO Box 10037 Erie PA 16514

DEMPSEY, JERRY EDWARD, retired service company executive; b. Landrum, S.C., Oct. 1, 1932; s. Adolphus Gerald and Willie Ceyattie (Lee) D.; m. Harriet Coan Calvert; children: Jerrie E., Harriet R., Margaret. BS, Clemson U., 1954; MBA, Ga. State Coll., 1968. With Borg-Warner Corp., Chgo., 1956-84, gen. mgr. York divsn., 1972-77, exec. v.p., 1977-79, pres., COO, 1979-84; sr. v.p. Waste Mgmt. Inc., Oak Brook, Ill., 1984-93; chmn., CEO PPG Industries, Inc., Pitts., 1993-97, chmn., 1997; bd. dirs. Navistar, PPG Industries, Inc., Eastman Chem. Co. Dean's adv. coun. Sch. Engring. Clemson U., chmn. pres.'s adv. coun.; bd. dirs. Pitts. Theol. Sem., Greenville Symphony, Greater Greenville Forum. Named Bus. Leader of Yr., Oak Brook (Ill.) Jaycees, 1989; recipient Bronze award Fin. World, 1989, 90, Pres.'s award Clemson U., 1990, Disting. Svc. award, 1992, Horatio Alger award, 1995, Am. Heritage award Anti-Defamation League, 1995. Mem. ASHRAE, Melrose Club, Duquesne Club (dir.), Laurel Valley Golf Club, Greenville Country Club, Fox Chapel Golf Club. Office: PPG Industries Inc 1 Ppg Pl Pittsburgh PA 15272-0001

DEMPSEY, MARY A., library commissioner, lawyer; m. Philip Corboy, Sept. 4, 1992. BA with honors, St. Mary's Coll., Winona, Minn., 1975; MLS, U. Ill., 1976; JD, DePaul U., 1982. Bar: Ill. 1982. Libr. Hillside (Ill.) Pub. Libr., 1976-78; assoc. Reuben & Proctor, Chgo., 1982-85; assoc. gen. counsel Michael Reese Hosp. and Med. Ctr., Chgo., 1985-86; pvt. practice, Chgo., 1987-89; counsel Sidley & Austin, Chgo., 1990-93; commr. Chgo. Pub. Libr., 1994—; adj. prof. law DePaul U. Coll. Law and Health Inst., Chgo., 1986-90; spl. counsel Chgo. Bd. Edn., 1987-89; mem. adv. bd. Dominican U. Grad. Sch. Libr. and Info. Sci., River Forest, Ill. Mem. State Street Commn., Chgo.; mem. exec. com. Greater State Street Coun.; bd. dirs. Big Shoulders Fund (for inner city Cath. schs.); bd. govs. Cath. Extension Soc.; trustee DePaul U., Chgo. Libr. scholar State of Ill. Mem. ALA, Pub. Libr. Assn., Ill. Libr. Assn., Chgo. Bar Assn. Office: Chgo Pub Libr 400 S State St Chicago IL 60605-1203

DEMPSEY, RAYMOND LEO, JR., radio and television producer, moderator, writer; b. Providence, June 18, 1949; s. Raymond Leo Sr. and Louise Veronica (Gambuto) D.; m. Patricia Batchelder (div. 1984); children: Joab, Jahdeam, Deezsha, Nathaniel, Talitha. BA in Liberal Arts, R.I. Coll., 1973; Cert. in Bus., U. R.I., 1979; cert., Blake Computer Programming Inst., 1977, Billy Graham Ashville N.C. Sch, Ashville, N.C., 1989. Lic. real estate agt., R.I.; lic. radio sta. operator FCC; cert. secondary tchr., videographer, contractor, R.I. Writer local and nat. publs., 1980-88; producer, moderator Chapter & Verse TV, Sta. RICA-TV, Providence, 1983—; tchr. R.I. Pub. High Schs., Providence and Cranston, 1988—; producer, moderator radio programs Ch. Focus and People, Sta. WRIB, East Providence, R.I., 1989—; bd. dirs. Blessing, Inc., Providence; spl. corr. Songtime U.S.A. Radio Network, 1988—, spl. reporter, spl. contbr., 1991; host Straight Talk, Sta. WKRI, 1989, dir. World Exch., 1991-93; co-host The Bible Answer Program, Sta. WARV, 1986; judge The Ace Awards, 1992, Cable Ace Awards, 1992; interviewer Gallup Poll, 1987; trainee N.E. Law Enforcement Officers Assn., 1991; elector Radio Hall of Fame, 1993, Stellar Awards, 1993; nursing asst. nursing homes, R.I., 1979; pvt. nurse's asst. R.I. Hosp., 1979; patient attendant R.I. Mental Hosp.; papers placed in permanent reference res. Brit. Libr., London, N.Y.C. Pub. Libr., Libr. Congress, Washington; donated reference libr. U. Steubenville, Ohio, 1995; preliminary judge Audio Pub. Assn. awards, 1996—. Bd. dirs. R.I. Right to Life, Cranston, 1973—; witness R.I. Gen. Assembly, 1973—, R.I. Bd. Health, 1973—; vol. ARC, R.I. Hosp.; registrar voters State of R.I., 1980, 91, 92; del. Rep. Nat. Conv. 1980; sponsor World Vision, Pasadena, Calif., 1981—, Compassion Internat., Colo. Springs, Colo., 1989—; chief boys instr. karate Mattson Acad., Providence, 1968-71; mem. Providence Sci. Outreach of Brown U.; del. Gov.'s Conf. on Libr. and Info. Svcs., 1991; elector White House Conf. on Libr. and Info. Svcs.; Justice of Peace, 1991; regional rep. Students Against Vietnam War, 1971, Taxpayers Action Network, 1991; ptnr. Food for the Hungry, 1984—; del. Ellen McCormack for Pres., 1976; vol. U.S. Fish and Wildlife Svc., R.I. Hosp., Providence, 1975, Providence Amb. Clinic, 1975; elected Rep. City Com. and Rep. State Ctrl. Com.; chmn. Issues and Rsch. Com. Rep. party Providence; numerous collection donations to libraries and Archdiocese of N.Y., 1975—; ret. dir. Ground Zero, Ams. Against Govt. Waste. Named One of Top 4 Local Cable TV Prodrs. in Nation, Nat. Assn. Local Cable Programming, 1987, ofcl. Jerusalem Pilgrim, State of Israel, 1990, Ptnr. in Philanthropy, 1995; recipient 2 Internat. Angel awards for excellence in Cable TV presentations, 1991, cert. U.S. SBA, 1990, Diamond award, 1992, 1st prize for excellence in pub. affairs in R.I. and Mass., 1992, Achievement award Dale Carnegie Orgn., 1992, 1st pl. award Mastermedia: The Spotlight award, 1993; nominated for J.C. Penney Golden Rule award. Mem. AAAS, ASCD, NRA, Am. Math. Soc., Coll. Sci. Tchrs., Sons Union Vets., Nat. Assn. H.S. Tchrs. English, Evangel. Theol. Soc., Soc. for Coll. Tchrs., Nat. Assn. Edn. of Young Children, Nat. Assn. Tchg. Sci., Modern Poetry Assn., Am. Soc. Oriental Rsch., Archaeol. Inst. Am., R.I. Assn. for Edn. Young Children, R.I. Assn. for Supervision and Curriculum Devel., Mental Health Assn. R.I., N.Y. Acad. Scis., Internat. Press Assn. (founding mem.), Nat. Geog. Soc., Nat. Assn. Broadcasters, Modern Poetry Assn., Nat. Assn. Radio Talk Show Hosts, Nat. Acad. Cable Programming, Near East Archaeol. Soc., Internat. Platform Assn., Nat. Assn. Tchrs. Sci., Jewish TV Inst. (charter), Smithsonian Air and Space Mus., Smithsonian Instn. (assoc.), Royal Inst. Pub. Health and Hygiene London (affiliate), Bread for the World, Evangs. for Social Action, Mus. Heritage Soc., Interscholastic Inst., Libr. Co. Phila., John Russell Bartlett Soc. (Brown U.), Intertel, Mensa, USCG Aux., Golden Key, Abraham Lincoln Soc., Internet Soc., Rel. Heritage Am., Providence Athenaeum, Toastmasters Internat., R.I. Pilots Assn., Phi Theta Kappa. Avocations: scuba diving, marksmanship, bibl. archeology. Home and Office: PO Box 41000 Providence RI 02940-1000 *Orthodoxy presumes orthopraxy, and correct knowledge must precede correct action: yet anything minus love equals zero.*

DEMPSEY, THOMAS JOSEPH, postmaster; b. Centralia, Pa., Mar. 16, 1945; s. William Anthony and Helen Agnes (Dewey) D.; m. Grace Mary Sewa, Nov. 24, 1973; children: Brian, Thomas Joseph Jr., Kevin. Grad., Postal Svc. Acad., Potomac, Md., 1984. Cert. postmaster trainer U.S. Postal Svc. Clk. U.S. Postal Svc., Centralia, 1968-77; mail carrier U.S. Postal Svc., Girardville, Pa., 1977-79; postmaster U.S. Postal Svc., Locustdale, Pa., 1979-81, Centralia, 1981-84, Girardville, 1984—; officer-in-charge selection bd. U.S. Postal Svc., Lancaster, Pa., 1992—, mem. postmaster selection bd. and customer svc. bd., 1994—. Author: History of Centralia, 1992. Sec. Centralia Ambulance Svc., 1970-73. Mem. Nat. Assn. Postmasters U.S., Nat. League Postmasters, Hist. Soc. Schuylkill County, KC. Democrat. Roman Catholic. Avocations: genealogy, history, fishing. Home: 204 W Main St Girardville PA 17935-1706 Office: US Postal Svc 210 W Main St Girardville PA 17935-9998

DEMSETZ, HAROLD, economist, educator; b. Chgo., 1930. BA, U. Ill., 1953; MBA, Northwestern U., 1954, PhD in Econs., 1959. Prof. econs. U. Chgo., 1963-71; sr. rsch. fellow Hoover Instn., Stanford, Calif., 1971-77; prof. econs. UCLA, 1971—, Arthur Anderson Alumni prof. bus. econs. 1988-95, emeritus, 1995—. Author: Economic, Legal, and Political Dimensions of Competition, 1982, The Organization of Economic Activity, Vol. I, 1988, Vol. II, 1989, The Economics of the Firm, 1995; contbr. numerous articles, book chpts. Fellow AAAS; mem. Mont Pelerin Soc., Am. Econs. Assn., WEA Internat. (pres. 1996). Office: UCLA Dept Econs 405 Hilgard Ave Los Angeles CA 90095-9000

DEMSKY, ISSUR DANIELOVITCH See DOUGLAS, KIRK

DEMUELLER, LUCIA, investment consultant; b. Manizales, Caldas, Colombia, Aug. 14, 1937; came to U.S., 1960; d. Ricardo Aristizabal and Soledad Villegas; m. Harold Charles Mueller, Feb. 26, 1966; children: Christine and Anne Marie (twins). Degree in journalism, U. Caldas, 1960; degree in bus. and fin., NYU, 1965; cert. in gerontology, Marymount Manhattan Coll., 1991. Editor Young Women's Mag., Bogota, Colombia, 1959-60; asst. export mgr. M & T Chems Inc., N.Y.C., 1963-66; mgr. banker acceptances Mitsui & Co., N.Y., N.Y.C., 1970-73; acct. exec. Conn. Mutual, N.Y.C., 1976-83; assoc. Cowan Agy., Mass. Fin., N.Y.C., 1983-86; investment cons. Chem. Investment Svcs., N.Y.C., 1993-94; internat. bus. cons., 1994—. Contbr. articles to profl. publs. Mgr. disaster assistance ctr. Fed. Emergency Mgmt., N.Y., 1985, 91. Mem. Nat. Def. Exec. Res. (mgr. various disaster sites), Latin Am. Progressive Group (pres. 1990—, founder). Home: 14003 SW 84th St Miami FL 33183-4423

DEMURO, PAUL ROBERT, lawyer; b. Aberdeen, Md., Mar. 21, 1954; s. Paul Robert and Amelia C. DeMuro; m. Susan Taylor, May 26, 1990; children: Melissa Taylor, Natalie Lauren, Alanna Leigh. BA summa cum laude, U. Md., 1976; JD, Washington U., 1979; MBA, U. Calif., Berkeley, 1986. Bar: Md. 1979, U.S. Dist. Ct. Md. 1979, D.C. 1980, U.S. Dist. Ct. D.C. 1980, U.S. Dist. Ct. (ea. dist.) Calif. 1986, U.S. Ct. Appeals (4th cir.) 1981, U.S. Tax Ct. 1981, Calif. 1982, U.S. Dist. Ct. (no. dist.) Calif. 1982; CPA, Md. Assoc. Ober, Grimes & Shriver, Balt., 1979-82; ptnr. Carpenter et al, San Francisco, 1982-89, McCutchen, Doyle, Brown & Enerson, San Francisco, 1989-93, Latham & Watkins, San Francisco, 1993—; bd. dirs. FMA Learning Solutions Inc. Author: The Financial Managers Guide to Managed Care and Integrated Delivery Systems, 1995, The Fundamentals of Managed Care and Network Development, 1999; co-author: Health Care Mergers and Acquisitions: The Transactional Perspective, 1996, Health Care Executives' Guide to Fraud and Abuse, 1998; editor, contbg. author Integrated Delivery Systems, 1994; article and book rev. editor Washington U. Law Qrtly., St. Louis, 1975-76. Mem. San Francisco Mus. Modern Art, 1985—; bd. dirs sch. health Calif. State U., 1992—. Fellow Healthcare Fin. Mgmt. Assn. (bd. dirs. No. Calif. chpt. 1990-93, 99—, sec. 1999—, nat. principles and practices bd. 1992-95, vice chair 1993-95, nat. bd. dirs. 1995-97, exec. com. 1996-97, chair compliance officers forum adv. coun. 1998—); mem. ABA (health law sect., chair transactional and bus. health care interest group 1998—), L.A. County Bar Assn. (health law sect.), Calif. Bar Assn., San Francisco Bar Assn., AICPA, Am. Health Lawyers Assn. (fraud and abuse and self-referral substantive law com. 1998—, task force on best practices in advising clients), The IPA Assn. Am. (mem. legal adv. coun. 1996—), Med. Group Mgmt. Assn. Republican. Office: Latham & Watkins 505 Montgomery St Ste 1900 San Francisco CA 94111-2552

DEMUTH, ALAN CORNELIUS, lawyer; b. Boulder, Colo., Apr. 29, 1935; s. Laurence Wheeler and Eugenia Augusta (Roach) DeM.; m. Susan McDermott; children: Scott Lewis, Evan Dale, Joel Millard. BA in Econs. & Gen. Studies magna cum laude, U. Colo., 1958, LLB, 1961. Bar: Colo. 1961, U.S. Dist. Ct. Colo. 1961, U.S. Ct. Appeals (10th cir.) 1962. Assoc. Akolt, Turnquist, Shepherd & Dick, Denver, 1961-68; ptnr. DeMuth & DeMuth, Denver, 1968—. Conf. atty. Rocky Mountain Conf. United Ch. of Christ, 1970-95; bd. dirs. Friends of U. Colo. Libr., 1978-86; bd. dirs., sponsor Denver Boys Inc., 1987-93, sec., 1988-89, v.p., 1989-90, pres., 1992-93; bd. dirs. Denver Kids, Inc., 1993—, Children's Ctr. for Arts and Learning, 1995—; mem. bd. advisors Lambuth Family Ctr. of Salvation Army, 1994—, chmn., 1994—; bd. advisors Metro Denver Salvation Army, 1988—, vice chmn. 1994-96. Mem. ABA, Colo. Bar Assn., Denver Bar Assn., Rotary (bd. dirs. 1996-98), Phi Beta Kappa, Sigma Alpha Epsilon, Phi Delta Phi. Republican. Mem. United Ch. of Christ. Office: DeMuth & DeMuth 990 S High St Denver CO 80209-4551

DEMUTH, CHRISTOPHER CLAY, lawyer, foundation executive; b. Evanston, Ill., Aug. 5, 1946; s. Harry Clay and Ethel Marie (Schaiell) DeM.; m. Susan Ann Shultis, June 9, 1973; children: Christopher Clay, Elizabeth Ann, Catherine Leas. A.B., Harvard Coll., 1968; J.D., U. Chgo., 1973. Bar: Ill. 1973, D.C. 1984. Staff asst. to Pres. Richard Nixon Washington, 1969-70; assoc. Sidley & Austin, Chgo., 1973-76; assoc. gen. counsel Consol. Rail Corp., Phila., 1976-77; lectr., dir. regulatory studies Harvard Sch. Govt., Cambridge, Mass., 1977-81; adminstr. info. and regulatory affairs U.S. Office Mgmt. and Budget, Washington, 1981-84, exec. dir. Presdl. Task Force on Regulatory Relief, 1981-83; mng. dir. Lexecon Inc., Washington, 1984-86; editor-in-chief, pub. Regulation mag., 1986; pres. Am. Enterprise Inst. for Pub. Policy Research, Washington, 1986—; chmn. bd. DeMuth Steel Products, 1993—, Clean Burn, Inc., 1993—. Mem. Am. Econ. Assn., Am. Law Econ. Assn. Republican. Episcopalian. Office: Am Enterprise Inst for Pub Policy Rsch 1150 17th St NW Washington DC 20036-4603*

DEMUTH, DANA ANDREW, umpire; b. Fremont, Ohio, May 30, 1956; m. Marjorie Whitaker, Dec. 2, 1978; 1 child, Dane. Umpire Calif. League, Tex. League, Pacific Coast League, Colombia and Dominican Republic Winter League, Nat. League, 1985—. Office: Nat League 350 Park Ave New York NY 10022 Office: Umpires Union 1735 Market St Philadelphia PA 19103

DEMUTH, VIVIENNE BLAKE MCCANDLESS, artist, illustrator; b. Nutley, N.J., Mar. 8, 1916; d. George Wilbur and Hazel Metcalfe Blake; m. Henry DeMuth, July 3, 1935 (div. Sept. 1957); children: Simon (dec.), Vivienne, Shelley, David; m. George Warren McCandless, May 12, 1984 (dec. May 1995). Diploma, Am. Sch. Design, 1932, 33. Designer, artist Norcross Pub. Co., N.Y.C. and West Chester, Pa., 1936-40, 50-75; designer, illustrator Fisher Price Toys, East Aurora, N.Y., 1957-80; freelance book illustrator many pub. cos., 1992-94; mem. newspaper panel cmty. newspapers Cape Cod, Mass.; artist, crafts tchr. presch. Cape Cod Mus. Natural History, Brewster, Mass., 1994—. Illustrator: Little Golden Book A to Z, 1945, Pre-School Science, 1996, many others. Mem. Nature Conservancy, Mass. Audubon Soc., Cape Cod Mus. Natural History (artist environ. posters). Avocations: early childhood education, grandchildren, cooking, travel, reading. Home: 2300 Herringbrook Rd PO Box 983 North Eastham MA 02651-0983

DEMY, TIMOTHY JAMES, military chaplain; b. Brownsville, Tex., Dec. 6, 1954; s. Millard Nile and Pauline Juanita (Owen) D.; m. Lyn Elizabeth Evans, Aug. 26, 1978. BA, Tex. Christian U., 1977; ThM, Dallas Theol. Sem., 1981, ThD, 1990; MA, U. Tex. at Arlington, 1994, Salve Regina U., 1990, Naval War Coll., 1999. Commd. lt. jr. grade USN, 1981, advanced through grades to cmdr., 1993; adj. instr. Naval War Coll., Newport, R.I., 1996—; co-dir. Ctr. for the Am. Family, Springfield, Va., 1995—. Co-author: When the Trumpet Sounds, 1995, The Coming Cashless Soc., 1996, Suicide: A Christian Response, 1998, Winning the Marriage Marathon, 1999, Genetic Engineering: A Christian Response, 1999, The Return on, 1999; contbr. articles to profl. jours. Mem. Nat. Assn. Evangelicals, Evangelical Theol. Soc., Soc. Biblical Lit., Ctr. for Bioethics and Human Dignity, Orgn. Am. Historians, Naval Order U.S. Avocations: reading, cartography, animals. Office: 7 Ellen Rd Middletown RI 02842-5504

DENACO, PARKER ALDEN, state official; b. Bangor, Maine, Apr. 19, 1943; s. Alden F. and Pauline (Newcomb) D. B.A., U. Maine, 1965; J.D., Washington and Lee U., 1968; M.B.A., U. Maine, 1975; postgrad. Air Command & Staff Coll., 1981. Bar: Maine 1968. Assoc. atty. Eaton & Peabody, Bangor, Maine, 1968-69; exec. dir. Maine Labor Relations Bd., Augusta, 1972—; adj. grad. instr. Thomas Coll., Waterville, Maine., 1977-80; staff judge advocate Maine Air N.G., Augusta, 1973-86. Contbr. articles to profl. jours. Bd. dirs. Acad. Collective Bargaining Info. Service, 1979-82, Pub. Employment Relations Services, 1978-81, New Eng. Consortium of State Labor Relations Agys., 1981—; pub. mem. Com. on Pub. Sector Bargaining, ABA, 1974—; neutral chair, 1987—; mem. Boston Adv. Council, Am. Arbitration Assn., 1978—; elected Nat. Acad. Arbitrators, 1987; corporator Maine Savs. Bank, 1982-84. Served to capt. U.S. Army, 1969-71, Air NG, 1973—. Recipient Harmon award USAF, 1986. Mem. Assn. Labor Relations Agys. (pres. 1978-79), Maine Bar Assn. (charter, labor sect. co-chmn. 1980-85), Soc. Profls. in Dispute Resolution, Indsl. Relations Research Assn., Nat. Acad. Arbitrators, Res. Officers Assn. (life), Nat. Guard Assn. of U.S. (life), fellow Coll. Labor and Employment Lawyers, Phi Delta Phi, Beta Gamma Sigma. Home: PO Box 1353 Bangor ME 04402-1353 Office: Maine Labor Relations Bd State St # 90 Augusta ME 04330-5610

DEN ADEL, RAYMOND LEE, classics educator; b. Pella, Iowa, Apr. 23, 1932; s. John J. and Nellie (DeGeus) D. BA, Ctrl. Coll., 1954; MA, U. Iowa, 1959; PhD, U. Ill., 1971. Latin tchr. Palla H.S., 1954-55; grad. student Am. Acad., Rome, 1960, Vergilian Sch., Cumae, Italy, 1960, 73; fellow U. Iowa, Iowa City, 1957-58, tchg. asst., 1962-63; Latin and English tchr. Proviso H.S., Hillside, Ill., 1958-62; v.p. Proviso Ednl. Assn., 1960-61; v.p. Am. Sch. Classical Studies, Athens, 1961, site participant, 1989, 90; fellow, asst. and instr. in classics U. Ill., Urbana, 1963-67; dir. Ill. H.S. Latin Conf., 1967; mem. faculty, chair classics dept. Rockford Coll., Ill., 1967-97; prof. Rockford Coll., 1975-97, prof. emeritus, 1997—; active Ill. Coun. Tchg. Fgn. Langs. Bd. dirs. Rockford Cmty. Concert Assn., 1979-85; mem. exec. com. Archtl. Inst. Am., 1976-82, governing bd., 1990-96, trustee, 1990-94, v.p., 1994-96, Disting. Svc. award, 1997. Served with CIC, U.S. Army, 1955-57. Fulbright grantee, 1960; named Vol. of Yr., Source Program, 1983; recipient Outstanding Coll. Latin Tchr. in Ill. award, 1987, Outstanding Fgn. Lang. Tchr. in Ill. award, 1989. Mem. AIA (coun. 1966—, Rockford Soc., Ctrl. Ill. Soc. sec.-treas. 1966-67, pres. 1968-70, 72-74, 91-93, sec. 1993-94, v.p. 1998-99), AAUP (coun. Ill. 1977-80), Am. Classical League (nat. coun. 1969-82), Am. Philol. Assn., Ill. Classical Conf. (v.p. 1968-69, pres. 1969-70), Classical Assn. Mid. West and South (1st v.p. 1980-81), Vergilian Soc. Am. (sec. 1978-80), Classical Soc. Am. Acad. Rome (sec. 1990-93), Rockford Rotary (bd. dirs. 1987-89, 91-95, dist. gov. rep. 1989-91, 94-97, v.p. 1992-93, pres. 1993-94, gov. Dist. 6420 1997-98, Svc. Above Self award Rockford Club and Dist. 6420), Am. Assn. Univ. Profs., (pres. Rockford chpt. 1974-76, sec. 1984-86, v.p. 1988-89), Assn. Dutch-Am. Studies, Eta Sigma Phi (nat. exec. sec. 1974-78), Chgo. Classical Club (pres. 1977-79), Phi Beta Kappa (pres. Eta Ill. chpt. 1989-92, triennial coun. 1988—), Phi Sigma Iota, Chi Gamma Iota, Sigma Tau Delta. Presbyterian. Avocations: photography, travel, reading, philately, music. Home: 2408 Eastmoreland Ave Rockford IL 61108-6373 Office: Rockford Coll 5050 E State St Rockford IL 61108-2393

DENARDIS, LAWRENCE J., academic administrator. Pres. U. New Haven, West Haven, Conn. Office: U New Haven Office of President 300 Orange Ave West Haven CT 06516-1916*

DENARO, ANTHONY THOMAS, psychiatrist; b. N.Y.C., Aug. 9, 1929; s. Joseph and Maria (DeGennaro) Denaro; m. Mitsuru Suzuki, Nov. 23, 1963. BS, CCNY, 1960; MD, U. Okla., 1969; MPA, U. Hartford, 1981. Diplomate Nat. Bd. Med. Examiners, Am. Bd. Psychiatry, Am. Bd. Gen. Psychiatry and Child Psychiatry, Adminstrv. Psychiatry. Intern Nassau County Med. Ctr., East Meadow, N.Y., 1969-70; resident in child psychiatry U. Pa., Phila., 1970-72, resident in gen. psychiatry, 1972-74; dir. child psychiatry U. Conn. Health Ctr., Farmington, 1974-78; dir. adolescent unit Natchaug Psychiat. Hosp., Willamantic, Conn., 1978-80; assoc. dir. child and adolescent service Mt. Sinai Hosp., Hartford, Conn., 1980-82; assoc. dir. child and adolescent psychiatry Elmcrest Psychiat. Inst., Portland, Conn., 1982-84; dir. outpatient psychiatry Woodhull Med. and Mental Health Ctr., N.Y.C., 1984-85; dir. child and adolescent psychiatry First Hosp. Wyoming Valley, Wilkes-Barre, Pa., 1985-98; med. dir. child and adolescent behavioral health svcs. Ea. Conn. Health Network, Inc., 1998-99; med. dir. Child Devel. Clinic, Scranton, Pa., 1999—; asst. prof. dept. psychiatry U. Conn. Sch. Medicine, Farmington, 1974-83. With U.S. Army, 1947-49. Fellow Am. Acad. Child and Adolescent Psychiatry; mem. AMA, Am. Psychiat. Assn., Am. Assn. Psychiat. Adminstrs., Northeastern Pa. Psychiat. Soc. (pres. 1990-91), Phi Beta Kappa. Republican. Office: Scranton Counseling Ctr Child Devel Clinic 326 Adams Ave Scranton PA 18503-1668

DENARO, GREGORY, lawyer; b. Rochester, N.Y., Dec. 10, 1954; m. Nancy Cardiff; children: Adrienne, Gregory, Madeline. BA, U. Rochester, 1976; JD, U. Miami, 1979. Bar: Fla. 1979, U.S. Dist. Ct. (so. dist.) Fla. 1979, U.S. Ct. Appeals (5th and 11th cirs.) 1981, U.S. Supreme Ct. 1984, N.Y. 1985, U.S. Dist. Ct. (mid. dist.) Fla. 1986, U.S. Ct. Appeals (D.C. cir.) 1989, U.S. Dist. Ct. (we. dist.) Tex. 1990, U.S. Ct. Appeals (4th cir.) 1992. Pub. defender Dade County, Miami, Fla., 1979-82; sr. ptnr. Gregory C. Denaro P.A., Miami, 1982—; advisor nat. mock trial U. Miami Law Sch., 1984—. Mem. ABA (criminal law sect.), Dade County Bar Assn., Assn. Trial Attys., Nat. Assn. Criminal Def. Lawyers, Fla. Assn. Criminal Def. Lawyers (bd. dirs. 1997, 98). Office: Coconut Grove Bank Bldg Ste 605 2701 S Bayshore Dr Coconut Grove FL 33133-5232

DE NATALE, ANDREW PETER, lawyer; b. Bklyn., July 7, 1950; s. Peter E. and Mary (Tamberino) DeN.; m. Lynn Susan Kennedy, July 28, 1973; children: Andrew, Christopher. BS in Econs., U. Pa., 1972; JD, Fordham U., 1975. Bar: N.Y. 1976, U.S. Dist. Ct. (so. dist.) N.Y. 1976, U.S. Dist. Ct. (ea. dist.) N.Y. 1977, U.S. Ct. Appeals (2d cir.) 1978, U.S. Supreme Ct. 1979, U.S. Dist. Ct. (no. dist.) N.Y. 1982. Assoc. Krause, Hirsch & Gross, N.Y.C., 1975-79; assoc. Stroock & Stroock & Lavan, N.Y.C., 1980-83, ptnr., 1984-91; ptnr. White & Case, N.Y.C., 1991—. Contbr. numerous articles to newspapers and profl. jours. Mem. ABA, N.Y. Yacht Club. Office: White & Case Bldg Ll 1155 Avenue Of The Americas New York NY 10036-2787

DENAULT, LINDA ELLEN STONE, educational administrator, educator; b. Mar. 13, 1945. BS, Worcester State Coll., 1968, MEd, 1973, CAGS, 1983; EdD, U. Mass., Amherst, 1998. Prin. Brookfield (Mass.) Elem. Sch., 1987-90, Burgess Elem. Sch., Sturbridge, Mass., 1990-95; instr., vis. prof. edn. dept. Worcester (Mass.) State Coll., 1995—; curriculum coord. Millbury (Mass.) Pub. Schs., 1997—. E-mail: ldenault@millburh.k12.ma.us. Office: 47 Osgood Rd Charlton MA 01508-0352

DENAVIT, JACQUES, retired physicist; b. Paris, Oct. 1, 1930; came to U.S., 1952; s. Georges and Marie (Arnould) D.; m. Catherine Dahlinger, Aug. 6, 1954; children: George, Paul, Mary. Degree in Gen. Math./Physics, U. Paris, 1952; MSEE, Northwestern U., 1953, PhD in Mech. Engring., 1956. Asst. prof. Northwestern U., Evanston, Ill., 1958-61, assoc. prof., 1961-66, prof. mech. and nuclear engring., 1966-82; rsch. physicist plasma physics divsn. Naval Rsch. Lab., Washington, 1969-71; rsch. physicist Lawrence Livermore Nat. Lab., Livermore, Calif., 1982-93. Author: (with R.S. Hartenberg) Kinematic Synthesis of Linkages, 1964; contbr. numerous articles on plasma physics and computer simulation to profl. jours. Fellow Am. Phys. Soc. Home: 3536 Gresham Ct Pleasanton CA 94588-3431

DENBY, DAVID, film critic. Film critic N.Y. Mag., 1993-98; film critic, feature writer New Yorker Mag., 1998—. Editor: Film Seventy-Two ato Seventy-Three: An Anthology by the Nat. Assn. of Film Critics, 1973; author: Great Books, 1996; contbr. articles to mags. Office: New Yorker MAgazine 20 W 23rd St New York NY 10036

DENCE, EDWARD WILLIAM, JR., lawyer, banker; b. Newport, R.I., Feb. 25, 1938; s. Edward William and Dorothea Margaret (Conway) D.; m. Claire A. Guertin, Nov. 14, 1970; children: Suzanne Lynn, Christine Anne. A.B. summa cum laude, Providence Coll., 1959; LL.B., Harvard U., 1963. Bar: Mass. 1963, R.I. 1965. Atty. New Eng. Electric System, 1963-68; sec., gen. counsel Fleet Fin. Group, Providence, 1968-85; v.p., mem. mgmt. com. Fleet Fin. Group, 1980-85, Ropes & Gray, Providence, 1985-92, Edwards & Angell, Providence, 1992—; Mem. stockholders' adv. com. Fed. Res. Bank, Boston, 1976-77. Mem. R.I. Commn. Inter-Govtl. Rels., 1970-71; chmn. Sargent Rehab. Ctr., 1991-92; bd. dirs. R.I. Pub. Expenditure Coun., 1969-85, R.I. Bar Found.; mem. Providence Roman Cath. Diocesan Bd. Edn., 1970-73; trustee, chmn. fin. com. St. Joseph Hosp.; trustee So. New Eng. Rehab. Ctr. Named One of Outstanding Young Men in Am., 1972. Mem. R.I. Bar Assn., Boston Bar Assn. (program chmn. banking com.). Home: 1485 High Hawk Rd East Greenwich RI 02818-1364

DENCE, MICHAEL ROBERT, retired research director; b. Sydney, Australia, June 17, 1931; s. Robert Cecil and Barbara Sidney (Laurence) D.; m. Carole E. Paintin, Sept. 24, 1967; children: Alexandra C., Victoria C. B.Sc., Sydney U., 1953. Geologist Falconbridge Nickel Mines Ltd., 1953-54; research asst. U. Toronto, Ont., Can., 1955-58; tech. officer Geol. Survey Can., 1959-61; sci. officer Dominion Obs., Ottawa, 1962-65; research scientist earth physics br. Can. Dept. Energy, Mines and Resources, Ottawa, 1966-81, dir. gravity and geodynamics div., earth physics br., 1981-82, dir. gravity, geothermics and geodynamics div., earth physics br., 1982-86; exec. sec. designate Royal Soc. Can., 1987, exec. dir., 1987-93, assoc. to pres., 1993-94; sec. Acad. Sci., 1994-97; prin. investigator NASA Lunar Sample Program. Recipient Public Service award Can. Public Service, 1973. Fellow AAAS, Royal Soc. Can., Meteoritical Soc. (Barringer medal 1988), Geol. Soc. Can.; mem. Am. Geophys. Union, Can. Geophys. Union. Home: 824 Nesbitt Pl, Ottawa, ON Canada K2C 0K1 Office: Royal Soc Can, 225 Metcalfe St Ste 308, Ottawa, ON Canada K2P 1P9

DENCH, JUDITH OLIVIA, actress; b. York, England, United Kingdom, Dec. 9, 1934; d. Reginald Arthur and Eleanora Olave (Jones) D.; m. Michael Williams, Feb. 5, 1971; 1 child, Tara Cressida Frances. Student, Ctrl. Sch. Speech Tng.; LittD (hon.), Warwick U., 1978, York U., 1983. Theatrical appearances include: (Old Vic) Hamlet, Midsummer Night's Dream, Twelfth Night, 1957-58, The Importance of Being Earnest, As You Like It, Romeo and Juliet, 1959-61; (Venice Festival) Romeo and Juliet (Paladino d'Argentino), 1961; (Royal Shakespeare Co., Stratford) The Cherry Orchard, Measure for Measure, Midsummer Night's Dream, A Penny for a Song, 1961-62; (Oxford Playhouse) The Alchemist, The Three Sisters, Romeo and Jeanette, 1964; (Oxford and London) The Promise, 1966-67; (London) Sally Bowles in Cabaret, 1968; (Royal Shakespeare Co., London) Twelfth Night, A Winter's Tale, London Assurance, 1970; (Royal Shakespeare Co., Stratford) The Merchant of Venice, The Duchess of Malfi, 1971; tour of Japan with Twelfth Night, 1972; (London) London Assurance, 1973; (Oxford and London) The Wolf, 1974; (London) The Good Companions, 1974-75, The Gay Lord Quex, 1975; (Royal Shakespeare Co., Stratford) Much Ado About Nothing, The Comedy of Errors, Macbeth (SWET Best Actress award for Lady Macbeth), King Lear, 1976-77; Cymbeline, 1979; (Royal Shakespeare Co., London) Pillars of the Community, The Way of the World, 1977-78, (Aldwych) Juno and the Paycock (SWET Best Actress award, Evening Std. Drama award for best actress, Plays and Players award for Best Actress, Variety Club award Actress of Yr.), 1981, A Kind of Alaska, The Importance of Being Earnest (Std. Best Actress award, Plays and Players award for best actress), Pack of Lies (Plays and Players award, SWET Best Actress award), Mr. and Mrs. Nobody, 1988, Antony and Cleopatra (Olivier award, Evening Std. Drama award, Drama mag. award), Gertrude in Hamlet, The Cherry Orchard, 1989, 90, The Blough and the Stars, The Sea, Coriolanus, 1992, The Gift of the Gorgon, 1992-93, The Seagull, 1994, Filumena in London, 1998, Amy's View in New York, 1999; dir. plays Much Ado About Nothing, Look Back in Anger, The Boys from Syracuse, Romeo and Juliet; TV appearances include: Major Barbara, Talking to a Stranger (Best TV Actress of Yr. award 1967), Jackanory, Luther, Nieghbours, Marching Song, Days to Come, The Comedy of Errors, Macbeth, Village Wooing, Love in a Cold Climate, A Fine Romance, The Cherry Orchard, Going Gently, Saigon, Mr. and Mrs. Edgehill, 1988 (ACE award), Ghosts, Make and Break, Behaving Badly, Can You Hear Me Thinking, Torch, Absolute Hell (Oliver award Best Actress 1996), As Time Goes By; films: He Who Rides a Tiger, A Study in Terror, Four in the Morning (Brit. Film Acad. Most Promising Newcomer award 1965), A Midsummer Night's Dream, The Third Secret, Deat Cert, Wetherby, 1985, A Room with a View, 84 Charing Cross Road, A Handful of Dust (Brit. Acad. Film and TV Arts award 1989), Henry V, 1989, Jack & Sarah, 1994, Golden Eye, 1995, A Little Night Music, 1995 (Oliver award Best Actress in a Musical 1996), Mrs. Brown (Brit. Acad. Film and TV Arts Sctoland award 1997, Critics Circle Film award 1997, Golden Globe award for best actress 1997, Acad. award nomination 1997), Amy's View, 1997 (Critics Circle Drama award 1997), Tomorrow Never Dies, 1997, Shakespeare in Love, 1998, Tea With Mussolini, 1999, The World is Not Enough, 1999. Recipient Rothermore award for lifetime achievement, 1997, Critics Circle award for outstanding svc. to the arts; decorated Order Brit. Empire; Dame Comdr. Brit. Empire. Mem. Religious Soc. Friends. *

DENDINGER, WILLIAM J., career officer, chaplain. BA in Philosophy and English, Immaculate Conception Sem., 1961; MA in Theology, Aquinas Inst., 1964; MS in Counseling, Creighton U., 1969; student, Squadron Officer Sch., 1973; postgrad., Sch. Applied Theology, 1978; student, Air War Coll., 1987. Commd. capt. USAF, 1970, advanced through grades to maj. gen., 1997; base chaplain Maxwell AFB, Ala., 1970-72, Yokota Air Base, Japan, 1972-74; cadet wing chaplain USAF Acad., Colorado Springs, Colo., 1974-78; base chaplain Osan Air Base, S. Korea, 1979-80, Mather AFB, Calif., 1980-82; mem. chaplain resource bd. USAF Chaplain Svc. Inst., Maxwell AFB, 1982-85; base chaplain Hahn Air Base, W. Germany, 1985-88; plans and programs officer then chief plans/programs div. Office Air Force Chief Chaplains, Bolling AFB, D.C., 1988-93; command chaplain Hdqs. Air Combat Command, Langley AFB, Va., 1993-95; dep. chief Air Force Chaplain Svc. Hdqs. USAF, Washington, 1995-97, chief Air Force Chaplain Svc., 1997—. Decorated Legion of Merit with oak leaf cluster. Named Prelate of Honor with title of Rev. Monsignor, His Holiness Pope John Paul II, 1994. Office: HQ USAF/HC 112 Luke Ave Ste 316 Bolling AFB DC 20332-9050

DENDRINOS, DIMITRIOS SPYROS, urban planning educator; b. Argostoli, Kefalonia, Greece, Sept. 2, 1944; came to U.S., 1969; s. Spyros H. and Iris Anninou (Kavalieratou) D. Diploma archtl. engring., U. Thessaloniki (Greece), 1968; M Urban Design, Washington U., St. Louis, 1971; PhD in City and Regional Planning, U. Pa., 1975. Prin. planner Middlesex County Planning Bd., New Brunswick, N.J., 1975; asst. prof. U. Kans., Lawrence, 1975-79, assoc. prof., 1980-83, prof. urban planning, 1983—, dir. urban and transp. dynamics lab., 1989—; vis. rsch. fellow U.S. Dept. Transp., Washington, 1979-80; sr. tech. advisor UN, People's Republic of China, 1988; vis. prof. Chiao-Tung U., Taiwan, 1995, Poly. of Turin, Italy, 1995-96; lectr. numerous univs., U.S. and abroad. Author: Urban Evolution, 1985, Chaos and Socio-Spatial Dynamics, 1990, The Dynamics of Cities, 1992; editor-in-chief Social-Spatial Dynamics, 1989-94; hon. editor, founder Jour. Discrete Dynamics in Nature and Society, 1996—; mem. editl. bd. Geog. Analysis, 1990-95, Sistemi Urbani, 1989—, Annals Regional Sci., 1993—; reviewer Math. Revs., 1989—; mem. editl. bd. Nonlinear Dynamics, Psychology and Life Scis., 1995—, Urban Sys.; contbr. numerous articles to sci. jours. Grantee U.S. Dept. Transp., Washington, 1980, NSF, Washington, 1981, 84, 85, IBM, 1990. Mem. Internat. Geographic Union. Nonlinear Sociospatial Dynamics Soc., Regional Sci. Assn.

DENDULURI, RAMARAO M., urologist; b. May 8, 1947. MD, Kurnool (India) Med. Coll. Pvt. practice, Morgan City, La., 1982—. E-mail: ramarao@iamerica.net. Home: 1011 8th St Morgan City LA 70380

DENDY, MARK, choreographer. BFA, N.C. Sch. Arts, 1983. Past young artist scholar Am. Dance Festival; founder Mark Dendy, Dance and Theatre, N.Y.C., 1983—. Appearances include (play) In Betweens; choreographer (film) Franchesca Page, 1997, (theatre) Ballet 1, 1990, Symmetries, 1994, Les Biches, 1997, Roman (1) Dream Analysis, Afternoon and the Faunes, 1998. NEA choreographer fellow; recipient Nat. Soc. Arts and Letters award for sustained achievement in the arts. Office: 279 E Houston St Apt 2B New York NY 10002-1033

DENEEN, PATRICK JOHN, political scientist, educator; b. Hartford, Conn., July 21, 1964; s. Richard P. and Irene M. (Dionne) D.; m. Inge M. Herre, Aug. 7, 1993; children: Francis Carey, Adrian John. BA in English, Rutgers U., 1986, PhD in Polit. Sci., 1995. Spl. adv. to dir. U.S. Info. Agy., Washington, 1995-97; educator Princeton (N.J.) U., 1997—. Author: The Odyssey of Political Theory, 1999. Recipient Leo Strauss award Am. Polit. Sci. Assn., 1995. Office: Dept Politics Princeton U Princeton NJ 08544

DENEGALL, JOHN PALMER, JR., construction company executive; b. Tarrytown, N.Y., Mar. 21, 1959; s. John P. Sr. and Edna D. (Kirkaldy) D.; m. Johnnie Lou Jarrett, Feb. 27, 1982 (div.); children: John P. III, Revisa Taylor. Student, Westchester Community Coll., Vahalla, N.Y., 1977-80. Mgr. Elmsford (N.Y.) Raceway Inc., 1976-80, Radio Shack, Yorktown Heights, N.Y., 1980-81; ins. claims adjuster Liberty Mut. Ins. Co., N.Y.C., 1981-85; sr. ins. claims rep. Crum & Forster Comml. Ins., N.Y.C., 1985-96; v.p., risk mgr. City Wide Asphalt Paving Co. Inc., Bklyn., 1996-99; v.p. Nico Asphalt Paving Inc., Astoria, N.Y., 1999—; arbitrator Ins. Arbitration

Forum, N.Y.C., 1986; pres. Denegell Properties, Inc., Jamaica, N.Y., 1986-89, Eva's Laundry Inc., Bronx, N.Y., 1989-94. Republican. Presbyterian. Avocations: bicycling, auto racing, basketball.

DENEGRE, GEORGE, lawyer; b. New Orleans, Oct. 10, 1923; s. Thomas Bayne and Alma (Baldwin) D.; m. Gayle Stocker, Oct. 4, 1950; children: Stanhope Bayne-Jones, Gayle Stocker Felchlin, George, John Gayle. BA, Yale U., 1943; LLB, Tulane U., 1948. Bar: La. 1948. With firm Chaffe, McCall, Toler & Philips, 1948-49; assoc. Jones, Walker Waechter, Poitevent, Carrère & Denègre, New Orleans, 1949-52; ptnr. Jones, Walker, Waechter, Poitevent, Carrère & Denègre, 1952—; asst. sec., dir. Canal Barge Co., Inc.; sec., dir. Cen. Gulf Lines, Inc.; sec. Internat. Shipholding Corp.; dir. Dr. G.H. Tichenor Antiseptic Co. Bd. dirs. Met. Crime Commn., 1965, Eugenie and Joseph Jones Family Found., 1963-93, Bus. Task Force for Edn., New Orleans Neighborhood Devel. Found., 1989-90, New Orleans Regional Med. Ctr., La. Assn. Mental Health, 1953-77, pres., 1960-61; bd. dirs., sec., exec. com., pres. World Trade Ctr.; bd. govs. Tulane Med. Ctr., 1969-83, vice-chmn., 1977-82, chmn., 1983; vice-chmn., bd. adminstrs. Tulane U., 1980-93; bd. dirs. Chamber New Orleans and River Region, chmn., 1991; vice-chmn. bd. dirs. Met. Arts Fund, 1989-90, New Orleans Coun.-Navy League U.S.; bd. dirs., sec. Bus. Coun.; mem. bd., exec. com. Pub. Affairs Rsch. Coun.; sec. La. Coun. for Fiscal Reform, 1987-96; bd. commrs. Downtown Devel. Dist., 1989-95, chmn., 1992; co-chmn. Mayor's Found. for Edn., 1987-91; chmn. Mayor's Com. for Charity Hosp.; founding mem. La. Partnership for Innovation and Tech. Metrovision Partnership; sec. bd. dirs. Orleans Intercmty. Coun.; vice-dean Consular Corps, 1988-91; Com. 100, 1993-95, Select Com. on Revenues and Expenditures in La. Future (SECURE), 1993-95; adv. bd. Coll. Bus. Adminstrn., U. New Orleans, 1994-96. Lt. USNR, 1943-46. Hon. Consul of India; Rex, King of Carnival, 1986. Mem. La. Bar Assn., New Orleans Bar Assn., Maritime Bar Assn., Boston Club of New Orleans, Pickwick Club, La. Club, New Orleans Country Club, Stratford Club. Home: 1525 Webster St New Orleans LA 70118-6134 Office: Jones Walker Waechter Poitevent Carrere Denegre 201 Saint Charles Ave New Orleans LA 70170-5100

DENENBERG, HERBERT SIDNEY, journalist, lawyer, former state official; b. Omaha, Nov. 20, 1929; s. David Aaron and Fannie (Rothenberg) D.; m. Naomi N. Glushakow, June 22, 1958. BS, Johns Hopkins U., 1958; JD, Creighton U., 1954; LLM, Harvard U., 1959; PhD, U. Pa., 1962; LLD, Allentown Coll. St. Francis de Sales, 1989; LHD, Spring Garden Coll., 1992. CLU; CPCU. Mem. firm Denenberg & Denenberg, Omaha, 1954-55; asst. prof. ins. U. Iowa, Iowa City, 1962; asst. prof. ins. Wharton Sch. Fin. and Commerce, U. Pa., 1962-65, assoc. prof., 1965-68, Harry J. Loman prof. ins., 1968-73; commr. ins. State of Pa., 1971-74; commr. Pa. Pub. Utility Commn., 1975; columnist Phila. Bull., 1975-79; consumer columnist Phila. Daily News, 1979-81, Phila. Jour., 1981-82, Del. County Daily and Sunday Times, 1987-90, Bucks County Courier Times, 1987-90, Pottstown Mercury, 1988-94, Burlington County Daily Times, 1987-90, Reading Eagle, 1989—, Doylestown Patriot, 1991—, Citizen's Choice of Wilkes-Barre, Pa., 1992—, Mainliner, 1992-94, Auto Insider, 1992-93, Collector's Guide, 1992-93, New Chester Jour., 1992— -94, Del. County Bus. Monthly, 1993-96, Hellenic News, 1993—, 1994; consumer columnist Phoenixville, Phoenix, 1994-96; consumer and investigative reporter Harron Cable Update 2nd Tri-State Media Network Cable System, 1999—, Sta. WCAU-TV (NBC), Phila., 1975-98; talk show host Sta. WCAU-AM CBS, Phila., 1976-80; columnist Sales and Mktg. Mag., 1976-80; regular on Real People, NBC-TV, 1979-80; consumer reporter Nat. Public Radio, 1979; Spl. counsel, rsch. dir. Pres.'s Nat. Adv. Panel on Ins. in Riot-Affected Areas., 1967-68; spl. adviser to Gov. Pa. on consumer affairs, 1974-75; assoc. dir. Wis. Ins. Laws Rev. Project, 1966-71; cons. Dept. Labor, 1965-68, Coop. Devel. Adminstrn. P.R., 1967-68, John F. Kennedy Ctr., Washington, 1966-71, Small Bus. Adminstrn., 1968-71, Dept. Justice, 1969, FTC, 1968, Dept. Transp., 1969-70, State of Nev., 1969-71; cons. Alaska Legislature, 1976; cons. U.S. Commn. Civil Rights, 1977-78; spl. cons. to Mayor Washington, 1968-69; mem. Bd. of Health Promotion and Disease Prevention of Inst. Medicine, Nat. Acad. Scis., 1973-74, sr. mem., 1973— ; vis. prof. law Temple U. Author: (with others) Risk and Insurance, 2d edit, 1973, (with Spencer L. Kimball) Insurance Government and Social Policy, 1969, (with J.R. Ferrari) Life Insurance and/or Mutual Funds, 1967, (with S.L. Kimball) Mass. Marketing of Property and Liability Insurance, 1970, The Insurance Trap, 1972, Shopper's Guide to Surgery, 1972, Shopper's Guide to Dentistry, 1973, Shopper's Guide to Insurance on Mobile Homes, 1973, A Citizens Bill of Hospital Rights, 1973, Shopper's Guide to Bankruptcy, 1974, Shopper's Guide Book, 1974, Herb Denenberg's Smart Shopper's Guide, 1980, Shoppers Guide to Medical Equipment, 1990, A Consumer's Guide to Herbal Medicines, 1999, A COnsumer's Guide to Herbal Medicines, 1999; columnist, mem. editorial bd. Caveat Emptor, 1971-79; mem. adv. bd. medicine and health newsletter The Dr.'s People, 1989-93. Dem. candidate for U.S. Senate, 1974; mem. adminstrv. bd. S.S. Huebner Found., 1968-71; bd. dirs. Consumers Union, 1973-76; mem. bd. trustees Ctr. for Proper Medication Use, 1994—. 1st lt. JAGC, AUS, 1955-58. Recipient awards for articles Jour. Risk and Ins., Lambert award, 1972, Nat. Press Club award, 1976, 77, 80, 84, 88, Journalism award Am. Osteo. Assn., 1976, Journalism award Am. Chiropractors Assn., 1977-80, 88, citation Columbia U., Media award Am. Trial Lawyers Assn., 1986, Enterprise Reporting award Phila. Press Club, 1986, 87, Grand Pub. Svc. award, 1987, 89, 96, 97, Best Feature award, 1995, 96, 97, award for lifetime achievement, 1998, Gov.'s Hwy. Safety award Pa., 1997, Enterprise Reporting award Pa. Associated Press, 1988, Nat. Headliner award, 1987-88, 90, 92, 40 Emmy awards, Best TV Pub. Svc. award Sigma Delta Chi, 1987, 88, 90, 92, 93, 94, 98, 99, TV Feature award, 1989, 94, 95, 96, 97, 98, TV Mag. Feature award, 1989, 92, Best Media Criticism, 1990, 93, Best Investigation, 1990, 92, 93, 94, 95, 96, 97, 98, 99, Best Health and Sci. Report, 1995, 96, 97, 98, 99, Breaking News award, 1998, Outstanding Media Consumer Svc. award Consumer Fedn. of Am., 1990, Sam Beber Disting. AZA Alumnus award B'nai B'rith, 1990, Outstanding Citizen award Firemen's Assn. Pa., 1991, Consumer of Yr. award Pa. Assn. Weights and Measures, 1991, Phila. award integrity in journalism, 1988, others; inducted Phila. Press Club Hall of Fame, 1995. Mem. Am. Risk and Ins. Assn. (2nd v.p. 1967-68, bd. dirs. 1967-71, pres. 1969-70), Med. Soc. Access to Physicians (blue ribbon panel Phila. County 1998—), Internat. Assn. Ins. Law (v.p. sci. sect. Am. chpt. 1967-71), Old Clunker Club (founder, pres. 1982—). Home: PO Box 7301 Saint Davids PA 19087-7301 Office: Sta WCAU-TV Philadelphia PA 19131 *Our governmental system is designed to make politicians fat and special interests groups rich. Government has become our number "one" consumer fraud. As a government official, educator, and author I have attempted to make government work for people instead of for special interests and politicians only. I have been willing to make waves and rock boats. I have tried to show that government can help people.*

DENES, MICHEL JANET, physical therapist, consultant in rehabilitation; b. Detroit, Apr. 29, 1950; d. Seymore Bernard and Clarine (Stierer) Swartz; m. George Denes, Jan. 22, 1984; 1 child, Zachary Todd. BS in Phys. Therapy, U. Mich., 1972. cert. in phys. therapy; cert. in neuro-devel. treatment in adult hemiplegia. Staff phys. therapist Sinai Hosp. of Detroit, 1972-77, supr., phys. therapist, 1977-78, chief phys. therapy supr., 1979-88; phys. therapist Rehab. Physicians, P.C., Birmingham, Mich., 1989; phys. therapy cons. closed head injury program Spl. Tree Rehab. Sys., Birmingham, 1989-98; coord. program devel. Great Lakes Rehab. Hosp., Southfield, Mich., 1998—; adj. instr. Wayne State U. Coll. Allied Health Professions, Detroit, 1982-90; lectr. in field. Mem. Neurodevel. Treatment Assn., Am. Acad. Oral Medicine. Avocations: tennis, travel, gardening and horticulture, American art, interior design. Office: Great Lakes Rehab Hosp 22401 Foster Winter Dr Southfield MI 48075-3724

DE NESNERA, ALEXANDER PETER, psychiatrist; b. Montclair, N.J., Feb. 9, 1957; s. Peter and Olia (Donn) de N.; m. Susan Carter Jarvis, May 30, 1987; 1 child, Christopher Lewis. Student, Johns Hopkins U., 1974-75; BA in Biology, NYU, 1978; diploma med. scis., St. George's U., Grenada, 1983; MD, Dartmouth Coll., 1986. Diplomate Nat. Bd. Med. Examiners; diplomate Am. Bd. of Psychiatry and Neurology; cert. geriat. Psychiatry, Am. Bd. Addiction Psychiatry; cert. forensic psychiatry. Escort interpreter U.S. Dept. State, Washington, 1978-86; research asst. Rockefeller U., N.Y.C., 1980-81; resident in psychiatry Dartmouth Hitchcock Med. Ctr., Hanover, N.H., 1986-90; asst. med. dir. Weekend Intoxicated Driver Intervention Program, Hanover, 1987-88; med. dir. Weekend Intoxicated Driver Intervention Program, 1988-89; cons. psychiatrist Hanover Terrace Nursing Home, 1988-89; cons. psychiatrist Alzheimer's disease clinic Mary Hitchcock Meml. Hosp., Hanover, 1988-89; staff psychiatrist Nashua (N.H.) Brookside Hosp., 1988-90; asst. prof. psychiatry Dartmouth Coll., 1990—; staff psychiatrist New Hampshire Hosp., 1990—; asst clerkship dir., med. student teaching Dartmouth Med. Sch., 1990—; cons. psychiatrist secure psychiat. unit Dept. Corrections, N.H. State Prison, 1997; bd. examiner Am. Bd. Psychiatry and Neurology, 1998. Mem. Am. Psychiat. Assn., Am. Coll. Physician Execs., N.H. Psychiat. Soc. (treas. 1997—), N.H. Med. Soc., Beta Lambda Sigma. Roman Catholic. Avocation: reading non-fiction history books. Office: New Hampshire Hosp 36 Clinton St Concord NH 03301-2359

DE NEUFVILLE, RICHARD LAWRENCE, engineering educator; b. N.Y.C., May 6, 1939; s. Lawrence Eustace and Adeline de N.; m. Virginia Lyons; children: Robert, Julie. SB, SM, MIT, 1961, PhD, 1965. Asst. prof. to assoc. prof. dept. civil engring. MIT, Cambridge, Mass., 1965-75; prof., chmn. Tech. and Policy Program MIT, Cambridge, 1975—; vis. prof. Ecole Centrale de Paris, 1981-82, U. Calif.-Berkeley, 1974-76, London Grad. Sch. Bus., 1973, Australian Bur. Transport and Comm. Econs., 1995; mem. vis. com. U. Va., Charlottesville, 1987, Tech. U., Delft, Eindhoven and Utrecht, The Netherlands, 1996-97; adj. prof. Ecole Nationale des Ponts et Chaussees of Paris, 1988—, U. Bristol, Eng., 1992-99. Author: Applied Systems Analysis, 1990, Airport Systems Planning, 1976, Systems Planning and Design, 1979, Systems Analysis for Engineers and Managers, 1971; editor Jour. Transp. Rsch., 1975-86, Jour. Air Transport Mgmt., 1993—. Bd. dirs. Geographic Data Tech., 1982-90, Urban Data Processing, 1970-80, Ecole Bilingue, French-Am. Internat. Sch. of Boston, 1992-97; trustee Kennedy Meml. Trust (U.K.), 1993-98; Consejo del Rector, Universidad Anahuac del Sur, Mexico, 1999—. 1st lt. C.E., U.S. Army, 1961-62. White House fellow, 1964-65, Guggenheim fellow, 1973, U.S.-Japan Leadership fellow, 1990; recipient Sys. Sci. prize NATO, 1974, Risk and Ins. prize Risk and Ins. Soc., 1976, Alpha Kappa Psi award, 1985, Engring. Excellence award Australia Instn. Engrs., 1986, Irwin Sizer award, 1988, FAA prize for tchg. excellence, 1990. Mem. ASCE, AAAS, Ops. Rsch. Soc. Am., Brit.-N.Am. Com., Am. Alpine Club, Cambridge Boat Club, Cambridge Skating Club, Cambridge Tennis Club, Internat. House of Japan. Office: MIT Rm E40-251 Cambridge MA 02139

DENEUVE, CATHERINE (CATHERINE DORLEAC), actress; b. Paris, Oct. 22, 1943; d. Maurice Dorleac and Renee Deneuve; m. David Bailey, 1965 (div. 1970); children: Christian Vadim, Chiara Mastroianni. Ed., Lycée La Fontaine, Paris. co-chair UNESCO campaign to protect World's Film Heritage, 1994—. Films include Les Petits Chats, 1956, Les Collegiennes, 1956, Les portes claquent, 1960, Les Parisiennes, 1961, Et Satan conduit le bal, 1962, Vacances portugaises, 1963, Le Vice et la Vertu, 1963, Les Parapluies de Cherbourg, 1964 (Golden Palm of Cannes Festival), La Chasse à l'homme, 1964, Les Plus belles escroqueries du monde, 1964, Un Monsieur de compagnie, 1964, Repulsion, 1965, Coeur à la gorge, 1965, Le Chant de Ronde, 1965, La Vie de Chateau, 1965, Les créatures, 1966, Les Demoiselles de Rochefort, 1966, Benjamin, 1967, Manon 70, 1967, Belle de Jour, 1967 (Golden Lion of Venice Festival), Meyerling, 1967, La Chamade, 1968, The April Fools, 1968, La Sirène du Mississippi, 1968, Tristana, 1969, It Only Happens to Others, 1971, Dirty Money, Hustle, 1975, Lovers Like Us, 1975, Act of Aggression, 1976, March or Die, 1977, La Grande Bourgeoise, 1977, The Last Metro, 1980, A Second Chance, 1981, Reporters, 1982, The Hunger, 1983, Fort Saganne, Scene of the Crime, Agent Trouble, 1987, FM-Frequency Murder, 1988, Drole d'endroit Pour Une Rencontre, 1988, Helmut Newton: Frames from the Edge, 1989, Indochine, 1992 (César award Best Actress, Acad. award nominee for Best Actress), Ma Saison Preferee, 1993, La Partie d'Echecs, 1994, Les Cent et Une Nuits, 1995, Les Voleurs, 1996, Place Vendome, 1997, Gènealogies d'un Crime, 1997, Pola X, 1998, Le Temps retrouvé, La Princesse de Clèves, 1999, The Last Napoleon, 1999, Est, ouest, 1999, Le Vent de la nuit, 1999, Belle Maman, 1999; prodr. A Strange Place to Meet, 1988. Office: care VMA, 10th Ave George, V 75008 Paris France*

DENEVAN, WILLIAM MAXFIELD, geographer, educator, ecologist; b. San Diego, Oct. 16, 1931; s. Lester W. and Wilda M. D.; m. Patricia Sue French, June 21, 1958; children: Curtis, Victoria. Ph.D. U. Calif.-Berkeley, 1963. Mem. faculty dept. geography U. Wis., Madison, 1963-94, prof., 1972-94, chmn. dept., 1980-83, dir. L.Am. Ctr., 1975-77, prof. emeritus, 1994—. Author: The Upland Pine Forests of Nicaragua, 1961, The Aboriginal Cultural Geography of the Llanos de Mojos of Bolivia, 1966, Adaptive Strategies in Karinya Subsistance, Venezuelan Llanos, 1978; editor: The Native Population of the Americas in 1492, 1976, Pre-Hispanic Agricultural Fields in the Andean Region, 1987, Swidden-Fallow Agroforestry in the Peruvian Amazon, 1988; contbr. articles to profl. jours. Served with USN, 1953-55. Fulbright grantee, 1957; NRC grantee, 1961-62; Ford Found. grantee, 1965-66; NSF grantee, 1972-73, 84-86; NEH grantee, 1989-90; Guggenheim fellow, 1977-78; Nat. Geog. Soc. grantee, 1985-86. Mem. Assn. Am. Geographers (Honors award 1987), Am. Geog. Soc., Am. Anthrop. Assn., Soc. for Am. Archaeology.

DENGEL, OTTMAR HUBERT, physicist; b. Kempten, Germany, Sept. 14, 1933. BS, Tech. U. Munich, 1954, MS, 1958, PhD, 1962. Rsch. asst. Tech. U. Munich, 1962-65; rsch. physicist Naval Surface Warfare Ctr., White Oak, Md., 1965-94; pres. Royal Systems, Front Royal, Va., 1994—. Achievements include 12 patents related to gas generators (hydrogen). Home: 6294 Browntown Rd Front Royal VA 22630-5133

DENGER, MICHAEL L., lawyer; b. Davenport, Iowa, Sept. 8, 1945; s. Ralph Henry and Bernice Marie (Cederberg) D.; m. Mary Elizabeth Colbert, Aug. 30, 1969; children: Lorna Marie, Mary Catherine, Rachel Anne. BS with highest distinction, Northwestern U., 1967; JD cum laude, Harvard U., 1970. Bar: D.C. 1970, U.S. Ct. Appeals (D.C. cir.) 1971, U.S. Supreme Ct. 1978. Assoc. atty. Sutherland, Asbill & Brennan, Washington, 1970-76, ptnr., 1976-92; ptnr. Gibson, Dunn & Crutcher, Washington, 1992—; speaker on antitrust, trade regulation numerous groups. Bd. editors Antitrust Report, 1992—; contbr. articles to profl. jours. Mem. nat. adv. coun. Northwestern U. Sch. Speech, Evanston, Ill., 1990—. 2d lt. USAR, 1970. Mem. ABA (vice chair antitrust law sect. 1985-86, sec. antitrust law sect. 1988-91, chair-elect antitrust law sect. 1991-92, chair antitrust law sect. 1992-93, chair edit. bd. antitrust sect. Federal and State Price Discrimination Law 1991, co-editor in chief antitrust sect. State Antitrust Practice and Statutes 3 vols. 1990, vice chair edit. bd. antitrust sect. Antitrust Law Devels. 2d edit. 1984), Columbia Country Club (Chevy Chase, Md.). Republican. Roman Catholic. Avocations: tennis, collecting military miniatures, military history, bridge. Home: 5802 Kirkside Dr Chevy Chase MD 20815-7118 Office: Gibson Dunn & Crutcher 1050 Connecticut Ave NW Ste 900 Washington DC 20036-5306

DENGLER, ROBERT ANTHONY, professional association executive; b. Upper Darby, Pa., Aug. 23, 1947; s. Anthony William and Harriet Josephine (Schneider) D.; m. Renee Faith Aird, Oct. 26, 1985. BS, Drexel U., 1970, MBA, 1972. Cert. assn. exec., mtg. profl. Cons. Orgn. Devel., Phila., 1972-73; dir. tng. & edn. Parkview Meml. Hosp., Ft. Wayne, Ind., 1973-76; dir. human resource mgmt. Americana Healthcare Corp., Chgo., 1976-82; corp. mgr. Human Resource Tng. and Devel. Means Svc. Inc., Chgo., 1982-83; dir. physician services West Suburban Hosp. Med. Ctr., Oak Park, Ill., 1983-85; assoc. dir. Assoc. Equipment Distributors, Oak Brook, Ill., 1985-88; exec. v.p. Internat. Reprographic Assn., Oak Brook, 1988-92; exec. dir. Data Processing Mgmt. Assn., Park Ridge, Ill., 1993-94; pres. R.A. Dengler & Assocs., 1994—; exec. dir. Nat. Assn. Med. Staff Svcs., Lombard, Ill., 1996-98. Bd. dirs. Riverside C. of C., 1996, Chgo. Mercedes-Benz Club, 1996; mem. Riverside Village Fin. Com., 1996; recording sec. Riverside Econ. Devel. Commn., 1996. Capt. USAR, 1972-80. Mem. Inst. of Mgmt. Consultants, Am. Soc. Assn. Execs., Chgo. Soc. Assn. Execs., Profl. Convention Mgmt. Assn., Mensa. Home and Office: 294 Lionel Rd Riverside IL 60546-2204

DENHAM, ALICE, writer; b. Jacksonville, Fla., Jan. 21, 1932; d. T.B. Simkins and Leila Meggs Denham; divorced; m. John Mueller. *In NY I'm known as the feminist Playmate Novelist! My 2nd novel, AMO, is about afeminist Centerfold from outer space. NY Press called AMO "a cult novel ripe forresurrection." Publishers, where are you? my 1st novel, My Darling from the Lions, is about the conflict between an independent wife and chauvinist husband. I've completed a family memoir, Shabby Genteel: A Southern Girlhood and a story collection. I'm the only Playmate to have a story published in the same issue of Playboy. That story, The Deal, became the film, Quizas which won festival prizes.* Author: My Darling from the Lions, 1967-68, Coming Together, 1969-70, AMO, 1974-75; contbr. articles and short stories various pubs. Home: 96 Grove St Apt 2 New York NY 10014-7021

DENHAM, CAROLINE VIRGINIA, retired college official; b. Detroit, June 22, 1937; d. Athel Fredric Denham and Emma Virginia (Franck) Kuhns. B.Mus., U. S.C., 1973. Sec. Shawnee Press, Inc., Delaware Water Gap, Pa., 1958-61, editorial asst., 1961-68; clk. typist U. S.C., Columbia, 1969-72, rsch. asst., 1972-76, dir. instnl. rsch., 1976-93; ret., 1994; libr. S.C. Philharm. Orch., 1970-82, pers. mgr., 1976-97, musician, 1968—. Treas. S.C. Assn. for Instl. Rsch., 1987-91, pres. 1992-93. Mem. S.C. State Employees Assn., Emeritus mem. Assn. for Instl. Rsch., Pi Kappa Lambda, Delta Omicron. Avocations: music, books, video movies, WWII history.

DENHAM, FREDERICK RONALD, management consultant; b. Middlebrough, Eng., Oct. 21, 1929; s. Frederick and Gladys (Tattersall) D.; m. Lynn Hughes, Sept. 19, 1953; children—John, Gillian, Michael. B.Sc., U. Durham, Eng., 1950, Ph.D., 1953; M.B.A., U. Buffalo, 1960. Registered profl. engr., Ont. cert. mgmt. cons. Sci. officer Def. Research Bd., Ottawa, Ont., Can., 1953-54; indsl. engr. Ford Motor Co. of Can., Ltd., Windsor, Ont., 1954-56; asst. supt. Union Carbide Can., Welland, Ont., 1956-61; cons. Thorne, Stevenson & Kellogg, Toronto, Ont., 1961-67; v.p. Stevenson, Kellogg, Ernst & Whinney, 1967-89; vice chmn. Peat, Marwick, Stevenson & Kellogg, Toronto, 1989-94; pres. Ron Denham & Assocs., Inc., 1994—; dir. Proctor & Redfern, Ltd., 1994—, A.T. Kearney, Toronto, 1994—; prof. Faculty Adminstrv. Studies York U., 1967-71. Trustee North York Bd. Edn., 1974-78. Fellow Engring. Inst. Can., Inst. Cert. Mgmt. Cons. Ont. (pres. 1982-83), Masons, Rotary (dist. gov. 1993-94). Anglican. Home and Office: 15 Danville Dr, North York, ON Canada M2P 1H7

DENHAM, RENA BELLE, lawyer, educator; b. Salina, Kans., Oct. 1956; d. Charles Morris and Alice Jane (Quandt) D. BA in Philosophy with honors, Mills Coll., Oakland, Calif., 1977; MA in Philosophy, U. Pa., 1979; JD, U. San Francisco, 1982. Bar: Calif. 1982, U.S. Dist. Ct. (No. Dist.) Calif. 1983, U.S. Ct. Appeals (9th cir.). Assoc. Burnhill, Morehouse, Burford, Schofield & Blunden, Walnut Creek, Calif., 1984-85, Daniel B. Schick, Walnut Creek, Calif., 1985-90; pvt. practice civil litigation Concord, Calif., 1991-92; ptnr. Mullin & Denham, Concord, Calif., 1992-93; pvt. practice Oakland, Calif., 1993-95; instr. legal asst. studies Truckee Meadows C.C., Reno, Nev., 1995—; instr. humanities Truckee Meadows C.C., Reno, 1999—; part-time instr. paralegal studies Calif. State U., Hayward, 1985-95; instr. bus. law Diablo Valley Coll., Pleasant Hill, Calif., 1984-85. Mem. Univ. and Cmty. Coll. Sys. of Nev. (mem. Status of Women com.), Sierra Nev. Celtic Soc. Avocation: golf. Office: Truckee Meadows CC Red Mt Bldg 334 700 Dandini Blvd Reno NV 89512

DENHAM, ROBERT EDWIN, lawyer, investment company executive; b. Dallas, Aug. 27, 1945; s. Wilburn H. and Anna Marie (Hughes) D; m. Carolyn Hunter, June 3, 1966; children: Jeffrey Hunter, Laura Maria. BA, U. Tex., 1966; MA, Harvard U., 1968, JD, 1971. Bar: Calif. 1972. Assoc. Munger Tolles and Olson, L.A., 1971-73; ptnr. Munger Tolles and Olson, L.A., 1973-85, 92-93; mng. ptnr. Munger Tolles and Olson, L.A., 1985-91; chmn., chief exec. officer Salomon Inc, N.Y.C., 1992-97; ptnr. Munger Tolles and Olson, L.A., 1998—. Pres. Pasadena (Calif.) Ednl. Found., 1977-79; bd. dirs. Pub. Counsel, L.A., 1981-84, United Way, N.Y.C., 1994-97; trustee Cathedral Corp. Diocese of L.A., 1986-92, Poly. Sch. Pasadena, 1989-93, v.p. bd. trustees, 1991-93; bd. trustees New Sch. Social Rsch., 1995—, Natural Resources Def. Coun., 1992—; adv. bd. of the pres. Calif. State U., Sonoma, 1993—; bd. trustees The Conference Bd., 1994—, Russell Sage Found., 1997—; pub. mem. Independence Stds. Bd., 1997—; former co-chmn. Subcoun. on Capital Allocation of the Competitiveness Policy Coun.; former mem. Bipartisan Commn. on Entitlement and Tax Reform; former U.S. rep. to the Asia Pacific Econ. Coun. Bus. Adv. Coun.; mem. bus. sector adv. group on corp. governance OECD; bd. dirs. U.S. Trust Co., AMKOR Tech., Inc. Mem. ABA, State Bar Calif., L.A. County Bar (bus. and corps. exec. com. 1985—). Democrat. Episcopalian. Avocations: soccer, cooking. Office: Munger Tolles and Olson 355 S Grand Ave # 3500 Los Angeles CA 90071-1560*

DENHAM, VERNON ROBERT, JR., lawyer; b. Atlanta, Apr. 18, 1948; s. Vernon Robert and Sara Elizabeth (Robertson) D.; m. Susan Elizabeth Willis, Mar. 19, 1974; children: Whitney Willis, Tyler Willis. Student, Rensselaer Poly. Inst., 1966-68; BSE, U. Mich., 1970, MSE, 1972; JD with honors, U. Fla., 1979. Bar: Fla. 1979, Ga. 1979, U.S. Dist. Ct. (no. dist.) Ga. 1979, U.S. Ct. Appeals (11th cir.) 1981. Engr. Ford Motor Co., Dearborn, Mich., 1972-73; assoc. Powell, Goldstein, Frazer & Murphy, Atlanta, 1979-86, ptnr., 1986—; mem. case notes com. U.S. Dist. Ct. (no. dist.) Ga., Atlanta, 1980-86, mem. magistrate merit selection panel, 1983. Lt. USNR, 1973-76. Mem. ABA (natural resources law sect., litigation sec., corp. and bus. sect.), Am. Chem. Soc., Internat. Soc. Regulatory Toxicology and Pharmacology, Fla. Bar (gen. practice trial sect., environ. and land use law sect.), State Bar Ga. (litigation and environ. sects.), Atlanta Bar Assn. (litigation, environ. sects., vice chair environ. sect. 1992-93, chair 1993-94), Order of Coif, Tau Beta Pi. Home: 1433 Sheridan Walk NE Atlanta GA 30324-3253 Office: Powell Goldstein Frazer & Murphy 191 Peachtree St NE Fl 16 Atlanta GA 30303-1740

DENHARDT, DAVID TILTON, molecular and cell biology educator; b. Sacramento, Feb. 25, 1939; s. David Burton and Edith (Tilton) D.; m. Georgetta Louise Harrar, July 1, 1961; children: Laura Jean, Kristin Ann, David Harrar. B.A. in Chemistry with high honors, Swarthmore Coll., 1960; Ph.D. in Biophysics, Calif. Inst. Tech., 1965. Instr. biol. labs Harvard U., 1964-66, asst. prof., 1966-70; assoc. prof. biochemistry McGill U., Montreal, Que., Can., 1970-77; prof. McGill U., 1977-80; prof. biochemistry, microbiology and immunology, dir. Cancer Research Lab., U. Western Ont., London, 1980-88; prof. biol. scis. Rutgers U., New Brunswick, N.J., 1988—, chmn., 1988-95, dir. Bur. Biol. Rsch., 1988-95, dir. cell devel. biology grad. program, 1991-94; mem. sci. adv. bd. Ctr. for Advanced Biotech. and Medicine, Piscataway, N.J., 1988-91, 1988-91. Editor: Jour. Virology, 1977-87, Gene, 1985-93, Exptl. Cell Rsch., 1994—; assoc. editor Jour. Cellular Biochemistry, 1994—; mem. editorial bd. Jour. Cancer Rsch. Methods and Clin. Oncology, In Vivo Internat. Jour. Fellow AAAS, Am. Acad. Microbiology, Royal Soc. Can.; mem. Am. Cancer Soc., Am. Soc. Biol. Chemists, Am. Microbiol. Soc., N.Y. Acad. Scis., Am. Soc. Cell Biology, Phi Beta Kappa. Office: Rutgers U Nelson Biol Labs 604 Allison Rd Piscataway NJ 08854-8000

DE NICOLA, PETER FRANCIS, photographic manufacturer; b. N.Y.C., Oct. 28, 1954; s. Louis Joseph and Nancy Eleanor (Maddi) DeN.; m. Charlotte Rebecca White, Sept. 2, 1998. BS, NYU, 1976, MBA, 1978. Pres., founder P.F. DeNicola, Inc., Stamford, Conn., 1976-84; acct. Main Hurdman, N.Y.C., Conn., 1978-81; tax mgr. Gen. Signal Corp., Stamford, Conn., 1981-83, Emery Air Freight Corp., Wilton, Conn., 1983-85; dir. taxes A.I. Internat. Corp., N.Y.C., Conn., 1985-88; tax mgr. Siemens Corp., N.Y.C., 1989-91; sr. tax analyst Fuji Photo Film U.S.A., Inc., Elmsford, N.Y., 1991-93, assoc. tax mgr., 1994-98, tax mgr., 1999—. Author: Legal Liability of Tax Return Preparers, 1978; contbr. articles to tax and investment periodicals. Recipient Ferdinand W. Lafrentz acctg. award, 1977 CPA, Conn., N.Y. Mem. Tax Soc. NYU, Assn. MBA Execs., Am. Mgmt. Assn., Stamford Tax Assn. (sec.-treas. 1988-89, v.p. 1989-90), Nat. Assn. Accts., NYU Commerce Alumni Assn. (dir. 1978-96 , corr. sec. 1978-79, rec. sec. 1979-81, chmn. budget com. 1987-88, chmn. Annual Bus. Conf. 1988-89, chmn. alumni admissions coun. 1989-96), AICPA (fed. tax and tax acctg. coms. 1984—), N.Y. Soc. CPAs (fed. and state tax com. 1983-85, depreciation and investment tax credit com. 1986-87), Conn. Soc. C.P.A.s, Tax Execs. Inst., Round Table Assn. of U.S. (co-founder 1986, nat. treas. 1987-88, 90-92, nat. pres. 1988-89, del. to internat. convention, 1987, 88), Estate Planning Council Westchester County, Round Table 3 of Greenwich (Conn.) (dir. 1984-90, 1985-86, pres. 1986-88), Internat. Platform Assn., Princeton Club, Rockefeller Ctr. Club (N.Y.C.), Landmark Club, Long Ridge Club (Stamford), Saw Mill River Racquet Club (Mt. Kisco, N.Y.), St. James's Club (Antigua), Capitol Hill Club (Washington), N.Y. Athletic Club,

Pelham (N.Y.) Country Club. Republican. Roman Catholic. Home: PO Box 4637 Stamford CT 06907-0637 Office: Fuji Photo Film USA Inc 555 Taxter Rd Elmsford NY 10523-2394

DENIHAN, WILLIAM M., city official. A in Bus. Law, Cuyahoga C.C., Cleve.; degree in urban studies, Cleve. State U. Dir. dept. pub. safety City of Cleve., 1993-99, exec. dir. dept. children and family svcs., 1999—; acting chief of police City of Cleve., 1994-95, 96. Trustee Bldg. Owners and Mgrs. Assn., 1993—, Substance Abuse Initiative of Greater Cleve., 1994—, Cleve. Police Hist. Soc. Mus., 1994—, ARC, 1995—, Historic Gateway Neighborhood, 1995—, Freedom House, 1993—, Ohio Canal Corridor, 1995—; pres. bd. dirs. Providence House, 1995-96; chmn. Byrne Com. of Criminal Justice Adv. Com., 1995—; mem. Greater Cleve. Safety Coun., 1992—, CPR Task Force, 1996, Campus Hosp. of Cleve., 1996, Rock and Roll Hall of Fame and Mus. Grand Opening Task Force, 1995, Gateway Grand Opening Task Force, Jacobs Field, 1994, Gund Arena, 1995; mem. adv. bd. Cuyahoga County Child Protection Coalition, 1994—. Recipient Downtown Recognition award Greater Cleve. Growth Assn., 1994, Outstanding Achievement award Caribbean Task Force, 1995. Mem. Cuyahoga County Chiefs of Police Assn., Safety Dirs. Assn. State of Ohio. Office: Dept Children and Family Svcs 3959 Euclid Ave Cleveland OH 44115*

DENIOUS, SHARON MARIE, publisher; b. Rulo, Nebr., Jan. 27, 1941; d. Thomas Wayne and Alma (Murphy) Fee; m. Jon Parks Denious, June 17, 1963; children: Timothy Scot, Elizabeth Denious Cessna. Grad. high sch. Operator N.W. Pipeline co., Ignacio, Colo., 1975-90; pub. The Silverton Standard & The Miner, Colo., 1990—. Mem. Colo. Press Assn., Nat. Newspaper Assn. Avocations: reading, hiking. Office: The Silverton Standard The Miner 1257 Greene St Silverton CO 81433

DE NIRO, ROBERT, actor; b. N.Y.C., Aug. 17, 1943; s. Robert and Virginia DeNiro; m. Diahnne Abbott; children: Raphael Eugene, Drina. Studied acting with, Stella Adler, Lee Strasberg. Motion pictures appearances include The Wedding Party, 1969, Hi, Mom!, 1970, Jennifer On My Mind, 1971, Bloody Mama, Born to Win, 1971, The Gang That Couldn't Shoot Straight, 1971, Bang the Drum Slowly, 1973, Mean Streets, 1973, The Godfather, Part II, 1974 (Acad. award best supporting actor), The Last Tycoon, Taxi Driver, 1976, New York, New York, 1900, 1977, The Deer Hunter, 1978, Raging Bull, 1980 (Acad. award best actor), True Confessions, 1981, The King of Comedy, 1982, Once Upon a Time in America, 1984, Falling in Love, 1984, Brazil, 1984, The Mission, 1985, Angel Heart, 1987, The Untouchables, 1987, Dear America: Letters Home From Vietnam, 1987 (documentary), Midnight Run, 1988, (also exec. prodr.) We're No Angels, 1989, Jacknife, 1989, Stanley & Iris, 1990, Goodfellas, 1990, Awakenings, 1991 (Acad. award nomination), Backdraft, 1991, Cape Fear, 1991, Guilty By Suspicion, 1991, Mistress, 1992, Night and the City, 1992, Mad Dog and Glory, 1993, This Boys Life, 1993, (also dir.) A Bronx Tale, 1993, Mary Shelley's Frankenstein, 1994, Casino, 1995, Heat, 1995, The Fan, 1996, Marvin's Room, 1996, Sleepers, 1996, (also prodr.) Wag the Dog, 1997, Copland, 1997, Great Expectations, 1998, 15 Minutes, 1999, Analyze This, 1999, Flawless, 1999 (also prodr.), The Adventures of Rocky and Bullwinkle, 1999 (also prodr.), Lenny Bruce: Swear to Tell the Truth, 1998 (TV, voice); prodr.: Entropy, 1999; co-prodr. Thunderheart, 1992; theater roles include Strange Show, 1982; Exec. producer: (TV) Tribeca, 1993, (film) Faithful, 1996. Recipient Hasty Pudding award Harvard U. 1979, D.W. Griffith award for best actor, 1990. Office: Creative Artists Agy 9830 Wilshire Blvd Beverly Hills CA 90212-1825*

DENIS, HEIDI ANFINSON, library administrator; b. Mar. 16, 1952. BA in Sociology, U. South Fla., 1981, MA in Libr. and Info. Sci., 1984. Asst. dir. Cen. Fla. Libr. Sys., Ocala, 1984-86, acting regional libr. dir., 1986-87; dir. Divsn. Libr. Svcs., Citrus County, Fla., 1987—, Dept. Comty. Svcs., Citrus County, 1997—. E-mail: heidid@cclib.org. Office: 425 W Roosevelt Blvd Beverly Hills FL 34465

DENISE, ROBERT PHILLIPS, consultant; b. Montreal, Que., Can., Nov. 13, 1936; s. Warren Edward and Lorena Hyacinth (Patterson) D.; m. Margaret Ellen Maloney, June 30, 1937; children: Robert Phillips, William Joseph, Christopher Andrew. AB, Duke U., 1959; postgrad., Northeastern U., Boston, 1970-71. Various mgmt. positions GE, 1959-77; treas. Hoffman-LaRoche Inc., Nutley, N.J., 1978-82; contr. Hoffman-LaRoche Inc., Nutley, 1982-85; v.p., treas. Becton Dickinson & Co., Franklin Lakes, N.J., 1985-89; chmn., pres., chief exec. officer Bucilla Corp., Hazleton, Pa., 1989-96; ind. cons., 1996—; mem. Mid-Atlantic adv. bd. Arkwright-Boston Ins. Co., 1985-89. Twp. committeeman, Millburn, N.J., 1981-86, vice chmn., dep. mayor, 1983-84, mayor, chmn. twp. com., 1984-86; mem. Planning Bd., 1979-86; v.p., bd. dirs. Nat. Soc. to Prevent Blindness-N.J., 1980-91; active Boy Scouts Am. With U.S. Army, 1960-62. Republican.

DENISE, THEODORE CULLOM, philosophy educator; b. Whitewater, Wis., Mar. 9, 1919; s. Malcolm F. and Margaret E. (Lawrence) D.; m. Kathleen W. Cowles, Oct. 4, 1942; children: Patricia Denise White, Theodore Cullom (dec.). BA, U. Mich., 1942, MA, 1947, PhD, 1955. Teaching fellow U. Mich., 1946-48; mem. faculty Syracuse U., 1948—, assoc. prof. philosophy, 1959-64, prof. philosophy, 1964-89, prof. emeritus philosophy, 1989—, chmn. dept., 1959-72, chmn. humanities depts., 1973-76; dir. liberal studies Inst. Univ. Adminstrs., 1961-63; dir. of semester in Italy, 1967-68, 76-77; dir. grad. studies in philosophy, 1976-84; mem. editorial com Univ. Press, 1972-78. Author: (with others) Great Traditions in Ethics, 1953, (with S.P. Peterfreund) Contemporary Philosophy and Its Origins, 1967; Editor: (with M.H. Williams) Retrospect and Prospect, 1956; Contbr. articles to philos. jours. Served with AUS, 1942-46. Mem. Assn. Symbolic Logic, Am. Philos. Assn., Alpha Kappa Lambda. Home: 301 Haddonfield Dr Syracuse NY 13214-1644 Office: Syracuse U Dept Philosophy Syracuse NY 13244

DENISON, DWIGHT VAL, educator; b. July 22, 1967. MPA, Brigham Young U., 1993; PhD, U. Ky., 1997. Asst. prof. NYU, N.Y.C., 1997—. E-mail: dwight.denison@nyu.edu. Office: 4 Washington Sq N # 5-44 New York NY 10003

DENISON, FLOYD GENE, insurance executive; b. N.Y.C., Nov. 28, 1943; m. Robin Denison, Mar. 5, 1978; children: Alana, Ian. BA, Siena Coll., 1965; MA, St. John's U., 1967; MBA, Bernard Baruch Coll., 1976. Acctg. mgr. Am. Fgn. Ins. Assn., N.Y.C., 1969-77; exec. v.p., dir. corp. assets Am. Bankers Ins. Group, Miami, Fla., 1977—. Mem. investment adv. com. Dade County (Fla.) Sch. Bd., 1984. Home: 9305 SW 117th Ter Miami FL 33176-4235 Office: Am Bankers Ins Group 11222 Quail Roost Dr Miami FL 33157-6543

DENISON, GILBERT WALTER, chemical engineer, administrator; b. Oklahoma City, Okla., Oct. 7, 1929; s. Henry Clark and Mary Ella (McBride) D.; m. Agatha Lorena Bitsche, Nov. 23, 1956; children: Brian, Gregory, Alice, Ronald. BS in Chem. Engring., U. Okla., 1957, MS in Chem. Engring., 1958, PhD, 1962. Registered profl. engr., Okla. Rsch. engr. Esso Rsch. & Engring., Linden, N.J., 1962-65; lab. mgr. J.M. Huber, Borger, Tex., 1965-66; sr. devel. engr. Continental Oil, Ponca City, Okla., 1966-69; R&D mgr. Dart Industries, Inc., Paramus, N.J., 1969-72; bus. cons. Raymond Chem. Co., Toledo, Ohio, 1972-73; various rsch. and engring. positons Chemical and Engring. Cos., Cleve., 1973-87; cons. in chem. engring. Cleve., also Okla., 1987-95; v.p. ops. and devel. Fed. Recycling Techs., Inc., Norman, Okla., 1995—. Inventor: formula for specialty adhesive for supporting mining roofs; co-inventor process for EPDM rubber, process method and system for recovering valuable products from scrap tires. With USMC, 1944-46, 50-52, PTO. Monsanto scholar, 1956-57, NSF fellow, 1957-59, NSF grantee, 1959-62. Mem. AIChE, Am. Chem. Soc. Republican. Achievements include development and design of process for manufacturing flame retardant; refinement, engineering and formulation of manufacturing process for ABS polymer; development of equipment and field test procedures for pipeline sealing process. Office: Fed Recycling Techs 3750 W Main St Ste Aa Norman OK 73072-4645

DENISON, RICHARD EUGENE, retired agricultural services company executive; b. Harrisburg, Pa., Aug. 24, 1932; s. Benjamin C. and Viola M. (Cramer) D.; m. Peggy A. Koskinas, Apr. 19, 1958; children: Richard E. Jr., Carol Denison Brame. BS, Pa. State U., 1954. Cert. agrl. cons. Asst. store mgr. Grange League Fedn., Youngsville, Pa., 1957-59; grain buyer Quaker Oats, Shiremanstown, Pa., 1959-62; assoc. editor, advt. salesman Pa. Farmer, Harrisburg, 1962-68, mgr., 1968-70; mgr. Pa. Farm Bur. Farm Mgmt. Svcs., Camp Hill, Pa., 1970-86; gen. mgr. Pa. Farm Bur. Mems. Svcs. Corp., Camp Hill, Pa., 1986-92; assoc. adminstr. Pa. Farm Bur., Camp Hill, 1992-94; pres. Pa. State Agrl. Adv. Coun., University Park, Pa., 1988-90, mem. 1984-94; mem. Pa. Adv. Coun. on Vocat. Edn., Harrisburg, 1982-85, Pa. Farm Show Com., Harrisburg, 1970-82. Various positions Keystone area coun. Boy Scouts Am., Mechanicsburg, Pa., 1945—, v.p., 1995-98; trustee Shiremanstown United Meth. Ch., 1977-87, adminstrv. bd. mem., 1960-87; past mem., chmn. adv. bd. Mechanicsburg Rainbow Assn., 1975-80; past mem. Shiremanstown Borough Coun., 1970-74; scouting coord. Ctrl. Pa. Conf. United Meth. Ch., 1998—. Served in USAF, 1955-57. Recipient Silver Beaver award Boy Scouts Am., 1977, award of merit, 1982, God and Svc. Recognition award, 1986, Disting. Commr. award, 1990, James E. West Fellowship award, 1994, Grand Cross of Color award Internat. Order of Rainbow for Girls, 1979, Dairy and Animal Sci. Disting. Animal Sci. Alumnus award Pa. State U., 1998. Mem. Am. Soc. Agrl. Cons., Harrisburg Consistory, Masons, Zembo Shrine, Coll. Agr. Alumni Soc. (bd. dirs., 1997—). Republican. Avocations: golf, scouting, hiking, gardening. Home: 211 E Walnut St Shiremanstown PA 17011-6768

DENISTON-TROCHTA, GRACE MARIE, educator, artist; d. Leopold and Amalie (Hotarek) Henzl; m. James Trochta; children: Paul Michael, Maria Suzanne. BA in Elem. Edn., U. Mich., 1962; MA in Art Edn., U. Iowa, 1984; PhD in Curriculum and Instrn & Art Edn., U. Wis., 1995. Cert. tchr art edn., elem. edn., Wis. 6th grade tchr. Colegio Franklin Roosevelt, Peru, 1963-64; art tchr., dept. chair St. Katharine's/St. Mark's Sch., Bettendorf, Iowa, 1975-82; art tchr. U. Chgo. Lab. Sch., The Dewey Sch., 1984-87, Graland Country Day Sch., Denver, 1987-88, Sewickley (Pa.) Acad., 1988-89, Greenfield (Wis.) Pub. Sch. Dist., 1990-91; adminstr. People's Rep. China vis. scholar exch. program U. Wis., Madison, 1982-84, career counselor, placement cons., tchg. asst., lectr. dept. art, 1989-96; asst. prof. art U. No. Iowa, Cedar Falls, 1996-98, U. Wis., OshKosh, 1998—; co-advisor Student Art Educator's Assn., 1996-98. Exhibited in group shows at U.Chgo. Lab. Sch., 1986, Women's Caucus for Art, Meml. Union, U. Wis., Madison, 1992, Milw. Inst. Art and Design, 1993, Milw. War Meml., 1992, Electronic Gallery, Chgo., 1993; contbr. articles to profl. jours. Mem. Am. Ednl. Rsch. Assn., Nat. Art Edn. Assn., Caucus on Social Theory and Art Edn. (comms. coord.), Seminar for Rsch. Art Edn., U.S. Soc. for Edn. Through Art, Women's Caucus for Art. Home: 300 S Shuman St Verona WI 53593-1347 Office: U Wis-Oshkosh 523 Arts and Comm Ctr Oshkosh WI 54901-8635

DENKE, CONRAD WILLIAM, motion picture producer; b. Cottonwood, Ariz., July 23, 1947; s. Lee Ernest and Barbara Ann (Russell) D.; m. Laura Lee Nielson; children: Alexander, Elisabeth. BA in Radio-TV Communications and Psychology, U. Wash., 1969. Dir. Sta. KCTS-TV, Seattle, 1967-69; dir. producer Cinema Assocs., Seattle, 1973-78; pres. Am. Motion Pictures, Seattle, 1978—, Am. Prodn. Svcs., Seattle, 1978—; bd. dirs. Am. Cinema Found., Whidbey Island Films. Dir., producer: (indsl. documentary) Tunnels Under Chicago, 1981 (Chris award 1981, Gold award, Silver award, Cine Golden Eagle award, 1981); dir. (ednl. documentary) More Than Bows and Arrows, 1978 (Best Western Documentary 1978); producer: (TV series) Adventures on Sinclair Island, 1986, (talk show series) Teens Talk, (PBS documentary) Educations Wars, 1996, National Desk, 1997, 99. Mormon bishop, stake presidency. With USAF, 1969-73. Recipient Cine Golden Eagle award Council on Internat. Nontheatrical Events, 1977, 79, 89, 95, Silver Cindy award Info. Film Producers Am., 1977, 98, Gold Camera award U.S. Indsl. Film Festival, 1978, Telly award, 1989, 95, 97, 2 Telly's, 1998, 2 Gold awards Emerald City awards, 1997, World medal N.Y. Film Festival, 1998, 2 Aegis awards, 1998, 2 Aurora awards, 1998. Mem. Internat. TV Assn. (dir. Seattle chpt. 1980-90, chpt. pres. 1983-84, Silver Reel, 1986, Gold Reel 1997), Wash. Motion Picture Coun. (pres. 1992-96), Assn. Ind. Comml. Producers (v.p. N.W. chpt. 1985-87, pres. 1987-90), Am. Cinema Found. in L.A. (bd. dirs., v.p. 1994—). Republican. Office: Am Motion Pictures 2247 15th Ave W Seattle WA 98119-2417

DENKE, PAUL HERMAN, aircraft engineer; b. San Francisco, Feb. 7, 1916; s. Edmund Herman and Ella Hermine (Riehl) D.; m. Beryl Ann Lincoln, Feb. 10, 1940; children: Karen Denke Mottaz, Claudia Denke Tesche, Marilyn Denke Oliver. BCE, U. Calif.-Berkeley, 1937, MCE, 1939. Registered profl. engr., Calif. Stress engr. Douglas Aircraft Co., Santa Monica, Calif., 1940-62, mgr. structural mechanics Long Beach, Calif., 1962-65, chief sci. computing, 1965-71, chief structures engr. methods and devel., 1972-78, chief scientist structural mechanics, 1979-84, staff mgr. Boeing fellow, 1985—; mem. faculty dept. engring. UCLA, 1941-50. Assoc. fellow AIAA; mem. Soc. Automotive Engrs. (Arch T. Colwell Merit award 1966, IAE Outstanding Engr. Merit award 1985), Sigma Xi, Chi Epsilon, Tau Beta Pi. Democrat. Pioneered and developed finite element method of structural analysis; author numerous technical papers. Home: 1800 Via Estudillo Palos Verdes Peninsula CA 90274-1908

DENKER, HENRY, playwright, author, director; b. N.Y.C., Nov. 25, 1912; s. Max and Jennie (Geller) D.; m. Edith Rose Heckman, Dec. 5, 1942. LL.B., N.Y. Law Sch., 1934. Bar: N.Y. 1935. Practiced law N.Y.C., 1935-38; exec. Research Inst. Am., N.Y.C., 1936-37; tax cons. Standard Stats. subs. Standard and Poor, N.Y.C., 1937-39; lectr. dramatic writing Am. Theatre Wing, 1961-63, Coll. of the Desert. Writer, dir., prodr.: (radio series) The Greatest Story Ever Told, N.Y.C., 1947-57; author: (Broadway plays) Time Limit, 1956, A Far Country, 1961, Venus at Large, 1962, A Case of Libel, 1964, What Did We Do Wrong, 1968, Something Old, Something New, 1976, Horowitz and Mrs. Washington, 1979; (off-Broadway) The Name of the Game, 1967, A Sound of Distant Thunder, 1969, The Headhunters, 1974; (screenplays) The Heartfarm, 1970, The Hook, Twilight of Honor, Time Limit, A Time for Miracles, 1980, Outrage, 1984; writer, dir., prodr. numerous TV dramas, 1950-66; TV spls. include Give Us Barrabas, 1964, Neither Are We Enemies, 1971, The Choice, The Court Martial of Lietenant Calley, Mother Seton, 1980, Love Leads the Way, 1985, Outrage, 1986, Case of Libel, 1986; author: I'll be Right Home Ma, 1949, My Son, The Lawyer, 1950, Salome, Princess of Galilee, 1954, That First Easter, 1956, The Director, 1970, The Kingmaker, 1972, A Place for the Mighty, 1973, The Physicians, 1975, The Experiment, 1976, The Starmaker, 1977, The Scofield Diagnosis, 1977, The Actress, 1978, The Error Judgement, 1979, Horowitz and Mrs. Washington, 1979, The Warfield Syndrome, 1981, Outrage!, 1982, The Healers, 1983, Kincaid, 1984, Love Leads the Way, 1985, A Case of Libel, 1985, Robert, My Son, 1985, Judge Spencer Dissents, 1986, The Choice, 1987, The Retreat, 1988, A Gift of Life, 1989, Payment in Full, 1990, Doctor on Trial, 1991, Labyrinth, 1994, This Child is Mine, 1995, To Marcy, With Love, 1996, A Place for Kathy, 1997, The Third Day, 1999. Recipient Peabody award, 1949; Christopher award, 1953; Emmy award, 1948. Mem. Acad. TV Arts and Scis. (coun.), Authors League (coun.), Dramatists Guild (mem. coun. 1967-69), Authors Guild, Writers' Guild. Jewish. Address: 241 Central Park W New York NY 10024-4530

DENKINGER, DONALD ANTON, umpire; b. Cedar Falls, Iowa, Aug. 23, 1936; married; 3 children. Student, Wartburg Coll., Al Somers Sch. Umpires. Supr. athletic programs White Sands Missile Range; former umpire Ala.-Fla. League, Northwest League, Tex. League, Internat. League; umpire maj. league baseball Am. League, N.Y.C., 1969—; with Umpires Union, Phila. With U.S. Army. Avocation: golfing. Office: Am League 350 Park Ave New York NY 10022 also: Umpires Union 1735 Market St Philadelphia PA 19103

DENKO, JOANNE D., psychiatrist, writer; b. Kalamazoo, Mich., Mar. 29, 1927; d. John S. and Marian Mildred (Boers) Decker; m. Charles Wasil Denko, June 17, 1950; children: Christopher Charles, Nicholas Charles, Timothy Charles. BA summa cum laude, Hope Coll., 1947; MD, Johns Hopkins U., 1951; MS in Psychiatry, U. Mich., 1963. Lic. psychiatrist Md., Ill., Mich., Ohio. Pvt. practice Columbus, Ohio, 1961-68; staff psychiatrist Fairview Gen. Hosp., Cleve., 1968-97, Cleve. Clinic Health Systems, 1997—; pvt. practice Rocky River, Ohio, 1968—; cons. Juvenile Diagnostic Ctr., Columbus, 1967-68, VA Hosp., Cleve., 1968-72, Cmty. Mental Health Ctrs., Greater Cleve., 1974-80; clin. instr. Case Western Res. U., Cleve., 1981-83. Author: Through the Keyhole at Gifted Men and Women, 1977, (monograph) The Psychiatric Aspects of Hypoparathyroidism, 1962; contbr. articles to profl. jours.; author poetry, 1960—. Mem. AAAS (reviewer children's books), Cleve. Astron. Soc. (bd. dirs. 1984-86, 96-98), Mensa (Cleve. area br. pres. 1986-87), Great Books Discussion Group (Rocky River, chmn. 1985-92, 94—), Kiwanis Internat. Russian Orthodox. Achievements include naming sexual deviance klismaphilia; research in special problems of adults of high intelligence, educating gifted girls, teenage alcoholism, mental illness in pre-literate peoples, psychiatric aspects of lupus. Home and Office: 21160 Avalon Dr Cleveland OH 44116-1120

DENLINGER, EDGAR JACOB, electronics engineering research executive; b. Lancaster, Pa., June 17, 1939; s. Victor Jacob and Marian Alice (Shoemaker) D.; m. Cynthia Della Wilson, June 24, 1967; children—Crystal Shereen, Craig Wesley. B.S. in Engring. Sci., Pa. State U., 1961; M.S.E.E., U. Pa., 1964, Ph.D. in E.E., 1969. Research engr. Applied Research RCA, Camden, N.J., 1961-65; research assoc. Moore Sch. U. Pa., Phila., 1965-67; mem. tech. staff MIT Lincoln Lab., Lexington, Mass., 1967-73; mem. tech. staff RCA Labs, Princeton, N.J., 1973-83, group head signal conversion systems research, 1983-87; group head microwave systems rsch. David Sarnoff Research Ctr., Princeton, N.J., 1987-92, sr. mem. tech. staff, 1992—; adj. prof. dept. elec. engring. Drexel U., Phila., 1982-88. Contbr. articles to profl. jours. Patentee microwave devices and circuits. Mem. Hickory Acres Civic Assn., East Windsor, N.J., 1973-81. Recipient Achievement award David Sarnoff Rsch. Ctr., Princeton, 1979, 94. Fellow IEEE (treas. sect. 1980-83, vice chmn. 1984, chmn. 1985). Republican. Presbyterian. Lodges: Mason, Tall Cedars, Shriners. Avocations: music; swimming. Home: 7 Wheatston Ct Princeton Junction NJ 08550-1936 Office: Sarnoff Corp Princeton NJ 08543-5300

DENLINGER, JOHN KENNETH, journalist; b. Lancaster, Pa., Mar. 25, 1942; s. John Emory and Elizabeth (Smith) D.; m. Nancy Dodson, July 29, 1995; children: Lauri, Scott. B.S. in Econs, Pa. State U., 1964. Mem. staff Pitts. Press, 1964-66; mem. staff Washington Post, 1966—; sports columnist, 1975-90. Author: For the Glory, 1994; co-author: Athletes for Sale, 1975, Redskin Country: From Baugh to the Super Bowl, 1983, Golf: The Mind Game, 1990, Tennis: The Mind Game, 1991, Skiing: The Mind Game, 1993. Office: The Washington Post 1150 15th St NW Washington DC 20071-0002

DENLINGER, VICKI LEE, secondary school physical education educator; b. Dayton, Ohio, June 13, 1961; d. David Lee and Barbara Ann (Zimmerman) D.; 1 child, David Micheal. Student, Ohio State U., 1979-82; BS in Edn., Wright State U., 1982-85; postgrad. studies, Miami U., Oxford, Ohio, 1986-87, U.S. Sports Acad., Daphne, Ala., 1996—. Cert. phys. edn. and health tchr., Ohio; lic. athletic trainer, Ohio. Student athletic trainer Wright State U., Dayton, Ohio, 1983-85; asst. athletic trainer Oakwood (Ohio) City Sch., 1984-86; grad. asst. athletic trainer Miami U., Oxford, Ohio, 1986-87; subst. tchr. Oakwood City Sch., Kettering Moraine City Schs., Ohio, 1987-89; athletic trainer Kettering Moraine City Schs., Kettering, Ohio, 1987-96; tchr. Kettering Moraine City Schs., Kettering, 1989—; owner InnerPrize, Kettering, 1996—; pub. speaker Greater Dayton Athletic Trainers, 1987—, InnerPrize, 1996—; advisor Kettering Fairmont Student Athletic Trainers Assn., Kettering Moraine City Schs., 1989-96; facilitator Student Assistance Support Group, Kettering-Moraine City Schs., , 1994—; instr. Kettering Awareness Tobacco Edn. Progra, 1997—; advisor Students Against Destructive Decisions, 1997—. Mem. PTA Assns. of various Kettering-Moraine Pub. Schs., 1989—; co-dir. Kettering 24-Hour Relay Challenge, 1999. Named Jaycee of the Month Region E, 1996, Ohio Jaycees, Most Outstanding Write-Up of the First Quarter, 1996, Ohio Jaycees. Mem. NEA, ASCD, Nat. Athletic Trainer's Assn. (cert. athletic trainer), Ohio Athletic Trainers Assn., Greater Dayton Athletic Trainers Assn., Nat. Strength and Conditioning Assn., Internat. Weight Lifting Assn. (cert. weight trainer), Ohio Edn. Assn., Kettering Edn. Assn., Ohio Assn. for Health, Phys. Edn., Recreation and Dance, Am. Coll. Sports Medicine, Nat. Fedn. Interscholastic Coaches Edn. Program/Am. Coaching Effectiveness Program, Sports First Aid Instr. Avocations: Christian studies, fitness, personal devel. and sports, athletics. Home: 3489 Valleywood Dr Kettering OH 45429-4234 Office: Kettering Fairmont HS 3301 Shroyer Rd Kettering OH 45429-2635

DENLOW, MORTON, federal judge; b. 1947. BA, Washington U., 1969; JD, Northwestern U., 1972. Pvt. practice Chgo., 1972-76; sr. lectr. Loyola U. Sch. Law, 1983-95; adj. prof. trial advocacy Northwestern U. Sch. Law, 1990-91; magistrate judge U.S. Dist. Ct. (no. dist.) Ill., 1996—. With USAR, 1970-76. FAX: 312-554-8547. Office: US Dist Ct 219 S Dearborn St Ste 2402 Chicago IL 60604-1802

DENMARK, BERNHARDT, manufacturing executive; b. Bklyn., June 6, 1917; s. William M. and Kate (Lazarus) D.; m. Muriel Schechter, Sept. 22, 1943; children: Richard J., Karen. A.B., NYU, 1941; postgrad., Am. U., 1941-42, Nat. Inst. Pub. Affairs, 1941-42. Vice pres. sales Telecoin Corp., N.Y.C., 1946-49; v.p. sales Internat. Latex Corp., N.Y.C., 1949-55; mgr. mktg. Playtex Co., N.Y.C., 1955-59; v.p., gen. mgr. family products div. Playtex Co., 1959-63, v.p. mktg., 1963-65; pres. Playtex Co. Playtex div., 1965-67, Internat. Playtex Corp., N.Y.C., 1968-69; chmn. bd. Internat. Playtex Corp., 1969; exec. v.p., dir., mem. exec. com. Glen Alden Corp., N.Y.C., 1969-72; pres. Bevis Industries, Inc., White Plains, N.Y., 1972-76, Bus. Mktg. Corp. for N.Y.C., 1977-78; chmn. Denmark, Donovan & Oppel Inc., N.Y.C., 1978-85; chmn. bd. dirs. Advanced Photonix, Inc., Camarillo, Calif., 1992—, Xsirius, Inc., Camarillo, 1992—; bd. dirs. Stanley Warner Corp., Schenley Industries, BVD Corp., Kleinerts Inc., Advanced Photonics Inc. Served to capt. AUS, 1942-46. Clubs: Fairview Country (Greenwich, Conn.); City Athletic (N.Y.C.). Home: 870 UN Plz New York NY 10017 Office: 1240 Avenida Acaso Camarillo CA 93012-8754

DENMARK, STANLEY JAY, orthodontist; b. Queens, N.Y., May 26, 1927; s. Jack and Frieda (Kirschenbaum) D.; m. Florence Levin, June 7, 1953 (div. June 1973); children: Valerie, Pamela (dec.) and Richard (twins); m. Anita Goodman, Jan. 2, 1983. BS, Queens Coll., 1950; MSc, NYU, 1955; DDS, U. Pa., 1955, orthodontics cert., 1957. Diplomate Am. Bd. Orthodontics. Practice dentistry specializing in orthodontics Westbury, N.Y., 1955-91; asst. prof. orthodontics Fairleigh Dickinson U., Hackensack, N.J., 1974-79; clin. asst. prof. growth and devel. scis. (orthodontics) Sch. Dentistry NYU, 1991—. With USN, 1945-47. Mem. ADA, Am. Assn. Orthodontists, Northeastern Soc. Orthodontists, Coll. Diplomates of Am. Bd. Orthodontists, Sigma Xi. Jewish. Avocations: painting, woodcuts, tennis, cross-country skiing. Home: 330 E 80th St New York NY 10021-0915 Office: NYU Coll Dentistry 345 E 24th St New York NY 10010-4086

DENN, CYRIL JOSEPH, insurance agent; b. Mankato, Minn., Jan. 23, 1948; s. Bertram Henry and Hildegard M. (Drummer) D.; m. Sandra Lee Jones, Oct. 22, 1966 (div. 1970); m. Darlene Kay Wittrock, Apr. 19, 1974; children: Darcy Ann, Amanda Kay, Cassandra Jo. BS, Mankato State U., 1977, 5-yr. cert., 1982; ChFC, Am. Coll., 1985. CLU, 1982. Factory laborer Kato Engring. Co., Mankato, 1971-74; sales rep. Met. Life, Mankato, 1974-76, sales mgr., 1976-79, sales rep., 1979-82; mktg. specialist Met. Life, Aurora, Ill., 1982-83; br. mgr. Met. Life, Sioux Falls, S.D., 1983-84, sales rep., 1984-86; regional mgr. Cath. Aid Assn., St. Paul, 1986-89; mgr. Prudential Ins. Co., Sioux Falls, 1989-91, Aberdeen, S.D., 1992-94; asst. mgr. Farm Bur. Fin. Svcs., Aberdeen, 1995-96; career agt. Farm Bur. Fin. Svcs., Mankato, Minn., 1996-97, Bus., Estate, Retirement & Ins. Planning, Mankato, 1996—; account rep. MetLife, Mankato, 1997—. Mem. St. Clair (Minn.) Pub. Sch. Bd., 1981-83. With U.S. Army, 1968-71. Fellow Life Underwriters Tng. Coun.; mem. Nat. Assn. Life Underwriters (nat. quality award 1975-89), nat. sales achievement award 1975-89), Sioux Falls Life Underwriters Assn. (bd. dirs. 1991-92, edn. chmn., co-chmn. life underwriting tng. coun.), Gen. Agy. Mgrs. Assn. (career devel. award 1994), Aberdeen Life Underwriters Assn. (bd. dirs. 1992-96, sec.-treas. 1994-95, pres. elect 1995-96), S.D. Life Underwriters Assn. (chmn. life underwriters tng. coun. 1993-96), Soc. Fin. Svc. Profls. (midwest liaison team 1992—, mem. devel. com. 1994-97, pres. Ea. S.D. chpt. 1992-93, video teleconf. coord. 1992-96, PACE com. 1991-94), S.D. Planned Giving Coun. (steering com. 1994-95, v.p. programs, chair 1995—), S.D. Ponies of Americas Club (bd. dirs. 1986-97, pres. 1987-89), Midwest Pony of Americas Club (pres. 1988-91, horse show chmn. 1989), Am. Legion, Mankato Area Chamber and Convention Bur. (bus. devel. com. 1996—, membership devel. com. 1998—).

Republican. Roman Catholic. Avocations: show horses, reading. Office: 424 Park Ln Mankato MN 56001-2038

DENN, MORTON MACE, chemical engineering educator; b. Passaic, N.J., July 7, 1939; s. Herbert Paul and Esther (Taub) D; m. Vivienne Roumani; children: Matthew Philip, Susannah Rachel, Rebekah Leah. BS in Engring., Princeton U., 1961; PhD, U. Minn., 1964. Postdoctoral fellow U. Del., Newark, 1964-65, from asst. prof. to prof. Chem. Engring., 1965-77, Allan P. Colburn prof., 1977-81; prof. U. Calif., Berkeley, 1981—, chmn. dept. chem. engring., 1991-94; Harry Pierce prof. chem. engring. Technion, Israel Inst. Tech., Haifa, 1979-80; Chevron Energy prof. chem. engring. Calif. Inst. Tech., 1980; vis. prof. chem. engring. U. Melbourne, Australia, 1985; program leader for polymers Ctr. for Advanced Materials Lawrence Berkeley Nat. Labs., 1983—; vis. Forchheimer prof. Hebrew U., Israel, 1998-99. Author: Optimization by Variational Methods, 1969, (co-author) Introduction to Chemical Engineering Analysis, 1972, Stability of Reaction and Transport Processes, 1975, Process Fluid Mechanics, 1980, Process Modeling, 1986; co-editor Chemical Process Control, 1976; contbr. numerous articles to profl. jours., author book chpts. Guggenheim fellow, 1971-72; William M. Lacey lectr. Calif. Inst. Tech., 1979, Fulbright lectr., 1979-80; Peter C. Reilly lectr. Notre Dame U., 1980; Bicentennial Commemoration lectr. La. State U., 1984; Arthur Kelly lectr. Purdue U., 1987; Stanley Katz lectr. CCNY, 1990. Fellow AIChE (editor jour. 1985-91, Profl. Progress award 1977, William H. Walker award 1984, Warren K. Lewis award 1998); mem. NAE, Am. Soc. Engring. Edn. (chem. engring. divsn. lectureship award 1993), Soc. Rheology (editor jour. 1995—, Bingham medal 1986), Brit. Soc. Rheology, Polymer Processing Soc., Sigma Xi. Office: U Calif Dept Chem Engring Berkeley CA 94720-1462

DENNARD, ROBERT HEATH, engineering executive, scientist; b. Terrell, Tex., Sept. 5, 1932; s. Buford Leon and Loma (Heath) D.; children—Robert (dec. Nov. 1998), Amy, Holly; m. Jane Bridges. BSEE, So. Methodist U., 1954, MSEE, 1956; PhD, Carnegie Inst. Tech., 1958. Staff engr. IBM, Yorktown Heights, N.Y., 1958-63; research staff mem. IBM Research Ctr., Yorktown Heights, N.Y., 1963-71, group mgr., 1971-79, fellow, 1979—. Contbr. articles to profl. jours.; patentee in field including basic dynamic RAM memory cell. Recipient Nat. Medal of Tech., Pres. U.S., 1988, Indsl. Rsch. Inst. Achievement award, 1989, Harvey prize Technion-Israel Inst. Tech., 1990; named Inventor of Yr., N.Y. Intellectual Property Law Assn., 1995; inducted into Nat. Inventors Hall of Fame, 1997. Fellow IEEE; mem. NAE, Am. Philos. Soc. Avocation: Scottish country dancing. Office: IBM Rsch Ctr PO Box 218 Yorktown Heights NY 10598-0218

DENNEEN, JOHN PAUL, lawyer; b. N.Y.C., Aug. 18, 1940; s. John Thomas Denneen and Pauline Jane Ludlow; m. Mary Veronica Murphy, July 3, 1965; children: John Edward, Thomas Michael, James Patrick, Robert Andrew, Daniel Joseph, Mary Elizabeth. BS, Fordham U., 1963; JD, Columbia U., 1966. Bar: N.Y. 1966, U.S. Ct. Appeals (2d cir.) 1974, U.S. Dist. Ct. (so. and ea. dists.) N.Y. 1975, Mo. 1987. Assoc. Seward & Kissel, N.Y.C., 1966-75; sr. v.p., gen counsel, sec. GK Techs., Inc., Greenwich, Conn., 1975-83; exec. v.p., gen. counsel, sec. Chromalloy Am. Corp., St. Louis, 1983-87; ptnr. Bryan Cave LLP, St. Louis, 1987—. Mem. ABA, Internat. Bar Assn., N.Y. State Bar Assn., N.Y.C. Bar Assn., Bar Assn. Met. St. Louis. Office: Bryan Cave LLP 211 N Broadway Ste 3600 Saint Louis MO 63102-2733

DENNEHY, BRIAN, actor; b. Bridgeport, Conn., July 9, 1939; m. Jennifer Dennehy; 3 children from previous marriage. Grad., Columbia U.; postgrad., Yale U. Appeared in motion pictures Semi-Tough, 1977, F.I.S.T., 1978, Foul Play, 1978, Butch and Sundance: The Early Days, 1979, 10, 1979, Little Miss Marker, 1980, Split Image, 1982, First Blood, 1982, Never Cry Wolf, 1983, Gorky Park, 1983, Twice in a Lifetime, 1985, Silverado, 1985, Cocoon, 1985, F/X, 1986, Legal Eagles, 1986, Best Seller, 1987, The Belly of an Architect, 1987, Return to Snowy River, 1988, Miles from Home, 1988, Cocoon: The Return, 1988, The Last of the Finest, Seven Minutes, Presumed Innocent, 1990, F/X 2, 1991, Gladiators, 1991, Midnight Movie, 1993, Gilligan's Island: The Movie, 1997, Tommy Boy, 1995, The Stars Fell on Henrietta, 1995, Romeo and Juliet, 1996, Dish Dogs, 1998, Out of the Cold, 1999, Deep River, Finders, Keepers, Looking for Mr. Goodbar; theatre appearances include Streamers, off-Broadway, 1976, The Rat in the Skull, Wisdom Bridge Theatre, Chgo., 1985, The Cherry Orchard, Bklyn. Acad. Music, 1988, The Iceman Cometh, Goodman Theatre, Chgo., 1990, Says I, Says He, Sea Plays, Bus Stop, Julius Caesar, Ivanov, The Front Page, Translations, Galileo, A Touch of the Poet, Goodman Theatre, Chgo., MacBeth, Romeo & Juliet, 1996; appeared in TV series Big Shamus, Little Shamus, 1979, Star of the Family, 1982-83, Birdland, 1993-94, (BBC series) Nostromo, 1995, A Season in Purgatory, 1996, Undue Influence, 1996, Larry McMurty's Dean Man Walk, 1996; numerous movies for TV including Annie Oakley, Showtime Cable TV Tall Tales and Legends series, 1985, Acceptable Risk, 1986, HBO prodn. The Lion of Africa, 1987, Perfect Witness, 1989 (Cable Ace nominee), The Last of the Finest, 1990, Shattered Vows, 1993, Murder in the Heartland, 1993 (Emmy nomination, Supporting Actor - Miniseries or Special, 1993), Prophet of Evil, 1993, Foreign Affair, 1993 (CableAce award, Best Actor in a movie or miniseries), Rising Son, Bloodfeud, Evergreen, Acceptable Risks, The Terrorist, A Rumor of War, In Broad Daylight, The Last Place on Earth, Teamster Boss: The Jackie Presser Story, Birdland, Leave of Absence, Jack Reed: An Honest Cop, Final Appeal, Pride and Extreme Prejudice, (miniseries) A Killing in a Small Town, 1990 (Emmy nominee for Outstanding Supporting Actor), To Catch a Killer, 1991 (Emmy nominee, Am TV awards nominee), The Burden of Proof, 1992 (Emmy nominee for Outstanding Supporting Actor), A Season in Purgatory, 1996, Nostromo, 1996, Dead Man's Walk, 1996, Day One, Undue Influence, 1996, Jack Reed: Death and Vengeance, 1996, ; dir., co-writer, actor, co-exec. prodr.: (TV movies) Jack Reed: Champion of the Cheap Homicide, Jack Reed: A Killer Amoungst Us, Jack Reed: One of Our Own, Shadow of A Doubt, Jack Reed: A Search for Justice, Jack Reed: Death and Vengeance, 1996, Netforce, 1999, Too Rich: The Secret Life of Doris Duke. Served with USMC, Vietnam. Won 1999 Tony Award, Best Actor, Drama, Death of a Salesman. Office: care Susan Smith & Assocs 121 N San Vicente Blvd Beverly Hills CA 90211-2303*

DENNEHY, LEISA JEANOTTA, company executive; b. Fairfield, Ohio, May 30, 1961; d. Will Robert and Rethel Jeanotta (Russell) Fights. BA in Chemistry, Miami U., Oxford, Ohio, 1982; BS in Med. Tech., Miami U., 1983; MBA, Duke U., 1991. Registered med. technologist. Med. technologist Mercy Hosp., Hamilton, Ohio, 1982-85; analytical chemist Procter & Gamble Co., Cin., 1985-87, products rsch. chemist, 1987-88; new products anlyst GlaxoWellcome, Research Triangle, N.C., 1988-90; internat. product mgr.-dermatology GlaxoWellcome, Research Triangle Park, N.C., 1990-91, mgr. new product market devel., 1991-95, sr. product mgr., 1995-96, internat. comml. strategy dir., 1996—. Co-author: Supercritical Fluid Extraction and Chromatography, 1988; contbr. articles to profl. jours. Named Women of the Day, 1979; recipient many acad. scholarships, 1980-82. Avocations: music, sports, cooking, reading, travel. Home & Office: Glaxo Wellcome Inc 5 Moore Drive Durham NC 27701-4613

DENNENY, JAMES CLINTON, JR., business consultant; b. Fayette, Mo., Nov. 10, 1924; s. James Clinton and Georgia M. (Pipes) D.; m. Betty Joyce Embrey, June 30, 1951; children: James Clinton III, John. AB in Econs., Ctrl. Meth. Coll., Fayette, 1947. With Southwestern Bell Telephone Co., 1947-89; gen. mgr. comml. dept. Southwestern Bell Telephone Co., Oklahoma City, 1966-77; v.p. customer svcs. Southwestern Bell Telephone Co., St. Louis, 1977-78, v.p. sales ops., 1978-81, v.p. bus. svcs., 1981-82, v.p. bus. sales, 1982-83, v.p. mktg., 1983-84, v.p. staff, 1984-87, v.p. Mo. ops., 1987-89; pres. Denneny & Assocs., 1989—. Trustee Oklahoma City Better Bus. Bur.; Soc. of fellows Nelson-Atkins Mus. of Art, 1987—; trustee U. Kansas City, 1987—; bd. dirs., exec. com. Econs. Devel. Corp.; pres. Kansas City Sch. Dist. Bldg. Corp.; bd. sec. treas. Kansas City Conv. and Visitors Bur.; mem. Lyric Opera of Kansas City Bus. Coun.; bd. dirs. KCPT-19 Pub. TV. With USMC, 1942-43. Mem. Greater Kansas City C. of C., Kansas City Rotary (found. pres. 1988—). Presbyterian. Fax: 816-822-8775.

DENNER, MELVIN WALTER, retired life sciences educator; b. North Washington, Iowa, Aug. 27, 1933; s. Norbert William and Petronella Nettie (Eischeid) D.; m. N. Anne Greer, June 19, 1965; children: Mark Andrew, Michael Alan (twins). BS, Upper Iowa U., 1961; MS (NSF fellow), U. Ky., 1963; PhD, Iowa State U., 1968. Asst. prof. life scis. U. So. Ind., Evansville, 1968-71, assoc. prof., 1971-76, prof., 1976-95, Disting. prof., 1989-90, pre-med. advisor, chmn. dept., 1969-95, assoc. chmn. div. scis. and math., 1975-77, acting chmn. div. scis. and math., 1976-77, chmn., 1979-87; dean Sch. of Sci. and Engring. Tech., 1994; coord. univ. self-study U. So. Ind., Evansville, 1976, 86, 96; Eucharistic minister Corpus Christi Ch., 1981—; panelist Ind. Com. Higher Edn., 1993. Contbr. articles to profl. jours.; editor USI Ret newsletter. Vice chmn. Iowa Young Dems., 1958-60; bd. dirs. Deaconess Hosp. Allied Health Programs, chmn. radiation tech. adv. com., 1987-95; bd. dirs. Evansville Mus. Arts and Scis.; mem. alumni adv. bd. U. So. Ind., 1982—; spl. minister Corpus Christi Ch., 1981—. With USN, 1953-57. Named Ind. Prof. of Yr., 1989, Sagamore of the Wabash, 1989; NSF fellow 1962, 64, NIH fellow, 1966-67, Alumni Achievement fellow, 1967-68. Fellow AAAS (film critic); mem. Internat. Soc. Invertebrate Pathology (founding), Am. Soc. Parasitologists, Am. Micros. Soc. (nat. treas.), North Ctrl. Assn. Colls. and Secondary Schs. (visitation team 1976-94), Am. Inst. Biol. Scis., Sigma Xi (pres. So. Ind. chpt.), Sigma Zeta. Home: 100 S Peerless Rd Evansville IN 47712-3043 Office: U So Ind Sch Sci & Engring Tech Evansville IN 47712 *The greatest gift we can have on earth is knowledge, for in knowledge we have truth.*

DENNERY, LINDA, newspaper publishing executive; b. Phila., July 7, 1947. Pres. Times-Picayune, New Orleans, 1997—. Office: Times-Picayune Mgmt 3800 Howard Ave New Orleans LA 70125-1429*

DENNETT, DANIEL CLEMENT, philosopher, author, educator; b. Boston, Mar. 28, 1942; s. Daniel Clement Jr. and Ruth Marjorie (Leck) D.; m. Susan Elizabeth Bell, June 8, 1962; children: Andrea Elizabeth, Peter Nathaniel. BA, Harvard U., 1963; PhD, Oxford U., 1965. Lectr. Oxford Coll. Tech., Eng., 1964-65; asst. prof. philosophy U. Calif., Irvine, 1965-70, assoc. prof. philosophy, 1970-71; assoc. prof. philosophy Tufts U., Medford, Mass., 1971-75, prof. philosophy, 1975-85, disting. arts and scis. prof., 1985—, dir. ctr. cognitive studies, 1985—; vis. prof. Harvard U., Cambridge, Mass., 1973, Pitts. U., 1975; co-dir. curricular software studio, Tufts U., Medford, 1985-89; John Locke lectr. Oxford U., 1983; Gavin David Young lectr. Adelaide U., Australia, 1985; Taft lectr. U. Cin., 1978; Luce disting. lectr. cognitive sci. U. Rochester, 1979; Herbert Spencer lectr. Oxford U., 1979; annual philosophy lectr. Princeton U., N.J., 1980; Sloan vis. scientist lectr. Yale U., New Haven, Conn., 1980; council philos. studies, summer inst. psychology, philosophy mind U. Wash., Seattle, 1981; Gramlich Meml. lectr. Dartmouth Coll., Hanover, N.H., 1985; vis. prof. Ecole Normale Superieure, Paris, 1985; disting. lectr. series, MIT Lab. Computer Sci., Cambridge, 1986. Author: Content and Consciousness, 1969, International Library of Philosophy and Scientific Method, paperback edit., 1986, Italian edit., 1992, Brainstorms: Philosophical Essays on Mind Psychology, 1978, Italian edit., 1990, Swedish edit., 1992, Elbow Room: The Varieties of Free Will Worth Wanting, 1984, German edit., 1986, Spanish edit., 1992, The Intentional Stance, 1987, French edit., 1990, Spanish edit., 1991, Consciousness Explained, 1991, Dutch, Italian, French, German edits., 1993, Darwin's Dangerous Idea, 1995, Kinds of Minds, 1996, BrainChildren, 1998; co-author: (with Douglas R. Hofstadter) The Mind's I: Fantasies and Reflections on Self and Soul, 1981, Japanese edit., 1984, Spanish and Italian edits., 1985, German and Dutch edits., 1986, Chinese, French edits., 1987; assoc. editor: Behavioral and Brain Sciences; contbr. numerous articles and reviews to profl. jours. Santayana fellow (hon.), 1974, NEH Younger Humanist fellow, 1974, Fulbright research fellow, 1978, All Souls Coll. vis. fellow, 1979, NEH sr. fellow, 1979, Ctr. Advanced Study Behavioral Scis., 1979-80, Guggenheim fellow, 1986-87. Mem. AAUP, Am. Acad. Arts and Scis., Am. Philos. Assn., Cognitive Sci. Soc., Coun. Philos. Studies, Soc. Philosophy Psychology (pres. 1980-81). Democrat. Club: Kollegewidgwok Yacht (Blue Hill, Maine). Avocations: sculpture, farming, sailing, scuba diving. Office: Tufts U Ctr for Cognitive Studies Medford MA 02155

DENNEY, LAURA FALIN, insurance company executive; b. Knoxville, Tenn., Sept. 23, 1948; d. Jack Gordon and Marilyn Frances (Ramsey) Falin; m. Richard Earl Buchannan, Feb. 14, 1970 (dec. Oct. 1972); m. Peter Michael Denney, Sept. 6, 1978. BS, East Tenn. State U., 1970. From underwriting asst. to mgr. personal lines underwriting Safeco Ins. Co., Atlanta, 1971-98, regional territory mgr., 1998—, regional territory mgr. personal lines, 1997—. Counselor St. Patrick's Episc. Ch., Dunwoody, Ga., 1983-86. Republican. Mem. Ch. of God. Avocations: golfing, reading, decorating. Office: Safeco Ins Co 1551 Juliette Dr Stone Mountain GA 30083-1519

DENNEY, LUCINDA ANN, retired relocation services executive; b. Akron, Aug. 7, 1938; d. Charles Andrew and Madora Heinretta (Frederick) Shetler; m. Jon E. Denney; children: Mary, Jon, Andrew. BA cum laude, Ohio Wesleyan U., 1960. Cons. Cleve., 1978-96; dir. corp. relocation Hackett & Arnold, Inc., Cleve., 1991-94. Mem. adv. coun. to pub. rels. com. Mus. Arts Assn.; exec. com. Cleve. Orch., jr. com. 1968-84; mem. adv. com. Rock'n Roll Hall of Fame, Cleve., 1986-94, Shaker Heights (Ohio) Citizens League, Cleve. Opera Coun., Shaker Heights Youth Ctr., 1982—, also v.p.; trustee Boy Scouts Am., 1984-97, Jr. League Cleve., 1968-95, Big Bros./Big Sisters of Greater Cleve., 1968-84, St. Luke's Hosp. Jr. Bd., 1968-84, St. Luke's Hosp. Assn., 1988—; mem. women's coun. Cleve. Mus. Art, 1997—; mem. Leadership Cleve., 1981-99, pres. 1993-94; mem. women's coun. bd. Cleve. Mus. Art. Named one of 1977 Most Interesting Persons, Cleve. Mag.; recipient Outstanding Pace Setter award Directory of Greater Cleve.'s Enterprising Women, 1985, Disting. Alumni award Cuyahoga Falls H.S., 1988. Mem. 20th Century Club, Mortar Bd., Alpha Theta Pi, Kappa Alpha Theta. Republican. Methodist. Avocations: tennis, golf, pub. speaking.

DENNIES, SANDRA LEE, city official; b. Buffalo, Dec. 26, 1951; d. Norman John and Shirley Edith (Dils) D.; m. Robert Francis Gilbane, Sept. 21, 1974 (div. Apr. 1987); children: Brandon Michael, Gianpatrick. AS in Dental Hygiene, U. Bridgeport, Conn., 1972, BS in Dental Hygiene Edn., 1973; MS in Health Scis., So. Conn. State U., 1979. Dental hygienist various orgns., New Haven, 1972-73, Leonard B. Zaslow, DDS, Westport, Conn., 1973-81; lectr. U. Bridgeport, 1973-76; planner City of Bridgeport, 1977-79, planning asst., 1979-81; grants dir. City of Stamford, Conn., 1981—; sec. Com. on Emergency Med. Disaster Planning, Bridgeport, 1978-79; dir., dep. dir. Stamford Coliseum Authority, 1982-91; dep. dir. Stamford Film Commn., 1986-88; v.p., sec. Stamford Sch. Readiness Found., Inc., 1998—. Editor, chief: Hy-Light Jour., 1973-76. Mem. Stamford Youth Planning and Adv. Bd., 1981-91, Stamford Youth Svc. Bur., 1991-95, United Way Corp., Stamford, 1986-93; pres., sec. Alcohol and Drug Abuse Coun., 1987-92; mem. bd. Christian outreach North Stamford Congl. Ch., 1988-92, 95—; mem. Coun. Chs. and Synagogues Assembly, Stamford, 1989; pres. Stamford Mcpl. Supervisory Employees Union, 1991—; v.p., sec. Stamford Sch. Readiness Found., 1998—. Democrat. Avocations: piano, clarinet, guitar, skiing. Home: 171 Shadow Ridge Rd Stamford CT 06905-1813 Office: City of Stamford PO Box 2152 888 Washington Blvd Stamford CT 06901-2902

DENNIN, JOSEPH FRANCIS, lawyer, former government official; b. N.Y.C., June 9, 1943; s. William Wilfred and Kathryn L (Sever) D.; m. Sandra Earl Peek, Dec. 28, 1968; children: Theresa Michel, Allison Kathleen, James Joseph. B.A. with great distinction, Stanford U., 1965, J.D., 1968; postgrad., U. Helsinki, Finland, 1968-69. Bar: Calif. 1969, N.Y. 1970, D.C. 1986, U.S. Supreme Ct. 1985, U.S. Ct. Appeals (fed. cir.) 1987, Ct. Internat. Trade 1987. Assoc. Simpson, Thacher & Bartlett, N.Y.C., 1969-75; counsel U.S. Senate Intelligence Com., Washington, 1975-76; staff asst. to Pres. White House, Washington, 1976-78; dir. ops. U.S. Internat. Trade Commn., Washington, 1978-79; dep. assoc. atty. gen. Dept. Justice, Washington, 1979-81; dep. asst. sec. for fin., investment and svcs. Dept. Commerce, Washington, 1981-82, dep. asst. sec. for Africa, the Near East and South Asia, 1982-84, asst. sec. for internat. econ. policy, 1984-86; ptnr. internat. dept. McKenna & Cuneo, L.L.P., Washington, 1986—; bd. dirs. U.S.-ROC (Taiwan) Bus. Coun.; mem. bd. advisors N.Am. Free Trade and Investment Report; mem. N.Am. Free Trade Agreement Article 19 Panel. Gen. editor Law and Practice of the World Trade Orgn. Fulbright grantee Inst. Internat. Edn., 1968. Mem. ABA. Home: 5108 Nahant St Bethesda MD 20816-2336 Office: McKenna & Cuneo LLP 815 Connecticut Ave NW Washington DC 20006-4004

DENNIN, ROBERT ALOYSIUS, JR., pharmaceutical research scientist; b. Newark, Mar. 5, 1951; s. Robert Aloysius Sr. and Elizabeth Jane (Cooney) D. B in Biology, Montclair State Univ., 1975, M in Biology, 1976. From asst. scientist II to sr. clin. rsch. coord. Hoffmann La Roche, Inc., Nutley, N.J., 1977-96; mgr. clin. ops. drug supply Hoffmann La Roche, Inc., Nutley, 1996—; rschr. in AIDS and cancer. Contbr. chpt. in book and articles to profl. jours. Mem. AAAS, Am. Soc. for Microbiology, N.Y. Acad. Scis. Avocations: piano, guitar. Office: Hoffmann-LaRoche Inc 340 Kingsland St Nutley NJ 07110-1199

DENNING, EILEEN BONAR, management consultant; b. Chester, Pa., June 24, 1944; d. Michael Bonar and Lucille J. Denbroeder. Postgrad., Greenwich U. Pres. Denning and Co., Castro Valley, Calif., 1975—; mem. adv. bd. Diablo Valley Coll. bus. div.; faculty adv. bd. Am. Inst. Banking. Designed and developed mgmt. tng. programs for various banks in California. Coord. Castro Valley Earthquake Preparedness, 1980—; fundraiser Castro Valley Schs., 1976—. Mem. Nat. Women's Polit. Caucus. Avocation: raising and training great pyrenees and german shepherd dogs. Home and Office: 20551 Forest Ave Apt 3 Castro Valley CA 94546-4575

DENNING, MICHAEL MARION, entrepreneur, computer company executive; b. Durant, Okla., Dec. 22, 1943; s. Samuel M. and Lula Mae (Waitman) D.; m. Suzette Karin Wallance, Aug. 10, 1968 (div. 1979); children: Lila Monique, Tanya Kerstin, Charlton Derek; m. Donna Jean Hamel, Sept. 28, 1985; children: Caitlin Shannon, Meghan O'Donnell. Student, USAF Acad., 1963; BS, U. Tex., 1966, Fairleigh Dickinson U., 1971; MS, Columbia U., 1973. Mgr. systems IBM, White Plains, N.Y., 1978-79; mgr. svc. and mktg. IBM, San Jose, Calif., 1979-81; nat. market support mgr. Memorex Corp., Santa Clara, Calif., 1979-81, v.p. mktg., 1981-82; v.p. mktg. and sales Icot Corp., Mountain View, Calif., 1982-83; exec. v.p. Phase Info. Machines Corp., Scottsdale, Ariz., 1983-84, Tricom Automotive Dealer Systems Inc., Hayward, Calif., 1985-87; pres. ADS Computer Svcs., Inc., Toronto, Ont., Can., 1985-87, Denning Investments, Inc., Palo Alto, Calif., 1987, Pers. Solutions Group, Inc., Menlo Park, Calif., 1990-96, Crystal Rsch. Corp., Scottsdale, Ariz., 1997-98; pres., CEO Landtech Environmental Inc., Scottsdale, Ariz., 1998—; adj. prof. Arizona State U. Coll. Bus., Tempe, 1997—. With USAF, 1962-66; Vietnam. Mem. Rotary, English Speaking Union, Phi Beta Kappa, Lambda Chi Alpha (pres. 1965-66). Republican. Methodist. Home: 9144 N 69th St Paradise Valley AZ 85253 Office: Crystal Rsch Corp 9144 N 69th St Paradise Valley AZ 85253-1930

DENNING, PETER JAMES, computer scientist, engineer; b. N.Y.C., Jan. 6, 1942; s. James Edwin and Catherine M. (Manton) D.; m. Dorothy Elizabeth Robling, Jan. 24, 1974; children—Anne, Diana. BEE, Manhattan Coll., 1964, ScD (hon.), 1985; MS in Elec. Engring., MIT, 1965, PhD, 1968; LL.D. (hon.), Concordia U., 1984. Asst. prof. elec. engring. Princeton U., 1968-72; assoc. prof. computer scis. Purdue U., 1972-75, prof., 1975-84, head dept., 1979-83; dir. Rsch. Inst. Advanced Computer Sci. NASA Ames Rsch. Ctr., Mountain View, Calif., 1983-90, rsch. fellow, 1990-91; assoc. dean, chair of computer sci. dept. George Mason U., 1991-97, dir. Ctr. for New Engr., 1993-98, vice provost for continuing profl. edn., 1997-98, univ. coord. for process reengring., 1998—; co-founder CSNET, 1981; bd. dirs. Charles Babbage Inst., Ctr. for Nat. Software Studies, 1996—; mem. tech. adv. bd. Sequent Computer Corp., 1985-91, Hewlett-Packard Labs., 1989-93. Author: Professional Development Seminars, 1968—, also textbooks and numerous rsch. papers; columnist Am. Scientist mag., 1985-93. Recipient Outstanding Faculty award Princeton U. Engring. Assn., 1971, Best Paper award Am. Fedn. Info. Processing Socs., 1972, Disting. Svc. to Computing Rsch. award Computing Rsch. Assn., 1989, Centennial Engring. award Manhattan Coll., 1992; NSF fellow, 1964-67. Fellow IEEE, AAAS, Assn. for Computing Machinery (pres. 1980-82, Karl Karlstrom Outstanding Educator award 1996, Outstanding Contbn. award 1998, Outstanding Computer Sci. Educator award 1999), Am. Soc. for Engring. Edn., Assn. for Computing Machinery (chmn. publs. bd. 1992-98, editor-in-chief Computing Surveys 1977-79, Comm. ACM 1983-92, Best Paper award 1968, Recognition of Svc. award 1974, Disting. Svc. award 1989), N.Y. Acad. Scis.; mem. Sigma Xi, Eta Kappa Nu, Tau Beta Pi. Office: George Mason U Computer Sci Dept 4A5 Fairfax VA 22030

DENNIS, ANTHONY JAMES, lawyer; b. Manchester, Conn., Feb. 11, 1963; s. Anthony James and Barbara Frances D. BA cum laude, Tufts U., 1985; JD, Northwestern U., Chgo., 1988. Bar: Conn. 1988, U.S. Dist. Ct. Conn. 1988, D.C. 1989. Assoc. Robinson & Cole, Hartford, Conn., 1988-89; atty. Aetna, Inc., Hartford, 1989-92, counsel, 1992—; TV and radio talk show guest. Author: The Rise of the Islamic Empire and the Threat to the West, 1996; co-author: Healthcare Antitrust: Strategies for Changing Provider Organizations, 1994; contbr. articles to profl. jours. Mem. Conn. Bar Assn. (subcom. chmn. 1990-93, exec. com. 1990—, com. chmn. 1990—, treas. 1993-94, vice-chmn. 1994-95, chmn. 1995—), D.C. Bar Assn., Nat. Health Lawyers Assn., Wadsworth Atheneum, KC (past grand knight). Home: PO Box 837 South Windsor CT 06074-0837 Office: Aetna Inc Hartford CT 06156-3124

DENNIS, DONALD DALY, retired librarian; b. Paris, Dec. 21, 1928; s. Alonzo Garcelon and Irene Eleanor (Daly) D.; m. Mary Lou Hartig, Oct. 17, 1964. BA, Bowdoin Coll., 1951, U. Calif., Berkeley, 1956; MLS, U. Calif., Berkeley, 1957; postgrad., U. Mich., 1966-67. Reference librarian Free Library of Phila., 1957-60; dept. head Drexel Inst. Library, 1960-62, adj. prof. library sci., 1963-67; head librarian Cedar Crest Coll., Allentown, Pa., 1962-66; head librarian Dearborn Campus Library, U. Mich., 1966-67, health scis. librarian, 1967-68; chief reference services div. Nat. Library of Medicine, Bethesda, Md., 1969-71; univ. librarian Am. U., Washington, 1971-88; lectr. Coll. Library and Info. Services, U. Md., College Park, 1980-83; library cons. Yarmouk U., Irbid, Jordan, 1983. Author: Simplifying Work in Small Public Libraries, 1965; Contbr. articles to profl. jours. Served to lt. USNR, 1951-55. Council on Library Resources grantee, 1963-65. Mem. ALA, D.C. Library Assn. (dir. 1973-75) library assns), , Omicron Delta Kappa. Home: 1107 Charles St Fredericksburg VA 22401-3803

DENNIS, DONNA FRANCES, sculptor, art educator; b. Springfield, Ohio, Oct. 16, 1942; d. Donald Phillips and Helen Frances (Hogue) D. BA in Art, Carleton Coll., 1964; student, Coll. Art Studies Abroad, Paris, 1964-65, Art Students League, N.Y.C., 1965-66. Instr. Skowhegan Sch. Painting and Sculpture, Maine, 1982, Sch. Visual Arts, N.Y.C., 1983-90, SUNY, Purchase, 1984-85, 87, Princeton U., N.J., 1984; assoc. prof. SUNY, Purchase, 1990-96, prof., 1996—; sculptor, art educator; b. Springfield, Ohio, Oct. 16, 1942; d. Donald Phillips and Helen Frances (Hogue) D. B.A. in Art, Carleton Coll., 1964; student Coll. Art Studies Abroad, Paris, 1964-65, Art Students League, N.Y.C., 1965-66. Instr. Skowhegan Sch. Painting and Sculpture, Maine, 1982, Sch. Visual Arts, N.Y.C., 1983-90, SUNY, Purchase, 1984-85, 87, Princeton U., N.J., 1984; assoc. prof. SUNY, Purchase, 1990-96, prof., 1996—. One-woman shows include Holly Solomon Gallery, N.Y.C., 1976, 80, 83, 98, Contemporary Arts Ctr., Cin., 1979, Neuberger Mus. of SUNY-Purchase, 1985, Univ. Gallery, U. Mass., Amherst, 1985, Bklyn. Mus., 1987, Del. Art Mus., Wilmington, 1988, Indpls. Mus. Art, 1991—, Sculpture Ctr., N.Y.C. 1993; exhibited in group shows Venice Biennale, Italy, 1982, 84, Whitney Mus., N.Y.C., 1979, 81, Tate Gallery, London, 1983, Hirshhorn Mus., Washington, 1979, 84, Biennial of Pub. Art, Neuberger Mus., 1997, Asheville (N.C.) Mus. Art, 1998; permanent commissions include decorative fence P.S. 234, N.Y.C., I.S. 5, Queens, N.Y., Wonderland Sta., MBTA, Boston, North Plaza, Klapper Hall, Queens Coll., Queens, N.Y., Am. Airlines Terminal, Kennedy Airport, N.Y.C. Recipient Art award for excellence in design N.Y.C. Art Commn., 1987, Art award Am. Acad. and Inst. of Arts and Letters, 1984, Bessie Set Design award, 1992; grantee N.Y. State Creative Artists, 1975, 81, N.Y. Found. for Arts, 1985, 92; fellow Guggenheim Found., 1979, Nat. Endowment Arts, 1977, 80, 86, 94. Democrat. One-woman shows include Holly Solomon Gallery, N.Y.C., 1976, 80, 83, 98, Contemporary Arts Ctr., Cin., 1979, Neuberger Mus. of SUNY-Purchase, 1985, Univ. Gallery, U. Mass., Amherst, 1985, Bklyn. Mus., 1987, Del. Art Mus., Wilmington, 1988, Indpls. Mus. Art, 1991—, Sculpture Ctr., N.Y.C., 1993; exhibited in group shows Venice Biennale, Italy, 1982, 84, Whitney Mus., N.Y.C., 1979, 81, Tate Gallery, London, 1983, Hirshhorn Mus., Washington, 1979, 84, Biennial of Pub. Art, Neuberger Mus., 1997, Asheville (N.C.) Mus. Art, 1998; permanent commissions include decorative fence P.S. 234, N.Y.C., I.S. 5, Queens, N.Y., Wonderland Sta., MBTA, Boston, North Plaza, Klapper Hall, Queens Coll., Queens, N.Y., Am. Airlines Terminal, Terminal One, Kennedy Airport, N.Y.C. Recipient Art award for excellence in design N.Y.C. Art Commn., 1987, Art award Am. Acad. and Inst. of Arts and Letters, 1984, Bessie Set Design award, 1992; grantee N.Y. State Creative Artists, 1975, 81, N.Y. Found. for Arts, 1985, 92; fellow Guggenheim Found., 1979, Nat. Endowment Arts, 1977, 80, 86, 94. Democrat. Home and Studio: 131 Duane St New York NY 10013-3850

DENNIS, EDWARD S(PENCER) G(ALE), JR., lawyer; b. Salisbury, Md., Jan. 24, 1945; s. Edward Spencer and Virginia (Monroe) D.; m. Lois Juliette Young, Dec. 27, 1969; 1 son, Edward Brookfield. BS, U.S. Mcht. Marine Acad., 1967; LLD, U. Pa., 1973. Bar: Pa. 1973. Law clk. Hon. A. Leon Higginbotham, Jr., U.S. Dist. Ct., Phila., 1973-75; asst. U.S. atty. U.S. Atty. Office, Phila., 1975-80, dep. chief. criminal div., 1978-80; chief narcotic and dangerous drug sect. U.S. Dept. Justice, Washington, 1980-83, asst. atty. gen. criminal div., 1988-90, acting dep. atty. gen., 1989; U.S. atty. Ea. Dist. Pa., Phila., 1983-88; ptnr., co-chair corp. investigations, criminal def. practice Morgan, Lewis & Bockius, Phila., 1990—; adj. prof. Law Sch. U. Pa., mem. bd. overseers. Fellow Am. Coll. Trial Lawyers; mem. ABA (mem. standing com. on fed. judiciary), Nat. Bar Assn., Phila. Bar Assn., Internat. Soc. Barristers. Office: Morgan Lewis & Bockius 1701 Market St Philadelphia PA 19103-2903 also: 1800 M St NW Washington DC 20036-5802

DENNIS, EVERETTE EUGENE, JR., foundation executive, journalism educator, writer; b. Seattle, Aug. 15, 1942; s. Everette Eugene and Kathryn Marie (Platt) D.; m. Emily Thompson Smith, 1988. B.S., U. Oreg., 1964; M.A., Syracuse U., 1966; Ph.D., U. Minn., 1974; postdoc., Harvard U., 1978-79. Info. officer dept. mental health State of Ill., Chgo., 1966-68; asst. prof. Kans. State U., Manhattan, 1968-72, head mental health mass communication program, 1968-72, acting head dept. journalism, 1971-72; asst. prof., assoc. prof. then prof. U. Minn., Mpls., 1972-81, dir. grad. program. Sch. Journalism and Mass Communication, 1972-81; prof., dean Sch. Journalism U. Oreg., Eugene, 1981-84; exec. dir. Freedom Forum Media Studies Ctr. Columbia U., N.Y.C., 1984-96; also v.p., 1989-94, sr. v.p., 1995-97; exec. dir. Internat. Consortiums Univs., 1996-97; pres. Am. Acad. in Berlin, 1996—; disting. prof. Grad. Sch. of Bus., Fordham U., 1997—; head Project on Future of Journalism and Mass Communication Edn.; trustee Internat. Mus. Photography at Eastman House, Rochester, N.Y., Internat. Inst. Communications, London, Ctr. Internat. Journalists. Reston, Va.; councillor Am. Antiquarian Soc., Worcester, Mass. Author: editor 35 books including: The Magic Writing Machine, 1971, Other Voices: The New Journalism in America, 1973, Justice Hugh Black and the First Amendment, 1978, Enduring Issues in Mass Communication, 1978, The Media Society, 1978, Reporting Processes and Practices, 1981, New Strategies for Public Affairs Reporting, 1983, Basic Issues in Mass Communication, 1984, Reshaping the Media, 1989, Media Freedom and Accountability, 1989, The Cost of Libel, 1989, Media Debates, 1991, 2d edit., 1996, Understanding Mass Communication, 6th edit. 1998, Media and the Environment, 1991, Beyond the Cold War, 1991, Of Media and People, 1992, Demystifying Media Technology, 1993, Higher Education in the Information Age, 1993, America's Schools and the Mass Media, 1993, Radio-The Forgotten Medium, 1995, The Culture of Crime, 1995, American Communication Research, 1996, Publishing Books, 1997, Media and Public Life, 1997, Media and Children, 1996, Media-Black and White, 1996, Media and Congress, 1997, Media and Democracy, 1998; editor-in-chief Media Studies Jour. 1987-96; contbr. articles to profl. jours. Summer fellow Stanford U., 1969, East-West Communication Inst., Hawaii, 1976; liberal arts fellow in law, Harvard U., 1978-79, vis. Nieman fellow, 1980, John F. Kennedy Sch. Govt. rsch. fellow, 1981; recipient H. Kreighbaum Under 40 award for nation's outstanding journalism educator, 1982, U. Oreg. Webfoot award, 1985. Fellow Am. Orthopsychiat. Assn.; mem. Assn. Edn. in Journalism & Mass. Comms. (pres. 1983-84), Am. Polit. Sci. Assn., Internat. Comm. Assn., Soc. Profl. Journalis ts, Internat. Mass Comm. Rsch. Soc., Internat. Inst. Comm., Coun. Fgn. Rels. Clubs: Century Assn. (N.Y.), Harvard Club (N.Y.). Office: Am Acad in Berlin Freedom Forum Studies 14 E 60th St New York NY 10022-1006 also: Fordham U. 113 W 60th St New York NY 10023-7404

DENNIS, FRANK GEORGE, JR., retired horticulture educator; b. Lyons, N.Y., Apr. 12, 1932; s. Frank George and Corinne Isabel (Smith) D.; m. Katharine Ann Merrell, June 5, 1954. BS in Agriculture, Cornell U., 1955, PhD in Pomology, 1961. Postdoctoral fellow NSF, Gif-sur-Yvette, France, 1961-62; asst. prof. Cornell U., Geneva, N.Y., 1962-68, assoc. prof., 1968—; assoc. prof. Mich. State U., East Lansing, 1968-72, prof., 1972-97. Contbr. articles to profl. jours. Fulbright fellow, Morocco, 1990. Fellow Am. Soc. for Hort. Sci. (v.p. 1985-86, Gourley award 1985); mem. Internat. Soc. Hort. Sci. (chmn. working group 1984-90, sci. editor HortSci 1997—), Sigma Xi. Office: Mich State U Dept Horticulture East Lansing MI 48824

DENNIS, GARY C., neurosurgeon, educator; b. Washington, Dec. 27, 1950; s. Creed and Yvonne (Bush) C.; m. Sharman Naomi Word Sept. 3, 1972; children: Gary Jr., Gina, Gregory. BA, Boston U.; MD, Howard U. Intern Johns Hopkins Hosp., Balt., 1976-77; residency Baylor Coll. of Medicine Affiliated Hosp., Houston, 1977-81; chief of neurosurgery Kern Med. Ctr., Bakersfield, Calif., 1981-83; clin. assoc. prof. U. Calif., San Diego, 1981-85; chief of neurosurgery Howard U., Washington, 1984—; asst. prof surgery Howard U., 1984-90, assoc. prof., 1990—; attending physician DC Gen. Hosp., Washington, 1990—; vis. lectr. neurosurgery Johns Hopkins Sch. Med., 1980-98; surg. cons. D.C. Gen . Hosp., 1986-89; mem. Mayors Commn. to oversee Med. Examiners Office, Washington, 1990, Mayors Transition Team for Health, Washington, 1990. Mem. Practicing Physicians Adv. Coun., Health Care Fin. Agy., Washington, 1991-99, Com. on Health Care Reform, Cong. Black Caucus, Washington, 1994—. Named One of Top Drs. S.E. Area, Washingtonian Mag., 1995. Fellow ACS; mem. Med. Soc. D.C. (pres. 1996-98), Nat. Med. Assn. (pres.-elect 1997—, pres. 1998-99), Am. Assn. Neurol. Surgeons (mem. chair 1994-95), Nat. Med. Assn. (bd. trustees 1992-97, 98—pres. 1998). Avocation: music, outdoor cooking, fishing. Office: Howard U Hosp 2041 Georgia Ave NW Washington DC 20060-0001

DENNIS, JACK BONNELL, computer scientist; b. Elizabeth, N.J., Oct. 13, 1931. SB, SM, MIT, 1954, ScD in Elec. Engring., 1958. Asst. prof. elec. engring. MIT, Cambridge, 1959-65; assoc. prof. MIT, 1965-69, prof. computer sci. and engring., 1969-87; prof. computer sci. and engring. emeritus, 1987—; pres. Dataflow Computer Corp., 1987—; chief scientist Acorn Networks, 1996—. Recipient Eckert-Mauchly award IEEE Assn. for Computing Machinery, 1984. Fellow IEEE, Assn. for Computing Machinery. Office: MIT Lab for Computer Sci 545 Technology Sq Cambridge MA 02139-3539

DENNIS, JAMES LEON, federal judge; b. Monroe, La., Jan. 9, 1936; s. Jenner Leon and Hope (Taylo) D.; m. Gwen Nicolich; children: Stephen James, Gregory Leon, Mark Taylo, John Timothy. B.S. in Bus. Adminstrn, La. Tech. U., Ruston, 1959; J.D., La. State U., 1962; LL.M., U. Va., 1984. Bar: La. 1962. Assoc. firm Hudson, Potts & Bernstein, Monroe, 1962-65; ptnr. Hudson, Potts & Bernstein, 1965-72; judge 4th Dist. Ct. La. for Morehouse and Ouachita Parishes, 1972-74, La. 2d Circuit Ct. Appeals, 1974-75; assoc. justice La. Supreme Ct., 1975-95; coord. La. Constnl. Revision Commn., 1970-72; del., chmn. judiciary com. La. Constnl. Conv., 1973; judge U.S. Ct. Appeals Fifth Cir., New Orleans, 1995—; Mem. La. Ho. of Reps., 1968-72; chmn. La. Commn. on Bicentennial U.S. Constn. With U.S. Army, 1955-57. Served with AUS, 1955-57. Mem. ABA (com. on appellate practice), La. Bar Assn., 4th Jud. Bar Assn. Methodist. Club: Rotary. Office: US Courthouse 600 Camp St New Orleans LA 70130-3425

DENNIS, JOHN DAVISON, minister; b. Pitts., Sept. 18, 1937; s. John Wellington and Helen Isabella (Davison) D.; m. Nancy Schumacher, Jan. 7, 1967; children: Michael, Andrew. AB, Wesleyan U., 1959; BD, Princeton Theol. Sem., 1962, ThM, 1965. Ordained to ministry United Presbyn. Ch. (USA), 1962. Asst. pastor First Presbyn. Ch., Germantown, Pa., 1962-69; sr. pastor First Presbyn. Ch., Corvallis, Oreg., 1969—; exch. min. St. Columbia's Presbyn. Ch., Johannesburg, Republic of South Africa, 1978. Chaplain Germantown Hosp., 1965-69; west coast dean Presbyn. Young Pastors Seminars, 1983-85; pres. Madison Ave. Task Force, 1975-77, pres. Corvallis Community Improvement, Inc., pres. USSR Sister City Assn., 1989-90; founder Corvallis Summer Music Festival, 1979, v.p., 1979-83; trustee, charter mem. Good Samaritan Hosp. Found., chmn., 1972-76; founder Corvallis Fish Emergency Aid Svc., 1969-76; trustee Ecumenical Ministries of Oreg., 1989—, chmn. bd. dirs. 1996-98; bd. dirs. United Way of Benton County, 1986-90; candidate U.S. Congress from Oreg. 5th dist., 1988; asst. squash coach Princeton Univ., 1959-62. Fellow Aspen Inst., 1987. Pacific coast doubles squash champions, 1972-73. Mem. Rotary (charter mem., dir. local club, Rotarian of Yr. 1998). Home: 2760 NW Skyline Dr Corvallis OR 97330-3168 Office: 114 SW 8th St Corvallis OR 97333-4546

DENNIS, KIMBERLY OHNEMUS, philanthropy consultant; b. Waltham, Mass., Aug. 3, 1957; d. Clifford Andrews and Jeanne (Kelley) Ohnemus; m. William Cullen Dennis, Aug. 20, 1991; children: D. William, Jesse Kelley. BA in Sociology, Bowdoin Coll., 1979. Child protective caseworker Maine Dept. Human Svcs., Caribou, Maine, 1979-80; adminstrv. asst. John M. Olin Found., N.Y.C., 1980-81, program officer, 1984-88; dir. of program devel. Pacific Rsch. Inst., San Francisco, 1988-89; dir. of public affairs Inst. for Humane Studies, Fairfax, Va., 1989-91; exec. dir. Philanthropy Roundtable, Indpls., 1991-96; philanthropy cons. Indpls., 1996—; exec. dir. D&D Found., Indpls., 1998—; commn. mem. Nat. Commn. on Philanthropy and Civic Renewal, Washington, 1996-97; bd. dirs. W.H. Brady Found., 1997—, Maggie Valley, N.C., Ind. Women's Forum, 1999—. Chmn. bd. Polit. Economy Rsch. Ctr., Bozeman, Mont., 1996—, mem. 1991—; adv. bd. Donner Found. New Leadershp Fellows Program, N.Y.C., 1995-97; judge Acton Inst. Samaritan Awards, Grand Rapids, 1994-97. Mem. The Phila. Soc. Republican.

DENNIS, RODNEY L., physician; b. Dec. 8, 1950. MD, U. Ala., 1981. Staff urologist Brookwood Med. Ctr., Birmingham, 1987—, chief of urology, 1998—.

DENNIS, STEVEN P., retail executive; b. Orange, N.J., Feb. 17, 1960; s. William Francis and Patricia Ann (Terhune) D.; m. Nancy Helen Pellowe, July 23, 1988; children: Elena Pellowe, Claire Pellowe. BA in Econs., Tufts U., 1982; MBA, Harvard U., 1984. Assoc. Booz Allen and Hamilton Inc, Chgo., 1984-86; mgr. strategic planning Nutra Sweet Co., Deerfield, Ill., 1986-87, dir. bus. devel., 1987-88, dir. bus. ventures group, 1988-90; mgr. bus. devel. Sears Splty. Retailing Corp., Chgo., 1991-92, contr., dir. strategic planning, 1992-93; dir. new bus. devel. Sears Mdse. Group, Hoffman Estates, Ill., 1993-94; nat. mgr. and dir. strategy and bus. devel. Sears Merchandising Group, Hoffman Estates, Ill., 1994, dir. fin. and bus. devel. HomeLife Furniture divsn., 1994-96; dir. bus. devel. Comml. Sales divsn. Sears Merchandising Group, Hoffman Estates, 1996-97, gen. mgr. appliances, 1997-98; v.p., gen. mgr. appliance divsn. Sears Comml. Sales, 1998—. Mem. Harvard Bus. Sch. Club of Chgo. (governing bd. Ravinia Music Festival Assocs.). Office: Sears Mdse Group 3333 Beverly Rd Hoffman Estates IL 60192

DENNIS, WALTER DECOSTER, suffragan bishop; b. Washington, DC, Aug. 23, 1932. BA, Va. State Coll., 1952; M.A., NYU, 1953; M.Div., Gen. Theol. Sem., 1958, D.D. (honoris causa), 1980; D.D. (honoris causa), Interdenominational Theol. Ctr.-Absalom Jones Theol. Inst., 1977; L.H.D. (hon.), Va. State U., 1983, Episcopal Sem. of S.W., 1983. Ordained deacon Protestant Episcopal Ch., 1956, ordained priest, 1958, ordained suffragan bishop, 1979. Curate St. Phillip's Ch., Bklyn., 1956; asst. min. Cathedral Ch. of St. John the Divine, N.Y.C., 1956-60, canon residentiary, 1965-79; vicar St. Cyprian's Ch., Hampton, Va., 1960-65; suffragan bishop of N.Y., 1979-99; adj. asst. prof. Am. history and constl. law Hampton Inst., 1961-65; adj. prof. Christian ethics Gen. Theol. Sem., 1975-79; lectr. U. of South Div. Sch., Sewanee, Tenn., 1974-75; mem. Nat. Task Force on Hunger, Episc. Ch., 1975-76; mem. adv. bd. Episc. Ch.'s Teaching Series: Ethics, 1975-99; convenor Black Caucus Diocese of N.Y., 1976-77; served as Diocese examining chaplain; mem. religious liberty com. Nat. Coun. Chs.; rsch. fellow Episc. Theol. Sem. of SW, 1978; N.Y. dep. Gen. Conv., 1979; mem. numerous coms. Diocese of N.Y.; adminstr. numerous programs for Cathedral Ch. of St. John the Divine; chmn. standing commn. Constn. and Canons; mem. Joint nominating com. for election of presiding bishop; mem. Standing Commn. on Structure of the Ch., 1995—; v.p. Province II, 1996—, mem. coun. of advice to presiding bishop, 1996—. Author: (booklets) Puerto Rican Neighbors, 1958, Mexican American Neighbors, 1960; contbg. author: (chpt.) On the Battle Lines, 1962; contbr. articles to profl. jours. Bd. dirs. Manhattanville Cmty. Ctr., Inc., Abortion Repeal Assn., Assn. For Study of Abortion, Inst. for Study of Human Resources, Homosexual Cmty. Counselling Ctr., Nat. Orgn. for Reform of Marijuana Laws, N.Y. Tng. Sch. for Deaconesses, Soc. Juvenile Justice and Sex Info. and Edn. Counsel of U.S., Planned Parenthood Fedn. of Am., Lenox Hill Hosp. Mem. Union Black Episcopalians, Guild of St. Ives (founder, sec.). Address: 502 Carters Grove Ct Hampton VA 23663 also: 171-B Atlantic Ave Hampton VA 23664*

DENNISON, DANIEL BASSEL, chemist; b. Gainesville, Fla., June 4, 1947; s. Raymond A. and Mary Louise (Grumbein) D.; m. Janet Gannaway. BS, Furman U., 1969, MS, 1974; PhD, Mich. State U., 1978. Rsch. scientist Coca-Cola Co., Atlanta, 1978-81; mgr. product devel. Coca-Cola USA, Atlanta, 1981-85, v.p. rsch. and quality assurance, 1985-88; dir. R & D, asst. v.p. Coca-Cola Co., Atlanta, 1988-94, v.p., dir. R&D, 1994-98, v.p., dir. sci. affairs, 1998—. 1st lt. U.S. Army, 1969-72. Mem. AAAS, Am. Chem. Soc., Inst. Food Technologists, Internat. Soc. Beverage Technologists. Office: The Coca-Cola Co One Coca-Cola Plaza NW Atlanta GA 30303

DENNISON, DAVID SHORT, JR., lawyer; b. Poland, Ohio, July 29, 1918; s. David Short and Cordelia (Whitman) D.; m. Dorothy Kelsey Houlette, May 11, 1973; children by previous marriage: Jennie, David Whitman. Student, Western Res. Acad., 1936; AB, Williams Coll., 1940; LLB, Western Res. U., 1945. Bar: Ohio 1946, D.C. 1959, Pa. 1975, Calif. 1977. Pvt. practice Warren, Ohio, 1946-70, 74-75; v.p., gen. counsel, sec. Wheeling-Pitts. Steel Corp., 1975-78; sole practice Monterey, Calif., 1978-95; mem. 85th Congress from Ohio, 1957-58; cons. (U.S. Civil Rights Commn.), 1959; mem. FTC, 1970-74. Chmn. Trumbull County (Ohio) Rep. Ctrl. and Exec. Coms., 1964-66; vice chmn. Monterey County (Calif.) Rep. Ctrl. Com., 1989; mem. Ohio Rep. Ctrl. Com., 1966-70, Trumbull County Bd. Elections, 1964-68; del. Rep. Nat. Conv., 1968; former bd. dirs. Carmel Found., Monterey Coll. Law; former trustee Western Res. Acad. With AFS, WWII. Home and Office: 200 Saint Andrews Pl NE Warren OH 44484-6731

DENNISON, GEORGE MARSHEL, academic administrator; b. Buffalo, Ill., Aug. 11, 1935; s. Earl Fredrick and Irene Gladys (McWhorter) D.; m. Jane Irene Schroeder, Dec. 26, 1954; children: Robert Gene, Rick Steven. AA, Custer County (Mont.) Jr. Coll., 1960; BA, U. Mont., 1962, MA, 1963; PhD, U. Wash., 1967. Asst. prof. U. Ark., Fayetteville, 1967-68; vis. asst. prof. U. Wash., Seattle, 1968-69; asst. prof. Colo. State U., Fort Collins, 1969-73, assoc. prof., 1973-77, assoc. dean Coll. Arts, Humanities and Social Sci., 1976-80, prof., 1977-87, acting acad. v.p., 1980-82, acting assoc. acad. v.p., 1982-86, assoc. acad. v.p., 1987; provost, v.p. acad. affairs Western Mich. U., Kalamazoo, 1987-90; pres. U. Mont., Missoula, 1990—; cons. U.S. Dept. Justice, 1976-84; bd. Community Med. Ctr, Missoula, 1st Bank, Missoula, Inst. Medicine and Humanities, Missoula. Author: The Dorr War, 1976; contbr. articles to jours. in field. Bd. dirs. Kalamazoo Ctr. for Med. Studies, 1989-90. With USN, 1953-57. ABA grantee, 1969-70; Colo. State U. grantee, 1970-75, Nat. Trust for Hist. Preservation grantee, 1976-78; U.S. Agy. for Internat. Devel. grantee, 1979—; Colo. Commn. on Higher Edn. devel. grantee, 1985. Mem. Am. Hist. Assn., Orgn. Am. Historians, Am. Assn. Higher Edn., Am. Soc. for Legal History. Avocations: handball, cross-country skiing. Office: U Montana Office of The Pres Univ Hall Rm 109 Missoula MT 59812

DENNISON, GERARD FRANCIS, economic analyst; b. Lewiston, Maine, Aug. 3, 1948; s. Alfred Alexandre Jr. and Regina Violet (Routhier) D.; m. Patricia Elaine Potter, June 24, 1989; stepchildren: Rochelle Elizabeth Fisher, Melanie Lois Potter. BS BA, Thomas Coll., 1970, MBA, 1986. Lic. stockbroker, Maine. Sr. econ. analyst Maine Dept. Labor, Lewiston, 1971—; mem. confs. in field. City councilor City of Auburn, Maine, 1994—; corporator, bd. dirs., mem. various coms. Auburn-Lewiston Boys/Girls Club; corporator Auburn Pub. Libr.; bd. dirs. Lewiston-Auburn Econ. Growth Coun., Lewiston-Auburn R.R.; mem. cmty. bldg. com. United Way; mem. Kittyhawk Indsl. Park Com.; chair Enhanced Cmty. Policing Com.; mem. adv. coun., planning com. Lewiston-Auburn Coll; mayor's rep. Auburn Sch. Com., Lewiston Auburn Edn. Coalition, dir. Auburn Exch. Club, dir. exec. com. Androscoggin Valley Coun. of Govts.; coord. Androscoggin County campaign for Gov. Angus S. King Jr., 1998. Mem. USA Forum Francophone des Affaires, Auburn Exch. Club, Auburn Bus. Devl. Corp., New Auburn Amer. Legion Post #153 Son's, Poland Spring Country Club, Prospect Hill Country Club. Democrat. Roman Catholic. Avocations: golf, reading, bowling. Home: 28 7th St Auburn ME 04210-5633 Office: Maine Dept Labor 5 Mollison Way Lewiston ME 04240

DENNISON, RAMONA POLLAN, special education educator; b. Floydada, Tex., Jan. 19, 1938; d. William C. and Anne M. (Tivis) Pollan; m. Bob Dennison, Oct. 12, 1956; 1 child, Tajquah. BS, MEd, E. Cen. U., 1972, cert. in psychometry, 1974, lic. in profl. counseling, 1975. Lic. psychometrist, profl. counselor. Tchr. Konawa (Okla.) Pub. Sch., 1972—. Mem. NEA, DAR, PEO, Okla. Edn. Assn., Okla. Assn. Children of Learning Disabilities, Konana Edn. Assn., Lic. Profl. Counselor Assn., Nat. Assn. Children Learning Disabilities, E. Cen. Alumni Assn., Tanti Study Club, Oak Hills Country Club, Delta Kappa Gamma, Phi Delta Kappa. Democrat. Baptist. Avocations: tennis, bridge, walking, cooking, gardening. Home: RR 4 Box 568 Ada OK 74820-9443

DENNISON, RICHARD LEON, entertainment company executive; b. Portland, Oreg., Aug. 13, 1939; s. Vernon L. and Georgia Pearl (Buchannan) D.; m. Kim Nga Khuu, Aug. 12, 1966; 1 child, John. Student, Portland State U., 1958-62. Seaman Merchant Marine, 1955-57; copywriter Fred Meyer Corp., Portland, 1958-60; sales rep. Am. Greetings Corp., Cleve., 1964-66; mng. dir. Muller & Phipps Ltd., N.Y.C. and Asia, 1966-75; pres. Riden Internat. Corp., Goleta, Calif., 1976—; mng. dir. All World Entertainment, Chgo., 1979—. Producer (TV documentary) JFK: Lost Pathway to Peace, 1986. Served with U.S. Army, 1960-63. Mem. AMVETS. Republican. Avocation: sports. Home: 6024 Paseo Palmilla Santa Barbara CA 93117-1717

DENNISON, RONALD WALTON, engineer; b. San Francisco, Oct. 23, 1944; s. S. Mason and Elizabeth Louise (Hatcher) D.; m. Deborah Ann Rutter, Aug. 10, 1991; children: Ronald, Frederick. BS in Physics and Math., San Jose State U., 1970, MS in Physics, 1972. Physicist, Memorex, Santa Clara, Calif., 1970-71; sr. engr. AVCO, San Jose, Calif., 1972-73; advanced devel. engr. Perkin Elmer, Palo Alto, Calif., 1973-75; staff engr. Hewlett-Packard, Santa Rosa, Calif., 1975-79; program gen. mgr. Burroughs, Westlake Village, Calif., 1979-82; dir. engring., founder EIKON, Simi Valley, Calif., 1982-85; sr. staff technologist Maxtor Corp., San Jose, 1987-90; dir. engring. Toshiba Am. Info. Systems, 1990-93, cons. engr., 1994—; materials. Author tech. publs. Served to sgt. USAF, 1963-67. Mem. IEEE, Am. Vacuum Soc., Internat. Soc. Hybrid Microelectronics, Internat. Disk Drive Equipment and Materials Assn. Republican. Methodist. Mem. Aircraft Owners and Pilots Assn., Internat. Comanche Soc. Home: 4050 Soelro Ct San Jose CA 95127-2711

DENNISON, TERRY ALAN, management consultant; b. Milw., Jan. 8, 1947; s. Willard Lawrence and Delphia Marie (Willis) D.; m. Lynn Celeste Kovacic, Mar. 30, 1974. BA, U. Wis., 1969, MBA, 1972. CPA, Ill. V.p. systems devel. Ins. Computing Corp., Madison, Wis., 1971-72; v.p., mgr. investment tech. and investment analytical services divs. Continental Ill. Nat. Bank & Trust Co., Chgo., 1972-84; v.p., mgr. data processing div. Wilshire Assocs., Santa Monica, Calif., 1984-87; prin. William M. Mercer, Inc., Deerfield, 1988—. Mem. Am. Inst. CPA's, Ill. Soc. CPA's. Office: William M Mercer Inc 1417 Lake Cook Rd Deerfield IL 60015-5223

DENNISS, JULIET DAWN, environmental specialist, geologist; b. Toledo, Aug. 5, 1962; d. Orlo Charles Hopkins and Nancy Lee (Stewart) Kinzel; m. Steven Karl Denniss, Aug. 31, 1991; 1 child, Jonathan Franklin. BA in Geology, U. Toledo, 1988. Teamleader asst., interviewer Nat. Family Opinion, Inc., Northwood, Ohio, 1984-90; geologist TolTest Inc. (also known as Environ. Cons. Inc.), Toledo, 1990-92; environ. specialist State of Ohio, Dept. of Transp., Columbus, 1992—. Avocations: historic folk tales, bridges, earthquakes, tornados, and congenital heart defects. Office: State Ohio Dept Transp Dept Transp 1980 W Broad St Columbus OH 43223-1102

DENNISTON, BRACKETT BADGER, III, lawyer; b. Oak Park, Ill., July 23, 1947; s. Brackett Badger Jr. and Frances Ann (Jones) D.; m. Kathleen Foley, Aug. 2, 1975; children: Alexandra, Brackett Badger IV, Elizabeth. AB, Kenyon Coll., 1969; JD, Harvard U., 1973. Bar: Mass. 1974, U.S. Dist. Ct. Mass. 1975, U.S. Dist. Ct. (we. dist.) Tex. 1987, U.S. Ct. Appeals (1st cir.) 1975, U.S. Ct. Appeals (D.C. cir.) 1976, U.S. Ct. Appeals (7th cir.) 1978, U.S. Ct. Appeals (10th cir.) 1981, U.S. Supreme Ct. 1981. Law clk. to judge U.S. Ct. Appeals for 9th Cir., Honolulu, 1973-74; assoc. Goodwin, Procter & Hoar, Boston, 1974-81, ptnr., 1981-82, 86-93, mem. exec. com., 1990-93; chief major frauds unit U.S. Atty.'s Office, Boston, 1982-86; chief legal counsel Gov. of Mass., Boston, 1993-96; v.p., sr. counsel litigation GE, Fairfield, Conn., 1996—. Class chmn. Kenyon Coll., Gambier, Ohio, 1979-90; mem. Duxbury (Mass.) Zoning Bd. Appeals, 1980-92, chmn., 1984-90. Recipient Dir.'s award for superior achievement U.S. Dept. Justice, 1986. Mem. Mass. Bar Assn. (chmn. coun. jud. adminstrn. sect. 1989-90, jud. adminstrv. coun. 1987-90, 95-96, criminal justice sect. 1986—, litig. sect. 1988—), Boston Found. (dir., supreme jud. ct. standing com. on substance abuse). Office: GE Co 3137 Easton Tpke Fairfield CT 06432-1008

DENNISTON, LYLE W., journalist. BA, U. Nebr., 1955; MA in History and Polit. Sci., Georgetown U., 1957. Reporter Nebr. City News-Press, 1948-51, Lincoln (Nebr.) Jour., 1951-55; Washington bur. reporter Wall St. Jour., 1957-60; editor law newsletters Prentice-Hall, Inc., Washington, 1960-63; Supreme Ct. reporter Washington Star, Washington, 1963-81; Supreme Ct. reporter, Washington bur. Balt. Sun, Washington, 1981—. Author: The Reporter and the Law: Techniques of Covering the Courts, 1980. Office: Baltimore Sun 1627 K St NW Ste 1100 Washington DC 20006-1792*

DENNISTON, MARJORIE MCGEORGE, retired elementary education educator; b. Coraopolis, Pa., Mar. 21, 1913; d. Chauncey Kirk and Elsie (George) McGeorge; m. Delbert Dicks Denniston, Dec. 25, 1942 (dec. 1973); 1 child, Robert Bruce. Student, Ohio U., 1931-33; BA, Westminster Coll., 1936; postgrad., U. Kans., 1959, Western Ill. U., 1962, 64. Elem. tchr. county schs. West Pittsburg, Pa., 1936-42, New Castle Sch. System, Pa., 1942, 51-78. Pres. Newcastle NEA, 1965-67; vol. aid Pa. Assn. Retarded Children, Jameson Hosp., Law County Home, 1984-96; trustee, elder Presbyn. Ch., New Castle, 1986-92, v.p. Ch. Women United, 1990-94. Named First Lady of New Castle, 1989, Outstanding Woman of Yr. for Community Svc. Jr. Woman's Club, 1990, Disting. Alumni Achievement Cmty. Svc. award Westminster Coll., 1990. Mem. AAUW, LWV (sec. New Castle chpt. 1986—), Coll. Club (parliamentarian), Woman's Club (parliamentarian Lawrence County fedn. 1984—, sec. 1986-88), Woman's Club of New Castle (parliamentarian 1990-99), Fedn. Jrs. (v.p. 1994-96), Pa. Assn. State Retirees (v.p. local chpt. 1994—), Cmty. Ch. Women Lawrence County (parliamentarian 1995—), Delta Kappa Gamma. Republican. Avocations: photography, coin and rock collecting, volunteering, book reviewing, traveling. Home: 331 Laurel Blvd New Castle PA 16101-2523

DENNISTON, MARTHA KENT, business owner, author; b. Phila., Feb. 8, 1920; d. Samuel Leonard and Elizabeth (Cryer) Kent; m. Edward Shippen Willing, May 14, 1942 (div. 1972); children: Peter, Matthew, Thomas, Stephen; m. George C. Denniston, July 5, 1974. BA, Bryn Mawr (Pa.) Coll., 1941; MA, U. Wash., Seattle, 1965. Clinic dir. Population Dynamics, Seattle, 1973-84; pvt. practice investor, 1950—; resort owner Ecologic Pl., Port Townsend, Wash., 1972—; sec. bd. dirs. Ctr. for Population Communications, N.Y.C., 1983-86. Author: Beyond Conception, Our Children's Children, 1971, (poems) The Bladed Quiet, 1994. Bd. dirs. Population Action Coun., Washington, 1977-80. Mem. Nat. Soc. Colonial Dames Am., Am. Farmlands Trust, Sigma Xi. Avocations: genealogy, environmental concerns. Home: 13030 12th Ave NW Seattle WA 98177-4109

DENNISTON, SCOTT F., federal agency administrator; b. Somerville, N.J.. BA in Econs., Waynesburg coll.; MS in Govt., So. Ill. U. With U.S. Customs Svc., 1974; various mgmt. positions Small Bus. Adminstrn., Washington, Seattle; breakout program mgr. Small Bus. Adminstrn.; dir. Office of Small and Disadvantaged Bus. Utilization Dept. Vets. Affairs, 1987—. Office: Dept Vets Affairs Small & Disadvantaged Bus Utilization 810 Vermont Ave NW Washington DC 20420-0001

DENNY, BREWSTER CASTBERG, retired university dean; b. Seattle, Sept. 5, 1924; s. Merle Wilson and Margaraith (Castberg) D.; m. Patricia

Virginia Sollitt, June 14, 1950; 1 child, Maria Janet. AB, U. Wash., 1945; MA in Law and Diplomacy, Tufts U., 1948, PhD, 1959. Instr. Mass. Inst. Tech., 1948-52; with Office of Sec. of Def., 1952-60; profl. staff mem. Sub-Com. on Nat. Policy Machinery, U.S. Senate, 1960-61; asso. prof. pub. affairs U. Wash., 1961-64, prof. pub. affairs, 1964—, 1st dir. Grad. Sch. Pub. Affairs, 1962-68, 1st dean, 1968-80, dean emeritus, 1980—, chmn. marine affairs bd., 1972-79, prof. Am. diplomatic history, 1991—; U.S. rep. to 23d Gen. Assembly UN, 1968; cons. RAND Corp., 1961-68; mem. vis. com. dept. govt. Harvard U., 1967-72; mem. Presdl. Adv. Coun. on Intergovtl. Pers. Policy, 1971-74; chmn. Gov.'s Task Force on Exec. Orgn., 1968-72; presdl. mem. U.S.-P.R. Commn. on Status of P.R., 1964-66; mem. bd. sci. and tech. in devel. NAS, 1976-81, co-chmn. Korean com. on sci. and tech., 1977-82; mem. Rsch. and Edn. Adv. Panel to Compt. Gen. U.S., 1979—. Author: Seeing American Policy Whole, 1985; contbr. to Am. Polit. Sci. Rev., Sci., Pub. Adminstrn. Rev.; author, co-author, editor articles, books, chpts., and reports. Trustee 20th Century Fund, 1975—, vice chmn., 1982-86, chmn., 1986-94; co-chair Children's Budget Coalition, 1991—. Mem. AAAS (com. on new directions 1975-78, charter mem. com. on sci. and pub. policy 1968-72, com. on arms control 1980-88), ASPA, UN Assn. U.S.A. (nat. policy panel on UN capabilities in the 1970s 1970-71), Nat. Acad. Pub. Adminstrn., Am. Hist. Assn., Coun. Fgn. rels., Nat. Assn. Schs. Pub. Affairs and Adminstrn. (pres. 1968-69). Home: 2021 1st Ave #F-12 Seattle WA 98121-2135

DENNY, COLLINS, III, lawyer; b. Richmond, Va., Dec. 5, 1933; s. Collins Jr. and Rebecca (Miller) D.; m. Anne Carples, June 28, 1957; children: Collins IV, William R., Katharine M. AB, Princeton U., 1956; LLB, U. Va., 1961. Bar: Va. 1961, U.S. Dist. Ct. (ea. dist.) Va. 1962, U.S. Ct. Appeals (4th cir.) 1962. U.S. Tax Ct. 1971, U.S. Ct. Claims 1976. Assoc. Denny, Valentine & Davenport, Richmond, 1961-67; ptnr. Mays & Valentine LLP, Richmond, 1967—, mng. ptnr., 1992-93; gen. counsel, corp. sec. Coastal Lumber Co., Weldon, N.C., 1980—; gen. counsel Bear Island Timberlands Co., L.L.C., Ashland, Va., 1985—, Bear Island Paper Co., L.L.C., 1985—. Contbr. chpt. to book, articles to profl. jours. Lt. USNR, 1956-66. Mem. ABA (chmn. exempt orgns. subcom., tax sect. 1971-86), Va. Bar Assn. (chmn. jr. bar 1965-66), Va. State Bar (com. chmn. 1981-83), Va. Tax Rev. (adv. bd. 1978—), Va. Forestry Assn., Richmond Feeder Cattle Assn. (pres. 1972-77), Princeton Alumni Assn. Va. (pres. 1974-78), Richmond-First Club (pres. 1969-70), Deep Run Hunt Club (pres. 1986-88), Va. Country Club. Episcopalian. Avocations: horse sports, tree farming, agriculture. Home: 1230 Millers Ln Manakin Sabot VA 23103-2720 Office: Mays & Valentine LLP 1111 E Main St PO Box 1122 Richmond VA 23218-1122

DENNY, FLOYD WOLFE, JR., pediatrician; b. Hartsville, S.C., Oct. 22, 1923; s. Floyd Wolfe and Marion Elizabeth (Porter) D.; m. Barbara H. Denny, Apr. 27, 1946; children: R. Zoe, Mark W., Timothy P. BS, Wofford Coll., 1944; MD, Vanderbilt U., 1946. Diplomate Am. Bd. Pediatrics. Intern Vanderbilt Hosp., Nashville, 1946-47; resident in pediatrics Vanderbilt Hosp., 1947-48; instr. pediatrics U. Minn., 1951-52, asst. prof., 1952-53; asst. prof. pediatrics Vanderbilt U. Sch. Medicine, 1953-55; asst. prof. preventive medicine and pediatrics Western Res. U. Sch. Medicine, 1955-60, asso. prof. preventive medicine, 1960; prof. Sch. Medicine, U. N.C., Chapel Hill, 1960—, chmn. dept. pediatrics, 1960-81, alumni disting. prof., 1974—; vis. scholar dept. epidemiology Sch. Pub. Health and Child Devel. Inst., 1977-78; vis. worker Med. Research Council Clin. Research Centre, London, 1970-71; mem. Commn. on Streptococcal and Staphylococcal Diseases Armed Forces Epidemiol. Bd., 1954-72, dep. dir., 1959-63; mem. Commn. on Acute Respiratory Diseases Armed Forces Epidemiol. Bd., 1960-73, dep. dir., 1963-67, dir., 1967-73; mem. Inst. Medicine, Nat. Acad. Scis., 1981—, Armed Forces Epidemiol. Bd., 1970-80. Mem. editorial bd.: Am. Rev. Respiratory Diseases, 1971-74; mem. publs. com.: Jour. Infectious Diseases, 1973-78; contbr. articles to med. jours. Served to maj. M.C. U.S. Army, 1948-51. Mem. Am. Acad. Pediatrics, Am. Assn. Immunologists, Am. Epidemiology Soc., Am. Fedn. Clin. Rsch., Am. Pediatric Soc. (pres. 1980-81, Howland award 1995), Am. Soc. Clin. Investigation, Am. Soc. Microbiology, Am. Thoracic Soc., Assn. Am. Physicians, Infectious Diseases Soc. Am. (pres. 1979-80), Soc. Exptl. Biology and Medicine, Soc. Pediatric Rsch. (pres. 1968-69), So. Soc. Clin. Rsch., So. Soc. Pediatric Rsch., Phi Beta Kappa, Alpha Omega Alpha. Home: 9210 Dodsons Crossroads Chapel Hill NC 27516-7681 Office: U NC Sch of Medicine Dept Pediatrics 358 Wing C CB # 7225 Chapel Hill NC 27599

DENNY, JUDITH ANN, retired lawyer; b. Lamar, Mo., Sept. 18, 1946; d. Lee Livingston and Genevieve Adelpha (Falke) D.; m. Thomas M. Lenard, May 29, 1976; children: Julia Lee, Michael William. BA, La. Tech. U., 1968; JD, George Washington U., 1972. Bar: D.C. 1973. Asst. spl. prosecutor Watergate Spl. Prosecution Force, Washington, 1973-75; pros. atty. U.S. Dept. Justice, Washington, 1975-78; dir. div. compliance U.S. Office Edn. HEW, Washington, 1978-80; acting asst. insp. gen. for investigations U.S. Dept. Edn., Washington, 1980; dep. dir. policy and compliance, office of revenue sharing U.S. Dept. Treasury, Washington, 1980-83, counselor to gen. counsel, 1983-89; insp. gen. ACTION, Washington, 1989-94; cons. Fed. Quality Inst., 1994-95. Mem. D.C. Bar Assn. Home: 2816 Arizona Ter NW Washington DC 20016-2642

DENNY, MARY CRAVER, state legislator, rancher; b. Houston, July 9, 1948; d. Kenneth and Lois (Skiles) Craver; m. Henry William Denny, Jan. 26, 1969 (div. Aug. 1990); 1 child, Bryan William. Student, U. Tex., 1966-70; BS in Elem. Edn. magna cum laude, U. North Tex., 1973. Cert. tchr., Tex. Owner, mgr. Craver Ranch, Aubrey, Tex., 1973—; mem. Tex. Ho. of Reps., Austin, 1993—. Vol. Tex. Rep. Com., 1964—; chmn. Denton County Rep. Com., Denton, Tex., 1983-91; bd. dirs. Tex. Com. for Humanities, 1990, YMCA, Denton, 1985—, Tex. Fedn. Rep. Women, 1988-92, 94-96; life mem. president's coun. U. North Tex., Denton, 1974—, chmn., 1983; del. state and nat. Rep. convs., 1972—; mem. Denton Benefit League, 1976—, Denton Arts Coun., 1986—; member numerous other civic orgns. Named Outstanding Rep. Vol., Denton County Rep. Com., 1985, One of 10 Outstanding Rep. Women, Tex. Fedn. Rep. Women, 1991, Outstanding Alumna in Edn., U. North Tex. Coll. Edn., 1993. Mem. Am. Legis. Exch. Coun., Nat. Conf. State Legislatures, Ariel Club, Delta Zeta. Episcopalian. Avocations: swimming, bridge. Address: 8684 FM 2153 Aubrey TX 76227-3010 Office: PO Box 2910 Austin TX 78768-2910 also: 1914 N Carroll Blvd Denton TX 76201-1831

DENNY, RICHARD ALDEN, JR., lawyer; b. Atlanta, Oct. 13, 1931; s. Richard Alden and Maybeth Sullivan (Graham) D.; m. Margaret Hunt, Aug. 1954; children: Margaret Denny Dozier, Richard Alden III, Dallas Hunt, Lee Denny Griffith. BA, Washington and Lee U., 1952; LLB, Emory U., 1954. Bar: Ga. 1954. Assoc. King & Spalding, Atlanta, 1954-60, ptnr., 1960-92. Chmn. bd. Met. Atlanta Crime Commn., 1972-73; bd. dirs. Woodruff Arts Ctr., 1991-97, life trustee, 1997—; bd. dirs. High Mus. of Art, Atlanta, 1971—, chmn., 1991-94; bd. dirs. Lovett Sch., Atlanta, 1969—, chmn., 1980-83. Mem. Lawyers Club Atlanta (pres. 1972-73), Atlanta Lawyers Found. (chmn. 1976-77), Washington and Lee Alumni Assn. (pres. 1980-81), Piedmont Driving Club (pres. 1982-84), Peachtree Golf Club, Omicron Delta Kappa. Episcopalian. Office: King & Spalding 191 Peachtree St NE Atlanta GA 30303-1740

DENNY, WILLIAM MURDOCH, JR., investment management executive; b. Schenectady, N.Y., June 10, 1934; s. William Murdock and Ione Elizabeth (Lundy) D.; m. Delores Gay Shillady, June 11, 1966; children: Ellen Gay, Nancy Beth, Linda Ann. ScB in Chemistry, Brown U., 1958; MBA in Fin., Drexel U., 1974. Mem. mgmt. staff chem. spltys. divsn. Pennwalt Corp., Phila., 1961-73; pres. Denny Fin. Enterprises, Paoli, Pa., 1974—; chmn. mgmt. com. Houston-Leon County Coal Co. Interests, Crockett, Tex., 1987—. Bd. dirs. United Way of North Central Chester County, 1980-83. Lt. comdr. USN, 1959-61. Mem. Fin. Analysts Fedn., Fin. Analysts Phila., Navy League U.S., corinthians Assn. (Phila. fleet capt. 1996-97), Phi Kappa Psi, Brown U. Club (pres. 1979-81, Phila.), Aronimink Golf Club (Newtown Square, Pa.), Yacht Club of Hilton Head Island (S.C.), Sea Pines Club. Office: PO Box 458 Paoli PA 19301 Home: Clover Mill Farm Chester Springs PA 19425

DENOMMÉ, ROBERT THOMAS, foreign language educator; b. Fitchburg, Mass., May 17, 1930; s. George Edward and Sara (Richards) D. BA, Assumption Coll., Worcester, Mass., 1952; MA, Boston U., 1953; Grad. Diploma, Sorbonne, U. Paris, 1959; PhD, Columbia U., 1962. Instr. in French St. Joseph's Coll., Phila., 1956-60; asst. prof. French U. Va., Charlottesville, 1962-64, U. Chgo., 1964-66; assoc. prof. French U. Va., Charlottesville, 1966-70, prof. French, 1970—, Douglas Huntly Gordon prof. French lit., 1991—, prof. and chmn. French dept., 1977-89; vis. prof. French U., Orléans, France, 1978. Author: The Naturalism of G. Geffroy, 1963, Nineteenth Century French Romantic Poets, 1969, French Parnassian Poets, 1972, Le Conte de Lisle, 1973, Alfred de Vigny, 1985. Decorated officier Ordre de Palmes Académiques (France); recipient All-Univ. Tchg. award U. Va. Bd. Visitors, 1994; Fulbright scholar, France, 1959. Mem. MLA (sec., chmn. 1971-72), Am. Assn. Tchrs. French, South Atlantic MLA (pres., past pres.), Assn. Internationale Études Françaises (Paris), Société des Amis d'Alfred de Vigny (Paris), Colonnade Club (Charlottesville), Phi Beta Kappa (hon., Beta Va. chpt.). Roman Catholic. Avocations: reading, classical music. Home: 119 Cameron Ln Charlottesville VA 22903-1707 Office: Univ Va Dept French 302 Cabell Hall Charlottesville VA 22903-3196

DENOON, DAVID BAUGH HOLDEN, economist, educator, consultant; b. Toledo, Apr. 12, 1945; s. Clarence E. and Eleanor (Kratz) D. B.A., Harvard U., 1966; M.P.A., Princeton U., 1968; Ph.D., MIT, 1975. Asst. to chmn. Pa. State Bd. Edn., 1968; program economist U.S. AID, Dept. of State, Jakarta, Indonesia, 1969-71; asst. to pres. Nat. Bur. Econ. Research, N.Y.C., 1971-72; asst. prof. politics and econs. NYU, 1975-78, 79-80, assoc. prof. politics and econs., 1982—; v.p. U.S. Export-Import Bank, Washington, 1978-79; dep. asst. sec. U.S. Dept. Def., Washington, 1981-82, cons., 1982-91; cons. U.S. Dept. State, Washington, 1992-93. Author: Devaluation Under Pressure: India, Indonesia, and Ghana, 1986, Real Reciprocity-Balancing U.S. Economic and Security Policies in the Pacific Basin, 1993, Ballistic Missile Defense in the Post-Cold War Era, 1995; editor, contbr.: The New International Economic Order: A U.S. Response, 1979, Constraints on Strategy: The Economics of Western Security, 1986, Changing Capital Markets and the Global Economy, 1988. Active Bucks County Land Use Task Force, 1975-78, Bucks Rep. Party, 1976—. Mem. Asia Soc., Am. Econ. Assn., Am. Polit. Sci. Assn., Coun. Fgn. Rels., Internat. Studies Assn., Internat. Inst. for Strategic Studies, Harvard Club (N.Y.C.), Cosmos Club (Washington). Home: 3609 Creamery Rd Wycombe PA 18980 Office: NYU 715 Broadway New York NY 10003-6860

DENSEN, PAUL MAXIMILLIAN, former health administrator, educator; b. N.Y.C., Aug. 1, 1913; s. Charles Edwin and Carrie (Weinberg) D.; m. Elizabeth A. Reed, Dec. 19, 1939; children—Rebecca E. (Mrs. John Rothfuss), Peter. A.B., Bklyn.Coll., 1934; D.Sc., Johns Hopkins U., 1939; M.A. (hon.), Harvard U., 1968. From instr. to assoc. prof. preventive medicine Vanderbilt U. Med. Sch., 1939-46; chief div. med. research statistics VA, Washington, 1946-49; assoc. prof., then prof. biometry Grad. Sch. Pub. Health, U. Pitts., 1949-54; dir. div. research and statistics Health Ins. Plan Greater N.Y., 1954-59; dep. commr. N.Y.C. Dept. Health, 1959-66; dept. adminstr. N.Y.C. Health Services Adminstrn., 1966-68; dir. Harvard Center Community Health and Med. Care, 1968-85; prof. community health Harvard Sch. Pub. Health, 1968-85, prof. emeritus, 1985—. Fellow Am. Statis. Assn., Am. Pub. Health Assn., AAAS; mem. Am. Epidemiol. Soc., Inst. Medicine. Home: PO Box 405 165 Fremont Rd Sandown NH 03873-2204

DENSEN-GERBER, JUDIANNE, psychiatrist, lawyer, educator; b. N.Y.C., Nov. 13, 1934; d. Gustave A. and Beatrice D.; m. Michael M. Baden, June 14, 1958; children: Trissa Austin Baden (dec.), Judson Michael, Lindsey Robert Baden, Sarah Densen Baden. AB cum laude, Bryn Mawr Coll., 1956; LLB, Columbia U., 1959, JD, 1969; MD, NYU, 1963. Bar: N.Y. 1961. Rotating intern French Hosp., N.Y.C., 1963-64; resident psychiatry Bellevue Hosp., N.Y.C., 1964-65, Met. Hosp., N.Y.C., 1965-67; ethics com. Park City Hosp., Bridgeport, Conn., 1988-93; mem. core staff Addiction Services Agy., N.Y.C., 1966-67; founder Odyssey House (psychiat. residence for rehab. narcotics addicts), N.Y.C., Mich., Maine, N.H., Utah, La., Australia, N.Z., 1967, from clin. dir. to pres. bd., 1967-82, exec. dir., 1967-74; courtesy physician Norwalk Hosp., N.Y.C., Mich., Maine, N.H., Utah, La., Australia, N.Z., 1974-82; pres., founder, CEO Odyssey Inst. Am., 1974-82; pres. Odyssey Inst. Australia, 1977-86, Odyssey Inst. Internat., Inc., 1978—; chair Odyssey Inst. Corp. Conn., 1974—; attending physician Gracie Sq. Hosp., N.Y.C., 1982-93, Park City Hosp., Bridgeport, Conn., 1985—, St. Vincents Hosp., Bridgeport, Conn., 1988-93; mem. ethics com. Bridgeport Hosp., attending physician, 1985—; attending physician Northwest Gen. Hosp., Detroit, 1985-86; active staff St. Vincent's Hosp., Bridgeport, 1987—; courtesy staff Norwalk Hosp., 1993—; assoc. vis. prof. law U. Utah Law Sch., 1973-75; adj. prof. law N.Y. Law Sch., 1973-76; chairperson plenary session drug abuse Am. Acad. Forensic Scis., 1972, sec. psychiatry sect., 1973, chmn. sect., 1974—; founder, 1973, since pres. Inst. Women's Wrongs; founder, since pres. Odyssey Inst. (health care for socially disadvantaged), 1974-80; bd. dirs. Simpson St. Devel. Assn., An Extraordinary Event (One to One for Mental Retardation), Bridge House; mem. Nat. Adv. Commn. Criminal Justice Standards and Goals, 1971-74, Pres.'s Commn. on White House Fellows, 1972-76; mem. drug experience adv. com. HEW, 1973-76; v.p. psychiat. sect. Internat. Forensic Medicine Conf., Budapest, 1967; pres. N.Y. Council Alcoholism, 1978—; co-chair com. on reproductive rights vs. best interest of the child Mich. State Senate, 1984-86; trustee Nat. Forensic Ctr., Princeton, N.J., 1985—, keynote speaker nat. conf., 1988, lectr., 1988; speaker Conf. for Multiple Personality Disorder, Chgo., 1985—; cons. to Mich. State Legislature to draft legislation on The Best Interests of the Child vs. the New Reproductive Techs., 1986; amicus curiae brief in Mary Beth Whitehead appeal Surrogate Mothering, 1987; sr. non-govt. psychiatrist L'Ambiance Plaza disaster, Bridgeport, 1987; guest lectr. narcotics addiction NYU Sch. Medicine, also Sch. Law.; in field dir. Daitch Shopwell, Inc.; cons. substance abuse device Insight Inc., Flint, Mich., 1987-88; guest speaker Cornell U., 1989, Internat. Hypnosis Soc. of Yale, 1989, Cumberland Law Sch., 1989, Sacred Heart U., 1994; founder, CEO, pres. The Family Maintenance Health Orgn., LLC; guest speaker Nat. Ctr. Forensic Scis. Author: (with Trissa Austin Baden) Drugs, Sex, Parents and You, 1972, We Mainline Dreams, The Odyssey House Story, 1973, Walk in My Shoes, 1976; (with David Sandberg) The Role of Child Abuse in Delinquency and Juvenile Court Decision-Making, 1984, Chronic Acting-Out Students and Child Abuse: A Handbook for Intervention, 1986, Shortened Forms: A Manual for Teachers On; (with John Dugan) Issues in Law and Psychiatry, 1988; contbr. articles to profl. jours.; editor: Jour. Corrective and Social Psychiatry, 1975; co-developer, co-inventor virocidal surface cleaner against AIDS, 1988. Mem. N.Y.C. Crime Control Commn., 1975-79, Gov.'s Task Force on Crime Control, Albany, N.Y., 1977-79, N.Y. State Crime Control Planning Bd., 1975-79; del. White House Conf. on Youth, 1971; bd. dirs. Nat. Coalition for Children's Justice, 1975—, Am. Soc. for Prevention of Cruelty to Children, 1979—, Mary E. Walker Found., 1978; psychiat. cons. Good Shepherd Home for Girls, 1989-90. Recipient Woman of Achievement award AAUW, 1970; Myrtle Wreath award Hadassah, 1970; B'nai B'rith Woman of Greatness award, 1971; Otty award for service to N.Y.C. Our Town Newspaper, 1977; named Dame of White Cross Australia, #1 Dame of Malta, Ky. Col., N.Y. State Hon. Fire Chief. Fellow Am. Coll. Legal Medicine (Congl. cert. merit 1990); mem. AMA, Conn. State Soc., Fairfield County Med. Soc., Soc. Med. Jurisprudence, Therapeutic Communities Am. (founding mem., 1st v.p. 1975—), Am. Acad. Psychiatry and Law (mem. AIDS ad hoc com 1988—), Am. Psychiat. Assn., Women's Forum N.Y. (founding mem.), Nat. Women's Forum, Internat. Women's Forum, Internat. Soc. Multiple Personality and Dissociative States, Conn. Med. Assn., Am. Orthopsychiat. Assn., ABA, N.Y. State Bar Assn., N.Y. County Women's Bar Assn., N.Y. Assn. Vol. Agys. Narcotics Addiction and Substance Abuse (dir. 1968—), Am. Psychiat. Assn., N.Y. Med. Assn., Post Traumatic Stress Syndrome Soc., Fairfield County Med. Soc. (physicians health subcom. 1986-92), Womens City Club N.Y.C. Republican. Unitarian. Office: Odyssey Inst Internat 5 Hedley Farms Rd Westport CT 06880-6335

DENSLEY, COLLEEN T., elementary education educator, curriculum facilitator; b. Provo, Utah, Apr. 12, 1950; d. Floyd and Mary Lou (Dixon) Taylor; m. Steven T. Densley, July 23, 1968; children: Steven, Tiffany, Landon, Marianne, Wendy, Logan. BS in Elem. Edn., Brigham Young U., 1986. Cert. elem. edn., Utah. Substitute tchr. Provo Sch. Dist., 1972-85; tchr. 6th grade, mainstreaming program Canyon Crest Elem. Sch., Provo, 1985-99; curriculum specialist Provo Sch. Dist., 1999—; tchr. asst., math tutor Brigham Young U., 1968-69; attendee World Gifted and Talented Conf., Salt Lake City, 1987, Tchr. Expectations and Student Achievement, 1988-89, Space Acad. for Educators, Huntsville, Ala., 1992; supr. coop. tchr. for practicum tchrs., 1987-90; co-chmn. accelerated learning and devel. com.; trainee for working with handicapped students in mainstreamed classroom, 1989; mem. elem. sch. lang. arts curriculum devel. com., 1990; mem. task force Thinking Strategies Curriculum, 1990-91; extensions specialist gifted and talented, 1990-91, math, 1991—; master tchr. Nat. Teacher Tng. Inst., 1993. Co-author (curricula) Provo Sch. Dist.'s Microorganism Sci. Kit, 1988, Arthropod Sci. Kit, 1988, Teaching for Thinking, 1990—. Recipient Honor Young Mother of Yr. award State of Utah, 1981; named Utah state Tchr. of Yr., 1992. Mem. NEA, Nat. Coun. Tchrs. Math., Utah Edn. Assn. Utah Coun. Tchrs. of Math, Internat. Space Edn. Initiative (adv. bd.), Provo Edn. Assn. (Tchr. of Yr. 1991-92). Republican. Mem. LDS Ch. Office: Provost Sch Dist 280 W 940 North Provo UT 84604-5429

DENSMORE, ANN, speech pathologist, audiologist, writer; b. L.A., Nov. 24, 1941; d. Ray B. and Margaret M. (Walsh) D.; children: Kristin Ann, Jennifer Ann. BS cum laude, UCLA, 1963; MA in Communicative Disorders, Calif. State U., 1975; student Cape Cod Conservatory of Arts, 1977-79, Harvard U. graphics-architecture program, 1980—; EdM in Human Devel. and Psychology, Harvard U., 1991; EdD, Clark U., Worcester, Mass., 1997. Office: 1628 Massachusetts Ave Lexington MA 02420-3802

DENSON, ALEXANDER BUNN, federal magistrate judge; b. Rocky Mount, N.C., Nov. 11, 1936; s. Samuel Leland and Elizabeth Pearl (Bunn) D.; children: Rebecca Anne Denson, Matthew Robert. BS, N.C. State U., 1959; LLB, Duke U., 1966. Bar: N.C. 1966. Assoc. Yarborough, Blanchard & Tucker, Raleigh, 1966-68; ptnr. Blanchard, Tucker, Twiggs & Denson, Raleigh, 1968-81; U.S. magistrate judge U.S. Dist. Ct. (ea. dist.), Raleigh, 1981—; OSHA adminstrv. law judge cons. N.C. Dept. Labor, Raleigh, 1978-81. Pres. Sir Walter Lions Club, 1982-83, Symphony Soc., Wake County chpt., 1975-76; founder Raleigh-Wake County Coalition for Homeless, 1987—; deacon Pullen Meml. Bapt. Ch., 1989-91; founding mem. Am. Shroud of Turin Assn., 1990-92; dir. Community Alternative Support Abodes for Mentally Ill Homeless, 1992—, chair 1996-98; elder Westminster Presbyn. Ch., 1998—. Lt. USNR, 1959-63. Recipient Outstanding Contbns. to Human Rels. and Human Svc. recognition, Gov., Raleigh Mayor, City Council, 1989. Mem. Wake County Duke Bar Assn. (past pres.). Republican. Avocations: gardening, chess. Office: US Dist Ct Po Box 25610 310 New Bern Ave Raleigh NC 27611-5610

DENSON, WILLIAM FRANK, III, lawyer; b. Birmingham, Ala., Aug. 1, 1943; s. William Frank Jr. and Martha Jane (Wilson) D.; m. Deborah Lynn Davis, July 6, 1974; 1 child, Patricia Lynn Pyle. BA, U. Montevallo, 1965; JD, Emory U., 1968. Bar: Ala. 1968. Atty. Spain, Gillon, Riley, Tate & Ansley, Birmingham, 1969-73; atty., asst. sec., sec. Vulcan Materials Co., Birmingham, 1973-88, sec., asst. gen. counsel, 1988-92, v.p., sec., asst. gen. counsel, 1992-94, v.p. law, sec., 1994-98, sr. v.p. law, sec., 1998—. Trustee U. Montevallo, 1987—; bd. dirs. Glenwood Mental Health Svcs., 1990-96. Mem. ABA, Ala. State Bar, Country Club of Birmingham, Willow Point Country Club (Alexander City, Ala.), Kiwanis Club Birmingham. Republican. Episcopalian. Avocations: golf, reading, travel. Home: 3215 E Briarcliff Rd Birmingham AL 35223-1304 Office: Vulcan Materials Co 1200 Urban Center Dr Birmingham AL 35242-2545

DENT, BUCKY (RUSSELL EARL DENT), professional baseball coach, former player; b. Savannah, Ga., Nov. 25, 1951; m. Stormy Dent (div.); children: Scott, Stacy; m. Marianne Dent. Player Chgo. White Sox, 1973-76; player N.Y. Yankees, 1977-82, mgr., 1989-90; player Tex. Rangers, 1982-83, Kansas City Royals, 1984; baseball coach Texas Rangers, Arlington, 1994-; tchr. Bucky Dent's Baseball Sch., Delray, Fla., 1990-. Office: care NY Yankees Yankee Stadium Bronx NY 10451*

DENT, CATHERINE GALE, secondary education educator; b. Salem, Mo., Apr. 20, 1953; d. James Ferguson and Virgina Gale (Martin) Dent; 1 son from previous marriage, M. Cole Schafer; m. Hobart E. Porter, Dec. 29, 1997. Student, U. Mo., 1971-74, 91—, Longview Commun. Coll., Lee's Summit, Mo., 1975, S.W. Bapt. U., Bolivar, Mo., 1985; MS in Ednl. Counseling, Columbia State U., 1997, PhD in Ednl. Adminstrn., 1997. Lic. funeral dir.; cert. secondary tchr., Mo. Feature writer, reporter Dent County Headliner, 1972-74; acctg. clk. Assn. of Unity Chs., Unity Village, Mo., 1974-77; graphic artist The Salem News, 1979; adminstrv. asst. Ozark Lead Co.-Kennecott Corp., Sweetwater, Mo., 1979-82; ch. organist United Meth. Ch., Salem, 1977-97; music tchr. Salem, 1983—; substitute tchr. Salem R-80 Sch. Dist., 1991—; owner Dent LLC. Bd. dirs. Salem Arts Coun., 1984—; mgr. Salem Community Jazz Band, 1985—; accompanist Salem Community Choir, 1984—, Salem R-80 Sch. Sys. Music Dept., 1990—; dir. Temple Carillons Handbell Choir, Salem, 1985-94; sec. Vocat. Edn. Adv. Com., 1996-99. Recipient Children's award Cosmopolitan Club; named to Outstanding Young Women in Am., 1985. Mem. Salem Computer Club, Dent County Hist. Soc., Order Ea. Star, Salem Rebekah Lodge, Fraternal Order of Eagles Ladies Aux., Internat. Order Rainbow for Girls (Grand Cross of Color 1968, supreme dep. 1998), Sorosis Club (pres. 1992-93), Cosmopolitan Club (sec. 1994-98, pres. 1998—). Democrat. Methodist. Avocations: playing piano, travel. Home: 1200 W Center St Salem MO 65560-2736

DENT, EDWARD EUGENE, manufacturing company specialist; b. Charleston, W.Va., Oct. 14, 1948; s. Eugene Franklin and Delcie Marie (Harper) D.; m. Karen Sue Smith, Nov. 21, 1968; children: Jason Edward, Joseph Andrew. BA, W.Va. Inst. Tech., 1973; MA, Va. State U., 1988; postgrad., Ind. U., 1998—. Cert. tchr., W.Va., Va. Fin. mgr. Ray Broyhill Ford, Hopewell, Va., 1973-75; bus. mgr. sales Strosnider Chevrolet, Inc., Hopewell, 1975-78; adminstr. crafts Brown & Root Constrn./Engrs., Richmond, Va., 1978-80; process spinning operator Kevlar spinning ops. E.I. duPont de Nemours & Co., Richmond, 1981—; chem. process operator Tyvek Union rep. Author: Race Relations in Hopewell, Va. 1635-1932, 1988, Betrayal: Employee Relations at DuPont, 1981-1994, 1995. Active So. Hist. Assn., Va. Hist. Soc., Chesterfield County Hist. Soc. Sgt. U.S. Army, 1967-69, Vietnam. Decorated Combat Inf. badge, Army Commendation medal with oak leaf cluster. Mem. Soc. First Inf. Divsn. (Big Red One), Am. Legion, Va. state U. Alumni (pub. rels. officer Chesterfield chpt. 1989-91), Phi Alpha Theta (alumni, treas. W.Va. Inst. Tech. chpt. 1972-73), Alpha Chi. Baptist. Avocations: reading, travel, teaching, fishing, writing. Home: 1105 Walnut Dr Chester VA 23836-6137 Office: E I duPont de Nemours & Co Richmond VA 23261

DENT, FREDERICK BAILY, mill executive, former ambassador, former secretary of commerce; b. Cape May, N.J., Aug. 17, 1922; s. Magruder and Edith (Baily) D.; m. Mildred C. Harrison, Mar. 11, 1944 (dec.); children: Frederick Baily, Mildred Hutcheson, Pauline Harrison, Diana Gwynn, Magruder Harrison. BA, Yale U., 1944. With Joshua L. Baily & Co., Inc., N.Y.C., 1946-47; with Mayfair Mills, Arcadia, S.C., 1947—, pres., 1958-88, treas., 1977—; chmn. Mayfair Mills, 1988—; also bd. dirs. Mayfair Mills, Arcadia, S.C.; sec. Dept. Commerce, Washington, 1973-75; amb., spl. rep. for trade negotiations, 1975-77; bd. dirs. Joshua L. Baily & Co. Chmn. Spartanburg County Planning and Devel. Commn., 1960-72; trustee Bus. Coun., Spartanburg Day Sch., Brevard Music Ctr.; past mem. corp. Yale U. Lt. USNR, 1943-46, PTO. Laureate, S.C. Bus. Hall of Fame. Mem. Spartanburg Area C. of C. (chmn. 1991). Episcopalian. Home: 221 Montgomery Dr Spartanburg SC 29302-3443 Office: Mayfair Mills Inc Arcadia SC 29320

DENT, LEANNA GAIL, secondary education educator; b. Manhattan, Kans., Oct. 21, 1949; d. William Charles and Maxine Madeline (Kackley) Payne; children: Laura Michelle, Jeffery Aaron; m. Robert Chester Koerner, Mar. 21, 1997. BS in Edn., U. Houston, 1973; postgrad., U. Tex., 1975-76; MS in Edn., Okla. State U., 1988. Cert. elementary and secondary art tchr., Okla., Tex. Tchr. art Popham Elem. Sch., Del Valle, Tex., 1973-77; graphic artist Conoco, Inc., Ponca City, Okla., 1987-88; tchr. art Garfield Elem. Sch., Ponca City, Okla., 1988-91, Reed Elem. Sch., Houston, 1991-92, Copeland Elem. Sch., Houston, 1992-94, Campbell Jr. High Sch., Houston, 1994—; cons. and specialist in field. Author: Using Synectics to Enhance the Evaluation of Works of Art, 1988. Vol. 1st Luth. Day Sch., Ponca City, 1977-91, Ponca City Inds. Sch. Dist., 1987-91; work com. Cy-Fair Ind. Sch. Dist., Houston, 1991-94. Acad. and Mem. scholar Okla. State U., 1986-88; named Spotlight Tchr. Yr., 1992-93. Mem. Nat. Art Edn., Tex. Art Edn. Assn. (judges commendation 1993), Assn. Tex. Profl. Educators, Houston Art Edn. Assn. (v.p. 1992-93, pres.-elect 1993-95, pres. 1995-97, past pres.

1997—), Phi Delta Kappa, Phi Kappa Phi. Republican. Lutheran. Avocations: riding horses, camping, art, museums, black and white movies. Office: Campbell Jr High Sch 11415 Bobcat Rd Houston TX 77064-3097

DENT, THOMAS G., lawyer; b. Chgo., May 2, 1942. Student, U. Ill., De Paul U.; LLB, De Paul U., 1970. Bar: Ill. 1970. Mem. Seyfarth, Shaw, Fairweather & Geraldson, Chgo. Office: Seyfarth Shaw Fairweather & Geraldson Mid Continental Plz 55 E Monroe St Ste 4200 Chicago IL 60603-5863*

DENTINGER, RONALD LEE, comedian, speaker, freelance writer; b. Milw., Feb. 14, 1941; s. William Cassel and Kathryn Faye (Ritzman) D.; m. Kaylee Ann Kasten, Aug. 28, 1965; children: Ronald Lee Jr., Joann Jean. Officer Milw. Police Dept., 1962-67; dist. mgr. Am. Automobile Assn., Madison, Wis., 1967-71; gen. mgr. Don Q Inn, Dodgeville, Wis., 1971-85; comedian, spkr. Dodgeville, 1976—. Humorist quoted in comedy mags., books; jokes sold to Rodney Dangerfield Joan Rivers, The Tonight Show, Saturday Night Live, 20/20 Show, Time Mag.; author: (with others) The Art of Communication, The Great Communicators II, (joke books) Down Time, How to Argue with Your Spouse. Pres. Hidden Valley Tourism Region, Wis., 1984. Named Funniest Person in Wis., Showtime-TV Network, 1985. Mem. Nat. Spkrs. Assn., Wis. Profl. Spkrs. Assn., Wis. Soc. Assn. Execs., Dodgeville C. of C. (pres. 1984). Home and Office: PO Box 151 Dodgeville WI 53533-0151

DENTLER, ROBERT ARNOLD, sociologist, educator; b. Chgo., Nov. 26, 1928; s. Arnold E. and Jennie (Munsen) D.; m. Helen Hosmer, Sept. 7, 1950; children: Deborah, Eric, Robin. B.S., Northwestern U., 1949, M.A., 1950; M.A., Am. U., 1954; Ph.D., U. Chgo., 1960. Reporter Chgo. City News Bur., 1949; tchr. Pomfret Sch., 1950-52; intelligence officer U.S. Govt., 1952-54; instr. Dickinson Coll., 1954-57; fellow U. Chgo., 1957-59; rschr. U. Kans., 1959-61; asst. prof. Dartmouth Coll., 1961-62; mem. faculty Tchrs. Coll., Columbia U., N.Y.C., 1962-72, prof. sociology, dep. dir. to dir. Ctr. for Urban Edn., 1966-72; dean Sch. Edn., Boston U., 1972-79; sr. sociologist Abt Assocs., Cambridge, Mass., 1979-83; prof. sociology U. Mass., Boston, 1983-92; sr. fellow McCormack Inst. Pub. Affairs, 1993-94; faculty assoc. Trotter Inst., 1994—; dir. Inst. for Learning and Teaching U. Mass., Boston, 1987, acting dean Coll. Edn., 1988. Author: (with Peter Rossi) The Politics of Urban Renewal, 1961, (with Nelson W. Polsby and Paul A. Smith) Politics and Social Life, 1963, (with Phillips Cutright) Hostage America, 1963, (with B. Mackler and M.E. Warshauer) The Urban R's: Race Relations as the Problem in Urban Education, 1967, Major American Social Problems, 1967, (with M.E. Warshauer) Big City Dropouts and Illiterates, 1967, American Community Problems, 1967, Major Social Problems, 1973, Urban Problems, 1977, (with M.B. Scott) Schools on Trial: An Inside Account of the Boston School Desegregation Case, 1981, (with D.C. Baltzell and D.J. Sullivan) University on Trial, 1983, (with A.L. Hafner) Hosting Newcomers, 1997; editor Sociol. Practice Rev., 1989-92. Home: 11 Childs Rd Lexington MA 02421-4517 Office: U Mass Dept Sociology Boston MA 02125-3393

DENTON, CHARLES MANDAVILLE, corporate consultant; b. Glendale, Calif., June 22, 1924; s. Horace Bruce and Marguerite (Mandaville) D.; m. Jean Margaret Brady, Dec. 3, 1955; children—Charles Mandaville II, Margot Elizabeth. Student, U. Calif., 1942, Okla. A. and M. Coll., 1943; B.A. in Journalism, U. So. Calif., 1949. Reporter San Fernando Valley Times, N. Hollywood, Calif., 1949-50, U.P., Los Angeles, 1950-52; reporter, sportswriter, columnist I.N.S., Los Angeles, 1952-59; reporter, feature writer, TV editor-columnist Los Angeles Examiner, 1959-62; free-lance TV and mag. writer, 1962-63; reporter Los Angeles Times, 1963; columnist San Francisco Examiner, 1963-68; communications dir. Leslie Salt Co., San Francisco, 1968-73; comm. dir. Crown Zellerbach Corp., San Francisco, 1973-83; v.p. Hilland Knowlton Inc., 1983-90. Author: (with Dr. W. Coda Martin) A Matter of Life, 1964. Pres. Greater Los Angeles Press Club Welfare Found., 1961. Served with USNR, 1943-46. Mem. Phi Beta Kappa, Phi Kappa Phi, Sigma Delta Chi, Blue Key. Clubs: Greater Los Angeles Press (pres. 1955-57), Tiburon Peninsula, Bohemian. Home and Office: 40 Seafirth Rd Belvedere Tiburon CA 94920-1125

DENTON, D. KEITH, management educator; b. Paducah, Ky., June 28, 1948; s. Derward and Bonnie Denton; 1 child, Shane. BS, Murray State U., 1971; M in Pub. Adminstrn., Memphis State U., 1974; PhD, So. Ill. U., 1981. Supr. Shelby Pre-Casting, Memphis, 1971-72; safety engr. Md. Casualty Corp., Memphis, 1972-76; instr. Draughn's Bus. Coll., Paducah, 1977; safety trainer Union Carbide Corp., Paducah, 1977-78; prof. So. Ill. U., Carbondale, 1978-83, S.W. Mo. State U., Springfield, 1983—; cons. Small Bus. Research Ctr., Springfield, 1985—, Springfield Remfg. Corp., 1986. Author: Safety Management, 1982, (with others) Safety Performance, 1985, Quality Service in America, 1989, The Production Game, 1990, Handling Employee Complaints, 1990, Horizontal Management, 1991, The Service Trainer, 1992, Recruitment Retention and Employee Relations, 1992, Did You Know?, Fascinating Facts and Fallacies, 1994, Enviro-Management: How Companies Turn Pollution Cost into Profits, 1994, The Toolbox for the Mind, 1999; contbr. over 120 articles to profl. jours. Mem. Acad. Mgmt., Nat. Assn. Purchasing, Am. Soc. Prodn. and Inventory Control, Inst. Indsl. Engrs. Office: SW Mo State U 901 S National Ave Springfield MO 65804-0088

DENTON, DAVID EDWARD, retired education educator; b. Crossville, Tenn., Feb. 4, 1935; s. David Pyle and Orbie Loraine (McLarty) D.; 1 dau., Mitzi Ann Mathenia. B.S. in English and Philosophy, U. Tenn., 1958, M.S. in Psychology, 1959, Ed.D. in Philosophy of Edn., 1963; studies for Episcopal priesthood, 1974-77; DSc (hon.), Isle of Man, 1993; PhD in Ancient Religions, N.Mex. Theol. Sem., 1997. Asst., then assoc. prof. psychology and philosophy Austin Peay State U., Tenn., 1962-66; prof. dept. social and philos. studies in edn. U. Ky., Lexington, 1966-86; chmn dept. U. Ky., 1979-83, prof. dept. policy studies and evaluation, 1986-93; ret., 1993; vis. prof. U. Tenn., 1964, W.Va. U., 1966, Ind. U., 1965; lectr. in field; bd. advs. N.Mex. Theol. Sem., 1998—. Author: Albert Camus and the Moral Dimensions of Education, 1964, The Philosophy of Albert Camus, 1967, The Language of Ordinary Experience, 1970, Existential Reflections on Teaching, 1972, Existentialism and Phenomenology in Education, 1974, What Is Educational Research, 1979, (novel) The Hallelujah Psychosis, 1986, Gaia's Drum: Ancient Voices and Our Children's Future, 1991; contbr. articles to profl. jours. Fellow Philosophy of Edn. Soc. (sec.-treas. 1982-84); mem. Ohio Valley Philosophy of Edn. Soc. (pres. 1970-71), Am. Edn. Research Assn., Soc. Phenomenology and Existential Philosophy, World Future Soc. Episcopalian.

DENTON, DAVID THOMAS, small business owner; b. Union, S.C., Nov. 22, 1949; s. William Richard and Margaret Louise (Mitchell) D.; m. Regina Yvone Canupp, Aug. 18, 1971; 1 child, David Thomas II. BA, U. S.C., 1990. Mgr. Denton Gas Co., Lockhart, S.C., 1967-93; owner Lockhart Car Wash, 1985—; v.p. Denton Gas Co., Inc., Lockhart, 1993-96; pres.% Denton Gas Co., Inc., 1996—. Lt. col. S.C. Army N.G., 1970—. Mem. Nat. Propane Gas Assn., Internat. Car Wash Assn., U.S. Army Armor Assn., Am. Legion (comdr. 1976), Shriners, Masons (sec. 1976). Presbyterian. Avocations: fishing, hunting, hiking. Home: 756 Mount Tabor Church Rd Union SC 29379-9599 Office: Denton Gas Co Inc 4636 Jonesville Lockhart Hwy Union SC 29379-7505

DENTON, DEREK ASHWORTH, medical researcher, foundation administrator; b. Launceston, Tasmania, Australia, May 27, 1924; s. Arthur A. and Catherine (Edwards) D.; m. Margaret Catherine Dame Scott, Mar. 13, 1953; children: Matthew, Angus. MBBS, Melbourne U., 1947. Haley Rsch. Fellow Walter and Eliza Hall Inst., Melbourne, 1948; med. rsch. fellow, sr. med. rsch. fellow Nat. Health and Med. Rsch. Coun., Melbourne, 1948—, prin. med. rsch. fellow, 1970; founding dir. Howard Florey Inst. Exptl. Physiology and Medicine, Melbourne, 1971-89, emeritus dir., 1990—; pres. Howard Florey Biomed. Found., Melbourne, 1997—; bd. dirs. David Syme Ltd. Pubs. "The Age", 1984-93; 1st v.p. Internat. Union of Physiol. Scis., 1983-89 (chmn. nominating com. and com. on commns. 1986-93), mem. jury Albert and Mary Lasker Found. awards in med. sci., 1979-90; fgn. assoc. NAS of U.S., 1995; adj. scientist Southwest Found. Biomed. Rsch., San Antonio, 1994—. Author: The Hunger for Salt, 1982, The Pinnacle of Life: Consciousness in Animals and Humans; editor: Olfaction and Taste, 1985. Fellow Royal Soc. (London), Royal Coll. Physicians (hon., London and Australia), Am. Physiol. Soc. (hon.), AAAS (hon., fgn.); mem. Royal Swedish Acad. Scis. (fgn. med. mem.), NAS (fgn. assoc.). Avocations: wine, tennis, fly fishing. Home: 816 Orrong Rd Toorak, 3142 Melbourne Australia Office: U Melbourne, Howard Florey Inst Exptl Physiology Medi, Parkville 3052, Australia

DENTON, FRANK M., newspaper editor; b. Tulsa, Mar. 30, 1945; s. Frank McCray and Eydith (Langley) D.; m. April Murphy, June 18, 1983; children: Langley Sara, Allegra Murphy. BA, U. Tex., 1968; MS, Columbia U., 1970; MBA, U. Wis., 1994, PhD, 1996. Sportswriter Austin Am. Statesman, 1964-66; reporter Stuart Long News Svc., Austin, Tex., 1966-69, Anniston (Ala.) Star, 1970-72, Cin. Enquirer, 1972-75; asst. lifestyle editor Detroit Free Press, 1976-78, lifestyle editor, 1978-81, asst. mng. editor, 1981-86; editor Wis. State Journal, Madison, 1986—; bd. dirs. Ind. Newspapers Inc., Mid-Am. Press Inst. Mem. Am. Soc. Newspaper Editors (bd. dirs.), Phi Kappa Phi. Home: 3005 Grandview Blvd Madison WI 53713-3435 Office: Wis State Journal 1901 Fish Hatchery Rd Madison WI 53713-1297

DENTON, JOAN CAMERON, reading consultant, former educator; b. Chgo.; d. Wallace William and Ruth Elizabeth (Nothof) Cameron; m. Robert Eastman Denton, Aug. 16, 1958; children: Marianne, Lynn, Robert. BS in Edn., Northwestern U., Evanston, Ill., 1954; MS in Spl. Edn. and Reading, U. Nebr., Omaha, 1982. Tchr. English and social studies Berwyn (Ill.) Pub. Schs.; tchr. devel. and advanced secondary reading Omaha Pub. Schs., reading diagnostician; lead tchr. Reading Svcs.; reading cons. Scholastic, Inc.; mem. external visitation team/reading Boys Town Schs., mem. external visitation team, Omaha Pub. Schs.; supr. summer literacy ctr., instr. U. Nebr., Omaha; mem. instrl. dist. coms.; former mem. rev. bd. Reading Tchr.; co-chair Metro Reading Coun. Lit. Project Listening Libr.; mem. reading leadership team Omaha Pub. Schs.; coord. OPS/AT&T Reading Pioneers Assisting Literacy in Schs. Program. Co-author computer-based reading comprehension course for Ind. Study H.S., U. Nebr. Coll. Continuing Edn. Chmn. Operation Sch. Bell, Assistance League Omaha. Recipient Disting. Alumni award U. Nebr. Coll. Edn., Omaha, 1998. Mem. AAUW, NEA, Nebr. Edn. Assn., Omaha Edn. Assn., Internat. Reading Assn., Nebr. Reading Assn., Met. Reading Coun., Phi Delta Kappa, Alpha Xi Delta.

DENTON, LAWRENCE MONETTE, consultant meteorologist, historian; b. Balt., Feb. 28, 1943; s. Paul Monette and Evelyn (Bayne) D.; m. Susan Thomas, Jan. 6, 1978. BA, Western Md. Coll., Westminster, 1965; MEd with honors, Johns Hopkins U., Balt., 1971. Dir. acad. svcs. Johns Hopkins U., Balt., 1968-78; spl. asst. to assoc. adminstr. NOAA, Dept. Commerce, Washington, 1978-81; pres. Denton & Assocs., Queenstown, Md., 1981—. Author: A Southern Star for Maryland, 1995. Mem. Am. Meteorol. Soc. Office: Denton & Assocs PO Box 468 Queenstown MD 21658-0468

DENTON, RAY DOUGLAS, insurance company executive; b. Lake City, Ark., May 16, 1937; s. Ray Dudney and Edna Lorraine (Roe) D.; BA, U. Mich., 1964, postgrad., 1969-70; JD, Wayne State U., 1969, postgrad., 1964-65; m. Cheryl Emma Borchardt, Mar. 9, 1964; children: Ray D., Derek St. Clair, Carter Lee (dec.). Claims rep. Hartford Ins. Co., Crum & Forster, Detroit, and Am. Claims, Chgo., 1962-73; partner Chgo. Metro Claims, Oak Park, Ill., 1974-75; founder, pres. Ray D. Denton & Assocs., Inc., Hinsdale, Ill., 1975—. Mem. Pi Kappa Alpha, Phi Alpha Delta. Office: 930 N York Rd Ste 14 Hinsdale IL 60521-2993

D'ENTREMONT, EDWARD JOSEPH, infosystems engineer, educator; b. Lynn Mass., June 25, 1954; s. Joseph Albenie and Gertrude Grace (Flattery) D'E. BA in Math., Salem State Coll., 1972-76; MS in Applied Math., Northeastern U., 1982. Floor supr. Jordan Marsh Co., Peabody, Mass., 1972-76; sci. programmer Electronics Corp. Am., Cambridge, Mass., 1977, Sulivan and Cogliano, Waltham, Mass., 1977; software engr. Raytheon Svc. Co., Burlington, Mass., 1977-86, Raytheon Missile Systems divsn., Bedford, Mass., 1986-96; software engr. Desktop Data Inc., Burlington, Mass., 1995-98, Newsedge Corp., 1998—; part-time instr. Fitchburg State at Raytheon Inst., Tewksburg, Mass, 1986-96, U. Lowell, Mass., 1991—; sr. software engr. Raytheon Co.; part-time instr. continuing edn. Salem State Coll., 1993-95. Editor-in-chief Salem State Coll. Yearbook, 1975, 76. Campaign worker presdl. campaigns, 1968-72, City Coun. and State Rep., Lynn, 1976, Dukakis for Gov., Lynn, 1982; vol. Aborn Elem. Sch. Tech. com. Mem. Am. Math. Soc., Math. Assn. Am., Soc. Indsl. and Applied Math., IEEE, IEEE Computer Soc., N.Y. Acad. Scis., Assn. Computing Machinery, St. Mary's High Sch. Alumni Assn., Salem State Alumni Assn., Northeastern Alumni Assn., Lexington Racquet and Swim Club. Democrat. Roman Catholic. Home: 50 York Rd Lynn MA 01904-1130

DENTZER, SUSAN, journalist; b. Phila., 1955. BA in English Lit., Dartmouth Coll., 1977; Nieman fellow, Harvard U., 1986-87. Reporter Southampton (N.Y.) Press/Hampton Chronicle-News, 1977-78; sr. writer Newsweek, N.Y.C., 1979-87; sr. writer/chief econ. corr. U.S. News and World Report, Washington, 1987-97, contbg. editor, 1997-99; health policy corr. The News Hour with Jim Lehrman, Arlington, Va., 1999—. Office: The News Hour with Jim Lehrman 2700 S Quincy St Arlington VA 22206*

DENUNZIO, RALPH DWIGHT, investment banker; b. White Plains, N.Y., Nov. 17, 1931; s. Frank and M. Winifred (Sandbach) DeN.; m. Jean A. Ames, Sept. 25, 1954; children: David Ames, Peter Dwight, Thomas Richard. AB, Princeton U., 1953. With Kidder, Peabody & Co., Inc., N.Y.C., 1953-87, exec. v.p., 1968-77, pres., 1977, chief exec. officer, 1980-87, chmn., chief exec. officer, 1986-1987, also dir.; bd. dirs. Fed. Express Corp., Memphis, Harris Corp., Melbourne, Fla., Nike, Inc., Beaverton, Oreg.; bd. govs. N.Y. Stock Exch., 1968, vice chmn. bd., 1969-71, chmn. bd., 1971-72. Past pres. bd. trustees Deerfield (Mass.) Acad.; past pres. bd. trustees Greenwich (Conn.) Country Day Sch.; past trustee Princeton U. Mem. Securities Industry Assn. (past chmn. 1980-81), Bond Club (N.Y.C.) (past pres., gov.), Links Club (N.Y.C.), Princeton Club (N.Y.C.), N.Y. Yacht Club, Stanwich Club (Greenwich), Riverside Yacht Club (Conn.), John's Island Club (Vero Beach, Fla.). Republican. Roman Catholic. Home: Bridle Path Ln Riverside CT 06878 Office: Harbor Point Assocs Inc 375 Park Ave Ste 2602 New York NY 10152-2699

DENUR, JACK BOAZ, scientific researcher, scientific consultant; b. N.Y.C., Sept. 12, 1951; s. Amnon Denur and Gail Levin. AS, El Centro Jr. Coll., Dallas, 1971; BS in Chemistry, U. Tex., Arlington, 1975; MS in Chemistry, Tex. A&M U., 1976; MS in Physics, U. North Tex., 1988. Sci. cons. Comml. Tech., Inc., Dallas, 1980—, Electric & Gas Tech., Inc., Dallas, 1985—, Atmospheric & Magnetics Tech., Inc., Dallas, 1996—, Reynolds Equipment Co., Inc., Dallas, 1997—. Mem. AAAS, Am. Phys. Soc., Astron. League, The Planetary Soc., Am. Assn. Physics Tchrs., Am. Assn. Weather Observers, Tex. Astron. Soc. Dallas, Dallas Paleontological Soc., Tex. Severe Storms Assn. Democrat. Jewish. Avocations: meteorology, astronomy, cats, science and technology, philosophy. Home: 5045 Royal Ln Dallas TX 75229-4310 Office: Comml Tech Inc 13636 Neutron Rd Dallas TX 75244-4410 also: Electric and Gas Tech Inc 13636 Neutron Rd Dallas TX 75244-4410

DENUZZO, RINALDO VINCENT, pharmacy educator; b. Cleve., Oct. 21, 1922; s. Luigi and Domenica Mary (Razzano) DiNuzzo; m. Lucy Bernadine Sneed, June 29, 1946; 1 child, Lisa Ann. BS, Albany Coll. Pharmacy, 1952; MS in Edn., SUNY-Albany, 1956. Registered pharmacist, N.Y., Fla., Vt. Prof. pharmacy N.Y. Coll. Pharmacy, Albany, 1952—, adminstrv. asst., 1963-80; pharmacist N.Y., Fla., Vt., 1968-95; sr. pharmacist inspector N.Y. State Dept. Health, 1966-95; field dir. Market Measures, Inc.; chmn. tech. pharmacy adv. com., 1977-95; lectr. drug product substitution and generic drugs. Author: Ann. Albany Coll. Pharmacy Prescription Survey, 1956-84, Substitution, The New York State Experience, 1980, RX Servcies, XIII Winter Olympic Games, 1980, Annual DeNuzzo Prescription Survey, 1985—, Impact of One-Line Prescription Form on Generic Drug Use, 1987, Cipro, Vasotec, Voltaren Post Biggest Gains, 1987, Using the Right Tools to Achieve Personal Success, 1990, Personal Selling, 1991, Annual Survey Tracks Drug Prescribing Trends, 1990, Consumer Prescription Prices Increase, 1991, Changes in Dental Prescribing, 1991, How to Reduce Prescription Medical Costs, 1992, Are Dental Prescriptions a Viable Target for RPhs?, 1992, Financial Success: A Challenge for the Future, 1996, A National Drug Expert Is Needed, 1999; editor: Albany Coll. Pharmacy Alumni News, 1961-81; mem. editl. bd. MMM, 1977-80. Instr. first aid, responding to emergencies, CPR ARC; mem. East Greenbush Ctrl. Sch. Dist. Bd. Edn., 1974-92, v.p., 1975-76, pres., 1976-78, 91-92, East Greenbush Edn. Found.; mem. adv. bd. Merrell-Dow Hosp., 1987; sec.-treas. Union U. Pharmacy Coll. Coun., 1970-80; cons. pharmacist, coord. pharm. svcs. XIII Olympic Winter Games, Lake Placid, N.Y., 1980; chmn. Albany Coll. Pharmacy Faculty, 1987-89, com. on coms., 1984-87, 96-97, promotions com. 1989-92, exec. com., grievance com., chair strategic planning steering com., 1995-96, faculty affairs chmn. and rev., 1990-94, mission statement com., 1995, sr. student status com., faculty ombudsman, 1991—; mem. profl. adv. com. Albany Vis. Nurses Assn.; mem. rev. panel on prescription payment rev. commn. of Office Tech. Assessment U.S. Congress, 1988; mem. ethics panel Siena Coll., 1992; mem., dir. So. Rensselaer County Taxpayers Assn.; liaison Health Sys. Mgmt. degree, Joint MS with Union Coll. With U.S. Army, 1941-46, USAF, 1946-47, capt. M.C. USAFR, 1948-63, ret., 1982. Named Francis J. O'Brien Pharmacy Man of Yr., 1979; recipient 25 Yr. Svc. citation ARC, 30 Yr. Svc. citation, Svc. plaque East Greenbush Ctrl. Sch. Dist., Svc. plaque East Greenbush Edn. Found., 25 Yr. Svc. award N.Y. State Dept. Health, Disting. Svc. citation Rensselaer County Taxpayers Assn. Mem. Am. Assn. Colls. Pharmacy (sec.-treas., coun. faculties 1979-80, coun., chmn. elect 1982-83, chmn. 1984-87, dir. 1984-89, roundtable presentation ann. meeting 1996, del. ann. meeting 1997), Am. Pharm. Assn., N.Y. State Pharm. Soc., N.Y. Sch. Bd. Assn., AARP, N.Y. State Pub. Employees Fedn., Albany Coll. Pharmacy Alumni Assn. (exec. dir. 1965-86, disting. svc. medal 1975), AAUP (pres. 1978—), Kappa Psi (2 Disting. Svc. Plaques 1988, Cert. of Commendation 1989, 96), Beta Delta (ann. Rinaldo V. DeNuzzo luncheon 1988—), Nat. Italian-Am. Found. (coun.), 46th and 72nd Recon Assn., Albany Coll. Pharmacy Pres.'s Club (chmn. bd. 1962-87), Army Five Star, Kappa Psi (dep. grand coun. Beta Delta chpt., Albany grad., sec.-treas., regent pro-temp), Officers Club (West Point, N.Y.). Republican. Roman Catholic. Home: 19 Alva St East Greenbush NY 12061-2027 Office: 106 New Scotland Ave Albany NY 12208-3425

DENVER, EILEEN ANN, magazine editor; b. N.Y.C., Nov. 16, 1942; d. Daniel Joseph and Katherine Agnes (Boland) D.; m. Duncan C. Stephens, July 2, 1988. B.A., Coll. New Rochelle, 1964; certificate, Radcliffe Sch. Pub., 1964; M.A., Ind. U., 1967. Editorial asst. Mass. Inst. Tech. Tech. Review, Boston, 1965-66; instr. English St. Peter's Coll., Jersey City, 1967-70; assoc. editor, writer Am. Home mag., N.Y.C., 1971-75; asst. editor Consumer Reports, Mt. Vernon, N.Y., 1975-77, asst. mng. editor, 1977-79, mng. editor, 1979-91, exec. editor, 1991-96, dir. editl. ops., 1997—. Office: Consumer Reports 101 Truman Ave Yonkers NY 10703-1044

DENWORTH, RAYMOND K., lawyer; b. Phila., Mar. 22, 1932; s. Raymond K. and Hilda (Lang) D.; m. Joanne Redmond, May 12, 1962; children: Michael R., Lydia L. BA, Wesleyan U., 1954; JD, U. Pa., 1961. Bar: Pa. 1962, U.S. Dist. Ct. (ea. dist.) Pa. 1962, U.S. Ct. Appeals (3d cir.) 1962, U.S. Supreme Ct. 1979. Assoc. Drinker Biddle & Reath, Phila., 1961-66; asst. dist. atty. City of Phila., 1967; ptnr. Drinker Biddle & Reath, 1968-97, of counsel, 1997—; bd. dirs. Shared Med. Sys., Inc., Malvern, Pa., AAA Mid-Atlantic, Inc., Phila., Keystone Ins. Co., Phila. Trustee Wesleyan U., Middletown, Ct., chmn. bd., 1992-97, Rosenbach Mus. & Libr.; pres. Samuel S. Fels Fund, Phila.; chmn. bd. United Way Southeastern Pa., 1988-90, gen. campaign chmn., 1990, dir. Mem. Union League Phila., Corinthian Yacht Club (Phila.). Republican. Avocation: sailing. Office: Drinker Biddle & Reath 1345 Chestnut St Ste 1300 Philadelphia PA 19107-3496

DENYES, JAMES RICHARD, industrial engineer; b. Detroit, Oct. 9, 1948; s. Heyward Thornton and Rosalie (Blair) D.; m. Pamela Brothers, Jan. 1, 1994; children: Amy Cheryne, Laura Michelle. BS in Indsl. Engring. and Ops. Rsch., Va. Tech. U., 1970. Indsl. engr., prodn. control engr., distbn. foreman Allied Chem. Corp., Moncure, N.C., 1970-72; quality control engr. Duke Constrn. Co., Norfolk, Va., 1972-75; command indsl. engr., staff indsl. engr. Navy Manpower and Material Analysis Ctr., Atlantic, Norfolk, 1975-84; head mgmt. engring. dept., Navy Manpower Analysis Ctr., Norfolk, 1981-84; dir. Navy Sch. Work Study, Navy Manpower Engring. Ctr., Norfolk, 1984-88; mgr. indsl. engring. Navy Manpower Analysis Ctr., Chesapeake, Va., 1988-89; dir. Navy Sch. Manpower Mgmt., 1989-94; tng. adminstr. Navy Occupational Safety, Health and Environ. Tng. Ctr., 1994—; co-founder Idea Assocs., 1983-94. Author: Work Smarter Not Harder--Methods Improvement Workbook, 1991; leadership staff Work Simplification Confs., 1992. Treas. VOKAL (Va. Orgn. to Keep Abortion Legal), 1977-79, bd. dirs., 1979-81; fin. adv. NOW, 1975-76; pres. B.M. Williams Elem. Sch. PTA, 1982-83, 1st v.p., 1983-84, 1st v.p., pres., 1984-85; mem. stds. of quality planning coun. Chesapeake Pub. Schs., 1982-83; pres. Crestwood Elem. Sch. PTA, 1986-87; founder, head steering com. couples group Unity Renaissance Ch., 1998, bd. dirs., 1998—, sec. 1998-99. Mem. ASTD (bd. dirs. chpt. 1992-97, bd. dirs. Hampton Roads quality mgmt. coun. 1989-91, exec. v.p. 1993-94, pres. 1995), Am. inst. Indsl. Engrs. (sr.; bd. dirs. 1977-91, prs. chpt. 1980-81, 88-89), Improvement Inst. (trustee 1982-85, 86-88, pres. 1989-92, Pres.'s Cup 1985), Creative Problem Solving Inst. (leadership staff 1985—), Va. Congress Parents and Tchrs. (hon. life)., Pi Delta Epsilon. Home: 2248 Bayberry St Virginia Beach VA 23451-1404 Office: NAVOSHENVTRACEN Norfolk VA 23511

DENYS, SYLVIA, lawyer; d. Joseph and Louise D. BA in Philosophy and English with honors, Duquesne U., 1970, MA in English, 1977, JD, 1979. Bar: Pa. 1979, U.S. Dist. Ct. (we. dist.) Pa. 1979, U.S. Ct. Appeals (3d cir.), 1994. Atty. Neighborhood Legal Svcs. Assn., Pitts., 1979-81; jud. law clk. Superior Ct. Pa., Pitts., 1981-82; asst. prof. Duquesne U. Grad. Sch. Bus. and Sch. Bus., 1982-89; pvt. practice Pitts., 1982-91, 93—; tchr. Acad. for the Advancement Sci., Pecs, Hungary, 1992-93; adj. prof. Duquesne U. Sch. Bus., 1990-91; vis. prof. Sch. Medicine, Pecs, 1991-92; adj. prof. Janus Pannonius Sch. Law, Pecs, Hungary, 1991-92lectr. and presenter in field. Mem. editl. bd. Duquesne Law Rev., 1978-79; contbr. articles to profl. jours. Legal coun., bd. dirs. Pitts. Deaf Theatre, Pitts., 1984-85; bd. dirs. YWCA, Pitts., 1984, Blind Outdoor Leisure Devel., Pitts., 1994-95; rev. com. United Way, Pitts., 1982-86; citizens assembly mem. Health and Welfare Planning Allegheny County, Pitts., 1982-85; v.p. UN Assn. Pitts., 1984-85, bd. dirs., 1982-85; vol. atty. Legal Resources for Women, Pitts., 1997, Neighborhood Legal Svcs. Assn., Pitts., 1994—; adv. bd. Radio Info. Svc., Pitts., 1994-95, vol. atty., 1996-97; govtl. activities com. United Cerebral Palsy, Pitts., 1994-96; dir. legal project for deaf and hard of hearing Pitts. Hearing, Speech and Deaf Svcs., 1995-96; tutor goodwill literacy program Allegheny County Jail, Pitts., 1995-96; membership com. World Affairs Coun., Pitts., 1983-85. Hunkele Found. grantee, Brussels, 1988, U.S. Info. Agy. grantee U. Pitts., 1992-93; Fulbright-Hayes fellow Coun. for Internat. Exch. of Scholars, 1990; selected mem. Team '92 Delegation of Commn. of European Communities, 1989-91. Mem. ABA (editor-in-chief Internat. Aspects of Antitrust Law newsletter 1984-86, del. to European Union 1989), ACLU (lawyers com. 1994-98), Fed. Bar Assn. (steering com., publicity chmn. Western Pa. chpt. 1995—), Am. Inns of Ct., Pa. Bar Assn. (legal svcs. to persons with disabilities com. 1994—, civil and equal rights com. 1994-98, LINK project for disabled children 1997-98), Allegheny County Bar Assn. (antitrust and class action com., court rules com., editl. bd. Pitts. Legal Jour. 1982-88, pub. svc. com., civil rights com., internat. twinning com. 1994-98), Womens Bar Assn. Allegheny County, World Federalists, Amnesty Internat., 1998—, Lawyers Com. for Human Rights. Avocations: languages, cultures, arts, nature, gourmet cooking. Home: 4609 Bayard St Pittsburgh PA 15213-2755 Office: 1710 Allegheny Bldg 429 Forbes Ave Pittsburgh PA 15219-1604

DENYSYK, BOHDAN, marketing professional; b. Kornberg, Germany, Feb. 13, 1947; came to U.S., 1949; s. John and Maria (Zelenewich) D.; m. Halina Bubela, June 28, 1969; children: Maria H., Danya L., Adrienne Y., Alexis M. BS, Manhattan Coll., 1968; MS, Cath. U. Am., 1971; PhD, Union Inst. (formerly Union for Experimenting Colls. and Univs.), Cin., 1981. Project mgr. Naval Weapons Lab., Dahlgren, Va., 1968-72; scientist Naval Med. Research Inst., Bethesda, Md., 1972-75; program mgr. Naval Surface Weapons Ctr., Dahlgren, 1975-78; dept. head E.G. & G. Inc., Rockville, Md., 1978-81; dep. asst. sec. U.S. Dept. Commerce, Washington, 1981-83; dir. civil programs IBM Corp., 1983-86; pres. DLR Assocs., Arlington, Va., 1972-80, 83—; pres. Global U.S.A., 1986—, also owner, bd. dirs.; mem. Congl. Adv. Panel on China, 1985—; bd. dirs. Mazak Corp.; mem. Def. Sci. Bd., 1990—. Contbr. articles to profl. jours. Mem. Presdl. Transition Team, Washington, 1991; regional dir. Rep. Nat. Com., 1980; dir. pub. rels. Ukrainian Nat. Info. Svc., 1976-80; mem. Pres.'s Export Coun.,

1981—, Presdl. Awards Commn., 1986-87; exec. dir. Md. Reagan-Bush Campaign, 1984, Bush-Quayle Campaign, 1992; mem. nat. policy forum Fgn. Affairs Coun., 1995—; pres. Phi Mu Alpha Sinfonia, 1967-68; nat. dir. for coalitions Dole for U.S. Pres. Campaign, 1987-88; dep. polit. dir. Dole for Pres., 1995-96; regional polit. dir. Gov. Bush for Pres. 2000, 1999. Navy fellow, 1969-72; Regents scholar, 1964-68. Fellow N.Y. Acad. Sci.; mem. AIAA, AAAS, Am. Def. Preparedness Assn., Am. Phys. Soc. Republican. Roman Catholic. Avocations: scuba, skiing, running. Office: Global USA Inc 2121 K St NW Ste 650 Washington DC 20037-1825

DENZLER, JAMES WYATT, pharmacist; b. Marion, Va., Jan. 30, 1958; s. Roger Vincent Denzler and Helen Margaret Lambert Williams. *Mother Helen retired after 30 years as a service representative for United Telephone Company. Her ancestry by way of her mother, Emma Leftridge Lambert, has been traced to 15th-century manor Leftwich Hall in Leftwich Village, Cheshire, England. Father Roger is a construction entrepreneur in Atkins, Virginia where a rural avenue bears his name. He is a relative of western movie star Randolph Scott for whom brother Randy is named. Sister Deborah's daughter Christa Ramsey recently graduated Magna Cum Laude from East Tennessee State University, where brother Roger also attained a degree in business management.* BS in Biology, East Tenn. U., 1981, U. Minn., 1988. Registered pharmacist, Va., Calif., N.Y. Pharmacist Longs Drugs, Santa Barbara, Calif., 1988-90, Thrifty Drugs, Santa Barbara, 1990-91, Eckerd/Revco, Virginia Beach, Va., 1991—, Norfolk (Va.) Gen. Hosp., 1998—; pres., owner Denzler Corp., Norfolk, 1996—. Mem. Am. Pharm. Assn., Aubudon Soc., U.S. Table Tennis Assn., Pi Kappa Alpha (chpt. pres.), Phi Delta Chi (chpt. pres.). Avocations: birding, table tennis, weight-lifting, photography. E-mail: jamz9260@aol.com.

DENZLER, NANCY J., artist; b. Newport, Ark., Apr. 17, 1936; d. Walter and Eathel (Faulkner) Blanchard; m. Ronald Ray Hopkins, Dec. 10, 1956; m. Arthur Henry Denzler, Dec. 31, 1969; m. Timothy Joseph Riordan, Apr. 10, 1989; children: Ronald Ray Hopkins Jr., Carrie Jayne Tel-Oren. BFA magna cum laude, SUNY, Buffalo, 1976, MFA, 1978. instr. sculpture, watercolor, acrylic, pastel and drawing, pvt. groups, 1971—. Works exhibited at Albright-Knox Gallery, Buffalo, 1976, 77, 79, Mainstreams, Marietta, Ohio, 1976, Erie (Pa.) Art Ctr., 1976, AAO Gallery and AC Gallery, Buffalo, 1977, 78, 79, Niagara Falls (N.Y.) Art Ctr., 1977, Patterson Art Gallery, Westfield, N.Y., 1979, Barn Workshop Gallery, Danvers, Mass., 1980, Union Gallery, Boston, 1982, Montserrat Gallery, Beverly, Mass., 1983, Copley Soc., 1997, others. Artists fellow Creative Artists Pub. Svc. Program, N.Y.C., 1980. Mem. Boston Visual Artists Union, The Copley Soc. of Boston. Address: 229 Ocean St Lynn MA 01902-3269

DEO, NARSINGH, computer science educator; b. Raniganj, Bihar, India, Jan. 2, 1936; s. Bihari Lal and Durga (Modi) Jee; m. Karen Ruth Baier, June 29, 1968. B.S., Patna U., India, 1956; Dip. I.I.Sc., Indian Inst. Sci., 1959; M.S., Calif. Inst. Tech., 1960; Ph.D., Northwestern U., 1965. Assoc. electronic engr. Burroughs Electro Data Div., 1960-62; sr. engr. Jet Propulsion Lab., Pasadena, 1966-69, mem. tech. staff, 1969-71; v.p. Britt Electronics Corp., Santa Monica, Calif., 1968-69; asst. prof. elec. engring. Calif. State Coll., 1971; assoc. prof. elec. engring. Indian Inst. Tech., Kanpur, 1971-74, prof., head computer ctr., 1975-77; vis. prof. computer sci. Wash. State U., Pullman, 1974-75, prof., 1977-87, chmn. dept. computer sci., 1980-84; Millican chair prof. U. Cen. Fla., Orlando, 1986—; dir. Ctr. for Parallel Computation, 1989—; electronics design cons. Ctr. Behavior Therapy, Beverly Hills, Calif., 1967-71; mem. faculty engring. extension UCLA, 1965-68; vis. assoc. prof. computer sci. U. Ill., Urbana; vis. prof. U. Nebr., Lincoln, 1977; vis. faculty IBM Thomas J. Watson Rsch., Yorktown Heights, N.Y., 1984. Author 4 textbooks, over 150 rsch. papers; patentee in field. Recipient Fla. Gov.'s award, 1989; grantee NSF, U.S. Dept. Transp., Army Rsch. Office, U.S. Army's PM-TRADE, Fla. High Tech. and Industry Coun. Fellow IEEE, Assn. Computing Machinery. Home: 3901 Orange Lake Dr Orlando FL 32817-1637

DEONES, JACK E., corporate executive; b. Mankato, Minn., Sept. 21, 1931; s. Nicholas H. and Beatrice R. (Viste) D.; m. Cleo Pat Peters, May 29, 1955; children—Gregg N., Alexa M. BSS, St. Mary's Coll., 1953; JD, Yale U., 1956. Bar: Minn. 1956, N.J. 1974. Spl. agt. FBI, 1960-62; atty. Pfizer, Inc., 1962-65; div. counsel Honeywell, Inc., 1965-69; asst. gen. counsel Foster Wheeler Corp., Livingston, N.J., 1969-77, corp. sec., 1977-96, v.p., 1984-96; chmn., pres. Castlerock Assocs., Parsippany, N.J., 1996—; dir. York Internat. Corp., Briarcliff Assocs., Inc. Served with USN, 1956-60. Mem. ABA, N.J. Bar Assn., Minn. Bar Assn. Home: 59 Briarcliff Rd Mountain Lakes NJ 07046-1304 Office: Castlerock Assocs PO Box 6133 Parsippany NJ 07054-7133

DEORCHIS, VINCENT MOORE, lawyer; b. N.Y.C., Aug. 25, 1949; s. Mario E. and Frankie (Moore) DeO.; m. Donna B., July 24, 1971; children: Vincent Scott, Dana Lauren. BA, Fordham Coll., 1971, JD, 1974. Bar: N.Y. 1975, U.S. Dist. Ct. (so. and ea. dists.) N.Y. 1975, U.S. Ct. Appeals (2d cir.) 1975, U.S. Supreme Ct. 1985, U.S. Ct. Appeals (3d cir.) 1989, U.S. Dist. Ct. (so. dist.) Tex. 1992, U.S. Ct. Appeals (4th cir.) 1996. Assoc. Haight, Gardner, Poor & Havens, N.Y.C., 1974-84; ptnr. DeOrchis & Ptnrs., N.Y.C., 1984-97, DeOrchis, Walker & Corsa, LLP, N.Y.C., 1997—. Co-author: Attorney's Practice Guide to Negotiations, 1985. Pres. North Stratmore Civic Assn., Manhasset, N.Y., 1978-82. Mem. ABA (com. on maritime litig.), Maritime Law Assn. (bd. dirs., chmn. com. on carriage of goods by sea), Assn. Transp. Practitioners, N.Y. County Lawyer's Assn. (com. on maritime and admiralty law), Propeller Club U.S. Avocation: sailing. Office: DeOrchis Walker & Corsa 2d Flr One Battery Park Plaza New York NY 10004-1480

DEORE, BILL, editorial cartoonist. Editorial cartoonist Dallas Morning News. Office: The Dallas Morning News Communications Ctr PO Box 655237 Dallas TX 75265-5237*

DEORIO, ANTHONY JOSEPH, surgeon; b. Chgo., June 27, 1945; s. Joseph John and Catherine Marie Deorio; m. Janet Ann Balskus, Jan. 10, 1970; children: Joseph, Catherine. BS, Loyola U., Chgo., 1967; MD, Loyola U., Maywood, Ill., 1971. Diplomate Am. Bd. Surgery. Intern St. Joseph Hosp., Chgo., 1971-72; resident in surgery Loyola Med. Ctr., Maywood, 1972-76, clin. instr. surgery, 1976-77, asst. prof. surgery, 1977—; pvt. practice Resurrection Hosp., Chgo., 1977—, dir. surg. edn., 1977—, chmn. dept. surgery, 1984-88, sec. med. staff, 1986-88; assoc. examiner Am. Bd. Surgery, 1993, 96. Contbr. articles to profl. jours. Fellow ACS (com. on applicants 1990-99); mem. AMA, Ill. Med. Soc., Chgo. Med. Soc., Chgo. Surg. Soc., Ill. Surg. Soc., Alumni Assn. Stritch Sch. Medicine (bd. govs.), Columbian Club, KC, Blue Key, Alpha Omega Alpha. Roman Catholic. Avocations: model railroads, sports, fishing. Office: 7447 W Talcott Ave Chicago IL 60631-3745

DEOUL, KATHLEEN BOARDSEN, executive; b. New London, Conn., May 5, 1944; d. Harry Kostrope Boardsen and Elizabeth (Conti) Dunham; m. Barry Melvyn Davis, May 21, 1966 (div. Jan. 1977), m. Neal Deoul, June 20, 1982; 1 child, Shannon Rae. Grad. high sch., New London, Conn. Br. mgr. Qwip Systems (divsn. Exxon), Balt.; br. ops. mgr. Exxon Office Systems, Pitts., 1977-81; owner, pres. Bus. Quars., Crystal City, Va., 1983-95, Wellness Alternatives, Balt., 1993—. Mem. adv. bd. Network Mktg. Lifestyles Mag.; mem. Team Diamond. Mem. President's Club Exxon, President's Club Nikken, Inc. Avocations: venture capitalist, travel, reading, interior decorating, public speaking.

DEOUL, NEAL, electronics company executive; b. N.Y.C., Feb. 27, 1931; s. George and Pearl (Hirschfield) D.; B.S. in Physics, Coll. City N.Y., 1952; postgrad. Rutgers U., 1954-55; JD, Bklyn. Law Sch., 1959; m. Bernice Kradel, Dec. 25, 1955 (div.); children: Cara Jan, Stefani Neva, Evan Craig; m., Kathleen B. Davis, June 20, 1982; 1 child, Shannon Rae. Engr., Signal Corps, U.S. Army, Evans Signal Lab., Belmar, N.J., 1952-55; engr. Airborne Instruments Lab., Deer Park, N.Y., 1955-56; sales mgr. FXR, Inc., Woodside, L.I., 1956-60; admitted to N.Y. State bar, 1960; pres. Microwave Dynamics Corp., Plainview, L.I., 1960-61, Paradynamics, Inc., Huntington Station, N.Y., 1961-64; mgr. Servo Corp. Am., Hicksville, N.Y., 1964-66; v.p. Trio Labs., Inc., Plainview, N.Y., 1966-69; exec. v.p. Microlab/FXR, Livingston, N.J., 1969-74; pres. Neal Deoul Assocs., Balt., Md., 1974—. Mem. IEEE (sr.), N.Y. State Bar Assn., Md. Bar Assn., Young Pres.'s Orgn., Profl. Group Engring. Mgmt., Am. Arbitration Assn. Home and Office: 2 Bellchase Ct Baltimore MD 21208-1300

DEPACE, NICHOLAS LOUIS, physician; b. Nutley, N.J., Oct. 18, 1953; s. Nicholas Frank and Rose (Piro) DeP.; m. Marilyn Tomaro, Jan. 17, 1981. BS, Seton Hall U.; MD, N.J. Sch. Medicine, Mt. Sinai, N.Y.C.; internal medicine cardiology, Hahnemann U., Phila. Diplomate Am. Bd. Internal Medicine and Cardiology. Intern in internal medicine Overlook Hosp., Summit, N.J., Columbia U., N.Y.C., 1978-79; resident internal medicine Hahnemann Med. Coll. and Hosp., Phila., 1979-81; practice medicine specializing in internal and cardiology medicine Phila., 1982—; with Sta. WPEN, Phila., 1990; clin. prof. medicine Thomas Jefferson U. Hosp., 1997—; chief divsn. preventive cardiology Grad. Hosp., 1996-97; dir. heart repair program Phila. Heart Inst., Presbyn. Med. Ctr., Phila., 1993-95; dir. Jefferson Heart Ctr. South, 1997—. Co-author: The Heart Repair Manual. Fellow Am. Coll. Cardiology, Am. Coll. Chest Physicians; mem. AMA, N.Y. Acad. Scis., Phila. Coll. Physicians. Republican. Roman Catholic. Avocations: reading, writing, travel, sports. Home: 109 Jefferson Ave Haddonfield NJ 08033-3411 Office: 188 Fries Mill Rd Ste N2 Turnersville NJ 08012-2055 also: 2422 24 S Broad St Philadelphia PA 19145

DE PALMA, BRIAN RUSSELL, film director, writer; b. Newark, Sept. 11, 1940; s. Anthony Fredrick and Vivenne (Muti) DeP.; m. Gale Anne Hurd, July 21, 1991; daughter, Lolita. BA, Columbia Coll., 1962; MA, Sarah Lawrence Coll., 1964. Dir. and writer: short film Woton's Wake, 1963 (Rosenthal Found. award 1963); documentary films Dionysus in '69, 1970, The Responsive Eye, 1966; feature films include Murder a la Mod, 1968, Greetings, 1968 (Silver Bear Berlin Film Festival award 1969), The Wedding Party, 1969, Hi Mom, 1970, Get to Know Your Rabbit, 1972, Sisters, 1973, Phantom of the Paradise, 1974 (Grand prize 1975), Obsession, 1976, Carrie, 1976 (Avoriaz prize 1977), The Fury, 1978, Home Movies, 1979, Dressed to Kill, 1980, Blow Out, 1981, Scarface, 1983, Body Double, 1984, Wise Guys, 1986, The Untouchables, 1987, Casualties of War, 1989, Bonfire of the Vanities, 1990, Raising Cain, 1992, Carlito's Way, 1993, Mission Impossible, 1996, Snake Eyes, 1998. Office: Paramount Pictures Lubitsch Annex # 119 5555 Melrose Ave # 119 West Hollywood CA 90038-3197*

DEPALMA, RALPH GEORGE, surgeon, educator; b. N.Y.C., Oct. 29, 1931; s. Frank and Maria (Sibilio) deP.; m. Maleva Tankard, Sept. 17, 1955; children: Ralph L., Edward F., Maleva B., Malinda G. AB, Columbia U, 1953; MD, NYU, 1956. Diplomate Am. Bd. Surgery, Am. Bd. Vascular Surgery. Resident in surgery Univ. Hosps., Cleve., 1962-64; from instr. to prof. surgery Case Western Res. U., Cleve., 1964-80; prof., chmn. surgery U. Nev., Reno, 1980-82, George Washington U. Sch. Medicine, Washington, 1982-92; Lewis B. Saltz prof. of surgery George Washington U. Med. Ctr., Washington, 1992-94; prof. surgery, vice-chmn. dept. surgery, assoc. dean U. Nev., Reno, 1994—. Editor: (with J.M. Giordano) Reoperative Vascular Surgery, 1987, Basic Science of Vascular Surgery, 1988; assoc. editor: Haimovici Vascular Surgery: Principles and Techniques, 1989; co-editor: Basic Science in Vascular Disease, 1997; assoc. editor Internat. Vascular Surgery, Internat. Jour. Impotence Rsch.; contbr. articles to profl. jours. Stroke liaison nat. chpt. Am. Heart Assn., 1992-94; bd. dirs. Reno Chamber Orch., 1999. Capt. USAF, 1958-61. Grantee USPHS, 1974-82. Fellow ACS; mem. Cleve. Vascular Soc. (pres. 1977-78), Rocky Mt. Vascular Soc. (pres. 1981-82), Am. Surg. Assn., Soc. Vascular Surgery, Washington Acad. Surgery (sec. 1991-92, v.p. 1992-93, pres. 1993-94), Am. Venous Forum (sec. 1991-94, bd. dirs. found. 1992-95), Am. Coll. Healthcare Execs. (assoc.), 1996. Cosmos Club (admissions com. 1992-94), Reno Rotary, Western Vascular Soc.

DEPALO, WILLIAM ANTHONY, JR., Latin American studies educator; b. N.Y.C., July 17, 1941; s. William Anthony and Elsie Elizabeth (Reighton) DeP.; m. Deborah Jean Borgmann, Dec. 30, 1983; children: Brian William, Katherine Elizabeth. BS in Microbiology, N.Mex. State U., 1963; MA in History, U. Okla., 1971; student, Interam. Def. Coll., Ft. McNair, Washington, 1985-86; PhD in Latin Am. Studies, U. N.Mex., 1994. Commd. 2d lt. U.S. Army, 1963, advanced through grades to col., 1985; comdr. 1st Bn., 10th Infantry, Ft. Carson, Colo., 1983-85, 4th Psychol. Ops. Group, Ft. Bragg, N.C., 1986-89, U.S. Army Sch. of the Ams., Ft. Benning, Ga., 1989-91; adj. prof. U. N.Mex., Albuquerque, 1995—. Author: The Mexican National Army, 1997; contbr. The United States and Mexico at War, 1998. Decorated Silver Star, Bronze Star for Valor, Purple Heart (2), Legion of Merit (3). Mem. Am. Hist. Assn. Republican. Roman Catholic. Avocations: triathlons, running, cycling. Home: 4009 Shenandoah Pl NE Albuquerque NM 87111-4157 Office: U NMex Latin Am Inst Albuquerque NM 87131

DEPAN, MARY ELIZABETH, civic volunteer, nurse; b. Boston, Oct. 5, 1927; d. Frank and Josephine Madeline (Lennon) Natter; m. Harry McCarthy Depan, Apr. 26, 1952 (div. Aug. 1981); children: Harry, Madeline, Mark, Andrew. Diploma in nursing, St. Elizabeth Hosp., Boston, 1948; student, Skidmore Coll., 1960—. RN, Mass. Oper. rm. supr. Gt. Lake Naval Sta., Chgo., 1949; staff nurse Beth Israel Hosp., Boston, 1949. Monitor, leader Gt. Books Found., Glens Falls, N.Y., 1960—, Adirondack C.C., Glens Falls, 1960—; vol., bd. dirs. Literacy Vols., Glens Falls, 1983—; vol. nurse ARC, Glens Falls, 1985—; active area sr. citizen's orgn., 1992—. Lt. (j.g.) USN, 1949-52. Recipient cert. for porcelain painting, 1991. Mem. Women in Arts (chartered), Porcelain Artists, Nat. Mus. Women in the Arts (charter), Women's Meml. (charter). Roman Catholic. Avocations: painting, travel, museums, volunteering. Home: 43 Quade St Glens Falls NY 12801-2706

DEPAOLA, DOMINICK PHILIP, academic administrator; b. Bklyn., Dec. 29, 1942; s. Dominick and Marie (DeStefano) DeP.; m. Rosemary Elizabeth Femiano, Aug. 2, 1969; 1 child, Alexis Jane. BS, St. Francis Coll., 1964; DDS, NYU, 1969; PhD, MIT, 1974; ScD (hon.), Baylor U., 1995. Assoc. prof. Va. Commonwealth U., Med. Coll. Va., Richmond, 1974-78; dean Dental Sch. U. Tex. Health Sci. Ctr., San Antonio, 1983-87, interim dean Grad. Sch. Biomed. Scis., 1986-87; dean Dental Sch. U. Medicine and Dentistry N.J., Newark, 1988-90; pres., dean Baylor Coll. Dentistry, Dallas, 1990-96; pres. Tex. A&M Univ. Sys.-Baylor Coll. Dentistry, Dallas, 1996-97; pres., CEO Forsyth Dental Ctr., Boston, 1998—; prof. Harvard U. Sch. Dental Medicine, Boston, 1999—; mem. Nat. Adv. Dental Rsch. Coun. for Nat. Inst. Dental Rsch., 1996—; mem. dental adv. com. Pew Commn. for Health Professions, 1991; bd. dirs. Oral Health Am., Block Drug Co.; mem. Commn. on Dental Accreditation, 1992-97. Recipient Presdl. award San Antonio Dist. Dental Soc., 1987, Alumni Achievement award NYU Coll. Dentistry, 1993. Fellow Am. Acad. Oral Medicine (hon.); mem. ADA, Am. Inst. Nutrition, Am. Assn. Dental Schs. (past pres. 1989-91), Am. Soc. for Clin. Nutrition (chair pub. info. com. 1995—), Am. Soc. Nutritional Scis. (chair pub. info. com. 1995—), Am. Assn. Dental Rsch., Internat. Assn. Dental Rsch., Hispanic Dental Assn. (hon.). Avocations: skiing, racquetball, tennis, golf, reading. Office: Forsyth Dental Ctr 140 Fenway Boston MA 02115-3799

DEPAOLIS, POTITO UMBERTO, food company executive; b. Mignano, Italy, Aug. 28, 1925; s. Giuseppe A. and Filomena (Macchiaverna) deP.; Vet. Dr., U. Naples, 1948; Libera Docenza, Ministero Pubblica Istruzione (Rome, Italy), 1955; m. Marie A. Caronna, Apr. 10, 1965. Came to U.S., 1966, naturalized, 1970. Prof. food service Vet. Sch., U. Naples, Italy, 1948-66; retired, 1966; asst. prof. A titre Benevole Ecole Veterinaire Alfort, Paris, France, 1956; vet. inspector U.S. Dept. Agr., Omaha, 1966-67; sr. research chemist Grain Processing Corp., Muscatine, Iowa, 1967-68; v.p., dir. product devel. Reddi Wip, Inc., Los Angeles, 1968-72; with Kubro Foods, Los Angeles, 1972-73, Shade Foods, Inc., 1975—; pres. Vegetable Protein Co., Riverside, Calif., 1973—, Tima Brand Food Co., 1975—, Dr. Tima Natural Foods, 1977—. Fulbright scholar Cornell U., Ithaca, N.Y., 1954; British Council scholar, U. Reading, Eng., 1959-60; postdoctoral research fellow NIH, Cornell U., 1963-64. Mem. Inst. Food Technologists, Italian Assn. Advancement Sci., AAAS, Vet. Med. Assn., Biol. Sci. Assn. Italy, Italian Press Assn., Greater Los Angeles Press Club. Contbr. articles in field to prol. jours. Patentee in field. Home: Bel Air 131 Groverton Pl Los Angeles CA 90077-3732 Office: 19428 Londelius St Northridge CA 91324-3511 also: 6878 Beck Ave North Hollywood CA 91605-6205

DEPAOLO, RONALD FRANCIS, editor, writer; b. Jamaica, N.Y., July 12, 1938; s. Francis Edward and Evelyn Helen (Turck) deP.; m. Meredith Nell Mass, Aug. 12, 1967; children—Britton, Damon, Baird. B.A. cum laude, Moravian Coll., Bethlehem, Pa., 1964; M.S., Northwestern U., 1965. Reporter, corr., writer Life mag., 1965-70; news editor, corr. Business Week mag., 1970-72; freelance writer and editor, 1972-76; editor-in-chief, asso. pub. I-AM mag., N.Y.C., 1976-78; sr. editor Boardroom Reports, N.Y.C., 1978-80; editor-in-chief M.D. Mag., N.Y.C., 1980-84; editor, pub. Kirkus Revs., N.Y.C., 1984-87; pres. Rock Lodge Devel. Corp., 1987—; adj. prof. communications Ramapo Coll., Mahwah, N.J., 1974-75. Author: Russia and the Independent States, 1992, The Presidency from A to Z, 1998, Elections from A to Z, 1998, Guide to Congress, 1999. Served with AUS, 1957-59, 60-61. Home: Hawks' Dance Farm 175 Rock Lodge Rd Stockholm NJ 07460

DE PAPP, ZSOLT GEORGE, endocrinologist; b. Windsor, Ont., Canada, Oct. 27, 1933; s. John L.E. and Emmy (Birgling) de P.; divorced; children: Anne, John, Erika. AB, Dartmouth Coll., 1955; MD, U. Rochester, 1959. Intern Strong Meml. Hosp., Rochester, N.Y., 1959-60, asst. resident in medicine, 1960-61; assoc. resident in medicine Yale New Haven Hosp., 1963-64; fellow in endocrinology Strong Meml. Hosp., 1964-65; head primary care ctr. St. Raphael's Hosp., New Haven, 1976-78; attending physician Yale New Haven Hosp., 1978-79; chief assoc. medicine U. Rochester (N.Y.) Sch. Medicine, 1980; head endocrine unit Highland Hosp., Rochester, 1980—. Capt. U.S. Army, 1961-63, Germany. Lutheran. Office: Highland Hosp 1000 South Ave Rochester NY 14620-2782

DEPARLE, NANCY-ANN MIN, federal agency administrator, lawyer; b. Rockwood, Tenn., Dec. 17, 1956; m. Jason DeParle. BA, U. Tenn., 1978; JD, Harvard U., 1983. Past pvt. practice in law; commr. human svcs. Gov. Ned McWherter State of Tenn., 1987-89; past assoc. dir. health and pers. office mgmt. and budget HHS; administr. Health Care Financing Adminstrn. HHS, Washington, 1997—. Rhodes scholar, 1979-81. Office: HHS Health Care Fin Adminstrn Rm 314G 200 Independence Ave SW Washington DC 20201-0004*

DEPASQUALE, LAURA, artist, art education administrator; b. Buffalo, Nov. 30, 1961; d. Anthony Charles and Virginia Anne (Burks) DeP.; m. Frank L. Foti, June 14, 1993. BA in Journalism, Am. U., 1984. Project coord. Bakehouse Children-at-Risk Art Workshops, Miami, Fla., 1992—; dir. edn. Bakehouse Children-at-Risk Art Workshops, Miami, 1997—; spl. presenter art for homeless children Assn. for Advancement of Social Work, Quebec City, Que., Can., 1997, for forming cmty. partnerships with Children-At-Risk, Miami, Fla., 1998. One-woman shows include Subculture Gallery, Phila., 1996, Art Ctr. South Fla., Miami Beach, 1997, Kirkland Art Ctr., Clinton, N.Y., 1997, Miami-Dade Cultural Resource Ctr., Miami, 1998, Am. Legion Park, Miami, 1998; group exhbn. at Mus. Art, Ft. Lauderdale, Fla., 1995. Ind. Artist fellow in vis. art Fla. State Dept. Cultural Affairs, 1995-96; Cultural Cmty. grantee Knight Ridder Found., South Fla., 1995-96; Round Robin Mural grantee Fifty of Fifty Found., South Fla., 1997, Wolfsonian Found., 1999. Studio: 739 NE 72nd Ter Miami FL 33138-5260

DEPASS, WILLIAM BRUNSON, JR., commercial and industrial real estate broker; b. Rock Hill, S.C., Sept. 8, 1947; s. William Brunson and Kathryn (Macaulay) DeP.; m. Susan Parker, May 17, 1975; children: William Brunson III, Martha Barham, Caroline Marshall. BA, Clemson U., 1969. cert. comml. investment broker. Polit. field rep. Supt. Edn. Campaign, Columbia, S.C., 1970; mail clk. Henderson Advt. Agy., Greenville, S.C., 1970-71; broker, agt. William Durham Co., Columbia, 1973-75, 80-88; asst. dir. Divsn. Adminstrn. Gov.'s Office, Columbia, 1975-76; state dir. Citizens for Reagan, Columbia, 1976; state liaison officer Heritage Conservation and Recreation Dept. Parks, Columbia, 1976-79; broker, agt. Wilson/Kibler, Inc., Columbia, 1988—. Pres. St. Andrew's Soc. of the City of Columbia, 1991; presdl. elector S.C. Rep. Party Exec. Com., Columbia, 1984; chmn. Richland County Rep. Orgn., Columbia, 1997—, State Election Com., Columbia, 1988-97; bd. dirs. Coop. Ministry, Columbia, 1995—. Capt. U.S. Army, 1971-73. Mem. Nat. Assn. Realtors, S.C. Assn. Realtors, Grtr. Columbia Assn. Realtors (chn. comml. divsn. 1991), Rotary (pres. Columbia chpt. 1996-97), Columbia Torch Club (sec. 1983, 90, v.p. 1984, 91, pres. 1985, 92). Republican. Presbyterian. Avocations: politics, genealogy, roses. E-mail: rdepass@wilsonkibler.com. Home: 1338 Sinkler Rd Columbia SC 29206 Office: Wilson/Kibler Inc 1111 Laurel St Columbia SC 29201

DEPATIE, DAVID HUDSON, motion picture company executive; b. Los Angeles, Dec. 24, 1930; s. Edmond LaVoie and Dorothy (Hudson) DeP.; m. Marcia Lee MacPherson, June 1972; children: David Hudson, Steven Linn, Michael Linn. Student, U. of South, 1947-48; A.B., U. Calif.-Berkeley, 1951. With Warner Bros. Pictures, Inc., 1951-63, v.p., gen. mgr. comml. and cartoon films div., 1963; pres. DePatie-Freleng Enterprises, Inc., Van Nuys, Calif., 1963—; founder, proprietor The DePatie Vineyards, 1983-90. Producer: Pink Panther and Inspector theatrical cartoon series; TV series The New Mr. Magoo; TV live-action and animation spl. The Hoober Bloob Highway; TV spl. Clerow Wilson Great Escape; TV series The Houndcats and the Barkleys; Christmas TV spls. The Tiny Tree; ABC aftersch. spl. My Mom's Having a Baby (recipient Emmy award); Dr. Seuss spl. Halloween Is Grinch Night (recipient Emmy award), Fantastic Four, Spider-Woman, The Pink Panther Christmas Special, The Bugs Bunny Christmas Special, Spider-Man & his Amazing Friends, The Pink Panther in Pink at First Sight, Pink Panther & Sons, 1985; Dr. Seuss Spls. The Grinch Grinchesthe Cat-In-The-Hat (Emmy award 1982); others.; nominated for Emmy award 1974-75; exec. producer: The Incredible Hulk, Pandamonium, Meatballs and Spaghetti, Dungeons and Dragons. Recipient First award for the Lorax Zagreb Internat. Film Festival, 1972; recipient Emmy Award for Dr. Seus special The Grinch Grinches The Cat-in-the Hat, 1982; Calif. State Fair Double Gold award for Best Zinfandel Wine of 1983, 1985, Wine & Spirits Mag. Am. Champion Zinfandel wine of 1984, 1986. Mem. Acad. Motion Picture Arts and Scis. (Oscar award for Pink Panther 1964), Soc. Motion Picture Editors, Phi Gamma Delta. Republican. Episcopalian. Office: DePatie-Freleng Enterprises Inc 3425 Stiles Ave Camarillo CA 93010-3900

DE PAUW, GOMMAR ALBERT, priest, educator; b. Stekene, Belgium, Oct. 11, 1918; came to U.S., 1949, naturalized, 1955; s. Desiré and Anna (Van Overloop) De P. Diplomate Classical Humanities, Coll. St. Nicholas, Belgium, 1936; JCB, U. Louvain, 1943, JCL, 1945; Juris Canonici Dr., Catholic U. Am., 1953. Ordained priest Roman Cath. Ch., 1942. Parish priest, chaplain Cath. Social Action, Ghent, Belgium, 1945-49, N.Y.C., 1949-52; successively prof. moral and fundamental dogmatic theology and canon law sem. div., assoc. prof. philosophy coll. div. Mt. St. Mary's Coll., Emmitsburg, Md., 1952-65, dean studies maj. sem. div., 1954-64, mem. council adminstrn., 1957-65; Theol. adviser II Vatican Ecumenical Council, 1962-65; founder-pres. Cath. Traditionalist Movement, Inc., 1964—. Author: The Educational Rights of the Church, 1953, The Rebel Priest, 1965, The Traditional Roman Catholic Mass, 1977, Bishops on War and Peace, 1983, The Traditional Requiem Mass, 1989, The Challenge of Peace Through Strength, 1989; co-author: New Catholic Ency.; Dictionary of the Bible, Ephemerides Theologicae Lovanienses; editor: Sounds of Truth and Tradition, Quote... Unquote; producer Latin radio mass, various religious phonograph records, audio and video cassettes. With Belgian Army inf. M.C., 1939-45, World War II Resistance and Free Polish Forces. Decorated Honor Cross (Free Polish Forces); recipient Achievement Citation, U.S. Army. Mem. AAUP, Internat. Platform Assn., Cath. Theol. Soc., Am. Canon Law Soc. Am., Am. Security Coun., Am. Cath. Philos. Assn., Nat. Cath. Ednl. Assn., Univ. Prof. for Acad. Order. Home and Office: Cath Traditionalist Movement 210 Maple Ave Westbury NY 11590-3117 *Especially since my founding of the Catholic Traditionalist Movement in 1964 has made me somewhat "controversial," I draw great inspiration from two sayings adorning the walls of my office. One, attributed to Davy Crockett: "Be sure you're right. Then go ahead!" The other, quoting Saint Athanasius: "If the whole world goes against the truth, then Athanasius must go against the whole world!" And when living by those axioms becomes heavy at times, I just brace myself and coin another one of my own: "It's better to be right alone, than to be wrong with a thousand others!".*

DE PAUW, LINDA GRANT, history educator, publisher; b. N.Y.C., Jan. 19, 1940; d. Phillip and Ruth (Marks) Grant. BA, Swarthmore Coll., 1961; PhD, Johns Hopkins U., 1964. Asst. prof. history George Mason Coll.-U.

Va., Fairfax, 1964-65; spl. asst. to archivist U.S. Nat. Archives, Washington, 1965-66; asst. prof. history George Washington U., Washington, 1966-69, assoc. prof., 1969-75, prof. Am. history, 1975-98, prof. emeritus, 1999—. Editor-in-chief, project dir. Documentary History of the First Fed. Congress, 1966-84; author: The Eleventh Pillar: New York State and the Federal Constitution, 1966, Founding Mothers: Women of America in the Revolutionary Era, 1975, Remember the Ladies, 1976, Seafaring Women, 1982; Baptism of Fire, 1993, Battle Cries and Lullabies, 1998; editor, pub. Minerva: Quar. Report on Women and the Mil., 1983—, Minerva's Bulletin Bd., 1988—; writer/producer Minerva on the Air (armed forces radio), 1987-89; editor H-Minerva, 1995—. Founder, pres. The Minerva Ctr., 1983—. Woodrow Wilson fellow, 1961. Mem. Am. Hist. Assn. (Beveridge award 1964). Home: 20 Granada Rd Pasadena MD 21122-2708

DEPERSIO, RICHARD JOHN, otolaryngologist, plastic surgeon; b. Oak Ridge, Tenn., July 10, 1949; s. John Dominick DePersio and Genevieve (Kellerman) Weinberg; m. Melissa Eddlemon, Nov. 23, 1994; children: Lauren Elizabeth, Katherine Genevieve, Gerard Edward. BS with honors, U. Tenn., Knoxville, 1971; MD, U. Tenn., Memphis, 1974. Diplomate Am. Bd. Facial, Plastic and Reconstructive Surgery, Am. Bd. Otolaryngology. Intern City of Memphis Hosps., 1975; surgery resident Meth. Hosp., Memphis, 1976-77; otolaryngology resident U. Tenn., Memphis, 1977-80; pvt. practice Knoxville Otolaryngology Facial Surgery Clinic, 1980—; clin. assoc. prof., U. Tenn. Dept. Surgery, Knoxville, 1980—. Fellow ACS, Am. Acad. Cosmetic Surgery, Am. Acad. Facial, Plastic and Reconstructive Surgery, Am. Acad. Otolaryngology-Head and Neck Surgery, Am. Rhinologic Soc., Am. Acad. Aesthetic and Restorative Surgery, Am. Soc. TMJ Surgeons, Am. Soc. Laser Medicine and Surgery; mem. AMA, Tenn. Med Assn., Knoxville Acad. Medicine (pres.-elect 1998, pres. 1999). Roman Catholic. Avocations: tennis, golf, basketball. Home: 6805 Shadow Ridge Dr Knoxville TN 37918-9530 Office: Knoxville Otolaryngology 939 E Emerald Ave Knoxville TN 37917-4540

DEPEW, CHARLES GARDNER, research company executive; b. Palmerton, Pa., July 21, 1930; s. Harlan A. and Mary Louise (Gardner) D.; m. Heloise Gilmore, June 16, 1956; children—Mark G., Jane L., Anne G., Henry C. BS in Edn; AB in Natural Sci., Wittenberg U., Springfield, Ohio, 1952; MBA, U. Mich., 1956. With Owens-Ill., Inc., 1956-87, v.p. adminstrv. div., 1969-72, v.p. glass container div., So. area mfg. mgr., 1972-73; v.p. glass container div., tech. dir. Owens-Ill., Inc., Toledo, 1973-79, v.p. corp. staff, energy and environ. tech., 1979-82; v.p., dir. govt. relations Owens-Ill. Inc., Toledo, 1982-87; pres., chief exec. officer Edison Indsl. Systems Ctr., Toledo, 1987-92; chmn. bd. NSF, Inc., Ann Arbor, Mich., 1995—. Trustee Toledo Symphony. Served to lt. (j.g.) USCGR, 1952-54. Presbyterian. E-mail: depew@nsf.org.; Fax: 419-882-7488. Office: NSF Internat PO Box 130 140 Ann Arbor MI 48113-0140*

DEPEW, MARIE KATHRYN, retired secondary school educator; b. Sterling, Colo., Dec. 1, 1928; d. Amos Carl and Dorothy Emelyn (Whiteley) Mehl; m. Emil Carlton DePew, Aug. 30, 1952 (dec. 1973). BA, U. Colo., 1950, MA, 1953. Post grad. Harvard U., Cambridge, Mass., 1962; tchr. Jefferson County Pub. Schs., Arvada, 1953-73; mgr. Colo. Accountability Program, Denver, 1973-83; sr. cons. Colo. Dept. Edn., Denver, 1973-85, ret., 1985. Author: (pamphlet) History of Hammil, Georgetown, Colorado, 1967; contbr. articles to profl. jours. Chmn. Colo. State Accountability Com., Denver, 1971-75. Fellow IDEA Programs, 1976-77, 79-81. Mem. Colo. Hist. Assn., Jefferson County Edn. Assn. (pres. 1963-64), Colo. Edn. Assn. (bd. dirs. 1965-70), Ky. Colonels (hon. mem.), Phi Beta Kappa. Republican. Methodist. Avocations: historical research, writing, travel, collecting antiques. Home: 920 Pennsylvania St Denver CO 80203-3157

DEPEW, MONETTE EVELYN, educator; b. Lindsborg, Kans., Nov. 5, 1956; d. Eugene and Arlene (Danielson) Kumle; m. Neil DePew, Aug. 12, 1979; children: Eric, Stefanie. BA, Ft. Hays State U., 1979, MA, 1994. Cert. tchr., Kans. Instr. Chase (Kans.) High Sch., 1978-84; substitute instr. Pratt (Kans.) High Sch., 1984-88; instr. Pratt C.C., 1988—. Mem. Nat. Coun. Tchrs. English, Midwest Reading & Devel. Edn. Assn., Pratt Higher Edn. Assn. (sec.), Modern Lang. Assn., Conf. Coll. Composition & Comm. Office: Pratt C C 348 NE State Road 61 Pratt KS 67124-8317

DE PIERO, NICHOLAS GABRIEL, anesthesiologist; b. New Castle, Pa., Nov. 29, 1915. BS, Geneva Coll., 1937; MD, Hahnemann U., Phila., 1942. Diplomate Am. Bd. Anesthesiologists. Intern Huron Rd. Hosp., Cleve., 1942-43, resident in anesthesiology, 1943-44; pvt. practice Garfield Heights, Ohio; dir. med. resource effectiveness marymount Hosp., Garfield Heights, med. dir. quality mgmt. Fellow Am. Coll. Anesthesiologists, Internat. Anesthesia Rsch. Soc.; mem. AMA, Am. Soc. Anesthesiologists (pres. 1967-68). Office: Marymount Hosp 12300 Mccracken Rd Garfield Heights OH 44125-2975

DEPINO, CHRIS ANTHONEY, state legislator; b. New Haven, July 10, 1952; s. Salvatore and Angela (Salemme) DeP.; m. Arlene Marie Porto, May 19, 1978; children: Angela, Joanna. AS in Edn., South Ctrl. C.C., New Haven, 1983. Condr. Metro-North Commuter R.R., N.Y.C., 1972-80. 83—, train master, 1980-83; mem. Conn. Ho. of Reps., Hartford, 1992—. Commr. Water Pollution Control Authority, New Haven, 1989-93; mem. New Haven Bd. Aldermen, 1989-93. Fed. Transp. Adminstrn. urban mass transp. planning fellow, 1982. Mem. Annex Young Men's Assn., St. Andrew Apostle Soc., UTU, Metro-North Commutr R.R. President's Club. Republican. Roman Catholic. Avocations: playing jazz harmonica, bicycling, swimming, music instructingg. Home: 1354 Dean St New Haven CT 06512-4000 Office: Conn Ho of Reps Legis Office Bldg Hartford CT 06106*

DEPIRO, MICHAEL FRANCIS, program analyst; b. Camp LeJeune, N.C., Mar. 10, 1968; s. Michael A. and Diane DePiro. BA, U. Tampa, 1990; MPA, Fla. State U., 1996. Staff intern Exec. Office Gov., Tallahassee, Fla., 1994; legis. intern Fla. C. of C., Tallahassee, 1995, Fla. Ho. Reps., Tallahassee, 1995-96; program analyst Dept. Agr., Alexandria, Va., 1996—. 1st. lt. U.S. Army, 1990-94. Mem. ASPA, Internat. City/County Mgmt. Assn. Avocations: reading, music, athletics. E-mail: michaeludepiro@yahoo.com. Office: USDA Food and Nutrition Svc 3101 Park Center Dr Alexandria VA 22302

DEPKOVICH, FRANCIS JOHN, retired retail chain executive; b. Anita, Pa., July 18, 1924; s. Michael John and Mary Elizabeth D.; m. Sophia S. Sokol, Jan. 28, 1950; children—Robert Francis (dec.), Diane Elizabeth. B.S. in Bus. Adminstrn, U. Pitts., 1949. With J.C. Penney Co. Inc., 1949-84; corp. ops. mgr. J.C. Penney Co. Inc., N.Y.C., 1966-79; dir., v.p. store and Facilities planning and constrn. J.C. Penney Co. Inc., 1979-84; seminar spkr.; adj. prof. retailing Fairleigh Dickinson U., Madison, N.J., 1985-94. Mem. master plan project Citizens Com. Morris Twp., N.J., 1970; mem. Morris Twp. Planning Bd., 1972-78, chmn., 1979-86. Served with AUS, 1943-45. Decorated Bronze Star; recipient Disting. Svc. award Greater Morristown area Jaycees, 1990; various certs. of appreciation. Republican. Roman Catholic.

DE PLANQUE, E. GAIL, physicist; b. Orange, N.J., Jan. 15, 1945; d. Martin William and Edna de Planque. AB, Immaculata Coll., 1967; MS, N.J. Inst. Tech., 1973; PhD, NYU, 1983. Physicist U.S. AEC, U.S. Dept. Energy, N.Y.C., 1967-82; dep. dir. environ. measurement lab. U.S. Dept. Energy, N.Y.C., 1982-87, dir. environ. measurement lab., 1987-91; adj. prof. NYU, N.Y.C., 1986—; pres. Pacific Nuclear Coun., 1989-91; mem. engring. sci. dept. adv. com., bd. trustees N.J. Inst. Tech., Newark, 1985-91. Contbr. articles to profl. jours. Commr. U.S. Nuclear Regulatory Commn., 1991-95; bd. trustees Northeast Utilities, 1995—; bd. dirs. British Nuclear Fuels, Inc., 1996—; Tex. Utilities Elec. Ops. Review Com., 1996—; cons. United Nation's Internat. Atomic Energy Agy., 1996—; mem. external adv. com., Amarillo Nat. Resource Ctr. for Plutonium, 1996—. Fellow Am. Nuclear Soc. (bd. dirs. 1977-80, 84-91, v.p. 1987-88, pres. 1988-89), Health Physics Soc., AAAS, Am. Phys. Soc., Assn. for Women in Sci. (v.p. N.Y. met. sect. 1980-82), Internat. Nuclear Energy Acad., (sec. 1996—). Achievements include research in environmental radiation, radiation protection, solid state dosimetry, thermoluminescence. *

DE PLANQUE, EMILE, III, computer consultant; b. Providence, Dec. 15, 1942; s. Emile de Planque Jr. and Dorothy M. (Rainalter) Baker; m. Rosanna Kathleen Bowden, Nov. 11, 1966; children: Suzanne Brigitte, Ian Christopher, Thomas James. Student, U. Va., 1960-65, Georgetown U., 1965; BA in English, George Mason U., 1969, postgrad., 1970-71, 88-89. Purchasing agent York Corrugating Co., Washington, 1965-66; comml. rep. C&P Telephone Co., Washington, 1966-70; staff assoc. C&P Telephone Co., Silver Spring, Md., 1970-77, staff analyst, 1977-81; mem. program staff AT&T, Oakton, Va., 1981-83; mgr. AT&T, Fairfax, Va., 1983-85; info. mgmt. specialist AT&T, Herndon, Va., 1985-89; sr. cons. Mindbank Cons. Group, Vienna, Va., 1990—; sec., treas. Kona Corp., Manassas, Va., 1979-83, bd. dirs., 1979—, v.p., 1984—; owner Innovation, Fairfax, 1984-91; prin. Presssmont Creative Enterprises, Fairfax, 1994—. Treas. Greenbriar West PTA, Fairfax, 1975-77, 80, v.p., 1978. Mem. Am. Assn. for Articifical Intelligence, Internat. Town and Country Club (nominating com. 1989). Avocations: golf, swimming, photography. Home: 3720 Center Way Fairfax VA 22033-2601 Office: Mindbank Cons Group 7800 Leesburg Pike Vienna VA 22182

DE POL, JOHN, artist; b. N.Y.C., Sept. 16, 1913; s. Joseph Zangrando and Theresa (Mariani) DeP.; m. Thelma June Roth, May 31, 1946; 1 dau., Patricia Gail. Student, Art Students League N.Y., Sch. Tech., Belfast, No. Ireland. Free lance wood engraver, printmaker, illustrator prints represented permanent collections, Cin. Mus., Library of Congress, N.Y. Pub. Library, Met. Mus. Art, Syracuse U. Library, others.; creator of, Woodcut Soc., presentation print, 1952, Miniature Print Soc., 1953, Albany Print Club, 1958-59; laureate, N.Y. Printers Wall of Fame, 1980. With USAAF, 1943-45. Recipient Richard Comyn Eames Mus. purchase prize, 1952, Kate W. Arms Meml. prize, 1955, 56, Albany Print Club Purchase prize, 1968, John Taylor Arms Meml. prize NAD, 1968, others; named Academician Nat. Acad. Design. Fellow Cleve. Med. Libr. Assn. (hon.); mem. Art Students League (life), Soc. Am. Graphic Artists, Albany Print Club, Rowfant Club Cleve. (hon.), The Typophiles (hon.). Address: 280 Spring Valley Rd Park Ridge NJ 07656-1018

DE POUZILHAC, ALAIN DUPLESSIS, advertising executive; b. Sete, Herault, France, June 11, 1945; s. Pierre and Jeanine (Caffarel) de P.; m. Carole de Pouzilhac, Sept. 6, 1969; children: Edouard, Cedric, Philippine. Asst. advt. mgr. Publicis, Paris, 1968; advt mgr. DDB, Paris, 1968-75; exec. v.p. Havas Conseil, Neuilly, France, 1976-82, chmn., CEO, 1982-87; chmn., CEO HDM, Neuilly and Puteaux, France, 1987-89; chmn., CEO Eurocom, Neuilly, 1989—, CEO, 1989—; chmn., CEO EURO RSCG, Neuilly, 1991—, Havas Advt., 1996—. Avocations: soccer, rugby. Home: 21 rue de Miromesnil, 75008 Paris France Office: Havas Advt. 84 rue de Villiers, 92300 Levallois-Perret France

DEPP, JOHNNY, actor; b. Owensboro, Ky., June 9, 1963; s. John and Betty Sue D.; m. Lori Anne Allison (div.). Guitarist; ex-member bands the Flame, the Kids, Rock City Angels, 1985; actor TV series 21 Jump Street, 1987-90; actor films Nightmare on Elm Street, 1984, Private Resort, 1985, Platoon, 1986, Cry-Baby, 1990, Edward Scissorhands, 1990, Freddy's Dead: The Final Nightmare, 1991, American Dreamers, 1992, Benny & Joon, 1993, What's Eating Gilbert Grape, 1993, Ed Wood, 1994, Arizona Dreamer, Don Juan DeMarco, 1995, Dead Man, 1995, Nick of Time, 1996, The Brave, Donnie Brasco, 1997, L.A. Without a Map, 1998, The Source, 1999, The Ninth Gate, 1999, The Libertine, 1999, Just to Be Together, 1999, The Astronaut's Wife, 1999, Sleepy Hollow, 1999; writer, dir., actor: The Brave, 1997, Fear and Loathing in Las Vegas, 1998, The Astronaut's Wife, 1998; TV movies include Slow Burn, 1986; TV guest appearance The Vicar of Dibley, 1994. Office: 500 Sepulveda Blvd Ste 500 Los Angeles CA 90049-3551 also: 2049 Century Park E Ste 2500 Los Angeles CA 90067-3127*

DEPP, (O.) RICHARD, III, obstetrician-gynecologist, educator; b. Glasgow, Ky., Sept. 26, 1938; s. Oren Richard II and Alma (Cates) D.; m. Kathleen Ann Kuhlman, Mar. 7, 1981; children: Oren Richard IV, Steven Christopher, Anna Bayles, Mary Cates. BS, Tulane U., 1960, MD, 1963. Diplomate Am. Bd. Ob-Gyn (examiner), Am. Bd. Maternal-Fetal Medicine. Resident in ob-gyn. Tulane U., New Orleans, 1967; sr. rsch. fellow U. Wash. Med. Sch., Seattle, 1967-69; assist. prof. ob-gyn. U. Wash., Seattle, 1969-71, U. Pitts., 1971-75; head maternal-fetal medicine, dir. perinatal ctr. Northwestern U. Med. Sch., Chgo., 1975-87, assoc. prof., 1975-81, prof., 1981-87; dir. obstetrics Prentice Women's Hosp., Chgo., 1975-87; prof. ob-gyn. Northwestern U. Med. Sch., 1987; prof. and chmn. ob-gyn. Jefferson Med. Coll., Phila., 1987-97; mem. attending staff, chmn. dept. ob-gyn. Thomas Jefferson U. Hosp., Phila., 1987—; chief dept. ob-gyn. Harborview Med. Ctr. King County Hosp., Seattle, 1969-71; dir. maternal-fetal intensive care unit, mem. attending staff Magee-Women's Hosp., Pitts., 1971-75; dir. div. obstetrics, mem. attending staff Prentice Women's Hosp. and Maternity Ctr. Northwestern Meml. Hosp., Chgo., 1975-87. Editor: The Ob-Gyn Resident, 1993; assoc. editor: Gynecology and Obstetrics, 1979; mem. editl. bd. Fetal Medicine; host Ob-Gyn Update Lifetime TV, 1992; contbr. chpts. to textbooks, articles to profl. jours. Major U.S. Army, 1963-71. Named One of Top 110 Outstanding Ob-Gyn's in U.S. Good Housekeeping mag., Sept. 1988; grantee NIH, March of Dimes Birth Defects Found. Fellow ACOG, Soc. Perinatal Obstetricians, Soc. Gynecologic Investigation, Am. Gynecol. and Obstetrics Soc., Chgo. Gynecol. Soc.; mem. Ctrl. Assn. Obstetricians and Gynecologists, Assn. Profs. Gynecology and Obstetrics (coun., sect. treas., pres.-elect), Phila. Cricket Club, Union League, Phi Eta Sigma, Alpha Epsilon Delta. Avocations: tennis, golf, travel. Office: Jefferson Med Coll 834 Chestnut St Ste 400 Philadelphia PA 19107-5100

DEPPERSCHMIDT, THOMAS ORLANDO, economist, educator; b. St. Louis, Dec. 3, 1935; s. Robert O. and Marcella C. (Meier) D.; m. Bertha Marie Waldman, Nov. 28, 1957; children: M. Susan, Mark, Joel, Andrew, Amy, Joan. A.B., Ft. Hays (Kans.) State U., 1958; Ph.D., U. Tex., 1965. Asst. prof., then asso. prof. W. Tex. State U., Canyon, 1961-66; prof. econs. Memphis State U., 1966—, chmn. dept., 1977-83; research assoc. study N.Y.C. elevator industry, 1996. Co-author: Encyclopedia of Economics, 1974, Assessing Family Loss in Wrongful Death Litigation, 1999; editor: Financial Policies in Transition, 1968; author over 40 tech. treatises. With AUS, 1954-56. Mem. Am. Econ. Assn., Nat. Acad. Forensic Economists, Am. Acad. Econ. and Fin. Experts (bd. dirs.), Soc. Litigation Economists. Home: 1957 Mt Repose Germantown TN 38139-3443 Office: U Memphis Dept Econs Memphis TN 38152

DEPPISCH, PAUL VINCENT, data communications executive; b. Madison, Wis., Dec. 15, 1950; s. Vincent Francis and Evelyn Catherine (Eichmeier) D. Cable splicing foreman GTE Calif., Santa Monica, 1968-73; gen. foreman DataCom Inc., Santa Monica, 1973-78; sr. project mgr. A.I.D.C.O., North Hollywood, Calif., 1978-84; cons. Systex Group Ltd., Phoenix, 1984-90; pres. Ambient Data Tech. Inc., Upland, Calif., 1990—; founder, dir. Boogere Prodns. Internat., Santa Monica, 1973—; bd. dirs. Systex Group Ltd. Min. Universal Life Ch., Modesto, Calif. Mem. Bldg. Industry Cons. Svc., Inc., C. of C., L.A. World Affairs Coun. Avocations: hunting, fishing, community service. Home: PO Box 1712 Santa Monica CA 90406-1712 Office: Ambient Data Tech Inc 517 N Mountain Ave # 101 Upland CA 91786-5016

DEPREIST, JAMES ANDERSON, conductor; b. Phila., Nov. 21, 1936; s. James Henry and Ethel (Anderson) De P.; m. Betty Louise Childress, Aug. 10, 1963; children: Tracy Elisabeth, Jennifer Anne; m. Ginette Grenier, July 19, 1980. Student, Phila. Conservatory Music, 1959-61; BS, U. Pa., 1958, MA, 1961, LHD (hon.), 1976; LHD (hon.), Reed Coll., 1990, Portland State U., 1993; MusD (hon.), Laval U., Quebec City, Can., 1980, Linfield Coll., 1986, Juilliard, 1993; DFA (hon.), U. Portland, 1983, Pacific U., 1985, Willamette U., 1987, Drexel U., 1989, Oreg. State U., 1990; Doctor of Arts and Letters (hon.), St. Mary's Coll., Moraga, Calif., 1985; HHD (hon.), Lewis and Clark U., 1986. Am. specialist music for State Dept., 1962-63; condr.-in-residence Bangkok, 1963-64; condr. various symphonies and orchs., 1964—; conductor, music dir. Oreg. Symphony, Portland, 1980—. Condr.: Am. debut with N.Y. Philharm., 1964, asst. condr. to Leonard Bernstein, N.Y. Philharm. Orch., 1965-66, prin. guest condr. Symphony of New World, 1968-70, European debut with Rotterdam Philharm., 1969; Helsinki Philharm., 1993; assoc. condr. Nat. Symphony Orch., Washington, 1971-75, prin. guest condr. Nat. Symphony Orch., 1975-76; music dir. L'Orchestre Symphonique de Que., 1976-83, Oreg. Symphony, 1980—, prin. guest condr. Helsinki Philharmonic, 1993, Mus. Dir. Monte Carlo Philharm., 1994; appeared with Phila. Orch., 1972, 76, 84, 85, 87, 90, 92, 93, 94, Chgo. Symphony, 1973, 90, 92, 94, Boston Symphony, 1973, Cleve. Orch., 1974; condr.: Am. premiere of Dvorak's First Symphony, N.Y. Philharm., 1972; chief condr. Malmö Symphony, 1991-94; author: (poems) This Precipice Garden, 1987, The Distant Siren, 1989. Trustee Lewis and Clark Coll., 1983—. Recipient 1st prize gold medal Dimitri Mitropoulos Internat. Music Competition for Condrs., 1964, Merit citation City of Phila., 1969, medal of City of Que., 1983; grantee Martha Baird Rockefeller Fund for Music, 1969, Insignia of Comdr. of Order of Lion of Finland, 1992. Fellow Am. Acad. Arts and Scis.; mem. Royal Swedish Acad. Music. Office: Oreg Symphony 921 SW Washington Ste 200 Portland OR 97205*

DEPTA, VICTOR MARSHALL, English educator, editor; b. Acoville, W.Va., Mar. 20, 1939; s. Andrew Steve and Opal Dama (Waugh) D.; m. Mary Sue Allen, Sept. 14, 1964 (div. Jan. 1984); 1 child, Helen Margaret. BA, Marshall U., 1965; MA, San Francisco State U., 1968; PhD, Ohio U., 1972. Prof. English, U. Tenn., Martin, 1972—; co-editor Blair Mountain Press, Martin, 1998—. Author: (books of poetry) The Creek, 1973, The House, 1978, A Doorkeeper in the House, 1993, The Helen Poems, 1994, the Silence of Blackberries, 1999, (novel) Idol and Sanctuary, 1993. With USN, 1956-60. Democrat. Home: 207 Elm St Martin TN 38237 Office: Blair Mountain Press PO Box 147 Martin TN 38237

DEPTULA, DAVID A., United States Air Force general. BS in Astronomy, U. Va., 1974, MS in Systems Engring., 1976; grad., Squadron Officer Sch., 1978, USAF Fighter Weapons Sch, Nellis AFB, Nev., Air Command and Staff Coll., 1983, Armed Forces Staff Coll., Norfolk Naval Air Sta., Va., 1987; MS in Nat. Security Strategy, Nat. War Coll., Ft. McNair, Washington, 1994. Commd. 2d lt. USAF, 1976, advanced through grades to Brig. Gen., 1998; tng. pilot to flight cmmdr. Kadena Air Base, Japan, 1976-83; chief wing weapons and tactics divsn., instr. pilot 325th Tactical Tng. Wing, Tyndall AFB, Fla., 1984-87; action officer, directorate Warfighting Concepts Devel. Hdqs. USAF, Washington, 1988-89; policy and issues analyst Office Sec. of Air Force, Washington, 1989-92; prin. offensive air campaign planner for dir. campaign plans USAF Operation Desert Shield, 1990-91; dir. Iraq target planning group USAF Operation Desert Storm, Riyadh, Saudi Arabia, 1990-91; team leader joint warfighting and deep attack issues Office Sec. Defense, Washington, 1994-95; commdr. 33rd Ops. Group, Eglin AFB, Fla., 1995-96; sr. air force rep. Nat. Defense Panel, Office Sec. Defense, Washington, 1997-98; cmmdr. combined task force operation no. watch U.S. European Command, Incirlik Air Base, Turkey, 1998—. Decorated Bronze Star medal, Air Medal, Combat Readiness medal with 2 oak leaf clusters, Legion of Merit, Defense Superior Svc. medal with oak leaf cluster. Office: Hdq CTF/CG USAF APO AE 09396

DERBES, ALBERT JOSEPH, III, lawyer, accountant; b. New Orleans, Mar. 18, 1940; s. Albert Joseph Jr. and Marcelle (Jourdan) D.; m. Shirley Brown, June 8, 1963; children: Albert Joseph IV, Eric Joseph. BBA, Tulane U., 1963, JD, 1966. Bar: La., Tex., U.S. Tax Ct., U.S. Supreme Ct., U.S. Ct. Appeals (5th cir.), U.S. Dist. Ct. (ea., mid. and we. dists.) La.; CPA, La., Miss., Ga., Fla. Ptnr. Derbes & Derbes, CPAs, New Orleans, 1964-69, Trahan, Kernion, & Derbes, CPAs, New Orleans, 1970-78, Hurdman & Cranston, CPAs, New Orleans, 1978-79, Main, Hurdman, CPAs, New Orleans, 1979-82, Windhorst, Pastorek & Gaundry, Attys. at Law, Harvey, La., 1982-88, Derbes & Co., CPAs, Metairie, La., 1982—; pvt. practice, 1988-95; with The Derbes Law Firm, LLC, Metairie, 1995—. Capt. USAF, 1966-69. Mem. ABA, AICPAs, La. State Bar Assn., La. Soc. CPAs, Miss. Soc. CPAs, Nat. Assn. State Bds. of Accountancy (bd. dirs. 1983-84, v.p. 1984-85, pres. 1986-87). Republican. Roman Catholic. Avocations: fishing, reading. Office: 3027 Ridgelake Dr PO Box 8176 Metairie LA 70011-8176

DERBES, DANIEL WILLIAM, manufacturing executive; b. Cin., Mar. 30, 1930; s. Earl Milton and Ruth Irene (Grauten) D.; m. Patricia Maloney, June 4, 1952; children: Donna Ann, Nancy Lynn (dec.), Stephen Paul. BS, U.S. Mil. Acad., 1952; MBA, Xavier U., Cin., 1963. Devel. engr. AiResearch Mfg. Co., Phoenix, 1956-58; with Garrett Corp., L.A., 1958-80, v.p., gen. mgr., then exec. v.p., 1975-80, dir., 1976-87; pres. Signal Cos., Inc., 1980-82, La Jolla, Calif., 1982-83; pres. Signal Advanced Tech Group, 1983-85, Allied-Signal Internat. Inc., 1985-88; exec. v.p. Allied-Signal, Inc., Morristown, N.J., 1985-88; pres. Signal Ventures, Solana Beach, Calif., 1990—; bd. dirs. San Diego Gas & Electric Co., chmn., 1998—; bd. dirs. Enova Corp., Oak Industries, Inc., WD-40 Co., Sempra Energy, So. Calif. Gas Co., Pacific Enterprises. Exec. bd. nat. coun. Boy Scouts Am., 1981-95; trustee U. San Diego, 1981—, vice-chmn., bd. trustees, 1990-93, chmn., 1993-96. With AUS, 1952-56. Republican. Roman Catholic. Office: Signal Ventures 777 S Pacific Coast Hwy Ste 107 Solana Beach CA 92075-2623

DERBY, ADELE, government agency administrator; b. Lynn, Mass., Apr. 1, 1932; d. Louis Irving and Pauline Marie (Zack) D.; m. David Keith Spielberger, Joan Ellen Spielberger. BS in Math., Tufts U., 1952; MS in Pub. Adminstrn., Fla. State U., 1976. Instr. Fla. State U., Tallahassee, 1967-71; chief Bur. Planning, Dept. Adminstrn., Tallahassee, 1971-77; gov.'s hwy. safety rep. State of Fla., Tallahassee, 1977-80; dir. driver and pedestrian rsch. Nat. Hwy. Traffic Safety Adminstrn., Washington, 1980-85, assoc. adminstr., 1985—. Recipient Presdl. Meritorious Exec. award Pres. of U.S., 1993, Disting. Exec. award, 1998, Hammer award V.P. of U.S., 1996. Mem. Fed. Exec. Alumni Assn. (pres. 1991-93), Women in Transp., Exec. Women in Govt. Home: 6308 Barrister Pl Alexandria VA 22307-1214 Office: US Dept Transp NHTSA 400 7th St SW Rm 5238 Washington DC 20590-0001

DERBY, ERNEST STEPHEN, federal judge; b. Boston, July 10, 1938; s. Elmer Goodrich and Lucy (Davis) D.; m. Gretel Hanauer, June 10, 1961; children: Anne Gray, Michael Stephen. AB with distinction, Wesleyan U., 1960; LLB cum laude, Harvard U., 1965. Bar: Md. Ct. Appeals 1965, U.S. Dist. Ct. Md. 1966, U.S. Ct. Appeals (4th cir.) 1968, U.S. Supreme Ct. 1973. Law clk. to presiding justice U.S. Dist. Ct. Md. and U.S. Ct. of Appeals 4th cir., 1965-66; assoc. Piper & Marbury, Balt., 1966-71, ptnr., 1973-87; asst. atty. gen. Atty. Gen. Md., 1971-73; judge U.S. Bankruptcy Ct., Balt., 1987—; adj. faculty U. Md. Sch. Law, 1987, 90—. Pres. Dismas Ho., Balt. Inc., 1969—; trustee Enoch Pratt Free Libr., Balt., 1977-93. Fellow Am. Coll. Bankruptcy, Md. Bar Found.; mem. Md. State Bar Assn., Anne Arundel County Bar Assn., Paca/Brent Am. Inn of Ct. (pres. 1993-94). Office: US District Court US Courthouse 101 W Lombard St Rm 9442 Baltimore MD 21201-2626

DERBY, SHELAH ANN NOVAK, English language educator; b. Syracuse, N.Y., May 10, 1961; d. Sidney and Gloria (Kahn) N.; m. Michael F. Derby, Aug. 20, 1988. BA, SUNY, Potsdam, 1983; MA, NYU, 1988. Cert. tchr. N.Y., Ala., N.C., Va. Tchr. English, Mexico (N.Y.) Acad. and Ctrl. Schs., 1984-88, Prince William County Schs., Manassas, Va., 1988-93, Sumter County Schs., York, Ala., 1993-97, Gates County Schs., Gatesville, N.C., 1997—; cons. No. Va. Writing Project, 1991-92. Participant SUPER Inst. Ala. Humanities Found., 1996, Confritute, 1999. Mem. Nat. Coun. Tchrs. English, N.C. Edn. Assn. Home: 107 Maury Pl Suffolk VA 23434-6217

DERBYSHIRE, WILLIAM WADLEIGH, language educator, translator; b. Phila., Dec. 30, 1936; s. Roger S. and Arline (Wadleigh) D.; m. Kathleen Derbyshire (div. 1981); children: Ann, Wesley, Lee. BA, U. Pa., 1958, MA, 1959, PhD, 1964. Cert. Russian-English translator. Instr. U. Pa., Phila., 1959-61; asst. prof. Lycoming Coll., Williamsport, Pa., 1961-63, SUNY-Binghamton, Vestal, N.Y., 1964-69; assoc. prof. Rutgers U., New Brunswick, N.J., 1969-76, prof., 1976-94; freelance translator, 1994—; cons. Thomas Edison Coll., Trenton, N.J., 1981-94. Author: Reference Grammar of Slovene, 1993; contbr. articles to profl. jours. Active Govs. Coun. ethnic Affairs, N.J., 1992-94. Fulbright fellow, 1972-73, N.J. Dept. Higher Edn. fellow, 1984-85; Rsch. grantee Dept. Edn., Washington, 1989-90, 95-96. Mem. Am. Assn. for the Advancement of Slavic Studies (bd. dirs. 1986-89), Am. Assn. Tchrs. Slavic and Eastern European Langs. (pres. 1985-86), Soc. Slovene Studies (sec., treas. 1982-86), Am. Translators Assn. Avocation: opera. Office: Rutgers U 227 Scott Hall New Brunswick NJ 08903

DERCHIN, DARY BRET INGHAM, writer; b. Camden, N.J., Sept. 15, 1941; d. Charles and Dorothy Roberta (Ingham) Lambiase; m. Michael Wayne Derchin, Dec. 29, 1970; children: Taylor-Leigh, Danielle Ashlin Lacey. BA, Montclair State Coll., 1962; postgrad., NYU, 1965, New Sch.,

1966. Tchr. Randolph, N.J., 1962-64; rsch. asst. NYU, N.Y.C., 1965-67, Bolivian Peace Corps Project, N.Y.C., 1966; co-head rsch. Derchin Enterprises, N.Y.C., 1970-75. Author: Real Talk, 1992; playwright Blue No More; contbr. articles to the N.Y. Times, Harper's and book the Big Picture, others; talk show host Sta. WALE, 1995, KFNY, WEVD; spkr., guest talk shows. Mem. Drama League, Lincoln Ctr. Film Soc., Am. Film Inst., Friends of Poets and Writers, Univ. Club, Nat. Art Club (lit. com., film com., Joseph Kesselring Playwright award com.). Home: Laurel Cove PO Box 200 Fair Haven NJ 07704-0200

DERCHIN, MICHAEL WAYNE, financial analyst; b. N.Y.C., Aug. 17, 1942; s. James and Rose (Minenberg) D.; m. Dary Bret Ingham, Dec. 29, 1970; children: Taylor-Leigh, Danielle-Ashlin Lacey. BA, Bklyn. Coll., 1964; MBA, CCNY, 1966; postgrad., Syracuse U., 1966-69. Sr. analyst Am. Airlines, N.Y.C., 1969-70; dir. mktg. Pan Am. World Airways, N.Y.C., 1970-74, Am. Airlines, N.Y.C., 1974-79; v.p. Oppenheimer & Co., Inc., N.Y.C., 1979-82, First Boston Corp., N.Y.C., 1982-88; mng. dir. Drexel Burnham Lambert, N.Y.C., 1988-90; sr. v.p., dir. rsch., chmn. stock selection com. Nat. West Securities, N.Y.C., 1990-95; columnist Travel Weekly, N.Y.C., 1984-90; spl. guest Wall St. Week, Owings Mills, Md., 1982-90, guest MacNeil Lehrer Newshour, N.Y., 1985; expert witness U.S. Senate Aviation subcom., 1984; lectr. Travel Research Assn., N.Y.C., 1981-84. Named to first team All Am. Analysts Instnl. Investor mag., 1983, 90. Mem. N.Y. Soc. Security Analysts, N.Y. Airline Analysts Soc. (chmn. mem. com. 1985, pres. 1986-87), Wings Club, Travel Tourism Rsch. Assn., Nat. Arts U. Club (N.Y.C.), Union League Club (N.Y.C.), Navesink Country Club (Crumson, N.J.).

DERDENGER, PATRICK, lawyer; b. L.A., June 29, 1946; s. Charles Patrick and Drucilla Marguerite (Lange) D.; m. Jo Lynn Dickins, Aug. 24, 1968; children: Kristin Lynn, Bryan Patrick, Timothy Patrick. BA, Loyola U., L.A., 1968; MBA, U. So. Calif., 1971, JD, 1974; LLM in Taxation, George Washington U., 1977. Bar: Calif. 1974, U.S. Ct. Claims 1975, Ariz. 1979, U.S. Ct. Appeals (9th cir.) 1979, U.S. Dist. Ct. Ariz. 1979, U.S. Tax Ct. 1979, U.S. Supreme Ct. 1979; cert. specialist in tax law. Trial atty. honors program U.S. Dept. Justice, Washington, 1974-78; ptnr. Lewis and Roca, Phoenix, 1978—; adj. prof. taxation Golden Gate U., Phoenix, 1983-87; mem. Ariz. State Tax Ct. Legis. Study Commn., Tax Law Specialist Commn., Ariz. Property Tax Oversight Commn.; appt. Ariz. Property Tax Oversight Commn., 1997—. Author: Arizona State and Local Taxation, Cases and Materials, 1983, Arizona Sales and Use Tax Guide, 1990, Advanced Arizona Sales and Use Tax, 1987-96, Arizona State and Local Taxation, 1989, 93, 96, Arizona Sales and Use Tax, 1988-96. Arizona Property Taxation, 1993-96, ABA Sales and Use Tax Deskbook, Property Tax Deskbook. Past pres., bd. dirs. North Scottsdale Little League; apptd. Ariz. Property Tax Oversight Commn. Served to capt. USAF, 1968-71. Recipient U.S. Law Week award Bur. Nat. Affairs, 1974. Mem. ABA (taxation sect., various coms.), Ariz. Bar Assn. (taxation sect., former chair sect. taxation, former treas., chmn. state and local tax com., chmn. continuing legal edn. com., tax adv. com., others, mem. tax law specialist commn.), Maricopa County Bar Assn., Inst. Sales Taxation, Nat. Tax Assn., Inst. Property Taxation Met. C. of C., Ariz. C. of C. (chair tax com.), U. So. Calif. Alumni Club (past pres., bd. dirs.), Phi Delta Phi. Home: 10040 E Happy Valley Rd Scottsdale AZ 85255-2395 Office: Lewis and Roca 2 Renaissance Plz 40 N Central Ave Ste 1900 Phoenix AZ 85004-4429

DERDERIAN, HOVNAN, church official; b. Beirut, Dec. 1, 1957. Student, Sem. of Catholicossate Cilicia, Antelias, Lebanon, 1983, Sem. Holy See of Etchmiadzin, Armenia; B of Theology, U. Oxford, Eng., 1983, M of Theology, 1987. Ordained celibate priest, 1980; ordained bishop, 1990, ordained archbishop, 1993. Pastor Holy Trinity Armenian ch., Toronto, Ont., Can., 1984-90; primate of diocese, bishop Armenian Ch. of Can., 1990-93, archbishop, 1993-94; v.p. Can. Coun. Chs., 1994—; primate Armenian Ch. Can. Office: Diocese of Armenian Ch Can, 615 Stuart, Outremont, PQ Canada H2V 3H2

DERDERIAN, JOHN A., systems analyst; b. Providence, Dec. 20, 1957; s. Roger and Sue (Tikiryan) D.; m. Terry Lynn Knox, May 11, 1984; children: Elizabeth, Michaela. BA in Psychology, U. R.I., 1979; MA in Devel. Psychology, R.I. Coll., 1981; MBA in Healthcare Adminstrn., Bryant Coll., Smithfield, R.I., 1989. Counselor, evening mgr. New Routes Runaway Program, Providence, 1980-81; psychotherapist Boston VA Med. Ctr., 1984-86, cancer registrar, 1987; chief data mgmt. Providence VA Med. Ctr., 1987-91, chief ambulatory care, 1990-91; software devel. analyst U.S. Dept. Vets. Affairs, Albany, N.Y., 1991—; vice-chmn. data validation com. Providence VA Med. Ctr., 1988-91. Fundraiser Walk for Life, Providence, 1985-91; vol., coach Spl. Olympics, Ft. Devens, Mass., 1982-83. With U.S. Army, 1981-83. Decorated Army Commendation medal. Diplomate Am. Coll. Healthcare Execs. (cert., regent's adv. coun. 1991). Avocations: computers, running, reading, skydiving. Office: US Dept Vets Affairs Albany CIOFO 113 Holland Ave Fl 4 Albany NY 12208-3410

DERE, WILLARD HONGLEN, internist, educator; b. Sacramento, Jan. 8, 1954; s. William Janson and Bessie Lon (Joe) D.; m. Julia Mei Lum, June 18, 1978; children: Melissa Ellen, Kathryn Elizabeth. AB, U. Calif., Davis, 1975, MD, 1980. Diplomate Nat. Bd. Med. Examiners. Intern Health Sci. Ctr., U. Utah, Salt Lake City, 1980-81, resident, 1981-83; instr. internal medicine, geriatrics U. Utah, Salt Lake City, 1985-87, asst. prof., 1987-89; rsch. fellow U. Calif., San Francisco, 1983-85; asst. prof. Ind. U. Sch Medicine, Indpls., 1989-98; clin. assoc. prof. Ind. U. Sch. Medicine, Indpls., 1998—; clin. rsch. physician Lilly Rsch. Labs., Indpls., 1989-91, dir. European regulatory affairs, 1991, dir. endocrine rsch., 1994-98, exec. dir. clin. rsch., 1998—; dir. emergency rm. VA Med. Ctr., Salt Lake City, 1985-86; cons. U. Utah Student Health Svc., Salt Lake City, 1985-89, acting dir., 1987-88. Editor: (book) Practical Care of the Ambulatory Patient, 1989; Contbr. articles to profl. jours. Vol. account exec. United Way, Ind., 1990. Hon. assoc. investigator VA, San Francisco, 1984. Mem. ACP, AAAS, Am. Geriatrics Soc., Am. Soc. Bone and Mineral Rsch., Assn. Osteobiology. Presbyn. Achievements include research in adrenocortical function in AIDS, oncogene regulation in thyroid cells; multi-center antibiotic trials, drug safety; health economics; and SERMs (selective estrogen receptor modulators). Office: Lilly Corp Ctr Lilly Rsch Labs Indianapolis IN 46285

DEREGIBUS, WILLIAM, artist; b. Mount Kisco, N.Y., May 21, 1954; s. Cleo and Diana (Douglass) DeR.; m. Surin Rungpanich, Oct. 30, 1986. BFA, Cornell U., Ithaca, N.Y., 1978. Artist, illustrator N.Y., Bangkok, 1978-86, 88—; gen. mgr. Vegas Hotel, Hua Hin, 1986-88. Illustrator: (books) Franklin and Sterling Hill Mines, N.J.-the World's Most Magnificent Mineral Deposits, 1995, The Silver Surf, 1995; painter, artist: (oil portrait) Mr. & Mrs. Edmund C. Lynch III, 1986, Aspen East: Home of D.H. Koch, Southampton, N.Y., 1993; curator Nassau County Ctr. for Cultural Devel., Muttontown, N.Y., 1996; mineral art included in the Steidle Mineral Art Collection/Pa. State U.; executed mural. Recipient Peacock Showcase award Visual Arts Alliance of Long Island, 1991. Episcopalian. Avocations: chess, martial arts, skiing, mineralogy, Asian studies. Home: Piping Rock Rd Locust Valley NY 11560

DE REINECK, MARIE, interior designer; b. Ellington, Mo.; d. Thomas Otto and Lessie (Deen) Buford; m. Baron Radu de Reineck, Mar. 30, 1933; 1 child, Claire; m. Radu Romanesco, Dec. 8, 1970. BS, Fordham U., 1941; grad., N.Y. Sch. Interior Design. Freelance interior designer, 1941—; tchr. interior design Finch Coll., N.Y.C., 1946-61, NYU, N.Y.C., 1949-54; founder Claymar Sch. Design, 1948-55. Author: How to Decorate Your Home, 1954. Mem. Am. Inst. Decorators, AIA/Am. Archtl. Found. (allied mem.). Republican. Roman Catholic.

DEREMEE, RICHARD ARTHUR, physician, educator, researcher; b. Red Wing, Minn., July 4, 1933; s. Arthur Eugene and Anna Helen (Vinquist) DeR.; m. E. Lucille Fogelstrom, Mar. 17, 1956; children—Lisa C., Brita L., Bo A. B.A., Gustavus Adolphus Coll., 1955; B.S., U. Minn., 1959, M.D., 1959. Diplomate Am. Bd. Internal Medicine. Intern William Beaumont Gen. Hosp., El Paso, 1959-60; resident Mayo Clinic, Rochester, Minn., 1962-66; fellow in internal medicine and pulmonary disease Mayo Clinic, 1962-66, cons. in internal medicine and pulmonary disease, 1966—; assoc. prof. medicine Mayo Med. Sch., Rochester, 1977-83, prof. medicine, 1983-96; ret., 1996; Friedrich Wegener Meml. lectr. Lübeck, Germany, 1992. Contbr. numerous articles to profl. jours. Served as capt. M.C., U.S. Army, 1959-62. Recipient cert. of achievement U.S. Army, 1962; Judson Daland travel award Mayo Found., 1966; Alumni citation Gustavus Adolphus Coll., 1982. Fellow ACP, Am. Coll. Chest Physicians; mem. Am. Thoracic Soc. Republican. Lutheran. Home: 2209 5th Ave NE Rochester MN 55906-4017

DEREMER, SUSAN RENÉ, artist; b. Atlanta, June 29, 1959; d. Lewis Emmett Rhoden and Beth Lee (Perkins) Keener; m. Randall Eugene Deremer, Apr. 7, 1990. Student, Inst. Fine Arts, Rio de Janeiro, 1977-78; BFA, U. Ga., 1982; postgrad., Atlanta Law Sch., 1987-88. Art dir. Exec. Printing, Inc., Marietta, Ga., 1988-90; graphic artist IBM, Atlanta, 1992-93; pres. Deremer Studio, Inc., Atlanta, 1993—. Illustrator/author: (book): Atlanta, An Historical Sketchbook, 1998; author: (newsletter) Folio, 1997—; one-woman shows include South Cobb Arts Alliance, Inc., Mableton, Ga., 1992, Smyrna (Ga.) Libr., 1996; exhibited in group shows 21st Ann. Atlanta Artists Club Mems. Traveling Show, 1993, 22d Ann., 1994, Atlanta Artist Club Show, 1994, Fine Arts Soc. of Kennesaw, Ga., 1995, Portrait Soc. of Atlanta, 1994-99; represented in permanent collections Bapt. Student Ctr., U. Ga., Athens, Robert L. Osborne H.S., Marietta, Glitsch Process Sys., Roswell, Ga. Mem. student adv. bd. High Mus. of Art, Atlanta, 1976-77, Ga. Gov.'s honors program Ga. State Bd. Edn., Macon, 1976. Recipient 1st pl. award Ga. Scholastic Press Assn., 1977, 2d pl. award Semana de Arte, 1977, Award of Excellence, Printing Industry Assn. of Ga., 1989. Mem. Am. Artists Profl. League Inc. (69th Grand Nat. Exhibition 1997, 70th Grand Nat. Exhibition 1998), Portrait Soc. Atlanta, Inc. (pres. 1992—), Am. Soc. Portrait Artists, Am. Soc. Classical Realism, Portrait Inst. N.Y. (charter). Presbyterian. E-mail: sderemer@worldnet.att.net. Office: Deremer Studio Inc PO Box 724023 Atlanta GA 31139-1023

DERESIEWICZ, HERBERT, mechanical engineering educator; b. Brno, Czechoslovakia, Nov. 5, 1925; s. William and Lotte (Rappaport) D.; m. Evelyn Altman, Mar. 12, 1955; children: Ellen, Robert, William. BME, CCNY, 1946; MS, Columbia U., 1948, PhD, 1952. Sr. staff engr. Applied Physics Lab., Johns Hopkins U., 1950-51; mem. faculty Columbia U., N.Y.C., 1951—, prof. mech. engring., 1962-94, chmn. dept. mech. engring., 1981-87, 90-93, emeritus, 1994—; cons. stress analysis, vibrations, elastic contact, wave propagation, mechanics granular and porous media., Fulbright sr. research scholar, Italy, 1960-61, Fulbright lectr., Israel, 1966-67; vis. prof., Israel, 1973-74. Editor Columbia Engring. Rsch., 1975-92; contbr. articles to profl. jours. Served with AUS, 1946-47. Univ. fellow Columbia U., 1949-50. Home: 336 Broad Ave Englewood NJ 07631-4304

DE REVERE, DAVID WILSEN, professional society administrator; b. Englewood, N.J., Nov. 13, 1937; s. Wilbur L. and Ethel M. (Gilchrist) De R.; m. Ellen B. Tompkins, June 7, 1958; children: Mark S., Roger T. BA, Colgate U., 1959; MDiv, Yale U., 1963. Cert. master chaplain Internat. Conf. Police Chaplains. Sr. pastor 1st Ch. of Christ in Saybrook, Old Saybrook, Conn., 1963-85; exec. dir. Internat. Conf. Police Chaplains, Destin, Fla., 1985—. Author, editor: Chaplaincy in Law Enforcement, 1989. Chaplain Old Saybrook (Conn.) Dept. Police Svcs., 1964-85, FBI, 1991—. Home and Office: PO Box 5590 Destin FL 32540-5590

DEREVLANY, JOHN, television writer/producer; b. Oct. 3, 1964. Writer, dir. (film) Leftovers, L.A., 1994; writer, performer TV Nation, N.Y.C., 1995; writer Nickelodeon, Burbank, Calif., 1996-97; writer, prodr. Jim Henson TV, L.A., 1998—; Founder Uke Til U Puke heavy metal ukulele band, 1988-91. Co-author: (book) Yuppies Invade My House at Dinnertime, 1988; contbg. editor: Nat. Lampoon nat., 1991. Recipient Grammy award nomination for TV Nation, 1995, Writer's Guild of Am. award for This Just In, 1994. Home: 171 Pier Ave #221 Santa Monica CA 90405

DERFNER, CAROL ANN, management consultant, fundraising counsel; b. San Diego, Aug. 8, 1944; d. Robert Raymond and Mildred Francis (Sherman) Parmley; m. John A. Derfner, Aug. 18, 1968 (div. Aug. 1975); 1 child, Tessa Leigh. AA, El Camino Coll., 1965; student, U. Alaska, NYU. Exec. dir. Anchorage (Alaska) Arts Coun., 1973-82; spl. asst. to the gov. State of Alaska, 1982-85; lobbyist, policy cons. Derfner & Assocs., Alaska, 1985-89; dir. fund devel. Inst. for East-West Security Studies, 1989-91; v.p. for fund devel. Cathedral Ch. of St. John the Divine, N.Y.C., 1991-92; cons. C.W. Shaver & Co. Inc., N.Y.C., 1992-97, chmn., CEO, 1997—; cons., advisor The Grantsmanship Ctr., Nat. Endowment for the Arts, Soroptimists Internat., Nat. Women's Polit. Caucus; presenter in field. Exec. com. Anchorage Bicentennial Commn.; dir. Alaska 25th Anniversary of Statehood Celebration; pres. Alaska Arts Coalition; chairperson Alaska Women's Polit. Caucus, Gov.'s Adv. Commn., Alaska. Recipient Outstanding Non-Profit Mgr. award Anchorage C. of C.; Gov.'s award for Leadership. Office: CW Shaver & Co Inc 654 Madison Ave Ste 1202 New York NY 10021

DERGALIS, GEORGE, artist, educator; b. Athens, Greece, Aug. 31, 1928; s. Demetrios and Zina (Alehina) D. m. Margaret Murphey; 1 child by previous marriage, Alexis. MFA, Accademia Belle Arti, Rome, 1951; diploma, Boston Museum Sch., 1956-59. Instr. Boston Mus. Sch., 1961-69, De Cordova Mus., Lincoln, Mass., 1961-94; pvt. instrn. Wayland, Mass., 1969—; chmn., curator Festival Bostonians for Art and Humanity, 1976; chmn. curator prisom art Inst. Contemporary Art Boston, 1975-76; artist-in-residence Ptnrs. of Ams., Colombia, 1979; lectr. Helicon, Harvard U., 1981; juror Once is Not Enough, Cambridge Art Assn., 1994. One-man shows include Woodstock Gallery, London, 1974, Cámera de Comercio de Medellin, Columbia, 1980, Galesburg (Ill) Civic Art Ctr., 1985, Hotel Meridien, Boston, 1987, Wayland Art/Space, 1994; exhibited in group shows Ariz. Nat., 1980, Tampa Mus., 1983-84, Danforth Mus., Framingham, Mass., 1988-90, Mus. Fine Arts, Boston, 1989 (merit award), Boston Pub. Libr., 1994-95, South Shore Art Ctr., 1994, Boston Corp. Art, 1995—, others; represented in permanent collections at Loomis and Sayles, Boston, Scudder, Steven and Clark, Boston, Sandoz Pharm. Corp., Hale & Dorr, Boston, Alliance Capital Mgmt., N.Y., Museo de Zea, Colombia, also pvt. collections; book It's All in Your Head, 1991. Trustee, Graham Jr. Coll., 1971; hon. dir. Boston Ballet, 1971. With USAF, 1951-54. William Paige scholar, 1959; recipient Prix de Rome, 1951; Civilian merit award U.S. Army Hist. Soc., 1969; Gold medal Accademia Italia delle Arte, 1980; Merit award Mus. of Fine Arts, 1989. Mem. Internat. Sculpture Assn., Alumni Assn. Boston Mus. Sch. (pres., 1966, 67), Copley Soc. Boston (v.p. and art chmn. 1978, Excellence in Technique award 1978), DeCordova Mus. Corp. Prgm. Home: 72 Oxbow Rd Wayland MA 01778-1009

DERGARABEDIAN, PAUL, energy and environmental company executive; b. Racine, Wis., Jan. 19, 1922; s. John and Mary (Hirmizian) D.; m. Mary A. Jansouzian, Dec. 27, 1947; children—Celeste, Claudia, Clarice, Paul. B.S., U. Wis., 1948, M.S., 1949; PhD (Shell Oil fellow), Caltech, 1952. Br. head U.S. Naval Weapons Center, Pasadena, Calif., 1952-55; lab. dir. TRW Systems, Redondo Beach, Calif., 1955-72; staff dir. TRW Systems (Energy Systems group), 1974-80; dir. The Aerospace Corp., El Segundo, Calif., 1972-74, 80-89, tech. cons., 1989—; vis. prof. aeros. Caltech, 1971-72; founder, dir. Frontier Savs. & Loan; cons. in field. Served with USAAF, 1943-46. Fellow Inst. Advancement of Engring., Am. Astron. Soc. (dir. 1971—, nat. pres. 1969-71); mem. Phi Beta Kappa, Sigma Xi. Democrat. Armenian Apostolic. Club: Stereophonic of So. Calif. (pres. 1967-69). Home: 22401 Canyon Crest Dr Mission Viejo CA 92692-4548 *As a scientist I have been moderately successful - and lucky - in doing what people in my field would consider creative work. The greatest contribution to this success, I feel, has been methodology which was gleaned from certain teachers and associates. If I have done the same for someone else, that would be the greater success.*

DERGRIGORIAN, RONALD, water microbiologist; b. Shiraz, Fars, Iran, Dec. 18, 1960; came to U.S., 1979; s. Arnold and Elma (Dror) D.; m. Ida Avanessian, Sept. 6, 1986; children: Tara, Mark. BA in Biology and Microbiology, Calif. State U., 1983, MS in Microbiology with distinction, 1989. Instr. Calif. State U., Northridge, 1983-86; from lab. technician I to water biologist Hyperion Treatment Plant, L.A., 1986-91; water microbiologist Dept. Water & Power, L.A., 1991—; hazardous materials mgmt. staff Dept. Water & Power, L.A., 1982—, emergency response team capt., 1993—, total quality mgmt. team, 1993-95. Co-author: Microbiology Laboratory Training Manual, 1989-90. Fund raising com. Armenian Gen. Benevolent Union, L.A., 1988, 94. Scholastic Achievement grantee Calif. State U., 1988-89. Mem. ASM, Am. Soc. Microbiology. Armenian Apostolic. Achievements include research in DNA base composition of Simonsiella and Alysiella; researched the validity of emerging method, MMO-MUG, in detection of indicator microorganisms in cooperation with other laboratories under the direction of the EPA. Office: Dept Water and Power 8501 Arleta Ave Rm 1f49 Sun Valley CA 91352-2958

DE RHAM, CASIMIR, JR., lawyer; b. N.Y.C., Sept. 5, 1924; s. Casimir and Lucy Lathrop (Patterson) de Rham; m. Elizabeth Moran Evarts, June 9, 1945; children: Elizabeth Morgan, Henry Casimir, Rufus Patterson, Jeremiah Evarts. Student, Yale U., 1943-44; AB, Harvard U., 1946, JD, 1949. Bar: Mass. 1949, U.S. Dist. Ct. Mass. 1949. Assoc. Palmer & Dodge, Boston, 1949-51, 52-55, ptnr., 1956-94, of counsel, 1994—; hon. dir. Cambridge Trust Co., Cambridge Bancorp, Controlled Risk Ins. Co. Trustee Mount Auburn Hosp., Cambridge, Mass., 1962-93, pres., 1966-77, chmn. bd. dirs., 1977-80, treas., 1993—, The Mount Auburn Found., Inc., 1985-91, 93-96, Commonwealth Sch., Boston, 1958—, chmn. bd. dirs., 1966-87, St. Mark's Sch., Southborough, Mass., 1962-74, Cambridge Cmty. Found., 1985—; overseer, dir. Boys and Girls Clubs of Boston Inc., 1956-93, sec., 1973-93, sr. adv. bd., 1993—; dir. Ctr. for Blood Rsch. Inc., Boston, 1964-90, clk., 1964-84, hon. trustee, 1990—; trustee, sec. Sterling and Francine Clark Art Inst., Williamstown, Mass., 1973-95, hon. trustee, 1995—; dir. Women's Ednl. and Indsl. Union, Boston, 1975-98; dir., treas. Florence Evans Bushee Found., Boston, 1982-94; trustee Campbell & Hall Charity Fund, Boston, 1981—; dir. Olivetti Found. Inc., Boston, 1960—, treas., 1983-94, clk., 1960-94; trustee Little Harbor Chapel, Portsmouth, N.H., 1959—; fin. adv. com. Cambridge Hist. Soc., 1980-91, chmn., 1988-90; chmn. Cambridge Rep. City Com., 1954-58; mem. Mass. Rep. State Com., 1960-69; alt. del. Rep. Nat. Conv., 1964, 68; mem. exec. com. Permanent Fund Soc., The Boston Found., 1993-94. Capt. USMC, 1943-46, 51-52. Mem. ABA, Mass. Bar Assn., Boston Bar Assn., Cambridge-Arlington-Belmont Bar Assn. (pres. 1982-83), Am. Bar Found., St. Botolph Club (Boston), The Country Club (Brookline, Mass.), Masons (Harvard Lodge), Am. Legion. Episcopalian. Avocations: reading, tennis, politics. Home: 47 Lakeview Ave Cambridge MA 02138 Office: Palmer & Dodge Ste 20 1 Beacon St Boston MA 02108-3190

DER-HOUSSIKIAN, HAIG, linguistics educator; b. Cairo, Aug. 16, 1938; s. Vagharsh and Adrine (Karalian) Der-H.; m. Gaylynne Hall, Aug. 27, 1961. Student, Am. U., Cairo, 1957-59; BA, Am. U., Beirut, 1961, MA, 1962; PhD, U. Tex., 1969. Research assoc. U. Dar-es-Salaam, Tanzania, 1966-67; asst. prof. linguistics U. Fla., Gainesville, 1967-72; dir. linguistics, 1971-72, 84-85; assoc. prof. U. Fla., Gainesville, 1972-77, dir. Ctr. for African Studies, 1973-79, prof., 1977—, chmn. dept. African and Asian langs. and lits., 1982-91; mem. grad. council U. Fla., 1988-91; sr. Fulbright lectr. Universidade de Luanda, Angola, 1972-73, Universite du Benin, Lome, Togo, 1979-81; vis. prof. African linguistics U. Zimbabwe, Harare, 1989; panelist, grant proposal reviewer U.S. Dept. Edn., Washington, 1976—; USIA Acad. Specialist Grant cons. to U. De Ouagadougou, Burkina Faso, 1981; USIA Acad. Specialist Grant lectr. U. Marien Ngouabi, Brazzaville, Congo, May-Aug. 1988; occasional grant proposal evaluator Social Sci. and Humanities Coun. Can. Author: TEM, Grammar Handbook, 1980, TEM, Communication and Culture, 1980, TEM, Special Skills, 1980; co-editor: Language and Linguistics Problems in Africa, 1977; compiler: A Bibliography of African Linguistics, 1972. ACTION grantee, 1980-81. Mem. MLA (African Linguistics bibliographer 1967-74), Linguistics Soc. Am., African Studies Assn., Southeastern Conf. on Linguistics, Phi Kappa Phi. Armenian Apostolic. Avocations: reading, hiking, traveling. Office: U Fla Dept African Asian Langs and Lit 470 Grinter Hall Gainesville FL 32611-2037 Mailing Address: Univ Station PO Box 14105 Gainesville FL 32604-2105

DERIC, ARTHUR JOSEPH, lawyer, management consultant, health coop trustee; b. Phila., July 20, 1926; m. Claire Brandt, June 26, 1954; children: John Mark, Beverly Joyce, Alexa Dru. BA in Polit. Sci., Temple U., 1950, JD, 1953; MBA, U. Pa., 1959. Bar: Pa. 1953, U.S. Dist. Ct. (ea. dist.) Pa. 1953. Law clk. Ct. of Common Pleas, Phila., 1953-55; claims atty. USF & G Ins. Co., Phila., 1955-59; adj. lectr. ins., risk mgmt. Wharton Sch. U. Pa., Phila., 1959; mgr. ins., risk mgmt. and employee benefit divsn. Am. Mgmt. Assn. Inc., N.Y.C., 1959-69; assoc. prof. Bucks County C.C., Newtown, Pa., 1965-70; v.p. Fred S. James & Co. Inc., N.Y.C., 1970-82; pres., gen. counsel Deric Assocs., Inc., Ft. Washington, Pa., 1982-96; founding trustee Am. Coop. Health Trust, Lansdale, Pa., 1996. Editor: The Total Approach to Employee Benefits, 1967; author, editor, cons. speeches, books, articles and monographs on bus., estate, and health risk mgmt. Capt. U.S. Army, 1944-56. Mem. ABA, Internat. Ins. Hall of Fame (emeritus elector), Scabbard and Blade, Conwell Inn of Phi Delta Phi (past pres.), Pi Gamma Mu. Avocations: golf, bridge, reading, swimming, grandparenting.

DERICCO, LAWRENCE ALBERT, college president emeritus; b. Stockton, Calif., Jan. 28, 1923; s. Giulio and Agnes (Giovacchini) DeR.; m. Alma Mezzetta, June 19, 1949; 1 child, Lawrence Paul. BA, U. Pacific, 1949, MA, 1971, LLD (hon.), 1987. Bank clk. Bank of Am., Stockton, 1942-43; prin. Castle Sch. Dist., San Joaquin County, Calif., 1950-53; dist. supt., prin. Waverly Sch. Dist., Stockton, 1953-63; bus. mgr. San Joaquin Delta Jr. Coll. Dist., Stockton, 1963-65, asst. supt., bus. mgr., 1965-77; v.p. mgmt. services San Joaquin Delta Jr. Coll. Dist., 1977-81; pres., supt. San Joaquin Delta Coll., 1981-87, pres. emeritus, 1988—. Bd. dirs. Pvt. Industry Coun. With AUS, 1943-46, PTO. Mem. NEA, Calif. Tchrs. Assn., Native Sons of Golden West (past pres.), Phi Delta Kappa. Office: 6847 N Pershing Ave Stockton CA 95207-2524

DERICKSON, STANLEY LEWIS, minister, writer; b. Lexington, Nebr., Feb. 19, 1940; s. George Henry and Mary LeOra Derickson; m. Faith Louann Diefenbach, Feb. 28, 1964; children: Stanley L. II, Laurie Lynn, Timothy James. BA, Denver Bapt. Bible Coll., 1973; ThB, Western Bapt. Bible Coll., Salem, Oreg., 1978; ThM, Trinity Theol. Sem., Newburgh, Ind., 1980; PhD, Trinity Theol. Sem., 1981. Ordained to ministry Berean Ch., 1976. Missionary WEF Ministries, 1982-87; tchr. Frontier Sch. of Bible, LaGrange, Wyo., 1987-91; interim pastor Immanuel Bapt. Ch., Salem, Oreg., 1996-97. Author: Mr. D.'s Notes on Theology, 1993, Mr. D.'s Notes on Missions, 1998, Mr. D.'s Notes on Regeneration, 1998; contbr. articles to Bapt. Bulletin, Voice mag. With USN, 1958-62.

DE RIEMER, DANIEL LOUIS, leasing company executive; b. San Antonio, Jan. 10, 1950; s. Sydney Daniel and Loraine (Neugebauer) De R.; m. Laura Rosen, Nov. 6, 1993. BS, U. Mo., Rolla, 1972. Engr. Cen. Soya Co., Chattanooga, 1976-78, Mark Controls Corp., Overland Park, Kans., 1978; gen. mgr. Pye Nissan, Inc., Dalton, Ga., 1978-82; pres. Total Leasing Systems, Inc., Chattanooga, 1982—. Editor Tennhorn newsletter, 1984-85. Bd. dirs. Chattanooga Riverbend Festival, 1990, 91, supr., 1992; mem. vol. staff 1996,97,98, 99 Centennial Olympic Games, Atlanta, 1996' vol. Atlanta Com. for Olympic Games, 1996; mem. engring. mgmt. adv. bd. U. Mo., 1998—, treas., 1999. Mem. Nat. Vehicle Leasing Assn., Nat. Vehicle Leasing Corp., Porsche Club Am. (treas. Tenn. chpt. 1982-84, pres. 1986-87, 89, membership chmn. 1992, Peach State Region co-chair Concours de Elegance 1995-96, 96-97), Lions (sec. 1987-88, 2d v.p. 1991, 1st v.p. 1992, pres. 1993, bd. dirs. 1997-99). Home: 735 Ashcreek Ct Roswell GA 30075-1385 Office: Total Leasing Systems Inc 107 Northgate Comml Ctr Chattanooga TN 37415-6913

DERISE, NELLIE LOUISE, nutritionist, educator, researcher; b. Jeanerette, La., Aug. 9, 1937; d. O'Niell Paul and Anita (Savoy) D. BS, U. Southwestern La., 1962; MS, U. Ala., 1964; PhD, Va. Poly. Inst., 1973. Grad. asst. U. Ala., Tuscaloosa, 1962-64; asst. prof. Iowa State U., Ames, 1968-70; asst. prof. U. Southwestern La., Lafayette, 1964-68, assoc. prof., 1973-81, prof. home econs., 1981-94; ret., 1994; Chmn La. State Nutrition Council, 1977-78. Contbr. articles to profl. jours. Mem. Am. Home Econs. Assn., Am. Dietetic Assn., U.S. Metric Assn., Soc. Nutrition Edn., La. Home Econs. Assn. (bd. dirs. 1973-75), La. Dietetic Assn. (bd. dirs. 1982-86), Inst. Food Tech., Sigma Xi. Democrat. Roman Catholic. Home: 1108 Highway 668 Jeanerette LA 70544-8611

DE RIVAS, CARMELA FODERARO, psychiatrist, hospital administrator; b. Cortale, Italy, Nov. 25, 1920; came to U.S., 1935, naturalized, 1942; d. Salvatore and Mary (Vaiti) Foderaro; m. Aureliano Rivas, Oct. 30, 1948; children: Carmen, Norma, Sandra, David. Student, U. Pa., 1940-42; M.D., Women's Med. Coll. Pa., 1946. Diplomate: Am. Bd. Psychiatry and Neurology. Intern women's Med. Coll. Pa. Hosp., 1946-47; gen. med. resident Chestnut Hill Hosp., Phila., 1947-48; gen. practice Tex., 1948-49; mem. staff Norristown (Pa.) State Hosp., 1949-63, supt., 1963-70, dir. family planning, 1979-87, clin. dir. spl. assignments, 1979-82; assoc. psychiatry U. Pa., 1963-75; psychiatrist Penn Found. Mental Health, Sellersville, Pa., 1970-72; dir. intake coping svcs. Ctrl. Montgomery Mental Health/Mental Retardation Ctr., Norristown, Pa., 1972-77, med. dir., 1977-82, psychiatrist, 1980-82; cons. surveyor HEalth Care Fin. Adminstrn., 1987—; dir. program evaluation Norristown State Hosp., 1979-82, med. dir., 1982-87. Named to Hall of Fame S. Phila. H.S., 1968; recipient citation Women's Med. Coll. Pa., 1968, Amita achievement award, 1976, achievement award Grad. Club Phila., 1976; named Woman of Yr. Pa. Fedn. Bus. and Profl. Women, 1979. Fellow Am. Psychiat. Assn., Pa. Psychiat. Soc. (rep. assembly of dist. brs. 1979-88); mem. AMA, Phila. Psychiat. Soc. (councilor), Montgomery County Med. Soc. (bd. dirs., past pres.), Pa. Med. Soc. (chmn. adv. com. to aux. 1981-88, mem. ho. of dels., mem. commn. on med. edn. 1991-94, mem. com. on continuing med. edn. 1994-98). Home: 700 Joseph Dr Wayne PA 19087-1021

DERKSEN, CHARLOTTE RUTH MEYNINK, librarian; b. Newberg, Oreg., Mar. 15, 1944; d. John Philip and Wanda Marie (Rohrbough) Meynink; m. Roy Arthur Derksen, Dec. 27, 1966; children: Kathryn Marie Lesedi, Elizabeth Charlotte. BS in Geology, Wheaton (Ill.) Coll., 1966; MA in Geology, U. Oreg., 1968, MLS, 1973. Faculty and librarian Moeding Coll., Ootse Botswana, 1968-70, head history dept., 1970-71; tchr. Jackson Pub. High Sch. (Minn.), 1975-77; sci. librarian U. Wis., Oshkosh, 1977-80; librarian and bibliographer Stanford (Calif.) U., 1980—, acting chief scis., 1985-86, head Sci. and Engring. Librs., 1992-97. Contb. author: Union List of Geologic Field Trip Guidebooks of North America, contbr. articles to profl. publs. Mem. ALA, Western Assn. Map Librarians, Geosci. Info. Soc. (v.p. 1997-98, pres. 1998-99), Cartographic Users Adv. Coun. (chair 1988-90), GeoRef Adv. Bd. (chair 1998—). Republican. Lutheran. Home: 128 Mission Dr Palo Alto CA 94303-2753 Office: Stanford U Branner Earth Scis Library Stanford CA 94305

DERLACKI, EUGENE L(UBIN), otolaryngologist, physician; b. Chgo., Mar. 16, 1913; s. Walter and Jadwiga (Pamulowna) D. BS, Northwestern U., 1936, MD, 1939; postgrad. otolaryngology, Rush Med. Coll., 1940, U. Ill., 1941-42. Diplomate: Am. Bd. Otolaryngology. Intern Cook County Hosp., Chgo., 1939-40, jr. resident, 1941, sr. resident, 1942-43; sr. attending staff Northwestern Meml. Hosp., 1946—; prof. otolaryngology Northwestern U. Med. Sch., from 1957, now prof. emeritus. Contbr. articles to profl. jours. Pres. Am. Hearing Research Found. Served with M.C. AUS, 1943-46. Mem. AMA, Am. Acad. Otolaryngology (past pres.), Coll. Allergists, Am. Otol. Soc. (past pres.), Am. Laryngol., Rhinol. and Otol. Soc. Home: Franklin St 1 The Mews Franklin St Geneva IL 60134-2654 Office: Northwestern Med Faculty Found 675 N Saint Clair St Chicago IL 60611-4807

DERMAN, CYRUS, mathematical statistician; b. Phila., July 16, 1925; s. Samuel and Bessie (Segal) D.; m. Martha Winn, Feb. 24, 1961; children: Adam Jason Winn (dec.), Hester Beth Rebecca. A.B., U. Pa., 1948, A.M., 1949; Ph.D., Columbia, 1954. Instr. Syracuse U., 1954-55; faculty Columbia U., 1955—, prof. operations research, 1965-94; prof. emeritus, 1994; vis. prof. Israel Inst. Tech., Haifa, 1961-62, Stanford, 1965-66; vis. prof. U. Calif., Davis, 1975-76, U. Calif., Berkeley, 1979. Author: (with Morton Klein) Probability and Statistical Inference for Engineers, 1959, Finite State Markovian Decision Processes, 1970, (with Leon Gleser and Ingram Olkin) A Guide to Probability Theory and Application, 1973, Probability Models and Applications, 1980, 2d edit., 1994, (with Shelton Ross) Statistical Aspects of Quality Control, 1996. Fellow Inst. Math. Statistics, Am. Statis. Assn. Research and publs. on theory of Markov chains, Brownian motion, statis. inference, mgmt. sci. and ops. research. Home: 15 Pond Hill Rd Chappaqua NY 10514-2531 Office: Columbia U Mudd Bldg New York NY 10027

DERMANIS, PAUL RAYMOND, architect; b. Jelgava, Latvia, Aug. 2, 1932; came to U.S., 1949; s. Pauls and Milda (Argals) D. BArch, U. Wash., 1955; MArch, MIT, 1959. Registered architect, Wash. Architect John Morse & Assocs., Seattle, 1961-62; assoc. Fred Bassetti & Co., Seattle, 1963-70; ptnr. Streeter/Dermanis & Assocs., Seattle, 1973-97; owner Paul Dermanis & Assoc., 1997—. Designs include Sunset house (citation 1984), treatment plant, 1992. Mem. Phinney Ridge Neighborhood Assn., Seattle, 1985—. With USN, 1955-57. Mem. AIA, Apt. Assn. Seattle and King County, U. Wash. Alumni Assn., MIT Club of Puget Sound, Phi Beta Kappa, Tau Sigma Delta. Democrat. Lutheran. Avocations: skiing, painting, photography.

DERMARDEROSIAN, DIRAN ROBERT, rug cleaning company executive; b. Boston, Oct. 29, 1940; s. Kevork George and Vartouhi (Belekian) DerM. BS, Curry Coll., Milton, Mass., 1964; MS, Emerson Coll., Boston, 1969. Vice prin. Billerica (Mass.) Sr. High Sch., 1975-86; pres. Brookline Rug Cleaning Co., Inc., Needham Heights, Mass., 1987—. Mem. Curry Coll. Alumni Assn., Emerson Coll. Alumni Assn., Billerica Elks. Avocations: boating, gardening. Home: 325 Hunnewell St Needham MA 02494-1340

DERMODY, FRANK, state legislator, lawyer; b. Scranton, Pa., May 29, 1951; m. Debra Hewetson. OBA, Columbia U., 1973; JD, Ind. U., 1982. Bar: Pa. Asst. dist. atty. Alegheny County (Pa.), 1984-90; dist. justice Oakmont-Verona, 1986-87; mem. Pa. Ho. of Reps., Harrisburg, 1991—; former instr. C.C. Alleghey County. Mem. Pa. Bar Inst. Continuing Legal Edn., Allegheny County Bar Assn., Oakmont Lions Club. Democrat. Address: 801 Freeport Rd Cheswick PA 15024-1209

DERN, LAURA, actress; b. Santa Monica, Calif., Feb. 10, 1967; d. Bruce Dern and Diane Ladd. Student, Lee Strasberg Inst., Royal Acad. Dramatic Art, London. Appeared in films Alice Doesn't Live Here Anymore, 1975, Foxes, 1980, Ladies and Gentlemen, The Fabulous Stains, 1982, Teachers, 1984, Mask, 1985, Smooth Talk, 1985, Blue Velvet, 1986, Haunted Summer, 1988, Fat Man & Little Boy, 1989, Wild At Heart, 1990, Rambling Rose, 1991 (Acad. award nomination for best actress, Golden Globe nomination for best actress in a drama), Jurassic Park, 1993, A Perfect World, 1993, Citizen Ruth, 1996, Bastard Out of Carolina, 1996; TV appearances include: Afterburn, 1992 (Golden Globe award for best actress in TV movie or mini series), Fallen Angels (Murder, Obliquely), 1993 (Emmy nomination, Best Actress - Drama, 1994), Ruby Ridge, 1996; stage appearances include The Palace of Amateurs (N.Y.), 1988, Brooklyn Laundry (L.A.); dir. The Gift. Office: ICM 8942 Wilshire Blvd Beverly Hills CA 90211-1934

DERNER, CAROL A., librarian; b. Evansville, Ind., May 12, 1934; d. Jacob Christopher and Catherine Loretta (Grant) Niedhammer; m. George Bendix Derner, May 4, 1957. BA in Am. Lit., Ind. U., 1956, MA in Libr. Sci., 1958. Children's libr. Monroe County Pub. Libr., Bloomington, Ind., 1958-59, Pub. Librs. of Lake County, Merrillville, Ind., 1959-60; sch. libr. Valparaiso (Ind.) Cmty. Schs., 1960-63; head popular libr. Gary (Ind.) Pub. Libr., 1963-64, head extension dept., 1964-67; head libr. Elmwood Park Pub. Libr., Elmwood, Ill., 1968-76; asst. dir. Lake County Pub. Libr., Merrillville, 1976-85, dir., 1985—; adj. faculty Ind. U. Sch. Libr. and Info. Sci., Bloomingron, 1982-94. Contbr. articles to profl. jours. Mem. edn. com. N.W. Ind. Forum, Portage, 1992—; mem., sec. Ednl. Referral Ctr., Highland, Ind., 1996—. Named Woman of Yr., Merrillville Bus. and Profl. women, 1990. Mem. ALA (coun. 1983-87), Ind. Libr. Fedn. (Libr. of Yr. 1997), Exec. Coun., Altrusa Club of Ind. Dunes (pres. 1998-99). Avocations: reading, travel, antiques. Home: 7260 Mckinley Cir Apt 208 Merrillville IN 46410-8200 Office: Lake County Pub Libr 1919 W 81st Ave Merrillville IN 46410-5382

DERNOVICH, DONALD FREDERICK, artist, educator; b. Rock Springs, Wyo., Apr. 9, 1942; s. Frank Donald and Francis Irene (Paternel) D.; m. Kathy Joan Fornengo, Aug. 1, 1970; children: Heath, Jessica, Kaitlyn. BA, U. Wyo., 1966, MA, 1967; MFA, Ft. Hays State U., 1983. Artist, illustrator U.S. Army, Ft. George G. Meade, 1967-69; comml. artist Penny Pincher Advtg., Grand Junction, Colo., 1969-70; art tchr. Decatur County Jr. H.S., Oberlin, Kans., 1970-74; tchr., head art dept. McCook (Nebr.) C.C., 1974—; bd. dirs. Assn. Nebr. Arts Clubs, 1986-90; juror art exhbns., 1980—; guest artist Wyo. Art Assn. annual conv., 1995. Artist: (watercolors) Splash Four, 1996, Splash Five, 1998; featured in publs. including Am. Artist Mag. Hon. life mem. McCook Arts Coun., 1976—. Work judged in top 100 Arts for the Parks, Jackson Hole, Wyo., 1994, 98, top 200, 1995, Best Watercolor award Western Spirits Art Show, Cheyenne, Wyo., 1994, 96, 98; quick draw artist C.M. Russell Art Auction, Great Falls, Mont., 1997, 98, 99. Mem. Nat. Watercolor Soc., Kans. Watercolor Soc., Assn. Am. Watercolor Soc. (assoc.), Oil Painters Am. Democrat. Roman Catholic. Avocations: fly fishing, travel, gallery hopping. Home: 210 Taylor PO Box 163 Culbertson NE 69024-0163 Office: McCook Community College 1205 E 3rd St Mc Cook NE 69001-2631

DE ROCCO, ANDREW GABRIEL, state commissioner, scientist, educator; b. Westerly, R.I., July 31, 1929; s. Joachim and Ida Lovat De R.; 1 son, J. Lovat. B.S. (Merit scholar), Purdue U., 1951; M.S., U. Mich., 1953, Ph.D. (Du Pont fellow), 1956; postdoctoral fellow, NRC, 1956-57. Mem. faculty U. Mich., Ann Arbor, 1957-62; vis. prof. U. Colo., Boulder, 1962-63; prof. molecular physics U. Md., College Park, 1963-79; First Disting. vis. prof. USAF Acad., 1975-76; vis. prof. Tufts U., 1968, 69; dean of faculty and Coll. prof. natural scis. Trinity Coll., Hartford, Conn., 1979-84; pres. Denison U., Granville, Ohio, 1984-89; dir. ind. coll. challenge program Ohio Bd. Regents, Columbus, 1988-89; cons. Ohio Found. Ind. Colls., 1989-91; commr. higher edn. State of Conn., Hartford, 1991—; mem. staff phys. scis. lab., div. computer research and tech. NIH, 1969-79; cons. Bendix Corp., Office of Sec. Def., Inst. for Def. Analysis, IBM, Dana Found., NIH, C.A. Johnson Found., Alfred E. Sloan Found., Am. Coun. on Edn., Assn. Am. Colls., Nat. Sci. Found., North Cent. Assn. Colls. and Secondary Schs.; pres. Nat. Collegiate Honors Coun., 1977-78. Contbr. numerous articles to profl. jours., chpts. to books; editorial cons., Acad. Press, Cambridge Univ. Press, Harper & Row, Holt, Rinehart & Winston, others. Bd. dirs. Greater Washington Coun. for Clean Air, 1967-71; mem. village coun. Friendship Heights, Chevy Chase, Md., 1974-76; bd. dirs. World Affairs Ctr., Conn., Innovations, Inc., CHESLA, Conn. Student Loan Found., Edn. Commn. of the States; chmn. bd. New Eng. Bd. Higher Edn., Shaliko Theatre Co., N.Y.C.; bd. dirs. Dworin Performance Ensemble, Chamber Music Plus, Sci. Ctr. Conn.; pres. North Coast Athletic Conf., 1986-88; bd govs. Rackham Sch. Grad. Studies, U. Mich.; mem. dean's adv. coun. Sch. Sci., Purdue U. Recipient William Raney Harper medal, 1988; NRC fellow, 1956-57; Am. Cancer Soc. fellow, 1956-57; NATO sr. fellow, 1964. Fellow AAAS, Random Soc.; mem. Ohio Found. Ind. Colls. (exec. com.), Conn. Acad. Sci. and Tech., Am. Chem. Soc., Am. Phys. Soc., Biophys. Soc., Am. Assn. Physics Tchrs. (com. internat. edn.), Md. Acad. Scis. (sci. coun. 1970-79), Engring. Acad. So. New Eng. (bd. govs.), State Higher Edn. Exec. Officers (exec. com.), The Compact for Faculty Diversity (nat. adv. com.), Sigma Xi, Phi Lambda Upsilon, Delta Rho Kappa, Sigma Pi Sigma, Omicron Delta Kappa. Office: Dept Higher Edn 61 Woodland St Ste 5 Hartford CT 06105-2391*

DEROCHE, KATHLEEN SAMROW, elementary educator, mathematics consultant; b. De Ridder, La., Sept. 29, 1952; d. Joseph Earl and Thekla Agnes (Meyer) Samrow; m. Nolan Joseph Deroche Jr., Aug. 7, 1971; children: Christopher, Juanita, Matthew, Sarah. BS in Elem. Edn., Nicholls State U., 1978, MEd, 1996. Cert. elem. edn., spl. edn., supervision of student tchrs. La. Elem. sch. tchr. St. James Pub. Schs., Lutcher, La., 1977—; tutor Gramercy, La., 1973-75; curriculum writer Nicholls State Univ. Region 3, Thibodaux, La., 1996-98; Fulbright Meml. tchr., Japan, 1998. Contbr. articles to profl. jours. Lectr. family life com. mem. St. Joseph Ch., Paulina, La., 1996-97; mem. quilt com., maypole coord. Centennial Com., Gramercy, Lutcher, 1993, 95; team leader La. Alliance Sch. Reform. Phys. edn. grantee STAR Enterprises, Convent, La., 1992, math. edn. grantee, 1993, sci. edn. grantee, 1994; recipient Presdl. Excellence award sci. & math. NSF, 1994, Making the Grade Tchr. award Freeport/McMoran & WVUE-TV, New Orleans, 1995, Excellence in Math Tchg. award La. Assn. Tchrs. Math., Baton Rouge, La., 1993, Greater New Orleans Math. Tchrs., 1993. Mem. Nat. Coun. Tchrs. Math. (cons. 1992—), La. Assn. Educators, St. James hist. Soc. (Hist. award 1994, ednl. chairperson 1985—), Phi Delta Kappa, Delta Kappa Gamma (v.p., pres. 1990-94), Phi Kappa Phi. Roman Catholic. Avocations: sewing, craftmaking, reading, quilting. Home: 2861 Admirals Landing St Paulina LA 70763-2504 Office: Gramercy Elem Sch PO Box 1518 Gramercy LA 70052-1518

DE RODON, MIRIAM NAVEIRA, supreme court justice; b. Santurce, P.R., July 28, 1934; married; 2 children. BA, Mount St. Vincent Coll., N.Y., 1956; JD, U. P.R. Law Sch., 1960; LLM, Columbia U., 1969; postgrad., Leiden U., Holland, 1971-72; LLD, U. Georgetown Sch. Law, 1990. Law clerk P.R. Supreme Ct., 1963-71, asst. atty. gen. Dept. Justice, 1966-73, asst. solicitor gen. Dept. Justice, 1973-76, assoc. justice, 1985—, pres. judicial commn. on gender bias, 1992—; tchr. Law Sch. U. P.R., 1971-72; atty. pvt. practice, 1976-85; prof. Sch. Law Inter-Am. U. Office: Supreme Ct PO Box 2392 San Juan PR 00902-2392*

DE ROEST, JAN MARIE, mental health counselor; b. Seattle, Wash., Oct. 9, 1965; d. Stanley Robert and Glenna Muriel (Bennett) Hagedorn; m. Gary Eugene De Roest, Apr. 26, 1987. BS in Microbiology, Oreg. State U., 1987; MA in Counseling Psychology, Lewis and Clark Coll., 1996. Cert. nursing asst. Med. asst. Met. Clinic, Portland, Oreg., 1987-89; tech. asst. Oreg. Health Sci. U., Portland, 1989-90; med. asst. Portland Clinic, 1991-92; tech. asst. VA Med. Ctr., Portland, 1992-93; med. asst. Neighborhood Health Clinic, Portland, 1995-96, master's intern, 1995-96; master's intern Delaunay Family of Svcs., Portland, 1995-96; geriatric mental health specialist Unity, Inc., Portland, 1997—. Mem. Am. Counseling Assn., Am. Aging and Devel. Assn., Am. Mental Health Counseling Assn., Am. Soc. Aging, Oreg. Gerontological Assn., Lewis and Clark Alumni Assn. Democrat. Roman Catholic. Office: Unity Inc 310 NW Flanders St Portland OR 97209-3941

DEROME, JACQUES FLORIAN, meteorology educator; b. Montreal, Que., Can., Apr. 20, 1941; s. Laurent and Marie Jeanne (Auger) D.; m. Monique Rose Hamelin, June 10, 1967; children: Julie, Bertrand. BS, McGill U., 1963, MS, 1964; PhD, U. Mich., 1968. Rsch. assoc. MIT, Cambridge, 1968-69; rsch. scientist Govt. of Can., Montreal, 1969-72; assoc. prof. meteorology McGill U., Montreal, 1972-85, prof., 1985—, chmn. dept., 1987-91, 94-98. Recipient Patterson medal Atmospheric Environ. Svc. Can., 1995. Mem. Can. Meteorol. and Oceanographic Soc. (v.p. 1993-94, pres. 1994-95, pres.'s prize 1983), Am. Meteorol. Soc. Office: McGill U, 805 Sherbrooke St W, Montreal, PQ Canada H3A 2K6

DEROMEDI, HERB, athletic director; b. May 26, 1939; m. Marilyn Deromedi; children: David, Tom, Lori. BS, U. Mich., 1960, MS, 1961. Asst. football coach Ctrl. Mich. U., Mt. Pleasant, 1967-78, head coach, 1978-94, athletic dir., 1994—. Office: Ctrl Mich U Rose Ctr Mount Pleasant MI 48859*

DERON, EDWARD MICHAEL, lawyer; b. Detroit, Dec. 18, 1945; m. Jana Lene Berlenbach, Aug. 12, 1977. BS, Wayne State U., 1968, JD cum laude, 1972; LLM in Taxation, NYU, 1973. Bar: Mich. 1972, U.S. Ct. Appeals (6th cir.) 1973, U.S. Tax Ct. 1974. Assoc. Evans & Luptak, Detroit, 1973-79, ptnr., 1980—. With U.S. Army, 1969-71, ETO, Germany. Mem. ABA, Mich. Bar Assn. (chmn. taxation sect., estates and trusts com. 1994-96, taxation sect. coun. 1996—, editor Mich. Tax Lawyer 1998-99) Detroit Bar Assn. (co-chmn. taxation com. 1984-86), Fin. and Estate Planning Coun. Detroit, Detroit Athletic Club, Rotary, KC. Office: Evans & Luptak 2500 Buhl Building Detroit MI 48226-3674

DE ROO, REMI JOSEPH, bishop; b. Swan Lake, Man., Can., Feb. 24, 1924; s. Raymond and Josephine (De Pape) De R. Student, St. Boniface (Man.) Coll.; STD, Angelicum U., Rome, Italy.; LLD (hon.), U. Antigonish, N.S., 1983, U. Brandon, Man., 1987; DD (hon.), U. Winnipeg, Man., 1990; LLD (hon.), U. Victoria, B.C., 1991. Ordained priest Roman Cath. Ch., 1950. Curate Holy Cross Parish, St. Boniface, 1952-53; sec. to archbishop of St. Boniface, 1954-56; diocesan dir. Cath. action Archdiocese St. Boniface, 1953-54; exec. sec. Man. Cath. Con., 1958; pastor Holy Cross Parish, 1960-62; bishop of Victoria, B.C., Can., 1962—; Can. Episcopal rep. Internat. Secretariat Apostleship Sea, 1964-78, Pontifical Commn. Culture, 1984-87; chairperson Human Rights Commn. B.C., 1974-77; mem. social affairs commn. Can. Conf. Cath. Bishops, 1973-87, 91-95, mem. theology commn., 1987-91; pres. Western Cath. Conf. Bishops, 1984-88; hon. pres. World Conf. for Religion and Peace for Can., 1994—. Hon. fellow Ryerson Poly. Inst., 1987. Address: 4044 Nelthorpe St # 1, Victoria, BC Canada V8X 2A1

DEROO, SALLY A., biology, geology and environmental science educator. BS, Eastern Mich. U., 1958; postgrad., 1958-63; MA, U. Mich., 1961, postgrad., 1963-92; postgrad., Wayne State U., 1964-68, Ohio State U., 1995—. Cert. elem. tchr., middle level, all subjects K-8; cert. high sch. level environ. scis., social studies, English, econs. 9-12; cert. tchr. mentally handicapped and emotionally impaired K-12; cert. Master Gardener, Mich. State U., 1997. Asst. prof. sci. Ea. Mich. U., Ypsilanti, 1958-63, asst. prof. biology and geology, 1968—, cons., 1958-89, tchr. spl. edn., cons., 1989—; tchr. sci. and geology Plymouth-Canton Cmty. Schs., 1963-95; curriculum specialist Ctrl. Mich. U., 1989-90; instr. dept. tchr. edn. Mich. State U., 1994-95; instr. sci. edn. Madonna U., asst. prof., mem. staff student tchr. edn. Dept. Edn., 1992—; asst. prof., mem. staff student tchr. edn. Dept. Edn. Madonna U.; advisor Salem H.S., 1990-95, Wayne State U., Detroit, 1995—, Pitts. State U., Kans. at Greenbush, 1995-97, Oakland U. Sci. Edn., 1997—; ednl. cons. Scholastic, Inc., 1996—; sci./ednl. cons. DTE Energy, Detroit, 1998—; mem. satellite conf. Tchrs. Making a Difference, 1990; mem. support team Sci. Teaching Edn. STEP adv. bd. Madonna U., Livonia, Mich.; mem. math. and sci. challenge grant design com. Wayne County, 1991; adv. bd. SEMSplus Mich. Envirothon, steering com. Nat. Envirothon, 1996—; mem. adv. com., issues author sci. curriculum support guides Mich. Dept. Edn., 1989-90; mem. adv. coun. Mich. Dept. Edn.; mem. Mich. curriculum frameworks joint steering com., 1992—, mem. writing com. h.s. proficiency exam., 1993, 94, 95—, mem. adv. com. h.s. sci. proficiency test, 1993, 94, 95-96; dist. commr. Wayne County Soil Dist. USDA, 1996—; project chair Project Cattail, Tchrs. and Students Making an Environ. Difference, 1992—; project dir. Gt. Lakes-Thunderbay Gt. Lakes Basin Work Shop, Alpena, Mich., 1990-93; cons. Detroit Edison (DTE) Solar Currents curricula, 1997—; facilitator numerous workshops; presenter in field. Author: (newsletter) Fledgeling, 1990—, (teaching manuals) Exploring Our Environment; contbg. writer Detroit Free Press sci. page; contbr. articles to sci. mags.; writer, dir. 26-week sci. TV series Explore with Me; sci. editor Ann Arbor Pubs., 1968-86; elem. publ. editor Mich. Sci. Tchrs.; adv. (tv waste mgmt. series) Neuton's Apple. Active Rouge River Restoration, 1988—, Friends of Mattaei Bot. Gardens Ann. Flower Show; established Model Adopt-a-Stream Project "River Watch" for Rough River Water Shed, 1994; planning asst. Cobo Ctr. 1st Annual etroit Bloomfest, 1999—. Recipient Outstanding Educator award Mich. Jaycees, 1963, Best of West Edn. award, 1984, Outstanding Svc. Recognition award Mich. Assn. Mid. Sch. Educators, 1989, 90, gov.'s citation State of Mich., 1990, 91, Tchr. of Yr. Program award IBM, 1990, Can Doers award Mich. Tech. Coun., 1993, Recognition of Support and Dedication dept. natural resources Builder's Assn. Southeastern Mich., 1990, 91, 92; named Outstanding Sci. Educator, Metro Detroit Sci. Tchrs. Assn., 1994; listed in Guinness Book of Records 1990-95 for snail racing. Mem. NEA, Nat. Sci. Tchrs. Assn. (presenter, local leader, chair publicity regional conf. 1999), Mich. Sci. Tchrs. Assn. (dir.-at-large, chair outreach conf., Outstanding Svc. award 1997, Disting. Svc. award 1998), Nat. Mid. Level Sci. Tchrs. Assn. (treas.), N t. Resource Def. Coun., Mich. Sci. Leaders Assn. (bd. dirs.), Mich. Edn. Assn., Sci. Curriculum Devel. Assn. (mid. sch. goal-based curriculum), Wayne County Task Force (intermediate sch. dist. writing team 1989, bd. dirs.), Mich. Alliance for Outdoor Edn., Detroit Zool. Inst., Internat. Joint Commn. (Gt. Lakes), Mich. Reading Assn. (sci. conf. chairperson 1992—), Phi Delta Kappa (editor newsletter U. Mich. chpt.). Address: Wayne State U Dept Edn, Gullen Ct Detroit MI 48202

DEROSA, DAVID FRANCIS, finance educator, trading company executive; b. Glen Ridge, N.J., July 20, 1950; s. Frank J. and Michelle A. DeRosa; m. Sibylle Schubach, May 23, 1986; children: Julia, Francesca. AB in Econs., U. Chgo., 1972, PhD in Fin. and Econs., 1978. Dir. fgn. exch. Swiss Bank Corp., N.Y.C., 1993-96; lectr. in fin. U. Chgo. Grad. Sch. Bus., 1995-96; mng. ptnr. Quadrangle Investments, Greenwich, Conn., 1996-97; pres. DeRosa Rsch. and Trading, New Canaan, Conn., 1997—; dir. MidWest ISO, 1998—; adj. prof. fin. Yale U. Sch. Mgmt., New Haven, 1996—; fellow yale Ctr. for Internat. Fin.; pres., owner Commodity Trading Advisor, 1997—; rschr. and cons. in internat. fin. markets; spkr. in field. Author: Options on Foreign Exchange, 1992, 2nd edit., 1999, Managing Foreign Exchange Risk, 1996, Currency Directives, 1998; contbr. articles to profl. jours. Avocation: financial columnist. E-mail: derosa@derosa-research.com.

DEROSA, FRANCIS DOMINIC, chemical company executive; b. Seneca Falls, N.Y., Feb. 26, 1936; s. Frank and Frances (Bruno) DeR.; m. Vivian DeRosa, Oct. 24, 1959; children: Kevin, Marc, Terri. Student, Rochester Inst. Tech., 1959-61; BS, Chadwick U., MBA; PhD, City U. L.A. Cert. med. photographer. CEO Advance Paper & Equipment Supply Inc., Mesa, Ariz., 1974—, Pottery Plus Ltd., Mesa, 1984—, Advance Tool Supply Inc., Mesa, 1989-94. Vice chmn. bd. adjustments City of Mesa, 1983-89, bd. dirs. dept. parks and recreation, 1983-86; pres. Christ the King Mens Club, 1983-84; bd. dirs. Mesa C. of C., 1983-88. Mem. Ariz. Sanitary Supply Assn. (pres. 1983-84), Internat. Sanitary Supply Assn. (coord. Ariz. chpt. 1994-96, sec. bd. 1994-96), Gilbert, Ariz. C. of C. (bd. dirs., v.p. 1992-96, pres. 1996-97, sec. internat. bd. 1994-96), Gilbert Heights Owners Assn. (pres. 1992-93), Mesa Country Club, Calif. Yacht Club, Santa Monica (Calif.) Yacht Club, Rotary (pres. Mesa Sunrise chpt. 1987-88, Paul Harris fellow 1988), Masons (32 degree, pres. 1973), Sons of Italy (pres. 1983-84), Shriners. Avocations: music, physical fitness, sailing, golf. Home: 513 E Horseshoe Ave Gilbert AZ 85296-1705 Office: Advance Paper & Maintenance Supply Inc 33 W Broadway Mesa AZ 85210-1505

DE ROSA, GUY PAUL, orthopedic surgery educator; b. Napoleon, Ohio, Oct. 25, 1939; married. BS, Notre Dame U., 1961; MD, Ind. U., 1965. Diplomate Am. Bd. Orthopedic Surgery (oral examiner 1983—, site investigator residency rev. com. 1983—, bd. dirs. 1990—, mem. credentials com. 1990-93, mem. oral examinations com. 1990—, mem. grad. edn. com. 1990—, chmn. 1995-97, mem. oral recertification examination com. 1992-93, mem. practice audit com. 1992-93, ABMS rep. alt. 1992-93, ACS adv. coun. 1992-94, sec. 1993-94, mem. exec. com. 1993-94, mem. cert. renewal com. 1993-94, mem. fin. com. 1993-94, vice chmn. residency rev. com. 1994—). Resident in gen. surgery Sch. Medicine, Ind. U., Indpls., 1965-66, resident in orthopedic surgery, 1966-70; fellow in pediat. orthopedics Hosp. for Sick Children, London, 1969-70; asst. prof. orthopedic surgery Sch. Medicine, Ind. U., Indpls., 1970-76, assoc. prof., 1976-82, dir. undergrad. edn. dept. orthopedic surgery, 1972—, chief neuromuscular disease, 1972—, coord. Garceau-Wayu Lectureships dept. orthopedic surgery, 1975—, dir. Cerebral Palsy Clinic, 1978-88, orthopedic cons. Hemophilia Clinic, 1978-91, prof. orthopedic surgery, 1981—, orthopedic cons. Rheumato-Orthopedic Clinic, 1984—, chmn. dept. orthopedic surgery, 1986-95; attending physician Wishard Meml. Hosp., Indpls., 1970-95, Ind. U. Med. Ctr., Indpls., 1970-95, James Whitcomb Riley Hosp. for Children, Indpls., 1970-95; cons. Ctrl. Ind. and So. Ind. State Bd. Health Programs, Scoliosis and Sch. Screening, 1977; mem. orthopedic surgery steering com. Children's Cancer Study Group, 1990; mem. residency rev. com. for orthopedic surgery Accreditation Coun. for Grad. Med. Edn., 1990—; vis. prof. Children's Hosp., Columbus, Ohio, 1977, St. Joseph Hosp., Ft. Wayne, Ind., 1977, Miami Valley Hosp., Dayton, Ohio, 1978, 82, 85, 86, Deaconess Hosp., Evansville, Ind., 1980, Bloomington (Ind.) Hosp., 1982, U. Tex., Galveston, 1982, U. Mo. Med. Ctr., Columbia, 1983, Southwestern Mich. Area Health Edn. Ctr., Kalamazoo, 1985, Newington (Conn.) Children's Hosp., 1988, Children's Hosp. Med. Ctr., Akron, Ohio, 1992, and numerous others; active Hemophilia Med. Adv. Coun., 1978—; presenter in field. Contbr. numerous articles to profl. jours. Bd. dirs. United Cerebral Palsy, 1973-85, Hemophilia Found., 1978—, New Hope of Ind., 1984-86, also mem. long range planning com. 1984-85, mem. task force on serving brain injured 1988, Ind. Found. Hand Surg. Rsch. and Edn., 1989-95; mem. adv. bd. Head Injury Found., 1983-95, Children's Limb Found., 1992—; mem. pub. rels. and promotion com. Ind. Gov. Coun. on Phys. Fitness and Sports Medicine, 1986-92, mem. promotion com. 1988-92; dir. State of Ind. Orthop. Rsch. and Edn. Found., 1993, bd. trustees, 1994. Maj. USAF, 1970-72. Grantee in field; recipient Ensminger award for rsch. in trauma, 1967, Willis Gatch award, 1968. Mem. AMA, Am. Orthop. Assn. (mem. nominating com. 1988-89, del.-at-large exec. com. 1988-89, mem. com. on N.Am. travelling fellowship 1989-93, mem. com. planning and devel. 1991—, 2nd pres.-elect 1994—), Am. Fracture Assn. (Wellmerling award 1982), Am. Acad. Pediats., Am. Acad. Orthop. Surgeons (mem. com. undergrad. edn. 1976-83, chmn. 1979-83, mem. com. pediat. orthopedics 1988-94, mem. subcom. on spine 1990, mem. subcom. on pediats program com. 1992, mem. coun. clin. resources 1993-94), Am. Acad. Cerebral Palsy and Devel. Medicine, Am. Orthop. Foot and Ankle Soc. (mem. com. biomechanics 1982-84, mem. program com. 1985—), Ind. Orthop. Soc. (mem. exec. com. 1986-95), Ind. State Med. Soc., Assn.

Orthop. Chmn., Clin. Orthop. Soc., Acad. Orthop. Soc. (mem. undergrad. edn. com. 1983-87), Little Orthop. Club, Marion County Med. Soc., Mid-Am. Orthop. Assn. (chmn. program com. 1986-87, bd. dirs. 1986—, sec. 1990-93, 2nd v.p. 1993-94, 1st v.p. 1994—), Orthop. Letters Club, Pediat. Orthop. Soc. N.Am. (mem. com. on fellowships 1986-92, bd. dirs. 1990-92, 2nd v.p. 1994, 1st v.p. 1995, pres. 1996), Russell Hibbs Soc., Scoliosis Rsch. Soc. (mem. edn. com. 1985—), Internat. Soc. Orthop. Surgery and Traumatology, Spectators Orthop. Letters Club, 20th Century Orthop. Assn., Alpha Omega Alpha, Alpha Epsilon Delta. Office: Am Bd Orthopedic Surgery 400 Silver Cedar Ct Chapel Hill NC 27514-1585*

DE ROSE, LOUIS JOHN, financial services executive; b. Elizabeth, N.J., Mar. 2, 1952; s. Ralph Anthony and Mary Rose (Di Leo) DeR.; m. Alejandrina Oriol, Jan. 20, 1982; children: Daniel A., Sandra M., Ralph A. III. AAS, Union Coll., 1972; BS, Rutgers U., 1980; postgrad., Pace U., 1980-84. Notary pub., N.J. Tax acct. U.S. Trust Co. N.Y., N.Y.C., 1972-79; tax acct. Fiduciary Trust Co., Inc., N.Y.C., 1979, asst. tax officer, 1979-80, tax officer, 1980-83; asst. v.p., dept. head Fiduciary Spl. Svcs., Inc., N.Y.C., 1983-86; v.p. Fiduciary Spl. Svcs., Inc., Jersey City, 1986-94, N.Y.C., 1994-97; mgr. profl. svcs. RIA Trust Svcs. Group, Iselin, N.J., 1997—. Coach Rahway (N.J.) Youth Soccer Assn., 1984-94; asst. den leader, com. chair Cub Scout Pack 47, Rahway, 1994-97, com. mem. Boy Scout Troop #49, Rahway, 1998-99. Mem. Computer Lang. Rsch. Fast Tax Users Group (pres. 1994-96). Democrat. Roman Catholic. Avocation: reading. Office: RIA Trust Svcs Group 100 Wood Ave S Iselin NJ 08830-2716

DE ROSEN, MICHEL, pharmaceutical company executive; b. Paris, Feb. 18, 1951; m. Laurence de Taisne de Rosen, June 29, 1979; children: Nicolas, Claire, Elie, Félix. Attended, Ecole Des Hautes Études Commerciales, Paris, 1972, Ecole Nationale D'Administration, Paris, 1976. Treasury official Govt. Treasury Dept., Paris, 1976-80, Treasury Dept., Paris, 1981-82; asst. to sec. of defense Dept. Defense, Paris, 1980-81; asst. to pres. Rhone-Poulenc Santé, Paris, 1982-84; gen. mgr. Pharmuka (RP Affiliate), Paris, 1984-86; chief of staff Min. Industry, Paris, 1986-88; dir. gen. Rhone-Poulenc Polymeres Fibres, Paris, 1988-90, Rhone-Poulenc Fibres, Paris, 1990-93; pres., COO, Rhône-Poulenc Rorer, Inc., Collegeville, Pa., 1993-95, pres., CEO, 1995-96; CEO, chmn. bd. Rhone-Poulenc Rorer, 1996—; mem. bd. dirs. Rhône-Poulenc Rorer Inc., Collegeville, 1993—, exec. coun. mem., 1993—; com. exec. mem. Rhône-Poulenc S.A., Paris, 1992—; mem. bd. dirs. PhRMA, Washington, 1994—. Home: 407 Pugh Rd Wayne PA 19087-1904 Office: Rhone-Poulenc Rorer Inc 500 Arcola Rd Collegeville PA 19426-3930*

DEROSIER, ARTHUR HENRY, JR., college president; b. Norwich, Conn., Feb. 18, 1931; s. Arthur Henry and Rose (Raymond) DeR.; m. Linda Preston Scott, Dec. 26, 1979; children: Deborah Ann, Marsha Carol, Brett Preston Scott, Melissa Estelle. BS, U. So. Miss., 1953; MA, U. S.C., 1955, PhD, 1959. Asst. prof. history The Citadel, 1956-57, Converse Coll., Spartanburg, S.C., 1957-59; asst. prof. U. So. Miss., 1959-60, assoc. prof., 1960-64, prof., 1964-65; assoc. prof. history U. Okla., 1965-67, asst. dean, Grad. Coll., 1966-67; dean Grad. Sch., prof. history East Tenn. State U., Johnson City, 1967-72; v.p. for adminstrn. East Tenn. State U., 1972-74; vice chancellor for acad. affairs, prof. history U. Miss., 1974-76, vice chancellor, 1976-77; pres. East Tenn. State U., 1977-80, Coll. of Idaho, Caldwell, 1980-87, Rocky Mountain Coll., Billings, Mont., 1987—; pres. Ind. Colls. of Mont., 1992—; vis. prof. history U. Mass., summer 1964; ednl. TV series on Am. history, 1966-72; bd. dirs. Rocky Mountain Bank. Author: Through the South with a Union Soldier, 1969, The Removal of the Choctaw Indians, 1970, (with others) Four Centuries of Southern Indians, 1975, Forked Tongues and Broken Treaties, 1975, Appalachia: Family Traditions in Transition, 1975, Pioneer Trails West, 1985, Institutional Revival: Case Histories, 1986; contbr. articles to hist. jours. Active numerous Indian philanthropies; mem. Idaho Commn. on Pardons and Parole, 1985-87; commr., U.S. Senate Commn. Online Child Proection, 1999—; bd. dirs. Deaconess Med. Ctr., 1988-92. With USAF, 1948-52. So. fellow, 1958; Am. Philos. Soc. grantee, 1964. Mem. Am. Hist. Assn., Orgn. Am. Historians, So. Hist. Assn., Western Hist. Assn., Nat. Assn. Ind. Colls. and Univs. (fin. com. higher edn. 1990-97), Coun. Ind. Colls., Western Ind. Colls. Fund, Nat. Assn. Sch. and Coll. of United Meth. Ch. (chmn. com. on internat. edn. 1993-96, bd. dirs. 1994-97), Rotary, Phi Beta Kappa. Home: 1809 Mulberry Dr Billings MT 59102-0601 Office: Rocky Mountain Coll Office of President 1511 Poly Dr Billings MT 59102-1739 *A college is a place where educational opportunities are available for all who treasure learning. The testing, challenging, and expanding of the mind is our primary responsibility, and we should be graded on how successfully we complete that task. A college is also an integral part of society. It helps us develop and clarify ideals and goals; it challenges us to develop a civilized set of principles; and it affords us an opportunity to test those principles and goals in the greater society. And it must teach us to approach life with a sense of humor. We are human: we are capable of significant achievements and bumbling failures. An educated person learns to live with both, allowing success and failure to meet each other with good grace and a smile.*

DE ROSIER, DAVID JOHN, biophysicist, educator; b. Milw., Feb. 22, 1939; s. Herman Francis and Adell Marie De Rosier; children: Elizabeth Anne, Charles David. BS, U. Chgo., 1961, PhD, 1965. Postdoctoral fellow Lab. Molecular Biology, Cambridge, England, 1965-69; asst. prof. chemistry U. Tex., Austin, 1968-72, assoc. prof., 1972-73; assoc. prof. physics Brandeis U., Waltham, Mass., 1973-78, prof., 1978-79, prof. biology, 1979—, chmn. grad. program biophysics, 1978-79, 80-83, chmn. dept. biology, 1984-87, Abraham S. and Gertrude Burg prof. life scis., 1993—; mem. study sci. NIH, 1983-86; chmn. Gordon Rsch. Conf., 1989; Bacaner rsch. lectr. U. Minn., 1990, Tom Garrar lectr., 1993; Blakeslee lectr. Smith Coll., 1996; dir. W.M. Keck Inst. for Cellular Visualization. Assoc. editor Jour. Molecular Biology, 1988-93; mem. editl. bd. Jour. Cell Biology, 1988-91, 96-99, Current Opinion in Structural Biology, 1991—, Biophys. Jour. Coordinator Mason-Rice Community Sch., Newton, Mass., 1975-77. Air Force Office Sci. Rsch. fellow, 1965, Am. Cancer Soc. fellow, 1966, NSF fellow, 1967, Guggenheim fellow, 1987; NIH grantee, 1970—; recipient Merit award NIH, 1991. Fellow AAAS, Am. Soc. Microbiology; mem. Biophys. Soc. (coun. mem., Elizabeth Robert Cole award 1993), Microscopic Soc. Am., Am. Soc. Cell Biologists. Home: 27 Chesterfield Rd Newton MA 02465-2343 Office: Brandeis U Rosenstiel Ctr Waltham MA 02465

DEROUCHEY, BEVERLY JEAN, investment company executive; b. Kenosha, Wis., Sept. 3, 1958; d. Dean Rodney and Doris May (Rasch) DeR. BS in Bus. Mgmt., U. Wis., 1982; MBA in Fin., Cornell U., 1984. Chartered fin. analyst, 1993. Acctg. asst. Kenosha (Wis.)-News Pub. Corp., 1979-81; polit. intern Office of Congressman Les Aspin, Racine, Wis., 1982; teaching asst. Cornell U., Ithaca, N.Y., 1983; audit intern Coopers and Lybrand, Syracuse, N.Y., 1983; staff cons. Peterson & Co., N.Y.C., 1984-86; assoc. Salomon Bros., N.Y.C., 1986-90, v.p., 1991; assoc. investment officer Dartmouth Coll., Hanover, N.H., 1992-94; v.p., dir. asset allocation CTC Consulting, Portland, Oreg., 1995; investment mgr. Constellation Investments, Inc., Balt., 1996-97; dir. rsch. Paradigm Cons. Svcs. LLC, Quechee VT. and Clifton NJ., 1998—. Alumni phonathons Cornell U., Ithaca, N.Y. and N.Y.C., 1982-87, co-chair new donor com., 1985-87; active Rep. Senatorial Inner Circle. Cornell U. scholar, 1982-84, BPW scholar, 1977, 82-83, AAUW scholar, 1981. Mem. Am. Film Inst., N.Y. Soc. of Security Analysts, Assn. for Investment Mgmt. and Rsch., Bus. and Profl. Women (bd. dirs. 1991-92), Film Soc. Lincoln Ctr., Quechee (Vt.)-Lakes Landowners' Assn. Republican. Lutheran. Avocations: tennis, golf, travel, writing. Home: PO Box 1309 Quechee VT 05059-1309

DEROUIN, JAMES G., lawyer; b. Eau Claire, Wis., July 11, 1944. BA cum laude, U. Wis., 1967, JD, 1968. Bar: Wis. 1968, Ariz. 1986. Ptnr. Steptoe & Johnson LLC, Phoenix, Ariz.; atty. Meyer, Hendricks, Victor, Osbonn & Maledon, Phoenix, Ariz.; ptnr. Dewitt, Ross & Stevens, Madison, Wis. PCB chair Wis. Dept. Natural Resources, 1976-78; mem. spl. com. on solid waste mgmt. Wis. Legis. Coun., 1976-79, ad hoc com. on hazardous waste mgmt., 1980-82, spl. com. on groundwater mgmt.; mem. Wis. Dept. Nat. Resources Metallic Mining Coun., 1978-85; chair Phoenix Environ. Quality Commn., 1986, Phoenix Environ. Quality Com., 1989-92; mem. Ariz. Govs. Regulatory Review Coun. 1986—; co-chair ADEQ/ADWR Groundwater Task Force, 1996-97. Chair. State Bar Ariz. (environ. and nat. resources law sect. 1989-90). Office: 40 N Central Ave Ste 2400 Phoenix AZ 85004-4453

DEROULET, DANIEL N., college dean; b. Livingston, N.J., Aug. 12, 1958; s. John N. and Ruth E. deRoulet; m. Teresa Lynn White, May 18, 1985; children: Jonathan, Eric, Kevin. BA, U. Calif., Irvine, 1980, MA, 1988, PhD, 1992. Assoc. prof. English, dept. chmn. North Park U., Chgo., 1992-98, dean undergrad. coll., 1998—. Grantee NEH, 1995. Mem. MLA. Office: North Park U 3225 W Foster Ave Box 11 Chicago IL 60625

DEROUSIE, CHARLES STUART, lawyer; b. Adrian, Mich., May 24, 1947; s. Stuart J. and Helia I. (Juntunen) DeR.; m. Patricia Jean Fetzer, May 31, 1969; children: Jennifer, Jason. BA magna cum laude, Oakland U., 1969; JD magna cum laude, U. Mich., 1973. Bar: Ohio, 1973, U.S. Dist. Ct. (so. dist.) Ohio 1974. Ptnr. Vorys, Sater, Seymour and Pease, LLP, Columbus, Ohio, 1973—. Trustee Ballet Met., Inc., Columbus, 1978-90, pres., 1986-88; trustee Gladden Community House, Columbus, 1975-81, pres., 1979-81; mem. Children's Hosp. Devel. Bd., Columbus, 1987—, pres. 1995-96; trustee Elder Choices of Ctrl. Ohio, Columbus, 1989-95, Heritage Day Health Ctrs., Columbus, 1992-98. Fellow Columbus Bar Found.; mem. ABA, Am. Health Lawyers Assn., Columbus Bar Assn., Ohio Bar Assn., Order of Coif. Office: Vorys Sater Seymour and Pease LLP PO Box 1008 52 E Gay St Columbus OH 43215-3161

DEROUX, DANIEL GRADY, artist; b. Juneau, Alaska, Oct. 25, 1951; s. Harold Edward DeRoux and Mary Elizabeth (Rice) Quist; m. JoAnn Marie Grady, Aug. 16, 1992; children: Eric, Katie. Curator of exhibits Alaska State Mus., Juneau, 1978-79; set designer Perseverance Theatre, Douglas, Alaska, 1988-91; owner Gallery Still Russian and Alaskan Contemporary Art, Juneau, 1991-92; artist, 1971—. Sole exhibns. include Natsoulas/Novelozo Gallery, Davis, Calif., 1989, Czar's Summer Palace, St. Petersberg, Russia, 1992, Somar Gallery, San Francisco, 1992, Mercer-Hood Gallery, Seattle, 1994, Ft. Mason Ctr., San Francisco, 1995. Recipient Gold medal for most accomplished artist, Bronze medal in Mixed Media, L.A. Internat. Art Competition, 1984, Third Place award N.Y. Internat. Art Competition, 1988; named Best of Show, Calgene West Coast Art Competition, Calif., 1988. Home and Studio: 19191 Randall Rd Juneau AK 99801-8209

DEROW, PETER ALFRED, publishing company executive; b. Boston, Apr. 18, 1940; s. Harry A. and Ruth D. (Dimond) Derow; m. Ruth C. Joffe, June 13, 1965; children: Jonathan, Polly, James. BA cum laude, Harvard U., 1963, MBA, 1965. Pres. Newsweek, Inc., N.Y.C., 1976-77; sr. v.p., dir. CBS, Inc., N.Y.C., 1977-78; v.p., dir. The Washington Post, 1978-81; chmn. Newsweek, Inc., N.Y.C., 1978-81; pres. CBS Pub. Group, N.Y.C., 1981-86; v.p. CBS, Inc., N.Y.C., 1981-86; pres. Goldmark Industries, N.Y.C., 1987-88; sr. v.p. Reed Pub. USA, Stamford, Conn. and Newton, Mass., 1988; pres. Instl. Investor, Inc., N.Y.C., 1988-97; dir. Global Decisions Group, LLC, N.Y.C., 1998—, 101 Comm., LLC, Pasadena, Calif., 1999—. Author: Successful Publishing on Campus, 1966; mem. editorial bd. Harvard Bus. Rev., 1981-95. Avocations: tennis, sculling, reading, running, bicycling. E-mail: derow@mindspring.com. Home: PO Box 534 Bedford NY 10506-0534 Office: 6 E 43d St 19th Fl New York NY 10017

DERR, DEBRA HULSE, advertising executive, publisher, editor; b. Newark, May 19, 1955; d. Edgar William and Mary Carway Hulse; m. David Derr, Oct. 6, 1984. Student, Fordham U., 1973-76. Lic. employment agy. operator, N.J. Prodn. coord. Telepages, Inc., Parsippany, N.J., 1976-79; credit investigator Hertz Corp., Parsippany, 1979-82; employment counselor Baker Pers., Pine Brook, N.J., 1982-84; copywriter Creative Mktg., Fairfield, N.J., 1984-87; pers. cons. Career Line, Inc., Morris Plains, N.J., 1987-92; v.p. D2 Studios, Inc., Parsippany, 1992—; Contbg. author: Journeys Into Self-Acceptance, 1994; pub., editor Tiny Lion, 1995. Activist, spkr. Nat. Orgn. to Advance Fat Acceptance, No. N.J. chpt., 1990—. Mem. NOW. Avocations: reading, historical researcher. Office: D2 Studios Inc PO Box 8112 Parsippany NJ 07054-8112

DERR, KENNETH T., oil company executive; b. 1936; m. Donna Mettler, Sept. 12, 1959; 3 children. BME, Cornell U., 1959, MBA, 1960. With Chevron Corp. (formerly Standard Oil Co. of Calif.), San Francisco, 1960—, v.p., 1972-85; pres. Chevron U.S.A., Inc. subs. Chevron Corp., San Francisco, 1978-84; head merger program Chevron Corp. and Gulf Oil Corp., San Francisco, 1984-85; vice-chmn. Chevron Corp., San Francisco, 1985-88, chmn., CEO, 1989—; bd. dirs. AT&T, Am. Productivity & Quality Ctr., Citigroup, Potlatch Corp. Trustee emeritus Cornell U. Mem. The Bus. Coun., Calif. Bus. Roundtable, Am. Petroleum Inst. (bd. dirs.), Nat. Petroleum Coun., San Francisco Golf Club, Orinda Country Clb, Pacific Union Club. Office: Chevron Corp PO Box 7643 575 Market St San Francisco CA 94105-2856

DERR, LEE E., chemical company executive; b. St. Joseph, Mo., June 12, 1948; s. LeRoyce Eugene and Helen Marie (Smith) D.; m. Mary Jo Saldi, Nov. 5, 1986; children: Lindsay, Marie. BS in Bus. Adminstrn., U. Mo., 1970. CPA, Kans., Mo. V.p., fin. and treas. Wulfsberg Electronics, Inc., Overland Park, Mo., 1976-84; group v.p. B.C. Christopher Securities, Kansas City, Mo., 1984-85; pres. Pyrotech Corp., Leawood, Kans., 1985—; pres. Interchem (N.A.) Industries, Inc., Overland Park, 1985—. Mem. AICPA. Home: 8690 Woodland Ave Shawnee Mission KS 66220-3106 Office: Interchem Industries Inc 9135 Barton St Overland Park KS 66214-1720

DERR, VERNON ELLSWORTH, retired government research administrator; b. Balt., Nov. 22, 1921; s. William Edward and Edith May D.; m. Mary Louise Van Atta, Mar. 6, 1943; children—Michael Edward, Katherine Mary, Louise Edith, Carol Jean. A.B. in Liberal Arts, St. John's Coll., Annapolis, Md., 1948; Ph.D., Johns Hopkins U., 1959. Student asst. Applied Physics Lab., Balt., 1950; research assoc. Johns Hopkins U., Balt., 1951-59; prin. scientist Martin Marietta, Orlando, Fla., 1959-67; physicist Environ. Rshc. Labs., Wave Propagation Lab. NOAA, Boulder, Colo., 1967-81, dep. dir. Wave Proagation Lab., 1981-83, dep., dir. Rsch. Labs., 1983-89; dir. Data Memt. Office, Chief Scientist Office, NOAA, Boulder, Colo., 1989-94; rsch. scientist Coop. Inst. Rsch. in Environ. Scis., U. Colo., 1994—; mem. Internat. Sci. Radio Union Commn. II; mem. Internat. Radiation Commn. Served to capt. U.S. Army 1942-46. Mem. Am. Geophys. Union, Optical Soc. Am., Am. Meteorol. Soc., IEEE (sr.), Internat. Assn. Meteorology and Atmospheric Physics (U.S. del. to Internat. Union Geodesy and Geophysics). Office: U Colo Coop Inst Environ Sci Campus Box 216 Boulder CO 80309-0216*

DERRICK, BUTLER CARSON, JR., lawyer, former congressman; b. Springfield, Mass., Sept. 30, 1936; s. Butler Carson and Mary English (Scott) D.; m. Beverly Davis; children: Lydia Gile, Butler Carson III, Charlotte Grantham, George Grantham. Student, U. S.C., 1954-58; LLB, U. Ga., 1965; hon. degree, Lander Coll., 1978, Erskine Coll., 1978; LLD (hon.), U. S.C., 1986; LHD (hon.), Med. U. S.C., 1988. Bar: S.C. 1965, D.C. 1988. Ptnr. Derrick & Byrd, Edgefield, S.C., 1970-75; mem. S.C. Ho. of Reps., 1969-74, 94th-103rd Congresses from 3rd S.C. dist., Washington, D.C., 1975-95; Dem. steering and policy com., house adminstrn. com., rules com., chief majority dep. whip; ptnr. Williams & Jensen, PC, Washington; assoc. Powell, Goldstein, Frazer & Murphy, Washington, 1999—; adv. bd. Sec. of Energy. Pres. Edgefield County Fish and Game Assn. Named Conservationist of Yr. S.C. Wildlife Fedn., 1977; Conservationist of Yr. Nat. Wildlife Fedn., 1977; one of Our Ten Best Friends in Congress Outdoor life mag.; recipient Disting. River Conservation award Am. Rivers Conservation Council, 1977. Mem. S.C. Bar Assn., ABA, D.C. Bar Assn., Edgefield County Bar Assn. (past pres.), Spl. Forces Assn. (hon., mem. Green Berets). Democrat. Episcopalian. Home: 48 S Battery St Charleston SC 29401-2327 Office: Powell Goldstein Frazer & Murphy 6th Fl 1001 Pennsylvania Ave NW Washington DC 20004*

DERRICK, GARY WAYNE, lawyer; b. Enid, Okla., Nov. 3, 1953; s. John Henry and Leota Elaine (Glenn) D.; m. Susan Adele Goodwin, Dec. 22, 1979 (div. June 1981); m. Francys Hollis Johnson, May 3, 1986; children: Meghan, Drew, Jane. BA in History, English, Okla. State U., 1976; JD, U. Okla., 1979. Bar: Okla. 1979. Assoc. Andrews, Davis, Legg, Bixler, Milsten & Price, Oklahoma City, 1979-84, ptnr., 1985-90; of counsel McKinney, Stringer & Webster, P.C., Oklahoma City, 1990-93; ptnr. Derrick & Briggs, Oklahoma City, 1994—; active Securities Law and Acctg. Group, Oklahoma City, 1979—; chmn. Gen. Corp. Act Commn., Okla., 1984—, chmn. Securities Liaison Com., Okla., 1985-86; lectr. sem. Okla. Corp. Act, 1986—. Conbg. author: Oklahoma Business Organizations. Mem. Okla. State U. Found., Stillwater, 1983-89, U. Okla. Found., Norman, 1982—; mem. condr.'s circle Okla. Symphony Orch., 1981-88; bd. dirs. Hist. Preservation, Inc., 1990—. Mem. ABA (taxation and corp. sect., banking and bus. law sect.), Okla. Bar Assn. (chmn. bus. assn. sect. 1985-87, outstanding contbn. to continuing legal edn., Earl Sneed award 1997), Oklahoma County Bar Assn. (bd. govs. young lawyers div. 1981-82), Am. Soc. Corp. Secs. (pres. Okla.-Ark. chpt. 1994-95), Oklahoma City Boat Club. Republican. Episcopalian. Avocations: sailing, violin. Home: 500 NW 15th St Oklahoma City OK 73103-2102 Office: Derrick & Briggs Bank One Ctr 20th Fl 100 N Broadway Ave Oklahoma City OK 73102-8606

DERRICK, JAMES V., JR., lawyer; b. Graham, Tex., Jan. 8, 1945. BA with honors, U. Tex., 1967, JD with honors, 1970. Bar: Tex. 1970. Jud. clk. U.S. Ct. Appeals (5th cir.), 1970-71; ptnr. Vinson & Elkins, Houston, from 1977; sr. v.p., gen. counsel Enron Corp., Houston, 1991—; adj. prof. U. Tex. Law Sch., 1984-90. Assoc. editor Tex. Law Rev., 1969-70. Mem. ABA, State Bar Tex., Houston Bar Found., Houston Bar Assn., Chancellors, Order of Coif, Houston Grand Opera (bd. dirs.), Soc. for Performing Arts, Found. for Jones Hall, U. Tex. Law Sch. Alumni Bd. (exec. com.). : Enron Global Power to Pipelines LLC PO Box 1188 Houston TX 77251-1188 also: Enron Corp 1400 Smith St Houston TX 77002*

DERRICK, JOHN MARTIN, JR., electric company executive; b. Washington, Mar. 14, 1940; s. John M. and Audrey (Robey) D.; m. Linda Denhofer, Oct. 14, 1961; 1 child, Mark Frederick. BSEE, Duke U., 1961; postgrad., George Washington U., 1969. Registered profl. engr., D.C., Md. Various engrng. positions Potomac Electric Power Corp., Washington, 1965-70, then mgr. various depts., then exec. v.p. and chief oper. officer, now pres., CEO. Pres. Duke Club Washington, 1974-75, Bethesda (Md.) Lions Club, 1978-79; trustee Md. Nature Conservancy; gov. Wesley Theol. Sem; chmn. YMCA, 1995-96, Jr. Achievement, 1994-95. Lt. (j.g.) USN, 1962-65. Mem. IEEE, NSPE, Washington Bldg. Congress (pres. 1985-86), Edison Electric Inst., U.S. Energy Assn. (treas.). Republican. Methodist. Avocations: boating, tennis, golf. Office: Potomac Electric Power Co 1900 Pennsylvania Ave NW Washington DC 20068-0002*

DERRICK, MALCOLM, physicist; b. Hull, Eng., Feb. 15, 1933; came to U.S., 1963, naturalized, 1976; s. Arthur Henry and Gladys (Hopkinson) D.; m. Kathleen Allen, 1957; 1 child, Matthew; m. Christa Zars Baumgardner, 1966; m. Eva Krebbers, 1995. B.Sc. with 1st class honours, U. Birmingham, 1954, Ph.D., 1959; M.A., Oxford U., 1961. Instr. Carnegie Inst. Tech., 1957-60; asst. prof. Oxford U., 1960-63; asst. physicist Argonne (Ill.) Nat. Lab., 1963-67, sr. physicist, 1967—, dir. high energy physics div., 1974-81; vis. prof. U. Minn., 1969-70, Univ. Coll., London, 1972-73; adv. com. Stanford U. Accelerator Center, Fermi Nat. Accelerator Lab.; mem. high energy physics adv. panel Dept. Energy. Author numerous research papers on high energy physics. Fellow Am. Phys. Soc. Home: 20 Equestrian Way Lemont IL 60439-9785 Office: Argonne Nat Lab Bldg 362 Argonne IL 60439 *The opportunity to spend a lifetime's career investigating the Fundamental physical basis of matter is one that has been given to relatively few people. Such research requires large and expensive accelerators and particle detectors and so can only be funded by government agencies. It is to the credit of the United States that such support has been generously given, and the resulting revolution in our understanding of nature is the outstanding intellectual achievement of our times.*

DERRICK, WILLIAM DENNIS, physical plant administrator, consultant; b. San Diego, Feb. 7, 1946; s. Charles Woodrow and Catherine Elizabeth (McCormick) D.; m. Lynda Ray Adams, June 15, 1964 (div. 1971); children: Tod Sean, Shannon Kay, Nicole Dione, Johnathon Robert; m. Frances C. Bouck, Nov. 19, 1979; children: Kaila June Warner, Bryan Charles. Student, U. Nebr., 1971-72, 73-74, U. Mont., 1974-77, 98-99, Internat. Corr., 1966-67, 81, Battelle Meml. Inst., 1985, Project Mgmt. Inst., 1986-95, 98—. Elec. draftsman City of Lincoln (Nebr.) Light Dept., 1964-65; asst. engr. to adjutant gen. Nebr. N.G. State of Nebr., Lincoln, 1965-66; owner, mgr., archtl. draftsman Lumberman's Plan Svc., Inc., Lincoln, 1966-70; owner, mgr. Lenny's Lounge, Missoula, Mo., 1978-80; engrng. technician, constrn. inspector, adminstr. USDA/Helena (Mont.) Nat. Forest, 1980-83; facilities project mgr. pub. office bldgs. div. City and County of Denver, 1984-86; supt. bldgs. and grounds Denver Pub. Libr., 1986-91; dir. phys. plant Red Rocks C.C., Lakewood, Colo., 1991-94; CEO Derrick, Inc., Stevensville, Mont.; chmn. bd. dirs. One Kind a Lady Ent. Elected commr. Local Govt. Study Commn., Stevensville, Mont., 1974; appointed bd. dirs. Lewis & Clark County Fair Bd., Helena, Mont., 1979-83. With U.S. Army, 1967-70, Vietnam. Mem. Project Mgmt. Inst. (cert. project mgr. profl. #619, v.p. programs Denver chpt. 1986-89, pres. 1990-91, v.p. pub. rels. 1992-93, bd. dirs., ex-officio). Independent. Avocations: computer technology, videography, photo journalism, ind. entrepeneurism. E-mail: L:wder181822@aol.com. Home: 313 11th St Apt 102B Stevensville MT 59870-2913

DERRICKSON, DENISE ANN, secondary school educator; b. Seaford, Del., Sept. 20, 1956; d. William Hudson and Patricia Ann (Adkins) D. BS, James Madison U., 1978; MEd in Counseling and Human Devel., George Mason U., 1990, MEd in Curriculum & Instrn., 1994. Social studies instr. Brentsville Dist. High Sch., Nokesville, Va., 1978-91, Woodbridge (Va.) Sr. High Sch., 1991—; faculty liaison Parent-Tchr. Action Coun., 1990-91; prin.'s adv. coun., 1994-96. Vol. Childrens Hosp., Washington, 1983-86, Action in the Community through Svc., Inc.-Helpline, Manassas, Va., 1988-92. Recipient Cert. Appreciation Prince William County Sch. Bd., 1989, Outstanding Educator award Va. Govs. Sch., 1990, ACTS-Helpline Outstanding Vol. Svc. award, 1990; presented with V.S. Flag Armed Svcs. Hall of Honor at the dedication of the U.S. Women's Meml., 1998. Mem. NEA, AAUW, ASCD, VFW, Am. Assn. Curriculum Devel., Nat. Soc. for Study of Edn., Va. Edn. Assn., Va. Assn. Supervision and Curriculum Devel., Prince William Edn. Assn., Internat. Platform Assn., Kappa Delta Phi, Phi Delta Kappa. Avocations: sewing, crafts, travel. Office: Woodbridge Sr High Sch 3001 Old Bridge Rd Woodbridge VA 22192-3299

DERRICKSON, SHIRLEY JEAN BALDWIN, elementary school educator; b. Balt., Aug. 7, 1943; d. James Francis and Dorothy Elizabeth (Jubb) Baldwin; m. Ernest Hughes Derrickson, Aug. 19, 1978. BA, Knox Coll., 1965; MEd, Goucher Coll., 1969; postgrad., Towson State U., 1970-77. Cert. profl. status elem. tchr., Del. Tchr. Howard Park Elem. Sch., Balt., 1969-70, Lida Lee Tall Learning Resource Ctr., Towson (Md.) State U., 1970-83, Selbyville (Del.) Middle Sch., 1983-84; tchr. East Millsboro (Del.) Elem. Sch., 1984—, lead tchr. in sci., 1995—. Foreign affairs chmn. Dagsboro (Del.) Century Club, 1990-96, sec., 1986-88; sec. Dagsboro Rep. Club, 1986-88; active Friends of Prince George's Chapel, 1994—, Del. Sr. Olympics, 1998. Recipient Washington Regional scholarship, 1961-64. Mem. NEA, Del. State Edn. Assn., Indian River Edn. Assn., PTO, Grace United Meth. Ch. Republican. Methodist. Avocations: canoeing, sailing, golf, tennis, volleyball. Office: East Millsboro Elem Sch 500 E State St Millsboro DE 19966-1199

DERRICKSON, WILLIAM BORDEN, manufacturing executive; b. Milford, Del., May 30, 1940; m. Patricia Jean Hayes, Feb. 1, 1964; children: Stephen Russel, Michael Scot. BSEE, U. Del., 1964; diploma, Harvard Bus. Sch., 1979. Registered profl. engr. Supr. elec. maintenance Delmarva Power, Salisbury, Md., 1964-68; instrumentation engr. Hercules, Inc., Wilmington, Del., 1968-69, Sun Shipbldg., Chester, Pa., 1969-70; dir. project Fla. Power & Light Co., Juno Beach, Fla., 1970-84; sr. v.p. Pub. Svc. Co. N.H., Manchester, 1984-85; pres. New Hampshire Yankee Electric Co., Seabrook, 1985-87; pres., COO WPD Assocs., Inc., 1986-88; pres., COO Quadrex Corp., Campbell, Calif., 1988-89, chmn. bd., CEO, 1989-93; also chmn. bd. dirs.; chmn. bd., CEO QES Inc., Palm City, Fla., 1994—; nuclear advisor Tenn. Valley Authority Bd. Dirs., 1987. Contbr. articles to profl. pubs. Named Constrn. Man of Yr. ENR/McGraw-Hill Publs., 1984. Mem. NSPE, Am. Nuclear Soc., Project Mgmt. Inst., N.H. Soc. Profl. Engrs., Internat. Platform Assn., Rep. Senatorial Inner Circle. Republican. Avocations: golf, travel, numismatics, piano. Home: 1864 SW Saint Andrews Dr

Palm City FL 34990-2208 Office: IBEX Group PO Box 2078 Palm City FL 34991-7078

DERRICOTTE, TOI, poet, educator; b. Hamtramck, Mich., Apr. 11, 1941; m. C. Bruce Derricotte, Dec. 30, 1967; 1 child. BA, Wayne State U., 1965; MA, NYU, 1984. Master tchr., poet N.J. and Md. State Couns. on The Arts, 1973-88; assoc. prof. English Lit. Old Dominion U., 1988-90; commonwealth prof. George Mason U., 1990-91; assoc. prof. U. Pitts., 1991-97, prof. English, 1998—; vis. prof. NYU, 1992; Delta Sigma Theta Endowed chair in poetry Xavier U., 1999; co-founder Cave Canem, 1996—. Author: The Empress of the Death House, 1978, Natural Birth, 1983, Captivity, 1989, Tender, 1997 (Paterson Poetry prize 1998), The Black Notebooks, 1997 (Notable Book of Yr., N.Y. Times); co-author: Creative Writing: A Manual for Teachers, 1985. Creative Writing fellow NEA, 1985, 90; recipient Pushcart prize, 1989, 98, Poetry Book award Folger Shakespeare Libr., 1990, Disting. Pioneering of the Arts award United Black Artists, USA, Inc., 1993, Anisfield-Wolf Book award Cleve. Found., 1998, Literary award ALA, 1998; named Ucross Found. resident, 1995, Yaddo resident, 1997. Mem. Poetry Soc. Am. (Lucille Medwick Meml. award 1985), Associated Writing Programs. Home: c/o Exec Support Svcs Inc 10436 Democracy Ln Potomac MD 20854-4036

DERSCH, CHARETTE ALYSE, marriage and family therapist; b. Houston, Feb. 21, 1971; d. Albert and Sharon Beth (Bradley) Rofé; m. John Stephen Dersch, May 27, 1995. BA in Psychology and French, Tex. Tech U., 1994, MS in Human Devel. and Family studies, 1996, postgrad., 1996—. Rsch. asst. Tex. Tech U., Lubbock, 1993—, instr., clin. intern, 1996—, rsch. cons. dept. psychiatry Health Sci. Ctr., 1999—; computer cons., Lubbock, 1994—; conf. presenter San Diego Cconf. on Responding to Child Maltreatment, 1996, Am. Assn. Family and Consumer Scis., 1996; program coord. Parent Empowerment Program, 1998—; transition counselor Transition to 7th Grade Program, 1998-99. Contbr. chpt. to book and articles to profl. jours. Vol. ccaseworker Family Outreach Ctr., Lubbock, 1995-96. Scholar Alpha Chi Omega, 1990-92, Family Outreach Ctr., 1995-96, Gladys M. Haley scholar, 1995-96, C.M. and Virginia Hucheson scholar, 1996-97, Lola Drew scholar, 1998-99. Mem. Am. Assn. for Marriage and Family Therapy (conf. presenter nat. conf. 1997, 98), Tex. Assn. for Marriage and Family Therapy, Lubbock Assn. for Marriage and Family Therapy (conf. presenter 1998, Golden Key, Phi Upsilon Omicron, Psi Chi, Pi Delta Phi. Office: Tex Tech U Dept Human Devel and Family Studies PO Box 41162 Lubbock TX 79409-1162

DERSH, RHODA E., management consultant, business executive; b. Phila., Sept. 10, 1934; civ; d. Maurice S. and Kay (Wiener) Eisman; m. Jerome Dersh, Dec. 23, 1956; children: Debra Lori, Jeffrey Jonathan. BA, U. Pa., 1955; MA, Tufts U., 1956; MBA, Manhattan Coll., 1980. Interpreter Consul of Chile, 1954-57; various teaching and staff positions Albright Coll., Mt. Holyoke Coll., Amherst Coll., Marple Newtown Sch., 1957-58; pres., chief exec. officer Profl. Practice Mgmt. Assocs., Reading, 1976—, Pace Inst., Reading, 1981—, Pace Mgmt., Inc., 1983—;, 1984-90; mem. regional adv. bd. Core States Bank, 1991—; mem., bd. dirs. Ctr. City Devel. Corp., 1992—. Author: The School Budget is Your Business, 1976, Business Management for Professional Offices, 1977, The School Budget: It's Your Money, It's Your Business, 1979, Improving Public School Management Practices, 1979, Part-Time Professional and Managerial Personnel: The Employers View, 1979; contbr. articles to profl. jours. Bd. dirs. Pa. State Bd. Pvt. Lic. Schs., 1987-93; cons. dir. pub. sch. budget study project City of Reading, 1967-78, chmn. comprehensive community plan task force, 1973-75; chmn. pub. svc. cons. project 1980-90; panel chmn. budget allocations United Way, 1974-76; del. White House Conf. on Children Youth, 1970; cofounder World Affairs Coun., Reading and Berks County, 1963-65; chmn. Berks County Com. for Children Youth, 1968-72; commr. Trial Ct. Nominating Commn. of Berks County (Pa.), 1982-84; bd. dirs. United Way of Berks County, 1984-89; chmn. programs Leadership Berks, 1986-87; bd. dirs. Reading Ctr. City Devel. Corp., Berks Bus.-Edn. Coalition Corp., 1991—. Recipient Trendsetter award YWCA, 1985. Mem. AAUW (ednl. found. grant.), LWV, Pa. Assn. Pvt. Sch. Bus. Adminstrs. (bd. dirs. 1985-89), Berks County C. of C. (bd. dirs. 1983-86, chmn. edn. com. 1983-85), Am. Acad. Ind. Cons. (pres. 1978-80), Reading and Berks C. of C (Entrepreneur of Yr. 1985), Rotary (bd. dirs. Reading, Pa., chpt. 1989-90). Office: 606 Court St Reading PA 19601-3542

DERSHOWITZ, ALAN MORTON, lawyer, educator; b. Bklyn., Sept. 1, 1938; s. Harry and Claire (Ringel) D.; m. Carolyn Cohen; children: Elon Marc, Jamin Seth, Ella Kaille Cohen Dershowitz. BA magna cum laude, Bklyn. Coll., 1959; LLB magna cum laude, Yale U., 1962; MA (hon.), Harvard Coll., 1967; LLD (hon.), Yeshiva U., 1989; PhD (hon.), Haifa U., 1993; JD (hon.), Syracuse U., 1997. Bar: D.C. 1963, Mass. 1968, U.S. Supreme Ct. 1968. Law clk. to chief judge David L. Bazelon, U.S. Ct. Appeals, 1962-63; to justice Arthur J. Goldberg, U.S. Supreme Ct., 1963-64; mem. faculty Harvard Law Sch., 1964—, prof. law, 1967—, Felix Frankfurter Prof. of Law, 1993—; fellow Ctr. for Advanced Study of Behavioral Scis., 1971-72; Cons. to dir. NIMH, 1967-69, (Pres.'s Commn. Civil Disorders), 1967, (Pres.'s Com. Causes Violence), 1968, (NAACP Legal Def. Fund), 1967-68, NIMH Pres.'s Commn. Marijuana and Drug Abuse, 1972-73, Coun. on Drug Abuse, 1972—, Ford Found. Study on Law and Justice, 1973-76; rapporteur Twentieth Century Fund Study on Sentencing, 1975-76. *Professor Alan Dershowitz of Harvard Law School has been described by Newsweek as "the nation's most peripatetic civil-liberties lawyer and one of its most distinguished defenders of individual rights." Time called him "the top lawyer of last resort in the country--a sort of judicial St. Jude." Business Week characterized him as "a feisty civil libertarian and one of the nation's most prominent legal educators." He has been profiled by every major magazine ranging from Life ("iconoclast and self-appointed scourge of the criminal justice system"); to Esquire ("the country's most articulate and uncompromising protector of criminal defendants").* Author: (with others) Psychoanalysis, Psychiatry and the Law, 1967, Criminal Law: Theory and Process, 1974, The Best Defense, 1982, Reversal of Fortune: Inside the von Bulow Case, 1986, Taking Liberties: A Decade of Hard Cases, Bad Laws and Bum Raps, 1988, Chutzpah, 1991, Contrary to Popular Opinion, 1992, The Abuse Excuse, 1994, The Advocate's Devil, 1994, Reasonable Doubts, 1996, The Vanishing American Jew, 1997, Sexual McCarthyism: Clinton, Starr and the Emerging Constitutional Crisis, 1998, Just Revenge, 1999; contbr. articles to profl. jours.; editor-in-chief Yale Law Jour., 1961-62. Chmn. civil rights com. New England region Anti-Defamation League, B'nai B'rith, 1980-85; bd. dirs. ACLU, 1968-71, 72-75, Assembly Behavioral and Social Scis. at Nat. Acad. Scis., 1973-76. Guggenheim fellow, 1978-79; recipient hon. doctorates from Hebrew Union, Monmouth. Mem. Order of Coif, Phi Beta Kappa. Jewish. Office: Harvard Law Sch 1575 Massachusetts Ave Cambridge MA 02138

DERSTADT, RONALD THEODORE, health care administrator; b. Detroit, June 9, 1950; s. Theodore Edward and Dorothy J. (Semko) D.; m. J. Gail Adamson, June 9, 1990. BA, U. Detroit, 1971; M of Hosp. Healthcare Adminstn., Xavier U., 1975. Mgr. shared svcs. Bethesda Hosp. North, Cin., 1975-76; asst. adminstr. McCullough-Hyde Meml. Hosp., Oxford, Ohio, 1977-79; pres. Hospice of Cin., Inc., 1979-82; dir. strategic planning St. Francis-St. George Hosp., Cin., 1982-84; v.p. Mgmt. Dynamics, Inc., Cin., 1984-85; sr. v.p. St. Francis-St. George Mgmt. Co., Cin., 1986-88; v.p. Franciscan Health System of Cin., 1988-91; dir. hosp. affairs ChoiceCare, Cin., 1991-95; CEO Medquest, Owensboro, Ky., 1995-98; pres. Strategic Defense Inc., Cin., 1998—; vice-chmn., bd. dirs. Franciscan Health Network, Cin., Franciscan Health Ventures, Cin. Treas., bd. dirs. Ohio Easter Seals Soc., Columbus, 1987-93; bd. dirs. S.W. Ohio Easter Seal Soc., Cin., 1986-92; adv. bd. Dater Jr. H.S., Cin., 1984-88. Fellow Am. Coll. Healthcare Execs.; mem. Healthcare Fin. Mgmt. Assn., Am. Hosp. Assn., Ohio Hosp. Assn. Avocations: boating, golf, radio control model building. Home: 3632 Shady Ln North Bend OH 45052 Office: 230 Northland Blvd Cincinnati OH 45024

DERTHICK, ALAN WENDELL, architect; b. Johnson City, Tenn., July 6, 1931; s. Lawrence Gridley and Helda Lee (Hannah) D.; m. Jane Bailey, Dec. 22, 1958; children: Mark Alan, Steven John. BArch, Auburn U., 1954. Registered architect, Tenn., Ga., Ala. Ptnr. Derthick, Henley & Wilkerson Architects, Chattanooga, 1960—. Prin. works include Miller Pla., 1989 (Honor award), Hunter Mus. Art, 1977-78 (Honor awards), Chattanooga Pub. Libr., 1977 (Honor award), Hamilton County Courts Bldg., 1992, Alexian Village, 1993, Covenant Transport Nat. Hdqrs., 1997. Chmn. Chattanooga Codes Rev. Bd., 1975-95, Mayor's Better Schs. Task Force, Chattanooga, 1984-85, Hamilton County Codes Appeals Bd., 1999; pres. First Christian Ch., 1978, 84, 98. With USAF, 1954-56. Recipient Nat. Concrete Reinforcing Steel Inst. Honor award, 1977. Mem. AIA (pres. Chattanooga chpt. 1966, 72, Honor award 1989; Gulf States Regional Honor award 1961, 77, 78), Tenn. Soc. Architects (pres. 1991), Mountain City Club. Home: 602 Marr Dr Signal Mountain TN 37377-2228 Office: Derthick Henley Wilkerson 1001 Carter St Chattanooga TN 37402-5014

DERTIEN, JAMES LEROY, librarian; b. Kearney, Nebr., Dec. 14, 1942; s. John Ludwig and Muriel May (Cooley) D.; m. Elaine Paulette Mohror, Dec. 26, 1966; children—David Dalton, Channing Lee. AB, U. S.D., 1965; MLS, U. Pitts., 1966; MPA, U. S.D., 1995. Head librarian Mitchell Pub. Library, S.D., 1966-67; head librarian Sioux Falls Coll., S.D., 1967-69; acting dir. libraries U. S.D., Vermillion, 1969-70; head librarian Vets. Meml. Pub. Library, Bismarck, N.D., 1970-75, Bellevue Pub. Library, Nebr., 1975-81; libr. dir. Siouxland Librs., S.D., 1981—. Pres., bd. dirs. Vol. and Info. Ctr., Sioux Falls, 1991-93. Mem. ALA, Mountain Plains Library Assn. (pres. 1978-79, editor newsletter 1982—), S.D. Library Assn. (pres. 1986-87). Unitarian. Lodge: Rotary. Avocations: backpacking, reading, fishing. Home: 800 E 14th St Apt 319 Sioux Falls SD 57104-5240 Office: Siouxland Librs 201 N Main Ave Sioux Falls SD 57104-6002

DERTOUZOS, MICHAEL LEONIDAS, computer scientist, electrical engineer, educator; b. Athens, Greece, Nov. 5, 1936; came to U.S., 1954, naturalized, 1965; s. Leonidas Michael and Rosana G. (Maris) D.; children: Alexandra, Leonidas. BSEE, U. Ark., 1957, MSEE, 1959; PhD, MIT, 1964; honorary doctorate, Nat. U. Athens, 1992. Head research and devel. Baldwin Electronics, Inc., 1958-60; research asst. MIT, Cambridge, 1960-64, asst. prof., 1964-68, assoc. prof., 1968-73, prof., 1973—, dir. Lab. for Computer Sci., 1968-74; founder, chmn. bd. Computek, Inc., 1964—; cons. in computers to industry, 1984—. Author: Threshold Logic: A Synthesis Approach, 1966, (with Athans, Spann and Mason) Systems, Networks and Computation: Multivariable Methods, 1974, Systems, Networks and Computation: Basic Concepts, 1972, (with Clark, Halle, Pool and Wiesner) The Telephone's First Century—and Beyond, 1977, The Computer Age; A Twenty Year View, 1979, (with others) Made in America: Regaining the Productive Edge, 1989; contbr. articles profl. jours. Trustee Athens Coll., Greece, 1973—, chmn. U.S. bd. trustees, 1992—; chmn. bd. Boston Camerata, 1976-80; dir. Cambridge Soc. Early Music, 1974-75. Recipient Terman Internat. Edn. award Am. Soc. Engring. Edn., 1975; Ford postdoctoral fellow, 1964-66; Fulbright scholar, 1954. Fellow IEEE (Thompson best paper prize 1968); mem. NAE, Acad. Athens, Sigma Xi, Tau Beta Pi, Pi Mu Epsilon. Greek Orthodox. Patentee in field. Office: MIT Lab Computer Sci 545 Technology Sq Cambridge MA 02139-3539*

DE RUSSY, CANDACE UTER, education reformer; b. Seattle, June 12, 1943; d. Lawrence Aloysius Uter and Sybil Ory Uter Morris; m. Cortes Eugene de Russy, Sept. 7, 1968; children: Gabrielle Voelkel, Andrè Ory. BA cum laude, St. Mary's Dominican Coll., 1964; MA in French, Middlebury Coll., 1965; PhD in French, Tulane U., 1971. Instr. St. John Fisher Coll., Rochester, N.Y., 1971-73; asst. prof. Dominican Coll. of Blauvelt, Orangeburg, N.Y., 1972-78; exec. officer Am. Found. for Resistance Internat., N.Y.C., 1986-88; adj. prof. New Sch. for Social Rsch., N.Y.C., 1991-93; contbg. editor Crisis Mag., Washington, 1995—; appeared on numerous TV and radio commentary programs, including 60 Minutes, 1998. Contbr. numerous articles to profl. jours. Trustee SUNY, Albany, 1995—, Westchester C.C., Valhalla, N.Y., 1993-95; mem. adv. bd. Am. Coun. Trustees and Alumni, Ind. Women's Forum, Washington, 1992—; mem. exec. com. Nat. Com. on Am. Fgn. Policy, N.Y.c., 1984-96. Recipient Frederick D. Wilhelmsen-L. Brent Bozell, Jr. award Cath. Social Action, 1998; NDEA grantee, 1966-71. Mem. Nat. Assn. Scholars, Soc. Cath. Social Scientists, Manhattan Inst. Republican. Roman Catholic. Avocations: study of ideas, iconography, current events, interior decorating, walking.

DERVAN, PETER BRENDAN, chemistry educator; b. Boston, July 28, 1945; s. Peter Brendan and Ellen (Comer) D.; m. Jackqueline K. Barton; children: Andrew, Elizabeth. BS, Boston Coll., 1967; PhD, Yale U., 1972. Asst. prof. Calif. Inst. Tech., Pasadena, 1973-79, assoc. prof., 1979-82, prof. chemistry, 1982-88, Bren prof. chemistry, 1988—; chmn. div. chemistry & chem. engring., 1994—; adv. bd. ACS Monographs, Washington, 1979-81. Mem. adv. bd. Jour. Organic Chemistry, Washington, 1981—; mem. editorial bd. Bioorganic Chemistry, 1983—, Chem. Rev. Jour., 1984—, Nucleic Acids Res., 1986—, Jour. Am. Chem. Soc., 1986—, Acct. Chem. Res., 1988—, Bioorganic Chem. Rev., 1988—, Bioconjugate Chemistry, 1989—, Jour. Med. Chemistry, 1991—, Tetrahedron, 1992—, Bioorganic and Med. Chemistry, 1993—, Chemical and Engineering News, 1992—; contbr. articles to profl. jours. A.P. Sloan Rsch. fellow, 1977; Camille and Henry Dreyfus scholar, 1978; Guggenheim fellow, 1983; recipient Arthur C. Cope Scholar award 1986, Maison de la Chimie Found. prize, 1996. Fellow Am. Acad. Scis.; mem. NAS, Am. Chem. Soc. (Nobel Laureate Signature award 1985, Harrison Howe award 1988, Arthur C. Cope award, 1993, Willard Gibbs medal, 1993, Rolf Sammet prize, 1993, William H. Nichols medal 1994, Kirkwood medal 1998, Alfred Bader award 1999), Inst. Medicine (Remsen award 1998). Office: Calif Inst Tech 1201 E California Blvd Pasadena CA 91125-0001

DERVARTANIAN, DANIEL VARTAN, biochemistry educator; b. Boston, July 16, 1933; s. Donabed and Nevart (Ouzounian) DerV.; m. Marie Elizabeth Ypma, May 15, 1964; children: Merle, Adrienne. AA, Boston U., 1953, BA, 1956; MS, Northeastern U., 1959; ScD, U. Amsterdam, The Netherlands, 1965. Wetenschappelijke medewerker U. Amsterdam, 1961-65; rsch. assoc. U. Wis., Madison, 1965-68; asst. prof. U. Ga., Athens, 1968-73, assoc. prof., 1973-78, prof. biochemistry, 1978—, assoc. dir. Sch. Chem. Scis., 1985-91, chmn. divsn. biol. scis., 1991—. Contbr. numerous articles to profl. jours.; editl. bd. Jour. Bioenergetics and Biomembranes, Boston, 1976-85, Jour. Bacteriology, Washington, 1980-82, Biochimica Et Biophysica Acta, Amsterdam, 1988-95. With U.S. Army, 1959-60. Recipient Rsch. Career award NIH, Bethesda, 1971-76; Rsch. grantee NSF, Washington, 1969-72, 84-87, 90-93, NIH, Bethesda, 1971-81, 85-95. Mem. Am. Soc. Microbiology, Am. Soc. Biochemistry and Molecular Biology. Armenian Gregorian (apostolic). Avocations: ancient European and American history, photography. Office: Univ Ga Divsn Biol Scis Biol Scis Bldg Rm 400 Athens GA 30602

DERVIN, BRENDA LOUISE, communications educator; b. Beverly, Mass., Nov. 20, 1938; d. Ermina Diluiso; adopted d. John Jordan and Marjorie (Sullivan) D. BS, Cornell U., 1960; MA, Mich. State U., 1968, PhD, 1972. Pub. info. asst. Am. Home Econ. Assn., Washington, 1960-62; pub. info. specialist Ctr. Consumer Affairs, U. Wis., Milw., 1962-65; instr., rsch. and teaching asst. dept. communications Mich. State U., E. Lansing, 1965-70; asst. prof., Sch. Info. Transfer Syracuse (N.Y.) U., 1970-72; asst. to assoc. prof. U. Wash., Seattle, 1972-85; prof. dept. communication Ohio State U., Columbus, 1985—. Co-author: The Mass Media Behavior of the Urban Poor, 1980; editor: Rethinking Communication, 1989; editor jour. Progress in Communication Sci., 1981-92; contbr. numerous articles to profl. publs. Grantee U.S. Office Edn., 1974-76, Calif. State Libr., 1974-84, Nat. Cancer Inst., 1984, Ameritech, 1992. Fellow Internat. Communication Assn. (pres. 1986-87); mem. Internat. Assn. Mass Communications Rsch. (governing coun. 1988-97). Home: 4269 Kenridge Dr Columbus OH 43220-4157 Office: Ohio State U Dept Comm 3016 Derby 154 N Oval Mall Columbus OH 43210-1330

DERVIS, KEMAL, bank executive; b. Istanbul, Turkey, Jan. 10, 1949. B in Econs., London Sch. Econs. and Polit. Sci., 1969, M in Econs., 1970; D in Econs., Princeton U., 1973. Mem. faculty dept. econs. Mid. East Tech. U., Ankara, Turkey; prof. econs. and internat. affairs Princeton U., 1976-78; mem. rsch. dept. The World Bank, 1978-82, divsn. chief for indsl. strategy and policy, 1982-86, chief economist for Europe, Mid. East and North Africa,, 1986-87, spl. ops. reorganization task force, 1987, dir. North Africa dept., dir. Ctrl. Europe dept., 1991-96, regional v.p. for Mid. East and North Africa,, 1996—; vis. prof. internat. econs. Bilkent U., Ankara, 1994; in charge World Bank's Bosnia Reconstruction Program, launched by Pres. James D. Wolfensohn, 1995. Author: (in Turkish) Foreign Trade in Planning Models, 1977, (with S. Robinson and J. de Melo) General Equilibrium Models for Development Policy, 1982; assoc. editor (jour.) Özgür Insan, 1974-76; contbr. articles to profl. jours. Office: The World Bank Main Complex 1818 H St NW Washington DC 20433-0002

DERWIN, JORDAN, lawyer, consultant, actor; b. N.Y.C., Sept. 15, 1931; s. Harry and Sadie (Baruch) D.; m. Barbara Joan Concool, July 4, 1956 (div. 1969); children: Susan Lee, Ellen; m. Joan Linda Wolfberg, May 6, 1973. BS, NYU, 1953, JD, 1959. Bar: N.Y. 1959, U.S. Dist. Ct. (so. and ea. dists.) N.Y. 1960, U.S. Ct. Appeals (2d. cir.) 1960, U.S. Supreme Ct. 1962. Arthur Garfield Hays rsch. fellow NYU, 1958-59, rsch. assoc. Duke U. Sch. of Law, Durham, N.C., 1959-60; assoc. Brennan, London, Buttenwieser, N.Y.C., 1960-64; sole practice Jordan Derwin, N.Y.C., 1964-70; gen. counsel N.Y.C. Off Track Betting Corp., 1970-74; assoc. gen. counsel Gen. Instrument Corp., N.Y.C., 1974-79; cons., 1980—; instr. basic life support, CPR and advanced 1st aid: ARC, 1988—, Am. Heart Assn., 1989—, Nat. Safety Coun., 1991—; instr. trainer basic cardiac lifesupport Am. Heart Assn., 1990—, mem. affiliate faculty, 1997—; emergency med. technician N.Y. State, 1990—; v.p., gen. counsel Cen. Park Med. Unit, Inc., N.Y.C., 1991—; del. N.Y.C. Ctrl. Labor Coun., 1996—. Author (with F. Hodge O'Neal), Expulsion or Oppression of Business Associates: Squeeze Outs in Small Business, 1960; actor in various films including Stardust Memories, 1980, Rollover, 1981, I'm Dancing as Fast as I Can, 1982, Hard Feelings, 1984, Cotton Club, 1984, One Down Two to Go, 1986, Cadillac Man, 1990, McBain 1991, Ambulance, 1992, Extreme Measures, 1996, Private Parts, 1997, TV programs including Nurse, Today's FBI, Another World, As The World Turns, Guiding Light, All My Children, One Life To Live, Loving, Saturday Night Live, Late Night and Late Show With David Letterman, Conan O'Brien Show, TV commls. 1980—; contbr. articles to prof. jours. Lt. j.g., USNR, 1953-56, Korea, Vietnam. Mem. SAG (dir. nat. bd. 1982—, nat. exec. com., 1983—, sec. N.Y. br. 1983-87, 12th nat. v.p. 1984-87, 4th nat. v.p. 1987-89, 1st v.p. N.Y. br. 1987-89, 2d v.p. N.Y. br. 1989-91, 95—, 3d v.p. N.Y. br. 1993-95), AFTRA (dir. N.Y. local bd. 1980-83, 87-90, dir. nat. bd. 1981-92, Ken Harvey award for outstanding svc. to the mem. 1998), Am. Soc. Mag. Photographers, Nat. Press Photographers Assn., Motion Picture Players Welfare Fund (trustee 1987—), Actors Equity Assn., Associated Actors and Artistes Am. AFL-CIO (del. internat. bd. 1984-94, 97—, ctrl. labor coun. N.Y.C. 1996—), Phi Delta Phi. Home and Office: 305 E 86th St New York NY 10028-4702

DERZON, GORDON M., hospital administrator; b. Milw., Dec. 28, 1934; married. B.A., Dartmouth Coll., 1957; M.H.A., U. Mich., 1961. Adminstrv. resident Bklyn. Hosp., 1960-61, adminstrv. asst., 1961-63, asst. exec. dir., 1963-65, exec. dir., 1966-67; exec. dir. State U. Hosp., Bklyn., 1967-68, Kings County Hosp. Center, Bklyn., 1968-74; CEO U. Wis. Hosps. and Clinics, Madison, 1974—; assoc. prof. SUNY, 1967-74; clin. prof. U. Wis.; mem. bd. Univ. Hosp. Consortium. Contbr. articles to profl. jours. Bd. dirs. Independent Living, Hospice Care, MATC Found. Mem. Am. Hosp. Assn. (past chmn. pub. gen. hosp. sect.). Home: 3440 Topping Rd Madison WI 53705-1439 Office: U Wis Hosp & Clinics 600 Highland Ave Madison WI 53792-0001

DE SÁ E SILVA, ELIZABETH ANNE, secondary school educator; b. Edmonds, Wash., Mar. 17, 1931; d. Sven Yngve and Anna Laura Elizabeth (Dahlin) Erlandson; m. Claudio de Sá e Silva, Sept. 12, 1955 (div. July 1977); children: Lydia, Marco, Nelson. BA, U. Oreg., 1953; postgrad., Columbia U., 1954-56, Calif. State U., Fresno, 1990, U. No. Iowa, 1993; MEd, Mont. State U., 1978. Cert. tchr., Oreg., Mont. Med. sec., 1947-49; sec. Merced (Calif.) Sch. Dist., 1950-51; sec., asst. Simon and Schuster, Inc., N.Y.C., 1954-56; tchr. Casa Roosevelt-União Cultural, São Paulo, Brazil, 1957-59, Coquille (Oreg.) Sch. Dist., 1978-96; music tchr. Cartwheels Presch., North Bend, Oreg., 1997—; tchr. piano, 1967-78; instr. Spanish, Southwestern Oreg. C.C., Coos Bay, 1991-94; pianist/organist Faith Luth. Ch., North Bend, Oreg., 1995—, vocal soloist, 1996—, voice tchr., 1997—. Chmn. publicity Music in Our Schs. Month, Oreg. Dist. VII, 1980-85; sec. Newcomer's Club, Bozeman, Mont., 1971. Quincentennial fellow U. Minn. and Found. José Ortega y Gasset, Madrid, 1991. Mem. AAUW (sec., scholarship chmn., co-pres., pres., treas., editor newsletter), Nat. Trust Hist. Preservation, Am. Coun. on Tchg. Fgn. Langs., Am. Assn. Tchrs. Spanish and Portuguese, Nat. Coun. Tchrs. English, Music Educators Nat. Conf., Oreg. Music Educators Assn., Oreg. Coun. Tchrs. English, Confedn. Oreg. Fgn. Lang. Tchrs., VoiceCare Network. Republican. Avocations: swimming, walking, travel, drama. Home: 3486 Spruce St North Bend OR 97459-1130

DESAI, ANITA, writer; b. Mussoorie, India, June 24, 1937; came to U.S., 1987; d. D.N. and Toni (Nime) Mazumdar; m. Ashvin Desai, Dec. 13, 1958; children: Rahul, Tani, Arjun, Kiran. BA, Delhi U., 1957. Tchr. Smith Coll., Mount Holyoke Coll.; prof. of writing MIT, Cambridge, 1993—. Author: Cry, the Peacock, 1963, Voices in the City, 1965, Bye-Bye Blackbird, 1968, The Peacock Garden, 1974, Where Shall We Go This Summer?, 1975, Cat on a Houseboat, 1976, Fire on the Mountain, 1977, Games at Twilight and Other Stories, 1978, Clear Light of Day, 1980, The Village by the Sea, 1982, In Custody, 1985, Baumgartner's Bombay, 1989, Journey to Ithaca, 1995, Fasting, Feasting, 1999. Recipient Winifred Holtby prize Royal Soc. Lit., 1978, Sahitya Acad. award, 1979, Guardian award for children's book, 1982, Lit. Lion award N.Y. Pub. Libr., 1993, Neil Gunn fellowship Scottish Arts Coun., 1994; Girton Coll. and Clare Hall fellow Cambridge U., Eng. Fellow Am. Acad. Arts and Letters (hon.), Royal Soc. Lit. Eng. Office: MIT 14E-303 Prog Writing/ Humanist Studies Cambridge MA 02139

DESAI, HIREN D., software engineer; b. Amravati, India, Oct. 24, 1959; came to U.S., 1982; s. Deovrat R. and Nilly D. Desai; m. Ketki H. Desai, Dec. 9, 1990; children: Rahul, Meera. BTech in Electronics Engring., Varanasi (India) Inst. Tech., 1982; MS in Computer Sci., U. Ctrl. Fla., 1985; MBA, Emory U., 1995. Systems mgr. Ultra Pink, N.Y.C., 1985-86; systems cons. Granada Systems Design, N.Y.C., 1987-90; sr. software engr. Estek Products-Kodak, Charlotte, N.C., 1990-92; project mgr., sr. mem. tech. staff Bellsouth Telecom., Atlanta, 1992-98; prin. cons. Oracle Cons. Svcs., Atlanta, 1998—. Recipient Mktg. Faculty Honor award and Decision & Info. Analysis award Emory U., Atlanta, 1996. Mem. IEEE, IEEE Computer Soc., Telephone Pioneers Am., Beta Gamma Sigma. Avocation: chess. Home and Office: 11650 Dunhill Place Dr Alpharetta GA 30005-6716

DESAI, KAVIN HIRENDRA, pediatrician; b. Bombay, Oct. 8, 1963. MD, Wayne State U., 1988. Resident in pediatrics Stanford U., Palo Alto, Calif., 1989-91, fellow in pediatric cardiology, 1991-94; staff pediat. cardiologist Stanford U., Palo Alto, 1994—. Recipient Clinician-Scientist award Am. Heart Assn., 1995-98. Office: Stanford U Pediat Cardio Divsn 750 Welch Rd Ste 305 Palo Alto CA 94304-1510*

DESAI, VEENA BALVANTRAI, obstetrician and gynecologist, educator; b. Karvan, Gujarat, India, Oct. 5, 1931; came to U.S., 1973; d. Balvantrai P. and Maniben (Vashi) Desai; m. Vinay D. Gandevia, Sept. 19, 1964. MBBS, Seth G.S. Med. Coll., Bombay, 1957, MD, 1961. Jr. resident Bombay U., 1957-59; house officer gyn. Chalmer's Hosp., Edinburgh, Scotland, 1962-63; registrar ob-gyn. Neath (U.K.) Gen. Hosp., 1963-64, Scunthorpe (U.K.) Gen. Hosp., 1964-66; chief resident ob-gyn. St. John (Can.) Gen. Hosp., 1973-74; attending ob-gyn. Portsmouth (N.H.) Hosp., 1975-84; assoc. prof. Boston U., 1985-86; sr. staff ob-gyn. Santa Clara (Calif.) Valley Med. Ctr., 1986-87; mem. sr. staff ob-gyn. West Anaheim (Calif.) Med. Ctr., 1988-98, chief dept. ob-gyn., 1992-93; ob/gyn Bay State Med. Ctr., Springfield, Mass., 1998-99; assoc. clin. prof. ob-gyn. U. Calif., Irvine, 1990-98, vice chmn. med. staff, 1994, 95; pres. Desai Med. Corp., Anaheim, 1989—. Chmn.'s advisor Nat. Security Coun.; charter mem. Presdl. Task Force; mem. Rep. Party Inner Cir., 1984-94. Recipient Presdl. Medal of Merit, 1982, award Spl. Congl. Adv. Bd., 1984, Order of Liberty, U.S. Congress, 1995, Medal of Freedom, U.S. Senate, 1994, medal Ronald Wilson Reagan Eternal Flame of Freedom, 1996. Fellow ACS, Internat. Coll. Surgeons, Am. Coll. Ob-Gyn., Royal Coll. Ob-Gyn. (chmn. Am. rep. com. 1997—); mem. Buena Park Rotary (pres. 1994, chair internat. svc. 1992-93). Avocations: latchhook work, internat. politics, traveling. Home: 149 Christopher Terr West Springfield MA 01089

DE SAINT PHALLE, PIERRE CLAUDE, lawyer; b. N.Y.C., July 21, 1948; s. Thibaut and Rosamonde (Frame) de Saint P. BA, Trinity Coll., 1970; JD, Columbia U., 1973. Bar: N.Y. 1974, U.S. Ct. Appeals (2d cir.)

1975, U.S. Dist. Ct. (so. and ea. dist.) N.Y. 1975, D.C. 1982. Assoc. Davis Polk & Wardwell, N.Y.C., 1973-82, European Office, 1976-77, ptnr., N.Y.C., 1983—; asst. gen. counsel U.S. Synthetic Fuels Corp., Washington, 1980-81. Mem. ABA, N.Y.C. Bar Assn., Internat. Bar Assn. River Club, Quoque Field Club, Quoque Beach Club, Nat. Golf Links of Am. Roman Catholic. Office: Davis Polk & Wardwell 450 Lexington Ave New York NY 10017-3911

DE SAINT PHALLE, THIBAUT, investment banker, educator, lawyer, financial consultant; b. Tuxedo Park, N.Y., July 23, 1918; s. Fal and Marie (Duryee) de Saint P.; m. Rosamond Frame, Jan. 12, 1946 (dec. 1960); children: Fal, Pierre, Thérèse; m. Elene Canrobert Isles, June 21, 1965 (div. 1983); children: Marc, Diane; m. Mariana M. Smith, April 24, 1983. Student, Harvard U., 1935-37; AB, Columbia U., 1939, JD, 1941. Bar: N.Y. 1942, D.C. 1984, U.S. Supreme Ct. 1945. Assoc. Chadbourne, Wallace, Parke & Whiteside, N.Y.C., 1941-50; ptnr., head corp. law dept. Lewis & McDonald, N.Y.C., 1950-58; v.p., treas. Becton, Dickinson and Co., Rutherford, N.J., 1958-62; dir. Becton, Dickinson and Co., 1958-67; sr. ptnr. Coudert Bros., N.Y.C., 1962-66; of counsel Coudert Bros., 1966-77, Vorys, Sater, Seymour & Pease, Washington, 1983-86; exec. prof. Fla. Gulf Coast U., 1998—; ltd. ptnr. Dean Witter & Co., pres. Dean Witter Overseas Fin. Corp., N.Y.C., 1967-68; investment banker Stralem, Saint Phalle & Co., Inc., N.Y.C., 1968-70, vice chmn. bd. dirs., 1968-70; mem. faculty, prof. internat. fin. and law Centre d'Etudes Industrielles, Geneva, 1971-76; dir. Export-Import Bank U.S., Washington, 1977-81; Scholl chair internat. bus. Georgetown U. Center Strategic and Internat. Studies, 1981-83; chmn. Saint Phalle Internat. Group, 1985—; dir. Atlantic Coun. of the U.S. Author: The Dollar Crisis, 1963, Multinational Corporations, 1976, U.S. Productivity and Competitiveness in International Trade, 1980, Trade Inflation and the Dollar, 1981, rev. edit., 1984, The Federal Reserve, an Intentional Mystery, 1985; contbr. numerous articles on internat. fin. and trade to profl. jours. Lt. comdr. USNR, 1942-46. Decorated Navy Commendation medal, Bronze Star, Legion d'Honneur (France). Mem. ABA, Met. Club, Jockey Club. Roman Catholic. Fax: 941-435-0667. Home and Office: Saint Phalle Internat Group 280 4th Ave N Naples FL 34102-8400

DE SALVA, SALVATORE JOSEPH, retired pharmacologist, toxicologist; b. N.Y.C., Jan. 14, 1924; s. Nicola Carlo and Frances Agnes (Caldarella) De S.; m. Elaine Mae Radloff, June 14, 1948; children: Salaine Claire De Salva Bonanne, Christopher Joseph, Stephanie De Salva Farrelly, Steven William, Gregory Vincent, Peter Nicholas, Philip Anthony, Deidre De Salva Berry. BS, Marquette U., 1947, MS, 1949; postgrad., U. Ill., Chgo., 1951-53; PhD, Stritch Sch. Medicine, Loyola U., Chgo., 1958. Research and teaching asst. Marquette U., Milw., 1947-49; research biochemist Milw. County Gen. Hosp., 1954; instr. U. Ill., Chgo., 1951-52; asst. prof. Chgo. Coll. Optometry, 1951-53; pharmacologist Armour Pharm. Lab., Chgo. 1953-59; sect. head Colgate Palmolive Co., Piscataway, N.J., 1959-66, sr. research assoc., 1966-72, mgr., 1972-76, assoc. dir. research for pharmacology and toxicology, 1976-83, dir. research pharmacology and toxicology, 1983-88, worldwide ops. dir., 1988-90, corp. dir. human and environ. safety worldwide, 1990-92; pres. Salva Cons. Svcs., Somerset, N.J., 1992-99; ret., 1999; lectr. Loyola U., 1957-59; mem. technician tng. N.J. Council for Research and Devel., Rutgers U., 1969-72. Editor: Symposium for Biomedical Electronic Instrumentation, 1965; contbr. articles to profl. jours.; patentee in field; current work in pharmaco-toxicology of flourides, sequestering agts. and surfactants, nitrosamine risk assessment, alternative safety testing method devel., safety of triclosan and use in dental therapeutic products. Mem. Park Forest (Ill.) Mosquito Abatement Program, 1952-55, Franklin Twp. (N.J.) Sch. Bd., 1969-70, Somerset (N.J.) Bd. Health, 1965-67, Cath. Youth Orgn., Somerset; v.p. Cedar Hill Swim Club, Somerset; active Boy Scouts Am., Somerset, 1965-67; trustee Franklin Twp. Day Care Ctr., 1969. Served with USN, 1942-46. Mem. AAAS, Soc. Exptl. Biology and Medicine, Am. Soc. Pharmacology and Exptl. Therapeutics, Soc. Toxicology, Internat. Union Pharmacology (toxicology sect.), N.Y. Acad. Scis., Internat. Soc. Regulatory Pharmacology and Toxicology, Internat. Soc. Study of Xenobiotics, Sigma Xi. Roman Catholic. Home: 83 Demott Ln Somerset NJ 08873-1604

DESANCTIS, ROMAN WILLIAM, cardiologist; b. Cambridge Springs, Pa., Oct. 30, 1930; s. Vincent and Margherita (Marini) DeS.; m. Ruth Ann Foley, May 7, 1955; children: Ellen Ruth, Lydia Marie, Andrea Jean, Marcia Louise. B.S. summa cum laude, U. Ariz., 1951, D.Sc. (hon.), 1999; M.D. magna cum laude, Harvard U., 1955; D.Sc. (hon.), Wilkes Coll., 1984. Diplomate: Am. Bd. Internal Medicine, Sub Bd. Cardiovascular Diseases. Successively intern, asst. resident, sr. resident in medicine Mass. Gen. Hosp., Boston, 1955-56, 58-60; fellow in cardiology Mass. Gen. Hosp., 1960-62; dir. CCU, 1967-80, dir. clin. cardiology, 1980-98, emeritus, 1998—, physician, 1970—; mem. faculty Harvard U. Med. Sch., 1964—, Evelyn and James Jenks and Paul Dudley White prof. medicine, 1998—. Co-author: Cardiac Clinico-Pathological Conferences of the Mass. Gen. Hosp, 1972, The Practice of Cardiology, 1989; contbr. articles to med. jours. Served as officer M.C. USNR, 1956-58. Decorated Order of Dynasty of Alouite (Morocco); recipient Excellence in Clin. Teaching award Harvard U. Med. Sch., 1990, Centennial Achievement award U. Ariz., 1989. Fellow ACP (master of the coll. 1994), Am. Coll. Cardiology (Gifted Tchr. award 1991, Disting. Fellow award 1999); mem. Am. Heart Assn. (David Littmann award 1996, Paul Dudley White award 1999), Assn. Am. Physicians, Inst. of Medicine, Assn. Univ. Cardiologists, New Eng. Cardiovasc. Soc. (pres. 1979-80), Am. Clin. and Climatol. Soc., Knights of Malta, Winchester Country Club, Aesculapian Club. Roman Catholic. Home: 5 Thoreau Cir Winchester MA 01890-3340 Office: Mass Gen Hosp 15 Parkman St # 467 Boston MA 02114-3117

DE SANCTIS, VINCENT, college president; b. Paterson, N.J., July 13, 1941; s. Vincent and Helen (Ruocco) De S.; m. Francine Barone, Aug. 19, 1967; children: Gregory, Stephanie. BA in Social Studies, William Paterson Coll., 1963; MA in Social Studies, Montclair State U., 1966; EdD in Adminstrn. and Supervision, Rutgers U., 1970. Tchr., dept. chmn. Passaic County Tech. and Vocat. High Sch., Wayne, N.J., 1963-68; rsch. asst. Grad. Sch. Edn. Rutgers U., New Brunswick, N.J., 1968-69; asst. dir. Adult Edn. Resource Ctr. Montclair State Coll., Upper Montclair, N.J., 1969-70, dir. Adult Edn. Resource Ctr., 1970-72, dir. HEW region II adult continuing edn. staff devel. project, 1972-75; dean community edn. Pa. Coll. Tech., 1975-78; asst. prof. Sch. Edn. So. Ill. U., Edwardsville, 1978-82; campus exec. officer Pa. State U.-Shenango Valley, Sharon, 1982-87; pres. Warren County Community Coll., Washington, N.J., 1988—; title III reader U.S. Dept. Edn. Mem. editorial bd. Adult Literacy and Basic Edn., 1977-82, Pitman Learning Series CBTE, 1978-79, Setting the Pace, 1980-82; editorial cons. Career Edn. quarterly, 1979-80; contbr. articles to profl. jours. Chmn. Commn. Adult Basic Edn., 1974; evaluator 70 001, Inc., 1979; mem. Warren County Human Rels. Commn. Mem. Am. Assn. C.C.s, Country C.C. Pres.'s Assn. N.J., Coun. County Colls. N.J. (chair fin. com. 1988—), Adult Edn. Assn. (cert. leadership), Hackettstown C. of C. (bd. dirs.), Rotary (chair youth exch. program Belvidere chpt.). Avocations: running, birding, reading. Home: 830 Lopatcong St Belvidere NJ 07823-2012 Office: Warren County Community Coll 475 State Route 57 W Washington NJ 07882-4343*

DESANDO, JOHN ANTHONY, humanities educator; b. Rochester, N.Y., Sept. 23, 1940; s. Carl James and Marie Louise (Notebaert) DeS.; children: Erik, Courtney, Rachel, Jessica, Thea, Gabrielle. BA, Georgetown U., 1962; MA, PhD, U. Ariz., 1972. Lic. auctioneer, Ohio. Asst. prof. English Norwich U., Northfield, Vt., 1967-74; dir. student activities U. Mass., Boston, 1975-77; dean of students U. Maine, Fort Kent, 1978-79; v.p. acad. affairs Franklin U., Columbus, Ohio, 1980-88; prof. humanities Franklin U., Columbus, 1988—; critic tv program World Film Classics TV series, Columbus, 1990—; acting pres. Franklin U., Columbus, 1985-86; reviewer Ohio Humanities Coun. Film Grants, 1994—; bd. dirs. Educable TV, Spillman Co., Film Coun. Greater Columbus Literacy Initiative; film host Columbus Mus. Art, Drexel Theatres. Assoc. editor Movies on Media Handbook, 1994—; cinema series host Columbus Mus. Art, 1994—; talk cinema critic Drexel Theatre, Columbus, 1996—; prodr. World Film Classics TV series, 1998. Chair humanities divsn. Columbus (Ohio) Internat. Film and Video Festival, 1994—; bd. dirs. Ohio State U. Mem. MLA, Nat. Coun. Tchrs. English, Nat. Auctioneers Assn., Ohio Auctioneers Assn., Ohio State U. Photography and Cinema Alumni Soc. (bd. dirs. 1997—), Nat. Euchre Players Assn. (bd. dirs.), Kiwanis Club Columbus (pres. 1994-95). Office: Franklin Univ 201 S Grant Ave Columbus OH 43215-5399

DE SANTI, SUSAN S., federal agency administrator; b. Glens Falls, N.Y., July 25, 1949. JD cum laude, Boston U., 1981. Ptnr. Hogan & Hartson, Washington; asst. dir. for policy and evaluation Bur. Competition Fed. Trade Commn., Washington, sr. atty. advisor to commr., sr. atty. advisor to chmn., dir. policy planning, 1995—; spkr. in field. contbr. articles to profl. jours. Mem. ABA. Office: Fed Trade Commn 6th and Pennsylvania Ave NW Washington DC 20580

DE SANTIS, MARK, osteopathic physician; b. Amityville, N.Y., Jan. 2, 1954; s. Vera De S.; m. Elizabeth Anne King, July 15, 1989; children: Mark Anthony, Matthew Robert. AS in Phys. Sci., Nassau C.C., 1975; BS in Nuclear Medicine, C.W. Post Coll., 1982; MS in Med. Biology, L.I. U., 1991; DO, Kirksville Coll. Osteo. Med., 1993. Registered nuclear medicine technologist. Asst. Brookhaven Nat. Lab., Upton, N.Y., 1978-87; staff nuclear medicine technologist Sloan-Kettering Meml. Med. Ctr., N.Y.C., 1977-78; asst. radiophysicist, nuc. cardiology tech. L.I. Jewish Med. Ctr., New Hyde Park, N.Y., 1978-88; med. intern Massapequa Gen. Hosp., Seaford, N.Y., 1993-94; osteopathic radiology resident St. Barnabas Hosp., Bronx, N.Y., 1994-95; nuclear medicine resident VA Med. Ctr., Northport, N.Y., 1995-97; diagnostic radiology resident Nassau County Med. Ctr., East Meadow, NY, 1997—; clin. instr. Sch. Allied Health Profls., Stony Brook U. Health Sci. Ctr., SUNY, 1986-87; medicine clerkship aerospace flight surgeon tng. course NASA, 1993. Contbr. articles to profl. publs. Founder Oil 4 Kids Project. With USN, 1982. Recipient Still Kickin' Editor award KCOM. Mem. Am. Osteo. Assn., Soc. Nuclear Medicine, Am. Roentgen Ray Soc., Am. Osteo. Coll. Radiology. Avocations: computer programming, flying, restoring antique autos, piano. Home: 55 Lincoln Blvd Bethpage NY 11714-5517 Office: Nassau County Medical Center Radiology Department East Meadow NY 11714

DE SANTIS, SYLVIA, library director; b. Palmer, Mass., Mar. 27, 1920; d. Ezio DeS. and Josephine Alonzo. BA in Chemistry, Mt. Holyoke Coll., 1942. Chem. rsch. libr. Jackson Lab., E.I. DuPont, Wilmington, Del., 1942-43; chem. rsch. libr. Naugatuck (Conn.) Chem., 1944-45, libr. dir., 1946-49; libr. dir. Monson (Mass.) Free Libr. & Reading Room Assoc., 1949-97; retired, 1997; cons. in field. Mem. Monson Arts Coun., Monson Hist. Soc. Mem. Western Mass. Libr. Club. Avocations: collecting art, books, photography, gardening. Home: 27 Margaret St Monson MA 01051-0358

DE SANTO, DONALD JAMES, psychologist, educational administrator; b. Bklyn., July 5, 1942; s. Vincent James and Rose Ann (Dowd) DeS.; m. Loretta DePippo, Aug. 25, 1962; children: Dolores, Jennifer, Marisa. BA cum laude, St. Francis Coll., N.Y., 1964; MA in Clin./Child Psychology, St. John's U., 1966; profl. diploma, 1976; hon. degree, Oglalalakota Coll., 1999. Asst. law libr. rsch. asst. Dewey, Ballantine, Bushby, Palmer & Wood, N.Y.C., 1960-64; rsch. asst. St. John's U., N.Y.C., 1964-65, tchg. fellow, 1965-66; project dir. 2 federally funded grants, 1975-76; dir. The Rugby Sch., Freehold, N.J., 1977—. Contbg. editor Channels jour. spl. educators, 1986-90, 96—. Mem. Nat. Trust Historic Preservation; mem. Youth Guidance; mem. Youth Guidance Com., Freehold, 1983—, chmn. econ. devel. com., 1984-86; mem. Econ. Devel. Com., Freehold, 1983-87; mem. Zoning Bd Adjustment, Freehold, 1985-86; commr. Lake Topanemus Commn., 1990-94; Rep. campaign chmn., Freehold, 1990, 91; bd. dirs. Monmouth County Transp. Assn., 1990, 91-92; mem. U.S. Selective Svc. Bd., 1991—; apptd. Selective Svc. Commn., 1992; v.p. Freehold Rep. Club, 1991-92; mem. adv. bd. Congl. Awards Com., 1994—; mcpl. chmn. Freehold Borough Rep. Party, 1995; appt. Rep. Nat. Com., 1995; participant, amb. People to People, Beijing, 1995; trustee Monmouth County Mental Health Assn. Recipient Fire Prevention medal, N.Y.C., 1954, citation for outstanding contbn. to arts in edn. N.J. Commr. Edn., 1981, Pres. award Assn. Schs. and Agys. for the Handicapped, 1995-96, N.J. Very Spl. Arts award, 1996, N.J. Gov's. Arts in Edn. award, 1996; Title VIb Fed. grantee, 1972-78. Mem. NRA (life), APA (pub. rels. com. div. 16), Nat. Assn. Pvt. Schs. Exceptional Children, Coun. Exceptional Children, N.J. Assn. Schs. and Agys. for handicapped (sec., conf. chmn. 1983-84, pub. rels. chmn. 1984-86, Pres. award 1995-96), nat. Soc. Psychologists in Mgmt., Assn. for Help Retarded Children, Monmouth County Hist. Assn., Internat. Platform Assn., N.J. Assn. Children With Learning Disabilities, Nat. Assn. Pvt. Schs. Exceptional Children (Coll. bd. 1992—), Optimists, Monmouth County Mental Health Assn. (bd. dirs.), Elks, Psi Chi, Phi Delta Kappa. Roman Catholic. Home: 222 Park Ave Freehold NJ 07728-2006 Office: care Rugby Sch at Woodfield PO Box 1403 Belmar NJ 07719-1403

DESANTO, WILLIAM ALLAN, marketing professional; b. Southampton, N.Y., June 14, 1972; s. William Allan and Carol Anne (Chiofaro) DeS. BSBA, Northeastern U., 1995. Mut. fund acct. State St. Bank & Trust Co., Boston, 1994-96; tech. analyst Salomon Smith Barney, Boston, 1996-98; v.p. mktg. ea. region Murray Johnstone Internat., Glasgow, Scotland, 1998—. Republican. Avocations: golf, squash, skiing, reading.

DE SAUSSURE, RICHARD LAURENS, JR., retired neurosurgery educator; b. Dec. 29, 1917; s. Richard Laurens and Margaret Hamilton De Saussure; m. Phyllis H. Falk; children: Alexis Laurens, Richard Laurens III, Denise Anita. AB, U. Va., 1939, MD, 1942. Diplomate Am. Bd. Neurol. Surgery (sec. 1970-73). Dean U. Tenn., Memphis, 1980-88; intern U. Va. Hosp., 1942-43, resident neurosurgery, 1946-47, 48-49; resident Cin. Gen. Hosp., Memphis, 1947-48; chief neurol. surgery VA Hosp., Memphis, 1949-50; instr. to prof. neurol. surgery U. Tenn., Memphis, 1950-88, dean, 1980-88, prof. emeritus, 1988—. Contbr. articles to med. jours. Maj. M.C., U.S. Army, 1943-46. Named Disting. Neurosurgeon, South Neurol. Surgery Soc., 1990; recipient Harvey Cushing medal Am. Assn. Neurol. Surgery, 1995. Republican. Episcopalian. Avocations: photography, golf, chess. E-mail: rldir DeSRichard@aol.com. Home: 4290 Heatherwood Ln Memphis TN 38117

DESBARATS, PETER HULLETT, journalist, academic administrator; b. Montreal, Que., Can., July 2, 1933; s. Hullett John and Margaret Ogston (Rettie) D. Student, Loyola Coll., Montreal, 1951. Feature writer The Gazette, Montreal, 1953-55; local reporter Reuters, London, 1955; feature writer The Winnipeg (Can.) Tribune, 1956, legis. reporter, 1957-60; polit. reporter, feature writer The Montreal Star, 1960-65; editor Parallel Mag., Montreal, 1965; host nightly news and pub. affairs show Sta. CBC-TV, Montreal, 1966-70; Ottawa editor Toronto Star, 1970-72; Ottawa bur. chief, host interview program Global TV, 1973-80; sr. cons. Royal Commn. on Newspapers, Ottawa, 1980-81; dean Sch. Journalism U. Western Ont., London, 1981-96, assoc. prof. journalism, 1981-86, prof., 1986-96, dir. Univ. Club, 1987, also mem. various coms.; mem. comms. adv. com. Can. Commn., UNESCO; cons. Task Force on Broadcasting Policy, 1985, Royal Commn. Electoral Reform, 1991, others; mem. selection com. Can. News Hall of Fame, 1986—; speaker on journalism and the role of the media, numerous sites throughout U.S., Can. and overseas; mem. Ont. Task Force Cardiovasc. Scis., 1991, Can. Observers' Mission to Romania, 1992; commr. Commn. of Inquiry Into Deployment of Can. Forces to Somalia, 1995-96. Author: (poetry) Halibut York, 1964, The State of Quebec, 1965, Gabrielle and Selena, 1966, René: A Canadian in Search of a Country, 1976, The Night the City Sang, 1977, The Hecklers, 1979, Canada Lost/Canada Found: The Search for a New Nation, 1981, Colin and the Computer, 1985, Guide to Canadian News Media, 1990, revised edit., 1996, Somalia Cover-up: A Commissioner's Journal, 1997, (play) The Great White Computer, 1966; editor: What They Used to Tell About Indian Legends from Labrador, 1969, Freedom of Expression and New Communication Technologies, 1998; former Can. corr. The Nat. Observer, Washington; freelance contbr. various mags.; co-host: PBS series The Editors Weekly, 1987-91; mem. edit. bd. Can. Jour. Comm., 1987—. Bd. dirs. Performing Arts Ctr. for Today, London, 1993-95, Orch. London, 1993—, London Mus. Archaeology, 1993—. Recipient Best News Broadcaster award Assn. Can. TV and Radio Artists, 1977, Best TV Interviewer award Assn. Can. TV and Radio Artists, 1980, 125th Anniversary Confedn. Can. medal, 1992. Mem. Can. Assn. Journalists, Can. Civil Liberties Assn. (bd. dirs. 1998—), Can. Journalism Found. (bd. dirs. 1997—).

DESCH, THEODORE EDWARD, retired health insurance company executive, lawyer; b. Chgo., Oct. 1, 1931; s. Louis G. and Dorothy (Prieb) D.; m. Donna K. Thorsell, Feb. 3, 1951; children: Theodore M. (dec. 1968), Steven R., Katherine S. Collins, Gregory S. AB, U. Ill., 1952, LLB, 1954. Bar: Ill. 1954; cert. employee benefits specialist, CLU, ChFC. Asst. gen. atty. C.,R.I.&P. R.R., 1956-59, gen. atty., 1959-65, gen. counsel, 1965-68, v.p. and gen. counsel, 1968-70, vice chmn. bd., 1970-73, chmn. bd., 1973-74, chief exec. officer, 1970-74, dir., 1970-75; ptnr. Kirkland & Ellis, Chgo., 1975-77; sr. v.p. law and pub. affairs Health Care Svc. Corp., a Mut. Legal Res. Co., Blue Cross and Blue Shield Ill., Chgo., 1977-86, sr. v.p. law and corp. affairs, 1986-97; sr. v.p. govt. contracts Chgo., 1997-98; ret., 1998; bd. dirs., chmn. Preferred Fin. Corp., Denver. Trustee North Cen. Coll., Naperville; bd. dirs., pres. Naperville Elderly Homes, Inc.; mem. adv. bd. dirs. Salvation Army, Chgo. 1st Lt., inf. U.S. Army, 1954-56. Mem. ABA, Ill. Bar Assn., Chgo. Bar Assn., Union League, Sky-Line Club, Cress Creek Country Club, Delta Sigma Phi (found. bd. trustees), Phi Alpha Delta. Home: 129 Springwood Dr Naperville IL 60540-7331

DESCOTEAUX, CAROL J., academic administrator; b. Nashua, N.H., Apr. 5, 1948; d. Henry Louis and Therese (Arel) D. BA, Notre Dame Coll., 1970; MEd, Boston Coll., 1975; MA, U. Notre Dame, 1984, PhD, 1985. Jr. high sch. instr., dir. religious studies St. Joseph's Sch., North Grosvenordale, Conn., 1970-73; jr. high sch. tchr., dir. religious edn. Notre Dame Sch., North Adams, Mass., 1973-77; jr. high sch. instr. Sacred Heart Sch., Groton, Conn., 1977-78; chairperson religious studies discipline U. Notre Dame, Grad. Theol. Union, Notre Dame, Ind., 1982-83, 84-85; pres. Notre Dame Coll., Manchester, N.H., 1985—; trustee King's Coll., Wilkes-Barre, Pa., 1987—; pres. Fedn. of Holy Cross Colls., 1985—; mem. adv. bd. Manchester Christian Life Ctr., 1978-80; treas. N.H. Coll. and Univ. Council, Manchester, 1985—; trustee N.H. Higher Edn. Assistance Found., 1986—. Mem. Manchester United Way campaign, 1985—; bd. incorporators, mem. ethics com., instl. research com. Cath. Med. Ctr., Manchester, 1986—. Named Disting. Woman Leader of Yr., So. N.H. region YWCA, 1985. Mem. Am. Acad. Religion, Coll. Theology Soc. Am., N.H. Women's Forum, Soc. Christian Ethics, AAUW, N.H. Women in Higher Edn. Democrat. Roman Catholic. Avocations: art, music, theater, fishing, bowling. Office: Notre Dame Coll Office of the President 2321 Elm St Manchester NH 03104-2213*

DESCY, DON EDMOND, library media technology educator, writer, editor; b. Hartford, Conn., Jan. 11, 1944; s. Henry Julian and Lillian D.V. (Svenson) D. BS in Biology Edn., Ctrl. Conn. State U., 1967, MS in Biology Edn., 1970; cert. in instrnl. media, U. Conn., 1981, PhD in Media and Tech., 1987. Tchg. asst. Ctrl. Conn. State U., New Britain, 1967-68; rsch. asst. Coll. Edn. U. Conn., Storrs, 1985-87; asst. adminstrv. dir. Conn. State Bar Examining Com., Hartford, 1987-89; adj. prof. Ea. Conn. State U., Willimantic, 1987-89, Ctrl. Conn. State U., New Britain, 1988-89; prof. Minn. State U., Mankato, 1989—; numerous presentations in field in 5 countries. Mem. editl. bd. Internat. Jour. Instrnl. Media, 1991—; columnist Techtrends, 1993—; contbr. over 80 articles to profl. jours., 4 chpts. to books. Scholar Conn. Ednl. Media Assn., 1984, rsch. scholar Japan, 1996. Mem. ALA, Internat. Soc. Tech. in Edn., Assn. Ednl. Comm. and Tech. (Twin Cities chpt.), Am. Assn. Sch. Librs., Minn. Ednl. Media Orgn., Minn. Soc. Tech. in Edn. Office: Minn State Univ Memorial Library PO Box 20 Mankato MN 56002-0020

DE SEAR, EDWARD MARSHALL, lawyer; b. Bradenton, Fla., Oct. 27, 1946; s. Robert Ashland and Shirley Ethelwyne (Griffin) De S.; m. Patricia Gail Healy, Aug. 8, 1970; children: Emily, Andrew. AB, Columbia Coll., 1968; JD, U. Va., 1973. Bar: N.Y. 1974. Ptnr. Brown & Wood, N.Y.C., 1973-82; v.p. Salomon Bros., Inc., N.Y.C., 1982-88; ptnr. Milbank, Tweed Hadley & McCoy, N.Y.C., 1988-93, Orrick, Herrington & Sutcliffe, N.Y.C., 1993—. Mem. Secondary Schs. Com., Columbia, N.Y.C., 1984—. Mem. ABA, Phi Gamma Delta. Republican. Episcopalian. Office: Orrick Herrington Sutcliffe 666 5th Ave New York NY 10103

DE SELDING, EDWARD BERTRAND, retired banker; b. Summit, N.J., June 15, 1926; s. Edward Fitzgerald and Alene (Rockwell) deS.; m. Joan Bulkley, Oct. 21, 1950; children—Peter, Ann, Edward Bertrand. B.A., Yale, 1950. With Spencer Trask & Co., Inc., N.Y.C., 1950-77, ptnr., 1962-68, sr. v.p., dir., 1968-77; sr. v.p., dir. Hornblower, Weeks, Noyes & Trask, Inc., N.Y.C., 1977-78; 1st v.p. Loeb Rhoades, Hornblower & Co., 1978-79; v.p. Bruns, Nordeman, Rea & Co., N.Y.C., 1979-81, Bache Halsey Stuart; Inc., 1981-82; v.p. Conn. Nat. Bank, 1982-91, ret. Served with USAAF, 1944-46. Mem. Nat. Assn. Securities Dealers Inc. (chmn. dist. 12 com. 1971, gov. 1972), Sawgrass Country Club, Tokeneke Club (pres. 1974-75). Republican. Episcopalian (vestryman 1961-63, 67-69, 77-79, warden 1984-87). Home: 9003 Lake Kathryn Dr Ponte Vedra Beach FL 32082-2919

DESER, STANLEY, physicist, educator; b. Rovno, Poland, Mar. 19, 1931. BS summa cum laude, Bklyn. Coll., 1949; MA, Harvard U., 1950, PhD, 1953; DPhil (hon.), Stockholm U., 1978. Mem. Inst. Advanced Study, Princeton, 1953-55, 93-94, Parker fellow, 1953-54; Jewett fellow Inst. for Advanced Study, Princeton, 1954-55; NSF postdoctoral fellow, mem. Inst. Theoretical Physics, Copenhagen, 1955-57; lectr. Harvard U., 1957-58; mem. faculty Brandeis U., Waltham, Mass., 1958—; prof. physics Brandeis U., 1965—, chmn. dept., 1969-71, 76-77, Ancell prof. physics, 1979—; E. Schrödinger prof. U. Vienna, 1996; vis. scientist European Ctr. Nuclear Rsch., Geneva, 1962-63, 76, 80-81, 94; mem. physics adv. com. NSF, 1982-86; Fulbright and Guggenheim fellow, vis. prof. Sorbonne, Paris, 1966-67, 71-72; Loeb lectr. Harvard U., 1975; S.R.C. sr. fellow Imperial Coll., 1976; vis. prof. College de France, Paris, 1976, 84; vis. fellow All Souls' Coll., Oxford (Eng.) U., 1977; investigator titular ad honorem CIDA (Venezuela); Fulbright prof. U. of the Republic Montevideo Uruguay, 1970. Mem. editl. bd. Annals of Physics, Jour. Geometry and Physics; mem. sci. bd. I.H.E.S., France, 1991-97, Inst. Theoretical Physics, Santa Barbara, 1989-93, chmn., 1992-93. Fellow NAS, Am. Phys. Soc., Inst. Physics (Dannie Heineman prize in math. physics 1994), Am. Acad. Arts and Scis. Spl. research on theoretical physics, field theory, gravitation. Office: Brandeis U Physics Dept MS 057 Waltham MA 02454

DE SERRES, FREDERICK JOSEPH, genetic toxicologist; b. Dobbs Ferry, N.Y., Sept. 24, 1929; s. Frederick J. and Helen Marie (Henshaw) de S.; m. Christine Marie Covone, Sept. 18, 1954; children: Mark, John, Paul, David, Jonathan, Lianne. BS in Biology, Tufts U., Medford, Mass., 1951; MS in Botany, Yale U., 1953, PhD, 1955; Doctorate (honoris causa), Cath. U. of Louvain, 1987. Research assoc. biology div. Oak Ridge Nat. Lab., 1955-57, sr. staff biologist, 1957-72; experimenters rep. NASA biosatellite program, 1964-68; coord. environ. mutagenesis program Oak Ridge Nat. Lab., 1969-72; lectr. U. Tenn., 1971-73; adj. prof. dept. pathology U. N.C., Chapel Hill, 1973-90; chief environ. mutagenesis br. Nat. Inst. Environ. Health Scis., Research Triangle Park, N.C., 1972-76, assoc. dir. genetics, 1976-86, guest rschr., 1994-98; rsch. dir. Ctr. for Life Scis. and Toxicology Rsch. Triangle Inst., Research Triangle Park, N.C., 1986-93, prin. sci., 1993-94; guest rschr. Nat. Toxicology program Nat. Inst. Environ. Health Scis., Research Triangle Park, N.C., 1994—; sr. cons. Tech. Planning & Mgmt. Corp., 1996-97, program mgr., 1998; U.S. coordinator biol. and genetic consequences project U.S.-USSR Environ. Protection Agreement, 1972-78; chmn. panel mutagenesis and carcinogenesis U.S.-Japan Coop. Med. Sci. Program, 1972-87; chmn. subcom. environ. mutagenesis, com. to coordinate toxicology and related programs Dept. Health and Human Services, 1972-85; mem. com. on assessment nitrate accumulation in environ., div. biology and agr. Nat. Acad. Scis./Nat. Research Council, 1970-72; mem. com. chemical toxicity and aging, commn. on life scis. Nat. Research Council, 1986-87; cons. in govt., chmn. workshops on environ. pollutants and mutagenesis, 1961-86; vis. prof. U. Zagazig, Egypt, Ain-Shams U., Cairo, 1982, Case Western Res. U., 1983. Editorial bd.: Radiation Botany, 1965-74, Mutation Research, 1969-72, Jour. Toxicology and Environ. Health, 1975-78, Carcinogenesis, 1979-85; editor: Jour. Environ. and Exptl. Botany, 1975-77, Mutation Research, 1973—; sect. editor: Jour. Environ. Pathology and Toxicology, 1979, Jour. Toxicology and Indsl. Health, 1984—; co-editor: Chemical Mutagens, Vol. 5, 1978, Vol. 6, 1980, Vol. 7, 1982, editor Vol. 8, 1983, vol. 9, 1985, vol. 10, 1986; cons. editor: Environmental Research, 1981—; contbg. editor: Environmental Mutagenesis, 1979-81; author 360 publs. including research papers, abstracts, book chpts., editorials research interests: environ. mutagenesis, microbial genetics, mutagenicity of carcinogens, radiation and chem. mutagenesis, space biology. Recipient Dir.'s award NIH, 1976; University Scholar Yale Univ., 1951-52, Wadsworth fellow, 1954-55; Nat. Cancer Inst. predoctoral fellow, 1952-54. Mem. AAAS, Genetic Soc. Am. (rep. to NRC 1970-73), Internat. Assn. Environ. Mutagen Socs. (v.p. 1985-89), Radiation Rsch. Soc., Am. Soc. Cancer Rsch.,

Environ. Mutagen Soc. (council 1969-72, v.p., 1972-73, pres. 1973-76, editor newsletter 1969-72, ann. award 1979, contbg. editor jour. 1979), Internat. Commn. Protection Against Environ. Mutagens and Carcinogensis (vice-chmn. 1976-84, commn. 1985-89), Environ. Mutagen Soc. (pres. 1991-93), European Environ. Mutagen Soc., Japanese Environ. Mutagen Soc., Alpha-1 Nat. Assn. (bd. dirs. 1998—), Alpha One Found. (med. and sci. adv. com. 1999—). E-mail: deserres@niehs.nih.gov. Home: 632 Rock Creek Rd Chapel Hill NC 27514-6716 Office: Lab Toxicology NIEHS MD Fl-06 Research Triangle Park NC 27709

DESEVE, G. EDWARD, federal official; m. Karren Purdy, Sept. 13, 1969; 1 child. BS in Labor Econs., Cornell U., 1967; M of Govt. Adminstrn. in Pub. Fin., U. Pa., 1971. With Vol. Svc. Am., 1968; dep. dir. model cities program City of Fresno, Calif., 1969; analyst community renewal program City of Phila., 1971, asst. to dir. fin., 1972, dep. dir. fin. for budget, 1974, dir. fin., 1980; pres. Pub. Fin. Mgmt., Inc., 1975, Am. Capital Group, 1985; mng. dir. Merrill Lynch Capital Markets, N.Y.C., 1983; spl. asst. to gov. State of Pa., 1990; dir. Drexel Partnership Interests Corp.; CFO HUD, Washington, 1993; contr. Office Mgmt. and Budget, Washington, 1995, dep. recruiter, 1997. Author: A Financial Management Handbook for Mayors and City Managers; contbr. to The Annals of the American Academy of Political and Social Sciences. Fellow Nat. Acad. Pub. Adminstrn. Office: 260 OEOB Washington DC 20503

DESFORGES, JANE FAY, medical educator, physician; b. Melrose, Mass., Dec. 18, 1921; d. Joseph Henry and Alice (Maher) Fay; m. Gerard Desforges, Sept. 11, 1948; children: Gerard Joseph, Jane Alice. BA cum laude (Durant scholar), Wellesley Coll., 1942; MD cum laude, Tufts U., 1945; ScD (hon.), Holy Cross Coll., 1990. Diplomate Am. Bd. Internal Medicine, Am. Bd. Hematology. Intern in pathology Mt. Auburn Hosp., Cambridge, Mass., 1945-46; intern in medicine Boston City Hosp., 1946-47, resident in medicine, then chief resident, 1948-50; USPHS research fellow in hematology Salt Lake Gen. Hosp., Salt Lake City, 1946-47; research fellow in hematology hosp. Thorndike Lab., 1950-52; physician-in-charge RH lab., 1952-53; mem. faculty Tufts U. Med. Sch., 1952—, prof. medicine, from 1972, disting. prof., from 1992, prof. emerita, 1994; asst. dir. Tufts Med. Svc., Boston City Hosp., 1952-67; assoc. dir. Tufts Med. Svc., 1967-68; acting dir., physician in charge, 1968-73; dir. Tufts Med. Svc., 1968-69; assoc. dir. Tufts hematology lab., 1954-67, asst. dir. hosp. labs., 1958-67, acting dir. labs., 1967-68; sr. physician in hematology, rsch. assoc. blood rsch. lab. New Eng. Med. Ctr. Hosp., Boston, 1973—; attending physician VA Hosp., Jamaica Plain; cons. in hematology to various area hosps., 1955-72. Assoc. editor New Eng. Jour. Medicine, 1960-93; mem. editl. bd. Blood, 1976-79; contbr. numerous articles to med. jours. Bd. dirs. Med. Found., Inc., 1976-82; trustee Boston Med. Libr., 1977-81; chmn. automation in med. lab. scis. rev. com. Nat. Inst. Gen. Med. Scis., 1974-76; chmn. consensus com. of infectious disease testing for blood transfusions NIH, 1995-96; mem. subcom. on hematology Am. Bd. Internal Medicine, 1976-82, bd. dirs., 1980-88, exec. com., 1984-88; chmn. blood diseases and resources adv. com. Nat. Heart, Lung and Blood Inst., 1978-81. Recipient Disting. Alumna award Wellesley Coll., 1981; NIH fellow, grantee, 1955-88. Fellow AAAS; mem. ACP (Master 1983, Disting. Tchr. award 1987, chmn. med. knowledge self assessment program IX 1989-92), Am. Fedn. Clin. Rsch., Am. Soc. Clin. Pathology, Am. Soc. Hematology (exec. com. 1975-78, adv. bd. 1980-82, v.p. 1982-83, pres. 1984-85), Internat. Soc. Hematology, Mass. Med. Soc. (mem. publs. com. 1995—), N.Y. Acad. Scis., Am. Assn. Physicians, Inst. Medicine, Phi Beta Kappa, Alpha Omega Alpha (Outstanding Tchr. award 1994). Home: 49 Lake Ave Melrose MA 02176-2701 Office: New England Med Ctr 750 Washington St Boston MA 02111-1526

DESHAZER, JAMES ARTHUR, agricultural engineer, educator, administrator; b. Washington, July 18, 1938; s. Grant Arthur and Velma DeShazer; m. Alice Marie Burton, Apr. 5, 1969; children: Jean Marie, David James. BS in Agriculture, U. Md., 1960, BSME, 1961; MS, Rutgers U., 1963; PhD, N.C. State U., 1967. Profl. engr., Idaho, Nebr. Assoc. prof. U. Nebr., Lincoln, 1967-75, prof., 1975-91, asst. dean, 1988-89; head agrl. engring. dept. U. Idaho, Moscow, 1991-95, head biol. and agrl. engring. dept., 1995—; chair animal care & use com. U. Nebr., 1989-90; program coord. North Cen. Sustainable Agrl., Washington, 1988-89; nat. chair Modeling Responses of Swine-CSRS, Washington, 1989-90, Systems Approach to Poultry Prodn.-CSRS, Washington, 1990-91. Editor procs. Optics in Agr., 1990, Optics in Agr. & Forestry, 1992, Optics in Agr., Forestry & Biol. Processing, 1994, Optics in Agr., Forestry & Biol. Processing II, 1996, Precision Agriculture and Biological Quality, 1998; contbr. chpt. to book. Recipient Livestock Svc. award Walnut Grove, Iowa, 1988. Fellow Am. Soc. Agrl. Engrs. (chair 1984-94, nat. medal 1979); mem. NSPE (chpt. chair 1986-87, 93-94, bd. dirs. 1994—, pres. Idaho chpt. 1998-99, Young Engr. award 1974), Am. Soc. for Engring. Edn. (chair 1993-94), Internat. Soc. Biometeorology, Lions (chpt dir. 1995-97). Home: 819 Nylarol St Moscow ID 83843-9313 Office: Biol & Agr Engring Dept Univ Idaho Moscow ID 83844-0904

DESHAZO, MARJORIE WHITE, occupational therapist; b. Syracuse, N.Y., Apr. 25, 1941; d. Rexford Everett and Joyce Winifred Ella (Brown) Young White; m. Del DeShazo, Dec. 22, 1966; stepchildren: Chad A., Karen A. Lynch. BS in Occupl. Therapy, U. Puget Sound, 1964. Lic. occupl. therapist, 1996. Occupl. therapist VA Med. Ctr., Roseburg, Oreg., 1965-70, Salisbury, N.C., 1970-78; occupl. therapist, co-chief VA Domiciliary, White City, Oreg., 1978-80; chief occupl. therapist VA Med. Ctr., Lexington, Ky., 1980-87; pvt. cons. occupl. therapy Camdenton, Mo., 1987—; coord. TV21 Art Collections, Springfield, Mo. Inventor in field; exhibited at Lexington Art League, 1986-87, Laurie Fine Arts Show, 1993, Ozark Art and Palette, 1996, Artery Gallery, 1996, Lloyd's Art Ctr. & Gallery, 1996, Lisa Frick Gallery, 1996-98; co-artist Osage Beach City Hall Mural. Active Greater Lake Area Arts Coun., Osage Beach, Mo., 1987—. Kappa Kappa Gamma scholar U. Puget Sound. Mem. Ozark Art and Palette Club (treas. 1998-99), Creative Artists Club (coord. art hanging 1998—). Democrat. Methodist. Avocations: sewing, art, gardening, gourmet cooking. Home: RR 82 Box 6225 5-58X Camdenton MO 65020

DE SHAZOR, ASHLEY DUNN, business consultant; b. Blackstone, Va., May 28, 1919; s. Francis Bertram and Carrie Lee (Joyner) DeS.; m. Margot Joy Best, Sept. 18, 1943 (dec. June 1966); children: Margot Joy DeShazor Brydon, Nancy De Shazor Bourke, Linda De Shazor Dunlosky; m. Shirley Dean Laffey, June 1, 1968; 1 son, Dean Laffey. BSBA, U. Richmond, Va., 1941. With Sears, Roebuck & Co., also pres. Sears, Roebuck de Colombia, 1941-63; with Montgomery Ward & Co., Chgo., 1963-80; procurement asst. to v.p. and gen. mdse. mgr. Montgomery Ward & Co., 1963-65, v.p., corp. credit mgr., 1966-80, also dir.; bd. dirs. Montgomery Ward Credit Corp., Signature Fin./Mktg. Inc., Montgomery Ward Auto Club, Jefferson Stores, Inc. Trustee, exec. com. Nat. Found. Consumer Credit; bd. govs. Credit Rsch. Ctr. and Privacy Rsch. Ctr., Purdue U.; trustee Farm Found.; bd. assocs. U. Richmond, 1972-80; mem. Fulbright grant selection com. for Colombia; mem. Ill. Electronic Funds Transfer Study Commn. Lt. comdr. USNR, ret., 1958. Mem. Nat. Retail Mchts. Assn. (bd. dirs., past chmn. credit mgmt. div.), Acad. Polit. Sci. (life mem.), The Retired Officers Assn. (life mem.), Rotary Club (Scottsdale, Ariz.), Camelback Golf Club (Scottsdale, Ariz.), Paradise Valley Country Club (Ariz.), Sigma Alpha Epsilon. Presbyterian. Home: 6712 E Maverick Rd Paradise Valley AZ 85253

DE SHIELDS, CARLA VEONECIA, county official; b. Huntsville, Ala., July 23, 1960; d. Harrison Francis and Theresa Anne (Powers) D. BS in Mktg., Ala. A&M U., 1989; MPA, Clark-Atlanta U., 1994, PhD candidate, present. Instr. Ala. A&M U., Normal, 1992; grants coord. Madison County, Huntsville, Ala., 1992. Mem. exec. com. Weed and Seed Com., Huntsville, 1996—; mem. Madison County Drug Commn., Huntsville, 1995—. Man to Man award Children's Trust Fund, 1996, 97, 98, Man to Man award Ala. Civil Justice, 1996, 97, 98; TAOD (Tobacco, Alcohol and Other Substances) Prevention Gov.'s grantee, Weed and Seed Dept., 1996, 97, 98. Mem. AAUW, AMA (Amer. Market Assn.), ASPA (Amer. Study of Public Admin.). Office: 3210 S HiLo Cir NE #B Huntsville AL 35811-1514

DESHIELDS BROOKS, DELORA, SR., medical technologist, medical writer; m. Eugene L. Brooks; children: DeLora D. Brooks II, Eugenia L. Brooks. Student, various colls., 1949-81. Medical technician, technologist Westchester County Dept. of Labs. and Rsch., Valhalla, N.Y., 1953, Grassland Hosp., County of Westchester Dept. Pub. Welfare, 1953-55, Scarsdale (N.Y.) Med. Group, 1958, Pvt. Med. Group of New Rochelle, N.Y., 1958, Greenwich (Conn.) Hosp., 1962, Ossining Med. Lab., 1960-61; rsch. asst. Columbia Presbyn., N.Y.C., 1962-63; med. technician, technologist Demir Lab., Mt. Vernon, N.Y., 1960-61; owner, dir. DeShields Med. Lab., New Rochelle, 1961-63; med. technician, technologist Harlem Valley State Hosp., Wingdale, N.Y., 1967; rsch. technologist Wassaic Devel. Ctr., 1982; with Hudson River Psychiat. Ctr. Contbr. articles to profl. jours. Chmn. ARC Blood Bank, New Rochelle, 1965, procurement disaster unit, 1965; mem. Civil Air Patrol; cons., leader Town of North East Dutchess County Girl Scout Troop; v.p. Millerton Day Care Ctr.; co-capt. Heart Fund; chmn. Am. Cancer Crusade; pres. Friends of the Millerton Free Libr., 1982, St. Patrick's Rosary Altar Soc., 1991; lectr. New Rochelle Girl Scout Coun., 1963; mem., lectr. New Rochelle Girl Scout Coun., 1963; mem., fund raiser North East Heart Assn., 1964. Scholarship Urban League of Westchester County, 1952. Mem. Am. Coll. of Med. Technology. Catholic. Home: PO Box 67 Millerton NY 12546-0067

DESHPANDÉ, ROHIT, marketing educator; b. Bombay, Dec. 7, 1951; came to U.S., 1973; s. Prabhakar and Vimala (Waglé) D.; m. Rebecca Schorin, Dec. 29, 1979; children: Jay Alexander, Neil Benjamin. BSc, U. Bombay, 1971, MMS, 1973; MBA, Northwestern U., Evanston, 1975; PhD, U. Pitts., 1979; MA (hon.), Dartmouth Coll., 1993. Asst. and assoc. prof. mktg. U. Tex., Austin, 1979-87; assoc. prof. mktg. Dartmouth Coll., Hanover, 1987-89, prof., 1989-93, E.B. Osborn prof. mktg., 1993-97; prof. Harvard Bus. Sch., Cambridge, Mass., 1997-98, Sebastian S. Kresge prof. mktg., 1998—; Thomas Henry Carroll Ford Found. vis. prof. bus. adminstrn. Harvard Bus. Sch., 1993; vis. scholar and prof. Stanford Bus. Sch., 1994, 96; exec. dir. Mktg. Sci. Inst., 1997-99. Contbr. articles to profl. jours. Recipient Jack Taylor Teaching Excellence award. Fellow (consortium) Am. Mktg. Assn.; mem. Assn. for Consumer Rsch., Am. Sociol. Assn., Omicron Delta Kappa, Beta Alpha Phi. Office: Harvard Bus Sch Cambridge MA 02163

DESI, LAURENCE, physician; b. N.Y.C., Jan. 16, 1950; m. George Ronald and Carol Diane (Eigenbrot) D.; m. Linda Ann Dziwulski, June 12, 1971; children: Ronald, Richard, Geoffrey, Jonathan, Laurence Jr. BS, Loyola Coll., 1971; MD, U. Md., 1975; MPH, Johns Hopkins U., 1976. Diplomate Am. Bd. Preventive Medicine. Plant physician Bethlehem Steel Corp., Sparrows Point, Md., 1981-83, plant med. dir., 1983-84; pvt. practice Balt., 1984-94; facility med. dir. PHP Healthcare, Newark, 1994—. Maj. USAF, 1978-81. Mem. Am. Coll. Occupl. and Environ. Medicine, Am. Coll. Preventive Medicine, Md. Coll. Occupl. and Environ. Medicine. Republican. Roman Catholic. Office: CRA c/o Drimler Chrysler 550 S College Ave Newark DE 19713

DESIATO, MICHAEL, periodical editor-in-chief; b. Rochester, N.Y., Dec. 9, 1955; s. Nicholas and Jenny Desiato; m. Lauren Desiato, Nov. 5, 1983; 1 child, Anthony. BSJ, Ohio U., 1977; postgrad., NYU. With Real Estate Forum, N.Y.C., 1978—, now editor-in-chief; also pub. dir. Real Estate N.Y. Mem. Nat. Assn. Real Estate Editors (bd. dirs.). Office: Real Estate Forum 111 8th Ave Ste 1600 New York NY 10011-5201*

DESIDERIO, DOMINIC MORSE, JR., chemistry and neurochemistry educator; b. McKees Rocks, Pa., Jan. 11, 1941; s. Dominic Morse and Jewell Aline (Hull) D.; m. Julie Marie Thomas, Oct. 9, 1965; children—Annette Marie, Dominic Michael. B.A., U. Pitts., 1961; S.M., MIT, 1964, Ph.D., 1965. Organic control chemist Pitts. Coke and Chem. Co., 1958-60; research chemist U. Pitts., 1960-61; teaching asst. MIT, Cambridge, 1961-62, research asst., 1962-65; research chemist Am. Cyanamid Co., Stamford, Conn., 1966-67; asst. prof. chemistry Baylor Coll. Medicine, Houston, 1967-71, assoc. prof. chemistry and biochemistry, 1971-78; prof. neurology (chemistry) and biochemistry, dir. U. Tenn., Memphis, 1978—; exch. student Internat. Assn. Exch. Students for Tech. Experience; polymer chemist Badische Anilin and Sodafabrik, Germany, summer 1962. Author and editor of books, chpts. in books and articles including Analysis of Neuropeptides by Liquid Chromatography and Mass Spectrometry, 1984, Mass Spectrometry of Peptides, 1990, Mass Spectrometry: Clinical and Biomedical Applications, vol. I, 1992, vol. II, 1994; co-editor (book series) Mass Spectrometry, 1997—; co-editor Mass. Spectrometry Revs., 1993—. Recipient 1st Ann. Internat. award Mass Spectrometry in Biochemistry and Medicine, Alghero, Italy, 1975; Intra-Sci. Research Found. fellow, 1971-75. Mem. Am. Soc. Biol. Chemistry, Am. Chem. Soc., Am. Soc. Mass Spectrometry, AAAS, Soc. for Neurosci., Memphis Neurosci. Soc. (pres. 1984-85), NIH (Metallobiochemistry study sect. 1985-89). Avocations: tennis, reading, ham radio, fishing, travel. Office: U Tenn Memphis Stout Neurosci Mass Spectrometry Lab 800 Madison Ave Memphis TN 38103-3400

DESILVA, ALAN W., physics educator, researcher; b. L.A., Feb. 8, 1932; s. Woodruff and Dorothy Belle (Cole) DeS.; m. Mochiko Yokoyama, July 27, 1959; children: Audrey Hope, Eric Woodruff, Eliot Gen. MS, UCLA, 1954; PhD, U. Calif., Berkeley, 1961. NSF postdoctoral rsch. fellow The Culham Lab., Abingdon, Berkshire, Eng., 1962-64; asst. prof. physics U. Md., College Park, 1964-68, assoc. prof., 1968-74, prof., 1974-97, prof. emeritus, 1997—; cons. Los Alamos Nat. Lab., 1963-81, U.S. Naval Rsch. Lab., Washington, 1973-90. Contbr. over 30 articles to sci. jours. With U.S. Army, 1954-56. Recipient sr. U.S. scientist award Alexander von Humboldt Found., Ruhr U., Bochum, Fed. Republic Germany, 1984-85. Fellow Am. Phys. Soc. Achievements include devel. of light scattering as a plasma diagnostic, light scattering observations of plasmas; rsch. on shock waves in plasmas and transport in strongly coupled plasmas. Office: U Md U Md Inst for Plasma Rsch College Park MD 20742

DESILVEY, DENNIS LEE, cardiologist, educator, university administrator; b. May 17, 1942; m. Kathleen Selkirk, Aug. 28, 1965; children: Ethan Selkirk, Caitlin O'Brian, Sarah Candace Shaw. BA in History and Religion magna cum laude, Yale U., 1964; MD, Columbia U., 1968. Lic. Vt., Va.; cert. Advanced Trauma Life Support instr. Intern medicine Cornell Med. Ctr., N.Y.C., 1968-69, resident medicine, 1969-71, resident medicine, cardiology, 1971; chief med. resident medicine North Shore U. Hosp., Manhasset, N.Y., 1972-73; instr. medicine North Shore U. Hosp., Manhasset, 1972-73; mem. staff Rancocas Valley Hosp., Willingboro, N.J., 1973-75; cardiologist Brachfeld Med. Assocs., Willingboro, N.J., 1974-75, Castleton (Vt.) Med. Assocs., 1975-77; attending physician Rutland Regional Med. Ctr., Rutland, Vt., 1975-92; pvt. practice Rutland, Vt., 1977-92; adj. asst. prof. clin. medicine Dartmouth Hitchcock Med. Ctr., Hanover, N.H., 1979-92; asst. prof. medicine U. Vt., Burlington, 1983-92; mem. staff Dwight David Eisenhower Med. Ctr., Ft. Gordon, Ga., 1991; dir. ambulatory cardiology, dir. cardiology consult svc., mem. clin. faculty cardiovascular divsn., dept. medicine Health Scis. Ctr. U. Va., Charlottesville, 1992—, assoc. prof. medicine Health Scis. Ctr., 1992—; cons. Southwestern Vt. Med. Ctr., Bennington, 1986—, Keller U.S. Army Hosp., West Point, N.Y., 1985—, internal medicine Veteran Affairs Med. Ctr., Salem, Va., 1993—; mem. critical care com. Rutland Regional Med. Ctr., pharmacy and therapeutics com., investigational review bd., ethics com.; mem. pharmacy and therapeutics com. Health Scis. Ctr. U. Va., nutrition com., health care evaluation com., ambulatory policy com.; bd. dirs., mem. profl. affairs com., mem. bylaws com. Blue Cross/Blue Shield Vt.; bd. dirs., founding mem. Vt. Cardiac Network; presenter New Eng. regional meeting Am. Coll. Physicians, Hanover, N.H., 1976, Advanced Concepts Shock and Trauma, Woodstock (Vt.) Inn, 1982; dir. ACLS Tng. Ctr.; chmn/. Resolution Com. Contbr. articles to profl. jours. Med. advisor skiing svcs. Killington Ski Area, 1975-92, Smokey House Found., 1975-80, Farm and Wilderness Camps, 1975-85; mem. steering com. Vt. Med. Practice Variation Assessment Program, 1988; mem. cardiology study sect. Vt. Program Quality Care, 1988-92, Vt. Gov.'s Coun. Phys. Fitness, 1985-88; vestry Trinity Episcopal Ch., 1986-89; bd. dirs. Vermont Diabetes Assn., 1975-79, Rutland Mental Health Svc., 1975-82, Rutland Area Vis. Nurses Assn., 1975-77, chmn. profl. affairs com., mem. utilization review com.; bd. dirs. Barstow Sch., 1986-90; town health officer Wallingford, Vt., 1975-80. Maj. U.S. Army, 1973-75; col. USAR, 1985—. Decorated Nat. Def. Svc. medal, Reserve Achievement medal, Army Commendation medal; recipient Physician Recognition award Am. Med. Assn., Exceptional Svc. award, Spiritual Aims award Kiwanis Club Am., 1983, U. Va. Pres.'s Report award, 1992. Fellow Am. Coll. Physicians, Am. Coll. Cardiology, N.Am. Soc. Pacing and Electrophysiology; mem. Am. Heart Assn. (ACLS instr., BCLS instr., nat. faculty ACLS Vt., mem. mil. tng. network ACLS, Advanced Trauma Life Support; bd. dirs. 1978-80, bd. dirs., at large appointee 1988-93, agenda planning com. 1986-89, affiliate relations com. 1986-88, sci. pub. com. 1989-93, "heart and stroke" planning com. 1989-90, participant edn. and inf. group heart guide consumer health and info. program, 1989-91, chmn. task force mission to elderly 1989-90; v.p.-elect New Eng. region 1986-87, regional v.p. 1987-88, fellow coun. clin. cardiology, bd. dirs. Charlottesville divsn. 1992—, bd. dirs. Va. affiliate 1992—, bd. dirs. Rutland, Vt. divsn. 1986-92, program coun. 1986-92, bd. dirs. Vt. affiliate 1975-92, exec. com. 1978-92, pres.-elect 1982-83, pres. 1983-85, co-chair capital campaign 1988-90, nominating com. 1984-86, cardiac rehab. com. 1982-85, program coun. 1978-90, ACLS com. 1978-90, cardiac critical care com. 1978-82, hypertension com. 1975-82, chmn. emergency cardiac care com. region V 1976-80, bd. dirs. N.J. affiliate 1973-75, BCLS com. 1973-75, mem. greater N.Y. affiliate 1966-72, BCLS instr. 1968-72, del. N.E. regional heart com. 1985-91, reaffiliation com. 1987-89, nominating com. 1987-88, Pysician of Yr. award 1992), Am. Soc. Echocardiology, N.Y. Acad. Scis., Vt. Cardiac Network (vice chmn. 1982-86), Phi Beta Kappa. Avocations: cycling, running, cross country skiing, hiking, mountain climbing, theology. Home: 1040 Winlergreenland Charlottesville VA 25903 Office: U Va Cardiovascular Dept Medicine PO Box 158 Charlottesville VA 22902-0158

DESIMONE, GLENN J., advertising executive; b. Passaic, N.J., Mar. 28, 1947; s. Joseph Anthony and Clara (Steinbach) DeS.; m. Virginia Mary Goett, Dec. 10, 1976; children: Glenn Jr., Grant, Christiann. BSME, Villanova (Pa.) U., 1969; MBA, Fairleigh Dickinson U., Rutherford, N.J., 1972. With E.I. DuPont de Nemours, Wilmington, Del., 1969-72; with Klemtner Advt., N.Y.C., 1972-75, MedCom, N.Y.C., 1975-82, Sutton Communications, N.Y.C., 1982-90; with DMB&B/Medicus Interon, 1991—, chmn. bd., chief exec. officer, 1996—. Bd. dirs. Friends of Nat. Libr. Medicine & Rsch. Am. Mem. Pharm. Advt. Club, Midwest Pharm. Advt. Council, Med. Advt. Agy. Assn. Club: Woodway Country (Darien, Conn.). Home: 24 Calhoun Dr Greenwich CT 06831-4437 Office: Medicus Group Internat Inc 1675 Broadway Fl 2 New York NY 10019-5865

DESIMONE, LIVIO DIEGO, diversified manufacturing company executive; b. Montreal, Que., Can., July 16, 1936; s. Joseph D. and Maria E. (Bergamin) De S.; m. Lise Marguerite Wong, 1957, children: Daniel J., Livia D., Mark A., Cynthia A. B.Chem. Engring., McGill U., Montreal, 957. Process engr. 3M Can., 1957-61; With 3M Co., St. Paul, 1961—; exec. v.p. life scis. sector 3M Can., St. Paul, 1981, exec. v.p. indsl. and consumer sector, 1984-86, exec. v.p. indsl. and consumer sector and pvt. svcs., 1986-89, exec. v.p. indsl. and electronic sector and corp. svcs., 1989-91, exec. v.p. info., imaging and electronic sector & pvt. svcs., 1991, exec. v.p., 1991; chmn. bd., CEO 3M Co., 1991—; bd. dirs. Cray Rsch. Inc., Dayton Hudson Corp., Gen. Mills Inc., Vulcan Materials Co. Bd. dirs. Jr. Achievement Inc. (nat.), Minn. Bus. Partnership, 3M Found.; trustee U. Minn. Found. Mem. Bus. Roundtable. Office: Minn Mining & Mfg Co 3 M Ctr Bldg 220 14W-05 Saint Paul MN 55144-0001*

DE SIMONE, LOUIS A., bishop; b. Phila., Feb. 21, 1922. Student, Villanova U., St. Charles Borromeo Sem., Pa. Ordained priest Roman Catholic Ch., 1952; ordained titular bishop of Cillium and aux. bishop of Phila., 1981-98, retired, 1998. Office: Chancery Office 222 N 17th St Philadelphia PA 19103-1202*

DESJARDINS, CLAUDE, physiologist, dean, administrator; b. Fall River, Mass., June 13, 1938; s. Armand Louis and Marguerite Jean (Mercier) D.; m. Jane Elizabeth Campbell, June 30, 1962; children: Douglas, Mark, Anne. BS, U. R.I., 1960; MS, Mich. State U., 1964, PhD, 1967. Fellow The Jackson Lab., Bar Harbor, Maine, 1967; asst. prof. dept. physiology Okla. State U., Stillwater, 1968-69, assoc. prof., 1969-72; assoc. prof. physiology U. Tex., Austin, 1970-75, prof. Inst. Reproductive Biology, Patterson Labs., 1975-86; NIH sr. fellow U. Va. Med. Sch., Charlottesville, 1983-84, prof. physiology, 1987-96, dir. Ctr. for Rsch. in Reproduction, 1990-96; prof. physiology & biophysics, sr. assoc. dean coll. of medicine, dir. office of rsch. U. Ill., Chgo., 1996—; mem. Ctr. for Advanced Studies, 1986; cons. NIH, ASA, VA, FDA, U.S. Dept. Agr. Danforth Found. fellow, 1960; C.F. Wilcox Found. scholar, 1958. Mem. Am. Physiol. Soc., Soc. Neurosci., Soc. Study Reprodn. (pres. 1982-83), Endocrine Soc., Am. Soc. for Cell Biology, The Microcirculatory Soc. Author: Cell and Molecular Biology of the Testis, 1993, Molecular Physiology of Testicular Cells, 1996; editor Am. Jour. Physiology: Endocrinology and Metabolism, 1991-95; editor in chief Jour. Andrology, 1989-91, Encyclopedia of Reproduction, 1997-98; mem. editl. bd. Biology of Reproduction, Endocrinology; contbr. articles to profl. jours.; patentee techs. for male contraception, mechanisms of peptide hormone transport in the microcirculation and ligand-dependent and ligand ind. actions of steroid hormones in peripheral vasculature. Office: U Ill at Chgo Office of Dean M/C 784 1853 W Polk St Chicago IL 60612-4316

DESJARDINS, ERIC, professional hockey player; b. Rouyn, Que., Can., June 14, 1969. Hockey player Montreal Canadiens, 1987-94, Phila. Flyers, 1995—. Named to play in NHL All-Star Game, 1996, QMJHL All-Star 2d team, 1986-87, 1st team, 1987-88; recipient Emile Bouchard Trophy, 1987-88. *

DESKINS, WILBUR EUGENE, mathematician, educator; b. Morgantown, W.Va., Feb. 20, 1927; s. Wilbur Lawrence and Avis (Creasy) D.; m. Barbara Brown, Apr. 18, 1953 (dec.); children—Lucinda Eugenie, Samantha Eugenie. B.S., U. Ky., 1949; M.S., U. Wis., 1950, Ph.D., 1953. Teaching asst. U. Wis., 1949-51, fellow, 1951-52, teaching asst., 1952-53, instr., 1953; instr. Ohio State U., 1953-55, asst. prof., 1955-56; asst. prof. Mich. State U., East Lansing, 1956-59, assoc. prof., 1959-63, prof. math., 1963-71; prof. math. U. Pitts., 1971-96, chmn. dept. math, 1971-87, assoc. dean Coll. Arts and Scis., 1988-96, prof. emeritus, 1996—. Author: Abstract Algebra, 1964. Mem. steering com. Pitts. Math. Collaborative, 1985-91; mem. exec. bd. Pitt. Sci. Inst., 1989-93. Mem. Math. Assn. Am. Research and articles on algebra and group theory. Office: Univ Pitts Pittsburgh PA 15260

DESLEY, JOHN WHITNEY, medical illustrator; b. Old Mystic, Conn., May 17, 1925; s. Clifford James and Hester (Walbridge) D.; m. Janice Reed, Dec. 22, 1951 (dec. Sept. 23, 1993); children: Christopher, Rebecca, Timothy, Rachel, Leah, Louisa; m. Margaret Wakeman, Aug. 31, 1996. BFA, Vesper George, Boston, 1950; M in Med. Illustration, Mass. Gen. Hosp., 1952; student, U. Conn., 1950. Asst. med. artist Mass. Gen. Hosp., Boston, 1951-52; chief med. artist VA Hosp., Birmingham, Ala., 1952-58; med. illustrator U. Minn., Mpls., 1958-63, Mayo Clinic, Rochester, Minn., 1963-90; freelance med. illustrator Rochester, 1990—. Illustrator for med. books, 1985—, (textbook) Cardiac Surgery, 1985; designer bicentennial medallion City of Rochester, 1976, bicentennial print design, 1977; author, illustrator: Persectives on Mayo (by John W. Desley), 1997. chmn. sch. bd. Bamber Valley Sch., Rochester, Minn., 1973-75. With USN, 1943-46. Home: 609 Sumac Rd Lewisville NC 27023-9555

DESLOGE, CHRISTOPHER DAVIS, SR., real estate and merchant banking executive; b. St. Louis, July 23, 1958; s. William Livingston and Loriel Martens (Johnson) D.; m. Mary Roberta Dubuque, May 22, 1981; children: William Livingston II, Christopher Davis Jr., Raymond Amadee Dubuque. *Mr. Desloge is descendant of Great Great Grandfather, Firmin Desloge who emigrated to America from Nantes, France, 1882. He formed Desloge Lead Company which became America's largest 5% ore mines. Firmin Desloge joined his uncle Firdinand Rozier, who emigrated to America in 1790 with friend John James Audubon. Mr. Desloge is related on his mother's side to American artist Norman Rockwell and General William Tecumseh Sherman. Mr. Desloge's children are related through their mother Mary Dubuque Desloge to U.S. President Ulysses S. Grant. Mr. Desloge is also descendant of the Livingstons, one of whom, Robert R. Livingston, was a signer of the Declaration of Independence.* Student, Drake U., 1977-79, Maryville Coll., 1979-80. V.p. Follman Properties, St. Louis, 1982-85; leasing mgr. Paragon Group, St. Louis, 1985-86; pres. Desloge Co., St. Louis, 1986-90; v.p. Hilliker Corp., St. Louis, 1990-92; pres. Braeburn Ptnrs., St. Louis, 1992-96; account mgr. Maritz, Stamford, Conn., 1996-98; mng. dir. Baytree Investors, Inc., 1998—; arbitrator BBB, St. Louis, 1991—. Author: Office Leasing: From the Tenants Point of View, 1995; contbg. editor St. Louis Bus. Jour., 1986-94. Mem. Real Estate Bd. Met. St. Louis, 1982-93; bd. dirs. St. Louis Psychoanalytic Inst., 1988-91, Internat. Tenant

Representation Alliance, St. Louis, 1992-94, Ctr. Head Injury Svcs., 1994-96; co-chmn. disaster svcs. ARC-Bi State Chpt., St. Louis, 1992-94; pres. bd. dirs. Desloge Found., St. Louis, 1993—. Recipient Recognition award for effort St. Louis Psychoanalytic Inst., 1992, Honor award for outstanding vol. ARC-Bi State Chpt., St. Louis, 1994. Mem. Nat. Coun. Consumer Arbitrators, Barnes Road Luncheon Group, Noonday Club, Veiled Prophet, St. Louis Country Club, Landmark Club, Darien Boat Club (bd. dirs. 1998—). Republican. Roman Catholic. Avocations: boating, shooting, golfing, tennis, automobiles.

DESLONGCHAMPS, PIERRE, chemistry educator; b. St.-Lin, Que., Can., May 8, 1938; s. Rodolphe and Madeleine D.; 3d m. Marie-Marthe Leroux; children: Patrice, Ghyslain. BS., U. Montreal, Que., Can., 1959; hon. doctorate, U. Montreal, 1984; PhD, U. N.B., 1964, hon. doctorate, 1985; hon. doctorate, U. Pierre et Marie, 1983, Bishop's U., 1984, Laval U., 1984; DSc, U. Moncton, N.B., Can., 1995. Research fellow Harvard U., 1964, postdoctoral fellow, 1965; asst. prof. chemistry U. Montreal, 1966-67; asst. prof. U. Sherbrooke, Que., 1967-68; assoc. prof. U. Sherbrooke, 1968-72, prof., 1972—. Author: Stereoelectronic Effects in Organic Chemistry, 1983; contbr. over 180 articles to profl. jours.; holder 9 patents in field. Decorated Officer Order of Can., 1989; recipient E.W.R. Steacie prize Nat. Rsch. Coun. Can., 1974, Can. Gold medal for sci. and engring. Nat. Scis. and Engring. Rsch. Coun. Can., 1993, Sci. prize Province Que., 1971-72, Marie-Victorian prize, 1987, Alfred Bader award Can. Soc. Chemistry, 1991, R.U. Lemieux award Chem. Soc. of Chemistry, 1994; Shell Can. Co. fellow, 1963, A.P. Sloan fellow, 1970-72, E.W.R. Steacie fellow, 1971-74, John Simon Guggenheim Meml. Found. fellow, 1979; Can. Coun. Izaak Walton Killam scholar, 1976-77. Fellow AAAS, Chem. Inst. Can. (Merck, Sharp and Dohme Lectrs. award 1976), Royal Soc. Can., Royal Soc. London; mem. Corp. Profl. Chemists Que., Am. Chem. Soc., New Swiss Chem. Soc., Assn. Harvard Chemists, Assn. Canadienne-Francaise pour l'Advancement des Sciences (medaille Vincent 1975, medaille Pariseau 1979), Assn. Advancement Scis. Can., Can. Com. Scientists and Scholars, Société Française de Chimie, Acad. des Scis. de Paris (foreign asst.). Inventor in field. Home: RR 1, 11 Ch McFarland, North Hatley, PQ Canada J0B 2C0 Address: Univ Sherbrooke Inst Pharm, 3001 12 North Ave, Sherbrooke, Canada J1H 5N4

DESMARAIS, CHARLES JOSEPH, museum director, writer, editor; b. N.Y.C., Apr. 21, 1949; s. Charles Emil and Helen Barbara (Young) D.; m. Sharon McLeod, May 1, 1970; m. Patricia Jon Carroll, June 15, 1979; m. Katherine Ann Morgan, Dec. 31, 1985. Student, Western Conn. State Coll., Danbury, 1967-71; B.S., SUNY-Rochester, 1975; M.F.A., SUNY-Buffalo, 1977. Curator Friends of Photography, Carmel, Calif., 1973-74; asst. editor Afterimage, Rochester, 1975-77; editor Exposure, Chgo., 1977-81; dir. Art Gallery, Columbia Coll., Chgo., 1977-79, Calif. Mus. Photography, U. Calif.-Riverside, 1981-88, Laguna Art Mus., Laguna Beach, Calif., 1988-94; Contemporary Arts Ctr., Cin., 1995—; guest curator Mus. Contemporary Art, Chgo., 1980, L.A. Ctr. Photog. Studies, 1981; arts adv. com. Riverside County Bd. Suprs., 1981-86; chair Orange County Arts Coun., 1989-91. Author, editor: Roger Mertin: Records 1976-1978, 1978, Michael Bishop, 1979, The Portrait Extended, 1980, Why I Got Into TV and Other Stories: The Art of Ilene Segalove, 1990, Proof: Los Angeles Art and the Photograph, 1960-1980, 1992, Humongolous: Sculpture and Other Works by Tim Hawkinson, 1996, Jim Dine Photographs, 1999; arts columnist Riverside Press Enterprise, 1987-88. Art Critic's fellow Nat. Endowment Arts, 1979. Mem. Assn. Art Mus. Dirs., Soc. Photog. Edn. (dir. 1979-83), Am. Assn. Museums, Coll. Art Assn. Office: Contemporary Arts Ctr 115 E 5th St Cincinnati OH 45202-3998

DESMARAIS, MAURICE, trade association administrator; b. Fall River, Mass., July 2, 1946; s. Armand Joseph and Lillian Anne (Moreau) D.; m. Lee Ann Sullivan; children: Ellen Marie, Elizabeth Ann. BA, Bridgewater State Coll., 1968; M in Mgmt., Cambridge Coll., 1993. Cert. ins. counselor; cert. assn. exec., chartered property casualty underwriter. Tchr. Tiverton Jr. Sr. High Sch., Tiverton, R.I., 1968-70; tchr. Bourne High Sch., Bourne, Mass., 1970-72; v.p., gen. mgr. Bryden & Sullivan et al. Ins. Agy., Hyannis, Mass., 1972-78; dir. edn. & conv. svcs. Profl. Ins. Agts. New Eng., Framingham, Mass., 1979-96; exec. v.p. New Eng. Wholesalers Assn. et al., Medway, Mass., 1996—; exec. dir. Am. Supply Assn., Chgo., 1996—, Northwest Distributor Assn., 1997-99; instr., spkr. New Eng. Wholesalers Assn. et al, Medway, Mass., 1985—; faculty adv. com. meeting mgmt. cert. program Bentley Coll., Waltham, Mass., 1987—, instr. risk mgmt., 1985-89; bd. trustees ASA Group Ins. Trust (ex-officio), Chgo., 1989—; spkr. Meeting World, N.Y.C., 1984, Nat. Assn. Exposition Mgrs., New Eng. Spkrs. Assn.; nat. chmn. edn. com. Nat. Assn. PIA Execs., Alexandria, Va., 1983; mem. adv. com. Ednl. Testing Svc., Princeton, N.J., 1983-85. Contbr. articles to Ins. Conf. Planning, 1981, Assn. Mgmt., 1982, Meeting News, 1983, Ins. Times, 1984, Supply House Times, 1990; author: Educational Training Systems, 1983-84. Chmn. vol. com. Spl. Olympics, Boston, 1984; author, cons. Nat. Assn. Profl. Ins. Agts., Alexandria, 1988—, The Saenger Orgn., Medway, Mass., 1988—; ind. meeting planner, pres. Assn. Mgmt. Svcs. Inc., Milford, Mass., 1991-97; pres. Wholesale/Retail Supplies Compensation Corp.; gen. mgr. ASA Ctr. for Advancing Tech. With USAR, 1968-74. Recipient Editors Choice award Meeting News, N.Y.C., 1985. Mem. Am. Soc. Quality Control, New Eng. Soc. Assn. Execs. (bd. dirs. 1984—, sec.-treas. 1991, chmn. 1993-94), Am. Soc. Assn. Execs. (spkr. contbg. author 11th ann. mgmt. conf.), Assn. Forum Chicagoland, Assn. for Quality and Participation. Roman Catholic.

DESMARAIS, PAUL, holding company executive; b. Sudbury, Ont., Can., Jan. 4, 1927; s. Jean-Noël and Lebea (Laforest) D.; m. Jacqueline Maranger, Sept. 8, 1953; children: Paul, André, Louise, Sophie. B.Comm., U. Ottawa, Ont., 1949. Chmn. exec. com. Power Corp. of Can., Montreal, Que., 1968—; bd. dirs. CLT-UFA, Electrafina S.A., The Great-West Life Assurance Co., Great-West Lifeco Inc., Groupe Bruxelles Lambert S.A., Investors Group Inc., London Ins. Group, London Life Ins. Co., Pargesa Holding S.A., Switzerland (chmn.), Petrofina S.A., Belgium, Power Broadcasting Inc., Power Corp. Can., Power Fin. Corp., La Presse Ltée, Telegraph Group Ltd.; chmn. Power Asia Capital Ltd.; mem. supervisory bd. AXA France, Internat. Adv. Com., Barrick Gold Corp., Can., Chase Manhattan Bank N.A., China Internat. Trust and Investment Corp., Compagnie Financière de Paribas, France. Decorated Companion Order of Can., Officer of Nat. Order of Que., Ordre Nat. de la Légion d'Honneur (France), Ordre de Léopold II (Belgium). Mem. Queen's Privy Coun. (Can.). Office: Power Corp Can, 751 Victoria Sq, Montreal, PQ Canada H2Y 2J3

DES MARAIS, PIERRE, II, communications holding company executive; b. Montreal, Que., Can., June 2, 1934; s. Pierre and Rolande (Varin) Des M.; m. Lise Blanchard, Jan. 21, 1956; children: Suzanne, Lison, Pierre III, Jean, Danielle, Stéphane, Sophie, Philippe, Anik. BA, Coll. St. Marie, 1954; grad. graphics arts course, Toronto, 1954; HEC in Bus. Adminstrn., U. Montreal, 1958. Pres., chief exec. officer Unimedia Inc., Montreal, 1987—; former chmn. Carling O'Keefe Ltd., dept. chmn., 1987; former chmn. Canadair Ltd., 1986; bd. dirs. Cognicase Inc., Hollinger Inc., Imperial Oil Ltd., Rothman's Inc., Sleeman Breweries Ltd., St. Lawrence Cement, Suzy Shier Ltd.; bd. dirs., chmn. Corp. de l'Hopital Maisonneuve-Rosemont. Former bd. dirs. Univ. de Montreal. Named hon. mem. Order of St. John, Que. Fellow Royal Geog. Soc.; mem. St. Denis Club, Mt. Royal Club, Forest and Stream Club. Avocation: skiing. Office: Unimédia Inc, 600 de Maisonneuve W Ste 3200, Montreal, PQ Canada H3A 3J2

DE SMET, LORRAINE MAY, artist; b. Passaic, N.J., May 5, 1928; d. Peter John and Mary (Lovas) Prevelige; m. Louis John de Smet, May 17, 1952; children: Mary Lizabeth, Jean Marie, Carolyn, Allise Marie. Student, Berkeley Sch., 1945, Art Students League, 1979-82. One woman show Pen and Brush Club, 1984 (Solo Show award). Bd. dirs. Art Ctr. of N.J., 1993—. Recipient 1st prize Livingston (N.J.) Art Assn., 1987, 88, Art Ctr. N.J., 1994, Am. Artist award at Ridgewood Art Inst., 1998, Caldwell Progress award, 1998, LAA merit award, 1998, 99, WEAA award Caldwell Coll., 1999, numerous other awards. Mem. U.S. Coast Guard Artists, Am. Artists Profl. League (Ann Waldron N.J. award award 1998), Pen and Brush Club of N.Y. (bd. dirs. 1985-92, v.p. 1989-92, dir. brush divsn. 1987-89, mem. dir. 1990-92, co-chair brush sect. 1994-95, 97), Art Ctr. of N.J. (bd. dirs., sec., membership chair), West Essex Art Assn. (bd. dirs. 1992-98, award 1999), Art Students League of N.Y. (life), Millburn-Short Hills Art Assn. Home: 33 Campbell Rd Fairfield NJ 07004-1735

DESMOND, JOHN JACOB, architect; b. Denver, Apr. 5, 1922; s. Timothy and Rose (Dvorak) D.; m. Blanche Russell, Sept. 29, 1951 (div.); children: John Michael, James Russell, Margaret; m. Nell Herring Lentz, Dec. 8, 1984. BArch, Tulane U., 1943; MArch., MIT, 1948. Archtl. draftsman Skidmore, Owings & Merrill, N.Y.C., 1947; archtl. designer, draftsman A. Hays Town, 1949-50, TVA, 1951-52; arch. Desmond & Davis, 1954-58, Desmond-Miremont-Burks, Baton Rouge, Hammond, La., from 1958; now pres. John Desmond & Assos., Baton Rouge. Author: Louisiana's Antebellum Architecture, 1970; contbr. articles to AIA Jour.; prin. works include Southea. La. Coll. Cafeteria, Hammond (1st honor award Gulf States region, Nat. Merit award AIA), St. Thomas More Ch. and Sch, Baton Rouge (honor award Gulf States region AIA), Cath. Student Ctr., Southea. La. Coll. (honor award Gulf States region AIA), La. State Libr., Baton Rouge (nat. AIA-ALA award, honor award Gulf States region AIA), Union Bldg, La. State U., Baton Rouge (1st honor award Gulf States region AIA), Cath. Life Ctr., Baton Rouge (honor award Gulf States region AIA); additions to Grace Meml. Episcopal Ch, Hammond (honor award Gulf States region AIA), D.C. Reeves Elem. Sch, Ponchatoula, La. (honor award Gulf States regional Nat. Honor award AIA), Tangipahoa Parish Courthouse, Amite, La. (honor award AIA and Office Civil Def., Gulf States Regional award 1997); design arch. Pennington Biomed. Rsch. Ctr. (Regional AIA Honor award), La. State Archives, U.S. Embassy, Monrovia, Liberia, Tulane U. Lindy Boggs Ctr., Baton Rouge Govtl. Ctr., Mobile County/City Courthouse Bldg. (honorable mention Nat. Archtl. Design Competition). Lt. USNR, 1943-46. Recipient Mayor Pres.'s medal for excellence in arts, 1994, award for hist. preservation of warden's home Found. for Hist. La., Outstanding Alumnus award Tulane U. Sch. Architecture. Fellow AIA (planning and urban design com., award for outstanding contbn. to design); mem. La. Archs. Assn., La. Landmarks Assn., Soc. Archtl. Historians, Nat. Trust for Hist. Preservation, Cosmos Club (Washington). Home: 1135 Carter Ave Baton Rouge LA 70806-7706 Office: John Desmond & Assocs 703 Laurel St Baton Rouge LA 70802-5635

DESMOND, LEIF, writer; b. Inglewood, Calif., Mar. 2, 1920; s. Guy Marion and Elma Agusta (Miller) Smith; m. Soledad Saenz, July 9, 1945 (div. Apr. 1982); children: Judith, Virginia, Marilyn Susan, Theresa, Loretta, Lawrence, Glenn; m. Yolanda Elkins Rambo, June 21, 1982. Student, Iowa State Coll., 1939-40, 42, San Fernando State Coll., 1959-65, U. Calif. Ext., 1961; AA in Bus. Adminstrn., Ventura (Calif.) Coll., 1959. Author: In the June of Summer, 1986, The Sparrow Safari, 1995, In Old October, 1996. Avocations: creative landscaping, agriculture, animals, philosophy, nature. Home: 2113 S Javelina Ave Yuma AZ 85364-6171

DESMOND, MABEL JEANNETTE, state legislator, educator; b. Lower Southampton, N.B., Can., Jan. 30, 1929; d. Charles Edward and Ada Gertrude (Ritchie) Lenentine; m. Jerry Russell Desmond, June 23, 1951; children: Jerry Russell Jr., Ronnee Beth, Jed Carey, Jennifer Shea. BS, Aroostock State Coll., 1964; MEd, U. Maine, 1975. Cert. prin., tchr., Maine. Tchr. Bridgewater (Maine) Elem. Sch., 1949-50, Gouldville Sch., Presque Isle, Maine, 1950-58, Mapleton H.S. and Mapleton Elem. Sch., Maine, 1958-63, 65-67, Gouldville Elem., Presque Isle, Maine, 1964-65, Ashland (Maine) Elem. Sch., 1969-70, Eva Hoyt Zippel Sch., Presque Isle, 1970-91; mem. adj. faculty U. Maine, Presque Isle, 1991—; rep. State of Maine, Augusta, 1995—; mem. tchr. edn. adv. com. U. Maine Presque Isle, 1995—, mem. edn. and cultural affairs com. in legislature. Contbr. editls. to newspapers and articles to profl. jours. Recipient Disting. Alumni award U. Maine, Presque Isle, 1995. Mem. AAUW, NEA, Maine Edn. Assn., U. Maine Presque Isle Alumni Assn. (exec. bd., pres. 1962-63, 74-75, sec. 1992-96), Delta Kappa Gamma (pres. 1984-86), Alpha Psi State (parliamentarian 1993-95). Democrat. Baptist. Avocations: writing, painting, reading. Home: PO Box 207 Mapleton ME 04757-0207 Office: Ho of Reps 2 State House Sta Augusta ME 04333-0002

DESMOND, PATRICIA LORRAINE, psychotherapist, writer, publisher; b. Boston, June 25, 1946; d. Francis X. and Mary L. (Donohue) D.; children: June, Timothy. AB, Stonehill Coll., 1968; MEd, U. Mass., Boston, 1994. Reporter The Patriot Ledger, Quincy, Mass., 1968-81; publisher Hingham (Mass.) Mariner, 1981-83, The Women's Jour., Hingham, 1985, Milton (Mass.) Times, 1995—; assoc. editor The Hingham Jour., 1985-86; copy editor Boston Herald, 1987-89; columnist Hull (Mass.) Times, 1988-94; editor Mariner Newspapers, Marshfield, Mass., 1989-91; pvt. practice Milton, Mass., 1993—; pub. Milton (Mass.) Times, 1995—; outpatient therapist High Point, Plymouth, Mass., 1994-96; case mgr. Harbor Light Ctr., Boston, 1995; columnist Tiny Town Gazette, Cohasset, Mass., 1993-96; publicist Share New Eng., Canton, Mass., 1993-95; therapist S. Bay Mental Health Ctr., Weymouth, 1995; relapse prevention counselor Nazareth Residence, Roxbury, 1995-96. Author: Cinnamon, 1988; co-author: How to Heal Your Heart, 1988; editor On the Edge, 1992-93; counselor/case mgr. St. Elizabeth's Comprehensive Alcoholism and Addictions Program, 1994-95. Recipient Honorary Mention Mass. Womens Press Assn., 1971, New England Press Assn., 1983. Mem. NOW (state coord. 1973-74), Am. Counseling Assn., Nat. Writers Union, Mass. Assn. Alcoholism and Drug Abuse Counselors, The Women's Poetry Collective. Avocations: poet, novelist.

DESMOND, WILLIAM J., lawyer; b. Boston, May 21, 1949; m. R. Christine Desmond Finke, July 1972. BA, Xavier U., 1973; JD, No. Ky. U., 1978. Assoc. Beirne and Withlin, Cin., 1978-83, Millikin and Fitton, Hamilton, Ohio, 1983-86; dir. legal affairs/risk mgmt. S.W. Ohio Regional Transit Authority, Cin., 1986—. Mem. Ohio State Bar Assn., Cin. Bar Assn. Office: SW Ohio Regional Transit 1014 Vine St Ste 2000 Cincinnati OH 45202-1116

DESNICK, ROBERT JOHN, human geneticist; b. Mpls., July 12, 1943; s. Theodore David and Celia Janice (Marcus) D.; m. Julie E. Herzig, Oct. 23, 1988; 1 child, Jonathan Phillips. B.A., U. Minn., 1965, Ph.D., 1970, M.D., 1971. Diplomate Am. Bd. Med. Examiners, Am. Acad. Pediatrics, Am. Bd. Med. Genetics (bd. dirs. 1990-93, treas. 1991-93). Rsch. assoc. U. Minn., Mpls., 1970-72, intern and resident dept. pediatrics, 1971-73, asst. prof. lab. medicine and pathology, 1973-75; assoc. prof. genetics and cell biology U. Minn. (Coll. Biol. Sci.), 1975-77; asst. prof. pediatrics U. Minn. (Dight Inst. Human Genetics), 1973-75, assoc. prof. pediatrics, 1975-77, prof. pediatrics, 1977; Arthur J. and Nellie Z. Cohen prof. pediatrics and genetics, 1977—, chief divsn. med. and molecular genetics Mt. Sinai Sch. Medicine, N.Y.C., 1977—, chair dept. Human Genetics, 1993—; dir. Mt. Sinai Ctr. Jewish Genetic Diseases, 1981—; program dir. Mt. Sinai Gen. Clin. Rsch. Ctr., 1990-99; attending physician pediatrics Mt. Sinai Hosp.; cons. physician pediatrics Beth Israel Med. Ctr., N.Y.C., City Ctr. Hosp. Elmhurst, N.Y.; med. adv. bd. Nat. Tay-Sachs and Allied Diseases Assn., 1975—, chmn. med. adv. bd., 1989-93; med. adv. bd. Nat. Neurofibromatosis Found., 1978-81; med. adv. bd. Nat. Found. Jewish Genetic Diseases, 1981—, Am. Porphyria Assn., 1984—, Mucolipidosis IV Found., 1984—, Nat. MPS Soc., 1987—; sci. adv. bd. Dysautonomia Found., 1990—; med. adv. bd. Internat. Incontinenta Pigmenti Found., 1993—; bd. dirs. Soc. Inherited Metabolic Diseases, 1983-92, pres., 1989-91; mem. N.Y. Gov.'s Adv. Com. on Genetics, 1982—; chmn. organizing com. Internat. Congresses Inherited Metabolic Diseases, 1990—; sci. adv. bd. Ara Parseghian Med. Rsch. Found., 1994—. Editor: Enzyme Therapy in Genetic Diseases, 1972, 79, Molecular Genetic Modification of Eucaryotes, 1978, Gaucher Disease: A Century of Delineation and Research, 1982, Animal Models of Inherited Metabolic Disorders, 1982, Recent Advances in Inborn Errors of Metabolism, 1987, Treatment of Genetic Diseases, 1991; mem. editl. bd. Enzyme, 1979—, Am. Jour. Human Genetics, 1980-84, Clinica Chemica Acta, 1984-96, Pediatrics, 1991-96, Human Mutation, 1991—, Biochem. Medicine and Metabolic Biology, 1991-97, Jour. Clin. Investigation, 1992-97, Jour. Inherited Metabolic Disease, 1996—, Jour. Human Genetics, 1998—, Molecular Genetics and Metabolism, 1998—; contbr. articles to profl. jours. Pres. 5th Internat. Congress of Inborn Errors of Metabolism, 1990. USPHS fellow, 1968-70; recipient Ross award Soc. Pediatric Rsch., 1972, C.J. Watson award U. Minn. Med. Sch., 1973, NIH Rsch. Career Devel. award, 1975-80, E. Mead Johnson award Am. Acad. Pediatrics, 1981, Outstanding Faculty award Mt. Sinai Sch. Medicine, 1991, NIH Merit award, 1992. Mem. AAAS, Am. Soc. Human Genetics, Genetics Soc. Am., Am. Acad. Pediatrics, Minn. Human Genetics League (dir. 1970-77), Soc. Complex Carbohydrates, Behavior Genetics Assn., Am. Fedn. Clin. Rsch., Am. Coll. Med. Genetics (founding fellow, chair hon. membership com. 1990-98, chair biochem. and molecular resource com. 1993—, chmn. accreditation com. 1998—), Am. Soc. Biochemistry and Molecular Biology, Assn. Profs. Human/Med. Genetics (pres-elect 1994, pres. 1996-98), Midwest Soc. Pediatric Rsch., Ea. Soc. Pediatric Rsch., Soc. Pediatric Rsch., Soc. Exptl. Biology and Medicine, Am. Soc. Exptl. Pathology, Cen. Soc. Clin. Rsch., Soc. Study Social Biology, Soc. Study Inborn Errors of Metabolism, N.Y. Acad. Sci., European Soc. Human Genetics, Harvey Soc. (sec. 1984-89), Soc. Inherited Metabolic Diseases (pres. 1989-90), Am. Pediatric Soc., Am. Soc. Microbiology, Am. Assn. Physicians, Am. Soc. Clin. Investigation, Assn. Patient-Oriented Rsch. (founding 1998—), Japanese Soc. Inherited Diseases (hon.), Societá Italiana di Pediatrica (hon.), Peripatetic Club, Sigma Xi. Office: Mt Sinai Sch Med Dept Human Genetics Fifth Ave & 100th St New York NY 10029

DESNOYERS, MEGAN FLOYD, archivist, educator; b. N.Y.C., Oct. 31, 1945; d. Lawrence Clifford and Frances Irene (Laffoon) Floyd; m. David George Desnoyers, Sept. 2, 1967; 1 child, Adam O'Neil. Postgrad., Am. U., 1972; AB, Vassar Coll., 1967; MLS, Rutgers U., 1968. Cert. archivist. Libr. John Jay H.S., Wappingers Falls, N.Y., 1968-69; archivist Franklin D. Roosevelt Libr., Hyde Park, N.Y., 1969; supervisory archivist John F. Kennedy Libr., Boston, 1970—, curator Ernest Hemingway Collection, 1987-96; instr. in archives adminstrn. Nat. Archives Modern Archives Inst., Washington, 1982—; lectr. archives adminstrn. U. Mass., Boston, 1978-80; lectr. on Hemingway, 1992-97; mem. Archives Adv. Commn., Boston, 1977—; archival advisor Girl Scouts U.S., N.Y.C., 1991—. Contbr. chpt. to book, articles to profl. jours. Mem. adv. bd., chmn. com. Voluntary Action Ctr., Mass. Bay United Way, Boston, 1974-80; mem., chair bd. trustees Randall Libr., Stow, Mass., 1976-80; ch. sch. tchr. St. Francis Xavier Ch., Bolton, Mass., 1982-84; mem. Mass. Hist. Records Adv. Bd., 1979—. Nat. Def. fellow, 1967-68. Fellow Soc. Am. Archivists; mem. New Eng. Archivists (sec. 1976-78), Soc. Am. Archivists (workshop instr.), Acad. Cert. Archivists (task force on recert. 1991-92), Beta Phi Mu. Democrat. Roman Catholic. Office: John F Kennedy Libr Columbia Point Boston MA 02125

DESOTO, LEWIS DAMIEN, art educator; b. San Bernardino, Calif., Jan. 3, 1954; s. Lewis Dan and Albertina (Quiroz) DeS. BA, U. Calif., Riverside, 1978; MFA, Claremont Grad. Sch., 1981. Tchr. Otis Parsons, L.A., 1982-85; chmn. art dept. Cornish Coll. of Arts, Seattle, 1985-88; prof. art San Francisco State U., 1988-93, 95—; dir. grad. studies Calif. Coll. Arts and Crafts, Oakland, 1993-95. Exhibited at New Mus., N.Y.C., 1992, Centro Cultural De La Raza, San Diego, 1993, Moderna Museet, Stockholm, Sweden, 1993, Christopher Grimes Gallery, Santa Monica, Calif., 1994, Denver Art Mus., 1994, Columbus Mus. Art, 1994, Des Moines Art Ctr., 1995, Fundacao Serralves, 1995, Oporto, Portugal, 1995, Metronòm, Barcelona, Spain, 1997, Public Art Commn., San Francisco Courthouse, 1998, Public Art Commn., San Francisco Internatl. Airport, 1999. Mem. photo coun. Seattle Art Mus., 1987-88, Eureka Fellowship, vis. arts, 1999. Recipient New Genres award Calif. Arts Coun., 1992, NEA fellow, 1996. Mem. L.A. Ctr. for Photographic Studies (bd. dirs. 1983-85), CameraWork (exec. bd. dirs. 1991-93), Ctr. for Arts (adv. bd. 1993-95), Friends of Photography (peer award bd. 1991-96). Office: San Francisco State U Art Dept 1600 Holloway Ave San Francisco CA 94132-1722

DE SOUSA, BYRON NAGIB, physician, anesthesiologist, clinical pharmacologist, educator; b. Goiania, Goias, Brazil, Jan. 15, 1949; came to the U.S., 1972; s. Lazaro Jose and Zarife (Chaul) de.; m. Ana Maria Soares, Nov. 15, 1991; stepchildren: Thiago M., Thais Martins; children: Daniela N., Elisabeth L. BS in Biology, U. Brasilia, Brazil, 1970, BS in Biology Edn., 1971, MD, 1973; PhD in Physiol. Chemistry, Ohio State U., 1976. Diplomate Am. Bd. Disability Analysis. Prin. CASEB & CSL biology tchr. Adult Sr. H.S., Brazil, 1969-71; instr. biochemistry U. Goias, Brazil, 1972; rsch. asst. prof. neurology UCLA-Wadsworth V.A. Med. Ctr., L.A., 1978-79; cons. physician Brentwood V.A. Med. Ctr., L.A., 1979-80; intern Wadsorth-Brentwood V.A. Med. Ctr., L.A., 1980-81; resident in Anesthesiology U. So. Calif. Med. Ctr., L.A., 1981-83; anesthesiologist Simi Valley Presbyn. Hosp., Calif., 1983-85, Simi Valley Community Hosp., Calif., 1983-85, Rio Hondo Meml. Hosp., L.A., 1983-85, Kaiser Permanente Med. Ctr., Orange County, Calif., 1983-84, Hollywood Presbyn. Med. Ctr., L.A., 1983-84, Pacoima Community Hosp., L.A., 1984; assoc. prof. biochemistry, pharmacology Fed. U. Goias, 1986-89; adj. prof. pharmacology U. North Tex. Health Sci. Ctr., Ft. Worth, 1993; anesthesiologist UTSMC affiliated hosps., Dallas, 1993; vis. prof. pharmacology, med. microbiology and immunology U. North Tex. Health Sci. Ctr., Ft. Worth; cons. Alcon Labs., Inc., 1989-90; adj. prof. dept. pharmacology U. North Tex. Health Sci. Ctr., Ft. Worth; dir. continuing med. edn. Am. Coll. Internat. Physicians-U. Tex. Southwestern Med. Ctr., Dallas; exec. dir. Internat. Inst. Medicine; organizer numerous symposia and seminars, U.S.A., Africa, Asia, Europe, S.Am.; exec. dir. Internat. Inst. Medicine, Ft. Worth, 1996—. Author, editor (book) Arts of Politics: Thoughts and Quotations, 1988; reviewer sci.and clin. jours. including Molecular and Chem. Neuropathology, 1989—, Internat. Med. Jour., 1994; contbr. over 60 articles to sci. jours.; inventor in field. Bd. dirs., sec. Substance Abuse Inst. N. Tex., 1993—; bd. dirs., mem. Longhorn coun. troop 17 Boy Scouts Am., Ft. Worth, 1995—, treas., 1995-97; mem. plan commn. Place 6 City of Ft. Worth, 1998; commr. Fort Worth City Planning Commn. NIA postdoctoral fellow Med. Coll. Pa., 1976-77, postdoctoral fellow U. Wis., 1977-78, Internal Medicine fellow UCLA Med. Ctr., 1979-80. Fellow Am. Coll. Internat. Physicians (trustee 1994—, pres. Dallas-Ft. Worth chpt.); mem. AAAS, AMA, Am. Soc. Anesthesiologists, Am. Soc. Neurochemistry, Western U.S.A. Pain Soc., Calif. Med. Assn., Calif. Soc. Anesthesiologists, Tex. Med. Assn., Tarrant County Med. Soc. Orange County Anesthesiology Soc., L.A. County Soc. Anesthesiologists, L.A. County Med. Soc., Internat. Anesthesia Rsch. Soc., Internat. Soc. Neurochemistry, European Brain and Behavior Soc., European Soc. Regional Anesthesia, Brazilian Coun. Ophthalmology, British Brain Rsch. Assn., Gerontological Soc., Soc. Neurosci. Avocations: biking, sailing, traveling, flying. Office: 7733 Blossom Dr Fort Worth TX 76133-7909

DESOUZA, JOAN MELANIE, psychologist; b. Bombay, Sept. 17, 1956; came to U.S., 1987; d. Anthony Julius and Natalia Marie (Alvares) deS.; m. John Alec Krzewinski, Sept. 7, 1990. BA in Psychology with honors, U. Bombay, 1976; BS in Guidance and Counseling, Wayne State U., 1984, MA in Psychology, 1986, PhD in Ednl. Psychology, 1991. Lic. psychologist, Mich.; cert. sch. psychologist. Grad. asst. Wayne State U., Detroit, 1984-85; editor, mem. part-time faculty Inst. Gerontology, Detroit, 1985-87; extern St. Joseph Mercy Hosp., Pontiac, Mich., 1986; psychologist Huron Valley Mens' Facility, Ypsilanti, Mich., 1987-96, Huron Valley Ctr., 1996—; cons. Arab-Am. cmty., Detroit, 1988, Ctr. Behavior and Medicine, 1994—. Co-author: (handbook) Medicare Survey Project: Effectiveness of DRG's, 1987; editor (newsletter) Info. on Aging, 1985-87. Intern Parents and Children Together, Detroit, 1984; activist for Laotian community and immigrants Internat. Inst., Detroit, 1983; asst. soup kitchen Mother Theresa's order, Detroit. Grad. profl. scholar Wayne State U., 1985, Rumble fellow, 1986-87, 87-88; parenting skills grantee for low-functioning child abusers Mich. Dept. Edn., Lansing, 1989-90, Spl. Edn. grantee, 1995; recipient Bob Richardson Meml. award for excellence in correctional edn. and rsch., 1995. Mem. APA, Mich. Psychol. Assn., Mich. Assn. Sch. Psychologists, Pi Lambda Theta (Detroit chpt.). Roman Catholic. Avocations: gardening, work with immigrants. Home: 203 Russell St Saline MI 48176-1133 Office: Huron Valley Ctr 3511 Bemis Rd Ypsilanti MI 48197-9373

DESPAIN, BECKY ANN, dental educator; b. Oklahoma City, July 14, 1948; children: Brian Thomas, Meredith Lynn. BS in Dental Hygiene, Baylor U., 1970; MEd, Cen. State U., Okla., 1982. Registered dental hygienist. Pvt. practice clin. dental hygienist Oklahoma City, 1970-73; instr. Coll. Dentistry, Okla. U. Health Scis. Ctr., Oklahoma City, 1973-82, asst. prof., 1982-85, acting chair dept. dental hygiene, 1984-85, clin. dental hygienist faculty practice, 1977-85; assoc. prof., dir. Caruth Sch. Dental Hygiene Baylor Coll. Dentistry, Dallas, 1985-93, assoc. prof. dept. pub. health scis., 1993—; clin. dental hygienist Drs. Israelson, Plemons & Jaynes, Richardson, Tex., 1995-97; clin. instr. Rose Jr. Coll., Midwest City, Okla., 1972; mem. affil. staff Okla. Children's Meml. Hosp., Oklahoma City, 1977-85; clin. dental hygienist North Tex. Periodontal and Implant Assn., Richardson, 1988-91; mem. test constrn. com. Nat. Bd. Dental Hygiene, ADA, Chgo., 1987-91, dental hygiene cons. Commn. on Dental Accreditation, 1989-96; investigator grants and contracts HHS, NIH. Editorial rev. bd.: Jour. Dental Hygiene, Chgo., 1982—; contbr. abstracts and articles to profl. jours. Spkr. sch. vols. program Oklahoma City Pub. Schs., 1976-85; project dir. Oral Healthlink: Dallas-Ft. Worth Coalition for Oral Health 2000; bd. dirs. Dallas chpt. ACLU of North Tex., pres., 1996-97; Tex. coord. nat. spit tobacco edn. program, Oral Health Am., 1996-97; bd. dirs. So.

Methodist U. YWCA, 1997-98. Recipient small grant award Rsch. Coun., OUHSC, Oklahoma City, 1985, Dental Hygiene Rsch. grant Oral-B Labs., Redwood City, Calif., 1985. Mem. APHA, Am. Assn. Dental Schs., Am. Assn. Dental Rsch., Am. Dental Hygienists Assn. (del. 1980-84), Am. Assn. Pub. Health Dentistry, Tex. Dental Hygienists Assn., Tex. Dental Hygiene Dirs. Assn. (sec. 1990-92), Dallas Dental Hygienists Soc. (v.p. 1994, pres.-elect 1995, pres. 1996), The Woman's Ctr. of Dallas (chair health care task force, bd. dirs. 1994-96, health com. Women's Coun. of Dallas County 1995-97), Sigma Phi Alpha, Kappa Delta Pi. Office: Baylor Coll Dentistry PO Box 660677 Dallas TX 75266-0677

DESPOMMIER, DICKSON DONALD, microbiology educator, parasitologist, researcher; b. New Orleans, June 5, 1940; s. Roland Medd and Beverly (Wood) D.; children—Bruce, Bradley. B.S., Fairleigh Dickinson U., 1962; M.S., Columbia U., 1964; Ph.D., U. Notre Dame, 1967. Postdoctoral fellow Rockefeller U., 1967-71; Asst. prof. pub. health Columbia U., N.Y.C., 1971-75, assoc. prof., 1975-77, prof. pub. health and microbiology, 1982—; cons. NIH, 1980-84, Gen. Food Corp., 1976, Cordis Corp., 1973-74, Bionetics Rsch. Inc., 1986-89, Eco-Chem, Inc., 1993; Theobald Smith lectr. 1993. Author: Parasitic Diseases, 3d edit., 1994, Parasite Life Cycles, 1988. Bd. dirs., chmn. edn. com. Catskill Flyfishing Ctr. and Mus., 1994—, dir., 1994—. Named Tchr. of Yr. Columbia U., 1980, 81, 83, 84; recipient Career Devel. award Nat. Inst. A.I.D., 1971-75, Disting. Tchr. award Med. Coll. Ohio, 1980, Deans' Disting. Tchr. award Columbia U., 1989. Mem. AAAS, Am. Soc. Parasitologists, Am. Soc. Tropical Medicine and Hygiene, Harvey Soc., N.Y. Soc. Tropical Medicine (pres. 1980), Internat. Commn. on Trichinellosis. Club: Trout Unltd. (bd. dirs. 1976-78) (Oradel, N.J.). Office: Room 124 Psychiat Inst Annex New York NY 10032

D'ESPOSITO, JULIAN C., JR., lawyer; b. N.Y.C., Aug. 6, 1944. BS, Loyola U., 1966; JD cum laude, Northwestern U., 1969. Bar: Ill. 1969, U.S. Dist. Ct. (no. dist.) 1969. Counsel to Gov. Ill., 1977-81; ptnr. Mayer, Brown & Platt, Chgo.; chmn. Winnetka Plan Commn., 1985-89; mem. Ill. Med. Ctr. Commn., 1987-94; dir. Taxpayers Fedn. Ill.; dir. Ill. Capital Devel. Bd., 1994-95; chmn. Ill. State Toll Hwy. Authority. Co-editor-in-chief Jour. Criminal Law, Criminology & Police Sci., Northwestern U., 1968-69. Mem. ABA. Office: Mayer Brown & Platt 190 S La Salle St Ste 3100 Chicago IL 60603-3441

DESPRES, LEO ARTHUR, sociology and anthropology educator, academic administrator; b. Lebanon, N.H., Mar. 29, 1932; s. Leo Arthur and Madeline (Bedford) D.; m. Loretta A. LaBarre, Aug. 22, 1953; children—Christine, Michelle, Denise, Mary Louise, Renee. B.A., U. Notre Dame, 1954, M.A., 1956; Ph.D., Ohio State U., 1960. Research assoc. Columbia Psychiat. Inst. and Hosp., 1957-60; postdoctoral fellow Social Sci. Research Council, Guyana, 1960-61; asst. prof. Ohio Wesleyan U., 1961-63; faculty Case Western Res. U., Cleve., 1963-74; prof. anthropology Case Western Res. U., 1967-74, chmn. dept., 1968-74; prof. sociology, anthropology U. Notre Dame, Ind., 1974-97; chmn. dept. U. Notre Dame, 1974-80, fellow Kellogg Inst. Internat. Studies, 1982—, prof. emeritus, 1997—; Cons. in field. Author: Cultural Pluralism and Nationalist Politics in British Guyana, 1968; editor: Ethnicity and Resource Competition in Plural Societies, 1975, Manaus: Social Life and Work in Brazil's Free Trade Zone, 1991. Fulbright scholar U. Guyana, 1970-71, Brazil, 1986; research grantee NSF, 1984. Mem. Am. Anthrop. Assn., Am. Ethnol. Soc., Latin Am. Studies Assn., Cen. States Anthrop. Soc. (pres. 1976-77), AAUP. Home: 17939 Bay Winds Dr South Bend IN 46635 Office: U Notre Dame Dept Anthropology Notre Dame IN 46556

DESPRES, LEON MATHIS, lawyer, former city official; b. Chgo., Feb. 2, 1908; s. Samuel and Henrietta (Rubovits) D.; m. Marian Alschuler, Sept. 10, 1931; children—Linda Baskin, Robert Leon. PhB, U. Chgo., 1927, JD, 1929; DLitt, Columbia Coll., 1990. Bar: Ill. 1929. Ptnr. Despres, Schwartz and Geoghegan, Chgo.; trial examiner NLRB, Chgo., 1935-37; instr. U. Chgo., 1936, U. Wis., summers 1946-49; alderman 5th Ward Chgo. City Council, 1955-75, parliamentarian, 1979-87. Mem. Chgo. Plan Commn., 1979-89. Mem. Am., Ill., Chgo. bar. assns., Chgo. Council Lawyers, Order of Coif, Phi Beta Kappa. Home: 5830 S Stony Island Ave Apt 10A Chicago IL 60637-2024 Office: 77 W Washington St Chicago IL 60602-2801

DESPRES, ROBERT LEON, urban planner; b. Chgo., Aug. 15, 1940; s. Leon Mathis and Marian (Alschuler) D.; m. Louise Fay, Feb. 16, 1974; 1 child, Frederick Leon. BA in Polit. Sci., U. Wis., 1961; MS in City and Regional Planning, U. Bridgeport, 1984. Urban renewal rep. HUD, Phila., 1961-68; reporter urban affairs The Telegram, Bridgeport, Conn., 1968-78, copy editor, 1978-79; copy editor The Hour, Norwalk, Conn., 1979-81; sr. planner Action for Bridgeport Community Devel., 1982-86, assoc. dir., 1986-87; comprehensive planner Greater Bridgeport Regional Planning Agy., 1987-94; lead planning analyst Conn. Dept. Social Svcs., 1994—; cons. Weston (Conn.) Planning and Zoning Commn., 1985; alt. commr. Westport (Conn.) Planning and Zoning Commn., 1986-88; apptd. to South Western Regional Planning Agy., 1987-93. V.p. Phila. Council Am. Youth Hostels, 1965-66. Named Outstanding Journalist, Hope Ctr., 1975. Mem. Am. Planning Assn., Am. Inst. Cert. Planners. Democrat. Jewish. Home: 3 Peters Ln Westport CT 06880-3937 Office: Conn Dept Social Studies 925 Housatonic Ave Bridgeport CT 06606-5717

DESPRIET, JOHN G., lawyer; b. Kortrijk, Belgium, Aug. 12, 1949. BS with honors, U. Fla., 1971, JD with honors, 1978; MBA, U. Utah, 1976. Bar: Ga. 1979, Fla. 1979. Mem. Smith, Gambrell & Russell, Atlanta. Sr. student editor U. Fla. Law Review, 1978. Capt. USAF, 1971-76. Mem. ABA, State Bar Ga., Fla. Bar. Office: Smith Gambrell & Russell 1230 Peachtree St NE Ste 3100 Atlanta GA 30309-3592*

DESROCHERS, ALAN ALFRED, electrical, computer and systems engineering educator, systems engineering consultant; b. Northampton, Mass., June 1, 1950; s. Alfred George and Helen Mary (Punska) D. B.S.E.E., U. Mass., Lowell, 1972; M.S.E.E., Purdue U., 1973, Ph.D., 1977. Assoc. engr. Lockheed Missiles & Space Co., Sunnyvale, Calif., 1974-75; asst. prof. Boston U., 1977-80; asst. prof. elec., computer and systems engring. Rensselaer Poly. Inst., Troy, N.Y., 1980-86, assoc. prof., 1986-90, prof., 1990—; summer faculty fellow USAF, Eglin AFB, Fla., 1978; cons. IBM, Cambridge, Mass., 1978-79, Alcoa, Pitts., 1983-85, Barron Assocs., Inc., Annandale, Va., 1985, Systolic Systems, Inc., San Jose, Calif., 1987, Kaiser Aluminum Co., Pleasanton, Calif., 1987, Law Offices of Frances E. Lehner, 1992—; vis. scientist Lab. for Info. and Decision Systems, MIT, 1987. Contbr. articles to profl. jours. Recipient V. L. Magoon Teaching award Purdue U., 1977, LEAD award Soc. Mfg. Engrs., 1987; research grantee NASA, Air Force Office Sci. Research, U.S. Army, IBM, Digital Equipment Corp., Alcoa, 1978-94. Fellow IEEE (sr., ednl. chmn. 1984-89); mem. Robotics and Automation Soc. of IEEE (elected officer 1989-95, editor Transactions on Robotics and Automation 1990-96), AAAS, N.Y. Acad. Scis., Sigma Xi, Eta Kappa Nu. Avocations: bicycling, sailing. Home: 30 Briarwood Rd Albany NY 12211-1222 Office: Rensselaer Poly Inst Elec Computer and Systems Engring Dept Troy NY 12180

DES ROCHES, ANTOINE, retired newspaper executive; b. Quebec, Que., Can., Jan. 9, 1924; s. Francis and Antoinette DesR.; m. Monique Nuytemans, Jan. 24, 1969. Reporter Le Soleil, 1942-47; news editor Le Soleil, also L'Evenement-Jour., Quebec, P.Q., 1947-52, Sta. CHLN, also Le Nouveau Jour., Montreal, P.Q., 1958-62; info. expert UNESCO, 1962-63; news editor La Presse, Montreal, 1964-67, 70-72, dir. pub. relations, 1972-88, asst to pres., 1982-88, spl. adv. to pres., 1988-95; pres. Les Editions La Presse, 1980-85, Assn. des Editeurs Canadiens, 1983-84. Roman Catholic. Home: 24 Buttonwood St, Dollard, PQ Canada H9A 2N2 *Be true, be kind, be thorough.*

DESROSIERS, ANNE BOOKE, performing arts administrator, consultant; b. Bradford, Pa., Sept. 30, 1938; d. Benjamin and Twila Mae (Schwab) Booke; m. Roger Isadore DesRosiers, Dec. 27, 1960 (div. 1994); children Marc (dec.), Diana, Berinthia. BA in English, U. Fla., 1960. Tchr. Rantoul (Ill.) Elem. Sch., 1961-63, Oogontz Jr. H.S., Phila., 1969-73; dir. adult edn. Guadaloupe Ctr., Salt Lake City, 1974-77; dir. devel. Repertory Theater of St. Louis, 1977-85, St. Louis Zoo, 1985-88; pres. DesRosiers & Assocs., Cleve., 1988—; mng. dir. Great Lakes Theater Festival, Cleve., 1993-98. Mem. Nat. Soc. Fund Raising Execs. (cert., Exec. Leadership Inst. 1990, Outstanding Fund Raising St. Louis chpt. 1988), Cleve. Cultural Coalition (vice chair 1995-98). Republican. Jewish. Avocations: golf, travel, sailing. E-mail: abdesr@megsinet.net. Fax: 216-541-0344. Home: 1 Bratenahl Pl Apt 1102 Bratenahl OH 44108-1155 Office: Ste 1102 One Bratenahl Pl Cleveland OH 44108

DESSASO, DEBORAH ANN, online communication specialist; b. Washington, Feb. 6, 1952; d. Coleman and Virginia Beatrice (Taylor) D. AS in Bus. Adminstrn., Southeastern U., 1986, BSBA, 1988; MA in English Composition and Rhetoric U. D.C., 1997. Clk.-stenographer FTC, Washington, 1969-70; sec. NEA, Washington, 1970-72; sec. AARP, Washington, 1972-79, assoc. adminstrv. specialist, 1979-80, adminstrv. specialist, 1979-89, legis. comm. specialist, 1989—; founding mem., sec. Andrus Fed. Credit Union, 1980. Mem. NAFE. Mem. Worldwide Ch. of God. Home: 3052 Stanton Rd SE Washington DC 20020-7883 Office: 601 E St NW Washington DC 20049-0001

DESSAUER, CARIN, journalist; b. Pottstown, Pa., Dec. 31, 1963; d. Ralph and Margot (Abrams) D.; m. Marc Richard Engel, May 29, 1988. BA cum laude, Bucknell U., 1985; postgrad., George Washington U., 1987. Reporter The Polit. Report, Washington, 1986-87; off-air reporter ABC News Polit. Unit, Washington, 1988; assoc. editor Congl. Quarterly's Politics in Am., Washington, 1989; contbg. editor Campaigns and Elections mag., Washington, 1989-91; head Washington polit. unit Cable News Network, 1990-91; assoc. polit. dir. CNN, Washington, 1991-95, dep. pol. dir., 1995-98, election dir., 1998—. Co-author: (monograph) Running to Win, 1988. Co-chair UJA Women's Bus. and Profl. Divsn., D.C. chpt., bd. dirs., cabinet, 1997—, exec. com., 1994-97; active Make A Wish Found., New Endeavors by Women. Mem. Phi Beta Kappa. Avocations: design, fitness, art, theatre, photography, travel. Office: CNN 820 1st St NE Washington DC 20002-4243

DESSAUER, JOHN PHILLIP, publisher, financial management company executive; b. Rochester, N.Y., Apr. 21, 1936; s. John H. and Margaret (Lee) D.; m. Marilynn White, Oct. 22, 1992; children: Theresa, Karen, Christine, Mary, John. BS in Physics, Le Moyne Coll., 1959; LLB, Cornell U., 1962. Bar: N.Y. 1962. Assoc. Harris, Beach et al, Rochester, 1962-67; trust officer Security Trust Co., Rochester, 1967-73, head trust dept., 1978-80; sr. investment officer Citibank, Zurich, Switzerland, 1974-77; editor Dessauer's Investors' World, Limmat Publs., Orleans, Mass., 1980—; pres. Limmat Publs., Orleans, Mass., 1980—; prin. Dessauer & McIntyre Asset Mgmt., Orleans, 1986—; panelist Wall Street Week, Owings Mills, Md., 1989—. Author: International Strategies for American Investors, 1987, Passport to Profits, 1990; columnist World Monitor mag., 1988-92. Office: Box 1718 Orleans MA 02653

DESSEM, R. LAWRENCE, dean, law educator; b. Berea, Ohio, May 16, 1951; s. Ralph Eugene and Jane Elizabeth (Brightbill) D.; m. Beth Ann Taylor, May 20, 1973; children: Matthew, Lindsay, Emily. BA, Macalester Coll., 1973; JD, Harvard U., 1976. Bar: Ohio 1976, D.C. 1979, Tenn. 1985. Law clk. to presiding judge U.S. Dist. Ct. (no. dist.) Ohio, Cleve., 1976-78; asst. gen. counsel NEA, Washington, 1978-80; trial atty. civil div. U.S. Dept. Justice, Washington, 1980-84, sr. trial counsel, 1984-85; assoc. prof. law coll. of law U. Tenn., Knoxville, 1985-92, prof. law coll. of law, 1992-95, assoc. dean, 1993-95; dean Mercer U., Macon, Ga., 1995—; mem. faculty Legal Edn. Inst., U.S. Dept. Justice, San Francisco, 1985, Nat. Inst. for Trial Adv., Chgo., 1987-90; reporter Adv. Group on Litigation Cost and Delay, Tenn., 1991-95; mem. Tenn. Supreme Ct. Commn. on Dispute Resolution, 1992-94. Author: Pretrial Litigation, 1991, 2d edit., 1996; contbr. articles to profl. jours. Nat. Merit scholar 1969. Fellow Am. Bar Found., Lawyer's Found. of Ga.; mem. ABA (co-chair dean's workshop 1998-99), Tenn. Bar Found., Am. Law Inst., Phi Beta Kappa. Office: Mercer U Law Sch 1400 Coleman Ave Macon GA 31207-0003

DESSER, KENNETH BARRY, cardiologist, educator; b. N.Y.C., Mar. 24, 1940; s. George and Sarah Ruth (Kaplan) D.; m. Carmen Yvonne Fletcher; children: Brett Karen, Lori Helene. BA, NYU, 1961; MD, N.Y. Med. Coll., 1965. Diplomate Am. Bd. Internal and Cardiovascular Disease. Intern Beth Israel Med. Ctr., N.Y.C., 1965-66, resident in medicine, 1968-70; cardiology fellow Inst. Cardiovascular Diseases, Phoenix, 1970-72; asst. dir. Inst. Cardiovasc. Diseases, Phoenix, 1977-83; fellowship dir. cardiology Good Samaritan Med. Ctr., Phoenix, 1983—; prof. medicine U. Ariz., Tucson, 1985—; editorial cons. to med. jours. Mem. emeritus Am. Jour. Cardiology, 1980-82; contbr. articles to profl. jours., chpts. to books. Capt. U.S. Army, 1966-68, Vietnam. Decorated Bronze Star with oak leaf, Purple Heart, Air medal, Cross of Gallantry; recipient Best Rsch. award Beth Israel Med. Ctr., 1966. Fellow ACP, Am. Coll. Cardiology (mem. editl. bd. 1983-85), Am. Coll. Chest Physicians, Am. Heart Assn.; mem. Am. Fedn. Med. Rsch. Avocations: scientific angling, collecting antique military books. Office: Cardiology and Internal Medicine 1144 E Mcdowell Rd Phoenix AZ 85006-2664

DESSER, MAXWELL MILTON, artist, art director, filmstrip producer; b. N.Y.C.; s. Solomon and Sadie (Franklin) Desser; m. Mary Alice Natkin, Mar. 7, 1953. Student, Pratt Inst., 1930-32; grad., Cooper Union U., 1940; student, Am. U., 1941-42, NYU, 1945-46, Am. U. Free lance art dir., filmstrip producer N.Y.C., 1935—; owner Desser Prodns., N.Y.C.; producer filmstrips Crawl (Internat. TV and Film Festival N.Y. Silver medal 1967), Dun's Market Identifiers (Internat. TV and Film Festival N.Y. gold medal 1968). Author: Using the Library, 1957; painting represented in International Waters Tour, Gt. Britain, Scotland, Can., U.S. Served to lt. USNR, 1942-45. Recipient Nat. Art League Gold medal, 1962, 64, 68, Spl. Tribute Gold medal honor Knickerbocker Artists, 1973, 87. Mem. Am. Watercolor Soc. (v.p. 1983—, Silver medal 1975, sec., dir. 1973-93, Dolphin fellow, ten awards 1975-89, rep. U.S., Gt. Britain and Can. Traveling Show 1991-93, U.S. in Internat. Waters exhbn. 1991-93, High Winds medal 1998), Allied Artists Am. (Silver medal 1978), Nat. Soc. Painters (Grumbacher Gold medal 1974, 91, Dr. Soloway award 1995), Audubon Artists (Silver medal 1981, bd. dirs. 1979-82), Allied Artists (Gold Medal honor 1989), Nat. Acad. Academician (cert. merit 1976, 90, 93, The Nat. Acad. Adolph and Clara Obrig prize 1997), Salmagundi Club (Emanuel Krueger award 1991, first prize 1994, Napoli award 1995, others). Office: Desser Prodns 85-28 168th Pl Jamaica NY 11432-2638

DESSI, ADRIAN FRANK, marketing and communications executive; b. Bklyn., Oct. 23, 1945; s. Adrian Lawrence and Marie Ann (Vastola) D.; m. Patricia Ann Larosa, Aug. 16, 1969; children: Mark Adrian, Christopher Guy. BBA, Pace U., 1969; MBA, St. John's U., 1975. Mktg. segment mgr. Chem. Bank, N.Y.C., 1969-78; v.p. mktg. Old Stone Corp., Providence, 1978-79; account supr. D.M. Group, Inc., N.Y.C., 1979-83, Rapp & Collins/DDB Co., 1983-84, Dancer, Fitzgerald & Sample Direct Advt. Agy., 1984-86; dir. mktg. comm. and rsch. Peat, Marwick, Main and Co., N.Y.C., 1986-90; group dir. mktg. Donnelley Mktg., Inc., 1990-93; sr. dir. direct mktg. new business Avon Products, 1993—. Mem. Mahopac Soccer Club, Lions. Home: 31 Kia Ora Blvd Mahopac NY 10541-4320 Office: 1251 Ave of Americas New York NY 10020

DESSLER, ALEXANDER JACK, space physics and astronomy educator, scientist; b. San Francisco, Oct. 21, 1928; s. David Alexander and Julia (Shapiro) D.; m. Lorraine Hudek, Apr. 18, 1952; children: Pauline Karen, David Alexander, Valerie Jan, Andrew Emory. B.S., Calif. Inst. Tech., 1952; Ph.D., Duke, 1956. Sect. head Lockheed Missiles & Space Co., 1956-62; prof. Grad. Research Center, Dallas, 1962-63, prof. space physics and astronomy, 1963-82, 86-93; chmn. dept. Rice U., Houston, 1963-69, 79-82, 87-92, campus bus. mgr., 1974-76; dir. space sci. lab. MSFC NASA, Huntsville, Ala., 1982-86; sr. rsch. scientist Lunar and Planetary Lab. U. Ariz., Tucson, 1993—; sci. adviser Nat Aeros. and Space Council, 1969-70; pres. Univs. Space Research Assn., 1975-81. Editor Jour. Geophys. Research, 1965-69, Revs. of Geophysics, 1969-74, The John Wiley Space Science Text Series, 1968-76, Geophys. Research Letters, 1986-89, Atmospheric and Space Science Series, 1986—; adv. bd.: Planetary and Space Sci., 1963-92; assoc. editor Space Solar Power Rev., 1980-85. Served with USN, 1946-48. Recipient Outstanding Young Scientist award Tex. wing Air Force Assn., 1964, medal for contbns. to internat. geophysics Soviet Geophys. Com., 1984, Stellar award for acad. devel., Rotary Nat., 1988. Fellow Am. Geophys. Union (Macelwane award 1963, John Adam Fleming medal 1993); mem. Am. Astron. Soc., Internat. Assn. Geomagnetism and Aeronomy (v.p. 1979-83), Royal Swedish Acad. Scis. (fgn. mem.). Home: 1434 E Seneca St Tucson AZ 85719-3645 Office: U Ariz Lunar Planetary Lab 901 Gould-Simpson Bldg Tucson AZ 85721

DESSLER, GARY S., business educator, author, consultant, administrator; b. N.Y.C., June 8, 1942; s. Alexander and Laura D.; m. Claudia Offman, Mar. 19, 1970; 1 child, Derek Carter. BSc, NYU, 1966; MSc, Rensselaer Poly., 1967; PhD, CUNY, 1973. Asst., assoc. prof. bus. Fla. Internat. U., Miami, 1971-78, assoc. dean coll. bus., 1971-79, prof. bus., 1979—, chmn. mgmt. and internat. bus. dept., 1992-97; cons. and corp. dir.; pres. Relsed Pub. Co., Inc., 1979—; columnist Miami Herald, 1979-91. Author: Human Behavior--Improving Performance at Work, 1980, Organization and Management, 1982, Applied Human Relations, 1983, Improving Productivity at Work, 1983, Management Fundamentals, 1985, Organization Theory, 1986, Human Resource Management, 7th edit., 1996 (also Spanish, Chinese, Indonesian, Russian, and internat. edit.), Winning Commitment, 1994, Managing Organizations in an Era of Change, 1995, Management: Leading People and Organizations in the 21st Century, 1998, Essentials of Human Resource Management, 1999; co-author: Introduction to Business, 7th edit., 1994; contbr. articles to profl. jours. Mem. Acad. Mgmt., Authors Guild. Office: Fla Internat U Coll of Bus Tamiami Trail Miami FL 33199-0001

DESSYPRIS, EMMANUEL NICHOLAS, hematologist-oncologist; b. Athens, Nov. 10, 1946; m. Chryssie Maria Cassiotis, Sept. 6, 1973; children: Margaret, Nicholas. MD with highest honors, Athens U. Sch. Medicine, 1970. Diplomate Am. Bd. Internal Medicine, Am. Bd. Hematology, Am. Bd. Oncology. Resident PG I & II dept. medicine and divsn. rheumatology Athens Naval and Vets. Hosp., 1971-73; resident PG III, 1st med. divsn. U. Thesalonica Affiliated Svc., E. Venizelos Meml. Hosp., Crete, Greece, 1973-74; resident Dept. Medicine, Yale U. Affiliated Svcs. St. Mary's Hosp., Waterbury, Conn., 1975-77; fellow in hematology Vanderbilt U Hosp. and VA Med. Ctr., Nashville, 1977-79; NIH rsch. fellow divsn. hematology, clin. fellow Vanderbilt U., 1979-80, instr. of medicine, 1980-81, asst. prof. medicine to assoc. prof., 1981-92; assoc. investigator to rsch. assoc. VA Med Ctr., Nashville, 1980-85, staff physician sects. of oncology and hematology, 1985-88, clin. investigator sects. of hematology and oncology, 1988-92; prof. medicine Med. Coll. Va., Richmond, 1992—, acting chmn. hematology, oncology, 1997—; chief hematology/oncology sect. McGuire Va. Med. Ctr., Richmond, 1992—; adv. com. Clin. Rsch. Ctr., 1985-88; interviewer Admission com. Sch. of Medicine, 1985—; mem. grad. med. edn. com., 1986-88; adv. coun. Dean's Faculty, 1987-88; mem. health scis. sect. Univ. IRB/CPHS, 1987-88, chmn. 1988-91; cons. to rev. br. NIH, NHLBI, 1991, cons. to spl. com. for clin. trials and tng. rev. sect. 1990; ad hoc Hematology Merit Rev. Bd. VA Med. Rsch. Svc., 1990. Editl. reviewer New Eng. Jour. Medicine, Annals of Internal Medicine, Blood, British Jour. of Haematology, Exptl. Hematology, Cancer Rsch., Cancer Treatment Reports, Jour. Lab. and Clin. Medicine, So. Med. Jour., Am. Jour. Med. Scis., Kidney Internat.; author: Synopsis of Internal Medicine, 1970, Pure Red Cell Aplasia, 1989; contbr. chpts. to book and numerous articles to profl. jours. Grantee VA Career Devel. award, 1980-82, 82-85, 91-94, 88-93. Fellow ACP; mem. AAAS, Am. Soc. Hematology, Am. Soc. Clin. Oncology, Internat. Soc. Exptl. Hematology, Am. Fedn. for clin. Rsch., Soc. for Exptl. Biology and Medicine, So. Soc. for Clin. Investigation, N.Y. Acad. Scis., Hellenic Soc. of Hematology. Office: McGuire VA Med Ctr Heatology/Oncology 111K 1201 Broad Rock Blvd Richmond VA 23249-0001

D'ESTE, MARY ERNESTINE, investment group executive; b. Chgo., Apr. 1, 1941; d. Ernest Gregory and Mary (Turcich) D'E. Student, Mundelein Coll., 1958-61. Sec. MMM, Bedford Park, Ill., 1961-69, Michael Reese Med. Ctr., Chgo., 1969-73; adminstrv. asst. Thomas Jefferson U., Phila., 1973-85, divisional adminstr., 1985-86; adminstr. dept. cardiothoracic surgery Hahnemann U., Phila., 1986-94, Med. Coll. Pa.-Hahnemann U. Hosps., Phila., 1994-96; exec. adminstr., bus. mgr. dept. cardiothoracic surgery Allegheny U. Hosps., 1997-98; v.p. CTS Cardiac & Thoracic Surgeons PC, Phila., 1986-98; adminstrv. coord. Scharf Investment Group, Phila., 1998—. V.p. archtl. review com. GTV Homeowners Assn., Marlton, N.J., 1979-85. Mem. Med. Group Mgmt. Assn., Am. Assn. Notaries, NAFE. Roman Catholic. Avocations: gardening, cooking, reading, needlepoint. Office: Scharf Investment Group 100 S Broad St 19th Fl Philadelphia PA 19110

DESTITO, ROANN M., state legislator; b. Jan. 15, 1956. BS, Le Moyne Coll. Assemblywoman dist. 116 N.Y. State Assembly. Mem. NOW, Bus. & Profl. Women. Office: NY State Assembly Rm 704 Legis Office Bldg State Capitol Albany NY 12248*

DESTLER, DAVE M., publisher, editor, journalist; b. Buffalo, Sept. 14, 1954. BA, Calif. State U., Northridge, 1979. Owner 2D Studio, Canoga Park, Calif., 1978-85, 2D Publishing, Canoga Park, 1985—. Publisher, editor (mags.) British Car Mag., 1985-96, Jr. Baseball, 1996—. Office: 2D Pub PO Box 9099 Canoga Park CA 91309-0099

DESVIGNES-KENDRICK, MARY, municipal official; m. Ernest A. Kendrick; children: Aziza, Jelani, Shomari. BA, NYU, 1974; MD, Meharry Med. Coll., 1978; MPH, U. Tex., 1988. Diplomate Nat. Bd. Med. Examiners, Am. Bd. Pediatrics. Intern Baylor Coll. Medicine Affiliated Hosps., Houston, 1978; resident in pediatrics Baylor Coll. Medicine Affiliated Hosps., 1979-81, staff pediatrician Martin Luther King Cmty. Clinic, 1982-86, instr. Dept. Cmty. Medicine, 1982-84, asst. prof. Dept. Cmty. Medicine, 1984-86; med. dir. Northside Health Ctr. City of Houston Dept. Health and Human Svcs., 1986-88, asst. dir. Personal Health Svcs., 1990-92, interim dir., 1992, dir., 1992—; adj. faculty U. Tex. Sch. Pub. Health, Houston, 1993—; chair City of Houston Dept. Health and Human Svcs. Com. for the Protection of Human Subjects, 1990-91, Exec. Quality Assurance Com., 1990-91; mem. Baylor Coll. of Medicine Affiliated Hosps. Affirmative Action Com., 1985-86, Com. on Adolescent Health Issues, 1985-86. Mem. Class XI Am. Leadership Forum, 1993, Leadership Tex. Class of 1991, adv. bd. Tex. Nurses Assn. Dist. 9, 1993, adv. bd. U. Houston Health Law and Policy Inst., 1992—, bd. dirs. Leadership Tex. Alumnae Assn., 1992-94, adv. bd. Greater HoAIDS Alliance, 1992, chair Houston Area Immunization Task Force, 1992, mem. adv. bd. Houston Assn. for Communication Disorders, 1991, mem. project adv. group U. Tex. Health Sci. Ctr. at Houston Sch. Pub. Health, 1991, bd. dirs. Children at Risk, 1991, Am. Lung Assn. Tuberculosis Ctrl., 1990-91, adv. bd. United Way of Tex. Houston/Gulf Coast chpt., 1993—, adv. bd. CORE, U. Houston Grad. Sch. Social Work, 1993—. Fellow Am. Acad. Pediatrics; mem. APHA (Milton and Ruth Roemer prize 1997), Nat. Med. Assn., Am. Coll. Physician Execs., Tex. Pediatric Soc., Nat. Forum Black Pub. Adminstrs. (cert. for Commitment to Excellence and Svc. to the Pub. 1993), Nat. Assn. County and City Health Officials (pres. 1997), Forum Club of Houston, Rotary. Office: Dept Health and Human Svcs City of Houston 8000 N Stadium Dr Houston TX 77054-1823*

DE SYON, GUILLAUME PAUL SAM, history educator; b. Paris, Mar. 2, 1966; came to U.S., 1994; s. Michel and Joelle Suzanne Juliette (Carpano) de S.; m. Maria Dee Mitchell, Aug. 27, 1994. BA, Tufts U., 1987; MA, George Washington U., 1989; PhD, Boston U., 1994. Contbg. editor Einstein Papers Project, Boston, 1992-94; asst. prof. history Albright Coll., Reading, pa., 1995—; coord. Johnson Ctr. for Interdisciplinary Studies, Reading, 1997-98. Contbg. editor: Collected Papers of Albert Einstein Vol. 8: Correspondence 1914-1918, 1998. With Swiss Air Force, 1984. Mem. Royal Aeronautical Soc., Soc. for the History of Tech., Am. Hist. Assn. Office: Albright Coll 13th & Bern Sts Reading PA 19612-5234

DE TABOAS, HILDA RIVERA, occupational health nurse; b. Coamo, P.R., Dec. 19, 1919; d. Dàmaso and Ramona (Zayas) Rivera; m. Julio Oscar Taboas; children: Julio Oscar, Alberto Jose, Carlos E. Cert., Bishop Willinger Sch. Nursing, 1941, Presbyn. Hosp., 1962, Met. Hosp., 1969, Coutinuos Edn., 1980. RN., P.R. RN U.S. Vet. Hosp., San Juan, P.R.; coronary care nurse Presbyn. Hosp., San Juan, P.R.; pvt. nurse Directory Nurses, San Juan, P.R.; first aid nurse Airport Internat. Islavarda, San Juan, P.R. Contbr. articles to profl. jours. Mem. Colegio Profesionales de Enfarmaria de P.R. Home: Purus 1687 Rp Hts San Juan PR 00926

DE TAKACSY, NICHOLAS BENEDICT, physicist, educator; b. Budapest, Hungary, Feb. 24, 1939; s. Constantin and Katalin (Jellenz) de T.; m.

Mickey Mary Dawson, June 16, 1962; children: Victoria, Christine, Frederica. B.Sc., Loyola Coll., Montreal, Que., Can., 1959; M.Sc., U. Montreal, 1963; Ph.D., McGill U., 1966. Rsch. assoc. Calif. Inst. Tech., Pasadena, 1966-67; asst. prof. Loyola Coll., Montreal, Montreal, 1967-68; mem. faculty McGill U., Montreal, 1968—, prof. physics, 1978—, chmn. dept., 1979-82, assoc. dean of sci., 1993-94, 95-98, acting dean sci., 1994-95, assoc. vice prin. acad., 1998—. Mem. Can. Assn. Physicists, Am. Phys. Soc. Roman Catholic. Office: 3600 University St Montreal PQ Canada H3A 2T8

DETELS, ROGER, epidemiologist, physician, former university dean; b. Bklyn., Oct. 14, 1936; s. Martin P. and Mary J. (Crooker) D.; m. Mary M. Doud, Sept. 14, 1963; children: Martin, Edward. BA, Harvard U., 1958; MD, NYU, 1962; MS in Preventive Medicine, U. Wash., 1966. Diplomate Am. Bd. Preventive Medicine. Intern U. Calif. Gen. Hosp., San Francisco, 1962-63; resident U. Wash., Seattle, 1963-66; med. officer, epidemiologist Nat. Inst. Neurol. Diseases, Bethesda, Md., 1969-71; assoc. prof. epidemiology Sch. Pub. Health UCLA, 1971-73, prof. Sch. Pub. Health, 1973—, dean, 1980-85, head div. epidemiology Sch. Pub. Health, 1972-80; guest lectr. various univs., profl. confs. and med. orgns., 1969—; sci. adv. com. Am. Found AIDS Rsch.; dir. UCLA/Fogarty AIDS Internat. Tng. & Rsch. Program, 1988—, Tng. Program in Epidemiology of HIV/AIDS, 1995—; cons. Ministries of Health, Thailand, Myanmar, The Philippines, 1989, Global Program on AIDS, 1995, Singapore, 1996, WHO, 1996, U.S. Agy. Internat. Devel., 1998, 99, Cambodia, 1998, 99, St. Thomas Med. Sch., London, 1993-94, Myanmar, 1997; mem. Nat. Adv. Environ. Health Scis. Coun., 1990-94; com. to study transmission of HIV through blood products Inst. Medicine, 1994-95. Editor: Oxford Textbook of Public Health, 1985, 2d edit. 1991, 3d edit., 1996; contbr. articles to profl. jours. Lt. comdr. M.C. USN, 1966-69. Grantee in field. Fellow AAAS, Am. Coll. Preventive Medicine, Am. Coll. Epidemiology (coun. 1987-89), Faculty Pub. Health Medicine Royal Coll. Physicians of U.K. (hon.); mem. Am. Epidemiol. Soc., Soc. Epidemiologic Rsch. (pres. 1977-78), Assn. Tchrs. Preventive Medicine (chmn. essay com. 1969-75), Am. Pub. Health Assn., Am. Assn. Cancer Edn. (membership com. 1978-85), Internat. Epidemiol. Assn. (exec. com. 1984—, treas. 1984-90, pres. 1990-93), Assn. Schs. Pub. Health (sec.-treas. 1980-85), Sigma Xi, Delta Omega. Fax: 310-206-6039. E-mail: detels@admin.ph.ucla.edu. Office: UCLA Sch Public Health Los Angeles CA 90095-1772

DETERMAN, JOHN DAVID, lawyer; b. Mitchell, S.D., Feb. 18, 1933; s. Alred John and Olive Gertrude (Lovinger) D.; m. Gloria Esther Rivas, Nov. 15, 1980; children by previous marriage: James Taylor, Mark Sterling. B.Engring. in Elec. Engring. cum laude, U. So. Calif., 1955; LL.D. magna cum laude, UCLA, 1961. Electronics engr. Hughes Aircraft Co., L.A., 1955-60; sr. ptnr. Tuttle & Taylor, Inc., L.A., 1961-86; gen. counsel Provena Foods Inc., Chino, Calif., 1986-92, CEO, 1992-98, chmn. bd., 1992—, also bd. dirs.; founder Carl D. Spaeth Scholarship Fund, Stanford U. Law Sch., 1972; mem. nat. panel arbitrators Am. Arbitration Assn., L.A., 1962—, mem. adv. coun., 1982—, mem. nat. panel of mediators, 1986—, mem. large complex case panel of arbitrators, 1993—. Mem. Am. Coll. Constrn. Arbitrators (charter 1982—), Order of Coif, Eta Kappa Nu, Tau Beta Pi. Home: 25 S El Molino St Alhambra CA 91801-4102 Office: Provena Foods Inc 5010 Eucalyptus Ave Chino CA 91710-9216 *Tolerate even intolerance but never cruelty.*

DETERS, JAMES RAYMOND, retired manufacturing and services company executive; b. Cin., June 18, 1937; s. Joseph Gerard and Elsie Marie (Murphy) D.; m. Jacklyne Florence Eaton, Feb. 20, 1960; children—James, Deborah. B.S.C., Ohio U., 1959; M.B.A., Ohio State U., 1963. Acctg. mgr. Procter & Gamble Co., Cin., 1963-66; asst. controller Boise Cascade Corp., Mpls., 1967; controller Lindsay div. TransUnion Corp., Mpls., 1968-69; group controller Borg-Warner Corp., Chgo., 1970-72; asst. corp. controller Borg-Warner Corp., 1973-75, corp. controller, 1975-82, v.p. human resources, 1982-85, v.p., chief fin. officer, 1985-87; sr. v.p., chief adminstrv. officer Material Scis. Corp., 1988-91; exec. in residence Purdue U., 1976; dir. Material Scis. Corp.; edn. cons. Abbott Labs., 1995—. Pres. Kidney Found. Ill., 1974-77; bd. dirs. Chgo. Youth Ctrs., 1974-76; trustee Grant Hosp., Chgo., 1978-85, Barat Coll., Lake Forest, Ill., 1978-82; chmn. Lake Forest Grad. Sch. Mgmt., 1985-87, prof., 1988—; adv. bd. U. Ill., 1983-90; mem. Leadership Coun. for Chgo. Open Communities, 1983-88. Capt. AUS, 1960-63. Mem. Fin. Execs. Inst., Ill. C. of C. (trustee 1980-82), Union League, Onwentsia Country Club, Delta Tau Delta. Republican. Roman Catholic. Home: 1300 Loch Ln Lake Forest IL 60045-3348

DETERT, MIRIAM ANNE, chemical analyst; b. San Diego, Calif., Sept. 16, 1925; d. George Bernard and Margaret Theresa Zita (Lohre) D. BS, Dominican Coll., San Rafael, Calif., 1947. Chem. analyst Shell Devel. Co., Emeryville, Calif., 1947-72, Houston, 1972-86. Photo participant Wax Rsch.: Quest, 1981; contbr. poetry to books including The National Library of Poetry - Best Poems of the 90's, Spirit of the Age, The Nightfall of Diamonds. Vol. Falkirk Cultural Ctr., San Rafael, 1987-91, M.D. Anderson Tumor Inst., Houston, 1978-86, Rep. Party, San Rafael, 1990, 94; mem. Jewish Comm. Ctr. Recipient Disting. Alumni award Dominican Coll., 1994. Mem. Marin Geneal. Soc. Republican. Roman Catholic. Avocations: etching, oil painting, geneal. rsch. on Detert name, swimming (Sr. Olympic Swimming award 1991).

DETGEN, AMY LYNN, copywriter; b. Summit, N.J., Nov. 9, 1970; d. Donald Charles Detgen and Susan Detgen Feldmann. BA in English and Spanish, Muhlenberg Coll., 1992; postgrad., U. N.H., 1998—. Publicity asst. Addison-Wesley Book Pub., N.Y.C., 1993-95; copywriter Farago Advt., N.Y.C., 1995-98; MPA dept. rep. U. N.H. Grad. Sch. Bd., Durham, 1998-99. Vol. tutor Hoboken (N.J.) Tutoring, 1997-98. Mem. ASPA. Democrat. Home: 113 State Rd Eliot ME 03903

DETHERO, J. HAMBRIGHT, banker; b. Chattanooga, Jan. 2, 1932; s. Jacob Hambright and Rosalie Frances (Gasser) D.; m. Charlotte Nixon Lee, Sept. 19, 1959; children: Dinah Lee, Charles Drew. BS in Bus. Adminstrn., U. Fla., 1953; BFT, Am. Grad. Sch. Internat. Mgmt., Phoenix, 1958. With Citibank, N.Y.C., P.R., Caracas, Venezuela, San Francisco, 1958-69; mgr. First Nat. City Bank (Internat.), San Francisco, until 1969; v.p. internat. div. Crocker Nat. Bank, San Francisco, 1969-75; sr. v.p. London, 1976-80, San Francisco, 1980-84; sr. v.p. Bank America World Trade Corp., San Francisco, 1984-85; 1st v.p. Security Pacific Nat. Bank, Los Angeles, 1986-87; regional mgr. Calif. Export Fin. Office, Calif. State World Trade Commn., San Francisco, 1988-93; sr. v.p. Comml. Bank of San Francisco, 1994-98; internat. bus. cons., instr., 1998—; adj. prof. Grad. Sch. Bus., St. Mary's Coll., Moraga, Calif., 1988—, John F. Kennedy U., Walnut Creek, Calif., 1997—. Author: Exporting Guide for California, 1993. Bd. dirs. Calif. Coun. Internat. Trade, 1972-77, 82-98, pres., 1974-76; trustee World Affairs Coun. No. Calif., 1971-77, 88-93; chmn. dist. Export Coun. No. Calif., 1983-93; dir. Internat. Diplomacy Coun., San Francisco, 1995—, treas., 1997—. Recipient Export Citizen of the Year award No. Calif. Export Coun./San Francisco Bus. Times, 1996. Home and Office: 694 Old Jonas Hill Rd Lafayette CA 94549-5214

DETHLOFF, HENRY CLAY, history educator; b. New Orleans, Aug. 10, 1934; s. Carl Curt and Camelia (Jordan) D.; m. Myrtle Anne Elliott, Aug. 27, 1961; children: Clay, Carl. B.A., U. Tex., Austin, 1956; M.A., Northwestern State U., Natchitoches, La., 1960; Ph.D., U. Mo., Columbia, 1964. Instr., then asst. prof. history U. Southwestern La., 1962-68; asso. prof. U. So. La., 1966-69; mem. faculty Tex. A&M U., 1969—, prof. history, 1975—, chmn. dept., 1980-85; pres. Intaglio, Inc. Author: Our Louisiana Legacy, 1968, The Centennial History of Texas A&M University, 1876-1976, 1975, Americans and Free Enterprise, 1979, A History of American Business, 1983, A History of the American Rice Industry 1685-1985, 1988, Suddenly, Tomorrow Came: A History of Johnson Space Ctr., 1993, The U.S. and the Global Economy, 1945-1995, 1997; co-author: A History of American Business, 1983, Timeless Heritage, A History of the Forest Service in the Southwest, 1988, Pattillo Higgins and the Search for Texas Oil, 1989, A Special Kind of Doctor: A History of Veterinary Medicine in Texas, 1991, Lousiana: A Study in Diversity, 1998; co-editor: American Business History: Case Studies, 1987. Served to lt. (j.g.) USNR, 1956-58. Mem. Agrl. History Assn., Econ. History Assn., So. Hist. Assn., Tex. Hist. Assn., La. Hist. Assn., Phi Kappa Phi, Phi Alpha Theta, Sigma Chi. Republican. Methodist. Home: 8709 Bent Tree Dr College Station TX 77845-5561 Office: Tex A&M U Dept History College Station TX 77843

DETHOMASIS, BROTHER LOUIS, college president; b. Bklyn., Oct. 6, 1940; s. Costantino and Anna (Maggio) DeT. B.S. in Fgn. Service, Georgetown U., 1963; Ph.D., Union Grad. Sch., 1982. Tchr. LaSalle Acad., Providence, 1969-71; assoc. headmaster LaSalle Mil. Acad., Oakdale, N.Y., 1971-73, pres., 1976-84; v.p. for fin. The Christian Brothers, Narragansett, R.I., 1973-76; pres. St. Mary's U., Winona, Minn., 1984—. Author: The Finance of Education, 1978; Investing With Options, 1981; Social Justice, 1982; My Father's Business, 1984. Recipient Pres.'s medal for Christian edn., St. John's Coll. High Sch., 1985, Christian Edn. award Franz W. Sichel Found., 1974. Roman Catholic. Home and Office: 700 Terrace Hts Apt 30 Winona MN 55987-1321*

DETIENNE, DARCY A., university administrator. BS in bus. Adminstrn., Eastern Mont. Coll., Billings, 1986; MS in Counseling and Human Devel., Moorhead (Minn.) State U., 1994. Program advisor Wichita (Kans.) State U., 1988-92; program dir. Idaho State U., Pocatello, 1992—. Mem. Nat. Assn. for Campus Activities (nat. conv. com. 1994-96, registration coord. Pacific N.W. region 1997-98). Office: Idaho State U Box 8118 8th Ave and Humboldt Pocatello ID 83209

DETJEN, ANN L., retired legal assistant; b. Ashland, Ky., Apr. 30, 1960; d. William Bennett and Elizabeth Goodman (Harrell) Lowe; m. John Carlyle Detjen, Aug. 8, 1981 (div. Sept. 1987); 1 child, Nicholas Michael Detjen. Exec. sec. Ashland (Ky.) Oil, Inc., 1979-81, legal sec., 1981-85; legal sec. Brown, Todd & Heyburn, Lexington, Ky., 1985-89, Landrum & Shouse, Lexington, Ky., 1989-90; office mgr., legal asst., legal sec. Brooks, Coffman & Fitzpatrick, Lexington, Ky., 1990; legal sec., legal asst. Gallion, Baker & Bray, Lexington, Ky., 1990-92, Dunn, Franklin & Riley, Lexington, Ky., 1992-94; disabled, ret., 1994—; prodr. orig. women's music CD; start-up bookselling bus. Author poetry. Democrat. Avocations: freelance writing, reading. Home: 1125 Centurian Rd Lexington KY 40517-3165

DETJEN, DAVID WHEELER, lawyer; b. St. Louis, Jan. 25, 1948; s. Don Wheeler and Shirley (Pence) D.; m. Barbara Louise Morgan, Jan. 6, 1973; children: Andrea Marlene, Erika Alexandra. *David Detjen is 3rd generation of lawyers in the Detjen family to represent European and American clients since his great-grandfather, Gustav Detjen, who emigrated to the U.S. from Germany in 1890 and became a lawyer. Gustav (who, at the end of his career, received the Bundesverdienstkreuz from the German government) and his son, C. Wheeler Detjen, carried on general law practice as Detjen and Detjen in St. Louis for nearly 50 years, handling matters for U.S. and European clients and also for German and Swiss consulates there, while David Detjen practices law in NYC, representing primarily clients from Germany and other European countries doing business in the U.S.* AB magna cum laude, Washington U., 1970, JD, 1973; postgrad., Eberhard-Karls-Universitaet, Tuebingen, Fed. Republic of Germany, 1969-70. Bar: Mo. 1973, U.S. Supreme Ct. 1976, U.S. Ct. Appeals (8th cir.) 1976, N.Y. 1981. Law clk. to chief judge U.S. Ct. Appeals (8th cir.), St. Louis, 1973-75; assoc. Lewis, Rice, Tucker, Allen & Chubb, St. Louis, 1975-80; assoc. Walter, Conston, Alexander & Green, P.C., N.Y.C., 1980-83, ptnr., 1983—; affiliate office resident Walter, Conston, Alexander & Green, P.C., Bangkok, 1991-92; lectr. in law Washington U., St. Louis, 1975-80. Author: Distributorship Agreements in the U.S., 1983, 2d edit., 1989, The Germans in Missouri, 1900-1918: Prohibition, Neutrality and Assimilation, 1985, Licensing Technology and Trademarks in the United States, 1988, 2d edit., 1997, Establishing a United States Joint Venture with a Foreign Partner, 1988, 3d edit., 1993, United States Joint Ventures with International Partners, 1999; bd. dirs. Felix Schoeller Tech. Papers Inc., 1998—. Mem. Wash. U. Law Sch. Nat. Coun., 1989—; sec. German Forum, N.Y.C., 1988—, bd. dirs. 1995—; mem. St. Louis County Rep Cen. Com., 1976-83, Am. Coun. on Germany; co-pres. King-Merritt Comty. Assn., Greenwich, Conn., 1997—; trustee Am. Inst. Contemporary German Studies at Johns Hopkins U., 1999—. Recipient Disting. Alumnus award Law Sch. Wash. U., 1998. Mem. ABA, N.Y. State Bar Assn. (exec. editor Internat. Law Practicum 1988—, mem. exec. com. internat. law and practice sect. 1999—), Assn. Bar City N.Y., German Am. Law Assn., German am. Round Table, William G. Eliot Soc. of Washington U. (N.Y. chmn. 1993—), Deutscher Verein Club N.Y.C. (bd. dirs. 1994-97, 99—), Order of Coif, Delta Phi Alpha. Presbyterian. Home: 35 Stonehedge Dr S Greenwich CT 06831-3220 Office: Walter Conston Alexander & Green 90 Park Ave Fl 14 New York NY 10016-1387

DETLEFSEN, WILLIAM DAVID, JR., chemicals executive; b. Scottsbluff, Nebr., Nov. 14, 1946; s. William David Jr. and Janette Fern (Tuttle) D.; m. Melba Kay Cunningham, Nov. 12, 1982; children: Michael David, Erika Lee, Whitney Anne. BS in Forestry, U. Idaho, 1970; PhD in Chemistry, U. Oreg., 1993. Chemist, applications technologist Borden, Adhesives and Resins, Springfield, Oreg., 1972-76, coord. tech. svc., 1976-78, supr. phenolic resins devel., 1983-87, mgr. R & D, 1987-94; dir. R & D, resins, adhesives specialties, 1994—; sr. devel. chemist Ga.-Pacific Resins, Crossett, Ark., 1978-83. Contbr. articles to profl. jours. 1st. lt. U.S. Army, 1970-72, Germany. Mem. AAAS, Am. Chem. Soc., Forest Products Rsch. Soc. Republican. Achievements include patents in field; co-discoverer first commercially feasible resins for gluing high moisture veneers into phenolic-bonded plywood. Office: Borden Chem Inc Adhesives & Resins Divsn 610 S 2nd St Springfield OR 97477-5398

DETMAR-PINES, GINA LOUISE, business strategy and policy educator; b. S.I., N.Y., May 3, 1949; d. Joseph and Grace Vivian (Brown) Sargente; m. Michael B. Pines, Sept. 11, 1988; 1 child, Drue Joseph Pines. BS in Edn., Wagner Coll., 1971, MS, 1972; MA in Urban Affairs and Policy Analysis, New Sch. for Social Rsch., 1987; MPhil, CUNY, 1995; PhD in Bus./Orgn. and Policy Studies, CUNY-Baruch Coll., 1996. Cert. adminstr. and supr., sch. dist. adminstr. Tchr. pub. schs. N.Y.C., 1971-82; coord. spl. projects, pub. affairs N.Y.C. Bd. Edn., 1982, spl. asst. to exec. dir. pupil svcs., 1983, asst. to chancellor, 1983-84, dir. Tchr. Summer Bus. Industry Program, 1984-93; prof. pub. adminstrn. and mgmt. John Jay Coll. Criminal Justice CUNY, 1992-93; vis. prof. Rensselaer at Hartford, 1993-98, Fairfield U., 1998—; liaison for the Tech. Industry Program, N.Y.C. Partnership, 1985-93. Mem. com. to re-elect Borough pres. Lamberti, S.I., 1985-86; chairperson Crystal Ball event Greater Hartford Easter Seals Rehab. Ctr., 1994, trustee, 1994—; bd. dirs. Hartford Symphony, com. mem. 50th Anniversary Gala, 1993. Mayor's scholar City of N.Y., 1984-96. Mem. ASPA, Fgn. Lang. Instrs. Assn., Strategic Mgmt. Soc., Acad. Mgmt., U.S. Seaplane Pilot's Assn., Internat. Orgn. for Lic. Women Pilots, Jr. League of Hartford, Hartford Task Force on Healthy Families, Chinese-Am. Soc., Am. Mgmt. Soc., Ea. Acad. Mgmt., Cambridge Flying Group Club. Episcopalian. Avocations: flying, scuba diving, skiing. Office: Fairfield U N Benson Rd Fairfield CT 06134

DETMER, DON EUGENE, health management and policy researcher, medical educator, surgeon; b. Winfield, Kans., Feb. 3, 1939; s. Lawrence Oscar and Esther Beulah (McCormick) D.; m. Mary Helen McFerson, Aug. 26, 1961; children: Mary Catherine, Emily Anne. Student, U. Kans., 1957-59, 60-61, U. Durham, 1959-60; MD, U. Kans., Kansas City, 1965. Intern, then resident in surgery Johns Hopkins U., Balt., 1965-67; clin. assoc. surg. br. Nat. Heart Inst. NIH, Bethesda, Md., 1967-69; resident in surgery Duke U., Durham, N.C., 1969-72; Global Cmty. Health fellow Dept. HEW, Inst. Medicine/NAS, Washington, 1972-73; prof. preventive medicine and surgery U. Wis., Madison, 1973-84; v.p. health scis., prof. surgery and med. info. U. Utah, Salt Lake City, 1984-88; univ. prof. health policy, prof. surgery and health evaluation scis. U. Va., Charlottesville, 1988-93, v.p., provost for health scis., 1988-96, sr. v.p., 1996-98, Louise Nurancy prof. health scis. policy, 1996-99, prof. emeritus, prof. med. edn., 1999—; Dennis Gillings prof. health mgmt. Cambridge U., 1999—; cons., Japan, China, Australasian Coll. Surgeons, U. Algeria, Robert Wood Johnson Found., Princeton, N.J.; bd. dirs. China Med. Bd. N.Y., Inc., NAS Inst. Medicine, Washington, chmn. bd. healthcare svcs., 1994—; chmn. nat. com. vital health stats. HHS, Washington, 1996-99; chair Blue Ridge Acad. Health Group, 1997—; regent Nat. Libr. Medicine, NIH, Bethesda, 1987-91; bd. dirs., developer adminstrv. medicine U. Wis. Contbr. articles on compartment syndromes, shin splints, health svcs. rsch. and policy to profl. jours. Chmn. pub. svc. com. bd. dirs. United Way, Salt Lake City, 1986-88, Charlottesville, Va., 1992-97; pres. Peace Luth. Ch., 1996-99. With USPHS, 1967-69, 72-73. Global Community Health fellow HEW, 1972-73. Fellow ACS (vice chmn. com. allied health pers. 1989-90, chmn. 1990-94, internat. health com. 1996—), Am. Coll. Sports Medicine, Am. Coll. Med. Info., Assn. Health Svcs. Rsch.; mem. AAAS, Am. Med. Informatics Assn. (bd. dirs. 1996-98), Assn. Acad. Health Ctrs. (bd. dirs. 1996-98), Inst. of Medicine of NAS, Soc. Med. Adminstrs. (treas. 1997—), Am. Acad. Physician Assts. (hon.), Am. Hosp. Assn. (chmn. coun. hosp. med. staffs 1984-87), Cosmos Club Washington, Alpha Omega Alpha. Lutheran. Avocations: fly fishing, painting, needlework. Home: 5245 Browns Gap Tpke Crozet VA 22932-1613 Office: Cambridge U, Judge Inst Mgmt Studies, Cambridge CB2 1AG, England

DETOLLA, LOUIS JAMES, research veterinarian; b. Phila., Nov. 18, 1947; s. Louis James and Linda (Liberatore) DeT.; m. Setsu Nakai, June 28, 1975; 1 child: Leonardo Nakai. BA, Temple U., 1970; MS, Rutgers U., 1974, PhD, 1978; VMD, U. Pa., 1982. Instr. biology Rutgers U., New Brunswick, N.J., 1975-78, teaching asst. in immunology, endocrinology, and genetics, 1973-78, postdoctoral fellow, 1978; NSF fellow U. Pa., Phila., 1979-82; rsch. veterinarian Sloan-Kettering Inst., N.Y.C., 1982-83; veterinarian Fox Chase Cancer Ctr., Phila., 1983-85; rsch. veterinarian Merck, Sharp & Dohme Labs., Rahway, N.J., 1985-88; dir. comparative medicine, chief vet. resources, assoc. prof. medicine pathology and comparative medicine U. Md. Sch. Medicine, vet. med. officer Balt. VA Med. Ctr., 1988—, sci. cons. Indicon, Inc., New Haven, 1983-85; bd. gov.'s, chmn. animal policy com. Nat. Aquarium, Balt., 1993—. Contbr. articles to profl. jours. Nat. Needs Manpower fellow NSF, 1980; NIH fellow in immunobiology, 1982; NIH grantee 1990—, Dept. of Def., 1995—; recipient Nat. Rsch. Svc. award NIH, 1983. Mem. AAAS, AVMA, Assn. Primate Veterinarians, Am. Soc. Lab. Animal Practitioners, Am. Soc. Zoologists, N.J. Acad. Scis., Am. Coll. Lab. Animal Medicine (bd. cert.), Phi Zeta. Office: U Maryland MSTF Bldg Rm G-100 10 S Pine St Baltimore MD 21201-1116

DE TOMASO, ERNEST PAT, general building contractor, developer; b. Pescara, Italy, July 27, 1915; s. Anthony and Frances Mary (Tarsa) DeT.; m. Lida Janet Sherlock, June 30, 1940; children: Ernest Patrick, John Anthony. Student, San Bernardino Valley Coll., 1961, Shabbarazzi Sch. Music, Rochester, N.Y., 1932. Musician Pat Thomas and His Orch., Rochester, 1931-37; baker Thrifty Drug Stores, L.A., 1938-46; ptnr. Anthony and Ernest P. DeTomaso Bldg. Contractors, Fontana, Calif., 1946-50; bldg. contractor Ernest P. DeTomaso Bldg. Contractor-Developer, Fontana, 1950-79; owner, lessor Towne Plaza Shopping Ctr., Fontana, 1987—; bd. dirs., v.p. Marygold Mut. Water Co., Bloomington, Calif. Mem. Greater Fontana United Fund, 1966-73, pres., 1973; mem. Planning Commn., Fontana, 1968-80, pres., 1970-71; founder, bd. dirs. Fontana Polit. Action Coalition, 1993—; trustee Eastern Star Homes of Calif., 1989-92. Recipient Devoted and Invaluable Svcs. award C. of C., Fontana, 1980, Outstanding Achievment award Greater Fontana United Fund, 1980, Svcs. Rendered award City of Fontana, 1981. Mem. Masons (Hiram award), Rotary, Order Eastern Star (worthy patron, grand officer, Exceptional Svc. award 1985). Republican. Avocations: music, fishing, travel. Home: 17155 Manzanita Dr Fontana CA 92335-5850

DE TONNANCOUR, PAUL ROGER GODEFROY, library administrator; b. Fall River, Mass., May 22, 1926; s. R. Godefroy and Emilie (St. Germain) de T.; m. Mary E. Fenno, Apr. 9, 1955; children—Paul Godefroy, Camille Marie. A.B. cum laude, Providence Coll., 1952; M.S., Simmons Coll., 1953; postgrad., Western Res. U., U. So. Cal. Asst. librarian Enoch Pratt Library, Balt., 1953-54; chief librarian, tech. analyst Armco Steel Corp., Balt., 1954-56; dir. rsch. library Gen. Dynamics (Ft. Worth div.), 1956—, dir. tech. information programs, 1964-87, with Proposal Devel. Ctr., 1987—; cons. MLA, U.S. Office Edn. on sci. info. pers.; John Cotton Dana lectr., 1966. Singer, Ft. Worth Opera Assn. Chorus. Author: The Exploitation of Technical Information, 1966; co-author: Science Information Personnel, 1963; Contbr. articles to profl. jours. Active United Fund and Community Council; mem. exec. com. Big Bros. Tarrant County.; Trustee Cosmopolitan Internat., 1961-63. Served with USNR, 1943-46. Named Boss of Year Am. Bus. Women's Assn., 1965. Mem. ALA, AAAS, Am., Nat. mgmt. assns., Ft. Worth Art Assn., Spl. Libraries Assn., Am. Soc. Information Sci., Delta Epsilon Sigma. Episcopalian. Clubs: Mason, Fort Worth Boat. Home: 6332 Genoa Rd Fort Worth TX 76116-2028 Office: PO Box 748 Fort Worth TX 76101-0748 *Above all, don't take yourself too seriously. Seek wisdom for itself and nurture a sense of humor. Together, they will serve you well.*

DE TORNYAY, RHEBA, nurse, former university dean, educator; b. Petaluma, Calif., Apr. 17, 1926; d. Bernard and Ella Fradkin; m. Rudy de Tornyay, June 4, 1954. Student, U. Calif., Berkeley, 1944-46; diploma, Mt. Zion Hosp. Sch. Nursing, 1949; A.B., San Francisco State U., 1951, M.A., 1954; Ed.D., Stanford U., 1967; Sc.D. (hon.), Ill. Wesleyan U., 1974; LHD (hon.), U. Portland, 1974, Georgetown U., 1994. Mem. faculty San Francisco State U., 1957-67, prof. nursing, 1966-67, chmn. dept., 1959-67; assoc. prof. U. Calif. Sch. Nursing, San Francisco, 1968-71; prof. U. Calif. Sch. Nursing, 1971; dean, prof. Sch. Nursing UCLA, 1971-75; dean emeritus, prof. U. Wash., Seattle, 1986—. Author: Strategies for Teaching nursing, 1971, 3rd edit., 1987, Japanese transl., 1974, Spanish edit., 1986; co-author: (with Heather Young) Choices: Making a Good Move to a Retirement Community, 1996. Trustee Robert Wood Johnson Found. Mem. ANA, Am. Acad. Nursing (charter fellow, pres. 1973-75), Inst. Medicine (governing coun. 1979-81). Home: 4540 8th Ave NE Apt 1001 Seattle WA 98105-4795

DETRE, KATHERINE MARIA, physician; b. Budapest, Hungary, Apr. 28, 1926; came to Can., 1949; d. Ignac and Irene (Lefkovits) Drechsler; m. Thomas P. Detre, Sept. 16, 1956; children: John, Anthony. Student, Pazmany Peter Med. Sch., Budapest, 1945-49; BA, Queens U., Kingston, Ont., Can., 1950, MD, 1952; MPH, Yale U., 1964, DPH, 1967. Rotating intern Kingston Gen. Hosp., Queens Kingston, Ont., 1952-53; resident in internal medicine Queen Mary Vets. Hosp. McGill, Montreal, Que., Can., 1953-56; research assoc. hematology Yale U., New Haven, 1956-60, lectr. in biometry, 1968-74; biostatistician VA Coop. Studies Program, West Haven, Conn., 1967-95; assoc. prof. U. Pitts., 1974-79, prof. epidemiology, 1979—; mem. clin. adv. bd. NIH, Bethesda, Md., 1977-78, mem. epidemiology and disease control com., 1983-87, mem. Fogarty Internat. Ctr. adv. bd., 1994—; mem. rsch. com. B, Nat. Heart, Lung and Blood Inst., Bethesda, 1978-82. Contbr. over 434 articles to profl. jours. Named Woman in Sci. Chatham Coll., 1987; internat. student scholar Queens U., 1949-52. Fellow AAAS (disting. scientist), Am. Coll. Cardiology (hon.), Coun. on Epidemiology (chmn. 1981-83), Am. Coll. Epidemiology; mem. Am. Statis. Assn. (Statistician of Yr. 1993), Biometric Soc. (regional adv. bd. 1993), Soc. Clin. Trials (bd. dirs. 1981-85, program com. 1994-95), Am. Epidemiology Soc. Office: U Pitts 130 Desoto St # A531 Pittsburgh PA 15261-2535*

DETRE, THOMAS, psychiatrist, educator; b. Budapest, Hungary, May 17, 1924; came to U.S., 1953, naturalized, 1958; m. Katherine Maria Drechsler, Sept. 15, 1956; children: John Allan, Antony James. BA, Gymnasium of Piarist Fathers, Kecskemet, Hungary, 1942; postgrad., Horthy Miklos U. and Pazmany Peter U., Hungary, 1945-47; MD, Rome U., 1952. Diplomate: Am. Bd. Psychiatry and Neurology (assoc. examiner). Intern Morrisania City Hosp., N.Y.C., 1953-54; resident in psychiatry Mt. Sinai Hosp., N.Y.C., 1954-55; resident in psychiatry Yale U., 1955-57, chief resident, instr., 1957-58, instr., 1958-59, asst. prof., 1959-62; dir. psychiat. inpatient service Yale-New Haven Hosp., 1960-68, assoc. prof., 1962-70, asst. chief psychiatry div., 1965-68, psychiatrist in chief, 1968-73, prof., 1970-73; prof., chmn. dept. psychiatry U. Pitts., 1973-82, assoc. sr. vice chancellor, 1982-84, disting. svc. prof. health scis., 1982—, disting. prof. psychiatry and neurosci., 1993-98, sr. v.p. health scis., 1984-92, sr. vice chancellor for health scis., 1992-98, pres. med. and health care div., 1986-90, pres. med. ctr., 1990-92; dir. Western Psychiat. Inst. and Clin. Western Psychiat. Inst. and Clin., 1973-94; exec. v.p. internat. and acadademic programs, dir. internat. med. affairs UPMC Health Sys., Pitts., 1998—; mem. Nat. Adv. Mental Health Coun., NIH, 1994-97. Author: (with H.G. Jarecki) Modern Psychiatric Treatment, 1971; contbr. chpts. to books. Fellow Am. Coll. Psychiatrists, Am. Coll. Neuropsychopharmacology (pres. 1994), Acad. Behavioral Medicine Rsch., Am. Psychiat. Assn. (life fellow); mem. AAAS, Inst. of Medicine (sr. mem.), Collegium Internat. Neuropsychopharmacologicum, Pan Am. Med. Assn., Am. Soc. Clin. Pharmacology and Therapeutics, Phi Beta Kappa. Office: U Pitts Western Psychiat Inst & Clinic 3811 Ohara St Pittsburgh PA 15213-2593

DETRICK, DONALD HOWARD, minister; b. Newberg, Oreg., Dec. 13, 1954; s. Howard Raymond and Madeline F. (Roth) D.; m. Jodi Lanette Dunlap, June 8, 1974; children: Kristina Lynne, Mark Andrew, Jana Kathleen. Student, Eugene Bible Coll., 1974-77; BA, Bapt. Christian Coll., 1985; MA in Counseling, Luther Rice Sem., 1990. Ordained to ministry Assemblies of God, 1980. Sr. pastor Dayton (Oreg.) Assembly of God, 1977-78; assoc. pastor First Assembly of God, Newberg, 1979-83; sr. pastor Abundant Life Ctr., Toledo, Oreg., 1983-91, Bethel Ch., Chehalis, Wash., 1991—; presbyter Oreg. Coun. Assemblies of God, Salem, 1986-91, exec. presbyter, 1987-91; presbyter NW Dist. Assemblies of God, 1994-96, exec. presbyter, 1996—. Contbr. articles to religious publs. Mem. Am. Assn. Christian Counselors. Republican. Office: Bethel Ch 132 Kirkland Rd Chehalis WA 98532-8724

DETTBARN, WOLF-DIETRICH, neurochemist, pharmacologist, educator; b. Berlin, Jan. 30, 1928; came to U.S., 1958, naturalized, 1968; s. Erwin Bruno and MariaMagdalena (Conrady) D.; children: Donata-Andrea, Henning-Christian. M.D.I, D. Göttingen, 1953. Intern Univ. Clinic, Göttingen, 1953-54; research assoc. biol. dept. Ciba Co., Basel, 1954-55; research assoc. Physiol. Inst., U. Saarland, Homburg, Saar, 1955-58; research assoc. neurology Columbia U., N.Y.C., 1958-61, asst. prof., 1961-67, assoc. prof., 1967-68; prof. pharmacology Vanderbilt U., Nashville, 1968-96, prof. pharmacology emeritus, 1996—, prof. neurology, 1985—; mem. com. on toxicology of anticholinesterase chems. NRC, 1981-83; cons. U.S. Army Med. R & D Command, 1981-82. Contbr. articles to profl. jours. Mem. internal rev. bd. Vanderbilt U., 1991-93. Recipient Career Devel. award, 1965; grantee NIH, 1958—. Mem. AAAS, Am. Physiol. Soc., Am. Soc. Pharmcology and Exptl. Therapeutics, Am. Soc. Neurochemistry, Soc. for Neurosci., Corp. Marine Biology Lab. (Woods Hole, Mass.). Home: 4422 Wayland Dr Nashville TN 37215-4024 Office: Vanderbilt U Med Ctr S 2100 Pierce Ave Nashville TN 37212-3162

DETTERMAN, ROBERT LINWOOD, financial planner; b. Norfolk, Va., May 1, 1931; s. George William and Jeanneille (Watson) D.; m. Virginia Armstrong; children: Janine, Patricia, William Arthur. BS in Engring., Va. Poly. Inst., 1953; PhD in Nuclear Engring., Oak Ridge Sch. Reactor Tech., 1954, postgrad., 1954; cert. in fin. planning, Coll. Fin. Planning, Denver, 1986. Registered investment advisor, Calif. Engring. test dir. Foster Wheeler Co., N.Y.C., 1954-59; sr. research engr. Atomics Internat. Co., Canoga Park, Calif., 1959-62; chief project engr. Rockwell Internat. Co., Canoga Park, Calif., 1962-68, dir. bus. devel., 1968-84, mgr. internat. program, 1984-87; pres. Bo-Gin Fin., Inc., Thousand Oaks, Calif., 1987—; owner Bo-Gin Arabians, Thousand Oaks, 1963—; nuclear cons. Danish Govt., 1960, Lawrence Livermore Lab., Calif., 1959. Trustee, mem. exec. com. Morris Animal Found., Denver, 1984—, chmn., 1984-88, now trustee emeritus; mem. pres.' adv. com. Kellog Arabian Ranch, U. Calif. Poly., Pomona; treas., trustee Arabian Horse Trust, Denver, 1979-94, now trustee emeritus; pres. Rolling Oaks Homes Assn., Thousand Oaks, Calif., 1980-82; chmn. Cal Bred Futurity. Named to Tent of Honor, Arabian Horse Trust, 1997. Mem. Nat. Assn. Personal Fin. Advisers, Internat. Assn. Fin. Planners, Inst. Cert. Fin. Planners, Am. Nuclear Soc., Acad. Magical Arts, Am. Horse Shows Assn., Am. Horse Coun., Magic Castle Club, Internat. Arabian Horse Assn. Club, Tau Beta Phi, Eta Kappa Nu, Phi Kappa Phi. Republican. Avocations: collecting stamps, growing orchids. Office: Bo-Gin Fin Inc Ste 220 3609 E Thousand Oaks Blvd Westlake Village CA 91362-6941

DETTINGER, GARTH BRYANT, surgeon, physician, retired air force officer, county health officer; b. Syracuse, N.Y., Dec. 23, 1921; s. Maurice and Maxine Bryant (giddings) D.; m. Gladys Ruth Hickingbotham, Aug. 5, 1939 (dec. Aug. 1996); children: Holly Maxine Dettinger Dixon-Keane, Ronald Mark, Michael James; m. Jeffa Taylor, July 26, 1997. A.B., Harvard U., 1948; M.D., Columbia U., 1952; M.S. in Surgery, Baylor U., 1956. Diplomate: Am. Bd. Surgery. Commd. officer U.S. Air Force, 1952, advanced through grades to maj. gen., 1977; intern Valley Forge Army Hosp., Phoenixville, Pa., 1952-53; resident in surgery Brooke Army Hosp., San Antonio, 1953-57; chief surgery MacDill Hosp., Tampa, Fla., 1957-59, Elmendorf Hosp., Alaska, 1959-62, Davis-Monthan Hosp., Tucson, 1962-64; hosp comdr. Roswell, N.Mex., 1964-67; chief profl. services Air Forces Europe, 1967-70; hosp. comdr. Vandenberg, Calif., 1970-72; surgeon Air Force Mil. Personnel Center, San Antonio, 1972-74; command surgeon Air Tng. Command, 1974-75; dir. plans and resources U.S. Air Force, Washington, 1975-77; dep. surgeon gen. U.S. Air Force, 1977-80; asst. health dir. Fairfax County, Va., 1980—; surg. cons. Surgeon Gen. U.S.; clin. assoc. prof. Georgetown U. Med. Sch., 1983—. Editor-in-chief: Surgeons Comments, 1967-70. Fellow A.C.S. (bd. govs.); mem. Soc. Med. Cons. to Armed Services, Alpha Omega Alpha. Republican. Episcopalian. Home: #M-116 9120 Belvoir Woods Pkwy # M-116 Fort Belvoir VA 22060-2721 Office: Fairfax County Health Dept 10777 Main St Ste 203 Fairfax VA 22030-6900 *I've always tried to leave anyone, anything or anyplace a little better than before I had been there.*

DETTKE, DIETER M., foundation executive; b. Brusendorf, Berlin, Germany, Jan. 15, 1941; s. Ferdinand and Marianne (Bartoschek) D.; m. Brigitte G. Ohm, June 27, 1969 (div.); 1 child, Nathalie; m. Gale A. Mattox, Aug. 20, 1983; 1 child, Elizabeth. Diplom-Politologe, Free U. Berlin, 1968, PhD, 1974. Rsch. assoc. German Soc. for Fgn. Affairs, Bonn, 1969-74; staff dir. German Fgn. Office, Bonn, 1982; fgn. policy advisor German Bundestag, Bonn, 1974-84; exec. dir. Friedrich-Ebert-Stiftung, Washington, 1984—. Author: Allianz im Wandel, 1976; editor book series International Political Currents, 1994. Expert and transatlantic activities in German-Am. dialogue. Fulbright scholar, 1967-68. Mem. Am. Polit. Sci. Assn., Internat. Studies Assn. (governing coun. internat. security studies sect. 1995—), Cosmos Club. German Social Dem. Party. Lutheran. Avocations: tennis, skiing, swimming. Office: Friedrich-Ebert-Stiftung 1155 15th St NW Ste 1100 Washington DC 20005-2706

DETTMER, ROBERT GERHART, retired beverage company executive; b. Parsons, Kans., Sept. 11, 1931; s. Ira Gerhart and Dema (Hinze) D.; m. Patricia Isabel York, Aug. 20, 1955; children: Stephanie, Constance, Robert Brantley. Student, U.S. Naval Acad., 1949-52; B in Bus. and Engring. Adminstrn., MIT, 1955; MBA, Harvard U., 1957. Engr. Lincoln Electric Co., Cleve., 1957-60; assoc. Booz, Allen & Hamilton, Cleve., 1960-64; propr. Robert G. Dettmer, Investment Mgmt., Cleve., 1964-66; v.p. ops. Tasa Corp., Pitts., 1966-68; pres. Scott Aviation div. A-T-O, Lancaster, N.Y., 1968-70, George J. Meyer Mfg. div., Milw., 1970-72, N.Am. Van Lines subs. PepsiCo, Inc., Fort Wayne, Ind., 1973-76; v.p. fin. mgmt. and planning PepsiCo, Inc., Purchase, N.Y., 1976-79; pres. Pepsi Cola Bottling Group subs., Purchase, N.Y., 1979-86; exec. v.p., CFO PepsiCo, Purchase, N.Y., 1986-96; Bd. dirs. Valero Energy, N.Am. Van Lines. Chmn. bd. Am. Movers Conf., 1974-76; trustee Miss Porter's Sch., 1978-84; trustee Manhattanville Coll., 1986-93, chmn. bd. trustees, 1988-92. Mem. Delta Tau Delta, Tau Beta Pi. Clubs: Harvard Bus. Sch. of Westchester-Fairfield County (chmn. bd. 1977-80), Harvard Bus. Sch. of Greater N.Y. (chmn. bd. 1982-83). Home: 80 Round Hill Rd Greenwich CT 06831-3743

DETUNO, JOSEPH EDWARD, lawyer; b. Chgo., Jan. 2, 1931; s. Robert and Sarah (Laurenzana) D. Student, De Paul U., 1949-51, LL.B., 1954. Bar: Ill. 1954. Atty. Security Mut. Casualty Co., Chgo., 1956-63; ptnr. Gifford, Detuno & Gifford, Chgo., 1963-91, Roddy, Power, Leahy, Guill, Zima & Gifford, 1991—. Served with AUS, 1954-56. Mem. ABA, Ill. Bar Assn., Chgo. Bar Assn. (chmn. com. indsl. commn. 1967-68), Am. Judicature Soc., Chgo. Trial Lawyers. Home: 201 E Chestnut St Chicago IL 60611-2358 Office: Roddy Power Leahy Guill et al 162 W Grand Ave Chicago IL 60610-4297

DETWEILER, DAVID KENNETH, veterinary physiologist, educator; b. Phila., Oct. 23, 1919; s. David Rieser and Pearl Irene (Overholt) D.; m. Inge E. A. Kludt, Feb. 2, 1965; children: Ellen, Diane, Judith, David, Inge, Kenneth. VMD, U. Pa., 1942, MS, 1949; ScD (hon.), Ohio State U., 1966; MVD (hon.), U. Vienna, Austria, 1968; DMV (hon.), U. Turin, Italy, 1969. Asst. instr. physiology and pharmacology Sch. Vet. Medicine, U. Pa., Phila., 1942-43; instr. Sch. Vet. Medicine, U. Pa., 1943-45, assoc. in physiology, pharmacology, 1945-47, asst. prof., 1947-51, assoc. prof., 1951-62; assoc. prof. Sch. Vet. Medicine, U. Pa. (Grad. Sch. Arts and Scis.); chmn. dept. vet. med. scis. Sch. Vet. Medicine, U. Pa. (Grad. Sch. Medicine), 1956-68, dir. comparative cardiovascular studies unit, 1960-90, prof., head lab. physiology and pharmacology, 1962-68, prof., head lab. physiology, 1968-90, prof. faculty arts and scis., 1968-90, chmn. grad. group comparative med. scis., 1971-87, prof. emeritus, 1990—; mem. Inst. Medicine, NAS, 1974—; guest USSR Acad. Sci.; cons. cardiovascular toxicology, 1950—. Contbr. numerous articles to various publs. Guggenheim fellow, 1955-56; recipient Disting. Veterinarian award Pa. Vet. Med. Assn., 1989, Disting. Practitioner award Nat. Acads. of Practice in Vet. Medicine, 1989; D.K. Detweiler prize in cardiology established in his honor German Group of World Vet. Med. Assn., 1982; David K. Detweiler Conf. Rm. named in honor Veterinary Sch. U. Pa., 1993, Centennial medal Veterinarian Sch. U. Pa., 1994; recipient FDA cert. appreciation, 1998. Fellow AAAS; mem. Am. Physiol. Soc., Am. Assn. Vet. Physiology and Pharmacology (pres.), N.Y. Acad. Scis., Am. Vet. Med. Assn. (Gaines award and medal 1960, Honor Roll award 1990), Coun. Basic Scis., Am. Heart Assn., Acad. Vet. Cardiology (pres.), Am. Coll. Vet. Internal Medicine (diplomate, cardiology group), Vet. Med. Alumni Soc. (Merit award U. Pa. 1981), Phi Zeta. Office: U Pa Sch Vet Medicine 3800 Spruce St Philadelphia PA 19104-6008

DETWELLER, RICHARD ALLEN, college president, psychology educator; b. Los Angeles, Nov. 14, 1946; s. James Irvin and Dorothy Elizabeth D.; m. Carol Sue D., Aug. 26, 1967; children: Jerusha, Natasha, Carrick. BA, Calif. Western U., 1968; MA, Princeton U., 1972, PhD, 1973. Structural draftsman Young's Iron Wroks, Burbank, Calif., 1962-64; peace corps volunteer U.S. Peace Corps, Truk, Caroline Islands; prof. psychology Drew U., Madison, N.J., 1973-92, vice pres., 1985-92; pres. Hartwick Coll., Oneonta, N.Y., 1992—, prof. psychology; vis. fellow Princeton (N.J.) U., 1973-74; internat. edn. cons. to various non-profit and govt. orgns., 1977—; vis. scholar U. Calif., Berkeley, Calif., 1980; profl. assoc. East West Ctr., Honolulu, HI, 1978. Contbr. numerous articles and speeches in the fields of psychology, edn. and info. tech. Recipient Outstanding Contribution and Leadership award Carnegie Mellon U., 1991. Mem. Coun. Ind. Colls., Ind. Col. Fund., Am. Coun. on Edn. Office: Hartwick Coll Oneonta NY 13820

DETWILER, JOSEPH ALDEN, artist; b. Goshen, Ind., Dec. 3, 1951. BA in Ceramics, U. Fla., 1980; MFA in Ceramics, George Washington U., 1982. Tchr. Cmty. Free Sch., Boulder, Colo., 1974-75, Creative Arts Workshop, New Haven, 1975-77, Wesleyan Potters Craft Ctr., Middletown, Conn., 1976-77, Roanoke Coll., Salem, Va., 1986, Mary Washington Coll., Fredericksburg, Va., 1987-88, 93-97; lectr. and spkr. in field. One-man show Hand Workshop, Richmond, 1989; group exhibits include Ctr. Culturel Mcpl., Frejus, France, 1989, Inst. Statale d'Arte F.A. Grue per la Ceramica, Castelli, Italy, 1989, Internat. Ceramics Festival Mino, Japan, 1990, 47 Concorso Internat. della Ceramica d'Arte--Faenza, Italy, 1991, Bedford Gallery, Longwood Coll., Farmville, Va., 1992, Md. Inst. Coll. Art, Balt., 1993, King Vaclav's Labyrinth of the State Castle, Cesky Krumlov, Czech Republic, 1994, Art Mus. of the Ams., Washington, 1994, San Angelo (Tex.) Mus. Fine Arts, 1995, Pewabic Pottery, Detroit, 1995, Internat. Ceramics Competition Mino, Tajimi City, Gifu, Japan, 1995, Frog Hollow Gallery, Manchester, Vt., 1996, Longwood Ctr. for the Visual Arts, Farmville, 1996, Oreg. Clay Nat., McMinnville, 1997, Monarch Nat. Ceramic Competition, Florence, Ala., 1997, Concours Internat. de Ceramique-Prix de la Ville de Carouge, Geneva, 1997, Kutani Internat. Ceramics Exhbn., Komatsu, Ishikawa, Japan, 1997, others; represented in permanent collections Nat. Mus. Am. Art, U. Fla., Del. Art Mus., U. Evansville, City of Portsmouth, Va., Waverly Hotel, Atlanta, Med. Coll. Va., Omni Hotel, Richmond, Ala. Power Corp., AmSouth Ctr., Huntsville, Ala., U. Va. Hosp., Charlottesville, Balch & Bingham, Birmingham, Monarch Tile Corp., World Bank, Washington, HealthSouth, Inc., Birmingham, others. Home: 13 River Ridge Ln Fredericksburg VA 22406-5318

DETWILER, SUSAN MARGARET, information brokerage executive; b. Bklyn., Dec. 8, 1953; d. Marshall and Anna (Dembrofsky) Pallas; m. Mark Fredrick Detwiler, Mar. 13, 1977; children: John Marshall, Elizabeth Ann. BS, SUNY, Albany, 1974; MBA, U. Mich., 1976. Market analyst Am. V. Mueller, Niles, Ill., 1976-80; mgr. market rsch. Zimmer Inc., Warsaw, Ind., 1980-85; pres. The Detwiler Group (formerly S.M. Detwiler & Assocs., Inc.), Ft. Wayne, Ind., 1985—. *Susan Detwiler consults to information providers on health and business content,and conducts business research for health and medical industries. The Detwiler Group maintains a database of health and medical resources, available online through Healthgate and Medical Data International, and in hard-copy through Dorland's Directories. Susan Detwiler is also a contributor to Medscape, writes regularly in both medical and information industry media, and offers several seminars on making the best use of information resources. Market and content analyses and competitive comparisons are based on research and 22 years of medical and information industry experience.* Prodr. and editor: Detwiler's Directory of Health and Medical Resources; contbr. Medscape online svcs. Mem. Med. Surg. Market Rsch. Group (past pres.), Assn. Ind. Info. Profls. (past v.p.), Regulatory Affairs Profl. Soc. Assn., Spl. Libraries Assn. Democrat. Avocations: choir, eclectic reading. E-mail: sdetwiler@detwiler.com. Office: PO Box 15308 Fort Wayne IN 46885-5308

DEUBLE, JOHN L., JR., environmental science and engineering services consultant; b. N.Y.C., Oct. 2, 1932; s. John Lewis and Lucille (Klotzbach) D.; m. Thelma C. Honeychurch, Aug. 28, 1955; children: Deborah, Steven. AA, AS in Phys. Sci., Stockton Coll., 1957; BA, BS in Chemistry, U. Pacific, 1959. Cert. profl. chemist, profl. engr., environ. inspector; registered environ. profl., registered environ. assessor. Sr. chemist Aero-Gen Corp., Sacramento, Calif., 1959-67; asst. dir. rsch. Lockheed Propulsion Co., Redlands, Calif., 1968-73; asst. div. mgr. Systems, Sci. and Software, La Jolla, Calif., 1974-79; gen. mgr. Wright Energy Nev. Corp., Reno, Nev., 1980-81; v.p. Energy Resources Co., La Jolla, 1982-83; dir. hazardous waste Aerovironment Inc., Monrovia, Calif., 1984-85; sr. program mgr. Ogden Environ. and Energy Svcs., San Diego, 1989-96; environ. cons. Encinitas, Calif., 1986-88, 97—. Contbr. articles profl. jours. With USAF, 1951-54. Recipient Tech. award Am. Ordnance Assn., 1969, Cert. of Achievement Am. Men and Women of Sci., 1986, Envrion. Registry, 1992. Fellow Am. Inst. Chemists; mem. ASTM, Am. Chem. Soc., Am. Inst. Chem. Engrs., Am. Meteorol. Soc., Am. Def. Inds. Assn., Air and Waste Mgmt. Assn., Calif. Inst. Chemists, Hazardous Materials Control Rsch. Inst., N.Y. Acad. Scis., Environ. Assessors Assn. Republican. Lutheran. Achievements include development and pioneering use of chemical (non-radioactive) tracers--gaseous, aqueous, and particulate in environmental and energy applications. Home and Office: Planning Asssocs 369 Cerro St Encinitas CA 92024-4805

DEUBLE, LOTTIE EDWARDS, missionary, receptionist; b. Franklinton, N.C., July 2, 1922; d. Kenneth Kenzie and Lizzie Patty (Oakley) Edwards; m. Harold William Deuble, Sept. 2, 1943; children: Maria Elizabeth Deuble Pries, Harolyn Mae Deuble Scherry, Janet Susan Deuble Larry. Saleslady McClennan's, Petersburg, Va., 1939-40, F.W. Woolworth, Petersburg, Va., 1940-41; operator, supr., instr. Chesapeake & Potomac Telephone Co., Petersburg, Va., 1941-43; test operator Diamond State Telephone Co., Dover, Del., 1948-53; PBX operator Kent Gen. Hosp., Dover, Del., 1953-54; part-time saleslady J.C. Penney Co., Dover, Del., 1955, Pierce's Pharmacy, Dover, Del., 1955-56; sec. R.C. Nehi Co., Dover, Del., 1956-60; time computor Internat. Playtex, Dover, Del., 1970-72; receptionist Dr. William Flanagan and Dr. Terry Bryan, Dover, Del., 1975-76; missionary to Crow Indians Am. Bapt. Ch., Pryor, Mont., 1976-78; speaker Am. Bapt. Ch., 1978—. Sunday sch. tchr. So. Bapt. Ch., Cambridge, Md., and Am. Bapt. Ch., Dover, 1940-88; v.p. programs, cir. leader, v.p. social concerns Am. Bapt. Women's Ministries, Dover, 1946—; bd. evangelism, prayer group leader 1st Bapt. Ch., Dover, 1957—, deaconess, 1970—, deacon emeritus, 1992; convenor, mem. of chpt. Order St. Luke the Physician, 1969-98; leader Camps Farthest Out; active End-Time Handmaidens Missionary work, 1980—, Ch. Women United, 1959-66; leader, hostess 7 Holy Land tours; spkr., slide presenter Indian studies Ednl. Resources Assn. in Schs.; mem. steering com. Good Shepherd Bapt. Ch., 1990-91. Mem. Christian Women's Club (various positions 1974—), DAR (chaplain 1992-95, regent col. Haslet chpt. 1998—). Am. Bapt. Avocations: writing, art, photography, traveling. Home: 519 Wyoming Ave Dover DE 19904-4352

DEUEL, THOMAS FRANKLIN, physician; b. Summit, N.J., Feb. 22, 1935; m. Ruthmary K. Deuel, Aug. 27, 1960; children: Julia S., Katherine S., Thomas A. AB in Biology, Princeton U., 1957; MD, Columbia U., 1961. Intern straight medicine U. Chgo. Hosps., 1961-62; rsch. fellow Ben May Lab. for Cancer Rsch., U. Chgo., 1962-63; resident in medicine U. Chgo. Hosps., 1963-64; asst. resident in medicine Mass. Gen. Hosp., Boston, 1964-65; various med. ednl. and rsch. positions, 1965-80; co-dir. hematology/oncology Wash. U., 1977-96; prof. medicine Wash. U. Sch. Medicine, St. Louis, 1979-96, prof. biochemistry and molecular biophysics, 1980-96; Lewis T. and Rosalind B. Apple prof. med. Wash. U. Sch. Medicine, Jewish Hosp., St. Louis, 1986-96; dir. oncology Barnes & Jewish Hosps., St. Louis, 1989-96; dir. divsn. growth regulation Beth Israel Hosp., Boston, 1996—; prof. medicine Harvard Med. Sch., Boston, 1996—; co-dir. div. hematology/oncology Wash. U., St. Louis, 1989—; mem. merit rev. bd. in hematology VA Dept. Medicine and Surgery, 1978-80; mem. rsch. com. Am. Heart Assn., Mo. affiliate, 1979-85; mem. hematology study sect. 1 NIH, 1980—; mem. pre-rev. panel for hematology programs Accreditation Coun. for Grad. Med. Edn., 1982-83; cons. grants rev. br. Nat. Cancer Inst., 1985; chmn. external sci. rev. com. U. Calif. San Francisco Cancer Rsch. Inst., 1988. Mem. editorial com. Jour. Clin. Investigations, 1982-87; mem. editorial bd. Oncogene Rsch., 1987, Bio Factors, 1987; assoc. editor Blood, 1988; contbr. articles to Biochim. Biophys. Acta, Biochem. Z., Archives Biochem. Biophys., Jour. Biol. Chemistry, Biochem. Biophys. Rsch. Commun., Proceedings NAS USA; author: (with others) The Enzymes of Glutamine Metabolism, 1973, Morris Hepatomas: Mechanisms of Regulation, 1978, Methods in Enzymology, Purine and Pyrimidine Nucleotide Metabolism, 1978. Mem. scientific adv. bd. Oridigm Corp., 1997. Recipient Nat. Heart, Lung & Blood Inst. Merit award NIH, 1988, Faculty Rsch. award Am. Cancer Soc., 1979, Spl. Recognition award Coun. on Arteriosclerosis Thrombosis and Vascualr Biology, 1997, Disting. Achievement award AHA, 1998. Mem. AAAS, ACS, Am. Fedn. for Clin. Rsch., Am. Soc. for Biochemistry and Molecular Biology, Am. Soc. Biol. Chemists, Am. Soc. for Clin. Investigation, Am. Soc. Hematology (publs. com. 1983—, chmn. sci. affairs com. 1985, Dameshek prize 1985), Assn. Am. Physicians, Internat. Soc. on Thrombosis and Haemostasis (Investigator Recognition award for contbns. to hemostasis 1985), N.Y. Acad. Scis., Cen. Soc. for Clin. Rsch. (hematology sub-specialty sect. 1983—), Protein Soc., Sigma Xi. Office: Beth Israel Deaconess Med Ctr Research East 213 PO Box 15732 Boston MA 02215-0015*

DEUKMEJIAN, GEORGE, lawyer, former governor; b. Albany, N.Y., June 6, 1928; s. C. George and Alice (Gairdan) D.; m. Gloria M. Saatjian, 1957; children: Leslie Ann, George Krikor, Andrea Diane. BA, Siena Coll., 1949; JD, St. John's U., 1952. Bar: N.Y. 1952, Calif. 1956, U.S. Supreme Ct. 1970. Mem. Calif. Assembly, 1963-67; mem. Calif. Senate, 1967-79, minority leader; atty. gen. State of Calif., 1979-82, gov., 1983-91; former dep. county counsel Los Angeles County.; partner Sidley & Austin, 1991—. Served with U.S. Army, 1953-55. Republican. Episcopalian. Office: Sidley & Austin 555 W 5th St Fl 40 Los Angeles CA 90013-1010

DEUNK, N. HOWARD, III, flying educator; b. Columbus, Ohio, July 31, 1952; s. Norman H. Jr. and Eileen G. (Gilson) D.; m. Linda Susan Letch, Feb. 14, 1976; children: Nathan, Jenny, David, Lori. BS in Engring. Sci., USAF Acad., 1974; student, USAF Basic Svc. Sch., 1979, USAF Inter Svc. Sch., 1981-82, USAF Sr. Svc. Sch., 1987-88; MS in Mgmt., Troy State U., 1991. Commd. 2d lt. USAF, 1974; advanced through grades to maj., 1986, ret., 1994; T-37 instr. pilot 71 Flying Tng. Wing Enid, Okla., 1980-85; chief learning ctr. 71 Flying Tng. Wing Enid, 1982-85; KC-135 instr. pilot 70th Air Refueling Squadron Grissom AFB, Ind., 1985-89; chief tactics divsn. 305 Strategic Wing Grissom AFB, 1988-89; unit move planner 306 Strategic Wing RAF Mildenhall, Eng., 1989-90; chief war plans RAF Mildenhall, 1991-92; airfield mgr. Tinker AFB, Okla., 1992-94; warehouse mgr., shipping and receiving supr. S.W. Wood, Oklahoma City, 1994-95; T-1 instr. pilot Boeing, Enid, 1995—. Mem. Am. Legion, Air Force Assn., Daedalians, VFW. Fax: (580) 237-7534. Home: 3910 Shenandoah Enid OK 73703-2017 Office: Boeing Co 173 Merritt Ave Ste 239 Enid OK 73705-5207

DEUPREE, MARVIN MATTOX, accountant, business consultant; b. Woodbine, Iowa, Oct. 8, 1917; s. Archie Orin and Pearl (Mattox) D.; m. Katherine Anita Beard, Aug. 18, 1951; children: Marvin Mattox, Meredith Ann. B.A. with high distinction, State U. Iowa, 1941; M.B.A. with distinction, U. Pa., 1948. C.P.A., N.Y., Ill., Mich., La., Iowa, Va., N.C. Instr. acctg. U. Pa., 1947-48; with Arthur Andersen & Co. (C.P.A.s), 1948-75, partner, 1960-75, mem. policy com. on acctg. and auditing, 1962-72; bus. cons., 1975—; pres. Emporium Specialties Co., Inc. 1977—; adj. asso. prof. NYU Grad. Sch. Bus. Adminstrn., 1973-76. Contbr. articles to profl. jours. Served as officer USNR, 1943-46. Mem. AICPA, N.Y. State, Ill. Socs. CPA's, Nat. Assn. Accts., Am. Acctg. Assn., Execs. Club (Chgo.), Wharton Grad. Bus. Sch. Club (Chgo.), Univ. Club (Chgo.), Phi Beta Kappa. Episcopalian. Home: 5 Academy Rd Ho Ho Kus NJ 07423-1301 Office: 1345 Avenue Of The Americas New York NY 10105-0302

DE URIOSTE, GEORGE ADOLFO, IV, software company executive; b. San Francisco, June 25, 1955; s. George Adolfo Sr. and Janet Germaine (Bruzzone) de U. BS, U. So. Calif., L.A., 1978; MBA, U. Calif., Berkeley, 1980. CPA, Calif. Auditor, cons. Deloitte Haskins & Sells, San Francisco, 1980-83; sr. fin. analyst Genstar Corp., San Francisco, 1983-85, Rolm Mil-Spec Computers, Inc., San Jose, Calif., 1986-88; mgr. fin. planning and analysis Ask Computer Systems, Inc., Mountain View, Calif., 1988-90; CFO TeamOne Systems, Inc., Sunnyvale, Calif., 1990-92; v.p. fin. and ops. Remedy Corp., Mountain View, Calif., 1992-98. Pres. U. So. Calif. Commerce Assocs., San Francisco, 1988-89. Mem. AICPA, Calif. Soc. CPAs, Churchill Club (bd. dirs., vice chmn. Palo Alto, Calif. 1989-94). Avocations: tennis, hunting, fishing, skiing, mountain bike riding, antique auto restoration. Home: 282 Walker Dr Mountain View CA 94043-2108 Office: Remedy Corp 1505 Salado Dr Mountain View CA 94043-1110

DEUSCHL, DENNIS ERWIN, communications executive; b. Bklyn., Nov. 25, 1940; s. Erwin A. and Dorothy E. (Peterson) D.; m. Vivian A. Sciaretta, Mar. 26, 1963; children: Lisa C., Piper J. BA in Journalism, Rutgers U., 1962; MS in Pub. Relations, Am. U., 1977. Dir. info. USAF, various bases, 1965-69; mgr. communications Prudential Ins. Co., Ft. Washington, Pa., 1969-71; dir. pub. relations 1st Va. Banks, Inc., Falls Church, 1971-75; dir. communications St. Lawrence Seaway Devel. Corp. U.S. Dept. Transp., Washington, 1976—; adj. prof. comms. Sch. of Comms. Am. U., Washington, 1994—. Coach Turnpike Basketball Club, Annandale, Va., 1982—. Capt. USAF, 1962-69, lt. col. USAFR, ret. Mem. Pub. Relations Soc. Am. (fully accredited), Nat. Assn. Govt. Communicators. Republican. Lutheran. Avocations: tennis, photography. Home: 4509 Weyburn Dr Annandale VA 22003-5627 Office: St Lawrence Seaway Devel US Dept Transp 400 7th St SW Rm 5424 Washington DC 20590-0001

DEUSCHLE, KURT WALTER, physician, educator; b. Kongen, Germany, Mar. 14, 1923; came to U.S., 1924, naturalized, 1949; s. John and Marie (Schaefer) D.; m. Jeanne Magagna, 1975; children by previous marriage—Kurt J., Sally, James. B.S. cum laude, Kent State U., 1944; M.D., U. Mich., 1948. Intern Colo. Gen. Hosp., Denver, 1948-49; resident medicine, fellow oncology Upstate Med. Ctr. SUNY, Syracuse, 1950-52; resident U.S.P.H.S. Navajo Indian Reservation, Ft. Defiance, Ariz., 1953; instr. medicine Upstate Med. Ctr. SUNY, Syracuse, 1954-55; asst. prof. pub. health and preventive medicine Cornell Med. Coll., 1955-60; prof., chmn. dept. community medicine U. Ky., 1960-68; Ethel H. Wise prof., chmn. and dir. dept. community medicine Mt. Sinai Sch. of Medicine, CUNY, 1968-90, prof. emeritus, 1990—; prof. emeritus, disting. svc. prof. Mt Sinai Hosp., 1993—; Ethel H. Wise chmn. emeritus Mt Sinai Sch. of Medicine, CUNY, 1993—, Disting. Svc. prof. dept. community medicine, 1993—; Merrimon lectr. U. N.C., Chapel Hill, 1975; mem. N.Y.C. Bd. Health, 1982-89; vis. prof. U. Lagos, Nigeria, 1977, Chinese Med. Assn., People's Republic China, 1986; mem. Tb control adv. com. Center Disease Control Dept. HEW; cons. manpower intelligence NIH; mem. Inst. Medicine of Nat. Acad. Scis., Washington; mem. rural health systems del. to China, 1978; mem. Nat. Adv. Environ. Health Scis. Coun. NIH, 1982-86; sr. advisor Report of U.S. Preventive Services Task Force, The Guide to Clinical Preventive Servcies, HHS, 1989; mem. com. pub. health N.Y. Acad. Medicine, 1983—, N.Y. State Council on Grad. Med. Edn., 1987—, adv. com. Am. Ba. Family Practice, 1986—. Author: (with J. Adair) The People's Health: Anthropology and Medicine in a Navajo Community, 1970, rev. and expanded edit., 1988; Contbr. to: (ed. John Norman) Medicine in the Ghetto, 1969, Community Medicine: Teaching, Research and Health Care, (ed. Lathem and Newberry), 1970. Served with AUS, 1943-46. Recipient Award of Honor, Mayor of N.Y.C., 1989, Jacobi award Associated Alumni Mt. Sinai Med.

Ctr., 1989, Alexander Richman Commemorative award Mt. Sinai Med. Ctr., 1991; Duncan Clark award Assn. Tchrs. Preventive Medicine, 1990; Commonwealth Fund sr. health fellow, 1966-67. Fellow AAAS, Am. Coll. Preventive Medicine (past pres., Disting. Svc. award 1975); mem. Am. Pub. Health Assn. (award for excellence in domestic health 1975), Alpha Omega Alpha. Home: 1212 5th Ave New York NY 10029-5210 Office: Fifth Ave New York NY 10029

DEUTCH, JOHN MARK, federal agency administrator, chemist, academic administrator; b. Brussels, Belgium, July 27, 1938; came to U.S., 1940, naturalized, 1946; s. Michael Joseph and Rachel Felicia (Fisher) D.; m. Pat Lyons; children: Philip, Paul, Zachary. B.A., Amherst Coll., 1961, D.Sc. and Humane Letters (hon.), 1978; B. Chem. Engring, M.I.T., 1961, Ph.D. in Phys. Chemistry, 1965; D.Litt. (hon.), U. Lowell, 1986. System analyst Office Sec. Def., 1961-65; fellow Nat. Acad. Scis./NRC, Nat. Bur. Standards, 1966-67; asst. prof. Princeton U., 1967-70; mem. faculty MIT, 1970—, prof. chemistry, 1971—, chmn. dept., 1976, dean sci., from 1982, provost, 1982-90, inst. prof., 1990—; under sec. for acquisition and technology Dept. of Defense, Washington, DC, 1993-94; dep. sec. Dept. of Defense, Washington, DC, 1994-95; dir. Central Intelligence, Washington, D.C., 1995-96; prof. MIT, 1996—; chmn. adv. panel on chemistry NSF, 1974; mem. Def. Sci. Bd., 1977—, Pres.'s Nuclear Safety Oversight Com.; dir. Office Energy Rsch., U.S. Dept. Energy, Washington, 1977-79, acting asst. sec. for energy tech., 1979, under sec., 1979-80; mem. Army Sci. Adv. Panel, 1975-78, Pres.'s Commn. on Strategic Forces, 1983, The White House Sci. Coun., 1985-89; mem. Pres.'s Fgn. Intelligence Adv. Bd., 1990—. Author research articles. Sloan fellow, 1969-71; Guggenheim fellow, 1974. Mem. Am. Phys. Soc., Am. Chem. Soc., Council Fgn. Relations, Am. Acad. Arts and Scis. Avocations: tennis, squash, reading. Office: MIT 77 Massachusetts Ave Cambridge MA 02139-4307*

DEUTSCH, ALLEEN DIMITROFF, university administrator; b. Cleve., Dec. 5, 1946; d. Joseph A. and Mildred A. (Dimitroff) D. BA, Bowling Green State U., 1969; MS, Miami U., Oxford Ohio, 1973, PhD, 1978. Asst. dean Coll. Arts and Scis., Miami U., Oxford, 1973-79; asst. to provost Bradley U., Peoria, Ill., 1979-83, dir. div. continuing edn. and profl. devel., adj. prof. Coll. Edn., 1983-87; dean div. continuing edn Auburn U., Montgonery, Ala., 1987-92; assoc. dir. CPD Fla. State U., Tallahassee, 1993—, interim dir., 1994-95. Pres. Planned Parenthood Greater Peoria, 1983-85, bd. dirs., 1981-87; mem. com. United Way, 1980-87; bd. dirs. Peoria YWCA, 1981-84, Planned Parenthood Ala., 1990-92. Mem. ASTD, Am. Assn. Higher Edn. (women's caucus), Am. Assn. Adult and Continuing Edn., Nat. Assn. Women Deans, Adminstrs. and Counselors, Univ. Continuing Edn. Assn. (region IV chmn. women's div., chmn. awards and honors com., bd. dirs., nat. membership chair, chmn. region III), Nat. Women's Studies Assn., Phi Delta Kappa, Phi Kappa Phi, Alpha Lambda Delta. Home: 2429 Beautyberry Ct Tallahassee FL 32308-6286 Office: Fla State U CPD/FSCC 555 W Pensacola St Tallahassee FL 32306-1640

DEUTSCH, ANNE, clinical nurse specialist; b. Leicester, England, Aug. 27, 1964; d. Robert and Pamela (Neale) G. BSN magna cum laude, U. Cin., 1986; MS, SUNY, Buffalo, 1992. Clin. nurse II U. Cin. Med. Ctr., 1986-88; staff nurse Buffalo Gen. Hosp., 1988-91; rsch. tng. asst. SUNY, Buffalo, 1988-90, rsch. cons., 1989-90, teaching asst., 1995-97; dir. edn. Uniform Data System, 1991-95, rsch. analyst, 1997—; clin. nurse Mt. Sinai Hosp., Toronto, 1991-92. Named one of Outstanding Young Woman of Am., Montgomery, Ala., 1987. Mem. APHA, Assn. Health Svcs. Rschrs., Assn. Rehab. Nurses (chpt. sec. 1988-90), Sigma Theta Tau. Home: 152 South Ln Grand Island NY 14072-1323

DEUTSCH, BARRY JOSEPH, consulting and development company executive; b. Gary, Ind., Aug. 10, 1941; s. Jack Elias and Helen Louise (La Rue) D. BS, U. So. Calif., 1969, MBA magna cum laude, 1970. Lectr. mgmt. U. So. Calif., L.A., 1967-70; pres., founder The Deutsch Group, Inc., L.A., 1970—; founder, CEO, chmn. bd. Investment Planning Network, Inc., 1988—. Author: Leadership Techniques, 1969, Recruiting Techniques, 1970, The Art of Selling, 1973, Professional Real Estate Management, 1975, Strategic Planning, 1976, Employer/Employee: Making the Transition, 1979, Managing by Objectives, 1980, Conducting Effective Performance Appraisal, 1982, Advanced Supervisory Development, 1984, Managing a Successful Financial Planning Business, 1988, How to Franchise Your Business, 1991. Chmn. bd. govs. Am. Hist. Ctr., 1980—. Mem. ASTD, Am. Mgmt. Assn., Am. Soc. Bus. and Mgmt. Cons., Internat. Mgmt. by Objectives Inst., Organization Devel. Network. Office: 1140 Highland Ave Ste 200 Manhattan Beach CA 90266

DEUTSCH, CLAUDE DAVID, physicist, educator; b. Paris, July 20, 1936; s. David and Caroline (Petrover) D.; m. Nimet Elabed, July 9, 1962; children: Alain, Eric. Degree in chem. engring., Ecole Nat. Supérieure, Paris, 1959; M in Theoretical Physics, U. Paris XI, Orsay, 1961; DSc, U. Paris VI, 1969. Mem. staff CNRS, Orsay, 1959-60, Inst. H. Poincaré, Paris, 1960-63; engr. CEA-EURATOM Nuclear Energy Ctr., Fontenay-aux-Roses, France, 1965-71; chief rsch. Nat. Ctr. Sci. Rsch. (CNRS), Orsay, 1973-80; dir. Plasma Physics Lab., Orsay, 1980-85, 94-99; chmn. Strongly Coupled Coolomb Systems 99, Saint-Malo, France, 1999—; vis. scientist U. Montreal, Can., 1973, U. Gainesville, Fla., 1974, MIT, Cambridge, 1976-78, ICTP, Trieste, Italy, 1981, Stanford U., Palo Alto, Calif., 1980, 83; vis. prof. Okayama (Japan) U., 1978-86, 89, Osaka (Japan) U., 1995, Weizmann Inst., Rehovot, Israel, 1983, GSI, Darmstadt, Germany, 1987; found. chmn. Internat. Workshop Atomic Physics Ion Driven Fusion, 1983; dir. Paris-Sud Info., Orsay, 1985-93, Ion-Plasma Interaction Rsch. Gathering, CNRS, Orléans, Orsay, 1989-96; mem. Nat. Com. on Plasma Sci., 1983; sci. dir. Les Houches (France) Winter Sch., 1995; chmn. Strongly Coupled Coolomb Systems 99, Saint Malo, 1999. Editor proc. for internat. confs. in field; mem. editl. bd. Jour. Physique, 1985-88; contbr. articles to profl. jours. With French Mil. Forces, 1963-64. Fellow Japan Soc. Promotion of Sci., 1978, 86, 89, NATO, 1980. Recipient bronze and silver C.N.R.S. medals. Fellow Am. Phys. Soc., French Phys. Soc. (prizes com. 1979-83, mem. coun. 1979-83); mem. European Com. Heavy Ion Fusion, 1993. Office: Plasma Physics Lab, Bat 212, 91405 Orsay France

DEUTSCH, DAVID ALLAN, artist; b. L.A., Aug. 8, 1943; s. Alex and Eleanor (Geller) D. BA in Econs., UCLA, 1965. Solo shows: Michael Walls Gallery, L.A., 1972, 112 Workshop Inc., N.Y.C., 1980, Annina Nosei Gallery, N.Y.C., 1981, 82, Blum Helman Gallery, N.Y.C., 1985, Galerie Montenay, Paris, 1988, Christine Burgin Gallery, N.Y.C., 1992, Jay Gorney Modern Art, N.Y.C., 1994, group shows: Annina Nosei Gallery, N.Y.C., 1980, Hayden Gallery, 1982, Contemporary Art at One Plaza, 1984, Bette Stoler Gallery, N.Y.C., 1984, John Weber Gallery, N.Y.C., 1986, Grace Borgenicht Gallery, 1988, Josh Baer Gallery, N.Y.C., 1991, Stuart Regan Gallery, L.A., 1992, Barbara Mathes Gallery, 1993, The Mus. of Modern Art, N.Y.C., 1994, Pfizer, Inc., 1995, artist: works contained in several mus. collections including Mus. Modern. Art., N.Y.C. Recipient Young Talent award L.A. County Mus., 1970.

DEUTSCH, DONNY, advertising executive. Chmn., CEO Deutsch, Inc., New York. Office: Deutsch Inc 111 8th Ave New York NY 10011-1603*

DEUTSCH, HAROLD FRANCIS, biochemist, researcher, educator; b. Sturgeon Bay, Wis., Sept. 2, 1918; s. Frank Joseph and Anna Catherine (Spahn) D.; m. Patricia Josephine Slidell, Aug. 8, 1942 (div. Nov. 1964); 1 child, Carolyn Frances; m. Regine Erika Merz, Dec. 15, 1965. PhB, U. Wis., 1940, PhD, 1944. Asst. prof. U. Wis., Madison, 1945-47, assoc. prof., 1947-54, prof., 1954-88, prof. emeritus, 1989—; vis. prof. U. Brazil, Rio de Janeiro, 1950, U. Sao Paulo, Brazil, 1954, Hokkado U., Japan, 1972, 81, U. Pretoria, 1988, Osako U., 1990, 1993, 99. Rockefeller fellow Nobel Med. Inst., Stockholm, 1950-51; Alexander von Humboldt prof. Fed. Republic of Germany, 1987. Mem. AAAS, Am. Soc. Biochemistry and Molecular Biology, Am. Chem. Soc., Am. Soc. Immunology. Office: Univ Wis 1300 University Ave Madison WI 53706-1510

DEUTSCH, HERBERT ARNOLD, music educator; b. Baldwin, N.Y., Feb. 9, 1932; s. Barnet Baruch and Miriam (Meyersburg) D.; m. Margaret Ann Carbray, Oct. 10, 1955 (dec.); children: Lisbeth Ann, Edmund Barnet; m. Nancy DiNapoli Blau, Sept. 14, 1997. BS in Edn., Hofstra U., 1956; MusM, Manhattan Sch. Music, 1961; postgrad., NYU, 1973-75. Music faculty East Meadow (N.Y.) Pub. Schs., 1959-60; freelance musician N.Y.C. area, 1960-61; lectr. music Hofstra Univ., Hempstead, N.Y., 1961-63, instr., 1964-68, asst. prof., 1969-73, assoc. prof., 1974-79, prof., 1983—, dept. chair, 1995—; dir. mktg. Moog Music div. Norlin Corp., Buffalo, 1980-81, dir. sales/mktg., 1981-83; cons. Pulse Concepts, L.I., N.Y., 1971—, Jim Henson's Muppets, N.Y.C., 1983-86, Norlin Corp., Chgo., 1976-79; edn. cons. Music and Computer Educator, 1989-91. Author: Synthesis, 1975, 2d rev. edit., 1984, Electroacoustic Music: Its First Century, 1993; composer numerous mus. works; contbr. articles to profl. jours., 1972—, Am. Record Guide, 1987-93. Mem. Huntington (N.Y.) Spl. Edn. PTA, 1976-88; bd. dirs. Huntington Symphony, 1973-75, Suffolk County (N.Y.) Family Services, 1975-77. Served with U.S. Army, 1956-58. Recipient grad. assistantship Manhattan Sch. Music, 1961; Meet the Composer grantee, 1976, 86, 87, 88, 90, 91, 92, 93, 94, 95, 96, 97, 98, Estabrook Disting. Alumni award Hofstra U., 1996. Mem. ASCAP (award 1992, 93, 94, 96, 97, 98), AAUP, L.I. Composers Alliance (founder, bd. dirs. 1972-91, v.p. 1991-95, pres. 1998-99), Am. Fedn. Musicians, Music and Entertainment Industry Edn. Assn.

DEUTSCH, JAMES BERNARD, lawyer; b. St. Louis, Aug. 24, 1948; s. William Joseph and Margaret (Klevorn) D.; m. Deborah Marie Hallenberg, June 26, 1976; children: Michael, Gabriel. BA, Southeast Mo. State U., 1974; JD, U. Mo., 1978. Bar: Mo. 1978, U.S. Dist. Ct. (we. dist.) Mo. 1978, U.S. Ct. Appeals (8th cir.), 1989, U.S. Supreme Ct., 1990. Assoc. Gt. Plains Legal Found., Kansas City, Mo., 1978-79; pvt. practice, Kansas City, 1979-81; gen. counsel Mo. Dept. Revenue, Jefferson City, Mo., 1981-83; commr. Mo. Adminstrv. Hearing Commn., Jefferson City, 1983-89; dep. atty.-gen State of Mo., Jefferson City, 1989-93; ptnr. Riezman & Blitz, P.C., Jefferson City, Mo., 1993—. Served to lance cpl. USMC, 1968-70, Vietnam. Named one of Men of Yr. in Constrn. Industry, Engring. News, McGraw-Hill Pub., N.Y.C., 1985. Mem. ABA (jud. adminstrn. com.), ASCE (hon. fellow), Mo. Bar Assn. (council mem. taxation com. 1985—, adminstrn. law and jud. adminstrn. coms.), Mo. Inst. for Justice (bd. dirs. 1977—), VFW. Office: Riezman & Blitz 308 E High St Jefferson City MO 65101-3237

DEUTSCH, LAWRENCE IRA, minister; b. Bklyn., June 17, 1939; s. Meyer Irving and Lillian (Ilkovitz) D.; m. Carolyn Ann Beaton, June 2, 1960 (div. Oct. 1986); children: Michael Keith, Eric Scott; m. Karol White, Dec. 31, 1987; stepchildren: Sharlotte Lester, Jason Lester. AAS, Bklyn. Coll., 1961; BTh, Calvary Bible Coll., Lake Charles, La., 1990; MA, Cornerstone U., 1991; Dr.Religious Edn., Moody Theol. Sem., 1992. Ordained to ministry Bapt. Ch., 1982. Pastor Congregation Beth Ha'Shem, Houston, 1988—; chaplain T.D.C. & Houston Downtown Med. Ctr., 1981—; bd. dirs. Jesus the Messiah Sem., 1990—, Beth Ha'Shem Christian Counseling Ctr. Author: (poetry) various publs. (silver award 1986, golden award 1987-89). Pub. rels. officer to mayor Gulfport, Miss., 1968-69. With USMC, 1958-64. Mem. So. Bapt. Messianic Alliance, Messianic Jewish Alliance Am., Internat. Writers Alive (v.p. 1990—). Republican. Mem. Messianic Ch. Home and Office: 3510 Greenwood Pl Deer Park TX 77536-5771 *LaChaim (To Life!). Life is very precious and very exciting. We need to make each day count to bring honor and glory to Yeshua Ha'Mashiach (Jesus the Messiah).*

DEUTSCH, MARSHALL E(MANUEL), medical products company executive, inventor; b. N.Y.C., Aug. 17, 1921; s. David and Madeline Lea (Roth) D.; m. Judith Greene, June 27, 1947; children: Pamina Margret, Ethan Amadeus, Freeman Sarastro. BS, CCNY, 1941; PhD, NYU, 1951. Tech. dir. NEN-Picker Radiopharms., Boston, 1966-68, Picker-Hoechst Inc., Bedford, Mass., 1968-70, Mead Diagnostics, Inc., Bedford, 1970-72, CIS Radiopharms., Bedford, 1972-74, Thyroid Diagnostics Inc., Bedford, 1972-85; chmn. Marshall Diagnostics Inc., Bedford, 1985-87; tech. adv. J&S Med. Assocs., Natick, Mass., 1988—; bd. dirs., corp. sec., v.p. Health Svcs. Internat., Washington, 1983-96; contractor Joint Publs. Rsch. Svc., Arlington, Va., 1984-92. Inventor self-contained technetium generator, 1971, various radiopharm. products, 1973, various clin. chem. test kits, devices, 1953-96; contbr. articles to mags. cons. AID, Zaire, 1979, UN Capital Devel. Fund, Benin, 1977. 1st lt. A.C., U.S. Army, 1942-45, ETO. Fellow AAAS (life); mem. Am. Assn. Clin. Chemistry (emeritus, chmn. pub. rels. com. 1962), Am. Chem. Soc. (sr., emeritus), N.Y. Acad. Scis., Sci. Rsch. Soc. Am. Unitarian Universalist. Avocations: folk dancing, growing exotic mushrooms. Home: 41 Concord Rd Sudbury MA 01776-2328 Office: J&S Med Assocs 35 Tripp St Ste 1 Framingham MA 01702-8780

DEUTSCH, MARTIN, emeritus physics professor; b. Vienna, Austria, Jan. 29, 1917; m. 1939, two children. BS, MIT, 1937, PhD, 1941; DHC (honorary), U. Algiers, Algeria, 1959. Instr. Physics MIT, Cambridge, Mass., 1941-45; scientist Los Alamos (Calif.) Sic. Lab., 1944-46, froms asst. prof. to prof., 1945-87, dir. Lab. Nuclear Sci., 1975-80; emeritus prof. Physics MIT, Cambridge, Mass., 1987—. Recipient Rumford Medal, AAAS, 1985. Fellow Am. Physical Soc., AAAS; mem. Nat. Acad. Scis. Office: Mass Inst Technology Dept Physics Cambridge MA 02139*

DEUTSCH, MARTIN BERNARD JOSEPH, editor, publisher; b. Karlsruhe, Fed. Republic of Germany, Apr. 7, 1931; came to U.S., 1939, naturalized, 1948; s. Benedikt and Margarethe (Zivi) D.; 1 son, Kenneth; m. Denise Elaine Brosius, Sept. 24, 1994. Student in history and journalism, CCNY, 1953; student in Eng. lit., Columbia U., summer 1955. CCNY coll. corr. N.Y. Times, 1953-55; mng. editor The Beachcomber, Long Beach Island, N.J., summers 1952, 53; reporter Southwest American, Ft. Smith, Ark., 1954-55; mng. editor Travel Courier and Travel Weekly, 1955-67; pres., editor, pub. travel mags. divsn. Ofcl. Airline Guides, N.Y.C., 1967-93; editor, pub. Reed Travel Mags., Secaucus, N.J., 1993-94; guest instr. U. Mass., 1975; cons., spkr. to travel and transp. industry. Monthly columnist: Up Front, Frequent Flyer mag., 1980-94; editor-at-large, monthly columnist Travel Agent mag., pres. trade show divsn.; pub. Selling North America, 1995—. Mem. Upper Manhattan Cmty. Planning Bd., 1965; mem. travel adv. bd. U.S. Dept. Commerce, U.S. Travel Svc., 1977-81; delegate White House Conf. on Travel and Tourism, 1995; officer Ctr. for Internat. Health and Coop., N.Y.C. With U.S. Army, 1953-55. Recipient various awards for travel journalism. Home: 15 W 72nd St New York NY 10023-3402 Office: 801 2nd Ave New York NY 10017-4706

DEUTSCH, NINA, pianist; b. San Antonio, Mar. 15; d. Irvin and Freda (Smukler) D. BS, Juilliard Sch. Music, 1964; MMA, Yale U., 1973. Concert pianist internat. and U.S. tours, 1965-82; entertainer, solo pianist Holland Am. Cruise Lines, 1987, 89-90; freelance pianist, lectr. on music, 1990—; exec. v.p. Internat. Symphony, N.Y.C., 1978-82. *Nina Deutsch achieved the first musical exchange on stage in the history of the People's Republic of China in 1982. As executive vice president of International Symphony for World Peace in 1982, she represented her organization in a series of concerts on that theme. ISWP had collected musical scores on the theme of Peace, Friendship, and Humanity. Her tour was endorsed by former U.S. President George Bush, and his brother Prescott Bush. Nina is also the first woman to have recorded the massive solo piano repertoire of Charles Ives. She presents lectures and lectures with musical illustrations.* Pianist: (records) Charles Ives, 1976, Vox Records; author: (book) Can You Afford Not to Be a Successful Private Teacher, 1994, (plays) Portrait of Liberace, 1995, Portrait of Clara Schumann, 1987; contbr. to mags. and newspapers. Bd. dirs. Metzner Found. for Overseas Relief; Ft. Lee coord. Channel 13, 1974. Tanglewood fellow Wulsin Fellowship, 1966; grantee Phillips Petroleum Found., 1982; recipient award for Am. music Nat. Fedn. Music Clubs, 1975; Oberlin Coll. scholar. Mem. Yale Alumni Assn. Bergen County. Avocations: swimming, hiking, baking. Home: Box 405 Leonia NJ 07605

DEUTSCH, PETER R., congressman, lawyer; b. Apr. 1, 1957; m. Lori Ann Coffino; children: Jonathan Michael, Danielle Brooke. BA in Psychology, Swarthmore Coll., 1979; JD, Yale U., 1982. Atty., 1983—; mem. 93rd-105th Congresses 20th Fla. dist., 1983—; mem. commerce com.; chmn. Privatization and Efficiency Com., 1986-88, Ins. Com., 1988-90, Congl. Reapportionment Subcom., 1990-92. Dir., founder Medicare Info. Program, Broward County, Fla., 1981-82. Recipient Humanitarian award Deborah Hosp., 1984, Torch of Liberty award Anti-Defamation League, 1985, Appreciation award Paralyzed Vets Assn., 1987, Scroll of Hon. Jewish Fedn., 1988; named Legislator of Yr. Broward County Chiropractic Soc., 1984, 85, Man of Yr. Lauderhill Regular Dem. Club, 1990, Alzheimer's Assn., 1990; Swarthmore Nat. scholar, 1975-79; J. Roland Pennock fellow, 1979. Mem. W. Broward Dem. Club, Broward Young Dems., Lauderhill Dem. Club, Pembrook Pines Dem. Club, Davie Dem. Club, United Dem. Club, Plantation Club, Sunrise C. of C., Tamarac C. of C., Margate Knights of Pythias, B'nai B'rith (Israeli award, Sunrise 1983), Jewish Fedn., Gold Key, Phi Beta Kappa. Office: US Ho of Reps 204 Cannon Bldg Washington DC 20515-0920

DEUTSCH, ROBERT WILLIAM, physicist; b. Far Rockaway, N.Y., Mar. 21, 1924; s. Nathan and Lena (Berger) D.; m. Florence Kadish, Sept. 11, 1949; children—Jane Lisa, David Jeffrey. B.S., MIT, 1948; Ph.D., U. Calif., 1953; LLD (hon.), U. Balt., 1999; LHD, Towson U., 1998. Registered profl. engr., Md., Mich. Physics cons. Martin-Marietta Corp., Balt., 1962-64; prof., chmn. dept. nuclear sci. and engring. Cath. U. Am., 1963-71; chmn. bd., chief exec. officer Gen. Physics Corp., Columbia, Md., 1966-87, RWD Tech. Inc., Columbia, 1988—; dir.; bd. dirs. Md. Sci. Contbr. articles to profl. jours.; author newspaper articles and pub. info. booklets on nuclear power. Bd. advisors U. Md. Tech. Advancement Program, 1988—; adv. bd. Sch. Continuing Studies Johns Hopkins U., 1994—; bd. visitors U. Md. Baltimore County, 1994—; trustee Md. Sci. Ctr., 1997—. Fellow Am. Nuclear Soc.; mem. NAE, AAAS, Am. Soc. Engring. Edn. Achievements include development and implementation of high tech. systems that improve human performance. Home: 8502 Arborwood Rd Baltimore MD 21208-1502 Office: RWD Tech Inc 10480 Little Patuxent Pkwy Columbia MD 21044-3530

DEUTSCH, SID, bioengineer, educator; b. N.Y.C., Sept. 19, 1918; s. Elias and Gussie (Hazen) D.; m. Ruth Appleman, Nov. 15, 1941 (div. June 1969), remarried, 1984; children: Alice, Phyllis, Naomi; m. Jane Arieti, Aug., 1969 (dec. Mar., 1978); m. Annette Page, Apr., 1979 (div. Dec., 1984). BEE, Cooper Union, 1941; MEE, Bklyn. Poly. Inst., 1947, PhD, 1955. Designer Fairchild Camera & Instrument Co., N.Y.C., 1943-44; instr. Madison Inst., Newark, 1946-50; engr. Poly. R & D Co., Bklyn., 1950-54; mem. faculty Bklyn. Poly. Inst., 1954-72, prof. elec. engring., 1962-72; prof. bioengring. Rutgers U. Med. Sch., Piscataway, N.J., 1972-79; vis. prof. U. S.Fla., Tampa, 1983-98; vis. prof. Tel Aviv U., Israel, 1977, prof. bioengring, 1979-84; cons. Lewyt Mfg. Corp., 1958-60; affiliate Rockefeller Inst., 1961-64. Author: Theory and Design of TV Receivers, 1951, Models of the Nervous System, 1967; co-author: Biomedical Instruments: Theory and Design, 1976, 2d edit., 1992, Neuroelectric Systems, 1987, Understanding the Nervous System: An Engineering Perspective, 1993; assoc. editor: IEEE Transactions on Biomedical Engring., 1991-96; patentee pseudorandom dot scan for TV. Mem. adult edn. com. Roslyn (N.Y.) Pub. Schs., 1955-58. With USNR, 1944-46. Fellow IEEE, Soc. for Info. Display; mem. Sigma Xi, Tau Beta Pi, Eta Kappa Nu. Home: 3967 Oakhurst Blvd Sarasota FL 34233-1447

DEUTSCH, STANLEY, anesthesiologist, educator; b. N.Y.C., Apr. 4, 1930; s. Elias and Estelle (Press) D.; m. Margaret R. Zuanic, July 11, 1971; children: Susan, Ellen, Nina, Eva. BA, NYU, 1950; MA, Boston U., 1951, PhD, 1955, MD, 1957. Diplomate Am. Bd. Anesthesiology. Rsch. and teaching fellow in physiology Boston U. Sch. Medicine, 1951-55; intern U. Pa. Grad. Hosp., 1957-58; resident in anesthesiology Hosp. U. Pa., 1958-61; asst. prof. anesthesiology U. Pa., 1963-65; asst. prof. Harvard U., 1965-69; prof. U. Chgo., 1969-71; prof., head. dept. anesthesiology U. Okla. Health Scis. Center, 1971-82; prof. anesthesiology U. Tex. Med. Sch., Houston, 1982-89; prof. anesthesiology George Washington Sch. Medicine, Washington, 1989-98, prof. emeritus, 1998—; cons. VA Med. Center, Oklahoma City. Contbr. articles to profl. publs. Capt., M.C. USAR, 1961-63. Mem. AMA, Am. Soc. Anesthesiologists, D.C. Med. Assn., Sigma Xi, Alpha Omega Alpha. Home: 1508 Colonial Ct Arlington VA 22209-1439 Office: George Washington U Hosp 901 23rd St NW Washington DC 20037-2327

DEUTSCH, THOMAS ALAN, ophthalmologist, educator; b. Nagoya, Japan, Aug. 11, 1954; (parents U.S. citizens); William E. and Natasha S. (Sobotka) D.; m. Judith Silverman, Dec. 6, 1986. AB, Washington U., 1975; MD, Rush Med. Coll., Chgo., 1979. Diplomate Am. Bd. Ophthalmology. Intern Presbyn.-St. Luke's Hosp., Chgo., 1979-80; resident U. Ill. Eye and Ear Infirmary, Chgo., 1980-83; asst. prof. ophthalmology U. Ill., Chgo., 1983-84; asst. prof. ophthalmology Rush Med. Coll., Chgo., 1984-87, assoc. prof., 1987-94, prof., 1994—, chmn. ophthalmology, 1996—; lectr., U. Ill., Chgo., 1984-96—; adj. asst. prof. biomed. engri., Northwestern U. Evanston, Ill., 1986-87, adj. assoc. prof., 1987-94, adj. prof., 1994-97. Assoc. editor Key Ophthalmology, 1986-88, Year Book Ophthalmology, 1986-88; author 6 books; contbr. articles to profl. jours. Recipient Chancellor's award Washington U., 1975, Henry Lyman award Rush Med. Coll, 1978, Mark Lepper tchg. award, 1994, Disting. Alumnus award Rush Med. Coll., 1998. Fellow ACS, Am. Acad. Ophthalmology (Honor award 1990); mem. Assn. Rsch. Vision Ophthalmology, Chgo. Ophthalmol. Soc. (chmn. clin. conf. 1986, councillor 1988-89, sec.-treas. 1989-91, pres. 1994-95), Rush Alumni Assn. (pres. 1990-93, James A. Campbell award 1990). Office: Rush Presbyn St Luke's Med Ctr 1725 W Harrison St Ste 918 Chicago IL 60612-3835

DEUTSCH, THOMAS FREDERICK, physicist; b. Vienna, Austria, Apr. 24, 1932; came to U.S., 1939; s. George and Sabina (Edel) D.; m. Judy Foreman, May 5, 1990. B. Engring Physics, Cornell U., 1955; AM, Harvard U., 1956, PhD, 1961. Prin. rsch. scientist Raytheon Co., Lexington, Mass., 1960-74; staff mem. Mass. Inst. Tech., Lexington, 1974-84; physicist Mass. Gen. Hosp., Boston, 1984—; assoc. prof. Harvard Med. Sch., Boston, 1987—. Contbr. articles to profl. jours.; patentee in field. Recipient of R.W. Wood Prize, 1991, Optical Soc. Am. Fellow Am. Phys. Soc., Optical Soc. Am. (Wood prize 1991), Am. Soc. for Lasers in Medicine; mem. IEEE (sr.). Office: Bar 703 Wellman Labs Mass Gen Hosp Boston MA 02114-2605*

DEUTSCHMAN, MRS. PAUL See RYAN, REGINA CLAIRE

DE VALERIA, DAVID ALAN, architect, sculptor; b. Indpls., July 31, 1955; s. Herman and Gina (Giusti) De V.; m. Patricia A. De Valeria, May 20, 1988; children: Bianca, Katya. BA, Ind. U., 1978; MArch, Columbia U., 1983. Registered architect, Calif., Ariz., Ind., Nev. Designer Buttrick White & Burtis, N.Y.C., 1983-84; sr. designer Skidmore Owings & Merrill, N.Y.C., 1984-85; prin. Device Projects, Hollywood, Calif., 1985-87; architect Herren & Damschen Architects, Berne, Switzerland, 1989-90; prin. Sperr/De Valeria Architects, Scottsdale, Ariz., 1990-93; assoc. prin. Schenkelshultz, Indpls., 1993-99; prin. Imirzian, De Valeria and Assocs., Phoenix, 1999—; adj. prof. Woodbury U., L.A., 1985-87; symposium on faculty planning and design Harvard U., 1998, Ariz. Biltmore Hotel, 1999. Sculptor Arroyo, 1992, The Fall, 1993, Globe, 1995, Luminous Corpse, 1996, The Harmony of the Spheres, 1997. Mem. parent coun. Mcpl. Sch. Dist. Washington Twp., Indpls., 1997; mem. long range planning com. Unitarian Universalist Ch., Ft. Wayne, Ind., 1997, Indpls., 1997-99. Recipient award for excellence in design Nat. Endowment for Arts, N.Y.C., 1981, Bronze award Am. Sch. and Univ., Ft. Wayne, 1996. Mem. AIA (citation allied arts 1992, allied arts award 1993). Office: Imiraizn and Assocs Architects 8906 N Central Ave Phoenix AZ 85020

DEVAN, DEBORAH HUNT, lawyer; b. Allentown, Pa., Jan. 22, 1950; d. Valerio R. and Audrey (Miller) H.; m. Mark S. Devan, May 30, 1981; children: Emily, David, Eric. BA in Econs. magna cum laude, U. Md., 1972, JD cum laude, 1975. Bar: Md. 1975, D.C. 1976, U.S. Dist. Ct. Md. 1976, U.S. Dist. Ct. D.C. 1987, U.S. Ct. Appeals (4th cir.) 1988, U.S. Ct. Appeals (2d cir.) 1991, U.S. Supreme Ct. 1980, Md. Ct. Appeals 1975, D.C. Ct. Appeals 1976. Ptnr. Weinberg and Green, Balt., 1974-94; prin. Neuberger, Quinn, Gielen, Rubin & Gibber, P.A., Balt., 1994—. Bd. dirs. Lutheran Hosp. Md., Inc., 1981-86, Cystic Fibrosis Found., 1983 (Community Svc. Gold award), Lutheran Health Care Corp., 1988-91, U. Md. Law Sch. Fund, 1991, Balt. Devel. Corp., 1999—; trustee Merry-Go-Round Enterprises, Inc. Mem. ABA (bus. bankruptcy com., subcommittee bankruptcy litigation, subcommittee claims and priorities), Am. Bankruptcy Inst., Turnaround Mgmt. Assn., Women's Bar Assn., Assn. Comml. Fin. Attys., Md. State Bar Assn., Inc. (subcommittee creditor's rights, bankruptcy and insolvency), Bankruptcy Bar Assn. Md. (corp. sec., bd. dirs., pres. 1996-97), Exec. and Profl. Women's Coun. Md. (1st v.p. 1984), Network 2000, Comml. Real Estate Women, Bar Assn. Balt. City (profl. ethics com. 1980, publicity com. 1981). Office: Neuberger Quinn Gielen Rubin & Gibber 1 South St Fl 27 Baltimore MD 21202-3282

DEVANE, DENIS JAMES, health care company executive; b. N.Y.C., Feb. 11, 1938; s. Eugene and Deborah (Courtney) D.; m. Margaret Mary Walsh, Oct. 14, 1961; children: Denise, Daniel, Deborah, Tara. BS, Fordham U., 1959. Asst. v.p. nat. sales mgr. C.I.T. Bldgs. Corp., N.Y.C., 1971-72, v.p., gen. mgr., 1973-74, pres., 1974-75; v.p. Lifemark Corp., Houston, 1975-80, sr. v.p., 1980-84; pres. Hosp. div. Health Group, Inc., Nashville, 1984; pres., chief operating officer Healthdyne, Inc., Marietta, Ga., 1985-86; pres., chief exec. officer Am. Rehab. Services Inc., Atlanta, 1987-88; chmn., CEO Rebound, Inc., Hendersonville, Tenn., 1989-92; exec. v.p. Healthsouth Corp., Birmingham, Ala., 1993-95; chmn. exec. com. Altria Healhcare Corp., Birmingham, 1997—, also bd. dirs. Mem. Summit Club, Greystone Golf Club. Home: 1097 Greymoor Rd Birmingham AL 35242-7211

DEVANE, JACKIE, head coach women's basketball; b. Phila.. BS in Phys. Edn., Delaware State U., Dover, 1983; MS, Pa. State U., Coll. Park, Pa., 1987. Head coach women's volleyball and basketball Cheyney (Pa.) State Coll., 1987-92; head coach women's basketball Del. State U., Dover, 1995—. Office: Del State U 1200 North DuPont Hwy Dover DE 19901*

DEVANE, PATRICIA ANN DOSS, educational administrator; b. Atlanta, June 15, 1945; d. Arthur Thomas and Mildred Elizabeth (House) D.; m. James Gordon DeVane, June 22, 1968; children: Jay, David, Patrick. AB in English, Elem. Edn., Ga. State U., 1968, MEd in Mid. Grades Edn., 1982, EdS in Ednl. Adminstrn., 1986. Cert. ednl. adminstr., supr. Tchr. DeKalb County Bd. Edn., Decatur, Ga., 1968-71, 73; tchr. mid. sch. Rockdale County Bd. Edn., Conyers, Ga., 1979-84; instrnl. lead tchr. Conyers Middle Sch., 1984-87; asst. prin. Conyers Mid. Sch., 1987-88; prin. Barksdale Elem. Sch., Conyers, 1988-93, Meml. Mid. Sch., Conyers, 1993—; presenter at profl. confs.; chmn. new prins. dinner Ga. State Prins. Ctr., Atlanta, 1988—; participant Internat. Invitational Conf., U. Oxford, Eng., 1991. Mem. ASCD, NAESP, Nat. Staff Devel. Coun., Nat. Mid. Sch. Assn., Ga. Mid. Sch. Assn., Ga. Assn. Ednl. Leaders. Baptist. Office: Meml Middle Sch 3205 Underwood Rd SE Conyers GA 30013-2309

DEVANE, WILLIAM, actor; b. Albany, N.Y., Sept. 5, 1939; m. Eugenie; children—Josh, Jake. Attended, Am. Acad. Dramatic Arts, N.Y.C. Movie appearances include: The Pursuit of Happiness, 1971, My Old Man's Place, 1971, McCabe and Mrs. Miller, 1971, Mortadella, 1971, Irish Whiskey Rebellion, 1973, Marathon Man, 1976, Family Plot, 1976, The Bad News Bears in Breaking Training, 1977, Rolling Thunder, Butch and Sundance: The Early Years, Yanks, Honky Tonk Freeway, 1980, Testament, 1983, Vital Signs, 1989; appeared in TV films The Missiles of October, Shirts/Skins, 1973, Crime Club, 1973, The Bait, 1973, Jane Doe, 1983, With Intent to Kill, 1984, Exception to the Rule, 1997, Forgotten Sins, 1997; TV miniseries From Here to Eternity, 1979, Black Beauty, A Women Named Jackie, 1991, Knots Landing: Back to the Cul-de-Sac, 1997, The Big Easy, Heavenly Curse, Chips, The War Dog; numerous other TV appearances, including Judgement: The Court Martial of the Tiger of Malaya-General Yamashita, on Stage, Medical Center, Ironside, Hawaii Five-O, Fear on Trial, The Snoop Sisters, Timestalkers, The Preppy Murder, 1989, Murder C.O.D., 1990, Death of Innocence, 1991, Nightmare in Columbia County, 1991, A Woman Named Jackie, 1991, Obsessed, 1992, The President's Child, 1992, Prophet of Evil: The Ervil Lebaron Story, 1993; actor in TV series Knots Landing, 1983-93, The Monroes, 1995—; TV movie The Absolute Truth, 1997, Doomsday Rock, 1997; stage appearances include: MacBird!, 1967, One Flew Over the Cuckoo's Nest, 1968, Are You Now Or Have You Ever Been?, 1980, The Changing Room, 1981, play: G.R. Point at Playhouse Theater, N.Y.C.; TV narrator The Most Dangerous Game, 1990. Office: Kazarian Spencer & Assocs Inc 11365 Ventura Blvd Ste 100 Studio City CA 91604-3148*

DEVANEY, CAROL SUSAN, management consultant; b. Panama City, Panama, May 8, 1954; d. James Henry DeVaney and Andrea Wong Mahoney; m. C. Eldon Taylor, July 30, 1978; 1 child, Taryne Jade Taylor; 1 stepchild, Deborah A. Taylor (dec. 1997). BA, Cath. U., 1974, MSW, 1975. Nat. Acad. cert. social worker; lic. clin. social worker, Va. Cmty. educator Prince George Health Dept., Cheverly, Md., 1975-76; coord. social svcs. Detox Ctr., Cocoa, Fla., 1976-77; psychiat. social worker Brevard County Mental Health, Melbourne, Fla., 1977-79; sr. clin. social worker Chesterfield (Va.) Mental Health, 1979-81; coord. bus. programs Chesterfield County, Chesterfield, 1981-86; adminstr. orgnl. devel. and tng. Henrico County, Henrico, Va., 1986-90; owner, pres. DeVaney-Wong Internat., Potomac, Md., 1990—; instr. Rollins Coll., Patrick AFB, Fla., 1977-79; cons. Coun. on Aging, Chesterfield, 1981-86; instr., vol. U. Richmond Women's Program, 1981-92; adv. bd. Bermuda Run, Chesterfield, 1983-86. Contbg. author: Prevention in Community M.H. Practice, 1992; author: (profl. manual) Stress Management, 1983; co-author: (book, manual, video) Let's Talk Diversity, 1992, Managing Diversity. Cons., vol. 1708 Gallery, Richmond, 1989-90; mem. adv. bd. Georgetown Hill Child Care, Potomac, 1994-95; mem. Brind (Europe) Register Customer Recommended Cons., 1993-99. Recipient program awards Nat. Assn. Counties, 1989-91. Mem. ASTD (v.p. comm. 1987-88, Richmond chpt. pres. 1989-90, founder/liaison nat. Ibero-Am. network 1990-97, D.C. met. v.p. programs 1997, v.p. programs Ft. Lauderdale chpt. 1998), NASW, Am. Bus. Women's Assn., Soc. for Human Resource Mgmt., World Future Soc., Brind Register Women's C. of C. Avocations: swimming, travel, ethnic cooking, languages, world philosophy.

DEVANEY, CYNTHIA ANN, elementary education educator, real estate broker; b. Gary, Ind., Feb. 6, 1947; d. Charles Barnard and Irene Mae (Nelson) Burner; m. Harold Verne DeVaney, Nov. 23, 1974 (dec. 1981). BS, Ball State U., 1970, MS, 1972; postgrad., Ind. U. and Purdue U., 1974-76. Cert. real estate broker, Ind. Real estate broker Century 21 McColly Realtors, Merrillville, Ind., 1979-86; real estate broker Better Homes and Gardens McColly Realtors, Merrillville, 1986—, with Pres.' Coun.; tchr. Merkley Elem. Sch., Highland, Ind., 1969—. Active Schubert Theater Guild, Chgo. Mem. N.W. Ind. Bd. Realtors (Million Dollar Club), Nat. Bd. Realtors, Jr. Ind Hist. Soc., Innsbrook Country Club, Match Point Tennis Club. Democrat. Methodist. Avocations: golf, tennis, traveling, gardening, theater. Home: 607 E 78th Pl Merrillville IN 46410-5624 Office: McColly Better Homes & Gardens 9143 Indianapolis Blvd Hammond IN 46322-2504

DEVANEY, DENNIS MARTIN, lawyer, educator; b. Cheverly, Md., Feb. 25, 1946; s. Peter Paul and Alice Dorothy (Duffy) D.; children: Jeanne Marie, Susan Theresa. BA in History, U. Md., 1968, MA in Govt. Politics, 1970; JD, Georgetown U., 1975. Bar: Md. 1976, D.C. 1976, Fla. 1977, U.S. Supreme Ct. 1980. Instr. European div. U. Md., Bremerhaven, Fed. Republic Germany, 1971-72; legis. asst. Md. Senate Jud. Commn., Annapolis, 1973-74; asst. gen. counsel U.S. Brewers Assn., Washington, 1975-77; counsel Food Mktg. Inst., Washington, 1977-79; ptnr. Randall, Bangert & Thelen, Washington, 1979-81; assoc. Tighe, Curhan & Piliero, Washington, 1981-82; mem. U.S. Merit System Protection Bd., Washington, 1982-88; gen. counsel Fed. Labor Relations Auth., Washington, DC, 1988; mem. NLRB, 1988-94; of counsel Winston & Strawn, 1995-97, Butzel Long, 1997—; adj. prof. George Washington U., Washington, 1982-90, Boston U., 1992-94, Cornell U., 1995, Tulane, 1995, assoc. prof. Wayne State U., 1995—. Served with USN, 1970-72, ETO. Mem. ABA, Md. Bar Assn., D.C. Bar Assn., Fla. Bar Assn., Fed. Bar Assn., Phi Alpha Theta, Pi Sigma Alpha, Delta Theta Phi, Omicron Delta Kappa. Democrat. Roman Catholic. Home: 500 River Place Dr Apt 5417 Detroit MI 48207-5051 Office: Butzel Long 150 W Jefferson Ave Ste 870 Detroit MI 48226-4415

DEVANEY, DONALD EVERETT, law enforcement official; b. Providence, Nov. 21, 1936; s. William Francis and Elizabeth Florence (Hill) D.; m. Tokiko Yoshida, May 19, 1960; 1 child, George Y. AA in Edn., El Paso Community Coll., 1973; BA, SUNY, Albany, 1979. Cert. healthcare protection adminstr. Internat. Healthcare Safety and Security Found. Sgt. maj. U.S. Army, 1954-83; customs inspector U.S. Customs Svc., Honolulu, 1983-84; provost marshal Tripler Army Med. Ctr., Honolulu, 1984—, regional chair Europe and Asia, 1989-93, 97—; past dir. Kalihi-Palama Immigrant Svc. Ctr.; extraordinary min. of the eucharist Tripler Catholic Cmty. Bd. dirs. USO, 1996, Coalition for a Drug Free Hawaii, 1996. Decorated Legion of Merit; recipient Disting Svc. award Hawaii Joint Police, 1977, 86, George Washington Honor medal Freedom's Found., 1973, Order Mil. Med. Merit, 1996, Elwood J. McGuire award Hawaii, 1997; elec. to Hawaii Jt. Police Assn. Hall of Fame, 1998, Nelson W. Aldrich Hall of Honor, 1998, Order of Military Medical Merit, 1997. Mem. USO (sec., bd. dirs. Hawaii chpt.), Hawaii Joint Police Assn. (pres. 1985, 98, 99), CID Agt. Assn., Nat. Assn. for Uniformed Svcs. (v.p. Hawaii chpt., nat. bd. dirs. 1996—), U.S. Army Retiree Coun. (U.S. Army Hawaii vice chmn.), Hawaii Law Enforcement and Pvt. Security (chmn. awards com.), Internat. Assn. for Healthcare Security and Safety (region 17 chairperson), Hawaii Coun. Police and Pvt. Security (bd. dirs. 1996—), Noncommd. Officer Assn. (life), Ret. Enlisted Assn. (life), DAV (life chpt. 3), Friend Med. Regt., Rotary (pres. Pearl Harbor chpt. 1991-92, dir. cmty. svc. dist. 5000, 1992-93), KC. Roman Catholic. Avocation: coin and stamp collecting. Fax: (808) 433-4465. Home: 98-911 Ainanui Loop Aiea HI 96701-2766 Office: Office Provost Marshal Tripler Army Med Ctr Honolulu HI 96859-5000

DEVANEY, JOHN GOODWIN, painter, muralist; b. Cin., May 17, 1946; s. John Parker Devaney and Martha Goodwin McCartney; children: Laurel MacDonald, Clover Lane. BFA, Marlboro (Vt.) Coll., 1969; MFA, Sch. of Mus. Fine Arts, Boston, 1990; student, N.Y. Studio Sch., 1969-70. Tchr. fellow Harvard U., Boston, 1984-86, 92-94; asst. prof. Art Inst. of Boston, 1984-93; prof. painting Marlboro Coll., 1991-92; designer/artist Marlboro Theatre Co., 1968-85, Actors Theatre, Nantucket, Mass., 1990-97. Muralist, Natatorium at U. Conn., Storrs, 1992, water garden mural Danehy Park, Cambridge, Mass., 1997, mural of Nantasket Beach, Hull, Mass. Mem., designer Friends of the Park, Cambridge, 1996—, Mid-Cambridge Neighborhood Assn., 1996—, Cambridge Arts Coun., Cambridge, 1994—. Visual Arts rsch. fellow Harvard U., 1975; artist fellowship residency MacDowell Colony, 1993, Yaddo Colony, 1993; Nat. Endowment grantee, 1993. Avocations: gardening, swimming, skiing, tennis. Home: 10 Pond View Dr Nantucket MA 02554-4403

DEVANTIER, PAUL W., communications executive, broadcaster; b. Wausau, Wis., Mar. 25, 1946; w. Walter Herman and Ella Marie (Mundt) D.; m. Ellen Stapel, Aug. 2, 1970; children: Richard, John, Andrew, Katie, Susan. BA, Concordia Coll., 1968; M in Divinity, Concordia Seminary, 1972; M in Mass Comm., So. Ill. U., Edwardsville, 1993; LLD, Concordia U., 1998. Radio announcer Sta. WXCO, Wausau, 1965-68, Sta. KRCH, St. Louis, 1968-72; dir. devel. Sta. KFUO-AM-FM, St. Louis, 1972-74, gen. mgr., 1974-82; exec. dir. communications Luth. Ch.—Mo. Synod, St. Louis, 1982—; speaker By the Way (internat. syndicated radio program) 1974—. Author: By the Way, 1993; exec. prodr.: (religious documentary film) Hymn A Celebration of Change, 1984 (Angel award), (TV spl.) Easter Alive 'Round the World, 1993 (Emmy award nomination), (TV spl.) Not Without Hope, 1994 (Angel award), Martin Luther Promo, 1998 (Telley award), Message of Hope, 1998 (Angel award DeRose Hinkhouse award), Just in Time For Christmas, 1999 (Angel award De Rose Hinkhouse award), (radio) Lutheran School Spots, 1999 (Angel award); exec. dir. Lutheran Witness mag., 1999 (Associated Ch. Press Best of Class award). Trustee, pres. Luth. Film Assocs., N.Y.C., 1982—. Mem. Religious Comm. Coun., World Assn. Christian Communicators, Nat. Religious Broadcasters, Phi Kappa Phi. Office: The Luth Ch—Mo Synod 1333 S Kirkwood Rd Saint Louis MO 63122-7226

DEVARIS, PANAYOTIS ERIC, architect; b. Lefkas Island, Greece, Dec. 29, 1932; came to U.S., 1960; M.Arch. Ecole des Beaux Arts, Paris, 1960; grad. cert. in bus. adminstrn., L.I. U., 1981. Registered architect; cert. Nat. Council Archtl. Registration Bds.; cert. profl. planner. Sr. corp. architect AT&T, N.Y.C., 1972-90; sr. corp. architect PSE&G, N.J., 1990-93, cons., 1990-93; pres. DeVaris/Workspace Planning & Design, Inc., 1990-97, Main St. South Orange Inc., 1997-99. Prin. works include projects in N.Y.C.: World Trade Ctr., Park Lane Hotel, The Gershwin Theatre, The Sovereign Apts., The Uris Office Bldg.; in Conn.: Wesleyan U. Dormitories, 1960-72; for AT&T: Microelectronics Hdqs., Berkeley Heights, N.J., Network Software Ctr., Lisle, Ill., AT&T Corp. Ctr., Chgo., Materials Mgmt. Ctrs., Sacramento, Calif., Wichita, Kans., Ramapo, N.Y., AT&T Techs. Offices, Tokyo, 1972-90; author, internat. lectr. in field of work environments; juror furniture design competition Corp. Design mag., Annual Design Awards N.Y. State Assn. Architects; contbr. articles to trade mags. Mem. exec. com. Architects for Social Responsibility, 1988-90. Recipient tech. excellence award Western Electric Co., Inc., 1983. Fellow AIA (chmn. corp. architects com. N.Y. chpt. 1978, nat. chpt. 1986, N.J. chpt. 1992, mem. steering com. 1983-90, rep. to Internat. Union of Architects 1985-91). Office: 18 Harding Dr South Orange NJ 07079-1203

DE VARON, LORNA COOKE, choral conductor; b. Western Springs, Ill., Jan. 17, 1921; d. Vernon Walter and Hazel Mildred (Watts) Cooke; m. Jose de Varon, May 14, 1944; children: David, Joanna, Cristina, Alexander. BA, Wellesley Coll., 1942; MA, Radcliffe Coll., 1945; MusD honoris causa, New Eng. Conservatory, 1988. Asst. condr. Radcliffe Choral Soc., Radcliffe-Harvard Choir, 1942-44; condr. Bryn Mawr Coll. Choir, 1944-47; condr. chorus, chmn. choral dept. New Eng. Conservatory Music, Boston, 1947-88; condr. chorus for concerts with Boston Symphony Orch. New Eng. Conservatory Music, 1952-86; concert performer New Eng. Conservatory Chorus, tours in U.S., Europe, Russia, Israel, China; condr. Israel Summer Festival, 1977-79; condr., tchr. choral conducting Tanglewood Festival Chorus, 1952-66; condr. New Eng. Conservatory Camerata, 1989—; prof. emerita New Eng. Conservatory; condr. Longy Chamber Chorus, 1989—; guest condr. Cameron Singers, Israel, 1984, Radio Chorus Beijing, 1987; chmn. Choral Inst. of Composers Conf., 1983-85; mem. choral adv. panel Nat. Endowment for Arts; condr. New Eng. Conservatory Chamber Singers, summers 1982-87, Monadnock Music Festival. Editor, arranger choral works, E.C. Schirmer and Galaxy Pubs., Boston. Mem. Cambridge Arts Council. Recipient medal for Disting. Achievement City of Boston, 1967, medal for Disting. Achievement Radcliffe Grad. Soc., 1972, medal for Disting. Achievement Wellesley Coll., 1978, medal of Israel, 1977, Ludi award New Eng. Conservatory, 1983, Harvard Glee Club medal, 1987. Mem. Am. Choral Condrs. Assn., Pi Kappa Lambda. Home: 94 Lake View Ave Cambridge MA 02138-3326

DE VASSAL, VLADIMIR, investment management executive; b. Phila., Dec. 10, 1959; s. Alexander and Miliza (Koster) de V.; m. Anna Hursky, June 6, 1987; children: Nina Elena, Paul Alexander. BA in Fin. and Acctg., Drexel U., 1982, MBA in Investment Mgmt., 1987. Chartered fin. analyst. Acct. Deloitte, Haskins & Sell, Phila., 1979; fin. analyst, cons., coord. RCA Govt. Comm., Camden, N.J., 1980-82; fin. analyst Corestates Fin. Corp., Phila., 1982-85, acctg. officer, 1985-88, asst. v.p., 1988-92, v.p. ALCO analysis, 1992-94, mgr. interest rate risk analysis, 1994-95; dir. quantitative analysis CoreStates Investment Advisers, Phila., 1995-98; dir. quantitative rsch. The Glenmede Trust Co., 1998—. Mem. AIMR, Fin. Analysts of Phila. Soc., Beta Gamma Sigma, Beta Alpha Psi. Avocations: travel, volleyball, hiking, chess, coin collecting. Home: PO Box 313 545 Station Ln Gwynedd Valley PA 19437 Office: The Glenmede Trust Co One Liberty Pl 1650 Market St Ste 1200 Philadelphia PA 19103-7391

DEVASSIE, TERRY LEE, newspaper executive; b. Columbus, Ohio, Oct. 27, 1939; s. Robert William and Laura Belle (VanOrsdel) DeV.; m. Lola Faye Sandifer, June 21, 1964; children: Trevor Lane, Thad Lamont. BA in Indsl. Design, Columbus Coll. Art & Design, 1964. Clk., sta. mgr. Columbus Dispatch, 1957-70, div. mgr., 1970-71, asst. to circulation dir., 1971-77, state circulation mgr., 1977-79, circulation mgr., 1979-81, asst. circulation dir., 1981—; ptnr. Preston-Strat Investments, 1993—; pres., CEO Creative Inserts Co., 1992—; owner, designer TLD Design, Columbus, 1964-69; architect-designer Eagle Real Estate/Builders, Columbus, 1968-70; extrusion designer Plaskolite, Inc., Columbus, 1968-69. Pub. speaker on newspapers and hosps.; designer of drive-up newspaper rack; patentee on graphic inserts for newspaper racks. Bd. dirs. St. Anthony Mercy Hosp., Columbus, 1987-91; bd. govs., exec. com. Shriners Hosp. Burn Ctr., Cin., 1986-96; bd. govs. Lexington Unit of Shriners Hosp., 1991; imperial bd. trustees Shriners Hosps. for Children, 1996—; endowment com. Simon Kenton Coun., Boy Scouts Am., 1998—. Mem. Ohio Circulation Mgrs. (pres. 1982, founder Pres.'s award 1982, Pres.'s award 1986), Ohio Newspaper Assn. (chmn. conv. 1983, Pres.'s award 1984), Internat. Circulation Mgrs. Assn. (chmn. Internat. Newspaper Carrier Day 1982-84, Pres.'s award 1992), Newspaper Assn. Am. (newspaper coun.), Press Club Ohio (pres. 1983-84), Charity Newsies, Masons (33 degree), Shriners (Illustrious Potentate Aladdin Temple 1995, imperial pub. rels. com. 1995, chmn. endowment, wills and gifts for Shriners hosps. for children 1998). Republican. Methodist. Avocations: landscaping, architectural building and designing, coin collecting, golf, children. Home: 5808 Lapaz Ct Westerville OH 43081-4112 Office: Columbus Dispatch 5300 Crosswind Dr Columbus OH 43228-3664

DEVAULT, DAVID V., bank executive; b. Worcester, Mass., Dec. 15, 1954. BBA, U. Mass., 1976. CPA, R.I. Various positions KPMG Peat Warwick, Providence, R.I., 1976-86; contr. Washington Trust Bancorp, Inc., Westerly, R.I., 1986-87, CFO, 1987-89, sr. v.p., CFO, 1990-98, exec. v.p., treas., CFO, 1998—. Chmn. YMCA, Westerly, R.I., 1999-2001. Mem. Fin. Execs. Inst. (pres. Providence chpt. 1996-97). Office: Washington Trust Bancorp Inc 23 Broad St Westerly RI 02891-1827

DEVAULT, JOHN LEE, oil company executive, geophysicist; b. Kansas City, Mo., Aug. 4, 1937; s. Isaac Henderson and Evelyn Margaret (Rowell) DeV.; m. Janet Ann Miller, Sept. 11, 1968; children: Bryan Charles, Chris Lee. B Chem. Engring., Case Inst. Tech., Cleve., 1959; BS, MacMurray Coll., Jacksonville, Ill., 1961; MS, U. Houston, 1975. Lic. geophysicist, Calif., Am. Assn. Petroleum Geologists, Am. Inst. Profl. Geologists, Soc. Ind. Profl. Earth Scientists. Geophysicist United Geophys., Europe, Africa, Middle East, Australia-Asia, Alaska and Houston, 1961-74; pres. Sercel Inc., Houston, 1974-88; chmn. Jade Corp., Houston, 1988—. Contbr. articles to Oil and Gas Jour. Dir. Jaycees, Springfield, Ill., 1960; downstate v.p. Young Rep. Club, Springfield, 1960; bd. dirs. Honors Coll., U. Houston, 1990—, MacMurray Coll.; trustee Culver Legion-Culver Academies. Mem. Geophys. Soc. Houston (hon. life, pres. 1987), Soc. Exploration Geophysics (1st v.p. 1993), Am. Inst. Profl. Geologists (pres. Tex. sect.), Culver Club of Greater Houston (pres.). Mem. Disciples of Christ Ch. Home: 703 Queensmill Ct Houston TX 77079-2411 Office: Jade Corp PO Box 218567 Houston TX 77218-8567

D'EVEGNEE, CHARLES PAUL, lawyer; b. Liege, Belgium, Aug. 4, 1939; came to U.S., 1959; s. Charles Clement and Fernande Francoise (Godet) Devignez; m. Marie-Therese L. Barnich, Apr. 17, 1962; children: Chantal E., Charles D. BA, Brigham Young U., 1966; MA, U. Conn., Storrs, 1969; JD, U. Conn., West Hartford, 1974. Bar: Va. 1991, U.S. Banktuptcy Ct. (ea. dist.-Richmond divsn.), U.S. Dist. Ct. 9ea. dist.) Va., U.S. Ct. Appeals (4th cir.), U.S. Supreme Ct. Group pension underwriter Conn. Gen. Life Ins. Co., Bloomfield, 1969-72; legal cons. Frank B. Hall & Co., N.Y.C., 1974-76; regional counsel Meidinger & Assocs., Richmond, Va., 1976-78; dir. Office Benefits Devel., Commonwealth of Va., Richmond, 1978-91; pvt. practice, Ashland, Va., 1991—. Co-author: European Antitrust Law, 1976. Mem. Va. Gov.'s U.S. Savs. Bond Com., Richmond, 1986; rep. exec. bd. State's United Appeals of Greater Richmond Community Chest, 1989. With U.S. Army, 1960-63. Mem. ABA, Va. State Bar Assn., Hanover Bar Assn., Richmond Bar Assn. Avocations: travel, landscaping, sports. Home: 6034 Northfall Creek Pkwy Mechanicsville VA 23111 Office: 130 Thompson St Ste D Ashland VA 23005-1512

DE VEIRMAN, GEERT ADOLF, engineer; b. St. Amandsberg, Belgium, Nov. 20, 1961; came to U.S., 1984; s. Marcel M. De V. and Hilda Verschueren; m. Michele Y. Mage, Dec. 31, 1994. MSEE, Cath. U. Leuven, Belgium, 1984; PhD, U. Minn., 1988. Sr. design engr. I Silicon Systems, Tustin, Calif., 1988-90, sr. design engr. II, 1990-93, group leader, 1992—, prin. engr., 1993-96, sr. prin. engr., 1996—. Contbr. articles to profl. jours. Mem. IEEE (sr.), Eta Kappa Nu, Phi Kappa Phi. E-mail: GEERT.DEVEIRMAN@TUS.ssi1.com. Home: 22 Festivo Irvine CA 92606 Office: Silicon Systems 14351 Myford Rd Tustin CA 92780

DEVELLANO, JAMES CHARLES, professional hockey manager; b. Toronto, Ont., Can., Jan. 18, 1943; came to U.S., 1979; s. James Joseph and Jean (Piter) D. Ont. scout St. Louis Blues NHL, Toronto, 1967-72; eastern Can. scout N.Y. Islanders, Toronto, 1972-74, dir. scouting, 1974-82; asst. gen. mgr. Islanders, L.I., N.Y., 1981-82; gen. mgr. Detroit Red Wings, 1982-90, sr. v.p., 1990—; v.p., gen. mgr. Indpls. Checkers, 1979-81; alternate gov. for Detroit Red Wings. Winner Stanley Cup with N.Y. Islanders, 1979-80, 80-81, 81-82, with Detroit Red Wings, 1996-97, 97-98, Pres.'s Trophy with Detroit Red Wings, 1994-95, 95-96. Mem. Nat. Hockey League (bd. govs.). Office: Detroit Red Wings Hockey Club Joe Louis Arena 600 Civic Center Dr Detroit MI 48226-4419

DEVENDORF, LOUISE MARIE, promoter, writer; b. LeRoy, Mich., Apr. 5, 1939; d. Louis George and Lucille Mariam (Dean) Hinkley; m. Richard George Devendorf, Aug. 10, 1974; 1 child, Laurie Anne Hinkley Walker. Grad. high sch., 1957. Underwriter asst. Mich. Mut. Liability, Grand Rapids, 1957-63; dance instr. Arthur Murray Studio, Grand Rapids, 1959-61; insp. Wolverine Worldwide, Big Rapids, Mich., 1965-85; office mgr. Advt. Assocs., Grand Rapids, 1985-89; free-lance writer and promoter Reed City, Mich., 1989—. Author: Some Nostalgia Pertaining to Pearls, 1995, (poetry) War in Haiti, 1996. Mem. City Coun., Reed City, 1988—; mem. ex officio Libr. Bd., Reed City, 1992—; bd. dirs. Osceola Cares, Osceola County, 1993—; active Phone Tree, Reed City, 1995—; musician Furniture City Orch., 1957-59. Recipient award Internat. Soc. Poets, 1996; elected to Internat. Poetry Hall of Fame, 1997. Avocations: reading, playing music, helping people. Home: 311 W Franklin PO Box 91 Reed City MI 49677-0091

DEVENNY, LILLIAN NICKELL, trophy company executive; b. Chesapeake, Ohio; d. Hayes Basil and Alice Irene (Noble) Nickell; m. John Paul DeVenny Jr., Dec. 31, 1955; children: Carrie DeVenny Paganini (dec.), John Hayes. Student, Covington Bus. Sch., 1954-55, Norfolk Coll., 1980-81. Office mgr., bookkeeper Nickell Electric Co., Covington, Va., 1950-55, exec., 1960-62; sec. 5th Naval Dist. Hdqtrs., Norfolk, Va., 1955-58, Profl. Realty, Virginia Beach, 1971; pub. rels. corp. sec. Hobby Industries, Virginia Beach, 1973-74; owner, mgr., instr., sec.-treas. Dete Corp. t/a Hobby Assoc., Virginia Beach, 1974—; singer, actress Tidewater Dinner Theater, Norfolk, part-time, 1971-75; involved numerous continuing edn. units. Writer column on Va. travel, 1978-79; editor newsletter, 1972-73. Founding mem., chmn. bd. dirs. Va. Opposing Drunk Driving, 1981—, state v.p., 1981-86, state pres., 1986—; mem. adv. bd. Va. Commn. on Alcohol Safety, 1987-91; participant Va. Assembly on Future of Va.'s Cts., U. Va., Commn. Pub. Svc., 1989; mem. spl. White House briefing on ways to combat tragedy of drunk driving, 1989; mem. Va. Civilian-Mil. Comty. Safety Com., 1988; mem. Va. Alcohol Safety Action Program Commn., 1991—; co-chmn. Va. Coalition Against Drunk Driving, 1989—; contbr. passage Omnibus Alcohol Safety Act, Va. Gen. Assembly, 1994; legis. liaison for CCATS Transp. Safety Coalition, 1998—. Recipient Cmty. Svc. award J.C. Penney Co., 1985, Hometown Hero, Sta. WVEC-TV, 1986. Mem. Internat. Ceramists Assn., Modern Woodmen Am. (regional sec. 1954), Beta Sigma Phi (mem.-at-large). Episcopalian. Avocations: singing, costume design, reading, theatre, herb gardening. Office: Deste Corp t/a Hobby Assocs 5815 Hargrove St Norfolk VA 23502-4636

DEVENS, JOHN SEARLE, natural resources administrator; b. Shickshinny, Pa., Mar. 31, 1940; s. John Ezra and Laura (Bulkley) D.; m. Sharon I. Snyder (div. 1979); children: John, Jerilyn, James, Janis. BS, Belmont Coll., 1964; MEd, Emory U., 1966; PhD, Wichita State U., 1975. Dir. speech and hearing Columbia (S.C.) Coll., 1967-70; head dept. audiology Inst. Logopedics, Wichita, Kans., 1970-71; supr. audiology State of Alaska, Fairbanks, 1971-73; asst. prof. U. Houston, Victoria, 1975-77; pres. Prince William Sound C.C., Valdez, Alaska, 1977-92, Sterling Coll., Craftsbury Common, Vt., 1993-96; dir. Valdez Hearing and Speech Ctr.; exec. dir. Prince William Sound Regional Citizens' Adv. Coun., 1997—; owner, operator Valdez Hearing and Speech Ctr., 1977—. Prodr. films on hearing problems; contbr. articles to profl. jours. Mayor City of Valdez, 1985-89, mem. city coun., 1980-89; nat. chmn. adv. com. Horsemanship for Handicapped, 1964-67; mem. Alaska Gov.'s Coun. for Handicapped, 1980-82; pres. Valdez chpt. Alaska Visitors Assn., 1980; mem. small cities adv. coun. Nat. League Cities, 1983-87, mem. internat. econ. devel. task force; mem. Nat. Export Coun.; bd. dirs. Resource Devel. Coun.; Dem. nominee U.S. Ho. Reps., 1990, 92; hosted internat. conf. on oil spills for mayors; exec. dir. Prince William Sound Regional Citizens Adv. Coun., 1997—. Mem. Am. Speech-Lang. Hearing Assn. (cert. clin. competence in audiology and speech and lang. pathology), Am. C. of C. in Korea, Valdez C. of C., Alaska Mcpl. League (bd. dirs. 1984-89), Elks, Eagles. Methodist. Avocation: charter boat operator. Home: 1241 W 27th Ave #865 Anchorage AK 99503-2318 Office: 750 W 2nd Ave Ste 100 Anchorage AK 99501-2167

DEVENS, PAUL, lawyer; b. Gary, Ind., June 8, 1931; s. Zenove and Anna (Brilla) Dewenetz; m. Setsuko Sugihara, Aug. 14, 1955; children: Paula, Vladimir, Mignon. BA in Econs. cum laude, Ind. U., 1954; LLB, Columbia U., 1957. Bar: N.Y. 1958, U.S. Dist. Ct. Hawaii 1960, Hawaii 1961, U.S. Ct. Appeals (9th cir.) 1962, U.S. Ct. Internat. Trade 1963, U.S. Supreme Ct. 1970. Pvt. practice law N.Y.C., 1958-60; ptnr. Lewis, Saunders & Key,

Honolulu, 1960-69; corp. counsel City and County of Honolulu, 1969-72, mng. dir., 1973-75; ptnr. Devens, Lo, Youth, Nakano & Saito, Honolulu, 1975-94, of counsel, 1994—; bd. dirs. Ctrl. Pacific Bank, Honolulu, CPB, Inc., Honolulu; judge Nuclear Claims Tribunal, Majuro, Republic of the Marshall Islands, 1988-90. Mem. Japan-Hawaii Econ. Coun., 1975—, Honolulu Charter Reorgn. Com., 1979-80, Pacific and Asian Affairs Coun., 1983; trustee Japan-Am. Soc. Honolulu, 1981—, pres., 1987-89; chmn. bd. dirs. Nat. Assn. Japan-Am. Socs., 1989-91; mem. bd. govs. Japanese Cultural Ctr., Hawaii, 1989-94, mem. bd. dirs., v.p., 1994-96, chmn. bd. dirs., 1996-97. Decorated Imperial Order of the Sacred Treasure, Gold Rays with Neck ribbon Govt. of Japan, 1993. Democrat. Eastern Orthodox. Office: Devens Lo Nakano Saito Lee & Wong 220 S King St Ste 1600 Honolulu HI 96813-4539

DEVENS, RICHARD MATHER, publishing executive, economist; b. Boston, Aug. 15, 1950; s. Richard M. and Sylvia (Pearson) D.; m. Rita Sheehan, June 29, 1986; children: Richard M. III, Timothy Joseph. BA in Internat. Rels. and Econs., Am. U., 1976, MA in Econs., 1979. Economist Bur. of Labor Stats., Washington, 1976-80, sr. economist, 1983-94; internat. fellow Columbia U., N.Y.C., 1980-81; corp. rschr. Horizon House, Dedham, Mass., 1982; exec. editor Monthly Labor Rev., Washington, 1994—. Editl. dir.: Report on the American Workforce, 1994, 95, 97; contbr. articles to profl. jours. Issues analyst Sears for Gov., Boston, 1982; mem. bd. of friends Boston Renaissance Sch., 1996. Sgt. USMC, 1969-72. Recipient Sec. of Labor Exceptional Achievement award, 1992, 93, 95. Mem. Am. Econ. Assn., Nat. Assn. Bus. Economists, Am. Soc. Mag. Editors. Avocations: rugby, history. Office: Monthly Labor Review 2 Massachusetts Ave NE Washington DC 20212-0022

DEVERE, RONALD, neurologist; b. Winnipeg, Can., Mar. 23, 1944; came to U.S., 1974; s. Leon and Sonya DeV.; divorced; children: Brent, Todd, Ross; m. Colleen Coleman, Sept. 12, 1993. MD, U. Manitoba, Can., 1968. Intern L.A. County-U. So. Calif. Med Ctr., 1968-69; resident in neurology U. Minn., Mpls., 1969-72; ptnr. Houston Neurology Assocs., 1980—. Fellow Am. Acad. Neurology, Am. Acad. Disability Evaluating Physicians, Am. Acad Eletromagnetic Medicine. Office: 15200 SW Fwy #395 Sugarland TX 77478

DEVEREUX, OWEN FRANCIS, metallurgy educator; b. Lexington, Mass., Aug. 23, 1937; s. George Francis and Mildred Anna (Gleeson) D.; m. Sally Williamson, June 15, 1957 (div. June 1969); children: Owen M., Amy L., Jonathan W., Nancy J.; m. Olivia Elaine Marin, June 13, 1969. BS, MIT, 1959, MS, 1960, PhD, 1962. Rsch. chemist Chevron Rsch. Co., La Habra, Calif., 1962-64; research chemist Corning (N.Y.) Glass Works, 1964-66, Chevron Oil Field Rsch. Col., La Habra, 1966-68; assoc. prof. U. Conn., Storrs, 1968-76, prof., 1976-99, head metallurgy dept., 1983-98. Author: Topics in Metallurgical Thermodynamics, 1983; contbr. articles to profl. jours. Rsch. grantee NSF, 1970-76, U.S. Dept. Energy, 1976-86, NSF Industry/Univ. Corp. Rsch. Ctr. for Grinding Rsch. and Devel., 1990-98. Mem. AIME, AAUP, Electrochem. Soc. (div. editor 1987-90), Nat. Assn. Corrosion Engrs. Avocations: quarter horses, carriage driving, saddle making, classical guitar. Home: PO Box 391 Storrs Mansfield CT 06268-0391 Office: Univ of Conn Box U-136 97 N Eagleville Rd Storrs Mansfield CT 06269-3136

DEVEREUX, TIMOTHY EDWARD, advertising agency executive; b. Chgo., Jan. 13, 1932; s. James Matthew and Nellie (Fitzmaurice) D.; m. Ann Sullivan, Apr. 2, 1956; children: Timothy Jr., Colette Marie, Jennifer Ann, Peter Gerard, Nora Marie, Matthew. BA in Communication Arts, U. Notre Dame, 1955. Copywriter Montgomery Ward & Co., Chgo., 1957-58; pub. relations dir. Victor Comptometer Corp., Chgo., 1958-60; sales promotion mgr. Bankers Life & Casualty Co., Chgo., 1960-61; dir. advt. and pub. relations Mid-America Foods, Inc., River Forest, Ill., 1961-62; mdse. mgr. Marshall John & Assos., Chgo. also Northbrook, 1962-65; acct. supr. Marshall John/Action Advt., Northbrook, Ill., 1965-70; exec. v.p., chief exec. officer Marshall John/Action Advt., 1970-77, also dir.; pres. Devereux Direct, Ltd., 1977-79; v.p. direct response group Frankel & Co., Chgo., 1979-85; pres. Timothy E. Devereux & Assocs., Oak Park, Ill., 1985—. Served to 1st lt. USMCR, 1955-57. Roman Catholic. Home and Office: 1185 S Oak Park Ave Oak Park IL 60304-2048

DEVERS, GAIL, track and field athlete; b. Seattle, Nov. 19, 1966. BA in Sociology, UCLA, 1988. Gold medalist, 100m Track and Field Barcelona Olympic Games, 1992; Gold medalist 100m, 100m Hurdles World Track and Field Championships, Stuttgart, Germany, 1993; Gold medalist, 100m Track and Field Atlanta Olympic Games, 1996, Gold medalist 4x100m relay, 1996; Gold medalist 4x100m relay World Championships, 1997. Nat. champion 100M hurdles, 1991, 92, 93, 95, 96; nat. indoor champion 60M, 1993; world indoor champion 60M, 1993; world champion 100M, 1993, 95; world champion 100M hurdles, 1993; Women's Sports Found. Athlete of Yr., 1997. Office: Elite Internat Sports Mktg 701 Market St Ste 1575 Saint Louis MO 63101-1899*

DEVERS, SUSAN MARIE, clinical nurse specialist, researcher; b. Richmond, Ind., Apr. 4, 1960; d. Elmer Harry Jr. and Martha Ann (Maurer) Fulton; 1 child, Shawnda L. ADN, Tulsa Jr. Coll., 1987; BSN, U. Tulsa, 1993; MSN, U. Okla., 1998. RN, Okla., Tex.; cert. ACLS. Unit nurse specialist med. ICU St. John's Med. Ctr., Tulsa, 1987-94; clin. nurse specialist, rschr. Cooper Aerobics Ctr., Cooper Clinic, Dallas, 1994—. Mem. AACN.

DEV FRIERSON, ROBERT, federal official. Assoc. gen. counsel Fed. Res. Sys., Washington; sec. of the bd. Fed Res. Systems. Office: Fed Res Sys Bd Members 20th & C Sts NW Washington DC 20551

DEVGAN, ONKAR DAVE N., technologist, consultant; b. Lahore, Panjab, India, Oct. 11, 1941; came to U.S., 1967; s. Thakar Dass Devgan and Sohag Wati Sharma; m. Veena Devgan, July 20, 1969; children: Sanjay, Pooja. BS, Panjab U., 1960; MS, Vikham U., 1963, PhD, 1966; MBA, Temple U., 1975. Instr., rsch. assoc. U. Pa., Phila., 1970-73; scientist C.E. Glass, Pennsauken, N.J., 1973-76; cons., vis. prof. U. Tex., Dallas, 1976-78; mgr. material devel., sr. engr. Tex. Inst., Dallas, 1978-83; engring. mgr. Fairchild Semiconductor, Palo Alto, Calif., 1983-84, 88; program mgr. Varian Assocs., Palo Alto, 1984-86; dir. microelectronics Northrup Corp., L.A., 1986-88; dir. tech. and ops. Polylithics Inc., Santa Clara, Calif., 1989-90; tech. and mgmt. cons. Devgan Assocs., Sunnyvale, Calif., 1991—; co-founder, pres. Paragon System Tech.; co-chmn. Semi GaAs Com., Mt. View, Calif., 1984-85; mem. Semi Automation Com., Mt. View, 1984-86; advisor Semi Equipment Uptime Com., Mt. View; chair session on process control and monitor Internat. Semiconductor Mfg. Sci. Symposium, San Francisco. Contbr. articles to tech. and bus. jours. PhD fellow Govt. of India, 1963-66, Coun. of Sci. and Indsl. Rsch. sr. fellow, 1966-67; NIH postdoctoral fellow, 1967-70. Mem. IEEE, Am. Chem. Soc. Achievements include inventions in key proprietary tech. in the areas of infra-red transmitting materials and semiconductor processing. Home and Office: 161 Butano Ave Sunnyvale CA 94086-7025

DE VIDO, ALFREDO EDUARDO, architect; b. N.Y.C., Mar. 19, 1932; s. Eduardo and Maria (Zanucco) DeV.; m. Catherine Nelligan, 1962; children—Roberto, Antonio J. B.Arch., Carnegie Mellon U., 1954; M.F.A., Princeton U., 1956. Registered architect, N.J., N.Y., Conn., Ma., Pa. Architect, Architects Collaborative, Rome, 1960-61, Marcel Breuer, N.Y.C., 1961-62, Ernest Kump, N.Y.C., 1963-67, MacFadyen & Knowles, N.Y.C., 1967-69, De Vido Assocs., N.Y.C., 1969—. Author: Designing Your Clients House, 1983, Innovative Management Techniques for Architectural Design and Construction, 1984, House Design: Art and Practice, 1996, also a monograph. Recipient Solar award HUD, 1979, Bard award City Club N.Y., 1983, 89, award Am. Solar Energy Soc., 1982, Design award Interfaith Forum on Religion, Art and Architecture, 1989, Design award Conn. Soc. of Architects, 1991, Queens C. of C. award 1993, Interior Design award Restaurants and Instns., 1997. Fellow AIA (honor award 1968, N.Y. chpt. design awards 1971, 77, 81, 94); mem. N.Y. State Assn. Architects (design awards 1980, 81, 82, 86, 92, 95), Am. Inst. Steel Constrn. (award 1977), Am. Wood Coun. award, 1993. Office: Alfredo De Vido Architects 412 E 85th St New York NY 10028-6302*

DEVIGNE, KAREN COOKE, retired amateur athletics executive; b. Phila., July 31, 1943; d. Paul and Matilda (Rich) Cooke; m. Jules Lloyd Devigne, June 26, 1965; children: Jules Paul, Denise Paige, Paul Michael. AA, Centenary Coll., Hackettstown, 1963; student, Northwestern U., 1963-65; BA, Ramapo Coll., Mahwah, 1976; MA, Emory U., Atlanta, 1989. Founder GYMSET, Marietta, Ga., 1981—. Cons. Girls Club Am. Marietta, 1989; vol. Cobb County Gymnastic Ctr., Marietta, 1976-95, Ga. Youth Soccer Assn., Atlanta, 1976-95; fundraiser Scottish Rite Children's Hosp., Atlanta, 1989. Recipient recognition awards from various youth groups, Atlanta, 1976—; named Nominee Woman of Yr. ABC News, Atlanta, 1984. Avocations: skiing, tennis, bridge. Home: 3701 Clubland Dr Marietta GA 30068-4006 also: 445 White Cloud Breckenridge CO 80424

DEVILBISS, JONATHAN FREDERICK, airline analyst; b. Saiburi, Pattani, Thailand, July 23, 1961; s. Frederick Henry and Iva Marie (Weidner) D.; m. Laura Anne Carr, June 4, 1994. BS in Aero. Engring., Purdue U., 1984; BA in Liberal Arts, Wheaton (Ill.) Coll., 1984. Sales engr. Brit. Aerospace Inc., Herndon, Va., 1985-88, tech. sales engr., 1988-89, sr. tech. sales engr., 1989-91, sr. product engr., 1991-92; mgr. product mktg. Jetstream Aircraft subs. Brit. Aerospace, Sterling, Va., 1993-94; mktg. analyst Mahalo Air Inc., Honolulu, 1997; reliability analyst Hawaiian Airlines, Honolulu, 1998—. Mem. AIAA, SAE (assoc.). Republican. Evangelical Christian. Home: 2816 Puumele Pl Honolulu HI 96817-1420

DEVILLE, DONALD CHARLES, accountant; b. New Roads, La., Sept. 18, 1953; s. Sterling Joseph and Barbara J. (Beaud) DeV.; m. Michelle L. Rinaudo, Apr. 14, 1984; children: Ariel Elizabeth, Stewart Charles, Olivia. BS in Acctg., La. State U., 1976. CPA, La. Auditor State of La., Baton Rouge, 1976-78; mgr. Hawthorn Waymouth & Carroll, Baton Rouge, 1978-89; pvt. practice acct. Baton Rouge, 1989—. Pres. Baton Rouge Work Exch., 1988; publicity dir. Baton Rouge Opera, 1989-90, treas., 1991—; liturg. min St. George Cath. Ch., Baton Rouge, 1987—; bd. dirs. Capital Area Safety Coun. La., treas., 1994-95; bd. dirs. Baton Rouge Boys Club. Recipient Freedom award La. Farm Bur. Mem. AICPA, La. Soc. CPAs, SAR (sec. 1990-93, pres. 1994, treas. La. 1998—, La. Meritorious Svc. award). Republican. Roman Catholic. Avocation: outdoor cooking. Home: 18002 Inverness Ave Baton Rouge LA 70810-5979

DE VILLE, WINSTON, genealogist; b. Evangeline Parish, La., Aug. 8, 1937; s. Dalvis Joseph De Ville and Olevia Johnson; div.; 1 child, Richard. BA, La. Coll., 1959; MA, La. State U., 1963. Tchr. English, French Berwick (La.) H.S., 1959-60; head dept. spl. collections Mobile (Ala.) Pub. Libr., 1963-64; coll. rep. Harper & Row, N.Y.C., 1964-66, Macmillan, N.Y.C., 1966-69; dir. Geneal. Publ. Co., Balt., 1969-71; founder, CEO Polyanthos, Inc., New Orleans, LA, 1971-85; cons. in field, 1985—; founding pres. Friends of the Archives of La.; cons. Alexandria (La.) Hist. Libr. and Mus., 1985—, U.S. Dept. Justice, 1992; cons. editor Provincial Press, Lafayette, La., 1996, The Talimali Band Appalache' Indians of La., 1997—. Founding trustee Assn. for the Promotion of Scholarship in Genealogy, Ltd., 1979-84; co-dir. Nat. Inst. on Geneal. Rsch. (nat. archives 1982-84). Fellow Am. Soc. Genealogists. Avocations: writing poetry, piano, collecting old prints, maps, books. Home: 1067 Rock Pit Rd Ville Platte LA 70586-8379

DEVILLERS, PAUL, member of parliament; b. Penetanguishene, Ont., Can., Mar. 11, 1946. LLB, U. Ottawa. Office: House of Commons, Confederation Bldg/Rm 172, Ottawa, ON Canada K1A 0A6

DEVIN, CARL ERIC, artist; b. Pitts., Jan. 31, 1946; s. Carl and Elizabeth (Munson) D.; m. Robin Sue Block, Mar. 8, 1980; children: C. Eric, Darton B. BA in Environ. Design, Pt. Park Coll., 1970; tchg. cert., U. R.I., 1981. Asst. art dir. Reuter and Bragdon, Pitts., 1966-67, Krebs United Publs., Indiana, Pa., 1967; artist, gallery owner Rick Devin Ltd., Hope Valley, R.I., 1985—; drawing instr. Ctr. for the Arts, Westerly, R.I., 1981-85, set designer, 1983-85; cons. regional art festivals, 1985-86. Artist (paintings) Butler Inst. Am. Art, 1989, (drawings) Foyer de Cultural Jeremie Haiti, 1993, (mural) Haitian Health Found., 1997. dem. Dem. Town Com., 1990—, Dem. Dist. Com., 1997—, Chariho Regional Sch. Com., 1994-98; mem. Hopkinton Town Coun., 1988-93, Hopkinton Hist. Dist. Commn., 1999—. Recipient 1st pl. award Newport Art Festival, 1985, Pawtucket Arts Coun., 1986, Glastonbury Art Guild, 1986. Mem. Wickford Art Assn. (Huzer award 1987, festival dir. 1984-88). Home: 1054 Main St Hope Valley RI 02832-0145 Office: 1059 Main St Hope Valley RI 02832-0145

DEVIN, (PHILIP) LEE, dramaturg, theater educator; b. Glendale, Calif., Apr. 28, 1938; s. Philip Lee Sr. and Bernice Hermoine (Rogers) D.; m. Barbara Kathleen Norton, June 22, 1958 (div. 1986); children: Siobhan Kathleen, Sean Michael. AB, San Jose State Coll., 1958; MA, Ind. U., 1961, PhD, 1967. Lectr. Ind. U. extension, Indpls., 1960-62; instr., tech. dir. U. Va., Charlottesville, 1962-66; instr., assoc. dir. Exptl. Theatre Vassar Coll., Poughkeepsie, N.Y., 1966-67; asst. prof., assoc. dir. Vassar Coll., 1967-70; assoc. prof., dir. theatre Swarthmore (Pa.) Coll., 1970-79, prof., dir. theatre, 1979-98, prof., 1998—; electrician, state mgr., prodn. stage mgr. Honey in the Rock, Beckley, W.Va., 1962-64; artist-in-residence Ball State U., Muncie, Ind., 1968, U. Calif. San Diego, La Jolla, 1973; assoc. artist People's Light and Theatre Co., Malvern, Pa., 1977—, dramaturg, 1985—. Author: (radio plays) Elegy for Irish Jack, 1973, When the Time Comes, 1978, Frankenstein, 1981 (WHA, Earplay Purchase awards); (with S. Hodkinson) (drama with music) Lament: for Guitar and Two Lovers, 1963; (active oratorio) Vox Populous, 1973; (opera) St. Carmen of the Main, 1987 actor various roles stage, film, TV; translator (with A. Adams) A Doll House, 1987, Oedipus, 1988. Recipient 1st prize WGBH Radio Drama, Boston, 1968, James S. Helms Playscript award, 1964, Calif. Olympiad of the Arts, 1965; librettist's grantee NEA, Washington, 1974, 75, 77; grantee Mellon Found., 1973, 77; Lang fellow 1990. Mem. Actors' Equity Assn., Assn. for Theatre in Higher Edn., Literary Mgrs. and Dramaturgs of the Ams. Avocation: fly fishing. Home: 603 Hillborn Ave Swarthmore PA 19081-1123 Office: The Theatre Swarthmore College 500 College Ave Swarthmore PA 19081-1306

DEVIN, RICHARD, film industry executive; b. Rochester, N.Y., Oct. 30, 1963; s. Patsy and Antoinette (Perrone) LaFica. AA, Monroe Coll., Rochester, 1983; BA, Cornell U., 1986. Actor N.Y.C., 1986-91; dir. project devel. Entertainment Mktg., Universal City, Calif., 1991-95; media advisor Simco & Assocs., L.A., 1995-96; exec. casting dir. Am. Film, L.A., 1996-98; exec. producer Devin Graham Entertainment, 1998—; producing dir. Light Opera of L.A., 1996—. Author: Actors' resumes, 1994, Do You Want to be an Actor?, 1996; playwright: My Mother's Coming, 1990 (Gypsy award 1995), Deceptive Peace, 1990. Recipient Vital Arts award Found. for Vital Arts, 1990. Avocations: polo, champion equestrian. Office: Entertainment Mktg Co PO Box 8559 Universal City CA 91618

DEVINATZ, ALLEN, mathematician, mathematics educator; b. Chgo., July 22, 1922; s. Victor and Kate (Bass) D.; m. Pearl Moskowitz, Sep. 16, 1956; children: Victor Gary, Ethan Sander. B.S., Ill. Inst. Tech., 1944; A.M., Harvard U., 1947, Ph.D., 1950. Instr. Ill. Inst. Tech., 1950-52; NSF Postdoctoral fellow, 1952-53; fellow Inst. Advanced Study, Princeton, 1953-54; asst. prof. U. Conn., 1954-55; mem. faculty Washington U., St. Louis, 1955-67, prof. math., 1961-67, acting chmn. dept., 1963-64; prof. math. Northwestern U., Evanston, Ill., 1967-92, prof. emeritus, 1992—, asst. chmn. dept., 1968-70, acting chmn. dept., 1991; vis. mem. Weizmann Inst., Israel, 1980, Inst. Hautes Etudes Sci., Paris, 1982, Inst. for Applications of Calculus-Mauro Picone, Rome, 1988; vis. scholar U. Calif., Berkeley, 1985; Disting. lectr. Hebrew U., Jerusalem, 1993. Contbr. articles profl. jours. Sr. NSF Postdoctoral fellow, 1960-61. Mem. Am. Math. Soc. (translation com. for Russian 1985-88), Sigma Xi, Tau Beta Pi. Office: Northwestern U Dept Math Lunt Bldg Evanston IL 60208

DEVINE, B. MACK, management consultant; b. Gadsden, Ala., Feb. 23, 1945; s. Charles Durwood and Ida Nell (Blanton) DeV.; m. Shirley Jean Fitzpatrick, Mar. 16, 1966; children: Charles, Cynthia. B.S. in Acctg., Jacksonville (Ala.) State U., 1968; postgrad., U. South Fla., Harvard U. Bus. Sch. Vice pres., dir. Bay-Con Industries, Tampa, Fla., 1971-74; v.p., treas. Automatic Mdsg. Co., Tampa, 1974-75; chief fin. officer So. Equipment Co., Tampa, 1975-76; v.p. Am. Agronomics Corp., Tampa, 1976-77; pres., dir. Am. Agronomics Corp., 1977-82; chmn., pres., dir. Key Energy Enterprises Inc., Tampa, 1982-88; chief exec. officer, pres. Devco Petroleum Co., Tampa, 1988-90; pres., chief exec. officer DeVine & Assocs., Inc., 1990-93; pres. The Holder Group, 1993-95, DeVine & Assocs., Inc., 1995—. Served with USAR, 1968-70. Decorated Army Commendation medal. Mem. Am. Mgmt. Assn. (president's assn.), Young Presidents Orgn. Republican. Clubs: Palma Ceia Country, Lodge: Rotary. Home and Office: 621 17th St Ste 1730 Denver CO 80293-1701*

DEVINE, BRIAN KIERNAN, pet food and supplies company executive; b. Washington, Mar. 1, 1942; s. William John and Rita Marie (Kiernan) D.; m. Silvija Viktorija Kutlets, June 13, 1964; children—Brian Jr., Brooke. BA, Georgetown U., 1963; postgrad., Am. U., 1964-65, Yale U., 1965. Statis. adv. USPHS, Washington, 1963-70; with Toys "R" Us, 1970-88; gen. mgr. San Jose, Calif., 1970-75; regional gen. mgr. Chgo., 1975-77; v.p. Saddle Brook, N.J., 1977-82; sr. v.p. Rochelle Park, N.J., 1982-88; pres. of furniture mfr./retailer Krause's Sofa Factory, Fountain Valley, Calif., 1988-89; pres., CEO Petco, San Diego, 1990—, chmn., pres., CEO pet food and supplies, 1994—; bd. dirs. Nat. Retail Fedn., Wild Oats Markets, Inc.; mem. coll. bd. advisers Georgetown U. Contbr. articles to profl. publs. Republican. Roman Catholic. Home: 6608 La Valle Plateada PO Box 1305 Rancho Santa Fe CA 92067-1305 Office: 9125 Rehco Rd San Diego CA 92121-2270

DEVINE, DONALD J., management and political consultant; b. Bronxville, N.Y., Apr. 14, 1937; s. John and Frances M. D.; m. Ann Delia Smith, Aug. 29, 1959; children: William, J. Michael, Patricia, Joseph. BBA, St. John's U., Jamaica, N.Y., 1959; MA, CUNY, 1965; PhD, Syracuse (N.Y.) U., 1967. Assoc. prof. govt. and politics U. Md., 1967-81; dir. U.S. Office Personnel Mgmt., 1981-85; pres. Donald Devine Co., 1985—; columnist Washington Times; adj. scholar Heritage Found. Author: The Attentive Public, 1970, The Political Culture of the United States, 1972, Does Freedom Work? Liberty and Justice in America, 1978, Reagan Electionomics, 1983, Reagan's Terrible Swift Sword, 1991, Restoring the Tenth Amendment, 1996. Parliamentarian, mem. exec. com. Md. Rep. Com., 1974-79; Md. chmn. Reagan for Pres., 1976, 80; sr. cons. Dole for Pres., 1988, 96; cons. Steve Forbes for pres., 1999; mem. rules com. Rep. Nat. Com., 1973-75, platform com., del., 1976-88, 96; treas. Am. Conservative Union; Rep. nominee Md. State Comptroller, 1976, 5th Congl. Dist., 1994. With USAR, 1960-66. Mem. Am. Polit. Sci. Assn., Am. Assn. Public Opinion Research, Mt. Pelerin Soc., Phila. Soc. Roman Catholic. Home: 4805 Idlewilde Rd Shady Side MD 20764-9768 Office: 919 Prince St Alexandria VA 22314-3008

DEVINE, DONN, lawyer, genealogist, former city official; b. South Amboy, N.J., Mar. 30, 1929; s. Frank Edward and Emily Theresa (DeRevere) D. m. Elizabeth Cecilia Baldwin, Nov. 23, 1951; children: Edward (dec.), Mary Elizabeth, Martin Joseph. BS, U. Del., 1949; JD with honors, Widener U., 1975. Bar: Del. 1975, U.S. Dist. Ct. Del. 1976, U.S. Supreme Ct. 1997; cert. genealogist and cert. genealogy instr. Bd. for Cert. Genealogists; cert. Am. Inst. Cert. Planners. Devel. chemist Allied Chem. Corp., Claymont, Del., 1950-52; newspaper writer, editor corp. publs. Atlas Powder Co., Wilmington, Del., 1952-60; mgmt. cons., 1960-68; dir. renewal planning City of Wilmington, 1968-79, dep. dir. planning, 1979-80, dir. planning, 1981-85; cons. Wilmington City Coun., 1985—; pvt. practice, 1985—; archival cons. Cath. Diocese Wilmington, 1989—; spl. counsel Del. Div. Alcoholism, Drug Abuse and Mental Health, 1990-93; trustee Bd. for Cert. Genealogists, 1992—; mediator Del. Superior Ct., 1998—. Author: Delaware National Guard, A Historical Sketch, 1968, DeRevere Family of Peekskill, New York, 1982; editor Del. Geneal. Soc. Jour., 1980-81, Cultural Resources Survey of Wilmington, Del., 1982-84; assoc. editor Del. Jour. Corp. Law, 1974-75. Past bd. dirs. Wilmington Small Bus. Devel. Corp., Wilmington Econ. Devel. Corp.; past officer Delmarva Ecumenical Agy.; emeritus bd. dirs., past officer Geriatric Svcs. Del.; past officer Christina Cultural Arts Ctr., Cath. Interracial Coun., Del. chpt. ACLU, Maplewood Housing for Elderly, St. Mary's-St. Patrick's Parish Coun. With USAR, 1950-54; brig. gen. Del. Army N.G., 1954-84, ret. Decorated Meritorious Svc. medal. Mem. Am. Planning Assn., Am. Chem. Soc., Del. Bar Assn., Del. Soc. SAR (past pres.), Nat. Geneal. Soc. (bd. dirs. 1994—), Assn. Cath. Diocesan Archivists (bd. dirs. 1993-95), Del. Geneal. Soc. (past pres.), Ft. Delaware Soc. (recognition award), Old Bohemia Hist. Soc. (bd. dirs. 1992—), Univ. and Whist Club, Chemists Club N.Y.C., Ancient Order Hibernians, Phi Kappa Phi, Delta Theta Phi. Democrat. Home: 2004 Kentmere Pky Wilmington DE 19806-2014

DEVINE, EDMOND FRANCIS, lawyer; b. Ann Arbor, Mich., Aug. 9, 1916; s. Frank B. and Elizabeth Catherine (Doherty) DeV.; m. Elizabeth Palmer Ward, Sept. 17, 1955; children: Elizabeth Palmer, Stephen Ward, Michael Edmond, Suzanne Lee. AB, U. Mich., 1937, JD, 1940; LLM, Cath. U. Am., 1941. Bar: Mich. 1940, U.S. Dist. Ct. (ea. dist.) Mich. 1940, U.S. Ct. Appeals (6th cir) 1974, U.S. Supreme Ct. 1975. Spl. agt. FBI, 1941-43; chief asst. prosecutor Washtenaw County (Mich.), Ann Arbor, 1947-53, prosecuting atty., 1953-58; ptnr. DeVine & DeVine, Ann Arbor, 1958-74, DeVine, DeVine, Kantor & Serr, Ann Arbor, 1974-84; sr. ptnr. Miller, Canfield, Paddock & Stone, Ann Arbor, 1984-92, of counsel, 1992—; lectr., asst. prof., adj. prof. U. Mich. Law Sch., 1949-79. Co-author: Criminal Procedure, 1960. Bd. dirs. Youth for Understanding, Inc., Ann Arbor, 1966-70. Lt. USNR, 1943-46, PTO. Decorated Bronze Star with combat v. Fellow Am. Bar Found. (cons. 1956-61), Am. Coll. Trial Lawyers, Mich. Bar Found.; mem. ABA, State Bar Mich. (bd. commrs., chmn. judiciary com. 1976-85, mem. rep. assembly, chmn. rules and calendar com.1971-76, co-chair U.S. Cts. com. 1986-87), Internat. Assn. Def. Counsel, U.S. Supreme Ct. Hist. Soc., Ann Arbor C. of C. (chmn. bd. 1971), Detroit Athletic Club, Barton Hills Country Club, Pres.'s Club, U. Mich., Varsity M Club, Order of Coif, Barristers, Phi Delta Phi, Phi Kappa Psi. Republican. Roman Catholic. Avocations: golf, jogging, reading. Home: 101 Underdown Rd Ann Arbor MI 48105-1078 Office: Miller Canfield Paddock & Stone 101 N Main St Fl 7 Ann Arbor MI 48104-5507

DEVINE, HUGH JAMES, JR., marketing executive, consultant; b. Buffalo, N.Y., May 8, 1938; s. Hugh James Sr. and Ruth D. Devine; m. Bernice Riley Cushing, May 27, 1984; children: Hugh James III, Thomas C., Catherine D. Whitaker, Kent T., Diane C. Alleborn, Linda C. Hughes, Karen C. Krueger. AB in Econs., Bethany Coll., 1961; MBA, U. Bridgeport, 1971. Mgr. mktg. intelligence Winchester-Western Div. Olin Corp., New Haven, 1961-71; sr. v.p., dir. mktg. Rsch. Data Svcs., Inc., Princeton, N.J., 1971-75; sr. v.p., dir. mktg. Total Rsch. Corp., Princeton, 1975-79, exec. v.p., dir. mktg., 1979-83, dir., 1978-97; pres. Total Rsch. Corp., Princeton, N.J., 1993-96, COO, 1996; mktg. cons., 1997—; speaker Am. Mgmt. Assn., N.Y.C., 1974-76, Assn. Nat. Advertisers, Washington, 1985, Fin. Independence Day, Princeton, 1986, U. N.C., Chapel Hill, 1989, 91. Author newsletter Strategic Goals Should Govern Mktg. Rsch. Budget, 1981; co-author newsletter The Value of Predictive Research, 1989; contbr. articles to mags. Sgt. USAR, 1961-67. Mem. Coun. Am. Survey Rsch. Orgn. (membership chmn. 1985, career planning chmn. 1986, survey quality com. 1990-91, 96), Am. Mktg. Assn., Am. Soc. Quality Control. Republican. Avocations: barbershop style singing, walking, reading, golf. Home and Office: 49 Krebs Rd Plainsboro NJ 08536-1104

DEVINE, JAMES JOSEPH, chemical products manufacturing company executive; b. Bklyn., Aug. 14, 1926; s. Peter Charles and Gertrude Marie (Flanagan) D.; m. Maud Hearn, Apr. 18, 1953; children: Lynn, Jeffrey, Drew, Douglas. BSChemE, Bucknell U., 1950; MBA, Rutgers U., 1959. Supr. Merck & Co., Elkton, Va., 1950-51, Danville, Pa., 1951-53; asst. plant mgr. Clorox Co., Jersey City, 1954-59; coating supt. Natvar Corp., Rahway, N.J., 1959-66; organic plant supt. Vulcan Materials Co., Newark, 1966-69; mfg. mgr. Shulton Inc., Clifton, N.J., 1969-72; chem. mfg. mgr. Fisher Sci. Co., Fair Lawn, N.J., 1972-87; engr. Heterene Chem. Co., Paterson, N.J., 1987-90, N.J. Dept. Environ. Protection, Trenton, N.J., 1993—. Served with USNR, 1944-46, PTO. Mem. Am. Chem. Soc., Am. Inst. Chem. Engrs., Alpha Chi Sigma, Sigma Chi. Republican. Roman Catholic. Home: 32 Terrill Rd Old Bridge NJ 08857-2144 Office: New Jersey Dept Env Protec 401 E State St Trenton NJ 08608-1501

DEVINE, KATHERINE, environmental consultant, educator; b. Denver, Oct. 15, 1951. BS, Rutgers U., 1973, MS, 1980; postgrad., U. Md., 1981-82. Lab. technician Princeton (N.J.) U., 1974-76; econ. and regulatory affairs analyst, program mgr. U.S. EPA, Washington, 1979-81, 82-89, cons., 1989—; exec. dir. Applied BioTreatment Assn., Washington, 1990-91; pres. DEVO Enterprises, Inc., Washington, 1990—; chair adv. bd. Applied Bioremediation Conf., 1993; co-chair Environ. Biotech. Conf., 1996, 97, others.

Author: N.J. Agricultural Experiment Station of Rutgers Uniersity, 1980, Bioremediation Case Studies: An Analysis of Vendor Supplied Data, 1992, Bioremediation Case Studies: Abstracts, 1992; co-author: Biomediation: Field Experiences, 1994, Bioremediation, 1994; founder, pub., editor (mag.) Biotreatment News, 1990-97; pub. The Gold Book; editor Indsl. Biotech. News, 1998; contbr. articles to profl. jours., chpts. to books; co-sponsor over 20 confs. Mem. Women's Coun. on Energy and the Environment, 1991-93. Recipient numerous fed. govt. and non- govt. awards. Mem. Am. Chem. Soc., Futures for Children, Alpha Zeta. Office: DEVO Enterprises Inc 704 9th St SE Washington DC 20003-2804

DEVINE, (JOSEPH) LAWRENCE, drama critic; b. N.Y.C., Sept. 21, 1935; s. John Justin and Hazel (Tippit) DeV.; m. Genevieve Christian, Aug. 29, 1959 (div. 1968); children: John Justin II, Ellen Morse; m. Lucy Memory Williamson, July 26, 1968 (dec. Oct. 1985); m. Lois Waterman, July 23, 1988. Student, Georgetown U., 1953-54, U. Mich., 1954; BS in Journalism, Northwestern U., 1957. Drama critic Miami (Fla.) Herald, 1962-67; entertainment editor, drama and film critic L.A. Herald-Examiner, 1967-68; entertainment editor, drama critic Detroit Free Press, 1968-98; assoc. dir. Critics Inst., Eugene O'Neill Meml. Theater Ctr., Waterford, Conn., 1973—; mem. faculty drama critics U. Detroit, 1974; NEH profl. fellow U. Mich., Ann Arbor, 1975-76; fellow NEH seminar for critics of arts, Washington, 1977; William Randolph Hearst vis. fellow U. Tex., Austin, 1995; mem. nat. new playwrights jury Am. Coll. Theatre Festival, critic-in-residence festivals, 1978-94; mem. Pulitzer prize nominating jury in drama, 1981-82, 91-92, 93-94; panelist Forums on Theater of the Absurd, London, 1986, Stanislavsky Anniversary, Moscow, 1988. Contbr. articles to profl. jours., revs. to newspapers, mags. Served with AUS, 1958-62. Recipient Amoco gold medal of excellence Am. Coll. Theatre Festivals, 1982, Mich. Gov.'s Art award, 1993, Outstanding Profl. Achievement award Mich. Allied Profl. Theatres, 1998, Lee Hills award for disting. career achievement, 1998; inducted Mich Journalism Hall of Fame, 1999. Mem. Am. Theater Critics ASsn. (chmn. exec. com. 1979-81), Internat. Assn. Theater Critics (U.S. del. biennial congresses Tel Aviv 1981, Mexico City 1983, E. Berlin 1987, Warsaw 1992, Gdansk, Poland 1998), N.Y. Drama Critics Cir., Beta Theta Pi, Sigma Delta Chi. Home: 657 Lincoln Rd Grosse Pointe MI 48230-1219

DEVINE, NANCY, postmaster; b. Hyannis, Mass., Feb. 8, 1949; d. Joseph Peter and Rose (Almeida) Cabral; m. Michael G. Devine, Mar. 20, 1971 (div. 1975); 1 child, Paul. Student, U. Mass., 1967-70. Postal clk. U.S. Postal Svc., Centerville, Mass., 1977-80; postmaster U.S. Postal Svc., West Hyannisport, Mass., 1980—; Affirmative Action planner U.S. Postal Svc., Brockton, Mass., 1979-80, prin. rep./exec. bd., Providence, 1993. Painter in acrylics. Art and Humanities grantee Barnstable Arts Coun., Mass. Art Coun., Nat. Endowment for the Arts. Mem. Nat. Assn. Women Artists, Cape Cod Art Assn., Smithsonian Instn. Home: PO Box 361 West Hyannisport MA 02672-0361

DEVINE, PATRICK CAMPBELL, urologist, educator; b. Norfolk, Va., June 7, 1925; s. Charles Joseph and Julia Campbell Devine; m. Linda Marie Dofflemoyer, June 13, 1953; children: Catherine, Patrick Jr., Michael, William. BA, Washington and Lee U., 1948; MD, U. Va., 1953. Diplomate Am. Bd. Urology. Intern surgery U. Va. Hosp., Charlottesville, 1953-54, resident urology, 1954-57; prof. dept. urology Ea. Va. Med. Sch., 1975—; cons. Lake Taylor City Hosp., Norfolk, Va., U.S. Navy Med. Ctr., Portsmouth, Va., VA Ctr., Hampton, Va.; active staff Med. Ctr. Hosps., Inc., DePau Hosp., Children's Hosp. of the King's Daughters; vis. prof. and presenter in field. Contbr. chpts. to books and articles to profl. jours. With U.S. Army, 1944-46. Fellow ACS, Am. Soc. Plastic and Reconstructive Surgeons, Inc. (assoc.), Am. Acad. Pediat.; mem. AAAS, AMA, Am. Assn. Clin. Urologists, Assn. Am. Med. Colls., Am. Urol. Assn. (pres. Mid-Atlantic sect. 1973-74, hon. mem. Southeastern sect.), Med. Soc. Va., Va. Urol. Soc., Norfolk Acad. Medicine, Tidewater Urol. Assn., Soc. Internat. D'Urologie, Confedn. Am. de Urologia, Soc. for Pediat. Urology, Soc. Univ. Urologists, So. Soc. Urologic Surgeons, So. Med. Assn., Seaboard Med. Assn., Norfolk Yacht and Country Club, Harbor Club, Norfolk C. of C., Norfolk German Soc., Princess Anne Country Club. Roman Catholic. Avocations: golf, hunting. Home: 1413 Berkshire Ln Virginia Beach VA 23451 Office: Devine-Fiveash Assocs Ltd Ste 100 400 W Brambleton Ave Norfolk VA 23510

DEVINE, SHANE, federal judge; b. Feb. 1, 1926. B.A., U. N.H., 1949; J.D., Boston Coll., 1952. Bar: N.H. 1952. Formerly ptnr. Devine, Millimet, Stahl & Branch, Manchester, N.H.; judge U.S. Dist. Ct. N.H., 1978—, chief judge, now sr. judge, 1992—. Mem. ABA, N.H. Bar Assn. (pres. 1973-74), Manchester Bar Assn. Office: US Dist Ct NH 55 Pleasant St Rm 511 Concord NH 03301-3954*

DEVINE, WALTER BERNARD, naval architect, marine engineer; b. Detroit, July 7, 1927; s. John Francis and Ethel Florence (Peoples) D.; m. Annemarie Jaggi, Dec. 29, 1956; children: Walter, Michael, Peter, David, Louise, Jessica, Andrew. BS in Marine Transp., U.S. Merchant Marine Acad., Kingspoint, N.Y., 1949; BS in Naval Arch., Marine Engring., U. Mich., 1953. 2nd mate Am. Presidents Lines, San Francisco, 1949-51; naval arch Md. Shipbldg., Balt., 1952-62, M. Mack Earle, Balt., 1962-65; v.p. Surface Separator Sys., Balt., 1963-65; naval arch. Exxon Corp., Houston, 1965-86; prin. Walter Devine & Sons, Escondido, Calif., 1986—; project mgr. Exxon, 1968-70, 1976-81, staff mgr., 1981-86. With USNR, 1945-51. Mem. Soc. Naval. Architecture and Marine Engring. (chmn. L.A. sect. 1992-93, chmn. Houstonsect. 1969-70). Roman Catholic. Achievements include patents for design of oil skimmer, design of large ice breaking vessel, design of oil tanker for extreme cold, design of access to pump room from engine room; research in conversion of tanker for oil processing, computer application in underwater inspection. Home & Office: Walter Devine & Sons 3621 Monte Real Escondido CA 92029-7911

DEVINEY, MARVIN LEE, JR., research institute scientist, program manager; b. Kingsville, Tex., Dec. 5, 1929; s. Marvin Lee and Esther Lee (Gambrell) D.; m. Marie Carole Massey, June 7, 1975; children: Marvin Lee III, John H., Ann-Marie K. Deviney Bowen. BS in Chemistry and Math., S.W. Tex. State U., San Marcos, 1949; MA in Phys. Chemistry, U. Tex., Austin, 1952, PhD in Phys. Chemistry, 1956. Cert. profl. chemist. Devel. chemist Celanese Chem. Co., Bishop, Tex., 1956-58; rsch. chemist Shell Chem. Co., Deer Park, Tex., 1958-66; sr. scientist, head group phys. and radio-chemistry Ashland Chem. Co., Houston, 1966-68, mgr. sect. phys. and analytical chemistry, 1968-71; mgr. sect. phys. chemistry div. rsch. and devel. Ashland Chem. Co., Columbus, Ohio, 1971-78; rsch. assoc., supr. applied surface chemistry Ashland Ventures Rsch. and Devel., Columbus, 1978-84, supr. electron microscopy, advanced aerospace composites, govt. contracts, 1984-90; inst. scientist, mem. internal R & D com. SW Rsch. Inst., San Antonio, Tex., 1990-97; pres. MLD Polymers/Composites, Inc., 1997—; R&D dir. Nuresco Polymers, 1998—; cons. polymer divsn. Southwest Tex. State U., 1998—; adj. prof. U. Tex., San Antonio, 1973-75, Ohio State U., 1990-91; mem. sci. adv. bd. Am. Petroleum Inst. Rsch. Project 60, 1968-74. Contbr. numerous articles to profl. jours.; patentee in field. Mem. ednl. adv. com. Columbus Tech. Inst., 1974-84, Cen. Ohio Tech. Coll., 1975-82, Hocking Tech. Coll., 1989-91. Lt. col., USAR, retired. Humble Oil Rsch. fellow, 1954. Fellow Am. Inst. Chemists (pres. Ohio Inst. 1978-82); mem. Tex. Acad. Sci., Am. Def. Preparedness Assn., Electron Microscopy Soc. Am., Materials Rsch. Soc., SAMPE Composite Soc., N.Am. Catalysis Soc., Am. Soc. Composites, Soc. Plastics Engrs., Soc. Automotive Engrs., Am. Chem. Soc. (chmn. chpt. exec. bd. 1969, bus. mgr. nat. div. Petroleum Chemistry, 1986-90, Best Paper award rubber div. 1967, 70, Hon. Mention awards 1968, 69, 73, symposia co-chmn., co-editor books on catalysis-surface chemistry 1985, carbon-graphite chemistry 1975), Engr.'s Coun. Houston (sr. councilor 1970-71), Sigma Xi, Phi Lambda Upsilon, Alpha Chi, Sigma Pi Sigma. Methodist. Office: 15934 Alsace San Antonio TX 78232-2790

DEVINO, WILLIAM STANLEY, economist, educator; b. Burlington, Vt., Nov. 17, 1926; s. William Arthur and Elaine Anna (Blaise) D.; m. Raphaella Frances Gillespie, Aug. 27, 1948; children: Bonnie Ann, Denise Marie. BA, U. Vt., 1951; MA, U. Conn., 1953; PhD, Mich. State U., 1959. Instr. econs. Mich. State U., 1955-57, Ford Found. dissertation fellow econs., 1957-58; from rsch. assoc. to lectr. Mich. State U. Sch. Labor and Indsl. Rels., 1958-60; from faculty to prof. bus. and econs. U. Maine, Orono, 1960-96; dir. U. Maine Sch. Bus. Adminstrn., 1963-65; dean U. Maine Coll. Bus. Adminstrn., Orono, 1965-96, dean emeritus, 1997—; Cons. Mich. Senate Labor Com., 1955; mem. Gov. Mich. Task Force on Labor, 1959; mem. arbitration roster Fed. Mediation and Concilation Svc.; mem. Gov. Maine Adv. Com. on Bus. Taxation, 1971-72; mem. fact finding panel Maine Labor Rels.Bd. Author: Exhaustion of Unemployment Benefits During a Recession, 1960; co-author: A Study of Textile Mill Closings in Selected New England Communities, 1966. Served with AUS, World War II. Mem. Nat. Acad. Arbitrators. Home: 358 Howard St Bangor ME 04401-4152 Office: U Maine Coll Bus Adminstrn Orono ME 04469

DE VISSCHER, FRANCOIS MARIE, investment banker; b. Louvain, Belgium, Sept. 24, 1953; s. Michel and Jacqueline (Velge) de V.; m. Maura Michaela Nicholson, Oct. 4, 1980; children: Patrick-Michel, Luke-Michel. BA in Applied Econs., U. Louvain, 1975; MBA, Rutgers U., 1977. CPA, N.Y. Staff asst. Coopers & Lybrand, Brussels, 1975-76; staff acct. Coopers & Lybrand, N.Y.C., 1977-79, sr. acct., 1979-80, supr. audit, 1980; assoc. Smith Barney, Harris Upham & Co., Inc., N.Y.C., 1981-82, 2nd v.p., 1983-84, v.p., 1985-88, mng. dir., 1988-90; pres. de Visscher & Co., Greenwich, Conn., 1990-98; ptnr. de Visscher, Olson & Allen LLC, Greenwich, 1998—; bd. dirs. Bekaert Corp. Pres. Family Firm Inst., Brookline, Mass.; trustee Whitby Sch., Greenwich, Conn. Mem. AICPA, Nat. Assn. Securities Dealers (registered rep.), N.Y. Soc. CPAs, Belgium Am. C. of C. (bd. dirs.), Bekaert N.V. Belgium (bd. dirs.), Larchmont (N.Y.) Yacht Club, Westchester Country Club (Rye, N.Y.), Pawling (N.Y.) Mt. Club. Avocations: sailing, shooting, fishing, golf. Office: de Visscher & Co 104 Field Point Rd Greenwich CT 06830-6464

DEVITA, M. CHRISTINE, foundation administrator. BA magna cum laude, Queens Coll., 1977; grad. cum laude, Fordham U., 1980. Bar: N.Y. 1981, U.S. Dist. Ct. (so. dist.) N.Y. 1982, U.S. Supreme Ct. 1986. With legal dept. Reader's Digest Assn., Inc., 1980-87, dep/ gen. counsel, 1984, also bd. dirs.; exec. dir. DeWitt Wallace and Lila Wallace Reader's Digest Funds, N.Y.C., 1987-89, pres., 1989—, also bd. dirs. Editor: Fordham Law Rev. Office: DeWitt Wallace Reader's Digest Found Inc 2 Park Ave Fl 23 New York NY 10016-9301*

DEVITA, VINCENT THEODORE, JR., oncologist; b. Bronx, N.Y., Mar. 7, 1935; s. Vincent Theodore and Isabel DeV.; m. Mary Kay Bush, Aug. 3, 1957; children: Teddy (dec.), Elizabeth. BS, Coll. William and Mary, 1957; MD, George Washington U., 1961; DSc (hon.), N.Y. Med. Coll., 1987, Georgetown U., 1989. Diplomate: Nat. Bd. Med. Examiners, Am. Bd. Internal Medicine (subspecialty hematology, med. oncology). Intern U. Mich. Med. Center, Ann Arbor, 1961-62; resident in medicine George Washington U. Med. Service D.C. Gen. Hosp., 1962-63; clin. assoc. Lab. Chem. Pharmacology, Nat. Cancer Inst. NIH, Bethesda, Md., 1963-65; sr. resident in medicine Yale New Haven Med. Center, 1965-66; sr. investigator solid tumor service, medicine br. Nat. Cancer Inst. NIH, 1966-68, head solid tumor service, medicine br., 1968-71, chief med. br., 1971-74, dir. div. cancer treatment, 1974-80, clin. dir. inst., 1975-80; dir. Nat. Cancer Inst., Nat. Cancer Program, NIH, 1980-88; physician-in-chief Meml. Sloan-Kettering Cancer Ctr., N.Y.C., 1988-91, attending physician, mem., 1988-93, Benno C. Schmidt chair clin. oncology, 1988-93; prof. medicine Cornell U. Med. Coll., 1989-93; dir. Yale Cancer Ctr., New Haven, 1993—; prof. medicine Yale U. Sch. Medicine, New Haven, 1993—; attending physician Yale-New Haven Hosp., 1993—; prof. epidemiology and pub. health, dir. of Yale Cancer Ctr. Yale U. Sch. Medicine, New Haven, 1994—; assoc. prof. medicine George Washington U. Med. Sch., 1971-75, prof. medicine, 1975-89; vis. physician Rockefeller U. Hosp., 1989-93; mem. expert advisory panel WHO, 1976-93; mem. Lasker Award Jury, 1974—; chmn. Com. French-Am. Agreement on Cancer Treatment Research, 1976; vis. prof. Stanford U. Med. Sch., 1972; 1st ann. Clowes lectr. Roswell Park Meml. Inst. Buffalo, 1973; mem. sci. com. 4th Internat. Congress on Anti-Cancer Chemotherapy, 1991-92, 5th Internat. Congress on Anti-Cancer Chemotherapy, also mem. internat. adv. bd., 1993—; mem. sci. adv. bd. Tobacco-Related Disease Rsch. Program State of Calif., 1991—, Hollings Cancer Ctr., 1991—; mem. adv. bd. Stop Cancer, 1991—; mem. sci. com. Italian-Am. Found. For Cancer Rsch., 1991—; mem. clin. adv. bd. Hybridon, Inc., 1993—; bd. dirs. Imclone Systems Inc., Oncotech Inc., Oncos Inc. Mem. editl. bd. Cancer Rsch., 1981-91, Gynecologic Oncology, 1981-91, Hematol. Oncology, 1981-87, Physicians' Drug Alert, 1982—, Jour. Clin. Oncology, 1983—; assoc. editor Online Jour. Current Clin. Trials, 1991—, Cancer Investigation, 1983-87, Am. Jour. Medicine, 1983-88; mem. extramural bd. assoc. editors Physicians Desk Query (PDQ), Nat. Cancer Inst., 1989—; mem. editl. bd. or adv. editor numerous other med. jours.; contbr. numerous articles to med. jours. Mem. awards assembly Gen. Motors Cancer Research Found., 1981-85, adv. council, 1984—; mem. Armand Hammer Cancer Award Com., 1983—. Served with USMCR, 1955-61. Tobacco Rsch. Industry fellow, 1959; decorated Oren del Sol en el Grando de Official, Govt. of Peru, 1970; recipient Albert and Mary Lasker Med. Rsch. award, 1972; Superior Svc. award HEW, 1975; Esther Langer Found. award, 1976; Alumni medallion Coll. William and Mary, 1976; Jeffrey Gottlieb award, 1976; Bronze medal Am. Soc. Therapeutic Radiology, 1978, Karnofsky prize and lecture, 1979, Griffuel prize Assn. for Devel. Rsch. on Cancer, 1980, James Ewing award Soc. Surg. Oncology, 1982; Meml. Sloan-Kettering Cancer Ctr. award, 1972; Disting. Svc. medal USPHS, 1983; Meyer and Anna Prentiss award, 1984; Second Emmanuel Cancer Found. award, 1984; Pierluigi Nervi award, Rome, 1985; Medal of Honor, Am. Cancer Soc., 1985; Barbara Bohen Pfeifer award Am.-Italian Found. Cancer Rsch., 1985; Stratton lectr. Am. Soc. Hematology, 1985; Leukemia Rsch. Fund lectr., London, 1985; Tenth Richard and Hilda Rosenthal Found. award, Am. Assn. Cancer Rsch., Inc., 1986; Stanley G. Kay Meml. award, D.C. Am. Cancer Soc., 1986, Sci. award Brady Cancer Rsch. Inst., 1987, Prix Cino del Duca, Paris, 1988, Pezcoller award Eur. Sch. Oncology, Trento, Italy, 1988, Surgeon Gen.'s Exemplary Svc. medal, 1988, Armand Hammer Cancer prize, 1990, Outstanding Achievement in Clin. Rsch. award Assn. Cmty. Cancer Ctrs., 1992; elected Conn. Acad. Sci. and Engring., 1994; recipient City of Medicine award, 1995. Fellow ACP, N.Y. Acad. Medicine; mem. AMA, Am. Soc. Clin. Oncology (chmn. program com. 1972, dir. 1973-76, pres. 1977-78), Am. Cancer Soc., Am. Soc. Hematology, Am. Assn. Cancer Rsch. (dir. 1976-79), Am. Fedn. Clin. Rsch., Am. Soc. Clin. Investigation, Assn. Am. Physicians, Soc. Surg. Oncology, Smith-Reed-Russel Med. Soc., Internat. Coun. for Coordinating Cancer Rsch. (pres. Am. bd. 1989-92), Alpha Omega Alpha. *

DEVITO, DANNY MICHAEL, actor, director, producer; b. Neptune, N.J., Nov. 17, 1944; s. Daniel and Julia DeV.; m. Rhea Perlman, Jan. 8, 1982; children: Lucy Chet, Gracie, Daniel Jacob. Grad., Am. Acad. Dramatic Arts, 1966. Theater appearances include The Man With a Flower in His Mouth, Sheridan Sq. Playhouse, 1969, The Shrinking Bride, 1971, One Flew Over the Cuckoo's Nest, 1971, DuBarry Was a Lady, 1972, A Phantasmagoria Historia of D. Johann Fauster Magister, Ph.D, M.D., D.D., D.L., etc., 1973, The Many Wives of Windsor (N.Y. Shakespeare Festival), 1974, Where Do We Go From Here?, 1974; motion picture appearances include Lady Liberty, 1971, Hurry Up, or I'll Be 30, 1973, Scalawag, 1973, One Flew Over the Cuckoo's Nest, 1975, Car Wash, 1976, Hot Dogs for Gaugin, Goin' South, 1978, Terms of Endearment, 1983, Romancing the Stone, 1984, Johnny Dangerously, 1984, Jewel of the Nile, 1985, Wise Guys, 1986, My Little Pony, 1986, Ruthless People, 1986, Tin Men, 1987, (dir. debut) Throw Momma from the Train, 1987, Twins, 1988, The War of the Roses (also dir.), 1989, Other People's Money, 1991, Batman Returns, 1992, Hoffa, (also producer, dir.) 1992, Jack the Bear, 1993, The Last Action Hero (voice), 1993, Renaissance Man, 1994, Junior, 1994, Get Shorty, (also prodr.), 1995, Matilda, (also dir.), 1996, Mars Attacks!, 1996, The Rainmaker, 1997, L.A. Confidential, 1997, Hercules, 1997; co-exec. prodr.: Reality Bites, 1994, Pulp Fiction, 1994; prodr.: Feeling Minnesota, 1996, Gattaca, 1997, Living Out Loud, 1998 (also prodr.), The Virgin Suicides, 1999, Stretch Armstrong, 1999, Pittsburgh, 1999, Hospitality Suite, 1999, Man On the Moon, 1999 (also prodr.); appeared in role of Louie in TV series Taxi, 1978-83; guest voice: The Simpsons, 1989; directed and appeared in cable TV movie The Ratings Game, 1984. Recipient Golden Globe award for TV series, Taxi, 1979; Emmy award 1981. Office: care Fred Specktor Creative Artists Agy Inc 9830 Wilshire Blvd Beverly Hills CA 90212-1804*

DEVITO, MATHIAS JOSEPH, retired real estate executive; b. Trenton, N.J., Aug. 23, 1930; s. Charles P. and Margaret L. DeV.; m. Rosetta Kormuth, July 28, 1956; children: Ann Margaret, Charles Michael. B.A., U. Md., 1954, LL.B. with highest honors, 1956; L.H.D., Salisbury State Coll., 1984. Bar: Md. Asst. atty. gen. State of Md., 1963-64; ptnr. Piper & Marbury, Balt., 1965-70; sr. v.p., gen. counsel, then exec. v.p. Rouse Co., Columbia, Md., 1968-73, pres., CEO, bd. dirs., 1973-84, chmn. bd. dirs., pres., CEO, 1984-93, chmn. bd. dirs., CEO, 1993-95, chmn. bd. dirs., 1995-97; chmn. emeritus, chmn. exec. com. of bd., 1997—; bd. dirs. Allfirst Fin. Corp. U.S. Airways Group, Inc.; chmn. Greater Balt. Com., 1990-92. Editor Md. Law Rev., 1955-56. Chmn. bd. trustees Md. State Colls., 1970-73; trustee Johns Hopkins U., 1983-89, Md. Inst. Coll. Art, 1995—. Mem. Adirondack League, Elkridge Club, Order of Coif. Roman Catholic. Office: Rouse Co 220 Village Sq 2 5100 Falls Rd Baltimore MD 21210-1935

DEVITT, AMY JOANNE, English educator; b. Ft. Collins, Colo., Feb. 14, 1955; d. Clayton Francis and Barbara Mary (Cadieux) D.; m. James W. Hartman, Aug. 6, 1991. BA, Trinity U., 1977; MA, U. Kans., 1979; PhD, U. Mich., 1982. Asst. prof. English U. Tulsa, 1982-85; asst. prof. English U. Kans., Lawrence, 1985-88, assoc. prof. English, 1988—, dir. freshman & sophmore English, 1994—. Author: Standardizing Written English, 1989; contbr. articles to profl. jours. Kemper Found. Teaching fellow, 1996. Mem. Am. Dialect Soc. (nominating com. 1991-93), Nat. Coun. Tchrs. English, Modern Lang. Assn., Writing Program Adminstrs, Phi Beta Kappa. Office: U Kans Dept English Lawrence KS 66045

DEVITT, JOHN LAWRENCE, consulting engineer; b. Denver, Sept. 27, 1925; s. Oliver Hinkley and Ellen Elizabeth (McPherson) D.; children: Jane, David, Ellen. BSEE, U. Colo., 1945, MS, 1949. Registered profl. engr., Colo. Engr. U.S. Bureau of Reclamation, Denver, 1947-50; plant mgr. AMF Corp., Colorado Springs, Colo., 1951-55; v.p., gen. mgr. Whittaker Corp. Power Sources div., Denver, 1955-61; chief engr. Metron Instrument Co., Denver, 1962-65; mgr. of electrochemistry Gates Corp., Denver, 1965-71; pvt. practice as a consulting engr. Denver, 1971—; profl. jazz musician (saxophone), Denver, 1946—. Co-inventor sealed lead-acid and lead-chloride batteries. Lt. USNR, 1943-52, PTO. Recipient Battery Research award, The Electrochem. Soc., 1986, Gaston Plantémedal Bulgarian Acad. of Scis., 1999. Mem. The Electrochem. Soc., Am. Chem. Soc., Inst. Elect. and Electronic Engrs., Colo. Mountain Club (pres. 1975), Am. Alpine Club, New York. Achievements include invention of first sealed lead-acid battery. Avocation: mountaineer. Office: Consulting Engr 985 S Jersey St Denver CO 80224-1418

DEVITT-GRASSO, PAULINE VIRGINIA, civic volunteer, nurse; b. Salem, Mass., May 13, 1930; d. John M. and Mary Elizabeth (Cologey) Devitt; m. Frank Anthony Grasso, Oct. 26, 1968; 1 stepson, Christopher Anthony. BSN, Boston Coll., 1952; student, Boston U., 1954-55, Boston State Tchrs. Coll., 1953-54. RN. Staff nurse J.P. Kennedy Jr. Meml. Hosp., Brighton, Mass., 1952-53; head nurse, day supr. J.P. Kennedy Jr. Meml. Hosp., Brighton, 1953-54, day supr., 1955, clin. instr., 1955-68, adminstrv. asst., 1968, dir. nursing edn., 1958-68; vis. instr. Boston Coll., Mass. State Coll., Meml. Hosp. Sch. Nursing, Newton, Mass. Meml. Hosp. Sch. Nursing, 1955-68, CUA S of N, 1990; bd. dirs. Behavioral Health Svcs. Inc., treas., 1996, 97, 98, 99. Pres. Project H.O.P.E., Manhattan Beach, Calif., 1982; pres. adv. coun. Meals on Wheels, Salvation Army, 1989, 90, 91, bd. dirs. Redondo Beach, 1992—, sec. bd. dirs., 1994; cons. Manhattan Beach Housing Found., 1986—, Manhattan Beach Case Mgr., 1982—; mem. adv. coun. South Bay Sr. Svcs., Torrance, Calif., 1986—, pres., 1995—, pres. adv. bd. 1995—; sr. advocate City of Manhattan Beach, 1982; bd. dirs. Ret. Sr. Vol. Program, Torrance, 1986-90; bd. dirs. Behavioral Health Svcs., 1992—, treas. 1996—, hosp. com., fin. com., exec. com.; neighborhood chair Girl Scouts U.S.; mem. Beach City Coun. on Aging, 1983-91; mem. Salvation Army Ladies Aux.; mem. adv. bd. Salvation Army Corps, Redondo Beach. Recipient Cert. of Appreciation, County of L.A., 1988, South Bat Sr. Svcs., 1998 Vol. of the Yr. award City of Manhattan Beach, 1988, Award of Honor County of L.A., 1989, State of Calif. Senate Rules Com. Resolution Commendation, 1988; named Outstanding Vol. Cath. Daus. of Am., 1986, Vol. of Yr. City Manhattan Beach, 1986-87; Rose and Scroll award Manhattan Beach C. of C., 1989, Art Michel Meml. Community Svc. award Manhattan Beach Rotary Club, 1989, Cert. of Appreciation KC's Queen of Martyrs Coun., 1989, Redondo Beach Lila Bell award Salvation Army, 1989, others, Manhattan Beach Vol. Appreciation award, 1982, 83, 84, 85, 86, 88, 90, 91, 92, 93, cert. South Bay Centinela Credit Union, 1990; nominated for Pres's. Vol. Action award Project H.O.P.E., 1987. Mem. AARP, South Bay Geneal. Soc., New Eng. Hist. and Geneal. Soc., Polish Genal. Soc. So. Calif., Am. Martyrs Altar Soc. (pres. 1983, coun. mem.-at-large 1992), Cath. U. Am. Nat. Alumni Assn. (hon.), Cath. U. Am. Sch. Nursing Alumni Assn. (hon.), Boston Coll. Alumni Assn., Manhattan Beach Sr. Citizens Club (pres. 1985-86, 88-89), Lions (Citizen of Yr. award Manhattan Beach club 1986), DAV (comdr.'s club 1990, 91, 92), Lady in Equestrian Order of Holy Sepulchre of Jerusalem. Democrat. Roman Catholic. Avocations: gardening, needlecraft, genealogy, volunteerism. Home: 329 3rd St Manhattan Beach CA 90266-6410

DEVIVO, ANGE, former small business owner; b. Bay Shore, N.Y., Oct. 20, 1925; d. Romeo Zanetti and Karolina (Hodapp) King; m. John Michael DeVivo, Dec. 30, 1950; 1 child, Michael. Student, Washington Sch. for Secs., N.Y.C., 1945-46. Sec. Am. Airlines, N.Y.C., 1946-51; exec. sec. W.C. Holzhauer, N.Y.C., 1951-52; dist. sales mgr. Emmons Jewelers, Inc., Bound Brook, N.J., 1952-53; exec. sec. N.J. Rep. State Com., 1960-64; adminstrv. sec. Mercy Hosp., Charlotte, N.C., 1973-81; pres. Secs., Plus, Convs., Plus, Charlotte, 1983-91; prin. Ange DeVivo & Assocs., Inc., Charlotte, 1991-92. Editor: The North Carolina Republican Woman, 2d edit., 1994, 3d edit., 1995. Mem. Human Svcs. Coun., Charlotte, 1984-88; mem. Emergency Med. Svc. Adv. Coun., Charlotte, 1981-92, chmn., 1988-90; mem. Charlotte Women's Polit. Caucus, 1972-96, Mecklenburg Evening Rep. Women's Club, Charlotte, 1970—, pres., 1973-74, 1993-94, Women's Roundtable, 1994, 95; mem. citizens adv. com. Conv. and Visitors Bur., 1986-90; coord. Women's Equality Day celebration Mecklenburg County Women's Commn., 1990, coord., fin. chair, 1991-92, co-chmn., fin. chair, 1993-96, mem. adv. bd. 1993-96, vice chair, 1995. Recipient Order of Long Leaf Pine award Gov. of N.C., 1974, Entrepreneur of Yr. award Women Bus. Owners, 1987, Spl. Recognition award for devotion, dedication and untiring efforts Mecklenburg County Women's Commn., 1996; honoree N.C. Fedn. Rep. Women, 1987; nominee for Cmty. Svc. award, 1994. Mem. Rep. Women Today. Roman Catholic. Avocations: politics, community volunteer work.

DEVIVO, DARREN DOUGLAS, broadcast executive, announcer; b. Yonkers, N.Y., Mar. 23, 1965; s. Frank James and Jeanette Johanna (Vietri) DeV.; m. Sharon Beth Fierro, Dec. 2, 1994. BS, Fordham U., 1987. Lic. FCC. Announcer, engr., prodn. dir. Sta. WFUV-FM, Bronx, N.Y., 1983-90, afternoon show host, 1991-92, morning drive host, asst. music dir., 1992-97, morning drive host, music promotions dir., 1997—; prodn. dept. asst. Sta. WNYW-TV, Manhattan, N.Y., 1989-90; announcer Sta. WEHM-FM, E. Hampton, N.Y., 1994-95; radio hour host Columbia Records, Manhattan, N.Y., 1995—; news announcer News 12--Neighborhood News, Syosset, N.Y., 1995-96. Democrat. Roman Catholic. Avocations: sports, music. Office: WFUV 90.7 FM Fordham U Keating Hall Bronx NY 10458

DE VIVO, DARRYL CLAUDE, pediatric neurologist; b. Everett, Mass., Aug. 28, 1937; m. Ruth Marie Crock, Feb. 6, 1965; children: Cynthia, Jessica, Kristin. BA, Amherst Coll., 1959; MD, U. Va., 1964. Diplomate Am. Bd. Psychiatry and Neurology (dir. for neurology 1991—). Intern Univ. Hosp., Boston, 1964-65; resident in pediatrics and neurology Mass. Gen. Hosp., Boston, 1965-67; clin. assoc. NIH, 1967-69; fellow in pediatric neurology St. Louis Children's Hosp., 1969-70; mem. faculty Wash. U. Sch. Medicine, St. Louis, 1970-78, prof. pediatrics and neurology, 1977-78; Sidney Carter prof. neurology and prof. pediatrics Coll. Physicians and Surgeons, Columbia U., N.Y.C., 1979—; dir. pediatric neurology Columbia-Presbyn. Med. Ctr., N.Y.C., 1979-98, assoc. chmn. child neurology & developmental neurobiology, 1998—; mem. coun. NANDS, 1997—; dir. neurology Am. Bd. Psychiatry and Neurology, 1991—. Assoc. editor: Rudolph's Textbook of Pediatrics, 17th edit., 1982, 18th edit., 1987, 19th edit., 1990, 20th edit., 1996; assoc. editor Annals of Neurology, 1979-83, Advances in Pediatrics, 1989—; contbr. articles to profl. jours. Mem. NANDS, 1997—. With USPHS, 1967-69. NIH grantee. Mem. Am. Neurol. Assn., Am. Acad. Neurology (sec. 1993-97, trustee Rsch. and Edn. Found. 1997—), Child Neurology Soc. (pres. 1989-91), Am. Pediatric Soc., Soc. Pediatric Rsch., Am. Soc. Neurochemistry, Internat. Child Neurology Assn., Soc. Neurosci., Alpha Omega Alpha. Office: Presbyn Hosp Neurology Inst 710 W 168th St New York NY 10032-2603*

DEVIVO, SAL J., newspaper executive; b. Saratoga Springs, N.Y., Feb. 3, 1937; s. Salvatore and Sabine (Lobombardo) DeV.; m. Carolyn Ann Turney, Dec. 17, 1961; children: Sally, Karen, Michael, Darin. B.A. in Journalism, St. Bonaventure U., 1962. Reporter The Saratogian, Saratoga Springs, 1956-58, Schenectady Gazette, 1959, Niagara Falls Gazette, N.Y., 1962; Reporter Sunday editor Niagara Gazette, 1964, city editor, 1966-68, editor, pub., 1974-75; mng. editor The Saratogian, 1968-72, editor, pub., 1972-74; editor Camden Courier-Post, N.J., 1975; pub. Camden Courier-Post, 1976-79; exec. editor, assoc. pub. Binghamton Press and Sun-Bull., N.Y., 1979-80; pres., pub. Utica Observer-Dispatch and Daily Press, N.Y., 1980-85, Wilmington Morning News and Evening Jour., Del., 1985-94, The Daily Jour., Vineland, N.J., 1994-96. Pres. Saratoga County United Way, 1973; gen. campaign chmn. Niagara Falls United Givers Fund, 1975, Utica United Way, 1985; pres. adv. council St. Bonaventure U., 1978-79; bd. dirs. Cooper Med. Center, Camden, 1978-79; trustee Wilmington Coll., 1989. Mem. N.Y. State Soc. Newspaper Editors (past pres.), Md., Del. , D.C. press assns., N.J. Press Assn. (dir.), Am. Newspaper Pubs. Assn., Am. Soc. Newspaper Editors. Roman Catholic. Home: 10 Summerknoll Cir Newark DE 19711-2488 Office: The Daily Journal PO Box 1504 Vineland NJ 08362-1504

DE VIZZIO, NICHOLAS JOSEPH, violinist, educator, conductor; b. Saratoga Springs, N.Y., Oct. 10, 1960; s. Benedetto Nicola and Assunta (Di Lauro) De V. AA in Music Performance, Ea. Nazarene Coll., 1982; advanced pedagogical studies with, Nathan Gottschalk, Raphael Bronstein, Roman Totenberg. Concert violinist U.S., Can., Europe, 1976—. *After recovering from polio, Nicholas De Vizzio started music lessons at the age of six and violin at the age of ten. Besides devoting his time and energy to giving public concert performances and teaching, he likes to donate his time giving performances to people who are not able to attend live performances, such as those in nursing facilities and hospitals. He is also available to do charity performances.* Public debut at age 11; internat. debut, 1976; profl. debut with mems. of Albany Symphony Orch., 1976; solo performance with Southeastern Philharmonic Orch., Weymouth, Mass., Quincy (Mass.) Symphony Orch.; conducting debut, 1981; performer with various orch. and ensembles, Music Performance Trust Fund-sponsored performances. Recipient Laureate and cert. Congress of Strings, Young Artists Assn., 1974-81, cert. Tchaikovsky Internat. Competition, 1990, Niccolo Paganini Internat. Competition, 1993, Jean-Frederic Perrenoud Found., 1996. Mem. Internat. Music Biographical Ctr. of Vienna, Am. Fedn. Musicians, Saratoga County Arts Coun. Avocations: reading, chess, museums, traveling music events, religious observations. Address: PO Box 1067 Saratoga Springs NY 12866-2206

DEVLIN, BARBARA JO, school district administrator; b. Milw., Oct. 6, 1947; d. Raymond Peter Seeley and Lois Elsa Young; m. John Edward Devlin, June 23, 1973; children: Christine Elizabeth, Kathleen Megan. BA, Gustavus Adolphus Coll., 1969; MA, U. Mass., 1971; PhD, U. Minn., 1978. Cert. tchr., sch. prin., supt., Minn.; cert. supt., Ill., Minn. Tchr. Worthington (Minn.) High Sch., 1971-75; rsch. assoc. Ednl. R & D, Mpls.-St. Paul, 1975-76, 76-77; coord. edn. svcs. Ednl. Coop. Svc., Mpls.-St. Paul, 1977-79; dir. personnel Minnetonka Pub. Schs., Excelsior, Minn., 1979-85, asst. supt., 1985-87; supt. Sch. Dist. 45, Villa Park, Ill., 1987-95, Ind. Sch. Dist. 280, Richfield, Minn., 1995—; editor working papers Gov.'s Coun. on Fluctuating Enrollments, St. Paul, 1976. Contbr. articles to ednl. jours. Bd. dirs. Richfield Found., 1995—. Ednl. Policy fellow George Washington U., 1977-78; mem. fellow program Bush Found. Pub. Schs., 1984-85; named Ill. Supt. of the Yr., 1994; recipient Disting. Alumni award Gustavus Adolphus Coll., 1994. Mem. Richfield C. of C. (bd. dirs. 1996—), Rotary Internat. (membership chair Villa Park unit 1989-91, vocat. dir. 1991-92, sec. 1992-93, pres. 1994-95), Optimists Internat. (pres. elect Richfield unit 1998-99). Methodist. Office: Richfield Pub Schs 7001 Harriet Ave Richfield MN 55423-3061

DEVLIN, DEAN, producer, writer, actor; b. Aug. 27, 1962. Prodr., writer Godzilla, 1998, Independence Day, 1996, Stargate, 1994 (Sci-Fi Universe Mag. Reader's Choice award); writer Universal Soldier, 1992; creator, exec. prodr. (TV series) The Visitor, 1997; actor (film) Total Exposure, 1991, Moon 44, 1990, Martians Go Home, 1990, City Limits, 1985, Real Genius, 1985, The Wild Life, 1984, My Bodyguard, 1980, (TV) Generations, 1989, Hard Copy, 1987, North Beach and Rawhide, 1985; guest appearances on L.A. Law, Happy Days, Misfits of Science. Recipient George Pal Meml. Award, 1998. Office: 1002 W Washington Blvd Culver City CA 90232*

DEVLIN, JAMES RICHARD, lawyer; b. Camden, N.J., July 7, 1950; s. Gerald William and Mary (Hand) D.; m. Louise Feeley; children: Grace, Jennifer, Kristen. BS in Indsl. Engring., N.J. Inst. Tech., 1972; JD, Fordham U., 1976. Bar: N.J. 1976, N.Y. 1977, U.S. Ct. Appeals (D.C. cir.) 1982. Various mgmt. positions in Long Lines Sect. AT&T, N.Y.C., 1972-76; counsel Long Lines Sect. AT&T, Bedminster, N.J., 1976-82; counsel AT&T, N.Y.C., 1982-83; gen. atty. comm. sect. AT&T, Basking Ridge, N.J., 1983-86; v.p., gen. counsel telephone United Telecomm., Inc., Westwood, Kans., 1987-88; exec. v.p. gen. counsel and external affairs Sprint Corp., Westwood, 1989—; bd. dirs. Transfinancial Holdings, Inc., Lenexa, Kans.; pres. bd. dirs. Ctr. Mgmt. Assitance, 1993-97; mem. bd. overseers N.J. Inst. Tech., 1997—. Past pres., bd. dirs. Ctr. for Mgmt. Assistance, Kansas City, Mo., 1993-96; bd. dirs. Heart of Am. United Way, Minority Supplier Coun., Kansas City; mem. bd. overseers N.J. Inst. Tech. Mem. ABA (past chmn. comm. com. pub. utility law sect.), Am. Arbitration Assn., Fed. Comm. Bar Assn. Home: 4104 W 123rd St Leawood KS 66209-2220 Office: Sprint Corp 2330 Shawnee Mission Pkwy Westwood KS 66205-2090

DEVLIN, JOHN GERARD, lawyer, author; b. Phila., Apr. 26, 1955; s. John and Catherine (Flannery) D.; m. Maureen Borneman, June 17, 1978; children: Caitlin, Colin, Courtenay, Conor. BA, Temple U., 1977, JD, 1980, LLM, 1996. Bar: Pa. 1980, N.J. 1992. Assoc. Spencer, Sherr & Moses, Norristown, Pa., 1980-82, Deasey, Scanlan & Bender, Phila., 1982-84; mng. atty. Devlin Assocs., P.A., Phila., 1984—. Author: Tort Liability for Bad Faith Claims, 1995. Mem. Union League Club, Phi Beta Kappa. Home: 123 S Broad St Philadelphia PA 19109-1029 Office: 1515 Market St Ste 2010 Philadelphia PA 19109-8908

DEVLIN, MICHAEL COLES, bass-baritone; b. Chgo., Nov. 27, 1942; s. John Stott and Jane (Coles) D. Mus.B., La. State U., 1965. Debut, N.Y.C. Opera, 1966, appeared with, Santa Fe Opera, Houston Opera and Symphony, San Francisco Symphony, symphonies in, Los Angeles, Phila., Boston, Chgo., New Orleans, Washington, N.Y. Philharm., opera cos. in, Boston, New Orleans, Washington, Ft. Worth, English debut, Glyndebourne Festival, 1974; appeared at, Covent Garden, 1975, 77, European debut, Holland Festival, 1977; appeared with, Frankfurt and Munich operas, 1977, Can. opera and symphony work in, Winnipeg, Toronto and Ottawa, debut, Met. Opera, 1978, San Francisco Opera, 1979, Hamburg and Paris operas, 1980, Miami and Monte Carlo operas, 1981, Dallas opera, 1983, Chgo. Opera, 1984, Los Angeles Opera, 1986.

DEVLIN, ROBERT MANNING, financial services company executive; b. Bklyn., Feb. 28, 1941; s. John Manning and Norma (Hall) D.; m. Katharine Bareis, Sept. 13, 1961; children: Michael Hall II, Matthew Bareis. BA in Econs., Tulane U., 1964. Various positions Mut. of N.Y., 1964-77; v.p., asst. to pres. Calif. Western States Life Ins. Co., Sacramento, 1977-80, sr. v.p., 1980; exec. v.p., dir. Am. Gen. Life and Accident Ins. Co., Nashville, 1980-85; exec. v.p. Am. Gen. Corp., Houston, 1986; pres., chief exec. officer, dir. Am. Gen. Life Ins. Co. Tex., Houston, 1986-93; vice chmn. Am. Gen. Corp., 1993-95, pres., 1995-96, pres., CEO, 1996-97, chmn. bd. dirs., CEO, 1997-98, chmn. bd. dirs., pres., CEO, 1998; chmn., dir. Am. Gen. Assurance Co., AGC Life Ins. Co., Am. Gen. Life & Accident Ins. Co., Knickerbocker Corp.; mem. Saratoga Reading Rms., Saratoga Springs, N.Y. Mem. Am. Soc. CLUs, Univ. Club (Houston), Winged Foot Golf Club (N.Y.), The Coronado Club (Houston), McGregor Links (Saratoga Springs, N.Y.), Belle Meade Country Club (Nashville), Met. Club (N.Y.), Univ. Club (N.Y.C.). Roman Catholic. Home: 2129 Brentwood Dr Houston TX 77019-3511 Office: Am Gen Corp The Variable Annuity Life Insurance Co 2929 Allen Pkwy Houston TX 77019-2197

DEVLIN, THOMAS JOSEPH, physicist; b. Jenkintown, Pa., Aug. 23, 1935; s. Thomas J. and Anne (Lyttle) D.; m. Nancy Sherry, July 28, 1962; children: Paul, Thomas E., Mark. BA, LaSalle U., 1957; MA, U. Calif., Berkeley, 1959, PhD, 1961. Rsch. assoc. U. Calif., Berkeley, 1961-62; from instr. to asst. prof. Princeton (N.J.) U., 1962-67; assoc. prof. Rutgers U., New Brunswick, N.J., 1967-78, prof., 1978—; guest scientist European Orgn. for Nuclear Rsch., Geneva, Switzerland, 1970-71, Fermilab, Batavia, Ill., 1980-81, 88-90. Contbr. sci. papers to profl. jours. John Simon Guggenheim fellow, 1991. Fellow Am. Phys. Soc. (W.K.H. Panofsky prize 1994). E-mail: devlin@physics.rutgers.edu. Fax: 732-445-4343. Office: Rutgers U Dept Physics & Astronomy 136 Frelinghuysen Rd Piscataway NJ 08854-8019

DEVLIN, THOMAS MCKEOWN, biochemist, educator; b. Phila., June 29, 1929; s. Frank and Ella Mae (McKeown) D.; m. Marjorie Adele Paynter, Aug. 15, 1953; children—Steven James, Mark Thomas. B.A., U. Pa., 1953; Ph.D., Johns Hopkins U., 1957. Rsch. assoc. Merck Inst., Rahway, N.J., 1957-61; sect. head Merck Inst., 1961-66, dir. enzymology, 1966-67; prof., chmn. dept. biochemistry Hahnemann U. Sch. Medicine, 1967-94, prof., 1994-95; prof. emeritus, 1995—; acting dean, Sch. Allied Health Professions Hahnemann U., 1972-74, 80-81; vis. scientist U. Brussels, 1964-65, Inst. Genetics, Naples, Italy, 1965; mem. NSF rev. panels, 1976-77; mem. coun. acad. soc. Assn. Am. Med. Colls., 1975-79; mem. com. on sci. and arts Franklin Inst., 1977-90; mem. test com. Nat. Bd. Med. Examiners, 1983-85; chair Med. Biochemistry Edn. Bd., 1986-93. Editor: (J. Wiley) Textbook of Biochemistry, 1982, 86, 92, 97; contbr. numerous articles to profl. jours. Mem. Commn. on Evaluation, Retention and Selection of Judges, Phila. Bar Assn., 1976-79, vice chmn., 1979; vis. com. Lehigh U., 1982-90; mem. selection panel for magistrate judges, 1993, 95; mem. tech. adv. com. Ben Franklin Tech. Ctr., 1991—. Mem. Am. Soc. for Biochemistry and Molecular Biology, Am. Assn. Cancer Research, Am. Soc. Cell Biology, Soc. Exptl. Biology and Medicine, Biophys. Soc., Biochem. Soc., Phi Beta Kappa, Sigma Xi. Episcopalian. Club: Ocean City (N.J.) Yacht. Home: 183 Beaumont Rd Devon PA 19333-1848 Office: MCP Hahnemann Sch Medicine Dept Biochemistry Philadelphia PA 19129

DEVLIN, WENDE DOROTHY, writer, artist; b. Buffalo, Apr. 27, 1918; d. Bernhardt Phillip Wende and Elizabeth May Buffington; m. Harry Devlin, Aug. 30, 1941; children: Harry, Wende, Jeffrey, Alexandra, Brian, Nicholas, David. BFA, Syracuse U., 1940. Author: (children's books) Old Black Witch, 1963, Old Witch and the Polkadot Ribbon, 1963, The Knobby Boys to the Rescue, 1965, Aunt Agatha, There is a Lion Under the Couch, 1968, How Fletcher was Hatched, 1970, (N.J. English Tchrs. award), A Kiss for a Warthog, 1970, Cranberry Thanksgiving, 1971, Old Witch Rescues Halloween, 1973 (Chgo. Book Fair award for excellence 1974), Cranberry Christmas, 1973, Cranberry Mystery, 1979, Hang on Hester, 1980, Cranberry Summer, 1991, Cranberry Valentine, 1986, Cranberry Autumn, 1994, The Trouble with Henriette, 1995; artist, painter comic strip Ragg Mopp, 1969-72; contbr. of many poems to Good Housekeeping mag.; one person show at Schering Plough, N.J.; represented in permanent collections at Midlantic Bank of N.J., Nat. Westminster Bank of N.J., also many private collections. Mem. Rutgers Adv. Coun. on Children's Lit., 1980—. Recipient Arents award Syracuse U., 1977; named to N.J. Literary Hall of Fame, 1989. Congregationalist. Home and Office: 443 Hillside Ave Westfield NJ 07090-2902 Office: Simon & Schuster 866 3rd Ave New York NY 10022-6221

DEVLIN, WILLIAM RUSSELL, newspaper owner; b. Northwood, N.D., Sept. 18, 1947; s. Russell T. and Marie E. D.; m. Marjorie Ann Offerdahl, Feb. 3, 1967; children: Russell, Patrick. Co-owner, co-pub. Steele County Press, Finley, N.D., 1970—. County Commr. Steele County, Finley, 1984-98; state rep. N.D., Bismarck, 1996—; mem. N.D. Rep. Party; House Rep. Caucus leader, 1999—; past pres. Finley Comm. Club. Mem. N.D. Newspaper Assn. (bd. dirs. 1973-79, state pres. 1978-79), Eagles, Sigma Delta Chi (state pres. 1972-73). Office: Steele County Press Inc PO Box 475 Finley ND 58230-0475

DEVOE, CHARLES LOUIS, II, sales and marketing consultant; b. Boston, July 22, 1943; s. Charles L. and Martha H. (Looney) D.; m. Marilyn Grady, June 21, 1969 (div. Mar. 1972); m. Candace Elizabeth Bell, Nov. 21, 1981 (div. July 1989); m. Amy Beth Abels, Oct. 5, 1992. Student, U. Mass., 1962-63, U. Beverly Hills, 1977-79. Sales rep. Nat. Airlines, Phila., San Francisco, 1967-72; sales mgr. Marriott Hotels, Berkeley, Calif., 1973; dist. mgr. Norwegian Caribbean Lines, L.A., 1974-75; mgr. customer com. Flying Tigers, L.A., 1975; dir. corp. mktg. Dollar Rent A Car, L.A., 1975-76; pres., sec.-treas. Innfields Inc., Beverly Hills, Calif., Los Angeles, Palm Harbor, Fla., 1976-94; pres. Hamilton Assocs., Clearwater, Fla., 1977—; v.p. mktg. Micro Bus. Software, Inc., Concord, N.H., 1983-84; exec. prodr. Opening Night Playhouse, Palm Harbor; chief investigator Coale & Van Susteren, PA, Washington, 1990-96. Mem. U.S. Senatorial Trust, Washington, 1986-89. Sgt. USMC, 1963-66. Recipient Ebony Club award, 1984, Viet Nam Svc. medal, Nat. Def. Svc. medal, Good Conduct medal, Honorable Discharge, OT Ambassador award Internat. Mgmt. Ch. Scientology, 1995—. Mem. Internat. Assn. Scientologists (awarded status of patron 1987) . Avocation: literature, arts, philosophy. Home: PO Box 10598 Clearwater FL 33757-8598 Office: 1114 Jackson Rd 5335 Wisconsin Ave NW Ste 720 Clearwater FL 33756

DEVOE, KENNETH NICKOLAS, food service executive; b. Mineola, N.Y., Sept. 13, 1944; s. Kenneth Pettit and Wykiena (Bos) D.; m. Linda Faye Mizer, May 7, 1965; children: Andrea W., Christina L., Kenneth C., Paula A. Student, Merced Coll., 1970-75. Police sgt. Merced (Calif.) Police Dept., 1966-75; sheriff sgt. Mariposa (Calif.) County Sheriff, 1975-81; pk. mgr. Am. Campgrounds Inc., Bellevue, Wash., 1981-83; owner DeVoe Enterprises, Atwater, Calif., 1983—. Chmn. Merced County Assn. Govts., 1990-98, Atwater 4th of July Com., 1983—; asst. mayor City of Atwater, 1987-94, mayor, 1994-98. With USAF, 1962-66. Mem. Atwater C. of C. (dir. 1991, dir.-at-large 1983-86, Citizen of Yr. 1987), Merced Trade Club (dir. 1991—), Castle Air Force Base Cols. Club., Kiwanis, Masons. Republican. Avocations: coin collecting, community activities. Home: 3302 Sextant Dr Atwater CA 95301-4725 Office: Devoe Enterprises 1898 Bellevue Rd Atwater CA 95301-2668

DEVOGT, JOHN FREDERICK, management science and business ethics educator, consultant; b. Detroit, Oct. 20, 1930; s. Leo Henry and Dorothy Helen (Gibbs) D.; m. Ann Marie Berby, Aug. 29, 1959; children—Joanne Elise, Linda Christine. B.S., U. N.C., 1957, Ph.D., 1966. Instr. Washington and Lee U., Lexington, Va., 1962-66; asst. prof. Washington and Lee U., 1966-67, assoc. prof., 1967-70, prof., 1970—, head dept., 1968-90; acad. dir. Washington and Lee Family Bus. Inst., 1987-89; state judge Blue Chip Enterprise Iniative, 1991-96; acad. Jonah A.Y. Goldratt Inst., 1991—; chmn. adv. bd. Lexington office CorEast Savs. Bank, Richmond, 1976-90. Chmn. Lexington City Sch. Bd., 1973; pres. Va. Sch. Bds. Assn., Charlottesville, 1974; v.p. Henry St. Playhouse, Lexington, 1985. Served to staff sgt. USAF, 1951-55. Vis. fellow Univ. Coll., Oxford, Eng., 1983. Mem. So. Mgmt. Assn. (pres. 1975-76), Phi Beta Kappa, Phi Eta Sigma, Beta Gamma Sigma. Presbyterian. Avocations: golf; amateur dramatics; singing. Home: 617 Stonewall St Lexington VA 24450-1947 Office: Washington and Lee Univ Lexington VA 24450

DEVOL, GEORGE CHARLES, JR., manufacturing executive; b. Louisville, Feb. 20, 1912; s. George C. and Elsa (Vance) D.; m. Evelyn R. Jahelka, Dec. 31, 1938; children: Christine, George C. III, Robert Vance, Suzanne. PhD in Sci., U. Bridgeport, 1985. Pres., United Cinephone Corp., N.Y., 1933-39; project engr. Sperry Gyroscope Co., Garden City, N.Y., 1939-41; gen. mgr. Gen. Electronic Industries, Greenwich, Conn., 1941-45; pres. Devol Rsch. Co., Ft. Lauderdale, Fla., 1947—, Automatic Mfg. Systems, Inc., Ft. Lauderdale, 1984—. Mem. Soc. of Mfg. Engrs. (life), Ocean Reef Club, Key Largo Club (Fla.), Lago Mar Club (Ft. Lauderdale, Fla.). Patentee in field of indsl. robots (40 patents). Home and Office: 1543 SE 13th St Fort Lauderdale FL 33316-2211

DEVOL, LUANA, dramatic soprano, consultant, arts administrator; b. San Mateo, Calif., Nov. 30, 1942. AA, Coll. San Mateo, 1960; postgrad., San Francisco State U., 1962, U.S. Internat. U., San Diego, 1970. Asst. to bd. dirs. Spring Opera Theatre, San Francisco, 1972-75; asst. gen. mgr. Paramount Theatre, Oakland, Calif., 1975-84; soprano Aachen (Germany) Stadttheater, Aachen, Germany, 1984-87, Mannheim Nat. Theater, Germany, 1987-91; opera singer Bayreuth, Hamburg, Munich, Dresden, Leipzig, San Francisco, La Scala, Italy, Paris, others; pvt. voice cons.; guest lectr. U. Md., Mannheim, 1991, 94 Seminar, European Singing Career, 1987, master class U. Nev., Las Vegas, 1996, 98, N.Y., 1999; mem. editl. bd. The Oakland Paramount, 1988. Made European debut as Leonore in Fidelio, Württembergische Staatsoper, 1983; roles include Isolde, Senta, Elsa, Elisabeth, Brunnhilde, Elektra, Faerberin, Kaiserin, Ariadne, Aida, Amelia, Tosca, Donna Anna and Donna Elvira. U.S. Internat. U. scholar, 1971; named Singer of Yr. Opern Welt, 1997. Mem. Am. Guild Musical Artists, Am.-German C. of C. Address: Weinstrasse 35, Forst 67147, Germany

DEVONE, DENISE, artist, educator; b. Newark, Sept. 13, 1953. BFA cum laude, Temple U., 1975; MFA, U. Hawaii, 1978. Instr. Newark Mus., 1990—; art tchr. Holy Cross Sch., Harrison, N.J., 1995—; adj. prof. County Coll. of Morris, Randolph, N.J., 1994—; cons. Donald B. Palmer Mus., Springfield, N.J., 1992-95. Executed murals Kaiser Hosp., Honolulu, 1985, Kaiser Pensacola Clinic, Honolulu, 1986, Distinctive Bodies Fitness, Warren, N.J., 1993, Ambulatory Pediatric Clinic, Overlook Hosp., Summit, N.J., 1994. Recipient Purchase awards Hawaii State Found. on Culture and the Arts, 1976, 78, 80, 86, award of merit City and County of Honolulu, 1988; N.J. State Coun. on Arts/Dept. State fellow, 1994-95. Mem. Nat. Assn. Women Artists, Inc., New Art Group/Watchung Arts Ctr., City Without Walls, Artists Space. Avocation: piano. Home: 33 Kew Dr Springfield NJ 07081-2530

DE VONE, JAMES MILTON, manufacturing company owner, entrepreneur; b. Durham, N.C., July 24, 1944; s. Louis Sherwood Sr. and Irene (Bell) De V.; children: James M., Jamie M. BS, N.C. Cen. U., 1966; MS, U. N.C., 1974. Dir. Windsor Ctr., Greensboro, N.C., 1970-71; recreation coord. Durham Housing Authority, 1971-78; pres. DeVone Mfg. Co., Inc., Durham, 1975—; founder, headmaster Sch. of Univ. Studies and Understanding, Durham, 1985—; founder Tornado Power, Durham, 1988—; U.S. cons. African Devel. Bank, Ivory Coast, W. Africa. Author: A Beautiful Dreamer, 1978, Global Warming Solutions; inventee in field. Mem. Middle East Assn., Internat. Platform Assn. Avocations: inventing, creative writing, reading. Home: 1827 Nixon St Durham NC 27707-4331 Office: Susu Products PO Box 51216-2916 Durham NC 27707-0024

DEVONS, SAMUEL, educator, physicist; b. Bangor, N.Wales, U.K., Sept. 30, 1914; came to U.S., 1959; s. David Isaac and Edith (Edlestein) D.; m. Celia Ruth Toubkin, Sept. 7, 1938; children—Susan Danielle, Judith Rosalind, Amanda Jane, Cathryn Ann Julie. B.A., Trinity Coll., Cambridge (Eng.) U., 1935, M.A., Ph.D. (Exhbn. 1851 scholar), 1939; M.Sc., Manchester (Eng.) U., 1959. Sr. sci. officer Air Ministry, Ministry Supply, U.K., 1939-45; fellow, dir. studies, lectr. physics Trinity Coll., 1946-49; prof. physics Imperial Coll., London, Eng., 1950-55; Langworthy prof. physics, dir. phys. labs. U. Manchester, 1955-60; prof. physics Columbia U., 1960-84, prof. emeritus, 1985—, chmn. dept., 1963-67; Royal Soc.-Leverhulme vis. prof., Andhra, India, 1967-68; Racah vis. prof. physics Hebrew U., Jerusalem, 1973; Balfour vis. prof. history of sci. Weizmann Inst., Israel, 1974, bd. govs., 1971—; Royal Soc. Rutherford Meml. Lectr., Australia, 1989; mem. Tech. Assistance-UNESCO Team of UN to S. Am., 1957. Author: Excited States of Nuclei, 1949; Editor: Biology and the Physical Sciences, 1969, High Energy Physics and Nuclear Structure, 1970. Served with RAF, 1944-45. Recipient Rutherford medal and prize Inst. Physics, U.K., 1970. Fellow Royal Soc. London, Am. Phys. Soc., The Joseph Priestley Assn. (founder, convenor 1986—), Phi Beta Kappa. Home: Lewis Rd Irvington NY 10533 Office: Columbia U Nevis Lab PO Box 137 Irvington NY 10533-0137

DEVORE, CARL BRENT, college president, educator; b. Zanesville, Ohio, Sept. 3, 1940; s. Carl Emerson and Helen Elizabeth (Van Atta) DeV.; m. Linda Mospens, July 2, 1966; children—Krista, Matthew. B.S.J., Ohio U., 1962; M.A., Kent State U., 1971, Ph.D., 1978. Dir. devel. Am. Heart Assn., Cleve., 1965-68; exec. dir. Kent State U. Found., Ohio, 1968-72; v.p. Hiram Coll., Ohio, 1972-82; pres. Davis and Elkins Coll., Elkins, W.Va., 1982-84, Otterbein Coll., Westerville, Ohio, 1984—; pres. Higher Edn. Coun., Columbus, 1985; trustee Nationwide Investing Found., 1990. Producer and moderator film series on liberal arts edn. Pres. Hiram (Ohio) Village Council, 1981; chmn. E. Cen. Colls., 1990; pres. Nat. Assn. Schs. and Colls., United Meth. Ch., 1991. Mem. Am. Assn. Advancement of Humanities, AAUP, Ohio Council of Fund Raising Execs. (pres. 1976), Ohio Coll. Assn. (pres. 1987), W.Va. Assn. Coll. and Univ. Pres. (pres. 1984), Westerville C. of C. (pres.). Clubs: University (Columbus, Ohio); University (N.Y.C.). Lodge: Rotary. Office: Otterbein Coll Pres Office Westerville OH 43081*

DEVORE, DAUN ALINE, lawyer; b. Ft. Worth; d. Jacques LeRoy and Madelyn Norma DeV. Student, U. Paris IV; BA magna cum laude, U. Calif., Irvine; JD, U. San Francisco; MPA, Harvard U.; postgrad., Oxford U. Bar: Calif., U.S. Ct. Appeals (fed. and 9th cirs.), U.S. Ct. Internat. Trade, U.S. Dist. Ct. (ctrl. dist.) Calif., U.S. Ct. Vets. Appeals. Law clk. U.S. Environ. Protection Agy. Region IX, Constitution Sub-Com., U.S. Senate Jud. Com.; honors clk. civil rights div. fed. enforcement U.S. Dept. Justice; summer atty. Office Pub. Defenders for the City and County, San Francisco; lectr. law coll. Seoul (Republic of Korea) Nat. U.; assoc. Cen. Internat. Law Firm, Seoul; U.S. prin. Othniel H.K. Ltd., Cambridge (Mass.), L.A., and Hong Kong; ptnr. Internat. Bus. Law Firm, Palm Springs, Calif. and Washington; conf. and seminar presenter, Korea, Singapore, Hong Kong. Contbr. articles to legal publs. Mem. legis. com. San Francisco Commn. on Status of Women; pub. rels. dir. Riverside County coun. Girl Scouts U.S.A.; hist. site commr. City of Palm Springs. Fulbright fellow, Seoul. Mem. ABA (com. internat. svcs., chmn. subcom. on Asia-Pacific sect. internat. law, internat. law com. gen. practice sect., chmn. 1992-97, mem. standing com. liaison to fgn. and internat. bars. 1992-97), Internat. Inst. Strategic Studies, Calif. Bar Assn. (com. internat. law), Armed Forces Comm. and Electronic Assn., Harvard Club (bd. dirs. Korea 1986), Toastmasters (numerous speech awards 1988, 89), Phi Delta Phi. Avocations: operatic singer, songwriter, flutist.

DEVORE, KIMBERLY, business executive; b. Louisville, June 19, 1947; d. Wendell O. and Shirley F. DeV. Student, Xavier U., 1972-76; AA, Coll. Mt. St. Joseph, 1979. Patient registration supr. St. Francis Hosp., Cin., 1974-76; cons., bus. mgr. Family Health Care Found., Cin., 1976-77; exec. dir. Hospice of Cin., Inc., 1977-80; pres. Micro Med, 1979-86; v.p. Sycamore Profl. Assn., 1979-86; ptnr. Enchanted House, 1979-86, sec., 1979-80, treas., 1980-83; dist. sales rep. Control-O-Fax, 1986; br. sales mgr., 1987, nat. dealer devel. rep., 1987, nat. computer field sales trainer, 1987-90; pres. U.S. Exec. Leasing and U.S. Med. Leasing, Inc., 1991—, Accu Svcs., Inc., 1993—, U.S. Med. Mgmt., Inc., 1994—; pres. U.S. Med. Mgmt. of Ga., Inc., 1994—. Pres. Humanity for World Inc., 1998—, pres. Saddle Creek Homeowners Assn., Inc., 1992-95, parliamentarian, 1995-96; chairperson Citizen's Police Adv. Com. City of Roswell, 1997-99; chairperson found. grants Orch. Atlanta, 1998-99, pres., 1999; bd. dirs., membership chairperson Smith Plantation City of Roswell, 1996-97; pres. Roswell Citizen's Police Acad., Inc., 1994-95; mem. City of Roswell Med. Devel. Dist. Coun., 1995—; mem. North Fulton Civic League, Inc., 1995-96; bd. dirs. Nat. Hospice Orgn., 1979-82, chmn. long-term planning com., fin. com., ann. meeting com., 1979-82, sec., 1980-81, treas., 1981-82; bd. dirs. Hospice of Miami Valley, Inc., 1982-86, also chmn. pers. com., by-laws com.; bd. dirs. Orch. Atlanta, 1998—. Mem. Greater Cin. Soc. Fund Raisers, Better Housing League; mem. service and rehab. com. Hamilton County Unit, Am. Cancer Soc., 1977-78; chair road com. Saddle Creek Homeowners Assn., 1991-92. Mem. Ohio Hospice Assn. (co-founder, state chmn., pres., 1978-83), Nat. League for Nursing, Ohio Hosp. Assn., Nat. Fedn. Bus. and Profl. Women's Clubs, Ohio Fedn. Bus. and Profl. Women's Clubs, Ohio Fedn. Bus. and Profl. Women's Clubs, Cin. Bus. and Profl. Women's Clubs (pres. 1973-75).

DEVORE, PAUL CAMERON, lawyer; b. Great Falls, Mont., Apr. 25, 1932; s. Paul Theodore and Maxine (Cameron) DeV.; m. Roberta Humphrey, Feb. 3, 1962; children: Jennifer Ross, Andrew Cameron, Christopher Humphrey. BA, Yale U., 1954; MA, Cambridge U., 1956; JD, Harvard U., 1961. Bar: Wash. 1961. Assoc. Wright, Innis, Simon & Todd, Seattle, 1961-66; ptnr. Davis Wright Tremaine, Seattle, 1967—, chmn. exec. com., 1983-95; mem. adv. bd. BNA Media Law Reporter, 1978—. Chmn. Seattle C.C., 1967-68, Bush Sch., Seattle, 1976-79, Virginia Mason Med. Found., 1984-85, Virginia Mason Rsch. Ctr., 1983-84, Seattle Found., 1985-87, Children's Hosp. Found., 1993-95; trustee Lakeside Sch., 1995—; chmn. bd. visitors U. Wash. Sch. Comm., 1989—; pres. A Contemporary Theatre, Seattle, 1972-74;

sec. Seattle Art Mus., 1973—. Mem. ABA (chmn. forum on comm. law 1981-84), Wash. State Bar Assn. (chmn. sect. corp. bus. and banking law 1981-82, bench, bar, press com. 1984-90), Seattle-King County Bar Assn. (trustee 1975-76), Seattle Tennis Club, Univ. Club, Phi Beta Kappa, Beta Theta Phi. Home: 5740 27th Ave NE Seattle WA 98105-5512 Office: Davis Wright Tremaine 2600 Century Sq 1501 4th Ave Ste 2600 Seattle WA 98101-1688

DE VORE, PAUL WARREN, technology educator; b. Parkersburg, W.Va., July 18, 1926; s. Harry and Eleanor Sarah (Dunn) De Vore; m. Eleanor Jean Condron, Apr. 7, 1952; children: Michelle Ann, Phillip Charles. BS, Ohio U., 1950; MA, Kent State U., 1954; EdD, Pa. State U., 1961; postgrad., Ohio State U., 1983. Postdoctoral fellow U. Md., 1965-66; instr. pub. schs. Chagrin Falls, Ohio, 1950-53; asst. prof. engring. Grove City Coll., 1953-56; asst. prof. SUNY-Oswego, 1956-60, dir. div. indsl. arts and tech., 1960-67; prof. tech. edn. W. Va. U., Morgantown, 1967-75, prof., chmn. tech. edn., 1975-85, prof., coord. rsch. project offices, dept. technology, 1985-92; dir. Appalachian Tech. Edn. Consortium, 1990-95; dir. div. edn. and tng. Nat. Tech. Transfer Ctr., 1992-93; tech. cons., pres. PWD Assocs., Morgantown, W.Va., 1974—; cons. NSF, U.S. Dept. Edn., AID, pub. schs., colls., univs.; mem. com. technol. literacy Nat. Acad. Engring., 1999—. Author: Technology: An Intellectual Discipline, 1964, Education in a Technological Society, 1971, Technology and the New Liberal Arts, 1976, Technology: An Introduction, 1980, Introduction to Transportation, 1983; cons. editor: Tech. Edn. Series, 1974-93. Mem. nat. commn. Tech. for All Ams., 1994-95; chmn. campaign United Fund, Oswego, 1962-63. Served with USN, 1944-46. Named Outstanding Tchr., W.Va. U., 1970-71, 89, W.Va. U. Coll. Resources and Edn., 1988; recipient Outstanding Rsch. award Phi Delta Kappa, 1978; recognized as one of individuals who has contbd. most to tech. edn., 1985, Internat. Tech. Edn. Assn. Acad. of Fellows, 1987. Mem. Coun. on Tech. Tchr. Edn., Soc. History of Tech., Internat. Tech. Edn. Assn., Epsilon Pi Tau (Disting. Svc. award 1976, Paul T. Hiser Exemplary Publ. award 1999). Home: 668 Colonial Dr Morgantown WV 26505-2423 Office: W Va U Tech Edn Rsch Proj Offices Morgantown WV 26506-6680 *Seek quality in all you do and conduct your personal and civic affairs in a responsible and civil manner.*

DEVORKIN, DAVID HYAM, historian, curator; b. L.A., Jan. 6, 1944; s. Howard and Judith (Schonberg) D.; m. Kunie Fujiki, June 2, 1970; 1 child, Hannah Fujiki. BS, UCLA, 1966; MS, San Diego State U., 1968; MPhil, Yale U., 1970; PhD, U. Leicester, Eng., 1978. Prof. astronomy Ctrl. Conn. State Coll., New Britain, 1970-80; cons. Am. Inst. Physics, N.Y.C., 1977-79; curator Nat. Air and Space Mus. Smithsonian Instn., Washington, 1980—. Author: History of Astronomy and Astrophysics, 1981, Race to the Stratosphere, 1988, Practical Astronomy, 1986, Science with a Vengeance, 1992; contbr. articles to profl. jours. Recipient NSF award, Sloan Found. award. Mem. Am. Astron. Soc. (Hist. Astronomy divsn. chair 1997-99), History Sci. Soc., Soc. History Tech., Internat. Astron. Union, Royal Astron. Society London. Office: Smithsonian Instn Nat Air & Space Mus Washington DC 20560

DE VOS, DANIEL G., sports team executive, marketing professional; b. Grand Rapids, Mich., Mar. 26, 1958; m. Pamella G. De Vos. Student, Northwood U. V.p., distbr. rels. N.Am. Amway Corp., Ada, Mich., v.p. Pacific divsn., v.p. corp. affairs, mem. policy bd. dirs., exec. com.; vice-chmn. governing bd. Orlando Magic basketball team; chmn., pres., CEO DP Fox/ Landquest Cos.; pres., CEO Grand Rapids Griffins; chmn., CEO Georgian Internat. Ltd.; chmn. Appliance Distributors Inc.; bd. dirs. Mercy Respite Ctr.; chmn., exec. com., bd. dirs. Genmar Industries, Mpls. Trustee First Union Real Estate Investments, Cleve., Butterworth Hosp., Grand Rapids, No. Mich. U., Marquette; bd. dirs., mem. exec. com., co-chair 1 million dollar capital campaign Family Outreach Ctr.; bd. dirs., chmn. ann. fund drive Grand Rapids Symphony, 1995-96. Mem. Econ. Club Grand Rapids. also Office: Orlando Magic Two Magic Pl 8701 Maitland Summit Blvd Orlando FL 32810*

DEVOS, DOUGLAS LEE, sales company executive; b. Grand Rapids, Mich., Oct. 6, 1964; m. Maria P. DeVos. BS, Purdue U., 1986. Sr. v.p. Asia Pacific, mem. policy bd.; bd. dirs. Nat. City Bank; vice chmn. Orlando Magic Governing Bd. Fundraising chair Downtown Macker Jam; bd. dirs., v.p. Grand Rapids Student Advancement Found.; nat. bd. dirs. Jr. Achievement; bd. dirs., vice chamn. Mich. Cities in Schs.; leadership giving co-chair United Way Campaign Cabinet, 1999; bd. mem. Holland Home. Mem. Grand Rapids Area C. of C. (bd. dirs.), Krannert Sch. Alumni Assn. (bd. dirs.), Rotary. Office: Amway Corp 7575 Fulton St E Ada MI 49355-0001

DEVOS, ELISABETH, political association executive; b. Holland, Mich., Jan. 8, 1958; d. Edgar Dale and Elsa D. (Zwiep) Prince; m. Richard M. DeVos Jr., 1979; four children. BS, Calvin Coll., 1979. Co-chmn. Kent County (Mich.) Rep. Finance Com., 1983-84, chmn., 1985-88, 96—; Rep. Nat. Committeewoman State of Mich., 1992-97; chmn. Mich. State Rep. Party, 1996—; mem. Nat. Rep. Com., 1996—; market rsch. analyst Amway Corp., 1979-81; pres. Windquest Group. Bd. dirs. Blodgett Meml. Med. Ctr., 1986—, Ada (Mich.) Christian Sch., 1992—; mem. Rep. Congl. Leadership Coun. Mem. Econ. Club of Grand Rapids. *

DE VOS, GEORGE ALPHONSE, psychologist, anthropologist; b. Detroit, July 25, 1922; s. Medard Joseph and Marina Marie (Tack) De V.; m. Suzanne Lake, Nov. 18, 1974; children: Laurie, Susan, Eric, Michael. BA in Sociology, U. Chgo., 1946, MA in Anthropology, 1948, PhD in Psychology, 1951. Chief psychologist, dir. psychol. tng. Elgin (Ill.) State Hosp., 1951-53; asst. prof. psychology U. Mich., Ann Arbor, 1955-57; assoc. prof. social welfare U. Calif., Berkeley, 1957-63, prof. anthropology, 1963-91, prof. emeritus, 1991—. Author: Oasis and Casbah, 1960, Japan's Invisible Race, 1966, Socialization for Achievement, 1973, Ethnic Identity, 1975, 3d edit., 1996, Responses to Change, 1976, Koreans in Japan, 1981, Heritage of Endurance, 1984, Religion and the Family, 1984, Culture and Self, 1985, The Rorschach Cross Culturally, 1989, Status Inequality, 1990, Social Cohesion and Alienation, 1993, Confucianism and The Family, 1998. Fulbright fellow, Nagoya, Japan, 1953-55; NIMN fellow French Min. Justice, 1963; NSF felow UN Social Def. Rsch. Inst., Rome, 1974—; Fulbright Sr. Rsch. Sch. Cath. U. Rio Grande do Sul, Brazil, 1992. Mem. APA (pres. Soc. for Psychol. Anthropology 1984-85), Assn. Asian Studies, Am. Anthropology Assn. Home: 2835 Morley Dr Oakland CA 94611-2547

DE VOS, PETER JON, ambassador; b. San Diego, Dec. 24, 1938. B.A., Princeton U., 1960; M.A., Johns Hopkins U., 1962. Consular officer Am. Consulate, Recife, Brazil, 1962-64; fgn. service officer for Brazil Dept. State, Washington, 1964-66; polit. officer Am. Consulate, Naples, 1966-68; dep. prin. officer Am. Embassy, Luanda, 1968-70; polit. officer Am. Consulate, Sao Paulo, 1970-71, Am. Embassy, Brasilia, 1971-73; spl. asst. Bur. Inter-Am. Affairs Dept. State, Washington, 1973-75; polit. officer Am. Embassy, Athens, 1975-78, Nat. War. Coll., 1978-79; dep. dir. So. African Affairs Dept. State, Washington, 1979-80; U.S. ambassador to Republic of Guinea-Bissau and to Republic of Cape Verde, 1980-83, Mozambique, Maputo, 1983-87; dep. asst. sec. of state U.S. Dept. State, Washington, 1987-89, prin. dep. asst. sec. state Bur. Oceans and Internat. Environ. and Sci. Affairsv, 1989-90, amb. to Republic of Liberia, 1990-92, appointed U.S. spl. envoy to Somalia, 1992; amb. to Republic of Tanzania U.S. Dept. State, 1992-94, amb. to Republic of Costa Rica, 1994-97; disting. guest lectr. U. Chgo., 1997—. Home: 8014 Riverside Dr Cabin John MD 20818-1627 Office: U Chgo Irving B Harris Grad Sch Chicago IL 60637

DEVOS, RICHARD MARVIN, JR. (DICK DEVOS), direct sales company executive, sports team executive; b. Grand Rapids, Mich., Oct. 21, 1955; s. Richard Marvin and Helen June (Van Wesep) DeV.; m. Elisabeth Dee Prince, Feb. 24, 1979; children: Richard Marvin III, Elisabeth Liane, Andrea Nichole, Ryan Edgar. BBA, Northwood U., 1981. Coordinator sales Amway Corp., Ada, Mich., 1973-75, coordinator meetings, 1975-77, mgmt. trainee, 1977-82, dir. spl. events, 1982-84, v.p. internat., 1984-89; bd. dirs. The Windquest Group, Inc., Grand Rapids, Mich., 1989—; pres. Amway Corp., Ada, Mich., 1993—; bd. dirs. USA DSA, 1993—, vice chmn. 1995-97, chmn. 1997, Old Kent Fin. Corp., 1994—; pres. Amway Asia Pacific Ltd., 1995—, pres., CEO Orlando Magic NBA, 1991-93; chmn. Amway Japan Ltd., 1995—, chmn. Direct Selling Edn. Found., 1998. Chmn. Kent Ottawa Muskegon Fgn. Trade Zone Bd., 1989-96, chmn. Coalition for Better Schs., 1993-94; bd. dirs. Grand Rapids Metro YMCA, 1984-90, Mackinac Ctr., 1990-95 (hon. chair bd. adv. 1995—), Kent Hosp. Fin. Authority, 1980-93, West Mich. Boy Scouts Am., 1985-93, chmn. Blodgett Health Care, Butterworth Found., 1994—; co-chmn. Grand Rapids Area Negro Coll. Fund, 1989-92; mem. by appointment of Pres. Bush Commn. on Presdl. Scholars, 1991-93; elected mem. Mich. State Bd. Edn., 1991-93; apptd. mem. Mich. Jobs Commn., 1993-97, Coun. La Grave Ave. Christian Reform Ch., 1983-86; bd. trustees Davenport Coll. Bus., 1991—, apptd. mem. bd. of control Grand Valley State U., 1995—; bd. dirs., exec. com. Project Rehab, 1978-84; participant Leadership Grand Rapids, 1985-86; mem. bd. dirs. Bus. Industry Political Action Com., 1995—, co-chmn. Grand Action Com., 1992—, bd. dirs., Right Place Prog., 1994—, co-chmn. Edn. Feedom Fund, 1994—, bd. dirs. Willow Creek Assoc., 1997—, Children's Scholarship Fund, 1998—, CEO America, 1998—, adv. bd. mem. Nat. Fatherhood Initiative, 1998, chmn. Restoring the Am. Dream, 1998—. Recipient Grand Rapids Jaycees Disting. Svc. award 1985, Disting. Svc. Citation Northwood U., 1991, Assn. Ind. Colls. and Univs. Mich. Disting. Svc. award, 1992. Mem. Nat. Assn. of Mfgs. (bd. dirs. 1994—), The Economic Club of Grand Rapids (bd. dirs.), nat. co-chmn. Republican Congrssional Leadership Coun., 1981-85, co-chmn. Grand Rapids Combined Arts Fund Drive, 1988-90, mem. Steering Com. Grand Valley State U. Water Resources Inst., 1989-93, bd. mem. World Trade Week Com., 1990-93, trustee, Federalist Soc., 1990-93, mem. Michigan 2000 Com., 1992. Lodge: Rotary. Avocations: sailing, skiing. Office: Amway Corp 7575 Fulton St E Ada MI 49355-0001*

DEVOSS, JAMES THOMAS, community foundation administrator, retired; b. Ocheyedan, Iowa, Mar. 22, 1916; s. Jesse Franklin and Ada Calista (Johnson) De V.; m. Dorothy Alberta Durr, Oct. 10, 1938; children: Richard Allan, Robert Neal, Rosalie Jean De Voss Starr. Student, U. Iowa, 1933-37; BS, U. Md., 1958. Circulation supr. Des Moines Register and Tribune., 1938-40; commd. 2d lt., inf., ORC U.S. Army, 1937, called to active duty, 1941, advanced through grades to col., 1961, grad. Command and Gen. Staff Coll., 1953, mem. mil. staff, Big Three Conf., Bermuda, 1953, spl. security officer, PTO, 1949-52, spl. security officer, U.S. Forces, Austria, 1954-55, spl. security officer, SHAPE, 1955-58, spl. security officer, joint chief staff and sec. of def., 1958-61; ret., 1961; asst. exec. sec. Am. Philatelic Soc., 1961-63, exec. dir., 1963-81; trustee Centre County Community Found., 1983-87, exec. sec., 1988-93; ret., 1993. Contbr. profl. handbooks.; editor: Am. Philatelic Congress Book, 1953. Pres. Phila. Internat. Philatelic Exhbn., 1974-86 ; pres. Am. Philatelic Rsch. Libr., 1980-83; trustee Philatelic Found., 1980-86. Decorated Legion of Merit; recipient Hanford Cup Garfield-Perry Stamp Club, Cleve., 1964; Outstanding Achievement in Philately award, 1967; Alfred F. Lichtenstein Meml. award for disting. svc. to philately, 1977; named to Roll of Disting. Philatelists Gt. Brit., 1981. Fellow Royal Philatelic Soc. (London) (Tilleard medal 1957), Royal Philatelic Soc. Can.; mem. Am. Philatelic Soc. (life, John N. Luff award 1955, 58), Am. Philatelic Congress (McCoy award 1953, 59, Jere Hess Barr award 1959), Collectors Club N.Y., Féderation Internationale de Philatélie (v.p. 1976-86), Postal History Soc. (hon.), Philatelic Found. (Mortimer L. Neinken award 1991), U.S. Philatelic Classic Soc. (Disting. Philatelist award 1993), Rotary. Presbyterian (elder). Home: 9 Nittany View Cir State College PA 16801-2403

DEVOTO, MARK BERNARD, music educator; b. Cambridge, Mass., Jan. 11, 1940; s. Bernard Augustine and Helen Avis (MacVicar) DeV.; m. Deanna Mirsky (div.); children: Emily Julia, Marya Ellen. BA, Harvard Coll., 1961; MFA, Princeton U., 1963, PhD, 1967. Tchr. Reed Coll., Portland, Oreg., 1964-68, U. N.H., Durham, 1968-81; tchr. dept. music Tufts U., Medford, Mass., 1981—; bd. mem. Internat. Alban Berg Soc., N.Y.C., 1975—; pres. Lili Boulanger Meml. Fund, Boston, 1985-96. Co-author: (with Walter Piston) Harmony, 5th edit., 1987; compiler: Mostly Short Pieces, 1992; translator, editor: Berg Guides, 1995 (ASCAP Deems Taylor 1995); mem. editl. bd. Perspectives of New Music, 1972—; composer many unpublished works. Mem. Am. Musicol. Soc., Soc. Music Theory, Soc. for Am. Music, New Eng. Conf. Music Theorists. Democrat. Jewish. Avocations: writing fiction, cooking. Home: 33 West St Medford MA 02155-4340 Office: Tufts U Music Dept 20 Professors Row Medford MA 02155-5807

DE VRIES, DAWN ANN, theology educator; b. Hammond, Ind., June 11, 1961; d. Martin Richard and Janet Ruth (Van Ramshorst) De V.; m. Brian Albert Gerrish, Aug. 3, 1990; 1 child, Heather Sylvia Gerrish. BA, U. Chgo., 1983, MA in Divinity, 1984, PhD in Divinity, 1994. Asst. prof. ch. history San Francisco Theol. Sem., San Anselmo, Calif., 1988-90; asst. prof. ch. history McCormick Sem., Chgo., 1990-93, assoc. prof., 1993-95; prof. theology Union Theol. Sem., Richmond, Va., 1995—. Author: Jesus Christ in the Preaching of Calvin and Schleiermacher, 1996; editor: Servant of the Word, 1987. E-mail: ddevries@utsva.edu. Office: Union Theol Sem 3401 Brook Rd Richmond VA 23227-4514

DE VRIES, DOUWE, oil company executive; b. Bussum, Netherlands, Oct. 25, 1922; came to U.S., 1952; naturalized, 1959; s. Pieter and Hiske (Hoekstra) DeV.; m. Robbie Ray Parsons, Apr. 2, 1953; children: Jessica, Peter. MSME, Delft (The Netherlands) U., 1952. Registered profl. engr., Netherlands, La. Drilling & prodn. engr. Shell Oil Co., Tex. N.Mex, 1954-58; spl. projects engr. Shell Devel. Co., Houston, 1958-60; project mgr. Shell Oil Co., La., 1960-68; pres., owner Project Engring., Inc., New Orleans, 1968-70; dir. engring. Stewart & Stevenson oilfield div., Houston, 1968-78; v.p. subsea prodn. NL Industries, Houston, 1978-81; pres., owner Oilfield Systems, Inc., Houston, 1981—; cons. Shell Oil Co., 1983-85, Fluor, 1986-87, Dailey Directional, 1988-89, Kvaerner Verft, Stavanger, Norway, 1990-92, Amoco Orient/CONHE, Houston, 1993-95, Brit. Borneo/McDermott, Houston, 1996-98; mentor Subsea Svcs., 1998—; expert witness product liability and patent infringement. Patentee: 14 patents including floating drilling and subsea completions, U.S., Brit., Internat., 1958-83. Elder Presbyn. Ch., New Orleans, 1960-69; sponsor U. Houston, Med. Ctr., Tex. A&M at Galveston, Houston Symphony, Mus. of Fine Arts; active in Rep. Orgn., Washington, 1980—; chmn. Houston-Baku Sister City Assn., 1970-80. Mem. ASME (com. mem., Holley medal 1979), Am. Petroleum Inst. (com. mem.), Marine Tech. Soc., Am. Coun. Master Mariners (hon.), Nat. Soc. Profl. Engrs., Tex. Soc. Profl. Engrs. Avocations: tennis, golf, fishing, yardwork, reading. Office: Oilfield Systems Inc 9219 Katy Fwy Ste 288 Houston TX 77024-1514

DE VRIES, KENNETH LAWRENCE, mechanical engineer, educator; b. Ogden, Utah, Oct. 27, 1933; s. Sam and Fern (Slater) DeV.; m. Kay M. McGee, Mar. 1, 1959; children: Kenneth, Susan. AS in Civil Engring., Weber State Coll., 1953; BSME, U. Utah, 1959, PhD in Physics, Mech. Engring., 1962. Registered profl. engr., Utah. Rsch. engr. hydraulic group Convair Aircraft Corp., Fort Worth, 1957-58; prof. dept. mech. engring. U. Utah, Salt Lake City, 1969-75, 1976-91, disting. prof., 1991—, chmn. dept., 1970-81; sr. assoc. dean U. Utah Coll. Engring., Salt Lake City, 1983-97, acting dean, 1997-98; program dir. div. materials rsch. NSF, Washington, 1975-76; materials cons. Browning, Morgan, Utah, 1972—; cons. 3M Co., Mpls., 1985—; tech. adv. bd. Emerson Electric, St. Louis, 1978—; mem. Utah Coun. Sci. and Tech., 1973-77; trustee Gordon Rsch. Conf., 1989-97, chair, 1992-93. Co-author: Analysis and Testing of Adhesive Bonds, 1978; contbr. chpts. to numerous books, articles and abstracts to profl. pubs. Fellow ASME, Am. Phys. Soc.; mem. Am. Chem. Soc. (polymer div.), Soc. Engring. Scis. (nat. officer), Adhesion Soc. (nat. officer). Mem. LDS Ch. Office: U Utah Coll Engring 2220 Merrill Engring Bldg Salt Lake City UT 84112

DE VRIES, MADELINE, public relations executive. Pres. DeVries Pub. Rels., N.Y.C. Office: DeVries Public Relations 30 E 60th St New York NY 10022-1008*

DE VRIES, RIMMER, economist; b. Utrecht, Netherlands, Jan. 20, 1929; came to U.S., 1951, naturalized, 1957; s. Jacob and Mettje (Verburg) de V.; m. Ruth Berg, May 24, 1958; children—Rimmer D., Jacqueline R., Joyce C. B.A., Netherlands Sch. Econs., 1951; M.A., Ohio State U., 1952, Ph.D., 1955. Economist Fed. Res. Bank N.Y., 1956-61; economist, then v.p. Morgan Guaranty Trust Co., N.Y.C., 1961-78, sr. v.p., 1978—, chief economist, 1988—; mng. dir. Morgan Guaranty Trust Co., 1990-94; cons. J.P. Morgan & Co. Inc., 1994—; bd. dirs. AGF Cos. Ltd. Mem. adv. com. Inst. Internat. Econs., Econ. Strategy Inst.; mem. adv. coun. Assn. Pub. Justice, Enterprise Devel. Internat.; mem. pres.'s coun. Calvin Coll. Mem. Coun. Fgn. Rels. Republican. Mem. Christian Reformed Ch. Home: 804 Holbeck Dr Camano Island WA 98292-7366

DEVRIES, ROBERT ALLEN, foundation administrator; b. Chgo., May 12, 1936; s. Robert and Mildred (Burgess) DeV.; m. Eleanor Rose Siems, Aug. 16, 1958; children: Susan E., Robert S., Laura H., Steven P. BS in Physiology, U. Chgo., 1958, MBA in Hosp. Adminstrn., 1961. Adminstrv. resident, asst. Miami Valley Hosp., Dayton, Ohio, 1959-61, asst. dir., 1961-67; adminstr. McPherson Community Health Ctr., Howell, Mich., 1967-71; program dir. W.K. Kellogg Found., Battle Creek, Mich., 1971-88, program dir., dir. Kellogg Internat. Fellowship Programs, 1988-90, program dir., dir. Internat. Study Grants and Exchanges, 1990-97, mem. adminstrv. coun., 1995-97, program dir., mem. fellowship com., 1997-99; ret., 1999; cons. on domestic and internat. programs W.K. Kellogg Founds., 1999—; bd. dirs. Lifecare Ambulance, Mich. Health Coun.; lectr. nursing orgn., adminstrn. Sch. Nursing Miami Valley Hosp., 1961-67, Grad. Sch. Pub. Health U. Mich., 1967—; adj. prof. Coll. Health and Human Svcs., Western Mich. U., 1986—; advisor Sch. Pub. Health Beijing Med. U., 1986—, Med. Coll. Health Staff, Shanghai, 1986—, 1st People's Hosp., Shanghai, 1986—; mem. nat. adv. com. on rural health U.S. Dept. Health and Human Svcs., Washington, 1988-92; mem. adv. panel acad. health scis. ctr. U.N.C., Chapel Hill, 1992-94; mem. policy coun. Nat. Inst. Rural Health Policy, 1987-90; mem. health planning and cert. of need workgroup Mich. Dept. Mgmt. & Budget, Mich. Dept. Pub. Health, 1986-87; vice chmn. adv. coun. Hosp. Rsch. & Ednl. Trust, Chgo., 1974-85; treas. coun. practice Am. Assn. Nurse Anesthetists, 1978-84; mem. Southwest Mich. Health Systems Agy. Bd., 1980-83; guest lectr. King's Fund Coll., London, U. Leeds, Eng., French Nat. Sch. Pub. Health, Rennes, U. Toronto, Pan Am. Health Orgn., Washington and Brasilia, Brazil, Katholieke Universiteit Leuven, Belgium, Internat. Hosp. Fedn., London, Elton Mayo Sch. Mgmt., Adelaide, Australia, Ministry Pub. Health, Beijing, Indian Hosp. Assn., New Delhi. Editorial bds. Inquiry, Hosp. & Health Svcs.; contbr. articles to profl. jours., also book chpts. Counselor Baxter Am. Found. Prize in Health Svcs. Rsch., 1986—; assoc. trustee Florence Nightingale Mus. Trust, London. Recipient Disting. Svc. award Am. Soc. Allied Health Professions, 1989, Med. Group Mgmt. Assn., Denver, 1990, Ohio State U. Alumni Assn., 1998; Monsignor Griffin award for disting. writing Ohio Hosp. Assn., 1965, Civic Achievement award Jr. C. of C., Chgo., 1955, recognition award for contbns. to svcs. to handicapped Commn. on Accreditation of Rehab. Facilities, 1976, Cmty. Health Leadership award Hosp. Rsch. and Ednl. Trust, 1994; named Outstanding Young Men in Am. Howell, Mich. Area C. of C. and Jaycees, 1970; Nat. Health Svcs. rsch. fellow, 1970-71. Fellow Am. Coll. Healthcare Execs., U.S. China Ednl. Inst., Can. Sch. Mgmt. (hon.); mem. APHA, Am. Hosp. Assn. (hon. life, vice chair R&D coun. 1974-85, adv. panel multi-hosp. systems 1977-85), Internat. Hosp. Fedn., Nat. Rural Health Assn., Mich. Hosp. Assn. (assn. governance and strategic planning com. 1986-89, pub. policy and govt. com. 1981-83), U. Chgo. Hosp. Adminstrn. Alumni Assn. (pres. 1982-83). Lutheran. Avocations: music, writing, travel, gardening. Office: WK Kellogg Foundations 1 Michigan Ave E Battle Creek MI 49017-4058

DE VRIES, ROBERT JOHN, investment banker; b. Pella, Iowa, Aug. 18, 1932; s. John G. and Anna (Kool) m. Patricia Lynn Jackson, Dec. 22, 1962; children: Robert John Jr., Garrett Andrew. BBA, U. Tex., Austin, 1958; MBA, Harvard Grad. Sch. of Bus., Boston, 1960. Registered principal. Security analyst Cyrus J. Lawrence & Sons, N.Y.C., 1960-64, Jas. H. Oliphant and Co., N.Y.C., 1964-66; investment banker William D. Witter Inc., N.Y., 1966-68; v.p. Mgmt. Planning Inc., Princeton, N.J., 1968-73; pres. Cryomed Devices, Inc., Princeton, 1973-80; v.p. Smith Barney, Harris Upham, 1981-84; pres., dir., founder Robert J. De Vries and Co., Inc., Kansas City, 1984—; dir. Aesculapian Concepts, Ltd. Served with USAF, 1952-56. Inst. of Chartered Fin. Analyst, Harvard Club of N.Y., Beta Gamma Sigma. Republican. Presbyterian. Avocations: photography, marathon running. Home: 6309 W 102nd St Shawnee Mission KS 66212-1719 Office: De Vries and Co 800 W 47th St Ste 319 Kansas City MO 64112-3022

DEVRIES, ROBERT K., religious book publisher; b. Sully, Iowa, July 6, 1932; s. Fred G. and Selena Irene (Willetts) DeV.; m. Carolyn Jo Schroeder, June 2, 1962 (div. 1978); children: Stephen Robert, Suzanne Mishael Dahill; m. Carolyn Gail Bergmans, May 26, 1979; children: Staci Ann McKellar, Keri Gail Bailey. AB, Wheaton Coll., 1954; ThM, Dallas Theol. Sem., 1958, ThD, 1969. Asst. registrar Dallas Theol. Sem., 1959-63; editor-in-chief Moody Press, Chgo., 1963-68; dir., v.p. pubs. Zondervan Pub. House, Grand Rapids, Mich., 1968-76, exec. v.p. book div., 1976-85; exec. v.p., publisher Zondervan Book Group, Zondervan Corp., Grand Rapids, Mich., 1985-86; pub. cons. Evang. Christian Pubs., 1987; pub., bd. dirs. Discovery House Pubs., Grand Rapids, 1987—; cons. Serendipity House, Littleton, Colo., 1990-99; bd. dirs. Serendipity House Found., Littleton, 1999—; bd. dirs. Oswald Chambers Pub. Assn. Ltd., Eng. Bd. dirs. Ligonier Valley Study Ctr., Stahlstown, Pa., 1979-83, Bd. Publ., Evang. Covenant Ch. Am., Chgo., 1989-94, chmn., 1992-94; advisor Internat. Coun. Bibl. Inerrancy, Walnut Creek, Calif., 1978-87. Recipient Outstanding Young Man in Am. award Jaycees, 1965. Mem. Evang. Christian Pubs. Assn. Republican. Mem. Evangelical Covenant Ch. Avocation: model railroading. Home: 7554 Lime Hollow Dr SE Grand Rapids MI 49546-7439 Office: 3000 Kraft Ave SE Grand Rapids MI 49512-2024

DEVRIES, WILLIAM CASTLE, surgeon, educator; b. Bklyn., Dec. 19, 1943; s. Hendrik and Cathryn Lucille (Castle) DeV.; children: Jon, Adrie, Kathryn, Andrew, Janna, William, Diana. B.S., U. Utah, 1966, M.D., 1970. Diplomate Am. Bd. Thoracic Surgery. Intern Duke U. Med. Ctr., 1970-71, resident in gen. and thoracic surgery, 1971-79; asst. prof. surgery U. Utah, 1979-84; pres. DeVries & Assocs., Elizabethtown, Ky., 1989—; asst. clin. prof. U. Louisville; mem. staff Bapt. Hosp. East, Louisville, Norton Hosp., Louisville, Southwest Hosp., Louisville, Audubon Regional Med. Ctr., Louisville, Suburban Med. Ctr., Louisville, Hardin Meml. Hosp., Elizabethtown, Ky., Jewish Hosp., Louisville; mem. courtesy staff St. Mary's and Elizabeth Hosp. Recipient Wintrobe award, 1970. Fellow ACS, Am. Coll. Cardiology, Am. Coll. Chest Physicians; mem. AMA, Ky. Heart Assn., Ky. State Med. Soc., Utah Heart Assn., Soc. Thoracic Surgeons, Alpha Omega Alpha. Mem. LDS Ch. Office: DeVries & Assocs PSC 906 Woodland Dr Ste 201 Elizabethtown KY 42701-2752*

DEW, CHARLES BURGESS, historian, educator; b. St. Petersburg, Fla., Jan. 5, 1937; s. Jack Carlos and Amy (Meek) D.; m. Robb Reavill Forman, Jan. 26, 1968. A.B., Williams Coll., 1958; Ph.D., Johns Hopkins, 1964. Instr. Wayne State U., 1963-64, asst. prof., 1964-65; asst. prof. La. State U., 1965-68; asso. prof. U. Mo., Columbia, 1968-72; prof. U. Mo., 1972-78; vis. asso. prof. U. Va., 1970-71; vis. prof. history Williams Coll., Williamstown, Mass., 1977-78, prof. history, 1978-85, Class of 1956 prof. Am. Studies, 1985-96, chmn. dept. history, 1986-92, dir. Francis C. Oakley Ctr. for Humanities and Social Scis., 1994-97; prof. social scis. W. Van Alan Clark Third Century, 1996—. Author: Ironmaker to the Confederacy: Joseph R. Anderson and the Tredegar Iron Works, 1966, The Meanings of American History, 1972, Bond of Iron: Master and Slave at Buffalo Forge, 1994; contbr. chpt. to Origins of the New South, 1877-1913 (C. Vann Woodward), rev. edit., 1972. Recipient Fletcher Pratt award N.Y. Civil War Round Table, 1966, award of merit Am. Assn. for State and Local History, 1967; finalist 1995 Lincoln prize. Mem. Am. Hist. Assn., Orgn. Am. Historians (Elliott Rudwick award 1995), Phi Beta Kappa, Delta Psi. Home: 218 Bulkley St Williamstown MA 01267-2023

DEW, THOMAS EDWARD, lawyer; b. Detroit, Feb. 13, 1947; s. Albert Nelson and Irene Theresa (Morris) D.; m. Gail Ruth Tuesink, June 27, 1970. BA, U. Mich., 1969; JD, Detroit Coll. Law, 1974. Bar: Mich. 1974, U.S. Dist. Ct. (ea. dist.) Mich. 1974, U.S. Tax Ct. 1980. Agt. IRS, Detroit, 1969-74; trust officer Ann Arbor (Mich.) Trust Co., 1974-75, asst. v.p., 1975-78; ptnr. Conner, Harbour, Dew, Ann Arbor, 1978-83, Harris, Lax, Guenzel & Dew, Ann Arbor, 1983-87; private practice Thomas E. Dew Profl. Corp., Ann Arbor, 1987-88; prin. Dever and Dew Profl. Corp., Ann Arbor, 1988—; lectr. Am. Coll., Bryn Mawr, Pa., 1979-82, Am. Inst. Paralegal Studies, Detroit, 1982. Mem. Ann Harbor Housing Commn., 1979-81, pres. 1981. Named Law scholar, Sigma Nu Phi, 1974. Fellow Mich. State Bar Found.; mem. State Bar Mich., Washtenaw County Bar Assn., Washtenaw Estate Planning Coun. (pres. 1979-80), New Enterprise Forum. Republican.

Presbyterian. Office: Dever and Dew Profl Corp 339 E Liberty St Ste 310 Ann Arbor MI 48104-2258

DEWALD, PAUL ADOLPH, psychiatrist, educator; b. N.Y.C., Mar. 12, 1920; s. Jacob Frederick and Elsie (Wurzburger) D.; m. Eleanor Whitman, Sept. 1, 1961; children: Jonathan S., Ellen F. B.A., Swarthmore Coll., 1942; M.D., U. Rochester, 1945; cert. psychoanalysis, SUNY, 1960. Intern, Strong Meml. Hosp., Rochester, N.Y., 1945-46; resident Strong Meml. Hosp., 1948-52; instr. U. Rochester, 1952-57, asst. prof. psychiatry, 1957-61; pvt. practice psychoanalysis St. Louis, 1961—; asst. clin. prof. psychiatry Washington U., St. Louis, 1961-65, 96—; asso. clin. prof. St. Louis U., 1965-69, clin. prof. psychiatry, 1969—; dir. treatment svc. Psychoanalytic Found. St. Louis, 1961-72, med. dir., 1972-83 St. Louis Psychoanalytic Inst., 1973-83, supervising and tng. analyst, 1973—; mem. faculty Chgo. Inst. Psychoanlysis, 1961-75, supervising and tng. analyst, 1965-73; vis. prof. U. Cin., 1968-80; mem. Mo. State Mental Health Commn., 1978-83, chmn., 1981-83; asst. prof. clin. psychiatry Washington U., 1995—. Author: Psychotherapy: A Dynamic Approach, 1964, 2d edit., 1969, The Psychoanalytic Process, 1972, Learning Process in Psycho-analytic Supervision, 1987; also articles. Served to capt. M.C., AUS, 1946-48. Fellow Am. Psychiat. Assn. (life); mem. Mo. Psychiat. Assn. (pres. 1970-71), Eastern Mo. Psychiat. Assn. (pres. 1969-70), Am. Psychoanalytic Assn. (life), St. Louis Psychoanalytic Soc. (pres. 1970-71, 86-88). Home: 60 Conway Ln Saint Louis MO 63124-1203 Office: 4524 Forest Park Ave Saint Louis MO 63108-2166 *I was encouraged by my parents to see my career as a potential source of creative enjoyment, fulfillment and self-esteem. I was fortunate to choose a field that encouraged those attitudes, and a wife who supported me in them. I have other interests and sources of fulfillment, but when there is nothing better or more enjoyable to do, I work.*

DEWALL, RICHARD ALLISON, retired surgeon; b. Appleton, Minn., Dec. 16, 1926; s. Herman H. and Grace G. (Gardner) DeW.; m. Diane B. Prettyman, Oct. 24, 1952; children—Beth B., Amy, Melissa. B.A., U. Minn., 1949, B.S., 1950, B.M., 1952, M.D., 1953, M.S. in Surgery, 1960; D.Sc. (hon.), Wright State U., 1986. Diplomate Am. Bd. Surgery, Am. Bd. Thoracic Surgery. Rsch. asst. dept. surgery U. Minn., 1954-56, instr. surgery, 1960-62, asst. prof., 1962-; rsch. fellow Am. Heart Assn., 1956-58, advanced rsch. fellow, 1958-60, established investigator, 1960-62; prof. surgery, chmn. dept. Chgo. Med. Sch., 1962-66; chief surgery Cox Heart Inst., Kettering, Ohio, 1966-82; mem. staff Kettering Hosp., 1982-87; ret., 1987; chmn. bd. Med., Inc., 1976—; coord. surgery residency tng. program Kettering Meml. Hosp., 1968-75; co-chmn. med. sch. planning com. Wright State U., Dayton, Ohio, 1968-73, clin. prof. surgery, 1975-87, clin. prof. emeritus, 1987—. Recipient award U.S. Jr. C. of C., 1957, Appreciation award Wright State U. Sch. Medicine, 1989. Fellow A.C.S., Am. Coll. Cardiology; mem. Soc. for Thoracic Surgery, AMA, AAAS (co-recipient Ida B. Gould Meml. award 1956), Soc. Univ. Surgeons, Am. Assn. Thoracic Surgery, Dayton Surg. Soc., Nu Sigma Nu, Sigma Chi., Rotary. Research on perfusion techniques as an aid to open heart surgery. Home: 421 Thornhill Rd Dayton OH 45419-2932

DEWALL-OWENS, KAREN MARIE, marketing consultant; b. Phoenix, May 31, 1943; d. Merle C. and Agnes M. (Larson) Feller; m. Charles E. DeWall, Sept. 3, 1963 (div. Feb. 1988); 1 child, Leslie Karen; m. John Dailor Owens, Apr. 16, 1995. AA, Phoenix Coll., 1969. Media buyer Wade Advt., Sacramento, 1964-66; media dir., Harwood Advt., Phoenix, 1967-71; co-owner, account exec. DeWall & Assocs. Advt. Co., 1971-87; dir. advt. Auto Media, Inc./Automotive Investment Group, Phoenix, 1987-93; owner Karen & Co. Advt., Phoenix, 1993—. Sustaining mem. Jr. League of Phoenix; mem. adv. bd. Heritage Sq., City of Phoenix. Named Ad-2 Advt. Person of Yr., Phoenix, 1984. Mem. Am. Women in Radio and TV (achievement award 1986), Phoenix Union Alumni Assn. (pres. 1997—). Republican. Home: 10847 N 11th St Phoenix AZ 85020-5836 Office: Karen & Co Advt 10847 N 11th St Phoenix AZ 85020-5836

DEWANE, JOHN RICHARD, retired manufacturing company executive, consultan; b. Cooperstown, Wis., Mar. 4, 1934; s. Clarence John and Arvilla Anne (Gannon) D.; m. Judith Anne Arnold, Mar. 17, 1974; 1 child, Kelly Susanne. BSME, U. Wis., 1957; MBA, U. Minn., 1973. Lic. pvt. pilot. Dir. mktg. planning Honeywell, Inc., Washington, 1974-76; dir. mktg. Honeywell, Inc., Mpls., 1976-78, v.p. svc. engrng., 1979-81, v.p. bus. devel., 1981-82, v.p., gen. mgr., 1982-87, group v.p., 1987-92; pres. space and aviation control Honeywell, Inc., Phoenix, 1992-97, pres. emeritus, 1997—; mem. NASA Aeronautics Adv. Com. Vice chmn. Cmty. Long-Range Improvement Com., Maple Grove, Minn., 1980-81, chmn. Econ. Devel. Commn., 1982-86; mem. Polit. Action com. Honeywell, 1979-83; mem. alumni adv. coun. U. Wis., mem. dean's indsl. liaison coun.; mem. tech. adv. com. on transp. equipment U.S. Dept. Commerce; bd. govs. Am. Def. Preparedness Assn., 1988-91; chmn. bd. dirs. Success By Six, Aris. Cities in Schs., Inc., Honeywell Found.; nat. bd. advisor U. Ariz. Keller Bus. Sch.; mem. deans 100 bd. Ariz. State U.; chmn. indsl. liaison coun. Embry-Riddle Aero U.; mem. State of Ariz. Gov.'s Tech. Commn., State of Ariz. Smart Beginnings Com.; mem. strategy coun. United Way of Phoenix, chair dirs. coun. conf. bd., 1995-97; bd. dirs. Asia Pacific Econ. Coun.; mem. Habitat for Humanity Endowment Com.; mem. APEC Satellite and Comm. Com.; mem. hon. bd. Phoenix Found. for the Blind. Served with USN, 1957-60. Holder four world airplane speed records. Navy scholar, 1952-57. Mem. U.S. Navy League, Air Force Assn., Assn. U.S. Army, Am. Def. Preparedness Assn., Aircraft Owners and Pilots Assn., Gen. Aviation Mfrs. Assn. (dir. 1983-97, chmn. forecasting com., chmn. airport ops. com.), Mpls. C. of C. (aviation com. 1980-88), Provost Club Ariz. State U. West, U. Wis. Engring. Sch. Adv. Coun. Office: Honeywell Space and Aviation Control PO Box 21111 Phoenix AZ 85036-1111

DEWAR, HELEN, reporter; b. Stockton, Calif., 1936. BA in Polit. Sci., Stanford U. Reporter The Northern Virginia Sun; metro reporter The Washington Post, Washington, 1961-77, nat. staff reporter, 1977—. Office: The Washington Post 1150 15th St NW Washington DC 20071-0001*

DEWAR, ROBERT EARL, artist; b. Chgo., May 18, 1943; s. William James and Dorothy Ann (Haupt) D.; m. Cynthia Ann Waldman, Apr. 24, 1982; 1 child, John Starr. BFA, Calif. State U., L.A., 1971. Computer analyst, programmer Jet Propulsion Lab., Pasadena, Calif., 1968-78, computer art specialist, 1981; computer graphics programmer CADAM, Inc., Burbank, Calif., 1983-90, computer graphics tech. support, 1990-91; computer graphics tech. support IBM, Santa Monica, Calif., 1992-94; artist, webmaster Tehachapi, Calif., 1994—. Author: A Technical Catalog of Computer Halftones, 1972; inventor in field. With U.S. Army, 1962-65. Home: 11600 Bonanza Dr Tehachapi CA 93561

DEWAR, THOMAS NORMAN, gastroenterologist; b. N.Y.C., May 20, 1961; s. Norman Russell and Monicka (Bessell) D.; m. Cindy Lawrence, Aug. 7, 1982; children: Robert Thomas, Emily Elizabeth. BA, U. Tex., 1982, MD, 1986. Resident, fellow U. Calif., San Francisco, 1986-92; physician Gastroenterol. Assn. North Tex., Ft. Worth, 1992—; chief of medicine All Saints Hosp., Ft. Worth, 1996—. Author: Bedside Procedures, 1992. Mem. Am. Coll. Physicians, Am. Soc. Gastrointestinal Endoscopy, Am. Coll. Gastroenterology. Office: 724 Pennsylvania Ave Fort Worth TX 76104-2221*

DEWART, CHRISTOPHER, architectural educator, furniture maker; m. Sarah Bradsahw, 1980; children: Seth W., Sarah R., Benjamin B. BA, Marlboro Coll., 1978. Architectural prof., tech. instr. MIT, Cambridge, Mass., 1980—; proprietor Wilder Woodworking. Recipient MIT Convocation Program award, 1992. Office: MIT Dept Architecture 77 Mass Ave Cambridge MA 02139-4307

DEWDNEY, ANTHONY EDWARD, quality assurance professional, auditor; b. Sidcup, Eng., May 27, 1940; s. William Stanley and Marjorie Alexandra (Selman) D.; m. Judith Midgley, July 31, 1965; children: Jacqueline Mary Bell, Andrew James. BS in Math., U. Southampton, Eng., 1962. Ops. rsch. officer Brit. Rlwys., London, 1962-67, freight liner planning asst., 1967-71, manpower planning asst., 1971-77; internal cons. BICC plc, Prescot, Eng., 1977-84; bus. cons. Invicta Bus. Consultancy, Formby, Eng., 1988-96; quality mgr. BBC-MEC Joint Venture, Old Saybrook, Conn., 1996—. Mem. parochial ch. coun. Holy Trinity Ch., Formby, 1988-96; mem. exec. coun. Royal Scottish Country Dance Soc., Edinburgh, 1985-96. Mem. Internat. Register Cert. Auditors. Anglican. Avocations: Scottish country dancing, railway modelling. Office: Balfour Beatty-Mass Elec Joint Venture 139B Mill Rock Rd E Old Saybrook CT 06475-4217

DE WEERDT, MARK MURRAY, retired judge; b. Cologne, Germany, May 6, 1928; arrived in Can., 1949,; s. Hendrik Eugen and Ina Dunbar (Murray) de W.; m. Linda Anne Alden Hadwen, Mar. 31, 1956; children: Simon André, Murray Hadwen, David Lockhart, Charles Dunbar. MA, Glasgow (Scotland) U., 1949; LLB, B.C. U., 1955. Cert. barrister and solicitor, B.C. 1956, N.W.T. 1958. Assoc. solicitor Cross & O'Grady, Victoria, B.C., 1956-57; adv. coun. Can. Dept. Justice, Ottawa, 1957-58; Crown Atty. Yellowknife, N.W.T., 1958-63; sr. counsel Can. Dept. Justice, Vancouver, 1976-79, gen. counsel and dir., 1979-81; sr. ptnr. deWeerdt, Searle, Finall et al., Yellowknife, N.W.T., 1958-71; magistrate and juvenile ct. judge N.W.T. Magistrate's Ct., Yellowknife, N.W.T., 1971-73; gen. solicitor Ins. Corp. B.C., Vancouver, 1974-76; justice N.W.T and Yukon Supreme Cts., Yellowknife & Whitehorse, 1981-96, Supreme Ct. of B.C., 1996-97, N.W.T and Yukon Cts. of Appeal, 1981-97, Ct. Martial Appeal Ct. of Can., 1995-97; ret., 1997; dep. judge Supreme Ct. N.W.T., 1996-97, 97—; chairperson judicial coun. N.W.T., Yellowknife, 1981-96; dir. Canadian Judges' Conf., 1982-89; alternating mem. Can. Judicial Coun., 1985-7, 89-91, 93-95. Author profl. papers. Vice-chmn. Yellowknife Sch. Dist. #1, 1964-68. Apptd. Queen's Coun., Can., 1968; recipient Commr.'s award for pub. svc. at highest level, 1997. Mem. Can. Bar Assn., Can. Inst. Administrn. Justice (life), N.W.T. Bar Assn. (pres. 1967-71), MacKenzie River and N.W.T. Progressive Conservation Assn. (pres. 1959-71). Avocations: gen. reading, walking. Home: 5459 Crown St, Vancouver, BC Canada V6N 4K1

DEWEES, DONALD CHARLES, securities company executive; b. Phila., Sept. 7, 1931; s. John Coleman and Elva (Burke) DeW.; m. Martha V. Folk, July 31, 1954; children: Donald C., Suzanne C., Gretchen F. BS in Commerce and Finance, Bucknell U., 1953; MBA, U. Pa., 1954. Data processing rep. Nat. Cash Register Co., Wilmington, Del., 1954-62; account rep. Francis I. duPont Co., Investments, Wilmington, 1962-67; br. mgr. Francis I. duPont Co., Investments, Balt., 1968; br. mgr. Butcher & Singer, Wilmington, 1969-71, v.p., 1971-76, 1st v.p., 1977, sr. v.p., 1978—, resident mgr., 1969-76, ltd. ptnr., 1976-87, exec. v.p., 1987, sr. exec. v.p., 1988-94, mng. dir., 1988-98, also bd. dirs.; mng. dir. Butcher & Singer, 1986-98, Wheat Securities, 1998-99; dir. Mgmt. Scis. Inc., 1978-92, Bus. Trends Inc., 1977-91, Computer Terminals and Tapes Ltd., 1970-98, Wheat Securities, mng. dir. Wheat Securities Butcher & Singer, 1986-99, Lloyds of London, 1985-99, First Union Bank, 1998-99; underwriting mem. Lloyds of London, 1985—; cons. in field. Author sales tng. publs. Active Wilmington YMCA; bd. dirs. Delawre Ctr. of Contemporary Arts, 1992-94, Ingleside Nursing Home, 1989-99, Ch. Home Found., 1986-92, Episcopal Hom of Del., 1983-90, Del. Symphony, 1995—, Del. Art Mus., 1996—; bd. dirs. Del Marva Boy Scouts of Am., 1989—, chmn. endowment com., 1993—; vice chmn. Nat. Assn. Christians and Jews, 1991-98; mem. allocation com. United Way, 1994; bd. dirs. Am. Cancer Soc., 1994—, Leukemia Soc., 1995—; chmn. Edgar A. Thronson Charitable Found., 1995—. Served with AUS, 1952-53, 58-59, Korea. Mem. Fin. Analysts Soc., Am. Philatelic Soc., Phi Kappa Psi, Univ. Club (Wilmington), Collectors Club (N.Y.), Rodney Square Club, Masons, Shriners, Greenville Country Club. Home: 4200 Pyles Ford Rd Wilmington DE 19807-1734 also: 25 Kelly Ln Bethany Beach DE 19930 Office: Wheat Securities 3801 Kennett Pike Greenville DE 19807-2321

DEWEESE, MARION SPENCER, educator, surgeon; b. Corydon, Ind., Aug. 17, 1915; s. Arville Otis and Vergie (Jenkins) DeW.; m. Helen Sosnoski, June 25, 1941; children—Diane Hope, Dawn Cheryl, Pamela Lea. B.A., Kent State U., 1935; M.D., U. Mich., 1939, M.S. in Surgery, 1948. Intern, then resident gen. surgery U. Mich. Hosp., 1939-41, 45-48; instr., then asst. prof. surgery U. Mich. Med. Sch., 1948-51, then assoc. prof. surgery, 1953-64, clin. prof. surgery, 1974—; practice gen. and vascular surgery Ann Arbor, retired 1988; pvt. practice gen. surgery San Diego, 1951-53; W. Alton Jones disting. prof. surgery, chmn. dept. U. Mo. Med. Sch., 1964-74; chief surgery Ann Arbor VA Hosp., 1953-56; chief staff St. Joseph Mercy Hosp., Ann Arbor, 1979-81. Contbr. profl. jours. Served to lt. col. M.C. AUS, 1941-45. Recipient Disting. Service award U. Mich. Med. Ctr. Alumni Soc., 1987. Mem. A.C.S., Am., Central, Western, So. surg. assns., Soc. Vascular Surgery, Internat. Cardio-Vascular Surgery Soc., AMA, Am. Assn. for Surgery Trauma, Am. Burn Assn., Soc. for Surgery Gastrointestinal Tract, others. Home: 2229 Glendaloch Rd Ann Arbor MI 48104-2831

DEWERD, LARRY ALBERT, medical physicist, educator; b. Milw., July 18, 1941; s. Anthony Lawrence and Dorothy M. (Heling) DeW.; m. Vada Mary Anderson, Sept. 14, 1963; children: Scott, Mark, Eric. BS, U. Wis., Milw., 1963; MS, U. Wis., 1965, PhD, 1970. Rsch. assoc. U. Wash., Seattle, 1970-72, rsch. asst. prof., 1973-75; vis. asst. prof. U. Wis., Madison, 1975-76, clin. asst. prof., 1976-79, clin. assoc. prof., 1979-86, prof., 1990—; mgr. product devel. Radiation Measurements, Middleton, Wis., 1986-90; dir. Radiation Calibration Lab., Madison, 1990—; cons. Instrumentarium, Milw., 1990; v.p. Standard Imaging, Madison, 1990—; presenter in field to sci. confs., seminars and workshops. Contbg. author: Brachytherapy, Ionization Chambers and Dosimetry, Thermoluminescence and Mammography; also numerous articles. Science chmn. Am. Cancer Soc. State of Wis., 1986-90. Grantee Nat. Cancer Inst., 1979-86, 94-98. Fellow Am. Assn. Physicists in Medicine (pres. 1990-92), Health Physics Soc., Am. Phys. Soc., Coun. Ionizing Radiation Measurements and Standards (pres. 1995-98), Sigma Xi (bd. dirs. 1984-86). Avocations: golf, fishing, backpacking, hunting. Home: 13 Pilgrim Cir Madison WI 53711-4033 Office: U Wis 1530 Med Sci Ctr 1300 University Ave Madison WI 53706-1510

DEWERTH, GORDON HENRY, management consultant; b. Milw., Sept. 3, 1939; s. Henry Andrew and Elizabeth Barbara (Schlitt) DeW.; m. Karen Lillian Overson, July 7, 1962; children: Julie, Christine, Amy. BBA, U. Wis., 1961; MBA, Bradley U., 1965. Asst. to treas. Jos. Schlitz Brewing Co., Milw., 1965-71; with ITT, N.Y.C., 1971-76; treas. Macmillan, Inc., N.Y.C., 1976-82; sr. v.p. fin. Cowles Media Co., Mpls., 1982-85; sr. v.p. fin., treas. U. Hartford, Conn., 1985-89; v.p., gen. mgr. Gestra Inc., West Caldwell, N.J., 1989-90; v.p. David Werner Internat. Corp., N.Y.C., 1990-94; mng. ptnr. Roundtable Ptnrs. Cons. Group, Pawtucket, R.I., 1994—. With U.S. Army, 1961-63. Mem. Assn. Corp. Growth, Mensa, Soc. Profl. Cons. Office: Roundtable Ptnrs Cons Group 545 Newport Ave Pawtucket RI 02861-3239

DEWEY, ANNE ELIZABETH MARIE, lawyer; b. Balt., Mar. 16, 1951; d. George Daniel and Elizabeth Patricia (Mohan) D.; children: Brendan M., Andrew P., Meghan E. BA, Mich. State U., 1972; JD, U. Chgo., 1975; grad., Stonier Grad. Sch. Banking, East Brunswick, N.J., 1983. Bar: D.C. 1976. Legal clk. and atty. FTC, Washington, 1975-78; atty. and sr. atty. Comptr. of Currency, Dallas and Washington, 1978-86; assoc. gen. counsel, gen. counsel, spl. counsel Farm Credit Adminstrn., McLean, Va., 1986-92; counsel, closed bank litig. and policy sect. FDIC, Washington, 1993-94; gen. counsel Office of Fed. Housing Enterprise Oversight, HUD, Washington, 1994—. Mem. ABA (bus. law sect., mem. banking law com., co-chair banking & fin. svcs. com., administrv. law & regulatory practice sect. 1997—), FBA (bd. dirs. D.C. chpt. 1988-91, banking law com. exec. coun. 1995—), Women in Housing and Fin. (bd. dirs. 1982-83, gen counsel 1991-93), D.C. Bar Assn., Exchequer Club. Roman Catholic. Office: Office Fed Housing Enterprise Oversight 1700 G St NW Fl 4 Washington DC 20552-0003

DEWEY, CLARENCE FORBES, JR., engineering educator; b. Pueblo, Colo., Mar. 27, 1935; s. Clarence F. and Elsie (Hafermalz) D.; m. Carolyn Miller, Aug. 3, 1963; 1 child, Devan Forbes. BE, Yale U., 1956; MS, Stanford U., 1957; PhD, Calif. Inst. Tech., 1963. Aero. rsch. scientist NASA-AMES, Moffet Field, Calif., summer 1956; tech. staff aeronutronic divsn. Ford, Newport Beach, 1957-59; rsch. asst. Calif. Inst. Tech., Pasadena, Calif., 1959-63; asst. prof. mech. engring. U. Colo., Boulder, 1963-68; assoc. prof. MIT, Cambridge, 1968-76, prof., 1976-98, prof. mech. engring. and bioengring., 1998—; assoc. in pathology Peter Brent Brigham Hosp., Boston, 1978-95; vis. scientist Inst. Plasma Physics, Garching, Germany, 1966-67; vis. prof. Harvard U. Med. Sch., 1978-79, Hefei Poly. U., China, 1986, Imperial Coll. Ctr. Med. and Biol. Sys., London, 1992; biomed. engr. Mass. Gen. Hosp., Boston, 1975-76, cons. in medicine, 1976-80; founder Mass. Computer Corp., 1981; bd. dirs. Saba Med. Imaging Tech., Nashville; co-dir. Internat. Consortium for Med. Imaging Tech., 1992-96; path. cons. Brigham and Women's Hosp., 1982—; cons. in field. Patentee in field; contbr. articles to profl. jours. Chmn. MIT United Way, 1996-97. Grantee NIH, Bethesda, Md., 1971—, Office Naval Rsch., San Diego 1970-75, 1987-89, Air Force Office Sci. Rsch., Washington, 1976-79. Fellow Am. Inst. Biomed. Engring. (founding); mem. Am. Phys. Soc., Biomed. Engring. Soc. (sr.). Avocations: tennis, trout fishing, skiing. Home: Marblehead MA 01945 Office: 77 Massachusetts Ave Cambridge MA 02139-4301

DEWEY, DONALD ODELL, university dean; b. Portland, Oreg., July 9, 1930; s. Leslie Hamilton and Helen (Odell) D.; m. Charlotte Marion Neuber, Sept. 21, 1952; children—Leslie Helen, Catherine Dawn, Scott Hamilton. Student, Lewis and Clark Coll., 1948-49; B.A., U. Oreg., 1952; M.S., U. Utah, 1956; Ph.D., U. Chgo., 1960. Mng. editor Condon (Oreg.) Globe-Times, 1952-53; city editor Ashland (Oreg.) Daily Tidings, 1953-54; asst. editor, assoc. editor The Papers of James Madison, Chgo., 1957-62; instr. U. Chgo., 1960-62; asst. prof., assoc. prof., prof. Calif. State U.-Los Angeles, 1962-96, dean Sch. Letters and Sci., 1970-84, dean Sch. Natural and Social Sci., 1984-96, dean emeritus, prof. emeritus, 1996—. Author: The Continuing Dialogue, 2 vols., 1964, Union and Liberty: Documents in American Constitutionalism, 1969, Marshall versus Jefferson: The Political Background of Marbury v. Madison, 1970, Becoming Informed Citizens: Lessons on the Constitution for Junior High School Students, 1988, revised edit., 1995, Invitation to the Dance: An Introduction to Social Dance, 1991, Becoming Informed Citizens: The Bill of Rights and Limited Government, 1995, That's a Good One: Cal State L.A. at 50, 1997; The Federalist and Antifederalist Papers, 1998; contbr. chpts. to books. Recipient Outstanding Prof. award Calif. State U., 1976. Mem. Am. Hist. Assn. (exec. coun. Pacific Coast br. 1971-74), Orgn. Am. Historians, Am. Soc. Legal History (adv. bd. Pacific Coast br. 1972-75), Gold Key, Phi Alpha Theta, Pi Sigma Alpha, Phi Kappa Phi, Sigma Delta Chi. Office: Calif State U Dept History 5151 State University Dr Los Angeles CA 90032-4226

DEWEY, DONALD WILLIAM, magazine publisher, editor, writer; b. Honolulu, Sept. 30, 1933; s. Donald William and Theckla Jean (Engeborg) D.; m. Sally Rae Ryan, Aug. 7, 1961; children: Michael Kevin, Wendy Ann. Student, Pomona Coll., 1953-55. With Pascoe Steel Corp., Pomona, Calif., 1955-56, div. Reynolds Aluminum Co., Los Angeles, 1956-58, Switzer Panel Corp., Pasadena, Calif., 1958-60; sales and gen. mgr. Western Pre-Cast Concrete Corp., Ontario, Calif., 1960-62; editor, pub. R/C Modeler Mag., Sierra Madre, Calif., 1963—, Freshwater and Marine Aquarium Mag., Sierra Madre, 1978—; pres., chmn. bd. R/C Modeler Corp., Sierra Madre, 1963—. Author: Radio Control From the Ground Up, 1970, Flight Training Course, 1973, For What It's Worth, Vol. 1, 1973, Vol. 2, 1975; contbr. articles to profl. jours. Sustaining mem. Rep. Nat. Com., 1981—; charter mem. Nat. Congl. Club, 1981—; mem. Rep. Presdl. Task Force, 1981—, U.S. Senatorial Club, 1983—, 1984 Presdl. Trust, Conservative Caucus, Nat. Tax Limitation Com., Nat. Conservative Polit. Action Com., Ronald Reagan Presdl. Libr. Served with Hosp. Corps, USN, 1951-55. Mem. Acad. Model Aeronautics, Nat. Aeronautic Assn.. Republican. Lutheran. Home: 410 W Montecito Ave Sierra Madre CA 91024-1716 Office: 144 W Sierra Madre Blvd Sierra Madre CA 91024-2435

DEWEY, DONNA, director, actress. Dir., actress A Story of Healing, 1997 (Acad. award for short subject documentary 1998). *

DEWEY, EDWARD ALLEN, retired construction company executive; b. Cleve., Feb. 27, 1932; s. Arthur Murray and Alice Virginia (Kellberg) D.; m. Joyce Knight, July 9, 1975; children by previous marriage—Anne Elizabeth Dewey, Jefferson Arthur. B.A. with distinction, Wesleyan U., Middletown, Conn., 1954; M.B.A., Harvard U., 1958. Trainee Ford Motor Co., Jersey City, 1958-59; fin. analyst Freeport Minerals, N.Y.C., 1959-62; v.p. fin. and adminstrn. Davy McKee Co., Lakeland, Fla., 1962-79; fin. mgr. Bechtel Group, San Francisco, 1979-82, contr., 1983-87, mgr. internal auditing, 1988-91, mgr. govt. ops., 1991-93, Latin Am. devel. mgr., 1994-97. Fund raiser Wesleyan U., Episcopal Ch., United Cerebal Palsy, Lakeland. Served to lt. USNR, 1954-56. Mem. Fin. Execs. Inst. Republican. Clubs: Bankers, Commerce. Home: 10647 Big Canoe Jasper GA 30143-5113

DEWEY, GEORGE WILLIS, III, non-profit corporation executive; b. May 2, 1960. Student, Luzerne County C.C. Founder, CEO Nationwide Patrol, Inc., Wilkes-Barre, Pa., 1985—. Democrat. Home: 61 E North Hampton St # 1110 Wilkes Barre PA 18701 Office: Nationwide Patrol PO Box 2629 Wilkes Barre PA 18703-2629

DEWEY, HENRY S., JR., elementary education educator; b. Buffalo, Dec. 31, 1944; s. Henry S. Dewey and Lavina V. (Malucci) McAvoy; m. Bernadine M. Kush, July 1, 1967; children: Andrea Lynn, Lauren Jennifer. BS in Edn., SUC, Buffalo, 1966; MS in Edn., State U. Coll., Buffalo, 1971; postgrad., SUNY, Buffalo, 1974-82, SUNY, Geneseo, 1974. Cert. tchr., elem. prin., sch. dist. adminstr., N.Y. Tchr. Maple West Elem. Sch., Williamsville, N.Y., 1966-70, asst. prin., 1970-71, adminstrv. asst., 1971-74, bldg. team leader, 1975-79, bldg. math. specialist, 1979—; prin. Coll. Learning Lab.-State Univ. Coll.-Buffalo, 1974-75; in-svc. lectr. Williamsville (N.Y.) Cen. Schs., 1972—; cons. Shaker Heights (Ohio) Sch., 1972; presenter programs at local sch. dists. Co-author curriculum guide to math., tchr. manual. Bd. dirs. Tifft Farm Nature Preserve, Buffalo, 1976-79. State award for excellence in math. teaching NSF, 1990. Mem. Am. Fedn. Tchrs., N.Y. State United Tchrs., Williamsville Tchrs. Assn. (2d v.p. 1968-70), Nat. Coun. Tchrs. Math., Assn. Math. Tchrs. N.Y. State, N.Y. State Assn. Computers and Tech. in Edn., N.Y. State Outdoor Edn. Assn. (treas. 1979-83, Svc. award 1981). Avocations: computers, cross-country skiing, camping. Office: Maple West Elem Sch 851 Maple Rd Buffalo NY 14221-3260

DEWEY, RALPH JAY, headmaster; b. N.Y.C., Feb. 8, 1944; s. Ralph Morris and Evelyn Elizabeth (Karle) D.; m. Vivian V. Barone Dewey, Dec. 20, 1970; children: Gabriella Maria, Meredith Elizabeth, Ralph Stephen. BS, Holy Cross Coll., Worcester, Mass., 1965; MAT, Brown U., Providence, 1968; EdS, Rutgers U., 1985. Teaching Cert., N.Y. Tchr. Moses Brown Sch., Providence, 1965-68; founding head of mid. sch. Portledge Sch., Locust Valley, N.Y., 1968-74; head of lower sch. Rutgers Preparatory Sch., Somerset, N.J., 1974-83; founding headmaster The Winston Sch., Summit, N.J., 1983-87; headmaster St. James Episc. Sch., Corpus Christi, 1987-95, Cape Fear Acad., Wilmington, N.C., 1995—; also bd. dirs.; regional coord. Southwestern Assn. Episcopal Schs., Corpus Christi, Tex., 1989-93, mem. stds. com. Southwestern Assn. Episcopal Schs., 1994-95, cons., Dallas, 1990-92; workshop presenter Nat. Assn. Ind. Sch., N.Y.C., 1991, Tex. Elem. Prins. and Suprs. Assn., 1991. Author, editor: Winston Newsletter, 1983-87, St. James Episcopal School Newsletter, 1987-95; author: Classical Vocabulary, 1990; contbr. articles to profl. jours. Treas. Coastal Bend Soc. Friends, 1988-95; sec., v.p. Harbor Playhouse, Corpus Christi, Tex., 1989-92; mem. Com. of 100, Wilmington, 1995; mem. exec. coun. Leadership Wilmington, 1996; bd. dirs. Ea. Plains Ind. Conf. Recipient U.S. Dept. Blue Ribbon Sch. Excellence award, Salute to Prins. award Nat. Assn. Elem. Sch. Prins. Mem. N.C. Assn. Ind. Schs. (chmn. membership 1999, membership chmn.), Sons of Am. Revolution, ASCD, Assn. Children with Learning Disabilities, Nat. Assn. for Edn. of Young Children, Nat. Coun. for Tchrs. English, Tex. ASCD, Network of Progressive Educators, Wilmington Rotary, Leadership Wilmington, Wilmington Execs. Club, City Club de Rossette. Mem. Soc. Friends. Avocations: Russian literature, furniture building. Home: 1010 Primivera Ct Wilmington NC 28409-4869 Office: Cape Fear Acad 3900 S College Rd Wilmington NC 28412-2098

DEWEY, SYLVIE PASCALE, French and Spanish language educator; b. Limoges, France, Mar. 26, 1947; came to U.S., 1969; d. Albert Emile and Simone Jeanne (Massonneau) Vergereau; m. Michael Thompson Dewey, Mar. 30, 1974; children: Daniel Albert, Caroline Nicole. MA, Rice U., 1974, PhD, 1976. Cert. in secondary edn., double cert. in French and Spanish. Instr. French U. Southwestern La., Lafayette, 1969-71, 74; tchg. asst. Rice U., Houston, 1972-74; tchr. Latin Rolla (Mo.) H.S., 1977-78; tchr. French and Spanish R.80 Salem (Mo.) Sch. Dist., 1978-84; instr. English U. Lyon, France, 1985-88; assoc. prof. French and Spanish Kutztown (Pa.) U., 1990—; vis. lectr. French and Spanish Pa. State U., State College, 1988-90; methodology specialist, student tchr. supr. Coll. Edn., Kutztown U., 1990-93. Contbr. articles to profl. jours. and books. Mem. MLA, Am. Assn. of Tchrs. of French (pres. Lehigh Valley chpt. 1991—), Alliance Française (v.p.

1993—), N.E. Am. Soc. for 18th-Century Studies, Women in French, French for Bus. and Internat. Trade, Mid. Atlantic and New Eng. Conf. for Can. Studies, Pa. State MLA, Pi Delta Phi, Phi Sigma Iota. Avocations: gardening, hiking. Home: 247 E Main St Kutztown PA 19530-1516 Office: Kutztown U DF 104 Dept Fgn Langs Kutztown PA 19530

DEWHURST, CHARLES KURT, museum director, curator, folklorist, English language educator; b. Passaic, N.J., Dec. 21, 1948; s. Charles Allaire and Minn Jule (Hanzl) D.;; m. Marsha MacDowell, Dec. 15, 1972; 1 dau., Marit Charlene. B.A., Mich. State U., 1970, M.A., 1973, Ph.D., 1983. Editorial asst. Carlton Press, N.Y.C., 1967; computer operator IBM, N.Y.C., 1968; project dir. Mich. State U. Mus., 1975, curator, 1976-83, dir., 1982—; guest curator Mus. Am. Folk Art, N.Y.C., 1978-83, Artrain, Detroit, 1980-83; dir. Festival of Mich. Folklife, 1987-95. Author: Reflections of Faith, 1983, Artists in Aprons, 1979, Rainbows in the Sky, 1978, Michigan Folk Art, 1976 (Am. Assn. State and Local History award 1977), Art at Work: Folk Pottery of Grand Ledge, Michigan, 1986, Michigan Quilts, 1987, Michigan Folklife Reader, 1988. Coun. mem. Mich. Humanities Coun., 1995—. Mus. profl. grantee Smithsonian Instn., Scandinavia, 1978, Fulbright, 1992; project grantee Mich. Coun. Humanities, 1990-96, NEH, 1991, NEA, 1982, 84-96, Disting. Svc. and Humanities award, 1994. Mem. Am. Folkore Soc., Mich. Folklore Soc. (mem. exec. bd.), Midwest Soc. Lit., Popular Culture Assn., Mich. Hist. Soc., Mich. Mus. Assn., Am. Assn. Mus., Internat. Coun. Mus., Mich. Coun. for Arts and Cultural Affairs. Home: 212 N Harrison Rd East Lansing MI 48823-4141 Office: Mich State U Mus W Circle Dr East Lansing MI 48824

DEWHURST, STEPHEN B., government official, lawyer; b. N.Y.C., Aug. 1, 1942; s. Henry S. and Jeanne A. (Dunne) D.; m. Miriam E. Petty, May 18, 1974. B.A., George Washington U., 1964, J.D., 1967. Bar: D.C. 1967. With Office Budget and Program Analysis, U.S. Dept. Agr., Washington, 1966-68, 70—, asst. dir. ops. revs., 1974-76, dep. dir. program revs., 1976-78, dir., 1978—. Served with U.S. Army, 1968-70. Decorated Army Commendation medal; recipient cert. of merit Dept. Agr., 1973, 77, Presdl. award as meritorious exec. Dept. Agr., 1980, 86, Presdl. award as Disting. Exec., Dept. Agr., 1991, 96. Mem. ABA, Am. Assn. for Budget and Program Analysis. Home: 3237 Dye Dr Falls Church VA 22042-3750 Office: USDA Budget & Program Analysis 14th & Independence Ave SW Washington DC 20250

DEWHURST, WILLIAM GEORGE, psychiatrist, educator, research director; b. Frosterley, Durham, Eng., Nov. 21, 1926; came to Can., 1969; s. William and Elspeth Leslie (Begg) D.; m. Margaret Dransfield, Sept. 17, 1960; children—Timothy Andrew, Susan Jane. B.A., Oxford U., Eng., 1947, B.M., B.Ch., 1950; MA, Oxford U., 1961; D.P.M. with distinction, London U., 1961. House physician, surgeon London Hosp., 1950-52, jr. registrar, registrar, 1954-58; registrar, sr. registrar Maudsley Hosp., London, 1958-62, cons. physician, 1965-69; lectr. Inst. Psychiatry, London, 1962-64, sr. lectr., 1965-69; assoc. prof. psychiatry U. Alta., Edmonton, Can., 1969-72, prof., 1972-92, prof. emeritus, 1992—, Hon. prof. pharmacy and pharm. scis., 1979-97, chmn. dept. psychiatry, 1975-90, dir. emeritus neurochem. rsch. unit, 1990—, hon. prof. oncology, 1983-97, chmn. med. staff adv. bd., 1988-90; mem. Atty. Gen. Alta. Bd. Rev., 1991, N.W.T. Bd. Rev., 1992-98, 95 Yukon Bd. Rev., 1994-98; pres.'s coun. U. Alta. Hosps., 1988-90, quality improvement coun., 1988-90, ethics consultative com., 1984-88, planning com. Vision 2000, 1985-87, hos ps.' planning com. and joint conf. com., 1971, 80, 87-90; cons. psychiatrist Royal Alexandra Hosp., Edmonton, Edmonton Gen. Hosp., Alberta Hosp., Ponoka, Ponoka Gen. Hosp.; chmn. med. coun. Can. Test Com., 1977-79, Royal Coll. Text Com. in Psychiatry, 1971-80, examiner, 1975-83. Co-editor: Neurobiology of Trace Amines, 1984, Pharmacotherapy of Affective Disorders, 1985; also conf. procs. Referee Nature, Can. Psychiat. Assn. Jour., Brit. Jour. Psychiatry; mem. editorial bd. Neuropsychobiology, Psychiat. Jour. U. Ottawa. Contbr. over 100 articles to profl. jours. Chmn. Edmonton Psychiat. Svcs. Steering Com., 1977-80; chmn. Edmonton Psychiat. Svcs. Planning Com., 1985-90; mem. Provincial Mental Health Adv. Coun., 1973-79, Mental Health Rsch. Com., 1973, Edmonton Bd. Health, 1974-76; Can. Psychiat. Rsch. Found., 1985— (also bd. dirs.); bd. dirs. Friends of Schizophrenics, 1980—, Alta., 1988; grant referee Health & Welfare Can., Med. Rsch. Coun. Can., Ont. Mental Health Found., Man. Health Rsch. Coun., B.C. Health Rsch. Found. Capt. Royal Army M.C., 1952-54. Fellow Can. Coll. Neuropsychopharmacology (pres. 1982-84, Coll. medal 1993), Am. Psychopathol. Assn., Am. Coll. Psychiatrists, Am. Psychiat. Assn., Royal Coll. Psychiatrist; mem. AAAS, Alta. Psychiat. Assn. (pres. 1973-74), Can. Psychiat. Assn. (pres. 1983-84), Alta Coll. Physicians and Surgeons, Alta. Med. Assn. (nominating coun. 1992-93, health issues coun. 1994-98, co-chmn. task force on drug info., 1996-98), Child and Adolescent Assn. (bd. dirs., v.p. 1992, pres. 1994-98), Assn. for Acad. Psychiatry, Brit. Med. Assn., Faculty Club. Anglican. Avocations: music, hockey, football, chess, athletics.

DEWHURST, WILLIAM HARVEY, psychiatrist; b. Huntington, W.Va., July 23, 1929; s. Richard Joseph and Grace Evelyn (Hollandsworth) D.; m. Katharine Ann Grigg, Apr. 2, 1955 (div. 1973); children: Cynthia, Katharine, Angela, William, Richard; m. Blanca Maria Peres, Nov. 22, 1974 (div. 1993); 1 child, Neil; m. Joan Diemer Wesley, 1993. BS, Marshall U., 1950, W.Va. U., 1952; MD, Med. Coll. of Va., 1954. Diplomate Am. Bd. Psychotherapy, Am. Bd. Psychiatry and Neurology; cert. med. examiner, Calif. Intern Med. Coll. of Va. Hosps., Richmond, 1954-55; jr./intermediate resident in psychiatry St. Elizabeths Hosp./George Washington U., Washington, 1955-56; intermediate/sr. resident in psychiatry Brentwood VA/UCLA and Mt. Sinai Hosps., L.A., 1958-60; pvt. practice Redondo Beach, Calif., 1960-72; pres. Torrance (Calif.) Mental Health Group, 1972-75, Dewhurst Med. Corp., Torrance, 1975-89; Bowling Green, Ky., 1989-95; chief of staff Del Amo Hosp., Torrance, 1972-76, clin. dir. alcohol and substance abuse svcs., 1975-78; med. dir. Charter Baywood Hosp., Long Beach, Calif., 1980-82; clin. instr. psychiatry U. Calif., 1968-72; asst. clin. prof. psychiatry UCLA, 1972-91; dir. eating disorders unit San Pedro Hosp., L.A., 1989-90, acting clin. dir. dept. psychiatry, 1990; med. dir. Rivendell Ky. Hosp., 1991-92, chief of staff, 1992-93; med. dir. Life Skills Inc., 1994—. Lt. USNR, 1956-68. Recipient Silver Bowl award Charter Med. Corp., Long Beach, 1982, awards in field. Mem. South Bay Psychiat. Soc. (pres. 1967-68), Warren County Med. Assn., Am. Psychiat. Assn., Ky. Psychiat. Soc. (Media award 1993), Bowling Green Rotary, others. Avocations: aquaristics, horticulture, reading, travel. Home: 1626 Cambridge Way Bowling Green KY 42103-1344 Office: 707 E Main St Bowling Green KY 42101-2337 *You've got to pitch till you win!.*

DEWILDE, DAVID MICHAEL, executive search consultant, financial services executive, lawyer; b. Bridgeton, N.J., Aug. 11, 1940; s. Louis and Dorothea (Donnelly) deW.; m. Katherine August, Dec. 30, 1984; children: Holland Stockdale, Christian DuCroix, Nicholas Alexander, Lucas Barrymore. AB, Dartmouth Coll., 1962; LLB, U. Va., 1967; MS in Mgmt., Stanford U., 1984. Bar: N.Y. 1968, D.C. 1972. Assoc. Curtis, Mallet-Prevost, Colt & Mosle, N.Y.C., 1967-69; assoc. gen. counsel HUD, Washington, 1969-72; investment banker Lehman Bros., Washington, 1972-74; dep. commr. FHA, Washington, 1974-76; pres. Govt. Nat. Mortgage Assn., Washington, 1976-77; mng. dir. Lepercq DeNeuflize & Co., N.Y.C., 1977-81; exec. v.p. policy and planning Fed. Nat. Mortgage Assn., Washington, 1981-82; pres. deWilde & Assocs., Washington, 1982-84; mng. dir., dir. fin. svcs. Boyden Internat., San Francisco, 1984-88; CEO Chartwell Ptnrs. Internat., San Francisco, 1989-97; mng. dir. LAI Worldwide, 1998—; bd. dirs. Berkshire Realty Investment Trust, Fritzi of Calif., Silicon Valley Bankshares, St. Luke's Pre-School, San Francisco. Editor-in-chief Va. Jour. Internat. Law, 1966-67. Lt. USN, 1962-64. Mem. Pacific Union Club (San Francisco), Met. Club (Washington), Belvedere Tennis Club. Republican. Office: LAI Ward Howell 275 Battery St Ste 2180 San Francisco CA 94111-3336

DEWINE, R. MICHAEL, senator, lawyer; b. Springfield, Ohio, Jan. 5, 1947; s. Richard and Jean DeWine; m. Frances Struewing, June 3, 1967; children: Patrick, Jill, Rebecca, John, Brian, Alice, Mark, Anna. BS in Edn., Miami U., Oxford, Ohio, 1969; JD, Ohio No. U., 1972. Bar: Ohio 1972, U.S. Supreme Ct. 1977. Asst. pros. atty. Greene County, Xenia, Ohio, 1973-75, pros. atty., 1977-81; mem. Ohio Senate, 1981-82, 98th, 99th, 100th, 101st Congress from 7th Ohio dist., Washington, 1983-90; lt. gov. State of Ohio, Columbus, Ohio, 1991-94; U.S. senator from Ohio, 1995—; mem. judiciary com., labor and human resources com., intelligence com., Health Edn. Com., Labor and Pensions Com. Republican. Roman Catholic. Home: 2587 Conley Rd Cedarville OH 45314-9525 Office: US Senate 140 Russell Senate Bldg Washington DC 20510*

DEWING, HENRY WOODS, SR., telecommunications executive; b. Argentia, Nfld., Can., Dec. 11, 1962; s. Bruce Warren and Martha Woods (Potter) D.; m. Sarah Brett Hurley, Sept. 12, 1992; children: Sarah Cameron, Henry Woods Jr., Margaret Blair, John Brett. BS, Washington and Lee U., 1985; MBA, U. Va., Charlottesville, 1991. Supr. Bell Atlantic, Washington, 1985-89; mgr. Bell Atlantic, Arlington, Va., 1991-94; cons. AT Kearney, Arlington, 1994-97; mgr. Compaq, Houston, 1997—. R.E. Lee scholar, 1983-85. Mem. Ky. Cols., Alumni Assn. of AOD of Chi Psi (v.p., pres., bd. dirs. 1985-93, Nelson T. Levings award 1985), Chi Psi Alumni Assn. of Nat. Capitol Area (pres. 1991-93), Washington and Lee Alumni Assn., Washington, 1985-97 (class rep. 1987-89). Episcopalian. Office: Compaq 20555 SH 249/MC 100103 Houston TX 77070

DEWING, LINDA THIMANN, sculptor; b. Boston, June 14, 1943; d. Kenneth Vivian and Ann Mary (Bateman) T.; m. J.T. Dewing Jr., Nov. 25, 1965 (div. June 1977); children: Christopher Bateman, Ginger Karin. BA, Radcliffe Coll., 1965; postgrad., New Eng. Sch. Art, 1969-71, Naguib Sch. Sculpture, 1977-79. Tchr. French Middletown (R.I.) H.S., 1965-69; interior designer David Kiel Interiors, Columbus, Ind., 1971-77; mold maker Paul King Foundry, Johnston, R.I., 1980-88; exec. asst. to pres. Wheaton Coll., Norton, Mass., 1988-96; network mktr. Cell Tech, Providence, 1996—. Mem. Providence Art Club. Avocations: nutrition and health, running, travel, reading, gardening. E-mail: linda@bluegreenalgae.com. Home and Office: 55 Modena Ave Providence RI 02908-2012

DEWITT, BARBARA JANE, journalist; b. Glendale, Calif., Aug. 5, 1947; d. Clarence James and Irene Brezina; m. Don DeWitt, Apr. 21, 1974; children: Lisa, Scarlett. BA in Journalism, Calif. State U., Northridge, 1971. Features editor The Daily Ind. Newspaper, Ridgecrest, Calif., 1971-84; fashion editor The Daily Breeze, Torrance, Calif., 1984-89; freelance fashion reporter The Seattle Times, 1990; fashion editor, columnist The Los Angeles Daily News, L.A., 1990—; instr. fashion writing UCLA, 1988, Am. Inter-Continental U., L.A., 1996—. Dir. Miss Indian Wells Valley Scholarship Pageant, 1980-84. Recipient 1st Pl. Best Youth Page, Calif. Newspaper Pubs. Assn., 1980, 1st Pl. Best Fashion, Wash. Press Assn., 1989, The Internat. Aldo award for fashion journalism, 1995, 96. Republican. Lutheran. Avocations: antiques, reading, swimming. Office: The Daily News 21221 Oxnard St Woodland Hills CA 91367-5081

DEWITT, BRYDON MERRILL, development consultant; b. Westernport, Md., June 9, 1943; s. Brydon Owens and Helen Naomi (Fike) DeW.; m. Louise Muriel Wampler, May 22, 1965; 1 child, Brydon Mark. BA, Bridgewater Coll., 1965; MFA, Va. Commonwealth U., 1973. Tchr. English, history, speech Luray (Va.) H.S., 1965-66; tchr. English, speech Harrisonburg (Va.) H.S., 1966-67; dir. student activities Va. Commonwealth U., Richmond, 1968-70, Albion (Mich.) Coll., 1970-72; asst. dir. Kline Campus Ctr. Bridgewater (Va.) Coll., 1972-73, dir. ann. giving/alumni, 1973-75, dir. devel., 1975-90; assoc. Gonser Gerber Tinker Stuhr, Naperville, Ill., 1990-95; pres. DeWitt & Assocs. Inc., Richmond, 1995—. Author, pub. quar. newsletter The Development Companion. Mem. Va. Assn. Fund Raising Execs., Va. Planned Giving Study Group, Nat. Assn. Fund Raising Execs. Republican. Baptist. Avocations: reading, writing, sports. Home and Office: 12701 Crimson Ct Richmond VA 23233-7657

DEWITT, CHARLES BARBOUR, federal government official; b. L.A., Mar. 13, 1950; s. Homer Charles and Gwenyth Deakin (Barbour) DeW.; m. Bonnie St. Clair; 1 child, Anna. BA with univ. distinction and dept. honors, Stanford U., 1972; postgrad., Cambridge U., 1972-73. Dep. sheriff City of San Jose, Calif., 1973-74, specialist regional crime bd., 1974-78, dir. justice div., 1978-84; fellow U.S. Dept. of Justice, 1984-89; advisor White House, Washington, 1989-90; dir. Nat. Inst. Justice, 1990-93; ptnr. Lafayette Group, Inc., Vienna, Va., 1993—; faculty Nat. Acad. Corrections, Boulder, Colo., 1986-90, Nat. Inst. Corrections, Washington, 1986-90; cons. Police Found., 1993-94. Author: National Directory of Corrections, 1986, 1988, Building on Experience, 1987, Prison Expansion, 1988. Adv. coun. The Ditchley Found. With USNCR, 1968-71. Recipient Atty. Gen.'s Achievement award, 1993, Dist. Attys. award, 1993, Am. Jails award, 1993. Mem. Am. Correctional Assn., Internat. Assn. Chiefs Police, Nat. Sheriffs Assn., Nat. Dist. Attys. Assn. Republican. Episcopalian. Avocations: jogging, skiing, tennis. Home: 5058 Sedgwick St NW Washington DC 20016-1940 Office: Lafayette Group Inc 8150 Leesburg Pike Ste 900 Vienna VA 22182-7749

DEWITT, CHARLES BENJAMIN, III, lawyer, educator; b. Glendale, Calif., Nov. 29, 1952; s. Charles Benjamin Jr. and Lucille Ann (Johnston) deW.; m. Karen Denise Blackwood, Dec. 29, 1979. BA magna cum laude, Pacific Union Coll., 1973; JD, U. So. Calif., 1976; MA, U. Memphis, 1995. Bar: Tenn. 1984, U.S. Dist. Ct. (we. dist.) Tenn. 1984, D.C. 1989. Atty., agy. mgr., v.p. SAFECO/Chgo. Title Ins., Memphis, 1980-91; regional underwriting counsel Commonwealth Land Title Ins. Co., 1991-93; asst. prof., instr. U. Memphis, 1986—, asst. dean paralegal, 1993-96., asst. dean law sch., 1996—. Contbr. articles to profl. jours. Registrar gen. Washington Family Descendants;. Mem. Memphis Bar Assn., Tenn. Land Title Assn. (sec.-treas. 1983-87), U. S.C. Alumni Assn. (life), Order Crown of Charlemagne, Kiwanis, Mensa, Phi Alpha Theta, Phi Kappa Phi, Phi Alpha Delta. Home: 2488 Cedarwood Dr Germantown TN 38138-5802 Office: U Memphis Sch Law Campus Box 526513 Memphis TN 38152

DEWITT, EDWARD FRANCES, artist; b. Jersey City, Aug. 1, 1938; s. Elmer and Linda (Kroll) DeW.; m. Cora Finn, Nov. 11, 1959 (separated 1970); children: April, Lenneice, Edward, Linda; m. Mary Golazizian, Sept. 17, 1972. artist cons. Bronx (N.Y.) Zoo, 1968-70, Aquarius Art Ltd., Fairview, N.J., 1971-73; artist, sculptor, v.p. Artistic Classics, Rutherford, N.J., 1974-77; artist, sculptor, Browns Mills, N.J., 1977-97. Artist 5-yr. silverplate series Anheuser Bush; commemorative works for Pub. Svc., Babe Ruth, Gen. Doolittle, Jim Thorpe PA; sculptures Ford Motor Co., GM Corp., Bicentennial Soc., Boy Scouts Am., Thomas Edison, NATO, Chesapeake Reproductions, Mappsville, Va.; award programs for Progresso Foods, Kentucky Fried Chicken; medallions John F. Kennedy, Dwight D. Eisenhower, Winston Churchill, Bobby Kennedy, Charles A. Lindbergh, Gerald ford: President; artist prints-sculptures models and collector plates Abundant Ocean Treasures, Saddlebrook, N.J.; represented in numerous pvt. collections; patentee on door striker plate. Avocations: the arts, music, guitar, fishing. Home and Studio: 411 N Carolina Trl Browns Mills NJ 08015-5405

DEWITT, EULA, accountant; b. Conway, S.C., Feb. 5, 1948; d. Joseph and Ethel Maude (Parmley) D.; m. John Ramos; children: Andre Carter, John Ramos III, David Carter. BS in Acctg., CUNY, 1981; cert., Bethlehem Missionary Bible Inst., 1990; ThM, Lighthouse Christian Coll., 1998. Jr. acct. Kenneth Leventhol, CPA Firm, N.Y., 1981; agent IRS, N.Y., 1981—, staff pub. speakers bur., 1985—, instr. for revenue agents, 1986—. Author newsletter; contbr. numerous articles to profl. jours. Tutor York Coll. CUNY, Jamaica, 1991—; guest spkr. Hunter Coll. 6th Ann. Conv., 1991, Exploring Divsn. Greater N.Y., 1991, Cath. Charities Archdiocese, N.Y., 1991, First Corinthian Bap. Ch., Bklyn., 1996—, various Bapt. chs., 1996; Sunday Sch. tchr. Bethlehem Missionary Ch., 1979—, leader altar workers ministry, 1991—, missionary to Belize, 1991, to Eng., 1993, to Guyana, 1995, Kano State, Nigeria, 1997, Jos State, Nigeria, 1997, Benue State, Nigeria, 1997. Mem. Inst. Mgmt. Accts. (bd. dirs. 1982—, v.p. profl. edn. 1994-95, pres.-elect 1996-97, pres. 1997—), Toastmaster's 21 Club (v.p., past pres., Able Toastmaster ATM 1996), Inst. Mgmt. Accts. (bd. dirs., pres. 1997-98). Avocations: photography, reading. Office: IRS 110 W 44th St New York NY 10036-4011

DEWITT, MARY THERESE, consultant; b. Chgo., Aug. 25, 1948; d. Robert Baldwin and Helen (Rossman) DeW. BA in Anthropology, U. Tex. at Arlington, 1995, MA in Interdisciplinary Studies, 1997. Dir. mktg. Homart Devel. Co., Florence, Ky., 1975-76, Melvin Simon & Assocs., Inc., Hurst, Tex., 1976-79; pres. Mary DeWitt Co., Ft. Worth, 1979-85; v.p. mktg. Southmark Comml. Mgmt., Dallas, 1986-87; prin. DeWitt Group and subs. Cat's-Eye Intelligence Svc., Dallas and Ft. Worth, 1988-98; faculty/staff U. N.Mex., Valencia, 1998—; acad. advisor dept. physics and astronomy U. N.Mex., 1998—; cons. logistics and documentation one team Internat. Group for Hist. Aircraft Recovery, The Phoenix Group South Pacific, 1989, U. N.Mex., Valencia Campus, 1998. Mem. Am. Coll. of Forensic Examiners, Archaeol. Inst. of Am., Internat. Assn. for Identification, Am. Assn. of Phys. Anthropologists, Lambda Alpha (v.p. 1994-97). Home: 612 6th St SW Albuquerque NM 87102-3808

DEWITT, MICHELE MIXNER, community planner; b. Key West, Fla., Sept. 18, 1969; d. Frank Lewis and Linda Louise (Anderson) Mixner; m. George Christopher DeWitt, Mar. 14, 1992. B in City Planning, U. Va., 1991. Draftsperson, asst. Alfonso & Assocs., Newport News, Va., 1992-94; environ. planner Middlesex County, Saluda, Va., 1994-96; regional planner Middle Peninsula Planning Dist. Commn., Saluda, 1996-98; community planner Ctr. Rural Devel. Va. Dept. Housing Community Devel., Richmond, Va., 1998; advisor Gloucester (Va.) Housing Adv. Bd., 1996—; indoor plumbing bd. mem. Chesapeake Bay Agy. on Aging, Urbanna, Va., 1997—. Sec. Friends of York River State Pk., Williamsburg, Va., 1996—. Econ. Devel. Inst. scholar Va. Econ. Developers Assn., 1997. Mem. Am. Planning Assn., Va. Microenterprise Network. Home: PO Box 389 Gloucester VA 23061-0389 Office: Va Dept Housing Commn Devel 501 N 2nd St Richmond VA 23219-1321

DEWITT, RALPH OGDEN, JR., military career history; b. Waynesville, Mo., June 30, 1942; m. Sheree Cully; children: Ogden, Ashley. DO, Kirksville Coll. Osteo., 1969. Diplomate Am. Bd. Family Practice. Pvt. practice; chief of staff Pulaski County Meml. Hosp., Waynesville; comdr. officer U.S. Army, 1973, advanced through grades to brig. gen., 1996—; family practice residency faculty Tripler Army Med. Ctr., Hawaii; family practice dep. dir. Womack Army Cmty. Hosp., Ft. Bragg, N.C.; divsn. surgeon 82nd Airborne Divsn. U.S. Army, Ft. Bragg; ctr. surgeon JFK Spl. Warfare Ctr., Ft. Bragg; chief dept. family practice and family practice residency Tripler Army Med. Ctr., Hawaii; med. advisor to comdr. 14th Coast Guard Dist. U.S. Army, Hawaii; ambulatory care cons. to Army surgeon gen., commdr. Womack Army Hosp., Ft. Bragg; surgeon XVIII Airborne Corps U.S. Army, Ft. Bragg; surgeon Joint Task Force South U.S. Army, Panama; comdr. William Beaumont Army Med. Ctr.; asst. surgeon gen., dep. chief staff Office Surgeon Gen., U.S. Army Med. Command, Ft. Sam Houston, Tex., 1997—; comdr. Brook Army Med. Ctr., Great Plains Regional Med. Command. Decorated Legion of Merit with three oak leaf clusters, Bronze Star, Meritorious Svc. medal with three oak leaf clusters, Army Commendation medal, Army Achievement medal, Armed Forces Expeditionary medal. Office: US Army Med Command Fort Sam Houston TX 78234

DEWITT, SALLIE LEE, realtor; b. Ft. Smith, Ark., Oct. 11, 1923; d. Lee and Claudia Cordelia Victoria (Vest) DeWitt. BS, U. Tex., 1944; student, U. Houston, 1971; postgrad. in Computers, Del Mar Coll., 1989. Real estate broker, Tex.; cert. profl. sec. Layout artist, copywriter Corpus Christi (Tex.) Caller-Times, 1945-56; exec. sec. to chief geologist Exxon Co., Houston, 1956-73; adminstrv. asst. to gen. mgr. Valley Telephone Coop., Inc., Raymondville, Tex., 1976-89; owner, mgr. Sallie Lee DeWitt Real Estate, Raymondville, Tex., 1980-89; broker assoc. Alfred Edge Realtors, Corpus Christi, 1990-95; broker, owner Sallie Lee DeWitt Real Estate, 1996—; property tax cons., Corpus Christi, 1992-94. Mem. Nueces County Hist. Soc., Corpus Christi, 1990—. Mem. AAUW, Women's Coun. Realtors, Corpus Christi Bd. Realtors, C.C. Town Hall, C.C. Bus. and Profl. Women, Civitan Internat., Tropical Trails Investment Club/Harlingen, Tex., Internat. Soc. Poets, Internta. soc. Photographers. Republican. Baptist. Avocations: poetry, piano, art, photography, genealogy.

DEWITT, WILLIAM O., JR., professional sports team executive; b. St. Louis, Aug. 31, 1941; s. William O. and Margaret H. DeW.; m. Katharine Cramer; children: Katie, Bill, Andrew, Margot. BA in Econs., Yale U., 1963; MBA, Harvard U., 1965. Pres. Reynolds, DeWitt & Co.; owner St. Louis Cardinals, 1996—; chmn. bd. dirs., CEO Gateway Group Inc., 1996—; co-chmn. Restaurant Mgmt. Inc.; bd. dirs. Sena Weller Rohe, Williams Inc., U.S. Playing Card Co. Pres. Fund for Ind. Schs. Cin., William O. and Margaret H. DeWitt Found.; pres. Rep. fin. com. Hamilton County; bd. dirs. Semple Found., Cin. Art Mus., Taft Mus., Salvation Army; mem. devel. bd. Yale U.; regional chmn. Yale Campaign; cabinet mem. Cin. Fine Arts Fund, United Way Cin., Multiple Sclerosis Soc. Office: St Louis Cardinals 250 Stadium Plz Saint Louis MO 63102

DEWITT-MORETTE, CÉCILE, physicist; b. Paris, Dec. 21, 1922; came to U.S., 1948; d. André and Marie Louise (Ravaudet) Morette; m. Bryce S. DeWitt, Apr. 26, 1951; children—Nicolette, Jan, Chris, Abigail. B.S., U. Caen, 1943; Ph.D., U. Paris, 1947. With Centre Nat. de la Recherche Sci., 1944-65, Maitre de Confs. prof., 1965-88; mem. Inst. Advanced Studies in Dublin, 1946-47, Copenhagen, 1947-48, Princeton, 1948-50; lectr. U. Calif. at Berkeley, 1952-55, U. N.C., Chapel Hill, 1956-71; prof. U. Tex., 1972-93, Jane and Roland Blumberg Centennial prof. physics, 1993—; founder, dir. Ecole d'ete de Physique Theorique, Les Houches, France, 1951-72. Author: Particules Elementaires, 1951, (with Y. Choquet-Bruhat and M. Dillard-Bleick) Analysis, Manifolds and Physics, 1977, rev. edit., 1982, (with A. Maheshwari, B. Nelson) Path Integration in Non Relativistic Quantum Mechanics, 1979, (with Y. Choquet Bruhat) Analysis, Manifolds and Physics, Part II, 92 Applications, 1989, also articles. Decorated chevalier Ordre Nat. du Mérite, chevalier Ordre des Palmes Académiques; Rask-Oersted fellow, 1947-48, Prix des Sciences Physiques et Mathematiques (Comite du Rayonnement Français, 1992). Fellow Am. Phys. Soc.; mem. Internat. Astron. Union, European Phys. Soc., Inst. Hautes Etudes Scientific (bd. trustees). Home: 2411 Vista Ln Austin TX 78703-2343 Office: U Tex Dept Physics Austin TX 78712

DE WOLF, DAVID ALTER, electrical engineer, educator; b. Dordrecht, The Netherlands, July 23, 1934; came to U.S., 1962; m. Peggy Louise Lumpkin; 1 dau., Sarah Eleonora; children by previous marriage: Naomi, Jiska. BS in Physics, U. Amsterdam, The Netherlands, 1955, MS in Physics, 1959; PhDEE, U. Eindhoven, The Netherlands, 1968. Rsch. scientist Edgewood (Md.) Arsenal U.S. Army Chem. Ctr., 1962; mem. tech. staff RCA Labs.-David Sarnoff Rsch. Ctr., Princeton, N.J., 1962-82; prof. elec. engring. Va. Tech., Blacksburg, 1982—; commn. B and F U.S. Nat. Com. Internat. Union Radio Sci., sec. 1985-89. Author 2 books and contbr. numerous articles on wave propagation, electron optics to profl. jours. Fellow IEEE, Optical Soc. Am. (assoc. editor JOSA 1969-81); mem. Am. Assn. Physics Tchrs., Dutch Physics Soc., Electromagnetics Acad., Sigma Xi, Eta Kappa Nu. Avocations: music, piano, literature, tennis. Office: Va Tech Dept Elec and Comp Engring Bradley Blacksburg VA 24061-0111

DEWOLF, SUSAN ULMER, operating room nurse; b. Williamsport, Pa., Sept. 1, 1953; d. Donald Hart and Helen Marie (Howery) Ulmer; m. C. Anson DeWolf, Sept. 1, 1979. BSN, Kennesaw (Ga.) State U., 1990. RN, Ga. Nurse oper. rm., 1st asst. Piedmont Hosp., Atlanta, 1990—; CEO, pres. Surg. First Assts., Inc., Marietta, Ga., 1998—; instr. endoscopic nursing edn., Marietta, Ga., 1990-92,. Mem. ANA, Assn. Oper. Rm. Nurses (Perioperative Nurse of Yr. suburban Atlanta chpt. 1998, pres. 1996-97), Soc. Vascular Nurses, Ga. Nurses Assn., RN 1st Assts. Ga., Sigma Theta Tau. Avocations: ballroom dancing, motorcycle touring, gardening. Home: 4542 High Rock Ter Marietta GA 30066-1606

DEWOLFE, JOHN CHAUNCEY, JR., lawyer; b. Chgo., June 9, 1913; s. John Chauncey and Mabel (Spafford) DeW.; m. Dorothy Fulton, May 9, 1942; children: John Chauncey, III, George F. B.S., U. Ill.; J.D., U. Wis., 1939. Bar: Wis. 1939, Ill. 1940. Ptnr. firm DeWolfe, Poynton & Stevens and predecessor firms, 1946—. Contbr. articles to profl. jours. Trustee Village of Riverside, Ill., 1963-70; Chmn. West Suburban Mass Transit Dist., 1974-76. Served from lt. to maj. AUS, 1942-45, 51-52; lt. col. USAR ret. Mem. Am., Ill., Wis. bar assns., Chgo. Bar Assn. (chmn. corp. law com. 1973-74), Bar Assn. 7th Fed. Circuit, Assn. Trial Lawyers Am., Sigma Phi Epsilon. Republican. Episcopalian. Club: University (Chgo.). Home: 1448 N Lake Shore Dr Chicago IL 60610-6655 Office: 135 S La Salle St Chicago IL 60603-4105

DEWOLFE, MARTHA ROSE, singer, songwriter, publisher; b. Arlington, Tex., Nov. 30, 1959; d. Homer C. and Grace R. DeWolfe. Student, N. Tex. State U., 1978-79, Larimer County Vocat.-Tech., Ft. Collins, Colo., 1983; cert. peace officer, Tarrant County Jr. Coll., Euless, Tex., 1984; student,

North Ctrl. Tex. Coun. Govts., 1984-94, Southwestern Law Enforcement Sch. of Police Supervision. Police officer Grand Prairie (Tex.) Police Dept., 1984-94, sgt., 1989-94, supr. crime prevention unit, 1991-92; mem. Police Employee Rels. Bd., 1990-91; BMI assoc.; estabished Maui Records, 1992, Midnight Tiger Music, BMI, 1994. Albums include That Flame Keeps Burning, 1992, Take Good Care of My Heart, 1995, Mama Look, 1997; songs include Adrianna, Worse Than Being Lonely, All the Blue, Patsy Come Home, River of Tears, Take Good Care of My Heart, Once a Year, The Drought; acting credits include Paramount's "Denton County Massacre", 1993, and commercials. Sec. Grand Prairie Police Assn., 1985-86. Recipient 1st place Tex. Comml. Art Skill Speed Competition, 1977-78. Mem. Fraternal Order Police, Grand Prairie Police Assn., Tex. Assn. Vet. Police Officers, Country Music Assn., Broadcast Music Internat., Nashville Songwriter's Assn. Internat., No. Calif. Songwriters Assn., Mensa. Avocations: pvt. pilot, cats, photography. Home: PO Box 266 Martinez CA 94553-0026

DE WOLFF, LOUIS, management consultant; b. N.Y.C., Dec. 21, 1929; s. Maurice and Minnie (Konrad) De W.; m. Grace Elise Sorrentino, Apr. 27, 1957; children: Douglas Louis, Cynthia Ann. AS, Bklyn. Coll., 1960; BS in Acctg., CCNY, 1962. Officer Lykes Bros. S.S. Co., New Orleans, 1950-57; export mgr. Cory Mann George Corp., N.Y.C., 1957-60; dist. supt. F&M Schaefer Brewing Co., N.Y.C., 1960-64; product and material mgr. Del Labs., Inc., Farmingdale, N.Y., 1965-69; exec. cons., exec. v.p. Pennington (N.J.) Industries, 1969-73; exec. v.p., dir. ops. Alexander Proudfoot Co., Chgo., 1973-86; mgr. ops. Metra Proudfoot Ltd., Brussels, 1986-87; CEO, chmn. DeWolff Boberg & Assocs., Charleston, S.C., 1987-97, chmn., 1998—. Lt. (j.g.) USMS and USNR, 1950-57, PTO. Republican. Lutheran. Avocations: carpentry, sailing, gardening. Home: 4723 Yachtsmans Dr Fernandina FL 32034-5550 Office: DeWolff Boberg & Assocs PO Box 21989 Charleston SC 29413-1989

DE WREE, EUGENE ERNEST, manufacturing company executive; b. Fairbanks, Alaska, June 26, 1930; s. Henry Joseph and Bertha Agnes DeWree; m. Shirley May Russo, Apr. 16, 1955 (dec. Sept. 1990); children: Angela Kathryn, Mary Rebecca, Thomas Albert, Babette Gabrielle, Jane Elizabeth; m. Jean Stanley Mack, Sept. 4, 1993; children: John Currie, Brigget Currie. BSME, Cogswell Engrng. Coll., 1955; MBA, Stanford U., 1979. Project engr. Heat and Control Co., San Francisco, 1955-59; chief appliations engr., then market mgr. Wesix Electric Heater Co., San Francisco, 1959-65; account mgr. Fisher Controls, San Francisco, 1965-76; market and sales mgr. TRW Mission, Houston, 1976-80; v.p. mktg.-sales Houston Heat Exch., 1980-82; mktg. mgr. Anderson, Greenwood & Co., 1982—; sr. ptnr. Affiliated Products, Inc.; pres. DeWree Enterprises, DeWree Rental Properties; ptnr., dir. Constrn. Info. Svcs., Cismap, TVMP; sr. v.p. Indsl. Market Rsch.; dir. Creative Capers, San Francisco and Houston. Mem. Belmont (Calif.) Pers. Bd., 1965; com. chmn. Boy Scouts Am., 1970; elected to bd. dirs. Cypress Forest Pub. Utility Dist. Harris County, Tex., 1981, 83, 85, 86-90, 92-96, Harris County Regional Water Supply; pres. Water Bd. Capt. arty. U.S. Army, 1951-53, Korea. Named Outstanding Jaycee of Yr., 1966. Mem. Am. Mgmt. Assn., Am. Nuc. Soc., Valve Mfg. Assn., Instrument Soc. Am. (sr.), Assn. Water Bd. Dirs., Water Pollution Control Fedn., Sales and Mktg. Execs., Houston Engrng. and Sci. Soc., KC (3d degree, dep. Grand Knight, 4th degree trustee), Inner Circle, Pine Forest Country Club, Plaza Club, Engrs. Club (San Francisco). Republican. Roman Catholic. E-mail: API77069@aol.com. Home and Office: Unit #610 5625 FM 1960 Rd W Houston TX 77069-4213

DEWS, HENRY, environmental educator, minister, recycler; b. Peoria, Ill., Feb. 7, 1948; s. Henry and Betty Ann (De Frees) D. AA in Arch. Design, So. Ill. U., 1968. Owner, mgr. Waste Not Paper Recycling, Carbondale, Ill., 1973—; min. Ministry of Salvation Ch., Carterville, Ill., 1978-98; environ. cons. Shawnee Cons., Carbondale, 1980—. Election judge Williamson County, 1990—; libr. vol., Carbondale Pub. Libr., 1993; cmty. vol., Newman Ctr., Carbondale, 1996—. Named Silver Poet, World of Poetry, 1989, Golden Poet, 1990. Mem. Unitarian Fellowship. Avocations: essayist, poet, musician, artist, volkswagon tinkerer. Home: 1504 Marion St Carterville IL 62918-5143 Office: 1261 Marion St Carterville IL 62918

DEWS, P(ETER) B(OOTH), medical scientist, educator; b. Ossett, Yorkshire, Eng., Sept. 11, 1922; s. G.A. and E. (Booth) D.; m. Grace Miller, Dec. 1949; children: Pamela, Kenneth, Alan, Michael. M.B.Ch.B., U. Leeds, Eng., 1944; PhD, MN, 1952; MA, Harvard U., 1959. House physician Grimsby Hosp., U.K., 1944-45; lectr. pharmacology U. Leeds, 1945-47; rsch. assoc. Wellcome Rsch. Labs., Tuckahoe, N.Y., 1948-49, Mayo Found., Rochester, Minn., 1950-52; from instr. to prof. Harvard Med. Sch., Boston, 1953-93, prof. emeritus, 1993—; mem. Nat. Adv. Mental Health Coun., Washington, 1985-88, Nat. Adv. Space Coun., Washington, 1982-86; v.p. Internat. Life Scis. Inst., Washington, 1977-97. Mem. Inst. of Medicine. Office: Harvard Med Sch NEPRC PO Box 9102 Southborough MA 01772-9102

DEWSBURY, DONALD ALLEN, historian of psychology, comparative psychologist; b. Bklyn., Aug. 11, 1939; s. Edwin Leroy and Carol Wieler (Neil) D.; children: Bryan Bradley, Laura Alison. A.B., Bucknell U., 1961; Ph.D., U. Mich., 1965. NSF postdoctoral fellow U. Calif., Berkeley, 1965-66; mem. faculty dept. psychology U. Fla., Gainesville, 1966—; prof. U. Fla., 1973—. Author: Comparative Animal Behavior, 1978, Comparative Psychology in the Twentieth Century, 1984; editor: (with D. Rethlingshafer) Comparative Psychology: A Modern Survey, 1973, (with T. McGill, B. Sachs) Sex and Behavior: Status and Prospectus, 1978, Mammalian Sexual Behavior, 1981; Foundations of Comparative Psychology, 1984; Leaders in the Study of Animal Behavior, 1985, Studying Animal Behavior, 1989, Contemporary Issues in Comparative Psychology, 1990, Unification Through Division: Histories of the Divisions of the American Psychological Association, vol. 1, 1996, vol. 2, 1997, vol. 3, 1998. Fellow APA (pres. divsn. 6 1992-93, pres. divsn. 26 1997-98), AAAS, Animal Behavior Soc. (pres. 1978-79); mem. Psychonomic Soc., History of Sci. Soc., Cheiron Soc., Phi Beta Kappa, Psi Chi. Home: 4004 NW 59th Ave Gainesville FL 32653-8358 Office: Univ Fla Dept Psychology Gainesville FL 32611-2250

DEWYN, KENNETH LEE, development executive, arts administrator, actor; b. Bellflower, Calif., Feb. 22, 1964; s. Evert and Irene (DeHoog) DeW.; m. Wynne A. Kroontje, Jan. 20, 1987; children: Brandon Alexander, Zachary Bryce, McKenna Vaughn. BA, Calvin Coll., 1986; MFA, Fla. State U., 1991. Dir. ann./planned giving Trinity Christian Coll., Palos Heights, Ill., 1994-98; dir. coll. rels. Trinity Christian Coll., Palos Heights, 1998-99; dir. devel. Chgo. Shakespeare Theater, 1999—; bd. dirs. Quarry Capital, Calgary, Alberta, Can., Pheasantback Resources, Calgary, 1997—. Mem. Christian Reformed Ch. N. Am. Office: Chgo Shakespeare Theater 820 N Orleans Ste 345 Chicago IL 60610

DEXHEIMER, LARRY WILLIAM, advertising agency executive; b. Hackensack, N.J., Aug. 8, 1941; s. Harold Dexheimer and Gretchen Bartell; m. Carol Frances Martin, May 1, 1965 (div. 1983); children—Lynda Anne, Susan Carol. B.S. in Mktg. and Advt., Fairleigh Dickinson U. Broadcast media buyer Doyle, Dane, Bernback, N.Y.C., 1964-67; media group head BBDO, N.Y.C., 1967-71; mktg. svcs. dir. Ally & Gargano, Inc., N.Y.C., 1972-89; ptnr., media dir. Messner, Vetere, Berger, McNamee & Schmetterer, 1989—. Mem. Internat. TV and Radio Soc. Avocations: tennis; reading; travel; fine arts. Home: 150 Overlook Ave Apt 6J Hackensack NJ 07601-2222 Office: Messner Vetere Berger McNamee Schmetterer 50 Hudson St New York NY 10013-3310*

DEXTER, DONALD HARVEY, surgeon; b. Maywood, Ill., Apr. 8, 1928; s. Harry Malcolm and Theodora Jane (Trelawny) D.; m. Esther Ruth Reeve, May 16, 1953; children: Donald Harvey, Scott Reeve, Bryce Malcolm, Margaret Helen. B.S., Tulane U., 1948; M.D., Northwestern U., 1950; LHD (hon.), Western Ill. U., 1993. Diplomate: Am. Bd. Surgery. Intern Cook County Hosp., Chgo., 1950-51; resident in surgery Ill. Central Hosp., Chgo., 1951-52, Cook County Hosp., 1955-58; practice medicine specializing in surgery Macomb, Ill., 1958-89; ret.; prof. dept. health scis. Western Ill. U., 1975-89; ret.; physician surveyor Joint Commn. on Accreditation Healthcare Orgns., 1989-93; chief of staff Beu Health Ctr., Western Ill. U., 1993—; sr. mem. Macomb Clinic; team physician; coroner McDonough County, Ill., 1964-76; mem. gov. bd., chmn. devel. coun. McDonough Dist. Hosp., 1995—. Mem. Western Ill. U. Found. Served with USNR, 1953-54. Named Outstanding Citizen of Macomb Jaycees, 1972, Outstanding Citizen of Macomb Macomb Area C. of C., 1973; recipient award of recognition Devel. Center of Western Ill. U. and Macomb Area C. of C., 1977; named to Hall of Fame Western Ill. U., 1991. Fellow ACS (pres. Ill. chpt. 1972, gov.-at-large Ill. chpt. 1983-88), state chmn. field liaison program commn. on cancer, 1983-89); mem. AMA, Ill. Med. Soc., (Outstanding Team Physician award 1985), Ill. Surg. Soc., M.W. Surg. Assn., Rotary (Paul Harris fellow 1987), Phi Beta Kappa. Republican. Episcopalian. Home: Tower Rd RR 1 Macomb IL 61455-9801

DEXTER, ROBERT PAUL, lawyer; b. Halifax, N.S., Can., Dec. 11, 1951; s. Carl Edmund and Jean Rankin (Collins) D.; 1 child, Angela Elizabeth. BComm, Dalhousie U., 1973, LLB, 1976. With firm Stewart McKelvey Stirling Scales, Halifax, 1977—, ptnr., 1982—; chmn., CEO, majority shareholder Maritime Travel Ltd., 1978—; vice chmn. N.S. Bus. Devel. Corp., 1992-94; bd. dirs. Empire Co. Ltd., Wajax Ltd., Sobeys Inc., High Liner Foods Inc., Maritime Life Assurance Co., Corpora Tel, Wajax Ltd., Maritime Tel. & Tel.; pres. Halifax Bd. Trade, 1993-94. Chmn. Metro United Way Campaign, 1997. I.W. Killam scholar, 1973, Sir James Dunn scholar, 1976. Mem. N.S. Barristers Soc., Can. Bar Assn., Young Pres. Orgn. Avocations: sailing, skiing, tennis. Home: 1028 Ridgewood Dr, Halifax, NS Canada B3H 3Y4 Office: Purdy's Wharf, 1959 Upper Water St PO Box 997, Halifax, NS Canada B3J 2X2

DEXTER, THEODORE HENRY, chemist; b. Preston, Cuba, June 1, 1923; s. Harry Malcolm and Theodora Jane (Trelawny) D. (parents Am. citizens); student Wheaton Coll., 1940-42; B.S., Tulane U., 1944, M.S., 1947; Ph.D., U. Ill., 1950; m. Marilyn Ann Cantara, July 26, 1952; children—Carol Dexter, Martha Dexter Rogala, John Dexter. Teaching asst. in chemistry, Tulane U., New Orleans, 1943-44, 46-47; chemist E.I. du Pont de Nemours, Inc., Okla. Ordnance Works, Pryor, 1944-45; Gen. Aniline research asst. U. Ill., Urbana, 1947-49; group leader chem. research Mathieson Chem. Corp., Niagara Falls, N.Y., 1949-55; sect. chief research Olin Mathieson Chem. Corp., Niagara Falls, 1955-60; research supr. Hooker Chem. Corp., Grand Island, N.Y., 1960-75, program leader, 1975-76, sr. research chemist, 1976-85 (now Hooker Indsl. and Specialty Chems. div. Occidental Chem. Corp.); cons. Dexter Cons. Services, 1986—; lectr., research adv. Joe Berg Found., 1960-61; mem. photoreactivity task force Mfg. Chemists Assn., 1966-68. Violinist Niagara Falls Philharm. Orch., 1950-72, Niagara Community Orch., 1988-92, Niagara Symphony, 1992—; group chmn. in-house steering com. United Givers Fund, 1970-73; exec. council Episcopal Diocese Western N.Y., 1977-81, nursing home ministry, 1972—; layreader, vestryman Episc. Ch., warden, 1967-68, 77-80, 92-94. With USN, 1945-46. Mem. Am. Chem. Soc. (Western N.Y. chmn. 1969-70, N.E. regional meeting divisional chmn. 1971, founder Western N.Y. Inorganic Chemistry Group 1967, Schoellkopf Award jury chmn. 1970-72), Soap and Detergent Assn. (del. internat. conf. 1979, com. chmn.), Electrochem. Soc., Sigma Xi, Alpha Chi Sigma (Niagara Frontier pres. 1954), Phi Lambda Upsilon. Contbr. articles to profl. publs.; lectr. in field; U.S. and fgn. patentee inorganic chemistry and processes. Home and Office: 850 Hillside Dr Lewiston NY 14092-1828

DEY, CAROL RUTH, secondary education educator; b. N.Y., Mar. 9, 1943; d. Robert Lewis Adelson and Anne Millman; m. John Peter Dey, Feb. 9, 1968 (div. Feb. 1978). AA, San Bernardino Valley Coll., 1965; BA, Calif. State U., Sacramento, 1969; MBA, Calif. State U., San Bernardino, 1983, postgrad., 1994-95. Sec. U.S. Dept of Interior, USAF, Retail Industry, San Bernardino, Sacramento, Calif., 1960-80; logistics mgr. USAF, San Bernardino, 1980-94; substitute tchr. San Bernardino Unified Sch. Dist., 1994—, Inland Empire Job Corp. Ctr., 1997—. Dancer Coppélia, San Bernardino, Calif., 1984; mem. St. Anne's Ch., San Bernardino, 1978—. Mem. Am. Bus. Women's Assn. (Calif. State Coll. scholar), Smithsonian Inst., AF Assn., Alumni Assn. Calif. State U. San Bernardino. Republican. Roman Catholic. Avocations: ballet, piano, sewing, cooking, singing.

DEY, CHARLOTTE JANE, retired community health nurse; b. Benson, Minn., Dec. 14, 1927; d. Elmer Ellsworth and Charlotte Iona (Eastman) Bowers; m. Thomas A. Dey, June 25, 1948 (dec. Mar. 1973); children: Thomas A. Jr., Scott E. Grad., St. Luke's Hosp. Sch. Nursing, 1948; student, Kansas City (Kans.) Jr. Coll., 1968; BS in Nursing with distinction, U. Kans., 1970; MPA, U. Mo., Kansas City, 1975. RN, Mo.; ordained deacon, Episcopal Ch., 1993. Head nurse communicable disease ward St. Luke's Children's Hosp., Kansas City, Mo., 1948-49; head nurse newborn nursery Providence Hosp., Kansas City, Kans., 1949-51; pub. health nurse Johnson County Health Dept., Olathe, Kans., 1951-52, 66-68, pub. health nurse, supr., 1970-72; evening supr. Olathe Community Hosp., 1953-55; office nurse B. Albert Lieberman, Jr., MD, Kansas City, Mo., 1960-66; coord. clin. confs. ANA, Kansas City, 1973-76; chief Bur. Community Health Nursing Mo. Dept. Health, Jefferson City, 1976-93; ret., 1993; sem. expert panel to review and update criteria to estimate future requirements for nursing pers. div. nursing Dept. Health and Human Svcs., 1984, mem. nat. adv. coun. nursing edn. and practice div. nursing, 1998—; chairperson Mid-Am. Community Health Nursing Leadership Group. Recipient award of merit Assn. State and Territorial Dirs. Nursing, 1992. Mem. ANA (cert. nursing adminstrn. advanced, chairperson exec. com. coun. community health nursing 1989-92), APHA, Nat. League Nursing, Nat. Perinatal Assn., Am. Acad. Health Adminstrn. (pres. Mo. chpt. 1980-82), Mo. State Nurses Assn. (coun. nursing svc. facilitors exec. com. 1983-92), Mo. Pub. Health Assn., Mo. League Nursing, Mo. Perinatal Assn., Kans. State Nurses' Assn. (vice chairperson community health conf. group), Kans. Pub. Health Assn. (legislative com.), Sigma Theta Tau. Mem. Episcopal Ch. Home: G102 1310 Swifts Hwy Jefferson City MO 64109

DEY, MARLENE MELCHIORRE, nursing educator, critical care nurse; b. L.I., N.Y., June 9, 1952; d. Ralph and Ann (Doria) Melchiorre; m. Theodore J. Dey, Jr.; children: Lauren, Michael. BSN, Fairleigh Dickenson U., 1974; MS in Nursing, Seton Hall U., 1983. RN, N.J.; cert. advanced practice clin. specialist in med.-surg. nursing ANCC, cert. nurse practitioner. Clin. coord. critical cardiac unit Newark Beth Israel Med. Ctr., 1980-81; instr. nursing Passaic County Community Coll., Paterson, N.J., 1984-87; staff relief nurse med. ICU, Hackensack (N.J.) Med. Ctr., 1988-94; assoc. prof. med.-surg. nursing Essex County Coll., Newark, 1988—, chairperson dept. nursing, 1997—; project dir. Karl Perkins Vocat.-Edn. grant nursing dept. Essex County Coll., 1990-92; cons. for computers in nursing edn., 1992—; per diem nurse practitioner family practice group Somerset Med. Ctr., Somerville, N.J.; adv. bd. Jack Ewing Acad. Charter Sch. Health Scis. and Tech. Recipient grant Helene Fulde Trust for Computer Lab. Enhancement, Essex County Coll., 1996. Mem. ANA, N.J. Nurses assn., Seton Hall U. Alumni Assn. (bd. dirs., svc. award 1993), Coll. Nursing Alumni Assn. (sec., pres.).

DEY, RADHESHYAM CHANDRA, cytologist; b. Calcutta, India, Jan. 30, 1950; came to U.S., 1978; s. Bhairab and Satyabala D.; m. Indrani Roy Chowdhury, July 5, 1981; children: Smita, Anita, Ishan. BSc, Bangabasi Coll., Calcutta, 1970; MSc, U. Calcutta, 1972, cert. in life sci., 1974; CT, Brooke Army Med. Ctr., San Antonio, 1983; cert. leaderhsip mgmt., ednl. devel., quality improvement and equal opportunity, Walter Reed Army Med. Ctr., 1989; postgrad., Laval U., Quebec City, Can., 1995, Albert Einstein Sch. Medicine, 1997. Registered cytotechnologist, Am. Soc. Clin. Pathologists, Internat. Acad. Cytology, Calif., Md. Rsch. fellow U. Calcutta, 1975-77; with Anthropol. Survey of India, Indian Mus. Calcutta, 1977-78; biol. science asst. Army Inst. Rsch., Washington, 1980-83; cytology specialist U.S. Army Hosp., Ft. Campbell, Ky., 1983-85, SHAPE Med. Ctr., SHAPE/Mons, Belgium, 1985-87; cytotechnologist Nat. Health Lab., Vienna, Va., 1988; supervisory cytologist Walter Reed Army Med. Ctr., Washington, 1988—; attended Indian Sci. Congress, U. New Delhi, Calcutta, Waltair, Gujarat, 1972-77, Internat. Congress of Cytology, Brussels, Belgium, 1987, Internat. Cytology Tutorials, Vienna, Austria, 1986, Tokyo, Japan, 1991, Harvard Med. Sch. Advances in Cytology, Boston, 1990, Coll. Am. Pathologists, Las Vegas, 1992, World Congress on Anthropol. & Ethnol. Scis., Mexico City, 1993, Williamsburg, Va., 1998, Am. Soc. Clin. Pathologists and Cytopathology, Seattle, Advanced Techniques in Human Identification-Armed Forces Inst. Pathology, Washington, 1994, Palaeopathology, 1993, Forensic Anthropology, 1995; participant New Directions for Leaders Focus 2000, Ft. Belvoir, Va., 1994, Immunol. Markers in Histopathology and Cytology, Inst. of Pathology, Ghent U. Hosp., Belgium, 1987, numerous seminars; mem. symposium for suprs. and team bldg. dynamics for mgrs. U.S. Army Walter Reed Med. Ctr., Washngton, 1995, 96; attended CAP/ASCP seminar L.A., 1998. Contbr. articles to profl. jours. Decorated U.S. Army Commendation medal, 1985, Achievement medal, 1984, Good Conduct medals, 1982, 85; recipient Decree of Merit for outstanding contbn. to medicine and health care, 1995, Excellence in Tchg. award Nat. Capital Region Consortium Pathology Residency, 1997, Comdr.'s award for civilian svc. U.S. Army Walter Reed Med. Ctr., 1997. Mem. AAAS, Internat. Acad. Cytology, Am. Anthropol. Assn., Am. Soc. Cytopathology, Am. Soc. Clin. Pathologists, N.Y. Acad. Scis., Soc. of Armed Forces Med. Lab. Scientists, Belge de Cytologie Clinique (del. visit to People's Repubblic China 1987, 91, internat. team cytologists exch. sci. knowledge with USSR 1990), Ind. Sci. Congress, Indian Anthropol. Soc., Washington Met. Assn. of Cytology. Avocations: soccer, swimming, running, traveling. Home: 2313 Snowflake Dr Odenton MD 21113-2237 Office: Walter Reed Army Med Ctr Dept Pathology Cytology Lab Washington DC 20307

DEY, SUHRIT K., mathematician, researcher; b. Calcutta, May 15, 1939; arrived in U.S., 1966; s. Gokul Das and Manimala D.; m. Sabita Kumar, Feb. 9, 1963 (wid. Oct. 1989); children: Sujata, Charlie; m. Roma Pratima Nath, Jan. 1, 1990. BA in Math with honors, Calcutta U., 1958, MA in Applied Math., 1960; PhD in Aerospace Engrng., Miss. State U., 1970. Lectr. in math. B.K.C. Coll., Calcutta, 1961-66; rsch. asst. aerospace engrng. Miss. State U., 1966-70; asst. prof. math. Ea. Ill. U., Charleston, 1970-77; prof. math. Ea. Ill. U., 1979—; sr. rsch. assoc. NASA/Ames Rsch. Ctr., Moffett Field, Calif., 1980-83; vis. prof. von Karman Inst. of Fluid Dynamics, Brussels, 1978, Boston U., Ramstein AFB, Germany, 1985-86, U. Seidlec, Poland, 1986; vis. scientist Indian Stats. Inst., 1991, Naval Underwater Warfare Ctr., New London, Conn., 1992, Colo. Sch. Mines, 1992, Tech. U. Denmark, Lyngby, 1993, Indian Inst. Tech., Delhi, 1996, S.N. Bose Ctr. Basic Scis., 1994, 96, U. Rome, 1997, U. Alicante, 1998, Eafit U., Medellin, Colombia, 1998, U. Vilnius, Lithuania, 1999, Inst. of Math & Informatics; vis. scientist Stanford U., 1980, Miss. State U. ERC, 1990, Wright Patterson AFB, 1991. Inventor in field (Hinemann Found. award, Germany 1978), (NRC fellowship 1981); editor jours. in field. Recipient Rsch. Associateship NRC, Washington, 1981-82, others; NRC fellow, 1982. Mem. Indian Acad. Math. (life), Inst. Applied Sci. and Computations, Phi Kappa Phi. Achievements include inventing perturbed functional iterations, a numerical method to solve nonlinear models accurately; D-matrices to analyze nonlinear stability of difference equations; D-Mappings for norm ind. contraction in a function space; massive parallel computations to solve large-scale nonlinear models with a fast speed of convergence in computers with a large number of parallel processors; accurate computations for stiff equations in chem. kinetics; scientific analysis of consciousness in nature, mathematical analysis of omnipresence and consciousness. Home: 1106 Timberlane Dr Charleston IL 61920-1767

DE YOUNG, DAVID SPENCER, astrophysicist, educator; b. Colorado Springs, Colo., Nov. 29, 1940; s. Henry C. and Zona L. (Church) DeY.; m. Mary Ellen Haney. BA, U. Colo., 1962; PhD, Cornell U., 1967. Rsch. physicist Los Alamos Nat. Labs., Los Alamos, N. Mex., 1967-69; astronomer Nat. Radio Astronomy Obs., Charlottesville, Va., 1969-80; astronomer Kitt Peak Nat. Obs., Tucson, 1980—, assoc. dir., 1983-88, dir., 1988-94; organizer numerous sci. confs.; mem. adv. bd. Aspen (Colo.) Ctr. Physics, 1977—, trustee, 1992—; mem. exec. com. steering com. San Diego Supercomputer Ctr., 1985—; bd. dirs. WIYN Telescope Consortium, Tucson. Contbr. articles to profl. jours. NASA grantee. Mem. Am. Phys. Soc., Am. Astron. Soc., Astron. Soc. Pacific, Internat. Astron. Union, Internat. Union Radio Soc., Phi Beta Kappa. Office: Kitt Peak Nat Obs 950 N Cherry Ave Tucson AZ 85719-4933

DEYSENROTH, PETER ALBIN, funeral director; b. Norwalk, Conn., Sept. 28, 1966; s. Paul Augustus and Elaine Frances (Albin) D.; m. Maria Holly Nichols, Aug. 5, 1995. Diploma, Simmons Sch. Mortuary Sci., Syracuse, N.Y., 1986; AAS, Herkimer (N.Y.) County C.C., 1987. Mgr. Raymond Funeral Home, Inc., Norwalk, Conn., 1988-94; lic. mgr., v.p., sec., co-owner Connell, Dow & Deysenroth, Inc., Cooperstown, N.Y., 1994—. Organist, asst. choir dir. First Presbyn. Ch., Cooperstown, 1996—; active Otsego County Rep. Com. Mem. Royal Coll. Organists, Am. Guild Organists, Lions Club of Cooperstown (sec. 1997—), Masons (worshipful master 1992-93, 96-97), Grand Lodge State of Conn. (assoc. grand marshall 1993-94), Grand Lodge State of N.Y. (grand dir. ceremonies, 1998—). Methodist. Avocations: music, reading, collecting books. Home: 82 Chestnut St Cooperstown NY 13326-1420 Office: Connell Dow & Deysenroth 82 Chestnut St Cooperstown NY 13326-1420

DE ZOETEN, GUSTAAF ADOLF, plant pathologist; b. Cepu, Indonesia, July 5, 1934; came to U.S., 1962; s. Jan Piet and Louise (Padt) de Z.; m. Catharina Marijka Okma, Jan. 14, 1961; three children. MS, State Agrl. U., Wageningen, The Netherlands, 1960; PhD, U. Calif., Davis, 1965. Postdoctoral fellow U. Calif., Berkeley, 1965-67; asst. prof. U. Wis., Madison, 1967-70, assoc. prof., 1970-74, prof., 1974-90; chair, head dept. botany & plant pathology Mich. State U., East Lansing, 1989—; cons. USAID, U. Porto Allegre, Brazil, 1978, N.Y. Found. Sci. amd Techj., Ithaca, 1984, 86, 88, 89-94, Biotech, Washington, 1993. Recipient career award NIH, 1969-74. Fellow Am. Phytopathol. Soc.; mem. Am. Soc. Virology, AAAS, Am. Inst. Biol. Scis. Avocations: skiing, hiking.

DEZON-JONES, ELYANE AGNES, French language educator, writer; b. Limoges, France; came to U.S., 1979; m. Alain Pillet, Nov. 14, 1970 (div. Jan. 1978); 1 child, Violaine Pillet; Alfred Haworth Jones, Sept. 21, 1978. MA in Comparative Lit., U. Poitiers, France, 1969, U. Va., 1973; PhD, U. Paris IV Sorbonne, 1976. Asst. prof. French U. Kans., Lawrence, 1979-81; asst. prof. Barnard Coll., N.Y.C., 1981-90; assoc. prof. Fordham U., Bronx, N.Y., 1990-91; prof. French Washington U., St. Louis, 1991—. Author: Proust et l'Amerique, 1982, Marie de Gournay, 1987, (novel) Meurtre Chez Tante Léonie, 1994, (under pseudonym Estelle Monbrun) Meurtre a Petite Plaisance, 1998; editor: Proust's Guermantes' Way, 1987, Proust's Swann Way, 1992; editor-in-chief Bull. Marcel Proust, 1989-95. Decorated Order Palmes Académiques (France). Mem. MLA, Soc. Friends of Proust, AAUW, SIEY. Office: Washington U 1 Brookings Dr Saint Louis MO 63130-4899

DEZURKO, EDWARD ROBERT, retired art educator; b. N.Y.C., Mar. 25, 1913; s. Edward and Hattie (Lehman) DeZ.; m. Madith Smith, July 30, 1938 (div. 1962); children: Robin Klein, Sandra Krchnak; m. Grace Crump, Sept. 5, 1964. BS in Edn., U. Ill., 1939, BS in Arch., 1940; MS in Arch., Columbia U., 1942; PhD, NYU, 1954. Tchr. Champaign (Ill.) H.S., 1941; tchr. arch. Kans. State Coll., Manhattan, 1942-47, Rice U., Houston, 1947-62; head dept. art Austin Coll., Sherman, Tex., 1962-66; prof. art U. Ga., Athens, 1966-79, emeritus prof. art, 1979—; draftsman, illlustrator U.S. Naval Ordnance Lab., Washington, 1943-44. Author: Early Kansas Churches, 1949, Origins of Functionalist Theory, 1957, Vistas and Mazes, 1997; contbr. articles to profl. jours. Recipient Ga. Poet of Yr. award Nat. League Am. Pen Women, 1997. Mem. AIA, Ga. Poetry Soc., Author's Club Athens, Pi Delta Phi, Zeta Zeta. Avocations: poetry, gardening, travel. Home: 220 Meadowview Rd Athens GA 30606-4226 Office: Lamar Dodd Sch Art U Ga Athens GA 30602

D'GABRIEL, CARLOS LEONARDO, retired travel executive; b. Havana, Cuba, Mar. 10, 1930; came to U.S., 1955; s. Zeidel and Hana (Schneider) D'G.; m. Judith Lobel, June 24, 1950 (div. 1971); children: Alexander P., Michelle E.; m. Prudence Saig, Dec. 4, 1971. Grad., Ga. Mil. Acad., 1944. Mgr. Shipairland Travel, Havana, 1945-50; corp. exec. Skycoach Internat. Airline, N.Y.C., 1950-55; mgr. Pan Am. World Airways, N.Y.C., 1955-62; v.p. Cophresi Travel Bur. Corp., N.Y.C., 1962-68; pres. Carber Travel Bur. Inc., N.Y.C., 1968-70, Superior Travel Bur., Inc., Miami Beach, Fla., 1970-95; regional v.p. Fla. Superior Travel, Castle Travel Group Co., Miami Beach, 1995-97. Recipient Shalom award Israel Ministry of Tourism, 1977, Willy Prestergard Meml. award Travel Industry Assn. Fla., 1980, Great Am. Traditions award B'nai B'rith Found. of U.S., 1993. Mem. Am. Soc. Travel Agts. (v.p. 1982), Inst. Cert. Travel Counselors, Assn. Retail Travel Agts. (bd. dirs. 1969), Turnberry Isle Resort and Club, Skal Club Internat. Republican. Jewish. Avocations: travel, tennis, golf. E-mail: cldg@usa.net. Home: 3762 NE 167th St Miami FL 33160-3538

DHALIWAL, HERB, Canadian government official; b. Ottawa, Ont., Can., Dec. 12, 1952. BCommerce, U. B.C., 1971. Min. of nat. revenue Ho. of Commons, Ottawa, 1997—. Office: Ho of Commons, Rm 121 E Block, Ottawa, ON Canada K1A 0A6*

DHANIREDDY, RAMASUBBAREDDY, neonatologist, researcher; b. Gunthachiyyapadu, India, July 8, 1951; s. Pedda Eswarareddy and Veeramma (Kasa) D.; m. Brezeetha Peddireddy Dhanireddy, Dec. 15, 1972; children: Shireesha, Kiran Kumar. MB, BS, Kurnool Med. Coll., 1974. Clin. asst. prof. of Pediatrics Georgetown U. Med. Ctr., Washington, 1982-84, asst. prof. Pediatrics, 1984-91, dir. Term Newborn Nursery, 1987-92, co-dir. Neonatal Intensive Care Unit, 1992-94; adjunct scientist NIH, Bethesda, Md., 1984-99; med. dir. Neonatal Pulmonary Function Testing Lab. Georgetown U. Hosp., Washington, 1991-99, dir. Nursery Quality Improvement, 1992-99, dir. Neonatal Intensive Care Unit, 1994-99, assoc. prof. pediat., 1991-97, prof. pediat., 1998—, chief sect. neonatology, med. dir. neonatal ICU; dir. neonatal-perinatal medicine fellowship program La. State U. Med. Ctr., Shreveport. Contbr. articles to profl. jours. Regional v.p. Telugu Assn. N.Am., Chgo., 1989-91; D.C. Mayoral Com. to Promote Breast Feeding, D.C. Mayor's Office, Washington. Lt. col. USAFR, 1993-97, col., 1997—. Recipient Surfactant Clin. Studies grant Burroughs Wellcome Co., 1989-93, Meritorious Svc. medal USAF, 1993, 98. Fellow Am.Acad. Pediatrics, Am. Coll. Nutrition; mem. Am. Fedn. for Clin. Rsch., Southern Soc. Pediatric Rsch., Soc. Pediatric Rsch. Democrat. Hindu. Avocations: travel, reading. Office: La State U Med Ctr Dept Pediats 1501 Kings Hwy Shreveport LA 71130

DHARA, VENKATA RAMANA, physician, educator; b. Gudivada, India, Nov. 14, 1953; came to U.S., 1985; s. Venkateswarlu and Sarojini Devi D.; m. Rosaline James Dodda, Feb. 16, 1979; children: Rahul, Vishal. MBBS, Pune (India) U., 1976; MD, Armed Forces Med. Coll., 1976; MPH, U. Medicine Dentistry N.J., 1987. Diplomate Am. Bd. Preventive Medicine. Intern Sion Hosp., Bombay, India, 1976-77; resident Robert Wood Johnson Med. Sch., Piscataway, N.J., 1985-87; med. dir. People's Clinic, Hyderabad, India, 1979-85; fellow in occupl. medicine Robert Wood Johnson Med. Sch., Piscataway, N.J., 1985-89; fellow Environ./Occpl. Health Scis. Inst., Piscataway, 1987-89; cons. Envirotech Cons., New Delhi, 1990-92; med. officer Agy. Toxic Substances Disease Registry, Atlanta, 1992-96; dir. occupl. medicine Choice Care, Atlanta, 1997—; clin. asst. prof. Morehouse Sch. Medicine, Atlanta, 1998—; cons. World Environment Ctr., N.Y.C., 1992-96, Internat. Labor Office, Geneva, 1992—; mem. Internat. Med. Commn. Bhopal, Toronto, Can., 1994—. *With over 20 years experience in the field of occupational and environmental medicine, Dr. Dhara practices in Atlanta and teaches at the Morehouse School of Medicine. He is involved in researching the health effects of the world's worst industrial disaster, which occurred in 1984 at the Union Carbide Plant in Bhopal, India. As a member of the International Medical Commission on Bhopal, Dhara was instrumental in designing and conducting the first long-term population studies on the disaster. Information from these studies led to an increased awareness of the toxicity of the disaster and resulted in improvments on health planning and treatment for the gas victims.* Contbr. articles to profl. jours. Active Forum Protection Environment, Hyderabad, 1982-85. Recipient Disting. Svc. award Meridian Med. Group, 1997; grantee Nat. Inst. Environ. Health Scis., 1998—. Mem. Am. Coll. Occpl. Environ. Medicine. Avocations: writing, reading, snorkeling. E-mail:rdhara@aol.com. Office: Choice Care 791 Oak St Hapeville GA 30354

D'HARNONCOURT, ANNE, museum director, executive; m. Joseph J. Rishel, June 19, 1971. B.A., Radcliffe Coll., 1965; M.A. with distinction, Courtauld Inst. Art, U. London, 1967. Curatorial asst. Phila. Mus. Art, 1967-69; asst. curator 20th Century art Art Inst. Chgo., 1969-71; curator 20th Century art Phila. Mus. Art, 1971-82, the George D. Widener dir., 1982—; bd. regents Smithsonian Instn. Organizer: (with McShine) exhbn. Marcel Duchamp, 1973-74, (with others) Philadelphia: Three Centuries of American Art, 1976, Eight Artists, 1978, (with Percy) Violet Oakley, 1979, Futurism and the International Avant-Garde, 1980, (with Sims) John Cage: Scores and Prints, 1982; author: (with Walter Hopps) Etant Donnes. Reflections on a New Work by Marcel Duchamp, 1969, The Cubist Cockatoo: Preliminary Exploration of Joseph Cornell's Hommages to Juan Gris, 1978, John Cage: Paying Attention, 1993, also prefaces for various books. Mem. vis. com. J. Paul Getty Mus., Malibu, Calif.; bd. dirs. Henry Luce Found., Inc., N.Y.C.; trustee Fairmount Park Art Assn. Phila.; mem. adv. com. Stuart Found., La Jolla, Calif., The Fabric Workshop, Phila.; mem. Mayor's Cultural Adv. Coun., Phila.; mem. Pa. Coun. on the Arts, Harrisburg. Fellow Am. Acad. Arts and Scis.; mem. Am. Philos. Soc., Assn. Art Mus. Dirs. Office: Phila Mus Art Benjamin Franklin Pkwy PO Box 7646 Philadelphia PA 19101-7646

D'HEURLE, FRANÇOIS MAX, research scientist, engineering educator; b. Paris, Nov. 23, 1925; came to U.S., 1946; s. Albert Emile and Odette (Valentini) d'H.; m. Adma Jeha, May 6, 1950; children: Amal, David, Alain. BSc Arts et Metiers, U. Paris, 1946; MS, Mich. Tech. U., 1948; PhD, Ill. Inst. Tech., 1958; D honoris causa, Royal Inst. Tech., Stockholm, 1995. Rsch. asst. U. Chgo., 1948-55; scientist IBM, Yorktown Heights, N.Y., 1958—; prof. Royal Inst. Tech., Stockholm, 1985—. Contbr. approximately 200 articles to profl. jours.; holder 10 patents. Recipient award Am. Inst. Physics, 1991, Theory to Practice Prize Minerals, Metals and Materials Soc., 1998. Fellow IEEE (Cledo-Brunetti award 1989); Am. Vacuum Soc. (Gaede-Langmuir award 1990); mem. Minerals, Metals and Materials Soc., Materials Rsch. Soc. Home: Spring Valley Rd Ossining NY 10562 Office: IBM Rsch PO Box 218 Yorktown Heights NY 10598-0218

DHILLON, AVTAR SINGH, psychiatrist; b. Sur Singh, Punjab, India, Aug. 10, 1952; came to U.S., 1980; s. Harbans Singh and Sukhwant D.; m. Inderbir Kaur Gill, Mar. 30, 1980; children: Sabrina, Megan. BSc, D.A.V. Coll., Amritsar, India, 1972; MD, Med. Coll., Amritsar, India, 1977. Diplomate Am. Bd. Psychiatry and Neurology, Am. Bd. Addiction Psychiatry. Intern Shri Guru Tegh Bahadur Hosp., Amritsar, India, 1977-78; resident Ea. State Hosp., Williamsburg, Va., 1982-85; psychiatrist Ea. State Hosp., Williamsburg, 1985-89, med. dir. acute psychiatry, 1989-99; med. dir. Colonial Svcs. Bd., Williamsburg, 1999—; pres. Ea. State Med. Staff, 1994-99. Treas. Guru Nanak Found. of Tidewater, Va. Beach, 1996. Mem. APA, Am. Soc. Addiction Medicine (cert.), Am. Soc. Clin. Pharmacology (cert.). Office: Colonial Svcs Bd 1657 Merrimac Trail Williamsburg VA 23185

DHIR, KRISHNA SWAROOP, business administration educator; b. Calcutta; s. Hari Das and Sushila Devi (Kochhar) D.; m. Shailaja Nair, July 3, 1983; children: Devika Dhir, Radhika Dhir. BTech, Indian Inst. of Tech., Bombay, 1966; MS, Mich. State U., 1967; MBA, U. Hawaii, 1968; PhD, U. Colo., 1975. Lectr. in bus. analysis U. Hawaii, Honolulu, 1967-69; devel. engr. Borg-Warner Corp., Parkersburg, W.Va., 1969-72; head dept. of bus. and industry W.Va. U., Parkersburg, 1969-72; asst. prof. mgmt. Clarkson U., Potsdam, N.Y., 1975-76; advisor Pharm. Divsn. Ciba-Geigy AG, Basle, Switzerland, 1976-82; assoc., prof. mgmt. sci. U. Colo., Boulder, 1979-82; v.p. strategic planning BioStar Med. Products, Inc., Boulder, 1984-86; dir. MIM degree program U. Denver, 1986-87; prof. health svcs. adminstrn. Med. U. S.C., Charleston, 1987-91; head, prof. dept. of bus. adminstrn. The Citadel, Charleston, 1987-91; dir., SBA prof. Sch. Bus. Adminstrn. Pa. State U., Harrisburg, 1991-96, prof. bus. adminstrn., 1991—; vis. prof. mgmt. and stats., U. Bombay, 1985, Swinburne U. of Technology, Melbourne, Australia, 1997; track chmn. Western Decision Scis. Inst., Monterey, Calif., 1988-89, Maui, Hawaii, 1993-94, 99—, San Francisco, 1994-95, The Big Island, Hawaii, 1996-97, Reno, Nev., 1997-98, Las Vegas, 1997-98, Athens, Greece, 1998-99, Nat. Decision Scis. Inst., Las Vegas, 1997-98, Internat. Decision Sci. Inst., Sydney, Australia, 1996-97, Athens, Greece, 1998-99; mem. adv. bd. Info. Resources Mgmt. Assn., 1988-93, others. Contbr. articles to profl. jours. Sen. Assn. of Students of U. of Colo., Boulder, 1973-74; pres. Internat. Club, Carnegie-Mellon U., Pitts., 1969. Lt. col. S.C. Militia, 1987-91. Grantee AMP, Inc., Harrisburg, Pa., 1992, 96, Ciba-Geigy AG, Basle, 1979-82; recipient 1st prize in radio-journalism, Art of Peace Competition, 1983, Merit Scholarship U.P. Bd. Edn., Allahabad, India, 1959, Gold medal St. John's Ambulance Assn., India, 1956, Best Paper award Western Decision Scis. Inst., 1994, Achievement award, 1993; Rama Watumull scholar, Honolulu, 1969. Mem. ASQC (bd. dirs. Mid-Ohio Valley chpt. 1972-73, edn. chmn. 1972-73), Decision Scis. Inst. (outstanding achievement award 1993 best theoretical/empirical rsch. paper). Avocations: photography, travel, camping. Office: Pa State Univ Middletown PA 17011

DHIR, VIJAY K., mechanical engineering educator; b. Giddarbaha, Panjab, India, Apr. 14, 1943; came to U.S., 1969; s. Harnand Lal and Parsinni Devi (Sofat) D.; m. Komal Lata Khanna, Aug. 31, 1973; children: Vinita, Vashita. BScME, Punjab Engrng. Coll., India, 1965; MTechME, Indian Inst. Tech., 1969; PhD in Mech. Engrng., U. Ky., 1972. Asst. devel. engr. Jyoti Pumps, Ltd., Baroda, India, 1968-69; postgrad. engr. Engrng. Rsch. Ctr. Tata Engrng. & Locomotive Co., Poona, India, 1969; rsch. asst. U. Ky., Lexington, 1969-72, rsch. assoc., 1972-74; asst. prof. chem., nuclear & thermal engrng. dept. UCLA, 1974-78, assoc. prof., 1978-82, prof. mech., aerospace & nuclear engrng. dept., 1982—, vice chmn. mech., aerospace & nuclear engrng. dept., 1988-91, chmn. dept., 1994—; cons. Nuclear Regulatory Commn., Seabulk Corp., Ft. Lauderdale, Fla., Argonne (Ill.) Nat. Lab., Pickard, Lowe & Garrick, Inc., Irvine, Calif., Rockwell Internat., Canoga Park, Calif., GE Corp., San Jose, Calif., Battelle N.W. Lab., Richland, Wash., Phys. Rsch., Inc., Torrance, Calif., Nat. Bur. Stds., Gaithersburg, Md., Los Alamos (N.Mex.) Nat. Lab., Sci. Applications Inc., El Segundo, Calif., Brookhaven Nat. Lab., Upton, N.Y.; chmn. numerous conf. sessions. Contbr. over 100 articles to profl. jours., over 100 papers to procs./conf. & symposia records; assoc. editor Applied Mechs. Rev., 1985-88, Jour. Heat Transfer, Transactions ASME, 1993-96, ASME Symposium Vol., 1978; referee numerous jours. Fellow ASME (Heat Transfer Meml. Award Sci. Category 1992), Am. Nuclear Soc. Office: Sch of Engrng & Applied Sc U Calif 46-147 K Engineering IV Los Angeles CA 90024

DHONDT, STEVEN THOMAS, marketing consultant; b. Xenia, Ohio, Aug. 4, 1944; s. Maurice Bernard and Madeline (Pierson) D.; m. Elizabeth Ann Emrick, June 11, 1966 (div. June 1972); 1 child, Jennifer Elizabeth; m. Patty Ruth Bayley, Jan. 9, 1982. BA, Adrian Coll., 1966; MA, Utah State U., 1967; Phd, Bowling Green State U., 1968, SUNY, Buffalo, 1971. Instr. English SUNY, Buffalo, 1968-74; assoc. dean of faculty SUNY, 1969-74; assoc. acad. dean Salem State Coll., Salem, Mass., 1974-77; dir. publishing Am.-Scandinavian Found., N.Y.C., 1977-79; prin. Dhondt Enterprises, N.Y.C., 1978-81; mgr. corp. communications Merck & Co., Inc., Rahway, N.J., 1981-83; sr. v.p., asst. dir. creative resources Shearson Lehman Bros. Inc., N.Y.C., 1983-93; sr. cons. Nagdeman & Co., Inc., N.Y.C., 1993-95; ind. mktg. cons., 1994-96; dir. corp. and found. rels. L.I. U., Brookville, N.Y., 1996-99; dir. found. rels. NYU, N.Y.C., 1999—; trustee N.J. Coun. on Econ. Edn., Trenton, 1981-83, Borough of Manhattan Community Coll. Fund, Inc., N.Y.C., Poets House, N.Y.C.; cons. Bayley, Leighton & Ryan, Inc., N.Y.C., 1988—. Author: First Reading, 1972, London Bridge, 1998, Yellow Monkey, 1999; mng. editor Coll. English Assn., Buffalo, 1972-74. Democrat. Methodist. Avocations: tennis, snorkeling, traveling. Home: 175 W 93rd St Apt 14C New York NY 10025-9340

DHRYMES, PHOEBUS JAMES, economist, educator; b. Cyprus, Oct. 1, 1932; s. Demetrios and Kyriaki (Neophytou) Dhrymiotis; m. Beatrice Bell Fitch, Dec. 10, 1972; children: Phoebus James, Philip Andrew, Alexander Robert. B.A. with highest honors, U. Tex., 1957; Ph.D., MIT, 1961. Asst. prof. econs. Harvard U., 1962-64; assoc. prof. econs. U. Pa., 1964-67, prof., 1967-73; prof. econs. Columbia U., N.Y.C., 1973—; vis. prof. fin. Wharton Sch. U. Pa., 1984. Author: Econometrics: Statistical Foundations and Applications, 1971, 74, Distributed Lags: Problems of Estimation and Formulation, 1971, 81, Russian edit., 1982, Introductory Econometrics, 1978, Mathematics for Econometrics, 1978, 2d edit., 1984, Topics in Advanced Econometrics: Probability Foundations, 1989, Tropics in Advanced Econometrics: vol. II Linear and Non Linear Simultaneous Equations, 1994, Theoretical and Applied Econometrics: The Selected Papers of Phoebus J. Dhrymes, 1995, Time Series, Unit Roots and Cointegration, 1998; mng. editor, editor Internat. Econ. Rev., 1965-72; co-editor Jour. Econometrics, 1972-77, exec. coun., 1993—. Served with U.S. Army, 1952-54. Fellow Econometric Soc., Am. Statis. Assn.; mem. Am. Econ. Assn. Office: Columbia U Dept Econs New York NY 10027

DIAISO, ROBERT JOSEPH, civil engineer; b. Jersey City, N.J., Jan. 3, 1940; s. Dominick A. and Marie M. (Sarno) DiA.; m. Elaine Ricca, June 8, 1963; 1 child, Michael. BS, U.S. Naval Acad., 1962; MCE, NYU, 1964; M in Urban and Regional Planning, U. Pitts., 1971; PhD, 1971, 1972. Engr. Clarke, Hartman & Dunn, 1955-57, 69; project dir. Inst. Urban Policy Analysis, 1970-71; assoc. partner Dewberry, Nealon & Davis, Annapolis, Md., 1971-81; sr. assoc. Dewberry & Davis, Annapolis, 1981-82; prin. Dewsberry & Davis, 1983-84; pres. Property Improvement Collaborative, Inc., 1984-90, LandScope, 1985—; dir. LandTech Corp., 1985-88, mng. dir., 1988-94; CEO, FM Tech Corp., 1991-94; pres., CEO The Tech Group, 1993—; organizer, dir. Bay Nat. Bank; Land Tech. Corp., 1986—; bd. dirs. Scotts Seaboard Corp.; pres. Peacock Mgmt. Systems. Pres., Crofton Civic Assn., 1973, trustee emeritus, 1998; chmn. bd. trustees by 3 govs. Anne Arundel C.C., 1974-98, trustee emeritus, 1998; mem. County Zoning Adv. Task Force, 1983-84; mem. county coun. adv. com. on adequate facilities, 1977-78; bd. dirs. Anne Arundel Trade Coun.; chmn. Public Works Rev. Bd.; mem. Sewer Allocation Task Force; chmn. County Exec. Transition Task Force, 1982; mem. County Exec. Transition Team, 1991, County Exec. USN David Taylor Naval Facility Reuse Com., 1996; mem. Gov's. com. on Affordable Housing, 1976-78; mem. adv. bd. Patuxent Water Reclamation Plant; mem. adv. com. Crofton on Municipal Incorp.; bldg. com. St. Elizabeth Ann Seton Ch. Served with USAF, 1962-69. Named Bus. Leader of Yr., Anne Arundel Trade Coun., 1982; HEW fellow, 1970-72. Mem. ASCE, Am. Planning Assn., Am. Inst. Certified Planners, Nat. Soc. Profl. Engrs., Assn. County Engrs. Roman Catholic. Office: 147 Old Solomons Island Rd Annapolis MD 21401-0903

DIAKIWSKY, NICHOLAS METRO, account executive; b. Ambridge, Pa., June 24, 1963; s. John and Frances (Weber) D. BSBA, Robert Morris Coll., Coraopolis, Pa., 1986; MBA, Robert Morris Coll., 1995. Asst. to cameraman Ind. News Svc., Ambridge, 1984-86; prodn. asst. Sta. KDKA-TV, Pitts., 1986-87; account exec. WRS Motion Picture and Video Lab., Pitts., 1986-96; program mgr. PHH Corp., Pitts., 1996-98; acct. mgr. Cendant Mobility, 1998—; bd. dirs. Urban Renewal Corp., 1998—; freelance cameraman, 1988—. Mem. Ukrainian Nat. Assn. (trustee 1990-92, fin. sec. 1992—, v.p. Pitts. dist. 1993, bd. advisors 1994—), Beaver County Hockey Club (team capt.), Alpha Tau Sigma. Byzantine Catholic. Avocations: running, ice hockey, hunting. Home: 2065 Ridge Road Ext Ambridge PA 15003-1037

DIAL, ELEANORE MAXWELL, foreign language educator; b. Norwich, Conn., Feb. 21, 1929; d. Joseph Walter and Irene (Beetham) Maxwell; *Dr. Dial's paternal great-great grandfather, Nicholas Clare, came from Berlin to Ulster County, New York in the 1830's. His son, Nicolas, became a shipbuilder and built a screw steamer, which was a dispatch ship for U.S. Grant during the Civil War. Paternal great grandfather, Joseph Beetham, a weaver from Yorkshire, England, sailed to Capetown where he married Ellen Cotton. Her father guarded Napoleon on St. Helena. Dr. Dial's grandfather, John E. Beetham (1859-1923) and his nine siblings, were born in England, Capetown and Tristan da Cunha. Some were whalermen when young, but they became farmers in New London County, Connecticut where they all settled* BA, U. Bridgeport (Conn.), 1951; MA in Spanish, Mexico City Coll., 1955; PhD, U. Mo., 1968; m. John E. Dial, Aug. 27, 1959. Mem. faculty U. Wisc.-Milw., 1968-75, Ind. State U., Terre Haute, 1975-78, Bowling Green (Ohio) State U., 1978-79; asst. prof. fgn. langs. and lits. Iowa State U., Ames, 1979-85, assoc. prof. 1985-96, emerita assoc. prof., 1996—; cons. pub. co.; participant workshops; del. 1st World Congress Women Journalists and Writers, Mex., 1975, also mem. edn. commn. NDEA grantee, 1967; Center Latin Am. grantee, 1972; Nat. Endowment Humanities summer seminar UCLA, 1981, U. Calif.-Santa Barbara, 1984; active Gov's. Commn. on Fgn. Langs. and Internat. Studies, 1988-95. Mem. Am. Assn. Tchrs. Spanish and Portuguese, Midwest MLA, MLA, N. Central Council Latin Americanists, Midwest Assn. Latin Am. Studies, Clermont County Geneal. Soc., Ohio Geneal. Soc., Story County (Iowa) Geneal. Soc., Caribbean Studies Assn., Phi Beta Delta, Phi Sigma Iota, Sigma Delta Pi. Contbr. articles, anthologies and revs. to scholarly jours. Home: 190 North St Batavia OH 45103-2911 Office: Iowa State U Ames IA 50011

DIAL, JOHN ELBERT, foreign language educator; b. Batavia, Ohio, Dec. 9, 1927; s. James Dial and Margaret (Cameron) Long; m. Eleanore Marjorie Maxwell, Aug. 27, 1959. *Shadrach Dial came to Ohio from North Carolina in 1810. His grandson, John Fielding Dial, served in the Civil War. Other ancestors served in the Revolutionary War, War of 1812 and Mexican War. John Dial purchased a house in Batavia, Ohio in 1876. His only son, James, was born there. A graduate of Ohio Military Institute, James also studied at Cincinnati College of Music. An accomplished pianist, he played drums in several bands and composed music under the name Robert Reynolds. He owned several small businesses, including a pre-World War I movie theatre. His children are: Ruth, Robert, Richard, and John Elbert.* BS in Edn., U. Cin., 1950; MA in Spanish, Mexico City Coll., 1955; PhD in Spanish, U. Mo.-Columbia, 1966. Instr. Marquette U., Milw., 1960-66, asst. prof., 1966-77, assoc. prof., 1977-92; ret., 1992; mem. adv. com. Ctr. Latin Am., U. Wis., Milw., 1983-85; lectr. in field. *Since retiring from Marquette University, John has continued research projects with his wife, Eleanore Maxwell Dial. John and Eleanore have had the pleasure of working together on numerous publishing projects. They have also lectured and read papers all over the United States in Vermont, Hawaii, Michigan, and Florida, and in many foreign countries such as Spain, Czechoslovakia, Egypt, Senegal, Canada, and Mexico. Their research trips have taken them to such places as Argentina, Germany, Italy, and Cuba. They are currently preparing an edition of memoirs of the Mexican War.* Co-author: Representative Work of Manuel Bennett, 1964, Romanzas de las Rejas, 1978, Women Writers of Spain, 1986; contbr. articles to profl. jours.; dir. numerous Spanish and Latin Am. plays. With U.S. Army, 1950-52. Recipient Cert. Honor, Inst. Hispánico, 1957. Mem. Am. Assn. Tchrs. Spanish and Portuguese, N. Ctrl. Coun. Latin Americanists, Caribbean Studies Assn., First Families of Clermont County, First Families of Ohio Descendants of Civil War, Batavia Alumni Assn. (v.p. 1996-97, pres. 1997-98), Phi Sigma Iota, Sigma Delta Pi (mem. Order of Discoverers 1992). Home: 190 North St Batavia OH 45103-2911

DIAL, MARSHALL REECE, library director; b. Tiptonville, Tenn., Apr. 17, 1925; s. William Wright and Addie Elizabeth Nobles Dial; m. Mary Lynn Marr, Sept. 23, 1960; children: Thomas Wayne, Dorothy Elizabeth Dial Dodson. BA, Goddard Coll., 1971; postgrad., S.E. Mo. State U., 1975. Dir. county libr. system New Madrid County, Portageville, Mo., 1955-96; cons. New Madrid County Libr., 1996-97. Author: Bootheel Swamp Struggle, 1961; editor: A Soldiers Life, 1963; contbr. articles to profl. jours. With U.S. Army, 1951-53. Democrat. Episcopalian. Avocations: coin collecting, civil war research, antiques. Home: 700 East Sixth St Portageville MO 63873

DIAMA, BENJAMIN, retired educator, artist, composer, writer; b. Hilo, Hawaii, Sept. 23, 1933; s. Agapito and Catalina (Buscas) D. *Benjamin Diama's parents were early immigrants from Cebu in The Philippines. In 1922, they sailed on the Tenya Maru to Hawaii seeking a better livelihood and employment in the Sugar Plantation of Hawaii. In addition to the strong faith instilled in them by their Catholic-Christian heritage and education, their American freedom and opportunities also played a significant role in their ability to establish and operate several successful businesses on Mamo Street in downtown Hilo, Hawaii. However, the 1960 Tidal Wave destroyed businesses; but fortunately, they could operate another Billiard Business before they retired, on Mamo Street.* BFA, Sch. Art Inst. Chgo., 1956. Cert. tchr., Hawaii. Tchr. art, basketball coach Waimea (Kauai, Hawaii) High Sch., 1963-67; tchr. music and art Campbell High Sch., Honolulu, 1967-68; tchr. math. and art Waipahu High Sch., Honolulu, 1968-69; tchr. art and music Palisades Elem. Sch., Honolulu, 1969-70; tchr. typing, history, art and music Honokaa (Hawaii) High Sch., 1970-73; tchr. music Kealakehe Sch., Kailua, 1973-74; ret., 1974. Author, writer, composer: Hawaii, 1983; author: Poems of Faith, 1983-88, School One vs. School Two On The Same School Campus, 1983, The Calendar-Clock Theory of the Universe with Faith -- Above and Beyond, 1984-90, Phonetic Sound-Musical Theory, 1990; contbr. author to book: Benjamin Diama -- The Calendar Clock Theory of the Universe, 1991, 92; producer, composer (Cassette) Hawaii I Love You, 1986; inventor universal clock, 1984, double floater boat, 1985. Recipient Achievement award Waimea Dept. Edn., 1964-67, Purchase award State Found. Arts on Culture and the Arts, 1984, State Found. Arts and Culture Acquisition Painting Art award State of Hawaii Govt. Art Collection. Mem. NEA, Hawaii Tchrs. Assn., Hawaii Edn. Assn., AAAS, Nat. Geog. Soc., Smithsonian Assocs., ASCAP, N.Y. Acad. Scis., Nat. Libr. Poetry (assoc.), Internat. Soc. Poets, Am. Geophysical Union. Mem. Salvation Army. Avocations: singing, writing science, coaching basketball. Home: PO Box 2997 Kailua Kona HI 96745-2997

DIAMANT, JOEL CHARLES, internist; b. N.Y.C., Oct. 11, 1963; s. Bernard and Alice Susan (Ruskin) D.; m. Caroline Ruth Taliaferro, Oct. 9, 1994. AB, U. Calif., Berkeley, 1985; MD with honors, U. Ill., 1990. Diplomate Am. Bd. Internal Medicine. Intern Scripps Clinic/Green Hosp., 1990-91; resident in internal medicine Scripps Clinic, La Jolla, Calif., 1991-93, chief resident in internal medicine, 1993-94, staff physician, 1994—; assoc. dir. internal medicine residency Scripps Clinic/Green Hosp., 1996-98, dir. internal medicine residency, 1998—. James scholar U. Ill. Coll. Medicine, 1990. Office: Scripps Clinic 10666 N Torrey Pines Rd La Jolla CA 92037-1092

DIAMOND, ABEL JOSEPH, architect; b. S.Africa, Nov. 8, 1932; naturalized, 1969; s. Jacob and Rachel (Werner) D.; m. Gillian Mary Huggins, Aug. 11, 1959; children: Andrew Michael, Alison Suzanne Katherine. BArch with distinction, U. Capetown, 1956; MA, U. Oxford, 1958; MArch, U. Pa., 1962; DEng honoris causa, Tech. U. of N.S., 1995. Certificate Nat. Registration Bds. U.S.A. Partner Diamond & Hallen, S.Africa, 1959-61; architect office of Louis Kahn, Phila., 1962-64; pvt. practice architecture Toronto, Ont., Can., 1965—; prin. A.J. Diamond and Ptnrs. (Architects and Planners), Toronto, 1975—; Graham prof. architecture U. Pa., 1996—; asst. prof. U. Pa., 1962-64; asso. prof. U. Toronto, 1964-69; adj. prof. York U., 1969-72; bd. dirs. Ontario Pl. Editl. bd.: Canadian Forum, 1976-79; archtl. works include York Sq., Toronto, Ont. Med. Assn. Hdqrs., Student Union Housing, U. Alta, Citadel Theatre, Edmonton, Innis coll. U. Toronto, Hydro Block Housing, Toronto, Arvida Med. Clinic for Alcan, Village Terraces Housing, Toronto Alcan Exec. Offices, Toronto, Montreal, Cleve., Cen. YMCA, Berkeley Castle, Burns Bldg., Calgary, nat. Ballet Sch. Theatre, Curtiss Hall, Arcadia Housing, Earth Scis. Rsch. Ctr., York U. Student Ctr., City Hall, Jerusalem, Richmond Hill Cen. Libr.; Baycrest Ctr. for Cognitive Disorders; St. Michaels Hosp.; Regent Park Community Health Ctr.; Riverdale Community Health Ctr.; Foreign Ministry, Jerusalem; Lundin House, Mustique; Garland House, Toronto; exhbn. of drawings and paintings, Toronto, 1996. Adv. bd. Taragon Theatre, 1978-79; registration bd. Ont. Assn. Architects, 1976-79; chmn. vis. com. Schs. of Architecture, Ont.; chmn. Nat. Capital Commn. Design Adv. Com., Ottawa, 1984-86; mem. Ont. Human Rights Commn., 1986-89; bd. dirs. Music Toronto, Ont. Place, 1996—; bd. govs. Mt. Sinai Hosp., Toronto, 1987—; mem. adv. bd. Sch. Architecture U. of Toronto, 1987—; Task Force Greater Toronto Area, 1995. Decorated officer Order of Can., officer Order of Ont., 1997; recipient Oxford Rugby Blue, Gov. Gen.'s design award, 1986, Credit Foncier award, 1986, Olympic Arts Festival Gold medal, 1988, Toronto Arts award, 1989, 5 Gov. Gen.'s awards Richmond Hill Cen. Libr. and Earth Scis. Ctr., York U. Student Centre, U. Toronto, 1976-97. Fellow Am. Inst. Archs. (hon.), Royal Archtl. Inst. Can., AIA (hon.), Royal Inst. Brit. Architects (assoc.); mem. Can. Inst. Planners, Am. Inst. of Planners, Royal Can. Acad. Arts. Clubs: Vincents (Oxford); University Club Toronto. Office: 2 Berkeley St Ste 600, Toronto, ON Canada M5A 2W3

DIAMOND, BERNARD ROBIN, lawyer; b. Bronx, N.Y., July 3, 1944; m. Elizabeth Heimbuch, Oct. 20, 1976; children: Jessica, Carey, Erin. BA, Rutgers U., 1966; JD, Bklyn. Law Sch., 1972. Bar: N.Y. 1973, U.S. Dist. Ct. (so. and ea. dists.) N.Y. 1973, U.S. Ct. Appeals (2d cir.) 1974. Gen. counsel The Trump Orgn., N.Y.C., 1995—. Mem. Assn. of the Bar of the City of N.Y. Office: Trump Orgn 725 5th Ave Fl 26 New York NY 10022-2520

DIAMOND, DANIEL LLOYD, surgeon. MD, Tulane U., 1970. Diplomate Am. Bd. Surgery (dir. 1995—). Intern U. Pitts. Health Ctr. Hosps., 1970-71, resident in surgery, 1971-76; dir. gen. surgery, divsn. surgery Allegheny Genl. Hosp., Pitts., 1976-95; assoc. prof. surgery Med. Coll. Pa., Pitts., 1976-95; chmn., prof. dept. surgery U. Tenn. Med. Ctr., Knoxville, 1995-98; Bd. dirs. Am. Bd. Surgery, 1994—. Mem. ACS (com. on trauma),

Assn. Program Dirs. (bd. dirs. 1994—). Office: 382 W Chestnut Ste 106 Washington PA 15301

DIAMOND, DAVID HOWARD, lawyer; b. N.Y.C., June 24, 1945; s. Philip and Betty (Resnikoff) D.; m. Barbara R. Jacobs, Sep. 6, 1969; children: John, Andrew, Jill. BA, SUNY, Binghamton, 1967; JD, Georgetown U., Washington, D.C., 1970. Bar: Va. 1970, D.C. 1971, N.J. 1972, N.Y. 1973, U.S. Supreme Ct. 1982, U.S. Dist. Ct. Asst. gen. counsel Nat. Treas. Employees Union, Washington, D.C., 1970-71; trial atty. Nat. Labor Relations Bd., Newark, N.J., 1971-73; assoc. Putney, Twombly, Hall & Hirson, N.Y.C., 1973-76; ptnr. Guggenheimer & Untermeyer, N.Y.C., 1976-86, Summit, Rovins & Felderman, N.Y.C., 1986-89, Patterson, Belknap, Webb & Tyler, N.Y.C., 1989-91, Proskauer, Rose LLP, N.Y.C., 1991—. Contbg. editor: Developing Labor Law, 1975-82. Pres., dir. Birchwood Civic Assn., Jericho, N.Y., 1985—; trustee Jericho Libr. Bd., 1994—. Mem. ABA (sect. labor and employment law, com. fed. labor standards), N.Y. State Bar Assn. (com. on individual and employee rights). Avocations: biking, tennis, whitewater rafting. Home: 18 Briar Ln Jericho NY 11753-2212 Office: Proskauer Rose LLP 1585 Broadway New York NY 10036-8200

DIAMOND, DAVID LEO, composer; b. Rochester, N.Y., July 9, 1915; s. Osias and Anna (Schildhaus) D. Student, Cleve. Inst. Music, 1927-29, Eastman Sch. Music, U. Rochester, 1930-34, Am. Conservatory, Fontainebleau, France, summers 1937, 38, New Music and Dalcroze Inst., N.Y. C., 1934-36; pvt. studies with Roger Sessions, N.Y.C.; pvt. studies with Nadia Boulanger, Paris; pvt. studies with Hermann Scherchen,, Switzerland. Tchr. composition Met. Music Sch., N.Y.C., 1950; lectr. on Am. music Seminar in Am. Studies Schloss Leopoldskron, Salzburg, Austria, 1949; Fulbright prof. U. Rome, 1951-52; Slee prof. music U. Buffalo, 1961, 63; prof., chmn. dept. composition Manhattan Sch. Music, N.Y.C., 1965-67; composer-in-residence Am. Acad. in Rome, 1971-72, Juilliard Sch. Music, 1973-97; Master Class Schola Cantorum, Paris, 1996, 97; vis. prof. U. Colo., Boulder, 1970, U. Denver, 1983, other univs.; composer-in-residence N.Y. Chamber Symphony, 1991—; hon. composer-in-residence Seattle Symphony, 1996. Contbr. to Jour. Modern Music, Music Quar., N.Y. Herald Tribune Decision; compositions include 12 symphonies, concertos for violin, cello, piano and flute, 11 string quartets, various chamber music, 52 preludes and fugues for piano, miscellaneous choral music and songs, solo symphony for organ, scores for motion pictures, and other forms of instrumental music; composer music for Columbia albums Fourth String Quartet, Romeo and Juliet, 4th Symphony (performed by Bernstein, N.Y. Philharm. Orch.) Quartet, Nonet, String Number 9, CRI Records, Two Sonatas for violin and piano, New World CD, Symphonies 1, 2, 3, 4, 8 and Concerto for small orch., Delos Records, Symphonies No. 5, New World Records, original score for Margaret Webster prodn. of The Tempest, 1944-45, incidental music for Cheryl Crawford prodn. of The Rose Tattoo, 1951, music for This Sacred Ground (Gettysburg Address, Delos Records, 1962; composer ballets TOM Delos Records, 1936, The Dream of Audubon, 1941, Formal Dance for Martha Graham; commd. works include: (opera) The Noblest Game, Nat. Opera Inst., 1975, Mirandolina, The Golden Slippers, Secular Cantata, N.Y. State Arts Coun.; cantata A Song for Hope, Elie Wiesel; Second Sonata for violin and piano, Libr. Congress McKim Fund; Second Sonata for cello and piano, Sonata for flute and piano, Trio for violin, clarinet, and piano for Verdehr Trio, Libr. Congress; Kaddish for cello and orch., Yo-Yo Ma; Symphony for organ Leonard Raver; Ode for orch., Tokyo Bunkamura; Fantasy on Old 100th for organ and brass quintet, Princeton U.; Concerto for string quartet and orch., Juilliard Sch.; works performed by major orchs. and other well known music orgns., throughout U.S. and abroad. Elfrida Whiteman scholar, 1935; recipient numerous major awards and prizes, 1935—, including: Prix de Rome, Paderewski award, Juilliard Pub. award, Stravinsky award ASCAP, Naumberg Rec. award for Nonet and String Quartet No. 9, William Schuman Lifetime Achievement award 1986, Gold Medal Am. Acad. Arts and Letters, 1991, Edward MacDowell Gold medal, 1991, Presdl. Medal of Honor, 1995; NEA grantee, Rockefeller Found. grantee, 1983; Guggenheim fellow, 1938, 42, 58. Mem. AAAL, Am. Acad. (Gold medal for eminence 1991, Nat. medal of Arts 1995). Address: 249 Edgerton St Rochester NY 14607-3315

DIAMOND, EUGENE CHRISTOPHER, lawyer, hospital administrator; b. Oceanside, Calif., Oct. 19, 1952; s. Eugene Francis and Rosemary (Wright) D.; m. Mary Theresa O'Donnell, Jan. 20, 1984; children: Eugene John, Kevin Seamus, Hannah Rosemary, Seamus Michael, Maeve Therese. BA, U. Notre Dame, 1974; MHA, St. Louis U., 1978, JD, 1979. Bar: Ill. 1979. Staff atty. AUL Legal Def. Fund, Chgo., 1979-80; adminstrv. asst. Holy Cross Hosp., Chgo., 1980-81, asst. adminstr., 1981-82, v.p., 1982-83, counsel to adminstr., 1980—, exec. v.p., 1983-91; exec. v.p., COO St. Margaret Mercy Healthcare Ctrs., Hammond, Ind., 1991-93, pres. CEO, 1993; cons. Birthright of Chgo., 1979—, mem. benefit com., 1981—; bd. dirs. Hammond C. of C., 1993, North West Ind. Forum. Mem. Ill. State Bar Assn., Chgo. Bar Assn. Mgmt. Roman Catholic. Office: St Margaret Mercy Healthcare Ctrs 5454 Hohman Ave Hammond IN 46320-1999

DIAMOND, FRED I., electronic engineer; b. Bklyn., Dec. 13, 1925; s. Joseph and Celia (Just) D.; m. Edna R. Hutt, Sept. 2, 1956; children: Celia, Joel, Shari. S.B.E.E., MIT, 1950; M.E.E., Syracuse U., 1953, Ph.D., 1966. Electronic engr. Rome Air Devel. Center, Griffiss AFB, N.Y., 1950-51; sr. scientist Rome Air Devel. Center, 1961-70, chief plans, 1970-73, tech. dir. communications and control div., 1973-81, chief scientist, 1981-91; dep. dir Rome Lab., 1991-94; chmn. avionics panel NATO Adv. Group for Aerospace R & D, 1975-86; exec. chmn. communications subgroup Australian, Canadian, N.Z., U.K., U.S. Tech. Coordination Program; instr. dept. math. Utica Coll., 1957-59; lectr. dept. elec. engring. Syracuse U., 1959-61; mem. ednl. coun. MIT, 1968-92; bd. dirs. N.Y. State Photonics Devel. Corp. Contbr. articles to profl. jours. Bd. dirs. Rome Community Concert Assn., 1968-80, Cen. Assn. for Blind and Vision Impaired; trustee Jervis Pub. Libr., 1977-89, pres., 1980-83; mem. indsl. adv. com. U. Mass. Sch. Engring., Syracuse U. Sch. Engring.; mem. coun. SUNY Inst. Tech.; ad hoc visitor Accreditation Bd. for Engring. and Tech. With U.S. Army, 1944-46. Recipient Meritorious Civilian Svc. medal USAF, 1968, Exceptional Civilian Svc. award, 1978, 84, Outstanding Civilian Career Svc. award, 1994; 7 Outstanding Performance awards Sr. Exec. Svc., 1982-87, 89, 90, 92, 93, Presdl. rank award as disting. exec. Fellow IEEE (life), AAAS, AIAA (assoc.); mem. Acad. of Sr. Profls. of Eckerd Coll.

DIAMOND, G. WILLIAM, former secretary of state; b. West Gardiner, Maine, Feb. 19, 1945; s. Elsie (Fellows) Emery; m. Jane Estes; children: Karyn, Kris. BS, Gorham State Coll., 1968; MS, U. So. Maine, 1972. Tchr. Field-Allen Elem. Sch., Windham Center, Maine, 1968-72; prin. Manchester Sch., North Windham, Maine, 1973-76; tchr. Windham Jr./Sr. High Sch., 1976-84; owner, founder Suburban Security, Inc., Windham, 1980—, Profl. Security Tng., Windham, 1985-87, Bill Diamond Assocs., Windham, 1987—; supt. schs. Raymond (Maine) Sch. Dept., 1987-88; sec. state State of Maine, Augusta, 1989-96; supt. schs. Elan Sch., Poland, Maine, 1996—; pres. Bill Diamond Assocs. State rep. Maine Legislature, Augusta, 1976-82, state senator, 1982-86; gubernatorial candidate State of Maine Primary, 1986. Ford Found. fellow, 1972-73. Mem. Nat. Assn. Secs. State. Democrat. Lutheran. Home: 261 Windham Center Rd Windham ME 04062-4390*

DIAMOND, GUSTAVE, federal judge; b. Burgettstown, Pa., Jan. 29, 1928; s. George and Margaret (Solinsky) D.; m. Emma L. Scarton, Dec. 28, 1974; 1 dau., Margaret Ann; 1 stepdau., Joanne Yoney. A.B., Duke U., 1951; J.D., Duquesne U., 1956. Bar: Pa. bar 1958, U.S. Ct. Appeals bar 1962. Law clk. to judge U.S. Dist. Ct., Pitts., 1955-61; 1st asst. U.S. atty. Western Dist. Pa., 1961-62, U.S. atty., 1963-69; partner firm Cooper, Schwartz, Diamond & Reich, Pitts., 1969-75; formerly individual practice law Washington, Pa.; former solicitor Washington County, Pa.; judge U.S. Dist. Ct. Western Dist. Pa.; chief judge U.S. Dist. Ct. (we. dist.) Pa., 1992-94, sr. judge, 1994—; chmn. Jud. Conf. Com. on Defender Svcs. Mem. ABA, Fed. Bar Assn., Pa. Bar Assn., Allegheny County Bar Assn., Washington County Bar Assn. Office: US Dist Ct 821 US Courthouse 7th St Rm 2 Pittsburgh PA 15219

DIAMOND, HARRIS, corporate communications executive, lawyer; b. N.Y.C., Feb. 5, 1953; m. Amy Simon, Mar. 26, 1956. BA, Drew U., 1975; MBA, Fairleigh Dickinson U., 1978; JD, Bklyn. Law Sch., 1983. Bar: N.Y., 1984. Various mgmt. positions Prudential Ins. Co., Newark, 1975-80; confidential asst. to dist. atty. Office Kings County Dist. Atty., Bklyn., 1982-85; ptnr., chmn. mgmt. com. Sawyer Miller Group, N.Y.C., 1986-93; COO Robinson, Lerer, Sawyer & Miller, 1993-95; chmn. and CEO BSMG Worldwide, 1996—; dir. Bozell Jacobs Kenyon Eckert, 1996—; chmn. True North Diversified Cos., 1999—; polit. analyst for network and local TV; frequent speaker on crisis comm. for industry and co. forums. Mem. N.Y.C. Cmty. Bd., 1980-83; bd. visitors Drew U., Madison, N.J., 1991—. Mem. Rolling Hills Country Club (Wilton, Conn.; bd. dirs.). Office: BSMG Worldwide 640 5th Ave New York NY 10019-6102

DIAMOND, HARVEY JEROME, machinery manufacturing company executive; b. Charlotte, N.C., Dec. 7, 1928; s. Harry B. and Jeanette (Davis) D.; m. Betty L. Ball, May 22, 1953 (dec. Nov. 1988); children: Michael, Beth, David Abby; m. Miriam Letey, 1989. BS, U. N.C., 1952. Sales mgr. Dixie Neon Supply House, Charlotte, 1950-61; pres., gen. mgr., chmn. bd., CEO Plasti-Vac, Inc., Charlotte, 1961—; pres., gen. mgr. Diamond Supply, Inc., 1971-84, chmn. bd. dirs., 1984—; pres. Plastic Prodn., Inc., 1973—, PVI Internat. Corp., 1980—; mem. dist. export coun. Dept. Commerce, 1979-93; del. White House Conf. on small Bus., 1980; bd. dirs. Maccabi USA/Sports for Israel. Author: (manual) Introduction to Vacuum Forming, 1976; patentee inverted clamping frame system for vacuum forming machines, process of vacuum forming plastics with vertical oven. Chmn. Mecklenburg Dem. Party, 1974-75, treas., 1972-74; del. Dem. Nat. Conv., 1972; bd. advisors Pfeiffer Coll., Misenheimer, N.C., 1977-89; participant White House conf. on Small Bus., 1978, White House Conf. on Anti-Inflation Initiatives, 1978; bd. dirs. U.S. Com. for Sports in Israel, 1995—. Recipient award for Activity in U.S. Trade Mission to S.Am., Dept. Commerce, 1967, March of Dimes award, 1966, Excellence in Exporting award N.C. Trade Club, 1981. Mem. Soc. Plastics Engrs., Soc. Plastics Industries, So. States Sign Assn. (bd. dirs. 1983-87), Southeastern States Sign Assn. (bd. dirs. 1991), Nat. Electric Sign Assn., Metrolina World Trade Assn. (v.p. 1982-83), Metrolina World Trade Club (pres. 1983-84), N.C. World Trade Assn. (bd. dirs. 1983-86, gen. chmn. ann. conv. 1984), US Comm. Sports in Isreal (bd. dirs. 1996—), Masons, Shriners. Jewish. Home: 9400 White Hemlock Ln Charlotte NC 28270-4403 Office: PO Box 5543 Charlotte NC 28299-5543

DIAMOND, IRENE, foundation administrator; b. Pitts., May 7, 1910; d. Horace and Leah (Grekin) Levine; m. Aaron Diamond, 1942 (dec.); 1 child, Jean. Ed., Pitts. Pub. Schs.; LHD (hon.), City Coll., CUNY, 1989, The Juilliard Sch., 1992; LLD (hon.), Queens Coll., CUNY, 1990, New Sch. Social Rsch., N.Y.C., 1994, Rockefeller U., 1997. Asst. editor story div. Warner Bros., Hollywood, Calif., 1934-35, editor, 1937-40; supr. dept. lit. Leland Hayward, Hollywood, 1935-37; editor story and talent div. Samuel Goldwyn-MGM, Hollywood and N.Y.C., 1940-41; editor story div., head talent div. Hal Wallis-Paramount Pictures, Hollywood and N.Y.C., 1941-70; pres., bd. dirs. Aaron Diamond Found., Inc., N.Y.C., 1986-96, Irene Diamond Fund, N.Y.C., 1996—. Bd. dirs. Aaron Diamond AIDS Rsch. Ctr., 1989—. Recipient Pres.'s medal Bank St. Coll., 1989, Liberty award Lambda Legal Def. and Edn. Fund, 1990, Disting. Community Svc. award United Hosp. Fund, 1990, medal Correctional Assn. of N.Y./Osborne Assn., 1990, Sybil C. Simon Disting. Patron award Arts and Bus. Coun., 1994. Mem. Film Soc. of Lincoln Ctr., Young Concert Artists, Human Rights Watch. Address: The Irene Diamond Fund 375 Park Ave Ste 3303 New York NY 10152-0002

DIAMOND, JARED MASON, biologist; b. Boston, Sept. 10, 1937; s. Louis K. and Flora K. D. B.A., Harvard U., 1958; Ph.D., Cambridge (Eng.) U., 1961. Jr. fellow Soc. Fellows Harvard U., 1962-65; assoc. in biophysics, 1965-66; asso. prof. physiology U. Calif. Med. Center, Los Angeles, 1966-68; prof. U. Calif. Med. Center, 1968—; cons. in conservation and nat. park planning govts., Papua New Guinea, Solomon Islands, Indonesia. Author: Avifauna of the Eastern Highlands of New Guinea, 1972, Ecology and Evolution of Communities, 1975; research and articles in membrane physiology and ecology. Recipient Burr medal Nat. Geog. Soc., 1979, Bowditch prize Am. Physiol. Soc., 1976, Disting. Achievement award Am. Gastroent. Assn., 1975. Fellow Am. Acad. Arts and Scis., MacArthur Found.; mem. Nat. Acad. Scis. Office: UCLA Med Ctr Dept of Physiology 10833 Le Conte Ave Los Angeles CA 90024*

DIAMOND, JESSICA, artist; b. Bronx, N.Y.. BFA, Sch. Visual Arts, N.Y.C., 1979; MFA, Columbia U., N.Y.C., 1981. One-woman shows include Standard Graphic, Cologne, Germany, 1990, Jablonka Gallery, Cologne, 1991, Gallery Fahnemann, Berlin, 1991, Gallery Massimo DeCarlo, Milan, 1993, Ynglingagatan 1, Stockholm, 1994, Rix, Linköping, Sweden, 1996, Deitch Projects, N.Y., 1996, le Consortium, Dijon, France, 1997, Vera Van Laer Gallery, Antwerp, Belgium, 1998, Ota Fine Arts, Tokyo, 1999; exhibited in group shows at Mus. van Hedendaagse Kunst Ghent, Belgium, 1993, Venice (Italy) Biennale, 1993, Vorarlberger Kunstverein, Bregenz, Austria, 1993, Corner House, Manchester, Eng., 1994, Deichtorhallen Hamburg, Germany, 1994, Mus. Contemporary Art, Sydney, Australia, 1994, Serpentine Gallery, London, 1994, Watari-um Mus., Tokyo, 1995, Kunsthalle Bern, Switzerland, 1995, Whitney Mus. Am. Art, N.Y.C., 1997, Stedelijk Mus. voor Actuele Kunst, Ghent, belgium, 1999, Paula Cooper Gallery, N.Y.C., 1999. Home and Studio: 549 83d St Brooklyn NY 11209-4503

DIAMOND, JOSEF, lawyer; b. L.A., Mar. 6, 1907; s. Michael and Ruby (Shifrin) D.; m. Violett Diamond, Apr. 2, 1933 (dec. 1979); children: Joel, Diane Foreman; m. Ann Dulien, Jan. 12, 1981 (dec. 1984); m. Muriel Bach, 1986. BBA, U. Wash., 1929, JD, 1931. Bar: Wash. 1931, U.S. Dist. Ct. (we. dist.) Wash. 1932, U.S. Ct. Appeals (9th cir.) 1934, U.S. Supreme Ct. 1944. Assoc. Caldwell & Lycette, Seattle, 1931-35; ptnr. Caldwell, Lycette & Diamond, Seattle, 1935-45, Lycette, Diamond & Sylvester, Seattle, 1945-80; ptnr. Diamond & Sylvester, Seattle, 1980-82, of counsel, 1982-88; of counsel Short, Cressman & Burgess, Seattle, 1988—; chmn. bd. Diamond Parking Inc., Seattle, 1945-70; cons. various businesses. Bd. dirs. Am. Heart Assn., 1960; chmn. Wash. Heart Assn., 1962. Col. JAGC, U.S. Army, WWII. Decorated Legion of Merit. Mem. Wash. Bar Assn., Assn. Trial Lawyers Wash., Seattle Bar Assn., Mil. Engrs. Soc., Wash. Athletic Club, Bellevue Athletic Club, Harbor Club, Rainier Club. Office: 3000 First Interstate Ctr 999 3d Ave Seattle WA 98104-4019

DIAMOND, M. JEROME, lawyer, former state official; b. Chgo., Mar. 16, 1942; s. Leo and Sonya (Pevsner) D.; m. Carol English Robinson; 8 children. AB, George Washington U., 1963; MA, U. Tenn., 1965, JD, 1968. Bar: Vt. 1968, U.S. Supreme Ct. 1975. Law clk. U.S. Dist. Judge Ernest Gibson, 1968-69; assoc. Kristensen, Cummings & Price, Brattleboro, Vt., 1969-70; state's atty. Windham County, Vt., 1970-74; atty. gen. State of Vt., 1975-81; atty., sr. ptnr. Diamond & Robinson, P.C., Montpelier, Vt., 1981—. Trustee Brooks Meml. Library, 1970-73; chmn. Putney Zoning Bd. Adjustment, 1971-74; mem. Vt. Criminal Justice Tng. Council, 1974-81, Vt. Commn. Adminstrn. of Justice, 1975-81; mem. Vt. Adv. Group, U.S. Civil Rights Commn.; gen. campaign chmn. United Way Washington County, 1986-87, 88-89; bd. dirs. Nat. Coun. on Aging, 1990-93, Vt. Bar Found., 1997—, Vt. State Employees Credit Union, 1997—; internat. commr. Anti-Defamation League, 1988-93. Mem. Vt. State's Attys. Assn. (past pres.), Vt. Bar Assn., Vt. Bar Found. (bd. dirs. 1997—), Washington County Bar Assn., Nat. Assn. Atty. Gens. (v.p. 1978-79, pres. 1980), Ea. Regional Conf. Attys. Gen. (chmn. 1975-76), B'nai B'rith (internat. commr. anti-defamation league 1988-93, internat. bd. govs. 1990-92), Jewish Inst. for Nat. Security Affairs (bd. dirs. 1993—), Am. Judicature Soc. (bd. dirs., Vt. rep. 1994—), Vt. State Employees Credit Union, 1997 (bd. dirs.), Shriners, Masons, Montpelier Rotary Club (bd. dirs. 1998—). Democrat. Jewish. Office: Diamond & Robinson PC PO Drawer D Montpelier VT 05601

DIAMOND, MARIAN CLEEVES, anatomy educator; b. Glendale, Calif., Nov. 11, 1926; d. Montague and Rosa Marian (Wamphler) Cleeves; m. Richard M. Diamond, Dec. 20, 1950 (div.); m. Arnold B. Scheibel, Sept. 14, 1982; children: Catherine, Richard, Jeffrey, Ann. AB, U. Calif., Berkeley, 1948, MA, 1949, PhD, 1953. With Harvard U., Cambridge, 1952-54, Cornell U., Ithaca, N.Y., 1954-58, U. Calif., San Francisco, 1954-58; prof. anatomy U. Calif., Berkeley, 1962—; asst. dean U. Calif., Berkeley, 1967-70, assoc. dean, 1970-73, dir. The Lawrence Hall of Sci., 1990-95, dir. emeritus, 1995—; vis. scholar Australian Nat. U., 1978, Fudan U., Shanghai, China, 1985, U. Nairobi, Kenya, 1988. Author: (with J. Hopson) Magic Trees of the Mind, 1998; author: Enriching Heredity, 1989; co-author: The Human Brain Coloring, 1985; editor: Contraceptive Hormones Estrogen and Human Welfare, 1978; contbr. 155 articles to profl. jours. V.p. County Women Dems., Ithaca, 1957; bd. dirs. Unitarian Ch., Berkeley, 1969. Recipient Calif. Gifted award, 1989, C.A.S.E. Calif. Prof. of Yr. award, Nat. Gold medalist, 1990, Woman of Yr. award Zonta Internat., 1991, U. medal La. Universidad Del Zulia, Maricaibo, Venezuela, 1992, Alumna of the Yr. award U. Calif.-Berkeley, 1995; Calif. Acad. Scis. fellow, 1991, 1st Senior Scholar award AAUW, 1997, Calif. Soc. Biomedical Rsch. Dist. Svc. award, 1998, Alumnae Resources-Women o fAchievement Vision and Excellence award, 1999, Benjamin Ide Wheeler award 1999. Fellow AAAS, AAUW (sr.; fellowship chair 1970-85); mem. Am. Assn. Anatomists, Soc. Neurosci., Philos. Soc. Washington, The Faculty Club (Berkeley) (v.p. 1979-85, 90-95). Avocations: hiking, sports, painting. Home: 2583 Virginia St Berkeley CA 94709-1108 Office: U Calif Dept Integrative Biology 3060 Valley Life Sciences Bldg Berkeley CA 94720-3141

DIAMOND, MICHAEL SHAWN, science and math educator, computer consultant; b. St. Louis, Jan. 26, 1960; s. Robert Dale Diamond and Jean Marie (Reutner) White. BSChemE, U. Mo., 1982; MEd, Hyles-Anderson Coll., 1989. Cert. engr.-in-tng.; lic., ordained to ministry Baptist Ch., 1989; endorsed advanced placement calculus and stats. tchr., S.C., qualified reader for advanced placement math. Nuclear engr. Charleston (S.C.) Naval Shipyard, Nuclear Engring. Dept., 1983-88, asst. shift test engr., 1983-85, asst. shift refueling engr., 1985-88; systems mgr. and sci. tchr. Faith Bapt. Ch. and Schs., Canoga Park, Calif., 1989-90, sci. tchr., 1989-92; programming asst., cons. Peterson Rsch., Costa Mesa, Calif., 1989-92; sci. dept. chmn. Gethsemane Bapt. Christian Sch., Long Beach, Calif., 1990-92; math. computer tchr. Pinewood Prep. Sch., Summerville, S.C., 1993-97, computer and tech. chair, 1994-97, 99; tng. splst. Software Tng. Ctr., North Charleston, S.C., 1997-98; quality assurance analyst in product devel. Blackbaud, Inc., Charleston, S.C., 1998; adj. instr. transfer chemistry, math. and engring. Trident Tech. Coll., North Charleston, S.C., 1993—; contract computer instr. Tng. Alliance, Charleston, 1993. Sunday sch. tchr. Gethsemane Bapt. Ch., Long Beach, 1990-92, Summerville (S.C.) Bapt. Ch., 1996—; mem. choir Trident Bapt. Ch., Charleston, S.C., 1993-96; singles Sun. sch. tchr. Summerville (S.C.) Bapt. Ch., 1996-99. Mem. NSPE, Am. Nuclear Soc., Nat. Sci. Tchrs. Assn., S.C. Sci. Coun., Nat. Coun. Tchrs. Math., S.C. Math. Tchrs. Assn., Low Country Math. Tchrs. Assn., S.C. Adv. Placement Math Tchrs. Assn., U.S. Judo Assn. (Winner's Cir. award 1987, 88, 89), Internat. Soc. of Tech. Educators, Pi Kappa Alpha. Republican. Avocations: reading, softball, personal computers, church work. Home: 1217 Texas Dr Apt B Ladson SC 29456

DIAMOND, PAUL STEVEN, lawyer; b. Bklyn., Jan. 2, 1953; s. George and Anna (Jaeger) D.; m. Robin Nilon. BA magna cum laude, Columbia U., 1974; JD, U. Pa., 1977. Bar: Pa. 1977, U.S. Dist. Ct. (ea. dist.) Pa, 1979, U.S. Ct. Appeals (3d cir.) 1979, U.S. Supreme Ct. 1983. Asst. dist. atty. Phila. Dist. Atty. Office, 1977-83; law clk. Supreme Ct. Pa., Phila., 1980; assoc. Dilworth, Paxson, Kalish & Kauffman, Phila., 1983-85, ptnr., 1986-91; ptnr. Obermayer, Rebmann, Maxwell & Hippel, Phila., 1992—; lectr. Temple U. Sch. Law, Phila., 1990-92; mem. civil prodecural rules com. Supreme Ct. Pa., 1995—, fed. judicial nominating commn., 1995—. Author: Federal Grand Jury Practice and Procedure, 1990, rev. 2nd edit., 1993; vice-chmn. Amicus Curiae Briefs Comm., 1995—. Mem. ABA (criminal justice sect., Amicus Curiae briefs subcom. 1983—, grand jury subcom. 1991—), Pa. Bar Assn., Phila. Bar Assn. Republican. Jewish. Office: Obermayer Rebmann Maxwell & Hippel One Penn Ctr 19th Fl 1617 John F Kennedy Blvd Philadelphia PA 19103*

DIAMOND, PHILIP ERNEST, lawyer; b. L.A., Feb. 11, 1925; s. William and Elizabeth (Weizenhaus) D.; m. Dorae Seymour (dec.); children: William, Wendy, Nancy; m. 2d, Jenny White Carson. B.A., UCLA, 1949, M.A., 1950; J.D., U. Calif., Berkeley, 1953. Bar: Calif. 1953, U.S. Dist. Ct. (no., ea. and cen. dists.) Calif. 1953, U.S. Ct. Appeals (9th cir.) 1953. Law clk. to presiding justice Calif. Dist. Ct. Appeals, 1953-54; assoc. Landels & Weigel, San Francisco, 1954-60; ptnr. Landels Weigel & Ripley, San Francisco, 1960-62; sr. ptnr. Landels, Ripley & Diamond, San Francisco. 1962-93—; pres. Diamond Wine Mchts., San Francisco, 1976—; bd. dirs. Yasutomo & Co. Pres. Contra Costa Sch. Bd. Assn., 1966-68. With USN, 1943-46. Mem. ABA, Am. Arbitration Assn., Calif. State Bar Assn., San Francisco Bar Assn., Phi Beta Kappa. Democrat. Clubs: Commonwealth, Mchts. & Exch. Office: 350 The Embarcadero San Francisco CA 94105-1204

DIAMOND, RICHARD, secondary education educator; b. N.Y.C., June 23, 1936; s. Oscar and Frieda (Rosenfeld) D.; m. Donna Jean Berkshire Wilson, June 14, 1961 (div. June 1974); m. Betty Ruth Jane Foster, Nov. 17, 1975; children: Thomas, Laura, Rick, Jeff. BA, U. Calif., Berkeley, 1958. Cert. tchr., Calif. Tchr. Riverside (Calif.) Unified Schs., 1959-67, 73—, coord. social studies, 1967-69, program dir. compensatory edn., 1969-72, attendance officer, 1972-73; author curriculum programs Afro-Am. history and Chicano studies, 1968; developer law and youth H.S. course, 1978, track coach, 1975-88. Contbr. articles and photographs to profl. jours. Co-creator nationally recognized h.s. vol. program, h.s. svc. learning coord., 1995—; mem. Riverside County Hist. Commn., 1997—; Dem. Party worker, 1964-72; Rep. Party worker, 1992—; historic commn. liaison Riverside County Archives Commn., 1998—. Named Social Studies Tchr. of Yr., Inland Empire Social Studies Assn., 1980, Tchr. of Yr., Arlington H.S., Riverside, 1992; recipient hon. svc. award Dist. Coun. PTA, Riverside, 1993, Johnny Harris Youth Action award City of Riverside,, 1998. Mem. NEA, Calif. Tchrs. Assn., Riverside County Tchrs. Assn. Presbyterian. Avocations: gardening, travel, reading, woodworking. E-mail: ddiamond@ix.metcom.com. Office: Arlington HS 2951 Jackson St Riverside CA 92503-5732

DIAMOND, RICHARD EDWARD, publisher; b. S.I., N.Y., May 24, 1932; s. Joseph H. and Gertrude (Newhouse) D.; m. Alice W. Blach, July 27, 1963; children: Caroline Harrison, Alison, Richard Edward. Student, Cornell U., 1953; LHD (hon.), Wagner Coll., 1991. With S.I. Advance, 1953—; publisher, 1979—; bd. dirs. Newspaper Advt. Bur. Trustee. S.I. Acad., 1967-89, pres. bd. dirs., 1977-87; bd. dirs. S.I. Hosp., 1978-88. Recipient Disting. Citizens award Wagner Coll., S.I., 1976. Mem. Am. Newspapers Pubs. Assn., Newspaper Assn. Am. (bd. dirs.). Jewish. Office: SI Advance 950 Fingerboard Rd Staten Island NY 10305-1453*

DIAMOND, RICHARD MARTIN, nuclear chemist; b. L.A., Jan. 7, 1924; divorced; 4 children. BS, UCLA, 1947; PhD in Nuclear Chemistry, U. Calif. Berkeley, 1951. Instr. chemistry Harvard U., 1951-54; asst. prof. Cornell U., 1954-58; mem. sr. staff Lawrence Berkeley Lab., U. Calif., 1958—, sr. scientist emeritus, 1995—; mem. U.S. Physics del. to Russia, 1966, rev. com. physics divsn. Oak Ridge Lab., 1972-74, Dept. of Energy rev. com. Brookhaven (n, gamma) Facility and Isotope Separator, 1983, 8pi Gamma Spect. Com., Chalk River, Canada, 1983, adv. com. Ind. Cyclotron Facility, 1980-83, Tandem-Linac Facility Argonne Nat. Lab., 1983-86, Holifield Rsch. Facility, 1988-90, Holifield Radioactive Ion Beam Facility, 1994-97; chmn. Gordon Conf. on Nuclear Chemistry, 1965, Conf. on Ion Exch., 1969, rev. com. UNISOR, Oak Ridge Nat. Lab., 1974-75, subcom. high spin and nuclei far from stability Dept. Energy-NSF, 1983; vis. fellow Japan Soc. for Promotion of Sci., 1981; co-organizer Int. Conf. Nuclear Physics, 1980, workshop on nuclear str., 1986, workshop Nat. Gamma-Ray Facility, 1987. Guggenheim fellow, 1966-67, Fullbright fellow, 1977. Fellow AAAS, Am. Phys. Soc. (shared Tom W. Bonner award 1980); mem. Am. Chem. Soc. (award in nuclear chemistry 1993). Achievements include research in nuclear spectroscopy, coulomb excitation, high-spin nuclear structure. Home: 574 Santa Clara Ave Berkeley CA 94707-1647 Office: Lawrence Berkeley Nat Lab Bldg 88 Nuclear Science Divsn Berkeley CA 94720

DIAMOND, RICKEY GARD, writer, educator; b. Benton Harbor, Mich., Dec. 21, 1946; d. Raymond Gard and Peggy M. (Thomas) Wall; m. F. Stephen McArthur III, Mar. 12, 1982. AA, Ind. U., 1981; BA, Vt. Coll., Norwich, 1982; MFA, Vt. Coll., Montpelier, 1984. Editor People's Voice, Barre, Vt., 1982-85, Vt. Woman, Burlington, 1985-88; devel. dir. C.V. Cmty. Action, Barre, 1988-90; asst. prof. Vt. Coll., Montpelier, 1995—; adj. prof. Vt. Coll., Johnson State C.C. Vt., 1985-95. Author: Second Sight, 1997; contbr. short stories, articles, columns to profl. publs., newspapers. Named Woman of Yr., Bus. and Profl. Women Vt., 1986, Susan B. Anthony award Vt. YWCA, 1987, Cmty. Action award AAUW Edn. Found. 1995. Mem.

AAUW (state sec. 1997—). Home and Office: 56 Browns Mill Rd Montpelier VT 05602

DIAMOND, ROBERT MICHAEL, lawyer; b. N.Y.C., Dec. 23, 1948; s. Meyer and Libby (Leventhal) D.; m. Amy B. Pullman, July 5, 1987; children: Michael Israel, Philip Brenner, Julia Rose. AB, Colgate U., 1970; JD, Columbia U., 1974. Bar: D.C. 1974, Va. 1976, Md. 1982. Assoc. Fried, Frank, Harris, Shriver & Kampelman, Washington, 1974-75; assoc., then ptnr. Hazel & Thomas, P.C., Falls Church, Va., 1975—. Contbr. articles to profl. jours. Trustee Cmty. Assns. Inst., Alexandria, Va., sec., 1993, treas., 1994, pres.-elect, 1995, pres., 1996, liason to jt. editl. bd. for Uniform Real Estate Acts, 1997—; mem. condominium subcom. Va. Housing Study Commn., 1993, 96. Recipient various awards Community Assns. Inst. including Outstanding Vol. 1989, Pres. Award for Outstanding Leadership, 1989-90. Mem. Coll. Cmty. Assn. Lawyers. Avocations: scuba diving, classic automobiles. E-mail: rdiamond@hazelthomas.com. Office: Hazel & Thomas PC 3110 Fairview Park Dr Ste 1400 Falls Church VA 22042-4503*

DIAMOND, SARA ROSE, writer, sociologist, lecturer; b. 1958. BA in Spanish, U. Calif., Irvine, 1979; MA in Sociology, U. Calif., Berkeley, 1988, PhD in Sociology, 1993. Lectr. U. Calif., Santa Cruz, 1988, 91, 94, U. Calif., Berkeley, 1994, Calif. State U. Hayward, 1995—. Author: Spiritual Warfare: The Politics of the Christian Right, 1989, Roads to Dominion: Right-Wing Movements and Political Power in the United States, 1995, Facing the Wrath: Confronting the Right in Dangerous Times, 1996, Not By Politics Alone: The Enduring Influence of the Christian Right, 1998. Home: PO Box 2439 Berkeley CA 94702-0439

DIAMOND, SEYMOUR, physician; b. Chgo., Apr. 15, 1925; s. Nathan Avruum and Rose (Roth) D.; m. Elaine June Flamm, June 20, 1948; children: Judi, Merle, Amy. Student, Loyola U., 1943-45; MB, Chgo. Med. Sch., 1948, MD, 1949. Intern White Cross Hosp., Columbus, Ohio, 1949-50; gen. practice medicine Chgo., 1950—; dir. Diamond Headache Clinic, Ltd., Chgo., 1970—; dir. inpatient headache unit Columbus Hosp., Chgo.; prof. neurology Finch U. Health Scis. Finch U. Health Scis., Chgo. Med. Sch., 1970-82, 85—, adj. prof. pharmacology and molecular biology, 1985—; awdn. prof. dept. family medicine U. Medicine and Dentistry N.J., Stratford, N.J., 1994; cons. mem. FDA Orphan Products Devel. Initial Rev. Group; lectr. dept. cmty. and family medicine Loyola U. Stritch Sch. Medicine, 1972-78; lectr. Falconbridge lecture series Laurentian U., Sudbury, Ont., Can., 1987; disting. lectr. neurology U. Tenn., 1992; AMA cons. on drug evaluation, 1993; mem. sci. com. neurology Internat. Jour. Pain Therapy, 1993. Author: A Pain Specialist's Approach to the Headache Patient, 1994; (with Bill and Cynthia Still) The Hormone Headache, 1995, Diagnosing and Managing Headaches, 1994; (with Donald J. Dalessio) The Practicing Physician's Approach to Headache, 5th edit., 1992, More Than Two Aspirin: Help for Your Headache Problem, 1976, Advice from the Diamond Headache Clinic, 1982; (with Judi Diamond-Falk) Coping with Your Headaches, 1982, 2d edit.; (with Mary Franklin Epstein), 1987; (with Arnold P. Friedman MD) Headache in Contemporary Patient Management series, 1983; (with Amy Diamond Vye) Headache and Diet, 1990; (with Michael Maliszewski) Sexual Aspects of Headaches, 1992; editor: Migraine Headache Prevention and Management; editor-in-chief Headache Quar., 1990—; editl. cons. BIOSIS, 1986-90; contbr. numerous articles on headache and related fields to profl. jours., chpts. to books. Bd. govs. Finch U. of Health/Chgo. Med. Sch. Recipient Disting. Alumni award Chgo. Med. Sch., 1977; Nat. Migraine Found. lectureship award, 1982, award Headache Consortium of New Eng., 1997, Cert. Appreciation, Chgo. Med. Soc., 1998; 1st recipient Migraine Trust lectureship, 1988; Brit. Migraine Trust 7th Internat. Migraine Symposium, London; Nat. Headache Found. Seymour Diamond fellow, 1993; Disting. lectr. in neurology U. Tenn., 1992. Fellow Royal Soc. Medicine; mem. AMA (Physicians Recognition awards 1970-73, 74, 77, 79, 82, 87, del. sect. clin. pharmacology and therapeutics 1987-89, mem. health policy agenda for Am. People, mem. Cost Effectiveness Conf., del. reference com. "C" on edn., reference com. C, 1988), mem. Bd. of Scientific and Policy Advs. for The Am. Council on Sci. and Health, So. Med. Assn., Am. Assn. Study of Headache (exec. dir. 1971-85, pres. 1972-74, #1 regent mem. 1984, svc. award 1971-85), Nat. Headache Found. (pres. 1971-77, exec. dir. 1977-95, exec. chmn. 1995—), World Fedn. Neurology (exec. officer 1980-95, research group on migraine and headache), Ill. Acad. Gen. Practice (chmn. mental health com. 1966-70), Ill. Med. Soc., Chgo. Med. Soc., Biofeedback Soc. Am., Internat. Assn. Study of Pain, Am. Soc. Clin. Pharmacology and Therapeutics (chmn. headache sect. 1982-89, mem. com. coordination sci. sects. 1983-89), Postgrad. Med. Assn. (pres. 1981). Office: 467 W Deming Pl Ste 500 Chicago IL 60614-1726 *I derive great satisfaction from helping a person who is totally disabled from pain to again lead a normal, functional life.*

DIAMOND, SHARI SEIDMAN, psychology educator, law researcher; b. Chgo., Mar. 17, 1947; d. Leon Harry and Rita (Wolff) S.; m. Stewart Howard Diamond, Nov. 1, 1970; 1 child, Nicole. BA in Psychology, Sociology, U. Mich., 1968; MA in Psychology, Northwestern U., 1970, PhD in Social Psychology, 1972; JD with honors, U. Chgo., 1985. Bar: Ill. 1985. Rsch. assoc. Sch. Law U. Chgo., 1972-73; asst. prof. psychology and criminal justice U. Ill., Chgo., 1973-79, assoc. prof., 1979-90, prof., 1990—; assoc. Sidley & Austin, Chgo., 1985-87; sr. rsch. fellow ABF, Chgo., 1987—; lectr. U. Chgo. Law Sch., 1994-96; prof. law and psychology Northwestern U., 1999—; cons. govtl. and pub. interests groups including Rsch. Adv. Panel for U.S. Sentencing Commn., 1987-91; acad. visitor dept. law London Sch. Econs., 1981; hon. fellow Ctr. for Urban Affairs Northwestern U., Evanston, Ill., 1973-73; hon. rsch. assoc. U. London, 1970; speaker, lectr. in field; mem. NAS panel on sentencing rsch., 1981-83, panel on forensic DNA evidence, 1994-96. Editor Law and Soc. Rev., 1988-91; past mem. editorial bd. Law and Soc. Rev., 1983-88, Law and Human Behavior, Crime and Justice Annual, Evaluation Rev.; reviewer NSF; contbr. articles to profl. jours. Chair Coll. Edn. Policy Com., 1979-80; dir. tng. grant NIMH Crime and Delinquency, 1979-80. Fellow Northwestern U., 1968-69, NIMH, 1969-71; grantee Spencer Found., 1972-74, disting. scholar, grantee, U. Ill., 1995-98, Law Enforcement Assistance Adminstrn., 1974-76, Ctr. for Crime and Delinquency NIMH, 1976-81, NSF, 1980-83, 90-92, 99—; B. Kenneth West U. scholar, 1995-98. Fellow APA (Award for Disting. Contbns. to Rsch. in Pub. Policy 1991), Am. Psychol. Soc.; mem. ABA, Am. Psychology-Law Soc. (pres. 1987-88), Law and Soc. Assn. (trustee 1979-82). Office: ABF 750 N Lake Shore Dr Chicago IL 60611-4403

DIAMOND, SIDNEY, chemist, educator; b. N.Y.C., Nov. 10, 1929; s. Julius and Ethel D.; m. Harriet Urish, May 2, 1953; children: Florence, Julia. B.S., Syracuse U., 1950; M.F., Duke U., 1951; Ph.D., Purdue U., 1963. Research engr. U.S. Bur. Public Rds. (now Fed. Hwy. Adminstrn.), Washington, 1953-61; research chemist U.S. Bur. Public Rds. (now Fed. Hwy. Adminstrn.), 1961-65; assoc. prof. engring. materials Purdue U., 1965-69, prof., 1969—; pres. Sidney Diamond and Assocs., Inc., engring. materials cons.; mem. Nat. Materials Adv. Bd. Com. on Status of Research in U.S. Cement and Concrete Industries; chmn. Internat. Symposium on Durability of Glass Fiber Reinforced Concrete, Chgo., 1985; mem. adv. com. NSF Ctr. for Advanced Cement-Based Materials, 1989—. Contbr. numerous articles on cement and concrete to profl. jours.; editor: Cement and Concrete Research. Served with U.S. Army, 1951-53. Fellow AM. Ceramic Soc. (past trustee, Copeland award), Am. Concrete Inst., Am. Concrete Inst. (anderson award 1993); mem. ASTM, Internat. Congress on Chemistry of Cement (pres. sect. 6 of 8th congress), Materials Rsch. Soc. Home: 819 Essex St West Lafayette IN 47906-1534 Office: Purdue U Sch Civil Engring West Lafayette IN 47907

DIAMOND, SIGMUND, editor, educator; b. Balt., June 14, 1920; s. Isidor and Yetta (Mirtenbaum) D.; m. Shirley Welson, Jan. 4, 1945; children—Stephen Mark, Betty. A.B., Johns Hopkins, 1940; Ph.D. in History, Harvard, 1953. With U.S. Govt., 1942-43; internat. rep. UAW-CIO, 1943-47; lectr. Am. history Sarah Lawrence Coll., 1955-56; mem. faculty Columbia U., 1955—, prof. history and sociology, 1964—, Giddings prof. sociology, 1978—, prof. emeritus, 1986—; editor Polit. Sci. Quar., 1963-75; Fulbright prof. Am. history Tel-Aviv U., 1975-76; vis. prof. Hebrew U. Jerusalem, 1969-70; panelist Com. on History as Social Sci., Behavioral and Social Scis. Survey Com., Nat. Acad. Scis. and Social Sci. Rsch. Coun. Author: The Reputation of the American Businessman, 1955, A Casual View of America: The Home Letters of Salomon De Rothschild, 1859-1861, 1961, In Quest: Journal of an Unquiet Pilgrimage, 1980, Compromised Campus: The Collaboration of the Universities with the Intelligence Community, 1945-55, 1992; editor: The Nation Transformed, 1963, The Creation of Society in the New World, 1963. Fellow Center Advanced Study Behavioral Scis., 1959-60; sr. research fellow Newberry Library, 1967. Mem. Am. Hist. Assn., Am. Sociol. Assn., Econ. History Assn., Conf. on Jewish Social Studies (editorial bd.). Home: 249 Darling Rd Salem CT 06420-3909

DIAMOND, STANLEY JAY, lawyer; b. Los Angeles, Nov. 27, 1927; s. Philip Alfred and Florence (Fadem) D.; m. Lois Jane Broida, June 22, 1969; children: Caryn Elaine, Diana Beth. B.A., UCLA, 1949; J.D., U. So. Calif., 1952. Bar: Calif. 1953. Practiced law Los Angeles, 1953—; dep. Office of Calif. Atty. Gen., Los Angeles, 1953; ptnr. Diamond & Tilem, Los Angeles, 1957-60, Diamond, Tilem & Colden, Los Angeles, 1960-79, Diamond & Wilson, Los Angeles, 1979—; lectr. music and entertainment law UCLA; Mem. nat. panel arbitrators Am. Arbitration Assn. Bd. dirs. Los Angeles Suicide Prevention Center, 1971-76. Served with 349th Engr. Constrn. Bn. AUS, 1945-47. Mem. ABA, Calif. Bar Assn., Los Angeles County Bar Assn., Beverly Hills Bar Assn., Am. Judicature Soc., Calif. Copyright Conf., Nat. Acad. Rec. Arts and Scis., Zeta Beta Tau, Nu Beta Epsilon. Office: 12304 Santa Monica Blvd 3d Fl Los Angeles CA 90025-2551

DIAMOND, STUART, educator, lawyer, business executive, consultant; b. Camden., N.J., June 20, 1948; s. Irving H. and Ruth (Safran) D. BA in English, Rutgers U., 1970; JD, Harvard U., 1990; MBA, U. Pa., 1992. Bar: N.J. 1990, N.Y. 1991. Mcpl. investigative reporter New Brunswick (N.J.) Daily Home News, 1969-73; mcpl., energy and environ. reporter Newsday, Long Island, N.Y., 1973-84; fin., tech., law, investigative reporter The N.Y. Times, N.Y.C., 1984-88; assoc. Morgan Stanley, N.Y.C., 1989, Sullivan & Cromwell, N.Y.C., 1989; assoc. dir. Harvard negotiation project, exec. dir. Conflict Mgmt. Group Harvard U. Law Sch., Cambridge, Mass., 1990-92; consultant United Nations, 1991—; pres. Global Strategy Group, N.Y.C., Calif., 1992—; prof. Wharton Sch. U. Pa., Phila., 1993—; contbg. editor Omni mag., 1978-81; lectr., TV commentator., 1978—. Author: It's In Your Power, 1978, No-Cost, Low-Cost Energy Tips, 1980; documentary films The Energy War, 1980, The Future is Now, 1981; also nat. mag. cover stories. Recipient Amos Tuck award nat. econ. reporting, 1978, 80, 82, Polk award nat. reporting, 1980, Scripps Howard Found. award, 1982, Pulitzer Prize, 1987. Mem. ABA, Sigma Delta Chi. Home: 26 Bevin Rd Northport NY 11768-1130

DIAMOND, SUSAN ZEE, management consultant; b. Okla., Aug. 20, 1949; d. Louis Edward and Henrietta (Wood) D.; m. Allan T. Devitt, July 27, 1974. AB (Nat. Merit scholar, GRTS scholar), U. Chgo., 1970; MBA, DePaul U., 1979; Cert. office automation prof. Dir. study guide prodn. Am. Sch. Co., Chgo., 1972-75; publs. supr. Allied Van Lines, Broadview, Ill., 1975-78, sr. account svcs. rep., 1978-79; pres. Diamond Assocs. Ltd., Bensenville, Ill., 1978—; Author: Records Management: A Practical Guide, 3rd edit., 1995; editor The Serpentine Muse, 1996—; condr. seminars Am. Mgmt. Assn., Can. Mgmt. Centre. Mem. Inst. of Mgmt. Accts., Assn. of Record Mgrs. and Adminstrs., Adventuresses of Sherlock Holmes, Baker St. Irregulars.

DIAMONSTEIN-SPIELVOGEL, BARBARALEE, writer, television interviewer/ producer; b. N.Y.C.; d. Rubin Robert and Sally H. Simmons; m. Alan A. Diamonstein, July 22, 1956; m. Carl Spielvogel, Oct. 27, 1981. BA, BC, MA, doctorate, NYU, 1963; DHL (hon.), Md. Inst. Coll. Art, 1990, Longwood Coll., 1995. Staff asst. The White House, 1963-66; 1st dir. dept. cultural affairs City of New York, 1966-67; dir. of Forums McCall Corp., 1967-69; editor spl. supplements, columnist Harper's Bazaar, 1969-71; spl. project dir., guest editor Art News, 1971-93; columnist Ladies Home Jour., 1979-84; contbr. to Saturday Rev., Vogue, Ms., Partisan Rev., N.Y. Times, Condé Nast, Traveller, House & Garden, others; mem. faculty Hunter Coll., CUNY, 1974-76, New Sch., 1976-84, Duke U. (Inst. Policy Scis.), 1978; arts cons. Sunday Morning CBS-TV, 1978-82; curator Buildings Reborn, Collaborations, Visions and Images, Remaking America, The Landmarks of N.Y. I, II & III (internat. travelling museum exhbns.), 1978—, and numerous others. TV interviewer, producer: About the Arts, WNYC-TV, 1975-79, ABC-TV Arts, 1980-88, A&E Network, 1980-89; videotape exhibitions Leo Castelli Gallery, 1978, 84, 88, 94; author: Open Secrets: 94 Women in Touch With Our Time, 1972, The World of Art, 1902-77, 75 Years of Art News, 1977, Buildings Reborn: New Uses, Old Places, 1978, Inside New York's Art World, 1979, American Architecture Now, 1980, Collaboration: Artists and Architects, 1981, Visions and Images: American Photographers on Photography, 1981, Interior Design: The New Freedom, 1982, Handmade in America, 1983, Fashion: The Inside Story, 1985, American Architecture Now, 1985, Remaking America, 1986, The Landmarks of New York, 1988, 18 Wonders of the New York World, 1992, The Landmarks of New York: Vol. II, 1993, Vol. III, 1998, Inside the Art World: Conversations with Barbaralee Diamonstein, 1994, Skills, Values, Dreams, 1995, Singular Voices: Americans Who Make a Difference, 1997; editor: Our 200 Years: Tradition and Renewal, 1975, MOMA at 50, 1980, and numerous others. Commr. N.Y.C. Landmarks Preservation Commn., 1972-87, N.Y.C. Cultural Commn., 1975-86, N.Y.C. Arts Commn., 1991-94; bd. dirs. Mcpl. Art Soc., 1973-83, Am. Coun. Arts, 1982-89, N.Y.C. Bicentennial Commn., 1973-77, Bklyn. Acad. Music, 1969-74, N.Y. Landmarks Conservancy, 1973-97, vice chmn., 1983-87; bd. advisors Film Anthology Archives, 1969—; bd. dirs. Fresh Air Fund, 1983—, Big Apple Circus, 1989-92; chmn. N.Y. Landmarks Preservation Found., 1987-95; mem. Pres.' coun. Rockefeller U., 1987—; bd. visitors Pub. Policy Inst. Duke U., 1987-93; mem. U.S. Nat. Commn. on the Holocaust, 1987-93, PEN Am. Ctr., 1980-96; chair Art Pub. Spaces com. Holocaust Mus., 1987-96, Hist. Landmarks Preservation Ctr., 1995—; bd. dirs. Corcoran Gallery Art, Washington, 1992—, N.Y. State Archive's Trust, 1994—; trustee N.Y. Hist. Soc., 1993-95, Ctrl. Pk. Conservancy, 1993-95; mem. drawing com. Met. Mus. Art, 1990—, Whitney Mus. Am. Art, 1995-98; mem. collector's com. Nat. Gallery of Art; bd. dirs. White House Endowment Fund, 1995-98; mem. U.S. Commn. Fine Arts, 1995—. Recipient Founder's Day award Pratt Inst., 1994, Outstanding Citizen award Citizen Ctrs., 1996, Heritage Trails award, 1998, Spirit of the City award Women's City Club, 1998, Manhausan award, 1999, New Millenium Humanitarian award HELP, 1999. Home: 720 Park Ave New York NY 10021-4954

DIANA, JOSEPH A., retired foundation executive; b. New Castle, Pa., June 26, 1924; s. Joseph Anthony and Emma (Eardly) D.; m. Kathryn June Matthews, June 26, 1946; children: Mark Steven, Chris Joseph, Todd Francis, Paul Jeffrey. Student, Notre Dame U., 1942; B.A., U. Mich., 1950, postgrad., 1950-51. Mem. adminstrv. staff U. Mich., 1950-56, sec. to faculty Med. Sch., 1956-69, asst. controller, 1969-70; v.p. fin. and mgmt. SUNY, Stony Brook, 1970-75; vice chancellor adminstrv. affairs, assoc. v.p. bus. affairs U. Ill., Champaign-Urbana, 1975-79; v.p., treas. emeritus John D. and Catherine T. MacArthur Found., Chgo.; pres. Dianaid Ltd., 1985-91; interim pub. Harper's mag.; sec., treas. Harper's Mag. Found., 1980-82. Republican. Roman Catholic. Home: 2310 Saint Francis Dr Ann Arbor MI 48104-4807

DIANGELO, JOSEPH ANTHONY, JR., management educator, academic dean; b. Phila., July 5, 1948; s. Joseph Anthony and Lucy (Lazzaro) D.; m. Frances R. Marcelli, Mar. 18, 1972; children: Deana, Kristen, Joseph Anthony III. BS, St. Joseph's U., 1970; MBA, Widener U., 1975; EdD, Temple U., 1985. Tchr. St. Thomas More H.S., Phila., 1970-75; archbishop Carroll H.S., Radnor, Pa., 1975-78; prof. mgmt. St. Joseph's U., Phila., 1978-80; prof., asst. dean Widener U., Chester, Pa., 1980-87, dean, 1985; asst. provost for grad. studies Widener U., Chester, 1986-88; dean Sch. Mgmt., 1987—; cons. Chespenn Health Service, Chester, 1984. Contbr. articles to profl. jours. Pres., bd. dirs. Children's Clinic Chester, 1983-86; gov.'s appointee Trial Ct. Nominating Com. of Delaware County, Pa., 1987—; pvt. industry coun. Del. County, 1990—; Delaware County Common Pleas Ct. appointee Sch. Dist. Bd. Control; chmn. edn. com., bd. dirs. Columbus Quincentennial Found., 1992-97; Pa. amb. Team Pa., 1999—. With USNG, 1970-76. Mem. ASTD, AACSB (bus. accreditation com. 1998—), Soc. Advancement Mgmt. (Disting. Prof. award 1980-81), Soc. Human Resource Mgmt., Acad. of Mgmt., Am. Arbitration Assn., Mid-Atlantic Assn. Colls. Bus. Adminstrn. (mem. exec. com. 1994—, 1st v.p. 1995, pres. 1996-97). Roman Catholic. Avocations: tennis, golf. Office: Widener U 14th Chestnut St Chester PA 19013

DIAS, KATHLEEN R. BRUNI-KERRIGAN, foreign language educator; b. Phila., Dec. 2, 1950; d. John Joseph and Dorothy (Bruni) K.; m. Lindolfo C. Dias. BA, Immaculata Coll., 1977; cert. acad. excellence, Istituto Italiano di Cultura, Lima, Peru, 1980; MA, Marywood U., 1983; postgrad., Temple U., 1984, U. Pa., 1986—; cert. proficiency, Berlitz Schs. Langs., 1983. Cert. secondary edn. tchr., elem. edn. tchr., 1984, elem./mid. and secondary sch. prin., Pa., 1996. Tchr., program dir. elem. edn. Phila., 1971-74, Chester County, Pa., 1976-78; tutor Fgn. Lang. Affairs, Delaware County, Pa., 1975-76; tchr., dir. Spanish elem. edn. Bucks County, Pa., 1978-79; tchr. ESL Lima, 1979-81; prof. Spanish Immaculata Coll., Pa., 1983; dir. L.Am. studies program Immaculata Coll., 1983-86; instr. fgn. lang. specialized tutoring program Delaware County, Pa., 1981—; vice-principal Drexel Hill Holy Child Acad., 1997—; chmn. VIP dept. U. Pa.; with Am. sect. Mus. Archaeology/Anthropology U. Pa., summers, 1986—, anthropology lab. analysis of Ctrl. and S.Am. artifacts; chmn., tchr. Latin, Spanish and English Holy Child Acad., Drexel Hill, adminstrv. asst., rep. various coms. bd. trustees.; coord. edn. dept. Mus. Anthropology and Archaeology, Univ. Pa., 1995-96; dir. curriculum devel. Holy Child Acad., 1996—, vice-prin., 1997—; guest spkr. U. Pa., 1996, Duke U. on Maya studies, 1999. Author 4-yr. lang. program Early Spanish learning for the Elementary School, 1982; Developing a Sensitivity to the Culture and History of Latin America, 1983, Mexico: Land, Culture and People, 1983, The Maya and Aztec Nations, 1984, The Inca Civilization: From Manco Capac to the Spanish Conquest, 1988, Manual for Teachers on Mesoamerican Cultures Grades 7-12, 1997; compilor, editor (study guide) for Hall of Ancient Mex. and Ctrl. Am. at Mus. of Natural History, N.Y.C., 1990; contbr. articles to scholarly jours. Mem. citizen's bd. Am. Cancer Rsch.; site mgr./facilitator Maya Quest Interactive Expedition, 1994-95. Italian Cultural Attaché scholar, Peru, 1979-81; State of Pa. grantee, 1980-81; recipient Disting. Leadership award, Comm. and Tech. award Pa. State U., 1995. Mem. MLA, Nat. Coun. Tchrs. English, Assn. Tchrs. Spanish and Portuguese, L.Am. Studies Assn., Pa. Assn. Edn., Pre-Columbian Soc. (bd. dirs. 1993—), Mus. Archaeology and Anthropology of U. Pa. E-mail: kerrigan@forum.swarthmore.edu.

DIASIO, ILSE WOLFARTSBERGER, volunteer; b. Linz, Austria, Nov. 12, 1946; came to U.S., 1967; d. D.I. Gettfried and Elfriede (Stuchlik) Wolfartsberger; m. Robert B. Diasio, July 4, 1970; children: Christoph, Thomas, Michael. Grad. in phys. therapy, U. Vienna, 1965-67. Phys. therapist Yale-New Haven Hosp., 1968-71, Vis. Nurse Assn., Rochester, N.Y., 1971-72; symposium coord. dept. pharmacology U. Ala., 1988; vol. tchr. German, Pemberton Elem. Sch., Richmond, Va., 1980-84, Vestavia Hills Elem. and H.S., 1985-93; organizer student exch. program between Vestavia Hills H.S. and Seebacher Gymnasium, Graz, Austria, 1990, 91, 94. Bd. dirs. Pemberton (Va.) Elem. Sch. PTA, 1979-84, pres., 1982-84; bd. dirs. Va. Commonwealth U. Faculty Woman's Club, 1978-84; pres. Childrens Svc. League, 1992-93, treas. 1991-92, asst. treas. 1990-91, 2d v.p., rec. sec., 1998-99; vol. Our Lady Queen of the Universe and Sacred Heart of Jesus Cath. Chs., 1988-90; St. Peter's rep. Alab. Arise, diocesan rep., rec. sec., 1988-94; mem. Peace and Justice Commn. of the Cath. Diocese of Birmingham, 1989-95, chair of commn., 1994-95; bd. dirs. Be an Apostle of Christ, 1988—; chair human concerns com. St. Peter's, 1988—; mem. Direct Svc. Network, 1989—; mem. Greater Birmingham Ministries program, 1989—; treas. Greater Birmingham UNA-USA chpt., 1992—; mem. COMPEER Bd., Birmingham, Ala., 1997—; bd. dirs. Greater Birmingham Ministries, 1998—, chmn. direct svcs. work group, 1999—; mem. WOC, Call to Action, Bread for the World, CALC, Pax Christi, Amnesty Internat., Nat. Conf. of Cmty. and Justice, Smithsonian Inst., UNICEF, Coalition Against Hate Crimes, 1997—, Birmingham Com. on Fgn. Rels., 1998—; bd. dirs. Ala. chpt. Fulbright Assn., 1999—; organizer Christmas gift drive for needy families Angel Tree project St. Peter's Cath. Ch., 1988—; bd. dirs. League Women Voters Greater Birmingham, 1999—. Recipient resolution City of Birmingham, 1999. Mem. AAUW, Nat. Mus. of Women in the Arts, U.S. Holocost Mus., Vereinigung Ehemaliger Körnerschülerinnen. Roman Catholic. Avocations: reading, music, skiing, cooking, travelling. Home: 1225 Branchwater Ln Vestavia Hills AL 35216-2001

DIASIO, RICHARD LEONARD, power transmission executive, sports facility executive; b. Bridgeport, Conn., Nov. 25, 1937; s. Daniel Joseph and Rose Sarah (Agasi) D.; m. Julia Ann Krhla, Oct. 14, 1961; children: Richard J., Laura L., Christopher S. AS in Mech. Engring., Bridgeport Engring. Inst., 1965. Engr. U.S. Elec. Motors, Milford, Conn., 1962-64; sales profl. Reliance Electric, Hamden, Conn., 1964-66; sales mgr. Dynamatic div. Eaton Corp., Fairfield, N.J., 1966-72; mgr. regional sales Harnischfeger Corp., Woodbridge, N.J., 1972-74; mgr. nat. sales Kanematsu-Gosho, South Plainfield, N.J., 1974-77; dir. mktg. Ind. Gear Works, Indpls., 1977-78, gen. mgr., 1978-80; pres. Ind. Power Transmission Systems, Inc., Indpls, 1980—; pres. Putnam Park Corp., Putnam County, Ind., 1990—, Diasio Car Co., 1999—. With USAF, 1955-59. Mem. Soc. Mfg. Engrs. (sr.), Dramatists Guild, Authors League Am. Republican. Roman Catholic. Avocations: auto sports, writing. Office: Ind Power Transmission Sys 470 Northfield Dr Brownsburg IN 46112-2113

DIAWARA, MANTHIA, film and literature educator, writer, filmmaker; b. Bamako, Mali, Dec. 19, 1953; came to U.S., 1974; m. Regina Austin (div. Aug. 1997); children: Mansita, Saman. BA, Am. U., 1977, MA, 1988. Asst. prof. U. Calif., Santa Barbara, 1985-89, assoc. prof., 1989-91; prof. film and lit. U. Pa., Phila., 1991-92, N.Y.C., 1992—. Author: African Cinema, 1992, In Search of Africa, 1998; editor: Black American Cinema, 1993; dir. film Rouch in Reverse, 1995. Office: NYU Dept Film 715 Broadway New York NY 10003-6860

DIAZ, CAMERON, actress; b. Long Beach, Calif., Aug. 30, 1972. Grad. high sch., Long Beach, Calif. Appeared in (films) The Mask, 1994, Feeling Minnesota, 1996, She's the One, 1996, The Last Supper, 1996, Keys to Tulsa, 1996, Head Above Water, 1996, My Best Friend's Wedding, 1997 (Blockbuster Entertainment award), a Life Less Ordinary, 1997, (television) Space Ghost Coast to Coast, 1994, Very Bad Things, 1998, Fear and Loathing in Las Vegas, 1998, There's Something About Mary, 1998 (N.Y. Film Critics Cir. award, MTV Movie award, Am. Comedy award), Invisible Circus, 1999, Being John Malkovich, 1999, Any Given Sunday, 1999. Named Female Star of Tomorrow, Nat. Theatre Owners Assn., 1996. *

DIAZ, CONSULEO, medical executive. BA, U. So. Calif., 1966, MS, 1989. CEO Rancho Los Amigos Med. Ctr., 1993—. Office: 7601 E Imperial Hwy Downey CA 90242

DIAZ, DAVID, illustrator; married; 3 children. Degree, Ft. Lauderdale (Fla.) Art Inst. Illustrator of children's books including Neighborhood Odes (Gary Soto), 1992, Smoky Night (Eve Bunting), 1994 (Caldecott medal 1995), Anansi's Narrow Waist (Len Cabral), 1994, Wilma Unlimited: How Wilma Rudolph Became the World's Fastest Woman (Kathleen Krull), 1996, Passing Strange: True Tales of New England Hauntings and Horrors (Joseph Citro), 1996, Just One Flick of the Finger (Marybeth Lorbiecki), 1996, The Inner City Mother Goose (Eve Merriam), 1996, Going Home (Eve Bunting), 1996, The Christmas Home (Eve Bunting), 1997, The Disappearing Alphabet (Richard Wilbur), 1999, The Little Scarecrow Boy (Margaret Wise Brown); one-man shows include Thurber Ctr. Gallery. Recipient awards Parents' Choice, Am. Illustrations, Comm. Arts, Am. Inst. Graphic Arts, N.Y. Art Dirs. Club. Office: care Harcourt Brace & Co 1697 Robin Pl Carlsbad CA 92009*

DIÁZ, ELENA R., community health nurse; b. Albuquerque; d. Maria E. Lopez. BSN, U. Ariz., 1975. RNC, ANA; cert. cmty. health nurse. Community health nurse Pima County Health Dept., Tucson, 1975—; ad hoc com. for minority recruitment and retention Coll. Nursing U. Ariz. Tucson; ct. appointed investigator for Pub. Fiduciary's Office, Pima County. Recipient St. Cyril's Clair Dunn/Judith Lovchik award Peace and Justice Com., 1987, La Esperanza award, 1987. Mem. Am. Assn. Hispanic Nurses, Am. Heart Assn., Nat. Coalition Hispanic Health and Human Svcs. Orgns., Tucson Assn. Hispanic Nurses.

DIAZ, FERNANDO GUSTAVO, neurosurgeon; came to U.S., 1971; s. Fernando Diaz Calderon and Susana (Barriga) D.; children: Fernando Austin, David Frederick, Sean Christopher, Patrick Aaron. BS, Centro Universitario Mex., 1963; MD, Univ. de Mex., 1969; MA, U. Kans., Kansas City, 1973; PhD, U. Minn., 1979; MA in Bus., Cen. Mich. U., Mt. Pleasant,

1987; JD, Wayne State U., 1995. Diplomate Am. Bd. Neurological Surgery; lic. physician and surgeon Mex., Can., Ill., Mich., Fla.; mem. Michigan Bar, 1995. Intern Regina Gen. Hosp., Sask., Can., 1969-70, resident in anethesia, 1971; resident in gen. surgery U. Kans., Kansas City, 1971-73; resident in neurosurgery U. Minn. Hosps., Mpls., 1973-78; staff neurosurgeon Henry Ford Hosp., Detroit, 1978-87; chmn. Neurosci. Inst. Santa Fe, Gainesville, Fla., 1987-90; prof., chmn. dept. neurol. surgery Wayne State U., Detroit, 1990—; neurosurg. nat. cons. to U.S. Surgeon Gen., USAF, 1991; coord. neurosurgery resident edn. Henry Ford Hosp., 1979—; clin. assoc. prof. surgery U. Mich., 1986—; mem. working group in neurosurgery WHO. Mem. editl. bd. Neurosurgery Jour.; contbr. articles to profl. jours. Lt. col. USAFR. Recipient awards Lily Pharms., Merck, Sharp & Dome Pharms., Organon Labs. Fellow ACS, Interam. Coll. Physicians, Internat. Coll. Surgeons (vice regent U.S. sect. 1985); mem. AMA, Neurosurg. Soc. Am., Soc. Neurol. Surgeons, Mich. Med. Soc., Wayne County Med. Soc., Am. Assn. Neurol. Surgeons (cerebrovascular sect.), Congress of Neurol. Surgeons, Mich. Assn. Neurol. Surgeons (sec.-treas. 1984-86, v.p. 1986, pres. 1997-98), Detroit Neurosurg. Acad. (v.p. 1986—), Soc. Critical Care Medicine, Mich. Heart Assn. (chmn. stroke com. 1984-86, community site ad-hoc com. 1984, community programs and edn. com. 1986), Mich. Assn. Neurosurgery (chmn. bd.), L.Am. Fedn. Neurosurgery (sec. gen.), U. Minn. Alumni Assn. Roman Catholic. Email: diaz@neurosurg.wayne.edu. Office: Wayne State U Neurol Surg 4201 Saint Antoine St Detroit MI 48201-2153

DIAZ, JAMES HENRY, public health physician; b. New Orleans, May 26, 1949; s. Abram Henry and Marjorie Lemann Diaz; m. Deborah Wright, Mar. 29, 1969; children: James Jr., Laura, Margaret. MD, Tulane U., 1975, D of Pub. Health, 1995, D in tropical medicine, 1998. Diplomate Am. Bd. Preventive Medicine, Am. Bd. Anesthesiology; bd. cert. Pub. Health, Pain Mgmt., Critical Care Medicine. Intern in gen. surgery Ochsner Clin. and Ochsner Found. Hosp., New Orleans, 1975-76; resident in ob-gyn. Health Scis. Ctr. U. Colo., Denver, 1976-77, resident in anesthesiology, 1977-79; fellow in pediat. anesthesiology and critical care Denver Children's Hosp., 1979-80; dir. ICU Ochsner Clinic, New Orleans, 1992-94, head pediatric anesthesia, 1980-95, co-dir., ICU, 1981-92; intern in gen. surgery Ochsner Clin. and Ochsner Found. Hosp., New Orleans, 1975-76; head preventitive medicine La. State U. Sch. of Medicine, New Orleans, 1996—, head MPH degree program, 1996—; sr. registrar in pediat. anaesthesia and critical care Hosp. for Sick Children, London, Eng., 1985; resident in gen. preventive medicine and pub. health Tulane U., 1995; pres. Lemann & Thibaut, Inc., Donaldsville, La., 1997—; adv. bd. respiratory care State of La., 1984-90; med. dir. La. Telemedicine Network State of La., 1995-97, Daus. of Charity Cmty. Health Partnership, New Orleans, 1996-98. Recipient Physician's Recognition award AMA, 1998—; named Top Doctors in New Orleans, 1998—. Fellow Am. Acad. of Pediatrics (sect. chair 1988-90); mem. La. Soc. for Respiratory Care (dir. 1992-93), New Orleans Anesthesia Soc. (pres. 1985-87), La. Soc. of Anesthesiologists (pres. 1987-89), La. State Med. Soc. (adv. bd. pain medicine 1996—). Office: La State U Sch of Medicine 1600 Canal St Ste 800 New Orleans LA 70112-2854

DIAZ, JAVIER VICENTE, bank executive; b. Nov. 11, 1969. BS in Marine Transp., U.S. Merchant Marine Acad., 1995. Assoc. Santander Investment Securities, N.Y.C., 1995-97; asst. v.p. Deutsche Bank Securities, N.Y.C., 1997—. Lt. USNR, 1995—.

DIAZ, JUSTINO, bass-baritone; b. San Juan, P.R., Jan. 29, 1940; m. Ilsa Rodriquez; children: Natascia, Katya. Student, U. P.R., 1958-59, New Eng. Conservatory Music, 1959-62; MusD (hon.), New Eng. Conservatory Music, 1986. Debut in Menotti's The Telephone, P.R., 1957; appearances with Fujiwara Opera, New Eng. Opera Theatre, 1961, Opera Co. Boston, 1966, Am. Opera Soc., 1963-64, 69, Dallas Civic Opera, opera cos. of New Orleans, Ft. Worth, San Juan, P.R., N.Y.C., Balt., Denver, Memphis, San Francisco, Boston, Miami, Fla., Washington, L.A., Seattle, Houston, symphony orchs. of N.Y.C., Cleve., Boston, Covent Garden, London, San Francisco, philharm. orchs. of Phila., Chgo., Dallas, Indpls., Detroit, N.Y.C., L.A., also Spoleto, Casals and Salzburg festivals and La Scala, Milan, Italy, Royal Opera House at Covent Garden, London, Gran Teatro del Liceo, Barcelona, Spain, Paris Opera Bastille, May Festival, Florence, Italy, San Francisco Opera Co., L.A. Music Ctr. Opera Co., Danish Royal Opera, Teatro Mcpl. Sao Paulo, Santiago de Chile, Teatro Colon, Buenos Aires, Bonn, Germany, Mexico City, Hamburg State Opera, Germany, Vienna (Austria) State Opera, Munich State Opera, Athens, Greece, Caracas (Venezuela) Opera, Rome Opera, Trieste (Italy) Opera, Verona (Italy) Summer Festival, Deutsches State Opera, Berlin, Edinburgh Festival, Mostly Mozart Festival, Lincoln Ctr., N.Y.C.; leading bass, baritone Met. Opera Co., 1963—, rec. artist for Columbia, London, Vanguard, ABC, RCA, Angel Records, ASV Records, EMI Records, Deutche Grammophone, Decca, Sony Classical; played Iago in Zeffirelli's film Othello. Recipient Handel medalion N.Y.C., 1966; recipient Family of Man citation Soc. Family of Man, 1966. Office: care John Miller 801 W 181st St Apt 20 New York NY 10033-4518

DIAZ, MANUEL, university tennis coach; m. Suzanne Rondeau; children: Manuel III, Eric, Alex. U. Ga., 1972-75. Profl. tennis player various cities, 1976-78; profl. tennis instr. various clubs, 1978-82; asst. tennis coach U. Ga., Athens, 1982-88, assoc. tennis coach, 1985, head tennis coach, 1988—; head coach Puerto Rico Davis Cup Team, 1992, 1994—. Coach of S.E. Conf. tennis champions, 1989, 91, 93, 95, 96, 97, NCAA finalist, 1989, 91, 93; named Wilson/ Intercoll. Tennis Assn. Nat. Coach of Yr., 1995. Office: U Ga Athletic Dept PO Box 1472 Athens GA 30603-1472*

DIAZ, NELSON ANGEL, lawyer; b. N.Y.C., May 23, 1947; s. Luis Diaz and Maria (Cancel) Rodriguez; m. Vilma D. Ortiz, June 21, 1969; children: Vilmarie, Nelson M.V., Delia Lee. AAS, St. John's U., 1967, BS, 1969; JD, Temple U., 1972; LLD (hon.), LaSalle Coll., 1982, St. John's U., 1987, Temple U., 1990, Albright Coll., 1995. Bar: Pa. 1972, D.C. 1978, U.S. Supreme Ct. 1978, N.Y. 1998. Legal intern Camden (N.J.) Regional Legal Svcs., 1970-71; asst. defender Defender Assn. Phila., 1972-73; asoc. counsel Temple U. Legal Aid Office, Phila., 1973-75; assoc. Fell, Spalding, Goff & Ruben, Phila., 1976-77; exec. dir. Spanish Mchts. Assn., Phila., 1973-77; White House fellow v.p. of U.S., 1977-78; assoc. Wolf, Block, Schorr & Solis-Cohen, Phila., 1978-81; adminstrv. judge Phila. Ct. of Common Pleas, 1981-93; gen. counsel HUD, Washington, 1993-97; ptnr. Blank, Rome, Comisky & McCauley, Phila., 1997—; lectr. Sch. Law Temple U., Phila., 1983—. Columnist Phila. Sun and Evening Bull., 1973-75; contbr. articles on Japanese, Peruvian legal system to various publs. Founder Phila. Leadership Prayer Breakfast, 1984-93; bd. dirs., com. chmn. Revitalized Neighborhood, 1983-87; participant, hon. chair Soviet Jewry Coun., 1985; com. mem. Charter Rev. Phila., 1986; chmn. Nat. Assn. Hispanic Elderly, L.A., 1978-93; trustee Young Life, 1989-93, Temple U., 1997—; bd. govs. Temple Hosp., Phila., 1975-93; founder, bd. dirs. Nat. P.R. Coalition, 1978-86; co-chmn., bd. dirs. Urban Affairs Partnership, Phila., 1984-90; bd. dirs. Midwest/N.E. Voter Registration Project, Chgo., 1982-93, 97—, World Affairs Coun., 1997—; chair Greater Phila. Billy Graham Crusade; active Found. Improvement Justice, 1992, Nat. Bar Assn. Jud. Coun., 1993, Frederick Douglass Soc. Found., 1995, Salvation Army, 1995, Boricua Coll., 1995; mem. Dem. Nat. Com. Recipient Life Achievement award Nat. Puerto Rican Coalition, Washington, 1988, Judge of the Yr. award Pa. Trial Lawyers Assn., 1989, Man of the Yr. award NAACP, North Phila., 1990, Cesar Chavez award, 1995; Japan Soc. fellow; Fulbright fellow, 1990. Mem. Pa. Bar Assn., Phila. Bar Assn., D.C. Bar Assn., Pa. Trial Lawyers Assn., State Conf. Trial Judges. Democrat. Avocation: sports. Office: Blank Rome Comisky & McCauley 1 Logan Sq Fl 3 Philadelphia PA 19103-6998

DIAZ, NILS JUAN, nuclear engineer, federal commissioner, regulator; b. Moron, Cuba, Apr. 7, 1938; came to U.S., 1961; s. Rafael Octavio Diaz and Rosa Dalia (Rojas) Chao; m. Zenaida G. Gonzalez, Oct. 9, 1960; children: NIls, Ariadne, Allene. BSME, U. Villanova, Havana, 1960; MS in Nuclear Engrng. Sci., U. Fla., 1964, PhD in Nuclear Engrng. Sci., 1969. Rsch. assoc. nuclear engrng. sci. U. Fla., Gainesville, 1965-69, asst. prof., reactor supr., 1969-74, assoc. prof., dir. nuclear facilities, 1974-79, prof., dir. nuclear facilities, 1979-84; assoc. dean for rsch. Sch. of Engrng. Calif. State U., Long Beach, 1984-86; prof. nuclear engrng. scis. U. Fla., Gainesville, 1986-96; dir. Innovative Nuclear Space Power and Propulsion Inst., Calif. and Fla., 1985-96; commr. U.S. Nuclear Regulatory Commn., 1996—; sr. cons. Exxon Nuclear, Fla. Power and Light-Fla. Power Corp., Bellevue, Wash. and Fla., 1974-79; pres., chief engr. Fla. Nuclear Assocs., Inc., Gainesville, 1976—; prin. advisor Nuclear Safety Coun., Madrid, 1981-83; internat. energy cons., Argentina, Brazil, Mex., Santo Domingo, Spain, Russia; commr. U.S. Nuclear Regulatory Commn. Contbr. articles to profl. jours. Chmn. Minority Engr. Program Adv. Bd., Long Beach, 1984-86. Recipient Disting. Svc. Award Math. Engrng. Sci. Achievements and Minority Engrng. Program State of Calif., Long Beach, 1983; named Hispanic Engr. of Yr. for Outstanding Tech. Contbns., Hispanic Engr. Nat. Achievement Com., Houston, 1990. Fellow AAAS, ASME, Am. Nuclear Soc.; mem. Am. Soc. for Engrng. Edn., Cuban-Am. Engrng. Soc. (Engr. of Yr. 1993), Hispanic Assn. Profl. Engrs. Republican. Roman Catholic. Achievements include patents for heterogeneous gas core reactors, gamma ray flaw detection system; invention of vapor core nuclear rocket propulsion system. Office: US Nuclear Regulatory Commn Offices of the Commr Washington DC 20555-0001

DIAZ, RAUL, psychologist; b. Phila., Aug. 23, 1957; s. Raul and Ofelia (Perez) D.; m. Connie M. Parsons, Jan. 17, 1957; children: Benjamin R., Samuel Alan, Natalie Lynn. BS, U. Fla., 1979; MA, Bowling Green (Ohio) State U., 1983, PhD, 1985. Lic. psychologist, Fla.; registered Nat. Register Health Svc. Providers in Psychology. Clin. psychology intern U. South Fla., Tampa, 1984-85; dir. psychol. svcs. Lake Hosp. of Palm Beaches, Lake Worth, Fla., 1985-89; clin. leader adult psychiat. unit Humana Hosp.—Palm Beaches, West Palm Beach, Fla., 1989-90; pres., co-dir. Woodlake Psychol. Assocs., P.A., Greenacres, Fla., 1990—; psychol. cons. to various police depts. including Office of Palm Beach County Sheriff, West Palm Beach, 1989—, to sheriff Broward County, Ft. Lauderdale, Fla., 1997—. Named Hijo Predilecto, Municipio de Candelaria, 1989. Mem. APA, Fla. Psychol. Assn., Coun. Police Psychol. Svcs. Avocations: running, weight lifting, nutrition, reading, travel. Office: Woodlake Psychol Assocs PA 3900 Woodlake Blvd Ste 211 Greenacres FL 33463-3045

DIAZ, SHARON, education administrator; b. Bakersfield, Calif., July 29, 1946; d. Karl C. and Mildred (Lunn) Clark; m. Luis F. Diaz, Oct. 19, 1968; children: Daniel, David. BS, San Jose State U., 1969; MS, U. Calif., San Francisco, 1973; PhD, St. Mary's Coll. Calif., 1999. Nurse Kaiser Found. Hosp., Redwood City, Calif., 1969-73; lectr. San Jose (Calif.) State Coll., 1969-70; nurse San Mateo (Calif.) County, 1970-71; instr. St. Francis Meml. Hosp. Sch. Nursing, San Francisco, 1973-76, asst. dir., 1976-78; dir. Samuel Merritt Hosp. Sch. Nursing, Oakland, Calif., 1978-84; founding pres. Samuel Merritt Coll., Oakland, 1984—; v.p. East Bay Area Health Edn. Ctr., Oakland, 1980-87; mem. adv. com. Calif. Acad. Partnership Program, 1990; mem. nat. adv. com. Nursing Outcomes Project. Bd. dirs. Head Royce Sch., 1990-98, vice chair, 1993-95, chair, 1995-97; bd. dirs. Ladies Home Soc., 1992—, sec. 1994-95, treas., CFO 1995-97, 2nd v.p. 1997-99; adv. bd. Ethnic Health Inst., 1997—; mem. commn. minorities higher edn. Am. Coun. Edn., 1998—. Named Woman of Yr., Oakland YWCA, 1996. Mem. Am. Assn. of Pres. Ind. Colls. and Univs., Sigma Theta Tau. Office: Samuel Merrritt Coll Office of Pres 370 Hawthorne Ave Oakland CA 94609-3108

DIAZ, WILLIAM ADAMS, political scientist; b. N.Y.C., Dec. 5, 1945; s. Carlos Rafael and Margarita (Adams) D.; BA, Fordham Coll., 1967; MA, Fordham U., 1969, PhD, 1978. Assoc. project dir. Fordham Inst. for Social Rsch., N.Y.C., 1970-74; rsch. assoc. 20th Century Fund, N.Y.C., 1974-77; sr. rsch. assoc. Manpower Demonstration Rsch. Corp., N.Y.C., 1977-83; program officer Ford Found., 1983—; chancellor search adv. com., N.Y.C. Bd. Edn., 1987-89; dir. N.Y.C. Nat. Service Corp., 1985—, N.Y.C. Outward Bound Ctr., 1989—. Chmn. bd. dirs. Aspira of N.Y., Inc., 1978-80; program com. Coun. on Founds., 1986-87, rsch. com., 1988-90. NDEA fellow, 1967-70. Mem. Am. Polit. Sci. Assn., Assn. for Pub. Policy Analysis and Mgmt., Alpha Mu Gamma, Pi Sigma Alpha. Home: 727 River Rd Teaneck NJ 07666-1619 Office: 320 E 43rd St New York NY 10017-4816

DIAZ-ARCE, RAUL, soccer player; b. San Miguel, El Salvador, Feb. 1, 1970. Player DC United, 1996-97, New England Revolution, 1998-99, San Jose Clash, 1999—; mem. El Salvadoran World Cup Nat. Team. also: US Soccer Fedn 1801 S Prairie Ave # 1811 Chicago IL 60616-1357*

DIAZ-ARRASTIA, GEORGE RAVELO, lawyer; b. Havana, Cuba, Aug. 20, 1959; came to U.S., 1968; s. Ramon Fuentes and Elihut (Ravelo) D.-A.; m. Maria del Carmen Gomez, Aug. 6, 1983. BA in History, Rice U., 1980; JD, U. Chgo., 1983. Bar: Tex. 1983, U.S. Dist. Ct. (so. dist.) Tex. 1985, U.S. Ct. Appeals (5th and D.C. cirs.) 1985, U.S. Supreme Ct. 1992, U.S. Dist. Ct. (no., we. and ea. dists.) Tex. 1994. Assoc. Baker & Botts, Houston, 1983-88, Deaton & Briggs (formerly Deaton, Briggs & McCain), Houston, 1988-90; ptnr. Gilpin, Paxson & Bersch, LLP, Houston, 1991-98, Schirrmeister Ajamie LLP, Houston, 1998—. Fellow Tex. Bar Found., Houston Bar Found.; mem. ABA, Am. Judicature Soc., Am. Soc. Internat. Law, State Bar of Tex., Houston Bar Assn., Coll. of State Bar Tex. Republican. Roman Catholic. E-mail: gdarrastia@shirr-aj.com. Home: 3794 Drake St Houston TX 77005-1118 Office: Schirrmeister Ajamie LLP 711 Louisiana Ste 2150 Houston TX 77002

DIAZ-BALART, LINCOLN, congressman; b. Havana, Cuba, Aug. 13, 1954; m. Cristina Fernandez; children: Lincoln Gabriel, Daniel. BA in Internat. Rels., New Coll. of U. So. Fla., 1976; diploma in Brit. Politics, Cambridge (Eng.) U.; JD, Case Western Res. U., 1979. Lawyer Legal Svcs. of Greater Miami, Fla.; asst. state atty. State of Fla.; mem. Fla. Ho. of Reps.from 110th Dist., 1986-89, Fla. State Senate from Dist. 34, 1989-92, Congress from 21st Fla. Dist., 1993—; mem. rules com.; vice chmn. subcom. on rules of the house. Mem. exec. com. Congl. Human Rights Caucus; vice chmn. Nat. Rep. Congl. Com. Mem. ABA, Fla. Bar Assn., Dade County Bar Assn., Cuban-Am. Bar Assn., Rep. Nat. Lawyers Assn., Lions. Republican. Roman Catholic. Office: US Ho of Reps Office of Ho Mems 404 Cannon Bldg Washington DC 20515-0921

DÍAZ DE GONZALEZ, ANA MARÍA, psychologist, educator; b. San Juan, P.R., July 26, 1945; d. Esteban Díaz-González and Petra (Guadalupe) De Diaz; m. Jorge Gonzalez Monclova, Jan. 7, 1968; children: Ana Teresa, Jorge, Julio Esteban. BS, U. P.R., Rio Piedras, 1965, MEd, 1973; MS, Caribbean Ctr. Advanced Study, San Juan, 1982, PhD, 1983. Lic. psychologist, P.R. Home economist U. P.R., Fajardo and San Juan, 1965-82; specialist in human devel. and gerontology U. P.R., San Juan, 1983—. Mem. APA, Assn. Economists Hogar (pres. 1965-92, Disting. Svc. award 1973), Assn. Specialists SEA (pres. 1982-93), Assn. Psychology P.R., Epsilon Sigma Phi (sec. 1970—), Gamma Sigma Delta. Roman Catholic. Avocations: piano, reading, exercise. Home: 1325 Calle 23 San Juan PR 00924-5249 Office: U PR Svc Extension Agr Terrenos Estacion Exptl Rio Piedras San Juan PR 00928

DIAZ-VERSON, SALVADOR, JR., investment advisor; b. Havana, Cuba, Dec. 31, 1951; s. Salvador and Metodia Diaz-V.; m. Patricia Dianne Floyd, Apr. 24, 1976; children: Salvador III, Patricia Elizabeth. BA in Fin., Fla. State U., Tallahassee, 1973. Chief investment officer Am. Family Life Assurance, Columbus, Ga., 1977-79; exec. v.p. Am. Family Corp., Columbus, 1980-83, pres., 1983-91, also dir.; pres. Diaz-Verson Capital Investment, 1991—; bd. dirs. Regions Bank, Ga.; pres., CEO Diaz-Verson Capital Investment Inc., 1992. Trsutee St. Francis Hosp., Fund Am. Studies; bd. dirs. United Way, Columbus, 1983—. Mem. Columbus C. of C. (bd. dirs. 1983—, chair 1989), Green Island Country Club, Country Club of Columbus. Roman Catholic. Office: Diaz-Verson Capital Investment Ste 105 1200 Brookstone Centre Pkwy Columbus GA 31904-2935

DIAZ-ZUBIETA, AGUSTIN, nuclear engineer, executive; b. Madrid, Spain, Mar. 24, 1936; came to U.S., 1953; s. Emilio Diaz Cabeza and Maria Teresa Zubieta Atucha; m. Beth Lee Fortune, Sept. 6, 1958; children: Walter Agustin, Michael Joel, Anthony John. B. U. Madrid, 1953; BSc in Physics, U. Tenn., 1958; MSc in Mech. Engrng., Duke U., 1960; PhD in Nuclear Engrng., U. Md., 1981. Nuclear engr. Combustion Engrng., Tenn., 1954-58; instr. engrng. Duke U., Durham, N.C., 1958-60; nuclear physicist Allis Chalmers Co., Washington, 1960-64; country mgr. South Africa Allis Chalmers Co., 1964-66; mgr. internat. power generation projects GE, N.Y.C., 1966-69, mgr. Europe and Middle East strategic planning, 1969-71; dir. internat. constrn. planning GE, Westport, Conn., 1971-75, dir. constrn., 1975-83; chief exec. officer GE Affiliate, Westport, 1983-87; v.p. internat. sales, devel. Internat. Tech. Corp., L.A., 1987-94; mng. dir. IT Italia S.P.A., IT Spain, S.A. Author: Measurement of Subcriticality of Nuclear Reactors by Stocastic Processes, 1981. Pres. Fairfield (Conn.) Assn. Condo Owners, 1983-87. Named Astronomer of Yr. Barnard Astronomical Soc., Chattanooga, 1957; fgn. exchange scholar U.S. Govt., 1953-58; grantee, NSF, 1958-60, U.S. Office of Ordinance Rsch. U.S. Army, 1958-60. Mem. Am. Nuclear Soc., Am. Soc. Mech. Engrs., Am. Soc. Profl. Engrs., Sigma Xi. Republican. Roman Catholic. Avocations: golf, tennis, swimming, sailing, music. Home: 47 Country Meadow Rd Rolling Hills Estates CA 90274

DIBACCO, RICHARD PAUL, vocational case manager; b. Thomas, W.Va., Dec. 21, 1954; s. Carmen P. and Mary Lou DiB.; m. Anabel Velazquez, June 22, 1991; children: Alexandra, Richard, Philip. BS in Psychology, W.Va. U., MS in Rehab. Counsel. Cert. disability mgmt. specialist, case mgr. Coord. residential svc. Western Dist. Guidance Ctr., Parkersburg, W.Va., 1979-82; account exec., rehab. specialist Intracorp, Maitland, Fla., 1982-88; CEO Workers Rehab., Winter Park, Fla., 1988—; bd. dirs. Threshold, Orlando, Fla., 1995—; rehab. planner State of Fla. Dept. of Labor, Tallahassee, 1983—. Mem. Nat. Assn. Rehab. Profls. in Pvt. Sector (treas. 1988), Brevard Claims Coun. (pres. 1986-87, v.p. 1985), Case Mgmt. Soc. Avocations: golf, basketball, reading, woodworking. Home: 229 Crooked Stick Ct Orlando FL 32828-8831 Office: Workers Rehab Inc 1 Purlieu Pl Ste 139 Winter Park FL 32792-4405

DIBATTISTE, CAROL A., lawyer; b. Phila., Dec. 28, 1951; d. Peter Martin DiBattiste and Hilda Yolanda (Battilana) Mignogna. BA, LaSalle U., 1976; JD, Temple U., 1981; LLM, Columbia U., 1986. Bar: Pa. 1982, N.Y. 1989, D.C. 1989, Fla. 1990, U.S. Ct. Mil. Appeals 1982, U.S. Supreme Ct. 1985. Commd. 2d lt. USAF, 1976, advanced through grades to maj., 1987, cir. trial counsel Pacific Region, 1982-85; mem. faculty USAF JAG Sch., Maxwell AFB, Ala., 1986-89; chief recruiting atty. Office of Judge Advocate Gen. USAF, Washington, 1989-91; asst. U.S. atty. So. Dist. Fla., Miami, 1991-92; dir. Office of Legal Edn. Dept. Justice, 1992-93; prin. dep. gen. coun. Dept. of Navy, 1993-94; dir. Exec. Office for U.S. Attys., Washington, 1994-98; dep. U.S. atty. So. Dist. Fla., Miami, 1998—; adj. faculty U. Miami Sch. Law Trial Skills, 1998—. Editor: The Reporter, 1986-87; mem. editorial bd. Air Force Law Rev., 1984, 85, 87; contbr. articles to profl. jours. Mem. bd. visitors Temple U. Sch. Law, 1996—; trustee USAF JAG Sch. Found., 1993-96. Mem. ABA (chmn. standing com. on mil. law 1989-91), Fed. Bar Assn. (Young Fed. Lawyer award 1985), Nat. Inst. for Trial Advocacy (faculty 1986-92), USAF Assn. Roman Catholic.

DIBB, DAVID WALTER, research association administrator; b. Draper, Utah, July 4, 1943; s. Walter and Mary (Lisinsky) D.; m. Vivian Berrett, Dec. 15, 1966; children: Stephanie, Gregory, Steven, Rebecca. BS, Brigham Young U., 1970; PhD, U. Ill., 1974. Cert. profl. agronomist, cert. profl. soil scientist. Rsch. asst. U. Ill., Urbana, 1970-74, teaching asst., 1971-74; vis. asst. prof. N.C. State U., Raleigh, 1974-75; rsch. dir. Potash and Phosphate Inst., Atlanta, 1982-89; regional dir. Potash and Phosphate Inst., Columbia, Mo., 1975-82; coord. Latin Am. Potash and Phosphate Inst., Atlanta, 1982-85; v.p. North Am. Potash and Phosphate Inst., West Lafayette, Ind., 1985-86, sr. v.p., 1987-88; pres. Potash and Phosphate Inst., Atlanta, 1989—; pres. Agronomic Sci. Found., Madison, Wis., 1983-85; mem. fertilizer industry adv. com. Food and Agrl. Orgn. of UN, Rome, 1988-94; exec. industry rev. group TVA, Muscle Shoals, Ala., 1989-94; adj. prof. Purdue U., West Lafayette, 1985-88; hon. prof. Chinese Acad. Agrl. Scis., 1996. Contbr. author: Potassium in Agriculture, 1985; editor: Fertilizer Research, 1989-90; contbr. articles to profl. jours. Instnl. rep. Boy Scouts Am., West Lafayette, 1982-85, asst. scoutmaster, Norcross, Ga., 1989-90; youth coach for basketball, baseball, and soccer, Mo., Ind., Ga., 1980-89; active PTA, Mo., Ind., Ga., 1978-96. Fellow Am. Soc. Agronomy (chmn. budget and fin. com. 1988), Soil Sci. Soc. Am.; mem. AAAS, Coun. for Agrl. Sci. and Tech., Internat. Soil Sci. Soc., Gamma Sigma Delta, Alpha Zeta. Office: Potash and Phosphate Inst 655 Engring Dr Ste 110 Norcross GA 30092

DIBELL, MARTA LEE, foreign language educator; b. Santa Barbara, Calif., July 3, 1964; d. David Lawrence Dibell and Helen Marie Smith. BA in German, Fla. State U., 1986. Rschr. Prentice Hall, Tallahassee, 1986-88; customer svc. rep. Prentice Hall, Santa Ana, Calif., 1988-90; tchr. Walnut (Calif.) Valley Unified Sch. Dist., 1991—. Mem. Am. Assn. Tchrs. German, U.S. Parachute Assn. (Falcon Relative Work award 1996), Fgn. Lang. Assn. Orange County. Avocations: gardening, cooking, skydiving, hiking. Home: 956 Rancho Cir Fullerton CA 92835-3337 Office: Walnut H S 400 Pierre Rd Walnut CA 91789-2535

DIBENEDETTO, ANTHONY THOMAS, engineering educator; b. N.Y.C., Oct. 27, 1933; s. Thomas and Mathilda DiB.; m. Rose Marie Lima, Feb. 12, 1955; children: Diane, Laura, Thomas, David, Stephen. B.Ch.E., CCNY, 1955; M.S., U. Wis., 1956, Ph.D., 1960. Chem. engr. Union Carbide Corp., 1954-55; prof. chem. engrng. U. Wis., 1960-67; prof., dir. materials research lab. Washington U., 1967-71; head dept. chem. engrng. U. Conn., 1971-77, v.p. grad. edn. and research, 1979-81, v.p. acad. affairs, 1981-86; Univ. prof. chem. engrng. U. Conn., Storrs, 1986-97, prof. emeritus, 1997, dir. Inst. Materials Sci., 1991-95, univ. prof. chem. engrng. emeritus, 1997—; cons. in field. Author: The Structure and Properties of Materials, 1967. Recipient Ednl. Service award Plastics Inst. Am., 1973; NSF profl. devel. award, 1977-79; Disting. Service award U. Wis., 1981, Outstanding Leadership award U. Conn., 1992, Plueddemann award, 1996. Mem. Soc. Plastics Engrs., Am. Inst. Chem. Engrng., Am. Chem. Soc., Sigma Xi, Tau Beta Pi. Home: 1 Brookside Ln Mansfield Center CT 06250-1109 Office: U Conn Inst Materials Sci # U136 Storrs Mansfield CT 06229

DIBERARDINO, MARIE ANTOINETTE, developmental biologist, educator; b. Phila., May 2, 1926; d. Henry and Adelina (Belfi) DiB. BS in Biology, Chestnut Hill Coll., 1948, JD (hon.), 1990; PhD in Zoology, U. Pa., 1962. Rsch. asst. Fox Chase Cancer Ctr. (formerly Inst. Cancer Rsch.), 1948-58, rsch. assoc., 1960-64, asst. mem., 1964-67; assoc. prof. anatomy Med. Coll. Pa. (MCP Hahnemann U.), Phila., 1967-71, prof. anatomy, 1971-81, prof. physiology, 1981-92, prof. biochemistry, 1992-96, prof. emerita, 1996—. Adv. bd.: Internat. Rev. of Cytology, 1976—, Differentiation, 1981—, Series: Developmental Biology, A Comprehensive Synthesis, 1982-94; assoc. editor Jour. Exptl. Zoology, 1984-86; Contbr. articles on devel., genetics and cell biology to sci. jours.; contbr. book revs. in field. Mem. NIH Fogarty Internat. Fellowship Study Group, 1984. NSF grantee, NIH grantee; recipient Jean Brachet Meml. award. Fellow AAAS; mem. Am. Soc. Cell Biology, Soc. for Devel. Biologists (treas., trustee 1975-78), Am. Soc. Zoologists, Internat. Soc. Devel. Biologists, Internat. Soc. of Differentiation (exec. com. 1978-85, 87-90, bd. dirs. 1980-94), Sigma Delta Epsilon. Office: Med Coll Pa Hahnemann Sch Med 2900 W Queen Ln Philadelphia PA 19129-1033

DI BERNADINIS, MICHAEL, commissioner recreation Philadelphia; b. July 14, 1949. BA in Polit. Sci., St. Joseph's U. Commr. recreation dept. City of Phila., 1992—. Office: Phila Recreation Dept 1600 Arch St Ste 6 Philadelphia PA 19103-2028*

DIBIAGGIO, JOHN A., university president; b. San Antonio, Sept. 11, 1932; s. Ciro and Acidalia DiBiaggio; children from previous marriage: David John, Dana Elizabeth, Deirdre Joan; m. Nancy Cronemiller, May 27, 1989. AB, Eastern Mich. U., 1954, D of Edn. (hon.), 1985; DDS, U. Detroit, 1958, LHD (hon.), 1985; MA, U. Mich., 1967; DSci. (hon.), Fairleigh Dickinson U., 1981; LLD (hon.), Sacred Heart U., Bridgeport, Conn., 1984, U. Md., 1985; DHL (hon.), U. New Eng., 1987, Tokyo U. Agr., 1991; LLD (hon.), U. Nigeria, Nsukka, 1992; LHD (hon.), Fitchburg State Coll., 1994, Amer. Coll. of Greece, 1998. Gen. practice dentistry New Baltimore, Mich., 1958-65; asst. prof., asst. to dean, dept. chmn. sch. dentistry U. Detroit, 1965-67; asst. dean student affairs U. Ky., Lexington, 1967-70; prof., dean sch. dentistry Va. Commonwealth U., Richmond, 1970-76; v.p. for health affairs, exec. dir. health ctr. U. Conn., Farmington, 1976-79; pres. U. Conn., Storrs, 1979-85, Mich. State U., East Lansing, 1985-92, Tufts U., Medford, Mass., 1992—; bd. dirs. Kaman Corp.; mem. Knight Found. Commn. on Intercollegiate Athletics, 1990—, PEW Health Professions Commn., 1990-93;. Author: (with others) Applied Practice Management: A Strategy for Stress Control, 1979; cons. Jour. ADA, 1967—; contbr. articles to profl. jours. Chmn. adv. com. dental scholars R.W. Johnson Found.; mem. Pres. Com. for Argonne Nat. Lab. 6, 1986—; trustee U. Detroit, 1979-86, Am. Film Inst., 1988—, Forsyth Dental Ctr., 1993—; trustee Am. Cancer Soc. Found., 1993—, pres. 1999; trustee Oral Health Am., 1995-97; mem. bd.

nominators Am. Inst. Pub. Svc., 1989-92; mem. coun. pres. Univs. Rsch. Assn., 1989-92; bd. dirs. Coun. for Aid to Edn., 1994-96, Mass. Nat. and Comty. Svc. Commn., 1994-97, Am. Coun. on Edn., 1995—, vice chmn., 1998, chmn., 1999, bd. dirs. Black Child and Family Inst., 1990, Mass. Campus Compact Exec. Com., 1995—, mem., exec. dir. search com., 1996, chair devel. com., 1996—, mem. governance com., 1996-98, chmn., 1998; mem. bd. assocs. Whitehead Inst. for Biomed. Rsch., 1995—, chmn., 1998; mem. Bus. Higher Edn. Forum, 1996—, WGBH Ednl. Found., 1992—, chmn. governance com., 1997—. Decorated Order of Merit, Italy; recipient Leadership award Sacred Heart U., Disting. Profl. of Yr. award Mich. Assn. Profls., 1985, Disting. Alumni award Eastern Mich. U., 1986; named Man of Yr., City of Detroit, 1985, Pierre Fauchard Gold Medal award, 1989. Fellow Am. Coll. Dentist, Internat. Coll. Dentists; mem. ADA (cons. jour.), APHA, Am. Assn. Dental Schs., Internat. Assn. Dental Rsch., Nat. Assn. State Univs. and Land Grant Colls. (chmn. 1986-87), NCAA Found. (bd. dirs. 1988—, mem. divsn. III pres.'s coun. 1997—), Am. Automobile Assn. (bd. dirs. 1994—), Am. Film Inst., Mass. Automobile Assn. (bd. dirs. 1992—), Nat. Italian Am. Found. (bd. dirs. 1988-94), Golden Key, Phi Kappa Phi, Omicron Kappa Upsilon, Beta Gamma Sigma, Alpha Omega Alpha (Achievement award 1993), Alpha Sigma Chi, Alpha Lambda Delta. Avocations: tennis, skiing, Packards. Office: Tufts U Office of Pres Medford MA 02155

DIBIANCO, GUSTAVE J., federal judge, eductor; b. 1941. BA, CUNY, 1966; JD, Bklyn. Law Sch., 1969. Bar: N.Y. 1969. With N.Y.C. Transit Authority, 1969; pvt. practice, 1970-71; asst. U.S. atty. U.S. Dept. Justice, Syracuse, 1972-82, ct. apptd. U.S. atty., 1972-82, chief asst. U.S. atty., 1982-87; magistrate judge for no. dist. N.Y., U.S. Magistrate Ct., Syracuse, 1987—; adj. prof. law Syracuse U. Coll. Law, 1989—. With U.S. Army, 1962-64. Office: 100 S Clinton St Rm C-219 Syracuse NY 13261

DIBICCARI, GRACE, pastor; b. White Plains, N.Y.; d. George Tsakanikas and Antoinette Buetti; children: Lawrence J. III, Christopher, Karen Fields, Sharon Esposito. Grad., Wynne Sch. Beauty Culture, White Plains, 1957; B of Divinity in Religion, So. Calif. Sch. Theology, 1994; M in Child Devel., Brighton U.; D in Devine Tech., Inventors Club of Am., 1998. Ordained min. Ind. Assemblies of God Internat., 1981. Pastor Grace Faith Assembly/Grace in Vessels of Christ Ministries, Danbury, Conn., 1981—; pres. Grace in Vessels of Christ Ministries, Danbury, 1981—; chancellor N.E. Bible Inst., Danbury, 1992—; chancellor, head of sch. bd. Grace Faith Christian Sch., Danbury, 1997—. Author 15 books including Victory in the Thought Life, Dealing with Your Problems, God Wants You to Be Happy; singer on 15 gospel albums including God of Miracles, Sacred Hymns, Behold the Lamb. 1st ofcl. pres. Little Ladies Softball League, Danbury, 1974. Recipient Menard Prison Ministry cert., 1990, award Brewster Rotary, 1988, Humanitarian award Internat. Hall of Fame, 1997; Bettermann fellow Nat. Religious Broadcasters, 1990. Mem. Am. Assn. Christian Counselors (charter). Office: Grace in Vessels of Christ Ministries Inc PO Box 3257 Danbury CT 06813-3257

DIBLASI, DIANNE CLARK, editor; b. Bklyn., May 3, 1960; d. Arthur J. and Constance C. (Clark) Mandick; m. Paul J. DiBlasi; 1 child, Bryan Gene. BA in Journalism, NYU, 1982. Asst. editor Random House/Fodor's Travel Guides, N.Y.C., 1983-85; writer, editor Constrn. Products Rev. Mag., Boston, 1986-88; prodn. editor Prentice Hall, Englewood Cliffs, N.J., 1988-91; owner, cons. D. DiBlasi Editl. Svcs., Hillsdale, N.J., 1991—. Copy editor: Take My Word For It, 1986; prodn. editor: Creativities! Elementary Curriculum Art Activities, 1991, Parenting Toward Solutions, 1997; editor, writer Constrn. Products Rev., 1986-88. Mem. Hillsdale Playground Assn., 1994-96, Hillsdale Centennial Com., 1996; mem., chair com. Meadowbrook Faculty and Family Assn., Hillsdale, 1996—. Mem. Editl. Freelancer Assn. Avocations: cooking contests, fundraising. Home and Office: 189 Everdell Ave Hillsdale NJ 07642-1922

DIBLASIO, DENIS, musician, educator; b. Camden, N.J., Feb. 27, 1954; s. William Rocco and Carmella Zita (Doganiero) DiB.; m. Hilda Yusko, Aug. 20, 1983; 1 child, Natalie Louise. BA, Glassboro (N.J.) State Coll., 1978; MusM, U. Miami, 1982. Dir. jazz studies Rowan U., Glassboro, 1987—; clinician Jamey Aebersold Jazz Camps, Elmhurst, Ill. and Louisville, 1987—, Bands of Am., Normal, Ill., 1988—, Villanova (Pa.) U., 1991—, U. Wis. Jazz Camps, Whitewater, 1990-94; adj. prof. Temple U., Phila., 1990-92, Phila. Coll. Performing Arts, 1990-92; musical dir. Maynard Ferguson Orch., Ojai, Calif., 1981-87; mem. adv. bd. Jazz Radio WRTI, Phila., 1986; advising editor Flute Talk mag., Northfield, Ill., 1989—; artist, clinician Yamaha Music of Am., Grand Rapids, Mich., 1984—. Author: DiBlasio's Bop Shop I, 1989, Diblasio's Bop Shop II, 1990, Survival Guide for Jazz Vocalists, 1991, Workouts for Creative Jazz Improvisation, 1993; CD's include Stormy Weather, Playing in the Yard, Catch Me, Seven Giant Steps to Heaven, Reflections of Childhood/Duets, Rhino. Mem., prodr. Denis Diblasio Quartet, 1987—. Recipient Outstanding Achievement award Phila. Jazz Soc., 1991, Festival Dedication, Willingboro Jazz Festival, 1996, Appreciation award Rowan Jazz Festival, 1997. Mem. ASCAP, Internat. Assn. Jazz Educators. Avocations: astronomy, yoga, swimming, movies. Home: 505 Highland Ter Pitman NJ 08071-1523 Office: Rowan U 201 Mullica Hill Rd Glassboro NJ 08028-1700

DIBNER, DAVID ROBERT, architect; b. N.Y.C., May 29, 1926; s. Harry Jesse and Masha Leah (Goldberg) D.; m. Dorothy Joyce Siegel, June 22, 1947; children: Mark Douglas, Amy Lauren. B.Arch., U. Pa., 1949. Registered architect, N.Y., Md., Va., D.C. Ptnr. Fordyce & Hamby Assocs., N.Y.C., 1956-66, The Grad Ptnrship., Newark, 1966-77; pres. Grad-Hoffman, Inc., 1971-75; v.p. Walker-Grad, N.Y.C., 1972-77; exec. v.p. Grad Assocs. P.A., Newark, 1975-77; asst. commr. design and constrn. GSA, Washington, 1977-82; sr. v.p. Bernard Johnson Inc., Bethesda, Md., 1982-89; v.p. and prin. architect Sverdrup Corp., Arlington, Va., 1989-92; adj. prof. Seton Hall U., South Orange, N.J., 1972-77; mem. Bldg. Rsch. Bd. of Nat. Acad. Sci., com. chmn., 1984-92. Author: Joint Ventures for Architects and Engineers, 1972, You and Your Architect, 1973, (with Amy Dibner-Dunlap) Building Additions Design, 1985; editor (with Andrew Lemer) The Role of Public Agencies in Fostering New Technology and Innovation in Building, 1992; chmn. editorial bd. Architecture/N.J., 1968-71; contbr. articles to profl. jours. Mem. West Orange Bd. of Adjustment, N.J., 1970-77, Bldg. Rsch. Bd., 1984-90; Nat. Trust for Historic Preservation. Served with USN, 1944-46, PTO. Fellow AIA (Washington chpt.).

DIBONA, CHARLES JOSEPH, retired trade association executive; b. Quincy, Mass., Feb. 26, 1932; s. Guido Ralph and Helen Elizabeth (Pangraze) DiB.; m. Evelyn Rauch, July 2, 1959; children: Caroline Anne, Charles J. BS, U.S. Naval Acad., 1956; MA (Rhodes scholar), Oxford U., Eng., 1962. Pres., chief exec. officer Center for Naval Analyses, 1967-73; spl. cons. to Pres. U.S., dep. dir.; White House Energy Policy Office, 1973-74; exec. v.p., chief oper. officer Am. Petroleum Inst., Washington, 1974-78; pres., chief exec. officer Am. Petroleum Inst., 1979-99; vice chmn. U.S. nat. com. World Petroleum Congress; mem. Fed. City Coun.; chmn. bd. dirs. Logistics Mgmt. Inst. Lt. comdr. USN, 1956-67. Mem. Am. Coun. for Capital Formation, World Econ. Forum (bd. govs.), Cosmos Club, F Street Club, Met. Club, Chevy Chase Country Club. Roman Catholic. Home: 9306 Georgetown Pike Great Falls VA 22066-2725*

DIBONAVENTURE, LORENZO, film company executive. Co-pres. Worldwide Theatrical Prodn. Warner Bros., Inc., Burbank, Calif. Office: Warner Bros Inc 4000 Warner Blvd Burbank CA 91522-0002*

DIBOS, DENNIS ROBERT, electronics industry executive; b. Chgo., Oct. 20, 1942; s. Jerome Lawrence and Edna Ida (Bach) D.; m. Janet Sue Kehl, Mar. 12, 1967; children: Gregory Cunningham, Emily Lair. BS in Mktg., U. Ill., 1963. Prodn. analyst Motorola, Chgo., 1967-68, prodn. control mgr., 1968, salesperson, 1968-70, market sales mgr., 1970-71, dist. sales mgr., 1971-75, area sales mgr., 1975-85, distbn. v.p., 1985-89, ops. mgr., v.p., 1989-91, gen. mgr., v.p. Mid-Atlantic div., 1991-93, gen. mgr., v.p. fed. govt. divsn., 1993—. Bd. dirs. Nat. Crime Prevention Coun., 1994. Lt. USNR, 1964-67, PTO. Mem. Internat. Assn. Chiefs Police, Assn. Pub. Safety Commn. Officers, Chartwell Country Club (Severna Park, Md.), Annapolis Yacht Club. Home: 3 St Andrews Close Severna Park MD 21146-1521 Office: Motorola 1301 E Algonquin Rd Schaumburg IL 60696

DIBRIENZA, STEPHEN, city councilman; b. Bklyn., Dec. 9, 1954; s. Joseph and Jeanette (Massulo) D.; m. Patricia Kabot, 1984; children: Stephanie Marie, Deanna Jean. BA magna cum laude, Pace U., 1976; JD, Fordham U., 1979. City councilman Dist. 30, N.Y.C.; city councilman Dist. 39, N.Y.C., chair legis. panel and subcom. waterfront devel., 1988-91, mem. land use com., chair subcom. landmarks, pub. siting and, 1992-93, contracts com., 1993, chair gen. welfare com., 1994—, mem. econ. devel. com. Office: 2903 Ford Hamilton Pky Brooklyn NY 11218*

DICAMILLO, GARY THOMAS, manufacturing executive; b. Niagara Falls, N.Y., Dec. 10, 1950; s. Joseph John and Olga Marie (Parenti) DiC.; m. Susan Christine Whitaker, Sept. 13, 1975; children: David, John, Benjamin. BSChemE, Rensselaer Poly. Inst., 1973; MBA, Harvard U., 1975. Brand mgr. Procter & Gamble, Cin., 1975-80; mgr. Mckinsey & Co., Chgo., 1980-83; v.p., gen. mgr. Culligan Internat. Co., Northbrook, Ill., 1983-86; pres. Worldwide Power Tools Group Black & Decker Corp., Towson, Md., 1986-95; chmn., CEO Polaroid Corp., Cambridge, Mass., 1995—; bd. dirs. Whirlpool Corp., Pella Corp., Sheridan Group. Mem. bd. govs. New Eng. Aquarium; commr. Md. Pub. Broadcasting Commn., 1988-93; trustee St. Paul's Sch., 1988-95, Greater Balt. Com., Md. Sci. Ctr.; bd. dirs. Leadership Balt., 1991-93; trustee Mus. of Sci., Boston. Recipient Albert Demers medal, Livingston Houston prize, Rensselaer Poly. Inst., 1973; Buffalo Alumni scholar Buffalo area Rensselaer Poly. Inst. Alumni, 1969; Chirurg Advt. fellow Harvard U. Bus. Sch., 1974; recipient Rensselaer Poly. Inst. Dirs. award, 1989. Mem. Water Quality Assn. (bd. dirs. 1985-86), Md. Acad. Scis. (bd. dirs. 1991-96), Rensselaer Poly. Inst. Club (bd. dirs. 1987-91, pres.), Rensselaer Alumni Assn. (bd. dirs. 1989-93, Alumni Key award 1990), Hardware Mktg. Coun., DIY Rsch. Inst. (bd. dirs. 1989-90), Skokie Country Club, Elkridge Club, Md. Club, L'Hirondelle Club, Willowbend Club, Wianno Club, Brae Burn Country Club, Harvard Club. Republican. Episcopalian. Avocations: golf, tennis, squash, antique furniture, Italian cooking. Home: 113 Cliff Rd Wellesley MA 02481-3017 Office: Polaroid Corp 784 Memorial Dr Cambridge MA 02139-3587

DICAPRIO, LEONARDO, actor; b. Hollywood, Calif., Nov. 11, 1974; s. George and Irmelin DiC. Actor: (films) Critters III, 1991, This Boy's Life, 1993, What's Eating Gilbert Grape?, 1993 (Academy award nomination best supporting actor 1993), The Quick and the Dead, 1995, The Basketball Diaries, 1995, Total Eclipse, 1996, Romeo and Juliet, 1997, Marvin's Room, 1997, Titanic, 1997, The Man in the Iron Mask, 1998, The Beach, 1999, Celebrity, 1998. (TV series) Parenthood, 1990, Growing Pains, 1991. Office: AMG 9465 Wilshire Blvd Beverly Hills CA 90212

DI CARLANTONIO, MARTIN, publishing executive. Editl. dir. Am. Jour. Nursing, N.Y.C., 1996. Office: Am Jour Nursing Co 555 W 57th St New York NY 10019-2925*

DICARLO, BERNARD, telecommunication executive; b. Bklyn., Oct. 27, 1946; s. Bernardo and Louise DiC.; divorced; childre: Dominic, Lisa Marie, Jeannine. Student, CCNY. V.p. Rockland MediLabs, Valley Cottage, N.Y., 1980-91, Profast Health & Diet Ctrs., Pomona, N.Y., 1987-92; pres. TNT, Inc., Bardonia, N.Y., 1992—; cons. in field. Pres. Rockland County Yough Football, N.Y., 1981-92. Sgt. U.S. Army, 1968-70. Mem. KC, Sons of Italy, Italian Am. Club. Roman Catholic. Home: 9 Village Green Bardonia NY 10954

DICARLO, DOMINICK L., federal judge; b. Bklyn., Mar. 11, 1928; m. Esther Hansen (dec.); children: Vincent, Carl, Robert, Barbara DiCarlo Basgaard; m. Susan L. Hauck. BA, St. John's Coll., 1950, LLB, 1953; LLM, NYU, 1957. Asst. U.S. atty. Eastern Dist. N.Y., 1959-62, chief organized crime and racketeering sect.; spl. asst. to U.S. atty., 1962; counsel to minority leader N.Y. Council, 1962-65; mem. N.Y. State assembly, 1965-81, dep. minority leader, 1975-78; vice chmn. N.Y. State Legis. Commn. Crime, 1969-70, Select Commn. Correctional Insts. and Programs, 1972-73; asst. sec. state for internat. narcotics matters Dept. State, Washington, 1981-84; rep. U.S. Commn. on narcotic drugs of econ. and social coun. UN, 1982-84; judge U.S. Ct. Internat. Trade, N.Y.C., 1984-91, chief judge, 1991-96, sr. status, 1996—. Office: US Ct Internat Trade 1 Federal Plz New York NY 10278-0001

DICARLO, LAURETTE MARY, nurse; b. Cleve., Aug. 19, 1950; d. Amerigo and Helen (Senuta) DiC. LPN, Willoughby-Eastlake Sch., 1976; AS in Nursing, Santa Fe C.C., Gainesville, Fla., 1982; BSN magna cum laude, U. South Fla., 1991, MS in Nursing, 1997. RN, Fla., advanced registered nurse practitioner. LPN Riverside Meth. Hosp., Columbus, Ohio, 1976-78, Lakeland (Fla.) Gen. Hosp., 1978-79, Alalhua Gen. Hosp., Gainesville, 1979-82; nurse mgr. progressive care Humana Northside Hosp., St. Petersburg, Fla., 1991-92; critical care nurse Columbia Largo (Fla.) Med. Ctr., 1982-91; med. supr. TGC Home Health, Clearwater, Fla., 1994-95; charge nurse cardiovascular intensive care, emergency nurse Columbia Largo Med. Ctr., 1992-98, nurse practitioner internal medicine and infectious disease, 1998—. Vol. Soc. for Prevention of Cruelty to Animals, Largo, 1991—. Santa Fe scholar, 1982, Joan K. Stout scholar Miami Heart Inst./U. South Fla., 1996-97. Mem. AACN, ANA, Am. Acad. Nurse Practitioners, Fla. Nurses Assn., Phi Kappa Phi, Sigma Theta Tau. Avocation: oil painting.

DICARLO, SUSANNE HELEN, financial analyst; b. Greensburg, Pa., Nov. 24, 1956; d. Wayne Larry and Clara Emogene (Weaver) Gower; m. John Joseph DiCarlo, June 21, 1980; children: Sarah Rose, Kristen Marie. BS in Acctg., Va. Poly. Inst. and State U., 1978. Auditor U.S. Army Audit Agy., Ft. Monroe, Va., 1978-79; acct. technician Fleet Combat Tng. Ctr., Virginia Beach, Va., 1980-82, supervisory auditor, 1982-83; fin. analyst Comml. Activity Mgmt. Team, Norfolk, Va., 1983—; fed. women's program mgr. Fleet Combat Tng. Ctr., 1980-83. Creator newsletter Fed. Women's Program Manager, 1980-83. Mem. Am. Soc. Mil. Comptrollers, Southeastern Assn. for Trailriders. Club: Seaside Mountaineers (Va. Beach) (treas. 1986-88). Home: 4013 Dillaway Ct Virginia Beach VA 23456-1257

DICE, BRUCE BURTON, exploration company executive; b. Grand Rapids, Mich., Dec. 24, 1926; s. William and Wilma (Rose) D.; children: Karen, Kevin, Kirk. BS in Geology, U. Mich., 1950; MS in Geology, Mich. State U., 1956. With El Paso Natural Gas, 1956-62, Drilling and Exploration Co., 1962-63, Ocean Drilling and Exploration, New Orleans, 1963-75; pres. Transco Exploration Co., Houston, 1975-82, Dice Exploration Co., Inc., Houston, 1982-95; cons. in field. Active Houston Symphony, Shepherd Soc. at Rice U., Houston Masterworks Chorus. Mem. Am. Assn. Petroleum Geologists, Houston Geol. Soc., Forum Club (Houston). Home: 1907 Grand Valley Dr Houston TX 77090-1052 Office: Wadi Petroleum Inc 14405 Walters Rd Houston TX 77014-1337 also: PO Box 73507 Houston TX 77273-3507

DICECCO, TONY, university head women's basketball coach; b. Niagara, N.Y.; m. Kristi DiCecco. Grad., Upper Iowa U. Head coach, tchr. phys. edn. and social studies West Ctr. in Maynard, Iowa, 1971-73; head girls basketball coach Montezuma (Iowa) Cmty. Schs., girls softball coach, tchr. phys. edn. and social studies, 1974-86; asst. coach Creighton U.; head women's basketball coach U. of Northern Iowa, Cedar Falls. Office: U Northern Iowa Upper NW UNI Dome Cedar Falls IA 50614-0314*

DICELLO, FRANCIS P., lawyer; b. Waukegan, Ill., May 5, 1941; s. Anthony M. and Mary Dicello; m. Mary Janice Dicello; children: Anthony, Andrew, Carlotta. BA, U. Notre Dame, 1963; JD, Fordham U., 1966. Bar: Conn. 1966, D.C. 1967, Md 1984, Va 1982. Trial atty. U.S. Dept. Justice, Washington, 1970-76; dep. asst., gen. counsel U.S. Railway Assn., Washington, 1976-78; asst., chief trial & settlement rev. sects. tax divsn. U.S. Dept. Justice, Washington, 1978-79; U.S. trustee Washington and, Va., 1979-82; ptnr., owner Hazel & Thomas, P.C., Washington, 1982-94; ptnr. Reed Smith Shaw & McClay, Washington, 1994—. Fellow Am. Coll. Bankruptcy; mem. Am. Bankruptcy Inst. Office: Reed Smith Shaw & McClay 1301 K St NW Ste 1100E Washington DC 20005-3373

DICELLO, JOHN FRANCIS, JR., physicist, educator; b. Bradford, Pa., Dec. 18, 1938; s. John Francis and Nicolina Camille (Costello) D.; m. Shirley Ann Rodgers, Aug. 25, 1962; children: John Francis III, Paul T. BS, St. Bonaventure U., 1960; MS, U. Pitts., 1962; PhD, Tex. A&M U., 1968. Instr. St. Bonaventure U., 1962-63; Univ. grad. fellow Tex. A&M U., College Station, 1963-65; AEC-Assoc. Western Univs. grad. fellow Los Alamos Nat. Lab., 1965-67, staff scientist, 1973-84; rsch. assoc., rsch. scientist Columbia U., N.Y.C., 1967-73; faculty U. N.Mex., Los Alamos, 1980-82; faculty fellowship Northwest Coll. and Univ. Assn. for Sci., Pacific N.W. Labs., 1989; prof. physics Clarkson U., Potsdam, N.Y., 1982-95; dir. med. physics and prof. oncology, joint appointment environ. health scis. Johns Hopkins U., Balt., 1995—. mem. peer rev. panel NASA specialized ctrs. of rsch. and tng., 1991; mem. ad hoc com. NIH/Dept. Energy, 1991—; vis. prof. Johns Hopkins Oncology Ctr., 1992-93. Bd. dirs. N.Mex. div. Am. Cancer Soc., 1978-82; mem. sci. com. #88 and #93, Nat. Coun. on Radiation Protection and Measurements, 1992—; mem. task group on biol. effects of space radiation Nat. Rsch. Coun. NAS, 1996. Mem. AAUP, IEEE (nuclear and plasma scis. div.), Am. Assn. Physicists in Medicine, Radiation Rsch. Soc. (editorial bd., assoc. editor Radiation Rsch. jour. 1992-96), Am. Inst. Biol. Scis. (radiation health peer rev. panel to NASA 1990-94), Am. Phys. Soc. (com. on space rsch.), Sigma Xi (pres. Clarkson U. chpt. 1991-92), Sigma Pi Sigma. Roman Catholic. Research in field of physics, dosimetry, microdosimetry, radiation biology, cancer research, integrated circuits, accelerator and nuclear physics, heavy-particle radiation therapy. Office: Johns Hopkins U Sch Medicine Oncology Ctr Divsn Radiation Oncology 600 N Wolfe St Baltimore MD 21287-0005

DICHARRY, JAMES PAUL, company official, retired air force officer; b. Burnside, La., June 29, 1953; s. Donald Joseph Sr. Dicharry and Rae Marie (Bourgeois) Dicharry-Tuttle; m. Debra Ann Hoagland, May 27, 1971 (div. Aug. 1973); 1 child, Eric Raymond; m. Betty May Hare, June 21, 1975; children: Charlotte Rene, Douglas Paul. BA cum laude in Acctg., Tex. Luth. Coll., 1978; MMA in Bus., Troy State U., 1985. Enlisted man USAF, 1973-79, commd. 2d lt., 1979, advanced through grades to maj., 1990; pers. specialist 27th Combat Support Group, Cannon AFB, N.Mex., 1973-75; pers. specialist hdqs. mil. pers. ctr. USAF, San Antonio, 1975-79, budget officer hdqs. officer tng. sch., 1979-81, budget analyst hdqs. air tng. command, 1981-82; chief budget br. 32d Tactical Fighter Squadron, The Netherlands, 1982-84; chief cost and mgmt. analysis br. USAF, The Netherlands, 1984-85; intern banker devel. United Bank Denver, 1985-86; air staff banking officer hdqs. acctg. and fin. ctr. USAF, Denver, 1986-87, exec. to commdr. acctg. and fin. ctr., 1987-89; fin. analyst Army and Air Force Exch. Svc., Dallas, 1989-93; ret., 1993; mgr. cash mgmt. dept. FootAction USA, 1993-94; pres. South Pork Ranch Miniatures, De Soto, Tex., 1993-95; owner, operator Southpork Ranch; v.p. Tint 'n More, Inc., Joplin, Mo., 1995—; past mem. and vice chmn. bd. dirs. Space Age Fed. Credit Union, Denver. Dr. adminstr. South Tex. Regional Blood Bank, San Antonio, 1981; asst. coach, coach various recreation depts., The Netherlands, Aurora, Colo., De Soto, 1983-92; asst. scoutmaster Boy Scouts Am., Aurora, Duncanville, Tex., 1985-91. Named one of Outstanding Young Men of Am., 1989. Mem. Am. Legion, Rotary Internat. Avocations: family, golf, racquetball, vietnamese pot-bellied pigs. Home: 2012 S Jackson Ave Joplin MO 64804-1846 Office: 300 N Main St Miami OK 74354-5920 also: 2230 S Main St Joplin MO 64804-2048

DI CHIERA, DAVID, performing arts impresario; b. McKeesport, Pa., Apr. 8, 1935; s. Cosimo and Maria (Pezzaniti) DiC.; m. Karen VanderKloot, July 20, 1965 (div. 1992); children: Lisa Maria, Cristina Maria. BA summa cum laude in Music, UCLA, 1956, MA in Composition (scholar), 1958, PhD in Musicology, 1962; certificate in composition and piano (Fulbright Research grantee), Naples Conservatory of Music, 1959; D (hon.), U. Mich., 1998. Instr. music U. Calif., Los Angeles, 1960-61; asst. prof. music Oakland U., Rochester, Mich., 1962-65; chmn. music dept. Oakland U., 1966-73; founder, gen. dir. Mich. Opera Theatre, Detroit, 1971—; founding dir. Music Hall Center for the Performing Arts, Detroit, 1973—; artistic dir. Dayton Opera Assn., 1981-92; founding gen. dir. Opera Pacific, Costa Mesa, Calif., 1985-97; trustee Nat. Opera Inst.; adj. prof. Oakland U., Wayne State U. Producer, dir.: Overture to Opera series for, Detroit Grand Opera series, 1963-71; Composer various works for piano, violin, orch., voice; author articles on Italian opera for various encyclopedias; contbr. revs. and articles to music jours. Mem. Arts Com. New Detroit, Inc.; trustee, mem. exec. com. Music Center for Performing Arts; mem. Arts Task Force City of Detroit. Recipient Atwater Kent award U. Calif., Los Angeles, 1961; Certificate of Appreciation City of Detroit, 1970; citation Mich. Legislature, 1976; Michaelangelo award Boys' Town of Italy, 1980; award Arts Found. of Mich., 1981; President's Cabinet award U. Detroit, 1982; George Gershwin fellow, 1958; named A Michiganian of Yr., 1980; cavaliere della Repubblica Italiana. Mem. Am. Arts Alliance (exec. com.), Nat. Opera Assn., Internat. Assn. Lyric Theatre (v.p.), Am. Symphony League, Am. Musicol. Soc., OPERA Am. (pres. 1979-83), AAUP, Phi Beta Kappa, Phi Mu Alpha Sinfonia. Club: Detroit Athletic. Office: Mich Opera Theatre Mich Opera Theatre 1526 Broadway Detroit MI 48202-2703

DICHTER, BARRY JOEL, lawyer; b. Brookline, Mass., Feb. 19, 1950; s. Irving Melvin and Arlene Dichter; m. Judith Rand, Oct. 22, 1972; children: Rebecca Lynn, Jason Benjamin. AB magna cum laude, Harvard U., 1972, JD cum laude, 1975. Bar: Mass. 1975, N.Y. 1976, U.S. Dist. Ct. (so. and ea. dists.) N.Y. 1976, D.C. 1980, U.S. Dist. Ct. D.C. 1980, U.S. Ct. Appeals (D.C. cir.) 1985. Assoc. Webster & Sheffield, N.Y.C., 1975-82; assoc. Cadwalader, Wickersham & Taft, N.Y.C., 1983-84, ptnr., 1984—; lectr. in field. Contbg. editor: Collier on Bankruptcy, 15th edit., rev. Vice chmn. Harvard Law Sch. Fund, Cambridge, Mass., 1984-88, class agt., 1988—; bd. dirs. Children's Corner, Inc., 1990-95, treas., 1992-95; mem. exec. com., bankruptcy and reorgn. group of lawyers divsn. N.Y. United Jewish Appeal. Mem. ABA (mem. task force on Sect. 110 1991-92, mem. task force on emerging issues in the transp. industry 1992-96, mem. task force on Article 9 securitization issues), Assn. of Bar of City of N.Y. (mem. bankruptcy com. 1986-89, 91-94). Office: Cadwalader Wickersham & Taft 100 Maiden Ln New York NY 10038-4818

DICHTER, MARK S., lawyer; b. Phila., Jan. 22, 1943; s. Harry B. and Mollie (Silverstein) D.; m. Tobey Gordon, Aug. 17, 1969; children: Aliza, Melissa. BSEE, Drexel U., 1966; JD magna cum laude, Villanova U., 1969. Bar: Pa. 1969, U.S. Ct. Appeals (3d cir.) 1969, U.S. Supreme Ct. 1979. Assoc. Morgan, Lewis & Bockius, LLP, Phila., 1969-76, ptnr., 1976—, chmn. labor and employment law sect. Co-author: Employee Dismissal Law: Forms and Procedures, 1986-91; editor-in-chief Ann. Supplement Employment Discrimination Law, 1984-89; co-editor: Employment-at-will, 1985, 86, State-by-State Survey, 1984-89; adv. bd. Disability Law Reporter. Bd. dirs., sec. Urban League Phila.; bd. dirs., v.p. Wilma Theater; bd. consultors Villanova U. Sch. Law; bd. dirs. Pub. Interest Law Ctr. Phila. Mem. ABA (labor and employment law sect. mgmt., mem. gov. coun. 1991—, co-chmn. equal opportunity com. 1986-89, litigation sect., employment law com.), Fed. Bar Assn. (equal employment com. vice-chmn. 1983-86), Nat. Employment Law Inst. (adv. bd. 1984—), Am. Employment Law Counsel (bd. dirs.), Am. Coll. Employment Lawyers, Def. Rsch. Inst. (chmn. employment law com. 1989-93). Fax: 215-963-5299. E-mail: dich5291@mlb.com. Home: 1017 Clinton St Philadelphia PA 19107-6016 Office: Morgan Lewis & Bockius 1701 Market St Philadelphia PA 19103-2921

DICHTER, MISHA, concert pianist; b. Shanghai, Peoples Republic of China, Sept. 27, 1945; came to U.S., 1947, naturalized, 1953; s. Leon and Lucy (Lhevine) D.; m. Cipa Glazman, Jan. 21, 1968; 2 children. Student, UCLA, 1963-64; B.S., Juilliard Sch., 1968. Performed world concert tours, 1966—; appeared with maj. world orchs. including Phila., Boston Symphony, Chgo. Symphony, L.A. Philharm., N.Y. Philharm., Cleve. orchs., Leningrad Symphony, Gewandhaus orchs., Leipzig, Vienna Philharm., Berlin Philharm., Israel Philharm.; appeared at major festivals including Aspen, Mostly Mozart, Ravinia; rec. artist with RCA, Philips, MusicMasters; contbr. articles to N.Y. Times, other mags. Recipient Silver medal Moscow Tschaikovsky Competition, 1966. Avocations: tennis, jogging, cartooning. Office: care CAMI Mushalla Divsn att Connie Shuman 165 W 57th St New York NY 10019-2201*

DICICCIO, FRANK J., city official; b. Phila., May 21, 1946; s. Arthur and Jean (Mortelliti) DiC.; divorced; children: Frank, Christine. Student, Temple U. Sch. Real Estate. City coun. 1st dist. Phila., 1996—. Pres. Citizen's Alliance for Better Neighborhoods. Recipient award Citizen's Crime Commn., 1997. Mem. Order Sons of Italy of Am., Italian Market

Civic Assn. Roman Catholic. Office: 332 City Hall Philadelphia PA 19107-3201

DICICCIO, SAL, city official; b. Youngstown, Ohio. Student, Ariz. State U. City coun. Phoenix, 1994—; chair internal policy subcom. Phoenix City Coun.; real estate agt. Active Ariz. Ctr. for Blind. Mem. Kiwanis. Roman Catholic. Office: 200 W Washington St Fl 11 Phoenix AZ 85003-1611*

DICICCO, TONY, soccer coach; b. Wethersfield, Conn., Aug. 5, 1948; m. Diane; children: Anthony, Andrew, Alex, Nicholas. Grad., Springfield Coll., 1970; M in Phys. Edn., Ctrl. Conn. State U.; advanced nat. diploma, Nat. Soccer Coaches Assn. Am. Lic. U.S. Soccer A. Profl. soccer player Conn. Wildcats, R.I. Oceaneers; asst. coach U.S. Women's Nat. Soccer Team, 1991-94, head coach, 1994—; asst. women's coach Under 20 Men's Nat. Team, 1993; founder Soccer Plus, Inc., Specialty Stores, 1981—, Soccer Plus Goalkeeper Schs., 1981—; region I boys goalkeeper dir.; goalkeeper specialist Nat. Soccer Coaches Assn. Am.; conductor U.S. Soccer and Nat. Soccer Coaches Assn. Am. nat. licensing camps. Recipient gold medal with team Olympics, Atlanta, 1996. Office: US Soccer Fedn US Soccer House 1801 S Prairie Ave Chicago IL 60616-1357*

DICIOCCIO, GARY FRANCIS, secondary education educator; b. Beaver Falls, Pa., Nov. 28, 1961; s. Americo M. and Rose (D'Ottavio) DiC. BS in Chemistry, Gannon U., 1985. Cert. tchr., Pa. Tchr. chemistry West Mifflin (Pa.) Area Sch. Dist., 1986-88, 90—; instr. chemistry C.C. Allegheny County, Pitts., 1988; lab. asst. INMETCO, Inc. Ellwood City, Pa., 1988; inorganic data control officer Roy F. Weston, Inc., West Chester, Pa., 1989-90; tchr. earth sci. West Shore Sch. Dist., Leymone, Pa., 1990; fellow Fermi Accelerator Nat. Lab., 1998-99. Proofreader Sci. Tchr. mag., 1992-94, western Pa. rep., 1994-96. Info. Tech. Edn. scholar Pa. Gen. Assembly, 1988; organic chemistry summer rsch. fellow Bucknell U., 1990, Dept. Energy fellow Argonne Nat. Lab., 1993, 94, ASCI fellow West Pa. Hosp., Pitts., 1993, H.S. Sci. Tchr. Inst. fellow U. Calif., Berkeley, 1995, Sci. and Soc. Inst. fellow U. Miami, Coral Gables, Fla., 1995, NASA Environ. program fellow Jesuit-Wheeling (W.Va.) Coll., 1995, Am. Assn. Immunologists fellow, 1997; grantee Mon Valley Edn. Consortium Great Ideas, 1993-96. Mem. Am. Chem. Soc., Am. Fedn. Tchrs., Am. Film Inst., Natural Sci. Tchrs. Assn., Pa. Sci. Tchrs. Assn., Theater Assn. Pa. Republican. Roman Catholic. Avocations: tennis, swimming, theater, reading. Office: West Mifflin Area H S 91 Commonwealth Ave West Mifflin PA 15122-2396

DICK, BERTRAM GALE, JR., physics educator; b. Portland, Oreg., June 12, 1926; s. Bertram Gale and Helen (Meengs) D.; m. Ann Bradford Volkmann, June 23, 1956; children—Timothy Howe, Robin Louise, Stephen Gale. B.A., Reed Coll., 1950; B.A. (Rhodes scholar), Wadham Coll., Oxford (Eng.) U., 1953, M.A., 1958; Ph.D., Cornell U., 1958. Rsch. assoc. U. Ill., 1957-59; mem. faculty U. Utah, 1959-98, prof. physics, 1965-98, prof. emeritus, 1998—, Univ. prof., 1979-80, chmn. dept., 1964-67, dean grad. sch., 1987-93; cons. Minn. Mining and Mfg. Co., 1960-67; vis. prof. Technische Hochschule, Munich, 1967-68; vis. scientist Max Planck Institut für Festkörperforschung, Stuttgart, Fed. Republic Germany, 1976-77; faculty Semester at Sea, fall 1983, 86. Mem. Alta Planning and Zoning Commn., 1972-76; pres. Chamber Music Salt Lake City, 1974-76; bd. dir. Citizen's Com. to Save Our Canyons, 1972—, Coalition for Utah's Future Project 2000, 1989-96. Served in USNR, 1944-46. Fellow Am. Phys. Soc.; mem. Am. Alpine Club, Phi Beta Kappa, Sigma Xi. Research in solid state theory. Home: 1377 Butler Ave Salt Lake City UT 84102-1803 Office: U Utah Dept Physics Salt Lake City UT 84112

DICK, DAVID E., construction company executive; b. 1948. With Dick Corp., Clairton, Pa., 1964—, now CEO; officer Dick Enterprises, Inc., Clairton. Office: Dick Corp PO Box 10896 Pittsburgh PA 15236-0896*

DICK, DOUGLAS PATRICK, construction company executive; b. Pitts., Jan. 5, 1953; s. Dorsey W. and Loretta L. D.; m. Deborah Genge, Dec. 11, 1976; children: Alexander Genge, Cameron Cora, Gavin Douglas. Student, Hawthorne Coll., 1971-72, Robert Morris Coll., 1972-73. Asst. sales mgr. Dick Corp., Pitts., 1971-75; constrn. mgr. Dick Corp., 1975-79, treas., 1979—, sr. v.p., 1985-93, pres., 1993—. Office: Dick Enterprises Inc 900 Route 51 Large PA 15025-3645 also: Dick Corp PO Box 10896 Pittsburgh PA 15236-0896*

DICK, ELLIOT COLTER, virologist, epidemiologist, educator; b. Miami, Fla., June 30, 1926; s. Elliot C. Dick and Helen Jean Cribb; m. Claire Rebecca Blumer, Sept. 23, 1967; children: Emily Diane, Elliot Mayhew, Frederic Krichton, Catherine Virginia. BA in Bacteriology, U. Minn., 1950, MS in Bacteriology, 1953, PhD in Bacteriology, 1955. Asst. prof. Bacteriology U. Kans., Lawrence, 1955-59; asst. prof. medicine Tulane U., New Orleans, 1959-61; asst. prof. Preventive Medicine U. Wis., Madison, 1961-64, assoc. prof., 1964-72, prof., 1972-96; cons. Kans. State Bd. Health, Topeka, 1955-59; mem. collaborative com. rhinoviruses WHO, 1966—; vis. scientist Delta Regional Primate Ctr., Tulane U., Covington, La., 1967-72; Sigrid Juselius Found. lectr., Turku, Finland, 1991. Contbr. articles, abstracts to profl. jours. including Jour. Infectious Diseases, Jour. Allergy and Clinical Immunology, Jour. Clinical Investigation, chpts. to books; patentee in field. With U.S. Army, 1944-46, ETO. Recipient Antarctic medal U.S., 1979; grantee U. Kans., 1956-59, Kans. State Bd. Health, 1957-58, USPHS, 1959-70, 71-73, 76, 79, 82, 85, 88, S.C. Johnson, 1966-67, 70-79, Smith, Kline & French, 1966-71, 74, 75, NASA, 1967-82, NSF, 1976-88, Kimberly-Clark, 1981-96, Hoffmann-LaRoche, 1986-96, Sterling Drug, 1989-96. Fellow Am. Acad. Microbiology (diplomat clin. microbiology), Infectious Disease Soc., Explorers Club; mem. AAAS, Am. Soc. Virology (founder), Am. Soc. Microbiology (Wis. legis. rep. 1970-96), Soc. Exptl. Biology and Medicine, N.Y. Acad. Scis., Phi Sigma, Sigma Xi. Mem. Unitarian Ch. Avocations: sailing, tennis, economics, history. Home: 11 Robin Cir Madison WI 53705-4929

DICK, HAROLD LATHAM, manufacturing executive; b. Wichita, Kans., Oct. 24, 1943; s. Harold G. and Evelyn (Spines) D.; m. Jeanne Marie Luczai, Aug. 25, 1973; children: Harold Campbell, Edward Latham. BA, Washburn U., 1966; MBA, Harvard U., 1968. Exec. asst. to treas. Skelly Oil Co., Tulsa, 1968-70; mgmt. cons. McKinsey & Co. Inc., Chgo., Dallas, Houston, 1970-77; dir. planning Frito-Lay Inc., Dallas, 1977-80; v.p. Norton Simon Inc., N.Y.C., 1980-83; founder Summit Ptnrs., Wichita, Kans., 1983-85; pres., chief exec. officer Doskocil Cos. Inc., Hutchinson, Kans., 1985-88; founder, pres. The Summit Group, Hutchinson, 1988—; adv. bd. dirs. Garvey Industries, Wichita, 1987-94, Petroleum Inc., Wichita, 1993—. Trustee Kanza coun. Boy Scouts Am., 1989-97, exec. bd., 1995-97, v.p. 1997—, exec. bd. dirs. Quivira coun., 1997—, v.p., 1997, coun. commr., 1998—; Stephen minister, 1987-94; mem. bd. regents Washburn U., 1995—, trustee endowment assn., 1990—, mem. presdl. search com., 1987-88, bd. dirs. alumni assn., 1986-89). Republican. Episcopalian. Office: The Summit Group 405 First National Ctr Hutchinson KS 67501

DICK, HAROLD MICHAEL, orthopedic surgeon; b. Buffalo, Dec. 22, 1933; s. Norman James and Helen (Ryan) D.; m. Schmidt, Apr. 12, 1977 (div. Jan. 1978); m. Joyce Ann Geller, Apr. 28, 1978; 1 child, Victoria Leigh. BA, Princeton U., 1956; MD, NYU, 1960. Diplomate Am. Bd. Orthopaedic Surgery; lic. dr. Hawaii, N.Y., Calif., N.J. Intern Queens Hosp., Honolulu, 1960-61; resident Roosevelt Hosp., N.Y.C., 1961-62; resident orthopaedic surgery Columbia-Presbyn. Med. Ctr., N.Y.C., 1962-66, hand fellow, 1966-67; tumor fellow NYU, 1967-68; chief pediat. orthopedics Columbia Presbyn. Med. Ctr., N.Y.C., 1973-83; prof. orthopaedic surgery Columbia-Presbyn. Med. Ctr., N.Y.C., 1965—, chmn. orthopaedic surgery, 1983-98, dir. orthopaedic surgery svc., 1983-98; cons. Harlem Hosp. Ctr., N.Y.C., 1967—, Helen Hayes Hosp., West Haverstraw, N.Y., 1967—, Nyack (N.Y.) Hosp., 1974—, Valley Hosp., Ridgewood, N.J., 1974—, Hyannis (Mass.) Hosp., 1976—, Greenwich (Conn.) Hosp. Assn., 1983—, Englewood (N.J.) Hosp., 1985—. Fellow ACS, Am. Acad. Orthopaedic Surgeons, N.Y. Acad. Medicine (Orthopaedic sect. sec. 1982-83, chmn. 1983-84, Hoar com. for rsch. fellowship 1993); mem. AMA, Am. Soc. for Surgery of the Hand, Am. Soc. for Surgery of Trauma, Musculoskeletal Oncology Soc., Am. Orthopaedic Assn. (pres.-elect 1994-95, pres. 1995-96), Orthopaedic Rsch. Soc., Orthopaedic Rsch. and Edn. Found. (bd. dirs., v.p. 1990-94), Pediatric Orthopaedic Soc. N.Am., Am. Bd. Orthopaedic Surgery Inc. (bd. dirs., bd. examiner for certifying exams, 1983—, pres.-elect 1995-96, pres. 1996-97), Acad. Orthopaedic Soc. (pres.-elect 1992-93, pres. 1993-94), Century Assn., Twentieth Century Orthopaedic Assn., Internat. Soc. Orthopaedic Surgery and Traumatology, Internat. Skeletal Soc., Internat. Soc. Orthopaedic Rsch. and Traumatology, Royal Soc. Med. (affiliate), Colombian Soc. Orthopaedic Surgery and Traumatology (hon.), Columbian Soc. Surgery of Hand (corr.), N.Y. Soc. for Surgery of Hand (charter, sec. 1975-77, v.p. 1977-79, pres. 1979-80), N.Y. Med. and Surg. Soc., N.J. Orthopaedic Soc., N.Y. State Soc. Orthopaedic Surgeons, N.Y. County Med. Soc., Pediatric Orthopaedic Club N.Y. (pres.-elect 1979-80, pres. 1980-81), Robert E. Carroll Hand Club, Frank E. Stinchfield Club. Avocation: sailing. Office: Presbyn Hosp Columbia-Presbyn Med Ctr 622 W 168th St New York NY 10032-3720*

DICK, HENRY HENRY, minister; b. Russia, June 1, 1922; s. Henry Henry and Mary (Unger) D.; m. Erica Penner, May 25, 1946; children—Janet (Mrs. Arthur Enns), Judith (Mrs. Ron Brown), James, Henry. Th.B., Mennonite Brethren Bible Coll., 1950. Ordained to ministry Mennonite Brethren Ch., 1950; pastor in Orillia, Ont., Can., 1950-54, Lodi, Calif., 1954-57, Shafter, Calif., 1958-69; faculty Tabor Coll., 1954-55; gen. sec. Mennonite Brethren Conf. of U.S.A., 1969-72; pres. Mennonite Brethren Bibl. Sem., Fresno, Calif., 1972-76; vice moderator Gen Conf. Mennonite Brethren Ch., 1975-78, moderator, 1979-84; pastor Reedley Mennonite Brethren Ch., 1976-88; ret., 1989; dir. ch. and constituency relations Mennonite Brethren Biblical Sem., 1987-89; moderator Pacific Dist. Conf., 1959-60, 61-63, 75-77; mem. exec. com. Mennonite Central Com. Internat., 1967-75, mem. bd. reference and counsel, 1966-69, 72-75, mem. bd. missions and services, 1969-72; exec. sec. Bd. Edn. Mennonite Brethren, 1969-72; chmn. Bd. Missions and Services, 1985-91; pastor emeritus Reedley Mennonite Brethren Ch., 1987. Columnist bi-weekly publ. Christian Leader, 1969-75. Bd. dirs. Bob Wilson Meml. Hosp., Ulysses, Kans., 1969-72; dist. minister Pacific Dist. Conf. Mennonite Brethren, 1989—. Recipient Humanitarian award Shafter C. of C., 1969, Citation bd. dirs. Bibl. Sem. Clubs: Kiwanis, Reedley Rotary. Home: 783 W Carpenter Ave Reedley CA 93654-3903 Office: 1632 L St Reedley CA 93654-3340

DICK, JAMES CORDELL, concert pianist; b. Hutchinson, Kans., June 29, 1940; s. George Gerhard and Dorothy Lois (Ulsh) D. 1958-63; Studied with, Dalies Frantz; MusB with spl. honors, U. Tex., 1963; studied with Sir Clifford Curzon, 1963-65; postgrad., Royal Acad. Music, London, 1963-65. Concert pianist Sol Hurok Presents, N.Y.C., 1968-70, Shaw Concerts, N.Y.C., 1970-75, Columbia Artists, N.Y.C., 1975-89, A.G. Declert and Assocs., Round Top, Tex., 1989—; founder, artistic dir. Internat. Festival-Inst., Round Top, 1971—; judge internat. recording competition Nat. Guild Piano Tchrs., 1970-71; nat. cons. music com. Inst. Internat. Edn., N.Y.C., 1971-72; mem. internat. jury Tschaikovsky Competition, Moscow, 1974, Van Cliburn Competition, Ft. Worth, 1975, 78; chmn. Fulbright Panel in Music, N.Y.C., 1978. Commd. (Am. piano concerto) Shiva's Drum, (nominated Pulitzer Prize in music), 1994. Recipient First Prize award Shreveport Symphony Competition, 1958-60, San Angelo Symphony Competition, 1958-60, Dallas Symphony, 1961-62, Nat. Guild Piano Tchrs., 1961-62, Tschaikovsky Internat. Competition, 1965-66, Leventritt Piano Competition, 1965-66, Busoni Internat. Piano Competition, 1965-66, Citation cert. Tex. Ho. Reps., 1975, award Japan Soc. Houston, 1975, Presdl. citation Nat. Fedn. Music Clubs, 1979, Round Top award Gov. William. P. Clements, Tex., 1980, Headliner of Yr. award Headliners Club, 1983; honoree Pres. Lyndon B. Johnson, 1965-66; nominee Pulitzer Prize in Music, 1974; commd. Ambassador of Goodwill, State of Tex., 1978; named Hon. Texan, Gov. Dolph Briscoe, 1978, Chevalier des Arts et Lettres French Ministry Culture, 1994; Fulbright scholar, Tobias Matthay fellow, Royal Acad. Music, Hon assoc., 1969, recipient Merit cert., 1965, Beethoven prize, Recital medal, Chevalier des Arts et Lettres, French Ministry of Cult., 1994. Mem. English Speaking Union, Philos. Soc. Tex. (treas. 1976—), Tex. Fedn. Music Clubs (hon. life), Tex. Lyceum Assn. (adv. dir. 1978—), Tuesday Mus. Club (hon.), Rotary Internat. (hon. life), Bohemians Club (N.Y.C.). Avocations: architecture, landscaping, literature, poetry, woodworking. E-mail: festhill@fais.net. Fax: 409-249-5078. E-mail: festhill@fais.net.

DICK, RAYMOND DALE, psychology educator; b. Toledo, Ohio, July 16, 1930; s. Floyd Edward and Clara Belle (Spilker) D.; m. Beverly Ann Sparks, June 18, 1955; children: Gregory Dale, Jeffrey Clayton. B.S., Northwestern U., 1952; M.A., U. Mo., 1955, Ph.D., 1958. Asst. prof. psychology Ft. Hays (Kans.) State Coll., 1958-62; assoc. prof. Fort Hayes (Kans.) State Coll., 1962-64, prof., 1964-66, acad. chmn. psychology dept., 1959-66; prof. psychology U. Wis., Eau Claire, 1966-81, dean Sch. Grad Studies, 1966-98, prof. emeritus, 1981—; assoc. Danforth Found., 1962-84, also chmn. Upper Midwest selection com., 1969-72; mem. com. liberal arts edn. North Central Assn. Colls. and Secondary Schs., 1963-66, coordinator liberal arts com., 1965-68, cons-examiner, 1971—. Contbr. profl. jours. Mem. Am., Midwestern, Wis. Psychol. Assns., AAUP, AAAS. Home: 2823 Irene Dr Eau Claire WI 54701-6692

DICK, RICHARD IRWIN, environmental engineer, educator; b. Sanborn, Iowa, July 18, 1935; s. Laurence Irwin and Lillian Marie (Riesser) D.; m. Delores Kay Den Beste, Aug. 31, 1958; children: Natalie Ann, Kevin Irwin, Laura Lynn, Craig David. B.S., Iowa State U., 1957; M.S., State U. Iowa, 1958; Ph.D., U. Ill., 1965. Sanitary engr. USPHS, Kansas City, Mo., 1958-60; sanitary engr. Clark, Daily and Dietz (Cons. Engrs.), Urbana, Ill., 1960-62; instr. to prof. civil engring. U. Ill., 1962-72; prof. civil engring. U. Del., Newark, 1972-77; Joseph P. Ripley prof. engring. Cornell U., Ithaca, N.Y., 1977—; Thomas R. Camp lectr. Boston Soc. Civil Engrs., 1981; disting. vis. scientist U.S. EPA Water Engring. Rsch. Lab., Cin., 1986-89; vis. engr. Water Pollution Rsch. Lab., Stevenage, Eng., 1970-71; hon. rsch. fellow Univ. Coll. London, 1990; vis. prof. U. B.C., Vancouver, 1991, McGill U., Montreal, 1991. Contbr. over 190 articles to profl. jours. Served with USPHS, 1958-60. Recipient Disting. Alumnus award U. Ill., 1996, Daniel M. Lazar '29 Excellence in Tchg. award. Mem. ASCE (Rudolph Hering medal 1986), Assn. Environ. Engring. Profs. (past pres., Disting. lectr. 1980, Outstanding Pub. award 1986, 87, Founder's award, 1998), Internat. Assn. Water Pollution Rsch. (past mem. exec. com., bd. govs.), Water Environment Fedn. (Harrison Prescott Eddy medal 1968), Am. Water Works Assn., Am. Pub. Health Assn., Charted Instn. Water and Environ. Mgmt., Sigma Xi, Tau Beta Pi, Chi Epsilon (U. Ill. Chpt. Honor mem. 1980, Cornell U. Prof. of Yr. 1995), Phi Kappa Phi. Home: 115 W Upland Rd Ithaca NY 14850-1415 Office: Cornell U 118 Hollister Hall Ithaca NY 14853-3501

DICK, SUSAN MARIE, English language educator; b. Battle Creek, Mich., Nov. 6, 1940; d. James Allen and Mildred Marie (Thomas) D. BA with honors, Western Mich. U., 1963; MA, Northwestern U., 1964, PhD, 1967. Prof. dept. English Queen's U., Kingston, Ont., 1967—. Editor: George Moore: Confessions of a Young Man, 1972, Virginia Woolf: Holograph of to the Lighthouse, 1982, Complete Shorter Fiction of V. Woolf, 1989, To the Lighthouse, 1992; co-editor: Essays for Richard Ellmann, 1989; author: Virginia Woolf, 1989; mem. editl. com. Virginia Woolf, 1989—.adr. Fellow Royal Soc. Can. Avocations: reading, gardening. Home: 177 Churchill Crescent, Kingston, ON Canada K7L 4N3

DICKASON, JOHN HAMILTON, retired foundation executive; b. Wooster, Ohio, June 3, 1931; s. Donald Eugene and Martha Himes (Hamilton) D.; m. Barbara Helen Fee, June 20, 1953; children: John Harold, Kathryn Helen. AB, Dartmouth Coll., 1953, MBA, 1954; grad., Inst. Orgn. Mgmt., Mich. State U., 1965, Advanced Mgmt. Program, Harvard U., 1980. With Scott Paper Co., 1954-58; personnel technician Ill. Civil Service Commn., Springfield, 1958-60; bus. mgr., then asso. dir. Ill. Bar Assn., 1960-70, exec. dir., 1970-85; v.p. fin. and adminstrn. Markey Charitable Trust, Miami, Fla., 1985-97; v.p. disolution adminstrn. Markey Charitable Trust, Miami, 1997-98. Pres. Springfield Mental Health Assn., 1965-66; sr. warden Christ Episc. Ch., Springfield, 1973-75, lic. lay reader, 1970-85, treas., 1966-69, 76-85; mem. fin. com. Diocese Springfield, 1975-77; treas. St. Philip's Episc. Ch., Coral Gables, Fla., 1986-93, sr. warden, 1988; chair St. Philips Found., 1998—; lic. eucharistic minister, 1997—; troop leader local Boy Scouts Am., 1966-85, mem. coun. exec. com., 1978-80; trustee Palmer Trinity Sch., 1999—. With AUS, 1954-56. Mem. ABA (assoc.), Ill. State Bar Assn. (hon.), Am. Soc. Assn. Execs. (life), Ill. Soc. Assn. Execs. (pres. 1972), Nat. Assn. Bar Execs. (pres. 1976-77, Man of Yr. 1983), Am. Judicature Soc., Found. Fin. Officers Group (steering com., editor newsletter), Coun. on Founds. (past chmn. legis. and regulations com., rsch. com.), Riviera Country Club, Dade Community Found. (fin. com.). Republican. Home: 751 Saldano Ave Miami FL 33143-6219

DICKAU, JOHN C., religious organization executive. V.p. global ch. enrichment Baptist Gen. Conf., Arlington Heights, Ill., to 1998. Office: Baptist General Conference 2002 S Arlington Heights Rd Arlington Heights IL 60005-4193

DICKE, JAMES FREDERICK, II, manufacturing company executive; b. San Angelo, Tex., Nov. 9, 1945; s. James Frederick and Eilleen (Webster) D.; m. Janet St. Clair, July 6, 1968; children: James F. III, Jennifer S. BS, Trinity U., 1968. Intern U.S. Ho. of Reps., Washington, 1966; sales coord. Crown Controls Corp., New Bremen, Ohio, 1968-69, v.p. internat., 1970-78; exec. v.p. Crown Equipment Corp., New Bremen, Ohio, 1979-80; pres. Crown Equipment Corp., New Bremen, 1980—; chmn. Crown Australia Pty. Ltd., Sydney, 1980—, Crown Ltd., Galway, Ireland, 1980—; bd. dirs. Dayton (Ohio) Power and Light Co. Chmn. bd. trustees Trinity U., San Antonio, 1980—, Dayton (Ohio) Art Inst., 1998—; trustee, sec. Culver (Ind.) Ednl. Found., 1981—; Midwest dir. Boys and Girls Clubs Am., Chgo., 1987—; co-chmn. Ohio Rep. Fin. Com., 1995—. Recipient Disting. Svc. award Culver Acads., 1989, Disting. Alumnus award Trinity U., 1991; honoree Nat. Acad. Design, 1999. Mem. Young Pres.' Orgn. (bd. dirs. 1985-94, internat. pres. 1992-93), Cum Laude Soc. Culver Acads., Key Largo Angelers CLub (chmn. bd. dirs. 1999—). Mem. United Ch. of Christ. Office: Crown Equipment Corp 40 S Washington St New Bremen OH 45869-1247

DICKENS, BERNARD MORRIS, law educator; b. London, Nov. 4, 1937; emigrated to Can., 1974; s. David and Rose (Jacobs) D.; m. Rebecca J. Cook, Apr., 1987. LL.B., King's Coll., U. London, 1961, LL.M., 1965, Ph.D., 1971; LL.D., U. London, 1978. Barrister, Inner Temple, 1963; barrister and solicitor, Law Soc. Upper Can. (Ont. bar), 1977. Tutorial student King's Coll., U. London, 1962-63; lectr. Coll. Law, London, 1964-68, sr. lectr., 1968-72, prin. lectr., 1972-74; research prof. law U. Toronto, Ont., Can., 1974-80, prof. law, 1980—; cons. panel human rsch. WHO/Coun. Internat. Orgns. Med. Scis., Geneva, 1979-83, 91-93, prin. investigator epidemiol. rsch. and human organ transplantation, 1990-91; legal cons. reproduction law Commonwealth Secretariat, London, 1976—; project cons. Ont. Law Reform, Toronto, 1982-84; cons. mem. com. on ethics Can. Med. Assn., Ottawa, 1982-89; mem. rsch. ethics com. NRC Can., Ottawa, 1992—, chair 1995—; adj. faculty Ctr. for Population and Family Health, Faculty Medicine, Columbia U., 1987—; mem. WHO task force on organ transplantation, 1996—. Author: Abortion and the Law, 1966, Medico-Legal Aspects of Family Law, 1979, (with R.J. Cook) Abortion Laws in Commonwealth Countries, 1979, Emerging Issues in Commonwealth Abortion Law, 1982, Medicine and the Law, 1993, (with D. Roy, J. Williams) Bioethics in Canada, 1993; mem. internat. editorial bd. Am. Jour. Law and Medicine; mem. editorial adv. bd. Bibliography of Bioethics, Kennedy Inst., 1978—; legal articles editor Jour. Law Medicine and Ethics, 1986—. Connaught grantee U. Toronto, 1974, 78; Julius Silver fellow Columbia Law Sch., 1987. Fellow Royal Soc. Medicine (London), Royal Soc. Can.; mem. Can. Bar Assn., Can. Assn. Law Tchrs., Am. Soc. Law, Medicine and Ethics (bd. dirs. 1986-92, sec. 1987-89, pres. 1990-91), World Assn. Med. Law (bd. dirs. 1994—, v.p. 1996—). Jewish. Home: 31 Walmer Rd #10, Toronto, ON Canada M5R 2W7 Office: U Toronto Faculty of Law, 84 Queen's Pk, Toronto, ON Canada M5S 2C5

DICKENS, CHARLES ALLEN, petroleum company executive; b. Mount Gilead, N.C., Nov. 26, 1932; s. Alonzo Newton and Elizabeth Ann (Haywood) D.; m. Helen Theresia Baudendistel, Jan. 4, 1958; children: Karen Ann, Constance Lynn, Pamela Jean, Kimberly Susan. BS, N.C. State U., 1954. Asst. chmn. engr., sr. chem. engr., project chmn. engr. Texaco, Inc., Beacon, N.Y., Port Arthur, Tex., 1954-63; sr. engr. Texaco UK Ltd., London, 1963-65; project engr. Brussels, 1965-67; mgr. additivie sales Texaco Europe Ltd., Brussels, 1969-72, Houston, 1972-84; v.p. mktg. and tech. South Coast Terminals Inc., Houston, 1984-96; cons., 1996—; ptnr. Chearlens Assocs., Compuo Ltd., 1996—. Served with USAF, 1955-57. Fellow Brit. Inst. Petroleum; mem. Am. Inst. Chem. Engrs., Am. Soc. Lubrication Engrs., SAE, Scabbard and Blade, Westador Residents Club, Plaza Club, Sigma Xi, Tau Beta Pi. Republican.

DICKENS, CHARLES HENDERSON, retired social scientist, consultant; b. Thomasville, N.C., Nov. 22, 1934; s. Argie Marshall and Edna (Sullivan) D.; m. Jane McClung, Aug. 27, 1965; children: Martha Jane, Anne Elizabeth. BS, Duke U., 1957, MEd, 1964, ED, 1966. Asst. prof. Wake Forest U., Winston-Salem, N.C., 1965-67; planning specialist NSF, Washington, 1967-69, assoc. program dir. undergrad. instrnl. program, 1969-73, study dir. sci. edn. studies group, 1973-83, sect. head scientific and tech. pers. studies sect., 1983-86, sect. head surveys and analysis sect., 1986-90; sr. policy analyst Fed. Coordinating Coun. for Sci., Engring., and Tech., Washington, 1990-92, exec. sec., 1992-93, ret., 1993; mem. adv. bd. Am. Men and Women of Sci., New Providence, N.J., 1991—, C.C. Cameron Applied Rsch. Ctr. U. N.C., Charlotte, 1994—. With U.S. Army, 1958-59. Recipient Angier B. Duke prize Duke U., 1953-57; Woodrow Wilson fellowship Woodrow Wilson Fellowship Found., 1963, James B. Duke fellowship Duke U., 1963, 64. Fellow AAAS; mem. Nat. Assn. Ret. Fed. Employees (mem. chpt. 156, v.p. 1995-96, pres. 1996-97, v.p. N.C. area I 1997—), N.Y. Acad. Scis. Republican. Presbyterian. Avocations: computing, reading. Home: One Arrow Pl Asheville NC 28805-9748

DICKENS, JUSTIN KIRK, nuclear physicist; b. Syracuse, N.Y., Nov. 2, 1931; s. Milton Clifford and Jennette Martin (Holmes) D.; m. Marcay Cosette Jordan, Dec. 21, 1957; children: Alan Russell, Leonard Raymond, Steven Kenneth, Michael Loren. AB in Physics, U. So. Calif., L.A., 1955, PhD in Physics, 1962; MS in Physics, U. Chgo., 1956. Engring. assoc. Collins Radio Co., Burbank, Calif., 1955; electronic technician Enrico Fermi Inst. for Nuclear Studies, Chgo., 1956-57; grad. teaching asst. U. So. Calif., L.A., 1957-61, rsch. assoc., 1961-62; rsch. staff mem. Oak Ridge (Tenn.) Nat. Lab., 1962-78, sr. rsch. staff mem., 1978-94; private cons., 1995; rsch. prof. physics U. Tenn., Knoxville, 1996—; gen. chmn. Internat. Conf. on Nuclear Data for Sci. and Tech., Gatlinburg, Tenn., 1994. Author: The Descendants of Ephraim Dickens (Jr.) and Thomas Dickens, 1992, rev. edit., vol. I, 1997, vol. II, 1998; co-author (tech. standard) Am. Nat. Standard on Decay Heat; contbr. 200 articles to profl. jours. Bd. dirs. Oak Ridge Community Playhouse, 1972, 85. With U.S. Army, 1950-52. Recipient Lifetime Achievement award Oak Ridge Comty. Playhouse, 1996, Lockheed Martin Energy Rsch. Tech. Achievement award, 1997. Mem. Am. Phys. Soc., Am. Nuclear Soc., Phi Beta Kappa, Sigma Xi. Office: Ctr of Exec Bldg 6010 Inst Heavy Ion Rsch MS 6354 Oak Ridge TN 37831-6354

DICKENS, MICHELE, registered nurse, educator; b. Chgo., Aug. 17, 1963; d. Ben Franklin and Trudy Emily (Allen) Tucker; m. Harvey Dickens, Oct. 12, 1985; children: Sarah and Danielle (twins). RN, Eastern Ky. U., 1984; BSN, U. Ky., 1997. RN, Ky.; cert. BLS instr., ACLS instr., HIV/AIDS instr., diabetes educator. RN Good Samaritan Hosp., Lexington, Ky., 1983-84; RN Taylor County Hosp., Campbellsville, Ky., 1984-93, RN, patient educator, 1993—; healthcare instr. orgns. in cmtys., chs., women's clubs, sr. clubs, among others. First aid instr., ARC, Ky., 1996—. Mem. Am. Assn. Diabetes Educators, Greater Louisville Assn. Diabetes Educators, Sigma Theta Tau. Home: 104 Buttercup Ln Campbellsville KY 42718-3301 Office: Taylor County Hosp 1700 Old Lebanon Rd Campbellsville KY 42718-9600

DICKENS, SHEILA JEANNE, family preservation educator; b. Cleve., Sept. 15, 1958; d. Joseph David and Stella Maureen (Brown) Cogdell; children: Randy, Laura, Rebecca. AA, Lakeland C.C., Mentor, Ohio, 1985; BA magna cum laude, Walsh U., 1993, MA, 1995. Nat. cert. counselor; lic. profl. clin. counselor; cert. chem. dependency counselor III. Tutor Lakeland Coll., Mentor, 1980-85; mgr. Wohl Shoe Co., St. Louis, 1985-89; merchandise asst. J.C. Penney, Kingsport, Tenn., 1989-91; grad. asst. Walsh U., North Canton, Ohio, 1994-96, instr., counselor-in-residence program coord., 1995-96; nat. cert. counselor Stark County, Ohio Domestic Violence Project, now women's counselor, clin. dir. Vol. Crisis Intervention Ctr., Canton, 1992-94; mem. disaster svc. team ARC, Canton, 1995—. Mem. Am. Acad. Experts in Traumatic Stress, Assn. Nat. Assn. of Alcohol and Drug Addiction Counselors, Chi Sigma Iota/Alpha Mu (liaison 1995-96). Office: PO Box 9432 Canton OH 44711-9432

DICKENS, WILLIAM THEODORE, economic researcher; b. Chgo., Dec. 31, 1953; s. William James and Estelle Geraldine (Schmidt) D.; m. Maureen Ellen Finegan, June 18, 1982; 1 child, Christopher James. BA, Bard Coll., 1976; PhD, MIT, 1981. Econometric computing cons. MIT, Cambridge, Mass., 1978-80; from asst. to assoc. prof. econ. U. Calif., Berkeley, 1980-95, prof. econ., 1995; vis. asst. prof. MIT, Cambridge, 1985-86; cons. World Bank, Washington, 1987-88, Calif. State Employees Assn., Oakland, Calif., 1988-89; sr. economist, pres. Coun. Econ. Advisors, 1993-94; vis. fellow The Brookings Instn., 1994-95, sr. fellow, 1995—; faculty rsch. fellow NBER, 1982-86, rsch. assoc., 1986-97. Editor, author: (with Laura Tyson) Dynamics of trade and Employment, 1988, Labor and an Integrated Europe, 1993, The U.S. Labor Market Effects of European Economic Integration, 1993, Looking Before We Leap: Social Science and Welfare Reform, 1995, (with Ronald Ferguson) Urban Problems and Community Development, 1999; contbr. articles to profl. jours. Grad. fellow NSF, 1976; recipient numerous grants. Mem. Am. Econs. Assn. Democrat. Avocation: flying. Home: 5913 Conway Rd Bethesda MD 20817-3428 Office: The Brookings Instn 1775 Massachusetts Ave NW Washington DC 20036-2188

DICKERMAN, JOHN MELVIN, lawyer; b. Hope, Ark., Aug. 21, 1914; s. Charles and Dorothy W. (Schultz) D.; m. Serafina Peoria, Oct. 26, 1956; 1 child, Dorothea W. BA, U. Ill., 1938, JD, 1940. Bar: Ill. 1940, Ohio 1942, U.S. Supreme Ct. 1944, U.S. Dist. Ct. (D.C. dist.) 1964. Atty. Rep. Steel Corp., Massillon, Ohio, 1940-42, U.S. Alien Property Custodian, Chgo., 1942-43; atty., Washington rep. Airline Pilot's Assn., 1943-47; legis. dir. Nat. Assn. Home Builders, Washington, 1947-52, exec. v.p., 1952-64; pres. John Dickerman & Assocs., Washington, 1964—. Mem. Nat. Assn. Home Builders (life, bd. dirs. 1964, named to Hall of Fame 1980), Am. Soc. Assn. Execs., Chgo. Bar Assn., D.C. Bar Assn., Lambda Alpha. Republican.

DICKERSON, BRIAN, columnist; b. Rochester, N.Y., Dec. 25, 1956; s. Donald Thomas and Shirley Wright D.; m. Andrea June Rowand, Dec. 6, 1986; 1 child, Zachary. BA History, Princeton U., 1979. Editor, reporter Miami (Fla.) Herald, 1979-88; editor mag. Detroit Free Press, 1988-97, columnist, 1997—; pres. Sunday Magazine Editors Assn., Phila., 1991-92. Office: Detroit Free Press 600 W Fort St Detroit MI 48226

DICKERSON, COLLEEN BERNICE PATTON, artist, educator; b. Cleburne, Tex., Sept. 17, 1922; d. Jennings Bryan and Alma Bernice (Clark) Patton; m. Arthur F. Dickerson; children: Sherry M., Chrystal Charmine. BA, Calif. State U., Northridge, 1980; studied with John Pike. presenter demonstrations Cayucos Art Assn., Morro Bay Art Assn., El Camino Real Art Assn. One-woman shows include Morro Bay Cmty. Bldg., Amandas Interiors, Arroyo Grande, Calif., 1996, Gt. Western Savs., San Luis Obispo, Calif.; exhibited in group shows; represented in permanent collections, including Polk Ins. Co., San Luis Obispo, Med. Ctr. MDM Ins. Co., L.A. Mem. Ctrl. Coast Watercolor Soc. (pres. 1986-87), Art Ctr., Oil Acrylic Pastel Group (chmn., co-chmn. 1989-98, prize Brush Strokes show 1999), Morro Bay Art Assn., San Luis Obispo Art Ctr. Avocations: Egyptology, Chinese painting, art history. Home and Studio: 245 Hacienda Ave San Luis Obispo CA 93401-7967

DICKERSON, CYNTHIA ROWE, marketing firm executive, consultant; b. Cin., Apr. 14, 1956; d. Richard Emmett and Frances Jeanette (Ellwanger) Rowe; m. Mark Alan Dickerson, Oct. 24, 1981; children: Shannon Gayle, Meredith Lynne. BSBA, U. So. Calif., 1979. Mgmt. asst. Computer Scis. Corp., Pasadena, Calif., 1974-78; rsch. asst. Dailey & Assocs., L.A., 1978-79; account exec. Young & Rubicam, L.A., 1979-81, Rowley & Linder Advt., Wichita, Kans., 1981-82, Chiat/Day Inc. Advt., San Francisco, 1983-85; product mgr. Sun-Diamond Growers of Calif., Pleasanton, 1985-88; mktg. cons. San Francisco, 1988-90; sr. bus. mgr. Del Monte Foods, San Francisco, 1990-93; dir. mktg. Yorkshire Dried Fruit & Nuts, Inc., San Francisco, 1993-94, Potlatch Corp., 1995-98; dir. category mgmt. Tri Valley Growers, 1999—. Named Outstanding Youth Women of Am., Jr. C. of C., 1985. Mem. Am. Mktg. Assn., Soc. Consumer Affairs Profls., Am. Rose Soc., Heritage Rose Group. Republican. Avocations: gardening, youth sports, playing piano, gourmet cooking. Fax: 925-327-6992. E-mail: Cynthia.Dickerson@TriValleyGrowers.com. Office: 12667 Alcosta Blvd Ste 500 San Ramon CA 94583-0587

DICKERSON, DENNIS CLARK, history educator; b. McKeesport, Pa., Aug. 12, 1949; s. Carl O'Neal and Oswanna (Wheeler) D.; m. Mary Anne Eubanks, Aug. 6, 1977; children: Nicole Denise, Valerie Anne, Christina Marie, Dennis Clark Jr. BA, Lincoln U., 1971; MA, Washington (Mo.) U., 1974, PhD, 1978; LHD (hon.), Morris Brown Coll., 1990; postgrad., Hartford Sem. Instr. history Forest Park C.C., St. Louis, 1974, Pa. State U. Ogontz, Abington, 1975-76; from asst. to assoc. prof. history Williams Coll., Williamstown, Mass., 1976-85, assoc. prof., 1987-88, prof., 1988-99, Stanfield prof. history, 1992-99; assoc. prof. history Rhodes Coll., Memphis, 1985-87; prof. history Vanderbilt U., Nashville, 1999—; mem. com. examiners GRE History test Ednl. Testing Svc., Princeton, 1990-96; corporator Williamstown Savs. Bank, 1992—; vis. prof. Payne Theol. Sem., Wilberforce, Ohio, 1992, 96, 98; vis. prof. Am. religious history Yale Div. Sch., 1995. Author: Out of the Crucible, 1986, Religion, Race and Region: Research Notes on A.M.E. Church History, 1995, Militant Mediator: Whitney M. Young, Jr., 1998; contbr. articles to profl. jours. Historiographer, African Meth. Episcopal Ch., 1988—, min. 1977—; trustee North Adams (Mass.) State Coll., 1992-95. Rockefeller Found. fellow U. Va., 1987-88. Mem. Am. Bible Soc. (trustee), Elks, Alpha Phi Alpha. Office: Vanderbilt U Dept History Nashville TN 37240

DICKERSON, ERIC DEMETRIC, former professional football player; b. Sealy, Tex., Sept. 2, 1960; s. Helen Dickerson. Student, So. Meth. U. Running back Los Angeles Rams, 1983-87; running back Indianapolis Colts, 1987-91, L.A. Raiders, 1992, Atlanta Falcons, 1993-94. Author: (with Richard Graham Walsh) Eric Dickerson's Secrets of Pro Power, 1989. Named All-America team, The Sporting News, 1982; NFL Player of Yr., 1983, Pro Football Writers Rookie of Yr., 1983; NFL All-Pro team, The Sporting News, 1983, 84, 86-88, played in Pro Bowl 1983-84, 86-89; set single season rushing yardage record, 1984; led NFL in rushing, 1983-84, 86. Inducted into the Pro Football Hall of Fame, 1999, Canton Ohio. NFL record for most consecutive seasons with 1,000 or more rushing yards, 1983-89); NFL record for most yards rushing (2,105), 1984; most games with 100 or more yards rushing (12), 1984; shares NFL record for most seasons with 2,000 or more yards rushing and receiving combined. Office: care Atlanta Falcons 2745 Burnette Rd Suwanee GA 30024-2127*

DICKERSON, EUGENIE ANN, writer, journalist; b. Chgo., Oct. 4, 1946; d. Hubert Eugene and Theresa Veronica (Tallarico) King; m. Brian W. Dickerson, Feb. 4, 1967. BA in History, U. Ill., 1968. Newsletter editor Sammamish Aero Modelers Soc., Redmond, Wash., 1976-79; freelance writer, 1977—, illustrator, 1981—, photographer, 1991—; speech writer for cmty. figures, 1992—; restaurant reviewer Seattle Times and others; columnist Bellevue (Wash.) Weekly News, 1990; book editor, cons. to various authors, 1988—. Contbg. author: Developing Arguments, 1990, The Writer's Handbook, 1993, The Writer's Handbook, 1998, The Writer's Journal Guide to the Writing Life, 1999. Recipient 3d place for editorial Nat. Fedn. Press Women, 1989. Mem. Washington Press Assn. (1st place for editorial 1989), Soc. Profl. Journalists. Office: 1212 146th Ave SE Bellevue WA 98007-5651

DICKERSON, JOE BERNARD, principal, educator; b. Marburg, Hesse, Germany, Mar. 24, 1951; came to U.S., 1954; s. Joseph Bernard and Eva Maria (Heitmann) D.; m. Joylyne Barbara Ginter, June 11, 1972; children: Alia Dawn, Aaron Mitchell. BSc in Edn., Valparaiso (Ind.) U., 1978; MSc in Edn., U. Mich., Dearborn, 1989; EdD, Nova Southeastern U., Ft. Lauderdale, Fla., 1996. Tchr. St. Joseph Sch., Adelaide, South Australia, 1972-74, St. John Bosco Sch., Adelaide, South Australia, 1974-76; prin. Zion Luth. Sch., Detroit, 1978-80, 86-91; tchr. Point Pearce (South Australia) Aboriginal Sch., 1980; prin. Trinity Luth. Sch., Southport, Queensland, Australia, 1980-82, Ceduna (South Australia) Luth. Sch., 1982-86; prof. of writing Purdue U., Ft. Wayne, Ind., 1992—; prin. Ctrl. Luth. Sch., New Haven, Ind., 1991-95; supt. Luth. Sch. Foothills, La Crescenta, Calif., 1995-96; prin. Pilgrim Luth. Sch., Santa Monica, Calif., 1996—. Editor: QBD Theatre mag., 1974; author monograph: Into the 80's - Lutheran Education in Australia, 1982. Mem. ASCD, Nat. Assn. Luth. Prins., Nat. Assn. Elem. Prins., Nat. Assn. Tchrs. Math., Nat. Assn. Luth. Dirs. of Devel., Ind. Luth. Prins. Assn. Lutheran. Avocations: outdoor activities, reading, fitness, vegetable gardening. Home: 7741 Apperson St Tujunga CA 91042-2110 Office: Acension Lutheran School 17910 S Prairie Ave Torrance CA 90504

DICKERSON, JOHN JOSEPH, JR., airport manager; b. N.Y.C., Aug. 21, 1923; s. John J. and Henrietta (Rund) D.; m. Alice M. Russhon, Feb. 9, 1946; children: Barbara, Kathleen, John, Ellen, George. BS in Aeronautical Engring., NYU, 1948. Various positions including gen. mgr. N.J. airports Port Authority, N.Y.C., 1948-85; ret., 1985. Mem. Palisades Park Bd. Edn.; mem. bd. trustees Englewood Hosp., pres. Capt. USAF, 1943-46. Mem. Am. Assn. Airport Execs. Republican. Roman Catholic. Home: 208 Penn View Dr Pennington NJ 08534-1919

DICKERSON, JOSEPH ALFRED, retired sales executive; b. Balt., Mar. 9, 1926; s. James Alfred and Clara Reed (Robinson) D.; m. Martha Cook Brooks, Apr. 7, 1951; children: Joseph, Katheryn Ann, Mark Reed. B of Engring., Johns Hopkins U., 1949. Sales engr., mgr. GE Supply Co., Balt., 1949-59; sales engr., mgr. wire and cable divsn. GE Supply Co., Indpls., 1959-66; nat. sales specialist wire and cable divsn. GE Supply Co., Laurel, Md., 1966-68; mgr. Atlantic dist. GE Supply Co., Phila., 1968-70; region mgr. GE Supply Co., Indpls., 1970-74; region mgr. GE Supply Co., Laurel, Md., 1974-76, utility sales specialist, 1976-86, ret., 1986; contract salesman GE Supply Co., Balt., 1986-91. Comdr. Am. Legion, Balt., 1963-64; officer Northwood Baseball League, Balt., 1951-63, mgr., 1951-63. With USAF, 1944-45. Mem. Upper Shore Geneaol. Soc. (chmn. 1997—, vendors 1998—). Republican. Roman Catholic. Avocation: genealogy. Home: RR 3 Box 272 Fenwick Island DE 19944

DICKERSON, JUSTIN BRANDT, financial and telecommunications policy analyst; b. July 27, 1976. BS, U. Utah, 1997; M of Mgmt., Willamette U., 1999. Legis. asst. Utah State Senate, Salt Lake City, 1997; telecomms. policy analyst State of Oreg., Salem, 1998-99; fin. analyst Mervyn's Calif., San Francisco, 1999—. E-mail: jdickers@willamette.edu.

DICKERSON, LON RICHARD, library administrator; b. Ypsilanti, Mich., Dec. 16, 1941; s. Lon E. and Maxine A. (Merryfield) D.; m. Anne Elizabeth Bryan, Aug. 24, 1968; children: Robert Lon, Sarah Elizabeth, Peter Bryan. AB, Albion Coll., 1964; MLS, U. Pitts., 1968. Dir. U. Liberia Librs., Monrovia, 1968-72, Lake Agassiz Regional Libr., Moorhead, Minn., 1972-85, Timberland Regional Libr., Olympia, Wash., 1985-92, Omaha Pub. Libr., 1993-96, Chatham-Effingham-Liberty Regional Libr., Savannah, Ga., 1996—; pres. Adv. Coun. to State Libr., Minn., 1977-78, Minn. Regional Pub. Libr. Systems Adminstrs., 1980, No. Lights Libr. Network Adv. Coun., Minn., 1981-82; v.p. Ga. Coun. Pub. Librs., 1998—. Contbr. articles to profl. jours. Libr. vol. Peace Corps Sierra Leone Libr. Bd., Freetown, 1964-67; mem. planning commn. City of Lacey, Wash.,1985-93; vice-chair planning commn. City of Lacey, 1991-93, mem. various sch. dist. coms.; bd. dirs. Clay-Wilkin Opportunity Coun., Moorhead, Minn., 1982-85; mem. steering com. Omaha 2000, 1993-96, Omaha Free-Net, 1994-96, United Way of the Midlands Com., Omaha, 1996. Mem. ALA (internat. rels. com. 1974-75), Wash. Libr. Assn. (co-chmn. legis. planning com. 1987-92, Pres.'s award 1988), Ga. Libr. Assn., Pub. Libr. Assn. (nominating com. 1989-90), Rotary, Tau Kappa Epsilon. Democrat. Congregationalist. Office: CEL Regional Libr 2002 Bull St Savannah GA 31401-8564

DICKERSON, MARIE HARVISON, nurse anesthetist; b. Leaf, Miss., Oct. 14, 1946; d. Thurman C. and Mary C. (Jarrell) Harvison; m. George T. Dickerson, Sept. 2, 1978; children: George H., Kathryn Marie. AA, Jones County Jr. Coll., 1967; BS, U. Ottawa, Kansas City, Kans., 1976; MEd, U. S. Ala., 1978. RN; cert. registered nurse anesthetist. Oper. rm. supr. George County Hosp., Lucedale, Miss., 1967-70; dir. Sch. Anesthesia, Mobile, Ala., 1972-79; chief anesthesia Wayne Gen. Hosp., Waynesboro, Miss., 1979-84; pres. Wayne Anesthesia, P.A., Waynesboro, 1984—. Maj. USAR. Mem. ANA, Miss. Nurses Assn. (dist. pres. 1983), Am. Assn. for Counseling and Devel., Miss. Assn. Nurse Anesthetists (bd. dirs.), Miss Counseling Assn. Baptist. Club: Waynesboro Home and Garden. Avocations: piano; voice; computers; antiques. Home: 824 Pou Dr Waynesboro MS 39367-2532

DICKERSON, MARTHA ANN, health facility administrator; b. Iowa City, Feb. 2, 1953; d. Wilbur R., Jr. and Phyllis (Schroeder) D. Diploma, Mass. Gen. Hosp. Sch. Nursing, Boston, 1975; BS, Iowa State U., 1978; MS, Rush U., 1983, postgrad. Head nurse, adminstrv. ednl. svcs. coord. Michael Reese Hosp. Med. Ctr., Chgo., 1978-87; clin. health edn. supr., corp. mgr., staff devel. Michael Reese Health Plan, Chgo., 1987-90; clin. svcs. mgr., nat. dir. nursing Buddy Systems, Inc., Chgo., 1990-92; corp. dir. clin. rsch. and spl. projects Cardiac Alliance, Inc., Chgo., 1992-95; mgr. cardiac care unit CareMed Chgo. (formerly Vis. Nurse Assn. Chgo.), 1995-98; adminstr./mgr. Coran Homecare, Des Plaines, Ill., 1998—; rsch. in field. Contbr. articles to profl. jours. Mem. AACN, Am. Soc. Health Edn. and Tng., Intravenous Nurses Soc., Am. Soc. Parenteral and Enteral Nutrition, Am. Heart Assn. (Chgo. divsn., chair CPR targeted activity group 1992-95, nat. CPR faculty 1992-95), Ill. Nurses Assn., Ill. League Nursing (pres. 1988-89), Sigma Theta Tau (eligibility com., by-laws com., rec. sec.). Home: 1522 W Thorndale Ave Chicago IL 60660-3311

DICKERSON, MONAR STEVE, city official; b. El Reno, Okla., Jan. 26, 1947; s. Monar Frank and Grace Elizabeth (Hooper) D.; m. Jean Rollins, May 16, 1969; 1 child, Kelli Leigh. Student, Oklahoma City U., 1965-69, Miss. Gulfcoast Jr. Coll., 1973-74; BS in Psychology, U. So. Miss., 1990. Cert. Meth. lay spkr. Asst. news dir. WVMI/WQID Radio, Biloxi, Miss., 1973-74, ops. mgr., 1974-75; news dir. WLOX-Radio, Biloxi, 1975-76; news anchor, reporter WLOX-TV, Biloxi, 1976-81; asst. to mayor City of Gulfport (Miss.), 1981-84; employee benefits specialist Stewart, Sneed, Hewes Inc., Gulfport, 1984-87; program specialist Area Agy. on Aging of So. Miss., Gulfport, 1987-90; bus. reporter Sun-Herald newspaper, Gulfport, 1990-93; asst. to mayor, pub. affairs mgr. City of Gulfport, 1993-97, bus. devel. coord., 1997—. Charter mem. strategic planning team Gulfport Sch. Dist., co-chair facilities planning com.; mem. devel. adv. com. U. So. Miss., Gulf Coast; mem. adv. bd. Salvation Army; lay leader 1st Meth. Ch. Gulfport; vol. Miss. Spl. Olympics. With USAF, 1969-73. Mem. Miss. Tourism Assn., Pub. Rels. Assn. Miss., Gulf Port Downtown Assn., Gulfport Bus. Club, Kiwanis. Avocations: sailing, horseback riding, bicycling, bowling. Home: 16 Independence Dr Gulfport MS 39507-1937

DICKERSON, RITA M., human resources professional; b. Phila., Oct. 7, 1946; d. Daniel Bryant Dickerson and Mary Rita (Dempsey) Moffa; m. Rocco John Albano, Jr., June 22, 1968 (div. Nov. 1990); children: Sharon Rita, Daniel Bryant. BS, La Salle U., 1994, MBA, 1995. Group claims examiner Aetna Ins. Co., Phila., 1965-69, Mass. Mut. Life Ins. Co., Phila., 1969-70; employee benefits coord. Nat. Liberty Corp., Phila., 1976; ins. plans claims examiner Guardian Life Ins. Co., Phila., 1979-80; group benefits examiner Bricklayers Benefit Plan, Phila., 1980-81; disability coord. and svcs. mgr. CIGNA Corp., Phila., 1981-91; benefits supr. Comcast Metrophone, Phila., 1993; cons. Lewis Co., Inc., Phila., 1994—; office mgr. Law Offices John W. Kormes, Phila., 1992—. Creator: (pamphlet) Terminal Digit Filing System, 1993, reports in field. Coord. Tacony Civic Assn., Phila., 1978; mem. regional bd. St. Martin of Tours, Phila., 1974-76. Recipient Twentieth Century award for Achievement Internat. Biographical Ctr., 1995. Mem. Soc. Human Resource Mgmt., St. Jerome's Ch. Republican. Roman Catholic. Avocations: gourmet cooking, gardening, interior decorating, antiques, reading. Home: 8122 Lister St Philadelphia PA 19152-3108

DICKES, ROBERT, psychiatrist; b. N.Y.C., Apr. 15, 1912; s. Benjamin and Anna (Adler) D.; m. Bernice Livingston, June 12, 1938; children: Richard A., Susan R. Dickes Hubbard. B.S., CCNY, 1933; M.S., Emory U., 1934, M.D., 1938. Diplomate: Am. Bd. Internal Medicine, Am. Bd. Psychiatry and Neurology. Intern L.I. Coll. Hosp., Bklyn., 1938-39; asst. resident in internal medicine L.I. Coll. Hosp., 1938-39, resident in medicine, 1939-41, dir. med. clinics, 1946-50; asso. in medicine L.I. Coll. Medicine, 1946, asst. prof. psychiatry, 1949; fellow in medicine Western Res. U.-Lakeside Hosp., 1941-42; fellow in psychiatry Kings County Hosp. Center-SUNY Bklyn., 1950-52, mem. staff, 1952—, pres. med. br., 1977-78; clin. assoc. prof. psychiatry Downstate Med. Center SUNY, Bklyn., 1950-54, assoc. prof., 1954-56, clin. assoc. prof., 1956-61, assoc. prof., 1961-63, prof., 1963, 78-82, prof. emeritus, 1982—, tng. and supervising analyst, 1965—, acting chmn. dept. psychiatry, 1965-66, 71-72, dir. infant behavior study lab., 1973, dir. center human sexuality, 1973—, chmn. dept. psychiatry, 1975-78; clin. prof. psychiatry NYU Coll. Medicine, 1982—; cons. VA hosps., Bklyn., Northport, N.Y.; v.p. Am. Bd. Sexology, 1989—. Contbr. articles to profl. publs. Bd. govs., mem. acquisitions com. Bklyn. Museum. Maj. M.C. U.S. Army, 1942-46. Commonwealth fellow, 1941-42, 48-49. Fellow A.C.P., Am. Psychiat. Assn., Am. Coll. Psychiatry; mem. Am. Psychoanalytic Assn., Psychoanalytic Assn. N.Y. (treas. 1962-64), Bklyn. Psychiat. Soc. (pres. 1967), Kings County Med. Soc., Kings County Psychiat. Soc. (pres. 1967-68), Soc. Sex Therapy and Research (pres. 1979-81), Am. Bd. Sexology (v.p. 1989—).

DICKESON, ROBERT CELMER, retired university president, foundation executive, political science educator; b. Independence, Mo., June 28, 1940; s. James Houston and Sophie Stephanie (Celmer) D.; m. Ludmila Ann Weir, June 22, 1963; children: Elizabeth Ann, Cynthia Marie. AB, U. Mo., 1962, MA, 1963, PhD, 1968; postgrad., U. No. Colo., 1971, 72; postgrad. inst. ednl. mgmt., Harvard U., 1973. Adminstrv. asst. U. Mo., Columbia, 1962-64, dir. student activities, 1964-68, asst. dean students, 1968-69; dean student affairs No. Ariz. U., Flagstaff, 1969-70, assoc. prof. polit. sci., 1970-76, prof., 1976-81, on leave, 1979-81, v.p. student affairs, 1970-79, v.p., univ. relations, 1973-79; dir. Ariz. Dept. Adminstrn., Phoenix, 1979-81; pres. U. No. Colo., Greeley, 1981-91, prof. polit. sci., 1981-87, 88-91; chief of staff to gov., exec. dir. Office of State Planning and Budgeting State of Colo., 1987; pres. Noel/Levitz Ctrs. Inc., Iowa City, IA, 1991-97; divsn. pres. USA Group, Inc., Indpls., 1995-97; sr. v.p. USA Group Found., 1997—; adj. prof. U. Colo., Denver, 1987, Ariz. State U., Tempe, 1979-81; nat. vice-chmn. Cert. Public Mgr. Policy Bd., 1980-81; planning and mgmt. cons.; mem. univ. adv. council Am. Council on Life Ins.; dir. United Bank of Greeley; mem. Pres.' Commn. NCAA, 1989-91; mem. Nat. Commn. on Minorities in Higher Edn., 1989-91; nat. cons. Office of Women in Higher Edn., Am. Coun. on Edn., 1989—. Author: Prioritizing Academic Programs and Services, 1999; contbr. articles to profl. jours. Active Boy Scouts Am., v.p. Grand Canyon council, Flagstaff, 1974-76, pres., 1976-79, mem. nat. council, 1976-81, T. Roosevelt council, 1979-81, v.p. Long's Peak Council, 1981-87; mem. state com. Ariz. Democratic Com., 1970-72; chmn. Gov.'s Commn. on Merit System Reform, 1979-80, Gov.'s Regulatory Rev. Council, 1980-81, Gov.'s Commn. Higher Edn., 1983-86; mem. Gov.'s Commn. Excellence in Edn., 1983-86, Gov.'s Coun. on Creative Schs., 1989-91; commr. from Colo. to Edn. Commn. of the States, 1987-91; internat. trustee Sigma Alpha Epsilon Found., 1993-97. Recipient Dist. award of Merit., 1973, Silver Beaver award, 1975, Disting. Service award Sigma Alpha Epsilon, 1969, Merit Key award 1997, Disting. Alumnus award U. Mo.-Columbia, 1988, Outstanding Pres. award Am. Assn. Colls. of Tchrs. Edn, 1991, Bus. Excellence award U. No. Colo., 1996; named to N. Crtrl. Athletic Conf. Hall of Fame, 1991. Mem. Am. Polit. Sci. Assn., Am. Soc. Public Adminstrn. (Ariz. exec. bd., Superior Svc. award 1981), Am. Acad. Polit. and Social Sci., Coll. Student Pers. Inst. (acad. coun. 1969-73), Assn. Pub. Coll. and Univ. Pres. (pres. 1985-87), Assn. Pub. Coll. and Univ. Pres. (pres. 1985-87), Nat. Assn. Student Pers. Adminstrs. (regional coun. 1974-79), Am. Assn. State Colls. and Univs. (chmn. coun. on doctoral granting instns., Meritorious Svc. award 1991), Columbia Club (Indpls.), Newcomen Soc., Phi Kappa Phi. United Methodist (pres. bd. trustees 1974). Lodges: Kiwanis (pres. 1975-76); Rotary. Office: USA Group 30 S Meridian Indianapolis IN 46204-3503

DICKEY, ARDEN, newspaper publishing executive. V.p. circulation The Miami Herald, Fla.; dir. circulation Knight-Ridder, Inc., Miami. Office: The Miami Herald Pub Co One Herald Plz Miami FL 33132-1693 Office: Knight-Ridder Inc Dept KRI Miami FL 33132*

DICKEY, GEORGE EDWARD, water resources consultant, economics educator; b. Sewickley, Pa., Jan. 27, 1940; s. George Otto and Frances Marie (Dougherty) D.; m. Susan Emma Veigel, July 14, 1966; children: Paul Edward, George Louis. BA, Johns Hopkins U., 1961; MA, Northwestern U., 1964, PhD, 1968. Operation rsch. analyst Office Sec. Def., Washington, 1967-69; asst. prof. U. Md., Balt., 1969-73; mem. staff Office Sec. of Army, Washington, 1973-75, econ. advisor, 1976-83; dep. for policy and evaluation Office of Asst. Sec. of Army for Civil Works, Washington, 1983-90, acting prin. dep., 1990-93; acting asst. sec., 1993-94; chief planning divsn. U.S. Army Corps of Engrs., Washington, 1994-98; prof. econ. Loyal Coll., Md., 1998—; vis. prof. Indsl. Coll. Armed Forces, Washington, 1967-70; cons. in field of water resources. Author: Money, Prices and Growth: The American Experience 1869-1896, 1977; contbr. articles to profl. publs. Capt. U.S. Army, 1965-67. Recipient award for Meritorious Civil Svc., 1981, Presdl. Rank award for Meritorious Svc., 1988, Presdl. Rank award for Disting. Svc., 1993, award for Exceptional Civilian Svc., 1998, Silver Order of the Fluery medal, 1998; Harold E. Stonier fellow, 1964-65. Mem. SAR, Am. Econ. Assn., Soc. of Sons of Revolution in State of Md., Cath. League for Religious and Civil Rights, The Nature Conservancy, Soc. Am. Mil. Engrs., Am. Water Resources Assn., Md. Hist. Soc., Johns Hopkins Club, Omicron Delta Epsilon. Home: 3 Stratford Rd Baltimore MD 21218-1145

DICKEY, GLENN ERNEST, JR., sports columnist; b. Virginia, Minn., Feb. 16, 1936; s. Glenn Ernest and Madlyn Marie (Emmert) D.; m. Nancy Jo McDaniel, Feb. 25, 1967; 1 son, Kevin Scott. B.A., U. Calif., Berkeley, 1958. Sports editor Watsonville (Calif.) Register-Pajoronian, 1958-63; sports writer San Francisco Chronicle, 1963-71, sports columnist, 1971—. Author: The Jock Empire, 1974, The Great No-Hitters, 1976, Champs and Chumps, 1976, The History of National League Baseball, 1979, The History of American League Baseball, 1980, (with Dick Berg) Eavesdropping America, 1980, America Has a Better Team, 1982, The History of Professional Basketball, 1982, The History of the World Series, 1984, (with Jim Tunney) Impartial Judgment: The Dean of NFL Referees Calls Football As He Sees It, 1988, San Francisco Forty-Niners: The Super Year, 1989; (with Bill Walsh) Building a Champion, 1990; Just Win, Baby, Al Davis and His Raiders, 1991; Sports Hero Kevin Mitchell (juvenile), 1993, Sports Hero Jerry Rice (juvenile), 1993; contbr. stories to Best Sports Stories, 1962, 68, 71, 75, 76. Home: 120 Florence Ave Oakland CA 94618-2249 Office: Chronicle Pub Co 901 Mission St San Francisco CA 94103-2905*

DICKEY, JAY W., JR., congressman, lawyer; b. 1939; s. Jay W. and Margaret D.; divorced; children: John, Laura, Ted, Rachel. BA, U. Ark., 1961, JD, 1963. City atty. Pine Bluff, Ark., 1968-70; mem. 103rd Congress from 4th Ark. dist., 1993—; mem. Appropriations Com. Past pres. Pine Bluff Jaycees (Disting. Svc. award); huddle leader Pine Bluff High Sch. Fellowship of Christian Athletes (mem. state bd.); mem. Pillars Club United Way, Century Club Boy Scouts Am.; past mem. LifeSavers of Ark. Childrens' Hosp.; state chmn. Christian Legal Soc. Republican. Office: US Ho of Reps Office of Ho Mems 2453 Rayburn Bldg Washington DC 20515-0404

DICKEY, JOHN HARWELL, lawyer; b. Huntsville, Ala., Feb. 22, 1944; s. Gilbert McClain and Marjorie Loucille (Harwell) D.; m. Nancy Margaret Eagar, Nov. 24, 1984; children: Marjorie Ruth, Gilbert Charles. BA, Samford U., 1966; JD, Cumberland Sch. of Law, 1969. Bar: Tenn. 1971, U.S. Dist. Ct. (ea. dist.) Tenn. 1972. Adminstrv. asst. Dist. Atty.'s Office, Huntsville, 1969-70; law clerk domestic and juvenille divsn. Cir. Ct., Huntsville, 1970-72; trial lawyer Legal Aid Soc., Chattanooga, 1972-75; pvt. practice Chattanooga, 1975-77, Fayetteville, Tenn., 1977-89; dist. pub. defender 17th jud. cir. State of Tenn., Fayetteville, 1989-98; pvt. practice, Fayetteville, Tenn., 1998—; mem. continuing edn. com. Pub. Defenders Conf., Tenn., 1990-92, mem. long range planning com., 1991-93, mem. legis. com., 1990-93, mem. exec. com., Mid. Tenn. rep., 1993-94. Lectr. Fayetteville-Lincoln County Leadership Tng. Program, 1989—; mem. adv. bd. Community Correction South Ctrl. Tenn., Fayetteville, 1989—; mem. Bedford County Dem. Club, 1989—. Mem. Nat. Assn. Criminal Def. Lawyers, Tenn. Bar Assn., Tenn. Assn. Criminal Def. Lawyers (membership com. 1989—, juvenile law com. 1988—, Disting. Svc. award 1990, 91, 92), Marshall County Bar Assn., Fayetteville-Lincoln County Bar Assn. (treas. 1977, sec. 1978, v.p. 1979, pres. 1980), Fayetteville-Lincoln County C. of C., Elks, Masons (jr. steward 1991, sr. steward 1992, jr. deacon 1993, jr. warden 1994, sr. warden 1995, worshipful master 1996), York Rite Mason, Scottish Rite Mason (32 degree), Shriners (sgt.-at-arms 1993, v.p. 1994, dir. pub. rels. 1994, 96—, pres. 1995), Internat. Platform Assn., Order of Ea. Star (chaplain 1993-94), Tenn. 4-H Found. Democrat. Methodist. Avocations: hunting, fishing, canoeing, kayaking. Home: 122 Brookmeade Dr Fayetteville TN 37334-2046 Office: 105 Main Ave S Fayetteville TN 37334-3057

DICKEY, JOHN SLOAN, JR., science association director; b. Washington, Jan. 24, 1941; s. John Sloan Sr. and Christina Margaret (Gillespie) D.; m. Joan Elizabeth Cass, Dec. 28, 1963 (div. 1977); 1 child, Nathaniel Hudson; m. Lynn McMath, June 6, 1978. BA, Dartmouth Coll., 1963; MS, Otago U., Dunedin, N.Z., 1966; PhD, Princeton (N.J.) U., 1969. Field geologist Brit. Newfoundland Exploration, Springdale, 1963; rsch. assoc. Smithsonian Astrophys. Obs., Cambridge, Mass., 1969-70; rsch. assoc. coll. obs. Harvard U., Cambridge, Mass., 1969-70, Carnegie Inst. of Washington, 1970-72; asst. prof. MIT, Cambridge, 1972-76, assoc. prof., 1976-79; program dir. geochemistry dept. NSF, Washington, 1979-81; prof. geology, head geology dept. Syracuse (N.Y.) U., 1981-88; dean sci., math. and engring. depts. Trinity U., San Antonio, 1988-98; dir. edn. and rsch. Am. Geophys. Union, Washington, 1998—; pres. Centaur Geol. Svcs. Inc., Boston, 1978-82. Author: (textbook) Lectures in Earth and Planetary Science, 1987, On the Rocks, 1996. Fulbright fellow N.Z., 1964-65. Fellow Mineral. Soc. Am.; mem. AAAS, Geochem. Soc. (treas. 1987-93), Am. Geophys. Union, Geol. Soc. Washington, Internat. Assn. Cosmology and Geochemistry, Lawrence Durrell Soc. Home: 1401 33d St NW Washington DC 20007 Office: Am Geophys Union 2000 Florida Ave NW Washington DC 20009-1231

DICKEY, JULIA EDWARDS, aviation consultant; b. Mar. 6, 1940; d. John Keith and Henrietta Barbara (Zerell) Edwards; m. Joseph E. Dickey, June 18, 1959; children: Joseph E., John Edwards. Student, DePauw U., 1958-59, MLS, 1967; AB, Ind. U., 1962. Asst. acquisitions libr. Ind. U. Regional Campus Librs., 1965-67; head tech. svcs. Bartholomew County Libr., Columbus, Ind., 1967-74; dir. reference svcs. Southeastern Ind. Area Libr. Svcs. Authority, Columbus, 1974-78, exec. dir., 1978-80; pres. Jedco Enterprises, 1981—; legis. strategy chmn. Ind. Libr. Coop. Devel., 1975; dir. Ind. Ind. Libr. Trustees Assn. Governance Project, 1982. Mem. Columbus exec. bd. Mayor's Task Force on Status of Women, 1973-76; del. Ind. Sch. Nominating Assembly, 1973-75, 75-77; bd. dirs. Human Svcs. Inc. (Bartholomew, Brown and Jackson Counties cmty. action program), 1975-79, sec., 1975, v.p., 1979, pres., 1976-78; ruling elder, session clk. First Presbyn. Ch. Aurora, Ind., 1996—, clk. of session, 1997—, chair pers., 1996—; mem. adv. coun. Ind./Nat. Network Study, 1977-78; mem. local adv. coun. Salvation Army, 1984-88; bd. dirs. Columbus Women's Ctr.; precinct coord. Vols. for Bayh, 1974; sheriff Columbus 1st precinct, 1975, clk., 1976-77, insp., 1978, judge, 1980-83; treas. Hayes for State Rep., 1978, 82-96; trustee Lawrenceburg Pub. Libr., 1998—. Named Outstanding Young Woman Am., 1973. Mem. ALA, AAUW (pres. 1973-75), Ind. Libr. Assn. (dist. chmn. 1972-73, chmn. libr. edn. divsn. 1980-81, ad hoc com. on legis. effectiveness 1982, various coms.), Libr. Assts. and Technicians Round Table (chmn. 1968-69), Tech. Svcs. Round Table (chmn. 1971-72, sec. libr. planning com. 1969-72), Bartholomew County Libr. Staff Assn. (pres. 1975-76), Exptl. Aircraft Assn. (charter pres. chpt. 729, Inc. 1981, advisor 1982, sec. 1984-85, treas. 1996—), Ind. EEA coun. (pres. 1982-88, advisor 1988—, internat. EAA conv. antique/classic mgmt. team 1988-98), Internat. Exptl. Aircraft Assn. (Major Achievement award 1983), Antique Airplane Assn., Dearborn County Hist. Soc. (bd. dirs. 1999—), First Tuesday, Rev. Club of Lawrenceburg, Ind. (corr. sec. 1996-97, ch. lit. com. 1998-99), Zonta Club (newsletter editor Tel-Zon 1981-89, rec. sec. 1984-85, treas. 1990-93, v.p. 1993-94), Psi Iota Xi (thrift shop steering 1985-94, v.p. thrift shop chmn. 1986-87, Mem. of Yr. 1988-89, pres.-elect 1991-92, pres. 1992-93, advisor 1993-94, mem. state assn. project com. 1992-93, constn./by-laws com. 1993-94); mem. bd. trustees Lawrenceburg Pub. Libr., 1998—. Home and Office: 55 Oakey Ave Lawrenceburg IN 47025-1538

DICKEY, KEITH WINFIELD, dentist, dental educator; b. South Bend, Ind., Jan. 13, 1949; s. Floyd Mitchell and Margaret Alice (Freeman) D.; m. Peggy Jo Graham, Jan. 25, 1975. B of Life Scis., Ind. State U., 1972; DDS, Ind. U., 1974; MBA, SO. Ill. U., 1987. Lic. dentist Ind., Ill. Dental practitioner pvt. practice, Mishawaka, Ind., 1974-80; educator dentistry Ind. U., South Bend, 1974-80, Ill. Ctrl. Coll., East Peoria, 1980-82; dental practitioner pvt. practice, Peoria, Ill, 1980-82; educator dentistry So. Ill. U., Alton, 1982—; dental practitioner pvt. practice, East Alton, Ill., 1983—; mem. dentistry aux. edn. bd. Ind. U., 1975-80, Ill. Ctrl. Coll., 1980-82; dentistry asst. edn. bd. Lewis & Clark C.C., Godfrey, Ill., 1983—; dentistry hygiene edn. bd. So. Ill. U., Carbondale, 1990—. Contbr. articles to profl. jours. Fellow Am. Coll. Ddentists; mem. ADA (cons. commn. dental edn. accreditation), Am. Acad. History Dentistry (Bremner Dental History award 1974), Am. Assn. Dental Schs. (sect. chair 1996-97), Ill. State Dental Soc. (del. 1994, trustee Paul W. Clopper Found. 1997), Madison Dist. Dental Soc. (pres. 1990-92), Orgn. Tchrs. Dental Practice Adminstrn. (pres. 1994-96), Ind. State U. Alumni Assn. (pres. 1998—), Xi Psi Phi (supreme pres. 1990-92), Omicron Kappa Upsilon (chpt. pres. 1995-96). Mem. Disciples of Christ. Avocations: flower gardening, piano. Home: 33 Glen Echo Dr Edwardsville IL 62025-3702 Office: Sch Dental Medicine 2800 College Ave Alton IL 62002-4742

DICKEY, NANCY EAGAR, social worker; b. Chattanooga, Dec. 11, 1947; d. Charles Harrison and Virginia Ruth (Genter) Eagar; m. John Harwell Dickey, Nov. 24, 1984; children: Marjorie Ruth, Gilbert Charles. BA, Webster Coll., St. Louis, 1969; MSSW, U. Tenn., 1977; MBA, Vanderbilt U., 1983. Vol. VISTA, Huntsville, Ala., 1970-71; probation officer, dist. supr. Hamilton County Juvenile Ct., Chattanooga, 1971-77; family individual counselor Cmty. Svcs., Chattanooga, 1978-80; supr. EPSDT Hamilton County Health Dept., Chattanooga, 1980-81; salesperson NCR, Nashville and Memphis, 1983-84; social worker Hosp. Home Health and Hospice, Fayetteville, Tenn., 1992-94; dir. social svcs. Lincoln County Health Facilities, Fayetteville, 1994—. Bd. dirs. Healthy Families/Children First, Shelbyville, 1996—, Sr. Citizens Adv. Bd., Fayetteville, 1997—, Lincoln County Cmty. Health Bd., 1996—, Hannah's House, Fayetteville, 1994—, sec., 1995-97, chmn., 1997—; team mem. Child Abuse Rev. Team, Fayetteville, 1994—; mem. multi-disciplinary cons. team Adult Protective Svcs., Fayetteville, 1996—; mem. 4-H Found., 1996—; mem. adv. bd. 4-H, Fayetteville, 1995-96. Mem. NASW (cert.), Tenn. Hosp. Assn., Tenn. Soc. Health Care Social Workers (bd. rep. 1994-95), Mid-South Coun. Health Care Social Wk. (sec. 1996), Pilot Club (corr. sec./rec. sec. 1994-96, sec. 1998—), Order Ea. Star. Avocations: crossword puzzles, logic problems. Home: 122 Brookmeade Dr Fayetteville TN 37334-2046 Office: Lincoln County Health Facilities 700 Maple St W Fayetteville TN 37334-3202

DICKEY, PHILLIP NELSON THEOPHILUS (PHILO DICKEY), poet, playwright; b. Cin., June 9, 1948; s. Phyllis Jean (Faul) D.; m. Valerie Mae Allen, June 11, 1971 (div. 1972); m. Lora Lynn Shaw, Sept. 15, 1975 (div. 1982). BFA in Theater Arts, Ohio U., 1975. Radio announcer various radio stas., 1964-77; radio/TV prodn., program analyst audio-visual instrn. svcs. The Pentagon, Washington, 1967-70; prin., owner Moot Enterprises, Chillicothe, Ohio, 1973—. Poet: Front Seat Revelations, 1973, Feng-Shu, 1989; author: (plays) Wordsmith, 1992, What Time Is It, Honey, 1996, 1-900-, 1996; actor outdoor drama Tecumseh, 1990-93, performances with Columbus Jr. Theatre, 1992-93. Staff sgt. USAF, 1966-70. Decorated Air Force Commendation medal, 1968, Purple Heart, 1969, Bronze star, 1969. Avocations: photography, reading, metaphysics, phenomenology. Home: PO Box 541 Chillicothe OH 45601-0541 Office: Moot Enterprises 33 N Paint St Ste 310 Chillicothe OH 45601-3116

DICKEY, ROBERT MARVIN (RICK DICKEY), property manager; b. Charleston, S.C., Dec. 3, 1950; s. John Lincoln II and Ruth (Marvin) D.; m. Teresa Ann Curry, Dec. 19, 1969 (div. 1979); 1 child, Gena Lynette. A of Computer Sci., USMC Degree Program, Washington, 1975. Cert. apt. property supr. Nat. Apt. Assn., Wash., occupancy specialist Nat. Ctr.for Housing Mgmt., Wash. Enlisted USMC, 1968, advanced through grades to staff sgt., 1968-78; shop mgr., bookkeeper Amalgamated Plant Co., Las Vegas, Nev., 1978-79; supr. constrn. Joseph Yousem Co., Las Vegas, 1979-80; apt. mgr. Robert A. McNeil Corp., Las Vegas, 1980, comml. bldg. mgr., leasing agt., 1980-82; asst. v.p., regional property mgr. Westminster Co., Las Vegas, 1982-87, Weyerhaeuser Mortgage Co., Las Vegas, 1988-89; pres., ptnr. Equinox Devel., Inc., Las Vegas, 1989-91; dir. residential properties R.W. Robideaux & Co., Spokane, Wash., 1992-97; mgr. residential divsn. G&B Real Estate Svcs., Spokane, 1997—. Contbr. articles to profl. jours. Mem. Nat. Assn. Realtors, Wash. Assn. Realtors, Spokane Assn. Realtors, Inst. Real Estate Mgmt. (accredited residential mgr., legis. chmn. 1987-88, Accredited Residential Mgr. award 1985, 86, 90), Nev. Apt. Assn. (v.p. 1985, pres. 1988—, bd. dirs.), So. Nev. Homebuilders Assn., Las Vegas Bd. Realtors (mgmt. legis. com. 1988).

DICKINSON, ALFRED JAMES, realtor; b. Eufaula, Ala., Dec. 19, 1916; s. Alfred J. and Bertha (Trotter) D.; m. Elsie Vick Mattingly, Mar. 21, 1942; children—Alfred James IV, Paul Mattingly, Elsie Stringfellow, Mary Bridgers. B.A., U. Richmond (Va.), 1937; M.B.A., Harvard, 1939. Asst. to comptroller Virginia-Carolina Chem. Corp., Richmond, Va., 1939-41; v.p. Virginia-Carolina Chem. Corp., 1952-56, v.p., asst. to pres., 1956-57; v.p. Freeport Sulphur Co., 1957-60; exec. v.p. W.M. Brown & Son, Inc., Richmond, 1960-63; chmn. bd. dirs. Alfred J. Dickinson, Inc., Richmond, 1963—; Spl. agt. FBI, 1941-44. Served as capt. USMCR, 1944-46. Mem. SAR, Soc. Cin. (Va.), Jamestowne Soc., Harvard Bus. Sch. Alumni Assn., Phi Beta Kappa, Omicron Delta Kappa, Phi Gamma Delta. Baptist. Clubs: Country of Virginia, Commonwealth. Home: 6101 Three Chopt Rd Richmond VA 23226-2731 Office: 4900 Augusta Ave Richmond VA 23230-3626

DICKINSON, BRADLEY WILLIAM, electrical engineering educator; b. St. Marys, Pa., Apr. 28, 1948; s. William Amos and Maxine I. (McDaniel) D.; m. Colette M. Aldrich, Mar. 12, 1983; children: James Aldrich, Betsy Rebecca. BS in Engring., Case Inst. Tech., 1970; MSEE, Stanford U., 1971, PhD in Elec. Engring., 1974. Asst. prof. dept. elec. engring. Princeton U., Princeton, N.J., 1974-80, assoc. prof., 1980-85, prof., 1985—; assoc. dean for acad. affairs Sch. Engring. and Applied Sci. Princeton U., 1991-94. Mng. coeditor: Mathematics of Control, Signals and Systems, 1988—; co-editor: Electronic Newsletter (E-Letter) On Systems, Control and Signal Processing, 1987-93, Selected Papers in Multidimensional Signal Processing, 1986, Concurrent Computations, 1988; author: Systems: Analysis, Design and Computation, 1991; contbr. over 60 tech. papers to profl. jours.; 2 patents on video compression. Fellow IEEE; mem. Tau Beta Pi. Office: Princeton U Dept Elec Engring Princeton NJ 08544-5263*

DICKINSON, CAROL RITTGERS, arts administrator, writer, executive director; b. Des Moines, Apr. 16, 1933; d. Robert Johnson and Cecil Marjorie (Snyder) Rittgers; m. Donald Ira Dickinson, June 6, 1959; 1 child, Lauren Lucy. BA in English with honors, Drake U., 1954; MA in Art History, U. Hawaii, 1964. Lydia Roberts fellow Columbia U., N.Y.C., 1954-56; instr. Iowa State U., U. Hawaii, Colo Women's Coll., U. Petroleum and Minerals, Dhahran, Saudi Arabia, Colo. Sc. Mines, Golden, 1956-76; dir. pub. programs Denver Art Mus., 1980-83; dir. publicity and edn. Mus. Western Art, Denver, 1985-86; freelance writer, 1979—; lectr., panelist numerous mus., univs. and profl. groups, Colo., 1980—. Co-editor, contbg. author: Colorado and the American Renaissance, 1980, Walking in Beauty, 1990; founding editor Denver Urban Design Forum Newsletter, 1984, 85; contbr. more than 400 articles to nat. and regional newspapers and mags.; art critic Denver Rocky Mountain News, 1990-92. Exec. dir. Foothills Art Ctr., Golden, 1992—. Mem. Colo. Press Women (first pl. award reviews features), Golden Fortnightly Club, Asian Art Assn. Democrat. Episcopalian. Avocations: Asian philosophies and history, Chinese brush painting, international hosting, films, felines. Office: Foothills Art Ctr 809 15th St Golden CO 80401-1813

DICKINSON, CHARLES ARTHUR, manufacturing company executive; b. Warroad, Minn., Oct. 30, 1923; s. Arthur J. and Josephine (Cohen) D.; m. Jean Louise Jenstad, Aug. 2, 1947; children: Peter, Joseph, Richard, Thomas, Anne. BEE, U. Minn., 1949, MBA, 1951. CEO Dataproducts Corp., Woodland Hills, Calif., 1980-85, Vt. Microsystems, Inc., Winooski, 1986-90; chmn. bd. Solectron Corp., Milipitas, Calif., 1986-90, 94-96; also bd. dirs. Solectron Corp., Milipitas; bd. dirs. Trident Microsystems, Mountain View, Calif., Vt. Microsystems, Winooski, Aavid Thermal Techs., Inc. 1st lt. USAF, 1943-46. Office: Solectron 604 Rood Pond Rd Williamstown VT 05679-9744

DICKINSON, CHARLES CAMERON, III, theologian, educator; b. Charleston, W.Va., May 13, 1936; s. Charles Cameron Jr. and Frances Ann (Saunders) D.; m. JoAnne Walton. BA cum laude, Dartmouth Coll., 1958; BD, Pitts. Theol. Sem., 1965; PhD, U. Pitts., 1973. Prof. English, Greek and N.T. Ecole de Theologie Kimbanguiste, Zaire, 1972; asst. prof. systematic theology and philosophy Union Theol. Sem., Richmond, Va., 1974-75; asst. prof. religion and philosophy Morris Harvey Coll., Charleston, 1975-79; prof. Am. Coll. of Rome, 1979; research prof. U. Charleston, 1980-81; curatorial assoc. manuscript collections Andover-Harvard Theol. Library, 1981-86; vis. scholar Christ Ch., Oxford (Eng.) U., 1979, Harvard U. Div. Sch., 1980; prof. linguistics and lit. Hebei Tchrs U., Shijiazhuang, Hebei Province, China, 1983-84; dir. Univ. Press Edits./Mountain State Press, Charleston, 1980-83; lectr. Harvard Med. Sch., 1985-88. Author: One Thing Necessary: The Word of God in Preaching, 1988; contbr. articles, revs. to profl. jours. Bd. dirs., mem. ednl. coun. River Sch., Charleston, 1978-81; bd. dirs. Charleston Chamber Music Soc., Kanawha Valley Youth Orch., Charleston Ballet, W.Va. Opera Theater, Kanawha Pastoral Counseling Ctr., Boston Conservatory, Boston Lyric Opera, Boston Camerata, Goethe Soc. New Eng.; mem. College des Conseillers, French Libr. and Cultural Ctr., Boston. With USMC, 1958-61. Entrance fellow Chgo. Theol. Sem., 1962; Chgo. U. Div. Sch. scholar, 1962. Fellow Royal Soc. Arts; mem. AAAS, Karl Barth Soc. N.Am. (dir.), Am. Acad. Religion, Soc. Bibl. Lit., Am. Theol. Soc., Am. Philos. Assn., Am. Assn. Advancement Humanities, W.Va. Philos. Soc., W.Va. Assn. Humanities, Internat. Bonhoeffer Soc., Edgewood Country Club (Charleston), Wichita Club, Univ. Club (Wichita Falls, Pitts.), Yale Club (N.Y.), Harvard Club (Boston, Dallas, France), Boston Athenaeum, Am. Club of Paris, Cercle de l'Union Interalliée, Rotary (chmn. Charleston Club student exchange com. 1978-79), Union Club, St. Botolph Club. Democrat. Home: 21 Chestnut St Boston MA 02108-3601 *On proud days, I swell with the Protestant spirit which brought the "rise of the West." On black days, I am glad I shall not live to see us kill all the animals, cut down all the trees, and crowd the earth with 20,000,000,000 people. Which shall it be? Earth's fate lies in our hands.*

DICKINSON, DONALD CHARLES, library science educator; b. Schenectady, N.Y., June 9, 1927; s. Charles William and Stella Barney (Sheldon) D.; m. Colleen Eleanor Schindler, Aug. 7, 1954; children: Ann, Jean, Ellen, Mary, Kathleen, Sheila. AB, SUNY, Albany, 1949; MLS, U. Ill., 1951; PhD, U. Mich., 1964. Ref. librarian Cen. Mo. State Coll., Warrensburg, 1951-53, Eastern Mich. U., Ypsilanti, 1953-56; asst. acquisitions U. Kans., Lawrence, 1956-58; head librarian Bemidji (Minn.) State Coll., 1958-66; dir. reader service U. Mo., Columbia, 1966-69; dir. grad. library sch. U. Ariz., Tucson, 1969-78, prof. grad. library sch., 1979-96, prof. emeritus, 1996—. Author: Bio-bibliography Langston Hughes, 1967, 2d edit., 1972, Hellmut Lehmann-Haupt, 1975, Dictionary of American Book Collectors, 1986, George Watson Cole, 1990, Henry E. Huntington's Library of Libraries, 1995, Dictionary of American Antiquarian Bookdealers, 1998. Grantee Am. Philos. Assn., 1969; Andrew W. Mellon fellow Henry E. Huntington Libr., 1989. Mem. ALA (coun. 1972-73, travel grantee 1960), Bibliographic Soc. Am., Ariz. Libr. Assn. (pres. 1978-79), Grolier Club (N.Y.C.), Zamorano Club (L.A.). Democrat.

DICKINSON, ELEANOR CREEKMORE, artist, educator; b. Knoxville, Tenn., Feb. 7, 1931; d. Robert Elmond and Evelyn Louise (Van Gilder) C.; m. Ben Wade Oakes Dickinson, June 12, 1952; children: Mark Wade, Katherine Van Gilder, Peter Somers. BA, U. Tenn., 1952; postgrad., San Francisco Art Inst., 1961-63, Académie de la Grande Chaumière, Paris, 1971; M.F.A., Calif. Coll. Arts and Crafts, 1982, Golden Gate U., 1984. Escrow officer Security Nat. Bank, Santa Monica, Calif., 1953-54; mem. faculty Calif. Coll. Arts and Crafts, Oakland, Calif., 1971—, assoc. prof. art, 1974-84, prof., 1984—, dir. galleries, 1975-85; artist-in-residence U. Tenn., 1969, Ark. State U., 1993; mem. faculty U. Calif. Ext., 1967-70; lectr. in field. Co-author, illustrator: Revival, 1974, That Old Time Religion, 1975; also mus. catalogs; illustrator: The Complete Fruit Cookbook, 1972, Human Sexuality: A Search for Understanding, 1984, Days Journey, 1985; commissions: University of San Francisco, 1990-92; one-person exhbns. include Corcoran Gallery Art, Washington, 1970, 74, San Francisco Mus. Modern Art, 1965, 68, Fine Arts Mus. San Francisco, 1969, 75, U. Tenn., 1976, Michael Himovitz Gallery, Sacramento, Calif., 1988, 89, 91, 93, 97, 98; touring exhbns. include Smithsonian Inst., 1975-81, Oakland Mus., 1979, Interart Ctr., N.Y.C., 1980, Tenn. State Mus., 1981-82, Galeria de Arte y Libros, Monterrey, Mex., 1978, Hatley Martin Gallery, San Francisco, 1986, 89, Gallery 10, Washington, 1989, Diverse Works, Houston, 1990, Ewing Gallery, U. Tenn., 1991, G.T.U. Gallery, U. Calif., Berkeley, 1991, Mus. Contemporary Religious Art, St. Louis, 1995; represented in permanent collections Nat. Collection Fine Arts, Corcoran Gallery Art, Libr. of Congress, Smithsonian Instn., San Francisco Mus. Modern Art, Butler Inst. Art, Oakland Mus., Santa Barbara Mus., Nat. Mus. Women in Arts, Washington; prodr. (TV program) The Art of the Matter-Professional Practices in Fine Arts, 1986—. Bd. dirs. Calif. Confedn. of the Arts, 1983-88; bd. dirs., v.p. Calif. Lawyers for the Arts, 1986—; mem. coun. bd. San Francisco Art Inst., 1966-91, trustee, 1964-67; sec., bd. dirs. YWCA, 1955-62; treas., bd. Westminster Ctr., 1955-59; bd. dirs. Children's Theater Assn., 1958-60, 93-94, Internat. Child Art Ctr., 1958-68. Recipient Disting. Alumni award San Francisco Art Inst., 1983, Master Drawing award Nat. Soc. Arts and Letters, 1983, Cert. of Recognition, El Consejo Mundial de Artistas Plasticos 2d Internat. Conf., 1993, Pres.'s award Nat. Womens Caucus for Art, 1995; grantee Zellerbach Family Fund, 1975, Calif. Coll. Arts and Crafts, 1994, NEH, 1978, 80, 82-85, Thomas F. Stanley Found., 1985, Bay Area Video Coalition, 1988-92, PAS Graphics, 1988, San Francisco Cmty. TV Corp., 1990, Skaggs Found., 1991. Mem. Coalition of Women's Art Orgns. (dir., v.p. 1978-80), Coll. Art Assn., AAUP, Calif. Confederation of Arts (bd. dirs. 1983-89), Calif. Lawyers for Arts (v.p. 1986—), San Francisco Art Assn. (sec., dir. 1964-67), NOW, Artists Equity Assn. (nat. v.p., dir. 1978-92), Arts Advocates, Women's Caucus for Art (nat. Affirmative Action officer 1978-80). Democrat. Episcopalian. Office: Calif Coll Arts and Crafts 1111 8th St San Francisco CA 94107

DICKINSON, GAIL KREPPS, educational administrator, educator; b. Lewistown, Pa., June 10, 1956; d. Harold and Esther (Bourdess) Krepps; m. Willis H. Dickinson, Dec. 22, 1979 (div. 1998); children: Margaret Lee, Elizabeth Ann. BS, Millersville U. Pa., 1977; MSLS, U. N.C., 1987; postgrad., U. Va., 1996—. Libr. Cape Charles (Va.) Pub. Sch., 1977-81, Broadwater Acad., Exmore, Va., 1981-85; instrnl. supervisor Union-Endicott Sch. Dist., Endicott, N.Y., 1987—; adj. prof. James Madison U., Harrisonburg, Va., 1997—. Mem. AAUW, ASCD, Am. Ednl. Rsch. Assn., Am. Assn. Sch. Librs. (bd. dirs. 1994-97), N.Y. Libr. Assn. (pres. sch. libr. media sect. 1994), Phi Delta Kappa. Avocations: reading, word and video games, outdoor activities.

DICKINSON, HENRY H., federal judge; b. 1934. LLB, Centre Coll., 1958. Law clk. to chief justice Ky. Ct. Appeals, 1958-59; pvt. practice Glasgow, Ky., 1959-87; city pros. atty. City of Glasgow, 1961-69, city atty., 1970-86; chief bankruptcy judge U.S. Dist. Ct. (we. dist.) Ky., Louisville, 1987—. Fax: (502) 625-7540. Office: US Dist Ct We Dist Ky 541 US Courthouse 601 W Broadway Louisville KY 40202

DICKINSON, JANE W., social services administrator; b. Kalamazoo, Sept. 27, 1919; d. Charles Herman and Rachel (Whaler) Wagner; student Hollins Coll., 1938-39; B.A., Duke U., 1941; M.Ed., Goucher Coll., 1965; m. E.F. Sherwood Dickinson, Oct. 23, 1943; children: Diane Jane Gray Clem, Carolyn Dickinson Vane. Exec. sec. Petroleum Industry Com., Balt., 1941-43; exec. sec. Sherwood Feed Mills Inc., Balt., 1943-79. Mem. exec. com. Children's Aid Md., 1960-61; mem. bd. women's aux. Balt. Symphony Orch., 1958-60; dist. chmn. Balt. Cancer Drive, 1958; dist. chmn. Balt. Mental Health Drive, 1957; co-chmn. Balt. United Appeal, 1968; bd. mgrs. Pickersgill Retirement Home. Mem. Alpha Delta Phi, Three Arts Club (Balt., sec. 1958-60, bd. govs. 1960-64, 67-70, pres. 1970-72), Women's Club of Roland Park (bd. govs. 1960-64, 86-88, 92-94), Cliff Dwellers Garden Club. Republican. Episcopalian. Home: 1055 W Joppa Rd Unit 609 Baltimore MD 21204-3748

DICKINSON, JANET MAE WEBSTER, relocation consulting executive; b. Cleve., Oct. 2, 1929; d. Richard and Gizella (Keplinger) Fisher; m. Rodney Earl Dickinson, June 18, 1965 (div. 1976); 1 child, Kimberly Cae. Grad., Larson Coll. for Women, New Haven; student, Portland State Coll. Lic. broker, Oreg. Pub. rels./promotion dir. KPTV-Channel 27, Portland, Oreg., 1951-54; exec. dir. Exposition-Recreation Commn., Portland, 1954-58; v.p. Art Lutz & Co., Realtors, Portland, 1975-79, Lutz Relocation Mgmt., Portland, 1977-79; corp. relocation mgr. Ga. Pacific Corp., Portland, 1979-82; pres., broker Ga. Pacific Fin. Co., Portland, 1980-82; pres., chief exec. officer The Dickinson Cons. Group, Portland, 1982—; pres. Wheatherstone Press, Lake Oswego, Oreg., 1983—, The Relocation Ctr., Portland, 1984—; cons. in field; lectr. in field; conductor workshops/seminars in field. Author: The Complete Guide to Family Relocation, The International Move, Building Your Dream House, Obtaining the Highest Price for Your Home, Have a Successful Garage Sale, Moving with Children, My Moving Coloring Book, The Group Move, Counseling the Transferee, Games to Play in the Car, Portland (Oreg.) Facts Book, Welcome to the United States, many others; contbr. articles to profl. jours. Mem. Pres.'s Com. to Employ Physically Handicapped, Oreg. Prison Assn.; established Women's Aux. for Waverly Baby Home; bd. dirs. Columbia River coun. Girl Scouts U.S.A., Salvation Army; active various polit. orgns.; chmn. ways and means com. Oreg. Symphony Soc., Portland Art Mus., Assistance League, Portland Jr. Symphony, March of Dimes, others. Mem. Employee Relocation Coun., City Club, Multnomah Athletic Club, Tualatin Valley Econ. Devel. Assn. (dir. 1988—). Republican. Episcopalian. Home: 20 Wheatherstone Lake Oswego OR 97035 Office: The Dickinson Cons Group Lincoln Ctr 10250 SW Greenburg Rd Ste 125 Portland OR 97223-5470

DICKINSON, JOSHUA CLIFTON, JR., museum director, educator; b. Tampa, Fla., Apr. 28, 1916; s. Joshua Clifton and Mary (Martin) D.; m. Lucy Jackson, Apr. 13, 1936 (wid. June 1997); children: Joshua Clifton III, Martin Freeman, Susan Ellissa; m. Sarah Donnovin Hadley, Nov. 1, 1997. Student, U. Va., 1936-39, Cornell U., 1938; BS, U. Fla., 1940, MS, 1946, PhD, 1950. Faculty U. Fla., 1946—, asst. prof. biology, 1950-55, assoc. prof. biology, 1955, prof. zoology, 1973-79; curator Fla. State Mus. (name changed to Fla. Mus. of Natural History), 1952-79, chmn. natural scis., 1953-60, acting dir., 1959-61, dir., 1961-79, dir. emeritus, 1979—; vis. investigator Woods Hole Oceanographic Inst., 1952; expdns. to, Honduras, 1946, Bahamas, 1958-62, 66-67, Jamaica, 1946, Baffin Island, 1955, Sombrero Island, 1964, Navassa Island, 1967, Turks and Caicos Islands, 1974. Contbr. articles to profl. jours. Chmn. Fla. Bd. Archives and History, 1967-69; mem. mus. adv. panel Nat. Endowment for Arts, 1970-72, co-chmn., 1972-74; panelist fellowship program NSF, 1966-68; mem. Nat. Council on Arts, 1976-82, also chmn. com. planning and policy; bd. dirs. Fla. Arts Celebration, 1984-92, vice chmn., 1985-86. Comdr. USCGR, 1942-46, ret. Grantee Nat. Park Service, 1954, NSF, 1955-57; Rsch. fellow Harvard U., 1951-52; recipient Disting. Alumnus award U. Fla., 1977, Presdl. Medallion U. Fla., 1979; Dickinson Hall named in his honor U. Fla. Mem. Am. Ornithologists Union, Am. Soc. Naturalists, Am. Assn. Museums (chmn. sci. mus. sect. 1961, mem. council 1964-70, sec. 1970), Am. Soc. Zoologists, Wilson Ornithol. Soc., Am. Assn. Sci. Mus. Dirs. (v.p. 1967-69), Assn. Systematic Collections (pres. 1972-75, bd. dir. 1974-76, chmn. membership com. 1976-79), Bahamas Nat. Trust, Assn. S.E. Biologists (sec. 1955-58), Fla. Acad. Scis. (chmn. biology sect. 1952, editor quar. jour. 1955-63), Conf. Dirs. Systematics Collections (pres. 1976-78), Fla. Audubon Soc. (bd. dir. 1958-64, 79-84), S.E. Museums Conf. (v.p. 1971-72, pres. 1972, James L. Shortt award 1987), Internat. Council Museums (exec. com. 1974-77), Am. Assn. Museums (vis. accreditation team 1973-75), Rotary (pres. Gainesville 1967-68), Sigma Xi, Phi Sigma, Alpha Tau Omega. Democrat. Presbyterian. Home: 9517 SW 40th Ln Gainesville FL 32608-4647 Office: U Fla Fla Mus Natural History Dickinson Hall Museum Rd Gainesville FL 32611

DICKINSON, NATHAN KILMER, writer; b. South Kingston, R.I., Feb. 2, 1973; s. Lance D. and Dorothy L. Powell D. BA in English, Wittenberg U., 1996; MS in Journalism, Columbia, 1999. Reporter Instl. Investor, N.Y.C., 1996-97, The Jersey Jour., Jersey City, N.J., 1997-98, Asbury Park Press/Ocean County Observer, Toms River, N.J., 1998—. Recipient News Feature award Working Press Assn. N.J., 1998. Mem. Soc. Profl. Journalists, Sigma Nu. Avocation: music. Home and office: 309 W 106th St Apt 2C New York NY 10025

DICKINSON, PETER, composer; b. Lytham St. Annes, Lancashire, England, Nov. 15, 1934; s. Frank and Muriel (Porter) D.; m. Bridget Jane Tomkinson, July 29, 1964; children: Jasper Edward Peck, Francis Charles Porter. BA, Cambridge (Eng.) U., 1956, MA, 1960; DMus, U. London, 1992; MusD (hon.), U. Keele, 1999; fellow Rotary Found., Juilliard Sch. Music, 1958-59. Freelance composer, writer, performer N.Y.C., 1959-61; lectr. Coll. St. Mark and St. John, London, 1962-66, Birmingham U., Eng., 1966-70; free-lance composer, writer, performer London, 1970-74; prof.

music Keele U., Staffordshire, Eng., 1974-84, emeritus prof., 1984; free-lance composer London, 1984—; prof. Goldsmiths U. London, 1991-97, emeritus prof., 1997; head music Inst. United States Studies U. London, 1997—; pres. London Concert Choir, 1987-97; bd. dirs. Trinity Coll. Music, London, 1985-98, Inst. U.S. Studies, London U., 1994—. Composer orchestra, chamber, choral, keyboard and vocal music; numerous recs.; recorder as pianist; author: The Music of Lennox Berkeley, 1989, Marigold: The Music of Billy Mayerl, 1999; editor: 20 British Composers, 1975; contbr. book chpts.; contbr. articles to profl. jours. John Stewart of Rannoch scholar, 1955. Fellow Royal Soc. Arts (hon.), Royal Coll. Organists, Trinity Coll. Music (hon.); mem. Royal Coll. Music (assoc.), Royal Acad. Music (licentiate), Assn. Profl. Composers (founder), Sonneck Soc., Royal Music Assn., Royal Soc. Musicians. Avocation: book collecting.

DICKINSON, RICHARD DONALD NYE, clergyman, educator, theological seminary administrator; b. Monson, Mass., Aug. 1, 1929; s. Richard Donald Nye and Phoebe Abigail (Naylor) D.; m. Nancy Leland Stone, Nov. 26, 1955; children: Elizabeth Stone, Richard Donald Nye III, Edward David McCrea. BA, Am. Internat. Coll., 1950, MA, 1951; STB, Boston U., 1954, PhD, 1959; cert., Institut Oecumenique, Geneva, 1955. Ordained to ministry United Ch. of Christ; chaplain, instr. Wheaton Coll., Norton, Mass., 1957-62; assoc. dir. Quaker Confs. in So. Asia, 1962-64; sr. research officer Inst. for Social Studies, The Hague, Netherlands, 1964-67; sec. for specialized assistance World Council Chs., 1967-68; now cons.; prof. Christian social ethics Christian Theol. Sem., Indpls., 1968-74, v.p., dean, 1974-86, acting pres., 1986-87, pres., 1987-97; chmn. devel. commn. World Coun. Chs.; mem. edn. commn. Nat. Coun. Chs., 1972-74; mem. ch. world service com.; incorporating mem. Center for Exploration Values and Meaning.; bd. dirs. internat. affairs div. Am. Friends Service Com., div. overseas ministries of Christian Ch. Author: The Christian College and National Development, 1967, Line and Plummet, 1968, The Christian College in Developing India, 1969, To Set at Liberty the Oppressed, 1975, Poor, Yet Making Many Rich, 1983. Bd. dirs. Ind. Opera Theatre, Internat. Ctr. Indpls., The Gemmer Found., Ind. Com. Econ. Edn., Martin Luther King Multiservice Ctr., Internat. Ctr. of Indpls., Ind.-Ky. Conf. United Meth. Ch., bd. dirs., chair fin. com.; mem. Greater Indpls. Progress Com. Mem. Am. Soc. for Christian Ethics, Soc. for Sci. Study Religion, Econs. Club of Indpls. (bd. dir.), Rotary. Home: 5173 N Kenwood Ave Indianapolis IN 46208-2619

DICKINSON, RICHARD HENRY, accountant; b. June 16, 1944; s. Everett I. and Gertrude T. (Frear) D.; m. Georgette M. Turner, Jan. 27, 1968 (div. June 1998); children: Eric, Christine, Brent. BS, U. Wis.; BBA, Siena Coll., 1973. Assoc. acct. Alexander Varga, CPA, Catskill, N.Y., 1973; contr. Hocker Power Brake Co., Inc., Evansville, Ind., 1974; dep. contr. Watervliet (N.Y.) Arsenal, Dept. Def., 1975-76; auditor Melvin I. Weiskopf, CPA, Saratoga Springs, N.Y., 1977; owner, prin. Richard H. Dickinson, CPA, Ballston Spa and Saratoga Springs, N.Y., 1978-83; owner Dickinson & Co., CPAs, Saratoga Spring, 1984-96; lectr. Siena Coll., Loudonville, N.Y., 1983-89, Skidmore Coll., 1990—. With U.S. Army, 1967-70. Decorated Silver Star, Bronze Star. Mem. Am. Inst. Corp. Contrs., N.Y. State Soc. CPAs, Inst. Mgmt. Accts., Masons, Rotary (pres. Ballston Spa chpt. 1979), Delta Epsilon Sigma, Alpha Kappa Alpha. Republican. Lutheran. Home: 4 Ritchie Pl Saratoga Springs NY 12866-2730 Office: 439 Maple Ave Saratoga Springs NY 12866-5503 also: 2 Washington Sq Greenwich NY 12834-1319

DICKINSON, RICHARD RAYMOND, retired oil company executive; b. Orange, Calif., Jan. 28, 1931; s. Raymond Russel and Florence Marie (Jacobson) D.; m. Barbara Jean Morrison, June 16, 1957; children: Roderick, Christine. B.S., Calif. Inst. Tech., 1952; M.S., U. So. Calif., 1960. Chem. engr. L.A. Refinery Texaco, 1952-68; gen. mgr. supply and distbn. Texaco, London, 1968-76; plant mgr. Eagle Point plant Texaco, Westville, N.J., 1976-79; gen. mgr. alternate energy group Texaco, White Plains, N.Y., 1979; v.p. strategic planning Texaco, 1979-82; sr. v.p. U.S. refining, mktg., supply and transp. Texaco U.S.A., Houston, 1982-87; v.p. tech. Texaco, Inc., White Plains, N.Y., 1988-94. Served with USNR, 1955-58. Home: 944 Hills Creek Dr Mc Kinney TX 75070-5232

DICKINSON, ROBERT EARL, atmospheric scientist, educator; b. Millersburg, Ohio, Mar. 26, 1940; s. Leonard Earl and Carmen L. (Ostby) D.; m. Nancy Mary Mielinis, Jan. 5, 1974. AB in Chemistry and Physics, Harvard U., 1961; MS in Meteorology, MIT, 1962, PhD in Meteorology, 1966. Rsch. assoc. MIT, Cambridge, 1966-68; scientist Nat. Ctr. Atmospheric Rsch., Boulder, Colo., 1968-73, sr. scientist, 1973-90, head climate sect., 1975-81, dep. dir. A.A.P. div., 1981-86, acting dir., 1986-87; prof. atmospheric physics U. Ariz., 1990-93; regents prof., 1993—; mem. climate rsch. com. NRC, Washington, 1985-90, chmn., 1987-90, com. earth sci., 1985-88, global change com., 1985-92; mem. WCRP sci. steering group GEWEX, 1988-92; UNU steering com. Climatic, Biotic and Human Interactions in Humid Tropics, 1984-88, steering com. Internat. Satellite Land Surface Climatology project, 1984-89. Editor: The Geophysiology of Amazonia, 1986; contbr. articles to profl. jours. Recipient G. Unger Vetlesen prize, 1996. Fellow AAAS, Am. Meteorol. Soc. (chmn. com. biometeorol. and aerobiol. 1987-89, Meisinger award 1973, Editors award 1976, Jule Charney award 1989, Walter Orr Roberts lectr. in interdisciplinary sci. 1995, Carl-Gustaf Rossby award 1997), Am. Geophys. Union (atmospheric sci. sect. 1986-88, pres.-elect 1988-90, pres. 1990-92, Revelle medal 1996); mem. NAS, Internat. Assn. Meteorol. and Atmospheric Physics (sec. climate commn. 1983-87). Democrat. Home: 9290 N Yorkshire Ct Tucson AZ 85742-9357 Office: U Ariz Inst Atmospheric Physics Tucson AZ 85721

DICKINSON, ROGER ALLYN, business administration educator; b. Bklyn., Sept. 8, 1929; s. Robert Albert and Esther (Odland) D.; m. Ruth Nordis, June 1, 1957; children: Robert Allyn, Roger Perry, Todd Charles, Bruce Gregory. A.B., Williams Coll., 1951; M.B.A., UCLA, 1955; Ph.D., Columbia U., 1967. Lectr., asst. prof. bus. adminstrn. U. Calif., Berkeley, 1964-69; assoc. prof. Rutgers Grad. Sch. Bus., Newark, N.J., 1969-70; prof. Rutgers Grad. Sch. Bus., 1970-75; prof. Coll. Bus. Adminstrn. U. Tex., Arlington, 1975-79, prof. mktg., 1979—; dean Coll. Bus., U. Tex., 1975-79. Author: Retail Management: A Channels Approach, 1974, (with others) A Basic Approach to Executive Decision Making, 1978, Retail Management, 1981; book note editor Jour. Retailing, 1970-92, Jour. Macromktg., 1992—; mem. editl. bd. Jour. Consumer Mktg., Jour. Mktg. Channels, Jour. Consumer Affairs, Jour. Macromktg.; contbr. chpts. to books and articles to profl. jours. Mem. Am. Collegiate Retailing Assn. (pres. 1980-82). Home: 2104 Tretorn Ct Arlington TX 76017-2763 Office: U Tex Coll of Bus Arlington TX 76019

DICKINSON, TEMPLE, lawyer; b. Glasgow, Ky., Mar. 13, 1956; s. Lewis and Selma (Goodman) D.; m. Jan Marie Wussow, Oct. 7, 1995. AB, Transylvania U., 1978; JD, Harvard U., 1984. Bar: Mass. 1985, N.Y. 1990, Ky. 1995, U.S. Dist. Ct. Mass. 1985, U.S. Ct. Appeals (1st cir.) 1988. Assoc. Casner, Edwards & Roseman, Boston, 1984-88; asst. dist. atty. Kings County Dist. Atty.'s Office, Bklyn., 1988-95; ptner. Gillenwater, Hampton and Dickinson, Glasgow, Ky., 1995—. Democrat. Mem. Disciples of Christ. Avocation: theater. Office: Gillenwater Hampton et al 103 E Main St Glasgow KY 42141-2835

DICKINSON, WADE, physicist, oil company executive, educator; b. Sharon, Pa., Oct. 29, 1926; s. Ben Wade Orr and Gladys Grace (Oakes) D.; m. Eleanor Creekmore, June 12, 1952; children: Mark, Katherine, Peter. Student, Carnegie Inst. Tech., 1944-45; BS, U.S. Mil. Acad., 1949; postgrad., Oak Ridge Sch. Reactor Tech., 1950-51. Commd. 2d lt. USAF, 1949, advanced through grades to capt., 1954, resigned, 1954; cons. physicist Rand Corp., Santa Monica, Calif., 1952-54; engring. cons. Bechtel Group, Inc., San Francisco, 1954-87; tech. advisor U.S. Congress, Washington, 1957-58; pres. Agrophysics, Inc., San Francisco, 1968—, Petrolphysics Inc., San Francisco, 1975—; ptnr. Radialphysics Ltd., San Francisco, 1980—, Robotphysics Ltd., San Francisco, 1983—; lectr. engring., bus. U. Calif., Berkeley, 1984—; cardiology cons. Mt. Zion Med. Ctr., U. Calif., San Francisco, 1970-95; chmn. bd. Calif. Med. Clin. Psychotherapy. Contbr. articles to profl. jours; patentee in field. Trustee World Affair Coun., 1958-62; mem. San Francisco Com. Fgn. Rels., Young Republicans, Calif. Mem. Am. Phys. Soc., Am. Soc. Petroleum Engrs. Episcopalian. Club: Bohemian (San Francisco). Lodges: Masons, Guardsmen. Home: 2125 Broderick St San Francisco CA 94115-1627 Office: Petrolphysics Inc 2101 3rd St San Francisco CA 94107-3188

DICKINSON, WILLIAM BOYD, JR., editorial consultant; b. Kansas City, Mo., Feb. 21, 1931; s. William Boyd and Aileen (Robinson) D.; m. Betty Ann Landree, Feb. 1, 1953; children: William Boyd IV, David Alan. A.B., U. Kans., 1953; student, George Washington U. Law Sch., 1957-58. With U.P.I., 1955-59; mem. staff overnight desk U.P.I., Washington, 1957-59; staff writer Editorial Research Reports, Washington, 1959-66; editor Editorial Research Reports, 1966-73; editor, v.p. Congl. Quar., Inc., 1972-73; gen. mgr., editorial dir. Washington Post Writers Group, 1973-91; cons., 1991-96, Biocentric Inst., 1991—; resident profl. Journalism Sch. U. Kans., 1993-99; manship chair Journalism Sch. La. State U., 1999—; Winston Churchill Traveling fellow, summer 1968. Supervisory editor: Congl. Quar.'s Complete Guide to Congress. Served with AUS, 1953-55. Press fellowship Knight Internat., 1998. Mem. William Allen White Found. (trustee), Alpha Tau Omega, Omicron Delta Kappa. (Washington). Home and Office: 1617 Alvamar Dr Lawrence KS 66047-1715 also: Univ Kansas Journalism Dept 200 Stauffer Flint Hall Lawrence KS 66045

DICKINSON, WILLIAM RICHARD, retired geologist and educator; b. Nashville, Oct. 26, 1931; s. Jacob McGavock and Margaret Adams (Smith) D.; m. Margaret Anne Palmer, 1953 (div. 1968); children: Ben William, Edward Ross; m. Jacqueline Jane Klein, Feb. 20, 1970. BS in Petroleum Engring., Stanford U., 1952, MS in Geology, 1956, PhD in Geology, 1958. Prof. geology Stanford U., Palo Alto, Calif., 1958-79; prof. geoscis. U. Ariz., Tucson, 1979-91; retired, 1991. Contbr. and editor articles to profl. jours. Lt. USAF, 1952-54. Guggenheim Meml. fellow, 1965. Fellow Geol. Soc. Am. (Penrose medal 1991); mem. Am. Geophys. Union, Am. Assn. Petroleum Geologists, Nat. Acad. Sci., Soc. for Sedimentary Geology.

DICKINSON, WILLIAM TREVOR, hydrologist, educator; b. Toronto, Ont., Can., Aug. 30, 1939; s. Clarence Heber and Katie Isobel (Kneen) D.; m. Sharon Lucille Tutt, Aug. 24, 1963; children: Michael Trevor, Cathryn Ruth. B.S.A., U. Toronto, 1961, B.A.Sci., 1962, M.S.A., 1964; Ph.D., Colo. State U., 1967. Research assoc. Colo. State U., 1964-67; asst. prof. engring. U. Guelph, Ont., 1967-70, assoc. prof., 1970-78, prof., 1978-94, prof. emeritus, 1995—, coordinator instructional devel., 1979-82; 3M teaching fellow, coord. univ. teaching program U. Guelph, 1991-93; pvt. cons. water resources engring. Contbr. articles to profl. jours. Mem. Assn. Profl. Engrs. Ont., Can. Assn. Univ. Tchrs., Soil Conservation Soc. Am., Soc. Tchrs. Learning High Edn., Can. Water Resources Assn. Mem. United Ch. of Can. Home: 68 Pine Ridge Dr, Guelph, ON Canada N1L 1J1 Office: Univ Guelph, Guelph, ON Canada N1G 2W1

DICKLER, HOWARD BYRON, biomedical administrator, research physician; b. Chgo., Jan. 2, 1942; s. Jerome Alvin and Josephine Rae (Sweet) D.; m. Ana Isabel Martinez, Sept. 20, 1986; children: Joanna, Carl. BA, Johns Hopkins U., 1964; MD with honors, George Washington U., 1968. Diplomate Am. Bd. Internal Medicine, Nat. Bd. Med. Examiners. Lt. comdr. USPHS, 1972, advanced through grades to capt., 1985; intern N.Y. Hosp.-Cornell U. Med. Ctr., N.Y.C., 1968-69, resident in internal medicine, 1969-71; rsch. assoc. Rockefeller U., N.Y.C., 1971-72; clin. assoc. Nat. Cancer Inst., Bethesda, Md., 1972-74, sr. investigator, 1974-89, instnl. rev. bd., 1982-84; acting dep. divsn. dir. Nat. Inst. Allergy and Infectious Disease, Bethesda, 1990-91, chief clin. immunology br., 1989-99; assoc. dean rsch. and grad. studies U. Md. Sch. Medicine, Balt., 1999—; leader trans-NIH initiative to develop hyper accelerated process to rev. and award grant applications; com. vice-chmn. WHO, Geneva, 1981-85; lectr., spkr. in field. Assoc. editor Jour. Immunology, 1976-79; contbr. articles to Jour. Exptl. Medicine, Advances in Immunology. Recipient Commendation medal USPHS, 1985, Outstanding Svc. medal, 1991. Mem. Am. Assn. Immunologists, Am. Soc. Clin. Investigation, Clin. Immunology Soc. (councilor 1991-94), Alpha Omega Alpha. Achievements include discovery of receptors for antibody on human cells, interactions between various immune cell receptors, and regulatory mechanisms which control antibody production; pioneering research on classification of human immune cell populations. Office: U Md Sch Medicine Rm 14-021 655 W Baltimore St Baltimore MD 21201-1559

DICKMAN, BERNARD HAROLD, statistics educator; b. Bklyn., Apr. 19, 1943; m. Esther Dickman, Mar. 26, 1970; children: Karen, Abraham, Joel, Rachelle. BS, Bklyn. Coll., 1964; MS, NYU, 1966, PhD, 1970. Mgmt. sci. cons. Celanese Corp., N.Y.C., 1969-84; assoc. prof. Hofstra U., Hempstead, N.Y., 1984—.

DICKMAN, CATHERINE CROWE, retired human services administrator; b. Talladega, AL, Jan. 27, 1931; d. William and Catherine Elizabeth (Graeber) Crowe; m. Frederick Norton Dickman Jr., May 19, 1956 (div. July 1975); children: Frederick Norton Dickman III, Catherine Dickman Houghton, Elizabeth Dickman Blank, Janet Dickman Campbell. AB with honor, Agnes Scott Coll., 1952; MS, Cleve. State U. Coll. Urban Affairs, 1976. Pub. info. officer Cuyahoga County, Ohio, 1975-77; dir. Friends of Shaker Sq., Cleve., 1979-81; rsch. assoc. Frank Porter Graham Child Devel. Ctr., Chapel Hill, N.C., 1984; pres. Dickman Placement Svcs., Chapel Hill, N.C., 1988-91; dir. The Women's Ctr., Chapel Hill, N.C., 1991-96; ret. Author (newsletter) The Partnership Paper, 1986. Field dir. Girl Scout coun., Wilmington, N.C., 1952-53; dir. christian edn. St. Charles Ave. Presbyn. Ch., New Orleans, 1956-57; co-founder Fair Housing, Inc., 1966-80; mem. Jr. League of Cleve, Inc., 1957—, pres. 1966-68, chair Assn. 12 Largest Jr. Leagues, 1967-68, Assn. Cmty. Agys., Chapel Hill, 1991-96, bd. dirs., 1995-96; chair nominating com., trustee The City Club of Cleve., 1979-82; trustee Health Mus. and Edn. Ctr., 1957-63, Karamu House, Cleve., 1968-70, Fedn. for Cmty. Planning, Cleve., 1979-82; adv. com. Health Profession Schs. in Svc. to the Nation, Chapel Hill, 1996—; elder Fairmount Presbyn. Ch., Cleve., 1970-73, Univ. Presbyn. Ch., Chapel Hill, 1986-89. Women's Ctr. established Catherine C. Dickman Ednl. fund in her honor, 1996. Mem. NOW (Chapel Hill chpt.), Nat. Audubon Soc., New Hope Audubon Soc. (bd. dirs. 1986-88), Chapel Hill Preservation Soc. (v.p., trustee 1989-90, sec. exec. com. 1997). Democrat. Avocations: bird watching, nature walks, writing. Home: 409 North St Chapel Hill NC 27514-3727

DICKMAN, FRANCOIS MOUSSIEGT, former foreign service officer, educator; b. Iowa City, Dec. 23, 1924; s. Adolphe Jacques and Henriette Louise (Moussiegt) D.; m. Margaret Hoy, June 3, 1947; children: Christine, Paul. BA, U. Wyo., 1947; MA, Tufts U., 1948. Rsch. asst. Brookings Instn., Washington, 1950; with U.S. Fgn. Svc., 1951-84; consular/comml. officer Barranquilla, Colombia, 1952-54; Arabic lang. trainee Beirut, Lebanon, 1955-57; econ./comml./consular officer Khartoum, Sudan, 1957-60; Egyptian-Syrian affairs desk officer Dept. State, 1961-65; econ. officer Tunis, Tunisia, 1965-68; student U.S. Army War Coll., Carlisle, Pa., 1968-69; econ. counselor Jidda, Saudi Arabia, 1969-72; dir. Arabian Peninsula affairs Dept. State, 1972-76; ambassador to United Arab Emirates, 1976-79, to Kuwait, 1979-83; diplomat in residence Marquette U., 1984; adj. prof. polit. sci. U. Wyo., Laramie, 1985—. Served with AUS, 1943-46, 50-51. Recipient Dept. State Meritorious Honor award, 1965, Disting. Alumni award U. Wyo., 1980, Exemplary Alumnus, 1993. Mem. VFW, U.S. Army War Coll. Alumni Assn., U. Wyo. Alumni Assn., Phi Beta Kappa, Phi Kappa Phi. Office: U Wyo Polit Sci Dept Laramie WY 82071-3197

DICKMAN, GLORIA JOYCE, geriatrics nurse; b. Hartford, Conn., Sept. 13, 1936; d. Otto Albert and Lillian Mae (Donovan) Kramer; m. Sam John Dickman, May 3, 1958; children: Jeanine Leah Barbara Crain, Kenneth William Otto. BA in Guidance Counseling, Bob Jones U., 1988; AS in Gen. Studies, Manchester C.C., 1992; ASN, U. of State of N.Y., 1993. LPN, Conn.; cert. profl. death educator and bereavement supporter. Staff charge nurse Salmon Brook Convalescent, Glastonbury, Conn., 1964-76; pool nurse Nursing Svcs. Inc., East Hartford, Conn., 1981—; RN supr. St. Elizabeth Health Ctr., East Hartford, Conn., 1993-95. Author: (children's book) Chuckles and Honey, 1991. Vol. Rep. election, East Hartford, 1992—; cons. sch. nurse Hartford Christian Acad., 1976—. Mem. Hospice Com. Conn., Conn. Authors Assn., Assn. Death Edn. & Counseling. Baptist. Avocations: chess, needlepoint, crafts. Home: 6268 Corbly Rd Apt 42 Cincinnati OH 45230-1544

DICKMAN, JAMES BRUCE, photojournalist; b. St. Louis, Mar. 25, 1949; s. Joseph Edward and Isabel Catherine (Brown) D.; m. Mary Kay Thomas, Sept. 23, 1968 (div.); children: Kristi Michele, Gavin Thomas; m. 2d Rebecca Lauren Skelton, Sept. 16, 1983; children: Matthew Benjamin, Margaret Catherine Anne. Student, U. Tex., 1967-69. Photographer McKinney Job Corps., Tex., 1969-70, Dallas Times Herald, 1970-86. Worked on photo projects Day in the Life of Can., Day in the Life of Am., Day in the Life of Spain, Day in the Life of the Soviet Union, Day in the Life of China; (book and CD-ROM) Passage to Vietnam, 1994; contbg. editor Am. Way Mag. Recipient Pulitzer prize for photography Columbia U., 1983; recipient World Press Photo of Yr. award World Press Photo Orgn., Holland, Amsterdam, 1983, 89, awards Dallas Press Club, AP and UPI, Tex. Headliners, Damascus Syria, Internat. Orgn. of Photography, 1st place, Sigma Delta Chi Disting. Service award, Bronze Medallion, others. Mem. Am. Soc. Mag. Photographers. *I've always felt that I've had a guardian angel pointing me in the correct directions. But it's always been up to me to do something with the opportunities once they're presented.*

DICKMAN, ROBERT LAURENCE, physicist, researcher; b. N.Y.C., May 16, 1947; s. Sidney and Eva (Goldberg) D.; m. Albertina Catharina Otter, Sept. 18, 1975; children: Joshua, Ilana. AB, Columbia U., 1969, PhD, 1976. Postdoctoral rsch. assoc. Rensselaer Poly. Inst., Troy, N.Y., 1975-77; mem. tech. staff The Aerospace Corp., L.A., 1977-80; faculty rsch. assoc. U. Mass., Amherst, 1980-85, assoc. prof., staff assoc., 1985-92; program mgr. Nat. Sci. Found., Washington, 1992—. Editor: Molecular Clouds in the Milky Way and External Galaxies, 1988; contbr. 80 articles to profl. jours. Recipient Ernest Fullam award Dudley Obs., 1986. Mem. Am. Phys. Soc., Am. Astron. Soc., Internat. Astron. Union. Office: NSF Div Astronomical Scis 4201 Wilson Blvd Arlington VA 22230-0001

DICKOW, JAMES FRED, management consultant; b. Chgo., Mar. 27, 1943; s. Fred H. and Margaret I. (Arnold) D.; m. Yvonne A. Zabilka, Aug. 20, 1966; children: Michael J., Christine Y. BSME, Purdue U., 1965, MSME, 1967. Cert. mgmt. cons. Mech. engr. CPC Internat., Argo, Ill., 1965-66; engr. dynamics McDonnell-Douglas Corp., St. Louis, 1967-70; cons. Drake Sheahan/Steward Dougal, Chgo., 1970-71; dir. distbn. planning Will Ross Div. G.D. Searle, Milw., 1971-80; dir. distbn. Gentec Healthcare, Milw., 1980-82, R&J Med. Supply, Milw., 1982-83; exec. v.p., ptnr. Kowaski-Dickow Assoc. Inc., Mequon, Wis., 1983—. Mem. Coun. Logistics Mgmt. (pres. Milw. roundtable 1978-79), Phi Kappa Theta (bd. dirs., nat. pres., pres. Ind. alumni 1980—). Home: 10011 N Miller Ct Thiensville WI 53092-6180

DICKS, JACK WILLIAM, lawyer; b. Tampa, Fla., Sept. 12, 1949; s. James R. and June (Simmons) D.; m. Linda Edmunds, Apr. 29, 1972; children: Jennifer, Lindsay. BSc, U. Fla., 1971; JD, George Mason U., 1980. Bar: Va. 1980, Fla. 1981; cert. mediator. Ptnr. Pino & Dicks, Orlando, Fla., 1987—; pres. Fin. Talk Network, Inc., 1990-92, J.W. Dicks Rsch. Inst., 1993—; pres. Delta First Fin., Inc.; nat. lectr. on real estate and fin. topics; instr. Nat. Assn. Relators, Chgo., 1982-86, Real Estate Securities and Syndication Inst., Chgo., 1982-87; pres. Delta Capital Properties; v.p. Delta Capital Devel. Corp. Author: Cash Management, 1984, Real Estate Forms, 1985, Questions and Answers on Real Estate, 1980, Syndicating Real Estate, 1985, Equity Sharing Solutions, 1985, The Option Strategy, 1984, Riches in Real Estate, 1980, Divorce and Money, 1989, Starting Out or Starting Over, 1989, The Other Side of Everyday, 1990, The Financial Success System, 1990, The Florida Investor, 1994, Financial CPR, 1993, The Small Business Legal Kit, 1995, Mutual Fund Investment Strategies, 1996, The 100 Best Investments for Your Retirement Account, 1996, The Entrepreneur Legal Companion, 1994, How to Incorporate and Start a Business, 50 state legal series, 1997, Moonlight Investing, 1998; (newsletters) Entrepreneur 2000, 1991—, The Mut. Fund Letter, 1987—, The Strategies Report, 1983-86, Strategic Investing, 1999. Mem. ABA, Nat. Assn. Realtors, Nat. Assn. Securities Dealers, Sigma Chi (v.p. 1970-71). Republican. Avocations: skiing, travel, boating. Office: Pino & Dicks 520 Crown Oak Centre Dr Longwood FL 32750-6187

DICKS, NORMAN DE VALOIS, congressman; b. Bremerton, Wash., Dec. 16, 1940; s. Horace D. and Eileen Cora D.; m. Suzanne Callison, Aug. 25, 1967; children: David, Ryan. BA, U. Wash., 1963, JD, 1968; LLD (hon.), Gonzaga U., 1987. Bars: Wash. 1968, D.C., 1978. Salesman, Boise Cascade Corp., Seattle, 1963; labor negotiator Kaiser Gypsum Co., Seattle, 1964; legis. asst. to Senator Warren Magnuson of Wash., 1968-73, adminstrv. asst., 1973-76; mem. 95th-106th Congress from 6th Wash. Dist., Washington, 1977—; mem. appropriations com. 95th-105th Congress from 6th Wash. Dist., Washington. Mem. U. Wash. Alumni Assn., Sigma Nu. Democrat. Lutheran. Office: US Ho Reps 2467 Rayburn Bldg Ofc Bldg Washington DC 20515-4706

DICKS, PATRICIA K., state senate employee; b. Detroit, Nov. 22, 1951. BS, U. Colo., 1973. Sec. Colo. Senate, Denver, 1998—. Office: State Capitol 200 E Colfax Ave Rm 250 Denver CO 80203

DICKSON, BRENT E(LLIS), state supreme court justice; b. July 18, 1941; m. Jan Aikman, June 8, 1963; children: Andrew, Kyle, Reed. BA, Purdue U., 1964; JD, Ind. U., Indpls., 1968; LittD, Purdue U., 1996. Bar: Ind. 1968, U.S. Ct. Appeals (7th cir.) 1972, U.S. Supreme Ct. 1975; cert. civil trial adv., NBTA. Pvt. practice Lafayette, Ind., 1968-85; sr. ptnr. Dickson, Reiling, Teder & Withered, 1977-85; justice Ind. Supreme Ct., Indpls., 1986—; adj. prof. Sch. of Law Ind. U., 1992—. Past pres. Tippecanoe County Hist. Assn.; mem. dean's adv. coun. Sch. Liberal Arts Purdue U., 1990-94; mem. adv. bd. Heartland Film Festival, 1995—. Office: Ind Supreme Ct 304 Statehouse Indianapolis IN 46204-2213*

DICKSON, DAVID WATSON DALY, retired college president; b. Portland, Maine, Feb. 16, 1919; s. David Augustus and Mary Marguerite (Daly) D.; m. Vera Mae Allen, Aug. 5, 1951 (dec. July 1979); children: David Augustus II, Deborah Anne, Deirdre Elizabeth; m. Barbara Childs Mickey, Feb. 14, 1981; children: Robert Warren, Sharon Marlissa. AB, Bowdoin Coll., 1941, LHD (hon.), 1974; MA, Harvard U., 1942, PhD, 1949; LHD (hon.), Bloomfield Coll., 1983; DLitt (hon.), Montclair State Coll., 1989. Instr. to assoc. prof. English Mich. State U., 1948-63; prof., head English dept. No. Mich. U., Marquette, 1963-66; dean No. Mich. U. (Sch. Arts and Sci.), 1966-67, v.p. acad. affairs, 1967-68; provost, v.p. acad. affairs, prof. English Fed. City Coll., Washington, 1968-69; prof. English, asst. to pres. State U. N.Y. at Stony Brook, 1969-72, dean continuing and developing edn., prof. English, 1972-73; pres. Montclair State Coll., Upper Montclair, N.J., 1973-84; pres. emeritus Montclair State Coll., 1989; Disting. Service prof. Montclair State Coll., Upper Montclair, N.J., 1984-88; prof. emeritus Montclair State Coll., 1989; cons. Nat. Found. for Humanities, 1969-71, Mott Found., 1973-74; speaker in field. Author: An Isolate of Isolates, 1995; contbr. articles to profl. jours. Chmn. lt. com. Mich. Coun. Arts, 1963-68; bd. dirs. Nat. Com. on Future of State Colls. and Univs.; trustee Montclair Art Mus., North Essex Devel. and Action Coun., Bloomfield Coll., 1984-89; bd. overseers Bowdoin Coll., 1966-75, trustee, 1975-82; mem. policy bd. Project Change; mem. bd. Commn. on Higher Edn. Mid. States Assn. Colls. and Secondary Schs., 1978-84; pres. Flagler County Auditorium, 1992-93. 1st lt. AUS, 1943-46. Recipient Disting. Teaching award Mich. State U., 1952; Disting. Educator award Bowdoin Coll., 1971; Austrian Cross of Honor for Letters and Arts; Rosenwald fellow, 1942-43; Smith Mundt fellow Syrian Nat. U. Damascus, 1958-59. Mem. MLA, Milton Soc., Am. Assn. State Colls. and Univs. (chmn. com. on undergrad. studies), Am. Assn. Colls. (commn. on liberal learning), Phi Beta Kappa, Omega Psi Phi, Sigma Psi Phi, Phi Kappa Phi, Rotary. Roman Catholic. Home: 125 Woodhaven Dr Palm Coast FL 32164-7979

DICKSON, EDGAR ROLLAND, gastroenterologist; b. Hackensack, N.J., June 10, 1933. MD, Ohio State U., 1959. Diplomate Am. Bd. Internal Medicine, Am. Bd. Gastroenterology. Intern Ohio State U. Hosp., Columbus, 1959-60; resident in internal medicine Mayo Clinic, Rochester, N.Y., 1960-63; asst. prof. medicine Mayo Med. Sch., Rochester, 1973-77, assoc. prof., 1977-80, prof., 1980—, Mary Loewll Leary prof. medicine, 1992—; dir. devel. Mayo Found. Edn. and Rsch., 1994—; mem. staff St. Mary's Hosp., Meth. Hosp.; mem. digestive disease adv. bd. NIH. Chair bd. dirs. Am. Liver Found., 1988-90. Fellow ACP; mem. Am. Gastroenterol. Assn., Am. Assn. Study of Liver Diseases (mem. fiscal audit com. 1991-94, ad hoc clinic com. 1992-96, chair fiscal com. 1994-97, mem. subcom. health care policy 1996—, abstract selection com.), Am. Fedn. Clin. Rsch., Internat. Assn. Study of the Liver, Sigma Xi. Office: Mayo Clinic 200 1st St SW Rochester MN 55905-0002*

DICKSON, EVA MAE, credit manager; b. Clarion, Iowa, Jan. 16, 1922; d. James and Ivah Blanche (Breckenridge) D. Grad. Interstate Bus. Coll., Klamath Falls, Oreg., 1943. Reporter, Mchts. Credit Service, Klamath Falls, 1941; credit dept. Montgomery Ward, Klamath Falls, 1941-42; bookkeeper Heilbronner Fuel Co., Klamath Falls, 1942; stenographer City of Klamath Falls, 1943, bookkeeper, office mgr., 1943-52; owner, operator All Star Bus. Service, Klamath Falls, 1953-58, Ace Mimeo Service, Klamath Falls, 1958-73; mgr. Mchts. Credit Service, 1973-87; customer service rep. CBI/Credit N.W., 1987-91. Bd. dirs. United Way, Klamath Falls, 1980-97; sec. Klamath Community Concert Assn., 1956-99; treas., memls. chmn. Klamath County chpt. Am. Cancer Soc.; bd. dirs., treas. Hope in Crisis; mem. Klamath County Centennial Com., 1982, Unification for Progress Joint Planning Com., 1985; mem. nursing adv. com. Oreg. Inst. Tech., 1982—; mem. Klamath Employment Tng. Adv. Com., 1983-86; bd. dirs., sec., treas. Klamath Consumer Council; sec. Unified City for Progress Task Force, 1983-84, Snowflake Winter Festival, 1984—; sec. First Presbyn. Ch., 1992—. Recipient Bronze Leadership award Assoc. Credit Burs., Inc., 1976. Mem. Daughters of Am. Colonists (past regent local chpt.), Consumer Credit Assn. Oreg. (pres. 1984-85), Credit Profl. Internat. (treas. dist. 10 1984-85, 2d v.p. dist. 10 1987-88, 1st v.p. 1988-89, pres. 1989-90, internat. bull. chmn. 1990-91, 92—), Assoc. Credit Bur. Pacific N.W. (pres. 1981-82), Assoc. Credit Bur. Oreg. (pres. 1978-80), Klamath Basin Credit Women-Internat. (pres. 1976-78), Soc. Cert. Consumer Credit Exec., Internat. Consumer Credit Assn., Klamath County C. of C. (pres. 1979, ambs. com. 1980—, Nat. Fedn. Bus. and Profl. Women's Club (chmn. nat. fin. com. 1983-84, nat. fin. com. 1982-83), Oreg. Fedn. Bus. and Profl. Women's Club (state pres. 1971-72), Klamath Falls Bus. and Profl. Women's Club (pres. 1966-67, 76-77, 1996—). Republican. Presbyterian. Club: Quota (pres. 1958-59, dist. gov. 1969-70). Avocations: painting, traveling.

DICKSON, GERI LENZEN, nursing educator, researcher; b. Milw., Feb. 28, 1932; d. Gilbert Ernst and Lily (Rehbein) Morong; m. LeRoy L. Lenzen, Apr. 1, 1950 (div. Nov. 1971); children: Lynnda Lenzen, Kathie Lenzen; m. Carlisle H. Dickson, June 8, 1979; children: Joel, Robert. BSN, Alverno Coll., 1974; MSN, Marquette U., 1978; PhD, U. Wis., 1989. RN, N.Y., N.J., Wis. Various nursing positions Milw. County Med. Complex, 1970-79, nurse instr., 1979-89; asst. prof. U. Wis., Milw., 1984-90; asst. prof. divsn. nursing NYU, N.Y.C., 1990-94; asst. prof. coll. nursing Rutgers U., Newark, 1994—; pvt. practice as ind. generalist nurse, Milw., 1977-80; mem. health cabinet Ctrl. Presbyn. Ch., N.Y.C., 1993-94. Contbr. articles to profl. jours and nursing texts. Mem. Nat. League Nursing, N.Y. State Nurses Assn., Women's Health Network, Soc. Rogerian Scholars, Sigma Theta Tau, Phi Theta Kappa. Presbyterian. Home: 30 Ernst Ave Bloomfield NJ 07003-4509

DICKSON, JAMES EDWIN, II, obstetrician, gynecologist; b. Pontiac, Mich., Feb. 18, 1943; s. James Edwin and Virginia (Farrar) D.; m. Joan Gayle Coonley, July 21, 1967; children: Alison, Andrew. BS, U. Mich., 1965; MD, Wayne State U., 1969. Diplomate Am. Bd. Ob-Gyn. Intern Harborview Med. Ctr., Seattle, 1969-70; resident U. Mich. Med. Ctr., 1972-75; pvt. practice Geneva, N.Y., 1975—; pres. Med. Assocs. Finger Lakes, Med. Assocs. of Finger Lakes; chmn. dept. ob-gyn. Geneva Gen. Hosp. Capt. M.C., USAF, 1970-72. Fellow Am. Coll. Obstetricians and Gynecologists; mem. Soc. Am. Laparoscopists, Miller Ob-Gyn Soc., N.Y. State Med. Soc., Buffalo Ob-Gyn Soc., Rotary (pres. Geneva 1988). Avocation: astronomy. Home: 16 Maplewood Dr Geneva NY 14456-1420 Office: Med Assocs Finger Lakes 200 North St Geneva NY 14456

DICKSON, JAMES FRANCIS, III, surgeon; b. Boston, May 4, 1924; s. James Francis Jr. and Mary Elizabeth (Rich) D.; m. Vivian Joan Franco, Dec. 23, 1977. A.B., Dartmouth Coll., 1944; M.D., Harvard Med. Sch., 1947. Diplomate Am. Bd. Surgery. Intern and resident Boston City Hosp., 1947-51; practice medicine specializing in thoracic surgery Boston, 1951-61; NIH spl. fellow MIT, Cambridge, 1961-65; dir. engring. in biology and medicine NIH, Bethesda, Md., 1965-75; dep. asst. sec. for health HEW, Washington, 1975-78; asst. surgeon gen. HHS, Washington, 1978-89; sr. advisor to dean Harvard Med. Sch., 1992—, vis. com., 1992—; bd. overseers Dartmouth Med. Sch., C. Everett Koop Inst. Fellow ACS, IEEE; mem. Inst. Medicine of NAS.

DICKSON, JIM, writer, producer; b. Chgo., Mar. 25, 1949; s. Vincent Brackley and Carol Lois (Schaffner) D.; m. Helen Denise McEachrane , Feb. 11, 1984 (div. 1988). B.A., Harvard U., 1970. Artistic adminstr. Santa Fe Opera, 1978-80; mng. dir. Chamber Opera Theatre, 1982; gen. mgr. Opera Festival of N.J., 1982-85; mng. dir. N.J. State Opera, 1985-89; exec. dir. Newark Arts Coun., 1989-95; propr. The Dickson Office, 1991—. Author: Monmouth, 1968, Fear of Success, 1971, Summer in the Midwest, 1975, Chiliasm, 1972, The Princess of the Suburbs, 1973, Banjo, 1981, A Couple Interviews With A Couple Czars, 1991; (musical) Pippin, 1969, Appetite and Embarrassment, 1998. Recipient Phyllis Anderson award, 1969. Office: PO Box 1337 Newark NJ 07101-1337*

DICKSON, MARK ALLAN, investment company executive; b. Alexandria, Va., May 17, 1954; s. John Allan and Sarah Shaw (Higgins) D.; m. Melody Mae Miner, Nov. 29, 1980; children: Camilla, Devin, Spencer, Maria, Eliza, Sarah, Palmer. BS, Brigham Young U., 1978. CPA, D.C. Sr. acct. M.B. Hariton & Co., Washington, 1978-83; tax acct. Arthur Young, Washington, 1983-84; asst. treas. TAG Group USA, Inc., Washington, 1984—. Mem. AICPA, Brigham Young U. Mgmt. Soc. (v.p. 1995—, treas. 1991-95). Home: 5821 Bent Twig Rd Mc Lean VA 22101-1807 Office: TAG Group USA Inc 1215 19th St NW Washington DC 20036-2401

DICKSON, MARKHAM ALLEN, wholesale company executive; b. Shreveport, La., June 10, 1922; s. Claudius Markham and Marjorie (Fields) D.; m. Margaret Shaffer, Sept. 4, 1943 (div. Mar. 1981); m. June Baldwin Dickson, Apr. 19, 1981; children: Louise Dickson Cravens, Claudius Markham, Markham Allen, Paul Meade. BS, MIT, 1947; MS, Calif. Inst. Tech., 1952, DD, Cranmer Theol. House Sem., 1996. Registered profl. engr., La.; ordained priest Episcopal Ch., 1973. Prodn. engr. Brewster Co., Shreveport, 1948-51; pres. Shreveport Druggists, 1951-52, Morris & Dickson Co. Ltd., Shreveport, 1952-95, also chmn. 1995—. Trustee Cranmer Theol. House Sem. Served to capt. USAAF, 1941-46. Recipient Conservationist of Yr. award DAR. Mem. Nat. Wholesale Druggists Assn. (Tech. award 1991). La Wholesale Drug Distbrs. (pres. 1981-90), La. Bd. Wholesale Drug Distbrs. (chmn. bd. 1988-92), Kappa Alpha, Shreveport Club, Masons (32nd degree, shrine). Office: Morris & Dickson Co Ltd 410 Kay Ln Shreveport LA 71115-3611

DICKSON, MAX CHARLES, retired career counselor, coordinator; b. Heber City, Utah, Oct. 15, 1924; s. Albert Douglas and Ruth (Hicken) D.; m. Darlene Newbold, May 22, 1944; children—Michael Kent, Dianne Dickson Smith, Ronald N., Kaylene Dickson Murray. B.S., U. Utah, 1950, M.S., 1966, M. Counseling, 1979. Cert. secondary tchr., adminstr., counselor, Utah. Tchr. Utah pub. schs., 1950-59; tchr., media coordinator, student govt. adviser Skyline High Sch., Salt Lake City, 1960-73, career ctr. coordinator/counselor, 1973-87; ret., 1987. Former bishop LDS Ch. Served with A.C., USN, 1943-45; PTO. Decorated Air medal. Named Tch. of Month, Granite Sch. Dist. Edn. Assn., Nov. 1961. Mem. Am. Vocat. Assn., Utah Sch. Counselors Assn., NEA, Utah Edn. Assn., Granite Edn. Assn., Sons of Utah Pioneers, Phi Delta Kappa. Democrat. Developer vocat. guidance program using micro computer.

DICKSON, ROBERT FRANK, nursing home executive; b. Carbondale, Ill., Oct. 23, 1933; s. Jason Milburn and Elizabeth (Krysher) D.; m. Roberta Joan Millican, May 16, 1964; children: Kevin, Craig, Angela, Rebecca. BS, So. Ill. U., 1960. With Farm Credit System, Ill., 1960-67; credit. rep. Fed. Intermediate Credit Bank, St. Louis, 1967-70; adminstr. Union County Hosp., Anna, Ill., 1970-72; v.p. Heritage Enterprises, Inc., Bloomington, Ill., 1972-85, exec. v.p., 1985—. Contbr. articles to mag. Served with USN, 1952-56. Mem. Ill. Health Care Assn. (bd. dirs. 1975-82, 85-86, pres. 1979, 85), Am. Health Care Assn. (bd. dirs. 1979-82, 86). Republican. Presbyterian. Lodge: Kiwanis. Avocations: boating, camping, gardening, reading. Home: 705 Bradley Dr Bloomington IL 61701-2203 Office: Heritage Enterprises Inc 115 W Jefferson St Ste 401 Bloomington IL 61701-3937

DICKSON, ROBERT LEE, lawyer; b. Hot Springs, Ark., Sept. 3, 1932; s. Constantine John and Georgia Marie (Allen) D.; m. Christina Farrar, Oct. 29, 1978; children—Robert Lee, Geoffrey, Alexandra, Christopher, George, John. BBA, U. Tex., 1959, LLB, 1960. Bar: Tex. 1960, Calif. 1965, U.S. Dist. Ct. (no. dist.) Tex. 1960, U.S. Dist. Ct. (ea. dist.) Wis. 1979, U.S. Supreme Ct. 1980, U.S. Dist. Ct. (ea. dist.) Calif. 1983, U.S. Ct. Appeals (7th cir.) 1983, U.S. Dist. Ct. (no. and so. dists.) Calif. 1984, U.S. Ct. Appeals (9th cir.) 1987, U.S. Ct. Appeals (1st and 10th cirs.) 1989. Assoc. to ptnr. Eplen, Daniel & Dickson, Abilene, Tex., 1960-65; assoc. to sr. ptnr. Haight, Dickson, Brown & Bonesteel, Santa Monica, Calif., 1965-88; sr. ptnr. Dickson, Carlson & Campillo, Santa Monica, 1988-98; ptnr. Arter & Hadden, L.A., 1998—; bd. advisors UCLA Sch Nursing. Contbr. articles to profl. jours. Fellow Am. Coll. Trial Lawyers; mem. Ind. Bar Com., Def. Rsch. Inst. (steering com. of drug and device litigation com.), Fedn. Ins. and Corp. Counsel (chmn. pharm. liability litigation sect. 1984-87, v.p. 1986-89, bd. dirs. 1989-95, sec.-treas. 1991-92, pres.-elect 1992-93, pres. 1993-94, chmn. 1994-95), Am. Bd. Trial Advocates, Assn. So. Calif. Def. Counsel (pres. 1976), Bel Air Country Club, Bel Air Bay Club (Pacific Palisades). Republican. Roman Catholic. Home: 14952 Alva Dr Pacific Palisades CA 90272-4401 Office: Arter & Hadden 725 S Figueroa St Ste 3400 Los Angeles CA 90017-5434

DICKSTEIN, CYNTHIA DIANE, international professional exchange specialist; b. Binghamton, N.Y., June 28, 1946; d. Simon and Marcella D. BA, Syracuse U., 1968; MA, Calif. State U., L.A., 1973. Peripatologist Braille Inst. Am., L.A., 1974-77, Perkins Sch. for the Blind, Boston, 1978, Mass. Assn. for the Blind, Boston, 1981-84; developer exch. programs Orgn. Internat. Profl. Exchs., Inc., Boston, 1980—, pres., 1981—; adminstr. dept. of ophthalmology Mass. Eye and Ear Infirmary Harvard Med. Sch., Boston, 1981-89; dir. fgn. exch. program New Eng. Soc. Newspaper Editors, Boston, 1984—. Contbr. articles to Boston Globe, various profl. publs. Developer program Citizen Exch. Coun., Boston, 1979-80.

DICKSTEIN, JACK, chemist; b. Phila., Dec. 14, 1925; s. Harry and Anna A. (Anselevitz) D.; m. Pauline M. Gotheif, Dec. 24, 1950; children: Jeffrey L., John F., Andrea E. BS in Biochemistry, Pa. State U., 1946; MA in Organic Chemistry, Temple U., 1951; PhD in Polymer Chemistry, Rutgers U., 1958. Rsch. assoc. E.R. Squibb & Sons, New Brunswick, N.J., 1951-56; lab. mgr. Borden Chem. Co., Phila., 1958-61; devel. mgr. thermoplastics divsn. Borden Chem. Co., Leominster, Mass., 1961-67; dir. R&D Borden Chem. Co., Phila., 1967-74; group mgr., mgr. R&D Haven Chem. Co., Phila., 1974-77; v.p., dir. R&D Seal Inc., Naugatuck, Conn., 1977-79; pres. Monomer-Polymer & Dajac Labs., Inc., Feasterville, Pa., 1979—; tech. cons. Avery Internat., Pasadena, Calif., 1978-81, Painesville, Ohio, 1981-83, Avmor Inc., Montreal, Can., 1982-84. Patentee in field; contbr. articles to profl. jours. 010Mem. AAAS, Am. Chem. Soc., Am. Inst. Chemists, N.Y. Acad. Scis., Franklin Inst., Sigma Xi. Jewish. Avocations: sports statistics, photography. Home: 318 Keats Rd Huntingdon Valley PA 19006-3029 Office: Monomer-Polymer & Dajac Labs 1675 Bustleton Pike Feasterville Trevose PA 19053

DICKSTEIN, JOAN BORTECK, arbitrator, conflict management consultant; b. Phila., June 20, 1919; d. Joseph and Mary (Leibovitz) Borteck; m. Benjamin Dickstein, Dec. 24, 1939; children: Howard, Kenneth, Mary. BA, Antioch Coll., 1974; MA in Sociology, U. Pa., 1978. Phila. coord. Gt. Books Found., Chgo., 1960-64; moderator, panelist Panel of Am. Women, Phila., 1964-73; trainer sensitivity courses Phila. Fellowship commn., 1966-69; rsch. assoc., cons. U. Pa. Human Resources Ctr., Phila., 1969-73; arbitrator comty. disputes Am. Arbitration Assn., Phila., 1969-82, Mcpl. Ct. of Phila., 1974-80, Commn. on Human Rels., Phila., 1979-82; facilitator interfaith dialogue Elkins Park (Pa.) Interfaith Dialogue, 1987—; guest lectr. conflict mgmt. La Salle Coll., Phila., 1971-74; mem. adv. com. Episcopal Comty. Svcs., Phila., 1972-73; cons. staff devel. Covenant House Health Svc., Phila., 1979-80. V.p. Phila. chpt. Am. Jewish Com., Phila., 1970-73; study tour mem. Scandinavia, World Future Soc., Washington, 1974; study tour mem. Mid. East, United Presbyn. Ch., Roman Cath. Conf., Am. Jewish Com., N.Y.C., 1976; bd. dirs. Or Hadash Congregation, Ft. Washington, Pa., 1990-93; peer counselor Women's Ctr., Jenkintown, Pa., 1987—. Recipient Human Rights award City of Phila. Commn. on Human Rels., 1982. Democrat. Jewish. Avocations: Great Books discussion programs, interfaith dialogue, aerobics, crossword puzzles, volunteering at women's ctr. Home: 8325 Fairview Rd Elkins Park PA 19027-2120

DICKSTEIN, SIDNEY, lawyer; b. Bklyn., May 13, 1925; s. Charles and Pearl (Stahl) D.; m. Barbara H. Duke, Sept. 20, 1953; children: Ellen Simeon, Matthew Howard, Nancy Joy. A.B., Franklin and Marshall Coll., Lancaster, Pa., 1947; J.D., Columbia U., 1949. Bar: N.Y. 1949, D.C. 1959. Law clk. to Joseph Richter, N.Y.C., 1949-50; assoc. law office Herman E. Cooper, 1950-53; founder Dickstein & Shapiro, N.Y.C., 1953; sr. ptnr. successor firm Dickstein, Shapiro, Morin & Oshinsky, Washington, 1953-97, sr. counsel, 1998—. Trustee Franklin and Marshall Coll., 1978—. Served with AUS, 1943-44, USNR, 1944-46. Mem. ABA, Bar Assn. D.C., Am. Jewish Com. (pres. Washington chpt. 1999—, mem. nat. bd. govs.). Home: 9050 Bradgrove Dr Bethesda MD 20817-3003 Office: Dickstein Shapiro Morin & Oshinsky 2101 L St NW Washington DC 20037-1526

DICLAUDIO, JANET ALBERTA, health information administrator; b. Monroeville, Pa., June 17, 1940; d. Frank and Pearl Alberta (Wolfgang) DiC. Cert. in Med. Rsch. Libr. Sci., Luth Med. Ctr., 1962; BA, Thiel Coll., 1975; MS, SUNY, Buffalo, 1978. Registered record adminstr. Dir. med. records Bashline Hosp., Grove City, Pa., 1962, St. Clair Meml. Hosp., Pitts., 1963-73; asst. prof. Ill. State U., Normal, 1976-81; corp. dir. med. records Buffalo Gen. Hosp., 1981-85; dir. med. records Candler Hosp., Savannah, Ga., 1985-94, med. records analyst, 1994-98; pres. prn Assocs., Savannah, Ga., 1998—; med. record cons. White Cliff Nursing Home, Greenville, Pa., 1973-75; mgmt. cons. Gifford W. Lorenz MD, Savannah, 1992-94. Contbr. articles to periodicals. Bd. dirs. Mid-Ill. Areawide Health Planning Corp., Normal, 1979-81. Mem. Am. Health Info. Mgmt. Assn., Ga. Health Info. Mgmt. Assn., S.E. Ga. Health Info. Mgmt. Assn. Avocations: painting, story telling, dancing, reading. Office: prn Assocs 7400 Abercorn St Ste 705-153 Savannah GA 31406-2447

DICLERICO, JOSEPH ANTHONY, JR., federal judge; b. Lynn, Mass., Jan. 30, 1941; s. Joseph Anthony and Ruth Adel (Cummings) DiC.; m. Laurie Breed Thomson, July 27, 1975; 1 child, Devon Thomson. BA, Williams Coll., Williamstown, Mass., 1963; LLB, Yale U., 1966. Bar: N.H. 1967, U.S. Dist. Ct. N.H. 1967, U.S. Ct. Appeals (1st cir.) 1973, U.S. Supreme Ct. 1975. Law clk. to presiding justice U.S. Dist. Ct. N.H., Concord, 1966-67, N.H. Supreme Ct., Concord, 1967-68; assoc. Cleveland Waters & Bass, Concord, 1968-70; asst. atty. gen. State of N.H., Concord, 1970-77; assoc. justice N.H. Superior Ct., Concord, 1977-91, chief justice, 1991-92; chief judge U.S. Dist. Ct. N.H., Concord, 1992-97; chmn. Superior Ct. sentence rev. disvn., 1987-92. Fellow Am. Bar Found. (life), N.H. Bar Found. (jud.); mem. N.H. Bar Assn (nat. conf. state trial judges 1986-92, nat. conf. fed. trial judges, 1992-96, mem. com. on codes of conduct jud. conf. of U.S. 1994—, dist. judge rep. from 1st cir. to Jud. Conf. of U.S. 1997—), Phi Beta Kappa. Republican. Roman Catholic. Avocation: gardening. Office: 55 Pleasant St Concord NH 03301-3954

DICONTI, MICHAEL ANDREW, trade organization executive; b. Glendale, Calif., Aug. 19, 1958; s. Andrew Raphael Jr. and Diane Rose (Carlotti) DiC.; m. Veronica Donahue, Aug. 6, 1988; 1 child, Nolan James. AB in Psychology magna cum laude, Occidental Coll., 1980; MBA in Acctg./Fin., UCLA, 1983; MA in Polit. Sci., Johns Hopkins U., 1987, PhD in Polit. Sci., 1990. Tax advisor Arthur Young, L.A., 1983-85; instr. C.C. of Balt., 1985-90, Johns Hopkins U., Balt., 1987-90; exec. asst. to pres. The Bus. Roundtable, Washington, 1990-93, dir. adminstrn., 1993—. Author: Entrepreneurship in Training, 1992. Asst. treas. Edn. Excellence Partnership, Washington, 1993—. Fellow Inst. for Study of World Politics, Washington, 1987-88. Mem. Phi Beta Kappa, Psi Chi (pres. Occidental Coll. chpt. 1979-80). Avocation: running. Home: 11621 Ayreshire Rd Oakton VA 22124-1207 Office: The Bus Roundtable 1615 L St NW Ste 1100 Washington DC 20036-5624

DICORCIA, EDWARD THOMAS, oil industry executive; b. Richmond Hill, N.Y., Oct. 16, 1930; s. Domenick and Emma DiCorcia; m. Madelyn Faress; children: Jeanette, Suzanne DiCorcia Shelby. BA, Columbia Coll., 1951; BCE, Columbia U., 1955, MCE, 1956. Registered profl. engr., Tex. Plant mgr. Esso Std. Oil Co., Bayonne, N.J., 1965-67; mgr. employee rels. Humble Oil & Refining Co., Houston, 1969-70; refinery mgr. Humble Oil & Refining Co., Baytown, Tex., 1970-73; exec. asst. to pres. Exxon Corp., N.Y.C., 1975-76, dep. mgr. corp. planning, 1976-79; v.p. supply Exxon Co. USA, Houston, 1979-81, v.p. refining, 1981-90; pres., CEO, The Uno-Ven Co., Arlington Heights, Ill., 1990-95; ret., 1995; gen. ptnr. Strategic Ptnrs., L.P., Houston, 1995—; dir. Am. Petroleum Inst., Washington, 1987-89, Nat. Petroleum Coun., Washington, 1994-95. Pub. Affairs fellow Brookings Instn., 1966. Home: 3439 Wickersham Ln Houston TX 77027-4133 Office: Strategic Ptnrs LP Ste 401 3614 Montrose Blvd Houston TX 77006-4651

DI CORCIA, PHILIP-LORCA, artist, photographer; b. Hartford, Conn., 1953. Diploma, Sch. Mus. Fine Arts, Boston, 1975, postgrad. cert., 1976; MFA, Yale U., 1979. One-man shows include Zeus Arts, Milan, 1985, Photographer's Gallery, London, 1991, 96, Galeria Palmira Suso, Lisbon, Portugal, 1993, Mus. Modren Art, N.Y.C., 1993, Ctr. Cultural Rocher, Lyon, France, 1993, Nikon Salon, Tokyo, 1994, Osaka, Japan, 1994, Art & Pub., Geneva, 1995, Galerie Klemens Gasser, Cologne, Germany, 1995, 96, 98, PaceWildensteinMacgill, N.Y.C., 1996, 98, Theoretical Events, Naples, 1996, PaceWildenstein, L.A., 1998, Mus. Nat. Ctr. Arts Reina Sofia, Madrid, 1998, Galerie Rodolphe Janssen, Brussels, Belgium, 1998, Galerie Almine Rech, Paris, 1998; group shows include Enjay Gallery Photography, Boston, 1977, Balt. Mus. Art, 1987, 91, Mus. Modern Art, N.Y.C., 1987, 91, Artists Space, N.Y.C., 1990, Art Gallery York U., Toronto, Can., 1991, Met. Mus. Art, N.Y.C., 1991, L.A. County Mus. Art, 1991, 92, Galeria Tanja Grunert, Cologne, 1992, Luhring Augustine Gallery, N.Y.C., 1993, San Francisco Mus. Modren Art, 1993, Robert Klein Gallery, Boston, 1994, Foto Manifestabe, Eindhoven, The Netherlands, 1994, Ansel Adams Ctr., San Francisco, 1995, Portland (Maine) Art Mus., 1995, 97, Art & Pub., Geneva, 1995, Inst. Contemporary Art, Boston, 1995, Galerie Agnes B, Paris, 1996, Whitney Mus. Am. Art, 1997, Reykjavik (Iceland) Mcpl. Art Mus., 1997, GementeMus., Helmond, Germany, 1997, Mus. Contemporary Art, Chgo., 1997, Howard Greenberg Gallery, N.Y.C., 1998, Galerie Fotohof, Salzburg, Austria; represented in permanent collections Boston Mus. Fine Arts, Chgo. Mus. Contemporary Photography, Dreyfus Corp., N.Y.c., L.A. County Mus. Art, Met. Mus. Art, Mus. Fine Art, Houston. Artist fellow Nat. Endowments Arts, 1980, 86, 89, John Simon Guggenheim Meml. Found. fellow, 1987. Office: Pace/Wildnestein/MacGill 32 E 57th St New York NY 10022

DI CORI, PAT MILLER, painter, sculptor; b. Cin., Nov. 15, 1929; d. Peter William and Ola (McCaffery) M.; m. Ferruccio di Cori, Nov. 18, 1963 (div. 1978). Studied with Robert Beverly Hale, 1960-64; Diploma, Inst. of Fin., N.Y.C., 1958. Tour guide, lectr. UN, N.Y.C., 1955-58; tour guide N.Y. Stock Exch., N.Y.C., 1958-60. *Surprise, humor, and discovery are the driving forces in DiCori's works in sculpture, drawing, and painting. Deceptively simple in it's play with form and content, each piece captures the viewer regardless of scale or media. The work provides a regenerative experience. What stands out is this quiet magnetic force, full of open spaces and terrains, created with essential line and form. DiCori's intent and exploration succeed by capturing the viewer and bringing them back again and again for a closer and deeper look. Collections: Terrence Gallowhur, Richard Kempe, George Klauber, Eric Nesbit, George Tooker, Nancy Walker.* Artist: (film documentary) Pat di Cori Reflections in the Mind's Eye, 1996; published in New York Art Review, 1988. Bd. dirs. Creative Arts Rehab. Ctr., N.Y.C., 1975-95, N.Y. Artists, Equity Assocs., Inc., 1991-95. Mem. Art Students League (life). Office: 102 Greene St New York NY 10012-3822

DICUS, BRIAN GEORGE, lawyer; b. Kansas City, Mo., Oct. 29, 1961; s. Clarence Howard and Edith Helen (George) D.; m. Vali Ann Venner, Dec. 14, 1985; children: Brian George, Cady Alyssa. BA, So. Meth. U., 1984, JD, 1987. Bar: Tex. 1987, U.S. Dist. Ct. (no. dist.) Tex. 1988; bd. cert. estate planning and probate law Tex. Bd. Legal Specialization. Assoc. Thorp & Sorenson, Dallas, 1987-89, Joseph E. Ashmore Jr., P.C., Dallas, 1989-92; pvt. practice Dallas, 1992—. Chmn. local alumni student recruiting program So. Meth. U., Dallas, 1989-90. Fellow Tex. Bar Found.; mem. Tex. Bar Assn., Dallas Bar Assn., Phi Alpha Delta, Pi Sigma Alpha. Home: 2336 Serenity Ln Heath TX 75032-1922 Office: 5910 N Central Expy Ste 920 Dallas TX 75206-5132

DICUS, DUANE A., physicist, educator; b. Okanogan, Wash., Nov. 23, 1938; m. Sandra; children: James, Steven, Richard. BS, U. Wash., 1961, MS, 1963; PhD in Physics, UCLA, 1968. Rsch. scientist Boeing Co., 1963-64; asst. prof. UCLA, 1968-69; rsch. assoc. MIT, 1969-71, U. Rochester, 1971-73; prof. of physics U. Tex. Fellow Am. Phys. Soc. Office: U Tex Dept Physics Ctr Particle Physics Bldg RLM Rm 9.204A Austin TX 78712*

DICUS, GRETA JOY, federal commissioner. BA in biol. scis., Tex. Woman's U., 1961; MA in radiation biology, U. Tex. Southwestern Med. Sch., 1967. Rschr. in radiation health effects Harvard Med. Sch., Rice U., U. Tex., Southwestern Med. Sch., 1961-77; with Divsn. Radiation Control & Emergency Mgmt. Ark. Dept. Health, 1980-82, chief of licensing, 1982-84, dir., 1984-93; confirmed by U.S. Senate as mem. bd. dirs. U.S. Enrichment Corp., 1994-95; confirmed by U.S. Senate as commr. U.S. Nuc. Regulatory Commn., 1995, commr., 1996—. Mem. Health Physics Soc., Conf. of Radiation Control Program Dirs., Sigma Xi. Office: Nuc Regulatory Commn 11555 Rockville Pike Rockville MD 20852-2738*

DICUS, JOHN CARMACK, thrift savings bank executive; b. Hutchinson, Kans., May 16, 1933; s. George Byron and Desda (Carmack) D.; m. Barbara Elizabeth Bubb, Feb. 4, 1956; children: Debra Elizabeth Kennedy, John Bubb. BS, U. Kans., 1955. With Capitol Fed. Savs. Bank, Topeka, 1959—; exec. v.p. Capitol Fed. Savs. Bank, 1963-69, pres., 1969—, chmn., 1989—; bd. dirs. Columbian Nat. Title Co., Topeka, Security Benefit Life Ins. Co., Topeka, Western Resources Inc., Topeka; treas. Scottish Rite Bodies Valley of Topeka; mem. Fed. Savs. and Loan Adv. Coun., 1973; mem. Fed. Res. Bd. Thrift Instns. Adv. Coun., 1986-87. Chmn. Shawnee County chpt. ARC, 1965; treas. Jayhawk area coun. Boy Scouts Am., 1967-68; pres. Topeka United Way, 1972-73; trustee Stormont-Vail Healthcare Inc., chmn. 1991-92; chmn. Menninger Fund; trustee Menninger Found.; vice chmn. Kans. U. Endowment Assn.; past pres. Native Sons of Kans. Lt. (j.g.) USN, 1956-59. Recipient Fred Ellsworth medallion U. Kans., 1990, Disting. Alumnus award U. Kans. Bus. Sch., 1998; Paul Harris fellow, 1992. Mem. Am.'s Comty. Bankers (past exec. com., past dir.), Heartland Comty. Bankers Assn. (pres. 1974-75), Topeka C. of C. (dir. 1962, v.p. 1965-66, 71, pres. 1978, pres. Indsl. Devel. Corp.), U. Kans. Alumni Assn. (nat. pres. 1987-88), Masons (33 degree), Kans. C. of C. and Industry (past dir.), Shriners (potentate Arab Temple 1975), Jesters, Rotary (past dir.), Topeka Country Club (dir., pres. 1972). Episcopalian (sr. warden, vestryman). Office: Capitol Fed Savings Bank 700 S Kansas Ave Fl 1 Topeka KS 66603-3894

DIDICH, JAN, hospice consultant; b. Lorain, Ohio, Nov. 20, 1952; d. Harry and Helen (Zaborniak) Murawski; m. Aaron N. Didich, May 12, 1979; 1 child, Aaron M. BSN, St. John Coll. of Cleve., 1975; MA in Community Psychology, N.E. Mo. State U., 1982. Asst. head nurse/charge nurse Cleve. Clinic Hosp., 1975-79; charge nurse neonatal ICU Kirksville (Mo.) Osteopathic Hosp., 1979-80; charge nurse ICU Grim-Smith Hosp., Kirksville, 1981-83; asst. instr. N.E. Mo. State U., Kirksville, 1980-83; hospice nurse Hospice of Cen. Iowa, Des Moines, 1984; community nurse Community Nursing Svcs., Mt. Holly, N.J., 1984; dir. patient svcs. Samaritan Hospice, N.J., 1985-86; advanced clin. nurse palliative care, 1986-87; dir. Tricare Hospice, Bellefontaine, Ohio; cons. Cleve. Clinic Found., 1988-90. Contbr. articles to profl. jours. Mem. ANA, Ohio Nurses' Assn., Nat. Hospice Orgn., Ohio Hospice Orgn., AAUW.

DIDION, JOAN, author; b. Sacramento, Calif., Dec. 5, 1934; d. Frank Reese and Eduene (Jerrett) D.; m. John Gregory Dunne, Jan. 30, 1964; 1 child, Quintana Roo. B.A. U. Calif., Berkeley, 1956. Assoc. feature editor Vogue mag., 1956-63; former columnist Saturday Evening Post, Life, Esquire; now contbr. The N.Y. Rev. of Books, The New Yorker. Novels include Run River, 1963, Play It As It Lays, 1970, A Book of Common Prayer, 1977, Democracy, 1984, The Last Thing He Wanted, 1996; books of essays: Slouching Towards Bethlehem, 1968, The White Album, 1979, After Henry, 1992; nonfiction Salvador, 1983, Miami, 1987; co-author: (with John

Gregory Dunne) Screenplays for films The Panic in Needle Park, 1971, Play It As It Lays, 1972, A Star Is Born, 1976, True Confessions, 1981, Hills Like White Elephants, 1991, Broken Trust, 1995, Up Close and Personal, 1996. Recipient 1st prize Vogue's Prix de Paris, 1956, Morton Dauwen Zabel prize AAAL, 1978, The Edward MacDowell medal, 1996. Mem. Am. Acad. Arts and Letters, Am. Acad. Arts and Scis., Coun. Fgn. Rels. Office: care Janklow & Nesbit 598 Madison Ave New York NY 10022-1614*

DIDISHEIM, PAUL, internist, hematologist; b. Paris, June 3, 1927; m. Ricarda Elizabeth Jahrreiss, Sept. 14, 1952; children: Melinda, Peter, Andrea. AB, Princeton U., 1950; MD, Johns Hopkins U., 1954. Intern in medicine Duke U.-Durham (N.C.) VA Hosp., Durham, 1954-55; instr., then asst. prof., chief coagulation lab. U. Utah Med. Ctr., Salt Lake City, 1958-65; dir. thrombosis rsch. lab. Mayo Clinic, Rochester, Minn., 1965-86, dir. hemostasis lab., 1974-86; head biomaterials program bioengring. rsch. group Nat. Heart, Lung and Blood Inst., NIH, Bethesda, Md., 1986-97; founder tissue engring. program Nat. Heart, Lung and Blood Inst., NIH, Bethesda, 1997; ind. cons., 1998—; assoc. physician, attending in internal medicine Salt Lake County Gen. Hosp., 1958-65; asst. prof. exptl. pathology Mayo Grad. Sch. Medicine, U. Minn., Rochester, 1966-70, assoc. prof. clin. pathology, 1970-73; assoc. prof. lab. medicine Mayo Med. Sch., Rochester, 1973-75, prof., 1975-86; mem. med. adv. bd. Utah and Intermountain chpts. Nat. Hemophilia Found., 1959-65, mem. med. and sci. adv. coun., 1964-77; mem. rsch. adv. com. ARC, 1967-73; founder, 1st chmn. subcom. on blood materials interactions Internat. Com. on Thrombosis and Haemostasis, 1982-85; mem. surgery and bioengring. study sect. NIH, 1982-86; chmn. working group on biol. evaluation med. devices Internat. Stds. Orgn., 1989-97; head U.S. del. to Conf. Biol. Evaluation Med. Devices, 1990-97; vis. prof. U. Paris XIII, 1992. Co-author: The Diagnosis of Bleeding Disorders, 1969, Mayo Clinic Laboratory Manual of Hemostasis, 1971; co-editor: Platelets, Thrombosis and Inhibitors, 1974, Vascular Diseases: Current research and Clinic Applications, 1987, Cardiovascular Biomaterials and Biocompatibility, 1993; assoc. editor Artery, 1974-82, Am. Jour. Hematology, 1982-85; editor Thrombosis Rsch., 1985-88; mem. editl. bd. Polymer edit. Jour. Biomaterials Sci., 1988—; contbr. over 300 articles and abstracts to med. jours. Pres., Unitarian Universalist Ch., Rochester, Minn., 1982-84; nat. adv. com. N.J. Ctr. for Biomaterials and Med. Devices, 1998—. With USN, 1945-46. Recipient Borden award for outstanding undergrad. med. rsch. Johns Hopkins U. Sch. Medicine, 1954, NIH Merit Award for outstanding leadership in biomaterials program NHLBI, 1992, C. William Hall award for outstanding support of biomaterials rsch. programs Soc. Biomaterials, 1995; postdoctoral fellow Life Ins. Med. Rsch. Fund, 1955-57, spl. rsch. fellow USPHS, 1957-58; grantee NIH, 1958-60, 71-83, Minn. Heart Assn., 1967-70, Japan Arteriosclerosis Rsch. Found., 1971-74. Fellow Am. Inst. for Med. and Biol. Enging. (founding); mem. Am. Fedn. Clin. Rsch., Am. Physiol. Soc., Am. Soc. Artificial Internal Organs, Am. Soc. Hematology, Am. Soc. Investigative Pathology, Ctrl. Soc. Clin. Rsch., Internat. Soc. Hematology, Internat. Soc. Thrombosis and Haemostasis (charter, internat. adv. com. 1980-86), Soc. for Biomaterials (liaison com. 1987-90, liaison to com. on std. reference materials 1992-97), Soc. Exptl. Biology and Medicine, Assn. Advancement Med. Instrumentation (com. for biol. testing med. and dental materials and devices 1989-97), Argentine Med.. Assn. (hon. corr.), Sigma Xi. Address: 3507 Rodman St NW Washington DC 20008-3118

DIDLO, LARRY L., security officer, educator; b. Manitowoc, Wis., Sept. 19, 1940; s. John Harvey Sr. and Clara Myrtle (Wood) D. BS, U. Wis., Oshkosh, 1963; MS in Edn., Ind. U., 1964. founder St. Lawrence Consortium, Oshkosh. Docent Exptl. Aircraft Assn.; vol. driver Disable Am. Vets.; mem., vol. Paine Art Ctr., Oshkosk. James E. West fellow Boy Scouts Am. Mem. VFW, Am. Legion, The "O" Club, Wisconsin State Reading Assn., Nat. Eagle Scout Assn., Phi Delta Kappa. Republican. Presbyterian. Avocations: photography, swimming, golf.

DI DOMENICA, ROBERT ANTHONY, musician, composer; b. N.Y.C., Mar. 4, 1927; s. Angelo and Philomena (Mosca) DiD.; m. Leona Knopf, Feb. 6, 1951 (dec. 1998); children—David, Peter Josef, Claude Robert; m. Ellen Bender, Apr., 1999. B.S., N.Y. U., 1951. Mem. theory-composition faculty New Eng. Conservatory, 1969-92, assoc. dean performing orgns., 1973-76, dean, 1976-78. Flutist, N.Y.C. Ctr. Opera, N.Y. Philharm., Symphony of Air, soloist, Composers Forum, 20th Century Innovations, rec. artist, RCA, Columbia, Colpix, MGM, Atlantic, Deutsche Grammophon records; recs. include Leona DiDomenica In Live First Performance of the Solo Piano Music of Robert DiDomenica, GM/200/CD; compositions include Symphony, 1961, Concerto for Violin and Chamber Orch., 1962, Quintet for Clarinet and String Quartet, 1965, Sonata for Violin and Piano, 1966; opera The Balcony, 1972, Black Poems (baritone, piano and tape), 1976, The Holy Colophon for Orch., Chorus, Soprano and Tenor, 1980, Piano Concerto No. 2, 1982, Dream Journeys for Orch., 1984, The Scarlet Letter (opera), 1986, Opera The Balcony given its world premier by The Opera Co. of Boston, 1990, performed at Moscow's Bolshoi Theater, 1991, (operatic trilogy) Francesco Cenci, 1996, Beatrice Cenci, 1993, The Cenci, 1995. Served with USNR, 1944-46. Guggenheim fellow, 1972-73; grantee Rockefeller Found., 1965; commd. by Goethe Inst., Boston, 1975. Mem. Broadcast Music Inc. Home: 159 Valley Rd Needham MA 02492

DIDOMENICO, MAURO, JR., communication executive; b. Bronx, N.Y., Jan. 12, 1937; s. Mauro and Elizabeth DiD.; m. Angela M. Carracino, Aug. 29, 1964; children—Catherine Lee, David M. BS, Stanford U., 1958, MS, 1959, PhD, 1963. Mem. tech. staff Bell Labs., Murray Hill, N.J., 1962-66; supr. Bell Labs., Murray Hill, 1966-70, head optical device dept., 1970-80; dept. head integrated circuit customer service dept. Bell Labs., Murray Hill, N.J., 1980-82; divsn. mgr. strategic planning AT&T, Basking Ridge, N.J., 1982-84; divsn. mgr. applied research BellCare, Morristown, N.J., 1984-85; exec. dir. tech. liaison office Bell Comms. Rsch., Morristown, N.J., 1985-92, ret., 1992; pres. CommTech Internat., Bernardsville, N.J., 1993-95; pres., founder FreeLinQ Comm., N.Y.C., 1995—. Contbr. numerous articles to profl. lit. Fellow IEEE, Am. Phys. Soc.; mem. N.Y. Acad. Scis., Sigma Xi, Tau Beta Pi. Roman Catholic.

DIE, ANN MARIE HAYES, college president, psychology educator; b. Baytown, Tex., Aug. 15, 1944; d. Robert L. and Dorothy Ann (Cooke) Hayes; m. Jerome Glynn Die, June 5, 1971; 1 child, Meredith Anne. BS with highest honors, Lamar U., 1966; MEd, U. Houston, 1969; PhD, Tex. A&M U., 1977. Lic. psychologist. Asst. prof. dept. psychology Lamar U., Beaumont, Tex., 1977-82, assoc. prof., dir. Psychol. Clinic, 1982-86, dir. grad. programs in psychology, 1981-86, Regents prof. psychology, 1986, pres. faculty senate, 1985-86; pvt. practice clin. psychology Beaumont, 1979-87; prof. Tulane U., New Orleans, 1988-92, dean Newcomb Coll., 1988-92, assoc. provost, 1991-92; pres., prof. psychology Hendrix Coll., Conway, Ark., 1992—; adminstr. adolescent residential unit Mental Health/Mental Retardation S.E. Tex., 1979-80, mem. cmty. adv. com., 1981-87; cons. in field; coordinating bd. Tex. Coll. and Univ. Sys. Internship, 1986; bd. dirs. Nat. Merit Scholarship Corp., Acxiom Corp., Found. for Ind. Higher Edn. Contbr. articles to profl. jours. Mem. cmty. adv. com. Beaumont State Ctr. Human Devel., 1981-88; chair So. Collegiate Athletic Conf., 1996-97; participant Nat. Identification Program for Women, Am. Coun. on Edn., 1985, mem. govt. rels. commn., 1993-96, chmn., 1994-96, chmn. coun. of fellow, 1995-96, bd. dirs., 1997— ; bd. dirs. Beaumont Civic Opera, Lamar U. Wesley Found., Tulane U. Wesley Found.; bd. govs. Isidore Newman Sch., 1991-92; trustee Robert Morris Coll., 1990-98, chmn. edn. com., 1990-94, chmn. pers. com., 1994-98; mem. univ. senate United Meth. Ch., 1993—, chair commn. on instnl. rev., 1997—; 1st v.p. Nat. Assn. Schs. & Colls. United Meth. Ch., 1996, pres. 1997-98; bd. dirs. Ouachita coun. girl Scouts U.S., 1996—; mem. Internat. Women's Forum, 1995—, Ark. Women's Leadership Forum, 1995—; mem. Ark. Commn. to Streamline State Govt., 1996—; mem. pres. commn. NCAA, 1997—, chmn. 1999—, mem. exec. com. 1999—; chair Assoc. Coll. of the South, 1997-99. Am. Coun. Edn. fellow Coll. William and Mary, 1986-87; recipient Regents Merit award, 1979, Coll. Health and Behavioral Sci. Merit award, 1982, Lamar U.; named one of Top 100 Women in Ark., Ark. Bus., 1995-99. Mem. APA, Southwestern Psychol. Assn., Family Svcs. Assn. (bd. dirs. 1988-89), Tex. Psychol. Assn. (dir. divsn. acad. psychologists 1986), S.E. Tex. Psychol. Assn. (treas. 1978-80, pres. 1983), Mental Health Assn. Jefferson County, Nat. Register Health Svc. Providers in Psychology, Nat. Assn. Ind. Colls. and Univs. (bd. dirs., vice chmn. 1995, chair 1996). Home: 1256 Winfield St Conway AR 72032-2741 Office: Hendrix Coll 1600 Washington Ave Conway AR 72032-4115

DIEBEL, NELSON, Olympic athlete, swimmer. Olympic swimmer Barcelona, Spain, 1992. Recipient 100m Breaststroke Gold medal Olympics, Barcelona, 1992, 4x100 Medley Relay Gold medal Olympics, Barcelona, 1992. Office: US Olympic Com 1750 E Boulder St Colorado Springs CO 80909-5724

DIEBOLT, JUDITH, newspaper editor; b. Atchison, Kans., Oct. 6, 1948; d. George Edward and Mary Lou (Hill) D.; m. John C. Aldrich, Oct. 25, 1985. BSJ, U. Kans., 1970. Reporter Detroit Free Press, 1970-80, columnist, 1980-82, asst. city editor, 1982-85; reporter Detroit News, 1986-88, asst city editor, 1988-89, suburban editor, 1989-91; mng. editor Burlington (Vt.) Free Press, 1991-94; city editor Detroit News, 1994-98. Recipient Pub. Svc. award AP, 1978. Mem. AP Mng. Editors, Detroit Press Club (bd. govs., 1990-91), Univ. Club Detroit. Roman Catholic. Office: The Detroit News 615 W Lafayette Blvd Detroit MI 48226-3197

DIEDERICH, FRANCOIS NICO, chemistry educator; b. Ettelbruck, Luxemborg, July 9, 1952; married, 1975; 2 children. Diploma in chemistry, U. Heidelberg, 1977; Dr rer nat in chemistry, 1979, Dr hab in organic chemistry, 1985. Rsch. fellow excimer interactions Max Planck Inst. Med. Rsch., Heidelberg, 1979; rsch. fellow reactive intermediates Dept. Chemistry U. Calif., L.A., 1979-81; rsch. assoc. host-guest chem. Dept. Organic Chemistry Max Planck Inst. Med. Rsch., Heidelberg, 1981-85; assoc. prof., 1985-89; prof. organic chemistry Dept. Chem. & Biochem. U. Calif., L.A., 1989-92, Organic Chemistry Lab., Fed. Inst. Tech., Zürich, Switzerland, 1992—. Mem. AAAS, Soc. German Chemists, Soc. German Naturalists & Physicians, Am. Chem. Soc., New Swiss Chem. Soc., Deutsche Akademie der Naturforshcer Leopoldina, Am. Acad. Arts and Scis. (hon. mem.), Sigma Xi. Research in synthetic host-guest chemistry; complexation of organic compounds in aqueous and organic solutions and in the solid state; hosts that catalyze and mimic the action of enzymes; hosts that complex enatioselectively; novel aromatic and heteroaromatic systems with material properties; molecular and polymeric carbon alltropes. Office: Organic Chem Lab ETH Zentrum, Universitaetstr 16, CH-8092 Zurich Switzerland

DIEDERICH, J(OHN) WILLIAM, internet publisher; b. Ladysmith, Wis., Aug. 30, 1929; s. Joseph Charles and Alice Florence (Yost) D.; m. Mary Theresa Klein, Nov. 25, 1950; children: Mary Theresa Diederich Evans, Robert Douglas, Charles Stuart, Michael Mark, Patricia Anne Diederich Irelan, Donna Maureen (dec.), Denise Brendan, Carol Lynn Diederich Weaver, Barbara Gail, Brian Donald, Tracy Maureen Diederich Jorgensen, Theodora Bernadette Diederich Davidson, Tamara Alice Diederich Williams, Lorraine Angela. PhB, Marquette U., Milw., 1951; MBA with high distinction, Harvard U., 1955. With Landmark Comm., Inc., Norfolk, Va., 1955-90, v.p., treas., 1965-73, exec. v.p. fin., 1973-78, exec. v.p. community newspapers, 1978-82, exec. v.p., CFO, 1982-90, fin. cons., 1990—; internet pub. Wide World Web Internat., Incline Village, 1996—; chmn. bd. dirs. Landmark Cmty. Newspapers, Inc., 1977-88; pres. Exec. Productivity Sys., Inc., 1982-88, LCI Credit Corp., 1991-93, Landmark TV Inc., 1991—, LTM Investments, Inc., 1991—; v.p., treas., KLAS, Inc., 1994-95; v.p. Internet Express, Inc., 1994—; pres., bd. dirs. Wide World Web Internat., 1995—, TWC Holdings, Inc., 1996—; instr. Boston U., 1954, Old Dominion U., 1955-59. Lt. col. USMC, 1951-53, USMCR, 1953-71. Baker scholar Harvard U., 1955. Mem. SAR, Nat. Assn. Accts., Am. Numismatic Assn., Nat. Geneal. Soc., Wis. Geneal. Soc., Pa. Geneal. Soc., Sigma Delta Chi. Roman Catholic. Home and Office: PO Box 7677 1466 Glarus Ct Incline Village NV 89451-7900*

DIEDRICH, RICHARD JOSEPH, architect; b. South Bend, Ind., May 8, 1936; s. Arthur Joseph and Lucille D.; Diploma in Architecture, Ecole Des Beaux Arts Americaines, Fountainbleau, France, 1960; BArch, U. Ill., 1961, MArch, 1962; m. Francyne L. Diedrich (div. 1980); children: Dawn Marie, Lisa Lee, Andrea Lynn; m. Linda P. Diedrich. Archtl. designer Richardson Severns Scheeler & Assos., Champaign, Ill., 1961-62; design critic U. Ill. Sch. Architecture, 1961-62; archtl. designer Swensson & Kott, Nashville, 1963-64; architect, v.p. Miller Waltz Diedrich, Architects, Milw., 1965-77; pres. MWD Archs., Atlanta, 1978-80, Diedrich Archs., 1980-97, Diedrich/NBA, Atlanta, exec. v.p., 1997—. Co-author: Golf Course Development and Real Estate. Mem. Whitefish Bay Bd. Appeals, 1968-71; v.p. North Decatur Youth Assn., 1975-76. Margaret T. Biddle scholar, 1960. Mem. AIA (past pres. Milw. chpt., six design awards, two S.E. regional award, three Ga. AIA award), Wis. Architect (past pres.). Archtl. works include: Avondale Sta., Med. Ctr. Sta., Atlanta Rapid Transit, S Miami Sta. of Miami Rapid Transit, Student Center, U. Ga., Bloomingdale's Stores, Boca Raton, Palm Beach Gardens, Mall of Am., Neiman Marcus Stores, Scotsdale, Ariz., Troy, Mich., Honolulu, Hawaii, Short Hills, N.J., King of Prussia, Pa., Paramus, N.J., Grand Cypress Clubhouse, Orlando, English Turn Clubhouse, New Orleans, Golf Club Ga., Atlanta, Country Club North, Dayton, Old Overton Club House, Birmingham, Cherokee Country Club, Atlanta, Naples Nat. Golf Club, Sun City Hilton Head amenity facilities, Aerial Tram, Stone Mountain Pk., Atlanta. Home: 8 Brookhaven Dr Atlanta GA 30319 Office: 1 Buckhead Plaza 3060 Peachtree Rd NW Ste 600 Atlanta GA 30305-2240

DIEDWARDO, MARY ANN PASDA, artist, writer; b. Sept. 19, 1953. BA in Theatre Arts, Pa. State U., 1975; MA in English, Lehigh U., 1980. Originator theatre program for sr. citizens and youth Northampton C.C., 1977-79; lectr. Allentown Coll. St. Francis de Sales, Center Valley, Pa., 1980-81, 89-90; artist-in-residence Pasda Studios Sch. of Art, Bethlehem, Pa., 1976—; dir. Mary Ann P. DiEdwardo Correspondence Sch. of Writing, Bethlehem, 1994—; tchr. Pa. Homeschoolers H.S. diploma program AP English Online, 1999—. Author numerous curriculum texts on writing instrn. Mem. Mortar Bd., Phi Beta Kappa, Phi Kappa Phi, Sigma Tau Delta. E-mail: diedwardo7@enter.net.

DIEFENBACH, DALE ALAN, law librarian, retired; b. Cleve., Aug. 14, 1933; s. Walter Ewald and Alice Naomi (Austin) D.; m. Olga Maspaitella, Jan. 20, 1973; 1 stepson, Andrew Ivan Ward. BA, Baldwin-Wallace Coll., 1955; MLS, U. Hawaii, 1970. Fgn. svc. officer U.S. Dept. State, 1961-68; reference libr. Cornell U. Law Libr., Ithaca, N.Y., 1970-87; sr. reference libr. Harvard U. Law Libr., Cambridge, Mass., 1987-97, ret., 1997; reference libr., adj. assoc. prof. law libr. Barry U. Orlando (Fla.) Sch. Law Euliano Law Libr., 1998—. Lt. (j.g.) USNR, 1956-60, Philippines. Recipient Ficken Meml. award Baldwin-Wallace Coll., Berea, Ohio, 1988. Mem. ALA, Am. Assn. Law Librs. Democrat. Fax: 407-275-3654. Home: 500 Windmeadows Altamonte Springs FL 32701-3572 Office: Barry U Orlando Sch Law Euliano Law Libr 6441 E Colonial Dr Orlando FL 32807-3673

DIEFENBACH, VIRON LEROY, dental, public health educator, university dean; b. Balt., Feb. 9, 1922; s. William Louis and Ardie Gertrude (Von Wachter) D.; m. Virginia Kent, Dec. 3, 1944 (div. Jan. 1956); children: Kathryn Louise, Arthur Karl; mem. Adele Larson Henderson, Apr. 18, 1956; children: William Henderson, Sue Henderson. Student, Western Md. Coll., 1940-42, Pratt Inst. Engring., 1943, Harvard U., 1944; DDS, U. Md., 1949; MPH, U. Pitts., 1954. Diplomate: Am. Bd. Dental Pub. Health. Dental intern USPHS Hosp., Norfolk, Va., 1949-50; various clin. assignments USPHS Hosp., 1950-52, dental pub. health field tng., 1954-55; asst. regional dental cons. USPHS, Chgo., Office Personnel, Office Surgeon Gen., USPHS, Washington, 1955-56; information dir. USPHS Dental Public Health, 1957-59; regional dental cons. USPHS, Denver, 1959-61; dep. chief div. USPHS (Dental Health), Bethesda, Md., 1962-65; acting chief and dir. USPHS (Dental Health), 1966; asst. surgeon gen. USPHS, 1966-70; asst. exec. dir. Am. Dental Assn., 1970-72; prof. health resources mgmt. Grad. Sch. Public Health, U. Ill., 1973-88, prof. emeritus, 1988—, assoc. dean, 1977, dean, 1978-83. With AUS, 1942-44; USPHS, 1949-70. Recipient Scholarship Gold medal U. Md., 1949, Meritorious Service medal USPHS, 1966, John W. Knutson Disting. Svc. award in dental pub. health, 1999. Fellow Am. Pub. Health Assn. (past sect. chmn., sec.), AAAS, Am. Coll. Dentists; mem. Commd. Officers Assn. USPHS (mem. exec. bd., past chmn. bd.), ADA, Am. Assn. Pub. Health Dentists, Fedn. Dentaire Internationale. Achievements include early scientific studies on use of fluorides in preventive dentistry, innovations in dental education and feasibility of dental care insurance. Home: Galena Territory 22 Vista Ridge Dr Galena IL 61036-9256 Office: U Ill at Chgo Grad Sch Pub Health Chicago IL 60612

DIEFENBACH, WILLIAM PAUL, neurosurgeon; b. N.Y.C., Dec. 11, 1949; s. William Carl Ludwig and Martha (Kahle) D.; m. Geraldine Musche, Apr. 10, 1977 (div. Oct. 1992); children: William Alexander, Katherine Murchdon; m. Tracey Jean Sandberg, Apr. 30, 1994. BA, Columbia U., 1972, MD, 1979. Resident in neurosurgery Neurol. Inst., N.Y.C., 1980-85; neurosurgeon Neurol. Assocs., Tucson, 1985-93, St. Vincent Health Ctr., Erie, Pa., 1993—. Capt. U.S. Army, 1973. Fellow ACS; mem. AMA, Congress Neurol. Surgeons, Am. Assn. Neurol. surgeons, Erie County Med. Soc. (pres.-elect 1995-96), Pa. Med. Soc. Republican. Presbyterian. Avocations: scuba diving, horseback riding, photography, travel. Office: St Vincent Neurol Surgery 311 W 24th St Erie PA 16502-2665

DIEFFENBACH, ALICEJEAN, artist; b. Nashville, Dec. 18, 1931; d. Bailey Everette and Elizabeth R. (Vinson) Thompson; m. Otto Weaver Dieffenbach, June 14, 1952; children: Otto W. III, Linda Madeleine Harrison, Susanne Elizabeth Hume. AB in Art History, Duke U., 1952; MS in Edn. Adminstrn., Johns Hopkins U., 1974. Soprano Balt. Opera Co., 1956-58; starring roles Met. Mus. Theatre, Actors Theatre, Balt., 1958-75; head art dept., tchr. Cockeysville (Md.) H.S., 1965-79; owner, designer Design Plus, Balt., 1972-80; real estate salesperson Merrill-Lynch/Cousins, Miami, Fla., 1980-82, Dieffenbach Real Estate, Rancho Santa Fe, Calif., 1982-89; artist, painter Solana Beach, Calif., 1992—. Soprano soloist Towson (Md.) Presbyn. Ch., 1955-80, Plymouth Congl. Ch., Coconut Grove, Fla., 1980-82, The Village Ch. Presby., Rancho Santa Fe, 1982—, The Handel Choir Balt., The Bach Soc. Balt.; soloist, performer San Diego Chamber Orch., 1985, 86, 89, 90, 91; soloist Balt. Symphony Orch.; solo show Rancho Santa Fe Libr., 1996. Mem. Rancho Santa Fe Libr. Guild, 1982—, Rep. Women, Rancho Santa Fe. Recipient 1st, 2d, and 3d Hon. Mention awards various juried art exhbns., 1993—. Mem. Artists Equity Assn. (treas. 1994-96), San Diego Art Inst. (numerous awards), San Dieguito Art Guild (numerous awards), San Diego Mus. Art Guild, San Diego Mus. Contemporary Art, Rancho Santa Fe Garden Club, Oil Painters Am., Rancho Santa Fe Art Guild. Presbyterian. Avocations: writing, needlepoint, dancing, traveling. Home: PO Box 261 Rancho Santa Fe CA 92067-0261 Studio: 444S Cedros Ave Solana Beach CA 92075-1915

DIEHL, CAROL LOU, library director, retired, library consultant; b. Milw., Aug. 10, 1929; d. Gilbert Fred and Erna Lou (Braeger) Doepke; m. Russell Phillip Diehl, Aug. 8, 1953; children: Holly Lou Diehl Nelson, Jeffrey Phillip. BS, U. Wis., Madison, 1951; MA, U. Wis., Oshkosh, 1971. Tchr. English, libr. Port Washington (Wis.) High Sch., 1951-54, Minoqua (Wis.) High Sch., 1954-55; libr. Ozaukee High Sch., Fredonia, Wis., 1964-65, Vernon County Tchrs. Coll., Viroqua, Wis., 1965-67; libr. media coord. Manawa (Wis.) Sch. Dist., 1973-77; dir. libr. media svcs. Sch. Dist. of New London, Wis., 1977-95; ret., 1995; lectr. U. Wis., Oshkosh, 1993, 95—; v.p. Coun. on Libr. and Network Devel., Madison, 1979; pres. Lake Forest Bd. Dirs., Eagle River, Wis., 1987-89; libr. cons. Thern Design Ctrs. Inc., 1994. Author: (with others) School Library Media Annual, 1985-87; news corr. Appleton (Wis.) Post Crescent, 1971-81; contbr. articles to profl. jours. Past mem. Fox Valley Symphony League; mem. exec. com. Waupaca County Grand Ole Party, chair, 1994-97, vice chmn., 1991-94; del.-at-large White House Conf. Libr. and Info. Svcs., 1991; trustee Sturm Meml. Libr., 1996—; mem. bd. edn. Sch. Dist. of Manawa, 1997—. Named Wis. Sch. Libr. Media Specialist of Yr. Assn. Ednl. Comm. and Tech., 1992. Mem. ALA (councilor-at-large 1998—, legis. com. 1986-91, ALA White House Conf. Libr. and Info. Svcs., 1995—, chairperson, 1992-95, legis. assembly chairperson 1989-90, membership com. 1995-99, ALTA legis. com. 1998-99, chair, 1999—), AASL (legis. chmn. 1987-95, planning and implementation task force White House Conf. 1990-92), Wis. Libr. Assn. (fed. rels. coord. 1990-91), Assn. Wis. Sch. Adminstr., Wis. Edn. Media Assn. (legis. com. 1986-93, Excellence award 1992), Futurae Club of Manawa, Phi Delta Kappa. Republican. Lutheran.

DIEHL, DEBORAH HILDA, lawyer; b. Troy, N.Y., Feb. 13, 1951; d. Warren S. and Norma K. (Apple) D.; m. Peter W. Hoffman, Feb. 29, 1980; 1 child, Alexandra Ellen. Student, U. de Rouen, France, 1971-72; BA, St. Lawrence U., 1973; JD, Syracuse U., 1976; postdoctoral, George Washington U., 1978-79. Bar: N.Y. 1977, D.C. 1981, Ohio 1982, Md. 1987. Atty. USDA, Washington, 1976-81; assoc. Thompson, Hine & Flory, Columbus, Ohio, 1981-87; assoc. Semmes, Bowen & Semmes, Balt., 1987-90, ptnr., 1990-95; ptnr. Whiteford, Taylor & Preston, Balt., 1995—. Pres. Mt. Royal Improvement Assn., 1995-97; pres. Midtown Cmty. Benefits Dist. Mgmt. Authority, 1998—, dir., 1995—; participant Leadership Md., 1997. Mem. ABA, Md. State Bar Assn., Bar Assn. City Balt. Avocations: gardening, running, historic preservation.

DIEHL, DIGBY ROBERT, journalist; b. Boonton, N.J., Nov. 14, 1940; s. Edwin Samuel and Mary Jane Shirley (Ellsworth) D.; m. Kay Beyer, June 6, 1981; 1 dau., Dylan Elizabeth. A.B. in Am. Studies (Henry Rutgers scholar), Rutgers U., 1962; M.A. in Theatre Arts, UCLA, 1966, postgrad., 1966-69. Editor Learning Center, Inc., Princeton, N.J., 1962-64; dir. research Creative Playthings, Los Angeles, 1964-66; editor Coast mag., Los Angeles, 1966-68, Show mag., Los Angeles, 1968-69; book editor Los Angeles Times, 1969-78; v.p., editor-in-chief Harry N. Abrams, Inc., N.Y.C., 1978-80; book editor L.A. Herald Examiner, 1981-86; movie critic, entertainment editor Sta. KCBS TV, Los Angeles, 1986-88; book columnist Playboy mag., Pasadena, Calif., 1988—; lit. corr. ABC-TV Good Morning America, N.Y.C., 1989—; instr. journalism UCLA, 1969-78; jurist Nat. Book Awards, 1972, Internat. Imitation Hemingway Contest, 1978—; mem. nominating com. Nat. Medal for Lit., 1972-75; v.p. Nat. Book Critics Cir., 1975-78, bd. dirs., 1981-87; jurist Am. Book Awards, 1981-85, v.p. programming, 1984-86; bd. dirs. Sun Valley Writers Conf., 1995—. Author: Supertalk: Extraordinary Conversations, 1974, Front Page, 1981, Tales From The Crypt: The Official Archives, 1996; author: (with Duane Clarridge) A Spy For All Seasons, 1996; lit. columnist IBM/Prodigy, 1987-96; columnist Modern Maturity, 1987—, Excite, 1995-97. Trustee KPFK-Pacifica Found. Recipient: Irita Van Doren award, 1977. Mem. AAUP, PEN (pres. L.A. Ctr. 1987, v.p. treas. 1988—), AFTRA, Am. Soc. Journalists and Authors, Writers Guild Am., Phi Beta Kappa, Phi Sigma Delta. Home: 788 S Lake Ave Pasadena CA 91106-3948*

DIEHL, DONNA RAE, education educator; b. Johnstown, Pa., Sept. 25, 1954; d. G. Edwin and Hilda M. (Batley) D. BS in Edn., Geneva Coll., 1976; MEd, U. Pitts., 1984; EdD, U. Ga., 1997. Cert. tchr., Pa. Substitute 2d and 3d grade tchr. Portage (Pa.) Elem./Mid. Sch., 1976-77, 3d grade tchr., 1977-86, 2d grade tchr., 1986-87; instr. Toccoa Falls (Ga.) Coll., 1987—; spkr. in field. Editor (newsletter) Chalk Talk; contbr. revs., articles to profl. publs., and ch. newsletter. Mem. choir First Alliance Ch., Toccoa, 1989-92, 96—; storyteller Stephens County Schs., Toccoa. Grantee U. Ga., 1991-92, Ga.'s Educators Profl. Devel. Mem. Internat. Reading Assn., Nat. Coun. Tchrs. English, Ga. Assn. Colls. Tchr. Edn., Ga. Assn. Ind. Colls. Tchr. Edn. Office: Toccoa Falls Coll PO Box 875 Toccoa Falls GA 30598

DIEHL, HARRY ALFRED, chemist, genealogist; b. York, Pa., Mar. 2, 1923; s. Ralph Eugene and Anna (Danner) D.; m. Margaret Marie Ehrhart, June 28, 1945; children: Rodney Eugene, Diane Susan Foster, Lori Elaine Vogan, Brian Eric. BA, Gettysburg Coll., 1948; MS, Pa. State U., 1951; MEd, U. Del., 1976. Tchr. chemistry William Penn Sr. High Sch., York, Pa., 1948-50; rsch. chemist E.I. DuPont, Wilmington, Del., 1951-83; genealogist pvt. practice, Wilmington, Del., 1977—. Author: Ancestors and Descendants of Francis & Lucinda Cornbower, 1982, Diehl-Deal-Dill-Dale Families of America, Vol. I, 1989. Cub Scout leader Boy Scouts Am., Wilmington, 1958-65, asst. scoutmaster, 1970-82; trustee, elder Presbyn. Ch., Wilmington, 1957-62, 95—. Sgt. USAF, 1941-46. Mem. Pa. Genealogy Soc. (bd. dirs. 1983-84), Del. Genealogy Soc. (bd. dirs., pres. 1981-82), Genealogy Soc. South Ctrl. Pa. (pres. 1992-93), Md. Genealogy Soc., Masons. Avocations: mineralogy, history.

DIEHL, JAMES HARVEY, church administrator; m. Dorothy Diehl; 4 children. BA, Olivet Nazarene U., 1959; DD, N.W. Nazarene Coll., 1960. Adminstr. MidAm. Nazarene Coll., 1973-76; dist. supt. Ch. of Nazarene, Nebr. and Colo., 1979-89; pastor Atlanta First Ch., 1976-79, Nazarene chs. in Iowa, Denver First Ch. of Nazarene, 1989-93; gen. supt. Ch. of the Nazarene, Kansas City, Mo., 1993—. Contbr. articles to Herald of Holiness, Preacher's Mag., Bread, World Mission, others; condr. daily radio program, weekly TV broadcast. Bd. trustees MidAm. Nazarene Coll., Nazarene Theol. Sem., Nazarene Bible Coll., N.W. Nazarene Coll.; chmn. bd. N.W. Nazarene Coll. Office: Ch of the Nazarene 6401 Paseo Blvd Kansas City MO 64131-1213

DIEHL, LOUIS F., hematologist; b. Trenton, N.J., Apr. 8, 1948; s. Louis and Anna D.; m. Anna Mae, Dec. 3, 1973; children: Megan, Erin. BS, Georgetown U., 1970, MD, 1975. Hematologist, oncologist Walter Reed Army Med. Ctr., Washington, 1975—.

DIEHL, PHILIP N., federal government official; m. Jacquita Pearson; children: Michael, Alex. BA, Austin Coll., Sherman, Tex.; MA in Govt., U. Tex. Dir. telephone regulation Tex. Pub. Utility Commn., Austin; v.p. regulatory affairs Internat. Telecharge Inc., Dallas; staff dir. U.S. Senate Fin.; legis. dir., counselor Senator Lloyd Bentsen; chief of staff U.S. Dept. of the Treasury, Washington, to 1994; dir. U.S. Mint, Washington, 1994—. Office: US Mint Judiciary Sq Bldg 633 3d St NW Washington DC 20220

DIEHL, RICHARD KURTH, retail business consultant; b. Chgo., July 6, 1935; s. George Henry and Agnes Martha (Kurth) D.; m. Barbara Louise Clark, June 9, 1957; children—Clark Kurth, Scott Richard, Stacy Louise. B.A., Beloit Coll., 1957; postgrad., Harvard U., 1957-58; M.B.A., U. Chgo., 1959. With brand mgmt. staff Procter & Gamble, Cin., 1959-62; v.p., account supr. Needham, Harper & Steers, Chgo., 1963-68; Dir. mktg. Kimberly-Clark Corp., Neenah, Wis., 1968-70; pres., chief exec. officer Purnell, Inc., Santa Monica, Calif., 1970-72; v.p., chief operating officer Theta Cable TV, Santa Monica, 1972-74; exec. v.p., chief savs. officer Western Fed. Savs. and Loan Assn., Los Angeles, 1974-80; exec. v.p., a founding officer Centurion Savs. and Loan Assn., Century City, Calif., 1980-82; founder Diehl & Assocs., Los Angeles, 1983—; pres., CEO Stockwell and Binney/Royale, La Habra, Calif., 1992—. Mem. Citizens Adv. Council Los Angeles Schs., 1970-72. Woodrow Wilson fellow, 1957-58; Harvard Austin fellow, 1957-58; Sears Roebuck Found. fellow, 1958-59. Mem. Phi Beta Kappa, Sigma Alpha Epsilon. Clubs: Riviera Tennis, Santa Monica Tennis Patrons. Lodge: Rotary. Home: 841 Bienveneda Ave Pacific Palisades CA 90272-2310

DIEHL, STEPHEN ANTHONY, human resources consultant; b. N.Y.C., Mar. 15, 1942; s. Anthony Stephen and Paula (Kula) D.; m. Barbara Lynn Marschman, Aug. 3, 1968. BS, L.I. U., 1963; postgrad. in bus., NYU, 1967-73. V.p. mktg. dir. Green Point Savs. Bank, Bklyn., 1969-77; sr. v.p., human resources dir. Green Point Bank, N.Y.C., 1977-95; dir. Human Resources N.Y. Road Runners Club (N.Y. City Marathon), 1996—; officer, dir. Soc. for Human Resources Mgmt., N.Y. chpt., 1995—. Mem. Savs. Banks Mktg. Forum N.Y. State (chmn. 1973-74), N.Y.C. Mktg. Forum (chmn. 1975-76), Human Resources Officers Forum (chmn. 1980-81), Savs. Banks Officers Forum (pres. 1986-87). Avocations: photography, video, stereo. Office: NY Road Runners Club 9 E 89th St New York NY 10128-0602

DIEHL, WILLIAM HENRY S., civil engineer; b. Washington, Dec. 14, 1930; s. John Richard Wilmot and Consuelo (Seggerman) D.; m. F. Wietske Hoogland, Sept. 7, 1968 (dec. Oct. 1993). BS in Civil Engring., Stanford (Calif.) U., 1952; MS, U. Tex., 1959; diploma in hydraulic engr., Internat. Inst. Hydraulic and Sanitary Engring., Delft, The Netherlands, 1960, diploma in sanitary engring., 1976. Registered profl. engr., Tex. Civil engr. Lance Engrs., Inc., El Paso, 1954-56, Tex. Hwy. Dept., El Paso, 1956-58, Morrison-Knudsen, San Francisco, 1961, Fed. Power Commn., Washington, 1962-76, Fed. Energy Regulatory Commn., Washington, 1985—; hydraulic engr. U.S. Geol. Survey, Austin, Tex., 1958-59; sr. civil engr. Haskoning Engrs., Nijmegen, The Netherlands, 1977-80; mem. Internat. Niagara Working Com., Buffalo, N.Y., 1972-76. 1st lt. U.S. Army, 1952-54, Korea. Mem. ASCE, U.S. Com. Large Dams, Am. Legion. Roman Catholic. Home: 13805 Piscataway Dr Fort Washington MD 20744-6637 Office: Fed Energy Regulatory Commn 888 1st St NE Washington DC 20426-0002

DIEHM, JAMES WARREN, lawyer, educator; b. Lancaster, Pa., Nov. 6, 1944; s. Warren G. and Verna M. (Hertzler) D.; m. Cathleen M. Hohmeier; children: Elizabeth Ann, Rebecca Jane. B.A., Pa. State U., 1966; J.D., Georgetown U., 1969. Bar: D.C. 1969, V.I. 1975, Pa. 1988. Asst. U.S. atty. Washington, 1970-74; asst. atty. gen. Atty. Gen.'s Office U.S. V.I., St. Croix, 1974-76; from assoc. to ptnr. Isherwood, Hunter & Diehm, St. Croix, 1976-83; U.S. atty. U.S. V.I., 1983-87; prof. law Widener U., 1987—; bar examiner U.S. V.I. Bar, 1979-87. Mem. ABA. Republican. Lutheran. Office: Widener U Sch Law 3800 Vartan Way Harrisburg PA 17110-9742

DIEHM, JAMIE RENEE, company official; b. Aug. 9, 1972. BA in Journalism, BA in English, Ind. U., 1994. Asst. spl. events planner, media liaison Little Professor Book Co., Ft. Wayne, Ind., 1994-95; copywriter Adcetera, Ft. Wayne, 1995; account mgr. Borshoff-Johnson & Co., Indpls., 1995-98; publs. mgr. Conner Prairie, Fishers, Ind., 1998—. E-mail: jdiehm@connerprairie.org. Home: 5172 N Broadway St Indianapolis IN 46205

DIEHR, DAVID BRUCE, social service administrator; b. Toledo, Ohio, June 4, 1939; s. Harlan E. and Lillis R. (Consaul) D.; m. Kathryn D. Welsh, Apr. 2, 1966; 1 child, Erik W. AB, Coll. William and Mary, 1961; postgrad., George Williams Coll., Chgo., 1961-63. Phys. dir. YMCA of Xenia-Greene County, Xenia, Ohio, 1964-68, YMCA of Joliet, Ill., 1968-74; exec. dir. N.W. YMCA of San Antonio, Tex., 1974-77; gen. dir. YMCA of Ctrl. Tex., Waco, 1977-86; group v.p. YMCA of Tucson, 1987-95; nat. field cons. YMCA of the USA-West, San Mateo, Calif., 1995—; treas., bd. dirs. Calif. Collaboration for Youth, Sacramento, 1995—. Mem. Assn. Profl. Dirs. (chpt. prs. 1980-83, dist. v.p. 1983-86), U.S. Power Squadron, Omicron Delta Kappa. Republican. Presbyterian. Avocations: sailing, tractor restoration. Office: YMCA of the USA 1650 S Amphlett Blvd Ste 314 San Mateo CA 94402-2516

DIEKEMA, ANTHONY J., college president emeritus, educational consultant; b. Borculo, Mich., Dec. 3, 1933; m. Jeane Waanders, Dec. 20, 1957; children: Douglas, David, Daniel, Paul, Mark, Maria, Tanya. BA, Calvin Coll., Grand Rapids, Mich., 1956; MA in Sociology and Anthropology, Mich. State U., 1958, PhD in Sociology, 1965. Field interviewer Bur. Bus. Research Mich. State U., East Lansing, 1955-56, asst. dir. housing, 1957-59; instr., lectr. sociology and anthropology Mich. State U., 1959-64, admissions counselor, 1959-61, asst. dir. admissions and scholarships, 1961-62, asst. registrar, 1962-64; asst. dean admissions and records, research assoc. in med. edn. and asst. prof. sociology U. Ill. Med. Center, Chgo., 1964-66; dir. admissions and records, asst. prof. sociology and edn. U. Ill. Med. Center, 1966-70, assoc. chancellor, asso. prof. med. edn., 1970-76; pres. Calvin Coll., 1976-96, pres. emeritus; mem. adv. bd. NBD Grand Rapids, 1983-95. Trustee Blodgett Meml. Med. Center, Grand Rapids, 1979-91; bd. dirs. Met. YMCA, 1979-93, Project Rehab, 1978-84; treas. Back-to-God Hour Radio Com., 1970-76; chmn. Synodical Com. on Race Relations, 1973-75; pres. Strategic Christian Ministry Found., 1969-73; mem. bd. curators Trinity Christian Coll., 1969-73, chmn., 1972-73, mem. presdl. search com., 1972-73, NCAA coun. 1983-87, Pres'. commn. 1987-91. Mem. Am. Assn. Pres.'s Ind. Coll. and Univs. (bd. dirs. 1978-84, 88-91), Nat. Assn. Ind. Colls. and Univs. (bd. dirs. 1991-94), Assn. Ind. Colls. and Univs. Mich. (exec. com. 1979-84), Am. Assn. Higher Edn., Am. Sociol. Assn., Soc. Health and Human Values, Soc. Values in Higher Edn., Nat. League Nursing (accreditation com. 1974-79), Alpha Kappa Delta, Rotary. Office: Calvin Coll Grand Rapids MI 49546

DIEKMANN, GILMORE FREDERICK, JR., lawyer; b. Evansville, Ind., Jan. 14, 1946; s. Gilmore Frederick Sr. and Mabel Pauline (Daniel) K.; m. Katherine Etta Westlake, July 12, 1969; children: Anne Westlake, Andrew Gilmore, Matthew Frederick. BSBA, Northwestern U., 1968, JD, 1971. Bar: Calif. 1972, U.S. Dist. Ct. Calif. (no., ea. and cen. dists.) Calif. 1972, U.S. Ct. Appeals (9th cir.) 1972, U.S. Supreme Ct. 1978. Assoc. Bronson, Bronson & McKinnon, San Francisco, 1971-78, ptnr. labor and employment law, 1979-99, chmn., mng. ptnr., 1991-93, chmn. labor, employment dept., 1993-99; ptnr. Seyfath, Shaw, Fairweather & Geraldson, San Francisco, 1999—. Author and speaker in field. Mem. ABA, American Bar Assn., Def. Rsch. Inst., Am. Emp. Law Coun., Order of Coif. Republican. Lutheran. Home: 51 Winship Ave Ross CA 94957 Office: Seyfarth Shaw Fairweather & Geraldson 101 California St Ste 2900 San Francisco CA 94111-5858

DI ELEUTERIO, JAMES, state official; b. Trenton, N.J., Feb. 9, 1953. BSA, Rider Coll., Lawrenceville, N.J., 1979; MBA, Widener U., Radner, Pa., 1987. Treas. State of N.J., Trenton, 1997—. Office: State of New Jersey Treasury Dept St HouseCN002 121 W State St Trenton NJ 08608-1101

DIELMAN, RAY WALTER, radiologic scientist, medical herbalist; b. Napoleon, Ohio, Dec. 25, 1938; s. Walter Carl and Gail Ann (Fenstermaker) D.; m. Diane Tahy, June 1961 (div. 1968); children: Joseph Scott, David Jon; m. Beverly Beavers, Oct. 16, 1994. Student, Defiance Coll., 1956-59; radiologic technologist diploma, St. Joseph Hosp. Sch., Ft. Wayne, Ind., 1962; nuclear medicine technologist cert., U. Mich., 1962; OPM, Harvard U., 1975; doctor of Naturopathy, Trinity Coll. Natural Health, 1997. Cert mgmt. cons., radiologic, nuclear medicine technologist. Supr. nuclear medicine U. Mich. Hosp., Ann Arbor, 1962-63; dir. nuclear medicine Mercy Hosp & Med. Ctr., Chgo., 1963-64; cons., nuclear medicine Picker Corp., White Plains, N.Y., 1964-67; pres. Dielman Cons., Inc., Chgo., 1967-88; dir. dept. of radiology Loyola U. Med. Ctr., Chgo., 1980-83; co-owner Island Cinema & Theatre, Sanibel Isle, Fla., 1983-87; mgr. Fla. Dept. Health Bur. Radiation Control, Tampa, 1988—; assoc. mem., com. Conf. Radiation Control Program Dirs., Frankfort, Ky., 1989-96; vice chmn. Radiation Control Rsch. and Edn. Found.; del. Internat. Com. of Radionuclide Metrology, London, 1976-85; mem. Manatee County Health Care Adv. Bd., 1995—. Co-editor/author: Essentials Nuclear Medicine Technology, 1970; contbr. articles to profl. jours. Recipient scholarship Am. Cancer Soc., 1962. Avocations: tennis, golf, sailing, skiing, travel. Home: PO Box 778 Anna Maria FL 34216-0778

DIEM, DEBRA R., elementary school educator; b. Ronceverte, W.Va., Dec. 31, 1956; d. Aubrey Wayne and Nancy E. (Feamster) Rickman; m. Dennis Keith Diem, Mar. 15, 1980; children: Laura, Nicole. BS in Elem. Edn. cum laude, Bluefield (W.Va.) State Coll., 1984; BS in Learning Disabilities, W.Va. Coll. Grad. Studies, Institute; AAS, Greenbrier Community Coll., Lewisburg, W.Va., 1977; MA in Learning Disabilities, U. W.Va., 1991. Tchr. 2d grade Greenbrier County Schs., Lewisburg. Mem. W.Va. Edn. Assn., Greenbrier County Edn. Assn., Greenbrier County Reading Assn. Home: HC 30 Box 106 Caldwell WV 24925-9708

DIEMAND, KIM EUGENE, human resources executive; b. Camden, N.J., Nov. 5, 1953; s. Eugene August and Ruth (Maute) D.; m. Jan Elizabeth Ratcliffe, Oct. 7, 1975; children: Megan, Michael, Andrew. AA, Coll. DuPage, 1977; BS, No. Ill. U., 1978. Office mgr. Diemand Printing Co., Chgo., 1978-79; indsl. engr., estimator Henry Pratt Co., Aurora, Ill., 1979-80; personnel mgr. Marmon/Keystone Corp., Lemont, Ill., 1980-81; plant personnel mgr. Gen. Mills Inc. Package Foods Div., Lodi, Calif., 1981-83; employee rels. mgr. The Gorton Group div. Gen Mills, Gloucester, Mass., 1983-90; dir. human resources McKesson Drug Co., Romeoville, Ill., 1990-94; distbn. ctr. mgr. McKesson Drug Co., St. Peters, Mo., 1994-96; v.p., gen. mgr. nat. customer support ctr. McKesson Drug Co., Westlake, Tex., 1996-97; v.p. human resources Tri-Gas Indsl. Gases, Irving, Tex., 1997-99; v.p., gen. mgr. D&K Healthcare Resources, Inc., Mpls., 1999—. Chief spokesman, mem. personnel bd. Town of Essex (Mass.), 1985-86. Sgt. USMC, 1971-75; dir. youth ministry Crown of Life Luth. Ch., Colleyville, Tex., 1997-98. Mem. Am. Soc. Human Resource Mgrs., Rolling Green Country Club. Office: D&K Healthcare Resources Inc 800 N Third St Minneapolis MN 55401 Address: 708 Heatherglen Dr Southlake TX 76092-8611

DIEMER, ARTHUR WILLIAM, real estate executive; b. Queens County, N.Y., Nov. 5, 1925; s. John and Elizabeth (Bernhard) D.; m. Opal Louise Droddy, Mar. 25, 1950; children: Paul A., Liddia E. Student, CCNY, 1943, St. Lawrence Univ., Canton, N.Y., 1944; BS, Dartmouth Coll., 1947; MS, Thayer Sch. of Engring., Hanover, N.H., 1948. Civil engr. Union Carbide, S. Charleston, W.Va., 1948-56; bldg. mgr. Union Carbide Realty Div., N.Y.C., 1960-67; v.p., pres. Cabot & Forbes Property Mgmt. Co., Boston, 1967-75; pres. Renaissance Ctr. Mgmt. Co., Detroit, 1975-77; co-founder, v.p. Renaissance Properties, Inc., Charlotte, N.C., 1977-84; pres. The Realty Evaluation Group, Inc., Charlotte, N.C., 1985—; Founder, pres. Discovery Assocs., Charlotte 1985—; mem. adv. commn. Ctr. for Bldg. Tech., U.S. Commerce Dept. Washington 1975-76, ad hoc com. U.S. Dept. Energy, Washington, 1974. Author articles in profl. jours. Incorporated Village of Bellerose, N.Y. commr. of parks, commr. of pub. works, elected trustee; bd. dirs. Lutheran Social Svcs., Detroit, 1976-77, Family Housing Svcs., Charlotte 1979-81. Mem. Internat. Grapho Analysis Soc., Dartmouth Club of Charlotte (pres. 1993-94). Republican. Lutheran. Home and Office: 4337 Silo Ln Charlotte NC 28226-5504

DIEMER, EMMA LOU, composer, music educator; b. Kansas City, Mo., Nov. 24, 1927; d. George Willis and Myrtle (Casebolt) D. MusB, Yale U., 1949, MusM, 1950; PhD, Eastman Sch. Music, 1960. Composer-in-residence Arlington (Va.) Schs., 1959-61; composer, cons. pub. schs., Arlington and Balt., 1964-65; prof. theory and composition U. Md., College Park, 1965-70, U. Calif., Santa Barbara, 1971-91; organist Ch. of the Reformation, Washington, 1962-71, Ch. of Christ, Santa Barbara, 1973-84, 1st Presbyn. Ch., Santa Barbara, 1984—. Composer of over 100 choral and instrumental compositions including Music for Woodwind Quartet, 1976, Four Poems of Alice Meynell for Soprano and Chamber Ensemble, 1977, Symphony No. 2, 1980, Suite for Orchestra, 1981, Suite of Homages, 1985, Church Rock, 1986, Variations for Piano, 4 Hands, 1987, String Quartet No. 1, 1987, Serenade for String Orch., 1988, Concerto for Marimba, 1990, Concerto for Piano, 1991, Sextet, 1992, Four Biblical Settings for Organ, 1992, Fantasy for Piano, 1993, Kyrie for Mixed Chorus, Organ, and Piano - 4 Hands, 1993, Santa Barbara Overture, 1995, Gloria for Mixed Chorus, 2 Pianos and Percussion, 1996, Psalm 122 for Bass Trombone and Organ, Psalm 121 for Organ, Brass and Percussion, Psalms for Flute and Organ, Psalms for Trumpet and Organ, Psalms for Percussion and Organ, 1998; composer-in-residence Santa Barbara Symphony, 1990-92. Fulbright scholar, 1952-53; grantee Ford Found. Young Composers, 1959-61, Kindler Found. Commn., 1963, Nat. Endowment Arts, 1980-81; Kennedy Ctr. Friedham award, 1992. Mem. ASCAP (ann. awards 1962—), Am. Guild Organists (composer of yr. 1995), Internat. Alliance for Women in Music, Am. Music Ctr., Mu Phi Epsilon (award of merit 1995). Democrat. Presbyterian. Avocations: reading, electronic and computer music. *A composer who succeeds in some measure must have talent, encouragement, strong self-motivation, an almost obsessive need for self-expression through music, a belief in the importance of one's own contribution, the ability to appraise one's own work, the desire, at least part of the time, to communicate.*

DIENER, BERT, former food broker, artist; b. N.Y.C., Mar. 21, 1915; s. Frederick and Lena (Rublin) D.; m. Hermine Van Baarn, Nov. 14, 1940; children: Francine Carol, Fredric Jay. BS, U. Va., 1937. Ptnr. Gold-Rose Diener, N.Y.C., 1939-45, Rich-Diener, N.Y.C., 1945-63; pres. Pratico-Diener Corp., Fort Lee, N.J., 1963-68; exec. v.p. Pratico, Diener & Stein, Inc., 1968-69, Diener & Stein, Inc., 1969-74; chief oper. officer Diener-Stein Sales, 1974-89; pres. Quad Media Concepts, 1978-79, Bert Diener, Inc., 1980-89; pres. Telestar Products Corp., Grocery Industry Svcs., Inc., Living Arts Force, chmn. emeritus; mem. mktg. adv. com. U.S. Banknote Corp.; contract adminstr. N.Y.C. Artists' Housing. One-man shows include Southold Gallery, L.I., 1967, Frankel Gallery, Roslyn, N.Y., 1968, Ctr. Art Gallery, N.Y.C., 1970, three man show, Sears-Vincent Price Gallery, Chgo., 1969; exhibited in group shows at Grand Prix Internat. D'Art Contemparin De la Principaute de Monaco, 1970, Sculpture Ctr., 1984-88, Nat. Arts Club, 1984, 87, Norton Gallery Art, Artists' Guild, 1989, 90, 92; pub. editor: Grocery Industry Directory Met. N.Y., 1961-65. Coord. Save Outdoor Sculpture, West Palm Beach and Palm Beach. Recipient Pres. Reagan's Commendation for community svc., 1984, 1st place awards Allied Artists of Am. for portrait sculpture, 1987, Artists Showplace Coop. for sculpture, 1992, Wisdom award of honor Wisdom Hall of Fame. Mem. Am. Arbitration Assn., Grocery Mfrs. Reps. N.Y.C. (past pres.), Nat. Food Brokers Assn. (past dir.), Assn. Food Distbrs. (past chmn. brokers divsn.), Artists Welfare Fund (past pres.), N.Y. Artists Equity (past pres.), Fine Arts Fedn. of N.Y. (past pres.), Sculpture Ctr. (past pres.), Met. Painters and Sculptors, Youth Art Program (founder, chmn.), Armory Art Ctr. (bd. dirs., instr. sculpture), Palm Beach County Cultural Coun., Mktg. Exec. Club N.Y., Norton Mus., Artists Guild. Home: 4236 Deste Ct Apt 301 Lake Worth FL 33467-4330 *The good that has come into my experience has only been meaningful when I in turn did some good. I am merely a medium through whom the good passes and the goods pass.*

DIENER, BETTY JANE, business educator; b. Washington, Sept. 15, 1940; d. Edward George and Minnie (Feild) D.; m. Robert D. Bell, 1987 (dec. 1993). AB, Wellesley Coll., 1962; MBA, Harvard U., 1964, DBA, 1974. Account exec. Young & Rubicam, Inc., N.Y.C., 1964-70; product mgr. Am. Cyanamid Co., Wayne, N.J., 1970-72; asst. dean, Sch. Bus. Case Western Res. U., Cleve., 1974-79; dean Sch. Bus. Adminstrn., Old Dominion U., Norfolk, Va., 1979-82; sec. commerce and resources Commonwealth of Va., Richmond, 1982-86; prof. mktg. Old Dominion U., Norfolk, Va., 1986-87; provost, vice chancellor acad. affairs U. Mass., Boston, 1987-88, prof. mktg., 1988—, spl. asst. to chancellor econ. devel., 1993-94; pres. Environ. Bus. Coun. New England, Inc., 1995-97. Contbr. articles to profl. publs. Commr. Norfolk Indsl. Devel. Authority, 1979-82; mem. Citizens Coun. for Chesapeake Bay, 1986-87; bd. dirs. Norfolk Conv. and Visitors Bur., 1979-82, Norfolk C. of C., 1979-82, Greater Norfolk Corp., 1986-87, Va. Orch. Group, 1982-87, Va. Stage Co., 1986-87, Karamu House, 1975-79, Womenspace, 1975-79, Rapid Recovery, 1975-79, Woodruff Hosp., 1975-79, Women's City Club Cleve., 1976-79; adviser Jr. Achievement, 1963-64, Plans for Progress, 1968-70, Leadership Met. Richmond, 1980-82; adv. com. on state and local govt. programs John F. Kennedy Sch. Govt., Harvard U., 1986-88; mem. Mass. gov.'s adv. com. on sci. and tech., 1988-90; arbitrator Am. Arbitration Assn., 1991—; mayor's task force empowerment zones, 1994. Named Outstanding Working Woman, Glamour Mag., 1979, one of 10 Outstanding Career Women of Decade, Glamour Mag., 1984; recipient Honor award Soil Conservation Soc., 1984. Democrat. Home: 50 Rogers Ln Eastham MA 02642-2559 Office: U Mass at Boston Harbor Campus Boston MA 02125

DIENER, ERWIN, immunologist; b. Lucerne, Switzerland, Jan. 6, 1932; arrived in Can., 1970; s. Reinhold and Alice (Treichler) D.; m. Eva Schaufelberger, 1957. PhD, U. Zurich, 1963. Rsch. fellow Inst. for Radiobiology, Zurich, 1960-64; Roche fellow Walter and Eliza Hall Inst., Melbourne, Australia, 1964-67, rsch. fellow, 1967-70; prof. U. Alta., Edmonton, Can., 1970-73, prof., head dept. immunology, 1973-88, prof. emeritus, 1989—. Fellow Royal Soc. Can.

DIENER, ROYCE, corporate director, retired healthcare services company executive; b. Balt., Mar. 27, 1918; s. Louis and Lillian (Goodman) D.; m. Jennifer S. Flinton; children: Robert, Joan, Michael, Dianne. BA, Harvard U.; LLD, Pepperdine U. Comml. lending officer, investment banker various locations to 1972; pres. Am. Med. Internat., Inc., Beverly Hills, Calif., 1972-75, pres., chief exec. officer, 1975-78, chmn., chief exec. officer, 1978-85, chmn. bd., 1986-88, chmn. exec. com., 1986-89; bd. dirs. Calif. Econ. Devel. Corp., Acuson, Inc., Advanced Tech. Venture Funds, Am. Health Properties, AMI Health Svcs., plc., Consortium 2000. Author: Financing a Growing Business, 1966, 4th edit., 1995. Bd. visitors Grad. Sch. Mgmt., UCLA; mem. governing bd., UCLA Med. Ctr.; mem. vis. com. Med. Sch. and Sch. Dental Medicine, Harvard U.; bd. dirs. L.A. Philharm. Assn., L.A. chpt. ARC, Heritage Sq. Mus., Santa Monica. Served to capt. USAF, 1942-46, PTO. Decorated D.F.C. with oak leaf cluster. Mem. L.A. C. of C. (bd. dirs.), Calif. C. of C. (bd. dirs.), Calif. Bus. Round Table (bd. dirs.), Harvard Club, Regency Club, Calif. Yacht Club, Riviera Country Club (L.A.), Marks Club (London), Outrigger Canoe Club (Oahu).

DIENER, THEODOR OTTO, plant pathologist; b. Zurich, Switzerland, Feb. 28, 1921; came to U.S., 1949, naturalized, 1955; s. Theodor Emanuel and Hedwig Rosa (Baumann) D.; m. Sybil Mary Fox, May 11, 1968; children by previous marriage: Theodor W., Robert A., Michael S. Diploma, Swiss Fed. Inst. Tech., 1946; DSc, Nat. Swiss Fed. Inst. Tech., 1948. Asst. Swiss Fed. Inst. Tech., Zurich, 1946-48; plant pathologist Swiss Fed. Exptl. Sta., Waedenswil, 1949-50; asst. prof. plant pathology R.I. State U., Kingston, 1950; asst. plant pathologist Wash. State U., Prosser, 1950-55; assoc. plant pathologist Wash. State U., 1955-59; rsch. plant pathologist agr. rsch. svc. USDA, Beltsville, Md., 1959-88, collaborator agr. rsch. svc., 1988-97; prof. botany, sr. staff sci. ctr. agr. biotech./dept. Botany U. Md., College Park, 1988—, acting dir. Ctr. Agr. Biotech., 1991-92, Disting. Univ. prof., 1994—; Disting. prof. U. Md. Biotech. Inst., 1998—; lectr. univs. and rsch. instr.; Regent's lectr. U. Calif., Riverside, 1970; A.W. Dimock lectr. Cornell U., 1975, Andrew D. White prof.-at-large, 1979-81, James Law disting. lectr. N.Y. State Coll. Vet. Medicine, 1981; disting. lectr. Boyce Thomson Inst. for Plant Rsch., 1987, Hong Kong U. Sci. and Tech., 1992; Ernest Everett Just Meml. lectr. Howard U., Washington, 1990; disting. prof. U. Md., Coll. Park, 1994—, Biotech Inst., 1998; guest lectr. Israel Soc. for Microbiology, Rehovot, 1994, Royal Swedish Acad. of Scis., Stockholm, 1997, Swedish Agrl. U., Uppsala, 1997, Royal Netherlands Acad. Arts and Scis., Amsterdam, 1998. Author: Viroids and Viroid Diseases, 1979; editor: The Viroids, 1987; assoc. editor: Virology, 1964-66, 74-76; editor: Jour., 1967-71; mem. editorial com.: Ann. Rev. Phytopathology, 1970-74, Annales de Virologie, 1980-88; contbr. articles to profl. jours.; discoverer novel class of pathogens (viroids), 1971. Recipient Campbell award Am. Inst. Biol. Scis., 1968; Superior Svc. award USDA, 1969, Disting. Svc. award, 1975; Alexander von Humboldt award, 1975, Wolf prize in Agr., 1987, U.S. Nat. medal of Sci., 1987, Gov.'s citation, State of Md., 1988, E.C. Stakman award U. Minn., 1988; inducted into USDA Sci. Hall of Fame, 1989. Fellow Am. Phytopath. Soc. (Ruth Allen award 1976), N.Y. Acad. Scis., Am. Acad. Arts and Scis.; mem. NAS, AAAS, Leopoldina, German Acad. Natural Scientists. Home: 11711 Battersea Dr PO Box 272 Beltsville MD 20704-0272 Office: U Md Ctr for Agrl Biotech College Park MD 20742

DIENSTAG, ELEANOR FOA, corporate communications consultant; b. Naples, Italy; d. Bruno Garibaldi and Lisa (Haimann) Foa; m. Jerome Dienstag (div. 1978); children: Joshua Foa, Jesse Paul. BA, Smith Coll., Northampton, Mass. Asst. editor Random House/Harper & Row, N.Y.C.; editor/writer Monocle Mag., N.Y.C.; cultural columnist Genesee Valley Newspapers, Rochester, N.Y.; sr. mgr., speechwriter Am. Express, N.Y.C., 1978-83; freelance journalist, N.Y.C., 1983—; lit. resident Yaddo Y., 1980, Va. Ctr. for Creative Arts, 1990-91, 95; lectr., book pub. columnist and reviewer in field. Author: Whither Thou Goest, 1976, In Good Company: 125 Years at the Heinz Table, 1994; contbr. articles, essays and feature stories to N.Y. Times, Harper's, N.Y. Observer, McCalls; columnist New Choices Mag., 1994-98. Recipient Merit award for speechwriting Internat. Assn. Bus. Comm., N.Y., 1981-82, Merit award Am. Express Mgmt. Newsletter, 1981, Outstanding Mem. award Women in Comm., 1984. Mem. Am. Soc. Journalists and Authors (pres.). Home and Office: Eleanor Foa Assocs 435 E 79th St New York NY 10021-1034

DIEPHOLZ, DANIEL R., real estate consultant, accountant; b. Calif., Aug. 25, 1964; s. Eugene L. and Ruby J. (Forsch) D. BSBA in Acctg., Valparaiso U., 1985; MS in Real Estate with acad. honors, NYU, 1990. CPA, Calif.; lic. real estate broker, Calif. Auditor Blue Cross Calif., Woodland Hills, 1986-87; corp. fin. assoc., v.p. Bateman Eichler, Hill Richards Inc., L.A., N.Y.C., 1987-89; real estate cons. Price Waterhouse, L.A., 1990-96; founder Diepholz & Co., Indian Wells, Calif., 1996—; chmn. bd. Taos Palms Inc., L.A., 1990—. Mem. ABA, Inst. of Mgmt. Accts., Nat. Assn. Accts. (bd. dirs. 1990-95). Democrat. Avocations: tennis, golf, sailing, swimming. Home: 592 West 1128 South Ovem UT 84058-7391 Office: Brigham Young Univ J Rueben Clark Law Sch Provo UT 84601

DIERCKS, CHESTER WILLIAM, JR., capital goods manufacturing company executive; b. Urbana, Ill., Oct. 15, 1926; s. Chester William and Anna (Gude) D.; children: Chester William, III, Lisa Beth; m. Elaine Hall, Oct. 3, 1992. BS in Gen. Engring., Iowa State U., Ames, 1950; M.S. in Indsl. Mgmt. (Sloan fellow), MIT, 1962. Gen. mgr. med. services, x-ray and splty. transformer div. Westinghouse Electric Co., Pitts., 1950-71; with Allis-Chalmers Corp. (and subs.), 1971-77, dir. Mgmt. Services, v.p., staff exec. Mgmt. Services, group exec., v.p. Indsl. Elec. Group, group exec., v.p. Elec. Products Group, sr. exec. v.p., chief fin. officer, 1976-77; pres., chief exec. officer Siemens-Allis, Inc., 1978-85; pres., chief exec. officer Utility Power Corp., Atlanta, 1978-89, ret., 1989; mem. Industry Sector Adv. Com. to 1974 Trade Reform Act, 1976-77; mem. mgmt. adv. coun. Coll. Mgmt., Ga. Inst. Tech. Bd. dirs. Japan Am. Soc.; mem. bd. visitors Emory U.; trustee emeritus Berry Coll., Mt. Berry, Ga.; past bd. govs. Soc. Alfred P. Sloan Fellows, MIT; elder Peachtree Presbyn. Ch., Atlanta. Served to 1st lt. U.S. Army, 1945-47. Mem. Nat. Elec. Mfrs. Assn. (past bd. govs. mem. long range planning com., chmn. govt. & internat. policy com.), Machinery and Allied Products Inc., Atlanta C. of C. (past exec. com. mem., 1st v.p. bd.

dirs.), Fla. Coun. 100, Fin. Execs. Inst., Capital City Club (Atlanta). Home: 4000 Brookside Dr Roswell GA 30076-5558

DIERCKS, EILEEN KAY, educational media coordinator, elementary education educator; b. Lima, Ohio, Oct. 31, 1944; d. Robert Wehner and Florence (Huckemeyer) McCarty; m. Dwight Richard Diercks, Dec. 27, 1969; children: Roger, David, Laura. BSEd, Bluffton Coll., 1962-66; MS, U. Ill., 1968. Tchr. elem. grades Kettering City Schs. (Ohio), 1966-67; children's libr. St. Charles County, St. Charles, Mo., 1968-69; libr. Rantoul (Ill.) High Sch., 1970-71; elem. tchr. Elmhurst (Ill.) Sch. Dist., 1971-72; media coordinator Plainfield (Ill.) Sch. Dist., 1980—; evaluator Rebecca Caudill Young Readers' Book Award, 1990-97. Founder, treas. FISH orgn., Plainfield, 1975-78; pres. Ch. Women United, 1974; sec. Plainfield Community TV Access League, 1987-89; treas. Plainfield Congl. Ch., 1983-88; bd. dirs. Cub Scouts, 1983-86; leader, mem. Girl Scouts U.S., Plainfield, 1985—; mem. Bolingbrook (Ill.) Community Chorus, 1986-90. Mo. State Libr. scholar, 1967, Naperville chpt. Valparaiso Univ. Guild, treas., 1993-95. Mem. ALA, NEA, Ill. Edn. Assn., Plainfield Assn. Tchrs., Ill. Sch. Libr. Media Assn. (membership chmn. 1992-93, mem. awards com. 1994-96, disaster relief chmn., 1996-97), Plainfield Athletic Club (sec. 1984-86), Rotary (Plainfield chpt., treas. 1994-95, v.p. 1995-96, pres. 1997-98), Delta Kappa Gamma (Beta Rho, treas. 1993-97), Pi Delta, Beta Phi Mu. Home: 13440 S Rivercrest Dr Plainfield IL 60544-8979 Office: Plainfield Sch Dist # 202 611 Fort Beggs Dr Plainfield IL 60544-1877

DIERCKS, FREDERICK OTTO, government official; b. Rainy River, Ont., Can., Sept. 8, 1912; s. Otto Herman and Lucy (Plunkett) D.; m. Kathryn Frances Transue, Sept. 1, 1937; children: Frederick William, Lucy Helena. B.S., U.S. Mil. Acad., 1937; M.S. in Civil Engring., MIT, 1939; M.S. in Photogrammetry, Syracuse U., 1950. Registered profl. engr., D.C. Commd. 2d lt. U.S. Army Corps Engrs., 1937; advanced through grades to col. U.S. Army, 1952; comdg. officer 656th Engr. Topographic Battalion, France and Germany, 1944-45, U.S. Army Map Service, Washington, 1957-61; asst. dir. mapping, charting, and geodesy Def. Intelligence Agy., 1961-63; dep. engr. 8th U.S. Army, Korea, 1963-64; dir. U.S. Army Coastal Engring. Research Ctr., 1964-67; ret., 1967; assoc. dir. U.S. Coast and Geodetic Survey, Rockville, Md., 1967-74; U.S. mem. commn. on cartography Pan Am. Inst. Geography and History, OAS, 1961-67, alt. U.S. mem. directing council, 1970-74, exec. sec. U.S. sect., 1975-87. Decorated Legion of Merit (U.S.), Grand Cross Order of King George II (Greece), Comdr. Most Exalted Order of White Elephant (Thailand), Bronze medal U.S. Dept. Commerce. Fellow ASCE, Soc. Am. Mil. Engrs. (Colbert medal); mem. Am. Soc. Photogrammetry (hon. mem., pres. 1970-71, Luis Struck award), Am. Congress on Surveying and Mapping, N.Y. Acad. Scis., Army-Navy Club, Cosmos Club (Washington), Masons (32 degree), Sigma Xi. Republican. Presbyterian. Home: 9120 Belvoir Woods Pkwy Apt 216 Fort Belvoir VA 22060-2724

DIERCKS, WALTER ELMER, lawyer; b. Irvington, N.J., July 6, 1945; s. Elmer Jules and Evelyn Sophie (Lauster) D.; m. Mary-Jane Atwater, Apr. 16, 1977; children: Emily Jane, Gillian Ruth. B.Chem. Engring., Rensselaer Poly. Inst., 1967; J.D., U. Va., 1972. Bar: Va. 1972, D.C. 1973, U.S. Supreme Ct. 1984. Engr. Bethlehem Steel Corp., Balt., 1968-69; Devel. engr. Diamond Shamrock Corp., Balt., 1969-70; pub. Charlottesville (Va.) Consumer, 1970-72; atty. FTC, Washington, 1972-76; dep. asst. dir. compliance Bur. Consumer Protection, 1976-77; gen. counsel, sec. Washington Star Co., 1977-81; ptnr. Rubin, Winston, Diercks, Harris & Cooke, LLP, Washington, 1981—. Chmn. Alexandria (Va.) Landlord-Tenant Relations Bd., 1976; mem. Alexandria Charter Rev. Commn., 1980-81, Alexandria Democratic Com., 1979-81, 83-85. Recipient award excellence FTC, 1977. Mem. ABA. Unitarian Universalist. Home: 304 Lamond Pl Alexandria VA 22314-4907 Office: 10th Fl 1333 New Hampshire Ave NW Washington DC 20036-1511

DIERDORF, DANIEL LEE (DAN DIERDORF), football analyst, sports commentator, former professional football player; b. Canton, Ohio, June 29, 1949; m. Debbie D.; children: Dana, Kelly (dec.), Katherine; children by previous marriage: Dan, Kristen. Student, U. Mich. Football player St. Louis Cardinals, 1971-83; with Sta. KMOX, St. Louis, 1974—; sports dir. Sta. KMOV-TV, St. Louis, 1987—; football analyst CBS NFL broadcasts, 1985-87, ABC Monday Night Football broadcasts, 1987-99; NHL football analyst CBS Sports, 99—. Mem. NFL Pro-Bowl Team, 1974-78, 80. Office: CBS Sports 51 W 52nd St New York NY 10019*

DIERDORFF, JOHN AINSWORTH, retired editor; b. Chgo., Feb. 1, 1928; s. John and Phoebe (Frary) D. B.A., Yale, 1949. Staff writer Yakima (Wash.) Morning Herald, 1950-52; staff writer Portland Oregonian, 1952-56; copy editor Bus. Week, N.Y.C., 1956-60, asst. editor, 1960-61, asst. mng. editor, 1961-66, 76-77, mng. editor, 1966-69, 77-93, sr. editor, 1969-76. Cons. editor Bus. Week Online, 1994—. Bd. dirs. Bard Coll. Music Festival. Mem. Am. Soc. Mag. Editors, Soc. Profl. Journalists, Coffee House Club, Dutch Treat Club, Overseas Press Club. Home: Grinnell St PO Box 108 Rhinecliff NY 12574-0108

DIERKER, LARRY, professional baseball team manager; b. Hollywood, Calif., Sept. 22, 1946; m. Judy; children: Ashley, Julia, Ryan. With Houston Colt .45s, 1964-77; dir. group and season sales office Houston Astros, 1977-79, mgr., color analyst, 1979—. Named to Nat. League All-Star Team, 1969, 71. Office: Houston Astros PO Box 288 Houston TX 77001-0288*

DIERKS, RICHARD ERNEST, veterinarian, educational administrator; b. Flandreau, S.D., Mar. 11, 1934; s. Martin and Lillian Ester (Benedict) D.; m. Eveline Carol Amundson, July 20, 1956; children—Jeffrey Scott, Steven Eric, Joel Richard. Student, S.D. State U., 1952-55; BS, U. Minn., 1957, DVM, 1959, MPH, 1964, PhD, 1964; MBA, U. Ill., 1985. Diplomate Am. Coll. Vet. Microbiologists, Am. Coll. Vet. Preventive Medicine. Supervisory microbiologist Communicable Disease Ctr., Atlanta, 1964-68; prof. coll. veterinary medicine Iowa State U., Ames, 1968-74; head dept. veterinary sci. Mont. State U., Bozeman, 1974-76; dean Coll. Veterinary Medicine U. Ill., Urbana, 1976-89; dean Coll. Veterinary Medicine U. Fla., Gainesville, 1989-97, prof., dean emeritus, 1997—; mem. tng. grant rev. com. Nat. Inst. Allergy and Infectious Diseases, 1973-74. Contbr. articles on virology, immunology and epidemiology to profl. jours. Served with USPHS, 1964-67. Career Devel. awardee Nat. Inst. Allergy and Infectious Diseases, 1969-74, Nat. Acad. Practitioners, 1995. Mem. Am. Vet. Medicine Assn., Am. Soc. Virology, Am. Soc. Microbiologists, Am. Assn. Immunologists, Am. Assn. Vet. Lab. Diagnosis, Colo. Vet. Medicine Assn., Fla. Vet. Medicine Assn., Soc. Exptl. Biology and Medicine, Gamma Sigma Delta, Phi Kappa Phi, Phi Zeta. Republican. Lutheran. Club: Rotary. Fax: (303) 678-1399. E-mail: redierks@worldnet.att.net. Office: 13651 N 115th St Longmont CO 80501-9303

DIERS, DONNA KAYE, nurse educator; b. Sheridan, Wyo., May 11, 1938; d. Don Carlos and Ilene Helen (Poffenberger) D. BSN, U. Denver, 1960; MSN, Yale U., 1964. Staff nurse Yale Psychiat. Inst., New Haven, 1960-62; mem. faculty Yale U. Sch. Nursing, New Haven, 1964—, Anne W. Goodrich prof., 1979—, dean, 1972-75; dir. Yale Health Services, Cmty. Health Care Plan, New Haven, 1972—. Author: Research in Nursing Practice, 1979. Mem. adv. com. Robert Wood Johnson Found., Princeton, N.J., 1980-86; mem. research rev. com. Nat. Ctr. Health Services Research, Washington, 1981-86. Recipient Henderson award Conn. Nurses Assn., 1980, Disting. Alumna award Yale U. Sch. Nursing, 1983. Fellow Am. Acad. Nursing; mem. Am. Nurses Assn. (J.M. Scott award 1986), Inst. Medicine of Nat. Acad. Scis. Home: 220 Osborn Ave New Haven CT 06511-2848 Office: Yale U Sch Nursing 100 Church St S PO Box 9740 New Haven CT 06536-0740*

DIERS, HANK H., drama educator, playwright, director; b. Dubuque, Iowa, Sept. 23, 1931; s. Hermann Henry and Elfriede Johanna (Langholz) D.; m. Doris Elaine Blumreich, Sept. 5, 1953; children: Daniel, Deborah, John, Alicia, David. BA, Wartburg Coll., 1953; postgrad., U. Dubuque, 1949, Loras Coll., 1953-54; MA, U. Ill., 1957, PhD, 1965; postgrad., Carnegie-Mellon U., 1987. Faculty drama dept. U. Miami, Coral Gables, Fla., 1960-86; chmn. dept. drama U. Miami, 1967-83, prof., 1968-86, dir. univ. theatres, 1973-83; acting dir. theatre, guest cons. SUNY, Old Westbury, 1983-86; dean fine arts and communications Susquehanna U., Selinsgrove, Pa., 1986-98; dir. theatre Florida Gulf Coast U., 1998—; exec. dir. So. Shakespeare Repertory Theatre, Coconut Grove Playhouse, 1961-68; exec. producer Ring Theatre Arts Festival Theatre, 1969—; founder Fumpets Puppet Theatre, ASTA Fair, Amsterdam, Netherlands, 1970. Dir.: (plays) Hamlet, 1968, The Royal Hunt of the Sun, 1968, The Boy Friend, 1971 (winner Am. Coll. Theatre Festival 1972), The Apple Tree, 1970, Jacques Brel (winner Am. Coll. Theatre Festival 1973), Anastasia, Miami New World Festival of Arts, 1982, Glass Menagerie, Equity, L.I., 1986; original producer: plays including Miami; playwright: Doctor, Doctor, 1971, 307 Defense of Hermann Goering, 1972, Mine Eyes Have Seen the Glory, 1976; (playwright, producer) This Is The Lord's Doing, 1987; creator (one man show) Muhlenberg, Middletown and Trappe, 1989, (prodr. PBS Spl., Emmy award nomination) Christmas from Susquehanpa; originator Noel, Cole, Ira and George, Sugden Theatre, Naples, Fla., 1999; exec. dir. Ft. Myers Classical Repertory Theatre, 1999; adaptor Chez Chez The Doctor, Foulds Theatre, Ft. Myers, 1999. Mem. alumni bd. Wartburg Coll., 1968—, Omni Theatre.; Trustee 3rd Century Bicentennial. Served with AUS, 1954-56. Recipient Silver medal for Photography N.Y. World's Fair, 1964, Angel award for Theatre The Miami Herald, 1966, 67, Iron Arrow U. Miami, 1970; Pa. Playwright fellow, 1988-89; grantee Luth. Ch. Am., 1986-87. Mem. Am. Theatre in Higher Edn., Soc. Collegiate Journalism (Medal of Merit 1996), Speech Communications Assn., Southeastern Theatre Conf. (sec. 1962-64), Fla. Theatre Conf. (v.p.), Pa. Theatre Assn., Internat. Coun. Fine Arts Deans, Fla. Arts Congress (dir.), Soc. Collegiate Journalists, Alpha Psi Omega, Alpha Phi Gamma, Omicron Delta Kappa, Alpha Epsilon Rho. Lutheran (Dade County council 1969-72). Office: Florida Gulf Coast U Fort Myers FL 33965-6565

DIERS, JAMES A., director department of neighborhoods Seattle; b. Burnaby, B.C., Can., Dec. 13, 1952; m. Sarah Driggs, 1976. BA in Third World Devel., Grinnell Coll., 1975. Organizer South End Seattle Cmty. Orgn., 1976-82; asst. dir. for comty. affairs Group Health Coop. of Puget Sound, Wash., 1982-88; dir. Dept. of Neighborhoods, Seattle, 1988—. Founder Sr. Caucus and Nuclear Awareness Group, Ptnrs. for Health; dir. Seattle Little City Halls program, mgr. 49 cmty. gardens, and the Historic Preservation Program overseeing adminstrn. of 200 bldgs. in seven hist. dists. Neighborhood Matching Fund under his adminstrn. named one of most innovative local govt. programs in nation, Ford Found. and Kennedy Sch. of Govt. Office: Dept Neighborhoods City of Seattle 700 3rd Ave Ste 400 Seattle WA 98104-1848

DIERSING, CAROLYN VIRGINIA, educational administrator; b. Rushville, Ohio, Sept. 13; d. Carl Emerson and Wilma Virginia (Neel) Deyo; m. Robert J. Diersing, Dec. 22, 1962; children: Robert, Timothy, Charles, Sheila, Christina. BA, Ohio State U., 1963; state cert., Ohio Dominican, 1985. Cert. tchr., Ohio. Libr. St. Mary's Sch., Delaware, Ohio, 1979-87; tech. svcs. asst. Beeghly Libr. Ohio Wesleyan U., Delaware, 1987-90, dir. curriculum resource dept. edn., 1990-96; libr. assoc. Westerville Pub. Libr., 1997—. Contbr. poetry to Voices. Mem. ALA, Del. Area Recovery Resources (bd. dirs. 1994-96, treas. 1995, sec. 1996), Ohio Libr. Coun. Office: Reference Dept 126 S State St Westerville OH 43081-2029

DIESCH, STANLEY LA VERNE, veterinarian, educator; b. Blooming Prairie, Minn., May 16, 1925; s. John Herman and Emma Lillian (Erickson) D.; m. Darlene Ardis Witty; July 22, 1956; children: Lauren, Stephanie. BS, U. Minn., 1951, DVM, 1956, MPH, 1963. Diplomate Am. Coll. Vet. Preventive Medicine and Epidemiology. Asst. prof. Coll. Vet. Med., U. Iowa, Iowa City, 1963-66; asst. prof. U. Minn. Coll. Vet. Medicine, St. Paul, 1966-69, assoc. prof., 1969-73, prof., 1973-95, prof. emeritus, 1995—, dir. internat. programs, 1985-98; prof. Sch. Pub. Health, U. Minn., Mpls., 1973-95; advisor Pan Am. Health Orgn., Washington, 1971—. Contbr. more than 100 articles to profl. jours., 4 chapters to books. Mem. East Buchanan County Sch. Bd., Winthrop, Iowa, 1960; Rep. del., Minn., 1970-85; co-chair nat. Outdoor Speedskating, St. Paul, 1973; bd. dirs. CENSHARE, Mpls., 1981-82; chmn. Veterinarians for Re-election of Durenberger, Minn., 1982, 88; bd. dirs. Minn.-Uruguay Ptnrs. Ams., 1981—, pres., 1990-94, chmn. bd., 1995-99; hon. consul of Uruguay in Minn., 1991-96. Recipient Am. Express award Nat. Assn. Ptnrs. Ams., 1984, Internat. Castricone U. Linkage award Nat. Assn. Ptnrs. Ams., 1998; WHO travel fellow, 1974; grantee EPA, 1968-71, USDA, 1978. Mem. AVMA (Pub. Svc. award 1987, Internat. Vet. Congress award 1998), APHA (coun. 1971-84), U.S. Animal Health Assn. (com. chair, Appreciation award 1986), Internat. Soc. Animal Hygiene (exec. bd. 1988-91, pres. 1991-94), Minn. Vet. Medicine Assn. (com. chair 1970-75, Disting. Svc. award 1996). Lutheran. Avocations: fishing, hunting, boating. Home and Office: 743 Heinel Dr Saint Paul MN 55113-2152

DIESEM, JOHN LAWRENCE, business executive; b. Albuquerque, July 16, 1941; s. Walter Franklin and Glen Ethel (Helpbringer) D.; m. Barbara Jane Willmarth, Feb. 25, 1967 (div. Oct. 10, 1976); m. Kathleen Terese Walsh, Feb. 2, 1979. BA with honors, George Washington U., 1964, MA, 1965; cert. in fin. mgmt., NYU, 1974; advanced profl. cert. in acctg., Pace U., 1992. Cert. prodn. and inventory mgmt., cert. mgmt. cons., cert. mgmt. acct. Group mgr. Electronic Data Sys., N.Y.C., 1970-74; dep. commr. N.Y. State, 1974-75; sr. mgr. Arthur Andersen, N.Y.C., 1975-80; v.p. bus. sys. devel. McGraw-Hill, N.Y.C., 1980-84; sr. mgr. Touche Ross & Co., N.Y.C., 1984-86; dir. strategic sys. planning KPMG Peat Marwick & Co., 1986-89; sr. v.p. sys. tech. Am. Stock Exch., N.Y.C., 1989-92; group v.p. sys. and tech. Simon & Schuster, 1992-93; COO Beta Systems/Kemper Securities, Brookfield, Wis., 1993-95; COO, CFO Guy & O'Neill, Inc., Fredonia, Wis., 1996-99; adj. prof. Bus. Sch., U. Mich., 1995-96, Cardinal Stritch U., Lakeland Coll., 1998—; dir. case study on microcomputer resource ctrs. Bus. Sch., Harvard U., 1981. Dir. George Washington U. dean's alumni adv. bd., 1981-83, mem. bd. vis. sch. bus. pub. mgmt., 1995—. Capt. USAF, 1965-69, Germany, Vietnam; to lt. col. USAFR; grad. Nat. Def. U., Air War Coll., Air Command and Staff Coll., Indsl. Coll. Armed Forces. Decorated Bronze Star, Vietnamese Cross of Gallantry with Palm, Air Force Commendation medal; named Bus. Sch. Alumnus of Yr. George Washington U., N.Y.C., 1991. Mem. Inst. Mgmt. Accts., Am. Prodn. and Inventory Control Soc., Royal Order of Jesters, Am. Arbitration Assn. (panel of arbitrators), N.Am. Coun. Info. Mgmt. Execs., Conf. Bd. (past chmn.), N.Y. Athletic Club, Army and Navy Club (Washington), Columbia Golf and Country Club, Cercle Sportif (Saigon, Vietnam), Nat. Sojourners (life; past pres.), Masons (past master), Grand Lodge Wis. (dist. dep. grand master dist. 10), Scottish Rite, Shriners, Omicron Delta Kappa, Sigma Chi, Phi Eta Sigma, Alpha Kappa Psi. Democrat. Episcopalian. Home: 11921 N Lantern Ln Mequon WI 53092-1567 also: Miller Rd Churchtown NY 12513

DIESTELKAMP, DAWN LEA, county superior court manager; b. Fresno, Calif., Apr. 23, 1954; d. Don and Joy LaVaughn (Davis) D. BS in Microbiology, Calif. State U., Fresno, 1976, MS in Pub. Adminstrn., 1983, cert. in tng. design and mgmt., 1992, MBA, 1995. Lic. clin. lab. technologist, Calif.; cert. clin. lab. dir. Clin. lab. technologist Valley Med. Ctr., Fresno, 1977-82, info. sys. coord., 1983-84, quality control coord., 1984-90, sys. and procedures analyst, 1990-91; sys. and procedures analyst Fresno County Superior Ct., 1991-98, ct. info. sys. mgr., 1998—; mem. faculty U. Phoenix, 1997; instr. Fresno City Coll. Tng. Inst., 1993—; mem. faculty Calif. State U., Fresno, 1999; cons., instr. in field. Mem. Calif. Ct. Clks. Assn. (co-chmn. tng. and cert. com.), Fresno Women's Network (bd. dirs., 2d v.p., historian), Fresno Met. Mus. Soc. Democrat. Office: 1100 Van Ness Ave Fresno CA 93724-0002

DIETCH, HENRY XERXES, judge; b. Bklyn., Nov. 13, 1913; s. Isadore J. and Mary (Krieg) D.; m. Shirley Friedman, Jan. 11, 1941; children: William A., Nancie I., James T. AA, Crane Coll., 1933; JD, John Marshall Law Sch., 1937; grad., Nat. Jud. Coll. Bar: Ill. 1937. Ptnr. firm Davis, Dietch & Ryan, Chgo., 1954-77; assoc. judge Circuit Ct. Cook County, 1977-84; ret., 1984—; hearing officer Dept. of Labor, Chgo., 1937-46; v.p., dir. Unity Savs. of Park Forest, Ill., to 1977, arbitrator, mediator, 1987—. Columnist: Judiciously Speaking, 1979—; Contbr. articles to profl. jours. Mayor City of Park Forest, 1949-55, corp. counsel, 1958-77, vice chmn. Chgo. adv. bd., Salvation Army, 1969-89, hon. bd. dirs. 1989—. Lt. USAAC, 1942-45, ETO. Recipient Citation of Merit John Marshall Law Sch., 1972. Mem. Am., Ill., Chgo. bar assns., Am. Judicature Soc., Nat. Inst. Mcpl. Law Officers. Clubs: Rotary, B'nai B'rith. Office: 18161 Morris Ave Homewood IL 60430-2108

DIETEL, JAMES EDWIN, lawyer, consultant; b. Dallas, Sept. 14, 1941; s. Bernhard Herman and Gladys Ellen D.; m. Elizabeth Nathan, May 9, 1964; 1 child, Elizabeth Lindsay. BSME, So. Meth. U., 1964; JD, George Washington U., 1969; LLM in Internat. Trade, Georgetown U., 1977; MBA, U. Pa., 1992. Bar: D.C. 1971, U.S. Dist. Ct. D.C. 1971, U.S. Ct. Appeals (D.C. cir.) 1975, U.S. Supreme Ct. 1975, Va. 1990. Engr. CIA, Washington, 1964-70; program evaluation officer CIA, 1970-73, assoc. gen. counsel, 1979-80, from assoc. dep. gen. counsel to insp., 1980-93, with office exec. dir., 1993-94; counsel for info. policy, 1994-95; participant ann. jud. conf. U.S. Ct. Appeals (D.C. cir.), 1986; speaker, ltr. and presenter in field. Author: Leading a Law Practice to Excellence, 1992, Sustaining Law Practice Excellence, 1992, Designing Effective Records Retention Compliance Program, 1993, Leaders' Digest: A Review of the Best Books on Leadership, 1995; contbr. articles to profl. jours. Mem. ABA (coun. mem. law practice mgmt. sect., chmn. govt. and pub. sector lawyers divsn.), Coll. Law Practice Mgmt., Cosmos Club, Pi Tau Sigma, Kappa Mu Epsilon, Kappa Alpha.

DIETEL, WILLIAM MOORE, former foundation executive; b. Islip, N.Y., Aug. 14, 1927; s. Frederick William and Zillah Yolanda (Vannuccini) D.; m. Linda Remington, June 16, 1951; children: Elizabeth Lynn, Cynthia Lyon, Lisa Remington, John Frederick, Victoria Moore. AB, Princeton U., 1950; MA, Yale U., 1952, PhD, 1959; postgrad., London U. Inst. Hist. Research, 1953-54. Instr. history U. Mass., Amherst, 1954-59; asst. dean of coll., asst. prof. humanities Amherst Coll., 1959-61; prin. Emma Willard Sch., Troy, N.Y., 1961-70; pres. Rockefeller Bros. Fund, N.Y.C., 1975-87; mem. Shell sustainable energy initiative expert adv. panel, London. Pres. Pierson-Lovelace Found., L.A., Brain Mapping Med. Rsch. Orgn., L.A.; trustee Idyllwild Arts, Calif.; mem. Am. Farmland Trust; mem. Philanthropic Rsch. Adv. Com. GuideStar. Mem. Univ. Club (N.Y.C.), Cosmos Club (Washington). Office: PO Box 309 Flint Hill VA 22627-0309

DIETER, GEORGE ELWOOD, JR., university official; b. Phila., Dec. 5, 1928; m. Nancy Joan Russell, June 21, 1952; children: Carol Joan, Barbara June. B.S. in Metall. Engring, Drexel Inst. Tech., 1950; Sc.D., Carnegie Inst. Tech., 1953. Research engr. E.I. duPont Engring Research Lab., Wilmington, Del., 1955-59; research supr. E.I. duPont Engring Research Lab., 1959-62; prof., head dept. metall. engring. Drexel Inst. Tech., 1962-69; dean Coll. Engring. Drexel U., 1969-73; dir. Processing Research Inst., Carnegie-Mellon U., 1973-77; dean Coll. Engring. U. Md., College Park, 1977-94, dir. continuous quality improvement, 1994—; cons. in field. Author: Mechanical Metallurgy, 1961, 3d edit., 1986, Engineering Design, 1983, 3d edit., 1999. Mem. 1953-55, AUS. Fellow AAAS, Am. Soc. Metals (A.E. White award 1986, Sauver award 1992), Am. Soc. Engring. Edn. (pres. 1993, Lamme award 1996), Minerals, Metals and Materials Soc. (educator award 1994); mem. NAE, AIME, Soc. Mfg. Engrs. (educator award 1987), Fedn. Materials Socs. (pres. 1990-92), Sigma Xi, Tau Beta Pi. Home: 1 Locksley Ct Silver Spring MD 20904-6321 Office: U Md Dept Continuous Quality Improvement College Park MD 20742

DIETER, RAYMOND ANDREW, JR., physician, surgeon; b. Chebanse, Ill., June 19, 1934; s. Raymond Augustus Sr. and Emma Rose (Witt) D.; m. Bette René Myers, Sept. 29, 1961; children: Raymond III, David, Lisa, Lynn, Deanna, Robert. Student, U. Ill., 1952-56, Olivet Nazarene Coll., 1954; MA in Physiology, U. Ill., 1966, BS in Chemistry, 1994; MD, Loyola U., 1960. Diplomate Am. Bd. Thoracic Surgery, Am. Bd. Surgery. Intern Cook County Hosp., Chgo., 1960-61; resident in gen. surgery VA Hosp., Hines, Ill., 1963-67, sr. resident in cardiopulmonary surgery, 1967-69; practice specializing in thoracic, cardiovascular surg. Glen Ellyn (Ill.) Clinic, 1969—, pres., 1982-85, also bd. dirs.; mem. staff Hines (Ill.) VA Hosp., 1963-74; mem. staff Cen. DuPage Hosp., Winfield, Ill., 1969—, pres. staff, 1987-89; mem. staff Loyola U. Med. Ctr., Maywood, Ill., 1969-80, Meml. Hosp. DuPage County, Elmhurst, Ill., 1969—, Delnor Hosp., St. Charles, Ill., 1970-79, Community Hosp., Geneva, Ill., 1970—, Alexian Bros. Med. Ctr., Elk Grove Village, Ill., 1975-79, 93—; mem. staff Good Samaritan Hosp., Downers Grove, Ill., 1976—, pres. staff, 1979; mem. staff Glendale Heights (Ill.) and Glen Oaks Cmty. Hosp., 1980—, St. Mary's Hosp., Streator, Ill., 1997—; clin. instr. Stritch Sch. Medicine Loyola U., 1966-71, clin. asst. prof., 1971-80; trustee Ctr. Bank, Glen Ellyn, 1978-90, Lake Shore Bank, Glen Ellyn Found.; internat. lectr. on med. topics; chmn. Glen Ellyn Clinic Facilities, 1987-98, Physicians Benefit trust, 1988-92; pres., chmn. bd. No. Ill. Surg. Ctr., 1989—; pres. DuPage Doctors, Inc., Ctr. for Surgery; bd. dirs., co-founder Cmty. Bank of Wheaton, Glen Ellyn, 1993—, Cmty. Bank Wheaton-Glen Ellyn, 1998; co-founder, pres. Northeast DuPage Surgicenters, 1997—; chmn. bd. dirs., CEO Masterile, Inc., 1997-99. Author: (with B.R. Dieter and A.C. Mickelson) Mickelson and Peterson Family Sketch, 1970, (with M.C. Sorensen and E.R. Dieter) A Sorensen and Jensen Family Tree, 1975, (with B.R. Dieter, C. Myers, U. Myers, and D. Dieter) A Myers and Remley Family Tree, 1978, (with others) A Witt and (von) Ruehle Family Sketch, 1976, A Hofeling, Janssen, Lehnert, and Meier Family Sketch, 1979, A Dieter Family Tree: Sketches of German Families, 1981, Thoracoscopy for Surgeons, 1994; editor: Thoracoscopy for Surgeons-Diagnostic and Therapeutic, 1995; contbr. numerous articles to profl. jours. and chpts. in med. book. Mgr. Glen Ellyn baseball team, 1970, 71, 78-82; asst. leader 4-H Club, 1975-83; mem. Glenbard South High Sch. Boosters, World Fedn. Drs. Who Respect Human Life, 1980—. Served with USPHS, 1961-63, with Res. 1982—. Fellow ACS, Internat. Coll. Angiology (editl. bd. 1995—), Internat. Coll. Surgeons (exec. com. 1991—, treas. 1993-94, pres. elect 1995-96, pres. 1997-98, U.S. sect., corp. sec. 1997— World body); mem. AMA (Physician's Recognition awards), Internat. Mus. Surg. Sci. (chmn. bd. dirs. 1991—), Internat. Soc. Circumpolar Health, Internat. Soc. Outdoor Health, Am. Coll. Angiology, Am. Coll. Chest Physicians, Assn. Acad. Surgeons, Am. Soc. Circumpolar Health (charter), Assn. Mil. Surgeons, Assn. Res. Officers, Am. Heart Assn. (coun. 1974—), Nat. Assn. Interns and Residents, Soc. Med. Hist. Chgo., Soc. Critical Care Medicine, Soc. Thoracic Surgeons (membership com.), Ill. State Med. Soc. (trustee 1983-92, chmn. Ill. hosp. med. staff sect. 1985-87, pres., med. adminstrs. ctr. for surgery 1994—), Ill. Thoracic Surg. Soc. (sec. 1981-83, pres. 1984-85), DuPage County Med. Soc. (pres. 1977, mem. numerous coms.), Chgo. Med. Soc., Charles B. Puestow Surg. Soc. (sec., treas. 1966-67, v.p. 1968), Good Samaritan Soc., Ala. Geographic Soc., Kankakee Valley Geneal. Soc., Ill. Geneal. Soc., U. Ill. Alumni Assn., Am. Rabbit Breeders Assn., Silver Marten Club. Republican. Roman Catholic. Club: Century (Elmhurst). Lodge: Lions (charter). Avocations: Alaska, large game animals, outdoor health, farming, fishing. Home: 22w240 Stanton Rd Glen Ellyn IL 60137-7111 Office: Glen Ellyn Clinic 454 Pennsylvania Ave Glen Ellyn IL 60137-4496

DIETER, RICHARD CHARLES, marketing and management professional; b. Northampton, Pa., Feb. 13, 1952; s. Roland George and Martha (Bierman) D.; m. Ann Elaine Urwin, May 21, 1983; children: Amara Katherine, Cary Richard. BA, Valparaiso U., 1973; MDiv, Luth. Sch. Theology, Chgo., 1974. Exec. dir. Orgn. NorthEast, Chgo., 1976-84; dir. pub. rels. Green Mountain Coll., Poultney, Vt., 1986-87; pres., performing artist mgr. and rep. Dieter Assocs., Pitts., 1984—; cons. on econ. devel. North Side Innovation Ctr., Pitts.; cons. bus. incubator Bus. Devel. Ctrs.; founder, dir. Horizon Inst.; ednl. reform and charter sch. cons. Bd. Dirs. Renewal Project; founder Ctr. Excellence. Editor: Neighborhood Development, 1978. Bd. dirs. People's Music Sch., Chgo., 1980-83. Mem. Phi Mu Alpha Sinfonia. Avocations: fishing, reading, travel, music. Home and Office: 289 W Prospect Ave Pittsburgh PA 15205-2027

DIETERICH, DOUGLAS THOMAS, gastroenterologist, researcher; b. Queens, N.Y., Mar. 1, 1951; s. Albert Frederick and Florence Anna (Kilroy) D. BS, Yale U., 1973; M in Health Adminstrn., C.W. Post, 1974; MD, NYU, 1978. Diplomate Am. Bd. Internal Medicine and Gastroenterology. Intern, then resident Bellevue Hosp., N.Y.C., 1978-81, fellow gastroenterology, 1981-83; attending physician NYU Hosp., 1983—; teaching asst. NYU, 1979-83, clin. instr. medicine, 1983-88, clin. asst. prof., 1988-93, clin. assoc. prof., 1993—; mem. AIDS Clin. Trials Group NIH, 1986-97, Internat. AIDS Soc. U.S.A.; pres. Liberty Med. LLP, N.Y.C., 1996—; chmn. HIV Ind. Physicians Assn.; chief divsn. gastroenterology Cabrini Med. Ctr. Contbr. articles to profl. jours. Bd. dirs. Cmty. Rsch. Initiative on AIDS, N.Y. chpt. Am. Liver Found. Fellow ACP, Am. Coll. Gastroenterology; mem. AMA, Am. Gastroent. Assn., Am. Soc. Gastrointestinal Endoscopy, Am. Soc. Internal Medicine, N.Y. County Med. Soc., N.Y. State Med. Soc., N.Y. Acad. Gastroenterology, Yale Club, Cherry Valley Club, Grand Harbor Club. Republican. Lutheran. Home: 62 Saint James St S Garden City NY 11530-6344 Office: 345 E 37th St New York NY 10016-3256

DIETERICH, RUSSELL BURKS, obstetrician, gynecologist; b. Springfield, Ill., May 9, 1943; s. Charles Russell and Irma Rebecca (Burks) D.; m. Lynn Ellen Heidinger (div. July 1976); 1 child, Kristen; m. Barbara Ann Browning (div. May 1990); children: Paula, Pamela, Patrick; m. Irene Lorraine Carroll, June 27, 1992; children: Kathleen Carroll, Jonathon Carroll. BA, Knox Coll., 1965; MD, U. Ill., 1970. Diplomate Am. Bd. Ob-Gyn., Nat. Bd. Med. Examiners. Intern Blodgett Meml. Hosp., Grand Rapids, Mich., 1970-71, residet, 1971-74; chief of staff ob-gyn. USAF Hosp., Whiteman AFB, 1975-76; chief ob-gyn. Barnes St. Peters (Mo.) Hosp., 1986-87; chief ob-gyn. St. Joseph Hosp., St. Charles, Mo., 1987-89, chief of staff, 1989-90; pres. Dieterich Ob/Gyn Assn., Inc., St. Charles, 1981-95; clin. instr. Sch. Medicine Mich. State U., 1973-74, Sch. Medicine Wash. U., St. Louis, 1988—; speakers bur. Syntex Labs.; adv. bd. Life Seekers, St. Charles. Prodr., condr. (mus. rec.) Sentimental Journey by Request, 1985. Bd. mgrs. St. Charles County YMCA, 1985—; internat. mem. Community YMCA, St. Charles, 1985—; bd. dirs. United Svcs. for the Handicapped, Inc., St. Charles, 1994—. Maj. USAF, 1974-76. Recipient Harvard Book prize Associated Harvard Clubs, 1960, Disting. Alumni award Sigma Nu. Fellow Am. Coll. Ob-Gyn. (presenter, Ephraim McDowell award 1974); mem. AMA, Internat. Soc. for Advancement of Humanistic Studies of Gynecology, Am. Assn. Gynecol. Laproscopists, Am. Fertility Soc., St. Louis Gynecol. Soc. Republican. Free Evangelical. Avocations: managing dance band, skiing, canoeing, hiking, sailing. Home: 6 Vicksburg Sta Saint Charles MO 63303-6143 Office: Heritage Ob-Gyn Assocs 2730 S Highway 94 Ste 202 Saint Charles MO 63303-5677

DIETERT, RODNEY REYNOLDS, immunology and toxicology educator; b. Ft. Lee, Va., Dec. 6, 1951; s. Ralph O. and Beverly (Reynolds) D.; children: Grant C., Matthew W. BS, Duke U., 1974; PhD, U. Tex., 1977. Asst. prof. immunogenetics Cornell U., Ithaca, N.Y., 1977-83, assoc. prof., 1983-89, prof., 1989—; prof. immunotoxicology Cornell U., Ithaca, 1997—; adj. prof. N.C. State U., 1992—; head grad. program in immunology Cornell U., Ithaca, N.Y., 1989-92, dir. Inst. for Comparative and Environ. Toxicology, 1992-97, prof. immunotoxicology, 1997—; sr. fellow Ctr. for the Environment, 1993-96; cons. pesticide program EPA, Washington, 1984-86, Embrex, Inc., Research Triangle Park, N.C., 1991-95; panelist Nat. Inst. Environ. Health Scis. (AIDS Therapeutics), Research Triangle Park, 1988, mem. oxidative damage panel, 1997; USDA grant panel mgr., Washington, 1993-94; mem. Am. Inst. Biol. Scis.-Gulf War Illnesses panel Dept. Def., 1995, 97; invited testimony U.S. Congress Clean Water Act, 1995; spkr. at profl. confs. Jour. editor CRC Press, Inc., Boca Raton, Fla., 1986-90, editor book series, 1990—; editor jour. Elsevier Sci. Publs., Ltd., Oxford, U.K., 1990-95; contbr. to profl. publs. Bd. dirs. Wesley Found., Ithaca, 1979-84; chmn. Minority Edn. Com., Ithaca, 1980; chmn. Environ. Com. on Native Americans, Ithaca, 1994-95. Mem. Am. Assn. Immunologists, Soc. Toxicology. Office: Cornell U Dept Microbiology/Immunol Coll Vet Med C5-135 UMC Ithaca NY 14853-5601

DIETHELM, ARNOLD GILLESPIE, surgeon; b. Balt., Jan. 13, 1932; s. Oskar Arnold and Grace (Gillespie) D.; m. Nancy Lee Lane, June 21, 1951; children: Nancy Elizabeth, Linda Lane, Eugene Arnold (dec.), Ellen Jeanette, Richard Gillespie. AB, Wash. State U., 1953; MD, Cornell U., 1958; DSc (hon.), U. Ala., 1993. Intern, then resident in surgery N.Y. Hosp., 1958-65; asst. in surgery, research fellow Peter Bent Brigham Hosp., Boston, 1965-66; research fellow surgery Harvard U. Med. Sch., 1966-67; instr. Cornell U. Med. Sch., 1964-65; mem. faculty U. Ala. Med. Center, Birmingham, 1967—; prof. surgery U. Ala. Med. Center, 1973—, vice chmn. dept., 1973-82, chmn. dept. surgery, 1982—; mem. residency rev. com. for surgery Accreditation Coun. for Grad. Med. Edn., 1994—, chmn., 1997-99. Contbr. articles med. jours. Mem. AAAS, ACS., AMA, Am. Soc. Nephrology, Am. Soc. Transplant Surgeons, Am. Surg. Assn., Am. Bd. Surgery (dir. 1987-93), Assn. Acad. Surgery, Transplantation Soc., So. Surg. Assn. Home: 3248 Sterling Rd Birmingham AL 35213-3508 Office: U Ala Hosp Dept Surgery 619 19th St S Birmingham AL 35233-0001

DIETLER, MICHAEL DAVID, archaeologist, educator; b. Washington, Mar. 19, 1952; s. Patrick C. and Dolores M. D.; m. Ingrid Herbich, 1985. AB, Stanford U., 1974; MA, U. Calif., Berkeley, 1976, PhD, 1990. Asst. prof. Yale U., New Haven, Conn., 1990-94, assoc. prof., 1994-95; assoc. prof. U. Chgo., 1995—. Contbr. articles to profl. jours. Fellow Royal Anthropological Inst.; mem. Am. Anthropological Assn., Archaeol. Inst. Am., Soc. Am. Archaeology, European Assn. Archaeologists, French Soc. Prehistory. Avocation: blues. Office: U Chgo Dept Anthropology 1126 E 59th St Chicago IL 60637-1580

DIETMEYER, DONALD LEO, retired electrical engineer, educator; b. Wausau, Wis., Nov. 20, 1932; s. Henry Joseph and Erna M. (Zastrow) D.; m. Carol White, Jan. 26, 1957; children: Karl Peter, Elizabeth Mary, Anne Katherine, Diana Lee. BSEE, U. Wis., Madison, 1954, MS, 1955, PhD, 1959. Mem. faculty U. Wis., Madison, 1958-63, 64-98, prof. elec. and computer engring., 1967-98, prof. emeritus, 1998—, assoc. dean Coll. Engring., 1983-95; sr. engr. IBM Corp., Poughkeepsie, N.Y., 1964. Author: Logic Design of Digital Systems, 1978, 3rd rev. edit., 1988, Conlan Report, 1983. With AUS, 1957. Recipient Western Electric Fund award, 1972. Fellow IEEE; mem. Computer Soc., Assn. Computing Machinery, Sigma Xi. Home: 2211 Waunona Way Madison WI 53713-1619 Office: 1415 Engineering Dr Madison WI 53706-1607

DIETRICH, BRUCE LEINBACH, planetarium and museum administrator, astronomer, educator; b. Reading, Pa., Oct. 10, 1937; s. Harold Richard and Emily Jeannette (Leinbach) D.; m. Renee Carol Long, Nov. 25, 1959; children: Dodson Bruce, Katie Ellen. BS, Kutztown U., 1960; MS, SUNY, Oswego, 1969. Tchr. Reading Pub. Schs., 1960-67; curator space sci. Reading Mus., 1967-69, dir. planetarium, 1969-92, dir., 1976-92, dir. emeritus, 1992—; instr. astronomy Reading Area Community Coll., 1972-75, asst. prof., 1975-82, prof., 1982—. Contbr. articles to profl. jours. Trustee Berks County Hist. Soc., 1994—, pres., 1996—; sec. Interactive Video Sci. Consortium; sec. Reading Musical Found., 1980-88, trustee, 1989—. Named Kellogg Mus. Profl., 1987; NSF grantee, 1965-67. Fellow Internat. Planetarium Soc.; mem. AAAS, Can. Assn. Planetariums, Mid-Atlantic Planetarium Soc., Am. Assn. Mus., Pa. Soc., Torch Club (Reading) (pres. 1987), Kiwanis (pres. 1969). Home and Office: 1546 Dauphin Ave Reading PA 19610-2118

DIETRICH, BRYAN DAVID, english educator, poet; b. Oklahoma City, OK, Dec. 30, 1965; s. Ross Brian and Betty Walker D., m. Darla Lee, June 6, 1986, (div., April 9, 1992), m. Alice Jeanette Stewart, Oct. 31, 1993. BA in English, Univ. of Sci. and Arts of Oklahoma, Chickasha, OK, 1986; MPW in Creative Writing, Univ. of Southern Calif., Los Angeles, CA, 1988; PhD in English, Univ. of North Tex., Denton, Tex., 1994. Grad. tchg. asst. Tex. A&M, Commerce, Commerce, Tex., 1990-91; instr. of eng. Univ. of Sci. and Arts, Chickasha, OK, 1989-90; grad. tchg. asst. Univ. of North Tex., Denton, TX, 1991-94; instr. of eng. Eastfield Com. Coll., Mesquite, Tex., 1991-94, Cowley Cty. Com. Coll., Mulvane, KS, 1994-95, Hesston Coll., Hesston, KS, 1994-96; assoc. prof. of eng. Newman Univ., Wichita, KS, 1995—; adv. bd., The MiltonCtr., Wichita, 1998—, The Newman Rev., 1998—, The Zenioth Acad., 1998—, judge, Kansas Voice Comp., 1999. Author, poem cycle, Quarterly West, 1996, poem, Negative Capability, 1998, editor, North tex. Rev., mag., 1991-93. vol., Mennonite Housing Proj., Wichita, 1994—, mem., Scottish Country Dancers, Wichita, 1994—. Writers at Work Fellowship Awd., 1996, Eve of St. Agnes Prize, 1998, finalist, Yale Younger Poets Prize, Yale Univ., 1996, 98, Paterson Prize in Poetry, 20th Century Fox, 1983, Tchr. of the Yr., Newman Univ., 1996, Mary Patchell Fellow, Univ. of Norht tex., 1992. Mem., Amer. Acad. of Poets, 1995—, Associated Writing Progs., 1995—, Modern Lang. Assn., 1995—, Semiotic Soc. of Amer., 1992—. Democrat, Buddhist. Avocations: camping, scottish country dancing, comic books, films. Home: 335 N Volutsia Wichita KS 67214 Office: Newman Univ Eng Dept 3100 McCormick Ave Wichita KS 67213

DIETRICH, CAROL ELIZABETH, educator, former dean; b. Pitts., Mar. 19, 1961; d. Herman Karl and Ruby Faye (Mast) D.; m. Christopher Gecik, Jan. 19, 1991. BA, Carnegie Mellon U., 1983; MA, Ohio State U., 1985, PhD, 1993, MEd, 1994. From asst. prof. to prof. DeVry Inst. Technology, Columbus, Ohio, 1988—, dean gen. edn., 1996-98; adj. faculty Coll. Mt. St. Joseph, Cin., 1997; co-founder, owner The Way We Word, Columbus, 1988—; cons. Reynoldsburg (Ohio) City Schs., 1994. Coun. Lutheran Ch., Upper Arlington, Ohio, 1996-97; pollworker Bd. Elections, Franklin County, Ohio, 1995. Mem. MLA, Am. Assn. Higher Edn., Nat. Coun. Tchrs. English. Avocations: poetry, violin, theology, gardening, writing. Home: 307 E Kanawha Ave Columbus OH 43214-1211 Office: DeVry Inst Technology 1350 Alum Creek Dr Columbus OH 43209-2764

DIETRICH, JONATHAN AUSTIN, chemical process engineer; b. Summit, N.J., June 3, 1966; s. Peter Kohler and Judith D.; m. Tisha Lee Arroyo, Mar. 25, 1995. BSChemE, U. R.I., 1988. Registered profl. engr. Specialty products mgr. Wheelabrator, Dallas, 1988-92; sr. engr. Metcalf & Eddy, Inc., Tampa, Fla., 1992-96; sr. engr. assoc. Montgomery Watson Americas, Cape Coral, 1997—; expert on packed-tower deaeration technology. Contbr. articles to profl. jours. Youth leader Wellspring United Meth. Ch., Tampa, 1995; vol. Muscular Dystrophy, Dallas, 1992, Cancer Soc., Tampa, 1996. Mem. AIChE, Water Environment Fedn., Fla. Engring. Soc., S.E. Desalting Assn. United Methodist. Achievements include development of ultra-low gas removal systems to less than 10 ppb; development of reverse osmosis membranes on municipal wastewaters. Office: Montgomery Watson Americas Inc 3501 Del Prado Blvd Cape Coral FL 33904

DIETRICH, JOSEPH JACOB, retired chemist, research executive; b. Bismark, N.D., Oct. 31, 1932; s. Jacob Peter and Elizabeth (Janzer) D.; m. Florence Kolodziejczak, June 27, 1959; children: Ann Marie, Michael, John, James. BA in Chemistry, St. John's U., Collegeville, Minn., 1953; PhD in Organic Chemistry, Iowa State U., 1957. Rsch. chemist PPG, Inc., Barberton, Ohio, 1957-59, Spencer Chem. Co., Kansas City, Kans., 1960-64; with Diamond-Shamrock Corp., Cleve., 1964-82, dir. rsch., 1973-78, dir. tech. devel., 1978-82; dir. tech. Eltech Systems Corp., Painesville, Ohio, 1982-85, dir. tech. and comml. devel./ Europe, Chardon, Ohio, 1986-90; pres. Eltech Internat. Corp., 1990-94, Elgard Corp., 1994; ret., 1994. Contbr. articles to profl. jours; patentee in field. Mem. Am. Chem. Soc., Soc. Plastic Engrs., Serra Club. Republican. Roman Catholic. Home: 6958 Pennywhistle Cir Painesville OH 44077-2141 Office: 470 Center St Chardon OH 44024-1068

DIETRICH, LAURA JORDAN, international policy advisor; b. Chgo., May 21, 1952; d. Leon Hubert and Mary Catherine (Kuhter) Jordan; m. Paul George Dietrich, Dec. 5, 1978. Student, Stephens Coll., Columbia, Mo., 1971-73. Dir. Nat. Ctr. for Legis. Research, St. Louis, 1977-81; bd. dirs. Nat. Ctr. for Legis. Research, Washington, 1981-89; congl. liaison U.S. Dept. Labor, Washington, 1981-82; dep. dir. external relations AID, Washington, 1982-83; spl. asst. to sec. Dept. Interior, Washington, 1983; dep. asst. sec. state U.S. Dept. State, Washington, 1984-87; dir. Found. Mgmt., Inc., Washington, 1982-85. Editor: (monographs) Legislative Policy, 1979, State Anti-Trust Laws, 1979, Public Employee Collective Bargaining, 1979, Nuclear Energy: The Legislative Issues, 1980, The Proposed Washington D.C. Amendment, 1981; author: U.S. Asylum Policy, 1986; contbr. editor Saturday Rev., 1984-85. Me. Rep. Nat. Com. Mem. Fgn. Policy Discussion Club, Sovereign Mil. Order of Malta, Marlborough Hunt Club, Middleburg Hunt. Roman Catholic. Avocation: fox hunting. Office: 1141 Custis St Alexandria VA 22308-1067

DIETRICH, RICHARD VINCENT, geologist, educator; b. LaFargeville, N.Y., Feb. 7, 1924; s. Roy Eugene and Mida Amy (Vincent) D.; m. Frances Elizabeth Smith, Dec. 28, 1946; children: Richard Smith, Kurt Robert, Krista Gayle Brown. AB, Colgate U., 1947; MS, Yale U., 1950, PhD, 1951. Geologist Iowa Geol. Survey, 1947, N.Y. State Sci. Service, summers 1949-50; asst. prof. geology Va. Poly. Inst., Blacksburg, 1951; asso. prof. Va. Poly. Inst., 1952-56, prof., 1956-69, mineral technologist Va. Engring. Exp. Sta., 1951-58; fulbright rsch. prof. Oslo U., Norway, 1959-60; asso. dean arts and scis. Va. Poly. Inst., 1966-69, dean, 1969; prof. geology Central Mich. U., Mt. Pleasant, 1969-86, prof. emeritus, 1986—, dean arts and scis., 1969-75; dir. Econ. Geol. Pub. Co., 1966-72. Author over 20 sci. books and textbooks in field (transl. into German, Malaysian, Russian, and Japanese); also poems, haiku, essays, cartoons; editor Mineral Industries Jour., 1953-61; mng. editor Bull. Econ. Geology, 1966-73; exec. editor Rocks and Minerals, 1980-88, petrology adv. editor, 1988—; mem. editl. bd. Mineral Record, 1969-74; contbr. over 300 articles to profl. jours.; composer, performer music. Organizer N. Am. for Mineral. Abstracts, 1976-80. Served with U.S. Air Corps, 1943-46. Recipient Acad. Citation Mich. Acad. Sci., Arts and Letters, 1978, Children's Sci. Book award N.Y. Acad. Scis., 1981; Fulbright rsch. prof. U. Oslo, 1958-59; Pres.'s scholar, 1941-42, Austin Colgate scholar Colgate U., 1943, Newton Lloyd Andrews scholar, 1943, Colgate U. scholar, 1946; Edward S. Binney fellow, 1948-49, James Dwight Dana fellow Yale U., 1950-51. Fellow Am. Mineral. Soc. (assoc. life), Soc. Econ. Geol. (sr.); mem. Norsk Geologisk Forening (life), Geol. Soc. Finland (life), Am. Geol. Inst. (gov. 1972-74), Assn. Earth Sci. Editors (pres. 1972-73), Phi Beta Kappa, Sigma Xi, Phi Kappa Phi, Sigma Gamma Epsilon. Presbyterian. Home: 1323 Center Dr Mount Pleasant MI 48858-4103 Office: Ctrl Mich U Geology Dept Brooks Hall Mount Pleasant MI 48859 *My parents were supportive although they had hoped for a different direction. Education, the work ethic, and retention of individualism and imagination were promoted.*

DIETRICH, ROBERT ANTHONY, pathologist, medical administrator, consultant; b. Buffalo, May 24, 1933; s. Charles Thomas and Mary Evelyn (Shoecraft) D.; m. Alison Elinor D'Arcy, June 13, 1959; children—Anne Marie, Alison D'Arcy, Karen Elizabeth, Kathleen Murray, Patricia Evelyn, Ellen Kiley. B.S., Canisius Coll., Buffalo, 1955; M.D., Georgetown U., Washington, 1959; M.S. in Surg. Pathology, U. Minn., Mpls., 1964; J.D., George Washington U., Washington, 1974. Diplomate Am. Bd. Pathology, Am. Bd. Nuclear Medicine. Intern D.C. Gen. Hosp., Washington, 1959-60; resident Mayo Clinic, Rochester, Minn., 1960-64; chief pathology svc. U.S. Army Hosp., Fort Gordon, Augusta, Ga., 1964-66; pathologist O.B. Hunter Meml. Lab., Washington, 1966-78; chmn. dept. pathology, chief div. nuclear medicine Montgomery Gen. Hosp., Olney, Md., 1972-78; vice chmn. dept. pathology, chief divsn. nuclear medicine Sibley Meml. Hosp., Washington, 1978-89; sec. Am. Soc. Clin. Pathologists, Chgo., 1981-88, exec. v.p./chief staff, 1982-92; cons., 1992—. Served to capt. U.S. Army, 1964-66. Noble Found. grantee Mayo Clinic, 1964. Fellow Am. Coll. Legal Medicine, Coll. Am. Path., Am. Soc. Clin. Path.; mem. Med. Soc. D.C. (sec. 1984-86, pres. 1988). Home and Office: 5506 Parkston Rd Bethesda MD 20816-3326

DIETRICH, SUZANNE CLAIRE, instructional designer, communications consultant; b. Granite City, Ill.; d. Charles Daniel and Evelyn Blanche (Waters) D. BS in Speech, Northwestern U., 1958; MS in Pub. Comm., Boston U., 1967; postgrad., So. Ill. U., 1973-83. Intern prodn. staf Sta. WGBH-TV, Boston, 1958-59; asst. dir., 1962-64; asst. dir. program invitation to instructional tv radio Ill. Office Supt. Pub. Instrn. Radio, Springfield, 1969-70; dir. program prodn. and distbn., 1970-72; instr. faculty call staff, speech dept. Sch. Fine Arts So. Ill. U., Edwardsville, 1972-73; grad. asst. for doctoral program office of dean Sch. Edn., 1975-78; rsch. asst. Ill. pub. telecomms. study Ill. Pub. Broadcasting Coun., 1979-80; cons., researchers in comm., 1980—; pub. advisor Bradly Pub., Inc., 1996. exec. prodr., dir. tv programs Con-Con Countdown, 1970, The Flag Speaks, 1971. Mem. sch. bd. St. Mary's Cath. Sch., Edwardsville, 1991-92; cable tv adv. com. City of Edwardsville, 1994—, co-chair, 1996-98; bd. dirs. Goshen Preservation Alliance, Edwardsville, 1992-94, pres., 1995-97; dir. Madison Hist. Mus., 1999—. Mem. Mdison County Hist. Soc. (bd. dirs. 1997-99). Roman Catholic. Home: 1011 Minnesota St Edwardsville IL 62025-1424

DIETRICH, WILLIAM ALAN, author, journalist; b. Tacoma, Sept. 29, 1951; s. William Richard and Janice Lenore (Pooler) D.; m. Holly Susan Roberts, Dec. 19, 1970; children: Lisa, Heidi. BA, Western Wash. U., 1973. Reporter Bellingham (Wash.) Herald, 1973-76, Gannett News Svc., Washington, 1976-78, Vancouver (Wash.) Columbian, 1978-82, Seattle Times, 1982-97; freelance writer, 1998—. Author: The Final Forest, 1992, Northwest Passage, 1995, Ice Reich, 1998. Recipient Paul Tobenkin award Columbia U., 1986, Pulitzer prize for nat. reporting, 1990; Nieman fellow Harvard U., 1987-88.

DIETRICH, WILLIAM GALE, lawyer, real estate developer, consultant; b. Kansas City, Mo., Mar. 6, 1925; s. Roy Kaiser and Gale (Gossett) D.; m. Marjorie Nell Reich, July 14, 1945; children: Meredith G. Dietrich Steinhaus, Ann E. Dietrich Cooling, Walter R. AB with high honors, Yale U., 1948, LLB, 1951. Bar: Mo. 1951. Ptnr. Dietrich, Davis, Dicus, Rowlands, Schmitt & Gorman (and predecessors), 1953-73; project dir., gen. counsel Blue Ridge Shopping Ctr., Inc., Kansas City, 1955-73, pres., gen. mgr., 1964-73; pres., gen. mgr. Blue Ridge Tower, Inc., Kansas City, 1967-73; sec.-treas. A. Reich & Sons, Inc., Kansas City, 1973-88, chmn., 1988—; pvt. practice law Kansas City, 1973—; sec., treas. A. Reich & Sons Gardens, Inc., 1973-89; pres. J&D Devel., Inc., 1987—; gen. ptnr. J & D Enterprises, 1986—; gen. mgr. The Farm Shopping and Office Ctr., 1994—; pres. BBJ Treats, L.L.C., 1994—. Sec., bd. dirs. Rsch. Med. Ctr., Kansas City, 1977, vice-chmn., 1980-83, chmn., 1983-87; bd. dirs. The Rsch. Found., 1980-91, vice-chmn., 1989-91; bd. dirs. Rsch. Health Svcs., 1980-81, vice chmn., 1983-87, chmn. 1987-89; bd. dirs. Mahana Condominium Assn., Maui, Hawaii, 1977-96, Blue Ridge Bank and Trust Co., Kansas City, 1982-94; vestry mem. Grace & Holy Trinity Cathedral, Kansas City, 1972-95, former treas. 1st lt. AUS, 1943-46, PTO. Mem. ABA, Mo. Bar Assn., Kansas City Bar Assn., Blue Ridge Mall Mchts. Assn. (dir. 1958-73), Internat. Coun. Shopping Ctrs. (past dir. for Mo., Kans, Iowa, cert. shopping ctr. mgr.), Lawyers Assn. Kansas City, Mission Hills Country Club, Yale Club, Kansas City (Mo.) Club, Rotary (bd. dirs., sec. found. Kansas City 1978—), Phi Beta Kappa (pres. Kansas City chpt. 1989-91), Phi Delta Phi. Home: 1000 Huntington Rd Kansas City MO 64113-1346 Office: 12125 Blue Ridge Blvd Ste A Grandview MO 64030-1195*

DIETZ, ARTHUR TOWNSEND, investment counseling company executive; b. Mt. Vernon, N.Y., Oct. 30, 1923; s. William Arthur and Adele Townsend (Dods) D.; m. Mary Archer, June 29, 1947 (dec. 1980); children: Adele Archer Dietz, Laura Townsend Stamm, Amelia Edmunds Williams; m. Mary Laura Peavy, Sept. 16, 1982 (dec. 1992); m. Margie Nell Lee Baghose, Oct. 4, 1992. AB, Wesleyan U., Middletown, Conn., 1946; MA, Princeton U., 1948, PhD, 1953. Instr. Princeton U., 1948-49; asst. prof. Wesleyan U., 1949-54; Mills Bee Lane prof. fin. and banking, dir. MBA program Emory U., Atlanta, 1959-88; dir. Alpha Funds, Atlanta, 1972-85, Enterprise Funds, Atlanta, 1985—, Enterprise Accumulation Trust, 1995—; pres. ATD Adv. Corp., 1996—, Strategic Portfolio Mgmt., 1988-95; bd. trustees Emory U. Resolution in Honor, 1983; vis. prof. IMEDE, 1965-66; Robert Morris prof., Va., 1984-85; chmn. First Atlanta Investments, LLC. Author books; contbr. articles to profl. jours. Pres. Fernbank PTA, DeKalb County, Ga., 1959-60; mem. DeKalb County Devel. Authority, 1980-84; Retirement Facility for Elderly Authority, DeKalb County, 1982-84. Sgt. AUS, 1942-45, ETO. Named one of Outstanding Educators of Am., 1972; recipient Emory Williams Disting. Teaching award Emory U., 1983; Woodrow Wilson fellow, 1946. Fellow Fin. Analysts Soc.; mem. Phi Beta Kappa (pres. Gamma chpt. 1964-65). Methodist. Avocations: tennis, bridge. Office: ATD Adv 1917 Chamdun Way Atlanta GA 30341-1770

DIETZ, CHARLTON HENRY, lawyer; b. LeMars, Iowa, Jan. 8, 1931; s. Clifford Henry and Mildred Verna (Eggensperger) D.; m. Viola Ann Lange, Aug. 17, 1952; children: Susan (Mrs. Jay Kakuk), Robin (Mrs. Jack Mayfield), Craig. BA, Macalester Coll., 1953; JD, William Mitchell Coll. Law, 1957, LLD, 1993. Bar: Minn. 1957. Mem. pub. rels. staff 3M, St. Paul, 1952-58, atty., 1958-70, assoc. counsel, asst. sec., 1970-72, asst. gen. counsel, 1972-75, sec., 1972-76, gen. counsel, 1975-92, v.p. legal affairs, 1976-88, sr. v.p., 1988-93; bd. dirs. Ea. Heights Bank, 1972—, chmn. bd., 1981-93; bd. dirs. Mairs & Power Mutual Funds, 1994—; mem. adv. bd. UFE; instr. William Mitchell Coll. Law, 1960-74, trustee, 1974-86, 87-96, pres., 1980-83. Bd. dirs. St. Paul Area YMCA, 1973-80, chmn. 1978-80, Minn. Citizens Coun. on Crime and Justice, 1976-88, pres., 1982-84, St. Paul United Way, 1980-95, Ramsey County Hist. Soc., 1979-86, St. Paul Lowertown Redevel. Corp., 1988-94, Minn. Hist. Soc., 1993—, Supreme Ct. Hist. Soc., 1991—, Children's Health Care, 1994—; trustee United Theol. Sem., 1976-82, Macalester Coll., 1983-89, Wilder Found., 1989—, chmn., 1996—; mem. Conferees of Minn. Citizens Conf. on Cts.; bd. dirs. Masonic Cancer Ctr. Fund, 1984—, pres. 1994-97. Fellow Am. Bar Found.; mem. ABA, Fedn. Bar Assn., Minn. Bar Assn., Ramsey County Bar Assn., Assn. Gen. Counsel, Am. Judicature Soc. (bd. dirs. 1989-95), Am. Law Inst., Masons, Shriners, Jesters. Republican. Mem. United Ch. of Christ. Home: 1 Birch Ln Saint Paul MN 55127-6402

DIETZ, DAVID W., elementary education educator. Tchr. Gainsville (Tex.) Jr. H.S. Recipient Tchr. Excellence award Internat. Tech. Edn. Assn., 1992. Office: Gainesville Jr HS 421 N Denton St Gainesville TX 76240-4016*

DIETZ, JANIS CAMILLE, business educator; b. Washington, May 26, 1950; d. Albert and Joan Mildred (MacMullen) Weinstein; m. John William Dietz, Apr. 10, 1981. BA, U. R.I., 1971; MBA, Calif. Poly. U., Pomona, 1984; PhD Claremont Grad. Sch., 1997. Customer svc. trainer People's Bank, Providence, 1974-76; salesman, food broker Bradshaw Co., L.A., 1976-78; salesman Johnson & Johnson, L.A., 1978-79, GE Co., L.A., 1979-82; regional sales mgr. Leviton Co., L.A., 1982-85; nat. sales mgr. Jensen Gen. div. Nortek Co., L.A., 1985-86; retail sales mgr. Norris div. Masco, L.A., 1986-88; nat. sales mgr. Thermador Waste King div. Masco, L.A., 1988-91; nat. accts. mgr. Universal Flooring div. Masco, 1991-92; western regional mgr. Peerless Faucet div. Masco, 1992-95; performance devel. cons., Delta Faucet, div. Masco, 1995—; assoc. prof. bus. adminstrn. U. LaVerne, 1995—; sales trainer, Upland, Calif., 1985—; instr. Calif. Poly. U., 1988-91; lectr. Whittier Coll., 1994. Dir. pub. rels. Jr. Achievement, Providence, 1975-76; bd. trustees Nat. Multiple Sclerosis Soc., So. Calif. chpt. Recipient Sector Svc. award GE Co., Fairfield, Conn., 1980, Outstanding Achievement award, 1988. Mem. NAFE, Sales Profls. L.A. (v.p. 1984-86), Toastmasters (adminstrv. v.p. 1985). Unitarian.

DIETZ, JOHN RAPHAEL, consulting engineer executive; b. Carbondale, Pa., Jan. 31, 1912; s. John A. and Bridget (Barrett) D.; m. Elizabeth Harding Bezilla, Mar. 15, 1983; children by previous marriage: Robert J., Elizabeth Dietz Brown. B.S. in Civil Engring., Drexel U., Phila., 1934. Registered profl. engr., Pa. Contract estimator J.A. Dietz Co., 1934-35; designer Pa. Dept. Hwys., 1935-38; designer, resident engr. Pa. Turnpike Commn., 1938-40; san. engr. for J.E. Greiner Co., Camp Meade, Md., 1940; designer Caribbean Architect-Engrs., 1941-42; chief designer for Gannett Eastman & Fleming, Inc., Andrews Air Field, Washington, 1942-43; civilian with U.S. Engr. Corps on study Potomac River Basin flood control, 1943-44; with Gannett Fleming Corddry and Carpenter, Inc., cons. engrs., 1942—; dir. hwy. div., then pres. Gannett Fleming Corddry and Carpenter, Inc., Harrisburg, Pa., 1950-76; chmn. bd. Gannett Fleming Corddry and Carpenter, Inc., 1970-83, chmn. emeritus, 1983—; dir. CCNB Bank (N.A.). Trustee Drexel U. Bd.; dirs. Holy Spirit Hosp., Camp Hill, Pa., 1965—, pres., 1983; bd. dirs. Villa Teresa Nursing Home, Harrisburg, Pa., 1973—, pres., 1973-75. Recipient A.J. Drexel Paul award Drexel U., 1973; named Knight of St. Gregory, Pope John Paul II, 1983; selected in 100 Most Outstanding Men Drexel U. Alumni, 1992. Life fellow ASCE (past pres. Central Pa. chpt.); mem. Am. Council Cons. Engrs., Nat. Soc. Profl. Engrs., Am. Road and Transp. Builders Assn. (past dir.), Pa. Hwy. Info. Assn. (past pres.), Pa. Soc. Profl. Engrs. (Profl. Engrs. Disting. Service award Harrisburg chpt. 1965). Roman Catholic. Home: PO Box 485 Camp Hill PA 17001-0485 Office: PO Box 67100 Harrisburg PA 17106-7100

DIETZ, PATRICIA ANN, engineering administrator; b. L.A., Nov. 30, 1958; m. Frank Raymond Dietz, July 1, 1978; children: Lindy K., Frank R. Jr. BA in Polit. Sci., U. Colo., 1983; MA in Psychology, Pepperdine U., 1993; Paralegal Cert., U. San Diego, 1988. Investment broker 1st Investors Corp., Colorado Springs, Colo., 1986-88; paralegal Law Offices of Ben Williams, Santa Monica, Calif., 1988-89; mgmt. analyst Bur. of Engring., City of L.A., 1989—; camp commandant Operation Safe Harbor-Haitian Humanitarian Relief Effort, 1992. Mem. Parent Tchr. Student Assn., Rosamond, Calif., 1992. With U.S. Army, 1983-86, capt. USAR, 1986-98, Retired Reserve Status, 1998—. Nat. Urban fellow, 1991. Mem. Civil Affairs Assn., Res. Officers Assn., Engrs. and Architects Assn. Republican.

DIETZ, PAUL T., company executive; b. Cin., Oct. 19, 1947; s. Harry John Edward and Paula Lecke D.; m. Debora Louise Smith, July 3, 1969; children: Erich, Heidi. BBA, U. Cin., 1969; MBA, Xavier U., 1974; CLU, ChFC, Am. Coll., 1992. Tchr., coach Forest Pk. H.S., Cin., 1989-90; sales mgr. SAFECO Ins., Cin., 1980-97; asst. v.p. Security Benefit, Topeka, 1997—. Avocations: golfing, boating, fishing, tennis, traveling. Home: 4107 Quail Pointe Ter Lawrence KS 66047

DIETZ, ROBERT BARRON, lawyer; b. San Diego, May 14, 1942; s. J. Thomas and Mary Agnes (Barron) D.; m. Grace Louise Purcell, Aug. 19,

1967; children: Thomas E., Michael B., Denis P., M. Alison. AB, Coll. Holy Cross, 1964; JD, Cornell U., 1968. Bar: N.Y. 1968, U.S. Dist. Ct. (no. dist.) N.Y. 1968, U.S. Dist. Ct. (so. and ea. dists.) N.Y. 1973, U.S. Supreme Ct. 1974. Asst. dist. atty. County of Dutchess, Poughkeepsie, N.Y., 1969-70, confidential law clk. to surrogate of Dutchess County, 1970-73; corp. counsel City of Poughkeepsie, 1973-75; assoc. Garrity & Dietz, Poughkeepsie, 1969-73, ptnr., 1973-75; assoc. Gellert & Cutler, P.C. and predecessor firms, Poughkeepsie, 1975-78, ptnr., 1978-86; pvt. practice law Poughkeepsie, 1986-94; ptnr. Dietz & Dietz, Poughkeepsie, 1995—; lectr. Dutchess C.C., Poughkeepsie, 1985—; mem. grievance com. 9th Jud. Dist., N.Y., 1987-95; bd. dirs. Youth Resource Devel. Corp., chmn., 1992-95. Bd. dirs. Mid Hudson Workshop for Disabled, Sports Mus. Dutchess County; chmn. Mid Hudson adv. bd. Salvation Army; bd. trustees Vassar-Warner Home; bd. counsellors The Children's Home of Poughkeepsie, Inc.; bd. dirs. Dutchess County coun. Boy Scouts Am.; former mem. City of Poughkeepsie Recreation Commn.; bd. dirs. Greystone Programs, Inc. Fellow Dist. 721 Rotary, Poughkeepsie, 1964-65. Mem. ABA, N.Y. State Bar Assn., Dutchess County Bar Assn., Poughkeepsie C. of C., Kiwanis (pres. Poughkeepsie club 1974-75). Republican. Roman Catholic. Avocations: golf, tennis, reading, baseball card collecting. Office: 2 Cannon St Poughkeepsie NY 12601-3224

DIETZ, ROBERT LEE, lawyer; b. Miami, Fla., Apr. 28, 1958; s. Edward William and Anna C. D.; m. Laura Sanders, May 8, 1982; children: John Edward, Stephanie Elizabeth. BA with honors, Eckerd Coll., St. Petersburg, Fla., 1979; JD, Vanderbilt U., 1982. Bar: Fla. 1984; cert. workers' compensation, 1992—; Supreme Ct. cert. cir. civil mediator, 1995—. Atty. Zimmerman, Shuffield, Kiser & Sutcliffe, P.A., Orlando, Fla., 1984—. Contbr. articles to profl. jours. Vice chair S.E. region bd. dirs. Canine Companions for Independence, Orlando, 1991-93; alumni bd. dirs., 1992-97, chair alumni capital campaign Eckerd Coll., 1994-97. Recipient McArthur Alumni award Eckerd Coll., 1993. Mem. ABA (nat. chair ABA TIPS, workers compensation and employer liability com. 1995-96), The Fla. Bar (workers compensation rules com. 1988-91), Orange County Bar Assn. (chmn. workers compensation com. 1996-97, Guardian ad Litem of the Yr. 1996), Fla. Def. Lawyers Assn. (chair workers compensation com. 1989-96, bd. dirs. 1991-95, sec.-treas. 1996-97, pres. 1998-99, Pro Bono award 1996), Civitan Internat. (Disting. gov. 1993-94, internat. mem. mktg. com. 1994-96, Club Honor key East Orlando club 1994, Winter Park Club 1996, College Park Club 1996, Dist. Honor key Sunshine dist. 1994, Region II Honor key 1995). Avocations: indoor soccer, speed chess, golf, tennis. Fax: 407-425-1537. E-mail: rdietz@zsks.com. Home: 2534 Shrewsbury Rd Orlando FL 32803-1336 Office: Zimmerman Shuffield Kiser & Sutcliffe PA 315 E Robinson St Ste 600 Orlando FL 32801-4308

DIETZ, WILLIAM, retired aeronautics engineer, consultant; b. Chgo., Apr. 17, 1919. BS, Aeronaut Inst., 1940. V.p. F16 engring. Gen. Dynamics Corp., 1972-78, v.p. Tomahawk Missile,, 1979-82, v.p. spl. projects, 1982-90, v.p. divsn., sr. tech. staff, 1990-93; cons. Lockheed Corp., Ft. Worth, 1993-99; ret. Mem. NAE, AIAA (Sylvanius Reed award).

DIETZ, WILLIAM RONALD, financial services executive; b. Seattle, Nov. 25, 1942; s. William Phillip and Helen Mae (Wilson) D.; m. Elizabeth R. Daoust; 1 child, David Phillip. BA, U. Wash., 1964; MBA, Stanford U., 1968. Fin. cons. 1st Nat. City Bank, N.Y.C., 1968-70; v.p., mgr. Citicorp Subs. Mgmt. Office, Citicorp, N.Y.C., 1971-74; chmn. Citicorp Factors, Inc., N.Y.C., 1974-75; v.p., mgr. N.Y., N.J. and Conn. comml. banking Citibank N.A., N.Y.C., 1976-78; sr. v.p., gen. mgr. Eastern region corp. banking Citibank N.A., 1978-81, sr. v.p., head Caribbean Basin div., 1982-84; pres. Charter Assocs. Ltd., 1985-89; chmn. and chief exec. officer CorEast Savs. Bank, Richmond, Va., 1989-91; pres., CEO Am. Savs. Bank, White Plains, N.Y., 1991-92, Mo. Bridge Bank, Kansas City, 1992-93, Anthem Fin., Inc., Indpls., 1993-96; mng. ptnr. Concord Ptnrs., 1997—; bd. dirs. Capital One Fin. Corp., Stratic Corp.; mem. policy com. Bank Mgmt. Inst., SUNY-Buffalo. Contbg. author: Customer-Focused Marketing of Financial Services; bd. advisors Jour. Consumer Lending. Trustee Children's Mus. of Indpls.; bd. advisors Ind. U./Purdue U., Indpls.; bd. trustees Indpls.-Marion County Pub. Libr. Found. Lt. USNR, 1964-66. Mem. Univ. Club (N.Y.C.), Woodstock Country Club, Delta Tau Delta. Home: 7925 Ridge Rd Indianapolis IN 46240-2539 Office: Concord Ptnrs 135 N Pennsylvania # 1400 Indianapolis IN 46204

DIETZE, GOTTFRIED, political science educator; b. Kemberg, Germany, Nov. 11, 1922; came to U.S., 1949; s. Paul and Susanne (Pechstein) D. Dr.Jur., U. Heidelberg, Germany, 1949; Ph.D., Princeton U., 1952; S.J.D., U. Va., 1961. Instr. polit. sci. Dickinson Coll., 1952-54; mem. faculty Johns Hopkins, 1954—, prof. polit. sci., 1962—; vis. prof. U. Heidelberg, 1956, 58-60, Brookings Instn., 1960-61, 67. Author: Ueber Formulierung der Menschenrechte, 1956, The Federalist, 1960, In Defense of Property, 1963 (Monks award), Magna Carta and Property, 1965, America's Political Dilemma, 1968, Youth, University and Democracy, 1970, Bedeutungswandel der Menschenrechte, 1971, Academic Truths and Frauds, 1972, Two Concepts of the Rule of Law, 1973, Deutschland-Wo Bist Du?, 1980, Kant und der Rechtsstaat, 1981, Kandidaten, 1982, El Gobierno Constitucional, 1983, Liberalism Proper and Proper Liberalism, 1984, Reiner Liberalismus, 1985, Konservativer Liberalismus in Amerika, 1987, Amerkanische Demokratie, 1988, Liberaler Kommentar zur Amerikanischen Verfassung, 1988, Politik-Wissenschaft, 1989, Der Hitler-Komplex, 1990, Liberale Demokratie, 1992, American Democracy, 1993, Problematik der Menschenrechte, 1995, Briefe aus Amerika, 1995, Begriff des Rechts, 1997, Deutschland, 1999; editor: Essays on the American Constitution, 1964. Lutheran. Office: Johns Hopkins U Dept Polit Sci Baltimore MD 21218

DIETZEL, LOUISE A., psychologist; b. Canton, Ohio, Nov. 18, 1937; d. Daniel Walter and Velma Irene Bender Miller; m. Cleason Samuel Dietzel, June 18, 1960; children: Laurie Christine, Rebecca Doreen, Beth Ann. BS, Goshen (Ind.) Coll., 1960; MS, St. Michaels Coll., 1976. Lic. Psychologist, lic. Clin. Mental Health Counselor, Vt. Dir. day care Mt. Pleasant, Mich., 1965-67, E. Lansing, Mich., 1967-71, Winooski, Vt., 1972-73; sch. cons. Essex Junction (Vt.) Schs., 1976-77; rsch. asst. U. Vt., Burlington, 1976-77; pvt. cons. practice Essex Junction, 1974—; chair counselor Vt. Clin. Mental Health Counselors, Montpelier, 1989-95, elem. counselor Essex Junction Schs., 1977-94, cons. Head Start, Burlington, Vt., 1992—. Author: Parenting With Respect and Peacefulness, 1995. Mem. Am. Mental Health Counselors Assoc., Vt. Psychol. Assn., Am. and Vt. Counseling Assn. Avocations: cooking, furniture refinishing, camping, antiqueing. Home: 37 Prospect St Essex Junction VT 05452-3612 Office: Psychol Svcs 6 Hillcrest Rd Essex Junction VT 05452-3611

DIFEDE, JOSEPH, retired judge; b. Sicily, Italy, Dec. 8, 1909; s. Alfonso and Concetta (Incardona) DiF.; m. Erma Carnosale, June 16, 1937; 1 child, Ann C. Crawshaw. BA, U. Rochester, 1933, MA, 1998; LLB, St. John's U., 1938, JD, 1940. Bar: N.Y. 1938. Mem. N.Y. Assembly, Albany, 1935; referee Dept. Labor, N.Y.C., 1936-44; chmn. N.Y. State Labor Rels. Bd., 1955-62; prof. law N.Y. Law Sch., 1962-88; justice civil ct. N.Y.C., 1968-71; justice N.Y. State Supreme Ct., N.Y.C., 1972-87; pvt. practice N.Y.C., 1942-55, 62-70; arbitrator, mediator N.Y.C. Office Collective Bargaining, 1987—. Contbr. articles to profl. jours. Active local and state Dem. Orgn., 1933-87. Recipient Medal of Freedom, 1947. Mem. ABA, N.Y. State Bar Assn. (ho. dels.), N.Y. Athletic Club, Phi Beta Kappa. Roman Catholic. Avocations: golf, bridge, tennis. Home: 3250 Perry Ave Bronx NY 10467-3207

DIFFIE, WHITFIELD, engineer; b. June 5, 1944. BS in Maths., MIT, 1965; postgrad. in elec. engring., Stanford U., 1975-78; D in Tech. Scis. honoris causa, Swiss Fed. Inst. Tech., Zurich, 1992. Rsch. asst. The Mitre Corp., Bedford, Mass., 1965-69; rsch. programmer artificial intellingence lab. Stanford U., Palo Alto, Calif., 1969-73, rsch. asst., 1975-78, rsch. programmer, 1975; self-supported researcher in cryptography, 1973-74; mgr. secure syss. rsch. No. Telecom, Mountain View, Calif., 1978-91; disting. engr., adv. computer and comm. security Sun Microsyss., Palo Alto, Calif., 1991—; organizer conf. Crypto '81, '83; mem. program com. Crypto 89; mem. program com. Status and Prospects of Rsch. in Cryptography '93, First ACM Conf. on Comms. and Computer Security, 1993; mem. adv. bd. Electronic Privacy Info. Ctr.; presenter in field. Contbr. numerous articles to scientific jours.; featured in Scientific Am., Sience, Time, Omni, Newsweek, N.Y. Times Mag., others. G.C. Steward fellow Gonville and Caius Coll., 1996; recipient award for Disting. Contbn. to Consumer Protection Calif. State Psychol. Assn., 1978, Nat. Computer Syss. Security award Nat. Inst. Stds. and Tech. and Nat. Security Agy., 1996, Louis E. Levy medal Franklin Inst., 1997, First Paris Kanellakis award ACM, 1997. Mem. IEEE (Info. Theory Soc. Paper award 1979, Donald G. Fink award 1981, conf. organizer 1983). Achievements include discovery of the concept fo public key cryptography, 1975; development of Mathlab symbolic manipulation system, of Lisp 1.6 systme; research on interactive debugging and extensible compiling, proof of correctnes of programs, proof checking and extensible compilers, on cryptography and its applications; patents (with Martin E. Hellman and Ralph Merkle) for cryptographic apparatus and method, 1980, (with Ashar Aziz) on security of mobile communications, 1993. Home: 288 Eleanor Dr Woodside CA 94062 Office: Sun Microsystems MAK 15-214 901 San Antonio Pkwy Palo Alto CA 94303*

DIFFRIENT, NIELS, industrial designer; b. Star, Miss., Sept. 6, 1928; s. Robert Ethan and Dovie Lee (Peacock) D.; m. Helena Hernmarck, May 29, 1976; children—(by previous marriage) Scott, Julie, Emily. Student, Wayne State U., 1951-52; B.F.A., Cranbrook Acad., 1954; hon. doctorate, Art Center Coll. of Design, 1975. Architect Eero Saarinen, Bloomfield Hills, Mich., 1948-53; with Walter B. Ford, Detroit, 1953-54, Marco Zanuso, Milan, Italy, 1954-55; gen. partner Henry Dreyfuss Assocs., N.Y.C., 1955-80; head ind. indsl. design studio Ridgefield, Conn., 1981—; mem. faculty indsl. design UCLA, 1961-69; mem. faculty Yale U., 1990. Co-author: Humanscale, 3 vols., 1974, 80; mem. editorial bd.: Indsl. Design mag, 1976-89; contbr. articles to profl. jours.; inventor, designer human engineered comml. chairs for Knoll Internat., 1979, 80, for Sunar Co., 1981, table system for Home Furniture Co., 1988, 92. Mem. bd. govs. Cranbrook Acad., Bloomfield Hills, Mich. Recipient nat. design award U.S. Dept. Transp., 1981, awards Resource Coun., 1979, 81, gold medal Inst. Bus. Designers, 1979, 80, 92, 93, best of show award, 1984, ann. award Design and Environ. mag., 1975, (with Marco Zanuso) Compasso d'Oro, 1957, awards Indsl. Design mag., 1981, 82, 85, 89, gold medal AIA, 1989; gold medal IDEA Bus. Week mag., 1993; named hon. royal designer for industry Royal Soc. Arts, London, 1987, Best of Show NEICON Furniture Exhbn., 1998; Fulbright fellow, 1954-55; grantee Nat. Endowment for Arts, 1975-80. Fellow Indsl. Design Soc. Am. (Design Excellence award 1980, Chrysler award for innovation 1996); mem. Internat. Design Conf. Aspen (bd. dirs. 1974-91), Internat. Design Edn. Found. (pres. 1976—), Am. Ctr. for Design (hon., bd. dirs.), Design Inst. New Zealand (hon.).

DIFORIO, ROBERT GEORGE, literary agent; b. Mamaroneck, N.Y., Mar. 19, 1940; s. Richard John and Mildred (Kuntz) D.; m. Birgit Rasmussen; children—Stephen Christopher, Danielle Alexandra. B.A., Williams Coll., 1964. From book sales rep. to v.p. book sales Kable News Co., 1964-72; with New Am. Libr./E.P. Dutton, N.Y.C., 1972-89, exec. v.p., 1980-81, pres., publisher, 1981-82; chmn., chief exec. officer New Am. Library/E.P. Dutton, 1983-89; sr. v.p. book sales and mktg. Arcata Graphics Co., 1990-91; prin. D4EO Unltd./Lit. Agy., D4EO Inc., 1991—. Bd. dirs., chmn. emeritus Weston (Conn.) Little League. Served with USCGR. Mem. Weston Field Club. E-mail: D4EO@home.com. Home: 7 Indian Valley Rd Weston CT 06883-1018

DIFRANCESCO, DONALD T., state senator, lawyer; b. Scotch Plains, N.J., Nov. 20, 1944; grad. Pa. State U., 1966; J.D., Seton Hall U., 1969; m. Diane Dragovic, June 17, 1967; children: Marie, Tracy, Marci. Bar: N.J. 1969. Practices in Warren, N.J.; ptnr. Bivona, Cohen, Kunzman, Coley, Yospin, Bernstein & DiFrancesco; mem. N.J. Assembly, 1976-79; mem. N.J. State Senate, 1979—, pres. State Senate, 1992—. Trustee N.J. Symphony; bd. dirs. Resolve Counseling Ctr., Children's Specialized Hosp., N.J.; mem. exec. com. Nat. Conf. State Legislators. Office: NJ Senate Senate Majority Office PO Box 99 Trenton NJ 08625-0099

DIFRANCESCO, JEFFREY JAMES, telecommunication and media executive; b. El Paso, Tex., Aug. 11, 1963; s. Salvatore Angelo and Margaret (Heigl) D.; m. Jennifer Jean Rapone, Apr. 11, 1987; children: Timothy Salvatore, Elizabeth Anne. BS in Math., Ill. Inst. Tech., Chgo., 1984; MEngring. in Computer Design, Pa. State U., 1991; MS in Bus., Johns Hopkins U., 1994; cert. of mergers & acquisitions, U. Pa., 1996. Sys. engr. Northrop Corp., Rolling Meadows, Ill., 1984-85; computer scientist Computer Scis. Corp., Moorestown, N.J., 1985-89; program mgr. AEL, Inc., Lansdale, Pa., 1989-91; pvt. practice cons. Fairfax, Va., 1991-93; dir. Bell Atlantic Tele-TV, Reston, —, 1993-95; prin. cons. Price Waterhouse LLP, N.Y.C., 1995-96; exec. v.p. strategic planning & bus. devel. Lenfest Comm., Inc., Oaks, Pa., 1996-98; CFO, exec. v.p. ops. & profl. svcs. Savera Systems Inc., Murray Hill, N.J., 1998—; bd. dirs. Telvue Corp., Smart Tone Authentication, Inc., CAM Systems, Inc.; keynote spkr., conf. chmn. AIC, SSPI, Internet Quality and Productivity Ctr., WEF, Salomon Smith Barney. Conbtr. articles to profl. pubs. Recipient Award of Excellence USN, 1987; featured as Next Generation, Cablevision mag. Home: 2592 Hillcrest Dr Lansdale PA 19446-6059 Office: Savera Systems Inc 535 Mountain Ave Murray Hill NJ 07974

DIGANGI, AL, marketing executive. V.p. mktg. Montgomery Ward & Co., Chgo., exec. v.p. Elec. Ave. and Auto Express, 1997—. Office: Montgomery Ward & Co Montgomery Ward Plz 619 W Chicago Ave Chicago IL 60610-2430*

DIGANGI, FRANK EDWARD, academic administrator; b. West Rutland, Vt., Sept. 29, 1917; s. Leonard and Mary Grace (Zafonti) DiG.; m. Genevieve Frances Colignon, June 27, 1946; children—Ellen (Mrs. Philo David Hall), Janet (Mrs. W. Dale Greenwood). B.S. in Pharmacy, Rutgers U., 1940; M.S., Western Res. U., 1942; Ph.D., U. Minn., 1948. Asst. prof. U. Minn. Coll. Pharmacy, 1948-52, asso. prof., 1952-57, prof. medicinal chemistry, 1957—, also asso. dean adminstrv. affairs. Author: Quantitative Pharmaceutical Analysis, 7th edit, 1977; Contbr. articles to pharm. jours. Served with USNR, 1943-46, PTO. Recipient Alumni Assn. Disting. Pharmacist award, 1977, Faculty Recognition award Coll. of Pharmacy Alumni Soc., 1981, Lawrence and Delores M. Weaver medal, 1997. Mem. Am. Pharm. Assn., Minn. Pharm. Assn. (pres. 1971, chmn. bd. 1972-73, Pharmacist of Yr. award 1972, Harold R. Popp Meml. award 1979, hon. mem. 1994), Mpls. Soc. Profl. Pharmacists (hon.), AAUP, Am. Chem. Soc., Am. Assn. Colls. Pharmacy, Sigma Xi, Phi Beta Phi, Phi Lambda Upsilon Rho Chi. Clubs: University Campus (Mpls.), University Faculty Golf (Mpls.), Gown-in-Town (Mpls.). Home: 1666 Coffman St Apt 234 Saint Paul MN 55108-1343 Office: Univ Minn College of Pharmacy Minneapolis MN 55455

DIGBY-JUNGER, RICHARD A, educator in English; b. Milw., Apr. 20, 1954; s. Eugene E. and Marjorie A. J.; children: Zachary, Casandra. BA in Journalism, English, U. Minn., 1976; MA in History, U. Wis., Milw., 1986; PhD in Mass Comm., U. Wis., 1989. Announcer, reporter WQFM-FM Radio, Milw., 1974-75; announcer, producer WWTC-AM, Mpls., 1975-77; news dir. WAKY-AM-FM, Duluth, Minn., 1977-81; announcer, rsch. specialist Wis. Pub. Radio, Madison, 1986-89; asst. prof. dept. journalism No. Ill. U., DeKalb, 1989-96; assoc. prof. dept. English and journalism Western Mich. U., Kalamazoo, 1996—. Author: (book) Journalist as Reformer, 1996; contbr. articles to Jour. of Ill. History and Chgo. History, 1999. Named Tchr. of Yr. Dept. Journalism, No. Ill. U., 1993-95. Mem. Soc. Profl. Journalists, Am. Journalism Historians Assn., Assn. for Edn. in Journalism and Mass Comm., Orgn. Am. Historians, Soc. for Am. Baseball Rsch., Phi Alpha Theta. Avocations: running, bicycling, swimming, reading. E-mail: richard.digby-junger@wmich.edu. Office: Western Mich U Dept English & Journalism Kalamazoo MI 49008

DIGENOVA, JOSEPH E., lawyer; b. Wilmington, Del., Feb. 22, 1945; s. Egidio Joseph and Elizabeth (Castelline) diG.; m. Victoria Toensing, June 27, 1981; children: Todd, Brady, Amy. BA, U. Cinn., 1967; JD, Georgetown U., 1970. Bar: D.C. 1970, U.S. Dist. Ct. D.C. 1970, U.S. Ct. Appeals (D.C. cir.) 1972. Law clk. to assoc. judge D.C. Ct. Appeals, 1970-71; dir., gen. counsel U. Cinn., 1971-72; asst. U.S. atty. Office of U.S. Atty., Washington, 1972-75, prin. asst. U.S. atty., 1982-83; U.S. atty. D.C., 1983-88; counsel for intelligence matters Office of U.S. Atty. Gen., Washington, 1976; counsel for select com. on intelligence U.S. Senate, Washington, 1975-76, counsel for subcommittee on D.C., com. govt. affairs, 1976, counsel for com. on judiciary, 1978, chief counsel, staff advisor for com. on rules and adminstrn., 1981; adminstrv. asst., legis. counsel U.S. Senator Charles Mathias, Washington, 1979; U.S. Atty. for D.C., 1983-88; ptnr. Bishop, Cook, Purcell & Reynolds, 1988-90, Manatt Phelps & Phillips, 1991-95; founding ptnr. diGenova & Toensing, 1996—; ind. counsel Clinton passport file search matter, 1992-95; apptd. grievance com. U.S. Dist. Ct. D.C., 1994. Contbr. articles to profl. jours. Mem. ABA (com. grand jury 1983-87, criminal justice sect. 1982—, white collar crime com. 1988—). Republican. Roman Catholic. Avocations: music, singing. Office: diGenova & Toensing 901 15th St NW Ste 430 Washington DC 20005-2327

DIGENOVA, SILVANO ANTONIO, rare coin and fine art dealer; b. Avellino, Italy, Mar. 20, 1962; came to U.S., 1964; s. Antonio and Maddalena (Moscarello) DeG.; m. Eve Remmer, Sept. 4, 1993. Student, U. Pa., 1980-84. Chmn., pres. Tangible Investments of Am., Phila. and Laguna Beach, Calif., 1984—. Mem. Am. Numismatic Assn., Profl. Numismatic Guild, Coin and Bullion Numismatic Accreditation Bd. (bd. dirs. 1986-89). Address: Tangible Asset Galleries Ste 103 1550 S Coast Hwy Laguna Beach CA 92651-3263

DIGERONIMO, DIANE MARY, nursing educator, psychotherapist; b. Montclair, N.J., Aug. 31, 1945; d. Daniel Sebastian and Carmela Marion (Arminio) DiG. RN, St. Mary's Hosp., Passaic, N.J., 1968; BA, Jersey City State Coll., 1969, MA in Spl. Edn., 1979; MSW, Rutgers U., 1981. Cert. sch. nurse.; cert. health educator; cert. clin. hypnosis; cert. diabetic educator; CCRN, Lic. Clin. Soc. Work. Nurse ICU Moutainside Hosp., Montclair, 1968-70, instr. nursing, 1970-74; nursing educator State Bds. Nursing Rev. Course LPN/RN, Montclair, 1974—; pres. Nursing Profl. Resources, Montclair, 1981—; vis. lectr. 1985—; pvt. practice psychotherapy, Montclair, 1981—; regional dir. N.J. Nurses Action Coalition, Essex County, 1976-81. Author: My Side of the Street, 1970, From Here To There, 1980, Care of the Critically Ill, 1994, Diabetic Screenings and Education, 1996; co-author: Machinary in Medicine, 1976; author poems (Golden Poet awad 1984); contbr. articles to profl. jours. Mem. ANA, NASW, N.J. Nurses Assn., N.J. Assn. Social Workers, Am. Legion Aux. Roman Catholic. Avocations: writing poetry, traveling, swimming, volunteer work. Home: 23 Stanford Pl Montclair NJ 07042-5009

DIGERONIMO, SUZANNE KAY, architect; b. Berwick, Pa., Mar. 27, 1947; d. George and Eleanor (Kapsak) Marcincavage; m. Louis Anthony DiGeronimo, Sept. 19, 1969; children: Marcello, Luciano. B.Arch., Cooper Union, 1971; Assoc. Applied Sci., Fashion Inst. Tech., N.Y.C., 1967; student, Pratt Inst., 1967-68, Columbia U., 1968-70. Registered architect, N.J., N.Y., Mich., Calif., N.H., Conn. Pres. DiGeronimo, P.A., Paramus, N.J., 1969—. Mem. AIA (chair practice com. 1991), Soc. Am. Mil. Engrs. (nat. v.p. 1994-97, pres. N.J. post 1989-90), Am. Arbitration Assn. (panel of arbitrators), Nat. Acad. Conciliators (conciliator), Colegio de Arquitectos P.R., N.J. Soc. Archs. (legislation com.), Arch.'s League of No. N.J., Chamber of Commerce and Industry of No. N.J. (legislation com.). Roman Catholic. Home: 16 Beekman Pl Fair Lawn NJ 07410-3604 Office: DiGeronimo PA 12 Sunflower Ave Paramus NJ 07652-3701*

DIGGES, EDWARD S(IMMS), JR., business management consultant; b. Pitts., June 30, 1946. AB, Princeton U., 1968; JD, U. Md., 1971; MBA, U. Pitts., 1998. Bar: Md. 1972, U.S. Supreme Ct. 1975. With staff of gov. State of Md., Annapolis, 1973; ptnr. Piper & Marbury, Washington and Balt., 1977-84; founding ptnr. Digges, Wharton & Levin, Annapolis, 1984-89; corp. cons. various corps., Towson, Md., 1989—; bd. dirs. Televest Comms., LLC, Corp. Comms. Mgmt. Group, LLC; instr. advanced bus. law Johns Hopkins U., 1975-78; lectr. civil procedure U. Balt. Law Sch., 1976-78; mem. govs. commn. to revise Md. code, 1978-90. Contbr. articles to profl. jours. Mem. Alumni Council Mercersburg Acad., 1982-88, pres. 1987-88; bd. advisors Indian Creek Sch., 1982-88, chmn. 1986-88; pres. Beacon Hill Community Assn., 1978-86. ROTC, U.S. Army, 1970-71. Mem. Md. State Bar Assn. (bd. govs. 1972-84), Am. Law Inst., Am. Bd. Trial Adv. (pres. Md. chpt. 1984-89), Inn XIII, Am. Inns of Ct. (Master of the Bench 1986-89), Scribes. Democrat. Roman Catholic. Clubs: So. Md. Soc. (bd. govs., pres. 1988), Mid Ocean (Bermuda), Princeton Club of N.Y. Home: PO Box 42737 Baltimore MD 21286

DIGGINS, DEAN RICHARD, dancer, artist; b. Hampton, Iowa, June 22, 1931; s. Mace Edson and Ruth Lois (Roberts) D. BS, Bklyn. Coll., 1967, MS, 1969; PhD, CUNY, 1971. Dance tchr. Diggins Dance Studio, Hampton, 1946-52; dancer Stone-Camryn Ballet Co., Chgo., 1954-55, Music Theater, Highland Park, Ill., 1955-56, Mattison Trio, N.Y.C., 1957-67; assoc. prof. psychology Bklyn. Coll., N.Y.C., 1971-90; tap dance soloist Morton Gould's Tap Dance Concerto, 1986-96; self employed artist Kittery, Maine, 1990—. One-man shows include Kittery (Maine) Art Assn., 1997, 98, Wentworth-Coolidge Mansion, Portsmouth, N.H., 1999. Sgt. U.S. Army, 1952-54. Home: 22 Trafton Ln Kittery ME 03904-5401

DIGGINS, JOHN PATRICK, history educator; b. San Francisco, Apr. 1, 1935; s. James Joseph and Anne (Naugton) D.; m. Jacy Battles (div. Sept. 1976); children: Sean, Nicole. AB, U. Calif., Berkeley, 1957; MA, San Francisco State U., 1959; PhD, U. So. Calif., L.A., 1964. Asst. prof. history San Francisco State U., 1966-69; prof. history U. Calif., Irvine, 1969-90; disting. prof. history Grad. Ctr. CUNY, N.Y.C., 1990—, acting dir. Ctr. for Humanities, Grad. Ctr., 1996-97; vis. fellow U. Cambridge, 1976-77; vis. prof. Princeton U., 1977-78; chair. Am. civilization L'Ecole des Hautes Etudes en Scis. Sociales, Paris, 1988-89; Commonwealth lectr. U. London, 1991; spkr. Lionel Trilling seminar, Columbia U., 1992; lectr. and cons. in field. Author: Mussolini and Fascism: The View From America, 1972, Italian edit., The American Left in the Twentieth Century, 1973, Up From Communism: Conservative Odysseys in American Intellectual History, 1975, The Bard of Savagery: Thorstein Veblen and Modern Social Theory, 1978, Spanish edit., The Lost Soul of American Politics: Virtue, Self-Interest and the Foundations of Liberalism, 1984, The Proud Decades: America in War and in Peace, 1941-1960, 1988, The Rise and Fall of the American Left, 1992, The Promises of Pragmatism: Modernism and the Crisis of Knowledge and Authority, 1994, Max Weber: Politics and the Spirit of Tragedy, 1996, The Liberal Persuasion: Arthur Schlesinger, Jr., and the Challenge of the American Past, 1997; co-editor: (with M. Kann) The Problem of Authority in America, 1982; contbr. articles to profl. jours. and newspapers. Recipient prizes Soc. for Italian Hist. Studies, 1965, Am. Studies Assn., 1966, John Dunning award Am. Hist. Assn., 1972; fellow Am. Philos. Soc., Social Sci. Rsch. Coun., Am. Coun. Learned Socs., NEH, John Simon Guggenheim Found., 1978; residence scholar Rockefeller Found., 1989; conf. grantee Rockefeller Found. Democrat. Office: Grad Ctr CUNY 33 W 42nd St New York NY 10036-8003

DIGGINS, PETER SHEEHAN, arts administrator; b. Rochester, N.Y., June 23, 1938; s. Bartholomew A. and Mona (Sheehan) D. BA in English, Georgetown U., 1959. guest artist cons. San Francisco Opera, 1997. Staff reporter Washington Post, 1960-65; asst. artistic adminstr. Met. Opera, N.Y.C., 1965-72; dir. dance programs N.Y. State Coun. on the Arts, 1972-75; gen. adminstr. The Joffrey Ballet, N.Y.C., 1975-79; pres. Peter S. Diggins Assocs., 1979—; Am. entertainment coord. Winter Olympics, Nagano, Japan, 1998; cons. in arts mgmt. dance and opera cos.; cons. for guest dancers San Francisco Opera, 1996; casting cons. Broadway and tour prodns. of Carousel, Titanic, Victor/Victoria, Cats, Red Shoes, Christmas Carol, 1993-98. Contbr. articles to Opera Mag. Recipient grant for European work-study tour Met. Opera, 1968. Home and Office: 133 W 71st St New York NY 10023-3834

DIGGS, BRADLEY C., lawyer; b. Missoula, Mont., Sept. 18, 1948. BA magna cum laude, Amherst Coll., 1970; JD cum laude, Harvard U., 1973. Bar: Wash. 1973. Mng. ptnr. Davis Wright Tremaine, Seattle. Mem. ABA, Phi Beta Kappa. Office: Davis Wright Tremaine 2600 Century Sq 1501 4th Ave Ste 2600 Seattle WA 98101-1688

DIGGS, MATTHEW O'BRIEN, JR., air conditioning and refrigeration manufacturing executive; b. Louisville, Jan. 11, 1933; s. Matthew O'Brien and Dorothy (Leary) D.; m. Nancy Carolyn Brown, Nov. 5, 1955; children: Elizabeth, Joan, Judith, Matthew III. Student, Hanover Coll., 1950-52; BSME, Purdue U., 1955; MBA, Harvard U., 1961. With Lincoln Electric, Cleve., 1957-59, Toledo Scale Corp., 1961-63; cons., assoc., v.p., then v.p. and mng. officer East Cen. Region Booz, Allen & Hamilton, Inc., Cleve., 1963-72; v.p. mktg. Copeland Corp., Sidney, Ohio, 1972-74, exec. v.p., 1974, pres., chief exec. officer, 1975-87, vice chmn., 1987-90; CEO The Diggs Group McClintock Ind., Dayton, Ohio, 1990—; bd. dirs. Cavert Wire Co., Inc., Tower Automotive, Inc., Dayton Superior Corp., Ripplewood Holdings L.L.C. Cmty. bd. trustees Wright State U., 1995—, Miami Valley Sch., 1990—; chmn. adv. bd. Herrick Labs. Perdue U., 1980—; former sr. warden St. Paul's Episcopal Ch. 1st lt. U.S. Army, 1955-57. Home: 1160 Lytle Ln Dayton OH 45409-2112 Office: 1630 Kettering Tower Dayton OH 45423-1005*

DIGGS, WALTER WHITLEY, health science facilty administrator; b. Memphis, Tenn., June 8, 1932; s. Lemuel Whitley and Beatrice (Moshier) D.; m. Ann C. Thobae, Nov. 29, 1958; children: Jennie, Thomas, Andrew. BS, Washington and Lee U., 1954; MHA, U. Minn., 1956. Adminstrv. resident Stormont-Vail Hosp., Topeka, 1955-56; asst. dir. The Johns Hopkins Hosp., Balt., 1959-66; adminstr. Med. Coll. Ga. Hosp., Augusta, 1966-70; asst. prof. Med. Coll. Ga., Augusta, 1970-71, U. Tenn. and U. Memphis, 1971-97; field rep. Joint Commn. Hosps., Chgo., 1981-88, 93—; supt. Memphis Mental Health Inst., 1987-93; cons. Tenn. Dept. Mental Health, 1993-95. Pres. Delta Found., Miss., 1987—, Ballet South, Memphis Ballet, Augusta Civic Ballet. Lt. USNR, 1956-59. Recipient Peter Cooper award, Unitarian Ch., Memphis, 1975, Forrest Fletcher, Washington and Lee, Lexington, Va., 1954. Fellow Am. Coll. Healthcare Execs. (life). Avocations: srs. track and field. Home: 5282 Shady Grove Rd Memphis TN 38120-2404

DIGIACINTO, GEORGE VINCENT, neurosurgeon; b. N.Y.C., Feb. 5, 1945; s. Albert George and Rose DiPerna D.; m. C. Ericson, July 13, 1968 (div. Sept. 1988); children: John, Catherine C.; m. Elizabeth Almeyda, May 7, 1989; children: Alexandra, Gregory. BA magna cum laude, Columbia Coll., 1966; MD, Harvard U., 1970. Attending Neurosurgeon St. Lukes Roosevelt Hosp. Ctr., N.Y.C., 1978—, dir. divsn. neurosurgery, 1992—. Lt. comdr., USN, 1972-74. Mem. AMA., Am. Assn. Neurosurgery. Avocations: skiing, listening to music, wood working. E-Mail: gudbrain@aol.com. Office: 425 West 59th St New York NY 10019-1128

DIGIAMARINO, MARIAN ELEANOR, realty administrator; b. Camden, N.J., July 23, 1947; d. James and Concetta (Biancosino) DiG. BS in Mgmt., Rutgers U., 1978. Clk. stenographer transp. div. Dept. of Navy, Phila., 1965-70, sec., 1970-73, realty asst. Profl. Devel. Ctr. program, 1973-75, realty specialist, 1975-81, supervisory realty specialist, head acquisition and ingrant sect., 1981-85, supervisory realty specialist, mgr. ops br., 1985-92, spl. asst. for real estate, 1992—; instr. USNR, Phila., 1983, 88. Contbr. articles to profl. jours. Mem. AAUW, Soc. Am. Mil. Engrs., Nat. Assn. Female Execs., Phi Chi Theta (pres. Del. Valley chpt. 1984-86, nat. councillor 1984, nat. fundraising com., pres. and corr. sec. (Alpha Omega chpt. 1976-78). Avocation: theatre, sports, needlework, reading, beach combing. Office: Dept Navy No Div Naval Facilities Base Closure Team 10 Indsl Hwy Mail Stop # 82 Lester PA 19113-2090

DI GIORGIO, ANTHONY J., college president. V.p. acad. affairs Trenton (N.J.) State Coll., until 1989; pres. Winthrop Coll., Rock Hill, S.C., 1989—. Office: Winthrop Coll Oakland Ave Rock Hill SC 29733*

DIGIOVACHINO, JOHN, special education educator; b. Newark, Mar. 20, 1955; s. John and Mary (Trapasso) Di G. BA, William Paterson Coll., 1977, MEd, 1981; EdD, Calif. Coast U., 1994. Dir. libr. skills program for mentally handicapped in East Orange (N.J.) Pub. Libr., 1978; tchr. handicapped Deron Sch., Livingston, N.J., 1978-80; tchr. handicapped Dover (N.J.) Pub. Schs., 1981-84, learning disability tchr., cons., 1984-89; dir. child study team Bedminster (N.J.) Pub. Sch., 1989-93; tchr. learning disabilities, cons. Town Dover (N.J.) Bd. Edn.; dir. spl. svcs. Oradell (N.J.) Pub. Sch., 1993-95; v.p., CST coord. Town of Boonton (N.J.) Bd. Edn., 1995-98; prin. Harrison Elem. Sch., Livington, N.J., 1998—; cons. to adv. bd. Bldg. Blocks Learning Child Care Svcs., Randolph, N.J., 1985-95. Coord. recreation program for handicapped Friends of East Hanover, N.J., 1977-83; mem. Hanover Park Regional High Sch. Dist. Bd. Edn., East Hanover, 1983-89; mem. East Hanover Twp. Bd. Edn., 1989-95, v.p., 1990-92, pres., 1993-95; chmn. East Hanover Drug Awareness Coun., 1987-96; bd. dirs. Morris County Dept. Human Svcs. CART and CIACC, 1996-97, UNICO, 1998—. Mem. ASCD, N.J. Assn. Pupil Pers. Svcs., N.J. Assn. Learning Cons., Coun. for Exceptional Children, Nat. Assn. of Pupil Svcs. Adminstrs., N.J. Assn. Sch. Adminstrs., N.J. Prins. and Suprs. Assn., North Jersey Spl. Edn. Adminstrs. Assn., K.C., Pi Lambda Theta, Kappa Delta Pi. Home: 26 Goldblatt Ter East Hanover NJ 07936-1416 Office: Harrison Elem Sch 148 N Livingston Ave Livingston NJ 07039-2121

DIGIOVANNA, EILEEN LANDENBERGER, osteopathic physician, educator; b. Columbus, Ohio, Nov. 24, 1933; d. Bernard Holman and Della Belle (Crabtree) Landenberger; m. Joseph Anthony DiGiovanna, Apr. 4, 1959; children: Michael, Mark, Gina, Geri, Vicki, Matthew, Kimberly. Student, Ohio State U., 1952-55; DO, Chgo. Coll. Osteopathy, 1959. Pvt. practice Massapequa Park, N.Y., 1960-81; asst. prof., assoc. prof. N.Y. Coll. Osteo. Medicine, Old Westbury, 1977-91, prof., 1991—, asst. dean student affairs, 1991-97, assoc. dean, 1997—. Author, editor: (textbook) Osteopathic Approach to Diagnosis and Treatment, 1991, 2d edit., 1997; contbr. articles to profl. jours. Lay speaker Meth. Ch., N.Y., 1988—, chmn. adminstrn. bd. 1993—. Fellow Am. Acad. Osteopathy (trustee 1992-94, pres. 1994-95); mem. Am. Osteo. Assn. (Educator of Yr. 1995), Am. Coll. Family Practice, N.Y. State Osteo. Med. Soc. (Physician of Yr. 1992). Republican. Avocations: reading, travel. Office: NY Coll Osteo Medicine Old Westbury NY 11568

DI GIOVANNI, ANTHONY, retired coal mining company executive; b. Phila., May 10, 1919; s. Charles and Josephine (Giacobbe) Di G.; m. Rose Persichetti, July 28, 1946; children: Joanne, Diane, Rosemary, Charles. B.S. in Bus. Adminstrn, St. Joseph's U., 1940. C.P.A., Pa. Acct. Service Supply Corp., Phila., 1940-42; account supr. Ernst & Ernst, 1942-51; mgr. Ernst & Ernst (Phila. Office), 1952-65; former v.p., dir. United Eastern Coal Sales Corp.; exec. v.p. finance and adminstrn. Barnes & Tucker Co., Valley Forge, Pa., 1965-72; pres., 1972-84, dir., 1972-85, 86—, v.p., 1990—; group pres. resources div. Alco Standard Corp., 1973-85, v.p., 1976-85; pres. Alco Standard Canadian Coal Corp., 1976-85; dir. Upshur Coals Corp. Bd. dirs. St. Joseph's U., 1983-85. Recipient ACE award, 1974, Spl. Dirs. award, 1976; both from Alco Standard Corp. Mem. AICPA, Nat. Coal Assn. (bd. dirs. 1973-85, fin. com. 1978-83), Pa. Inst. CPAs (past. bd. dirs., chmn. com.), Sons of Italy (treas., mem. policy com. Commonwealth lodge # 1949 1989-91), Overbrook Italian Am. Club, Phoenixville Country Club. Roman Catholic.

DIGIROLAMO, GLEN FRANCIS, actor; b. Paterson, N.J., Sept. 16, 1961; s. Frank and Phyllis (Vanecek) DiG. Pres., CEO, chmn. bd. Ultimate Assocs., Wayne, N.J.; pres., CEO Centillion Group Internat., Wayne; v.p., sec., treas. F. DiGirolamo & Son, Inc., Wayne; actor TV comml., Aruba, W.I., 1989. Actor: (film) Gremlins II, 1989, Cadillac Man, 1989, Long Time Companions, 1989, Ambulance, 1989, Mo Better Blues, 1989, Godfather III, 1990, Other Peoples Money, 1990, Jersey Girls, 1991, The Sinatra Story, 1992. Elected candidate Dem. County Com., Bergen County, N.J., 1989, 90, 91, 92; legis. aide Assemblyman Thomas Duch, Bergen County, 1989. Mem. AFTRA, Harley Owners Group (charter mem., Bergen and Passaic county chpts.). Roman Catholic. Avocations: guitar, photography, travel, billiards, motorcycles, boating.

DI GIROLAMO, ROSINA E., education educator; b. Monterey, Calif., Aug. 3, 1945; d. Anthony and Frances (Lucido) DiG. AA, Monterey Peninsula Coll., 1965; BA, Calif. State U., Hayward, 1967; MA, Calif. Polytech., San Luis Obispo, 1975. Tchr. Monterey (Calif.) Pub. Unified Sch. Dist., 1968—. Polit. action chairperson Monterey Bay Tchrs. Assn., 1993-94; mem. City's Youth Task Force, 1997. Nominee for Outstanding Tchr., Lori Flagg Found., Monterey, 1991-92, Outstanding Middle Sch. Tchr. of Yr. Rotary Club, 1998. Mem. Calif. Reading Assn., Calif. Tchrs. of English, Nat. Tchrs. of English, Calif. Leadership Team, Calif. Assn. Student Leaders (advisor). Democrat. Roman Catholic. Avocations: reading, com. work, travel. Home: 77 Via Chualar Monterey CA 93940-2528 Office: Walter Colton Mid Sch 100 Toda Vis Monterey CA 93940-4237

DIGIULIO, CINZIA, Italian language educator; b. Brescia, Italy, Apr. 2, 1961; came to U.S., 1988; d. Gustavo DiGiulio and Nilde Giovagnoli. Laurea cum laude, U. Cath., Milan, 1987; MA in Comparative Lit., Purdue U., 1990; PhD in Italian, U. N.C., 1997. Instr. Latin Purdue U., West Lafayette, Ind., 1988-90; instr. Italian U. N.C., Chapel Hill, 1991-97; vis. asst. prof. Italian Wesleyan U., Middletown, Conn., 1997-98, Purdue, West Lafayette, 1998—. Contbr. articles to profl. jours. Dissertation fellow U. N.C., 1996. Mem. MLA, Am. Assn. Italian Studies, Am. Assn. Tchrs. of Italian, Am. Comparative Lit. Assn. Office: Purdue U Stanley Coulter Hall West Lafayette IN 47907

DIGMAN, LESTER ALOYSIUS, management educator; b. Kieler, Wis., Nov. 22, 1938; s. Arthur Louis and Hilda Dorothy (Jansen) D.; m. Ellen Rhomberg Pfohl, Jan. 15, 1966; children: Stephanie, Sarah, Mark. BSME, U. Iowa, 1961, MSIE, 1962, PhD, 1970. Registered profl. engr., Mass. Mgmt. cons. U.S. Ameta, Rock Island, Ill., 1962-67; mgmt. instr. U. Iowa, Iowa City, 1967-69; head applied math. dept. U.S. Ameta, Rock Island, Ill., 1969-74, head managerial tng. dept., 1974-77; assoc. prof. mgt. U. Nebr., Lincoln, 1977-84, dir. grad. studies in mgmt., 1982—, prof. mgmt., 1984-87, Leonard E Whittaker Am. Charter disting. prof. mgmt., 1987-93, Met. Fed. Bank disting. prof. mgmt., 1993-95, First Bank disting. prof. mgmt., 1995-98, U.S. Bank disting. prof. mgmt., 1998—; dir. Ctr. for Tech. Mgmt. and Decision Scis., 1992-94; interim dir. Gallup Rsch. Ctr., 1994-95; mem. adv. bd. Ctr. for Albanian Studies, 1992—; cons. various orgns., 1963-72; sec. treas. Mgmt. Svcs. Assocs. Ltd., Davenport, Iowa, 1972-77; owner L.A. Digman and Assocs., Lincoln, 1977—; gen. ptnr. Letna Properties, Madison, Wis., 1978—. Author: Strategic Management, 1986, 5th edit., 1999, Network Analysis for Management Decisions, 1982; contbr. articles to profl. jours. Recipient Dist. award SBA, 1980, Certs. of Appreciation Dept. of Def., 1972. Fellow Decision Scis. Inst. (charter, program chmn. 1986, pres. 1987-88, coord. doctoral consortium 1989, strategy/policy track chmn. 1991, v.p. 1992-94, strategic mgmt. track chmn. internat. meeting 1993, chair long-range planning com. 1995-96, adv. com. for internat. meeting 1997); mem. IEEE, Strategic Mgmt. Soc. (founding), Acad. of Mgmt., Strategic Leadership Forum, Pan Pacific Bus. Assn., Inst. for Ops. Rsch. and Mgmt. Scis. (founding), MBA Roundtable (charter, steering com.), Lincoln Univ. Club, Firethorn Country Club, Confrerie de la Chaine Rotisseurs. Roman Catholic. Avocations: gardening, photography, wine tasting. Home: 7520 Lincolnshire Rd Lincoln NE 68506-1635 Office: U Nebr 277 CBA Lincoln NE 68588

DIGNAC, GENY (EUGENIA M. BERMUDEZ), sculptor; b. Buenos Aires, Argentina, June 8, 1932; came to U.S., 1954; d. Jose Victor Marenco and Margarita Eugenia D.; m. Jose Y. Bermudez, Apr. 7, 1958; children—Alexander, Melanie. Ed., U. Buenos Aires, 1952-54. lectr. in field. Exhibited in one-woman shows at Galeria 22, Caracas, Venezuela, 1967, Michael Berger Gallery, Pitts., 1969, Cinema 2, Caracas, 1971, Pyramid Gallery, Washington, 1971; exhibited in numerous group shows including Corcoran Gallery of Art, Washington, 1958, 59, Inst. Contemporary Arts, Washington, 1967, Bklyn. Mus., 1968, Mus. Modern Art, Buenos Aires, 1971, Mus. Fine Arts, Boston, 1971, Palais des Beaux Arts, Brussels, 1974, Inst. Contemporary Arts, London, 1974; represented in permanent collections including Fundacio Joan Miro, Barcelona, Spain, Palazzo Dei Diamanti, Ferrara, Italy, Museo La Tertulia, Cali, Colombia, Galeria del Banco Central, Guayaquil, Ecuador, The Latinoamerican Art Found., San Juan, P.R., and others in Argentina, Chile, Germany, Italy, Ireland, Spain, U.S. and Venezuela; works include 27 Fire Gestures-, 1970-89; radio and TV interviews, U.S. and abroad; works with lights, fire and temperatures; subject of profl. articles, films. Recipient prize for light sculpture IX Festival of Art, 1969. Home: 4109 E Via Estrella Phoenix AZ 85028-4515

DIGNAM, ROBERT JOSEPH, retired orthopaedic surgeon; b. Manchester, N.H., July 8, 1925; s. Walter Joseph and Margaret Veronica (Lowe) D.; m. Evelyn Pettitt, Aug. 4, 1951; children—Stephen Mark, Lyn Shore, Margaret Gale. B.S., Bates Coll., 1945; M.D., Tufts U., 1949. Intern Boston City Hosp., 1949-50, resident in orthopedic surgery, 1954-57; resident in orthopedic surgery Lahey Clinic, Boston, 1953-54; practice medicine specializing in orthopedic surgery Santa Monica, Calif., 1960-82; mem. staff St. Johns Hosp. UCLA Med. Center; clin. prof. orthopedic surgery UCLA. Served to lt., M.C. USN, 1951-54. Fellow A.C.S.; mem. AMA, Mass. Med. Soc., Calif. Med. Assn., Am. Acad. Orthopedic Surgeons. Home: 821 Alma Real Dr Pacific Palisades CA 90272-3705

DIGNAM, WILLIAM JOSEPH, obstetrician, gynecologist, educator; b. Manchester, N.H., Aug. 11, 1920; s. Walter Joseph and Margaret Veronica (Lowe) D.; m. Winifred Kennedy, June 7, 1947; children—Mary Brett, Kevan Jean, Erin Margaret, Meighan Ann. A.B., Dartmouth Coll., 1941; M.D., Harvard U., 1943. Intern Boston City Hosp., 1944; resident in ob-gyn U. Kans. Med. Ctr., Kansas City, 1947-50; from asst. prof. to prof. ob-gyn UCLA, 1951—; affiliated with UCLA Med. Ctr., Cedars-Sinai Med. Ctr., Harbor-UCLA Med. Ctr. Roman Catholic. Home: 820 Alma Real Dr Pacific Palisades CA 90272-3704 Office: UCLA Sch Medicine Dept Ob-Gyn 10833 Le Conte Ave Los Angeles CA 90095-3075

DIGNAN, THOMAS GREGORY, JR., lawyer; b. Worcester, Mass., May 23, 1940; s. Thomas Gregory and Hester Clare (Sharkey) D.; m. Mary Anne Connor, Sept. 16, 1978; children: Kellyanne E., Maryclare E. BA, Yale U., 1961; JD, U. Mich., 1964. Bar: Mass. 1964, U.S. Supreme Ct. 1968. Assoc. firm Ropes & Gray, Boston, 1964-74; ptnr. firm Ropes & Gray, 1974—; spl. asst. atty. gen. State of Mass., 1974-76; dir. Boston Edison Co.; trustee BEC Energy. Asst. editor: Mich. Law Rev., 1963-64; contbr. articles to profl. jours. Bd. dirs. Family Counseling and Guidance Ctrs., Inc., 1967-76, 78-94, v.p., 1983-87, pres., 1987-89; trustee Cath. Charitable Bur. of Boston, Inc., 1994-97, Dana Hall Sch., 1994—; bd. dirs. Gov.'s Mgmt. Task Force, 1979-81, Mass. Moderator's assn., 1994—; mem. fin. com. Town of Sudbury, 1982-85, moderator, 1985—; bd. advisors Environ. Law Ctr., Vt. Law Sch., 1981—; mem. vis. com. U. Mich. Law Sch.; corporator Emerson Hosp., 1989—. Mem. ABA, Mass. Bar Assn., Boston Bar Assn., Assn. Internationale du Droit Nucleaire, Am. Nuclear Soc., Am. Law Inst., Downtown Club, Nashawtuc Country Club, Order of the Coif, Phi Delta Phi. Republican. Roman Catholic. Home: 8 Saddle Ridge Rd Sudbury MA 01776-2772 Office: Ropes & Gray One International Pl Boston MA 02110

DIGREGORY, NICHOLAS A., secondary educator, coach; b. Phila., July 14, 1954; m. Kathleen A. McNamara, June 27, 1987; children: Megan Nicole, Sarah Elizabeth, Evan John. BA, East Stroudsburg (Pa.) U., 1976; MA, West Chester (Pa.) U., 1991; supr.'s cert., Rowan Coll., Glassboro, N.J., 1992. Substitute tchr. pub. schs., Pa., 1976-82; tchr. social studies Delsea Regional High Sch., Franklinville, N.J., 1982—, instrnl. supr. English and social studies dept., 1997. Mem. Collingdale (Pa.) Parks and Recreation Com., 1988-91. Named All-American scholar U.S. Achievement Acad., 1990. Mem. Nat. Coun. for Social Studies, Mid. States Coun. for Social Studies, East Stroudsburg U. Alumni Assn. (bd. dirs., coord. Delaware County, Pa. chpt. 1987—), Phi Alpha Theta. Avocations: tennis, biking, gardening. Office: Delsea Regional High Sch Blackwoodtown Rd Franklinville NJ 08322

DIGUIDO, AL, publishing executive; m. Chris DiGuido; children: Rosemarie, George, Diana. BA in Political Science, St. Francis Coll., Bklyn. Outdoors advtg. salesperson Foster and Kleiser; various advtg./sales pos. Training Mag. and 3M; nat. acct. exec. Parade Mag.; with mag. divsn. Children's Television Network; advtg. mgr. for PC Mag. Ziff-Davis Publishing, assoc. pub., pub. Computer Shopper Mag., exec. v.p. Office: Computer Shopper Ziff-Davis 28 E 28th St 10th Fl New York NY 10016*

DIJKSTRA, EDSGER WYBE, computer science educator, mathematician; b. Rotterdam, The Netherlands, May 11, 1930; came to U.S., 1984; s. Douwe Wijbe and Brechtje Cornelia (Kluyver) D.; m. Maria Cornelia Debets, Apr. 23, 1957; children: Marcus Joost, Femke Elisabeth, Rutger Michael. Candidaats degree, U. Leyden, The Netherlands, 1951; doctoral degree, U. Leyden, 1956; PhD, U. Amsterdam, 1959; DSc (hon.), Queen's U. Belfast, No. Ireland, 1976. Staff mem. Math. Centre, Amsterdam, The Netherlands, 1952-62; prof. math. Tech. U., Eindhoven, The Netherlands, 1962-73; rsch. fellow Burroughs Corp., Nuenen, The Netherlands, 1973-84; prof., Schlumberger Centennial chair in computer sci. U. Tex., Austin, 1984—. Editor Acta Informatica. Disting. fellow Brit. Computer Soc.; mem. Royal Netherlands Acad. Arts and Scis., Am. Acad. Arts and Scis. (hon. fgn.), Assn. for Computing Machinery (Turing award 1972). E-mail: dijksta@cs.utexas.edu. Home: 6602 Robbie Creek Cv Austin TX 78750-8138 Office: U Tex Dept Computer Scis Austin TX 78712

DIKEMAN, MAY, writer; b. Baldwin, N.Y., Sept. 8, 1923; d. James Bradley and Elsie Isabel (Helmrich) Dikeman; m. Norman Edward Hoss, Sept. 12, 1946; children: Antonie Kyrie, Kurt, Talara Kristin. BA, Vassar Coll., 1945. Instr. writers workshops New Sch. Social Rsch., N.Y.C., 1968-69. Author: (novel) The Pike, 1954, The Angelica, 1971, The Devil We Know, 1973; author of short stories. Atlantic "First" Ingram Merrill grantee Atlantic Monthly. Home: 70 Irving Pl New York NY 10003-2205

DIKTAS, CHRISTOS JAMES, lawyer; b. Hackensack, N.J., June 17, 1955; s. Christos James and Elpiniki (Angelou) D. Student U. Salonika (Greece), 1976, U. Copenhagen (Denmark), 1976. BA, Montclair State U., 1977; JD, Calif. Western Sch. Law, 1981; diploma, Rutgers U., 1992. Bar: N.J. 1982, U.S. Dist. Ct. N.J. 1982, N.Y. 1989, U.S. Supreme Ct. 1989. Law sec. Honorable James F. Madden, Superior Ct. Judge, Hackensack, N.J., 1981-82; sr. assoc. Klinger, Nicolette, Mavroudis & Honig, Hackensack, 1982-85; ptnr. Montecallo & Diktas, Hackensack, 1985-86; ptnr., Biagiotti, Marino, Montecallo & Diktas, Hackensack, 1986-89; ptnr., Diktas & Habeeb, North Bergen, N.J., 1989-94; ptnr. Diktas Gillen, 1995—. asst. counsel Bergen County, 1986-87; atty. zoning bd. adjustment Borough of Cliffside Park, N.J., 1986-94; atty. planning bd. Borough of Ridgefield, N.J., 1987—, Borough atty. Bogota, N.J., 1989-91; bd. edn. atty., Bogota, 1992-95; labor counsel Bergen County, N.J., 1990—; borough atty. Fairview, N.J., 1994-95; borough atty., Cliffside Park, 1994—; atty. planning bd. City of Garfield, N.J., 1994—; adj. prof. law Montclair (N.J.) State U., 1988—. Editor lead articles Calif. Western Internat. Law Jour., 1980-81. Campaign dir. Kingman for Senate Com., Bergen County, N.J., 1983; mcpl. coord. Kean for Gov. campaign, 1985; asst. treas. Arthur F. Jones for Congress, 9th Congl. Dist., 1986. Mem. ABA, N.J. Bar Assn., Bergen County Bar Assn., Order of Am. Hellenic Edn. Progressive Assn., Phi Alpa Delta (parliamentarian Campbell E. Beaumont chpt. 1978-81). Greek Orthodox. Lodge: Sons of Pericles (5th dist. gov. 1976-77, supreme gov. 1977-78). Home: 445 Oncrest Ter Cliffside Park NJ 07010-2814 Office: Diktas Gillen 596 Anderson Ave Cliffside Park NJ 07010-1831

DI LASCIA, ALFRED PAUL, philosophy educator; b. Chelsea, Mass., Jan. 6, 1924; s. Anthony Di Lascia and Concetta Pote; widowed; children: Gian-Maria, Paul. BA, Queens Coll., 1946; MA, Fordham U., 1949, PhD, 1967. From instr. to assoc. prof. philosophy Manhattan Coll., Riverdale, N.Y., 1949-72, prof. philosophy, 1972—; adj. prof. Hunter Coll., N.Y.C., 1965-82. Assoc. editor Cross Currents, 1950-90; mem. adv. bd. The Encyclopedia of Philosophy, 1967—; contbr. articles to profl. jours. Named Premio Internazionale Luigi Sturzo, City of Caltagisone, Italy, 1993; grantee Danforth Found., 1960-61, 63-64. Roman Catholic. Office: Manhattan Coll Riverdale NY 10471

DILBECK, CHARLES STEVENS, JR., real estate company executive; b. Dallas, Dec. 2, 1944; s. Charles Stevens Sr. and Betty Doris (Owens) D.; 1 child, Stephen Douglas; m. Carolyn Jane DeBoer, Sept. 4, 1994. BS, Wichita State U., 1968; MS, Stanford U., 1969, postgrad., 1970-71. Engr. United Tech. Ctr., Sunnyvale, Calif., 1971-72; cons. Diversicom, Inc., Santa Clara, Calif., 1972-73; engr. Anamet Labs., San Carlos, Calif., 1973-75; cons. real estate investment Cert. Capital Corp., San Jose, Calif., 1975-82; pvt. practice in real estate, San Jose, 1981—; prin. Am. Equity Investments, San Jose, 1982—; mem. Los Gatos (Calif.) Rent Adv. Com., 1988. Mem. Nat. Apt. Assn., San Jose Real Estate Bd., Tri-County Apt. Assn., Gold Key Club, Tau Beta Pi (pres. 1968), Sigma Gamma Tau. Republican. Avocation: ocean yacht racing. Home: 301 Alta Loma Ln Santa Cruz CA 95062-4620 Office: Am Equity Investments 301 Alta Loma Ln Santa Cruz CA 95062-4620

DILCHER, DAVID LEONARD, paleobotany educator, research scholar; b. Cedar Falls, Iowa, July 10, 1936; m. Katherine Swanson, 1961; children: Peter, Ann. BS in Natural History, U. Minn., 1958, MS in Botany, Geology and Zoology, 1960; postgrad., U. Ill., 1960-62; PhD in Biology, Geology, Yale U., 1964; participant OTS course field dendrology, Costa Rica, 1968. Teaching asst. U. Minn., Mpls., 1958-60, U. Ill., Urbana, 1960-62, Yale U., New Haven, Conn., 1962-63; Cullman-Univ. fellow Yale U., 1963-64, instr. biology, 1965-66; NSF postdoctoral fellow Senckenberg Mus., Frankfurt am Main, Fed. Republic of Germany, 1964-65; asst. prof. botany Ind. U., Bloomington, 1966-70, assoc. prof., 1970-76; Guggenheim fellow Imperial Coll., Univ. London, 1972-73; assoc. prof. geology Ind. U., Bloomington, 1975-77, prof. paleobotany, 1977-90, adj. prof. biology, adj. prof. geology, 1990—; grad. rsch. prof. Fla. Mus. Natural History, U. Fla., Gainesville, 1990—; panel mem. for systematic biology program, NSF, 1977, 78, 79, panel mem. for selecting NATO postdoctoral fellow, 1982, mem. adv. com. Earth Sys. History, 1997—; vis. lectr. to People's Republic of China Nat. Acad. Sci. com. on scholarly communications with China, 1986; corr. mem. Senckenberg Mus., Frankfurt, Fed. Republic Germany, 1989; hon. prof. Nanjing Inst. Geology and Paleontology, Acad. Sinica, China, 1998—. Author: (with D. Redmon, M. Tansey and D. Whitehead) Plant Biology Laboratory Manual, 1973, 2d edit., 1975; editor: (with Tom Taylor and Theodore Delevoryas) Plant Reproduction in the Fossil Record, symposium vol., 1979, (with T. Taylor) Biostratigraphy of Fossil Plants: Successional and Paleoecological Analysis, 1980, (with William L. Crepet) Origin and Evolution of Flowering Plants, Symposium Volume, 1984, (with Michael S. Zavada) Phylogeny of the Hamamedidae, symposium vol., 1986, (with Patrick S. Herendeen) Advances in Legume Systematics Part 4, The Fossil Record, 1992; contbr. numerous articles and abstracts to profl. jours. and books. Mem. utilities bd. City of Bloomington, 1974-76; ruling elder First Presbyn. Ch. Bloomington, 1975-77; bd. dirs. United Campus Ministries, 1971-72, Smithsonian Mus. Natural History, 1998—; mem. coun. Monroe County United Ministries, 1975-77. Dist. vis. rsch. scholar U. Adelaide, Australia, 1981, 88; vis. rsch. scholar Birbal Sahn Palaeonbot. Inst., Lucknow, India, 1992; grantee Sigma Xi, 1961, 62, 66, Ind. U., 1967-68, Orgn. Tropical Studies, 1971; travel grantee Ind. U., 1968, 71, 77, 80; rsch. grantee NSF, 1966-69, 69-71, 71-74, 75-77, 77-79, 79, 79-80, 79-84, 82-83, 83-84, 85-89, Amax Coal Found., 1980-81; Eaton-Hooker fellow, 1963, Cullman-Univ. fellow, 1963-64, Guggenheim fellow, Giessen, Fed. Republic of Germany, 1972-73, Ind. U., 1972-73, Brit. Mus. Natural History, London, 1988-89, NATO coop. rsch. grantee, 1991-93; recipient Tracey M. Sonneborn award for disting. rsch. and excellence in tchg. Ind. U., 1978-88, Bot. Soc. Am. Merit award, 1991, Birbal Sahni Found. award, 1998. Fellow Ind. Acad. Sci.; mem. NAS, AAAS, Bot. Soc. Am. (chmn. paleobot. sect. 1974, sec.-treas. 1975-77, rep. to jour. editl. bd. 1978-79, jour. editl. bd. 1981-82, conservation com. 1978-81, chmn. conservation com. 1981, 82, program dir. 1982-84, exec. bd. 1982-91, sec. 1984-88, pres.-elect 1988-89, pres. 1989-90), Paleontol. Soc., Paleontol. Assn., Internat. Orgn. Paleobotany (N.Am. rep. 1975-81, v.p. 1987-93), Assn. Tropical Biology, Am. Inst. Biol. Scis., Am. Assn. Stratigraphic Palynologists, Internat. Assn. Angiosperm Paleobotany (pres. 1977-80), Geol. Soc. Am. (com. on collection and collecting 1978-85), Ky. Acad. Scis., Senckenberg Natur Mus. und Forschungsgeshellshaft Frankfurt am Main (corr. mem. 1990), Sigma Xi (pres.-elect Ind. chpt. 1985-86, pres. 1986-87). Office: U Fla Dept Natural Sci Fla Mus Natural History PO Box 117800 Gainesville FL 32611-7800

DI LELLA, ALEXANDER ANTHONY, biblical studies educator; b. Paterson, N.J., Aug. 14, 1929; s. Alessandro and Adelaide (Grimaldi) Di L. B.A., St. Bonaventure U., 1952; S.T.L., Cath. U. Am., 1959, Ph.D., 1962; S.S.L., Pontifical Bibl. Inst., Rome, 1964. Entered Franciscan Order, Roman Catholic Ch., 1949; ordained priest, 1955. Lectr. O.T. and bibl. Greek Holy Name Coll., Washington, 1964-67; asst. prof. Semitic lang. Cath. U. Am., 1966-68, assoc. prof., 1968-76, assoc. prof. Bibl. studies, 1976-77, prof., 1977-92, Andrews-Kelly-Ryan disting. prof. bib. studies, 1992—; adj. prof. O.T., Washington Theol. Union, 1969-72; mem. Rev. Standard Version Bible Com., 1982—; chmn. bd. of control New Am. Bible, 1988—. Assoc. editor, translator New American Bible, 1965-87; editor New Revised Standard Version Bible Cath. Edit., 1993; author: The Hebrew Text of Sirach: A Text-Critical and Historical Study, 1966, The Book of Daniel, 1978, Proverbs in the Old Testament in Syriac According to the Peshitta Version, 1979, The Wisdom of Ben Sira, 1987, II Libro di Daniele (1-6), 1995, (7-14), 1996, Daniel: A Book for Troubling Times, 1997; contbr. articles and revs. to scholarly and popular publs. Mem. instnl. rev. bd. Dubroff Eye Ctr., Silver Spring, Md., 1982-94; cancer care continuum group Washington Hosp. Ctr., 1995-96. Am. Sch. Oriental Research fellow, 1962-63; Guggenheim fellow, 1972-73; Assn. Theol. Schs. in U.S. and Can. fellow, 1979-80. Mem. Soc. Bibl. Lit. (pres. Chesapeake Bay region 1972-73), Cath. Bibl. Assn. (pres. 1975-76, del. to Council on Study of Religion 1971-72). Home: Curley Hall Cath U Am Washington DC 20064 Office: Cath U Am Rm 420 Caldwell Hall Washington DC 20064 *Most of my adult life I have been a student of Biblical languages and literatures, interpretation and theology. Teaching, research and publications enable me to convey to others the value of the Bible as a primary document of Judaism and Christianity and as a significant factor in Western culture and civilization.*

DILEO, DANIEL, social sciences educator; b. N.Y.C., Nov. 9, 1953; s. Joseph H. and Joan (McTague) DiL. BA, Temple U., 1986, PhD, 1994. Staff nurse Grad. Hosp., Phila., 1976-81, Frankford Hosp., Phila., 1982-90; asst. prof. Bucknell U., Lewisburg, Pa., 1992-94, Pa. State U., Altoona, 1994—; mem. adv. bd. Home Nursing Agy., Altoona, 1997—. Contbr. articles to profl. jours. Roman Catholic.

DILFER, TRENT, professional football player; b. Mar. 13, 1972; m. Cassandra; 1 child, Madeleine. Student, Fresno State U. Quarterback Tampa Bay Buccaneers, 1994—. Active Fellowship Christian Athletes, Athletes in Action, United Way, Big Bros./Big Sisters, Police Athletic League, Hardy's Huddle. Broke Doug Williams 1982 record by throwing 138 consecutive passes without interception. Office: Tampa Bay Buccaneers One Buccaneer Pl Tampa FL 33607*

DILIBERTO, RICHARD ANTHONY, JR., lawyer; b. Hazleton, Pa., July 19, 1961; s. Richard A. Sr. and Marija (Vukcevich) D.; m. Faith Ann Petrovich, Sept. 4, 1982. BS in Edn. cum laude, Bloomsburg U. of Pa., 1982; JD cum laude, Widener U., Wilmington, Del., 1986. Bar: Del. 1986, Pa. 1987, N.J. 1987, U.S. Dist. Ct. Del. 1987. Law clk. Superior Ct. Del., Wilmington, 1986-87; ptnr. Young, Conaway, Stargatt & Taylor, Wilmington, 1987—; adj. prof. paralegal program Widener U., 1987-90; rep. Del State House of Reps., 1992—. Contbr. articles to profl. jours. Coach basketball YMCA, softball, 1994—. Recipient Assn. Trial Lawyers Am. Advocacy award, 1986, Del. State Bar Assn. Disting. Legis. Svc. award, 1999. Mem. ABA, Del. Bar Assn. Roman Catholic. Fax: (302) 571-1253. E-mail: rdiliberto@ycst.com. Home: 2 Philip Ct Newark DE 19711-5681 Office: Young Conaway Stargatt & Taylor Rodney Sq 11th Fl PO Box 391 Wilmington DE 19899-0391

DILKS, PARK BANKERT, JR., lawyer; b. Phila., Mar. 25, 1928; s. Park Bankert and Gertrude Scott (Hilton) D.; children: Jonathan Park, Jennifer Robin. AB, U. Pa., 1948, JD, 1951. Bar: Pa. 1952, D.C. 1951, U.S. Supreme Ct. 1962. Asst. dist. atty. Phila., 1952; assoc. firm Souser & Schumacker, Phila., 1953-60; assoc. firm Morgan, Lewis & Bockius, Phila., 1961-63, ptnr., 1964-95, of counsel, 1996—; chmn. bd. U.S. Investment Fund, 1973—; dir. Broadstone Group, Inc., N.Y.C. Served as 1st lt. USAR, 1952-58. Mem. ABA, Pa. Bar Assn., Phila. Bar Assn., D.C. Bar Assn., Fed. Bar Assn., Assn. Bar City N.Y., Phi Beta Kappa. Club: Union League. Home: 605 W Gravers Ln Philadelphia PA 19118-4127 Office: 1701 Market St Philadelphia PA 19103-2921

DILKS, SATTARIA S., mental health nurse, therapist; b. Iola, Kans., Oct. 12, 1955; d. Paul J. and Janice E. (McHenry) Smith; m. Lawrence S. Dilks, Feb. 24, 1990; children: Jason Kaine Alexander, Cameron Gray Alexander, Russell Morris Alexander, Michelle Elizabeth Dilks. BSN, West Tex. State U., 1978; MA in Psychology, McNeese State U., 1988. Cert. psychiat./mental health nurse; lic. profl. counselor, La. Mental health technician Killgore Children's Psychiat. Hosp., Amarillo, Tex.; nurse mgr. psychiat. unit St. Patrick Hosp., Lake Charles, La.; DON, clin. coord. Charter Hosp. of Lake Charles, adolescent svcs. program adminstr.; pvt. practice mental health counseling and consultation. Pres. adv. bd. Lake Charles Mental Health Ctr., 1990; active Girl Scouts U.S. Mem. La. Counseling Assn., La. Mental Health Counseling Assn., Girl Scouts U.S., Sigma Theta Tau. Home: 1901 Rosedown Dr Lake Charles LA 70605-9700 Office: 2829 4th Ave Ste 150 Lake Charles LA 70601-7897

DILL, CHARLES ANTHONY, manufacturing and computer company executive; b. Cleve., Nov. 29, 1939; s. Melville Reese and Gladys (Frode) D.; m. Louise T. Hall, Aug. 24, 1963 (dec. Sept. 28, 1983); children: Charles Anthony, Dudley Barnes; m. Mary M. Howell, Jan. 17, 1987. BSME, Yale U., 1961; MBA, Harvard U., 1963. With Emerson Electric Co., 1963-88, corp. v.p. internat., 1973-77; pres. A.B. Chance Co. subs. Emerson Electric Co., 1977-80; corp. group v.p. Emerson Electric Co., St. Louis, 1980-82; sr. v.p. office of chief exec., adv. dir. Emerson Electric Co., 1982-88; pres., COO, bd. dirs. AVX Corp., N.Y.C., 1988-90; pres., CEO, bd. dirs. Bridge Info. Systems, Inc., St. Louis, 1990-95; gen. ptnr. Gateway Equity Ptnrs. IV, St. Louis, 1995—; bd. dirs. Stout Industries, Eck Adams Corp., Digital Concepts of Mo., Zoltec Inc., Stifel Nicholaus Inc., Pinnacle Automation Inc., Transact Techs., DT Industries. Mem. St. Louis Country Club, Log Cabin Club. Republican. Home: 807 S Warson Rd Saint Louis MO 63124-1258 Office: Gateway Equity Partners 8000 Maryland Ave Ste 1190 Saint Louis MO 63105-3910

DILL, ELLEN RENÉE, minister; b. Detroit, Jan. 2, 1949; d. Clarence Lorenzo and Melvin Elizabeth (Knowles) D.; divorced; children: Christopher Edward Brown, Crystal Elizabeth Brown. BA, Nazareth Coll. Mich., 1972; MDiv, Garrett Evang. Sem., Evanston, Ill., 1979; postgrad., Northwestern U., Evanston, Ill., 1979-82; DMin, Chgo. Theol. Sem., 1995. Lic. to ministry United Meth. Ch., 1974, ordained 1985. Teaching asst. Head Start St. Agnes Ch., Detroit, 1966-68; tchr. Eastside Vicariate Sch., Detroit, 1972-77; pastor St. Luke United Meth. Ch., Chgo., 1980-82; assoc. pastor First United Meth. Ch., Chgo., 1982-84; pastor Clair-Christian United Meth. Ch., Chgo., 1984-88, Community United Meth. Ch., Markham, Ill., 1988-90, Woodlawn United Meth. Ch., Chgo., 1990-93, Immanuel United Meth. Ch., 1993—; pastor United campus ministry chaplain Winona (Minn.) State U., 1995—; condr. seminar on women in ministry Garrett Evang. Sem., 1981, condr. seminar on ch. and soc., 1980, instr. continuing edn. seminar for clergy in adminstrn., 1987; bd. dirs. So. Dist. Bd. Ordained Ministry, Bd. Ch. Bldg. Location; mem. So. Dist. Coun. on Ministries, So. Dist. Strategy Com.; former chmn. No. Ill. Conf. Bd. Edn., So. Dist. Bd. Edn.; former asst. chmn. bd. edn. United Meth. Ch.; mem. Detroit Conf. Elders Orders, 1985; asst. spiritual dir. Walk to Emmaus, 1988-90, 92, spiritual dir. men's walk, 1991; mem. No. Ill. Conf. Commn. on Status and Role of Women, 1991-93, United Meth. Found., U. Chgo., 1990-93; mem. monitoring com. Ill. Conf. Configuration; mem. planning com. Western Dist. Lab. Sch.; invocation Chgo. City Coun. meetings, 1990, 91, 93; chairperson Minn. Conf. Commn. on Religion and Race, 1995; mem. Minn. Conf. Coun. on Ministries, 1995—; mem. Ethics Minority Concerns Commn., Minn. Conf., 1993—; mem. med. ethics com. Cmty. Meml. Hosp., Winona, Minn., 1995—; active Winona Area Ministerium, 1995—, Winona Cultural Diversity Task Force, 1997—; bd. mem. Project Fine, 1997—. Co-author: Teachers Guide: Two Hundred Years of American Methodism, 1981; editorial advisor The Christian Ministry jour., 1987—; contbr. articles to profl. jours. Bd. dirs. Carroll M. Felton Jr. Housing Found., 1992-93; asst. dean Pembroke Inst., 1992; bd. dirs. Austin Christian Law Ctr., 1983-93, Child Serve Cmty. Coun., Chgo., 1984-88, Garrett-Evang. Sem., 1978; area chair Mayor's Com. to Keep Detroit Beautiful, 1965. Recipient citation Mayor's Com. To Keep Detroit Beautiful, 1966, citation for excellence in journalism Mich. Press Assn., 1978; Hartman scholar, 1979; Dempster Grad. fellow, 1980, Hartman fellow, 1981. Mem. NAFE, Nat. Assn. Bus. and Profl. Women, Internat. Platform Assn., Black United Meths. for Ch. Renewal (citation for svc. 1982, planning com. jurisdictional meeting, bd. dirs.), Clergy Cluster, Ecumenical Ministerial Assn., Women of the 90s (exec. com. 1992-93), Minn. Coun. of Chs. (bd. dirs. 1994—), Mpls. Initiative AgainstRacism, Mpls. Coun. Ch. (ministries divsn.). Avocations: reading, sewing, teaching, writing, studying. Home and Office: 457 S Baker St Winona MN 55987-2626 *In my life I have found that the power of evil is impotent when confronted by that which is good.*

DILL, ELLIS HAROLD, university dean; b. Pittsburg County, Okla., Dec. 31, 1932; s. Harold and Mayme Doris (Ellis) D.; m. Cleone June Granrud, Sept. 12, 1953; children—Michael Harold, Susan Marie. A.A., Grant Tech. Jr. Coll., 1951; B.S. in Civil Engring, U. Calif. at Berkeley, 1954, M.S. in Civil Engring, 1955, Ph.D., 1957. Asst. prof. to prof. aeros. and astronautics U. Wash., 1956-77, chmn. dept. aeros. and astronautics, 1976-77; dean engring. Rutgers U., New Brunswick, N.J., 1977-98, univ. prof., 1998—. Mem. Soc. Natural Philosophy. Research, numerous publs. on mechanics of solids. Home: 436 Brentwood Dr Piscataway NJ 08854-3608 Office: Rutgers U Coll Engring New Brunswick NJ 08903

DILL, FREDERICK HAYES, electrical engineer; b. Sewickley, Pa., Mar. 1, 1932; s. Frederick H. and Caroline (Rankin) D.; m. Amanda Brown, Feb. 26, 1968; children: Kevin A., Janet L., Stephen M. BS in Physics, Carnegie Inst. Tech., 1954, MSEE, 1956, PhDEE, 1958. Mem. rsch. staff IBM Rsch., Yorktown Heights, N.Y., 1958-82, sr. tech. staff, 1990—; sr. tech. staff gen. tech. div. IBM, East Fishkill, N.Y., 1983-89. Co-inventor solid state laser, video RAM memory; contbr. articles to profl. jours. Trainer, coach Westchester (N.Y.) Putnam Spl. Olympics, 1980-97, bd. dirs., 1982-92. 1st lt. U.S. Army, 1958-59. Fellow IEEE (Centennial medal 1984, bd. dirs. 1990-91); mem. NAE (chair electronics sect. 1999—), Electron Devices Soc. IEEE (v.p. 1980-81, pres. 1982-83), IBM Acad. Tech. (v.p., 1992, pres. 1993). Home: 28 Twin Lakes Rd South Salem NY 10590-1009 Office: IBM Rsch Ctr PO Box 218 Yorktown Heights NY 10598-0218

DILL, JOHN FRANCIS, retired publishing company executive; b. Hempstead, N.Y., May 3, 1934; s. Samuel Leland and Jeanne Marie (Dorsch) D.; m. Joan Eileen Shipps, Aug. 22, 1959 (div. 1973); m. Virginia Rae Dapson, Nov. 23, 1973; children: Patricia, Diane, Kevin, Catherine, Glenn. *John Francis Dill is the second son of Samuel Leland Dill (1896-1971). Samuel Dill descended from Caleb Dill (d. 1756), who about 1730 had immigrated from the North of Ireland and bought the McIntosh present in the town of Hamptonburgh, Orange County in the State of New York. Caleb had four sons: David, John, Caleb and Samuel Leland Dill's ancestor Robert (1721-1794). Robert Dill's son David (1759-1841) was a soldier in the Revolutionary War and fought at Fort Montgomery. In 1888 Samuel Leland Dill's grandfather, Samuel Dill (1838-1921), was elected Sheriff in Ulster County, New York.* BA, Oberlin Coll., 1957; MBA, NYU, 1963; LHD (hon.), Logan Coll., 1995, U. Mo., St. Louis, 1996. Mgmt. trainee Mut. Life Ins., N.Y.C., 1959-63; mgr. McGraw Hill Book Co., N.Y.C., 1963-68, dir. mktg., 1969-77, pub., gen. mgr., 1977-81; pres., CEO Year Book Med. Pubs., Chgo., 1981-89; pres., chief exec. officer CRC Press Inc., Boca Raton, Fla.; chmn., CEO, pres. Mosby Year Book, 1989-95, chmn. emeritus, 1995—. Bd. dirs. Copyright Clearance Ctr., 1989-95, Mathews Dickey Boy's Club, U. Mo., St. Louis, Chancellor's Coun., pres. 1994-95. Mem. Am. Med. Pubs. Assn. (pres. 1987-88), Am. Assn. Pubs. (chmn. profl. divsn. 1981, chmn. librs. com. 1979), Internat. Assn. Sci. Tech., Med. Pubs. of the World (bd. dirs., treas., chmn. 1994-96), St. Louis Club, Country Club of St. Albans. E-mail: vfdill@aol.com. Home: 216 Carlyle Lake Dr Saint Louis MO 63141-7544

DILL, KENNETH AUSTIN, pharmaceutical chemistry educator; b. Oklahoma City, Dec. 11, 1947; s. Austin Glenn and Margaret (Blocker) D. S.B., Mass. Inst. Tech., 1971, S.M., 1971; Ph.D., U. Calif.-San Diego, 1978. Fellow Damon Runyon-Walter Winchell Stanford (Calif.) U., 1978-81; asst. prof. chemistry U. Fla., Gainesville, 1981-82; asst. prof. pharm. chemistry and pharmacy U. Calif., San Francisco, 1982-85, assoc. prof., 1985-89, prof., 1989—; adj. prof. pharmaceutics U. Utah, 1989—. PEW Found. scholar; recipient Hans Neurath award Protein Soc., 1998. Contbr. numerous sci. articles to profl. publs.; patentee in field. Fellow Am. Phys. Soc., AAAS; mem. Am. Chem. Soc., Biophys. Soc. (Nat. lectr. 1996, pres. 1998). Office: Univ Calif Pharm Chemistry Dept San Francisco CA 94143

DILL, LADDIE JOHN, artist; b. Long Beach, Calif., Sept. 14, 1943; s. James Melvin and Virginia (Crane) D.; children: Ariel, Jackson Caldwell. BFA, Chouinard Art Inst., 1968. Chmn. of visual arts The Studio Sch., Santa Monica, Calif.; lectr. painting and drawing UCLA, 1975-88. Exhbns. include: San Francisco Mus. Modern Art, 1977-78, Albright Knox Mus., Buffalo, 1978-79, Charles Cowles Gallery, N.Y.C., 1983-85, The First Show, Los Angeles; represented in permanent collections: Mus. Modern Art, N.Y.C., Laguna Mus. Art, Los Angeles County Mus., Mus. Contemporary Art, Los Angeles, Santa Barbara Mus., San Francisco Mus. Modern Art, Seattle Mus., Newport Harbor Art Mus., Oakland Mus., Smithsonian Instn., IBM, Nat. Mus., Seoul, Republic of Korea, San Diego Mus. Art, La. Mus., Denmark, Am. Embassy, Helsinki, Finland, Corcoran Gallery Art, Washington, Chgo Art Inst., Greenville County (S.C.) Mus., Palm Springs Desert Mus., Phoenix Art Mus., William Rockhill Nelsen Mus., Kansas City, Phillips Collection. Nat. Endowment Arts grantee, 1975, 82; Guggenheim Found. fellow, 1979-80; Calif. Arts Council Commn. grantee, 1983-84.

DILL, LESLEY, sculptor; b. Bronxville, N.Y., 1950. Student, Skidmore Coll., 1968-70; BA in English cum laude, Trinity Coll., 1972; MA in Art Edn., Smith Coll., 1974; MFA in Painting, Md. Inst. Art, 1980. curator fall show Condeso/Lawler Gallery, N.Y., 1984; artist-in-residence Altos de Chavon, Dominican Republic, 1984; curator Traps: Elements of Psychic Seduction, Carlo Lamagna Gallery, N.Y., 1987; faculty Parsons Sch. Design, 1991—; instr. art St. Ann's Sch., Bklyn., 1984-91, Parsons Sch. Design, 1990-91. One-person shows include Queens Mus. Bulova, N.Y., 1992, Arthur Roger Gallery, New Orleans, 1993, 94, Ann Jaffe Gallery, Miami, Fla., 1993, Sandler Hudson Gallery, Atlanta, 1993, Bernard Toale Gallery, Boston, 1993, Frumkin/Adams Gallery, N.Y., 1993, Gracie Mansion Gallery, N.Y., 1994, Aldrich Mus. Contemporary Art, 1993, Nohra Haime Gallery, N.Y., 1994, Rotunda Gallery, Bklyn., 1994, Castle Gallery, Coll. New Rochelle, N.Y., 1994, Valparaiso Biennial, Chile, 1994-95, Frumkin/Adams Gallery, N.Y.C., 1993, 95, Gallery at Dieu Donne Papermill, N.Y.C., 1995, George Adams Gallery, , N.Y.C., 1995, 97, Orlando Mus. Art, Fla., 1996, Creteil Maison des Arts, 1996, Cohen Berkowitz Gallery, Kansas City, 1996, Susan Cummins Gallery, Mill Valley, Calif., 1996; Art Mus. U. Memphis, 1997, Equinox Gallery, Vancouver, Can., 1997, Galleru Cohn Edelstein, São Paulo, Brazil, 1997, Locus Gallery, St. Louis, 1998; two person shows include Nature Morte Gallery, New Delhi, 1998; represented in permanent collections Libr. Congress, Washington, Met. Mus. Art and Mus. Modern Art, N.Y., RISD, Providence, Prudential Ins. Co. Am., Newark, Achenbach Found., MH de Young Meml. Mus., San Francisco. Recipient Zaner Corp. Purchase award Small Works, 1983, Patterson Sims, 1983, Project Residency award Hillwood Art Mus. and N.Y. State Coun. Arts, 1992; fellow Nat. Endowment Arts, 1990. Home: 6 Greene St New York NY 10013-5814 Office: Frumkin/Adams Gallery 50 W 57th St New York NY 10019-3914

DILL, SHERI, publishing executive. Assoc. pub. Wichita (Kans.) Eagle, v.p. mktg. Office: The Wichita Eagle PO Box 820 Wichita KS 67201-0820*

DILL, VIRGINIA S., accountant; b. Ilion, N.Y., June 19, 1938; d. Marhlon G. and Beatrice M. (Suffern) Dapson; m. John F. Dill, Nov. 23, 1973; children: Patricia, Diane, Kevin, Catherine, Glenn. Student, U. Rochester, 1956-58; BA, Upsala Coll., 1976. CPA. Sales assoc. Lauten Realty, Middletown, N.J., 1971-73; staff mem. Arthur Young & Co., Newark, 1976-81; mgr. Arthur Young & Co., Chgo., 1981-85, prin., 1985-88, ptnr., 1988-89; ptnr. Ernst & Young, Chgo., 1989-90, St. Louis, 1990; v.p. fin. Felco AutoLease, St. Louis, 1991-92, exec. v.p., cfo, 1992-98; bd. dirs. Citizens Nat. Bank of Greater St. Louis. Bd. dirs., treas. Chgo. City Ballet, 1985-87; co-founder Ballet Chgo., 1987-91; treas. Dance St. Louis, 1991—, United Way Gtr. St. Louis; vice chmn. Inventions, 1986—, St. Louis Forum, 1992—. Mem. AICPA, Fin. Execs. Inst. (bd. dirs. St. Louis chpt. 1992—, pres. 1998-99), St. Louis Club. Home: 216 Carlyle Lake Dr Saint Louis MO 63141-7544

DILL, WILLIAM RANKIN, college president; b. Sewickley, Pa., Aug. 18, 1930; s. Frederick Hayes and Caroline (Rankin) D.; m. Jean McLeod, June 13, 1953; children: Jens McLeod, Holly Ruth, Harrison Rankin, Cynthia Wightman. AB, Bates Coll., 1951, LLD (hon.), 1987; MS, Carnegie Inst. Tech., 1953, PhD, 1956; postgrad., U. Oslo, 1953-54; LHD (hon.), Babson Coll., 1991. Faculty mem. Carnegie-Mellon U., Pitts., 1955-65; program dir. edn. R & D IBM, White Plains, N.Y., 1965-70; dean Grad. Sch. Bus. Adminstrn., NYU, N.Y.C., 1970-80, U.S.-Chinese Nat. Ctr. for Mgmt. Devel., Dalian, China, 1980-81; pres. Babson Coll., Wellesley, Mass., 1981-89; dir. Office of Global Enterprise U. So. Maine, Portland, 1989-91, cons., 1991-94; pres. Anna Maria Coll., 1995-96, Boston Arch. Ctr., 1996-97; bd. dirs. Salomon Bros. Mut. Funds; trustee Bradford Coll., Maine Coll. of Art. Author: The New Managers, 1962, The Carnegie Tech. Management Game, 1964, The Organizational World, 1973, Running the American Corporation, 1978, Planning in the US and USSR, 1978. Fulbright scholar, 1953-54; recipient Disting. Achievement award Carnegie-Mellon U., 1989. Fellow AAAS; mem. Phi Beta Kappa, Sigma Xi, Delta Sigma Rho, Beta Gamma Sigma. Unitarian. Home: 25 Birch Ln Cumb Foreside ME 04110-1225

DILLABER, PHILIP ARTHUR, budget and resource analyst, economist, consultant; b. Springfield, Mass., Aug. 24, 1922; s. Ralph E. and Grace (Holman) D.; m. Jacqueline M. Bertin, July 16, 1946; children: Anne Erline (Mrs. Donald Youngblood), Katherine Marie, John Philip, Patricia Elizabeth (Mrs. Joseph Mickley). *Brother, Private Ralph E. Dillaber, Selectee, was the first western Massachusetts casualty on maneuvers, June 6, 1941. Sister Maria Raphael has been a member of the St. Joseph order for 50 years. Wife, Jacqueline has a BA from George Mason University and is a music teacher. Daughter, Anne, has a BA and MA in Education from Old Dominion and George Mason Universities and is a teacher. Daughter, Katherine, has a BA in Communications from James Madison University and is an Army program analyst. Son, John, has a BA in Photography from George Mason University and is a photographer for the Smithsonian. Daughter, Patricia, has a BS in Business from Virginia Polytechnic Institute and State University and is a defense budget analyst.* BA with honors, Am. Internat. Coll., 1949; MBA, Ind. U., 1950; postgrad., U. Mich., Ind. U., 1950-54; PhD, Pacific Western U., 1985. Cert. govt. fin. mgr. Clk. rsch. and devel. div. Springfield Armory, 1946-47; rsch. asst. dept. econs. Ind. U., 1951, lectr. econs., 1955-57; orgn. and methods examiner USAF, Gulfport, Miss., 1952-53; mgmt. analyst 5th U.S. Army, Chgo., 1954-61; program progress and resources mgmt. analyst Continental Army Command, Ft. Monroe, Va., 1962-66; adminstrv. officer U.S. Army NIKE-X System Office, Alexandria, Va., 1967; program analyst Office Asst. Chief Staff Force Devel. Dept. Army, Washington, 1967-71, budget analyst Office Dep. Chief Staff Logistics, 1971-74; budget analyst Office Dep. Chief Staff Rsch., Devel. and Acquisition, Washington, 1974-80; sr. analyst Info. Spectrum, Inc., Arlington, Va., 1980-87; mem. Nat. Def. Exec. Reserve, Washington, 1985-97; cons. Profl. Group, Inc., 1992—; del. Citizen Amb. Program Pub. Budgeting and Fin. Mgmt., People's Republic of China, 1995; mem. Nat. Exec. Svc. Corp., N.Y.C., 1997; guest lectr. econs. Purdue U., 1959-61. *Dr. Dillaber started in the Springfield Armory on the production line. He was a member of the Service Army Finance Corps as part of the D-Day Normandy landings. He returned to Research and Development and to college through his PhD in Economics. He worked in the Air Force and Army training commands on major issues. Later he was an administrative officer in the Nike-X Office (ABM). Next, as a program analyst for the Combat Vehicles Office (the first Army effort system wide development), in the Air Defense Office, a coordinator for the Army production base budget and a budget preparer for the entire Army Major Equipment program from 1972 to 1980. For the next seven years, he was with a private firm contracting with the Navy. Since his second retirement he has continued activity with the National Defense Executive Reserve, from 1985 to 1997, and National Executive Service Corps, from 1997 to the present.* Decorated Commendation medal Regional Coun., Normandy, France, 1994, Wall of Liberty Meml. Mus., Caen, France, 1994; mem. Exceptional WWII Fin. Unit displayed U.S. Army Fin. Corps Mus., Ft. Jackson, S.C. Mem. Am. Econ. Assn., Nat. Contract Mgmt. Assn., Nat. Def. Indsl. Assn., Am. Assn. Budget Program Analysis, Project Mgmt. Inst., Assn. Govt. Accts. (cert. govt. fin. mgr.), Am. Soc. Pub. Adminstrn., Sons. of Am. Revolution, Assn. Def. and Emergency Resources, Beta Gamma Sigma. Home: 3003 Arkendale St Woodbridge VA 22193-1223

DILLAHUNTY, WILBUR HARRIS, lawyer; b. Memphis, June 30, 1928; s. Joseph S. and Octavia M. (Jones) D.; 1 child, Sharon K. JD, U. Ark., 1954. Bar: Ark. 1954. City atty. West Memphis, Ark., 1958-68; U.S. atty. (ea. dist.) Little Rock, 1968-79; exec. asst. adminstr. SBA, Washington, 1979-80; prin. Dillahunty Law Firm, Little Rock, 1980—; chancery and probate judge 6th Jud. Dist., 6th Divsn., Little Rock, 1997—. Served to lt. U.S. Army, 1945-48, ETO. Mem. ABA, Pulaski Bar Assn., Nat. Assn. Former U.S. Attys. (pres. 1991—), Am. Inns of Ct. (pres. William R. Overton chpt. 1989-90). Home: 9710 Catskill Rd Little Rock AR 72227-5562

DILLARD, ANNIE, author; b. Pitts., Apr. 30, 1945; d. Frank and Pam (Lambert) Doak; m. R.H.W. Dillard, 1965 (div.); m. Gary Clevidence, 1980 (div.); 1 child, Cody Rose; stepchildren: Carin, Shelly; m. Robert D. Richardson, Jr., 1988. BA, Hollins Coll., 1967, MA, 1968. Contbg. editor Harper's Mag., N.Y.C., 1974-81, 83-85; scholar-in-residence Western Wash. U., Bellingham, 1975-78; disting. vis. prof. Wesleyan U., 1979-83, adj. prof., 1983—, writer-in-residence, 1987—, bd. dirs. Writers Conf., 1984—, chmn., 1991—; fellow Calhoun Coll., Yale U., New Haven, Conn.; Phi Beta Kappa orator Harvard-Radcliffe U., 1983; mem. U.S. writers del. UCLA US-Chinese Writers Conf., 1982; mem. U.S. cultural del. to China, 1982; bd. dirs. The New Press, Key West Writers Conf., Wesleyan Writers Conf., Key West Literary Seminars; mem. usage panel Am. Heritage Dictionary. Author: Tickets for a Prayer Wheel, 1974, Pilgrim at Tinker Creek, 1974 (Pulitzer prize for gen. non-fiction 1975, Best Fgn. Book Pub. in France 1990), Holy the Firm, 1978, Living by Fiction, 1982, Teaching a Stone to Talk, 1982, Encounters with Chinese Writers, 1984, An American Childhood, 1987 (Nat. Book Critics award finalist 1987), The Writing Life, 1989 (English-speaking union Amb. Book award 1990), The Living, 1992, The Annie Dillard Reader, 1994, Mornings Like This, 1995, For the Time Being, 1999, For the Time Being, 1999; editor: (with Robert Atwan) Best Essays, 1988; (with Cort Conley) Modern American Memoirs, 1995. Mem. Nat. Com. on U.S.-China Rels., 1982—, Cath. Commn. Intellectual and Cultural Affairs, St. Mary's Soup Kitchen, Key West, Fla.; bd. dirs. Milton Ctr., Authors League Fund. Recipient N.Y. Presswomen's award for excellence, 1975, Wash. Gov.'s award for contbn. to lit., 1978, Appalachian Gold medallion U. Charleston, 1989, Found. award St. Botolph's Club, 1989, History Maker award Hist. Soc. Western Pa., 1993, Conn. Gov.'s award in the arts, 1993, Milton Ctr. prize, 1994, Campion award Am. Mag., 1994, Am. Arts and Letters award in Lit., 1998; grantee NEA, 1980-81, Guggenheim Found., 1985-86. Mem. NAACP, Soc. Am. Historians, Poetry Soc. Am., Authors Guild, Nat. Citizens for Pub. Librs., Am. Acad. Arts and Letters, Phi Beta Kappa. Democrat. Address: c/o Timothy Seldes Russell & Volkening 50 W 29th St New York NY 10001-4227

DILLARD, DEAN INNES, English language educator; b. Melvern, Kans., Aug. 13, 1947; s. Alva Everett and Dorothy Marie (Whitney) D. BS in Edn., Emporia (Kans.) State U., 1969, MA, 1975, postgrad., 1977; postgrad., Ft. Hays State U., Hays, Kans., 1980. Tchr. English Unified Sch. Dist. 379, Clay Center, Kans., 1969-70; tchr. English and social studies Unified Sch. Dist. 208, WaKeeney, Kans., 1972-84; instr. English Neosho County C.C., Chanute, Kans., 1984—, chair divsn. liberal arts, 1996—, interim v.p. acad. and student affairs, 1997-98; fine arts task force Neosho County C.C., Chanute, 1990-91. With U.S. Army, 1970-71. Mem. MLA, ASCD, Nat. Coun. Tchrs. English, Nat. Coun. Instructional Adminstrs., The Assn. Lit. Scholars and Critics, Assembly on Lit. for Adolescents (life), Midwest Modern Lang. Assn., Kans. Assn. Tchrs. English (exec. bd. 1981-84), Neosho County C.C. Educators Assn., Am. Legion, VFW, Chanute Lions Club (zone chmn. 1988-90), Kappa Delta Pi. Republican. Home: 732 S Washington Ave Chanute KS 66720-2713 Office: Neosho County C C 800 W 14th St Chanute KS 66720-2639

DILLARD, JOHN MARTIN, lawyer, pilot; b. Long Beach, Calif., Dec. 25, 1945; s. John Warren and Clara Leora (Livermore) D.; student U. Calif., Berkeley, 1963-67; BA, UCLA, 1968; JD, Pepperdine U., 1976; m. Patricia Anne Yeager, Aug. 10, 1968; children: Jason Robert, Jennifer Lee. Instr. pilot Norton AFB, Calif., 1973-77. Bar: Calif., 1976. Assoc. Magana, Cathcart & McCarthy, L.A., 1977-80, Lord, Bissell & Brook, L.A., 1980-85; of counsel Finley, Kumble, Wagner, 1985-86, Schell & Delamer, 1986-94, Law Offices of John M. Dillard, 1986—, v.p., gen. counsel, dir. Resort Aviation Svcs, Inc., Calif., 1988-93; mng. ptnr. Natkin & Weisbach, So. Calif., 1988-89; arbitrator Orange County Superior Ct.; atty. settlement officer U.S. Dist. Ct. Ctrl. Dist. Calif. Active Am. Cancer Soc.; bd. dirs. Placentia-Yorba Linda Edn. Found., Inc. Capt. USAF, 1968-73, Vietnam. Mem. ATLA (aviation litigation com.), Am. Bar Assn. (aviation com.), Orange County Bar Assn., Fed. Bar Assn., L.A. County Bar Assn. (aviation com.), Century City Bar Assn., Internat. Platform Assn., Res. Officers Assn., Orange County Com. of 100, Sigma Nu. Home: 19621 Verona Ln Yorba Linda CA 92886-2858 Office: 313 N Birch St Santa Ana CA 92701-5263

DILLARD, MARILYN DIANNE, property manager; b. Norfolk, Va., July 7, 1940; d. Thomas Ortman and Sally Ruth (Wallerich) D.; m. James Conner Coons, Nov. 6, 1965 (div. June 1988); 1 child, Adrienne Alexandra Dillard Coons (dec.). Studied with Russian prima ballerina, Alexandra Danilova, 1940's; student with honors at entrance, UCLA, 1958-59; BA in Bus. Adminstrn. with honors, U. Wash., 1962. Modeling-print work Harry Conover, N.Y.C., 1945; ballet instr. Ivan Novikoff Sch. Russian Ballet, 1955; model Elizabeth Leonard Agy., Seattle, 1955-68; mem. fashion bd., retail worker Frederick & Nelson, Seattle, 1962; retail worker I. Magnin & Co., Seattle, 1963-64; property mgr. Seattle, 1961—; antique and interior designer John J. Cunningham Antiques, Seattle, 1968-73; owner, interior designer Marilyn Dianne Dillard Interiors, 1973—; rsch. bd. advisors Am. Biog. Inst., Inc., 1990—. Author: (poetry) Flutterby, 1951, Spring Flowers, 1951; contbr., asst. chmn. (with Jr. League of Seattle) Seattle Classic Cookbook, 1980-83. Charter mem., pres. Children's Med. Ctr., Maude Fox Guild, Seattle, 1965—, Jr. Women's Symphony Assn., 1967-73, Va. Mason Med. Ctr. Soc., 1990—, Nat. Mus. of Am. Indian, Smithsonian Instn., 1992; mem. Seattle Jr. Club, 1962-65, 97—; bd. dirs. Patrons N.W. Civic, Cultural and Charitable Orgns., chmn. various coms., Seattle, 1976—, prodn. chmn., 1977-78, 84-85, auction party chmn., 1983-84, exec. com., 1984-85, chmn. bd. vols., 1990-91, adv. coun., 1991—; mem. U. Wash. Arboretum Found. Unit, 1966-73, pres., 1969; bd. dirs. Coun. for Prevention Child Abuse-Neglect, Seattle, 1974-75; bd. dirs., v.p., mem. coms. Seattle Children's Theatre, 1984-90, asst. in lighting main stage plays, 1987-93, adv. coun., 1993—; asst. in lighting main stage plays Bathhouse Theatre, 1987-90; adv. bd. N.W. Asian Am. Theatre, 1987—, Co-Motion Dance Co., 1991—; organizer teen groups Episcopal Ch. of Epiphany, 1965-67; provisional class pres. Jr. League Seattle, 1971-72, next to new shop asst. chmn., 1972-73, bd. dirs. admissions chmn., 1976-77, exec. v.p., exec. com., bd. dirs., 1978-79, sustaining mem., 1984—; charter mem. Jr. Women's Symphony Assn., 1967-73; mem. Seattle Art Mus., 1975-90, Landmark, 1990—, Corp. Coun. for Arts, 1991—; founding dir. Adrienne Coons Meml. Fund, 1985, v.p., 1985-92, 95—, pres. 1992-95; mem. steering com. Heart Ball Am. Heart Assn., 1986, 87, auction chmn., 1986; mem. steering com. Bellevue Sch. Dist. Children's Theatre, 1983-85, pub. rels. chair, 1984, asst. stage mgr., 1985; mem. Hist. Seattle Preservation and Devel. Authority, 1997—; mem. Eastlake Cmty. Coun., 1997—. Named Miss Greater Seattle, 1964. Mem. U. Wash. Alumnae Assn. (life), Pacific N.W. Ballet Assn. (charter), Progressive Animal Welfare Soc., Associated Women (student coun. U. Wash. 1962), Profl. Rodeo Cowboys Assn. (assoc.), Seattle Tennis Club. Republican. Episcopalian. Avocations: needlepoint, horseback riding, theatre, travel, antique restoration. Home and Office: 2053 Minor Ave E Seattle WA 98102-3513

DILLARD, NANCY ROSE, naval officer; b. Rosebud, Tex., Oct. 31, 1950; d. Hilyard Blanchard and Rose Lee (Kuhn) D. BSEd, Ga So. Coll., 1973, MEd, 1974, EdS, 1978; MS, Naval Postgrad. Sch., 1990; MA, Naval War Coll., 1997. Field agt. N.Y. Life Ins. Co., Savannah, 1979-81; commd. ensign USN, 1982, advanced through grades to comdr., 1999; with U.S. Naval Comms. Sta., Nea Makri, Greece, 1982-85, Naval Telecomms. Command, Washington, 1985-88, Naval Comms. Detachment, Cheltenham, Md., 1990-92, Bur. Naval Pers., Washington, 1992-94, Naval Computer & Telecomms. Sta., New Orleans, 1994-96, U.S. Cen. Command, Tampa, Fla. Decorated Joint Svc. Achievement medal, Naval Commendation medal with 3 gold stars, Naval Achievement medal with gold star. Mem. Ga. Assn. Intercollegiate Athletics for Women (chmn. ethics and eligibility com., bd. dirs. 1976-78), Ga. Assn. Health, Phys. Edn., Recreation and Dance (v.p. for health 1977), U.S. Naval Inst., Pilot Club, Delta Kappa Gamma. Roman Catholic. Avocations: reading, golf, travel. Home: 3605 Elk Ridge Ln Valrico FL 33594-6390

DILLARD, RICHARD, director of public affairs. Dir. pub. affairs Milliken & Co., Spartanburg, S.C. Office: Milliken & Co PO Box 1926 Spartanburg SC 29304-1926

DILLARD, RICHARD HENRY WILDE, English language professional, educator, author; b. Roanoke, Va., Oct. 11, 1937; s. Benton Oscar and Mattie Lee (Mullins) D.; m. Cathy Anne Hankla, Mar. 24, 1979. B.A., Roanoke Coll., 1958; M.A. (Woodrow Wilson fellow), U. Va., 1959, Ph.D., 1965. Instr. in English, Roanoke Coll., summer 1961; Instr. in English U. Va., 1961-64; asst. prof. English, Hollins Coll., 1964-68, assoc. prof., 1968-74, prof., 1974—. Author: The Day I Stopped Dreaming About Barbara Steele, 1966, News of the Nile, 1971, After Borges, 1972, The Book of Changes, 1974, Horror Films, 1976, The Greeting: New and Selected Poems, 1981, The First Man on the Sun, 1983, Understanding George Garrett, 1988, Just Here, Just Now, 1994, Omniphobia, 1995; (with others) A New Pléiade: Seleacted Poems, 1998, (screenplay) Frankenstein Meets the Space Monster, 1965; editor Hollins Critic, 1996—; editorial bd. Hollins Critic, 1966-77; editor-in-chief Children's Literature, 1992—. Ford Found. grantee, 1972; recipient Acad. Am. Poets award, 1961, O.B. Hardison, Jr. Poetry prize, 1994; named CASE Va. Prof. of Yr., 1987. Mem. Authors Guild, Bibliog. Soc. U. Va., Thoreau Soc., Poe Studies Assn., Internat. PEN, Melville Soc., Truman Library Inst., Phi Beta Kappa. Democrat. Baptist. Office: PO Box 9671 Roanoke VA 24020-1671

DILLARD, ROBERT LIONEL, JR., lawyer, former life insurance executive; b. Corsicana, Tex., Sept. 30, 1913; s. Robert Lionel and Mattie Sam (Jack) D.; m. Dundee Sheeks, Jan 30, 1937; children: Robert Lionel III, Diane Dillard More, Deborah (Mrs. John B. Cullen III). B.S. in Commerce, So. Meth. U., 1934, J.D., 1935; LL.M., Harvard U., 1936. Bar: Tex. 1935. With firm Saner, Saner & Jack, Dallas, 1936-41; asst. city atty. Dallas, 1941-45; with Southland Life Ins. Co., Dallas, 1945—; v.p., gen. counsel, sr. v.p., gen. counsel Southland Life Ins. Co., 1966-70, exec. v.p., gen. counsel, 1970-78, also dir.; with firm Saner, Jack, Sallinger & Nichols (now Nichols, Jackson, Dillard, Hager & Smith), Dallas, 1978—; city atty. Carrollton, Tex., 1947-75. Author articles in field. Mem. bd. edn. Dallas Ind. Sch. Dist., 1953-62, pres., 1961-62, trustee pub. TV, Dallas, 1957-74; pres. Dallas Council Social Agys., 1963-65, Dallas Council Camp Fire Girls, 1960-61; chmn. nat. bd. Camp Fire Girls, 1965-68; officer, dir. Dallas Symphony Orch., 1961-74. Recipient Disting. Law Alumnus award So. Meth. U., 1958, Disting. Alumnus award, 1963. Fellow Am. Bar Found.; mem. ABA (ho. of dels. 1956-58), Inter-Am. Bar Assn., Tex. Bar, Dallas Bar Assn. (pres. 1948), Am. Judicature Soc., Nat. Legal Aid Soc., Assn. Life Ins. Counsel (pres. 1973—), Alpha Tau Omega, Delta Theta Phi (past dist. chancellor), Order Woolsack. Methodist (chmn. ofcl. bd., tchr. adult Sunday sch.). Club: Mason (33 deg.; grand master Tex. 1961-62). Home: 6624 Lakewood Blvd Dallas TX 75214-3747 Office: 500 N Akard St Ste 1800 Dallas TX 75201-3350

DILLARD, ROBERT PERKINS, pediatrician, educator; b. Ft. Benjamin Harrison, Ind., June 7, 1941; s. Harry Knight and Anna Frances (Perkins) D.; children: Robert Perkins, Ann Michele, Christopher Stevens, Catherine Colleen; m. Roberta L. Schaffner, Oct. 20, 1991; 1 child, Preston Fielding. AB, Transylvania U., 1963; MD, U. Ky., Lexington, 1967. Diplomate Am. Bd. Pediatrics, subbd. pediatric gastroenterology; lic. physician, Ky., Fla., N.C. Rotating intern U. Okla. Med. Ctr., Oklahoma City, 1967-68; resident in pediat. Children's Meml. Hosp., U. Okla. Med. Ctr., Oklahoma City, 1968-71; fellow pediatric gastroenterology and nutrition Children's Hosp. Med. ctr., Cin., 1989-90; clin. asst. prof. pediatrics U South Fla. Coll. Medicine, Tampa, 1975-77; asst. prof. pediatric medicine, assoc. dir. ambulatory peds. East Carolina U., Greenville, N.C., 1977-83, dir. pediatric nutrition support svcs., 1981-83; assoc. prof. pediatrics U. Ky. Coll. Medicine, Lexington, 1983, dir. level I nursery, asst. dir. gen. pediatrics, 1983-89, assoc. prof., dir. pediatric gastroenterology and nutrition, 1990-94, assoc. prof. multidisciplinary PhD program, 1993-94; dir. pediatric gastroenterology and nutrition Sacred Heart Children's Hosp., 1994-97, Nemours Children's Clinic, 1997—; cons. pediatrician Children's Hosp. at Sacred Heart, Pensacola, Fla., 1971-73; attending physician St. Joseph's Hosp., Tampa Gen. Hosp., Women's Hosp., Tampa, 1973-77, Pitt County Meml. Hosp., Greenville, 1977-83, U. Ky. Med. Ctr., Lexington, 1983-94, Children's Hosp. at Sacred Heart, 1994—; pvt. practice, Tampa, 1973-77; rsch. asst. dept. animal pathology U. Ky., 1959-62, dept. anatomy, 1963, summer rsch. fellow dept. ob/gyn., 1964; extern Ctrl. Bapt. Hosp., Lexington, 1965; sr. aviation med. examiner FAA, Lexington, 1983-94, Pensacola, 1994—. Author: Newborn Care Manual, 1981, Parent's Guide to Newborn Care, 1986, Parent's Guide to Newborn Care/Resident and Student Handbook, 1986; (videotape) Care of the Newborn, 1980; author exam questions subbd. pediat. gastroenterology Am. Bd. Pediatrics; contbr. articles to profl. jours., chpts. to books. With USN, 1971-73, capt. Res. Grantee Ross Labs., 1981-82, Mead-Johnson, 1982, Children's Miracle Network, 1990, 92, 94-96, Nat. Dairy Coun., 1984, 87. Fellow Am. Acad. Pediat., N.Am. Soc. Pediat. Gastroenterology and Nutrition; mem. NRA, Sons Confederate Vets., Am. Gastroenterology Assn., Aerospace Med. Assn., Soc. USN Flight Surgeons, U. Ky. Coll. Medicine Alumni Assn., So. Gut Club. Republican. Avocations: flying, shooting, sailing, scuba diving, drawing. Office: Nemours Childrens Clin W C Payne Bldg 5149 N 9th Ave Ste 308 Pensacola FL 32504-8778

DILLARD, SUZANNE, interior designer; d. Jerome Wallace and Mary Mae (Price) Sorenson; m. Warren Marcus Dillard; 1 child, Jeremy Blake. Student, Tex. A&M U., 1961-64; BS, U. Tex., 1965; student, Pepperdine U., 1974, UCLA, 1977-78. Interior designer Pepperdine U., Malibu, Calif., 1982-95, exec. bd. dirs. Ctr. Arts, 1993-97; cons., interior design Neptune and Thomas, Architects, Pasadena, Calif., 1979-80; pres. Suzanne Dillard Interiors, Pacific Palisades, Calif., 1974—; prin. on camera designer TV pilot, Dream House, Forecast Group Prodns., 1983; speaker in field. Treas. Nat. Arts Assn., L.A., 1982-83, benefit chair, 1992; pres. Fine Arts aux., Assistance League So. Calif., L.A., 1984; patron, sponsor, prodn. chmn. The Footlighters, L.A., 1985-86, pres., 1992-93; pres. League for Children, 1991-93, Achievement Awards Coll. Scientists, 1994-96; benefit chair Freedoms Found., 1995, 1st v.p., 1997-98, pres., 1998—; bd. dirs. Ctr. for Arts Pepperdine U. Mem. SAG, AFTRA, NATAS, Acad. TV Arts and Scis., Internat. Platform Assn. (pres. 1997—, adv. bd.), Internat. Found. for Ednl. and Performing Arts (adv. bd.), Delta Delta Delta (pres. L.A. chpt. 1970-72, pres. sleighbell 1993-94). Republican. Mem. Ch. of Christ. Avocations: piano, voice, oil painting, reading, skiing. Office: 9620 Arby Dr Beverly Hills CA 90210

DILLARD, W. THOMAS, lawyer; b. Dothan, Ala., Nov. 28, 1941; s. William T. and Gladys (Harris) D.; m. Susan Jean Jakuboski, Oct. 26, 1974. BA, U. Tenn., 1963, JD, 1964. Bar: Tenn. 1965; cert. criminal trial specialist Nat. Bd. Trial Advocacy. Asst. U.S. atty. Dept. Justice, Knoxville, Tenn., 1967-76; chief asst. U.S. atty. Dept. Justice, Knoxville, 1978-83, U.S. atty., 1981; U.S. atty. Dept. Justice, Tallahassee, 1983-86; ptnr. Ritchie, Fels, and Dillard, P.C., Knoxville, Tenn., 1987—; U.S. magistrate, 1976-78; adj. prof. East Tenn. State U., Knoxville, 1979-80, U. Tenn. Coll. Law, 1993-98; instr. Knoxville Police Acad., 1979-82, Nat. Inst. Trial Advocacy, Chapel Hill, N.C., 1985—, U. Tenn. Trial Advocacy Program, 1992, 94. Deacon Presbyn. Ch., Knoxville, 1972-76, elder, 1978-82, 88-91, 95-98; mem. Mayor's Commn. on Police. Fellow Am. Coll. Trial Lawyers, Tenn. Bar Found.; mem. ABA, Am. Judicature Soc., Knoxville Young Lawyers (pres. 1972-73), Nat. Assn. Criminal Def. Lawyers, Tenn. Assn. Criminal Def. Lawyers (bd. dirs.), Nat. Assn. Former U.S. Attys. (bd. dirs.), Knoxville Bar Found. (bd. govs.). Avocations: reading, hiking, travel. Home: 4800 Santa Monica Rd Knoxville TN 37918-4528 Office: Ritchie Fels & Dillard 606 W Main Ave Knoxville TN 37902-2603

DILLARD, WILLIAM T., department store chain executive; b. Mineral Springs, Ark., 1914; s. Thomas Dillard. BBA, U. Ark., 1935; MS, Columbia U., 1937. With Sears Roebuck & Co., Tulsa, 1937; opened own dept. store Nashville, 1938; then with Wooten's Dept. Store (later Wooten & Dillard, then Dillard's), Texarkana; pres. Dillard Dept. Stores Inc., Little Rock, until 1977, chmn. bd., 1977—, CEO, 1998—; chmn. bd. dirs. Dillard Investment Co., Dillard Travel; mem. nat. adv. bd. First Comml. Bank, Little Rock. Mem. Nat. Retail Mchts. Assn. (dir.). Office: Dillards Inc 1600 Cantrell Rd Little Rock AR 72201-1110*

DILLASHAW, EULA CATHERINE, artist, graphic artist; b. Memphis, Feb. 19, 1947; d. John Clemons and Catherny Livingston (Murdock) Ballew; m. Stanley Neil Williams, July 29, 1968 (div. Sept. 1982); children: John C., Eric N., Heather L.; m. William Alfred Dillashaw, Oct. 22, 1986. Student, Art Instrn. Sch., 1959-63, Memphis State U., 1965-67, Daytona Beach C.C., 1986-89. Exec. sec. Franklin Simon, N.Y.C., 1973-78, Benefit Providers for Local Unions, Memphis, 1979-82; tchr. Eula's Art Studio & Gallery, Lake Helen, 1993—; tchr. pvt. art classes for children and adults. One-person shows include Daytona Beach Airport, 1996, Daytona Beach Shores City Hall/C. of C., 1997; represented in pvt. collections. Supt. fine arts Volusia County Fair, Deland, 1995—; pres. Lake Helen League of Artists & Crafters, 1994—. Recipient Best in Show profl. divsn. Volusia City Fair, 1997. Mem. NAFE, Internat. Platform Assn., Lake Helen C. of C., Jaycees. Democrat. Avocations: gourmet cooking, raising pedigree birds, traveling. Home and Studio: 291 S Euclid Ave Lake Helen FL 32744-2920

DILLE, EARL KAYE, utility company executive; b. Chillicothe, Mo., Apr. 25, 1927; s. George Earl and Josephine Christina (Kaye) D.; m. Martha Virginia Merrill, Sept. 8, 1951; children—Thomas Merrill, James Warren. BS, U.S. Naval Acad., 1950; MS, St. Louis U., 1961. With Union Elec. Co., St. Louis, 1957-92, pres., 1988-92; cons. engr. St. Louis, 1992—; pres. Assoc. Industries Mo., 1974-76; chmn. North Am. Elect. Reliability Coun., 1991-93. Adv. coun. Coll. Engring., U. Mo.; exec. bd. St. Louis Area coun. Boy Scouts Am.; bd. dirs. Bethesda Hosps. and Homes, chmn., 1987-90; chmn. Mo. Hist. Soc., 1987-90. With USN, 1950-57. Recipient Disting. Svc. in Engring. award U. Mo., 1973, Alumni Merit award St. Louis U., 1974, Outstanding Engr. in Industry award Mo. Soc. Profl. Engrs., 1976, Disting. Svc. award Mo. Soc. Profl. Engrs., 1992, Silver Beaver award Boy Scouts Am., 1987. Mem. IEEE (sr.), Engrs. Club St. Louis (pres. 1977-78), Bellerive Country Club, St. Louis Club, Masons (grand master Mo. 1982-83), Scottish Rite (SGIG Mo. 1989—), Sigma Xi, Sigma Chi. Episcopalian.

DILLE, JOHN ROBERT, physician; b. Waynesburg, Pa., Sept. 2, 1931; s. Charles Emanuel and Ruth Emma (South) D.; m. Joan Marie Sirtosky, Dec. 17, 1955 (wid. Mar. 1996); children: Paul Andrew, John Alan. BS, Waynesburg Coll., 1952; MD, U. Pitts., 1956; M in Indsl. Health, Harvard U., 1960. Diplomate Am. Bd. Preventive Medicine; cert. Correctional Health Profl. Intern Akron City Hosp., 1956-57; resident in aerospace medicine USAF Sch. Aerospace Medicine, San Antonio, 1960-62; program adv. officer FAA Civil Aeromed. Rsch. Inst., Oklahoma City, 1961-64; western region flight surgeon FAA, L.A., 1965; chief FAA Civil Aeromed. Inst., U.S. Dept. Transp., Oklahoma City, 1966-87, ret., 1987; med. dir. Okla. Dept. Corrections, Oklahoma City, 1990-93; assoc. prof. U. Okla., 1961-98, dir. tng. residency in aerospace medicine, 1967-72; state surgeon Okla. Army N.G., 1990-91; surveyor Nat. Commn. on Correctional Health Care. Assoc. editor: Ag Pilot Internat. mag., 1980-98, Conservation Aeronautics mag., 1989-92, Above All mag., 1992; mem. editorial bd. Aviation, Space and Environ. Medicine, 1987-94; contbr. articles to profl. jours. With USAF, 1957-59; col. M.C., U.S. Army N.G., 1976-91. Recipient Meritorious award William A. Jump Found., 1968; named Army N.G. Flight Surgeon of Yr. 1987, Master Flight Surgeon, 1987. Fellow Aerospace Med. Assn. (mem. exec. coun. 1978-81, 93-98, chmn. history and archives com. 1982-90, chmn. sci. program com. 1985, 1st v.p., 1990-91, pres. 1992-93, Theodore C. Lyster award 1978, Harry G. Moseley award 1987, Armstrong lectr. 1997, chmn. nominating com. 1997-98), Am. Coll. Preventive Medicine (regent 1974-77); mem. Internat. Acad. Aviation and Space Medicine, Soc. U.S. Army Flight Surgeons (bd. govs. 1990-92, Order Aeromed. Merit), Mil. and Hospitaller Order St. Lazarus of Jerusalem, Am. Air Mail Soc. (bd. dirs. 1990-92), Res. Officers Assn., Soc. Correctional Physicians (cert. correctional health profl.), Sigma Xi, Nu Sigma Nu. Presbyterian. Home and Office: 335 Merkle Dr Norman OK 73069-6429

DILLE, ROLAND PAUL, college president; b. Dassel, Minn., Sept. 16, 1924; s. Oliver Valentine and Eleanor (Johnson) D.; m. Beth Hopeman, Sept. 4, 1948; children—Deborah, Martha, Sarah, Benjamin. B.A. summa cum laude, U. Minn., 1949, Ph.D., 1962, LHD (hon.), 1995. Instr. English U. Minn., 1953-56; asst. prof. St. Olaf Coll., Northfield, Minn., 1956-61; asst. prof. English Calif. Lutheran Coll., Thousand Oaks, Calif., 1961-63; mem. faculty Moorhead (Minn.) State U., 1964-94, pres., 1968-94; ret., 1994; chmn. Commn. on Instns. Higher Edn. of N. Cen. Assn. of Colls. and Schs., 1991. Author: Four Romantic Poets, 1969; contbr. numerous articles and revs. to profl. jours. Treas. Am. Assn. State Colls. and Univs., 1977-78, bd. dirs., 1978-80, chmn., 1980-81; mem. Nat. Coun. for Humanities, 1980-86; vice-chair Commn. on Higher Edn., North Cen. Assn., 1989-91, chair, 1991-93. With inf. AUS, 1944-46. Disting. Svc. to Humanities award given by Minn. Humanities Commn. named in his honor; named one of 100 most effective Am. coll. pres., 1987. Mem. Phi Beta Kappa. Home: 516 9th St S Moorhead MN 56560-3519 Office: Moorhead State U 11th St S Moorhead MN 56560-9980

DILLENBERG, JACK, public health officer; m. Marianna Dillenberg. BA in Psychology, Tulane U., 1967; DDS, NYU, 1971; MPH, Harvard Sch. Pub. Health, 1978. Dentist Southbury (Conn.) Tng. Sch., 1973-75; mgr. Rural Dental Health Clinic, Jamaica, 1975-77; vis. lectr. Cape Cod C.C., 1978-84; tutor dept. population scis. Harvard Sch. Pub. Health, 1978-81; cons. Mass. Dept. Mental Health, 1978-84; pvt. practice Beacon St. Dental Assocs., Brookline, Mass., 1980-84; instr. Harvard Sch. Dental Medicine, 1980-84; cons. Pan Am. Health Orgn., 1980—; dir. Ariz. Dept. Health Svcs., 1993—; area health officer L.A. County Dept. Health Svcs., Santa Monica, Calif., 1999—; founder, dir. Project S.H.I.P., 1979-84; pres. Dentanomics, Inc., 1984-86; pub. health cons. World Bank, 1978—; clin. instr. Harvard Sch. Dental Medicine, 1988—; mem. faculty U. Phoenix, 1989—. Recipient Presdl. Citation ADA, 1992, Nat. Fluoridation award CDC, 1991, Alunmi award of Merit, Harvard Sch. Pub. Health, 1997, Marketer of the year, Am. Mktg. Assn., 1997. Mem. ADA, Assn. State and Territorial Dental Dirs., Ariz. Pub. Health Assn., Pres. Assoc. State and Ter. Health Officials, 1997. Office: 5743 E Indian School Rd Phoenix AZ 85018-6103 also: LA County Dept Health Svcs 2509 Pico Blvd Santa Monica CA 90405*

DILLER, BARRY, entertainment company executive; b. San Francisco, Feb. 2, 1942; s. Michael and Reva (Addison) D. Vice pres. feature films and movies of week ABC, 1971-73, ABC (prime time TV), 1973-74; chmn. bd. Paramount Pictures Corp., 1974-84; pres. Gulf & Western Entertainment Group, 1983-84; chmn., chief exec. officer Twentieth Century Fox Film Corp., TCF Holdings, L.A., 1984-85, Fox, Inc., 1985-92, QVC Network Inc., 1992-94; chief exec. officer, bd. chair Silver King Comm., Inc., 1995-98; bd. chmn. Home Shopping Network, 1995-98; chmn., CEO USA Networks, Inc., N.Y.C., 1998—; bd. dirs. News Corp Ltd., FCC Adv. Com. on Advanced TV Svcs., Mus. TV and Radio, Calif. Inst. Arts, Acad. Arts and Scis. Found. Mem. Pres. Export Coun. Office: USA Networks Inc 152 W 57th St 42nd Fl New York NY 10009*

DILLER, EDWARD DIETRICH, lawyer; b. Pandora, Ohio, Aug. 7, 1947; s. Hiram D. and Selma G. (Warkentin) D.; m. Karen Esmonde, June 1, 1968; children: Jason, Anna. BA, Bluffton Coll., 1969; postgrad., U. Oreg., 1969-70; JD cum laude, Harvard U., 1976. Assoc. Taft, Stettinius & Hollister, Cin., 1976-84, ptnr., 1984—, chmn. gen. dept., 1998—; chmn. Gen. Conf. Coun. on Higher Edn., 1990-93, 96—, vice chmn., 1993-94; lectr. numerous seminars. Tchr. Mennonite Ctrl. Com., Frankfield, Jamaica, 1970-73; trustee Mental Health Svcs. East, 1977-85, Bluffton Coll., 1979—, mem. exec. com., 1987—, co-chmn. $6,000,000 Capital Campaign, 1987-90, chmn. bd., 1991—; mem. Family Svc. of the Greater Cin. Area, 1989-96, chmn., 1992-95; trustee Habitat for Humanity (Southwestern Ohio and No. Ky. affiliate), 1995—; trustee Working in Neighborhoods, 1991-94, Dan Beard Coun. Boy Scouts of Am., 1996; mem. Leadership Cin. Class XVI; trustee Found. Family Svc., 1997—. Mem. Ohio State Bar Assn., Cin. Bar Assn., Ohio Harvard Law Sch. Assn. (past treas.). Office: 1800 Firstar Tower 425 Walnut St Cincinnati OH 45202-3923

DILLER, ELIZABETH E., artist, educator. BArch, The Cooper Union. Assoc. prof. arch. design Princeton (N.J.) U.; ptnr. Diller & Scofidio, N.Y.C. Co-pub.: Back to the Front: Tourisms of War, Flesh: an anti-monograph; co-creator JETLAG, 1998. Office: Princeton U Sch Architecture 5116 Architecture Princeton NJ 08544-5264

DILLER, JOHN C., professional athletics executive; m. Holly Diller; children: Raegan, Corey, Mary Clare. Grad., Georgetown U., Yale U. Law Sch. Atty. Simpson Thacher and Bartlett; v.p. legal and bus. affairs Madison Sq. Garden Corp., N.Y.C., 1969-74, sr. v.p. adminstrn., 1987-89; former pres. N.Y. State Sports Authority; former operator mgmt., cons. and bus. adv. practice; project mgr., then exec. v.p., chief oper. officer RCTV, 1979-84; former exec. v.p., pres. MSG Sports Group, N.Y.C.; former pres. N.Y. Knickerbockers, NBA, N.Y. Rangers, NHL; exec. v.p. N.Y. Mets; pres., CEO San Antonio Spurs, to 1998; pres., COO Nashville Predators, 1998—. Office: Nashville Predators 501 Broadway Nashville TN 37203-3932

DILLER, KARL CONRAD, linguistics educator; b. Wooster, Ohio, Jan. 24, 1939; s. Oliver Daniel and Eunice Miriam (Conrad) D.; m. Elizabeth Holsinger Ginsburg, May 4, 1984; children: John Andrew, David Daniel. BA, U. Pitts., 1961; EdM, Harvard U., 1964, PhD, 1967. Asst. prof. Coll. Militaire Royal de St. Jean, Que., Can., 1967-68; English lectr. Harvard U., Cambridge, Mass., 1968-72; from assoc. prof. to prof. U. N.H., Durham, 1972—, chair faculty senate, 1995-96, pres. faculty union, 1992-93, 98-99; vis. prof. U. Hawaii, Honolulu, summer 1974, 79-80, Kobe (Japan) Shoin Women's U., 1990-92. Author: Generative Grammar, Structural Linguistics and Language Teaching, 1971, The Language Teaching Controversy, 1978, Rationalism and Empiricism in Language Teaching, 1982; editor, author: Individual Differences and Universals and Language Learning Aptitude, 1981. Hon. adv. prof. Beijing U. Aeronautics and Astronautics, 1993. Mem. AAUP (nat. coun. 1993-99), AAAS, ACLU, Linguistic Assn. Am., Cognitive Sci. Soc., TESOL. E-mail: karl.diller@unh.edu. Office: U NH Hamilton Smith Hall Durham NH 03824

DILLER, PHYLLIS, actress, author; b. Lima, Ohio, July 17, 1917; d. Perry Marcus and Frances Ada (Romshe) Driver; m. Sherwood Anderson Diller, Nov. 4, 1939 (div. Sept. 1965); children: Peter III, Sally, Suzanne Diller Mills, Stephanie Diller Waldron, Perry; m. Warde Donovan, Oct. 7, 1965 (div. July 1975). Student, Sherwood Music Conservatory, Chgo., 1935-37, Bluffton (Ohio) Coll., 1938-39; D.H.L., Nat. Christian U., 1973; PhD (hon.), Bluffton Coll., 1993. (Best TV Comedienne award TV Radio Mirror 1965); Author: Phyllis Diller Tells All About Fang, 1963, Phyllis Diller's Housekeeping Hints, 1966, Phyllis Diller's Marriage Manual, The Complete Mother, The Joys of Aging and How to Avoid Them, 1981; Accompanied Bob Hope entertainment group to, South Vietnam, Christmas, 1966, symphony appearances soloing on piano.; Theatrical prodns. include Dark at the Top of the Stairs, 1961, Wonderful Town, 1962, Happy Birthday, 1963, Hello, Dolly!, 1970, Everybody Loves Opal, 1972, What Are We Going to Do With Jenny, 1977, Nunsense, 1989, The Wizard of Oz, 1990-92; numerous appearances TV and radio, concerts, supper clubs and hotels, 1955—; producer, writer: Phyllis Diller Shows, 1963, 64; rec. artist, Verve Records, Columbia Records, pres., BAM Prodns., Ltd., from 1965, PhilDil Prodns., Ltd., 1966—; motion pictures include Eight on the Lam, 1967, The Private Navy of Sergeant O'Farrell, Hungry Reunion, 1981, Pink Motel, 1983, The Nutcracker Prince, 1990, The Boneyard, 1991, The Perfect Man, 1993, The Silence of the Hams, 1994, A Bug's Life (voice), 1998, Everything's Jake, 1999, The Debtors, 1999; star: TV series The Pruitts of Southampton, 1966-67, Beautiful Phyllis Diller Show, 1968-69 (Recipient honors including Star of Year award Nat. Assn. Theatre Owners), The Bold and the Beautiful (recurring role), 1995—; video appearance: How to Have a Moneymaking Garage Sale, 1987. Recipient Minuteman award U.S. Treasury Dept., Disting. Service citation Ladies Aux. VFW, Woman of Year award Variety Club Women Balt.; Golden Apple Hollywood Women's Press Club, 1967, Woman of Year award St. Louis chpt. Nat. Bus. and Profl. Women's Club, 1971; named hon. mayor Brentwood, Calif., 1971; Hon. life mem. San Francisco Press and Union League Club; named Walk of Fame Star on Hollywood Blvd., 1975, Hon. Chair for Outstanding Svc. to Calif. State U. at Los Angeles, Friends of Music Scholarship Auction, 1982; recipient Doctor of Comedy award Kent State U., 1980, AMC Cancer Rsch. Ctr. Humanitarian award, 1981, Child-Help USA Woman of Yr. award, 1989; City of Los Angeles Proclamation of Phyllis Diller Week Mayor Tom Bradley, 1979; named to Ohio's Hall of Fame, 1981; Commonwealth scholar, 1964. Office: The Suchin Co 12747 Riverside Dr Apt 208 North Hollywood CA 91607-3303

DILLEY, BARBARA JEAN, college administrator, choreographer, educator; b. Chgo., Mar. 13, 1938; d. Robert Vernon and Jean Phyllis (Fairweather) D.; m. Lewis Lloyd, May 1961 (div.); 1 child, Benjamin Lloyd; m. Brent Bondurant, Mar. 1977 (div.); 1 child, Owen Bondurant. BA, Mt. Holyoke Coll., 1960. Dancer Merce Cunningham Dance Co., N.Y.C., 1963-68; ind. dancer, choreographer N.Y.C. and Boulder, Colo., 1966-82; dancer Yvonne Rainer Co., N.Y.C., 1967-70; dancer, choreographer The Grand Union, N.Y.C., 1970-76; mem. faculty dance program Naropa Inst., Boulder, 1974—, dir. dance program, 1974-84; condr. pvt. workshops Toronto, Ont.,

Can., Montreal, Que., Can., Halifax, N.S., Can., The Netherlands, Eng., Switzerland, Germany, 1978—; vis. faculty European Dance Devel. Ctr., Arnheim, The Netherlands, 1993-94; artistic dir. Crystal Dance, Boulder, 1978-81; mem. vis. faculty NYU, Radcliffe Coll., Cornell U., U. Colo., George Washington U., others; dir. dance symposium, 1981; adjudicator S.W. divsn. Am. Coll. Dance Festival, Loretto Heights, Colo., 1986. Mem. grants selection panel Colo. Coun. of Arts and Humanities, 1981, mem. panel on policy devel. for individual grants, 1983. NEA Choreographic fellow, 1974, 76, 81; Boulder City Arts Coun. grantee, 1981. Democrat. Buddhist. Office: Naropa Inst 2130 Arapahoe Ave Boulder CO 80302-6697

DILLEY, WILLIAM GREGORY, aviation company executive; b. Sterling, Colo., June 6, 1922; s. William Gregory and Ethel Marie (Chandler) D.; m. M. Jean McCarthy, May 14, 1944; children: Gregory Dean, Karen Kay. BEng, U. Colo., 1951. Founder Spectra Sonics, Ogden, Utah, 1963—; cons., lectr. in field; investigator USAF Directorate of Flight Safety Rsch.. Contbr. over 300 articles to profl. jours.; patentee in field. Organizing mem. Minutemen. With USAF, Colo. Air N.G. Recipient Disting. Engring. Alumnus award U. Colo., 1977, Centennial medal; named one of prominent engrs. in U.S. Sci. and Tech. div. Libr. of Congress; fellow Audio Engring. Soc., 1970. Holder U.S. and world aircraft speed records. Office: Spectra Sonics 3750 Airport Rd Ogden UT 84405-1599

DILLIN, JOHN WOODWARD, JR., newspaper editor, correspondent; b. Miami, Fla., July 6, 1936; s. John Woodward and Alberta (Thompson) D.; m. Gay Andrews, Oct. 1, 1966 (div. 1988); 1 child, Katherine. B.S.J. with honors, U. Fla., 1958, postgrad. in U.S. history, 1961-63. Reporter St. Augustine Record, Fla., 1958, Tampa Tribune, Fla., 1960-61; with Christian Sci. Monitor, 1964—; reporter Christian Sci. Monitor, Boston, 1964-66; corr. Christian Sci. Monitor, Vietnam, 1966-67; city editor Christian Sci. Monitor, Boston, 1967-71; corr. Christian Sci. Monitor, Atlanta and Washington, 1971-79; mng. editor for news Christian Sci. Monitor, Boston, 1979-83; nat. polit. corr. Christian Sci. Monitor, Washington, 1983-94; mng. editor Christian Sci. Monitor, Boston, 1994-99; assoc. editor, Washington bur. chief Christian Sci. Monitor, Washington, 1999—. Served with AUS, 1958-59. Recipient Sigma Delta Chi award for Washington Corr., 1993. Christian Scientist. Home: 5525 15th St Arlington VA 22205 Office: 910 16th St NW Washington DC 20006

DILLIN, S. HUGH, federal judge; b. Petersburg, Ind., June 9, 1914; s. Samuel E. and Maude (Harrell) D.; m. Mary Eloise Humphreys, Nov. 24, 1940; 1 child, Patricia Wright. A.B. in Govt, Ind. U., 1936, LLB, 1938, LLD, 1992; D of Civil Law (hon.), Ind. State U., 1990. Bar: Ind. 1938. Ptnr. Dillin & Dillin, Petersburg, 1938-61; U.S. dist. judge So. Dist. Ind., 1961—, chief judge, 1982-84; mem. Jud. Conf. U.S., 1979-82, mem. exec. com., 1980-82, mem. Jud. Conf. Com. on Ct. Adminstrn., 1983-89, chmn. subcom. on fed.-state rels., 1983-89; mem. Jud. Panel on Multidist. Litigation, 1983-92; sec. Pub. Svc. Commn. Ind., 1942; mem. Interstate Oil Compact Commn., 1949-52, 61. Mem. Ind. Ho. of Reps. from Pike and Knox Counties, 1937, 39, 41, 51, floor leader, 1951; mem. Ind. Senate from Pike and Gibson Counties, 1959-61, pres. pro tem, 1961. Capt. AUS, 1943-46. Recipient Disting. Alumnus award Ind. U. Coll. Arts and Scis., 1985, Ind. U. Sch. Law, 1987. Mem. Am. Bar Assn., Ind. State Bar Assn., Fed. Bar Assn., 7th Cir. Judges Assn. (pres. 1977-79), Am. Judicature Soc., Delta Tau Delta, Phi Delta Phi. Democrat. Presbyn. Club: Indianapolis Athletic. Office: US Dist Ct 255 US Courthouse 46 E Ohio St Indianapolis IN 46204-1903

DILLING, KIRKPATRICK WALLWICK, lawyer; b. Evanston, Ill., Apr. 11, 1920; s. Albert W. and Elizabeth (Kirkpatrick) D.; m. Betty Ellen Bronson, June, 1942 (div. July 1944); m. Elizabeth Ely Tilden, Dec. 11, 1948; children: Diana Jean, Eloise Tilden, Victoria Walgreen, Albert Kirkpatrick. Student, Cornell U., 1939-40; BS in Law, Northwestern U., 1942; postgrad., DePaul U., 1946-47, L'Ecole Vaubier, Montreux, Switzerland; Degré Normal, Sorbonne U., Paris. Bar: Ill. 1947, U.S. Dist. Ct. (no. dist.) Ill., Ind., Mich., Md., La., Tex., Okla., Wis., Idaho, U.S. Ct. Appeals (2nd, 3rd, 5th, 7th, 8th, 9th, 10th, 11th, fed. and D.C. cirs.), U.S. Supreme Ct. Ptnr. Dilling and Dilling, Chgo., 1948—; counsel Cancer Control Soc., Nat. Coun. for Improved Health; bd. dirs. Klaire Labs., Nutradelle Labs., Ltd., V.E. Irons, Inc.; v.p. Midwest Medic-Aide, Inc.; spl. counsel Herbalife (U.K.) Ltd., Herbalife Australasia Pty., Ltd.; lectr. on pub. health law. Contbr. articles to pub. health publs. Bd. dirs. Adelle Davis Found., Liberty Lobby. 1st lt. AUS, 1943-46. Recipient Humanitarian award Nat. Health Fedn. Mem. ABA, Ill. Bar Assn., Chgo. Bar Assn., Assn. Trial Lawyers Am., Cornell Soc. Engrs., Am. Legion, Air Force Assn., Pharm. Advt. Club, Rolls Royce Owners' Club, Tower Club, Cornell U., Chicago Club, Delta Upsilon. Republican. Episcopalian. Home: 1120 Lee Rd Northbrook IL 60062-3816

DILLINGHAM, JOHN ALLEN, marketing professional; b. Kansas City, Mo., Jan. 9, 1939; s. Jay B. and Frances (Thompson) D.; m. Nancy Jane Abbott, Sept. 4, 1965; children: Allen Edwards, William Kemp. *John Dillingham is the 9th generation in America. He is a member of Southern Branch of Dillingham family that came from Maryland in 1708, to Southern Virginia, to Bluegrass area in Kentucky, to Kansas City area in 1850s. He is the 7th generation, consisting of civic, business, agricultural and political leaders to resides in Clay and Platte Counties, now a part of Kansas City North.* AS, Wentworth Mil. Acad., 1958; AB in Polit. Sci., U. Mo., 1961, MS in Pub. Adminstrn., 1962. Br. mgr. Rudy-Patrick divsn. W.R. Grace Co., Mt. Vernon, Ill., 1964-68; pres. Sho-Hawk Industries, Kansas City, Mo., 1968-72; v.p. comml. loans Traders Nat. Bank, Kansas City, 1972-79; sr. v.p. sales and mktg. Garney Constrn. Co., Kansas City, 1979-95; pres., bd. dirs. Jo Dill, Inc., 1985—, Dillingham Enterprises, 1997—; bd. dirs. United Funds, Inc., Kansas City; chmn. Clay County Indsl. Devel. Authority, 1980—, Clay County EDC, 1972-74; mem. pres. adv. bd. for extension U. Mo., 1972-80; cons. CMSU Grad. Sch., Warrensberg, Mo., 1996-97; dir., cons. McDougal Constrn., Kansas City, 1996-97; adv. dir. Northland Bd. United Mo. Bank, 1998—, Synergy Svcs. Trustee Wentworth Mil. Acad., Lexington, 1978-80, 93—; state chmn. Mo. 4H Found., Columbia, 1985-90; mem. ctrl. governing bd. Children's Mercy Hosp., Kansas City, 1987-92; bd. dirs. Kansas City Conv. and Vis. Bur., 1976-80, Northland Cmty. Fund, Kansas City, 1988-97, Kansas City Sports Commn., 1990-93; treas. Harry S. Truman Scholarship Nat. Alumni Assn., 1979-90; mem., v.p. Kansas City Bd. Police Commrs., 1990-95; chmn. Kansas City Mcpl. Asst. Corp., 1984—, Alex Doniphan Meml. Hwy. Naming; hon. co-chair St. Plus X H.S. Capital campaign, 1998-99; coordinating bd. task force on affordability of higher edn. State of Mo., 1999; mem. Nat. 4H Resource Devel. Com., 1990-92, Kansas City Mayor's Fast Forward Commn., 1996—, Metro C. C. Found., Kansas City, 1996—; exec. bd. Heart of Am. coun. Boy Scouts Am., 1993—; 1st bd. dirs. alumni assn. U.S. Command and Gen. Staff Coll., Ft. Leavenworth, Kans., 1993—; dir. DARE of Greater Kansas City, 1995-98, CMSU Found. Warrensburg, 1995-97, Am. Royal, Kansas City, Mo., 1997—; co-chmn. K.C. Storm runoff campaign. With U.S. Army, 1964. Recipient Faculty Alumni award U. Mo., Columbia, 1981, Silver Beaver award Boy Scouts Am. Heart Am. coun., 1992, Harry S. Truman Scholarship Appreciation plaque, 1993, Cmty. Svc. award Park Coll., 1993, Pub. Svc. award Ctrl. Mo. State Univ., 1994; named one of 100 Most Influential Kans. Citizens, Ingrams Mag., 1993. Spirit award Kansas City, 1999. Mem. SAR, VFW, Am. Legion, Sons of the Confederate Officers, Decendents of Magna Charta, Plantenegent Soc., Northland C. of C. (Quality of Life award 1990), KC Kings, Gold Coaters (pres. 1979-89), Mt. Vernon Ill. C. of C. (pres. 1968), Native Sons Kansas City (bd. dirs. 1991-92, 98—), Sigma Alpha Epsilon (KC Alumni Assn. pres. 1976, Honor Man 1988, trustee Nat. Found. 1987-93, Nat. Disting. Svc. award 1993). Democrat. Mem. Disciples of Christ Ch. Avocations: fishing, landscaping, family genealogy. Fax: 816-842-6803. Home: 4040 NW Claymont Dr Kansas City MO 64116-1751 Office: 924 Livestock Exch Bldg Kansas City MO 64102

DILLINGHAM, MARJORIE CARTER, foreign language educator; b. Bicknell, Ind., Aug. 20, 1915; m. William Pyrle Dillingham, (dec. 1981); children: William Pyrle (dec.), Robert Carter, Sharon Dillingham Martin. PhD in Spanish (Delta Kappa Gamma scholar and fellow), Fla. State U., 1970. High sch. tchr. Fla.; former instr. St. George's Sch., Havana; former mem. faculty Panama Canal Zone Coll., Fla. State U., Duke U., Univ. Ga.; dir. traveling Spanish conversation classes in Spain, Ctrl. and S. Am.; U.S. rep. (with husband) Hemispheric Conf. on Taxation, Rosario, Argentina. Named to Putnam County Hall of Fame, 1986. Mem. Am. Assn. Tchrs. Spanish and Portuguese (past pres. Fla. chpt.), Fla. Edn. Assn. (past pres. fgn. lang. div.), La Sociedad Honoraria Hispanica (past nat. pres.), Fgn. Lang. Tchrs. Leon County, Fla. (pres.), Delta Kappa Gamma (pres.), Phi Kappa Phi, Sigma Delta Pi (pres.), Beta Pi Theta, Kappa Delta Pi, Alpha Omicron Pi, Delta Kappa Gamma. Home: 2109 Trescott Dr Tallahassee FL 32312-3331

DILLINGHAM, RUTH ELAINE, lawyer, nurse; b. Buffalo, Dec. 15, 1956; d. Bernard Thomas and Betty Lou (Haley) Quigley; m. Scott Edward Dillingham, June 5, 1982. BSN, D'Youville Coll., Buffalo, 1979; JD, Syracuse U., 1994. Neonatal nurse Children's Hosp. Med. Ctr., Cin.; regional adminstr. Empire State Peer Rev. Orgn., Syracuse, N.Y.; dir. N.Y. State quality assurance Empire State Med. Sci. Edn. Found., Syracuse, dir. upstate ops. Mem. Legis. Rsch. Bur., Sigma Theta Tau (Nat. Nursing Honor Soc.). Home: 4541 Ridge Rd Cazenovia NY 13035-9304

DILLINGHAM, WILLIAM BYRON, literature educator, author; b. Atlanta, Mar. 7, 1930; s. Cornelius Howard and Emerald (Storey) D.; m. Marion Elizabeth Joiner, July 3, 1952; children: Rebecca Lynn, Judith Ann, Paul Christopher. BA, Emory U., 1955, MA, 1956; PhD, U. Pa., 1961. Instr. Emory U., Atlanta, 1956-62, asst. prof., 1962-66, assoc. prof., 1966-68, prof., 1968-84, chair. dept. English, 1979-82, 85-86, 90-91, Charles Howard Candler prof. Am. lit., 1984-96; prof. emeritus, 1996—. Author: Frank Norris: Instinct and Art, 1969, An Artist in the Rigging, 1972, Melville's Short Fiction, 1977, Melville's Later Novels, 1986, Melville and His Circle: The Last Years, 1996; co-author: Humor of the Old Southwest, 1964, 2d edit., 1975, 3d edit., 1994, Practical English Handbook, 10th edit., 1995; mem. editl. bd. Nineteenth-Century Lit., 1990-97, South Atlantic Rev., 1986-89, Frank Norris Studies, 1986-94. Served with U.S. Army, 1950-52. Recipient Fulbright award U.S. Govt., 1964-65, Sr. fellowship NEH, 1978-79, Guggenheim Found., 1982-83. Mem. MLA (mem. adv. coun. Am. lit. sect. 1988-90), Soc. Lit. Scholars and Critics, South Atlantic MLA, Frank Norris Soc., Melville Soc. (pres. 1987), Kipling Soc., Phi Beta Kappa, Omicron Delta Kappa. Avocations: bass fishing, beach walking. Home: 1416 Vista Leaf Dr Decatur GA 30033-2012 also: 3258 Esperanza Ave Daytona Beach FL 32118-6231

DILL-KOCHER, LAURIE, textile artist; b. Sharon, Pa., June 10, 1953; d. William Allen and Marjorie (Croft) Dill; m. Thomas Earl Kocher. BS, Edinboro (Pa.) State U., 1975, BFA, 1976; MFA in Weaving and Textile Design, Rochester Inst. Tech., 1979. Fiber artist, 1976—; mem. faculty fibers, dept. art Nazareth Coll. Rochester, N.Y., 1992—; vis. artist Rochester Inst. Tech., 1989, 93; adj. assoc. prof. art Roberts Wesleyan Coll., Rochester, 1993-95; area program coord./instr. dept. fine and applied arts U. Akron, Ohio, 1981-83. Exhibited in solo shows at Wallace Meml. Gallery/ Rochester Inst. Tech., 1979, Hubert Art Ctr., Shippensburg (Pa.) State U., 1982, Rochester Inst. Tech., 1982, Doshi Ctr. Contemporary Art, Harrisburg, Pa., 1981, Carnegie Art Inst., Leavenworth, Kans., 1993, Nazareth Coll., Roberts Wesleyan Coll., 1994, others; exhibited in group shows at Arrowmont Sch. of Crafts, Gatlinburg, Tenn., 1975, Three Rivers Arts Festival Internat., Pitts., Marietta Crafts Coll. Nat., Trumbull Art Guild Ann., Ohio Ceramic, Sculpture and Craft Show/Butler Inst. Am. Art, Youngstown, Ohio, Tweek Mus. Art/U. Minn.-Duluth, Cleve. Mus. Art, DelMano Gallery, L.A., Dawson Gallery, Rochester, Univ. Coll. at Buffalo, Curtiss Mus., Hammondsport, N.Y., Nazareth Coll., Rochester, Burchfield-Penney Art Ctr./Buffalo State Coll., N.Y. State Mus., Albany, numerous others; represented in collections at Wallace Meml. Libr./Rochester Inst. Tech., Genessee Hosp., Rochester, Bell Comms. Rsch., Red Bank, N.J., The Hewett Corp., Bedminster, N.J., Burchfield Art Ctr., Buffalo, ARC Permanent Collection, Rochester, Lederle-Praxis Biols., Rochester, Jewish Assn. on Aging/Weinberg Village, Pitts., Kaiser Permanente Med. Ctr., Baldwin Park, Calif., others; subject of numerous articles. Grantee Ruth Chenven Found., 1987, Empire State Craft Alliance, 1998. Home: 70 Lafayette Pkwy Rochester NY 14625

DILLMAN, DONALD ANDREW, sociologist, educator, survey methodologist; b. Chariton, Iowa, Oct. 24, 1941. BS, Iowa State U., 1964, MS, 1966, PhD, 1969. Rsch. assoc. Iowa State U., Ames, 1967-69; asst. prof. Wash. State U., Pullman, 1969-73, assoc. prof., dept. chair, 1973-81, prof., 1978—, dir. social and econ. scis. rsch. ctr., 1986-96, dep. dir. R&D Social Econ. Scis. Rsch. Ctr., 1996—; guest prof. German Ctr. for Survey Methods Rsch., Mannheim, Fed. Republic of Germany, 1985, 87; sr. survey methodologist Office of Dir. U.S. Bur. Census, 1991-95; cons. and lectr. in field. Author: Mail and Telephone Surveys, 1978; co-author 5 books; contbr. articles to profl. jours. Kellogg fellow, 1981-83; grantee in field. Fellow AAAS, Am. Statis. Assn.; mem. Am. Sociol. Assn., Rural Sociol. Soc. Am. (pres. 1983-84, Outstanding Svc. award 1983, Excellence in Rsch. award 1998), Am. Assn. Pub. Opinion Rsch. (sec.-treas. 1985-87). E-mail: dillman@wsu.edu. Home: 705 SW Mies St Pullman WA 99163-2056 Office: Wash State U Wilson Hall 133 Pullman WA 99164-4014

DILLMAN, GRANT, journalist; b. Columbus, Ohio, May 4, 1918; s. Herschel and Daisy L. (Fothergill) D.; m. Audrey Maslow, June 30, 1945 (dec. June 1984); children: Darryl, Craig; 1 child by previous marriage, Jo Kunkle; m. Gwen Gibson, Jan. 15, 1987. Student, Franklin U., Columbus, 1940-41. With Columbus Dispatch, 1939-42; with pub. relations div. Curtiss-Wright Co., 1942; with UPI (and predecessor), 1942-83, night editor, then news editor Washington bur., 1950-73, v.p. and Washington mgr., 1973-83; exec. dir. Nat. Press Found., 1983-84, bd. dirs., 1984-96, dir. emeritus, 1996—; dir. SPJ SDX First Amendment Ctr., 1984-86; sr. editorial advisor Maturity News Svc., 1989-95, contbg. editor, 1996-97; freelance writer, 1998—; chmn. com. on nat. reporting The Pulitzer Prize, 1983. Named to Sigma Delta Chi Washington Hall of Fame, 1978. Mem. Sigma Delta Chi (chmn. nat. freedom of info. com. 1973-76). Clubs: Gridiron (pres. 1980), Nat. Press. Home: 304 Cloudes Mill Way Alexandria VA 22304-3023*

DILLMAN, JOSEPH JOHN THOMAS, electric utility executive; b. Shenandoah, Pa., July 30, 1941; s. Joseph Bartholomew and Mary (Tomcho) D.; m. Beverly Carol Ann Holmes, Oct. 5, 1963; children: Thomas, Alan, Janice. BSME, Drexel U., 1963; MS, SUNY, Buffalo, 1969. Asst. to supt. Dunkirk (N.Y.) Steam Sta. Niagara Mohawk Power Corp., 1965-73, asst. ops. supr., 1973-74; gen. foreman mech. maintenance C.R. Huntley Sta. Niagara Mohawk Power Corp., Tonawanda, N.Y., 1974-75, supt. mech. maintenance, 1975-82, plant mgr., 1982—. Dir. Town of Tonawanda Devel. Corp., 1991—, chmn. Waterfront Com., 1992—; mem. Niagara River Remedial Adv. Com., 1994—. 1st lt. U.S. Army, 1963-65. Mem. ASME, N.Y. Utility Power Generation Com. (chmn. 1986-87). Roman Catholic. Avocations: canoe tripping; whitewater canoeing, gardening, 4-H judging. Home: 24 Cree Ton Dr Amherst NY 14228-1607 Office: Niagara Mohawk Power Corp CR Huntley Sta 3500 River Rd Tonawanda NY 14150-7781

DILLMAN, KRISTIN WICKER, middle school educator, musician; b. Ft. Dodge, Iowa, Nov. 7, 1953; d. Winford Lee and Helen Caroline (Brown) Egli; m. Kirk Michael Wicker, Jan. 1, 1982 (dec. June 1982); m. David D. Dillman, Apr. 13, 1990; adopted children: Alek Joseph, Andrew Mikhail. AA, Iowa Cen. Coll., 1974; B in Music Edn., Morningside Coll., 1976; M in Mus., U. S.D., 1983. Cert. tchr., Iowa. Tchr. instrumental music Garrigan Affiliated Schs., Algona, Iowa, 1976-77, Sioux City (Iowa) Community Schs., 1977—. Asst. prin. bassist Sioux City Symphony, 1974-93, 95—; prin. bassist, 1993-95; freelance bassist Sioux City, 1976—. Named Tchr. of Yr. Sioux City Community Schs., 1988-89. Mem. NEA, Iowa Edn. Assn., Sioux city Edn. Assn., Iowa Bandmasters Assn., Sioux City Musicians Assn., Zeta Sigma, Mu Phi Epsilon. Republican. Lutheran. Avocations: golf, walking, gardening, skiing. Office: Woodrow Wilson Mid Sch 1010 Iowa St Sioux City IA 51105-1711

DILLMAN, ROBERT JOHN, academic administrator; b. Brooklyn, N.Y., June 30, 1941; s. George amd Emma (Drago) D.; m. Roseann Farley Morris; children: Deirdre, John, Siobhan, James. BS, SUNY, New Paltz, 1963; MS, Pa. State U., 1970; PhD, Clark U., 1976. Tchr. Connetquot High Sch., Bohemia, N.Y., 1963-64, 66-67; faculty mem. Bridgewater (Mass.) State Coll., 1967-78, chairperson, 1978-82, v.p. acad. affairs, 1982-87, acting pres., 1987-88; pres. Fairmont (W.Va.) State Coll., 1988-96, E. Strudsburg (Pa.) U., 1996—; bd. dirs. C.B. & T. Fin. Corp., Fairmont, W.Va. Bd. dirs. United Way, Fairmont, 1989. Materials sci. faculty fellow NSF, Clark U., 1971-72. Mem. Am. Assn. Colls. and Univs., Am. Assn. Higher Edn., C. of C. of Marion City. Office: E Stroudsburg U 200 Prospect St East Stroudsburg PA 18301*

DILLOFF, NEIL JOEL, lawyer; b. Apr. 3, 1948; s. Marvin M. and Gertrude S. (Kraus) D.; m. Beverly A. Berd, June 6, 1971; children: Danielle, Shani, Scott. AB, U. N.C., 1970; JD, Georgetown U., 1973. Bar: Md. 1973, Pa. 1974, D.C. 1983, U.S. Dist. Ct. Md. 1977, U.S. Ct. Appeals (4th cir.) 1979, U.S. Supreme Ct. 1987. Assoc. Piper & Marbury, Balt., 1977-82, ptnr., 1982—; head comml. lit. practice group, 1994—; instr. Md. Inst. for Continuing Legal Edn., Balt., 1983—. Author: Civil Pretrial Practice - Maryland Institute for Continuing Education in the Law; contbr. articles to profl. jours. Served to lt. JAGC, USN, 1973-77. Mem. ABA (assoc. editor litigation news 1980-82), Md. Bar Assn., Balt. City Bar Assn., Phi Beta Kappa, Balt. Ctr. Club. Democrat. Jewish. Office: Piper & Marbury 36 S Charles St Baltimore MD 21201-3020*

DILLON, CLARENCE DOUGLAS, retired investment company executive; b. Geneva, Switzerland, Aug. 21, 1909; s. Clarence and Anne McE. (Douglas) D.; m. Phyllis C. Ellsworth, Mar. 10, 1931 (dec.); children: Phyllis Ellsworth (Mrs. Phyllis Collins), Joan Douglas (Duchesse de Mouchy); m. Susan S. Sage, Jan. 1, 1983. Grad., Groton Sch., 1927; A.B., Harvard U., 1931, LL.D., 1959; LL.D., NYU, 1956, Lafayette Coll., 1957, U. Hartford, 1958, Columbia U., 1959, Williams Coll., 1960, Rutgers U., 1961, Princeton U., 1961, U. Pa., 1962, Middlebury Coll., 1963, Tufts U., 1982. Mem. N.Y. Stock Exchange, 1931-36; dir. U.S. & Foreign Securities Corp. and U.S. & Internat. Securities Corp., 1937-53; pres. U.S. & Fgn. Securities Corp. and U.S. & Internat. Securities Corp., 1947-53, pres., dir., 1967-71, chmn. bd., 1971-84; dir. Dillon, Read & Co., Inc., 1938-53, chmn. bd., 1946-53, chmn. exec. com., dir., 1971-81; ambassador to France, 1953-57; under sec. of state for econ. affairs Dept. State, 1958-59, under sec. of state, 1959-61, sec. of treasury, 1961-65. Pres. Met. Mus. Art, N.Y.C., 1970-78, chmn., 1978-83; hon. gov. N.Y. Hosp.; chmn. Rockefeller Found., 1972-75, Brookings Instn., 1970-76, pres. bd. overseers, Harvard Coll., 1968-72. Served from ensign to lt. comdr. USNR, 1941-45. Decorated Air medal, Legion of Merit, Presdl. medal of freedom. Mem. Soc. Colonial Wars N.Y., Soc. of Cincinnati. Clubs: Racquet and Tennis, Knickerbocker, Links, Century, Pilgrims (N.Y.C.); Metropolitan (Washington). Office: 27th Fl 1330 Ave of Americas New York NY 10019-5422

DILLON, CLIFFORD BRIEN, retired lawyer; b. Amarillo, Tex., Oct. 25, 1921; s. Clifford Newton and Leone (Brien) D.; m. Audrey Catherine Johnson, Jan. 16, 1945; children: Audrey Catherine Dillon Peters (dec. Nov. 1997), Robert Brien, Douglas Johnson. B.B.A., U. Tex., 1943, LL.B. with honors, 1947. Bar: Tex. 1947. Practiced in Houston, 1947-87; ptnr. Baker & Botts, 1957-87, ret. ptnr., 1987—; mem. faculty Southwestern Legal Found., 1968-87. Author articles in field. Life mem., bd. dirs. U. Tex. Health Sci. Ctr., Houston; past mem. antitrust adv. bd. Bur. Nat. Affairs; past bd. dirs. Houston Vis. Nurses Assn.; bd. visitors, life mem. Mc Donald Obs. and Astronomy, 1986—. Fellow ABA (chmn. sect. antitrust law 1975-76, Ho. of Dels. 1974-75, 85-87, bd. govs. 1985-87), State Bar Tex., Am. Judicature Soc., Tex. Bar Found., Houston Bar Found.; mem. Houston Bar Assn., Houston C. of C., U.S. C. of C. (past mem. adv. coun. antitrust policy), Phi Kappa Psi, Phi Delta Phi. Presbyterian. Clubs: Houston Country (Houston), Petroleum (Houston); Riverhill Country (Kerrville, Tex.), Old Baldy (Saratoga, Wyo.).. Office: Baker & Botts 3000 One Shell Plaza Houston TX 77002

DILLON, DAVID ANTHONY, journalist, lecturer; b. Fitchburg, Mass., Aug. 24, 1947; s. John Joseph and Lauretta Irene (Morris) D.; m. Sally Ann Hall, June 5, 1971; children: Christopher, Catherine. BA, Boston Coll., 1963; MA, Harvard U., 1965, PhD, 1970. Asst. prof. So. Meth. U., Dallas, 1970-77; mag. editor D Mag., Dallas, 1978-81; archtl. editor Dallas Morning News, 1981—. Author: Experience and Expression, 1976, Dallas Architecture, 1986, Extending the Legacy: Planning America's Capital in the 21st Century, 1997; contbg. editor Texas Architect, Architecture, 1982—, Landscape Architecture, 1990—, Archtl. Record, 1996—. Loeb fellow Harvard U., 1986-87; NEA Critic's grantee, 1980; recipient AP award for criticism, 1988, 90, 91. Democrat. Roman Catholic. Home: PO Box 3323 Amherst MA 01004-3323 Office: The Dallas Morning News 508 Young St Dallas TX 75202-4828*

DILLON, DAVID BRIAN, retail grocery executive; b. Hutchinson, Kans., Mar. 30, 1951; s. Paul Wilson and Ruth (Muirhead) D.; m. Dee A. Ehling, July 29, 1973; children: Jefferson, Heather, Kathryn. BS, U. Kans., 1973; JD, So. Meth. U., 1976. V.p. Fry's Food Stores of Ariz. Inc. div. Dillon Cos. Inc., Phoenix, 1978-79, exec. v.p., 1979-83; v.p. Dillon Cos. Inc. (subs. of Kroger Co.), Hutchinson, 1983-86, pres., 1986-95; exec. v.p. Kroger Co., Cin., 1990-95; chmn. bd. Dillon Cos., Inc. (subs. Kroger Co.), Cin., 1993—; pres., COO The Kroger Co., Cin., 1995—; also bd. dirs., 1995—; bd. dirs. 1st Nat. Hutchinson, Bethesda, Inc., 1996—. Chmn. Leadership Hutchinson, 1986-87, Leadership Kans., 1988; bd. dirs. Bethesda Hosp., Cin., 1996—; bd. trustees U. Kans. Endowment Assn., 1993—, U. Cin. Found., 1997—, Den Beard Coun. of Boy Scouts Am., 1996—; bd. advisors U. Kans. Bus. Sch., 1990—. Recipient Brotherhood-Sisterhood award Kans. region NCCJ, 1992. Mem. U. Kans. Alumni Assn., Urban League of Greater Cin. (trustee 1998—), Order of Coif, Sigma Chi (Balfour award 1973). Republican. Presbyterian. Office: The Kroger Co 1014 Vine St Ste 1000 Cincinnati OH 45202-1100

DILLON, DONALD WARD, management consultant; b. Wichita, Kans., Jan. 31, 1936; s. Maurice B. and Helen M. (Ward) D.; m. Jacquelyn A. Hicks, Dec. 28, 1958; m. Brenda Marie Rager, July 9, 1983. B.Music Edn., Wichita State U., 1959, M.Music Edn., 1961; D.Music. Edn., U. Okla., 1970. Tchr. music Derby (Kans.) public schs., 1959-66; mem. faculty Southeastern La. U., Hammond, 1968-69; exec. dir. Okla. Arts and Humanities Council, 1969-73; asst. dir. fed.-state partnership Nat. Endowment Arts, Washington, 1973-79; dir. grants office Nat. Endowment Arts, 1979; exec. dir. Music Educators Nat. Conf., Reston, Va., 1979-83; pres. Don Dillon Assocs. Inc., Dallas, 1983—; exec. mgmt. cons., bd.dirs. Fund Advancement Music Edn., 1979—. Exec. editor: Music Educators Jour, 1979—, Design for Arts Edn, 1980—; Contbr. articles profl. jours. Bd. dirs. Nat. Com. Arts for Handicapped, 1980—. Mem. Am. Soc. Assn. Execs., Inst. Assn. Mgmt. Cos., Meeting Planners Internat. Methodist. Home: 6204 Trailwood Dr Plano TX 75024-6023 Office: 4020 Mcewen Rd Ste 105 Dallas TX 75244-5019

DILLON, FRANCIS PATRICK, human resources executive, management and personnel sales consultant; b. Long Beach, Calif., Mar. 15, 1937; s. Wallace Myron and Mary Elizabeth (Land) D.; B.A., U. Va., 1959; M.S., Def. Fgn. Affairs Sch., 1962; M.B.A., Pepperdine U., 1976; m. Vicki Lee Dillon, Oct. 1980; children: Cary Randolph, Francis Patrick Jr., Randee, Rick. Traffic mgr., mgr. pers. svcs. Pacific Telephone Co., Sacramento and Lakeport, Calif., 1966-69; asst. mgr. manpower planning and devel. Pan-Am. World Airways, N.Y.C., 1969-71; mgr. pers. and orgn. devel. Continental Airlines, L.A., 1971-74; dir. human resources Bourns, Inc., Riverside, Calif., 1974-80; v.p. employee and cmty. relations MSI Data Corp., 1980-83; pres. Pavi Enterprises, 1983—; cons. mgmt. Pers. Outplacement Counseling/Sales/ Mgmt., fin. svcs. and estate planning, 1983—; pres., CEO Pers. Products & Svcs., Inc., 1984-91; v.p. Exec. Horizons, Inc., 1988-94; sr. profl. svcs. cons. Right Assocs., 1994-97; pres. Meditrans Inc., 1977-80. Bd. dirs. Health Svcs. Maintenance Orgn., Inc., Youth Svcs. Ctr., Inc.; vol. precinct worker. Served to lt. comdr. USN, 1959-66; asst. naval attaché, Brazil, 1963-65. Recipient Disting. Svc. award Jaycees, 1969; Jack Cates Meml. Vol. of Year award Youth Svc. Ctr., 1977. Mem. Assn. Internal Mgmt. Cons.'s, Am. Soc. Personnel Adminstrn., Personnel Indsl. Rels. Assn., Am. Soc. Tng. and Devel., Am. Electronics Assn. (human resources com., chmn. human resources symposium), Lake Mission Viejo Assn. (sec., bd. dirs. 1990-94). Republican. Episcopalian. Clubs: Mission Viejo Sailing, YMCA Bike, Mission Viejo Ski, Caving, Toastmasters (pres. 1966-67), Have Dirt Will Travel, Capo Valley 4 Wheelers. Office: Pavi Enterprises 27331 Via Amistoso Mission Viejo CA 92692-2410

DILLON, FRANCIS RICHARD, retired air force officer; b. Hartford, Conn., Nov. 3, 1939; s. Frank Clifford and Margaret Elizabeth (Drohan) D.; m. Judith Wheeler, June 15, 1963; children: Christopher R., Douglas C. BS in Mktg., U. Conn., 1962; MS in Polit. Sci., Troy (Ala.) State U., 1978. Commd. 2d lt. USAF, 1962, advanced through grades to brig. gen., 1988; various command and staff positions in U.S. and Europe, European area specialist responsible for counterintelligence and anti-terrorism for Air Force pers. in Europe, 1976-79; comdr. Air Force Office Spl. Investigations, Bolling AFB, D.C., 1988-93; retired, 1993; mng. dir. ops., COO MPC Telcom, LP, Annandale, Va., 1993-94; v.p. Background Rsch. Internat. L.L.C., Falls Church, Va., 1995-97; cons. DS/FX Internat., Falls Church, Va., 1997—. Mem. Am. Soc. Indsl. Security, Internat. Narcotics Enforcement Officer Assn., Internat. Assn. Chiefs of Police. Roman Catholic. Avocations: sailing, skiing, reading, tennis. Home: 47 W Chops Point Rd Bath ME 04530-9313

DILLON, FRANCIS XAVIER, anesthesiologist; b. August, Ga., July 11, 1959; s. John Francis and Frances Joanne (Niehaus) D.; m. Elizabeth Faye New, Sept. 14, 1985; 1 child, John Francis. AB with distinction, Ind. U., 1980; MD with highest distinction, Ind. U., Indpls., 1985. Diplomate Am. Bd. Anesthesiology. lic. M.D., Ind. Intern Ind. U. Med. Ctr., Indpls., 1985-86, 98, resident, 1986-89, 98-99; attending anesthesiologist Ind. U. Hosps., Indpls., 1989-92; asst. prof. dept. anesthesia Ind. U. Sch. Medicine, Indpls., 1989-92; attending anesthesiologist Winona Meml. Hosp., Indpls., 1992—; assoc. instr. organic chemistry and human anatomy Ind. U., Bloomington depts. chemistry and med. studies, 1981-82; vis. investigator dept. neurobiology Northeastern Ohio Univs. Coll. Medicine, Rootstown, Ohio, 1988; adj. mem. com. on standards of care Am. Soc. Anesthesiologists, 1989-92; med. dir. anesthesia sect. Winona Meml. Hosp., Indpls., 1994-97. Contbr. articles and abstracts to profl. jours. including Anesthesiology, Jour. Clin. Anesthesiology, Anesthesia Analgesia, Clin. Laser Monthly. Recipient Merit scholarship, Ind. U., 1977, Mayor's Vol. partnership award, City of Indpls., 1996, Blue Horizon award Blue & Co., L.L.C., Indpls. Mem. Internat. Anesthesia Rsch. Soc., Assn. Anesthesia Clin. Dirs., Soc. Physics Students Am. Inst. Physics, Am. Soc. for Testing and Materials, Phi Beta Kappa, Phi Eta Sigma (Fred H. Turner scholarship), Sigma Pi Sigma, Alpha Omega Alpha. Roman Catholic. Avocations: golf, music, blacksmithing. Home: 5221 N Washington Blvd Indianapolis IN 46220-3060 Office: Ind U Med Ctr Dept of Med Residency Prog 1001 W 20th St W Bld M200 Indianapolis IN 46202

DILLON, HERB LESTER, critical care and emergency room nurse; b. Duluth, Minn., June 7, 1948; m. Sharon Dillon, July 12, 1969; children: Herb T., Travis M. BA in Nursing, Coll. of St. Scholastica, Duluth, 1973. RN, Minn.; cert. in ACLS, BCLS; CEN; EMT, BCLS instr.; cert. trauma nursing critical care. Nurse emergency room, supr. U.S. Army Hosp., Ft. Riley, Kans., 1973-76; head nurse emergency rm. St. Mary's Med. Ctr., Duluth, 1981-82, critical care transport nurse, 1984-85, EMT instr., 1985—. Nurse dir. Grandma's Marathon, 1979—; Lt. col. USAR, 1971-94, ret. Mem. Emergency Nurses Assn. (cert., EMS Nurse of Yr. 1997). Home: 5127 Dodge St Duluth MN 55804-2436

DILLON, HOWARD BURTON, civil engineer; b. Hardyville, Ky., Aug. 12, 1935; s. Charlie Edison and Mary Opal (Bell) D.; m. Bonny Jean Garard, May 19, 1962; 1 child, Robert Edward. BCE, U. Louisville, 1958, MCE, 1960; postgrad., Okla. State U., 1962, Mich. State U., 1962-65. Registered profl. engr., Ind. Instr. U. Louisville, Ky., 1958-60; from assoc. prof. to prof. Ind. Inst. Tech., Ft. Wayne, 1960-62; NSF fellow Okla. State U., Stillwater, 1962; NSF grantee, instr. Mich. State U., East Lansing, 1962-67; head civil engring. dept. MW Inc. Cons. Engrs., Indpls., 1967-83; project mgr. civil divsn. SEG Engrs. & Cons., Indpls., 1983-91; pvt. practice Howard B. Dillon, Cons. Engr., Indpls., 1991—; asst. dir. to local pub. road needs study for Ind., 1970; mem. design com. for dams in Ind., 1974—; spl. cons. to Ind. Dept. Nat. Resources on dams, 1980—; mem. infrastructure com. for State of Ind., 1984—. Contbr. articles to profl. jours. Committeeman Wayne 52 precinct, Indpls., 1972-86; vice-ward chmn. Wayne South Twp., Indpls., 1986-87. Hazelett and Erdal scholar, 1957-58, W.B. Wendt scholar U. Louisville; recipient Order of Engr. award Purdue U., 1993. Mem. ASCE (Outstanding Civil Engring. Grad. award 1958), NSPE, Am. Soc. Engring. Edn., ASTM, Internat. Soc. Found. Engrs., Mil. Engrs., Internat. Acad. Sci. Ind. Water Resources Assn., Am. Water Works Assn., Nat. Audubon Soc., Optimists (pres. Suburban West chpt. 1972-74, bd. dirs. 1974-78, sec. 1992-94, lt. gov. ind. dist. 1972-74, Optimist of Yr., 1995); Chi Epsilon. Democrat. Baptist. Avocations: fishing, travel, photography, lecturing, coin collecting. Home and Office: 6548 Westdrum Rd Indianapolis IN 46241-1843

DILLON, JAMES JOSEPH, lawyer; b. Rockville Ctr., N.Y., June 18, 1948; s. James Martin and Rosemary (Peter) D.; m. Martha Stone Wiske, Mar. 19, 1977; 1 child, Eleanor. BA, Fordham U., 1970, Oxford U., 1972; JD, Harvard U., 1975; MA, Oxford U., 1982. Bar: Mass. 1975, U.S. Dist. Ct. Mass. 1976, U.S. Ct. Appeals (1st cir.) 1978, U.S. Ct. Appeals (5th cir.) 1986, U.S. Ct. Appeals (6th cir.) 1996, U.S. Ct. Appeals (11th cir.) 1995, U.S. Supreme Ct. 1990. Assoc. Goodwin, Procter & Hoar LLP, Boston, 1975-83, ptnr., 1983—; dir. Beth Israel Deaconess Med. Ctr. Obstetrics and Gynecology Found., Inc., overseer Huntington Theatre Co. Mem. ABA, Mass. State Bar Assn., Boston Bar Assn. Democrat. Club: St. Botolph (Boston). Office: Goodwin Procter & Hoar LLP Exchange Pl Boston MA 02109-2881

DILLON, JAMES JUDE, arts educator; b. N.Y.C., Nov. 16, 1948; s. James and Katherine Veronica (O'Gara) D. BA in History, CUNY, Flushing, 1975; MS in Labor Rels., Cornell/Baruch Univs., 1987. Sr. investigator N.Y.State Health Dept., N.Y.C., 1980-85; chmn. Cmty. Planning Bd., L.I., 1986-87; pres. Allied Irish Artists, L.I., 1989—. Vice-pres. Gateway Cmty. Restoration, Inc., Sunnyside, N.Y., 1988-93; pres. Queens Coalition for Good Govt., L.I., 1989—; candidate N.Y.C. Coun., Western Queens; rep. candidate for U.S. Congress, 7th C.D., 1998. Republican. Roman Catholic. Avocations: travel, weightlifting, collecting Irish and Am. art. Home: 48-50 37 St Long Island City NY 11101

DILLON, JAMES MCNULTY, retired banker; b. Buffalo, Nov. 6, 1933; s. Robert E. and Marion Alice (McNulty) D.; m. Susan Ray, Aug. 27, 1954; children: Katharine, Timothy, Brian, James M. Jr., Anne, John, Margaret. BA, Amherst Coll., 1955. Acct. exec. Merrill Lynch Pierce Fenner & Smith, Buffalo, 1960-61; sr. v.p. in charge Western region trust dept. Marine Midland Bank, Buffalo, 1961-77; exec. v.p. Fleet Nat. Bank, Providence, 1977-88; sr. v.p. Bankers Trust Co., N.Y.C., 1988-92; exec. dir. pvt. & trust banking Swiss Bank Corp., 1992-93; dir. Devel. Diocese Bridgeport, 1993-94; bd. trustees Cath. Cmty. Found., Santa Rosa, Calif., 1997—; bd. dirs. Valley Resources, Inc., Cumberland, R.I. Bd. trustees R.I. Sch. Design, 1985-92; chmn. Jack F. Kemp Congl. Campaign Com., 1970, 72, 74, 76. With USAF, 1956-59. Decorated knight grand cross Equestrian ORder Holy Sepulchre, Jerusalem. Mem. Am. Banker Assn. (chmn. trust divsn. 1988), Knight of Malta. Republican. Home: 3920 Peterson Dr Calistoga CA 94515-9621

DILLON, JEAN KATHERINE, executive secretary, small business owner; b. Birmingham, Ala., May 18, 1925; d. Andrew Crawford and Nell (Cook) Dillon; m. Roy Lerone Morris, June 12, 1946 (div. May 1969); children: Norma Jean, Elizabeth Annell. *Married in Scotland, William and Jeanie Cook immigrated to the U.S. in 1887. They helped develop the coal mining industry in North Central Alabama (1895-1923), enabling Birmingham Industrial Heritage District to play important roles in both World Wars. Their historic William Cook House in Nauvoo, Alabama, represents the economic impact of the coal mining era in the U.S. and embodies Cook's Scottish/coalmining heritage. The home was listed on the Alabama Register of Landmarks and Historic Places on March 23, 1990, on the Birmingham Industrial Heritage District in 1995, and in the Congressional Record in 1995. Granddaughter/ owner Jean K. Dillon has commissioned a play about their lives to be written and staged.* BA in Bus. and Edn., Huntingdon Coll., 1950. Cert. tchr. secondary edn., Ala. Sec./bookkeeper H.T. Fitzpatrick CPA, Atty., Montgomery, Ala., 1948-50; sec., budget technician Dir. Budget, HQ Air Univ., Maxwell AFB, Ala., 1950-58; exec. sec., adminstrv. asst. Comptroller, HQ Air Univ., Maxwell AFB, Ala., 1958-86; adminstrv. asst. Family Violence Program, State Coalition, Montgomery, 1986; owner/ operator The William Cook House, Nauvoo, Ala., 1989—. Pres. Nauvoo Hist. Soc., Inc., 1989-98, bd. dirs., 1998—; mem., patron Birmingham Hist. Soc., 1991—; mem. Nat. Hist. Preservation Forum, 1995—; sec., bd. dirs. Ala. Highland Games, Inc., Montgomery, 1992—; bd. dirs. St. Andrew's Soc., Montgomery, 1995-98, Walker County Arts Coun., 1996—, Montgomery Landmarks Found., Nat. Trust for Hist. Preservation, Nat. Parks Svc.; treas. Capital City Rep. Women, 1995-96, chmn. budget and fin. com. 1997—, v.p. 1997-98; mem. Montgomery County, Ala. Rep. Exec. Com., 1998—; mem.-at-large, bd. dirs. Heart of Dixie Scottish Heritage Soc., 1999—; mem. Walker County Geneology Soc., 1999—; mem. planning com. Heart of Dixie Highland Games and Scots-Irish Festival, Jasper, Ala. and Ofcl. State Ala. Highland Games, Montgomery, 1999—. Mem. AAUW, Huntingdon Coll. Alumni Assn. (life), Walker County C. of C. (sec.-treas., vice chair tourism task force 1990—). Methodist. Avocations: travel, geneology, historical research, writing, heritage. Home and Office: 929 Parkwood Dr Montgomery AL 36109-1228

DILLON, JOHN T., paper company executive; b. Schroon Lake, N.Y., 1938. Grad., U. of Hartford, 1965, Columbia U., 1971. Chmn., CEO, dir. Internat. Paper Co., Purchase, N.Y., 1996—; bd. dirs. Carter Holt Harvey, Ltd. Trustee Nat. Coun. on Econ. Edn. Office: Internat Paper Co 2 Manhattanville Rd Purchase NY 10577-2118*

DILLON, JOSEPH NEIL, pastor; b. Fresno, Calif., July 31, 1945; s. Howard Arthur and Blanch Marie (Nichols) D.; m. Paula Ann Gunovich, June 17, 1973; children: Chandra M., Ryan A. 0BA, Pacific Luth. U., 1970; MDiv, Northwestern Luth. Theol. Sem., 1976. Ordained to ministry, Luth. Ch., 1976. Pastor 1st Luth. Ch., Anconda, Mont., 1976-82, Messiah Luth. Ch., Billings, Mont., 1982-85; assoc. pastor Messiah Luth. Ch., Auburn, Wash., 1985-88; sr. pastor Messiah Luth. Ch., 1988-90; dean, Evergreen Conf., South King Coun., Wash., 1990—; regional coun. Region I ELCA Southwest Wash., 1987-90, pres., 1988-90; pres., Auburn Ministrial Assn., 1988-90; sec. SWW Synod ELCA, 1990—; chair Lutheran Pub. Policy Bd. Washington, 1998—. Mem. Gov. Coun. Employment Planning, Anaconda, 1980-83; pres., bd. dirs., Anaconda Devel. Disabled, 1978-82; bd. dirs., Auburn Youth Resources, 1987—; mem. Human Resources Commn., City Auburn, 1987—. Sgt. U.S. Army, 1963-66. Mem. Lions. Home: 6307 37th Pl SE Auburn WA 98092-7391 Office: Messiah Luth Ch 805 4th St NE Auburn WA 98002-5088

DILLON, LAURA WHITE, communications executive; m. Paul J. Dillon; 3 children. BA, Allegheny Coll., 1974; MA in English, U. Pa., 1977. Writer, editor Instnl. Investor mag., N.Y.C.; comms. officer J.P. Morgan & Co., N.Y.C., 1980-83, asst. to chmn. and CEO, 1985-89, mng. dir. corp. comm. group, 1989—, founding diversity steering com. Trustee Oak Knoll Sch., Summit, N.J. Mem. Pub. Rels. Seminar. Fax: (212) 648-5984. Office: JP Morgan Co Inc 60 Wall St New York NY 10260*

DILLON, MATT, actor; b. New Rochelle, N.Y., Feb. 18, 1964; s. Paul and Mary Ellen Dillon. Appeared in films including Over the Edge, 1979, Little Darlings, 1980, My Bodyguard, 1980, Liar's Moon, 1982, Tex, 1982, The Outsiders, 1983, Rumblefish, 1983, The Flamingo Kid, 1984, Target, 1985, Rebel, 1986, Native Son, 1986, Big Town, 1987, Kansas, 1988, Bloodhounds of Broadway, 1989, Drugstore Cowboy, 1989, A Kiss Before Dying, 1991, Singles, 1992, The Saint of Fort Washington, 1993, Mr. Wonderful, 1993, Golden Gate, 1994, To Die For, 1995, Frankie Starlight, 1995, Grace of My Heart, 1996, Beautiful Girls, 1996, Albino Alligator, 1996, In and Out, 1997; TV appearances include The Great American Fourth of July, Women and Men 2; actor stage play Boys of Winter, 1985. Office: c/o Elaine Goldsmith ICM 40 W 57th St New York NY 10019-4001*

DILLON, MERTON LYNN, historian, educator; b. nr. Addison, Mich., Apr. 4, 1924; s. Henry J. and Cecil Edith (Sanford) D. B.A., Mich. State Normal Coll., 1945; M.A., U. Mich., 1948, Ph.D., 1951. Asst. prof. history N.Mex. Mil. Inst., Roswell, 1951-56; asst. prof. Tex. Tech. Coll., Lubbock, 1956-59; asso. prof. Tex. Tech. Coll., 1959-63, prof., 1963-65; asso. prof. Northern Ill. U., DeKalb, 1965-67; prof. Ohio State U., Columbus, 1967-91, prof. emeritus, 1991—. Author: Elijah P. Lovejoy, Abolitionist Editor, 1961, Benjamin Lundy and the Struggle for Negro Freedom, 1966, The Abolitionists, the Growth of a Dissenting Minority, 1974; Ulrich Bonnell Phillips, Historian of the Old South, 1985, Slavery Attacked: Southern Slaves and Their Allies, 1619-1865, 1990; contbr. articles to profl. jours. NEH fellow, 1973-74. Mem. Am. Hist. Assn., Orgn. Am. Historians, So. Hist. Assn. (bd. editors 1959-63), ACLU, Phi Beta Kappa. Home: 10460 Addison Rd Jerome MI 49249-9723 Office: Ohio State U Dept History Columbus OH 43210

DILLON, MICHAEL EARL, engineering executive, mechanical engineer, educator; b. Lynwood, Calif., Mar. 4, 1946; s. Earl Edward and Sally Ann (Wallace) D.; m. Bernardine Jeanette Staples, June 10, 1967; children: Bryan Douglas, Nicole Marie, Brendon McMichael. BA in Math., Calif. State U., Long Beach, 1978, postgrad. Registered profl. engr., Calif., Colo., Tex. Nev., Utah, Ariz., Wyo., Pa., Hawaii, N.Y., Wash., Oreg., Idaho, Mo., La., Minn., Mont., Nebr., Mich., Ind., Okla., Tenn., N.J., Ga., Fla., Ohio, Va., Wis., Ill., Arks., Iowa, Okla., others; chartered engr., U.K. Journeyman plumber Roy E. Dillon & Sons, Long Beach, 1967-69, ptnr., 1969-73; field supr. Dennis Mech., San Marino, 1973-74; chief mech. official City of Long Beach, 1974-79; mgr. engr. Southland Industries, Long Beach, 1979-83; v.p. Syska & Hennessy, L.A. and N.Y., 1983-87; prin. Robert M. Young & Assoc., Pasadena, Calif., 1987-89; pres. Dillon Cons. Engrs., Long Beach, 1989—; mech. cons. in field; instr. U. Calif., Irvine, San Diego and L.A., U. So. Calif., L.A., Calif. State U., Long Beach, U. Tex., Arlington; lectr. in field. Contbr. over 160 poems to various publs., co articles to profl. jours. Vice chair Mechanical, Plumbing, Elec. and Energy Code Adv. Commn. of Calif., Bldg. Stds. Commn.; bd. examiners Appeals and Condemnations, Long Beach; mem. State Fire Marshals Adv. Bd., Sacramento, Calif.; mem. adv. bd. City of L.A.; mem. bus. adv. bd. City of Long Beach. Recipient Environ. Ozone Protection award U.S. EPA, 1993, John Fies award Internat. Conf. Bldg. Ofcls., 1995. Fellow ASHRAE (Disting. Svc. award 1991), Chartered Inst. Bldg. Svc. Engrs. Gt. Britain and Ireland, Inst. Refrigeration, Heating, Air Conditioning Engrs. of New Zealand, Inst. Advancement Engring.; mem. ASCE, NSPE, ASTM, ASME, Am. Cons. Engrs. Coun., Am. Soc. Plumbing Engrs., Internat. Soc. Fire Safety Sci., Nat. Acad. Forensic Engrs., Nat. Inst. for Engring. Ethics, Nat. Fire Protection Assn., Internat. Conf. Bldg. Ofcls. (John Fies award 1995), Internat. Platform Assn., Internat. Fire Code Inst., So. Bldg. Code Congress Internat., Bldg. Ofcls. and Code Adminstrn. Internat., Cons. Engrs. and Land Surveyors Calif., Soc. Fire Protection Engrs., Tau Beta Pi, Pi Tau Sigma, Chi Epsilon, others. Avocation: poetry. Home: 1107 E 46th St Long Beach CA 90807-1003 Office: Dillon Cons Engrs 1165 E San Antonio Dr Ste D Long Beach CA 90807-2374 *Rather I live and love in coventry than lust and rust in the public reign of insouciant sycophancy.*

DILLON, MILLICENT GERSON, writer; b. May 24, 1925. AB, Hunter Coll., 1944; MA, San Francisco State U., 1966. Author: Baby Perpetua and Other Stories, 1971, The One in the Back Is Nedea, 1973, A Little Original Sin: The Life and Work of Jane Bowles, 1981, After Egypt, Isadora Duncan and Mary Cassatt, 1990, The Dance of the Mothers, 1991, You Are Not I: A Portrait of Paul Bowles, 1998. Home: 83 6th Ave San Francisco CA 94118

DILLON, PATRICIA ANNE, state legislator; b. Flushing, N.Y., July 9, 1948; d. Raymond Walter and Patricia Marie (Kuhlmann) D.; m. John Schley Hughes, July 5, 1977; 1 child, Patrick John. BA, Marymount U., 1970; MA, Ohio State U., 1974; MPH, Yale U., 1998. Researcher Yale Sch. Medicine, New Haven, Conn., 1974-77; dir., founder New Haven Project Battered Women, 1977-80; devel. adminstr. City of Norwalk (Conn.), 1980-82; state legislator State of Conn., Hartford, 1984—; chmn. pub. health com. State of COnn., Hartford, 1990—; chmn. appropriations subcom. health and hosps. State of Conn., Hartford, 1992—, dep. majority leader, 1992—. Contbr. articles on family violence, health, taxation, solid waste, AIDS and Irish issues to various publs.; author: (with others) Blood Feuds, 1999. Ward chmn. Dem. Town Com., New Haven, 1976-86; alderwoman New Haven Bd. Alderman, 1979-85. Roman Catholic. Avocations: bibliophile, gardening. Home: 68 W Rock Ave New Haven CT 06515-2221 Office: Lt Gen Assembly Legion Office Bldg Capitol Ave Hartford CT 06106

DILLON, PATRICIA HARRINGTON, medical/surgical nurse; b. Covington, Va., Apr. 1, 1937; d. John Lawrence and Sally Ellen (Atkinson) Harrington; m. Donald T. Dillon, Sept. 17, 1966; children: Kathleen Marie, Donald Clark. BSN, Cath. U. Am., 1959; student, Adelphi Coll., 1985. Cert. cardiopulmonary resuscitation, perioperative nursing. Staff nurse Providence Hosp., Washington; instr. in operating room Mt. Sinai Hosp., N.Y.C.; staff nurse St. John's Queens Hosp., Elmhurst, N.Y., CentraState Med. Ctr., Freehold, N.J. Mem. Assn. Operating Room Nurses. Home: 28 Mariners Cv Freehold NJ 07728-3705

DILLON, PHILLIP MICHAEL, construction company executive; b. Ypsilanti, Mich., July 15, 1944; s. Robert Timothy and Maxine Helen (Elliott) D.; student Mich. State U., 1962-66; m. Phyllis Louise Brooks, Jan. 21, 1978; children: Richard, Debora, Michael, Robert, Karen. Store mgr. Morse Shoe, Inc., Detroit, 1964-68, asst. dir. store planning and constrn., Canton, Mass., 1968-72; dir. store planning and constrn. Stride Rite Corp., Boston, 1972-74; sr. v.p. Capitol Cos., Inc., Arlington Heights, Ill., 1974-81; chmn. bd., chief exec. officer Standard Cos., Inc., Palatine, Ill., 1982-83; co-owner, sr. v.p. Eagle Constrn. Corp., 1983-88; chief exec. officer Dillon Enterprises Ltd., Lemont, Ill., 1988—; bd. dirs. Dillon Enterprises, Ltd.; co-owner, bd. dirs., chmn. Ominitech, Inc.; co-owner, bd. dirs., sr. ptnr. Internat. Developers Partnership, Dillon Farm Partnership Mich., Dillon Yo Ranch Partnership Tex. Mem. Inst. Store Planners, Assn. Gen. Contractors Am., Builders Assn. Chgo., Land Owners Assn. (archtl. rev. com.), Green Acres Sportsman Club, Tex. Longhorn Breeders Assoc. Roman Catholic. Office: 15850 New Ave Ste 100 Lemont IL 60439-3680

DILLON, ROBERT MORTON, retired association executive, architectural consultant; b. Seattle, Oct. 27, 1923; s. James Richard and Lucille (Morton) D.; m. Mary Charlotte Beeson, Jan. 6, 1943; children: Robert Thomas, Colleen Marie Dillon Brown, Patrick Morton. Student, U. Ill., 1946-47; BArch., U. Wash., 1949; MA in Architecture, U. Fla., 1954. Registered architect, Fla. Designer-draftsman Williams and Longstreet (Architects), Greenville, S.C., 1949-50, William G. Lyles, Bissett, Carlisle & Wolff (Architects), Columbia, S.C., 1949-50, Robert M. Dillon and Wm. B. Eaton (Architects), Gainesville, Fla., 1952-55; staff architect Bldg. Rsch. Adv. Bd., Nat. Acad. Scis.-NRC, Washington, 1955-56, project dir., 1956-58, exec. dir., 1958-77; exec. sec. U.S. nat. com. for Conseil Internat. du Batiment, 1962-74; Sec. U.S. Planning Com. 2d Internat. Conf. on Permafrost, Yakutsk, USSR, 1972-74; exec. asst. to pres. Nat. Inst. Bldg. Scis., Washington, 1978-81, v.p., 1982-84, acting contr., 1983-84; exec. v.p. Am. Coun. Constrn. Edn., Washington, 1984-89, cons., 1989—; asst. prof. arch. Clemson Coll., 1949-50; instr., asst. prof. arch. U. Fla., 1950-55; lectr. structural theory and design Cath. U. Am., 1956-62; guest lectr. Air Force Inst. Tech., Wright-Patterson AFB, 1964-65; disting. faculty Acad. Code Adminstrn. and Enforcement U. Ill., 1972, professorial lectr. George Washington U., 1977-77, 81-82; vis. prof. Coll. Environ. Design U. Okla., 1984, adj. assoc. prof. bldg. sci., 1985-89, grad. sch. arch. Univ. Utah, 1978. Author: (with S.W. Crawley) Steel Buildings: Analysis and Design, 1970, 4th edit., 1993 (also 3d edit. pub. in Spanish 1992); contbg. author: Funk and Wagnall's New Ency., 1972, Ency. of Architecture, 1989; editor-in-chief: Guide to the Use of NEHRP Provisions in Earthquake Resistant Design of Buildings, 1987, Building Seismic Safety Coun., Nat. Inst. Bldg. Scis. Cons. Ednl. Facilities Labs., N.Y.C., 1958-71; mem. adv. com. low-income housing demonstration program HUD, Washington, 1964-67; mem. working groups U.S.-USSR Agreement on Housing and Other Constrn., 1975-85; mem. sub-panel housing White House Panel on Civilian Tech., Washington, 1961-62; mem. advs. to F. Stuart Fitzpatrick Meml. Award Trustee, 1969-84, chmn., 1974-78; mem. adv. panel Basic Homes Program OEO and HUD, 1972-77; mem. Nat. Adv. Coun. Rsch. Energy Conservation, 1975-78; mem. adv. com. Coun. Am. Bldg. Ofcls., 1976-86; mem. tech. coun. on bldg. codes and stds.; sec. Home and Land Owners Assn., Angel Fire, N.Mex., 1991-95; co-chmn., sec. initial bd. dirs. Assn. Angel Fire Property Owners, 1995-96; mem. master plan task force Angel Fire Planning and Zoning Commn., 1997. Mem. AIA (com. rsch. for architecture 1962-67, chmn. 1969, chmn. com. archtl. barriers 1967-68, nat. housing com. 1970-72, 84-85, mem. emeritus 1990—), ASCE (life, task com. cold regions 1977-79, tech. coun. cold regions engring., exec. com. 1976-84, chmn. 1981, stds. com. 1987-94,), DAV (life), Nat. Acad. Code Adminstrn. (life, trustee 1976-80, exec. com. 1978-82, new bd. dirs. 1980-82, 83-84, sec.-treas. 1982-82), Am. Inst. Steel Constrn., Am. Inst. Constructors, Am. Coun. Constrn. Edn. (trustee 1990-96), Nat. Inst. Bldg. Scis. (cons. coun. 1984-93, honor award 1997). Home and Office: PO Box 232 Gold Beach OR 97444-0232

DILLON, ROBERT SHERWOOD, retired government official; b. Chgo., Jan. 7, 1929; s. Dale Crowell and Viola May (Sherwood)D.; m. Caroline Sue Burch, June 16, 1951; children: Dale, Robert Jr., John, Elizabeth, Thomas. BA, Duke U., 1951; postgrad., Princeton U., 1958-59. Ops. officer CIA, 1951-56; fgn. svc. officer (including U.S. Amb. Lebanon, 1981-83) Dept. State, Washington, 1956-84; asst. sec. gen. UN, Vienna, Austria, 1984-88; pres. Am.-Mideast Ednl. & Tng. Svcs., Washington, 1988-95; UN spl. envoy for Rwanda and Burundi, 1994; advisor Dept. of State, 1995—. Cpl. U.S. Army, 1947-48. Recipient Presdl. Honor award, White House, 1983.

DILLON, RODNEY LEE, lawyer; b. Vincennes, Ind., Feb. 25, 1938; s. Ray E. and Jeanne E. (O'Conner) D.; m. N. Swarts (div. May 1975); children: Vicki, Terri, Jacki, Kelli; m. Rebecca Boyer, Mar. 28, 1981; co-guardian: Zachary, Shawn Michelle, Justin and Michael Dillon. BA in Econs., U. Cin., 1960; JD, U. Louisville, 1972. Bar: Fla. 1973, U.S. Dist. Ct. (mid. dist.) Fla. 1973, U.S. Ct. Appeals (5th cir.) 1977, U.S. Supreme Ct. 1977, U.S. Ct. Appeals (11th cir.) 1988; bd. cert. consumer bankruptcy law. Pvt. practice, Sarasota, Fla., 1973—. Recipient awards of appreciation Lawyers Referral Svc., Sarasota County Bar Assn. Mem. ABA, Fla. Bar Assn. (lawyer referral svc. 1994-95), Am. Bankruptcy Inst., Tampa Bay Bankruptcy Bar Assn., Sarasota County Bar Assn., Columbus Assn. (pres. 1978-80), Sarasota Outboard Club (commodore 1991-92), Eagles, Elks, KC (adv. 1983-89). Republican. Roman Catholic. Avocations: boating, fishing, diving. E-mail: rdillonl@mindspring.com. Office: 2831 Ringling Blvd Ste 210D Sarasota FL 34237-5352

DILLON, WILTON STERLING, anthropologist, foundation administrator; b. Yale, Okla., July 13, 1923; s. Earl Henry and Edith Holland (Canfield) D.; m. Virginia Leigh Harris, Jan. 20, 1956; 1 child, James Harris. BA, U. Calif.-Berkeley, 1951; postgrad., Inst. Ethnology, U. Paris, U. Leyden, 1951-52; PhD, Columbia U., 1961. News reporter Holdenville (Okla.) Daily News, 1936-41; info. specialist, civilian mem. Civil Info. and Edn. Sect. SCAP, Tokyo, 1946-49; vis. lectr. sociology and anthropology Hobart and William Smith colls., Geneva, N.Y., 1953-54; staff anthropologist Japan Soc. N.Y.; also lectr. Japanese studies Fordham U., 1954; dir. Clearinghouse for Research in Human Orgn., Soc. Applied Anthropology, N.Y.C., 1954-56; exec. sec., dir. research Phelps-Stokes Fund N.Y.; including dir. research project on higher edn. and African nationhood U. Ghana, 1957-63; vis. lectr. Columbia U., New Sch. Social Research, 1957-63; staff dir. Nat. Acad. Scis., 1963-69; dir. symposia and seminars Smithsonian Instn., Washington, 1969-85, dir. interdisciplinary studies, 1986-90, sr. scholar, 1990—; dir. internat. commemoration of 250th anniversary of birth of Thomas Jefferson, 1992—; adj. prof. U. Ala., 1971—; chmn. Oxford U.-Smithsonian Seminars, 1985. Author: Gifts and Nations, 1968; editor: (with John F. Eisenberg) Man and Beast: Comparative Social Behavior, 1971, The Cultural Drama, 1974, (with Neil G. Kotler) The Statue of Liberty Revisited: Making a Universal Symbol, 1993; contbr. articles to profl. jours.; editl. bd. Ala. Heritage. Del. numerous internat. confs. including UNESCO, Pugwash; mem. adv. coun. on Africa Dept. State, 1964-68; hon. commr. Internat. Year of Child, 1979-80; pres. bd. dirs. Inst. Intercultural Studies, N.Y.C.; trustee emeritus Phelps-Stokes Fund, 1985—; sec.-treas., bd. dirs. Inst. Psychiatry and Fgn. Affairs; bd. visitors Wake Forest U., 1978-81; adv. com. Hubert Humphrey Inst. for Pub. Affairs, 1988-94; bd. dirs. Delta Rsch. and Ednl. Found., 1987-95; trustee Friends of Raoul Wallenberg Found., 1995-97, Lives and Legacies Inc., 1995—; advisor Nation's Capital Bicentennial Celebration 1999-2000, Margaret Mead Centenary 2001, Historic Mt. Vernon 1999. With USAAF, 1943-46. Decorated Chevalier de l'ordre des arts et lettres, 1983; Woodrow Wilson Internat. Center for Scholars guest scholar, 1970. Fellow Am. Anthrop. Assn., AAAS, Royal Soc. Arts; mem. Lit. Soc. Washington (pres. 1990), Anthrop. Soc. Washington. Episcopalian (lay reader N.Y. diocese 1958-60). Club: Cosmos (Washington). Home: 1446 Woodacre Dr Mc Lean VA 22101-2536 Office: Smithsonian Instn Washington DC 20560

DILLON-MARCOTTE, KATHRYN ANNE, Lawyer; b. Apr. 20, 1969. BA, Colgate U., 1991; JD, U. Denver, 1994. Intern U.S. Securities and Exch. Commn., Denver, 1993-94; ptnr. Lanphear & Dillon, Cranston,

R.I., 1995—. E-mail: marcotte@prodigy.net. Office: 2100 Broad St Cranston RI 02905-3342

DILLON-MCHUGH, CATHLEEN THERESA, librarian, consultant; b. Newark, Jan. 31, 1951; d. William David and Rose (Baker) Dillon; m. Joseph F. McHugh, Apr. 16, 1988. BA cum laude, Bloomfield (N.J.) Coll., 1973; MLS, Rutgers U., 1976. Reference-cataloging libr. Neptune (N.J.) Pub. Libr., 1976-77; indexer Popular Periodical Index, Wayne, N.J., 1979-95; sch. libr. Hudson Cath. High Sch., Jersey City, 1980-81; govtl. reference libr. N.J. State Libr., Trenton, 1981-82, law reference libr., 1982-83, referral libr., 1983-87; tech. reference libr. Bell Communications Rsch., Red Bank, N.J., 1987; reference libr. Middletown Twp. Pub. Libr., N.J., 1988-89; libr./info. specialist, cons. various corps., N.J. and Maine, 1990-94; libr. Gov. Baxter Sch. for the Deaf, Falmouth, Maine, 1994-99; freelance writer, content developer, 1999—; cons. Quantum Enterprises, Inc., Middletown, 1985-86; dir. Edith Belle Libby Meml. Libr., Old Orchard Beach, Maine, 1991-94. Mem. Maine Libr. Assn. Avocations: needlework, ceili dancing, American Sign Language.

DILLON-RIDGLEY, DIANNE GRANVILLE, mediator, consultant, association executive; b. Dallas, Tex.; d. Harold Bishop and Evelyn (Hardin) Dillon; children: Karima Afia, Dasal Hardin. BA in Philosophy, Howard U., 1972; student, Iowa Mediation Svc., 1986, 90, 91. Cert. farmer/creditor and family matrimonial mediator. Mediator The Iowa Mediation Svc., 1986—, edn. mktg. specialist, 1991; workshop instr. Kettering Family Found., Dayton, Ohio, 1988—, cons., 1991-94; with office of student affairs U. Iowa, 1991-94; pres., dir. Zero Population Growth, Washington, 1994—; chmn., Human Rights Commn., Burlington, Iowa, 1986-90; mem. Iowa Humanities bd. state divsn. of NEH, 1984-90, v.p. prog. com., exec. com., chmn. mem. com.; com. profl. ethics Iowa Supreme Court, Iowa Bar Assn.; U.S. del. to UNCED, 1991, N.Y.C., adv. and mem. U.S. del. to the UN conf. on environ. and devel., Rio de Janeiro, 1992; bd. dirs. Child & Family Policy Ctr., Iowa divsn., 1989—; chair target small bus. bd. Iowa Dept. Econ. Devel., 1987—; vice chmn. bd. dirs. Nat. Summit on Africa, Washington, 1997—; mem. coun. sustainable devel. U.S. Pres.'s Coun., Washington, 1994—; sr. policy analyst WEDO, N.Y.C., 1993—; bd. dirs. Interfac Inc., Atlanta, 1997—; adj. lectr. U. Ind. Sch. Pub. and Environ. Affairs, 1997—; interim dir. WEDG, N.Y.C. Mem. nat. bd. dirs. YWCA of the U.S.A., N.Y.C., 1988—, pub. policy com., 1988-91, co-chair racial justice com., 1991—, rep. to UN conf. on environ. and devel. for YWCA of U.S.A., bd. dirs. YWCA Burlington, 1981-87, chair adult com., fin. com. chair bldg. corp. bd.; friends devel. coun. U. Iowa Mus. of Art, Burlington Fine Arts League, scholarship com. 1986-89, bd. dirs. Mus. African Am. Hist., Boston, 1976-89; bd. dirs. Burlington Civic Mus. Assn., v.p. 1985-91; bd. dirs. U. Iowa libs., 1991—, mem. human needs commn. Episcopal Diocese of Iowa; vestry bd. Christ Episcopal Ch., Burlington; bd. dirs., selection com., Martin Luther King Scholarship of Iowa, 1987—; co-chair racial justice YWCA, N.Y.C., 1994—; mem. internat. steering com. Global Water Partnership, Stockholm, 1998—. Recipient of Outstanding Woman of the Year in Politics award, 1985. Mem. Assn. Iowa Human Rights Agys. (lobbyist 1990, pres. 1986-90). Office: Zero Population Growth 1400 16th St NW Ste 320 Washington DC 20036-2290*

DILLS, JAMES ARLOF, retired publishing company executive; b. Guelph, Ont., Can., Aug. 11, 1930; s. George Arlof and Isma Marie (MacPherson) D.; m. Shirley Jean Elliott, Aug. 16, 1952; children—Steven George, James Mark, Paul David, Catherine Jane, Carolyn Shirley. Grad. in journalism, Ryerson Poly. Inst., 1951. Pub. The Can. Champion, Milton, Ont., 1966-78, The Georgetown (Ont.) Ind., 1973-78; sec.-treas. Dills Printing and Pub. Co. Ltd., Acton, Ont., 1954—; exec. dir. Can. Community Newspapers Assn., Toronto, Ont., 1979-87; mem. adv. com. journalism program Sheridan Coll., 1965-78; pres. Ont. Weekly Newspapers Assn., 1975-76; pub. County Chronicles Press, 1992—; dir. Milton Evergreen Cemetery Co., 1997. Author: Moments in History, 1993. Vice Chair, Mackenzie Heritage Printery, Queenston.,1998; pres. Milton Hist. Soc., 1977-80. Named Citizen of Yr. Milton, 1978.

DILLY, MARIAN JEANETTE, humanities educator; b. Vining, Minn., Nov. 7, 1921; d. John Fredolph and Mabel Josephine (Haagenson) Linder; m. Robert Lee Dily, June 22, 1946 (dec. Oct. 1987); children: Ronald Lee, Patricia Jeanette Dilly Vero. Studetn, U. Minn., 1944-45; grad., John R. Powers Finishing Sch., N.Y.C., 1957, Zell McC. Fashion Career Sch., Mpls., 1957, Estelle Compton Models Inst., Mpls., 1966, Nancy Taylor Charm Sch., N.Y.C., 1967, Patricia Stevens Career Sch., Mpls., 1968; BS in English cum laude, Black Hills State U., Spearfish, S.D., 1975. Instr. Nat. Coll., Rapid City, S.D., 1966-68; instr., dir. Nancy Taylor Charm Sch., 1966-68; hostess TV shows, 1966-74; lectr. in personality devel., dir., prodr. beauty and talent pageants, freelance coord. in fashion shows, judge beauty and talent pageants of local, state and nat. levels, 1966—. Actress bit parts Nauman Films Inc., 1970. Active ARC; dir., 1st v.p. Black Hills Girl Scout Coun., 1967-72; chmn. bd. dirs., pres. Luth. Social Svc. Aux., Western S.D. and Eastern Wyo., 1960-65; chmn. women's events Dakota Days and Nat. Premiere, 1968; bd. dirs. YMCA, 1976-81; mem. Dallas Symphony Orch. League, 1987-90, Dallas Mus. of Art League, 1987-90, Women's Club, Dallas County, Tex., Inc., 1987-90. Recipient award Rapid City C. of C., 1968, Fashion awards March of Dimes, 1967-72, Svc. award Black Hills Girl Scout Coun., award of appreciation Yellowstone Internat. Toastmistress Club. Mem. AAUW (sec., mem. exec.b d. 1988-90), Nu Tau Sigma (past advisor), Delta Tau Kappa, Singing Tribe of Wahoo. Avocations: golf, bridge, music, skiing. Address: 1607 Woodward St Erie CO 80516

DILMORE, CINDY CORLEY, special education educator; b. Laurel, Miss., Oct. 15, 1959; d. John Edward and Shelby (Dickerson) Corley; m. David Dilmore, June 17, 1978; children: Matthew, Cortnee. BS in Elem. Edn., U. So. Miss., 1980, BS in Spl. Edn., 1982, MEd in Handicapped Edn., 1990. Cert. tchr., spl. edn. tchr., Miss. Specific learning disabilities tchr. Taylorsville (Miss.) Elem. Sch., 1980-97, also tchr. mentally retarded and hearing impaired students; functional living skills tchr. Taylorsville (Miss.) H.S., 1997—. Troop leader Taylorsville area Girl Scouts U.S., 1989-94. Mem. NEA, Miss. Assn. Educators, Miss. Assn. Children and Adults with Learning Disabilities. Baptist. Avocations: reading, cross stitch, cooking, crafts. Home: 107 Abe Gentry Rd Mount Olive MS 39119-9106 Office: Taylorsville HS PO Box 8 Taylorsville MS 39168-0008

DILORENZO, FRANCIS X., bishop; b. Philadelphia, PA, Apr. 15, 1942. ordained priest May 18, 1968. Titular bishop of Tigia, 1988; aux. bishop Diocese of Scranton, 1988; Most Rev. Bishop Diocese of Honolulu, 1993-94, bishop, 1994—. Office: Bishop of Honolulu 1184 Bishop St Honolulu HI 96813-2858*

DI LORENZO, JOHN FLORIO, JR., lawyer; b. Paterson, N.J., May 18, 1940; s. John F. and Ida (Cona) Di L.; m. Ernestine R. De Rose, Nov. 15, 1969; children: Christina P., Roberta J. BA, Seton Hall U., 1962; LLB, Columbia U., 1966, MBA, 1966. Bar: N.J. 1967, N.Y. 1968, Ohio 1981. Assoc. Stryker, Tams & Dill, Esqs., Newark, 1966-68; atty. Am. Electric Power Svc. Corp., N.Y.C., 1968-79, asst. gen. counsel, asst. v.p., exec. asst. to pres., 1979-81; assoc. gen. counsel, v.p., sec. Am. Electric Power Svc. Corp., Columbus, Ohio, 1981—; sec. various Am. Electric Power Systems cos., 1987—, asst. sec. 1979. Trustee Ballet Met. Columbus, 1981-87. Mem. ABA (chmn. subcom. on pub. utility holding co. act of fed. regulation of securities com. 1985-94), Scioto Country Club. Roman Catholic. Avocations: skiing, travel. Home: 2756 Elginfield Rd Columbus OH 43220-4248 Office: Am Electric Power Svc 1 Riverside Plz Columbus OH 43215-2355

DILTS, DAVID MICHAEL, management researcher, university facility director; b. Flint, Mich., Oct. 8, 1950; s. Carl O. and Lorraine D. Dilts; m. Barbara Jean Gonnella; children: Matthew, Andrew, Philip, Simon, Joanna. BS, Calif. Poly. State U., 1972; MBA, U. Oreg., 1973, PhD, 1983. Ops. analyst Simpson Plastics Co., Eugene, Oreg., 1974-76, mgr. planning and devel., 1976-77, mgr. strategic planning, 1977-78; bus. specialist Specialized Tng. Program, Eugene, 1980-81; asst. prof. Grad. Sch. Bus. Adminstrn. Mich. State U., East Lansing, 1984-86; assoc. prof. mgmt. scis., engring. faculty U. Waterloo (Ont.), 1986-96, dir. Centre for Integrating Mfg., 1988-91, prof. mgmt. scis., 1996—; dir. Mgmt. of Integrated Mfg., 1991; co-dir. SEEPAC, 1994—; ptnr. D&D Cons., Eugene, 1978-84; cons. Lockheed Martin, TRW, CAM-I, Govt. Can.; bd. dirs. Advanced Info. Techs., East Lansing; vis. prof. Vanderbilt U., Nashville, 1999—. Author: Accounting Information Systems, 1987; co-author: Shop Floor Control, 1985, Computer Integrated Manufacturing Notes, 1986, Shop Floor Control: Principles and Practices, 1987, The Competitively Integrated Enterprise, 1992, vol. 2, 1993, vol. 3, 1993; editor: Operations Management Review, 1995-97. Treas. MidMich. Lekotek, East Lansing, 1984-85, pres. 1986. Recipient Disting. Theoretical Paper award Am. Inst. for Decision Scis., 1982, AT&T Found. award Am. Assembly Collegiate Schs. Bus., 1985. Mem. Am. Acctg. Assn., Acad. Mgmt., Decision Scis. Inst. (Instructional Innovation award 1992, Disting. Application Paper award 1997), Inst. for Operations Rsch. and the Mgmt. Scis.

DILTS, JON PAUL, law educator; b. Monterey, Ind., Sept. 7, 1945; s. Charles Albert and Janet Cecilia (Keitzer) D.; m. Anne Williams Avirett, Aug. 21, 1971; children: Christopher, Andrew. BA, Saint Meinrad Coll., 1967; MA, Ind. U., 1974; JD, Valparaiso U., 1981. Bar: Ind. 1981, U.S. Dist. Ct. (so. dist.) Ind. 1981. Reporter Peru (Ind.) Daily Tribune, 1972-73, wire editor, 1973-76, city editor, 1976-78; law clk. Ind. Ct. Appeals, Indpls., 1981-82; asst. prof. Ind. U., Bloomington, 1982-88, assoc. prof., 1988—, assoc. dean, 1985—. Author: The Magnificent 92 Indiana Courthouses, 1992; co-author: Media Law, 1994, 97; mem. editl. bd. Comms. Law & Policy, 1998—. Trustee Saint Meinrad Coll., Sch. Theology, 1996-98; mem. exec. bd. dirs. Hoosier Trails Coun., Boy Scouts Am., Bloomington, 1992-93. With U.S. Army, 1968-71. Mem. Assn. for Edn. in Journalism and Mass Comm. (head law divsn. 1987-88), Soc. Profl. Journalists, AP Mng. Editors Assn., Rotary. Democrat. Roman Catholic. Avocations: skiing, hiking, backpacking, canoeing, sailing. Office: Ind U Sch Journalism 940 E Seventh St Bloomington IN 47405

DILUOFFO, SANTINA, chiropractor; b. Yonkers, N.Y., Aug. 29, 1958; d. Leone and Anna (Lanzara) DiL. BS in Biology, Mercy Coll., Dobbs Ferry, N.Y., 1980; D Chiropractic, N.Y. Chiropractic Coll., 1986. Pvt. practice Hempstead, N.Y., 1986—, Glen Cove, N.Y., 1988—; lectr. on chiropractic to pub. schs. and chs. Hempstead Police Dept., 1988—; promoter growing up drug free U.S. Dept. Edn., Washington, 1992—; treating doctor for Cedric Harris at Olympics, Atlanta, 1996; appid. to perform scoliosis screenings to Hempstead Pub. Schs.; Amway distbr.; spkr. in field. Columnist Caribbean Am. Athlete newspaper, 1996—; contbr. articles to newspapers. Active Father Flanagan's Boys' Home, Hempstead Health Coun., 1998. Mem. MADD. Avocations: stamp collecting, reading, exercise, nature walks, meditation. Office: 33 Front St Hempstead NY 11550-3601

DILWORTH, EDWIN EARLE, retired obstetrician, gynecologist; b. Jasper, Ala., June 28, 1914; s. Tranny and Bertie (Caldwell) D.; m. Neida May Humphrey, June 17, 1939; children: John Edwin, Robert Earle, Nancy. AB, U. Ala., 1936; MD, Tulane U., 1940. Diplomate Am. Bd. Ob-Gyn. Intern, then resident in ob-gyn. Shreveport (La.) Charity Hosp., 1940-44; pvt. practice Shreveport, 1959-60; chief ob-gyn. Schumpert Meml. Med. Ctr., 1951, pres. staff, 1954; chief ob-gyn. Confederate Meml. Med. Ctr. (now La. State U. Med. Ctr.), Shreveport, 1954-76, pres. staff, 1959; clin. prof. ob-gyn. La. State U., Shreveport, 1967-90, prof. emeritus, 1990—. Contbr. articles to profl. jours. Head med. divsn. Shreveport United Way, 1972. Capt. M.C., AUS, 1944-46. Recipient Disting. Svc. award Shreveport Med. Soc., 1980. Fellow ACOG (founding), ACS; mem. Cen. Assn. Ob-Gyn., Southeastern Assn. Ob-Gyn., So. Gynecol. and Obstet. Soc., Shreveport Photog. Soc. Home: 660 Thora Blvd Shreveport LA 71106-1822

DILWORTH, ROBERT LEXOW, career military officer, adult education educator; b. Chgo., Aug. 19, 1936; s. Robert Oliver and Linda Agnes (Lexow) D.; m. Doris Elthea Smith, Sept. 1, 1981; children by previous marriage: Alexa, Robert. BS in Advt., U. Fla., 1959; MS in Mil. Sci., U.S. Army Command and Gen. Staff Coll., 1971; MA in Pub. Adminstrn., U. Okla., 1975; MEd, Columbia U., 1993, EdD, 1993. Commd. 2nd lt. U.S. Army, 1959, advanced through grades to brig. gen., 1986; chief adminstrn. div. office chief of staff U.S. Army, Washington, 1968-70, chief mgmt. analysis br. office chief of staff, 1971-75; chief of staff 2nd infantry div. U.S. Army, Republic of Korea, 1975-76; chief mgmt. div. adj. gen. ctr. U.S. Army, Washington, 1976-77, chief compt. div. Nat. Guard Bur., 1978-81; dep. comdr. 1st pers. command U.S. Army, Schwetzingen, Fed. Republic of Germany, 1981-84; dir. resource mgmt. U.S. Mil. Acad. U.S. Army, West Point, N.Y., 1984-86; adjutant gen. army U.S. Army, Alexandria, Va., 1986-88; dep. chief staff pers. adminstrn. and logistics, tng. and doctrine command U.S. Army, Ft. Monroe, Va., 1988-91; asst. prof. adult edn., human resource devel. Va. Commonwealth U., Richmond, 1993—; guest lectr. Hungarian Mil. Acad., 1989. Contbr. articles to profl. jours. Mem. ASPA (exec. com. mgmt. sci. and policy analysis sect. 1992-96), ASTD (nat. rsch. com. 1997-99), Acad. Human Resource Devel., Assn. U.S. Army, Retired Officer Assn., Internat. Soc. Quality Govt. (nat. dir. 1992-93). Methodist. Avocation: writing for publication. Home: 12400 Northlake Pl Richmond VA 23233-6636 Office: Va Commonwealth U Sch Edn PO Box 842020 1015 W Main St Richmond VA 23284-9061

DIMACHKIE, MAZEN MOHAMMAD, health care educator; b. Beirut, Mar. 30, 1962; came to the U.S., 1988; s. Mohammad Cha'ban Dimachkie and Siham Ghalayini; m. Mary Frances Greenwell, Jan. 24, 1992; children: Mohamad Dave, Dena Catherine. BS in Chemistry with distinction, Am. U. Beirut, 1984, MD, 1988. Diplomate Am. Bd. Neurology and Psychiatry with added qualification in clin. neurophysiology. Intern internal medicine Stagnes Hosp., Balt., 1988-90; neurology resident U. Tex., Houston, 1990-93, neuromuscular fellow, 1993-94, instr., 1993-94, asst. prof., 1995—; asst. prof. U. Okla. Health Sci. Ctr., Oklahoma City, 1994-95; cons. Med. Mktg. Conf., Livingston, N.J., 1998—, Vistalink Med. Cons., 1998—. Contbr. chpts. to books and articles to profl. jours. Recipient Spl. Action Svc. award VA Med. Ctr., Oklahoma City, 1995, Appreciation cert. Muscular Dystrophy Assn., Houston, 1996-98. Mem. AMA (Physician Recognition award 1997—), Am. Acad. Neurology, Am. Assn. for Electrodiagnostic Medicine, Am. Bd. Med. Specialties, So. Med. Assn., Harris County Med. Soc. Avocations: fishing, movies. E-mail: mdimachkie@dnamail.com. Office: Univ Tex 6431 Fannin MSB 7044 Houston TX 77030

DIMAGGIO, FRANK LOUIS, civil engineering educator; b. N.Y.C., Sept. 2, 1929; s. Serafino and Maria (Barbuto) DiM.; m. Irene C. Koehn, Dec. 15, 1963; children: Samuel, Peter. B.S., Columbia U., 1950, M.S., 1951, Ph.D., 1954. Registered profl. engr., N.Y. Prof. civil engring. Columbia U., 1956—, chmn. dept., 1975-78, Carleton prof., 1978—; cons. in field, 1956—. Served with AUS, 1954-56. NSF sr. postdoctoral fellow, 1962-63; guest scholar Kyoto U., Japan, 1986. Fellow ASCE (chmn. exec. com. engring. mech. div. 1982-83, chmn. adv. bd. engring. mechanics div. 1985-86); mem. Sigma Xi. Home: 138 Van Orden Ave Leonia NJ 07605-1521 Office: Columbia Univ Dept Civil Engring and Engring Mechanics New York NY 10027

DIMAIO, VIRGINIA SUE, gallery owner; b. Houston, July 6, 1921; d. Jesse Lee and Gabriella Sue (Norris) Chambers; m. James V. DiMaio, 1955 (div. 1968); children: Victoria, James V. AB, U. Redlands, 1943; student, U. So. Calif., 1943-45, Scripps Coll., 1943, Pomona Coll., 1945. Owner, dir. Galeria Capistrano, San Juan Capistrano, N.Mex., 1979—, Santa Fe, 1979—; founder Mus. Women in Arts, Washington; cons., appraiser Southwestern and Am. Indian Handcrafts; lectr. Calif. State U., Long Beach; mem. Heard Mus.; established ann. Helen Hardin Meml. scholarship for woman artist grad. Inst. Am. Indian Art, Santa Fe, also ann. Helen Hardin award for outstanding artist at Indian Market, S.W. Assn. on Indian Affairs, Santa Fe; bd. dirs. Mus. of Man, San Diego, 1989, Am. Diabetes Assn. Santa Fe, 1996—, Appraisals, Etc., 1996—; mem. Intertribal Coun. U. Calif., Irvine, 1990; founder Inst. Am. Indian Art, Santa Fe, 1993, bd. dirs., 1992—, chmn. devel. com., 1996—; mem. task force San Juan Capistrano City, 1995; bd. dirs. Futures for Children, 1996. Author: (foreword to Mus. of Man exhibit catalogue) Paths Beyond Tradition. Recipient Bronze Plaque Recognition award Navajo Tribal Mus., 1977. Mem. Am. Soc. Appraisers, Indian Arts and Crafts Assn. (chmn. devel.), S.W. Assn. Indian Affairs, San Juan Capistrano C. of C. Republican. Roman Catholic. Office: Am Soc Appraisers PO Box 22868 Santa Fe NM 87502-2868

DIMANCESCU, MIHAI D., neurosurgeon, researcher, educator; b. Maidenhead, Berkshire, Eng., Mar. 27, 1940; came to U.S., 1956, naturalized, 1963; s. Dimitri D. and Alexandra Irina (Radulescu) D.; m. Joan E. Brenner, Mar. 17, 1966; children: Stefan, Marc-Mihai. BA, Yale U., 1962; MD, U. Toulouse, France, 1968. Diplomate Am. Bd. Neurol. Surgery. Rotating intern Purpan Hosp., Toulouse, 1968-69; jr. resident in gen. surgery Hartford (Conn.) Hosp., 1969-70; jr. resident in neurosurgy Albert Einstein-Montefiore Hosp., Bronx, N.Y., 1970-72; rsch. fellow in spasticity and movement disorders U. Miami (Fla.)-VA Hosp., 1972-74; sr. resident in neurosurgery U. Miami, 1972-76, asst. instr. in neurol. surgery, 1975-76; pvt. practice in medicine specializing in neurosurgery Freeport and Garden City, N.Y., 1976—; dir. Internat. Coma Recovery Inst., Garden City, 1977—; mem. faculty, dir. brain studies Internat. Sch. of Evan Thomas Inst., Phila., 1980—; mem. staff, assoc. dir. dept. neurosurgery Franklin Gen. Hosp., Valley Stream, N.Y.; mem. staff, pres. med. bd. South Nassau Cmtys. Hosp., Oceanside, N.Y.; chief divsn. neurosurgery Mercy Med. Ctr., Rockville Ctr., N.Y., St. Francis Hosp., Roslyn, N.Y., Winthrop U. Hosp., Mineola, N.Y., North Shore U. Hosp., Manhasset, N.Y.; continuing med. edn. lectr., 1977—; cons. neurosurgery Inst. for Achievement of Human Potential, Phila., 1977—; mem. surg. core faculty Health Sci. Ctr., Sch. Medicine, SUNY-Stony Brook, 1980—. Contbr. articles to profl. jours. Bd. dirs. Inst. Achievement Human Potential, 1990—, Princess Margarita Romania Found., chmn., 1998—. Recipient Golden medal World Orgn. Human Potential, 1978; VA grantee, 1972-74. Fellow ACS, Royal Soc. Arts; mem. AMA, Am. Assn. Neurol. Surgeons, Congress Neurol. Surgeons (Sci. Exhibit award 1974), Coma Recovery Assn. (chmn. bd. dirs. Garden City chpt. 1983), N.Y. State Neurosurg. Soc. (bd. dirs. 1983-88, pres.-elect 1986-87, pres. 1988), Med. Soc. State of N.Y. (neurosurg. del. interspity. com. 1983-88), N.Y. State Head Injury Providers' Coun. (rotating chmn. 1986-87), World Med. Assn., Nassau County Med. Soc., Nassau Physicians' Rev. Orgn. Office: Neurol Surgery PC 88 S Bergen Pl Freeport NY 11520-3510 also: Neurol Surgery PC 950 Franklin Ave Garden City NY 11530-2906

DIMANT, JACOB, internist; b. Rehovot, Israel, Apr. 27, 1947; came to U.S., 1972, naturalized, 1977; s. Simcha and Ita D.; m. Rose Bea Jearolmen, Sept. 11, 1974. MD, Hebrew U., Jerusalem, 1972. Diplomate Am. Bd. Internal Medicine and Rheumatology and Geriatric Medicine, Am. Bd. Quality Assurance and Utilization Rev. Physicians. Intern Maimonides Med. Ctr., Bklyn., 1972-73; resident in medicine Maimonides Med. Ctr., 1973-75; chief resident in medicine Maimonides Med. Ctr., Bklyn., 1975-76; fellow in rheumatology Downstate Med. Ctr., Bklyn., 1976-78; practice medicine specializing in internal medicine and rheumatology Bklyn., 1975—; dir. rheumatology Maimonides Med. Ctr., Bklyn., 1978-89, assoc. dir. med. edn., 1978-80; med. dir. Clove Lakes Nursing Home, S.I., N.Y., 1985-97; med. dir. Prospect Park Nursing Home, Bklyn., 1977-87, Crown Nursing Home, Bklyn., 1983—, Hillside Manor Nursing Ctr., Queens, N.Y., 1993-98, Augustana Luth. Home, Bklyn., 1996—; pres. Crown Nursing Home Assocs., Inc., Bklyn., 1989—; asst. prof. medicine SUNY, Bklyn., 1978—. Contbr. articles to profl. jours. Named hon. police surgeon N.Y.C. Police Dept., 1982; fellow Arthritis Found. of N.Y., 1977-78. Fellow ACP; mem. Am. Geriatric Soc., Am. Med. Dirs. Assn. (bd. dirs. 1995-97, treas. 1997-99), N.Y. Med. Dirs. Assn. (pres. 1994-96). Office: Crown Nursing Home 3457 Nostrand Ave Brooklyn NY 11229-5194

DI MARCO, ANTHONY SABATINO, retired educational administrator; b. Castelnuovo di S Pio, Delle Carmere, L Aquila, Italy, Jan. 27, 1934; came to U.S., 1947; s. Berardino and Anna M. Di Marco; m. Filomena Agatha Benincasa, July 21, 1962; children: Laura, Diane, Michael, Carl. BS, NYU, N.Y.C., 1956, MA, 1967; postgrad., SUNY, 1969-71. Tchr. Bd. Edn., Yonkers, N.Y., 1956-61, Monticello, N.Y., 1961-64; tchr. Mid. Country Cen. Sch. Dist., Centereach, N.Y., 1964-71, dir. vocational edn., 1971-80, dir. occupational edn., 1980-84, dir. occupational and continuing edn., 1984-91; ret., 1991; cons. N.Y. State Edn. Dept. Bur. Trade, Tech. and Tech. Edn., Albany, 1987. With U.S. Army, 1957-59. Mem. Am. Vocat. Assn., N.Y. State Occupational Edn. Assn., Vocat. Edn. Adminstrs. N.Y. State (sec. 1984-91), L.I. Assn. Vocat. Edn. Adminstrs. (officer 1974-81, Leadership award 1981). Republican. Roman Catholic. Home: 7 Hofstra Dr Farmingville NY 11738

DI MARCO, BARBARANNE YANUS, multiple handicapped special education educator; b. Jersey City, Nov. 16, 1946; d. Stanley Joseph and Anne Barbara (Dalack) Yanus; m. Charles Benjamin DiMarco, Mar. 15, 1986; 1 child, Charles Garrett. BA in Music Edn., Trenton State Coll., 1968; MA in Spl. Edn., Kean Coll., 1971, elem. edn. cert., 1974, adminstrv. cert., 1976. Cert. elem., music, adminstrn., spl. edn., N.J. Vocal music educator Roselle (N.J.) Bd. Edn., 1968-69, tchr. trainable mentally retarded, 1969-76, tchr. multiple handicapped, 1976—; color guard instr. Roselle Bd. Edn., 1973-88, elem. tutor, 1976-92, adminstrv. asst. to supt., 1980-85; program dir., sec., Expanded Dimensions in Gifted Edn., Westfield, N.J., 1978—. Vestryperson St. Luke's Ch., Roselle, 1989-91. Recipient Govs. Tchr. Recognition award, Gov. Florio, N.J., Trenton, 1992-93. Mem. NEA, N.J. Edn. Assn., Roselle Edn. Assn., N.J. Assn. for Retarded Children, Eastern Star (25-yr award 1991), Delta Omicron. Republican. Episcopalian. Avocations: skiing, flying, oil painting, travel, swimming, music, golf. Home: 13 Gentore Ct Edison NJ 08820-1029 Office: Dr Charles C Polk Sch 1100 Warren St Roselle NJ 07203-2736

DI MARIA, CHARLES WALTER, mechanical and automation engineer, consultant; b. Phila., May 3, 1927; s. Giuseppi and Antoinette Di Maria; m. Gloria Josephine Sarcone, June 14, 1958; children: Karen Marie, Lori Ann. BA in Physics, Temple U., 1968. Mech. designer Globe Holst Co., Wyndmoor, Pa., 1956-65; mfg. engr. Elco Corp., Willow Grove, Pa., 1965-72; project mgr. The Budd Co., Phila., 1972-81; adv. mfg. unit mgr. RCA Corp./GE Aerospace, Moorestown, N.J., 1981-93; mem. coop. edn. program Rensselaer Poly. Inst., Troy, N.Y., 1987-90. Contbr. articles to profl. jours. Mem. fund raising com. United Way, 1991. Mem. Soc. Mfg. Engrs. (cert.), Ind. Order Odd Fellows. Roman Catholic. Achievements include patent in Coax to Waveguide Transition. Home and Office: 2008 Grace Ln Flourtown PA 19031-1708

DIMARIA, ROSE ANN, nursing educator; b. Bronx, N.Y., Nov. 14, 1964; d. Angelo and Julia (Ingenito) DiM. BSN cum laude, Hunter Coll., 1986, MS in Nursing, 1990; PhD in Nursing, NYU, 1998. RN, N.Y.; cert. nutrition support nurse. Staff nurse gen. surgery unit Bronx Mcpl. Hosp. Ctr., 1986-87, staff nurse SICU/burn unit, 1987-89, nutrition nurse clinician, 1989-93, asst. DON surg. critical care, 1993-95; asst. prof. Sch. Nursing W.Va. U., 1995—. Mem. AACN, Am. Soc. Parenteral and Enteral Nutrition, W.Va. State Nurse Assn., W.Va. Soc. for Parenteral and Enteral Nutrition, N.Y.C. Soc. Parenteral and Enteral Nutrition (pres. 1992-93).

DI MARIA, VALERIE THERESA, public relations executive; b. Bronx, N.Y., Apr. 5, 1957; d. Victor Joseph and Vivian Roslyn (D'Amico) Di Maria. BA in Journalism, NYU, 1978. Asst. dir. U.S. Div. Sidonie S. Ltd., N.Y.C., 1978-79; acct. supr. The Rowland Co., N.Y.C., 1979-82, Ketchum Pub. Rels., N.Y.C., 1982-83; pub. rels. dir. Charles of the Ritz Group Ltd., N.Y.C., 1983-84; sr. v.p. Porter/Novelli Pub. Rels., N.Y.C., 1984-89; mng. dir. GCI Group, N.Y.C., 1989—, now pres., 1996; v.p. pub. rels. & advt. GE Capital, Stamford, Conn. Mem. Pub. Rels. Soc. Am. (Silver Anvil award 1986), The Fashion Group, Am. Film Inst., Women Execs. in Pub. Rels. (bd. dirs.), Women in Comms., Advt. Women of N.Y., Women's Sports Found., Phi Beta Kappa. Office: GE Capital 260 Long Ridge Rd Stamford CT 06927*

DIMARIO, MICHAEL FRANCIS, federal agency official, lawyer; b. N.Y.C., May 30, 1937; s. Philip Salvatore and Frances (Pizzoferrato) DiM.; m. Priscilla Carolyn Weaver, June 25, 1960; children: Michael Gregory (dec.), Stephen Robert, Christopher James. BA, Davis and Elkins Coll., 1960, LLD (hon.), 1994; JD, Georgetown U., 1971. Bar: D.C. 1972, Md. 1972. Part-time assoc. Ross, Locte, Murray & Redding Law Firm, Bowie, MD, 1971-75; labor mgmt. rels. specialist GPO, Washington, 1973-75; prin. Sherry & DiMario Chartered, Bowie, Md., 1975-77; labor mgmt. rels. specialist U.S. Govt. Printing Office, Washington, 1977-78, dep. gen. counsel, 1979-80, dep. asst. pub. printer, 1981-82, asst. pub. printer, info. diss./supt. docs., 1983-84, adminstrv. judge, 1984-90, asst. pub. printer ops. and procurement, 1990-92, dir. procurement svcs., 1992-93, dep. pub. printer, 1993, pub. printer, 1993—. Active City Coun., Bowie, Md., 1977-90, Md. Mcpl. League, 1977-90, Prince George's County Mcpl. Assoc., 1977-90; trustee Davis & Elkins Coll. Capt. USAF, 1960-67. Mem. ABA, D.C. Bar

Assn., Md. Bar Assn., Prince George's County Bar Assn. Office: US Govt Printing Office 732 N Capitol St NW Washington DC 20401

DIMARTINO, CHRISTINA, writer. Student, Palm Beach Jr. Coll., Fla. Atlantic U. Owner Kornhauser of Palm Beach, Inc., 1976-92, Seminole Sandals, Inc., 1993; retail cons. Robert Bindschedler, Paris, 1994-95; creater TV programming, rsch., mktg. plan N.Am. Media Corp., 1994-95; author newsletter Glenn-Kelly Pub. Co., 1995—; writer Anderson Pub. Co., 1995—; lectr. in field; writing lectr., tutor City of West Palm Beach. Contbr. numerous articles to profl. jours.; lead contbg. writer for 6 nat. mags.; author/collaborator 24 books. Exec. bd. Palm Beach Crime Watch; mem. Palm Beach Pub. Sch. PTA, past pres.; mem. Preservation Found. of Palm Beach County; active Cystic Fibrosis Found.; chmn. Kravis Ctr. Children's Com.; founder, pres. Royal Poinciana Bus. Assn.; mem., spl. events com. Palm Beach County Sch. Arts; coord. fgn. exch. students Interant. Edn. Forum. Named Mem. of the Yr. Palm Beach County Transp. Found., 1974; recipient Outstanding Mem. award Palm Beach Crime Watch, Inc., 1994, Appreciation award, 1989, Chmn. award Cystic Fibrosis Found., 1984, Adminstrv. Appreciation award Palm Beach Pub. Sch., 1989, Acknowledgement for authoring nat. award winning article Am. Bus. Press Assn., 1999, Jesse H. Neal Lit. Achievement award, 1999. Home: PO Box 925 Palm Beach FL 33480-0925

DI MARTINO, DAVID, legislative staff member. Student, Cath. Meml., 1987; BA in Comm., U. N.H., 1991. Staff asst. Senator John F. Kerry, Washington, 1993-94; personal asst. Senator John F. Kerry, Boston, 1994-97; prof. staff mem. U.S. Senate Com. on Small Bus., Washington, 1997; press sec. U.S. Rep. Thomas M. Barrett, Washington, 1997—; press advance coord., lead advance The Kerry Com., Boston, 1996; press vol. John Edwards for U.S. Senate Campaign, Raleigh, N.C., 1998. Fax: 202-225-2185. Home: 606 Constitution Ave NE Washington DC 20002 Office: Rep Tom Barrett 1224 Longworth House Bldg Washington DC 20515

DIMAS, TRENT, Olympic athlete, gymnast; b. Albuquerque, Nov. 10, 1970. Grad., U. Nebr. Olympic gymnast Barcelona, Spain, 1992. Recipient Men's Horizontal Bar Gold medal Olympics, Barcelona, 1992. Office: care USA Gymnastics Pan Am Plz 201 S Capitol Ave Ste 300 Indianapolis IN 46225-1058*

DI MASCIO, JOHN PHILIP, lawyer; b. Bklyn., Feb. 4, 1944; s. Eugenio and Stella (Scheuermann) Di M.; m. Angela Piccininni, Apr. 2, 1967 (div. 1980); children: John Philip, Jr., Christine, Thomas; m. Linda Nick, Oct. 19, 1997. BA, C.W. Post Coll., 1975; MA, L.I. U., 1976; postgrad., NYU, 1976-79; JD, St. John's U., 1983. Bar: N.Y. 1984, U.S. Dist. Ct. (ea. and so. dists.) N.Y. 1984, U.S. Ct. Appeals (2d cir.) 1984, U.S. Supreme Ct. 1997, U.S. Ct. Appeals for Armed Forces 1997, U.S. Ct. of Fed. Claims, 1997, U.S. Ct. Appeals (fed. cir.) 1997. Sr. ct. officer N.Y. State Supreme Ct., Mineola, 1970-82; assoc. Joel R. Brandes, P.C., Garden City, N.Y., 1984; pvt. practice N.Y., 1984-87; ptnr. Di Mascio, Meisner & Koopersmith, Carle Place, 1987-93; sole practice Garden City, 1993—. Contbg. author Ann. Survey. With USN, 1962-69. Recipient various acad. awards. Mem. ABA (bus. law, health law and family law sects.), N.Y. State Bar Assn. (family law com. 1982), Nassau County Bar Assn. (vice-chmn. matrimonial com. sup. ct. com., fam. ct. com. 1984, co-editor monthly publ. Recent Decisions), Am. Inns of Ct. (N.Y. family law chpt.). Avocations: photography, boating. Office: 300 Garden City Plz Garden City NY 11530-3302

DIMASI, SALVATORE FRANCIS, state legislator; b. Boston, Aug. 11, 1945; s. Joseph and Celia (Mele) D.; m. Kathleen DiMasi. BS, Boston Coll., 1967; JD, Suffolk U., 1971. Fin. mgmt. trainee Raytheon, Lexington, Mass., 1967-68; asst. dist. atty. Suffolk County, 1974-76; ptnr. DiMasi, Donabed & Karll, 1980-88; rep. 3d Dist. Mass. State Rep., Suffolk, 1979—, mem. judiciary com. and vice chmn. state adminstrv. com., 1979—, chmn. crime justice com., 1985-88, chmn. judiciary com., 1988—; owner DiMasi Law Offices, 1988—; mem. Pierendello Lyceum, 1988. Past pres. Neighborhood Task Force, Boston; mem. Neighborhood Justice Network; pres. bd. dirs. Sobriety, Treatment, Edn. and Prevention;. Mem. ABA, Mass. Bar Assn., Boston Bar Assn., Justinian Law Soc., Sons of Italy, Chinese Cultural Soc., K.C., Delta Sigma Pi. Address: 114 State St Boston MA 02109-1339*

DIMATTEO, RHONDA LYNN, speech-language pathologist, audiologist; b. Easton, Pa., Sept. 12, 1955; d. Michael John and Betty Lenora (O'Brien) DiM. Assoc. in Gen. Edn., Northampton County Area Community Coll., 1981; BS, Trenton State Coll., 1983; MA, Hahnemann U., 1985. Cert. clin. competence in speech-lang. pathology and audiology; registered therapy dogs trainer and handler Comfort Caring Canines. Lead tchr. The Nursery Sch. of Easton, Inc., 1974-83; speech-lang. pathologist, audiologist Warren Hills Regional Bd. Edn., Washington, N.J., 1985—, child study team mem., 1985—; speech-lang. pathologist, audiologist, lang. devel. tchr. Mountainview Youth Correctional Facility, Annandale, N.J., 1990—, theater instr., child study team mem., 1990—; dir. speech and hearing screening ARC, Easton, 1982—; coach cross-country and track Warren Hills Regional Bd. Edn., Washington, N.J., 1987—. Author several poems; actress several theatre co.'s. Operation Search screening dir. ARC Hearing Screenings, Easton, 1982—; trainer dogs Northampton County Soc. for The Prevention of Cruelty to Animals, Easton, 1970—; mem. hearing ear dog program New Eng. Assistance Dog Svcs., West Boylston, Mass., 1985—; mem. adoption svc. Northampton County SPCA, Easton, 1970—. Recipient Proudly We Hail cmty. award Easton, Pa., 1993. Mem. ASHA (cert., Project Enhance media campaign recruiter 1989), NEA (profl.), Pa. Speech-Lang.-Hearing Assn. (profl.), N.J. Speech-Lang.-Hearing Assn. (profl.), N.J. Edn. Assn. (profl.), N.J. Interscholastic Coaching Assn. (profl.), Nat. Coun. Tchrs. English (profl.), Nat. Student Speech-Lang.-Hearing Assn., Comm. Workers Am. (profl.), Warren County Edn. Assn., Warren Hills Edn. Assn., The Drama League. Lutheran. Avocations: dog shows, theatre, journalism, poetry, organized sports. Home and Office: 803 Cattell St Easton PA 18042-1524

DIMAURO, NANCY MARION, nursing administrator; b. N.Y.C., July 18, 1951; d. James F. and Antoinette (Grimaldi) DiM. BSN, L.I. U., Bklyn., 1973; MA, NYU, N.Y.C., 1982. Cert. in continuing edn. and staff devel., ANCC, BLS instr., trainer, Am. Heart Assn. Sr. staff nurse, charge nurse N.Y. Hosp., N.Y.C., 1973-81; dir. staff devel. Victory Meml. Hosp., Bklyn., 1981-86; acting asst. dir., instr. nursing edn. Beth Israel Med. Ctr., N.Y.C., 1986-89; dir. continuing edn. Am. Jour. Nursing Co., N.Y.C., 1989-96, Lippincott Williams & Wilkins, 1996—; bd. dirs. Nurses House, 1994-98, v.p., 1998—; rep. Am. Bd. Nursing Spltys., 1995-98, sec., 1996-98, site vis. Am. Nurses Credentialing Ctr. Commn. on Accreditation, 1995—, commr. 99—. Recipient Cert. of Appreciation for Svc., ARC, 1984-85. Mem. ANA (coun. on continuing edn. 1995 chair ANCC nursing continuing edn. and staff devel., test devel. com. and bd. on cert. 1993-97), Met. Continuing Edn. Assn., N.Y. State Nurses Assn. (N.Y.C. regional CE rev. com. 1996—), Sigma Theta Tau (treas. chpt. 1989-93, Pres.' award Upsilon chpt. 1992, pub. com., eligibility com. 1994).

DI MEDIO, GREGORY LAWRENCE, writer, English language educator, information analyst; b. Columbus, Ohio, Nov. 17, 1963; s. Gabriel Silvio and Patricia Ann (Kennedy) Di M.; m. Rebecca Westmoreland Brown, Mar. 22, 1991. BA in English, U. Colo., 1987; MA in English, U. S.C., 1994. Tech. writer/editor Ctr. Rsch. in Human Devel. and Edn., Temple U., Phila., 1988-91; adj. mem. faculty dept. arts and scis. Midlands Tech. Coll., Columbia, 1992-94, writing ctr. coord., 1993-94; prof. English dept. arts and scis. Denmark (S.C.) Tech. Coll., 1994-95; freelance tech. writer/editor Pitts., 1995-97; writer/project mgr. Agnew Moyer Smith, Pitts., 1998—; grants cons. WQED Pub. TV and Radio, Pitts., 1996; writing ctr. tutor U. S.C., Columbia, 1993. Contbr. articles to profl. jours. Mem. Sierra Club (newsletter editor 1986-87, freelance editor 1989-91, lobbyist 1990-91), Soc. for Tech. Comm., Trout Unltd., Sigma Tau Delta, Alpha Phi Gamma. Democrat. Avocations: nature walks and writing, fly fishing, live jazz, Internet. E-mail: gdimedio@amsite.com. Home: 14 4th St Pittsburgh PA 15215-2914 Office: Agnew Moyer Smith 503 Martindale St Pittsburgh PA 15212

DIMEGLIO, NICOLAS JOSEPH, real estate broker, small business owner; m. Robin White. AS in Paralegal Scis., Mercer County C.C., Trenton, N.J., 1981; Real Estate Sales Qualification course, Mercer County C.C., 1988; BS in Polit Sci., Trenton State Coll., 1984; Broker Qualification course, Real Estate Sch., Princeton, N.J., 1991. Accreditd buyer rep. real estate buyers agt. Sr. paralegal McCarthy & Schatzman P.A., Princeton, N.J., 1982-88; sales rep. Century 21, Robert M. Goldberg Realtors, North Brunswick, N.J., 1988-89, Fox & Lazo Realtors, Jack Burke Real Estate, Inc., North Brunswick, N.J., 1989-91; broker, assoc. Gloria Zastko Realtors, North Brunswick, N.J., 1991-94; pres., broker Prudential DiMeglio Realtors, Somerset, N.J., 1994-97; pres. DiMeglio Realty Group, Somerset, N.J., 1997—. Corp. sponsor Heritage Day Com., No. Brunswick, 1996, 97, 98, Toys for Tots Drive, 1996, 97, 98. Recipient cert. of commendation Mercer County Vol. Lawyers Project, 1987, cert. of merit Nat. Paralegal Assn., 1988; named to NJAR Million Dollar Club, 1990, 91, 92, 93, 94, N.J. Bd. Realtors, Silver level 92, 94, gold level 93. Mem. Soc. Hill of Somerset (pres.), MIddlesex-Somerset Realtors Assn., Nat. Assn. Realtors (real estate buyer's accreditation). Home: 87 Chelsea Ct Franklin Park NJ 08823-1504 Office: DiMeglio Realty Group 1711 Rte 27 Somerset NJ 08873

DIMELFI, RONALD J., materials scientist; b. N.Y.C.; s. Gerard J. and Yolanda DiMelfi; m. Elizabeth S. DiMelfi, July 11, 1982. BS, SUNY, Stony Brook, 1967, MS, 1969; PhD, Stanford U., 1975. Materials scientist Argonne (Ill.) Nat. Lab., 1977-84, 90—, mgr. materials behavior sect. reactor engring. divsn., 1997—; assoc. prof. U. N.Mex., Albuquerque, 1984-86; pres. Materials Engring. R&D, San Diego, 1986-90; materials scientist Naval Ocean Systems Ctr., San Diego, 1988-90. Contbr. articles to profl. jours. Vol. Daley for Mayor Campaign, Chgo., 1993, 96. Rsch. grantee Office of Naval Rsch., 1988, Air Force Office of Scientific Rsch., 1989-91; recognized for significant contbn. for rsch. for reactor safety Am. Nuclear Soc., 1978. Mem. Materials Soc., Am. Soc. for Materials (chmn. computer simulating com. 1995-97, chmn. Chgo. chpt. 1995-96), Materials Rsch. Soc., MENSA, Sigma Xi. Avocation: film studies. Office: Argonne Nat Lab 9700 Cass Ave Argonne IL 60439-4803

DI MEO, DOMINICK, artist, sculptor, painter; b. Niagara Falls, N.Y., Feb. 1, 1927; s. Antonio and Michelina (Sandonato) Di M.; m. Judith S. Cousins, Dec. 26, 1963. B.F.A., Sch. Art Inst., Chgo., 1952; M.F.A., State U. Iowa, 1953. vis. artist Sch. of Art Inst. Chgo., 1977; instr. Chgo. Acad. Fine Arts, 1967-69. One man shows include Lake Forest (Ill.) Coll., 1955, Bemidji (Minn.) Coll., 1963, Fairweather-Hardin Gallery, Chgo., 1964, 68, 71, Barat Coll., Lake Forest, 1966, Chgo. Public Library, 1966, Kendall Coll., Evanston, Ill., 1967, Westbroadway Gallery, N.Y.C., 1973, 75, 76, Project Studios One, Long Island City, N.Y., 1982, group exhbns. include, Albright-Knox Art Gallery, Buffalo, 1953, 54, Art Inst. Chgo, 1959, 60, 61, 63, 65, 66, 67, 68, 71, 76, 79, 89-90, Ann. Exhbn. of Contemporary Am. Painting, Whitney Mus. of Am. Art, N.Y., 1967-68, Mus. Contemporary Art, Chgo., 1969, Joan Miro Internat. Drawing Prize Competition, Barcelona, Spain, 1977, 78, 79, 80, Centro Cultural/Arte Contemporaneo, Mexico City, Nov. 1986-Jan. 1987, Art Inst. Chgo., 1989-90; represented in permanent collections, Art Inst. Chgo., Whitney Mus. Am. Art, N.Y.C., U. Mass., Amherst, Nat. Collection Fine Arts, Smithsonian Instn., Elmhurst (Ill.) Coll. Fellow Guggenheim Found., 1972, sculpture fellow Nat. Endowment for Arts, 1983. Mem. Momentum (founding mem.), Participating Artists Chgo.), Artists Collaborative. Address: 429 Broome St New York NY 10013-2686

DI MINO, ANDRÉ ANTHONY, manufacturing executive, consultant; b. Bklyn., Aug. 24, 1955; s. Alfonso and Nancy (Zarbo) DiM.; m. Jenny DiCapua, May 30, 1981. BS in Indsl. Engring., Fairleigh Dickinson U., 1978, MBA in Fin., 1981. Engr. ADMTronics Inc., Emerson, N.J., 1977-79; dir. tech. ADMTronics Inc., Emerson, 1979-82; sec./treas. ADMTronics Inc., Northvale, N.J., 1982-86; exec. v.p. and dir. ADMTronics Inc., Northvale, 1986—; founder, dir. Enviro-Pack Devel. Corp., Northvale, N.J., 1991—; ptnr., cons. Tech. Mgmt. Cons., Woodcliff Lake, N.J., 1978-94; v.p., dir. Pegasus Labs., Inc., Northvale, N.J., 1989—, Sonotron Med. Sys., Inc., Northvale, 1988—, VET-Sonotron Sys., Inc., Northvale, 1988—; pres. AA-Northvale Med. Assocs., Inc., 1998—. Inventor in field. Mem. coun. Borough of Woodcliff Lake, 1984-97, pres., 1987-93, 97, mem. cable adv. com., 1999; corr. sec. Office N.E. Rep. Orgn. (NERO), 1989—, treas., 1992-93, vice chmn., 1993; co-chmn. privatization subcom. Bergen County Cost Containment Rev. Team, 1991; mem. open space com. Bergen County, 1997, 98; fundraising dir. Our Lady Mother of the Ch., Woodcliff Lake; founding mem., 1st v.p. Woodcliff chpt. Unico Nat. Svcs. Orgn., 1990-92, pres., 1992-94, 97-99; dep. dist. gov., 1993-94, dist. gov., 1994-96; founder, pres. Cmty. Access TV studio WCL-TV, 1990—; pres. Woodcliff Lake Rep. Club, 1994-96; devel. chmn. NW Bergen chpt. Am. Heart Assn. (vice chmn. 1995-96), 1994; founder, chmn. Woodcliff Lake Sr. Assn., 1989—; trustee Pascack Hist. Soc., 1995—; vice chmn. Pascack Valley Region Cmty. Devel. com., 1997. Named Vol. of Yr. Bergen County, N.J., 1991, 93, Citizen of Yr. Passack Valley C. of C., 1993. Mem. Woodcliff Lake Vol. Fire Assn. (hon.). Republican. Roman Catholic. Avocations: classic cars, antiques, video and photography. Office: ADMTronics Inc 224S Pegasus Ave Northvale NJ 07647-1904

DIMINO, SYLVIA THERESA, elementary and secondary educator; b. N.Y.C., June 6, 1955; d. John Anthony and Elena (Berardesca) D. BA, St. John's U., 1977; MPA, NYU, 1980, MA in Elem. and Secondary Edn., 1982, cert. advance studies in ednl. adminstrn., 1986, cert. in advanced studies in mgmt., 1992; MA in Tchg. ESL, Adelphi U., 1984; MA in Libr. Sci., Pratt Inst., 1998; cooking cert., Nat. Gourmet Cooking Sch., 1999. Cert. elem. and secondary tchr., sch. adminstr., in mgmt. practices, social studies, math., N.Y.; cert. Prana yoga tchr., 1999. Traffic coord. Creamer Inc., N.Y.C., 1977-79; tchr. St. Patrick's Sch., N.Y.C., 1979-82; tchr. IS 131, Manhattan, N.Y.C., 1984-90, adminstr., coord., 1985-90, asst. prin., 1990-99; tchr. H.S. ESL N.Y.C. Bd. Edn., 1995-99, libr. sci. tchr., 1999—. Named to 2000 Most Notable Women. Mem. NAFE, AAUW, Nat. Orgn. Women in Adminstrn., Bus. Cir. N.Y., Nat. Coun. Adminstrv. Women in Edn., Nat. Orgn. Italian-Am. Women (mentoring dir.), Yoga Tchrs. Assn. Roman Catholic. Avocation: walking, hiking, yoga. Office: Park West High Sch 525 W 50 St New York NY 10019

DIMITRIADIS, ANDRE C., health care executive; b. Istanbul, Turkey, Sept. 29, 1940; s. Constantine N. and Terry D. BS, Robert Coll., Istanbul, 1964; MS, Princeton U., 1965; MBA, NYU, 1967, PhD, 1970. Analyst Mobil Oil Internat., N.Y.C., 1965-67; mgr. TWA, N.Y.C., 1967-73; dir. Pan Am. Airways, N.Y.C., 1973-76; asst. treas. Pan Am. Airways, 1976-79; v.p., chief fin. officer Air Calif., Newport Beach, 1979-82; exec. v.p. fin. and adminstrn., chief fin. officer Western Airlines, Los Angeles, 1982-85; dir. Western Airlines; sr. v.p. (fin) Am. Med. Internat., from 1985, chief fin. officer, 1985-89, exec. v.p., 1988-89; dir., exec. v.p. fin., chief fin. officer Beverly Enterprises Inc., Ft. Smith, Ark., 1989-92; chmn., CEO LTC Properties, Inc., 1992—; bd. dirs. Magellan Health Svc. Democrat. Greek Orthodox. Home: 4470 Vista Del Preseas Malibu CA 90265-2540 Office: Ltc Properties Inc 300 E Esplanade Dr Ste 1860 Oxnard CA 93030-1286

DIMITRY, JOHN RANDOLPH, academic administrator; b. Detroit, Feb. 15, 1929; s. Dracos Alexander and Elizabeth Stanton (Bisland) D.; m. Audrey Oktavec, Aug. 20, 1952; children: Mark, Jane, Kate. Student, Spring Hill Coll., 1948-49; B.A., Wayne State U., 1952, M.S., 1954, Ed.D., 1966. Tchr., Highland Park (Mich.) Jr. Coll., 1954-61; asst. to pres. Macomb County C.C., Warren, Mich., 1963-65; dean center campus Macomb County Community Coll., 1966-67, pres., 1967-75; pres. Northern Essex Community Coll., Haverhill, Mass., 1975—; mem. Gov.'s Commn. on Higher Edn., 1973-75; pres. Mich. C.C. Assn., 1972-73; mem. Mass. Gov.'s State Job Tng. Coordinating Coun., 1983-91; mem. Mass. Commn. for Occupational Edn., 1982-88; chmn. NE Consortium of Colls. and Univs. in Mass., 1985-86, Mass. C.C. Pres. Assn., 1986-87, New England Regional Student Exch. Program ADv. Coun., 1992—. Bd. dirs. Lawrence Boys Club, Lawrence Yough Commn. Lt. U.S. Army, 1947-48, 52-53. Kellogg Found. fellow Community Coll. Adminstrn., 1961-63; recipient Leadership award Prudential Ins. Co. Am., 1992. Mem. Greater Haverhill C. of C. (pres. 1985-86). Home: Old Wharf Rd West Newbury MA 01985 Office: No Essex Community Coll Office of the Pres Elliott Way Haverhill MA 01830-2399

DIMITRY, THEODORE GEORGE, retired lawyer; b. New Orleans, Jan. 15, 1937; s. Theodore Joseph and Ouida Marion (Seiler) D.; m. S. Elizabeth Warren; children: Mary Elizabeth Hyry, Theodore Warren. B.S., Tulane U., 1958, J.D., 1960. Bar: La. 1960, Tex. 1964. Assoc. firm Phelps, Dunbar, Marks, Claverie & Sims, New Orleans, 1965-69, ptnr., 1969-75; ptnr. firm Vinson & Elkins, Houston, 1975-98; ret., 1998, pvt. practice arbitrator and mediator, 1999—; rsch. fellow Southwestern Legal Found., Dallas, 1973-98; spkr. on maritime law, offshore contracting, ins. and resource devel. at profl. seminars, 1975—. Contbr. articles to profl. jours. Mem. permanent adv. bd. Tulane U. Admiralty Law Inst., 1985—. Served with USN, 1960-64. Mem. Maritime Law Assn. U.S., Southeastern Admiralty Law Inst., Am. Soc. Internat. Law, ABA. Fax: 713-467-7153.

DIMMA, WILLIAM ANDREW, real estate executive; b. Montreal, Que., Can., Aug. 13, 1928; s. William Roy and Lillian Norine (Miller) D.; m. Katherine Louise Vacy Ash, May 13, 1961; children: Suzanne Elizabeth Irene, Katherine Lillian Louise. BA in Sci., U. Toronto, Can., 1948; postgrad., Harvard U., 1956, DBA, 1973; MBA, York U., Toronto, 1969; LLD (hon.), York U., 1998; D of Commerce (hon.), St. Mary's U., 1991. Registered profl. engr., Ont. With Union Carbide Can Ltd., 1948-70, exec. v.p., bd. dirs., 1967-70; prof., dean faculty adminstrv. studies York U., 1974-76; pres., bd. dirs. Torstar Corp., Toronto Star Newspapers Ltd., Toronto, 1976-78; pres. A.E. LePage Ltd., Toronto, 1979-84; pres., CEO Royal LePage Ltd., Toronto, 1984-86, dep. chmn., 1986-93; bd. dirs. Am. Eco Co., CBOC Continental Ltd., Enbridge Corp., Magellan Aerospace Corp., Monsanto Can. Innovation & Growth Coun., Silcorp Ltd., Sears Can., Sears Can. Acceptance Co. Ltd., Swiss Re Life and Health Can. Ltd., Trilon Fin. Corp.; chmn. bd. dirs. Home Capital Group, Can. Bus. Media, Ltd., The Swiss Reins. Can. Group, Royal Le Page Comml. Adv. Bd., Perigee Inc. Author: Canada Development Corporation: Diffident Experiment on a Large Scale. Hon. dir. Niagara Inst., chmn. 1983-86; hon. gov. York U., chmn., 1992-97; hon. trustee Hosp. for Sick Children; gov. Jr. Achievement of Met. Toronto, chmn., 1992-93; gov., bd. dirs. Can. Journalism Found. Decorated knight comdr. Order of St. Lazarus of Jerusalem; Elmslie Meml. scholar, 1944; Stevens gold medal Harvard Bus. Sch., 1971; Can. Coun. fellow, 1970-73; apptd. to Order of Can., 1996; recipient York Univ. award Outstanding Corp. Leadership, 1992. Fellow Inst. Corp. Dirs.; mem. Toronto Club, Toronto Golf Club, York Club, Beta Theta Pi. Avocations: cross-country skiing, swimming, cycling. Home: Apt 302, 407 Walmer Rd, Toronto, ON Canada M5R 3N2

DIMMICK, CAROLYN REABER, federal judge; b. Seattle, Oct. 24, 1929; d. Maurice C. and Margaret T. (Taylor) Reaber; m. Cyrus Allen Dimmick, Sept. 10, 1955; children: Taylor, Dana. BA, U. Wash., 1951, JD, 1963; LLD, Gonzaga U., 1982, CUNY, 1987. Bar: Wash. 1953. Asst. atty. gen. State of Wash., Seattle, 1953-55; pros. atty. King County, Wash., 1955-59, 60-62; sole practice Seattle, 1959-60, 62-65; judge N.E. Dist. Ct. Wash., 1965-75, King County Superior Ct., 1976-80; justice Wash. Supreme Ct., 1981-85; judge U.S. Dist. Ct. (we. dist.) Wash., Seattle, 1985-94, chief judge, 1994-97, sr. judge, 1997—; chmn. Jud. Resources Com., 1991-94, active, 1987-94. Recipient Matrix Table award, 1981, World Plan Execs. Council award, 1981, Vanguard Honor award King County of Washington Women Lawyers, 1996, Honorable mention U. Wash. Law Rev., 1997, Disting. Alumni award U. Wash. Law Sch., 1997. Mem. ABA, Am. Judges Assn. (gov.), Nat. Assn. Women Judges, World Assn. Judges, Wash. Bar Assn., Am. Judicature Soc., Order of Coif (Wash. chpt.). Office: US Dist Ct 713 US Courthouse 1010 5th Ave Ste 713 Seattle WA 98104-1189

DIMMICK, CHARLES WILLIAM, geology educator; b. Elizabeth, N.J., Feb. 16, 1940; s. Byron Orme and Claire Louise (Pilger) D.; m. Charleen Fristoe, Aug. 30, 1963; children: Byron Wesley, Edward Arthur. Geol. Engr., Colo. Sch. Mines, 1962; MS in Geology, U. Fla., 1964; PhD, Tulane U., 1969. Lic. geologist, N.C. Asst. prof. geology Stephen F. Austin State U., Nacogdoches, Tex., 1967-70, Austin Peay State U., Clarksville, Tenn., 1970-72; prof. geology Cen. Conn. State U., New Britain, 1972—; cons. and assoc. dir. Environ. Mgmt. Corp., Kensington, Conn., 1974-94. Contbr. articles to profl. jours. Vice chmn. Cheshire Inland Wetlands Commn., Conn., 1974—; pres. Cheshire Fair Assn., 1984-87, pres. Conn. Agrl. Fair, 1994-97. NSF fellow, 1963-64, 66-67. Mem. Am. Inst. Profl. Geologists (cert., pres. N.E. sect. 1988-90, del. nat. adv. bd. 1990-92—, nat. editor 1993-94), Paleontologic Rsch. Inst., Soc. Econ. Paleontologists and Mineralogists, Sigma Xi. Democrat. Episcopalian. Clubs: Assn. Conn. Fairs. Lodge: Patrons of Husbandry. Avocations: gardening, agrl. fairs. Home: 60 Broadview Rd Cheshire CT 06410-4202 Office: Cen Conn State U Dept Physics And Earth Scis New Britain CT 06050

DIMMITT, CORNELIA, psychologist, educator; b. Boston, Mar. 16, 1938; d. Harrison and Martha Fredericka (Read) D.; m. (div.); children: Colin Barclay Church, Jeffrey Harrison Church. BA, Harvard U., 1958; MA, Columbia U., 1966; PhD, Syracuse U., 1970; diplomate, C. G. Jung Inst., Zurich, Switzerland, 1985. Asst. prof. Am. U., Washington, 1970-71; from asst. to assoc. prof. (with tenure) Georgetown U., Washington, 1971-82; pvt. practice Boston, 1985—; Mem. admissions com. Coll. Arts and Scis., Georgetown U., Washington, 1974-76, mem. rank and tenure com., 1977-78; dir. admissions com. C. G. Jung Inst., Boston, 1986-89, pres. tng. bd., 1989-91; pres. NESJA, 1993-97. Author: Classical Hindu Mythology, 1978. NEH fellow, 1979-80. Mem. Am. Oriental Soc., New England Soc. Jungian Analysts, Assn. Grads. in Analytical Psychology (Switzerland), Internat. Assn. for Analytical Psychology. Home and Office: 4 Otis Pl Boston MA 02108-1036

DIMMITT, LAWRENCE ANDREW, lawyer; b. Kansas City, Kans., July 20, 1941; s. Herbert Andrew and Mary (Duncan) D.; m. Lois Kinney, Dec. 23, 1962; children: Cynthia Susan, Lawrence Michael. BA, Kans. State U., 1963, MA, 1967; JD, Washburn U., 1968. Bar: Kans. 1968, U.S. Dist. Ct. Kans. 1968, U.S. Ct. Appeals (10th cir.) 1969, Mo. 1973, N.Y. 1975, U.S. Supreme Ct. 1986. Atty. Southwestern Bell Telephone Co., Topeka, 1968-73; atty. Southwestern Bell Telephone Co., St. Louis, 1973-74, gen. atty. regulation, 1979; atty. AT&T, N.Y.C., 1974-79; gen. atty. Kans. Southwestern Bell Telephone Co., Topeka, 1979-94; ret., 1994; adj. prof. telecomms. law Washburn U. Sch. Law, 1996-99. Bd. dirs. First United Meth. Ch., Topeka, 1979-84, mem. nominating com., 1985-87; bd. dirs. Sunflower Music Festival, 1993-94; mem. master planning com. Historic Ward-Meade Park, 1998-99. Recipient commendation Legal Aid Soc. Topeka, 1986, 90, 93. Mem. Kans. Bar Assn. (pres. adminstrv. law sect. 1985-86, bd. editors newsletter), Topeka Bar Assn., Phi Alpha Delta (alumni bd. 1986-88, 1993-97), Rotary (bd. dirs., 2d vice-pres. 1999—). Home: 3123 SW 15th St Topeka KS 66604-2515

DIMMOCK, JOHN OLIVER, university research center director; b. Mineola, N.Y., Nov. 24, 1936; s. Clarence Oliver and Eleanor Stevens (Waste) D.; m. Barbara Welch Clark, June 21, 1958 (div. Nov. 1973); children: Leanne, Cynthia, John; m. Cynthia Kalliope Vouros, May 12, 1974; children: Jonathan, Justin, James. BS in Physics, Yale U., 1958, PhD in Physics, 1962. Mem. staff rsch. div. Raytheon, Waltham, Mass., 1962-63; mem. staff rsch. div. MIT Lincoln Lab., Lexington, 1963-66, leader applied physics group, 1966-71, leader applied optics group, 1971-74; dir. electronics and solid state scis. Office Naval Rsch., Arlington, Va., 1974-81, dep. dir., dir. tech. programs, 1981-84; tech. dir. Air Force Office Sci. Rsch., Washington, 1984-89; staff v.p. for rsch. McDonnell Douglas Corp., St. Louis, 1989-92; tech. dir. strategic technologies McDonnell Douglas Corp., St. Louis, 1992-93; dir. ctr. applied optics U. Ala., Huntsville, 1993—. Author: Properties of the Thirty-Two Point Groups, 1963; contbr. over 60 articles to sci. jours.; patentee in field. Recipient Superior Civilian Svc. award USN, 1984. Fellow AIAA (assoc.), Am. Phys. Soc.; mem. IEEE (sr.), AAAS, Sigma Xi. Office: U Ala Huntsville Ctr Applied Optics Huntsville AL 35899

DIMON, JAMES, financial services executive; b. N.Y.C., Mar. 13, 1956; s. Theodore and Themis Dimon; m. Judith Kent, May 21, 1983; children: Julia, Laura, Kara. BA, Tufts U., 1978; MBA, Harvard U., 1982. V.p., asst. to pres. Am. Express Co., N.Y.C., 1982-85; pvt. practice investor, 1985-86; sr. v.p., CFO Comml. Credit Co., Balt., 1986-88; exec. v.p., CFO Primerica Corp., N.Y.C., 1991-93, pres., 1993—; pres., COO Travelers Inc.; pres., COO, CFO The Travelers Inc, 1993—. Office: Travelers Group Inc 388 Greenwich St New York NY 10013-2362

DIMOND, EDMUNDS GREY, medical educator; b. St. Louis, Dec. 8, 1918; s. Edmunds Grey and Gertrude Ruth (Schmidt) D.; m. Mary Dwight Clark, Nov. 28, 1968 (dec. June 1983); children: Sherri Grey Byrer, Lea

Grey, Lark Grey Dimond-Cates. Student, Purdue U., 1938-39; BS, Ind. U., 1942, MD, 1944. Mem. faculty Med. Ctr., U. Kans., Kansas City, 1950-60, prof., chmn. dept. medicine, 1953-60, dir. cardiovascular lab., 1950-60; mem., dir. Inst. for Cardiopulmonary Diseases, Scripps Clinic and Rsch. Found., 1960-67; rsch. assoc. physiology Scripps Inst. Oceanography, La Jolla, Calif., 1960-68; prof. in residence Sch. Medicine, U. Calif., San Diego, 1967-68; scholar in residence Nat. Libr. Medicine, 1967; spl. asst. to asst. sec. HEW, Washington, 1968; Disting. prof. medicine U. Mo., Kansas City, 1968-98, provost for health scis., 1968-79; Fulbright prof., The Netherlands, 1956; vis. prof., Israel, 1978; scholar in residence Rockefeller Found. Study Ctr., Bellagio, Italy, 1978; chmn. overseas edn. team Dept. State, 1962, 64-66, 73; guest lectr. Chinese Med. Assn., 1971-73, 76-80, 82-92; pres. Edgar Snow Fund, Inc., Diastole-Hospital Hill, Inc. Author: Electrocardiography, 1952, rev. edits., 1955, 60, 64, Digitalis, 1957, Exercise Electrocardiograms, 1961, More Than Herbs and Acupuncture, 1975, Inside China Today, 1981, Take Wing, 1991, Dr. Horse of China, 1992, Reverend Whitehead, Mississippi Pioneer, 1987, Letters from Forest Place, 1993, Essays By An Unfinished Physician, 1995; editor: Diastole on Hospital Hill Audiotape, 1980-86; editor-in-chief Accel, 1968-77; contbr. articles to profl. jours. Bd. dirs. Truman Med. Ctr., Kansas City, Mo., Eye Found., Kansas City, Sci. Edn. Partnership, Kansas City. With M.C., AUS, 1945-47. Paul Dudley White Traveling scholar, 1956-57. Master Am. Coll. Cardiology (pres. 1962, Disting. Svc. award 1969). Home and Office: 2501 Holmes St Kansas City MO 64108-2742

DIMOND, ROBERT EDWARD, publisher; b. Washington, Dec. 12, 1936; s. James Robert and Helen Marie (Murphy) D.; m. Patricia Berger (div.); children: Mark Edward, Michele Lynn Keating, Melinda Ann. B.A. in Journalism, George Washington U., 1961. Mng. editor Nat. Automobile Dealers Assn. Mag., Washington, 1955-63; editor, pub. Bus. Products Mag., Washington, 1963-69; v.p. Hitchcock Pub. Co.; pub. Infosystems Mag., Office Products Mag., Wheaton, Ill., 1969-81; pres. R.E. Dimond & Assocs., Hinsdale, Ill., 1981-83; pub. Networking Mgmt. Mag., Westford, Mass., 1983-89, Home Improvement Ctr. Mag., Lincolnshire, Ill., 1989-90; v.p., pub. dir. mining and constrn. group Intertec; pub. Coal, Rock Products, Internat. Construction, Concrete Products, Engring. and Mining Jour., C&D Materials Recycling and Keystone Directory, 1990-96; group v.p. Intertec Pub. Co., 1996-99; pres. R.E. Dimond & Assocs., 1999—. Served with USAF, 1961-62. Democrat. Roman Catholic. Home and Office: 400 Bentley Pl Buffalo Grove IL 60089-2500 *Never lose your sense of humor. Everyone has been helped in life somewhere along the way by an unselfish act; don't forget this when you have the opportunity to extend a hand.*

DIMOND, THOMAS, investment advisory company executive; b. Scarsdale, N.Y., Jan. 24, 1916; s. George A. and Jessie (Kennedy) D. BA magna cum laude, Princeton U., 1939; MBA, Harvard U., 1941. Mem. faculty Wharton Sch. Fin., U. Pa., 1948; economist, account mgr. Lionel D. Edie & Co., 1948-50; economist, mgr. comml. rsch. Youngstown Sheet & Tube Co., Ohio, 1951-56; sr. account mgr., security analyst deVegh & Co., N.Y.C., 1956-60; pres. Humes-Schmidlapp Assocs., N.Y.C., 1960—; bd. dirs. Mercer Mgmt. Corp., co-mgr. Mercer Fund, 1963-67; bd. dirs. Scudder Spl. Fund, 1967-72, Scudder Duv-Vest, 1968-71; gen. ptnr. HS Spl. Fund. Contbr. articles to profl. publs. Trustee, Humes Found., 1963—. Capt. USAAF, 1941-46. Mem. N.Y. Soc. Security Analysts, Racquet & Tennis Club, Down Town Assn. (N.Y.C.). Episcopalian. Home: 200 E 66th St Apt C1703 New York NY 10021-6728 Office: Humes-Schmidlapp Assoc 375 Park Ave Ste 3505 New York NY 10152-0002

DIMOS, HELEN, landscape designer; b. Washington, Dec. 14, 1942; d. Louis C. and Vasiliki (Mallos) D.; m. Benjamin Kuhn Oko, 1981; stepchildren: Daniel, Michael. BA in History, Bryn Mawr Coll., 1964; BS in Landscape Architecture, CCNY, 1994. Asst. landscape architect Cen. Park Conservancy, N.Y.C., 1994-96; pres. Hendler & Dimos, Inc., N.Y.C., 1995-90; landscape and site designer, 1996—; mem. archtl. adv. com. and Ridgefield design coun., Ridgefield, Conn. Mem. Am. Soc. Landscape Architects. Office: 11 Barlow Mt Rd Ridgefield CT 06877

DI MUCCIO, MARY-JO, retired librarian; b. Hanford, Calif., June 16, 1930; d. Vincent and Theresa (Yovino) DiMuccio. BA, Immaculate Heart Coll., 1953, MA, 1960; PhD, U.S. Internat. U., 1970. Tchr. parochial schs. Los Angeles, 1949-54, San Francisco, 1954-58; tchr. Govt. of Can., Victoria, B.C., 1959-60; asst. librarian Immaculate Heart Coll. Library, Los Angeles, 1960-62; head librarian Immaculate Heart Coll. Library, 1962-72; adminstrv. librarian City of Sunnyvale, Calif., 1972-88; ret., 1988. Exec. bd., past pres. Sunnyvale Community Services. Mem. ALA, ICF (past pres.), Spl. Libr. Assn., Cath. Libr. Assn. (past pres.), Calif. Libr. Assn., Sunnyvale Bus. and Profl. Women, Peninsula Dist. Bus. and Profl. Women (pres.). Home: 736 Muir Dr Mountain View CA 94041-2509 *My goal has been to become a universal person, and that is my responsibility as a professional person-to see that the society we are building for tomorrow is appropriate to the needs of the people we serve.*

DIMURA, LINDA HART, healthcare organization administrator; b. West Palm Beach, Fla., June 2, 1962; d. Norman Browning Hart Jr. and Margo Jean (Tew) Hart; m. John Samuel DiMura, Jan. 22, 1989. Student, Eckerd Coll., St. Petersburg, Fla., 1979-81; BA, U. Fla., 1985. Ops. dir. The Fla. Orch., Tampa, Fla., 1985-90; v.p., gen. mgr. Print 'n Go, Inc., Tampa, 1986-91, Shandra, Tampa, 1990-92; dir. devel. Nat. Easter Seal Soc., St. Petersburg, 1992-94, Am. Cancer Soc., Tampa, 1994-96; sr. cons. The Lighter Co., Clearwater, Fla., 1996-97; dir. devel. and mktg. Tampa Bay History Ctr., 1997-98; exec. dir. Watson Clinic Found., Lakeland, Fla., 1998—; presenter Am. Lung Assn., 1997. Dir. devel. and mktg. The Fla. Orch., Tampa, 1990; exec. prodr. telethon Easter Seal Soc. of Fla., Tampa, 1982-83, prodr., 1989-90; mem. exec. com. Hillsborough County Reps., 1992-94; fundraising cons. Rep. candidates, Pinellas and Hillsborough Counties, Fla.; hon. bd. dirs. Hillsborough Animal Health Found., Tampa, 1996-98. Mem. Nat. Soc. Fund Raising Execs. (cert., v.p. Suncoast chpt. 1997—, bd. dirs. 1995—, chair Nat. Philanthropy Day 1995, presenter major gifts seminar 1996, mentor major gifts 1995, planned giving 1996, Suncoast Signature award 1995), Assn. for Healthcare Philanthropy. Baptist. Avocations: snow skiing, scuba diving, horse showing, piano, orchestral conducting. E-mail: ldimura@watsonclinic.com. Home: 1704 S Miller Rd Valrico FL 33594-4736 Office: Watson Clinic Found 1430 Lakeland Hills Blvd Lakeland FL 33805

DINAN, DONALD ROBERT, lawyer; b. Nashua, N.H., Aug. 28, 1949; s. Robert J. and Jeanette F. (Farland) D.; m. Amy Littlepage, June 24, 1978. BS in Econs., U. Pa., 1971; JD, Georgetown U., 1974; LLM, London Sch. Econs., 1975. Bar: Mass. 1976, D.C. 1977, N.Y. 1986, U.S. Supreme Ct. 1979, U.S. Ct. Internat. Trade 1982. Atty. advisor U.S. Internat. Trade Commn., Washington, 1976-81, chief patent br., 1981-82, chief unfair imports investigation div., 1981-82; ptnr. Adduci Dinan & Mastriani, Washington, 1982-88, Fitzpatrick, Cella, Harper & Scinto, Washington, 1988-90, O'Connor & Hannan, Washington, 1990-98, Hall Estill, 1998—; prof. internat. trade Georgetown U., Wharton Econs. Soc.; prin. Coun. for Excellence in Govt. Mem. Mayor's Internat. Adv. Coun., Washington, D.C. Regulatory Reform Com.D.C. Stadium Com.; chmn. Adv. Neighbor Commn.-Capitol Hill, Washington Dem. State Com., gen. counsel, 1988-92, 94—. Mem. ABA, Fed. Bar Assn., ITC Trial Laywers Assn., Am. Intellectual Property Law Assn. (chmn. internat. trade com., export lic. com.). Democrat. Roman Catholic. Home: 221 9th St SE Washington DC 20003-2112 Office: Hall Estill Hardwick Gable Goldin & Nelson 1120 20th Pl NW Ste 750 Washington DC 20036-3483

DINAN, ROBERT MICHAEL, lawyer; b. Quebec City, Que., Can., Aug. 12, 1956; s. John H.T. and Lorraine (Matte) D.; m. Alicia Soldevila, June 11, 1983; children: Karina, Philippe, John. LLB, U. Laval, Que., 1978. Bar: Que., 1980. Assoc. Pothier Begin et al, Quebec City, 1980-87, ptnr., 1987-94; ptnr. Lepage Dinan, Quebec City, 1994—; chmn. bd. TeleFilm Can., Montreal, 1993-98. Mem. exec. com., v.p., pres. Jeffery Hales Hosp., Quebec City, 1992-95, bd. dirs., 1992—, chmn. bd. dirs., 1996—; bd. dirs. Duke of Edinburgh's award, bd. dirs. Voice of English Que., 1992-98, mem. exec. com., 1995-98, v.p., 1997-98; St. Brigid's Home, 1985-89, Danse Partout, 1989-91, Morrin Coll. Found., 1997—, fin. com. 1997—, bldg. com. 1997—; mem. Centre Aide Que., 1985—, Assemblée Regie Régional Santé et Svcs. Sociaux, 1992-97, appt. Queen's Coun., 1992; bd. dirs. Can. TV and Cable Prodn. Fund, 1996-98. Recipient Bursery award Minister of Justice, Can., 1978. Mem. Can. Bar Assn., Que. Bar Assn. (external rels. com. 1993-96, libr. com. 1986-88), Que. C. of C. Avocations: gardening, oil painting, skiing, cycling. Home: 2391 Marie-Victorin, Sillery, PQ Canada G1T 1K2

DINAN, SUSAN EILEEN, history educator; b. Buffalo, May 15, 1965; d. Thomas Edward and Judy (Cleary) Dinan; m. Benson Sutherland Hawk, Sept. 16, 1970. BS, Cornell U., 1987; MA, U. Ill., 1989; PhD, U. Wis., 1996. Tchg. asst. U. Wis., Madison, lectr., to 1996; asst. prof. history L.I. U., Brookville, N.Y., 1996—; co-dir. Merit Fellowship Program, Brookville, 1998—. Mem. Amnesty Internat., Tchg. Tolerance. L.I. U. devel. grantee, 1998; Inst. fellow Folger Shakespeare Libr., 1998; Sumner Inst. fellow NEH, 1998. Mem. Am. Hist. Assn., Soc. Early Modern Scholars, French Hist. Assn., Soc. Early Modern Women, Soc. for History of Women Religious. Avocations: tennis, biking, skiing, cooking, knitting. Email: sdinan@liu.edu. Home: 93-16 68th Ave Forest Hills NY 11375 Office: L I U Dept History 720 Northern Blvd Greenvale NY 11548

DINARDO, GERRY, coach; b. Nov. 10, 1952; m. Terri Brown; children: Kate, Michael. BA, Univ. Notre Dame, 1975; MEd, Univ. Maine, 1977. Asst. coach Maine Univ., 1975-77, Eastern Mich. Univ., 1978-81, Colorado Univ., 1982-90; head coach Vanderbilt Univ., 1991-94, La. State Univ., 1995—. Named Nat. Assn. Coach of Yr., 1989, Southeastern Conf. Coach of Yr., 1991, Kodak Regional Coach of Yr., 1991, Blue-Gray Classic coach of winning South team, 1991. Office: La State Univ PO Box 25095 Baton Rouge LA 70894-5095*

DINCULEANU, NICOLAE, mathematician; b. Padea, Romania, Feb. 26, 1925; came to U.S., 1976; s. Nicolae and Frusina (Lusca) Dobrescu; m. Elena Constantinescu, Feb. 9, 1959. Engr., Poly. Inst., Bucharest, 1950; licencie math., U. Bucharest, 1951; Ph.D. in Math, U. Bucarest, 1957. Prof. math. U. Bucharest, 1950-77; vis. prof. Queen's U., Kingston, Ont., Can., 1966-67, U. Rennes, France, U. Erlangen, Germany, 1970; Disting. vis. prof. U. Pitts., 1970-71; vis. research prof. U. Fla., Gainesville, 1972-77; prof. math. U. Fla., 1977—. Author: Vector Measures, 1967, Integration on Locally Compact Spaces, 1974, Textbook of Mathematical Analysis, 2 vols, 1962; also articles. Recipient Stoilov prize Romanian Acad., 1964. Mem. Am. Math. Soc. Mem. Romanian Orthodox Ch. Club: Torch. Office: U Fla Math Dept Little Hall # 475 Gainesville FL 32611-2082

DINE, THOMAS ALAN, foreign policy expert; b. Cin., Feb. 29, 1940; s. Stanley and Eunice (Cohen) D.; m. Joan Corbett, Mar. 19, 1967; children: Amy Eleana, Laura Rachel. BA, Colgate U., 1962; MA, UCLA, 1966. Vol. U.S. Peace Corps, Philippines, 1962-64; congl. liaison U.S. Peace Corps, Washington, 1966-67; personal asst. to Am. ambassador Am. Embassy, New Delhi, India, 1967-69; legis. asst. to U.S. Senator Frank Church, Washington, 1970-74; sr. analyst U.S. Senate Budget Com., Washington, 1975-78; fgn. policy advisor to U.S. Senator Edward Kennedy, Washington, 1979-80; exec. dir. Am. Israel Pub. Affairs Com., Washington, 1980-93; asst. adminstr. Europe and New Ind. States U.S. Agy. Internat. Devel., Washington, 1993-97; pres. Radio Free Europe/Radio Liberty, Prague, Czech Republic, 1997—. Contbr. articles to profl. jours. Harvard U. fellow, 1974-75, Brookings Instn. sr. fellow, 1979. Mem. Council on Fgn. Relations, Am. Hist. Assn., Soc. Historians of Am. Fgn. Policy, Cosmos Club. Jewish. Office: RFE/RL Inc, Vinohradska 1, 110 00 Prague 1, Czech Republic

DINEEN, JOHN K., lawyer; b. Gardiner, Maine, Jan. 21, 1928; s. James J. and Eleanor (Kelley) D.; m. Carolyn Foley Reardon (dec. 1982); children: Jane, Martha, Louisa, Jessica, John; m. Susan Lowell Wales, Aug. 15, 1986; children: Theodore, Ralph, Andrew. BA, U. Maine, 1951; JD, Boston U., 1954. Bar: Maine 1954, Mass. 1954. Ptnr. Weston, Patrick & Stevens, Boston, 1954-67, Peabody & Arnold, Boston, 1967-70, 91—, Gaston & Snow, Boston, 1970-91; spl. asst. atty. gen. Commonwealth of Mass., Boston, 1965-67; bd. dirs. exec. com. Fiduciary Trust Co., Boston, P&O Properties Boston, Inc., London; dir. Dingle Am. Properties Ltd., Dingle, County Kerry, Ireland, 1973—; pres., trustee Boston Local Devel. Corp., 1982—. Trustee emeritus Waring Sch., Beverley, Mass., 1981—, Cambridge (Mass.) Coll.; trustee U.S.S. Constn. Mus., 1993—; trustee, chmn. Nahant (Mass.) Pub. Libr., 1996—; former trustee Boston U. Med. Ctr., Winsor Sch. Emmanuel Coll., Boston, Hebron Acad., Maine; trustee Boston Aid to the Blind, 1994—. With U.S. Army, 1946-48. Mem. Boston Bar Assn., Mass. Bar Assn., Boston Law Sch. Alumni Assn. (exec. com. 1989-91), Marshall Street Hist. Soc., Tavern Club, Union Club, Cary Street Club, Apollo Club, Norway Weary Club. Republican. Roman Catholic. Home: 40 Pleasant St Nahant MA 01908-1632 Office: Peabody & Arnold 50 Rowes Wharf Fl 7 Boston MA 02110-3342

DINEEN, JOSEPH LAWRENCE, legal compliance professional, consultant; b. Jersey City, Sept. 25, 1942; s. Cornelius P. and Dolores (Fitzsimmons) D.; m. Andrea J. Manzone, Nov. 20, 1965; children: Jacqueline, Kimberley A. BA in Polit. Sci., Fordham U., 1964; MBA in Human Resources, St. John's U., Springfield, La., 1984, PhD in Indsl. Psychology, 1988. Tchr. Xavier H.S., N.Y.C., 1964-67; adminstrv. mgr. Royal Globe Ins., N.Y.C., 1967-72; pers. mgr. U. Ga., Athens, 1972-74; v.p., dir. Fowler Products Co., Athens, 1974-85; sr. v.p. Scovill, Inc., Clarksville, Ga., 1985-88; dir. human resources Charter Med. Corp., Macon, Ga., 1988-93, G&O Mfg. Co., Jackson, Miss., 1993-96; chief compliance officer Union Hosp. Dist., Union, S.C., 1996—; dir., chmn. bd. N.E. Ga. Employee Assistance Program, Athens, 1974-85, Employer Assistance Group-Dept. of Labor, Athens, 1988-93; mem., cert. tchr. Dept. Labor, 1986—; budget dir. United Way of N.E. Ga., Athens, 1985-88; cons. Gov.'s Com., Jackson, 1995-96. Author: Management in 21st Century, 1995. Dir. United Way, Athens and Jackson, 1974-93, Employee Assistance Program, Athens, 1974-85; mem. Pres. Carter's Roundtable of Businessmen, Dept. of Commerce, 1978. Mem. Soc. Human Resource Mgmt. Avocations: teaching seminars, racquetball, tennis, reading. Home: PO Box 992 Union SC 29379-0992

DINER, STEVEN JAY, history educator; b. N.Y.C., Dec. 14, 1944; s. Dave and Helen (Fenster) D.; m. Hasia R. Schwartzman), July 12, 1970; children: Shira Miriam, Eli Moshe, Matan David. BA, SUNY, Binghamton, 1966, MA, 1968; PhD, U. Chgo., 1972. Asst. prof. urban studies U. D.C., Washington, 1972-76, assoc. prof., 1976-81, prof., 1981-85, chair dept. urban studiees, 1978-83, dir. Ctr. for Applied Rsch. and Urban Policy, 1984-85; prof. history George Mason U., Fairfax, Va., 1985-98, vice provost, 1985-89, assoc. sr. v.p., 1990-94; prof. history, dean faculty arts & scis. Rutgers U., Newark, 1998—; chair Edn. Licensure Commn. D.C., Washington, 1988-93; bd. dirs. D.C. Cmty. Humanities Coun., Washington, 1983-87. Author: A City and Its Universities, 1980, Housing Washington's People, 1983, A Very Different Age, 1998; mem. editl. bd. Washington History, 1993—, Historians of the Guilded Age and Progressive Era, 1995—. Mem. Am. Hist. Assn., Orgn. Am. Historians, Hist. Soc. Washington. Democrat. Jewish. Office: Rutgers U Office Dean Arts & Scis Newark NJ 07102-1801

DINERMAN, MIRIAM, social work educator; b. N.Y.C., Apr. 13, 1925; d. Abraham J. and Frances (Shostac) Goldforb; m. Harold Dinerman, June 12, 1951 (dec. June 1976); children: David, Ellen, Ruth. BA with honors, Swarthmore Coll., 1945; MSW, Columbia U., 1949, D Social Work, 1972. Youth dir. Jewish Assn. for Neighborhood Ctrs., N.Y.C., 1949-50, program dir., 1951-54; various social work partime positions, 1955-60; asst. prof. Rutgers U. Grad. Sch. Social Work, New Brunswick, N.J., 1961-72, assoc. prof., 1972-76, prof., 1976-99, asst. dean for acad. planning, 1973-75, assoc. dean, 1975-81, acting dean, 1978, chmn. health care sequence, mem. New Brunswick faculty coun., 1989-93, chair, 1991-92; dir. PhD program Rutgers U. Sch. Social Work, New Brunswick, N.J., 1992-97, emerita, 1999—; mem. grants rev. panel Office Human Devel. Svcs., HHS, 1986-90; cons. on health and social svcs. N.J. Legis. Task Force on 21st Century; mem. task force on standard of need N.J. Divsn. Econ. Assistance, 1989-91; manuscript rev. editor Longman's Press, Methuen Press; dir. Ctr. for Internat. and Comparative Social Work, 1977—. Editor: Social Work Futures, 1983; mem. editl. bd. Affilia: Jour. Women and Social Work, 1985-94, 95—, book rev. editor, 1995—; contbr. articles to profl. jours., chpts. to books. Bd. dirs. Def. for Children Internat., 1980-88. Grantee NIMH, 1966-67, Rutgers U. Rsch. Coun. and Samuel Silberman Fund, 1979-80. Mem. NASW (profl. pres. 1984-86, nat. com. on nominations and leadership identification 1988-97, mem. editl. com. 1991-95, steering com. polit. action for candidate election 1996—, bd. dirs. N.Y.C. chpt. 1999—), AAUP (N.J. task force on health care policy), Acad. Cert. Social Workers, Internat. Assn. Schs. Social Work (bd. dirs., agt. 1988-95), Coun. on Social Work Edn. (program planning com. 1984-89, ednl. policy and planning commn. 1989-94), Group for Advancement of Doctoral Edn. (sec. steering com. 1990-96). Home: 353 W 29th St New York NY 10001-4784

DINERSTEIN, MARC J., career military officer; b. New Haven, Nov. 24, 1948; s. Janice Fay Sipple, Nov. 29, 1977 (div. 1988); 1 child, Ann Marie; m. Laurel Ann Matheson, Aug. 1, 1990. BA, U. Conn., 1970; MA, Ctrl. Mich. U., 1984, Webster U., 1987; DMgmt, Colo. Tech. U., 1996. Enlisted USAF, 1970, advanced through grades to col.; dir. ops. Detachment 6 1st Spare Wing USAF, Kapaun Air Station, Germany, 1982-85; chief space sys. Air Force Space Command USAF, Colorado Springs, 1985-87; dir. ops. 4th Space Warning Squadron USAF, Holloman AFB, N.Mex., 1987-90; comdr. 7th Space Warning Squadron USAF, Beale AFB, Calif., 1990-92; dep. comdr. 21st Ops. Group USAF, Colorado Springs, 1992-93, chief tng. testing & configuration Air Force Space Command, 1993-94, chief mission ops. U.S. Space Command, 1994-97; sr. analyst Scitor Corp., 1997—. Mem. Air Force Assn., Armed Forces Comms./Electronics Assn., Freemasons, Nat. Sojourners. Avocations: flying, swimming, scuba diving. Home: 8435 Camfield Cir Colorado Springs CO 80920-7030 Office: Scitor Corp 1250 Academy Park Loop Ste 208 Colorado Springs CO 80910-3707*

DINERSTEIN, ROBERT DAVID, lawyer; b. N.Y.C., May 3, 1953; s. Irving and Helen (Risch) D.; m. Joan Patricia Fread, June 4, 1983; children: Michael Fread, Jonathan Fread. AB in History magna cum laude, Cornell U., 1974; JD, Yale U., 1977. Bar: N.Y. 1978, D.C. 1983, Md. 1984, U.S. Dist. Ct. D.C. 1984, U.S. Dist. Ct. Md. 1985, U.S. Supreme Ct. 1988. Trial atty. U.S. Dept. Justice, Washington, 1977-82; clin. lectr., supervising atty. Am. U., Washington, 1983-84, acting dir. criminal justice clinic, 1984-85, dir. 1985-86, dir. Office Clin. Programs, 1985-88, acting dir. Office Clin. Programs, 1987-88; dir. Office Clin. Programs Am. U., 1989-96; assoc. prof. Am. U., Washington, 1988-90, prof., 1990—, assoc. dean for acad. affairs, 1997—; bd. dirs. D.C. Law Students in Ct., Washington, 1983-96, chmn., 1995-96; Fair Employment Coun. Greater Washington; appted. mem. President's Com. on Mental Retardation, 1994, civil rights cluster Dept. Justice Clinton Transition Team, 1992, hearing officer Va. Dept. Edn. v. Riley, 1994-95. Author: (with others) Report on the Chilean Electoral Process, 1987, (with others) A Guide to Consent, 1998; contbr. chpts. to books, articles to profl. jours.; mem. bd. editors, co-founder Clinical Law Rev., 1992-99. Recipient Spl. Commendation award U.S. Dept. Justice, 1979, 80, Meritorious Service award U.S. Dept. Justice, 1981, Outstanding Performance Ratings 1978-82, Pro Bono Service award Internat. Human Rights Law Group, Washington, 1988, bd. mem. svc. award Md. Disability Law Ctr., 1997. Mem. ABA (skills tng. com., sect. on legal edn. and admissions to the bar 1991-94), Assn. Am. Law Schs. (mem. exec. com. sect. on clin. legal edn. 1987-88, chair 1992, award for contributions 1994, com. on clin. legal edn., 1996), Clin. Tchr. Conf. (planning com. 1988, 90, 95), Washington Legal Clin. for the Homeless (bd. dirs. 1988—, legal coun. for the elderly 1990-92), Am. Assn. Mental Retardation (pres. legal process and adv. div. 1990-91, legis. and social issues com. 1992-95). Democrat. Jewish. Avocations: piano, sports, reading, politics. Home: 5909 Cranston Rd Bethesda MD 20816-1115 Office: Am U Washington Coll of Law Ste 366 4801 Massachusetts Ave NW Washington DC 20016-8180

DING, CHEN, investment banker; b. Wuxi, Jiangsu, Peoples Republic of China, Feb. 10, 1919; came to U.S., 1985; s. Zugeng and Shu (Feng) D.; m. Fuzhen Tang, Sept. 30, 1950; children: Dahai, Dadi. BA, Jiaotong U., Shanghai, Peoples Republic of China, 1939; MA, U. Pa., 1943; PhD, Harvard U., 1946. Corp. sec., chief fin. officer Sung Sing Textile Corp., Shanghai, 1947-49; vice chmn. Shanghai Fedn. Industry and Commerce, 1949-85; N.Y. rep. China Internat. Trust & Investment Corp., Beijing and N.Y.C., 1985-93, also bd. dirs., 1983-97. Office: CITIC NY Rep Office 2 World Trade Ctr Ste 2250 New York NY 10048-2298

DING, DAN XIONG, English educator; b. Zhengzhou, Henan, China, July 14, 1961; s. William Yiying and Jane Yamin (Zhang) D.; m. Karen Min Lo, June 3, 1995; 1 child, Daphne Fenny. BA in English, Shanghai Internat. Trade U., 1981; MA in English, Calif. State U., Dominguez Hills, 1989; PhD in English, Ill. State U., 1998. Tech. interpretator, writer Ministry Machine-Bldg. Industry, Beijing, 1982-84; tech. translator, writer Link and Pan. Enterprises, Inc., Torrance, Calif., 1989-92; tchg. asst. Ill. State U., Normal, 1992-98; asst. prof. English Ferris State U., Big Rapids, Mich., 1998—. Contbr. articles to profl. jours. Avocation: classical music. Office: Ferris State U ASC 3080 Big Rapids MI 49307

DINGELL, JOHN DAVID, congressman; b. Colorado Springs, Colo., July 8, 1926; s. John D. and Grace (Bigler) D. BS in Chemistry, Georgetown U., 1949, JD, 1952. Bar: D.C. 1952, Mich. 1953. Pk. ranger U.S. Dept. Interior, 1948-52; asst. pros. atty. Wayne County, Mich., 1953-55; mem. 84th-88th Congresses from 15th dist., Mich., 1955-65, 89th-106th Congresses from 16th dist., Mich., 1965—; mem. migratory bird conservation commn.; ranking mem. commerce com. 2nd lt. inf. AUS, 1945-46. Office: US Ho of Reps 2328 Rayburn Bldg Washington DC 20515-2216*

DINGES, CHARLES V., professional association executive. BA in Govt., Wesleyan U., 1979. Legis. asst. Office of Sidney Yates-Ho. of Reps., Washington, 1979-80; Washington rep. Nat. Audubon Soc., 1980-82; dir. pub. affairs Environ. Fund, Washington, 1982-85; mng. dir. ASCE, Washington, 1985—. E-mail: cdinges@asce.org. Office: 1015 15th St NW Ste 600 Washington DC 20005

DINGES, RICHARD ALLEN, entrepreneur; b. Englewood, N.J., June 17, 1945; m. Kathie A. Headley; children: Kelly, Courtney, Daniel. Grad., Jersey City State Coll., 1967; MEd, U. Hawaii, 1972; postgrad., William Peterson Coll., 1974-79. Cert. sch. adminstr.; cert. sch. spl. services dir., N.J., Ariz., Hawaii. Pres. Def. Industry Assocs., Sierra Vista, Ariz., 1979—, Fed. Career Cons., Sierra Vista, Ariz., 1985; dir. Nat. Scholarship Locators, Sierra Vista, 1985—; spl. needs counselor Pinelander Regional Sch. Dist. Editor: Guide to U.S. Defense Contractors, 1985, 87, 10 Step Guide to College Selection, Salary Negotiations for Military, How to Survive the Job Interview. Vice prin. Little Egg Harbor Primary Sch.; founder Families in Touch, 1992. Mem. Cochise County Merit Commn. (vice-chmn.), Platform Soc. Speakers' Assn. Office: 3 White Oak Ln Tuckerton NJ 08087-9775

DINGLE, ALBERT NELSON, meteorology educator; b. Bismarck, N.D., May 22, 1916; s. Victor Stanley and Nanna Bergetha (Nelson) D.; m. Eleanor Amelia Nelson, Nov. 20, 1941 (dec. Dec. 1994); children: Karen Louise, Timothy Nelson; m. Florence Ellen Altenbernt Miller, Oct. 15, 1996. BS in Agrl. Engring., U. Minn., 1939; MS in Agrl. Engring., Iowa State Coll., 1940; SM in Meteorology, MIT, 1945, ScD, 1947. Asst. prof. physics Hampton (Va.) Inst., 1941-43; rsch. assoc. meteorology MIT, Cambridge, 1943-47; asst. prof. physics Ohio State U., Columbus, 1947-54; rsch. assoc. meteorology U. Mich., Ann Arbor, 1954-55, assoc. prof. meteorology, 1955-63, prof. atmospheric sci., 1963-81, prof. emeritus, 1981—; cons. Pres. Adv. Com. Weather Control, Washington, 1951-55; lectr. Am. Meteorol. Soc., 1952-56; mem. NCAR Aviation Adv. Com., Boulder, Colo., 1965-78; pres. Air Surround, Inc., Dexter, Mich., 1968-83; rschr. in field. Inventor optical raindrop-size spectrometer. Active various bds., coms. Zion Luth. Ch., Ann Arbor, 1954-96; councilman City Coun. Ann Arbor, 1958-60; bd. dirs. Luth. Social Svcs. Mich., Detroit, 1983-92. NSF grantee, 1952. Fellow AAAS; mem. Sigma Xi. Democrat. Avocations: golf, skiing, bridge, handcrafts. Home: 728 W Union Bell Dr Green Valley AZ 85614-5926

DINGLE, MARK EDWARD, management consultant; b. N.Y.C., Aug. 11, 1967; s. David Howard Dingle and Celia Burnaby (Drayson) Ryan. BS in Indsl. Engring., Cornell U., 1989, MBA, 1991. Sr. assoc. IBM, Endicott, N.Y., 1991-93; cons. 24/7 Media, N.Y.C., 1994-95; sr. bus. cons. Bristol-Myers Squibb, N.Y.C., 1995-97; assoc. dir. Viant Corp., 1995—. Bd. dirs. Earth Day So. Tier, Endicott, 1991-93; mentor Minds Matter, N.Y.C., 1995-97. Avocations: squash, singing, mountain biking. Home: 40 E 78th St 9H New York NY 10021 Office: Viant Corp 625 Avenue Of The Americas New York NY 10011

DINGMAN, MICHAEL DAVID, industrial company executive, international investor; b. New Haven, Sept. 29, 1931; s. James Everett and Amelia (Williamson) D.; children from 1st marriage: Michael David, Linda Channing (Mrs. Michael S. Cady), James Clifford; m. 2d, Elizabeth G. Tharp; children: James Tharp, David Ross, Patrick Michael. Student, U. Md., DSc Bus. Mgmt. (hon.). Various mgmt. positions Sigma Instruments, Inc., Braintree, Mass., 1954-64; gen. and ltd. ptnr. Burnham & Co., N.Y.C., 1964-70; pres., CEO, bd. dirs. Wheelabrator-Frye Inc., Hampton, N.H., 1970-83, chmn. bd., 1977-83; pres., bd. dirs. The Signal Cos., Inc., La Jolla, Calif., 1983-85, AlliedSignal, Morristown, N.J., 1985-86; chmn. bd., CEO The Henley Group, Inc. and affiliates, Hampton, N.H., 1986-92; chmn. bd. Fisher Sci. Internat. Inc., Hampton, 1991-98; chmn. bd., CEO Abex Inc., Hampton, 1992-95; pres., CEO Shipston Group Ltd., Nassau, Bahamas, 1994—; bd. dirs. Ford Motor Co., Fisher Sci. Internat. Inc. Trustee The John A. Hartford Found. Mem. IEEE (adv. bd.). Clubs: Links, Yacht (N.Y.C.); Union (Boston); Cruising of Am. (Conn.); Bohemian (San Francisco); Lyford Cay (Nassau); La Jolla Country, San Diego Yacht. Office: Shipston Group Ltd Lyford Cay, PO Box N7776, Nassau Bahamas

DINGS, FRED, poet; b. Lancaster, Pa.; m. Maria Marin. MA in English, U. Del., 1981; MFA in Creative Writing, U. Iowa, 1985; PhD in English, U. Utah, 1991. Asst. prof. Wichita (Kans.) State U., 1997—. Author: Eulogy for a Private Man, 1999, After the Solstice, 1993. Avocation: playing piano. Office: English Dept Box 14 Wichita State Univ Wichita KS 67260-0014

DINGWALL, DAVID C., Canadian government official; b. South Bar, N.S., Canada, June 29, 1952; s. George R. and Isabell I. (Schaump) D.; children: Jay David, Leigh Anne, Jennifer Rae. BComm; LLB, Dalhousie U., N.S., 1974. Spl. asst. office of the min. of pub. health, atty. gen. govt. N.S., min. resp. N.S. human rights com. and task force status of women Canada, 1974-76; pvt. law practice, 1979-80; parliamentary sec. to min. energy, mines and resources House of Commons, Canada, 1982-84, M.P. from Cape Breton-East Richmond, 1980-93; vice-chmn. standing com. natural resources and pub. works House of Commons; chair liberal caucus Parliament Can., 1985-86, nat. exec., 1986-87; chief opposition whip House of Commons, 1990-93, opposition leader, 1990-91; min. Atlantic Can. Opportunities Agy., Pub. Works and Gov. Svcs. Canada, 1993-96; mem. Privy Coun., 1993-97; min. of health Canada, 1996-97; founder, lobbyist Wallding Internat., Ottawa, 1997—. Office: Wallding Internat, 350 Sparks St Ste 1208, Ottawa, ON Canada K1R F58*

DINH, ANTHONY TUNG, internist; b. Jan. 1, 1938; s. Hoan B. and Phieu T. (Nguyen) D.; m. Lisa L. Tran, Jan. 8, 1971; children: Andrew A., Thomas A. BS, U. Saigon, Vietnam, 1959, MD, 1967. Diplomate Am. Bd. Internal Medicine, Am. Bd. Infectious Disease, Am. Bd. Med. Microbiology. Intern in internal medicine Phila. Gen. Hosp., 1976-77; resident in internal medicine Wayne State U., 1977-79; fellow in infectious diseases U. Pa., 1979-81; asst. prof. U. Saigon, 1970-75; chief infectious disease VA Med. Ctr., Beckley, W.Va., 1981-82, chief med. svc., 1982-85, chief staff, 1985—; adj. clin. prof. medicine W.Va. Sch. Osteopathic Medicine, Lewisburg, 1987—; cons. in infectius disease. Contbr. articles to profl. jours. Mem. ACP, N.Y. Acad. Scis., Am. Soc. Microbiology, Raleigh County Med. Soc. (chmn. continuing med. edn. 1987—), W.Va. State Med. Assn. Office: Beckley Med Arts 2401 S Kanawha St Beckley WV 25801-6905

DINH, THIN VAN, electronics specialist; b. Saigon, Vietnam, Apr. 7, 1939; came to U.S., 1975; s. Hoi Dinh and Ut Thi Tran; m. Mo Tran Dinh, Dec. 10, 1962; children: Truong An, Uyen, Huan, Tram. LLB, U. Saigon, 1974; PhD in Counseling (hon.), Progressive Universal Life Ch., 1994. Tchr. Dept. Edn., Danang, Vietnam, 1959-63, Lythaito Sch., Saigon, 1972-75; garage worker Car Body Clinic, portland, Oreg., 1975-78; electronic technician Tektronix, Beaverton, Oreg., 1978-95; specialist, tester Maxim Integrated Cir., Beaverton, 1995—. Author Tung Canh Dieu Bay, also articles in Vietnamese. Spkr. to chs., schs. and Vietnamese cmty. Officer Vietnamese Army, 1963-72. Avocations: music, economics research. Home: 6704 SE 82d Ave Portland OR 97266 Office: Maxim Integrated Products 14320 SW Jenkins Rd Beaverton OR 97005

DINI, JOSEPH EDWARD, JR., state legislator; b. Yerington, Nev., Mar. 28, 1929; s. Giuseppe and Elvira (Castellani) D.; m. Mouryne Landing; children: Joseph, George, David, Michael. BSBA, U. Nev., Reno, 1951. Mem. Nev. State Assembly, Carson City, 1967—; majority leader Nev. State Assembly, 1975; speaker Nev. State Assembly, Carson City, 1977, 87, 89, 91, 93, 97, 99; minority leader Nev. State Assembly, 1985; interim fin. com. mem., 1985-99, speaker pro tem, 1973; co-spkr. Nev. State Assembly, Carson City, 1995; chmn. water policy com. Western Legis. Conf., 1993-94, 96-98; pres. Dini's Lucky Club Casino, Yerington, Nev., 1972—; mem. legis. com. Nev. State Assembly, 1971-77, 91, 93, 95, 97, vice chmn., 1981-82, 96-97, chmn., 1982-83, 93-94. Mem. Yerington Vol. Fire Dept.; mem. Lyon County Dem. Ctrl. Com., Nev. Am. Revolution Bicentennial Commn.; past dist. gov., active mem. 20-30 Club. Recipient Outstanding Citizen award Nev. Edn. Assn., 1973, Friend of Edn. award Nev. State Edn. Assn., 1986, Citizen of Yr. award Nev. Judges Assn., 1987, Dedicated and Valued Leadership award Nat. Conf. State Legislatures, 1989, Excellence in Pub. Svc. award Nev. Trial Lawyers Assn., 1990, Silver Plow award Nev. Farm Bur., 1991, Skill, Integrith, Responsibility award Assoc. Gen. Contractors, 1994, Guardian of Small Bus. award Nat. Fedn. Ind. Bus., 1996, Spl. Recognition award Nev. State Firefighters Assn., 1998, Appreciation award Nev. Emergency Preparedness Assn., 1998; named Conservation Legislator of Yr. Nev. Wildlife Fedn., 1991, Alumni of Yr., U. Nev. Alumni Assn., 1997, Legislator of Yr. Mem. Mason Valley C. of C. (pres.), Rotary (pres. Yerington 1989), Lions (pres. Yerington chpt. 1975), Masons, Shriners, York Rite, Scottish Rite, Order Ea. Star, Gamma Sigma Delta, Phi Sigma Kappa (Disting. Alumna award 1993). Home: 104 N Mountain View St Yerington NV 89447-2239 Office: Dini's Lucky Club Inc 45 N Main St Yerington NV 89447-2230

DINI, JOSEPH J., aircraft leasing and finance executive; b. Somerville, Mass., Apr. 25, 1941; s. John Paul and Rose C.; m. Teresa C. Dini, Apr. 26, 1964; 1 child, Lisa M. BS in Fin., Northeastern U., 1973; MS in Mgmt., Lesley Coll., 1984. Lic. real estate broker. Br. mgr. Arlington Nat. Bank, Bedford, Mass., 1963-66; fin. and mktg. adminstr. Bankers Leasing, Inc., Boston, 1967-73; v.p. Integrated Resources, Inc., Lexington, Mass., 1973-85; pres. First NH Resources, Inc., Boston, 1985-87; v.p. Airfund Corp., Lexington, Mass., 1987-88; v.p. aircraft DPF Group, Ltd., Waltham, Mass., 1988-92; chmn., CEO United Aircraft Finance, Inc., 1992-94; v.p. Gen. Aviation/Finova Capital Corp., Lexington, Mass., 1994—; prin. United Fin. Svcs., 1992; founder Morgaid Corp., 1990; seminar dir. Integrated Resources Equity Mktg., Lexington, Mass., 1984-85; instr. mktg. mgmt., Merrimack Coll., N. Andover, Mass., 1985-87, fin. (masters level) Lesley Coll. Nat. Outreach, Cambridge, Mass., 1987-90. Author: Equipment Leasing, Encyclopedia of Investments 2nd edit., 1990, 2nd edit. update, 1991. Master tchr. Archdiocese of Boston, 1977-86; chmn. sch. com., Lexington, 1993-94; trustee Cary Meml. Libr., Lexington, 1993—. Mem. Sigma Epsilon Rho (spkr. Geneva 1998). Roman Catholic. Avocations: writing, running, woodworking, teaching.

DINICOLA, ROBERT, consumer products company executive. With Macy's Dept. Store, N.Y.C., 1973-89, Federated Stores, N.Y.C., 1989-91; chmn. bd., ceo Bon, Seattle, 1991-94; chmn. bd., CEO Zale Del. Inc., 1991—. Office: Zale Delaware Inc 901 W Walnut Hill Ln Irving TX 75038-1003

DI NICOLO, ROBERTO, allergist; b. Trieste, Italy, Mar. 29, 1958; s. Michele and Maria (Universo) Di N.; m. Lisa Joy Goetz, Sept. 1, 1984; 1 child, Calvin Alexander. Grad., Superior Sch. Sci., Trieste, Italy, 1977; MD, U. Trieste, 1985. Diplomate Am. Bd. Pediats., Am. Bd. Internal Medicine, Am. Bd. Allergy and Immunology. Intern SUNY, Winthrop Univ. Hosp., Stony Brook, N.Y., 1986-87; resident dept. pediats. All Children's Hosp., U. South Fla., 1987-89; clin. fellow adult and pediat. allergy and immunology U. South Fla. Tchg. Hosps., St. Petersburg and Tampa, Fla., 1989-91; pvt. practice allergy and immunology Volusia Asthma and Allergy Specialists, Ormond Beach, Fla., 1991-93; dir. The Asthma, Allergy and Sinus Clinic, Daytona Beach, Fla., 1993—; part-time emergency room physician Bayfront Med. Ctr., St. Petersburg, Fla., 1990-91; part-time pvt. practice allergy and immunology Drs. W. Schmid and R. Doyle, St. Petersburg, 1990-91. Med. columnist Daytona Beach (Fla.) News Jour., 1992—. Recipient McCarthy award Halifax Med. Ctr., 1991. Fellow Am. Acad. Pediats.; mem. Am. Coll. Allergy and Immunology, Fla. Med. Assn. (Physician Communicator of Yr. 1994), Volusia County Med. Soc. Home: 86 Hollow Branch Xing Ormond Beach FL 32174-4814 Office: The Asthma Allergy & Sinus Clinic 353 N Clyde Morris Blvd Ste 1 Daytona Beach FL 32114-2732

DINKEL, JOHN GEORGE, magazine editor; b. Bklyn., Aug. 1, 1944; s. Charles Ernest and Loretta Gertrude D.; m. Leslie Hawkins, Oct. 25, 1969; children: Meredith Anne, Kevin Carter. BS in Mech. Engring, U. Mich., 1967, MS in Mech. Engring, 1969. Staff engr. Chrysler Corp., Highland Park, Mich., 1967-69; engring. editor Car Life Mag., Newport Beach, Calif., 1969-70; engring. editor Road & Track Mag., Newport Beach, 1972-79, editor, 1979-88, editor in chief, 1988-91, editor at large, 1991-92; dir. product communications Hill-Holliday, 1991-92; pres. John Dinkel & Assocs., 1991—; editor-at-large Sports Car Internat., 1992—; v.p. editl. ops. Calcar, 1995-97; group mgr. member info. and comm. svcs. Automobile Club So. Calif., Costa Mesa, 1998—; pub. Westways, 1998—; commencement speaker U. Mich., Dearborn, 1987; hon. judge Meadow Brook Hall Concourse D'Elegance, 1985-86, Hillsborough Concourse D'Elegance, 1989, Palo Alto Concours D'Elegance, 1990; v.p. editl. ops., Calcar, 1994—; spkr. Direct Mktg. Club So. Calif., 1992. Author: Road & Track Auto Dictionary, 1977; co-author: RX-7: Mazda's Legendary Sports Car, 1991, Mazda MX-5 Miata, 1998; editor-at-large European Car, 1997—; co-host daily radio show Auto Report, 1986-88; host weekly radio show Drive Time, 1996—; contbr. articles to profl. jours. Nat. chmn. U. Mich. Ann. Fund, 1988—; commr. Irvine (Calif.) Baseball Assn.; sec. Irvine Pony Baseball-Softball, 1995—; organizer clothing drive victims of Armenia earthquake, 1988; soccer coach AYSO, 1984-90, Irvine Soccer Club, 1991—; baseball coach Northwood Little League, 1994—; basketball coach Irvine Boys and Girls Club, 1993—. Honored by Colden Ctr. for the Performing Arts, Queens Coll., N.Y.C., 1990. Mem. SAE (panelist conf. on impacts of intelligent vehicle hwy. systems 1990, organizer, chmn. sessions on fuel economy and small cars 1978-79, chmn. pub. affairs Future Transp. Conf. 1997), Am. Racing Press Assn., Internat. Motor Press Assn., Sports Car Club Am., Internat. Motor Sports Assn., Automobile Club So. Calif. (group mgr. mem. info. and comm. svcs. 1998—), Motor Press Guild (pres. 1991), Pi Tau Sigma. Four-time winner of SCCA Nelson Ledges 24-hour endurance auto race. Office: Automobile Club So Calif 3333 Fairview Rd Costa Mesa CA 92626-1699

DINKHA, MAS KH'NANYA, IV, church administrator. Catholic patriarch Apostolic Catholic Assyrian Ch. of the E. Office: Apostolic/Cath Assyrian Ch, 3d Ave # 32, Tehran 14, Iran also: Apostolic & Cath Assyrian Ch East 7201 N Ashland Chicago IL 60626*

DINKINS, CAROL EGGERT, lawyer; b. Corpus Christi, Tex., Nov. 9, 1945; d. Edgar H. Jr. and Evelyn S. (Scheel) Eggert; m. Bob Brown; children: Anne, Amy. BS, U. Tex., 1968; JD, U. Houston, 1971. Bar: Tex. 1971. Prin. assoc. Tex. Law Inst. Coastal and Marine Resources, Coll. Law U. Houston, Tex., 1971-73; assoc., ptnr. Vinson & Elkins, Houston, 1973-81, 83-84, 85—, mem. mgmt. com., 1991-96; asst. atty. gen. environ. and natural resources Dept. Justice, 1981-83, U.S. dep. atty. gen., 1984-85; chmn. Pres.'s Task Force on Legal Equity for Women, 1981-83; mem. Hawaiian Native Study Commn., 1981-83; dir. Nat. Consumer Coop. Banks Bd., 1981, mem. Texas Parks Wildlife Com. Author articles in field. Chmn. Tex. Gov.'s Flood Control Action Group 1980-81; commr. Tex. Parks and Wildlife Dept., 1997—; bd. dirs. The Nature Conservancy, 1996—, Oryx Energy Co., 1990-95, U. Houston Law Ctr. Found., 1985-89, 96-98, Environ. and Energy Study Inst., 1986-98, Houston Mus. Natural Sci. 1, 1986-98, Tex. Nature Conservancy, 1985—, chair, 1996—. Mem. ABA (ho. of dels., past chmn. state and local govt. sect., immediate past chair sect. nat. resources, energy, and environ. law, standing com. on Fed. Judges 1997-98; bd. editors ABA Jour.), Fed. Bar Assn. (bd. dirs. Houston chpt. 1986), State Bar Tex., Houston Bar Assn., Tex. Water Conservation Assn., Houston Law Rev. Assn. (bd. dirs. 1978). Republican. Lutheran. Office: Vinson & Elkins 2300 First City Tower 1001 Fannin St Ste 3300 Houston TX 77002-6706

DINMAN, BERTRAM DAVID, consultant, retired aluminum company executive; b. Phila., Aug. 9, 1925; s. Meyer and Minnie (Kaufman) D.; m. Gabrielle Stamm, June 11, 1950; children: Stefanie, Jonathan David, Emily, Joshua. Student, Temple U., 1944, 46-51, MD, 1951; ScD, U. Cin., 1957. Asst. prof. to prof. Ohio State U. Coll. Medicine, 1957-65; prof., dir. Inst. Indsl. Health, U. Mich. Sch. Pub. Health, 1965-73; corp. med. dir. Aluminum Co. Am., Pitts., 1973-78, v.p. health and safety, 1978-87; clin. prof. dept. environ. and occupational health U. Pitts., 1987—; trustee Am. Bd. Preventive Medicine, vice chmn., 1976-85; cons. U.S. Army, USN, WHO; mem. U.S. del. ILO, 1980-81, 84-85; vis. fellow Green Coll. U. Oxford, 1986-92. Served with C.E. U.S. Army, 1944-46. Fellow Am. Coll. Occupl. and Environ. Medicine (A.G. Kammer Merit in authorship award 1972, S. Knudsen award 1988, Health Achievement in Occupl. Medicine award 1992); mem. Permanent Commn. and Internat. Assn. Occupational Health (dir., emeritus), Am. Acad. Occupational Medicine (pres. 1973-74, Kehoe award, G. H. Gehrmann Lectr. 1982). Home: 4710 Bayard St Pittsburgh PA 15213-1708 Office: Dept Occuaptional and Environ Health U Pitts Pittsburgh PA 15261

DINNEEN, GERALD PAUL, electrical engineer, former government official; b. Elmhurst, N.Y., Oct. 23, 1924; s. Walter James and Anna Constance (Costello) D.; m. Mary Purington, June 28, 1947; children: Patricia Dinneen Mooney, Barbara Dinneen Sehr, Michael. BS, Queens Coll., 1947; MS, U. Wis., 1948, PHD, 1952. Teaching asst. U. Wis., 1947-51; sr. devel. engr. Goodyear Aircraft, 1951-53; with MIT, Lexington, 1953-77, prof. elec. engring., dir. Lincoln Lab.; asst. sec. of def., 1977-81; corp. v.p. sci. and tech. Honeywell Inc., Mpls., 1981-89; fgn. sec. NAE, Washington, 1988-95; chair policy divsn Nat. Rsch. Coun., Washington, 1997—; cons. Def. Dept. NASA, USN, USAF. Served with AC, AUS, 1943-46. Recipient Disting. Pub. Service award Dept. Def., 1981. Mem. NAE, Engring. Acad. Japan, Swiss Acad. of Engring. Scis., Royal Acad. of Engring. (U.K.), Am. Math. Soc., Math. Assn. Am., Cosmos Club (Washington), Sigma Xi, Phi Beta Kappa. Home: 7611 Gleason Rd Minneapolis MN 55439-2561 Office: Nat Rsch Coun 2101 Constitution Ave NW Washington DC 20418-0007

DINNERSTEIN, HARVEY, artist; b. N.Y.C., Apr. 3, 1928; s. Louis and Sarah (Kobilansky) D.; m. Lois Behrke, May 25, 1951; children: Rachel, Michael. Student of, Moses Soyer, 1944-46; student, Art Students League, 1946-47, Tyler Art Sch., Temple U., 1950; D (hon.), Lyme Acad. Fine Arts, 1998. Instr. drawing and painting Sch. Visual Arts, N.Y.C., 1963-80, N.A.D., 1974-92, Art Students League, 1980—. One-man shows include Davis Galleries, N.Y.C., 1955, 60-61, 63, Kenmore Galleries, Phila., 1964, 66, 69-70, F.A.R. Galleries, N.Y.C., 1972, 79, Sindin Galleries, 1983, Deutsch Galleries, 1989, Capricorn Galleries, 1990, Butler Inst. Am. Art, Youngstown, Ohio, 1994, Gerold Wunderlich Galleries, 1997; exhibited in group shows at Whitney Mus. Am. Art, N.Y.C., 1955, New Britain (Conn.) Mus. Am. Art, 1964, Am. Acad. and Inst. Arts and Letters, N.Y.C., 1974, Pa. State U. Mus. Art, 1974, others; works represented in collections Met. Mus. Art, Lehman Coll., Whitney Mus. Am. Art, Martin Luther King Labor Ctr., N.Y.C., New Britain Mus. Art, Fleming Mus. at U. Vt., Burlington; author: A Portfolio of Drawings, 1968, Harvey Dinnerstein-Artist at Work, 1978. Served with U.S. Army, 1951-53. Recipient Temple Gold medal Pa. Acad. Fine Art, 1950; Allied Artist Gold medal, 1977; President's award Audubon Artists, 1978; Arthur Ross award Classical Am., 1983; others; Tiffany Found. grantee, 1948, 61. Mem. N.A.D. (Obrig prize 1986). Home and Studio: 933 President St Brooklyn NY 11215-1603

DINNERSTEIN, LEONARD, historian, educator; b. N.Y.C., May 5, 1934; s. Abraham and Lillian (Kubrik) D.; m. Myra Anne Rosenberg, Aug. 20, 1961; children: Andrew, Julie. B of Social Scis., CCNY, 1955; MA, Columbia U., 1960, PhD, 1966. Instr. N.Y. Inst. Tech., N.Y.C., 1960-65; asst. prof. Fairleigh Dickinson U., Teaneck, N.J., 1967-70; prof. Am. history U. Ariz., Tucson, 1970—, dir. Judaic studies, 1993—; adj. prof. Columbia U., summers 1969, 72, 74, 81, 87, 89, NYU, summers 1969-70, 82, 86. Author: The Leo Frank Case, 1968 (Anisfield-Wolf award 1969), America and the Survivors of the Holocaust, 1982, Uneasy at Home, 1987; (with David M. Reimers) Ethnic Americans: A History of Immigration and Assimilation, 1987; (with R.L. Nichols, D.M. Reimers) Natives and Strangers, 1996, Antisemitism in America, 1994 (Nat. Jewish Book prize 1994); contbr. articles to profl. jours.; editor: (with Fred Jaher) The Aliens, 1970; (with Kenneth T. Jackson) American Vistas, 1971, 7th edit., 1995; (with Mary Dale Palsson) Jews in the South, 1973; (with Jean Christie) Decisions and Revisions: Interpretations of t20th Century American History, 1975, America Since World War II, 1976. Mem. Orgn. Am. Historians, Am. Hist. Assn., Am. Jewish Hist. Assn. Democrat. Jewish. Home: 1981 E Miraval Cuarto Tucson AZ 85718-3032 Office: U Ariz Dept History Tucson AZ 85721-0027

DINNERSTEIN, SIMON ABRAHAM, artist, educator; b. Bklyn., Feb. 16, 1943; s. Louis and Sarah (Kobilansky) D.; m. Renée Sudler, Aug. 28, 1965; 1 child, Simone. BA, CCNY, 1965; postgrad., Bklyn. Mus. Art Sch., 1964-67, Hochschule für Bildende, Kassel, Fed. Republic Germany, 1970-71. Instr. in fine arts New Sch. Social Rsch., Parsons Sch. of Design, N.Y.C., 1975—; adj. lectr. N.Y.C. Tech. Coll., Bklyn., 1979-89; vis. prof. Pratt Inst., Bklyn., 1986-87; vis. artist Calhoun Sch., N.Y., 1988-89; lectr. Am. Acad. Rome, 1977-78, USIS, Barcelona and Madrid, Spain, 1979, Pa. State U., 1984, Pt. Washington Pub. Libr., 1990, St. Paul's Sch., Concord, N.H., 1991, Nassau C.C., 1994, Nat. Acad. of Design, 1997. One-man shows include Staempfli Gallery, N.Y.C., 1975, 79, 88, Inst. Internat. Edn., 1976-77, 79, Am. Acad. Rome, 1977, Pratt Inst., 1987, New Sch. Social Rsch., 1981, 93, Martin Luther King Labor Ctr., N.Y.C., 1985, St. Paul's Sch., Concord, 1991, N.J. Ctr. for Visual Art, Summit, 1994, ACA Galleries, N.Y., Bread and Roses Gallery, N.Y. and St. Peters Church, N.Y., 1999, Walton Arts Ctr., Fayetteville, Ark., Texarkana Regional Arts Ctr., Texarkana, U. Richmond, 2000; subject of book The Art of Simon Dinnerstein, 1991; included in anthology Drawing from Life, 1992, 97, Centennial Directory, 1997, Am. Acad. Rome, 1995, Hooked on Drawing: Illustrated Lessons and Exercises for Grades 4 and up, by Sandy Brooke, 1996, Community of Creativity, A Century of Mac Dowell Colony Artists, 1996; represented by ACA Galleries, N.Y.C.; author: Simon Dinnerstein: Painting and Drawing, 1999. Recipient Rome prize Am. Acad. in Rome, 1976-78, Ingram Merrill Found. award for painting, 1978-79, Cannon prize NAD, 1988, Ralph Fabri prize NAD, 1997, Bertelsen award NAD, 1998; Childe Hassam purchase award Am. Acad. Arts and Letters, 1976, 77, 78; fellow Fulbright Found., Germany, 1970-71, Louis Comfort Tiffany Found., 1976, MacDowell Colony, 1969, 79, N.Y. Found. for Arts, 1987; E.D. Found. grantee, 1977, 78. Mem. NAD, Soc. Fellows Am. Acad. Rome. Democrat. Jewish. Avocations: reading, film, walking, travel, dreaming. Home and Office: 415 1st St Brooklyn NY 11215-2507

DINNIMAN, ANDREW ERIC, county commissioner, history educator, academic program director, international studies educator; b. New Haven, Oct. 10, 1944; s. Harold and Edith (Stephson) D.; m. Margo Portnoy, June 8, 1969; 1 dau., Alexis. BA, U. Conn., 1966; MA, U. Md., 1969; EdD, Pa. State U., 1978. Student pers. worker U. Md., 1969-71, U. Denver, 1971-72; prof. West Chester (Pa.) State U., 1972—; dir. Ctr. for Internat. Programs, 1986—; commissioner Chester County, 1992—. Chmn. Chester County Dem. Com., 1979-85; mem. Pa. Dem. State Com., 1982-89, mem. exec. com., 1984-89; chmn. Eastern Pa. Dem. County Chmn. Assn., 1982-85; mem. Dem. Nat. Com., 1984-89; del. Dem. Nat. Conv., 1984, 88, 92, 96; pres. Pa. Coun. on Internat. Edn., 1989-91; v.p. Downingtown Area (Pa.) Sch. Bd., 1975-79; mem. Central Chester County Vocat.-Tech. Sch. Bd., 1978-79; mem. Chester County Conservation Dist., 1992—; mem. Pa. State Transp. Adv. Com., 1992-95, mem. Chester County Econ. Devel. Bd., 1992-96; mem. Nat. Assn. Counties Com. on Globalization, 1997-98. Recipient Bicentennial award Pa. Sch. Bds. Assn., 1976, Outstanding Acad. Service award Commonwealth Pa., 1977, Human Rights award W. Chester State U. chpt. NAACP, 1980, Cmty. Svc. award Coatesville NAACP, 1997, Mil. Order of Purple Heart Nat. citation for outstanding svc., 1998, Excellence in Local Govt. award Commonwealth of Pa., 1998. Mem. Chester County Hist. Soc., Pa. Soc. Jewish. Author: Book of Human Relations Readings, 1980, Education for International Competence in Pennsylvania, 1988; also articles. Home: 467 Spruce Dr Exton PA 19341-2025 Office: Courthouse 2 N High St West Chester PA 19380-3025

DINNING, WOODFORD WYNDHAM, JR., lawyer; b. Demopolis, Ala., Aug. 15, 1954; s. Woodford W. and Gladys (Brown) D.; m. Tammy E. Cannon, May 27, 1994. AS, U. Ala., 1976, JD, 1979. Bar: Ala. 1979, U.S. Dist. Ct. (so. dist.) Ala. 1980. Mcpl. judge City of Demopolis, 1980-93, 98—; ptnr. Lloyd, Dinning, Boggs & Dinning, Demopolis, 1979—; mcpl. judge City of Linden, Ala., 1997—; pres. and bd. dirs. Tenn. Tom Motel, Inc.; atty. Marengo County Commn. and City of Linden, Ala. Mem. U. Ala. Alumni Assn. (chmn. 1985-86). Avocations: water skiing, snow skiing. Office: Lloyd Dinning Boggs & Dinning PO Drawer Z Demopolis AL 36732

DINOS, NICHOLAS, engineering educator, administrator; b. Tamaqua, Pa., Jan. 15, 1934; s. Christophoros and Calliope (Haralambos) D.; m. Lillian Gravell, June 18, 1955; children: Gwen Elizabeth, Christopher Nicholas, Janet Kay. BS, Pa. State U., 1955; MS, Lehigh U., 1966, PhD, 1967. Engr. E.I. duPont Co., Terre Haute, Ind., 1955-57, rsch. engr., Augusta, Ga., 1957-64; assoc. prof. Ohio U., Athens, 1967-72, prof., 1972—, chmn., 1976-89; vis. prof. Chubu U., Nagoya, Japan, 1976. Contbr. articles to profl. jours. Elder Presbyn. Ch., Athens, 1967—. NASA fellow Lehigh U., Stanford U., 1966, 72, 74, U.S. Steel fellow Lehigh U., 1965; Danforth Found. assoc. Ohio U., 1978—. Mem. AAUP, AAAS, Am. Inst. Chem. Engrs., Am. Chem. Soc., Am. Soc. Engring. Edn., Sigma Xi, Phi Kappa Phi, Tau Beta Pi. Democrat. Avocations: reading, music, outdoors, travel. Home: 29 Briarwood Dr Athens OH 45701-1302 Office: Ohio U Dept Chem Engring Athens OH 45701

DINOSO, VICENTE PESCADOR, JR., physician, educator; b. San Marcelino, Philippines, Oct. 17, 1936; came to U.S., 1961, naturalized, 1973; s. Vicente Dinoso and Eugenia Corpus (Pescador) D.; m. Alice M. Dinoso, June 19, 1965; children—Vincent, David. B.S., U. Philippines, 1955, M.D., 1960. Intern Mt. Sinai Hosp., Hartford, Conn., 1961-62; resident St. Mary's Hosp., Waterbury, Conn., 1962-64, Lahey Clinic Found., Boston, 1964-65; research fellow Temple U. Sch. Medicine, Phila., 1965-66, 68-69; instr. medicine Temple U. Sch. Medicine, 1969-72, asst. prof., 1972-74; assoc. prof. medicine Hahnemann U. Sch. Medicine, Phila., 1974-78, prof. medicine, assoc. prof. physiology, 1978—; practice medicine specializing in gastroenterology, 1969—. Co-editor: Gastrointestinal Emergencies, 1976; contbr. articles to med. jours. Mem. Am. Gastroenterol. Assn., Am. Physiol. Soc., Am. Fedn. for Clin. Research, AAAS, Sigma Xi. Republican. Home: 1421 Granary Rd Blue Bell PA 19422-2124 Office: Hahnemann U Hosp Broad and Vine St Philadelphia PA 19102-5087

DINSE, JOHN MERRELL, lawyer; b. Rochester, N.Y., June 26, 1925; s. Frank John and Lois Vanlora (Merrell) D.; m. Ann Thompson (Goodenough), Dec. 27, 1948; children—Jeffrey P., Pamela D. Johnston. A.B., U. Rochester, 1947; LL.B., Cornell U., 1950. Bar: N.Y. 1950, Vt. 1951, U.S. Dist. Ct. Vt. 1952, U.S. Ct. Appeals (2d cir.) 1957. Assoc. firm Austin & Edmunds, Burlington, Vt., 1950-57; ptnr. Dinse, Erdmann, & Clapp (and predecessor firms), Burlington, 1957-90; of counsel Dinse, Knapp, & McAndrew (and predecessor firms), Burlington, 1990—. Mem. Vt. Waterways Commn., 1962-63; chmn. Vt. Jud. Nominating Bd., 1967-77; fin. chmn. Vt. Rep. Com., 1967, campaign chmn. Gov. Deane C. Davis, 1968, 70; mem. Med. Ctr. Hosp. Assocs.; dir. Vt. Mcpl. Bond Bank, 1980-93; mem. waterways com. Interstate Commn. on Champlain Basin; past trustee Burlington YWCA; past bd. govs. Med. Ctr. Hosp. Vt.; past bd. dirs. Vt. Diabetes Assn., Arthritis Found.; bd. dirs. Vt. Symphony Orch., 1993—, v.p., 1995—. With U.S. Army, 1943-46. Decorated Bronze star. Fellow Am. Coll. Trial Lawyers, Am. Bar Found., Am. Coll. Trust and Estate Counsel; mem. ABA, New Eng. Bar Assn. (bd. dirs. 1977-80), Chittenden County Bar Assn., Vt. Bar Assn. (bd. mgrs. 1974—, pres. 1978-79), Am. Bd. Trial Advs. (bd. dirs. 1990-92), Am. Judicature Soc. (dir. 1975-79), Am. Acad. Hosp. Attys., No. New Eng. Def. Counsel Assn. (pres. 1971-72), Assn. Def. Attys., Internat. Assn. Def. Counsel, Def. Research Inst. (dir. 1975-81, pres. 1980, chmn. bd. 1981), Am. Law Inst., Nat. Assn. Coll. and Univ. Attys. Club: Lake Champlain Yacht (commodore 1961-62); Malletts Bay Boat (master 1957-58). Home: Harbor Rd Shelburne VT 05482 Office: Dinse Knapp & McAndrew PO Box 988 209 Battery St Burlington VT 05402

DINSMOOR, JAMES ARTHUR, psychology educator; b. Woburn, Mass., Oct. 4, 1921; s. Daniel Stark and Jean Erskine (Masson) D.; m. Anne Darrow Berninger, July 17, 1943 (div. Mar. 1953); 1 son, Daniel Stark; m.

Marise Kay Sawyer, Jan. 1, 1956; children: Mara Jean, Robert Scott. B.A., Dartmouth Coll., 1943; M.A., Columbia U., 1945, Ph.D., 1949. Instr. Newark Colls., Rutgers U., 1945-46; lectr. Columbia U., N.Y.C., 1946-51; asst. prof. Ind. U., Bloomington, 1951-58, assoc. prof., 1958-63, prof. psychology, 1963-86, prof. emeritus psychology, 1987—. Author: Operant Conditioning: An Experimental Analysis of Behavior, 1970. Mem. nat. bd. Nat. Com. for a Sane Nuclear Policy, Washington, 1966-68. Fellow APA (divsn. v.p. 1977-80, divsn. pres. 1992-93); mem. Soc. Exptl. Analysis of Behavior (pres. 1979-81), Midwestern Psychol. Assn. (coun. 1973-82, pres. 1980-81), Assn. for Behavior Analysis (orgnl. com. 1974-76). Home: 1511 E Maxwell Ln Bloomington IN 47401-5144 Office: Ind U Dept Psychology 1101 E Tenth St Bloomington IN 47405-7007

DINSMOOR, ROBERT DAVIDSON, judge; b. El Paso, Tex., May 19, 1955; s. William Bell Jr. and Mary (Higgins) D. BA in Polit. Sci., Brigham Young U., 1979, JD, 1982. Bar: Tex. 1983, U.S. Dist. Ct. (we. dist.) Tex. 1985, U.S. Ct. Appeals (5th cir.) 1986, U.S. Supreme Ct. 1987. Rsch. assoc. J. Reuben Clark Law Sch., Brigham Young U., Provo, Utah, 1981-82; asst. dist. atty. El Paso (Tex.) Dist. Atty., 1983-90; dist. ct. judge State of Tex., El Paso, 1991—; spkr. Tex. County Judges Assn., 1992, 1992 Ann. Mex. Am. Bar Assn. of Tex. Conf., 1992, 97, St. Mary's U. Law Sch. Ethics Seminar, 1999, El Paso Bar Assn. Ethics Seminar, 1997-99, also various h.s. and mid. schs., El Paso, 1988—; co-founder El Paso Criminal Law Study Group. Contbr. articles to profl. jours. Bd. dirs. S.W. Repertory Orgn., El Paso, 1994-95; Sunday Sch. pres. Latter Day Saints Ch., 5th ward, El Paso, 1993-95; exec. sec. to bishop, 1995—. Recipient Outstanding Achievement award El Paso Young Lawyers Assn., 1990, Outstanding Jurist award, 1999. Mem. State Bar Tex. (mem. indigent representation com. 1994-98, 99—, victim/witness com. 1992-95, 97-98), El Paso Bar Assn. (mem. legal bar com., libr. com., criminal law com.; others 1986—, bd. dirs. 1993-96, sec. 1996-97, treas. 1997-98, v.p. 1998-99, pres.-elect 1999—). Democrat. Avocations: playing piano, writing music, bicycle riding, basketball, accordion playing. Office: 120th Dist Ct County Bldg Rm 605 500 E San Antonio Ave El Paso TX 79901-2419

DINSMORE, PHILIP WADE, architect; b. Gilroy, Calif., Nov. 4, 1942; s. Wilbur Allen and Elizabeth Eleanor (Hill) D.; m. Mary Kathryn Mead; children: Robert Allen, Kerry Philip. BArch, U. Ariz., 1965. Registered arch., Ariz., Calif., Nev., S.C., N.C., Wyo. Nat. Coun. Archtl. Registration Bds. Designer William L. Pereira & Assocs., L.A., 1965-67; assoc. CNWC Archs., Tucson, 1967-69; prin., ptnr. Arch. One Ltd., Tucson, 1970-90; pres. Durrant Archts. Ariz., Phoenix, Tucson, 1995—; bd. dirs. Durrant Group, 1992—. Mem., chmn. Archtl. Approval Bd., City of Tucson, 1974-75, 77; bd. dirs. Tucson Met. YMCA, 1993—, U. Ariz. Coll. Arch., environ. design coun.; trustee AIA Benefit Ins. Trust, 1997—. Recipient Tucker award Bldg. Stone Inst., 1986. Fellow AIA (nat. bd. dirs. 1981-84, nat. sec. 1984-88, regional fellows rep. 1990-96, Ariz. Archs. medal 1985, Western Mountain Region Citation award 1973, 76, 78, Award of Honor 1983, Silver medal 1992); mem. Am. Archtl. Found. (bd. regents 1988-92), Constrn. Specifications Inst., Ariz. Soc. Archs. (citation 1977-80, 89). Office: Durrant Ariz 2980 N Campbell S-130 Tucson AZ 85719-2897

DINSMORE, SUSAN MARIE, secondary education educator; b. Albia, Iowa, June 11, 1952; d. John Raymond and Kathryn Mae Conway; m. Larry Deane Dinsmore, Apr. 5, 1980; stepchildren: Brook, Jana. AA, Ottumwa (Iowa) Heights, 1972; BA, N.W. Mo. State, 1974; MA, N.E. Mo. State, 1985. Elem. libr. Ottumwa Cmty. Schs., 1974-80, jr. high libr., 1980-84, tchr., 1984—. Mem. Iowa Assn. Mid. Level Edn., Ottumwa Fedn. Tchrs. (sec. 1986—). Roman Catholic. Home: PO Box 286 Fremont IA 52561 Office: Evans Jr HS 812 Chester Ave Ottumwa IA 52501-4192

DINTENFASS, MARK, writer, English educator; b. Appleton, Wis., Nov. 15, 1941; s. Sidney Dintenfass and Gerri Berger; m. Phyllis Schulman; children: David, Nathan, Mark. BA, Columbia U., 1963, MA, 1964; MFA, U. Iowa, 1968. Prof. English Lawrence U., Appleton, 1968-99. Author: Make Yourself An Earthquake, 1969, Montgomery Street, 1978, Old World, New World, 1982, A Loving Place, 1986. Recipient Disting. Achievement award Wis. Libr. Assn., 1987; named Notable Wis. Writer, Wis. Libr. Assn., 1986. Mem. PEN, Author's Guild. Avocations: music, computing. E-mail: mldin@execpc.com and dintenfm@lawrence.edu. Office: Lawrence Univ Main Hall Appleton WI 54911

DINTENFASS, TERRY, art dealer; b. Atlantic City, N.J.. Pres. Terry Dintenfass, Inc., N.Y.C., 1960—. Office: 20 E 79th St New York NY 10021-0106*

DI NUNZIO, DOMINICK, educational administrator; b. Bristol, Pa., Mar. 7, 1931; s. Anthony and Mary (Minni) Di N.; m. Helen Mae Appleton, Dec. 29, 1953; children: Dominick, Mark, Douglas, Celeste. BS, Millersville (Pa.) U., 1953; MEd, Rutgers U., 1960, postgrad., 1960-63; postgrad., U. Pa., 1965-68, Temple U., 1969-71, Lehigh U., 1983; PhD, Walden U., 1972. Tchr., basketball coach Bristol H.S., 1955-61; vice prin. Pemberton Twp. (N.J.) H.S., 1961-65, prin., 1965-73; prin. Pemberton Twp. H.S. No. 2, 1973-76, Pemberton Twp. Elem. Schs., 1976-84; prin. Mid. Schs., 1984-91, asst. supt., 1991—; mem. acad. policy bd. Walden U., 1978-83. With U.S. Army, 1953-55. Recipient Legion of Honor, Chapel of Four Chaplains, 1982, Disting. Alumnus award Walden U., 1982; named Secondary Educator of Am., 1973. Mem. ASCD, NEA, N.J. Edn. Assn., Nat. Assn. Secondary Sch. Prins., N.J. Assn. Secondary Sch. Prins., Am. Assn. Sch. Adminstrs., Nat. Doctorate Assn., N.J. Schoolmasters Club, South Jersey Schoolmens Club, Coun. for Basic Edn., Nat. Soc. for Study Edn., Millersville U. Alumni Assn. (exec. com. 1972—, v.p. 1978-80, pres. 1980-82, Disting. Svc. award 1987), Walden U. Alumni Assn. (pres. 1978-84), Walden U. Mid. States Regional Assn. (pres. 1983-85), Order Sons of Italy in Am., Pemberton Rotary (pres. 1976-77, Paul Harris fellow 1996), Masons (worshipful master 1987, dist. G chmn. Masonic edn. 1988-91, facilitator dist. C Hirami leadership program 1990—, chmn. dist. C membership devel. and retention 1992—), Phi Delta Kappa. Presbyterian. Home: 37 Underwood Rd Levittown PA 19056-2601 Office: PO Box 98 Browns Mills NJ 08015-0098

DIOKNO, ANANIAS C., urologic surgeon, educator; b. San Luis, Batangas, The Philippines, Aug. 13, 1942; came to the U.S., 1966; s. Pedro B. and Rosario M. Diokno; m. Lourdes M. Herrero, Apr. 29, 1967; children: Dennis, Donna, David, Deana. AA, U. Santo Tomas, Manila, 1960, MD, 1965. Diplomate Am. Bd. Urology. Urology resident U. Mich., Ann Arbor, 1970, instr. urology, 1971-72, asst. prof. urology, 1972-76, assoc. prof. urology, 1976-82, prof. urology, 1982-84, clin. prof. urology, 1984—; chief urology William Beaumont Hosp., Royal Oak, Mich., 1984—; cons. Pharmacia Upjohn, Kalamazoo, Mich., 1996—; adv. bd. Alza Pharm., Palo Alto, Calif., 1998—. Author: Current Urologic Tx, 1994, Fact and Research-Gerontology, 1995; co-editor: Lower G.U. Radiology, 1997; editor Urology: Index and Reviews, 1997—; mem. editl. bd. Jour. Gerontologic Nephrology and Urology, 1990—. Lectr. AARP, Southfield, Mich., 1996; cons. IC Support Group, Royal Oak, 1996. Recipient Merit award NIH, Bethesda, Md., 1989; rsch. grantee NIH, Bethesda, 1990-99. Mem. ACS, Internat. Coll. Surgeons, Am. Urol. Assn. (pres. north ctrl. sect. 1996-97), Philippine Am. Urol. Soc. (pres. 1983-84), Mich. Urol. Soc. (pres. 1984-85), Reed M. Nesbit Urol. Soc. (pres.-elect 1998—). E-mail: adiokno@beaumont.edu. Office: William Beaumont Hosp Dept Urology 3535 W 13 Mile Rd Royal Oak MI 48073-6710

DION, CELINE, musician; b. Charlemagne, Quebec, Can., Mar. 30, 1970. Albums include: Unison, 1990 (album of the year 1990), Celine Dion, 1992, Colour of My Love, 1993 (multi-platinum 1994), Premieres Anees, 1994, Dion Chante Plamondon, 1994, Des Mots Qui Sonnent, 1995, Power of Love, 1995, French Album, 1995, Live A Paris, 1996, Falling Into You (Grammy award 1997), Let's Talk About Love, 1997, S'il suffisait d'aimer, 1998, These are Special Times, 1998 (Grammy & Juno awds. 1999); apperances include Real Love, 1979, Beauty & the Beast, 1991 (Grammy award 1992, best selling single 1992, Acad. award 1992), Sleepless in Seattle, 1993, Through the Fire, 1994. Office: Sony Music 550 Madison Ave New York NY 10022-3211

DION, MARC MUNROE, newspaper columnist; b. Fall River, Mass., May 10, 1957; s. Eugene Wilfred and Margaret Munroe Dion. BA in English, U. Mo., 1980. Newsman AP, Kansas City, Mo., 1983—; book reviewer Kansas City Star, 1992—; columnist Fall River Herald News, 1992—. Author: To Veronicas New Lover, 1984. Bd. dirs. Arts Unltd., 1995. Recipient 1st Pl. Humor Column award New England Press Assn., 1995, 3d Pl Editorials award New England Associated Press News Execs. Assn. Mem. Nat. Soc. Newspaper Columnists, Vets. Assn. of Bristol (bd. dirs. 1997—), Soc. of Profl. Journalists, Boxing Writers Assn. of Am. Roman Catholic. Avocation: boxing. Home: 631 Walnut Fall River MA 02720 Office: Herald News 207 Pocasset Fall River MA 02721

DION, STÉPHANE, federal official; b. 1955; married; 1 daughter. BA in Polit. Sci., U. Laval, 1977, MA in Polit. Sci., 1979; D in Sociology, Inst. Polit. Paris. Prof. polit. sci. U. Moncton, Can., 1984, U. Montréal, Can., 1984-96; pres. Privy Coun., Can., 1996—; min. Intergovernmental Affairs, Can., 1996—; vis. prof. Lab. Econ. Pub., Paris; sr. rsch. fellow Brookings Inst., Washington; rsch. fellow Can. Ctr. Mgmt. Devel. Co-dir. Can. Jour. Polit. Sci.; contbr. articles to profl. jours. Office: Privy Coun Langevin Bl 8th Fl, Intergovtl Affairs 66 Slater St, Ottawa, ON Canada K1A 0A3

DIONG, BILLY MING, control engineering researcher; b. Singapore, Singapore, Oct. 22, 1962; came to U.S., 1983; s. Woong-Siew and Soo-Eng (Ting) D.; m. Temmy King, July 22, 1989; 1 child, Stephanie. BS with univ. honors, U. Ill., 1986, MS, 1988, PhD, 1992. Engr. Automation Applications Ctr., Singapore, 1988; rsch. asst. dept. gen. engring. U. Ill., Urbana, 1988-91, rsch. asst. coord. sci. lab., 1991-92; researcher Sundstrand Aerospace, Rockford, Ill., 1992-95; asst. prof. elec. engring. U. Tex.-Pan Am., Edinburg, 1995-99, U. Tex., El Paso, 1999—. Contbr. articles to sci. jours. Engring. scholar Sundstrand Corp., 1983-87; Conf. Travel grantee U. Ill., 1991, Faculty Rsch. Coun. grantee U. Tex.-Pan Am., 1995, 96, NSF grantee, 1997; Air Force Office of Sci. Rsch. summer fellow, 1997; Univ. Rsch. Initiative grantee U. Tex., El Paso, 1999. Mem. IEEE, Am. Soc. Engring. Edn., Tau Beta Pi (hon.), Eta Kappa Nu (hon.), Phi Eta Sigma (hon.). Avocations: computers, music, chess, swimming. Home: 535 S Mesa Hills Apt 1026 El Paso TX 79912 Office: U Tex-El Paso Elec and Computer Engring 500 W University Ave El Paso TX 79902

DIONISOPOULOS, GEORGE ALLAN, lawyer; b. Santa Monica, Calif., July 31, 1954; s. P. Allan and Christine (Nassios) D.; m. Sandra Doreen Jordan, June 11, 1977; children: Sarah, Elaina. BA summa cum laude, U. Ill., 1976; JD cum laude, Harvard U., 1980. Bar: Wis. 1980, U.S. Dist. Ct. (ea. and we. dists.) Wis. 1980. Ptnr. Foley & Lardner, Milw., 1980—. Mem. ABA (real property and probate sect., taxation sect.), Wis. Bar Assn. (speaker 1984—), Milw. Young Lawyers Assn., Phi Beta Kappa. Greek Orthodox. Home: W304n2978 Hawksnest Ct Pewaukee WI 53072-4279 Office: Foley & Lardner 777 E Wisconsin Ave Ste 3800 Milwaukee WI 53202-5367

DIONNE, GERALD FRANCIS, research physicist, educator, consultant; b. Montreal, Feb. 5, 1935; came to U.S., 1964, naturalized, 1980; s. Louis Philip and Clare Isabel (Flood) D.; m. Claudette Leblanc, June 29, 1963; 1 child, Stephen. BS summa cum laude, Loyola Coll., U. Montreal, 1956; B of Engring. magna cum laude, McGill U., Montreal, 1958, PhD in Physics, 1964; MS, Carnegie-Mellon U., 1959. Jr. engr. IBM Corp., Poughkeepsie, N.Y., 1959-60; sr. engr. Sylvania Electric Products, Woburn, Mass., 1960-61; rsch. asst., lectr. McGill U., 1964; sr. rsch. assoc. Pratt & Whitney Aircraft, North Haven, Conn., 1964-66; mem. rsch. staff Lincoln Lab., MIT, Lexington, Mass., 1966-96; expert svcs. pers. Lincoln Lab., MIT, Lexington, 1996—; grad student rsch. advisor, sci. and tech. advisor to industry and govt. Contbr. articles to sci. jours.; rschr. in magnetism, magnetoelastic and magneto-optic phenomena, superconductivity theory and devices, microwave, submillimeter-wave, optical and surface physics; holder patents for microwave, superconducting, and magnetic devices. NRC of Can. fellow. Fellow IEEE; mem. Am. Phys. Soc., Corp. Profl. Engrs. Que., Sigma Xi. Home: 182 High St Winchester MA 01890-3366 Office: 244 Wood St Lexington MA 02421-6426

DIONNE, JOSEPH LEWIS, publishing company executive; b. Montgomery, Ala., June 29, 1933; s. Antonio Ernest Joseph and Myrtle Mae (Armstrong) D.; m. Joan F. Durand, June 12, 1954; children: Marsha Joan Dionne Guerin, Gary Joseph, Darren Durand. B.A., Hofstra U., 1955, M.S., 1957; Ed.D., Columbia U., 1965. Guidance counselor L.I. Public Schs., 1956-61; asst. prof. Hofstra U., Hempstead, N.Y., 1962-63; dir. instrn., project dir. Ford Found. Sch. Improvement grant Brentwood (N.Y.) Pub. Schs., 1963-66; v.p. research and devel. Ednl. Developmental Labs., Huntington, N.Y., 1966-68; v.p., gen. mgr. CTB/McGraw-Hill, Monterey, Calif., 1968-73; sr. v.p. corp. planning McGraw-Hill, Inc., N.Y.C., 1973-77, exec. v.p. ops., 1979-81; pres. McGraw-Hill Info. Systems Co., N.Y.C., 1977-79; former pres. McGraw Hill, Inc., N.Y.C., 1981—, chmn., CEO, 1988-98, chmn., 1998-99; bd. dirs. The Equitable Life Assurance Soc. of U.S., The Equitable Coms. Inc., Harris Corp., Ryder System, Inc. Elder Presbyn. Ch. New Canaan; past pres. Soc. To Advance Retarded; past chmn. bd. trustees Hofstra U. 2d lt. U.S. Army, 1955-56. Mem. Phi Alpha Theta, Kappa Delta Pi, Phi Delta Kappa. Clubs: Woodway Country (Darien, Conn.), Blind Brook Club, Inc. (Purchase, N.Y.). Office: The McGraw Hill Cos 1221 Ave of Americas New York NY 10020-1001

DIORIO, EILEEN PATRICIA, medical technologist, retired, philosophy educator; b. Pitts., Mar. 17, 1938; d. Charles Frederick and Elizabeth (Maturkanich) Kozlowski; m. David Robert Kaslewicz, June 21, 1958 (div. May 1965); m. Alfred Frank Diorio, June 11, 1983; children: Suzanne C. Kaslewicz Ickes, Fredric C. Kaslewicz, Warren G. Kaslewicz, Jennifer Kaslewicz Dalessandro. Student, Duquesne U., 1956-58. Reg. Med. Technologist, Pa. Microbiology technician Presbyn. U. Hosp., Pitts., 1967-70; supr. virology/immunology lab. Allegheny Gen. Hosp., Pitts., 1970-90; co-dir. Himalayan Inst. Yoga Science & Philosophy of Pitts., 1977-96. Vol. med. lab. mgr. Himalayan Inst. Hosp., India, 1992-96. Avocations: playing violin, cooking, tchg. meditation and relaxation.

DIORIO, ROBERT JOSEPH, psychotherapist, consultant; b. Chgo., Dec. 21, 1945; s. Joseph and Mary Jane (Christopher) DiO.; m. Diane Rose Belcastro, Sept. 30, 1967; children: Jason, Adam. BA, St. Mary's Coll., Winona, Minn., 1967; MA in Biology, Edn., U. Chgo., 1969; PhD in Clin. Psychology, U. for Humanistic Studies, Las Vegas, Nev., 1984. Supervising probation officer 18th Jud. Cir. Ct., Wheaton, Ill., 1970-78; cons., adminstr. Nat. Med. Svc., Las Vegas, 1978-82; out-patient dir. Western Counseling Assn., Las Vegas, 1982-84; adminstr., psychotherapist Assn. Counselors of So. Nev., Las Vegas, 1984—; bd. dirs. Ctr. for Independent Living, Las Vegas, Las Vegas Exec.'s Assn.; mem. adv. bd. Compassionate Friends, Las Vegas, 1996—. Fellow Am. Bd. Med. Psychotherapists (diplomate), Am. Bd. Cert. Managed Care Providers; mem. ACA, Las Vegas Exec.'s Assn. (pres. 1990-91), Am. Coun. Hypnotist Examiners (hypnotherapist), Nat. Assn. Drug and Alcohol Counselors (master addiction counselor 1995—), Thought Field Therapy. Avocations: poetry, soccer, walking, fishing. Office: Health Care Cons Inc 2860 E Flamingo Rd Ste H Las Vegas NV 89121-5270

DIPADOVA, LAURIE NEWMAN, educator; b. Portsmouth, Va., July 31, 1945; d. Everett Hale Newman Jr. and Evelyn Naomi Moore; m. Theodore Anthony DePadova, Mar. 25, 1972 (div. Nov. 1994); children: Audra Mae, Joseph Russell; m. Hugh Grant Stocks, July 8, 1995. BA in Sociology, U. Va., 1967; MS in Sociology, U. Utah, 1970; PhD in Pub. Adminstrn. & Policy, SUNY, Albany, 1995. Instr. sociology Ricks Coll., Rexburg, Idaho, 1969-71, Old Dominion U., Norfold, Va., 1971-76; trainer human svcs. grad. sch. social work SUNY, Albany, 1980-81; tng. assoc. N.Y. State Dept. Social Svcs., Albany, 1981-83; rsch. asst. dept. pub. adminstrn. SUNY, Albany, 1987-91; assoc. faculty SUNY, Saratoga Springs, N.Y., 1991-95; depugy dir., adj. assoc. prof. polit. sci. U. Utah, Salt Lake City, 1987—; vis. asst. prof. polit. sci. U. Utah, 1995-97; cons. in field. Contbr. articles to profl. jours. Bd. dirs. Pk. Pl. Cmty. Mental Health Ctr., Norvolf, 1974-75, Citizen's Assn. Justice Va., 1975; elected ofcl. Holiday Cmty. Coun., Salt Lake City, 1998. Mem. Am. Soc. Pub. Adminstrn., Utah Nonprofits Assn., Acad. Mgmt., Assn. Rsch. Nonprofit & Voluntary Assns., Pi Alpha Alpha. Mem. LDS Ch. Avocations: Am. Civil War, Genealogy, running, travel. Office: U Utah Ctr Pub Policy Rm 2120 1901 E South Campus Dr Salt Lake City UT 84112

DI PALMA, JOSEPH ALPHONSE, investment company executive, lawyer; b. N.Y.C., Jan. 17, 1931; s. Gaetano and Michela May (Ambrosio) Di P.; m. Joycelyn Ann Engle, Apr. 18, 1970; children: Joycelyn Joan, Julianne Michelle. BA, Columbia U., 1952; JD, Fordham U., 1958; LLM in Taxation, NYU, 1959. Bar: N.Y. 1959. Tax atty. CBS, N.Y.C., 1960-64; v.p. tax dept. TWA, N.Y.C., 1964-74; pvt. practice law N.Y.C., 1974-87; investor, exec. dir. Di Palma Family Holdings, Las Vegas and N.Y.C., 1987—; cons. in field; head study group Comprehensive Gaming Study, N.Y.C. and Washington, 1990—; think tank exec. dir. Di Palma Position Papers; founder Di Palma Forum, U. Nev., Las Vegas; established The Di Palma Ctr. for Study of Jewelry and Precious Metals at Cooper-Hewitt, Nat. Design Mus., Smithsonian Instn., N.Y.C. Contbr. articles to profl. jours.; author: Di Palma Postion Papers. Bd. dirs. Friends of the Henry St. Settlement, N.Y.C., 1961-63, Outdoor Cleanliness Assn., N.Y.C., 1961-65; chmn. Air Transport Assn. Taxation Com., 1974. With U.S. Army, 1953-54. Recipient Disting. Svc. and Valuable Counsel commendation award Air Transport Assn., 1974, spl. commendation from N.Y.C. mayor Rudolph Giuliani, 1997. Mem. Internat. Platform Assn., N.Y. State Bar Assn., N.Y. Athletic Club. Roman Catholic. Home: 3111 Bel Air Dr Apt 21B Las Vegas NV 89109-1506 Office: PO Box 72158 Las Vegas NV 89170-2158 also: 930 5th Ave # 4 J&H New York NY 10021-2651

DIPALMA, JOSEPH RUPERT, pharmacology educator; b. N.Y.C., Mar. 21, 1916; s. Frank and Anna (Attanasio) DiP.; m. Mary Solowey, June 26, 1948; children: Maria, Dorothea, Joan, Yvonne, Mary-Jo. BS, Columbia U., 1936; MD, SUNY, Bklyn., 1941; DSc (hon.), Hahnemann U., 1980. Intern, resident in internal medicine Kings County Hosp., Bklyn., 1942-44; asst. prof. medicine and pharmacology State U. N.Y. Downstate Med. Sch., 1946; prof. pharmacology, chmn. dept. Hahnemann Med. Coll. and Hosp., Phila., 1951-67; dean Hahnemann Med. Coll. and Hosp., 1967-82, v.p., 1971-82, sr. v.p., 1972-82, prof. pharmacology and medicine, 1982-86, emeritus prof. pharmacology and medicine, 1986—, emeritus dean, 1986—; mem. bd. Regional Med. Program Southeastern Pa., 1967-75, Health Systems Agy., 1977—. Editor: Pharmacology in Medicine, 1971, Basic Pharmacology in Medicine, 1976, 4th edit., 1994; contbr. med. jours. Recipient Alumni medallion SUNY, Downstate Med. Sch., 1966, Corp. medal Hahnemann U., 1990. Mem. Coll. Physicians Phila. (council 1969-78), AMA, Pa., Phila. County Med. socs., Am. Physiol. Soc., Am. Soc. Pharmacology and Exptl. Therapeutics, Am. Soc. Clin. Investigation, Am. Soc. Clin. Pharmacology, Alpha Omega Alpha. Home: 100 Pembroke Ave Wayne PA 19087-4819 Office: 235 N 15th St Philadelphia PA 19102-1101 *The creation of new ideas and approaches is always the ultimate goal.*

DI PAOLA, ROBERT ARNOLD, mathematics and computer science educator; b. N.Y.C., Nov. 28, 1933; s. Anthony and Lucy Philomena (Parente) Di P. BS, Fordham U., 1956, MA, 1959; PhD, Yeshiva U., 1964. Mathematician Grumman Aircraft Corp., Bethpage, N.Y., 1957-59; asst. prof. UCLA, 1964-66; mathematician The Rand Corp., Santa Monica, Calif., 1966-72; prof. math. and computer sci. CUNY, 1975—; vis. prof. U. Siena, 1976-77, 84, 85, 89, 93, 94, 96, U. Oxford, Eng., 1989; cons. in field. Contbr. rsch. papers to math. jours. Grantee, NSF, 1982-85, 85-92. Mem. Am. Math. Soc., Assn. Symbolic Logic. Republican. Roman Catholic. Avocations: jogging, military, sports and Italian history, Roman Catholic philosophy, theology. Office: Grad Sch Univ Ctr 33 W 42nd St New York NY 10036-8003

DI PAOLO, MARIA GRAZIA, language educator, writer; d. Alfredo and Giosina (Di Cicco) Di P.; m. Gianroberto Sarolli; 1 child, Giandomenico Sarolli. BA, Hunter Coll., 1969; MA, Columbia U., 1972, PhD, 1977. Instr. Columbia U., N.Y.C., 1973-77; asst. prof. Vassar Coll., Poughkeepsie, N.Y., 1977-85, CUNY, N.Y.C., 1985-90; assoc. prof. CUNY, 1990-94, prof., 1994—; mem. pers. & budget com. Lehman Coll., CUNY, 1986—; chair Italian Rev. Panel CUNY Rsch. Found., 1988-89, 90-91, 96-97; mem. editl. bd. Can. Jour. Italian Studies, 1988—; pres. Italian Culture Soc. Lehman Coll., 1996—. Author: B. Fenoglio, 1988; translator: Fenoglio's a Private Matter, 1988; editor: D'Annunzio's Correspondence with Son Veniero, 1994; contbr. articles to various publs. Recipient Faculty fellowship Columbia U., 1970-75, Sabbatical grant Vassar Coll., 1982-83, PSC-CUNY Rsch. award, 1988-89, 90-91. Mem. MLA, Am. Assn. Tchrs. Italian. Roman Cath. Avocations: tennis, reading club, opera going.

DIPAOLO, PETER THOMAS, engineering executive, educator; b. Phila., Sept. 4, 1937; s. Peter T. and Erma (Palestini) DiP.; m. Josephine M. Mercurio, Apr. 28, 1962; children: Louis Joseph, Michael Louis. BSME, Villanova U., 1971; MBA, Nova U., 1980, D of Bus. Adminstrn., 1987. Mech. designer RCA Corp., Camden, N.J., 1955-66; project engr. Boeing Corp., Morton, Pa., 1966-68; mech. engr. Burroughs Corp., Paoli, Pa., 1968-70; sect. mgr. Gould-Systems Engring. Labs, Ft. Lauderdale, Fla., 1970-76; corp. fellow Modular Computer Systems, Ft. Lauderdale, 1976-86; sr. dir. hardware engring. Datapoint, Inc., San Antonio, 1986-88; pres. Sanford Rose Assocs., Ft. Lauderdale, 1988—, Integrated Consulting Internat., Ft. Lauderdale, 1990—; prof. mgmt. grad. sch. Nova U., Ft. Lauderdale, 1981—. Patentee in field. Served to cpl. USMCR, 1959-65. Mem. Fin. Execs. Inst. (Award for Excellence 1985), Epsilon Tau Lambda. Republican. Roman Catholic. Avocations: hunting, photography. Home and Office: Integrated Cons Internat 1797 Pine Bay Dr Lake Mary FL 32746-7101

DIPASQUALE, PAUL ALBERT, sculptor; b. Perth Amboy, N.J., June 29, 1951; m. Kelly Kennedy, Oct. 3, 1981; children: Kate, Mary. BA, U. Va., 1973; MFA, Va. Commonwealth U., 1976. Arts instr. No. Va. C.C., Annandale, 1979-81; vis. artist Md. Inst. Art, Balt., 1982; owner DiPasquale Studio, Richmond, Va., 1985—; vis. artist, prof. Coll. William & Mary, Williamsburg, Va., 1991-92; adj. instr. Va. Commonwealth U., Richmond, 1987-98; vis. artist Am. Acad. Rome, 1998, vis. artist Va. Mus. Arts, 1987-89; resident artist Va. Commn. for Arts, Richmond, 1989-91. cons. Time Life Books, Washington, 1981-82, Smithsonian Instn., Washington, 1982-83, prin. works include Headman Monument, Richmond, VA, 1991, Arthur Ashe Monument, Richmond, 1996, bronze installation of Oliver Hill, Black Hist. Mus. VA, 1997, Gov. and Mrs. Godwin, VA Wesleyan Col., 1998; represented in permanent collections: Baltimore Aquarium, Smithsonian Instn., Washington, Richmond Braves Ballpark, VA Hist. Soc. Bd. dirs. Black History Mus. Va., Richmond, 1993-98, Arts Coun. Richmond, 1991; pres. Fulton Hill Civic Assn., Richmond, 1990-91.3. Mem. Soc. Friends. Avocations: canoeing, cross country skiing, motivational speaking.

DIPBOYE, MARILYN JOYCE, publisher, editor, writer; b. Detroit, June 29, 1938; d. Frank Artemus and Elizabeth Ione (Rumford) Welch; m. Donald Lee Dipboye, June 15, 1972. BA, Eastern Mich. U., Ypsilanti, 1960. Tchr. Cherry Hill Schs., Westland, 1960-62, USAF, Tokyo, Japan, 1962-64, Ferndale Sch., 1967-75; publisher, editor, writer Warren, Mich., 1976—. Pub., Cat Talk, Cat Collectors Catalogue. Mem. Cat Writers Assn. Avocations: collecting cat memorabilia, alpine skiing, working out. Home: 33161 Wendy Dr Sterling Heights MI 48310-6473

DIPENTIMA, RENATO ANTHONY, systems executive; b. Jan. 17, 1941; s. Victor and Mary (Cadolino) DiP.; m. Ellen Gillespie, July 24, 1965; children: Margaret Ellen, Katherine Alice. BA, NYU, 1963; MA, George Washington U., 1979; PhD, U. Md., 1984. With Social Security Adminstrn., N.Y.C., 1963, 68-69; ops. analyst Social Security Adminstrn., Balt., 1969-70; sr. planning specialist Pres.'s Welfare Reform Task Force, HEW, Washington, 1970-72; chief mgmt. info. Bur. of Supplement Security Income Social Security Adminstrn., Balt., 1972-73, dir. sys., 1973-75, mem. strike force, 1975, dir. control and coord. Office of Advanced Sys., 1975-79, dir. assistance payments Office of Policy, 1979-82, exec. officer Nat. Commn. Social Security Reform, 1982, dep. assoc. commr. for sys. requirements, 1982-84, dep. assoc. commr. for sys. integration, 1984-88, assoc. commr. for sys. design and devel., 1988-90, dep. commr. for sys., 1990-95; v.p., chief info. officer Sys. Rsch. and Applications Corp., Arlington, Va., 1995-97; pres. SRA Fed. Sys.; adj. faculty mem. U. Md., 1981-95, Loyola Coll., 1991-95; lectr. in field; bd. dirs. WRInc. Adv. bd. Sybase Inc., Tivoli Inc. Mem. Coun. on Excellence; mem. internat. adv. bd. Loyola Coll. Recipient Under Sec.'s Spl. citation HEW, 1972, Sec.'s citation, 1974, Commr.'s citation Social Security Adminstrn., 1974, Dir.'s citation, 1979, Dep. Commr.'s citation, 1984, Commr.'s citation, 1991, Sec.'s Exec. Mgmt. citation Health and Human Svcs., 1987, Presdl. Meritorious Rank award, 1989, Presdl. Disting. Rank award, 1990. Home: 11434 Cedar Ridge Dr Potomac MD 20854-3761

DIPERNA, FRANK PAUL, photographer, educator; b. Pitts., Feb. 4, 1947; s. Frank Paul and Virginia Carmella (DeRenna) DiP. BS in Mech. Engring.,

Va.Polytech. Inst., 1970; student, Visual Studies Workshop, 1971-72; MA in Photography, Goddard Coll., 1977. Assoc. prof. art and photography Corcoran Sch. Art, Washington, 1974-94, prof., 1994—, chmn. photography dept., 1978-81, 84-87; instr. photography No. Va. C.C., Alexandria, 1973-78, George Washington U., Washington, summer 1974; lectrs. and workshops Smithsonian Inst., 1976, Maine Photog. Inst. Rockport, 1977, Am. U., Washington, 1977, 78, 79, Internat. Ctr. Photography, N.Y.C., 1979, U. Del., 1981, James Madison U., Harrisonburg, Va., 1982, Rice U., Houston, No. Va. C.C., Sterling, 1991, 93. Solo exhbns. include Kathleen Ewing Gallery, Washington, 1982, 84, 89, 95, 98, Diane Brown Gallery, Washington, 1977, 78, 80, Bird in Hand Gallery, Alexandria, 1973, Corcoran Gallery Art, 1974, 77, Recontres Internationales de la Photographie, Arles, France, 1981, Rice Univ., Houston, 1986; group exhbns. include Athenaeum Mus., Alexandria, 1972, Photo Impressions Gallery, Washington, 1974, Va. Mus. Fine Arts, Richmond, 1973, 75, 80, The Franklin Inst., Phila., 1978, Susan Spiritus Gallery, Newport Beach, Calif., 1979, Mus. Fine Arts, Houston, 1979, Decordova Mus., Lincoln, Mass., 1979, Mpls. Inst. Arts, 1979, L.A. Inst. Contemporary Art, 1979, Denver Art Mus., 1979, Art Inst. Chgo., 1979, Phila. Coll. Art, 1980, Brown U., Providence, R.I., 1980, Arlington (Va.) Arts Ctr., 1981, Everson Mus. Art, Syracuse, N.Y., 1985, Comfort Gallery Haverford (Pa.) Coll., 1986, Washington Ctr. Photography, 1992, Nat. Mus. Am. Art, 1992, Smithsonian Inst., 1992, Carnegie Mus. Art, 1992, New Orleans Mus. Art, 1992, Corcoran Gallery of Art, 1994, 96, 98, Virginia's Photographers, Longwood Ctr. for the Visual Arts, Farmville, Va., 1997, many others; represented in permanent collections Recontres Internationale de la Photographie, Arles, France, Bibliotheque Nationale, Paris, Libr. Cong., Washington, Polaroid (Euopa) Amsterdam, The Netherlands, Corcoran Gallery of Art, Va. Mus. Fine Arts, Smithsonian Inst., Balt. Mus. Art, Nat. Mus. Am. Art, Washington. Artist-in-Residence Lightwork, Syracuse, N.Y., 1982, Camargo Found., Cassis, France, 1980; Graduate fellow Va. Mus. Fine Arts, 1975. Avocations: tennis, fishing, playing guitar, birdwatching, furniture making. Office: Corcoran Sch Art 500 17th St NW Washington DC 20006-4804

DIPIAZZA, MICHAEL CHARLES, insurance company executive; b. N.Y.C., Aug. 22, 1953; s. Carmelo and Grace (Vassallo) DiP.; m. Lillian Dugan, Dec. 21, 1979. CLU. Asst. v.p. sales Nat. Benefit Life Ins. Co., N.Y.C., 1975-79, asst. v.p. product devel., 1979-81; pres. Wm. B. Smith Agy., N.Y.C., 1979; cons. Ins. Sales Support Systems, Piscataway, N.J., 1981-82; asst. v.p. merchandising MONY, N.Y.C., 1982-86; v.p. merchandising Home Life Ins. Co., N.Y.C., 1986-92; asst. v.p. product devel. and mktg. MetLife, Bridgewater, N.J., 1992-97; asst. v.p. mktg. and merchandising MONY, N.Y.C., 1998—. Mem. Nat. Assn. Life Underwriters, Am. Soc. CLU's. Avocations: music, model railroading, wood working, Am. history.

DIPIETRO, FRANCIS, writer; b. Cambridge, Mass., Apr. 7, 1970; s. Francis Charles and Marie Amelia (Oliveira) DiP. Student, Harvard U., 1985-86, U. Hawaii, 1988. Author Francis DiPietro Literary Svcs., Medford, Mass., 1984—; contbr. Medford Citizen, 1992—, Medford Transcript, 1992—. Author: Portobello Road, 1994, The Orange Phoenix, 1996, Holland & Bonni, 1997, The Afterlife of Trisha Bumwood, 1999, (screenplay) The Hawaii Brothers, 1997. Chmn. Hillcrest Assocs., Medford, 1992-93; dir. Cmty. Theatre, Medford, 1994; contbr. Nat. Diabetes Fund, 1997, Handgun Control, 1997, Nat. Children's Cancer Soc., 1997, Disabled Am. Vets., 1997. Recipient Mayor's citations City of Medford, 1987, 88. Mem. ACLU, The Authors Guild, The Authors League Am., Acad. Am. Poets. Avocations: scrabble, reading fiction, chess, tennis, hiking. Home: Four Luther Rd Medford MA 02155-2910

DIPIETRO, MARK JOSEPH, lawyer; b. Memphis, Aug. 25, 1947; s. Joseph Mark and Anne E. (Dorsey) DiP.; m. Kathleen Ann (Rafferty), June 22, 1968; children: Mark, Lora, Matthew. BA in Chemistry, So. Ill. U., 1969; JD, John Marshall Law Sch., 1976. Bar: Ill. 1976, Minn. 1983. Chemist Univ. Conn. Med. Sch., Hartford, 1969-70, VA Hosp., Indpls., 1970-71, U.S. Steel Corp., Gary, Ind., 1971-76; atty. Standard Oil of Ind. (now BP-Amoco), Chgo., 1976-81; from assoc. to ptnr. Merchant and Gould PA, Mpls., 1981-91; sr. v.p., sec. Merchant & Gould PA, St. Paul, 1992—. Mem. Met. Airport Sound Abatement Com., Mpls., 1984. Mem. ABA, AAAS, Internat. Bar Assn., Am. Intellectual Property Assn., Minn. Intellectual Property Assn., Ramsey County Bar Assn. Roman Catholic. Avocations: reading, bicycling, aerobics, piano. Home: 815 Fairview Ave S Saint Paul MN 55116-2161 Office: Merchant & Gould 3100 Norwest Ctr Minneapolis MN 55402-4131

DIPIETRO, MICHELE A., insurance underwriter; b. Meadowbrook, Pa., Aug. 11, 1967; d. Edward Joseph and Joyce Ann DiPietro. BSBA, Shippensburg U., 1989. CPCU. Reports control coord. U.S. Healthcare, Bluebell, Pa., 1990-91; account coord. Nat. Risk Mgmt., Valley Forge, Pa., 1991-93; dir. ops. Consol. Risk Svcs., Inc., Wayne, Pa., 1993—. Avocations: reading, movies, theater, learning. E-mail: Mpetie@aol.com. Office: Consol Risk Svcs Inc 985 Old Eagle Sch Rd #504 Wayne PA 19087

DIPIETRO, RALPH ANTHONY, marketing and management consultant, educator; b. N.Y.C., Oct. 27, 1942; s. Joseph and Marie (Borelli) DiP. BBA, CUNY, 1964, MBA, 1966; PhD, NYU, 1972. Chmn., prof. mktg. and internat. bus. dept. Sch. Bus. Montclair State U., Upper Montclair, N.J., 1972—; adj. prof. mgmt. NYU, 1976-97, mgmt. tng. dir. Inst. Retail Mgmt., 1976-86; cons. Mfrs. Hanover Trust, N.Y.C., 1979-85, Sharp Electronics, N.Y.C., 1980-94, Battus Corp., N.Y.C., 1982-85, AT&T Bell Labs., 1989-91; program dir. Bally of Switzerland, N.Y.C., 1981-93, Fortunoff's, N.Y.C., 1984-86. Author: Managerial Effectiveness: A Review and an Empirical Testing of a Model, 1973; contbr. articles to profl. jours. Mem. Am. Mktg. Assn., Acad. Mktg. Scis., Internat. Assn. Applied Psychology, Omicron Delta Epsilon. Avocations: tennis, swimming, opera. Home: 361 Green Briar Ct Mountainside NJ 07092-1407

DIPKO, THOMAS EARL, minister, national church executive; b. St. Michael, Pa., June 26, 1936; s. John and Sarah Jane (Gittins) D.; m. Sandra Jane Faust, Nov. 19, 1960; children: Lisa Renee, Sarah Marie. BA, Otterbein Coll., 1958; MDiv, United Theol. Sem., 1961; PhD in Ecumenical Theology, Boston U., 1969; LLD (hon.), Heidelberg Coll., 1987; DD (hon.), United Theol. Sem. of the Twin Cities, 1992; LHD (hon.), The Defiance Coll., 1992; DD (hon.), Elmhurst Coll., 1993, Ursinus Coll., 1994. ordained min. Youth min. First United Methodist Ch., Dayton, Ohio, 1958-61; ecumenical intern social action office Ch. Rhineland-Westphalia, Germany, 1962; asst. pastor First Ch. Congregational, Swampscott, Mass., 1963-64; pastor First United Methodist Ch., East Conemaugh, Pa., 1964-66; asst. pastor South Ch. Congregational, Andover, Mass., 1966-68; sr. pastor Christ Ch. United in Lowell, Mass., 1969-77, Grace Congregational Ch., Framingham, Mass., 1977-84; conf. min. and exec. Ohio conf. United Ch. of Christ, Columbus, 1984-92; exec. v.p. United Ch. Bd. for Homeland Ministries, Cleve., 1992—; mem. bd. trustees The Defiance Coll., 1985—; mem. exec. com. Consultation on Church Union, Princeton, N.J., 1989—; del. Seventh Assembly World Coun. Churches, Canberra, Australia, 1991; mem. bd. dirs. Ryder Meml. Hosp., Humacao, Puerto Rico, 1993-96. Author: (first draft, book) United Church of Christ Book of Worship, 1986; contbr. chpts. to books, articles to profl. jours. chmn. Lowell Drug Action Com., 1971-74; mem. bd. dirs. Internat. Inst., 1971-77. Samaritans (suicide intervention), 1983-84; del. gen. coun. World Alliance Reformed Chs., Debrecen, Hungary, 1997. Fellow Coll. Preachers, 1983. Mem. N.Am. Acad. Ecumenists (mem. exec. com. 1981-83), Christians Associated for Rels. in Eastern Europe, Consultation on Common Texts. Avocations: swimming, perennial gardening, canoeing. Office: United Ch Bd Homeland Ministries 700 Prospect Ave E Cleveland OH 44115-1131*

DI PRIMA, STEPHANIE MARIE, educational administrator; b. Chgo., Aug. 29, 1952; d. Joseph and Ann Marie (Albate) Di P. BA in English, Rosary Coll., 1974; MEd in Adminstrn. and Supervision, Loyola U., Chgo., 1979. Tchr. St. Vincent Ferrer Sch., River Forest, Ill., 1974-78; prin. Our Lady of Hope Sch., Rosemont, Ill., 1978-81, Sacred Heart Sch., Winnetka, Ill., 1981-84, St. Monica Sch., Chgo., 1984-91, St. Martha Sch., Morton Grove, Ill., 1991-97; asst. prin. for student svcs. St. Viator H.S., Arlington Heights, Ill., 1997—; instr. Rosary Coll., River Forest, Ill., Dominican U., River Forest, Ill., 1988—. Mem. ASCD, Nat. Assn. Secondary Sch. Prins., Nat. Cath. Ednl. Assn., Ill. Prins. Assn., Ill. Assn. Supervision and Curriculum Devel., Women in Mgmt., Nat. Assn. Secondary Sch. Principals. Avocations: piano, reading, theatre and fine arts, needlecrafts, travel. Office: St Viator High Sch 1213 E Oakton St Arlington Heights IL 60004-5099

DIR, DAVE, professional soccer coach; b. June 23, 1959. Student, Western Ill. U. Profl. soccer player Chgo. Sting, 1980-84; soccer coach Trinity Prep Luth. Sch., Orlando, Fla., 1984-90; coach Regis U., Denver, 1990-92; head coach Colo. Foxes, 1992-93; dir. player devel. Major League Soccer, 1993-95; head coach Dallas Burn, 1995—; goalkeeper coach U.S. Youth Soccer Assn. Region IV Olympic Devel. Program. Named Coach of the Yr., Colo. Athletic Conf., 1991. Office: c/o Dallas Burn 2602 McKinney #200 Dallas TX 75204*

DIRCKS, PHYLLIS TOAL, English language educator; b. N.Y.C., Jan. 8, 1935; d. John Joseph and Catherine Henderson (Whyte) T.; m. Richard Joseph Dircks, Aug. 17, 1963; children: Cathy, Laurie, Deirdre, Richard, Joseph, Gillian. BA summa cum laude, St. John's U., N.Y.C., 1957; MA, Brown U., 1960; PhD, N.Y. U., 1967. Instr. Coll. New Rochelle, N.Y., 1958-61, St. John's U., 1961-63; instr. to prof. Long Island U., Brookville, N.Y., 1963—; exec. sec Long Island British Studies Group, 1974-80. Author: David Garrick, 1985, Two Burlettas of Kane O'Hara, 1987, The Eighteenth Century English Burletta, 1999; contbr. numerous articles to profl. jours. Assoc. Danforth Found., 1976-92. Grantee Danforth Found., 1965, 66, 67; NEH, 1993, 94; fellow Am. Coun. Learned Societies, 1972, Nat. Woodrow Wilson Fellowship Found., 1957. Mem. MLA, Am. Soc. Theatre Rsch. (exec. com. 1973—, editor newsletter 1973-94, archivist 1980—), Soc. Theatre Rsch., Am. Soc. 18th Century Studies. Home: 5 Edwin Ln Huntington NY 11743-2332 Office: Long Island Univ CW Post Campus Greenvale NY 11548

DIRCKS, RICHARD JOSEPH, English language educator, writer; b. N.Y.C., May 22, 1926; s. Curt and Georgette Elizabeth (Middleton) D; m. Phyllis Ann Toal, Aug. 17, 1963; children: Cathy, Laurie, Deirdre, Richard, Gillian, Joseph. BA, Fordham U., 1949, MA, 1950, PhD, 1961. Asst. prof. Seton Hall U., South Orange, N.J., 1950-56; from asst. prof. to prof. English, St. John's U., Jamaica, N.Y., 1956—, chmn. dept., 1964-67, 94-95, assoc. dean grad. sch., 1973-75, dir. humanities rsch. ctr., 1975-77; departmental rep., St. John's Coll., 1962-64; lectr. in writing Fordham Sch. Adult Edn., 1963-69; cons. on writing Union Carbide Corp., N.Y.C., 1968-69. Author: Richard Cumberland, 1976, Henry Fielding, 1983; co-author: Functional English, 1959; editor: Letters of Richard Cumberland, 1988, The Unpublished Plays of Richard Cumberland, 2 vols., 1991-92, The Memoirs of Richard Cumberland, 1999; contbr. numerous articles to profl. jours. With U.S. Army, 1944-45. Shell Rsch. Grantee, 1967; Assoc. Danforth Found., 1978-86. Mem. MLA, Am. Soc. 18th-Century Studies, Am. Soc. For Theatre Rsch. Avocations: sailing, photography. Home: 5 Edwin Ln Huntington NY 11743-2332 Office: St John's U 8000 Utopia Pkwy Jamaica NY 11432-1343

DIRDA, MICHAEL, book critic; b. Lorain, Ohio, 1948; m. Marian Peck; children: Christopher, Michael, Nathaniel. BA in English with highest honors, Oberlin Coll., 1970; MA, Cornell U., 1974, PhD in Comparative Lit., 1977. Sr. asst. editor, writer Washington Post Book World, 1978—. Author: Caring for Your Books. Recipient Pulitzer Prize for disting. criticism, 1993. Mem. Nat. Book Critics Circle (former bd. dirs.), hon. Doctor of Letters, Wash. Coll., 1997. Office: Washington Post 1150 15th St NW Washington DC 20071-0002

DIRECTOR, STEPHEN WILLIAM, electrical and computer engineering educator, academic administrator; b. Bklyn., June 28, 1943; s. Murray and Lillian (Brody) D.; m. Lorraine Schwartz, June 20, 1965; children: Joshua, Kimberly, Cynthia, Deborah. BS, SUNY, Stony Brook, 1965; MS, U. Calif., Berkeley, 1967, PhD, 1968. Prof. elec. engring. U. Fla., Gainesville, 1968-77; vis. scientist IBM Rsch. Labs., Yorktown Heights, N.Y., 1974-75; prof. elec. and computer engring. Carnegie-Mellon U., Pitts., 1977-96, U.A. and Helen Whitaker Univ. prof. electrical and computer engring., 1980-96, prof. computer sci., 1981-96, head dept. elec. and computer engring., 1982-91; univ. prof., 1992-93; dean Carnegie Inst. Tech. Carnegie-Mellon U., Pitts., 1991-96; Robert J. Vlasic Dean of Engring. U. Mich., Ann Arbor, 1996—, prof. elec. engring. and computer science, 1996—; cons. Intel Corp., Santa Clara, Calif., 1977-84, Digital Equipment Corp., Hudson, Mass., 1982-88, Calma Corp., 1985-86, Mentor Graphics Corp., 1988-91; sci. adv. bd. Nextwave, Inc., 1990—; bd. dirs. OrCAD, Inc., 1991—, CAD Framework Initiative, 1991-93, Aspect Devel. Corp., 1991-92; tech. adv. bd. JW2 Inc., 1991— LSI Logic 1994—, Autogate Logic, 1994—; sr. research fell. IC2 Inst, 1996—, bd. dirs. Accredation Bd. for Engring. and Tech., Inc. 1996—; sr. cons. editor McGraw-Hill Book Co., N.Y.C., 1976—; dir. Rsch. Ctr. Computer-Aided Design, Pitts., 1982-89. Author: Introduction to System Theory, 1972, Circuit Theory, 1975, VLSI Design for Manufacturing: Yield Enhancement, 1989, Principles of VLSI System Planning: A Framework for Conceptual Design, 1991; editor: Computer-Aided Design, 1974; co-editor: Advances in Computer-Aided Design for VLSI: vol. 8, Statistical Approach to VLSI, 1994. Recipient Frederick Emmons Terman award Am. Soc. Engring. Edn., 1976; named Distinguished Alumnus, SUNY, Stony Brook, 1984; Aristotle Award Semiconductor Rsch. Corp., 1996, Outstanding Alumnus award in Elec. Engring. U. Calif., Berkeley, 1996. Fellow IEEE (W.R.G. Baker prize 1979, Centennial medal 1984, Edn. Soc. Outstanding Achievement award 1995, Edn. medal 1998); mem. NAE, IEEE Cirs. and Sys. Soc. (pres. 1981, assoc. editor jour. 1973-75, best paper award 1970, 85, 89, 92, soc. award 1992). Office: Univ Michigan Coll Engring Robert H Lurie Engring Ctr Ann Arbor MI 48109

DIRENZO, GORDON JAMES, sociologist, psychologist, educator; b. North Attleboro, Mass., July 19, 1934; s. Santo and Giulia (Petti) DiR.; m. Mary Kathleen Ryan, July 6, 1968; children: Maria Giulia, Chiara Veronica, Marco Santo. BA, U. Notre Dame, 1956, MA, 1957, PhD, 1963; postgrad., Harvard U., 1959, Columbia U., 1963-65, U. Colo., 1964. Lic. psychologist, Del.; cert. social psychologist. Instr. Coll. of St. Rose, Albany, N.Y., 1957-59; Instr. U. Portland, Oreg., 1961-62; asst. prof. Fairfield (Conn.) U., 1962-66; asso. prof. Ind. U., South Bend, 1966-70; prof. sociology U. Del., Newark, 1970—; mem. faculty Siena Coll., Albany (N.Y.) Med. Center, 1958-59, U. Notre Dame, 1960-61, Coll. White Plains, 1963-65, Bklyn. Coll., 1965, Western Conn. State U., 1964; mem. faculty SUNY, Stony Brook, 1980, Cortland, 1966; affiliate mem. med. and dental staff Med. Center Del., Wilmington, 1976-80, St. Francis Hosp., Wilmington, 1980—, Northeastern Hosp., Phila., 1982-85, Rockford Ctr., Wilmington, 1995—; pres. Behavior Cons., Newark, Del., 1975—; dir. Sociol. Cons. Group, North Attleboro, Mass., 1963-75; Fulbright-Hays prof. U. Rome, 1968-69, U. Bologna, Italy, 1980-81; mem., sec., bd. examiners psychologists State of Del., 1991-99. Author: Personality, Power and Politics, 1967, Concepts, Theory and Explanation in the Behavioral Sciences, 1966, Personality and Politics, 1974, We, the People: American Character and Social Change, 1977, Sociological Perspectives, 1987, Human Social Behavior, 1990, The Social Individual, 1996, Personality and Society, 1998; contbr. articles to profl. jours. Recipient Disting. Svc. award Am. Assn. Family Practice, 1980, 82, 84, Excellence in Teaching award U. Del., 1991; fellow U. Notre Dame, 1959-60, Italian Ministry Edn., 1960, NSF, 1964; grantee Ford Found., 1960, NEH, 1975, Del. Inst. Med. Edn. and Rsch., 1975. Fellow Am. Sociol. Assn. (diplomate); mem. APA, AAUP, AAAS, Assn. Behavioral Scis. in Med. Edn., Soc. Personality and Social Psychology, Soc. for Advancement Social Psychology (bd. dirs. 1988-94), Am.-Italian Hist. Assn. (nat. exec. council 1977-80), Fulbright Alumni Assn., Internat. Sociol. Assn., Clin. Sociology Assn., Internat. Soc. Polit. Psychology (charter), Soc. Psychologists in Medicine, Internat. Polit. Sci. Assn., Soc. for Study Social Problems, Soc. Psychol. Study Social Issues, Eastern Sociol. Soc., Am. Sociol. Assn., Alpha Kappa Delta. Home: 28 Deer Run Little Baltimore Farms Newark DE 19711 Office: U Del Dept Sociology Newark DE 19716

DIRIENZO, MARGARET HELEN, nursing administrator; b. Tampa, Fla., May 17, 1962; d. Raymond Thomas and Helen Irene (Fortier) Connors; m. James Basilio Dirienzo, Sept. 21, 1984; children: James, Kaitlyn. AAS, Pace U., 1982, BSN, 1985. Cert. emergency nurse; ACLS, PALS; RN, Pa. From staff nurse to asst. mgr. emergency dept. Danbury (Conn.) Hosp., 1982-92; patient care mgr. asst. ER Geisinger Med. Ctr., Danville, Pa., 1992-94; sr. mgr. customer access svcs. Penn State Geisinger Health Sys., Danville, 1994-99; clin. mgr. Call Ctr., Seton Healthcare Sys., Austin, 1999—; acting trauma coord. Danbury Hosp., 1991-92. Mem. Emergency Nurses Assn., Assn. Ambulatory Care Nurses. Democrat. Roman Catholic. Avocations: cross stitch, camping, travel, craft making. Home: 1553 Jerusalem Dr Round Rock TX 78664 Office: Penn State Geisinger Tel-A-Nurse Svc Academy Dr Danville PA 17822-1518

DIRKS, KENNETH RAY, pathologist, medical educator, army officer; b. Newton, Kans., Feb. 11, 1925; s. Jacob Kenneth and Ruth Viola (Penner) D.; m. Betty Jean Worsham, June 9, 1946; children: Susan Jan, Jeffrey Mark, Deborah Anne, Timothy David, Melissa Jane. M.D., Washington U., St. Louis, 1947. Diplomate: Am. Bd. Pathology. Rotating intern St. Louis City Hosp., 1948, asst. resident in gen. surgery, 1948-49; resident in pathology VA Hosp., Jefferson Barracks, Mo., 1951-53; resident in pathology, asst. chief lab. service VA Hosp., Indpls., 1953-54; resident in pathology Letterman Army Hosp., San Francisco, 1956-57; fellow in tropical medicine and parasitology La. State U., Central Am., 1958; asst. in pathology Washington U. Sch. Medicine, 1952-53; asst. chief lab. service VA Hosp., Jefferson Barracks, 1953; instr. pathology U. Ind. Med. Center, Indpls., 1953-54; commd. capt. M.C. U.S. Army, 1954, advanced through grades to maj. gen., 1976; dir. research Med. Research and Devel. Command, Washington, 1968-69; dep. comdr. Med. Research and Devel. Command, 1969-71, comdr., 1973-76; asst. surgeon gen., research and devel. U.S. Army, 1973-76; dep. comdr., comdr. Med. Research Inst. Infectious Diseases, Ft. Detrick, Frederick, Md., 1972-73; comdr. Fitzsimons Army Med. Center, Denver, 1976-77; supt. Acad. Health Scis., Ft. Sam Houston, Tex., 1977-80; assoc. prof. to prof. pathology and lab. medicine Coll. Med. Tex. A&M U., College Station, 1980-95; interim head dept. Coll. Medicine, Tex. A&M U., College Station, 1990-91; prof. emeritus pathology, 1995—; asst. dean coll. Coll. Medicine, Tex. A&M U., College Station, 1985-88; dir. dept. student health svcs. and A.P. Beutel Health Ctr. Tex. A&M U., College Station, 1989-95; dir. student health svcs. emeritus, 1995—. Contbr. articles to med. jours. Decorated D.S.M., Legion of Merit with oak leaf cluster, Meritorious Service medal, Army Commendation medal with oak leaf cluster. Fellow Coll. Am. Pathologists, Internat. Acad. Pathology. Address: 2513 Oak Cir Bryan TX 77802-2009 *1) Know your job and work hard. 2) Respect all persons. 3) Be candid and honest always. 4)Persevere in the face of adversity. 5) Love God, country, and other people. 6) Help others.*

DIRKS, LEE EDWARD, newspaper executive; b. Indpls., Aug. 4, 1935; s. Raymond Louis and Virginia Belle (Wagner) D.; m. Barbara Dee Nutt, June 16, 1956 (div. Jan. 1985); children: Stephen Merle, Deborah Virginia, David Louis. B.A., DePauw U., 1956; M.A., Fletcher Sch. Law and Diplomacy, 1957. Reporter Boston Globe, 1957, Nat. Observer, Washington, 1962-65; news editor Nat. Observer, 1966-68; securities analyst specializing in newspaper stocks Dirks Bros., Ltd., Washington, 1969-71, Delafield, Childs, Inc., Washington, 1971-75, C.S. McKee & Co., Washington, 1975-76; asst. to pres. Detroit Free Press, 1976-77, v.p., gen. mgr., 1977-80; chmn. Dirks, Van Essen & Assoc., Santa Fe, N.Mex., 1980—. Author: Religion in Action, 1965; pub.: Newspaper Newsletter, 1970-76. Bd. dirs. Nat. Ghost Ranch Found., Santa Fe, 1973-97, Santa Fe Opera, 1998— . Served to capt. USAF, 1957-61. Named Religion Writer of Yr. Religious Newswriters Assn., 1964. Fellow Religious Pub. Relations Council; mem. Phi Beta Kappa, Lambda Chi Alpha. Unitarian. Clubs: Nat. Press (Washington); Oakland Hills (Detroit); Las Campanas (Santa Fe). Home: 11 E Arrowhead Cir Santa Fe NM 87501-8248 Office: 119 E Marcy St Ste 100 Santa Fe NM 87501-2046

DIRKS, LESLIE CHANT, communications and electronics company executive; b. New Ulm, Minn., Mar. 7, 1936; s. Emerald Francis and Eva Gay (Fabianke) D.; m. Janet Church; children: Anthony, Jason, Elizabeth. BS in Physics, MIT, 1958; BS, Oxford (Eng.) U., 1960. Registered elec. engr., Calif. Instr. physics Philips Acad., Andover, Mass., 1960-61; with office directorate of Sci. & Tech. U.S. Govt., Washington, 1961-71, dir. Office of Spl. Projects., 1971-76, dep. dir. Sci. and Tech., 1976-82; corp. v.p. of research and devel. Raytheon Corp., Lexington, Mass., 1982-84; v.p. Space and Communications group Hughes Aircraft Co., El Segundo, Calif., 1984-90, ret., 1990. Recipient Nat. Security Metal Pres. U.S., 1978. Mem. Nat. Acad. Engring., Nat. Research Council (mem. Army-Space com. 1986—). Unitarian. Avocations: hiking, bicycling. *

DIRKS, MIKE, golf coach; m. Susan; 1 child, David. BA in Bus. Adminstrn., Lamar U., 1985. Coach Lamar U., 1986-90, Tulane U., 1990-94; head golf coach U. Houston, 1994—. Named Coach of Yr. Metro Conference, 1994. Office: Univ Houston Athletic Dept 3100 Cullen Blvd Houston TX 77004*

DIRKS, NICHOLAS B., cultural research organization administrator/history educator. Dir. Ctr. for South & Southeast Asian Studies, U Michigan, Ann Arbor; prof. History, prof. Anthropology U Michigan, Ann Arbor; prof. anthropology and history Columbia U., N.Y.C., chmn. dept. anthropology. Office: Columbia University Dept Anthropology New York NY 10027*

DIRKSEN, RICHARD WAYNE, canon precentor, organist, choirmaster; b. Freeport, Ill., Feb. 8, 1921; s. Richard Watson and Maude (Logemann) D.; m. Joan Milton Shaw (dec. 1995); children: Richard Shaw, Geoffrey Paul, Laura Gail, Mark Christopher. C.O.C., Peabody Conservatory, 1942; D.F.A. (hon.), George Washington U., 1981; Mus.D. (hon.), Mount Union Coll., 1986. Asst. organist-choirmaster Washington Cathedral, 1942-47, assoc. organist-choirmaster, 1947-69, dir. program, 1964-69, precentor, 1969-91, organist-choirmaster, 1977-88, ret., 1991, canon precentor emeritus, 1993—. Composer sacred music and secular operettas. Served to sgt. U.S. Army, 1942-45. Named Disting. Alumnus Peabody Conservatory, 1980. Mem. ASCAP, Am. Guild Organists, Assn. Anglican Musicians, Rock Creek Golf Club. Episcopalian.

DIROSA, STEVEN JOSEPH, primary and secondary school educator; b. Phila.; s. Joseph and Patricia (Bealer) D. BS, Temple U., 1989; MS in Ednl. Technologies, Rosemont Coll., 1996. Cert. elem., secondary tchr., Pa. Tchr., dept. head Chester-Upland (Pa.) Sch. Dist., 1989—; tech. dir. STEP Summer Student Prog., Chester, Pa., 1990-95; intramural sports asst. dir. Chester-Upland Sch. Dist., 1993-96. Author: Travel Tales (Billy the Shoe), 1989 (best children's short story award Pa. Tchr. Pages 1990). Recipient Pres.' award Pres.' Acad. Excellence Com., Rosemont, Pa., 1992, outstanding svc. award S.E. Pa. STEP Prog., Chester, Pa., 1994. Fellow Smithsonian Instrn.; mem. World Wildlife Fund, Nat. Coun. Tchrs. of Math, Sierra Club. Home: 232 Talbot Dr Broomall PA 19008-3729 Office: Chester-Upland Sch Dist Main St Sch 704 Main St Brookhaven PA 19015-2608

DIRR, JOHN CHARLES (JACK DIRR), television producer and director; b. Queens, N.Y., Aug. 4, 1949; s. Peter George and Marie Christine (Haggarty) D.; m. Barbara Wianecki, June 3, 1972; children: Pamela, Michael, Robert. AA, Thomas A. Edison Coll., Trenton, N.J., 1978. Producer, dir. Bergen Community Coll., Paramus, N.J., 1972—, adj. instr., 1981-85; host TV series N.J. Issues, 1986-88. Producer TV series On Campus at Bergen Community College, 1989-91 (N.J. Press Club award 1990); dir. March of Dimes Telethon, Fifty Years of Achievement, 1986-87; producer, dir. fundraisers Scholastic All-Stars '88 (N.J. Press Club award 1989, 90), Scholastic All-Stars '89; dir., technician TV sports series Sports Innerview, 1989-90. Mem. Planning Bd., Bogota, N.J., 1987-89; borough liaison N.J. Film and Motion Picture Commn., Bogota, 1986-89. With U.S. Army, 1970-72. Named Prodr. of Yr. Cable TV Network N.J., 1995. Mem. NATAS, Internat. TV Assn., N.J. Edn. Assn. Roman Catholic. Avocations: avid camper, scoutmaster, youth coach. Office: Bergen Community Coll 400 Paramus Rd Paramus NJ 07652-1508

DIRUSCIO, LAWRENCE WILLIAM, advertising executive; b. Buffalo, Jan. 2, 1941; s. Guido Carmen and Mabel Ella (Bach) DiR.; m. Gloria J. Edney, Aug. 19, 1972; children: Lawrence M., Lorie P., Darryl C., Teresa M., Jack D. With various broadcast stas. and instr., adminstr. Bill Wade Sch. Radio and TV, San Diego, San Francisco, Los Angeles, 1961-69; account exec. Sta. KGB Radio, San Diego, 1969, gen. sales mgr., 1970-72; pres. Free Apple Advt., San Diego, 1972-94, Fin. Mgmt. Assocs., Inc., San Diego, 1979-84, Self-Pub. Ptnrs., San Diego, 1981—, Media Mix Assocs. Enterprises, Inc., 1984-86; pres. Press-Courier Pub. Co., Inc., 1985-86; pres. Media Mix Advt. and Pub. Relations, 1985—, Taking Care of Bus. Pub. Co., 1990—; pres. Formula Mktg. Co., 1993. Chmn. bd. Quicksilver Enterprises,

Inc., A Public Corp., 1992-93; lectr., writer on problems of small bus. survival. Served with USN, 1958-60. Five Emmy nominations for T.V. commercial writing and prodn. Mem. Nat. Acad. TV Arts and Scis. Democrat. Roman Catholic. Office: Media Mix Advt and Pub Rels 726 W Kalmia St San Diego CA 92101-1311

DIRVIN, GERALD VINCENT, retired consumer products company executive; b. Phila., Mar. 28, 1937; s. Vincent A. and Mary (Fitch) D.; m. Polly Burnett, June 27, 1959; children: John, David, Barbara. BA, Hamilton Coll., Clinton, N.Y., 1959. With Procter & Gamble Co., 1959-94, sales mgt., then v.p. coffee divsn., 1975-80; sr. v.p. Procter & Gamble Co., Cin., 1980-89, exec. v.p., 1990-94, dir., 1981-94; bd. dirs. Fifth Third Bank and Bancorp., Cintas Corp. Chmn. bd. trustees Cin. Med. Ctr. Fund; vice-chmn., bd. trustees Hamilton Coll., Johnny Bench Scholarship Fund. Mem. Comml. Club, Plantation Golf Club, Commonwealth Club, Camargo Club, Pine Valley Golf Club (bd. dirs.), Double Eagle Golf Club, Confrerei des Chevaliers du Tastevin, Pablo Creek Golf Club, Ponte Vedra Club. Republican. Roman Catholic.

DISAIA, PHILIP JOHN, gynecologist, obstetrician, radiology educator; b. Providence, Aug. 14, 1937; s. George and Antoinette (Vastano) DiS.; divorced; children: John P., Steven D.; m. Patricia June; children: Dominic J., Vincent J. BS cum laude, Brown U., 1959; MD cum laude, Tufts U., 1963; MD (hon.), U. Genoa, Italy, 1999. Diplomate Am. Bd. Ob-Gyn. (examiner 1975—, bd. dirs. 1994, v.p. bd. dirs. 1997—), Am. Bd. Gynecologic Oncology (bd. dirs. 1987—). Intern Yale U. Sch. Medicine, New Haven Hosp., 1963-64, resident in ob-gyn., 1964-67, instr. ob-gyn., 1966-67; fellow in gynecologic oncology U. Tex. M.D. Anderson Hosp. and Tumor Inst., Houston, 1969-70, NIH sr. fellow, 1969-70, instr. ob-gyn., 1969-71; asst. prof. ob-gyn. and radiology U. So. Calif. Sch. Medicine, L.A., 1971-74, assoc. prof., 1974-77; prof., chmn. dept. ob-gyn. U. Calif., Irvine Med. Ctr. Calif. Coll. Medicine, 1977-88, prof., 1977—, prof. radiology, radiation therapy div., 1978—, assoc. vice chancellor for health scis. Irvine Coll. Medicine, 1987-89, Dorothy Marsh chair of reproductive biology, 1989—, dep. dir. cancer ctr., 1989—, pres. med. staff, 1993-97; pres. UCI Clin. Practice Group, 1994—; dir. div. gynecol. oncology Am. Bd. Obstetrics & Gynecology, 1995—, bd. dirs., 1994—; bd. dirs. U. Calif. Irvine Med. Ctr., 1995, chair health sys. steering com., 1995, chair health sys. capital planning group, 1995, health sys. bd. dirs., 1995; clin. enterprise adv. coun. to pres. U. Calif., 1995; academic planning task force U. Calif. Irvine, 1994, continuing med. edn. com., 1991-94; cancer liaison commn. on cancer Am. Coll. Surgeons, 1981-94; bd. dirs., dir. at large Am. Cancer Soc., 1985—; clin. prof. dept. ob-gyn. U. Nev. Sch. Medicine, Reno, 1985—; chmn. site visit team for surgery br. Nat. Cancer Inst. NIH, 1983, subcom. surg. oncology rsch. devel., 1982-83, mem. sci. counselors div. cancer treatment, 1979-83; mem. gov.'s adv. coun. on cancer State of Calif., 1980-85; vis. prof., lectr., speaker various sci. meetings, confs., courses. Author: (with E.J. Quilligan) Ovarian Tumors, Current Diagnosis, 1974, (with others) Synopsis of Gynecologic Oncology, 1975, (with W.T. Creasman) Clinical Gynecologic Oncology, 1980, 4th edit. 1993, 5th edit. 1997; contbr. numerous articles to profl. jours., book chpts.; assoc. editor Gynecologic Oncology, Endocurietherapy/Hyperthermia Oncology, Danforth's Textbook of Obstetrics & Gynecology; mem. editorial adv. bd. Am. Jour. Reproductive Immunology, Cancer Clinical Trials, The Female Patient, New Trends in Gynecology and Obstetrics (Italian publ.); reviewer Am. Jour. Ob-Gyn., Med. and Pediatric Oncology, New Eng. Jour. Medicine, Ob-Gyn. jour., Cancer; physician cons. Patient Care Standards jour.; sci. adv. bd. The Clin. Cancer Letter. Recipient Disting. Alumnus award M.D. Anderson Hosp. and Tumor Inst. U. Tex., 1980, Silver Apple award U. Calif. Med. Students, 1983, Lauds and Laurels Profl. Achievement award U. Calif. Alumni Assn., 1983, Hubert Haussel's award Long Beach Meml. Hosp., 1983, Dist. Faculty Lectureship award for Teaching, U. Calif. Irvine Acad. Senate, 1993-94, also various rsch. awards. Fellow Am. Coll. Obstetricians and Gynecologists (com. on human rsch. for cancer 1979—, chmn. 1984—, chmn. subcom. on gynecologic oncology 1984-85, prolog editorial and adv. com. 1986—, v.p. 1997-99, various others), ACS (bd. govs. 1998—), Commn. on Cancer Liaison, Western Assn. Gynecologic Oncologists (founder 1971, pres. 1978-79), Am. Gynecol. and Obstet. Soc. (exec. coun. 1986—), Am. Gynecologic Soc., Pacific Coast Ob/Gyn Soc., South Atlantic Assn. Obstetricians and Gynecologists (hon.); mem. AMA, Am. Cancer Soc. (bd. dirs. L.A. County unit 1975-77, Orange County 1979, unit pres. 1993—; bd. dirs. Calif. div. 1985—, chmn. med. scientific com. 1993-94), Nat. Am. Cancer Soc. (dir.-at-large, bd. dirs. 1985—, chmn. program com. for nat. conf. 1986, vice-chmn. detection and treatment adv. group gynecol. cancer 1993-94, active in others), Am. Coll. Radiology (commn. on cancer 1984-85), Am. Soc. Clin. Oncologists, Soc. Gynecologic Oncologists (exec. coun. 1975-80, pres. 1982-83), Internat. Gynecologic Oncology Cancer Soc., Italian Soc. Ob-Gyn. (Camillo Golgi prof. U. Brescia 1991), Calif. Med. Assn., other profl. orgns., Alpha Omega Alpha. Office: U Calif Irvine Med Ctr 101 The City Dr S Rm 403 Orange CA 92868-3201

DISALLE, MICHAEL DANNY, secondary education educator; b. Denver, May 16, 1945; s. Michael and Agnes Marie (Kulik) DiS.; m. Marikaye Lucas, June 22, 1968; children: Katharine Marie, Kristin Jean, Michael Charles, Matthew Gregory. BA, Regis Coll., 1967; MEd, Lesley Coll., 1992. Cert. tchr., Colo. Tchr. Assumption Sch., Welby, Colo., 1968-74, Cherry Creek High Sch., Englewood, Colo., 1974-95; poet, writer, 1995—. Author: (computer program/tchr.'s guide) Adventures of Tom Sawyer, 1983, One Day in the Life of Ivan Denisovich, 1984. Asst. den leader Boy Scouts Am., Aurora, Colo., 1988-89. Mem. ASCD, Nat. Coun. Tchrs. of English, Nat. Scholastic Press Assn., Journalism Edn. Assn., Colo. Lang. Arts Soc., Colo. State High Sch. Press Assn., Columbia Scholastic Press Assn. Avocations: fly fishing, gardening, cooking, fly tying.

DI SALVATORE, CHRIS ALLEN, mechanical engineer; b. Bangor, Maine, Oct. 7, 1960; s. Colombo and Margaret (Kane) Di S. BS in Mech. Engring., U. Maine, Orono, 1982. Mech. engr. Singer Kearfott Divsn., Wayne, N.J., 1982-84; sr. engr. Northrop Corp., Hawthorne, Calif., 1984-91; design engr., mgr. Control Micro Sys., Orlando, Fla., 1995-96; cons., 1989—. Achievements include conceptual design and engineering of hardware for "on-th-fly" galvonometric low-inertia scanning laser marking system; component design for laser gyroscope navigation systems contributing to further advancement in laser navigation accuracy; development of computer aided three dimension concept design, lumped parameter thermal analysis and finite element structural analysis for various electronic systems with applications for missile guidance systems, laser weapon systems, electronic countermeasure systems, military land system electronics, electronic display systems, military, civil and commercial satellite electronics, and locomotive brake system electronics. Home: PO Box 2193 Pinellas Park FL 33780-2193

DI SALVO, NICHOLAS ARMAND, dental educator, orthodontist; b. N.Y.C., Nov. 2, 1920; s. Frank and Mary (Ruberto) DiS.; m. Pauline Rose Pluta, June 2, 1945; children—Allan, Donald. B.S., CCNY, 1942; D.D.S., Columbia U., 1945, Ph.D. in Physiology, 1952, cert. in orthodontics, 1957. Diplomate Am. Bd. Orthodontics. Fellow Inst. Dental Research, Columbia U., 1950-52; instr. physiology Coll. Physicians and Surgeons, Columbia U., 1948-51, asst. prof. physiology, 1952-57, assoc., 1957-58, prof. dentistry, 1958-87, dir. orthodontics, 1957-87, prof. emeritus dentistry, 1987—; attending dentist Presbyterian Hosp., N.Y.C., 1975-87, cons. emeritus dentistry, 1987—; cons. N.Y. State Dept. Health, 1970—, VA, N.Y.C., 1975, Project/HOPE/Egypt, Alexandria and Cairo, 1976, Nat. Def. Med. Ctr., Taipei, Taiwan, 1982. Contbg. editor book chpts. Contbr. articles to profl. jours. Pres., Hartsdale-Fels Civic Assn., 1960-66. Served to lt. USNR, 1945-50. Recipient Disting. Service award Orthodontic Alumni Soc. Columbia U., 1973; fellow 8th Inst. Advanced Edn. in Dental Research. Mem. Am. Assn. Orthodontists (del. 1970-76), Northeastern Soc. Orthodontists (pres. 1974-75, Disting. Svc. award 1995), Angle Soc. of Orthodontists (pres. 1977-79), Internat. Soc. Craniofacial Biology (pres. 1965-66). Republican. Roman Catholic. Home: 145 Princeton Dr Hartsdale NY 10530-2010 Office: Columbia U Dental Sch 630 W 168th St New York NY 10032-3702

DISANDRO, LINDA ANITA, counselor; b. Phila., Aug. 23, 1950; d. Anthony and Frances Helen (Lopinski) D. BA, Holy Family Coll., 1972. Exec. sec. dept. radiology Episcopal Hosp., Phila., 1972-77; sr. sssssssec. dept. radiology Hosp. U. Pa., Phila., 1977-89; faculty Cheltenham Township Adult Evening Sch., Wyncote, Pa., 1982-84; admissions counselor Holy Family Coll., Phila., 1989-96, assoc. dir. admissions, 1996-98; dir. coll. counseling St. Basil Acad., Fox Chase Manor, Pa., 1998—. Mem. AAUW, Nat. Assn. Coll. Admission Counselling (co-chair Phila. Nat. Coll. Fair 1995-97), Pa. Assn. Secondary Sch. and Coll. Admissions Counselors, Pa. Assn. Cath. Colls. Admission Officers (adv. bd. 1991-98), Phila. Area Cath. Colls. (adv. bd./transp. coord., 1991-98), Polish Am. Congress, Assoc. Polish Home Phila. Democrat. Roman Catholic. Avocations: arts and crafts, travel, theater. Home: 4542 Edgemont St Philadelphia PA 19137-2002 Office: Saint Basil Acad 711 Fox Chase Rd Jenkintown PA 19046-4197

DISARCINA, GARY THOMAS, baseball player; b. Malden, Mass., Nov. 19, 1967. BS, U. Mass. Shortstop Calif. Angels (now Anaheim Angels), 1989—. Named to Am. League All-Star Team, 1995. Office: Anaheim Angels 2000 Gene Autry Way Anaheim CA 92806-6100*

DISBROW, MICHAEL RAY, aerospace supplier company executive; b. Highland Park, Mich., June 12, 1959; s. Arthur Ray and Vivian (Childress) D.; m. Lynn Marie Lodyga, July 14, 1984; children: Matthew Ray, Nicole Marie. BSME, Purdue U., 1981; MBA, Harvard U., 1986. Co-op. assoc. BFGoodrich Co., Akron, Ohio, 1978-81; axle engr. Bendix Automotive Brake Sys. divsn. Allied Signal, Inc., South Bend, Ind., 1982-83, R & D engr., 1983-84, disc brake engr., 1984, mgr. strategic planning, 1986-87, mgr. Far East bus. planning, 1987-88, mgr. N.Am. joint venture programs, 1988; internal cons. Fram divsn. Allied Signal, Inc., East Providence, R.I., 1985; dir. svc. ctr. Hartzell Propeller, Inc., Piqua, Ohio, 1988-94, v.p. Dornier 328 program, 1994-95, v.p. product support, 1995-97, v.p. mktg. and customer support, 1997—; mem. indsl. adv. com., dept. aviation tech. Purdue U., 1996—. Prodn. advisor Jr. Achievement of Michiana, South Bend, 1982-83, exec. advisor, 1983-84; mem. bus. adv. bd. Oakwood (Ohio) City Bd. Edn., 1996—; bd. dirs. Miami County YMCA, 1997—, Jr. Achievement of Dayton, 1998—. Named Prodn. Advisor of Yr., Jr. Achievment of Michiana, 1983; fellow The Little Family Found., 1984, 85, Allied Signal Inc., 1984-86. Mem. Regional Airline Assn. (assoc. mem. coun. 1996—), Tau Beta Pi. Republican. Methodist. Home: 820 Shafor Blvd Dayton OH 45419-3450 Office: Hartzell Propeller Inc One Propellar Pl Piqua OH 45356

DISCEPOLA, NUNZIO (NICK), Canadian government official; b. Italy, Nov. 27, 1949. BS, McGill U., MBA. Mem. Parliament, Ottawa, Ont., Can., 1993—. Office: Ho of Commons, 498 W Block, Ottawa, ON Canada K1A 0A6*

DISCH, THOMAS M(ICHAEL), author; b. Des Moines, Iowa, Feb. 2, 1940; s. Felix H. and Helen Margaret (Gilbertson) D. Student, NYU, 1959-62. Drama critic The Nation, N.Y.C., 1987-91, N.Y. Daily News, 1992-93; artist-in-residence Coll. of William and Mary, 1996. Author: The Genocides, 1965, Mankind Under the Leash, 1966, The House That Fear Built, 1966, Echo Round His Bones, 1967, Black Alice, 1968, Camp Concentration, 1968, The Prisoner, 1969, 334, 1974, Clara Reeve, 1975, Getting Into Death and Other Stories, 1976 (O'Henry prize 1975), On Wings of Song, 1979 (John W. Campbell Meml. award 1980), Xmas, 1979 (O'Henry prize 1979), Neighboring Lives, 1981, The Businessman: A Tale of Terror, 1984, Amnesia, 1985, The M.D.: A Horror Story, 1991, The Priest: A Gothic Romance, 1994, The Dreams our Stuff is Made of: How Science Fiction Conquered the World, 1998, The Sub: A Study in Witchcraft, 1999, (juvenile) A Tale of Dan de Lioni, 1986, The Brave Little Toaster: A Bedtime Story For Small Appliances, 1986 (Brit. Sci. Fiction award 1981), The Brave Little Toaster Goes to Mars, 1988, (poetry) The Right Way To Figure Plumbing, 1972, ABCDEFG HIJKLM NOPQRST UVWXYZ, 1981, Orders of the Retina, 1982, Burn This, 1972, Here I Am, There You Are, Where Were We, 1984, Yes Let's: New and Selected Poems, 1989, Dark Verses and Light, 1991 (story collections) One Hundred and Two H-Bombs and Other Science Fiction Stories, 1966, Under Compulsion, 1968, Getting Into Death: The Best Short Story or Thomas M. Disch, 1973, The Early Science Fiction Stories of Thomas M. Disch, 1977, Fundamental Disch, 1980, The Man Who Had No Idea, 1982, (short stories) Ringtime, 1983, Torturing Mr. Amberwell, 1985, The Castle of Indolence, 1995; scriptwriter: (TV episode) Miami Vice, 1987; editor: The Ruins of the Earth: An Anthology of Stories of the Immediate Future, Bad Moon Rising: An Anthology of Political Foreboding, 1975, New Constellations: An Anthology of Tomorrow's Mythologies, 1976, Strangerness: A Collection of Curious Tales, 1977; contbr.: numerous poems and articles, lit. criticism to publs. including Poetry; libretto opera The Fall of the House of Usher, Frankenstein; dramatic adaptation Ben Hur, 1989, The Cardinal Detoxes, 1990. Recipient Michael J. Braude award Am. Acd. Arts and Letters, 1999. Mem. PEN, Writer's Guild East.

DISCORFANO, SHARON MARIE, English literature educator; b. Hackensack, N.J., July 1, 1970; d. Kenneth and Sharon (Latour) D. BA in English, Rice U., 1992; MA in English, Georgetown U., 1994. Educator Austin (Tex.) C.C., 1995, St. Stephen's Sch., Austin, 1995-96, Episcopal H.S., Houston, 1996-97, St. David's Sch., N.Y.C., 1997—; copy-editor Disney Press-Hyerion Books, N.Y.C., 1994. Author: From There to Here, 1997; author of poetry. Recipient Melville Study award NEH, 1996, Common Ground Study award NEH/Duke Energy Corp., Houston, 1997. Mem. Nat. Coun. Tchrs. English, Phi Beta Kappa. Avocations: singer, choreographer, dancer. Office: St Davids Sch 12 E 89th St New York NY 10028-1327

DISERAFINO, RENEÉ MARIE, elementary education educator; b. Jan. 3, 1957. BS, Gwynedd-Mercy Coll., 1979. Tchr. 1st and 2d grades Royal Palm Acad., Naples, Fla.; tchr. 4th grade St. Francis Xavier Sch., Newark. Home: 28996 Seton Ct Bonita Springs FL 34134

DISERIO, FRANK JOSEPH, pharmaceutical company executive, consultant; b. N.Y.C., Oct. 3, 1931; s. Anthony and Catherine (Solimando) DiS.; m. Lauretta Brunck, 1954 (div. May 1984); children: Anthony Mark, Francis Joseph, Paul James; m. Marjatta Niemioja, Oct. 19, 1985). BS, NYU, 1963; MBA, Fairleigh Dickinson U., 1970; PhD, Union Inst., 1979. Ptnr. Foam Age Lounge, Inc. and Dawn W.W. Co., N.Y.C., 1956-59; from sales rep. to clin. rsch. dir. Sandoz Pharmaceuticals, Inc., East Hanover, N.J., 1959-80, dir. CNS med. rsch., 1985-90; exec. dir. clin. rsch., head OTC/analgesia clin. rsch. dept. Sandoz Rsch. Inst., East Hanover, 1988-95; pharm. devel. cons. Morristown, N.J., 1995—; assoc. prof. U. Medicine & Dentistry N.J. Sch. Osteopathic Medicine, 1998—. Contbr. articles to profl. jours. Capt. USAF, 1952-56. Mem. Internat. Headache Soc., Am. Assn. for Study Headache, Am. Acad. Neurology (non-clin. assoc.), Am. Soc. Clin. Pharmacology and Therapeutics, N.Y. Acad. Scis., Rock Spring Club. Republican. Roman Catholic. Avocations: golf, travel, arts. Home: 24 Pippins Way Morristown NJ 07960-6971

DISHAROON, LESLIE BENJAMIN, retired insurance executive; b. Phila., Aug. 6, 1932; s. Theodore Lee and Sally (Oglesby) D.; m. Ann Merriwether, June 26, 1954; children: Lee Ann Disharoon Tolzmann, Beth Disharoon Morris, Martha Disharoon Wright, Carrie Disharoon Souter. B.A., Brown U., 1954; M.B.A., Columbia U., 1956. C.L.U. With Conn. Gen. Life Ins. Co., 1956-60, Conn. Mut. Life Ins. Co., Hartford, Conn., 1960-77; chmn. bd. Monumental Life Ins. Co., Balt., 1977-83; pres., dir. Monumental Corp., 1978-89, chmn. bd., 1979-89; chmn. bd. MSD&T Funds Inc., Balt.; bd. dirs. Travelers, Inc., Aegon, USA, Inc., GRC Internat. Trustee Johns Hopkins Hosp., Balt. Mem. Farmington Country Club (Charlottesville, Va.), Green Spring Valley Hunt Club (Garrison, Md.), Swan Island Club (Currituck, N.C.), Caves Valley Golf Club, Beta Gamma Sigma. Address: care Caves Valley Golf Club 2910 Blendon Rd Owings Mills MD 21117-2360

DISHER, DAVID ALAN, lawyer, geophysical research consultant; b. Chgo., Apr. 15, 1944; s. Hugh George and Beatrice Rose (Selmanovitz) D.; children: Karl Theodore, Carol Ann; m. Clara Hoffman, Sept. 17, 1991. BS in Elec. Engring., MIT, 1965, MS in Elec. Engring., 1966; JD, U. Houston, 1983. Bar: Tex. 1984, U.S. Ct. Appeals (5th cir.) 1984, U.S. Tax Ct. 1984, U.S. Dist. Ct. (so. dist.) 1986, U.S. Supreme Ct. 1987. Mathematician Shell Devel., Houston, 1966-68; sr. engr. Tex. Instruments, Stafford, 1968; dir. rsch. GEOCOM, New Orleans, 1969-70; cons., inventor Disher Consulting Svc., Houston, 1970-73; pres., chmn. bd. Seismic Programming Internat., 1973-84, 1974-84; pvt. practice law LaMarque, Tex., 1984-99; pvt. prac. Houston, TX, 1999—; v.p. St. Vincent's House, Galveston, Tex.; ind. geophys. rsch. cons. Contbr. articles to Geophysics. Mem. Concerned Citizens Galveston County, 1986—; precinct chmn., Galveston, 1980-84. Mem. ABA, NAACP, ACLU, Mainland Bar (treas.), Galveston Family Law Bar (treas.). E-mail: disherdave@aol.com; fax: 713-961-9402. Office: 3318 Mercer Houston TX 77027

DISHEROON, FRED RUSSELL, lawyer; b. Hot Springs, Ark., Nov. 21, 1931; s. Andrew Russell and Ruth Fayrene (Bearden) D.; m. Laurel Joan Picou, Apr. 1, 1961 (div. Dec. 1977); children: Terri Suzanne, John Frederick; m. Diane L. Donley, Apr. 8, 1989; 1 child, Travis William. AB, Hendrix Coll., 1953; JD, So. Meth. U., 1956; LLM in Environ. Law, George Washington U., 1976. Bar: Tex. 1956, U.S. Ct. Appeals (1st, 5th, 6th, 8th, 9th, 10th, 11th D.C. and fed. cirs.), U.S. Supreme Ct. 1964, Va. 1974. Atty. Superior Ins. Co., Dallas, 1960-64; claims atty. Sentry Ins. Co., Dallas, 1964-67; litigation counsel Stigall, Maxfield & Collier, Dallas, 1967-69; sole practice Dallas, 1969-70; asst. gen. counsel for litigation C.E. U.S. Army, Washington, 1970-75; spl. litigation counsel Dept. Justice, Washington, 1975—; instr. environ. law U. Ala.-Huntsville, 1979-82; lectr. law George Washington U., 1981-86; vis. rsch. specialist U. Calif., Davis, 1990. Co-author: Sustainable Environmental Law, 1993, Water Law, Trends, Policies and Practice, 1995; editor Southwestern Law Jour., 1955-56. Col. JAGC, USAR. Recipient numerous outstanding performance awrds U.S. Army, Dept. Justice, Sr. Exec. Svc. meritorious award Dept. Justice, 1984, Outstanding Civilian Svc. medal Dept. Army. Mem. Sr. Execs. Assn. Home: 3508 Riverwood Rd Alexandria VA 22309-2720 Office: Dept Justice Environ & Natural Resources Divsn 601 Pennsylvania Ave NW Ste 110 Washington DC 20004-2601

DISHMAN, CRIS EDWARD, professional football player; b. Louisville, Aug. 13, 1965. Student, Purdue U. Cornerback Houston Oilers, 1988-96, Washington Redskins, 1997-98, Kansas City Chiefs, 1998—. Played in Pro Bowl, 1991. Office: c/o Kansas City Chiefs One Arrowhead Dr Kansas City MO 64129*

DISHMAN, ROSE MARIE RICE, academic administrator, researcher. BS in Physics with honors, U. Mo., 1966; MS in Physics, U. Calif., Riverside, 1968, PhD, 1971; MBA, San Diego State U., 1979. Physics instr., elem. particle rsch. assoc. U. Tenn., Knoxville, Oak Ridge, 1968-71; computer programmer, analyst Signal Processing Divsn. Sys. Ctrl., Inc., Palo Alto, Calif., 1971-72; instr. physics San Diego State U., 1974-75; instr. algebra, calculus, physics San Diego C.C., Navy Tng. Ctr., Marine Corps Recruit Depot, 1975-78; instr. Grossmont Coll., San Diego, 1976-77; prof., dept. head Sch. Engring. and Applied Sci. U.S. Internat. U., San Diego, 1977-92, dean Sch. Engring. and Applied Sci., 1989-92, acting provost, v.p. acad. affairs, 1991-92; dean acad. affairs DeVry Inst. Tech., Pomona, Calif., 1992-94; pres. DeVry Inst. Tech., Pomona, Long Beach, Calif., 1994—; supr. world-wide acad. progs. including campuses in Mex., Eng., Kenya, U.S. Internat. U., primary supr. deans Schs. of Edn., Bus., Visual and Performing Arts, Human Behavior, Hotel and Restaurant Mgmt., Libr., Learning Resource Ctr., developer civil engring., engring. mgmt., electronics tech., elec. engring. progs. resulting in Engring. Accreditation Commn. of the Accreditation Bd. for Engring. and Tech. accreditation for civil engring. prog. for San Diego, London campuses, mem. curriculum coun. for all univ. progs., advisor U.S. Internat. U. Engring. Club; elected mem. Calif. Engring. Liaison Com., pres. pvt. univ. segment. Named outstanting engring. educator Am. Soc. Engring. Edn., 1989; rsch. grantee Fulbright-Hayes, 1972-73, grantee Am. Soc. Engring. Edn., NASA, 1979, Am. Soc. Engring. Edn., Dept. Energy, 1981, 82, 1984-85, Fed. Emergency Mgmt. Agy., 1983, 86. Fax: 909-623-5666. Office: DeVry Inst Tech Univ Ctr 901 Corp Ctr Dr Pomona CA 91768-2642

DISHON, CRAMER STEVEN, sales executive; b. Craven County, N.C., June 21, 1953; s. Harley Cramer and Sylvia Elaine (McCroskey) D.; m. Patricia Jenkins, June 25, 1977; children: Sarah Marie, Elizabeth Dawn. Student, Dundalk Cmty. Coll., 1972-73, Va. Western Cmty. Coll., 1985. Bonded weighmaster Am. Smelting and Refining, Balt., 1972-73; time keeper Bethlehem Erection, Balt., 1973-74; permit ironworker Ironworks Local 16, Balt., 1974-75; sanitary op. technician Back River WWTP, Balt., 1975-77; svc. technician Fairbanks Weighting Divsn., Balt., 1977-79; sales engr. Security Scale Svc., Roanoke, Va., 1979-90; sales mgr. Am. Scale and Equipment, Balt., 1990—; agt.-ins. Primercia Fin. Svcs., Balt., 1993—. Bd. dirs. Vinton Dem. Com., Roanoke, 1988-90, Highshire Cmty. Orgn., Dundalk, Md., 1990-93; chmn. CBMC, Rosedale, Md., 1993-95; chmn. deacons North Point Bapt., Balt., 1993-96; various positions Vinton Bapt. Ch., Roanoke, 1980-90; Sundy sch. dir. Woolford Meml. Bapt. Ch., Dundalk, 1990, ch. coun., budget com.; Sunday sch. dir. North Point Bapt. Ch., Dundalk, 1991-96, ch. coun., fin., budget chmn, other coms. Mem. Internat. Soc. of Weighting and Measurement (lt. gov. 1996—, chmn. Potomac divsn. 1993-95, vice chmn. Potomac divsn. 1991-93, Svc. award 1995), Gideons Internat., Christian Bus. Mens Caleb Group. Baptist. Avocations: softball player, baseball fan, church service, walking, baseball collectibles. Home: PO Box 4044 117 Highshire Ct Baltimore MD 21222-3054 Office: Am Scale & Equipment Co Inc 8839 Kelso Dr Baltimore MD 21221-3141

DISHONG, DIANE ELIZABETH, medical/surgical nurse, rehabilitation nurse; b. Massillon, Ohio, Aug. 8, 1958; d. Theodore William and Judith Anne (Hoisington) Weiand; m. Morris William Dishong, Sept. 11, 1984; 1 child, Jeffrey William. Lic. practical nurse summa cum laude, Canton Practical Nursing Sch., 1984. Cert. in CPR, first aid. LPN, office nurse Canton, Ohio; LPN Timken Mercy Med. Ctr.; staff LPN Akron (Ohio) Gen. Med. Ctr.; LPN in chem. rehab. Massillon Cmty. Hosp.; staff nurse Stark County Eye Care Clinic; owner, CEO Bill's Beer Barn Beverage Drive Thru, Inc., Canton. Recipient hwy. safety award Nat. Hwy. Council. Mem. MADD, LPN Assn. Ohio.

DISHY, BOB, actor; b. Bklyn.; s. Nathan and Amy (Barazani) D.; m. Judy Graubart; 1 child, Samuel Nathan. Ed. in drama, Syracuse U. Appeared in Broadway plays Damn Yankees, 1955, From A to Z, Flora The Red Menace, The Unknown Soldier and His Wife, Something Different, The Goodbye People, A Way of Life, The Creation of the World and Other Business, An American Millionaire, Sly Fox, Murder at the Howard Johnsons, Grown Ups, Cafe Crown, The Tenth Man; off-Broadway plays Chic, There Is A Play Tonight, Can-Can, By Jupiter, The Shawl; actor, dir. N.Y. Second City Co.; also appeared in various regional theaters, Stratford Shakespeare Festival, Mark Taper Forum, Am. Repertory Theatre, The Public Theatre, Berkshire Theatre Festival, Williamson Theatre Festival; appeared in films including The Tiger Makes Out, Lovers and Others Strangers, The Big Bus, Last Married Couple in America, First Family, Author, Author, Brighton Beach Memoirs, Critical Condition, Stay Tuned, Used People, My Boyfriend's Back, Don Juan DeMarco and the Centerfold, Jungle 2 Jungle, The Fish in the Bathtub, Judy Berlin, Labor Pains; numerous network and PBS shows including Frasier, Columbo, Law and Order, All in the Family, Mary Tyler Moore, Barney Miller, The Good Doctor, The Cafeteria; mem. TV series co. That Was The Week That Was; actor, dir. TV series Story Theatre. Served with U.S. Army 1957-59. Winner All-Army Entertainment Contest; Tony award nomination; recipient Drama Desk award, Chancellor's medal for disting. achievement Syracuse U. Mem. Acad. Motion Picture Arts and Scis.

DI SIMONE, ROBERT NICHOLAS, radiologist, educator; b. Canton, Ohio, Nov. 15, 1937; s. Nicholas Joseph and Margaret Elizabeth (Karas) DiS.; m. Patricia Anne Zwigard, June 22, 1963; children: Christopher, Angela, Elizabeth. BSc summa cum laude, Ohio State U., 1959, MSc, 1963, MD cum laude, 1963. Diplomate Am. Bd. Radiology, Am. Bd. Nuclear Medicine. Intern, fellow Johns Hopkins U. Hosp., Balt., 1963-64, asst. resident, fellow in internal medicine, 1964-65, asst. resident, fellow in radiology, 1967-70, instr., radiologist, 1970-71; dir. nuclear medicine Aultman Hosp., Canton, 1971-95, pres., med. staff, 1986-87, vice-chmn. dept. radiology, 1988-96, sec.-treas. med. staff, 1977-79; chmn. nuclear medicine sect. Northeastern Ohio Univs. Coll. Medicine, Rootstown, 1979-97; chmn. dept. radiology Northeastern Ohio Univs. Coll. of Medicine (NEOUCOM), Rootstown, 1992-93; diagnostic radiologist Aultman Health Found., Canton, Ohio, 1971—. Author: Imaging of the Endocrine System in Organ System Radiology, 1984; contbr. articles to profl. jours. Fellow Am. Coll. Radiology; mem. AMA, Soc. Nuclear Medicine, Ohio State Med. Soc. (del. 1983-95), Radiol. Soc. N.Am., Stark County Med. Soc. (trustee 1979-95, chmn.

bd. censors 1980-82, pres. 1993), Unique Club Stark County, Phi Beta Kappa, Sigma Xi, Alpha Omega Alpha, Phi Lambda Upsilon. Avocations: playing bluegrass guitar music, collecting antique old trains, traveling, hiking. Home: 2465 Oakway St NW Canton OH 44720-5886 Office: Aultman Hosp 2600 6th St SW Canton OH 44710-1702

DISINGER, JOHN FRANKLIN, natural resources educator; b. Lockport, N.Y., July 7, 1930; s. Allan Eugene and Grace (Meeks) D.; m. Norma Jean Vescovi, June 25, 1960; children: David C., Douglas A. BS, SUNY, Brockport, 1952; MEd, U. Rochester, 1960; PhD, Ohio State U., 1971. Lic. sci. tchr., N.Y. Tchr., chmn. mid. sch. sci. dept. West Irondequoit Cen. Sch. Dist., Rochester, N.Y., 1955-70; prof. Sch. Natural Resources Ohio State U., Columbus, 1971-95, prof. emeritus, 1995—, acting dir., 1988-89; faculty Ohio State U. Coll. Edn., Columbus, 1971-95; assoc. dir. Ednl. Resources Info. Ctr. Clearinghouse for Sci., Math, Environ. Edn., Columbus, 1971-91; cons. TVA, Knoxville, 1985-88, N. Am. Assn. Environ. Edn., 1993. Mem. editl. bd. The Environmentalist, 1984—; contbr. articles to profl. jours. Mem. Environ. Lit. Coun., 1996—. Recipient Pres.' award Ohio Alliance for Environ., 1984, Alumni award for disting tchg. Ohio State U., 1995. Fellow Ohio Acad. Sci.; mem. N.Am. Assn. Environ. Edn. (pres. 1985-86, Walter Jeske award 1984, Pres. award, 1991). Presbyterian. Office: Ohio State Univ Sch Natural Resources 2021 Coffey Rd Columbus OH 43210-1044

DISIPIO, ROCCO THOMAS, writer; b. Phila., Dec. 17, 1949; s. Rocco Benjamin and Rita Elizabeth Bilotti; m. Jane Heeres Newell, Nov. 1974 (div. 1981). BS in Police Adminstrn., Mich. State U., 1971. Chief tour guide Mich. State U., 1970-71; probation, parole officer Pa. Ct. Common Pleas, 1971-79; gen. mgr. Poniard Books, Inc., Broomall, Pa., 1980-82; ops. mgr. Myles Med. Equip., Ardmore, Pa., 1982-85; editor-in-chief Merit Industries, Bensalem, Pa., 1985-87; freelance writer, 1987—; prodr. Fgn. Films Enterprises, L.A., 1995—. Author: (world's 1st internet novel) Arcadia Ego, 1996 (USA Today award), (novel) Darkness. Paradise. 1997. Avocation: target shooting. Office: c/o Aleph Pub Chgo PO Box 414 Alburg VT 05440-0414

DISKANT, GREGORY L., lawyer; b. Phila., June 7, 1948; s. Robert and Eda (Grunberg) D.; m. Sandra S. Baron, Feb. 29, 1980; children: Edward, Benjamin. AB, Princeton U., 1970; JD, Columbia U., 1974. Bar: N.Y. 1975. Law clk. to Hon. J. Skelly Wright, U.S. Ct. Appeals for D.C. Cir., Washington, 1974-75; law clk. to Hon. Thurgood Marshall, U.S. Supreme Ct., Washington, 1975-76; asst. U.S. atty. for so. dist. N.Y., Dept. Justice, N.Y.C., 1976-80, chief appellate atty., 1980; assoc. Patterson, Belknap, Webb & Tyler, N.Y.C., 1981-82, ptnr., 1982—, co-chair, 1997—. Editor-in-chief Columbia Law Rev., 1973-74. Kent scholar, 1972, Stone scholar, 1973, 74. Fellow Am. Coll. Trial Lawyers; mem. ABA, N.Y. State Bar Assn., Assn. Bar of City of N.Y. Office: Patterson Belknap Webb & Tyler 1133 Avenue Of The Americas New York NY 10036-6710

DISKIN, MICHAEL EDWARD, plastics industry executive; b. Dallas, Aug. 8, 1946; s. William Michael and Edna Patricia (Loughran) D.; m. Mary Jean Fraser, Oct. 8, 1972; children: Robyn Kristine, Karyn Marie, Michael Alexander, Stephen James, Alisyn Krystal. BS in Bus. Adminstrn & Econs., No. Mich. U., 1971. Sales rep. Lincoln Nat. Life, Fort Wayne, Ind., 1971-73, Durkee Foods, Dayton, Ohio, 1973-75; sales mgr. Durkee Foods, Cleve., 1975-78; from product mgr. asst. to sr. mktg. mgr. Durkee Foods, Westlake, Ohio, 1978-87; bus. mgr. Engelhard Corp., Cleve., 1987-88; dir. mktg. Master Builders Technologies, Cleve., 1988-92; exec. v.p. Specrete-Ip, Inc., Cleve., 1992-98; pres., owner Four Seasons Industries, Garrettsville, Ohio, 1998—. V.p. Put-in-Bay (Ohio) Property Owners Assn.; cpl. USMC, 1966-68. Mem. Lake Erie Islands Hist. Soc., Put-in-Bay Yacht Club, Crews Nest Club. Republican. Roman Catholic. Avocations: trap and target shooting, boating, fishing, travel. Home: 1745 Halls Carriage Path Westlake OH 44145-2030 Office: Four Seasons Industries 10426 Industrial Dr Garrettsville OH 44231-9764

DISMUKE, LEROY, special education educator, coordinator; b. Camden, Ark., Aug. 18, 1937; s. Roy Dismuke and Edna Mae (Bragg) Byrd; m. Gladys Monroe Cangle, Apr. 8, 1961; 1 child, Alan. BA, Lane Coll., 1960; MA, Ea. Mich. U., 1968, Ea. Mich. U., 1979. Cert. spl. edn. tchr., Mich. Tchr. Flint (Mich.) Pub. Schs., 1960-78, tchr. cons., 1979-84, dept. chmn., 1985-91, coord. dept. spl. edn., 1991—, steward in spl. edn., 1997—. Treas. NAACP, Flint, 1982-88; mem. Urban League, Flint, 1970-90. Mem. NEA (nat. rep. 1980-90), Mich. Edn. Assn. (state rep. 1975-90, voted into Hall of Fame region 10, 1997), United Tchrs. Flint (local rep. 1967-75, exec. bd. dirs. 1970-78), Coun. for Exceptional Children (Person of Yr. award 1989), Kappa Alpha Psi (Man of Yr. award 1990, 97). Democrat. Methodist. Home: 1701 Laurel Oak Dr Flint MI 48507-2210

DISNEY, ANTHEA, publishing executive; b. Dunstable, Eng., Oct. 13, 1946; came to U.S., 1973; d. Alfred Leslie and Elsie (Wale) Disney; m. Peter Robert Howe, Jan. 28, 1984. Ed., Queen's Coll., Eng. Fgn. corr. London Daily Mail, N.Y.C., 1973-75; features editor London Daily Mail, London, 1975-77; bur. chief London Daily Mail, N.Y.C., 1977-79; columnist London Daily Express, N.Y.C., 1979-84; dep. mng. editor N.Y. Daily News, N.Y.C., 1984-87; editor Sunday Daily News, 1984-87, US Mag., 1987-88; editor-in-chief Self mag., 1988-89; mag. developer Murdoch Mags., 1988-90; exec. producer Fox TV's A Current Affair, 1990-91; editor-in-chief TV Guide mag., N.Y.C., 1991-95; editorial dir. Murdoch Mags., 1993-95; editor-in-chief I-Guide, Newscorp's Internet Svc., 1995-96; pres., CEO Harper Collins Publishers, 1996-97; chmn., CEO News Am. Pub. Group, N.Y.C., 1997—, TV Guide, Inc., 1999; exec. v.p. content News Corp., N.Y.C., 1999—. Office: News Corp 1211 Avenue Of The Americas New York NY 10036-8701

DISNEY, KAREN C., critical care nurse; b. Blount County, Tenn., Sept. 6, 1961; d. William E. and Betty G. (Miller) D. LPN, Blount Occupation Ednl. Ctr., Maryville, Tenn., 1981; ADN, Walter State C.C., Morristown, Tenn., 1987. Cert. critical care nurse, nephrology nurse; RN, Tenn. Respiratory technician Blount Meml. Hosp., Maryville, 1979-81, LPN, critical care, med./surgical, 1981-87, RN critical care, 1987-89; dialysis RN relief charge nurse Dialysis Clinic, Inc., Knoxville, Tenn., 1989—. Home: 954 Lee Delia Ln Alcoa TN 37701-1549

DISNEY, MICHAEL GEORGE, financial services executive; b. Harvey, Ill., Nov. 30, 1955. Grad. h.s., Harvey; grad., Life Underwriters Tng. Coun. Sales mgr. Met. Life Ins. Co., Naperville, Ill., 1979-84; regional dir. Firemens Fund Ins. Co., San Diego, 1984-85; owner, mgr. Disney Fin., Inc., San Diego, 1985—; pres., founding mem. Grossmont Letip, 1992—. Founding mem., pres. Grossmont Letip, 1993-94. Mem. Nat. Assn. Life Underwriters, Life Underwriters Tng. Coun. (moderator-cons. 1986-87), Million Dollar Round Table (coord., chmn. San Diego chpt. 1987-89), La Mesa (Calif.) C. of C., San Diego C. of C., El Cajon C. of C., Toastmasters. Grossmont Letip (founder, pres. 1994-96). Avocations: photography, camping, fishing. Home: 3910 Dorsie Ln La Mesa CA 91941-7335 Office: 2615 Camino Del Rio S Ste 308 San Diego CA 92108-3713

DISNEY, RALPH L(YNDE), retired industrial engineering educator; b. Balt., Feb. 27, 1928. BE, Johns Hopkins U., 1952, MSE, 1955, DEng., 1964. Engr. Industrial Diecraft Inc., 1953-55, rsch. analyst Ops. Rsch. Office, 1955-56; asst. prof. Lamar State Coll., Beaumont, 1956-59; assoc. prof. U. Buffalo, 1959-63; vis. assoc. prof. U. Mich., Ann Arbor, 1963-64, assoc. prof., 1964-68, prof. indsl. engrng., 1968-77; Charles O. Gordon prof. indsl. engrng. Va. Polytech Inst. & State U., Blacksburg, 1977-87; prof. indsl. engrng. dept. Tex. A&M U., College Station, 1988-96; ret., 1996; OAS vis. prof. Inst. Aeron. Tech., Brazil, 1970-71; disting. vis. prof. Grad. Sch. Ohio State U., Columbus, 1974-75; vis. prof. dept. math. and stats. U. São Paulo, Brazil. Author 2 books; editor sects. in books; contbr. more than 70 articles to profl. jours. Erskine fellow Canterbury U., Christchurch, New Zealand, 1995. Fellow Am. Inst. Indsl. Engrs. (A.G. Holzman award 1986, David Baker award 1972, Frank and Lillian Gilbreth Indsl. Engrng. award 1993); mem. ORSA (mem. coun. 1978-82), INFORMS (founder sect. on applied probabilities, sect. pres. 1979), Nat. Acad. Engrng. Summer Home: 1395 Locust Ave Blacksburg VA 24060-5626 Winter Home: 8445 Charter Club Cir Apt 5 Fort Myers FL 33919-6827

DISNEY, ROY EDWARD, broadcasting company executive; b. Los Angeles, Jan. 10, 1930; s. Roy Oliver and Edna (Francis) D.; m. Patricia Ann Dailey, Sept. 17, 1955; children: Roy Patrick, Susan Margaret, Abigail Edna, Timothy John. B.A., Pomona Coll., 1951. Guest relations exec. NBC, Hollywood, Calif., 1952; apprentice film editor Mark VII Prodns., Hollywood, 1942; asst. film editor, cameraman prodn. asst., writer, producer Walt Disney Prodns., Burbank, Calif., 1954-77, dir., 1967—; pres. Roy E. Disney Prodns. Inc., Burbank, 1978—; chmn. bd. dir. Shamrock Broadcasting Co., Hollywood, 1979—; chmn. bd. dir., founder Shamrock Holdings Inc., Burbank, 1980—; trustee Calif. Inst. Arts, Valencia, 1967—; vice chmn. Walt Disney Co., Burbank. Author: novelized adaptation of Perri; producer (film) Pacific High, Mysteries of the Deep (TV show) Walt Disney's Wonderful World of Color, others; exec. producer Cheetah; writer, dir., producer numerous TV prodns. Bd. dirs. Big Bros. of Greater Los Angeles; mem. adv. bd. dirs. St. Joseph Med. Ctr., Burbank; mem. U.S. Naval Acad. Sailing Squadron, Annapolis, Md.; fellow U. Ky. Recipient Acad. award nomination for Mysteries of the Deep. Mem. Dirs. Guild Am. West, Writers Guild Am. Republican. Clubs: 100, Confrerie des Chevaliers du Tastevin, St. Francis Yacht, Calif. Yacht, San Diego Yacht, Transpacific Yacht, Los Angeles Yacht. Office: Walt Disney Co 500 S Buena Vista St Burbank CA 91521-1890

DISPENZA, JOAN MARIE, ambulatory care nurse, administrator; b. Buffalo, May 10, 1955; d. Frank J. and Madeline (Miano) D. BSN, D'Youville Coll., Buffalo, 1976, MSN in Cmty. Health, 1989. Staff nurse, CCU Millard Fillmore Hosp., Buffalo, 1976-85, head nurse CCU, 1985-89, DON, 1989-96; mgr. ambulatory care Millard Fillmore Health Sys., Buffalo, 1996—. Mem. AACN, Nat. League Nursing, Am. Coll. Healthcare Execs. (assoc.), Am. Orgn. Nurse Execs., N.Y. State Nurses Assn., Sigma Theta Tau. Office: Kaleida Health 3 Gates Cir Buffalo NY 14209-1120

DISSETTE, ALYCE MARIE, television newsmedia and theatrical producer, non-profit foundation executive; b. Flint, Mich., Mar. 16, 1952; d. Leland Richard and Carol A.R. (Scott) D. Student, U. Mich., Flint, 1972-73, U. Wis., 1975-76. Personal asst. Gilbert V. Helmsly Jr., Madison, Wis., 1975-78; adminstrv. asst. Presentations, Met. Opera, N.Y.C., 1977-79; exec. dir. ODC/Dance, San Francisco, 1983-86; producer, exec. dir. David Gordon/Pick Up Co., N.Y.C., 1986-89; founder/dir., ptnr. 501C3 Inc., N.Y.C., 1994-96; dir. Top Shows Inc., N.Y.C., 1997—; dir. computer art competitition New Voices, New Visions, 1994. Exec. prodr. (PBS series) Alive TV/Alive from Off-Center, 1991-93, Cable Ace Award ALIVE/MTV Co-prodn., 1994; prodr. websites including Hugo Boss Wordslam, 1996, Roden Crater, 1997; prodr. Art Spiegelman's Three Panel Opera, 1997—; assoc. prodr. Monsters of Grace, 1998-99. Office: Top Show Inc 584 Broadway Rm 1008 New York NY 10012-3253

DISTELHORST, GARIS FRED, trade association executive; b. Columbus, Ohio, Jan. 21, 1942; s. Harold Theodore and Ruth (Haywood) D.; m. Helen Cecilla Gillen, Oct. 28, 1972; children: Garen, Kristen, Alison. BSc, Ohio State U., 1965. V.p. Smith, Bucklin & Assocs., Washington, 1969-80; chief staff exec., CEO, pres. Nat. Assn. Coll. Stores, Oberlin, Ohio, 1980-98; pres. Assn. Initiatives, Inc., Westlake, Ohio, 1998—; mem. book and libr. adv. com. USIA, 1990-93; bd. dirs. First Merit Corp., Holcombs, Inc. Pres. Oberlin Cmty. Improvement Corp., 1985-88; bd. dirs. Leadership Lorain County, 1988-89, Access Program, 1994-97, Conv. and Visitors Bur. Greater Cleve., 1995—, Lorain County C.C. Found.; bd. dirs. Lorain County United Way, 1991-97, v.p., 1993-94, pres., 1994-96, campaign chmn., 1993. Decorated USN Achievement medal, 1969. Mem. Inst. Assn. Mgmt. Soc. (treas. 1979-80, award of merit), Am. Soc. Assn. Execs. (bd. dirs. 1981-84, vice chmn. 1985, chmn.-elect 1994, chmn. 1995-96, bd. dirs. found. 1990-94, vice chmn. found. 1991-92, chmn. found. 1992-93, Key award 1984, chmn. Assn. Advance Am. 1993-94), TEC (The Exec. Com.), Oberlin Area C. of C. (pres. 1987-90, bd. dirs. 1987-90), Greater Cleve. Soc. Assn. Execs. Republican. Roman Catholic. Office: Assn Initiatives Inc 30400 Detroit Rd Westlake OH 44145-1855 *Leadership isn't about having followers, but rather about providing an inspiring vision of a better future that people can buy into, participate in, and find reward from.*

DISTENFELD, ARIEL, hematologist, educator; b. Jerusalem, Oct. 10, 1931; came to U.S., 1950; s. Akiva and Jenia (Locker) D.; m. Joy Alpert, July 3, 1955 (dec.); children: Rona Distenfeld Statman, M. Suzan Distenfeld Crabb, Elana Distenfeld Gitter. BA, NYU, 1953, MD, 1957. Diplomate Am. Bd. Internal Medicine, Am. Bd. Hematology. Pvt. practice N.Y.C., 1963-97; intern, then resident Bellevue Hosp., N.Y.C., 1957-60; fellow NYU Med. Ctr., N.Y.C., 1960-61; chief hematology divsn. Cabrini Med. Ctr., N.Y.C., 1965—, dir. blood bank, 1967—; clin. assoc. prof. medicine NYU, N.Y.C., 1980—; med. dir. Cabrini Hospice, N.Y.C., 1996—; assoc. Tisch Univ. Hosp., N.Y.C., 1963—. Pvt. inf., Israeli Army, 1948-49. Fellow ACP, Am. Soc. Hematology; mem. Am. Soc. Clin. Oncology, Internat. Soc. Hematology; mem. Am. Soc. Internal Medicine, Internat. Soc. Blood Transfusion, N.Y. Acad. Medicine, Soc. Study Blood, Bellevue Alumni (v.p. 1997-98). Republican. Jewish. Avocations: bicycling, swimming, gardening, music, theatre. Office: 227 E 19th St New York NY 10003-2602

DI SUVERO, MARK, sculptor; b. Shanghai, Sept. 18, 1933; s. Vittorio and Matilde (Millo) DiS. B.A., U. Calif., Berkeley, 1957. Co-founder Park Place Gallery, N.Y.C., 1963. Founder Socrates Sculpture Pk., N.Y.C., 1986; one-person shows include Green Gallery, N.Y., 1960, Park Place Gallery, N.Y., 1966, Van Abbemuseum, Eindhoven, Netherlands, 1972, City of Chalon-sur-Saone, France, 1974, Jardin des Tuileries, Paris, 1975, Whitney Mus., N.Y.C., 1975, Oil and Steel Gallery, N.Y.C., 1983, Storm King Art Ctr., 1985, 95, 96, Wurttembergischer Kunstverein, Stuttgart, 1988, City of Valence, France, 1990, Musee d'Art Moderne et d'Art Contemporain de Nice, France, 1991, City of Chalon/Saône, France, 1992, IVAM Centre Julio Gonzalez, Valencia, Spain, 1994, XLVI Venice Biennial, 1995, others; group exhbns. include Palais des Beaux-Arts, 1981, Construct Gallery, Chgo., 1982, San Francisco Mus. Modern Art, 1982; represented in permanent collections, Art Inst. Chgo., Whitney Mus., N.Y.C., Museum of Modern Art, N.Y.C., Wadsworth Atheneum, Hartford, Conn., City Art Mus., St. Louis, others. Grantee Longview Found., Walter K. Gutman Found.; recipient Art Inst. Chgo. award, 1963, Creative Arts award Brandeis U., 1969, Skowhegan Sch. award, 1974. Office: c/o Spacetime 3040 Vernon Blvd Box 2128 Long Island City NY 11102*

DITHRICH, MARIE, elementary education educator; b. Pitts., Jan. 5, 1950; d. Aloysius Martin and Vera (Leszunova) D. BS in Edn., U. Pitts., 1971, MEd, 1974. Cert. elem. tchr., Pa. Tchr. math. and computers 19th Ave Elem. Sch., Steel Valley Sch. Dist., Munhall, Pa., 1971-76, Barrett Elem. Sch., Steel Valley Sch. Dist., Homestead, Pa., 1976—; cons. D.C. Health-Math., 1994—. Bd. dirs. Carnegie Libr. of Homestead, 1997—, asst. treas., 1998—. Recipient Presdl. award for Excellence in Sci. and Math. Teaching, NSF, 1990; named Steel Valley C. of C. Educator of Yr., 1991. Mem. Nat. Coun. Tchrs. Math., Pa. Coun. Tchrs. Math. (award Merit 1991), Coun. Presdl. Awardees in Math., Soc. Elem. Presdl. Awardees, Pa. State Edn. Assn., Steel Valley Edn. Assn. (mem. negotiationg team 1985-86, 90—, faculty rep. 1987—, v.p. 1991—, treas. 1994-96), Delta Zeta. Mem. Eastern Orthodox Ch. Office: Barrett Elem Sch 221 E 12th Ave Homestead PA 15120-1690

DITIBERIO, JOHN KESLEY, psychotherapist, educator, consultant; b. Hendersonville, N.C., Oct. 30, 1944; s. Joseph C. and Carolyn S. DiTiberio; m. Lisa K. Sharrard, June 21, 1975; children: Cynthia J., Anne C. BA, Kalamazoo Coll., 1966; MA, Mich. State U., 1970, PhD, 1976. Lic. psychologist and health svc. provider, Mo. Tchr. E. Lansing (Mich.) H.S., 1966-72; asst. prof. Mich. State U., E. Lansing, 1976-77; staff psychologist U. Ill., Chgo., 1977-85; assoc. dir. St. Louis U., 1985-87, assoc. prof., chair, 1987—; mem. rsch. adv. bd. Consulting Psychologists Press, Palo Alto, Calif., 1995—. Mem. editl. bd. Jour. Psychol. Type, 1984—; co-author: Personality and the Teaching of Composition, 1989, Writing and Personality, 1995, MBTI Manual, 3d edit., 1998. Dir. Family Devel. Ctr., St. Louis, 1993—. Focus on Families grantee Danforth Found., 1993-96. Mem. APA, ACA, Assn. Psychol. Type (trainer 1985—). Mem. United Ch. of Christ. Avocations: camping, music. E-mail: ditiberi@slu.edu. Home: 624 Spring Meadows Dr Ballwin MO 63011 Office: Saint Louis U 3750 Lindell Blvd Saint Louis MO 63108

DITKA, MICHAEL KELLER, professional football coach; b. Carnegie, Pa., Oct. 18, 1939; s. Mike and Charlotte (Keller) D.; m. Margery Ditka, Jan. 21, 1961 (div. 1973); children: Michael, Mark, Megan, Matthew; m. Diana S. Ditka, July 8, 1977. Student, U. Pitts. Profl. football player Chgo. Bears, 1961-66, Phila. Eagles, 1967-68; profl. football player Dallas Cowboys, 1969-72, asst. coach, 1973-81; head coach Chgo. Bears, 1982-93; coach Chgo. Bears Superbowl Championship Team, 1985; owner Ditka's Restaurant, Chgo., 1986—; head coach New Orleans Saints, 1997—. Named Rookie of Yr., NFL, 1961; named to Pro Bowl, 1962-66; inducted into Hall of Fame, 1988; named coach of the year, NFL, 1988. Roman Catholic. Office: New Orleans Saints 5800 Airline Hwy Metairie LA 70003-3876*

DITKOWSKY, KENNETH K., lawyer; b. Chgo., July 12, 1936; s. Samuel J. and Lillian (Plavnik) D.; m. Judith Goodman, Aug. 9, 1959; children—Naomi, Deborah, R. Benjamin. B.S., U. Chgo.; J.D., Loyola U., Chgo. Bar: Ill. 1961, U.S. Dist. Ct. (no. dist.) Ill. 1962, U.S. Ct. Apls. (7th cir.) 1973, U.S. Tax Ct. 1973, U.S. Sup. Ct. 1975. Ptnr., Ditkowsky & Contorer, Chgo., 1961—. Mem. Ill. Bar Assn. Office: Ditkowsky & Contorer 2626 W Touhy Ave Chicago IL 60645-3110

DITLOW, CLARENCE M., think-tank executive. Exec. dir. Ctr. for Auto Safety, Wash., D.C. Office: Ctr Auto Safety 2001 S St NW Ste 410 Washington DC 20009-1160*

D'ITRI, FRANK MICHAEL, environmental research chemist; b. Flint, Mich., Apr. 25, 1933; s. Dominic and Angelina (Costanza) D'I.; m. Patricia Ann Ward, Sept. 10, 1955; children: Michael Payne, Angela Kathryn, Patricia Ann, Julie Lynn. BS in Zoology, Mich. State U., 1955, MS in Analytical Chemistry, 1966, PhD, 1968. Lab. technician Dow Industry Service Labs., Midland, Mich., 1960-62; research asst. dept. chemistry Mich. State U., East Lansing, 1963-68, asst. prof. dept. fisheries and wildlife, 1968-72, assoc. prof. dept. fisheries and wildlife, 1973-76, prof. dept. fisheries and wildlife, 1977—; assoc. dir. Inst. Water Rsch., 1987—; asst. dir. Mich. Agrl. Exptl. Sta., 1996—; cons. U.S. Dept. Energy, Washington, 1983-85, EEC, UN, Geneva, 1982—; vis. prof. U. Bahia, Brazil, 1978, Tokyo U. Agr., 1980, 84-85, 87, 94; mem. adv. bd. Lewis Pubs., Inc., Springer-Verlag. Author: The Environmental Mercury Problem, 1972, (with P.A. D'Itri) Mercury Contamination: A Human Tragedy, 1977, (with A.W. Andren, R.A. Doherty, J.M. Wood), Assessment of Mercury in the Environment, 1978, Acid Precipitation, 1982, Artificial Reefs, 1985; editor (with J. Aguirre M., M. Athie L.), Municipal Wastewater in Agriculture, 1981, Land Treatment of Municipal Wastewater: Vegetation Selection and Management, 1982, Acid Precipitation: Effects on Ecological Systems, 1982, (with M.A. Kamrin) PCBs: Human and Environmental Hazards, 1983, Artificial Reefs: Marine and Freshwater Applications, 1985, A System Approach to Conservation Tillage, 1985, (with H.H. Prince) Coastal Wetlands, 1985; (with L.G. Wolfson) Rural Groundwater Contamination, 1987, Chemical Deicers And The Environment, 1992, (with H.W. Belcher) Subirrigation and Controlled Drainage, 1995, Zebra Mussels and Aquatic Nuisance Species, 1997, (with Y. Itakura) Integrated Environmental Management, 1999; contbr. numerous articles to profl. jours. Mem. critical materials adv. subcom. Mich. Water Resources Commns. Mich. Dept. Natural Resources, 1971-79, mem. solid waste com., 1971-79; mem. subcom. Mich. State U. Waste Control Authority Chem. Waste, 1971—; mem. tech. adv. com. Great Lakes Protection fund tech. adv. com., 1990-93; mem. Great Lakes Commn., 1992—; mem. subirrigation steering com. Mich. Soil Conservation Svc., 1986—; mem. fluctuating lake levels com. Internat. Joint Commn., 1992-93; mem. internat. rsch. group mercury pollution in Amazon, Brazil, 1992—. NIH summer fellow, 1964-67, Socony-Mobil fellow Mich. State U., 1967-68, Japan Soc. Promotion Sci. fellow, 1980; Rockefeller Found. Bellagio Resident scholar, 1972, 75. Mem. Am. Chem. Soc., Am. Soc. Limnology and Oceanography, Assn. Analytical Chemists, Water Pollution Research Soc., Midwest Univs. Analytical Chemists Conf., Mich. Acad. Sci., Arts and Letters, Sigma Xi, Setac. Home: 4395 Elmwood Dr Okemos MI 48864-3034 Office: Mich State U 115 Manly Miles 1405 S Harrison Rd East Lansing MI 48823-5289

DITTENHAFER, BRIAN DOUGLAS, banker, economist; b. York, Pa., Aug. 15, 1942; s. Nathaniel Webster and Evelyn Romaine (Myers) D.; m. Miriam Marcy, Aug. 22, 1964; 1 child. BA, Ursinus Coll., 1964; MA, Temple U., 1966, postgrad., 1967-71. Personnel asst. Philco Corp., Phila., 1965-66; teaching asst. Temple U., Phila., 1966-67; research asso. Temple U., 1968-69; bus. economist Fed. Res. Bank of Atlanta, 1971-76; v.p., chief economist Fed. Home Loan Bank of N.Y., N.Y.C., 1976-79, sr. v.p., chief fin. officer, 1979-80, exec. v.p., 1980-85, pres., 1985-92; pres. Collective Fed. Savs. Bank, 1992-94, Collective Bancorp, 1992-94; chmn. MBD Mgmt. Co., 1994—; vice chmn. Fin. Instns. Thrift Plan, 1991-92, chmn., 1992; trustee Fin. Instns. Retirement Fund, 1985-92, vice chmn., 1991, chmn., 1992; bd. dirs. Investors Savs. Bank. bd. dirs. Social Compact, 1990—, sec., 1995—; mem. FNMA Found. Adv. Group, 1994; deacon Ctrl. Presbyn. Ch., 1981-84; bd. dirs. N.Y. Coun. Econ. Edn., 1983-89; chmn. Resolution Funding Corp., 1989-92. Temple U. fellow, G.E. Found. fellow Temple U. Mem. Nat. Assn. Bus. Economists, Am. Econ. Assn., Am. Fin. Assn., Am. Real Estate and Urban Econ. Assn., N.Y. Assn. Bus. Econs., Omicron Delta Epsilon. Club: Forecaster's of N.Y. (sec.-treas. 1982-84).

DITTER, J. WILLIAM, JR., federal judge; b. Phila., Oct. 19, 1921. *Father a congressman from 1933 until his death in 1943, lead the efforts before World War II to obtain legislation for a two ocean navy. The USS J. William Ditter (DM31), a destroyer mine-layer, was named in his honor as is the chapel at the Naval Air Station, Willow Grove, Pennsylvania. Cousin, Dorothy Gondos Beers, was full professor and dean of women at American University, Washington, DC. Cousin, Edward G. Biester, was a state judge, 1949-70, and his son, Edward G. Biester, Jr., a member of congress, Attorney General of Pennsylvania, and is now a state judge in Bucks County, Pennsylvania.* B.A., Ursinus Coll., 1943, LL.D., 1970; LL.B., U. Pa., 1948. Bar: Pa. 1949. Clk. Ct. Common Pleas, Montgomery County, Pa., 1948-51; asst. dist. atty. Montgomery County, 1951, 53-55, 1st asst. dist. atty., 1956-60; mem. firm Ditter and Jenkins and predecessor firm, Ambler, Pa., 1953-63; judge Ct. Common Pleas, Montgomery County, 1964-70; judge U.S. Dist. Ct. Ea. Dist. Pa., Phila., 1970-86, sr. judge, 1986—; lectr. Villanova U. Past pres. bd. trustees Calvary Methodist Ch.; charter pres. Ambler Jaycees, 1954-55; bd. dirs. Riverview Osteo. Hosp., Norristown, Pa., 1964-71; bd. consulters Villanova U. Sch. Law, 1977—. Served to capt. USNR, 1943-68. Recipient Disting. Alumnus award Ambler High Sch., 1986; named Alumnus of Yr., Ursinus Coll., 1980. Mem. Am., Fed., Pa., Montgomery County bar assns., Hist. Soc. U.S. Dist. Ct. Eastern Dist. Pa. (incorporator, bd. dirs.). Office: US Dist Ct 3118 601 Market St Philadelphia PA 19106-1713

DITTES, JAMES EDWARD, psychology of religion educator; b. Cleve., Dec. 26, 1926; s. Mercein Edward and Mary (Freeman) D.; children: Lawrence William (dec.), Nancy Eleanor, Carolyn Ann, Joanne Frances; m. Anne Hebert Smith, Nov. 27, 1987. A.B., Oberlin Coll., 1949; B.D., Yale U., 1954, M.S., 1955, Ph.D., 1958. Instr. Am. Sch., Talas, Turkey, 1950-52; ordained to ministry United Ch. Christ, 1954; mem. faculty Yale U., 1955—, prof. psychology of religion, 1967-84, prof. pastoral theology and psychology, 1984—, chmn. dept. religious studies, 1975-82; chmn. Council on Grad. Studies in Religion in U.S. and Can., 1970-71. Author: The Church in the Way, 1967, Minister on the Spot, 1970, Bias and the Pious, 1973, When the People Say No, 1979, The Male Predicament, 1985, When Work Goes Sour, 1987, Men at Work, 1996, Driven by Hope, 1996, Pastoral Counseling, 1999, Re-Calling Ministry, 1999, (with Robert Menges) Psychological Studies of Clergymen, 1965, (with Donald Capps) The Hunger of the Heart, 1990. Served with USNR, 1945-46. Guggenheim fellow, 1965-66; Fulbright Research fellow Rome, 1965-66; sr. fellow NEH, 1972-73. Mem. Soc. Sci. Study of Religion (exec. sec. 1959-63, editor jour. 1966-71, pres. 1971-73). Home: 1157 Whitney Ave Hamden CT 06517-3434 Office: 409 Prospect St New Haven CT 06511-2167

DITTMAN, DEBORAH RUTH, real estate broker; b. Sacramento, Apr. 15, 1932; d. Charles Harwood and Ruth (Potter) Kinsley; m. John Alvin Cardoza, Sept. 1950 (div. 1964); children: Harold Cardoza, Nancy Jongeward, John Allan Cardoza, Gregory Cardoza, Janice Boswell; m. Edgar Marshall Dittman, Jan. 22, 1967 (dec. Jan. 1982); m. Philip George Vrieling, July 7, 1990. Student, Humprey's Coll., 1966; cert. in real estate, San Joaquin Delta Coll., 1977; grad. real estate sales, Anthony Schs., 1978. Lic. real estate assoc., Calif., 1974-78, lic. real estate broker, 1978; cert. residential specialist. Sec. Calif. Dept. Water Resources, Patterson and Tracy, 1966-72;

hostess Welcome Wagon, Tracy, 1973-74; assoc. realtor Reeve Assocs., Tracy, 1975-80; broker Allied Brokers, Tracy, 1980-83; ptnr. real estate Putt, Fallavena, Willbanks & Dittman, Tracy, 1983-98; mem. adv. bd. Tracy Fed. Bank (formerly Tracy Savings & Loan), 1989-97, Women's Coun. Realtors, 1990—. Mem. Residential Sales Coun., 1989, Women's Coun. Realtors, 1990. Mem. Nat. Assn. Realtors, Ctrl. Valley Assn. Realtors, Calif. Assn. Realtors (dir. 1980-81, 85), Tracy Bd. Realtors (dir. 1976, 77, 80-83, 85-86, pres. 1981, 85), Cert. Real Estate Specialists (v.p. no. Calif. chpt. 1990, pres. 1991), So. Alameda Assn. Realtors, Tracy C. of C. (bd. dirs. 1988-90). Home: 12134 Midway Dr Tracy CA 95376-9113 Office: 1045 Tracy Blvd Tracy CA 95376

DITTMAN, KATHRYN ANNE, veterinarian; b. Lawton, Okla., Feb. 18, 1960; d. Donald Mathew Opel and Margaret Anne (Rulon) Powell; m. Mark Frederick Dittman, Mar. 13, 1983; children: Matthew Frederick, Margaret June (dec. Jan. 1998). BS, Tex. A&M U., 1983, DVM, 1985. Veterinarian Altas Palmas Animal Clinic, Harlingen, Tex., 1985—. Sunday Sch. supt. 1st United Meth. Ch., La Feria, Tex., 1997. Mem. Valley Veterinary Med. Assn. (pres. 1988), Tex. Veterinary Med. Assn. (bd. dirs. 1990-91), Am. Veterinary Med. Assn., Assn. Avian Veterinarians. Republican. Methodist. Office: Altas Palmas Animal Clinic 8369 W Business 83 Harlingen TX 78552-9602

DITTMER, BILLIE SPRUILL, school psychologist; b. Aurora, N.C., Dec. 19, 1935; d. Leonard Alston and Elizabeth (Peele) Spruill; m. Bill Dittmer, Apr. 11, 1968; 1 child, Dana. BS in Elem. Edn., East Carolina U., 1957; MA in Edn1. Psychology, U. Nebr., 1967, cert. in Sch. Psychology, 1976. Cert. sch. psychologist, Nebr. Elem. sch. tchr. Schs. in N.C., La., Minn., Nebr., 1957-69; counselor Lincoln (Nebr.) Pub. Schs., 1969-72, Bryan Extension Ctr. LPS, Lincoln, 1972-77; sch. psychologist Lincoln Pub. Schs., 1977—; chmn. curriculum com., English tchr. Bryan Extension Ctr. LPS, Lincoln, Nebr., 1971-72, dir. summer sch., 1973; vocat. counselor Job Employment Training Cmty. Employment Training Assn., 1973-78, gifted evaluator Lincoln (Nebr.) Pub. Schs., 1979-94. Sec. Lincoln unit U.S. Coast Guard Auxiliary, 1969-79, state sec., Omaha, Nebr., 1970-76. Named Outstanding Woman Auxiliarist, No. Region U.S. Coast Guard Aux., Mpls., 1974. Mem. NEA, Nebr. Edn. Assn., Nat. Assn. Sch. Psychologists, Lincoln Edn. Assn. (bldg. rep. 1967), Phi Delta Kappa. Democrat. Lutheran. Avocations: gardening, reading, boating, outdoor activities. Home: RR 1 Box 21A Denton NE 68339-9705 Office: Lincoln Pub Schs 5901 O St Lincoln NE 68510-2235

DITTMER, JOHN AVERY, history educator; b. Seymour, Ind., Oct. 30, 1939; s. J. Avery and Melba Roberta (Ahlbrand) D.; m. Ellen Ann Tobey, June 3, 1961; children: Julia Susan, John David. BS in Edn., Ind. U., 1961, MA in History, 1964, PhD in History, 1971. Asst. prof. Tougaloo (Miss.) Coll., 1967-68, acad. dean, 1968-70, assoc. prof., 1971-79; assoc. prof. history DePauw U., Greencastle, Ind., 1985-92; prof. —, —, —, 1993—; vis. assoc. prof. Brown U., Providence, R.I., 1979-80, 81-82, 83-84, MIT, Cambridge, 1982-84; cons. NEH, Washington, 1980-83, PBS Series, Eyes on the Prize, Boston, 1986. Author: Black Georgia in the Progressive Era, 1900-1920, 1977, Local People: The Struggle for Civil Rights in Mississippi, 1994 (Lillian Smith book award, 1994, Bancroft prize Columbia Univ. 1995); contbr. articles to profl. jours. Recipient Younger Humanist fellowship NEH, 1973-74, fellowship-in-residence NEH, Vanderbilt U., 1976-77, fellowship Rockefeller Foun., 1980-81, Am. Coun. Learned Socs., 1983-84, Ctr. for Study of Civil Rights, U. Va., 1988-89. Mem. Orgn. of Am. Historians (Frederick Jackson Turner award finalist 1972), So. Hist. Assn., Am. Hist. Assn. Avocations: tennis, golf, jazz music. Home: 230 Westwood Rd Fillmore IN 46128-9621 Office: DePauw U Dept History Greencastle IN 46135

DITTMER, LINDA JEAN, retired photojournalist, photographer, computer artist; b. Detroit, 1950; d. Max Gene Witherow and Julienne Heldegarde Sikorski; m. Dennis Robert, July 11, 1970 (div. Feb. 1987); 1 child, Jesse Michael. Student, Coll. Art and Design, Detroit, 1988-90; AAS, Oakland Coll., 1993; student, Wayne State U., 1994—. Prodr. Greater Media, Detroit, 1985-87; broadcaster Wismer Broadcasting, Port Huron, Mich., 1987-89; sports writer UPI, Detroit, 1992-93; freelance photojournalist AP, Detroit News, Detroit Free Press, 1989—; pvt. practice computer cons., Detroit, 1996—. Recipient Recognition award Children's Hosp. Detroit, 1986, Cert. Appreciation, Easter Seal Soc., Detroit, 1986, Presdl. Phys. Fitness Instr. award, 1990, Disting. Svc. award Arthritis Found., Detroit, 1992. Mem. Nat. Press Photographers Assn., Soc. Profl. Journalists, Golden Key Nat. Honor Soc. Avocations: snowshoeing, hiking, skiing, music, theatre.

DIULUS, FREDERICK ALFONSO-EDWARD, business educator; b. Cleve., Oct. 1, 1941; s. Frederick Edward Diulus and Ellen Delores (San Gregorio) Diulus-Rohatsch; m. Esther Jeanette Brickey, Dec. 20, 1969 (div. 1977); m. Sharon Bonenberger, Sept., 1980 (div. 1983); m. Sally Evan White, May 4, 1991; 1 child, Danielle Marie-Fay. BS, Fla. State U., 1962; MBA, Golden Gate U., 1971; PhD, The Union Inst., 1999. Registered investment adviser. CEO SPQR Ltd., 1971-77; dir. rsch., chief economist Inst. of Econ. Analysis, 1978-80; sr. fin. adviser for v.p. Rep. of Ghana, Accra, 1980-82; dir. fin. svcs. Guardian Ptnrs. Investment Transaction Corp., Los Altos, Calif., 1983-85, pres., CEO, 1985-88; regional dir. Edn. and Tng. Inst., Detroit, 1989-91; mng. gen. ptnr. King of Hearts Comm., Atlantic Beach, Fla., 1989-92; pub., editor Anastasia Gazette, St. Augustine, Fla., 1991-94; adj. prof. U. Ctrl. Fla., Orlando, 1996; founder, exec. dir. Ctr. Ethics In Free Enterprise, Jacksonville, Fla., 1997—; adj. prof. U. North Fla., Jacksonville, 1989—; founder, bd. dirs. Delta Pacific Bank, Pittsburg, Calif., 1973-76. Author: 21st Century Entrepreneurship: Venturing Outside the Box, 1998; author, editor (quarterly books) The Federal Financial Register, 1985-88, The Federal Financial Digest, 1984-88; editl. bd. Acad. of Free Enterprise Education, 1997—, Acad. Entrepreneurship Edn., 1998—. Mem. citizen's critique com. Orlando Sentinel, 1997. Capt. USAF, 1966-68, Vietnam. Decorated Bronze Star; named One of America's Leading Educators, Walton Found., 1997, 98; named to Very Important Prof. program Promotional Products Assn., 1997; Samuel Walton Free Enterprise fellow at UNF, 1996—. Mem. Nat. Assn. Credit Union Svc. Orgns. (founder), Credit Union Govt. Securities Mutual Funds (founder), Pyramid Savings and Loan Assn. (founder), Knights of Columbus (scribe), Delta Theta Phi, Pi Kappa Phi (nat. sec. 1975-79). Roman Catholic. Avocations: golf, tennis, fly fishing. Home: PO Box 352079 Palm Coast FL 32135-2079 Office: U North Fla 4567 Saint John's Bluff Rd Palm Coast FL 32135

DIVELY, DWIGHT DOUGLAS, finance director; b. Spokane, Wash., Sept. 24, 1958; s. Richard Lorraine and Marie Eleanor (Barnes) D.; m. Susan Lorraine Soderstrom, June 13, 1987; children: Nathan Douglas, Natalie Lorraine. BSChemE, Rose-Hulman Inst. Tech., 1980; MPA of Pub. Affairs, Princeton U., 1982; PhC in Civil Engring., U. Wash., 1986. Rsch. scientist Battelle, Seattle, 1982-84; policy analyst, staff dir. Wash. High Tech. Coord. Bd., Seattle, 1984-86; cons. Bellevue, Wash., 1986-87; legis. analyst Seattle City Coun., 1987-90, supervising analyst, 1990-92, staff dir., 1992-94; dir. Seattle Fin. Dept., 1994-96, Seattle Exec. Svcs. Dept., 1997—; cons. We. Interstate Commn. on Higher Edn., Boulder, Colo., 1986-91; affiliate prof. U. Wash., 1989—; instr. South Seattle C.C., 1992—; mem. faculty Cascade Ctr., Seattle, 1992—. Co-author: Benefit-Cost Analysis in Theory and Practice, 1994. Chmn. interview panel Truman Scholarship Found., Washington, 1989—. Recipient Elmer B. Staats award Truman Scholarship Found., 1994. Mem. Govt. Fin. Officers Assn. Lutheran. Avocations: cooking, rose gardening. Office: Fin Dept 600 4th Ave Ste 103 Seattle WA 98104-1874

DIVER, COLIN S., law educator, dean; b. 1943. BA, Amherst Coll., 1965; LLB, Harvard U., 1968; MA, U. Pa., 1989; LLD, Amherst Coll., 1990. Bar: Mass. 1968. Spl. counsel Office of the Mayor, Boston, 1968-71; asst. sec. consumer affairs Exec. Office Consumer Affairs, Boston, 1971-72; undersec. adminstrn. Exec. Office Adminstrn. and Fin., Boston, 1972-74; assoc. prof. Boston U., 1975-81, prof., 1981-89, from assoc. dean to dean, 1985-89; dean, Bernard G. Segal prof. U. Pa., Phila., 1989—; cons. Adminstrv. Conf. of U.S., 1980-88. Chmn. Mass. State Ethics Com., 1983-89; mem. adv. com. on enforcement policy NRC, 1984-85. Office: U Pa Law Sch 3400 Chestnut St Philadelphia PA 19104-6204

DIVINE, ROBERT ALEXANDER, history educator; b. Bklyn., May 10, 1929; s. Walter E. and Emily (Mable) D.; m. Barbara C. Renick, Aug. 6, 1955 (dec.); children: J. Douglas, Elisabeth T., Richard L., Kirk M.; m. Darlene S. Harris, June 1, 1996. B.A., Yale U., 1951, M.A., 1952, Ph.D., 1954. Instr. U. Tex., Austin, 1954-57; asst. prof. U. Tex., 1957-61, assoc. prof., 1961-63, prof. history, 1963—, chmn. dept. history, 1963-68, Piper prof., 1972, George W. Littlefield prof. Am. history, 1981-96, prof. emeritus, 1996—; fellow Center for Advanced Study in Behavioral Scis. Stanford, Calif., 1962-63; Albert Shaw lectr. in diplomatic history, Johns Hopkins, 1968. Author: American Immigration Policy, 1924-52, 1957, The Illusion of Neutrality, 1962, The Reluctant Belligerent, 1965, Second Chance, 1967, Roosevelt and World War II, 1969, Foreign Policy and U.S. Presidential Elections, 1940-60, 2 vols., 1974, Since 1945: Politics and Diplomacy in Recent American History, 1975, Blowing on the Wind, 1978, Eisenhower and the Cold War, 1981, The Sputnik Challenge, 1993; co-author: America Past and Present, 1984, 3d edit., 1991, 4th edit., 1995, 5th edit., 1999. Mem. Orgn. Am. Historians, Soc. for Historians of Am. Fgn. Rels. Democrat. Methodist. E-mail: rdivine@austin.rr.com. Home: 10617 Sans Souci Pl Austin TX 78759-6185

DIVINE, THEODORE EMRY, electrical engineer; b. Hailey, Idaho, May 27, 1943; s. Theodore Clyde and Muriel Juanita 9Kirtley) D.; m. Roberta Louise Erickson, Mar. 19, 1966; children: Timothy Shannon, Brianna Kristine, Rachel Melissa. BSEE, U. Wash., 1966, MBA, 1970. Engr. Gen. Telephone Co. of N.W., 1968-69; mem. tech. staff. N.W. ops. Computer Scis. Corp., 1970-72; rsch. engr. Battelle Pacific N.W. Labs., Richland, Wash., 1973—; rsch. sect. mgr. Battelle pacific N.W. Labs., Richland, Wash., 1978, staff engr., def. programs, 1980-89; program mgr., spl. programs Idaho Nat. Engr. Lab., Idaho Falls, 1989—, mgr. Nat. Security Programs Office, 1992-93, spl. programs mgr., 1993-96; staff scientist Battelle pacific N.W. Nat. Labs., Richland, 1996-97, spl. programs sector dep. Battelle Meml. Inst., 1997—. Mem. editl. adv. bd. Internat. Jours. Computers & Electronics in Agr., The Netherlands, 1983-95. Ruling elder First Presbyn. Ch., Prosser, Wash., 1982-84; pres. Mid-Columbia Sci. Fair Assn., 1975-76. With Signal Corps USAR, 1966-84, Vietnam. Decorated Bronze star. Mem. IEEE, Am. Soc. Agrl. Engrs. (com. chmn. 1977-78, 82-83, chmn. nat. conf. on electronics in agr. 1983), Beta Gamma Sigma.

DIVITTO, SHARON FAITH, mental health nurse, administrator; b. Worcester, Mass., Dec. 7, 1960; d. Edward Ronald and Elizabeth Ann (Carey) Lamusta; m. Michael Francis DiVitto, June 14, 1987. B in Nursing magna cum laude, Fitchburg State Coll., 1982; MA in Psychology magna cum laude, Assumption Coll., 1990; MSN in Psychiat. Nursing, U. Mass., 1998. RN, Mass.; cert. emergency nurse, emergency med. technician, BCLS, ACLS; cert. clin. specialist in mental health in adult nursing. Flight nurse U. Mass. Med. Ctr., Worcester, critical care nurse surg.-trauma ICU, psychiat. nurse inpatient unit, mem. com. psychiat. nursing practice, 1990-97; patient svcs. coord.-nurse mgr. inpatient psychiat. units St. Joseph's Hosp. Psychiat. Svcs., Providence, 1997, 99; outpatient psychiat. nurse Valley Adult Counseling Svcs., Milford, Mass., 1990-91; clin. specialist, cons. liaison U. Mass. Med. Ctr., 1994-97; psychiat. clin. specialist VNA Ctrl. Mass., 1994—. Mem. ANA, AACN, Mass. Nurses Assn. (sec. U. Mass. Med. Ctr. chpt., mem. dist. II bylaws com., cabinet on nursing practice 1992-95), Emergency Nurses Assn., Nat. Flight Nurses Assn., New Eng. Flight Nurses Assn., Internat. Soc. Psychiat. Cons. and Liaison Nurses, Nat. Inst. for Human Caring, Sigma Theta Tau (rec. sec., newsletter editor, com. chmn., del. nat. conf. Epsilon Beta chpt., v.p. 1991-93, chmn. programs com. 1991-93, pres.-elect 1993-94, pres. 1994-96, del. internat. conv. 1985, 93, 95), Internat. Assn. Forensic Nurses. Avocations: piano, sports, stained glass and country crafts, reading. Home: 128 Heights Of Hill St Whitinsville MA 01588-1050

DIVON, MICHAEL Y., obstetrican and gynecologist; b. Cheb, Czechoslovaki, Oct. 6, 1947; s. David and Friei D.; m. Ruth Divon Barkai, Jan. 3, 1956 (div.). BS summa cum laude, Northrop Inst. Tech., 1973; MD cum laude, Technion Israel Inst., 1978. Dir. ob-gyn Albert Einstein Coll. Medicine, Bronx, N.Y., 1989-97, Lenox Hill Hosp., N.Y.C., 1997—. Maj. USAF, 1966-83.

DIVONE, LOUIS VINCENT, aerospace engineer, educator, author, government official; b. N.Y.C., July 24, 1934; s. Dominic and Christina Agnes (Cassa) D.; B.Aero. Engring., Poly. Inst. Bklyn., 1955; M.S., M.I.T., 1956; m. Judene Frances Smith, Aug. 10, 1968. Mem. tech. staff Jet Propulsion Lab., Calif. Inst. Tech., 1956-67, 69-72; program mgr. NASA, 1962-63; cons. Dept. Transp., 1968-69; dir. wind energy systems NSF, 1973-74; dir. wind energy systems ERDA, 1975-76; dir. Wind Energy Tech. div. Dept. Energy, Washington, 1977-83, dir. Office Solar Electric Techs., 1982-84, 86-90; assoc. dep. asst. sec. Transp. Tech., 1990-91; assoc. dep. asst. sec. for Bldgs. Tech., 1992-94; acting dep. asst. sec. bldg. techs., 1994-95, acting dep. asst. sec. bldg. tech., state and cmty. programs, 1996, assoc. dep. asst. sec. for indsl. techs., 1997—; spl. asst. to dir. market planning and research Grumman Aerospace Corp., 1984-85; professorial lectr. George Washington U., 1976-84; cons. Wind Energy Working Group, UN, 1979-81; chmn. wind energy exec. com. Internat. Energy Agy., 1978-82. Co-editor Energy series Inst. Elec. Engrs., 1990—; contbr. papers to profl. symposia; patentee variable area rocket nozzle, self-attaching fluid coupling. Recipient Apollo Achievement award NASA, 1970, Spl. Achievement award ERDA, 1976. Pres.'s. Exec. Exchange Program appointment, 1984-85. Fellow AAAS, AIAA (assoc. fellow); mem. Sr. Exec. Assn., Smithsonian Assos., Antique Airplane Assn., Nat. Trust for Hist. Preservation, Nat. Aviation Club, Cessna 180 Owners Club, Sigma Xi, Tau Beta Pi. Home: 2530 Leeds Rd Oakton VA 22124-1406 Office: 1000 Independence Ave SW Washington DC 20585-0001

DIWAN, ROMESH KUMAR, economics educator; b. Sabathu, India, Dec. 20, 1933; came to U.S., 1967; naturalized, Aug. 17, 1988; s. Fatehchand and Lila D.; m. Joyce Johnson, Oct. 25, 1970. M.S., Delhi Sch. Econs., 1955; Ph.D. in Ecns., U. Birmington (Eng.), 1965. Lectr. dept. econs. Panjab U., Chandigarh, India, 1958-61; lectr. econometrics U. Glasgow, Scotland, 1964-65; cons. to UN, N.Y.C., 1965-66, 67-68; vis. assoc. prof. dept. econs. U. Hawaii, Honolulu, 1966-67; assoc. prof. dept. econs. Rensselaer Poly. Inst., Troy, N.Y., 1968-73, prof., 1973—, chmn. dept., 1982-87; vis. prof. Washington U., St. Louis, 1971; mem. exec. bd. N.Y. State Conf. for Asian Studies, 1974-77; acad. vis. London Sch. Econs. and Polit. Sci., 1976-77; vis. scholar Gadjah Mada U., Indonesia, 1991; chmn. bd. trustees Assn. Indian Econs. Study; mem. adv. bd. The Other Econ. Summit, N.Am.; mem. Nat. Bur. Econ. Rsch. Conf. on Rsch. in Income and Wealth, India Internat. Ctr. Author: (with Dennis Livingston) Alternative Development Strategies and Appropriate Technology, 1979; (with Mark Lutz) Essays in Gandhian Economics, 1985; (with Renu Kallianpur) Productivity and Technological Change in Foodgrains, 1986; (with Chandana Chakraborty) High Technology and International Competitiveness, 1991; mem. editorial bd. Easter Econ. Jour., Gandhi Marg, Asian Thought and Society; contbr. numerous articles on prodn. function and econ. devel. to profl. jours. NSF grantee, 1978, 81; hosted Fullbright scholar, 1989-90. Mem. Econometric Soc., Assn. for Social Econs., Am. Econ. Assn., Assn. for Asian Studies, Assn. for Indian Econ. Studies (chmn. 1975-81), Fedn. Am. Scientists, Friends of Earth Internat. (editorial bd.), N.Y. State Assn. for Asian Studies, Internat. Inst. Social Econs. Office: Rensselaer Poly Inst 110 8th St Dept Econs Troy NY 12180-3522

DIWU, ZHENJUN, chemist; b. Xunyi, China, June 29, 1962; came to U.S., 1993; s. Junxue Diwu and Qiaoyun Zhang; m. Cailan Zhang, Dec. 18, 1962; children: Y. Allan, X. Brooks. PhD, Chinese Acad. Scis., Beijing, 1988. Patent examiner The Chinese Patent Office, Beijing, 1989-90; postdoctoral fellow U. Alta., Edmonton, Can., 1990-93; prin. scientist Molecular Probes, Inc., Eugene, Oreg., 1993—; grant reviewer The Israel Sci. Found., 1993—; mem. drug rev. panel The Current Drugs, 1996—. Contbr. articles to profl. jours.; article reviewer Jour. Photochemistry and Photobiology, 1992—, Tetrahedron, 1993—. Mem. Am. Chem. Soc., Am. Photobiology Soc., Am. Oxygen Soc. Achievements include exploration of the therapeutic and diagnostic applications of hypocrellins and hypericin, development of a number of fluorescent probes for biomedical application. Office: Molecular Probes Inc 4849 Pitchford Ave Eugene OR 97402-9165

DIX, GARY ERROL, engineering executive; b. Bieber, Calif., Jan. 10, 1942; s. Errol Alvin and Evelyn Nadine (Miller) D.; m. Lanaya Diane Easley, Jan. 4, 1964. BS in Mech. Engring., U. Calif., Berkeley, 1963, MS in Mech. Engring., 1965, PhD in Mech. Engring., 1971. Engr. Gen. Electric Nuclear, San Jose, Calif., 1965-71; mgr. thermal devel. Gen. Electric Nuclear, San Jose, 1971-75, mgr. safety and hydraulics, 1975-82, mgr. core methods, 1982-85, mgr. automation sys., 1985-89, mgr. quality assurance and automation, 1989-94, mgr. devel. programs, 1994-97; code rev. group cons. Nuclear Regulatory Commn., Washington, 1976-85; cons. in field, 1997—. Contbr. articles to profl. jours.; patentee in field. Fellow Am. Nuclear Soc. (exec. com. Thermal Hydraulics divsn. 1981-91, chmn. 1986-87); mem. ASME. Avocations: computers, wine, motorcycles, basketball, movies. Office: PO Box 2394 Saratoga CA 95070-0394

DIX, ROLLIN C(UMMING), mechanical engineering educator, consultant; b. N.Y.C., Feb. 8, 1936; s. Omer Houston and Ona Mae (Cumming) D.; m. Elaine B. VanNest, June 18, 1960; children: Gregory, Elisabeth, Karen. BSME, Purdue U., 1957, MSME, 1958, PhD, 1963. Registered profl. engr., Ill. Asst. prof. mech. engring. Ill. Inst. Tech., Chgo., 1964-69, assoc. prof., 1969-80, prof., 1980—, assoc. dean for computing, 1980-96; pres. Patpending Mktg., Inc., 1996—. Patentee road repair vehicle, method for vestibular test. 1st lt. U.S. Army, 1960-61. Fellow ASME; mem. Soc. Mfg. Engrs. Home: 10154 S Seeley Ave Chicago IL 60643-2037 Office: Ill Inst Tech 10 W 32d St Chicago IL 60616-3729

DIXIT, BALWANT NARAYAN, pharmacology and toxicology educator; b. Kerawade, India, Jan. 7, 1933; came to U.S., 1962; s. Narayan V. and Janakibai N. (Gokhale) D.; m. Vidya B. Ghanekar, Dec. 26, 1969; children: Sunil, Sanjay. B.S. in Chemistry and Biology, Fergusson Coll., Poona, India, 1954; B.S. in Chemistry with honors, U. Poona, 1955; M.S. in Biochemistry with honors, U.Poona, 1956; M.S. in Pharmacology with honors, U. Baroda, India, 1962; Ph.D., U. Pitts., 1965. Sr. research fellow Baroda U., 1960-61; asst. prof. pharmacology U. Pitts., 1965-68; assoc. prof., 1968-74, prof., 1974—, asst. chmn., 1969-74, acting dean, 1976-78, chmn., 1974-87, assoc. dean, 1974-84; dir. Ctr. for the Performing Arts of India, 1992—. Recipient Disting. Alumnus award U. Pitts. Sch. Pharmacy, 1982; fellow Internat. Union Physiological Scis., 1962. Mem. Am. Soc. Pharmacology and Explt. Therapeutics, Soc. Neurosci., N.Y. Acad. Sci., Internat. Soc. Xenobiotic Metabolism. Home: 608 Ravencrest Rd Pittsburgh PA 15215-1120 Office: U Pitts 541 Salk Hall Pittsburgh PA 15261-1905

DIXIT, VISHVA M., pathology educator. MD, U. Nairobi, Kenya, 1980; postgrad., Washington U., St. Louis, 1982-86. Intern dept. medicine Kenyatta Nat. Hosp., 1980-81; resident pathology and medicine Barnes Hosp., St. Louis, 1981-86; asst. prof. pathology Med. Sch. U. Mich., Ann Arbor, 1986-91, assoc. prof., 1991—, prof. pathology, 1995-97; dir. molecular oncology Genentech, San Francisco, 1997—. Contbr. articles to profl. jours. Recipient Best Pathology Student award Kenya Med. Assn., 1980, Best Overall Med. Student Kamala Meml. award, 1980, Warner-Lambert/Parke-Davis Exptl. Pathology award Am. Soc. Investigative Pathology, 1996; Josiah Macy Found. fellow, 1989. Office: Genentech 1 Dna Way South San Francisco CA 94080-4990*

DIXON, ALBERT KING, II, retired university administrator; b. Savannah, Ga., Dec. 28, 1936; s. Albert King and Katharine Blanchard (Simmons) D.; m. Augusta Lee Mason, Mar. 27, 1959; children: Albert King III, Augusta Mason, Lee Simmons. BA in Polit. Sci. cum laude, U. S.C., 1959; postgrad., Furman U., 1984, U. Okla., 1985, Am. Inst. Banking, 1984-85. Commd. 2d lt. USMC, 1959, advanced through grades to lt. col., 1975; exec. officer USMC, Camp Pendleton, Calif., 1961, Okinawa, Japan, 1961-62; series officer Recruit Depot, athletic officer, head football coach USMC, San Diego, 1962-65; commdg. officer USMC, Vietnam, 1966-67; instr., Marine Corps Devel. and Edn. Commd., head platoon tactics sect. Basic Sch. USMC, Quantico, Va., 1967-70; schs. officer, staff sec. to commdg. gen. Pacific Fleet Marine Force USMC, Camp Smith, Hawaii, 1970-73; head football coach Quantico Marines, 1968; ops. and ground tng. officer USMC, Okinawa, 1973-74; officer in charge recruiting sta. USMC, Oklahoma City, 1974-77; ground support tng. and equipment officer Hdqs. Marine Corps USMC, Washington, 1977-81, retired, 1981; exec. dir. Laurens (S.C.) Family YMCA, 1981-83; v.p., city exec. Palmetto Bank, Laurens, 1983-88; assoc. v.p. alumni affairs U. S.C., Columbia, 1988, dir. athletics, 1988-92, spl. asst. to pres. for univ. promotion and leadership devel. 1993-97; ret., 1997. Active Boy Scouts Am.; Sunday Sch. tchr., elder, mem. com. various Presbyn. chs., Hawaii, Okla., S.C., Va.; Chmn. capital campaign Laurens County Libr., 1987-88; past pres. Laurens Dist. H.S. Booster Club, Laurens County Touchdown Club; past bd. visitors Lander Coll.; past mem. U. S.C. Edn. Found.; past mem. found. bd. Piedmont Tech.; bd. dirs. Dixie Youth Baseball, 1987, vice chmn., player agt., bd. dirs., Laurens, 1982-88; bd. dirs. Upper Savannah Coun. Govts., 1988; pres. Laurens 100 Club, 1984, 88; vice chmn. Laurens County Hist. Soc., 1985-87, Laurens County Bicentennial Com., 1985-86, Palmetto Partnership, Found. for Drug Abuse, Columbia, 1989-91; mem. study com. City of Columbia Baseball Stadium, 1989-90; mem. adv. bd. Midlands chpt. Nat. Football Found. and Hall of Fame; mem. steering com. Future Group Richland County; gov. Rotary Dist. 7750., 1987-88. Recipient Dist. award of Merit, Silver Beaver award and Scoutmaster of Yr. award Boy Scouts Am.; named to U. S.C. Athletic Hall of Fame, State of S.C. Athletic Hall of Fame. Mem. S.C. Assn. Regional Couns. (bd. dirs. 1992—, pres. 1995), So. Ind. Collegiate Ofcls. Assn. (athletic dirs. representative 1989-90), Greater Columbia C. of C. (mem. coun. on edn.), Coll. Football Assn. Athletic Dirs. (mem. com. 1989-90), VFW, Am. Legion, Laurens 100 Club (pres. 1984, 88), Masons, Shriners, Rotary Club of Laurens (dist. 7750 gov. 1987-88), Phi Beta Kappa, Sigma Alpha Pi, Omicron Delta Kappa (past pres.), Kappa Sigma Kappa (past pres.), Kappa Alpha. Avocations: reading, jogging, yardwork. Home: 1200 Dixon Rd Laurens SC 29360-9803

DIXON, ANDREW DERART, retired academic administrator; b. Belfast, No. Ireland, Oct. 27, 1925; came to U.S., 1963, naturalized, 1972; s. Andrew and Martha (Stewart) D.; m. Mary Elizabeth Henderson, Oct. 14, 1948; children: Penelope Jane, Melinda Sara, Alison Mary. Licentiate in Dental Surgery, Queens U., Belfast, 1948, B in Dental Surgery, 1949, M.Dental Surgery, 1953, B.S. (Nuffield Found. dental fellow), 1954, D.Sc., 1965; Ph.D., U. Manchester, 1958. Asst. lectr. anatomy U. Manchester, 1954-56, lectr., 1956-62, sr. lectr., 1962-63; vis. assoc. prof. anatomy U. Iowa, 1959-61; prof. dental sci. U. N.C., Chapel Hill, 1963-65, prof. dental sci., anatomy, 1965-69, prof. oral biology and anatomy, 1969-73, asst. dean, coordinator research Sch. Dentistry, 1966-69, dir. Dental Research Ctr., 1967-73, assoc. dean research, 1969-73; prof., dean UCLA, 1973-80, assoc. dean for faculty affairs, 1985-92, assoc. dean adminstrn., 1989-92; prof. emeritus, 1993—; chmn. dental tng. com. Nat. Inst. Dental Rsch., 1972-73; mem. No. Ireland Partnership. Author, editor sci. texts; contbr. numerous articles to profl. jours. Studies on early devel. and growth of the jaws, sex chromatin in oral smears as a diagnostic tool, nerve supply to oral mucous membrane, facial tissues and temporomandibular joint, facial skeletal growth, trigeminal pathway, including trigeminal ganglion, using histological histochem. and electron microscopy methods. Fulbright Sr. Fellow award, 1959-61, Commonwealth Fund Travel fellow, 1961. Fellow Am. Coll. Dentists, Internat. Coll. Dentists, AAAS; mem. ADA, Inst. of Medicine (sr.), Pacific Coast Soc. Orthodontists (hon.), Western Conf. Dental Examiners and Dental Deans (pres. 1979-80), Anat. Soc. Gt. Britain and Ireland (sr.), Am. Assn. Anatomists, Internat. Assn. Dental Rsch., AAAS, Am. Soc. Cell Biology, N.Y. Acad. Sci., Internat. Soc. Craniofacial Biology, Pierre Fauchard Acad., Sigma Xi, Omicron Kappa Upsilon, Psi Omega. Home: Box 8169 501 Portola Rd Portola Valley CA 94028

DIXON, ANN RENEE, writer; b. Richland, Wash., Feb. 26, 1954; d. David Sherman and Barbara Mae (Cook) Dixon; m. Walter Raymond Pudwill, May 30, 1982; children: Linnea Clare, Noranna Noel. BA in Swedish Lang. and Lit., U. Wash., 1976. Libr. Willow (Alaska) Pub. Libr., 1987-97. Author: (children's books) How Raven Brought Light to People, 1991, The Sleeping Lady, 1994, Merry Birthday, Nora Noel, 1996, Trick-or-Treat!, 1998, The Blueberry Shoe, 1999. Mem. Author's Guild, Soc. Children's Book Writers and Illustrators, Alaska Libr. Assn., Alaska Ctr. for the Book. Avocations: gardening, cross country skiing, swimming, walking, reading.

DIXON, ARMENDIA PIERCE, school program administrator; b. Laurel, Miss., July 15, 1937; d. L.E. and Denothras (Pickens) Pierce; m. Harrison D. Dixon Jr., Aug. 28, 1971; 1 child, Harrison D. III. BS in Edn., Jackson (Miss.) State U., 1960; postgrad., No. Ill. State U., 1965-66; MEd, Edinboro (Pa.) U., 1978; PhD, Kent State U., 1994, Kent State U., 1994. Cert. English and secondary edn., Miss. Tchr. English, libr. Laurel City Schs.,

1962-67; tchr. English, dir. summer pre-sch. Erie (Pa.) Pub. Schs., 1967-72; tchr. English, drama, journalism, forensic coach Crawford Cen. Schs., Meadville, Pa., 1972-85, asst. prin., facilitator sch. improvement coun., 1985-89, coord. successful student partnership, 1988—; prin. Meadville Area Sr. High, 1993; exec. dir. Meadville Latch-Key Program, 1985—; coord. Urban Tchrs. Project, Kent State U., adj. asst. prof., 1989—, dir. Prospective Tchrs. Program for Phi Delta Kappa; charter mem. Results chpt., Kent State U., 1990; dir. high sch. edn. Sch. dist. City of Erie, 1993—; dir. of high sch. edn., The Sch. Dist. of the City of Erie, Pa., 1993—. Fundraiser Cystic Fibrosis Found., Pitts., 1976, 79, 81, Sickle Cell Anemia, Erie, 1978-83; pres. Martin Luther King Jr. Scholarship Fund, Inc., 1979-89; bd. dirs. ARC, Erie, 1996—, Villa Marie Coll., Erie, 1995—, Internat. Inst., 1994—; mem. adv. bd. Am. Enterprise, Erie, 1993—. Mem. NAACP (pres. Meadville chpt. 1984—), Nat. Assn. Secondary Sch. Prins., Pa. Assn. Secondary Sch. Prins., Order Eastern Star (worthy matron), Navy Mothers, Rainbow Ill, Burres, Phi Delta Kappa, Alpha Kappa Alpha. Methodist. Avocations: collecting dolls, writing, gardening. Home: PO Box 561 Meadville PA 16335-0561 Office: Crawford Ctrl Schs 847 N Main St Meadville PA 16335-2655

DIXON, BILLY GENE, academic administrator; b. Benton, Ill., Oct. 25, 1935; s. John and Stella (Prowell) D.; m. Judith R. McCommons, June 7, 1957; children: Valerie J., Clark A. BS, So. Ill. U., 1957, PhD, 1967; MS, Ill. Wesleyan U., 1961. Tchr. math., chmn. dept. Cahokia (Ill.) High Sch., 1960-61; tchr. Univ. Sch., So. Ill. U., Carbondale, 1961-67, chmn. dept. math., 1963-67; dir. rsch. and evaluation ESEA Title II Project Uplift, Mt. Vernon, Ill., 1967-69; coordinator profl. edn. experiences Coll. Edn. So. Ill. U., Carbondale, 1968-75, mem. faculty, coord. grad. program in secondary edn., 1975-78, departmental exec. officer curriculum and instrn., 1978—. Pres. Benton Cmty. Pk. Dist., 1974-95. Named Citizen of Yr., Benton C. of C., 1982; recipient Liberty Bell award, 1995. Mem. Ill. Assn. Tchr. Educators (pres. 1973, exec. coun. 1976-79, Disting. mem. 1984), Assn. Tchr. Educators (chmn. nat. rev. panel Disting. Program in Tchr. Edn. 1976-86, exec. bd. 1983-86, pres. 1988-89, Pres.'s award 1983, 84, 95, Disting. mem. 1992), Pi Mu Epsilon, Phi Kappa Phi, Phi Delta Kappa, Kappa Delta Pi. Democrat. Methodist. Home: 9793 Stuyvesant St Benton IL 62812-5916 Office: So Ill U Dept Curriculum Instrn Carbondale IL 62901-4610

DIXON, CARL FRANKLIN, lawyer; b. Mansfield, Ohio, Feb. 17, 1948; s. Carl Hughes and Elizabeth (Kauffman) D.; m. Barbara Wagner, Dec. 27, 1969 (div. 1990); children: Clare Elizabeth, Jane Allison. B.A., Ill. Wesleyan U., 1970, B.S., 1970; M.A. Fletcher Sch. Law and Diplomacy div. Tufts U., 1971; JD, U. Chgo., 1974. Bar: Ill. 1975, U.S. Dist. Ct. (no. dist.) Ill. 1975, Ohio 1983. Assoc., Keck, Mahin & Cate, Chgo., 1974-78; ptnr. Dixon & Kois, Chgo., 1978-82; assoc. Porter, Wright, Morris & Arthur, Cleve., 1982-85, ptnr., 1986-87; v.p., sec., gen. counsel Weston, Inc., Cleve., 1987-90; counsel Beeler, Schad & Diamond, P.C., Chgo., 1990-93; nat. exec. dir. Nat. Kidney Cancer Assn., Evanston, Ill., 1994—. Recipient Adlai E. Stevenson award UN Assn., 1970; Edward R. Murrow fellow, 1971. bd. dirs. Chgo. Opera Theatre, 1992—. Mem. ABA, Am. Lung Assn. (trustee 1986—), Chgo. Regional Alumni Assn. Ill. Wesleyan U. (pres. 1997—), Kennilworth (Ill.) Club, North Shore Country Club (Glenview, Ill.), Phi Kappa Phi. Republican. Episcopalian. Home: 628 Brier St Kenilworth IL 60043-1061

DIXON, CAROL ANN, writer, educator; b. Huntington, W.Va., Jan. 24, 1959; d. Karl Albert and Ann (Watts) Brooks; m. Stephen Andrew Dixon, Dec. 22, 1978; 1 child, Joseph. BA, Marietta Coll., 1991. Cert. tchr., Ohio. Tchr. Marietta (Ohio) City Schs., 1991-99. Author: Aradus, 1994, Roll Call, 1996. Recipient Martin Luther King Jr. award Martin Luther King Jr. Elem. Sch., Tuscaloosa, Ala., 1991. Pentecostal. Avocations: writing, reading, art, computers. E-mail: carol.dixon@usa.net. Home and Office: 62A Rt 4 Marietta OH 45750

DIXON, DANIEL ROBERTS, JR., retired tax lawyer; b. Rocky Mount, N.C., Feb. 22, 1911; s. Daniel Roberts and Ida Louise (Mason) D.; children: Daniel Roberts III, Carolyn Roy Dixon Dyess. AB, Coll. William and Mary, 1937; JD, Duke U., 1941; LLM in Taxation, NYU, 1951. CPA, N.C.; bar: N.C. Atty. Hamel, Park & Saunders, Washington, 1951-52; asst. prof. N.C. State U., Raleigh, 1954-76; pvt. practice Raleigh, 1953—. Author: Graphic Guide Fundamental Accounting; inventor building block; contbr. articles to profl. jours. Mem. Internat. Visitors Coun., Raleigh, N.C. Capt. U.S. Air Corps., 1942-46. Mem. Navy League of U.S. (judge advocate 1990-96), N.C. Triangle Coun., N.C. Bar Assn., Wake County Bar Assn., Phi Beta Kappa (pres. Wake County), Omicron Delta Epsilon. Avocations: carpentry, organist. Home: 1022 Shelley Rd Raleigh NC 27609-4332 Office: Dixon & Hunt 7 N Bloodworth St Raleigh NC 27601-1101

DIXON, FRANK JAMES, medical scientist, educator; b. St. Paul, Mar. 9, 1920; s. Frank James and Rose Augusta (Kuhfeld) D.; m. Marion Edwards, Mar. 14, 1946; children: Janet Wynne, Frank, Michael. BS, U. Minn., 1941, MB, 1943, MD, 1944; DS (hon.), Med. Coll. Ohio, 1983; DSc (hon.), Washington U., 1992. Diplomate: Am. Bd. Pathology. Intern U.S. Naval Hosp., Great Lakes, Ill., 1943-44; research asst. dept. pathology Harvard, 1946-48; instr. dept. pathology Washington U., 1948-50, asst. prof., 1950-51; prof., chmn. dept. pathology U. Pitts. Med. Sch., 1951-60; chmn. dept. exptl. pathology Scripps Clinic and Research Found., La Jolla, Calif., 1961-74; chmn. biomed. research depts. Scripps Clinic and Research Found., 1970-74, dir. research inst., 1974-86, dir. emeritus, 1987—; rsch. assoc. dept. biology U. Calif., San Diego, 1961-64, prof. in residence dept. biology, 1965-68, adj. prof. dept. pathology, 1968-96; sci. advisor NIH, Nat. Found., Helen Hay Whitney Found., St. Jude's Med. Ctr., Christ Hosp. Inst., Cin.; mem. expert adv. panel on immunology WHO; sci. adv. bd. Nat. Kidney Found.; Pahlavi lectr. Ministry of Sci. and Higher Tech., Iran, 1976; mem. adv. com. Lupus Rsch. Inst., Nat. Multiple Sclerosis Soc., Harold C. Simmons Arthritis Rsch. Ctr., Irvington House Inst., Mass. Gen. Hosp. Editor: Advances in Immunology; mem. editorial bd. Excerpta Medica, Jour. Exptl. Medicine, Am. Jour. Pathology, Cellular Immunology, Kidney Hosp. Practice, Perspectives in Biology and Medicine, Jour. Exptl. Clin. Cancer Rsch., Springer Seminars in Immunopathology, Immunological Revs.; contbr. articles to profl. jours. Served with M.C. USNR, 1943-46. Recipient Theobald Smith award, 1952, Parke-Davis award in exptl. pathology, 1957, Disting. Achievement award Modern Medicine, 1961, Martin E. Rehfuss award in internal medicine, 1966, Von Pirquet medal Ann. Forum on Allergy, 1967, Bunim medal Am. Rheumatism Assn., 1968, Internat. award Gairdner Found., 1969, Mayo Soley award Western Soc. Clin. Research, 1969, Albert Lasker Basic Med. Research award, 1975, Dickson prize U. Pitts., 1975, Homer Smith award N.Y. Heart Assn., 1976, Rous-Whipple award Am. Assn. Pathologists, 1979, So. Calif. Permanente Med. Group Immunology award, 1979, Regents award U. Minn., 1985, H.P. Smith award Am. Soc. Clin. Pathologists, 1985, Gold-Headed Cane award, 1987, Distinguished Service award Lupus Found. Am., 1987, 88; Flame of Hope award Terri Gotthelf Rsch. Inst., 1987, Paul Klemperer award N.Y. Acad. Medicine, 1989, Jean Hamburger award Internat. Soc. Nephrology, 1990. Fellow Am. Coll. Allergists, Am. Acad. Allergy, Royal Coll. Pathologists (hon.); mem. NAS, N.Y. Acad. Scis. Western Assn. Physicians, Western Soc. Clin. Research, Soc. Exptl. Biology and Medicine, Transplantation Soc., AAAS, Am. Soc. Clin. Investigation, Am. Acad. Allergists, Interurban Path. Soc., Harvey Soc. (lectr. 1962), Am. Soc. Exptl. Pathology (pres. 1966), Am. Assn. Immunologists (pres. 1972), Am. Assn. for Cancer Research, Assn. Am. Physicians, Am. Acad. Arts and Scis., Am. Heart Assn., Coun. on the Kidney in Cardiovascular Disease, Fedn. Am. Scientists, Internat. Acad. Pathology, U.S. Acad. Pathologists, Can. Acad. Pathologists, Scandinavian Soc. for Immunology (hon.), Japanese Nephrology Soc. (hon.), Sigma Xi, Nu Sigma Nu, Alpha Omega Alpha. Office: Scripps Rsch Inst 10550 N Torrey Pines Rd La Jolla CA 92037-1000

DIXON, FREDERICK DAIL, architect; b. Raleigh, N.C., Dec. 18, 1942; s. Frederick Dail (dec.) and Mary Isabel (Richbourg)(dec.) D.; m. Artemis Markatos, July 7, 1968; children: Frederick Markatos. BArch, Clemson (S.C.) U., 1966; MFA in Sculpture, U. N.C., 1970. Intern Leslie H. Boney, Architects, Wilmington, N.C., 1966-68; architect John D. Latimer & Assocs., Durham, N.C., 1968-72, Cogswell/Hausler Assocs., Chapel Hill, N.C., 1972-74; founding ptnr. Designworks, Carrboro, N.C., 1974-82; pres. Dixon Weinstein Architects, PA, Chapel Hill, N.C., 1982—; instr. Boston Archtl. Ctr., 1970-71; vis. studio instr., critic Sch. Design N.C. State U., Raleigh, 1983—. Author: (teaching manual) Building An Energy Efficient Home, 1979. HUD grantee. Fellow AIA, South Atlantic Region AIA (award for excellence in arch. 1991, 92, Merit award 1998), N.C. AIA (Merit award 1991, 92, 95, 98). Democrat. Office: Dixon Weinstein Architects PA #25 The Courtyard 431 W Franklin St Chapel Hill NC 27516-2319

DIXON, GALE HARLLEE, drug company executive; b. Florence, S.C., Sept. 13, 1944; d. Hammond Alfred and Geraldine (Young) H.; m. Lawrence Rembert Dixon III, Aug. 22, 1963; children: Elizabeth Teal, Sarah Anne. Student, Winthrop Coll., 1962-63, Richmond Profl. Inst., 1963-64. Receptionist Mead Corp., Durham, N.C., 1964-66; sec., bookkeeper Dixon Drug Co., Inc., Florence, S.C., 1966-85, v.p., sec., 1985—; adv. bd. mem. Quality Bus. Credit, Florence, S.C., 1988-96. Author: (booklet) Brief History of United Methodist Women. Pres. United Meth. Women, 1981-82, mem. adminstrv. bd., 1981—, chmn. coun. on ministries, 1990-94; chmn. 125th Ann., Ctrl. United Meth. Ch., Florence, 1995; treas. Florence Jr. Welfare Legue, 1978, bd. dirs., 1978-81; mem. Hist. Soc. S.C.; sustaining mem. jr. Welfare League of Florence, S.C., 1986—. Recipient Service award Florence Heart Assn., 1974; named Florence's Outstanding Young Woman, Florence Jaycees, 1980. Mem. DAR (treas. 1989-90, sec. 1996—), Florence C. of C., Huguenot Soc. S.C., Colonial Dames of XVII Century, Florence Heritage Found. (sec. 1988), Forget Me Not Garden Club (pres. 1979-80), Garden Club of S.C. (life). Methodist. Home: 1210 W Claremont Ave Florence SC 29501-5624 Office: Dixon Drug Co Inc 160 S Dargan St Florence SC 29506-2532

DIXON, GEORGE DAVID, radiologist; b. Valley City, N.D., Mar. 27, 1936; s. George Sherman and Isabel Ruth (Eaton) D.; m. Carol Marie Vennerstrom, Feb. 28, 1958; children: Barbara Sarah, George David Jr. Student, Willamette U., 1954-55; BA, U. N.D., 1959; MD, Tulane U., 1961. Diplomate Am. Bd. Radiology (added qualifications 1997). Intern St. Luke's Hosp., Duluth, Minn., 1961-62; gen. practice Lenont-Peterson Clinic, Cook, Minn., 1962-64; resident in radiology Mayo Clinic, Rochester, Minn., 1964-66, 68-70; radiologist St. Luke's Hosp. Radiol. Group, Inc., Kansas City, Mo., 1970—, sec., 1971—; clin. prof. radiology U. Mo. Sch. Medicine, Kansas City, 1985—; sec.-treas. med. staff St. Lukes Hosp., 1992, v.p. med. staff, 1993, pres. med. staff, 1995. Mem. edit. adv. bd. Miller-Freeman Pubs., Inc., 1979—; contbr. articles to med. jours. Pres. Interdenominational Christian Youth Council, Fargo, N.D., 1953-54; lay leader Indian Heights United Meth. Ch., Overland Park, Kans., 1977-79. Served to capt. U.S. Army, 1966-68, Vietnam. Fellow Am. Coll. Radiology (alt. councilor Mo.), Am. Heart Assn., Soc. Cardiovasc. and Interventional Radiology; mem. AMA, Mo. State Med. Soc., Mo. Radiol. Soc. (bd. dirs.), Met. Med. Soc., Greater Kansas City Radiol. Soc. (sec. 1978-79, treas. 1977-78, pres.), Radiol. Soc. N.Am. (counselor Western Mo. dist. 1988-92, 98—), Am. Roentgen Ray Soc., New Eng. Hist. Geneal. Soc., Wally Byan Caravan Club (Kansas City), Masons, Phi Beta Kappa, Beta Theta Pi, Phi Beta Pi. Republican. Avocations: traveling by trailer, genealogy. Home: 10416 Mohawk Ln Shawnee Mission KS 66206-2551 Office: St Lukes Hosp Dept Radiology PO Box 119000 Kansas City MO 64171-9000 *Personal philosophy: Words by which I have come to live by - "All I really need to know I learned in kindergarten and Sunday School."*

DIXON, GORDON HENRY, biochemist; b. Durban, South Africa, Mar. 25, 1930; Can. citizen; s. Walter James and Ruth (Nightingale) D.; m. Sylvia W. Gillen, Nov. 20, 1954; children: Frances Anne, Walter Timothy, Christopher James, Robin Jonathan. M.A. with honors, U. Cambridge, Eng., 1951; Ph.D., U. Toronto, 1956. Research asso. U. Wash., 1956-58; research asso. U. Oxford, Eng., 1958-59; asst. prof. biochemistry U. Toronto, 1959-61, asso. prof., 1961-63; prof. U. B.C., 1963-72; prof., chmn. dept. biochemistry U. Sussex, Eng., 1972-74; prof. med. biochemistry U. Calgary, Alta., Can., 1974-94; emeritus, 1994—; chmn. U. Calgary, Alta., Can., 1983-88. Contbr. articles to profl. jours. Recipient Steacie prize Steacie Found., 1966, Killam Meml. prize Can. Coun., 1991; named Officer of the Order of Canada, 1993. Fellow Royal Soc. London, Royal Soc. Can. (Flavelle medal 1980); mem. Am. Soc. Biol. Chemists, Am. Soc. Cell Biology, Can. Biochem. Soc. (pres. 1982-83, Ayerst award 1966), Pan-Am. Assn. Biochem. Socs. (v.p. 1984-87, pres. 1987-90), Internat. Union Biochemistry (exec. coun. 1988-94). E-mail: gdixon@islandnet.com.

DIXON, HARRY D., JR., prosecutor; b. Waycross, Ga., Nov. 6, 1953; s. Harry D. Sr. and Ruth (Starling) D.; m. Elizabeth Tonning, Apr. 19, 1980; 2 children. AB in History, Valdosta State Coll., 1974; JD, U. Ga., 1977. Bar: Ga. 1977, U.S. Dist. Ct. Ga. 1978, U.S. Ct. Appeals 1979. Law clk. to Hon. Marvin Hartley, Jr. Superior Ct. for Mid. Jud. Cir., 1977-78; asst. dist. atty. Waycross Jud. Cir., 1977-79, dist. atty., 1983-94; atty. Bennett, Pedrick and Bennett, 1979-83; U.S. atty. for so. dist. Ga. U.S. Dept. Justice, Savannah, 1994—. Office: US Atty So Dist GA 100 Bull St Ste 201 Savannah GA 31401-3305*

DIXON, JACK EDWARD, biological chemistry educator, consultant; b. June 16, 1943. BA, UCLA, 1966; PhD, U. Calif., Santa Barbara, 1971. NSF Found. postdoctoral rsch. fellow U. Calif., San Diego, 1971-73; from asst. prof. to assoc. prof. biochemistry Purdue U., West Lafayette, Ind., 1973-82, prof. biochemistry, 1982-86, Harvey W. Wiley disting. prof. biochemistry, 1986-91; Minor J. Coon prof. biol. chemistry, chmn. dept. U. Mich., Ann Arbor, 1991—; adj. asst. prof. biochemistry, Ind. U. Sch. Medicine, 1976-78, assoc. prof. biochemistry, 1978-91, adj. prof. biochemistry, 1983-91; part-time prof. medicine Ind. U. Sch. Medicine, 1985-91; vis. lectr. Wash. State U., 1985; cons. Wyeth-Ayurst Co., Phila., 1985—, Monsanto Chem. Co., St. Louis, 1985—, Mitotix Inc., Cambridge, Mass., 1993—; P.T. Varandani Meml. lectr. Wright State U., Dayton, Ohio, 1987; chmn. rsch. rev. com. Ind. affiliate Am. Heart Assn., 1983; spl. reviewer alcohol study NIH, 1983, 84, endocrine study sect., 1985-90: Nathan O. Kaplan lectr. U. Calif., San Diego, 1991; Vestling lectr. U. Iowa, 1991; Edmund Fischer lectr. U. Wash., Seattle, 1993; Arets Novo Nordisk lectr. U. Copenhagen, 1994; presenter in field. Mem. editl. bd.: Archives Biochem. Biophysics, 1981-84, Am. Jour. Physiology, 1985—, Jour. Biol. Chemistry, 1989—, Endocrinology, 1993—, Biochemistry, 1994—, Analytical Biochemistry, 1985—, exec. editor. Recipient Rsch. award Ind. affiliate Am. Diabetes Assn., 1985-86, MERIT award NIH, 1987, 96, Lions award for cancer rsch., 1990. Fellow Mich. Soc. Fellows, U. Mich. (sr.), Am. Acad. Arts and Sci.; mem. AAAS, NAS (elected mem. Inst. Medicine 1993), Am. Chem. Soc., Am. Physiol. Soc., Am. Soc. Biochemistry and Molecular Biology (program chmn. 1994—, pres. 1996-97), Am. Soc. Cell Biology, Am. Soc. Neurosci., Soc. Sigma XI, Phi Kappa Phi. Office: U Mich Biochem Dept M5416 Med Sci 1 0606 Ann Arbor MI 48109-0606*

DIXON, JO-ANN CONTE, management consultant; b. Orange, N.J., Aug. 5, 1942; d. Rocco Louis and Antoinette (DeRosa) Conte; m. Michael Eugene Dixon, July 26, 1964; children: Christopher Michael, Peter Eugene. Student, Paterson State Coll., 1960-63; AA, Thomas A. Edison Coll., 1976; BA, 1978. Tchr. St. Raphael's Sch., Livingston, N.J., 1963-68; owner Orgn. Unltd., Glen Ridge, N.J., 1972-76; market rsch. analyst Harkness & Assoc., San Francisco, 1976-78; adminstr. corp. tng. dept. Rapidata, Inc., Fairfield, N.J., 1978-80; mgr. corp. tng. dept., 1980-81; pres., prin. cons. Q, Inc., Essex Fells, 1980-89; pres. MatchPlay Internat., Inc., 1992-96; regional dir. Am. Mgmt. Assoc., 1996-98, dir. bus. devel., 1999—; bd. trustees Mt. St. Dominic Acad., 1989-95; dir. alumni rels. N.J. Inst. Tech., Newark, 1981-83, West Essex Cmty. Health Svcs., devel. chair, 1988-93, pres. 1993-95; dir. mgmt. devel. Rutgers U. Grad. Sch. Mgmt., 1983-84; bd. dir. alumni affairs/devel. officer Seton Hall Law Sch., Newark, 1984-85; chmn. bd. trustees Nat. Inst. for Orgnl. and Mgmt. Rsch., Essex Fells, N.J., 1987-92. Chmn. bd., sec. Passaic River Coalition, Basking Ridge, N.J., 1976-83, vice chmn. bd., 1983-88, regional coord., 1971-76; chmn. mayor's com. on environ., Glen Ridge, 1974-75; mem. N.J. Gov.'s Task Force for Passaic River, 1976-78; mem., pres. Home and Sch. Bd., Glen Ridge, 1978-79; mem. Nat. Trust Hist. Preservation scholar, 1977. Recipient citation Borough of Glen Ridge, 1975, Kiwanis award for excellence in citizen involvement, 1974, Charles T. Morgan award for excellence in tng. and devel., 1989. Mem. Am. Soc. Tng. and Devel. (v.p. comms. profl.) excellence award 1980), LWV, Knights of malto-Order St. John of Jerusalem (Dame of Malta 1986), Glen Ridge Hist. Soc. (founder), West Essex C. of C. (bd. dirs. 1988-89, v.p. 1990-91, pres. 1991-92), Kiwanis (bd. dirs. 1990-93, N.J. found. bd. trustees 1990-92, sec. 1996—, v.p. Caldwell/West Essex chpt. 1996-97, pres. elect 1997-98, pres. 1998—). Home and Office: 97 Lane Ave West Caldwell NJ 07006-7426

DIXON, JOANNE ELAINE, music educator; b. Lancaster, Pa., July 3, 1944; d. William Russell and Anna Mary (Allen) D. B Music Edn., Westminster Choir Coll., Princeton, N.J., 1966; MEd, Trenton State Coll., 1982. Cert. music tchr., N.J. Music tchr. Warren (N.J.) Twp. Sch. Dist., 1966-67; vocal music tchr. Branchburg Twp. Sch. Dist., Somerville, N.J., 1967—, handbell dir., 1985—; music edn. handbell cons. Somerset County Dept. Edn., 1988-90; handbell dir., cons. Music Educator's Nat. Conf., Washington, 1990; N.J. rep. Com. for Handbells in Music Edn., Dayton, Ohio, 1990—. Handbell ringer First United Meth. Ch., Somerville, 1985—, mem. visions com., 1992-94, substitute handbell dir., 1992—; condr. N.J. Schs. Handbell Festival, 1995, 96. Recipient Excellence in Tchg. award State of N.J. Dept. Edn., 1988. Mem. Am. Guild English Handbell Ringers (area II N.J. rep. 1993-96, N.J. state rep. 1993-96, handbell workshop dir. 1993—), Branchburg Fedn. Tchrs. Democrat. Avocations: ringing handbells, painting, reading, stitchery. Home: 977 Robin Rd Somerville NJ 08876-4440 Office: Old York Sch 580 Old York Rd Somerville NJ 08876-3785

DIXON, JOHN FULTON, village manager; b. Bellingham, Wash., Dec. 17, 1946; s. Fulton Albert and Patricia (Broderick) D.; m. Karen Elizabeth Creagh, May 19, 1973; children: Neil, Craig. BS, Bradley U., 1971; M in Mgmt., Vanderbilt U., 1973. Asst. village mgr. Village of Hoffman Estates, Ill., 1974-76, village mgr., 1980-86; dir. village svcs. Village of Roselle, Ill., 1976-79; asst. village mgr. Village of Schaumburg, Ill., 1979-80; village adminstr. Village of Lake Zurich, Ill., 1986-87; village mgr. Village of Mt. Prospect, Ill., 1987-92; village adminstr. Village of Lake Zurich, 1992—; mgr. exec. bd. dirs. N.W. Suburban Mcpl. Joint Action Water Agy., Hoffman Estates, 1980-92; mem. exec. bd. dirs. N.W. Cen. Dispatch, Arlington Heights, Ill., 1987-92. Troop com. chmn. Boy Scouts Am., 1989-93; bd. dirs. Marklund Chilren's Home. Recipient Chief Scout's award Gov. Gen. of Jamaica, Kingston, 1970; Adminstrv. fellow Woodrow Wilson Found., 1973-74, Houston fellow Vanderbilt U., 1972-73; Baker scholar Vanderbilt U., 1971-73. Mem. Met. Chgo. City Mgrs. Assn. (bd. dirs., pres. 1986-87), Ill. City Mgmt. Assn. (bd. dirs., pres. 1990-91), Rotary (bd. dirs. 1989—, pres. Lake Zurich chpt. 1997-98). Roman Catholic. Avocations: golf, travel. Home: 248 Sebby Ln Lake Zurich IL 60047-1358 Office: Village of Lake Zurich 70 E Main St Lake Zurich IL 60047-3204

DIXON, JOHN MORRIS, magazine editor; b. Long Branch, N.J., June 22, 1933; s. Abram C. and Emily (Minton) D.; m. Carol Ruth Nipomnich, Dec. 27, 1959; children: Peter, Susannah. B.Arch., MIT, 1955. From asst. editor to sr. editor Progressive Architecture, 1960-65, editor, 1971-96; sr. editor Archtl. Forum, 1965-71. Author: Architectural Design Preview, U.S.A, 1962, (with N. White and E. Willensky) A.I.A. Guide to New York City, 1967. Served to 1st lt. AUS, 1955-57. Fellow A.I.A. (chmn. exhibits com. N.Y. chpt. 1964-65, co-chmn. visitors com. N.Y. chpt. 1965-66, chmn. pub. relations com. N.Y. chpt. 1970-71, mem. design com. 1978—, chmn. 1983). Home: 382 Sound Beach Ave Old Greenwich CT 06870-2223

DIXON, JOHN MORRIS, JR., lawyer; b. Hopkinsville, Ky., Apr. 3, 1940; s. John Morris Sr. and Margaret (Herndon) D.; m. Myrna R. Dixon, Sept. 3, 1960 (div. 1981); children: John M. III, Kathryn D.; m. Linda Palmer, Mar. 25, 1995; stepchildren: Eric Scowden Jr., Brent Scowden. BS, U. Ky., 1962, JD, 1965. Bar: Ky. 1965, Ark. 1968. Assoc. Bridges, Young, Matthews & Davis, Pine Bluff, Ark., 1968-70; ptnr. Turner & Dixon, Hopkinsville, 1970-75, Turner, Dixon, Kemp & Fletcher, Hopkinsville, 1975-77, Turner, Dixon & Kemp, Hopkinsville, 1977-89; prin. John M. Dixon Jr., Atty., Hopkinsville, 1989; ptnr. Dixon & Kemp, Hopkinsville, 1989-91; U.S. magistrate judge Bowling Green, Ky., 1991—. Capt. U.S. Army, 1965-68. Mem. ABA, Ky. Bar Assn. Office: US Courthouse 241 E Main St Bowling Green KY 42101-2170

DIXON, JOHN SPENCER, international executive; b. London, Apr. 23, 1957; s. Richard Kennedy and Elizabeth Ann (Flaxman) D.; m. Karen Beth Swanson, Aug. 18, 1984; children: Katherine Elizabeth, John Spencer Jr. BA with honors, Oxford U., 1979, MA, 1985; MBA, Harvard U., 1982. Supply exec. Hi-Tec Sports Ltd., Essex, England, 1982-86; pres. Hi-Tec Internat. Ltd., Taichung, Taiwan, 1983-84; founder, ptnr. Transatlantic Mktg. Co., Essex, England, 1985—; exec. v.p. Decipher, Inc., Norfolk, Va., 1988-90; pres. Waller Whittemore & Co., Virginia Beach, Va., 1992—, PH Internat., Virginia Beach, Va., 1997—. Mem. Brit. Toy and Hobby Mfrs. Assn. Presbyterian. Avocations: music, sports. Home: 4829 Berrywood Rd Virginia Beach VA 23464-5874 Office: 1060 Laskin Rd Ste 22B Virginia Beach VA 23451-6381

DIXON, JOHN WESLEY, JR., retired religion and art educator; b. Richmond, Va., Aug. 18, 1919; s. John Wesley and Margaret (Denny) D.; m. Vivian Ardelia Slagle, Jan. 9, 1943; children: Susan Raglan, Judith Ann, Miriam Elizabeth. B.A., Emory & Henry Coll., 1941; Ph.D., U. Chgo., 1953. Instr. Mich. State U., East Lansing, 1950-52; asst. prof. Emory U., Atlanta, 1952-57; exec. dir. Faculty Christian Fellowship, N.Y.C., 1955-57; assoc. prof. Dickinson Coll., Carlisle, Pa., 1957-60; prof. Fla. Presbyn. Coll., St. Petersburg, 1960-63; prof. religion and art U. N.C., Chapel Hill, 1963-87, prof. emeritus, 1987—. Author: Nature and Grace in Art, 1964, Art and the Theological Imagination, 1978, The Physiology of Faith, 1979, The Christ of Michelangelo, 1994, Images of Truth, 1996. Served to 1st lt. U.S. Army, 1941-45. Recipient Tanner Teaching award, 1967. Democrat. Episcopalian. Home: 216 Glenhill Ln Chapel Hill NC 27514-5916 Office: U NC Dept Religion Chapel Hill NC 27514

DIXON, JULIAN CAREY, congressman; b. Washington, Aug. 8, 1934; m. Bettye Lee; 1 child, Cary Gordon. BS, Calif. State U., L.A., 1962; LLB, Southwestern U., L.A., 1967. Mem. Calif. State Assembly, 1972-78; mem. 96th-106th Congresses from Calif. 28th (now 32nd) Dist.; mem. House Appropriations Com. 96th-106th Congresses from Calif. 32d Dist.; mem. subcom. on D.C.; mem. subcom. Commerce, Justice, State and Judiciary; ranking mem. select com. on intelligence, mem. subcom. on nat. security, mem. appropriations subcom. on D.C.; bd. dirs. CBC Found., Inc., pres., 1986-90. With U.S. Army, 1957-60. Mem. NAACP, Urban League, Calif. Arts Commn. Democrat. Office: House of Representatives 2252 Rayburn Bldg Washington DC 20515-0532

DIXON, KATHLEEN GRACE, English educator; b. Richland, Wash., Jan. 23, 1955; d. John Wesley and Donna Rae (Rummer) D. BA, U. Wash., 1978, MA, 1983; PhD, U. Mich., 1991. Instr. Chadron (Nebr.) State Coll., 1983-84; asst. prof. Eastern Oreg. State Coll., LaGrande, 1986-85, Ohio State U., Lima, 1989-91; from asst. prof. to assoc. prof. U. N.D., Grand Forks, 1991—; reader Coll. Composition & Comm., 1995—, Jour. Advanced Composition, 1996—. Author: Making Relationships, 1997, Outbursts in Academe, 1998. Mem. MLA, Nat. Coun. Tchrs. English, Nat. Women's Studies Assn. Democrat. Avocations: gardening, traveling, cross-country skiing. Office: English Dept U ND PO Box 7209 Grand Forks ND 58202-7209

DIXON, LANI GENE, critical care nurse; b. Elgin, Ill., Aug. 7, 1942; d. Hubert Leroy and Luella Evadine (Causey) Fredrickson; m. Vincent Dale Dixon, July 5, 1966; children: Daniel Lee, Darin Lance. Diploma, Evanston Hosp. Assn., 1963; BA, St. Mary's Coll., 1987, MS, 1991. Courier nurse Sante Fe R.R., Chgo.; critical care staff nurse Good Samaritan Hosp., San Jose, Calif.; dept. mgr. Good Samaritan Hosp., San Jose, dir. patient care; nurse recruiter Kaiser Permanente Med. Ctr., Santa Clara, Calif.; dir. prime care Watsonville (Calif.) Cmty. Hosp.; clin. rsch. assoc. Abbott Labs., Morgan Hill, Calif. Recipient Mgrs. Innovation award Good Samaritan Hosp., 1988; named Bus. Assoc. of Yr., Am. Bus. Womens Assn., 1991. Mem. Assn. Clin. Rsch. Profls., Soc. Critical Care Medicine, Orgn. Nurse Execs., Calif. Nurses Assn. Home: 17392 Tassajara Cir Morgan Hill CA 95037-7022

DIXON, LARRY DEAN, state legislator; b. Nowata, Okla., Aug. 31, 1942; s. Chesley Lafayette and Charlene (Walker) D.; m. Gaynell Kimbrough, Dec. 23, 1967; children: Katherine Dixon Hert, Elizabeth Walker. AAS, Columbia Basin Jr. Coll., 1966; BS in Police Sci., Wash. State U., 1968, MA in History, 1970. Cons., Ala. State Dept. Edn., 1970-72; dir. dept. edn. Med. Assn. State of Ala., Montgomery, 1972-76; dir. Montgomery Family Practice Residency Program, 1976-78, Jackson Hosp. Found., Montgomery, 1978-81; exec. dir. Ala. Bd. Med. Examiners, Montgomery, 1981—. Mem. Montgomery City Council, 1975-78, Ala. Ho. of Reps., 1978-82, Ala. Senate, 1982—; past mem. steering com. Nat. Clearinghouse on Licensure,

Enforcement and Regulation; past bd. dirs. Fedn. State Med. Bds.; presdl. appointee Intergovt. Agy. Coun. on Edn., 1986-90, 90-94; mem. legis. adv. bd. So. Regional Edn. Bd., 1986-90; mem. Med. Scholarship Bd., State of Ala., 1988—; past trustee Tuskegee U. Served with U.S. Army, 1961-64. Mem. Nat. Conf. State Legislatures, Adminstrs. in Medicine Soc. (pres. 1984-85), Edn. Commn. of the States, Ala. Ex POWs (hon.). Republican. Methodist. Clubs: Blue Gray Assn. Lodge: Lions (Montgomery). Home and Office: 820 E Fairview Ave Montgomery AL 36106-1818 also: PO Box 946 Montgomery AL 36101-0946

DIXON, LORRAINE, city official; b. Chgo., June 18, 1950. BS in Secondary Edn., Chgo. State U., 1972. Alderman, ward 8 Chgo., 1991—. chmn. Com. on Budget and Govt. Ops., 1994—; pres. pro-tempore Chgo. City Coun.; bd. dirs. Open Hands Chgo. and Jackson Park Hosp. Mem. United Negro Coll. Fund, Cook County Dem. Women, Ill. Majority Women's Caucus, Operation PUSH, 87th St. C. of C. (bd. dirs.). Office: 8539 S Cottage Grove Ave Chicago IL 60619-6115

DIXON, MARGUERITE ANDERSON, retired nursing educator; b. Pitts., May 18, 1930; d. William Orlando and Ida Mary (Taylor) Anderson; m. Relyea M. Dixon, June 15, 1952 (dec.); children: Marguerite Elise Dixon-Roper, Relyea Paul. BSN, U. Ill., Chgo., 1959; BA, Andrews U., Berrien Springs, Mich., 1952; MSN, U. Ill., Chgo., 1971, PhD, 1982. Rsch. asst. Coll. Dentistry U. Ill.; adminstrv. nurse I, II & III U. Ill. Hosp., asst. dir. nursing; asst. prof., coord. grad. program psychiat. nursing U. Ill., Chgo., 1985-90; acting dean Chgo. State U., 1990-93. Contbr. articles to profl. jours. Mem. Mayor's Task Force on Women's Health, Chgo., 1993—; pres. local host. bd., 1994. Mem. ANA, Ill. Nurses Assn., Sigma Theta Tau Internat.

DIXON, MICHAEL WAYNE, designer, writer, researcher; b. Honolulu, Hawaii, May 3, 1942; s. Gordon Alvin and Terry (Mendes) D.; m. Janis Marie Travis, Jan. 4, 1963 (div. 1977); children: Kimberlee Ann, Gregory Page, Morgan Ashley; m. Harlene Miller, Dec. 15, 1997. Tech. illustrator Rockwell Internat., Anaheim, Calif., 1962-66, Western Gear Corp., Lynwood, Calif., 1966-69; owner Unisex Clothing Store, Norwalk, Calif., 1969-71; mgr. Am. Health Industries, Downey, Calif., 1971-72; police officer Vernon Police Dept., L.A. Police Dept., 1972-81; designer, pres. Dornaus and Dixon Enterprises, Inc., Huntington Beach, Calif., 1979-88; freelance writer Huntington Beach, 1986—. *Michael Dixon has a strongly varied and prolific background in several disciplines: principally human biology, physics, chemistry, ballistics and mechanical design engineering. As an independent researcher with more than thirty years experience, he discovered the cause and cure for atherosclerosis (the main cause of cardiovascular disease), conducted and directed all of the research in the development of the patented potentiated magnesium, developed and patented world's first double ligand, compound coordination which produces orthomolecular homeastasis. He has five United States patents and twenty-nine foreign patents to his name. He is the founder, director of research and CEO of Maxcelint (1999) and founder and CEO of Gusty Winds Corporation (1991).* Inventor firearm safety devices, 10mm auto cartridge, Just'n Case police holster, MAWB cutter police bullet, BodyHugger holsters and ammunition holders, piper nigrum and acetic acid lachrymator, nutritional supplement formula that prevents arteriosclerosis, potentiated magnesium (patentee); author: Bren Ten Owner's Manual, 1982, BodyShaping, 1985, BodyQuest, 1993, BodySense, 1993, BodyLanguage, 1993, Courtroom Rapport, 1993, Naked Truth, 1995, There is a Magic Bullet After All, 1996, Cardiovascular Disease, Potentiated Magnesium and the True Fountain of Youth, 1999. Founder, dir. Street Smart Pepper Spray Hdqs. of Calif., 1994—, CEO Gusty Winds Corp., 1991—, founder, CEO Maxcelint, 1999. With USN, 1959-62. Mem. N.Y. Acad. Scis., Am. Film Inst., Rsch. Coun. Scripps Clinic and Rsch. Found., Smithsonian Instn., L.A. County Mus. Art, Linus Pauling Inst. Sci. and Medicine.

DIXON, MICHEL L., educational administrator; b. Norman, Okla., Oct. 2, 1945; s. Gerald R. and Erma M. (Fischer) D.; m. Mary Dee Brown, July 12, 1970 (div. 1995); children: Terri, Kelly, Kristi, Johanna. BA, Athens Coll., 1968, BE, 1972; MEd, U. Ala., 1976. Ins. adjustor Gen. Adjustment Bur., Birmingham, Ala., 1968-71; tchr. Adamsburg Sch., DeKalb County, Ala., 1971-72, Decatur (Ala.) City Schs., 1972-80; pubs. rep. Economy Pub. Co., Oklahoma City, 1980-82, Jostens Printing & Pub. Div., Mpls., 1982-84; course dir. AS100 Air Force ROTC, Maxwell AFB, Ala., 1984-85; pub. Civil Air Patrol News Aux. USAF, Maxwell AFB, 1985-86; tng. specialist, course mgr. Corps Engrs. Tng. div. U.S. Army, Huntsville, Ala., 1986-89; adminstr. Lawrence County High Sch., Moulton, Ala., 1989-90, Dept. Defense Dependent Sch., Nuernburg, Fed. Repub. Germany, 1990-91; dir. edn. programs in all western states U.S. Army 6th Recruiting BDE, Ft. Baker, Calif., 1991-94; prin. Round Valley H.S., Covelo, Calif., 1994-95; asst. prin. Calexico (Calif.) H.S., 1996-97, Capistrano Adult Sch., 1997-98; dir. cmty. edu. Mt. Brook (Ala.) Schs., Ala., 1998—. Author: textbook AS 100, 1984; editor The Air Force Today, 1985; author, editor 3 slide briefings Aircraft and Weapons of AF, Vietnam, Korea, 1984-85; pub. Civil Air Patrol News, 1985-86. Test proctor Am. Mensa Soc. Presbyterian. Avocations: photography, electronics, country dancing, woodworking, bicycling. Home: 1501 Cedar Crest Dr Birmingham AL 35216-5322 Office: Mountain Brook High Sch 3650 Bethune Dr Mountain Brook AL 35223-1499

DIXON, NEIL EDWARD, elementary school educator, paleoanthropologist; b. Inglewood, Calif.; s. Thomas Francis and Margaret (Donovan) D. BA, Pepperdine U., 1968, teaching credential, 1969; cert. sci. lang., U. So. Calif., 1987. Engr. trainee N.Am. Aviation Inc., Miami, Fla., 1964; elem. educator Woodcrest Sch., L.A. Unified Sch. Dist., 1969-98; curriculum developer L.A. Zoo, 1987-90; tchr. inservice leader L.A. Dept. Water and Power; curriculum developer L.A. County Museum Natural History, 1991; mem. rsch. expdn. to Amazon (Peru), 1981, 87, 98-99, to Sudan, 1982-83, rsch. expdn. to Amazon/Andes, 1987, 98. Author: (books) Chinese Golden Monkey, 1987, Stones and Bones Elementary Pathways, 1989. Named Tchr. of Yr., L.A. County, 1994, Tchr. of Yr., NAACP, 1990, participant Tchr. in Space, 1985-86; grantee Urban Quail Farm Project, 1986, L.A. Ednl. Partnership, 1989, computer tech. grantee Calif. A.B. 803, 1988, Louis B. Leakey Rsch. grantee, 1985-87; Advances in Biol. Sci. Program fellow NSF, 1987, 88, Smithsonian Inst./Nat. Acad. of Scis. Nat. Sci. Resources Ctr./Elem. Sci. Inst., 1992; recipient Toberman award Black-Foxe Mil. Inst., 1965. Mem. NSTA, World Aerospace Educators Orgn., Mentor Sci. Tchr. Home: 1105 Van Buren Ave Venice CA 90291-5028

DIXON, N(ORMAN) REX, speech and hearing scientist, educator; b. Ecorse, Mich., Feb. 24, 1932; s. Theodore Roosevelt and Mary Ann (Barnes) D.; m. Barbara Allen Rose, Sept. 19, 1968; 1 child, Lara Britton. BA, Western Mich. U., 1958; MA, Ind. U., 1960; PhD, Stanford U., 1966. Instr. Cornell U., Ithaca, N.Y., 1960-61; research staff mem. IBM Corp., San Jose, Calif., 1963-67; adv. scientist IBM Corp., Raleigh, N.C., 1967-72; research staff mem. IBM Corp., Yorktown Heights, N.Y., 1972-83; assoc. editor Jour. Research and Devel. IBM Corp., White Plains, N.Y., 1983-84; editor IBM Corp., 1984-89, cons., 1989—; asst. prof. San Jose State U., Calif., 1964-65; adj. prof. N.C. Central U., Durham, 1967, N.C. State U., 1969-70; vis. prof. Brown U., Providence, 1980—; mem. com. computerized speech recognition NRC, 1983-84. Editor: (with others) Automatic Speech and Speaker Recognition, 1979; contbr. articles to profl. jours. Fellow IEEE (chmn. tech. program Internat. Conf. Acoustics, Speech and Signal Processing 1977, assoc. editor, mem. editorial bd. Jour. Transactions on Acoustics Speech and Signal Processing 1977-81, gen. chmn. Workshop on Automatic Speech Recognition, gen. chmn. Internat. Conf. Acoustics, Speech and Signal Processing 1985, co-chmn. IEEE-Academia Sinica Workshop on Acoustics, Speech and Signal Processing 1986, bd. dirs. 1986-87, Meritorious Service award 1979, 86, vice chmn. pubs. bd. 1987, v.p. tech. activities 1988, chmn. tech. activites bd. 1988); mem. Acoustics Speech and Signal Processing Soc. of IEEE (mem. adminstrv. com. 1976-79, chmn. tech. com. on speech processing 1977-80, chmn. standing com. on conf. standards 1977-81, v.p. 1979-81, pres. 1982-83, Meritorious Service award 1979), Internat. Platform Assn., 1991. Home and Office: 1325 Pembroke Jones Dr Wilmington NC 28405-5205

DIXON, PAUL EDWARD, lawyer, metal products and manufacturing company executive, lawyer; b. Bklyn., Aug. 27, 1944; s. Paul Stewart and Bernice (Mathisen) D.; BA, Villanova U., 1966; JD, St. Johns U., 1972; m. Kathleen Constance Kayser, Sept. 23, 1967; children: Jennifer Pyne, Paul Kayser, Meredith Stewart. Admitted to N.Y. State bar, 1972, U.S. Supreme Ct., 1976; assoc. mem. firm Rogers & Wells, N.Y.C., 1972-77; sec., asst. gen. counsel Volvo of Am. Corp., Rockleigh, N.J., 1977-79, v.p., gen. counsel, 1979-81; v.p., gen. counsel, sec. Reichhold Chems. Inc., 1981-88; sr. v.p., gen. counsel, sec. The Warnaco Group Inc., 1988-91; v.p., gen. counsel, sec. Handy & Harman, N.Y.C., 1992—; chmn. Teeches Ltd., Bermuda. Mem. ABA, Assn. Bar City N.Y., N.Y. State Bar Assn., U.S. Supreme Ct. Hist. Soc., Am. Corp. Counsel Assn. Club: Bedford Golf and Tennis Club. Office: Handy & Harman 555 Theodore Fremd Ave Rye NY 10580-1437

DIXON, RICHARD N., state legislator; b. Apr. 17, 1938; married; 2 children. BS, Morgan State U., 1960, MBA, 1975; LLD, Western Md. Coll., 1988. Asst. v.p. Merrill Lynch Pierce Fenner & Smith, Inc.; del. Dist. 5A Md. State Delegation, 1983-94, del. Dist. 5, 1995—, mem. appropriations com., 1983—, chmn. joint budget and audit com., co-chmn. spl. joint com. on pensions; treas. State of Md. Mem. Carroll County Bd. Edn., 1970-78, pres., 1975-77; trustee Mid-States Assn. Colls. and Schs., Commn. on Secondary Schs. Decorated Bronze Star. Mem. NRA, VFW, Aircraft Owners and Pilots Assn., Kappa Alpha Psi. Address: 109 Goldstein Treasury 80 Calvert St Rm 109 Annapolis MD 21401-1907*

DIXON, RICHARD WAYNE, retired communications company executive; b. Hubbard, Oreg., Sept. 25, 1936; s. Harlow C. and Mabel (Nilsson) D.; m. Rosina O. Berry, July 4, 1970; children: Erica, Douglas, Andrew. BA, Harvard U., 1958, MA, 1960, PhD, 1964. Tech. staff mem. AT&T Bell Labs., Murray Hill, N.J., 1965, supr. lightwave lasers group, 1968-79, head optoelectronics devices dept., 1979-83, dir. lightwave devices lab., 1983-90, dir. platforms and new products labs., 1991-93; now expert witness and tech. cons., Bernardsville, N.J. Contbr. articles to various publs. Nat. scholar Harvard U., 1955-58; NSF fellow, 1959-63. Fellow IEEE (editor Electronic Device Letters 1980-90, Medal of Engring. Excellence 1993); mem. AAAS, Am. Phys. Soc. Home: 43 Old Wood Rd Bernardsville NJ 07924-1416

DIXON, ROBERT F., telecommunications executive; b. Newport, R.I., July 5, 1948; s. Robert and Helen (Dowd) D. BFA, R.I. Sch. Design, 1970, BArch, 1971. Intern architect State of Conn., Hartford, 1971-72, engring. asst., 1972-73, mgmt. analyst I, 1973-75, mgmt. analyst II, 1975-78, mgmt. analyst assoc., 1978-80; prin. analyst telecommunications Office of the Comptroller, Hartford, 1980-83, dir. telecommunications div., 1983-89; dir. telecommunications Office of Info. and Tech., Hartford, 1989-96; dir. planning and architecture dept. info. tech. State of Conn., 1997—. Trustee, vice chair ednl. policy com. R.I. Sch. Design, Providence, 1989—; dir. Rope Ferry Commons, a part of the Jordan Village Historic Dist., Waterford, 1987—. Mem. R.I. Sch. Design Alumni Assn. (pres. 1989-91), Coun. of State Govts. (strategic planning com. 1991—), Nat. Assn. State Telecommunications Dirs. (pres. 1991-93), Conn. Telecommunications Assn. (pres. 1985-86). Avocation: whitewater paddle-rafting. Office: State of Conn Dept of Info Tech 340 Capitol Ave Rm 302 Hartford CT 06106-1415

DIXON, ROBERT JAMES, aerospace consultant, former air force officer, former aerospace company executive; b. N.Y.C., Apr. 9, 1920; s. William H. and Mary A. (Smith) D.; m. Elizabeth Harriman (dec.); m. Lamana M. Kelly, July 19, 1958; children: Kelly Lee, Thomas Fries, Roland Cahill, Mary Lucinda. Grad., Collegiate Sch., N.Y.C., 1937; A.B., Dartmouth Coll., 1941; grad., Air War Coll., 1959. Enlisted RCAF, 1941; trans. USAAF, 1943; advanced through grades to gen. USAF, 1973; served as pilot ETO, World War II, Korea; vice comdr. 7th Air Force, Vietnam, 1969-70; dep. chief staff personnel Hdqrs. USAF, Washington, 1970-73; comdr. TAC Air Command, Langley, Va., 1973-78; ret., 1978; pres. Fairchild Republic Co., Farmingdale, N.Y., 1978-81, chmn., 1982, ret., 1982. Decorated D.S.C., D.S.M. (4), Legion of Merit (2) U.S.; D.F.C. (2) U.S. and U.K.; Legion of Honor France; recipient Collier trophy, 1978. Home and Office: 29342 Ridgeview Trl Fair Oaks Ranch TX 78015

DIXON, ROSINA BERRY, physician, pharmaceutical development consultant; b. Columbus, Ohio, Dec. 3, 1942; d. Loren C. and Florence H. (Bateson) Berry; m. Richard W. Dixon, July 4, 1970; children: Erica H., Douglas R., Andrew D. BA in Chemistry, Radcliffe Coll., 1964; MD, Columbia U., 1968. Diplomate Am. Bd. Internal Medicine. Intern, resident, and chief med. resident Roosevelt Hosp., N.Y.C., 1968-72; from sr. assoc. to exec. dir. Ciba-Geigy, Summit, N.J., 1972-81; med. dir. Schering Labs., Kenilworth, N.J., 1981-84; v.p. Med. Market Spltys., Boonton, N.J., 1985-86; cons. pharm. devel. Bernardsville, N.J., 1986—; bd. dirs. Cambrex Corp., East Rutherford, N.J., Enzon, Inc., Piscataway, N.J., Church & Dwight Co., Inc., Princeton, N.J.; instr. medicine Coll. Phys. and Surg., Columbia U., 1972—; preceptor in family practice Overlook Hosp., Summit, 1979—; mem. governing bd. Daytop at Mendham, N.J., 1991—; trustee Bonnie Brae, N.J., 1992. Mem. Am. Coll. Clin. Pharmacology, Am. Soc. Clin. Pharmacology and Therapeutics, Nat. Assn. Corp. Dirs. Episcopalian. Home and Office: 43 Old Wood Rd Bernardsville NJ 07924-1416

DIXON, SHEILA, councilwoman; married; 2 children. BA, Towson State U., 1976; MS, Johns Hopkins U., 1982. Mem. Dem. State Century Com. Dist 40 City of Balt., 1986-87; city councilwoman Dist 4 Balt. City Coun., 1987—, mem. Drug and Substance Abuse Com., mem. Housing Authority; internat. trade specialist dept. bus. and econ. devel. Md. Office Internat. Bus., Baltimore; tchr. Stuart Hill Elem. Sch. Recipient Legis. Achievement award Greater Balt. Bd. of Realtors, 1991. Mem. NAACP (Md. State Enolia P. McMillan award 1993), African Am. Women's Caucus, Women Power, Assn. Study Afro-Am. Life and History Inc., Rainbow Coalition, Nat. Forum Black Pub. Adminstrn. Democrat. Office: Baltimore City Hall Rm 525 Baltimore MD 21202*

DIXON, SHIRLEY JUANITA, restaurant owner; b. Canton, N.C., June 29, 1935; d. Willard Luther and Bessie Eugenia (Scroggs) Clark; m. Clinton Matthew Dixon, Jan. 3, 1953; children: Elizabeth Swanger, Hugh Monroe III, Cynthia Owen, Sharon Henson. BS, Wayne State U., 1956; postgrad., Mary Baldwin Coll., 1958, U. N.C., 1977. Acct. Standard Oil Co., Detroit, 1955-57; asst. dining room mgr. Statler Hilton, Detroit, 1958-60; bookkeeper Osborne Lumber Co., Canton, N.C., 1960-61; bus. owner, pres. Dixon's Restaurant, Canton, 1961—; judge N.C. Assn. Distributive Edn. Assn., state and dist., 1982—; owner Halbert's Family Heritage Ctr., Canton. Past Pres. Haywood County Assn. Retarded Citizens Bd., 1985-94, past v.p., chmn. bd. dirs.; bd. commrs. Haywood Vocats. Opportunities, 1985-94, treas. bd. dirs.; Haywood Sr. Leadership Council; dist. dir. 11th Congl. Dist. Dem. Women, 1982-85; state Teen-Dem. advisor State Dem. party, 1985-90; del. 1988 Dem. Nat. Conv., Atlanta; alderwoman Town of Canton, N.C.; vice-chair Gov.'s. Adv. Coun. on Aging, State N.C., 1982-89; 1st v.p. crime prevention Community Watch Bd., State N.C., 1985, 86; mem. Criminal Justice Bd., N.C. Assembly on Women and the Economy; chair Western N.C. Epilepsy Assn., Haywood County N.C. Mus. History, 1987—; co-chair Haywood County Commn. on the Bi-Centennial of Constn., 1987-92; Haywood County Econ. Strategy Commn.; v.p., b.d. dirs. Haywood County Retirement Coun., Region A Coun. on Aging; bd. dirs. Haywood County Sr. Housing, C.B.C. United Way (mem. chair); chair bd. Canton Sr. Citizen's Ctr.; mem. Haywood County Ease Retirement Com.; pres., chairwoman bd. Haywood County Assn. Retarded Citizens; pres. N.C. coun. Alzheimer's Disease and Related Disorders Assn.; bd. dirs. Canton Recreation Dept., Western N.C. Alzheimer's Disease and Related Disorders Assn., 1987-91, v.p., C.B; bd. dirs. Haywood Literary Coun., Haywood Sr. Leadership Coun., W.N.C. Econ. Devel. Com., United Way, 1991—, drive chmn.; mem. legis. subcom. Alzheimer's-State of N.C.; bd. dirs. N.C. Conf. for Social Svcs., 1987-91; v.p. bd. Western N.C. Alzheimer's Assn., 1987-91; pres. State Coun. on Alzheimer's; apptd. mem. Legis. Study Com. on Alzheimer's; apptd. mem. State of N.C. Adv. Bd. on Community Care and Health; mem. Habitat for Humanity Haywood County; bd. chair Pigeon Valley Optimist Club; apptd. by Senate Western N.C. Econ. Devel. Commn.; appointee Haywood County Econ. Devel. Commn., Canton Hist. Commn.; judge U.S. Olympic Torch Bearers. Recipient Outstanding Svc. award Crime Prevention from Gov., 1982, Gov.'s Spl. Vol. award, 1983, Outstanding Svc. award N.C. Cmty. Watch Assn., 1984, Cmty. Svc. award to Handicapped, 1983-84, Outstanding Svc. award ARC, 1988; named Employer of Yr. for Hiring Handicapped N.C. Assn. for Retarded Citizens, 1985, Cmty. Person of Yr. Kiwanis Club, 1991, Citizen of Yr. in Western N.C., 1995; Rec. Outstanding award Haywood Co. Sr. Games, 1992; inducted into N.C. Softball Hall of Fame, 1997. Mem. AAUW, NAFE, Women's Polit. Caucus (So. Women's Leadership award 1998) , Internat. Platform Assn., Women's Forum N.C., Nat. Bd. Alzheimers Assn. (regional del.), Canton Bus. and Profl. Assn. (pres. 1974-79, Woman of Yr. 1984), Altrusa (Woman of Yr. in N.C. 1989). Democrat. Episcopalian. Avocation: softball club. Home: 104 Skyland Ter Canton NC 28716-3718 Office: Dixons Restaurant 30 N Main St Canton NC 28716-3805

DIXON, SHIRLEY LEE, emergency physician; b. N.Y.C., Dec. 10, 1947; d. Henry Ester and Ethel Mae (Samuels) D. BS in Biology, CCNY, 1969; MD, Howard U., 1976; MPH, Columbia U., 1983. Diplomate Am. Bd. Forensic Examiners (mem., fellow). Intern Harlem Hosp. Ctr., N.Y.C., 1976-77, resident in internal medicine, 1979-81, attending physician dept. ambulatory care, 1981-83; attending physician La Guardia Med. Group PC, 1983-85; emergency rm. attending Interfaith Med. Ctr., 1985-87; med. dir. U.S. Postal Svc., Bklyn., 1986-93; med. officer U.S. Postal Svc., 1993-96; attending emergency room VA Hosp., Bronx, 1993-96; mem. cmty. adv. bd. Harlem Hosp., 1981-83; attending physician night screening clinic Lincoln Hosp., 1989-91. Active People to People Citizen Amb. Program, Spokane, Wash., 1991. Served with USPHS, 1977-79. Health Professions scholar, USHPS scholar; Nat. Med. fellow. Mem. Am. Profl. Practice Assn. (life), Am. Acad. Experts in Traumatic Stress, N.Y. Acad. Scis., Assn. Clinicians for Underserved (charter). Home: 752 West End Ave New York NY 10025-6230

DIXON, STEVEN MICHAEL, university administrator; b. McMinnville, Ohio, Apr. 20, 1957; s. Leonard Ray and Margaret Elizabeth Dixon; m. Teresa Sue Mendenhall, Aug. 5, 1980; children: Alexa Michelle, Jason Scott, Kaylene Elizabeth. BA, Graceland Coll., 1979; MA, U. Mo., Kansas City, 1985. Exec. min. RLDS Ch., St. Joseph, Mo., 1983-84; asst. dean, coord. residence life Park Coll., Parkville, Mo., 1984-87; coord. residence life Oreg. Inst. of Tech., Klamath Falls, Oreg., 1987-88; asst. dean, dir. residence life Pacific U., 1988-90; asst. dean of students Simpson Coll., Indianola, Iowa, 1990-92, assoc. dean of students, 1992-97; dir. housing and residence life Eastern N.Mex. U., Portales, 1997—; comprehensive tng. com. UMR-ACUHO, 1990-97, residential first yr. experience task force, 1994-97, profl. devel. com., 1990-92. Counselor to pastor Reorganized LDS, Clovis, N.Mex., 1997—, ch. youth leader, 1981-84, 95—; adult vol. Boy Scouts Am., Indianola, 1995-97; mem. non-jud. human rels. com., 1994-97. Mem. Nat. Assn. of Student Pers. Adminstr. Avocations: travel, camping, photography, cross stitch, reading. E-mail: steve.dixon@enmu.edu. Home: 1120 Concord Rd Clovis NM 88101 Office: Enmu Housing and Residence Life Station 39 Portales NM 88130

DIXON, STEWART STRAWN, lawyer; b. Chgo., Nov. 5, 1930; s. Wesley M. and Katherine (Strawn) D.; m. Romayne Wilson, June 24, 1961 (dec. July 1993); children: Stewart S. Jr., John W., Romayne W. Thompson; m. Ann Wilson Grozier, Sept. 15, 1997. BA, Yale U., 1952; JD, U. Mich., 1955. Bar: Ill. 1957, U.S. Dist. Ct. 1957, U.S. Ct. Appeals 1974, U.S. Supreme Ct. 1974. Ptnr. Kirkland & Ellis, Chgo., 1957-67, Wildman, Harrold, Allen & Dixon, Chgo., 1967—; dir. Lord, Abbett & Co. Managed Mut. Funds, N.Y.C., 1976—; dir. Otho Sprague Inst., Chgo. Trustee, past chmn. Chgo. Hist. Soc., 1982-87. 1st lt. U.S. Army, 1955-60. Mem. Am. Bar Assn., Am. Law Inst., Ill. Bar Assn., Chgo. Bar Assn. Republican. Episcopalian. Clubs: Chgo., Commonwealth, Commercial, Met., Univ., Old Elm, Onwentsia, Rolling Rock. Office: Wildman Harrold Allen & Dixon 225 W Wacker Dr Chicago IL 60606-1224

DIXON, TAMECKA, professional basketball player; b. Dec. 14, 1975. Grad., Kans. State U., 1997. Basketball player Los Angeles Sparks Women's NBA, Inglewood, Calif., 1997—. Mem. Olympic Festival Team South, 1995. Avocations: dancing, shopping. Office: Los Angeles Sparks Gt Western Forum 3900 W Manchester Blvd Inglewood CA 90305-2200*

DIXON, TERRY PHILLIP, academic administrator, educational consultant; b. Cin., May 8, 1946; s. Henry Phillip and Annabel (Kincaid) D.; m. Evelyn Bowman, Dec. 23, 1969. BS in Chemistry, Biology, Cumberland Coll., 1968; MS in Elem. Edn., Ill. State U., 1978; EdD., U. Nebr., 1988. Cert. elem. tchr., Mo., Ill.; cert. secondary sci. tchr. Tchr. biology, coach Cissna Park (Ill.) High Sch., 1968-69; tchr. Gilman (Ill.) Elem. Sch., 1969-78; chmn. div. Tarkio (Mo.) Coll., 1978-89; cons. higher edn. Williams Dixon Assocs., Tarkio, 1979-86; cons. Dixon & Assocs., Killeen, Tex., 1989—; v.p. acad. affairs U. Cen. Tex., Killeen, 1989-93; v.p. acad. affairs, provost Clarkson Coll., Omaha, 1997—; instnl. evaluator Am. Coun. of Edn. and Sch. Coun. of Small Bus.; v.p. bd. dirs. Lewis, Dixon and Assocs., 1992—. Mem. Community Revitilization Com., Tarkio, 1985-89; vice chmn. bd. dirs. N.W. Mo. Learning Ctr., Tarkio, 1986-89; mem. fin. com. Ctrl. Tex. Alcoholic Rehab. Ctr., Temple, 1990-93. Mem. Assn. Tchr. Educators, Rotary, Nebr. Educators Assn., Mo. Unit Assn. Tchr. Edn., Greater Killeen C. of C. (mem. small bus. coun.), Phi Delta Kappa. Baptist. Avocations: software design, writing, research. Home: 101 S 42nd St Omaha NE 68131-2715 Office: Clarkson Coll 101 S 42nd St Omaha NE 68131-2715

DIXON, WALLACE WADE, federal judge; b. 1943. BS, U. N.C., 1965; JD, Wake Forest U., 1972. Bar: N.C. 1972, U.S. Dist. Ct. (ea. and we. dists.) N.C., U.S. Ct. Appeals (4th cir.). Assoc. Twiford & Abbott, Elizabeth City, N.C., 1972; ptnr. Collier, Harris & Homesley and Homesly, Jones Gaines & Dixon, Statesville, N.C., 1973-80; asst. U.S. atty. and 1st asst. for ea. dist. N.C., U.S. Magistrate Judge, Raleigh, 1983—. Capt. USMC, 1965-69, Vietnam. Dedocrated Bronze Star, Purple Heart (2) with oak leaf cluster. Mem. N.C. State Bar, N.C. Bar Assn., Masons (master). Office: Fed Bldg 310 Bern Ave Raleigh NC 27601

DIXON, WHEELER WINSTON, film and video studies educator, writer; b. New Brunswick, N.J., Mar. 12, 1950; s. Percival Vincent and Hilda-Barr (Wheeler) D.; m. Gwendolyn Audrey Foster, Dec. 23, 1985. AB, Livingston Coll., 1972; MA, MPhil, Rutgers U., 1980, PhD, 1982. Instr. English Rutgers U., New Brunswick, 1974-84; lectr. film studies The New Sch. for Social Rsch., 1983, 97, 98; asst. prof. English and art U. Nebr., Lincoln, 1984-88, chmn. film studies program, assoc. prof. English, 1988-92, chmn. film studies program, prof. English, 1992—; series editor Cultural Studies in Cinema Video Series SUNY Press, 1995—; guest programmer, lectr. Nat. Film Theatre of Brit. Film Inst. and Mus. of Moving Image, London, 1991; guest programmer Nat. Film Theatre of Brit. Film Inst., London, 1992; mem. ad hoc curriculum rev. com. dept. English, U. Nebr., Lincoln, 1992, mem. faculty devel. fellowship com., 1992-95, chmn. Robinson Prize com., spring 1994, chmn. faculty devel. fellowship com., 1994, mem. various MA thesis and PhD coms.; panelist NEH, 1993—; presenter papers in field; lectr. Lincoln Ctr., 1997. Author: The "B" Directors: A Bibliographical Directory, 1985, The Cinematic Vision of F. Scott Fitzgerald, 1986, The Films of Freddie Francis, 1991, The Charm of Evil: The Films of Terence Fisher, 1991, The Films of Reginald Le Borg: Interviews, Essays and Filmography, 1992, The Early Film Criticism of François Truffaut, 1993, Re-Viewing British Cinema 1900-1992: Essays and Interviews, 1994, It Looks at You: The Returned Gaze of Cinema, 1995, The Films of Jean-Luc Godard, 1997, The Exploding Eye: A Re-visionary History of 1960s Experimental Cinema, 1997, The Transparency of Spectacle, 1998, Disaster and Memory, 1999; guest editor Film Criticism, Fall-Winter 1991-92, mem. editl. bd., 1991—, article reviewer, 1991—; article reviewer Jour. of History of Sexuality, 1991-93, Cinema Jour., 1993—; mem. adv. bd. Jour. Popular Brit. Cinema; manuscript reviewer SUNY Press, 1993—; contbr. articles and revs. to profl. jours. and essays to various publs., including Film Criticism, Films in Rev., Cineaste, Interview, others; writer, dir., prodr. Coming Attractions: A History of the Motion Picture Trailer, 1986-88, (feature film) What Can I Do?, 1993 (Layman Found. award 1993-94); co-prodr., co-dir., co-writer: Women Who Made The Movies, 1988-90; dir./prodr.: (feature film) Squatters, 1994; exhibited in group shows at U. Nebr.-Lincoln, 1985-86, 87-88, 89-90, Syracuse U., 1986, W.Va. U., 1986, Lincolnshire Coll. Art, Lincoln, Eng., 1988-89; performances include That's Different: Tales of Nebraska, 1987; exhibitions of films include Whitney Mus. Am. Art, 1972, Mus. Modern Art, 1994, Mus. Moving Image, London, 1994, Millennium Film Workshop, 1997, and others. Grantee Royal Film Archive of Belgium, 1974, N.J. State Arts Coun., 1972, Rsch. Coun., U. Nebr., 1984-85, Ind. Filmmaker, S.W. Alt. Media Project, 1985, Interdisciplinary Arts Fellowship Program, Rockefeller Found. and NEA, 1987, Rsch. Coun., 1987, 89, S.W. Alt. Media Project Ind. Prodn. Fund, 1993; George Holmes Faculty fellow, 1989. Office: U Nebraska Dept English 202 Andrews Hall Lincoln NE 68588-0333

DIXON, W(ILLIAM) ROBERT, retired educational psychology educator; b. Hudson, Pa., Sept. 16, 1917; s. William Robert and Mary (George) D.; m. Carol Everson Lewis, Dec. 20, 1940; children: William R., Barbara Ann. A.B., Syracuse U., 1938, M.A., 1939; Ph.D. (Horace H. Rackham fellow 1947-48, Burke Aaron Hinsdale scholar 1948), U. Mich., 1948. Tchr., prin. W. Canada Valley Central Schs., Middleville, N.Y., 1940-42; asst. prof. U. Ill., 1948-49; asst. prof. U. Mich., 1949-52, asso. prof., 1952-56, prof. ednl. psychology, 1956-86, ret., 1986; vis. prof. edn. U. Bombay, India, 1964-65. Contbr. articles to profl. jours. Dir. Mich. Interdisciplinary Research Tng. Program, 1967-72. Served with USAAF, 1942-45. Decorated Air Medal with 10 oak leaf clusters, D.F.C. Fellow Am. Psychol. Assn., AAAS; mem. Am. Ednl. Research Assn. Nationally ranked tennis player Men's Singles, 1945, Vets. Singles, 1962. Home: 2793 W Fairway Loop Dunnellon FL 34434-4829

DIXON, WILLIAM ROBERT, musician, composer, educator; b. Nantucket, Mass., Oct. 5, 1925; s. William Robert and Louise Ann (Wade) D.; children: William, Claudia Gayle, William. Diploma, Hartnette Conservatory Music, 1951. Clk., internat. civil servant UN Secretariat, N.Y.C., 1956-62; free lance musician, composer N.Y.C., 1962-67; mem. faculty Columbia U. Tchrs. Coll., 1967-70; composer-in-residence George Washington U., Washington, 1967; dir. Conservatory of Univ. of the Streets, N.Y.C., 1967-68; guest artist in residence Ohio State U., 1967; mem. faculty dept. dance Bennington (Vt.) Coll., 1968-95, chmn. dept. black music, 1973-86; vis. prof. U. Wis., Madison, 1971-72; lectr. painting and music Mus. Modern Art, Verona, Italy, 1982, Palast, Nuremberg, Fed. Republic Germany, 1990; lectr. workshop on contemporary music Pori, Finland, 1991, Jerusalem, Tel Aviv, Israel, 1990; lectr. in Black Art Music Maison du Livre et du Son, Villeurbanne, France, 1994; tchr. Master Classes in Improvisation Ecole Nationale de Musique, Villeurbanne, France, 1994, Master Class Composition and Performance NYU, 1996. Recs. include Archie Shepp-Bill Dixon Quartet, 1962, Bill Dixon 7-Tette, 1963, Intents and Purposes: The Bill Dixon Orchestra, 1967, For Franz, 1976, New Music, Second Wave, 1979, Bill Dixon in Italy, 2 vols., 1980, considerations 1 and 2 Bill Dixon, 1980, 82, November: 1981, 1982, Bill Dixon in the Labyrinth, 1983, Collection, 1985, Thoughts, 1986, Son of Sisyphus, 1990, Bill Dixon: Vade Mecum, 1994, Vade Mecum II, 1996, (6-CD set) Bill Dixon: Solo Trumpet, 1998, PAPYRUS vol. 1 and 2, compositions for trumpet, percussion & piano, 1999; retrospective of music compositions 1963-91 by Radio Sta. WKCR, Columbia U., 1991-92; trumpet soloist Celebration Orchestra, Berlin, Germany, 1994; concert performance of original compositions Espace Tonkin, Villeurbanne, France, 1994, Teatro Colosseo, Rome, Italy, 1996, Nickelsdorf, Austria, 1997; composed orch. piece Cologne (Germany) Radio Sta., 1998; paintings exhibited, Ferrari Gallery, Verona, Italy, 1982, Multimedia Contemporary Art Gallery, Brescia, Italy, 1982, Palast, Nuremberg, Germany, 1990; exhibited lithographs Villeurbanne, France, 1994, Chittenden Bank, Bennington, Vt., 1994-95, Skoto Gallery, N.Y.C., 1996; retrospective of paintings 1968-91, So. Vt. Coll., 1991; author: L'Opera, (biodiscography by Ben Young) Dixonia, 1998; prodr. lithographs Union Regionale pour le Devel. de la Lithographie d'Art, Lyon, France, 1994; lithograph exhibn. Skoto Gallery, N.Y.C., 1996. Mem. adv. com. New Eng. Found. of the Arts. Served with U.S. Army, 1944-46. Recipient Disting. Visitor in the Arts Middlebury Coll., 1986. Fellow Vt. Acad. Arts and Scis.; mem. Am. Fedn. Musicians, Duke Ellington Jazz Soc. (hon.). *Were it possible to live for three thousand years, one could lay around the house and do nothing for the first five hundred years, go to school for the next five hundred and then have two thousand years left to find a way to do work, etc., of substance. Since that is NOT the case (and even if one crosses with the green and not in between and manages to live to be one hundred--in cosmic or universal time akin to attempting to spit in the Atlantic Ocean from a height of 50,000 feet and expecting a ripple to follow) there is another reality extant. And from the time THAT reality dawned on me, I have endeavoured (albeit not always with success) to do everything one hundred percent. Those things I felt I COULDN'T (for whatever reason) expend that kind of energy upon, I have left alone.*

DIXON, WRIGHT TRACY, JR., lawyer; b. Raleigh, N.C., Oct. 7, 1921; s. Wright T. and Marion Jefferson (Homes) D.; m. Elizabeth Prince Nufer, June 3, 1950; children: Wright III, William N., Elizabeth Prince. AB, Duke U., 1947; LLB, U. N.C., 1951. Bar: N.C. 1951, U.S. Dsit. Ct. (ea., mid. and we. dists.), N.C. 1951, U.S. Ct. Appeals (4th cir.) 1956; cert. mediator, N.C. Ptnr. Bailey & Dixon, Raleigh, N.C., 1956—; mem. Bd. of Adjustments, Raleigh, 1960-74, chmn., 1969-74. Jr. warden, sr. warden, mem. vestry St. Michael's Episcopal Ch., Raleigh; trustee So. Sem. Va., 1961-81, N.C. Clinent Security Fund, 1986-91. With USMC, 1943-59. Fellow Am. Bar Found.; mem. ABA (del. 1984-88), N.C. State Bar (counselor 1979-86, pres. 1985-86, Gen. Practice Hall of Fame 1997), Wake County Bar Assn. (pres. 1976, mem. N.C. commn. on code recodification 1979-81, hon. bd. mem. 1995, Joseph Branch professionalism award 1996), Raleigh Kiwanis Club (pres.), Sphinx Club (pres.), Carolina Country Club, Capital City Club. Avocations: golf, woodworking, genealogy, tennis, reading. Home: 414 Marlowe Rd Raleigh NC 27609-7018 Office: Bailey & Dixon PO Box 1351 2 Hannover Sq Raleigh NC 27602

DIXON-SHOMETTE, DONNA M., medical paralegal; b. Munich, Germany, Dec. 17, 1963; d. Thomas Joe Pitts and Maria T. (Meier) Gibbs; m. C. Douglas Shomette, Dec. 5, 1995 (div. Nov. 1998). Paralegal Real Estate, Criminal Law, Southeastern Paralegal Inst., 1994; cert. paralegal, La. State U., 1995; computer studies, Collin County C.C., Plano, Tex., 1998. Cert. notary, Tex. Legal adminstr., paralegal Graves & Allison PC, Shreveport, La., 1982-83; import coord., dept. mgr., model Jerell Inc., Dallas, 1985-87; sales rep. John Robert Powers, Dallas, 1986-90; ops. mgr., designer Dasha Designs, Dallas, 1992; med. paralegal Baron & Budd PC, Dallas, 1993; paralegal Fanning, Harper & Martinson, PC, Dallas, 1997; freelance paralegal Dallas, 1997—. Poet: Four poems published in Nat. Libr. Poetry, 1995 (Editor's Choice award for all 4). Mem. Save the Whales-Orca Adoption Program, 1993-96, Nat. Trust for Hist. Preservation, 1995. Art award Holiday in Dixie, 1974. Mem. ABA (assoc.), ATLA (assoc.), State Bar of Tex. (assoc.), Nat. Assn. Legal Assts., Dallas Assn. Legal Assts., Dallas Opera Guild, Dallas Mus. of Art, Dallas Arboretum and Botanical Gardens. Republican. Presbyterian. Avocations: fgn. travel, skiing, sailing, art, poetry. Home: 3932 18th St Plano TX 75074

DI XX MIGLIA, GABRIELLA, artist, conservationist; b. Genoa, Italy, June 10, 1949; d. Walter and Maria Giovanna (Lupo) Repetto Carboneschi di Ventimiglia; m. Fredi Chiappelli Zdekauer, June 10, 1980 (dec. Mar. 1990). Student, Acad. Ligustica of Art, Genoa, 1970, Acad. Ligustica of Art, Genoa, 1974-77; degree in painting conservation, Lab. di Restauro, 1997. Owner G. Di XX Miglia Painting, L.A., 1980—; conservationist/restorationist paintings L.A., 1979-85, China, 1985-91; cons. in art conservation, 1990—. One woman shows include La Piccola Gallery, Esther Robles Gallery, L.A., City art Mus., Florence, UCLA Faculty Ctr.; group shows include L.A. Art Orgn., 1990-93, What's Women Got to do With It, SCLA, 1993, Gallery 825, West Hollywood, Calif., 1996, World Contemporary Art, L.A. Conv. Ctr., 1998, Galerie Internat., Palo Alto, 1998, Galerie Everart, Paris, 1999. Patron LACMA Custume Coun., 1989—, Hammer Mus., L.A., 1995-99. Recipient Gold medal for best drawing Genoa, 1972, Cert. of Commendation County of L.A. Bd. Suprs., 1991, arts award UCLA, 1995. Mem. Westwood Art Assn. (bd. dirs. 1983-84), AFEA (bd. dirs. 1983-86), L.A. Art Assn. Galleries (bd. dirs. 1990—), Am. Portrait Assn., UCLA Medieval and Renaissance Ctr. (hon.), Nat. Art Assn. Roman Catholic. Avocations: gardening, tennis, interior decorating, fashion design, cooking. E-mail: dixxmiglia@earthlink.net. Office: 600 N Kenter Ave Los Angeles CA 90049-1918

DIYORIO, JOHN SALVATORE, chemistry educator; b. Charleston, S.C., Jan. 23, 1943; s. George Francis and Lucia (Stanziola) D.; m. Linda Carol Pratt, June 20, 1970; children: John Christopher, Ashley Diane. BS in Chemistry, Coll. of Charleston, 1964; PhD in Chemistry, U. S.C., 1969. Prof. chemistry Wytheville (Va.) C.C., 1969—; dir. Govs. Magnet Sch. for Sci. and Tech., Wytheville, 1985-86, 91-93; acting adminstrv. asst. to pres. Wytheville C.C., 1986-87. Contbr. articles to profl. jours. Chair 9th Dist. Dem. Com., Va., 1981-85, pres. Wytheville Jaycees, 1969-80; mem. Va. Dem. Ctrl. Com., Richmond, 1976-85; state v.p. Va. Jaycees, Lynchburg, 1972-73; improvement of instrn. Wytheville C.C., 1990; vice-chair Wythe County Local Emergency Planning Com., vice chair, sec. 1990—; elder Wytheville Prebyn. Ch., 1998—. Recipient Disting. Svc. award Wytheville C.C. Ednl. Found., 1991. Mem. Wytheville Rotary Club (program chair, pres. 1994-95, Paul Harris fellowship 1997). Democrat. Presbyterian. Avocations: reading, stamps, photography. Fax: 540-223-4778. E-mail: wcdiyorio@wc.cc.va.us. Office: Wytheville CC 1000 E Main St Wytheville VA 24382

DIZARD, WILSON PAUL, JR., international affairs consultant, educator; b. N.Y.C., Mar. 6, 1922; s. Wilson Paul and Helen Marie (Oliver) D.; m. Lynn Margaret Wood, Mar. 11, 1944; children: John William, Stephen Wood, Wilson Paul III, Mark Christopher. BS, Fordham Coll., 1947; postgrad., Columbia U., 1947-49. Writer, editor Time Inc., N.Y.C., 1947-51; with Dept. State and USIA, 1951-80; vice consul Istanbul, Turkey, 1951-53; chief Greece-Turkey-Iran br., 1953-55; info. officer Am. embassy, Athens, Greece, 1955-60; pub. affairs officer consulate-gen. Dacca, 1960-62; spl. asst. dep. dir., 1964-65, asst. dep. dir., 1966-67; 1st sec. Am. Embassy, Warsaw, Poland, 1968-70; asst. dir. Pub. Affairs Office, Saigon, Vietnam, 1970; spl. adviser polit. sect. U.S. Embassy, Saigon, 1971; comm. adviser to dir. USIA, Washington, 1971-73; chief plans and program policy USIA, 1973-77; vice-chmn. U.S. del. to 1979 World Adminstrv. Radio Conf. Dept. State, Washington, 1978-79; v.p. Kalba-Bowen Assocs., Cambridge, Mass., 1980-86; adj. prof. internat. affairs Georgetown U., 1975-95, sr. fellow, 1983-89; sr. assoc. Ctr. for Strategic and Internat. Studies, 1989—; cons. comm. policy U.S. Dept. State, 1984-88; mem. U.S. del. and exec. asst. to conf. dir. Internat. Telecom. Satellite Conf., Washington, 1968-69; rsch. assoc. Ctr. Internat. Studies, MIT, 1962-63; vis. lectr. polit. sci. dept. MIT, 1981. Author: The Strategy of Truth, 1961, Television-A World View, 1966, The Coming Information Age, 1981, Mikhail Gorvachev's Information Revolution, 1987, Old Media, New Media, 1994, Meganet: Building the Global Information Highway, 1997; contbr. articles to profl. jours. Cons. Carnegie Found. Commn. on Endl. TV; mem. adv. bd. Pacific Telecom. Coun., 1990-91. With AUS, 1943-46. Rsch. fellow Assn. Diplomatic Studies and Tng., 1997—. Mem. Am. Polit. Sci. Assn., Assn. for Diplomatic Studies and Tng., Global Telecom. Soc., Soc. Historians Am. Fgn. Rels., Internet Soc., Am. Fgn. Svc. Assn., Soc. Satellite, Profls., Washington Inst. Fgn. Affairs. Clubs: Cosmos (Washington). Home: 2811 28th St NW Washington DC 20008-4109 Office: Ctr Strategic & Internat Studies 1800 K St NW Washington DC 20006-2202

DI ZEREGA, THOMAS WILLIAM, former energy company executive, lawyer; b. Round Hill, Va., Sept. 27, 1927; s. Augustus and Susan Martha (Nichols) diZ.; m. Mary Howe Glascock, Sept. 15, 1956; 1 child, Mary Bryan. B.A., U. Wichita, 1953; J.D., George Washington U., 1956. Bar: Va. 1958, D.C. 1964, U.S. Supreme Ct. 1965, Pa. 1968, N.Y. 1971, Utah 1980. V.p. Atlantic Richfield Co., Los Angeles, 1968-74; exec. v.p. Northwest Energy Co., Salt Lake City, 1974-80, also dir., pres., 1980-83; pres. Apco Oil Corp., Houston, 1975-78, also dir.; pres. Apco Argentina, Inc., 1975-83 also dir; pres. Marshall Nat. Bank, 1986-91: trustee Apco Liquidating Trust; dir. Marshall Nat. Bank, Alpha Land Co., Apco Trust, Carrtown Investments. Trustee Va. Mil. Inst. Found., Inc., 1986-91. Served in U.S. Army, 1946-47. Democrat. Episcopalian. Clubs: Calif. (Los Angeles); Fauquier (Warrenton); Met. (Washington), Chevy Chase (Washington), Commonwealth (Richmond). Home: Oakdale Farm Upperville VA 20185 Office: PO Box 247 Upperville VA 20185-0247

DJEDDAH, RICHARD NISSIM, investment banker; s. Joseph N. and Nelly (Serper) D.; m. Rachel Ruth Baron; 1 child, Esteevered. BS in Physics, CCNY, 1971; MBA, CUNY, 1986, PhD in Fin., 1990. Notary pub., N.Y. Prin., pres. Richard N. Djeddah & Assocs., N.Y.C., 1976—. Author: The Impact of Advertising on Security Prices, 1990. Mem. N.Y. Acad. Scis., Alliance Francaise, Baron Rothchild Golf and Country Club (Caesaria). Republican. Avocations: skiing, golf, chess, collecting ancient coins and art. Home: 346 Heathcote Rd Scarsdale NY 10583-7132 Office: RN Djeddah & Assocs 4 Park Ave New York NY 10016-5339

DJERASSI, CARL, chemist, educator, writer; b. Vienna, Austria, Oct. 29, 1923; s. Samuel and Alice (Friedmann) D.; m. Virginia Jeremiah (div. 1950); m. Norma Lundholm (div. 1976); children: Dale, Pamela (dec.); m. Diane W. Middlebrook, 1985. AB summa cum laude, Kenyon Coll., 1942, DSc (hon.), 1958; PhD, U. Wis., 1945; DSc (hon.), Nat. U. Mex., 1953, Fed. U., Rio de Janeiro, 1969, Worcester Poly. Inst., 1972, Wayne State U., 1974, Columbia U., 1975, Uppsala U., 1977, Coe Coll., 1978, U. Geneva, 1978, U. Ghent, 1985, U. Man., 1985, Adelphi U., 1993, U. Wis., 1995, U. S.C., 1995, Swiss Fed. Inst. Tech., 1995, U. Md.- Balt. County, 1997, Bulgarian Acad. Scis., 1998. Rsch. chemist Ciba Pharm. Products, Inc., Summit, N.J., 1942-43, 45-49; assoc. dir. rsch. Syntex, Mexico City, 1949-52; rsch. v.p. Syntex, 1957-60; v.p. Syntex Labs., Palo Alto, Calif., 1960-62; v.p. Syntex Rsch., 1962-68, pres., 1968-72; pres. Zoecon Corp., 1968-83, chmn. bd. dirs., 1968-86; prof. chemistry Wayne State U., 1952-59, Stanford (Calif.) U., 1959—; founder, pres. Djerassi Resident Artists Program, Woodside, Calif. Author: The Futurist and Other Stories, 1988, (novels) Cantor's Dilemma, 1989, The Bourbaki Gambit, 1994, Marx Deceased, 1996, Menachem's Seed, 1997, NO, 1998; (poetry) The Clock Runs Backward, 1991, (drama) An Immaculate Misconception, 1998, (autobiography) The Pill, Pygmy Chimps and Degas' Horse, 1992, also 9 others; mem. editl. bd. Jour. Organic Chemistry, 1955-59, Tetrahedron, 1958-92, Steroids, 1963—, Proc. of NAS, 1964-70, Jour. Am. Chem. Soc., 1966-75, Organic Mass Spectrometry, 1968-91; contbr. numerous articles to profl. jours., poems, memoirs and short stories to lit. publs. Recipient Intrasci. Rsch. Found. award, 1969, Freedman Patent award Am. Inst. Chemists, 1970, Chem. Pioneer award, 1973, Nat. Medal Sci. for first synthesis of oral contraceptive, 1973, Perkin medal, 1975, Wolf prize in chemistry, 1978, John and Samuel Bard award in sci. and medicine, 1983, Roussel prize, Paris, 1988, Discovers award Pharm. Mfg. Assn., 1988, Nat. Medal Tech. for new approaches to insect control, 1991, Nev. medal, 1992, Thomson medal Internat. Soc. Mass Spectroscopy, 1994, Prince Mahidol award, Thailand, 1995, Sovereign Fund award, 1996, Austrian Cross of Honor First Class, 1999; named to Nat. Inventors Hall of Fame. Mem. NAS (Indsl. Application of Sci. award 1990), NAS Inst. Medicine, Am. Chem. Soc. (award pure chemistry 1958, Baekeland medal 1959, Fritzsche award 1960, award for creative invention 1973, award in chemistry of contemporary tech. problems 1983, Esselen award 1989, Priestley medal 1992, Gibbs medal 1997), Royal Soc. Chemistry (hon. fellow, Centenary lectr. 1964), Am. Acad. Arts and Scis., German Acad. (Leopoldina), Royal Swedish Acad. Scis. (fgn.), Royal Swedish Acad. Engring. Scis. (fgn.), Am. Acad. Pharm. Scis. (hon.), Brazilian Acad. Scis. (fgn.), Mexican Acad. Scis., Bulgarian Acad. Scis. (fgn.), Phi Beta Kappa, Sigma Xi (Proctor prize for sci. achievement 1998), Phi Lambda Upsilon (hon.). E-mail: djerassi@stanford.edu. Office: Stanford U Dept Chemistry Stanford CA 94305-5080

DJERASSI, ISAAC, physician, medical researcher; b. Sofia, Bulgaria, July 27, 1925; came to U.S., 1954, naturalized, 1962; s. Rahamim and Adela (Tadjer) D.; m. Nira Eskenazy, Jan. 31, 1954; children—Ram Isaac, Ady Lynn. Student, Sofia U. Med. Sch., 1944-49; M.D., Hebrew U., Jerusalem, 1952; D.H. (hon.), Villanova U., 1977. Intern Hadassah Hosp., Tel Aviv, 1951-52; resident Hadassah Hosp., 1953-54; research asso. Harvard U. Med. Sch., Boston, 1955-60; asst. prof. pediatrics U. Pa., Phila., 1960-69; dir. research Mercy Cath. Med. Center, Phila., 1969—; also dir. hematology Mercy Cath. Med. Center; prof. oncology U. Tel Aviv Med. Sch., 1986, dir. Djerassi-Elias Oncology Inst., 1987. Contbr. articles to profl. jours. Mem. med. advisory bd. Nat. Hemophilia Found., Phila., 1964—; mem. med. advisory bd. Leukemia Soc., 1970—. Recipient Albert Lasker award Albert and Mary Lasker Found, 1972, E. Cohn-De Laval award, 1990. Mem. Am. Soc. Cancer Research, Soc. Pediatric Research, Am. Soc. Exptl. Pathology, Am. Assn. Blood Banks. Inventor filtration leukophersis system and machine for white blood cell transfusions, 1970; discoverer high methotrexate-citrovorum rescue chemotherapy of cancer, 1964-77; developer platelet transfusions, 1955-62. Home: 2034 Delancey Pl Philadelphia PA 19103-6510 Office: Mercy Cath Med Ctr PO Box 19709 Philadelphia PA 19143-0709

DJEREJIAN, EDWARD PETER, institute administrator, former diplomat; b. N.Y.C., Mar. 6, 1939; s. Peter Minas and Mary (Yazudjian) D.; m. Francoise Andrée Haelters, July 31, 1971; children: Gregory, Francesca. BS in Fgn. Svc., Georgetown U., 1960, hon. doctorate, 1992. Staff asst. to sec. of state U.S. Dept. of State, 1963-64; Political officer Am. Embassy, Beirut, Lebanon, 1965-69; political/labor officer Am. Consulate Gen., Casablanca, Morocco, 1969-72; spl. asst. Under Sec. of State, Washington, 1973-75; prin. officer Am. Consulate Gen., Bordeaux, France, 1975-77; political counselor Am. Embassy, Moscow, USSR, 1979-81; dep. chief of mission Am. Embassy, Amman, Jordan, 1981-84; dep. spokesman & dep. asst. sec. Dept. of State, Washington, 1984-85; spl. asst. to the pres., dep. press sec. The White House, 1985-86; prin. dep. asst. sec. for Near East/South Asia, 1987-88; Am. ambassador Am. Embassy, Damascus, Syria, 1988-91; asst. sec. Near Eastern and South Asian Affairs bur. Dept. State, Washington, 1991-93; amb. to Israel Tel Aviv, 1993-94; dir. James A. Baker III Inst. for Pub. Policy Rice U., Houston, 1994—; bd. dirs. Occidental Petroleum Corp., Global Industries, Ltd. 1st Lt. U.S. Army, 1961-62 (Korea). Recipient Presdl. award, Presdl. Meritorious Svc. award, 1988, Superior Honor award Dept. State, 1984, Disting. Honor award, 1993, Presdl. Disting. Svc. award, 1994, Ellis Island medal of honor, Moral Statesman award ADL, 1994. Mem. Coun. on Fgn. Rels. Armenian Apostolic. Avocations: writing, skiing. Office: Baker Inst Pub Policy Rice Univ 6100 Main St Houston TX 77005-1827

DJORDJEVIC, BORISLAV BORO, materials scientist, researcher; b. Brezice, Slovenia, Aug. 25, 1951; came to U.S., 1968; s. Branislav Branko and Cirila (Antolovic) D.; m. Nancy Grant, June 29, 1974; children: Julie Owen, Christine Antolovic. BS in Physics, Coll. William and Mary, 1973; MSE in Materials Sci., Johns Hopkins U., 1978, PhD in Materials Sci., 1979. Rsch. asst. Coll. William and Mary, Williamsburg, Va., 1971-72; grad. rsch. asst. Johns Hopkins U., Balt., 1973-79; tech. cons. Nat. Bureau of Standards, Gaithersburg, Md., 1979; postdoctoral fellow Johns Hopkins U., Balt., 1979; scientist Martin Marietta Labs., Balt., 1980-84, sr. scientist, group leader, 1984-88, mgr. rsch., engring., 1988-93; prin. rsch. scientist Ctr. Nondestructive Evaluation, Johns Hopkins U., Balt., 1993—, assoc. dir., 1995—; dir. of univ. Johns Hopkins U., 1980-93; pres. Materials and Sensors Tech., Inc., 1994—. Contbr. articles to profl. jours. Mem. ASTM, AAAS, IEEE, Am. Soc. for Nondestructive Testing (com. chmn. 1981-86, chmn. rsch. coun. 1997—, bd. dirs. 1996—), ASM, Am. Phys. Soc., Acoustical Soc. Am. Achievements include patent for ultrasonic liquid jet probe; development of high power ultrasonics for thick multilayer structures, through body ultrasonic test methods for solid rocket motors and robotic fully automated ultrasonic test system; subsystem for launch vehicles, embedding of sensors for health monitoring of advanced composite structures, nondestructive evaluation of civil structures, laser-optic sonar; rsch. in optical probing of stress waves in-process NDE. Home: 1110 Bellevista Ct Severna Park MD 21146-4846 Office: Johns Hopkins U Ctr Nondestructive Evaluation 3400 N Charles St Baltimore MD 21218-2680

DJORDJEVIC, DIMITRIJE, historian, educator; b. Belgrad, Yugoslavia, Feb. 27, 1922; came to U.S., 1970, naturalized, 1977; s. Vladimir and Jelena (Rasic) D.; m. Nan Fletcher, June 1981; 1 child, Jelena. Student, U. Beograd, 1950-54, Ph.D., 1962. Sr. staff mem. Inst. History, Serbian Acad. Scis. and Arts, 1958-69, Inst. Balkan Studies, 1969-70; prof. U. Calif., Santa Barbara, 1970-91, prof. emeritus, 1991—; chmn. Russian area studies U. Calif., 1976-82; mem. Nat. Com. to Promote History of Habsburg Monarchy, 1973-79. Author: Austro-Serbian Customs War 1906-1911, in Serbian, 1962, Revolutions nationales des peuples balkaniques, 1804-1914, 1965, Scars and Memory, 1997; co-author: The Balkan Revolutionary Tradition, 1981, also papers, essays, revs.; editor: The Creation of Yugoslavia, 1914-1918, 1980; editorial bd. profl. jours. Mem. Am. Hist. Assn., Am. Assn. Advancement Slavic Studies, Conf. Slavic and East European History (pres. 1984), Serbian Acad. Scis., N. Am. Assn. Serbiam Studies (pres. 1986-88). Serbian Orthodox.

DJORDJEVICH, MICHAEL, insurance company executive; b. Belgrade, Yugoslavia, Aug. 24, 1936; came to U.S., 1956, naturalized, 1961; s. Dragoslav R. and Ruzica J. Georgevich; m. Marie Louise Hohman, Jan. 20, 1963; children—Marie, Alexander, Michelle. B.S., U. Calif., Berkeley, 1960; M.B.A., San Francisco State U., 1963. With Fireman's Fund Ins. Co., San Francisco, 1962—; supr. cost and standards Fireman's Fund Ins. Co., 1965-70, asst. treas., 1970-74, v.p. investments, 1974-78, v.p., treas., 1978-83, v.p. fin. ins., dir., 1983-84; pres., chief exec. officer USF&G Fin. Sec. Co., 1985-86, dir., chief exec. officer; pres., chief exec. officer Capital Guaranty Corp., 1986-95; pres., dir. Studenica Found., 1995—; dir. Fin. Assurance Holdings Ltd., 1996-98; pres., CEO Monad Fin., 1997-98; pres., CEO Bank of S.E. Europe Internat. Inc., 1998—. Author: (essays) About Happy Living, 1985. State pres. Calif. Young Republicans, 1965-66; vice chmn. United Republicans of Calif., 1968-69; dir. First Serbian Benevolent Soc., 1976-80; commr. Statue of Liberty Ellis Island Centennial Commn., 1986—; pres. Serbian Unity Congress, 1990-93; pres. and founder Coun. for Democratic Changes in Serbia, 1998—. Served with U.S. Army, 1962-63. Republican. Serbian Orthodox. Home: 8 Loch Haven Ct San Rafael CA 94901-2402 *In the dark shadows of Nazi and Communist tyranny and then in the steady glow of freedom in America, I have grown to understand: that human dignity and integrity can be maintained even under most adverse conditions; that one can remain true to oneself regardless of outside forces; that we have a choice to do or not to do what is right, just and noble.*

DLAB, VLASTIMIL, mathematics educator, researcher; b. Bzi, Czech Republic, Aug. 5, 1932; came to Can., 1968; s. Vlastimil Dlab and Anna (Stuchlikova) Dlabova; m. Zdenka Dvorakova, Apr. 27, 1959 (div.); children—Dagmar, Daniel Jan; m. Helena Briestenska, Dec. 18, 1985; children: Philip Adam, David Michael. R.N.Dr., Charles U., Prague, Czech Republic, 1956, C.Sc., 1959, Habilitation, 1962, DSc, 1966; PhD, U. Khartoum, Sudan, 1962. Research fellow Czechoslovak Acad. Scis., Prague, 1956-57; lectr., sr. lectr. Charles U., Prague, 1957-59, reader, 1964-65; lectr., sr. lectr. U. Khartoum, Sudan, 1959-64; research fellow, sr. research fellow Inst. Advanced Studies, Australian Nat. U., Canberra, 1965-68; prof. math. Carleton U., Ottawa, Ont., Can., 1968-98; dir. Grad. Inst. Charles U., 1992-94; chmn. dept. Carleton U., Ottawa, Ont., Can., 1971-74, 94-97, disting. rsch. prof., 1998—, prof. emeritus; professorem hospitem Charles U., 1995—; vis. prof. U. Paris VI, Brandeis U., U. Bonn, Monash U., U. Tsukuba, U. Sao Paulo, U. Stuttgart, U. Poitiers, Nat. U. Mex., U. Essen, U. Bielefeld, Hungarian Acad. Scis., Budapest, U. Warsaw, U. Normal Beijing, U. Vienna, UCLA, U. Va., Czechoslovak Acad. Scis., U. Trondheim, U. Paderborn, U. St. Petersburg, U. Reims, U. Sao Paulo, Osaka U., Yamaneashi U., Shinshu U., Eotvos U., Budapest, Charle U., Prague. Author: Representations of Valued Graphs, 1980, An Introduction to Diagrammatical Methods, 1981, Quasi-hereditary Algebras, 1994; editor: Algebra and Representation Theory, 1998—; editor procs. internat. confs., 1974, 79, 84, 87, 90, 92, 93, 94, 96; contbr. numerous articles to profl. jours. Recipient Diploma of Honour Union Czechoslovak Mathematicians, 1962; Can. Council fellow, 1974; Japan Soc. Promotion of Sci. sr. rsch. fellow, 1981; sci. exchange grantee Nat. Scis. and Engring. Rsch. Coun. Can., 1978, 81, 83, 85, 88, 91. Fellow Royal Soc. Can. (convenor 1977-78, 80-81, coun. mem. 1980-81, editor Comptes rendus mathematiques-Math. Reports 1997—); mem. Am. Math. Soc., Math. Assn. Am., Can. Math. Soc. (coun., chmn. rsch. com. 1973-77, editor Can. Jour. Math. 1988-93), European Math. Soc., London Math. Soc. Roman Catholic. Avocations: sports, music. Home: 277 Sherwood Dr, Ottawa, ON Canada K1Y 3W3 Office: Carleton U Sch Math & Stat, Math Dept, Ottawa, ON Canada K1S 5B6

DLESK, GEORGE, retired pulp and paper industry executive; b. Chgo., Dec. 13, 1914; s. John J. and Anna (Dedic) D.; m. Jacquelyn McCredie, Mar. 16, 1940 (div. Jan. 1985, remarried Jan. 1997); children: Lynn, Devi, Andrea. B.S. in Indsl. Mgmt, U. Ill., 1939; postgrad., U. Calif., Berkeley, 1942, Inst. Paper Chemistry, Appleton, Wis., 1955, U. Sarasota, 1979; grad., Advanced Mgmt. Program, Harvard, 1967. With Booz, Allen & Hamilton, Chgo., 1943-46, Packaging Corp. Am., 1946-75; v.p. paperbd. div. Packaging Corp. Am., Evanston, Ill., 1956-67, sr. v.p., 1967-74; sr. v.p. mills, dir. Consol. Packaging Corp., Chgo., 1975-76; pres. Mgmt. Services for Paper Industry, Chgo., 1976-78; with Am. Inst. Fin. and Mgmt., 1979-81; pres. Computer Program Builders, Inc., 1981-89; ret., 1989. Mem. Sarasota Power Squadron. Mem. Sarasota Power Squadron. Episcopalian. Clubs: Sarasota Sailing Squadron, Sarasota Yacht. Home: The Fountains 7979 S Tamiami Trl Apt 250 Sarasota FL 34231-6819

D'LOWER, DEL, manufacturing executive; s. Max and Estere (Gerlatky) D.; m. Helen Fuchs, June 5, 1937 (dec. Mar. 1980); 1 child, Esther Ann. Student, U. Tulsa, 1942-44, New Sch., N.Y.C., 1960-63, 81-82. Cosmetologist, Seligman & Latz, N.Y.C., 1936-41, Del's, Tulsa, 1941-46; beauty salon owner Delby, N.Y.C., 1946-75; greeting card mfr., 1972; diversified bus. exec., pres., CEO Delby System, N.Y.C., 1975—, personal care products mfr., 1976. Author: Ginny the Pretty White Doe, 1973; composer:

High Cheek Bones, 1960, Only the Ashes Remain, The Wedding Waltz; Goodby Diane, 1990, m'Dina, Dinosaurian Coquette, 1993; patentee in field. Fellow ASCAP, 1992. Jewish. Avocations: creative writing, composing, poems, plays. Office: Delby System 47 W 34th St Ste 959 New York NY 10001-2121

DLUGOSZEWSKI, LUCIA, artistic director; b. Detroit, June 16, 1934. Student, Wayne State U.; studied with, Carl Beutel, Edward Bredshall, Ktja Andy, Grete Sultan, Felix Salzer, Edgard Varese. Composer Structure for the Poetry of Everyday Sound, 1949, Archaic Timbre Piano Music, 1958, Space Is a Diamond, 1970, Tender Theatre Flight Nageire, Densities, Nova, Corona, Clear Core, Amos Elusive Empty August, Strange Tenderness of naked Leaping, (commd. by Mikhail Baryshnikov) Disparate Stairway Radical other Quartet, 1994, Radical Quidditas Dew Tear Duende; artist dir. Erik Hawkins Dance Co., 1998—; recording artists various labels. Recipient Koussevitzky Internat. Recording award, 1979, Phoebe Kechum Thorne award, others; named Musician of Yr. Musical Am., Village Voice, 1975; Guggenheim fellow. Office: Erick Hawkins Sch Dance PO Box 1117 New York NY 10013-0866*

DLUHY, DEBORAH HAIGH, college dean; b. Summit, N.J., Mar. 4, 1940; d. Richard Hartman Haigh and Elin Frederika Anderson Neumann; m. Robert George Dluhy, June 11, 1962; 1 child, Leonore Alexandra. BA, Wheaton Coll., 1962; postgrad., Boston U., 1962-63, U. Heidelberg, Germany, 1963-65; PhD, Harvard U., 1976. Instr. fine arts Wheaton Coll., Norton, Mass., 1975-76, Radcliffe Coll., Cambridge, Mass., 1977, Boston Coll., Newton, Mass., 1976-77, 78; devel. officer Mus. Fine Arts, Boston, 1978-84, asst. dir. devel., 1984-86; assoc. dean adminstrn. Sch. Mus. Fine Arts, Boston, 1986-87, dean acad. programs and adminstrn., 1987-93, dean, 1993—. Trustee Wheaton Coll., Norton, Mass., 1988—, pres. Alumni Assn. 1994-2000; trustee Cultural Edn. Collaborative Boston, 1987-90; visitor Walnut Hill Sch., Natick, Mass., 1996—; pres. Pro Arts Consortium, 1999-01, Woodrow Wilson fellow, 1963. Mem. Nat. Assn. Schs. Art and Design (evaluator 1996—, rsch. com. 1990-96, bd. dirs. 1996—), Copley Soc. Boston (hon. trustee 1997—), Assn. Ind. Coll. Art and Design (bd. dirs., mem. exec. com., chair, program com.). Home: 104 Fletcher Rd Belmont MA 02478-2018 Office: Sch Mus of Fine Arts 230 Fenway Boston MA 02115-5534

D'LUHY, JOHN JAMES, investment banker; b. Passaic, N.J., Sept. 18, 1933; s. John George and Leonora (Fila) D'L.; m. Gale Rainsford, Dec. 7, 1968; children: Amanda, Pamela. AB, Trinity Coll., 1955; MBA, U. Pa., 1959. Lic. amateur radio operator K2EXI, comml. pilot (instrument-rated). Jr. exec. trainee Merrill Lynch, N.Y.C., 1956-58, with over-the-counter research dept., 1959-60; assoc. syndicate dept., investment mgmt., investment banking Lazard Freres & Co., N.Y.C., 1960-68; sr. v.p., ptnr., dir. money mgmt. and venture capital divs. R.W. Pressprich & Co., N.Y.C., 1968-72; dir. money mgmt. and fin. placements Wood Walker & Co., N.Y.C., 1972-73; pres. U.S. Oil Co., 1973-83, founder, pres., 1983-84; pvt. investor Dominick & Dominick, N.Y.C., 1983-86; fin. advisor Robert Thomas Securities divsn. Raymond James Assocs., N.Y.C., 1990—; trustee Collier Svcs. Found., Marlboro, N.J., 1986-92; bus. coun. Monmouth Univ., West Long Branch, N.J., 1994-98. Hon. usher St. Patrick's Cath., N.Y.C., 1969—, chief hon. usher, 1975-76; founding mem. U.S. Naval War Coll. Found., Newport, R.I.; co-chmn. Spring Lake Centennial Com., 1990-92; pres. Spring Lake Chorus, 1990-92; mem. Bond Club N.Y., 1963-91, Thursday Evening Club, 1981-87. Served with USNR, 1955. Mem. Investment Assn. N.Y. (bd. dirs. 1967, chmn. capital and money mktgs. com.), Assn. Investment Mgmt. and Rsch., N.Y. Soc. Security Analysts (sr. analyst), Am. Radio Relay League, Aircraft Owners and Pilots Assn., Univ. Club N.Y.C. (coun. 1977-83, exec. com., treas. 1979-83), Spring Lake (N.J.) Bath and Tennis Club, Jersey Aero Club (chmn. rules com. 1992), Blue Hill (N.Y.C.) Troupe. Roman Catholic. Home: 115 Ludlow Ave Spring Lake NJ 07762-1547

DLUHY, ROBERT GEORGE, physician; b. Montclair, N.J., Jan. 23, 1937; s. John George and Leona (Fila) D.; m. Deborah Haigh; 1 child, Leonore Alexandra. AB magna cum laude, Princeton U., 1958; MD, Harvard Med. Sch., 1962. Intern/resident Peter Bent Brigham Hosp., Boston, 1962, 65-67, endocrine fellow, 1967-69; instr. med. Harvard Med. Sch., Boston, 1969-74, asst. prof. med., 1974-80, assoc. prof. med., 1980-98, prof. med., 1998—. Capt. med. corp. U.S. Army, 1964-66, Germany. Fellow, Hypertension Coun. AHA, Endocrine Soc.; mem. Phi Beta Kappa. Office: Endocrine Hypertension Divs 221 Longwood Ave # Rfb2 Boston MA 02115-5822

DMOCHOWSKI, JAN RAFAL, surgeon, researcher; b. Warsaw, Poland, Aug. 27, 1927; came to U.S., 1968; s. Antoni and Teresa (Choloniewska) D.; m. Aleksandra Zylewicz, Dec. 31, 1953; 1 child, Maciej. MD, Med. Acad., Lodz, Poland, 1952, PhD, 1962. Assoc., sr. assoc., adj. prof. Med. Acad., Lodz, Poland, 1950-68, docent, 1967-68; res. fellow in surg. Harvard Med. Sch., Boston, 1963-65, 68-70, instr. surgery, 1970-76; dir. blood transfusion svc. Peter Bent Brigham Hosp., Boston, 1973-77; attending surgeon transplant svc. Peter Bent Brigham Hosp., 1975-76; assoc. surgery Peter Bent Brigham Hosp., Boston, 1975-77, dir. blood transfusion svc., 1973-77; surg. coord. St. Vincent's Hosp., Worcester, Mass., 1977-87, dir. surg. ICU, 1984-87; assoc. prof. surgery U. Mass Med. Sch., Worcester, 1977-81; sr. surgeon Lahey Clin. Med. Ctr., Burlington, Mass., 1987-92, cons. breast svc., 1987-92, ret. Contbr. numerous articles to profl. jours. Capt. M.C., Polish Resistance, Home Army. Fellow ACS. Avocations: photography, sailing, travel.

DMOWSKI, W. PAUL, obstetrician, gynecologist; b. Lodz, Poland, May 17, 1937; came to U.S., 1964; naturalized 1988; s. Thaddeus and Mirona (Jakubowska) D.; m. May 20, 1967 (div. 1975); 1 child Andrzej. T. MD, The Warsaw (Poland) Med. Acad., 1962; PhD in Endocrinology, Med. Coll. Ga., 1971. Diplomate Am. Bd. Ob. and Gyn., Reproductive Endocrinology/Infertility. Intern Warsaw U. Hosps., 1961-62; resident dept. ob-gyn Ottawa (Can.) Gen. Hosp., 1962-64, Beth Israel Med. Ctr., N.Y.C., 1964-67; Population Coun. rsch. fellow in gynecologic endocrinology Med. Coll. Ga., Augusta, 1967-69; asst. prof. dept. ob-gyn Pritzker Sch. Medicine U. Chgo., 1971-74, assoc. prof. dept. ob-gyn Pritzker Sch. Medicine, 1974-79; prof. U. Ark. for Med. Scis., Little Rock, 1979-81, Rush Med. Coll., Chgo., 1981—; assoc. attending physician dept. ob-gyn Michael Reese Hosp. and Med. Ctr., Chgo., 1971-76, attending physician, 1976-79; attending physician U. Ark. for Med. Scis., 1979-81; sr. attending physician Rush-Presbyn.-St. Lukes Med. Ctr., Chgo., 1981—; attending physician Grant Hosp. Chgo., 1982—; mem. cons. staff dept. ob-gyn. Christ Hosp., Oak Lawn, Ill., 1982—; mem. courtesy staff MacNeal Hosp., Berwyn, Ill., 1989—; cons. staff dept. ob/gyn Elmhurst (Ill.) Hosp., 1994—; founder, dir. fertility unit Michael Reese Med. Ctr., 1973-79, co-dir. sect. reproductive endocrinology and infertility, 1976-79; dir. div. reproductive endocrinology and infertility U. Ark. for Med. Scis., 1979-81; founder, dir. fellowship tng. program in reproductive endocrinology and infertility Rush Med. Coll., 1982-88, dir. sect. reproductive endocrinology and infertility, 1981-88; founder, dir. in vitro fertilization and embryo transfer program Rush-Presbyn. St. Luke's Med. Ctr., 1983-88; founder, dir. family fertility ctr. Grant Hosp., 1988-95, Inst. for Study and Treatment Endometriosis, 1988—; presenter sci. exhibits in endometriosis and immunology to over 176 profl. meetings. Contbr. over 129 articles to profl. jours., 40 chapts. to books; numerous invited articles, letters to editor in field. Recipient Cert. Appreciation ACS, 1979; grantee, clin. investigator Winthrop Rsch. Inst., 1967—, Ill. Inst. Tech., 1971-72Program Applied Rsch. on Fertility Regulation, 1973-75, Nat. 1st. Child Health and Human Devel., 1973-75, Carnrick Labs., 1975-79, Organon Internat., 1979-82, Abbott Labs., 1984—, Hoechst-Roussel Pharm., 1985-90, ICI Pharm., 1988-92, Syntex Labs., 1992-94, Ostex Internat., 1993-95, Serono Labs., 1998—, Praecis Pharms., 1998—. Fellow Am. Coll. Ob-Gyn. (Prize award 1975, 76, Coll. award 1969); mem. AMA (Cert. Merit 1969, 76, 78), Am. Assn. Gynecologic Laparoscopists, Am. Assn. Tissue Banks, Am. Soc. Reproductive Medicine (Cert. award 1977, Ortho Symposium Award 1980, Poster award 1992), Am. Soc. for Immunology of Reprodn., Ark. Med. Soc., Assn. Profs. Gynecology and Obstetrics, Chgo. Assn. Reproductive Endocrinologists, Chgo. Gynecol. Soc., Chgo. Med. Soc., Endocrine Soc., Ill. State Med. Soc., Little Rock Gynecol. Soc., N.Y. Acad. Scis., Soc. for Advancement Contraception, Soc. for Gynecologic Investigation, Soc. Reproductive Endocrinologists, Soc. Reproductive Surgeons, Soc. for Study Reprodn., Soc. for Assisted Reproductive Tech. Office: 2425 W 22nd St Ste 102 Oak Brook IL 60523-4643

DMYTRYSHYN, BASIL, historian, educator; b. Poland, Jan. 14, 1925; came to U.S., 1947, naturalized, 1951; s. Frank and Euphrosinia (Senchak) Dmytryshyn; m. Virginia Roehl, July 16, 1949; children: Sonia, Tania. BA, U. Ark., 1950; MA, U. Ark, 1951; PhD, U. Calif.-Berkeley, 1955; hon. diploma, U. Kiev-Mohyla Acad., 1993. Asst. prof. history Portland State U., Oreg., 1956-59; assoc. prof. Portland State U., 1959-64, prof., 1964-89, prof. emeritus, 1996—; assoc. dir. Internat. Trade and Commerce Inst., 1984-89; vis. prof. U. Ill., 1964-65, Harvard U., 1971, U. Hawaii, 1976, Hokkaido U., Sapporo, Japan, 1978-79; adviser U. Kiev-Mohyla Acad., 1993. Author books including: Moscow and the Ukraine, 1918-1953, 1956, Medieval Russia, 900-1700, 3d edit., 1990, Imperial Russia, 1700-1917, 3d edit., 1990, Modernization of Russia Under Peter I and Catherine II, 1974, Colonial Russian America 1817-1832, 1976, A History of Russia, 1977, U.S.S.R.: A Concise History, 4th edit., 1984, The End of Russian America, 1979, Civil and Savage Encounters, 1983, Russian Statecraft, 1985, Russian Conquest of Siberia 1558-1700, 1985, Russian Penetration of the North Pacific Archipelago, 1700-1799, 1987, The Soviet Union and the Middle East, 1917-1985, 1987, Russia's Colonies in North America, 1799-1867, 1988, The Soviet Union and the Arab World of the Fertile Crescent, 1918-1985, 1994, Imperial Russia, 1700-1917, 1999; contbr. articles to profl. jours. U.S., Can., Yugoslavia, Italy, South Korea, Fed. Republic Germany, France, Eng., Japan, Russia, Ukraine. State bd. dirs. PTA, Oreg., 1963-64; mem. World Affairs Council, 1965-92. Named Hon. Rsch. Prof. Emeritus, Kyungnam U., 1989—; Fulbright-Hays fellow W. Germany, 1967-68; fellow Kennan Inst. Advanced Russian Studies, Washington, 1978; recipient John Mosser award Oreg. State Bd. Higher Edn., 1966, 67; Branford P. Millar award for faculty excellence Portland State U., 1985, Outstanding Retired Faculty award, 1994; Hillard scholar in the humanities U. Nev., Reno, 1992. Mem. Am. Assn. Advancement Slavic Studies (dir. 1972-75), Am. Hist. Assn., Western Slavic Assn. (pres. 1990-92), Can. Assn. Slavists, Oreg. Hist. Soc., Nat. Geog. Soc., Conf. Slavic and East European History (nat. sec. 1972-75), Am. Assn. for Ukrainian Studies (pres. 1991-93), Ctr. Study of Russian Am. (hon.), Assn. Study Nationalities (bd. mem.-at-large USSR & Ea. Europe 1993—), Czechoslovak Soc. Arts and Scis., Soc. Jewish-Ukraine Contacts, Assn. Home: 2745 S Via Del Bac Green Valley AZ 85614-1071

DOAN, HERBERT DOW, technical business consultant; b. Midland, Mich., Sept. 5, 1922; s. Leland Ira and Ruth Alden (Dow) D.; m. Donalda Lockwood, 1946 (div.); children: Jeffrey W., Christine Mary, Ruth Alden, Michael Alden; m. Anna Junia Cassell, July 16, 1979; 1 child, Alexandra Anne Alden. B Chem. Enging., Cornell U., 1949. Founder, owner Doan Assocs., Midland, 1971-85; chmn., dir. Neogen Corp., Lansing, Mich., 1983-99; pres. Mich. High Tech. Task Force, Lansing, 1981-90; nat. adv. com. dept. engring. U. Mich., Ann Arbor, 1984-95; chmn. Midland Molecular Inst., 1971—; dir. Mich. Materials and Processing Inst., Ann Arbor, 1984-92; trustee, sec. Herbert H. and Grace A. Dow Found., Midland, 1951—; researcher Dow Chem. Co., Midland, 1949-60, exec. v.p., 1960-62, pres., 1962-71; pres. The Herbert H. and Grace A Dow Found., Midland, 1996—; dir. Applied Intelligent Systems, Inc., Ann Arbor, Chem. Bank and Trust Co., Arch Devel. Corp., Chgo.; mem. engring. coun. Cornell U., Ithaca, N.Y., 1964-85, emeritus, 1985—; mem. Nat. Sci. Bd., Washington, 1976-82, vice chmn., 1981-82; mem. Commn. on Phys. Scis., Math. and Applications, NRC of NAS, Washington, 1987-91; bd. govs. Argonne Nat. Lab., U. Chgo., 1984-90; tech. assessment adv. coun. Office Tech. Assessment, Washington, 1992-95. Staff sgt. USAF, 1942-45; PTO. Mem. Am. Inst. Chem. Engrs., Am. Chem. Soc., Sigma Xi. Home: 3801 Valley Dr Midland MI 48640-6601 Office: Herbert H and Grace A Dow Found PO Box 169 Midland MI 48640-0169

DOAN, MARY FRANCES, advertising executive; b. Vallejo, Calif., Apr. 16, 1954; d. Larry E. and Dudley (Harbison) D.; m. Timothy Warren Hesselgren, Mar. 19, 1988; children: Edward Latimer, Clinton Robert. BA in Linguistics, U. Calif., Berkeley, 1976; M in Internat. Mgmt., Am. Grad. Sch. Internat. Mgmt., 1980. Trading asst. The Capital Group, L.A., 1980-81; fin. analyst Litton Industries, Beverly Hills, Calif., 1981-82; account exec. Grey Advt., San Francisco, L.A., 1982-84, J. Walter Thompson, San Francisco, 1984-85, Lowe Marshalk, San Francisco, 1985-86; account supr. Young & Rubicam, San Francisco, 1986-89; CEO, pres. Saatchi & Saatchi, San Francisco, 1989-96, worldwide dir. client svc. applications, 1996—. Office: Saatchi & Saatchi 735 Battery St Ste 400 San Francisco CA 94111-1538

DOAN, MICHAEL FREDERICK, editor; b. Oakland, Calif., Feb. 5, 1942; s. Philip Melville and Agnes Blair (Gee) D.; m. Mary Pickett Craddock, May 11, 1985; 1 child, Sara. BA in Journalism, U. Calif., Berkeley, 1963. Corr. AP, Las Vegas, 1968-69; econs. corr. AP, Washington, 1970-79; assoc. editor U.S. News and World Report, Washington, 1979-87; editor Satellite Orbit mag., Vienna, Va., 1987-92; assoc. editor Kiplinger Washington Editors, 1992—. Trustee United Meth. Ch., Washington, 1998. With USAR, 1964-70. Mem. Nat. Press Club, Washington Press Club (mem. chmn., sec. 1980-87). Methodist. Avocations: skiing, jazz piano. Home: 3316 21st Ave N Arlington VA 22207-3821 Office: Kiplinger Washington Editors 1729 H St NW Washington DC 20006-3904

DOAN, PATRICIA NAN, librarian; b. Fayetteville, Ark., Oct. 27, 1930; d. William Rader and Olga (White) Rogers; B.A., U. Ark., 1951; m. John Cannon Doan, Apr. 2, 1950; children—William Curtis, Sarah Cannon, Mary Virginia. Librarian, Okmulgee (Okla.) Public Library, 1967-94. Treas. Okmulgee Art Guild, 1969-71; sec. Okmulgee County Devel. Council, 1971—, Creek Nation Council House Bd., 1975-93. Mem. Okmulgee Meml. Hosp. Found.; mem. Okmulgee Task Force, county chmn. Okmulgee County History Book Com.; bd. dirs., mem. adv. bd. Okmulgee Main Street, 1987-94. Mem. ALA, Okla. Library Assn. (sec. public library div. 1970), Okmulgee County Geneal. Soc. (v.p. 1970), Sigma Alpha Iota, Zeta Tau Alpha. Democrat. Episcopalian. Compiler: Index of the 1907 Census of Okmulgee, Oklahoma, 1971. Home: 6920 Hwy 56 Okmulgee OK 74447-9403

DOAN, PATRICK TOAI VAN, writer, foundation administrator; b. Sept. 14, 1946. Rsch. assoc. Fletcher Sch. of Law and Diplomacy, Medford, Mass., 1979-82; vis. scholar U. Calif., Berkeley, 1982-84; dir. Inst. South East Asian Policy Analysis, Boston, 1984-86; pres. Inst. for Democracy, Washington, 1986-96; v.p. Am. Edn. Found., Irvine, Calif., 1997—; lectr. MIT, Yale U., Stanford U., Cornell U., Harvard U. Author: Vietnamese Gulag, 1986, France, 1979, Germany, 1980, Portrait of Enemy, 1988, Eng., 1996; co-author: A Vietcong Memoir, 1988; contbr. numerous articles to Washington Post, N.Y. Times, L.A. Times, Wall St. Jour., Christian Sci. Monitor, others. dir. Vietnam free-market edn. project CIPE, U.S.C. of C., 1992-94. E-mail: scupsint@aol.com. Office: PO Box 4995 Irvine CA 92616-4995

DOAN, PETRA LEISENRING, urban planner, educator; b. Concord, Mass., Oct. 23, 1955; s. Foster Quaril and Elizabeth (Leisenring) D.; m. Rebecca Shoemaker Miles, Aug. 8, 1981; children: Jessamyn Jessup, Daniel Miles. BA, Haverford Coll., 1977; M of Regional Planning, Cornell U., 1984, PhD, 1988. Mgmt. analyst U.S Dept. Justice, Washington, 1980-81; planning cons. Min. Planning, Amman, Jordan, 1984-85; instr. Cornell U., Ithaca, 1986-88; vis. asst. prof. U. N.C., Chapel Hill, 1988-89; asst. prof. Fla. State U., Tallahassee, 1989-96, assoc. prof., 1996—; cons. U.S. Agy. Internat. Devel. Contbr. articles to profl. jours. Vol. U.S. Peace Corps., Aneho, Togo, cons.: mem. Am. Friends Svc. Com., Phila., 1995—. Sage Grad. fellow Cornell U., 1981-84; Sr. Fulbright scholar Coun. Internat. Exch. Scholars, 1995-97. Mem. Am. Planning Assn., Middle East Studies Assn., African Studies Assn., Assn. Collegiate Scholars Planning, Regional Sci. Assn. Internat. Soc. of Friends. Home: 3342 Nottingham Dr Tallahassee FL 32312-1442 Office: Dept Urban Regional Planning Fla State U Tallahassee FL 32306-2280

DOAN, XUYEN VAN, lawyer; b. Hadong, Vietnam, Apr. 1, 1949; came to U.S., 1975; s. Quyet V. Doan and Binh T. Kieu: m. Binh Thanh Tran, 1980; children: Quy-Bao, Ky-Nam. Licence en droit, U. Saigon Law Sch., Vietnam, 1971; MBA, U. Ark., 1977; JD, U. Calif. Hastings, 1982. Bar: Saigon 1972, Calif. 1982. Sole practice Costa Mesa and San Jose, Calif., 1982-84; ptnr. Doan & Vu, San Jose 1984-90; prin. Law Offices of Xuyen V. Doan, 1990-95; ptnr. Doan & Tran, San Jose, 1995—; founder, coord. VietLawyers Com., Calif. and Vietnam. Author: Of the Seas and Men, 1985, also other publs. in English and Vietnamese. Named Ark. Traveler Ambassador of Good Will, State of Ark., 1975. Email: JD@VietLawyers.com. Office: 2114 Senter Rd Ste 20 San Jose CA 95112

DOANE, J. WILLIAM, physics educator and researcher, science administrator; b. Bayard, Nebr., Apr. 26, 1935; married, 1958; 2 children. BS, U. Mo., 1956, MS, 1962, PhD in Physics, 1965. From asst. to assoc. prof. Kent State U., 1965-74, prof. physics, 1974-96, prof. emeritus, 1996—, assoc. dir. Liquid Crystal Inst., 1979-83, dir. Liquid Crystal Inst., 1983-96, dir. emeritus, 1996—; v.p. R&D, chief sci. officer Kent Displays, Inc., Ohio, 1996—; prin. investigator def. agy. and industry grants NSF. Contbr. over 200 articles to profl. jours; holder of 10 patents. Fellow Am. Phys. Soc.; mem. Am. Assn. Physics Tchrs., Sigma Xi. Achievements includes research on liquid crystal display and nuclear magnetic resonance in liquid crystals. Office: Kent Displays Inc 343 Portage Blvd Kent OH 44240-7284

DOANE, WOOLSON WHITNEY, internist; b. Worcester, Mass., Mar. 21, 1939; s. Whitney Randall and Mary Helen (Woolson) D.; m. Patricia Louise Morse, June 21, 1962; children: Melinda L., Morse W., Seth J. BA, U. Vt., 1962, MD, 1965. Diplomate Am. Bd. Internal Medicine. Lt. USNR, 1966-68; gen. med. officer Force Troops Fleet, Camp Lejeune, N.C., 1966-68; pvt. practice Franklin Meml. Hosp., Greenfield, Mass., 1971-82; assoc. med. dir. respiratory therapy Maine Med. Ctr., Waterville, 1982-84; med. dir. Knolls Atomic Power Lab., Schenectady, N.Y., 1984-87; area med. dir. GE Plastics-GE Aerospace, Pittsfield, Mass., 1987-90; med. dir. GE Plastics, Pittsfield, 1991-93; corp. med. dir. Reynolds Metal Co., Richmond, Va., 1993-97; chief of medicine VAMROC, Togus, Maine, 1997—; bd. dirs. Ctr. and Mass. Am. Lung Assn., Worcester, 1973-82; trustee, bd. dirs. Franklin Meml. Hosp., Greenfield, 1975-79. Bd. dirs. Franklin County Community Action Coun., Greenfield, 1978-81; corporator Berkshire Med. Ctr., Pittsfield, 1987-93; mem. GE Elfan Soc., Pittsfield, Schenectady, 1984-93. Recipient Woodbury Alumni prize U. Vt., 1965. Mem. Am. Coll. Physician Execs. Republican. Episcopalian. Achievements include communication program for lay persons on risks of polychlorinated biophenols; program devel. in respiratory therapy, cardiopulmonary lab., cardiac-rehab.; design and management of care practice models including EAP integration with managed mental health benefits.

DOBBERSTEIN, ERIC, lawyer; b. Las Vegas, Sept. 19, 1961; s. Herbert Emil and Ruth Ferris (Young) D.; children: Eric Rashon, Ian Cordell, Nyles Elijah. Student, U. Nev., 1981; BA, U. Nev., Las Vegas, 1985; JD, Thurgood Marshall Sch. of Law, 1988. Bar: Nev. 1989, U.S. Dist. Ct. Nev. 1989, U.S. Ct. Appeals (9th cir.) 1990. Asst. law libr. Libr. Mgmt. Svc., Houston, 1987-88; lawyer, law clk. Zervas & Evans, Las Vegas, 1986-89; lawyer Keith Gregory, Ltd., Las Vegas, 1989, Morton & McCullough, Las Vegas, 1990-91; pvt. practice Henderson, Nev., 1991—; arbitrator Eighth Jud. Dist. Ct., Las Vegas, 1992—; Justice of Peace Pro Tempore, 1999—; referee small claims ct., traffic court, 1998-99. Editor (notes) Thurgood Marshall Law Rev., 1988. Planning commr. City of Henderson, Nev., 1994-97. Mem. ABA, State Bar of Nev., Nev. Trial Lawyers Assn., Clark County Bar Assn., State Bar of Nev. (mem. fee dispute com., atty. disciplinary bd. 1998—). Democrat. Avocation: sports. Office: 1399 Galleria Dr Ste 201 Henderson NV 89014

DOBBERT, DUANE LLOYD, forensic psychologist, educator, consultant; b. Detroit, Jan. 22, 1946; s. Lloly Louis and Enid Louise D.; m. Joyce Elaine Till, Sept. 12, 1992; 1 child, Kelley Lynn Dobbert Jones. BA, Albion Coll., 1967; MA, Mich. State U., 1971; postgrad., Grad. Sch. Am. Diplomate Am. Bd. Forensic Examiners, Am. Coll. Forensic Examiners. Dir. children's svcs. Calhoun County Juvenile Ct., Marshall, Mich., 1969-88; v.p. Vestil Mfg. Co., Angola, Ind., 1989-94; prof. Tri-State U., Angola, 1994—; pres. Tri-State Cons., Angola, 1994—; cons. Mich. Dept. Corrections; cons. educator Nat. Coun. Juvenile and Family Ct. Judges, Reno, 1973—; educator Mich. Jud. Inst., E. Lansing, Mich. Editor: Forensic Psychology Textbook, 1993; contbr. articles to profl. jours. Avocations: fly fishing, waterfowl hunting. E-mail: dldobbert@dmci.net. Home: 95 LN 230 A Jimmerson Lake Angola IN 46703

DOBBIE, GEORGE HERBERT, retired textile manufacturing executive; b. Galt, Ont., Can., Nov. 15, 1918; s. George Alexander and Edith (Scott) D.; m. Marie L. Reiser, Mar. 15, 1941; children—George C., Murray S., Brian H., Alexander M. Student, Bishop Ridley Coll., 1934-35, McGill U., 1936-39. With Newlands & Co., Galt, 1939—; sales mgr. hand knit div. Newlands & Co., 1947-51, pres., 1951-63; pres. Dobbie Industries Ltd., 1963-77; past chmn. bd. Glenelg Textiles Ltd., Galt, Agatex Devel. Ltd., Galt; hon. dir. Domtar, Inc., Montreal. Past chmn. Can. Textile Inst., Galt Bd. Trade, Galt Bd. Edn.; past bd. govs. U. Waterloo, Lakefield Coll. Sch., Ont. Served from pvt. to capt. Royal Canadian Army, 1941-45. Mem. Can. Woolen and Knit Goods Mfrs. Assn. (pres. 1956-58), Primary Textiles Inst. Can. (chmn.), Can. Mfrs. Assn. (past v.p.), Pacific Basin Econ. Coun. (past v.p.), Can. Bus. and Industry Adv. Coun. (past v.p.). Home: 45 Blair Rd, Galt, ON Canada N1S 2H8

DOBBIN, EDMUND J., university administrator; b. Bklyn., 1935. BA in Philosophy, Villanova U., 1958; MA, Augustinian Coll., 1962; SDT, U. Louvain, Belgium, 1971. ordained priest Roman Cath. Ch., 1962. Tchr. math. and religion, prefect of students Malvern Prep. Sch., 1962-67; tchr. systematic theology Washington Theol. Union, 1971-87, asst. prof., assoc. prof.; assoc. prof. Villanova (Pa.) U., 1987—, pres., 1988—. Trustee Villanova U., 1979-87, Merrimack Coll., North Andover, Mass., 1971-89, chmn. bd., 1986-89; mem. provincial coun. Augustinian Province of St. Thomas of Villanova, 1982-89. Mem. Am. Acad. Religion, Cath. Theol. Soc. Am. Office: Villanova U Office of the President 800 E Lancaster Ave Villanova PA 19085-1603*

DOBBINS, BRENDA LORRAINE ADAMS, secondary school educator; b. Elkin, N.C., Apr. 20, 1949; d. James Everett Archie and Margaret Ophelia (Petty) Adams; m. Spencer Ray Dobbins, Apr. 13, 1974; 1 child, Bryan Reece. BS, N.C. A&T State U., 1970; MS, U. N.C., Greensboro, 1989. Cert. vocat. bus. tchr., N.C. Life. N.C. Nat. Bank, Greensboro, 1970; sec. GE, Phila., 1970-71, N.C. A&T State U., Greensboro, 1971; tech. aide Wilkes County Bd. Edn., Wilkesboro, N.C., 1971-72, tchr. bus. edn., 1972—; coord. staff devel. East Wilkes H.S., Ronda, N.C., 1973-85, new tchr. mentor, 1985—, advisor Future Bus. Leaders Am. 1972—; sch. rep. Appalachian State U.-Pub. Sch. Partnership, Boone, N.C., 1987-96. Mem. N.C. Ext. Homemakers, Wilkesboro, 1983-93; sec. bd. dirs. Clingman Med. Ctr., Ronda, 1979-81; bd. dirs. Lincoln Heights Recreation Corp., Wilkesboro, 1987—; youth supr., teen Sunday sch. tchr. Poplar Spring Bapt. Ch., vacation Bible sch. dir. 1973-98, local missionary pres., 1992-94, sec., 1998—; special worker Wilkes County Union Missionary, 1997—; bd. dirs. Woman's Home and Fgn. Missionary Aux., 1999—; 4-H advisor; vol. Wilkes One-on-One, 1991; vice chair Wilkes County Coop. Ext. Adv. Coun., 1987-88; Citizen's Ambassador, del. to China People to People, Oct. 1995. Mem. NEA, Nat. Bus. Edn. Assn., N.C. Bus. Edn. Assn., Am. Vocat. Assn., N.C. Assn. Educators (local treas. 1988-89, local treas. 1993-96), Delta Pi Epsilon. Democrat. Baptist. Avocations: camping, bible study, reading, crafts, computers. Home: 10879 E US Highway 421 Roaring River NC 28669-8303 Office: East Wilkes High Sch PO Box 368 Ronda NC 28670-0368

DOBBINS, JAMES FRANCIS, JR., foreign service officer; b. N.Y.C., May 31, 1942; s. James Francis and Agnes Ann (Bent) D.; m. Toril Kleivdal, Dec. 31, 1969; children: Colin, Christian. BSFS, Georgetown U., 1963. Commd. fgn. svc. officer Dept. State, 1967; staff U.S. del. Vietnam Peace Talks, Paris, 1968; policy planning staff Dept. State, Washington, 1969-71; consul Strasbourg, France; spl. asst. to U.S. rep. UN, N.Y.C., 1973-75; polit.-mil. officer Am. Embassy, London, 1975-80; dep. asst. sec. U.S. Dept. State, Washington, 1982-85; dep. chief mission Am. Embassy, Bonn, Fed. Republic Germany, 1985-89; prin. dep. asst. Sec. of State for Europe, 1989-91; amb. to the European Communities, 1991-93; spl. coord. Somalia Dept. State, Washington, 1993, spl. Haiti coord., 1994-96; sr. dir. Inter-Am. affairs White House, Washington, 1996—. Lt. (j.g.) USN, 1963-66. Recipient Superior Honor award Dept. State, 1982, Presdl. award 1989, 92, 97, Expeditionary medal Vietnam, 7 sr. performance awards Dept. State, 1993. Office: White House Rm 361 Old Exec Office Bldg Washington DC 20504

DOBBINS, JAMES TALMAGE, JR., analytical chemist, researcher; b. Chapel Hill, N.C., June 13, 1926; s. James Talmage and Lila (Shore) D.; m. Jacqueleene Bowen, Dec. 22, 1951; children: James Talmage III, Steven Earl. BS in Chemistry, U. N.C., 1947, PhD in Analytical Chemistry, 1958. Chief indsl. hygiene sect. Med. Gen. Lab., Tokyo, 1953-55, head dept.

chemistry, 1955-6; rsch. chemist II R.J. Reynolds Tobacco Co., Winston-Salem, N.C., 1958-65; rsch. sect. head II R.J. Reynolds Tobacco Co., Winston-Salem, 1965-72; mgr. analytical rsch. div. R.J. Reynolds Industries, Winston-Salem, 1972-75; master scientist RJR Nabisco, Winston-Salem, 1975-83; master chemist Bowman Gray Tech. Ctr., Winston-Salem, 1983-89; retired, 1989. Contbr. articles to Jour. Assn. Official Agrl. Chemists, Jour. Assn. Official Analytical Chemists, Spectroscopy, Encyclopedia Ind. Chem. Analysis. Fellow Am. Inst. Chemists; mem. AAAS, Soc. for Applied Spectroscopy, N.Y. Acad. Sci., N.C. Acad. Sci., Am. Chem. Soc. (sec., chmn. elect and chmn. ctrl. N.C. sect. 1964, 65, 66), Sigma Xi (sec. Wake Forest chpt. 1986-90). Democrat. Baptist. Achievements include conception of column-elutive sample prep for plant matter analysis; design of clean room facilities for ICP spectrometry of trace inorganics, and of first-of-its-kind computer intelligent auto-dilution by flow injection/ICP analysis. Home: 2838 Bartram Rd Winston Salem NC 27106-5105

DOBBINS, MICHAEL A., city planning and development commissioner; b. Denver. BArch, Yale U., MArch. Lic. arch.; cert. planner, Am. Inst. Cert. Planners. Asst. prof. architecture Tulane U. Sch. Architecture, New Orleans; tech. dir. New Orleans Comprehensive River Transp. Study; dep. dir. City of N.Y. Urban Design Group; planning dir. Borough of S.I., N.Y.C.; dir. urban planning City of Birmingham, Ala.; campus planning dir. U. Calif., Berkeley, lectr., dept. city and regional planning; commr., dept. planning, devel. and neighborhood conservation City of Atlanta; frequent participant in planning in design forums, various cities and states. Active supporter cmty. and neighborhood-based activities. Recipient numerous honors and awards. Fellow Am. Inst. Archs. Office: Dept Planning Devel & Conservation 68 Mitchell St SW Atlanta GA 30303-3520*

DOBBS, DAN BYRON, lawyer, educator; b. Ft. Smith, Ark., Nov. 8, 1932; s. George Byron and Gladys Pauline (Stone) D.; m. Betty Jo Teeter, May 31, 1953 (div. 1978); children: Katherine, George, Rebecca, Jean. B.A., U. Ark., 1956, LL.B., 1956; LL.M., U. Ill., 1961, J.S.D., 1966. Bar: Ark. 1956. Partner firm Dobbs, Pryor & Dobbs, Ft. Smith, 1956-60; asst. prof. law U. N.C., Chapel Hill, 1961-63; assoc. prof. U. N.C., 1963-66, prof., 1967, Aubrey L. Brooks prof. law, 1975-77; Rosenstiel prof. law U. Ariz., 1978—, Regents prof., 1992—; vis. asst. prof. U. Tex., summer 1961; vis. prof. U. Minn., 1966-67, Cornell Law Sch., 1968-69, U. Va. Law Sch., 1974, U. Ariz. Law Sch., 1977-78. Author: Handbook on the Law of Remedies, Damages, Equity, Restitution, 1973, Problems in Remedies, 1974, The Law of Remedies, 3 vols., 2d edit., 1993; co-author: Prosser and Keeton on Torts, 5th edit., 1984, Torts and Compensation, 1985, 2d edit., 1993, 3d edit. (with Paul Hayden), 1997; contbr. articles to legal jours. Office: U Ariz Law Coll Tucson AZ 85721

DOBBS, GEORGE ALBERT, funeral director, embalmer; b. Atlanta, Oct. 16, 1943; s. Albert F. and Ruby Lee (Haynes) D. Student Fla. Bapt. Theol. Coll., 1963-67; BA, Cornell U., 1974; AA in Mortuary Sci. and Adminstrn., John A. Gupton Coll., 1990. Cert. funeral svc. practitioner. Retail store mgr. Alterman Foods, Atlanta, 1962-74; ind. mng. agt. George A. Dobbs & Assocs., Decatur, Ga., 1974-78, motivational spkr., Hermitage, Tenn., 1992—; retail mgr. K-Mart Corp., Decatur, 1978-91; funeral dir., embalmer, SCI Nashville Group, , 1991-97; svc. ctr. coord. Nashville Family Funeral Homes, SCI Nashville Group, 1997—. Named Small Bus. Mgr. of Year, Dekalb Businessman's Assn., 1974, 76. Mem. Ga. Lodge of Rsch., Scottish Rite Rsch. Soc., Mo. Lodge of Rsch., Capital City Club, Mason (past master Ga. and Tenn.), Grotto, Knights of Mecca, Shriner (Ky. col. 1996—), Hon. Order of Ky. Cols. Baptist. Republican. Office: Woodlawn Funeral Home 660 Thompson Ln Nashville TN 37204-3608 Address: PO Box 290275 Nashville TN 27229-0275

DOBBS, GREGORY ALLAN, journalist; b. San Francisco, Oct. 9, 1946; s. Harold Stanley and Annette Rae (Lehrer) D.; m. Carol Lynn Walker, Nov. 25, 1973; children: Jason Walker, Alexander Adair. B.A., U. Calif., Berkeley, 1968; M.S.J., Northwestern U., 1969. Assignment editor, reporter Sta. KGO-TV, San Francisco, 1966-68; news dir. San Francisco Tourist Info. Program Service, 1968; editor ABC Radio, Chgo., 1969-71; producer ABC News, Chgo., 1971-73; corr. ABC News, 1973-77, London, 1977-82, Paris, 1982-86, Denver, 1986-92; host The Greg Dobbs Show/Sta. KOA Radio, 1992—; lectr. Northwestern U. Sch. Journalism, 1975, 76; prof. U. Colo. Sch. Journalism, 1996—. Columnist The Denver Post, 1996—. Recipient Sigma Delta Chi Disting. Svc. award for TV reporting Soc. Profl. Journalists, 1980, Emmy award for outstanding documentary, 1989, award of excellence Colo. Broadcasters Assn., 1993, 94, award for best talk show Colo. Soc. Profl. Journalists, 1994; Lippmann fellow Ford Found., 1975. Office: 1153 Bergen Pkwy Ste M150 Evergreen CO 80439-9525

DOBBS, JOHN BARNES, artist, educator; b. Nutley, N.J., Aug. 2, 1931; s. John Montgomery and Catherine (Barnes) D.; m. Anne Baudement, 1959; children: Nicolas, Michel. Student, R.I. Sch. Design, 1949, Bklyn. Mus. Art Sch., 1950-52, Skowhegan Sch., 1952. Prof. studio art John Jay Coll. CUNY, N.Y.C., 1974-96. Twenty-three one-man shows in U.S. and France; group exhbns. include Am. Acad. Arts and Letters (Childe Hassam purchase prize 1972, Art award 1994), Whitney Mus., Nat. Acad. Design (Ranger Fund purchase prize 1966, 90, Benjamin Altman prize 1980, Edwin Palmer prize 1991), Mus. Modern Art, Butler Inst. Am. Art, Salon des Independents. Cpl. U.S. Army, 1952-54, ETO. Louis Comfort Tiffany grantee, 1967. Mem. NAD (academician), Century Club. Home: 463 West St Apt B339 New York NY 10014-2032

DOBBS, LOU, television executive, managing editor; b. Childress, Tex., Sept. 24, 1945; m. Debi Segura; children: Chance, Jason, Hilary, Heather. Degree in econs., Harvard U., 1967. Copy reader L.A. Times; chief econs. corr., anchor Moneyline CNN, N.Y.C., 1980-81, anchor Primenews, 1981, v.p., mng. editor bus. news, 1984-97, pres. news, exec. v.p., 1997—; anchor Moneyline CNN, Tokyo, 1989; host TV spl. Nobel Minds Stockholm, 1993; anchor Moneyline Chgo., 1992; sr. v.p., 1992-97, exec. v.p., 1997—; mem. Loeb Award judges com. Recipient George Foster Peabody award for coverage of 1987 stock market crash, Luminary award Bus. Journalism Rev., 1990, CableAce award, Front Page award, N.Y. Film Festival award, Janus award, Daniel Webster award, Emmy awards; named Father of Yr., Nat. Father's Day Com., 1993. Mem. NATAS, Investigative Reporters and Editors Assn., Am. Econ. Assn., Sigma Delta Chi. Office: Cable News Network 20th Fl 5 Penn Plz Fl 22 New York NY 10001-1878*

DOBBS, RITA MARIE, travel company executive; b. Chgo., May 12, 1965; d. Frank R. and Mary Ann (Kalata) D. BA in French, U. Houston, 1992, BA in Russian Studies, 1996. Assoc. Macy's, Houston, 1984-87, 88-91; travel assistance coord. Am. Internat. Assistance Svcs., Houston, 1993-97; travel agt. CUC Internat., Inc., Houston, 1998; customer care cons. PrimeCo Personal Comms., Houston, 1998—. Pi Delta Phi scholar, 1987. Mem. MLA, Am. Translators Assn., L'Alliance Francaise Houston, Tex. Fgn. Lang. Assn., Russian Studies Club, Pi Delta Pi (sec. 1987). Home: 2222 Primwood Ct Pearland TX 77584-9817 Office: PrimeCo Personal Comms 5959 Corporate Dr Ste 2500 Houston TX 77036

DOBELIS, GEORGE, manufacturing company executive; b. July 31, 1940; s. John and Dorothy Dobelis; m. Dolores Ann Nagle, Dec. 2, 1972; children: Sally Ann Berg, Christian Eric Berg, Kurt Conrad Berg. AA in Engring., Santa Monica Coll., 1963; student, Control Data Inst., 1970. Engring. Masterite Ind., Torrance, Calif., 1969-70; engring. mgr. Elco Corp., El Segundo, Calif., 1964-76, mgr. new products, 1976-77; pres. Connector Tech. Inc., Anaheim, Calif., 1977—. Patentee in field; contbr. articles to profl. jours. Served as sgt. N.G., 1963-69. Mem. IEEE. Republican. Avocations: golf, skiing, camping, hiking.

DOBELIS, INGE NACHMAN, editor; b. Würzburg, Germany, Nov. 16, 1933; came to U.S., 1938, naturalized, 1951; d. Rudolf Hugo and Resi (Hamburger) Nachman; BA in English, U. Ga., 1956; m. Miervaldis C. Dobelis, May 4, 1969; 1 son, Arthur N. Editorial positions Buttenheim Publs. and Crowell-Collier, 1956-64; copy editor Gen. Book div. Readers Digest, N.Y.C., 1965-72, assoc. editor, 1973-79, sr. editor, 1979-85, sr. staff editor, 1985-97; freelance writer, editor, 1998—. Exec. bd., officer Murray Hill Democratic Club, 1968-74; exec. bd. Community Bd. No. 6, N.Y.C., 1973-78, sec., 1976, chmn. health and hosps. com., 1974-78; trustee, officer Brotherhood Synagogue, 1983—, pres. 1993-95; mem. N.Y. Dem. County Com., 1967-74. Mem. Phi Beta Kappa. Assoc. editor: Reader's Digest Family Encyclopedia of American History, 1975; Reader's Digest Family Health Guide and Medical Encyclopedia, 1976; Reader's Digest Illustrated Guide to Gardening, 1978; editor: Readers Digest Family Legal Guide, 1981; Quick and Thrifty Cooking, 1984; Magic and Medicine of Plants, 1986; Great Recipes for Good Health, 1988; America: Land of Beauty and Splendor, 1992, Legal Problem Solver, 1994, Know Your Rights, 1995. Club: Nat. Arts (N.Y.C.). Home: 201 E 17th St New York NY 10003-3607 Office: Reader's Digest Gen Books 260 Madison Ave Fl 6 New York NY 10016-2490

DOBELL, BYRON MAXWELL, magazine consultant; b. Bronx, N.Y., May 30, 1927; s. Jacob and Marie (Schaeffer) D.; m. Edith Spielberg, 1952 (div. 1957); m. Ande Rubin, 1958 (dec. 1967); 1 dau., Elizabeth; m. Elizabeth Rodgers Dempster, 1969 (dec. 1992). AB, Columbia U., 1947. Picture editor U.S. Camera, 1952-55; asso. editor Popular Photography, 1956-57; feature editor Pageant, 1957-58, This Week, 1958-60; sr. editor Time-Life Books, 1960-62, asso. dir. editorial planning, 1971-72; mng. editor Esquire mag., N.Y.C., 1962-67, 79-82, editor-in-chief, 1977; editor-in-chief Book World (weekly lit. supplement Chgo. Tribune and Washington Post), 1967-69; editor-in-chief book div. McCall Pub. Co., 1969-71; editorial dir. New York mag., 1972-77; sr. editor Life mag., N.Y.C., 1978-79; editor-in-chief Am. Heritage mag., 1982-90, Am. Heritage of Invention & Tech. mag., 1984-90; mag. cons. N.Y.C., 1990—; bd. dirs. Am. Soc. Mag. Editors, 1987-91. Editor: Life Guide to Paris, A Sense of History. Served with AUS, 1946-47. Named to Am. Soc. of Mag. Editor's Hall of Fame, 1998. Mem. PEN (N.Y.C.), Century Assn. Home and Office: 150 E 69th St New York NY 10021-5704

DOBELLE, EVAN SAMUEL, college administrator; b. Washington, Apr. 22, 1945; s. Martin and Lillian (Mendelsohn) D.; m. Edith Huntington Kit, June 7, 1970; 1 child, Harry Huntington. BA, U. Mass., 1983, MEd, 1970, EdD, 1987; MPA, Harvard U., 1984. Exec. asst. U.S. Senator Edward Brooke, Boston, 1971-73; mayor City of Pittsfield, Mass., 1973-76; commr. environ. mgmt. State of Mass., Boston, 1976-77; chief protocol U.S., Washington, 1977-78; treas. Dem. Nat. Com., Washington, 1978-79, dep. chair, 1980-81; chairman Carter-Mondale Presdl. Com., Washington, 1979-80; v.p. Bear Stearns and Co., N.Y.C., 1984-87; pres. Middlesex (Mass.) Community Coll., 1987-90; chancellor City Coll. San Francisco, 1991—; pres. Trinity College, Hartford, Conn., 1995—. Bd. dirs. Jacobs Pillow Dance Festival, Conn. Pub. TV; bd. govs. Jewish Fedn. of Hartford. Jewish. Avocations: golf, swimming, reading, travel, U.S. history. Office: Trinity College Office of the President Hartford CT 06106

DOBER, RICHARD PATRICK, campus and facility planner, writer; b. Phila., Mar. 30, 1928; s. Lawrence Joseph and Veronica (Brake) D.; m. Betty Edwards, Dec. 28, 1957 (Sept. 1958); m. Eleanor Lee Lyman, Sept. 23, 1961; children: Patrick Lee, Claire Brake Danaher. BA in Design, Bklyn. Coll., 1953; M of City Planning, Harvard U., 1957. Cert. planner. Exec. dir. Sasaki, Walker and Assocs., Watertown, Mass., 1958-62; sr. cons. Dober and Assocs., Inc., Cambridge, Mass., 1962-92, Dober, Lidsky, Craig and Assocs., 1992—; cons. Bush Found., World Bank, U.S. Dept. of Edn., UNESCO, Ford Found., others; v.p. Boston Architectural Ctr., 1969-72; lectr. Grad. Program Urban Design, MIT, 1972; vis. critic Beijing U., 1985, MIT, 1980, Coll. of Design, Iowa State U., 1979, U. Ill., 1974, Harvard U., 1963-65; faculty Inst. of Ednl. Mgmt. Harvard Grad. Sch. Edn., 1991-92. Author: Campus Planning, 1964, Campus Design, 1992, Campus Architecture, 1996; contbr. numerous articles to profl. jours. With U.S. Army, 1953-55. Recipient Award of Merit Am. Assn. of Jr. Colls., 1968, 1st Prize Coun. for Advancement and Support of Edn., 1983, Disting. Alumnus award Bklyn. Coll., 1992, Founder's award for Disting. Achievement and Exceptional Contbns. to Higher Edn. Planning Soc. for Colls. and Univs. Planning, 1992. Mem. Am. Inst. of Cert. Planners, Soc. for Coll. and Univ. Planning (founding mem., bd. dirs. 1969-72), The Renaissance Soc. of Am., Assn. of Collegiate Schs. of Architecture, Internat. Coun. of Mus., Can. Arts Coun. (cons. 1972). Avocations: travel, opera, books on Georgian architecture. E-mail: rpd@dlca.com. Office: Dober Lidsky Craig and Assocs Inc 385 Concord Ave Belmont MA 02178

DOBERENZ, ALEXANDER R., nutrition educator, chemist; b. Newark, Aug. 17, 1936; s. Alexander J. and Marie (Zink) D.; m. Angela Rajoppi, June 7, 1958; children: Annamarie, Judith Lynn, Hoke Jr. B.S. in Chemistry, Tusculum Coll., 1958; M.S., U. Ariz., 1960, Ph.D. in Biochemistry and Nutrition, 1963. Research assoc. dept. physics U. Ariz., Tucson, 1963-69; vis. assoc. prof. nutrition U. Hawaii, 1969; assoc. prof. nutritional scis. U. Wis., Green Bay, 1969-71; prof. U. Wis., 1971-76, assoc. dean Coll. and Sch. Profl. Studies, 1969-76, prof. growth and devel., 1975-76; prof. food sci. and human nutrition U. Del., Newark, 1976-97; dean Coll. Human Resources U. Del., 1976-93, coord. home econs. rsch., 1978-93, spl. asst. to the pres., 1993, interim v.p. for student life, 1994-95; prof. nutritional scis., Coll. of Health and Nursing Scis. U. Del., Newark, 1997—; cons. food industry, 1976-93; mem. nat. steering com. new initiatives for home econs. U.S. Dept. Agr., 1979-81, USDA Planning com. Workshops on Improving Health Maintenance, 1984-87. Contbr. numerous articles on food chemistry and nutrition to profl. publs. Head underwater recovery unit Pima County Sheriff's Dept., 1966-68; warrant officer CAP, 1965-69; mem. Brown County Comprehensive Health Planning Council, 1973-76; bd. dirs. Pima County Sheriff's Search and Rescue, 1968. Recipient Research Career Devel. award NIH, 1966-69, Outstanding Educator Am., 1971, 72. Fellow Am. Inst. Chemists; mem. Am. Chem. Soc., Am. Home Econs. Soc., Am. Inst. Nutrition (Mead Johnson award nominating com. 1973-76), Nutrition Soc. Today, Soc. for Nutrition Edn., Nutrition Soc. London Soc. Exptl. Biology and Medicine, Am. Soc. Clin. Nutrition, AAAS, Assn. Adminstrs. of Home Econs., Del. Gerontol. Soc. (exec. com. 1978), Nat. Council Adminstrs. Home Econs. (exec. bd. 1982-83), Am. Pub. Health Assn., Del.-Panama Ptnrs. of Ams., Assn. for Devel. Computer Based Instruction, Del. Acad. Sci., Sigma Xi, Phi Lambda Upsilon., Phi Kappa Phi. Roman Catholic. Clubs: University and Whist. Office: U Del 222 Alison Hall Newark DE 19716

DOBERSTEIN, AUDREY K., college president; b. June 12, 1932; m. Stephen C. Doberstein; children: Carole, Stephen, Anne, Curt. B.S., East Stroudsburg State Coll., 1953; M.Ed., U. Del., 1957; Ed.D., U. Pa., 1982. Exec. dir. Title I ESEA, Del. Dept. Public Instrn., 1965-69; pres. Ednl. Research and Services, Inc., 1969-79; asso. prof. Cheyney State Coll., 1969-79; pres. Wilmington Coll., New Castle, Del., 1979—. Mem. NEA, Am. Assn. Higher Edn., AAUW, Del. Assn. Bus. and Profl. Women, Phi Delta Kappa. Office: Wilmington Coll Office of the President 320 Dupont Hwy New Castle DE 19720*

DOBES, WILLIAM LAMAR, JR., dermatologist; b. Atlanta, Apr. 16, 1943; s. William Lamar and Sara (Wilson) D.; m. Martha Husmann, June 16, 1966; children: Margaret Alison, William Shane. BA, Emory U., 1965, MD, 1969. Diplomate Am. Bd. Dermatology. Intern Grady Meml. Hosp., Atlanta, 1969-70; fellow in dermatology Mayo Clinic, 1970-71; fellow U. Miami, 1971-73; clin. instr. Emory U. Sch. Medicine, Atlanta, 1973-77, asst. prof. dermatology, 1977-83, assoc. prof., 1983—; dir. immunofluorescense lab., 1978-85; mem. staff Crawford Long, Grady Meml., Piedmont hosps., Atlanta; dir. Skin Cancer Project, Emory U., 1981-89; chmn. profl. edn. unit Atlanta chpt. Am. Cancer Soc., 1980-86, also bd. dirs., pres., 1986-87, chmn. bd. dirs., 1987-88; pres. Carter's Atlanta, project chmn. Physicians Com., 1992-95. Contbr. articles to profl. jours. and texts. Chmn. Ga. med. bd. Lupus Found., 1988, bd. dirs. Whitney Rsch. Lab., 1998—. Dermatology Found. Rsch. award, 1979. Fellow Am. Dermatol. Assn.; mem. AMA, ACP, Soc. Investigative Dermatology, Am. Acad. Dermatology (chmn. com. quality assurance 1982-84, adv. coun. 1985-95, ad coun. exec. com. 1991-95, com. on stds. of care 1987-91, chmn. CLIA task force 1993-97), So. Med. Assn. (vice chmn. 1983), Pan Am. Med. Assn., Am. Soc. Dermatologic Surgery, Ga. Dermatol. Assn. (pres. 1986-87), Atlanta Dermatol. Assn. (pres. 1979), N.Am. Clin. Dermatologic Soc., Soc. Tropical Dermatology, Med. Assn. Atlanta (bd. dirs. 1985-92, chmn. comm. com. 1985-90, sec. 1988-89, pres.-elect 1989-90, pres. 1990-91), Med. Assn. Ga. (Interspltу. Coun. 1984-97, com. on cancer 1988-93, pub. rels. com. 1988-94, del. to Ga. Med. Assn. 1985—, Outstanding Svc. award 1993), Atlanta Clin. Soc., Atlanta Olympic Med. Com. (chmn. dermatology sect. 1996), Emory U. Med. Alumni Assn. (pres. 1980, 86, exec. com. 1992-97), Phi Delta Theta (past pres.), Phi Chi (past pres.), Cherokee Town & Country Club (Atlanta). Home: 2898 Rivermeade Dr NW Atlanta GA 30327-2010 Office: 2045 Peachtree St NE Atlanta GA 30309-1414 also: Emory U Sch Medicine Dept Dermatology Atlanta GA 30308

DOBEY, JAMES KENNETH, banker; b. Vallejo, Calif., June 20, 1919; s. Austin E. and Margaret (Hansen) D.; m. Jean Smith, Apr. 18, 1942; children: James A., Peter M. AB, U. Calif., Berkeley, 1940; postgrad., Rutgers U., 1956. With Shell Oil Co., Comml. Credit Corp., 1940-42; with Wells Fargo Bank, San Francisco, 1946-72, exec. v.p., 1965-72, vice chmn. bd., 1973, chmn. bd., 1977-80, ret. Capt. airborne inf. AUS, 1942-46. Mem. Delta Chi. Office: PO Box 1419 Aptos CA 95001-1419

DOBIE, ROBERT ALAN, otologist; b. Annapolis, Md., July 26, 1945. AB in Biology with great distinction, Stanford U., 1967, MD, 1971. Intern Stanford (Calif.) U. Sch. Medicine, 1971, resident in otolaryngology, 1971-75; asst. prof. dept. otolaryngology-head and neck surgery U. Wash., Seattle, 1975-80, assoc. prof., 1980-85, prof., 1985-90; rsch. fellow in auditory physiology Kresge Hearing Rsch. Lab. La. State U. Med. Ctr., New Orleans, 1977-78; T.W. Folbre prof., chmn. dept. otolaryngology U. Tex. Health Sci. Ctr., San Antonio, 1990—; attending otolaryngologist Med. Ctr. Hosp. (name now Univ. Hosp.), Audie L. Murphy Meml. Vets. Hosp., San Antonio, 1990—; dir. Virginia Merrill Bloedel Hearing Rsch. Ctr. U. Wash., 1988-90; rsch. affiliate Child Devel. & Mental Retardation Ctr., 1988-90; cons. in otology Madigan Army Med. Ctr., Tacoma, Wash., 1987-90, Kaiser Aluminum and Chem. Corp., Oakland, Calif., 1976-86; chief otolaryngology svc. VA Med. Ctr., Seattle, 1978-83, 75-77; clin. fellow in otoneurosurgery Univ. Hosp., Zurich, 1983-84; mem. Coun. for Accreditation in Occupl. Hearing Conservation, 1990—; mem. program adv. com. Nat. Inst. on Deafness and Other Communicative Disorders, 1996—; bd. dirs. Deafness Rsch. Found. Author: Medical-Legal Evaluation of Hearing Loss, 1993, (with others) Guide for the Evaluation of Hearing Handicap, 1981, Guide for Conservation of Hearing in Noise, 1982; editor: Approach to Swallowing Disorders, 1984; mem. editl. bds. Am. Jour. Otology, Laryngoscope, Otolaryngology-Head and Neck Surgery; contbr. articles to profl. jours. and chpts. to books. Mem. ACS, AMA, Am. Acad. Otolaryngology-Head and Neck Surgery (chair noise subcom. 1981-87, 95-98), Am. Laryngological, Rhinological and Otological Soc., Am. Otological Soc., Am. Neurotology Soc., Am. Auditory Soc., Am. Soc. for Head and Neck Surgery, Am. Speech-Lang.-Hearing Assn., Collegium Oto-Rhino-Laryngologicum Amicitiae sacrum, Politizer Soc., Assn. for Rsch. in Otolaryngology (pres. 1993-94), Am. Coll. Occupational Medicine, Bexar County Med. Soc., San Antonio Soc. Otolaryngology-Head and Neck Surgery, So. Med. Assn., Tex. Med. Assn. Office: U Tex Health Sci Ctr 7703 Floyd Curl Dr San Antonio TX 78284-6200

DOBKIN, JAMES ALLEN, lawyer, engineer, artist; b. N.Y.C., Sept. 9, 1940; s. Louis Robert and Eve (Gartner) D.; m. Irma Laufer, Aug. 4, 1964; children: Jill, David. BChemE (nuclear), Poly. U., 1961; JD, NYU, 1964; LLM, Georgetown U., 1968. Bar: N.Y. 1965, U.S. Supreme Ct. 1968, D.C. 1969. Assoc. Arnold & Porter, Washington, 1968-72, ptnr., 1973—; atty. advisor Pres.'s Commn. on Govt. Procurement, Washington, 1972-73; adj. prof. law, Georgetown U. Author: Contracting with the U.S. Government, 1986; co-author: International Joint Ventures, 1986, 2d edit., 1989, Dow Jones Handbook of Joint Venturing, 1988, Intellectual Property Counseling and Litigation, 1987, The Defense-Space Market: A How-To Guide for Small Business, 1985; editor, co-author: International Technology Joint Ventures in the Countries of the Pacific Rim, 1988, Joint Ventures with International Partners, vol. 1, 1989, vol. 2, 1991, Intellectual Property Considerations in the Formation and Operation of Joint Enterprises for U.S. Major Defense Systems Acquisitions, 1993, Joint Ventures with International Partners: Structuring and Negotiation with Forms, 1994, Federal Privatization and Outsourcing of Information Technology Functions: A Practitioner's Perspective, 1996, Fundamental Principles for Organizational Compliance Programs: A Practitioner's Perspective, 1997; contbr. numerous articles to legal and econ. jours., chpts. to texts and treatises; numerous group and one-man art exhbns. throughout U.S. Served to capt. U.S. Army, 1964-68. Mem. ABA, Fed. Bar Assn., D.C. Bar Assn. Democrat. Jewish. Home and Studio: 8810 Fernwood Rd Bethesda MD 20817-3014 Office: Arnold & Porter 555 12th St NW Washington DC 20004-1206*

DOBKIN, JOHN HOWARD, art administrator; b. Hartford, Conn., Feb. 19, 1942; s. Louis P. and Ruth D.; children: Carlos, Leopoldo, Anthony. B.A., Yale U., 1964; cert., Institut d'etudes Politiques, 1965; J.D., NYU, 1968. Exec. asst. to sec. Smithsonian Inst., Washington, 1963-71; adminstr. Cooper-Hewitt Mus., N.Y.C., 1971-78; dir. Nat. Acad. Design, N.Y.C., 1978-89; pres. Hist. Hudson Valley, Tarrytown, N.Y., 1990—. Bd. dirs. Sch. Am. Ballet, Mcpl. Art Soc., Arthur Ross Found., Alliance Capital Mgmt. Corp., Westchester Partnership for Econ. Devel. Named to the Order of the Lion, Govt. of Finland; recipient Smithsonian Instn. Exceptional Service award, 1969. Mem. Conn. Bar Assn. Club: Century Assn. (N.Y.C.). Office: Hist Hudson Valley 150 White Plains Rd Tarrytown NY 10591-5535

DOBLE, RICHARD DEGARIS, editor, publisher, photographer; b. Sharon, Conn., July 24, 1944; s. Enoch Hall II and Winifred Rene (deGaris) D.; m. Janet Lois Harriman, Feb. 17, 1991. BA with honors, U. N.C., 1966, MAC, 1975. Instr., grant writer Child Devel. Ctr., Chapel Hill, N.C., 1966-69; dir. Photography Workshop, Durham, N.C., 1973-75; photographer, writer, owner Creative Still Photography, Durham, 1975-94; editor, pub., founder $avvy Discount$ Newsletter, Smyrna, N.C., 1994—; pres. PhotoCarolina, Durham, 1977-85; dir. Durham Photog. Archive Project, 1978-81. Author: How to Get the Best Buys, 1997, $avvy Discount$, 1997; contbr. article series to Freebies Mag., 1995—, Health and Money Mag., 1997-99; exhibited various artworks at Perth (Australia) Inst. Contemporary Arts, 1999, Orlando Mus. Art, 1998, Greenville Mus. Art, 1995, also 8 one-man shows of photographs; contbr. poetry to lit. publs. Chmn. bd. dirs. St. Joseph's Historic Found., Durham, 1978-83. Recipient Best in Show award Durham Arts Coun., 1975; Photography Archive grantee Nat. Endowment for the Arts, 1978, Comty. Edn. grantee N.C. Humanities Com., 1977. Mem. Carteret Arts Coun. Office: $avvy Discount$ Newsletter 195 Old Nassau Rd PO Box 96 Smyrna NC 28579

DOBLER, DONALD WILLIAM, retired college dean, consultant, corporate executive; b. Rocky Ford, Colo., Apr. 18, 1927; s. William L. and Anna (Nelson) D.; m. Elaine Carlson, Dec. 27, 1951; children: Kathleen, David, Daniel. BS in Engring., Colo State U., 1946-50; MBA, Stanford U., 1958, PhD, 1960. Application and sales engr. Westinghouse Elec. Corp., Pitts. and Phila., 1950-53; mgr. purchasing and materials FMC Corp., Green River, Wyo., 1953-57; guest lectr. Stanford Sch. Bus., 1960; asst. prof. mgmt. State U. Utah, Logan, 1960-63; assoc. prof. State U. Utah, 1964-66, head dept. bus. adminstrn., 1964-66; vis. prof. mgmt. Dartmouth Coll., 1963-64; dean Coll. Bus., Colo. State U., Ft. Collins, 1966-86; ind. mgmt. cons. Ft. Collins, 1986-91; corp. v.p. for cert. and program devel. Nat. Assn. Purchasing Mgmt., Tempe, Ariz., 1990-94; past bd. dirs. U. Nat. Bank, Home Fed. Savs. Bank; pres. Parklane Arms, Inc., 1967-77; part-time mgmt. cons., 1960-86; cons. European Logistics Mgmt. Program, 1970, 72, 77, European Fedn. Purchasing, 1970; faculty Mgmt. Center Netherlands, 1972; dean's adv. coun. logistics mgmt. program Ariz. State U., 1991-94; mem. adv. bd. Mgmt. Inst. U. Wis., 1992-97. Sr. author: Purchasing and Supply Management, 1965, 6th edit., 1996; co-author: The Purchasing Handbook, 1993; mem. editl. bd. European Jour. Purchasing and Supply Mgmt., 1993—; contbr. articles on mgmt. to profl. jours., chpts. to books. Mem. Colo. Gov.'s Adv. Com., 1968-77, Ft. Collins Mayor's Budget Com., 1968-71; dist. chmn. Boy Scouts Am., 1974-77; mem. adv. council Colo. Region, SBA, 1973-79, No. Region, Colo. Div. Employment, 1975-77; bd. dirs., div. chmn. Ft. Collins United Way, 1973-80, pres., 1977; bd. dirs. Ft. Collins Jr. Achievement, 1973-87; bd. dirs. Colo. Assn. Commerce and Industry Ednl. Found., 1988-91. Served with USNR, 1945-46. Mem. Acad. Mgmt., Nat. Assn. Purchasing Mgmt. (Shipman Medalist 1987, chmn. nat. acad. plan com. 1976-81, mem. profl. cert. bd. 1981-86, chmn. 1985-86, assoc. editor Internat. Jour. Purchasing and Materials Mgmt. 1975-80, editor 1980-97), Denver Purchasing Mgmt. Assn. (dir. 1975-83, v.p. 1977, pres. 1979), Am. Prodn. and Inventory Control Soc., Green River Jr. C. of C. (pres. 1955), Am. Assn. Collegiate Schs. Bus. (nat. com. continuing accreditation 1972-78, nat. standards commn. 1978-81, dir. 1980-83, chmn. fin. and audit com.

1983), Sigma Tau, Phi Kappa Phi (editorial cons. Nat. Forum, 1988-94), Rotary, Beta Gamma Sigma (nat. gov. 1975-78). Methodist.

DOBOS, SISTER MARION, parochial school educator; b. McKeesport, Pa., Oct. 14, 1940. BS in Edn., Youngstown State U., 1969; MA in Religious Edn., Dayton U., 1981. Tchr. Chgo. Archdiocese Cath. Schs., 1961-64, Queen of Peace Sch., Wichita Falls, Tex., 1964-65, St. Theresa Sch., Pitts., 1975-76, Sts. Peter and Paul Sch., Warren, Ohio, 1965-75, 77-86, St. Anne Ukranian Sch., Austintown, Ohio, 1986-87, Blossom Montessori Sch., Warren, 1987-88, Sts. Peter and Paul Sch., 1988—; adminstr. Benedictine Early Learning Ctr. Nursing Sch. & Day Care, Warren, 1989-95, Archdiocesan dir. religious edn., 1996—; formation dir. Benedictine Sisters, Warren, 1979-89; dir. religious edn. Sts. Peter and Paul Sch., Byzantine Archdiocese Pitts., 1996. Mem. Nat. Cath. Educators Assn., Ohio Cath. Educators Assn., Assn. for Edn. of Young Children, Greek Cath. Union, Jednota Cath. Lodge, Ohio Cosmetology. Democrat. Avocations: aerobics, crafts, walking. Home: 3605 Perrysville Ave Pittsburgh PA 15214-2229 Office: Office of Religious Edn 3605 Perrysville Ave Pittsburgh PA 15214-2229

DOBRIANSKY, PAULA JON, business executive; b. Alexandria, Va., Sept. 14; d. Lev Eugene and Julia Kusy D. BS summa cum laude, Sch. Fgn. Service, Georgetown U., 1977; MA, Harvard U., 1980, PhD, 1991. Adminstrv. aide Dept. Army, Washington, 1973-76; staff asst. Am. Embassy, Rome, 1976; rsch. asst. joint econ. com. U.S. Congress, Washington, 1977-78; NATO analyst Bur. Intelligence and Rsch., Dept. State, Washington, 1979; staff mem. NSC, White House, Washington, 1980-83, dep. dir. European and Soviet affairs, 1983-84, dir. European and Soviet affairs, 1984-87; dep. asst. sec. of state for Human Rights and Humanitarian Affairs, 1987-90; dep. head U.S. Del. to Conf. on Security and Cooperation in Europe, Copenhagen, 1990; assoc. dir. for policy and programs U.S. Info. Agy., 1990-93; co-chair internat. TV coun. Corp. Pub. Broadcasting, 1993-94; sr. internat. affairs and trade advisor Hunton and Williams, Washington, 1994-97; v.p., dir. Washington Office Coun. on Fgn. Rels., 1997—. Host Freedom's Challenge, Nat. Empowerment Television, 1994-96; co-host Worldwise, 1997; commr. U.S. Adv. Commn. on Pub. Diplomacy, 1997—; adj. fellow Hudson Inst., 1993—. Bd. dirs. Congl. Human Rights Found., 1994-95, Western NIS Enterprise Fund, 1994—, Am. Com. for Aid to Poland, 1994-95; bd. vis. George Mason U., 1994-98, Horton Internat. Inc., 1998—. Fulbright-Hays scholar, 1978; Rotary Found. fellow, 1979, Ford Found. fellow, 1980; named one of ten Most Outstanding Young Women in Am., 1982, one of ten Outstanding Working Women of 1990, Ethnic Woman of Yr., 1990; recipient Georgetown U. Alumni Achievement award, 1986, State Dept. Superior Honor award, 1990. Mem. Internat. Inst. Strategic Studies, Coun. Fgn. Rels., Am. Polit. Sci. Assn., Fulbright Assn., Phi Beta Kappa, Phi Alpha Theta, Pi Sigma Alpha, U.S. Environ. Tng. Inst. (bd. adv. 1992-93), Harvard Club (bd. dirs. 1982-85), Nat. Endowment for Democracy (bd. dirs. 1993—, vice chmn. 1995—), Am. Coun. of Young Polit. Leaders (trustee 1993—), University Club (Washington). Office: Coun on Fgn Rels 1779 Massachusetts Ave NW Washington DC 20036-2109

DOBRICK, JO-ANNE, business executive, environmental consultant; b. Sept. 19, 1945; d. Nathan Shaye and Lillian (Davis) Shaye-Hirsch; 1 child, Rebecca Dobrick. Student, Ohio State U., Art Inst. Chgo.; BA, Roosevelt U., 1972. Dir. Dobrick Gallery, Chgo., 1974-84; exec. search nationally, 1984-86; cons. Laventhol & Horwath, Chgo., 1986-90; sales and mktg. Splty. Advt., 1992-97; cons. EPA and SCAA, Washington, 1997—; CEO Basket Classics, Chgo., 1997—; v.p. Indsl. Water, Waste and Sewage Group, Chgo., 1988-90; assoc. bd. mem. Film Festival, Chgo. Bd. dirs. Chgo. Art Dealers ASsn., 1980-84, Steppenwolf Theatre, Chgo., 1986-91; chair for auction WTTW, Chgo., 1976. Home: 2128 N Bissell St Chicago IL 60614-4202

DOBRIN, SHELDON L., architect; b. Chgo., June 2, 1945; s. Max and Sophie (Schuman) D.; m. Marlene K. Smith, Jan. 26, 1969; children: Stefanie, Jonathan. BArch, Ill. Inst. Tech., 1969, BS, 1970. Registered architect, Ill., Ind., Mich., Wis., Mo. Architect Form Assocs., Chgo., 1969; tchr. Chgo. Bd. Edn., 1969-72; architect Robert L. Friedman & Assocs., Ltd., Chgo., 1972-78; v.p. Robert L. Friedman, Chgo., 1978-90; prin. Friedman, Dobrin and Assocs., Northbrook, Ill., 1984-90; pres. Dobrin Assocs., Ltd., Lincolnshire, Ill., 1991—. Contbr. articles to profl. jours. Docent Chgo. Archtl. Found., 1971-78; mem. caucus bd. Highland Park Sch. Dist., 1988; mem. Highland Park Historic Preservation Commn., 1988-96. Recipient Spl. Recognition for Archtl. Design awards, 1985, 88, 89. Mem. AIA (Chgo. chpt. voting del. convs. 1985, 88, 89, com. chair 1993 conv.), COCA Internat., Nat. Coun. Archtl. Registration Bds. (cert.), Art Inst. Chgo., Alpha Epsilon Pi. Avocations: bicycling, travel. Office: Dobrin Assocs Ltd Ste 140 75 Tri-State Internat Lincolnshire IL 60069

DOBRINSKY, HERBERT COLMAN, university administrator; b. Montreal, Quebec, Can., Apr. 6, 1933; came to U.S., 1962; s. Victor and Lillian D.; m. Dina Loebenberg, Dec., 1954; children—Deborah Kramer, Tova Cohen, Aaron David. B.A., Yeshiva U., 1954, M.S. in Edn., 1959, D. in Edn., 1980; Semikha (rabbinic ordination), Rabbi Isaac Elchanan Theological Sem., Yeshiva U., 1957. Rabbi, Beth Israel Synagogue, Halifax, N.S., Can., 1958-62; assoc dir. div. communal services Yeshiva U., N.Y.C., 1962-73, dir. rabbinic placement, 1964-73, dir. Sephardic community activities program div. of communal service, 1964-80, exec. asst. to pres., 1973-80, v.p. univ. affairs, 1980—. Author: A Treasury of Sephardic Laws and Customs, 1986. Office: Yeshiva U Univ Affairs 500 W 185th St New York NY 10033-3299

DOBRINSKY, SUSAN ELIZABETH, human resources director; b. Warren, N.J., Sept. 25, 1943; d. Samuel Henry Jr. and Janet Adeline (Ryder) Christie; m. Stanley Dobrinsky, Feb. 12, 1972; children: David Stanley, Mark Alan. BA, Lycoming Coll., 1965. Cert. for Sr. Execs., John F. Kennedy Sch. of Govt. of Harvard U., 1994, PHR Cert. by SHRM, Profl. in Human Resources, 1997. Pers. asst. County of Somerset, Somerville, N.J., 1970-74, pers. mgr., 1974-82, pers. dir., 1982-90; dir. adminstrn. County of Somerset, Somerville, 1991-95, dir. human resources, 1995—; gov. apptd. Pub. Employees Occupl. Safety and Health Adv. Bd., Dept. of Labor, Trenton, N.J., 1984—; bd. trustees, treas. N.J. Pub. Employer Labor Rels. Assn., Somerville, N.J., 1993—; mem. Soc. Human Resource Mgmt. Cen. Jersey, Somerset, 1978—; pres. Comty. Indsl. Rels. Orgn., Somerset, 1990-92; apptd. senate pres., mem. Pension Commn., Trenton, 1992—. Mem., dep. mayor Green Brook Twp. Commn., 1987-88, mayor, 1989-92; v.p. Somerset County Governing Offcls., 1990, pres., 1991; sec. Rep. Club, Green Brook, 1977. Recipient N.J. Alumni award 4-H Youth Devel. Program, 1992. Mem. Nat. Pub. Employer's Labor Rels. Assn., N.J. Pub. Employer Labor Rels. Assn. (bd. trustees, treas. 1993—), Soc. Human Resource Mgmt., Ctrl. N.J. Soc. Human Resource Mgmt., Internat. Personnel Mgmt. Assn., N.J. Pension and Health Commn., Cmty. Indsl. Rels. Orgn. (treas. 1988-90, pres. 1990-92), Pub. Pers. Orgn. (pres. 1990—), DAR (Elizabeth Snyder chpt. regent 1998). Republican. Methodist. Avocations: skiing, genealogy, reading, crafts. Home: 11 Glenn Ave Green Brook NJ 08812-2431 Office: County of Somerset 20 Grove St Somerville NJ 08876-2306

DOBRITT, DENNIS WILLIAM, physician, researcher, pain management specialist; b. Detroit, July 13, 1953; s. Walter Peter and Catherine Janet (Auito) D.; m. Kitty Louise Burros, June 21, 1980; children: Carol Ann, Julie Marie, Diane Elizabeth. BS magna cum laude, Western Mich. U., 1975; DO, Phila. Coll. Osteopathic Medicine, 1981. Diplomate Nat. Bd. Osteopathic Examiners, Am. Bd. Anesthesiology, Am. Bd. Pain Medicine, Am. Bd. Pain Mgmt. Intern Garden City (Mich.) Hosp., 1981-82, emergency physician, 1982-83; emergency physician McPherson Hosp., Howell, Mich., 1983-84; resident physician Providence Hosp., Southfield, Mich., 1983-85, fellow, 1985-86, chief resident, 1985, attending anesthesiologist, 1986—; attending physician Botsford Hosp., Farmington Hills, Mich., 1986-87; asst. clin. prof. coll. osteopathic medicine Mich. State U., Ann Arbor, 1987—; dir. Ctr. for Pain Control, Farmington Hills, 1986-87, Farmbrook Pain Control Ctr., Southfield, 1987-96; chief pain medicine Providence Hosp., 1994—, dir. pain ctrl. ctr., 1996—. Editor newsletter Osteo. Pain Mgmt. News, 1987-88; guest editor Mich. Osteo. Jour., 1987-88; contbr. articles to profl. jours. Active Mich. Osteopathic Polit. Action Com., 1987-88. Mem. AMA, Am. Osteo. Assn., Am. Soc. Anesthesiology, Internat. Anesthesiology Research Soc., Am. Pain Soc., Internat. Assn. for Study of Pain. Roman Catholic. Avocations: computers, reading, basketball, water-skiing, softball. Office: Providence Hosp Pain Control Ctr 22301 Foster Winter Dr Ste 200 Southfield MI 48075-3707 also: 16001 W 9 Mile Rd Southfield MI 48075-4818

DOBROF, ROSE WIESMAN, professor; b. Denver, Nov. 11, 1924; d. Jerome and Mildred (Hornbein) W.; m. Alfred Dobrof, June 8, 1948; children: Marilyn, Joan, Susan, Judy. BA, U. Colo., 1945; MSW, U. Pitts., 1948; DSW, Columbia U., 1976; DHL (hon.), SUNY, 1996. Lect. div. social svcs. Ind. U., Bloomington, 1952-60; dir. group svc. and vol. dept. The Hebrew Home for the Aged at Riverdale, Bronx, N.Y., 1961-63, asst. dir., 1966-70; assoc. prof. Hunter Coll. CUNY, 1975-78, prof. Hunter Coll., 1979-96; Brookdale prof. gerontology CUNY, N.Y.C., 1979—; exec. dir. Brookdale Ctr. on Aging Hunter Coll., N.Y.C., 1974-93, acting v.p., 1993-94; doctoral faculty grad. ctr. CUNY, 1979-96; profl. lectr. in community medicine Mt. Sinai Sch. Medicine, 1982—, co-dir. long-term gerontological ctr., 1979-81, co-dir. geriatric edn. ctr., 1985-96; cons. N.Y. State Moreland Act Commn., 1975-76, VA, 1977, Ark. Dept. Health and Social Svcs., 1976-80; chair gov.'s task force on long term care in year 2000, 1986; mem. gov.'s task force on older women, 1986-87; adv. com. sr. citizen affairs for Congresswoman Nita M. Lowey, 1990—; adj. prof. gerontology, Coll. of Optometry, SUNY, 1990—; mem. N.Y. State Pub. Health Coun., 1991-95, Gov.'s Health Care Adv. Bd., 1991-94; mem. policy com. White Ho. Conf. Aging, 1995, Fed. Coun. on Aging, 1994-96. Editor-in-chief The Jour. of Gerontological Social Work, 1977—. Co-chmn. com. on aging Fedn. Jewish Philanthropies, 1979-81; trustee Jewish Assn. for Svcs. of the Aged, N.Y.C., 1977-83; statewide adv. coun. N.Y. State Dept. Social Svcs., 1977-79; bd. dirs. N.Y.C. chpt. Nat. Caucus and Ctr. for the Black Aged, 1982—; exec. com., adv. bd. N.Y. Cmty. Trust Ctr. on Policy in Aging, 1985—, vice chmn., 1987—; bd. dirs. St. Margaret's House, 1987-90, New York Found., 1996—; bd. mem. Am. Fedn. Aging Rsch., 1996—; sr. fellow The Brookdale Found., 1985—; co-chair U.S. Com. for Celebration of UN Yr. of Older Persons, 1997—. Named One of Five Outstanding Alumni, U. Pitts., 1979; recipient Outstanding Alumnus award for excellence in social work edn., U. Pitts., 1981, award for outstanding leadership in the field of social work, Nat. Assn. Soc. Workers, 1983, Robert Ray Parks award, 1986, Alice Brophy award, The Burden Ctr., 1987, The Gift of Life award, Parker Jewish Geriatric Inst., 1989, The Walter M. Beattie Jr. award N.Y. State Assn. Gerontol. Educators Inst., 1989, 1990 Social Worker in Aging award Nat. Assn. Social Workers, 1990, The Pres.'s medal Hunter Coll., 1991, Gerontology Educator Merit award, 1991, award of Merit Older Women's League Greater N.Y., 1993, Elinor Guggenheimer award Coun. Sr. Ctrs. and Svcs., 1995, Lifetime Achievement award Sr. Action in a Gay Environment, 1997, Lifetime Achievement award Presbyn. Sr. Svcs., 1999. Fellow N.Y. Acad. Medicine; mem. Friends and Relatives of the Institutionalized Aged (pres. 1976-80, bd. dirs. 1980-88), Acad. for the Humanities and Scis., Nat. Assn. Social Workers, Nat. Coun. on Aging, N.Y. Acad. Sci., Am. Soc. in Aging, Gerontological Soc., Phi Beta Kappa, Delta Sigma Rho, Pi Gamma Mu. Democrat. Jewish. Avocations: bridge, swimming, gardening. Office: Brookdale Ctr on Aging 425 E 25th St New York NY 10010-2547

DOBRONSKI, MARK WILLIAM, judge, justice of the peace; b. Detroit, Oct. 8, 1957; s. Clarence Robert and Jean (Shotey) D.; m. Susan Kay Roach, Sept. 12, 1980; children: Clarence Robert III, Juli E. AS, Crery Ford C.C., 1980. Cert. engr. Nat. Assn. Radio and Telecomm. Engrs. V.p. Mobilfone, Inc., Dearborn, Mich., 1977-79; asst. v.p. RAM Broadcasting Corp., N.Y.C., 1979-86; adminstr. State of Ariz., Phoenix, 1986-88, 89-97; divsn. comdr. City of Peoria (Ariz.) Police Dept., 1991; cons., expert witness Teletech, Inc., Dearborn, 1980-98. Mem., bd. dirs. Congl. Ch. of the Valley, United Ch. of Christ, Scottsdale, Ariz., 1994-98; mem. Maricopa County Sheriff's Exec. Posse, Phoenix, 1996-98. Mem. Am. Pvt. Radio Assn. (dir. 1989-98). Republican. Office: Scottsdale Justice Ct 3700 N 75th St Scottsdale AZ 85251

DOBROV, GREGORY W., adult education educator, researcher; b. San Mateo, Calif.; s. Wadim Ivanovich and Barbara Jane (Lyon) D.; m. Tamara Alita Osipoff, Feb. 23, 1986; children: Joni Marielle, Alexandra Vera. BTh, Holy Trinity Sem., 1981; MA in Classics, Syracuse U., 1983; MA in Classics/Linguistics, Cornell U., 1985, PhD in Classics, 1988. Asst. prof. classics Syracuse (N.Y.) U., 1988-92; asst. prof. U. Mich., 1992-98, Loyola U., Chgo., 1998—. Author: Figures of Play, 1999; editor: Beyond Aristophanes, 1995, The City As Comedy, 1997; contbr. articles to profl. jours. Recipient Whitney Humanities Ctr. fellow Yale Univ., 1992, Inst. for Humanities fellow U. Mich., 1994. Mem. Am. Philological Assn. Avocations: jazz guitarist. E-mail: dobrov@orion.it.luc.edu. Home: 6749 N Caldwell Ave Chicago IL 60646-1354 Office: Crown Ctr 555 Classical Studies Loyola U Chicago IL 60626

DOBROVOLNY, JERRY STANLEY, engineering educator; b. Chgo., Nov. 2, 1922; s. Stanley and Marie (Barone) D.; m. Joan Gretchen Baker, June 14, 1947; children: James Lawrence, Janet Lee. BSME, U. Ill., 1943, MS, 1947. Registered profl. engr., Ill. Mem. faculty U. Ill., Urbana, 1945-87, assoc. prof. Coll. Engring., 1957—, prof., head dept. gen. engring., 1959-87, prof. emeritus, 1987—; geophys. rsch. engr. Ill. Geol. Survey, summers 1949-52; design and traffic survey engr. Ill. Divsn. Hwys., summers 1948, 53, 54; cons. soil mechanics, 1955—; mem. Ill. Adv. Coun. on Vocat. Edn., 1969-72, Nat. Adv. Coun. on Vocat. Edn., 1970-73. Author: (with others) Basic Drawing for Engineering Technology, (with R.P. Hoelscher and C.H. Springer) Graphics for Engineers, 1985, (with D.C. O'Bryant) 2nd edit., 1991. Chmn. Champaign County Mass Transit Dist., 1986-98, bd. dirs., 1995-98, chmn. bd. dirs., 1992-95; past pres. Champaign County Young Rep. Club; mem. Champaign County Rep. Ctrl. Com.; mem. Champaign-Urbana Mass Transit Dist., 1987-98, chmn., 1992-98. Fellow AAAS; mem. Am. Legion, 40 and 8, Soc. for History and Tech., Ill. Acad. Sci., Am. Soc. Engring. Edn. (Arthur Williston award 1971), Am. Soc. C.E., Am. Tech. Edn. Assn. (trustee 1964-67, 69-74, pres. 1967-68), Nat. Soc. Profl. Engrs., Ill. Soc. Profl. Engrs. (pres. Champaign County chpt. 1964-65, state v.p. 1971-73, pres. 1974-75, Ill. award 1983, Disting. Service award 1986), Champaign County Soc. Profl. Engrs., Newcomen Soc. N.Am., Sigma Xi, Scabbard and Blade, Sigma Iota Epsilon, Tau Nu Tau. Home: 1104 S Prospect Ave Champaign IL 61820-6322 Office: U Ill Dept Gen Engring Urbana IL 61801

DOBRY, ALIKI CALIRROE, artist; b. Alexandria, Egypt, Sept. 11, 1929; came to U.S., 1953; d. Apostolos and Irene (Papassinessiou) Zafiriadis; m. Edward Adams Dobry, July 2, 1954 (dec. July 1985); children: Mary M., Dorothy Ann., Alice Elizabeth. BA in Arts, U. Alexandria, Egypt, 1950; M in Arts, U. Ga., 1953; BA in Fine Arts, St. Mary's Coll., St. Mary's City, Md., 1992. Mgr. mail dept. Ford Motor Co., Alexandria, Egypt, 1952; English tchr. Great Mills H.S., Md., 1954-55; mgr., co-owner St. Mary's Vet. Hosp., Lexington Park, Md., 1955-87. One-woman shows include Gallery N. Psychico, Athens, Greece, 1995, Loffler Ctr., Gt. Mills, Md., 1997; exhibited in group shows at Internat. Bienale, Paris, 1993, Chapelle de la Sorbonne, Paris, 1994, Mattawoman Creek Art Ctr., Md., 1994 (supr. artist award 1994), Paris, 1994 (grand prix de Paris award 1994), Michael Stone Gallery, Washington, 1994, Gallery N. Psychico, 1995, Agora Gallery, N.Y.C., 1996, State of Art Gallery, Ithaca, N.Y., 1996, Nat. Soc. Artists, League City, Tex., 1997, Musée des Beaux Arts D'Unet of France, Sapporo, Japan, 1997, So. Md. Higher Edn. Ctr., California, 1998, Gov.'s Mansion, Annapolis, 1998. Brownie leader Greek Girl Scouts, Alexandria, Egypt, 1949-50, hon. mem., 1990—; vol. March of Dimes, Leukemia Soc., Cancer Soc., Calif., Md., 1993—. Recipient scholarship Rotary Club Knights Templar, 1953; 2d prize Aurora Artists, 1995. Mem. Md. Fedn. Arts, Arts Alliance, Mattawoman Art Creek. Home: 23187 Falling Leaf Ln California MD 20619-6104

DOBRZYN, JANET ELAINE, quality management professional; b. Allentown, Pa., Oct. 9, 1956; d. Frank John and Doris (Ross) D. Diploma, Pottsville Hosp. Sch. Nursing, 1977; AA, L.A. Valley Coll., 1984; BSN, Calif. State Coll., Long Beach, 1985; MSN, Azusa (Calif.) Pacific U., 1991. RN, Calif., Okla., Pa., Ky., Ga.; cert. profl. healthcare quality. Charge nurse evenings Allentown (Pa.) Osteo. hosp., 1977-80; charge nurse relief Encino (Calif.) Hosp., 1980-81; registry nurse Profl. Staffing, Northridge, Calif., 1981-82; clin. nurse II pediatric ICU Childrens Hosp. of L.A., 1982-86, clin. info. specialist, 1986-89; quality mgmt. specialist PacifiCare of Calif., Cypress, 1989-91, quality mgmt. spl. projects coord., 1991-92; mgr. quality mgmt. PacifiCare of Okla., Tulsa, 1992-93, sr. project specialist quality mgmt., 1993-95; accreditation facilitator Humana, Louisville, Ky., 1995-96; mgr. quality mgmt. Healthwise of Ky., Lexington, 1996-97; mgr. nat. medicare med. svcs. Prudential Healthcare, Atlanta, 1997—; adj. faculty Sch. Nursing U. Louisville; guest lectr. Spaulding U.; cons., reviewer of prototype pub. Commerce Clearing House, Inc., Riverwoods, Ill., 1993; mem. ANA/GHAA task force to develop nursing curriculum in managed care for nursing students, 1994; speaker in field. Camp nurse vol. Forest Home Conf. Ctr., San Bernardino, Calif., 1988. Mem. Am. Assn. Managed Care Nurses, Nat. Assn. for Healthcare Quality, Nat. Assn., Prolife Nurses Assn., Sigma Theta Tau (newsletter editor). Republican. Avocations: reading, travel, walking, swimming, videos. Home: 2931 Torreya Way SE Marietta GA 30067-6028 Office: Prudential Healthcare 2859 Paces Ferry Rd SE Ste 750 Atlanta GA 30339-5701

DOBRZYNSKI, JUDITH HELEN, journalist, commentator; b. Rochester, N.Y., Mar. 8, 1949; d. Francis Anthony and Theresa (Contino) D. BS cum laude, Syracuse U., 1971. Corr. McGraw-Hill, San Francisco and N.Y.C., 1971-75; corr. Bus. Week, Washington, 1976-79, London, 1979-83; corp. strategies editor, assoc. editor Bus. Week, N.Y.C., 1983-88, sr. writer, 1988-91, sr. editor, 1991-94; bus. reporter N.Y. Times, 1995-97, culture reporter, 1997—; mem. New Founds. Corp. Governance Group, Harvard U., Boston, 1992-95; mem. adv. panel Corp. Investment Project, U.S. Coun. on Competitiveness, Washington, 1990-92. Author articles and book revs. Trustee CEC Internat. Ptnrs., N.Y.C., 1993-96; bd. dirs. City Lights Youth Theatre, N.Y.C., 1994-96. Mem. Century Assn., Syracuse U. Newhouse Sch. Alumni Assn. (bd. dirs. 1991-94, pres. 1992-93). Office: NY Times 229 W 43rd St New York NY 10036-3959

DOBSON, ALAN, veterinary physiology educator; b. London, Dec. 20, 1928; s. Albert Percy and Dorothy Blanche D.; m. Marjorie Jean Masson, Mar. 29, 1954; children: Ian, Janet, Graham, Barry. BA in Biochemistry with honors, Cambridge (Eng.) U., Eng., 1952; MA, Cambridge (Eng.) U., 1970; ScD in Physiology, Cambridge (Eng.) U., Eng., 1982; PhD in Physiology of Nutrition, Aberdeen U., Scotland, 1956. Exhibitioner Corpus Christi Coll., Cambridge U., Eng., 1949-52; sci. officer Rowett Research Inst., Aberdeen, 1952-57, sr. sci. officer, 1957-64, prin. sci. officer, 1964; vis. prof. N.Y. State Vet. Coll. Cornell U., 1961-62, assoc. prof. vet. physiology N.Y. State Vet. Coll., 1964-70, prof. Coll. of Vet. Medicine, 1970-95, emeritus prof., 1995—; Wellcome fellow Sch. Vet. Medicine, Cambridge U., 1970-71; vis. worker Physiol. Lab., Cambridge, 1977-78, 79, 80, 82, 84-85; vis. prof. Faculty of Agr. and Forestry, U. Alta, Edmonton, Can., 1984; ICEC-Carnegie fellow Carnegie-Mellon U., Pitts., 1986, Quartercentenary rsch. fellow Emmanuel Coll., Cambridge, 1990; bd. dirs. Transonics Systems, Inc., Measurements Innovations Corp. Contbr. articles to profl. jours. Bd. dirs. Cornell Rsch. Found., 1989-95. With RAF, 1947-49. Mem. Biochem. Soc. (U.K.), Physiol. Soc. (U.K.), Am. Physiol. Soc. Home: PO Box 458 21 Etna Ln Etna NY 13062 Office: Cornell Univ Coll Vet Medicine Dept of Biomed Scis Ithaca NY 14853

DOBSON, BRIDGET MCCOLL HURSLEY, television executive and writer; b. Milw., Sept. 1, 1938; d. Franklin McColl and Doris (Berger) Hursley; m. Jerome John Dobson, June 16, 1961; children: Mary McColl, Andrew Carmichael. BA, Stanford U., 1960, MA, 1964; CBA, Harvard U., 1961. Assoc. writer General Hospital ABC-TV, 1965-73, head writer General Hospital, 1973-75; producer Friendly Road Sta. KIXE-TV, Redding, Calif., 1972; head writer Guiding Light CBS-TV, 1975-80, head writer As the World Turns, 1980-83; creator, co-owner Santa Barbara NBC-TV, 1983—, head writer Santa Barbara, 1983-86, 91, exec. producer Santa Barbara, 1986-87, 91, creative prodn. exec. Santa Barbara, 1990-91; pres. Dobson Global Entertainment, L.A., 1994—; bd. dirs. Emory U. Carlos Mus.; bd. advisors Atlanta Internat. Sch., 1997—. Author, co-lyricist: Slings and Eros, 1993; prodr. Confessions of a Nightingale, 1994; exhibited in gallery show acrylic paintings Swan Coach House, Atlanta, 1997, exhibited oil paintings Raymond Lawrence Gallery, Atlanta, 1999, Fay Gold Gallery, Atlanta, 1999. Bd. dirs. Carlos Mus., 1998—. Recipient Emmy award, 1988. Mem. Nat. Acad. TV Arts and Scis. (com. on substance abuse 1986-88), Writers Guild Am. (award for Guiding Light 1977, for Santa Barbara 1991), Am. Film Inst. (mem. TV com. 1986-88). Office: PO Box 52813 Atlanta GA 30355-0813

DOBSON, DONALD ALFRED, retired electrical engineer; b. Evanston, Ill., Feb. 19, 1928; s. Alfred Topping and Agnes Lucille (Park) D. BSEE, Northwestern U., 1950, PhD, 1955; MSEE, MIT, 1951. Research assoc. Northwestern U., Evanston, 1951-54; engr. Indsl. Research Products, Franklin Park, Ill., 1952; sr. engr. Sperry Gyroscope Co., Great Neck, N.Y., 1954-59; sr. tech. specialist N.Am. Aviation, Columbus, Ohio, 1959-63; research staff mem. Inst. for Def. Analyses, Arlington, Va., 1963-90, adj. staff mem., 1990-98; ret. Inst. for Def. Analyses, Arlington, 1998; instr. physics Adelphi Coll., Garden City, N.Y., 1956. Mem. IEEE, Sigma Xi, Tau Beta Pi, Eta Kappa Nu, Pi Mu Epsilon. Home: 6800 Fleetwood Rd Apt 420 Mc Lean VA 22101-3607

DOBSON, JAMES LANE, bank executive; b. Elizabeth, N.J., Sept. 13, 1966; s. James Lane and Patricia Dietz D.; m. Gopa Gohel, Aug. 8, 1998. BA, Cath. U. Am., 1988. Chartered fin. analyst. Assoc. Paine Webber, N.Y.C., 1988-90, analyst, 1991-93; v.p. Smith Barney Webber, N.Y.C., 1993-94, Donaldson, Lufkin & Jenrette, N.Y.C., 1994—. Patron Met. Opera, N.Y.C., 1994—; contbr. Mus. Nat. History, N.Y.C., 1996—. Mem. Assn. Investment Mgmt. & Rsch. Democrat. Roman Catholic. Avocations: running, fitness, trap shooting. E-mail: jdobson dlj.com.

DOBSON, JANET LOUISE, writer; b. Columbus, Ohio, Aug. 10, 1951; d. Vernon Richard and Betty Jean (Hames) Schmitt; m. John William Dobson, Dec. 22, 1973; children: Evan Michael, Colin Richard. BA in Music with high distinction, U. Mich., 1973; postgrad., Ohio State U., 1975-77; MD, Med. Coll. of Ohio, 1980. Diplomate Am. Bd. Pathology. Pathology resident Mercy Hosp., Toledo, 1980-84; pathology fellow Ohio State U., Columbus, 1984-85, rschr., flow cytometry, 1985-86; in-house med. cons. Porter, Wright, Morris & Arthur Attys., Columbus, 1987-92; medicolegal cons., freelance Springfield, Ohio, 1992—; med. writer Springfield, 1995—. Author: (book) Rolf Armstrong - Giant of American Glamour Art, 1997, (booklet) Learn to Type This Weekend, 1997. Trustee Planned Parenthood of the Greater Miami Valley, Dayton, Ohio, 1995—; mem. Springfield Mus. of Art, 1989—, Nature Conservancy, Columbus, 1991—. Fellow Coll. of Am. Pathologists; mem. Am. Soc. Clin. Pathologists, Western Ohio Watercolor Soc. (Best of Show award 1995, Hon. Mention 1997). Avocations: painting, gardening, antiques. Office: 2330 E High St Springfield OH 45505-1322

DOBSON, JOANNE ABELE, English language educator; b. N.Y.C., Mar. 27, 1942; d. Charles Louis and Mildred Frances (McKinley) Abele; m. David Eugene Dobson, July 28, 1963; children: Elisabeth, David, Rebecca. BA in English, Kings Coll., 1963; MA in English, SUNY, Albany, 1977; PhD in English, U. Mass., 1985. Asst. prof. Fordham U., Bronx, 1987-93, assoc. prof., 1993—; vis. asst. prof. Amherst (Mass.) Coll., 1985-86, Tufts U. Medford, Mass., 1986-87. Author: Dickinson and the Strategies of Reticence, 1989; editor: The Hidden Hand, 1988; co-editor Legacy: Jour. Am. Women Writers, 1983-93; gen. editor Am. Women Writers Reprint Series, 1985-92; contbr. articles to profl. jours.; mem. editorial bd. Am. Lit., 1995-98. Rsch. fellow NEH, 1990-91. Mem. Am. Lit. Assn., Modern Lang. Assn. Office: Fordham U English Dept Bronx NY 10458

DOBSON, MICHAEL P., publishing executive; b. Easton, Md., Apr. 29, 1947. BA, U. Md., 1969. Gen. mgr. Anthroposophic Press Inc., Hudson, N.Y., 1986—; cons. Social Ecology Assocs., Southfield, Mich., 1982-86. Office: Anthroposophic Press Inc 3390 Route 9 Hudson NY 12534-4322*

DOBSON, REBECCA ELIZABETH, secondary education educator, retired; b. Kinston, Ala., Jan. 31, 1925; d. Marcus F. and Henrietta (Fleming) Newsom; m. Clem M. Martin, Jr., Aug. 2, 1940 (div. May 1959); m. Bernard D. Dobson, Nov. 21, 1964. AA, St. Petersburg Coll., 1954; BA, BS, U. Tampa, 1959, MA, 1963. Cert. tchr., Fla. Clerk State of Ala., Montgomery, 1943-44; info. specialist Dept. of State, Washington, 1944-45; substitute tchr. Pinellas Sch., ST. Petersburg, Fla., 1955-58; tchr. Hillsboro Sch. Sys., Tampa, 1958-80; genealogical cons. Ozark, Ala., 1984—. Author: Woe and Giddiup, 1980, Possums Run Over Their Graves, 1999, Grits, Greens, Gumbo, 1999; co-author: Southern Ancestors Cookbook, 1999. Mem. AAUW, Fla. Ret. Educators Assn., U. Tampa Alumni Assn., DeSoto DAR,

United Daus. of Confederacy. Democrat. Baptist. Avocations: computers, gardening, genealogy, gourmet cooking, history research. Home: 611 S Union Ave Ozark AL 36360-1836

DOBSON, RICHARD LAWRENCE, dermatologist, educator; b. Boston, Apr. 12, 1928; s. Joseph William and Celia Beatrice (Siegler) D.; m. Marie C. Mollomo, Aug. 19, 1950; children: Richard Lawrence, Pamela Blair, Lisa Marie. M.D., U. Chgo., 1953; B.S., U. N.H., 1981. Diplomate Am. Bd. Dermatology (v.p. 1987-88, pres. 1988-89). Intern Cin. Gen. Hosp., 1953-54; resident Hitchcock Clinic, Hanover, N.H., 1954-57; asst. prof. dermatology U. N.C., Chapel Hill, 1957-61; prof. U. Oreg., Portland, 1961-72, SUNY-Buffalo, 1972-79; prof. Med. U. S.C., Charleston, 1980-98, acting dean, 1985-86, chmn. dept. anatomy and cell biology, 1991-92, prof. emeritus, 1998—; vis. prof. U. Nijmegen, The Netherlands, 1969-70; hon. prof. Shanghai 2d Med. U.; hon. cons. Royal Prince Alfred Hosp., Sydney, Australia; bd. dirs. Medicis Corp. Inc. Editor: Year Book of Dermatology, 1979-82, Clinical Dermatology, 1972-82, Contemporary Review, 1973-87; asst. editor: Jour. Am. Acad. Dermatology, 1979-87, editor, 1988-98; mng. editor Arch. Dermatol. Research, 1982-87 . Served with USN, 1946-47. Fellow ACP, Am. Acad. Dermatology (pres. 1983-84); mem. Am. Dermatologic Assn. (treas. 1977-82), Soc. Investigative Dermatology (pres. 1975-76), Oreg. Dermatol. Soc. (pres. 1971-72); hon. mem. Brit. Assn. Dermatology, Spanish Assn. Dermatology, French Dermatology Soc., Polish Dermatology Soc., Finnish Dermatology Soc., Dutch Dermatology Soc., German Dermatology Soc., N.Am. Dermatology Soc., Ga. Dermatology Soc., Iowa Dermatology Soc., Snee Farm Club. Republican. Roman Catholic. Home: 3356 Olympic Ln Mount Pleasant SC 29466-8998 Office: Med U SC 171 Ashley Ave Charleston SC 29425-0001

DOBSON, ROBERT ALBERTUS, III, lawyer, executive, volunteer; b. Greenville, S.C., Nov. 27, 1938; s. Robert A. Jr. and Dorothy (Leonard) D.; m. Linda Josephine Bryant, Nov. 18, 1956; children: Robert, William, Michael, Daniel, Jonathan, Laura (dec.); m. Catherine Elizabeth Cornmesser, Sept. 17, 1983; children: Andrew, Thomas. BS in Acctg. summa cum laude, U. S.C., 1960, JD magna cum laude, 1962. Asst. dean of students U. S.C., 1960-62; pvt. practice pub. acctg. Greenville, 1962-64; ptnr. Dobson & Dobson, Greenville, 1964-93; chmn., bd. trustees Limestone Coll., 1987-89. *Practiced tax and corporate law for thirty years pioneering the professional corporation concept for physicians, dentists and other professionals in South Carolina. Left his law practice in 1993 to devote full time to Christian ministry. Dobson Ministries supplies spiritual materials, support and encouragement to the elderly in nursing homes and to children in orphanages and shelters throughout the United States. Partners with and supports other ministries, including Homeless Children International and Campus Crusade for Christ. Extensively involved in numerous philanthropies.* Contbr. articles on tax and acctg. to profl. jours. Lay minister St. Francis Episcopal Ch., Greenville; chmn. bd. Dobson Tape Ministry, Homeless Children Internat., Inc.; bd. dirs. A Child's Haven, Inc., Found. for the Multihandicapped, Deaf and Blind, Spartanburg, S.C.; mem. adv. bd. Salvation Army, Greenville; chmn. fund raising com. Sch. Ministries, Inc., 1997-98; mem. history's handful Campus Crusade for Christ. Mem. ABA, S.C. Bar Assn., AICPAs, Am. Assn. Attys. and CPAs, S.C. Assn. Pub. Accts., Block C Assn. The Group, U. S.C. Alumni Assn. (cir. v.p.), Kappa Sigma (chmn. legal com. 1989-93, dist. grand master 1971—, Nat. Dist. Grand Master of the Yr. 1986, John G. Tower Disting. Alumni award 1997, Stephen Alonzo Jackson award 1998), Phi Beta Kappa. Episcopalian. Lodges: Sertoma Internat. (dist. treas.), Sertoma Sunrisers (pres. Greenville club). Home: 1207 Pelham Rd Greenville SC 29615-3643 Office: 1306 S Church St Greenville SC 29605-3814

DOBSON, ROBERT ALBERTUS, IV, corporate executive; b. Greenville, S.C., June 16, 1957; s. Robert Albertus III and Linda (Bryant) D.; m. Belinda Joy Jolly, July 21, 1984; children: Robert Albertus V, Jourdan Marie, Lauren Priscilla. BS in Mgmt., U. S.C., 1981. Gen. mgr. Winners Corp., Greenville, 1984-87; pres., CEO Foothills Family Properties Inc., Greenville, 1987-94, Model Train Techs., LLC, Greenville, 1994—. Republican. Episcopalian. Office: Model Train Techs LLC 2435 E North St Ste 240 Greenville SC 29615-2173

DOBY, JOHN THOMAS, social psychologist; b. Gray, Ky., May 29, 1920; s. Daniel W. and Minnie (Farris) D.; m. Rose Catherine Hopper Doby, Dec. 21, 1942; children: Mary Catherine, Nancy H. AB cum laude, Union Coll., Barbourville, Ky., 1946; MS, U. Wis., 1950; PhD, 1956. Assoc. prof., prof. Sociology and Anthropology Wofford Coll., Spartanburg, S.C., 1950-57; assoc. prof. Sociology and Anthropology Emory U., Atlanta, 1958-63; prof. Emory U., 1963-85, chmn. Dept. Sociology and Anthropology, 1960-69, chmn. Dept. Sociology, 1980-85, prof. emeritus of Sociology, 1985; cons. Engring. Ga. Inst. Tech., Atlanta, 1960-62; cons. Ednl. Testing Svc., Princeton, N.J., 1969; mem. faculty Grad. Sch. Consumer Banking U. Va., summer 1972-75; vis. scientist lectr. NSF Am. Sociological Assn., 1965-66; chair Tech. Scientific Adv. Com. on Mental Retardation, Ga. Dept. Health, 1965-66; dir. NSF Summer Inst. for Coll. Tchrs. of Sociology, Emory U., 1965-66; mem. NSF fellowship panel Nat. Acad. Sci., adv. com. Divsn. Mental health, Ga. Dept. Health, 1966-72, Sci. faculty Panel Am. Coun. Learned Soc., Nat. Sci. Postdoctoral Panel, 1976-77; pres. So. Sociological Soc., 1969-70; chair Com. on Undergraduate Curriculum and teaching, Am. Sociological Assn., 1968-70; dir. Nat. Sci. Found. Emory U., 1970-71, program on skill conversion tng. of aerospace engrs., 1970-71. Author: Introduction to Social Research, 1954, Introduction to Social Psychology, 1966, Introduction to Social Research, 1967; editor, author: Sociology: A Study of Man in Adaptation, 1973; contbr. articles to profl. jours., chpt. to Science, Mind, and Psychology, 1989. Maj. USAF, 1941-46. Grantee NIMH, 1960, NSF, 1964, 65, 71, Office of Econ. Opportunity, 1966-67, Nat. Inst. Child Health and Human Devel., 1979-80. Methodist. Home: RR 3 Box 82H Corbin KY 40701-9469

DOBYNS, BROWN MCILVAINE, surgeon, educator; b. Jacksonville, Ill., May 14, 1913; s. Henry D. and Leah (McIlvaine) D.; married; children—Mary Meredith, Courtney Sara, Brown McIlvaine. BA, Ill. Coll., 1935; MD, Johns Hopkins, 1939; MS, U. Minn., 1944, PhD, 1946. Diplomate: Am. Bd. Surgery. Intern surgery Johns Hopkins Hosp., 1939-40; fellow surgery Mayo Found., 1940-43; resident surgery Kahler Hosp., Mayo Clinic, 1943-45, 1st asst. surgery, 1945-46, asst. surg. staff, 1946; research fellow surgery, med. sch. Harvard, 1946-48, asst. prof. surgery, 1948-51; grad. asst. surgery Mass. Gen. Hosp., 1946-48, asst. surgery, 1946-51; asso. prof. surgery Western Res. U. Med. Sch., 1951-58, prof. surgery, 1958-84, prof. emeritus, 1984—; asst. chief surg. service Cleve. Met. Gen. Hosp., 1951-66, assoc. chief surg. service, 1967-88; asst. surgeon Univ. Hosp., Cleve., 1951-88; Fulbright lectr., Australia, 1966. Mem. fellowship subcom. Com. on Growth NRC, 1950-54; mem. fellowship com. NSF, 1954-61, chmn., 1955-61; adv. screening com. med. scis. Fulbright, 1955-58; adv. com. research on etiology cancer Am. Cancer Soc., 1956-59, chmn. adv. com. on instnl. grants, 1963-65; mem. Dernham Scholarship com. Calif. Cancer Soc., 1964-74. Recipient Van Meter prize, 1946, award of merit, 1954, Disting. Service award, 1978; all Am. Thyroid Assn.; citation for disting. public service Ill. Coll.; elected to Cleve. Med. Hall of Fame, 1997. Fellow ACS; mem. AAAS, Soc. Univ. Surgeons, Am. Soc. Clin. Investigation, Am. Surg. Assn., Ctrl. Surg. Assn., Am. Thyroid Assn. (pres. 1956-57), Cleve. Surg. Soc. (pres. 1966-67), Halstead Soc., Societé Internationale de Chirurgie, Endocrine Soc., Sigma Xi. Home: 9930 Kirtland Rd Chardon OH 44024-9746 *Try to have a new experience every day.*

DOCHERTY, ROBERT KELLIEHAN, II, minister; b. Newton, Mass., May 27, 1935; s. Alexander Harper and Mary (Campbell) D.; m. Eileen Joyce Rockefeller, June 14, 1958; children: Robert K. III, Scott Rockefeller, Stacy Jean. BA, Sterling Coll., 1961, Moody Bible Inst., 1970; MS, Pittsburg (Kans.) State U., 1972; PhD, Kans. State U., 1981. Ordained to ministry Presbyn. Ch. (U.S.A.), 1977. Min. 1st Bapt. Ch., Frederick, Kans., 1959-63, Russell, Kans., 1964-67; campus min. Pittsburg State U., 1967-72; mem. State Staff Kans. Bapt. Conv., Topeka, 1972-77; min. United Presbyn. Ch., Pittsburg, 1977-85; co-pastor The Presbyn. Ch., Pittsburg, 1985-87; organizing pastor John Knox Presbyn. Ch., Wichita, Kans., 1988, pastor, 1988-95; pastor St. Andrew Presbyn. Ch., Kimberling City, Mo., 1995—; moderator Synod Ministries Divsn., Overland Park, Kans., 1990-96, Church Related Colls. Com., Overland Park; moderator com. on ministry Presbytery of John Calvin, 1996—. Author: Community Education with School Superintendents, 1980. Founder Help NOW Inc., Pittsburg, 1972; bd. dirs. Elm Acres Youth Home, Girard, Kans., 1973-79; chmn. United Way, Pittsburg, 1974, co-chmn., 1983; treas. Mt. Carmel Hosp. Found., Pittsburg, 1984-87; chaplain CAP, Wichita, 1988—; trustee Presbyn. Manors of Mid-Am., Wichita, Kans., Presbyn. Children's Svcs., St. Louis; pres. bd. Christian Assocs. of Tablerock Lake, Inc. Nat. Coun. Chs. Christ fellow, 1976; C.S. Mott Found. fellow Kans. State U., 1978. Mem. Kiwanis (gov. Kans. 1972-73). Office: St Andrew Presbyn Ch 30 James River Rd Kimberling City MO 65686-9702 *Life is a quest, made up of many relationships, the most important one is to the giver of Life, God.*

DOCKEN, EDSEL ARDEAN, SR. (DEAN DOCKEN), urban planner; b. Jasper, Minn., Mar. 7, 1928; s. Edwin Alexander and Audrey (Norton) D.; m. Helen Jane Stokes, Oct. 10, 1954; children: Edsel A. Jr., Robin J. BS, U. Md., 1963; postgrad., Boston U., 1966, George Washington U., 1972; AA in Bus. Adminstrn. with honors, Harford Community Coll., 1981, cert. Real Estate Brokerage, 1983. Cert. real estate salesman. Enlisted U.S. Army, 1951, advanced through grades to lt. col., 1967, retired, 1971; insp. Test and Evaluation Commn., Aberdeen, Md., 1969-70; payroll mgr. Bata Shoe Co. Inc., Belcamp, Md., 1971-76; urban planner Town of Bel Air, Md., 1976-90; founder, exec. dir. Ordnance Mus. Found., Inc., Aberdeen, Md., 1991-93; exec. sec. The U.S. Ordnance Corps Assn., 1992—; mem. Md. Energy Office, Balt., 1977-83. Key man United Way of Ctrl. Md., 1978-87; chmn. tennis March of Dimes, 1978-79; bd. dirs. Rolling Green Community Assn., 1985-91; life mem. nat. com. for motor fleet ops. Mich. State U. Mem. Internat. Adminstrv. Mgmt. Soc., Am. Planning Assn. (charter), Mt. Ararat Lodge. Democrat. Lutheran. Avocations: hunting, fishing, gardening. Home: 3109 Rolling Green Dr Churchville MD 21028-1313 Office: US Ordnance Corps Assn PO Box 377 Aberdeen Proving Ground MD 21005-0377

DOCKERY, J. LEE, retired medical school administrator; b. Amity, Ark., 1932. MD, U. Ark., 1957. Rotating intern Jackson Meml. Hosp., Miami, Fla., 1957-58, active attending staff, 1963-75; resident in ob-gyn. U. Miami, 1958-61; active staff Doctor's Hosp. Miami, 1963-75; active staff, chmn. dept. ob-gyn. Bapt. Hosp. Miami, 1972-73; staff Shands Hosp., Gainesville, Fla., 1975-91; prof. ob-gyn. U. Fla., Gainesville, 1980-92, assoc. dean, 1980-86, exec. assoc. dean, 1986-88, interim dean, assoc. v.p. clin. affairs, 1988-91; exec. v.p. Am. Bd. Med. Specialties, 1991-97; clin. adj. prof. dept. ob-gyn. Northwestern U. Med. Sch., 1992—; clin. prof. dept. ob-gyn. U. Fla. Coll. Medicine, 1992—; mem. Accreditation Coun. for Grad. Med. Edn., 1984-89; mem. Liaison Com. for Med. Edn., 1989-91; mem. Fla. Bd. Medicine, 1988-92; mem. exam. bd. Fed. State Med. Bds., 1991-94. Mem. AMA (mem. coun. med. edn. 1983-92, chmn. 1987-88), So. Med. Assn. (pres. 1987-88), Fla. Med. Assn. (pres. 1983-84), Alpha Omega Alpha.

DOCKERY, ROBERT GERALD, minister; b. Fayetteville, Ark., Nov. 2, 1948; s. Geroge Lawson and Zelen (Bradley) D.; m. Meredy Jane Roberts, July 15, 1971; children: Jared Nathan, Rachael Marie, Robert Luke. BA, Harding U., 1971. Ordained to ministry Ch. of Christ, 1970. Min. Habberton Ch. of Christ, Fayetteville, 1968-69, Baldwin Ch. of Christ, Fayetteville, 1971—; dir. Ozark Christian Leadership Program, Fayetteville, Gospel Tracts Internat., Fayetteville. Author: Sermons For Special Occassions, 1977, The Holy Spirit: Unraveling the Mystery, 1990, Reasons for Believing, 1997; contbr. articles to profl. jours. Co-founder Pro-Life Edn. Alliance, 1983; speaker Ark. Right To Life Rally, Little Rock, 1983. Home: 17572 Lake Sequoyah Rd Fayetteville AR 72701-9554 Office: 4377 E Huntsville Rd Fayetteville AR 72701

DOCKING, THOMAS ROBERT, lawyer, former state lieutenant governor; b. Lawrence, Kans., Aug. 10, 1954; s. Robert Blackwell and Meredith (Gear) D.; m. Jill Sadowsky, June 18, 1977; children: Brian Thomas, Margery Meredith. BS, U. Kans., 1976, MBA, JD, 1980. Bar: Kans. 1980. Assoc. Regan & McGannon, Wichita, Kans., 1980-82, ptnr., 1983-90; ptnr. Ayesh, Docking, Herd & Theis, Wichita, 1990, Morris, Laing, Evans, Brock & Kennedy, Wichita, 1990—; lt. gov. State of Kans., Topeka, 1983-87; Dem. nominee for Gov. of Kans., 1986; chmn. adv. bd. Docking Inst. Pub. Affairs, Ft. Hays State U. Mem. steering com. Campaign Kans.; chmn. campaign com. Coll. Liberal Arts and Sci., 1988-91; bd. dirs. Kans. Easter Seals-Goodwill Industries, 1987-93, chmn. 1989 Telethon, vice-chair, 1991-93; bd. dirs. Wichita Conv. and Visitors Bur., chmn.; bd. dirs. St. Francis Found., 1988-94; trustee Emporia State Univ. Sch. Bd.; chmn. Wichita Water Conservation Task Force, 1991—; mem. Wichita/Brookes Water Task Force, 1997; mem. allocation com. United Way of the Plains, 1997—; mem. U. Ks. Law Sch. bd. govs., 1998—. Mem. ABA, Kans. Bar Assn., Pi Sigma Alpha, Beta Gamma Sigma, Beta Theta Pi. Presbyterian. Home: 125 S Crestway St Wichita KS 67218-1309 Office: Morris Laing Evans Brock & Kennedy 200 W Douglas Ave Fl 4 Wichita KS 67202-3013

DOCKSTEADER, KAREN KEMP, marketing executive; b. Salisbury, Md., Feb. 11, 1953; d. Robert George and Laverne (Briggs) Kemp; children: Daniel Richard Arrington IV, James William Arrington; m. Gerald Hugh Docksteader, Apr. 3, 1997. BS, Iowa State U., 1975; MEd, Salisbury State U., 1979. Dir. horticultural project Chesapeake Rehab. Ctr., Easton, Md., 1975-76; mgr. greenhouses Bountiful Ridge Nurseries, Inc., Princess Anne, Md., 1976-77; instr. horticulture Dorchester Bd. Edn., Cambridge, Md., 1978-80, Fredrick (Md.) Bd. Edn., 1980-87; instr. agronomy Frederick Community Coll., 1985; treas. Kemp's Ltd., Inc., Martinsburg, W.Va., 1985-87; pres. Kemp's Ltd., Inc., Frederick, Md., 1987—; cons., mgr. U.S. retail sales Kord Products, Ltd., Brampton, Ont., Can., 1995-98; keynote speaker Vocat. Counseling Orgn., Md., 1980-88; cons. retail and comml. mktg. groups, 1977-91; dir. Russian-Georgian Rose Project, Tblissi, Georgia (USSR), 1993. Editor newsletter The Spreader, 1990; featured narrator documentary Our Land, Our Future, 1980 (Gold award 1980); exhibitor Assn. Nurserymen, Balt. and King of Prussia, Pa., 1986-91. Coach 4-H, FFA, NJHA, and other youth orgns., Md., 1977-91; state chair Soil Conservation Poster Competition, Md., 1990-91; judge horticulture county fairs, state and nat. 4-H and FFA activities, 1977-91. Named Conservation Tchr. of Yr., State Soil and Water Conservation Svc., Annapolis, Md., 1984, Outstanding Young Co-Operator, Md. and Va. Coop., Lancaster, Pa., 1988. Mem. DAR, Md. Greenhouse Growers Assn., New Market Grange, Md. Hist. Soc., Hackers Creek Hist. Soc., Somerset Pa. Hist. Soc. Avocations: genealogy and historical research, writing, needlework, gardening. Office: Kemp's Ltd Inc 5009 Camelback Ln Frederick MD 21703-6901

DOCKTERMAN, MICHAEL, lawyer; b. Davenport, Iowa, Dec. 14, 1954; s. Jerome and Elaine (Epstein) D.; m. Laura Di Giantonio, Sept. 25, 1983; 1 child, Eliana. BA, Yale U., 1975; JD, Duke U., 1978. Bar: Ill. 1978, U.S. Dist. Ct. (no. dist.) Ill. 1978, U.S. Dist. Ct. (ea. dist.) Mich. 1986, U.S. Dist. Ct. (ctrl. dist.) Ill. 1988, U.S. Dist. Ct. (so. dist.) Ill. 1991, U.S. Dist. Ct. (we. dist.) Mich. 1995, U.S. Dist. Ct. (ea. dist.) Mo. 1996, U.S. Ct. Appeals (7th cir.) 1978, U.S. Ct. Appeals (4th, 6th and fed. cirs.) 1990, U.S. Ct. Appeals (2d cir.) 1993, U.S. Supreme Ct. 1992. Ptnr. Wildman, Harrold, Allen and Dixon, Chgo., 1978—. Co-author: IICLE Class Actions, 1986, 92; contbg. author: ABA Criminal Antitrust Litigation Manual, 1999; contbr. articles to profl. jours. Active Chgo. Vol. Legal Svcs., 1983—; adult bd. dirs. Greater Midwest region B'nai B'rith Youth Orgn., 1985—; bd. dirs. KAM Isaiah Israel Congregation, 1993-96, Duke Law Alumni Assn., sec.; trustee Max and Gretel Janowski Fund, Chgo., 1992—; mem. The Chgo. Com., Chgo. Coun. on Fgn. Rels., Am. Refugee Com. Recipient Award for Advocacy Internat. Acad. Trial Lawyers, Leadership Devel. award B'nai B'rith Youth Orgn. Fellow Pvt. Adjudication Found.; mem. ABA (chair corp. governance subcom. Corp. Counsel com. Bus. Law Sect.), Chgo. Bar Assn., Legal Club Chgo., B'nai B'rith Justice Lodge. Office: Wildman Harrold Allen Dixon 225 W Wacker Dr Chicago IL 60606

DOCTER, CHARLES ALFRED, lawyer, former state legislator; b. Hamburg, Germany, Aug. 5, 1931; s. Alfred Joseph and Annie Beatrice D.; m. Marcia Kaplan, Nov. 27, 1958; children: Will Henry, Michael Warren, Adina Jo. BA magna cum laude, Kenyon Coll., 1953; JD, U. Chgo., 1956. Bar: D.C. 1959, Md. 1962, U.S. Supreme Ct. 1959. Former aide to late Sen. Paul H. Douglas; practice law, specializing in bankruptcy and reorgn. Washington, 1959—; sr. partner firm Docter, Docter, Lynn, P.C., Washington, 1967—; presdl. appointee to bd. Pa. Ave. Devel. Corp., 1995-96; pres. Montgomery County (Md.) Com. for Fair Representation, 1962-65. Pres. Western Suburban Democratic Club, 1965-66; mem. Md. Ho. of Dels., 1967-78; serving variously as chmn. Montgomery and Prince George's counties Bi-County Dels.; bd. dirs. Met. Washington Coun. Govts., 1970, Downtown D.C. Bus. Improvement Dist., 1997—. Served to lt. USNR, 1956-59. Fellow Am. Coll. Bankruptcy, Walter Chandler Am. Inn of Ct. (master emeritus). Sponsor Md. tenants' rights laws, Md. Pub. campaign financing law, Md. revolving credit law and other consumer measures. Home: 1101 Market Sq W 801 Pennsylvania Ave NW Washington DC 20004-2615 Office: Docter Docter & Lynn PC 666 11th St NW Ste 1010 Washington DC 20001-4525

DOCTOR, KENNETH JAY, editor; b. L.A., Jan. 5, 1950; s. Joseph and Ruth (Kazdoy) D.; m. Katherine Conant Francis, June 14, 1971; children: Jenika, Joseph, Katy. BA in Sociology, U. Calif., Santa Cruz, 1971; MS in Journalism, U. Oreg., 1979. Editor, pub. Willamette Valley Observer, Eugene, Oreg., 1975-82; mng. editor Oreg. Mag., Portland, 1982-84; mng. editor, features Boulder (Colo.) Daily Camera, 1984-86; assoc. editor, features St. Paul Pioneer Press, 1986-90, mng. editor, features, 1990-94, mng. editor, 1994-97; v.p. editl. Knight Ridder New Media, San Jose, Calif., 1997—; chair Knight-Ridder Task Force on Family Readers, Miami, Fla., 1991. Recipient Achievement award Oreg. Civil Liberties Union, Eugene, 1982. Mem. Soc. Newspaper Design, Am. Soc. Newspaper Editors. Avocations: baseball, travel. E-mail: kdoctor@realcities.com. Office: Knight Ridder New Media 50 W San Fernando St Ste 700 San Jose CA 95113-2413

DOCTOROFF, MARK GUNTHER, bank officer; b. Boston, Jan. 28, 1972; s. Frederic Steven and Cynthia (De Long) D. BA in Polit. Sci. and Japanese Lang., Bates Coll., 1994. Analyst Chem. Bank Corp., N.Y.C., 1994-95, sr. fin. analyst, 1995-96; assoc. Chase Manhattan Bank, N.Y.C., 1996-97, Singapore, Singapore, 1997-99. Alumni agt., class pres. Choate Rosemary Hall AAF, Wallingford, Conn., 1994-99; mentor, tutor Children's Aid Soc., N.Y.C., 1995-97. Mem. Capital Markets Credit Analyst Soc. Republican. Home: 2 Leedon Rd # 12-06, Singapore 267829, Singapore Office: Chase Manhattan Bank, 150 Beach Rd Gateway W, Singapore 189720, Singapore

DOCTOROFF, MARTIN MYLES, judge; b. Cambridge, Mass., Jan. 27, 1933; s. Abraham M. and Rose (Blackstone) D.; m. Allene Ruth Miller, Aug. 26, 1956; children: Daniel Louis, Mark Howard, Andrew Seth, Thomas David. BA, Harvard Coll., 1954; JD, U. Mich., 1957. Spl. agt. FBI, 1957-60; ptnr. Bellinson & Doctoroff, Oak Park, Mich., 1960-65, Bellinson, Doctoroff & Wartell, Southfield, Mich., 1965-74, Zussman, Doctoroff & Wartell, Southfield, Mich., 1975-80, Bushnell, Gage, Doctoroff & Reizen, Southfield, 1980-87; appellate judge Mich. Ct. of Appeals, Southfield, 1987—, elected chief judge, 1992-97; spl. asst. atty. gen. State of Mich., 1969-87, mem. atty. discipline bd., 1984-90, chmn., 1986-87; pub. adminstr. Oakland County, Mich., 1975-87; spl. prosecutor Oakland County Grand Jury, 1979. Chmn. Birmingham Planning Bd., 1973-75; mem. exec com. Coun. of Chief Judge, Intermediate Cts. of Appeal, pres., 1997-98; mem. Birmingham Cable Bd. Mem. ABA (standing com. jud. selection 1986-92, appellate practice com., jud. adminstrn. div., sec., mem. exec. com. appellate judges conf.), FBA, Mich. Bar Assn. (standing com. on jud. qualifications 1982-87, bd. commrs. 1990—, sec. 1993-96), Mass. Bar Assn., Oakland County Bar Assn. (bd. dirs.), Southfield Bar Assn., Am. Acad. Matrimonial Lawyers, Soc. Former Spl. Agts. Democratic. Jewish. Avocations: gourmet cooking, reading, travel. Fax: (248) 358-3782. Office: Mich Ct Appeals 27777 Franklin Rd 760 American Center Bldg Southfield MI 48034

DOCTOROW, EDGAR LAWRENCE, novelist, English educator; b. N.Y.C., Jan. 6, 1931; s. David Richard and Rose (Levine) D.; m. Helen Esther Setzer, Aug. 20, 1954; children: Jenny, Caroline, Richard. AB in Philosophy with honors, Kenyon Coll., 1952, LHD (hon.), 1976; student, Columbia U., 1952-53; LittD (hon.), Hobart and William Smith Coll., 1979; LHD (hon.), Brandeis U., 1989. Script reader Columbia Pictures, Inc., N.Y.C.; sr. editor New Am. Libr., N.Y.C., 1959-64; editor-in-chief Dial Press, N.Y.C., 1964-69; v.p., pub. Dial Press, 1968-69; mem. faculty Sarah Lawrence Coll., Bronxville, N.Y., 1971-78; creative writing fellow Sch. Drama Yale U., New Haven, 1974-75; Glucksman Prof. English and Am. Letters NYU, 1982—; writer-in-residence U. Calif, Irvine, 1969-70; vis. prof. U. Utah, 1975; vis. sr. fellow Coun. on Humanities Princeton U., 1980. Author: (novels) Welcome to Hard Times, 1960, Big as Life, 1966, The Book of Daniel, 1971 (Nat. Book award nominee 1972), Ragtime, 1975 (Nat. Book Critics Circle award 1976, Arts and Letters award 1976), Loon Lake, 1980 (Nat. Book award nominee 1980), Lives of the Poets: Six Stories and a Novella, 1984, World's Fair, 1985 (Nat. Book award 1986), Billy Bathgate, 1989 (Nat. Book award nominee 1989, Nat. Book Critics Circle award 1990, PEN/Faulkner award 1990, William Dean Howells medal Am. Acad. and Inst. Arts and Letters 1990), The Waterworks, 1994, Ragtime, 1994; (play) Drinks Before Dinner, 1979; (screenplay) Daniel, 1983; (essays) Jack London, Hemingway, and the Constitution: Selected Essays 1977-92, 1993. With AUS, 1953-55. Recipient Arts and Letters award Am. Acad. and Nat. Inst. Art, 1976; Guggenheim fellow, 1973, Creative Artists Program Svc. fellow, 1973-74; Edith Wharton citation of merit for fiction and N.Y. State Author, 1989-91. Mem. Authors Guild (bd. dir.), Am. Acad. and Inst. Arts and Letters, Am. Acad. Arts and Scis., Am. PEN, Writers Guild Am. East, Century Assn. Office: Random House Pubs 201 E 50th St New York NY 10022-7703 also: NYU English Dept New York NY 10003-6607*

DODABALAPUR, ANANTH, electrical engineer; b. Bangalore, Karnataka, India, Feb. 17, 1963; came to U.S., 1985; s. Krishna Rao; m. Rati Chitnis, Aug. 15, 1991; children: Sonia, Siddharth. BTech, Indian Inst. Tech., Madras, India, 1985; MS, U. Tex., 1987, PhD, 1990. Grad. rsch. asst. Microelectronics Rsch. Ctr. U. Tex., Austin, 1985-90; postdoctoral mem. of tech. staff AT&T Bell Labs., Holmdel, N.J., 1990-92; mem. tech. staff optical physics rsch. dept. Bell Labs., Lucent Techs., Murray Hill, N.J., 1992—. Mem. IEEE, Materials Rsch. Soc. (co-chair rsch. symposia on organic electronics 1997, 98). Achievements include research in white light emitting diodes, organic led based color displays, organic lasers, transport in molecular solids, organic transistors, organic transistor complementary circuits, pioneering research on photonic-bandgap based lasers, integrated organic optoelectrics, and molecular circuits. Office: Lucent Technologies 600 Mountain Ave New Providence NJ 07974-2008

DODD, ALAN CHARLES, art educator; b. Milford, Conn., Nov. 10, 1945; s. John Abbott and Kathryne Jean (Legeyt) D.; m. Dorothy Anne Magee, Aug. 16, 1968; children: Sara, Peter, Elizabeth. BS, So. Conn. State U., 1978, MS, 1989, postgrad., 1992. Cert. tchr. art K-12. Tchr. art Milford Pub. Schs., 1968—; scenic designer Black Rock Congl. Ch., Fairfield, Conn., 1982—. Pottery exhibited Milford Pub. Libr., 1989; designer, prodr. Display for Valley C. of C. Expo, 1997. Mem. Milford Fine Arts Coun., Milford Hist. Soc., Milford C. of C. (edn. com. 1995—). Avocations: potter, musician. Home: 14 George St Milford CT 06460-4809

DODD, CHARLES GARDNER, physical chemist; b. St. Louis, Jan. 26, 1915; s. Harry Gardner and Ruth Esther (Hauskins) D.; m. Edel Marie Bovbjerg, June 10, 1943; children—Sally Little, Karen Elise, Mary Bartlett, Frederick Porter. B.S., Rice U., 1940; M.S., U. Mich., 1945, Ph.D., 1948. In academic work and indsl. rsch. with Fed. Bur. Mines, Bartlesville, Okla., 1953-74; with Warner Lambert Co., Milford, Conn., 1974-80; pres. CTC Technologies, Inc. (formerly Conn. Tech. Cons., Inc.), Tucson, 1980—; vis. scholar dept. chem. U. Ariz., 1991—; importer, distbr. sci. instruments. Contbr. articles to sci. and tech. publs. Fellow AAAS; mem. Am. Vacuum Soc., Am. Chem. Soc., Clay Minerals Soc., Chemists Club. Office: CTC Technolgies Inc 1295 N Oracle Rd Ste 141 Tucson AZ 85737

DODD, CHRISTOPHER J., senator; b. Willimantic, Conn., May 27, 1944; s. Thomas J. and Grace (Murphy) D. B.A. in English Lit., Providence Coll., 1966; J.D., U. Louisville, 1972. Bar: Conn. 1973. Vol. Peace Corps, Dominican Republic, 1966-68; atty. Suisman, Shapiro, Wool & Brennan, New London, Conn., 1973-74; mem. 94th-96th Congresses from 2d Conn. Dist., 1975-80; sen. from Conn. U.S. Senate, Washington, 1980—, mem. fgn. rels., banking, housing & urban affairs coms., rules com., 1981—, mem. subcom. edn., arts & humanities, founder & co-chmn. Senate Children's Caucus, 1983—, ranking mem. Western Hemisphere subcom., mem. subcom. children & families, labor com., randing mem. subcom. securities, banking com.; chmn. Dem. Nat. Com.; mem. Whitewater com. Served with AUS, 1969-75. Recipient Hubert H. Humphrey Pub. Svc. award, Outstanding U.S. Senator award, Nathan Davis award AMA, Head Start Senator of

Decade award. Democrat. Roman Catholic. Office: US Senate 444 Russell Senate Bldg Washington DC 20510-0702*

DODD, DARLENE MAE, nurse, retired air force officer; b. Dowagiac, Mich., Oct. 11, 1935; d. Charles B. and Lila H. Dodd. Diploma in nursing, Borgess Hosp. Sch. Nursing, Kalamazoo, 1957; grad., USAF Flight Nurse Course, 1959, USAF Squadron Officers Sch., 1963, Air Command and Staff Coll., 1973; BS in Psychology and Gen. Studies, So. Oreg. State Coll., 1987, postgrad., 1987. Commd. 2d lt. USAF, 1959, advanced through grades to lt. col., 1975; staff nurse USAF, Randolph AFB, Tex., 1959-60, Ladd AFB, Alaska, 1960-62, Selfridge AFB, Mich., 1962-63, Cam Rahn Bay Air Base, Vietnam, 1966-67, Seymour Johnson AFB, N.C., 1967-69; staff nurse USAF Acad., Colorado Springs, Colo., 1971-72; flight nurse 22d Aeromed. Evacuation, Tex., 1963-66; chief nurse USAF, Danang Air Base, Vietnam, 1068; flight nurse USAF, Yokotu AFB, Japan, 1969-71; clin. coord. ob-gyn., flight nurse USAF, Elmendorf AFB, Alaska, 1973-76; clin. nurse coord. ob-gyn. and pediatric svcs. USAF Med. Ctr., Keesler AFB, Miss., 1976-79; ret., 1979; with Bear Creek Corp., Medford, Oreg. Decorated Bronze Star. Mem. DAV, VFW, Am. Legion (life), Soc. Ret. Air Force Nurses, Ret. Officers Assn., Vietnam Vets. Am., Uniformed Svcs. Disabled Retirees, Air Force Assn., Women of Moose, Psi Chi, Phi Kappa Phi. Home: 712 1st St Phoenix OR 97535

DODD, DAVID K., banker; b. Hartford, Conn., Oct. 31, 1932; s. Thomas K. and Florence E. Dodd. BA, Yale U., 1954; MBA, Harvard U., 1958. Dir., sr. v.p. Merrill Lynch Internat., London, N.Y.C., 1958-79; internat. mktg. dir. CEDEL, London, 1979-81; dep. dir. NatWest Capital Markets, London, 1981-85; dep. mng. dir. Sakura Fin., London, 1985-90; sr. cons. D.C. Gardner, London, 1990-91; mng. ptnr. The Kilburn Partnership, Avon, Conn., 1991-95, 97—; sr. advisor Sporitelni Invest, Prague, Czech Republic, 1995-97. Contbr. articles to profl. jours. Lt. (j.g.) USN, 1954-56. Mem. Assn. Investment Mgmt. and Rsch., N.Y. Soc. Security Analysts, Bond Club N.Y. Avocations: tennis, golf, skiing, traveling. E-mail: dkdodd@usa.net. Office: The Kilburn Partnership 40 Byron Dr Avon CT 06001

DODD, DONALD BRADFORD, museum administrator, historian; b. Manchester, Ala., Feb. 6, 1940; s. Benjamin Garland and Alta Savannah (Weaver) D.; m. Sandra Ellen Whitten, June 10, 1961 (div. June 1983); children: Donna Ellen, Donald Bradford Jr.; m. Amelia Jane Bartlett, Dec. 7, 1985; 1 child, Anna Lorene. BS, U. North Ala., 1961; MA, Auburn U., 1966; PhD, U. Ga., 1969. Prof. history Auburn U., Montgomery, Ala., 1969-95, prof. history emeritus, 1995—; adminstr. So. Mus. Flight, Birmingham, Ala., 1996—. Author: Alabama Now and Then: A Contemporary Look, 1994; co-author: Alabama History: An Annotated Bibliography, 1998; co-editor: State and Local Government Administration, 1987; compiler: Historical Statistics of the States of the United States, 1993; also others. Col., USAFR, 1961-92. Mem. Orgn. Am. Historians (life), Air Force Assn. (life), So. Hist. Assn. (life), Ala. Hist. Assn. (life), Phi Alpha Theta, Phi Kappa Phi. Avocations: writing, editing. Home: 3308 Saddlebrook Cir Birmingham AL 35210-4200 Office: Southern Mus of Flight 4343 73rd St N Birmingham AL 35206-3642

DODD, GERALDA, metal products executive; children: T. Edward Sellers III, Madison Dodd Sellers. U. Toledo, Ohio. Receptionist Heidtman Steel, Toledo, OH, 1978-79, various positions, 1979-88, dir. purchasing, 1988; vp HS Processing (subs. Heidtmann Steel), Balt., 1988-90; pres., CEO Thomas Madison Inc., Detroit. Bd. dirs. Detroit Regional Chamber, Detroit Econ. Growth Corp., Workforce Devel. Music Hall, Nataki Talibath Sch., United Way Cmty. Svcs., Nat. Kidney Found. of Mich. and New Detroit, Inc. Mem. Womens Econ. Club, Nat. Assn. Women Bus. Owners, Nat. Assn. Black Automotive Suppliers, Assn. Women in Metals Industry, Greater Wayne County chpt. of The Links, Inc. Fax: 313-273-8052. Office: Thomas Madison Inc 12301 Hubbell St Detroit MI 48227-2777

DODD, JACK GORDON, JR., physicist, educator; b. Spokane, Wash., June 19, 1926; s. Jack Gordon and Mary Ida (Stuart) D.; m. Mary Ann Howell, June 11, 1951; children—Jeffrey John, Laura Jean. Student, State Coll. Wash., 1946-48; B.S. in Physics, Ill. Inst. Tech., 1951; M.S. in Physics, U. Ark., 1957, Ph.D. in Physics, 1965. With Argonne (Ill.) Nat. Lab., 1951-53; tchr. Fourche Valley High Sch., 1953-55, 56-57; asst. prof. Drury Coll., 1957-60; assoc. prof. Ark. Poly. Coll., 1960-65, U. Tenn., Knoxville, 1965-69; Charles A. Dana prof. physics and astronomy Colgate U., Hamilton, N.Y., 1969-87; ret. Colgate U., 1988; v.p. Spectrum Sq., Ithaca, N.Y., 1987—; chmn. bd. trustees McCrome Rsch. Inst., Chgo., 1999—; cons. on phys. optics, microscopy, detonation theory, spectral and image data processing. Served with USN, 1944-46. Mem. Am. Assn. Physics Tchrs., Am. Phys. Soc., Am. Astron. Soc., Optical Soc. Am., Sigma Xi. Office: 213 Sears Pond Rd Sherburne NY 13460-5018

DODD, JOE DAVID, safety engineer, consultant, administrator; b. Walnut Grove, Mo., Jan. 22, 1920; s. Marshall Hill and Pearl (Combs) D.; m. Nona Bell Junkins, Sept. 17, 1939; 1 dau. Linda Kay Dodd Craig. Student S.W. Mo. State U., 1937-39, Wash. U., 1947-55. Cert. profl. safety engr. Calif. Office asst. retail credit co., Kansas City, Mo., 1939-42; bus driver City of Springfield (Mo.), 1945-47; ops., engring., and personnel positions Shell Oil Co., Wood River (Ill.) Refinery, 1947-66; health and safety dept. mgr. Martinez Mfg. Complex, Calif., 1966-83, retired 1983; exec. dir. Fire Protection Tng. Acad., U. Nev.-Reno; rep. Shell Oil Co., Western Oil and Gas Assn., 1970-81. Mem. Republican Presdl. Task Force. Served with USMC, 1942-45. Decorated Presdl. Citation. Mem. Western Oil and Gas Assn. (Hose Handler award 1972-81, Outstanding mem. award), Am. Soc. Safety Engrs., Veterans Safety, State and County Fire Chiefs Assn., Peace Officers Assn., Nat. Fire Protection Assn. Presbyterian (elder). Established Fire Protection Tng. Acad., U. Nev.-Reno, Stead Campus.

DODD, JOHN ROBERT, non-profit organization administrator; b. Dallas, Oct. 15, 1951; s. Carlos Lestor and Betty (Ayers) D.; m. Mary Teresa Parsons, Nov. 12, 1983; children: Katherine Howard, Mary Alexandra. BA, Coll. William and Mary, 1975; MA, U. N.C., 1980. Tchr. Cinnaminson (N.J.) H.S., 1975-78; grad. asst. U. N.C., Chapel Hill, 1978-80; PAC coord. Nat. Congl. Club, Raleigh, N.C., 1981-82; v.p. Coalition for Freedom, Raleigh, 1982-85; pres. J & T Dodd Assocs., Fairfax, Va., 1985-94, Jesse Helms Ctr, Wingate, N.C., 1994—; cons. to various mems. of Congress. Bd. dirs. Fellowship of Christian Athletes, Washington, 1991-94; head Lacrosse coach Wingate U. Named Coach of Yr., Washington Post, 1985, 87, Connection Papers, 1991, 92. Mem. Nat. Soc. Fund Raising Execs. (D.C. chpt. membership com. 1985-89). Republican. Office: Jesse Helms Ctr PO Box 247 Wingate NC 28174-0247

DODD, LOIS, artist, art professor; b. Montclair, N.J., Apr. 22, 1927; d. Lawrence Dodd and Margaret Vanderhoff; m. William Dickey King (div.); 1 child, Eli Benjamin. Student, Cooper Union, 1945-48. Tchr. art Bklyn. Coll., 1971-92. One woman shows include Tanager Gallery, N.Y.C., 1954-62, Green Mountain Gallery, N.Y.C., 1969-76, Fischbach Gallery, N.Y.C., 1978—, Washington (Conn.) Art Assn., 1977, Cape Split Pl., Maine, 1977-83, N.J. State Mus., Trenton, 1981, Lyman Allyn Mus., Conn., 1980, La. State U., Baton Rouge, 1984, Anne Weber Gallery, Maine, 1987, Caldbeck Gallery, Maine, 1980, 95, 98, Dartmouth (N.H.) Coll., 1990, Rider (N.J.) Coll., 1993, Montclair Art Mus., N.J., 1996, Farnsworth Art Mus., Rockland, Maine, 1996, Trenton City Mus.; represented in permanent collections at Colby Coll. Mus., Cooper Hewitt Mus., Farnsworth Mus., Kalamazoo Art Ctr., NAD, AT&T, Chase Manhattan Bank, Commerce Bancshares Inc., Met. Life Ins. Co., Readers Digest, R.V. Reynolds Security, Pacific Nat. Bank, First Nat. City Bank. Bd. govs. Skowhegan Sch. of Painting and Sculptures, 1980—. Recipient award Am. Acad. Arts and Letters, 1986, Disting. Alumni citation Cooper Union, 1987; Ingram Merrill Found. grantee, 1971. Mem. NAD, Am. Acad. Arts and Letters. Home and Studio: 30 E 2nd St New York NY 10003-8906

DODD, SARA MAE PALMER, executive assistant; b. Cin.; d. Charles Austen and Ruth Halsey (Miller) Palmer; m. Edward Dodd, Mar. 31, 1953 (dec.); children: J. Edward, Diane Dodd Peterson. BA, Hiram Coll., 1949; postgrad., Rutgers U., 1968. Exec. dir. Camp Fire Girls, Inc., Indpls., 1949-53; regional field advisor Camp Fire Girls, Inc., N.Y.C., 1973; substitute tchr. Piscataway (N.J.) Sch. Dist., 1974-79; asst. to pres. Ctr. for Profl. Advancement, East Brunswick, N.J., 1979-89. Active LWV, Piscataway, N.J., 1957-87, pres., fin. chmn., newsletter editor, 1957-87, v.p., 1985-87, leadership com., 1987-89; adv. Piscataway Twp. Sr. Citizen Adv. Commn.; vol. tutor in ESL program Literacy Vols. of Am. Mem. Honor Roll of Women, Piscataway. Methodist. Avocations: oil painting, creative writing.

DODD, STEVEN LOUIS, systems engineer; b. Gainesville, Ga., Aug. 19, 1953; s. Oscar Louis and Vivian Irene (King) D.; m. Laureen Tyler, Apr. 8, 1989; children: Kevin Forrest, Emma Catherine. BS in Math., Davidson (N.C.) Coll., 1975; MS in Applied Math., N.C. State U., 1977, PhD in Ops. Rsch., 1982. Cons. EPA, Research Triangle Park, N.C., 1976-77; systems engr. AT&T Bell Labs., Holmdel, N.J., 1982-86, supr., systems engr. and developer, 1986-90; dist. mgr., tech. mktg. AT&T Bus. Communications Svcs., Bridgewater, N.J., 1990-91; dir. strategic planning Cin. Bell Info. Systems, Fairfax, Va., 1991-92, dir. platform mgmt., 1992; dir. gas and electric group Cin. Bell Info. Systems, 1993, dir. comm. solutions group, 1993-96; v.p. Win Star Telecomm., Tysons Corner, Va., 1996-99, sr. v.p., 1999—. Contbr. articles to profl. jours. Mem. Phi Beta Kappa, Omicron Delta Kappa, Omega Ro, Upsilon Pi Epsilon, Pi Mu Epsilon. Achievements include research in performance evaluation review, IEEE computer graphics and applications and numerische mathematik. Office: Win Star Comms 2545 Horse Pen Pen Rd Herndon VA 22071

DODD, THOMAS J., ambassador, educator; b. Washington, Mar. 29, 1935; 3 children. Student, Georgetown U., 1957; BS in Fgn. Svc., U. Barcelona, Spain; student, U. Santander, Spain, U. Iberoamericana, Mex., Johns Hopkins U., 1958-59; MA, George Washington U., 1961, PhD in History, 1966. Asst. prof. history sch. fgn. svc., grad. sch. Georgetown U., Washington, 1966-74, assoc. prof., 1974-93, dir. Latin Am. studies program grad. sch., 1966-73, assoc. faculty ctr. strategic and internat. studies, 1981; amb. to Republic of Uruguay, 1993—; faculty adviser The Ctrl. Am. Inst. Labor Studies AID, Guatemala, Costa Rica, Nicaragua and Panama, 1969; cons. policy and coordination staff office of sec. Dept. State, 1970-72; lectr. Inter-Am. Def. Coll., Def. Intelligence Coll., Nat. Def. U., Fgn. Svc. Inst., Dept. State, 1971-86; mem. Latin Am. discussion group The Brookings Instn., Washington, 1973; commentator The Panama Canal Treaties Debate Pub. Affairs Radio, 1974-78; pres. Inter-Am. Coun. of U.S., 1976-77, 85; chmn. advanced seminar Ctrl. Am. and Spanish Caribbean Fgn. Svc. Inst., Washington, 1981-86; mem. faculty adv. bd. inst. study diplomacy sch. fgn. svc. Georgetown U., 1982-93; lectr. Smithsonian Instn., Washington, 1982, 85; lectr. bus. coun. internat. understanding Am. U., Spain, Mex., Ctrl. Am., 1984-93; vis. prof. Def. Intelligence Coll., Sch. Strategic Intelligence, Washington, 1984-93; mem. Europe acad. rev. panel Acad. Ednl. Devel., USIA, 1986; mem. examining bd. Latin Am. scholarship program Am. Univs., 1987; mem. examining bd. Candidates for Fulbright Awards, Republic of Honduras, 1987. Author: (with others) Latin American Foreign Policies: An Analysis, 1975; author: The Letters of Tomas Herran: Colombian Diplomat and the Panama Crisis, 1903-04, 1985, Managing Democracy in Central America, United States and Nicaragua, 1927-1933, 1992; contbr. articles and book revs. on Latin Am. to profl. jours. Active Trinity Players Theater Group, La Commn. Nacional del Centenario del Descrubrimiento de Am. Capt. U.S. Army, 1958-61. Decorated Commendation medal; recipient Disting. Alumni award Chesire Acad., 1993; grantee Delmar Found., 1971, Gawaina Luster Faculty grantee Instituto Colombiano del Historia, Instituto Caro y Cuervo, 1978, Joint Faculty Summer grantee Georgetown U., 1982, grantee Ford Found., 1982, Fulbright grantee, 1986, Edmund A. Walsh Faculty Travel and Rsch. grantee, 1987, grantee New Eng. Circle Found., 1989, Walsh Faculty grantee, 1991, 92; Calouste Gulbenkian fellow, 1966, Rsch. fellow Orgn. Am. States, 1987, Fulbright fellow Republic of Honduras, 1987. Mem. Am. Hist. Assn., Latin Am. Studies Assn., Mid-Atlantic Assn. Latin Am. Studies, Conf. Latin Am. History, Ctr. Inter-Am. Rels., N.Y.C. Caribbean Studies Assn., World Affairs Coun., Washington Area Modern Latin Am. Historians Forum, Coun. Ambs., Pi Gamma Mu, Delta Phi Epsilon. Roman Catholic. Avocations: squash, tennis, hiking, reading biographies. Office: American Embassy, Lauro Muller 1776, Montevideo Uruguay

DODD, VIRGINIA, medical/surgical and endoscopy nurse; b. Gadsden, Ala., Sept. 7, 1928; d. Clayton Daniel and Lois Roberta (Morgan) Bridges; m. J.W. Dodd, Jr., July 29, 1951; children: Susan Dodd Tankersley, Mark S., Joseph K. Diploma, Erlanger Sch. Nursing, Chattanooga, 1950. RN, Ga., Tenn.; cert. gastroenterology clinician. Staff nurse obstet. dept. and surg. unit Erlanger Hosp., Chattanooga, 1951; staff nurse surg. unit Hucheson Med. Ctr., Ft. Oglethorpe, Ga., 1953-56, staff nurse clin. instr. lic. practical nursing, 1960-61; head nurse recovery room Hutcheson Med. Ctr., Ft. Oglethorpe, Ga., 1967-80, head nurse gastrointestinal lab., 1981-92, part-time staff nurse, 1992—. Mem. Ga. Nurses Assn., Soc. Gastroenterology Nurses. Home: 29 Williams Ln Rossville GA 30741-4039

DODD, VIRGINIA MARILYN, veterinarian; b. Battle Creek, Mich., Oct. 14, 1950; d. George Vernon and Marilyn Ottilie (Johnson) D. BS cum laude, Mich. State U., E Lansing, 1972; DVM cum laude, Mich. State U., East Lansing, 1974. Diplomate Am. Bd. Vet. Practitioners, Companion Animal Practice, 1982, 91. Veterinarian Butler Animal Hosps. Pa., Charlotte, N.C., 1975-83; medicine resident U. Tenn., Knoxville, 1983-86; asst. prof. medicine U. Saskatchewan, Canada, 1986-87; veterinarian Vet. Referral Service, Charlotte, N.C., 1988-89, After Hours Vet. Emergency Clinic, Greensboro, N.C., 1989-92, Dodd Vet. Svcs., Madison, Tenn., 1992-95; pres. Eco-Systems, 1992-94; veterinarian Forsyth County Vet. Emergency Clinic, 1993-98; owner Dodd Vet. Imaging Svcs., 1994—; veterinarian Vet. Cons. & Relief Svcs., 1988-91; spkr. U. Tenn., Knoxville, 1984-91, U. Sask., 1986-87, CCVMA, 1991; mem. credentials com. Am. Bd. Vet. Practitioners, 1990—, official photographer, 1992-94. Author: Med. Case Report A.V.M.A. Jour. 1986, Radiology Case Report Vet. Radiology 1987. Pres. Greater Charlotte Vet. Med. Assn., 1980-82; advisor Vet. Med. Tech. Adv. Com. Cen. Carolina Tech. Coll., Sanford, N.C., 1981-83; coord. Nat. Pet Wk., Mecklenburg County, N.C., 1982. Mem. Am. Vet. Med. Assn., Am. Assn. Vet. Clinicians, Am. Heartworm Soc., Am. Inst. of Ultrasound in Medicine, Soc. of Diagnostic Med. Sonographers, Vt. Cancer Soc., Vet. Emergency and Critical Care Soc., Vet. Ultrasound Soc., Nashville Striders, Knoxville Track Club, Sierra Club, Triathlon Club, Twin City Track Club, Friends of Triad Pets (pres.), Nature Conservancy, Phi Zeta. Avocations: road running, fly fishing, skiing, tennis, nature photography. Home and Office: Dodd Vet Svcs 504 Gayron Dr Winston Salem NC 27105-1715

DODDS, BRENDA KAY, nurse; b. Wheeling, W.Va., July 14, 1961; d. Ray Charles and Kathryn June (Ries) D. BS, Graceland Coll., 1983; A in Child Devel., 1990. RN. Staff nurse Resthaven Retirement Home, Independence, Mo., 1983-84; staff nurse telemetry unit Columbia Independence Regional Health Ctr., 1983—; camp nurse Mo-Kan Salvation Army Camp, Kansas City, Mo., 1984; dental asst. Ronald E. Jennings, DDS P.C., Independence, 1985-87; sch. nurse Noland Child Devel. Ctr., Independence Pub. Sch. Dist., 1988-96, head tchr., 1990-96, morning supr., 1993-96; staff Independence Head Start program Independence Sch. Dist., 1997—. Vol. ARC, Independence, 1983—, Voluntary Action Ctr., 1987-95; vocalist Independence Messiah/Festival Choir, 1983—; musician Independence Symphony Band, 1988—. Mem. Nat. Assn. for Edn. Young Children, Mo. Nurses Assn., Profl. Nurses Assn., Mensa. Avocations: hand crafts, gardening, spinning, weaving.

DODDS, CHRISTINE J., nursing administrator; b. Glen Ridge, N.J., Apr. 15, 1954; d. John M. and Frances L. (Marden) Sellar; m. John L. Dodds, Dec. 14, 1985. BSN, Bloomfield Coll., 1979; BA, Monmouth Coll., 1982; MS in Health Adminstrn., Cen. Mich. U., 1988. Staff nurse pediatrics St. Michael's Med. Ctr., Newark; clin. instr. Burlington County Vo-Tech High Sch., Mt. Holly, N.J.; adj. faculty Mercer County C.C., East Windsor, N.J.; nursing supr. Deborah Heart and Lung Ctr., Browns Mills, N.J. Author: (with others) Handbook of Pediatric Nutrition, Heart to Heart Surgical Book. Mem. AACN, ANA.

DODDS, DALE IRVIN, chemicals executive; b. Los Angeles, May 3, 1915; s. Nathan Thomas and Mary Amanda (Latham) D.; m. Phyllis Doreen Kirchmayer, Dec. 20, 1941; children: Nathan E., Allan I., Dale I. Jr., Charles A. AB in Chemistry, Stanford U., 1937. Chem. engr. trainee The Texas Co., Long Beach, Calif., 1937-39; chemist Standard Oil of Calif., Richmond, 1939-41; chief chemist Scriver and Quinn Interchem., L.A., 1941-46; salesman E.B. Taylor and Co. Mfg. Rep., L.A., 1947-53, Burbank (Calif.) Chem. Co., 1953-57, Chem. Mfg. Co./ICI, L.A., 1957-68; pres., CEO J.J. Mauget Co., L.A., 1969-97; CEO J.J. Mauget Co., Arcadia, Calif., 1998—. Inventor: Systemic Fungicide, 1976; patentee in field; contributed to devel. Microinjection for Trees. Fellow Am. Inst. Chemists; mem. Am. Chem. Soc., L.A. Athletic Club, Sigma Alpha Epsilon Alumni (pres. Pasadena, Calif. chpt. 1973, 90). Republican. Christian Scientist. Office: JJ Mauget Co 5435 Peck Rd Arcadia CA 91006-5847

DODDS, DAVID WILLIAM, superintendent; b. Lakewood, Ohio, June 15, 1945; s. David William and Jean Margaret (Curtis) D.; m. Barbara Joyce Andelman, Aug. 17, 1968; children: Amy Lynn Dodds Layton, Emily Margaret, Elizabeth Joy. BA, Millikin U., 1967; MS, Ind. U., 1968; EdD, No. Ill. U., 1992. Tchr. speech and English Mt. Prospect (Ill.) H.S. Dist. 214, 1968-72; asst. prin. McHenry (Ill.) H.S. Dist. 156, 1972-77, prin., 1977-92; supt. McHenry Sch. Dist. 15, 1992—. Co-chair McVotes, McHenry County, 1995-97; mem. econ. devel. com. City of McHenry, 1993-99. Inst. Devel. of Edn. Activities fellow, 1976, 93-99, NEH fellow. Mem. SAR, Kiwanis (past pres. 1977-99). Avocations: singing, music. Office: Sch Dist 15 1011 N Green St Mchenry IL 60050

DODDS, LAWRENCE DONALD, lawyer; b. Ogdensburg, N.Y., Mar. 31, 1967; s. Donald Wilbur and Virginia Ann (Moore) D.; m. Amy Elizabeth Haugh, June 17, 1995. AB, Hamilton Coll., 1989; MA, Hahnemann U., 1997, PhD, 1999; JD, Villanova U., 1997. Clin. counselor Wediko Children's Svcs., Hillsboro, N.H., 1989-90, clin. coord., 1990-91; legal intern Defender Assn. Phila., 1993-94, Schnader Harrison Segal & Lewis, Phila., 1996; psychology intern Settlement Music Sch., Phila., 1993-94, Hahnemann Univ., Phila., 1994-95, The Devereux Found., 1997-98; atty. Schader Harrison Segal & Lewis, LLP, Phila., 1998—. Mem. ABA, APA, Am. Psychology Law Soc., Order of Coif, Phi Beta Kappa, Phi Kappa Phi.

DODDS, LINDA CAROL, insurance company executive; b. Tucson, June 2, 1957; d. George A. and Bette R. (Bell) D. AA, U. Md., 1979; BA, Tex. Tech U., 1982; MBA, Our Lady of the Lake U., 1986, postgrad., 1998—. Svc. rep. USAA, San Antonio, 1982-84; portfolio asst. USAA-IMCO, San Antonio, 1984-85; sr. rep. USAA, San Antonio, 1985-86; asst. area mgr. USAA, Tampa, Fla., 1986-88, area mgr., 1988-92, dist. mgr., 1992-97; dist. mgr. USAA, San Antonio, 1997-98; spkr. in field. Treas. Forest Hills Homeowners Assn., Tampa, 1992-93; mem. Tex. Fedn. Rep. Women, San Antonio, 1985; co-chair United Way, 1995-96; active USAA Vol. Corp., Tampa, 1989—. Mem. Soc. CPCU, Delta Mu Delta, Sigma Iota Epsilon.

DODDS, ROBERT JAMES, III, lawyer; b. San Antonio, Sept. 19, 1943; s. Robert James Jr. and Kathryn (Bechman) D.; m. Deborah N. Detchon, June 25, 1966 (div. Mar. 1989); children: Zachary Bechman, Seth Detchon; m. D.J. Knowles, Dec. 27, 1990. BA, Yale U., 1965; LLB, U. Pa., 1969. Assoc. Reed Smith Shaw & McClay, Pitts., 1969-77, ptnr., 1978-91; ptrn. Davenport & Dodds, LLP, Santa Fe, 1992—; of counsel Strassburger, McKenna, Gutnick & Potter, Pitts., 1991—; bd. dirs. ATP Inc., Davison Sand & Gravel Co., Pitts.; pres. Homewood Cemetery, Pitts., 1980-91, bd. dirs. Trustee Mus. Art, Carnegie Inst, 1974-84, Westmoreland Mus. Art, Greensburg, Pa., YMCA of Pitts., Carnegie-Mellon U.; dir., pres. Pitts. Plan for Art, 1981-85; dir., chmn. West Pa. Hosp. Found., Carnegie Mellon Art Gallery; bd. dirs. Western Pa. Hosp., Western Pa. Healthcare Systems Inc., Pitts. Athletic Assn., Inst. Am. Indian Arts Found., Santa Fe. Democrat. Episcopalian. Home: 3101 Old Pecos Trl Unit 687 Santa Fe NM 87505-9547 Office: Davenport & Dodds LLP 312 Montezuma Ave Santa Fe NM 87501-2627*

DODERER, MINNETTE FRERICHS, state legislator; b. Holland, Iowa, May 16, 1923; d. John A. and Sophie S. Frerichs; m. Fred H. Doderer, Aug. 5, 1944 (dec. 1991); children: Dennis, Kay Lynn. BA, U. Iowa, 1948. Mem. Iowa Ho. of Reps., 1964-69, 80—, minority whip, 1967-68, chairperson ways and means com., 1983-88, chair commerce com., 1989-90, chair small bus., econ. devel. and trade com., 1991-92; mem. Iowa Senate, 1970-79, pres. pro tem, 1975-76; vis. prof. Stephens Coll., Iowa State Univ. (both 1979); vice-chairwoman Iowa Interstate Cooperation Commn., 1965-66; vice-chairwoman Democratic Party Johnson County, 1957-60; vice chairperson com. on budget and taxation Nat. Conf. State Legislator's; mem. Dem. Nat. Com., 1968-70, Dem. Nat. Policy Council Elected Ofcls., 1973-76; chairwoman Iowa del. Internat. Women's Yr. Del. Bd. fellows Iowa Sch. Religion. Recipient Disting. Svc. award Iowa Edn. Assn., 1969, Wilson award Commn. on Status of Women, 1989, Gold Seal award Iowa Coalition Against Domestic Violence, 1995, Friend of Nursing award, 1996, citation Am. Acad. Pediat., 1996, Woman of Achievement award Bus. and Profl. Women, 1997, medal of honor Vet. Feminists Am., 1999; named to Iowa Women's Hall of Fame, 1978, Woman of Yr., Iowa City Sr. Ctr., 1995. Mem. LWV, Pioneer Lawnmakers (pres. 1993-95), Delta Kappa Gamma (hon.). Democrat. Methodist.

DODGE, ARTHUR BYRON, JR., business executive; b. Lancaster, Pa., June 13, 1923; s. Arthur Byron and Marion Frances (Cochran) D.; m. Margaretha Gerbert, Dec. 28, 1954; children: Arthur B., Andrew Nikolaus. Student, Williams Coll., 1942; BS in Econs., Franklin and Marshall Coll., 1947. With Dodge Cork Co., 1947—, product mgr., 1947-50, factory mgr., 1952-57, mgr. fgn. divsn., 1958-61, v.p., sec., 1961-81, pres., 1981-90; bd. dirs. Dodge-Regupol, Inc., 1989—, chmn., 1990—; bd. dirs., sec. Gerbert, Ltd., Lancaster, 1979—, Intertrade, Inc., Lancaster, 1979-91. Trustee Episcopal Ch. Sch. Found., 1958-85, Lancaster Theol. Sem., 1998—; pres. Friends of SOS Children's Villages, 1979-85, bd. dirs., 1979—; bd. dirs., treas. SOS Children's Villages USA, 1993-98; bd. dirs. 88th Inf. Divsn. Assn., 1988—, pres., 1996-97; pres. Meml. Trust, 1992—. Capt. AUS, 1942-45, 50-52. Decorated Bronze Star with cluster, Purple Heart with cluster, Meritorious Svc. award; battlefield commn. Italy, 1944. Mem. ASTM, Cork Inst. Am. (treas. 1980—), Newcomen Soc., Pa. Soc., Pa. Commn. Employment of Handicapped, Delta Upsilon, Hamilton Club, Lancaster Country Club. Republican. Office: 715 Fountain Ave Lancaster PA 17601-4547

DODGE, CLEVELAND EARL, JR., manufacturing executive; b. N.Y.C., Mar. 7, 1922; s. Cleveland Earl and Pauline (Morgan) D.; m. Phyllis Boushall, Dec. 19, 1942; children: Alice Berkeley, Sally Mole, Cleveland Earl III. B.S. in Mech. Engring., Princeton U., 1943; D Humanics, Springfield Coll., 1996. With DeLaval Steam Turbine Co., 1942, Gen. Electric Co., 1946-51; v.p., dir. Warren Wire Co., Pownal, Vt., 1951-55; pres., dir. Dodge Industries, Inc., Hoosick Falls, N.Y., 1955-67; v.p., dir. Engineered Yarns, Inc., 1962-68; pres. Internat. Dodge, Inc., 1968—, also treas., dir.; pres., dir. Dodge Machine Co., 1968—; pres., bd. dirs. Alta Energy Corp., 1980-89, Amex Plastics Inc., 1972-74, Amm. Hydride Corp., 1991—; bd. dirs. Display Sys., Inc., Imetrix Corp.; pres., bd. dirs. Banded Hub, Internat. Dodge, Inc., Cleeland Corp., Am. Hydride Corp., Dodge Machine Co., Inc., Wild Goose Island Corp. Patentee in field. Pres., bd. dirs. Cleveland H. Dodge Found.; trustee Thousand Island Shipyard Mus.; trustee emeritus, vice chmn. YMCA Retirement Fund, Springfield Coll., Bennington Mus. Lt. USNR, 1943-45. Mem. Princeton Engring. Assn., Princeton Rowing Assn., Laurentian Lodge (Shawbridge, Que., Can.), Taconic Golf Club (Williamstown, Mass.), Kiwanis. Congregationalist. Avocations: skiing, golf, travel. Office: Internat Dodge Inc PO Box 178 Hoosick Falls NY 12090-0178

DODGE, CLIFFORD HOWLE, geologist; b. Lancaster, Pa., Aug. 20, 1950; s. Richard Keller and Nancy Howle D.; m. Christine Miles, Apr. 4, 1981 (div. Aug. 1995). BA, Lehigh U., Bethlehem, Pa., 1972; MS, Northwestern U., Evanston, Ill., 1976. Registered profl. geologist, Pa.; cert. profl. geologist Am. Inst. Profl. Geologists. Hydrologist/geologist U.S. Geol. Survey/Water Resources Divsn., Harrisburg and Meadville, Pa., 1976-79; geologist Pa. Geol. Survey/Dept. Conservation and Natural Resources, Harrisburg, 1979—; expert witness Pa. Dept. Environ. Resources, Harrisburg, 1991, The Carbon/Graphite Group, Inc., Saint Marys, Pa., 1991. Contbr. numerous articles to profl. jours. and publs. Mem. Friends of the Lancaster Cemetery. Mem. Geol. Soc. Am., SEPM Soc. for Sedimentary Geology, History of Earth Sci. Soc., Harrisburg Area Geol. Soc., Demuth Found., Nat. Geog. Soc., Pa. Soc. Sons of the Revolution, Lancaster County Hist. Soc., Elk County Hist. Soc., Beverly Hist. Soc., Friends of the R.R. Mus. Pa., Sigma Xi, Theta Chi. Episcopalian. Home: 145 Primrose Dr Hershey PA 17033-2638 Office: Pa Geol Survey/DCNR PO Box 8453 Harrisburg PA 17105-8453

DODGE, EDWARD JOHN, retired insurance executive; b. Malone, N.Y., Mar. 28, 1935; s. Harry Gilman and Marjorie Dietz (Wright) D.; m. Ann Louise Cupps, Aug. 21, 1932. *Edward's ancestor, Peter Doidge, of Stopworth, Chester, England was knighted and granted a coat of arms on April 8, 1273 by Edward I. The family moved to America in 1629. Family helped establish Beverly, Massachusetts. The family was the largest of financial contributors to Harvard University at its inception. The family fought in every war America was involved in. The family was awarded a Congressional Medal of Honor. His family helped establish the underground railroad. They have been noted for their philanthropy, education, legal, medical, clergy, literary, and business successes. They also surveyed and laid every major railroad west of Mississippi River and in Mexico.* Grad., Phoenix Union H.S., 1953. Map clk. N.Y. Underwriters, San Francisco, 1956-57; underwriter Reliance Ins., San Francisco, 1957-58; agt. Am. Hardware Mut., San Francisco, 1958; investigator Retail Credit Co., 1963-68; claims adjuster Allstate Ins., Arlington Heights, Ill., 1968-70, Epiic Ins., Phoenix, 1974; claims examiner GEICO, Chgo., 1970-73; multi-line adjuster Ariz. Adjustment, Phoenix, 1973-74; investigator Equifax, Chgo., 1974-78; sales br. mgr. Hooper Holmes, Chgo. and Springfield, Ill., 1978-80; multi-line agt. Met. Ins., Springfield, 1980-81; subrogation examiner Horace Mann Ins., Springfield, 1982-97; ret., 1997. *Edward has been involved in progressive industrial education. He trained and worked as a safety engineer and performed criminal investigation, product liability, fire, traffic accident, and disability investigations in and out of the country. He developed a current industry wide theory of psychological dependence on disability payments. He also served in various management positions with different companies and worked with various law enforcement agencies on national, foreign, and local levels to Interpol.* Author: Relief is Greatly Wanted, The Battle of Fort William Henry, 1998; contbr. articles to hist. publs. Commr. Boy Scouts Am., Arlington Heights, Ill., 1971-78, Springfield, 1981-92, Phoenix, 1983-84, vice chmn. scouting, Arlinton Heights, 1977-79, vice chmn. exploring, 1988-90. Sgt. USMC, 1952-56, USAF, 1958-62. Recipient Dist. Commrs. award Boy Scouts Am., 1978, Bronze Big Horn award Boy Scouts Am., 1989, Scouter of Month award Boy Scouts Am., 1978. Mem. Masons, The Queen's Regimental Assn. (hon. life mem.), The Princess of Wale's Royal Regimental Assn. (hon. life mem.). Republican. Methodist. Avocations: historical research, historical writing. Home: 1223 N Rutledge St Springfield IL 62702-2524

DODGE, GEOFFREY A., magazine publisher; b. Newburyport, Mass., Aug. 14, 1960; s. Edward and Sandra (Whitley) D. BA, Babson Coll., Wellesley, Mass., 1983. Ad sales rep. IDG, Boston, 1985-86; pub. Boston Computer News, 1986; sales rep. Fortune, N.Y.C., 1987-89, Washington mgr., 1989-92, N.Y. advt. dir., 1992-94, eastern advt. dir., 1994-95; pub. Money mag., n.Y.C., 1995—. Mem. exec. com. Jr. Achievement, N.Y.C., 1988—. Mem. N.Y. Athletic Club, Rockefeller Center Club, Sleepy Hollow Country Club (Scarborough, N.Y.). Office: Money Time Inc Rockefeller Center New York NY 10020-1393*

DODGE, JAMES WILLIAM, lawyer, educator; b. Springfield, Ill., Sept. 14, 1967; s. James U. and Nancy C. (Donaldson) D.; m. Cynthia Joy Selby, July 19, 1991; children: James A., Adrienne R.M. BS, U. Ill., 1989; JD, So. Ill. U., 1992. Bar: Ill. 1992, U.S. Dist. Ct. (ctrl. dist.) 1992, U.S. Ct. Appeals (7th cir.) 1993, U.S. Tax Ct. 1993. Pvt. practice Springfield, 1992-93; asst. atty. gen. Ill. Atty. Gen.'s Office, Springfield, 1993-97; first asst. state's atty. Christian County State's Atty.'s Office, Taylorville, Ill., 1997-99; legal counsel judiciary com. Ill. Senate Dem. Leader's Office, Springfield, Ill., 1999—; instr. MacMurry Coll., Jacksonville, 1998—; instr. Robert Morris Coll., Springfield, 1993-99. Author: A Brief Survey of Limited Liability Partnership Law in Illinois, 1996; contbr. articles to profl. jours. Ky. Col., Commonwealth of Ky., 1994. Fellow Ill. Bar Found.; mem. ABA, Ill. State Bar Assn. (mem.law-related edn. to pub. com. 1994-97, Christian County Bar Assn. (v.p. 1998—), Ask a Lawyer Day vol. 1994—, h.s. mock trial evaluator 1994—), Sangamon County Bar Assn. (dir. Young Lawyer's divsn. 1993-98), Acad. Legal Studies in Bus., Sangamo Club, Masons, Phi Alpha Delta. Episcopalian. Office: Ill Senate Dem Leader's Office Rm 309 State Capitol Springfield IL 62706

DODGE, PAUL CECIL, academic administrator; b. Granville, N.Y., Mar. 25, 1943; s. Cecil John Paul and Elsie Elizabeth Dodge Rogers; m. Margaret Mary Kostyun, June 6, 1964 (div. Sept. 1985); 1 child, Cynthia Ruth; m. Cynthia Dee Bennett, Apr. 26, 1986; children: Michelle Lynn, Jason Paul, Benjamin Charles. BA in Math., U. Vt., 1967. Mgr. data processing Thermal Wire & Electronics, South Hero, Vt., 1967-70, DDSV divsn. Vt. Cos., Burlington, 1970-73, Revere Copper & Brass, Clinton, Ill., 1973-78, Angelica Corp., St. Louis, 1978-81; pres. chief ops. officer Dodge Mgmt., St. Louis, 1981-82; mgr. systems and programming Terra Internat., 1982-87; pres. chief ops. officer Mo. Tech. Sch., 1987—. Mem. Mo. Assn. Pvt. Career Schs. (pres. 1993-94), Nat. Rehab. Assn., Mo. Rehab. Assn. Republican. Presbyterian. Avocations: amatuer radio, chess. Office: Mo Tech Sch 1167 Corporate Lake Dr Saint Louis MO 63132-1716*

DODGE, PHILIP ROGERS, physician, educator; b. Beverly, Mass., Mar. 16, 1923; s. Israel R. and Anna (McCarthy) D.; children: Susan, Judith. Student, U. N.H., 1941-43, Yale, 1943; M.D., U. Rochester, 1948. Diplomate: Am. Bd. Psychiatry and Neurology. Intern Strong Meml. Hosp., 1948-49; asst. resident neurology Boston City Hosp., 1949-50, resident, 1950, sr. resident, 1951-52; practice medicine, specializing in child neurology Boston, 1956-67, St. Louis, 1967—; teaching fellow neurology Harvard Med. Sch., 1950, 51-53, instr. neurology, 1956-58, assoc. in neurology, 1958-61, asst. prof., 1962-67; asst. neurologist Mass. Gen. Hosp., 1956-59, dir. pediatric neurology program, 1958-67, assoc. neurologist, 1959-63, neurologist, 1963-67, assoc. pediatrician, 1961-62, pediatrician, 1962-67; investigator Joseph P. Kennedy, Jr. Meml. Labs. for Study Mental Retardation, 1962-67; pediatric neurologist Boston Lying-In Hosp., 1961-67; cons. in neurology Walter E. Fernald State Sch. for Retarded Children, 1963-67; med. dir. St. Louis Children's Hosp., 1967-84, pediatrician-in-chief, 1967-86; assoc. neurologist Barnes Hosp., 1967—; chmn. Mallinckrodt Dept. Pediatrics, Washington U. Sch. Medicine, 1967-86, prof. pediatrics and neurology, 1967-93; prof. emeritus pediatrics and neurology Washington U. Sch. Medicine, 1993—; lectr. in pediatrics, 1993—; vis. scientist Clin. Research Center, U. P.R., 1965-66, hon. vis. prof. physiology, 1967; cons. collaborative project on cerebral palsy Nat. Inst. Neurol. Diseases and Blindness, 1958; bd. dirs., chmn. research adv. com. Mass. Soc. for Prevention Cruelty to Children, 1961-67; mem. sci. research adv. bd. Nat. Assn. for Retarded Children, 1963-67; bd. dirs. Central Midwestern Regional Lab., Inc., 1968-70; mem. gen. clin. research centers adv. com. USPHS, 1971-74; mem. Mo. Gov.'s Council on Developmental Disabilities, 1971-74; chmn. Mo. Mental Health Commn., 1974-78; mem. nat. adv. child health and human devel. council NIH, 1974-77; chmn. panel on neurol. disorders, developmental, long-range program strategies NINCDS, 1977-79; panel chmn., consensus devel. conf. on diagnosis and treatment of Reye's Syndrome, 1981; vis. prof. pediatrics and adolescent medicine, Royal Postgrad. Med. Sch., U. London, 1986—; hon. vis. fellow dept. pathology U. Western Australia, Nedlands, Australia, 1986-87; vis. prof. neurology Columbia U. Coll. Physicians and Surgeons, N.Y.C., 1987-88; spl. asst. to dir. for mental retardation Nat. Inst. Child Health and Human Devel., NIH, Washington, 1987-88. Author: (with others) Nutrition and the Developing Nervous System, 1975; Editorial bd.: (with others) Jour. Developmental Medicine and Child Neurology, 1965—, Jour. Pediatrics, 1970-80, Pediatric Research, 1970-78, Current Problems in Pediatrics, 1969-84, Neurology, 1973-76; Contbr. (with others) articles to profl. jours. Served from 1st lt. to maj. M.C. U.S. Army, 1950-56. Mem. Am. Pediatric Soc. (coun. 1972-78, chmn. coun. 1978-79), Am. Acad. Neurology (past com. chmn.), Am. Neurol. Assn., Child Neurology Soc., Assn. for Rsch. in Nervous and Mental Disease, Soc. Pediatric Rsch., Soc. Biol. Psychiatry, St. Louis Soc. Neurol. Scis., Assn. Med. Sch. Pediatric Dept. Chmn. (pres. 1975-77), Alpha Omega Alpha. Home: 410 N Newstead Ave Saint Louis MO 63108-2654 Office: 1 Childrens Pl Saint Louis MO 63110-1002

DODGE, RICHARD EUGENE, oceanographer, educator, marine life administrator; b. Machias, Maine, Mar. 4, 1947; m. Barbara McFadden; children: Kelley, Nathan. BA, U. Maine, 1969; MPhil, Yale U., 1973, PhD in Geology and Geophysics, 1978. Curator paleontology Peabody Mus. Natural History Yale U., 1978; from asst. prof. to assoc. prof. ocean sci. Nova U. Oceanography Ctr., Dania, Fla., 1978-93, prof. ocean sci., 1993—, dir. Inst. Marine & Coastal Studies, 1985, assoc. dir., 1985-98; dean Nova U. Oceanography Ctr., Dania, 1998—; cons. damage to coral reefs from ship groundings; subcontractor dept. energy-ocean thermal energy conversion, U. Miami, 1980-81; field work Red Sea-Saudi Arabia, Vicques, P.R., St. Croix and U.S. V.I. Geol. editor: Coral Reefs. Grantee Geol. Soc. Am., 1974-75, NSF, 1975-77, 79-81, 84-85, 85-86, 89-90, EPA, 1980-82, Nat. Oceanic Atmospheric Adminstrn., 1980-82, Exxon, Bermuda Biol. Sta., 1981-82, Am. Petroleum Inst., 1984-86, White Hall Found., 1985-86, Seagrant, 1989-92, USCS, 1989-91. Mem. AAAS, Am. Soc. Shore and Beach, Internat. Soc. Reef Studies. Achievements include research in ecology, paleoecology, paleoclimatology, and paleobiology of corals and coral reefs; relation of coral growth rate to environment for recent and fossil ecology studies; geology of coral reefs to include structure, zonation, morphology, dating, sea level changes. Office: Nova Southeastern University Instit Marine & Coastal Studies 8000 N Ocean Dr Dania FL 33004-3033

DODGE, STEVEN B., broadcast executive; b. New Haven, Conn.; m. Anne Dodge; children: Tom, Kristen, Ben. BA in English, Yale U., 1967. Founder, CEO Am. Cablesyss. Corp., 1978-88; now chmn., CEO Am. Radio Syss. (now Am. Tower Corp.), 1988—; bd. dirs. Am. Media, Inc., Sensitech, Inc., PageMart Wireless, Inc., Jobson Pub. Trustee Dana Farber Cancer Inst. Lt. USN, 1967-71. Mem. Nat. Assn. Broadcasters (bd. dirs.). Avocations: gardening, reading, biking, building. Office: Am Tower Corp 116 Huntington Ave Fl 11 Boston MA 02116-5749*

DODGE, WILLIAM DOUGLAS, insurance company consultant; b. Savannah, Ga., Sept. 26, 1937; s. Kenneth Douglas and Bettie Wilbur (Sadler) D.; m. Susan Penny, Dec. 27, 1958 (div. 1976); children: Gregory D., Phillip C., Warren D., Andrew L.; m. Marian Elizabeth Monroe, Apr. 2, 1983. BS, Ga. Inst. Tech., 1959; MBA, Ga. State U., 1966. CPCU, ARM. Underwriter Liberty Mutual Ins. Co., Atlanta, 1960-66; ins. adminstr. Lockheed Corp., Marietta, Ga., 1966-78; risk mgr. Schlumberger Ltd., Atlanta, 1978-79; v.p. ins. Fuqua Industries, Inc., Atlanta, 1979-90, v.p. ins. and benefits, 1991-92; pres. Fuqua Ins. Co. Ltd., Hamilton, Bermuda, 1978-92, Fuqua Risk Retention Group, Atlanta, 1989-92; ind. risk mgmt. cons. Atlanta, 1992-95; adv. bd. Risk Mgmt. Inc., N.Y.C., 1978-92; chmn. bd., mem. investment com. J&H WF Syndicate B., N.Y. Ins. Exch., N.Y.C., 1984-88. Co-author: The Hold Harmless Agreement, 1968. Mem. Exec. Com. Reorgn. and Mgmt. Improvement State of Ga., 1971, Agts. Licensing Exam. Revision Bd. State Ga., 1970; bd. dirs. Ednl. Found., 1980-88; lt. comdr. USPS/Tubee Light Power Squadron, 1998-99, comdr., 1999—. Republican. Methodist. Avocations: gardening, boating. Home: 12 Pipers Pond Ln Savannah GA 31404-1122 Office: Mickey Dodge & Assocs Inc 12 Pipers Pond Ln Savannah GA 31404-1122

DODGEN, LARRY J., career officer; b. June 12, 1949. Commd. U.S. Army, advanced through grades to brig. gen., 1998; dep. dir. Joint Theater Air Missile Def. Orgn., Washington, 1998—. Office: Joint Theater Air Missile Def Orgn 8000 Joint Staff Pentagon Washington DC 20318-8000

DODGE ROBBINS, DOROTHY ELLIN, English educator; b. Aug. 16, 1958. MA, U. S.D., 1991; PhD, U. Nebr., 1999. Lectr. Tex. A&M, College Station, 1987-88; asst. prof. English Dakota Wesleyan U., Mitchell, S.D., 1995—. E-mail: dododge@DWU.edu. Office: 1504 Elizabeth Ruston LA 71270

DODOHARA, JEAN NOTON, music educator; b. Monroe, Wis., Feb. 21, 1934; d. Albert Henry and Eunice Elizabeth (Edgerton) Noton; BA, Monmouth (Ill.) Coll., 1955; MS, U. Ill., 1975, adminstrv. cert., 1980, EdD, 1985; m. Laurence G. Landers, June 7, 1955 (div.); children: Theodore Scott, Thomas Warren, Philip John; m. Edward R. Harris, Nov. 27, 1981 (dec.); stepchildren: Adrianne, Erica; m. Takashi Dodohara, Aug. 7, 1988; 1 stepchild, Eve D. Dodohara. Tchr. music schs. in Ill. and Fla., 1955-76; tchr. ch. music for children, 1957-72; tchr. music Dist. 54, Schaumburg, Ill., 1976-93; teaching asst. U. Ill., 1979. Named Outstanding Young Woman of Yr., Jaycee Wives, St. Charles, Mo., 1968; charter mem. Nat. Mus. Women in Arts. Mem. NEA (life), AAUW, Music Educators Nat. Conf. (life), Ill. Educators Assn. (life), Elgin Area Ret. Tchrs. Assn., U. Ill. Alumni Assn. (life), Mortar Bd., Mensa, Delta Kappa Pi. Mem. United Ch. of Christ. Home: 1068 Hampshire Ln Elgin IL 60120-4905

DODS, WALTER ARTHUR, JR., bank executive; b. Honolulu, May 26, 1941; s. Walter Arthur Sr. and Mildred (Phillips) D.; m. Diane Lauren Nosse, Sept. 18, 1971; children: Walter A. III, Christopher L., Peter D., Lauren S. BBA, U. Hawaii, 1967. Mktg. officer 1st Hawaiian Bank, Honolulu, 1969, asst. v.p. mktg. div., 1969-71, v.p., chmn. mktg. and rsch. group, 1971-73, sr. v.p. mktg. and rsch. group, 1973-76, exec. v.p. retail banking group, 1976-78, exec. v.p. gen. banking group, 1978-84, pres., 1984-89, chmn., ceo, 1989—; chmn., pres., CEO First Hawaiian, Inc., 1989-90, chmn., CEO, 1989—; chmn., CEO First Hawaiian Creditcorp., 1989-92; bd. dirs. First Hawaiian Inc., 1st Hawaiian Bank, First Hawaiian Creditcorp Inc., First Hawaiian Leading, Inc., Alexander & Baldwin Inc., A&B-Hawaii Inc., Duty Free Shoppers Adv. Bd., Matson Navigation Co. Inc., 1st Ins. Co. Hawaii Ltd., GTE Calif., GTE Hawaiian Telephone Co., GTE Northwest, Grace Pacific Corp., Oceanic Cablevision Inc., Pacific Guardian Life Ins. Co., Princeville Adv. Group, RHP, Inc., Restaurant Suntory USA, Inc., Suntory Resorts, Inc. Bd. dirs. Ahahui Koa Anuenue, East-West Ctr. Found.; past sec., treas. The Rehab. Hosp. of the Pacific; exec. bd. mem. Aloha Coun., Boy Scouts Am.; trustee, past chmn., trustee Blood Bank Hawaii; past chmn. bd. Aloha United Way; past chmn. Bd. Water Supply; bd. govs., v.p. fin. Ctr. for Internat. Comml. Dispute Resolution; bd. dirs., treas. Coalition for Drug-Free Hawaii; trustee Contemporary Mus. co-chmn. corp. campaign com.; mem. Duty Free Shoppers Adv. Bd.; past chmn. Gubernatorial Inauguration, 1974, 82; bd. govs. Hawaii Employers Coun.; trustee Hawaii Maritime Ctr; mem. Gov.'s Adv. Bd. Geothermal/Inter-Island Cable Project, Gov.'s Blue Ribbon Panel on the Future of Healthcare in Hawaii; dir., past chmn. Hawaii Visitors Bur.; exec. com. Hawaiian Open; past spl. dir. Homeless Kokua Week; bd. gov. Honolulu Country Club, Japanese Cultural Ctr. Hawaii, Pacific Peace Found.; trustee Japan-Am. Inst. Mgmt. Sci., The Nature Conservancy Hawaii, Punahou Sch.; Hawaii chmn. Japan-Hawaii Econ. Coun.; chmn., dir. Pacific Internat. Ctr. for High Tech. Rsch.; past co-chmn., chmn. bldg. fund St. Louis High Sch.; treas. The 200 Club; dir. World Cup Honolulu 1994. Named Outstanding Jaycee in Nation, 1963, Outstanding Young Man Am. from Hawaii, 1972, Marketer of Yr., Am. Mktg. Assn., 1987; recipient Riley Allen Individual Devel. award, 1964, Hawaii State Jaycees 3 Outstanding Young Men award, 1971, Am. Advt. Fedn. Silver medal, 1977, St. Louis High Sch.'s Outstanding Alumnus award, 1980. Mem. Am. Bankers Assn., Bank Mktg. Assn., Hawaii Bankers Assn., Hawaii Bus. Roundtable, C. of C. of Hawaii, Honolulu Press Club. Office: 1st Hawaiian Bank PO Box 3200 Honolulu HI 96847

DODSON, BRUCE J., funeral director; b. Alma, Mich., Oct. 9, 1937; s. Floyd S. and Bertha M. (Van Vynck) D.; m. Carolyn K. McCracken, Jan. 24, 1970; children: Eric, Joshua. AA, Northwood Inst., Midland, Mich., 1961; cert. Mortuary Scis., Wis. Inst. Mortuary Scis., Milw., 1962. Automobile dealer Edmore, Mich., 1955-58; mgr. Stebbins Funeral Home, Stanton, Mich., 1962-69; owner Dodson Funeral Home, St. Ignace, Mich., 1969—; pres. Dist. Funeral Dirs. 9, 1974-78. Mem. Stanton City Coun., 1963-68, St. Ignace City Coun., 1981-83; mem. Gov.'s Task Force for Mackinac Bridge Fin., 1986-87; mayor City of St. Ignace, 1983—; chmn. Mackinac Straits Hosp. Bd., 1989-91, vice chmn., 1991-92; co-founder St. Ignace Antique Auto Show, 1976—; mem. Mackinac County Bldg. Authority, 1993-98; chair, 1995-96. Named St. Ignace Citizen of the Yr. C. of C., 1992. Mem. Nat. Funeral Dirs. Assn., Mich. Funeral Dirs. Assn. (bd. govs. 1978-81), Mich. Assn. Mayors, Automobile Club Am. (life, nat. judge), Classic Car Club Am., Motor City Packard Club (charter), Family Motor Coach Assn. (life), Great Lakes Cruising Club. Methodist. Avocations: antique automobiles, model trains, Great Lakes boating. Home and Office: 240 Mccann St Saint Ignace MI 49781-1651

DODSON, CARL EDWARD, nuclear engineer, real estate agent, executive, minister, assistant superintendent; b. Chgo., July 8, 1956; s. John Eddie and Birdie (Dodson) Allen; m. Peggy E. Dodson; children: LaTressa, Letiticia, LaTonya, Carl Jr., Barry. A in Engring., State Tech. Inst. at Memphis, 1980. Lic. FCC 3d class, lic. Tenn. Bd. Realtors; ordained elder. Engring. aide Spl. Design, Knoxville, Tenn., 1980-82, Sequoyah Nuclear Plant, Knoxville, Tenn., 1982-84; design engr. Sequoyah Nuclear Plant, Soddy, Tenn., 1985-88; real estate agt. Holmes Real Estate Co., Knoxville, Tenn., 1989-91; pres., chief exec. officer Ezra Inc., Knoxville, 1990-91; sr. technician, analyst Weston Gulf Coast, University Park, Ill., 1992-94; pharm. technician Centeon, Kankakee, Ill., 1994-96; assoc. pastor Shiloh Full Gospel Bapt. Ch., Kankakee; asst. superintendent Public Works, Kankakee, 1996—. Author (software): New Student, 1980. Mem. Nat. Inst. Certification in Engring. Technologies, Jaycees (Chattanooga). Avocations: chess, reading, computer programming, bowling, photography. Home: 354 S 5th Ave Kankakee IL 60901-3647

DODSON, D. KEITH, engineering and construction company executive; b. Greenville, Tex., Nov. 2, 1943; s. Durwood R. and Louise (Amos) D.; m. Johnette Foster, Aug. 31, 1968; children: J. Marshall, Chandos A. B in Bus. and Engring., U. Tex., 1966; postgrad. in bus., U. Houston. Various positions leading to pres. internat. land ops. div. Brown & Root Inc., Houston, 1966-88; pres., chief exec. officer petroleum and chems. U.S.A. John Brown E&C, Houston, 1988-94; v.p. venture op. M.W. Kellogg Co., Houston, 1994-95; CEO M.W. Kellogg, London, 1995-97; pres. Dresser Kellogg Energy Svcs., Houston, 1997-98; mng. dir. Kellogg Devel. Corp., Houston, 1998-98; sr. v.p. Stone & Webster Engring. Corp., Houston, 1998—; mem. engring. found. adv. coun. U. Tex., Austin, 1991—, chmn. 1994—; chmn. U. Tex. Austin, 1994-95. Chmn. exec. com. Constrn. Industry Inst., Austin, Tex., 1991; bd. dirs. world trade divsn. Greater Houston Partnership, 1993-94; chmn. Gov. Forum Club Houston, 1993-94. Mem. Am. Inst. Chem. Engrs. (exec. bd. dirs. engring. and constrn. conf. 1985-89), Petroleum Club (Houston), Lakeside Country Club (Houston), Royal Automobile Club (London). Home: 32 W Oak Dr Houston TX 77056-2118 Office: Stone & Webster Engring Corp 1430 Enclave Pkwy Houston TX 77077-2023

DODSON, DARYL THEODORE, ballet administrator, arts consultant; b. Warrensburg, Mo., Oct. 9, 1934; s. Theodore and Ada Marie (Ayres) D. BS, Cen. Mo. State U., 1956. mem. Gov. S.C.'s Coun. of the Arts, 1974; mem. adv. panel Vt. Coun. on Arts, 1978; mgr. Am. tour 1st cultural exch., People's Republic of China and U.S., 1978, Nat. Ballet Cuba, 1979, Royal Ballet Eng., 1981; pres. Pine Cone Enterprises, Ltd., 1977-81; propr. Pine Cone Inn, Haverhill, N.H., 1978-81; mgr. Opera House, John F. Kennedy Ctr., Washington, 1981; mgr. U.S. and Can. tour Sweeney Todd, 1982; mgr. U.S. tours Amadeus, 1982-83, The Wiz, 1983-84, Les Miserables, 1988-92, Phantom of the Opera, 1992-99; mgr. N.Y. engagement The Golden Land, 1985; mgr. Porgy and Bess, 1986-87, La Cage Aux Folles, 1987, N.Y. and U.S. tour Paris Opera Ballet, 1988; gen. mgr. John Curry Skating Co., 1984. Asst. dir. The Mikado, N.Y.C. Opera, 1959; regisseur Chgo. Opera Ballet, 1960, asst. stage mgr. Am. Ballet Theatre, N.Y.C., 1960, stage mgr., 1961, prodn. stage mgr., 1961, prodn. mgr., 1963, gen. mgr., 1968-77. Served with U.S. Army, 1957-59. Mem. Theta Chi, Theta Alpha Phi. Episcopalian. Home: On The Commons Haverhill NH 03765 Office: 1650 Broadway Ste 800 New York NY 10019-6833

DODSON, DONALD MILLS, restaurant executive; b. Shamrock, Tex., Nov. 2, 1937; s. Freeman Mills and Marvie Hazel (Rives) D.; m. Sharon Jane Webb, Feb. 6, 1961; children—Randal, Stephanie, Kendal. Student, Tex. Tech. Trainee Furrs Bishops Cafeteria, Odessa, Tex., 1958, asst. mgr., 1958-59; mgr. Furrs Cafeteria, Odessa, Lubbock, Tucson, Denver, 1959-68; dist. mgr. Furrs Cafeteria, Lubbock, Tex., 1968-75, v.p. region, 1975-77, v.p. personnel devel., 1977-82, exec. v.p. ops., 1982—, sr. exec. v.p. ops., chief oper. officer support depts., 1987-90, regional v.p. West Tex. and Ea. New Mex., 1990—; sr. v.p. food and beverage Furrs Cafeteria, Lubbock, 1990—, divisional v.p., 1991-92; v.p. ops. Furrs Cafeteria, Richardson, Tex., 1993—. Mem. Nat. Restaurant Assn., Tex. Restaurant Assn. *

DODSON, GEORGE WAYNE, computer company executive, consultant; b. Danville, Ill., Jan. 21, 1937; s. Maurice Keith and Marjorie Ruth (Ingalsbe) D.; m. Evandra May Mendenhall, Aug. 4, 1957; children: Michael, Curtis, Janet. BS in Math., U. Ill., 1966; MS in Ops. Rsch., Union Coll., 1970. Statis. mgr. U. Ill., Urbana, 1960-66; sr. performance anayst IBM Corp., Poughkeepsie, N.Y., 1966-70, performance mgr., 1970-79; lab. performance mgr. IBM Corp., Tucson, 1979-85; program mgr. IBM Corp., Roanoke, Tex., 1987-91, prin. info. systems mgmt. cons., 1991-93; prin. info. systems mgmt. cons. IBM Consulting Group, Dallas, 1994-96; dir. tech. svcs. Morino Assocs., Vienna, Va., 1985-86; dir. performance products UCCEL Corp., Dallas, 1986-87; prin. IBM Global Svcs., 1996-97; dir. info. tech. mgmt. consulting Candle Corp., Dallas, 1997—. Mem. Computer Measurement Group (chmn. 1983, 89, pres. 1983-85, bd. dirs. 1985-89, treas. 1990-95, A.A. Michelson award lifetime achievement 1997). Avocations: softball, music, photography. Office: Candle Corp 12790 Merit Dr Dallas TX 75251-1226

DODSON, HERSHA RHEE, psychiatric-mental health nurse; b. Pecos, Tex., Feb. 18, 1939; d. Herschel W. and Marjorie E. (Jarrell) Woods; m. Louis Dean Dodson, July 2, 1962 (dec. Nov. 1973); children: Raina Elise, Farley Duane. Diploma, Shannon Sch. Nursing, San Angelo, Tex., 1963; B in Applied Arts and Sci., Midwestern State U., Wichita Falls, Tex., 1986; M in Counseling, St. John's U., Springfield, La., 1996. RN, Tex.; cert. psychiat. and mental health nurse. Shift nurse supr. Wichita Falls State Hosp.; adolescent nurse coord. Red River Psychiat. Hosp.-HCA, Wichita Falls; staff nurse adolescent unit Sun Valley Regional Hosp.-HCA, El Paso, Tex.; coord., psychiat. nurse Tex. Dept. Mental Health and Mental Retardation, Van Horn, 1990—; part-time nurse El Paso (Tex.) State Ctr., 1994-98, El Paso Psychiat. Ctr., 1998. Home: PO Box 234 Van Horn TX 79855-0234

DODSON, SAMUEL ROBINETTE, III, investment banker; b. Nashville, Feb. 24, 1943; s. Samuel Robinette and Helen Elizabeth (Maiden) D.; m. Marsha Robertson Moody, Aug. 2, 1969; children—Bradley John, Andrew Caldwell. Student, Yale U., 1961-63; B.S., Vanderbilt U., 1966; M.B.A., U. Chgo., 1968; M.S., London Sch. Econs., 1968. Various fin. and planning positions Exxon Corp. and Affiliates, Houston, 1968-81; v.p. First Boston Corp., 1981-84, mng. dir., 1984-93; mng. dir. Merrill Lynch, Houston, 1993—. Served to 1st lt. U.S. Army, 1963-64.

DODSON, VERNON NATHAN, physician, educator; b. Benton Harbor, Mich., Feb. 19, 1923; m. Shirley Jane Wheelihan; children: Martha Ione, Kathryn Anne, Christine Louise, John Nathan, Elizabeth Marie. Student, Mich. State Coll., 1941-43, 46, Northwestern U., summer 1942, Compton (Calif.) Coll., 1943, U. Oreg., 1943-44, Corpus Christi Coll., U. Oxford, Eng., 1945, U. Mich., 1946-47, 48, 51-52; BS, U. Mich., 1952; MD, Marquette U., 1951. Intern in surgery Henry Ford Hosp., Detroit, 1952-53; asst. in pathology Johns Hopkins U. Hosp., Balt., 1953-54, asst. pathologist, 1953-54; resident in internal medicine Univ. Hosp., Ann Arbor, Mich., 1954-57; rsch. assoc. U. Mich. Med. Sch., Ann Arbor, 1957-60, 60-71, lectr., 1959, from jr. clin. instr. to assoc. prof., 1956-64, assoc. prof. Dept. Indsl. Health, Sch. Pub. Health, 1965-71; attending physician U.S. VA Hosp., Ann Arbor, 1961-70; mem. med. staff Milw. County Gen. Hosp., 1971-72; rsch. assoc. U.S. VA Ctr., Wood, Wis., 1971-72; prof. medicine and environ. medicine Med. Coll. Wis., Milw., 1971-72; vis. prof. dept. preventive medicine U. Wis. Med. Sch., Madison, 1973-74, prof. medicine, sect. internal medicine, and preventive medicine, 1977-94, prof. emeritus medicine and preventive medicine, 1994—; lectr. Sch. Dentistry, U. Mich., Ann Arbor, 1957-58, Sch. Nursing, U. Mich., 1958-60, Coll. Lit., Sci. and Arts, Inst. Social Work, U. Mich., 1957-58; cons. staff physician Rochester, Minn. Meth. Hosp., 1974-77; dir. Univ. Employee Health Svc., U. Wis., Madison, 1977-80, mem. staff Ctr. Health Sci., 1978-95, hon. staff, 1995—; physician cons. VA Hosp., Madison, 1978-95; mem. interdepartmental program in toxicology, U. Mich., 1965-71, vice chair, 1969-71; mem. Environ. Toxicology Ctr., Divsn. Health Scis., U. Wis., Madison, 1972-74, 77-94, acting dir., 1974-76, 78-79, assoc. dir. Sch. Biotron., 1979-84; vis. prof. U. Tex. Health Sci. Ctr., Sch. Pub. Health, Houston, 1986, So. Occupational Health Ctr., U. Calif., Irvine, 1986; mem. com. on edn. and libr., Trinity Meml. Hosp., Cudahy, Wis., 1971-71, assoc. med. staff, 1972-73; mem. assoc. med. staff St. Lukes Hosp., Milw., 1972-73; cons. Joint Commn. on Hosp. Accreditation, Chgo., 1974-76; cons. in preventive medicine and internal medicine, Mayo Clinic, Mayo Found., Rochester, 1974-77; cons. GM, Warren, Mich., 1963-65, 72-84, med. dir. GM, Oak Creek, Wis., 1971-72; cons. Oscar Mayer Co., 1973-74; cons. plant physician, IBM, Rochester, 1976-77; cons. med. dir. George A. Hormel co., Austin, Minn., 1977; mem. occupational health adv. bd. GM, UAW, 1982-85; cons. Owens-Corning Fiberglas, Toledo, 1968—, Gen. Mills, Mpls., 1980—; bd. dirs. Nat. Biogerontology Inst., 1984—; cons. USPHS, Dept. Natural Resources, Wis., Dept. Health and Social Svcs., Wis., U.S. Dept.

Agr., OSHA, Wis., Nat. Inst. Occupational Safety and Health, Ctr. for Disease Control, Dept. Industry, Labor and Human Rels., Wis.; mem. Gov.'s Task Force on Occupational Health and Safety, State of Wis., Extramural Ctr. Adv. Rev. Panel, Nat. Inst. for Occupational Health and Safety, Sentinel Event Notification System for Occupational Risks, Divsn. Health, State Dept. Health and Social Svc., Madison, Wis.; vice chair Residency Rev. Com. for Preventive Medicine, Accreditation Coun. for Gen. Med. Edn. Edn. cons. editor Am. Jour. Occupational Medicine, 1979-89; assoc. editor Am. Jour. Indsl. Medicine, 1986-80; author 2 books, 17 book chpts., 44 sci. rsch. papers, 119 abstracts and presentations, 4 TV programs; co-editor 1 book. Mem. spl. citizen's adv. com. on safety Ann Arbor Bd. Edn., 1969, gov.'s com. on crime detection and law enforcement, ad hoc com. on lab. svcs., State of Mich., 1969; chmn., mem. com. on sch. safety, King Sch., Ann Arbor, 1969-70; mem. Kettle Moraine High Sch. Band Parents, Wales, Wis., 1972-74, v.p., 1973-74, citizen's com. on drug abuse, Waukesha County, Wis., 1973-74. With U.S. Army, 1942-45, ETO. Recipient Disting. Svc. award, Occupational Health award UAW, GM, 1988. Fellow ACP, Am. Coll. Occupl. Medicine (bd. dirs. 1987—, award 1988), Am. Coll. Medicine, Am. Occupl. Medicine Assn. (bd. govs. 1985, award 1988), Am. Coll. Occupl. and Environ. Medicine, Am. Coll. Preventive Medicine, Soc. Occupl. and Environ. Health; mem. AAAS, AMA (rep. residency rev. com., vice chair accreditation coun. for gen. med. edn., Physician's Recognition award 1981—), Am. Fedn. for Clin. Rsch., The Biochem. Soc. (London), Wis. State Med. Soc. (environ./occupl. health commn., legis. affairs commn., continuing med. edn. commn., Meritorious Svc. award 1991, 96), Ctrl. States Occupl. Medicine Assn. (bd. govs.), Dane County Med. Soc., Am. Pub. Health Assn., Wis. Pub. Health Assn., Am. Cancer Soc. (award 1987), Internat. Commn. for Occupl. Health (Geneva), alumnae orgns. Mich. State U., U. Mich., Marquette U., Johns Hopkins U., Mayo Clinic, Med. Coll. Wis., U. Wis., Henry Ford Hosp., VFW, 11th Armored Divsn. Assn., Friends of WHA-TV, Smithsonian Instn., Nat. Geog. Soc., World Wildlife Fund, Sierra Club, Natural Resource Def. Coun., Sigma Xi. Office: U Wis Dept Medicine 504 Walnut St Madison WI 53705-2335

DODSON, W(ILLIAM) EDWIN, child neurology educator; b. Durham, N.C., Dec. 23, 1941; s. Howard William and Mildred (Sorrell) D.; m. Doreen Carol Davis, June 4, 1964 (div. May 1976); children: Anna Elizabeth, William Edwin Jr., Jason David; m. Sandra Schorr (div.); children: Steven Gage, Matthew Sorrell. AB, Duke U., 1963, MD, 1967. Intern Children's Hosp., Boston, 1967-68, resident in pediat., 1970-71; resident, fellow in child neurology Barnes Hosp. and St. Louis Children's Hosp., 1971-75; asst. prof. child neurology Washington U., St. Louis, 1975-80, resident in pediat., 1970-71, assoc. prof., 1980-86, prof. child neurology, 1986—; assoc. dean admissions and fin. aid Washington U. Sch. Medicine, St. Louis, 1990—; assoc. vice-chancellor for continuing edn. Washington U. Sch. Medicine, St. Louis, 1997—; bd. dirs. Family Resource Ctr., St. Louis, Physicians Corp., Washington U. Alliance Corp., First Tier Health Corp., Grace Hill Health Ctr., Nat. Com. to Prevent Child Abuse, Mo.; pres. bd. dirs. St. Louis Child Abuse Network. Mem. editorial bd. Annals of Neurology and Clinical Neuropharmacology; contbr. articles to profl. jours. Bd. dirs. City St. Louis Bd. Children's Welfare, 1984-86; mem. profl. adv. bd. Epilepsy Found. Am., 1987-94, chmn.-elect, 1991-93, pres.-elect, 1993-95, pres. 1995-97, chmn. bd., 1997-98; co-chmn. Blue Ribbon Commn. on Future Svcs. to Children & Families, Mo., 1987-88; chmn. Children's Trust Fund Mo., 1989-91, bd. dirs., 1985-91. Recipient Spl. Recognition award State of Md., 1971, Career Acad. Devel. award NIH, 1975, Disting. Social Svcs. award Mo. Dept. Social Svcs., 1988, Child Adv. award St. Louis Child Abuse Network, 1990, Child Adv. award Family Resource Ctr., 1991, Spl. Recognition award Epilepsy Fedn. St. Louis, 1992, Guardian Angel award St. Louis Family Support Network, 1999, Samuel Clemmens award Epilepsy Found., St. Louis, 1999. Fellow Am. Acad. Neurology, Am. Acad. Pediatrics; mem. Child Neurology Soc. (bd. dirs. 1985-87), Am. Neurol. Assn., Soc. Pediatric Research, Cen. Soc. Neurol. Research (sec., treas. 1985, pres. 1989), Alpha Omega Alpha. Avocations: fly fishing, water sports, photography. Office: St Louis Childrens Hosp One Childrens Pl Saint Louis MO 63110-1014

DOEBLER, BETTIE ANNE, language educator, researcher, writer; b. Atlantic City, N.J.; d. Willoughby Foster and Ann Bailey (Ratledge) Young; m. John W. Doebler, Sept. 1, 1954 (dec. Aug. 26, 1994); 1 child, Mark B. BA, Duke U., 1953, MA, 1955; PhD, U. Wis., 1961. From instr. to assoc. prof. Dickinson Coll., Carlisle, Pa., 1961-70; assoc. prof. Ariz. State U., Tempe, 1971, prof., 1975, prof. emeritus, 1994—, dir. interdisciplinary humanities program, 1989-94. Author: The Quickening Seed: Death in the Sermons of John Donne, 1974, Rooted Sorrow: Dying in Early Modern England, 1994; contbr. articles to profl. jours.; author of poems to literary jours. Angier B. Duke Grad. fellow Duke U., 1954; recipient Faculty Rsch. award Ariz. State U., 1984. Episcopalian. Office: Ariz State U Dept English Tempe AZ 85287

DOEBLER, PAUL DICKERSON, publishing management executive; b. Milw., July 3, 1930; s. Paul Henry and Grace Elizabeth (Whittaker) D.; m. Aileen Mary Hunt, May 15, 1958 (dec. 1966); m. Terry Gerda Moss, Dec. 15, 1967. B.S. in Journalism, Northwestern U., 1953; B.S. in Printing Mgmt., Carnegie-Mellon U., 1956. Editor-in-chief Book Prodn. Industry mag. Penton Pub. Co., N.Y.C., 1965-71; pub. mgmt. cons. N.Y.C., 1972-80; mgr. bus. devel. R.R. Bowker subs. Xerox, N.Y.C., 1980-82, editor-in-chief profl. books, 1983-84; pub. cons. Xerox Systems Group, El Segundo, Calif., 1984-85, mgr. documentation systems, 1985-86, mgr. documentation systems mktg., 1986-89; pres. Paul Doebler Enterprises, Camarillo, Calif., 1990—; instr. Assn. Am. Pubs., 1985, CCNY, 1980-85; guest lectr. The Writing Program MIT, 1988-90; instr. learning Tree U., 1997—. Contbr. articles to mags. Mem. Carnegie Printers Alumni Assn. (pres. 1972). Home: 6343 Gitana Ave Camarillo CA 93012-8135

DOEDE, JOHN HENRY, investment company executive; b. Chgo., Sept. 29, 1937; s. Clinton Milford and Dorothy Ruth (Hagemeyer) D.; m. Jean Anne Dabbs, May 6, 1983; children: Danna, Tina, Timothy. AB in Chemistry, Harvard U., 1959; MS in Phys. Chemistry, U. Chgo., 1962, PhD in Phys. Chemistry, Physics, 1963. Physicist Argonne (Ill.) Nat. Lab., 1963-65; mgr. EMR computer div. (electro magnetic rsch.) Schlumberger Corp., Mpls., 1965-67; pres. Data Internat. Inc., Mpls., 1967-70; v.p. Heizer Corp., Chgo., 1970-72; v.p., dir. 1st Chgo. Investment Corp., 1972-83; pres. The Polaris Capital Group, San Diego, 1983-88; chmn. JDJD, Inc., Palm Beach, Fla., 1992-97, Blue Eagle Golf Ctrs., Inc., Wayne, Pa., 1996-98, AIG Silk Road Fund, N.Y.C., 1997—. Republican. Home: 8480 N Canta Bello Paradise Valley AZ 85253-8118

D'OENCH, RUSSELL GRACE, JR., publishing consultant; b. N.Y.C., Feb. 16, 1927; s. Russell Grace and Dorothie (Sharp) D'O.; m. Ellen Gates, Sept. 10, 1949; children: Peter, Ellen, Russell Grace III. LittD (hon.), Wilcox Coll. Nursing, 1993. Reporter Berkshire Eagle, Pittsfield, Mass., 1947-52; pub., editor Sunnyvale (Calif.) Standard, 1952-56; pres. Sagamore Press, Inc., N.Y.C., 1956-58; editor, chmn. bd. dirs. Middletown (Conn.) Press, 1959-91; chmn. Dormers Corp., Middleton, 1992—; mem. Middletown adv. bd. Conn. Nat. Bank, chmn., 1982-86; vis. lectr. Wesleyan U., 1967-71; corporator Farmers and Mechanics Bank, Middletown, 1960-93; bd. dirs. Middlesex Mutual Assurance Co., Conn. Acad. for Edn. in Math., Sci. and Tech., Middlesex County Cmty. Found.; chmn. Middletown 2000. Contbg. author: Read All About It. Chmn. bd. dirs. Wilcox Coll. Nursing, 1991-94; mem. trustees coun. Conn. Conf. Ind. Colls., 1992-94; bd. dirs. Goodspeed Opera Found., Conn. Pub. Expenditure Coun., 1965-67, 89-93; past bd. dirs. Conn. Student Loan Found., Conn. Humanities Coun., Conn. Hosp. Assn.; bd. dirs. Govs. for Higher Edn., 1983-88, chmn., 1983-85; pres. Middleton Found. for Arts, 1984—; active Commn. to Study Higher Edn., Conn. Gov.'s Commn. on Higher Edn. and Economy; past chmn. Conn. Joint Com. on Edn1. Tech. With USMC, 1945-46. Mem. Am. Soc. Newspaper Editors, Sigma Delta Chi (Conn. chpt., past sec.). Home: 147 Phedon Pky Middletown CT 06457-2450 Office: Dormers Corp PO Box 271 Portland CT 06480-0271

DOENECKE, JUSTUS D., history educator; b. Bklyn., Mar. 5, 1938. BA magna cum laude, Colgate U., 1960; MA, Princeton U., 1962, PhD, 1966. Instr. history Colgate U., 1963-64; instr. history Ohio Wesleyan U., 1965-66, asst. prof. history, 1966-69; asst. prof. history New Coll., Sarasota, Fla., 1969-71; assoc. prof. history New Coll., Sarasota, 1971-75; assoc. prof. history New Coll. Univ. South Fla., Sarasota, 1975-77, prof. history, 1977—. Author: Not to the Swift: The Old Isolationists in the Cold War Era, 1979, The Diplomacy of Frustration: The Manchurian Crisis of 1931-1933 as Revealed in the Papers of Stanley K. Hornbeck, 1981, The Presidencies of James A. Garfield and Chester A. Arthur, 1981, When the Wicked Rise: American Opinion-Makers and the Manchurian Crisis of 1931-33, 1984, Anti-Intervention: A Bibliographical Introduction to Isolationism and Pacifism from World War I to the Early Cold War, 1987, In Danger Undaunted: The Anti-Interventionist Movement of 1940-41 as Revealed in the Papers of the America First Committee, 1990, From Isolation to War, 1931-1941, 1991, The Battle Against Intervention, 1939-41, 1997; contbr. articles to profl. jours. Woodrow Wilson Nat. fellow, 1960, Danforth fellow, 1960, Non-resident summer fellow Inst. for Humane Studies, 1970, 71, resident summer fellow Inst. for Humane Studies, 1975, 76, 78, 81, sr. rsch. fellow acad. yr. Inst. for Humane Studies, 1977-78, summer fellow NEH, 1971, fellow John Anton Kittridge Ednl. Fund, 1973-80, Harry S. Truman Libr., 1973, Earhart Found., 1995, vis. fellow New Coll., Oxford, 1991; Shell Oil Rsch. grantee, 1975. Mem. Soc. for Historians Am. Fgn. Rels. (program co-chair 1986, Link award com. 1992—, Arthur S. Link prize for documentary editing 1991), Am. Hist. Assn., Am. Soc. Ch. History, Hist. Soc. Episcopal Ch., Hist. Soc., Conf. on Peace Rsch. in History (coun. 1966-69, 75-89), Phi Beta Kappa. E-mail: doenecke@virtu.sar.usf.edu. Fax: 941-359-4475. Office: New Coll Univ South Fla Sarasota FL 34243-2197

DOENGES, BYRON FREDERICK, economist, educator, former government official; b. Ft. Wayne, Ind., June 18, 1922; s. Arthur Philip and Elsie (Mesing) D.; m. Elaine Aiken, June 15, 1947. Diploma, Internat. Bus. Coll., 1941; student, DePauw U., 1943-44; AB, Franklin (Ind.) Coll., 1946; MBA, Ind. U., 1948, PhD, 1962; DLtrs (hon.), Franklin Coll. of Ind., 1985. Instr., headmaster boarding dept. Punahou Sr. Acad., Honolulu, 1948-50; dir. scholarships and loans Ind. U., Bloomington, 1951-56, asst. dean Coll. Arts and Scis., 1955-65; prof. econs., dean Coll. Liberal Arts Willamette U., 1965-71; econ. cons. Gov. Oreg., 1971-72; dep. asst. dir. ACDA, Washington, 1972-73; chief econs. and spl. studies div. ACDA, 1973-76; sr. econs. advisor U.S. Arms Control and Disarmament Agy., 1976-93; ind. writer and internat. econ. cons., 1993—; program devel. head Title II NDEA, U.S. Office Edn., Washington, 1958-59; assoc. dir. Salzburg (Austria) Seminar Am. Studies, 1962-64; mem. Higher Commn. N.W. Assn. Secondary and Higher Schs., 1968-71; mem. exec. bd. N.W. Assn. Pvt. Colls. and Univs., 1969-70; chmn. planning com. Navy V-12 Nat. Colloquium, 1989; conduct spl. rsch. on internat. capital movements, econs. higher edn., econs. arms control, Soviet and successor states to former Soviet Union economies, econ. impact of def. spending. Editor: Accountability, 1973, World Military Expenditures and Arms Transfers, 1981-84, Arms Control Ann. Report, 1981-91, Arms Control Impact Statement for the Congress, 1991; contbr. articles to profl. jours. Lt. comdr. USNR, 1943-46, PTO. Recipient alumni citation Franklin Coll., 1977. Mem. Am. Econ. Assn., Cosmos Club (Washington), Lambda Chi Alpha (mem. nat. fellowship bd. 1965—, Meritorious Svc. award 1984), Pi Gamma Mu, Omicron Delta Kappa. Home: 1002 Fearrington Post Pittsboro NC 27312-5503 Office: 4 E Madison Pittsboro NC 27312

DOENGES, RUDOLPH CONRAD, finance educator; b. Tonkawa, Okla., Dec. 7, 1930; s. Rudolph Soland and Helen Elizabeth (Lower) D.; m. Ellen Ione Gummere, Oct. 5, 1963; children: Rudolph Conrad, John Soland, William Gummere. A.B. magna cum laude (scholar 1948-54), Harvard U., 1952, M.B.A., 1954; D.B.A. (Ford Found. fellow 1963-64), U. Colo., Boulder, 1965. Mktg. analyst Ford Motor Co., Dearborn, Mich., 1954; gen. mgr. Doenges-Long Motors and Western Auto Rentals, Colorado Springs, 1958-61; mem. faculty U. Tex., Austin, 1964—; prof. fin. U. Tex., 1974—, Arthur Andersen & Co. prof. fin., 1983—, assoc. dean Grad. Sch. Bus., 1972-76, chmn. dept. fin., 1976-80, assoc. dean Coll. Bus. Adminstrn., 1987-97. Author: (with E. W. Walker) Case Problems in Financial Management, 1968, Consumer Credit in Texas, 1970; editor: Readings in Money and Banking, 1968, (with H. A. Wolf) Corporate Planning Models, 1971; contbr. articles in field to profl. jours. Gen. Bd. Pensions United Meth. Ch., 1988-96; trustee Iliff Sch. Theology, 1992-96. Served with USN, 1955-58. Mem. Austin C. of C., Fin. Mgmt. Assn. (dir. 1980-82), Southwestern Fin. Assn. (pres. 1973-74), Southwestern Fedn. Adminstrv. Disciplines (pres. 1975-76), Austin Soc. Fin. Analysts, El Paso Club (Colorado Springs), Austin Club, Garden of the Gods Club. Republican. Methodist. Home: 3500 Hillbrook Cir Austin TX 78731-4036 Office: U Tex Dept Finance Austin TX 78712*

DOEPKE, KATHERINE LOUISE GULDBERG, choral director, former music educator; b. Suttons Bay, Mich., Dec. 18, 1921; d. Gottfred Johannes and Aasta Agnethe (Kalstad) Guldberg; m. Henry August Doepke, Aug. 13, 1944; children: Karen Sernett, Chris, Bruce, Barbara Potuck. BS, U. Minn., 1944, MA, 1967, postgrad. Tchr. music Mpls. Pub. Schs., 1963-83; choral dir. Trinity First Luth. Ch., Mpls., 1953-92; cons./mentor Mpls. Pub. Schs., 1984-87; organizer, producer 3 jr. high sch. honors choirs Am. Choral Dirs. Assn., 1986, 88, 89. Editor monograph; author curriculum materials; composer children's musicals for sch. and ch., 1966-96; contbr. articles to profl. jours. Vol. Courage Ctr., Mpls., 1983-86, Food at Your Door, 1984-88; dir. Gray Aires Chorus, Mpls. 1986-95; bd. dirs., publicity chair, mem. various coms. Thursday Musical, 1984—, pres., 1998—. Named composer in residence Mpls. Pub. Schs., 1985. Mem. AAUW (chair coms., prodr. anniversary video 1997), Am. Choral Dirs. Assn. (state sec.-treas., historian, sec. F.M. Christiansen Endowment Fund com.), Music Educators Nat. Conf. (clinician 1976, 78, 80), Mu Phi Epsilon (internat. pres. 1992-95). Lutheran. Avocations: computer composing, walking, reading. Home: 8300 Golden Valley Rd #329 Minneapolis MN 55429

DOERFLER, LEO G., audiology educator; b. N.Y.C., June 25, 1919; s. Gustav S. and Anna (Steiner) D.; m. Alice Laura Turechek, Dec. 19, 1943; children—Dennis Lee, Donald Lee, David Lee, Ann Laura. A.B., N.Y.U., 1939; M.S., Washington U., St. Louis, 1941; Ph.D., Northwestern U., 1948. Tchr.- psychologist Iowa Sch. Deaf, Council Bluffs, 1941-43; instr. audiology Northwestern U., 1946-48; chief dept. audiology-speech pathology Latrobe Area Hosp., 1976—; prof. audiology emeritus (Sch. Medicine); dir. doctoral program bioacoustics U. Pitts., 1948-76; dir. dept. audiology Eye and Ear Hosp., Pitts., 1948-76; pres. Westmoreland Hearing Assocs.; chmn. bd. Audiology Coop.; Cons. in field, 1946—, Nat. Inst. Neurol. and Communicative Diseases and Stroke. Contbr. articles to profl. jours. Bd. dirs. Cerebral Palsy Assn. Pitts., 1958—. Served with AUS, World War II. C.C. Bunch fellow Northwestern U., 1946-47. Fellow AAAS, Am. Speech and Hearing Assn. (pres. 1967); mem. Am. Indsl. Hygiene Assn. (com. on noise), Indsl. Med. Assn. (com. on noise), Am. Acad. Ophthalmology and Otolaryngology (com. on hearing and equilibrium), Am. Bd. Examiners in Speech Pathology and Audiology (pres. 1960), Acad. Dispensing Audiologists (pres. 1978-79), Sigma Xi. Inventor D-S test for psychogenic deafness. Home: 4533 W Barlind Dr Pittsburgh PA 15227-1131

DOERING, CHARLES HENRY, research scientist, educator, editor, publisher; b. Munich, Germany, Jan. 7, 1935; came to U.S., 1950; s. Heinrich and Marianne (Fleischmann) D.; m. Panayiota Maria Thliveris, June 17, 1961; children: Andreanna, Erika, Stefan, Anselm. BS in Chemistry, U. San Francisco, 1956; MS in Organic Chemistry, U. Munich, 1959; PhD in Biochemistry, U. Calif., San Francisco, 1964. Postdoctoral fellow Harvard Med. Sch., Boston, 1964-67; rsch. scientist Stanford (Calif.) U. Sch. Medicine, 1967-76; rsch. assoc. prof. SUNY, Stony Brook, 1976-86; editor Springer Verlag Publs., N.Y.C., 1986-90, Oxford Univ. Press, N.Y.C., 1990-91; exec. editor VCH Publs., Inc., N.Y.C., 1991-94; sr. editor Am. Inst. Physics Press, Woodbury, N.Y., 1994—. Contbr. over 30 articles to profl. jours. Mem. AAAS, Am. Chem. Soc., N.Y. Acad. Scis., Soc. Scholarly Pub. Home: 21 Dyke Rd Setauket NY 11733-3014 Office: Am Inst Physics 500 Sunnyside Blvd Woodbury NY 11797-2924

DOERING, WILLIAM VON EGGERS, organic chemist, educator; b. Ft. Worth, June 22, 1917; s. Carl Rupp and Antoinette (von Eggers) D.; m. Ruth Haines, 1947 (div. 1954); children: Christian, Peter, Margaretta; m. Sarah Cowles Bullitt, 1969 (div. 1981). BS, Harvard U., 1938, PhD, 1943; DSc (hon.), Tex. Christian U., 1974; D in Natural Sci. (hon.), Karlsruhe U., Fed. Republic Germany, 1987. Faculty, Columbia U., 1943-52; prof. Yale U., 1952-67, dir. div. sci., 1962-65; prof. Karlsruhe U., 1967-86; prof. emeritus Harvard U., 1986—; hon. prof. Fudan U., Shanghai, China, 1980; research chemist Nat. Def. Research Council, Harvard U., 1941-42, Polaroid Corp., 1943, Office Prodn. Research and Devel., 1944-45; dir. Hickrill Chem. Research Found., Katonah, N.Y., 1947-59. Contbr. articles to profl. jours.; hon. regional editor: Tetrahedron, 1958-60. Chmn. Council for Livable World, Washington, 1962-72, pres., 1973-78. Recipient John Scott award City of Phila., 1945; Pure Chemistry award Am. Chem. Soc., 1953, Synthetic Organic Chem. Mfrs. Assn.; medal for creative work in synthetic organic chemistry Am. Chem. Soc., 1966; Hofmann medal German Chem. Soc., 1962; William C. DeVane medal Yale Phi Beta Kappa, 1967; Theodore William Richards medal, 1970; James Flack Norris award in phys. organic chemistry, 1989 both N.E. sect. Am. Chem. Soc.; Welch Found. award, 1990, Kosolapoff award Auburn U., 1995. Mem. Nat. Acad. Sci., Am. Acad. Arts and Scis. Home: 53 Francis Ave Cambridge MA 02138-1911 Office: Harvard U Dept Chemistry 12 Oxford St Cambridge MA 02138-2902

DOERMANN, HUMPHREY, economics educator; b. Toledo, Nov. 13, 1930; s. Henry John and Alice (Robbins Humphrey) D.; m. Elisabeth Adams Wakefield, Jan. 7, 1956; children: Elisabeth M., Eleanor H., Julia L. AB, Harvard U., 1952, MBA, 1958, PhD, 1967; LLD (hon.), Xavier U., La., 1990, U. Minn., 1997; LHD (hon.), Coll. St. Scholastica, 1993, U. St. Thomas, 1996, Ctrl. Coll., 1998. Asst. to com. on admissions and scholarships Harvard, 1955-56; reporter Mpls. Star, 1958-60; asst. to bus. mgr. Mpls. Star & Tribune Co., 1960-61; dir. admissions Harvard, 1961-66; asst. to dean Harvard (Faculty of Arts and Scis.), 1966-69, asst. dean for financial affairs, 1970-71; lectr. on edn. Harvard (Grad. Sch. Edn.), 1967-71; exec. dir. Bush Found., St. Paul, 1971-78; pres. Bush Found., 1978-97; vis. prof. Macalester Coll., 1997—; cons. Coun. Higher Edn. Va., 1969, W. Va. Bd. Regents, 1970; bd. overseers Harvard Coll., Harvard U., 1973-79; trustee St. Paul Acad. and Summit Sch., 1997—; bd. dirs. Coun. on Founds., Washington, 1985-92, chmn. bd. 1990-92; trustee Found. Ctr., N.Y.C., 1975-83, chmn. bd. 1982-83; chmn. Minn. Coun. on Founds., 1981-85, Coll. Bd., N.Y.C., 1994—; chmn. Minn. Legis. Task Force on Student Aid, 1993; chair regents candidate adv. coun. U. Minn. Author: Crosscurrents in College Admissions, rev. edit, 1970, Toward Equal Access, 1978; cons. editor Change mag., 1991—; contbr. articles to Found. News, other jours. Mem. Belmont (Mass.) Town Meeting, 1969-70; dist. chmn. Rhodes Scholarship Selection Com., 1995. Served to lt. (j.g.) USN, 1952-55. Home: 736 Goodrich Ave Saint Paul MN 55105-3524 Office: Macalester Coll 1600 Grand Ave Saint Paul MN 55105-1801

DOERMANN, PAUL EDMUND, retired surgeon; b. Kodaikanal, India, Aug. 3, 1926; s. Carl M. and Cora (Knupke) D.; m. W. Ernestine McPherson, May 3, 1953; children—William McPherson, Marcia, Paula Michelle, Diana, Charles. Student, Ohio State U., 1944; B.S., Capital U., 1947; M.D., U. Mich., 1951. Diplomate Am. Bd. Surgery. Intern Louisville Gen. Hosp., 1951-52, resident in surgery, 1952-53; resident in surgery Milw. County Hosp., 1955-58; med. missionary Lutheran Mission Hosp., Madang, New Guinea, 1958-69; surgeon Linvill Clinic, Columbia City, Ind., 1960-61; practice medicine specializing in surgery Huntington, Ind.; ret., 1990; pres. med. staff, chief surg. service Huntington Meml. Hosp.; pres. Huntington Surg. Corp. Served from 1st lt. to capt., AUS, 1953-55. Luth. Acad. scholar. Fellow ACS; mem. Huntington County Med. Soc., Christian Med. Soc., Am. Assn. Physicians and Surgeons, Pvt. Doctors Am., Huntington C. of C. Lutheran. Lodge: Rotary (Paul Harris fellow). Home: 5503 W 500 N Huntington IN 46750-8022

DOERPER, JOHN ERWIN, publisher, editor; b. Wuerzburg, Germany, Sept. 17, 1943; came to U.S., 1963, permanent resident, 1973; s. Werner and Theresia (Wolf) D.; m. Victoria McCulloch, Dec. 2, 1970. BA, Calif. State U., Fullerton, 1968; MA/ABD, U. Calif., Davis, 1972. Writer/author Seattle, 1984—; food columnist Washington, Seattle, 1985-88, Seattle Times, 1985-88; food editor Wash.-The Evergreen State Mag., Seattle, 1989-94, Pacific Northwest mag., 1989-94, Seattle Home and Garden, 1989-91; pub., editor, founder Pacific Epicure, Quarterly Jour. Gastronomy, Bellingham, Wash., 1988—; dir. Annual N.W. Invitational Chef's Symposium. Author: Eating Well: A Guide to Foods of the Pacific Northwest, 1984, The Eating Well Cookbook, 1984, Shellfish Cookery: Absolutely Delicious Recipes from the West Coast, 1985; author, illustrator: The Blue Carp, 1994, Wine Country: California's Napa and Sonoma Valleys, 1996, Pacific Northwest, 1997, Coastal California, 1998 (Lowell Thomas Travel Journalism Competition Gold medal 1999); contbr. articles to profl. jours., intro. and chpts. to books; co-author: Washington: A Compass Guide, 1995. Recipient Silver medal, White award for city and regional mags. William Allen White Sch. Journalism, U. Kans. Mem. Oxford Symposium Food and Cookery (speaker 26th Ann. Pacific N.W. Writer's Conf. 1982, 92). Avocations: food, wine, travel, painting, printmaking. Home: 610 Donovan Ave Bellingham WA 98225-7315

DOERR, BARBARA ANN, health facility director; b. Poteet, Tex., Apr. 2, 1951; d. William Ira and Margaret Sophia (Lozano) Potts; m. Michael F. Doerr, Aug. 19, 1984 (divorced); 1 child, Jennifer. BSN, U. Tex., 1975. RN, Tex.; cert. nursing adminstr. Am. Nurses Credentialing Ctr. Nursing house supr. Brackenridge Hosp., Austin, Tex., 1980-84, clin. coord., 1984-87, dir. med./surg. nursing, 1987-93, acting asst. adminstr., 1989-90, dir. nursing adminstrn., 1993-95; dir. nursing practice Seton Healthcare Orgn., Austin, 1996—. Mem. ANA, Tex. Nurses Assn. (dist. V, Nurse of Yr. 1990-91), U. Tex.-Austin Sch. Nursing Alumni Assn. (pres.), Tex. Orgn. of Nurse Execs., Sigma Theta Tau (Epsilon chpt.). Home: 202 Lakeway Dr Austin TX 78734 Office: Seton Healthcare Orgn 601 E 15th St Austin TX 78701

DOERR, EDD, religious liberty organization executive; b. Indpls., Dec. 21, 1930; s. Eugene Henry and Mary Catherine (Burk) D.; m. Herenia Isabel Osma, Apr. 21, 1956; children: Eric E., Helena T. BS, Ind. U., 1956. Cert. secondary educator, Ind.; counselor Am. Humanist Assn. Exec. dir. Americans for Religious Liberty, Silver Spring, Md., 1982—; pres. Am. Humanist Assn., Amherst, N.Y., 1995—; bd. dirs. Internat. Humanist and Ethical Union, London, 1985—, N.Am. Com. for Humanism, Farmington Hills, Mich., 1985—. Author: The Conspiracy That Failed, 1968, Religious Liberty in Crisis, 1988, (fiction) Eden II, 1974, A Hitch in Time, 1988, (poems) Images, 1991, Catholic Schools: The Facts, 1993, (poems) Dancing on the Wall, 1993; Vox Populi: Letters to the Editor, 1999; co-author: Religion and Public Education: Common Sense and the Law, 1991, Church Schools and Public Money: The Politics of Parochiaid, 1991, Religious Liberty and State Constitutions, 1993, The Case Against School Vouchers, 1995; editor: Timely and Timeless: The Wisdom of E. Burdette Backus, 1998; co-editor: Abortion Rights and Fetal "Personhood," 1989, The Great Quotations on Religious Freedom, 1991. Campaign leader Md. Coalition for Pub. Edn. and Religious Liberty, Silver Spring, 1972, 74; bd. dirs. Religious Coalition for Reproductive Choice, Washington, 1973—, Nat. Com. Pub. Edn. and Religious Liberty, 1970—. Mem. Md. ACLU (bd. dirs.), Fellowship Religious Humanists (bd. dirs. 1989—), Phi Delta Kappa. Democrat. Office: Americans for Religious Liberty PO Box 6656 Silver Spring MD 20916-6656 *If full religious liberty for every American is to survive and grow, it is imperative that we halt every effort to erode our constitutional principle of separation of church and state.*

DOERRIE, BOBETTE, secondary education educator; b. Albuquerque, June 22, 1944; d. Neill and Dorothy Madelyn (Jones) Patterson; m. Edward Lewis Horton, Aug. 21, 1966 (div. 1990); children: Leah, James, Carol, Neill; m. Jerome Lee Doerrie, July 28, 1991; children: Jennifer, Elena. BA, McMurry Coll., 1966; MEd, DePaul U., 1977. Cert. sec. broadfield sci. Tchr. physics and phys. sci. G/T coord. Perryton (Tex.) H.S.; tchr. Summit Sch., Dundee, Ill., 1974-77, Lamesa Middle Sch., 1980-85, Lamesa H.S., 1968-69, 85-91, Perryton High Sch., 1991-98; co-dir. Dawson County Sci. Fair, 1981-91; coach Odyssey of the Mind, 1988-91; mem. McMurry U. Ednl. Adv. Bd., 1991-97, engring. team faculty advisor, 1998-99, sci. olympiad coach, 1998-99; mem. Mus. Bd. Dawson County, 1983-90; mem. Libr. Bd. Ochiltree County, 1993-95, v.p., 1994-95. Recipient Excellence in Teaching award Tex. State Assn. for Physics Tchrs., 1992, Tchr. of Yr., Region XVI Gifted and Talented Tchrs., 1994; NSF/Tex. Edn. Assn. Christa McAuliffe grantee, 1993. Mem. South Plains Sci. Soc. (pres. 1988, recipient Sharon Christa McAuliffe Tchr. of the Yr., 1987), Sci. Tchrs. of Tex. (treas. 1998—), Delta Kamma Gamma (past pres.). Avocations: amateur radio, painting, poetry writing, archaeology, reading. Home: RR 2 Box 504 Booker TX 79005-9713 Office: Perryton High Sch 1200 S Jefferson St Perryton TX 79070-3700

DOERRIES, REINHARD RENÉ, modern history educator; b. Berlin, Sept. 25, 1934; came to U.S., 1954; s. Hermann and Annemarie (Kochendoerffer)

D.; m. Elaine Linda Sulli, Jan. 20, 1963; 1 child, Chantal-Aimée. BA, Concordia Coll., 1958; MFA, Ohio U., 1960; MA, Yale U., 1962; MBA, Inst. Européen d'Adminstrn. des Affaires, Fontainbleau, France, 1965; PhD, Bochum U., 1971; habilitation, U. Hamburg, 1982. With internat. divsn. 1st Nat. Bank of Boston, 1962-64; internat. mgmt. cons. Booz Allen & Hamilton Intenrat., Zurich, Switzerland, 1965-68; asst. prof. modern history Hamburg U., Germany, 1970-73, 75-83; prof. Hamburg U., 1983-86, U. Kassel, Germany, 1986-88, U. Erlangen-Nuremberg, Germany, 1988—; guest prof. U. Southampton, Eng., 1986; internat. fellow Am. Council Learned Socs., N.Y.C., 1973-75; lectr. in field. Authro: Washington-Berlin 1908/1917, 1975, Iren und Deutsche in der Neuen Welt, 1985, Imperial Challenge, 1989, Prelude to the Easter Rising, 1999; co-editor: Amerikastudien, 1990—; co-editor: American Studies Book Series, 1990—; adv. editor: Perspectives in Intelligence History, 1991-95; contbr. articles to profl. publs. Bd. dirs. Internat. Sch., Hamburg, 1979-80, Am. House Nuremburg, 1995—, vice chmn., 1996—. Danforth Found. fellow Yale U., 1962. Mem. German Soc. for Am. Studies (dir. 1976-84, pres. 1987-90, dir. 1990—), Am. Hist. Assn., German Soc. for Can. Studies, Immigration History Soc., Intelligence History Study Group (dir. 1993—), Soc. for Historians of Am. Fgn. Rels., German Hist. Assn., Group 65 Club (founder), Yale Club. Avocation: painting. Office: U Erlangen-Nuremberg, Findelgasse 9, 90402 Nuremberg Germany

DOERSAM, CHARLES HENRY, JR., engineer; b. N.Y.C., Nov. 1, 1921; s. Charles Henry, Sr. and Mary Emily (Davenport) D.; m. Cynthia Ann Wick, Dec. 7, 1954 (div. dec. 1980); children: Charles Henry III, Donna Davenport, Dean Robert. BS in Engr., Columbia U., 1942, MSME, 1944; post grad., MIT, U. Mich., N.Y.U. Registered profl. engr., N.Y. Indsl. engr. Pratt & Whitney, East Hartford, Conn., 1941-42; tech. staff Bell Telephone Labs, N.Y.C., 1942-44; sr. project engr Specl. Devices Ctr., Sands Pt., N.Y., 1946-53; project mgr. Sperry Gyroscope Co., Lake Success, N.Y., 1953-60; new product planning mgr. Potter Instrument Co., Plainview, N.Y., 1960-62; dir. mktg. chief engr. Instruments for Industry, Hicksville, N.Y., 1962-64; prof. Polytech. Instit. of Bklyn., 1964-69; pres. Com Comp Inc, Hauppauge, N.Y., 1969-71; chief engr. Fiber Optic Sensors, Inc., Old Lyme, Conn., 1983—; pres. DOERCO Cons., CUB Computer Co., NUTEK Corp., Princeton Automated Labs., Pedagogy Rsch. Inst.; nat. chmn. IRE Profl. Group on Space Electronics, 1950. Pantentee in field; contbr. articles to profl. jours. Bd. Advisors Waldorf Sch., Garden City, N.Y., 1964-68, Portledge Sch., Locust Valley, N.Y., 1977. Mem. North Shore Yacht Club (commn. 1968-69), Point O'Woods Club. Republican. Congregationalist. Avocations: tennis, sailing, woodworking, gardening, constrn. Home and Office: 67 Shore Rd PO Box 927 Old Lyme CT 06371-0927

DOERSHUK, CARL FREDERICK, physician, professor of pediatrics; b. Warren, Ohio, Dec. 24, 1930; s. Carl Frederick and Eula Blanche (Mahan) D.; m. Emma Lou Plummer, Aug. 21, 1954; children: Rebecca Lee, John Frederick, David Plummer. BA, Oberlin Coll., 1952; MD, Case Western Res. U., 1956. Intern U.S. Naval Hosp., Camp Pendleton, Ohio, 1956-57; resident in pediat. Cleve. Met. Gen. Hosp. and Babies and Children's Hosp., Cleve., 1959-61; postdoctoral pulmonary fellow Babies and Children's Hosp. USPHS, Cleve., 1961-63; sr. instr. to prof. pediatrics specializing in academic pediatric pulmonary medicine Case Western Res. U., Cleve., 1963-98, emeritus prof., 1998—. Co-editor Pediatric Respiratory Therapy, 1974, 3d edit., 1986; contbr. articles to profl. jours. Chmn. med. adv. coun. Cystic Fibrosis Found., Washington, 1966-72, bd. trustees, 1969-81, exec. com., 1969-74, v.p. med. affairs Cleve. chpt., 1965-90. Lt. M.C., USN, 1957-59. Named Young Man Yr. Cystic Fibrosis Found., 1970; recipient Richard C. Talamo Clinician Scientist award Cystic Fibrosis Found., 1997. Mem. Am. Pediatric Soc., Soc. Pediatric Research, Am. Acad. Pediatrics (exec. com. chest sect.), Am. Thoracic Soc. (chmn. pediatric pulmonary sect. 1971), No. Ohio Pediatric Soc., Acad. Medicine. Avocations: sailing, raising dahlias. Office: Rainbow Babies and Childrens Hosp 2101 Adelbert Rd Cleveland OH 44106-2624

DOESBURG, JOHN C., military career officer; b. Milw., May 15, 1947; m. Denise Doesburg; children: Sean, Russell. Grad., U. Okla., 1970, Command & Gen. Staff Coll., Army War Coll. Commd. officer U.S. Army, 1970, advanced through grades to maj. gen., battery exec. officer A Battery, 1st Battalion, 10th Field, brigade chem. officer 2nd Brigade, 82nd Airborne Divsn., comdr. hdqrs. co., 2nd Brigade, 82nd Airborne Divsn.; comdr. 21st Chem. Co., 82nd Airborne Divsn., career program mgr. MILPERCEN; mem. U.S. Negotiations Team for a Chem. Weapons Treaty U.S. Arms Control and Disarmament Agy.; exec. officer U.S. Army Chem. Activity Western Command U.S. Army, divsn. chem. officer 25th Infantry Divsn., comdr. 84th Chem. Battalion, comdr. U.S. Army Chem. Activity Pacific, chief chem. and NBC def. divsn., Office Dep. Chif Staff Ops., dir. Joint Program Office for Biol. Def.; commanding gen. U.S. Army Soldier and Biol. Chem. Command, Aberdeen Proving Ground, Md., 1998—. Decorated Def. Superior Svc. medal, Legion of Merit, Def. Meritorious Svc. medal, Army Meritorious Svc. medal with five oak leaf clusters, Army Commendation medal with oak leaf cluster. Office: US Army Soldier & Biol Chem Command Aberdeen Proving Ground MD 21010

DOESCHER, WILLIAM FREDERICK, communications executive; b. Utica, N.Y., Dec. 9, 1937; s. Frederick William and Katherine Ann (Kipp) D.; m. Linda Blair, Nov. 25, 1977; children: Michelle Blair, Douglas C., Marc H. Blair, Cinda L. BA in Econs., Colgate U., 1959; MS in Journalism, Syracuse (N.Y.) U., 1961; postgrad. in advanced mgmt., Columbia U., 1973. Pub. rels. assoc., editor Chase Manhattan News Chase Manhattan Bank, N.Y.C., 1961-65; mgr. press rels. Inmont Corp., 1965-66; asst. corp. rels. mgr. U.S. Plywood Corp., 1966-67; pub. affairs mgr. ea. region Champion Internat. Corp., 1967-69, mgr. advt. svcs., then dir. corp. advt., 1969-71; v.p. pub. rels. and advt. Drexel Heritage Furnishings, Inc., 1971-78; v.p. comms. Dun & Bradstreet, Inc., 1978-83, v.p. pub. rels. and advt., 1983-96, sr. v.p. global comm., 1992—; sr. v.p., chief comm. officer Dun & Bradstreet Corp., 1996—; also pub. D&B Reports mag., N.Y.C., 1978-94. Author numerous articles in mags., periodicals; pub. D&B Reports mag., N.Y.C., 1978-94. Bd. dirs. Colgate U. Alumni Corp., Direct Mktg. Assn., Jackie Robinson Found., BBBonline; mem., adv. com. S.I. Newhouse Sch. Pub. Comm. Distant Learning Program at Syracuse U.; bd. govs. Scarsdale (N.Y.) Golf Club; past pres. Nat. Combined Health Appeal; past pres. Scarsdale, N.Y. Civic Club; past bd. dirs. Nat. Easter Seal Soc., N.Y. Easter Seal Soc., N.Y.C. divsn. Am. Cancer Soc. With USAR, 1959-65. Mem. Pub. Rels. Seminar, Arthur Page Soc., Pub. Rels. Soc. Am. Office: 1 Diamond Hill Rd Murray Hill NJ 07974-1200

DOETSCH, VIRGINIA LAMB, former advertising executive, writer; b. N.Y.C., Oct. 12, 1920; d. Andrew Thomas and Cameola Weeden (Burns) Lamb; m. Gunter H. Doetsch, Oct. 12, 1953 (div. Feb. 1972); 1 child, Hugo. BS, Northwestern U., 1941; postgrad., Columbia U., 1943-44, 46-47. Writer, dir. pub. rels. J. Walter Thompson, Frankfurt, Germany, 1953-56; v.p., creative group head Tatham-Laird Y Kudner (now RSCG Euro-Tatham), Chgo., 1959-76, Needham Harper Steers (now DDB-Needham), Chgo., 1976-83; free-lance advt. writer and prodr. Chgo., 1983—; writer, rschr. OmniTech Cons. Group, Chgo., 1992—. Bd. dirs. Better Bus. Bur., Chgo., 1973-76, Jr. Achievement, Chgo., 1973-76; fundraiser Chgo. Symphony Orch., 1990—, Women's Assn., 1990—. With ARC, China, Burma, India, 1944-46 (Bronze star). Mem. Nat. Am. Advt. Fedn. (Woman of Yr. award 1973), Women's Advt. Club (Woman of Yr. award 1973), Chgo. Advt. Club (bd. dirs. 1973-76). Avocations: arts, swimming, walking, health, work. Home: 400 E Randolph St Apt 828 Chicago IL 60601-7309

DOEZEMA, MARIANNE, art historian; b. Grand Rapids, Mich., Sept. 8, 1950; d. Charles William and Geraldine Frances (Slopsema) D.; m. Michael Andrew Marlais, Dec. 29, 1977. B.A., Mich. State U., 1973; M.A., U. Mich., 1975, PhD, Boston U., 1990. Instr. dept. art history and edn. Cleve. Mus. Art, 1976-79, asst. curator, 1980-81; curator of edn. Ga. Mus. Art, Athens, 1981-83, assoc. dir., 1983-85; asst. prof. Randolph-Macon Women's Coll., 1992-94; dir. Mt. Holyoke Coll. Art Mus., 1994—. Author: American Realism and the Industrial Age, 1980, George Bellows and Urban America, 1997; co-editor: Reading American Art, 1998. Contbr. articles to profl. jours. Presdl. U. Grad. fellow Boston U., 1985-86; Luce Found., 1987—. Mem. Coll. Art Assn. Am. Office: Mount Holyoke Coll Art Mus Lower Lake Rd South Hadley MA 01075-1499

DOGANÇAY, BURHAN C., artist, photographer, sculptor; b. Istanbul, Turkey, Sept. 11, 1929; s. Adil and Hediye Dogançay; m. Angela Hausmann, Dec. 11, 1978. Student, Acad. de la Grande Chaumière, 1955; PhD in Econs., U. Paris, 1956. Dir. Dept Tourism Govt. of Turkey, Ankara, 1959-62; dir. Turk Info. Govt. of Turkey, N.Y.C., 1962-64; artist N.Y.C., 1964—. Photographer: Bridge of Dreams, 1999; exhibited works at Centre Georges Pompidou, Paris, 1982, Palais des Beaux-Arts, Brussels, 1982, Musée St.-Georges, Liège, Belgium, 1982, Musée d'Art Contemporain, Montreal, 1983, Seibu Mus. Art, Tokyo, 1989, State Russian Mus., Leningrad, 1992, Artists' Union, Moscow, 1992, JKF Internat. Airport, 1998—; designed Aubusson tapestry; executed Alucobond Shadow sculpture; author monograph, 1986; author: Dessine-moi L'Amour, 1992; photographer in over 100 countries. Recipient Cert. of Appreciation, City of N.Y., 1964, medal of appreciaiton Ministry of Culture Russia, 1992, Nat. Medal of Arts for Lifetime Achievement and Cultural Contbn., Pres. of Turkey, 1995; fellow Tamarind Lithography Workshop, 1969; design selected for UNICEF cards, 1974, 96. *Mostly unshattered self-confidence, hard work and the willingness to meet new challenges are the basis of my success and happiness.*

DOGGETT, AUBREY CLAYTON, JR., real estate executive, consultant; b. Greensboro, N.C., Nov. 8, 1928; s. Aubrey Clayton and Ann (Blevins) D.; m. Judy Perier, July 26, 1952; children: Aubrey Clayton III, Kathryn Ann, Russell Lee, Robert Keith, Karen Michelle. B.S., U. N.C., 1950, grad. exec. program, 1960. Salesman Richardson Realty, Inc., Greensboro, 1950, 52-53; reviewing appraiser Prudential Ins. Co. Am., Greensboro, 1953-58; exec. v.p., dir., mem. exec. com. Kavanagh-Smith and Co., Greensboro, 1958-63; v.p. mortgage loan dept. Wachovia Bank & Trust Co., Winston-Salem, N.C., 1963-66; sr. v.p. Wachovia Bank & Trust Co., 1966-70; pres., founder Wachovia Mortgage Co., 1970-71; pres., trustee, founder Wachovia Realty Investments, 1970-71; pres., dir. Wingreen Corp., Winston-Salem, 1971—; sr. v.p., bd. dirs. AMIC Corp. (now G.E. Mortgage Ins. Co.), 1981-83; mem. Gov. N.C. Com. Low Income Housing, 1964-68; chmn. ad hoc com. Winston-Salem Model Cities Commn., 1969; bd. dirs., mem. investment com. Richardson Corp., 1989-93; past mem., past chmn. N.C. Housing Adv. Coun.; past adv. asset mgr. Mo. Savs. Assn., Preferred Savs. Bank. Past mem. bd. dirs. Winston-Salem Housing Found. Exec. Bd., Granville Place Inc., Koerner Place, Inc., East Salem Homes, Inc. (housing for elderly); chmn. Greater Greensboro Open Golf Tournament, 1960. Lt. Col. USMCR, 1950-52; lt. col. Res. ret. Decorated Purple Heart. Mem. Mortgage Bankers Assn. Am. (hon., gov. at large 1971-82, legis. exec. com., income property com., chmn. mortgage bankers polit. action com.), Mortgage Bankers Assn. Carolinas (pres. 1970, bd. dirs. 1966-71), Western Piedmont Bd. Realtors (hon.), SAR, Sigma Chi. Episcopalian. Home: 382 Hanover Arms Ct Apt C Winston Salem NC 27104-4154 Office: PO Box 21523 Winston Salem NC 27120-1523

DOGGETT, LLOYD, congressman, former state supreme court justice; b. Austin, Tex., Oct. 6, 1946; s. Lloyd A. and Alyce (Freydenfeldt) D.; m. Elizabeth Belk, 1969; children: Lisa, Catherine. BBA in Bus., U. Tex., 1967, JD with honors, 1970. Bar: Tex. 1971, U.S. Ct. Appeals (5th cir.) 1972, U.S. Dist. Ct. (we. dist.) Tex. 1972. Mem. Tex. State Senate, Dist. 14, 1973-85; ptnr. Doggett and Jacks, Austin, 1975-88; justice Tex. Supreme Ct., Austin, 1989-94; mem. 104th-106th U.S. Congresses from 10th Tex. dist., Washington, DC, 1995—; mem. budget com., resources com. 104th-106th U.S. Congresses from 10th Tex. dist.; mem. various coms. U.S. Ho. of Reps., including budget com., sci. com. and subcom con basic rsch., Dem. caucus task force on crime, Dem. caucus parliamentary group, co-chair Dem. caucus task force on budget; adj. prof. U. Tex. Sch. of Law, 1989-94; chair Supreme Ct. Task Force on Jud. Ethics, 1992-94. Named one of Five Outstanding Young Texans Tex. Jaycees, 1977, Outstanding Young Lawyer of Austin, 1978, one of Best Legislators, Tex. Monthly, 1979, 81, Outstanding State Senator, Common Cause, 1980, Disting. Alumnus, Bus. Adminstrn. Honors program U. Tex., 1989, Outstanding Jurist in Tex., Mex. Am. Bar Assn., 1993; recipient James Madison award Freedom of Info. Found. Tex., 1990, First Amendment award Nat. Soc. Profl. Journalists, 1990, Arthur B. DeWitty award for outstanding achievement in human rights Austin NAACP, others. Mem. Consumers Union U.S. (bd. dirs. 1976-79, 80-81, 86-89), Tex. Consumer Assn. (pres. 1973). Methodist. Office: US House Reps 328 Cannon HOB Washington DC 20515-4310*

DOGLIONE, ARTHUR GEORGE, data processing executive; b. Bklyn., May 24, 1938; s. Francis and Georgia (Smith) D.; m. Maryann Laurette Bonfanti, Sept. 3, 1960; children: Dana Ann, Arthur Todd, Lora Michele. AA, Scottsdale (Ariz.) Community, 1978; AAS, Maricopa Tech. Coll., Phoenix, 1984; BS, Ariz. State U., 1985. Salesman Columbus Realty Co., Trenton, N.J., 1962-65; appraiser J.H. Martin Appraisal Co., Trenton, 1965-68; office mgr. Mcpl. Revaluations, Avon-by-the-Sea, N.J., 1968-69; pres., broker Area Real Estate Agy., Wall, N.J., 1969-76; property appraiser Ariz. Dept. Revenue, Phoenix, 1976-78; investment appraiser Continental Bank, Phoenix, 1978-79; appraisal systems specialist Ariz. Dept. Revenue, Phoenix, 1979-80; project dir. Ariz. Dept. Adminstrn., 1980-83; pres. Logical Models, Scottsdale, Ariz., 1983-95; founder Genus Tech., Scottsdale, 1989—; tax assessor Upper Freehold Twp., N.J., 1974-75, Borough of Bradley Beach, N.J., 1975; lectr. in field. Author various software. Counselor SCORE, SBA, Mesa, Ariz., 1986-90. Mem. Phi Theta Kappa. Republican. Roman Catholic. Office: GENUS Tech PO Box 725 Scottsdale AZ 85252-0725

DOHANIAN, DIRAN KAVORK, art historian, educator; b. Somerville, Mass., Mar. 26, 1931; s. Hagop Mardiros and Esther (Babigian) D. B.F.A., Mass. Sch. Art, 1952; A.M. in Teaching, Harvard, 1953, M.A., 1955, Ph.D., 1964. Instr. art Eastern Nazarene Coll., Wollaston, Mass., 1952-55; reader in fine arts Harvard U., Cambridge, Mass., 1954-55, 56-57, teaching fellow fine arts, 1955-57; vis. asst. prof. history art U. Ala., 1957-58; vis. asst. prof. history Oriental art U. Mich., 1959-60; asst. prof. fine arts, dir. course in Oriental humanities U. Rochester, N.Y., 1960-65, assoc. prof. fine arts, 1965-71, prof., 1971-87, prof. art history, 1988—, acting chmn. dept. fine arts, 1977-78, chmn. dept. fine arts, 1980-83, mem. faculty coun. Coll. Arts & Sci., 1991-94, sec. faculty coun., 1992-94; cons. curator Oriental art The Meml. Art Gallery, Rochester, 1976-88, bd. mgrs., 1977-78, 80-83; Cooke-Daniels Meml. lectr. art Cooke-Daniels Found. and Denver Art Mus., 1965; Louise Weiser lectr. Mt. Holyoke Coll., 1983; cons. Choice, Jour. Assn. Coll. Research Libraries. Author: The Mahayana Buddhist Sculpture of Ceylon, 1977, also articles in profl. jours. C.R.B. fellow Belgian Art Seminar, Brussels and Antwerp, 1956; Fulbright fellow India, 1958-59; sr. research fellow Am. Inst. Ceylonese Studies, Colombo, 1968; Am. Council Learned Socs. fellow India, 1973. Fellow Am. Philos. Soc.; mem. Am. Inst. Indian Studies (trustee 1964-65), Am. Com. for History South Asian Art (dir. 1969-71). Home: 269 Payson Rd Belmont MA 02478-3406 Office: U Rochester Dept Art and Art History Rochester NY 14627

DOHERTY, BARBARA WHITEHURST, chemical purchasing manager; b. Charlotte, Jan. 18, 1935; d. Frank Joseph and Geneva Kathryn (Pease) Whitehurst; m. Martin William Doherty, Sr., June 23, 1956 (div. June, 1975); children: Martin William, Jr., Frank Whitehurst. BA in Religion magna cum laude, Duke U., 1956. Cert. notary pub., 1982-97. Rsch. asst., dept. sociology Duke U., Durham, N.C., 1953-56; sec. Pelham (N.Y.) Visiting Nurse & Family Svc., 1958-59; adminstrv. asst. Mecklenburg Times, Charlotte, N.C., 1972-73; bookkeeper Carolina Waterbed Co., Charlotte, N.C., 1972-74; mgr., purchasing and inventory control Reagents, Inc., Charlotte, N.C., 1974-97. Author: poems appear in: Southern Poetry Review, 1992, 1993, 1995, Charlotte Observer, 1993, Sparrowgrass Poetry Forum, 1997. Treas. Charlotte (N.C.) Fair Housing, 1968-70; mem. Charlotte-Mecklenburg Schs. Emergency Sch. Assistance Adv. Com., 1972; Co-chair Paul Leonard for City Council Campaign, Charlotte, 1970; friend of the ct. Swann vs. Bd. Edn., Charlotte, 1972; vol. Marylyn Huff for Sch. Bd., Charlotte, 1970, 74; founder ACLU, Charlotte, 1980 (sec., 1980-82, treas., 1982-84); vol. Harvey Gantt for Mayor campaign, Charlotte, 1983, 85; co-founder, treas. Parents and Friends of Lesbians and Gays, Charlotte, 1988-90; bd. mem. Metrolina Cmty. Svc. Project, Charlotte, 1990-93 (treas., 1992-93). Mem. Phi Beta Kappa, Sigma Delta Pi. Democrat. Avocations: politics, African travel. Home: 1419 Ferncliff Rd Charlotte NC 28211-2002

DOHERTY, BRIAN GERARD, alderman; b. Chgo., Oct. 25, 1957; s. Daniel Joseph and Kathleen (McDonagh) D.; m. Rose Mary Gillespie, 1986; children: Kathleen Marie, Kevin Michael. BA, U. N.E. Ill., 1984. Alderman 41st Ward, Chgo., 1991—. Boxing champ Chgo. Pk. Dist., 1972, 73, Chgo. Golden Gloves champion Tribune Charities, 1973. Mem. Alpha Chi Honor Soc. Roman Catholic. Home: 7805 W Catalpa Ave Chicago IL 60656-1640 Office: 7818 W Higgins Rd Chicago IL 60631-3325

DOHERTY, CHARLES VINCENT, investment counsel executive; b. Pitts., Dec. 17, 1933; s. Charles V. and Emma (Lager) D.; m. Marilyn Bongiorno, Oct. 17, 1964; children: Charles, Michelle, Kristen. BS, U. Notre Dame, 1955; MBA, U. Chgo., 1967. CPA, Ill. Tax specialist Haskins & Sells, CPA, Chgo., 1960-67; ptnr. Lamson Bros. & Co., Chgo., 1968-73; pres. Doherty Zable & Co., Chgo., 1974-85, Chgo. Stock Exch., Inc., 1986-92; mng. dir. Madison Asset Group, Chgo., 1993—; bd. dirs. Lakeside Bank, Howe Barnes Securities, Inc., NationsBanc Fin. Products, Brauvin Capital Corp., Knight Trimark Group Inc.; trustee Wayne Hummer Money Market Trust, Wayne Hummer Income Trust. Mem. chancellor's adv. coun. U. Ill., Chgo., 1991—; bd. dirs. West Suburban Health Care Corp. Roman Catholic.

DOHERTY, EVELYN MARIE, data processing consultant; b. Phila., Sept. 26, 1941; d. James Robert and Virginia (Checkley) D. Diploma, RCA Tech. Inst., Cherry Hill, N.J., 1968. Freelance data processing programmer N.J., 1978-81; data processing cons. N.J., 1981—; cons. collection agy., brokerage, banking, med., edn., transp., pub., food wholesaleing, utility systems, mfg.; reseller of PC's and software; lectr. data processing Camden County (N.J.) Coll. Contbr. articles to profl. jours. Chair Collingswood (N.J.) Dems., 1968; founder Babe Didrikson Collingswood Softball Team for Women; organizer Erlton South Town Watch (pub. cmty. notebook); mem. budget com. Cherry Hill Sch. Dist.; adv. for vol. firefighters. Mem. Data Processing Mgmt. Assn. (chmn., mem. ednl. com., bd. dirs. N.J. chpt. 1980—). Roman Catholic. Avocations: tennis, bridge, chess, charitable activites. Office: PO Box 3780 Cherry Hill NJ 08034-0584

DOHERTY, GLEN PATRICK, lawyer; b. Toledo, Ohio, Jan. 3, 1963; s. Daniel Owen and Elaine (May) D.; m. Rhonda Jo Hugick, Nov. 18, 1998. BS, Cornell U., 1986; LLD cum laude, Cornell Law Sch., 1989. Bar: Bar: N.Y. 1990, U.S. Dist. Ct. (no. dist.) N.Y. 1990, U.S. Dist. Ct. (so. and ea. dists.) N.Y., 1991. Assoc. Bond, Schoeneck & King, Syracuse, N.Y., 1989-91; assoc. Degraff, Foy, Holt-Harris & Kunz, LLP, Albany, 1991-96, ptnr., 1996—. Co-editor N.Y. Employment Law, 1997—; contbr. articles to profl. jours. Committeeman N.Y. State Reps., Colonie, 1991; designer Albany County Flag, 1979; bd. dirs. Albany Symphony Orch., 1999—. Mem. Lake George Club, Cornell Club of N.Y., Fort Orange Club, Phi Kappa Phi. Republican. Roman Catholic. Avocations: sailing, squash. Fax: 518-436-0210. E-mail: GPD@Degraff-Foy.com. Office: Degraff Foy Holt-Harris & Kunz LLP 90 State St Albany NY 12207

DOHERTY, JOHN L., lawyer; b. Pitts., Dec. 17, 1934; s. John A. and Carmella G. (Conte) D.; m. Diane J. Passetti, Aug. 10, 1963; children: John F., Kathleen A. BA, Duquesne U., 1960, JD, 1966. Bar: Pa. 1966. Law clk. to chief judge U.S. Dist. Ct. Western Dist. Pa., 1966-67; asst. Livingston, Miller & Haywood, Pitts., 1967-75; asst. city solicitor Pitts., 1969-70; law clk. to judge Allegheny County Ct. Common Pleas, Pitts., 1971-73; ptnr. Manifesto, Doherty & Donahoe, P.C., Pitts., 1975-92; chief disciplinary counsel Disciplinary Bd. of the Supreme Ct. Pa., 1992—. Served with U.S. Army, 1954-56. Fellow Am. Coll. Trial Lawyers, Acad. Trial Lawyers (past pres.); mem. Allegheny County Bar Assn., Pa. Trial Lawyers Assn. (past chmn. criminal trial sect.), Assn. Trial Lawyers Am., Pa. Criminal Def. Assn., Pa. Bar Assn. (bd. govs.), Assn. Trial Lawyers in Criminal Ct. (past pres.).

DOHERTY, KAREN ANN, corporate executive; b. Elizabeth, N.J., July 6, 1952; d. Eugene Nason Godfrey and Helen L. (Andersen) D.; m. Jonathan Kent Tillinghast, June 17, 1972 (div. Oct. 1978); 1 child, Robert. Account exec. The John O'Donnell Co., N.Y.C., 1979-80; nat. conservation rep. Sierra Club, N.Y.C., 1980-81; dir. membership and top mgmt. programs Am. Mgmt. Assn., N.Y.C., 1981-97; program mgr. Am. Mgmt. Assn. Pres. Assn., N.Y.C., 1998-99; v.p. mktg. Internat. Inst. Learning, Inc., N.Y.C., 1999, Exaclair Inc., N.Y.C., 1999—; bd. dirs. Coop. Jamestown Tenants Assn., 1990—. Bd. dirs. Old Mill Landowners Assn. Mem. Trinity Coll. Alumnae Assn. (bd. dirs. Com. N.Y.C. group 1979-82), Women in Need (corp. adv. coun.). Democrat. Roman Catholic. E-mail: kdoh138@aol.com. Home: 138 71st St Apt F1 Brooklyn NY 11209-1141 Office: Exaclair Inc 616 W 46th St 4th Fl New York NY 10036

DOHERTY, KATHERINE MANN, librarian, writer; b. N.Y.C., July 11, 1951; d. Jack Howard Mann and Glenn (Ellis) Andrews; m. Craig A. Doherty, June 16, 1973; 1 child, Meghan Corinne. BA, U. N.Mex., 1973; MSLS, Simmons Coll., 1976. Cataloger Mass. Hist. Soc., Boston, 1976-79; libr. media specialist Zuni (N.Mex.) Pub. Sch.s, 1982-86; libr. dist. Zuni Pub. Schs., 1985-86; unified media specialist Nantucket (Mass.) Elem. Sch., 1986-87; dir. learning resources Fortier Libr., N.H. Cmty. Tech. Coll., Berlin, 1987—. Author: (children's books) Apaches and Navajos, 1989, Iroquois, 1989, (young adult books) Benazir Bhutto, 1990, The Zunis, 1993, Arnold Schwarzenegger, 1993, The Huron, 1994, The Narragansett, 1994, The Chickasaw, 1994, The Ute, 1994, The Chuilla, 1994, The Sioux, 1994, The Golden Gate Bridge, 1995, Hoover Dam, 1995, Mount Rushmore, 1995, Washington Monument, 1995, Gateway Arch, 1995, The Wampanoag, 1995, The Penobscot, 1995, The Astrodome, 1996, The Erie Canal, 1996, the Empire State Building, 1997, The Alaska Pipeline, 1997; pub. Field Trial Mag. Office: NH Tech Coll Coll Libr 2020 Riverside Dr Berlin NH 03570-3717

DOHERTY, PATRICIA ANN, computer systems analyst; b. Perth Amboy, N.J., Jan. 21, 1959; d. William Urban and Marion Ann (Mazola) O'Brien; m. Stephen Joseph Doherty, Feb. 12, 1983; children: Kathleen Elizabeth, Brian Stephen. BA summa cum laude, Rutgers U., 1981, MS in Math., 1987. Cert. tchr. math., N.J. Bank teller Nat. State Bank, Elizabeth, N.J., 1979; intern Merck & Co., Inc., Rahway, N.J., summer 1980, programmer technician, 1981-82, from programmer to sr. systems assoc./project mgr., 1982—; math. workshop tutor, Rutgers U., New Brunswick, 1978-81. Advisor St. James Youth Group, St. James Ch., Woodbridge, N.J., 1985-86; computer advisor Rutgers U., pres., 1979-80; leader North Edison coun. Girls Scouts U.S., 1992-99. Recipient award for excellence Merck & Co., Inc., 1990, 95; named Leader of Yr. N. Edison Girl Scouts U.S., 1995-96. Mem. Am. Math. Soc., Phi Beta Kappa, Pi Mu Epsilon (sec. 1980-81, Jr. award in Math. 1980), Kappa Delta Pi (v.p. 1980-81). Roman Catholic. Avocations: oil painting, skiing, crafts, decorating. Home: 7 Old Hickory Ln Edison NJ 08820-1124

DOHERTY, PATRICIA ANNE, psychologist; b. Ottumwa, Iowa, May 25, 1947; d. Russell S. and Dorotha L. (Moehle) Cadwallader; m. Michael Doherty, Sept.6, 1969; 1 child, David M. BA in History, U. Iowa, 1969, MA, 1974, PhD in Counselor Edn., 1979. Cert. prof. counselor, Wis.; nat. cert. counselor. Grad. asst. U. Iowa, Iowa City, 1974-78; counseling intern Colo. State U., Ft. Collins, 1978-79; sr. psychologist U. Wis., Stevens Point, 1979—. Author chpt. Women, Power and Relationships; contbr. articles to profl. jours. Mem. Wausau (Wis.) Lyric Choir, 1994—, bd. dirs., 1999—; ofcl. Wis. Spl. Olympics, Stevens Point, 1989—. Mem. ACA, Am. Coll. Pers. Assn., Silvan Tompkins Inst., Phi Delta Kappa, Phi Kappa Phi, Pi Lambda Theta. Avocations: singing, tennis, swimming, running, skiing. Home: 217 Saint Paul St Apt B Stevens Point WI 54481-2291 Office: U Wis Stevens Point Counseling Ctr 317 Delzell Hall Stevens Point WI 54481

DOHERTY, PATRICK WILLIAM, city official; b. Amityville, N.Y., May 24, 1951; s. Patrick John and Catherine Anne (Lydon) D. BA, Hofstra U., Hempstead, N.Y., 1976; JD, Hofstra Law Sch., Hempstead, N.Y., 1983; MIA, Columbia U. Sch. Internat. and Public Affairs, N.Y.C., 1984. Bar: N.Y. 1985. Editor, writer N.Y.S. Assembly, Albany, 1976, regional coord., 1977-80; adminstrv. assoc. N.Y.C. Comptroller's Office, 1984-88, dir. investment responsibility, 1988—; assoc. editor Hofstra Law Review, Hempstead, N.Y., 1982-83. Recipient Atty. of the Yr. award Kings County Dist. Atty's. Office, 1994, Sean MacBride Human Rights award City of N.Y., 1994, Irish Am. Top 100 award Irish Am. Mag., 1994. Mem. bd. advisors Britain and Ireland Human Rights Ctr., London. Mem. Coun. Instnl. Investors, Social Investment Forum, Brehon Law Soc. Democrat. Avocation: antiquarian books and coins. Home: 43 Simon St Babylon NY

11702-2325 Office: Office Comptroller City NY 1 Centre St Rm 729 New York NY 10007-1602

DOHERTY, PETER CHARLES, immunologist; b. Brisbane, Australia, Oct. 15, 1940; came to U.S., 1988; s. Eric C. and Linda Doherty; m. Penelope Stephens, 1965; children: James, Michael. B.V.Sc (hons), U. Queensland, Australia, 1962, MVSc, 1966; PhD, U. Edinburgh, Scotland, 1970; DVs (hon.), U. Queensland; DSc (hon), Australian Nat. U. Vet. officer Animal Rsch. Inst., Brisbane, Australia, 1963-67; sci. officer Moredun Rsch. Inst., Edinburgh, 1967-71; postdoctoral fellow John Curtin Sch. Med. Rsch., Canberra, Australia, 1972-75, prof., head dept. exptl. pathology, 1982-88; from assoc. prof. to prof. The Wistar Inst., Phila., 1975-82; mem., chmn. dept. immunology St. Jude Children's Rsch. Hosp., Memphis, 1988—; Bd. dirs. Internat. Lab. Animal Diseases, Nairobi, 1986-92; mem. NIH exptl. virology study sect., 1982-83, 1990—. Contbr. chpts. to books, articles to profl. jours. Recipient Paul Ehrlich prize Fed. Republic Germany, 1983, Gairdner Internat. award for med. sci. Can., 1986, Lasker award for Basic Med. Rsch., 1995; Co-recipient Nobel Prize for medicine, 1996; Royal Soc. London fellow, 1987. Fellow Australian Acad. Sci. Avocations: walking, reading, skiing. Office: Saint Jude Children's Rsch Hosp 332 N Lauderdale St Memphis TN 38105-2794*

DOHERTY, REBECCA FEENEY, federal judge; b. Ft. Worth, June 3, 1952; d. Charles Edwin Feeney and Annabelle (Knight) Smith; divorced; 1 child, George Jason. BA, Northwestern State U., 1973, MA, 1975; JD, La. State U., 1981. Bar: La. 1981, U.S. Dist. Ct. (mid., ea. and we. dists.) La. 1981, U.S. Ct. Appeals (5th cir.) 1981, U.S. Dist. Ct. (so. dist.) Tex. 1986, U.S. Dist. Ct. (ea. dist.) Tex. 1989. Assoc. Onebane, Donohoe, Bernard, Torian, Diaz, McNamara & Abell, Lafayette, La., 1981-84, ptnr., 1985-91; U.S. dist. ct. judge We. Dist. La., Lafayette, 1991—; adj. instr. Northwestern State U., Natchitoches, La., 1975; co-dir. secondary level gifted and talented program Webster Parish, La., 1978. Contbr. articles to profl. jours.; mem. La. Law Rev., 1980, 81. Recipient Am. Jurisprudence award Lawyers Coop. Pub. Co., 1980, Career Achievement award 1991; inducted into La. State U. Law Ctr. Hall of Fame, 1987. Mem. ABA, La. Bar Assn., La. Assn. Def. Counsel, La. Assn. Trial Lawyers, Acadian Assn. Women Attys., Order of Coif. Office: US Dist Ct 800 Lafayette St Ste 4900 Lafayette LA 70501-6936

DOHERTY, ROBERT CHRISTOPHER, lawyer; b. Elizabeth, N.J., Sept. 3, 1943; s. Christopher Joseph and Marie Veronica (McLaughlin) D.; m. Sarajane Frances Doherty, June 12, 1965; children: Dennis Michael, Amy Elizabeth, Tracey Carolan. AB, St. Peter's Coll., 1965; JD, Seton Hall U., 1970. Bar: N.J. 1970, U.S. Ct. Appeals (3rd cir.) 1982, U.S. Supreme Ct. 1977. Asst. prosecutor Union County, Elizabeth, N.J., 1971-72; mem. Schumann, Hession, Kennelly & Dorment, Jersey City, 1972-73, Robert D. Younghans, Westfield, N.J., 1973-76; ptnr. Doherty & Kopnicki, Westfield, 1976-87; county counsel Union County, Elizabeth, 1981-88; assoc. Nelinson, Roche & Carter, East Orange, N.J., 1988-92, Stanley Marcus, Newark, 1992-98, Weiner Lesniak, Parsippany, N.J., 1998—. Mem. ABA, N.J. Bar Assn., Union County Bar Assn., Essex County Bar Assn., N.J. Assn. County Counsels. Republican. Roman Catholic. Home: 771 Fairacres Ave Westfield NJ 07090-2027 Office: Weiner Lesniak 299 Cherry Hill Rd Parsippany NJ 07054-1111

DOHERTY, ROBERT CUNNINGHAM, advertising executive, retired; b. N.Y.C., Sept. 30, 1930; s. Francis Joseph and Helen (Utley) D.; m. Brucie Rial (div. 1961); children: Michael Bruce, Robert Kelly; m. Kerstin Brigetta Karlsson; children: Andrew Seger, Thomas Nils. BA, Princeton U., 1952. Account exec. Needham Harper Steers, N.Y.C., 1958-62, v.p., account supr., 1962-65; exec. v.p. John Rockwell and Assocs., N.Y.C., 1965-73, ptnr., chmn. bd., 1973-75; v.p. mgmt. group Wells, Rich & Greene, N.Y.C., 1975-79; sr. v.p. McKinney & Silver, Raleigh, N.C., 1979-83, exec. v.p., 1983-87, pres., 1987-90, chief exec. officer, 1991-97, chmn., 1993-98; ret., 1998. Trustee N.C. Symphony, 1991—, N.C. Mus. History, 1997—. Served to 1st lt. USMC, 1952-54, Korea. Mem. Figure Eight Yacht Club (Wilmington, N.C.), Princeton Club (N.Y.C.), Ivy Club (Princeton, N.J.), Cardinal Club (Raleigh, N.C.). Episcopalian. Office: First Union Capital Ctr Ste 1700 150 Fayetteville Street Mall Raleigh NC 27601-2919

DOHERTY, ROBERT FRANCIS, JR., aerospace industry professional; b. North Quincy, Mass., Aug. 7, 1954; s. Robert Francis and Rose Virginia (Wheeler) D. BS in Mgmt., U. Mass., Dartmouth, 1977. Sales mgr. Jordan Marsh Co., Boston, 1977-78; ops. mgr. Cramer Electronics, Newton, Mass., 1978-79; from d/e supr. to sect. mgr. nat. accts. Data Gen. Corp., Westboro, Mass., 1979-84; sales ops. mgr. Printronix, Inc., Malden, Mass., 1984-87; sales/contracts adminstrn. mgr. M/A-Com, Inc., Burlington, Mass., 1987-89; mktg. mgr. M/A-Com, Inc., Chelmsford, Mass., 1989-92; mgr. customer satisfaction M/A Com Inc., Lowell, Mass., 1992-94, internal cons. sys. applications products, 1994-95; program mgr. AMP M/A-COM, Inc., Lowell, Mass., 1995-99, dir. program mgmt., 1999—; newspaper corr., chair various restructuring coms.; cons. internal reengring. Active human rights groups, health founds. Mem. Nat. Contract Mgmt. Assn., Assn. of Old Crows, M/A-Com Mgmt. Club, Air Force Assn., Nat. Def. Indsl. Assn., Air Force Assn. Roman Catholic. Avocations: jogging, swimming, skiing, antiques, travel. Home: 27 Dwight St # 1 Boston MA 02118-3608

DOHERTY, SHANNON, actress; b. Memphis, Apr. 12, 1971; d. Tom and Rosa D.; m. Ashley Hamilton, 1993 (div. 1994). TV series: Little House: A New Beginning, 1982-83, Our House, 1986-88, Beverly Hills, 90210, 1990-94; TV movies: The Other Lover, 1985, Robert Kennedy and His Times, 1985, Obsessed, 1992, Rebel Highway: Jailbreakers, Showtime, 1994, A Burning Passion: The Margaret Mitchell Story, 1994, Gone in the Night, 1996; films: Night Shift, 1982, (voice) The Secret of Nimh, 1982, Girls Just Want to Have Fun, 1985, Heathers, 1989, Blindfold: Acts of Obsession, 1993, Almost Dead, 1994, Mallrats, 1995.TV series: Charmed, 97-. Baptist. Office: care ICM 8942 Wilshire Blvd Beverly Hills CA 90211-1934

DOHERTY, STEVE, lawyer, state legislator; b. Great Falls, Mont., May 5, 1952; s. Arthur Frederick and Myra M. (Sheldon) D. BA, U. Pa., 1975; JD, Lewis & Clark Law Sch., 1984. Assoc. Spears, Lubersky, Campbell, Bledsoe, Anderson & Young, Portland, 1984-86; from assoc. to ptnr. Graybill, Ostrem, Warner & Crotty, Great Falls, Mont., 1986-92; assoc. Smith & Guenther, Great Falls, Mont., 1992-97; senator Mont. Senate, Great Falls, Mont., 1991—, majority whip, chmn. jud. com., 1993-94, mem. taxation and nat. resources com., 1991-94, mem. environ. quality coun. com., 1991-94, mem. edn. com., 1995, mem. fish and game and ethics com., 1997; ptnr. Smith & Doherty, Great Falls, Mont., 1998—. Bd. dirs. Rural Employment Opportunities, Helena, 1990-92. Mem. Great Falls Pub. Radio Assn. (bd. dirs. 1986-91). Democrat. Avocations: hunting, fishing, hiking, skiing, Western history. Fax: (406) 452-9787. Office: Smith & Doherty 410 Central Ave Ste 522 Great Falls MT 59401-3128*

DOHERTY, THOMAS, publisher; b. Hartford, Conn., Apr. 23, 1935; s. Thomas and Elizabeth (Story) D.; m. Tatiana Pachina, July 19, 1992; children: Linda, Kathleen, Thomas W.; 1 stepchild, Leana Cavallo. Student, Trinity Coll., 1953-57. From salesman to divsn. sales mgr. Pocket Books, 1958-69; nat. sales mgr. Simon & Schuster, 1969-70; pub. Tempo Books, 1971-75; pub., gen. mgr. Ace and Tempo divsns. Grossett & Dunlap Inc., 1976-80; founder, pres. Tom Doherty Assocs., Inc., N.Y.C., 1980-87; pres., pub. Tor/Forge Books, N.Y.C., 1987—. Winner Skylark award, Locus award for Best Pub. sci. and fantasy, 12 yrs. Mem. World Sci. Fiction Assn. (charter), Nat. Space Inst. Republican. Roman Catholic. Home: 280 Park Ave S Apt 15A New York NY 10010-6131 Office: Tor Books 175 5th Ave New York NY 10010-7703

DOHERTY, THOMAS JOSEPH, financial services industry consultant; b. Cambridge, Mass., Oct. 20, 1933; s. Thomas Joseph and Margaret Cecelia (O'Connell) D.; m. Carol Anne Conroy, Jan. 5, 1957; children: William, John, Robert, Susan. AB cum laude, Suffolk U., Boston, 1961. With Merrill Lynch & Co., Inc., N.Y.C., 1958-90; v.p. Merrill Lynch, Pierce, Fenner & Smith Inc., 1978-90; mng. dir. Merrill Lynch White Weld Capital Markets Group, 1979-83, Merrill Lynch Capital Markets, 1989-90; pres., chief exec. officer Merrill Lynch Specialists, Inc., 1985-90; trustee Cin. Stock Exch., 1979-83; past mem. Am. Stock Exch., N.Y. Stock Exch.; bd. govs Pacific Stock Exch., 1984-90. Served with AUS, 1953-55. Mem. Security Traders Assn. N.Y., Nat. Security Traders Assn. (chmn. exchange liaison com. 1986-87), Gen. Alumni Assn. Suffolk U. (bd. dirs. 1976-77). Republican. Roman Catholic.

DOHLMAN, DENNIS RAYE, oil company executive; b. Iowa Falls, Iowa, Mar. 16, 1946; s. Lowell L. and Harmina (Ploeger) D.; m. Mary Ilene Ontjes, Sept. 2, 1966; children: John Bradley, Rebecca Ralene. BSChemE, Iowa State U., 1968. Process engr. No. Petrochem. Co., Morris, Ill., 1968-70, maintenance engr., 1970-72, utility area asst. supt., 1972-74, utility area supt., 1974-76; plant supt. Aminoil U.S.A., Inc., Tioga, N.D., 1976-79; project engr. Fenix & Scisson Inc., Casper, Wyo., 1979-80; sr. gas engr. ARCO Oil & Gas Co., Crane, Tex., 1980-81, ops. supr., 1981-84, sr. plant engr., 1984-90; sr. mech. engr., 1990—. Trustee Crane Ind. Sch. Bd., 1989—, pres., 1995-96. Mem. AIChE, Permian Basin Sch. Bd. Assn. (v.p. 1994-95, pres. 1995-97), Lions (Lion of Yr. award Crane 1992). Avocations: carpentry, singing, reading, vehicle maintenance. Home: 300 E 19th St Crane TX 79731-4404 Office: ARCO Permian FM1601 HC-65 PO Box 55 Crane TX 79731-0055

DOHMEN, FREDERICK HOEGER, retired wholesale drug company executive; b. Milw., May 12, 1917; s. Fred William and Viola (Gutsch) D.; BA in Commerce, U. Wis., 1939; m. Gladys Elizabeth Dite, Dec. 23, 1939 (dec. 1963); children: William Francis, Robert Charles; m. Mary Alexander Holgate, June 27, 1964. With F. Dohmen Co., Milw., 1939-82, successively warehouse employee, sec., v.p., 1944-52, pres., 1952-82, dir., 1947—, chmn. bd., 1952-82; travel lectr. various orgns., 1980—. Bd. dirs. St. Luke's Hosp. Ednl. Found., Milw., 1965-83, pres., 1969-72, chmn. bd., 1972-73; bd. dirs. U. Wis., Milw. Found., 1976-79, bd. visitors, 1978-88, emeritus mem. 1988—; assoc. chmn. Nat. Bible Week, Laymen's Nat. Bible Com., N.Y.C., 1968-82, council of adv., 1983—; elder Presbyn. Ch.; bd. dirs. Riveredge Nature Ctr., Newburg, Wis., 1993-94. Mem. Nat. Wholesale Druggists Assn. (chmn. mfr. relations com. 1962, resolutions com. 1963, mem. of bd. control 1963-66), Nat. Assn. Wholesalers (trustee 1966-75), Druggists Service Council (dir. 1967-71), Wis. Pharm. Assn., Miss. Valley Drug Club, Beta Gamma Sigma, Phi Eta Sigma, Delta Kappa Epsilon, University Club, Town Club (Milw.) Avocations: travel, photography. Home: 3903 W Mequon Rd Mequon WI 53092-2727

DOHMEN, MARY HOLGATE, retired primary school educator; b. Gary, Ind., July 28, 1918; d. Clarence Gibson and Margaret Alexander (Kinnear) Holgate; m. Frederick Hoeger Dohmen, June 27, 1964; children: William Francis, Robert Charles. BS, Milw. State Tchrs. Coll., 1940; M of Philosophy, U. Wis., 1945. Cert. tchr., Wis. Tchr. primary grades Baraboo (Wis.) Pub. Schs., 1940-43, Whitefish Bay (Wis.) Pub. Schs., 1943-64. Contbr. articles, story, poems to various pubs. Bd. dirs. Homestead H.S. chpt. Am. Field Svc., Mequon, Wis., 1970-80; mem. Milw. Aux. VNA, 1975—, 2d v.p., 1983-85, Milw. Pub. Mus. Enrichment Club, 1975—, Boys and Girls Club of Greater Milw., 1986—; vol. Reading is Fun program, 1987—, Milw. Symphony Orch. League, 1960—, Ptnrs. in Conservation, World Wildlife Fund, Washington, 1991—, Milw. Art Mus. Garden Club, 1979—, com. chmn., 1981-86; mem. Chancellor's Soc. U. Wis.-Milw., 1991—; travel lectr. various orgns., 1980—. Mem. AAUW, Milw. Coll. Endowment Assn. (v.p. 1987-90, pres. 1991-93), Bascom Hill Soc. (U. Wis.), Woman's Club Wis., Alpha Phi (pres. Milw. alumnae 1962-64), Pi Lambda Theta (pres. Milw. alumnae 1962-64), Delta Kappa Gamma. Republican. Presbyterian. Avocations: writing, travel, nature. Home: 3903 W Mequon Rd Mequon WI 53092-2727

DOHNANYI, CHRISTOPH VON, musician, conductor; b. Berlin, Sept. 8, 1929; s. Hans and Christina (Bonhoeffer) von D. Student, U. Munich, Hochschule fuer Musik, Munich, Fla. State U., Berkshire Music Ctr.; doctorate (hon.), Oberlin Coll., Cleve. Inst. Music, Case Western Res. U., Eastman Sch. Music, 1998. Coach, condr. Frankfurt (Germany) Opera, 1952-57, gen. music dir., artistic dir., 1968-77; gen. music dir. Lubeck, Germany, 1957-63, Kassel, Germany, 1963-66; dir. West German Radio Symphony, Cologne, 1964-70; artistic dir., chief condr., intendant Hamburg (Germany) State Opera, 1977-84; music dir. designate Cleve. Orch., 1982-84, music dir., 1984—; prin. condr. Philharmonia Orch., London, 1997—; guest condr. in U.S. and Europe, including Salzburg Festival, Chatelet Paris, Zurich Opera House, Israel Philharmonic, Orchestre de Paris, Vienna Philharmonic; prin. guest condr. Philharmonia Orch., London, 1994—. Recordings with Vienna Philharmonia include opera: Wozzeck, Lulu, Fidelio, Flying Dutchman, Salome, 5 Mendelssohn symphonies, works by Stravinsky, Tschaikovsky, Glass, Schnittke; recordings with Cleve. orch. include symphonies of Beethoven, Brahms, Schumann, Bruckner, Dvorak, Mahler, Mozart, Schubert; orchestral works by Bartok, Lutoslawski, R. Strauss, Webern, Ives, Ruggles, Birtwistle; opera Rheingold, Walkure. Recipient Scopus award Am. Friends of Hebrew U. in Jerusalem, 1996, Scroll of Remembrance for Von Dohnányi and Bonhoeffer Families in German resistance U.S. Holocaust Mus., Washington, 1995, Condr. of Yr. award Musical Am., 1992, Comdr.'s Cross Republic of Austria, 1992, Comdr. de L'Ordre des Arts et des Lettres, France, Cross Order of Merit, Germany, Bartok prize, Hungary, 1982, Goethe medal City of Frankfurt, 1979, Richard Straus prize Munich, 1951. Office: Cleve Orch 11001 Euclid Ave Cleveland OH 44106-1713 Address: Colbert Artists Mgmt 111 W 57th St New York NY 10019-2211*

DOHR, DONALD R., metallurgical engineer, researcher; b. Rio de Janeiro, Niteroi, Apr. 12, 1924; came to U.S., 1944; s. Nicholas and Candida (Caramuru) D.; m. Virginia Marion O'Donnell, Mar. 30, 1960 (dec. Feb. 1987). ME, Stevens Inst. Tech., 1952, MS in Metallurgy, 1968. Jr. metallurgist Crucible Steel Co., Harrison, N.J., 1952-54; metallurgist Engelhard Industries, Newark, 1954-56, Foster Wheeler Corp., Carterei, N.J., 1956-60, Weston Instruments, Inc., Newark, 1960-66; sr. metallurgist Singer Co., Denville, N.J., 1966-71; unit head materials and processes lab. Kearfott Guidance & Navigation Corp. (formerly Singer Co.), Little Falls, N.J., 1971-91. Author: Liquid Phases Sintering Mechanisms, Magnetic Properties of Metals & Alloys. Staff sgt. U.S. Army, 1944-46, PTO. Mem. Am. Soc. Metals-Internat., Nat. Soc. Profl. Engrs., Soc. Mfg. Engrs. Republican. Roman Catholic. Achievements include patents in Magnetic Field Force Application and Threat Tensioner. Home: 410A Troy Towers Bloomfield NJ 07003-3370

DOHRENWEND, BRUCE PHILIP, psychiatric epidemiologist, social psychologist, educator; b. N.Y.C., July 26, 1927; s. Gustav John and Gertrude Elise (Funke) D.; m. Barbara Anne Snell, Sept. 21, 1951 (dec. June 1982); m. Catherine J. Douglass, June 1, 1985. B.A., Columbia U., 1950, M.A., 1952; Ph.D., Cornell U., 1955. Cert. psychologist, N.Y. Research assoc. Cornell U., Ithaca, N.Y., 1954-58; research assoc. Columbia U., N.Y.C., 1958-63, asst. prof., 1963-67, assoc. prof., 1967-70, prof., 1970—; chief of rsch. dept. social psychiatry N.Y. State Psychiat. Inst., N.Y.C., 1979—; mem. task panel on problems, scope and boundaries Presl. Commn. on Mental Health, Washington, 1977-78; head task group on behavioral effects Presl. Commn. on Accident at Three Mile Island, Washington, 1979; mem. tech. evaluation bd. Vietnam Era Veterans study, VA, Washington, 1983-89. Author: (with others) Social Status and Psychological Disorder, 1969, Mental Illness in the United States, 1980, (with others) Socioeconomic Status and Psychiatric Disorders, 1992; editor: (with others) Stressful Life Events, 1974, Stressful Life Events and Their Contexts, 1981. Served with USNR, 1945-46. Recipient Research Scientist award NIMH, 1971, 76, 81, 86, 91, Emily Mumford award Columbia U., 1992; NIMH grantee, 1964-82, 77—. Fellow Am. Psychol. Assn. (co-recipient disting. contbns. div. community psychology award 1980), AAAS (co-recipient prize for behavioral rsch. 1990), Am. Psychopathol. Assn. (Hamilton award 1994); mem. Am. Pub. Health Assn. (co-recipient Rema Lapouse Mental Health Epidemiology award 1981), Am. Sociol. Assn., Soc. for Study of Social Problems (Disting. Contbrs. award divsn. psychiat. sociology 1994). Home: 1056 5th Ave New York NY 10028-0112 Office: NY State Psychiat Inst 1051 Riverside Dr Unit 8 New York NY 10032*

DOHRING, DOUG, marketing executive. Chmn. Dohring Co., Calif. Office: Dohring Co 412 W Broadway Ste 300 Glendale CA 91204

DOHRING, LAURIE, marketing executive. CEO Dohring Co., Glendale, Calif. Office: Dohring Co 412 West Broadway Ste 300 Glendale CA 91204

DOHRMANN, RICHARD MARTIN, computer software publishing executive; b. Washington, Mo., Jan. 25, 1947; s. Leonard Benjamin and Helen Emma Fronie (Zeiler) D.; m. Marie Lyle Howell, Aug. 30, 1980; children: Helen Alexandra, Elizabeth Howell, Mary Lyle. BA, U. Ill., 1969; MBA, Vanderbilt U., Nashville, 1987. Owner Fat Chance Prodns., Nashville, 1973-80; journalist Sta. WPLN-FM, Nashville, 1973-79; software engr., analyst S&H Computer Systems, Inc., Nashville, 1979-81, systems analyst, 1980-81, asst. gen. mgr., 1981-82, v.p. mktg. and sales, 1982-96, bd. dirs.; founder, pres., chmn., CEO Express Media Corp., Nashville, 1996—; spkr. at confs. in field. Composer various music works; author poetry, film criticism; contbr. articles on computer software to profl. jours. Dir. Solstice Festival, Nashville; chmn. adv. coun. Susan Gray Sch. for Children, Nashville; pres. Nashville New Music Consort; bd. dirs. Nashville Chamber Orch. Mem. Beta Gamma Sigma. Episcopalian. Home: PO Box 120804 Nashville TN 37212-0804 Office: Express Media Corp 1419 Donelson Pike Nashville TN 37217-2957

DOHRMANN, RUSSELL WILLIAM, manufacturing company executive; b. Clinton, Iowa, June 29, 1942; s. Russell Wilbert and Anita Doris (Miller) D.; m. Rita Marie Meade, Dec. 26, 1964 (dec. Feb. 1978); m. M. Jean Stapleton, Aug. 18, 1979. BS, Upper Iowa U., 1965; MBA, Drake U., 1971. Acct. Chamberlain Mfg. Corp., Clinton, 1965-66; plant controller Chamberlain Mfg. Corp., Derry, Pa., 1967-68; fin. analyst Frye Copysystems Inc., Des Moines, 1968-71, v.p., controller, 1971-77, pres., 1980-97, also bd. dirs.; internat. controller Wheelabrator-Frye, N.Y.C., 1977-78; pres. Fry-eTech, Inc., Des Moines, 1997-98; group controller Wheelabrator-Frye, Des Moines, 1978-80; cons., 1998—. Mem. Nat. Assn. Accts., Des Moines C. of C. Republican. Methodist.

DOI, LOIS, psychiatric social worker; b. Honolulu, Oct. 24, 1951; d. James Masato and Thelma Kimiko Miyamoto; m. Brian Doi, May 26, 1972; children: Michael, Lorian. BS, U. Hawaii, 1974, MSW, 1978. Lic. clin. social worker, Calif. Psychiat. social worker, child specialist Desert Community Mental Health Ctr., Indio, Calif., 1979-92, coordinator children's day treatment program, 1982-91; pvt. practice psychiat. social worker 1-2-1 Counseling, Palm Springs, Calif., 1992—; owner, ptnr. 1-2-1 Counseling, Rancho Mirage, Calif.; psychiat. social worker, adult case mgr. Desert Community Mental Health Ctr., Palm Springs, Calif., 1992-93; clin. dir. Barbara Sinatra Children's Ctr., Rancho Mirage, Calif., 1998; expert examiner, Bd. of Behavioral Sci. Examiners, 1987—. Vol. advisor Community Recreation Ctr. Youth Group, Hawaii, 1967-69; vol. interviewer ARC Food Stamp Program, Hawaii, 1973; vol. asst. YWCA Programs Young Mothers and Teens, Hawaii, 1973; vol. group leader YWCA Juvenile Delinquent Program, Hawaii, 1973; placement counselor Vols. In Service to Am., L.A., 1975; VISTA counselor L.A. Urban League, 1975-76. Mem. Nat. Assn. Social Workers. Avocations: needlework, reading. Office: 1-2-1 Counseling # 409 42-600 Bob Hope Dr Rancho Mirage CA 92270

DOIDA, STANLEY Y., dentist; b. Kalamath Falls, Calif., Dec. 15, 1944; s. Sam S. and Mae M. (Nakao) D.; m. Eileen M. Crilly; children: Stanley Jr., Scott Samuel. Student, Knox Coll., 1965-67; DDS, Northwestern U., 1970. Asst. prof. Sch. Dentistry Northwestern U., Chgo., 1970-71; CEO Midtown Dental, Denver, 1971—; instr. U. Colo. Dental Sch., Denver, 1972-74. Mem. ADA, Acad. Operative Dentistry, Acad. Gold Foil Operators, Glenmoor Country Club, Club at Cordillera. Home: 9638 E Maplewood Cir Englewood CO 80111-7016 Office: Midtown Dental 1800 Vine St Denver CO 80206-1122

DOIG, BEVERLY IRENE, systems specialist; b. Bozeman, Mont., Oct. 21, 1936; d. James Stuart Doig and Elsie Florence (Andes) Doig Townsend. AA, Graceland Coll., 1956; BA, U. Kans., 1958; MS, U. Wis., 1970; cert. in Interior Design, UCLA, 1993, tng. classes Windows NT oper. sys., 1996. Aerodynamic technician II Ames Labs.-NACA, Moffett Field, Calif., 1957; real time systems specialist Dept. of Army, White Sands Missile Range, N.Mex., 1958-66; large systems specialist computing ctr. U. Wis., Madison, 1966-70; sr. systems analyst Burroughs, Ltd., Canberra, Australia, 1970-72; systems specialist Tech. Info. Office Burroughs Corp., Detroit, 1973-78; sr. systems specialist Burroughs Gmbh, Munich, 1978-79, Burroughs AB, Stockholm, 1979-80; networking cons. Midland Bank, Ltd., Sheffield, Eng., 1980-83; networking specialist Burroughs Corp. (now UNISYS), Mission Viejo, Calif., 1983-98; tchg. asst. Canberra (Australia) Coll., 1972; tchr. Wayne State U. Ext., Detroit, 1976-77; freelance interior designer, 1992-98; with Homeworks Decorating Showroom, Farmington, N.Mex., 1998—; part-time tchr. computer application San Juan Coll., Farmington, 1998—. Vol. youth groups and camps Reorganized LDS Ch., N.Mex., Wis., Australia, Mich., Calif., Germany, U.K.; inner youth worker, Detroit; mentor Saddleback H.S. Scholar Mitchell Math., 1956-58, Watkins Residential, 1956-58. Mem. Assn. Computing Machinery (local chpt. chmn. membership 1969), Lambda Delta Sigma. Republican. Avocations: working with junior high, doing craft projects, designing. Office: HOMEWORKS 1008 N Butler Ave Farmington NM 87401-6865

DOIG, JAMESON WALLACE, political science educator; b. Oakland, Calif., June 12, 1933; s. James Rufus and Mary (Jameson) D.; m. Joan Nishimoto, Oct. 8, 1955; children: Rachel, Stephen, Sarah. A.B., Dartmouth Coll., 1954; M.P.A., Princeton U., 1958, M.A., 1959, Ph.D., 1961. Research asst. N.J. Republican Com., 1957; staff mem. Brookings Instn., 1959-61; from asst. prof. to prof. politics and pub. affairs PrincetoN U., 1961—; assoc. dean Woodrow Wilson Sch., Princeton U., 1972-73, dir. univ. research program in criminal justice, 1973-93; dir. Grad. Studies Polit. Dept. Princeton, 1988-90, chair Undergrad. Studies, 1991-94, chair politcs. dept., 1997—; cons. Fels Fund, 1966-68, Daniel and Florence Guggenheim Found., 1970—, Nat. Prison Overcrowding Project, 1983, Lavenburg Found., 1983-90; vis. prof. John Jay Coll. Criminal Justice, 1967-68, 70-72; mem. adv. com. Gov. N.J., 1965-70, ABA 1974-78, Supreme Ct. N.J., 1980-92, Vera Inst. Justice, 1986-92, NRC/Trans. Rsch. Bd., 1990-92; mem. adv. bd. Police Found., 1977-78, Rockefeller Ctr., Dartmouth Coll., 1990-96, Taubman Ctr. Harvard U., 1996—; mem. adv. coun. N.J. Dept. Corrections, 1974-82, vice-chmn., 1980-82; cons. on parole to gov. of N.J., 1975-78; bd. dirs. N.J. Assn. on Correction, 1971-74, 80-82, N.J. Bar Inst. & Law Ctr., 1974-78, Nat. Ctr. for Adminstrv. Justice, 1979-82, S. Forty Corp., 1980-82. Author: Metropolitan Transportation Politics and the New York Region, 1966, (with D.E. Mann) The Assistant Secretaries, 1965, (with D.T. Stanley and D.E. Mann) Men Who Govern, 1967, (with M. Danielson) New York: The Politics of Urban Regional Development, 1982, Empire on the Hudson, 1999; co-author, editor: Criminal Corrections: Ideals and Realities, 1983, Leadership and Innovation, 1987, 90, Combating Corruption/Encouraging Ethics, 1990; contbr. Governing the States and Localities, 1969, Agenda for a City, 1970, Metropolitan Politics, 1971, Urban Politics and Policy-Making, 1973, Crime and Criminal Justice, 1975, Public Administration of Law Enforcement Policies, 1979, Politics of Urban Development, 1987, Public Authorities and Public Policy, 1991, Landscape of Modernity, 1992, Studies in American Political Development, 1993, Technology and Culture, 1994, Building the Public City, 1995. Served to lt. (j.g.) USNR, 1954-56. Recipient Herbert Kaufman award, 1989, A. P. Usher prize, 1995, A. Wildavsky award, 1997. Mem. Am. Correctional Assn., Am. Polit. Sci. Assn., Am. Soc. Pub. Adminstrn., Law and Soc. Assn., Soc. History of Technology, Policy Studies Orgn., Phi Beta Kappa. Office: Princeton U Corwin Hall Robertson Hall Princeton NJ 08544

DOJKA, EDWIN SIGMUND, civil engineer; b. Niagara Falls, N.Y., Dec. 20, 1924; s. Zygmunt Joseph and Felixa (Pasek) D.; BCE, Rensselaer Poly. Inst., 1951; m. Jean L. Keller, July 9, 1949; children: Paul, Gail Dojka Hoesterman, Jay. Structures engr. Bell Aircraft Corp., Wheatfield, N.Y., 1951-52; design engr. Hooker Electro Chem. Corp., Niagara Falls, N.Y., 1952-55; civil engr. City of Niagara Falls (N.Y.), 1955-58, asst. city engr., 1958-60, dep. city engr., 1960-63, city engr., 1963-79; city engr. City of North Tonawanda, 1979-85; mem. sewer commn., plumbing bd., 1963-85, mem. planning bd., 1963-66, bd. equalization rev., 1963-71; mem. Niagara County Planning Bd., 1978-91, Traffic Safety Commn., 1979-85. Mem. United Fund Community Budget Com., 1962-68; mem. Community Ambassador Gen. Com., 1958, 59; Fleet Safety adv. commr., Niagara Falls, 1960-68; bd. assocs. Mt. St. Mary's Hosp., 1969-70. With inf. AUS, World War II; ETO. Decorated Bronze Star, Purple Heart, Combat Infantryman's badge. Registered profl. engr., land surveyor, N.Y. Fellow ASCE; mem. NRA, Soc. Am. Mil. Engrs., Am. Pub. Works Assn., Am. Water Works Assn.,

Nat. Soc. Profl. Engrs., The Heritage Found., Water Pollution Control Fedn., Am. Planning Assn., Inst. for Engring., Am. Arbitration Assn. (comml. panelist 1978—), DAV, Internat. Platform Assn., Am. Legion, 102d Inf. Div. Assn., AMVETS, Meml. Day Assn., Boys Club Alumni Assn., VFW, Pulaski Civic League, Polish Legion Am. Vets., Royal Canadian Legion (hon.), Mil. Order Purple Heart, 40 and 8, 2d Armored Div. Assn., 25th Bomb Group Assn., Hon. Order Ky. Cols., Kosciuszko Found., Dom Polski Club, First Friday Club, Echo Club, Sertoma Club, K.C. (hon.), Elks, Sigma Xi, Chi Epsilon, Tau Beta Pi. Roman Catholic. Home: 509 80th St Niagara Falls NY 14304-2301

DOJNY, RICHARD FRANCIS, publishing company executive; b. Norwalk, Conn., Apr. 24, 1940; s. Francis Joseph and Mary (Ross) D.; m. Brooke Maury, July 16, 1966; children: Matthew, Maury. B.A., Dartmouth Coll., 1962. Sales rep. McGraw-Hill Book Co., N.Y.C., 1964-69, editor, 1969-73, field mgr., 1973-76, regional mgr., 1976-77, dir. mktg., 1977-79, v.p., gen. mgr., 1979-84; v.p. mktg. Macmillan Pub. Co., N.Y.C., 1984-85, v.p., dir. trade sales, 1985-86, v.p. adult trade pub., 1986-87, v.p. sales and mktg. div., 1987-91, pres., college div., 1991-94; pres. Prentice Hall edn., career and tech. divsn. Simon & Schuster Higher Edn. Group, Upper Saddle River, N.J., 1994—. 1st lt. U.S. Army, 1962-64. Mem. Assn. Am. Pubs. (higher edn. divsn. exec. com.), Nat. Assn. Coll. Stores (bd. dirs. 1991-94). Roman Catholic. Home: 39 Burr Farms Rd Westport CT 06880-3818 Office: Simon & Schuster Higher Edn Prentice Hall 1 Lake St Upper Saddle River NJ 07458-1813

DOKE, MARSHALL J., JR., lawyer; b. Wichita Falls, Tex., June 9, 1934; s. Marshall J. and Mary Jane (Johnson) D.; m. Betty Marie Orsini, June 2, 1956; children: Gregory J., Michael J., Laetitia Marie. BA magna cum laude, Hardin-Simmons U., 1956; LLB magna cum laude, So. Meth. U., 1959. Bar: Tex. 1959. Assoc. Thompson, Knight, Wright & Simmons, Dallas, 1959, 62-65; founding ptnr. Rain Harrell Emery Young & Doke, Dallas, 1965-87, Doke & Riley, Dallas, 1987-92; ptnr. McKenna & Cuneo, 1993-96, Gardere & Wynne, L.L.P., Dallas, 1996—; gen. counsel Tex. Rep. Party, 1976-77; mem. adv. coun. U.S. Ct. Fed. Claims, 1982—. Author: Ann. Procurement Rev., Govt. Contractor Briefing Papers, Contract Changes, Fed. Contract Mgmt., 1982—, also articles; editor-in-chief: Southwestern Law Jour., 1958-59; editor: ABA Ann. Devels. in Govt. Contract Law, 1975-78 . Pres. Hope Cottage-Children's Bur., Inc., 1969-70, Hope Cottage Found., 1997—; mem. bd. visitors Law Sch., So. Meth. U., 1966-69, McDonald Obs., U. Tex., 1990—; dir. Tex. Hist. Found., 1993—, v.p., 1996-98; mem. law com., bd. trustees So. Meth. U., 1977-78; bd. dirs., pres. World Trade Assn., Dallas-Ft. Worth, 1979-80; chmn. bd. dirs. Internat. Trade Assn. Dallas/Ft. Worth, 1993-94; bd. dirs., sec. Theater Trustees Am., 1983-93; chmn. Mayor's Internat. Com., City of Dallas, 1984-87, mem. Judicial Nominating Commn., 1997—. 1st lt. JAGC, U.S. Army, 1959-62. Fellow Am. Bar Found., Tex. Bar Found.; mem. ABA (chmn. sect. pub. contract law 1969-70, ho. of dels. 1970-72, 74—, bd. govs. 1980-82, nominating com. 1988-91, chmn. conf. sect. dels. 1991—), Tex. Bar Assn., U.S. Ct. of Fed. Claims Bar Assn. (bd. govs. 1987—, pres. 1996), Bd. of Contract Appeals Bar Assn. (pres. 1988-90, bd. govs. 1988—), Am. Bar Retirement Assn. (bd. dirs., trustee 1980-84, pres 1982-90), Nat. Conf. Lawyers and CPAs (co-chmn. 1983-85), Nat. Contract Mgmt. Assn. (nat. bd. advisors 1983—), Dallas C. of C. (chmn. internat. com. 1979-83). E-mail: dokm@gardere.com. Home: 6910 Dartbrook Dr Dallas TX 75240-7926 Office: Gardere & Wynne Thanksgiving Tower Ste 3000 Dallas TX 75201-7254

DOKURNO, ANTHONY DAVID, lawyer; b. Gardner, Mass., Mar. 14, 1957; s. Anthony Chester and Damey Anteena (Aleson) D.; m. Andee J. Rappazzo. BA, Holy Cross Coll., 1979; JD, Vt. Law Sch., 1982; postgrad., Johns Hopkins U., 1993-94. Bar: Mass. 1982, U.S. Ct. Appeals for the Armed Forces 1986, U.S. Supreme Ct. 1987. Pvt. practice law Fitchburg, Mass., 1982-86; appellate counsel Navy-Marine Corps Appellate Rev. Activity, Washington, 1986-88; atty. admiralty div. JAG, Washington, 1988-90, atty. ops. and mgmt., 1991-93. Assoc. counsel, bd. vets. appeals Dept. Vets. Affairs, 1994-96; analyst Dept. of Def., 1996—. Comdr. USNR, 1998—. Mem. Maritime Law Assn., Nat. Cryptologic History Found., Am. Legion, Naval Res. Assn., Mensa, Phi Beta Kappa. Home: 200 N Pickett St Apt 1504 Alexandria VA 22304-2127

DOLAMORE, MICHAEL JOHN, physician; b. London, July 27, 1958; came to U.S., 1986; s. John David and Myra Rosemary (Wisson) D.; m. Jeanne Marie Porcino, Sept. 2, 1984; children: Matthew, Christina, Sophie. MB BS, London U., 1982. Diplomate Am. Bd. Family Practitioners, Am. Bd. Family Physicians; cert. added qilifications in geriatric medicine; diplomate Royal Coll. Gen. Practitioners; cert. med. dir. Resident Colchester, England, 1983-86; attending physician Mid Hudson Family Health Svcs. Inst., Kingston, N.Y., 1988—; assoc. clin. prof. N.Y. Med. Coll., Valhalla, N.Y., 1991-98; med. dir. Ten Broeck Commons, Lake Katrine, N.Y., 1995—. Geriatric Medicine fellow Mt. Sinai Sch. Medicine, N.Y.C., 1986-87. Fellow Am. Acad. Family Physicians (cert. med. dir.); mem. Am. Med. Dirs. Assn., Am. Geriatric Soc., N.Y. State Med. Soc., Med. Soc. Ulster County, Royal Coll. Gen. Practitioners U.K., N.Y. Med. Dirs. Assn. Avocations: fly fishing, skiing, history, outdoors, music. Office: Mid-Hudson Family Health 20 Ricks Rd Woodstock NY 12498-1114

DOLAN, ANDREW KEVIN, lawyer; b. Chgo., Dec. 7, 1945; s. Andrew O. and Elsie (Grafner) D.; children: Andrew, Francesca, Melinda. BA, U. Ill., Chgo., 1967; JD, Columbia U., 1970, MPH, 1976, DPH, 1980. Bar: Wash. 1980. Asst. prof. law Rutgers-Camden Law Sch., N.J., 1970-72; assoc. prof. law U. So. Calif., L.A., 1972-75; assoc. prof. pub. health U. Wash., Seattle, 1977-81; ptnr. Bogle & Gates, Seattle, 1988-93; pvt. practice law, 1993—. Commr. Civil Svc. Commn., Lake Forest Park, Wash., 1981; mcpl. judge City of Lake Forest Park, 1982-98. Russell Sage fellow, 1975. Mem. Order of Coif, Washington Athletic Club. Avocation: book collecting. Office: 5800 Columbia Ctr 701 5th Ave Seattle WA 98104-7016

DOLAN, CHARLES FRANCIS, media, entertainment company executive; b. Oct. 16, 1926; m. Helen Burgess; children: Patrick, Tom, James, Mari-Anne, Kathleen, Deborah. Student, John Carroll U. Founder Sterling Manhattan Cable, 1961, Teleguide, Inc., HBO, 1971, Cablevision, Sterling Manhattan Cable, 1973; mng. gen. ptnr. Cablevision and predecessor firms, 1973-85; founder, chmn. Cablevision Systems Corp., Woodbury, N.Y., 1985—; majority owner Madison Square Garden Properties, 1995—, also bd. dirs. Bd. dirs. St. Francis Hosp., L.I., N.Y., Cold Spring Harbor Lab., ; trustee Fairfield (Conn.) U.; mng. dir. Met. Opera, N.Y.C. Avocation: sailing. Office: Cablevision Systems Corp 1111 Stewart Ave Bethpage NY 11714-3581

DOLAN, DAN, communications executive; b. Passaic, N.J., Aug. 3, 1949. Sports writer Star Ledger, Newark, 1970-73, invesitgative reporter, 1973-79; copy editor N.Y. Post, N.Y.C., 1980-84; asst. editor Nat. Enquirer, Cantara, Fla., 1984-87; assoc. editor Globe Mag., 1989—; founding editor Luxury Lifestyles, 1991; editor Globe, 1994-96, Nat. Examiner, 1992-94; dep. editl. dir. Globe Comm., Boca Raton, Fla., 1996—. Office: Globe Comm 5401 Broken Sound Blvd NW Boca Raton FL 33487-3512

DOLAN, EDWARD CHARLES, lawyer; b. N.Y.C., Sept. 25, 1953; s. Eamonn Ignatius and Mary Theresa (Golden) D.; m. Margaret Mary Vaughan, Nov. 29, 1980; children: Caroline, William. BA, Columbia U., 1975; JD, Georgetown U., 1978. Bar: Md. 1978, D.C. 1979, U.S. Dist. Ct. Md. 1980, U.S. Dist. Ct. D.C. 1980, U.S. Supreme Ct. 1983, U.S. Ct. of Appeals (4th cir.), U.S. Dist. Ct. Colo. 1997. Intern Office of U.S. Atty., ea. dist., N.Y., 1977; law clk. Dept. Justice Drug Enforcement Adminstrn., Washington, 1978; assoc. Beckett Cromwell & Myers, Bethesda, Md., 1978-84; assoc. Hogan and Hartson L.L.P., Washington, D.C., 1984-87, counsel, 1987-89, ptnr., 1989—; Chandler Bankruptcy Inn of Ct., Washington, 1990—; mem. standing com. local rules Bankruptcy Ct., Md., 1984—, chair, 1996-97. Author: (with others) The Law of Distressed Real Estate, 1988, Practice Manual for the Maryland Lawyer, 1989, 2d edit., 1992; contbg. author: Environmental Aspects of Real Estate Transactions, 1995. Pres. De Chantal Parish Home and Sch. Assn., Bethesda, 1990-92; active De Chantal Parish Sch. Bd., Bethesda, 1992-96, pres., 1994-96; mem. parents' coun. St. Anselm's Abbey Sch., Washington, 1995—; active Columbia Coll. Secondary Schs. Com., N.Y.C., 1978-92; class co-chmn. Columbia Coll. Club, Washington, 1990-92. Mem. ABA, Md. State Bar Assn., Montgomery County Bar Assn. (chmn. bankruptcy com. 1990-91), Prince George's County Bar Assn. (spl. com. on professionalism 1988-90), Bankruptcy Bar Assn. (Md. pres. 1989-90, dir. 1988—), D.C. Bar Assn. (chmn. bus. bankruptcy com. 1995—). Office: Hogan and Hartson LLP 555 13th St NW Ste 800E Washington DC 20004-1161

DOLAN, EDWARD FRANCIS, writer; b. Oakland, Calif., Feb. 10, 1924; s. Edward Francis Sr. and Zelda Olympia (Vieira) D.; m. Rose Esther Pudfedoot, Nov. 17, 1945 (dec.); children: Timothy L., Wendy Anne Irving. Student, U. So. Calif., L.A., 1942-43, U. San Francisco, 1958-59. Freelance writer KRON-TV, Bay Area Pub. Schs. TV Coun., Pub. Svc. telecasts for Archdiocese, San Francisco, 1949-53; instr. dept. speech and drama Monticello Coll., Alton, Ill., 1953-56; writer, 1957—. Author: Pasteur and the Invisible Giants, 1958, White Battleground: The Conquest of the Arctic, 1961, Disaster 1906: The San Francisco Earthquake and Fire, 1967, Legal Action: A Layman's Guide, 1972; A Lion in the Sun: The Rise and Fall of the British Empire, 1973, Amnesty: The American Puzzle, 1976, Gun Control: A Decision for Americans, 1978, Child Abuse, 1980, revised edit., 1992, Adolf Hitler: A Portrait in Tyranny, 1981, History of the Movies, 1983, The Simon & Schuster Sports Question and Answer Book, 1984, Hollywood Goes to War, 1985, Drugs in Sports, 1986, revised edit., 1992, The Old Farmer's Almanac Book of Weather Lore, 1988, MIA: Missing in Action, 1989, America after Vietnam: Legacies of a Hated War, 1989, (with M.M. Scariano) Nuclear Waste: The 10,000-Year Challenge, 1990, Our Poisoned Sky, 1991, America in World War II: 1941, 1991, America in World War II: 1942, 1992, America in World War II: 1943, 1992, Animal Folklore: From Black Cats to White Horses, 1992, The American Wilderness and Its Future, 1992, America in World War II, 1944, 1993, Folk Medicine: Cures and Curiosities, 1993, America in World War II: 1945, 1994, Your Privacy: Protecting It in a Nosy World, 1994, Teenagers and Compulsive Gambling, 1994, (with M.M. Scariano) Illiteracy in America, 1995, The American Revolution: How We Fought the War of Independence, 1995, America in World War I, 1996, (with M.M. Scariano) Shaping U.S. Foreign Policy, 1996, In Sports, Money Talks, 1996, Our Poisoned Waters, 1997, The Civil War: A House Divided, 1997, America in the Korean War, 1998, Beyond the Frontier: the Story of the Trails West, 1999, 102 non-fiction titles. With U.S. Army, 1943-45, ETO. Mem. Calif. Writers Club (pres. Redwood br. 1976-77, 83-84). Avocation: golf.

DOLAN, ELLEN MARIE, library director; b. Marlboro, Mass., Mar. 23, 1959; d. Gerald John and Ann (Perry) D.; m. James Golden, May 21, 1993; 1 child, Catherine Dolan Hayden. BA in Edn., Anna Maria Coll., Paxton, Mass., 1981; M Libr. and Info. Sci., Simmons Coll., 1990. Cert. librarianship, Mass. Young adult libr. Marlborough (Mass.) Pub. Libr., 1981-82, children's libr., 1982-86, asst. dir., 1986-93; libr. dir. Beaman Meml. Pub. Libr., West Boylston, Mass., 1993—; mem. interlibr. loan task force, mem. bibliographic record procurement com., mem. strategic planning com. Ctrl.-Western Mass. Automated Resource Sharing Network, Paxton, 1991-96; chmn. tech. utilization com. Ctrl. Mass. Regional Libr. Sys., Shrewsbury, 1996, mem. exec. bd., 1998—. Mem. ALA, New Eng. Libr. Assn., Mass. Libr. Assn., Phi Beta Mu. Avocation: storytelling.

DOLAN, JAMES, communications executive; 5 children. Past advt. sales v.p. Cablevision Sys. Corp., past advt. corp. dir. Rainbow Advt. Sales Corp., past CEO Rainbow Programming Holdings, Inc.; CEO, pres. Cablevision Sys. Corp., Woodbury, N.Y., 1995—, also bd. dirs.; CEO Rainbow Holdings, Inc.; creator Rainbow Advtsg. Sales Corp.; bd. dirs. Hazelden N.Y., Cable Labs, Colo., Madison Sq. Garden; creator, past mgr. Sta. WKNR-AM, Cleve. Hon. co-chmn. L.I. Film and TV Found.; active capital campaign com. Friends Acad. Mem. Nat. Cable TV Assn. (bd. dirs., mem. exec. com., chmn. com. music licensing). Avocations: yachting, music. Office: Cablevision Sys Corp 111 Stewart Ave Bethpage NY 11714*

DOLAN, JAMES MICHAEL, JR., zoological society executive; b. N.Y.C., Feb. 27, 1937; s. James Michael and Emily Catherine (Wackerbauer) D. BS, Mt. St. Mary's Coll., Emmitsburg, Md., 1959; PhD, Inst. fur Haustierkunde, U. Kiel, Fed. Republic Germany, 1963. Asst. curator birds San Diego Zoo, 1963-64, assoc. curator birds, 1964-73, dir. animal sci., 1973-74; gen. curator San Diego Wild Animal Pk., 1974-81; gen. curator mammals Zool. Soc. San Diego, 1982-85, dir. collections, 1986—; advisor Econ. Rsch. Assocs.; adj. prof. zoology San Diego State U.; tech. asst. UN in Malaysia, 1970, Indian Zool. Gardens, 1976, Kuwait Zool. Garden, 1978, Seoul (Korea) Zool. Garden; mem. Survival Svc. Commn., Faro, Portugal, 1978; zoo advisory for U.S. Fish & Wildlife Svc. to India, 1980; del. internat. confs. including Conv. on Internat. Trade in Endangered Species Wild Fauna and Flora, Buenos Aires, 1985, Internat. Conf. Rupricaprines, Japan, 1987. Collecting expdns. to Cen. Am. countries, 1965, Australia, 1966, Papua-New Guinea, 1966, Java and Borneo, 1969, Fiji, 1970, Costa Rica, 1976; participant giant eland capture expdn. Senegal and Mali, 1979; mem. adv. bd. Internat. Zoo Yearbook, London. Fellow Am. Assn. Zool. Pks. and Aquariums (coordinator Arabian oryx group species survival plan); mem. Internat. Union Dirs. Zool. Gardens, Internat. Union for Conservation of Nature & Natural Resources (active several species survival commn. specialist groups, del. meetings and confs. Eng., Australia, Czechoslovakia, Hong Kong 1980-84, Fed. Republic Germany, 1987, reintroduction program Przewalski's horse Republic of China and Tibet, 1987, conf. Arabian oryx Saudi Arabia, 1987, com. to review new Taipei Zoo 1987), Am. Pheasant and Waterfowl Assn., African Lovebird Soc., Avicultural Soc., Explorer's Club, Fauna Preservation Soc., Found. Protection and Preservation of Przewalski Horse, Internat. Crane Found., World Pheasant Assn., Zooculturists, German Soc. Mammalogists. Avocations: book collecting, aviculture. Home: 18836 Paradise Mountain Rd Valley Center CA 92082-7430 Office: San Diego Zoo PO Box 551 San Diego CA 92112-0551*

DOLAN, JAMES VINCENT, lawyer; b. Washington, Nov. 11, 1938; s. John Vincent and Philomena Theresa (Vance) D.; m. Anne McSherry Reilly, June 18, 1960; children: Caroline McSherry, James Reilly. AB, Georgetown U., 1960, LLB, 1963. Bar: U.S. Dist. Ct. 1963, U.S. Ct. Appeals (D.C.) cir. 1964, U.S. Ct. Appeals (4th cir.) 1976. Law clk. U.S. Ct. Appeals D.C., 1963-64; assoc. Steptoe & Johnson, Washington, 1964-71, ptnr., 1971-82; mem. Steptoe & Johnson Chartered, Washington, 1982-83; v.p. law Union Pacific R.R., Omaha, 1983—. Co-author: Construction Contract Law, 1981; contbr. articles to legal jours.; editor-in-chief: Georgetown Law Jour., 1962-63. Mem. ABA, Nebr. Bar Assn., D.C. Bar Assn., Barristers, Congl. Country Club (v.p. 1982, pres. 1983), Omaha Country Club. Republican. Roman Catholic. Home: 1909 County Road 8 Yutan NE 68073-5013 Office: Union Pacific RR 1416 Dodge St Omaha NE 68179-0002

DOLAN, JAN CLARK, former state legislator; b. Akron, Ohio, Jan. 15, 1927; d. Herbert Spencer and Jean Risk Clark; m. Walter John Dolan, Apr. 22, 1950 (dec. July 1986); children: Mark Raymond, Scott Spencer, Gary Clark, Todd Alvin. BA, U. Akron, 1949. Home svc. rep. East Ohio Gas Co., Akron, 1949-50; dietitian Akron City Hosp., 1950-51; tchr. Brecksville (Ohio) Sch. Dist., 1962-66; adminstr. Orchard Hills Adult Day Ctr., West Bloomfield, Mich., 1978-83; mem. Farmington Hills (Mich.) City Coun., 1975-88, Mich. Ho. of Reps., Lansing, 1989-96. Mayor City of Farmington Hills, 1978, 85; elder Presbyn. Ch. Republican. Home: 22587 Gill Rd Farmington Hills MI 48335

DOLAN, JIM, broadcast executive. Gen. mgr. Sta. WPOC-FM, Balt. Office: WPOC Radio 711 W 40th St Baltimore MD 21211-2120*

DOLAN, JOHN E., consultant, retired utility executive; b. N.Y.C., May 9, 1923; s. John A. and Marie C. (Comiskey) D.; m. Anne Dolan, Feb. 16, 1952; children—John E., Bryan, Vincent, Robert, Raymond, Philip, Lawrence, Paul. Student, Rensselaer Poly. Inst., 1946-47; B.S.M.E., Columbia U., 1950. With Am. Electric Power Service Corp., Columbus, Ohio, 1950-88, chief mech. engr., 1966, chief engr., 1967, sr. exec. v.p. engring., 1975-79, vice chmn. engring. and constrn., 1979-88; ret.; bd. dir., v.p. subs. cos. and Am. Electric Power Service Corp.; cons., 1988—; bd. dirs. Dravo Corp. Served to 1st lt. USAAF, 1942-46. Decorated Air medal (4). Fellow ASME (James N. Landis medal 1990); mem. NAE, Tau Beta Pi. Roman Catholic. Home: 14448 Mark Dr Largo FL 33774-5102

DOLAN, JOHN RALPH, retired corporation executive; b. Peabody, Mass., Apr. 20, 1926; s. John L. and Ethel M. D.; m. Lois M. Burkhart, Jan. 24, 1948 (dec.); children: Mary Ellen, Geraldine, Dorothy, John, Peter; m. Barbara C. Gleason, Dec. 22, 1995; stepchildren: Janet Rogers, Barry, David, Julie Doyle. Student, Boston Coll., 1943, Bryant and Stratton Coll., 1945-46, Bentley Coll., 1948-50. Passenger accountant Cunard Steamship Co., 1947-50; office mgr. Dolan Tanning Co., 1950-56; gen. mgr. Flash Sportswear, 1957-59; budget mgr. CBS Electronics Co., 1959-62; controller/treas. Am. Polymer & Chem. Co., 1962-63; dir. financial planning E.G. & G., Inc., Bedford, Mass., 1963-71, controller, 1971-86; sr. v.p., chief fin. officer EG&G Inc., Wellesley, Mass., 1986-91. Mem. Town Meeting, Danvers, Mass., 1964-70, Sch. Bldg. Com., Danvers, 1966-69. Served with USNR, 1943-45. Mem. Financial Execs. Inst. Home: 56 Summer St Danvers MA 01923-1549

DOLAN, JUNE ANN, health facility administrator; b. Oakland, Calif., June 24, 1942; d. Edward Joseph and Pauline (McCune) D. AA, Orange Coast Coll., 1969; B of Religion and Philosophy, Loyola-Mary Mount U., Orange, Calif., 1965. MICN, ACLS. Asst. head nurse med./surg. ICU and neuro surg. ICU Riverside (Calif.) Gen. Hosp., head nurse med./surg. ICU, asst. dir. of nurses; care provider handicapped, 1987—. Vol. Spl. Olympics, 1987-91; mem. Inland AIDS project; adult advisory mem. Ability Counts Sheltered Workshop; Sister at St. Joseph of Orange, 1960-65. Mem. RGH Aux., Nursing Mgmt. Coun. Avocation: sports, arts and crafts, music, cooking, gardening.

DOLAN, KAY FRANCES, human resources administrator. Grad. with honors, U. Oreg. Dir. rsch. and demonstration divsn. Office of Personnel Mgmt., Washington, dep. asst. dir. Office of Retirement Programs, Honolulu area mgr.; dir. human resource mgmt. FAA; dep. asst. sec. human resources Dept. of Treasury, Washington, 1997—. Mem. Phi Beta Kappa. Office: Dept of Treasury Human Resources 15th and Pennsylvania NW Washington DC 20220

DOLAN, MICHAEL JOHN, psychologist; b. Ashland, Pa., June 16, 1958; s. William J. and Elizabeth A. (Bolich) D.; m. Debra Lee Sharpless, May 16, 1987; children: Jamie Elizabeth, Michael John. BA in Psychology, Penn State U., 1980; MA in Counseling Psychology, Kutztown U., 1988. Diplomate addiction counseling Pa. Chem. Abuse Cert. Bd.; cert. of proficency in substance use disorders Bd. Govs. APA Profl. Psychology. Counselor On Drugs Inc., State Coll., Pa., 1979-81; drug and alcohol counselor Good Samaritan Hosp., Pottsville, Pa., 1981-82; counselor, program dir. Endeavor Inc., Bethlehem, Pa., 1982-88; clin. supr. Lehigh Valley Behavioral Health Ctr., Allentown, Pa., 1988-91; psychologist Community Psychol. Svcs. Consultants Inc., Allentown, 1989—. Mem. APA. Avocations: reading, my kids. Home: 3155 Shakespeare Rd Bethlehem PA 18017-2731 Office: Community Psychol Svcs 2341 Walbert Ave Allentown PA 18104-1351

DOLAN, MICHAEL WILLIAM, lawyer; b. Kansas City, Mo., Dec. 13, 1942; s. William Michael and Vivian (Bush) D.; m. Laurel C. Cummings, June 13, 1964 (div. 1984); children: Matthew, Abigail. BA, U. Kans., 1964; JD with honors, George Washington U., 1969; MLT, Georgetown U., 1981. Bar: Va. 1969, D.C. 1970, U.S. Ct. Claims 1981, U.S. Tax Ct. 1981, U.S. Supreme Ct. 1973. Atty. Dept. Justice, Washington, 1971-73, dep. legis. counsel, 1973-79, dep. asst. atty. gen., 1979-85; with Fed Exec. Devel. Program, 1978-79; assoc. Winthrop, Stimson, Putnam & Roberts, Washington, 1985-94; chief Article III Judges divsn. Adminstrv. Office of U.S. Ct., Washington, 1994—. Contbr. numerous articles to profl. jours. 1st lt. U.S. Army, 1964-66. Recipient John Marshall award Dept. Justice, 1978. Democrat. Office: One Columbus Circle NE Washington DC 20544

DOLAN, PATRICK THOMAS, English educator; b. Evanston, Ill., Apr. 17, 1948; s. Patrick Thomas and Mary Agnes (Dobyns) D.; m. Bonnie Kay Longworth, Dec. 20, 1976; children: Sydney Alison Webster, Anna Foster. BA in English, Met. State Coll., Denver, 1971; MA in English, Colo. State U., 1972. Lectr. in English Arapahoe Cmty. Coll., Littleton, Colo., 1973-75; mem. dept. English Arapahoe Cmty. Coll., 1975—; dir. honors program Arapahoe Cmty. Coll., 1996-98. Mem. Colo. Right to Life Com., Denver, 1994—. Mem. SAR, AAUP (state steering com., pres. chpt. 1979-82), Nat. Assn. Scholars (stae exec. com. 1990—), Colo. Edn. Assn. (chpt. exec. com. 1976-78), Christian Leadership Ministries, Colo. C.S. Lewis Soc. (dir. 1980—), Soc. Colonial Wars, Rocky Mountain G.K. Chesterton Soc. (dir. 1993—). Republican. Anglican. Office: Arapahoe Cmty Coll 2500 W College Dr Littleton CO 80120-1956

DOLAN, PETER BROWN, lawyer; b. Bklyn., Mar. 25, 1939; s. Daniel Arthur and Eileen Margaret (Brown) D.; m. Jacqueline Elizabeth Gruning, Sept. 9, 1961; children: Kerry Anne, Peter Brown Jr. BS, U.S. Naval Acad., 1960; JD, U. So. Calif., 1967. Bar: Calif. 1967, U.S. Ct. Appeals (9th cir.) 1968, U.S. Dist. Ct. (no. and ctrl. dists.) Calif. 1967, U.S. Dist. Ct. (ea. dist.) Calif. 1972, U.S. Dist. Ct. (so. dist.) Calif. 1973, U.S. Claims Ct. 1982, U.S. Supreme Ct. 1986. Dep. L.A. County counsel, 1967-69; assoc. Macdonald, Halsted & Laybourne, L.A., 1969-71, ptnr., 1972-77; ptnr. Overton, Lyman & Prince, L.A., 1977-87, Morrison & Foerster, L.A., 1987-93, Morgan, Lewis & Bockius LLP, L.A., 1993—. Active Pasadena (Calif.) Tournament of Roses Assn., 1973—; pres. West Pasadena Residents Assn., 1979-81. Served to lt. USN, 1960-64, comdr. USNR, 1964-86. Mem. ABA, Fed. Bar Assn., State Bar Calif., Assn. Bus. Trial Lawyers, L.A. County Bar Assn., Bel-Air Bay Club, Chancery (L.A.), City Club on Bunker Hill, Phi Delta Phi. Democrat. Roman Catholic. Fax: (213) 612-2554.

DOLAN, PETER J., corporate financial consultant; b. N.Y.C., July 22, 1927; s. Peter Dolan and Mary Fitzpatrick; m. Ruth E. Bachop, Aug. 26, 1950; children: Robert, Kevin, Paul, James, William, Eileen, Elizabeth, Mary. MS, Columbia U., 1954; BBA, Manhattan Coll., 1949. CPA, N.Y. Ptnr., nat. dir. Ernst & Young, N.Y.C., 1954-83; vice-chmn., dir. Universal Matchbox Ltd., Hong Kong, 1985-89; prin. P. J. Dolan Assocs., Algonquin Assocs., Fla., 1985—; dir. Springer-Verlag USA, N.Y., 1983-88, Hodder Assocs. LLC, N.Y., 1998—. Chmn. fin. com., dir. Marymount Manhattan Coll., 1988-92; mem. fin. com., dir. Calvary Hosp., N.Y., 1985-94; dir., pres. S.E. Yonkers Comty. Assn., N.Y., 1968-70; dir. Armonk (N.Y.) Pub. Schs., 1971-75. Recipient Ann. Outstanding award Campfire Girls, N.Y., 1970-72.

DOLAN, PETER ROBERT, company executive; b. Salem, Mass., Jan. 6, 1956; s. John Ralph and Lois (Burkhart) D.; m. Katherine Helen Lange, Sept. 12, 1981; children: Christopher Lange, Timothy Lange. B, Tufts U., 1978; MBA, Dartmouth Coll., 1980. Asst. product mgr. Gen. Foods Corp., White Plains, N.Y., 1980-81, assoc. product mgr., 1982-83, product mgr., 1983-84, sr. product mgr., 1985, group product mgr., 1986-87, category mgr., 1987-88; v.p. mktg. Bristol-Myers Co., N.Y.C., 1988-90; sr. v.p. mktg. & sales Bristol-Myers Co., 1990-91, sr. v.p. mktg., sales & ops., 1991-92, exec. v.p., 1992, pres., 1993-94; pres. Mead Johnson Nutritional Group, Evansville, Ind., 1995-96; group pres. nutritionals and med. devices Bristol-Myers Squibb Co., 1997—, pres. Europe, Worldwide medicines, 1998—, sr. v.p. strategy, 1999—; bd. dirs. Old Nat. Bank; bd. overseers Tufts Medical Sch. Bd. Co-author Insider's Guide to the Top Ten Business Schools, 1982. Mem. Non-Prescription Drug Mfrs. Assn. (bd. dirs. 1993), Young Pres. Orgn. Avocations: triathlons, tennis, scuba diving.

DOLAN, RAYMOND BERNARD, insurance executive; b. Chgo., Feb. 13, 1923; s. Christopher P. and Florence M. (Taylor) D.; m. Theresa, May 25, 1946; children—Paul, Ronald, Donald, Sharon. Student, No. Mich. U., 1942; D.Arts and Scis. (hon.), Mt. Marty Coll., Yankton, S.D., 1980. With Equitable Life Assurance Soc. U.S., 1946—; v.p., chief line ops. Equitable Life Assurance Soc. U.S., N.Y.C., 1971-74; sr. v.p. corp. communications Equitable Life Assurance Soc. U.S., 1974-79, exec. v.p., chief agy. officer, 1979—; chmn. bd. Equitable of Del., 1985—; Inst. Life Ins. prof. in residence, econs. dept. St. Olaf Coll., 1975; dir. Equitable Variable Life Ins. Co., Equitable Capitol Mgmt. Corp., Equitable Life Leasing Corp., Equico Securities Corp., Donaldson, Lufkin & Jennette Inc., U.S. Marshalls Found. Vice chmn. Holy Spirit Ch. Parish Council, Stamford, Conn., 1968-71; chmn. Stamford dist. Boy Scouts Am., 1970-73; past trustee, vice chmn. bd. dirs. Teledaga Coll., Ala.; chmn. bd. dirs. Nat. Council Better Bus. Burs. Served to lt. col. USAF, 1942-45, 51-52, 61-62. Decorated D.F.C., Air medal with 4 oak leaf clusters. Mem. Nat. Assn. Life Underwriters, C.L.U.'s N.Y., Nat. Guard Assn. (life), Consumer Council, Am. Council Life Ins., Res. Officers

Assn., Conf. Bd., Pub. Affairs Research Council. Republican. Roman Catholic. Club: K.C. (4th deg.). Home: 5 Kings Grant 377 Main St New Canaan CT 06840-5941 Office: Equitable Life Assurance Soc US 787 7th Ave Fl 38 New York NY 10019-6082

DOLAN, THOMAS CHRISTOPHER, professional society administrator; b. Chgo., Dec. 31, 1947; s. Thomas Christopher and Bernice Mary (Doyle) D.; m. Georgia Ann Siebke, Feb. 14, 1983; children: William, Barbara, Lauren. BBA, Loyola U., Chgo., 1969; PhD, U. Iowa, 1977. Instr. U. Iowa, Iowa City, 1971-72; vis. fellow U. Wash., Seattle, 1973-74; asst. prof. U. Mo., Columbia, 1974-79; assoc. prof., dir. St. Louis U., 1979-86; v.p. Am. Coll. Healthcare Execs., Chgo., 1986-87, exec. v.p., 1987-91, pres., 1991—; mem. Accrediting Commn. on Edn. for Health Svcs. Adminstrn., Washington, 1985-86; chmn. Assn. Univ. Programs in Health Adminstrn., Washington, 1983-84; cons. HEW, Kansas City, Mo., 1974-79, State of Mo., Jefferson City, 1974-79. Author: Systems for Health Care Administration: A Model for the Education of Health Manpower, 1975; contbr. articles to profl. jours. Pres. Mental Health Assn. Boone County, Columbia, Mo., 1977-78, Mental Health Assn. Mo., Jefferson City, 1980-82; bd. mem. Nat. Mental Health Assn., Washington, 1982-83, Alexian Bros. Hosp., St. Louis, 1980-86, Assn. Forum, 1995—, Am. Soc. Assn. Execs. Found., Washington, 1995—. Fellow Am. Coll. Healthcare Execs., Am. Soc. Assn. Execs. (cert. assn. exec.); mem. APHA. Roman Catholic. Avocations: golf, motorcycling, reading. Office: Am Coll Healthcare Execs 1 N Franklin St Ste 1700 Chicago IL 60606-3421

DOLAN, THOMAS JOSEPH, judge; b. Bronx, N.Y., Oct. 24, 1943; s. Joseph William and Helen Winnifred (Hannigan) D.; m. Barbara Louise Nuesell, Apr. 6, 1968; children—Claire Jean, Claudia Barbara. B.S., Fordham U., 1965; J.D., St. John's U., 1968. Bar: N.Y. 1968, U.S. Ct. Mil. Appeals 1969, U.S. Dist. Ct. (so. and ea. dists.) N.Y. 1975, U.S. Supreme Ct. 1980. Asst. dist. atty. Office of Dist. Atty. Dutchess County, Poughkeepsie, N.Y., 1973-92, county court judge, Dutchess County, 1993—. Served to capt. JAGC, U.S. Army, 1968-73, Vietnam. Decorated Bronze Star (2), Army Commendation medal (2). Mem. N.Y. State Bar Assn., Dutchess County Bar Assn. Republican. Roman Catholic. Clubs: So. Dutchess Exchange (Fishkill, N.Y.). Home: Neville Rd Wappingers Falls NY 12590 Office: County Court 10 Market St Ste 7 Poughkeepsie NY 12601-3230

DOLAN, TOM, Olympic athlete; b. Sept. 15, 1978. Student in liberal arts and econ., U. Mich., 1998—. Swimmer; gold medalist 400m individual medley Olympic Summer Games, 1996; 7-time U.S. nat. champion; sponsor Carl-Burke. Spokesperson Am. Lung Assn. World record-holder 400m individual medley, Am. record-holder 500y, 1650 freestyle and 400y individual medley. Office: c/o USA Swimming 1 Olympic Plz Colorado Springs CO 80918*

DOLAN, WILLIAM DAVID, JR., physician; b. Westerly, R.I., Apr. 30, 1913; s. William David and Mary E. (Dunn) D.; m. Christine Shea, Nov. 25, 1942; children—William David, III, Mary Anne, John Patrick. B.S., U. R.I., 1935; M.D., Georgetown U., 1942; D.Sc. (hon.), Marymount U., 1975, Georgetown U., 1983. Intern Georgetown U. Hosp., 1942-43, resident, 1943-45; practice medicine specializing in pathology Arlington, Va., 1947-95; dir. pathology Arlington Hosp., 1947-95; pres. med. staff Arlington Hosp., 1982-87, trustee; asst. dean sch. medicine affairs at Arlington Hosp. Georgetown U., clin. prof. dept. pathology. Council to dean Georgetown U., 1977—. Served to maj., M.C. AUS, 1942-47. Recipient Distinguished Service to Pathology award Am. Soc. Clin. Pathologists and Coll. Am. Pathologists, 1976, The Brent award Diocese of Arlington, 1989. Mem. AMA (council on sci. affairs, chmn. 1985), So. Med. Assn., Med. Soc. Va. and D.C., Arlington County Med. Soc. (past pres.), Am. Cancer Soc. (bd. dirs.), Am. Soc. Clin. Pathologists (past pres., disting. svc. award honoring Israel Davidsohn 1991), Am. Blood Commn. (past pres.), Coll. Am. Pathologists, Internat. Acad. Pathology, Va. Soc. for Pathology, Arlington County C. of C. (past dir.), Am. Registry of Pathology (pres. 1991-93), Alpha Omega Alpha. Roman Catholic. Club: Washington Golf and Country. Office: 1701 N George Mason Dr Arlington VA 22205-3610

DOLBERG, DAVID SPENCER, business executive, lawyer, scientist; b. L.A., Nov. 28, 1945; s. Samuel and Kitty (Snyder) D.; m. Katherine Blumberg, Feb. 22, 1974 (div. 1979); 1 child, Max; m. Sarah Carnochan, May 23, 1992 (div. 1995); m. Elana Mann, June 15, 1997; 1 child, Kayla. BA in Biology with honors, U. Calif., Berkeley, 1974; PhD in Molecular Biology, U. Calif., San Diego, 1980; JD, U. Calif., Berkeley, 1989. Bar: Calif. 1989, U.S. Dist. Ct. (no. dist.) Calif. 1989, U.S. Patent and Trademark Office, 1990. Staff biologist, postdoctoral fellow Lawrence Berkeley Lab. U. Calif., 1980-85; assoc. Irell & Manella, Menlo Park, Calif., 1989-91; v.p. EROX Corp., Menlo Park, Calif., 1991-92; v.p. sci. and patents Pherin Corp., Menlo Park, Calif., 1992-94; pvt. practice Berkeley, 1994-98, N.Y.C., 1996-97, Richmond, Calif., 1998—; speaker in field. Contbr. articles to Jour. Gen. Virology, Jour. Virology, Nature, Science, Psychoneuroendocrinology. Address: 37 Terrace Ave Richmond CA 94801

DOLBIN, STEVEN MICHAEL, sculptor, educator; b. Mt. Union, Pa., June 4, 1958; s. David A. and Margaret Grace (Welker) D.; m. Robin Ann Howells, June 4, 1988; children: Reece, Collin. BA, Shippensburg U., 1983; MFA, Pratt Inst., 1989. Cert. secondary edn. art tchr., Pa. Art tchr., artwork dir. West Shore Sch. Dist., Camp Hill, Pa., 1984-87; grad. asst., student union mgr. Pratt Inst., Bklyn., 1987-89; adj. prof. Curry Coll., Milton, Mass., 1989-90; adj. prof. U. Conn., Storrs, 1989-93, vis. prof., 1994-95; sculptor, lectr., art cons., owner, mng. dir. Elliott Sta. Sculpture Studio, Pomfret Center, Conn., 1992—; adj. prof. Amherst Coll., Mass. Prin. works include sculpture U. Tenn., 1994-95, Willliam Benton Mus. Art, Storrs, Conn., 1994, The Frances Colburn Gallery U. Vt., Burlington, 1995, The Empire State Park, Bklyn., 1997. RISD scholar for Advancement of Art Edn., 1987; Pollock-Krasner grantee, 1991. Avocations: philosophy, writing, travel, sports.

DOLBY, RAY MILTON, engineering company executive, electrical engineer; b. Portland, Oreg., Jan. 18, 1933; s. Earl Milton and Esther Eufemia (Strand) D.; m. Dagmar Baumert, Aug. 19, 1966; children—Thomas Eric, David Earl. Student, San Jose State Coll., 1951-52, 55, Washington U., St. Louis, 1953-54; BSEE, Stanford U., 1957; Ph.D. in Physics (Marshall scholar 1957-60, Draper's studentship 1959-61, NSF fellow 1960-61), Cambridge (Eng.) U., 1961, ScD (hon.), 1997. Comml. pilot instrument rating FAA. Electronic technician/jr. engr. Ampex Corp., Redwood City, Calif., 1949-53; engr. Ampex Corp., 1955-57, sr. engr., 1957; PhD research student in physics Cavendish Lab., Cambridge U., 1957-61, research in long wavelength x-rays, 1957-63; fellow Pembroke Coll., 1961-63; cons. U.K. Atomic Energy Authority, 1962-63; UNESCO adviser Central Sci. Instruments Orgn., Chandigarh, Punjab, India, 1963-65; owner, chmn., CEO Dolby Labs. Inc., San Francisco and Wootton Bassett, U.K., 1965—. Trustee Univ. High Sch., San Francisco, 1978-84; bd. dirs. San Francisco Opera; bd. govs. San Francisco Symphony; mem. Marshall Scholarship selection com., 1979-85. Served with U.S. Army, 1953-54. Decorated officer Most Excellent Order of Brit. Empire; recipient Beech-Thompson award Stanford U., 1956, Emmy award, 1957, 89, Trendsetter award Billboard, 1971, Top 200 Execs. Bi-Centennial award, 1976, Lyre award Inst. High Fidelity, 1972, Emile Berliner Maker of the Microphone award Emile Berliner Assn., 1972, Sci. and Engring. award Acad. Motion Picture Arts and Scis., 1979, Oscar award, 1989, Pioneer award Internat. Teleprodn. Soc., 1988, Edward Rhein Ring award Edward Rhein Found., 1988, Life Achievement award Cinema Audio Soc., 1989, Grammy award NARAS, 1995, Nat. Medal Tech., U.S. Dept. Commerce, 1997, Medal of Achievement, Am. Electronics Assn., 1997; named Man of Yr. Internat. Tape Assn., 1987; hon. fellow Pembroke Coll., Cambridge U., 1983. Fellow Audio Engring. Soc. (bd. govs. 1972-74, 79-84 Silver Medal award 1971, Gold medal award 1992, pres. 1980-81), Brit. Kinematograph, Sound and TV Soc. (outstanding tech. and sci. award 1995), Soc. Motion Picture and TV Engrs. (Samuel L. Warner award 1979, Alexander M. Poniatoff Gold Medal 1982, Progress award 1983, hon. mem. 1992), Inst. Broadcast Sound; mem. IEEE (Ibuka award 1997), St. Francis Yacht Club, Pacific Union Club, Tau Beta Pi. Achievements include inventions, research, publs. in video tape recording, x-ray microanalysis, noise reduction and quality improvements in audio and video systems; holder 50 U.S. patents. Office: Dolby Labs 100 Potrero Ave San Francisco CA 94103-4886

DOLCE, CARL JOHN, education administration educator; b. New Orleans, June 3, 1928; s. John and Nina (Puglia) D.; m. Nancy Lockwood, July 27, 1955; children: Carla, John. BA, Tulane U., 1947; MEd, Loyola U., New Orleans, 1955; EdD, Harvard U., 1963. Elem. sch. tchr. New Orleans Pub. Schs., 1948-54, secondary sch. tchr., 1954-55, jr. high sch. prin., 1955-63, supt. schs., 1965-69; rsch. assoc., lectr. Harvard Grad. Sch. Edn., Cambridge, Mass., 1963-65; dean Coll. Edn. and Psychology, N.C. State U., Raleigh, 1969-88, dean emeritus, prof. edn. adminstrn., 1989—; chair adv. com. aesthetic edn. Cen. Midwest Regulatory Lab., St. Louis, 1968-71; chair exptl. schs. selection com. Office Edn., Washington, 1971-72; pres. Coun. Basic Edn., Washington, 1972-79; vice chmn. nat. assn. Elem. and Secondary Edn. Act Title IV state adv. councs., 1978-79. Editorial bd. Ednl. Forum, 1988; author book chpts., monograph, articles. Chmn. Wake County (N.C.) Sch. Study Com., Raleigh, 1978-79; chmn. tech. advisors Durham City/County Merger Task Force, 1988. Sgt. U.S. Army, 1950-52. U.S Office Edn. grantee, 1971-78, 81-82, 86-87. Mem. Raleigh Chamber Music Guild (pres. 1978-1980, Phi Kappa Phi (pres. N.C. State U. chpt. 1982-83). Avocations: gardening, reading, mysteries, puzzles. Home: 801 Macon Pl Raleigh NC 27609-5552 Office: NC State U Coll Edn and Psychology Box 7801 Raleigh NC 27695-7801

DOLD, ROBERT BRUCE, journalist; b. Newark, Mar. 9, 1955; s. Robert Bruce and Margaret (Noll) D.; m. Eileen Claire Norris, July 10, 1982; children: Megan, Kristen. BS in Journalism, Northwestern U., 1977, MS in Journalism, 1978. Reporter Suburban Trib, Hinsdale, Ill., 1978-83; reporter Chgo. Tribune, 1983-90, mem. editl. bd., 1990-95, dep. editl. page editor, columnist, 1995—; Pulitzer prize juror, 1997-98. Columnist Chgo. Enterprise, 1991-95; critic: Downbeat Mag., 1980-84; commentator: Chgo. Week in Rev., 1987—. Bd. dirs. Jazz Inst. Chgo., 1980-83. Recipient Peter Lisagor award Sigma Delta Chi, 1988, Pulitzer prize for editorial writing, 1994, Scripps Howard Found. Nat. award Commentary, 1999. Mem. Am. Soc. Newspaper Editors. Roman Catholic. Avocations: golf, basketball, jazz music. Home: 501 N Park Rd La Grange Park IL 60526-5516 Office: Chgo Tribune 435 N Michigan Ave Chicago IL 60611-4066

DOLE, ARTHUR ALEXANDER, psychology educator; b. San Francisco, Oct. 25, 1917; s. Arthur Alexander and Ella Elizabeth (Duncan) D.; m. Marjorie Elizabeth Welsh, Mar. 19, 1949; children: Peter, Steven, Barbara. BA, Antioch Coll., 1946; MA, Ohio State U., 1949, PhD, 1951; MA (hon.), U. Pa., 1973. Diplomate Am. Bd. Examiners in Profl. Psychology. Asst. psychology and edn. Antioch Coll., 1946-48; counselor Ohio State U., 1948-51; dir. Bur. Testing and Guidance, U. Hawaii, 1951-60, from asst. prof. to prof. psychology, 1951-67; prof. psychology in edn. U. Pa., 1967-88, chmn. dept., 1967-88, prof. emeritus, 1988—; mem. internat. adv. bd. Univ MSG, Romero, El Salvador. Author articles in field.; cons. editor profl. jours. Bd. dirs. Am. Family Found.; pres. PEACE, Internat. Fellow APA; mem. AAAS, AAUP, ACA, Am. Ednl. Rsch. Assn., Internat. Coun. Psychologists, Internat. Assn. Applied Psychology, Nat. Rehab. Assn., Sigma Xi.

DOLE, ELIZABETH HANFORD, former charitable organization administrator, former secretary of labor, former secretary of transportation; b. Salisbury, N.C., July 29, 1936; d. John Van and Mary Ella (Cathey) Hanford; m. Robert Joseph Dole (former U.S. Senator from Kans.), Dec. 6, 1975. BA with honors in Polit. Sci., Duke U., 1958; postgrad., Oxford (Eng.) U., summer 1959; MA in Edn. and Govt., Harvard U., 1960, JD, 1965. Bar: D.C. 1966. Staff asst. to asst. sec. for edn. HEW, Washington, 1966-67; practiced law Washington, 1967-68; assoc. dir. legis. affairs, then exec. dir. Pres.'s Com. for Consumer Interests, Washington, 1968-71; dep. asst. to Pres. The White House, Washington, 1971-73; commr. FTC, Washington, 1973-79; chmn. Voters for Reagan-Bush, 1980; dir. Human Services Group, Office of Exec. Br. Mgmt., Office of Pres.-Elect, 1980; asst. to Pres. for pub. liaison, 1981-83; sec. U.S. Dept. Transp., 1983-87; with Robert Dole Presdl. Campaign, 1987-88; participant 1988 Presdl. and Congl. campaigns; sec. U.S. Dept. Labor, 1989-90; pres. ARC, 1991-99; mem. nominating com. Am. Stock Exch., 1972, N.C. Consumer Coun., 1972. Trustee Duke U., 1974-88; mem. coun. Harvard Law Sch. Assocs., mem. vis. com. Harvard Sch. Pub. Health, 1992-95; mem. bd. overseers Harvard U., 1989-95. Recipient Arthur S. Flemming award U.S. Govt., 1972, Humanitarian award Nat. Commn. Against Drunk Driving, 1988, Disting. Alumni award Duke U., 1988, N.C. award, 1991, Lifetime Achievement award (Breaking The Glass Ceiling) Women Execs. in State Govt., 1993, North Carolinian of the Yr. award N.C. Press Assn., 1993, Radcliffe medal, 1993, Leadership award LWV, 1994, Maxwell Finland award Nat. Found. Infectious Diseases, 1994, Disting. Svc. award Nat. Safety Coun., 1989, Raoul Wallenberg award for Humanitarian Svc., 1995, Christian Woman of Yr. award, 1996; named one of Am.'s 200 Young Leaders, Time mag., 1974, one of World's 10 Most Admired Women, Gallup Poll, 1988, one of 10 most fascinating people 1996 Barbara Walter's Spl., most inspiring polit. figure 1996 MSNBC, 3d most admired woman in Am. Good Housekeeping, 1996, 98; selected for Safety and Health Hall of Fame Internat., 1993; inducted into Nat. Women's Hall of Fame, 1995. Mem. Phi Beta Kappa, Pi Lambda Theta, Pi Sigma Alpha. Office: PO Box 58247 Washington DC 20037

DOLE, ROBERT J., lawyer, former senator; b. Russell, Kans., July 22, 1923; s. Doran R. and Bina Dole; m. Elizabeth Hanford, Dec. 1975. Student, U. Kans., 1941-43, U. Ariz.; A.B., Washburn Mcpl. U., Topeka, 1952, LL.B., 1952; LL.D. (hon.), Washburn U., Topeka, 1969. Bar: Kans. 1952. Mem. Kans. Ho. of Reps., 1951-53; sole practice Russell, Kans., 1953-61; Russell County atty., 1953-61; mem. 87th Congress from 6th Dist., Kans., 88th-90th congresses from 1st Dist., Kans., U.S. Senate from Kans., 1969-96; chmn. Rep. Nat. Com., 1971-73; Senate majority leader U.S. Senate from Kans., 1985-86, Senate Rep. leader, 1987-96; of counsel Verner, Liipfert, Bernhard, McPherson & Hand, 1999—; Rep. vice-presdl. candidate, 1976; Rep. presdl. candidate, 1996. Chmn. Dole Found. Served with AUS, 1943-48, World War II. Decorated Purple Heart (2), Bronze Star with 2 clusters. Recipient Horatio Alger award Horatio Alger Assn. Disting. Ams., 1988, Presdl. medal Freedom. Mem. Am. Legion, VFW, DAV, 4-H Fair Assn., Masons, Shriners, Elks, Kiwanis, Kappa Sigma. Methodist. Office: Verner Liipfert Bernhard McPherson & Hand 901 15th St NW 4th Fl Washington DC 20005-2301*

DOLE, ROBERT PAUL, retired appliance manufacturing company executive; b. Freeport, Ill., Nov. 12, 1923; s. Herman Walter and Louise Marie (Bornemeier) D.; m. Joyce Lindsay, Mar. 14, 1947; 1 child, Luanne Dole Cloyd. BA, Cornell Coll., Mt. Vernon, Iowa, 1948. Personnel mgr. Green Giant Co., Lanark, Ill., 1948-50; controller Green Giant Co., 1951-52; asst. treas. Henney Motor Co., Inc., Freeport, 1952-53, Eureka Williams Corp., Bloomington, Ill., 1954-62; v.p. and asst. gen. mgr. The Eureka Co., Bloomington, 1962-79; sr. v.p. The Eureka Co., 1980, pres., 1980-88; exec. v.p., dir. parent co. Nat. Union Electric Corp., 1980-84, pres., dir., 1984-85, chmn. bd., pres., dir., 1985-88, chmn. bd., 1985-88; group v.p., dir. Dometic Inc., Bloomington, Ill., 1984-86; group pres., dir. White Consol. Industries, Cleve., 1987-88; trustee Internat. Assn. Machinists Nat. Pension Fund, 1972-80; dir. First Fed. Savs. and Loan Assn., Bloomington, Ill., 1982—, Eagle Bank Group, 1996—. Served in U.S. Army, 1943-46. Republican. Lodges: Masons, Elks.

DOLE, VINCENT PAUL, medical research executive, educator; b. Chgo., May 8, 1913; s. Vincent Paul and Anne (Dowling) D.; m. Elizabeth Ann Strange, May 23, 1942 (div. 1965); children: Vincent Paul III, Susan, Bruce; m. Marie Nyswander, 1965 (dec. 1986); m. Margaret E. Cool, 1992. AB, Stanford U., 1934; MD, Harvard U., 1939. Intern Mass. Gen. Hosp., Boston, 1940-41; mem. staff Rockefeller U., N.Y.C., 1941—, prof., 1951—. Developer methadone maintenance treatment program for heroin addiction. Office: Rockefeller U Dept of Medicine 1230 York Ave New York NY 10021-6399*

DOLEAC, CHARLES BARTHOLOMEW, lawyer; b. New Orleans, Sept. 20, 1947; s. Cyril Bartholomew and Emma Elizabeth (St. Clair) D.; m. Denise Kilfoyle, Feb. 2, 1972; children: Keith Gabriel, Jessa Lee. BS cum laude, U. N.H., 1968; JD, NYU, 1971. Bar: Mass. 1972, N.H. 1972, Maine 1973. Law clk. to Justice Grimes N.H. Supreme Ct., Concord, 1972-73; assoc. Boynton, Waldron, Dill & Aeschliman, Portsmouth, N.H., 1973-76; ptnr. Boynton, Waldron, Doleac, Woodman & Scott, Portsmouth, 1977—; appointed mediator N.H. Superior Ct., 1992—; del. to tour Chinese legal system Chinese Ministry Justice, 1982; del. to People's Republic of China/U.S. joint session on trade investments and econ. law Chinese Ministry Justice/U.S. Dept. Justice, Beijing, 1987; propr. Portsmouth Athenaeum; moderator seminars on ethics for Leaders & Comparative Cultures and Values/East & West Aspen Inst., 1990-95; mem. faculty Southwestern Legal Found. Ctr. for Law Enforcement Ethics, 1993—; adv. bd. mem. Southwestern Law Enforcement Inst., 1995—; mem. faculty Southwestern Legal Found. Internat. & Comparative Law Ctr., 1997—. Contbr. articles to profl. jours. Mem. citizens adv. coun. Portsmouth Cmty. Devel. Program, 1976-77; incorporator N.H. Charitable Found.; pres., bd. dirs. Seacoast United Way; chmn. Portsmouth Bd. Bldg. Appeals, 1976-77; chmn. stewardship com. Soc. Preservation New Eng. Antiquities, 1980-84, also trustee; pres. bd. trustees Strawbery Banke Mus., 1985-88; founder Daniel Webster Inn of Ct., 1993, Charles C. Doe Inn of Ct., 1994, Portsmouth Peace Treaty Forum, 1994; founder, pres. Japan-Am. Soc. N.H., 1988. NEH fellow, Aspen Inst.; named Citizen of Yr. Portsmouth, N.H., 1991. Fellow N.H. Bar Found; mem. ATLA, Mass. Bar Assn., Maine Bar Assn., N.H. Bar Assn., N.H. Trial Lawyers Assn., Maine Trial Lawyers Assn. Avocations: masters swimming. Home: Little Harbor Rd Portsmouth NH 03801 Office: Boynton Waldron Doleac Woodman & Scott PA 82 Court St Portsmouth NH 03801-4414

DOLEN, WILLIAM KENNEDY, allergist, immunologist, pediatrician, educator; b. Memphis, Oct. 16, 1952; s. William Smith and Dorothy DeWitt (Kennedy) D.; m. Carolyn Canon, Dec. 21, 1974; children: John William, Susan Elizabeth. BS in Biology with distinction and honors, Rhodes Coll., 1974; MD, U. Tenn., 1977. Cert. Nat. Bd. Med. Examiners, Am. Bd. Pediatrics, Am. Bd. Allergy and Immunology. Commd. 2d lt. U.S. Army, 1974, advanced through grades to maj., 1982; intern in pediatrics U. Tenn. Hosp., Knoxville, 1977-78; med. officer SHAPE Med. Ctr., Belgium, 1978-79; commdr. U.S. Army NATO Health Clinic, Belgium, 1979-80; resident in pediatrics Letterman Army Med. Ctr., San Francisco, 1980-82; pediatrician Bassett Army Community Hosp., Ft. Wainwright, Alaska, 1982-84; fellow allergy and clin. immunology Fitzsimons Army Med. Ctr., Aurora, Colo., 1984-86; clin. instr. pediatrics F. Edward Hébert Sch. Medicine Uniformed Svcs. U. Health Scis., Bethesda, Md., 1986-87, clin. asst. prof. pediatrics, 1988-89; allergist, immunologist Ochsner Clinic, New Orleans, 1988-89, Allergy Respiratory Inst. Colo., Denver, 1989-92; chief pediatric allergy sect. allergy-immunology svc. Fitzsimons Army Med. Ctr., Aurora, Colo., 1986-88; clin. assoc. prof. medicine Ctr. for Health Scis. U. Colo., Denver, 1990-92; assoc. prof. pediatrics and medicine Med. Coll. Ga., Augusta, 1992-98, prof., 1998—; chair subcom. on allergen selection, practice parameters task force Joint Coun. Allergy and Immunology, 1992—; presenter in field. Author: (with others) Rhinolaryngoscopy, 2d edit., 1989, Rhinitis, 2d edit., 1991; mem. editl. bd. Annals of Allergy, 1993—, ad hoc reviewer, 1990-93; author (audiovisual programs) Allergy Case Studies, 1992, The Upper Airway, 1992, Asthma is an Allergic Disease, 1994; contbr. articles to profl. jours., chpts. to books. Assoc. dir. Augusta Choral Soc. Fellow Am. Coll. Allergy, Asthma and Immunology (bd. regents, 1993-96, exec. com. 1995-96, chair comm. coun. 1993-96, chair workshop com. 1990-97, mem. ann. program com. 1986-87, 90—, CME com. 1988-94, chair Rhinitis com. 1988-93, workshop com. 1989-90), Am. Acad. Allergy and Immunology (chair com. on in vivo testing 1991-93, com. computers and tech. 1994-97, workshop com. 1993-96); mem. AMA, Ga. Soc. Allergy and Immunology, European Acad. Allergology and Clin. Immunology (subcom. skin testing 1992—), Am. Guild of Organists. Episcopalian. Office: Sect Allergy Immunology Med Coll GA Augusta GA 30912

DOLES, JOHN HENRY, III, retired telecommunications company manager; b. Youngstown, Ohio, Nov. 20, 1943; s. John Henry and Wanda Fay (Castor) D. BS in Math., Case Inst. Tech., Cleve., 1965; PhD in Math., MIT, 1969. Mem. tech. staff Bell Labs., Whippany, N.J., 1969-85, tech. supr., 1986-88; project mgr. AT&T Advanced Tech. Sys., Arlington, Va., 1989-95, ret., 1996; chmn. bd. dirs. Whippany Fed. Credit Union, 1979-89. Contbr. articles to profl. jours. Mem. MIT Club of Wash. Home: 1201 S Eads St Apt 1612 Arlington VA 22202-2844

DOLEZAL, LEO THOMAS, telecommunications executive; b. Perry, Okla., Aug. 3, 1944; s. Leo Frank and Evalena Augusta (Pursley) D.; m. Derrla Mae Lawhon, Oct. 21, 1963 (dec.); children: Corinna, Rohmona, Consuela, Derral, Kyle; m. Lynda M. Manley, Nov. 11, 1994. AS in Electronics, No. Okla. Coll., 1964. Licensed gen. radiotelephone operator FCC. Aircraft radio technician Serv Air Inc., Enid, Okla., 1964-69; frame attendant S.W. Bell Tel., Enid, 1969-70, comm. technician, 1970-74; combination technician S.W. Bell Tel., Billings, Okla., 1974-78, Ponca City, Okla., 1978-80; mgr. network ops. S.W. Bell Tel., Enid, 1980—; mem. O.T. Autry Vo-Tech Tech. Electronics Adv. Com., Enid, 1987—. Pres. Billings Housing Authority, 1990-94, Billings Sch. Bd., pres. 1999—. Lt. col. USAR, ret. Mem. NRA (life), Res. Officers Assn. (life), Lions (pres. 1977, 90-92), Billings Rotary (pres. 1978, 92, sec. 1991-92), Masons (past master Billings lodge), Billings C. of C. (v.p.). Republican. Mem. Ch. of The Brethren. Avocations: hunting, camping, running. Office: PO Box 392 Enid OK 73702-0392

DOLGEN, JONATHAN L., motion picture company executive. Ed., Cornell U., grad., 1966; JD, N.Y.U. Law Sch., 1969. Lawyer Fried, Frank, Harris, Shriver & Jacobson, N.Y.C, 1969-76; asst. gen. counsel, deputy gen. counsel Columbia Pictures Industries, 1976-85, sr. v.p. Worldwide Bus. Affairs, 1979, exec. v.p., 1980; sr. exec., v.p. fox Inc., 1985-90; pres. Columbia Pictures, 1990-94; chmn., CEO Viacom Entertainment Group, 1994; pres. TV div. 20th Century-Fox Film Corp., Beverly Hills, Calif.; sr. exec. v.p. telecommunications Fox Inc., Beverly Hills, 1985-88, pres., 1988-91; pres. motion picture group Columbia Pictures, Culver City, Calif., 1991—; chmn., CEO Viacom Entertainment Group, N.Y.C., 1994—; bd. fellows Claremont U. Ctr. and Grad. Sch.; founder Friends of the Cornell U. Theater Arts Ctr.; mem. Alumni Coun. N.Y.U. Law Sch.; founding mem. Edn. First; adv. Calif. State Summer Sch. for the Arts.; pres. Columbia's Pay Cable & Home Entertainment Group, 1983; chmn. Twentieth TV, 1988-90; mem. bd. dirs. Sony Pictures. *

DOLGER, JONATHAN, editor, literary agent; b. N.Y.C., Sept. 3, 1938; s. Henry and Laura (Zeck) D. A.B., Brown U., 1960. Asst. publicity dir. Simon and Schuster, 1962-65; assoc. editor Fawcett Crest Books, 1965-66; mng. editor Dell Books, 1966-68; sr. editor New Am. Library, 1968; v.p., mng. editor Simon and Schuster, 1968-78; editor-in-chief Fireside Paperbacks, 1968-78; sr. editor Trade div. Harper & Row, 1978-79; pres. The Jonathan Dolger Agy., N.Y.C., 1980—; lectr. pub. procedures course Radcliffe Coll., New Sch. Social Rsch.; faculty mem. The Writing Ctr., Marymount Coll., N.Y.C.; pub. course NYU, U. Pa. Pub. Inst., S.W. Writers Workshop, U. So. Maine Writers Conf., Tennessee Williams Writers' Festival; cons. Brown U. Alumni/Student Profl. Network. Author: The Expense Account Diet, 1969; also articles. Mem. Am. Soc. Journalists and Authors, Assn. Author's Reps. Office: 49 E 96th St New York NY 10128-0782

DOLGIN, MARTIN, cardiologist; b. N.Y.C., Apr. 12, 1919; s. Samuel and Bertha (Brodsky) D.; m. Jeanne Rydell, Feb. 12, 1950; children: Barbara, Deborah, Stuart. A.B., NYU, 1939, M.D., 1943. Diplomate: Am. Bd. Internal Medicine: cert. cardivascular disease. Intern, resident in medicine Lincoln Hosp., N.Y.C., 1943, 44; fellow in internal medicine Lahey Clinic, Boston, 1945, 46; fellow in cardiovasc. disease rsch. Michael Reese Hosp., Chgo., 1947; instr. to assoc. prof. medicine NYU, N.Y.C., 1948-73, prof. clin. medicine, 1973—; attending physician Bellevue Hosp. and Tisch Univ. Hosp., N.Y.C., 1973—; adj. attending physician Montefiore Hosp., N.Y.C., 1948-68; cons. in cardiology Will Rogers Hosp., Saranac Lake, N.Y., Columbus Hosp., N.Y.C., 1960-70; chief cardiology sect. N.Y. VA Hosp., 1955-89, cons. cardiology, 1989—. Editorial bd.: Jour. Electrocardiology; contbr. articles in electrocardiography to publs. Served with M.D. U.S. Army, 1952-54. Fellow ACP, Am. Coll. Cardiology, N.Y. Acad. Sci.; mem. Am. Fedn. Clin. Research, Am. Heart Assn., AAAS, Alpha Omega Alpha. Home: 32 Mountainview Ave Ardsley NY 10502-2010 Office: NY VA Hospital 423 E 23rd St New York NY 10010-5050

DOLGOW, ALLAN BENTLEY, consulting company executive; b. N.Y.C., Dec. 14, 1933; divorced; children: Nicole, Marc, Ginger, Kimbie. BIE, NYU, 1959, MBA, 1972; postgrad., Hunter Coll., 1976, U. Calif., 1991. With Republic Aviation Corp., Farmingdale, N.Y., 1959-60, Internat. Paper

Co., N.Y.C., 1960-73, J.C. Penney Co., Inc., N.Y.C., 1973-76, Morse Electro Products, N.Y.C., 1976-77, Morse Electrophonic Hong Kong Ltd., N.Y.C., 1976-77, Revlon, Inc., Edison, N.J., 1977-79, SRI Internat., Menlo Park, Calif., 1979-96, Dolgow Cons. Group, Menlo Park, Calif., 1996-99, Dolgow Cons., Redwood City and Stockton, Calif., 1996-99. With U.S. Army, 1954-56, Germany. Office: 3722 EWS Wood Blvd Stockton CA 95206-5246

DOLIAN, ROBERT PAUL, lawyer; b. Terre Haute, Ind., Jan. 11, 1948; s. Frank Eugene and Edith Alice (Prentice) D.; m. Lauren Elizabeth Haggerty, July 5, 1975; children: Matthew W., Brad L., Andrew R. BA, Duke U., 1969; JD cum laude, Harvard U., 1975. Bar: Conn. 1975, U.S. Dist. Ct. Conn. 1976, U.S. Dist. Ct. (so. dist.) N.Y. 1976, U.S. Ct. Appeals (2d cir.) 1976. Assoc. Cummings and Lockwood, Stamford, Conn., 1975-83, ptnr., 1983—; spl. master U.S. Dist. Ct. Conn., 1988—; atty. trial referee Conn. Superior Ct., 1989—; dir. Conn. Legal Svcs. Mem. vestry St. Francis Episc. Ch., Stamford, 1990-93; dir. United Way, Stamford, 1997—. Mem. ABA, Conn. Bar Assn., Stamford Regional Bar Assn., Phi Beta Kappa. Office: Cummings and Lockwood Four Stamford Place Stamford CT 06901-3240

DOLIBOIS, ROBERT JOSEPH, trade association administrator; b. Hamilton, Ohio, Aug. 26, 1947; s. John E. and Winifred E. (Englehart) D.; m. Susan K. Lallathin, June 16, 1973; children: Ryan, Sara. BA, Miami U., Ohio, 1969. Lt. USN, 1969-74; v.p. Nat. Assn. Life Underwriters, Washington, 1974-88; pres. Assn. Mgmt. Group, 1988-91; exec. v.p. Am. Assn. Nurserymen, 1991—; chmn. bd. dirs. Am. Soc. Assn. Execs., Washington, 1992-99. Elder McLean (Va.) Presbyn. Ch., 1990-93. Lt. USN, 1969-74. Named Cert. Assn. Exec. Am. Soc. of Assn. Execs., Washington, 1979. Mem. Am. Soc. Assn. Execs. Presbyterian. Home: 2709 N Brandywine St Arlington VA 22207-2722 Office: Am Nursery & Landscape Assn 1250 I St NW Ste 500 Washington DC 20005-3922

DOLICE, JOSEPH LEO, multimedia art publisher, exhibition director; b. Newark, Oct. 12, 1941; s. Leon Louis and Mary Sabina (Lewandowski) D. BA, Iona Coll., 1963; MA, Hunter Coll., 1978. Dir., stage designer F. Richard Love Theatrical Prodns., White Plains, N.Y., 1969; stage designer various theater companies, N.Y., 1969-73; exhbn. dir. New Rochelle (N.Y.) Coun. on the Arts, 1977—; art dir. Stan Rose Assocs., N.Y.C., 1980-90; exhbn. dir. Fulton Gallery, N.Y.C., 1980-92; theater mgr. Village Gate, N.Y.C., 1987-92; art dir. Dezer Enterprises, N.Y.C., 1987-89; exhbn. dir. Janapa Gallery, N.Y.C., 1990; prodn. dir. Ruff Theatrical, Bklyn., 1991-95; publisher Dolice Graphics, N.Y.C., 1980—; a/v corporate and events tech. mgmt., various companies in N.Y.C. and Calif., 1994—. Author: Old New York Remembered, 1982; author, pub. Demo Directory, 1994-95, Free Computer Media, 1996, Vintage New York, 1998; exec. editor N.Y. Downtown News, 1987-89; contbr. articles to various pubs. Publicity dir. Putnam County Bicentennial Commn., Carmel, N.Y., 1976; exhbn. dir. Danbury (Conn.) State Arts & Crafts Fair, 1979-83; dir. Putnam Arts Coun. annual profl. art exhibit, 1976; advt. dir. TheARTgallery Mag., 1974-76; exhbn. dir. New Rochelle Coun. on Arts. With U.S. Army, 1964-66, U.S., Korea. Mem. Entertainment Svcs. and Tech. Assn., Montauk Artists Assn. Avocations: writing, theatrical and performance work. E-mail address: techman@erols.com. Fax: 212-260-9217. Office: Dolice Graphics 163 3d Ave Ste 321 New York NY 10003-2523

DOLICH, ANDREW BRUCE, sports marketing executive; b. Bklyn., Feb. 18, 1947; s. Mac and Yetta (Weiselter) D.; m. Ellen Andrea Fass, June 11, 1972; children: Lindsey, Caryn, Cory. BA, Am. U., 1969; MEd, Ohio U., 1971. Adminstrv. asst. to gen. mgr. Phila. 76ers, NBA, 1971-74; v.p. Md. Arrows Lacrosse, Landover, 1974-76; mktg. dir. Washington Capitals, NHL, Landover, 1976-78; exec. v.p., gen. mgr. Washington Diplomats Soccer, 1978-80; v.p. bus. ops. Oakland A's Baseball, Calif., 1980-92, exec. v.p., 1993-95; pres., COO Golden State Warriors NBA, Oakland, Calif., 1995-98; pres. Dolich & Assoc. Sports Mktg., Alameda, Calif., 1996—; exec. v.p. Advantix, 1998—; nat. fundraising chmn. sports adminstrs. program Ohio U., Athens, dir., 1978-82; lectr. sports mktg. U. Calif. Ext. Bd. dirs. Bay Area Sports Hall of Fame, 1982—. Celebrate Oakland Com., Internat. Sports Mktg. Coun., Oakland Zoo Adv. Coun. Recipient Alumni of Yr. award Ohio U. Sports Adminstrs. Program, Athens, 1982; recipient Clio award Am. Advt. Fedn., 1982. E-mail: adolich@advantix.com. *

DOLIN, SAMUEL JOSEPH, composer, educator; b. Montreal, Can., Aug. 22, 1917; s. Joseph and Freda (Levin) D.; m. Inthia Leslie Pidgeon, Mar. 7, 1953; children: Leslie Elizabeth, John Joseph. MusB, U. Toronto, 1942, MusD, 1956. Tchr., Royal Conservatory of Music, Toronto, 1945—, also lectr.; mem., assoc. Can. Music Center, 1970-75; artistic dir. Can. Contemporary Music Workshop, 1983-88; gov. North Simcoe Arts Coun., 1986; chmn. emeritus Composition Dept. Royal Consevatory Music, Toronto, also bd. examiners; tchr. composition Glenn Gould Profl. Sch. Compositions include: (for orch.) Symphony No. 2, (chamber music) Sonatina, (for flute, violin and violoncello with tape) 3 sonatas, 1973, (opera) Casino, (guitar solo) Ricercar, 1974, Concerto for Piano and Orch., 1974, (for 1-5 accordions and tape) Adikia, (for guitar solo) Fantasy, Symphony No. 3, (for violoncello) Prelude, Interlude and Fantasy, Sonata for Violoncello and Piano, 1978, (for flute and voice) Deuteronomy XXXII, (for 2 pianos and percussion) Concerto for 4, Sonata Fantasia for Baroque Flute and Forte Piano, Trio for Piano, Violin and Cello, (for various instruments, dancer, slides) Golden Section, 1981, (for trombone and cello) Kinesis I and II, 1981, Quintet for Brass, 1981; Hero of Our Time, Cantata for Baritone, Male Chorus and Orch., 1985, Concerto for Accordion and Orchestra, Double Concerto for Oboe, Cello and Orchestra, 1987, (for film) The Meeting Point; recs. include Concerto for Four, Sonata for Accordion, Fantasy, Sonata for Violin and Piano, Double Concerto for Oboe, Violoncello and Orch., 1988, Intermezzo (cello and piano), 1989, Quartet No. 2 (string quartet), 1990, 2 vocalises for 2 cellos, 1990, Toccata for piano, 1990, Giant's Tomb-Suite for Organ and Trumpet, 1991, 2x3—Two pieces for violin and piano, 1992, Variables for Cello and Piano, 1993, (recorded CD, 1994), Slightly Square Round Dance (orchestra), April March (CBC-CD); commd. Georgian Bay-Ont. Arts Coun. Commn. Can. Council grantee (5); recipient numerous commns. Mem. Can. League Composers (pres. 1979-83), Internat. Soc. Contemporary Music (v.p. 1972-75), Drakkar Music and Tech. (v.p. 1994).

DOLINER, NATHANIEL LEE, lawyer; b. Daytona Beach, Fla., June 28, 1949; s. Joseph and Asia (Shaffer) D.; m. Debra Lynn Simon, June 5, 1983. BA, George Washington U., 1970; JD, Vanderbilt U., 1973; LLM in Taxation, U. Fla., 1977. Bar: Fla. 1973, U.S. Tax Ct. 1973, U.S. Dist. Ct. (mid. dist.) Fla. 1974. Assoc. Smalbein, Eubank, Johnson, Rosier & Bussey, P.A., Daytona Beach, Fla., 1973-76; vis. asst. prof. law U. Fla., Gainesville, 1977-78; assoc. Carlton, Fields, Ward, Emmanuel, Smith & Cutler, P.A., Tampa, Fla., 1978-82; shareholder Carlton, Fields, Ward, Emmanuel, Smith & Cutler, P.A., Tampa, 1982—, chmn. corp. and securities dept., 1984-96, treas., 1985-86, co-chair bus. transactions dept., 1996-98, chair bus. transactions dept., 1998—; spkr. NYU Real Estate Tax Inst., 1989, 94, Advanced Tax Inst., Balt., 1994, ABA Presdl. Showcase Programs ABA Ann. Conv., 1993-96; co-chmn., spkr. ABA mergers and Acquisitions Inst., N.Y.C., 1996 2d Ann. Inst. Negotiating Bus. Acquisitions, Chgo., 1997, 3d Ann. Inst., New Orleans, 1998. Adv. bd. Mergers and Acquisitions Law Report. Bd. dirs. Big Bros./Big Sisters Greater Tampa, Inc., 1980-82, Child Abuse Coun., Inc., 1986-95, asst. treas., 1987-88, treas., 1988-89, pres.-elect 1989-90, pres., 1990-91; dist. commr. Gulf Ridgecoun. Boy Scouts Am., 1983; bd. dirs. Tampa Jewish Fedn. Bd., 1988-91, Mus. Sci. and Industry, Tampa, 1994—, exec. com., 1994—, sec. 1995-97, first vice chair, 1997—; mem. alumni bd. Vanderbilt Law Sch., 1998—, bd. dirs., exec. com. Hillel Sch. Tampa, 1998—, first vice chair, 1999—. Fellow Am. Bar Found., Am. Coll. Tax Counsel; mem. ABA tax sect. (vice chmn. continuing legal education com. 1986-88, chmn. 1988-90, mem. bus. law sect. com. negotiated acquisitions, vice chair 1997-98, chair 1998—, chmn. task force preliminary and ancillary agreements, 1992-95, mem. acquisition rev. subcom. 1992-95, chair program letters of intent in bus. transactions 1993, chair programs subcom. 1995-98, exec. com. 1995—, co-chair program mergers of for-profit and not-for-profit hosps. 1996, spkr. not for profit corps. 1997), Am. Law Inst., Fla. Bar Assn. (mem. exec. coun. tax sect. 1980-83, tax cert. com. 1987-88, vice chair 1988-89, chair 1989-90), Greater Tampa C. of C. (chmn. Ambassadors Target Task Force of Com. of 100 1984-85, 87-88, chair geographic task force 1989-90, vice chmn. govt. fin. and taxation coun. 1987-88, chmn. 1988-89, bd. govs. 1990-93, exec. com. 1992, chmn. govtl. affairs dept., 1992), Anti-Defamation League (regional bd. mem. 1986-90, exec. com. 1987-90), Tampa Club (bd. dirs. 1987-92, sec. 1987-89, pres. 1990-91). Home: 13341 Golf Crest Cir Tampa FL 33624-4648 Office: Carlton Fields Ward Emmanuel Smith & Cutler PA Ste 500 777 S Harbour Island Blvd Tampa FL 33602-5729

DOLINGER, MICHAEL H., federal judge; b. 1946. BA magna cum laude, Columbia U., 1968, JD, 1972. Bar: N.Y. 1972. Law clk. to Hon. Wilfred Feinberg, U.S. Ct. Appeals for 2d Circuit, N.Y.C., 1972-73; assoc. Nickerson Kramer Lowenstein Nessen Kamin & Soll, N.Y.C., 1973-76; asst. U.S. atty. U.S. Dept. Justice, N.Y.C., 1978-84; chief magistrate judge for so. dist. N.Y., U.S. Magistrate Ct., N.Y.C., 1984—. Office: 1670 US Courthouse 500 Pearl St New York NY 10007-1316

DOLL, DAVID MICHAEL, journalist; b. West Allis, Wis., Apr. 13, 1933; s. B. Luke and Thelma Nelly (Dings) D.; m. Kathleen Blasi, June 11, 1960; children: D. Michael (dec.), Bernard L., Elizabeth K.M. BS, Marquette U., Milw., 1956, MA, 1958; ABD, U Birmingham, 1960. Instr. Modesto (Calif.) Jr. Coll., 1963-65; asst. prof. tech. dir. Western Ky. U., Bowling Green, 1964-65; asst. prof. Northland Coll., Ashland, Wis., 1967-69; sr. sys. analyst NML, Milw., 1970-72; contbg. writer Sensible Sound, Snyder, N.Y., 1976—; prof. outreach program Mt. Senario Coll., Ladysmith, Wis., 1983-96; contbg. writer, substitute tchr. Racine (Wis.) Unified Sch. Dist. Home: 1028 Blaine Ave Racine WI 53405-2902

DOLL, LYNNE MARIE, public relations agency executive; b. Glendale, Calif., Aug. 27, 1961; d. George William and Carol Ann (Kennedy) D.; m. David Jay Lans, Oct. 11, 1986. BA in Journalism, Calif. State U., Northridge, 1983. Freelance writer Austin Pub. Rels. Systems, Glendale, 1978-82; asst. account exec. Berkhemer & Kline, L.A., 1982-83; exec. v.p., ptnr. Rogers & Assocs., L.A., 1983—; exec. dir. Suzuki Automotive Found. for Life, Brea, Calif., 1986-91; mem. strategic planning com. Gateway to Indian Am. Corp. for Am. Indian Devel., San Francisco, 1988-90. Pub. rels. cons., Rape Treatment Ctr., L.A., 1986—. Mem. Ad Club L.A. (bd. dirs., pres. 1994-95), Pub. Rels. Soc. Am., So. Calif. Assn. Philanthropy, Coun. on Founds., Internat. Motor Press Assn., Nat. Conf. for Cmty. and Justice (bd. dirs. 1996—). Democrat. Office: Rogers & Assocs 1875 Century Park E Ste 300 Los Angeles CA 90067-2504

DOLLAR, ALISON CATHLEEN, business official; b. Silver Spring, Md., Nov. 8, 1971; d. Joseph Tilmon Jr. and Diane Elaine Dollar. BS in Polit. Sci., Frostburg (Md.) State U., 1993; MPA, U. Balt., 1998. Settlement adminstrn. Safford Lincoln Mercury, Silver Spring, 1993—. precinct chmn. dist. 19, Montgomery County Young Reps., Rockville, Md., 1998. Mem. ASPA, Pi Alpha Alpha. Republican. Roman Catholic. Home: 3805 Gawayne Ter Silver Spring MD 20906

DOLLEN, CHARLES JOSEPH, clergyman, writer; b. Rochester, N.Y., Apr. 14, 1926; s. Charles Joseph Dollen and Cecilia Margaret (Pfeiffer) Kelly. BA, St. Bernard's Coll., Rochester, 1948; MS in LS, U. So. Calif., 1956; MDiv, St. Bernard's Inst., Rochester, 1985. Ordained priest Roman Cath. Ch., 1954, domestic prelate, 1985. Libr. dir. U. San Diego, 1954-73; pastor St. Gabriel's Cath. Ch., Poway, Calif., 1973-96, ret., 1996; book rev. editor The Priest, 1973—; book reviewer Cath. News Svc., 1973—. Author: Book of Catholic Wisdom, 1986, Traditional Catholic Prayers, 1990, The Holy Eucharist, 1994, On The Love of God, 1996, Psalms: Prayerbook of the King, 1998; contbr. numerous articles to religious publs. Mem. Poway Unified Sch. Dist. Sch. Bd., 1977-82. Lt., chaplain, USNR, 1956-60. Mem. ALA, Calif. Libr. Assn. (various offices), Cath. Libr. Assn. (various offices). Democrat. Avocations: stamps, coins, swimming, gardening. Home: 12841 Amber Hill Ln Poway CA 92064-3701*

DOLLENS, RONALD W., pharmaceuticals company executive; b. Ind., Dec. 17, 1946; s. William Franklin and Louise Anna (Davis) D.; m. Susan Stanley, Aug. 30, 1969; children: Stephanie, Grant. BS, Purdue U., 1970; MBA, Ind. U., 1972. From sales rep. to dir. bus. devel. Eli Lilly & Co., Indpls., 1972-85; from sr. v.p. to ceo Advanced Cardiovasc. Sys., Santa Clara, 1985-91; pres. med. devices divsn. Eli Lilly & Co., 1991-94; pres., ceo Guidant Corp., Indpls., 1994—. Office: Guidant Corp PO Box 44906 Indianapolis IN 46244-0906*

DOLLIVER, JAMES MORGAN, retired state supreme court justice; b. Ft. Dodge, Iowa, Oct. 13, 1924; s. James Isaac and Margaret Elizabeth (Morgan) D.; m. Barbara Babcock, Dec. 18, 1948; children: Elizabeth, James, Peter, Keith, Jennifer, Nancy. BA in Polit. Sci. with high honors, Swarthmore Coll., 1949; LLB, U. Wash., 1952; D in Liberal Arts (hon.), U. Puget Sound, 1981. Bar: Wash. 1952. Clk. to presiding justice Wash. Supreme Ct., 1952-53; pvt. practice Port Angeles, Wash., 1953-54, Everett, Wash., 1961-64; adminstrv. asst. to Congressman Jack Westland, 1955-61, Gov. Daniel J. Evans, 1965-76; justice Supreme Ct. State of Wash., 1976-99, chief justice, 1985-87; adj. prof. U. Puget Sound Sch. Law, 1988-92. Chmn. United Way Campaign Thurston County, 1975; chmn. Wash. chpt. Nature Conservancy, 1981-83; pres. exec. bd. Tumwater Area coun. Boy Scouts Am., 1972-73, Wash. State Capital Hist. Assn., 1976-80, 85—, also trustee, 1983-84; trustee Deaconess Children's Home, Everett, 1963-65, U. Puget Sound, 1969—, chair exec. com., 1990-93, Wash. 4-H Found., 1977-93, Claremont (Calif.) Theol. Sem., assoc. mem., Community Mental Health Ctr., 1977-84; bd. mgrs. Swarthmore Coll., 1980-84; bd. dirs. Thurston Mason Community Health Ctr., 1977-84, Thurston Youth Svcs. Soc., 1969-84, also pres., 1983, mem. exec com. 1970-84, Wash. Women's Employment and Edn., 1982-84; mem. jud. coun. United Meth. Ch., 1984-92, gen. cong., 1970-72, 80—, gen. bd. ch. and soc., 1976-84; adv. coun. Ret. Sr. Vol. program, 1979-83; pres. Wash. Ctr. Law-related Edn., 1987-89, bd. dirs. 1987-95; bd. dirs. World Assn. for Children and Parents, 1987-93; trustee U. Wash. Law Sch. Found., 1982-90, Olympic Park Inst., 1988-94; mem. bd. visitors U. Wash. Sch. Social Work, 1987-93; chair bd. visitors U. Puget Sound Sch. Law, 1988-90, bd. visitors, 1988-93; chmn. bd. dirs. Pub. Lands Employee Recognition Fund, 1994—; mem. bd. dirs. St. Peter Hosp. Med. Rehab. Community Adv. Bd., 1993—. With USN, 1943-45; ensign USCG, 1945-46. Recipient award Nat. Council Japanese Am. Citizens League, 1976; Silver Beaver award, 1971; Silver Antelope award, 1976. Mem. ABA, Wash. Bar Assn., Am. Judges Assn., Am. Judicature Soc., Pub. Broadcast Found. (bd. dirs. 1982-95), Masons, Rotary, Phi Delta Theta, Delta Theta Phi.

DOLLIVER, ROBERT HENRY, psychology educator; b. Fort Dodge, Iowa, Oct. 15, 1934. B.A., Cornell Coll., 1958; M.A., Ohio State U., 1963, Ph.D., 1966. Social worker Bd. Child Welfare, Elyria, Ohio, 1958-59; social worker Cleve. Boys Sch., 1959-61; asst., then assoc. prof. psychology U. Mo., Columbia, 1966-77, prof., 1977—. Office: U Mo Dept Psychology Columbia MO 65211

DOLMAN, JOHN PHILLIPS (TIM), JR. (TIM DOLMAN), communications company executive; b. Phila., May 22, 1944; s. John Phillips and Dodie Lewis (Porter) D.; m. Rebecca Critchlow, Oct. 29, 1977; children—John P. III, Timothy Chadwick (dec.). AB in History, Wagner Coll., 1966; MBA. in Internat. Bus, U. Pa., 1971. Asst. account exec. Benton & Bowles Inc., N.Y.C., 1971-72, account exec., 1972-73; account dir Benton & Bowles Inc., Amsterdam and London, 1973-75, v.p., account supr., 1975-78; pub. Motor Boating & Sailing mag., 1978-80; gen. mgr. mag. devel. Hearst Mags., N.Y.C., 1980-82; v.p., asst. pub. Pub. div. Playboy Enterprises, Inc., Chgo., 1983-84, sr. v.p., 1984-88; pres. Dolman & Co., New Canaan, Conn., 1988-92; sr. v.p. mktg. Championship Auto Racing Teams, Inc. dba IndyCar, 1992-94; v.p. mktg. and bus. devel. OCC Sports Inc. subs. ESPN, Inc. subs. ABC, Inc. subs. Walt Disney Co., 1994—. Contbr.: Marine Bus. mag, 1977-78. 1st lt. U.S. Army, 1966-69, Vietnam; lic. capt. USCG, 1988. Decorated Bronze Star. Mem. VFW, N.Y. Yacht Club. Republican. Episcopalian.

DOLMATCH, THEODORE BIELEY, management consultant; b. N.Y.C., Apr. 22, 1924; s. Aaron and Diana (Bieley) D.; m. Blanche Ormont, Dec. 28, 1948; children: Karen Ann, Stephen Joseph. BA, NYU, 1947, MA, 1948; student, Columbia U., N.Y.C., 1948-50. Tchr. Queens Coll., 1948-50; asst. supr. Sch. Gen. Studies, Bklyn. Coll., 1950-55; publs. bus. mgr. Am. Mgmt. Assn., 1955-62; pres. Pitman Pub. Corp., N.Y.C., 1962-71, Intext Publishers Group, N.Y.C., also Intext Ednl. Devel. Group, N.Y.C., 1971-75, Info. Please Pub., Inc., N.Y.C., 1976-80, Dolmatch Publs., Inc., N.Y.C., 1979-85; cons. to govt. agys. and corps., 1981—; chmn. ISD/Shaw, Inc., Washington, 1986—; bd. dirs. Pragmatix, Inc. Author (sometimes under pseudonym Stephen Josephs) books and articles. Home: 298 Law Rd Briarcliff Manor NY 10510-2115

DOLNICK, IRENE, financial services company official; b. El Paso, Tex., Oct. 2, 1948; d. Apolonio and Inez (Martinez) Rivera; m. Peter Dolnick, Apr. 8, 1970. BA summa cum laude, U. Mass., Boston, 1995; postgrad., Boston Coll., 1996—. Br. mgr. Western Temp. Svcs., Worcester, Mass., 1987-88; pres., owner PI Pers. Svcs., Randolph, Mass., 1988-90; bilingual tutor and counselor Thomas Gardner Sch., Boston, 1996; tng. specialist Boston Fin. Data Svcs., North Quincy, Mass., 1996—. Author: Perceived Mother-Daughter Interaction Amoung Aggressive Female Adolescents, 1998. Counselor, rschr. Hyde Park Sch., Boston, 1992-93, 94-95, Boston Latin Sch., 1994-95; bilingual tutor and counselor Thomas Gardner Sch., Boston, 1996. Mem. Golden Key (pres. Boston chpt. 1995-96), Psi Chi, Inst. for the Recruitment of Tchrs. Avocations: theater, tennis, physical education, reading classics, astronomy.

DOLPH, WILBERT EMERY, lawyer; b. Palatka, Fla., Dec. 29, 1923; s. Wilbert Emery and Ophelia (Reynolds) D.; m. Roberta Hundley; children: Wilbert Emery III, Kenneth Alan, Scott Marshall, Cheryl, Karlsson. Student, U. Ariz., 1941-42, LL.B., 1949. Bar: Ariz. 1949. Asst. city atty. Tucson, 1949-50; asst. atty. gen. Ariz., 1950-51; pvt. practice Tucson, 1951-94; counsel. jud. com. Ariz. Senate, 1952; shareholder Bilby & Shoenhair, P.C., 1953-89; ptnr. Snell & Wilmer, Tucson, 1989-93, of counsel, 1992-93; ret., 1993. Pres. Pima County Young Dems., 1952-53; v.p. Ariz. Young Dems., 1952-53; trustee Tucson Med. Ctr., pres., 1973-75; mem. U. Ariz. Found., U. Ariz. Pres.'s Club; chmn. bd. dirs. Friends of Libr., U. Ariz., 1995-97; past bd. visitors U. Ariz. Law Coll.; past bd. dirs. Ariz. Sonora Desert Mus., Ariz. Heart Assn., So. Ariz. Heart Assn., Tucson Festival Soc., Ariz. Children's Home Assn., Tucson YMCA, Ariz. Coun. Econ. Edn.; past vestryman, parish warden St. Phlips in the Hills Episcopal Ch., 1974-76. With USNR, 1942-44, to capt. USMCR, 1944-46. Decorated Air medal. Mem. ABA, Ariz. Bar Assn., Pima County Bar Assn. (exec. com., pres. 1974-75), Navy League, Foothills Forum, Tucson Fgn. Rels. Com., Phi Delta Phi, Sigma Chi, Grad. Club (pres. 1987), Skyline Country Club, U.S. Power Squadron (sec. 1995). Home: 4749 Cherry Hills Dr Tucson AZ 85718-2634

DOLT, FREDERICK CORRANCE, lawyer; b. Louisville, Oct. 10, 1929; s. O. Frederick and Margaret A. (Corrance) D.; m. Lucy M. Voelker, Dec. 8, 1960; 1 child, Frederick C. Jr. JD, U. Louisville, 1952. Bar: Ky. 1952, U.S. Ct. Appeals (6th cir.) 1955, U.S. Supreme Ct. 1972, La. 1982. Assoc. Morris & Garlove, Louisville, 1955-59; sole practice Louisville, 1959-70, 79—; ptnr. Leibson, Dolt & McCarthy, Louisville, 1970-73. Mem. Inner Circle Advocates, 1981. Served with U.S. Army, 1953-55. Mem. ABA, Ky. Bar Assn. (chmn. ins. negligence sect. 1968-70, mem. Ho. of Dels. 1970-80), Assn. Trial Lawyers Am. (state del. 1965-70), Ky. Trial Lawyers Assn. (pres. 1970). Republican. Presbyterian. Avocation: golf. Home: 19634 Lost Creek Dr Fort Myers FL 33912-5539 Office: 310 Starks Bldg Louisville KY 40202

DOLUISIO, JAMES THOMAS, pharmacy educator; b. Bethlehem, Pa., Sept. 28, 1935; s. Dominic and Sue (Powell) D.; m. Phyllis M. Sabolski, June 20, 1959; children—Thomas, James, Rebecca. B.S. in Pharmacy, Temple U., 1957, M.S., 1959; Ph.D., Purdue U., 1962; DSc, Phila. Coll. Pharmacy and Sci., 1983; DSc (hon.), Purdue U., 1995. From asst. prof. to assoc. prof. pharmacy Phila. Coll. Pharmacy and Sci., 1961-67, also assoc. dir. dept., 1965-67; prof., chmn. dept. pharmacy U. Ky., Lexington, 1967-73; prof., dean U. Tex., Austin, 1973-98; bd. dirs. Eckerd Corp., 1986-96, COR Therapeutics; cons. Smith Kline & French Labs., Phila., 1962-67, McNeil Labs., Ft. Washington, Pa., 1967-72, Hoechst Labs., Somerville, N.J., 1973-93, Nat. Inst. Drug Abuse, 1976-78, HEW, U.S. Surgeon Gen., 1975-83. Contbr. to profl. and sci. jours. Active Pharmacists Against Drug Abuse Found, 1984; chmn. U.S. Pharmacopeial Conv., Inc., 1990-95; v.p. Fedn. Internat. Pharmaceutique, 1994-98. NSF fellow, 1959-61; Am. Found. Pharm. Edn. fellow, 1957-59. Mem. Am. Pharm. Assn. (Remington Honor medal 1995), Am. Assn. Colls. Pharmacy, Am. Soc. Hosp. Pharmacy, Am. Assn. Pharm. Scientists, Rho Chi. Office: U Texas College of Pharmacy Austin TX 78712

DOMAHIDY, MARY RODGERS, public policy educator; b. Ft. Eustis, Va., Sept. 14, 1945; d. James Maxey and Adelaide Louise (Cox) Rodgers; m. Steve E., July 28, 1973. BA, Vanderbilt U., 1967; MA, St. Louis U., 1978, PhD, 1990. Cert. secondary social studies tchr., Mo. Spol. programs dir. YWCA, Greenville, S.C., 1967-69; program coord. YWCA, Greenville, 1974-76; social studies tchr., dept. chair Greenville County Schs., 1969-74; rsch. asst. St. Louis U., 1977-80, asst. prof., 1990—, dept. chair, 1996—; planner St. Louis County Govt., 1980-84; exec. bd. St. Louis-Jefferson Solid Waste Dist., St. Louis, 1993—. Contbr. articles to profl. jours. Mem. Planning Commn., Chesterfield, Mo., 1988-95, chair 1991-93; bd. dirs. Mo. Goodwill Industries, St. Louis, 1991—; bd. dirs., exec. bd. Focus - St. Louis, 1996—. Recipient Gov.'s award for Excellence in Tchg., Mo. Coord. Bd. for Higher Edn. Office: Dept Pub Policy Studies 3663 Lindell Blvd Ste 180 Saint Louis MO 63108-3342

DOMAN, NICHOLAS R., lawyer; b. Budapest, Hungary, Apr. 10, 1913; s. Odon and Irene (Parkany) D.; m. Katharine Huntington Bigelow, 1951 (dec.); children: Daniel Bigelow, Alexander Macdonald; m. Judith Nicely Perrin, 1992. Student, London Sch. Econs., 1932; M.A. in Law, U. Colo., 1935; J.D., U. Budapest, 1936; postgrad., Geneva Sch. Internat. Studies, 1937. Bar: D.C. 1947, N.Y. 1948, U.S. Supreme Ct 1948. Mem. research faculty U. Chgo., 1939-40; lectr. Rotary Internat. Inst., Chgo., 1940-41, 46-47; asst. prof. govt. and econs. Coll. William and Mary, 1941-42; asst. to U.S. Chief Prosecutor Nuremberg Trial, 1945-46; practice law N.Y.C. and Washington, 1948—; adj. prof. Sch. Law, NYU, 1959-77; founder Nicholas R. Doman Soc. Internat. Law U. Colo., 1967; symposium leader on internat. transactions Am. Law Inst.-ABA, Am. Soc. Internat. Law, World Peace Through Law; v.p., dir., gen. counsel Assn. to Unite the Democracies, Washington; panelist, commentator on internat. politics for TV and radio. Author: The Coming Age of World Control, 1942; Contbr. articles to profl. jours., popular publs. Trustee Pitzer Coll., 1975—. Served to 1st lt. AUS, 1942-45, Italy. Recipient George Washington award, 1979; Norlin award U. Colo., 1980. Mem. Internat. Law Assn. (exec. com. 1965—, hon. v.p. U.S. br.), Am. Law Inst. (life), Internat. Bar Assn., Union Internationale des Avocats, Order Coif (hon.), Shelter Island Yacht Club, Gardiner's Bay Country Club, Univ. Club (N.Y.C.). Office: 420 Lexington Ave New York NY 10170-0002*

DOMARADZKI, THEODORE FELIX, Slavic studies educator, editor; b. Warsaw, Poland, Oct. 27, 1910; s. Joseph and Maria (Tomaszewska) D.; m. Maria Teresa Dobija, Apr. 20, 1954 (dec. Oct. 1997). Baccalaureat, Polish Coll., Zakopane, 1930; MA, U. Warsaw, 1939; LittD, U. Rome (Italy), 1941; diploma, Acad. Polit. Sci., Warsaw, 1936. Asst. in diplomatic history Acad. Polit. Sci., 1936-39; assoc. prof. Pontificio Inst. Orientale, Gregorian U., Rome, 1943-47; prof. Polish lit., prof. Slavic studies U. Montreal, Que., Can., 1948-76, dir. dept. Slavic studies, 1948-63, hon. life prof., 1996—; prof., hon. pres. Inst. Comparative Civilizations Montreal, 1976—; dir. Polish Rsch. Ctr. Inst. Comparative Civilizations, 1963—; dir. Polish program and Paderewski collection, chairperson Polish studies U. Montreal, 1948-76; vis. prof. Fordham U., 1948-50; prof., dir. dept. Slavic studies U. Ottawa, 1949-53; lectr. Polish lang. State U. Rome, 1941-47. Author: Les Considerations de C.K. Norwid sur la liberte de la parole, 1971, Le Symbolisme et L'Universalisme de C.K. Norwid, 1974, Norwid poet of Christianity, 1984, Échos Romantiques Et Les Maisons D'Auteurs Au Canada, 1990, Personalités Ethniques du Québec, 1991; editor: Slavic and East European Studies, 1956-76, Slavic Publications/Publications Slaves, 1976—. Head demographical divsn. Warsaw City Hall, 1932-35; chief edn. divsn. for Poles Brit. Embassy, Rome, 1945-46; pres. Can. Com. for Orgn. World U., 1971-84; dir. gen. Inst. Comparative Civilizations. Maj. Polish Red Cross (2nd Polish corps of Brit. Army in Italy), 1944-46. Decorated Order of Can.; knight Order Polonia Restituta; Golden Cross of Merit (Poland); comdr. Papal Order St. Gregory the Great, comdr. Royal Order St. Sava; knight French Underground Forces. Mem. Pen Club Internat.-Can. Francophone Ctr., Assn. Can. Writers, Can. Soc. Comparative Study Civilizations (hon. life mem., pres. 1972-76), Can. Internat. Acad. Humanities and Social Scis. (v.p. 1975-95), Can. Assn. Slavists (hon. life), Com. for Can.-Polish Univ. and Sci. Cooperation (pres. Que. sect. 1969-93), Que. Ethnic Press Assn.

(v.p. 1979-81), Royal Canadian Legion (officer sect. filiale Jean Brilliant). Home and Office: Inst Comparative Civil, 60 Ave Willowdale Apt 702, Outremont, Montreal, PQ Canada H3T 2A3

DOMBALIS, CONSTANTINE NICHOLAS, minister; b. Norfolk, Va., July 29, 1925; s. Nicholas John and Helen Constantine (Matinos) D.; m. Mary Christine Fourgis, June 6, 1954; children: Nicholas, Christopher. BTh, Hellenic Coll., 1947; BD, Holy Cross Sem., 1949; STB, Gen. Theol. Sch., 1951; DD (hon.), U. Richmond, 1988; DHL (hon.), Randolph Macon Coll., 1996. Ordained to ministry Greek Orthodox Ch., 1954. Pastor Greek Orthodox Ch., Richmond, Va., 1954-71; dean Greek Orthodox Cathedral, Richmond, Va., 1971-96; dean emeritus Greek Orthodox Cathedral, Richmond, 1996—; vicar Archdiocese of Va., Richmond, 1976-96; exec. com. Va. Coun. of Chs., Richmond, 1978-96; U.S. del. to UN 38th Gen. Assembly, 1983; mem. coun. religious leaders U.S. Holocaust Meml., Washington, 1989-94; exec. bd. dirs. Sts. Cosma and Damianos Sr. Residence, Richmond, 1988—. Contbr. articles to profl. jours. Chmn. Va. Dept. of Rehab., 1979-83; chmn. religious com. Va. Statute for Religious Freedom, 1989—; mem. bd. visitors Va. Commonwealth U., 1991-96; founder Richmond Internat. Airport Interfaith Chapel, 1996; mem. Ctr. for Study of Religious Freedom, Va. Weslyan Coll., 1995. Recipient DAR award, 1968, NCCJ award 1974, B'nai Brith Torch of Liberty award 1976; named one of 100 Most Influential Richmonders 1986, one of 100 Power Players of Richmond, 1998. Mem. UNESCO (bd. dirs. 1980-82), Holy Cross Theol. Sch. Alumni Assn. (pres. 1978-82). Home: 304 Sandalwood Dr Richmond VA 23229-7637

DOMBECK, HAROLD ARTHUR, insurance company executive; b. Bronx, N.Y., Mar. 23, 1941; s. Max J. and Rose R. (Schefren) D.; m. Cynthia E. Kofoed, May 14, 1983; children: Mark J., Glenn D., David S. B of Civil Engring., NYU, 1962, M of Civil Engring., 1963. Profl. engr., N.Y., N.J., Conn., Ga. Instr. San Antonio Coll., San Antonio, Tex., 1964-65, SUNY, Farmingdale, 1965-68; project mgr. H2M Group, Melville, N.Y., 1965-74, dir. environ. engring., 1971-81, dir. mktg., 1982-85, exec. v.p., 1986-88, pres., 1989-91, pres., chief exec. officer, chmn., 1991-94; CEO Dombeck Assocs. Inc., Duluth, Ga., 1995—; chmn., CEO Archs. and Engrs. Ins. Co., Greenville, Del., 1987—; v.p., CFO, Dod/Pritchard Comms. Inc., Norcross, Ga., 1998—; chmn. bd. dirs. Am. Cons. Engrs. Pension Trust, St. Louis, 1991-94; bd. dirs. Archs. and Engrs. Loss Control, Inc., Northbrook Ill., 1990-95; chmn. ACEC Bus. Inst. Trust, St. Louis, 1994-96. Pres. High Woods Civic Assn., St. James, N.Y., 1971-73. 1st lt. USAF, 1963-65. Fellow ASCE, Am. Cons. Engrs. Coun. (pres. L.I. 1982-84); mem. Am. Acad. Environ. Engrs. (diplomate), NSPE (dir. 1982-85), N.Y. State Water Pollution Control Assn. (dir. 1980-83), N.Y. State Soc. Profl. Engrs. (pres. 1983-84, pres. Suff County chpt. 1978-80, Engr. of Yr. 1989, 90, Outstanding Svc. awards 1988, 89). Avocations: gardening, reading, golf. Office: AEIC 2 Greenville Crossing 4001 Kennett Pike Greenville DE 19807-2315

DOMBECK, MICHAEL PAUL, fisheries biologist; b. Stevens Point, Wis., Sept. 21, 1948; s. Leonard Barney and Estelle Evelyn (Gross) D.; m. Patricia Ann Rider, July 25, 1975; 1 child, Mary Rider. BS in Biology and Gen. Sci., U. Wis., Stevens Point, 1971, MST in Biology and Edn., 1974; MS in Zoology, U. Minn., 1977; PhD in fisheries biology, Iowa State U., 1984. Fishing guide Hayward, Wis., 1966-77; instr. zoology U. Wis., Stevens Point, 1971-73; research specialist Bell Mus., Mpls., 1975-77; staff columnist Visitor Mag., Hayward, 1975—; fisheries biologist USDA Forest Svc., Milw., 1978-85; regional fisheries program mgr. Pacific S.W. Region USDA Forest Svc., San Francisco, 1985-87; mgr. Nat. Fisheries Program, Washington, 1987-89; sci. advisor, spl. asst. to dir. Bur. Land Mgmt., Washington, 1989-92, acting dir., 1994-97; acting asst. sec., dep. asst. sec. Land and Minerals Mgmt. Dept. of Interior, Washington, 1993, chief to staff to asst. sec. Land and Minerals Mgmt., 1993-94; chief USDA Forest Svc., 1997—; cons. Freshwater Fishing Hall of Fame, Hayward, 1984—, bd. govs. (life); program chmn. Internat. Muskellunge Symposium, 1984. Contbr. articles to profl. jours.; inventor oxygen stratification (nat. award 1985), artificial turf fish egg incubator (nat. award 1986). Legislative fellow, 1988, T. Roosevelt fellow Am. Mus. Natural History, 1975; recipient "Ding" J.N. Darling Conservation Writers award, 1981, 82, 83, Outdoor Writer's Assn. Am. scholarship, 1983. Mem. Soc. Am. Foresters, Am. Fisheries Soc. (cert., sec./treas. Wis. chpt. 1983-85), Am. Inst. Fisheries Research Biologists, Freshwater Fishing Hall of Fame, Sigma Xi, Gamma Sigma Delta. Avocations: fishing, camping, hiking, oil painting, music. Office: USDA Auditor Bldg 4 NW 1400 Independence Ave SW Washington DC 20090-6090*

DOMBKOWSKI, THOMAS RAYMOND, public health administrator; b. Rochester, N.Y., June 28, 1950; s. Bernard Albert and Helene Marie (Skurski) D. BA, U. Notre Dame, 1972; JD, DePaul U., 1977. Bar: Ill., 1977. Revenue officer IRS, Chgo., 1974-81, supervisory revenue officer, 1981-83, program analyst, 1983-86; exec. dir. Chgo. House, 1986-90; staff writer Howard Brown Health Ctr., Chgo., 1990-92; program dir. Chgo. Dept. Health, 1992—; co-founder, chmn. bd. dirs. Chgo. House, 1985-86. Mem. Adv. Coun. on Gay and Lesbian Issues, Chgo., 1990-92; founder Chgo. Gay and Lesbian Hall of Fame, 1991, co-chair selection com., 1993-97; mem. MACS study, Chgo., 1983—; founding bd. dirs. IMPACT, Chgo., 1987-88; mem., sustainer Gerber-Hart Libr., Chgo., 1990—; chief judge Internat. Mr. Leather, Chgo., 1992—. Recipient Pearl Hart Humanitarian award Mattachine Midwest, 1986, Man of Yr. award Gay/Lesbian Physicians, 1987, Sudbery Cmty. Svc. award IVI/IPO of Ill., 1989, Tree of Life award AIDS Pastoral Care Network, 1998; named to Hall of Fame, Gay Chgo. Mag., 1991, Chgo. Gay and Lesbian Hall of Fame, 1992. Avocations: travel, history, theater, leather. Home: # 404 920 W Sheridan Rd Chicago IL 60613 Office: Chgo Dept Pub Health 333 S State St # 2-148 Chicago IL 60604-3900

DOMBROWSKI, ANNE WESSELING, microbiologist, researcher; b. Cin., Jan. 26, 1948; m. Allan Wayne Dombrowski, Apr. 17, 1982; children: Amy, Alicia. BA summa cum laude, Xavier U., 1970; MS, U. Cin., 1972, PhD, 1974. Fellow Scripps Clinic & Rsch. Found., La Jolla, Calif., 1974-76; sr. rsch. microbiologist Merck & Co., Inc., Rahway, N.J., 1976-87, rsch. fellow, 1987-96, sr. rsch. fellow, 1996—. Patentee in field; contbr. articles to profl. jours. Mem. AAAS, Soc. Indsl. Microbiology (sec. 1982-85, dir. 1998—), Am. Soc. Microbiology, Mycol. Soc. Avocations: reading, gardening. Home: 51 Landsdowne Rd East Brunswick NJ 08816-4156 Office: Merck & Co Inc PO Box 2000 Rahway NJ 07065-0900

DOMBROWSKI, BOB, artist, publisher; b. Buffalo, Feb. 16, 1944; s. Edward A. and Mary Ann Dombrowski. BS, SUNY, Buffalo, 1965; postgrad., Cornish Inst., Seattle, 1975-76. Artist, N.Y.C., 1976—; owner, mgr. GB Art Co., N.Y.C., 1994—; cons. Cementex Corp., N.Y.C., 1989—. Creator, prodr. Ode to Birth of Shiva, 1987, Elegy for the Republic, 1991, Hwy. 17, 1993, On Thinking Thoughts, 1997; exhibited in group shows at Albright-Knox Art Mus., Buffalo, 1980, Ashford Hollow (N.Y.) Found., 1980, Storefront for Art and Architecture, N.Y.C., 1985, Franklin Furnace, N.Y.C., 1986, Nelson-Atkins Mus., Kansas City, 1989, Shedhalle (Rote Fabrik), Zurich, 1989, Barking Legs Dance Theater, Chattanooga, 1995; represented in permanent collections including Cmty. Bd. #3, Nico Smith Gallery, N.Y.C., Mus. Modern Art Libr., N.Y.C., Bettina Riedel Ltd., Phila., Pernod Corp., N.Y.C., La Perla Garden, N.Y.C., Francis Pratt Usui, Nicholson, Pa., Cleve. Art Inst. Mem. Internat. Sculpture Ctr., N.Y. Artists Equity (bd. dirs. 1989-90). Avocations: photography, walking. Home and Office: 805 6th Ave New York NY 10001

DOMBROWSKI, DAVID, baseball team executive; b. Chgo., July 27, 1956; s. Ronald Edward and Laurie Bernadine Dombrowski. B of Adminstrn., Western Mich. U., 1979. Adminstrv. asst. Chgo. White Sox, 1978-79, asst. dir. player devel. and scouting, 1979-80, asst. gen. mgr., 1980-85, v.p. baseball ops., 1985-86; dir. player devel. Montreal Expos, 1986-87, asst. gen. mgr., 1987-88, gen. mgr., 1988-91; exec. v.p., gen. mgr. Fla. Marlins, Miami, 1991—. Bd. dirs. Chgo. Baseball Cancer Charities, 1981—. Named Exec. of Yr., UPI, 1990. Avocations: sports, jogging, movies, theatre. Office: Fla Marlins 2267 NW 199th St Miami FL 33056-2600*

DOMBROWSKI, MITCHELL PAUL, physician, inventor, researcher; b. Detroit, Apr. 24, 1953; s. Mitchell Stanley and Dorothy Julia (Silarski) D.; m. Jocelyn McKinley, Mar. 7, 1981; children: Michael, Jacqueline, David, Elizabeth. BS, U. Mich., 1975; MD, Wayne State U., 1979. Diplomate Am. Bd. OB-Gyn, Am. Bd. Perinatology. Resident in obstetrics and gynecology Detroit, 1979-84, fellow in perinatology, 1984-86; from asst. to assoc. prof. Wayne State U. Sch. Medicine, Detroit, 1986-98, prof., 1998, chmn., chief, 1996-98; prin. investigator maternal fetal medicine network units Nat. Inst. Child Health and Human Devel., 1996. Contbr. articles to med. publs.; patentee fetal blood sampling device, suction sampling device, reagent test strip, digital medication device, self-capping needle assemblies, amnicentises needle. Recipient Research award Nat Insts Hlth. Recipient Nat. Inst. Alcohol Abuse and Alcoholism award, AMA; grantee Nat. Heart, Lung and Blood Inst./NICHD, 1994; fellow Am. Coll. Obstetrics and Gynecologists, Soc. Perinatal Obstetricians; Diabetes Rsch. Office: Hutzel Hosp 4707 Saint Antoine St Detroit MI 48201-1498

DOMENICI, PETE V. (VICHI DOMENICI), senator; b. Albuquerque, May 7, 1932; s. Cherubino and Alda (Vichi) D.; m. Nancy Burk, Jan. 15, 1958; children: Lisa, Peter, Nella, Clare, David, Nanette, Helen, Paula. Student, U. Albuquerque, 1950-52; BS, U. N.Mex., 1954, LLD (hon.); LLB, Denver U., 1958; LLD (hon.), Georgetown U. Sch. Medicine; HHD (hon.), N.Mex. State U. Bar: N.Mex. 1958. Tchr. math. pub. schs. Albuquerque, 1954-55; ptnr. firm Domenici & Bonham, Albuquerque, 1958-72; chmn., ex-officio mayor Albuquerque, 1967; mem. U.S. Senate from N.Mex., 106th Congress, N.Mex., 1972—; city commr. Albuquerque, 1966-68; mem. appropriations com., energy and natural resources com., chmn. subcom. on energy rsch. and devel.; mem. com. on environ. and pub. works, mem. govtl. affairs com.; chmn. budget com., com. on Indian affairs; mem. Presl. Adv. Com. on Federalism; senate Rep. policy com. Mem. Gov.'s Policy Bd. for Law Enforcement, 1967-68; chmn. Model Cities Joint Adv. Com., 1967-68. Recipient Nat. League of Cities award Outstanding Performance in Congress; Disting. Svc. award Tax Found., 1986, Legislator of Yr. award Nat. Mental Health Assn., 1987, public sector leadership award, 1996. Mem. Nat. League Cities, Middle Rio Grande Council Govts. Office: US Senate 328 Hart Senate Office Bldg Washington DC 20510-3101

DOMEÑO, EUGENE TIMOTHY, elementary education educator, principal; b. L.A., Oct. 22, 1938; s. Digno and Aurora Mary (Roldan) D. AA, Santa Monica (Calif.) City Coll., 1958; BA, Calif. State U., 1960, MA, 1966. Cert. elem. tchr., gen. sch svcs, special secondary tchr. Elem. tchr. L.A. Unified Sch. Dist., 1960-70; asst. prin. Pomona (Calif.) Unified Sch. Dist., 1970-71, prin., 1971—; cons. testing and evaluation Pomona Unified Sch. Dist., 1990—. With USNR, 1957-65. Recipient PTA Hon. Svc. award Granada Elem. PTA, Granada Hills, Calif., 1960, Armstrong Sch. PTA, Diamond Bar, Calif., 1990, Calif. Disting. Sch. Calif. Dept. Edn., 1989, Nat. Blue Ribbon Sch. U.S. Dept. Edn., Washington, 1990, Prin. and Leadership award, 1990. Mem. ASCD, Nat. Assn. Elem. Sch. Prins. (Prin. of Leadership award with Nat. Safety Com., 1991), Nat. Assn. Year Round Sch., Assn. Calif. Sch. Administrs., Pomona Elem. Prin.'s Assn., Diamond Bar C. of C. (edn. com.). Avocations: golf, dancing, tennis, playing the flute. Office: Neil Armstrong Elem Sch 22750 Beaverhead Dr Diamond Bar CA 91765-1566

DOMER, FLOYD RAY, pharmacologist, educator; b. Cedar Rapids, Iowa, July 12, 1931; s. William Ray and Caroline Anne (Zimmer) D.; m. Judith Elaine Kofroth, 1965. B.S., State U. Iowa, 1954, M.S., 1956; Ph.D., Tulane U., 1959. Life Ins. Med. Research Fund postdoctoral fellow Nat. Inst. Med. Research, London, 1959-60; with USAF Research and Devel. Command Istituto Superior di Sanita, Rome, 1960-61; asst. prof. pharmacology U. Cin., 1961-62; asst. prof. pharmacology Tulane U., New Orleans, 1963-64, assoc. prof., 1965-74, prof., 1974-97; adj. prof. biology Appalachian State U., Boone, N.C., 1998—. Author: Animal Experiments in Pharmacological Analysis, 1971, Practical Anesthetic Pharmacology, 2d edit. 1986. Recipient award for teaching Owl Club, 1982, 83, 91, 94, 96. Mem. Am. Soc. Pharmacology and Exptl. Therapeutics, Soc. Neurosci., Soc. Exptl. Biology and Medicine. Club: Trojan. Home: # 2 194 Hillbeck Rd Boone NC 28607-7955 Office: Appalachian State U Dept Biology Boone NC 28608-2027

DOMESHEK, SOL, aeronautical engineer; b. N.Y.C., 1920; m. Florence Schnepf, 1942; 2 children. BS, CCNY, 1940; B in Mech. Engring., NYU, 1956. Lic. profl. engr. N.Y., N.J. Photo-mapper U.S. Geol. Survey, Washington, 1942-44; various engring. mgmt. assignments U.S. Naval Tng. Device Ctr., Port Washington, N.Y., 1946-66; dir. display and navigation devel. divsn. U.S. Army Avionics Lab., Fort Monmouth, N.J., 1966-86; pvt. practice Scotch Plains, N.J., 1986—; mem. U.S. Civil Svc. Bd. Engring. Examiners, N.Y., 1956-64; chmn. symposium on cockpit environment NATO, 1968; co-sponsor Internat. Symposium on Geographic Orientation in Flight, 1969; presenter sch. workshops engring. in cmty. life, 1990—. Lt. (j.g.) USN, PTO, 1944-46; with U.S. Navy Rsch. Reserve, 1946-52. Mem. NSPE, Am. Soc. Photogrammetry, Optical Soc. Am., Army Aviation Assn. Am. Achievements include 17 patents in areas of photo-mapping, projection systems for training, terrain modeling, day/night map displays for drivers and pilots. Office: 2320 Edgewood Ter Scotch Plains NJ 07076-2107

DOMEYKO, CECILIA, television producer; b. Santiago, Chile, May 1, 1950; came to U.S., 1975; d. Juan Ladislao and Paz (Lea-Plaza) D.; m. Luis Fernando Vera, Nov. 29, 1969 (div. 1982); children: J. Cristobal, Rodrigo A.; m. Jackson Johnstone Jorgens, June 4, 1988; children: Elisabeth, Catherine. BA in Journalism, Cath. U., Santiago, 1971; MA in Film and Prodn., Am. U., 1982. On-camera host Sta. WJLA-TV, Washington, 1982-87; on-camera reporter U.S. Info. Agt., Washington, 1984-87, Univision-TV, Washington, 1987-88; pres. Accent Media Prodns., Mc Lean, Va., 1988—; Hispanic cons. AARP, Washington, 1989-95; scriptwriter World Bank, Washington, 1982-84; dir., producer World Bank Econ. Recovery in Involuntary Resettlement, 1995, Education in Chile, 1996; fgn. corr. Channel 13 Cath. U., 1989-96. Scriptwriter: Lily, 1982, A Day in Srishnagar, 1984, Dandora, 1985; dir., producer: (documentary videos) Portrait of Ana Maria Vera, 1982, Magic Wool, 1996. Recipient Cindy award Discovery Channel, 1996, Silver Apple award Nat. Ednl. Media Assn., gold cert. for La Familia Unida and hon. mention for Uganda Edn., Worldfest Flagstaff Internat. Film Festival, 1998, Communicator award, Crystal award of excellence for Urgnda Edn. Reform and Crystal award of distinction for Chilean Edn., 1998, Summit bronze statue and cert. for La Familia Unida, 1999, silver plaque for Uganda Edn., Internat. Cinema in Industry Competition, 1999. Mem. NATAS, AFTRA, SAG, Women in Film and Video. Roman Catholic. Avocations: photography, gardening. Office: Accent Media Prodns 1350 Beverly Rd Ste 213 Mc Lean VA 22101

DOMINGO, ESTHER, music educator; b. Havana, Cuba, July 13, 1954; d. Silverio and Esther (Benitez) D. MusB in Music Edn., Mercer U., Atlanta, 1978, MusB in Piano Performance, 1978; MusM in Piano Pedagogy, Ga. State U., 1985. Cert. Yamaha music in edn. sys.; cert. music tchr., Ga. Sec., Spanish/ESOL tchrs. asst. Atlanta Pub. Schs., 1978-81; pvt. piano and Yamah music edn. tchr. Atlanta Music Ctr., 1983-89; piano and music theory tchr. Mercer U., Atlanta, 1980-91; piano and group music classes tchr. The Children's Sch., Atlanta, 1989-92; ESL tchr. Internat. Edn. Ctr., Atlanta, 1991-92; piano, theory and group classes tchr. pvt. home music studio, Atlanta, 1976—; pvt. piano and music theory tchr. Ga. Acad. Music, Atlanta, 1992—; gen. music, choral tchr. Atlanta Pub. Schs., 1992—; pianist Spanish Mission, Second-Ponce de Leon Bapt. Ch., Atlanta, 1970—. Neighborhood rep. Hispanic cmty. Ga. Power Co., Atlanta, 1978-79. Fine Arts grantee Atlanta Pub. Schs., 1998. Mem. Atlanta Music Tchrs. Assn. (program chmn. 1990-91, membership chmn. 1991-92, v.p. 1992-93, pres. 1993-94. Baptist. Avocations: handbell performer/choir, swimming, softball, travel. Office: Morningside Elem Sch 1053 E Rock Springs Rd NE Atlanta GA 30306-3099

DOMINGO, PLACIDO, tenor; b. Madrid, Spain, Jan. 21, 1941; s. Placido and Pepita (Embil) D.; m. Marta Ornelas; children: Jose, Placido, Alvaro Maurizio. Student, Conservatory in Mexico City; hon. degree, Royal Coll. Music, 1982, Complutense de Madrid, 1989. Artistic dir. Washington Opera, 1994—; co-founder, music adv., prin. guest condr. L.A. Music Ctr. Opera. Made operatic debut in La Traviata, 1961; debut, Met. Opera, 1968; star tenor with opera cos. including, La Scala, Covent Garden, Hamburg State Opera, Vienna State Opera, N.Y.C. Opera, San Francisco Opera, Nat. Hebrew Opera in Tel-Aviv; leading roles: 109 operas including Don Rodrigo, Tosca, Andrea Chenier, Don Carlo, Carmen, La Boheme, Errani, Parsifal, Idomeneo; appeared in films: Traviata, 1983, Carmen, 1984, Otello, 1986; made more than 100 recs., including 93 full-length operas, for BMG (formerly RCA), DGG, Sony, Decca/London, Philips, Time Warner, EMI (Angel); made more than 50 videos; performed in concert, PBS TV spl. (with José Carreras & Luciano Pavorotti) The Three Tenors, L.A., 1994; condr. numerous performances at major opera houses, including Met. Opera, London's Covent Garden, Vienna State Opera; music dir. Seville World's Fair; active Operalia internat. vocal competition. Performed concerts to benefit victims of 1985 Mexican earthquake. Recipient 8 Grammy awards. Address: care Vincent & Farrell Assocs 157 W 57th St Ste 502 New York NY 10019-2210*

DOMINGO-FORASTÉ, DOUGLAS, classics educator; b. L.A., May 4, 1954; s. Pedro and Maureen Vaughn D.; m. Diana Joy Lukenbach, June 23, 1973; children: Chrysia, Cynthia. AB, U. Calif., Davis, 1976; MA, U. Calif., Santa Barbara, 1981, PhD, 1988. Author: (with others) Byzantine Defenders of Images, 1998; editor: Claudii Aeliani Epistulae Et Fragmenta, 1994. Office: CSULB Classics 1250 Bellflower Blvd Long Beach CA 90840

DOMINGUE, EMERY, consulting engineering company executive, retired; b. Scott, La., Jan. 9, 1926; s. Lucien and Mathilde (Hebert) D.; m. Beatrice Broussard, Dec. 30, 1950; children: Dave, Cal James, Kevin Drew. BS, U. Southwestern La., 1949; MS, U. Ill., 1955. Engr. La. Dept. Hwys., 1949-50, East Tex. Constrn. Co., 1950-51; tchr. civil engring. U. Southwestern La., 1951-61; prin. Domingue, Szabo & Assocs., Inc., Lafayette, La., 1957-96, ret., 1996. Mem. Lafayette Parish Planning Commn.; pres. La. Intracoastal Seaway Assn. With U.S. Army, 1944-46, ETO. Fellow ASCE (pres., cert. of appreciation Baton Rouge br.), Am. Cons. Engrs. Coun.; mem. Am. Soc. Profl. Engrs., Profl. Engrs. Pvt. Practice, Am. Concrete Inst., Am. Congress Surveying and Mapping, Am. Pub. Works Assn., Am. Ry. Engring. Assn., Cons. Engrs. Coun. La. (A.E. Wilder award), C. of C. (exec. com., dir.), Kiwanis (Lafayette) (pres.), Ragin Cajun Club. Democrat. Roman Catholic. Home: 203 Beverly Dr Lafayette LA 70503-3107 Office: 400 E Kaliste Saloom Rd Lafayette LA 70508-8508

DOMINGUE, GERALD JAMES, medical scientist, microbiology, immunology and urology educator, researcher, clinical bacteriologist; b. Lafayette, La., Mar. 2, 1937; s. Edgar Paul and Sarah Ann (Prejean) D.; m. Marie H. Dugas, Aug. 30, 1958 (div. 1980); children: Andrea, Yvonne, Michelle, Gerald Jr., Marcel; m. Kathryn H. Colbert, June 20, 1981 (div. 1985). BS in Bacteriology, U. Southwestern La., 1959; PhD in Med. Microbiol. and Immunology, Tulane U., 1964. Post-doctoral research fellow Children's Hosp., asst. research instr. pediatrics SUNY, Buffalo, 1965-66; dir. microbiol. Snodgras Lab. of Pathology and Bacteriology, St. Louis, 1966-67; instr. microbiology St. Louis U., 1966-67; asst. prof. microbiology, immunology and urology Tulane U., New Orleans, 1967-70, assoc. prof. microbiology, immunology and urology, 1970-74, prof. microbiology, immunology and urology, 1974-97, prof. emeritus, 1997—; lectr. microbiology sch. dentistry Washington U., St. Louis, 1966-67; vis. prof., lectr. Peruvian Urol. Assn., Lima, 1973, First Internat. Congress Bacteriology, Jerusalem, 1973, Internat. Convocation Immunology, Buffalo, 1974, World Health Orgn. Conf. on Sperm Immunology, Aarhus, Denmark, 1974, European Soc. Exptl. Urol. Research, Wurzburg, Fed. Republic Germany, 1976, Internat. Seminar L-Forms, Montpellier, France, 1976, U. Melbourne, Royal Melbourne Hosp., Australia, 1978, XII Internat. Congress Microbiology, Munich, 1978, Internat. Symposium Vaccines and Vaccinations, Institut Pasteur, Paris, 1985; speaker U. Montpellier Sch. Medicine, 1985, 4th Internat. Congress on Pyelonephritis, Goteborg, Sweden, 1986, Orion Diagnostica, Helsinki, Finland, 1986, Nat. Inst. Hygiene, Warsaw, Poland, 1986, Symposium on Molecular Biology and Infectious Diseases, Institut Pasteur, 1987; mem. com. for infection control So. Bapt. Hosp., 1971-75, Charity Hosp. La., 1977—, Tulane U. Hosp., 1977—; mem. infectious disease com. St. Louis City Hosp., 1966-67; mem., reviewer, visitor project sites NIH Grant Review Study Sects., 1967—, NSF, Kaiser Rsch. Found., Kidney Found. of Can.; cons. bacteriology So. Bapt. Hosp., New Orleans, 1968-84, Tulane U. Hosp., 1978-83, Med. Tech. Corp., Somerset, N.J., 1983—; research cons. VA Hosp., New Orleans, 1970-78; cons., mem. tech. adv. bd. Analytab Products, Inc., N.Y.C., 1972-77, cons. Chiron Corp., Emeryville, Calif.; expert witness to subcom. on dept. investigation oversight and research for Animal Cancer Research Act, U.S. Ho. of Reps., 1980. Author, editor: Cell Wall-Deficient Bacteria, 1962; editorial bd. cons. numerous jours.; contbr. over 100 articles to profl. jours. and chpts. to books. Pres. France-Louisiane de la Nouvelle Orleans, 1985—, pres. fondateur, 1988; apptd. mem. Gov.'s Council for Devel. of French Lang. in La., 1985, 88; mem. Met. Area Com., New Orleans, 1987, Bur. Govtl. Research, New Orleans, 1987; mem. Mayor's Com. New Orleans-Paris Cultural Exchange, 1988; chmn. scholar's com. La. COm. on French Revolution, 1988; mem. Alliance for Good Govt., 1980-84; mem. Greater New Orleans French Bd., 1987—; rep. Coun. for Devel. French and France Louisiane for celebration of French Bicentennial, 1989. Served with La. N.G., USAR, 1955-63. Guaranty scholar U. Southwestern La., 1958; grantee NIH, 1970—, Schlieder Found., Armour Pharm. House, VA, Cadwallader Family Sonation, Med. Tech. Corp., Orion Diagnostica; named to Chevalier in the Order of Palmes Academiques, French Prime Minister; recipient French Medal, 1996. Fellow Am. Acad. Microbiology, Infectious Disease Soc. Am.; mem. Am. Soc. Microbiology (divisional lectr. 1978, found. lectr. 1979-80, symposium lectr. 1994), Soc. Basic Urologic Rsch. (state of art lectr. 1994), Soc. for Exptl. Biology and Medicine, AAAS, Am. Assn. Univ. Profs., Fedn. Am. Scientists, Southwestern Assn. Clin. Microbiology (editor newsletter 1983-85, pres. 1985-86), N.Y. Acad. Scis., Am. Assn. Lab. Animal Sci., Soc. Basic Urological Research (nominating com. 1988), Am. Urological Assn. (affiliate mem.), French-Am. Bus. Assn., 1988, Sigma Xi. Republican. Roman Catholic. Avocations: painting, writing. Home: PO Box 51999 New Orleans LA 70151-1999 Office: Tulane U Sch Medicine 1430 Tulane Ave New Orleans LA 70112-2699

DOMINGUEZ, DANIEL R., judge; b. 1945. BA, Boston U., 1967; LLB cum laude, U. P.R., 1970. Bar: P.R. Atty. Hector M. Laffitte Law Offices, 1970-72; ptnr. Laffitte, Dominguez & Totti, 1973-84, Dominguez & Totti, 1983-94; judge U.S. Dist. Ct. P.R., San Juan, 1994—; gov. Adv. Com. on Labor Policy, 1984; mem. bd. Fed. Bar Examiners U.S. Dist. Ct. P.R., 1989-94, mem. Civil Justice Reform Act Adv. Group, 1991-94; mem. merit selection com. for Appointment of U.S. Magistrate Judges, 1993; mem. com. for jud. reform Gov. P.R., 1993-94. Mem. Berwind Country Club, Hyatt Dorado Beach Country Club. Office: US Dist Ct PR US Courthouse CH-129 150 Ave Carlos Chardon San Juan PR 00918-1703

DOMINGUEZ, EDDIE, artist; b. Tucumcari, N.Mex., Oct. 17, 1957. BFA, Cleve. Inst. Art, 1981; MFA, Alfred U., 1983. Grad. asst., ceramics and visual design courses Alfred (N.Y.) U., 1981-83; artist-in-residence, lectr. Ohio State U., Columbus, 1984; artist-in-edn. N.Mex. Arts Divsn., Santa Fe, 1985-86; artist-in-residence Cleve. Inst. Art, 1986; artist-in-residence, lectr. U. Mont., Missoula, 1988; asst. prof. art U. Nebr., Lincoln, 1998—; Lectr., presenter workshops, mem. panels Ill. Arts Coun., Chgo., 1994, NEA, Washington, 1994, Ariz. Commn. on the Arts, 1994, Concordia U., Montreal, Que., Can., 1994, Mass. Coll. Art, Boston, 1994, Bennington (Vt.) Coll., 1994, 95, 96, Peters Valley, Layton, N.J., 1994, Firehouse Art Ctr., Norman, Okla., 1994, Haystack Mountain Sch. Arts & Crafts, Deer Isle, Maine, 1994, Ghost Ranch, Abiquiu, N.Mex., 1995, We. States Arts Fedn., Santa Fe, 1995, Colo. Coun. on the Arts, Boulder, 1995, Durango (Colo.) Art Ctr., 1995, Tamarind Inst., Albuquerque, 1995, 96, Kansas City (Mo.) Ar Inst., 1995, Hallmark Cards, Kansas City, 1996, Wichita (Kans.) Ctr. Arts, 1996, La. State U., Baton Rouge, 1996, Idaho State Arts Coun. Grants, Boise, 1996, Mattie Rhodes Counseling and Art Ctr., Kansas City, 1996, Southwest Ctr. Crafts, San Antonio, 1997, Very Spl. Arts, Albuquerque, 197, Topeka (Kans.) and Shawnee County Pub. Libr., 1997, numerous others. Solo exhbns. include Pro Art Gallery, St. Louis, 1990, Mobilia Gallery, Cambridge, Mass., 1990, Munson Gallery, Santa Fe, 1990, 92, 94, 95, 97, Mariposa Gallery, Albuquerque, 1990, Joanne Rapp Gallery, Scottsdale, Ariz., 1991, 93, 95, Felicita Found., Escondido, Calif., 1991, Tucumcari (N.Mex.) Area Vocat. Sch., 1992, Manchester Art Ctr., Pitts., 1993, Wetsman Collection, Detroit, 1993, Clovis (N.Mex.) C.C., 1993, Firehouse Art Ctr., 1994, Kavesh Gallery, Sun Valley, Idaho, 1995, Jan Weiner Gallery, Kansas City, 1995, 96, numerous others; group exhbns. include Fred Jones Mus. Art, U. Okla., Norman, 1995, Roswell (N.Mex.) Mus. & Art Ctr., 1995, Nancy Margolis Gallery, N.Y.C., 1995, Sharadin Art Gallery, Kutztown (Pa.) U., 1995, Richard Kavesh Gallery, 1995, Jan Weiner Gallery, 1995, Ariz. State U. Art Mus., Tempe, 1995, Islip (N.Y.) Mus., 1995, Bruce Kapson Gallery, Santa Monica, Calif., 1996, Site Sante Fe

Gallery, 1996, Johnston County C.C., Overland Parks, Kans., 1996, Jane Haslem Gallery, Washington, 196, Karen Ruhlen Gallery, Santa Fe, 1996, Margo Jacobson Gallery, Portland, Oreg., 1996, Very Spl. Arts Gallery, Albuquerque, 1997, Joanne Rapp Gallery, 1997, numerous others; pub. art project include, among others, murals at Great Brook Valley Health Ctr., Worcester, Mass., 1994, Mass. Gen. Hosp., 1996; represented in many permanent collections, including Cooper-Hewitt, N.Y.C., Mus. Fine Arts, Santa Fe, Cleve. Inst. Art, Fed. Reserve Bank, Dallas, Roswell Mus. and Art Ctr., Albuquerque Mus. Fine Arts, City of Tucson (Ariz.), Phoenix Airport, Renwick Gallery Nat. Mus. Am. Art Smithsonian Inst., Washington, Detroit Inst. Art, Hallmark Cards Corp., Kansas City, State Capitol Art Collection, Santa Fe, pvt. collections. Recipient numerous grants, including NEA fellowships, 1986, 88, Kohler Arts-in-Industry grant, Sheboygan, Wis., 1988, Percent for Art Project grant, Phoenix Arts Coun., 1990, 1992; recipient various prizes, including Clay, Fiber and Wood Best in Show, Albuquerque, 1984, Clay in '87 1st place award, Albuquerque St. Fair Exhbn., 1987.

DOMINGUEZ, EDWARD ANTHONY, physician, medical educator, consultant; b. San Antonio, Tex., July 22, 1960. AB, Rice U., 1982; MD, Baylor Coll. Medicine, 1986. Diplomate Am. Bd. Internal Med. Intern Baylor Coll. Med., Houston, 1986-87; resident in internal medicine Baylor Coll. Medicine, Houston, 1987-89, fellow in infectious diseases, 1989-92; chief resident Veterans Affairs Med. Ctr., Houston, 1990; assoc. prof. medicine Creighton U., Omaha, Nebr., 1998—; asst. prof. medicine U. Nebr., Omaha, Nebr., 1998—, assoc. prof. medicine, 1998—; med. corr. KETV-TV Omaha, 1994—. Author: (with others) Clinical Oncology, 1995, Conn's Current Therapy, 1996; contbr. articles to profl. jours. Assoc. advisor Rice U., Houston, 1989-92, pres. Assn. Rice Alumni, 1999—; minister St. Vincent de Paul Catholic Ch., Omaha, 1995—. Recipient Leadership award Multiple Sclerosis Soc., Omaha, 1997. Fellow Am. Coll. Physicians, Infectious Diseases Soc. Am., Am. Soc. Microbiology; mem. Am. Soc. Transplantation. Avocations: guitar, snow skiing, am. history, history of medicine. Office: Univ Nebraska Medical Center 985400 Nebraska Med Ctr Omaha NE 68198-5400

DOMINGUEZ, JORGE IGNACIO, government educator; b. Havana, Cuba, June 2, 1945; came to U.S., 1960; s. Jorge Jose and Lilia Rosa (de la Carrera) D.; m. Mary Alice Kmietek, Dec. 16, 1967; children: Lara Lisa, Leslie Karen. AB, Yale U., 1967; AM, Harvard U., 1968, PhD, 1972. From asst. prof. to prof. govt. Harvard U., Cambridge, Mass., 1972-93; Frank G. Thomson prof. govt. Harvard U., Cambridge, 1993-96; chmn. Latin Am. and Iberian studies Harvard U., Cambridge, Mass., 1979-83, 90-93, acting dir. ctr. for internat. affairs, 1995; Clarence Dillon prof. internat. affairs Harvard U., Cambridge, 1996—, dir. Weatherhead Ctr. for Internat. Affairs, 1996—, Harvard Coll. prof., 1998—; active Coun. on Fgn. Rels., Inter-Am. Dialogue, 1982—, sr. fellow, 1993-94, assoc. fellow, 1995—. Author: Cuba: Order and Revolution, 1978, Insurrection or Loyalty, 1980, To Make the World Safe for Revolution: Cuba's Foreign Policy, 1989, Democratic Politics in Latin America and the Caribbean, 1998; editor, author: Economic Issues and Political Conflict, 1982, Mexico's Political Economy, 1982, Democracy in the Caribbean, 1993, Essays on Mexico, Central and South America: Scholarly Debates from the 1950s to the 1990s, (7 vols.), 1994, Constructing Democratic Governance: Latin America and the Caribbean in the 1990s, 1996, Technopols: Freeing Politics and Markets in Latin America in the 1990s, 1997, Democratic Transitions in Central America, 1997; co-author: Democratizing Mexico: Public Opinion and Electoral Choices, 1996; mem. editl. bd. Am. Polit. Sci. Rev., 1979-81, Mexican Studies, 1983—, Polit. Sci. Quar., 1984—, Cuban Studies, 1991—; series editor Crisis in Central America: A Four-Part Special Report, Frontline, PBS, 1985 (Peabody award); chief editl. adv. three-part spl. report Mexico, 1988. Chmn. bd. trustees Latin Am. Scholarship Proglram of Am. Univs., Cambridge, Mass., 1981-82. Recipient Joseph Levenson Meml. Teaching award Harvard U., 1991; mem. Antilles Rsch. Program Yale U., New Haven, 1974-75; jr. fellow Harvard U., 1969-72, Fulbright-Hays fellow, 1983-88. Mem. Latin Am. Studies Assn. (pres. 1982-83), New Eng. Council Latin Am. Studies (pres. 1980), Pan Am. Soc. New Eng. (gov. 1979-82), Inst. Cuban Studies (pres. 1990-94). Club: Elihu (New Haven). Office: Harvard U Ctr Internat Affairs 1737 Cambridge St Cambridge MA 02138-3016

DOMINGUEZ, KATHRYN MARY, educator; b. Santa Monica, Calif., Nov. 26, 1960; d. Frederick A. and Margaret M. (McGauren) D. AB, Vassar Coll., 1982; MA, Yale U., 1984, M in Philosophy, 1985, PhD, 1987. Researcher Congl. Budget Office, Washington, summer 1984; rsch. scholar bd. of govs. FRS, Washington, 1985-86; asst. prof. pub. policy Kennedy Sch. Govt. Harvard U., Cambridge, Mass., 1987-91, assoc. prof. pub. policy, 1991-97; assoc. prof. pub. policy U. Mich., Ann Arbor, 1997—; rsch. cons IMF, Washington, 1989; vis. asst. prof., asst. dir. internat. fin. sect. dept. econs. Princeton U., 1990-91; Nat. Bur. Econs. Rsch. Olin fellow, 1991-92. Author: (monograph) Oil and Money, 1989; Exchange Rate Efficiency and the Behavior of International Asset Markets, 1992; (with Jeff Frankel) Does Foreign Exchange Intervention Work?, 1993. Mem. Nat. Bur. Econ. Rsch. (faculty rsch. fellow 1989—), Am. Econ. Assn., Am. Fin. Assn., Phi Beta Kappa. Democrat. Office: U Mich Sch Pub Policy Lorch Hall 611 Tappan Ave Ann Arbor MI 48109-1220

DOMINI, AMY LEE, trustee; b. N.Y.C., Jan. 25, 1950; d. Enzo Vice and Margaret Cabot (Colt) D.; m. Peter D. Kinder, Sept. 28, 1980 (div.); 1 child, Peter D. CFA. Stockbroker Tucker Anthony & RL Day, Cambridge, Mass., 1975-80, Moseley Securities, Cambridge, 1980-85; portfolio mgr. Franklin R & D Corp., Boston, 1985-87; pvt. trustee Loring, Wolcott & Coolidge, Boston, 1987—; pres. Domini Social Equity Fund, N.Y.C., 1996—; chair of bd. Linder, Lydenberg, Domini & Co., Cambridge, 1991—; ptnr. Domini Social Investments LLC, Boston, 1997—. Co-author: (books) Ethical Investing, 1984, Challenges of Wealth, Social Investment Almanac, 1992, Investing for Good. Bd. dirs. Social Investment Forum, Washington, 1994—, ch. pension fund Episcopal Ch., N.Y.C., 1994—; governing bd. Interfaith Ctr. on Corp. Responsibility, N.Y.C., 1985-95; mem. social responsibility investments com. Episcopal Ch., N.Y.C., 1985-91. Recipient Accioniste award Accion Internat., 1992, Money's 100 Best Mut. Funds award Money Mag., 1998, SRI Svc. award 1st Affirmative Fin. Network, 1996. Mem. Nat. Comty. Capital Assn. (assoc., bd. dirs. 1987-91), Boston Security Analysts Soc., Social Investment Forum, Somerset Club, Cambridge Boat Club. Democrat. Episcopalian. Avocations: day-sailing, gardening. Office: Loring Wolcott & Coolidge 230 Congress St Fl 12 Boston MA 02110-2437

DOMINIAK, GERALDINE FLORENCE, accounting educator; b. Detroit, Sept. 28, 1934; d. Benjamin Vincent and Geraldine Esther (Davey) D. BS, U. Detroit, 1954, MBA, 1956; PhD, Mich. State U., 1966. CPA, Mich. Audit supr. Coopers & Lybrand, 1958-63; asst. prof. U. Detroit, 1965-68; assoc. prof. Mich. State U., 1968-69; prof. acctg. Tex. Christian U., Ft. Worth, 1969-97, chmn. dept. acctg., 1974-83; Arthur Young prof. acctg. Fla. A&M U., 1977. Author: (with J. Edwards and T. Hedges) Interim Financial Reporting, 1972; (with J. Louderback) Managerial Accounting, 1975, 8th edit., 1997. Ford Found. fellow, 1964-65. Mem. AICPA, Am. Acctg. Assn., Assn. Govt. Accts., Inst. Mgmt. Accts., Am. Woman's Soc. CPAs, Tex. Soc. CPAs, AAUP, ACLU, Beta Alpha Psi, Beta Gamma Sigma. Roman Catholic. Home: 4401 Cardiff Ave Fort Worth TX 76133-3513 *To teach is to learn.*

DOMINICK, CHARLES ALVA, college official; b. Canton, Ohio, Mar. 31, 1943; s. Joseph and Dorthy (Hawkins) D.; m. Nancy Unkefer, July 26, 1969; 1 child, Timothy Joseph. BA, Coll. of Wooster, 1965; MA, Ohio State U., 1968; PhD, U. Mich., 1987; postgrad., Harvard U., 1988. Admissions counselor Davis and Elkins (W.Va.) Coll., 1965-67, Mt. Union Coll., Alliance, Ohio, 1967-68; admissions asst. U. Mich., Ann Arbor, 1977-78, rsch. assoc. Project Choice, 1978-79; asst. dean admissions Wittenberg U., Springfield, Ohio, 1972-77, assoc. dir. for univ. advancement, 1979-80, asst. to pres., 1980-85, v.p. for instnl. rels., 1985—. Contbg. author: Managing Change in Higher Education, 1990, Student Recruitment, 1991. Mem. Community Housing Resources Bd., Springfield, 1986-92; bd. dirs. Clark County Labor-Mgmt. Rels. Com., Springfield, 1987-90, Jr. Achievement, 1990-95, Aid for Coll. Opportunities; trustee Oakwood Village, Springfield, 1988-96; trustee Clark County Hist. Soc., 1986-94, pres., 1989-92, bd. dirs. Cmty. Hosp. Found., 1996—. Mem. Springfield Univ. Club (v.p. 1991-92), Rotary, Springfield Polo Club (pres. 1999—), Springfield Country Club. Home: 829 Linmuth Ct S Springfield OH 45503-1903 Office: Wittenberg U PO Box 720 U Ward St at N Wittenberg Springfield OH 45501

DOMINICK, PETER HOYT, JR., architect; b. N.Y.C., June 9, 1941; s. Peter Hoyt and Nancy Parks D.; m. Philae M. Carver, Dec. 9, 1978; children—Philae M., James W. B.A., Yale U., 1963; M.Arch., U. Pa., 1967. Registered architect, Colo. Project designer John R. Wild, Pty., Ltd., Papau, New Guinea, 1968-69, Spence Robinson, Hong Kong, 1969-71, W.C. Muchow & Ptnrs., Denver, 1971-74; pres. Wazee Design/Devel., Denver, 1973-75; prin. Dominick Architects, Denver, 1975-88; sr. prin. Urban Design Group, Inc., 1988—. Trustee Downtown Denver, Inc., Civic Ventures, 1984-94 , Met. Denver Arts Alliance, 1983-84; mem. Mayor's Commn. on the Arts, 1983; juror Gov.'s awards, Denver, 1982. Fellow AIA (nat. com. on design, bd. dirs.); mem. Colo. Soc. Architects. Republican. Episcopalian. Club: Cactus, Arapahoe Tennis. Office: Urban Design Group Inc 1621 18th St Ste 200 Denver CO 80202-1267*

DOMINICK, RAYMOND HUNTER, III, history educator; b. Atlanta, Oct. 8, 1945; s. Raymond Hunter Jr. and Anne (Lawler) D.; m. Gayle Babin, Jan. 17, 1968; 1 child, David; m. Lynn Murphy, Aug. 17, 1979. BA, La. State U., 1968; PhD, U. N.C., 1973. Instr. U. N.C., Chapel Hill, 1973-74; from asst. prof. to assoc. prof. Ohio State U., Mansfield, 1974-92, prof., 1992—. Author: Wilhelm Liebknecht and the Founding of the German Social Democratic Party, 1982, The Environmental Movement in Germany: Prophets and Pioneers, 1871-1971, 1992 (Outstanding Pub. of 1992). Mem. citizens adv. coun. GM, Mansfield, 1992-96; co-mgr. McClain for Congress Campaign, Mansfield, 1998. Fulbright sr. scholar, 1995. Mem. German Studies Assn., Am. Soc. Environ. History. Avocations: tennis, golf, sailing, carpentry, gardening. E-mail: dominick.1@osu.edu. Office: Ohio State U 1680 University Dr Mansfield OH 44906

DOMINIK, JACK EDWARD, lawyer; b. Chgo., July 9, 1924; s. Ewald Arthur and Gertrude Alene (Crotzer) D.; children: Paul, David, Georgia Lee, Elizabeth, Sarah, Clare. BSME with distinction, Purdue U., 1947; JD, Northwestern U., 1950. Bar: Ill. 1950, U.S. Patent Office 1953, Wis. 1959, Fla. 1964, U.S. Dist. Ct. (ea. dist.) Wis. 1959, U.S. Supreme Ct. 1965, U.S. Dist. Ct. (no. dist.) Ohio 1962, U.S. Dist. Ct. (so. dist.) Ill. 1965, U.S. Ct. Appeals (7th and 9th cirs.) 1965, U.S. Ct. Appeals (4th cir.) 1973, U.S. Dist. Ct. (so. dist.) Fla. 1974, U.S. Ct. Appeals (5th cir.) 1977, U.S. Dist. Ct. (mid. dist.) Fla. 1979, U.S. Ct. Appeals (fed. cir.) 1983, U.S. Ct. Appeals (11th cir.) 1984, U.S. Ct. Appeals (2d cir.) 1987. Assoc. Carlson, Pitzner, Hubbard & Wolfe, Chgo., 1950-54; ptnr. Ooms and Dominik, Chgo., 1954-59, White & Hirshboeck, Milw., 1959-62; ptnr. Dominik, Knechtel, DeMeur & Samlan, Chgo., 1962-78, Miami, Fla., 1978—. Served to 1st lt., C.E. AUS, 1943-46, ETO. Mil. govt. judge, 1945-46. Mem. ABA, Wis. Bar Assn., Fla. Bar Assn., Chgo. Bar Assn., Am. Patent Law Assn., Chgo. Patent Law Assn. (chmn. taxation com. 1966, 69-70), Milw. Patent Law Assn., Patent Law Assn. So. Fla. (founder, dir. 1982—, past pres.), Chgo. Yacht Club, Union League Club, Tau Beta Pi, Pi Tau Sigma, Tau Kappa Alpha. Avocation: flying. Home: 14751 Lewis Rd Miami Lakes FL 33014-2731 Office: 6175 NW 153rd St Hialeah FL 33014-2435

DOMINIK, JOHN JULIUS, retired advertising company executive; b. St. Cloud, Minn., Oct. 9, 1922; s. John and Mary (Appert) D.; m. Shirley Ann Moline, Sept. 3, 1962; five children. BA, St. John's U., 1946. Reporter, photographer St. Cloud Sentinel, 1947-49; acct. exec. The Stockbridger Co., St. Cloud, 1949-61; advt. mgr. The Liturgical Press, Collegeville, Minn., 1962-92. Author: Cold Spring Granite, Three Towns into One City, 1976, St. Cloud: The Triplet City, 1980, That You May Find Healing, 1982. Home: 2298 Rodeo Rd Sartell MN 56377

DOMINO, FATS (ANTOINE DOMINO), pianist, singer, songwriter; b. New Orleans, Feb. 26, 1928. Pianist since youth; performed with groups in clubs, for dances, in theaters; composer blues; recording artist numerous albums including: Here Comes Fats Domino, 1963, Fats on Fire, 1965, Fats '65, Getaway With Fats Domino, 1966, Fats Domino, 1966, Stompin' Fats Domino, 1967, Trouble in Mind, Fats is Back, 1968, Live in Montreux, 1973, Sleeping on the Job, 1978, The Best of Fats, 1990, All Time Greatest Hits, 1991, Fats Domino, 1991, Best of Fats Domino Live, 1992, Antoine "Fats" Domino, 1992, The Fat Man, 1995; toured Britain, 1967; appeared in films: Shake, Rattle & Rock, Disc Jockey Jamboree, The Big Beat, The Girl Can't Help It, Any Which Way You Can; appeared on TV spl. Fats Domino & Friends, 1987. Inducted Rock and Roll Hall of Fame, 1986, recipient Grammy Lifetime Achievement award, 1987. Recipient Nat. Medal Arts, 1998. Office: care Steve Cooper Willard Alexander Agy 9229 W Sunset Blvd Fl 4 Los Angeles CA 90069-3402 also: SMS Records 14134 NE Airport Way Portland OR 97230-3443*

DOMJAN, JOSEPH (SPIRI DOMJAN), artist; b. Budapest, Hungary, Mar. 15, 1907; s. Paul and Maria (Lika) D.; m. Evelyn A. Domjan, Mar. 13, 1944; children—Alma Domjan Melbourne, Michael P., Daniel G. B.A., Hungarian Royal Acad. Fine Arts, 1940, M.A., 1942. founder Domjan Mus., Sarospatek, Hungary, 1977. Exhibited in over 550 one-man shows including Ernst Mus., Budapest, 1955, Mus. Art and History, Geneva, 1975, Cin. Art Mus., 1958, 74, N.J. State Mus., Trenton, 1966, 73, Dallas Pub. Libr., 1964, 77, Mueo della Bellas Artes, Mexico City, 1966, Cuyuga Mus., Auburn, N.Y., 1975; represented in numerous permanent collections including Met. Mus., Victoria and Albert Mus., Tate Gallery, London, Mus. Modern Art, Paris, Albertina Graphische Sammlung, Vienna, Nat. Gallery Fine Arts, Libr. of Congress, Washington, Nat. Mus., Stockholm, Mus. Modern Art, Tokyo; author, illustrator 24 books; author: The Proud Peacock, 1966, The Little Cock, 1966, The Artist and the Legend, 1975, Bellringer, 1975, Wing Beat, 1976, Edge of Paradise, 1979. Rockefeller Found. grantee, 1958; Recipient numerous prizes Soc. Illustrators, numerous prizes Am. Inst. Graphic Arts, numerous prizes Print Club of Albany, numerous prizes Am. Color Print Soc. Mem. Nat. Acad. Design, Soc. Am. Graphic Artists, Soc. Illustrators, Print Council Am., Silvermine Guild, Internat. Platform Assn. Address: West Lake Rd Tuxedo Park NY 10987

DOMJAN, LASZLO KAROLY, newspaper editor; b. Kormend, Hungary, Apr. 19, 1947; came to U.S., 1956; s. Frank and Violet Domjan; m. Louise Replogle, June 6, 1969; children: Andrew P., Eric S. BJ, U. Mo., 1969. Copy editor St. Louis Globe-Democrat, 1969; reporter, bureau chief UPI, St. Louis, 1969-81; reporter, night city editor St. Louis Post-Dispatch, 1981—, exec. city editor, 1987-96, projects editor, 1996-97, asst. mng. editor, 1997-99, editor, 1999—. Author, editor: Dioxin: Quandary for the 80s, 1983 (numerous awards); author: (reporter series) Hungary: Thirty Years After, 1986; editor: (series) Prosecutorial Corruption (1993 Pulitzer prize finalist). Active Leadership St. Louis. Recipient Herb Trask award Sigma Delta Chi, St. Louis, 1968. Mem. Press Club of Met. St. Louis, Investigative Reporters and Editors. Roman Catholic. Avocations: reading, freelance writing, music. Office: St Louis Post-Dispatch 900 N Tucker Blvd Saint Louis MO 63101-1099 *Always do right. Always do your best. Always make time for romance.*

DOMJAN, SPIRI See DOMJAN, JOSEPH

DOMMEL, DARLENE HURST, writer; b. Charles City, Iowa, July 11, 1940; d. Roy and Elsie (Hopkes) Hurst; B.S. with high distinction, U. Minn., 1963; m. James H. Dommel, Oct. 15, 1961; children: Diann, Christine, David. MS, 1965, grad. exec. program Grad. Sch. Bus. Administrn., 1972; postgrad. So. Meth. U., 1976-77. Pub. health nurse Combined Nursing Service, Mpls., 1963-64; author: (book) Collector's Encyclopedia of the Dakota Potteries, Collectors Encyclopedia of Howard Pierce Porcelain; contbr. articles on pottery to various collectors and antiques mags., 1967—; organizer, exhibitor of art pottery display touring fin. instns. in upper midwest, 1976-82; lectr. and cons. health care, antiques, journalism; health care specialist Health Services Research Center, St. Louis Park Med. Center, 1978-79; instr. Augsburg Coll., 1979-81. Mem. Minn. Adv. Task Force on Epilepsy, 1981-83, State Council for Handicapped, 1982-84, Dept. Pub. Welfare Adv. Council on Mental Retardation and Phys. Disabilities, 1982-84; mem. profl. adv. bd. Epilepsy Found. Minn., 1984-95. Mem. Mpls. Inst. Arts. USPHS trainee, 1964-65; Sigma Theta Tau scholar, 1962-63; Martha Ripley scholar, 1961-62; U. Minn. Sch. Nursing Found. scholar, 1962. Mem. U. Minn. Alumni Assn., Nat. Writers Club, Nat. League for Nursing (regional assembly constituent leagues for nursing. exec. com. 1985-87), Minn. League for Nursing (pres. 1983-85). Gethsemane Luth. Ch. Women, Am. Art Pottery Collectors Assn., Sigma Theta Tau, Delta Delta Delta. Lutheran. Home: 510 Westwood Dr N Minneapolis MN 55422-5266

DOMMEN, ARTHUR JOHN, agricultural economist; b. Mexico City, Mexico, June 24, 1934; came to U.S., 1940, naturalized, 1958; s. John Henry and Sarah (Hall) D.; m. Phan Thi Hong Loan. B.Sc., Cornell U., 1955; Ph.D., U. Md., 1975. Mem. staff UPI, 1957-63; bur. chief UPI, Saigon, 1959-61, Hong Kong, Hong Kong, 1961-63; mem. staff Los Angeles Times, 1965-71; bur. chief Los Angeles Times, New Delhi, India, 1966-68, Saigon, Vietnam, 1968-71; agrl. economist Intech, Inc., Silver Spring, Md., 1975-77; mem. AID Mission to, Tunisia, 1977-79; with USDA, Washington, 1980-96; affiliate prof. Indochina Inst. George Mason U., Fairfax, Va., 1996—. Author: Conflict in Laos, The Politics of Neutralization, 1964; Laos: Keystone of Indochina, 1985. Served with AUS, 1955-57. Press fellow N.Y. Council Fgn. Relations, 1963-64. Home and Office: 7716 Radnor Rd Bethesda MD 20817-6282

DOMMERMUTH, WILLIAM PETER, marketing consultant, educator; b. Chgo.; s. Peter R. and Gertrude Dommermuth; m. H. Joan Hasty, June 6, 1959; children: Karin, Margaret, Jean. BA, U. Iowa; PhD, Northwestern U., 1964. Advt. copywriter Sears, Roebuck & Co., Chgo.; sales promotion mgr. Sears, Roebuck & Co.; asst., then asso. prof. mktg. U. Tex., Austin, 1961-67; asso. prof. U. Iowa, Iowa City, 1967-68; prof. So. Ill. U., Carbondale, 1968-86, U. Mo., St. Louis, 1986—; CEO Optiphonics, Inc.; Cons. bus. firms. Author (with Kernan and Sommers): Promotion: An Introductory Analysis, 1970, (with Andersen) Distribution Systems, 1972, (with Marcus and others) Modern Marketing, 1975, Modern Marketing Management, 1980, Promotion: Analysis, Creativity and Strategy, 1984, 2d edit., 1989; contbr. articles to profl. jours. Mem. Am. Mktg. Assn., Am. Psychol. Assn., So. Mktg. Assn., Midwest Mktg. Assn., Phi Beta Kappa, Beta Gamma Sigma, Theta Xi, Delta Sigma Pi. Home: 11 Paris Ct Lake Saint Louis MO 63367-1506

DOMNING, DARYL PAUL, paleontologist, educator; b. Biloxi, Miss., Mar. 14, 1947; s. Emile Frederick and Maud Louise (Mugnier) D.; m. Katherine Hubbell, July 10, 1987; 1 child, Charlotte Roxanna. BS, Tulane U., 1968; MA, U. Calif. Berkeley, 1970, PhD, 1975. Rsch. biologist Inst. Nacional de Pesquisas da Amazonia, Manaus, Brazil, 1976-78; asst. prof., assoc. prof. Howard U., Washington, 1978-92, prof., 1992—; mem. sci. advisors com. U.S. Marine Mammal Commn., Washington, 1982-85, 93-97; mem. manatee tech. adv. coun. Fla. Dept. Environ. Protection, Tallahassee, 1981—; mem. sci. adv. com. Save the Manatee Club, Maitland, Fla., 1986—. Fellow Linnean Soc. London; mem. Am. Soc. Mammalogists, Soc. Marine Mammalogy, Soc. Systematic Zoology, Soc. Vertebrate Paleontology, Fla. Paleontol. Soc. Democrat. Roman Catholic. Home: 9211 Wendell St Silver Spring MD 20901-3533 Office: Howard Univ Dept Anatomy 520 W St NW Washington DC 20059

DOMOWITZ, IAN, economics educator; b. N.Y.C., Nov. 29, 1951; s. Jacob and Marilyn (Raffer) D.; m. Marguerite Morton, Sept. 25, 1984. BA, U. Conn., 1977; PhD, U. Calif., San Diego, 1982. Asst. prof., assoc. prof., prof. econs. Northwestern U., Evanston, Ill., 1982-98, mem. rsch. faculty Inst. for Policy Rsch., 1987-98; Mary Jean and Frank P. Smeal chaired prof. fin. Pa. State U., University Park, 1998—; rsch. dir. K2 Capital Mgmt., 1992-94; cons. IMF, 1992, World Bank, 1993-96, 98-99, to various internat. fin. markets with respect to automated exch. structures, 1991-97; cons. U.S. Commodity Futures Trading Commn., 1991, 95-96; scientific adv. bd. ITG, Inc., 1997—. Contbr. over 50 articles to profl. jours., chpts. to books. Sgt. U.S. Army, 1972-75, Germany. NSF grantee, 1984, 85, 87, 90. Mem. Am. Fin. Assn., Am. Statistical Assn., Nat. Assn. Securities Dealers (econ. ad. bd. 1998—, bond market transparency com. 1998—), Econometric Soc. Home: 115 Picadilly Rd Port Matilda PA 16870 Office: Pa State U Smeal Coll Bus Adminstrn University Park PA 16802

DOMPKE, NORBERT FRANK, retired photography studio executive; b. Chgo., Oct. 16, 1920; s. Frank and Mary (Manley) D.; m. Marjorie Gies, Dec. 12, 1964; children: Scott, Pamela. Grad. Wright Jr. Coll., 1939-40; student Northwestern U., 1946-49. Cost comptroller, budget dir. Scott Radio Corp., 1947; pres. TV Forecast, Inc., 1948-52, editor Chgo. edit. TV Guide, 1953, mgr. Wis. edit., 1954; pres. Root Photographers, Inc., Chgo., 1955-91, also chmn. bd. dirs; bd. dirs. Root Studio, Inc., 1991-96, ret., 1996. Adv. com. photography & audiovisual tech., So. Ill. U., 1980-81; adv. bd. Gordon Tech. High Sch., 1979-86. Co-founder TV Guide, 1947. With USAAC, 1943-47. CPA, Ill. Mem. NEA, Nat. Sch. Press Assn., Nat. Collegiate Sch. Press Assn., United Photographers Orgn. (pres. 1970-71), Profl. Photographers Am., Profl. Sch. Photographers Am. (v.p. 1966-67, 87-88, sec.-treas. 1967-69, pres. 1969-70, dir. 1971-78, treas. 1985-86, sec. 1986-87, pres. 1988-89), Photo Mktg. Assn. (recipient disting. svc. award 1992), Photographic Art & Sci. Found. (hall of fame elector 1969-96), Ill. Small Bus. Men's Assn. (dir. 1970-73), Chgo. Assn. Commerce and Industry (edn. com. 1966-94), Ill. High Sch. Press Assn., North Cen. Assn. (visitation com. 1986), Chgo. Bible Soc. (bd. advisors), Ill. C. of C., Internat. Club. Home: 175 N Harbor Dr Apt 2602 Chicago IL 60601-7345

DOMZELLA, JANET, library director; b. Marquette, Mich., Mar. 22, 1935; d. Jack Carl and Alice Margaret (Blom) Messenger; m. Theodore S. Wodzinski (div. 1974); children: Christopher, Joseph, Daniel; m. Perry Landon Domzella, July 15, 1977; stepchildren: Perry, Pamela. BS, No. Mich. U., 1973; MLS, U. Buffalo, 1979. Sch. libr. media specialist Niagara Falls (N.Y.) Bd. Edn., 1974-75, Iroquois Ctrl. Sch., Elma, N.Y., 1975-77; dir. Lewiston (N.Y.) Pub. Libr., 1977—. Co-author: Lewiston: Self Guided Tour, 1986. Vol. firefighter Upper Mountain Vol. Fire Co., Lewiston, 1980-90, treas., 1984-90; mem. Town of Lewiston Bur. Fire Prevention, 1988-90; mem. adv. bd. Documentary Heritage Program, 1991-93; mem. pub. libr. program Coll. of Charleston (S.C.) Conf., 1998. Mem. ALA, N.Y. Libr. Assn. Democrat. Roman Catholic. Avocations: rosemaling, watercolor. Office: Lewiston Pub Libr 305 S 8th St Lewiston NY 14092-1744

DONABEDIAN, AVEDIS, physician; b. Beirut, Lebanon, Jan. 7, 1919; came to U.S., 1955, naturalized, 1960; s. Samuel and Maritza (Der Hagopian) D.; m. Dorothy Salibian, Sept. 15, 1945; children: Haig, Bairj, Armen. BA, Am. U., Beirut, 1940, MD, 1944; MPH, Harvard U., 1955. Physician, acting supt. English Mission Hosp., Jerusalem, 1945-47; instr. physiology, clin. asst. dermatology and venereology Am. U. Med. Sch., 1948-51, univ. physician, dir. univ. health service, 1949-54; med. assoc. United Community Services Met. Boston, 1955-57; asst. prof., then assoc. prof. preventive medicine N.Y. Med. Coll., 1957-61; mem. faculty U. Mich. Sch. Pub. Health, Ann Arbor, 1961—, prof. med. care orgn., 1964-79, Nathan Sinai disting. prof. public health, 1979-89, emeritus. Author: A Guide to Medical Care Administration: Medical Care Appraisal--Quality and Utilization, 1969, Aspects of Medical Care Administration, 1973, Benefits in medical Care Programs, 1976, The Definition of Quality and Approaches to Its Assessment, 1980, Medical Care Chartbook, 1986, The Criteria and Standards of Quality, 1982, The Methods and Findings of Quality Assessment and Monitoring, 1985; co-author: Striving for Quality in Health Care: An Inquiry into Policy and Practice, 1991. Recipient Dean Conley award Am. Coll. Hosp. Adminstrs., 1969; Norman A. Welch award Nat. Assn. Blue Shield Plans, 1976; Elizur Wright award Am. Risk and Ins. Assn., 1978; Nat. Merit award Delta Omega, 1978; Richard B. Tobias award Am. Coll. Utilization Rev. Physicians, 1984; Outstanding Contbns. in Health Services Research award Assn. Health Services Research, 1985, Baxter Am. Found. Health Services Research prize, 1986, Gold Medal award Med. Alumni Assn., Am. U. of Beirut, 1986, The Ernest A Codman award of The Joint Commn. on Accreditation of Healthcare Orgns., 1997. Fellow APHA, Am. Coll. Utilization Rev. Physicians (hon.), Royal Coll. Gen. Practitioners (hon.), Am. Coll. Med. Quality, Am. Coll. Healthcare Execs. (hon.); mem. Inst. Medicine of NAS, Nat. Acad. Medicine of Mex. (hon.), Internat. Soc. Quality Assurance in Health Care (hon.), Avedis Donabedian Found. (Barcelona, hon. pres. 1990—, Buenos Aires, hon. pres. 1994—). Home: 1739 Ivywood Dr Ann Arbor MI 48103-4523 Office: HMP-SPH II 109 Observatory St Ann Arbor MI 48109-2029

DONAGHY, CHRISTINE ANN, English language educator; b. Allentown, Pa., June 16, 1966; d. James Gerard and Jacqueline M. (Devlin) D.; m. Christopher J. Kopas, Aug. 1 1997. BA, Trenton State Coll., 1989; M in

English, William Paterson U., 1999. Sales supr. Sears & Roebuck, Rockaway, N.J., 1983-97; tchr. English Parsippany Bd. of Edn., Parsippany, N.J., 1992—. Mem. Nat. Coun. of Tchrs. of Eng. Home: 86 Clover Hill Dr Flanders NJ 07836-9559 Office: Brooklawn Mid Sch 250 Beachwood Rd Parsippany NJ 07054-2459

DONAHO, JOHN ALBERT, consultant; b. Chgo., Sept. 9, 1917; s. John and Pauline (Langdon) D.; m. Patricia A. Maguire, Sept. 23, 1961. BA, Ctrl. YMCA Coll., 1943; cert. pub. adminstrn., U. Chgo., MA. Asst. to contr. Commonwealth Edison Co., Chgo., 1935-42; asst. dir. work simplification and measurement U.S. Bur. Budget, Exec. Office of the Pres., Washington, 1943-47; v.p. devel. Roosevelt U., Chgo., 1947-48; budget dir., city mgr. City of Richmond, Va., 1948-52; pres. John A. Donaho & Assocs. Inc., Reisterstown, Md., 1953—; cons. to Mayor of Balt. and Gov. of Md., 1952-54, 74-87, 88-89; chmn. Md. Local Govt. Ins. Trust, 1987-88; ins. commr. State of Md., 1989-93; lectr., mem. faculty Am. U., Washington, Washington (D.C.) U., Goucher Coll., Balt., Johns Hopkins U., Balt., U. Balt., Fgn. Svc. Inst., Va. Commonwealth U., Roosevelt U., Chgo.; chmn. Va. State Commn. on Uniform Fin. Reporting. Contbr. articles to profl. jours. Pres., dir. Univ. Club, Balt.; dir. United Reisterstown Residents; pres. Lakeview Club, Inc., Reisterstown, Civitan Club Balt., Md., Civitan Club Richmond, Va.; mem., sec. Balt. (Md.) City Com. on Workers' Compensation, Balt. (Md.) City Com. on Ins. and Risk Mgmt.; mem. Md. Gov.'s Task Force on Liability Ins., Md. Gov.'s Blue Ribbon Task Force on Self-Ins., Gov.'s Blue Ribbon Commn. on Ins., Gov.'s Prescription Drug Commn.; chmn. Ad Hoc Com. on Liability Ins. for Md.; others; trustee Balt. Internat. Culinary Coll. Fellow Soc. for Advancement Mgmt. (pres. Balt. regional chpt., v.p. Richmond chpt., chmn. round table on work simplification D.C. chpt.), Am. Soc. Pub. Adminstrn. (sr. mem., pres. Md. chpt., dir. Olympia chpt.); mem. Nat. Assn. Ins. Commrs. Office: 120 Cockeysville Rd # S100 Cockeysville MD 21030-2132

DONAHOE, DAVID LAWRENCE, state and city official; b. Pitts., June 5, 1949; s. Thomas Kernan and Anna Mae (Lawrence) D.; m. Judith DiNardo, June 5, 1971; children: Jennifer, Jeffrey. B.A. in Secondary Edn., U. Pitts., 1971; M.A. in Pub. Adminstrn., U. Pitts, 1978. Asst. dir., adminstr. Allegheny County, Pitts., 1974-76, dep. controller, 1976-77, county clk., 1977-78, dir. aviation, 1980-83; sch. treas. City of Pitts., 1978-80, exec. sec. to Mayor, 1986-88; exec. dir. Urban Redevel. Authority of Pitts., 1988-89; sec. of revenue State of Pa., 1989-91; exec. dir. Pitts. Schs., 1991-95, Allegheny Regional Asset Dist., 1995—; sec. bd. Port Authority Allegheny County, 1975-80; teaching asst. U. Pitts, 1976, instr., 1985. Exec. dir. Pa. Econ. League, Pitts., 1983-85; bd. dir. Community Coll. Allegheny County, 1988. Mem. ASPA, Mcpl. Fin. Officers Am. (debt. com. 1979), Airport Operators Council Internat., League Municipalites (bd. dirs. Pitts. 1975-76). Democrat. Roman Catholic. Office: 1 Smithfield St Pittsburgh PA 15222-2221

DONAHOE, JIM, broadcast executive. V.p., gen. mgr. Sta. KYXY-FM, San Diego, 1998; pres. Pacific Star Comms. Office: KYXY Radio 8033 Linda Vista Rd San Diego CA 92111-5197*

DONAHOE, MAUREEN ALICE, accounting consultant; b. N.Y.C., June 9, 1959; d. William A. and Alice P. (O'Connor) D. BA in Acctg., Belmont Abbey Coll., 1982; MBA in Fin., Fordham U., 1992. CPA, N.Y. Staff acct. Bankers Trust Co., N.Y.C., 1982-85; sr. auditor Feldman Radin and Co., N.Y.C., 1985-87; valuation svcs. mgr. Ernst & Young, N.Y.C., 1987-91; mgr. cons. Policano and Manzo, Saddlebrook, N.J., 1991—; dir. 417 E. 90th St. Corp., N.Y.C., 1995—. Mem. alumni bd. Belmont Abbey Coll., 1994—. Mem. AICPA, Assn. Insolvency Accts., N.Y. State Soc. CPAs (mem. insolvency and reorgn. com. 1993-94). Republican. Roman Catholic. Avocation: golf. Home: 12 Upper Mountain Ave Montclair NJ 07042-1814 Office: Policano and Manzo LLC Plz II Ste 200 Park 80 W Saddle Brook NJ 07663

DONAHOE, PETER ALOYSIUS, lawyer. BA in Polit. Sci., U. Wash., Seattle, 1957; JD, Harvard U., 1960. Bar: Hawaii 1961. Assoc. Carlsmith, Carlsmith, Wichman & Case, Hilo, Hawaii, 1960-63; staff Senate Majority Hawaii State Senate, Honolulu, 1963; dep. Atty. Gen. anti-trust divsn. State of Hawaii, Honolulu, 1963-65; asst. U.S. Atty. U.S. Dept. Justice, Honolulu, 1965-67; ptnr. Robertson, Castle & Anthony, Honolulu, 1967-71; pvt. practice Honolulu, 1973-91; dir. Atty.'s and Judge's Assistance Program Supreme Ct. for State of Hawaii, Honolulu, 1993—; vis. prof. polit. sci. Am. Coll. Switzerland, Leysan, 1971-73; chmn. liquor commn., City and County of Honolulu, 1969; lectr. Hawaii Inst. CLE. Contbr. articles to profl. jours. Mem. Hawaii State Bar Assn. Home: 47-516 Hui Iwa St Kaneohe HI 96744-4615

DONAHOO, JAMES SAUNDERS, cardiothoracic surgeon; b. Jackson, Tenn., Sept. 30, 1937; s. Henry Amos and Ruby Burt (Welch) D.; m. Rose Carol Manasco, June 24, 1961; children: Paige, James. AB, Birmingham So. Coll., 1959; MD, Med. Coll. Ala., 1963. Chief resident surgeon Vanderbilt U. Hosp., Nashville, 1969; chief resident cardiac surgery Johns Hopkins U., Balt., 1971, asst. prof. surgery, 1971-75, assoc. prof. surgery, 1975-82; assoc. prof. surgery Jefferson Med. Coll., Phila., 1983-89; prof. cardiothoracic surgery Univ. Medicine Dentistry N.J., Newark, 1989—; chief thoracic surgery East Orange (N.J.) VA Hosp., 1989—. Editor: Practical Reviews in Surgery, 1975-82; contbr. articles to profl. jours. Col. USAR, 1964-92, Op. Desert Storm, 1991. Recipient Gold Medal Paper award S.E. Surg. Conv., 1967. Fellow ACS; mem. Am. Assn. Thoracic Surgery, So. Surg. Assn., So. Thoracic Surg. Assn. (coun. mem., Osler Abbott award 1982), N.Y. Soc. Thoracic Surgery, N.J. Soc. Thoracic Surgeons (pres. 1994), Elkridge Harford Hunt Club (exec. com. 1980), Alpha Omega Alpha. Episcopalian. Avocations: polo, fox-hunting, opera, oriental carpets, 19th century paintings. Home: 71 Hillcrest Ave Summit NJ 07901-2012 Office: Univ Medicine and Dentistry NJ 185 Bergen St # G-595 Newark NJ 07103-2426

DONAHUE, ARTHUR THOMAS, television producer; b. Adams, Mass., Nov. 30, 1954; s. Arthur William and Jeanne Claire (Roulier) D.; m. Mary Virginia Lawson, Sept. 9, 1978; children: Erin Marion, Sean Lawson. BA in Comm. Studies, U. Mass., 1976. Lic. 1st class radiotelephone operator FCC, 1979. Photographer, editor WWLP-TV, Springfield, Mass., 1972-77, WBZ-TV, Boston, 1977-80; prodr., photographer WFSB-TV, Hartford, Conn., 1980-86; prodr. WCVB-TV, Boston, 1987—; cons. TV news, 1986—. Prodr., writer, photographer 50 "Chronicle" news mag. programs, 1989—; prodr. (documentary) New England Portrait, 1995 (Emmy award 1996), Mill River Disaster, 1993 (Telly award 1994). Named New Eng. TV News Photographer Yr. Boston Press Photographers Assn., 1977-85. Mem. NATAS (Emmy awards 1980-96), Nat. Press Photographers Assn. (TV documentary Greetings From the Grange 1993, Nat. TV News Photographer Yr. 1985). Avocations: hiking, cross country skiing, photography, amateur radio, writing. Office: WCVB-TV 5 Tv Pl Needham MA 02494-2302

DONAHUE, CHARLES LEE, JR., health network executive; b. Norwood, Mass., Mar. 31, 1943; s. Charles and Katherine (Gallagher) D.; m. Nancy Turner, Aug. 15, 1971; children: Jessica, Charles, Morgan, Caroline, Matthew. AB, Brown U., 1965; MA, Cornell U., 1973. Vol. U.S. Peace Corps, Trengganu, Malaysia, 1967-68; project co-dir. Mass. Health Rsch. Inst., Boston, 1973-75; health planning analyst Boston U., Boston, 1976-80; regional program analyst U.S. Pub. Health Svc., Boston, 1980-81; exec. dir. Health Planning Coun., Boston, 1981-89; pres. Healthcare VALUE Mgmt., Norwood, Mass., 1990—; pres. Mass. Health Coun., 1990-91; adj. asst. prof. Pub. Health Boston U., 1990—. Contbr. articles to profl. jours. Recipient Schlesinger award Am. Pub. Health Assn. and Am. Health Plan Assn., 1987. Avocations: coaching youth hockey, golf, fatherhood. Home: 407 Gay St Westwood MA 02090-1729

DONAHUE, DONALD FRANCIS, secondary education educator; b. Miami, Fla., June 1, 1953; s. Charles Francis and Emma ALetta (Solan). BA, Trenton (N.J.) State U., 1975; Rider Army ROTC, Trenton, N.J., 1971-75. Cert. Tchr. of History, N.J. Sch. bd. mem. Twp. Hamilton, 1973-80, democratic com., 1976—; tchr. St. James Sch., Trenton, N.J., 1985—, coach, athletic dir., 1985—; drug abuse coord. St. James PTA, Trenton, N.J., 1988-93. Sch. bd. mem., pres. Hamilton Bd. Edn., 1973-80, 1978, 80, 81; basketball coach, softball coach Cath. Youth Orgn. Trenton, N.J., 1986—; P.J. Hill basketball coach, 1998-99; mem. Mercer County Consortium, 1999. 1st Lt. U.S. Army, 1971-75. Grantee Ptnrs. in Learning, N.J. Dept. Edn., 1987-80, 88-89, George Ahr Endowment Diocese of Trenton, 1988, 91. Mem. Hamilton Democratic Club, N.J. State Democratic Com., Cath. Youth Orgn., Mercer County Young Democratics, Hamilton Twp. Young Democrats. Democrat. Roman Catholic. Avocations: basketball, politics, football. Home: 416 E Howell St Hamilton NJ 08610-5841 Office: P J Hill Sch 1010 E State St Trenton NJ 08609-1506

DONAHUE, DONALD JORDAN, mining company executive; b. Bklyn., July 5, 1924; s. John F. and Florence (Jordan) D.; m. Mary Meyer, Jan. 20, 1951 (dec. June 1990); m. Carol Ann Pascal, Sept. 16, 1992; children: Mary G., Judith A., Donald Jordan, Thomas, Nicholas P. BA, Georgetown U., 1947; MBA, NYU, 1951. With Chem. Corn Exch. Bank, N.Y.C., 1947-49, Am. Metal Climax Inc. (name changed to AMAX, Inc.), N.Y.C., 1949-75; treas. Am. Metal Climax Inc. (name changed to AMAX, Inc.), 1957-67, v.p., 1963-65, exec. v.p., 1965-69, pres., 1969-75, also dir., 1964-75; vice chmn. Continental Can Co., Inc. (name changed to Continental Group, Inc.), N.Y.C., 1975-84; chmn. KMI Continental Can Co., Inc. (formerly Continental Group, Inc.), 1987-96, Magma Copper Co., San Manuel, Ariz., 1987-96; bd. dirs. Pioneer Cos., Inc., Chase Brass Industries, Inc. Mem. Greenwich Country Club, University Club (N.Y.C.), Loblolly Pines Country Club. Office: 27 Signal Rd Stamford CT 06902-7921

DONAHUE, JOHN DAVID, public official, educator; b. Alexandria, Ind., June 17, 1956; s. Thomas Edward and Judith Ann (Wheatley) D.; m. Margaret Ann Pax, Aug. 23, 1986; children: Kathleen, Benedict. BA, Ind. U., 1979; M in Pub. Policy, Harvard U., 1982, PhD, 1987. From asst. prof. to assoc. prof. Harvard U., Cambridge, Mass., 1987-93; asst. sec. U.S. Dept. Labor, Washington, 1993-94, counselor to sec., 1994-95; assoc. prof. public policy Harvard University, Cambridge, Mass., 1995—; cons. econ., Cambridge, 1985-99; adv. com. on shareholder responsibiity Harvard U., 1998-99.
Author: The Privatization Decision, 1989, Disunited States, 1997, Hazardous Crosscurrents, 1998; co-author: New Deals: The Chrysler Revival, 1985; editor: Cost-Benefit Analysis and Project Design, 1980, Jamming in the Symphony-Innovation in the Federal Government, 1999. Advisor Clinton Presdl. Transition, Washington, 1993. Doctoral fellow NSF, 1980, fellow Dively Found., 1984. Office: Harvard University 79 Jfk St Cambridge MA 02138-5801

DONAHUE, JOHN EDWARD, physician; b. Revere, Mass., Apr. 27, 1966; s. Edward Francis and Camille (Santoro) D. BS summa cum laude, Tufts U., 1988, MD, 1992. Diplomate Am. Bd. Psychiatry and Neurology, Nat. Bd. Med. Examiners. Intern St. Elizabeth's Med. Ctr., Boston, 1992-93; resident New Eng. Med. Ctr., Boston, 1993-96; fellow R.I. Hosp., Providence, 1996-99. *Dr. Donahue won the 1999 Gustaf Retzius Neuroanatomy Competition (East Coast) with the highest score ever in the East Coast competition to date. Being a neuropathologist and board-certified neurologist makes him particularly adept at clinical-pathologic correlations, as he brings a unique clinical perspective to the neuropathologic material. He is engaged in Alzheimer's disease research, but enjoys practicing all aspects of neuropathology. Dr. Donahue anticipates completing his neuropathology fellowship in June of 1999, and he has accepted a position to become Director of Neuropathology at the New Jersey Neuroscience Institute (part of J.F.K. Medical Center) in Edison, N.J. starting in July, 1999.* Contbr. articles to profl. jours. Recipient David L. Kasdon prize Tufts U. Sch. Medicine, 1992, Second Place award Gustaf Retzius Neuroanatomy Competition, 1997, 98, champion 1999. Mem. AMA, Mass. Med. Soc., Am. Acad. Neurology, Am. Assn. Neuropathologists, Coll. Am. Pathologists, Phi Beta Kappa. Avocations: swimming, computers. Office: NJ Neurosci Inst JFK Med Ctr 65 James St Edison NJ 08818-3059

DONAHUE, JOHN EDWARD, lawyer; b. Milw., Aug. 22, 1950; s. Joseph Robert and Helen Ann (Kelly) D.; m. Maureen Dolores Hart, Sept. 20, 1974; children: Timothy Robert Hart, Michael John Hart. BA with honors, Marquette U., 1972; JD, U. Wis., Madison, 1975. Bar: Wis. 1975, U.S. Dist. Ct. (we. and ea. dists.) Wis. 1975. Assoc. Weiss, Steuer, Berzowski and Kriger, Milw., 1975-80; ptnr. Weiss, Berzowski, Brady & Donahue LLP, Milw., 1981—; guest lectr. Marquette U. Law Sch., Milw., 1976-90; presenter programs Wis. Inst. CPAs, 1984—, Minn. Soc. CPAs, 1992—; expert witness The Best Lawyers in Am., 1995-96, 97-98, 99—. Past chmn. bd. trustees, past chmn. bd. dirs., past chmn. bd. govs., trustee, exec. com., com. chmn. Mt. Mary Coll., Milw., 1984—, past pres., bd. dirs. com. chmn. Met. Milw. Civic Alliance, 1980—, Children's Hosp. Found., Milw., 1984—; mem. steering com. Greater Milw. Initiative, 1989-92; v.p., bd. dirs. Future Milw., 1984-88; council bd., com. chmn., scoutmaster, Boy Scouts Am., 1990—. Recipient citation Milwaukee County Bd. Suprs., 1990, spl. svc. award Met. Milw. Civil Alliance, 1990, silver beaver award Boy Scouts Am., 1995; named outstanding instr. AICPA, 1991. Mem. ABA, Wis. Bar Assn., Milw. Bar Assn., Wis. Retirement Plan Profls., Greater Milw. Employee Benefits Coun., Kiwanis Club (pres. Milw. unit 1989-90, Outstanding Kiwanian 1989-97, Kiwanian of Yr. 1993). Office: Weiss Berzowski Brady & Donahue LLP 700 N Water St Milwaukee WI 53202-4206

DONAHUE, JOHN F., insurance executive; b. Phila., Mar. 23, 1936; s. Charles William and Marie Binigna (Carr) D.; m. Joyce A. Endt, Apr. 23, 1960; children: Cheryl, Bryan. CPCU. Underwriting dir. ITT Hartford, Hartford, Conn., 1967-69, asst. sec., 1969-73, sec., 1973-76, asst. v.p., 1976-81, v.p., 1981-89, sr. v.p., 1989—; chmn. Hartford Reins. Co., 1987, Gen. Policy Com. on U.S. Aviation Ins. Group, N.Y.C., 1990, Am. Nuclear Insurers, Farmington, Conn., 1990, Nat. Coun. on Compensation, Boca Raton, Fla., 1990; ins. svcs. ofcl. Comml. Risk Svcs., N.Y.C., 1990. Bd. dirs. ARC, Hartford, 1991, Bushnell, Hartford, 1991, Conn. Community Care, Inc., Hartford, 1991. Republican. Roman Catholic. Avocations: golf, tennis. Office: ITT Hartford 690 Asylum Ave Hartford CT 06105-3845

DONAHUE, JOHN FRANCIS, investment company executive; b. Pitts., 1924. Grad., U.S. Mil. Acad., 1946. Chmn. Federated Investors, Pitts. Office: Federated Investors Federated Investors Tower 1001 Liberty Ave Ste 2100 Pittsburgh PA 15222-3779

DONAHUE, JOHN JOSEPH, park and recreation director; b. Bklyn., Nov. 20, 1952; s. John and Anna Donahue; m. Sarah Grassi, July 2, 1977; 1 child, John Vincent. Degree in natural resource mgmt., Calif. State U., Sonoma, 1986. Instr. Bklyn. Bot. Garden, 1977-78; supr. N.Y.C. Parks Dept., 1978-79; gardener Cape Cod Nat. Seashore, 1980-83, John Muir Nat. Hist. Site, 1983-86; specialist nat. resource mgmt. Morristown (N.J.) Nat. Hist. Park, 1986-89; specialist environ. protection Nat. Park Svc., Washington, 1989-94; supt. Thomas Stone Nat. Hist. Site, Charles County, Md., 1994—, George Washington Birthplace Nat. Monument, Washington's Birthplace, Va., 1994—; adv. bd. mem. Olmsted Ctr. Landscape Preservation, Valley Forge Archeol. Ctr.; bd. dirs., treas. George Wright Soc.; chief visitor protection and resource mgmt. Cape Cod Nat. Seashore, 1993. Spkr. in field; contbr. articles to profl. jours. Fax: 804/224-2142. Office: George Washington Birthplace Nat Monument RR 1 Box 717 Washingtons Birthplace VA 22443

DONAHUE, JOHN LAWRENCE, JR., paper company executive; b. Chgo., Nov. 9, 1939; s. John Lawrence Sr. and Margaret (Bollinger) D.; m. Maureen Anne Forbes, June 20, 1964; children: John L. III, Thomas James, Michael Patrick, Margaret Anne. BS in Marine Engring., U.S. Merchant Marine Acad., 1961. Lic. marine engr. Marine engr. Am. Export Lines, N.Y.C., 1961-64; chief engr. Gen. Box Co., Des Plaines, Ill., 1964-74; dir. engring. Mead Container Corp., Cin., 1974-82; pres. Donahue & Assocs. Internat., Inc., Milford, Ohio, 1982—. Trustee, treas. Milford Community Fire Dept. Inc., 1983—. Served to lt. USNR. Mem. Tech. Assn. Pulp and Paper Industry, Assn. Ind. Corrugated Converters. Republican. Roman Catholic. Avocation: yachting. Office: 2002 Ford Cir Ste H Milford OH 45150-2748

DONAHUE, JOHN M(ICHAEL), lawyer; b. Phila., Apr. 20, 1952; s. Joseph Henry (dec.) and Helen Catherine (Fitzpatrick) D. BA in English, LaSalle Coll., 1974; JD, John Marshall Law Sch., 1978. Bar: Pa. 1978, U.S. Dist. Ct. (ea. dist.) Pa. 1979, Calif. 1994. Legal examiner Transam. Ins. Co., Phila., 1978-82; trial atty. Transamerica Ins. Cos., Phila., 1982-88; assoc. Law Offices of Thomas J. McNally, Phila., 1982-88, Harris & Silverman, Phila., 1988—; trial atty. CIGNA, Phila., 1988—. Mem. Phila. Bar Assn., Phila. Assn. Def. Counsel, John Marshall Law Sch. Alumni Assn. (rep. 1985—). Republican. Roman Catholic. Avocations: photography, golf, cycling. Home: 870 N 28th St Apt 216 Philadelphia PA 19130-1729 Office: Harris & Silverman 1601 Chestnut St Ste 3600 Philadelphia PA 19192-0003

DONAHUE, MARY ROSENBERG, psychologist; b. N.Y.C., Dec. 20, 1932; d. Lester and Ethel (Hyman) Rosenberg; children: Laurie, Rachel. BA, Adelphi U., 1954; MA, N.Y. U., 1958; PhD, St. John U., 1968. Tchr. Elmont, N.Y., 1954-57, sch. psychologist, 1957-63; cons. psychologist NIMH, 1964-65; sch. psychologist Mamaroneck, N.Y., 1966-67; pvt. practice psychology Bethesda, Md., 1971—; expert witness local jurisdictions regarding domestic issues, womens issues, abuse, 1974—; speaker on custody evaluations and expert witness considerations; cons. Washington Hosp. Ctr. Co-author: On Your Own, 1993, 2d edit. 1996. NIMH grantee, 1962-63, 64-65. Mem. APA, Md. Psychol. Assn., D.C. Psychol. Assn., Am. Orthopsychiat. Assn., Assn. Pvt. Practitioners, Montgomery County Round Table. Home: 12017 Edgepark Ct Potomac MD 20854-2138 Office: 5902 Hubbard Dr Rockville MD 20852-4823

DONAHUE, PATRICIA TOOTHAKER, retired social worker, administrator; b. Alamo, Tex., Sept. 6, 1922; d. Henry Tull and Minnie Elizabeth (Scott) Toothaker; m. Hayden Hackney Donahue, Feb. 22, 1947; children: Erin Kathleen, Kerry Shannon, Patricia Marie. BA, U. Okla., 1977, MSW, 1978. Lic. social worker with specialty in clin. social work, Okla. Clin. social worker Cen. Okla. Community Mental Health Ctr., Norman, 1979-91; participant VII World Congress Mental Health, Vienna, Austria, 1983; adj. asst. prof. U. Okla. Sch. Social Work, Norman, 1989—. Vol. counselor Woman's Resource Ctr., Norman, 1978-79; active Cleve. County Aging Svcs. Adv. Coun., 1988-91. Mem. Nat. Alliance for Mentally Ill, Cleve. County Mental Health Assn., Cleve. County Med. Aux. (pres. 1970-71), Reviewers Club Norman (pres. 1970). Home: Rm # 218 750 S Canadian Trails Dr Norman OK 73072-7640

DONAHUE, RICHARD JAMES, secondary school educator; b. New Rochelle, N.Y., Dec. 11, 1950; s. Raymond Douglas and Helen Andrea (Garibaldi) Silva. BS in Math., SUNY, Oneonta, 1972; MS (spl.), Coll. New Rochelle, 1977; MS in Ednl. Computing, Iona Coll., 1986. Cert. spl. edn. tchr., N.Y., tchr. secondary math., N.Y. Tchr. spl. edn. Adams Sch., N.Y.C., 1973-75, curriculum coord., 1976-77; tchr. math. and computer literacy Eastchester (N.Y.) Jr. H.S., 1975-76, 77—; tchr. math. SAT preparation New Rochelle H.S., 1981-83, tchr. Gen. Ednl. Devel. math., 1981—; tchr. computers Coll. New Rochelle, 1988, adj. asst. prof., 1988-92; tchr. computers Manhattanville Coll., Purchase, N.Y., 1983-85; mem. challenge gifted and talented program Concordia Coll., Bronxville, N.Y., 1988-89; tchr. tng. courses in computer applications Eastchester Union Free Sch. Dist., 1993-94; tchr. mentor on use of telecom. Am. Online's Scholastic Network, 1994; adv. bd. world wide web Scholastic Network; participant Waikoloa Sci. Project, Hawaii, 1997. Author: BASIC Number Theory Programs, 1985-86, PASCAL Number Theory Programs, 1987, also computer software series in math. edn., 1982-83; also articles and internet column. Recipient N.Y. State Model Schs. Tchr. Integration award Madison-Oneida Bd. Coop. Edn. Svcs., 1998, N.Y. Wired Applied Tech. award The N.Y. Jour. News, 1999; NSF Math. Devel. Program grantee, 1981, NEWMAST grantee Ednl. Workshop NASA, 1994, Tchr. Resource Agt. grantee Am. Astron. Soc., 1996, Reader's Digest Found. Interdisciplinary Learning PRoject grantee, 1998, BEPT mini grantee, 1998, Impact II grantee BOCES N.Y. State Edn. Dept. Mem. Nat. Coun. Tchr. Math. (reviewer and referee for Math. Tchr. publ.), Assn. Math. Tchrs. N.Y. State, Math. Assn. Am., Eastchester Tchrs. Assn. (treas. 1983-97), N.Y. State Congress of Parents and Tchrs. (life, Jenkins award 1994), Eastchester Tchrs. Inst. (treas. 1983-85), Nat. Sci. Tchrs. Assn., N.Y. State Assn. for Computers and Tech. in Edn., N.Y. State Tech. Edn. Assn., Film Soc. Lincoln Ctr., Am. Film Inst., Bronxville, Eastchester, Pelham and Tuckahoe Consortium, Westchester Amateur Astronomers, Internat. Tech. Edn. Assn. Home: 60 Locust Ave Apt A201 New Rochelle NY 10801-7360

DONAHUE, RICHARD KING, athletic apparel executive, lawyer; b. Lowell, Mass., July 20, 1927; s. Joseph P. and Dorothy F. (Riordan) D.; m. Nancy Lawson, Sept. 19, 1953; children: Gail M., Timothy J., Michael R., Nancy C., Richard K., Daniel J., Alicia A., Stephen J., Christopher P., Tara E., Philip A. A.B., Dartmouth Coll., 1948; J.D., Boston U., 1951. Bar: Mass. 1951. Ptnr. Donahue & Donahue, Attys., P.C., Lowell, Mass., 1951-60, 63-90; v.p., chmn. bd., Nike, Inc., 1990— ; asst. to Pres. Kennedy, Washington, 1960-63. Served with USNR. Recipient Herbert Harley award Am. Judicature Soc., 1981. Mem. Am. Bd. Trial Advs., ABA (gov., ho. of dels. 1972—), Am. Coll. Trial Lawyers, Mass. Bar Assn. (past pres., Gold medal 1979), New Eng. Bar Assn. (past pres.). Clubs: Union League (Boston); Vesper Country (Tyngsboro, Mass.); Fed. City (Washington); Yorick (Lowell). Office: Nike Inc 1 Bowerman Dr Beaverton OR 97005-6453*

DONAHUE, ROSS DONALD, state official; b. DuBois, Pa., Dec. 4, 1945; s. Thomas Charles and Lois Bowes (Forsyth) D.; m. Mary Ann Morrison, June 6, 1970; children: Garth T., Zachary M. BS, Pa. State U., 1967, MEd, 1971, PhD, 1994. Cert. rehab. counselor. Tchr. St. Mary's (Pa.) Sch. Dist., 1967-68; rehab. counselor Commonwealth of Pa., DuBois, 1968-70, 71-77, rehab. supr., 1977-85, rehab. adminstr., 1995—; sec. exec. com. North Ctrl. Regional Planning & Devel. Coun. for Pvt. Industry, Ridgway, Pa., 1990—; treas. St. Mary's H.S. Transition Bd., 1994—. Chair Exec. Planning Com., Harrisburg, Pa., 1988-93; co-chair Pa. Job. Creation Project, DuBois, Pa. and statewide, 1991-94. Recipient Nat. Rehab. fellowship Rehab. Svcs. Adminstrn., University Park, Pa., 1971. Mem. ASTD, Pa. Rehab. Counselor's Assn. (pres. 1981-83), Pa. Rehab. ASsn. (treas. 1976-82), Nat. Rehab. Adminstrs. Assn., Overall Econ. Devel. Assn., North Ctrl. Loan Rev. Com., DuBois Ednl. Assn. (bd. dirs.). Republican. Presbyterian. Avocations: music, travel. Home: 21 Treasure Lake DuBois PA 15801 Office: Office Vocat Rehab 199 Beaver Dr Du Bois PA 15801-2515

DONAHUE, SHIRLEY OHNSTAD, elementary education educator; b. Darlington, Wis., Aug. 29, 1937; d. Joseph and Edna L. (Peterson) Ohnstad; m. John V. Donahue, Aug. 20, 1960; children: Roger K., Jeffrey J. BS, U. Wis., Platteville, 1959; MS, No. Ill. U., 1978. Cert. tchr., Ill. Tchr. Freeport (Ill.) Sch. Sys., 1959-62, Belvidere (Ill.) Sch. Sys., 1962-64, Pecatonica (Ill.) Sch. Sys., 1964-66, Orangeville (Ill.) Sch. Sys., 1966-67, Rock Falls (Ill.) Sch. Sys., 1967-93; ret. Rock Falls (Ill.) Sch. System, 1993. Co-author gifted student curriculum materials. Mem. Liturgical com. St. Mary's Ch., Sterling, Ill., 1980-84, aux. min., 1980-94; mem. Friends of Sterling Pub. Libr., v.p. 1990-93, 96, pres. 1995; bd. dirs. YWCA, sec. bd. dirs., 1994-95; mem. Cmty. Gen. Hosp. Med. Aux., 1993—, co-chair sr. health ins. program, 1994—; pres. Community Gen. Hosp. Aux., 1995-99; pres. YWCA, 1997-99; bd. dirs. ARC, Lincolnland chpt., 1996—. Recipient Western Ill. Master Tchr. award, 1991. Mem. Rock Falls Elem. Edn. Assn. (chmn. polit. action com. for edn. 1985-87), Ill. Edn. Assn., NEA, AAUW, Sterling Democratic Women. Roman Catholic. Avocation: bicycling. Home: 1720 Avenue E Sterling IL 61081-1124

DONAHUE, THOMAS MICHAEL, physics educator; b. Healdton, Okla., May 23, 1921; s. Robert Emmett and Mary (Lyndon) D.; m. Esther Marie McPherson, Jan. 1, 1950; children: Brian M., Kevin E., Neil M. A.B., Rockhurst Coll., 1942, D.Sc. (hon.), 1981; Ph.D., Johns Hopkins U., 1947. Rsch. assoc., asst. prof. Johns Hopkins U., 1947-51; asst. prof. U. Pitts., 1951-53, assoc. prof., 1953-57, prof., 1957-74, dir. Lab. Atmospheric and Space Sci., 1966-74, dir. Space Rsch. Coordination Ctr., 1966-74; chmn. dept. atmospheric and oceanic sci. and Space Physics Rsch. Lab., U. Mich., Ann Arbor, 1974-81, prof., 1981-87, Edward H. White II disting. univ. prof. planetary sci. dept. atmospheric oceanic and space scis., dept. physics, 1987-94; disting. univ. prof. emeritus, 1994—; dir. ctr. for integrated study global change U. Mich., 1990-93; mem. phys. scis. com. NASA, 1972-77, adv. coun., 1982-88, solar system exploration com., 1981-82; mem. Arecibo adv. bd. Cornell U., 1971-76, 86-89, chmn. 1989; mem. Space Telescope Sci. Inst. Adv. Com., 1986-89, chmn., 1987-89; chmn. solar terrestrial rels. com. NAS, mem. atmospheric scis. com., mem. geophysics rsch. bd., mem. climate bd., chmn. space sci. bd. 1982-88, mem. nominating com., 1987-88; chmn. space sci. in the 21st Century study NAS, 1984-87, com. for U.S.-USSR workshop on planetary scis., 1988-91, com. on planetary and lunar exploration, 1992-93; chmn. sci. steering groups Pioneer Venus multi-probe and orbital missions to Venus, 1974-93, pub. affairs com. Am. Geog. Union; trustee-at-large Upper Atmosphere Rsch. Corp., 1975-87; vice-chmn. exec. com., trustee Univ. Corp. for Atmospheric Rsch., 1978-85; chmn. bd. trustees Univs.

Space Rsch. Assn., 1978-82; mem. vis. com. Max Planck Gesellschaft fur Aeronomie, 1989-96; mem. nat. tech. adv. com. Nat. Inst. for Global Environ. Change, 1992; Marcel Nicolet lectr. Am. Geophys. Union, 1993. Editor: Space Research X, 1969; assoc. editor numerous publs., particularly specializing in atomic physics and properties of planetary atmospheres; editor: Venus, 1983; assoc. editor: Planetary and Space Sci. Served with AUS, 1944-46. Guggenheim fellow, Paris, 1960; recipient Public Svc. award NASA, 1977, 88, 8, achievement awards Disting. Public Svc. medal, 1980, Wellock Disting. Rsch. Accomplishments award U. Mich., 1981, Stephen S. Attwood award Excellence in Engring., U. Mich., 1994; Arctowski medal Nat. Acad. Sci., 1981, Fleming medal Am. Geophys. Union, 1981; Rsch. Excellence award Coll. Engring., 1981; Henry Russel lectr. U. Mich., 1987; Space Sci. award AIAA, 1988; 1st Space Sci. medalist Nat. Space Club, 1989. Fellow AAAS, Am. Phys. Soc., Am. Geophys. Union (pres. solar-planetary rels. 1972-75, v.p. 1969-72, chmn. pub. policies com. 1990-93, Marcel Nicolet lectr. 1993), Mich. Soc. Fellows; mem. NAS, Internat. Acad. Astronautics. Achievements include participation in Voyager mission to outer planets, Galileo mission to Jupiter, Cassini Mission to Saturn, Planet B Mission to Mars, Spacelab 1, Apollo 17, Apollo-Soyuz, chmn. sci. steering group Pioneer Venus multiprobe/orbiter missions. Home: 1781 Arlington Blvd Ann Arbor MI 48104-4105

DONAHUE, THOMAS REILLY, trade union official; b. N.Y.C., Sept. 4, 1928; s. Thomas Reilly and Mary E. (Purcell) D.; children: Nancy Angela, Thomas Reilly III. BA, Manhattan Coll., 1949; JD, Fordham U., 1956; LLD (hon.), U. Notre Dame, 1980, Loyola U., Chgo., 1984, SUNY, 1988, Manhattan Coll., 1988, U. Mass., 1990. Dir. edn., bus. agt. local 32B Bldg. Svc. Employees Internat. Union, AFL-CIO, 1949-52, dir. contract dept., 1952-57; European labor program coord. Free Europe Com., Paris, 1957-60; asst. to pres. Bldg. Svc. Employees Internat. Union, AFL-CIO, 1960-67; asst. sect. for labor-mgmt. rels. U.S. Dept. Labor, 1967-69; exec. sec. Svc. Employees Internat. Union, 1969-71, v.p., 1971-73; exec. asst. to pres. AFL-CIO, 1973-79; sec.-treas. AFL-CIO, Washington, 1979-95, pres., 1995-96, assoc., 1996—; co-chmn. Found. for Prevention and Early Resolution of Conflict, 1996-97. Former mem., bd. dirs. U.S. Cath. Conf. Com. on Social Devel., Carnegie Corp., Nat. Urban League, Brookings Instn., Muscular Dystrophy Assn., African Am. Inst.; bd. dirs. Work in Am. Inst., Pres. Coun. on Sustainable Devel., Nat. Planning Assn., Coun. on Fgn. Rels., Nat. Endowment for Democracy, Inst. Multi-Track Diplomacy. With USNR, 1945-46. Sr. fellow Work in Am. Inst., 1997—. Democrat. Home: 613 G St SW Washington DC 20024-2439 Office: AFL-CIO 1717 K St Ste 707 Washington DC 20006-4145

DONAHUE, TIMOTHY M., communications executive. Pres. McCaw Cellular Comm., 1986-91; pres., gen. mgr. AT&T Wireless of N.Y. and N.J., 1991-96; pres. Nextel Comms. Inc., Rutherford, N.J., 1996—. Office: Nextel Comm Inc 1505 Farm Credit Dr Ste 100 Mc Lean VA 22102-5091*

DONALD, ALEXANDER GRANT, psychiatrist, educator; b. Darlington, S.C., Jan. 24, 1928; s. Raymond George and Chesnut Evans (McIntosh) D.; m. Emma Louise Coggeshall, Oct. 25, 1958; children: Sandy, Mary Chesnut, Marion Lide. BS, Davidson Coll., 1948; MD, Med. U. S.C., 1952. Diplomate: Am. Bd. Psychiatry and Neurology. Intern Jefferson Med. Coll., 1952-53; resident in psychiatry Walter Reed Hosp., 1956-59; dir. Mental Health Clinic, Florence, S.C., 1962-66; dept. commr. S.C. Dept. Mental Health, 1966-67; dir. William S Hall Psychiat. Inst., Columbia, 1967-90; prof., chmn. dept. neuropsychiatry and behavioral scis. Sch. Medicine, U. S.C., Columbia, 1975-90, Disting. prof. neuropsychiatry, assoc. dean ednl. planning, 1990-91; Disting. prof. emeritus Sch. Medicine, U. S.C., 1991—; bd. dirs. Health Resource Found. Bd. trustees Richland Meml. Hosp., 1993—, vice chmn., 1997, chmn., 1999; bd. dirs. S.C. Inst. for Med. Edn. and Rsch., pres., 1992-96. Fellow Am. Coll. Psychiatrists, Am. Psychiat. Assn. (pres. S.C. chpt. 1967), So. Psychiat. Assn. (v.p.); mem. AMA, Columbia Med. Soc. (v.p. 1981, del. 1981, pres. 1989-90), Evening Music Club (pres. 1989-90), Alpha Omega Alpha. Presbyterian. Office: U SC Sch Medicine 3555 Harden Street Ext Ste 104 Columbia SC 29203-6894 *Accepting responsibility for ones' actions - using one's mind to understand one's self is the highest function of mankind.*

DONALD, BERNICE B., judge; b. Miss., Sept. 17, 1951; d. Perry and Willie Bell (Hall) Bowie; m. W. L. Donald, Oct. 9, 1973. BA in Sociology, Memphis State Univ., 1974, JD, 1979; student, Nat. Judicial Coll., 1983, 84. Bar: Tenn. 1979, U.S. Fed. Ct. 1979, U.S. Supreme Ct. 1989. Clk. South Central Bell Telephone Co., 1971-75, mgr., 1975-80; staff atty. Memphis Area Legal Svcs., 1980, Shelby County Public Defenders Office, 1980-82; judge Gen. Sessions Criminal Ct. of Shelby County, Tenn., 1982-88; bankruptcy judge U.S. Bankruptcy Ct. (we. dist.) Tenn., Memphis, 1988-96; U.S. dist. judge U.S. Dist. Ct. (we. dist.) Tenn., 1996—; faculty mem. Fed. Judicial Ctr., 1991—, Nat. Judicial Coll., 1992—; adj. prof. Cecil C. Humphreys Sch. of Law. Recipient Cmty. Svcs. award Nat. Conf. on Christians and Jews, 1986, Martin Luther King Cmty. Svc. award, Young Careerist award State of Tenn. Raleigh Bureau of Profl. Women; named Citizen of Yr. Excelsior Chpt. of Eastern Star, Woman of Yr. Pentecostal Ch. of God in Christ. Mem. Nat. Assn. of Women Judges (pres. 1990-91), Am. Judges Assn., Nat. Ctr. for State Cts., Am. Bar Assn., Nat. Bar Assn., Tenn. Bar Assn. (bd. dirs. 1997—), Memphis County Bar Assn., Shelby County Bar Assn., Am. Trial Lawyers Assn., Assn. of Women Attys. (pres. 1991, bd. dirs.), Nat. Conf. of Bankruptcy Judges (bd. dirs. 1993), Nat. Conf. of Women's Bar Assn. (bd. mem.), Nat. Conf. of Spl. Ct. Judges (sec.), Leadership Memphis (pres. 1987, bd. dirs.), Internat. Women's Forum. Avocations: reading, crossword puzzles, music, bicycling, walking. Office: Federal Building 167 North Main StSte 341 Memphis TN 38103*

DONALD, DAVID HERBERT, author, history educator; b. Goodman, Miss., Oct. 1, 1920; s. Ira Unger and Sue Ella (Belford) D.; m. Aida DiPace, 1955; 1 son, Bruce Randall. Student, Holmes Jr. Coll., 1937-39; AB, Millsaps Coll., 1941, LHD, 1976; AM, U. Ill., 1942, PhD, 1946, LHD (hon.), 1992; MA (hon.), U. Oxford, 1959, Harvard U., 1973; LittD (hon.), Coll. Charleston, 1985; D in History, Lincoln U., 1996. Teaching fellow U. N.C., 1942; research asst. history U. Ill., 1943-45, research assoc., 1946-47; fellow Social Sci. Research Council, 1945-46; instr. history Columbia U., 1947-49; assoc. prof. history Smith Coll., 1949-51; asst. prof. history Columbia U. Grad. Faculty, 1951-52, assoc. prof., 1952-57, prof. history, 1957-59; prof. history Princeton U., 1959-62; prof. Am. history Johns Hopkins U., Balt., 1962-73; Harry C. Black prof. Johns Hopkins U., 1963-73, dir. Inst. So. History,, 1966-72; Charles Warren prof. Am. history and prof. Am. civilization Harvard U., 1973-91, prof. emeritus, 1991—, chmn. grad. program in Am. civilization, 1979-85; vis. assoc. prof. Amherst Coll., 1950; Fulbright lectr. Am. history U. Coll. North Wales, 1953-54; mem. Inst. Advanced Study, 1957-58; Harmsworth prof. Am. history Oxford U., 1959-60; John P. Young lectr. Memphis State U., 1963; Walter Lynwood Fleming lectr. La. State U., 1965; Benjamin Rush lectr. Am. Psychiat. Assn., 1972; Commonwealth lectr. Univ. Coll., London, 1975; Samuel Paley lectr. Hebrew Univ. of Jerusalem, 1991. Author: Lincoln's Herndon, 1948, Divided We Fought, A Pictorial History of the War, 1861-65, 1952, Inside Lincoln's Cabinet: The Civil War Diaries of Salmon P. Chase, 1954, Lincoln Reconsidered: Essays on the Civil War Era, 1956, rev. 1961, A Rebel's Recollections, (G.C. Eggleston), 1959, Charles Sumner and the Coming of the Civil War, 1960 (Pulitzer prize in biography), Why the North Won the Civil War, 1960, rev. edit., 1996, (with J.G. Randall) The Civil War and Reconstruction, 2d edit., 1961, rev., enlarged edit., 1969, The Divided Union, 1961, The Politics of Reconstruction, 1863-67, 1965, The Nation in Crisis, 1861-1877, 1969, Charles Sumner and the Rights of Man, 1970, (with Sidney Andrews) The South Since the War, 1970, Gone for a Soldier, 1975, (with others) The Great Republic, 1977, rev. edit., 1981, 3rd edit., 1985, 4th edit., 1992, Liberty and Union, 1978, Look Homeward: A Life of Thomas Wolfe, 1987 (Pulitzer prize 1988), Lincoln, 1995 rev. edit., 1996, Charles Sumner, 1997; editor: War Diary and Letters of Stephen Minot Weld, 1979; gen. editor: Documentary History of American Life, The Making of America Series, 6 vols.; co-editor: (with wife) Diary of Charles Francis Adams, 2 vols., 1964; contbr. articles to periodicals. Recipient Abraham Lincoln Lit. award Union League Club N.Y.C., 1977, C. Hugh Holman prize MLA, 1988, Benjamin L.C. Wailes award Miss. Hist. Soc., 1994, Barondess-Lincoln prize, 1996, Christopher award, 1996, Lincoln prize Gettysburg Coll., 1996, Jefferson Davis award Mus. of Confederacy, 1996; Guggenheim fellow, 1964-65, 85-86, fellow Am. Coun. Learned Socs., 1969-70, Ctr. for Advanced Study Behavioral Scis., 1969-70, George A. and Eliza G. Howard fellow, 1957-58, sr. fellow NEH, 1971-72. Fellow Am. Acad. Arts and Scis.; mem. Orgn. Am. Historians, Am. Hist. Assn., So. Hist. Assn. (v.p. 1968, pres. 1969), Soc. Am. Historians, Mass. Hist. Soc., Am. Antiquarian Soc., Phi Beta Kappa, Phi Kappa Phi, Pi Kappa Delta, Pi Kappa Alpha, Omicron Delta Kappa. Episcopalian. Clubs: Harvard (N.Y.C.); Cosmos, Signet, Fox. Home: 41 Lincoln Rd PO Box 6158 Lincoln MA 01773-6158

DONALD, EDWARD MILTON, JR., marketing company executive; b. Detroit, Jan. 11, 1947; s. Edward Milton Sr. and Rosa Marie (Stockell) D.; divorced; children: Christopher Jarrod, Emily Hope, Joshua Andrew.

DONALD, ERIC PAUL, aeronautical engineer, inventor; b. Sunderland, Eng., Feb. 23, 1930; came to U.S., 1964, naturalized, 1970; s. Norman and Dorothy (Dobson) D.; m. Christine Juliet Allen, Dec. 26, 1966; children: April Elise America, Paul Allen Hertford. Student, Sunderland Tech. Coll., 1949; H.N.C., Acton Tech. Coll., 1957; M.Sc., Cranfield Inst. Tech., 1974. Engr. Fairey Aviation Co., London, 1953-59; research engr. English Electric Co., 1959-64; indsl. engring. cons. N.Y.C., 1965-66; cons. engr. Lockheed Corp., 1966-67, Boeing, 1967-69, Grumman, 1969-70, Hawker Siddeley, 1970-71; chief stress analyst Guided Weapons div. Brit. Aircraft Corp., 1973-79; sr. engring. scientist Douglas Aircraft Co., Long Beach, Calif., 1979—; prin. scientist and engr. spl. projects Douglas Aircraft Co.; retired, 1992, ret., ; cons. Northrop Aircraft Co., 1992-93, Donald-Hathaway Assocs., 1996—; founder Donald Rsch., 1978, E.P. Donald Ltd., 1979; mng. dir. Blee-Bolt Indicators Ltd., 1979—. Pub. TransAtlantic Traveller, 1993—, The Bus. Calendar for the American Republic, 1999; contbr. articles to profl. jours.; patentee in field. Served with RAF, 1950-52. Nominated for Nobel prize, 1998; Nominated for Poet Laureate, 1999. Fellow AIAA (assoc.); mem. Royal Aero. Soc., Inst. Patentees and Inventors (Richardson gold medal 1977), Soc. Genealogists, World Affairs Coun. Orange County, Soc. for Advancement of Mgmt. Orange County (v.p. edn. univs. and colls.). Anglican. Home: PO Box 15111 Long Beach CA 90815-0111 *If I had done no more than solve the world metal fatigue detection problem, I should have considered my life worthwhile.*

DONALD, JACK C., oil company executive; b. Edmonton, Alta., Can., Nov. 29, 1934; s. Archibald Scott and Margaret Catherine (Cameron) D.; m. Joan M. Schultz, Oct. 29, 1955. Student, Southern Alberta Inst. Tech., 1959. Owner, operator Parkdale Auto Svc., Edmonton, 1957-60; sales mgr. Sanford Oil Ltd., Edmonton, 1960-63, Pacific Petroleums, Edmonton, 1963-64; pres., gen. mgr. Parkland Oil Products, Red Deer, Alta., 1964-71; v.p. mktg. Turbo Resources, Calgary, Alta., 1971-76; pres., chief exec. officer Parkland Industries Ltd., Red Deer, 1977—; chmn., bd. dirs. Can. Western Bank, Edmonton, Can. Western Trust; v.p., bd. dirs. Brandt Industries Ltd., Regina, 1984—; bd. dirs. TransAlta Utilities Corp., Ensign Resources Svc. Group Inc., Can. Petroleum Products Inst.; pub. mem. coun. Inst. Chartered Accts. Alta. Alderman City of Red Deer, 1971-77. Mem. Rotary. Office: Parkland Industries Ltd, 4919 59th St # 236, Red Deer, AB Canada T4N 6C9

DONALD, JAMES, supermarket chain executive. Trainee Publix Super Mkts., Inc., 1971-76; mgmt. exec. Fla., Ala. and Tex. divsns. Albertson's, 1976-91; key exec. Wal-Mart, 1991-94; sr. v.p., mgr. 130 store ea. divsns. Safeway, Inc., 1994-96; CEO Pathmark Stores, Inc., Carteret, N.J., 1996—, also chmn. bd. dirs. Office: Pathmark Stores Inc 200 Milik St Carteret NJ 07008-1102 also: PO Box 5301 Woodbridge NJ 07095-0915*

DONALD, JAMES E., military career officer; b. Jackson, Miss., Apr. 20, 1949; m. August S. Green; children: Jeff, Cheryl. BA in Polit. Sci. and History, U. Miss., 1970; MPA, U. Mo., 1983; grad., Command Gen. Staff Coll., Nat. War Coll. Commd. 2d lt. U.S. Army Inf., 1970, advanced through grades to maj. gen.; bn. adj./comdr. C Co. 1st Bn., 87th Inf. Regiment U.S. Army Inf., Baumholder, Germany; inf. advisor Readiness Group Stewart U.S. Army Inf., N.Y.; inspector gen., inspection team chief 101st Airborne Divsn. U.S. Army Inf., Ft. Campbell, Ky.; bn. exec. officer 2d Bn., 502d Inf. Regiment U.S. Army Inf., bn. comdr. 1st Bn., 502d Inf. Regiment, chief forces team War Plans divsn., Office Dep. Chief Staff, comdr. 1st Brigade, 101st Airborne divsn., chief mil. support divsn.; dep. dir. ops./JE U.S. Pacific Command U.S. Army Inf., Camp Smith, Hawaii; asst. divsn. comdr. ops. 25th Inf. Divsn. U.S. Army Inf., Schofield Barracks, Hawaii; dep. commdg. gen. U.S. Army Pacific, Ft. Shafter, 1998—. Decorated Def. Superior Svc. medal, Legion of Merit with oak leaf cluster, Bronze Star, Meritorious Svc. medal with four oak leaf clusters, Army Commendation medal with oak leaf cluster, Nat. Def. Svc. medal with svc. star, Armed Forces Expeditionary medal, Kuwait Liberation medal, S.W. Asia Svc. ribbon. Office: US Army Pacific Fort Shafter HI 96858

DONALD, JAMES ROBERT, federal agency official, economist, outdoors writer; b. Omega, Ga., Dec. 31, 1933; s. Clinton Ernest and Lorena (Branan) D.; m. Nancy Ripple, Sept. 16, 1961; children: James Gordon, Mary Carol. Cert., Abraham Baldwin Agrl. Coll., 1952; BS, U. Ga., 1954; MS, N.C. State U., 1956; cert. in govt. tng., Mich. State U., 1975. Economist Econ. Rsch. Svc., USDA, Washington, 1957-76, outlook officer World Agrl. Outlook Bd., 1977-81; retired, 1994; chairperson USDA, Washington, 1982-94; freelance writer on fishing affairs, Mineral, Va., 1972—. With U.S. Army, 1957-63. Recipient Superior Svc. award USDA, 1968, Presdl. rank award, 1989. Mem. Am. Agrl. Econs. Assn. (Best Info. Bull. award 1976), Bass Angler's Soc. Am. Home: 584 Laurelwood Dr Mineral VA 23117-4734

DONALD, JOHN HEPBURN, II, quality assurance professional, consultant; b. Goffstown, N.H., July 14, 1921; s. John Hepburn and Doris Lillian (Mudge) D.; m. Jeanette Leone Fanshaw, Nov. 13, 1947; children: Ruth Elizabeth Donald Sousa, John Hepburn III, Lloyd Gordon. Diploma, Northeastern U., 1962. Lab. technician Monsanto Co., Everett, Mass., 1941-50; lab. supr. Monsanto Co., Everett, 1950-62, quality engr., statistician, 1962-78; audit cons. Reflectone Inc., Tampa, Fla., 1979-83; project mgr. quality assurance Singer Co., Link Divsn., Houston, 1983-87; quality assurance cons. Quality Control Svcs., Inc., Monticello, Fla., 1988—. Vice chmn. Town Conservation Commn., Reading, Mass., 1977-79; cubmaster, scoutmaster and dist. commr. Boy Scouts. With USN, 1942-45, 47-51. Mem. Am. Soc. for Quality Control (sr. mem., founding chmn., sect. chmn. 1984—, cert. quality engr.), Inst. Cert. Profl. Mgrs. (cert. mgr.). Republican. Lutheran. Avocations: genealogy, photography. Office: Quality Control Svcs 263 Pearl St Reading MA 01867-1739

DONALD, NORMAN HENDERSON, III, lawyer; b. Denver, Nov. 1, 1937; s. Norman Henderson Jr. and Angelene (Pell) D.; m. Alice Allen, Oct. 31, 1970 (div. Aug. 1980); children: Norman H. IV (dec.), Helen P.; m. Kathryn Akers, Sept. 26, 1981 (div. Jan. 1998). AB, Princeton U., 1959; LLB, Harvard U., 1962. Bar: N.Y. 1962. Assoc. Davis, Polk & Wardwell, N.Y.C., 1962-67; assoc. Skadden, Arps, Slate, Meagher & Flom, N.Y.C., 1967-68, ptnr., 1968-94; chmn. bd. dirs. Norwil Holdings, Inc., N.Y.C., Atlanta and Sarasota, Solarmax Corp., Sarasota. Mem. Assn. of Bar of City of N.Y., Practising Law Inst. (editor Reit Restructuring 1977—), St. Paul's Sch. Alumni Assn. (v.p., bd. dirs. 1984-86), Union Club (N.Y.C.), Racquet Club (N.Y.C.), Gold Creek Club (Dawsonville, Ga.). Republican. Episcopalian. Home: Mistral Farms 1544 Bailey Waters Rd Dawsonville GA 30534-1807 Office: care Brock Fensterstock et al 153 E 53rd St New York NY 10022-4611

DONALD, ROBERT GRAHAM, retail food chain human resources executive; b. Vancouver, B.C., Can., May 22, 1943; came to U.S., 1946; s. H. Graham and Marion O. (Benoit) D.; m. Patricia K. Shea, Oct. 17, 1970; children: Linda M., Lisa A. Student Delaware Valley Coll., Doylestown, Pa., 1961-63; B.S., Iowa State U., 1965; grad. exec. program food industry mgmt., Cornell U., 1972. With Grand Union Co., Wayne, N.J., 1968—; labor relations asst. Grand Union Co., Elmwood Park, N.J., 1974-75, dist. sales mgr., 1976-78, dir. personnel, 1978-81, v.p.-personnel and adminstrv. services, 1981-86; v.p. compensation and benefits Grand Union Co., 1986—. Served in U.S. Army, 1966-68. Mem. Soc. for Human Resources Mgmt., Internat. Found. of Employee Benefits, Am. Compensation Assn., Food Mktg. Inst. Benefits Coun., Health Care Equity Action League, Health Care Payor's Coalition N.J., Vt. Employer's Health Alliance. Office: The Grand Union Co 201 Willowbrook Blvd Fl 1 Wayne NJ 07470-7010

DONALDSON, COLEMAN DUPONT, aerodynamics and aerospace consulting engineer; b. Phila., Sept. 22, 1922; s. John W. and Renee (duPont) D.; m. Barbara Goldsmith, Jan. 17, 1945; children: B. Beirne, Coleman duPont, Evan F., Alexander M., William M. BS in Aero. Engring., Rensselaer Poly. Inst., 1943; MA, Princeton U., 1954, PhD, 1957. Staff, NACA, Langley Field, Va., 1943-44; head aerophysics sect. NACA, 1946-52; gen. aerodynamics USAC, Wright Field, Ohio, 1945-46; aerodynamic evaluation Bell Aircraft, Niagara Falls, N.Y., 1946; sr. cons., pres. Aero Research Assos. of Princeton, N.J., 1954-79, chmn. bd., 1979-86; group gen. mgr. Aero Research Assocs. Princeton Inc., 1986-87; v.p. Titan Systems, Inc., 1986-87; ret., 1987; cons. missile guidance and control Gen. Precision Equipment Corp., 1957-68; cons. magnetohydro-dynamics Thompson Ramo Wooldridge, Inc., 1958-61; cons. aerodynamic heating, gen aerodynamics Martin Marietta Corp., 1955-72; gen. editor Princeton series on high speed aerodynamics and jet propulsion, 1955-64; cons. boundary layer stability, aerodynamic heating, missile and ordnance systems dept. GE Co., 1956-72; cons. Grumman Aerospace Corp., 1959-72; Robert H. Goddard vis. lectr. with rank of prof. Princeton U., 1970-71; mem. rsch. tech. adv. coun. panel on rsch. NASA, 1969-76, hypersonic tech. com., 1986-90; mem. indsl. profl. adv. com. Pa. State U.; mem. Pres.' Air Quality Adv. Bd., 1973-74; chmn. lab. adv. bd. for air warfare Naval Rsch. Adv. Com., 1986-89, DARPA Tech. Adv. Panel on Hydrodynamics and Acoustics, 1991-94; chmn. adv. coun. dept. aerospace and mech. scis. Princeton U., 1973-78; cons. Ctr. for Naval Analysis, 1990-98; adv. devel. and tech. ops. Martin Marietta Corp., 1989-96; mem. adv. panel NASA Ctr. Turbulence Rsch., 1993-95. Author articles on aerodynamics. Recipient Meritorious Pub. Svc. award Chief Naval Rsch., 1990. Fellow AIAA (Dryden Rsch. lecture award 1971, gen. chmn. 13th aerospace scis. meeting 1975), NAE, Am. Phys. Soc., Sigma Xi, Delta Phi. Home: 7 Merry Point Ter Newport News VA 23606-2824

DONALDSON, EDWARD MOSSOP, research scientist emeritus, aquaculture consultant; b. Whitehaven, Cumbria, England, June 25, 1939; arrived in Can., 1961; s. Edward and Margaret Elizabeth (Mossop) D.; m. Judith Denise Selwood, Aug. 8, 1964; 1 child, Heather Jean. BSc with honors, Sheffield (Eng.) U., 1961, DSc, 1975; PhD, U. B.C., Vancouver, Can., 1964. Rsch. scientist Dept. Fisheries and Oceans, West Vancouver, B.C., 1965-97, sect. head fish culture rsch., 1981-89, sect. head biotech., genetics and nutrition, 1989-97, head Ctr. of Disciplinary Excellence for Biotech. and Genetics in Aquaculture, 1987-97; scientist emeritus Dept. Fisheries and Oceans, West Vancouver, 1997—; cons. in aquaculture and the environment, 1997—; hon. rsch. assoc. U. B.C., 1979-88, adj. prof., 1988—; cons. finfish aquaculture FAO, UN Devel. Program, Can. Internat. Devel. Agy., Internat. Devel. Rsch. Ctrs., U.S. AID, Office of Tech. assessment of the U.S. Congress, Can. Exec. Svc. Overseas, Sci. Com. on Problems of Environment, WHO, U.S. Seagrant, others; mem. Nat. Scis. and Engring. Rsch. Coun. Can., mem. strategic grant selection com. for food agriculture and aquaculture, 1988-93; mem., active in strategic planning for applied rsch. and knowledge com. biotech. B.C. Sci. Coun. mem. editorial bd. Gen. and Comparative Endocrinology, 1971-78, Can. Jour. Fisheries and Aquatic Sci., 1985-88, Aquaculture, 1983—, Can. Jour. Zoology, 1986-91, Revista Italiana de Acquacoltura, 1991—; contbr. over 400 articles to sci. jours. and conf. procs.; contbr. to books on endocrinology, biotech. and aquaculture; patentee in field. Recipient award for best publs. in Transactions of Am. Fisheries Soc., 1977, Ministerial Merit award Min. of Fisheries and Oceans, 1989, B.C. Sci. Coun. Gold medal, 1992, Ministries Commendation award, 1997; B.C. Sugar Co. scholar, 1961; NIH fellow, 1964-65; recipient Thomas W. Eadie medal Royal Soc. Can., 1995. Fellow Acad. Sci. of Royal Soc. Can. (mem. Rowmanoswky medal com. 1994, Thomas W. Eadie medal com. 1995-96); mem. Can. Soc. Zoologists (councilor 1980-83), World Aquaculture Soc., Aquaculture Assn. Can. Office: Dept Fisheries & Oceans, 4160 Marine Dr, West Vancouver, BC Canada V7V 1N6

DONALDSON, GEORGE BURNEY, environmental consultant; b. Oakland, Calif., Mar. 16, 1945; s. George T. and L. M. (Burney) D.; m. Jennifer L. Bishop, Feb. 16, 1974; children: Dawn Marie, Matthew George. AS in Criminology, Porterville Coll., 1972. Registered environ. assessor, Calif.; cert. transp. specialist. Police officer City of Lindsay, Calif., 1966-67; distbn. mgr. Ortho divsn. Chevron Chem. Co., Lindsay, 1967-73; safety specialist Wilbur-Ellis Co., Fresno, Calif., 1973-77, safety dir., 1977-79, dir. corp. regulatory affairs, 1979-97; sr. environ. cons. Geomatrix Cons., Inc., Fresno, 1997—; industry rep. to White House Inter-Govtl. Sci. Engring. and Tech. Adv. Panel, Task Force on Transp. of Non-Nuclear Hazardous Materials, 1980; industry rep. Transp. Rsch. Bd.'s Nat. Strategies Conf. on Transp. of Hazardous Materials and Wastes in the 1980s, NAS, 1981, Hazardous Materials Transp. Conf., Nat. Conf. of State Legislatures, 1982; spkr. and moderator in field; dir. Western Fertilizer and Pesticide Safety seminar, Sacramento, 1979; spkr. Southeastern Agrl. Chem. Safety seminar, Winston-Salem, N.C., 1986. Chmn. industry/govt. task force for unique on-site hazardous waste recycling, devel. task force for computerized regulatory software and data base sys., devel. task force modifying high expansion foam tech. for fire suppression; hazardous materials adviser, motor carrier rating com. Calif. Hwy. Patrol, 1978-79; bd. dirs., mem. exec. com. Californians for Food & Shelter. With U.S. Army, 1962-65. Mem. VFW, Western Agrl. Chems. Assn. (past chmn. transp., distbn. and safety com., outstanding mem. of yr. 1981, govtl. affairs com., regulatory affairs com., trustee polit. action com.), Nat. Agrl. Chems. Assn. (past chmn. transp. and distbn. com., occupl. safety and health com., environ. mgmt. com., state affairs com., moderator spring conf. 1989), U.S. Inter-Regional Coordinating Coun. (trans. and distbn. com.), Am. Soc. Safety Engrs., Calif. Fertilizer Assn. (transp. and distbn. com., environ. com.), Fresno Agrl. Round Table, Fresno City and County C. of C. (agrl. steering com., govt. affairs com.), Calif. C. of C. (environ. policy com.), Am. Legion, Elks. Office: Geomatrix Cons Inc 2444 Main St Ste 215 Fresno CA 93721-2734

DONALDSON, JAMES NEILL, banker; b. Washington County, Pa., Mar. 25, 1940; s. James Reed and Mary Alice (Neill) D. BA in Polit. Sci., Westminster Coll., 1962; MEd, U. Pitts., 1965, postgrad. in law, 1962-64. cert. trust and fin. advisor; accredited esteate planner. Trust adminstr. Bankers Trust Co., N.Y.C., 1967-70, asst. trust officer, 1970-73; trust officer Bankers Trust Co., White Plains, N.Y., 1973-76, officer-in-charge Trust Adminstrv. Unit, 1976, v.p., 1976-78, head trust office, 1978-82, with Trust Adminstrn. Unit, 1982-83; head new bus. devel., trust and estates group Chem. Bank, N.Y.C., 1983-88, head trust and estates adminstrn. mgmt., 1989-90; sect. head mgr. trust and estates adminstrn. Chase Manhattan Bank, N.Y.C., 1990-96, personal trust sales Global Trust and Fiduciary Unit, 1996—; Chase rep. to Corp. Fiduciaries Assn. of N.Y.C.; editl. mini-adv. bd. Trusts & Estates Mag., 1997—; lectr. Bank Mktg. Assn. Conf., 1995, 99; mem. Estate Planning Coun. Westchester County (N.Y.), 1975—, bd. dirs., 1980-85, treas. 1986-87, v.p., 1988-89, pres. 1989; mem. Estate Planning Coun. Rockland County (N.Y.), 1973—, pres., 1984-85; mem. Estate Planning Coun. N.Y.C., 1983—, bd. dirs., 1988-91, 97—; lectr. estate adminstrn. Trust Div., N.Y. State Bankers Assn., 1975, 90, 93, 96, mem. estate planning com., 1980-83, mem. mktg. com., 1984—, chmn. 1989-94. Mem. Planned Giving Coun., U. Pitts.; mem. planned giving com. N.Y. chpt. Arthritis Found. Mem. Phi Kappa Tau. Office: Chase Manhattan Pvt Bank 1211 Avenue Of The Americas New York NY 10036-8701

DONALDSON, JAMES OSWELL, III, neurology educator; b. Butler, Pa., July 19, 1942; s. James Oswell Jr. and Estelle Mathilda (Unverzagt) D.; m. Mary Hoopingarner, Aug. 23, 1969 (div. Dec. 1983); 1 child, Andrew Robert; m. Susan McKernin, Nov. 3, 1984; stepchildren: Brendan McDonald, Ian McDonald. BS, Haverford Coll., 1964; MD, U. Pa., 1968. Diplomate Am. Bd. Psychiatry and Neurology, Am. Bd. Internal Medicine. Intern in medicine Hosp. of U. Pa., Phila., 1968-69, resident, 1969-70, resident in neurology, 1974-76; hon. house physician Nat. Hosp. for Nervous Diseases, London, 1973-74, sr. vis. fellow, 1991; asst. prof. neurology U. Conn. Sch. Medicine, Farmington, 1977-82, assoc. prof., 1982-88, prof., 1988—. Author: Neurology of Pregnancy, 1978, 2nd edit., 1989. Maj. M.C., U.S. Army, 1970-73. Fellow ACP, Am. Acad. Neurology; mem. Am. Neurol. Assn. Office: U Conn Health Ctr 263 Farmington Ave Farmington CT 06030-0002

DONALDSON, JOHN CECIL, JR., consumer products company executive; b. Bklyn., Dec. 8, 1933; s. John Cecil and Josephine (Greason) D.; m. Marilyn J. Smith, Aug. 29, 1959; children: Susan, John III. AB, Brown U., 1956; MBA, U. Pa., 1959; postgrad., Bentley Sch. Acctg., 1957, LaSalle Law Sch., 1959. Various positions Gen. Motors Corp., Flint, Mich., 1960-71;

zone mgr. Gen. Motors Corp., Buffalo, 1971-76; zone mgr. Gen. Motors Corp., Newark, 1976-77, mgr. forward product planning, 1977-78; from dir. sales and mktg. to v.p. Corbin Ltd., 1979-85; exec. v.p. and gen. mgr. TMG Corp., N.Y.C., 1986—; pres. Gen. Motors Exec. Club, Newark, N.J., 1977-78. Mem. Am. Mktg. Assn. Republican. Avocations: ice skating, tennis, golf. Address: 806 Shoot Flying Hill Rd Centerville MA 02632

DONALDSON, MARCIA JEAN, lay worker; b. Wilmington, Del., June 20, 1925; C. Aubrey Smith and Marcia Allen (Hall) Whitman; m. Robert Donald Donaldson, Jan. 8, 1944; children: Robert Gary, Pamela Lynn, David Keith. Student pub. schs., Wilmington. Sunday Sch. tchr. Del., N.J., 1943-70; tchr. Child Evangelism Fellowship, Wilmington, 1943-55; tchr., bd. dirs. Child Evangelism Fellowship, N.J., 1955-64; dir. Child Evangelism Fellowship, Ocean County, N.J., 1964-73; pres., exec. dir. Christian Children's Assocs., Toms River, N.J., 1973—. Writer radio and TV syndicated programs worldwide for children; producer, hostess radio and TV program Adventure Pals. Mem. Nat. Religious Broadcasters Assn., Gideons Aux. Office: PO Box 446 Toms River NJ 08754-0446 *Of all the important achievements one can accomplish in this life I believe the most rewarding is to be able to introduce another person to the one true and living God, who alone can give us real joy and hope and peace.*

DONALDSON, PENNY L., library director; b. Dodge City, Kans., Feb. 9, 1944; d. Harley Philip and Eunice Maxine Gover; m. Ervin George Donaldson, June 12, 1965; children: Pamela Johnston, Bruce, Jyrel, Arlee. BS, U. Kans., 1967; MLS, Emporia State U., 1993. Mem. interlibr. loan staff U. Kans. Librs., Lawrence, 1986-94, interlibr. loan libr., 1994-96; dir. Atchison (Kans.) Libr., 1996—. Bd. dirs. Kans. Interlibr. Loan Coun., 1994-96. Mem. DAR, AAUW, Bus. and Profl. Women (corr. sec. 1997—), Kans. Libr. Assn., Magna Charta Dames, Rotary (newsletter editor 1996—), Atchison C. of C. (quality coun. 1996—, amb. 1996—). Republican. Presbyterian. Avocations: knitting, crocheting, sewing. Home: 622 N 4th Atchison KS 66002 Office: Atchison Libr 401 Kansas Ave Atchison KS 66002

DONALDSON, PETER SAMUEL, humanities educator; b. N.Y.C., Nov. 21, 1942; s. John J. and Constance (Stalberg) D.; m. Alice Kaplan, Aug. 1965; children: J. Caleb, Ethan, Emily. BA, Columbia U., 1964, PhD, 1973; BA, Cambridge (Eng.) U., 1966. Preceptor in English, Columbia U., N.Y.C., 1967-69; instr. lit. MIT, Cambridge, 1969-73, asst. prof., 1973-78, assoc. prof., 1978-88, prof., 1988-93, Ann Fetter Friedlaender prof. humanities, 1993—, head lit. faculty, 1990—, dir. Shakespeare electronic archive, 1992—. Author: Machiavelli and Mystery of State, 1988, Shakespearean Films/Shakespearean Directors, 1990; editor, translator: A Machiavellian Treatise, 1976. Columbia U. Euretia J. Kellett fellow Clare Coll., Cambridge, Eng., 1964-66, fellow NEH, 19731 Am. Coun. Learned Socs., 1973; grantee NEH, 1992—, Mellon Found., 1995—. Fellow Royal Hist. Soc. (U.K.); mem. MLA, Shakespeare Assn. Am., Internat. Shakespeare Assn. Democrat. Avocation: photography. Home: 40 Rindge Ave Cambridge MA 02140-1914 Office: MIT 77 Massachusetts Ave Cambridge MA 02139-4307

DONALDSON, REBECCA S., elementary education educator, reading specialist; b. Price, Utah, Feb. 8, 1955; d. Joseph Fazzio and Martha Beatrice Cook; m. Brady Evan Donaldson, Jan. 14, 1978; children: Megan, Brady Christopher, Alyssa Nichole. BS, Brigham Young U., 1977; MEd, Utah State U., 1993. Cert. elem. tchr., Utah, reading endorsement. Educator Carbon Sch. Dist., Price, 1979-96; reading specialist S.E. Edn. Svc. Ctr., Price, 1996—; state sec. Utah Coun. Internat. Reading Assn., Salt Lake City, 1996—. Co-author: Understanding Nonfiction, 1999. Mem. ASCD, Internat. Reading Assn., Nat. Coun. Tchrs. English, Assn. Edn. Young Children. Avocations: reading, writing, baking, gardening, home decorating, music. E-mail: rebecca@m.sesc.kiz.ut.us. Office: SE Edn Svc 685 E 200 S Price UT 84501

DONALDSON, ROBERT FROST, minister; b. Charlevoix, Mich., May 29, 1945; s. Howard Earl and Lois Marie (Frost) D.; m. Suzanne Alzina Trowbridge, Dec. 22, 1973 (div. Nov. 1986); children: Samantha, Roberta; m. Karen Mae Hoisington, Feb. 14, 1987; children: Cathy, David, Laura. DDiv, Universal Life Ch., 1994, PhD in Religion, 1995; BS in Pastoral Counseling, Am. Internat. U., 1996. Ordained minister Am. Fellowship, 1988, Ministers for Christ Assembly of Churches, 1994. Owner East Jordan Zephyr Svc., 1965-67; mechanic, assembler East Jordan (Mich.) Iron Works, Inc., 1967—; owner Donaldson Machine Shop, Ellsworth, Mich., 1975-90; pastor, counselor Discovery Ministries, East Jordan, 1988—. Sec. South Arm Twp. Planning and Zoning Bd., East Jordan, 1986-89; candidate for sch. bd. Ellsworth Schs., 1984; mem. arts couns. East Jordan, Petoskey, Traverse City and Cadillac, Mich. Mem. UUCOP (founder, sec. 1993-97). Avocations: protection of children, wellness in the workplace. Home: 701 Division St East Jordan MI 49727-9747

DONALDSON, ROBERT MACARTNEY, JR., physician; b. Hubbardston, Mass., Aug. 1, 1927; s. Robert Macartney and Helen Mildred (Morrow) D.; m. Priscilla Hurd, Sept. 1, 1950; children: Robert M., John H.; m. Phyllis Bodel, Jan. 14, 1974; m. Ellen Garvey, Jan. 5, 1986. B.S., Yale U., 1949; M.D., Boston U., 1952. Diplomate Am. Bd. Internal Medicine (bd. govs. 1984-90). Intern Montreal (Que., Can.) Gen. Hosp., 1952-53; resident Boston VA Hosp., 1955-57; fellow in gastroenterology Peter Bent Brigham Hosp., Boston, 1957-59; instr. Harvard U. Med. Sch., 1957-59; asst. prof. medicine Boston U., Med. Sch., 1959-64, prof., chief gastroenterology, 1967-73; assoc. prof. U. Wis. Med. Sch., 1964-67; prof. medicine, dept. internal medicine Yale U. Med. Sch., 1973-97, dep. dean, 1987-91; acting dean, 1991-92; chmn. adv. bd. Nat. Center Ulcer Research and Edn., 1975-88; chmn. adv. tng. grant com. NIH, 1967-73; chmn. adv. research com. VA, 1968-71. Editor: Jour. Gastroenterology, 1970-77; contbr. chpts. med. textbooks. Served with USNR, 1953-55. Recipient Clin. Investigator award VA, 1959-64; spl. fellow NIH, 1957-59; named Disting. VA Physician, 1995-97. Master ACP; mem. Am. Gastroenterol. Assn. (pres. 1979-80), Am. Fedn. Clin. Research, Am. Soc. Clin. Investigation, Assn. Am. Physicians. Office: Yale U Sch Medicine 333 Cedar St New Haven CT 06510-3206*

DONALDSON, ROGER, film director; b. Ballarat, Australia, Nov. 15, 1945. Dir. (films): Sleeping Dogs, 1977, Smash Palace, 1981, The Bounty, 1984, Marie, 1985, No Way Out, 1987, Cocktail, 1988, Cadillac Man, 1990, White Sands, 1992, The Getaway, 1993, Species, 1996, ((TV) Winners and Losers. Office: Creative Artists Agency 9830 Wilshire Blvd Beverly Hills CA 90212-1825*

DONALDSON, SAMUEL ANDREW, journalist; b. El Paso, Tex., Mar. 11, 1934; s. Samuel Andrew and Chloe (Hampson) D.; m. Billie Kay Butler, Nov. 30, 1963; children: Samuel, Jennifer, Thomas, Robert; m. Janice Claire Smith, Apr. 16, 1983. BA, U. Tex., El Paso, 1955; postgrad., U. So. Calif., 1955-56. Radio/TV news reporter/anchorman WTOP, Washington, 1961-67; Capitol Hill corr. ABC News, Washington, 1967-77; White House corr. ABC News, 1977-89; panelist This Week With David Brinkley, 1981-96; coanchor This Week With Sam Donaldson and Cokie Roberts, 1996-98, Prime Time Live, ABC, 1989-98; chief White House corr. ABC News, 1998—; coanchor 20/20 ABC, 1998—. Author: Hold On Mr. President, 1987. Served to capt. AUS, 1956-59. Recipient Broadcaster of Yr. award Nat. Press Found., 1998; named Best Television White House Corr. in Bus., The Washington Journalism Rev., 1985, Best Television Corr. in Bus., 1986, 87, 88, 89; recipient three Emmy awards, George Foster Peabody award, others. Mem. AFTRA (past pres. Washington-Balt. chpt.). Office: 20/20 ABC 1717 Desales St NW Washington DC 20036-4401*

DONALDSON, SARAH SUSAN, radiologist; b. Portland, Oreg., 1939. BS, RN, U. Oreg., 1961; MD, Harvard U., 1968. Intern U. Wash., 1968-69; resident in radiol. therapy Stanford (Calif.) Med. Ctr., 1969-72; fellow in pediatric oncology Inst. Gustave-Roussy, 1972-73; prof. radiol. oncology Stanford U. Sch. Medicine., 1973—. Office: Stanford U Med Ctr Dept Radio/Oncology 300 Pasteur Dr Palo Alto CA 94304-2203

DONALDSON, SCOTT, English language educator, writer; b. Mpls., Nov. 11, 1928; s. Frank Arthur and Ruth Evelyn (Chase) D.; m. Janet Kay Mikelson, Apr. 12, 1957 (div.); children—Matthew Chase, Stephen Scott, Andrew Wilson; m. Vivian Lee Baker, Mar. 5, 1982; stepchildren—Janet Breckenridge, Britton Donaldson. BA in English, Yale U., 1951; MA in English, U. Minn., 1952, PhD in Am. Studies, 1966. Reporter Mpls. Star, 1956-58; editor, pub. Bloomington Sun, Minn., 1958-61; exec. editor Sun Newspapers, Twin City suburbs, Minn., 1961-64; asst. prof. English Coll. William and Mary, Williamsburg, Va., 1966-69, assoc. prof., 1969-74, prof., 1974—, Louise G.T. Cooley prof. English, 1984-92. Author: The Suburban Myth, 1969, Poet in America: Winfield Townley Scott, 1972, By Force of Will: The Life and Art of Ernest Hemingway, 1977, (with Ann Massa) American Literature: Nineteenth and Early Twentieth Centuries, 1978, Fool for Love, F. Scott Fitzgerald, 1983, John Cheever: A Biography, 1988, Archibald MacLeish: An American Life, 1992 (Ambassador Book award); editor: On the Road, 1979, Critical Essays on F. Scott Fitzgerald's The Great Gatsby, 1984, Conversations with John Cheever, 1987, New Essays on a Farewell to Arms, 1990, Cambridge Companion to Hemingway, 1996; also numerous revs. and articles on Am. lit. and Am. culture. Served with U.S. Army, 1953-56. Recipient Mid Am. award Soc. for Study of Midwestern Lit., 1996; Fulbright Sr. lectureship, 1970-71, 79-80; fellow Bruern Found., 1972-73, MacDowell Colony, 1980-81, Rockefeller Found., 1982, NEH, 1984-85, 90—. Mem. MLA, Am. Studies Assn., Fulbright Alumni Assn. (bd. dirs. 1977-80), Authors Guild, Hemingway Soc., PEN, Nat. Book Critics Cir., Mpls. Club, Minikahda Club (Mpls.), Cosmos Club (Washington), Phi Beta Kappa. Avocations: tennis, golf, duplicate bridge. Home and Office: Desert Highlands 303 10040 E Happy Valley Rd Scottsdale AZ 85255-2395

DONALDSON, STEPHEN REEDER, author; b. Cleve., May 13, 1947; s. James R. and Mary Ruth (Reeder) D. BA, Coll. of Wooster, 1968; MA, Kent State U., 1971; LittD (hon.), Coll. of Wooster, 1993. Asst. dispatcher Akron City Hosp., 1968-70; tchg. fellow Kent State U., 1971; acquisitions editor Tapp-Gentz Assos., West Chester, Pa., 1973-74; instr. Ghost Ranch Writers Workshops, N.Mex., 1973-77. Author: Lord Foul's Bane, 1977, The Illearth War, 1977, The Power That Preserves, 1977, The Wounded Land, 1980, The One Tree, 1982, White Gold Wielder, 1983, Daughter of Regals, 1984, The Mirror of Her Dreams, 1986, A Man Rides Through, 1987, The Real Story, 1991, Forbidden Knowledge, 1991, A Dark and Hungry God Arises, 1992, Chaos and Order, 1994, This Day All Gods Die, 1996, Reave The Just, 1999, (as Reed Stephens) The Man Who Killed His Brother, 1980, The Man Who Risked His Partner, 1984, The Man Who Tried to Get Away, 1990; editor: Strange Dreams, 1993. Recipient John W. Campbell award best new writer World Sci. Fiction Conv., 1979, Best Novel award Brit. Fantasy Soc., 1979, Balrog award for best novel, 1981, 83, for best collection, 1985, Saturn award for best fantasy novel, 1983, Book ofYr. award Sci. Fiction Book Club, 1987, 88. Mem. Am. Contract Bridge League, Internat. Assn. for the Fantastic in the Arts, Anshin Budo Kai, SSLF Dojo. Club: Duke City Bridge. Office: care Howard Morhaim Rm 604 841 Broadway New York NY 10003-4704

DONALDSON, SUE KAREN, dean, nursing educator; b. Detroit, Sept. 16, 1943. BSN, Wayne State U., 1965, MSN, 1966; PhD, U. Wash., 1973. Asst. assoc. prof. physiology and nursing U. Wash., Seattle, 1973-78; assoc. prof. physiology and nursing Rush U., Ill., 1978-84, dir. clin. nursing rsch. program, 1980-84; former assoc. dean rsch. Sch. Nursing, U. Minn., Mpls.; now dean Sch. Nursing, Johns Hopkins U., Balt., 1994—. Grantee Wash. State Heart Assn., 1973-74, NIH, 1973—, USPHS, 1980—, Muscular Dystrophy Assn., 1981—. Mem. ANA, NAS, Am. Heart Assn., Coun. Nurse Rschrs. Office: Johns Hopkins U Sch Nursing 525 N Wolfe St Baltimore MD 21205*

DONALDSON, WILLIAM FIELDING, JR., orthopedic surgeon; b. May 12, 1921; s. William Fielding and Isabel (McGranahan) D.; m. Jean Marguerite Waechter, Jan. 21, 1946; children—Susan, Anne, William Fielding, Nancy. BS, U. Pitts., 1942, MD, 1943. Diplomate Am. Bd. Orthopedic Surgery. Intern St. Francis Gen. Hosp., Pitts., 1944; resident orthopaedic surgery VA Hosp., Aspinwall, Pa., 1946-49, Children's Hosp., Pitts., 1949-50; Gibney fellow in scoliosis Hosp. Spl. Surgery, N.Y.C., 1952-53; sr. staff mem. emeritus Presbyn.-Univ. Hosp., Pitts., 1951—; sr. staff mem., med. dir. Children's Hosp. Pitts., 1951-93, emeritus, 1994, bd. trustees, 1981—; sr. staff mem. emeritus St. Margaret Meml. Hosp., Pitts., 1964-70; attending cons. VA Hosp., Pitts., 1970—; mem. courtesy staff St. Francis Gen. Hosp., 1961-86, mem. emeritus staff, 1990; mem. courtesy staff Shadyside Hosp., 1961—; practice medicine specializing in orthopedic surgery Pitts.; prof. emeritus; clin. instr. U. Pitts., 1951-58, asst. prof., 1958-62, clin. assoc. prof., 1962-67, clin. prof., 1967—, bd. trustees, 1981-87, trustee emeritus, 1989—; mem. Coordinating Council Med. Edn., 1978-80; cons. grad. med. edn. Nat. Adv. Com. to Sec. HEW, 1975-80; pres. Adv. Council for Orthopedic Resident Edn.; mem. Nat. Commn. on Arthritis and Related Musculoskeletal Diseases, 1975-77; orthopaedic adv. bd. chmn. Shriners Hosp. Crippled Children, 1981-93, chmn. emeritus 1993—; mem. adv. com. Allegheny County chpt. Nat. Found. Mar. of Dimes, 1968; mem. search com. for dir. Allegheny County health Dept., 1969; mem. health adv. council Community Action Pitts., 1965; bd. dirs. Western Pa. Comprehensive Health Planning Agy., 1960-77; 2d vice chmn. Hosp. Council Western Pa., 1974-77; bd. dirs. Hosp. Utilization Project, 1970, many others. Contbr. articles to profl. jours. Served with USN, 1944-46. Recipient Frederick M. Jacob Physician's Merit award Allegheny County Med. Soc., 1976, Man of Yr. award Pitts. Acad. Medicine, 1977. Mem. ABA (com. on med. profl. liability 1976-80), Council Med. Splty. Socs. (rep. of ACS), Am. Acad. Orthopedic Surgeons (dir. 1970-79, pres. 1975-76), ACS (bd. regents 1976-85, v.p.-elect, v.p. 1986-87), AMA, Am. Orthopedic Assn., Am. Rheumatism Assn., Pan Pacific Surg. Assn. (v.p. 1975), Rocky Mountain Traumatologic Soc. (pres. 1986), Pa. Med. Soc. (ho. of dels. 1964-70, pres. 1987-88), Pa. Orthopedic Soc. (pres. 1961-62), Allegheny County Med. Soc. (pres. 1970), Am. Assn. Surgery of Trauma, Assn. Bone and Joint Surgeons (hon.), Can. Orthopedic Assn., Central Surg. Assn., New Eng. Orthopedic Soc., N.Y. Acad. Sci., Pediatric Soc., Scoliosis Research Soc., Soc. Research in Hydrocephalus and Spina Bifida, S.C. Orthopedic Soc. (hon.), Pitts. Acad. Medicine, Pitts. Pediatric Soc., Pitts. Surg. Soc., Pitts. Rheumatism Assn. Republican. Presbyterian. Office: Childrens Hosp Pitts 3705 5th Ave Pittsburgh PA 15213-2524

DONALDSON, WILLIAM HENRY, financial executive; b. Buffalo, June 2, 1931; s. Eames and Guida (Marx) D.; m. Sept. 17, 1960; children: Adam, Kimberly, Matthew. BA, Yale U., 1953, MA (hon.), 1970; MBA with distinction, Harvard U., 1958; LLD (hon.), Webster U., 1992; DPhil (hon.), St. Lawrence U., 1995; DHL (hon.), Alfred U., 1995. Chmn., chief exec. Donaldson, Lufkin & Jenrette, Inc., N.Y.C., 1959-73; undersec. of state U.S. Dept. State, Washington, 1973-74; spl. cons. to v.p. of U.S. Washington, 1974; dean, Beinecke prof. mgmt. Yale Grad. Mgmt. Sch., New Haven, 1975-80; chmn., CEO Donaldson Enterprises, Inc., N.Y.C., 1980-90; chmn., chief exec. N.Y. Stock Exch., N.Y.C., 1990-95; founder, sr. advisor Donaldson, Lufkin and Jenrette, Inc., 1996—; bd. dirs. Aetna Life & Casualty, Honeywell Inc., Philip Morris Cos. Inc., Bright Horizons Family Solutions, Inc. Trustee, chmn. fin. com. Ford Found., N.Y.C., 1968-80; trustee Yale U., New Haven, 1970-75; ptnr. N.Y.C. Partnership; bd. dirs. Bus. Coun. of State of N.Y., 1990-96, Lincoln Ctr. for Performing Arts, N.Y.C.; trustee N.Y. Police Found., Marine Corps Univ. Found., Aspen Inst.; gov. Fgn. Policy Assn.; chmn. Carnegie Endowment for Internat. Peace, 1999—, Carnegie Endowment for Internat. Peace. 1st lt. USMC, 1953-55. Recipient Pres.'s Disting. Svc. award SUNY, 1976; named Businessman of Yr., AP, 1969. Mem. Inst. CFAs, Yale Mgmt. Sch. (chmn. bd. advisors 1995—), Coun. on Fgn. Rels., Aspen Inst. (trustee). Office: Donaldson Lufkin & Jenrette Inc 277 Park Ave New York NY 10017-2016

DONALDSON, WILLIAM L., retired newspaper publishing company executive; b. Yankton, S.D., Apr. 16, 1932; m. Beverly Buhn, May 31, 1958; children: Mary Jo Donaldson Langstraat, Will, John (dec.). BSBA, U. S.D., 1958. Printer, advt. mgr. Vermillion (S.D.) Plain Talk, 1955-58; advt. account exec. Sioux Falls (S.D.) Argus Leader, 1958-60; nat. advt. account exec. Omaha World-Herald Co., 1960-62, pers. mgr., 1963-72, mgr. employee rels., 1972-81, dir. curculation, 1981-87, v.p. sales, 1987-94, sr. v.p., gen. mgr., 1994-96, corp. sec., 1980-95, also bd. dirs. Vice chmn. Allen H. Neuharth Adv. Com., 1987—. With U.S. Army, 1952-54, Korea. Mem. Omaha Fedn. Advt. (Silver Medal Life Time Achievement award 1994), Rotary. Office: Omaha World-Herald Co World-Herald Sq Omaha NE 68102

DONALDSON, WILLIS LYLE, research institute administrator; b. Cleburne, Tex., May 1, 1915; s. Charles Lyle and Anna (Bell) D.; m. Frances Virginia Donnell, Aug. 20, 1938; children: Sarah Donaldson Seaberg, Susan Donaldson Pollock, Sylvia Donaldson Nelson, Anthony Lyle. B.S., Tex. Tech. U., 1938. Registered profl. engr., Pa., Tex. Distbn. engr. Tex. Electric Service Co., 1938-42, supervisory engr., 1945-46; asst. prof. elec. engring. Lehigh U., 1946-51, assoc. prof., 1953-54; with S.W. Research Inst., San Antonio, 1954—; v.p. S.W. Research Inst., 1964-72, v.p. planning and program devel., 1972-74, sr. v.p. planning and program devel., 1974-85, sr. cons., 1985—. Bd. dirs. San Antonio Chamber Music Soc., pres., 1962-72, 87-93, mem., 1954—. Capt. USNR, 1942-45, 51-53. Named Disting. Engr. Tex. Tech. U., 1969. Fellow IEEE, Am. Soc. Nondestructive Testing; mem. Armed Forces Communications and Electronics Assn. (disting. life), Sigma Xi, Tau Beta Pi, Eta Kappa Nu, Alpha Chi. Home: 104 Pontiac Ln San Antonio TX 78232-3507 Office: 6220 Culebra Rd San Antonio TX 78238-5166

DONALDSON, WILMA CRANKSHAW, elementary education educator; b. Havre de Grace, Md., Aug. 28, 1942; d. John Hamilton and Wilma Chaffee (Thurlow) Crankshaw; m. James Neill Donaldson, Aug. 5, 1967. BA in Edn. cum laude, Westminster Coll., 1964; MA in Edn., Fairfield U., 1976. Educator Hurlbutt Elem. Sch., Weston, Conn., 1964-78, 92—, Weston Mid. Sch., 1979-91; team leader Hurlbutt Elem. Sch., 1967-68, 76-78, sci. rep., 1992—; judge Odyssey of the Mind, Conn., 1995—; presenter to various tchrs. orgns.; developer of curriculum Hurlbutt Elem. Sch. Author: (filmstrip script) Science Series, 1972, Metric Math Series, 1973. Chairperson fine arts New England Sch. Accreditation Com., Weston, 1990-91; trainer Project CHEM, Exxon Corp., 1991—; state planning com. and chair site/workshop com. Conn. Elem. Sci. Day Conf., 1994—. Recipient Faculty Mem. Presdl. Recognition Sch. award U.S. Dept. Edn., 1987-88, Celebration of Excellence award State of Conn., 1989, 92, 95, 98. Mem. NEA, Nat. Sci. Tchrs. Assn. (workshop presentor Moscow 1991, NASA-NEWEST awardee 1997), ASCD, Conn. Edn. Assn., Conn. Alliance Arts Edn. (Weston Tchr. of Yr. 1994-95, Conn. Alliance of the Arts Disting. Tchr. of Yr. 1995), Coun. Elem. Sci. Internat. (com. chmn. 1991—), Delta Zeta. Avocations: art, theater, photography, travel.

DONATELLI, DANIEL DOMINIC, JR., medical/surgical and oncological nurse; b. Youngstown, Ohio, May 29, 1958; s. Daniel D. Sr. and Nerina J. Donatelli; m. Deborah I. Pihonsky, May 17, 1986; children: Danamarie, Danielle, Deborah. BS in Zoology and Biology, Ohio U., 1981; BSN, Kent (Ohio) State U., 1986; MBA, Youngstown State U., 1999. RN, Ohio; cert. med./surg. nurse, clin. nurse II, oncology nurse. Resident dir. Bromly Corp., Athens, Ohio; asst. mgr. Tel Star Restaurant, Youngstown, 1991-96; asst. clin. nurse mgr. oncology unit Western Res. Care System, Youngstown, Ohio, 1996—, nurse clinician dept. quality mgmt. Vol. Athens Mental Health Ctr., 1977-81. Named Nurse of Hope for Mahoning County, Am. Cancer Soc., 1992-94. Mem. ANA, Ohio Nurses Assn. (dist. 3), Sigma Theta Tau. Home: 7483 Salinas Trl Boardman OH 44512

DONATH, THERESE, artist, author; b. Hammond, Ind.; student Monticello Coll., 1946-47; BFA, St. Joseph's Coll., 1975; additional study Oxbow Summer Sch. Painting, Immaculate Heart Coll., Hollywood, Calif., Penland, N.C., Haystack, Maine; radio/TV personality, 1978-92. Interviewer, producer Viewpoint, Sta. WLNR-FM, Lansing, Ill., 1963-64; reporter, columnist N.W. Ind. Sentinel, 1965; freelance writer Monterey Peninsula Herald, 1981-85; contbg. author Monterey Life mag. 1981-85; asst. dir. Michael Karolyi Meml. Found., Vence, France, 1979; one-woman shows include: Ill. Inst. Tech., Chgo., 1971; group shows include: Palos Verdes (Calif.) Mus., 1974, L.A. Inst. Contemporary Art, 1978, Mus. Contemporary Art, Chgo., 1975, Calif. State U., Fullerton, 1973, No. Ill. U., DeKalb, 1971, Bellevue (Wash.) Mus. Art, 1986-87; represented in permanent collections including Kennedy Gallery, N.Y.C., also pvt. collections; creative cons. Aslan Tours and Travel, 1983-85; instr., lectr. Penland, N.C., 1970, Haystack Mountain Sch., Deer Isle, Maine, 1974, Sheffield Poly., Eng., 1978. Bd. dirs., sec. Mental Health Soc. Greater Chgo., 1963-64; exec. dir. Lansing (Ill.) Mental Health Soc., 1963-64. Recipient awards No. Ind. Art Mus., 1966, 70, 71, 73; grantee Ragdale Found., Lake Forest, Ill., 1982. Represented in The Mirror Book, 1978; author: Screams and Laughter, 1992; author, illustrator: Before I Die, A Creative Legacy, 1989; contbr. articles to profl. jours., newspapers; illustrator: Run Computer Run, 1983. *I am settling into old age like a thumb in the mouth. Comfort, not conformity, loom like figures on tapestry. I read my life between the lines.*

DONATI, ENRICO, artist; b. Milan, Italy, Feb. 19, 1909; came to U.S., 1934, naturalized, 1945; s. Federico and Marianna (Vita) D.; m. Claire Javal, 1934; children: Marina, Sylviane (Mrs. Claude Mahias); m. Adele Schmidt, 1965; 1 dau., Alexandra. D. Econs. and Social Scis., U. Pavia, Italy, 1929. vis. lectr., critic Yale U., 1960—; mem. jury Fulbright Scholarship Program, 1954-56, 61-64; mem. Yale Coun. Arts and Architecture, 1962-72; mem. adv. bd. Parsons Sch. Design, N.Y.C., 1959; chmn. nat. com. Univ. Art Mus., Berkeley, Calif., 1970-72; adv. bd. regents Brandeis U., 1956-65. Mem. Surrealist group, until 1950; one-man shows include Passedoit Gallery, N.Y.C., 1942, 44, New Sch. Social Rsch., 1943, The Arts Club, Chgo., 1944, G. Place Gallery, Washington, 1944, Durand-Ruel Galleries, N.Y.C., 1945, 46, 47, 49, Galerie Drouant-David, Paris, 1947, Gallery Studio, Chgo., 1947, Krouse Coll., Syracuse (N.Y.) U., 1947, A. Weil, Paris, 1949, Galleria Corso Bittorio Emanuele II, Milan, 1950, Galleria del Milione, Milan, 1950, Paul Rosenberg Gallery, N.Y.C., 1950, Galleria dell'Obelisco, Rome, 1950, Alexandre Iolas Gallery, N.Y.C., 1952, Galleria d'arte del Cavallino, Venice, 1952, 53, Galleria del Naviglio, Milan, 1952, 56, Betty Parsons Gallery, N.Y.C., 1954, 55, 57, 59, 60, Lowe Art Gallery, Syracuse U., 1958, Palais des Beaux-Arts, Brussels, 1961, Neue Galerie im Kunstlerhaus, Munich, 1962, Staempfli Gallery, N.Y.C., 1962, 63, 66, 68, 70, 72, 74, 76, J.L. Hudson Gallery, Detroit, 1964, 66, Hayden Gallery, MIT, Cambridge, 1964, Obelisk Gallery, Washington, 1965, Ankrum Gallery, L.A., 1977, 79, 82, Minn. Mus. Art, St. Paul, 1977, Chrysler Mus., Norfolk, Va., 1977, Fairweather Hardin Gallery, Chgo., 1977, Tenn. Fine Arts Ctr., Nashville, 1977, Davenport Mcpl. Art Gallery, Iowa, 1978, Hunter Mus. Art, Chattanooga, 1978, Wildenstein Art Ctr., Houston, 1978, Norton Gallery Art, West Palm Beach, Fla., 1979, Osuna Gallery, Washington, 1979, Phillips Collection, Washington, 1979, Palm Springs (Calif.) Desert Mus., 1980, Internat. Art Fair, Grand Palais, FIAC, Paris, 1980, Carone Gallery, Ft. Lauderdale, Fla., 1984, 90, 92, 94, Gimpel & Weitzenhoffer Gallery, N.Y.C., 1984, 86, 87, Georges Fall, Paris, 1985, Louis Newman Gallery, Beverly Hills, Calif., 1986, 89, 91, 94, Zabriskie Gallery, N.Y.C., 1987, Galerie Zabriskie, Paris, 1989, Horwitch Newman Gallery, Scottsdale, Ariz., 1995, 96, Maxwell Davidson Gallery, N.Y.C., 1995, 97, Boca Raton (Fla.) Mus. Art, 1997, Alter & Gil, L.A., 1998; represented in permanent collections Albright Knox Art Gallery, Buffalo, N.Y., Balt. Mus. Art, Musees royaux des Beaux-Arts de Belgique, Brussels, U. Art Mus., U. Calif., Berkeley, Detroit Inst. Arts, Doane Coll., Crete, Nebr., Mus Art, Ft. Lauderdale, Solomon R. Guggenheim Mus., N.Y.C., High Mus. Art, Atlanta, Hirshborn Mus. and Sculpture Garden, Smithsonian Instn., Washington, Housatonic C.C., Bridgeport, Conn., Mus Internat. Ctr. Aesthetic Rsch., Turin, Italy, Israel Mus., Jerusalem, Johns-Hopkins Hosp., Balt., Lowe Mus., U. Miami, MIT-Last Visual Art Ctr., Cambridge, U. Mich. Art Gallery, Ann Arbor, Mus Modern Art, N.Y.C., Mus. Fine Arts, Houston, Neuberger Mus. Art, SUNY, Purchase, Newark Mus., Galleria Nazionale d'arte Moderne, Milan, Orlando (Fla.) Mus. Art, Palm Springs Desert Mus., Phila. Mus. Art, Rockefeller U., N.Y.C., Galleria Nazionale d'arte Moderne, Rome, Mus. Fine Arts, St. Petersburg, Fla., Oklahoma City Art Mus., Arturo Schwarz Surrealist Found., Milan, Seattle Art Mus., Swarthmore (Pa.) Coll. Art Collection, Tacoma Art Mus., U. Tex. Austin, Archer M. Huntington Art Gallery, Tougaloo (Miss.) Coll., Vassar Coll., Poughkeepsie, N.Y., Washington U. Gallery Art, St. Louis, Whitney Mu. Am. Art, N.Y.C., Yale U. Art Gallery, New Haven, Conn., also collections numerous bus. corps., pvt. collections. Lt. Italian Mountain Troops. Decorated cavaliere Della Corona D'Italia. Mem. New Canaan Country Club (Conn.), Bohemian Club (San Francisco). Studio: 222 Central Park S New York NY 10019-1408 Address: Zabriskie Gallery 724 5th Ave New York NY 10019-4106 also: Max Davidson Gallery 41 E 57th St New York NY 10022-1908 also: 622 Barrington Ave Ste 107 Los Angeles CA 90049

DONATI, ROBERT MARIO, physician, educational administrator; b. Richmond Heights, Mo., Feb. 28, 1934; s. Leo S. and Rose Marie (Gualdoni) D. BS in Biology, St. Louis U., 1955, MD, 1959. Diplomate

Am. Bd. Nuclear Medicine. Intern St. Louis City Hosp., 1959-60; asst. resident John Cochran Hosp., St. Louis, 1960-62; fellow in nuclear medicine St. Louis U., 1962-63; pvt. practice specializing in nuclear medicine St. Louis, 1963-93; mem. staff St. Louis VA Med. Ctr., 1963-83, chief nuclear medicine svc., 1968-79, chief of staff, 1979-83; mem. staff St. Louis U. Hosps., 1963-93, interim chief exec. officer, 1987-88; mem. staff St. Mary's Health Ctr., 1984-93; mem. faculty Sch. Medicine St. Louis U., 1963—, asst. prof. internal medicine, 1965-68, assoc. prof., 1968-74, prof., 1974-93, prof. emeritus internal medicine, 1993—, prof. radiology, 1979-93, prof. emeritus radiology, 1993—, dir. div. nuclear medicine Sch. Medicine, 1968-87, sr. assoc. dean Sch. Medicine, 1983-93; exec. assoc. v.p. Med. Ctr., 1985-93, acting v.p., 1986; adj. prof. medicine Washington U. Sch. Medicine, 1979-83; rschr. in clin. investigative nuclear medicine and humoral control of cellular proliferation; fin. com. del. Am. Bd. Med. Spltys., 1984-90. Editor: (with W.T. Newton) Radioassay in Clinical Medicine, 1973, (with J. Edwards) Current Medical Practice, 1992; contbr. articles to profl. jours. Mem. Presdl. Adv. Commn. on VA, 1972, Inst. Medicine com. to estimate VA physician needs, 1988-90; bd. dirs. Alliance for Cmty. Health, Inc., 1986-96, Ind. Colls. and Univs. of Mo., 1985, Affiliated Med. Transport, Inc., 1985-89, Healthline Mgmt. Svcs., Inc., 1986-94, chmn., 1988-93, Healthline Corp. Health Metro St. Louis, 1992-94, Ctrl. Med. Ctr., Inc., 1988-89, Healthlink, Inc., 1987-93, Abbott Ambulance Co., Inc., 1989-94, chmn., 1992-94; mem. HEW Task Force on Health Effects Ionizing Radiation, 1978-79; mem. desegregation monitoring and adv. com. U.S. Dist. Ct., 1980. Decorated Army Commendation medal; recipient VA Disting. Service award, 1983, alumni Merit award St. Louis U., 1996. Mem. AMA (residency rev. com. for nuclear medicine 1978-80, coun. on med. schs. 1984-94), AAUP, Am. Bd. Nuclear Medicine (life, bd. dirs. 1980—, vice chmn. 1984-85, chmn. 1985-86), St. Louis Med. Soc., Am. Fedn. for Clin. Rsch. (councilor 1967-70), Ctrl. Soc. Clin. Rsch., N.Y. Acad. Scis., Soc. Exptl. Biology and Medicine, Soc. Nuclear Medicine (acad. coun. 1970—, trustee 1977-81, 90-92, assoc. chmn. sci. program 1978, mem. publs. com. 1979-83, chmn. 1982-83, mem. bus. advisors com. 1989-93, chmn. 1990-92), Am. Coll. Nuclear Physicians, Internat. Socs. Hematology, Soc. Med. Cons. to Armed Forces, Cosmos Club, Phi Beta Kappa, Sigma Xi, Alpha Omega Alpha. Roman Catholic. Home: 5335 Botanical Ave Saint Louis MO 63110-3123 Office: St Louis U Sch Medicine 1402 S Grand Blvd Saint Louis MO 63104-1004

DONDANVILLE, JOHN WALLACE, lawyer; b. Moline, Ill., Nov. 29, 1937; s. Laurence A. and Eva C. (Ender) D.; m. Maureen C. Ryan, Apr. 16, 1966; children: Edward John, Julie Ann. AB in History, Holy Cross Coll., 1959; JD, Northwestern U., 1962. Bar: Ill. 1962. Ptnr. Baker & McKenzie, Chgo., 1965-97; ret., 1997; pres., mem. B&D Devel. LLC. Author: Product Liability Trends & Implications, 1970. Bd. advisors Marillac House, Chgo., 1986—. Mem. ABA, Ill. Bar Assn., Chgo. Bar Assn., Am. Mgmt. Assn. (mem. ins. and risk mgmt. coun.). Avocation: hiking.

DONDER, PAULINE VERONICA, legal secretary; b. Torrington, Conn., Apr. 2, 1951; d. Charles Hansen and Veronica Donder Pavek; m. Manuel Angel Guillen, July 17, 1976 (div. 1996); children: Veronica, Juliana. Grad., Wykeham Rise, Washington, Conn., 1969; student, Ithaca Coll., 1969-70, Denver U., 1970-71. With Vagabond Ranch, Granby, Colo., 1951-74. Author: Crisis Paper for Colorado Parents, 1993; co-author: Youth on the Edge, 1994. Mem. juvenile justice subcom. Safe City Summit, Denver, 1994, Homeless and Runaway Youth Adv. Group, Denver, 1994, homeless youth subcom. Colo. Children's Code Recodification, 1995, Denver SafeNite Curfew Adv. Group, 1995-99; mentor Denver Kids, Inc., 1996-99; vol. reader Colo. Ctr. for the Book, 1997; choral reading tchr. Denver Summer Scholars, 1997. Avocation: open adoption. Home: 4180 Wolff St Denver CO 80212-2228 Office: Kutak Rock 717 17th St Ste 2900 Denver CO 80202-3329

DONE, ROBERT STACY, consultant; b. Tucson, Apr. 7, 1965; s. Richard Avon Done and Nancy Jane (Meeks) Burks; m. Michele Renae Barwick, May 17, 1987 (div. Mar. 1990); m. Elizabeth Evans Robinson, Feb. 20, 1993; children: Rachel Evans, Ethan James. AS in Law Enforcement, Mo. So. State Coll., 1987, BS in Criminal Justice Adminstrn., 1987; MPA, U. Ariz., 1992, MS in Mgmt., 1998. Criminal investigator Pima County, Tucson, 1988-99; pres. Data Methods Corp., Tucson, 1984—. Contbr. articles to profl. jours. Mem. Am. Evaluation Assn., Acad. Mgmt. Home: PO Box 64967 Tucson AZ 85728-4967

DONEGAN, CHARLES EDWARD, lawyer, educator; b. Chgo., Apr. 10, 1933; s. Arthur C. and Odessa (Arnold) D.; m. Patty Lou Harris, June 15, 1963; 1 son, Carter Edward. B.S.C., Roosevelt U., 1954; M.S., Loyola U., 1959; J.D., Howard U., 1967; LL.M., Columbia, 1970. Bar: N.Y. 1968, D.C. 1968, Ill. 1979. Pub. sch. tchr. Chgo., 1956-59; with Office Internal Revenue, Chgo., 1959-62; labor economist U.S. Dept. Labor, Washington, 1962-65; legal intern U.S. Commn. Civil Rights, Washington, summer 1966; asst. counsel NAACP Legal Def. Fund, N.Y.C., 1967-69; lectr. law Baruch Coll., N.Y.C., 1969-70; asst. prof. law State U. N.Y. at Buffalo, 1970-73; assoc. prof. law Howard U., 1973-77; vis. assoc. prof. Ohio State U., Columbus, 1977-78; asst. regional counsel U.S. EPA, 1978-80; prof. law So. U., Baton Rouge, 1980—; sole practice law Chgo. and Washington, 1984—; arbitrator steel industry, 1972, U.S. Postal Svc., New Orleans, D.C. Superior Ct., 1987—, Fed. Mediation and Conciliation Svc., 1985—, N.Y. Stock Exch.; vis. prof. law La. State U., summer 1981, N.C. Cen. U., Durham, 1988—, So. U., Baton Rouge, spring 1992; real estate broker; mem. bd. consumer claims Dist. D.C., 1988—; mem. Mayor's Transition Task Force, Washington, 1995; moot ct. judge Georgetown U. Law Sch., Washington, 1987—, Howard U. Law Sch., Washington, 1987—, Balsa, 1987—; spkr., participant nat. confs. on law, edn. and labor rels. Author: Discrimination in Public Employment, 1975; Contbr. articles to profl. jours., to Dictionary Am. Negro Biography. Active Ams. for Dem. Action; me. adv. com. D.C. Bd. of Edn. Named one of Top 42 Lawyers in Washington Area, Washington Afro-Am. Newspaper, 1993, 94, 95, 96' Ford Found. scholar, 1965-67. Columbia U., 1972-73, NEH Postdoctoral fellow in Afro-Am. studies Yale U., 1972-73. Mem. ABA (vice chmn. edn. and curriculum com. local govt. law sect. 1972-80, pub. edn. com. sect. local govt. 1974-84, chmn. liaison com. AALS, 1984, chair arbitration sect.), Nat. Bar Assn. (labor and employment law sect., steering com.), D.C. Bar Assn., Washington Bar Assn. (chmn. legal edn. com.), Chgo. Bar Assn., Fed. Bar Assn., Cook County Bar Assn., Am. Arbitration Assn. (arbitrator), D.C. Fee Arbitration Bd. (bd. govs. 1990—), Nat. Conf. Black Lawyers (bd. organizers), Nat. Futures Assn. (arbitrator), Nat. Assn. Securities Dealers (arbitrator), Assn. Henri Capitant, Roosevelt U. Alumni Assn. (rep. at George Washington U. 175th anniversary charter day convocation 1996), Loyola U. Alumni Assn. (v.p. Washington), Howard U. Alumni Assn. (rep. at Hunter Coll. Centennial 1970), Columbia U. Alumni Assn. (v.p. law Washington), Alpha Phi Alpha, Phi Alpha Kappa, Phi Alpha Delta. Home: 4315 Argyle Ter NW Washington DC 20011-4243 Office: Ste 900 South Bldg 601 Pennsylvania Ave NW Washington DC 20004-2601 also: 311 S Wacker Dr Ste 4550 Chicago IL 60606-6622 *I have always tried to do my best and never give in to obstacles. I have also been blessed with wonderful parents, relatives, friends, teachers and mentors who had confidence in me.*

DONEGAN, CHERYL, artist; b. New Haven, 1962. BFA in Painting, R.I. Sch. Design, 1984; MFA, Hunter Coll., 1990. artist-in-residence Banff Ctr. Fine Arts, Alberta, Can., 1985. One-woman shows include Elizabeth Koury Gallery, N.Y.C., 1993, Studio Guenzani, Milan, Italy, 1994, All Girls, Berlin, 1994, Galerie Rizzo, Paris, 1994, Nice Fine Arts, France, 1994, Basilico Fine Arts, N.Y.C., 1996, 97, Baumgartner Galleries, Washington, 1997, Lotta Hammer, London, 1998; exhibited in group shows at The Walter Philips Gallery, Banff, Can., 1985, Jon Gerstadt Gallery, N.Y.C., 1986, P.S. 122, N.Y.C., 1987, Althea Viafora Gallery, N.Y.C., 1990, Simon Watson Gallery, N.Y.C., 1990, 91, 522 Lafayette St. Space, 1991, Dooley Le Cappelaine Gallery, N.Y.C., 1992, Kim Light Gallery, L.A., 1993, Mus. Contemporary Art, Chgo., 1994, Whitney Mus. Am. Art, 1995, Trans Hudson Gallery, Jersey City, N.J., 1996, 98, Mus. Modern Art, N.Y.C., 1997, ACC Galerie Wiemar, 1998, Bard Ctr. Curatorial Studies, N.Y., 1999, numerous others; author: The Power of Feminist Art, 1994; contbr. articles to profl. jours. Recipient Grand Prix, 7th Internat. Festival of Saint-Gervais, Geneva, 1997. Fax: 212-334-5187. Office: care Basilico Fine Arts 26 Wooster St New York NY 10013

DONEHUE, JOHN DOUGLAS, interdenominational ministries executive; b. Cramerton, N.C., July 5, 1928; s. John Sidney and Annie (Shepherd) D.; m. Mary Phelps, Jan. 9, 1952 (dec. 1964); children: Teresa Jean, Marilyn Phelps; m. Sylvia Loise McKenzie, Feb. 11, 1966 (dec. Nov. 1971); children: Hayden Shepherd, John Douglas; m. Virginia Kirkland, June 28, 1975; children: Anne Mikell, Robertson Carr. Student, Am. Press Inst., Columbia U., 1965, 71-73; LHD (hon.), Charleston So. U., 1985. Sports editor Orangeburg (S.C.) Times and Dem., 1948-50; polit reporter Montgomery (Ala.) Advertiser, 1954-55; sports editor Charleston (S.C.) News and Courier, 1956, copy editor, 1958, state editor, 1959-62, city editor, 1962-68, mng. editor, 1968-71, promotion dir., 1971-75, v.p. for corp. pub. rels., 1975-96; v.p. corp. comm., adminstr. The Post and Courier Found., 1996—; bd. dirs. Star Gospel Mission, Charleston, 1962-80, chmn. bd. dirs., 1980-96, exec. dir., 1996—; faculty advisor Student Newspaoer, Charleston So. U.; lectr.; spl. adviser comdt. 7th USCG dist. for establishment of dist.-wide pub. info. program, 1960-61; journalism lectr. Charleston So. U.; sec. 1st bd. founders, 1969. Compiler: News and Courier Style Books, 1969; guest commentator Nat. Pub. Radio. Chmn. adv. bd. Salvation Army; chmn. regional adv. coun. S.C. Dept. Youth Svc.; chmn. planning bd. United Way; bd. dirs. Charleston Mus., S.C. Tricentennial Prade Com., 1972; pres. Palmetto Safety Coun.; lay reader, vestryman, sr. warden Episc. Ch.; chmn. bd. Charleston County Libr. Found. Recipient Freedoms Found. award, 1969, S.C. Family of Yr. award, Am. Advt. Fedn. Silver Medal award, 1987, FA citation for meritorious svc., 1971. Mem. John Ancrum Soc. of Soc. Prevention Cruelty to Animals, Carolina Art Assn., Internat. Newspaper Promotion Assn., S.C. Press Assn. (pres. 1985), Air Force Assn. (dir. Charleston coun.), Naval Civilian Mgrs. Assn., Navy league (v.p. Charleston coun.), Charleston Trident C. of C. (pres. 1983), Toastmasters Internat. (charter mem. Okinawa club), Okinawa Soc., Downtown Athletic Club, Pacific Stars and Stripes Alumni Assn. (bd. dirs.), Rotary Charleston (pres. 1974-75). Home: 66 Bull St Charleston SC 29401-1303 Office: Star Gospel Mission PO Box 20235 474 Meeting St Charleston SC 29403-4831

DONELAN, MARK ANTHONY, physicist; b. Grenada, West Indies, Mar. 27, 1942; came to Can., 1960, naturalized, 1969; s. William Gregory and Ivy (Payne) D.; B.Engring., McGill U., 1964; Ph.D., U. B.C., 1970; m. June Lynch, June 10, 1967; children: Laura, Maxwell. Project engr. Procter & Gamble Can., Hamilton, Ont., 1964-66; Killam postdoctoral fellow Cambridge (Eng.) U., 1970-71; rsch. scientist Environ. Can., Burlington, Ont., 1971-96; prof. Rosenstiel Sch. Marine and Atmospheric Sci. U. Miami, 1996—; asso. prof. civil engring. McMaster U., Hamilton, Ont., 1979-85, prof. civil engring., 1985-93; adj. prof. Waterloo (Ont.) U., 1979—, Laval U., Que., 1990-94, U. Miami, Fla., 1992-96; emeritus scientist Environ. Can., Burlington, Ont., 1997—. Humboldt research fellow Max-Planck-Institut für Meteorologie, Germany, 1984. Fellow Am. Meteorol. Soc. (Sverdrup Gold medal 1994), Royal Soc. Can.; mem. AAAS, Can. Meteorol. and Oceanographic Soc., Am. Geophys. Union, The Oceanography Soc. Office: U Miami Rosenstiel Sch Marine/Sci 4600 Rickenbacker Cswy Miami FL 33149-1098

DONELAN, PETER ANDREW, dermatologist; b. Memphis, Nov. 13, 1953; s. Richard T. and Irene M. (Jacobson) D. BA in Chemistry, Wake Forest U., 1975; MD, U. South Fla., 1978. Diplomate, Am. Bd. Dermatology. Intern U. South Fla., Tampa, Fla., 1978-79; resident in internal medicine U. South Fla., Tampa, 1979-80, resident in dermatology, 1980-83, assoc. clin. prof. medicine, 1984—; instr. dermatologic surgery VA Hosp., 1993—; pvt. practice, Tampa, 1983—; chief dermatology Tampa Gen. Hosp., 1987-88, U. Conn. Hosp., 1993—. Mem. editorial bd. Bull. Hillsboro County Med. Soc., 1987—. Named to Best Doctors in Am., 1996-97. Fellow Am. Acad. Dermatology, Am. Soc. Dermatol. Surgery; mem. Fla. Dermatol. Soc., Leaders Soc. of Dermatology Found., Fla. Med. Soc., Green Jacket Club, Pres.'s Coun. Avocations: golf, skiing. Office: 3000 E Fletcher Ave Ste 200 Tampa FL 33613-4644

DONELIAN, ARMEN, pianist, composer, author; b. N.Y.C., Dec. 1, 1950; s. Khatchik Ohannes and Lillian (Sarkisian) D. Artists cert., Westchester Conservatory Music, 1968; BA in Music, Columbia U., 1972; studies with, Carl Bamberger, Ludmila Ulehla, Harold Seletsky, Richard Beirach. Jazz pianist, composer, 1972—; pvt. tchr. piano and theory N.Y.C., 1965—; instr. piano Westchester Conservatory Music, White Plains, N.Y., 1972-75, 83-87, instr. theory, 1974-75; instr. piano, ear tng., jazz ensemble Mannes/New Sch. Jazz Program, N.Y.C., 1986—, William Paterson Coll., N.J., 1993—. Composer: (albums) The Wayfarer, Stargazer, Secrets, Trio 87, Sofrito, A Reverie, Hurricane, Positively Armenian 2, others; (film) Passion City (Best Film Score, 1988, Tisch Sch. of Arts, N.Y.U.); performer numerous worldwide tours, TV, radio and film appearances, 1976—; pianist with many jazz artists including Sonny Rollins, Mongo Santamaria, Billy Harper, Lionel Hampton, Chet Baker, Dave Liebman, Paquito D'Rivera, Anne-Marie Moss, Night Ark; author: Training the Ear: For the Improvising Musician, 1992; contbr. articles to Jazz World mag. and Op mag., Downbeat mag., Keyboard mag., Rutgers Ann. Rev. of Jazz Studies. Meet the Composer grantee, 1979, 83, 87, 99; Jazz Performance fellow Nat. Endowment for the Arts, 1983, 86, 90, 92, 94, 96. Mem. Am. Fedn. Musicians (local 802), Steinway Affiliated Artist. Office: Mannes/New Sch Jazz Program 55 W 13th St Fl 5 New York NY 10011-7958

DONELSON, JOHN EVERETT, biochemistry educator, molecular biologist; b. Ogden, Iowa, May 23, 1943; s. Mervin E. and Christine (James) D.; m. Linda Meyers, Sept. 16, 1966; children: Christina, Loren, Lyn, Emory. BS, Iowa State U., 1965; PhD, Cornell U., 1971. Postdoctoral fellow MRC Lab. Molecular biology, Cambridge, Eng., 1971-74, Stanford (Calif.) U., 1974; from asst. prof., assoc. prof. to prof. biochemistry U. Iowa, Iowa City, 1975-89, Disting. prof. biochemistry, 1989—; chmn. dept. biochemistry U. Iowa, 1998—; investigator Howard Hughes Med. Ctr. Howard Hughes Med. Inst., Iowa City, 1989-97. Contbr. numerous articles to profl. jours., sci. mags. Vol. Am. Peace Corps, Dormaa, Ghana, 1965-67. Recipient Molecular Parasitology award Burroughs-Wellcome Found., N.C., 1983, Medal of Sci. Achievement award Iowa Gov., 1990. Office: U Iowa Howard Hughes Med Inst Dept Biochemistry Iowa City IA 52242

DONELY, GEORGE ANTHONY THOMAS, III, economist, consultant; b. New Orleans, Aug. 14, 1934; s. George A.T. and Valerie Clare (Burmaster) D.; m. Lisa Suzanne Young, June 30, 1963; 1 child, Valerie Jennie Young. AB in Econs. cum laude, Williams Coll., 1956; MA in Econs., Columbia U., 1958; PhD, U. Mashad, Iran, 1967. Economist Lionel D. Edie & Co., N.Y.C., 1959-60; instr. La. State U., New Orleans, 1960-61; joined Fgn. Service, Dept. State, 1961-69; economist IMF, Washington, 1969-91; cons. Miss Lisa's Sugarless Foods, Inc., Washington, 1985-92. Contbr. articles to profl. jours. Mem. steering com. Friends of Music at Smithsonian, Washington, 1972—; vol. Md. Hist. Trust, Annapolis, 1982-85; bd. dirs., treas. Chamber Orch. So. Md., 1998—; mem. restoration adv. bd. Patuxent River NAS. Ford Found. fellow Columbia U., 1958. Mem. Am. Econ. Assn., Econ. History Assn., Round Table, St. Mary's River Yacht Club, Met. Club, Williams Club, Rotary (Paul Harris fellow). Home: St Richard's Manor 22880 Old Manor Ln Lexington Park MD 20653-2146

DONEN, STANLEY, film director; b. Columbia, S.C., Apr. 13, 1924. Ed., U. S.C. Co-dir.: (films) On the Town, 1949, Singin' in the Rain, 1952, It's Always Fair Weather, 1955, The Pajama Game, 1957, Damn Yankees, 1958; dir.: (films) Royal Wedding, 1951, Love Is Better Than None, 1952, Fearless Fagan, 1952, Give a Girl a Break, 1953, Seven Brides for Seven Brothers, 1954, Deep in My Heart, 1954, Funny Face, 1957, Kiss Them for Me, 1957, Indiscreet, 1958, Once More with Feeling, 1960, Surprise Package, 1960, The Grass Is Greener, 1971, Charade, 1964, Arabesque, 1966, Two for the Road, 1967, Bedazzled, 1967, Staircase, 1969, The Little Prince, 1974, Lucky Lady, 1975, Movie Movie, 1978, Saturn 3, 1980, Blame It on Rio, 1984, (TV movie) Love Letters, 1999. Recipient Lifetime Achievement award (hon. Oscar) Acad. Motion Picture Arts and Scis., 1998, Golden Eddie award Am. Cinema Editors, 1998, Lifetime Achievement award Palm Beach Internat. Film Festival, 1999. Mem. Dirs. Guild Am. Office: c/o LaGrange Group 11828 La Grange Ave Los Angeles CA 90025*

DONENFELD, KENNETH JAY, management consultant; b. Bklyn., Nov. 2, 1946; s. Israel James and Anne (Puretz) D.; BA, CUNY, 1967; MA, Syracuse U., 1968; postgrad. N.Y. Inst. Fin., 1971; m. Sharon Etta Kamer, June 23, 1968; children: Elissa Meredith, Jonathan Lloyd. Mgmt. cons. Georgeson & Co., N.Y.C., 1969-79; exec. v.p., dir. investor rels. div. Robert Marston and Assocs., N.Y.C., 1979-89; pres. Robert Marston Investor Rels., Inc., 1988; exec. v.p. D.F. King and Co., Inc., N.Y.C., 1989-91; pres. The Donenfeld Group, Inc., N.Y.C., 1991—, DGI Investor Relations, Inc., N.Y.C., 1996—. N.Y. State Regents scholar, 1963-67. Mem. Nat. Investor Rels. Inst. (adv. bd. IR mag.), N.Y. Assn. for Internat. Investment, Swedish C. of C., N.Y. Soc. Security Analysts, The Bd. Rm. Club, Media Club. Republican. Home: 90 Emerson Dr Great Neck NY 11023-1831

DONER, GARY WILLIAM, lawyer; b. Louisville, Nov. 3, 1951; s. Charles and Billie (Miller) D.; m. Cynthia Ann Herman, July 7, 1973; 1 child, Laura. BS, Wright State U., 1974; JD cum laude, U. Toledo, 1990. CPA, Ohio. Tax analyst NCR Corp., Dayton, Ohio, 1975-80; tax mgr. Dayco Corp., Dayton, 1980-85; tax dir. Cooper Tire & Rubber Co., Findlay, Ohio, 1985-99; mgr. fed. taxes Dana Corp., Toledo, Ohio, 1999—; part-time instr. Ownes Coll., Toledo, 1985-86, acctg. adv. com., 1985—; mem. operating com. Ohio Pub. Expenditures Coun.; pres. Tax Forum, Toledo, 1993—. Named Ky. Col. Mem. ABA, AICPA, Ohio Soc. CPAs, Tax Execs. Inst., Ohio Bar Assn., Ohio C. of C. (tax com., adv. on taxes). Roman Catholic. Avocations: tennis, weightlifting. Home: 26065 Edinborough Cir Perrysburg OH 43551-9545 Office: DANA Corp 4500 Dorr St Toledo OH 43615

DONESA, ANTONIO BRAGANZA, neurosurgeon; b. Manila, July 27, 1935; came to U.S., 1959, naturalized, 1969; s. Alfonso Pinson and Flora (Braganza) D.; m. Barbara Louise Quinn, Nov. 30, 1962; children: Carmen, Christopher. BS, U. Philippines, 1955, MD, 1959. Intern St. Mary's Hosp., Waterbury, Conn., 1959-60; resident Huron Road Hosp., 1960-61, U. Ala. Med. Ctr., Birmingham, 1961-65; pvt. practice neurosurgery Ft. Wayne, Ind., 1966—; pres., dir. Neurosurgery, Inc., Ft. Wayne, 1971—; mem. staff Parkview Hosp., Ft. Wayne, St. Joseph's Hosp., Ft. Wayne, Luth. Hosp., Ft. Wayne; cons. Marion (Ind.) Gen. Hosp.; founder, past pres. Liberty for Am. Minority Physicians, LAMP Legal Fund. Founder UPMASA Permanent Endowment Fund. Recipient Leadership award March of Dimes, 1972, Cert. of Appreciation, Heart Fund, 1971, others. Mem. Assn. Philippine Physicians in Am. (Community Svc. award 1983), Ft. Wayne Acad. Medicine and Surgery, Ind. Philippine Med. Assn. (past. pres.), Am. Coll. Internat. Physicians (founder, exec. dir. 1978-90, chmn. 1985, Leadership award 1975, Disting. Fellow award 1982), Ind. State Med. Assn., Allen (Ft. Wayne, pres. 12th dist. 1985-86) County Med. Soc. (pres. 1990-91), Congress Neurol. Surgeons, Soc. Philippine Neurol. Surgeons in Am. (past pres.), Neurosurg. Soc. Ind., Soc. Philippine Surgeons Am., U. Philippines Med. Alumni Soc. in Am. (nat. pres. 1985-87, Disting. Alumnus Overseas 1985), Masons, Shriners, Summit Club. Office: 3030 Lake Ave Fort Wayne IN 46805-5428

DONEY, WILLIS FREDERICK, philosophy educator; b. Pitts., Aug. 19, 1925; s. Willis Frederick and Ora (Powell) D. B.A., Princeton, 1946, M.A., Ph.D., 1949; M.A., Dartmouth, 1966. Instr. Cornell U., Ithaca, N.Y., 1949-52; vis. lectr. U. Mich., Ann Arbor, 1952; asst. prof. Ohio State U., Columbus, 1953-56, 57-58; George Santayana fellow Harvard U., Cambridge, Mass., 1956-57, vis. lectr., 1963; mem. faculty Dartmouth Coll., Hanover, N.H., 1958—, prof. philosophy, 1966—; mem. Inst. for Advanced Study, Princeton, N.J., 1972-73; vis. lectr. Harvard, 1963; vis. prof. Edinburgh U., 1980. Author articles on 17th Century philosophy.; Editor: Descartes: A Collection of Critical Studies, 1967, Malebranche: Entretiens sur la Métaphysique, 1980, (with Vere Chappell) Twenty Five Years of Descartes Scholarship 1960-1984: A Bibliography, 1987, Eternal Truths and the Cartesian Circle, 1987, Berkeley on Abstraction and Abstract Ideas, 1989. Ford-Dartmouth fellow, 1970; Camargo Found. fellow, 1978-79. Home: 6 Union Village Rd Norwich VT 05055-9643 Office: Philosophy Dept Dartmouth Coll Hanover NH 03755

DONFRIED, KARL PAUL, minister, theology educator; b. N.Y.C., Apr. 6, 1940; s. Paul and Else (Schmuck) D.; m. Katharine E. Krayer, Sept. 10, 1960; children: Paul Andrew, Karen Erika, Mark Christopher. AB, Columbia U., 1960; BD, Harvard U., 1963; STM, Union Theol. Sem., 1965; ThD, U. Heidelberg, Fed. Republic Germany, 1968. Ordained to ministry Lutheran Ch. in Am., 1963; named ecumenical canon Christ Ch. Cathedral, Springfield, Mass., 1977. Assoc. pastor ch. N.Y.C., 1963-64; acting Luth. chaplain (Columbia U.), 1963-64; mem. faculty Smith Coll., Northampton, Mass., 1968—, prof. N.T. and early Christianity, 1968—, chmn. dept. religion and mem. N.T. panel Nat. Luth.-Roman Cath. Dialogue, 1971-73, 75-78, dir. ancient studies, 1994-95; chmn. Columbia Seminar for Study of N.T., 1976-77; vis. prof. Assumption Coll., Worcester, Mass., 1975, Amherst Coll., 1976, 78, 85, St. Hyacinth Coll. and Sem., Granby, Mass., 1976, Brown U., 1979, Mt. Holyoke Coll., 1983, U. Hamburg, 1985, Yale Univ. Div. Sch., New Haven, 1993; Fulbright vis. prof. Hebrew U., Jerusalem, 1997. Author: (with R.E. Brown, J. Reumann) Peter in the New Testament, 1973, The Setting of Second Clement in Early Christianity, 1974, (with others) Mary in the New Testament, 1978, The Dynamic Word, 1981; editor: The Romans Debate, 1977, The Romans Debate: New and Expanded Edition, 1991, (with I.H. Marshall) The Shorter Pauline Epistles, 1993, (with Peter Richardson) Judaism and Christianity in First-Century Rome, 1998; mem. editorial bd.: Jour. Bibl. Lit., 1975-81. Mem. Am. Acad. Religion (dir. 1972-73, pres. New Eng. region 1971-72), Studiorum Novi Testamenti Societas (chmn. Paul seminar 1975-78, exec. com. 1979-83, chmn. New Testament Texts in Their Cultural Environment seminar 1990-94, chmn. Thessalonian Correspondence seminar 1995—), Soc. Bibl. Lit. (pres. New Eng. region 1975-76), Cath. Bibl. Assn. (participant internat. congresses scholars in Aberdeen, Basel, Bern, Bielefeld, Cambridge, Canterbury, Copenhagen, Edinburgh, Einhoven, Göttingen, Heidelberg, Frankfurt, Jerusalem, Louvain, Milan, Newcastle, Oxford, Prague, Rome, Sigtuna, Strasbourg, Toronto, Tubingen). Office: Smith Coll Dept Religion Northampton MA 01063 *As the son of immigrant parents, I learned early the value of hard and honest work, the necessity for integrity in all human relations and the blessings of generosity to those less fortunate. These values, together with my commitment to Christianity, have shaped, and continue to shape, my life.*

DONG, GANGYI, acupunturist, medical researcher; b. Xian, Shanxi, China, Dec. 14, 1954; came to U.S., 1987; s. Zheng-Jun and Qiying Zheng D.; m. Xinxin Guo, Nov. 15, 1983; 1 child, Sarah. Diploma, Boji Secondary Med. Sch., 1974; MD, Anhui (China) Med. Coll. TCM, Anhui, China, 1983; MA, West Chester (Pa.) U., 1989. Cert. acupuncturist. Asst. prof. acpuncture dept. Anhui Med. Coll. TCM, Hefei, 1983-87; physician Tchg. Hosp. of Anhui Med. Coll., Hefei, 1983-87; rsch. asst. Med. Sch., Temple U., Phila., 1989-92, postdoctoral rsch. fellow, 1992-93; rsch. assoc. Children Hosp. Phila., 1993—; pres. Alternative Med. One Inc., West Chester, Pa., 1995—; owner, Chinese herbalist Acupuncture Assocs. Chester County, West Chester, 1989—. Author, prodr., editor: (video tapes) Chinese Self-Acupressure Massage, 1996-97. Mem. Endocrinology Soc. Pa., Acupuncture Soc. Pa., Acupuncture Soc. Am. Avocations: painting, music, travel, sports. Fax: (610) 896-7254. Office: Acupuncture Assocs Chester County 1505 Mcdaniel Dr West Chester PA 19380-6671

DONG, QIAN, radiologist, researcher; b. Kunming, Yunnan, China, Mar. 8, 1968; s. Hua Zhao and Heyu (Wang) D.; m. Bing Chen, Jan. 28, 1994. MD, Kunming Med. Coll., 1991. Resident No. 1 Hosp. Kunming Med. Coll., 1991-95, attending radiologist, 1995—; rsch. fellow U. Mich., Ann Arbopr, 1996—. Contbr. articles to profl. jours. Recipient Outstanding Electronic Exhibit bronze award Am. Roentgen Ray Soc., 1998, cert. merit for electronic excellence, 1998. Avocations: music, travel, sports, reading. E-mail: bingch@umich.edu. Office: U Mich Dept Radiology 1500 E Medical Center Dr Ann Arbor MI 48109-0030

DONG, ZHAOQIN, materials and testing engineer, researcher; b. Dingtao, China, Apr. 19, 1963; s. Guanghan Dong and Limei Tian Dong; m. Jie Gao, Jan. 9, 1987. BS, Jiangxi (China) Inst. Metall., 1982; MS, Inst. Aero. Materials, Beijing, 1985, Calif. Inst. Tech., 1992. Engr. Inst. Aero. Materials, 1985-90; grad. rschr. Calif. Inst. Tech., Pasadena, 1990-93, U. Calif., Irvine, 1993-95; adv. bds., cons. Beijing Union Soc. Materials Testing, 1984-97, Longxiang (China) Inst. Gen. Tech., 1995-97. Author: Selection and Use of Engineering Materials, 1990; contbr. articles to profl. jours., including Acta Aero. et Astronautical Sinica, Jour. Aerospace Power, Jour. Mech. Engring. Fellow Soc. Aeronautics and Astronautics (Beijing); mem. ASME, AIAA, ASTM. Achievements include criterion: the guide of strain energy time-dependent fatigue life prediction methods, strain energy-frequency separation model, aeronautical industry criterion HB/Z 217-92.

DONIE, SCOTT, Olympic athlete, platform diver; b. Vicenza, Italy, Oct. 10, 1968. BA in communication/advt., So. Meth. U., 1990. Olympic platform diver Barcelona, Spain, 1992; Olympic springboard diver Atlanta, 1996. Recipient Silver medal platform diving Olympics, Barcelona, 1992, 4th place medal springboard diving Olympics, Atlanta, 1996. Home: 13315 Apple Tree Rd Houston TX 77079-7107

DONIGER, WENDY, history of religions educator; b. N.Y.C., Nov. 20, 1940; d. Lester L. and Rita (Roth) Doniger; m. Dennis M. O'Flaherty, Mar. 31, 1964; 1 child, Michael Lester O'Flaherty. BA summa cum laude, Radcliffe Coll., 1962; PhD, Harvard U., 1968. Lectr. U. London Sch. Oriental and African Studies, 1968-75; vis. lectr. U. Calif., Berkeley, 1975-77; prof. history of religions Div. Sch., dept. South Asian langs., com. on social thought U. Chgo., 1978-85, Mircea Eliade prof., 1986—. Author: (under name of Wendy Doniger O'Flaherty) Asceticism and Eroticism in the Mythology of Siva, 1973, Hindu Myths, 1975, The Origins of Evil in Hindu Mythology, 1976, Women, Androgynes and Other Mythical Beasts, 1980, The Rig Veda: An Anthology, 1981, Karma and Rebirth in Classical Indian Traditions, 1980, Dreams, Illusion and Other Realities, 1984, Other Peoples' Myths, 1988, (under name of Wendy Doniger), The Laws of Manu, 1991, Mythologies, 1991, Purana Perennis, 1993, The Implied Spider, 1998, Splitting the Difference, 1999; editor Jour. Am. Acad. Religion, 1977-80, History of Religions, 1979—; mem. editl. bd. Ency. Britannica, 1987-98, Daedalus, 1990-98. Recipient Lucy Allen Paton prize, 1961, Phi Beta Kappa prize, 1962; Jonathan Fay Fund scholar, 1962, Am. Inst. Indian Studies fellow, 1963-64, NEH summer stipend, 1980, Guggenheim fellow, 1980-81. Fellow Soc. for the Arts, Religion and Culture, Am. Philos. Soc., Am. Acad. Arts and Scis.; mem. Am. Acad. Religion (pres. 1984), Am. Soc. for Study Religion, Am. Oriental Soc., Assn. Asian Studies (pres. 1998), Phi Beta Kappa. Home: 1319 E 55th St Chicago IL 60615-5301 Office: U Chgo Div Sch 1025 E 58th St Chicago IL 60637-1509

DONKER, RICHARD BRUCE, health care administrator; b. Modesto, Calif., Sept. 29, 1950; s. Luverne Peter and Ruth Bernice (Hoskenga) D.; m. Elizabeth Gail Content, May 3, 1986; children: Elizabeth Anne, Danica Ruth. AA, Modesto Jr. Coll., 1970; BS, Calvin Coll., Grand Rapids, Mich., 1972; MA, Calif. State Coll., Turlock, 1978; EdD, U. Pacific, 1980. Grant dir. Yosemite Community Coll. Dist., Modesto, 1975-77; dir. flight ops. Meml. Hosps. Assn., Modesto, 1980-85, adminstrv. coord., 1985-87, v.p. bus. systems, 1987-89; v.p. clin. svcs. Meml. Hosp. Assn., Modesto, 1989-92; prin. Global Bus. Network, Emeryville, Calif., 1992—; divisional pres. Coastal Health Care Group, Inc., Durham, N.C., 1993—; exec. dir. MediPLUS Health Plans, Inc., Modesto, 1986-92; pres. Calif. Aeromed. Rescue and Evacuation, Inc., Modesto, 1985—; lectr. Am. Hosp. Assn., Chgo., 1984—; bd. dirs. Synergistic Sys., Inc.; cons. in field, 1984—. Author: Emergency Medical Technician Outreach Training, 1977, (with others) The Hospital Emergency Department: Returning to Financial Viability, 1987, Restructuring Ambulatory Care, A Guide to Reorganization, 1990, The Hospital Emergency Department, 1992, Implementing an Emerbency Department Capitation Program, 1997. Bd. dirs. Stanislaus Paramedic Assn., Modesto, 1978-82, Head Rest, Inc., Modesto, 1980; bd. dirs. regional occupational program Stanislau County Dept. Edn., 1980; del. People-to-People Citizen Amb. Program, People's Republic of China, 1988. Mem. Am. Acad. Med. Adminstrs., Nat. Acad. Scis. Inst. Medicine (com. pediatric emergency med. svcs. 1991-92), Phi Delta Kappa, Commonwealth Club. Presbyterian. Avocations: sailing, flying, scuba diving, piano. Home: 1322 Edgebrook Dr Modesto CA 95354-1537 Office: 2828 Croasdaile Dr Durham NC 27705-2505

DONKERVOET, RICHARD CORNELIUS, architect; b. Detroit, Oct. 8, 1930; s. Cornelius and Anna Eva Hendrika (Boer) D.; m. Carolyn Eugenia Moore, May 4, 1957; children: Carolyn Daralice Donkervoet Boles, Sharon Elisabeth Donkervoet Credit, John Cornelius. BArch, U. Mich., 1952; MArch, MIT, 1953. Fulbright fellow Tech. U., Delft, Holland, 1954-55; architect Cochran, Stephenson & Wing, Balt., 1957-63; ptnr. Cochran, Stephenson & Donkervoet, Inc., Balt., 1963-68, exec. v.p., 1968-83, pres., 1983-96, chmn., 1996—. Trustee Roland Park Country Sch., Balt., 1968-75, Balt. Mus. Art., 1970—; pres. bd. trustees Westminster House, Balt., 1975—; pres. bd. dirs. Citizens League Balt., 1980-82. Served with U.S. Army, 1956-58. Fellow AIA (pres. Balt. chpt., bd. dirs. 1973, treas. 1966, Disting. Svc. award 1977); mem. Md. Club, Hamilton St. Club (mem. steering com. 1983-88), Ctr. Club (Balt.). Avocations: reading, travel, tennis. Home: 200 Bolton Pl Baltimore MD 21217-4105 Office: C S & D Inc 323 W Camden St Ste 700 Baltimore MD 21201-8601

DONLAN, THOMAS GARRETT, journalist; b. N.Y.C., Mar. 31, 1945; s. Thomas Garrett and Elizabeth May (Beard) D.; m. Carol Knopes Donlan, Feb. 5, 1972; children: Nicholas G., Alice E. AB, Hamilton Coll., 1967; MA, Ind. U., 1968. Reporter The Record, Hackensack, N.J., 1969-74; newsman AP, Trenton, N.J., 1974-79; assoc. editor Barron's Mag., N.Y.C., 1979-81; Washington editor Barron's Mag., Washington, 1981-91, editor editorial page, 1992—. Author: Supertech: How America Can Win the Technology Race, 1991, Don't Count On It: Why Your Pension May Be In Jeopardy and How to Protect Yourself, 1994. Mem. Nat. Press Club, Severn Sailing Assn., Sailing Club of the Chesapeake, Annapolis Yacht Club. Avocations: sailing, squash. Home: 6516 Jay Miller Dr Falls Church VA 22041-1135 Office: Barron's Mag 1025 Connecticut Ave NW Ste 800 Washington DC 20036-5419

DONLEAVY, JAMES PATRICK, writer, artist; b. Bklyn., Apr. 23, 1926; m. Valerie Heron (div.); children: Philip, Karen; m. Mary Wilson Price (div.); children: Rebecca, Rory. Student, Trinity Coll., Dublin, Ireland. Author: novel, later adapted as play The Ginger Man, 1955; drama Fairy Tales of New York, 1960; A Singular Man novel, later adapted as play, 1963, Meet My Maker the Mad Molecule, short stories, sketches, 1964, The Saddest Summer of Samuel S, novella, later adapted as play, 1966, The Beastly Beatitudes of Balthazar B, novel, later adapted as play, 1968, The Onion Eaters, 1971, The Plays of J.P. Donleavy, 1972; novel A Fairy Tale of New York, 1973; The Unexpurgated Code, A Complete Manual of Survival and Manners, 1975, The Destinies of Darcy Dancer, Gentleman, 1977; novel Schultz, 1979, Leila, 1983, Are You Listening Rabbi Löw, 1987; De Alfonce Tennis, The Superlative Game of Eccentric Champions. Its History, Accoutrements, Rules, Conduct and Regimen, 1984, J.P. Donleavy's Ireland. In All Her Sins and in Some of Her Graces, 1986 (Gold award Worldfest Houston 1993, Cine Golden Eagle award), A Singular Country, 1989, That Darcy, That Dancer, That Gentleman, 1990, The History of the Ginger Man, 1994, Wrong Information is Being Given Out at Pinceton, 1998, (novella) The Lady Who Liked Clean Rest Rooms, 1996, An Author and His Image, 1997; contbr. to numerous mags. and jours. including Times of London, N.Y. Times, Washington Post, Atlantic Monthly, The Daily Telegraph, The New Yorker, Rolling Stone, others; art exhbns.: Painter's Gallery, St. Stephen's Green, Dublin, 1950, 51, Bronxville, N.Y., 1959, Langton Galleries, London, 1975, Godolphin Gallery, Dublin, 1986, Caldwell Galleries, Belfast, 1987, Anna Mei Chadwick Gallery, London, 1989, 91, 94, Alba Fine Art Gallery, London, 1991, Front Lounge Gallery, 1995. Served with USNR, World War II. Recipient Creative Arts award Brandeis U., 1961-62; AAAL grantee, 1975. Home: Levington Park, Mullingar County Westmeath, Ireland

DONLEVY, JOHN DEARDEN, lawyer; b. Chgo., May 29, 1933; s. Frank and Alice Genevieve (O'Connor) D.; m. Kristin Bach Minnick, Apr. 20, 1963 (div. Sept. 1985); 1 son, John Dearden. Student, Stanford U., 1950-52; BS, Northwestern U., 1954; JD, U. Chgo., 1957; postgrad., Northwestern U., 1958. Bar: Ill. 1957, U.S. Dist. Ct. (no. dist.) 1957, U.S. Ct. Appeals (7th cir.) 1969, U.S. Supreme Ct. 1972. Asst. state's atty. Cook County Criminal Divsn., Chgo., 1958-61; city prosecutor City of Evanston, Ill., 1961; assoc. Mayer, Brown & Platt, Chgo., 1962-73, ptnr., 1973-90; pvt. practice law Chgo., 1990—; participant Hinton Moot Ct. Competition U. Chgo., 1955-56, judge, 1972. Bd. dirs. English-Speaking Union, Chgo., 1964-65; active Rep. Orgn., 1958-60. Recipient Disting. Legal award Am. Legion, Chgo., 1960; named spl. prosecutor-labor racketeering Cook County State's Atty., Chgo., 1959-61; profiled in Lindberg "Summerdale--35 Year Anniversary", 1995. Mem. ABA, Ill. Bar Assn., Chgo. Bar Assn. (criminal law com., chair def. of prisoners com.), Chgo. Athletic Assn. Office: 30 N La Salle St Ste 2140 Chicago IL 60602-2502 *I have always sought to examine problems carefully in order to obtain the fullest possible understanding of them, as I believe that with proper understanding, there is nothing in life which need be feared.*

DONLEY, DENNIS LEE, school librarian; b. Port Hueneme, Calif., July 19, 1950; s. Mickey Holt and Joan Elizabeth (Smith) D.; m. Ruth Ann Shank, June 10, 1972; children: Eric Holt, Evan Scott. AA, Ventura Coll., 1970; BA with honors, U. Calif., Santa Barbara, 1973; MLS, San Jose State U., 1976. Cert. secondary tchr., Calif. Libr. media tchr. San Diego Unified Sch. Dist., 1975—; lectr. Calif. State U., L.A., 1987-89; libr. cons. San Diego C.C. Dist., 1990; chmn. sch. adv. com. Point Loma H.S., San Diego, 1986-87; coop. book rev. bd. San Diego County, 1984-86; creator adult sch. curriculum, 1984-86; contbr. Deadbase X, Deadbase 94, The Deadhead's Taping Compendium, Vols. 1-3. Mem. ALA, Calif. Libr. Media Educators Assn. Avocations: reading, music, fitness. Office: Hoover HS 4474 El Cajon Blvd San Diego CA 92115-4312

DONLEY, EDWARD, manufacturing company executive; b. Highland Park, Mich., Nov. 26, 1921; s. Hugh and Frances (Gavin) D.; m. Inez Cantrell, Oct. 24, 1946; children: Martha Donley Robb, Thomas, John. BME, Lawrence Tech. U., 1943; grad. Advanced Mgmt. Program, Harvard U., 1959. V.p. Air Products and Chems., Inc., Allentown, Pa., 1950-66, exec. v.p., 1966, pres., 1966-78, chief exec. officer, 1973-86, chmn. bd., 1978-86, chmn. exec. com., 1986-92; chmn. bd. Am. Standard, Inc., 1992-93; former chmn. bd. of mems. Lawrence Tech. U.; past chmn. bus. higher edn. forum Am. Coun. Edn.; bd. dirs., former chmn. Ctr. for Workforce Preparation and Quality Edn.; bd. dirs. Nat. Assessment Governing Bd. Chmn. bd. Pa. Cmty. Learning and Info. Network; mem. Pa. Bd. Edn.; chmn. StandardsWork (formerly Coalition for Goals 2000); bd. dirs. Nat. Endowment for Democracy, Ctr. for Workforce Preparation and Quality Edn., Lehigh ValleyBus.-Edn. Partnership, Pa. Partnerships for Children, Coun. for Higher Edn. Accreditation, Tchr. Edn. Accreditation Coun.; emeritus trustee Carnegie Mellon U.; former trustee Am. Coll. Testing; chair Edn. Policy and Leadership Ctr. Mem. Soc. Chem. Industry, Middle States Assn. (commr. elem. schs.). Home: 326 N 27th St Allentown PA 18104-4871 Office: 7201 Hamilton Blvd Allentown PA 18195-1526

DONLEY, JAMES WALTON, management consultant; b. Cleve., June 27, 1934; s. Howard Russell and Mary Louise (Mullikin) D.; m. Frances Elizabeth Jordan, July 5, 1963 (div. Oct. 1983); children: Dana, Elizabeth; m. Mary Todd Mann Goodspeed, May 25, 1985; children: Bennett, Mary Todd, Emily, Jonathan Goodspeed. BA, Denison U., 1958; MBA, U. Pa., 1960. Asst. to pub. Time Mag., N.Y.C., 1960-67; sr. v.p. Thomas J. Deegan Co., N.Y.C., 1967-71; asst. commr. N.Y.C. Dept. Commerce, 1971-72; asst. sec. U.S. Dept. Treasury, Wash., 1972-74; chmn. Donley Comm., N.Y.C., 1974—; country dir. Bulgaria Internat. Exec. Svc. Corps, Sofia, 1995-97; bd. dirs. Technoserve, Inc. Mem. bd. visitors Western Res. Acad., Hudson, Ohio. With U.S. Army, 1954-56, Germany. Mem. Round Hill Club, Belle Haven Club. Republican. Congregationalist. Home: 28 Wooddale Rd Greenwich CT 06830-3824

DONLEY, RUSSELL LEE, III, former state representative; b. Salt Lake City, Feb. 3, 1939; s. R. Lee and Leona (Sherwood) D.; m. Karen Kocherhans, June 4, 1960; children: Tammera Sue, Tonya Kay, Christina Lynn. BSCE with honors, U. Wyo., 1961; MS in Engring., U. Fla., 1962. From mem. to spkr. of house Wyo. Ho. of Reps., 1969-84; chmn. bd. Nat. Ctr. Constl. Studies, Wyo. region, 1983-87; CEO Constitution Schs. Inc., Casper, 1987—; owner Russell L. Donley & Assocs., 1988—; v.p. Nat. Bus. Solutions, LLC, 1997—; chmn. appropriations com. Wyo Ho. of Reps., 1975-78, chmn. legis. mgmt. coun., 1983-84. Chmn. Western Region Coun. State Govts., 1982-83; Rep. candidate for gov. Wyo, 1986; precinct committeeman Rep. Cen. Com., 1987-96; chmn. Wyo. Young Reps., 1968; fin. chmn. Natrona County Rep. Cen. Com., 1970; pres. bd. dirs. YMCA, Casper, 1976-77; state chmn. Initiative # 3 dr. Invest in Wyo. not Wall St., 1994. Recipient award for engring. excellence Am. Cons. Engrs. Council; recipient Legislator of Yr. award Nat. Republican Legislators Assn., 1981; named Wyo. Outstanding Young Engr. Sigma Tau, 1974, Disting. Wyo. Engr. Tau Beta Pi., 1976. Former mem. Am. Water Works Assn., Nat. Soc. Profl. Engrs., Wyo. Soc. Profl. Engrs., Wyo. Engring. Soc., Wyo. Assn. Cons. Engrs. and Surveyors. LDS Church. Home: 1140 Ivy Ln Casper WY 82609-2702 Office: 240 S Wolcott St Ste 234 Casper WY 82601-2552

DONLON, JOSEPHINE A., diagnostic and evalution counseling therapist, educator; b. N.Y.C., Apr. 3, 1921; d. Henry R. and Josephine V. (Klarer) Janssen; R.N., Englewood (N.J.) Hosp., 1941; B.A. in Psychology, Colo. Coll., Colorado Springs, 1945; M.Ed., Nat. Coll. Edn., Evanston, Ill., 1975; m. William James Donlon; children—William James, Gregory A., Michele L., DruAnn. Pediatric psychiat. nurse N.Y. State Psychiat. Inst., N.Y.C., 1941-42; supr. psychiat. nursing Colo. U. Psychiat. Inst., 1945-47; pub. health nurse Denver Sch., 1947-48; diagnostic educator Schaumburg (Ill.) Sch. Dist. 54, 1969-78; pvt. practice diagnostic evaluation and counseling, Brookeville, Md., 1979-87, Pineland, Fla., 1987—. Leader, Girl Scouts U.S.A., 1958-62; previously active PTA's in Colo. and Ill. Mem. Council Exceptional Children, Council for Children with Behavioral Disorders, Council for Ednl. Diagnostic Services. Research in genetic endocrine diseases of pancreas and thyroid and relation to learning and behavior. Certified in nursing, spl. edn., Ill., Colo.; specialist in social maladjusted, learning disabled, educable mentally handicapped. Home: PO Box 2212 Pineland FL 33945-2212

DONLON, WILLIAM JAMES, lawyer; b. Colorado Springs, Colo., Apr. 22, 1924; s. John Andrew and Kathleen M. Donlon; m. Josephine A. Janssen, July 19, 1946; children—William James, Gregory A., Michele, Dru Ann Gazelle. Student Colo. Coll., 1941-43; B.S., U. Denver, 1949, J.D., 1950. Bar: Colo. 1950, Ohio 1964, Ill. 1969, U.S. Dist. Ct. Colo. 1956 (no. dist.) Ill. 1974, U.S. Ct. Apls. (10th cir.) 1957, U.S. Ct. Apls. (5th cir.) 1970, U.S. Ct. Apls. (7th cir.) 1974, U.S. Ct. Apls. D.C. 1979, U.S. Supreme Ct. 1965. Dep. clk. Dist. Ct. Denver, 1949-50; solo practice, Denver, 1953-63; gen. counsel Brotherhood Ry., Airline and S.S. Clks., Freight Handlers, Express and Sta. Employees, Rosemont, Ill., 1963-84, Rockville, Md., 1963-86; instr. labor U. Ill., 1972-78. Served with USAAF, 1942-45. Decorated Air medal with 2 oak leaf clusters. Mem. ABA (council sect. labor and employment law 1977-86), Ill. Bar Assn., D.C. Bar Assn., Am. Legion, VFW, KC (Grand Knights coun. 10329 1991-93), Phi Alpha Delta, Phi Delta Theta. Democrat. Roman Catholic. Office: PO Box 2212 Pineland FL 33945-2212

DONNALLY, PATRICIA BRODERICK, newspaper editor; b. Cheverly, Md., Mar. 11, 1955; d. James Duane and Olga Frances (Duenas) Broderick; m. Robert Andrew Donnally, Dec. 30, 1977; 1 child, Danielle Christine; BS, U. Md., 1977. Fashion editor The Washington Times (D.C.), 1983-85, The San Francisco Chronicle, 1985—. Recipient Atrium award, 1984, 87-89, 90, 94, 95, 96, 97, Lulu award, 1985, 87, award Am. Cancer Soc., 1991, Aldo award, 1994. Avocation: travel. Office: Chronicle Pub Co 901 Mission St San Francisco CA 94103-2905

DONNALLY, ROBERT ANDREW, lawyer, real estate broker; b. Washington, July 10, 1953; s. Reaumur Stearnes and Katherine Ann (Sutliff) D.; m. Patricia Kane Broderick, Dec. 30, 1977; 1 child, Danielle Christine. BA in Psychology, U. Md., 1976; JD, U. Balt., 1980; cert. in bus., Stanford U., 1996. Bar: Md. 1980, Calif. 1986. Pvt. practice Oxen Hill, Md., 1980-81; rsch. contract staff officer Dept. Def., Ft. Meade, Md., 1981-85; with legal and contractual ops. ARGOSystems, Inc., Sunnyvale, Calif., 1985-90; asst. dir. Inst. Def. Analyses, San Diego, 1990-91; dep. chief counsel ARGOSystems, Inc., 1991-93, chief counsel, corp. sec., 1993-98; chief counsel comms. and infomanagement divsn. Boeing Co., 1997-98; gen. counsel, mng. ptnr. BT Comml. Real Estate, Palo Alto, Calif., 1998—. Editor-in-chief The Forum, 1979-80. Active The Pillars Soc./United Way, 1991—. Waxter Legal scholar U. Baltimore, 1978. Mem. Am. Corp. Counsel, Nat. Contract Mgmt. Assn., Md. Bar Assn., Calif. Bar Assn., Assn. of Silicon Valley Brokers, Tae Kwon Do Assn. (Black Belt), Black Belt, Kukkiwon World Tae Kwon Do Assn. Avocations: martial arts, marathons, hiking, travel, reading. Office: BT Comml Real Estate 2445 Faber Pl Ste 250 Palo Alto CA 94303-3316

DONNELL, HAROLD EUGENE, JR., professional society administrator; b. Balt., Mar. 12, 1935; s. Harold Eugene and Ruth Elizabeth (Meeth) D.; m. Rosemary Gatch, Apr. 25, 1959; children—David Crawford, Laurette Butler. BA, Amherst Coll., 1957. Field asst., agt. Equitable Life Assurance Soc., Balt., 1958-61; salesman Eastern Products Corp., Balt., 1961-64; asst. nat. sales mgr. Eastern Products Corp., 1964-66; exec. dir. Md. State Dental Assn., Towson, 1966-74, Acad. Gen. Dentistry, Chgo., 1974—. Trustee Am. Fund for Dental Health, 1976-84 . Served with U.S. Army, 1957-58. Recipient Disting. Service award N.C. Acad. Gen. Dentistry, 1980; ann. Walter E. Levine Meritorious Service award Alpha Omega, 1970. Fellow Acad. Gen. Denistry (hon.); mem. ADA, Am. Soc. Assn. Execs. (cert. assn. exec.), Assn. Forum, Acad. Gen. Dentistry. Republican. Lutheran. Office: Academy of General Dentistry 211 E Chicago Ave Chicago IL 60611-2637 *Any degree of success I have achieved in this life is a result of dedicatedly applying the talents I have been given or acquired with single minded drive to accomplish specific goals.*

DONNELL, JOHN RANDOLPH, retired petroleum executive; b. Findlay, Ohio, June 22, 1912; s. Otto Dewey and Glenn (McClelland) D.; m. Margaret Louise Watt, Feb. 1, 1939 (dec.); children: John Randolph, Ann (Mrs. R. Kennedy Davis), William Watt, Thomas Blakeman, Richard Holmes; m. Maureen Nahas, July 31, 1981. BS, Case Inst. Tech., 1934. Spl. rep. Marathon Oil Co., Findlay, 1938; asst. to mgr. prodn. Marathon Oil Co., 1944-50, treas., 1950-54, v.p. supply and transp., 1954-61, dir., 1954-73, v.p. charge internat. activities, 1961-65, sr. v.p. internat., 1965-67, sr. v.p. corporate planning, 1967-69, sr. v.p. finance and planning, 1969-73; pres. Marathon Internat. Oil Co., 1961-67; dir. First Nat. Bank Findlay, 1939-83, chmn. bd., 1947-83; dir. Toledo Trust Co., 1958-80, Toledo Trustcorp., Inc., 1970-80. Pres. Bd. Edn. Findlay, 1944-54; Trustee Case Western Res. U., Cleve.; Regional chmn. Boy Scouts Am., 1953-56, mem. nat. exec. bd., 1953-83; bd. dirs. World Scout Found., 1980-88. Mem. Findlay Country Club, Toledo Club, Belmont Country Club (Toledo), The Country Club, Union Club (Cleve.), Rolling Rock Club (Ligonier, Pa.), Bath and Tennis club, Beach Club, Everglades Club (Palm Beach, Fla.), Bailey's Beach Club, Country Club, Chagrin Valley Hunt Club (Cleveland, OH.), Newport (R.I.) Sigma Xi, Tau Beta Pi. Presbyterian. Home: 300 Parc Monceau Palm Beach FL 33480-5113

DONNELL, WILLIAM RAY, small business owner, communications executive; b. Lewiston, Maine, Oct. 3, 1931; s. William Thomas and Gladys Mae (Spinney) D.; m. Mayra Cintia Colon, June 16, 1962 (div. Jan., 1996); children: William Thomas, Jose Ismael, Ariadne Elizabeth. BA, U. Maine, 1959. Comml. capt.'s lic. 1954. Comml. fisherman Maine, 1948-52, 55-60; tchr. Bath (Maine) Jr. H.S., 1962, substitute tchr., 1963; tchr. Deer Isle (Maine) H.S., 1965, 71, tchr. adult edn., 1976; tchr. St. Jude Integrated H.S., St. Finians, Nfld., Can., 1972, Stonington (Maine) Elem. Sch., 1973; v.p., bd. dirs. Fisheries Comm., Inc., 1977—; owner, operator Donnell's Clapboard Mill, Sedgwick, Maine, 1983—; recreational dir. City of Bath, 1963; capt. prin. comml. passenger schooner, 1965-71; remedial instr. Harpwell Islands Sch., Maine, 1983—; farmer Deer Isle, 1968-71, 72-78, Highlands, NFld. 1971-72, Sedgwick, 1978—; lectr. in field, guest speaker TV Can.-U.S. offshore boundary issue. Contbg. editor Comml. Fisheries News, 1981-83; editor Maine Comml. Fisheries, 1979-80, Fisheries Fed. Register Rev., 1981-82; author numerous poems. Mem. Gov.'s Lobster Adv. Coun., Maine, 1980-85; candidate state legislature from Bath Area, Sagadahoc County, Maine, 1969; charter mem., bd. dirs. Maine Fisherman's Forum, Inc., 1985; lectr. discussion team Theleme's Laguna Beach, Calif., 1985; co-chmn. Hancock County 4-H Citizenshp Com., 1987-88; mem. exec. com. Hancock County Extension, 1988—; mem. Downeast Resource Conservation & Devel. Coun., 1994—; moderator Sedgwick Town Meeting, 1993-94; mem. Sedgwick Budget Com., 1995—. Sgt. U.S. Army, 1952-54, Korea. Decorated Bronze Star, Korean Svc. medal with 2 bronze stars; recipient Poetry award Nfld. and Labrador Arts and Letters Contest, 1972. Mem. Sigma Chi (pres.). Avocations: antique vehicles, vessels and machinery. Home and Office: Donnells Clapboard Mill County Rd Sedgwick ME 04676

DONNELLA, MICHAEL ANDRE, lawyer; b. Great Lakes, Ill., Oct. 16, 1954; s. Joseph Anthony and Jacqueline (Reddick) D. BA in Mathematics, Wesleyan U., Middletown, Conn., 1976; JD, U.Chgo., 1979. Bar: Ga. 1979, U.S. Ct. Appeals (D.C. and 11th cirs.) 1980, N.J. 1987. Assoc. Troutman, Sanders et al, Atlanta, 1979-83; atty. AT&T So. Region, Atlanta, 1983-86; sr. atty. AT&T Internat., Basking Ridge, N.J., 1986-95; divsn. counsel Am. Home Products Corp., St. Davids, PA, 1995—; vis. prof. Nat. Urban League Black Exec. Exchange Program, 1986, Huston-Tillotson Coll., Austin, Tex. Interviewer Wesleyan Schs. Com., Middletown, 1976—; counsel Ga. Legis. Black Caucus, Atlanta, 1982-86; mem. visitors com. U. Chgo. Law Sch., 1989-92. Named to 100 Black Men of N.J., Inc. Black Elected Ofcls. Found. Roman Catholic. Avocations: jazz, sports. Office: Am Home Products Corp 170 Radnor Chester Rd Wayne PA 19087-5252

DONNELLAN, ANDREW B., JR., lawyer; b. Rockville Centre, N.Y., Jan. 24, 1952. AB cum laude, Georgetown U., 1973; MBA, Rensselaer Polytechnic Inst., 1977; JD cum laude, Albany Law Sch., 1977. Assoc. Dewey, Ballantine, Bushby, Palmer & Wood, N.Y.C., 1977-86; with Reliance Group Holdings, Inc., N.Y.C., 1986—, v.p., chief litigation counsel, 1995—; bd. dirs. Larchmont Shore Club Corp. Office: Reliance Group Holdings Inc 55 E 52nd St New York NY 10055

DONNELLEY, JAMES RUSSELL, printing company executive; b. Chgo., June 18, 1935; s. Elliott and Ann (Steinwedell) D.; m. Nina Louis Herrmann, Apr. 11, 1980; children: Niel J., Nicole C. BA, Dartmouth Coll., 1957; MBA, U. Chgo., 1962. With R.R. Donnelley & Sons Co., Chgo., 1962—, v.p., 1974-75, group pres. fin. svcs. group, 1985-87, group pres. corp. devel., 1987-90, vice chmn. bd., 1990—, also bd. dirs. Office: RR Donnelley & Sons Co 77 W Wacker Dr Fl 8 Chicago IL 60601-1696

DONNELLY, ANNA, hospital administrator; b. Aug. 20, 1961. BS, St. John's U., Jamaica, N.Y., 1984, MD in Edn., 1989. Counselor HEOP divsn. St. John's U., 1986-90, asst. dir. HEOP divsn., 1990-92, assoc. dir., 1992-94, dir., 1994—. Office: St Johns Univ HEOP Divsn 8000 Utopia Pky Jamaica NY 11432-1343

DONNELLY, BARBARA, artist, educator; b. Somerville, Mass.; d. Russell Winfield and Pearl Marie (Cameron) Chick; m. Robert Boag Donnelly, May 29, 1954; children: Kathleen, Sharon, Robert Jr., Patricia, Michael, Brian. AA, Boston U., 1954. Tchr. oil painting, watercolors Beverly (Mass.) Adult Edn., 1969-80, 83-90, tchr. basic drawing, 1970-90; tchr. Lakes Region Outdoor Painting, N.H., 1977-85; tchr. pen, ink No. Essex C. C., Newburyport, Mass., 1986-88; court rm. artist Channel 56, Boston, 1987—; tchr. watercolor Gloucester, Mass., 1993—. Illustrator: The Little Book Shop, 1989; cover artist: Palette Talk, 1990; one-woman shows include French Embassy, Washington, 1998; contbr. articles to profl. jours. Asst. chmn. Beverly Bicentennial Arts Festival, 1975, chmn. 1976. Named Internat. Artist-in-Residence, Dinan, France, "Les Amis de La Grande Vigne" Mus., 1996. Mem. Am. Artists Profl. League, Acad. Artists Assn., North Shore Arts Assn., Rockport Art Assn., New England Watercolor Soc. (Paul Strisik Meml. award 1998), Guild of Beverly Artists, Copley Soc. of Boston. Roman Catholic. Avocations: photography, computer art, architecture. Office: Barbara Donnelly Art Gallery 19 Harbor Loop Gloucester MA 01930-5003

DONNELLY, BARBARA SCHETTLER, medical technologist, retired; b. Sweetwater, Tenn., Dec. 2, 1933; d. Clarence G. and Irene Elizabeth (Brown) Schettler; A.A., Tenn. Wesleyan Coll., 1952; B.S., U. Tenn., 1954; cert. med. tech., Erlanger Hosp. Sch. Med. Tech., 1954; postgrad. So. Meth. U., 1980-81; children—Linda Ann, Richard Michael. Med. technologist Erlanger Hosp., Chattanooga, 1953-57, St. Luke's Episcopal Hosp., Tex. Med. Ctr., Houston, 1957-58, 1962; engring. R &D SCI Systems Inc., Huntsville, Ala., 1974-76; cons. hematology systems Abbott Labs., Dallas, 1976-77, hematology specialist, Dallas, Irving, Tex., 1977-81, tech. specialist microbiology systems, Irving, 1981-83, coord. tech. svc. clin. chemistry systems, 1983-84, coord. customer trng clin. chemistry systems, 1984-87, supr. clin. chemistry tech. svcs., 1987-88, supr. clin. chemistry customer support ctr., 1988-93, supr. clin. chemistry and x-systems customer support ctr., 1993-97, ret., 1997. Mem. Am. Soc. Clin. Pathologists (cert. med. technologist), Am. Soc. Microbiology, Nat. Assn. Female Execs., U. Tenn. Alumni Assn., Chi

Omega. Contbr. articles on cytology to profl. jours. Republican. Methodist. Home: 204 Greenbriar Ln Bedford TX 76021-2006

DONNELLY, CAROL BURNS, education educator; b. Worcester, Mass., Sept. 15, 1946; d. Francis A. and Loretta (Chisholm) Burns; m. James C. Donnelly Jr., June 28, 1968; children: James C. IV, Sarah Y. BA, Wellesley Coll., 1968; MA, U. Miami, 1970; MEd, Harvard U., 1980; EdD, Boston U., 1988. High sch. tchr., guidance counselor Auburn (Mass.) Pub. Schs., 1971-74; parent liaison Cambridge (Mass.) Pub. Schs., 1980; kindergarten tchr. Newton (Mass.) Pub. Schs., 1982-84; early childhood coord. Auburn (Mass.) Pub. Schs., 1984-92, dir. spl. edn., 1992-97; asst. prof. edn. Worcester State Coll., 1997—; adj. instr. Bridgewater (Mass.) State Coll., 1978-79, Quincy (Mass.) Jr. Coll., 1974-79, Curry Coll., Milton, Mass., 1980-81, Boston U., 1979-80; mem. adv. bd. PEAK Program, Worcester Pub. Schs., 1985-87. Co-author: Streams and Puddles: A Comparison of Two Young Writers, 1980. Trustee Elm Park Ctr. for Early Childhood Edn., Worcester, 1988-91, pres., 1991; trustee Worcester Children's Theatre, 1986-88, Worcester Ctr. for Crafts, 1994—; pres., mem. coun. Worcester Art Mus., 1990-91; v.p. Preservation Worcester, 1990-92; trustee, incorporator Worcester Park Spirit Inc., 1987-90. Mem. ASCD, Mass. Tchrs. Assn., Mass. Assn. Early Childhood Tchr. Educators, Nat. Assn. Edn. Young Children, Pi Lambda Theta, Kappa Delta Pi. Office: 5 West St Auburn MA 01501-1301

DONNELLY, CHARLES ROBERT, retired college president; b. Allen, Mich., Apr. 3, 1921; s. Peter Joseph and Florence Veronica (Stitt) D.; m. Marilynn Elaine Jones, Sept. 15, 1945; children—Maureen, Michael, Mark, Bridget, Patrick, Kathleen. B.A., Hillsdale (Mich.) Coll., 1941; M.A., U. Mich., 1947, Ph.D., 1961. Tchr. English Rockwood (Mich.) High Sch., 1941-42; tchr. English, baseball coach Flint (Mich.) Community Jr. Coll., 1947-60, dean, then pres., 1960-70; pres. Community Colls. of U. Nev. System, 1970-77; pres. Alpena (Mich.) Community Coll., 1977-88, pres. emeritus, 1988—; interim pres. Mott C.C., Flint, Mich., 1992; mem. Western States Regional Manpower Adv. Com., 1970-74; pres. Mich. Assn. Jr. Colls., 1964-65. Served with AUS, 1942-46. Recipient Alumni Achievement award Hillsdale Coll., 1968; Athletic award Nat. Assn. Jr. Colls., 1970. Mem. Am. Vocat. Assn., Mich. Community Coll. Assn. Democrat. Roman Catholic. Clubs: Kiwanis, K.C. Home: 4420 E Shomi St Phoenix AZ 85044-4005

DONNELLY, EDWARD JAMES, JR., medical services company executive; b. Windsor, Ont., Can., May 16, 1946; s. Edward James and Hilda Rae (Cornwall) D.; m. JoDell Tamborello, Dec. 20, 1972 (div. 1982); children: Edward James III, Anna Mistelle. BS, U. Houston, 1973. Pres. Perfusion Assocs., Houston, 1970-85; pres., chief exec. officer Allied Cardiac Svcs., Houston, 1985-95; dir. ops. Tex. SETA/Baxter, Houston, 1995-96, Baxter/New Bus. Initiatives, 1996-97, Baxter CVG Perfusion Svcs., San Diego, 1997—; bd. dirs. Taylor Made Homes. Contbr. articles to profl. publs. Mem. Am. Soc. Extracorporeal Technologists (pres. so. region 1978-80, 84-86), Houston Bd. Realtors, Houston Jaycees. Republican. Episcopalian. Home: 2331 Dorrington St Houston TX 77030-3211 Office: Baxter CVG Perfusion Svcs 16818 Via Del Campo Ct San Diego CA 92127-1714

DONNELLY, GERARD KEVIN, marketing and retail executive; b. N.Y.C., July 2, 1933; s. Joseph R. and Margaret M. (Siefert) D.; m. Maria McAllister, Aug. 29, 1964; children: Gerard K., Peter F., Deirdre A., Patrick J., James V. BBA in Acctg., Pace U., 1957; cert. in indsl. rels., Colgate U., 1966. Asst. contr. Allied Stores Corp., N.Y.C., 1957-65; gen. auditor Lone Star Industries, N.Y.C., 1965-67; contr., asst. sec. Computer Applications Inc., N.Y.C., 1967-70; pres. Rhodes S.W., Phoenix, 1970-75; sr. v.p. Hart Schaffner & Marx, Chgo., 1975-81; CEO, chmn. bd. dirs. Hughes & Hatcher Inc., Phila., 1981-83; sr. v.p., dir. Macys-N.E. Inc., N.Y.C., 1983-90; pres., CEO H.C. Prange Co., Green Bay, Wis., 1990-94; with Edison Power Tech., Paramus, N.J., 1996—; mng. cons. Houlihan, Lokey, Howard & Zukin, N.Y.C., 1994—; CEO Princeton (N.J.)-Middletown Ptnrs., 1994—; bd. dirs. Frederick Atkins, Inc., N.Y.C., Younkers Inc., Des Moines, Princeton Mgmt. and Logistics Group, Inc., H.C. Prange Co., Green Bay, Innovative Power Techs., Inc., New Monmouth, N.J., Edison Power Techs., Inc., Proffitt's, Inc., Birmingham, Ala. Mem. County Com., Queens County, N.Y., 1955-64; commr. pks. and recreation, Manalapan Twp., N.J., 1967-68; bd. dirs. Ctrl. Bus. Dist. Assn., Detroit, 1981-83, U. Wis. Green Bay Founders Assn., 1991—. With USN, 1951-53. Mem. Nat. Retail Fedn., Am. Mgmt. Assn., Internat. Coun. Shopping Ctrs., Menswear Retailers Am., Cherry Valley Country Club, U.S. Power Squadron, N.Y. Athletic, Celtic Soc. Football (referee), KC (4 degree). Roman Catholic. Home: 160 Spring Hill Rd Skillman NJ 08558-1418 Office: PO Box 662 New Monmouth NJ 07748-0662

DONNELLY, JAMES CORCORAN, JR., lawyer; b. Newton, Mass., June 10, 1946; s. James C. Sr. and Margery J. (MacNeil) D.; m. Carol R. Burns, June 28, 1968; children: James C. IV, Sarah Y. BA, Dartmouth Coll., 1968; JD, Boston Coll., 1973. Bar: Mass. 1973, U.S. Dist. Ct. Mass. 1974, U.S. Ct. Appeals (7th cir.) 1979, U.S. Ct. Appeals (1st cir.) 1983, U.S. Tax Ct. 1988, U.S. Dist. Ct. (no. dist.) Ohio 1991, U.S. Ct. Appeals (2d cir) 1994. From assoc. to prin. Hale & Dorr, Boston, 1973-84; sr. ptnr. Mirick, O'Connell, DeMallie & Lougee, Worcester, Mass., 1985—, chmn. litigation dept., 1993-97; bd. dirs. C.P. Bourg, Inc., New Bedford, Mass. Editor-in-chief 1972 Annual Survey of Mass. Law. Corporator Greater Worcester Cmty. Found., 1986—, mem. monitoring and evaluation com., 1997—; trustee Higgins Armory Mus., Worcester, 1985—, pres. 1994-97, Worcester Art Mus., 1987-88; treas. Am. Antiquarian Soc., 1997—. Fellow Mass. Bar Found., 1994; mem. ABA, Mass. Bar Assn., Worcester County Bar Assn. (co-chmn. fed. ct. com. 1995—), Dartmouth Lawyers Assn., Worcester Club (bd. dirs. 1995—), Dartmouth Club Ctrl. Mass. (exec. com. 1996—, pres. 1997—), Dartmouth Coll. Club (Officers exec. com. 1997—, v.p. 1998—).que. Avocations: sailing, skiing, bicycling, hiking, history. Home: 285 Salisbury St Worcester MA 01609-1661 Office: Mirick O'Connell 1700 Bank Boston Tower 100 Front St Worcester MA 01608-1402

DONNELLY, JAMES OWEN, state legislator, bank executive; b. N.Y.C., Apr. 10, 1967; s. James William and Antoinette (Orlowski) D.; m. Melissa Beth Small, Sept. 2, 1991; children: James B., Joshua. BA in Polit. Sci., U. Maine, Presque Isle, 1990; postgrad., U. Maine, Orono, Husson Coll. Automobile salesman Norsworthy's Chrysler-Dodge, Presque Isle, 1990-93; mem. Maine Ho. Reps., Augusta, 1990—; mem. appropriations and fin. affairs com. Maine Ho. Reps., 1995—; leader Maine Ho. Reps., Augusta, 1996—; cmty. mid. market relationship mgr. Key Bank, Presque Isle, Maine, 1993—. Bd. dirs. Temporary Shelter for the Homeless, Presque Isle, 1992—, Aroostook County Action Program, 1993—, chmn. EEOC subcom.; mem. alumni bd. U. Maine at Presque Isle, 1992—; mem. del. Rep. City & County Com., vice chair Aroostook County Del., 1995-97, chair, 1997—, Presque Isle-Aroostook County, 1990—; notary public State of Maine, 1990—; active Leaders Encouraging Aroostook Devel., 1990—; apptd. by Gov. of Maine to Am. Coun. Young Polit. Leaders. Mem. Rotary Internat. Republican. Roman Catholic. Avocations: fishing, reading, camping, cross country skiing. Home: PO Box 176 Bangor ME 04402 Office: Key Bank 23 Water St Bangor ME 04402-1144

DONNELLY, KEVIN WILLIAM, lawyer; b. Rockville Centre, N.Y., Sept. 25, 1954; s. William Lorne and Marie Grace (Busch) D.; m. Judith Marcia Brier, July 19, 1986; children: Lisa, Jennifer. BS, Boston Coll., 1976, JD, 1979; MBA, Dartmouth Coll., 1982. Bar: N.Y. 1980, Mass. 1980. Tax atty. Exxon Corp., N.Y.C., 1979-80; assoc. Hemenway & Barnes, Boston, 1982-83; v.p., gen. counsel The Yankee Cos. Inc., Boston, 1983-88, Nortek, Inc., Providence, 1988—. Mem. ABA, Mass. Bar Assn. Home: 11 Foxhunt Trl Walpole MA 02081-2270 Office: Nortek Inc 50 Kennedy Plz Ste 1700 Providence RI 02903-2360

DONNELLY, LESLIE FAYE HARRIS, psychologist, psychology educator; b. Washington, Nov. 16, 1960; d. Virdin Hoyle and Nancy Lee (Burgess) Harris; m. Alan Scott; children: Nicholas Scott, Julia Lee. BA in Psychology, Salisbury State U., 1983; MA in Psychology, No. Ariz. State, 1988, EdD in Counseling Psychology, 1992. Lic. psychologist, Md. Counselor Adventure Discovery, Flagstaff, Ariz., 1984-86; grad. asst. No. Ariz. U., Flagstaff, 1987-91; pre-doct. intern Coconino Guidance Ctr., Flagstaff, 1991-92; postdoct. intern New Hope Counseling, Salisbury, Md., 1995-96; asst. prof. Salisbury (Md.) State U., 1993—; pvt. practice psychologist Salisbury, 1997—. Mem. Am. Psychol. Assn., Am. Soc. Clin. Hypnosis, Coun. Nat. Register Health Svc. Providers, Md. Psychol. Assn. Avocations: flying, running, parenting.

DONNELLY, MARIAN CARD, art historian, educator; b. Evanston, Ill., Sept. 12, 1923; d. Harold S. and Ethel (Gates) Card; m. Russell J. Donnelly, Jan. 21, 1956; 1 child, James Armstrong. AB summa cum laude, Oberlin Coll., 1946, MA, 1948; PhD, Yale U., 1956. Instr. fine arts Upsala Coll., 1948-50; art librarian U. Rochester, 1951-53; research asso. decorative arts Art Inst., Chgo., 1956-57; vis. lectr. U. Chgo., 1965; asst. prof. dept. art history U. Oreg., Eugene, 1966-68; asso. prof. U. Oreg., 1969-73, prof., 1973-81, prof. emeritus, 1981—; participant Attingham (Eng.) Summer Sch., 1972, 75; vis. research scholar in art history U. Copenhagen, 1972; lectr. U. Oreg. Center for Internat. Music, Stuttgart, Germany, 1972. Author: The New England Meeting Houses of the Seventeenth Century, 1968, A Short History of Observatories, 1973, Architecture in the Scandinavian Countries, 1992, Oregon Bach Festival 1970-94, 1994, A History, Society of Architectural Historians, 1998; contbr. articles to profl. jours. Bd. dirs.-at-large Oreg. Bach Festival. Am. Council Learned Socs. grantee, 1959-60. Fellow Royal Soc. Arts (London); mem. Archeol. Inst. Am., Nat. Trust for Scotland, Soc. for Preservation of New England Antiquities, Soc. Archtl. Historians (bd. dirs. 1964-67, 78-81, assoc. editor newsletter 1966-72, 2nd v.p. 1972-74, 1st v.p. 1974-76, pres. 1976-78, gen. chmn. Bicentennial programs 1975-76), Phi Beta Kappa. Home: 2175 Olive St Eugene OR 97405-2837

DONNELLY, MICHAEL JOSEPH, management consultant; b. Montreal, Quebec, Can., Dec. 28, 1951; s. Terrence James and Beatrice Miriam (Faloon) D.; m. Barbara Lynne Webb. BA in Commerce, Simon Fraser U., 1976. Chartered acct. Acct. Campbell, Sharp, Chartered Accts., Victoria, B.C., Can., 1973-76, KPMG, Victoria, 1976-79; controller Park Pacific Group of Cos., Victoria, 1979-80; gen. mgr. Indsl. Plastics (A subs. of the Park Pacific Group of Cos.), Victoria, 1980-83; chief fin. officer Action Group of Cos., Ft. Lauderdale, 1984-85; pres. Beacon Mgmt. Group, Inc., Pompano Beach, Fla., 1985—; trustee, mem. bd. trade PAC Inc., 1990-95; dir. Enterprise Amb. Program, 1991, chmn. adv. bd., 1995-98; dir. NatBank, 1996-97. Contbr. articles to profl. pubs. Chmn. Uptown Bus. Coun., 1996; chmn. adv. bd. Fla. Atlantic U. Small Bus. Devel. Ctr., 1993-96; mem. Coll. Bus. exec. adv. bd. Fla. Atlantic U., 1996-98. Mem. Nat. Assn. Accts. (bd. dirs. Ft. Lauderdale chpt. 1988-90), Inst. Chartered Accts. B.C., Can. Am. Bus. Alliance South Fla. (pres. 1989-95), Fla. Small Bus. Devel. Ctr. Network (adv. bd. 1990—, chmn. 1995—), Turnaround Mgmt. Assn., Assn. Insolvency Accts., Uptown Bus. Assn. (pres. 1989-90, chmn. CEO adv. coun. 1991-94, chmn. Uptown Bus. Coun. 1996), Greater Ft. Lauderdale C. of C. (bd. govs. 1995-96, 98—, bd. dirs. 1996, 99, v. chmn. govt. affairs, 1999). Avocations: bicycling, walking, golf. Office: Beacon Mgmt Group Inc 1000 W Mcnab Rd Pompano Beach FL 33069-4719

DONNELLY, ROBERT TRUE, retired state supreme court justice; b. Lebanon, Mo., Aug. 31, 1924; s. Thomas John and Sybil Justine (True) D.; m. Wanda Sue Oates, Nov. 16, 1946; children: Thomas Page, Brian True. Student, Tulsa U., 1942-43, Ohio State U., 1943; J.D., U. Mo., 1949. Bar: Mo. 1949. Mem. firm Donnelly & Donnelly, Lebanon; city atty. Lebanon, 1954-55; asst. atty. gen. Mo., 1957-61; justice Supreme Ct. Mo., Jefferson City, 1965-89; chief justice Supreme Ct. Mo., 1973-75, 81-83; bd. govs. Mo. Bar, 1957-63. Mem. Lebanon Bd. Edn., 1959-65; trustee Sch. Religion, Drury Coll., Springfield, Mo., 1958-66, Mo. Sch. Religion, Columbia, 1971-72. Served with inf. AUS, World War II. Decorated Purple Heart, Bronze Star. Mem. Mo. Bar Assn., Phi Delta Phi. Presbyterian. Home: 3112 Wiliamsburg Way Jefferson City MO 65109-5732

DONNELLY, ROBERT WILLIAM, bishop. Attended, St. Meinard (Ind.) Sem. Coll., Mt. St. Mary's West Sem., Norwood, Ohio. Ordained priest Roman Cath. Ch., 1957; ordained titular bishop Gasba, aux. bishop, Toledo, 1984. Home: 2544 Parkwood Ave Toledo OH 43610-1317*

DONNELLY, RUSSELL JAMES, physicist, educator; b. Hamilton, Ont., Can., Apr. 16, 1930; s. Clifford Ernest and Bessie (Harrison) D.; m. Marian Card, Jan. 21, 1956; 1 son, James. BSc, McMaster U., 1951, MSc, 1952, LLD, 1999; MS, Yale U., 1953, PhD, 1956. Faculty U. Chgo., 1956-66, prof. physics, 1965-66; prof. physics U. Oreg., Eugene, 1966—; chmn. dept. U. Oreg., 1966-72, 82-83; vis. prof. Niels Bohr Inst., Copenhagen, Denmark, 1972; co-founder Pine Mountain Obs., 1967; cons. GM Co. Rsch. Labs., 1958-68, NSF, 1968-76, 79-84, mem. adv. panel for physics, 1970-73, chmn., 1971-72; mem. adv. coms. on matls. rsch., 1979-84; mem. Task Force on Fundamental Physics and Chemistry in Space, Space Sci. Bd., NRC; cons. Jet Propulsion Lab., Calif. Inst. Tech., Pasadena, 1973-82; chmn. Sci. Adv. Com. for Low Temp. Facilities in Space, 1990-91; mem. fluid dynamics discipline working group, NASA, 1992-95; gen. chmn. 20th Internat. Conf. on Low Temp. Physics, 1993. Author: (with Parks, Glaberson) Experimental Superfluidity, 1967, (with Francis) Cryogenic Science and Technology: Contributions of Leo Dana, 1985, Quantized Vortices in Helium II, 1991; editor: (with Herman, Prigogine) Non-Equilibrium Thermodynamics Variational Techniques and Stability, 1966, High Reynolds Number Flows Using Liquid and Gaseous Helium, 1991, Procs. 20th Internat. Conf. Low Temperature Physics, Physica B, 1994; editor: (with Sreenivasan) Flow at Ultra-High Reynolds and Rayleigh Numbers; mem. editorial bd. Physics of Fluids, 1966-68, Phys. Rev. E, 1978-84, assoc. editor, 1987-93; mem. editorial bd. Jour. Phys. and Chem. Ref. Data, 1989-92, Handbook of Chemistry and Physics, 1998-98; contbr. articles to profl. jours. Bd. dirs. U. Oreg. Found., 1970-72, 88-91, investment com., 1990-91; bd. dirs. Oreg. Mus. Park Commn., 1975-87, chmn., 1975-82; bd. dirs. Oreg. Bach Festival, 1975-87, Oreg. Mozart Players, 1990-93. Alfred P. Sloan fellow, 1959-63; sr. vis. fellow Sci. Rsch. Coun., U.K., 1978; recipient Disting. Alumnus award McMaster U., 1992, Lars Onsager medal Norwegian U. Sci. and Tech., 1996; 1995 Chia-Shun Yih lectr. U. Mich., 1996 Fritz London Meml. lectr. Duke U, Howard Vollum award Reed Coll., 1997. Fellow AAAS, Am. Phys. Soc. (exec. com. div. fluid dynamics 1966-72, 80-84, 88-91, sec.-treas. 1967-70, 88-91, chmn. 1971-72, 82-83, APS Otto Laporte award 1974), Inst. of Physics (London); mem. Nat. Trust for Scotland, Soc. Archtl. Historians, Cosmos Club. Episcopalian. Research on physics fluids, especially hydrodynamic stability, turbulence and superfluidity. Home: 2175 Olive St Eugene OR 97405-2837 Office: Univ Oreg Dept Physics Eugene OR 97403-1274

DONNELLY, THOMAS JOSEPH, lawyer; b. Pitts., Mar. 4, 1925; s. Thomas E. and Ruth L. (Beitzer) D.; m. Marilyn A. Pfohl, Apr. 16, 1955; children: Thomas C., Elizabeth A., Daria, Heather, Michael, Marilyn, Peter. Student, MIT, 1943-44; BS in Engring., U. Mich., 1946, JD, 1950. Bar: Pa. 1951. Student engr. Westinghouse Electric Corp., 1946-47; since practiced in Pitts. Trustee Carlow Coll., Pitts., Weston Jesuit Sc. Theology, Cambridge, Mass.; bd. dirs. United Way Allegheny County. With USNR, 1943-46. Mem. Barristers Soc., Am., Pa., Allegheny County Bar assns., Tau Beta Pi. Roman Catholic. Clubs: Knight of Malta, Toastmasters U. Mich. Lawyers (Ann Arbor); University, Duquesne, Chatham (Mass.) Yacht. Home: 1085 Shady Ave Pittsburgh PA 15232-2912 Office: 1810 Centre City Tower Pittsburgh PA 15222-3907

DONNELLY-KEMPF, MOIRA ANN, nursing administrator; b. Toledo, June 11, 1963; d. Gerald M. and Ruth Ann (Crawford) Donnelly; m. Ronald W. Kempf, Aug. 31, 1985. Diploma, Mercy Sch. Nursing, Toledo, 1983; student, Eastern Mich. U., St. Joseph's Coll., 1992. RN. Clin. rehab. nurse Meml. Hosp., South Bend, Ind., 1983-84, U. Mich. Med. Ctr., Ann Arbor, 1985-87; med. claims nurse analyst Kapner Wolfberg & Assocs., Van Nuys, Calif., 1988-89; sr. auditing specialist Intracorp, Southfield, Mich., 1989-94, sr. early intervention specialist, 1994-97; mktg. assoc. The Lakeland Ctr, Southfield, 1997—. Mem. Mercy Sch. Nursing Alumnae Assn.

DONNEM, ROLAND WILLIAM, board of directors, hotel owner, developer; b. Seattle, Nov. 8, 1929; s. William Roland and Mary Louise (Hughes) D.; m. Sarah Brandon Lund, Feb. 18, 1961; children: Elizabeth Prince, Sarah Madison. BA, Yale U., 1952; JD magna cum laude, Harvard U., 1957. Bar: N.Y. 1958, U.S. Dist. Ct. (ea. and so. dists.) N.Y. 1959, U.S. Ct. Appeals (2d cir.) 1959, U.S. Ct. Claims 1960, U.S. Tax Ct. 1960, U.S. Supreme Ct. 1963, U.S. Ct. Appeals (3d cir.) 1969, D.C. 1970, U.S. Ct. Appeals (D.C. cir.) 1970, Ohio 1976, U.S. Dist. Ct. (no. dist.) Ohio 1980, U.S. Ct. Appeals (7th cir.) 1980, U.S. Ct. Appeals (6th cir.) 1984. With Davis Polk & Wardwell, N.Y.C., 1957-63, 64-69; law sec. appellate divsn. N.Y. Supreme Ct., N.Y.C., 1963-64; dir. policy planning antitrust divsn. Justice Dept., Washington, 1969-71; v.p., sec., gen. counsel Standard Brands Inc., N.Y.C., 1971-76; from v.p. law to sr. v.p. law and casualty prevention Chessie System, Cleve., 1976-86; ptnr. Meta Ptnrs., real estate devel., 1984-89, mng. ptnr., 1989—, registered security rep., 1985-90; bd. dirs., gen. counsel Acorn Properties, Inc., Cleve., 1985—, pres., 1989—; bd. dirs., gen. counsel Meta Devel. Corp., Cleve., 1985—, pres., 1989—; bd. dirs., gen. counsel Meta Properties, Inc., Cleve., 1988—, pres., 1989—; founding mem., bd. dirs. Assn. Sheraton Franchisees N.Am., 1997—. Mem. editl. bd. Harvard Law Rev., 1955-57. Bd. dirs., fin. v.p. Presbyn. Home for Aged Women, N.Y.C., 1972-76; bd. dirs., treas. James Lenox Ho., Inc., 1972-76; trustee Food and Drug Law Inst., 1974-76; trustee, sec. Brick Presbyn. Ch., N.Y.C., 1974-76; sec. class of 1952, Yale U., 1992-97; bd. dirs. Yale Alumni Fund, 1990-95; chmn. Cleve. Area Yale Campaign, 1991-97. Lt. (j.g.) USNR, 1952-54. Fellow Timothy Dwight Coll., Yale U., 1987—. Mem. D.C. Bar Assn., Ohio Bar Assn., Greater Cleve. Bar Assn., Am. Law Inst. (life), Am. Arbitration Assn. (nat. panel arbitrators), Def. Orientation Conf. Assn. (bd. dirs. 1996—), Yale U. Alumni Assn. Cleve. (treas. 1982-84, del. 1984-87, trustee 1984-93, adv. coun. 1993—), Yale U. Alumni Assn. (bd. govs. 1987-90), Union Club (N.Y.C. and Cleve.), Capitol Hill Club (Washington), Washington Chevy Chase Club, Cleve. Racquet Club, Kirtland Club (Cleve.), Met. Club (Washington), Phi Beta Kappa. Republican. Presbyterian. Home: 2945 Fontenay Rd Shaker Heights OH 44120-1726 Office: 3619 Park East Dr Ste 214 Beachwood OH 44122-4309

DONNEM, SARAH LUND, financial analyst, non-profit and political organization consultant; b. St. Louis, Apr. 10, 1936; d. Joel Y. and Erle Hall (Harsh) Lund; m. Roland W. Donnem, Feb. 18, 1961; children: Elizabeth Prince Donnem Sigety, Sarah Madison. BA, Vassar Coll., 1958. Tech. aide, computer programmer Bell Labs., Whippany, N.J., 1959-60; chmn. placement vol. opportunities N.Y. Jr. League, 1972-73, asst. treas. 1974-75, chmn. urban problems relating to mental health, 1967-69, mem. project rsch. com., 1967-71, chmn., 1973-74, mem. bd. mgrs. 1973-74; chmn. cmty. rsch. Washington Jr. League, 1970-71, mem. bd. mgrs., 1970-71; mem. Stratford Hall (N.Y.) Com., 1970—; bd. dirs. East Side Settlement House, Bronx, N.Y., 1972—, v.p., 1975-76, chmn. Nat. Horse Show Benefit, 1976, winter antiques show com., 1994—, co-chmn. adv. com., 1991-94, mem. nominating com., 1990—, mem. investment com., 1993—; bd. dirs. Stanley M. Isaacs Neighborhood Ctr., N.Y.C., 1973-76, v.p., 1975-76; bd. dirs. Presbyn. Home for Aged Women, N.Y.C., 1974-76, v.p., 1976; mem. exec. bd. N.Y. Aux. of Blue Ridge Sch., 1971-75, sec., 1965-67, pres., 1973-75; budget and benevolence com. Brick Presbyn. Ch., N.Y.C., 1973-76, mem. social svc. com., 1973-74, chmn. fgn. students com., 1963-64. Bd. dirs. Search and Care, N.Y.C., 1973-76, Project LEARN, Cleve., 1990-96; chmn. Literacy Fund, 1991-95, mem. 1995—; Friends of Project LEARN, 1986—; mem. Fedn. Cmty. Planning, Cleve., Coun. on Older Persons, 1978-82, mem. Future Planning Task Force, 1980-81, Commn. on Social Concerns, 1982-84; trustee Golden Age Ctrs. Greater Cleve., 1979-92, investment com., 1993, 1st v.p., 1980-81, pres., 1981-85, chmn. Western Res. Antiques Show, 1979, 80, exec. com., 1981, 97, antiques show adv. com., 1997—; women's adv. coun. Western Res. Hist. Soc., 1977, coord. sec. 1978; mem. women's com. Cleve. Orch., 1979-85, Vassar Coll. Cleve. sec. 1980-82, v.p. 1983, pres. 1984-86; AAVC Club Liason Com. 1986-89, chmn. regional program com., 1987-89, chmn. Vassar in Chgo. Conf. 1989; bd. dirs. Cleve. Ballet, 1980—, exec. com., 1981, 96—, fin. com., 1982-88, 95—, mem. ballet sch. com., 1985-88, nominating com., 1988-90, 95—, co-chair, 1997—; co-chmn. Yale Ball, 1983; bd. advisers Ret. Sr. Vol. Program, 1982, trustee, 1983-90, chmn. long range planning comm., 1986, sec. 1987-89; mem. Family Friends Adv. Coun., 1987-89; trustee Fairmount Presbyn. Ch., 1985-88; mem. long range planning com. United Way, Cleve., 1985-87; coord. Friends of Voinovich, 1987-89; womens advisory com. Voinovich for Governor, 1990, Voinovich for Senate, 1997-98, chmn. Voinovich Task Force On Aging, 1990-91, Ohio Adv. Coun. on Aging, 1991—, legis. com., 1994—, chmn., Cuyahoga County Republican policy Com., 1999—, Plain Dealer adv. counsel for elderly coverage, 1991-93; chmn. Johns Hopkins Parents Fund, 1986-88, Project LEARN 15th Anniversary celebration (with Barbara Bush, hon. chmn.), 1989-90; coord. Decorative Arts Trust Cleve. Symposium, 1996; mem. Leadership Cleve. Class 1992; del White House Conf. on Aging, 1995. Named Vol. of Yr. N.Y. Jr. League, 1975; recipient Sustainer Svc. award Jr. League Cleve., 1990. Mem. Nat. Inst. Social Scis. (mem. memberships com. 1972-92, trustee 1984-96). Nat. Soc. of Colonial Dames. Republican. Clubs: Colony (N.Y.C.); Chevy Chase (Washington); Intown, Vassar, Jr. League Cleve., Kirtland (Cleve.). Address: 2945 Fontenay Rd Shaker Heights OH 44120

DONNER, RICHARD, film director, producer; b. N.Y.C., 1939. Dir.: X-15, 1961, Salt and Pepper, 1968, Twinky, 1969, The Omen, 1976, Superman, 1978, Inside Moves, 1981, Radio Flyer, 1991; exec. prodr.: The Final Conflict, The Lost Boys, 1991, Delirious, 1991, Free Willy, 1993; dir., exec. prodr.: The Toy, 1982; dir., prodr.: Ladyhawke, 1985, Goonies, 1985, Lethal Weapon, 1987, Scrooged, 1988, Lethal Weapon 2, 1989, Lethal Weapon 3, 1992, Maverick, 1994, Assassins, 1995, Lethal Weapon 4, 1998; prodr.: Blackheart, 1999 (TV); dir., prodr.: Made Men, 1999); dir. (TV episodes) Have Gun Will Travel, Perry Mason, Cannon, Get Smart, The Fugitive, Kojak, Bronk, Lucas Tanner, Gilligan's Island, Man From U.N.C.L.E., Twilight Zone, The Banana Splits, Combat, Tales from the Crypt, Two Fisted Tales, Conspiracy Theory, 1997; (TV movies) Portrait of a Teenage Alcoholic, Senior Year, A Shadow in the Streets. Office: Richard Donner Prodns 4000 Warner Blvd Bldg 102 Burbank CA 91522-0001 also: CAA 9830 Wilshire Blvd Beverly Hills CA 90212-1804*

DONNER, WILLIAM TROUTMAN, psychiatrist; b. Sharon Pa., Jan. 8, 1921; s. Raymond H. and Edna (Troutman) D.; student U. Pa., 1939-42, MD, 1946; m. Alice Easby Wilkinson, Apr. 12, 1946; children: William W., Marda Elisa, Mary Alice, Margot Ramona. Intern, Allegheny Gen. Hosp., Pitts., 1945-46; resident Friends Hosp., Phila., 1948-50, Hosp. of U. Pa., 1950-51; practice medicine specializing in psychiatry, Abington, Pa., 1951-95; psychiatrist Neuropsychiat. Assocs. of Old York Rd., Abington, 1962-64; dir. mental health clinic Abington Meml. Hosp., 1958-64, interim chmn. dept. psychiatry, 1983-85; instr. U. Pa., 1951-58, assoc. psychiatry, 1958-78; clin. asst. prof. Hahnemann Med. Coll., 1978-96; acting chmn. Dept. Psychiatry, Abington (Pa.) Meml. Hosp., 1988-95, chmn. dept. Psychiatry Abington (Pa.) Meml. Hosp., 1994-95, emeritus chair, 1995. Pres. bd. dirs. Family Svc. Montgomery County, 1966-67. Served with AUS, 1946-48. Mem. Am. Geriatric Soc., Am. Psychiat. Assn., Am. Assn. Geriatric Psychiatrists, Pa. State, Montgomery County Med. Socs. Contbr. articles to tech. jours. Home: 314 Wellington Ter Jenkintown PA 19046-3832

DONNESON, SEENA SAND, artist; b. N.Y.C.; d. Max and Ann (Silber) S.; m. Sam Gershwin; children: Erika Donneson, Lisa Donneson. Attended, Pratt Inst., Art Students League. art staff NYU, Nassau County Office Cultural Devel., New Sch. for Social Rsch., N.H. Coll.; guest artist Tamarind Lithography Workshop; vis. artist Clayworks, N.Y.C. One-person shows include Lauren Rogers Mus. Art, Laurel, Miss., Greenville (N.C.) Mus. Art, Galerie #836, Sante Fe, N.Mex., Lehigh U., Princeton U., Portland (Maine) Mus. Art, Piertrantonio Gallery, N.Y.C., U. Calif., L.I. U., George Washington U., Danville (Va.) Mus. Fine Arts and History, others; exhibited in group shows at SUNY, N.Y.C., Quietude Sculpture Garden, N.J., Sculpture in Color, N.Y.C., Ft. Lauderdale (Fla.) Mus., Norfolk Mus. Arts and Scis., Bklyn. Mus., San Francisco Mus. Art, DeCordova Mus., fgn. traveling exhbns., USIS, Mcpl. Art Mus., Tokyo, also on tour throughout Japan, Musseo de Belles Artes, Buenos Aires, Argentina, Scotland, Eng.; represented in permanent collections Va. Mus. Fine Art, Bklyn. Mus., Norfolk Mus., USIA Art in Embassies, L.A. County Mus. Art, Mus. Modern Art, N.Y.C., Smithsonian Mus., N.J. State Mus., Ft. Lauderdale Mus. Fine Art, Snug Harbor Cultural Ctr., N.Y.C., N.Y. Pub. Libr., Cornell Med. Sch., N.Y.C., others, also numerous colls., univs. and bus. corps.; also pvt. collections; revs. Newsday, The N.Y. Times, The N.Y. Post, Art News, Conran Octypus Ltd., others. Recipient numerous art awards; fellow Edward MacDowell Found., guest artist Tamarind Lithography Workshop, Creative Artists Pub. Svc. grant N.Y. State Coun. on Arts, 1983-84; grantee Mcpl. Art Soc., N.Y. Art in Park, 1974, Queens Coun. on Arts, 1992. Mem. Artists Equity, Nat. Assn. Women Artists, L.I.C. Artists (bd. dirs.). Studio: 43-49 10th St Long Island City NY 11101-6923

DONNICI, PETER JOSEPH, lawyer, law educator, consultant; b. Kansas City, Mo., Sept. 5, 1939; s. Albert H. and Jennie (Danubio) D.; m. Diane DuPlantier, July 27, 1985; children: JuliaAnn Donnici Clifford, Joseph A.,

Joann Donnici Powers. BA, U. Mo., Kansas City, 1959, JD, 1962; LLM, Yale U., 1963. Bar: Mo. 1963, U.S. Supreme Ct. 1966, Calif. 1969. Asst. prof. law U. San Francisco, 1963-65, assoc. prof., 1965-68, prof., 1968-91, prof. emeritus, 1992—; assoc. Law Offices Joseph L. Alioto, San Francisco, 1967-72; sole practice San Francisco, 1974—; ptnr. Donnici & LuPo, San Francisco, 1982-92, Donnici, Kerwin, Phillips & Donnici, San Francisco, 1993—; chmn. L.L. Hillblom Found. & Charitable Trust, 1995—; asst. prosecutor Jackson County Prosecutor's Office, Mo., 1963; cons. to Office of Mayor of San Francisco, 1966-72; No. Calif. bd. dirs. Coun. on Legal Ednl. Opportunity, San Francisco, 1969-70; conciliator for housing discrimination cases HUD, San Francisco, 1976; cons. Calif. Consumer Affairs' Task Force on Electronic Funds Transfer, Sacramento, 1978-79; bd. dirs. Air Micronesia, Inc., DHL Internat., Ltd., Bermuda, Continental Micronesia; spl. counsel and del. to internat. confs. Commonwealth of No. Mariana Islands, 1983-84; faculty adviser U. San Francisco Law Rev., 1966-91; bd. counselors U. San Francisco, 1993—. Editor-in-Chief: U. Mo., Kansas City Law Rev., 1961-62; contbr. articles to profl. jours., 1964—. Lawyers' com. for Urban Affairs, San Francisco, 1965-68. Wilson scholar U. Mo.-Kansas City, 1956-62; Sterling fellow Law Sch., Yale U., 1962-63. Mem. Bench and Robe, Phi Delta Phi. Democrat. Roman Catholic. Home: 190 Cresta Vista Dr San Francisco CA 94127-1635 Office: One Post St Ste 2450 San Francisco CA 94104

D'ONOFRIO, MARY ANN, medical transcription company executive; b. Detroit, Jan. 24, 1933; d. Charles Henry and Cecilia Rose (Levan) Clifford; m. Dominic Armando D'Onofrio, Apr. 19, 1958; children: Margaret Clement, Anthony, Elizabeth, Maria Spurgeon. BA, Marygrove Coll., 1954; MLS, U. Mich., 1955. Cert. med. transcriptionist. Reader's advisor Detroit Pub. Libr., 1955-58; cataloger Willow Run (Mich.) Pub. Libr., 1959-61, St. Thomas Grade and High Sch., Ann Arbor, Mich., 1968-72; med. record analyst Chelsea (Mich.) Community Hosp., 1972-79; pres. Meditranscript Svc., Ann Arbor, 1979-81; asst. office mgr. Dr. Maxfield, D.O., Tucson, 1981-82; quality assurance analyst, utilization rev. Tucson (Ariz.) Gen. Hosp., 1983-86; exec. asst. Dr. McEldoon M.D., Tucson, 1986-88; pres. Meditranscript Svc., Tucson, 1986-88; co-owner Med-Comm Assocs., Tucson, 1989—; co-owner, assoc. designer EMA of Tucson custom apparel and jewelry design co. Co-author: Psychiatric Words & Phrases, 1990, 2d edit., 1998; contbr. articles to profl. jours; co-developer Cross-Search. Block leader Infantile Paralysis Assn., Ann Arbor, 1975-80, Easter Seal Assn., Tucson, 1983-86, Am. Heart Assn., 1994, Am. Cancer Soc., 1992, 96, Leukemia Soc. of Am., 1997, 98. Mem. Am. Assn. for Med. Transcription (parliamentarian Sonora Desert chpt. 1984-86, 90-93, 95, bylaws com. 1996-97, compiler/editor AAMI Annotated Bibliography 1981, Named Disting. Mem. 1984, treas. Sonora Desert chpt. 1987, 98, 99, jour. columnist 1982-86, by-laws com. 1995-97, policies & procedures panelist 1997-98), Ednl. Honor Soc., Pi Lambda Theta (life). Avocations: desert gardening, sunset/landscape photography, reading.

DONOFRIO, NICHOLAS M., computer engineer. BS, Rensselaer Polytech.; MS, Syracuse Univ. Designer Internat. Bus. Mach., 1967-83; dir. Semiconductor Devel. Lab., Burlington, Vt., 1983-85, sec., exec. mgr., 1985-86; gen. mgr. site ops. Semiconductor Devel. & Mfg., 1986-87; dir. hardware devel. Corp. Headquarters, 1987-88; v.p., corp. v.p., pres. Personal Computer Prod. Devel., 1988-91; sr. v.p., group exec. Server Group Internat. Bus. Mach., 1995-97, sr. v.p. tech., mfg., 1997—. Fellow IEEE; mem. Nat. Acad. Engr., Sigam Xi, N.Y. Acad. Sci. Office: IBM New Orchard Rd Armonk NY 10504*

DONOFRIO, PETER DANIEL, neurology educator; b. Syracuse, N.Y., June 5, 1950; s. Carmin Peter and Donna Marie (Powers) D.; m. Kathleen Ann Fitzgerald, May 29, 1976; children: Molly, Emily, Julie. BS, U. Notre Dame, 1972; MD, Ohio State U., 1975. Diplomate Am. Bd. Internal Medicine, Am. Bd. Neurology, Am. Bd. Emergency Medicine. Resident internal medicine Good Samaritan Hosp., Cin., 1978; resident neurology U. Mich. Med. Ctr., Ann Arbor, 1981, instr., 1982-84; instr. V.A. Hosp., Ann Arbor, 1982-84, asst. prof., 1984-85; asst. prof. U. Mich. Med. Ctr., Ann Arbor, 1984-85; asst. prof. neurology Wake Forest U. Sch. Medicine, Winston-Salem, N.C., 1986-89, assoc. prof., 1989-97, prof., 1997—, vice chmn. dept., 1993—; cons. in neurology, Winston-Salem, 1984—. Contr. articles to profl. jours. Dept. rep. United Way, Winston-Salem, N.C., 1989—. Scholar U. Notre Dame U., 1968. Fellow Am. Acad. Neurology; mem. Am. Assn. Electrodiagnostic Medicine, Am. Neurological Assn. Roman Catholic. Avocations: woodworking, piano, hi-fidelity, landscaping. Home: 3509 Donegal Dr Clemmons NC 27012-8678 Office: Wake Forest Univ Medical Center Blvd Winston Salem NC 27157

D'ONOFRIO, VINCENT PHILIP, actor. Appeared in films Full Metal Jacket, 1987, Adventures in Babysitting, 1987, Mystic Pizza, 1988, The Blood of Heroes, 1990, Naked Tango, 1990, Crooked Hearts, 1991, Dying Young, 1991, Fires Within, 1991, The Player, 1992, Household Saints, 1993, Being Human, 1994, Imaginary Crimes, 1994, Ed Wood, 1994, Stuart Saves His Family, 1995, Strange Days, 1995, Feeling Minnesota, 1996, Men in Black, 1997, The Velocity of Gary, 1998, The Newton Boys, 1998, Claire Dolan, 1998, The Championship Season, 1999, The 13th Floor, 1999, Steal This Movie, 1999, Spanish Judges, 1999, Impostor, 1999; on TV in The Taking of Pelham One Two Three, 1998. Office: ICM 8942 Wilshire Blvd Beverly Hills CA 90211-1934*

DONOGHUE, GEORGE EDWARD, retired secondary educator; b. Saginaw, Mich., July 7, 1943; s. George and Florine (Dodge) D.; m. Carolyn Jane Brown, Apr. 3, 1964; two children. BS, Western Mich. U., 1966, MA, 1976. Mgr. Valley Lanes, Midland, Mich., 1963-64; tchr. Portage (Mich.) Pub. Schs., 1966-91. Author: (poems) Poetry Motel, 1995, Sunday Suitor, 1997, The Dirty Word, 1997, Lou Daniels Nature Anthology, 1998. Mem. The Writers Voice of the YMCA, Met. Detroit. Mem. NEA, Mich. Edn. Assn., Portage Edn. Assn. (contract negotiator 1970-76), Kalamazoo Friends of Poetry, Acad. of Am. Poets. Home: 4006 Rockwood Dr Kalamazoo MI 49004-3148

DONOGHUE, JOHN, communications executive. Sr. v.p. mktg. MCI Comm. Corp., Washington. Office: MCI Comm Corp 1801 Pennsylvania Ave NW Washington DC 20006-3606*

DONOGHUE, JOHN CHARLES, software management consultant; b. Oswego, N.Y., Sept. 19, 1950; s. James Charles and Marion Louise (Farrell) D.; m. Ann Marie Perry, Dec. 20, 1969; children: John Charles II, Kelly Anne. BS in Electronic Tech., Chapman Coll., 1981; student, U. Calif., Irvine, 1981-82; MA, U. Redlands, 1987; postgrad., Western State U. Coll., 1988-89, Azusa Pacific U., 1991-93. Enlisted USAF, 1969, advanced through grades to staff sgt., 1977, resigned, 1979; mgr. Lockheed Aircraft, Ontario, Calif., 1979-85; project engr. Northrop Corp., Pico Rivera, Calif., 1985—; cons., Fontana, Calif., 1981—; mem. software coun. Northrop Corp., Hawthorne, Calif., 1987-97, software improvement network U. Calif., Irvine, 1988—, capability maturity model corr. group Software Engring. Inst., Pitts., 1993—, L.A. software improvement network U. So. Calif., 1994—; charter mem. Software Inspection and Rev. Orgn., Sunnyvale, Calif., 1981—. Vol. cons. S.W. Anthropol. Assn. Calif. State U., L.A., 1996-97, Resource Conservation Dist., Rancho Cucamonga, Calif., 1996—, Southwest Mus., L.A., 1997—. Mem. IEEE, Northrop Gruman Mgmt. Club, N.Y. Acad. Scis., Nat. Space Soc. Avocations: motorcycling, snorkeling. Office: Northrop Gruman Corp Mil Aircraft Sys Divsn 8900 Washington Blvd Pico Rivera CA 90660-3765

DONOGHUE, JOHN FRANCIS, archbishop; b. Washington, Aug. 9, 1928. Student, St. Mary's Sem., Cath. U. Ordained priest Cath. Ch., 1955. Chancellor and vicar gen. Washington Archdiocese, 1973-84; bishop Charlotte, N.C., 1984-93; archbishop archdiocese of Atlanta, 1993—. Home: 136 W Wesley Rd NW Atlanta GA 30305-3523 Office: Archdiocese of Atlanta Chancery Office 680 W Peachtree St NW Atlanta GA 30308-1931*

DONOGHUE, MILDRED RANSDORF, education educator; b. Cleve.; d. James and Caroline (Sychra) Ransdorf; m. Charles K. Donoghue (dec. 1982); children: Kathleen, James. Ed.D., UCLA, 1962; J.D., Western State U., 1979. Asst. prof. edn. Calif. State U.-Fullerton, 1962-66, assoc. prof., 1966-71; prof. Calif. State U., Fullerton, 1971—. Author: Foreign Languages and the Schools, 1967, Foreign Languages and the Elementary School Child, 1968, The Child and the English Language Arts, 1971, 75, 79, 85, 90; co-author: Second Languages in Primary Education, 1979; contbr. articles to profl. jours. and Ednl. Resources Info. Ctr. U.S. Dept. Edn. Mem. AAUP, AAUW, TESOL, Nat. Network for Early Lang. Learning, Nat. Coun. Tchrs. English, Am. Dialect Soc., Am. Ednl. Rsch. Assn., Nat. Soc. for Study of Edn., Am. Assn. Tchrs. Spanish and Portuguese, Internat. Reading Assn., Nat. Assn. Edn. Young Children, Orange County Med. Assn. Women's Aux., Authors Guild, Assn. for Childhood Edn. Internat., Phi Beta Kappa, Phi Kappa Phi, Pi Lambda Theta, Alpha Upsilon Alpha. Address: Prof of Education 800 State College Blvd Fullerton CA 92834

DONOHO, TIM MARK, entrepreneur; b. St. Louis, Sept. 25, 1955; s. James O. and Jean (Dace) D.; m. Deborah Ann Peeples, Feb. 27, 1981; children: Drew Morgan, Jourdan Alexis. BABA, Columbia Coll., 1979. Editor U.S. Army, Okinawa, Japan, 1973-77; sales mgr. Unival Investments, Okinawa, 1975-77; nat. dir. mktg. Pyramid Life Ins. Co., Springfield, Mo., 1978-82; chmn., owner Ins. Mktg. Group, Springfield, 1982-90; pres., owner Am. Dental Program, Inc., Ft. Lauderdale, Fla., 1984-97, Donoho Gruppe Cos., Ft. Lauderdale, 1985—; owner Advantage Dental Health Plans, Ft. Lauderdale, Fla., 1984-97; pub., editor, owner Prime Years News Mag., Ft. Lauderdale, 1985-92; chmn., owner Bus. Healthcare Coalition Inc., 1995-98, Healthfirst Dental Practices Inc., 1997—; chmn. Express Bakery, 1998—. Bd. dirs. So. Fla. chpt. Nat. Multiple Sclerosis Soc., 1996-97; founder, chmn. bd. dirs. Pastors Closet, 1989—, Film the Bible Mins., Inc., 1996—; bd. govs. Graves Archael. Mus., 1998—. With U.S. Army, 1973-77. Mem. Nat. Assn. Dental Plans (chmn. bd. dirs. 1996-97). Republican. Baptist. Avocations: tennis, golf, loudspeaker design. Home: 1075 Hillsboro Mile Hillsboro Bch FL 33062-2142 Office: Donoho Gruppe Cos 8100 N University Dr Ste 200 Fort Lauderdale FL 33321

DONOHOE, CATHRYN MURRAY, journalist; b. Bronx, N.Y.; d. Harry and Helen (Crowley) Murray; m. Thomas W. Donohoe, Dec. 1, 1962. BA in Am. Lit. cum laude, Middlebury Coll., 1958; grad. student in Russian lit., Columbia U., 1958-60; grad. student in journalism, American U., 1983-84; cert. in Russian lang. and culture, Gornyi Inst., St. Petersburg, Russia, 1993. Rsch. and policy coord. Radio Liberty, N.Y.C., 1963-74; freelance journalist, 1977-84; reporter Potomac (Md.) Almanac, 1985; reporter Washington Times, 1985-94, deputy editor, features, 1994—. Recipient Nat. Mag. award for pub. svc., 1985. Office: Washington Times 3600 New York Ave NE Washington DC 20002-1996

DONOHOE, JEROME FRANCIS, lawyer; b. Yankton, S.D., Mar. 17, 1939; s. Francis A. and Ruth D.; m. Elaine Joyce Bush, Jan. 27, 1968; 1 child, Nicole Elaine. BA, St. John's U., 1961; JD cum laude, U. Minn., 1964. Bar: Ill. 1964, S.D. 1964. Atty. Atchison, Topeka & Santa Fe Ry. Co., Chgo., 1967-73, gen. atty., 1973-78; gen. counsel corp. affairs Santa Fe Industries Inc., Chgo., 1978-84; v.p. law Santa Fe Industries, Inc., Chgo., 1984-90, Santa Fe Pacific Corp., Chgo., 1984-94; ptnr. Mayer, Brown & Platt, Chgo., 1990—. Mem. corp. coun. Interlochen (Mich.) Ctr. for Arts, 1987—; bd. dirs. Better Govt. Assn., 1989—. Capt. JAGC, U.S. Army, 1964-67. Fellow Ill. Bar Found.; mem. ABA (sect. vice chair, chair membership and railroad coms., pub. utility, comm. and transp. law sect.), Northwestern U. Assocs., Northwestern U. Corp. Counsel Ctr., Chgo. Club, Chgo. Athletic Assn., Michigan Shores Club (Wilmette, Ill.). Office: Mayer Brown & Platt 190 S La Salle St Ste 3100 Chicago IL 60603-3441

DONOHUE, CARROLL JOHN, lawyer; b. St. Louis, June 24, 1917; s. Thomas M. and Florence (Klefisch) D.; m. Juanita Maire, Jan. 4, 1943 (div. July 1973); children: Patricia Carol, Christine Ann Donohue Smith, Deborah Lee Donohue Wilucki; m. Barbara Lounsbury, Dec., 1978. AB, Washington U., St. Louis, 1939, LLB/JD magna cum laude, 1939. Bar: Mo. 1939. Ptnr. Husch, Eppenberger, Donohue, Cornfeld & Jenkins, St. Louis, 1949—. Contbr. articles to profl. jours. Campaign chmn. ARC, St. Louis County, 1950; mem. ad. com. Child Welfare, St. Louis, 1952-55; mem. exec. com. Slum Clearance, 1949, bond issues coms., 1995; mem. bond issue com. St. Louis County Bond Issue, screening and supervisory coms., 1955-61, county citizen's com. for better law enforcement, 1953-56, chmn. com. on immigration policy, 1954-56; mayor City of Olivette, Mo., 1953-56; chmn. St. Louis County Bd. Election Commrs., 1960-65; chmn. com. Non-Partisan Ct. Plan; vice chmn. bd. Regional Commerce and Growth Assn. (lifetime recognition award 1996); pres. St. Louis C.C. Found.; bd. dirs. Downtown St. Louis, Inc. (leadership award 1996), Civil Entrepreneurs Orgn., Caring Found., Gateway Mayors Emeritus Inc., Anti-Drug Abuse Edn. Fund, P.T. Boat. Comdr. USN, WWII. Decorated Bronze Star medal, Navy and Marine Corps medal; recipient Disting. Alumni award Washington U., 1991, Good Guys award NOW, 1995. Mem. ABA, Mo. Bar Assn. (past bd. govs., chmn. ann. meeting, editor jour. 1940-41), St. Louis Bar Assn. (past pres., v.p., treas., Disting. Lawyer award 1992), Order of Coif, Mo. Athletic Club, Univ. Club, Omicron Delta Kappa, Sigma Phi Epsilon, Delta Theta Phi. Office: Husch & Eppenberger 100 N Broadway Ste 1300 Saint Louis MO 63102-2789*

DONOHUE, DAVID PATRICK, engineering executive, retired navy rear admiral; b. N.Y.C., May 7, 1931; s. Patrick Joseph and Beatrice Anna (Bligh) D.; m. Dolores Theresa Bowen, Nov. 24, 1956; children: Christine, David, Steven, Joanne, Denise. AB, Holy Cross Coll., 1953; MSEE, U.S. Naval Postgrad. Sch., 1961; postgrad., Harvard Bus. Sch., 1969, Kennedy Sch. Nat. Security, 1986. Design advisor Vietnam Naval Shipyard, Saigon, Vietnam, 1965-66; plan/estimating supt. Puget Sound Naval Shipyard, Bremerton, Wash., 1966-69; ship projects officer, supr. shipbuilding USN, Seattle, 1969-71; ship systems engr. Staff Naval Air Forces Pacific, San Diego, 1971-75; exec. dir. surface platforms Naval Sea Systems Command, Washington, 1975-77; prodn., planning officer Pearl Harbor (Hawaii) Naval Shipyard, 1977-80; shipyard commdr. Norfolk Naval Shipyard, Portsmouth, Va., 1980-83; rear adm., dir. maintenance U.S. Atlantic Fleet USN, Norfolk, Va., 1983-89; engring. mgr. The Jonathan Corp., Norfolk, 1989-91; program mgr. The Jonathan Corp., 1991-93; v.p., gen. mgr. shipyard The Jonathan Corp., Norfolk, 1993-95; corp. tech. dir. Integrated Syss Analysts, Inc., Chesapeake, Va., 1995—; exec. adv. coun. Old Dominion U. Coll. Bus. and Pub. Adminstrn., 1996-99. Pres. Portsmouth Area United Way, 1981-82, com. mem. South Hampton Roads chpt. , Norfolk, 1983-88; chmn. Portsmouth Armed Svcs. YMCA, 1981-82. Mem. Am. Soc. for Quality Control (vice-chmn. Tidewater, Va. sect. 1995-97, chmn. 1997-98, sec. 1998—), Am. Soc. Naval Engrs. (councillor Tidewater, Va. sect. 1981-84, nat. councillor 1990-93), Soc. Naval Architects and Marine engrs. (Hampton Rds. sect. chmn. 1985-86, chmn. ship prodn. com. nat. shipbuilding rsch. program 1990-95, Va. gov.'s commn. on base retention 1995), VA Assn., Norfolk Naval Shipyard Portsmouth Assn. (pres. 1998—). Republican. Roman Catholic. Home: 216 Brackenridge Ave Norfolk VA 23505-4322 Office: Integrated Syss Analysts Inc 1717 S Park Ct Chesapeake VA 23320-8911

DONOHUE, EDITH M., human resources specialist, consultant; b. Balt., Nov. 10, 1938; d. Edward Anthony and Beatrice (Jones) McParland; m. Salvatore R. Donohue, Aug. 23, 1960; children: Kathleen, Deborah. BA, Coll. Notre Dame, Balt., 1960; MS, Johns Hopkins U., 1981, CASE, 1985, PhD in Human Resources, 1990. Dir. pub. relations Coll. Notre Dame, Balt., 1970-71, asst. dir. continuing edn., 1978-81, dir. continuing edn., 1981-86; coord. program bus. and industry Catonsville C.C., Baltimore County, Md., 1986-88; mgr. tng. and devel. Sheppard Pratt Hosp., Balt., 1988-90; assoc. prof. Barry U., advisor grad. program, 1993-98; adj. faculty Loyola Coll. Grad. Studies Program, Fla. Inst. Tech., Indian River C.C. Co-author: Communicate Like a Manager, 1989; co-editor, contbg. author career devel. workshop manual, 1985; contbr. articles to profl. jours. Pres. Cathedral Sch. Parents Assn., 1972-74; asst. treas., treas. Md. Gen. Hosp. Aux., 1975-78; dir. Homeland Assn., 1978-81; regional rep., leader Girl Scouts Cen. Md., 1975-76; dir. sect. Exec. Women's Network, Balt., 1983-85; adv. bd. Mayor's Com. on Aging, 1981-86; dir. Md. Assn. Higher Edn., 1985-88; vol. trainer United Way Martin County, co-chair campaign, 1994—, strategic planning com., 1998—; mem. steering com. Chautauqua South. Recipient Mayor's Citation, City of Balt. Council, 1985. Mem. Am. Assn. Tng. and Devel (bd. dirs.), Am. Counseling Assn., AAUW (dir., v.p. 1980-83), Soc. Human Resources Mgmt., Martin County Personnel Mgt. Assn. (edn. chmn. 1991-94), Martin County C. of C. (edn. com. 1991-94), Friends of Lyric (bd. dirs., chmn., strategic planning, pres.), Chi Sigma Iota (pres.), Phi Delta Kappa. Republican. Roman Catholic. Avocations: tennis, performing arts, reading, wellness. Home: Apt 3103 144 NE Edgewater Dr Stuart FL 34996-4477

DONOHUE, GEORGE L., federal aviation educator, former government official, mechanical engineer; b. Wichita, Kans., July 8, 1944; s. George Edward and Dorothy Mae (Cunningham) Custer; m. Andreana Grillis, June 7, 1969; children: Carmen, Kathleen, Georgiana, Caroline. Student, Ga. Inst. Tech., Atlanta, 1962-64; BSME, U. Houston, 1967; MS, Okla. State U., 1968, PhD, 1972. Coop student NASA, Clear Lake, Tex., 1963-67; postdoctoral fellow Naval Undersea Ctr., Pasadena, 1972-73; br. head Naval ocean Sys. Ctr., San Diego, 1973-76; prog. mgr. DARPA, Arlington, Va., 1976-77; div. head Naval Ocean Sys. Ctr., San Diego, 1977-79; v.p. Dynamics Tech. Inc., Torrance, Calif., 1979-84; prog. mgr. The Rand Corp., Santa Monica, Calif., 1984-88; office dir. Def. Adv. Rsch. project Agy., Arlington, 1988-89; v.p. The Rand Corp., Santa Monica, 1989-94; assoc. adminstr. rsch. and acquisition FAA, Washington, 1994-98; mem. profl. adv. com. Aerospace Engring. dept. Pa. State U., 1988-91; FAA vis. prof. air-transp. tech. and policy Sch. IT & Engring. George Mason U., Fairfax, Va., 1998—. Contbr. articles to profl. jours.; patentee in field. Adult advisor Girl Scouts U.S.A., Torrance, 1987-88; treas. YMCA Girls Gymnastics Team, San Pedro, Calif., 1983. Dept. Def. Merit Civil Svc. medal, 1977; NRC fellow, 1972; NDEA fellow, 1967. Fellow AIAA (policy com. 1990-94); mem. Aircraft Owners & Pilots Assn., Exptl. Aircraft Assn., Air Traffic Control Assn., Elks, Tau Beta Pi, Sigma Xi, Omicron Delta Kappa, Pi Tau Sigma. Roman Catholic. Avocations: flying, skiing, sailing, backpacking.

DONOHUE, JAMES J., lawyer; b. N.Y.C., Dec. 3, 1947; s. Joseph P. and Constance (Anderson) D.; m. Carol A. Mager, July 29, 1973; children: Jay Mager, Megan Constance. AB, Dartmouth Coll., 1969; JD, U. Pa., 1972. Atty. Fed. Defender Phila., 1972-76; ptnr. White and Williams, Phila., 1976—. Mem. ABA (chair trial evidence com., litigation sect. 1995—), Phila Bar Found. (trustee 1992-97), Phila. Racquet Club, Phila. Cricket Club, Rotary Club Phila. (bd. dirs. 1993-95), WYCK (bd. dirs. 1996—, treas. 1998—). Avocations: skiing, golf. Office: White and Williams 1800 One Liberty Pl 1650 Market St Philadelphia PA 19103-7395

DONOHUE, JOHN JOSEPH, law educator; b. Alexandria, Va., Jan. 30, 1953; s. Mildred (Sileo) Donohue; m. Marijke Rijsberman, Dec. 27, 1986 (div.); 1 child, Lauren Elizabeth; m. Maureen O'Kicki, Oct. 25, 1995; 1 child, Aidan John. BA, Hamilton Coll., 1974; JD, Harvard U., 1977; PhD, Yale U., 1986. Bar: Conn. 1977, D.C. 1978. Assoc. Covington & Burling, Washington, D.C., 1978-81; fellow Civil Liability Program, Law Sch. Yale U., New Haven, 1985-86; rsch. fellow Am. Bar Found., Chgo., 1986-95; Class of 1967 James B. Haddad prof. law Northwestern U., Chgo., 1994-95; prof. Stanford (Calif.) Law Sch., 1995—. Contbr. articles to profl. jours. Mem. ABA, Am. Econ. Assn., Phi Beta Kappa. Office: Stanford Law Sch Crown Quad Stanford CA 94305

DONOHUE, JOHN PATRICK, lawyer; b. N.Y.C., Sept. 16, 1944; s. Joseph Francis and Catherine Elizabeth (Feeney) D.; m. Patricia Ann Holly, June 11, 1977; children—Eileen Mary, Anne Catherine. B.A., Providence Coll., 1966; J.D., Catholic U. Am., 1969. Bar: N.Y. 1973, U.S. Ct. Appeals (2d cir.) 1973, U.S. Ct. Appeals (fed. cir.) 1974, N.J. 1975, U.S. Dist. Ct. N.J. 1975, U.S. Dist. Ct. (so., ea. dists.) N.Y. 1975, U.S. Supreme Ct. 1978, D.C. 1981, Pa. 1986. Spl. agt. FBI, Washington, 1969-71; assoc. Donohue & Donohue, N.Y.C., 1971-74, ptnr., 1974—; adj. prof. law internat. bus. transactions Seton Hall U. Sch. Law, Newark, 1986-94. Author book sect. Customs Fraud Section on Business Crimes, 1982; co-author: The Prevention and Prosecution of Computer and High Technology Crime. Bd. dirs. Maritime Exch. Delaware River and Bay; mem. bd. regents Cath. U. Am., 1990—, chmn. 1997—; trustee Rosemont (Pa.) Sch., chmn. 1996—; mem. bd. visitors Cath. U. Sch. Law, 1998—. Named Man of Yr., Phila. Customs, Brokers and Forwarders Assn., 1984. Mem. Customs and Internat. Trade Bar Assn., Pa. State Bar Assn. Republican. Roman Catholic. Office: Donohue & Donohue 232 S 4th St Philadelphia PA 19106-3704

DONOHUE, JOYCE MORRISSEY, biochemist, toxicologist, nutritionist, educator; b. Holyoke, Mass., Jan. 27, 1940; d. Richard Charles and Anna Elizabeth (Joyce) Morrissey; m. John Thomas Donohue, Jan. 27, 1973; children: Maura Joyce, John Thomas, Sean Richard, Eric Patrick. BS, Framingham (Mass.) State Coll., 1961; MS, U. Mass., 1964; PhD, U. N.H., 1972. Cert. secondary sch. tchr., Mass. ; registered dietitian. Tchr. West Springfield (Mass.) H.S., 1962-66; instr. Framingham State Coll., 1966-68, asst. prof. biochemistry and nutrition, 1971-72, assoc. prof., 1972-73; adj. prof. No. Va. C.C., Annandale, 1974—, Va. Poly. Inst. and State U., Falls Church, 1979-97; health scientist VJ Cicconi & Assocs., Woodbridge, Va., 1981-89; toxicology svc. mgr. Law Environ. Washington Svc. Ctr., Woodbridge, Va., 1989-90; program mgr., prin. scientist ICAIR/Life Sys. Inc., Arlington, Va., 1990-94; mgr. toxicology NSF Internat., Washington, 1994-96; sr. toxicologist Office Water U.S. EPA, Washington, 1996—; mem. adv. com. Prince William County Sch. Food Svc., 1983-85. Vice chmn. citizens adv. com. for debris landfill and solid waste mgmt., Prince William County, 1987—; mem. Prince William County Wetlands Bd., 1989—; mem. dietetics program adv. com. James Madison U., Va., 1997—. Recipient Alumni Achievement award Framingham State Coll., 1986. Mem. AAAS, Am. Dietetic Assn. (cert.), No. Va. Dietetic Assn., Sigma Xi. Home: 11979 William And Mary Cir Woodbridge VA 22192-1314 Office: USEPA 401 M St SW Mail Code 4304 Washington DC 20460

DONOHUE, MARC DAVID, chemical engineering educator; b. Watertown, N.Y., Sept. 10, 1951; s. Paul Francis and Beverly Gertrude (Hodge) D.; m. Mary Ann Chamberlain, July 20, 1974; children: Paul, Megan, Ian. BS, Clarkson Coll. Tech., 1973; PhD, U. Calif., Berkeley, 1977. Asst. prof. chem. engring. Clarkson Coll. Tech., Potsdam, N.Y., 1977-79; asst. prof. Johns Hopkins U., Balt., 1979-83, assoc. prof., 1983-87, prof., 1987—, chmn. dept., 1984-95. Recipient Adminstr.'s Pollution Prevention award for Region III, U.S. EPA, 1992, Md. sect. Outstanding Engring. Achievement award NSPE, 1989. Mem. Am. Inst. Chem. Engrs., Am. Chem. Soc., Am. Soc. Engring. Edn. (Outstanding Young Engr. award 1984), Tau Beta Pi.

DONOHUE, MARY, state official; b. Rensselaer County, N.Y.; children: Sara, Justin. B.Edn., Coll. New Rochelle, 1968; MS in Edn., Russell Sage Coll., Troy, N.Y., 1973; JD, Union U., 1983. Bar: N.Y. 1983. Tchr. elem., jr. h.s. Rensselaer and Albany County (N.Y.) sch. dists., Albany, 1969-78; law clk., intern U.S. Atty.'s Office, Albany, 1980-83; assoc. O'Connell & Aronowitz, Albany, 1983-88; pvt. practice Troy, 1988-92; asst. county atty. Rensselaer County, 1990-92, dist. atty., 1992-96; justice N.Y. Supreme Ct., 3rd Jud. Dist., 1996-98; lt. gov. State of N.Y., Albany, 1998—. Chair Capital Dist. Women's Adv. Coun., 1996; mem. Gov.'elect Pataki's Transition Team for Criminal Justice, 1994-96. Office: Office of Lt Governor State Capitol Rm 326 Albany NY 12224*

DONOHUE, PATRICIA CAROL, academic administrator; b. St. Louis, Jan. 11, 1946; d. Carroll and Juanita Dohonue; m. James H. Stevens Jr., Aug. 27, 1966 (div. Mar. 1984); children: James H. III, Carol Janet. AB, Duke U., 1966; MA, U. Mo., 1974, PhD, 1982. Tchr. math, secondary schs. Balt., St. Louis and Shawnee Mission, Kans., 1966-71; lectr. U. Mo., Kansas City, 1975-76, rsch. asst. affirmative action, 1976-79, coord. affirmative action, 1979-82, instl. rsch. assoc., 1982-84, acting dir. affirmative action and acad. pers., 1984; dir. instl. rsch. Lakeland C.C., 1984-86; asst. dean acad. affairs, math., engring. and tech. Harrisburg Area C.C., 1986-89, dean sch. bus., engring., and tech., 1989-93, dean Lebanon campus, v.p. cmty. devel. and external affairs, 1993; vice chancellor edn. St. Louis C.C., 1993—, acting pres. Florissant Valley campus, 1998-99; active Pa. Coun. on Vocat. Edn., 1989-93; bd. dirs. St. Louis Sch. to Work, Inc., 1994—, v.p., 1994-96, pres., 1996—; chairperson Pa. Occupl. Deans, 1988-93; bd. dirs., chmn. edn. com. Humane Soc. Mo., 1997—. Bd. dirs., v.p. Am. Cancer Soc. Jackson County, 1975-84; mem. adv. coun. Ben Franklin Partnership, 1988-93; leader Hemlock coun. Girl Scouts U.S.A., bd. dirs. 1986-93; bd. dirs. PTA, 1975-77, Cmty. Lebanon Assocs., Ctrl. Pa. Tech. Coun., 1989-93, sec., 1992-93; bd.d irs. Mantec, 1988-93; mem. steering com. New Baldwin Corridor Coalition, 1991-93, chair edn. task force, 1992-93; mem. Leadership St. Louis, 1996-97. Recipient Outstanding Service and Achievement award U. Mo. Kansas City, 1976, Outstanding Svc. award Ctrl. Pa. Tech. Coun., 1993; Jack C. Coffey grantee, 1978; named Outstanding Woman AAUW, 1989, one of Outstanding Leaders Nat. Inst. Leadership Devel., 1986, Exec. Leadership Inst., 1990. Mem. ASCD, Nat. Coun. Tchrs. of Math., Math. Assn. Am., Am. Vocat. Assn., Am. Assn. Cmty. Colls. (mem. coun. affiliated chairpersons 1994—, chairperson coun. 1996—, mem. commn. on cmty. and workforce devel. 1995-98), Nat. Coun. for Occupl. Edn. (chairperson diversity task force 1991, chairperson job tng. 2000 task force 1992, bd. dirs. 1992—, v.p. programs 1992-93, v.p. membership 1993-94, pres. 1995-96, past pres. 1996-97), Am. Assn. Women in Cmty. and Jr. Colls. (Pa. state coord. 1988, bd. dirs. Region 3 1989-91), Soc. Mfg. Engrs. (chmn. 1989-90), Women's Equity Project, Nat. Assn. Student Pers. Adminstrs., Women's Network, Assn. Inst. Rsch., Phi Delta Kappa (pres. 1975, Read fellow 1989), Phi Kappa Phi, Pi Lambda Theta, Delta Gamma (v.p., del. nat. conv. 1988, pres. 1989-91, Cream Rose Outstanding Svc. award 1070). Home: 6235 Washington Ave Saint Louis MO 63130-4847 Office: St Louis C C 300 S Broadway Saint Louis MO 63102-2800

DONOHUE, STACEY LEE, English language and literature educator; b. Patchogue, N.Y., Dec. 1, 1963; d. Harold E. and Janice C. (Devine) Mahneke; m. Steven B. Huddleston, Dec. 15, 1996. BA in English, SUNY, Binghamton, 1985; PhD in English, CUNY, 1995. Instr. English, Borough of Manhattan C.C., CUNY, 1988-95; assoc. prof. English, Ctrl. Oreg. C.C., Bend, 1995—; adj. instr. NYU, 1990-93. Editor: (newspaper) The Lookout, Bend, 1995-96. Bd. dirs. Cen. Oreg. Forest Issues Com., Bend, 1995-96, Human Dignity Coalition, Bend, 1998—; mem. Friends of the Libr., Bend, 1996—. Mem. MLA, Pamla MLA, Multi Ethnic Lit. of U.S., Eugene O'Neill Soc. Avocations: hiking, backpacking, movies. E-mail: sdonohue@cocc.edu. Office: Ctrl Oreg CC Humanities Dept 2600 NW College Way Bend OR 97701-5933

DONOIAN, GEORGE, association executive; b. Detroit, Apr. 12, 1931; s. John H. and Irma Helen (Mekhitarian) D.; m. Eleanor Amanda Hall, July 29, 1961 (div. Feb. 1986); 1 child, John Hayden. BA, Wayne State U., 1954, MEd, 1955, EdD, 1963, postgrad., 1965. Cert. tchr. elem. and secondary edn., Mich. Elem. tchr. Detroit Pub. schs., 1954-65, reading coord., 1965-66, adminstr. h.s., 1966-67, program devel. adminstrn., 1967-71, bus. adminstr. schs., 1971-86; faculty Wayne County C.C., Detroit, 1970-71, prof. dept. psychology, 1971-72; prof. psychology and sociology St. Mary's Coll., Orchard Lake, Mich., 1991-94; prof. psychology/edn. No. Mich. U., Marquette, 1965. Contbr. articles to profl. jours. Field rep. Am. Diabetes Assn., Dearborn Heights, Mich., 1991—. Sgt. U.S. Army, 1951-59. Recipient Anthony Wayne award Wayne State U., 1983. Mem. APA (emeritus mem.), Soc. for Armenian Studies, Armenian Numismatic Soc., Ret. Orgn. for Suprs. and Adminstrs., Wayne County Sch. Bus. Ofcls. (pres. 1982), Knights of Vartan (comdr. 1987-92). Republican. Presbyterian. Avocations: collecting miniature books, pocket knives and coins, travel, photography, jewelry making. Home: 26005 Joy Rd Dearborn Heights MI 48127-1100

DONOVAN, ALAN BARTON, college president; b. Rochester, N.Y., Dec. 16, 1937; s. John Arnold and Rosalie (Kreag) D.; m. Carol Henning, Aug. 15, 1975; children: Timothy B., Leah. AB, Williams Coll., 1959; PhD, Yale U., 1964. Instr., asst. prof. Temple U., Phila., 1963-65; asst. to assoc. prof. Kenyon Coll., Gambler, Ohio, 1965-70; dean SUNY Coll. at New Paltz, 1970-73; dean arts and scis. Giassboro (N.J.) State Coll., 1973-84; v.p. acad. affairs No. Mich. U., Marquette, 1984-88; pres. SUNY Coll. at Oneonta, 1988—; mem. N.J. com. for humanities, New Brunswick, 1979-84, chmn. 1983-84; mem. Mich. coun. for humanities, East Lansing, 1986-88. Woodrow Wilson Found. fellow, 1959-60. Mem. Phi Beta Kappa. Office: SUNY Office of Pres Oneonta NY 13820*

DONOVAN, ANDREW JOSEPH, financial consultant; b. N.Y.C., Nov. 22, 1952; s. Andrew Joseph and Marion (Cooley) D.; m. Margaret Mary Dowd, June 17, 1984; children: Andrew, John, Daniel. BA, Fordham U., 1974, MA, 1976, PhD, 1983. Adj. instr. Fordham U., Bronx, N.Y., 1976-78; ops. mgr. Merrill Lynch, Pierce, Fenner & Smith, N.Y.C., 1978-79; stockbroker Merrill Lynch, Pierce, Fenner & Smith, Mt. Kisco, N.Y., 1984-88, Kidder Peabody, White Plains, N.Y., 1988-89; dir. devel. N.Y. Med. Coll., Valhalla, 1989-93, U.S. Merchant Marine Acad. Found., Inc., Kings Point, N.Y., 1993-96; fin. cons. Chase Investment Svcs. Corp., 1996—; chmn. N.Y. State 4-H Found., Inc., 1990-92. Author: The Political Clock, 1983. Councilman Town of Yorktown, N.Y., 1990-93; legislator Westchester County, N.Y., 1994-97. Lt. cmdr. USNR, 1979—. Fellow H.B. Earhart Found., 1976. Republican. Roman Catholic. Avocation: collecting books. Home: 3195 Radcliffe Dr Yorktown Heights NY 10598-2520 Office: Chase Investment Svcs Corp 2035 Crompond Rd Yorktown Heights NY 10598-4230

DONOVAN, ANNE, coach; b. Ridgewood, N.J., Nov. 1, 1961. Asst. coach Old Dominion U.; head coach women's basketball E. Carolina U., Greenville, 1995-98; head coach Phila. Rage, 1998-99. Recipient Naismith Player of Yr. award, 1983, Olympic Team Gold medal, 1984, 88, World Championship Team Gold medal, 1986. Mem. USA Basketball Com. (exec. bd. dirs. 1996—). Three time All-Am. selection; led nation in rebounding, 1982; all-time leading scorer, blocker and rebounder Old Dominion Univ.; Olympian, 1980, 84, 88; World Championship team, 1983, 86. Office: c/o USA Basketball 5465 Mark Dabling Blvd Colorado Springs CO 80918-3842*

DONOVAN, BILLY, university basketball boach; b. May 30, 1965; m. Christine D'Auria; children: William, Hasbrouck, Bryan. BA, Providence Coll., 1987. Profl. basketball player N.Y. Knicks, NBA, 1987-88; grad. asst. coach U. Ky., Lexington, 1989-90, asst. coach, 1990-93, assoc. coach, 1993-94; head coach Marshall U., 1994-96, U. Fla., Gainesville, 1996—; [. Named Nat. Rookie Coach of Yr., Basketball Times, 1994, W.Va. Coll. Coach of Yr., 1994, So. Conf. Coach of Yr., 1994. Office: U Fla Basketball Office PO Box 14485 Gainesville FL 32604*

DONOVAN, BRIAN, reporter, journalist; b. Syracuse, N.Y., Mar. 11, 1941; children: Gregg, Becky.; BA, Syracuse U., 1963. With Democract & Chronicle, Rochester, N.Y., 1964-67; investigative reporter Newsday, Melville, N.Y., 1967—. Recipient Pulitzer Prize for investigative reporting, 1995, George Polk award for Nat. Reporting, 1980, John Hancock award for Fin. Reporting, 1985, others. Office: Newsday 235 Pinelawn Rd Melville NY 11747-4250*

DONOVAN, BRIAN JOSEPH, oil industry executive; b. Paterson, N.J., Feb. 12, 1953; s. John Harold and Helen (Cheevers) D.; m. Rachael Cecile Couvillon, Jan. 16, 1982; children: Meaghan Marie, Michael John. Student, Villanova U., 1970-71; BS in Marine and Nuclear Engring., U.S. Merchant Marine Acad., 1975; JD, Syracuse U., 1997. Lic. chief engr. USCG. Marine engr. J. Ray McDermott, U.K., 1975-77; sr. project mgr. Offshore Logistics, Inc., various fgn. cities, 1977-82; prin. B. Donovan and Assocs., Inc., Lafayette, La., and Riyadh, Saudi Arabia, 1982—; chmn., chief exec. officer Internat. Drilling and Exploration, Inc., Lafayette, Montevideo, Uruguay, 1987—; del. U.S.-China Joint Session on Industry, Trade, and Econ. Devel., China, 1988; founder The Mercosur Group, Buenos Aires, 1992. Author: Vessel Preservation, 1986; patentee oil and gas well blowout suppression system. Mem. ABA, Fla. Bar, Internat. Bar Assn., Inter-Am. Bar Assn., Am. Soc. Naval Architects and Marine Engrs., U.S. Mcht. Marine Acad. Alumni Assn. Roman Catholic. Avocations: golf, skiing, karate, world travel. E-mail: donovanb@gte.net. Home: 28736 Skyglade Pl Wesley Chapel FL 33543-6415 Office: The Mercosur Grp PO Box 7455 Wesley Chapel FL 33543-7455

DONOVAN, BRUCE ELLIOT, classics educator, university dean; b. Lawrence, Mass., Mar. 8, 1937; s. Harry Albert and Ruth Hannah (Kent) D.; m. Doris Louise Stearn, Sept. 7, 1959; children: Gregory Stearn, Erika Ruth. AB, Brown U., 1959; postgrad., U. Bristol, Eng., 1959-60; MA, Yale U., 1961, PhD, 1965; postgrad., Rutgers Center for Alcohol Studies, 1976. Instr. Yale U., 1962-65; from instr. to prof. classics Brown U., Providence, 1965—; assoc. dean for chem. dependency Brown U., 1977—, dean freshmen and sophomores, 1981-87, assoc. dean coll., 1977—; instr. summer sch. alcohol studies Rutgers U.; cons. on collegiate alcoholism and other drug abuse. Author: Euripides Papyri from Oxyrhynchus, 1969; author articles and revs. on ancient Greek lit. and alcohol and other drug issues. Bd. dirs. Vols. in Action, 1975-90, R.I. Coun. on Alcoholism and Other Drug Dependence, 1973-94, New Eng. Inst. Alcohol Studies, 1978-91; founding mem. New Eng. Coll. Alcohol Network, Academics Recovering Together; steering com. Network Colls. and Univs. Committed to the Elimination of Substance Abuse, 1988-93. Fulbright fellow, 1959-60; Woodrow Wilson fellow, 1960-61; fellow Center for Hellenic Studies, Washington, 1971-72. Mem. Am. Philol. Assn., Employee Assistance Profl. Assn. Home: 261 President Ave Providence RI 02906-5537 Office: Brown U PO Box 1865 Providence RI 02912-1865*

DONOVAN, CAROL ANN, state legislator; b. Lynn, Mass., June 5, 1937; d. John Barrows and Virginia Mary (Pearce) D. AB, Regis Coll., Weston, Mass., 1959, MA, 1980. Tchr. home econs. Woburn (Mass.) Sch. System, 1959-74, spl. edn. tchr., 1974-84, spl. edn. liaison, 1984-90; mem. Mass. Ho. of Reps., Boston, 1991—; vice chair Post Audit and Oversight Com., Boston; polit. cons. Mass. Tchrs. Assn., Boston, 1985-89. Mem. Mass. Caucus of Women Legislators, 1991—; mem. Nat. Women's Polit. Caucus, 1989—; bd. dirs. Winchester (Mass.) Hosp., 1992—, New Horizons Woburn; bd. dirs. Ctrl. Middlesex Assn. Retarded Citizens, Woburn, 1984—, also past pres.; sec. Woburn Dem. City Com., 1984—. Recipient Elder Advocacy award Minuteman Home Care, Burlington, Mass., 1993, Disting. Citizen award ARC Mass., Waltham, 1993, Legislator of Yr. award Mass. Disabilities Coun. and ARC, 1994. Mem. Women's Legis. Lobby, Woburn Middlesex Lions Club. Roman Catholic. Avocation: travel. Office: State House Rm 473B Boston MA 02133*

DONOVAN, CHARLES STEPHEN, lawyer; b. Boston, Feb. 28, 1951; s. Alfred Michael and Maureen (Murphy) D.; m. Lisa Marie Dicharry, Apr. 21, 1979; children: Yvette, Martine, Neal. BA, Haverford Coll., 1974; JD, Cornell U., 1977. Bar: Mass. 1977, La. 1977, Calif. 1982, U.S. Supreme Ct. 1988. Atty. Phelps, Dunbar, Marks, Claverie & Sims, New Orleans, 1977-81, Dorr, Cooper & Hays, San Francisco, 1981-84, Walsh, Donovan, Lindh & Keech LLP, San Francisco, 1984—; instr. maritime law Calif. Maritime Acad., Vallejo, 1982—; spl. advisor U.S. State Dept., 1993-96. Contbr. numerous articles to profl. jours. Recipient Gustavus H. Robinson prize Cornell Law Sch., 1977. Mem. ABA (chmn. admiralty and maritime law com. Chgo. 1989-90), Internat. Bar Assn., Maritime Law Assn. U.S. (chmn. com. on maritime criminal law 1998—, chmn. subcom. on maritime liens and mortgages 1994—), Tulane Admiralty Inst. (permanent adv. bd.), Marine Exch. (bd. dirs. San Francisco Bay region 1993-96). Avocations: skiing, hiking, mandolin, guitar, sailing. Office: Walsh Donovan Lindh & Keech LLP 595 Market St Ste 2000 San Francisco CA 94105-2831

DONOVAN, CRAIG POULENEZ, public administration educator; married; 3 children. BA, U. Calif., 1979, 80; MA, San Francisco State U., 1985; PhD, U. Wash., 1994. Mem. faculty various colls., Calif., Wash., and, N.J., 1983-94; sr. cons., mgr. Parallel Lines/Quantum Svcs., San Francisco, 1984-89; asst. prof., dir. BA/MPA honors program Kean U., Union, N.J., 1994—; adv. City of Plainfield, N.J., 1996—, Union County Devel., N.J., 1997—. Author: Director of Journals in Public Affairs, Public Administration and Political Science, 1999; co-author: Psychologically Speaking: A Self-Assessment, 1996; editor: A Guide to Graduate Education in Public Affairs and Public Administration, 1997; creator, prodr.: (tv series) The Reinvention Machine, Part of the Communicating Commitment: The Public Service Excellence and Leadership Program, 1997—; contbr. articles to profl. jours. Recipient Rsch. award Wash. Dept. of Transp., 1993, 94. Mem. Am. Soc. Pub. Adminstrn. (nat., N.J. chpts.), Nat. Assn. Schs. Pub. Affairs and Adminstrn. (spl. projects editor), N.J. Rsch. Consortium (exec. coun.), Acad. Mgmt. Office: Kean U Sch Bus Govt Tech 1000 Morris Ave Union NJ 07083-7133

DONOVAN, DENIS MILLER, psychiatrist, author, lecturer; b. Chgo., June 5, 1946. BA in Edn., Psychology, Social Sci. and French, Antioch Coll., 1969, MEd in Psychology and Social Sci., 1969; MD, McMaster U., Hamilton, Ont., Can., 1975. Diplomate Am. Bd. Med. Psychotherapists; lic. psychiatrist Fla., Va., N.C.; cert. tchr. Gt. Britain, Calif. Tchr. French Corvallis (Oreg.) Sch. Dist., 1969-70; rsch. psychologist dept. clin. psychology VA O.P. Clinic, L.A., 1970; psychotherapist children's svcs. Camarillo (Calif.) State Hosp., 1970-71; resident in psychiatry Inst. for Social Psychiatry, London, 1971-72, U. N.C., Chapel Hill, 1977-79; psychiat. cons., trainer office edn. and staff devel. S.C. State Dept. Social Svcs., 1975-81; med. dir. child and family svcs. Area Mental Health Program of Vance, Granville, Franklin and Warren Counties, 1979-83; psychiat. cons. region IV adoption resource ctr. U. N.C., Chapel Hill, 1979-80; pvt. practice child, adolescent and gen. psychiatry Chapel Hill, 1979-83; dir. Rsch. Triangle Ctr. for Psychotherapy, Research Triangle Park, N.C., 1981-83; dir. adult impatient svc. Community Mental Health Ctr. and Psychiat. Inst., Norfolk, Va., 1983; med. dir. The Children's Ctr. for Devel. Psychiatry, St. Petersburg, Fla., 1983—; cons. Nat. Coun. for Adoption, Guardian ad Litem Program Juvenile Ct. 6th Jud. Dist., Fla., Child Protection Team All Children's Hosp., St. Petersburg, Pinellas County Sch. System, Fla. Diagnostic and Learning Recources System, Early Childhood Coun. Pinellas County, Pinellas County Assn. for Learning Disabilities; trainer Fla. Inst. Law Enforcement, Fla. Dept. Law Enforcement Crime Against Children Div.; adj. prof. Union Grad. Sch., 1973; adj. faculty St. Petersburg Jr. Coll., 1987; founder co-founder Kairos Ventures, Ltd.; chair New Traumatology Conf.; prof. psychiatry & traumatology Psychosocial Stress Rsch. Lab. & Clinic, Fla. State U. Co-author: Healing the Hurt Child: A Developmental-Contextual Approach, 1990, What Did I Just Say!?! How New Insights into Childhood Thinking Can Help You Communicate More Effectively With Your Child, 1999. W.S. Hall Psychiatric Inst. fellow, 1975-77. Fellow Am. Assn. Social Psychiatry, Am. Psychol. Soc., Am. Assn. Applied Preventive Psychology, Brit. Assn. Social Psychiatry; mem. AAAS, Am. Acad. Child and Adolescent Psychiatry (book reviewer), Met. Washington Soc. Adolescent Psychiatry, Am. Soc. Adolescent Psychiatry, Am. Acad. Psychiatry and the Law (book reviewer), Fla. Acad. Forensic Psychiatry, N.Y. Acad. Scis., Childhood Trauma Soc. (founder), Soc. for Rsch. in Child Devel., Soc. for Social Studies of Sci., Soc. for Rsch. on Adolescence, Cognitive Sci. Soc., Internat. Soc. for Traumatic Stress Studies. Office: Children's Ctr Devel Psychiatry 6675 13th Ave N Ste 2-a Saint Petersburg FL 33710-5483

DONOVAN, DENNIS DALE, priest; b. Nyack, N.Y., Feb. 26, 1954; s. Thomas A. and Helen I. (Rudolph) D. BA in Philosophy, Don Bosco Coll., 1977; MA in Theology, Pontifical Coll. Josephinum, 1983, MDiv in Theology, 1983. Joined Soc. St. Francis de Sales, Roman Cath. ch., 1973, ordained priest, 1983; cert. tchr. N.Y., N.J. Asst. adminstr. Salesian Sch., Goshen, N.Y., 1983-85; adminstr. Salesian Ctr., Columbus, Ohio, 1985-94, vicar, 1998—; dir. devel. Salesians of Don Bosco Province of St. Philip the Apostle, New Rochelle, N.Y., 1994-98; assoc. pastor St. Anthony Ch., Nanuet, N.Y., 1994-98; vicar Salesian Provincial House, New Rochelle, N.Y., 1994-98, Salesian Ctr., Columbus, Ohio, 1998—; assoc. pastor St. Joseph Cathedral, Columbus, 1998—; assoc., youth min. St. Andrew Parish, Upper Arlington, Ohio, 1985-94; mem. Nat. Cath. Devel. Conf., 1995—; chmn. Ea. province Salesian Centennial Com., 1995-98. Chaplain Ohio Senate, Columbus, 1987-94, Don Bosco Ladies Guild, Larchmont, N.Y., 1994—; trustee Salesian Boys and Girls Club Columbus, 1993—; mem. Juvenile Delinquency Task Force, Franklin County, 1988-90; mem. Westchester chpt. Crohn's and Colitis Found. Am., 1980—; exec. dir. Salesian Boys & Girls Club, Columbus, Ohio, 1998—; mem. Profl. Adv. Coun. United Way Franklin County, Columbus, 1998—, Ohio Alliance of Boys & Girls Clubs, 1998—; bd. trustees Discovery Dist. Devel. Corp., Columbus, 1998—; mem. race rels. vision coun. United Way Franklin County, 1999—, Columbus Met. Area Ch. Coun., 1999—. Recipient Senate Resolution award Ohio Senate, 1988. Mem. Acad. Boys & Girls Club Profls., Nat. Soc. Fundraising Execs., Am. Guild Organists (bd. dirs., chaplain 1986—), KC (chaplain 1987—), Assn. Boys and Girls Club Profls. Home: 80 S 6th St Columbus OH 43215-4726

DONOVAN, DIANNE FRANCYS, journalist; b. Houston, Sept. 30, 1948; d. James Henry and Doris Elaine (Simerly) D.; m. Anthony Charles Burba; children: Donovan Anthony, James Donovan. Student, Trinity Coll., Dublin, Ireland, 1969; BA, Spring Hill Coll., 1970; MA, U. Mo., 1975, U. Chgo., 1982. Copy editor Chgo. Sun-Times, 1977-79; fgn./nat. copy desk supr. Chgo. Tribune, 1979-80, asst. editor for news/features, 1980-83, lit. editor, 1985-93, mem. editorial bd., 1993—; vis. prof. U. Oreg. Sch. Journalism, Eugene, 1983-85; adj. faculty Northwestern U. Sch. Journalism, 1980-81, 89-90; bd. dirs. Chgo. Tribune Found. Bd. dirs. Nelson Algren/Heartland lit. awards, Chgo., 1986-93; judge Nat. Headliners' Club Awards, Atlantic City, N.J., 1983. Episcopalian. Office: Chgo Tribune Co 435 N Michigan Ave Chicago IL 60611-4066

DONOVAN, DONNA MAE, newspaper publisher; b. Jersey City, Mar. 14, 1952; d. William Clayton and Elizabeth Dorothy (Hanley) Hagemann; m. Jerome Francis Donovan, Nov. 6, 1982; children: Matthew James, Andrew William, Erin Elizabeth. BA in Journalism, Syracuse U., 1974. Pub. Burlington (Vt.) Free Press, 1986-91, Utica (N.Y.) Observer-Dispatch, 1991—; v.p. East region Gannett Co., 1986-88. Bd. dirs. Chittenden County United Way, 1987-91, also chmn. cmty. svc. div.; bd. dirs. Leadership Champlain, 1987-91; bd. dirs. Leadership Mohawk Valley, 1992-98, pres., 1995-96, sec., 1997-98; bd. dirs. Ctrl. N.Y. Cmty. Arts Coun., 1994—, Downtown Utica Devel. Assn., 1992-98, sec., 1996-98; bd. dirs. Oneida County Indsl. Devel. Corp., 1993-97; bd. dirs. Oneida County EDGE, 1998—, Mohawk Valley C.C. Found., 1997—; mem. nat. adv. bd. Syracuse U. Sch. Journalism; mem. Our Lady of Lourdes Parents Adv. Bd., 1992-98. Mem. Newspaper Assn. Am., N.Y. Newspaper Pubs. Assn. (bd. dirs. 1993-96), Mohawk Valley C. of C. (bd. dirs. 1999—), United Way of Greater Utica (bd. dirs. 1999—). Roman Catholic. Office: Observer-Dispatch 221 Oriskany Plz Utica NY 13501-1201

DONOVAN, DOROTHY DIANE, adult nurse practitioner; b. Red Bank, N.J., Apr. 26, 1961; d. John J. and Elsie H. (Carey) D. BSN, Seton Hall U., 1986, MSN, 1995. RN, N.J.; ANP, N.J.; cert. med.-surg. nurse; cert. adult nurse practitioner; cert. in infection control. Adult nurse practitioner HIP Healthplan of N.J., Edison, N.J.; nurse dept. emergency Riverview Med. Ctr., Red Bank, N.J. Mem. ANA, AANP, N.J. Nurses Assn., Sigma Theta Tau.

DONOVAN, GEORGE JOSEPH, industry executive, consultant; b. Jersey City, Apr. 15, 1935; s. Matthew T. and Jean (Wilson) D.; m. Susan M. Tamborini; children—Marybeth, George Joseph Jr., Amy. BS in Chemistry, St. Peter's Coll., Jersey City; postgrad. in organic chemistry, Seaton Hall U.; postgrad. in fin. and mktg., NYU; postgrad. in internat. relations, U. Pa. Research chemist Reaction Motors, Inc., Denville, N.J., 1956-58; research and devel. tech. rep. Thiokol Corp., Washington, 1961-63, asst. mgr. midwest regional office, 1963-65, mgr., dir. aerospace mktg., 1965-74, asst. to pres., 1974-75, corp. dir. mktg., 1975-77, v.p., 1977-82; dep. asst. sec. for systems Office of Asst. Sec. Air Force for Research Devel. and Logistics, Washington, 1983-85, prin. dep. asst. sec., 1985-86; pres. Prime Resources, 1986-87; v.p. Washington ops. Tex. Instruments Inc., 1988-91; v.p. govtl Relations Smiths Industries, 1991—, also bd. dirs.; cons. to industry and govt., Def. Sci. Bd.; mem. Naval Rsch. Adv. Com.; bd. dirs. USO Capital. Patentee liquid and solid propellant ingredients and formulations (13); contbr. articles to profl. jours. Recipient Exceptional Civilian Svc. award USAF. Mem. AIAA, Navy League, Air Force Assn. (bd. dirs.), Navy League (exec. com.), Assn. U.S. Army, Navy League (bd. dirs.), Nat. Def. Indsl. Assn. (bd. dirs., chmn. pub. policy com.), Congression Country Club. Club: Congression Country. Avocations: hunting, fishing, golf, boating, reading. Home: 4632 Charleston Ter NW Washington DC 20007-1900

DONOVAN, GERALD ALTON, retired academic administrator, former university dean; b. Hartford, Conn., Feb. 10, 1925; s. Gerald Joseph and Alice Gertrude (Gleason) D.; m. Barbara Ann Hue, Feb. 1, 1948; children: Deborah E. (Mrs. Alan Abare), Clayton H., Bruce G. BA, U. Conn., 1950, MS, 1952; PhD, Iowa State U., 1955. Poultry nutritionist Charles Pfizer & Co., Inc., Terre Haute, Ind., 1955-60; prof., chmn. poultry sci. dept. U. Vt., 1960-66; asso. dir. U. Vt. (Vt. Agrl. Expt. Sta.); asso. dean Coll. Agr. and Home Econs., U. Vt., 1966-73; dean Coll. Resource Devel., U. R.I., Kingston, 1973-89, dir. Internat. Ctr. Marine Resource Devel., 1975-89, ret., 1989—; exec. dir. Northeastern Region Aquaculture Ctr., Southeastern Mass. U., 1988-90, ret., 1990; mem. U.S. AID/BIFAD Joint Research Council, 1979-83. Contbr. articles to profl. jours. Bd. dirs. Vt. C.C., 1970-73, Operation Clean Govt., 1997—; tech. specialist AARP-Tax Aide Program, 1993—; chairperson Narragansett Rep. Com., 1991-93; vol. tax cons. to the elderly. With USN, 1943-46. Mem. Am. Inst. Nutrition, Agrl. Research Inst., Assn. Agrl. Expt. Sta. Dirs., Sigma Xi, Alpha Zeta, Alpha Gamma Rho. Home: 65 Wyndcliff Dr Saunderstown RI 02874-2408

DONOVAN, GREGORY STEARN, human services administrator; b. Sept. 11, 1962. BA, Grinnell Coll., 1984; MPA, U. Mo., 1990. Clin. counselor Youth Opportunities Upheld, Worcester, Mass., 1985-87; dir. agy. rels. Heart of Am. United Way, Kansas City, Mo., 1987-94; budge analyst Nebr. Unicameral Legis., Lincoln, Nebr., 1994-97; dir. spl. initiatives Lincoln Action Program, 1997—. Home: 6056 Cross Creek Rd Lincoln NE 68516-3779

DONOVAN, HELEN W., newspaper editor. Exec. editor Boston Globe, 1993—. Office: Boston Globe Newspapers PO Box 2378 Boston MA 02107-2378*

DONOVAN, JOHN ARTHUR, lawyer; b. N.Y.C., Apr. 11, 1942; children: Lara, Alex. AB, Harvard U., 1965; JD, Fordham Law Sch., 1967. Bar: N.Y. 1967, U.S. Tax. Ct. 1968, U.S. Ct. Appeals (2nd cir), 1968, U.S. Dist. Ct. (so., no. dists.) N.Y. 1969, U.S. Supreme Ct. 1971, U.S. Ct. Appeals (10th cir.) 1972, U.S. Ct. Appeals (9th cir.) 1976, Calif. 1982, U.S. Dist. Ct. (so., no. dists.) Calif. 1982, U.S. Ct. Appeals (5th cir.) 1983, Alaska 1993. Assoc. Hughes, Hubbard & Reed, N.Y.C., 1967-74; ptnr. Hughes, Hubbard & Reed, N.Y.C., L.A., 1974-85, Skadden, Arps, Slate, Meagher & Flom, L.A., 1985—; mem. adj. faculty law sch. U. So. Calif., L.A., 1986-87. Office: Skadden Arps Slate Meagher & Flom 300 S Grand Ave Ste 3400 Los Angeles CA 90071-3109

DONOVAN, JOHN VINCENT, consulting company executive; b. Chgo., May 13, 1924; s. Timothy Vincent and Mabel (Hederman) D.; m. Patricia Hasselhorn, Dec. 29, 1950; children: James, Timothy, Walter. AB, DePauw U., 1947, postgrad. in law, 1947-48; postgrad. in bus., Northwestern U., 1949-54. Mem. adminstrv. staff Swift-Brazil, 1947-50; asst. treas. Mid State Corp. Mobil Homes, Union City, Mich., 1951-55; gen. mgr. Bailey Corp., cosmetics, Chgo., 1955-58; sales mgr. Dole Corp., Honolulu, Ill., 1961-63; chmn. Intercon Rsch. Assocs. Ltd., Lincolnwood, Ill., 1963—. Past bd. dirs. Ind. Voters Ill., Chgo. Lt. (j.g.) USNR, 1942-45. PTO. Mem. AAAS, Licensing Execs. Soc., Assn. Corp. Growth, World Future Soc., Chgo. Athletic Assn., Mich. Shores Club. Home: 431 Laurel Ave Wilmette IL 60091-2809 Office: Intercon Rsch Assocs Ltd 6865 N Lincoln Ave Lincolnwood IL 60646-2697

DONOVAN, LESLIE ANN, honors division educator, consultant; b. Kansas City, Mo., July 9, 1957; d. Richard Wayne and Marilyn (Lovelady) D. BA in English, U. N.Mex., 1982, MA in English, 1986; diploma with honors, U. Coll., Dublin, Ireland, 1987; PhD in English, U. Wash., 1993. Tchg. asst. dept. English U. Wash., Seattle, 1989-90; asst. dir. English computer-integrated courses, Seattle, 1990-92; instr. Albuquerque TV-I, 1993-96; instr. dept Women Studies U. N.Mex., Albuquerque, 1994-96; instr. English U. N.Mex., 1994-96, instr. gen. honors program, 1995-96, asst. prof. gen. honors divsn., 1996—; Legacy Curriculum, U. N.Mex., 1993, chair com. gen. honors, 1996—, mem. coun. women studies, 1995-96; freelance editor, proofreader, Albuquerque, 1987—. Contbr. articles, poetry to jours. in field. ITT Internat. fellow Internat. Exch., 1986. Mem. AAUW, MLA, Rocky Mountain Modern Lang. Assn. (chair Old English 1996—). Avocations: computers, science fiction, fantasy. Office: U NMex Gen Honors Program Humanities Bldg Albuquerque NM 87131

DONOVAN, MARION CONRAN, school social worker; b. Quincy, Mass., Oct. 11, 1926; d. Joseph and Ellen (Fitzgerald) Conran; m. Francis Joseph Donovan, Nov. 22, 1952; children: Jeanne Francis Jr., Darilyn, Judith, Kenneth, Brian, David. AB, Emmanuel Coll., 1948; MSW, Boston Coll., 1950. Lic. social worker. Family caseworker Newark Family Svc., 1953; family svc. worker Boston Family Svc., 1950-52, 54; sch. social worker Plainville (Mass.) Pub. Sch. System, 1977-78; sch. social worker Needham (Mass.) Pub. Schs., 1978-91, ret., 1991. Chmn. child abuse study LWV, 1989-90; founding pres. St. Elizabeth's Hosp. Aux., Brighton, Mass., 1969—; bd. dirs. Tufts Med. Sch. Faculty Wives, 1968-75, Mass. Hosp. Assn. Aux., 1970-73. Mem. NEA, LWV, Nat. Assn. Social Workers, Mass. Tchrs. Assn. Roman Catholic. Avocations: reading, quilting, water activities.

DONOVAN, MAUREEN DRISCOLL, lawyer; b. N.Y.C., Dec. 2, 1940; d. Bartholomew Driscoll and Josephine (Keohane) Driscoll. AB, Coll. of New Rochelle, 1962; LLB with honors, Fordham U., 1966. Bar: N.Y. 1966, U.S. Supreme Ct. 1971, U.S. Ct. Appeals (2d cir.) 1975, U.S. Dist. Ct. (so. dist.) N.Y. 1976. Assoc. White & Case LLP, N.Y.C., 1966-75, ptnr., 1975—. Trustee St. Barnabas Hosp., Bronx, N.Y., 1992—, chair fin. com. 1997—, vice chair bd., 1998—; trustee N.Y. Urban Coalition, N.Y.C., 1990-94. Mem. ABA, Princeton Club (N.Y.), Coral Beach Club (Paget, Bermuda), Englewood (N.J.) Field Club. Office: White & Case LLP 1155 Avenue of the Americas New York NY 10036-2711

DONOVAN, MAUREEN HILDEGARDE, librarian, educator; b. Boston, Dec. 13, 1948; d. Alfred Michael and Maureen Hildegarde (Murphy) D.; m. James Richard Bartholomew, Sept. 9, 1978; 1 child, Thomas Alfred Bartholomew. BA, Manhattanville Coll., 1970; MA in East Asian Langs. and Cultures, Columbia U., 1973, MS in Libr. Svc., 1974. Asst. editor R.R. Bowker Co., N.Y.C., 1973; librarian I Gest Oriental Libr. Princeton (N.J.) U., 1974-77, libr. II, 1977-78; instr., Japanese studies libr. Ohio State U., Columbus, 1978-88, asst. prof., Japanese studies libr., 1988-94, assoc. prof., Japanese studies libr., 1994—; vis. lectr. Sch. Libr. and Info. Sci. Keio U., Tokyo, 1995-96; cons. U. Wis., Madison, 1991, McGill U., Montreal, Que., 1993, RMG, Inc., Chgo., 1993; webmaster East Asian Librs. Cooper WWW, 1994—. Editor mailing list Asian Database Online Cmty., 1993-97, editor electronic newsletter, 1998—. Fellow Japan Found., Tokyo, 1995-96; grantee U.S. Dept. Edn., 1994-96, Japan-U.S. Friendship Commn., 1994-96, Sun Microsystems, Inc., 1995; inductee Matignon H.S. (Cambridge, Mass.) Achievement Hall of Fame, 1999. Mem. ALA, Assn. for Asian Studies (chair com. on East Asian librs. 1991-94), Internat. Assn. Orientalist Librs. Home: 2372 Lytham Rd Columbus OH 43220-4640 Office: 328 Main Libr 1858 Neil Ave Columbus OH 43210-1225

DONOVAN, MOLLY WALSH, clinical psychologist; b. Northampton, Pa., June 19, 1946; d. William James and Helen Madeline (Farren) Walsh; m. Joseph R. Donovan, Sept. 6, 1969 (div. June 1983); m. Barry Jay Wepman, Apr. 8, 1989. BA in Psychology, Chestnut Hill Coll., 1968; PhD in Clin. Psychology, George Washington U., 1976. Lic. psychologist, D.C. Pvt. practice Washington, 1976—; co-founder, co-dir. Washington Women's Psychotherapy Ctr., Washington, 1979-91; adj. faculty George Washington U., 1994-98, Washington Soc. Psychoanalytic Psychology, 1993-96. Guest editor Jour. Am. Acad. Psychotherapists, 1997; author: (with others) Mothers & Daughters, 1998. Mem. Women, Gender and Psychoanalysis (pres. 1996-97), Washington Soc. Psychoanalytic Psychology (pres. 1993-95). Avocation: photography. Office: 1301 20th St NW Washington DC 20036-6023

DONOVAN, PAUL V., former bishop; b. Bernard, Iowa, Sept. 1, 1924; s. John J. and Loretta (Carew) D. Student, St. Joseph Sem., Grand Rapids, Mich.; BA, St. Gregory Sem., Cin., 1946; postgrad., Mt. St. Mary Sem. of West, Cin.; JCL, Pontifical Lateran U., Rome, 1957. Ordained priest Roman Catholic Ch., 1950; asst. pastor St. Mary Ch., Jackson, Mich., 1950-51; sec. to bishop of Lansing Mich.; adminstr. St. Peter Ch., Eaton Rapids, Mich., 1951-55; sec. to bishop, 1957-59; pastor Our Lady of Fatima Ch., Michigan Center, Mich.; and St. Rita Mission, Clark Lake, Mich., 1959-68; pastor St. Agnes Ch., Flint, Mich., 1968-71; bishop of Kalamazoo, 1971-94; mem. liturgical commn. Diocese of Lansing, chmn., 1963; mem. Cath. Bd. Edn., Jackson and Hillsdale counties; mem. bishop's personnel com., priests' senate. Bd. dirs. Family Services and, Mich. Children's Aid. Office: 2131 Aberdeen Dr Kalamazoo MI 49008-1759 Address: 238 Falkirk Ct Kalamazoo MI 49006*

DONOVAN, R. MICHAEL, management consultant; b. Worcester, Mass., Aug. 30, 1943; s. George F. and Ethel May (Dowell) D.; m. Sarah Jean Lawrence, Dec. 19, 1992; children: James M., Thomas M., Kandace H., R. Michael II. BSBA, Northeastern U., Boston, 1965; MBA, Calif. Western. U., 1978. Exec. v.p. Donovan, Zappala Assocs., Inc., N. Andover, Mass., 1970-74; v.p. ops. SW Industries, Providence, R.I., 1974-77; dir. Touche Ross & Co., Boston, 1977-79; sr. mgr. Peat, Marwick, Mitchell & Co., Boston, 1979-83; pres. R. Michael Donovan, Inc., Natick, Mass., 1983—; bd. dirs. Am. Inst. Mfg., Boston, 1991—. Author: Planning and Controlling Manufacturing Resources, 1978, Time-Based Manufacturing Performance: Guidelines for Quick Response, 1993, Reengineering the Manufacturing Enterprise, 1994, Supply Chain Management: Strengthening Manufacturing's Weak Links, 1996, Demand-Based Flow Manufacturing to Achieve Quick Reponse, 1997, Cycle Time Reduction: Faster Is Better, 1998. Dir. Contact-Boston, 1987-88; pres. Natick Baseball League, 1979-85. Mem. Am. Prodn. & Inventory Control Soc., Soc. Mfg. Engrs., Inst. Industrial Engrs. Office: R Michael Donovan Inc 945 Concord St Framingham MA 01701-4613

DONOVAN, ROBERT ALAN, English educator; b. Chgo., Sept. 27, 1921; s. John Elmer and Dorothy (Dickey) D.; m. Hope Elaine Taussig, Sept. 15, 1942; children: Faith, Peter Alan, Brian Roger. PhB, U. Chgo., 1948, MA, 1950; PhD, Washington U., St. Louis, 1953. Instr. English Cornell U., Ithaca, N.Y., 1953-56, asst. prof., 1956-62; prof. English SUNY, Albany, 1962-91, prof. emeritus, 1991—, chmn. dept. English, 1981-84. Author: The Shaping Vision: Imagination in the English Novel from Defoe to Dickens, 1966; contbr. articles to profl. jours. Sgt. U.S. Army, 1942-46, ETO. Mem. MLA, Phi Beta Kappa. Home: 5945 State Farm Rd Guilderland NY 12084-9531 Office: SUNY Dept English Albany NY 12222

DONOVAN, ROBERT JOHN, retired journalist; b. Buffalo, Aug. 21, 1912; s. Michael J. and Katherine (Sullivan) D.; m. Martha Fisher, May 9, 1941 (dec.); children: Patricia, Peter, Amy; m. Gerry Van der Heuvel, Mar. 17, 1978. Litt.D. (hon.), Am. Internat. Coll., 1962, Stonehill Coll., 1983. Mem. staff Buffalo Courier-Express, 1933-37; with N.Y. Herald Tribune, 1937-63, on European edit., 1945; mem. N.Y. Herald Tribune, Washington Bur., 1947-63; chief N.Y. Herald Tribune, 1957-63; chief Washington bur. Los Angeles Times, 1963-70; assoc. editor Los Angeles Times, Los Angeles, 1970-77; fellow Woodrow Wilson Internat. Center for Scholars, 1978-79; sr. fellow Woodrow Wilson Sch. Pub. and Internat. Affairs, Princeton, N.J., 1979-80; Ferris prof. journalism Princeton U., 1980-81; guest scholar Woodrow Wilson Internat. Ctr. for Scholars, 1990-91. Author: The Assassins, 1955, Eisenhower: The Inside Story, 1956, (with Joseph W. Martin, Jr.) My First Fifty Years in Politics, 1960, PT 109: John F. Kennedy in World War II, 1961, The Future of the Republican Party, 1964, Conflict and Crisis: The Presidency of Harry S Truman, 1945-48, 1977, Tumultuous Years: The Presidency of Harry S Truman, 1949-53, 1982, Nemesis: Truman and Johnson in the Coils of War in Asia, 1984, The Second Victory: The Marshall Plan and the Postwar Revival of Europe, 1987, Confidential Secretary: Ann Whitman's Twenty Years with Eisenhower and Rockefeller, 1988, (with Ray Scherer) Unsilent Revolution: Television News and American Public Life, 1948-1991, 1992; also mag. articles. Served AUS, World War II; staff Stars and Stripes in Paris. Mem. White House Corrs. Assn. (pres. 1954), Gridiron Club, Army-Navy Country Club, Isla del Sol Yacht and Country Club. Home: Shoreham West 2700 Calvert St NW # 311 Washington DC 20008-2621

DONOVAN, SHARON ANN, educator; b. Balt., Feb. 17, 1944; d. Jesse F. and Ruth Elizabeth (Keller) D. BA, U. Md., Balt., 1969. Cert. profl. tchr. Assoc. Coppin-Hopkins Humanities Program, Balt., 1986-91; asst. dean arts and humanities UMBC, Catonsville, Md., 1973-76; asst. to dean fine arts Towson (Md.) State U., 1977-85; tchr. Balt. City Schs., 1986—. Contbr. articles to publs.; founding mem., bd. dirs. The Feminist Press; founder "Herstory" MS Mag., 1976. Grantee Fund for Endl. Excellence. Mem. NCTE, MCTELA, Md. State Conf. on Women's Studies (chairperson, Tchr. of Yr. 1994, 95). Home: 2039 E Lombard St Baltimore MD 21231-1924 Office: 2555 Harford Rd Baltimore MD 21218-4837

DONOVAN, TATE, actor; b. N.Y.C., Sept. 25, 1963. Appeared in films North Beach and Rawhide, 1985, Into thin Air, 1986, Spacecamp, 1986, Nutcracker: Money, Madness and Murder, 1987, Clean and Sober, 1988, Dead-Bang, 1989, Memphis Belle, 1990, Little Noises, 1991, Love Potion #9, 1992, Holy Matrimony, 1994, Hercules (voice), 1997, 98, America's Dream, 1996, The Only Thrill, 1997, Murder at 1600, 1997; (TV) Partners, 1996, Tempting Fate, 1998, Trinity, 1998. Office: c/o United Talent Agy Inc 9560 Wilshire Blvd Ste 500 Beverly Hills CA 90212-2427*

DONOVAN, THOMAS B., judge; b. Oakland, Calif., Oct. 9, 1935; m. Shirley Ann Rapaport, Aug. 12, 1956; children: Thomas B., Robin. BA, U. Calif., Berkeley, 1957, JD, 1962. Bar: Calif., D.C., U.S. Dist. Ct. (no. and ea. dists.) Calif., U.S. Dist. Ct. D.C., U.S. Ct. Appeals (9th and D.C. cirs.), U.S. Supreme Ct. Assoc. Covington & Burling, Washington, 1962-63; assoc., then ptnr. Dinkelspiel & Dinkelspiel, San Francisco, 1964-69; ptnr., mng. ptnr Dinkelspiel, Donovan & Reder, San Francisco, 1969-93; judge U.S. Bankruptcy Ct., L.A., 1994—; judge pro tem Mcpl. Ct. and Superior Ct., San Francisco, Oakland and Berkeley, Calif., 1979-93. Author, editor Calif. Law Rev., 1960-62. Bd. dirs. Berkeley Repertory Theatre, 1977-87, Drama Studio London, Berkeley, 1982-84, Aurora Theatre Co., 1992-94, Women Empowering Women, 1987-94, Entrade, 1991-94; mem. Fair Campaign Practices Commn., Berkeley, 1977-79. Office: US Bankruptcy Ct 255 E Temple St Ste 1352 Los Angeles CA 90012-3334

DONOVAN, VICKI A., elementary school teacher; m. Jack W. Donovan, 1986; children: Brett Cameron, Marissa Leigh (twins). AA in Math. and Sci., Cape Cod (Mass.) C.C., 1979; BS in Elem. and Spl. Edn., Fitchburg (Mass.) State Coll., 1981; MEd in Curriculum and Instrn., Lesley Coll., 1996. 3d grade tchr. Mashpee (Mass.) Elem. Sch., 1982-83; chpt. 1 tchr. Ezra Baker Elem. Sch., Dennis, Mass., 1983-85, 1st grade tchr., 1985-86; 2d grade tchr. Paul Smith Elem. Sch., Franklin, N.H., 1986-87; 5th grade tchr. Belmont (N.H.) Elem. Sch., 1987-94, 4th grade tchr., 1994—; methods I tchg. mentor, Plymouth State Coll., 1991, 92, 95, 96, 97, 98, student tchr. mentor, 1996, workshop presenter, Math. 1987, Multiple Intelligence's 1998; yearbook advisor Belmont Elem. Sch., 1987—; mem. lang arts curriculum com., 1994—, health fair com., 1997—. Mem. Belmont (N.H.) Civic Pride Orgn., 1993. Belmont Youth and Edn. Com., 1995, Govt. Study Com., 1996; mem. Shaker Regional Edn. com., 1997. Recipient Acad. of Applied Sci. and Ctrl. N.H. Ednl. Collaborative award. 1993; named Outstanding Young Citizen, New Hampshire C. of C., 1998, N.H. Tchr. of Yr., 1998. Mem. NEA (negotiation com. 1988-89). ASCD. Office: Belmont Elem Sch 96 Gilmanton Rd Belmont NH 03220

DONOVAN, WILLARD PATRICK, retired elementary education educator; b. Grand Rapids, Mich., Sept. 1, 1930; s. Willard Andrew and Thelma Alfreda (Davis) D.; m. Dorothy Jane Nester, Nov. 27, 1954 (dec. May 1981); children: Cindy Jane, Kimberly Sue. BS, Ea. Mich. U., 1965, MA, 1969. Cert. grades K-8, Mich. Enlisted U.S. Army, 1947, advanced through grades to master sgt., 1953; platoon sgt. U.S. Army of Occupation, Korea, 1947-48, Japan, 1948-50; platoon sgt. U.S. Army Korean War Svc., 1950-51; ret. U.S. Army, 1964; pharm. sales Nat. Drug Co., Detroit, 1964-66; tchr. Cromie Elem. Sch. Warren (Mich.) Consol. Schs., 1966—, ret., 1995; reading textbook and curriculum devel. com. Warren (Mich.) Consol. Schs., 1969-73, sci. com., 1970-95; curriculum and textbook com. Macomb County Christian Schs., Warren, 1982-95. Decorated Combat Infantry badge U.S. Army, Korea, 1950, Purple heart with three clusters U.S. Army, Korea, 1950-51, Korea-Japan Svc. medal, 1951, Presdl. citation, 1951, Korean medal with three campaign clusters, 1951, Nat. Def. Svc. medal, 1951, Bronze star, Silver star; named Chosen few Army and Marines 31st Infantry Assn. Mem. NRA, Am. Quarterhouse Assn., Assn. U.S. Army, Detroit Area Coun. Tchrs. Math., Met. Detroit Sci. Tchrs. Assn., The Chosin Few, Nat. Edn. Assn., Mich. Edn. Assn., Warren (Mich.) Edn. Assn. Avocations: theatre, arts, horsemanship, traveling, pistol shooting. Home: PO Box 563 8440 Mission Hills Arizona City AZ 85223

DOOB, JOSEPH LEO, mathematician, educator; b. Cin., Feb. 27, 1910; s. Leo and Mollie (Doerfler) D.; m. Elsie Haviland Field, June 26, 1931 (dec. Jan. 1991); children: Stephen, Peter, Deborah. B.A., Harvard U., 1930, M.A., 1931, Ph.D., 1932; D.Sc. (hon.), U. Ill., 1981. Faculty U. Ill., Urbana, 1935—; successively assoc., asst. prof., assoc. prof. U. Ill., 1935-45, prof. math., 1945—, now emeritus prof. Recipient Nat. Medal of Sci., 1979. Mem. NAS, Am. Acad. Arts and Scis., Acad. Scis. (Paris) (fgn. assoc.). Home: 101 W Windsor Rd # 1104 Urbana IL 61802-6663

DOOB, LEONARD WILLIAM, psychology educator, academic administrator; b. N.Y.C., Mar. 3, 1909; s. William and Florence (Lewis) D.; m. Eveline Bates, Mar. 21, 1936; children: Christopher Bates, Anthony Newcomb, Nicholas Ellsworth. AB, Dartmouth Coll., 1929; AM, Duke U., 1930; postgrad., U. Frankfurt, Germany, 1930-32; PhD, Harvard U., 1934. Asst. instr. psychology Duke U., Durham, N.C., 1929-30; instr. sociology Dartmouth Coll., 1932-33; mem. faculty Yale U., New Haven, 1934-78, prof. psychology, 1950-77, also div. social scis., chmn. African studies, Sterling prof. emeritus psychology, rsch. scholar, assoc. dir. South African Rsch. program, 1977-94; various positions, to policy coord. overseas br. Office of War Info., 1941-45. Editor Jour. of Social Psychology, 1965—; author 15 books, co-author 3 books on comm., pub. opinion, acculturation, ethics, conflict resolution and sustainability; contbr. articles to profl. jours. Home: 6 Clark Rd Woodbridge CT 06525-1609 Office: PO Box 208205 New Haven CT 06520-8205*

DOODY, AGNES G., communications educator, management and communication consultant; b. New Haven; d. Daniel M. and Carrie Mae (Goodrich) D.; m. Arthur D. Jeffrey, Dec. 22, 1962 (dec. Sept. 1985); children: Andrew N., Jill; m. Ellis H. Maris, Jr., June 28, 1991. BA, Emerson Coll., 1952; MA, Pa. State U., 1954, PhD, 1961; cert. program on negotiation, Harvard U. Prof. communications U. R.I., Kingston, 1958—; pres. Arthur Assocs.; bd. dirs., co-chairperson PierBank, Narragansett, R.I., 1994. Mem. Soc. Profls. in Dispute Resolution, Internat. Comm. Assn., Nat. Comm. Assn., Ea. Comm. Assn. (pres. 1967-68), Rotary (newsletter editor Wakefield 1989-90). Avocations: photography, travel, gardening. Home: One Post Rd Wakefield RI 02879

DOODY, LOUIS CLARENCE, JR., accountant; b. New Orleans, Feb. 5, 1940; s. Louis Clarence and Elsie Clair (Connors) D.; BCS, Tulane U., 1963; m. Barbara Virginia Pettett, Oct. 9, 1982; children by previous marriage: Dana Lori, Mary Lyn, Kathleen Louise. Accountant, Louis C. Doody, C.P.A., 1963-68, partner Doody and Doody, C.P.A.'s, 1969—. C.P.A., La., Tex., Miss. Mem. AICPA, La. Soc. C.P.A.'s. Home: 36 Cypress Rd Covington LA 70433-4306 Office: 3838 N Causeway Blvd Ste 2525 Metairie LA 70002-8317

DOODY, MARGARET ANNE, English language educator; b. St. John, N.B., Can., Sept. 21, 1939; came to U.S., 1976; d. Hubert and Anne Ruth (Cornwall) D. B.A., Dalhousie U., Can., 1960; B.A. with 1st class hons., Lady Margaret Hall-Oxford U., Eng., 1962, M.A., 1965, D.Phil., 1968; LLD (hon.), Dalhousie U., 1985. Instr. English U. Victoria (B.C., Can.), 1962-64, asst. prof. English, 1968-69; lectr. Univ. Coll. Swansea, Wales, 1969-76; assoc. prof. English U. Calif.-Berkeley, 1976-80; prof. English dept. Princeton U., N.J., 1980-89; Andrew W. Mellon prof. humanities, prof. English Vanderbilt U., Nashville, 1989—, dir. comparative lit. program, 1992—. Author: A Natural Passion: A Study of the Novels of Samuel Richardson, 1974; (novels) Aristotle Detective, 1978, The Alchemists, 1980; (play) (with F. Stuber) Clarissa, 1984; The Daring Muse: Augustan Poetry Reconsidered, 1985; Frances Burney: The Life in the Works, 1988, The True Story of the Novel, 1996; editor: (with Peter Sabor) Samuel Richardson Tercentenary Essays, 1989; co-editor: (with Douglas Murray) Catharine and Other Writings by Jane Austen, 1993, (with Wendy Barry and Mary Doody Jones) Anne of Green Gables, 1997. Guggenheim postdoctoral fellow, 1979; recipient Rose Mary Crawshay award Brit. Acad., 1986. Episcopalian. Office: Vanderbilt U Comparative Lit PO Box 63 Sta B Nashville TN 37240

DOOLEY, ANN ELIZABETH, freelance writers cooperative executive, editor; b. Mpls., Feb. 19, 1952; d. Merlyn James and Susan Marie (Hinze) Dooley; m. John M. Dodge, May 8, 1983; children: Christopher Dooley Dodge, Kathryn Dooley Dodge. BA in Journalism, U. Wis., 1974. Freelance journalist, 1974-75; photo editor C.W. Communications, Newton, Mass., 1975-77, writer, photographer, 1977-79; editor Computerworld O A, Framingham, Mass., 1979-83; editorial dir. Computerworld Focus, Framingham, 1983-92; pres. freelance writers coop. Dooley & Assocs., West Newbury, Mass., 1992—; speaker, chmn. mem. editorial adv. bd. various computer confs. Mem. Pub. Relations Soc. Am., Women in Communications (sec. 1982-84). Democrat. Home and Office: 1 Old Parish Way West Newbury MA 01985-1222

DOOLEY, BETTY PARSONS, educational association administrator. Student, Tex. Inst. Tech., Tex. U. Lobbyist Austin, Tex., 1969-70; dir. regional orgns. Health Security Action Coun., 1971-77; exec. dir. Congl. Caucus Women's Issues, 1977-79; pres. Women's Rsch Edn. Inst., Washington, 1979—; mem. women's health adv. bd. Duke Med. Sch.; mem. adv. com. employment tng. Vets. Sec. Labor; mem. outreach com. Ctr. Cross Cultural Rsch. on Women, Oxford, Eng. Washington corr. Tex. Monthly Mag., 1974-75. Candidate Tex. State Legis., 1970, U.S. Congress, 1964. Mem. Nat. Coun. Rsch. Women (charter). Office: Womens Rsch Edn Inst 1750 New York Ave NW Ste 350 Washington DC 20006-5301*

DOOLEY, CALVIN MILLARD, congressman; b. Visalia, Calif., Jan. 11, 1954. BS, U. Calif., Davis, 1977; MA, Stanford U., 1987. Mem. 102nd-105th Congresses (now 106th Congress) from Calif. Dist. 17 (now 20th), 1991—; mem. agriculture com., mem. natural resources com. Democrat. Methodist. Office: Ho of Reps 1201 Longworth Bldg Washington DC 20515-0520

DOOLEY, DAVID J., elementary school principal. Prin. Aquila Primary Ctr., St. Louis Park, Minn., 1984-99, Field's Sch., Mpls., 1999—. Recipient Elem. Sch. Recognition award U.S. Dept. Edn., 1989-90. Office: Field's Sch 4645 4th Ave S Minneapolis MN 55409*

DOOLEY, DONALD JOHN, retired publishing executive; b. Des Moines, Aug. 16, 1921; s. Martin and Anne Marguerite (Barger) D.; m. Beverly Frederick, Dec. 21, 1955 (div. 1977); children—Nancy Elizabeth, Katherine Anne (dec.), Mary Bridget, Robert Frederick. B.A., U. Iowa, 1947; postgrad., Drake U., 1949-50. Gen. Promotion and pub. relations mgr. Meredith Corp., Des Moines, 1953-59, dir. pub. relations, 1960-65; art and editorial dir. Better Homes & Gardens Books & Spl. Interest Publs., Des Moines, 1965-77; dir. editorial planning and devel. Better Homes and Gardens Books (Meredith Corp.), Des Moines, 1977-84; cons., 1985. Chmn. bd. adv. com. Sch. Vol. Program, Des Moines; steering com. Intercultural Affairs program to Desegregate Dist. Schs., 1975-77; treas. Iowa U. Parents Assn., 1977-79; bd. dirs. Iowa Cystic Fibrosis Found., 1979-87, v.p., 1981-85; trustee Citizens Scholarship Found. Am., 1976-85, Iowa Freedom of Info. Council, 1977-87; adv. bd. Adult and Community Edn., Des Moines Pub. Sch., 1982—; cons. White House Conf. on Families, 1981. Served with USAAF, 1942-46. Decorated 2 battle stars; recipient Dorothy Dawe award, 1973. Mem. Pub. Rels. Soc. Am. (accredited, pres. chpt. 1969, dir. chpt. 1965-76), ACLU, Beyond War (co-dir. Iowa office 1987-88), Friendship Force, Ams. for Dem. Action, Sigma Nu (comdr. chpt. 1946-47), Found. for Global Community, 1991—. Democrat. Club: Echo Valley Country. Home and Office: 3711 Oak Creek Pl West Des Moines IA 50265-7968

DOOLEY, GEORGE JOSEPH, III, metallurgist; b. Greenwich, Conn., Aug. 8, 1941; s. George Joseph and Susan Marilyn (Robustelli) D.; children: Deborah Susan, Jennifer Ann, Daniel Paul; m. Marye Khrys Von Tellrop, Oct. 27, 1984; children: Samantha Joel, Charles Douglas, Anastacia Halley, James Huston, Cynthia Maureen, Sandra Robin, Karen Linn, Kimberly Marie. BS, U. Notre Dame, 1963; MS, Iowa State U., 1966; PhD, Oreg. State U., 1969. Research asst. Ames (Iowa) Lab. AEC, 1963-66; research metallurgist U.S. Bur. Mines, Albany, Oreg., 1966-68, dir. Albany Research Ctr., 1984—; research scientist Aerospace Research Labs. USAF, Wright Patterson AFB, Ohio, 1968-72; dir. research and devel. Oreg. Metall. Corp., Albany, 1974-83, dir. metall. and quality assurance, 1983-84; mem. metallurgy adv. bd. Linn Benton Community Coll., Albany, 1976—. Contbr. articles to profl. jours. Served to capt. USAF, 1968-72. Democrat. Roman Catholic. Home: 8804 NW Arboretum Rd Corvallis OR 97330-9571 Office: US Dept Energy Albany Rsch Ctr 1450 Queen Ave SW Albany OR 97321-2152

DOOLEY, J. GORDON, food scientist; b. Nevada, Mo., Nov. 15, 1935; s. Howard Eugene and Wilma June (Vanderford) D.; B.S. with honors in Biology, Drury Coll., Springfield, Mo., 1958; postgrad. (NSF grantee) U. Mo., Rolla, 1961, (NSF grantee) Kirksville (Mo.) State Coll., 1959; M.S. in Biology (NSF grantee), Brown U., 1966; postgrad. bus. mgmt. Alexander Hamilton Inst., 1973-75, No. Ill. U., 1964. Tchr. sci. Morton West High Sch., Berwyn, Ill., 1963-64; dairy technologist Borden Co., Elgin, Ill., 1964-65; project leader Cheese Products Lab., Kraft Corp., Glenview, Ill., 1965-73; sr. food scientist Wallerstein Co. div. Travenol Labs., Inc., Morton Grove, Ill., 1973-77; mgr. food sci. GB Fermentation Industries, Inc., Des Plaines, Ill., 1977-79, mgr. product devel., 1979-82; group leader Food Ingredients div. Stauffer Chem. Co., Clawson, Mich., 1982-84; sr. research scientist Schreiber Foods, Inc., Green Bay, Wis., 1984-87, DMV Ridgeview, LaCrosse, Wis., 1987-92; mgr. regulatory affairs, info. svcs., DMV USA, LaCrosse, 1992-95; rsch. scientist, Iowa, 1996-98; regulatory compliance officer Colo. Biolabs, Inc., Aurora, Colo., 1999—; sci. lectr. seminars, Mexico, 1975; assoc. mem. Ad Hoc Enzyme Tech. Com., 1978—; dairy research adv. bd. Utah State U.; del. in field. Recipient Spoke award Nevada (Mo.) Jr. C. of C., 1960. Speaker, reporter People to People Sanitarians del. to China, 1989. Mem. Am. Dairy Sci. Assn., Inst. Food Technologists, Am. Chem. Soc., Cousteau Soc., Am. Inst. Biol. Scis., Nat. Sci. Tchrs. Assn., Whey Products Inst., Beta Beta Beta, Phi Eta Sigma. Republican. Presbyterian. Clubs: Toastmasters Internat. (pres. Baxter Labs. club 1976-77); Brown U. (Chgo.). Patentee in food and enzyme tech. field; contbr. sci. articles to profl. jours. Home: 4280 30th St Greeley CO 80634 Office: Colo Biolabs Inc PO Box 6296 Aurora CO 80045-0296

DOOLEY, JAMES C., newspaper editor, director of photography; m. Susan Levy; children: David, Marc, Steven, Thomas. From reporter to state editor The Ariz. Republic, 1966-78; photo assignment editor, dep. dir. photography L.A. Times, 1978-86; chief photo editor Newsday, N.Y.C., 1986—. Office: Newsday Inc 235 Pinelawn Rd Melville NY 11747-4250

DOOLEY, JO ANN CATHERINE, retired publishing company executive; b. Cin., Nov. 24, 1930; d. Joseph Frank and Margaret Mary (Flynn) D. Ed. U. Cin., 1966. Clk. Castellini Co., Cin., 1949-52; IBM operator Kroger Co., Cin., 1952; asst. acct. Gardner Publs., Inc., Cin., 1953-67, treas., sec., 1967-95, bd. dirs., 1983-99, v.p. fin., 1986-95, ret., 1995; also trustee employees profit sharing trust, trustee retirement trust; cons., 1996—. Mem. Am. Soc. Women Accts. (advt. mgr. Woman CPA 1979-81, nat. pres. 1982-83, exec. com., Achievement award). Roman Catholic. Office: 6915 Valley Ave Cincinnati OH 45244-3029

DOOLEY, JOHN AUGUSTINE, III, state supreme court justice; b. Nashua, N.H., Apr. 10, 1944; s. John A. and Edna Elizabeth (Elwell) D.; m. Sandra C. Sapp, Dec. 19, 1970. BS, Union Coll., 1965; LLB, Boston Coll., 1968. Bar: Vt. 1968. Law clk. to presiding judge U.S. Dist. Ct. Vt., 1968-69; asst. dir. Vt. Legal Aid, 1969-72, dir., 1972-78; legal counsel to gov. of Vt., 1985; sec. of adminstrn. State of Vt., 1985-87; assoc. justice Vt. Supreme Ct., 1987—; part-time U.S. magistrate for Vt., from 1971. Co-author: Cases and Materials on Urban Poverty Law, 1974. Mem. Vt. Bar Assn. Office: Vt Supreme Ct 109 State St Montpelier VT 05609*

DOOLEY, KARLA JEANETTE, reporter; b. Hopkinsville, Ky., Feb. 2, 1977; d. Carlos Lee and Mildred Jeanette Bilbrey; 1 child, Carson Dooley. BA, U. Ky., 1999. Reporter, photographer News-Dem. Leader, Russellville, Ky., 1996-97; archival asst. U. Ky. M.I. King Libr., Lexington, 1996-98; reporting intern Lexington Herald-Leader, 1998, 99; lab. technician Dermatology Assocs. Ky., Lexington, 1998-99; asst. news editor Ky. Kernel, Lexington, 1999. Contbg. photographer U. Ky. Jour. Artistic Renderings, 1997, 98. Otis A. Singletary scholar U. Ky., 1995. Mem. Soc. Profl. Journalists (treas. U. Ky. chpt. 1999). Avocations: reading, cross-training, aerobics. E-mail: kjbilb0@pop.uky.edu. Home: 3337 Royal Wood Rd Lexington KY 40515

DOOLEY, LENA ROSE (NELSON), writer, editor; b. Hot Springs, Ark., Nov. 13, 1942; d. Bennel Alden and Frances Arabella (Brians) Nelson; m. James Allan Dooley, Nov. 7, 1964; children: Marilyn Van Zant, Jennifer Waldron. BA in Speech and Drama, Howard Payne Coll., Brownwood, Tex., 1964; student, Ouachita Bapt. Coll., Arkadelphia, Ark., 1960-62, Abilene Christian U., 1970-71. Cert. tchr., Tex. Tchr. Schleicher County Ind. Sch. Dist., El Dorado, Tex., 1964-65; aux. rural mail carrier U.S. Postal Svc., Colleyville, Tex., 1982-84; mng. editor The Christian Informer, Dallas, 1991; video script writer Accelerated Christian Edn., Lewisville, Tex., 1991-93; instr. Fine Arts Acad., Bedford, Tex., 1996—; adminstrv. editor curriculum divsn. The Paradigm Alternative Ctrs., Dublin, Tex., 1996-97; project coord., adminstrv. editor F.L.A.M.E.S. Curriculum, FUMC, Bedford, Tex., 1998—; freelance writer/editor, Hurst, Tex., 1985—; clown Granny Pockets, Hurst, 1989—. Author: Home to Her Heart, 1993; asst. movie prodr., dir. To Love Enough, 1990; play writer, dir. Sleeping Beauty,

1986. Developer Write Right seminar, Hurst, 1996; dir. Bedford FUMC Players, 1982—; leader writer's group AAUW, Abilene, 1970-72; chmn. book sale Friends of Hurst Libr., 1985-88, chmn. craft sale, 1987-88. Mem. RWA, NTRWA (mem. chmn. 1998), Gospel Artists and Musicians Assn. (bd. dirs. 1990-92), Mid-Cities Christian Writers (coord. 1997), Christians in Theatre Arts, Trinity Valley Christian Writers (coord. seminars 1984-87). Republican. Methodist. Avocations: travel, needlework, volunteering with children, reading. Home and Office: 1913 Sage Trl Hurst TX 76054-3138

DOOLEY, MICHAEL P., law educator; b. 1939. BA, U. Iowa, 1960, JD, 1963. Bar: Iowa 1963, N.Y. 1964, Ill. 1971, Va. 1979. Assoc. Dewey, Ballantine, Bushby, Palmer & Wood, 1963-68; assoc. prof. U. Ill., 1968-71, prof., 1971-72; vis. prof. U. Va., 1971-72, prof., 1972-80, Doherty prof., 1980-90, William S. Potter prof. and dir. grad. studies, 1990—; mem. Saltzburg Seminar in Am. Studies, 1986; mem. legal adv. com. N.Y. Stock Exch. Mem. ABA (com. on corp. laws 1983-91, 96—, corp. practice com. 1995—), Am. Law Inst. (reporter Model Bus. Corp. Act 1996—). Office: U Va Sch Law 580 Massie Rd Charlottesville VA 22903-1738

DOOLEY, PATRICK JOHN, graphic designer, design educator; b. Cleve., May 29, 1950; s. John William and Edna Ann (Mellick) D.; m. Mary Leah Spicer, Apr. 3, 1982; children: Claire Adele, Grace Ellen, James Joseph. BFA, U. Iowa, 1975, MA, 1977, MFA, 1978. Designer J. Paul Getty Mus., L.A., 1980-89; design mgr. J. Paul Getty Mus., J. Paul Getty Trust, L.A., 1987-89; designer, owner Patrick Dooley Design, Santa Monica, Calif., 1989-93, Lawrence, Kans., 1993—; mem. faculty Otis Parsons Sch. Art and Design, L.A., 1988-93; mem. faculty dept. design Sch. Fine Art U. Kans., Lawrence, 1993—, Gretchen Van Bloom Budig tchg. prof., 1997; freelance graphic designer, L.A., 1978-80, designer, cons. Walt Disney Co., Burbank, Calif., 1989-93, Lannan Lit. Found., L.A., 1991—, The Lapis Press, Venice, Calif., 1989-93, Nelson-Atkins Mus., Kansas City, Mo., 1995-96; spkr. Assn. Am. U. Presses ann. conf., 1994, Art Dirs. Club Tulsa, 1996; judge 42nd Art Dirs. Club L.A. Show, 1988. Designer: (poster) Illuminated Manuscripts, 1984 (N.Y. Type Dirs. Club award of excellence 1985), (books) Whisper of the Muse, 1986 (N.Y. Art Dirs. Club award of merit 1987), Pierre Dubreuil, 1988 (Am. Inst. Graphic Arts Book Show cert. of excellence 1989), The Surrealists Look at Art, 1990 (N.Y. Art Dirs. Club award of merit 1991), Explorations, 1992 (Am. Inst. Graphic Arts 50 Books of 1992), Pacific Wall, 1992 (Am. Inst. Graphic Arts Cover Show 1994), Walter Evans: The Getty Museum Collection, 1996 (Assn. Am. Univ. Presses cert. of excellence 1996). Recipient over 60 awards from Comm. Arts Mag., Print Mag., Am. Assn. Museums, Art Mus. Assn. Am., Am. Fedn. Arts, Univ. and Coll. Designer's Assn., others. Mem. Am. Inst. Graphic Arts, Univ. and Coll. Designers Assn. Avocation: gardening. Office: U Kans Dept Design 300 Art and Design Bldg Lawrence KS 66045

DOOLEY, THOMAS E., telecommunications company executive. BS, St. John's U., 1978; MBA, NYU, 1984. From sr. v.p. corp. devel. to deputy chmn. Viacom, Inc., N.Y.C., 1980—; bd. dirs. Starsight Telecomms., Inc. Bd. dirs. Laurie Strauss Leukemia Found. Mem. Cable TV Adminstrn. Assn., Mus. TV & Radio, Am. Mgmt. Assn., Internat. Radio & TV Soc. Office: Viacom Inc 1515 Broadway New York NY 10036-8901*

DOOLEY, TIMOTHY KEVIN, retail professional; b. Bloomington, Ind., Mar. 11, 1958; s. Robert Owen and Donna Simon Dooley; m. Karen Lea Hembach, Feb. 26, 1981; children: Robert Lee, Heather Marie, Daniel Owen. BS in Govt. and Politics, U. Md., 1991; MPA, Troy State U., 1995; AA in Microcomputers, N.Mex. State U., 1996. Retail asst. mgr. K-Mart Inc., Palmer, Mass., 1982-85; collections mgr. Bank of Am., Denver, 1985-87; commd. officer U.S. Army, 1987, advanced through grades to staff sgt.; emergency room tech. Womack Army Hosp., Ft. Bragg, N.C., 1987-88; office mgr. Army Dental Clinic, Augsburg, Germany, 1988-92, White Sands, N.Mex., 1992-97, Illesheim, Germany, 1997-98; ret. Army Dental Clinic, 1998; retail asst. mgr. Sears Roebuck & Co., Chgo., 1998—. Sgt. USAF, 1977-82. Decorated Army Achievement medal U.S. Army, 1988, 88, 89, Army Commendation medal U.S. Army, 1988, 90, Meritorious Svc. medal U.S. Army, 1992, 97, 98. Mem. ASPA, Colonial Williamsburg Found., U. Md. Alumni Assn., N.Mex. State U. Alumni Assn., Troy State U. Alumni Assn., Kappa Delta Pi. Republican. Methodist.

DOOLING, RICHARD PATRICK, writer, lawyer; b. Omaha, Mar. 20, 1954. BA in English, Art History, St. Louis U., 1976; attended respiratory therapy, med. scis., U. Nebr., 1982-83; attended adv. respiratory therapy program, U. Chgo. Hosps. & Clinics, 1983; JD, St. Louis U., 1987. Reg. respiratory therapist; cert. respiratory therapy technician. Assoc. labor and employment rels. Bryan, Cave, St. Louis, 1987-91; solo practitioner U.S. Ct. Appeals (8th cir.), 1991-94; tchr. English lit. Europe, Africa, 1981-82. Author: (novels) Critical Care, 1992, White Man's Grave, 1994 (Nat. Book award nomination 1994), (nonfiction) Blue Streak: Swearing, Free Speech and Sexual Harassment, (fiction) Brainstorm, 1998; short fiction pub. in The New Yorker, Story, and Smoke mags. *

DOOLITTLE, JAMES H., retired cable television systems company executive. BA, High Point Coll. System mgr. Am. TV & Communications Corp., Fayetteville, N.C., 1970-72, regional mgr., 1972-77, ea. div. mgr. of N.C. and mid-states regions, 1977-80, v.p. ea. ops., 1980-82, sr. v.p. cable ops., 1982-84, exec. v.p., 1984-85, with office of pres., 1985-87, exec. v.p., chief oper. officer, Englewood, Colo., 1987—; pres. Time Warner Cable, Stanford, Conn., 1998, Glen Britt, 1999—. *

DOOLITTLE, JESSE WILLIAM, JR., lawyer; b. Wheaton, Ill., May 19, 1929; s. Jesse William and Selma Caroline (Schacht) D.; m. Annette Danforth Bush, May 5, 1962; children: Danforth Bush, Alice Walters. AB, DePauw U., 1951; LLB magna cum laude, Harvard, 1954. Bar: D.C. 1954. Law clk. to U.S. Supreme Ct. Justice Felix Frankfurter, 1957-58; asso. firm Covington & Burling, Washington, 1958-61; asst. to solicitor gen. of U.S. Dept. Justice, Washington, 1961-63; 1st asst. civil div. Dept. Justice, 1963-66; gen. counsel Dept. Air Force, Washington, 1966-68; asst. sec. for manpower and res. affairs Dept. Air Force, 1968-69; partner firm Prather Seeger Doolittle & Farmer, Washington, 1969-94; editl. cons. Lexis-Nexis, 1995-98. Mem.: Harvard Law Rev, 1952-54. Pres. bd. trustees Nat. Child Rsch. Ctr., Washington, 1972-74; mem. bd. overseers com. to visit ROTC programs Harvard, 1967-69; com. to visit Law Sch., 1969-75; mem. governing bd. Nat. Cathedral Sch. for Girls, Washington, 1979-85, vice-chmn., 1981-82, chmn., 1982-85; mem. chpt. Washington Nat. Cathedral, 1982-85; mem. policy bd. Legal Counsel for the Elderly, Washington, 1992-97. 1st lt. AUS, 1954-57. Recipient Career Service award Nat. Civil Service League, 1968, Exceptional Civilian Service award Dept. Air Force, 1969. Mem. Am. Law Inst., Harvard Law Sch. Assn. (coun. 1964-68), Harvard Law Rev. Assn. (bd. overseers 1967-72, 92-98), Phi Beta Kappa, Delta Chi. Democrat. Episcopalian (sr. warden 1973-75, past vestryman). Clubs: Metropolitan, Chevy Chase. Home: 4000 Cathedral Ave NW Apt 444B Washington DC 20016-5282

DOOLITTLE, JOHN TAYLOR, congressman; b. Glendale, Calif., Oct. 30, 1950; s. Merrill T. and Dorothy Doolittle; B.A. in History with honors, U. Calif., Santa Cruz, 1972; J.D., McGeorge Sch. Law, U. Pacific, 1978; m. Julia Harlow, Feb. 17, 1979; children: John Taylor Jr., Courtney A. Bar: Calif. 1978. Mem. Calif. State Senate, 1980-90; mem. 102nd-105th Congresses (now 106th Congress) from Calif. 4th dist., 1991—; mem. agriculture com., mem. resource com., chair water and power resources subcom. Republican. Mem. LDS Ch. Office: Ho of Reps 1526 Longworth Bldg Washington DC 20515-0504

DOOLITTLE, MICHAEL JIM, lawyer; b. Boise, Idaho, Feb. 29, 1956; s. Wallace Gale and Jean Mary (Fisher) D.; m. Jeanette Lynn Johnson, Aug. 16, 1980; children: Bradford Nicholas, Holly Anne, Nicole Jeanette. BBA, Boise State U., 1979; JD, U. Idaho, 1982. Bar: Idaho 1982, U.S. Dist. Ct. Idaho 1982, U.S. Ct. Appeals (fed. cir.) 1987, U.S. Ct. Appeals (9th cir.) 1988. Pvt. practice legal researcher Boise, 1982-83; assoc. Dennis J. Sallaz, Boise, 1983-87; ptnr. Sallaz and Doolittle, Boise, 1988-89, Sallaz, Doolittle & Gordon, Chtd., Boise, 1989-94, Ringert Clark Chartered, Boise, 1996—. Bd. dirs. Ada County Youth Baseball, Inc., 1986—; mem. Bogus Basin Ski Racing Alliance, 1992—. Recipient Am. Jurisprudence award Lawyers Coop. Pub., Moscow, Idaho, 1981, Outstanding Adv. award Idaho Assn. Def. Counsel, 1982, Pro Bono Svc. award Idaho State Bar, 1989. Mem. Idaho Assn. Criminal Def. Lawyers, Nat. Assn. Retail Collection Attys., Idaho Bar Assn., Boise Bar Assn., Idaho Trial Lawyers Assn., Idaho Attys. for Criminal Justice. Roman Catholic. Avocations: reading, golf, weight-lifting, travel, gardening. E-mail: mjd@ringertclark.com. Office: Ringert Clark Chartered PO Box 2773 455 S 3d St Boise ID 83701-2773

DOOLITTLE, RUSSELL FRANCIS, biochemist, educator; b. New Haven, Jan. 10, 1931; s. Russell A. and Mary Catherine (Bohan) D.; m. Frances Ann Tynan, June 6, 1931; children: Lawrence Russell, William Edward. BA, Wesleyan U., 1952; MA, Trinity Coll., 1957; PhD, Harvard U., 1962. Instr. biochemistry Amherst (Mass.) Coll., 1961-62; asst. research biologist U. Calif.-San Diego, La Jolla, 1964-65, asst. prof. biochemistry, 1965-67, assoc. prof., 1967-72, prof., 1972—, chmn. dept. chemistry, 1981-84, rsch. prof. biology and chemistry, 1994—; advisor Can. Inst. for Advanced Rsch. Author: of Urfs and Orfs, 1987; contbr. articles to profl. jours. Served as sgt. U.S. Army, 1952-54. Guggenheim fellow, 1984-85, Non-Resident fellow Salk Inst., 1990-98. Fellow AAAS; mem. NAS, Am. Soc. Biol. Chemistry, Am. Acad. Arts and Scis., Am. Philos. Soc. (Paul Ehrlich prize 1989, Stein and Moore award 1991). Office: Univ Calif San Diego Ctr Molecular Genetics La Jolla CA 92093

DOOLITTLE, SIDNEY NEWING, retail executive; b. Binghamton, N.Y., Sept. 7, 1934; s. Raymond Luvurn and Helen Esther (Newing) D.; m. Barbara Mae Colsten, Sept. 12, 1954; children: Scott Sidney, Craig Francis, Sally Anne. Student, Rensselaer Poly. Inst., 1954-56; A.A. in Advanced Mgmt, Harvard U., 1977. With Montgomery Ward & Co., 1955-83, dir. internat. ops., 1970-73; v.p., dir. Montgomery Ward & Co. (Montgomery Ward Internat. Inc.), 1972; corp. v.p., div. mgr. catalog mdse. Montgomery Ward & Co., Chgo., 1978-83; exec. v.p., mdse. mgr., dir. Warehouse Club, Inc., 1983-84; pres. SND Enterprises, 1984-85; founding ptnr. McMillan/Doolittle, 1986—; bd. dirs., chmn. compensation and audit com. Otasco Inc., 1986-88; bd. dirs. High Performance Appliances, 1992-96. Vice chmn. bd. dirs. Henrotin Hosp., Chgo., 1980-97; vice-chmn. Mid-Am. chpt. Red Cross. Mem. Mail Order Assn. Am. (chmn. bd. 1981-83), Chgo. Fgn. Relations Council. Presbyterian. Office: McMillan Doolittle 350 W Hubbard St Chicago IL 60610-4098*

DOOLITTLE, WARREN T., retired federal official; b. Webster City, Iowa, July 24, 1921; s. Edward and Rhoda Leone (McGuire) D.; m. Jane Anne Beddow, July 5, 1920; children: Linda Jane, Randolph James, Steven Eric. BS in Forestry, Iowa State U., 1946; MS in Forestry, Duke U., 1950; PhD in Forestry, Yale U., 1955. Enlisted USAF, 1943, advanced through grades to lt. col., 1969; navigator USAF, Europe, 1943-45, South Korea, 1951-52; rsch. scientist USDA Forest Svc., Asheville, N.C., 1946-57, Washington, 1957-59; from asst. dir. to dir. USDA Forest Svc., Upper Darby, Pa., 1959-74; assoc. dep. chief USDA Forest Svc., Washington, 1974-80, ret., 1980. Contbr. articles to profl. jours. Moderator Congrl. Ch., Asheville, N.C., 1956-57. Lt. col. USAF, 1943-69. Decorated DFC. Fellow Soc. Am. Foresters (pres. 1986, John Beale Meml. award 1983); mem. Am. Forests (B.E. Fernow award 1993), Internat. Soc. Tropical Foresters (pres. 1984—), Res. Officers Assn. Republican. Avocations: golfing, skiing. Home: 16112 Berkeley Dr Haymarket VA 20169-1824

DOONER, JOHN JOSEPH, JR., advertising executive; b. Mt. Vernon, N.Y., Aug. 3, 1948; s. John Joseph and Elizabeth Ann (Forrest) D.; m. Cynthia Ann Stewart, Aug. 16, 1975; children: Miriam, Jaclyn. B.A., St. Thomas Villanova Coll., Miami, Fla.; postgrad., Iona Coll. Advt. media supr. Grey Advt., N.Y.C., 1970-73; assoc. media dir. The Marschalk Co., N.Y.C., 1973-74, account mgr., 1974-84; exec. v.p. McCann-Erickson, N.Y.C., 1984—, gen. mgr. N.Y. office, 1984-88, pres. N.Am. region, 1988-94; pres., COO McCann-Erickson Worldwide, N.Y.C., 1992-94, chmn., CEO, 1994—; bd. dirs. The Interpublic Group. Mem. bd. govs. Tri State United Way campaign, 1994-95; bd. trustees New Rochesste Med. Ctr., 1993—. Mem. Pelham Country Club, Lago Mar Club (Ft. Lauderdale, Fla.). Avocations: tennis, boating. Office: McCann-Erickson Worldwide 750 3rd Ave Fl 3 New York NY 10017-2798*

DOORISH, JOHN FRANCIS, physicist, mathematician, educator; b. Bklyn., Jan. 13, 1957; s. Thomas Joseph Anthony and Annunciata Ann (Longobardi) D. BS in Physics, St. John's U., 1980; MS in Applied Physics, Columbia U., 1985, EdD in Math. and Astrophysics, 1988. Rsch. physicist N.Y.C. Bur. Noise Abatement Dept. Environ. Protection, 1981; adj. asst. prof. Boro. Manhattan Community Coll., N.Y.C., 1991-94; assoc. prof. physics Wagner Coll., S.I., N.Y., 1994-96; rsch. scientist eye radiation and environ. rsch. lab. Columbia U. Coll. Physician and Surgeons, N.Y.C., 1996-99; prin. investigator Artificial Retina Package Project, Eye Radiation Lab., Columbia U.; pres., founder Second Sight of N.Y., Inc., 1999—; assoc. rsch. scientist Princeton (N.J.) U., 1992-93; pres. Second Sight N.Y. Inc. Contbr. articles to profl. jours. and internat. sci. confs. Mem. ASCPA, N.Y.C., Internat. Fund Animal Welfare, Boston. St. John's scholar. Mem. AAAS, Am. Astron. Soc., Am. Phys. Soc., Assn. Rsch. in Vision and Ophthalmology, N.Y. Acad. Scis., Planetary Soc. Republican. Roman Catholic. Office: Columbia U Eye Radiation Environ Rsch Lab 160 Fort Washington Ave New York NY 10032

DOORLEY, THOMAS LAWRENCE, III, management consulting firm executive; b. Sewickley, Pa., Aug. 15, 1944; s. Thomas Lawrence and Emma Lou (Sage) D.; m. Gail Lynn Schwartz, Feb. 3, 1968; children: Christopher Sage, Scott Frederick. BSChemE, Pa. State U., BA in Arts and Sci., 1967; MBA in Mktg., Columbia U., 1969. Cons. Westvaco, N.Y.C., 1968-69; sr. cons. A D Little, Cambridge, Mass., 1969-74, bus. unit mgr., 1974-76; founder, exec. v.p. Braxton Assocs., Boston, 1977-82, sr. ptnr., 1996—. Author: Teaming up for the 90's; contbr. articles to profl. jours. Chmn., bd. dirs. The Soccer Network, Boston, 1987—; mem. leadership club United Way Mass., Boston, 1986-90; coach Wellesley (Mass.) United Soccer Club, 1977-90; deacon Wellesley Congregational Ch., 1970's, sr. high youth advisor, 1970's. Woodrow Wilson fellow Columbia U., 1969. Mem. Columbia Bus. Sch. Club, Wellesley Country Club, Alliance Analyst and World Econ. Found. (advisory bd.). Avocations: running, fitness, reading, children. Home: 34 Arnold Rd Wellesley MA 02481-2841 Office: Braxton Assocs 200 Clarendon St Ste 2000 Boston MA 02116-5021

DOPF, GLENN WILLIAM, lawyer; b. N.Y.C., June 6, 1953; s. William Bernard and Doris Virginia (Roxby) D. BS cum laude, Fordham Coll., 1975; JD, Fordham U., 1979; LLM, NYU, 1983. Bar: N.J. 1979, U.S. Dist. Ct. N.J. 1979, N.Y. 1980, U.S. Dist. Ct. (so. and ea. dists.) N.Y. 1980, U.S. Ct. Appeals (2d cir.) 1980, U.S. Ct. Internat. Trade 1981, U.S. Supreme Ct. 1983. Assoc. Martin, Clearwater & Bell, N.Y.C., 1980-81; ptnr. Kopff, Nardelli & Dopf, N.Y.C., 1982—. Mem. ABA, Assn. Bar City N.Y. Office: Kopff Nardelli & Dopf 440 9th Ave Fl 15 New York NY 10001-1688

DOR, CAPLYN, artist; b. Buffalo, Nov. 13, 1952; d. Triest Joseph and Josephine Lenore (Condello) Cappello; m. Kenneth James Doerfler, Nov. 17, 1979; 1 child, Daniel Allen Sheehy. One-woman shows include J.C. Mazur Gallery, Buffalo, 1989, Hilbert Coll., Hamburg, N.Y., 1990, Arts Coun. Buffalo and Erie County, 1991, Castellani Art Mus., Niagara U., Niagara Falls, N.Y., 1992, Waligur-Doering Gallery, Hamburg, N.Y., 1997; featured artist Clary-Miner Gallery, Buffalo, 1991, Albright-Knox Art Gallery/Mus., Buffalo, 1992, 94, Del Bello Gallery, Toronto, 1995-96; exhibited in group show Soho Internat. Art Competition, Ariel Gallery, N.Y.C., 1990 (award), 92 (award), Trans-Hudson Gallery, N.Y.C., 1998, Abraham Lubelski Gallery, N.Y.C., 1998. Active Arts Coun. Buffalo and Erie County, 1988—, Castellani Art Mus., 1992—. Recipient Hon. Mention Art Calendar's Crabbie Awards, 1997, Internat. "Gold" Computer, Animation, Photography, Illustration award, 1998, Artistic Excellence Achievement award TINT mag., 1998, Best of Show award Artistic Impressions Spring Art Competition, 1998, Judges Choice award Art Career, 1999, others; Creative arts fellow N.Y. State Coun. Arts, 1992. Mem. Internat. Registry Artists and Artwork, Renaissance 2001, Western N.Y. Artists Group. Avocations: computers, reading, photography, travel, cooking. Home and Studio: 4246 Twinmeadow Ln Hamburg NY 14075-1336

DOR, YORAM, accountant, firm executive; b. Tel Aviv, Apr. 17, 1945; came to U.S., 1974; s. Simon and Shulamit (Remple) D.; m. Ofra Lipshitz, Apr. 9, 1967; children: Gil, Ron. Diploma in Acctg., Hebrew U. Jerusalem, 1969; BA in Econs., Tel Aviv U., 1971; MBA, UCLA, 1977. CPA, Calif. Sr. auditor Somekh Chaikin, CPA, Tel Aviv, 1969-72; CFO East African Hotels, Dar-es-Salaam, Tanzania, 1972-74; staff acct. Hyatt Med. Enterprises, Inc. (name now Nu Med, Inc.), Encino, Calif., 1974-75, asst. contr., 1975-77, corp. contr., 1977-79, v.p. fin., 1979-82, sr. v.p. fin., CFO, 1982-87, exec. v.p. fin., CFO, 1987-95; ptnr. Sloman and Dor, Encino, 1995—; also bd. dirs. Mem. AICPA, Calif. Soc. CPA's. Office: Sloman & Dor 16633 Ventura Blvd Ste 913 Encino CA 91436-1849

DORADO, MARIANNE GAERTNER, lawyer; b. Neptune, N.J., May 18, 1956; d. Wolfgang Wilhelm and Marianne L. (Weber) Gaertner; m. Richard Manuel Dorado, Oct. 1, 1982; children: Marianne Christine, Kathleen Gina. BA, Yale U., 1978; JD, U. Mich., 1981. Bar: N.Y. 1982, U.S. Supreme Ct. 1993. Ptnr. Chimel Dorado, N.Y.C., 1998—; bd. dirs. Blue Heron Theater, N.Y.C. Contbr. articles to profl. jours. Extern office legal advisor U.S. Dept. State, Washington, 1980. Republican. Roman Catholic. Office: Chimel Dorado 14th Fl 1180 Ave of Americas New York NY 10036

DORAN, CHARLES EDWARD, textile manufacturing executive; b. Hartford, Conn., Mar. 31, 1928; s. Charles Edward and Josephine Catherine (Maher) D.; m. Anne Marie McGovern, May 18, 1957; children—Charles Francis, John Francis, Pamela Anne. BA, Hamilton Coll., 1951; MA, Yale U., 1952. Trainee Gen. Elec. Co., 1953-56, financial mgmt. positions, 1956-65; asst. treas. Collins & Aikman Corp., N.Y.C., 1965-71; treas. Collins & Aikman Corp., 1971-88; mem. adv. bd. Arkwright-Boston Ins. Co., 1981-87. Served with USNR, 1946-48. Mem. Fin. Execs. Inst., Nat. Assn. Corp. Treasurers, Yale Club, Union League Club (N.Y.C.), Phi Beta Kappa, Chi Psi. Republican. Roman Catholic.

DORAN, JAMES MARTIN, retired food products company executive; b. Toronto, Ohio, Apr. 21, 1933; s. Hugh John and Mary Agnes (Murray) D.; m. Peggotty Hanks Namm, Dec. 9, 1967 (dec. Dec. 1978); children—Beth Namm, Wendy Harrison. B.S. in Bus. Adminstrn., John Carroll Univ., 1955. C.P.A., Pa., Ohio. Sr. acct. Deloitte, Haskins & Sells, Pitts., 1956-60; sr. corp. acct. Revere Copper & Brass, Rome, N.Y., 1960-64; contr. A.C. Gilbert Co., New Haven, 1964-67, Heublein Spirits & Wine, Farmington, Conn., 1967-83; sr. v.p. fin. Heublein, Inc., Farmington, 1983-89, ret.; v.p., dir. Arebec Corp., N.Y.C., 1969—. V.p., trustee Namm Found., N.Y.C., 1970—; mem. Leadership Greater Hartford, 1977—; trustee McAuley Retirement Community, 1991—, Julie Edn. Ctr., 1996—. Mem. AICPA. Roman Catholic. Avocations: investing, tennis, golf. Home: 83 Rumford St West Hartford CT 06107-3754

DORAN, KAY JOANN, Spanish language educator; b. Clintonville, Wis., Aug. 6, 1935; d. Joseph Nathaniel and Rosetta Louise (Wotruba) K.; m. Roger Douglas Doran, Aug. 10, 1957. BS in Secondary Edn., U. Wis., 1957. Cert. tchr., Wis. Spanish/English tchr. Stoughton (Wis.) H.S., 1957-60, West H.S., Green Bay, Wis., 1960-63; Spanish tchr. Antigo (Wis.) H.S., 1963-64, Elcho (Wis.) H.S., 1985—. Bd. dirs. U. Wis. Madison Alumni Assn., Antigo, 1996—; mem. Ice Age Trail Coun., 1990-97. Fellowship to Mexico, Rockefeller Found., 1988; participant Spain Today NEH, U. Va., Madrid, 1994; participant Wis. Tchr. World, Dept. Pub. Instrn., 1991. Mem. Am. Assn. Tchrs. of Spanish and Portuguese (Wis. chpt. pres. 1990-91), Wis. Assn. of Fgn. Lang. Tchrs. (bd. dirs. 1990-91, cert. of recognition 1997), Delta Kappa Gamma (v.p. 1989). Avocations: skiing, hiking, reading, study of art, knitting. Home: 1503 Clermont St Antigo WI 54409-2312 Office: Elcho High Sch PO Box 800 Elcho WI 54428-0800

DORAN, MARK RICHARD, real estate financial executive; b. Chgo., June 17, 1954; s. Paul George and Mae (Olson) D.; m. Wendy Carole Beckham, Dec. 17, 1977; children: Blake, Barrett, Hayley. BBA in Acctg., Baylor U., 1975, MBA, 1976. From asst. acct. to supr. Peat, Marwick, Mitchell & Co., Dallas, 1977-81; sr. v.p. fin. Lincoln Property Co., Dallas, 1982-89; exec. v.p., CFO Prentiss Properties Trust, Dallas, 1990-98; exec. v.p., CFR Transwestern Comml. Svcs., 1999—. Deacon Park Cities Bapt. Ch., Dallas, 1988—. Mem. Nat. Assn. Real Estate Investment Trusts, Nat. Assn. Indsl. and Office Pks., The Urban Land Inst., The Real Estate Coun., University Park Dads Club, Baylor U. Alumni Assn. Avocations: basketball, golf, snow skiing. Office: Transwestern Comml Svcs 12221 Merit Dr Dallas TX 75251

DORAN, THOMAS GEORGE, bishop; b. Rockford, IL, Feb. 20, 1936. Licentiate in Sacred Theology, Pontifical Gregorian U., Rome, 1962, Ph.D. in Canon Law, 1975-78. Ordained priest, 1961, ordained bishop, 1994. Asst. pastor St. Joseph Parish, Elgin, IL, St. Peter Parish, South Beloit; various admin. duties Diocese of Rockford, rector diocesan cathedral; prelate auditor Roman Rota, 1986-1994; bishop Roman Rota, Rockford, Ill., 1994—. Office: Diocese of Rockford PO Box 7045 Rockford IL 61125-7044*

DORAN, TIMOTHY PATRICK, educational administrator; b. N.Y.C., July 1, 1949; s. Joseph Anthony and Claire (Griffin) D.; m. Kathleen Matava, Aug. 1, 1981; children: Claire Marie, Bridget Anne. BA in Econs., Le Moyne Coll., 1971; MA in Teaching, U. Alaska, 1984, Education Specialist, 1990. Cert. type A secondary, econs., type B K-12 prin., supt. Svc. rep. Emigrant Savings Bank, N.Y.C., 1971-72; exec., dir. Project Equality Northwest, Seattle, 1972-73; exec. dir. Jesuit Vol. Corps., Portland, Oreg., 1973-75, adminstv. advisor Kaltag City (Alaska) coun., 1975-77; program developer Diocese Fairbanks, Alaska, 1978-81, adminstr., supt. St. Mary's Cath. High Sch., 1981-83; prin. intern U. Alaska, Fairbanks, 1984, vis. instr., 1990-94; tchr. Anthony A. Andrews Sch., St. Michael, Alaska, 1984-86; prin., tchr. James C. Isabell Sch, Teller, Alaska, 1986-88; prin. Unalakleet (Alaska) Schs., 1988-90, Denali Elem. Sch., Fairbanks, 1992—; acad. coord. U. Alaska, summers 1984-86, Elderhostel instr., 1991—, sch. edn. curr. adv. bd., 1998—; docent U. Alaska Mus., 1991. Active nat. com. Campaign for Human Devel., 1980-83; mem. manpower planning coun. Tanana Chiefs Conf., 1976-77, parish coun. Sacred Heart Cathedral, 1979-81; Sunday Sch. tchr. St. Mark's Univ. Parish, 1990-97, adv. coun., 1998—; mem. com. Fairbanks Arts Coun. for Edn., 1995—; bd. dirs. Literacy Coun. Alaska, 1997-98. Recipient Merit awards Alaska Dept. Edn., 1986-90. Mem. ASCD, Nat. Assn. Elem. Sch. Prins., Alaska Assn. Elem. Sch. Prins. (v.p.), Fairbanks Prins. Assn. (v.p., pres.-elect), Alaska Math. Consortium (bd. dirs.). E-mail: tdoran@northstar.k12.ak.us. Home: 512 Windsor Dr Fairbanks AK 99709-3439 Office: Denali Elem Sch 1042 Lathrop St Fairbanks AK 99701-4124

DORAN, WILLIAM MICHAEL, lawyer; b. Albany, N.Y., May 26, 1940; s. James R. and Lorene Tinsley (Nees) D.; m. Susan Coryell Lloyd; children: Melissa, Heather, Leigh. BS in Journalism, Northwestern U., 1962; LLB, U. Pa., 1966. Assoc. Morgan, Lewis & Bockius, Phila., 1967-76, ptnr., 1976—; dir. SEI Corp.; trustee SEI Liquid Asset Trust, SEI Daily Income Trust, SEI Tax Exempt Trust, SEI Instl. Managed Trust, SEI Index Funds, SEI Internat. Trust, The Advisors Inner Cir. Fund, The Arbor Fund, Inventor Funds, Incs. Vice chmn. World Affairs Coun. Phila. Mem. ABA, Pa. Bar Assn., Phila. Bar Assn., Nat. Assn. Bond Lawyers. Home: 27 Druim Moir Ln Philadelphia PA 19118-4134 Office: Morgan Lewis & Bockius LLP 1701 Market St Philadelphia PA 19103-2903*

DORATO, PETER, electrical and computer engineering educator; b. N.Y.C., Dec. 17, 1932; s. Fioretto and Rosina (Lachello) D.; m. Marie Madeleine Turlan, June 2, 1956; children: Christopher, Alexander, Sylvia, Veronica. BEE, CCNY, 1955; MSEE, Columbia U., 1956; DEE, Poly. Inst. N.Y., 1961. Registered profl. engr., Colo. Lectr. elec. engring. dept. CCNY, 1956-57; instr. elec. engring. Poly. Inst. N.Y., Bklyn., 1957-61, prof., 1961-72; prof. elec. engring., dir. Resource System Analysis U. Colo., Colorado Springs, 1972-76; prof. elec. and computer engring. U. N.Mex., Albuquerque, 1984—, chmn. dept., 1976-84; hon. chaired prof. Nanjing Aero. Inst., 1989; vis. prof. Politecnico di Torino, Italy, 1991-92. Co-author Linear Quadratic Control, 1995, Robust Control for Unstructured Perturbations, 1992, Robust Control-System Design, 1996; editor: Robust Control, Recent Results in Robust Control and Advances in Adaptive Control, reprint vols., 1987, 90, 91, IEEE Press Reprint Vol. Series, 1989-90; assoc. editor Automatica Jour., 1969-83, 89-92, editor rapid publs., 1994—; assoc. editor IEEE Trans on Edn., 1989-91; contbr. articles on control systems theory to profl. jours. Recipient John R. Ragazzini edn. award Am. Automatic Control Coun., 1998. Fellow IEEE; mem. IEEE Control Systems Soc. (Disting. Mem. award). Democrat. Home: 1514 Roma Ave NE Albuquerque NM 87106-

4513 Office: U NMex Dept Elec Computer Eng Albuquerque NM 87131-1356

DORDELMAN, WILLIAM FORSYTH, food company executive; b. Glen Ridge, N.J., Oct. 18, 1940; s. Wilbert E. and Dorothy F. (Forsyth) D.; m. Barbara Ann Gaddis, Sept. 16, 1959; children: Dorothy Ann, William Edward, Patricia Lynne, Lauren Forsyth. BA in Econs, U. Va., 1962; MBA, Harvard U., 1964. With Gen. Foods Corp., White Plains, N.Y., 1965—; advt. and merchandising mgr. Birdseye div. Gen. Foods Corp., White Plains, 1972-73, gen. mgr. main meal strategic bus. unit, 1973-77, v.p. corp., pres. Food Products div., 1977-80, corp. group v.p., 1980-86; pres. Fairfield Capital, Rowayton, Conn., 1986-92; co-CEO B. Manischewitz Co., 1992-93; chmn., CEO Colo. Prime Foods, 1993-98; prin. Kohlberg & Co., Mcht. Bankers, 1998—; bd. dirs. Bailey & Alling Lumber Co., Oscar Mayer, Entemanns, B. Manischewitz Co., Color Spot Nursery, United Signature Foods, Colo. Prime Food. Bd. dirs. Mid-Fairfield Youth Hockey Assn., 1973-77, St. Vincent's Hosp. Mem. Am. Mgmt. Assn., Am. Mktg. Assn., Young Pres. Orgn. (bd. dirs. N.Y. chpt. 1982), Weeburn Country Club, Ocean Reef Club, Westchester/Fairfield County Club, Harvard Bus. Sch. Club (dir. 1978—), Zeta Psi. Episcopalian. Home: 9 Woodley Rd Darien CT 06820-2622

DORE, ANITA WILKES, English educator; b. N.Y.C., Dec. 16, 1914; d. Abraham P. and Rose (Hirsch) Wilkes; m. Robert M. Dore, June 26, 1938; children: Marjorie Dore Allen, Elizabeth. BA, Vassar Coll., 1935; MA with honors, Columbia U., 1937. Cert. English tchr., N.Y. Tchr. H.S. English, Bd. Edn., N.Y.C., 1937-41, 56-59, TV broadcaster, producer, 1961-65, coordinator English jr. high sch. div., 1959-61, chair English dept., 1965-67, asst. dir. English, 1967-73, dir. English, N.Y.C. schs., 1973-83, cons., 1983—; cons. Young Playwrights Dramatists Guild, N.Y.C., 1983-87. Author: Premier Book of Major Poets, 1970, Emerging Woman, 1974; co-author: Distrust of Authority, 1981; also articles. Pres., bd. dirs. Sch. Settlement House, Bklyn., 1951-53; mem. edn. com. NOW, N.Y.C., 1972-75; chair Child Study Children's Book Com. Bank St. Coll., 1983-98; sec., bd. dirs. Westport-Westport Arts Ctr., Conn., 1983-93; trustee Westport Libr.ss, Conn.; 1985-92; chair adv. com. young poets and playwrights festivals of Conn. Westport Arts Ctr., 1983—. Recipient Elizabeth Dana prize in English, Vassar Coll., 1934; named Honoree Salute to Women YWCA, 1991. Fellow N.Y. State English Council (v.p. 1970-75); mem. Nat. Council Tchrs. English Lit. Commn., N.Y.C. Assn. Tchrs. English (v.p. 1962-70), Alumnae Assn. Vassar (class 1935 pres. 1996—). Democrat. Avocations: theatre, traveling, politics. Home: 36 E 36th St New York NY 10016-3463

DORE, STEPHEN EDWARD, JR., retired civil engineer; b. Providence, Apr. 1, 1918; s. Stephen Edward and Anna Caroline (Chace) D.; m. Evelyn Mae Andrews, Mar. 14, 1942 (dec. Jan. 1995); children: Linda Jane, Jeffrey Stephen, Sherrill Ann. B.S. in Engring, Brown U., 1940. Registered profl. engr., Conn., Maine, Mass., N.H., R.I. registered land surveyor, Maine. Surveyor Met. Dist. Hartford County, Conn., 1940; engring. draftsman design dept. U.S. Navy, Quonset Point, R.I., 1940-42; draftsman R.I. Dept. Pub. Works, Providence, 1946; hydraulic engr. C.E., Providence, 1946; structural designer E.B. Badger Co., Boston, 1946-47; with Coffin & Richardson Inc. (Cons. Engrs.), Boston, 1947-83; sr. project engr. Coffin & Richardson Inc. (Cons. Engrs.), 1958-62, v.p., chief engr., 1962-73, exec. v.p., 1973-79, pres., 1979-83, also bd. dirs.; ret., 1983. Treas. Cedarcrest Civic Assn., Canton, Mass., 1952-55. Served to capt. C.E. U.S. Army, 1942-46. Fellow ASCE, Cons. Engrs. Council; mem. Am., New Eng. water works assns., Soc. Mil. Engrs., Boston Soc. Civil Engrs. Unitarian. Home: 1438 W Schwartz Blvd Lady Lake FL 32159-6115

DOREMUS, ROBERT HEWARD, glass and ceramics processing educator; b. Denver, Sept. 16, 1928; s. Francis Heward and Elsie Marion (Segelke) D.; m. Germaine Briancon, Mar. 19, 1956; children—Marc Francis, Elaine, Carol, Natalie. B.S., U. Colo., 1950; M.S., U. Ill., 1951, Ph.D., 1953; Ph.D. (Fulbright fellow), U. Cambridge, Eng., 1956. Phys. chemist Gen. Electric Research and Devel. Ctr., Schenectady, 1956-71; N.Y. State prof. glass and ceramics Rensselaer Poly. Inst., Troy, N.Y., 1971—, chair materials engring. dept., 1986-95; cons. in field. Author: Glass Science, 1973, 94, Rates of Phase Transformations, 1985. Co-editor: Growth and Perfection of Crystals, 1958; Contbr. articles to profl. jours. Bd. dirs. Phila. Luth. Sem., 1967-76. Fellow Am. Ceramic Soc.; mem. AAAS, Sigma Xi, Sigma Tau, Tau Beta Pi. Lutheran. Office: Materials Dept Rensselaer Poly Instit Troy NY 12181

DORER, FRED HAROLD, chemistry educator; b. Auburn, Calif., May 3, 1936; s. Fred H. and Mary E. (Fisher) D.; m. Marilyn Pearl Young, Sept. 6, 1958; children: Garrett Michael, Russell Kenneth. B.S., Calif. State U.-Long Beach, 1961; Ph.D., U. Wash., 1965; postgrad., U. Freiburg, (Germany), 1965-66. Rsch. chemist Shell Devel. Co., Emeryville, Calif., 1966-67; prof. chemistry Calif. State U., Fullerton, 1967-75; assoc. program dir. chem. dynamics NSF, Washington, 1974-75; chmn., prof. chemistry San Francisco State U., 1975-81; dean natural sci. Sonoma State U., Rohnert Park, Calif., 1981-82, provost, v.p., 1982-84; acad. v.p. Calif. State U., Bakersfield, 1984—, provost v.p., 1996—. Contbr. articles to profl. jours. Served with USMC, 1954-57. Grantee Research Corp., 1968; grantee NSF, 1969-75, Petroleum Research Fund, 1978, 80; fellow NSF, 1965. Mem. AAAS, Am. Assn. Higher Edn., Am. Chem. Soc. Home: 5704 Muirfield Dr Bakersfield CA 93306 Office: Calif State U 9001 Stockdale Hwy Bakersfield CA 93311-1022

DORF, RICHARD CARL, electrical engineering and management educator; b. N.Y.C., Dec. 27, 1933; s. William Carl and Marion (Fraser) D.; m. Joy H. MacDonald, June 15, 1957; children: Christine, Renée. BS, Clarkson U., 1955; MS, U. Colo., 1957; PhD, U.S. Naval Postgrad. Sch., 1961. Registered profl. engr., Calif. Instr. Clarkson U., Potsdam, N.Y., 1956-58; instr., asst. prof. U.S. Naval Postgrad. Sch., Monterey, Calif., 1958-63; prof., chmn. U. Santa Clara, Calif., 1963-69; v.p. Ohio U., Athens, 1969-72; dean of extended learning U. Calif., Davis, 1972-81, prof. in mgmt. and elec. engring., 1972—; lectr. U. Edinburgh, Scotland, 1961-62; cons. Lawrence Livermore (Calif.) Nat. Lab., 1981—; chmn. Sacramento Valley Venture Capital Forum, 1985-90. Author: The Mutual Fund Portfolio Planner, 1988, The New Mutual Fund Advisor, 1988, Electric Circuits, 3d edit., 1996, Modern Control Systems, 8th edit., 1998; editor: Ency. of Robotics, 1987, Circuits, Devices and Systems, 1991, Handbook of Electrical Engineering, 2d edit., 1997, Handbook of Manufacturing and Automation, 1994, Handbook of Technology Management, 1999. Bd. dirs. Sta. KVIE, PBS, Sacramento, 1976-79; ruling elder Davis Cmty. Ch., 1973-76; chmn. Sonoma Valley Econ. Devel. Assn., 1993—; mem. City Coun., City of Sonoma, 1994-98; vice mayor City of Sonoma, 1994, 98, mayor, 1996. With U.S. Army, 1956. Recipient Alumni award Clarkson U., 1979, Disting. Alumni award Colo. U., 1998. Fellow IEEE; mem. Am. Soc. Engring. Edn. (sr., chmn. div. 1980—), University Club (bd. dirs. 1988-91), Rotary (bd. dirs. 1978-80). Presbyterian. Office: U Calif Elec Engring Dept Davis CA 95616

DORFMAN, ALLEN BERNARD, international management consultant; b. N.Y.C., Mar. 30, 1930; s. Harry and Jean (Schreiber) D.; m. Elaine Turbé, Jan. 9, 1955; children: Nancy Ann, Jeffrey David. BBA summa cum laude, 1952; postgrad. mgmt. studies, Harvard Bus. Sch. From mem. exec. tng. squad to sr. mgmt. R.H. Macy's, N.Y.C., 1954-67; asst. gen. mdse. mgr., v.p., mem. mgmt. com. N.Y. div. Allied Stores Corp., N.Y.C., 1967-69; v.p., gen. mdse. mgr. hard and soft goods, mem. exec. com. Town & Country Full Line Discount Stores div. Lane Bryant Corp., N.Y.C., 1969-71; pres., dir. Nat. Bellas Hess Inc., Kansas City, Mo., 1971-73; corp. sr. v.p. and pres., CEO retail div. Jewelcor, Inc., N.Y.C., 1973-77; corp. sr. v.p., dir. corp. ops., mem. exec. com. Vornado, Inc., Garfield, N.J., 1977-78; chmn. bd. dirs., CEO Allen B. Dorfman, Mgmt. Consulting Co., 1978—; prof. Grad. Sch., L.I. U., evenings. Bd. dirs., exec. v.p. Am. Cancer Soc.; bd. dirs. Kings Point Civic Assn. With AUS, 1952-54. Recipient award Advt. Club N.Y., Torch of Liberty award Nat. Anti-Defamation League. Mem. Mass. Retailing Inst., Nat. Retail Mchts. Assn., Nat. Assn. Catalog Showroom Merchandisers, Inc., Adelphi Coll. Found., Boy Scouts Am., Boys Club, Philhamonics Assn., Police Athletic League, Polo Club (mem. adv. bd. govs.-exec. com., chmn. emeritus coun. of pres.), Wildwood Country Club (pres., bd. dirs., Kings Point, N.Y.), Beta Gamma Sigma, Eta Mu Pi, Sigma Alpha. Patent pending zippered ice and roller skates. Office: Allen B Dorfman Mgmt Consulting Co Polo Club-Penthouse Villa 17588 Ashbourne Ln # C Boca Raton FL 33496-2461

DORFMAN, HOWARD DAVID, pathologist, educator; b. N.Y., July 20, 1928; s. Louis and Helen (Weingarten) D.; m. Esther Novick, June 21, 1952; children: Richard H., Peter W., Leslie Jane. BA, NYU, 1947; MD, SUNY, Bklyn., 1951. Resident in pathology Mt. Sinai Hosp., N.Y., 1952-54, Columbia Presby. Medical Ctr., N.Y., 1954-58; dir. pathology Sharon (Conn.) Hosp., 1958-60; assoc. pathologist Sinai Hosp. Balt., Baltimore, Md., 1960-64; dir. pathology Hosp. Joint Diseases, N.Y., 1964-74; pathologist-in-chief Sinai Hosp. Balt., 1974-85; prof. orthopedic pathology Johns Hopkins Sch. of Medicine, Balt., 1985; prof. pathology, radiology and orthopaedic surgery Albert Einstein Coll. Medicine, Bronx, N.Y., 1985—; Walter Putschar lectr. Mass. Gen. Hosp. Harvard Med. Sch., 1983; vis. prof. Wayne State U. Sch. Medicine, 1984, Baylor Coll. Medicine, Houston, 1984, Cleve. Clinic, 1984, SUNY, Stonybrook, 1994, Johns Hopkins U. Sch. Medicine, 1995, U. Mich. Sch. Medicine, 1997, Cornell U. Sch. Medicine, Meml.-Sloan Kettering Cancer Ctr., 1998, U. Pitts. Sch. Medicine, 1998, Brigham and Women's Hosp., Harvard Med. Sch., 1998. Author: Bone Tumors, 1998; co-author: Tumors of Bone and Cartilage, 1971. Recipient Henry Jaffe award Hosp. Joint Diseases, 1984. Mem. N.Y. Pathological Soc. (pres. 1989-91), Internat. Skeletal Soc. (pres. 1986-88). Home: 530 E 72nd St Apt 5G New York NY 10021-4844

DORFMAN, JOHN CHARLES, lawyer; b. Wilkinsburg, Pa., Feb. 3, 1925; s. Leo O. Dorfman; m. Ruth B. Davison; children: Beverly (Dorfman) Lenci, Laura, Carolyn, Bradley. BEE, Yale U., 1945; JD, Cornell U., 1949. Bar: N.Y. 1949, Conn. 1950, Pa., 1956, U.S. Dist. Ct. (ea. dist.) Pa. 1957, U.S. Ct. Appeals (fed. cir.) 1982, U.S. Supreme Ct. 1959, U.S. Patent & Trademark Office 1949. Patent counsel Machlett Labs. Inc., Springdale, Conn., 1949-54; assoc. Pennie & Edmonds, N.Y.C., 1954-55; assoc. Howson & Howson, Phila., 1955-59, ptnr., 1960-73; ptnr., chmn. Dann, Dorfman, Herrell & Skillman, Phila., 1974—. Elder Wayne Presbyn. Ch. Served to lt. (j.g.) USNR, 1943-46. Mem. ABA (chmn. sect. patent, trademark and copyright law 1984-85, hon. mem. coun.), Nat. Coun. Patent Law Assn. (chmn. 1978-79), Am. Intellectual Property Law Assn. (bd. dirs. 1973-76), Phila. Patent Law Assn. (pres. 1974-76), Nat. Inventors Hall of Fame Found. (pres. 1977-78, bd. dirs. 1979—, mem. joint bd. NIHF and Inventure Place 1995—), Union League Club (Phila.), St. David's Golf Club (Wayne, Pa.), Yale Club of Phila. (pres. 1980-81), Tau Beta Pi, Delta Tau Delta (bd. Cornell U. house corp. 1969—). Republican. Avocations: skiing, golf, travel. Home: 215 Midland Ave Wayne PA 19087-4108 Office: Dann Dorfman Herrell & Skillman 1601 Market St Ste 720 Philadelphia PA 19103-2307

DORFMAN, PAUL MICHAEL, bank executive; b. Chgo., Mar. 16, 1939; s. Isaiah Sol. and Lillian M. D.; m. Janet Ruth Vogel, June 18, 1961; children: Judith A. Mendelsohn, Jeffrey H., Eric M., Benjamin K. BA in Econs., Princeton Univ., 1961; JD, Yale Univ., 1964. Bar: Ill. 1964. Attorney Mayer, Brown and Platt, Chgo., 1964-69; v.p. Continental Ill. Venture Corp., Chgo., 1969-71; exec. v.p. JMB Realty Corp., Chgo., 1971-73; v.p. transportation sect., client info. svcs., others Bank Am., San Francisco, 1973-79, v.p. strategic planning world banking divsn., 1979-80; group v.p., head credit adminstrn. Europe Middle East Divsn Bank Am., London, 1980-82; sr. v.p. Asia divsn. Bank Am., Tokyo, 1982-85; sr. v.p. world banking divsn. Bank Am., San Francisco, 1985-86, sr. v.p. credit policy, 1986-90, exec. v.p. credit risk mgmt., 1990—, chmn. country risk com., 1986—; vice chmn. credit policy com. Bank Am., 1986-98; dir., office, Robert Morris Assocs., 1993—, nat. chmn. 1997-98. Contbr. articles to profl. jours. Mem. bd. dirs. San Francisco Chpt. Am. Jewish Com., 1987—; dir. Japan Soc. No. Calif., 1996—, v.p., 1997—; trustee World Affairs Coun. of No. Calif., 1999—. Mem. Phi Beta Kappa. Office: Bank Am 555 California St San Francisco CA 94104-1590

DORFMAN, ROBERT, economics educator; b. N.Y.C., Oct. 27, 1916; s. Samuel M. and Mina Ruth (Gordon) D.; m. Nancy Schelling, Nov. 6, 1949; children: Peter J., Ann E. BA, Columbia U., 1936, MA, 1937; PhD, U. Calif., Berkeley, 1950. Asst. statistician Bur. Labor Stats., Dept. Labor, Washington, 1939-41; statistician OPA, Washington, 1941-43; ops. analyst U.S. Air Force, S.W. Pacific and Washington, 1943-50; assoc. prof. econs U. Calif., Berkeley, 1950-55; prof. econs. Harvard U., Cambridge, Mass., 1955-87; prof. emeritus Harvard U., Cambridge, 1987—; mem. clean air sci. adv. com. EPA, 1978-84; mem. environ. studies bd. NRC, 1974-77; mem. Presdl. Commn. on Waterlogging and Salinity in West Pakistan, 1961-63, Presdl. Commn. on Employment and Unemployment Stats., 1962-63. Author: Prices and Markets, 1967, Economic Theory and Public Decisions, 1997; co-author: Linear Programming and Economic Analysis, 1958; co-editor: Economics of the Environment: Selected Readings, 1972, 3d edit. 1993; editor Quar. Jour. Econs., 1976-84. Guggenheim fellow, 1970-71. Fellow Am. Acad. Arts and Scis., Econometric Soc. (coun. 1962-64); mem. Am. Econs. Assn. (v.p. 1982, Disting. fellow 1993), Inst. Mgmt. Sci. (pres. 1965-66), Assn. Resource and Environ. Economists (v.p. 1981). Home: 81 Kilburn Rd Belmont MA 02478-2464 Office: Harvard U Dept Econs Littauer Ctr 325 Cambridge MA 02138

DORGAN, BYRON LESLIE, senator; b. Dickinson, N.D., May 14, 1942; s. Emmett P. and Dorothy (Bach) D.; m. Kimberly Olson Dorgan; children: Scott, Shelly (dec.), Brendon, Haley. BBA, U. N.D., 1965; MBA, U. Denver, 1966. Exec. devel. trainee Martin Marietta Corp., Denver, 1966-67; dep. tax commr., then tax commr. State of N.D., 1967-80; mem. 97th-102nd congresses from N.D., Washington, 1981-92, U.S. Senate from N.D., Washington, 1992—; asst. Dem. floor leader U.S. Senate, Washington, 1996—; mem. commerce, sci. and transp. com., select com. on Indian affairs, Dem. policy com., 1992—, appropriations com., energy and natural resource com.; instr. econs. Bismarck (N.D.) Jr. Coll., 1969-71. Contbr. articles to profl. jours. Recipient Nat. Leadership award Office Gov. N.D., 1972. Mem. Nat. Assn. Tax Adminstrs. (exec. com. 1972-75). Office: US Senate 713 Hart Senate Off Bldg Washington DC 20510*

DORIA, ANTHONY NOTARNICOLA, college dean, educator; b. Savona, Italy, June 2, 1927; s. Vito Sante and Jolanda (Giampaolo) Notarnicola. M.B.A., Wharton Sch., U. Pa., 1953; LL.M. (equivalent), U. Paris, 1960; D.Jr., U. Rome, 1962. Prof. history, bus. and internat. law Community Coll. at Suffolk County, Selden, N.Y., 1960-65, L.I. U., Southampton, N.Y., 1964-65; founder, pres. Royalton Coll. Sch. Internat. Affairs, S. Royalton, Vt., 1965-72; founder, dean Vt. Law Sch., 1972-74; dean Royalton Coll. Sch. Internat. Affairs (Royalton Coll. Law Study Center), 1974-92; prof. internat. law U. China, Beijing, 1992—; dir. grad. sch. program Internat. Bus. and Law - Hong Kong Ctr.; dir. grad. sch. program internat. bus. and law Hong Kong Ctr.; cons. internat. law and orgns.; panelist Am. Arbitration Assn.; mem. Vt. Gov.'s Commn. on Student Affairs, 1972-75. Author: Italy and the Free World, 1945, The Conquest of the Congo, 1947, Influences in the Making of Foreign Policy in the United States of America, Great Britain and France, 1953, Introduction to the Study of International Law, 1990. Candidate for U.S. Senate, 1986. Served with underground resistance movement World War II. Recipient Merit cert. UN; citation Boy Scouts Am., 1965. Mem. Am. Judicature Soc., Internat. Bar Assn., Internat. Law Assn., Am. Soc. Internat. Law, AAUP, Acad. Polit. Sci., Noble Assn. Chevaliers Pontificaux (life), Elysee (Paris), Penn and Pencil, Rotary (pres. 1990-91). Home: The Royalton Inn South Royalton VT 05068 Office: Royalton Coll Law Study Ctr South Royalton VT 05068

DORIA, JOSEPH V., JR., state legislator; b. June 28, 1946; m. Maribeth Keselica. AB, St. Peter's Coll., 1968; MA, Boston Coll., 1969; postgrad., Columbia Tchrs. Coll. Assembly mem. dist. 31 N.J. State Assembly; speaker N.J. State Assembly, 1990-91, chmn. higher edn. & regulated professions com. Past pres. Bayonne Bd. Edn.; dir. edn. svc. St. Peter's Coll.; vol. Bayonne coun. Boy Scouts Am., Urban League. Mem. Rotary. Office: PO Box 1408 Bayonne NJ 07002-6408*

DORIAN, BRETT J., federal judge; b. 1934. BA, San Francisco State U., 1959; JD, Boalt Hall, 1962. Apptd. bankruptcy judge ea. dist. U.S. Dist. Ct. Calif., 1988. With U.S. Army, 1952-54. Fax: (209) 498-7344. Office: 2656 US Courthouse 1130 O St Fresno CA 93721-2201

DORIANI, BETH MACLAY, English language educator; b. Pitts., Jan. 6, 1961; d. William N. and Betty (Boucher) Maclay; m. Christopher W. Doriani, June 4, 1983; children: Kara E., Andrew C., Joelle M. BA in English, Calvin Coll., 1983; MA, Kent State U., 1986; PhD, U. Notre Dame, 1990. Assoc. prof. English Northwestern Coll., Orange City, Iowa, 1990-98; academic dean Malone Coll., Canton, Ohio, 1998—. Author: Emily Dickinson, Daughter of Prophecy, 1996; contbr. articles to profl. jours. Grantee Pew Evangelical Scholars, 1997. Mem. MLA (Am. Lit. sect.), Emily Dickinson Internat. Soc. Avocations: boating, reading, swimming, flute. Office: Malone Coll 515 25th St NW Canton OH 44709 Address: 4814 Elberta Ave NW Canton OH 44709-1934

DORIN, DENNIS DANIEL, political science educator, researcher; b. Bklyn., May 11, 1942; s. Michael M. and Marie E. D.; m. Jo Ann Cannon, June 15, 1968; children: Daniel Brooks, Catherine Ann. BA in Polit. Sci. summa cum laude, Ariz. State U., 1964; MA in Govt., U. Va., 1965, PhD in Govt., 1974. Asst. prof. Am. U., Washington, 1967-72; from instr. to prof. polit. sci. U. N.C., Charlotte, 1972—. Contbr. articles to profl. jours., numerous newspapers. Mem. Supreme Ct. Hist. Soc. Guest scholar Brookings Instn., Washington, 1966-67; NDEA fellow, U.S. Govt., 1964-67. Mem. Am. Polit. Sci. Assn., Am. Soc. Criminology, So. Polit. Sci. Assn., Southea. Assn. Pre-Law Advisors, John Marshall Found., Golden Key, Phi Beta Kappa, Phi Kappa Phi, Pi Sigma Alpha. Home: 6601 Wheeler Dr Charlotte NC 28211 Office: Dept Polit Sci U NC Charlotte 9201 University City Blvd Charlotte NC 28223

DORIO, MARTIN MATTHEW, material handling company executive; b. Bklyn., Nov. 12, 1945; s. Martin M. and Josephine V. (Marsala) D.; m. Gayle M. Morris, June 16, 1968; children: Paul, Jay. BS, SUNY, Stony Brook, 1967; PhD, U. Mass., 1975. Rsch. chemist Diamond Shamrock Corp., Painesville, Ohio, 1975-76; group leader Diamond Shamrock Corp., Painesville, 1977-79; venture mgr. Gen. Electric Lighting Bus., Cleve., 1979-81, quality and mfg. tech. mgr., 1981-87; dir. quality and productivity FMC Corp., Chgo., 1987-90; v.p. worldwide product mgmt. and market strategy Case Corp., Racine, Wis., 1990-91; v.p. corp. planning and devel. J.I. Case Corp., Racine, Wis., 1992-95; pres., CEO, dir. CLARK Material Handling Co., Lexington, Ky., 1995—; mem. adv. com. Dept. Energy, Washington, 1977-79, Am. Productivity and Quality Ctr., Houston, 1988-90; mem. adv. com. on quality Ency. Brittanica, 1988-90; mem. bd. examiners Malcolm Baldrige Nat. Quality Award, 1988-90. Author: Multiple Electron Resonance Spectroscopy, 1979; contbr. articles to profl. jours.; patentee in field. Adv. bd. dirs. Mus. Culture and Diversity, 1997—; bd. dirs. Lexington Arts & Cultural Coun., 1996—; co-chair advanced divsn. Lexington: Strides Ahead, 1998—. Capt. USAF, 1968-71. Recipient Nat. Svc. award Nat. Inst. Sci. and Tech., 1988-90. Mem. Am. Soc. Quality Control (exec. com. 1984-85), Am. Mgmt. Assn., Assn. Mfg. Excellence, World Future Soc., Planetary Soc. Avocations: tennis, raquetball, photography, reading, writing. Home: 2105 Wiltshire Pl Lexington KY 40515-1167 Office: Clark Material Handling Co 172 Trade St Lexington KY 40511-2620

DORION, ROBERT CHARLES, entrepreneur, investor; b. N.Y.C., Dec. 28, 1926; s. William J. and Adelaide (Bacardi) D.; m. Ana Maria Ferber, Nov. 26, 1954; children: Robert Patrick, Marianne Michelle, Nicholas Christian, Kristel Alexia. Student, Columbia U., 1943-44; B of Naval Scis., Dartmouth Coll., 1946. Buyer Balfour, Guthrie and Co. Ltd., 1948-49; capt. M/V Assault Shark Industries div. Borden & Co., 1950-51; pres. Dorion, Rubio and Cia, 1952-57; mgr., ins., mining and chem. dept. Grace & Co., 1954-59; sales mgr. Gen. Tires, Guatemala, 1960-61; chmn. El Salto, S.A., 1962-78; pres. Tecnicos En Seguros, S.A., 1979—, Marcas Mundiales, S.A., 1978—; dir. Bacardi Ltd., Bermuda, Marcas Mundiales S.A., Industrias Rio Dulce S.A. Contbr. articles to profl. jours. Friend Am. Mus. of Nat. History, N.Y.C.; field assoc. Fla. Mus., Gainesville, Mote Marine Lab., Sarasota, Fla., USN Meml. Found., dir., Interamer. Scout Found., US Navy Meml. Found. Fellow Internat. Oceanographic Found. (life); mem. Rotary (Paul Harris fellow), World Scout Orgn. (Baden-Powell fellow), Interam. Scout Found. (dir.), U.S. Navy Memorial Found. (dir.), U.S. Naval Inst. (life), Audubon Soc. (life), Internat. Wildlife Soc., Order of The Bronze Wolf. Avocations: Pre-Columbian archaeology, cryptozoolical studies, shark research, deep sea fishing. Office: care Bacardi Martini Ltd 2100 Biscayne Blvd Miami FL 33137-5014 also: Kristel SA Apt 195A, Guatemala City Guatemala

DORIS, ALAN S(ANFORD), lawyer; b. Cleve., June 18, 1947; s. Sam E. and Rebecca (Sunshine) D.; m. Nancy Rose Spitzer, Jan. 10, 1976; children: Matthew, Lisa. AB and BS in Bus. cum laude, Miami U., Oxford U., 1969; JD cum laude, Harvard U., 1972. Bar: Ohio 1972, U.S. Dist. Ct. (no. dist.) Ohio 1972, U.S. Tax Ct. 1972, U.S. Ct. Appeals (6th cir.) 1972. Assoc. Stotter, Familo, Cavitch, Elden & Durkin, Cleve., 1972-77; ptnr. Elden & Ford, Cleve., 1978-79, Benesch, Friedlander, Coplan & Aronoff, Cleve., 1980—. Editor: Ohio Transaction Guide. Treas. Hawthorne Valley Country Club, Cleve., 1984-85; chmn. Cleve. Tax Inst., 1994. Mem. ABA (chmn. capital recovery com. taxation sect. 1994-96). Avocation: golf. Office: Benesch Friedlander Coplan & Aronoff 2300 American Rd Cleveland OH 44144-2301*

DORIS, EUGENE PATRICK, athletics director; b. Nov. 1, 1948. BA in History, Fordham U., 1970, MAT in Social Studies, 1974. Social studies tchr. Archbishop Molloy High Sch., Jamaica, N.Y., 1974-77, Archbishop Stepinca High Sch., White Plains, N.Y., 1977-84; asst. dir. athletics Fordham U., N.Y.C., 1984-85; assoc. dir. athletics Fordham U., 1985-89; dir. athletics Marist Coll., Poughkeepsie, N.Y., 1989-94, Fairfield U., Fairfield, Conn., 1994—. Home: 245 Unquowa Rd Unit 110 Fairfield CT 06430-5057

DORITY, DOUGLAS H., association executive; b. Marion, Va., Dec. 9, 1938; s. Douglas H. and Lucille (Johnson) D.; children: Susan Lynn Colbert, Sheri Denise Drawdy, Tracy Shannon; m. Denise B. Brown, Feb. 17, 1979; children: Brooke Renee, Matthew Douglas. Student, Nat. Bus. Coll., 1958-59. From internat. rep. to adminstrv. asst. to internat. pres. Retail Clks. Internat. Union, Cin., Phila., Washington, 1961-1976; dir. region II, internat. v.p. Retail Clks. Internat. Union, N.Y.C., N.J., 1976-86; internat. dir. orgn. United Food and Comml. Workers Internat. Union, Washington, 1986—, exec. v.p., 1989-94, internat. pres., 1994—. Del. Dem. Conv., San Francisco, 1980. Avocation: home renovations. Office: United Food & Comml Workers Internat Union 1775 K St NW Washington DC 20006-1502*

DORKEY, CHARLES EDWARD, III, lawyer; b. Phila., June 23, 1948; s. Charles Edward and Peggy O'Neal D.; children: Charles Edward IV, John Hilliard, Marjorie Lyddon. AB cum laude, Dartmouth Coll., 1970; JD, Univ. Pa., 1973. Bar: Pa. 1974, N.Y. 1975, D.C. 1977. Law clk. to hon. Samuel J. Roberts Supreme Ct. of Pa., 1973-74; assoc. Sullivan & Cromwell, N.Y.C., 1975-81; ptnr. Reboul, MacMurray, Hewitt, Maynard & Kristol, N.Y.C., 1981-84, Richards & O'Neil, N.Y.C., 1984-91, Haythe & Curley, N.Y.C., 1992—; bd. dirs. Empire State Devel. Corp., N.Y.C. Water Fin. Auth., N.Y. State Job Devel. Auth., N.Y. State Sci. and Tech. Found., Harlem Cmty. Devel. Corp., 42d St. Devel. Project, N.Y. State Mortgage Loan Enforcement and Adminstrn. Corp., N.Y. Parks and Conservation Assn.; trustee Citizens Budget Commn., 1993-98; trustee N.Y. Hist. Soc., 1998—; mem. First Dept. Jud. Screening Com.; mem. State Ct. of Claims Jud. Screening Com.; mem. Departmental Disciplinary Com. of the First Jud. Dept.; mem. alumni coun. Dartmouth Coll., 1990-93, pres. class 1970, 1991-95; approved mediator U.S. Dist. Ct. (so. dist.); mediator N.Y. Panel Disting. Neutrals for Ctr. for Pub. Resources, Supreme Ct., N.Y. County, Judicial Hearing Office, State of N.Y., Banking Dept. Overseer U. Pa. Law Sch., 1993-99; nat. chmn. Law Annual Giving, 1991-93; trustee N.Y. Hist. Soc. Mem. ABA, N.Y. State Bar Assn. (exec. com. comml. and fed. litigation sect. 1986—, fed. judiciary com. 1989—, internat. law and practice sect., com. internat. dispute resolution 1987—) Assn. of Bar of City of N.Y. (products liability com. 1983-86. fed. legis. com. 1990-93, state cts. of superior jurisdiction 1993-96, coun. jud. adminstrn. 1996-99), Heights Casino Club, N.Y. Athletic Club. Republican. Congregationalist. Home: 205 E 69th St Apt 6C New York NY 10021-5402 also: 74 Pascal Ave Rockport ME 04856-5919 Office: Haythe & Curley 237 Park Ave New York NY 10017-3140

DORKIN, FREDERIC EUGENE, lawyer; b. Bridgeport, Conn., Feb. 1, 1932; s. William and Selma (Kraus) D.; m. Harriette A. Garfinkel, June 14, 1959; children: Rosalyn Gail, David Ira, Deborah Ruth. AB, Dartmouth Coll., 1953; LLB, Duke U., 1956; LLM, George Washington U., 1968. Bar: Conn. 1956, D.C. 1968, Wash. 1979. Atty. SEC, Washington, 1956-57; pvt. practice Bridgeport, 1960-61; asst. sec. CT Corp. Sys., N.Y.C., Washington, 1961-68; assoc. counsel, asst. sec. Susquehanna Corp., Alexandria, Va., 1968-

69; sec., counsel Microdot Inc., Greenwich, Conn., 1969-72; gen. counsel Boeing Computer Svcs., Inc., Morristown, N.J., 1972-78; corp. counsel Boeing Co., Seattle, 1978-82, sr. corp. counsel, 1982-83; asst. gen. counsel Boeing Co., 1984-85; divsn. chief counsel Boeing Electronics Co., 1985-90; sr. counsel Boeing Def. & Space Group, Seattle, 1991-93, ret., 1993; legal cons., arbitrator-mediator Seattle, 1993—. With JAGC, U.S. Army, 1957-60. Mem. Phi Delta Phi, Tau Epsilon Phi. Home: 501 Kirkland Ave Apt 207 Kirkland WA 98033-6248

DORLAND, BYRL BROWN, retired civic worker; b. Apr. 25, 1915; d. David Alma and Ethel Myrle (Peterson) Brown; m. Jack Albert Dorland, June 11, 1944; children: Lynn Dorland Ballinger, Lee Allison. *In 1620, ancestor Edward Fuller, with wife, Marian, and son, Samuel, sailed from England to America on the Mayflower. Shortly after docking, both parents died, leaving twelve-year old Samuel to fend for himself. Samuel's progeny, George Austin Brown, migrated to Utah and married a Morman. This couple (paternal grandparents) and Frans ans Christina Petersen (maternal grandparents) were the first Caucasians to penetrate Utah's mid-Rocky Maountains--Ute territory. On this frigid, hostile mountaintop, these pioneers founded a settlement called "Koosharem." It is here that Mrs. Dorland's father, mother and their nine children grew up. Amoung Samuel Fuller's latest descendants are Byrl's grandchildren: Dawn Carolyn, Mitsi Mary, Charles Chance.* Cert. AA, Snow Jr. Coll., Ephraim, Utah, 1936; tchg. cert., Brigham Young U., 1937; BS, Utah State Coll., Logan, 1940; grad., Family Inst. Vassar Coll., Poughkeepsie, N.Y., 1978, John Robert Powers, Sch. Profl. Women, N.Y.C., 1980. Sch. tchr. Utah, 1937-39, 40-42; restored Washington Irving's graveplot in Sleepy Hollow (N.Y.) Cemetery (named Nat. Hist. Landmark 1972); nat. dir. Washington Irving Graveplot Restoration Program, 1968—, designer landmark plaque for grave; mem. Nat. Coun. State Garden Clubs,1959—; pres. Potpourri Garden Club, Westchester, N.Y., 1966—; nat. chmn. for graveplot programs Washington Irving Bicentennial, 1983-84; dir. Dorland Family Graveyard Restoration, N.J. Hist. Landmark, 1983—. Recipient Disting. Alumni award for Cmty. Svc. Snow Coll., 1989; recipient May Duff Walters trophy Nat. Coun. State Garden Clubs, 1974; nat. trophy Nat. Historic Landmark Com., 1974; citation Keep Am. Beautiful, 1974. Mem. Nat. Trust for Historic Preservation (assoc., Pres.'s award 1977), Nat. Historic Soc. Am., Gen. Soc. Mayflower Desc., Am. Mus. Natural History (hon.), Internat. Washington Irving Soc. (founder, pres. 1981—), Nat. Assn. for Gravestone Studies (hon.), Herb Soc. Am., DAR, Internat. Platform Assn., Old Dutch Churchyard Restoration Assn., Am. Mus. Natural History (hon. mem.). Home: 20802 N Cave Creek Rd Apt 60 Phoenix AZ 85024-4438

DORLAND, DODGE OATWELL, investment advisor; b. N.Y.C., Feb. 27, 1948; s. Joseph Warner and Marion (Dodge) D.; m. Bonita Gillette Zeese, Jan. 9, 1971. Diploma, Choate Sch., 1966; BA, Colgate U., 1970; MBA, NYU, 1975. Chartered market tech., 1994. With Mfrs. Hanover Trust Co., N.Y.C., 1970-77, asst. sec., 1974-77; with Bank of Montreal Trust Co., N.Y.C., 1977-86, v.p., 1979-86, v.p. communications unit, 1982-86, U.S. industry coord. for communications, 1983-86; v.p. Shearson Lehman Bros., Inc., N.Y.C., 1986-88, GE Capital Corp., 1988-90; mng. gen. ptnr. Continental Cellular, 1989-90; prin. Landor Investment Mgmt., Inc., 1990—; U.S. and fgn. investment market commentator NBC, CNBC, CNN-FNN, Bloomberg and Reuters TV; bd. dirs. So. Telecom, Inc., West Ga. Cable, Inc.; US, internat. market commentator NBC, CNBC, CNN-FNN, Bloomberg, Reuters tv. Author: The Communications Industry: An Informational Overview, 1983; contbr. papers in field to profl. jours. Treas. Learning for Living Inst., N.Y.C., 1977-81; chmn. bd. dirs. 325 E. 72d St. Apts., N.Y.C., 1978-81; participant NYU Grad. Sch. Bus. Mgmt. Decision Lab., 1977-79, bd. dirs.; mem. investment com. Assn. for Relief of Elderly Inc., 1984—; bd. dirs., chmn. Edn. Com. Mem. Internat. Soc. Fin. Analysts, Assn. for Investment Mgmt. & Rsch., Soc. Quantitative Analysts, N.Y. Soc. Security Analysts (CFA com., bd. dirs.), Market Technicians Assn. (columnist newsletter, bd. dirs.), Soc. Quantitive Analysts, SAR, Nat. Cable TV Assn., Nat. Assn. Broadcasters, Cellular Telecommunications Industry Assn., The Elfun Soc. N.Y., Communications Tech. Analysts Assn., Drama League N.Y., Broadcast Fin. Mgmt. Assn., Telocator Network Am., Internat. Platform Assn., Media and Entertainment Analysts Assn. N.Y., Am. Film Inst., Smithsonian Inst., Vets Corp. Arty., Soc. Colonial Wars, Mil. Order Loyal Legion U.S., Knickerbocker Greys Vets. Corp., Holland Soc., World Univ. Roundtable, Yale Club (N.Y.C.), Meadow Club, Bathing Corp. Club (Southampton, N.Y.), Toastmasters (v.p. Mfrs. Hanover chpt. 1975-78). Republican. Episcopalian.

DORLAND, JOHN HOWARD, international management consultant; b. Washington, July 23, 1940; s. Gilbert Meding and Lillian (Okkerse) D.; m. Harriet Etter, June 12, 1965; children—John Henry, Howard Etter. BS, USMA, 1963; MS, U. So. Miss., 1968; MBA, U. Tenn., 1978. Commd. 2d lt. U.S. Army, 1963, advanced through grades to maj., 1973, ret. col., USAR, 1985; exec. v.p. Commerce Union Bank, Nashville, Tenn., 1973-81, FCB/FCBI, Pompano Beach, Fla., 1981-82; pres. Fla. Coast Bank, Pompano Beach, 1982-84; pres., CEO Hollywood (Fla.) Bank, 1984-90; CEO interim Suburban Bankshares, Inc., 1993-94; prin. Gemini Cons., 1994-95; pres. Dorland & Assocs., 1990—; dir. FCCS, Margate, Fla., FCB, Pompano Beach. Author: Duty, Honor, Company-West Point Fundamentals for Business Success, 1992. Commr. Mid. Tenn. coun. Boy Scouts Am., 1979; with Leadership Nashville, 1979; bd. dirs. YMCA, Ft. Lauderdale, 1983-89, Honda Golf Classics, Broward Econ. Devel., Com. of 100, United Way of Broward County. Decorated Bronze Star with 5 oak leaf clusters, Air medal with 5 oak leaf clusters, Purple Heart. Mem. Am. Bankers Assn., BEDC Broward County, Fla. Bankers Assn. (bd. dirs.), Fla. League Fin. Instns., Hollywood C. of C. Republican. Episcopalian. Home: 103 Heatherset Close Franklin TN 37069-7068 Office: Dorland & Assocs 103 Heatherset Close Franklin TN 37069-7068

DORLEAC, CATHERINE See DENEUVE, CATHERINE

DORMAN, ALBERT A., consulting engineer executive, architect; b. Phila., Apr. 30, 1926; s. William and Edith (Kleiman) D.; m. Joan Bettie Heiten, July 29, 1950; children: Laura Jane, Kenneth Joseph, Richard Coleman. BS, Newark Coll. Engring., 1945; MS, U. So. Calif., 1962; ScD (hon.), N.J. Inst. Tech., 1999. Registered profl. engr., Calif., N.Y., Ill., Oreg., Ariz., Pa., Nev., registered architect, Calif., Oreg. Owner firm Albert A. Dorman, Hanford, Calif., 1954-66; v.p. Daniel, Mann, Johnson & Mendenhall, Los Angeles, 1967-73; pres., chief oper. officer Daniel, Mann, Johnson & Mendenhall, 1974-77, pres., chief exec. officer, 1977-84, chmn., chief exec. officer, 1984-91; chmn. Daniel, Mann, Johnson & Mendenhall, Los Angeles, 1991-99; chmn., chief exec. officer AECOM Tech. Corp., L.A., 1984-91, chmn., 1991-92; founding chmn. AECOM Tech Corp., L.A., 1992—; chmn. Holmes & Narver, Inc., Orange, Calif., 1991-97, Frederic R. Harris, Inc., N.Y.C., 1988-91, Consoer, Townsend and Assocs., Inc., Chgo., 1988-91; pres., chmn. bd. dirs. Hanford Savs. & Loan Assn., 1963-72. Contbr. articles to profl. jours. Pres. Cmty. Concerts Assn., 1962-64; past mem. bd. councilors Sch. Urban and Regional Planning, U. So. Calif.; trustee Harvey Mudd Coll., J. David Gladstone Found., 1988—, Nat. Found. Advancement in Arts, 1988-99; bd. overseers N.J. Inst. Tech., 1989—; vice chmn. Los Angeles County Earthquake Fact-Finding Commn., 1980. With U.S. Army, 1945-47. Recipient Civil Engring. Alumnus award U. So. Calif., 1976, Edward F. Weston medal N.J. Inst. Tech., 1986, Golden Beaver Engring. award, 1991, Eponym, Albert Dorman Honors Coll., N.J. Inst. Tech., 1993, Disting. Award of Merit, ACEC, 1996, Medal, U. Calif., San Francisco, 1996. Fellow AIA, (hon. mem.) ASCE (Harland Bartholomew award 1976, NAE, Parcel-Sverdrup Civil Engring. Mgmt. award 1987, pres. L.A. sect. 1984-85), Am. Cons. Engrs. Coun. (life); mem. Real Estate Constrn. Industries (Humanitarian award 1986), Am. Pub. Works Assn., Cons. Engrs. Assn. Calif. (bd. dirs. 1982-88, pres. 1985-86), Am. Water Works Assn. (life), Water Pollution Control Fedn. (life), Calif. C. of C. (bd. dirs. 1986-94), L.A. Area C. of C. (bd. dirs. 1983-88, exec. com. 1985-87), Calif. Club, Met. Club, Kiwanis (pres. 1962), Tau Beta Pi, Chi Epsilon. Office: AECOM Tech Corp 3250 Wilshire Blvd Los Angeles CA 90010-1577

DORMAN, CRAIG EMERY, oceanographer, academic administrator; b. Cambridge, Mass., Aug. 27, 1940; s. Carlton Earl and Sarah Elizabeth (Emery) D.; m. Cynthia Eileen Larson, Aug. 25, 1962; children: Clifford Ellery, Clark Evans, Curt Emerson. BA, Dartmouth Coll., 1962; MS, Navy Post Grad. Sch., 1969; PhD, MIT/WHOI Joint Prog. Oceanog., 1972. Commd. ensign USN, 1962, advanced through grades to rear admiral, 1987, ret., 1989; CEO Woods Hole (Mass.) Oceanographic Instn., 1989-93; dep. dir. Def. Rsch. and Engring. for Lab. mgmt., Washington, 1993-95; sr. scientist Applied Rsch. Lab. Pa. State U., 1995—; chief scientist, tech. dir. internat. field office Office Naval Rsch., 1995-98, ONROID, 1998—; dir. Maritrans, Phila.; vis. prof. Imperial Coll., London, 1996-97. Corp. mem. WHOI, Bermuda Biol. Sta. for Rsch., SEA Edn. Assn. Decorated Legion of Merit (2). Mem. Russian Acad. Natural Sci. Home: 4107 27th Rd N Arlington VA 22207-5116 Office: 800 N Quincy St Arlington VA 22217-1906

DORMAN, JEFFREY LAWRENCE, lawyer; b. Akron, Ohio, Feb. 6, 1949; s. Milton and Belle (Handler) D.; m. Bernadette Marie Pawlik, Sept. 2, 1988. BA, U. Mich., 1971; JD, Case Western Res. U., Cleve., 1974; MS, U. Wis., 1976. Bar: Ohio 1975, Ill. 1979, U.S. Dist. Ct. (no. dist.) Ill. 1980. Staff atty. U.S. Dept. Justice, Washington, 1976-79; assoc. Sonnenschein Nath & Rosenthal, Chgo., 1979-82; ptnr. Sonnenschein Nath & Rosenthal, 1982—. Mem. ABA, Ohio Bar Assn., Chgo. Bar Assn. Avocation: mountain climbing. Home: 2639 N Southport Ave Chicago IL 60614-1227 Office: Sonnenschein Nath Rosenthal 8000 Sears Tower 233 S Wacker Dr Ste 8000 Chicago IL 60606-6342

DORMAN, JOHN FREDERICK, genealogist; b. Louisville, July 25, 1928; s. John Frederick and Sue Carpenter (Miller) D. B.A., U. Louisville, 1950; M.A., Emory U., 1955. Asst. archivist Coll. William and Mary, 1953-55; genealogist, 1955—; editor The Virginia Genealogist, 1957—; lectr. Nat. Inst. Geneal. Research, 1963-74, 77-93, Inst. Geneal. and Hist. Research Samford U., 1977-88; trustee Bd. for Cert. of Genealogists, 1964-84, pres., 1979-82, exec. dir., 1983-96. Fellow Am. Soc. Genealogists (treas. 1959-66, pres. 1982-85), Va. Geneal. Soc.; mem. Soc. Cincinnati, Soc. Colonial Wars (dep. registrar gen. 1969-81, D.C. gov. 1980-82), SR (gen. registrar 1976-85, pres. D.C. chpt. 1982-84), SAR (D.C. pres. 1967-68), Nat. Geneal. Soc. (v.p. 1958-59, 68-70, libr. 1959-60), Children Am. Revolution (sr. nat. registrar 1960-62, sr. nat. treas. 1962-64, 66-68, sr. nat. 2d v.p. 1968-70), Descs. Colonial Govs. (gov. gen. 1973-76), Descs. Lords Md. Manors (pres. 1985-89), Sovereign Mil. Order Temple Jerusalem. Republican. Episcopalian. Club: Cosmos (Washington). Home: 175 Hulls Chapel Rd Fredericksburg VA 22406-5218

DORMAN, LINNEAUS CUTHBERT, retired chemist; b. Orangeburg, S.C., June 28, 1935; s. John Albert and Georgia (Hammond) D.; m. Phae Louise Hubble, June 21, 1958; children: Evelyn Suzanne, John Albert III. BS, Bradley U., 1956; PhD, Ind. U., 1961; DSc(hon.), Saginaw Valley State U., 1988. Chemist No. Regional Lab., U.S. Dept. Agr., Peoria, Ill., summers 1956-59; research chemist Dow Chem. Co., Midland, Mich., 1960-68; research specialist Dow Chem. Co., 1968-76, research assoc., 1976-83, assoc. scientist, 1983-93, sr. assoc. scientist, 1993-94; ret., 1994; Lawrence lectr. Bradley U., 1990, mem. adv. bd., 1994; active Centurion Soc., 1993, Burgess award selection com., 1996—, chemistry dept. adv. bd.; adv. panel Dow Corning Midland Plant. Contbr. articles to profl. jours. Mem. NAACP, Midland Commn. on Cmty. Rels., 1963-73, vice-chmn., 1967; mem. Black Exec. Exch. Program, Urban League, 1971, 75; trustee Midland Found., 1980-90, v.p., 1987-90; dir.-at-large Midland Ctr. for the Arts, 1984, 85; bd. fellows Saginaw Valley State Coll., 1975-87, emeritus mem., 1987, v.p., 1981-83, pres., 1983-85, ann. fund drive, 1985-95, presdl. search com., 1989; chmn. Cen. Rsch. and Devel. Scientists Orgn., 1992. Paul Harris fellow Rotary, 1989; co-recipient Bond award Am. Oil Chemists Soc., 1960; recipient Cen. Rsch. Inventor of Yr. award Dow Chem. Co., 1982. Mem. AAAS, Nat. Orgn. Black Chemists and Chem. Engrs. (Percy L. Julian award 1999), Am. Chem. Soc. (sect. treas. 1966, sec. 1967, dir. 1968-70, councilor 1971-76, 80-81, 84-92), Midland Rotary (sec. 1980-81, v.p. 1981-82, pres. 1982-83), Saginaw Valley Torch Club, Sigma Xi (chpt. treas. 1969, sec. 1970, pres. 1975), Phi Lambda Upsilon, Pi Kappa Delta, Omega Psi Phi. Mem. United Ch. of Christ. Patentee in field. Home: PO Box 1732 Midland MI 48641-1732

DORMAN, N.B., writer; b. Iowa, 1927; divorced; 2 children. BA, Calif. State U., Chico, 1963. Various clerical and sales positions, asst. county libr., free-lance typesetter and copy editor, writer, 1972—. Author: (juvenile) Laughter in the Background, Elsevier/Nelson, 1980, (juvenile) Petey and Miss Magic, Linnet/Shoe String, 1993; contbr. stories to mags. Vol. in alcohol recovery programs. Address: PO Box 775 Chico CA 95927-0775

DORMAN, RICHARD FREDERICK, JR., association executive, consultant; b. Peoria, Ill., June 3, 1944; s. Richard Frederick and Pauline Elizabeth (Dryfus) D.; children: Richard F., Kevin M.; m. Anne Marie Carlton, May 28, 1976. Student, Franklin U., Columbus, Ohio, 1963-65, 68-69, New Sch. Social Reform, N.Y.C., 1979-80, U. Md., 1982. Field rep. Ohio Civil Service Employees Assn., Columbus, 1972-75; regional dir. St. Jude Children's Research Hosp., N.Y.C., 1975-80; exec. dir. Assembly Govtl. Employees, Washington, 1980-85; with Quality Mgmt. Inst., Washington, 1985-86; exec. dir. Am. Congress on Surveying and Mapping, Falls Church, Va., 1986-90, Ohio Coun. for Home Care, 1991-93; exec. v.p., COO Assn. for Profls. in Infection Control and Epidemiology Inc., Washington, 1993-95; v.p. Assn. Mgmt. Group, Arlington, Va., 1995-96; ptnr. McIntoch & Dorman, Washington, 1982-86; pres. Catalyst Group, Alexandria, 1996—. Founder, pres. Columbus Ind. Jr. High Football League, Ohio, 1970. Recipient Recognition for Contbn. to Women's Sports Ohio Ho. of Reps., 1975, 76. Mem. Am. Soc. Assn. Execs. (cert. assn. exec., fellow 1988), Greater Washington Soc. Assn. Execs. Republican. Presbyterian.

DORMAN, THOMAS ALFRED, internist, orthopaedist; b. Nairobi, Kenya, Nov. 16, 1936; came to U.S., 1977; s. Charles and Elizabeth D.; m. Allison Margaret Millar, Oct. 24, 1970; children: Jill, Michael, Andrew, Erin. Student, Liverpool U., 1959-62; MB, BChir, Edinburgh U., 1965. Diplomate Am. Bd. Internal Medicine. Staff gen. surgery Leith Hosp., Edinburgh, 1965-66; staff gen. medicine Western Gen. Hosp., Edinburgh, 1966; staff Elsie Inglis Maternity Hosp., Edinburgh, 1966-67, Norway House Hosp., Northern Manitoba, 1967; resident in medicine Union Meml. Hosp., Balt., 1967; staff anaesthetics dept. Sir Patrick Duns Hosp., Dublin, 1967-68; staff gen. surgery Naas Hosp., Ireland, 1968; staff pediat. neurology Royal Hosp. Sick Children, Edinburgh, 1968-69; registrar cardiology, gen. medicine Western Gen. Hosp., Edinburgh, 1969-71; staff internal medicine and cardiology Ft. Frances Clinic, Ontario, 1971-77; resident in internal medicine Winnipeg Gen. Hosp./U. Manitoba, 1972-73; pvt. practice San Luis Obispo, Calif., 1977—; staff Sierra Vista Hosp., San Luis Obispo, French Hosp., San Luis Obispo, San Luis Obispo Gen. Hosp. Editor, columnist Jour. Orthop. Medicine; contbr. articles to profl. jours. Fellow Royal Coll. Physicians; mem. Assn. Am. Physicians and Surgeons, Am. Back Soc. (bd. dirs.), British Med. Assn., British Inst. Manual Medicine, Am. Assn. Orthop. Medicine (charter mem., bd. dirs., chmn. rsch. com., newsletter editor), Cyriax Found., N.Am. Spine Soc., Assn. Musculoskeletal Medicine, Coll. Physicians and Surgeons Ontario, Calif. Med. Assn., San Luis Obispo County Med. Soc.. Office: 929 291st St Federal Way WA 98003-7300

DORME, PATRICK JOHN, electronic company executive; b. N.Y.C., Nov. 6, 1935; s. Nunzio and Mary Dorme; m. Alice M. Frenza, Sept. 8, 1957; children: Patrick John, Kathleen, Donna, Robin, Allison. BBA, Iona Coll., 1957. CPA, N.Y. Acct. Alexander Grant & Co., N.Y.C., 1957-60; chief acct. Hawthorne (N.Y.) Lumber Co., 1960-62; asst. contr. John Wiley & Sons, N.Y.C., 1962-68; v.p. fin. Dynamics Corp. Am., Greenwich, Conn., 1968-98; bd. dirs. CTS Corp., Elkhart, Ind., Dynamics Corp. Am. Mem. Am. Inst. CPAs, N.Y. State Soc. CPAs, Nat. Assn. Accts. Republican. Roman Catholic. Home: 300 Loring Ave Pelham NY 10803-2230 Office: Dynamics Corp of Am 475 Steamboat Rd Ste 5 Greenwich CT 06830-7197

DORMINEY, HENRY CLAYTON, JR., allergist; b. Tifton, Ga., May 15, 1949; s. Henry Clayton and Virginia (Petty) D.; m. Diane Louise Thiel, Sept. 29, 1978. BS, Davidson Coll., 1971; MD, U. Iowa, 1975. Diplomate Am. Bd. Internal Medicine, Am. Bd. Allergy and Immunology; lic. physician, Ga. Med. intern, U. Iowa Hosps. and Clinics, Iowa City, 1975-76, med. resident, 1976-78, allergy and immunology fellow, 1978-80; practice medicine specializing in allergy and clin. immunology Allergy and Dermatology Assocs. P.C., Tifton, Ga., 1981—; mem. staff Tifton Gen. Hosp.; bd. dirs. Brumby's Crossing, Dorminey Enterprises; chmn. and founder Tifton Mus. Arts and Heritage, 1991. Assoc. editor, contbg. author Vital Signs, 1969-71. Bd. dirs. Tift County Found. Ednl. Excellence, Tifton Heritage Found., pres., 1992, Treas. Tift County Foun. Edn. Excellence, 1996—. Recipient Physician's Recognition award AMA, 1979, 85, Lee Willingham III trophy Davidson Coll., 1987 Tifton Main Street Program award, 1989, Best Adaptive Re-Use Project, Tifton Historic District, The Coco Cola Bldg., 1993; The Am. Numismatic Soc., VA grantee, 1978-80, Am. Coll. Allergy grantee, 1980. Mem. ACP, Am. Acad. Allergy (travel grantee 1980), Allergy & Dermatology Assoc. Tifton, Tift County Med. Soc. (sec., treas. 1983-84, v.p. 1984-85, pres. 1985-86), Med. Assn. Ga., Forward Tifton, Tifton C. of C. Democrat. Lodge: Rotary (Spl. Merit award, founder Tifton Directory, bd. dirs. 1988-93, pres.-elect 1989-90, pres. 1990-91, Paul Harris fellow 1993). Home: 1001 N Ridge Ave Tifton GA 31794-3953 Office: 820 Love Ave Tifton GA 31794-4071

DORN, ALFRED, poet, retired English educator; b. N.Y.C., Dec. 9, 1929; s. Frederick and Julia (Memminger) D.; m. Anita Lorenz Paslack, Sept. 11, 1971. BS, NYU, 1953, MA, 1956, PhD, 1966. Grad. asst. NYU, N.Y.C., 1956-60; English prof. Rider Coll., Trenton, N.J., 1963-64, Queensborough C.C., Bayside, N.Y., 1966-92; ret.; bd. dirs. World Order Narrative and Formalist Poets, Flushing, N.Y. Co-editor: New Orlando Poetry Anthologies, 1958, 63, 68; author of poetry. Penfield fellow NYU, N.Y.C., 1957. Mem. Poetry Soc. Am. (bd. mem. 1963-66, v.p. 1969-72, conf. fellow 1966), Nat. Trust for Hist. Preservation. Avocations: art history, writing art criticism, antiques, psychic research, cats. Office: World Order Narrative & Formalist Poets PO Box 580174 Sta A Flushing NY 11358-0174

DORN, CHARLES MEEKER, art education educator; b. Mpls., Jan. 17, 1927; s. Melville Wilkinson and Margaret (Meeker) D.; m. Virginia Josephine Coble, July 11, 1947; children: Mary Jan, Charles Meeker. B.A., M.A., George Peabody Coll. Tchrs., 1950; Ed.D., U. Tex., 1959. Asst. prof. art Union U., Jackson, Tenn., 1950-54; instr. art and edn. Memphis State U., 1954-57; lectr. edn. U. Tex., 1957-59; head art dept. Nat. Coll. Edn., Evanston, Ill., 1959-61; assoc. prof. art No. Ill. State U., 1961-62; exec. sec. Nat. Art Edn. Assn., Washington, 1962-70; prof., chmn. dept. art Calif. State U., Northridge, 1970-72; prof. creative arts Purdue U., Lafayette, Ind., 1972-86, head dept., 1972-76; prof., dir. Ctr. for Arts Adminstrn. Fla. State U., Tallahassee, 1986—, chmn. dept. art edn., 1986-90. Served with AUS, 1945-46. Recipient 25th Anniversary award for disting. service Nat. Gallery Art, 1966. Mem. Fla. Art Edn. Assn., Nat. Art Edn. Assn. (pres. 1975-77, Disting. Svc. award 1979, Disting. fellow 1982, Southeastern Higher Edn. Art Educator award 1990), Internat. Soc. Edn. Through Art, Phi Delta Kappa, Kappa Phi Kappa. Home: 1736 Silverwood Dr Tallahassee FL 32301-6779 Office: Fla State U Dept Art Edn Tallahassee FL 32306

DORN, DOLORES, actress; b. Chgo., Mar. 3; d. Edward Dorn Heft and Alice Ellen Eagmin; m. Franchot Tone, May 14, 1966 (dec. 1968); m. Ben Piazza, Aug. 6, 1969 (dec.). Studied with, Uta Hagen, 1964-66, Lee Strasberg, N.Y.C., 1967-82; BFA, Goodman Theater, Chgo., 1962. Pvt. coach to stars Los Angeles, 1974—; tchr. Am. Film Inst., Los Angeles, 1977-89, Lee Strasberg Theater Inst., Los Angeles, 1983-86; coach Star Search 1984, Los Angeles, 1984; mem. The Actor's Studio, N.Y.C. Appeared in TV shows Divorce Court, Studio 5B, Family Med. Ctr., Superior Ct., Simon and Simon, Night Cries, Intimate Strangers, Charlie's Angels, Jigsaw John, Tenafly, Girls of Huntington House, Run for Your Life, Strawberry Blonde, Capitol, Sisters, Picket Fences; appeared in motion pictures Tell Me a Riddle, The Stronger, The Candy Snatchers, Thirteen West Street, Underworld U.S.A., The Bounty Hunter, Uncle Vanya (Best Actress award San Francisco Internat. Film Festival 1967), Murders of the Rue Morgue, In the Line of Fire; appeared in Broadway plays The Midnight Sun, Starward Ark, Hide and Seek, (off-Broadway plays) The Pinter Plays, To Damascus, Plays for Bleeker Street, Lime Green Khaki Blue, Between Two Thieves, Uncle Vanya, A Mighty Man Is He, Catch As Catch Can, L.A., Dancing on the Table; contract actress Warner Bros., Columbia Film Studios; dir., playwright On the Telephone at The Actor's Studio, 1995, Actor's Studio, 1996; playwright Throw-Away Woman, 1997, Throw-Away Baby, 1998, Throw Her in the Trash Can, 1998. Mem. Women in Flim, Actor's Studio, Am. Film Inst. (hon.).

DORN, GORDON JOSEPH, artist, art educator; b. Sheboygan, Wis., Dec. 5, 1943; s. Frank and Olive G. (Rollman) D. BA in Edn., Wis. State U., 1966; MFA in Painting, U. Wis., 1969. Prof. art No. Ill. U., Dekalb, 1969—; state v.p. AAUP of Ill., 1990-92, state pres., 1992-96. One-man shows include Roy Boyd Gallery, Chgo., 1977, 79, 82, 85, 88, 91, 95, 97, 98, group exhbns. include Art Inst. Chgo., 1977, 79, Chgo. Internat. Art Exposition, 1997, 98, 99; patentee in field. Recipient prize Art Inst. Chgo., 1977; exhbns. reviewed in Chgo. Tribune, 1991, 95, 98, Chgo. Sun Times, 1982, 84. Avocations: writing education materials, inventing. Home: 806 S 1st St De Kalb IL 60115-4122 Office: Sch Art No Ill Univ Dekalb IL 60115

DORN, JAMES ANDREW, editor; b. Buffalo, Aug. 26, 1945; s. Andrew William and Mary Carol (Gannon) D.; m. Carol Evans Cronmiller, Sept. 5, 1970; children: Andrea Yvonne, Heather Katherine. BS in Econs., Canisius Coll., 1967; MA in Econs., U. Va., 1969, PhD, 1976. Prof. Towson U., Balt., 1973—, 1989—; editor Cato Jour. Cato Inst., Washington, 1982—, v.p. for acad. affairs, 1989—; research fellow Inst. Humane Studies George Mason U., Fairfax, Va., 1986-95. Editor: The Future of Money in the Information Age, 1997, China in the New Millennium, 1998; co-editor: (with Henry G. Manne) Economic Liberties and the Judiciary, 1987, (with Anna J. Schwartz) The Search for Stable Money, 1987, (with William A. Niskanen) Dollars, Deficits and Trade, 1989, (with Wang Xi) Economic Reform in China, 1990, (with Roberto Salinas-León) Money and Markets in the Americas, 1996, (with Steve Hanke and Alan Walters) The Revolution in Development Economics, 1998; contbr. articles to profl. jours. Mem. White House Commn. on Presdl. Scholars, Washington, 1984-90. Hayek Fund grantee Inst. for Humane Studies, 1986-87, Earhart grantee 1969-70, 81; Thomas Jefferson Ctr. fellow U. Va., 1969-70. Mem. Am. Econ. Assn., Mont Pelerin Soc., West Side Rowing Club (Buffalo). Avocations: Alpine hiking, photography, geology, jogging. Office: Cato Inst 1000 Massachusetts Ave NW Washington DC 20001-5400

DORN, JENNIFER LYNN, charitable organization administrator; b. Grand Island, Nebr., Dec. 7, 1950; d. Harold Clarence and Ethel Agnes D.; m. Kurt Pfotenhauer. BA, Oreg. State U., 1973; MPA, U. Conn., 1977. Legis. asst. Senator M. Hatfield, Washington, 1977-81; com. staff Senate Appropriations, Washington, 1981-83; spl. asst. Sec. Elizabeth Dole, Washington, 1983-84; dir. Comml. Space Transp., Washington, 1984-85; assoc. dep. sec. U.S. Dept. Transp., Washington, 1985-87; asst. sec. policy U.S. Dept. Labor, Washington, 1989-91; sr. v.p. pub. support ARC, Washington, 1991-98; pres. Nat. Health Mus., 1998—. Mem. Washington Women's Forum, Cosmos Club. Republican. Lutheran. Home: 2041 Beacon Pl Reston VA 20191-4842 Office: 1331 h St NW Ste #600 Washington DC 20005-3814*

DORN, LOUIS OTTO, minister, editor; b. Detroit, July 1, 1928; s. Theodore Herman and Thekla Maria (Frederking) D.; m. Erna Ruth Koessel, June 14, 1953; children: Margaret Ligaya Dorn White, Peter Bayani, Martin Louis, Judith Anne Dorn. BA, Concordia Theol. Sem., St. Louis, 1951, BD, 1962; MA in Linguistics, Ateneo de Manila U., Quezon City, The Philippines, 1974; PhD, Luth. Sch. Theology, Chgo., 1980. Ordained to ministry Luth. Ch.-Mo. Synod, 1953. Missionary Luth. Ch. in The Philippines, Manila, 1953-74; candidate Ohio dist. Luth. Ch. -Mo. Synod, 1975-80; candidate N.J. dist. Luth. Ch.-Mo. Synod, 1980—; transls. rsch. assoc. Am. Bible Soc., N.Y.C., 1979-90; transl. cons. United Bible Socs., N.Y.C., 1990—; chmn. Luth. Philippine Mission, Manila, 1962-63, 71-72; sec. Luth. Ch. in The Philippines, Manila, 1962-63, commn. for ecumenical affairs, 1964-74, dir. transls. dept., 1966-74; hon. transls. advisor Philippine Bible Soc., Manila, 1968-74; bd. dirs. Interchurch Lang. Sch., Quezon City, 1964-74, chmn. bd., 1967-74. Contbr. articles and revs. to religious publs. Grantee Cen. dist. Luth. Ch.-Mo. Synod, 1944-53; scholarship grantee Luth. Sch. Theology, Chgo., 1974-78. Mem. Soc. Bibl. Lit. Office: Am Bible Soc 1865 Broadway New York NY 10023-7503 *People often don't know how to live under God's grace because they can't forgive themselves and know only God's law. To accept God's grace, to be willing to be forgiven, results in an amazing life of freedom that honors the Savior.*

DORN, MARIAN MARGARET, educator, sports management administrator; b. North Chicago, Ill., Sept. 25, 1931; d. John and Marian (Petkovsek) Jelovsek; m. Eugene G. Dorn, Aug. 2, 1952 (div. 1975); 1 child, Bradford Jay. BS, U. Ill., 1953; MS, U. So. Calif., 1961. Tchr., North Chicago Cmty. H.S., 1954-56; tchr., advisor activities, high sch., Pico-Rivera, Calif., 1956-62; tchr., coach Calif. H.S., Whittier, 1962-65; prof. phys. edn., chmn. dept., coach, asst. chmn. div. women's athletic dir. Cypress (Calif.) Coll., 1966—; men's, women's golf coach; mgr. Billie Jean King Tennis Ctr., Long Beach, Calif., 1982-86; founder King-Dorn Golf Schs., Long Beach, 1984; pres. So. Calif. Athletic Conf., 1981; curriculum cons. Calif. Dept. Edn., 1989-92; spkr. Citizen Amb. Program China Conf. women, 1995; coach golf team state champions Women's Cypress Coll., 1997. Mem. del. to China Citizens Ambassador Program, 1995. Recipient cert. of merit Cypress Elem. Sch. Dist., 1976; Outstanding Svc. award Cypress Coll., 1986; named Women's Coach of Yr. Orgn. Empire Conf., 1995, Master Profl., 1996, Coll. Women's Golf Coach of Yr., Calif. Coaches Assn., 1998, L.P.G.A. Western Sect. Coach of Yr., 1998; nominated Coach of Yr., L.P.G.A. Western Sect., 1991-96. Mem. Calif. (v.p. So. dist.), San Gabriel Valley (pres.) Assns. Health, Phys. Edn. and Recreation, So. Calif. C.C. Athletic Coun. (sec., dir. pub. rels.), NEA, Calif. Tchrs. Assn., AAHPERD, Ladies Profl. Golf Assn. Conglist. Author: Bowling Manual, 1974. Office: 9200 Valley View St Cypress CA 90630-5805

DORN, NATALIE REID, consultant; b. N.Y.C.; d. John A. and Marianna (Tresenberg) Borokhovich; m. Ed Reid, July 31, 1938 (div. Apr. 1963); children: Michael John, Douglas Paul; m. Robert M. Dorn, Nov. 28, 1964. Student, Bklyn. Coll., 1937-40, Pepperdine Coll., 1969-70. Model Conover Agy., N.Y.C., 1940-54; columnist Westchester (N.Y.) Recorder, 1954-59; ptnr. Dateline, Las Vegas, Nev., 1957-61; mgr., buyer Joseph Magnin, Las Vegas, Nev., 1961-62; ptnr., cons. Personnel Placement Employment Agy. and Conv. Coords., Las Vegas, 1961-63; acct. exec. John A. Tetley Co., L.A., 1963-65; cons. Sport Ct. Am., Salt Lake City, 1975--; realtor, Va., Calif., 1974--. Exec. v.p. Clark County Mental Health Assn., 1961-63; ednl. chmn. Hollywood Wing, Greek Theatre Assn., 1965, mem. hospitality com. LWV, 1969; co-founder Child Abuse Listening Line, 1973—; sponsor Ashland (Oreg.) Sheakespearean Festival, 1984; concertmaster Sacramento Opera; patron, Davis Art Ctr.; docent Internat. House, Davis, 1987—; bd. dirs. El Macero Niners, Davis Art Ctr. Guild. Mem. AMA Aux., Los Angeles County Med. Assn. Aux. (chmn. publs. dist. 5, 1970-72, program chmn. 1972), Nat. Trust for Historic Preservation, Nat. Mus., Women in Arts, Crocker Art Mus., Crocker Art Mus. Assocs. Corps, Crocker Soc., El Macero Country Club. Avocations: golf, painting, writing.

DORN, NORMAN PHILIP, management consulting firm executive; b. Ithaca, N.Y., Jan. 29, 1945; s. Saul James and Pearl Dorn; m. Evelyn Mary Samonas, July 3, 1966; children: Paul, Ian, Nathan, Mark. BS, Carnegie-Mellon U., 1966; MS, U. Pitts., 1969. Engr. Westinghouse Electric, Pitts., 1969-78; sr. engr. GPU Svc. Corp., Forked River, N.J., 1978-79; mng. dir. Accountable Systems Co. Internat. Inc., Toms River, N.J., 1979—. Mem. Telephone Pioneers, Masons, Toastmasters. Achievements include inventions, quality improvements, requirements process engineering, process controls development instruction, system stability analysis procedures, telecommunications technology, systems (applications) architecture and manufacturing management. Office: 1358 Hooper Ave # 137 Toms River NJ 08753-2882 Mailing: PO Box 2808 Chapel Hill NC 27515-2808

DORN, SAMUEL O., endodontist; b. N.Y.C., Jan. 1, 1946; s. Benjamin and Mae (Baylin) D.; m. Linda Frances Neuger, Dec. 23, 1984; children: Lanelle, Brian, Adam, Dawn. BA, Queens Coll., 1966; DDS, Fairleigh Dickinson U., 1970; cert., Nassau County Med. Ctr., 1976. Diplomate Am. Bd. Endodontics. Capt. USAF, Washington, 1970-72; pvt. practice Forest Hills, N.Y., 1972-76, Ft. Lauderdale, Fla., 1976—; clin. instr. Fairleigh Dickinson U. Dental Sch., Hackensack, N.J., 1973-74; cons. in field; chmn. advanced endodontics Dade County Dental Rsch. Clinic, Miami, 1977-93; clin. assoc. prof. U. Fla. Sch. Dentistry; clin. asst. prof. U. Miami Sch. Medicine, 1977-93; dir., treas. Am. Bd. Endodontics, 1991-98; prof., dir. postgrad. endodontics Nova Southeastern U. Sch. Dental Medicine; lectr. in field. Trustee Endowment & Meml. Found., Chgo., 1987-88. Named Dentist of Year East Coast Dental Soc., 1987. Fellow Am. Coll. Dentists, Internat. Coll. Dentists; mem. Am. Assn. Endodontists (bd. dirs. 1988-91, sec.), Fla. Assn. Endodontists (pres. 1990-92), Greater Hollywood Dental Soc. (pres. 1988-89), South Fla. Endodontic Soc. (pres. 1982-83), East Coast Dist. Dental Soc. (pres. 1996-97), Am. Assn. Dental Rsch. Jewish. Avocations: tennis, travel, cycling. Home: 1031 SW 91st Ave Fort Lauderdale FL 33324-3817 Office: 8200 W Sunrise Blvd Fort Lauderdale FL 33322-5426 also: Nova Southeastern U Coll Dental Medicine 3200 S University Dr Fort Lauderdale FL 33328-2018

DORN, SUE BRICKER, consultant, retired hospital administrator; b. Seattle, Apr. 1, 1934; d. Barney and Frances B. (Schnitzer) Bricker; m. Philip Henry Dorn, Dec. 31, 1955 (dec.); children: Charles, Martha Dorn Maurer. BA, Stanford U., Palo Alto, 1955; MA, Bank St. Coll., 1973. Cert. tchr., N.Y. Dir. promotion exec. compensation svc. Am. Mgmt. Assn., N.Y.C., 1956-58; tchr. spl. edn. N.Y.C. Bd. of Edn., 1969-77; assoc. dir. Yale U., New Haven, 1977-79; v.p. Bank St. Coll. of Edn., N.Y.C., 1979-81, Aspen Inst. for Humanistic Studies, N.Y.C., 1981-82; assoc. v.p. Yale U., New Haven, 1982-87; dep. dir. devel. and pub. affairs Mus. of Modern Art, N.Y.C., 1987-94; v.p., vice provost for devel. The N.Y. Hosp.-Cornell Med. Ctr., 1994-98; mem. maj. gifts com. Stanford U.; bd. advisors Catalyst; cons. in field. Pres. LWV, Warren, Mich., 1962-65, Stanford Alumni Club of N.Y., N.J. and Conn., N.Y.C., 1968-70, 25 East 86th St. Corp., N.Y.C., 1989-93, 95—; mem. dirs. adv. bd. Yale Comprehensive Cancer Ctr., Yale U., 1990-94. Named Citizen of the Yr., Warren C. of C., 1962; recipient Citation, City of Warren, 1963, Gold Spike award and Cert. of Outstanding Achievement, Stanford U., 1976. Mem. Stanford Assocs. Home: 25 E 86th St New York NY 10028-0553

DORN, VIRGINIA ALICE, artist, art gallery director; b. Mpls., June 22, 1916; d. Raymond Edwin and Ruth Virginia (Nylander) Henneman; m. John Emil Dorn, Feb. 22, 1937 (dec. Sept. 1971); children: John Robert, Michael Raymond. BS, U. Minn., 1937. Mgr. med. lab. Orinda, Calif., 1955-61; instr. art Orinda Civic Ctr., 1980-81; mgr., tchr. San Francisco Women Artists Gallery, 1984—. One woman shows include Lucien LaBaudt Gallery, San Francisco, 1975, St. Paul's Towers, Oakland, Calif., 1976, Contemporary Arts, Berkeley, Calif., 1977, 80, Trinity Gallery, Berkeley, 1982, Valley Arts Gallery, Walnut Creek, Calif., 1982, Univ. Club, San Francisco, 1983, Holy Names Coll. Gallery, Oakland, 1987, Wellness Cmty. Gallery, Walnut Creek, 1991, Vincent's Ear Gallery, Orinda, Calif., 1994, also many juried and invitational shows in Calif. Recipient Lifetime Achievement award Women's Caucus for Art, 1996. Mem. San Francisco Women Artists (bd. dirs., fund raiser, mgr., instr., coord.), Oakland Art Assn., Valley Art Assn., Berkeley Art Ctr., East Bay Women Artists. Avocations: travel, music. Home: 95 Evergreen Dr Orinda CA 94563-3114

DORNAN, KEVIN WILLIAM, lawyer; b. Rockville Centre, N.Y., Apr. 13, 1952; s. William G. and Grace M. (Maher) D. BA, Johns Hopkins U., 1973; student, U. Heidelberg, Germany, 1973-74; MA, U. N.C., 1975, Catholic U., 1979; JD, U. Md., Balt., 1987. Bar: Md. 1988, U.S. Dist. Ct. Md. 1988, U.S. Ct. Appeals (2nd, 4th, and D.C. cir.) 1988, U.S. Dist. Ct. (ea. and we. dist.) Ark. 1992, D.C. 1993, U.S. Dist. Ct. D.C. 1994, Fla. 1996, U.S. Ct. Appeals (11th cir.) 1996, U.S. Dist. Ct. (mid. dist.) Fla. 1997, U.S. Dist. Ct. (we. dist.) Tex. 1999, U.S. Supreme Ct. 1999. Assoc. Finley, Kumble, Wagner, Washington, 1987-88, Pillsbury, Madison & Sutro, Washington, 1989-91; sr. assoc. Winthrop, Stimson, Putnam & Roberts, Washington, 1991-94; prin. Law Offices of Kevin W. Dornan, North Bethesda, Md., 1994-96; sr. assoc. Salem, Saxon & Nielsen, PA, Tampa, Fla., 1997; gen. counsel Internat. Carrier Exch., Inc., Jacksonville, Fla., 1997—; adj. prof. Eckerd Coll. Bus. and Environ. Law, St. Petersburg, Fla., 1996—, St. Leo Coll. Bus. Ethics, St. Leo, Fla., 1996-97. Editor Md. Law Rev., 1986-87; contbr. article to profl. jour. Mem. adv. bd. Clinton-Gore Com., Washington, 1995-96; chair nat. alumni sch. com. Johns Hopkins U., Washington, 1976-82. Asper fellow U.S. Dist. Ct. Md., 1986, fellow U. N.C., 1974-75, Boston U., 1975-76; Rothenberg scholar U. Md., 1986-87. Mem. ABA, FBA, Md. State Bar Assn., D.C. Bar Assn., Fla. Bar. Democrat. Roman Catholic. Home: 700 Boardwalk Dr Apt 721 Ponte Vedra Beach FL 32082-6261 Office: 8421 Baymeadows Way Ste 1 Jacksonville FL 32256-8223

DORNAN, ROBERT KENNETH, former congressman; b. N.Y.C., Apr. 3, 1933; s. Harry Joseph and Gertrude Consuelo (McFadden) D.; m. Sallie Hansen, Apr. 16, 1955; children: Robin Marie, Robert Kenneth II, Theresa Ann, Mark Douglas, Kathleen Regina. Student, Loyola U., Westchester, Calif., 1950-53. Nat. spokesman Citizens for Decency Through Law, 1973-76; mem. 95th-97th Congresses from 27th Calif. dist., 1977-83, 99th-103rd Congresses from 38th Calif. dist., 1985-93, 103rd Congress and 104th Congress from 46th Calif. dist., 1993-96; chmn. Nat. Sec. Subcom. on Military Personnel, chmn. Tech. and Tactical Intelligence. Host TV polit. talk shows in Los Angeles, 1965-73; host, producer: Robert K. Dornan Show, Los Angeles, 1970-73; combat photographer/broadcast journalist assigned 8 times to Laos-Cambodia-Vietnam, 1965-74; originator POW/MIA bracelet. Served to capt., fighter pilot USAF, 1953-58, fighter pilot, amphibian rescue pilot and intelligence officer USAFR, 1958-75. Mem. Am. Legion, Navy League, Air Force Assn., Res. Officers Assn., AMVET, Assn. Former Intelligence Officers, Am. Helicopter Soc. Special Forces Assn., AFTRA. Republican. Roman Catholic. Lodge: K.C. Address: 12755 Broohurst St Garden Grove CA 92840*

DORNBUSCH, ARTHUR A., II, lawyer; b. Peru, Ill., Nov. 8, 1943; s. Arthur A. Sr. and Genevieve C. (Knudtson) D.; children: Kimberly, Brendan, Courtney, Eric; m. Jacqueline Bahrs Montanus, Feb. 10, 1996. BA, Yale U., 1966; LLB, U. Pa., 1969. Bar: N.Y. 1970, U.S. Ct. Appeals (2d cir.) 1971, U.S. Dist. Ct. (so. and ea. dists.) N.Y. 1971. Assoc. Dewey, Ballantine, Bushby, Palmer & Wood, N.Y.C., 1969-72; asst. gen. counsel Boise Cascade Corp., N.Y.C., 1972-75; asst. gen counsel Teleprompter Corp., N.Y.C., 1975-76; asst. gen. counsel Engelhard Industries div. Engelhard Minerals and Chem. Corp., Edison, N.J., 1976-80; v.p., gen. counsel Minerals and Chems. divsn. Engelhard Corp., Edison, 1980-84; v.p., gen. counsel, sec. Engelhard Corp., Iselin, N.J., 1984—. Mem. Pelham (N.Y.) Union Free Sch. Bd., 1979-82. Mem. ABA, N.Y. State Bar Assn., Assn. Bar City N.Y., Am. Corp. Counsel Assn., Am. Intellectual Property Law Assn., Am. Soc. Corp. Secs., Mfrs. Alliance for Productivity and Innovation. Office: Engelhard Corp PO Box 770 101 Wood Ave S Iselin NJ 08830-2703

DORNBUSCH, RUDIGER, economics educator; b. Krefeld, Germany, June 8, 1942; came to U.S., 1967; s. Paul and Josefine (Buhner) Dornbusch. Lic., U. Geneva, 1966; Ph.D., U. Chgo., 1971; Dr. honoris Causa, U. Basel. Asst. prof. econs. U. Chgo., 1971, U. Rochester, N.Y., 1972-73; assoc. prof. MIT, Cambridge, Mass., 1975-77, prof. econs. and internat. mgmt., 1977—, now Ford prof. econs. and internat. mgmt.; hon. prof. Univ. del Pacifico, Lima, Peru; advisor Inst. Internat. Econs., Washington, 1982—. Author: Open Economy Macro-economics, 1980, (with Stanley Fischer) Macroeconomics, 1977, Economics, 1983, Dollars, Debts and Deficits, 1987, Exchange Rates and Inflation, 1988, Stabilization, Debt and Reform, 1993. Fellow Guggenheim Found., 1979. Fellow Am. Acad. Arts and Scis., Econometric Soc., Am. Econs. Assn. (v.p. 1990). E-mail: rudi@mit.edu. Office: MIT Dept Econs E52-357 Cambridge MA 02139

DORNBUSH, K. TERRY, former ambassador, consulting company executive; b. Atlanta, Oct. 31, 1933; m. Marilyn Pierce; 3 children. BA magna cum laude, Vanderbilt U.; postgrad., Emory U., N.Y. Inst. Fin. Former CEO, Hipolex Corp.; former pres. DOAG USA Inc.; former vice chmn. Am. Western Corp.; former ptnr. Courts & Co. & Investment Bankers; amb. to The Netherlands, Am. Embassy, The Hague, 1994-98; CEO, Dornbush Advisers BV, cons., Amsterdam, The Netherlands, 1998—; hon. chmn. bd. RAND Europe. Office: Concertgebouwplein 15, 1071 LL Amsterdam The Netherlands also: Am Embassy The Hague Psc 71 Box 1000 APO AE 09715-0011

DORNBUSH, VICKY JEAN, medical billing systems executive; b. Willowick, Ohio, Aug. 12, 1951; d. Charles W. and Josephine H. (Palumbo) Rader; m. Eric D. Erickson, Oct. 22, 1972 (div. June 1974); 1 child, Dana; m. Thomas Dornbush, Dec. 29, 1979 (div. 1987). Student, Kent State U., 1969-72, San Jose State U., 1982-84. Accounts receivable clk. MV Nursery, Richmond, Calif., 1975-76; accounts receivable and computer supr. Ga. Pacific, Richmond, 1976-78; acct. Ga. Pacific, Tracy, Calif., 1978-79, Crown-Zellerbach, Anaheim, Calif., 1979-80; acct. Interstate Pharmacy Corp., San Jose, Calif., 1981-83, contr., 1983-85; gen. ptnr. Med. Billing Systems, San Jose, 1984-89; regional billing mgr., co-ordinator St. Joseph's Med. Resources, Stockton, Calif., 1997—; seminar trainer Systems Plus, Mountain View, Calif., 1987-89, MD Solutions, 1989-97; instr. med. program Sawyer Coll. Mem. San Jose Civic Light Opera, 1987—, San Jose Repertory Co., 1987-89; pres., bd. dirs. San Jose Stage Co., 1990—. Mem. AGPAM, Exec. Sales Women, Nat. Soc. Pub. Accts., Women in Bus., Univ. Women. Dem. Methodist. Office: St Joseph's Med. Resources 49 W Yokuts Ave Stockton CA 95207-5728

DORNEMANN, MICHAEL, book publishing executive. With Internat. Business Machines, Germany, 1970-76, BMW, Munich, Germany, 1977-78, The Boston Consulting Gourp Inc., Boston, 1978-82; chmn., ceo Bertelsmann Music Group, N.Y.C., 1987—. Office: BMG Entertainment 1540 Broadway New York NY 10036-4039*

DORNER, KENNETH R., plastic surgeon; 3 children. BA, U. Mich., 1953, MD, 1956. Diplomate Am. Bd. Plastic Surgery, Am. Bd. Gen. Surgery. Pvt. practice Kalamazoo, Mich., 1968—. Mem. AMA, ACS, Acad. Plastic Surgeons, Am. Soc. Plastic and Reconstruction Surgeons, Am. Soc. Aesthetic Plastic Surgery, Am. Mzxillo Facial Soc., Lypoplasty Soc., Mich. Acad. Plastic Surgeons, Mich. State Med. Soc. Avocations: tennis, sailing, reading, photography, piano. Office: 252 E Lovell Ste 220 Kalamazoo MI 49007

DORNER, PETER PAUL, retired economist, educator; b. Luxemburg, Wis., Jan. 13, 1925; s. Peter and Monica (Altmann) D.; m. Lois Cathryn Hartnig, Dec. 26, 1950. BS, U. Wis.-Madison, 1951; MS, U. Tenn., Knoxville, 1953; PhD, Harvard U., 1959. Asst. prof. agrl. econs. U. Tenn., 1953-54; asst. prof. U. Wis.-Madison, 1954-56, assoc. prof., 1959-62, prof., 1962-89, dir. Land Tenure Center, 1965-66, 68-71, chmn. dept. agrl. econs., 1972-76, dean internat. studies and programs, 1980-89, prof., dean emeritus, 1989—; prof. U. Chile, Santiago, 1963-65; sr. staff economist Pres.'s Coun. Econ. Advisors, Washington, 1967-68; cons. UN, UN food, agrl. orgns., World Bank, U.S. Govt., state govtl. agys., InterAm. Devel. Bank. Author: Land Reform and Economic Development, 1972, Latin American Land Reforms in Theory and Practice: a Retrospective Analysis, 1992; editor: Cooperative and Commune: Group Farming in the Economic Development of Agriculture, 1977, Resources and Development: Natural Resource Policies and Economic Development in an Interdependent World, 1980; contbr. numerous articles to profl. jours., popular mags. Served with inf. U.S. Army, 1944-46. Mem. AAUP. Home: 1555 Gray Owl Ct Oregon WI 53575-2581

DORNER-ANDELORA, SHARON AGNES HADDON, computer technical consultant, educator; b. Morristown, N.J., Nov. 3, 1943; d. William P. and Eleanor (Dygert) Haddon: BA in Bus. Edn., Montclair State Coll., 1965, MA in Bus. Edn., 1970, MA in Guidance and Counseling, 1978; EdD in Vocat.-Tech. Edn., Adminstrn. and Supervision, Rutgers U., 1982; m. Robert Andelora, Feb. 17, 1985; children: Wendy, Meridith. Tchr., Morris Knolls High Sch., 1965-70; tchr. Katherine Gibbs Sec. Sch., Montclair, N.J., 1973-74; tchr. Leonia (N.J.) High Sch., 1974-75; tchr. bus. Woodcliff Sch., Woodcliff Lake, N.J., 1976—, adminstrv. intern to supt., 1980-82; computer tech. cons., 1992—; tchr. adult sch. Sussex Vocat. Sch., County Coll. Morris, Randolph, N.J. Judge, Election Bd., Montclair, 1972-82. Author Southwestern Pub. Co., 1992—, Glencoe McGraw-Hill Book Co., 1997—. Mem. ASCD, Am. Vocat. Assn., Am. Vocat. Research Assn., N.J. Vocat. Assn., NEA, N.J. Edn. Assn., Bergen County Edn. Assn., Woodcliff Lake Edn. Assn. (sec. 1976-84, treas. 1991—), N.J. Bus. Edn. Assn. (co-editor Observer 1988-90, historian/photographer 1990-92, sec. 1992-94, 1st v.p. 1994-95, pres.-elect 1995-96, pres. 1996-97, webmaster 1997—, Educator of the Yr. award 1996), Internat. Soc. Bus. Edn., Nat. Bus. Edn. Assn. (mem. telecomm. com. 1995—, mem. publs. com. 1996—), Ea. Bus. Edn. Assn. (Educator of the Yr. 1996), Consumers League (dir. 1979-85), N.J. Coll. Ednl. Leaders (v.p. 1985-89, treas. 1983-84, Northeastern regional rep. 1982-83, chairperson membership com. 1989-93), Northeast Coalition Ednl. Leaders, N.J. Assn. Ednl. Tech., N.J. Macintosh Users' Group, Delta Pi Epsilon (pres. Beta Phi chpt. 1979-80, v.p. 1978-79, sec. 1976-78, newsletter editor 1974-76, 89—, nat. com. 1980-84, nat. council rep. 1981-88, nat. historian 1987-89, chmn. nat. com. 1982-84, nat. pubs. com. 1996—), Sigma Kappa (nat. alumnae province officer 1977-81, nat. alumnae dist. dir. 1981-87, Nat. Colby award 1994), Phi Delta Kappa (pres. 1980-82 treas. 1975-79, 82-84, council del. 1977-80, 84-86, research rep. 1986-88, found. rep. 1988—), Omicron Tau Theta (pres. Delta chpt. 1987-88, v.p. 1986-87, nat. parliamentarian 1986-88). Lodges: Daus. of Nile, N.J. Eastern Star, Women of the Moose. Mem. adv. bd. Today's Sec., 1981-82. Home: 28 College Ave Montclair NJ 07043-1604 Office: 134 Woodcliff Ave Westwood NJ 07675-8296

DORNETTE, W(ILLIAM) STUART, lawyer, educator; b. Washington, Mar. 2, 1951; s. William Henry Lueders and Frances Roberta (Hester) D.; m. Martha Louise Mehl, Nov. 19, 1983; children: Marjorie Frances, Anna Christine, David Paul. AB, Williams Coll., 1972; JD, U. Va., 1975. Bar: Va. 1975, Ohio 1975, U.S. Dist. Ct. (so. dist.) Ohio, 1975, D.C. 1976, U.S. Ct. Appeals (6th cir.) 1977, U.S. Supreme Ct. 1980. Assoc. Taft, Stettinius & Hollister, Cin., 1975-83, ptnr., 1983—; instr. law U. Cin., 1980-87, adj. prof., 1988-91. Co-author: Federal Judiciary Almanac, 1984-87. Mem. Ohio Bd. Bar Examiners, 1992-93, Hamilton County Republican Exec. Com., 1982—; bd. dirs. Zool. Soc. Cin., 1983-94, Cin. Parks Found., 1995—. Mem. Cin. Bar Assn., Fed. Bar Assn., Ohio State Bar Assn., Am. Phys. Soc. Republican. Methodist. Home: 329 Bishopsbridge Dr Cincinnati OH 45255-3948 Office: 1800 Star Bank Ctr 425 Walnut St Cincinnati OH 45202-3923

DORNEY, PAULETTE SUE, critical care nurse, consultant, educator; b. Easton, Pa., Sept. 2, 1959; d. Paul H. and Carolyn (Freeman) D. Diploma, St. Luke's Sch. of Nursing, 1979; BSN, Cedar Crest Coll., 1984; MSN, U. Pa., 1989. RN, Pa. Asst. prof. nursing Lehigh County C.C., Schencksville, Pa., 1990-92; staff devel. critical care educator North Penn Hosp., Lansdale, Pa., 1992-95; cardiology clin. nurse specialist Easton Cardiovasc. Assocs., 1995-97; critical care clin. nurse specialist Easton (Pa.) Hosp., 1997—; freelance clin. editor Springhouse (Pa.) Corp. Mem. AACN, Sigma Theta Tau. Home: 125 Red Haven Dr North Wales PA 19454-1441

DORNFELD, DAVID ALAN, engineering educator; b. Horicon, Wis., Aug. 3, 1949; s. Harlan Edgar and Cleopatra D.; Barbara Ruth Dornfeld, Sept. 18, 1976. BS in Mech. Engrng. with Honors, U. Wis., 1972, MS in Mech. Engrng., 1973, PhD in Mech. Engrng., 1976. Asst. prof. dept. Systems-Design U. Wis., Milw., 1976-77; asst. prof. Mfg. Engrng. U. Calif., Berkeley, 1977-83, assoc. prof. Mfg. Engrng., 1983-89, vice-chmn. instrn. dept. Mech. Engrng., 1987-88, dir. Engrng. Systems Rsch. Ctr., 1989-98, prof. Mfg. Engrng., 1989—; assoc. dir. rsch. École Nationale Superieure des Mines de Paris, Berkeley, 1983-84; invited prof. École Nationale Superieure D'Arts et Metiers, Paris, 1992-93; cons., expert witness for intellectual property issues, sensor systems, mfg. automation. Contbr. articles to profl. jours., chpts. in books; presenter numerous seminars, confs.; patentee in field. Fellow ASME (past editor, mem. editl. bd. Mfg. Rev. Jour., pres advisory com., Blackall Machine Tool and Gage Award 1990), Soc. Mfg. Engrs. (fellow editl. bd. Jour. Mfg. Systems, Outstanding Young Engr. award 1982); mem. Am. Soc. Precision Engrng., Nat. Rsch. Coun. (nat. inst. stds. & tech. review panel for mfg. engrng. lab.), Nat. Inst. Stds. and Tech., Acoustic Emission Working Group, N.Am. Mfg. Rsch. Inst. (past pres., scientific com.), Japan Soc. Precision Engrng., Coll. Internat. pour l'Etude Scientifique des Techniques de Production Mechanique (CIRP). Avocations: hiking, travelling, reading. Office: U Calif Dept Mech Engrng Berkeley CA 94720-1740

DORNFELD, SHARON WICKS, lawyer; b. Detroit, Jan. 22, 1952; d. John Hoddard and Mary Catherine (Hogan) Wicks; m. William Harlan Dornfeld, Dec. 30, 1977; children: Christopher David, Catherine Ann. BA, U. Mich., 1974, JD, 1981. Bar: Conn. 1982, U.S. Dist. Ct. Conn. 1983, U.S. Supreme Ct. 1996. Pvt. practice Danbury, Conn., 1988—. Bd. dirs. A Better Chance in Ridgefield, Conn., 1985-91; parking violations hearing officer Town of Ridgefield, 1988—; mem. Office of Child Advocate Adv. Com., 1996—. Mem. ABA, Nat. Assn. Counsel Children, Conn. Bar Assn., Danbury Bar Assn. (pres. 1995). Democrat. Christian Scientist. Office: 42 Main St Danbury CT 06810-8047

DORNFEST, BURTON SAUL, anatomy educator; b. N.Y.C., Oct. 31, 1930; s. Irving and Yetta (Rosengarten) D.; BA, N.Y.U., 1952, MS, 1954, PhD, 1960; m. Eveline Drucker, June 13, 1954; children: Michael, Barry. *Immediate family consists of his devoted wife, Eveline, and caring sons, Barry and Michael, along with Michael's compassionate wife, Jodi.* Rsch. asst. dept. biostats. Sloan-Kettering Inst. and Meml. Hosp., N.Y.C., 1952-53; rsch. asst. dept. biology N.Y.U., 1953-54, 56-58, instr. gen. sci., 1958-63; instr. anatomy N.Y. Med. Coll., 1963-64; instr. anatomy SUNY Health Sci Ctr. at Bklyn., 1964-67, asst. prof., 1967-73, assoc. prof., 1973-91; cons. study sect. Nat. Heart and Lung Inst., 1975; adj. prof. Med. Sch. CUNY, 1974-97; adj. prof. hematology sch. health scis. Hunter Coll., 1978-82, 90-91, anatomy Inst. Continuing Biomed. Edn., 1979-86, N.Y. Med. Coll., 1982-85, 91-96, Touro Coll. Ctr. Biomed. Edn., 1983-88, Einstein coll., Medicine, 1991—. NIH fellow, 1958-60, 61-63; Leukemia Soc., 1960-61; Nat. Inst. Arthritis and Metabolic Diseases grantee, 1964-71; Nat. Cancer Inst. grantee, 1973-75; Mildred Werner League for Cancer Research grantee, 1976-77; co-prin. investigator NIH Heart, Blood and Lung Inst., 1982-85. Served with U.S. Army, 1954-56. Mem. AAAS, N.Y. Acad. Scis., Am. Soc. Hematology, Am. Assn. Clin. Anatomists, Internat. Soc. Exptl. Hematology, Am. Assn. Anatomists, Sigma Xi. Jewish. Contbr. articles in field to profl. jours. Home and Office: 96 Everett Rd Demarest NJ 07627-1225

DORNHECKER, SANDRA LEE, human resources executive, consultant; b. Chgo., Mar. 15, 1958; d. Robert Joseph and Joan Edith (Bechtel) Dagenais; m. James J. Kukuczka, Sept. 5, 1981 (div. June, 1988); m. Mark S. Dornhecker, Aug. 4, 1992. BA, Nat. Coll Edn., 1986; postgrad. studies, DePaul U., 1987-88, Gov.'s State U., 1991—. Correspondent N. Am. Life Ins., Chgo., 1975-76; paralegal James Wilton, Atty., Chgo., 1977-78; word processing mgr. Pullman Trailmobile, Chgo., 1978-80; human resource mgr. Ill. Cancer Coun., Chgo., 1980-86, human resources dir., 1986-92; human resources dir. Brookfield (Ill.) Zoo, 1992—; owner, mgr. Resumes, Inc., Frankfort, Ill, 1989—; cons. The Mgmt. Team, Highland Park, Ill., 1989-93. Mem. Soc. Human Resource Mgmt., Soc. Human Resource Profls. Lutheran. Office: Chgo Zoological Soc 3300 Golf Rd Brookfield IL 60513-1060

DORNING, JOHN JOSEPH, nuclear engineering, engineering physics and applied mathematics educator; b. Bronx, N.Y., Apr. 17, 1938; s. John Joseph and Sarrah Cathrine (McCormack) D.; m. Helen Marie Driscoll, July 27, 1963; children: Michael, James, Denise. B.S. in Marine Engring., U.S. Mcht. Marine Acad., 1959; M.S. (AEC fellow), Columbia U., 1963, Ph.D. (AEC fellow), 1967. Marine engr. U.S. Mcht. Marine, 1960-62; asst. physicist Brookhaven Nat. Lab., Upton, N.Y., 1967-69, assoc. physicist, group leader, 1969-70; assoc. prof. nuclear engring. U. Ill., Urbana, 1970-75, prof., 1975-84; Whitney Stone prof. nuclear engrng., engrng. physics and applied math. U. Va., Charlottesville, 1984—; NRC vis. prof. math. physics U. Bologna, Italy, 1975-76, 81, 85, 87; internat. prof. nuclear engring. Italian Ministry of Edn., 1983, 84, 86; physicist plasma theory group, div. magnetic fusion energy Lawrence Livermore (Calif.) Nat. Lab., 1977-78; cons. to U.S. nat. labs. and indsl. research labs., 1970—. Contbr. articles to various publs. Served as ensign USN, 1959-60. Recipient Ernest O. Lawrence award U.S. Dept. Energy, 1990. Fellow AAAS, Am. Phys. Soc., Am. Nuclear Soc. (Mark Mills award 1967, Arthur Holly Compton award 1998); mem. Am. Soc. for Engring. Edn., (Glenn Murphy award 1988), Soc. Indsl. and Applied Math., N.Y. Acad. Scis., Sigma Xi. Office: U Va Reactor Facility Thornton Hall Charlottesville VA 22903-2442

DOROCKE, LAWRENCE FRANCIS, lawyer; b. Chgo., Oct. 4, 1946; s. Walter P. and Effie M. (Gillis) D.; m. Diane L. Roberts, June 22, 1968; children: Todd D., Rob L., Jill A. BS in Econs., Purdue U., 1968, MS in Indsl. Relations, 1970; JD magna cum laude, Ind. U., 1973. Bar: Ind. 1973, U.S. Dist. Ct. (so. dist.) Ind. 1973, Iowa 1974, U.S. Ct. Appeals (7th cir.). Asst. mgr. personnel Comml. Solvents Corp., Terre Haute, Ind., 1970-71; law clk. to chief justice U.S. Dist. Ct. (so. dist.) Iowa, Des Moines, 1973-75; ptnr. Dann, Pecar, Newman & Kleiman P.C., Indpls., 1975—. Mem. ABA, Ind. Bar Assn., Indpls. Bar Assn. Roman Catholic. Home: Apt 1316 308 W Haydn Dr Carmel IN 46032 Office: Dann Pecar Newman & Kleiman PO Box 82008 1 American Sq Ste 2300 Indianapolis IN 46282-0001

DORPAT, THEODORE LORENZ, psychoanalyst; b. Miles City, Mont., Mar. 25, 1925; s. Theodore Ertman and Eda (Christiansen) D.; married; 1 child, Joanne Katherine. B.S., Whitworth Coll., 1948; M.D., U. Wash., 1952; grad., Seattle Psychoanalytic Inst., 1964. Resident in psychiatry Seattle VA Hosp., 1953-55, Cin. Gen. Hosp., 1955-56; instr. in psychiatry U. Wash., 1956-58, asst. prof. psychiatry, 1958-59, asso. prof., 1969-75, prof., 1976—; practice medicine specializing in psychiatry Seattle, 1958-64; practice psychoanalysis, 1964; instr. Seattle Psychoanalytic Inst., 1966-71, tng. psychoanalyt, 1971—, dir., 1984; chmn. Wash. Gov.'s Task Force for Commitment Law Reform; trustee Seattle Community Psychiat. Clinic; pres., trustee Seattle Psychoanalytic Inst. Contbr. numerous articles, revs. to profl. books and jours. Served to ensign USNR, 1943-46. Fellow Am. Psychiat. Assn.; mem. Am. Psychoanalytic Assn., AMA, Seattle Psychoanalytic Soc. (sec.-treas. 1965-67, pres. 1972-73), AAAS, Alpha Omega Alpha, Sigma Xi. Home: 7700 E Green Lake Dr N Seattle WA 98103-4971 Office: Blakely Bldg 2271 NE 51st St Seattle WA 98105-5713

DORR, DANIEL ALAN, personal and professional development facilitator; b. Cherokee, Iowa, Oct. 4, 1946; s. Ronald Dorr and Dora Dean (McManus) Kahl; m. Mildred Ann Clark Edwards, 1967 (div. Nov. 1969); children: Christopher, Kara; m. Mary Jo Steele, Feb. 20, 1972; children: Molly, Gabriel. Student, U. No. Iowa, 1965-69, Rudolf Steiner Coll., Sacramento, 1980-82, Calif. Coast U., 1993—. Cert. PSI World facilitator. Divsn. gen. mgr. U.S. Solar Corp. West, Sacramento, 1980-81; sales and mktg. dir. precious metals and jewelry mfg. co. Sausalito, Calif., 1981-83; lead instr. PSI World Seminars, San Rafael, Calif., 1983-90; owner, CEO Ptnrs. in Excellence seminars, 1990-94; pres. Mastering Peak Performance series seminars, 1994—; designer, facilitator numerous profl. and personal performance seminars and workshops including Creating Abundance in All Areas of Your Life, The Vision-Mission Workshop, Ptnrs. in Excellence, Mastering Peak Performance: The Personal Leadership Programme. Contbr. articles to profl. publs. Bd. dirs. Marin Waldorf Sch., San Rafael, 1977-80. Recipient Award of Acknowledgement and Appreciation, Gov. of Guam, 1993, Award of Appreciation, Portuguese-Am. Conf., 1990, Award of Appreciation, Manitoba (Can.) Sales Assn., 1989, Award of Appreciation, Dr. John Hall, The Options for Youth Orgn., 1988. Mem. ASTD, Am. Soc. for Transpersonal Psychology, Assn. Transpersonal Psychology, Nat. Assn. for Self-Employed, Inst. Noetic Scis., C. of C. Avocations: musician, listening to music, reading, hiking, jewelry design. Office: Dan Dorr Assocs Inc 836 McFarlane Ave Sebastopol CA 95472

DORR, ROBERT CHARLES, lawyer; b. Denver, Jan. 7, 1946; s. Owen and Rose Esther (Tudek) D.; m. Sandra Leah Gehlsen, Feb. 26, 1972; children: Bryan, Aric. BSEE, Milw. Sch. Engring., 1968; MSEE, Northwestern U., 1970; JD, U. Denver, 1975. Bar: Colo. 1975, U.S. Dist. Ct. Colo. 1975, U.S. Patent Office 1975. Mem. tech. staff Bell Labs., Naperville, Ill., 1968-72, patent staff, Denver, 1975-76; ptnr. Dorr, Carson, Sloan & Birney, P.C., Denver, 1976-86, sr. ptnr., 1986—; ptnr. Internat. Practicum Inst., Denver, 1979—; seminar speaker various profl. orgns. Co-author: Protecting Trade Secrets, Patents and Copyrights, 1995, 3rd edit., 1999, Protecting Trade Dress, 1992, 2d edit., 1999; contbr. articles to profl. jours. Active Citizens Com. for Retention of Judges, Denver, 1984. Milw. Sch. Engring. scholar, 1964-68; named Outstanding Young Man Am., 1976. Mem. ABA, Colo. Bar Assn. (pres. patent, trademark, copyright sect.), Douglas-Elbert County Bar Assn. (pres. 1983), IEEE, AAAS, Sigma Xi. Roman Catholic. Home: 1755 S Hwy 83 PO Box 116 Franktown CO 80116-0116 Office: Dorr Carson Sloan & Birney PC 3010 E 6th Ave Denver CO 80206-4328

DORR, STEPHANIE TILDEN, psychologist; b. Orlando, Fla., Sept. 21, 1950; d. Luther Willis Tilden II and Lillian Murfee (Grace) Owen; m. Darwin Dorr, May 21, 1986. AA, El Camino Coll., 1975; BA, U. N.C., 1985; MA, Western Carolina U., 1991. Cons. psychologist Sylva (N.C.) Psychol. Assocs., 1991-92; staff psychologist Park Ridge Hosp., Naples, N.C., 1992, Blue Ridge Ctr., Asheville, N.C., 1991-93; pvt. practice psychology Asheville, 1991-93; project mgr. Sedgwick County Dept. Mental Health, Wichita, Kans., 1993-95; pvt. practice psychotherapy and psychol. assessment Counseling and Mediation Ctr., Wichita, Kans., 1995-98; therapist United Meth. Youthville Clinic, Wichita, 1998—; adj. faculty Kans. Newman Coll., Wichita, 1995—, Butler County (Kans.) Cmty. Coll., 1996—; Assertive Cmty. Treatment (ACT) team clinician United Meth. Youthville, Wichita, 1997-98; presenter in field. Contbr. articles to profl. publs. Recipient Excellence in Tchg. award Butler County C.C., 1997, Outstanding Faculty Mem. award Butler County C.C., 1998. Mem. APA, Internat. Rorschach and Projective Techniques Soc., Soc. for Personality Assessment, Soc. for Psychologists in Mgmt., Psychoanalytic Study Group (sec. 1989-93, award 1993), Western N.C. Psychol. Assn. (mem.-at-large 1985-93, pres.-elect 1993), Psi Chi, Pi Gamma Mu. Episcopalian. Avocations: sewing, rock collecting, travel. Office: United Meth Youthville Clinic 811 E Douglas Ave Wichita KS 67202-3507

DORRANCE, DEBRA ANN, secondary school educator; b. N.Y.C., Oct. 13, 1961; d. William Joseph and Dorothy Patricia (Anderson) Clark; m. Paul Dorrance, Dec. 30, 1986. BA in English and Lit., SUNY, Binghamton, 1983; postgrad., Carroll Coll., Helena, Mont., 1985; BS in Libr. Sci., U. Utah, 1987; MA in Edn., Lesley Coll., Boston, 1996; postgrad., Seattle Pacific U., 1996—. Tchr. english Helena H.S., 1986, Broadwater H.S., Townsend, Mont., 1987; tchr. English and writing Headmaster Distance Learning, Helena, 1988-92; tchr. English Capital H.S., Helena, 1993—. Mem. Nat. Coun. Tchrs. English, Arts Plus. Home: 150 Horseshoe Bend Rd Helena MT 59602-7417 Office: Capital High School 100 Valley Dr Helena MT 59601-0199

DORRILL, WILLIAM FRANKLIN, political scientist, educator; b. Dallas, July 25, 1931; s. William Cumbie and Ruth (Esther Webb) D.; m. Martha Jeanne Brawley, Mar. 3, 1951; children: Jennifer Ruth, William Sidney, Rebecca Jeanne, Lisa Kathryn. BA, Baylor U., 1952; MA, U. Va., 1954; postgrad., Australian Nat. U., Canberra, 1954; PhD, Harvard U., 1972. Fgn. affairs analyst U.S. Govt., Washington, 1961-63; polit. scientist RAND Corp., Santa Monica, Calif., 1963-67; project chmn., sr. staff mem. Rsch. Analysis Corp., McLean, Va., 1967-68; dir. Asian Studies Ctr., assoc. prof. polit. sci. U. Pitts., 1969-77, chmn. dept. East Asian langs. and lits., 1972-77; dean Coll. Arts and Sci., prof. polit. sci. Ohio U., Athens, 1977-84; provost, prof. polit. sci. U. Louisville, 1984-88; pres. Longwood Coll., Farmville, Va., 1988-96, pres. emeritus, 1996—, prof. polit. sci. and history, 1988-96, bd. visitors, disting. prof., 1996—; vis. lectr. Fgn. Svc. Inst., U.S. Dept. State, Washington, 1962-80; mem. faculty coll. mgmt. program Carnegie-Mellon U. and Nat. Ctr. for Higher Edn. Mgmt. Systems, Summer 1980; vis. lectr. univ. adminstrn. Chinese univs., 1980, 84, 85, 87, 89; program cons. La. Bd. Regents, Baton Rouge, summers 1982-83, U. Tenn., Knoxville, 1988; mem. com. on internat. edn. Am. Coun. on Edn., 1990, U.S. AID Univ. Ctr. Program Adv. Group, 1991. Contbr. articles on East Asian politics and internat. relations to profl. jours., chpts. on Chinese politics and history to scholarly books. Mem. Athens County Bd. Mental Retardation and Devel. Disabilities, Ohio, 1982-84; chmn. bd. dirs. Kentuckiana Metroversity, 1986-88. Recipient Disting. Achievement medal Baylor U., 1980; Fulbright scholar, 1954; Soc. for Values in Higher Edn. Kent fellow, 1957-58; Ford Found. fgn. area fellow Taiwan, Hong Kong, 1959-61. Fellow Soc. for Values in Higher Edn.; mem. Am. Conf. Acad. Deans (vice chmn. 1981-82, chmn. 1982-83, bd. dirs. 1980-84), Assn. Asian Studies, Asia Soc. (adv. com. performing arts 1977-85), Nat. Com. on U.S.-China Rels., Am. Assn. State Colls. and Univs. (com. on accreditation and instl. assessment 1989-96, chmn. 1990-96, nominating com. 1993-94, governor's commn. to propose recommendations to improve and enhance econ. devel. in Southside Region of Commonwealth Va. 1990-96), So. Assn. of Colls. and Schs. (commn. on colls. 1986-88, 91-96, Southside Va. Bus. and Edn. Com. 1991-96, exec. coun. 1992—), Nat. Assn. State Univs. and Land Grant Colls. (acad. coun., exec. com. 1987-88), Gov.'s Bus. Edn. Commn., Coun. for Internat. Exch. of Scholars (bd. dirs. 1992-96), Coun. on Postsecondary Edn. Environ. Task Force, Salzburg sem. U. prgm., 1998, Va. C. of C. (Va. emissary 1993-96), Rotary. Democrat. Presbyterian. Home: 1007 Fayette St Farmville VA 23901-2029 Office: Longwood Coll Dept History & Polit Sci Farmville VA 23909

DORRIS, CARLOS EUGENE, chemicals executive; b. Sugarland, Tex., Aug. 25, 1935; s. T.J. and Laura Mae D.; m. Karen Ruth Wood, Aug. 17, 1969; children: Twanda, Kristen, Anthony, Jeffery, Thomas. BS, U. Tex., 1959. Chemist Dow Chem. Co., Freeport, Tex., 1959-63; from chemist to corp. mgr. Jones Blair Co., Dallas, 1963—. Mem. Nat. Paint & Coating Assn., Soc. Coatings Tech. (pres. 1986-87), Dallas Soc. Coatings Tech. (pres.). Avocations: ranching, outdoor activities. Office: Jones Blair Co 2728 Empire Central Dallas TX 75235-4409

DORROS, IRWIN, consultant, retired telecommunications executive; b. Bklyn., Oct. 3, 1929; s. Harry and Irene (Shapiro) D.; m. Janet Eve Levine, Sept. 12, 1954; children: Robert, Mark, Gail, Gerald. BS, MS, MIT, 1956; D in Engring. Sci., Columbia U., 1962. Exec. dir. Bell Telephone Labs., Holmdel, N.J., 1956-78; asst. v.p. AT&T, Basking Ridge, N.J., 1978-83; exec. v.p. tech. svcs. Bell Communications Rsch. (Bellcore), Livingston, N.J., 1984-93; bd. dirs. Vertex Industries, Clifton, N.J.; mem. com. on electronic mail NRC, 1979-81, mem. telecomm. bd. computer applications, 1980-82; mem. sci. com. SIP San Salvador Ctr., Venice, 1993-94; chmn. engring. coun. Columbia U. Sch. Engring. and Applied Sci.; vice chmn., bd. overseers N.J. Inst. Tech.; chmn. sys. subcom. FCC Adv. Com. on Advanced TV Svc., 1987-95; chmn. N.J. Commn. on Sci. and Tech., 1995—. Contbr. numerous articles to profl. jours.; holder 5 patents in telecommunication circuits and systems. Trustee Congregation B'nai Israel, Rumson, N.J., 1979-82; mem. Jewish Cmty. Housing Bd., 1991—. With U.S. Army, 1950-51. Recipient N.J. Sci. & Tech. medal N.J. R&D Coun., 1992, Egleston medal Columbia U., 1995. Fellow IEEE (mem. awards bd., Leadership recognition 1990, Founders medal 1990); mem. IEEE Comm. Soc. (policy bd. 1976-82), Nat. Acad. Engring., Fairmount Country Club. Republican. Jewish.

DORSCH, JEFFREY PETER, journalist; b. Rockville Ctr., N.Y., July 12, 1956; s. Frederick John and Elinor (Eilhardt) D.; m. Vicki Lynne Rice, Jan. 16, 1993; 1 child, Cali Sierra. BA, Fordham Coll., The Bronx, N.Y., 1978. Staff reporter Bay City News Svc., San Francisco, 1979, Healdsburg (Calif.) Tribune, 1979-82; correspondent Electronic News, San Francisco/Palo Alto, Calif., 1982-86; sr. editor Electronic News, N.Y.C., 1986-90; mng. editor Electronic News, N.Y.C. and Mountain View, Calif., 1991-95; editor-in-chief Electronic News, Mountain View, 1995—; editor-at-large Electronic News, Cedar Park, Tex., 1998—. Avocations: reading, traveling, family life. Office: Electronic News 1600 Coltonway Cedar Park TX 78613*

DORSEN, NORMAN, lawyer, educator; b. N.Y.C., Sept. 4, 1930; s. Arthur and Tanya (Stone) D.; m. Harriette Koffler, Nov. 25, 1965; children: Jennifer, Caroline Gail, Anne. BA, Columbia U., 1950; LLB magna cum laude, Harvard U., 1953; postgrad., London Sch. Econs., 1955-56; LLD (hon.), Ripon Coll., 1981, John Jay Coll. Criminal Justice, 1992. Bar: D.C. 1953, N.Y. 1954. Law clk. to chief judge Calvert Magruder U.S. Ct. Appeals, Boston, 1956-57; law clk. to Justice John Marshall Harlan U.S. Supreme Ct., Washington, 1957-58; assoc. Dewey, Ballantine, Bushby, Palmer & Wood, N.Y.C., 1958-60; prof. law NYU Sch. Law, N.Y.C., 1961-81, Stokes prof., 1981—, dir. Hays civil liberties program, 1961—, dir. global law sch. program, 1994-96, chmn., 1996—; vis. prof. law London Sch. Econs., 1968, U. Calif., Berkeley, 1974-75, Harvard U., 1980, 83, 84; cons. U.S. Commn. on Violence, 1968-69, Random House, 1969-73, B.B.C., 1969-73, U.S. Commn. on Social Security, 1979-80, Native Am. Rights Fund, 1978-89; exec. dir. spl. com. on courtroom conduct Assn. Bar N.Y.C., 1970-73; chmn. Com. for Pub. Justice, 1972-74; vice chmn. HEW sec.'s rev. panel on new drug regulation, 1975-76, chmn., 1976-77; mem. N.Y.C. Commn. on Status of Women, 1978-80; chmn. Sec. of Treasury's Citizen Rev. Panel on Good O' Boy Round-up, 1995-96. Author: (with others) Political and Civil Rights in U.S., 3d edit, 1967, 4th edit., Vol. I, 1976, Vol. II, 1979, Frontiers of Civil Liberties, 1968, Discrimination and Civil Rights, 1969, (with L. Friedman) Disorder in the Court, 1973, (with S. Gillers) Regulation of Lawyers, 1985, 2d edit., 1989; editor: The Rights of Americans, 1971, (with S. Gillers) None of Your Business, 1974, Our Endangered Rights, 1984, The Evolving Constitution, 1987, (with others) Human Rights in Northern Ireland, 1991. 1st lt. JAGC, U.S. Army, 1953-55. Recipient medal French Minister of Justice, 1983; Fulbright Disting. Prof., Argentina, 1987, 88. Fellow Am. Acad. Arts and Scis.; mem. ABA (chmn. com. free speech and press 1968-70), ACLU (gen. counsel 1969-76, pres. 1976-91), Am. Law Inst., Coun. on Fgn. Rels., Lawyers Com. Human Rights (chmn. bd. dirs. 1995—), Lawyer Com. Civil Rights, U.S. Assn. Constnl. Law (pres. 1996—), Soc. Am. Law Tchrs. (pres. 1973-75), Thomas Jefferson Ctr. for Free Expression (trustee). Home: 146 Central Park W New York NY 10023-2005 Office: NYU Sch Law 40 Washington Sq S New York NY 10012-1005

DORSET, PHYLLIS FLANDERS, technical writer, editor; b. Tacoma, Wash., Sept. 10, 1924; d. William Winchell and Rhea Louise (MacDougall) Flanders; m. Donald Edward Dorset, Apr. 20, 1963. BA, U. Wash., 1948, MA, 1949; postgrad., U. N.Mex., 1949-50. Tech. writer Sandia Corp., Albuquerque, 1952-56; tech. writer/editor SRI Internat. (formerly Stanford Rsch. Inst.), Menlo Park, Calif., 1956—. Author: Historic Ships Afloat, 1967, The New Eldorado, 1970; editor: Fluid Dynamics; contbr. articles to profl. jours. Mem. Arts Commn., Menlo Park, 1970-73. Mem. Authors Guild. Home: 460 Sherwood Way Menlo Park CA 94025-3716

DORSETT, JUDITH A., elementary education educator; b. Tacoma, Oct. 18, 1944; d. Lyall Edgar and Elnora (Hutton) Templin; m. Nick A. Dorsett, Aug. 28, 1965; children: Charles, Drew. BA, Cen. Washington U., 1967. Tutor K-adult edn., Yakima Valley, Wash., 1968—; elem. tchr. and tech. resource tchr., reading specialist Yakima (Wash.) Dist. 7, 1967—, reading specialist; ednl. seminar leader in Northwest, 1971—. Author: Bulletin Board Activity Centers, Creative Calling and Effective Follow-Up, Handbook of Creativity, Bulletin Board Builders, #2, #3, #4; contbr. articles to children's and tchrs.' mags. Recipient PTA Golden Acorn award, 1985; named Tchr. of Yr., 1985, Vol. of Yr., 1984. Home: 2606 Draper Rd Yakima WA 98903-9216 Office: Whitney Elem Sch 4411 W Nob Hill Blvd Yakima WA 98908-3740

DORSEY, BENJAMIN WILLIAM, engineering/construction company executive; b. New London, Conn., May 14, 1936; s. Thomas Francis Jr. and Helen Collins Dorsey; m. Chari Liles, Sept. 26, 1980; children: Scott. Matthew, Alison, Julie. BA, Bowdoin Coll., 1959; MBA, U. Maine, 1967. Instr. Kents Hill (Maine) Prep. Sch., 1963-66; dep. commr. State of Maine Dept. Commerce and Industry, Augusta, 1968-74; mng. dir. Fluor Daniel Cons., Greenville, S.C., 1974—. Lt. USN, 1959-63. Republican. Roman Catholic. Avocations: cooking, gardening, sailing. E-mail: bill.dorsey@fluordaniel.com. Home: 103 River Oaks Rd Greer SC 29650 Office: Fluor Daniel Cons 100 Fluor Daniel Dr Greenville SC 29607

DORSEY, DAVID FREDERICK, dean, humanities educator; b. Phila., June 30, 1934; s. David Frederick Dorsey and Isabel Barbara Miller. BA in Latin, Haverford Coll., 1956; MA in Latin and Greek, U. Mich., 1957, Princeton U., 1965; PhD in Latin and Greek, Princeton U., 1967; MLS, Clark Atlanta U., 1996. Instr., asst. prof. Howard U., Washington, 1960-69; assoc. prof. NYU, N.Y.C., 1969-72; assoc. prof. Atlanta U., 1972-89, assoc. dean arts and scis., 1983-86, acting dean, 1986-89; chair African and African studies Clark Atlatna U., 1994—, dean grad. studies, 1997—. Editor: Design and Intent in African Literature, 1982; contbr. articles and revs. to jours. Named Danforth tchr., 1963-66; Woodrow Wilson fellow, 1956, Ford fellow Ford Found., Uganda, Kenya, 1970-71, Fulbright prof. U.S. Govt., Tanzania, 1991-93, Fulbright rschr. U.S. and Egypt Govts., Cairo, 1995; UNCF disting. scholar, 1986. Mem. MLA (del. assembly 1998—), African Lit. Assn., Coun. Grad. Schs., Coll. Lang. Assn., Phi Beta Kappa. Democrat. Avocations: swimming, stained glass. Home: 1197 Avon Ave SW Atlanta GA 30310 Office: Clark Atlanta Univ 223 James P Brawley Dr Atlanta GA 30314

DORSEY, DOLORES FLORENCE, corporate treasurer, business executive; b. Buffalo, May 26, 1928; d. William G. and Florence R. D. B.S., Coll. St. Elizabeth, 1950. With Aerojet-Gen. Corp., 1953—; asst. to treas. Aerojet-Gen. Corp., El Monte, Calif., 1972-74; asst. treas. Aerojet-Gen. Corp., 1974-79, treas., 1979—. Mem. Cash Mgmt. Group San Diego (past pres.), Nat. Assn. Corp. Treas., Fin. Execs. Inst. (v.p.). Republican. Roman Catholic. Office: 10300 N Torrey Pines Rd La Jolla CA 92037-1020

DORSEY, EUGENE CARROLL, former foundation and communications executive; b. Springfield, Ill., Feb. 7, 1927; s. Prentiss Eugene and Reta Mae (Bennett) D.; m. Rita LaVerne Sutzer, June 18, 1949; children—David Eugene, Philip Alan. BS in Journalism, U. Ill., 1949; hon. doctorate, Coll. of Idaho, 1987, Keuka Coll., 1990. Program dir. Sta. WSOY, Decatur, Ill., 1953-57; sta. mgr. Sta. WVLN, Olney, Ill., 1957-59; gen. mgr. Metro-East Jour., East St. Louis, Ill., 1959-63, Idaho Statesman, Boise, 1963-65; pub. Idaho Statesman, 1965-71, State Jour., Lansing, Mich., 1971; dir. Federated Publs., Inc., Battle Creek, Mich., 1966-71; v.p. Federated Publs., Inc., Battle Creek, 1969-71; gen. mgr. Gannett Rochester Newspapers, N.Y., 1971; pub. Gannett Rochester Newspapers, 1972-79; v.p. spl. divs. Gannett Co., 1978-79; pres. Gannett N.W. div. pub. Idaho Statesman, 1979-81; mem. adv. bd. UPI, 1979; pres., chief exec. officer, trustee Gannett Found., Rochester, N.Y., 1981-89; ret.; chmn. Ind. Sector, Washington, 1989-92; bd. dirs. 17 Prudential Mut. Funds. Trustee emeritus Coll. Idaho; hon. bd. dirs. Meml. Art Gallery, Internat. Mus. of Photography at George Eastman House; past pres. Rochester Grantmakers Forum; past chmn. Am. Coun. for Arts, Ind. Sector's Give Five campaign to encourage donation of 5%income and 5 hrs. vol. work; past dirs. Family Svc. Am. With USNR, 1945-46. Named Outstanding Young Man of Ill., Ill. Jr. C. of C., 1961; recipient Honor medal Freedom Found., 1968. Mem. Country Club Rochester, Longboat Key Club. Home: 2010 Harbourside Dr Unit 2003 Longboat Key FL 34228-4236 also: 68 Winding Creek Ln Rochester NY 14625-2175

DORSEY, JAMES BAKER, surgeon, lawyer; b. Saratoga Springs, N.Y., Aug. 29, 1927; s. Francis Edward and Katherine (Baker) D.; m. Patricia Ann Walsh, June 10, 1950; children: Katherine, Mary Lee, Pamela, Suzanne, James B., Jr., Alison. BA, Brown U., 1949; LLB, Union U. Sch., 1952, JD, 1991; MD, N.Y. Med. Coll., 1957. Bar: N.Y. 1953, Mass. 1988, U.S. Supreme Ct. 1982; lic. physician, N.Y., Mass., Calif. Intern Greenwich Hosp., Conn., 1957-58; resident White Plains Hosp., N.Y., 1958-59, Lenox Hill Hosp., N.Y.C., 1961-64; chmn. dept. surgery Saratoga Hosp., Saratoga Springs, 1976-79, 85-87; cons. surgeon Wesley Nursing Homes, Saratoga Springs, 1964—. Bd. dirs. Saratoga YMCA, Saratoga Springs, 1971-72; pres. Saratoga Springs Hist. Soc., 1972-74. Diplomate Am. Bd. Surgery. Fellow ACS, Am. Coll. Legal Medicine; mem. Saratoga County Bar Assn., Saratoga County Med. Soc. (pres. 1982-85), Med. Soc. N.Y., Mass. Med. Soc., N.Y. State Bar Assn., Mass. Bar Assn., AMA. Republican. Roman Catholic. Lodge: Elks, K.C. Office: 112 S Broadway Adirondack Trust Bldg St 1 Saratoga Springs NY 12866

DORSEY, JAMES FRANCIS, JR., naval officer; b. Balt., May 28, 1934; s. James Francis Sr. and Elizabeth Rosalee (MacNamara) D.; m. Jeanne Lynch Hobbs, Aug. 16, 1958; children: James Francis III, Timothy Walker. Grad. in naval aviation, USN, Pensacola, Fla., 1956; degree in Polit. Sci., Naval Postgrad. Sch., Monterey, Calif., 1967. Commd. ensign USN, 1956, advanced through grades to VADM, 1991, comdg. officer 3 fighter squadrons, 1971-76, exec. officer USS Midway, 1976-78, comdg. officer USS Caloosehatchee, 1978-80, comdg. officer USS America, 1981-82, dir. joint program office, undersec. def. policy, dep. dir. def. mobilization systems planning activity, 1982-84, comdr. carrier group FOUR, and NATO comdr. carrier striking force Atlantic, 1984-85, dir. ops. U.S. European Command, 1985-87, dep. asst. chief naval ops. for plans, policy and ops., dep. ops. dep. for joint chief staff matters, 1987-89, comdr. 3d Fleet, 1989-91, ret., 1991; CEO Flag Ltd., Alexandria, Va., 1991—. Mem. Assn. Naval Aviation, U.S. Naval Inst., Chesapeake Bay Soc., Harbor Pt. Hoa (v.p.), Golden Eagle--The Early Pioneer Naval Aviators Assn. Office: PO Box 1119 Solomons MD 20688

DORSEY, JEREMIAH EDMUND, pharmaceutical company executive; b. Worcester, Mass., Oct. 15, 1944; s. Jeremiah Edmund and Mary Theresa D.; m. Nadia S. Vidach, Dec. 6, 1970; children: Todd Edmud, Jaime Erin, Megan Elizabeth, Kelly Ann. AB, Assumption Coll., 1966; MBA, Farleigh Dickinson U., 1978. With Johnson & Johnson, New Brunswick, N.J., 1969-88; nat. indsl. engring. mgr. Johnson & Johnson, New Brunswick, 1975-76, supt. ops. and maintenance, 1976-88, dir. ops. mem. mgmt. bd., 1976-88; v.p. mktg., ops., gen. mgr. sales Johnson & Johnson Dental Products Co., New Brunswick, 1976-88; exec. v.p. The Kaelin Group, Bridgeton, N.J., 1988; pres. Towle Housewares Co., Newburyport, Mass., 1988-90; pres., CEO Foster Med. Supply, Inc., Dedham, Mass., 1990-92; group pres. Carvel Hall Corp., Crisfield, Md., 1990—; pres., COO West Pharm. Svcs. Inc., Lionville, Pa., 1992—; corp. officer J.E. Dorsey Co., Carvel Hall Corp., Crisfield, Md.; bd. dirs. West Co. de Mex., Daikyo Seiko, Tokyo, Schubert Seals, Horsens, Denmark, DanBioSyst, Nottingham, Eng., Geschaftsfuherer West Co., Europe. Editor: Spl. Forces Assn. News. Active N.J. Commn. for Discharge Upgrade, Appalachian Trail Conf.; mem. alumni bd. dirs. Assumption Coll., adv. com. U. P.R. Sch. of Pharmacy; mem. mil. acad. selection com. U.S. Senate; vice chmn. N.J. Vietnam Vets Leadership Program; mem.Mercer County Pvt. Industry Coun. (N.J.), N.J. SR-92 Coalition. With U.S. Army, 1966-69, Vietnam. Decorated Silver Star, Bronze Star, 2 oak leaf clusters, Purple Heart, 4 oak leaf clusters, Army Commendation medal, Air medal with oak leaf cluster, Medal of Honor., Gallantry Cross, Vietnam; recipient Corp. Affirmative Action award 1981. Mem. DAV, KC, Sierra Club, Spl. Forces Assn., Smithsonian Assocs., Soc. First Divsn., Tiger Karate Soc., (Black Belt), Johnson & Johnson Mgmt. Club, Delta Epsilon Sigma. Roman Catholic. Home: 30 Fox Ridge Dr Malvern PA 19355-2876 Office: 101 Gordon Dr Exton PA 19341-1320

DORSEY, JOHN RUSSELL, journalist; b. Balt., Dec. 17, 1938; s. Charles Howard and Emma (Deputy) D. A.B., Harvard U., 1961. Mem. staff Balt. Sun, 1962-81, 83-99, Sunday Sun book rev. editor, 1967-69, Sunday Sun restaurant critic, 1971-81, 84-86, Sun art critic, 1983-84, 86-99. Author: (with James D. Dilts) A Guide to Baltimore Architecture, 1973; Mount Vernon Place, 1983; editor: On Mencken, 1980. Mem. Md. Club, 14 West Hamilton Street Club, Harvard-Radcliffe Club. Home: 600 Edgevale Rd Baltimore MD 21210-1904

DORSEY, JOHN VICTOR, poet, screenwriter, editor; b. Waipahu, Hawaii, Nov. 27, 1976; s. John Victor and Donna Marie (Maggio) D. Stuent, Westmoreland C.C., Youngwood, Pa., 1995-97. Editor Heaven Train, Greensburg, Pa., 1996-98; judge Poet's Fantasy, Rice Lake, Wis., 1995. Author: When It's Over and Other Poems, 1995; co-author: (screenplay) Wish All you Want..., 1997. Recipient Editor's Choice award Nat. Libr. Poetry, 1994. Avocations: reading, hiking, watching films. Home: RR 1 Box 858 Greensburg PA 15601-9674

DORSEY, JOHN WESLEY, JR., university administrator, economist; b. Hagerstown, Md., June 13, 1936; s. John Wesley and Abbie Virginia (Wy) D.; m. Jeanne Ascosi; 1 child, Rachel Lynette. B.S., U. Md., 1958; cert., London Sch. Econs., 1959; M.A., Harvard U., 1962, Ph.D., 1964. Teaching fellow Harvard U., 1961, 62-63; asst. prof. econs. U. Md., 1963-66; asso. prof., dir. U. Md. (Bur. Bus. and Econ. Research), 1966-70; vice chancellor for adminstrv. affairs U. Md., College Park, 1970-77; acting chancellor U. Md., 1974-75, prof. econs., 1976—; chancellor U. Md., Baltimore County, 1977-86; asst. to pres. U. Md., 1986-89; cons. to govt. Md. Employees Credit Union Bd., 1975—. Rotary Found. scholar, 1958-59; Brookings research fellow, 1961-63. Mem. Am. Econs. Assn., Phi Beta Kappa, Phi Kappa Phi, Omicron Delta Kappa. Home: 8234 Bubbling Spring Laurel MD 20723-1079 Office: Univ Maryland Dept Econs College Park MD 20742

DORSEY, LORAINE, English educator; b. Navasota, Tex., Sept. 5, 1943; d. Ira and Mae Ester (Amerson) D. BA, Prairie View A & M U., 1964; MA, Tex. A & M U., 1971. Lang. arts educator George Washington Carver Jr. H.S., Navasota, 1964-66, lang. arts, Spanish educator, 1968-69; sec., English educator George Washington Carver H.S., Navasota, 1966-68; English educator Navasota H.S., 1969—. Adv. bd. Friends of the Libr., Navasota. Recipient Chalk Bd. award 29th Masonic Dist., 1992, Appreciation award Truevine Bapt. Ch., 1997. Mem. NEA, Nat. Coun. Tchrs. English, Tex. State Tchrs. Assn., Grimes County Local Assn. (pres., sec.), Delta Kappa Gamma, Alpha Delta Kappa. Democrat. Baptist. Avocations: reading, writing short stories, gardening, walking, aerobics.

DORSEY, MARY ELIZABETH, lawyer; b. Florissant, Mo., July 4, 1962; d. Richard Peter Jr. and Dolores Irene (McNamara) D. BA in Acctg., Benedictine Coll., 1984; JD, St. Louis U., 1987. Bar: Mo. 1989, U.S. Dist. Ct. (we. dist.) Mo. 1989, U.S. Dist. Ct. (ea. dist.) Mo. 1990, U.S. Supreme Ct. 1994, U.S. Ct. Appeals (8th cir.) 1997. Rschr. Ind. Legal Rsch., Florissant, 1987-89; atty. assoc. Deeba Sauter Herd, St. Louis, 1989-98; ptnr. Ahlheim & Dorsey, LLC, St. Charles, 1998—; bd. dirs. North County, Inc. Merit badge counselor St. Louis Area coun. Boy Scouts Am., 1988—, mem.

com. Troop 748, mem. Order of the Arrow, 1992, Brotherhood, 1994; corr. sec. Florissant Twp. Open Dem. Club, 1989-91, sgt. at arms, 1991—; treas. Friends of Rick Dorsey, St. Louis, 1988, 90, 92, 96; mem. Dem. Com., Florissant Twp., 1996—. Mem. ABA, ATLA, Mo. Assn. Trial Attys., Bar Assn. Met. St. Louis (lectr. law related edn. com. 1988—), St. Louis County Bar Assn., Mo. Jaycees (state legal counsel 1997—, dist. dir. 1998-99), Florissant Valley Jaycees (dir. 1993-94, treas. 1994-95, state dir. 1995-97, v.p. 1997-98). Democrat. Roman Catholic. Avocations: golf, camping, theatre. Office: Ahlheim & Dorsey LLC 2209 1st Capitol Dr Saint Charles MO 63301-5809

DORSEY, PETER COLLINS, federal judge; b. New London, Conn., Mar. 24, 1931; s. Thomas F., Jr. and Helen Mary (Collins) D.; m. Cornelia McEwen, June 26, 1954; children: Karen G., Peter C., Jennifer S., Christopher M. B.A., Yale U., 1953; J.D., Harvard U., 1959. Ptnr. Flanagan, Dorsey & Flanagan, New Haven, 1963-74; U.S. atty. Dept. Justice, New Haven, 1974-77; ptnr. Flanagan, Dorsey & Mulvey; New Haven, 1977-83; judge U.S. Dist. Ct. Conn., New Haven, 1983-99, chief judge, 1994-98, now sr. judge; mem. Jud. Conf. of U.S. Cts., 1995-98. Councilman Town of Hamden, Conn., 1961-69; town atty., 1973-74; commr. Bd. of Police, Hamden, 1977-81. Served to lt. comdr., USNR, 1953-56. Fellow Am. Coll. Trial Lawyers; mem. ABA (mem. house of dels. 1974-78), Conn. Bar Assn. (bd. govs. 1968-70, 74-78, pres. 1978), Am. Coll. Trial Lawyers, Conn. Def. Lawyers Assn. (pres. 1974), Am. Inns of Ct. Hartford (pres. 1991-93). Roman Catholic. Office: US Dist Ct 141 Church St New Haven CT 06510-2030*

DORSEY, RHODA MARY, retired academic administrator; b. Boston, Sept. 9, 1927; d. Thomas Francis and Hedwig (Hoge) D. BA magna cum laude, Smith Coll., 1949, LLD, 1979; BA, Cambridge (Eng.) U., 1951, MA, 1954; PhD, U. Minn., 1956; LLD, Nazareth Coll. Rochester, 1970, Goucher Coll., 1994; DHL (hon.), Mount St. Mary's Coll., 1976, Mount Vernon Coll., 1979, Coll. St. Catherine, 1983, Johns Hopkins U., 1986, Towson State U., 1987, Coll. Notre Dame of Md., 1995, Coll. of Notre Dame Md., 1995. Mem. faculty Goucher Coll., Balt., Md., 1954-94; prof. history Goucher Coll., 1965-68, dean, v.p., 1968-73, acting pres., 1973-74; pres. Goucher Coll., Balt., 1974-94, pres. emeritus, 1994—; lectr. history Loyola Coll., Balt., 1958-62, Johns Hopkins U., Balt., 1960-61; bd. trustee Roland Park County Sch., 1995—. Bd. dirs. Friends of Cambridge U., 1978—, sec., 1989-93; bd. dirs. Gen. German Aged Peoples Home, Balt., 1984—, Greater Balt. Med. Ctr., 1990—, Md. Humanities Coun., Baltimore County Landmarks Preservation Commn., 1994—; bd. dirs., chair Hist. Hampton, Inc., 1992—; trustee Loyola, Notre Dame Libr., Balt., 1994—, Roland Park Country Sch., 1995—; chair Gov.'s Commn. Svc., 1994—. Named Outstanding Woman Mgr. of 1984 U. Balt. Women's Program in Mgmt. and WMAR-TV, Woman of Yr. Balt. County Commn. for Women, 1993; recipient Outstanding Achievement award U. Minn. Alumni Assn., 1984, Andrew White medal Loyola Coll., Balt., 1985; named in peer survey as one of 100 Most Effective Coll. and Univ. Pres. in U.S., Chronicle of Higher Edn., 1986. Mem. Internat. Women's forum, Smith Club, Hamilton St. Club (Balt.), Cosmopolitan Club (N.Y.C.).

DORSEY, WILLIAM WALTER, aerospace engineer, engineering executive; b. Long Branch, N.J., Dec. 23, 1934; s. Walter Gorman and Esther (Smith) D.; m. Lorraine Shirley Sanders, June 26, 1962; children: William W., Suzanne E. BSME, George Washington U., 1958, MS in Engring., 1965. Aerospace engr. Nat. Bur. Standards, Washington, 1960-65; sr. engr. Fairchild Hiller Corp., Germantown, Md., 1965-69; spacecraft mgr. European Space Agy., Noordwijk ann Zee, Holland, 1970-76; prin. engr. Fairchild Industries, Germantown, 1977-79; mem. tech. staff INTELSAT, Washington, 1979-85; dir. engring. Fairchild Space & Def. Co., Germantown, 1985-94; mech. systems mgr. Lockheed Martin Svcs., Lanham, Md., 1995; v.p. engring. Astral Inc., Rockville, Md., 1995-97; v.p. Kris Engring., North Potomac, Md., 1997—. Contbr. articles to sci. jours. Capt. USAF, 1958-60. Mem. AIAA, ASME. Achievements include development of unique design for the deployment control of the GEOS spacecraft 20 meter cable boom, of an analytical approach to the station keeping problem of colocating communication satellites in the same orbital location; design of numerous spacecraft thermal control subsystems including ATS-F, SERT-II, NIMBUS-D, and IMP-I using large computer programs; management of design, development and manufacture of instrument module for TOPEX Scientific Spacecraft. Home: 11832 Goya Dr Potomac MD 20854-3307 Office: Kris Engring Inc 14120 Stonecutter Dr North Potomac MD 20878-4803

DORSHER, PETER T., physician; b. Chgo., May 21, 1958; s. Robert Peter and Mary Ruth (McGee) D. BS in Biomed. Engring., Case Inst. Tech., 1980; MS in Biomed. Engring., Northwestern U., 1982; MD, Rush Med. Coll., 1985. Cert. Am. Bd. Phys. Medicine and Rehab. Intern, then resident in phys. medicine and rehab. Mayo Clinic, Rochester, Minn., 1985-89, sr. assoc. cons., 1989-91; sr. assoc. cons. Mayo Clinic, Jacksonville, Fla., 1995—; physician Rehab. Medicine Cons. of La., Baton Rouge, 1991-95; cons. Mayo Clinic, 1995—. Contbr. chpts. to books. Mem. Alpha Omega Alpha, Sigma Xi, Mortar Bd. Avocations: music/guitar, cooking, computer based education. Office: Mayo Clinic Jacksonville 4500 San Pablo Rd S Jacksonville FL 32224-1865

DORSKY, NATHANIEL, filmmaker; b. N.Y.C.. Student, Antioch Coll., 1961, NYU, 1962. instr. U. Calif. Berkeley, Stanford U. Filmmaker Bend in the River, 1955, Ingreen, 1964, A Fall Trip Home, 1965, Summerwind, 1965, Hours for Jerome, 1966-82, Gaugerion in Tahiti, 1968 (Emmy award), Pneuma, 1976-83, Ariel, 1983, 17 Reasons Why, 1985-87, Alaya, 1976-87, Triste, 1974-96, What Happened to Kerouac?, 1985 (Emmy award), Variations, 1992-98, Night Waltz: The Music of Paul Bowles, 1999 (Emmy award). Guggenheim fellow, 1997; grantee NEA; grantee Calif. Arts Coun.

DORTCH, CARL RAYMOND, former association executive; b. nr. Hanson, Ky., Sept. 14, 1914; s. Walter B. and Delia (Baldwin) D.; m. Anna Gale Greenland, Nov. 17, 1950; children: Walter A., David J. A.B., DePauw U., 1936, D.Public Service (hon.), 1979; M.A. in Pub. Adminstrn, U. Cin., 1938; LL.D. (hon.), Marian Coll., 1981. With Indpls. C. of C., 1937-79, asst. gen. mgr., 1950-62, gen. mgr., 1962-64, exec. v.p., 1964-75, pres., 1976-79; chmn. Ind. White River Park Devel. Commn.; chmn. bd. Indpls. Local Improvement Bond Bank. Bd. dirs. Indpls. chpt. ARC Consortium for Urban Edn., Indpls. Ednl. TV, Greater Indpls. Progress Com., Cmty. Svc. Coun., New Hope of Ind., Starlight Musicals, Ctr. for Leadership Devel.; pres., chmn. bd. dirs. United Fund Greater Indpls.; bd. advisers Christian Theol. Sem.; found. mem. Univ. Heights Hosp. Served to 1st lt. USAAF, 1943-45. Recipient John N. VanDerVriew award U.S. C. of C., 1947, Disting. Svc. award U.S. Jr. C. of C., 1949; named Man of Yr. Indpls. Times, 1956, Man of Yr. Indpls. Press Club, 1978, Man of Yr. Ind. Acad., 1980. Mem. Am. C. of C. Execs. (vice chmn., bd. dirs.), Ind. Commerce Execs. Assn. (past pres.), S.K. Lacy Leadership Series, Indpls. Execs. Svd. Corps, DePauw Alumni Assn., Edward Rector Alumni Assn. (past pres.), Indpls. Press Club, Meridian Hills Country Club, Masons (33 degree). Presbyterian (elder). Home: 2726A Marquette Manor West Dr Indianapolis IN 46268-3813

DORTON, TRUDA LOU, medical, surgical and geriatrics nurse; b. Elkhorn Creek, Ky., Aug. 26, 1949; d. Earl D. and Joyce (Kidd) Marshall; m. Eugene Anderson, Nov. 26, 1966 (dec. Apr. 1971); children: Gena Lynn, Richard Eugene; m. Leon Dorton, Dec. 15, 1972; children: Leondra Michelle, Jerald Thomas, Jonathan Layne. AS, Pikeville Coll., 1993, student, 1993. RN, Ky. Instr. computer usage Lookout (Ky.) Elem. Sch., 1983; water/sewage technician McCoy & McCoy Environ. Cons., Pikeville, Ky., 1984; owner Signs of the Times, Elkhorn City, Ky., 1979-89; sec.'s asst. humanities and social scis. divsns. Pikeville Coll., 1989-92; nurse aide Mud Creek Clinic, Grethel, Ky., 1992-93; charge nurse Jenkins (Ky.) Cmty. Hosp., 1993-94; case mix coord. Parkview Manor Nursing Home, 1994-95, minimum data set and nursing care plan coord., 1995; acute care nurse Harrison Meml. Hosp., Cynthiana, Ky., 1996—; vol. nurse aide Mud Creek Clinic, Grethel, 1989-92. Founder free blood pressure clinic H.E.L.P.S. Community Action Program, Hellier, Ky., 1983; co-founder H.E.L.P.S. Community Action Group, Hellier, 1983; mem. Ellis Island Centennial Commn., N.Y., 1986. Appalachian Honors scholar Pikeville Coll., 1989-92. Mem. Nat. Geog. Soc., Ky. Nursing Assn., Order Ky. Cols. (Honorable Ky. Col. 1989), Smithsonian Inst., Pikeville Coll. Alumni Assn. Democrat. Mem. Worldwide Ch. of God. Avocations: creating Indian jewelry and wall hangings, classical music. Home: RR # 5 Box 313A Union Pike Cynthiana KY 41031-9033 Office: Harrison Meml Hosp Acute Care 150 Miller Ct Cynthiana KY 41031-1603

DORWARD, JUDITH A., association executive; b. Hazleton, Pa., Apr. 16, 1941; d. Eugene Joseph and Dorothy Cecelia (Shields) McNertney; m. Douglas Dean Owens, Apr. 15, 1961 (div. 1968); children: Kevin Patrick, Kelly Shawn; m. Clifford Neal Dorward, July 4, 1969 (div. 1974). AA, Lehigh County Community Coll., 1979; BA, Muhlenberg Coll., 1984; grad. in statis. process control, Process Mgmt. Inst., Inc., Mpls., 1986. Customer svc. clk. Pa. Power & Light Co., Allentown, 1959-61; mgr. Merle Norman Cosmetic Studios, Allentown and Bethlehem, Pa., 1968-70; adminstrv. clk. Pillsbury Co., East Greenville, Pa., 1970-85; ops. prodn. mgr. Pillsbury Co., East Greenville, 1985-87, mgr. distbn. and prodn. control, 1987-93, chair labor rels. com., 1987-91, customer svc., vender liaison mgr., 1993-94; Pillsbury customer svc. rep. Americold Corp., Fogelsville, Pa., 1994-95; exec. field rep. Better Bus. Bureau Ea. Pa., 1996—. Former voting machine operator Lehigh County, Slatington, Pa.; held various offices Gen. Fedn. of Women's Clubs. Mem. Exec. Women Internat. (dir. publs. 1991, dir. membership 1992-93, v.p., pres.-elect 1994, pres. 1995), Phi Beta Kappa. Democrat. Roman Catholic. Avocation: foreign travel. Home: 2830 Linden St 3C Bethlehem PA 18017-3962 Office: BBB Lehigh Valley Divsn 528 N New St Bethlehem PA 18018-5715

DORWART, DONALD BRUCE, lawyer; b. Zanesville, Ohio, Dec. 12, 1949; s. Walter G. and Katherine (Kachmar) D.; m. Judith K. Coleman, Aug. 21, 1971; children: Claire Lauren, Hillary Beth. BA, Vanderbilt U., 1971; JD, Washington U., St. Louis, 1974. Bar: Mo. 1974, U.S. Dist. Ct. (ea. dist.) Mo. 1974. Assoc. Thompson Coburn LLP, St. Louis, 1974-79, ptnr., 1980—; dir. New Energy Corp. Ind., 1992-95. Contbr. articles to profl. jours. Mem. ABA, Maritime Law Assn. U.S. (proctor, mem. maritime fin. com. 1980—), Bar Assn. Met. St. Louis (chair securities regulation com. 1979), Focus St. Louis (mem. selection com. 1990-91, mem. fin. com. 1990—, mem. implementation steering com. 1988-90), Noonday Club. Office: Thompson Coburn 1 Mercantile Ctr Ste 3300 Saint Louis MO 63101-1643

DOSAMANTES-BEAUDRY, IRMA, psychology educator; b. Mexico City; m. Walter A. Beaudry. BS, CUNY, 1959, MA, 1962; PhD, Mich. State U., 1967; postgrad., UCLA, 1972-73; grad. psychoanalyst, L.A. Inst./Soc. Psych. Studies, 1993. Assoc. dir., counselor SUNY, Stonybrook, 1968-71; assoc. prof. U. No. Colo., 1973-74, Calif. State U., L.A., 1974-77; prof. UCLA, 1977—; dir. dance/movement therapy program UCLA, 1977—. Author: (book) Body-Image: A Cross-Cultural Perspective, 1993; editor-in-chief: (profl. jour.) The Arts in Psychotherapy Jour., 1998—, mem. editl. bd., 1986-87; mem. editl. bd. Am. Dance Therapy Jour., 1988-97. U. Calif. Pacific Rim Rsch. grantee, 1991-92. Mem. APA, Am. Dance Therapy Assn. (bd. dirs. 1974-84, pres. 1980-82, Chace Found. award 1997), Am. Assn. for Study of Mental Imagery (bd. dirs. 1982-86, pres. 1983-84), Internat. Psychoanalytic Assn., L.A. Inst. and Soc. for Psychoanalytic Studies. Avocations: tennis, gardening. Office: UCLA World Arts & Cultures Dept PO Box 951608 Los Angeles CA 90095-1608

DOSANJH, DARSHAN S(INGH), aeronautical engineer, educator; b. Sultanwind, Punjab, India, Feb. 21, 1921; came to U.S., 1946, naturalized, 1965; s. S. Arur and Inder (Hundal) D.; B.Sc. (honours) Physics, Punjab U., India, 1944, M.S., 1945; M.S. in Aero. Engring., U. Mich., 1948; Ph.D. in Aeros., Johns Hopkins U., 1953; m. Harwant K. Gill, Mar. 18, 1957; children—Amrita K., Kiren K., Rajit S. Research assoc. U. Md. Inst. Fluid Dynamics and Applied Math., 1955-56; assoc. prof. mech. and aerospace engring. Syracuse (N.Y.) U., 1956-62, prof., 1962-91, prof. emeritus, 1992—; vis. prof. Coll. Aeros., Cranfield, Eng., 1961-62; Fulbright-Hayes sr. faculty research fellow and vis. prof. Southampton (Eng.) U., 1971-72. NATO fellow, 1967. Mem. AIAA (aeroacoustics tech. com.; assoc. fellow); mem. Acoustical Soc. Am., Am. Phys. Soc., ASME, Am. Soc. Engring. Edn., AAUP. Editor: Modern Optical Methods in Gas Dynamics Research, 1971; Effects of Noise on Hearing, 1976; contbr. numerous articles to sci. jours. Home: 5176 Brockway Ln Fayetteville NY 13066-1704

DOSCHER, RICHARD JOHN, protective services official; b. Livermore, Calif., Aug. 31, 1952; s. Henry John and Violet Mary (Sutton) D.; m. Kathryn Laura Vierria, May 5, 1979; children: Cameron, Shannon. AS in Adminstrn. Justice, Yuba C.C., Maryville, Calif., 1987; BPA, U. San Francisco, 1991, MPA, 1993. From police officer to sgt. Yuba City (Calif.) Police Dept., 1977-85, sgt., watch commander, 1985-86, lt., divsn. commdr., 1986-89, lt., divsn. cmmdr. tech. svcs. and support, 1989-91, capt., divsn. cmmdr. field ops, 2d in command agy., 1991-93, capt., divsn. cmmdr. investigation, 2d in commd. agy., chief of police, 1995—; adj. prof. ethics Yuba C.C., 1997—. Bd. dirs. Yuba/Sutter Easter Seal Soc., 1988—; vol. Calif. Prune Festival, 1988—, Spl. Olympics, 1987—, Bok Kai Chinese Cultural Festival, 1993—, Yuba City Cmty. Theater, 1992—; adv. com. Adminstrn. of Justice Yuba Coll., 1993—; eucharistic min. St. Isidore's Cath. Ch., 1984—. With USAF, 1972-76. Mem. Am. Soc. for Pub. Adminstrn., Calif. Assn. Police Tng. Officers, Calif. Police Chiefs Assn. (bd. dirs. 1998—), , Calif. Peace Officers Assn., Peace Officers' Rsch. Assn. Calif., Yuba City Police Officers Assn. (past officer 1978-80), Kiwanis Club (bd. dirs., 2d v.p. Yuba City), Yuba City Health and Racquet Club. Avocation: astronomy. Office: Yuba City Police Dept 1545 Poole Blvd Yuba City CA 95993-2615

DOSÉ, FREDERICK PHILIP, JR., art historian, art and antiques appraiser, consultant, liquidator; b. Chgo., Sept. 9, 1946; s. Frederick P. and Alfa Elaine (Bahr) D.; m. Dee Hampton Keehn, June 8, 1985. BA, Northwestern U., 1968, MA, 1981. Faculty, art historian Northeastern Ill. U., Chgo., 1974-75, Colgate U., Hamilton, N.Y., 1976-80, Ray Coll., Chgo., 1984-97; fine arts & antiques appraiser for ins., probate, donation, estate, 1980—; art critic Chgo. Journal, 1982-85; curator, dir. Chgo. br. Daniel B. Grossman Gallery, 1983; agt., broker Charles Lipson Antiquities, Jamaica Plain, Mass., 1985—; ct. apptd. liquidator, 1987—; expert, witness in field. Co-author: (with Dennis Minichello) Appraisal and Insurance of Fine Art and Antiques, 1997; author (catalogue) Wilson Irvine, 1984; contbr. articles to profl. jours. Judge Old Town Art Fair, Chgo., 1991. Mem. Coll. Art Assn., Internat. Soc. Appraisers (contbg. editor bull. 1981—), Newberry Libr. Assocs., Friends of Victoria & Albert Mus., Furniture History Soc. London, Soc. for Ancient Numismatics, Am. Numismatics Assn., Archaeol. Inst. Am., Napoleonic Soc. Am.

DOS REIS, LUCIANO SÉRGIO LEMOS, surgeon; b. Aveiro, Portugal, Feb. 5, 1927; s. Joaquim and Maria da Purificação Lemos dos Reis; m. Maria Fernanda Cardielos, June 12, 1960; children: Miguel, Helena. Grad., U. Coimbra, Portugal, 1952, MD, 1952, PhD, 1961. Asst. gen. pathology faculty medicine Coimbra U., 1952-54; gen. intern Bridgeport (Conn.) Hosp., 1954-55; resident in gen. surgery Albert Einstein Med. Ctr., Phila., 1955-57, 60-61; asst. gen. surgery faculty medicine Coimbra Univ. Hosp., 1957-60; resident thoracic and cardiovascular surgery U. Md., Balt., 1961-62; agreg. prof. surgery U. Coimbra, 1965—; prof. surgery U. Luanda, Angola, Portugal, 1968-71; dir. surgery Centro Hosp. Coimbra, 1972-95; dir. jour. Médico Hospitalar, 1995-98; organizer, pres. postgrad. courses on gastric surgery and in surgery; tchr. Escola Superior de Tecnologia de Saude-Coimbra, 1994-99. Author: Etiopatogenia e Fisiopatologia da Pancreatite Aguda, 1960, Atelectasia Pulmonar (pulmonary function after bronchial recanalization), 1968; contbr. numerous articles to profl. jours. mainly on acute pancreatitis (distant visceral lesions in acute pancreatitis; blood volume in acute pancreatitis), cancer of colon, cancer of stomach. Nat. bd. dirs. Assn. Portuguesa dos Medicos da Carreira Hosp., 1991-96; mem. Group Archaeology and Art of Coimbra, 1980—; organizer, pres. Simposio Internacional de Cirurgia de Urgência, 1983. Grantee Fundação Calouste Gulbenkian, 1960-61, 92, Deutscher Akademischer Austauschdienst, 1980, 83, Brit. Coun., 1962. Mem. Sociedade Portuguesa de Cirurgia. Avocations: history, history of Portuguese navigation, painting. Home: R D Afonso II 43, P3030396 Coimbra Portugal Office: Edifício Topázio, Rua Olivença 9-Sala 408, P3000306 Coimbra Portugal

DOSS, AMANDA D., producer; b. May 10, 1970. BFA, RISD, 1992. Prodr. Citron Haligman Bedecarr @48, San Francisco, 1995-97, Foote Cone & Belding, N.Y.C., 1997—; prodr., ptnr. Ugly Betty Prodns., San Francisco and N.Y.C., 1995—. E-mail: uglybetty@earthlink.net. Home: 618 Carroll St 2d Fl Brooklyn NY 11215

DOSS, RIANNE SIMONE, juvenile protection officer, business executive; b. Dec. 25, 1970. BS, Grand Valley State U., Allendale, Mich., 1992, MPA, 1997. Asst. juvenile officer 3d Jud. Circuit Ct., Detroit, 1995—; v.p. Fire-Stal Concepts, Inc., Detroit, 1996—. Home: 19335 Mendota St Detroit MI 48221-1451

DOSSETT, LAWRENCE SHERMAN, professional services company official; b. Santa Ana, Calif., May 11, 1936; s. Wheeler Sherman and Eunice Elizabeth (Bright) D.; student U. Ariz., 1957-58, U. Calif., Irvine, 1973-75, Loyola Marymount Coll., 1974; m. Joanne Kallisch; children: Todd Sherman, Garrick Robert (dec.), Dana Shelene, Ryan William. Engring. draftsman Hughes Aircraft Co., Tucson, 1955-57, John J. Foster Mfg. Co., Costa Mesa, Calif., 1958, Standard Elec. Products, Costa Mesa, 1959; engring. mgr. Electronic Engring. Co., Santa Ana, 1959-79; product quality mgr. Farwest Data Systems, Irvine, Calif., 1979-82; dist. mgr. profl. svcs., nat. cons. mgr., sr. industry cons. Comserv/MSA/DBSoftware, L.A., 1982-92, sr. manufacturing industry cons., 1992-93; mfg. cons. Marcam Corp., Irvine, Calif., 1993-94; sr. industry cons. Cincom Sys., Inc., Irvine, Calif., 1994—. Mem. Western Electronic Mfrs. Assn., Am. Prodn. and Inventory Control Soc., Computer Mfrs. Conf., Cert. in mgmt. Am. Mgmt. Assn. Author: MRPXXI Asset/Liability Management System, 1993; co-author patent reel spindle, 1972. Office: Cincom Sys Inc 18101 Von Karman Ave Ste 1200 Irvine CA 92612-1012

DOSSEY, RICHARD LEE, accountant; b. Peoria, Ill., May 11, 1937; s. Arthur B. and Mary A. Dossey; m. Judy D. Humphries; children: Richard, Christine, Craig, Lynda. BS, Bradley U., 1959. CPA, Ill. From audit staff to mgr. Arthur Young & Co., Chgo., 1959-67; asst. contr. Sangamo Electric Co., Springfield, Ill., 1967-68; with KPMG Peat Marwick, 1968-94; mgr., ptnr. KPMG Peat Marwick, Chgo., 1968-74; mng. ptnr. KPMG Peat Marwick, Indpls., 1974-88, Cleve., 1988-93; area mng. ptnr., mem. mgmt. com. KPMG Peat Marwick, Chgo., 1990-93. Bd. dirs. Chgo. Commons Assn., 1971-74, Econ. Club, Indpls., 1974-88, Multiple Sclerosis Soc., Indpls., 1983-85, Crossroads Rehab. Ctrs., Indpls., 1986-88, Marion County Healthcare Ctr., Indpls., 1986-88, INROADS, Inc., Indpls., 1986-88, Greater Cleve. Growth Assn., 1989-93, Vis. Nurse Assn., 1989-95, Am. Cancer Soc., 1989-94, Gt. Lakes Theatre Festival, 1990-94, The Cleve. Playhouse, 1992-94; chmn. acctg. adv. bd. Case Western Res. U., 1988-94; mem. vis. com. Sch. Bus., Cleve. State U., 1992-94; mem. Cleve. Opera Coun., Cleve. Coun. Fgn. Rels. Mem. AICPA, Ill. Soc. CPAs, Ind. Soc. CPAs, Crooked Stick Golf Club, Wigwam Country Club. Republican. Methodist. Avocations: golf, tennis, bridge. Office: KPMG Peat Marwick LLP 1500 National City Ctr Cleveland OH 44114

DOSSIN, ERNEST JOSEPH, III, credit consulting company executive; b. Detroit, May 24, 1941; s. Ernest Joseph and Jean (Dickson) D.; m. Mary Jane Mortimore, July 24, 1965; children: Ernest Joseph IV, Tobias Alfred. BA in Bus., Valparaiso U., 1963; MBA in Fin., Fairleigh Dickinson U., 1978; postgrad., Walden U., 1995-98. Asst. store mgr. W.T. Grant, Norfolk, Va., 1967-68; dir. acctg. Am. Express, Trenton, N.J., 1968-72; corp. dir. credit Americana Hotels, N.Y.C., 1972-79; v.p. Myers Group, Rouses Point, N.Y., 1979-92; exec. v.p. Global Collections Inc., Plattsburgh, N.Y., 1985-93; pres. Dossin's Consulting Assocs., Plattsburg, N.Y., 1993—; guest lectr. Plattsburgh State U., 1995; leader seminars in improving credit practices, 1985-91; adj. faculty SUNY, Plattsburgh, 1993—, C.C. of Vt., 1993—. Author: Strictly Business, 1991. Corp. bd. mem. Champlaine Valley Physicians Hosp., 1998—; treas. New Eng. Synod Evang. Luth. Ch. Am., 1997—; congl. pres. Redeemer Luth. Ch., Plattsburh, 1985-8 9, congl. v.p., 1990-93; bd. dirs. Oratorio Soc., pres. 1996-98; bd. dirs. Plat tsburgh, 1986-90; treas. Luth. Coll., Teaneck, N.J., 1975-79; mem. exec. com. Boy Scouts Am., Clinton County, 1994—. Mem. Nat. Assn. Credit Mgrs. (cited 1984, 85), Internat. Credit Assn. (exec.), Soc. Cert. Consumer Credit Execs. (cert. exec.), Plattsburgh C. of C., Soc. for Preservation Barbershop Quartet Singing (v.p. 1990-93), Mgmt. Club Plattsburgh (bd. dirs. 1987-91). Republican. Lutheran. Avocations: boating, barbershop quartet singing, football. Home: 1318 Lake Shore Rd Chazy NY 12921-1912 Office: Dossin's Consulting Assocs Plattsburgh NY 12901

DOSTAL, ROBERT JOSEPH, philosophy educator; b. Ft. Benton, Mont., June 12, 1947; s. Elmer and Mary Patricia (Carr) D.; m. Kathleen Ruth Sprengard, June 24, 1947; children: Kerstin Ursula, Christopher John, Patrick Joseph. BA, Cath. U. Am., 1969, MA, 1971; PhD, Pa. State U., 1977. Asst. prof. Memphis State U., 1976-80; prof. Bryn Mawr Coll., 1980—, Rufus Jones prof. philosophy, 1994—, provost, 1994—; chmn. dept. philosophy Bryn Mawr (Pa.) Coll., 1987—; asst. dir. Phila. Philosophy Consortium, 1982-87. contbr. articles to profl. jours. NEH summer rsch. fellow, 1986, Ethics and Values in Sci. and Tech. grantee NSF, 1984-86, Humboldt fellow, 1981-82, 87. Mem. Am. Philos. Assn., Soc. for Phenomenology and Existential Philosophy, Metaphysical Soc., N.Am. Kant Soc. Roman Catholic. Office: Bryn Mawr Coll Provost 101 N. Merion Ave Bryn Mawr PA 19010*

DOSTER, DANIEL HARRIS, retired counselor, minister; b. Moultrie, Ga., Dec. 15, 1934; s. Percy James and Juanita (Huff) D.; m. Robin Baker, Mar. 29, 1964; children: Christopher Robin Eagy, Sally Sheppard Powell. BA, Fla. State U., 1961; MS, Ft. Valley State U.., 1984. Ordained minister, 1980; cert. criminal justice specialist with master addiction cert.; ordained deacon Episcopal Ch., 1980, ordained priest Episcopal Ch., 1997. Min., deacon Christ Episcopal Ch., Dublin, Ga., 1980-97, min., 1997—; counselor Dodge Correctional Instn. (now Dodge State Prison), Chester, Ga., 1984-87, Community Mental Health Ctr. Mid. Ga., Dublin, 1987-96; pres. Ga. Retail Bakers Assn., Atlanta, 1964-65; chaplain Parkside Lodge Dublin, 1984-92, Al Sihah Shrine Temple, Macon, 1991—. Pres. Cmty. Concert Assn., Dublin, 1985, 86, 87, bd. dirs., 1984-92; membership chmn. Al Sihah Shrine Temple, 1993-95, chaplain, 1992—. Mem. Kiwanis (pres. Dublin-Shamrock Club 1981, Kiwanian of Yr. 1981), Masons, Shriners, Laurens Shrine Club (Dublin, Ga., sec. 1992-93), Fla. State U. Mid. Ga. Seminole Club (bd. dirs. 1993, v.p. acad. affairs 1994, pres. 1998-99, master gardener), Kappa Alpha. Republican. Avocations: music, cookbook collecting, cooking, gardening. Home: 724 Victoria Cir Dublin GA 31021-5542

DOSTER, ROSE ELEANOR WILHELM, artist; b. Balt., May 11, 1938; d. Lewis Milford and Leeanora A. (Naylore) Wilhelm; cert. illustration and design Art Instrn. Sch. Mpls., 1956; cert. design and painting Md. Inst. Coll. Art, 1960, postgrad., 1960-62; m. Jesse Alfred Doster, Feb. 22, 1958; children: Jeffrey Allen, Roxane Elana. Exhibited in one-woman shows: Hampstead Library Gallery, 1969, 70, Aurora Fed. Gallery, Balt., 1969, Goodman Gallery, Ellicott City, Md., 1971, Central Savs. Gallery, Towson, Md., 1971, Parkville (Md.) Library Gallery, 1972, Equitable Trust Bank Reisterstown Gallery, Balt., 1973, Hanover Art Guild, 1981, Md. Ctr. Pub. Broadcasting, 1982, Kent Island Fedn. of Art Gallery, 1990, others; exhibited in group shows: St. John's Coll., Johns Hopkins, Goodman Gallery, Slayton House, Columbia, Md., Paynter Gallery, Rehoboth, Del., Hilltop House, Harpers Ferry, W.Va., 1974-86, Balt. Mus. Art Downtown Gallery, 1976, Towsontowne Arts Festival, 1977-79, 82, 84, McDonough Sch.'s Cleve. Gallery, 1978, Unicorn Gallery, 1979, Canon Bldg. U.S. Ho. of Reps., Washington, 1981-82, Md. State NLAPW, Art Exhibit, Balt., 1983, Annapolis, 1985, Md. chpt. Nat. League Am. Penwomen, 1983, Easton Art Acad., 1987, 88, 89, 90, 91, 92, 93, 94, 95, 96, 97, Invitational Craft Show, Cordova, 1988, Dorchester County Art Showcase, 1989, 90, 91, 92, 93, 94, 95, 96, 97, Salisbury-Wicomico Arts Festival, 1993, St. Michaels Maritime Mus. Show 1992-93, 94, 95, Chesapeake Coll. Art Show, 1987, 88, 89, 90, 91, 92, 93, 94, 95, Dorchester Educators Art Show, 1990, 91, 92, 94, 95, 96, 97, Working Artists Forum Juried Show, 1995, 96, 97, 98, 99; tchr. drawing, painting and ceramics, 1968—; craft supt. Carroll County 4H Fair, 1982, 83, 84, 85. Active Boy Scouts Am., Girl Scouts U.S.; leader Shiloh Clovers 4-H Club, Shiloh Clover's 4-H Club, 1983-84; trustee Balt. Mus. Art; pres. Carroll County Arts Coun., 1975-76, 94; v.p. Caroline County Arts Coun., 1993, pres. 1994; judge Montgomery County Fair, 1984, 86, 87, Howard County Fair, 1985, Balt. County 4-H Fair, Frederick County Fair, 1988, Caroline County Fair, 1989, 90, Easton Art Acad. Children's Exhibit, 1994, Federation Woman's Club of Denton Children's Competition, 1992-93, 94, Md. State Fair, 1993, 94, 95; mem. bd. Carroll County Farmers Market—crafts; elected mem. Working Artists Forum 1987-88, 89, 90, 91, 92, 93—, sec., 1992-93, treas., 1993-94, 95, 96, 97, 98, 99. Recipient numerous awards including George Peabody award, 1960, Judges Choice award Dorchester

Educators Art Show, 1990, Best of Painters award Artisan's Fair Queen Anne Rotary Club, 1992, Nat. Potpourri Contest winner Floral and Nature Crafts Mags., 1995, 96, medal from Gov. and First Lady of Md., 1998. Mem. Nat. League Am. Pen Women (br. art chmn. 1970-72, 1st v.p. 1972-74, pres. Carroll br. 1974-76, br. historian 1976-88, 89, 90, 91-94, 95, 96, branch achievement chmn., 1988-90, 92-94, br. newsletter editor 1992-93, 94, state historian 1982-84, 88-90, 93, chmn. tri-state miniature art show 1993, chmn. 50th Anniversary Show, 1995), Working Artist Forum (treas. 1994, 95, 96, 97, 98, chmn. miniature painting show 1997), Kent Island Fedn. of Art, Chestertown Art League, Rehoboth Art League, Md. Inst. Art Alumni Assns., Balt. Watercolor Soc. (assoc.), Carroll County Hist. Soc. (bd. dirs. 1986—), Caroline County Hist. Soc., Betsy Patterson Doll Club, Lady Baltimore Doll Club, Miss Carroll's Doll Study Club (founder, pres.), Ea. Shore Miniature Enthusiasts Club (founder, pres.), Ea. Shore Doll Study Club (historian 1993, libr. 1995, 96). Home: 9472 Quail Run Rd Denton MD 21629-1731

DOSTI, ROSE, newspaper columnist, author; b. N.Y.C., Feb. 6, 1931; m. Luan Dosti, Apr. 22, 1951 (dec. Oct. 1992); 3 children. Student, Hunter Coll., 1949-51, Ithaca Coll., 1952-53. Staff writer L.A. Times, 1964-92, columnist, 1992—. Author: (cookbooks) Light Style, 1979, rev., 1991, New California Cuisine, 1986, Mid East Mediterranean, 1982, rev., 1993, Dear SOS, 1994, Dear SOS Desserts, 1996. Bd. dirs. Nat. Women's Polit. Caucus, L.A., 1992—; mem. World Affairs Coun., L.A., 1994—, Internat. Visitors Br., L.A., 1992-96, Hollywood Women's Polit. Com., L.A., 1993-96. Recipient award Carnation Co., 1981, 83, R.T. French Co., 1983, Calif. Diabetic Assn., 1985. Mem. Assn. Food Journalists, PEN West, Internat. Women's Media Found., L.A. Press Club. Democrat. Avocations: art, sculpture, piano, singing, exercise.

DOSWALD, HERMAN KENNETH, German language educator, academic administrator; b. Oakland, Calif., Mar. 24, 1932; s. Herman and Caroline Josephine (Mello) D.; m. Ruth Eugenie Hannes, Dec. 21, 1956; children: Caroline Susan, Stephanie Ann. AA, U. Calif., Berkeley, 1952, BA, 1955; MA, U. Wash., 1959, PhD, 1965. Instr., dept. German and Russian Oberlin (Ohio) Coll., 1959-60; instr., dept. German U. Wash., Seattle, 1960-61; instr., dept. fgn. langs. Seattle U., 1961-62; asst. prof. German U. Kans., Lawrence, 1964-67; asst., then assoc. prof., dept. fgn. langs. Fresno (Calif.) State U., 1967-72; prof., chmn. dept. German and Russian Kent (Ohio) State U., 1972-79; head dept. fgn. langs. Va. Poly. Inst. and State U., Blacksburg, 1979-84, assoc. dean adminstrn., Coll. Arts & Scis., 1984-86, interim dean Coll. Arts & Scis., 1986-87, dean, 1987-93, prof. German, 1993-96, prof. German, dean Coll. Arts & Scis. emeritus, 1996—. Contbr. articles to profl. jours. Served to 1st lt. U.S. Army, 1962-64. Adenauer scholar, Munich, Fed. Republic Germany, 1953-54; Fulbright fellow, Vienna, Austria, 1958-59. Mem. Phi Beta Kappa, Phi Kappa Phi, Omicron Delta Kappa. Home: 4592 Preston Forest Dr Blacksburg VA 24060-8660

DOTI, JAMES L., academic administrator. Dean Chapman U., pres., 1991—. Office: Chapman U Office of President 333 N Glassell St Orange CA 92866-1099*

DOTO, IRENE LOUISE, statistician; b. Wilmington, Del., May 7, 1922; d. Antonio and Teresa (Tabasso) D. BA, U. Pa., 1943; MA, Temple U., 1948, Columbia U., 1954. Engring. asst. RCA-Victor, 1943-44; research asst. U. Pa., 1944; actuarial clk. Penn Mut. Life Ins. Co., 1944-46; instr. math. Temple U., 1946-53; commd. lt. health services officer USPHS, 1954, advanced through grades to capt., 1963; statistician Communicable Disease Ctr., Atlanta, 1954-55, Kansas City, Kans., 1955-67; chief statis. and publ. services, ecol. investigations program Ctr. for Disease Control, Kansas City, 1967-73, chief statis. services, div. hepatitis and viral enteritis, Phoenix, 1973-83; statis. cons., 1984—; mem. adj. faculty Phoenix Ctr., Ottawa U., 1982-98. Mem. Am. Statis. Assn., Biometrics Soc., Am. Pub. Health Assn., Ariz. Pub. Health Assn., Ariz. Council Engring. and Sci. Assn. (officer 1982-90, pres. 1988-89), Primate Found. Ariz. (mem. animal care and use com. 1986—), Bus. and Profl. Women's Club Phoenix, The Retired Officers Assn. (state sec.-treas. 1995-96), Sigma Xi, Pi Mu Epsilon. Office: PO Box 22197 Phoenix AZ 85028-0197

DOTO, PAUL JEROME, accountant; b. Newark, July 22, 1917; s. Anthony and Edith Margaret (Mascellaro) D. BS, NYU, 1947. CPA, N.J., N.Y.; registered mcpl. acct., N.J.; registered pub. sch. acct., N.J. Acct. John Hewitt Foundry Co., East Newark, N.J., 1941-43; acct. S.D. Leidesdorf & Co., N.Y.C., 1947-56; CPA Peat Marwick Mitchell & Co., N.Y.C., 1956-64; asst. controller Lincoln Ctr. for the Performing Arts Inc., N.Y.C. 1964-69; controller Seton Hall U., South Orange, N.J., 1969-74, Belart Products, Applied Coatings, Maddock, Inc., N.J., 1974-80, Internat. Trading Sales, Inc., Pan Atlantic Paper Co., N.Y.C., 1980; cons. Controller's Office, City N.Y., 1966. Bd. dirs. Parkway, Ltd., 1973-78. Served with AUS, 1943-46. Mem. Nat. Police Hall of Fame. Mem. N.Y. State Soc. CPA's (chmn. govtl. accounting com. 1963-64, chmn. internal control quest on aid of municipalities N.Y. State), AICPA (40 yr. mem.), Cath. Accts. Guild (bd. govs. 1961-64), N.J. Soc. CPA's, Fin. Exec. Inst., Am. Acctg. Assn., N.Y. Assn. Profs., Smithsonian Assocs. (charter), Nat. Wildlife Fedn., Am. Legion, Am. Mus. Natural Hist. N.Y.C. (assoc.). Address: PO Box 13 Claymont DE 19703-0013

DOTRICE, ROY LOUIS, actor; b. Guernsey Channel Isles, U.K., May 26, 1929; came to U.S., 1967; s. Louis and Neva (Wilton) D.; m. Kay Newman, May 8, 1947; children: Michele, Karen, Yvette. Student, Elizabeth Coll., Guernsey Channel Isles. Actor in leading roles Royal Shakespeare Co., Eng., 9 yrs.; actor West End of London, Broadway; actor: (TV series) Beauty and the Beast, Going to Extremes, Picket Fences, Mr. and Mrs. Smith, Sliders, The Promised Land. With RAF, 1940-45, ETO. Recipient award Guiness Book of World Records for World's Longest Running One-Person Show "Brief Lives", Best Actor award "B.A.F.T.A.", 1969, Emmy award "Caretaker", 1966, Tony nomination "A Life", 1982. Mem. Garrick Club (London). Avocations: fishing, riding. Office: Award Assocs 9720 Wilshire Blvd Beverly Hills CA 90212-2021

DOTSON, DONALD L., lawyer; b. Rutherford County, N.C., Oct. 8, 1938; s. Herman A. and Lottie E. (Hardin) D. AB, U. N.C., 1960; JD, Wake Forest U., 1968. Bar: N.C., Pa., D.C., U.S. Supreme Ct. Atty. NLRB, 1968-73, chmn., 1983-87; labor counsel Westinghouse Electric Corp., 1973-75; labor atty. Western Electric Co., 1975-76; chief labor counsel Wheeling-Pitts. Steel Corp., 1976-81; asst. sec. labor, 1981-83; pvt. practice law, Washington, 1987-91; sr. v.p. Beverly Enterprises, 1991—. Served with USN, 1960-65. Republican. Episcopalian. Office: 5111 Rogers Ave Ste 40-a Fort Smith AR 72919-9002

DOTSON, GEORGE STEPHEN, drilling company executive; b. Okemah, Okla., Dec. 25, 1940; s. Hilmer C. and Alma Lucille (McGee) D.; m. Phyllis A. Nickerson, Aug. 17, 1963; children: Sarah, Grant. B.S., M.I.T., 1963; M.B.A., Harvard U., 1970. Asst. to pres. Helmerich & Payne, Inc., Tulsa, 1970-73; v.p. Helmerich & Payne (Peru) Drilling Co., 1974-75; v.p. Helmerich & Payne Internat. Drilling Co., 1976-77, pres., chief operating officer, 1977—; v.p. drilling Helmerich & Payne, Inc., 1977—, also bd. dirs.; bd. dirs. Atwood Oceanics, Inc., Varco Internat.; chmn. Internat. Assn. Drilling Contractors, 1995. Served to capt. U.S. Army, 1964-68. Decorated Bronze Star. Office: Helmerich Payne Internat Drilling Co 1579 E 21st St Tulsa OK 74114-1303

DOTSON, JOHN LOUIS, JR., newspaper publisher; b. Paterson, N.J., Feb. 5, 1937; s. John Louis and Evelyn Elizabeth (Nelson) D.; m. Peggy Elaine Burnett, Apr. 4, 1959; children: John, Damon, Christopher, Brandon, Leslie. B.S., Temple U., 1958, Doctor of Journalism (hon.), 1981. Reporter Newark News, 1959-64; gen. assignment reporter Detroit Free Press, 1965; with Newsweek Mag., 1965-83; corr. Detroit, 1965-69; corr. L.A., 1969-70, bur. chief, 1970-75; news editor N.Y.C., 1976-77, sr. editor, 1977-83; asst. to exec. editor Phila. Inquirer, 1983-84; exec. asst. to pres. Phila. Newspapers, Inc., 1984-85, dir. night ops., 1986-87; pres., pub. Daily Camera, Boulder, Colo., 1987-92; pub. Akron (Ohio) Beacon Jour., 1992—; bd. dirs. Robert C. Maynard Inst. Journalism Edn., 1974—, treas., 1974-78, chmn., 1980-84, 93—; mem. Pulitzer Prize Bd., 1991—; bd. dirs. Inventure Place; mem. nat. adv. bd. Poynter Inst. for Media Studies. Mem. bd. visitors John S. Knight Fellowships, Stanford U., 1983—, Sch. Journalism, U. N.C., Chapel Hill, 1987—; mem. adv. bd. Sch. Journalism and Mass Comms., U. Colo., Boulder; trustee Akron Cmty. Found., 1993—, chmn., 1995—; mem. exec. com. Akron Regional Devel. Bd.; mem. governing bd. Summit Edn. Initiative; joint operating bd., exec. com. Inventure Place. Office: Akron Beacon Jour 44 E Exchange St Akron OH 44328-0001*

DOTSON, JOHN RAY, oil painter; b. Charles City, Iowa; s. John Bernard and Lorraine Shirley (Wilson) D.; m. Barbara Ann Vetter; 1 child, James R. Cert. medication aide, North Iowa C.C., 1981; student, North Iowa Area C.C., 1997—. Medication aide County Care Facility, Iowa, 1971-96; CEO Artsoft Portraitures, Mason City. Avocations: computer programming, computer aided design. Home: 210 6th St SE Mason City IA 50401-4042

DOTSON, LIBBY, foundation executive; b. Nashville, Feb. 18, 1950; d. Cornelius Franklin Watts and Jean Bass Scott; widowed; children: Jennifer Lynn, Christopher Lee. BS, Vanderbilt U., 1972. Comml. loan asst. Ft. Worth Nat. Bank, 1972-75; asst. v.p., corp. officer Tex. Am. Bank/Tex. Am. Bancshares, Inc., Ft. worth, 1975-90; asst. v.p. Bank One, Ft. worth, 1990-93; dir. cmty. devel. All Saints Health System, Ft. Worth, 1993-95, chief devel. officer, 1996-99; pres. Child Study Ctr. Found., 1999—; mem. Funding Info. Ctr., Ft. Worth, 1997—. Bd. dirs. Cancer Care Svcs., 1992—, chair, 1993-94; bd. dirs. Prevent Blindness Tex., v.p. pub. rels., 1994-96; bd. dirs. Am. Red Cross Tarrant County, 1995, Cmty. Health Found of Tarrant County, 1995-96. Recipient Algernon Sydney Sullivan award for altruism Peabody Coll./Vanderbilt U., 1972, Women in Bus. award YWCA, Ft. Worth, 1997, NSFRE Agy. Vol. of Yr./Cancer Care Svcs. award, 1998, Vol. of Yr./Prevent Blindness award, 1995. Mem. Assn. for Healthcare Philanthropy, Nat. Soc. Fund Raising Execs., Rotary Internat. Avocations: performing arts, reading, aerobics. Office: Child Study Ctr Found 1300 W Lancaster Ave Fort Worth TX 76102

DOTSON, ROBERT CHARLES, news correspondent; b. St. Louis, Oct. 3, 1946; s. William Henry and Dorothy Mae (Bailey) D.; m. Linda Gay Puckett, July 1, 1972; 1 child, Amy Michelle. BS in Journalism and Polit. Sci., Kans. U., 1968; MS in TV, Syracuse U., 1969. News dir. Sta. KANU-FM, Lawrence, Kans., 1966-68; reporter, photographer, documentary producer KMBC-TV, Kansas City, Mo., 1968; dir. spl. projects WKY-TV, Oklahoma City, 1969-75; corr. WKYC-TV, Cleve., 1975-77; network corr. NBC News, Dallas, 1977-79; corr. Prime Time Saturday Atlanta, 1979-80, corr. Today Show, 1980-85; nat. corr. NBC Nightly News, Atlanta, 1985—, Dateline NBC, 1985—; vis. prof. journalism U. Okla., 1969-73; faculty affiliate Colo. State U., Ft. Collins; writer, host Bob Dotson's Am., travel channel and NBC Superchannel, 1996-98. Author: ...in Pursuit of the American Dream, 1985 (George Washington Honor medal Freedom Found. 1985); documentaries include Through the Looking Glass Darkly, 1974 (Emmy award, RFK award), The Urban Reservation, 1975 (RFK award DuPont-Columbia Journalism award), Still Got Life to Go, 1972, (Emmy nomination), Smoke and Steel, 1973 (Emmy nomination), The Sunshine Child, 1983 (Emmy nomination), People Who Make a Defference, 1987 (Emmy nomination), Bob Dotson's NBC Nightly News Stories, 1987 (Gabriel award 1987), Bob Dotson, 1987 (Media Acess award 1987), Assignment Am., 1989 (Nat. Headliners award 1990, Emmy nomination, 1989, Ohio State award 1989), El Capitan's Courageous Climbers, 1990 (Cine Golden Eale, Italian Film Festival grand prize, Union of Mountain Climbers grand prize, Wilbur award U.S. Film Festival 1990, 91, Cine Grand Prize Best Am. Non-Fiction Film, 1991, Bombay, India Internat. Film Festival Grand Prize, 1991, Japan, Spain Internat. Sprots Film Fest. Grand Prize, 1991, Juan Antonio Samaranch Spl. Citation, 1991), The River's Edge, Dateline NBC, 1994 (Emmy award), Susan Smith Coverage, 1994 (Clarion award), Bob Dotson's America Closeup, 1994 (Clarion award), The River's Edge, 1994 (Emmy award), Bob Dotson's Am., 1996. Recipient numerous awards including Elec. Media Grand Prize Nat. Assn. Yr. Round Edn., 1993, Gabriel Grand Prize Bob Dotson's Am. Diary, 1992, TV of Merit award DAR, 1985, Gabriel award Nat. Cath. Assn. Broadcasters, 1984, Clarion award Women in Communications, 1983, Epilepsy Found. Am. award, 1977, Silver medal Internat. Film and TV Festival of N.Y., 1976. Mem. Nat. Acad. TV Arts and Scis., Nat. Press Photographers Assn. (The Sprague Meml. award 1989), Writers Guild Am., Internat. Platform Assn., Sigma Delta Chi. Avocation: writing. Office: NBC News 1175 Peachtree St NE Ste 1140 Atlanta GA 30361-6208

DOTT, ROBERT HENRY, JR., geologist, educator; b. Tulsa, June 2, 1929; s. Robert Henry and Esther Edgerton (Reed) D.; m. Nancy Maud Robertson, Feb. 1, 1951; children: James, Karen, Eric, Cynthia, Brian. Student, U. Okla., 1946-48; BS, U. Mich., 1950, MS, 1951; PhD, Columbia U., 1956. Exploration geologist Humble Oil & Refining Co., Ariz., Oreg., Wash., 1954-56, So. Calif., 1958; mem. faculty U. Wis.-Madison, 1958-94, prof. geology, 1966-84, Stanley A. Tyler Disting. prof., 1984—, chmn. dept. geology and geophysics, 1974-77, emeritus prof., 1994—; vis. prof. U. Calif., Berkeley, 1969; Cabot disting. vis. prof. U. Houston, 1986-87; NSF sci. faculty fellow Stanford U. and U.S. Geol. Survey, 1978, U. Colo., 1979; acad. visitor Oxford U., Imperial Coll., London, 1985-86, Adelaide U., Australia, 1992; cons. Roan Selection Trust, Ltd., Zambia, 1967, Atlantic-Richfield Co., 1983-85, Hubbard Map Co., 1984-86; lectr. Bur. Petroleum and Marine Geology, People's Republic of China, 1986; Erskine fellow and vis. prof. Canterbury U., N.Z., 1987; Woodford-Ellis lectr. Pomona Coll., 1994. Co-author: Evolution of the Earth, 5th edit. 1994; contbr. articles on sedimentology, tectonics, geology of So. Andes and history of geology to profl. jours. Served to 1st lt. USAF, 1956-57. Recipient Outstanding Tchr. award Wis. Student Assn., 1969, Ben H. Parker award Am. Inst. Profl. Geologists, 1992; AEC fellow Columbia U., 1956. Fellow Geol. Soc. Am. (chmn. history of geology divsn. 1990, councilor 1992-94, History of Geology award 1995), Edinburgh Geol. Soc. (hon. corr. 1997); mem. AAAS, Am. Assn. Petroleum Geologists (Pres's award 1956, Disting. Svc. award 1984, Disting. Lectr. 1985), Soc. Econ. Paleontologists and Mineralogists (sec.-treas. 1968-70, v.p. 1972-73, pres. 1981-82, hon. mem. 1987, William H. Twenhofel medal 1993), Internat. Assn. Sedimentologists, History of Earth Sci. Soc. (pres. 1990), Sigma Xi (Disting. lectr. 1988-89). Unitarian. Office: U Wis Dept Geology and Geophysics 1215 W Dayton St Madison WI 53706-1600 *To understand the earth's past, which no human could witness, has long seemed to me the most exciting challenge imaginable. It is like a great Sherlock Holmes mystery story.*

DOTTEN, MICHAEL CHESTER, lawyer; b. Marathon, Ont., Can., Feb. 23, 1952; came to U.S., 1957; s. William James and Ona Adelaide (Sheppard) D.; m. Kathleen Curtis, Aug. 17, 1974 (div. July 1991); children: Matthew Curtis, Tyler Ryan; m. Cheryl Calvin, Apr. 16, 1994. BS in Polit. Sci., U. Oreg., 1974, JD, 1977. Bar: Idaho 1977, Oreg. 1978, U.S. Dist. Ct. Idaho 1977, U.S. Dist. Ct. Oreg. 1978, U.S. Ct. Appeals (9th cir.), U.S. Ct. Appeals (D.C. cir.) 1987, U.S. Ct. Claims 1986, U.S. Supreme Ct. 1996. Staff asst. U.S. Senator Bob Packwood, Washington, 1973-74; asst. atty. gen. State of Idaho, Boise, 1977-78; chief rate counsel Bonneville Power Adminstrn., Portland, 1978-83; spl. counsel Heller, Ehrman, White & McAuliffe, Portland, 1983-84, ptnr., 1985-98, 99—; gen. counsel PG&E Gas Transmission, N.W. Corp., Portland, 1998-99; utility com. mem. Ctr. for Pub. Resources, N.Y.C., 1992—. Coun. Emanual Hosp. Assocs., Portland, 1988-92; bd. dirs. William Temple House, 1995—, chmn. devel. com., 1996-98, v.p., 1997-98, pres., 1998—; active Portland Interneighborhood Trans. Rev. Commn., 1986-88. Hunter Leadership scholar U. Oreg., 1973, Oreg. scholar, 1970. Mem. ABA (chmn. electric power com. sect. natural resources 1985-88, coun. liaison energy com. 1990-93, coordinating group on energy law 1992-96), Fed. Bar Assn. (pres. Oreg. chpt. 1989-90, Chpt. Activity award 1990, Pres. award 1988-89), Oreg. State Bar (chmn. dispute resolution com. 1986-87), U. Oreg. Law Sch. Alumni Assn. (pres. 1989-92), Multnomah Athletic Club. Democrat. Episcopalian. Avocations: snow skiing, golf, hiking, travel, racquetball. Office: PG&E Gas Transmission NW Corp 2100 SW River Pky Portland OR 97201-8009

DOTTIN, ERSKINE S., education educator; b. St. Michael, Barbados, July 21, 1940; s. Grafton Howard and Beryl Dottin; m. Cynthia E. Dottin, Apr. 25, 1970; 1 child, Farrell S. BS, U. West Fla., 1973, MEd, 1974; PhD, Miami U., Oxford, Ohio, 1976; AA, Pensacola (Fla.) Jr. Coll., 1972. Tchr. Pensacola Sch. Liberal Arts; from instructional specialist to assoc. prof. edn. U. West Fla., Pensacola, 1977-92; prof. Fla. Internat. U., 1992—. Author: Thinking About Education, 1989, Teaching as Enchancing Human Effectiveness, 1994. Mem. ASCD, Global Alliance for Transformation of Edn., Am. Edn!. Rsch. Assn., Am. Ednl. Studies Assn., S.E. Philosophy Edn. Soc., Fla. Founds. Edn. Soc. (past pres.), NCATE Bd. Examiners (unit accreditation bd.), Coun. Learned Socs. in Edn. (pres.), Phi Kappa Phi, Phi Delta Kappa. Home: 14810 SW 149th Ave Miami FL 33196-2334 Office: Fla Internat Univ Coll Edn Dept Founds University Park Miami FL 33199

DOTY, DALE VANCE, psychotherapist, hypnotherapist; b. Rochester, N.Y., Apr. 11, 1954; s. Charles F. and E. Alta (Smith) D.; m. Krisinte R. Krystan, Aug. 19, 1989; children: Bryce, Kimberly, David. BS, U. Rochester, 1974, MA, 1976; PhD, City U., 1990. Registered hypnotist. Tchr. N.Y. State Edn. Dept., Albany, N.Y., 1974—; psychotherapist Confidential Interpersonal Counseling, Hemlock, N.Y.; prof. psychology Monroe C.C., Rochester, St. John Fisher Coll., Rochester Inst. Tech., SUNY, Geneseo; coord./cons. AKSED Rehab.; cons. Highland Hosp.; drug edn. coord. Marketview Heights Assn.; speaker weekly radio program, 1990. Contbr. articles to profl. jours.; author ednl. progs. in field. EMT Henrietta (N.Y.) Vol. Ambulance, 1975-90, Honeoye Falls (N.Y.) Vol. Ambulance, 1979-85; counseling specialist Chances and Changes/Domestic Violence, Geneseo, N.Y., 1990—; instr. Nat. Red Cross. Mem. Am. Assn. Counseling (assoc.), Am. Mental Health Counselors, Am. Coll. Pers. Assn., Am. Psychol. Practitioners Assn., Internat. Counselors and Therapists ASsn., Nat. Headache Found. Avocations: fishing, hunting, camping, music. Home: 5310 Curtis Rd Hemlock NY 14466-9619 Office: Confidential Interpersonal Counseling 5310 Curtis Rd Hemlock NY 14466 also: 94 Main St Geneseo NY 14454-1228

DOTY, DAVID SINGLETON, federal judge; b. Anoka, Minn., June 30, 1929. BA, U. Minn., 1961, LLB, 1961; LLD (hon.), William Mitchell Coll. Law. Bar: Minn. 1961, U.S. Ct. Appeals (8th and 9th cirs.) 1976, U.S. Supreme Ct. 1982. V.p., dir. Popham, Haik, Schnobrich, Kaufman & Doty, Mpls., 1962-87, pres., 1977-79; instr. William Mitchell Coll. Law, Mpls., 1963-64; judge U.S. Dist. Ct. for Minn., Mpls., 1987—. Mem. Adv. Com. on Civil Rules, 1992-98, Adv. Com. on Evidence Rules, 1994-98; trustee Mpls. Libr. Bd., 1969-79, Mpls. Found., 1976-83. Fellow ABA Found.; mem. ABA, Minn. Bar Assn. (gov. 1976-87, sec. 1980-83, pres. 1984-85), Hennepin County Bar Assn. (pres. 1975-76), Am. Judicature Soc., Am. Law Inst. Home: 23 Greenway Gables Minneapolis MN 55403-2145 Office: US Dist Ct 14 W US Courthouse 300 S 4th St Minneapolis MN 55415-1320

DOTY, DELLA CORRINE, organization administrator; b. Marshalltown, Iowa, Mar. 12, 1945; d. Edwin Francis and Della Edna (Keller) Mack; m. Philip Edward Doty, Dec. 23, 1967; children: Sarah Corrine, Anne Elizabeth. BSBA in Acctg., Drake U., 1967. CPA, Colo. Audit staff mem. Alexander Grant & Co. CPAs, Denver, 1967-71; controller Valley View Hosp. and Med. Ctr., Denver, 1971-75; rate rev. specialist Colo. Hosp. Assn., Denver, 1975-79; dir. Colo. Medicare Group Appeal Program, Littleton, 1979-91; assoc. dir. Comms. Inst., 1992-94; lectr. in field. Contbr. articles to profl. jours. Dir., asst. treas. YWCA of Metro Denver, 1972-74; bd. dirs. Colo. Heart Assn., 1974-82; dir. Families First, Inc., 1987-89, chmn., bd. dirs., 1988-89; trustee Colo. Children's Chorale, 1988-94, 95—, chmn., 1992-94; pres. Denver Symphony Debs, 1996, Alpha Phi Nat. Housing Corp., 1999—; mem. Jr. League of Denver, 1979—, v.p. mktg., 1985-86; sec. Littleton Pub. Schs. Bldg. Authority, 1983-86; active various charitable orgns.; v.p. fin. and housing Alpha Phi Internat., 1974-78, trustee, 1980-86; dir., treas. Alpha Phi Found., 1978-86. Recipient Founders Merit award Healthcare Fin. Mgmt. Assn., 1976, 83, Outstanding Vol. award Jr. League of Denver, 1984, Sustainer Cmty. Svc. award, 1994. Mem. Alpha Phi (nat. housing corp. pres. 1999—, Ursa Major award 1980). Republican. Baptist. Address: 5981 S Coventry Ln W Littleton CO 80123-6706

DOTY, DONALD D., retired banker; b. Independence, Kans., June 30, 1928; s. Laton L. and Dorothy (Russell) D.; m. Cheri F. Montgomery, June 14, 1952; children: John Scott, Susan Dorothy, Mark Montgomery. BS, Okla. State U., 1950; postgrad., U. Wis. Grad. Sch. Banking, 1963. Rancher nr. Bartlesville, Okla., 1950-94; asst. cashier First Nat. Bank, Bartlesville, 1956-58; asst. v.p. First Nat. Bank, 1958-60, v.p., 1964-69, exec. v.p., 1969-74; pres. WestStar Bank, n.a. (formerly First Nat. Bank), Bartlesville, 1974-93; also bd. dirs., retired, 1993; pres. First Bancshares, Inc., Bartlesville, 1974-93, bd. dirs.; chmn. S.W. Cattlemen's Credit Corp., 1979-90; pres. Bartlesville Credit Bur., 1972—; pres. Bartlesville-Area Indsl. Devel. Co., 1970—; chmn. First Okla. Life Ins. Co., Oklahoma City, 1990-95; chmn. Coll. Bus. Assocs., Okla. State U., 1991-92. Chmn. trustees Jane Phillips Episcopal Meml. Med. Ctr., 1970—; trustee Washington County Indsl. Devel. Trust Authority, 1973-80; chmn. Frank Phillips Found., bartlesville, 1975—; bd. trustees St. John Hosp., Tulsa. Capt. USAF, 1953-55. Named to Okla. State U., Coll. of Bus. Hall of Fame, 1994; recipient Disting. Svc. award Bartlesville, 1957. Mem. Am. Bankers Assn., Okla. Bankers Assn. (pres. 1984-85), Bartlesville C. of C. (v.p., bd. dirs. 1965-81, pres. 1981-82), Jaycees (Outstanding Young Man Bartlesville 1957, Okla. 1958), Masons, Shriners, Rotary, Sigma Alpha Epsilon. Republican. Episcopalian. Avocations: skiing, hunting, golf. Home: 1915 Hillcrest Dr Bartlesville OK 74003-6231

DOTY, GRESDNA ANN, education educator; b. Oelwein, Iowa, Feb. 22, 1931; d. James William and Gresdna (Wood) D.; m. James G. Traynham, Nov. 28, 1980. AA, Monticello Coll., Alton, Ill., 1951; BA, U. No. Iowa, 1953; MA, U. Fla., 1957; PhD, Ind. U., 1967. Instr. S.W. Tex. State U., San Marcos, 1957-61, asst. prof., 1964-65; asst. prof. La. State U., Baton Rouge, 1967-73, assoc. prof., 1973-79, dir. theatre, 1973-77, 81-91, prof., 1979-84, alumni prof., 1984—, alumni prof. emeritus, 1996—, chair dept. theatre, 1991-93. Author: Anne Brunton Merry in the American Theatre, 1971; co-editor: (with Billy J. Harbin) Inside the Royal Court Theatre, 1956-81: Artists Talk, 1990; contbr. articles to profl. jours. Bd. dirs. Arts Coun. Greater Baton Rouge, 1987—, pres., 1990-91. Rsch. grantee Nat. Endowment Humanities, 1981, Exxon Edn. Found., 1981. Fellow S.W. Theatre Assn.; mem. Am. Theatre Assn. (bd. dirs. 1977-80), Am. Coll. Theatre Festival (nat. chmn. 1976-79), Am. Soc. Theatre Rsch. (mem. exec. com. 1988-91, v.p. 1994-97), Nat. Theatre Conf., Assn. Theatre Higher Edn., Coll. of Fellow of Am. Theatre. Home: 122 Highland Trace Baton Rouge LA 70810-5061 Office: La State U Theatre 217 Da Bldg M Baton Rouge LA 70803

DOTY, HORACE JAY, JR., theater administrator, arts consultant; b. St. Petersburg, Fla., May 25, 1924; s. Horace Herndon and Mabel (Bruce) D.; student Sherwood Music Sch., Chgo., 1942-43; BA in Music, Pomona Coll., 1950; cert. La Verne Coll., 1969; MA in Edn., Claremont Grad. Sch., 1972; cert. in Bus. Adminstrn., 1984; m. Wanda L. Flory, Dec. 27, 1947; 1 child, Janet. Propr. Jay Doty's Inc., Claremont, 1960-68; concert mgr. Claremont Colls., 1968-73, supr. Garrison Theater, U. Ctr. Box Office, dir. Auditorium, theater events, coordinator programs, 1973-79, 81-90; exec. dir. Flint Ctr. for Performing Arts, Cupertino, Calif., 1979-81. Mem. blue ribbon com. Fox Theater Restoration, Pomona, Calif., 1982; mem. Claremont Bicentennial Com. for Performing Arts, 1975-76; mem. touring adv. panel, cons. and site visitor Calif. Arts Council; mem. exec. bd., Calif. Presenters. Served with inf. AUS, 1943-46. NEA fellow, 1986. Mem. Assn. Coll., Univ. and Community Arts Adminstrs. (dir. 1983-86), Western Alliance Arts Adminstrs. (pres. 1975-77), Internat. Assn. Auditorium Mgrs., Claremont C. of C. (pres. 1965-66). Office: Jay Doty Arts Cons 4145 Oak Hollow Rd Claremont CA 91711-2329

DOTY, JAMES EDWARD, pastor, psychologist; b. Lakewood, Ohio, May 8, 1922; s. Ordello Luce and Margaret (McCurdy) D.; m. Mary Merciel Smith, Sept. 8, 1943; children: Mark Allen, David Wesley, Martha Suzanne. AB, Mt. Union Coll., Alliance, Ohio, 1944, DD (hon.), 1965; MDiv cum laude, Boston U., 1947, PhD, 1959; postgrad., Harvard U., Oxford U.; DD (hon.), DePauw U., 1966. Ordained to ministry Meth. Ch., 1945. Pastor in Salem, Mass., 1947-51, Lynn, Mass., 1951-57; founder, dir. Greater Lynn Pastoral Care and Counselling Ctr., 1954-57; dir. pastoral care and counselling Ind. Area Meth. Ch., 1957-66; pres. Baker U., 1966-73; pvt. practice pastoral psychology Corpus Christi, Tex., 1973—; exec. dir. Corpus Christi Pastoral Counselling Ctr., 1973-84; interim sr. pastor First United Methodist Ch., Corpus Christi, 1988-89; interim pastor 1st Presbyn. Ch., Portland, Tex., 1991-98; mem. staff Boston Ctr. Adult Edn., 1949-53; spl. lectr. Union Theol. Sem., Buenos Aires, 1962, Meth. Theol. Sem., Sao Paulo, Brazil, 1962, Epworth Theol. Sem., Salisbury, Rhodesia, 1963, Meth. Theol. Sem.,

Mulungwishi, Congo, 1964, Trinity Theol. Coll., Singapore, 1967, Union Theol. Sem., Manila, The Philippines, 1967, Gbanga Meth. Theol. Sem., Monrovia, Liberia, 1975, Meth. Theol. Sem., Suva, Fiji, 1986; mem. First Student Christian Movement Conf. in postwar Germany, Heidelberg U., summer 1947; del. World Family Life Consultation, Birmingham, Eng., 1966; chmn. World Family Life, 1981-86; mem. World Meth. Coun., London, 1966, Denver, 1971, Dublin, 1976, Honolulu, 1981; del. World Meth. Coun., Nairobi, Kenya, 1986, Singapore, 1991—; chmn. exec. com., chmn. bd. visitors Sch. Theology Boston U. Author: The Pastor as Agape Counselor, 1964, Postmark Lambarene: A Visit with Albert Schweitzer, 1965; editor: Authentic Man Encounters God's World, 1967, Students Search for Meaning, 1971, (with Merciel S. Doty) For Heaven's Sake, 1993, Albert Schweitzer: Reverence for Life, 1993, With Schweitzer in Africa, 1994; producer, moderator weekly program Focus, Sta. KEDT-TV, 1984—. V.p. Pike Twp. Sch. Bd., Marion County, Ind., 1960-66. Recipient Alumni of Year award Mt. Union Coll., 1963, Alumni award of merit, Boston U., 1969. Mem. APA, S.W. Conf. United Meth. Ch., Tex. Bd. Profl. Counselors, Am. Bd. Sexology (diplomate), Am. Assn. Pastoral Counselors (diplomate, bd. dirs.), Am. Assn. Marriage and Family Therapy, Am. Assn. Sex. Educators, Counselors and Therapists, Town Club, Rotary, Sigma Alpha Epsilon, Zeta Chi. Home: 102 Lakeshore Dr Corpus Christi TX 78413-2635 Office: 4838 Holly Rd Ste 204 Corpus Christi TX 78411-4754

DOTY, JAMES ROBERT, lawyer; b. Houston, May 14, 1940; s. Robert Earl and Vivian (Weaver) D.; m. Joan Stewart Richardson, June 10, 1972; children: Katherine Brooks, Robert Daniel. BA, Rice U., 1962; AB, Oxford U., Eng., 1964; MA, Harvard U., 1966; LLB, Yale U., 1969. Bar: Tex. 1969, D.C. 1988, U.S. Supreme Ct., U.S. Ct. Appeals (D.C. cir.). Ptnr. Baker & Botts, Washington, 1977-90; gen. counsel SEC, Washington, 1990-92; sr. ptnr. Baker & Botts, Washington, 1992—. Contbr. articles to profl. jours. Rhodes scholar Oxford U., 1962-64. Mem. ABA, Fed. Bar Assn. (exec. bd.), State Bar Tex., Houston Bar Assn., D.C. Bar Assn., Am. Law Inst., D.C. Bar Ct.

DOTY, MAXENE STANSELL, psychologist, retired; b. May 13, 1935. BA, Ohio State U., 1978, MA, 1980, PhD, 1984. Psychologist Southwest Cmty. Health Ctr., Columbus, Ohio, 1983-85; pvt. practice Columbus, Ohio, 1985-87; staff Counseling Ctr., U. Maine, Orono, 1987-97, ret., 1997. Mem. Phi Beta Kappa. E-mail: mdoty@acadia.net. Home: RR 1 Box 790 Surry ME 04684-9710

DOTY, PAUL MEAD, biochemist, educator, arms control specialist; b. Charleston, W.Va., June 1, 1920; s. Paul Mead and Maud (Stewart) D.; m. Margaretta Elenor Grevatt, Oct. 31, 1942 (div. Aug. 1953); 1 child, Gordon Sutherland; m. Helga Boedtker, Feb. 27, 1954; children: Marcia, Rebecca, Katherine. BS, Pa. State Coll., 1941; MA, Columbia U., 1943, PhD, 1944; DSc, U. Chgo., 1966. From instr. to asst. prof. chemistry Poly. Inst. Bklyn., 1943-46; Rockefeller fellow Cambridge (Eng.) U., 1946-47; asst. prof. chemistry U. Notre Dame, South Bend, Ind., 1947-48; asst. prof. chemistry Harvard U., Cambridge, Mass., 1948-50, prof. chemistry, 1950-68, Mallinckrodt prof. biochemistry, 1968-88, prof. pub. policy Kennedy Sch., 1988-90, prof. biochemistry emeritus, 1988—, prof. pub. policy emeritus, 1990—; dir. Ctr. for Sci. and Internat. Affaris, Harvard U., 1973-85, dir. emeritus, 1985—; mem. Pres.'s Sci. Adv. Commn., White House, Washington, 1961-64; mem. gen. adv. com. on arms control to Pres., White House, 1976-80; bd. dirs., vice chmn. Mitre Corp., Bedford, Mass., 1975-92; bd. dirs. Internat. Sci. Found., Washington, 1993-97. Editor: Defending Deterrence: Managing the ABM Treaty, 1989; founder, editor quar. jour. Internat. Security, 1975-85; author more than 350 articles. Bd. dirs. Aspen Inst. Berlin, 1981—, Harriman Inst., Columbia U., 1986—; mem. Aspen Inst. for Humanitsic Studies, Wye, Md., 1969-85; mem. Pugwash Confs., 1957-97. Recipient Pure Chemistry award Am. Chem. Soc., 1956. Mem. Am. Acad. Arts and Sci. (commn. on internat. security), Nat. Acad. Sci. (com. on internat. security and arms control), Am. Philos. Soc. Home: 4 Kirkland Pl Cambridge MA 02138-2034 Office: Kennedy Sch Govt Harvard U 79 Jfk St Cambridge MA 02138-5801

DOTY, PHILIP EDWARD, accountant; b. Red Oak, Iowa, Dec. 9, 1943; s. Wade Bryan and Vera Mae (Dodd) D.; m. Della Corrine Mack, Dec. 23, 1967; children: Sarah, Anne. BSBA, Drake U., 1967. CPA, Colo. Ptnr. Arthur Andersen LLP, Denver, 1967—, dir. oil and gas practice and tng., 1987-89. Treas. Mile High United Way, Denver, 1984-88, bd. dirs., 1998—; treas. Mile High br. Girl Scouts U.S.A., 1987-92; bd. dirs. Leadership Denver Assn., 1987-89, Artreach, Inc., Denver, 1986-89, Colo. Ballet, 1992-98; mem. exec. bd. Denver Area coun. Boy Scouts Am., 1998—. With USAR, 1967-73. Mem. AICPA (nat. coun. 1994-97), Am. Petroleum Inst., Petroleum Accts. Soc. (pres. 1989), Ind. Petroleum Assn. Mountain States (bd. dirs. 1987-97, treas. 1991-92), Colo. Soc. CPA's (pres. 1994), Denver Petroleum Club (sec.-treas. 1988-91, Man of Yr. award 1993, bd. dirs. 1997—), Columbine Country Club, Classic Car Club Am. (dir. Colo. region 1996-98), Beta Gamma Sigma. Republican. Baptist. Avocations: classic cars, skiing, hunting.

DOTY, RICHARD LEROY, medical researcher; b. Boulder, Colo., Oct. 14, 1944; s. George David and Frances Amelia (Bradley) D. BS, Colo. State U., 1966; MA, Calif. State U., 1968; PhD, Mich. State U., 1971; postgrad., U. Calif., Berkeley, 1973. Instr. dept. psychology Calif. State U., San Francisco, 1971-72, U. San Francisco, 1971-72; asst. mem. Monell Chem. Senses Ctr., Phila., 1974-76, assoc. mem., head human olfaction sect., 1976-78; dir. smell and taste ctr. Hosp. U. Pa., Phila., 1979—; dir. smell and taste ctr. Sch. Medicine, U. Pa., Phila., 1980—, asst. prof. dept. otorhinolaryngology, human communication, 1983-89, assoc. prof., 1989-93; prof. dept. otorhinolaryngology U. Pa., Phila., 1994—; cons. in field; lectr. in field; editorial cons. for numerous profl. jours.; external adv. bd. Taste and Smell Ctr. U. Conn./Yale U., 1982-84, Rocky Mountain Taste and Smell Ctr., U. Colo. Sch. Medicine, 1985, Mayo Found. Project, 1989; internat. adv. bd. 1st Internat. Congress on Food and Health, Salsomaggiore Terme, Italy, 1985. Author: The Smell Identification Test (TM) Administration Manual, 1983, 2d edit., 1989, 3d edit., 1995; editor: Mammalian Olfaction, Reproductive Processes and Behavior, 1976, Handbook of Olfaction and Gustation, 1995; co-editor: (with T.V. Getchell, E.P. Koster) Chemical Senses, spl. edit., 1981, (with D.G. Laing, W. Breopohl) Human Olfaction, 1990, (with L.M. Bartoshuk, T.V. Getchell and J.B. Snow) Smell and Taste in Health Disease, 1991, (with D. Muller-Schwartze) Chemical Signals in Vertebrates VI, 1992. NIH postdoctoral rsch. fellow, 1973-75; grantee Nat. Inst. on Aging, 1989-91, Nat. Inst. Deafness and Other Comm. Disorders, 1980—. Mem. European Chemoreception Rsch. Orgn. (mem. organizational com. 1981), Assn. for Chemoreception Scis. (mem. program com. 1985, 87, mem. elections com. 1987), AAAS, N.Y. Acad. Scis., Assn. for Rsch. in Otolaryngology, Am. Acad. Otolaryngology (head and neck surgery), Am. Psychol. Assn., Internat. Soc. for Chem. Ecology, Phila. Coll. Physicians (mem. adv. com., sect. on geriatrics and gerontology). Home: 125 White Horse Pike Haddon Heights NJ 08035-1909 Office: U Pa Smell & Taste Ctr 5 Ravdin Bldg 3400 Spruce St Philadelphia PA 19104-4204

DOTY, ROBERT WALTER, lawyer; b. Aliquippa, Pa., Sept. 19, 1942; s. David Lucien and Iona (Fox) D.; m. Joyce Marie Shaffalo, Sept. 10, 1961; children: Genie, Merrie Beth. BA cum laude, Wheaton Coll., 1963; JD, Vanderbilt U., 1966. Bar: Pa. 1966, U.S. Supreme Ct. 1982. Assoc. Eckert Seamans Cherin & Mellot, Pitts., 1966-74, ptnr., 1975-91; dir. Cohen & Grigsby, P.C., Pitts., 1991—; solicitor Crescent Township, Allegheny County, Pa., 1969—; arbitrator Am. Arbitration Assn., nat. panel, 1978—, speaker at seminars; lectr. Westinghouse Internat. Sch. Environ. Mgmt., Ft. Collins, Colo., 1980-82. Mem. nat. com. on wills and trusts centennial campaign Vanderbilt U., 1977-81. Recipient Archie B. Martin Meml. scholarship medal Vanderbilt U., 1964, Robert F. Jackson Meml. scholarship prize, 1965, Founder's medal, 1966; 3 Am. Jurisprudence awards in contracts, civil procedure and criminal law The Lawyers Co-operative Pub. Co., Rochester, N.Y., 1964, 65; Mark Woodworth Walton scholar Vanderbilt U., 1965. Mem. Pa. Bar Assn., Allegheny County Bar Assn. (governing coun. civil litigation sect.), Duquesne Club, YMCA, Wheaton Club (past pres.), Fox Chapel Racquet Club, Order of Coif, Phi Kappa Delta, Phi Alpha Delta. Avocations: swimming, hiking, tennis. Office: 11 Stanwix St 15th Floor Pittsburgh PA 15222

DOTY, ROBERT WILLIAM, neurophysiologist, educator; b. New Rochelle, N.Y., Jan. 10, 1920; s. Earle Birdsell and Ethel Laurette (Mack) D.; m. Elizabeth Natalie Jusewich, Aug. 30, 1941; children—Robert William, Mary E., Cheryl A., Richard M. B.S., U. Chgo., 1948, M.S., 1949, Ph.D., 1950. Postdoctoral fellow U. Ill., Chgo., 1950-51; asst. prof. U. Utah, Salt Lake City, 1951-56; from asst. to assoc. prof. U. Mich., Ann Arbor, 1956-61; prof. U. Rochester, N.Y., 1961—; vis. prof. U. Mex., 1975, U. Osaka, Japan, 1981; sci. adviser NIMH, Bethesda, Md., 1975-79, Yerkes Inst., Atlanta, 1975-78. Assoc. editor: Acta Neurobiologiae, Warsaw, 1971—, Behavioral Brain Research, 1981—; contbr. articles to profl. jours. Served to capt. U.S. Army, 1942-46. Recipient Javits award, Nat. Inst. Neurol. and Communicative Disorders and Stroke., NIH, 1986. Fellow AAAS; mem. Am. Psychol. Soc. (pres. div. 6, 1984), Internat. Brain Research Orgn., Current Anthropology (assoc.), Soc. for Neurosci. (pres. 1975-76, councilor 1970-74). Avocations: photography; history; langs. Office: Box 603 U Rochester Med Ctr Neurobiology and Anatomy Rochester NY 14642

DOTY, SHAYNE TAYLOR, organist; b. Memphis, Aug. 19, 1961; s. Robert Allen and Janice Moffet Doty. BA, Duke U., 1983; diploma, Conservatoire Nat. Superieur Musique Lyon, 1986; MM, So. Meth. U., 1991. Rsch. assoc. Capital Campaign for Arts and Scis., Duke U., 1983-84; organist, choirmaster St. Paul's Episcopal Ch., Washington, 1991-98; organist Am. Cath., Paris, 1995-96; asst. dir. corp. and found. rels. U. Md., College Park, 1997-98; sr. major gift officer Met. Opera Assn., N.Y.C., 1998—. Organ recitalist including St. Denis, Paris, St. Paul's, Toronto, Nat. Cathedral, Washington; ensembles Les Arts Florissants, Washington Bach Consort, N.C. Symphony and Winston-Salem Symphony. Mary Duke Biddle scholarship Duke U., 1979-83; Frank Huntington Beebe fellow, 1984-86. Mem. Assn. of Anglican Musicians, Royal Sch. of Ch. Music, Am. Guild of Organists. Episcopalian. Office: Met Opera Assn Lincoln Ctr New York NY 10023

DOTY, WILLIAM GUY, religious studies/humanities educator; b. Ratón, N.Mex., Aug. 7, 1939; s. William Henry and Marcia Constance (Freeman) D.; m. Joan T. Mallonée, Sept. 7, 1965. BA, U. N.Mex., 1961; MDiv, San Francisco Theol. Sem., 1963; PhD, Drew U., 1966. Instr. religion Rutgers U., 1965-66; instr. Garrett Theol. Sem., 1966-67; lectr. Vassar Coll., Poughkeepsie, N.Y., 1967-68; asst. prof. Douglass Coll., Rutgers U., New Brunswick, N.J., 1968-75; vis. lectr. in classics U. Mass., Amherst, 1976-77; mem. faculty Goddard Coll., Plainfield, Vt., 1978-80; assoc. prof. dept. religious studies U. Ala., Tuscaloosa, 1981-82, prof., 1982—, dept. chair, 1983-88, rsch. prof., 1991—; vis. assoc. prof. Hampshire Coll., Amherst, 1978; mem. faculty, program advisor Beacon Coll., Boston, 1978-82; vis. scholar Emory U., 1988, adj. faculty, 1989-90, 1992-93, 97-99; judge Carlie Meml. Prize. Author: Contemporary New Testament Interpretation, 1972, Letters in Primitive Christianity, 1973, Mythography: The Study of Myths and Rituals, 1986 (named Outstanding Acad. Book, Choice mag. 1987); also articles; editor: The Daemonic Imagination: Biblical Text and Secular Story, 1990; (with Wendell C. Beane) Myths, Rites, Symbols: A Mircea Eliade Reader, 1976; translator: Candid Questions Concerning Gospel Form Criticism: A Methodological Sketch of the Fundamental Problematics of Form and Redaction Criticism (Erhardt Güttgemanns), 1979; editor (with Norman R. Petersen) Semeia jour., 1976; guest editor Archê jour., 1981; co-editor Issues in Integrative Studies, 1991; exhbns. include Festival for the Arts, Somerset County Coll., Bicentennial History Exhbn., 1976; contbr. photography and photog. reproductions to: Portrait of a Village: A History Of Millstone. Pres. exec. com. Friends of Arboretum, Tuscaloosa; bd. dirs. com. on traditional arts of Ams., Africa, and Oceania Birmingham Mus. Art, 1987-88. Recipient Alumni Achievement award Alumni Soc. of Grad. Sch./ Drew U., 1991; San Francisco Theol. Sem., Drew U., Alumni fellow San Francisco Theiol. Sem., Presbyn. Grad. fellow, B'nai B'rith fellow, 1970, Soc. for Religion in Higher Edn fellow, 1971-72, Woodrow Wilson Inst. fellow, 1986, 90; Mellon grantee, 1984, NEH grantee, 1984, 91; Goodwin-Philpott Eminent Scholar in History, Auburn U., 1997-98. Fellow Soc. for Values in Higher Edn. (editorial bd. Soundings: An Interdisciplinary Jour. 1980-93, bd. dirs. cen. com. 1987-90, guest editor 1988), mem. Am. Acad. Religion (coord. juries awards for excellence in study of religion com. 1987-93, rsch. grants selection com. 1999—), So. Humanities Coun. (del.-at-large exec. com. 1988-91). Home: 4343 Springhill Dr Tuscaloosa AL 35405-4746 Office: U Ala Dept Religious Studies Box 264 Tuscaloosa AL 35487-0264

DOUBLEDAY, CHARLES WILLIAM, dermatologist, educator; b. Houston, Oct. 1, 1954; s. Leonard Charles and Margaret (Walker) D.; m. Verlinde Van den Berge Hill, June 22, 1985; children: George Marchant, Julia Van den Berge, Walker Hill. BA with honors, U. Tex., Austin, 1976; MD, U. Tex., Houston, 1981. Diplomate Am. Bd. Dermatology, 1987. Rotating intern John Peter Smith Hosp., Ft. Worth, 1981-82; resident in dermatology U. Tex. Med. Sch., 1982-83, 85-87, fellow in dermatology, 1985; clin. asst. prof. dermatology, 1988—; pvt. practice, Houston, 1987—. Contbr. articles to med. jours. Recipient high sci. quality award Soc. for Investigative Dermatology, 1986; rsch. fellow Dermatology Found., 1985. Fellow Am. Acad. Dermatology; mem. Tex. Med. Assn., Harris County Med. Soc., Tex. Dermatol. Soc., Houston Dermatol. Soc., U. Tex. Houston Health Sci. Ctr. (devel. coun., 1994-96), bd. dirs. Republic Nat. Bank, The Park People, mem. Houston Country Club. Republican. Episcopalian. Avocations: tennis. golf. Office: 515 Post Oak Blvd Ste 535 Houston TX 77027-9494

DOUBLEDAY, NELSON, professional baseball team executive. Grad., Princeton, 1954. With Doubleday & Co. Inc., N.Y.C., 1954-56, from 59, former pres., chief exec. officer, chmn. bd. dirs.; chmn. bd., majority owner N.Y. Mets Baseball Team, 1980—. Served with USAF, 1956-59. Office: NY Mets 123-10 Roosevelt Ave Flushing NY 11368-1600*

DOUBLEDAY, SIMON RICHARD, historian; b. Bournemouth, Eng., Sept. 24, 1966; came to U.S., 1989; s. E. Richard and C. Alison (Chaplin) D. BA in History with 1st class honours, Cambridge (Eng.) U., 1988; PhD in History, Harvard U., 1996. Asst. prof. Hamilton Coll., Clinton, N.Y., 1996—. Home: 3805 Harding Rd Clinton NY 13323 Office: Hamilton Coll Dept History Clinton NY 13323

DOUCETTE, BETTY, public and community health and geriatrics nurse; b. Mosinee, Wis., Jan. 29, 1924; d. Wenzel and Margretta (Brietenstein) Vavra; m. Nieland R. Doucette, Nov. 12, 1949; children: Tom, Bob, Dan, John, Carol, Bill, Jeanne, Sue, Judy. Diploma, St. Marys Hosp. Sch. Nursing, Wausau, Wis., 1945; student, Nicolet Coll. and Tech. Inst., Rhinelander, Wis., 1971-81, Viterbo Coll., LaCrosse, Wis., 1982. Cert. pub. health nurse. Supr. med. ward St. Marys Hosp., Wausau, 1945-49; indsl. nurse Owens-Ill. Mill, Tomahawk, 1964-69; nurse supr. Golden Age Nursing Home, Tomahawk, Wis., 1969-78; home care nurse Lincoln County Nursing Svcs., Merrill, Wis., 1978-91; RN Lincoln County Health Bd., 1994—.

DOUCETTE, DAVID ROBERT, computer systems company executive; b. Pitts., Feb. 2, 1946; s. Adrian Robert and Mary Alyce (Newland) D. BSEE cum laude, Poly. Inst. Bklyn., 1968, MSEE, 1970, PhD, 1974. Asst. prof. electrical engring. Poly. Inst. N.Y. (now Poly. U.), 1973-74, assoc. prof. computer sci., 1975-82, prof., 1982—, dir., 1994—, assoc. dean, 1997—; sr. staff specialist advanced planning Gruman Data Sys. Corp., Bethpage, N.Y., 1979-80, program mgr., 1979-80, mgr. graphics sys., 1980-84, from asst. dir. to dir. interactive sys. support, 1984-86; dir. interactive sys. Gruman Data Sys., Corp., Bethpage, N.Y., 1986-94; pres., CEO D3Software Corp., 1994—. Active Friends of L.I. Heritage, Nassau County Hist. Soc., Garden City Hist. Soc. Recipient Achievement award Engrs. Joint Coun. L.I., 1999. Mem. IEEE (past sect. chmn., Centennial medal), Assn. Computing Machinery (past chpt. chmn.), L.I. Forum for Tech. (past dir.), AIAA (past sect. dir.), Nat. Space Soc., Planetary Soc., Nat. Eagle Scout Assn., Sigma Xi, Tau Beta Pi, Eta Kappa Nu, L.I. Early Fliers Club. Office: Poly U Dept Computer/Info Sci 901 Route 110 Farmingdale NY 11735-3906

DOUCETTE, MARY-ALYCE, computer company executive; b. Pitts., Feb. 12, 1924; d. Andrew George and Alice Jane (Sloan) Newland; m. Adrian Robert Doucette, Feb. 6, 1945 (dec. June 1983); children: David Robert, Regis Robert. BS cum laude, U. Pitts., 1945. Mgr. Newland Bros., Millvale, Pa., 1946-53; gen. mgr. Newland-Ludlo, Pitts., 1953-72; mgmt. cons. D3 Software, Garden City, N.Y., 1972-80, sec., corp. officer, 1980—. Fin. sec. Cerebral Palsy Assn., Garden City, Helen Keller Svcs. for Blind, Garden City; mem. Winthrop-U. Hosp. Aux., Mercy League, Friends of Adelphi Univ. Libr., Friends of Hist. St. George Ch. of Hempstead, N.Y., Adv. Coun. for Continuing Edn., Garden City Sch. Dist., 1988—. Mem. AAUW, L.I. Panhellenic, Univ. Club, Nassau County Hist. Soc. (life), Garden City Hist. Soc., Community Club Garden City-Hempstead, Woman's Club Garden City, Alpha Delta Pi, Pi Lambda Theta. Home: 146 Washington Ave Garden City NY 11530-3013 Office: D3 Software PO Box 8051 Garden City NY 11530-8051

DOUD, WALLACE C., retired information systems executive; b. Bellingham, Wash., Feb. 25, 1925; s. Forrest Roy and Florence (Pollock) D.; m. Marjorie K. Fenton, Oct. 25, 1949 (dec. 1962); children: Forrest J., Mary, Margaret, Barbara, Melissa; m. Janice F. Freudenberg, June 15, 1963 (dec. 1978); children: Michael, Karen; m. Jean A. Kennedy, Oct. 13, 1979. BBA, U. Wis., 1948; DHL (hon.), Mercy Coll., 1983. Salesman IBM Corp., Milw., St. Paul, Detroit; dir. patent relations IBM Corp., Armonk, N.Y., 1960-71, v.p. services staff, 1971-77, v.p. comml. and industry rels., 1977-85. Chmn. Bd. Parks and Recreation White Plains, N.Y., 1983-84; chmn., pres. United Way, White Plains, 1975-80. Recipient Youth Services award B'nai B'rith, 1972, Medallion Westchester Community Coll., 1980. Mem. Whippoorwill Club, Country Club of Fla., Little Club, Megunticook Golf Club, St. Andrews Club. Republican. Presbyterian.

DOUDS, VIRGINIA LEE, elementary education educator; b. Pitts., Jan. 17, 1943; d. Leland Ray and Virginia Helen (Dodds) Frazier; m. William Wallace Douds, June 20, 1964; children: William Stewart Douds, Michael Leland Douds. BA in Elem. Edn., Westminster Coll., New Wilmington, Pa., 1964; MA (Master's Equivalency), Dept. Edn., State of Pa., 1990. Cert. elem. tchr., Pa. Elem. tchr./non-graded Good Hope Elem. Sch., Glendale-Riverhills, Wis., 1964-65; elem. tchr./1st grade Carlisle Elem. Sch., Delaware, Ohio, 1965-66; elem. tchr./3rd grade Meml. Elem. Sch., Bethel Park, Pa., 1973-74; elem. tchr./1st and 3rd grades Logan Elem. Sch., Bethel Park, 1974-91; elem. tchr./3rd grade Neil Armstrong Elem. Sch., Bethel Park, 1991—; software cons. Coal Kids, U.S. Dept. Mines, 1993; mem. lang. arts, reading com. Bethel Park Schs., 1989—, SIP scholarship com. Bethel Park Fedn. Tcrhs., 1973—; cooperating tchr. Bethel Parks Schs., 1986—; mentor tchr. Bethel Park Schs., 1992-93, 95—; mem. instrnl. support team Bethel Park Schs., 1988-91; mem. Mid. States Accreditation com., 1993-94, strategic planning com., 1994-95. Mem. alumni coun. exec. bd. Westminster Coll., 1979-83; mem. exec. bd. Parents Assn., 1985-89. Recipient mini grant/ writing, publishing ctr. Bethel Park Schs., 1989, Gift of Time tribute Am. Family Inst., 1990, 91, All Star Educator award U. Pitts./Pitts. Post Gazette, 1996. Mem. Nat. Coun. Tchrs. of English, Bethel Park Fedn. Tchrs., PTO. Republican. Presbyterian. Avocations: reading, gardening, golf. Home: 2679 Burnsdale Dr Bethel Park PA 15102-2005

DOUGAL, ARWIN ADELBERT, electrical engineer, educator; b. Dunlap, Iowa, Nov. 22, 1926; s. Adelbert Isaac and Goldya (White) D.; m. Margaret Jane McLennan, Sept. 3, 1951; children: Catherine Ann, Roger Adelbert, Leonard Harley, Laura Beth. B.S., Iowa State U., 1952; M.S., U. Ill., 1955, Ph.D., 1957. Registered profl. engr., Tex. Radio engr. Collins Radio Co., Cedar Rapids, Iowa, 1952; research asst., research asso., asst. prof., asso. prof. U. Ill., Urbana, 1952-61; prof., mem. grad. faculty, dir. labs. for electronics and related sci. research U. Tex., Austin, 1961-67; prof. U. Tex., 1969—; dir. Electronics Research Center, 1971-77, sec. grad. assembly, 1972-74; dir. Austron, Inc., 1977-82; asst. dir. def. research and engring. for research Office Sec. Def., Washington, 1967-69; cons. Tex. Instruments, Inc., Dallas, Gen. Dynamics Corp., Ft. Worth, U. Calif. Los Alamos Sci. Lab. Contbr. articles to profl. jours. Faculty sponsor U. Tex. Conservative Democrats Club, 1966-67; sr. mem. CAP, 1984—; elder local Presbyn. Ch. With USAF, 1946-49. Recipient Teaching Excellence awards U. Tex. Students Assn., 1962, 63, Spl. award for outstanding service as program chmn. S.W. IEEE Conf. and Exhbn., 1967; Outstanding Grad. Adviser award Grad. Engring. Council, U. Tex., 1971; Disting. Advisor award Grad. Engring. Council, U. Tex., 1977, 84; Teaching Achievement award Grad. Engring. Council, U. Tex., 1977; Profl. Achievement citation in engring. Iowa State U. Alumni Assn., 1975. Fellow Am. Phys. Soc., IEEE (dir. 1980-81, Centennial medal 1984, Student Br. citation 1988, Outstanding Br. Counselor award, 1991, chmn. ctrl. Tex. sect. 1993-94); mem. Am. Soc. Engring. Edn., Hill Country Yacht Club, Sigma Xi, Phi Kappa Phi, Tau Beta Pi, Eta Kappa Nu, Pi Mu Epsilon, Phi Eta Sigma. Home: 6115 Rickey Dr Austin TX 78757-4437

DOUGAN, DEBORAH RAE, neuropsychology professional; b. Urbana, Ill., Jan. 22, 1952; d. Francis William and Barbara Belle (Ash) D. BA in Psychology, U. Ill., 1973; MA in Counseling, Gov.'s State U., 1978; PhD in Neuropsychology, Oreg. State U., 1982. Lic. psychol. assoc., Tex. Staff therapist Ozark Community Mental Health, Joplin, Mo., 1982-85; neuropsychol. cons. Tex. Commn. for Blind, Austin, 1985-87; psychol. assoc. Warm Springs Rehab. Hosp., Gonzales, Tex., 1987-88, Rehab. Hosp. South Tex., Corpus Christi, 1988-89; psychosocial dir. New Medico Rehab. Ctr., Lindale, Tex., 1989-90; clin. coord. Rainbow Rehab. Ctrs., Ft. Worth, 1991-93; neuropsychology profl. Cypress Creek Rehab. Ctr., Houston, 1993-95; coord. Strategic Stress Mgmt. Seminars, Houston, 1996—; predoctoral intern State Hosp., Vinita, Okla., 1981-82. Mem. APA, Tex. Head Injury Assn. (North Ctrl. chpt. bd. dirs., survivors coun. liaision 1991-93, survivors group leader Corpus Christi head injury chpt. 1988-89, Tyler (Tex.) head injury chpt. 1989-90, survivors group leader Ft. Worth head injury chpt. 1991-93, vice chair chpt. rels. state orgn. 1994-96, bd. dirs., sec. Houston chpt. 1995-96), Toastmasters Internat. Avocations: jazzercise, computer, house plants. Home and Office: Apt 3110 21717 Inverness Forest Blvd Houston TX 77073-1354

DOUGHERTY, BARBARA LEE, artist, writer; b. L.A., Apr. 25, 1949; d. Cliff and Muriel Tamarra (Rubin) Beck; m. Michael R. Dougherty, Feb. 10, 1970; children: Jessie, Luke, Elvi. BS in Fine Art, N.Y. State Coll., 1975. Staff writer South Coast Cmty. Newspapers, Santa Barbara, Calif., 1988-90; contbg. editor Art Calendar, Upper Fairmont, Md., 1991—; dir. mktg. Art Calendar, Frenchtown, Md., 1993-96, publ., 1997—; instr. art programs, 1975—; mem. City Adv. Bd. on Art, Santa Barbara, 1979-89, chmn., 1991-94; producer KCTV, Santa Barbara, 1990-94; CEO Harvest Am. Publs., 1992-93; judge for art shows Va. Ctr. for the Arts, 1998, Arts Atlantica, 1998, others. Author, artist: In Search of a Sunflower, 1992, Harvest California, 1990, Getting the Word Out, 1996, Getting Exposure, 1996; prodr. 4 videos on art, 1990—; contbr. articles to Mktg. Art, Sunshine Artists, 1996; one-woman show at Salisbury State U. Galleries, 1994. Fundraiser Boys and Girls Club of Am., Carpinteria, Calif., 1977-93; bd. dirs. Somerset County Art Coun., 1999. Recipient Best of Show award Hosp. Aux., Boulder, Nev., 1991, 1st place award Death Valley 49ers Club, 1989, 2d place award, 1990. Democrat. Roman Catholic. Home and Office: Babara Dougherty Inc PO Box 170 Upper Fairmount MD 21867-0170

DOUGHERTY, BETSEY OLENICK, architect; b. Guanatamo Bay, Cuba, Oct. 25, 1950; (parents Am. citizens); d. Everett and Charlotte (Kristal) Olenick; m. Brian Paul Dougherty, Aug. 25, 1974; children: Gray Brenner, Megan Victoria. AB in Architecture, U. Calif., Berkeley, 1972, MArch, 1975. Registered architect, Calif.; cert. Nat. Coun. Archtl. Registration Bds. Designer, drafter Maxwell Starkman, L.A., 1972-73, HO & K, San Francisco, 1975-76; job capt. Wm. Blurock & Ptnrs., Newport Beach, Calif., 1976-78; assoc. architect U. Calif., Irvine, 1978-79; arch. Dougherty & Dougherty, Costa Mesa, 1979—. Author: Green Architecture, 1995; contbr. articles to profl. jours. Mem. Newport Beach Specific Area Plan Com., 1985, Career Edn. Adv. com., Newport Beach, 1986; leader Girl Scouts U.S.A., Orange County Bd. Recipient Gold Nugget grand award Pacific Coast Builders Conf., 1998, Coalition for Adequate Sch. Housing award of excellence, 1992, 94, 96, Calif. Masonry award, 1992, So. Calif. Edison award of excellence, 1994, Disting. Svc. citation AIACC, 1994. Fellow AIA (pres. Orange County chpt. 1984, Calif. chpt. 1988, nat. bd. dirs. 1989-91, nat. sec. 1992-94, design awards Orange County chpt. 1981-86, 89-90, 98, Nathaniel Owings award Calif. Coun. 1997), Calif. Archtl. Found. (pres. 1995-97). Avocations: family, sailing, camping. Email: www.ddaia.com. Office: Dougherty & Dougherty 3194D Airport Loop Dr Costa Mesa CA 92626-3405

DOUGHERTY, CHARLES HAMILTON, pediatrician; b. St. Louis, June 1, 1947; s. Charles Joseph and Suzanne Louise (Hamilton) D.; m. Mary

Laverty Peckham, July 7, 1972; children: Bridget, Matthew, Erin, Kelly. BA in Biology, Coll. of the Holy Cross, 1969; MD, U. Rochester Sch. of Medicine, N.Y., 1973. Pediatric resident St. Louis Children's Hosp., 1973-76; pvt. practice pediatrics Primary Pediatric Care Group, St. Louis, 1976-86, Esse Health, St. Louis, 1986—. Fellow Am. Acad. Pediatrics. Roman Catholic. Avocations: marathon running, adventure vacations, computers, water sports, powered parachute pilot. Office: Esse Health 13303 Tesson Ferry Rd Saint Louis MO 63128-4062

DOUGHERTY, CHARLES JOHN, university administrator, philosophy and medical ethics educator; b. N.Y.C., June 28, 1949; s. Charles Aloysius and Mary Elizabeth (Quinn) D.; m. Sandra Lee Drabik; children: Constance Marie, Justin Charles. BA, St. Bonaventure U., 1971; MA, U. Notre Dame, 1973, PhD in Philosophy, 1975. Prof. philosophy Creighton U., Omaha, 1975-88, dir., Ctr. for Health Policy and Ethics, 1988-95, v.p. acad. affairs, 1995—. Author: Ideal, Fact, and Medicine, 1985, (with R.P. Heaney) Research for Health Professionals, 1988, American Health Care: Realities, Rights and Reforms, 1988, (with Jerry Cederblom) Ethics at Work, 1990, (with A. Haddad and B. Edwards) Ethical Dilemmas in Perioperative Nursing, 1990, Back to Reform, 1996; contbr. articles to profl. jours.; mem. bd. editors Health Progress, 1989—. Chmn. Nebr. Com. for the Humanities, Lincoln, 1987-88; bd. dirs. Fedn. of State Humanities Couns., 1986-89; mem. disciplinary rev. bd. Nebr. Supreme Ct., 1988—, Nebr. Accountability and Disclosure Commn., 1991—; bd. dirs. Sisters of Charity Health Sys. of Cin., 1994-96; bd. trustees Cath. Health Assn., 1995—. Mem. Am. Philos. Assn., Am. Catholic Philos. Assn. (exec. council mem. 1987-90), Alpha Sigma Nu. Democrat. Roman Catholic. Office: VP for Acad Affairs Creighton Univ Omaha NE 68178

DOUGHERTY, CHARLOTTE ANNE, financial planner, insurance and securities representative; b. Canton, Ohio, Nov. 9, 1947; d. Myron Martin and Wilma Rose Brown; m. John Edwin Dougherty, Jr., Feb. 14, 1976; 1 child, John Edwin. BA, Miami U., Oxford, Ohio, 1969; postgrad. Kent State U. (Ohio), 1971-73. Cert. fin. planner. Social worker Summit County Welfare, Akron, Ohio, 1971-73; research coordinator Tufts U., Medford, Mass., 1973-74; corp. recruiter Lincoln Nat. Sales Corp., Ft. Wayne, Ind., 1976-79; registered rep. Lincoln Nat. Life, Cin., 1980—, LNC Equity Sales Corp., Cin., 1989—. Contbr. articles to profl. jours. Mem. Inst. Cert. Fin. Planners, Internat. Assn. Fin. Planners (v.p. Cin. chpt. 1990—), Internat. Assn. for Fin. Planning (pres.-elect Cin. chpt. 1991, pres. 1992-93), Nat. Assn. Life Underwriters, Cin. Assn. Life Underwriters. Office: Oxford Fin Group 8044 Montgomery Rd Ste 400W Cincinnati OH 45236-2919

DOUGHERTY, DANA DEAN LESLEY, television producer, educator; b. Birmingham, Ala.; d. Paul Russell and Daisy Dean (Dunham) Lesley; m. Floyd Wallace Dougherty; 1 child, Lesley Dean. BS in Secondary and Bus. Edn., Speech Therapy, Drama, Auburn U., 1968. Cert. elem. tchr., Ala. Tchr. speech, drama, computer typing, shorthand, acctg., bus. law Jefferson State Jr. Coll., Birmingham, 1968-73; office mgr. Baker, McDaniel & Hall, Birmingham, 1973-78; tchr. Mountain Brook Bd. Edn., Birmingham, 1979—; producer, dir. drama and music TV show Dean and Company, Birmingham, 1980—; corp. sec. F.W. Dougherty Engrs. and Assocs. Inc., 1987—. Composer various songs. Mem. Arlington Hist. Soc.; mem. women's com. Ala. Ballet, Salvation Army Women's Aux. Recipient numerous awards Birmingham Cable TV, 1981-89, Cable TV Vulcan award, 1989-90, 90-91, World Poetry Golden Poet award, 1990, 91, Silver poet award, 1991. Mem. ALA, Poetry Soc., Actors and Theatre Guild, So. Bus. Edn. Assn., Ala. Assn. Legal Secs., Ala. Theater Orgn. Soc., Ala. Cable Network Affiliates, Nat. Theater Orgn. Soc., Jr. Women's C. of C., Thalian Lit. Club (Woman of Yr. award 1994—), Arlington Hist. Soc., Nat. Bus. Edn. Assn., Quill Club (libr. award, libr. writing award), Beta Sigma Phi. Baptist. Avocations: children's puppet workshops, crocheting, costuming puppets, piano and organ music, singing. Office: Dean and Co 2441 Old Springville Rd Birmingham AL 35215-4053

DOUGHERTY, DENNIS A., chemistry educator; b. Harrisburg, Pa., Dec. 4, 1952; s. John E. and Colleen (Canning) D.; m. Ellen M. Donnelly, June 3, 1973; children: Meghan, Kayla. BS, MS, Bucknell U., 1974; PhD, Princeton U., 1978. Postdoctoral fellow Yale U., New Haven, 1978-79; asst. prof. Calif. Inst. Tech., Pasadena, 1979-85, assoc. prof. chemistry, 1985-89, prof., 1989—. Contbr. articles to sci. jours. Recipient ICI Pharms. award for excellence in chemistry, 1991, Arthur C. Cope Scholar award, 1992; Alfred P. Sloan Found. fellow, 1983; Camille and Henry Dreyfus Tchr. scholar, 1984. Fellow Am. Acad. Arts and Scis.; mem. Am. Chem. Soc., Phi Beta Kappa. Home: 1817 Bushnell Ave South Pasadena CA 91030-4905 Office: Calif Inst Tech Div Chemistry & Chem Engring Calif Inst Tech # 164-30 Pasadena CA 91125

DOUGHERTY, ELMER LLOYD, JR., retired chemical engineering educator, consultant; b. Dorrance, Kans., Feb. 7, 1930; s. Elmer Lloyd and Nettie Linda (Anspaugh) D.; m. Joan Victoria Benton, Nov. 25, 1952 (div. June 1963); children: Sharon, Victoria, Timothy, Michael (dec.); m. Ann Marie Da Silva. Student, Ft. Hays State Coll., 1946-48; B.S. in Chem. Engring., U. Kans., 1950; M.S. in Chem. Engring., U. Ill., 1952, Ph.D. in Chem. Engring., 1955. Chem. engr. Esso Standard Oil Co., Baton Rouge, 1951-52; chem. engr. Dow Chem. Co., Freeport, Tex., 1955-58; research engr. Standard Oil of Calif., San Francisco, 1958-65; mgr. mgmt. sci. Union Carbide Corp., N.Y.C., 1965-68; cons. chem. engring. Stamford, Conn. and Denver, 1968-71; founder and owner Maraco, Inc., Monarch Beach, Calif., 1980—; prof. chem. engring. U. So. Calif., L.A., 1971-95, prof. emeritus, 1995—; cons. OPEC, Vienna Austria, 1978-82, SANTOS, Ltd., Adelaide, Australia, 1980—, Kuwait Oil Co., 1995—. Contbr. numerous articles to profl. jours. Mem. Soc. Petroleum Engrs. (Disting. mem., chmn. Los Angeles Basin sect. 1984-85, Ferguson medal 1964, J.J. Arps award 1989), Am. Inst. Chem. Engrs., Internat. Assn. Energy Economists, Inst. Mgmt. Sci. Republican. Clubs: El Niguel Country (bd. dirs. 1976-78) (Laguna Niguel, Calif.). Avocation: golf. Home: 33531 Marlinspike Dr Monarch Beach CA 92629-4426 Office: Maraco Inc 33531 Marlinspike Dr Monarch Beach CA 92629-4426

DOUGHERTY, FLOYD WALLACE, design engineer; b. Birmingham, Ala., Oct. 25, 1942; s. Floyd Patrick and Mary Josephine (Wallace) D.; m. Dana Dean Lesley, Sept. 2; 1 child, Lesley Dean. BS, Auburn U., 1966; BSCE, U. Ala., 1970. Registered prof. engr., Ala., Miss., Ga. Design engr. Paul B. Krebs & Assocs., Birmingham, Ala., 1967-87; pres., owner F.W. Dougherty Engring. & Assocs., Birmingham, Ala., 1987—. Dir. Dean & Co. Cmty. TV Show, Birmingham, 1980—. Sgt. U.S. Army Corp Engrs. Mem. ASCE, Am. Water Works Assn., Ala. Water & Pollution Control Assn., Water Environment Fedn. (George W. White award 1996). Republican. Baptist. Avocations: fishing, skiing.

DOUGHERTY, F(RANCIS) KELLY, data processing executive; b. Lubbock, Tex., May 15, 1953; s. Francis Kelly and Mary Ann (Odell) D.; m. Bonnie Lee Burch, June 14, 1975; children: Anne Katherine, Margaret Erin, Mary Bridget, Kerry Meaghan, Frances Cara. BA in Math. and Physics summa cum laude, U. Dallas, 1975; MS in Computer Sci., U. Tex., Dallas, 1998; cert. assoc. customer svc. Life Office Mgmt. Inst., 1992. CLU; cert. computing profl.; chartered fin. cons.; Microsoft cert. programmer. Actuarial trainee Ranger Nat. Life Ins., Houston, 1976-77; mgr. time sharing services Phila. Life Ins. Co., Houston, 1977-81; systems engr. Electronic Data Systems, Dallas, 1981-85; tech. specialist J.C. Penney Direct Mktg. Svcs., Inc., Plano, Tex., 1985—. U. Dallas scholar, 1971-75; Rice U. fellow, 1975-76. Pres. St. Elizabeth Seton Parish Bd. Edn., 1989-92. Fellow Life Mgmt. Inst. (master); mem. IEEE, Assn. for Computing Machinery, Am. Assn. for Artificial Intelligence, KC. Republican. Roman Catholic. Home: 2713 S Cypress Cir Plano TX 75075-3154 Office: JC Penney Direct Mktg Svcs Inc 2700 W Plano Pky Plano TX 75075-8205

DOUGHERTY, GERARD MICHAEL, lawyer; b. Glen Cove, N.Y., May 11, 1959; s. Joseph John and Gina (DeGeorge) D.; m. Sherry Dougherty, Oct. 15, 1988; children: Briana Kristin, Danielle Caitlyn. BS in Mktg. and Econs., St. Johns U., 1981; JD, Southwestern U., 1984. Bar: Calif. 1985. Assoc. Matthew Biren & Assocs., L.A., 1984-87, Alfonso, Klonsky & Sternberg, Woodland Hills, Calif., 1987-89, Anderson Krehbiel McCreary, Westlake Village, Calif., 1989-95; ptnr. Dougherty and Waters, Simi Valley, Calif., 1995-97; prin. Dougherty & Landon, P.L.C., Westlake Village, Calif., 1997-98; sr. ptnr. Dougherty & Landon, P.L.C., Thousand Oaks, 1999—. Co-host Law Talk, KVEN Radio, Ventura, Calif. Coach Simi Valley Boys and Girls Club, 1995—; v.p. Simi Valley Rep. Club, 1996-97; bd. mem. Calif. Congress Reps., 1997—. Mem. Ventura County Bar Assn., Bus. Networking Internat., Westlake Village, Entrepreneurs United (Conejo Valley), Kiwanis. Roman Catholic. Avocations: ice and roller hockey, boating, camping. Office: Dougherty & Landon 2660 Townsgate Rd Ste 400 Thousand Oaks CA 91361-5715

DOUGHERTY, JAMES, orthopedic surgeon, educator, author; b. Lawrence, Mass., July 31, 1926; s. James A. and Maude D. (Dillard) D.; m. Marilyn Hays (dec.); m. Rita Buchman; children: James (dec.), Charles, Janice, Jonathan, Christopher. *Wife, Rita Buchman Dougherty. Pioneer woman home builder. Property manager and real estate broker. Winner "People's Choice" National Needlepoint Guild Convention, 1991. Editor national needlepoint teacher's programs. President ANG Southwestern chpt.* BS, Trinity Coll., Hartford, Conn., 1950; MD, Albany Med. Coll., N.Y., 1951. Diplomate, examiner and monitor Am. Bd. Orthopaedic Surgery, 1965-82; diplomate Am. Bd. Forensic Examiners, Am. Bd. Forensic Medicine. Intern U. Chgo. Clinics, 1951-52, resident, 1951-56, instr., 1955-56; chmn. divsn. orthop. surgery SUNY, Syracuse, 1958-60; prof. clin. surgery Albany Med. Coll., 1960-96, attending surgeon, 1961-94, chief of staff, 1987-89, prof. emeritus, 1996—; trustee Albany Med. Ctr., 1993-95; cons. Subacute Care Alternative Project, Washington. Author: Ponies In The Window, 1998, (hymns) Life's Narrow Pathways, A Babe Was Born; mem. editl. bd. Techniques in Orthops.; contbr. articles to profl. jours. Mem. Bd. Edn. Ravena-Coeymans-Selkirk Ctrl. Schs., Ravena, N.Y., 1960-75; med. dir. N.Y. Sr. Games, 1986-89; trustee Schaeffer Meml. Libr., 1990-92, Albany Med. Ctr., 1993-95; bd. dirs. Inst. for Study of Aging, 1990—. Served with U.S. Army, 1944-46. Recipient Alumni medal Albany Med. Coll., 1951. Fellow Am. Acad. Orthopaedic Surgeons; mem. Crawford Campbell Soc. (founder, pres. 1978-88), U. Chgo. Surg. Soc., Northeastern Regional Assn. Sports Medicine (chmn. 1984-89), Albany Med. Coll. Alumni Assn. (trustee 1990—, pres. 1994-96, Meritorious Svc. award 1996), Internat. Platform Assn., Sr. and Ret. Physicians' Assn. of Lee County Fla. (founder, pres. 1997-98), Alpha Omega Alpha, Sigma Psi, Sigma Nu. Presbyterian. Home: 3510 Pine Fern Ln Bonita Springs FL 34134-1918 Office: 1444 Western Ave Albany NY 12203-3495 *As an orthopaedic surgeon I have sometimes been tempted to exaggerate my role and massage my ego. But then I am reminded that I merely treated - God healed and the patient made it work!.*

DOUGHERTY, JOHN CHRYSOSTOM, III, lawyer; b. Beeville, Tex., May 3, 1915; s. John Chrysostom and Mary V. (Henderson) D.; m. Mary Ireland Graves, Apr. 18, 1942 (dec. July 1977); children: Mary Ireland, John Chrysostom IV; m. Bea Ann Smith, June 1978 (div. 1981); m. Sarah B. Randle, 1981 (dec. June 1997). BA, U. Tex., 1937; LLB, Harvard U., 1940; diploma, Inter-Am. Acad. Internat. and Comparative Law, Havana, Cuba, 1948. Bar: Tex. 1940. Atty. Hewit & Dougherty, Beeville, 1940-41; ptnr. Graves & Dougherty, Austin, Tex., 1946-50, Graves, Dougherty & Greenhill, Austin, 1950-57, Graves, Dougherty & Gee, Austin, 1957-60, Graves, Dougherty, Gee & Hearon, Austin, 1961-66, Graves, Dougherty, Gee, Hearon, Moody & Garwood, Austin, 1966-73, Graves, Dougherty, Hearon, Moody & Garwood, Austin, 1973-79; ptnr. Graves, Dougherty, Hearon & Moody, Austin, 1979-93, sr. counsel, 1993—; ret., 1997; spl. asst. atty. gen., 1949-50; Hon. French Consul, Austin, 1971-86; lectr. on tax, estate planning, probate code, community property problems; mem. Tex. Submerged Lands Adv. Com., 1963-72, Tex. Bus. and Commerce Code Adv. Com., 1964-66, Gov.'s Com. on Marine Resources, 1970-71, Gov.'s Planning Com. on Colorado River Basin Water Quality Mgmt. Study, 1972-73, Tex. Legis. Property Tax Com., 1973-75. Co-editor: Texas Appellate Practice, 1964, 2d edit., 1977; contbr. Bowe, Estate Planning and Taxation, 1957, 65; Texas Lawyers Practice Guide, 1967, 71, How to Live and Die with Texas Probate, 1968, 7th edit., 1995, Texas Estate Administration, 1975, 78; mem. bd. editors: Appellate Procedure in Tex., 1964, 2d edit., 1982; contbr. articles to legal jours. Bd. dirs. Tex. Beta Students Aid Fund, 1949-84, Grenville Clark Fund at Dartmouth Coll., 1976-90, Umlauf Sculpture Garden, Inc., 1990-91, New Life Inst., 1993—; past bd. dirs. Advanced Religious Study Found., Holy Cross Hosp., Sea Arama, Inc., Nat. Pollution Control Found., Austin Nat. Bank; trustee St. Stephen's Episcopal Sch., Austin, 1969-83, Tex. Equal Access to Justice Found., 1986-90, U. Tex. Law Sch. Found., 1974—; mem. adv. com. Legal Assts. Tng. Inst., U. Tex., 1990—; mem. vis. com. Harvard Law Sch., 1983-87. Capt. C.I.C., AUS, 1941-44, JAGC, 1944-46, maj. USAR. Decorated Medaille Française, France, Medaille d'honneur en Argent des Affairs Etrangeres, France, chevalier l'Ordre Nat. du Merite. Fellow Am. Bar Found., Tex. Bar Found., Am. Coll. Trust and Estate Counsel, Am. Coll. Tax Counsel; mem. ABA (ho. of dels. 1982-88, standing com. on lawyers pub. responsibility 1983-85, mem. spl. com. on delivery legal svcs. 1987-91, com. legal problems of the elderly 1997—), Am. Arbitration Assn. (nat. panel arbitrators 1958-90), Travis County Bar Assn. (pres. 1979-80), Internat. Acad. Estate and Trust Law (exec. coun. 1988-90), State Bar Tex. (chmn. sect. taxation 1965-66, pres. 1979-80, com. legal svcs. to the poor 1986-94), Am. Judicature Soc. (bd. dirs. 1985-87), Am. Law Inst. (adv. com. project law governing lawyers 1990-97), Tex. Supreme Ct. Hist. Soc. (trustee), Philos. Soc. Tex. (pres. 1989, bd. dirs. 1989—), Harvard Law Sch. Assn. (mem. com. on pub. svc. law 1990-95, chmn. 1990-95, coun. 1991-95, exec. com. 1992-95), Tex. Appleseed, Inc. (bd. dirs. 1996—), Rotary. Presbyterian. E-mail: cdougherty@gdhm.com. Home: 6 Green Ln Austin TX 78703-2515 Office: 515 Congress Ave Ste 2300 Austin TX 78701-3503 also: PO Box 98 Austin TX 78767-0098

DOUGHERTY, JOHN ERNEST, judge; b. Jan. 29, 1924; s. John Edwin and Margaret Moss (Colwell) D.; m. Ivy Patricia Morris, Dec. 28, 1949; children: David M., Margaret Dougherty Roberts, John R., Elizabeth Dougherty Poole. BA, Emory U., 1948, LLB, 1950. Bar: Ga. 1950, U.S. Dist. Ct. (no. dist.) Ga. 1959, U.S. Ct. Appeals (11th cir.) 1967. Sole practice Atlanta, 1950-53; assoc. Arnold & Gambrell, Atlanta, 1954-63; sole practice Atlanta, 1963-77; assoc. city atty. City of Atlanta, 1963-77; magistrate judge U.S. Dist. Ct. No. Dist. Ga., Atlanta, 1977—, chief magistrate judge, 1984-88. Served to col. USAF, 1943-46. Mem. Atlanta Bar Assn., State Bar Ga., Atlanta Lawyers Club, Druid Hills Civic Assn. Republican. Episcopalian. Office: 1629 US Courthouse 75 Spring St SW Atlanta GA 30303-3309*

DOUGHERTY, JOHN JAMES, computer software company executive, consultant; b. Phila., Aug. 15, 1924; s. John James Sr. and Hilda Margaret (Belmont) D.; m. Marjorie Theresa Coyle, June 28, 1947; children: John J., Moira A., Marjorie T., Brian P., Hilda M., Eileen M., Ann J. BSEE, Villanova (Pa.) U., 1950. Registered profl. engr., Pa. Jr. engr. Phila. Electric Co., 1951-53, engr., 1953-56, sr. engr., 1956-62, engr. in charge, 1972-75; div. dir. Electric Power Rsch. Inst., Palo Alto, Calif., 1975-79, v.p., 1979-86; cons. Electric Power Rsch. Inst., 1986—, Forensic Techs. Inc., San Francisco, 1986—. Lt. USN, 1943-46. Fellow IEEE (Herman Halpern award 1988). Roman Catholic. Avocations: golf, bowling, bridge. Home: 4766 Calle De Lucia San Jose CA 95124-4848

DOUGHERTY, JOHN MARTIN, bishop; b. Scranton, Pa., Apr. 29, 1932. Student, St. Charles Coll., Cantonsville, Md., 1951, St. Mary's Sem. Balt., 1957, U. Notre Dame, 1956; LLD, U. Scranton. Ordained priest Roman Cath. Ch., 1957. Titular bishop Diocese of Sufetula, 1995—; auxiliary bishop Diocese of Scranton, 1995—. Office: Chancery Office 300 Wyoming Ave Scranton PA 18503-1242*

DOUGHERTY, JUDE PATRICK, dean; b. Chgo., July 21, 1930; s. Edward Timothy and Cecilia Anastasia (Loew) D.; m. Patricia Ann Regan, Dec. 28, 1957; children: Thomas, Michael, John, Paul. BA, Cath. U. Am., 1954, MA, 1955, PhD, 1960; LHD (hon.), Thomas More Coll., 1995. Instr. Marquette U., 1957-58; instr. Bellarmine Coll., 1958-60, asst. prof., 1960-63, assoc. prof., 1963-66; assoc. prof. Cath. U. Am., 1966-76, prof., 1976—; dean Cath. U. Am. (Sch. Philosophy), 1967—; vis. assoc. prof. Georgetown U., summer, 1965; vis. prof. Katholieke Universiteit te Leuven, Belgium, 1974-75. Author: Recent American Naturalism, 1960; co-author: Approaches to Morality, 1966; Editor: Theological Directions of the Ecumenical Movement, 1964, The Impact of Vatican II, 1966, The Good Life and Its Pursuit, 1985; editor: Rev. of Metaphysics, 1971—; gen. editor: Studies in Philosophy and the History of Philosophy, 1978—. Mem. bd. advisors Franklin J. Matchette Found., 1971—; trustee Bellarmine Coll., 1972-75, U. Bridgeport, 1995—; mem. Pontifical Acad., St. Thomas, Rome, 1981—; mem. Academia Scientiarum et Artium Europae, Salzburg, 1991—. Mem. Am. Philos. Assn. (program chmn. ea. divsn. 1988, exec. com. ea. divsn. 1989-93), Am. Cath. Philos. Assn. (pres. 1974-75, Aquinas medal 1994), Washington Philosophy Club (pres. 1968-69), Soc. for Philosophy Religion (pres. 1978-79), Metaphys. Soc. Am. (pres. 1983-84), Fellowship Cath. Scholars (exec. sec. 1994-97, treas. 1994-97, Cardinal Wright award 1994). Home: 9036 Rouen Ln Potomac MD 20854-3130 Office: Cath U Am Sch Philosophy 620 Michigan Ave NE Washington DC 20064-0001

DOUGHERTY, JUNE EILEEN, librarian; b. Union City, N.J., Mar. 27, 1929; d. Robert John and Jane Veronica (Smith) Beyrer; B.A. in Edn., Peterson State Coll., 1967; postgrad. Rutgers U. Sch. Library Sci., 1959-69; m. Donald E. Dougherty, Dec. 2, 1946; 1 son, Glen Allan. With A. B. Dumont, Paterson, N.J., 1950-54; sch. librarian St. Paul's Elementary Sch., Prospect Park, N.J., 1957—; dir. North Haledon (N.J.) Free Pub. Library, 1957—; sec.-treas. Dougherty & Dougherty, Inc., North Haledon, 1968—. Den mother Boy Scouts Am., 1954-57; mem. Gov. N.J.'s Tercentenary Com., 1962-64. Mem. Am., N.J., N. Haledon library assns., Cath. Library Assn., N.J. Libraries Roundtable, Bergen-Passaic Library Club, Friends N. Haledon Library. Roman Catholic. Club: St. Paul's Social. Home: 155 Westervelt Ave Haledon NJ 07508-3074 Office: 129 Overlook Ave North Haledon NJ 07508-2570

DOUGHERTY, NEIL JOSEPH, physical education educator, safety consultant; b. Elizabeth, N.J., Apr. 7, 1943; s. Neil Joseph and Doris Burnett (Lindsay) D.; m. Margaret Ruth Quaranta, July 17, 1965; 1 child, Margaret Elizabeth. BS, Rutgers U., 1964, EdM, 1965; EdD, Temple U., 1970. Tchr. phys. edn. St. Joseph's Sch., Bound Brook, N.J., 1964-65; teaching assoc. Temple U., Phila., 1967-70; prof. Rutgers U., New Brunswick, N.J., 1970—; mem. adv. bd. Youth Sports Rsch. Coun., New Brunswick, 1987—; nat. faculty mem. U.S. Sports Acad., 1988—. Co-author: Understanding and Assessing Human Movement, 1980, Management Principles in Sport and Leisure Sciences, 1985, Contemporary Approaches to the Teaching of Physical Education, 1979, 87, Sport, Physical Activity and the Law, 1993; editor: Physical Education and Sport for Secondary School Students, 1983, 93, Principles of Safety in Physical Education and Sport, 1987, 93, Outdoor Recreation Safety, 1998, (jour.) The Reporter, 1977-81, (monograph series) Briefings, 1974-75; mem. editl. bd. Leisure Times Focus, 1984-88, Jour. of Tchg. in Phys. Edn., 1981-85, Safety Notebook, 1998—; contbr. to profl. jours. 1st lt. U.S. Army, 1965-67. Recipient Merit award Ea. Assn. for Health, Phys. Edn., Recreation and Dance, 1980, Honor award, 1982, Honor award Soc. for Study of Legal Aspects of Sport and Phys. Activity, 1998. Mem. Nat. Assn. Phys. Edn. Higher Edn. (pres. 1984-86), Sch. and Comty. Safety Soc. Am. (pres. 1996-98, Profl. Svc. award 1991, 97, Scholar award 1994), N.J. Assn. of Dirs. of Health, Phys. Edn. and Recreation (pres. 1976-78), N.J. Assn. for Health, Phys. Edn., Recreation and Dance (pres. 1979-80, Honor fellow award 1983, Disting. Leadership award 1982), Coll. and Univ. Phys. Edn. Coun. (chmn. 1985-88). Avocations: fishing, water sports, golf. Home: 1655 East Dr Point Pleasant NJ 08742-5117 Office: Rutgers U Dept Exercise Sci/Sport Stu New Brunswick NJ 08903

DOUGHERTY, RALEIGH GORDON, manufacturer's representative; b. Saginaw, Mich., Aug. 19, 1928; s. Raleigh Gordon and Helen Jean (McCrum) D.; 1 child, Karen Kealani. Salesman H.D. Hudson Mfg. Co., Chgo., 1946-48; field sales rep. Jensen Mfg. Co., Chgo., 1948-50; field sales mgr. Regency Idea, Indpls., 1950-54; mgr. Brenna & Browne, Honolulu, 1954-56; owner, pres. Dougherty Enterprises, Honolulu, 1956—; manufacturer's representative; b. Saginaw, Mich., Aug. 19, 1928; s. Raleigh Gordon and Helen Jean (McCrum) D.; 1 child, Karen Kealani. Salesman, H.D. Hudson Mfg. Co., Chgo., 1946-48; field sales rep. Jensen Mfg. Co., Chgo., 1948-50; field sales mgr. Regency Idea, Indpls., 1950-54; mgr. Brenna & Browne, Honolulu, 1954-56; owner, pres. Dougherty Enterprises, Honolulu, 1956—. With U.S. Army, 1950-52. Mem. Hawaii Hotel Assn., Internat. Home Furnishings Reps. Assn., Air Force Assn., DAV (life), Navy League U.S., Am. Legion, Korean Vet., Elks (past trustee Hawaii). Republican. Methodist. With U.S. Army, 1950-52. Mem. Hawaii Hotel Assn., Internat. Home Furnishings Reps. Assn., Air Force Assn., DAV (life), Navy League U.S., Am. Legion, Korean Vet., Elks (past trustee Hawaii). Republican. Methodist. Home and Office: 1326 Lunalilo Home Rd Honolulu HI 96825-3216

DOUGHERTY, RICHARD MARTIN, library and information science educator; b. East Chicago, Ind., Jan. 17, 1935; s. Floyd C. and Harriet E. (Martin) D.; m. Ann Prescott, Mar. 24, 1974; children—Kathryn E., Emily E.; children by previous marriage—Jill Ann, Jacquelyn A., Douglas M. B.S., Purdue U., 1959, LHD honoris causa, 1991; M.L.S., Rutgers U., 1961, Ph.D., 1963; LHD honoris causa, U. Stellenbosch, South Africa, 1995. Head acquisitions dept. Univ. Library, U. N.C., Chapel Hill, 1963-66; assoc. dir. libraries U. Colo., Boulder, 1966-70; prof. library sci. Syracuse U., N.Y., 1970-72; univ. librarian U. Calif-Berkeley, 1972-78; dir. univ. library U. Mich., Ann Arbor, 1978-88, acting dean. Sch. Library Sci., 1984-85, prof. sch. info., 1978-98; pres. Dougherty & Assocs., 1994—; cons., change mgmt. librs.; founder, pres. Mountainside Pub. Corp., 1974—. Author: Scientific Management of Library Organizations, 2d edit., 1982; co-author: Preferred Futures for Libraries II, 1993; editor Coll. and Research Libraries jour., 1969-74, Jour. Acad. Librarianship, 1975-94, Library Issues, 1981—. Trustee Ann Arbor Dist. Libr., 1995—, pres. bd. trustees, 1998—. Recipient Esther Piercy award, 1968, Disting. Alumnus award Rutgers U., 1980, Acad. Librarian Yr., Assn. Coll. and Research Libraries, 1983, ALA Hugh C. Atkinson Meml. award, 1988, Blackwell Scholarship award, 1992, Joseph Lippincott medal, 1997; fellow Council on Library Resources. Mem. ALA (coun. 1969-76, 89-92, exec. bd. 1972-76, 89-92, endowment trustee 1986-89, pres. 1990-91), Assn. Rsch. Librs. (bd. dirs. 1977-80), Rsch. Librs. Group, Inc. (exec. com. 1984-88, chmn. bd. govs. 1986-87), Soc. Scholarly Pub. (bd. dirs. 1990-92, exec. com. 1991-92), Internat. Fedn. Libr. Assns. (round table of editors of library jours. 1985-87, standing com. univ. libr. sect. 1981-87). E-mail: rmdoughe@umich.edu. Home: 6 Northwick Ct Ann Arbor MI 48105-1408 Office: U Mich Sch Info Ann Arbor MI 48109

DOUGHERTY, ROBERT ANTHONY, manufacturing company executive; b. St. Louis, May 3, 1928; s. Joseph A. and Venita E. (Gretline) D.; m. Rosemary Schmertmann, Jan. 29, 1955; children: Kevin, Patrick, Michael, Mary Ann, Timothy. B.S. in Mech. Engring, U. Notre Dame, 1952. Registered profl. engr., Calif. cert. mfg. engr. Sales engr. Robert R. Stephens Machinery Co., St. Louis, 1952-60; dist. mgr. Robert R. Stephens Machinery Co., 1961-72; pres. Dougherty & Assocs., Prairie Village, Kans., 1972—; bd. dirs. Tech-Industry Cons., Lenexa, Kans.; exec. com. Kans. Industry/Univ./Govt. Engring. Edn. Consortium. Mem. adv. com. Pittsburg, Kans. Sch. Sci. and Tech., 1987—; coord. cons. Kans. U. Ctrs. Excellence for Kans. Tech. Enterprise Corp., 1991—. Served with U.S. Army, 1946-48. Recipient Productivity award Coll. and Univ. Mfg. Edn. Council, 1979, Soc. Mfg. Engrs. Joseph A. Siegel Meml. honor award, 1992; Outstanding Engring. Achievements award San Fernando Valley Engrs. Council, 1980. Fellow Instn. Prodn. Engrs. Gt. Britain (life); mem. ASME (state legis. fellow), Am. Soc. for Metals, Soc. Mfg. Engrs. (pres. 1980-81, dir. 1971-82, Region 5 award of merit 1969). Roman Catholic. Clubs: Round Hill Bath and Tennis (pres. 1971), Hillcrest Country (v.p. 1982, pres. 1983—). Office: PO Box 8149 Shawnee Mission KS 66208-0149

DOUGHERTY, URSEL THIELBEULE, communications and marketing executive; b. Rotenburg, W. Ger., July 30, 1942; naturalized U.S. citizen, 1965; d. Hugo and Margarete (Marquardt) Thielbeule; m. Erich A. Eichhorn, Jan. 3, 1979. BA summa cum laude in Polit. Sci., Cleve. State U., 1971; MA in Polit. Sci., U. Wis., 1972; MBA in Fin., Case Western Res., 1982. Journalist maj. daily, women's mag., Germany, 1962-66; assoc. editor Farm Chems., 1967; publs. mgr. Trabon Systems, 1967-68; rsch. analyst Legis. Coun., State of Wis., 1972; pub. rels. adminstr. to mgr. pub. info. Eaton Corp., Cleve., 1972-84; dir. pub. affairs Freightliner/Mercedes-Benz Truck Co., Portland, Oreg., 1984-87, v.p. chmn.'s office Daimler Benz N.A. Holding Co., Inc., Washington, 1987-90; v.p. bus. devel., corp. affairs Penske Corp., Cleve.; v.p. investor rels. Detroit Diesel Corp.; founder, prin. USCH Internat. Fin. Comms. Firm; cons. small bus. Trustee, Lake Erie coun. Girl Scouts U.S., 1975-82, Sr. Citizen Resources, 1978-81; amb. Jr. Achievement, 1979; steering com. YWCA Career Women of Achievement, 1981; adv. bd.

Women's Career Networking, 1980-84; trustee, chmn. fin. com. Young Audience Greater Cleve. Mem. Nat. Investor Rels. Inst., Pub. Rels. Soc. Am. Office: 1510 Crest Rd Cleveland OH 44121-1722

DOUGHTY, A. GLENN, minister; b. Somers Point, N.J., Aug. 30, 1942; s. Alfred and Irene Dorothy (Colhouer) D.; m. Carole True, June 17, 1967; children: Matthew Glenn, Lynn Carole. BS in Bible Studies, Phila. Coll. of Bible, 1965; MDiv, Faith Theol. Sem., 1968. Ordained to ministry Fellowship Fundamental Bible Chs., 1970. Pastor Community Bible Ch., Barrington, N.J., 1968-70, The Bible Ch. of Westville, N.J., 1970—; chmn. Bible Protestant Ch. Ext., 1970-73; sec. Fellowship of Fundamental Bible Chs., 1976-95, Ministerial Qualifications Com., 1980-95. Chmn. Cmty. Dispute Resolution Com., Westville, 1986—. Mem. Am. Coun. Christian Chs. (mem. exec. com. 1990—), Fellowship of Fundamental Bible Chs. (trustee 1985-95, pres. trustees 1985-91, chmn. trustees 1993-95, sec. Fundamental Bible Missions 1996-98, pres. 1998—). Home and Office: 134 Delsea Dr Westville NJ 08093-1159

DOUGHTY, GEORGE FRANKLIN, airport administrator; b. Wheeling, W.Va., Mar. 11, 1946; s. Ernest Heyward and Elizabeth Gertrude (Dei) D.; m. Jennifer L. Tyma; children: Susan Elizabeth, Jennifer Anne, Patrick George, Shannon Marie. B.S. in Aerospace Engring., W.Va. U., 1968. Asst. mgr. Cedar Rapids Mcpl. Airport, Iowa, 1975-78; dep. dir. Balt.-Washington Internat. Airport State of Md., 1978-80; dir. port control City of Cleve., Ohio, 1980-84; dir. aviation Stapleton Internat. Airport City and County of Denver, 1981-92; exec. dir. Lehigh-Northampton Airport Authority, Allentown, Pa., 1992—. Recipient Laurels award Aviation Week and Space Tech., 1988. Mem. Am. Assn. Airport Execs. (dir. 1980), Airports Coun. Internat. N.Am. (chmn. govtl. affairs com. 1985-86, bd. dirs. 1986-89, 1st vice chmn. 1992, chmn. 1993). Home: 2131 Stonewall Dr Macungie PA 18062-9064 Office: Lehigh Valley Intl Airport 3311 Airport Rd Allentown PA 18103-1040

DOUGHTY, JULIAN ORUS, mechanical engineer, educator; b. Tuscaloosa, Ala., June 11, 1933; s. Orus and Blonnye (Deavours) D.; m. Barbara Ann Parr, Jan. 28, 1956; children: Glen Edward, Diane Marie. BSAE, Miss. State U., 1956, MSAE, 1960; PhD in Engring. Sci., U. Tenn., 1966. Registered profl. engr., Ala. Design engr. McDonnell Aircraft Corp., St. Louis, 1956-57; instr. engring. graphics Miss. State U., Starkville, 1957-60; instr. basic engring. U. Tenn., Knoxville, 1960-63; instr. engring. mechanics U. Tenn., 1963-66; asst. prof. aerospace engring. U. Ala., Tuscaloosa, 1966-70; assoc. prof. aerospace engring. U. Ala., 1970-77, prof. aerospace engring., 1977-81, prof. mech. engring., 1981—; engring. cons., expert witness. Contbr. articles to profl. jours. Recipient Spl. Svc. award, Ala. sect. AIAA, 1979, Herbert Kuenzel award, Engring. Coll., U. Ala., 1988. Assoc. fellow AIAA; mem. ASME, SAE, Am. Soc. Engring. Edn., Sigma Xi, Sigma Gamma Tau. Avocations: golf, painting, reading. Home: 10521 Winding Way Tuscaloosa AL 35405-9719 Office: U Alabama PO Box 870276 Tuscaloosa AL 35487-0154

DOUGHTY, MARK EDWARD, environmental consultant; b. Phila., Jan. 11, 1959; s. Clarence Edward and Barbara Jean Doughty; m. Katharine Rachel Brewster, Dec. 18, 1982; children: Dakotah, Emily, Elijah, Hannah, Abraham. BS in Biology, The Citadel, 1980. Pres. environ. divsn. Testwell Craig Testing Labs., Mays Landing, N.J.; pres. Testwell Craig Environ. Cons., Mays Landing; v.p. MDS Environmental, Thorofare, N.J.; pres. Doughty Environ. Hygiene Assocs., Mays Landing. Mem. Weymouth Twp. Zoning Bd., Dorothy, N.J., 1995—; chmn. Weymouth Twp. Environ. Commn., Dorothy, 1995-97. Mem. Am. Indsl. Hygiene Assn. (N.J. chpt.), Soc. Environ. Profls. (membership com. chair N.J. chpt. 1994-95), Nat. Asbestos Coun. (sec. N.J. chpt. 1989-91, exec. bd. mem. N.J. chpt. 1991-94). Avocations: Appalachian trail thruhiker, wilderness exploration, photography, skiing. Office: Doughty Environ Hygiene Assocs 6066 Main St Mays Landing NJ 08330-1852

DOUGHTY, MICHAEL DEAN, insurance agent; b. Oklahoma City, Nov. 7, 1947; s. Charles Dean and Francis Jean (Schumpert) D.; m. Sherrie Lynn Perkins, May 30, 1970; children: Steven Kyle, Brian Edward. BS in Edn., Okla. State U., 1971; postgrad., Command Sgts. Maj. Acad.; Assoc. in Risk Mgmt., Ins. Inst. Am., 1993. Cert. prof. ins. agt.; cert. ins. counselor; cert. profl. ins. agt. Tchr., coach Perry (Okla.) Pub. Schs., 1971-80; asst. v.p., field agt. Coaches Ins. Assn. Am., Memphis, 1980-84; v.p., officer mgr. Albright Ins. Agy., Inc., Perry, Okla., 1984-88; prodr. Holt Ins. Agy., Perry, 1988—, co-owner, 1992—; instr. Indian-Meridian Voc. Tech., Stillwater, Okla., 1985, new ins. edn. program Excellence in Svc., Ava, Moa., 1996-98; faculty instr. Cert. Ins. Svcs. Rep. Program, Soc. Cert. Ins. Couns., 1992—, Excellence in Svc. Comml. Ins. courses, 1996—. Bd. dirs. United Fund Perry, 1983-86, 94-96, 97-99; youth sports cons. Noble County Family YMCA, Perry, 1985; vocat. bus. adv. bd. Perry H.S., 1990-95; mem. fin. adv. com. on taxes Noble County, 1993; mem. bus. devel. com. Perry Devel. Coalition, 1994-96; trustee First Bapt. Ch., 1997-99, chmn. 1999. Command sgt. maj. Okla. Army N.G., 1970-96, ret. 1996. Mem. Profl. Ins. Agts. Okla. (bd. dirs. 1998—), Okla. Assn. Ins. Agts. (discussion leader 1988, mem. pub. rels. com. 1988-91, chmn. 1990-91, rural and small agts. com. 1992-93), Ind. Ins. Agts. Am., Ins. Inst. Assn. (assoc. risk mgmt.), Stillwater Life Underwriters Assn. (pres. 1982-83), Jaycees (past chpt. pres. 1992-93), Perry C. of C. (bd. dirs. 1993-96, v.p. 1994, pres. 1995, 96), Am. Legion (adj.), N.G. Assn. Okla. (life), Non-Commd. Officers Assn., Assn. U.S. Army, Perry Quarterback Club (pres. 1990-92), Perry Diamond Club (v.p. 1990-91), Elks (chmn. Americanism 1989-94), Perry C. of C. (v.p. 1993-94, pres. 1994-96). Democrat. Avocations: golf, volleyball, hunting, fishing. Home: 915 Jackson St Perry OK 73077-3012 Office: Holt Ins Agy 718 Delaware St Perry OK 73077-6425

DOUGLAS, ANDREW, legal nurse; b. N.Y., N.Y., Mar. 27, 1948; s. Lloyd James and Paula (Levine) D.; m. Lauren Gail Gentile, Aug. 6, 1988. AS in Nursing, Coll. of the Desert, 1976; Ryan teaching credential, Calif. State U., 1979, MA in Bioethics, 1985; BS in Health Sci., Health Care, Redlands U., 1982. RN, Fla.; diplomate Am. Bd. Disability Analysts; CCRN; cert. disability mgmt. specialist; cert. case mgr.; cert. rehab. RN; Am. Bd. Disability Analysts. Orderly ER Desert Hosp., Palm Springs, Calif., 1972-74; charge nurse CCU, founder terminal illness program Desert Hosp., 1974-78; head nurse ICU, shock unit cardiac lab. Weil & Shubin Hollywood Presbyn. Med. Ctr., U. So. Calif. Med. Ctr., L.A., 1978-83; critical care instr. ethics com. Queen of Angels Hosp., L.A., 1983-84; pres., owner Med. Systems Designs, L.A., 1984-89; case mgr. Nancy Sapp & Assocs., Orlando, Fla., 1989-93, Resource Opportunities, Orlando, 1992-93, Med. Mgmt. & Re-Employment, Orlando, 1993—; pres., owner, med.-legal expert Health Care Adv. Cons., Inc., Boca Raton, Fla., 1989—; founder, cons., speaker Profls. Assisting the Dying, L.A., 1988-89; educator AACN, FARN, 1983—; cons. brain injuries Goodwill Industries, West Palm Beach, Fla., 1994—; cons. adv. bd. Pinecrest Rehab. Hosp., Delray Beach, Fla., 1993-94. Author: (books) Socialization, Sexism & Stereotyping, 1982, Stress and Bioethics in Critical Care Units, 1985; contbr. articles to jours. in field. Speaker Greiving Parents, Boca Raton, Fla., 1992—, Profls. Assisting the Dying, L.A., 1984-89. Mem. AACN, Assn. Rehab. Nurses, Assn. & Soc. of Law and Medicine, Individual Cas Mgmt. Assn., Hastings Ctr. for Human Ethics, Thanatology Soc. Avocations: diving, boating, cinema, travel. Home: 3199 NE 8th Ave Boca Raton FL 33431-6912

DOUGLAS, ANDREW, state supreme court justice; b. Toledo, July 5, 1932; 4 children. J.D., U. Toledo, 1959. Bar: Ohio 1960, U.S. Dist. Ct. (no. dist.) Ohio 1960. Former ptnr. Winchester & Douglas; judge Ohio 6th Dist. Ct. Appeals, 1981-84; justice Ohio Supreme Ct., 1985—; mem. nat. adv. bd. Ctr. for Informatics Law John Marshall Law Sch., Chgo.; former spl. counsel Atty. Gen. of Ohio; former instr. law Ohio Dominican Coll. Served with U.S. Army, 1952-54. Recipient award Maumee Valley council Girl Scouts U.S., 1976, Outstanding Service award Toledo Police Command Officers Assn., 1980, Toledo Soc. for Autistic Children and Adults, 1983, Extra-Spl. Person award Central Catholic High Sch., 1981, Disting. Service award Toledo Police Patrolman's Assn., 1982, award Ohio Hispanic Inst. Opportunity, 1985, Disting. Merit award Alpha Sigma Phi, 1988, Gold "T" award U. Toledo, First Amendment award Cen. Ohio Chpt. Soc. Profl. Journalists Sigma Delta Chi, 1989; named to Woodward High Sch. Hall of Fame. Mem. Toledo Bar Assn., Lucas County Bar Assn., Ohio Bar Assn., Toledo U. Alumni Assn., U. Toledo Coll. Law Alumni Assn. (Disting. Alumnus award 1991), Internat. Inst., North Toledo Old Timers Assn., Old Newsboys Goodfellow Assn., Pi Sigma Alpha, Delta Theta Phi. Office: Ohio Supreme Ct 30 E Broad St Fl 3 Columbus OH 43266*

DOUGLAS, BRUCE LEE, oral and maxillofacial surgeon, medical director, educator, workplace health consultant, gerontology consultant; b. N.Y.C., July 14, 1925; s. William and Carrie (Basescu) D.; m. Janet Ramsden; children: Clifford, Steven, Jennifer, Sarah, Sandra. A.B., Princeton U., 1947; D.D.S., NYU, 1948; postgrad. in oral surgery, Columbia U., 1949-51, M.A. in Edn, 1955, diploma in higher edn, 1957; M.P.H., U. Calif. at Berkeley, 1962. Diplomate Am. Bd. Oral and Maxillofacial Surgery. Dental intern Queens Gen. Hosp., Jamaica, N.Y., 1948-49; oral surgery resident Queens Hosp. Center, Jamaica, 1953-54; practice oral surgery Rego Park, N.Y., 1954-59; Fulbright prof. oral surgery and anesthesiology Japan, 1959-61; prof. oral medicine and community dentistry Coll. Dentistry U. Ill., 1962-72, prof. preventive medicine Coll. Medicine, 1962-72; prof. health adminstrn. Sch. Pub. Health, 1972-98; prof. dental and oral surgery Rush Med. Coll., 1970-76, clin. prof. surgery, 1979—; sr. fellow aging and applied gerontology Chgo. Med. Sch., 1993-96; prof. environ. and occupl. health Sch. Pub. Health, 1998—; chief dentistry and oral surgery Rush-Presbyn.-St. Luke's Med. Ctr., Chgo., 1968-75; dir. Office Dental Manpower Distbn., Ill. Dept. Pub. Health, 1975-76, chief divsn. dental health, 1976-77, chief health manpower devel., 1977-78; chief dept. dentistry and oral surgery Chgo. Ctr. Hosp., 1978-81; chief sect. dentistry and oral surgery Grant Hosp. Chgo., 1980-90, attending oral and maxillofacial surgeon, 1980—; pres. Chgo. Dental Group, 1978-90; dental columnist Chgo. Sun-Times, 1977-78; Fulbright prof. oral surgery and anesthesiology Okayama (Japan) U. and Tokyo Med.-Dental U., 1959-61; WHO cons. to U. Antioquia, Colombia, Nat. U. and U. Zulia, Venezuela, 1964-69, Mahidol U., Bangkok, Thailand, 1973, Gt. Britain, 1977; vis. prof. Northwestern U. Coll. Dentistry, 1982-84; mem. transition team on health policy, chmn. com. on occupational health Mayor Harold Washington, 1983; cons. occupational health and safety Chgo. Dept. Health, 1983-84; cons. St. Petersburg State U., Russia, 1990, 93; cons. ADA Coun. Hosp. Dental Svcs., 1959-68, Dept. State Internat. Scholars Program, Inst. of Internat. Edn., W.K. Kellogg Found.; cons. Russian Mil. Med. Acad., dept. of traumatology, 1993, med. affairs cons. Ministry of Health, St. Petersburg, Russia, 1994-98; med. dir. Integra Comp, Deerfield, Ill., 1996-99, Sedgwick (Marsh) CMS, Chgo., 1996-99; sr. cons. Lake County (Ill.) Sheriff's Dept., 1996-97. Author: Guide to Hospital Dental Procedure, 1964, Dental Care for Special Patient, 1966, Introduction to Hospital Dentistry, 1970, Criteria for Quality Assessment of Oral Surgery Services, 1982, 85, 87; contbr. (with Clifford E. Douglas) Medical and Hospital Negligence, 1988, 90; contbg. author: Safety and Preventive Medicine in the Workplace, Managing Workers' Compensation, 1996; editor Am. Assn. Hosp. Dentists, 1966-71; assoc. editor Jour. Oral Surgery, 1959-67; assoc. editor (USA) Internat. Med. Revs., Russia, 1994-96. Mem. Ill. Ho. of Reps., 11th Dist., 1971-72, 12th Dist., 1973-74; chmn. Am. Indian Commn., State of Ill., 1973-74; bd. dirs. Chgo. Easter Seal Soc., Hemophilia Found., Infant Welfare Soc.; chmn. Ill. Coalition Against Tobacco, 1991-93; mem. AARP State of Ill. Legis. Com., 1991-92; AARP/Vote, 1992-94, pres. North Shore chpt., 1992-94, works dept., 1992-95, cmty./employer outreach coord., 1994-95; bd. dirs. Fulbright Assn. Task Force on Intercultural Exch. with Ea. Europe; coord. humanitarian med. aid mission to Russia, 1993-95. With USNR, 1943-45, lt. Dental Corps, 1951-53. Recipient William J. Gies Nat. Dental Editorial award, 1969, Best Legislator award Ind. Voters Ill., 1972, 74, Profl. Bus. Person of Yr. award Lincoln Park C. of C., 1987, hon. commendations from Ill. Pub. Health Assn., Ill. Interagy. Coun. on Smoking & Disease, United Blood Svcs. Chgo., Hemophilia Found., Ill. Ho. Reps., Ill. Vet. Med. Assn., numerous other awards. Fellow APHA, Internat. Coll. Dentists, Chgo. Inst. Medicine (bd. dirs. 1970-80, chair com. intercultural exch. with Russia 1994-95), Am. Dental Soc. Anesthesiology (past pres.); mem. ADA (life), Am. Assn. Hosp. Dentists (past pres.), Am. Soc. on Aging (chair task force on the older worker 1998—), Fulbright Assn. (pres. Chgo. chpt. 1990-92), Internat. Assn. Oral and Maxillofacial Surgeons, Sigma Xi, Phi Delta Kappa, Omicron Kappa Upsilon. Home: 2401 Duffy Ln Riverwoods IL 60015-1729
A health professional career can be the portal through which an educated person can pass to a fuller and richer life. My health professional, education, and public health degrees made it possible for me to broaden my involvement in the affairs of my community, my nation, my world, and now the world of business, and to serve individuals in need as well.

DOUGLAS, CHARLES W., lawyer; b. Chgo., Apr. 1, 1948. BA, Northwestern U., 1970; JD, Harvard U., 1974. Bar: Ill. 1974, U.S. Dist. Ct. (no. dist.) Ill. 1974, U.S. Ct. Appeals (6th cir.) 1978, U.S. Ct. Appeals (9th cir.) 1981, U.S. Ct. Appeals (2nd cir.) 1983, U.S. Ct. Appeals (7th cir.) 1984. Ptnr. Sidley & Austin, Chgo. Office: Sidley & Austin 1 First Natl Plz Chicago IL 60603-2003*

DOUGLAS, CINDY HOLLOWAY, mortgage company executive; b. Queens, N.Y., Aug. 8, 1960; d. Richard Stephen and Beverly Bunny (Harris) Tannenbaum; m. David Milton Holloway (div. Mar. 1986); 1 child, Benjamin Jerome; m. Michael William Douglas, Mar. 21, 1998. BA, Calif. State U., Fullerton, 1981. Lic. real estate broker. Waitress Bob's Big Boy, San Bernardino, Calif., 1984-85; receptionist RNG Mortgage Co., San Bernardino, 1985; loan processor Quality Mortgage Co., Colton, Calif., 1985-88, loan officer, 1988-91; loan officer RNG Mortgage, 1991-92; v.p., br. mgr. Mountain West Fin., 1992-97; prodn. and mktg. mgr. South Pacific Fin., 1997-97; real estate loan mgr. Arrowhead Credit Union, 1998—. Mem. San Bernardino Bd. Realtors (spl. events com. 1988—, comm. com. 1990—), Nat. Trust for Hist. Preservation, San Bernardino Execs. Assn., Assn. Profl. Mortgage Women (bd. dirs. 1989-90, v.p. 1992-93, Affiliate of Yr. award 1990), San Bernardino Execs. Group (bd. dirs. 1994—). Home: PO Box 3187 Crestline CA 92325-3187

DOUGLAS, CLARENCE JAMES, JR., corporation executive, management consultant; b. Corry, Pa., May 9, 1924; s. Clarence James and Pearl Vivian (Rager) D.; m. Barbara M. Creighton, Jan. 30, 1949; children: Stephen, James, Jeffrey, Shawn Lynn, Robert, Heather. BBA magna cum laude, U. Pitts., 1958; postgrad., Indsl. Coll. of Armed Forces, Washington, 1965; MBA, George Washington U., 1966. Commd. 2d lt. U.S. Army Air Corps., 1944; advanced through grades to brig. gen. USAF, 1970, ret., 1975; successively navigator, radar observer U.S. Army Air Corps; sr. pilot USAF, 1943-66, dir. programs def. comm. planning group DCA, 1966-70, chief of staff U.S. Taiwan Def. Command, 1970-72, comdr. 1st Composite Wing, 1972-75; program dir Decisions and Designs Inc., McLean, Va., 1975-85; asst. to pres. PSC, Inc., Fairfax, Va., 1985-86; CEO Carr Techs. Inc., Oklahoma City, 1988-91; sr. mgmt. cons., 1986—; pres. J3 Investment Group, Herndon, Va., 1988-91; sec., bd. dirs. Seamast, Inc., Fairfax, PSC, Inc., 1988—, Internat. Video Broadcasts, Inc., Fairfax, 1988-94; founder., sec., bd. dirs. Internat. Privatization Enterprises, 1994-96; sec., bd. dirs. The Adler Cos., 1992—. Pres. PTA, Colton, Calif., 1963; deacon Presbyn. Ch., Erie, Pa., 1940. Decorated Disting. Svc. medal USAF, 2 Legions of Merit, Medal of Cloud and Banner Govt. Republic of China; named Disting. Citizen State of Md., 1974; U. Pitts. scholar, 1957. Mem. DAV (life), Ret. Officers Assn., Air Force Assn., Army Navy Country Club (Arlington Va.), Evergreen Country Club, (Haymarket, Va.), Am. Legion, Beta Gamma Sigma. Avocations: tennis, golf. Home: 3518 Woolman Dr Haymarket VA 20169-1821

DOUGLAS, CRERAR, religious studies educator; b. Sept. 4, 1944. BA, Columbia U., 1966; MDiv, Hartford Sem., 1969, PhD, 1973. Prof. dept. religious studies Calif. State U., Northridge, 1971—, chair dept. religious studies, 1998—. Author: Positive Negatives: A Motif in Christian Tradition, 1991. E-mail: crerar.douglas@csun.edu. Office: Calif State U Dept Religious Studies Northridge CA 91330-8316

DOUGLAS, DARCY, special education educator; b. Ft. Belvoir, Va., Apr. 17, 1950; d. James Shepard and Jeanne Marie (Dupré) D.; m. John H. Carpenter, Sept. 27, 1975 (div. June 1980); children: Troy Douglas, Angela. BS in Spl. Edn. summa cum laude, James Madison U., 1972; MA in Edn. summa cum laude, George Washington U., 1975. Cert. mental retardation tchr., interrelated tchr. Multi-handicapped tchr. Martinsburg, W.Va., 1972-74; resource tchr. Md., 1975; edn. dir. Pearl St. House, Framingham, Mass., 1976; nursery worker YMCA, Cin., 1977-78; day care dir. Atlanta, 1980; staff devel., mgmt., tchr. Ga. Retardation Ctr., Atlanta, 1980-88; resource tchr., tchr. self-contained learning disabilities, lead tchr. Cobb County Pub. Schs., Marietta, Ga., 1988—. Fellow State of W.Va., 1974-75, Washington, 1974-75. Mem. Coun. Exceptional Children, Benton Mackaye Trail Assn. (treas. 1985-86, pres. 1987-89, 99—, newsletter editor 1989-91, Maintenance 1991-94), Appalachian Trail Club, Nature Conservancy. Avocations: teaching private piano, back packing, trail building, bread baking, computers. Home: 3233 Rangers Gate Dr Marietta GA 30062-1472 Office: Cobb County Pub Schs Marietta GA 30060

DOUGLAS, DWIGHT OLIVER, university administrator; b. Mt. Carmel, Ill., May 7, 1941; s. Dwight Oliver and Jeannette Elizabeth (Moyer) D.; m. Carol Jane Brunson, June 2, 1963; children: Terri, Staci, Dana. B.S., Eastern Ill. U., 1962, M.S., 1966; D.Ed., U. Tenn., 1972. Asst. dir. residence halls U. Tenn., Knoxville, 1969-71, dir. residence halls, 1971-72; dir. housing U. Ga., Athens, 1972-74, dean student affairs, 1975-78, assoc. v.p. acad. affairs, 1978-80, v.p. student affairs, 1980—. Contbr. articles to profl. jours.; mem. editorial bds. Pres. PTA Council Clarke County, 1978; pres. Gaines Sch. PTA, 1977-78. Mem. Nat. Assn. Student Personnel Adminstrs. (state dir. Ga. 1982-84), So. Assn. Coll. Student Affairs, Ga. Personnel Assn., Phi Delta Kappa, Kappa Delta Pi, Omicron Delta Kappa, Demosthenian Literary Soc. Methodist. Club: Gridiron. Office: U Ga 201 Academic Bldg Athens GA 30602

DOUGLAS, FRANK FAIR, architect, graphic designer; b. Mansfield, La., Oct. 27, 1945; s. Edward Osler and Minnie Merle (Flanders) D.; m. Judith Catherine Wainwright, Sept. 6, 1969; 1 child, Samuel Wainwright. Student, NYU; BArch, La. State U., 1968. Registered architect. Designer Eggers & Higgins, N.Y.C., 1968-69; designer Neuhaus & Taylor, Houston, 1969-70, dir. graphics, 1970-72, assoc., 1972-75, sr. assoc., 1975-77; v.p. 3D/Internat., Houston, 1977-81, sr. v.p., 1981-86, exec. v.p., 1986-87; chmn., pres. Douglas/Gallagher, Houston, Washington, Nashville, 1987—; exhibit design and environ. prgaphic projects include Miss. Pavilion/Expoo '84, Singapore Pavilion/Expo '86, Conoco Retail Facilities Studies, 1987, Hotel Cheyenne and Santa Fe Disneyland Park, 1992, Environ. Graphics Stds. Entergy, Inc., 1994, Rangers Ballpark, 1994, N.Y. Yankees Spring Home Facility, 1996, Philippine Centennial Internat. Environ. Graphic, Anaheim Stadium for Disney Sports, Urban Graphics Syss. for cities of Mobile, Ala., San Antonio, San Juan, P.R., Salt Lake City, Galveston, Tex.; image cons. GM at Renaissance Ctr., Detroit, Mus. of Jewish Heritage, N.Y., 1997; Janet Annenberg Hooker Hall of Fame, Smithsonian, Independance Hall Visitors Ctr., Phila., Triple A Stadium for Oklahoma City Redhawks, Memphis Redbirds. Bd. dirs. Tex. Film Commn., Austin, 1982—; multi-media panelist Cultural Arts Coun. Houston, 1982-84; co-chair visual com. Houston Econ. Summit Host Com., 1990. Recipient awards for exhbns., 1985, 86, 88. Fellow AIA (bd. dirs. 1997—, exec. com. Houston chpt. 1989-90, pres. 1992, honor award 1985), Tex. Soc. Architects (v.p. 1994-96); mem. Soc. Environ. Graphic Designers (bd. dirs. 1971-72, Design award 1974), Rice Design Alliance (pres., bd. dirs. 1981-88, 91—), Soc. Mktg. Profl. Svcs. (bd. dirs. Houston chpt. 1982-92, Design award 1980O, Ind. Design Soc. Am., Houston City Club, Houston Club. Republican. Presbyterian. Home: 3822 Olympia Dr Houston TX 77019-3032 Office: Douglas Gallagher 3040 Post Oak Blvd Ste 510 Houston TX 77056-6589

DOUGLAS, FRED ROBERT, cost engineering consultant; b. Newark, N.J., Apr. 25, 1924; s. Nathan and Sara (Schneider) D.; m. Lenore Berger, Mar. 20, 1954; children: Neil Richard, David Nathaniel. BSChemE, N.J. Inst. Tech., 1945; MSChemE, Poly. Inst. N.Y., 1949. Asst. to prodn. mgr. Bristol-Myers Corp., N.Y.C., 1948-52; chem. engr. Jefferson Chem. Co. Inc., N.Y.C., 1952-53; technologist Texaco Inc., Beacon, N.Y., 1953-88; pvt. practice cons., 1988—; lectr. in cost engring. Contbr. articles to profl. jours. Pres. Hudson Valley Community Concerts Assn., 1968-69. With U.S. Army, 1945-47. Named Engr. of Distinction, Engrs. Joint Coun., 1970. Fellow Am. Assn. Cost Engrs. Internat. (sec. 1968-69, bd. dirs. 1983-84, v.p. 1985-89); mem. Rsch. Soc. Am. (treas. 1958-59). Home: PO Box 193 Glenham NY 12527-0193

DOUGLAS, HOPE M., psychotherapist, forensic hypnotist; b. Marblehead, Mass., Jan. 14, 1947; d. W.I. and Beatrice B. Kenerson. BA in Psychology, Mich. State U., 1969, MA in Rehab. Counseling, 1970. Cert. mental health counselor, Fla.; cert. Ericksonian hypnotist. With Bur. Narcotics and Dangerous Drugs, U.S. Dept. Jusitce, Denver, 1971; with narcotics investigation, officer Glendale Police Dept., Denver, 1971-74; exec. dir., dir. edn., nat. speaker Child and Family Agy. of S.E. Conn., 1974-84; evidence technician, instr. homicide investigation Naples (Fla.) Police Dept., 1984-90; founder, exec. dir. wildlife rehab. svcs. and edn. Wind Over Wings, Inc., Westbrook, Conn., 1990—; instr. wildlife rehab. Conn. Dept. Environ. Protection, 1991-92, 95, 96, 98; adj. faculty Conn. Coll., Mitchell Coll. Contbr. articles to profl. jours. Mem. adv. bd. Child Welfare League Am. Recipient J. Edgar Hoover award for excellence, 1985. Mem. Conn. Wildlife Rehab. Assn. (pres. 1992, bd. dirs. 1996—), Internat. Wildlife Rehab. Coun. (v.p. 1993-94, 97, acting exec. dir. 1995, bd. dirs. 1995-96, illustrator rehab. book series and disability book series 1995, 96). Mailing: PO Box 30 Westbrook CT 06498 Home: 26 Chittenden Hill Rd Westbrook CT 06498-1411

DOUGLAS, ILEANA, actress; b. Brockton, Mass., July 25, 1965. Appeared in films Guilty By Suspicion, 1991, Cape Fear, 1992, To Die For, 1995, Search & Destroy, 1995, Grace Of My Heart, 1996, Picture Perfect, 1997, Wedding Bell Blues, 1997, Bella Mafia, CBS Mow, 1997, Hacks, 1998, Happy Texas, 1999, Can't Stop Dancing, 1999, Message in a Bottle, 1999, Lansky (TV), 1999. Office: Rogers & Cowen Publicity C/O Michelle Bega 1888 Century Park E Ste 500 Los Angeles CA 90067-1709*

DOUGLAS, JAMES (BUSTER), boxer; b. Columbus, Ohio; s. Billy and Lula Douglas; children: Lamar, Cardaé. Profl. boxer 1981—;, defeated Mike Tyson, Feb. 1990 to become undisputed heavyweight champion. Office: Attn Lawrence Nallie 465 Waterbury Ct Ste A Gahanna OH 43230-5312

DOUGLAS, JAMES M., universtiy president. BA in Math., Tex. So. U., 1966, JD, 1970; JSM, Stanford U., 1971. Programmer analyst Singer Gen. Precision, Houston, 1971-72; asst. prof. law Thurgood Marshall Sch. Law, Tex. So. U., 1972-74; asst. prof. law Cleve.-Marshall Coll. Law, Cleve. State U., 1974-75, asst. prof. law, asst. dean for student affairs, 1974-75; assoc. prof. law, assoc. dean Syracuse U. Coll. Law, 1975-80; prof. law Northeastern U. Sch. Law, Boston, 1980-81; dean, prof. law Tex. So. U., 1981-95, interim provost, sr. v.p. for acad. affairs, 1995, interim pres., 1995, pres., 1995-99, prof. Law Sch. Contbr. numerous articles to profl. jours. Bd. dirs. Sickle Cell Found. Tex., 1988-94, pres., 1990-91; mem. steering com. Houston Campaign for Homeless, 1988-89; bd. dirs. Boy Scouts Am., 1993—, Greater Houston Partnership, 1996—. Mem. ABA, State Bar Tex., Tex. Supreme Ct. Hist. Soc. (trustee 1990-95), Houston Bar Assn. (chair law practice mgmt. sect. 1995—), Nat. Bar Assn., Houston C. of C. life), others. Office: Tex So U 3100 Cleburne St Houston TX 77004-4501*

DOUGLAS, JANICE GREEN, physician, educator; b. Nashville, July 11, 1943; d. Louis D. and Electa Green. BA magna cum laude, Fish U., 1964; MD, Meharry Med. Coll., 1968. Intern Meharry Med. Coll., 1968-71; NIH tng. fellow in endocrinology, instr. internal medicine Vanderbilt U., Nashville, 1971-73; sr. staff fellow sect. on hormonal regulation NIH, 1973-76; asst. prof. medicine Case Western Res. U. Sch. Medicine, Cleve., 1976-81, assoc. prof. medicine, 1981-84, prof. medicine, 1984—; dir. hypertension renal ambulatory care svc. Univ. Hosps. Cleve., 1976-80; dir. divsn. endocrinology and hypertension dept. medicine Univ. Hosps. Cleve. and Case Western Res. U., 1988-93, vice chair acad. affairs dept. medicine, 1991—, dir. divsn. hypertension dept. medicine, 1993—; mem. numerous grant rev. coms.; lectr., presenter in field; atteding physician in medicine and endicrinology U. Hosps., 1987; vis. prof. SUNY, Kings County Hosp. and Health Sci. Ctr., Bklyn., 1987, Med. U. S.C., 1989, Harlem Hosp., N.Y.C., 1993, N.Y. Med. Coll., Valhalla, 1994. mem. editl. rev. bd. Jour. Clin. Investigation, 1990—, Am. Jour. Physiology, Renal Fluid and Electrolytes, 1989-91; editl. bd. Hypertension, 1994—, Am. Soc. Clin. Investigation, 1990—, Ethnicity and Disease, 1990—, Circulation, 1993—; guest editor Jour. Clin. Investigation, U. Calif., San Diego, 1992—; assoc. editor Jour. Lab. and Clin. Medicine, 1986-90; reviewer numerous manuscripts and abstracts.; contbr. numerous articles, abstracts to profl. publs., chpts. to books. Fellow High Blood Pressure Coun., Am. Heart Assn., 1993—. Mem. Assn. Am. Physicians, Cleve. Med. Assn., Am. Soc. Hypertension, Kidney Found. Ohio, Women in Endocrinology, Inter-Am. Soc. Hypertension, Women in Nephrology, Assn. for Acad. Minority Physicians, Am. Physiology Soc.,

Endocrine Soc., Ctrl. Soc. for Clin. Rsch., Internat. Soc. Hypertension in Blacks, Inst. Medicine of NAS, Internat. Soc. Nephrology, Am. Soc. Nephrology, Am. Soc. Clin. Investigation, Am. Fedn. Clin. Rsch., Am. Heart Assn., Phi Beta Kappa, Alpha Omega Alpha (pres. Meharry chpt. 1968), Beta Kappa Chi. Office: Case Western U Sch Medicine 10900 Euclid Ave # 165 Cleveland OH 44106-1712*

DOUGLAS, JOANNE M. KAERWER, elementary education educator; b. St. Paul, Mar. 20, 1949; d. Richard F. and Betty A. (Hoelscher) Kaerwer; children: Jeremy F., Katherine E. BA summa cum laude, Tufts U., 1971, MEd, 1972; CAGS, Fitchburg State Coll., 1999. Cert. elem. edn. Tchr. primary level Mass. Hosp. Sch., Canton, 1971-85; elem. tchr. Sharon (Mass.) Alternative Sch., 1985—. Mem. NEA, ASCD, Mass. Tchrs. Assn., Sharon Tchrs. Assn., Phi Beta Kappa. Home: 12 Robs Ln Sharon MA 02067-1436 Office: Sharon Alternative Sch 45 Wilshire Dr Sharon MA 02067-1529

DOUGLAS, J(OCELYN) FIELDING, toxicologist, consultant; b. Delta, Utah, Jan. 25, 1927; s. Benjamin and Amelia (Fielding) D.; m. Rose Mary Terrazzino, Sept. 16, 1951; children: David Benjamin, Pamela Susan, Jason Terrell. BS with high honors, U. Ill., 1948; MA, Columbia U., 1950, PhD, 1953. Project leader Johnson & Johnson, New Brunswick, N.J., 1952-58; dir. biochemistry Carter-Wallace, Cranbury, N.J., 1958-74; dep. dir. carcinogenesis testing program Nat. Cancer Inst., Bethesda, Md., 1976-80; chief ops. Nat. Toxicology Program, Bethesda, 1980-84; pres. Sci. Svcs., Inc., Front Royal, Va., 1984—; expert cons. NIH, Bethesda, 1976-81; cons. in field. Author, editor: Carcinogenesis and Mutagenesis Testing, 1984; contbr. numerous articles to profl. jours. Pvt. U.S. Army, 1944-46. Recipient Richard Neff award Richard Neff Soc., 1966, Dir. award Nat. Cancer Inst., 1979; USPHS fellow, 1950-52. Fellow AAAS; mem. Soc. Toxicology, Am. Soc. Pharmacology and Exptl. Therapeutics, Am. Chem. Soc. (chmn. biochem. sect. 1954). Avocations: gardening, reading, meditation. Home and Office: Sci Svcs Inc PO Box 533 Front Royal VA 22630-0533

DOUGLAS, JOHN LEWIS, lawyer; b. Atlanta, Sept. 23, 1950; s. Charles Lewis Jr. and Bettye Lee (Phelps) D.; m. Rebecca Ann Peterson, Aug. 16, 1974; children: Amber Lynne, Dianna Michelle, John Lewis Jr., Scott Foster, Charles Tillman, Alexander Peterson, Michael Lawrence, Jolanta Kuuzik, Tomas Kuuzik. BA in Econs., Davidson (N.C.) Coll., 1972; JD, U. Ga., 1977. Bar: Ga. 1977. Assoc. Alston and Bird, Atlanta, 1977-83, ptnr., 1983-87, 90—; gen. counsel FDIC, Washington, 1987-89. Contbr. articles to profl. jours. Republican. Mem. LDS Ch. Office: Alston & Bird LLP 1 Atlantic Ctr 1201 W Peachtree St NW Ste 4200 Atlanta GA 30309-3424

DOUGLAS, JOHN PAUL, recruiter, lawyer, commercial and family law media; b. Louisville, Jan. 6, 1939; s. John Sammuel and Margaret Mary (Wagner) D.; m. Laura Christine Welborn, Feb. 17, 1968; children: Constance, John, Robert, D. Bear. AB, Regis U., Denver, 1968; JD, No. Ky. U., 1976. Bar: Ohio 1976, Tex. 1981, U.S. Supreme Ct. 1982. Program officer Cath. Relief Svcs., India, 1968-70; adminstr. Hamilton County, Cin., 1970-76, trial atty., 1976-80; gen. counsel Gen. Exploration Co., Dallas, 1980-86; pvt. practice Douglas & Assocs., Dallas, 1989-90, 92—; Legal Search Internatl. (pres. 1998—), adj. prof. law U. Dallas, 1989-91. Contbr. articles to various publs. Pres. Maria Kannon Zen Ctr., Dallas, 1996. With USN, 1958-62, 90-92, capt. USNR, 1973-90, 93-96. Mem. Am. Arbitration Assn. (arbitrator 1990—), Soc. Hindu-Christian Soc., Camaldolese Oblate. Roman Catholic. Avocations: backpacking, arctophie. Home and Office: PO Box 851521 Richardson TX 75085-1521

DOUGLAS, KARIN NADJA, engineer; b. Berlin, Sept. 2, 1931; came to U.S., 1963; d. Fritz and Irma (Rutke) Kruse; m. Karl Vonmoos, May 21, 1955 (div. Dec. 1961); m. Robert P. Douglas, Dec. 13, 1969. AS in Legal Adminstrn. magna cum laude, Sacred Heart U., Fairfield, Conn., 1984. Apprentice in tech. drafting and design Hasler AG., Bern, Switzerland, 1961-63; elec. designer UOP Air Correction Divsn., Norwalk, Conn., 1968-83; engrng. cons. various engrng. corps., Fairfield County, Conn., 1983-87; agy. compliance coord. ITT Flygt Corp., Trumbull, Conn., 1987—. Creator Evelyn Conley scholarship for Sacred Heart U., 1988; bd. dirs. Nat. Lymphedema Network, San Francisco, 1997—, creator lymphedema alert bracelet, 1997, creator 1st lymphedema support group in Conn., 1996-97, also patient adv.; sec., trustee Friends of Boothe Park, Inc., mus. and rose garden, Stratford, Conn., 1985—. Recipient D-Day award Nat. Lymphedema Network, 1996. Avocations: sailing, fishing, cooking. Home: 96A Seminole Ln Stratford CT 06614-8149

DOUGLAS, KATHLEEN MARY HARRIGAN, psychotherapist, educator; b. Boston, Apr. 24, 1950; d. John Joseph and Kathleen Margaret (Connolly) Harrigan; m. Dr. Robert E. Douglas, Feb. 24, 1977; children: David, Pamela, Elizabeth. Student, Uxbridge, England; BA in Psychology, Sophia U., Tokyo, 1972; MA in Counseling Psychology, Chapman U., Orange, Calif., 1983; PhD in Counselor Edn., U. Fla., 1990. Elem tchr. Marymount Prep Sch., Palos Verdes, Calif., 1973-99; pvt. practice Orlando, Fla., 1985-95; psychology prof. Valencia C.C., Orlando, Fla., 1989-93; prof. Fla. Inst. Tech., 1990-94; asst. prof., grad. acad. advisors, clin. internship supr. Troy State U., Orlando, Fla., 1993-97; software developer of clinically oriented software, 1994—; assoc. prof. Barry U., Orlando, 1999—; drug/alcohol counselor Ft. Belvoir, Va., 1981-82; counselor Orange County Mental Health Ctr., Winter Park, Fla., 1982-83; child abuse therapist Thee Door, Orlando, 1983-84; presenter in field. Author: The Therapeutic Superhighway, 1995. Counselor Winter Park Towers Nursing Home, 1985; vol. group counselor Hillcrest Halfway House, Orlando, 1985. 1st Lt. U.S. Army, 1976-80. Recipient Marion medal Cath. Ch., Boston, 1966, Civic award Spouse Abuse, Inc., Orlando, 1984. Mem. Am. Assn. for Counseling and Devel., Kappa Delta Phi, Pi Lambda Theta, Chi Sigma Iota. Roman Catholic. Home: 1781 Lake Berry Dr Winter Park FL 32789-5911

DOUGLAS, KENNETH JAY, food products executive; b. Harbor Beach, Mich., Sept. 4, 1922; s. Harry Douglas and Xenia (Williamson) D.; m. Elizabeth Ann Schweizer, Aug. 17, 1946; children: Connie Ann, Andrew Jay. Student, U. Ill., 1940-41, 46-47; J.D., Chgo. Kent Coll. Law, 1950; grad., Advanced Mgmt. Program, Harvard, 1962. Bar: Ill. 1950, Ind. 1952. Spl. agt. FBI, 1950-54; dir. indsl. relations Dean Foods Co., Franklin Park, Ill., 1954-64, v.p. fin. and adminstrn., 1964-70, chmn. bd., chief exec. officer, 1970-87, chmn. bd., 1987-89, vice-chmn., 1989-92; bd. dirs. Richardson Electonics, Ltd., Andrew Corp.; bd. dirs., vice chmn. Loyola Univ. Health System. Chmn. bd. trustees West Suburban Hosp. Med. Ctr., Oak Park, Ill.; mem. bd. overseers Ill. Inst. Tech./Chgo.-Kent Coll. Law; mem. Chgo. Com. With USNR, 1944-46. Mem. Chgo. Club, Econ. Club, Execs. Club, Comml. Club (Chgo.), Oak Park Country Club, River Forest Tennis Club, Old Baldy Country Club (Wyo.). Republican. Office: 1440 W North Ave Ste 207 Melrose Park IL 60160-1425

DOUGLAS, KIRK (ISSUR DANIELOVITCH DEMSKY), actor, motion picture producer; b. Amsterdam, N.Y., Dec. 9, 1916; s. Harry and Bryna (Sanglel) Danielovitch; m. Diana Dill (div. Feb. 1950); children: Michael, Joel; m. Anne Buydens, May 29, 1954; children: Peter, Eric Anthony. A.B., St. Lawrence U., 1938, D.F.A. (hon.), 1958; student, Am. Acad. Dramatic Arts, 1939-41. Appeared on Broadway in Spring Again, Three Sisters, Kiss and Tell, Wind is Ninety, Alice in Arms, Man Bites Dog; producer, star Broadway play One Flew over the Cuckoo's Nest; appeared in films: The Strange Love of Martha Ivers, 1946, Morning Becomes Electra, 1947, I Walk Alone, 1947, Out of the Past, 1947, Walls of Jericho, 1948, My Dear Secretary, 1948, A Letter to Three Wives, 1948, Champion, 1949, Young Man with a Horn, 1950, The Glass Menagerie, Ace in the Hole, Along the Great Divide, Detective Story, 1951, The Big Sky, 1951, The Big Trees, The Bad and the Beautiful, 1952, Equilibrium, 1952, The Story of Three Loves, The Juggler, 1953, Act of Love, Ulysses, 20,000 Leagues Under the Sea, 1954, Man Without a Star, The Racers, 1954, Lust for Life, 1956, Top Secret Affair, Gunfight at O.K. Corral, Paths of Glory, 1957, Last Train for Gunhill, 1958, Strangers When We Meet, 1958, The Devil's Disciple, 1959, Town Without Pity, The Last Sunset, 1961, Two Weeks in Another Town, 1962, The List of Adrian Messenger, For Love or Money, The Hook, 1963, In Harm's Way, Heroes of Telemark, 1965, Cast a Giant Shadow, Is Paris Burning?, 1966, War Wagon, The Way West, 1967, A Lovely Way to Die, 1968, The Arrangement, 1969, There Was a Crooked Man, 1970, The Light at the Edge of the World, Catch Me A Spy, 1971, A Man To Respect, 1972, Master Touch, 1972, Scalawag, 1973, Jekyl & Hyde, 1973, Posse, 1975, Once is Not Enough, 1975, Holocaust 2000, 1977, The Fury, 1978, The Villain, Saturn 3, Home Movies, 1979, The Man from Snowy River, 1982, Eddie Macon's Run, 1983, Tough Guys, 1986, Oscar, 1991, Greedy, 1994, Welcome to Veraz, 1990, A Song for David, 1996; producer, dir. films Scalawag, 1973, Posse, 1975; pres. Bryna Co.; producer, actor films: The Final Countdown, Indian Fighter, 1955, Vikings, 1964, Spartacus, 1960, The Last Sunset, 1961, Lonely are the Brave, 1962, Summertree, 1963, Seven Days in May, 1964, The Brotherhood, 1968, A Gunfight, 1971, Oscar, 1991, The Secret, 1991, Take Me Home Again, 1994; co-producer film One Flew Over the Cuckoo's Nest, 1975, The Final Countdown, 1979; TV miniseries appearance: Queenie, 1987; TV film appearance: Mousy (also dir.), 1973, The Money Changers, Victory at Entebbe, 1976, Remembrance of Love, 1982, Draw!, 1984, Amos, 1985, Inherit the Wind, 1988; author: (autobiography) The Ragman's Son, 1988; (novels) Dance with the Devil, 1990, The Gift, 1992, Last Tango in Brooklyn, 1994, The Broken Mirror, 1997. Nominated for Acad. Award, 1949, 52, 56; recipient N.Y. Film Critics award, 1956, Hollywood Fgn. Press award, 1956, Heart and Torch award Am. Heart Assn., 1956, Splendid Am. award of merit George Washington Carver Meml. Found., 1957, cited in Congl. Record for service as goodwill ambassador, 1964, Cecil B. DeMille award for contbns. in entertainment field, 1967, Presdl. Medal of Freedom, 1981, elected to Cowboy Hall of Fame, 1984, Lifetime Achievement award Am. Film Inst., 1991; decorated Legion of Honor (France), 1985, Chevalier de la Legion d'Honneur, 1985, Officer de la Legion d'Honneur, 1990; Kennedy Center Honor, 1994; HonoraryOscar, Lifetime Achievement, 1997. Mem. UN Assn. (dir. Los Angeles chpt.). Made State Dept.-USIA tours around world. Office: CAA 9830 Wilshire Blvd Beverly Hills CA 90212-1804

DOUGLAS, (CHARLES) LEE, executive vice president basketball team; b. Atlanta, Ga., Aug. 23, 1952; m. Nancy; children: Brent, Kelly. BA in Indsl. Mgmt., Ga. Tech., 1974; MBA, Ga. State U., 1978. From sales rep. to exec. v.p. Atlanta Hawks, 1978-89, exec. v.p., 1989—; cons. Atlanta Braves, 1992—; mem. Mktg. Advisory Bd. NBA Properties. Bd. dirs. Atlanta Hawks Found. Office: One CNN Ctr Ste 405 S Tower Atlanta GA 30303*

DOUGLAS, LESLIE, investment banker; b. Enon Valley, Pa., Mar. 14, 1914; s. Robert R. and Margaret M. (Mc Anlis) D.; m. Jean Wallace, Oct. 12, 1946; children—David, Ann and Joan (twins). B.S., Geneva Coll., Beaver Falls, Pa., 1935; M.B.A., Harvard U., 1937. Investment mgr. Royal Liverpool Group, N.Y.C., 1937-41; investment banker Folger Nolan Fleming Douglas, Inc., Washington, 1946—; v.p. Folger Nolan Fleming Douglas, Inc., 1955—; bd. govs. Assn. Stock Exchange Firms, 1969-72, Securities Industry Assn., 1972-75. Trustee Holton Arms Sch., Washington, Landon Sch., Vis. Nurses Assn., Washington. Served to lt. comdr. USN, 1941-46. Republican. Presbyterian. Clubs: Chevy Chase; Met. (Washington). Home: 4733 Woodway Ln NW Washington DC 20016-3240 Office: 725 15th St NW Washington DC 20005-2109

DOUGLAS, MARY TEW, anthropology and humanities educator; b. San Remo, Italy, Mar. 25, 1921; came to U.S., 1977; m. James Douglas, 1951; children: Janet, James, Philip. BA, U. Oxford, Eng., 1943, MA, 1947, BSc, 1948, PhD, 1951; hon. doctorate, U. Uppsala, U. Notre Dame, Jewish Theol. Sem., U. East Anglia, U. of Essex, U. Warwick. Rsch. fellow Internat. African Inst. for Fieldwork, Belgian Congo, 1949-50, 53, 87; lectr. anthropology Univ. Coll., London, 1951-62, prof. social anthropology, 1971-78; reader U. London, 1963-70; dir. rsch. on culture Russell Sage Found., N.Y.C., 1977-81; Avalon Found. prof. in humanities Northwestern U., Evanston, Ill., 1981-85; vis. prof. depts. religion and anthropology Princeton U., 1985-88. Author: Lele of the Kasai, 1966, Purity and Danger, 1966, Natural Symbols, 1970, Implicit Meanings, 1975, Risk and Culture, 1982; In the Active Voice, 1982; editor: Essays in the Sociology of Perception, 1982, How Institutions Think, 1986, Risk Acceptability, 1987, Risk and Blame, 1992, In the Wilderness, 1993, Thought Styles, 1996, Missing Persons, 1998. Hon. fellow U. Coll. London, 1994; decorated Comdr. British Empire, 1992. Mem. AAAS, Academia Europaea, Brit. Acad. Address: 22 Hillway, Highgate, London N66QA, England

DOUGLAS, MICHAEL, publishing executive; b. Corpus Christi, Tex., Nov. 19, 1955; s. Phyllis Marie (Blackshear) Fusillier; children: Kenneth Muhammad, Michelle Muhammad, Gabrielle Muhammad, Phenix Muhammad, Aaron Muhammad. Student, Ariz. State U., 1979-82. Pres. Mecca Publs., Phoenix, 1986—; owner Re-Creation Enterprises, Phoenix, 1990—. Author: Brotherhood, War, Revolution, 1986, Jabril—God, Man, Angel, 1990, Apocalypse Now 1997-2007, 1995. Pres. Neighborhood Agrl. Program, Phoenix, 1988; with operation paintbrush City of Phoenix, 1988; head of unknown writer's workshop Mecca Publ., Phoenix, 1994—; homeless counselor Prodigal Son, Phoenix, 1995. With U.S. Army, 1972-74. Muslim. Avocations: community service, reading. Office: Mecca Publs PO Box 28238 Tempe AZ 85285-8238

DOUGLAS, MICHAEL KIRK, actor, film producer, director; b. New Brunswick, N.J., Sept. 25, 1944; s. Kirk and Diana Douglas; m. Diandra Morrell Luker, Mar. 20, 1977; 1 child, Cameron Morrell. B.A., U. Calif., Santa Barbara, 1967. Actor: films including (film debut) Hail Hero, 1969, Summertime, 1971, Napoleon and Samantha, 1972, Coma, 1978, Running, 1979, It's My Turn, 1981, Star Chamber, 1983, A Chorus Line, 1985, Black Rain, 1989, The War of the Roses, 1989, Shining Through, 1992, Falling Down, 1993, Disclosure, 1994, The American President, 1995, The Ghost and the Darkness, 1996, A Song for David, 1996, The Game, 1997; TV series: Streets of San Francisco; producer: (films) One Flew Over the Cuckoo's Nest, 1975 (Acad. award for best picture), The China Syndrome; exec. producer: (film) Starman, 1984; producer, actor: (films) Romancing the Stone, 1984, Jewel of the Nile, 1985, Fatal Attraction, 1987, Wall Street, 1987 (Golden Globe award for best actor, Acad. award for best actor), A Perfect Murder, 1998, Wonder Boys, 1999, Still Life, 1999; producer Flatliners, 1990, Radio Flyer, 1992, Face/Off, 1997, The Rainmaker, 1997; co-exec. producer The Tender, Made in America; founder record label Third Stone/Atlantic. Office: care Creative Artists Agy Inc 9830 Wilshire Blvd Beverly Hills CA 90212-1804*

DOUGLAS, P C, producer, director, reporter, editor; b. Houston; s. Hilda Florence Carrithers. BA in Broadcast Journalism, Tex. Tech. U., 1994. Reporter/photographer KCBD-TV, Lubbock, Tex., 1992-93; copy editor La Ventana, Tex. Tech. U., Lubbock, 1993-94; reporter The Independent, Gallup, N.Mex., 1994; radio announcer KDLK/KLKE, Del Rio, Tex., 1994; reporter Del Rio News-Herald, 1994; reporter/photographer KOSA-TV, Odessa, Tex., 1994-96; radio announcer KQRX-FM, Odessa, 1995-96; flight attendant Southwest Airlines, Dallas, 1996-97; polit./govtl. reporter Houston News Today, 1997-98; media coord. Motivators, Inc., Houston, 1998-99; prodr., dir., reporter, editor Houston Internat. Bus. Ch, 1999—. Co-prodr.: (TV documentary) Lubbock Hispanic Women Leaders, 1993 (1st place award 1993). Media vol. Make-A-Wish Found. West Tex., Odessa, 1994-96. Recipient 1st place award Soc. Profl. Journalists, 1993. Avocations: Hawaiian culture and history research, travel, stamp collecting. Home: #211 1341 Castle Ct Houston TX 77006 Office: Houston Internat Bus Ch Ste 100 3013 Fountainview Houston TX 77057

DOUGLAS, PAUL WOLFF, retired mining executive; b. Springfield, Mass., Sept. 12, 1926; s. Paul Howard and Dorothy (Wolff) D.; children: Philip LeBreton, Carolyn Jory Jacobs, Christine Sanders Tansey, Paul Harding (dec.). AB, Princeton U., 1948; student, Leeds (Eng.) U., 1948. Dir. internal finance sect. ECA Mission to France, 1948-52; with Freeport Minerals Co., 1952—, exec., v.p., dir., 1970-75, pres., chmn. exec. com., 1975—; pres., chief exec. officer Freeport-McMoran Inc., 1981-83; chmn., chief exec. officer Pittston Co., 1984-91; ret., 1991; bd. dirs. Phelps Dodge Corp.; chmn. Cmty. Planning Bd., N.Y.C., 1966-68. Served with USNR, 1944-46. Home: Ste 4600 45 E 62nd St New York NY 10021-8025 Office: Rm 4600 60 E 42nd St Ste 4600 New York NY 10165-0006

DOUGLAS, ROBERT GORDON, JR., physician; b. N.Y.C., Apr. 17, 1934; s. Robert Gordon and Alice (Lewis) D.; m. Ann Castle Moses, Dec. 22, 1956; children: Robert Gordon, 3d, Timothy Stuart, Catherine Lewis. AB, Princeton U., 1955; MD, Cornell U., 1959. Diplomate Am. Bd. Internal Medicine. Successively intern, asst. resident in internal medicine, resident N.Y. Hosp., 1959-61, 62-63; asst. resident Johns Hopkins Hosp., 1961-62; USPHS clin. assoc., clin. investigator Nat. Inst. Allergy and Infectious Disease, 1963-66; asst. prof. microbiology and medicine Baylor Coll. Medicine, Houston, 1966-70; mem. faculty Sch. Medicine and Dentistry U. Rochester, N.Y., 1970-82, prof. medicine and microbiology Sch. Medicine and Dentistry, 1974-82, head infectious disease unit Sch. Medicine and Dentistry, 1970-82, sr. assoc. dean edn. Sch. Medicine and Dentistry, 1979-82; prof., chmn. dept. medicine Med. Coll. Cornell U., 1982-90; physician in chief N.Y. Hosp., 1982-90; sr. v.p. medi. and sci. affairs Merck Sharp & Dohme Internat., 1990-91; pres. Merck Vaccines, 1991-99; cons. in field; adj. prof. medicine Cornell U. Med. Coll., 1990—; hon. attending physician N.Y. Hosp., 1990—. Editor: Principles and Practices of Infectious Diseases, 1979, 2d edit., 1985, 3d edit., 1990; contbr. articles to profl. jours. Recipient Hawkins award Assn. Am. Pubs., 1980. Fellow ACP, Infectious Diseases Soc. Am. (pres. 1991-92, Feldman award); mem. Inst. Medicine, Am. Soc. Clin. Investigation, Assn. Am. Physicians, Am. Clin. Climatol. Assn. Home: 8 Windermere Way Princeton NJ 08540-7553 Office: One Merck Dr PO Box 100 Whitehouse Station NJ 08889-0100

DOUGLAS, ROBERT LEE, lawyer; b. Chgo., Nov. 12, 1936; s. Clinton Arnold and Blance Omara (Perkins) D.; m. Ida Marie Chalstrom, Mar. 18, 1960; 1 child, Clinton Arnold II. BA, Eastern Ill. U., 1961; LLB, U. Ill., 1965. Bar: Ill. 1965, U.S. Dist. Ct. (no. dist.) 1966, U.S. Ct. Appeals (7th cir.) 1966, U.S. Dist. Ct. (ea. dist.) 1968, U.S. Dist. Ct. (so. dist.), U.S. Supreme Ct. 1983. Assoc. Peterson, Lawry, Rall, Barber & Ross, Chgo., 1965-67; pvt. practice Robinson, Ill., 1967—; mem. U. Ill. Pres. Coun. Del. Thomas Jefferson Constnl. Conv., Chgo., 1985; profl. chmn. Am. Cancer Soc., Robinson, 1967; del. Crawpac, Robinson, 1985—. With USN, 1954-57, PTO. Mem. ABA, ATLA, Ill. Trial Lawyers Assn. (bd. mgrs. 1985-87), Crawford County Bar Assn. (ad. 1967, pres. 1978, 96-97), Ill. State Bar Assn., Am. Angus Assn., Am. Legion, Quail Creek Country Club, Elks, Moose. Democrat. Methodist. Avocation: cattle breeding.

DOUGLAS, ROBERT OWEN, writer; b. Aberdeen, S.D., Feb. 18, 1940; s. James Garrison and Lorene Augusta (Soper) D. BA, Claremont McKenna Coll., 1962. Maritime editor San Pedro (Calif.) News Pilot, 1968-70; freelance photographer Nat. Geog. Mag., Washington, 1969; pvt. practice writer Tacoma, 1977—. Lyricist Bravo, You're High Voltage, 1996, The Vacation Song, 1996, Writer The Seven Seals, 1999, Heart of Gold, 1999, Secret Pandemonium, 1999, Holy Moses!, 1999; inventor Douglas Tower Turbine, 1996. Lt. USN, 1963-68. Recipient Song of the Month award Chapel Rec. Co., Wollaston, Mass., 1996. Mem. The Camelot Soc. (dir.). Avocations: photography, music. Address: The Camelot Soc PO Box 1633 Tacoma WA 98401-1633

DOUGLAS, WILLIAM ERNEST, retired government official; b. Charleston, S.C., Nov. 26, 1930; s. William Ernest and Helen A. (Fortune) D.; m. Nancy Anne Gibson, July 18, 1980. AB, The Citadel, 1956; postgrad., U. S.C., 1956-59. Asst. dist. dir. Jackson dist. IRS, Miss., 1972-73, Atlanta dist. IRS, 1973-74; asst. regional commr. S.E. region IRS, Atlanta, 1974-78; dir. Regional Service Ctr. S.E. Region IRS, Atlanta, 1978-80; commr. fin. mgmt. svc. U.S. Treasury Dept., Washington, 1980-91. With U.S. Army, 1948-52, Korean War, 1950-51. Recipient Rec. Sec. of Treasury's Disting. Svc. award, 1991, Presdl. Exec. Rank award, 1991. Home: 205 Settlers Rd Saint Simons GA 31522

DOUGLASS, BETTY JEAN, executive secretary; b. Oil City, Pa., June 5, 1928; d. Nelson Earl and Hazel Vesta (Graham) Stover; m. Paul James Douglass, Jan. 15, 1946; children: Paul James Jr., Linda Jean Wolfe, Timothy Earl, Gary Arthur. Student, Diablo Valley Coll., Pleasant Hill, Calif., 1973-74, Cerritos (Calif.) Coll., 1975-76; AS, L.A. Harbor Coll., 1982. Auditor Gen. Dynamics/Astro., Kearney Mesa, Calif., 1958-60; sec. Gen. Dynamics, Topeka, 1960-62; co-owner 7-11 Southland, Del Mar, Calif., 1965-69; pers. U. S.C., Charleston, 1969-71; bookkeeper Breuner's, Concord, Calif., 1972-75; office adminstr. 4 Seasons Cabinet, Vancouver, Wash., 1976-79, Nat. Nursing, Inc., Carson, Calif., 1979-81, Quality Mgmt. Cons., Ormond Beach, Fla., 1987—. Contbr. poems to anthologies. Vol. Long Beach (Calif.) Rape Crisis Ctr., 1985-86; treas. Bapt. Ch., Walnut, Calif., 1972; mem. visitation com. Tomoka Christian Ch., Ormond Beach, 1997. Mem. Internat. Poetry Soc., Alpha Gamma Sigma. Republican. Avocations: 12 grandchildren, 14 great-grandchildren, oil painting, computers, bicycling.

DOUGLASS, BRUCE E., physician; b. Berwyn, Ill., Sept. 26, 1917; s. Frank Lionel and Helen Mary (Eccles) D.; m. Charlotte Maurer Natwick, Oct. 14, 1942; children: Jean N., Bruce G., John F. B.A., U. Wis., 1938, M.D., 1942; M.S. in Medicine, U. Minn., 1949. Intern Med. Coll. of Va., Richmond, 1942-43; resident in internal medicine Mayo Clinic, Rochester, Minn, 1947-50; mem. staff Mayo Clinic, 1949—, chmn. div. preventive medicine, 1962—; dir. Mayo Clinic (Mayo sect. of Patient and Health Edn.), 1976—; dir. Occupational Health Inst., Chgo., 1968—. Author: Anatomy of the Portal Vein and Its Tributaries, 1949, The Problem of Benign Bronchial Obstruction, 1954, Predicting Disease: Is It Possible? 1971, Health Problems of Hospital Employees, 1971, Examining Healthy Persons: How and How Often? 1980. Chmn. Rochester Music Bd., 1960-70; v.p. Minn. Zool. Soc., 1974-77. Served to capt. M.C. AUS, 1944-47. Fellow Am. Acad. Occupational Medicine (Keogh award 1981), Am. Occupational Med. Assn. (pres. 1977-78, Meritorious Service award 1979); mem. AMA (Physician's Recognition award 1974-77, chmn. sect. council on preventive medicine 1978-80, del. for occupational med. to ho. of dels. 1978-85), Minn. Med. Assn. (chmn. com. on public health edn. 1979), Ramazzini Soc., Assn. Tchrs. Preventive Medicine, Am. Coll. Preventive Medicine, Minn. Zool. Soc., Sigma Xi, Phi Kappa Phi, Sigma Phi, Nu Sigma Nu. Home: 9851 Watertower Rd Interlochen MI 49643-9526 Office: Mayo Clinic Rochester MN 55905

DOUGLASS, CARL DEAN, biochemistry consultant, former government official; b. Little Rock, Apr. 27, 1925; s. Dennie and Elizabeth (Rives) D.; m. Vera Davis, Jan. 23, 1946; children—Joseph Dean, Katherine Elizabeth. B.S., Hendrix Coll., Conway, Ark., 1947; M.S. in Chemistry, U. Okla., 1949, Ph.D., 1952. From instr. to asso. prof. biochemistry U. Ark., 1952-59; chief nutrition research br. FDA, Washington, 1959-61; with NIH, Bethesda, Md., from 1961, asso. dir. statistics, analysis and research evaluation, div. research grants, 1970-71, dep. dir. div., 1971-76, dir., 1976-85; pvt. practice cons. Md., 1985—. Served with USNR, 1943-46. Fellow Oak Ridge Inst. Nuclear Studies, 1951-52. Fellow Am. Inst. Chemists, AAAS; mem. Am. Chem. Soc., Soc. Exptl. Biology and Medicine, Am. Inst. Nutrition, Am. Inst. Biol. Scis., Sigma Xi, Alpha Chi Sigma, Phi Lambda Upsilon. Home and Office: 15107 Interlachen Dr Silver Spring MD 20906-5625

DOUGLASS, ELLEN HEATHER, humanities educator; b. Oceanside, N.Y., May 1, 1959; d. Richard Edmond and Amy Carolyn (Smith) D.; m. William Jesse Biddle. BA in History, Carleton Coll., 1982; MA in Comparative Lit., Brown U., 1987, PhD in Comparative Lit., 1994. Asst. prof. comparative lit. and women's studies Pa. State U., State College, 1985—; tchg. asst. Brown U., Providence, 1985-87, 90-93; vis. scholar, prof. Fed. U. Rio de Janeiro, 1987-88; vis. scholar U. West Indies, Kingston, Jamaica, 1989. Contbr. chpts. to books and articles to profl. jours. Fulbright fellow, Rio de Janeiro, 1987-88. Mem. MLA, Northeastern MLA, Am. Comparative Lit. Assn., Nat. Women's Studies Assn.

DOUGLASS, ENID HART, educational program director; b. L.A., Oct. 23, 1926; d. Frank Roland and Enid Yandell (Lewis) Hart; m. Malcolm P. Douglass, Aug. 28, 1948; children: Malcolm Paul Jr., John Aubrey, Susan Enid. BA, Pomona Coll., 1948; MA, Claremont (Calif.) Grad. Sch., 1959. Research asst. World Book Ency., Palo Alto, Calif., 1953-54; exec. sec., asst. dir. oral history program Claremont Grad. U., 1963-71, dir. oral history program, 1971—, lectr. history, 1977—; mem. Calif. Heritage Preservation Commn., 1977-85, chmn. 1983-85. Contbr. articles to hist. jours. Mayor pro tem City of Claremont, 1980-82, mayor, 1982-86; mem. planning and rsch. adv. coun. State of Calif.; mem. city coun. City of Claremont, 1978-86; founder Claremont Heritage, Inc., 1977-80; bd. dirs., 1986-95; bd. dirs. Pilgrim Pla., Claremont; founder, steering com., founding bd. Claremont Cmty. Found., 1989-95, pres., 1990-94. Mem. Oral History Assn. (pres. 1979-80), Southwest Oral History Assn. (founding steering com. 1981, J.V. Mink award 1984), Nat. Council Pub. History (sounding com. 1980), LWV (bd. dirs. 1957-59, Outstanding Svc. to Community award, 1986). Democrat. Avocation: tennis. Home: 1195 N Berkeley Ave Claremont CA 91711-3842

Office: Claremont Grad U Oral History Program 710 N College Ave Claremont CA 91711-3921

DOUGLASS, FRANK RUSSELL, lawyer; b. Dallas, May 29, 1933; s. Claire Allen and Caroline (Score) D.; m. Carita Calkins, Feb. 5, 1955 (div. 1983); children: Russell, Tom, Andrew, Cathy; m. Betty Elwanda Richards, Dec. 31, 1983. BBA, Southwestern U., 1953; LLB, U. Tex., 1958. Bar: Tex. 1957, U.S. Dist. Ct. (we. dist.) Tex. 1960, U.S. Dist. Ct. (so. dist.) Tex. 1981, U.S. Dist. Ct. (no. dist.) Tex. 1985, U.S. Dist. Ct. (ea. dist.) Tex. 1987, U.S. Supreme Ct. 1964, U.S. Ct. Appeals (5th cir.) 1985; cert. in civil trial law, and oil, gas and mineral law. Various positions to ptnr. McGinnis, Lochridge & Kilgore, Austin, Tex., 1957-76; sr. ptnr. Scott, Douglass & McConnico, Austin, 1976—; bd. dirs. Mallon Resources, Denver, Rio Petroleum Co., Amarillo, Tex; trustee Southwestern U., Georgetown, Tex. (distinguished alumnus 1999). Contbr. articles to profl. jours. City atty., Westlake Hills, Tex., 1968. Served as airman USAF, 1953-55. Named Dist. Alumus Southwestern U., 1999. Fellow Am. Coll. Trial Lawyers; mem. ABA (natural resources law sect., coun. 1987-90, litig. sect.), Am. Inns of Ct., State Bar of Tex., Tex. Bar Found., The Tex. Ctr. for Legal Ethics and Professionalism (founding), Dallas Bar Assn., The Littlefield Soc. U. Tex. (charter). Home and Office: 10424 Woodford Dr Dallas TX 75229-6317

DOUGLASS, GUS RUBEN, state agency administrator; b. Leon, W.Va., Feb. 22, 1927; s. Gus Rodney and Fannie Elizabeth (Grimm) D.; m. Anna Lee Roush, Oct. 23, 1947; children: Steve, Thomas, Mary Lee, Cynthia. BA, W.Va. U., 1985. Asst. commr. agr. W.Va. Dept. Agr., 1957, commr. agr., 1964-88, 92—; bd. dirs. Banc One Holdings Co., Bank One Point Pleasant; trustee Pleasant Valley Hosp.; trustee, adminstr. W. Va. Rural Rehab. Loan Fund; chmn. so. regional com. Food and Agr. under Pres. Jimmy Carter; pres. So. U.S. Trade Assn.; mem. adv. com. fgn. animal and poultry diseases U.S. Sec.; mem., past chmn. W.Va. Rural Devel. Coun.; chmn. State Soil Conservation Com.; past chmn. W.Va. Air Pollution Control Commn., State Forestry Commn.; mem. W.Va. Housing Devel. Fund; co-operator 400 acre beef and grain farm. Gubernatorial candidate W.Va., 1988; bd. dirs. State Farm Mus., State Fair W.Va.; mem. Leon Bapt. Ch. Recipient Disting. Svc. award Gamma Sigma Delta, Man of Yr. award Progressive Farmer Mag.; named to Agriculture and Forestry Hall of Fame, 1990. Mem. Future Farmers Am. (state and nat. pres.), Nat. Future Farmers Am. Alumni Assn. (past pres.), Nat. Assn. State Depts. Agriculture (past. pres.), So. Assn. State Depts. Agriculture (past pres.), Farm Bureau (county pres.), Poultry Assn., Livestock Assn., Masons, Shriners. Democrat. Avocations: carpentry, gardening, hunting, fishing, reading. Office: WVa Dept Agriculture Rm E-28 State Capitol Charleston WV 25305*

DOUGLASS, JANE DEMPSEY, theology educator; b. Wilmington, Del., Mar. 22, 1933; d. Hazell Brownlie and Ethel Katherine (Smith) Dempsey; m. Gordon Klene Douglass, Aug. 23, 1964; children: Alan Bruce, Anne Lorine, John Gordon. AB, Syracuse U., 1954; postgrad., U. Geneva, Switzerland, 1954-55; AM, Radcliffe Coll., 1961; PhD, Harvard U., 1963; ThD (hon.), U. Geneva, 1994; LHD (hon.), Franklin and Marshall Coll., 1992; DD (hon.), U. St. Andrews, Scotland, 1992. Assoc. dir. Presbyn. Student Ctr., Columbia, Mo., 1955-58; teaching fellow Harvard Divinity Sch., Cambridge, Mass., 1959-62; from instr. to prof. Sch. of Theology at Claremont and Claremont Grad. Sch., Claremont, Ca., 1963-85; Hazel Thompson McCord prof. hist. theology Princeton (N.J.) Theol. Sem., 1985-98, emerita, 1998—; pres. Am. Soc. Ch. History, 1983; v.p. World Alliance of Reformed Chs., 1989-90, pres. 1990-97, mem. exec. com., 1997—. Author: Justification in Late Medieval Preaching: A Study of John Geiler of Keisersberg, 1966, 2d edit., 1989, Women, Freedom and Calvin, 1985; editor: (with Jack L. Stotts) To Confess the Faith Today, 1990, (with James F. Kay) Women, Gender and Christian Community, 1997, (with Páraic Réamonn) Partnership in God's Mission in the Middle East, 1998; contbr. articles to profl. jours. Presbyterian. Office: Princeton Theol Seminary PO Box 821 Princeton NJ 08542-0803

DOUGLASS, LAURA LEE, pharmaceutical company official; b. Dixon, Ill., June 3, 1964; d. Robert R. and Helen C. (Heuerman) Johnson; m. John W. Douglass, Sept. 3, 1988; children: Alissa C., Amanda M. ADN, SUNY, Albany, 1986; postgrad., U. Wis., La Crosse, U. Wis., Madison. RN, Wis. Staff nurse Norrell Critical Care Svcs., Madison, 1986-88; float staff nurse U. Wis. Hosp., Madison, 1988-90; staff nurse, charge nurse Meriter Hosp., Madison, 1986-90; dir. nursing Oreg. (Wis.) Manor and Adult Group Home, 1990-91; rsch. project mgr. Corning Besselaar Clin. Rsch., Madison, 1991-93, assoc. dir. clin. ops., 1993-96; sr. rsch. specialist Med. Sch. U. Wis., Madison, 1993-94; dir. clin. rsch. Bone Care Internat., Madison, 1997—; grad. alumni advisor for nursing students SUNY, Albany; presenter in field. Mem. ANA, Wis. Biotech. Assn., Wis. Nurses Assn., Assocs. of Clin. Pharmacology (cert. clin. rsch. coord.).

DOUGLASS, MARY CLEMENT, retired curator, historian; b. McAlester, Okla., Dec. 5, 1944; d. Albert Bittick and Mary Agnes (Hamilton) Clement; m. Errol Dwight Douglass, June 24, 1966; children: John Vodette, Aran Bittick. Student, East Ctrl. State U., 1963-66; BA in Edn., Ctrl. State U., 1967; postgrad., Kans. State U., 1988, U. Tex., 1990. Social studies tchr. Ell-Saline H.S., Brookville, Kans., 1967-69; archtl. historian City of Salina (Kans.) Heritage Commn., 1984-88; registrar Smoky Hill Mus., Salina, 1986-88, curator of collections, 1989-97; ret.; dist. 1 rep. Kans. Mus. Assn., Topeka, 1991-92, v.p., program chair, 1993-94; mem. Landon grants com. Kans. State Hist. Soc., Topeka, 1992-93, mem. deaccession rev., 1993—; mem. program com. Mountain-Plains Mus. Assn., 1992-93. Author: Clement Chronicles, 1982, Salina Kansas Historical Resources, 1984 (also video); editor Tree Climber, 1982-87. Grad. Leadership Salina C. of C., 1987; bd. mem., pers. com. Salina Rescue Mission, 1992-93, City of Salina Heritage Commrs., 1998-99. Recipient medal of appreciation Kans. Soc. SAR, Salina, 1988, Martha Washington medal Kans. Soc. SAR, Salina, 1989, Seaton award for Prose, Kans. Quarterly, 1989, award for Outstanding Quarterly, Kans. Coun. Geneal. Socs., 1988, Mus. accreditation Am. Assn. Mus., Washington, 1997; grantee Salina Arts and Humanities, 1986, 87. Mem. DAR (regent Mary Wade Strother chpt. 1985-86), United Daus. of the Confederacy, Inst. Mus. Svcs. (surveyor MAP program 1992—), Christian Motorcyclists Assn. (sec. chpt. 363 1997-98), Smoky Valley Geneal. Soc. (bd. mem., v.p. 1995-98), Salina Heights Christian Ch. (libr. 1997—). Republican. Avocations: family history research, needle arts, motorcycle touring, painting, ministry. Home: 259 N Kansas Ave Salina KS 67401-8515

DOUGLASS, RAMONA ELIZABETH, medical sales professional; b. N.Y.C., Aug. 15, 1949; d. Howard William and Lena Verona (Belle) D. Student, Colo. Sch. Mines, 1966-68; BS in Physical Sci., Colo. State U., 1970. Adminstrv. asst. S.E. Queens Community Corp., Queens, N.Y., 1970-71; research editor Encyclopedia Britannica, Chgo., 1971-73; sales rep. Scott Foresman Co., Glenview, Ill., 1973-75, Am. Sci. Products, McGaw Park, Ill., 1975-78; mgr. New Eng. territory Hollister, Inc., Libertyville, Ill., 1978-81; mgr. midwest region Precision Dynamics Corp., San Fernando, Calif., 1981-95, mgr. Western region, bar code specialist, 1995—, mng. editor sales and mktg. newsletter, 1998—; ptnr. Douglass/Sherod-Winter Assocs., Chgo., 1986-88, DMB Group, Internat., 1990-91; mem. Nat. Network Women in Sales, 1986-93, v.p. corp. rels., 1989-90; co-founder Healthy Concepts, Inc., 1993, mktg. v.p., cons., 1998—; apptd. to Fed. 2000 Census Adv. Com., 1995—, mem. Fed. Working Group on Racial and Ethnic Tabulations, 1997—; lectr., spkr. in field; appearances on radio and TV programs, including Oprah Winfrey Show, Jerry Springer Show, Mark Walberg Show, CBS Sunday Morning, Aaron Freeman Show, others. Contbr. poetry Great Am. Poetry Anthology, 1987; subject in The Rainbow Effect: Interracial Families, 1987, Heroes of Conscience: A Biographical Dictionary, 1996; contbg. author: The Multiracial Experience: Racial Borders as the New Frontier, 1995. Founding mem. The Nat. Alliance Against Racist & Polit. Repression, Chgo., 1972; bd. dirs., chair publicity The Biracial Family Network, Chgo., 1987-90, v.p., 1990-92, pres., 1992-93; v.p. pub. rels. Assn. Multi-Ethnic Ams., 1988-90, v.p. midwest region, 1991-94, pres., 1994—. Recipient Pioneer award for outstanding contbn. to multiracial issues U. Calif., Berkeley, 1997, Building Bridges award Racial Harmony award Multiracial Ams. of so. Calif., 1996. Mem. NAFE. Democrat. Avocations: creative writing, music, gourmet cooking, sailing. Office: Precision Dynamics Corp 13880 Del Sur St San Fernando CA 91340-3490

DOUGLASS, ROBERT LEE, electronics association executive, city councilman; b. Winnsboro, S.C., June 23, 1928; s. John Douglass and Jannie B. (Stevenson) D.; m. Bernice Viola Sales, 1947; children: Beverly E., Ronald K., Eric L., Loren R. BS, Morgan State Coll., 1953; BSEE, Johns Hopkins U., 1962. Commd. 2d lt. U.S. Army, 1953, advanced through grades to 1st lt., 1955; instr. Balt. City Pub. Schs., 1955-64; elec. design engr. Bendix Corp., Towson, Md., 1962-64; systems engr. IBM Corp., Gaithersburg, Md., 1965-67; pres., founder Balt. Electronics Assn., Inc., 1968—. City councilman, Balt., 1967-74, 96—; state sen. 45th dist., Md., 1975-82; chmn. Md. Legis. Black Caucus, 1975-77, 79; del. Dem. Nat. Conv., 1976; mem. state ctrl. com., 1993-96. Recipient Nat. Svc. medal. Mem. East Balt. Cmty. Corp., Eastside Dem. Orgn., Nat. Assn. Black Mfrs., Balt. Urban Coalition, Paul Laurence Dunbar Cmty. Sch., Omega Sigma Chi. African Methodist Episcopalian. Home: 2111 Homewood Ave Baltimore MD 21218-6104 Office: City Hall Rm 509 Baltimore MD 21202*

DOUGLASS, ROBERT ROYAL, banker, lawyer; b. Binghamton, N.Y., Oct. 16, 1931; s. Robert R. and Frances (Behan) D.; m. Linda Ann Luria, June 2, 1962; children: Robert Royal, Alexandra Brooke, Andrew. B.A. with distinction, Dartmouth Coll., 1953; LL.B., Cornell U., 1959. Bar: N.Y. Asso. Hinman, Howard & Kattell, 1959-64; 1st asst. counsel to Gov. N.Y. State, Albany, 1964-65; counsel to gov. Gov. N.Y. State, 1965-70, sec. to gov., 1971-72; partner Milbank, Tweed, Hadley & McCloy, 1972-76; exec. v.p., gen. counsel Chase Manhattan Bank, N.Y.C., 1976-83; exec. v.p. Chase Manhattan Bank, 1983-85, vice chmn., 1985-93; of counsel Melbank Tweed Hadly & McCloy, N.Y.C., 1994—; dir. Rockefeller Ctr., Inc., 1976-82, HRE Properties, 1990—, Gryphon Holdings, 1993-95, Home Ins. Co., 1993—; chmn. Nelson Rockefeller's Campaign for Rep. Presdl. Nomination, 1958; commr. Port Authority of N.Y. State and N.J., 1972-76; trustee N.Y.C. Pub. Libr., 1972-86; bd. dirs., chmn. exec. com. Downtown-Lower Manhattan Assn., N.Y.C., 1973-91, chmn., 1991—; mem. vis. com. John F. Kennedy Sch. Govt., Harvard U., 1974-79; mem. N.Y. Landmarks Conservancy, 1977-80; chmn. Cedel Internat., 1994—, Alliance for Downtown N.Y., 1995—. Trustee Dartmouth Coll., 1983-93, Mus. of Modern Art, 1989-94. Served with M.C., U.S. Army, 1954-56. Recipient Wallace award Am.-Scottish Found., 1974. Mem. ABA, N.Y. State Bar Assn., Coun. Fgn. Rels. Roman Catholic. Clubs: Century Assn, World Trade Center, Round Hill, Seal Harbor, Blind Brook. Office: Milbank Tweed Hadley & Mc Cloy 1 Chase Manhattan Plz Fl 47 New York NY 10005-1401*

DOUMA, HARRY HEIN, social service agency administrator; b. Richmond, N.Y., Mar. 12, 1933; s. Hein and Ida D. (Van Der Veer) D.; m. Carole Marie Piening; June 21, 1958; children:Daniel H., Deborah Joy, Crystal A. BA in Philosophy, Shelton Coll., 1960; MDiv, Faith Theol. Sem., 1965. Ordained to ministry, 1965. Pastor Port Monmouth (N.J.) Ch., 1955-60; chaplain Edward R. Johnstone Tng. and Research Ctr., Bordentown, N.J., 1960-65; pastor Times Beach (Mo.) Bible Ch., 1965-67, 1st Bapt. Ch., Pilot Knob, Mo., 1967-76; founder, pres., pastor Penuel, Inc., Ironton, Mo., 1973—. Author The Book of Revelation for the Layman, 1971. Mem. Rep. Presdl. Task Force. Served with USN, 1953-55. Recipient Dir.'s Cmty. Leadership award FBI of St. Louis, 1995. Avocations: travel, swimming, fishing, music. Home: Rt 1 Box 593 326 Michael Ln Ironton MO 63650-8202 Office: Penuel Inc PO Box 367 Ironton MO 63650-0367

DOUMAR, ROBERT GEORGE, judge; b. Feb. 17, 1930; m. Dorothy Ann Mundy; children: Robert G., Charles C. BA, U. Va., 1951, LLB, 1953, LLM, 1988. Assoc. Venable, Parsons, Kyle & Hylton, 1955-58; sr. ptnr. Doumar, Pincus, Knight & Harlan, 1958-81; judge U.S. Dist. Ct. (ea. dist.) Va., Norfolk, 1981—; now sr. judge U.S. Dist. Ct. (ea. dist.) Va. Lt. USAF. Mem. ATLA, Am. Judicature Soc., Def. Rsch. Inst., Internat. Soc. Barristers, Va. Conf. of Local Bar Assns., Va. Assn. Trial Lawyers. Roman Catholic. Office: US Dist Ct US Courthouse 600 Granby St Ste 344 Norfolk VA 23510-1923

DOUMLELE, RUTH HAILEY, communications company executive, broadcast accounting consultant; b. Charlotte County, Va., Nov. 6, 1925; d. Clarrie Robert Hailey and Virginia Susan (Slaughter) Ferguson; m. John Antony Doumlele, May 8, 1943; children: John Antony, Suzanne Denise Doumlele Owen. Cert. in commerce, U. Richmond, 1968; BA, Mary Baldwin Coll., 1982. Sta. acct. WLEE-Radio, Richmond, Va., 1965-67, bus. mgr., 1967-73; area bus. mgr. Nationwide Communications Inc., Richmond, 1973-75; corp. bus. mgr., Neighborhood Communications Corp., Inc., Richmond, 1978-86, asst. v.p., 1981-86; owner Broadcast Acctg. Cons., Midlothian, Va., 1986-95; treas., dir. Guests of Honor, Ltd., Richmond, 1984-89; sec., Inner Light, Inc., 1984-96; docent Va.'s Gov.'s Mansion, 1997—. Contbr. articles to profl. jours., hist. and astrol. publs.; mem. editorial rev. bd. The Woman C.P.A., 1980—. Mem. Am. Soc. Women Accts. (chpt. pres. 1974-76, contbg. editor The Coord. 1990, Chgo., Woman of Achievement award 1991), Broadcast Fin. Mgmt. Assn., Nat. League Am. Pen Women (br. pres. 1984-86), Am. Fedn. Astrologers, Va. Assn. Amateur Athletic Union (records chmn. 1959-62), Women's Club of Powhatan, Selective Svc. System Local Bd., Powhatan Hist. Soc. Episcopalian. Avocations: salt water fishing, Civil War history, travel, astrology. Home and Office: 2510 Chastain Ln Midlothian VA 23113-9400

DOUSKEY, THERESA KATHRYN, health facility administrator; b. New Haven, Conn., Nov. 30, 1938; d. Stanley Anthony and Wadia (Mekdeci) D. RN, Grace New Haven Sch. Nursing, 1959; BS in Nursing, So. Conn. State U., 1962; MPA in Health Care, U. New Haven, 1979. Various positions Yale New Haven Hosp., 1959-80; asst. dir. nursing Meriden (Conn.) Wallingford Hosp., 1980-81; nurse Regional Visiting Nurse Agy., North Haven, Conn., 1983-87; home care coord. Milford (Conn.) Hosp., 1990-93; case mgr., nurse Cmty. Care, Inc., New Haven, 1988-90, 93-97; nurse cons. Anthem Blue Cross/Blue Shield, North Haven, Conn., 1997-98; nurse case mgr. home care program for elderly South Ctrl. Area Aging, New Haven, Conn., 1998—. Mem. Am. Nurses Assn., Conn. Nurses Assn. (nominating com. 1972-74), Conn. Assn. Continuity of Care, Sigma Theta Tau. Republican. Avocations: needle crafts, gardening, working with animal humane groups, established social ministries outreach program at local church. Home: 412 Narrow Ln Orange CT 06477-3315

DOUTHAT, JAMES EVANS, college administrator; b. Petersburg, Va., Oct. 24, 1946; s. Robert Hoilman and Thelma (Evans) D.; m. Emily Esther Christenberry, Dec. 30, 1972; children: Mark Evans, Anna Christenberry. AB, Coll. of William and Mary, 1969; M of Divinty, Duke U., 1972, EdD, 1977. Asst., assoc., then dean student life Duke U., Durham, N.C., 1972-80; v.p. student life Albion (Mich.) Coll., 1980-84, adminstrv. v.p., 1984-85, exec. v.p., 1985-89; pres. Lycoming Coll., Williamsport, Pa., 1989—, also bd. dirs.; corp. dir. No. Cen. Bank, 1992—. Pres. United Way, Albion, 1983; bd. dirs. Lycoming Found., 1990—; adv. bd. Williamsport-Lycoming Found., Sch. Theology, Claremont, Calif., 1991—; bd. mgrs. Williamsport Hosp. and Med. Ctr., 1992—. Mem. Williamsport/Lycoming C. of C. (chmn. 1997—). Methodist. Avocations: antiques, travel. Home: 325 Grampian Blvd Williamsport PA 17701-1859 Office: Lycoming Coll Office of Pres Campus Box 156 Williamsport PA 17701-5192*

DOUTHITT, SHIRLEY ANN, insurance agent; b. Mexia, Tex., Feb. 21, 1947; d. Othello Young and Hazel Lorene (Corley) Thompson; m. A. Dwane Douthitt, Nov. 24, 1966; 1 child, Steven Dwane. Student, Leonard's Tng Sch., Houston, 1979; student Tex. local recording agts. licensing course, Austin, Tex., 1980; student farmers ins. group tng. program, Austin, 1980; student life underwriters trng course, Tyler, Tex., 1987. Lic. ins. agt. Sec. Lindsey & Newsom Ins. Adjusters, Palestine, Tex., 1965-73, J. Herrington Ins. Agy., Palestine, 1973-76, Ramsey Ins. Agy., Palestine, 1976-79; agt. Farmers Ins. Group, Palestine, 1979—. Recipient Bus. Woman of Yr. Palestine Profl. Bus. Women, 1983. Mem. NAFE, Women's Club. Avocations: reading, gardening, concerts, home decorating. Office: Shirley Douthitt Ins Agy 3507 W Oak St Palestine TX 75801-8417

DOUTT, GERALDINE MOFFATT, retired educational administrator; b. Warren, Mich., Apr. 16, 1927; d. Stanford and Wilhelmine (Ewaldt) Moffatt; m. Robert G. Doutt; children: Eric Robert, Gerald George. B.S. in Occupational Therapy, Eastern Mich. U., Ypsilanti, 1952, M.A. in Edn., 1959; E.D.S. in Spl. Edn., Wayne State U., Detroit, 1968. Tchr., Van Dyke Pub. Schs., Warren, 1963-65, tchr. educable mentally impaired, 1965-67, tchr. cons. for emotionally impaired, 1967-69, dir. spl. edn., 1969-90, ret. Chmn. Macomb County Interagy. Council, 1968-69. Mem. Mich. Assn. Dirs. Spl. Edn., Nat. Council Exceptional Children, Delta Kappa Gamma. Home: 22919 Playview St Saint Clair Shores MI 48082-2085 also: Treasure Island Higgins Lake PO Box 412 Higgins Lake MI 48627-0412

DOUTT, RICHARD LEROY, entomologist, lawyer, educator; b. La Verne, Calif., Dec. 6, 1916; s. Mace and Adele (Bussey) D.; m. Lucinda Margaret Killian, Mar. 21, 1942 (dec.); children: Richard Jonathan, Jeffrey Thomas (dec.); m. Betty Mann, Apr. 20, 1979. B.S., U. Calif. at Berkeley, 1939, M.S., 1940, Ph.D., 1946; LL.B., San Francisco Law Sch., 1959, J.D., 1968. Bar: Calif. bar 1960. Faculty U. Calif. at Berkeley, 1946—, prof. entomology, 1960-75, prof. emeritus, 1975—, chmn. div. biol. control, 1964-69; acting dean Coll. Agrl. Scis., 1969-70; mem. firm Foley, Saler & Doutt, Albany, Calif., 1960-67; environ. counsel firm Henningson, Durham and Richardson, Santa Barbara, Calif., 1975-81; entomologist Santa Barbara County, Calif., 1981-83. Author: Cape Bulbs, 1994; contbr. articles to profl. jours. Served to lt. comdr. USNR, 1941-45. Fellow Calif. Acad. Scis.; mem. Entomol. Soc. Am., Calif. Bar, Sigma Xi. Democrat. Home: 1781 Glen Oaks Dr Santa Barbara CA 93108-2111

DOUTY, ROBERT WATSON, minister, educator; b. Phila., June 20, 1943; m. MarshaLee Wood, Apr. 22, 1972. BA in Psychology, Calif. State U., Long Beach, 1969; MS in Edn., U. Bridgeport, 1974; MDiv, Alliance Theol. Sem., Nyack, N.Y., 1993. Ordained to ministry Am. Bapt. Chs., 1990; teaching cert., N.Y. Tchr. Garrison (N.Y.) Sch., 1980—; chmn. bd. deacons 1st Bapt. Ch., Ossining, N.Y., 1980-82, dir. Christian edn., 1985-91; assoc. pastor 1st Bapt. Ch., Ossining, 1990-96; dir. Christian edn. St. Philip's Episc. Ch., Garrison, N.Y., 1996-98; pastor Cold Spring (N.Y.) Bapt. Ch., 1998—; deacon 1st Bapt. Ch., 1973-82, chmn. missions, 1990-95; chaplain Phelps Hosp., Tarrytown, N.Y., 1988—. Author: Star City: A Classroom Management System, 1989; author: (with others) In The Footsteps of Birdy Edwards, 1980; contbr. articles to mags. Victory 94 team leader to elect Gov. George Pataki, 1994. With U.S. Navy, 1962-65. Mem. Am. Assn. Christian Counselors, Baker St. Irregulars (The Priory Sch.). Republican.

DOUVAN, ELIZABETH, social psychologist, educator; b. South Bend, Ind., Nov. 3, 1926; d. John and Janet F. (Powers) Malcolm; m. Eugene Victor Douvan, Dec. 27, 1947; children: Thomas Alexander, Catherine Des Ormiers. AB, Vassar Coll., 1946; MA, U. Mich., 1948, PhD, 1951. Study dir. Survey Rsch. Ctr., U. Mich., Ann Arbor, 1950-58; lectr. dept. psychology U. Mich., Ann Arbor, 1951-61, assoc. prof., 1961-65, Kellogg prof. psychology, 1965-96, Kellogg prof. emerita, 1996—, also program dir. Inst. for Social Rsch., 1970—; assoc. dir. Inst. for Social Rsch., 1994—; dir. residential coll. U. Mich., 1985-88; mem. faculty Fielding Inst., 1983—; cons. NIMH, NSF, various founds.; mem. Ann Arbor Bd. Health, 1972-76. Author: The Adolescent Experience, 1966, Feminine Personality and Conflict, 1970, The Inner American, 1981, Mental Health in America, 1981, Marital Instability, 1995; contbr. articles to profl. jours. Recipient various grants. Mem. AAAS, APA (pres. divsn. 35, 1970-71), Am. Psychol. Soc., Assn. for Women in Psychology, Nat. Women's Studies Assn. Democrat. Office: U Mich Inst for Social Rsch 426 Thompson St Rm 5102 Ann Arbor MI 48104-2321

DOVALE, FERN LOUISE, civil engineer; b. Ft. Leavenworth, Kans., May 11, 1956; d. Riel Stanton and Beatrice Marie (Mayor) Crandall; m. Antonio Joseph DoVale Jr., Oct. 17, 1981; children: Antonio Joseph III, Elizabeth Rose, Jennifer Louise. BSCE, MIT, 1978; MSCE, Columbia U., 1982. Registered profl. engr., N.J. Assoc. engr. M.W. Kellogg Co., Hackensack, N.J., 1978-80; engr. Nuclear Power Svcs., Inc., Secaucus, N.J., 1980-83, sr. engr., 1983-85, lead engr., 1985-86, project engr., 1986-88; project mgr. NPS Technologies Group, Inc., Secaucus, 1988-89; engring. mgr. NPS Technologies Group, Inc., Elmwood Park, N.J., 1989-92, Integrated Engring. Software, Inc., Englewood Cliffs, N.J., 1992-93; ret., 1993. Author, editor computer manuals. Mem. ASCE, ASME, NSPE, Am. Nuc. Soc. (mem. exec. com. No. N.J. sect. 1986-89, 91-94), MIT Alumni Club No. N.J. (bd. dirs. 1979-95, membership v.p. 1982-84, 89-92, program v.p. 1984-85, 92-94, pres. 1985-86, 94-95), MIT Ednl. Coun. Home: 430 Mckinney Rd Wexford PA 15090-8538

DOVE, LORRAINE FAYE, gerontology nurse; b. West Reading, Pa., Feb. 20, 1960; d. Blaine Hoye Sr. and Faye Louise (Heisey) D. Diploma, Reading Hosp. Sch. of Nursing, 1982. RN, Fla., Pa., Ga.; cert. gerontol. nurse. Asst. dir. nursing Leader Nursing and Rehab. Ctr., Lebanon, Pa., 1983-84; dir. nursing Sunrise Manor, Ft. Pierce, Fla., 1986-88, Vero Beach (Fla.) Care Ctr., 1988-92, Okeechobee (Fla.) Health Care Facility, 1992-94; regional nurse cons. Patient Care Pharmacy, Pompano Beach, Fla., 1994-95; CQI/RA coord. Colonial Palms East, Pompano Beach, 1995; dir. nursing Atlantis, Lantana, Fla., 1995-96, Springtree, Sunrise, Fla., 1996-97; quality assurance coord./corp. clin. svcs. dir./educator Premiere/Integrated Health Svcs., Pembroke Pines, Fla., 1997—; past mem. FHCA AIDS task force, Health and Human Svcs. Bd., Aging and Adult Com., AIDS Consortium of the Treasure Coast. Mem. Nat. Assn. Dirs. Nursing Adminstrn., Fla. Assn. Dirs. Nursing Adminstrn.

DOVE, RITA FRANCES, poet, English language educator; b. Akron, Ohio, Aug. 28, 1952; d. Ray A. and Elvira E. (Hord) D.; m. Fred Viebahn, Mar. 23, 1979; 1 child, Aviva Chantal Tamu Dove-Viebahn. BA summa cum laude, Miami U., Oxford, Ohio, 1973; postgrad., Universität Tübingen, Fed. Republic Germany, 1974-75; MFA, U. Iowa, 1977; LLD (hon.), Miami U., Oxford, Ohio, 1988, Knox Coll., 1989, Tuskegee U., 1994, U. Miami, Fla., 1994, Washington U., St. Louis, 1994, Case Western Res. U., 1994, U. Akron, 1994, Ariz. State U., 1995, Boston Coll., 1995, Dartmouth Coll., 1995, Spelman Coll., 1996, U. Pa., 1996, U. N.C., 1997, U. Notre Dame, 1997, Northeastern U., 1997, Columbia U., 1998. Asst. prof. English Ariz. State U., Tempe, 1981-84, assoc. prof., 1984-87, prof., 1987-89; prof. U. Va., Charlottesville, 1989-93, Commonwealth prof. English, 1993—; U.S. poet laureate/cons. in poetry Libr. of Congress, Washington, 1993-95; writer-in-residence Tuskegee (Ala.) Inst., 1982; lit. panelist Nat. Endowment for Arts, Washington, 1984-86, chmn. poetry grants panel, 1985; judge Walt Whitman award Acad. Am. Poets, 1990, Pulitzer prize in poetry, 1991, Ruth Lilly prize 1991, Nat. Book award in poetry 1991, 98, Anisfield-Wolf Book awards, 1992—, Shelley Meml. award, 1997, Amy Lowell fellowship, 1997; poetry panel chmn. Pulitzer prize, 1997; final judge Brittingham and Pollack prizes, 1997; juror Christopher Columbus Fellowship Found., 1998. author: (poetry) Ten Poems, 1977, The Only Dark Spot in the Sky, 1980, The Yellow House on the Corner, 1980, Mandolin, 1982, Museum, 1983, Thomas and Beulah, 1986 (Pulitzer Prize in poetry 1987), The Other Side of the House, 1988, Grace Notes, 1989 (Ohioana award 1990), Selected Poems, 1993 (Ohioana award 1994), Lady Freedom Among Us, 1994, Mother Love, 1995, Evening Primrose, 1998, On the Bus with Rosa Parks, 1999; (verse drama) The Darker Face of the Earth, 1994 (W. Alton Jones Found. grant 1994, Kennedy Ctr. Fund for New Am. Plays award 1995, Geraldine Dodge Found. grant, 1997), completely rev. 2d edit., 1996 (first performance Oreg. Shakespeare Festival 1996); (novel) Through the Ivory Gate, 1992 (Va. Coll. Stores Book award 1993); (short stories) Fifth Sunday , 1985 (Callaloo award 1986); (essays) The Poet's World, 1995; mem. editorial bd. Nat. Forum, 1984-89, Iris, 1989—; mem. adv. bd. Ploughshares, 1992—, N.C. Writers Network, 1992—, Civilization, 1994-97; assoc. editor Callaloo, 1986-98; adv. and contbg. editor Gettysburg Rev., 1987—, TriQuarterly, 1988—, Ga. Review, 1994—, Bellingham Rev., 1996—, Internat. Quarterly, 1997—, Callaloo, 1998—, Mid-Am. Rev., 1998—. Commr. The Schomburg Ctr. for Rsch. in Black Culture, N.Y. Pub. Libr., 1987—; mem. Renaissance Forum Folger Shakespeare Libr., 1993-95, Coun. of Scholars Libr. of Congress, 1994—; mem. nat. launch com. AmeriCorps, 1994; mem. awards coun. Am. Acad. Achievement, 1994—; mem. adv. bd. Thomas Jefferson Ctr. Freedom of Expression, 1994—, U.S. Civil War Ctr., 1995—, Va. Ctr. Creative Arts, 1995—; The Poets Corner elector Cathedral Ch. St. John the Divine, N.Y.C., 1991—; bd. govs. Humanities Rsch. Inst. U. Calif., 1996—. Presdl. scholar, 1970, Nat. Achievement scholar, 1970-73; Fulbright/Hays fellow, 1974-75, rsch. fellow U. Iowa, 1975, teaching/writing fellow U. Iowa, 1976-77, Guggenheim Found. fellow, 1983-84, Mellon sr. fellow Nat. Humanities Ctr., 1988-89, fellow Ctr. for Advanced Studies, U. Va., 1989-92, fellow Shannon Ctr. for Advanced Studies, U. Va., 1995—; grantee NEA, 1978, 89; recipient Lavan Younger Poet award Acad. Am. Poets, 1986, GE Found. award, 1987, Bellagio (Italy) residency Rockefeller Found., 1988, Ohio Gov.'s award 1988, Literary Lion citation N.Y. Pub. Libr., 1991, Women of Yr. award Glamour Mag., 1993, NAACP Great Am. Artist award, 1993, Golden Plate award Am. Acad. Achievement, 1994, Disting. Achievement medal Miami

U. Alumni Assn., 1994, Renaissance Forum award for leadership in the literary arts Folger Shakespeare Libr., 1994, Carl Sandburg award Internat. Platform Assn., 1994, Heinz award in arts and humanities, 1996, Nat. Medal in the Humanities Pres. of U.S. and NEH, 1996, Duke Ellington awards, 1999; inducted Ohio Women's Hall of Fame, 1991, Nat. Assn. of Women in Edn. Disting. Woman award, 1997, Sara Lee Frontrunner award, 1997, Barnes & Noble Writers for Writers award, 1997, Levinson prize Poetry mag., 1998; named Phi Beta Kappa poet Harvard U., 1993. Mem. PEN, ASCAP, Am. Philos. Soc., Poetry Soc. Am., Associated Writing Programs (bd. dirs. 1985-88, pres. 1986-87), Am. Acad. Achievement (mem. golden plate awards coun. 1994—), Phi Beta Kappa (senator 1994—), Phi Kappa Phi. Office: U Va Dept English 219 Bryan Hall Charlottesville VA 22903

DOVER, BENJAMIN FRANKLIN, writer, correspondent; b. Waco, Tex., Apr. 23. BS in Bus., Tex. Christian U., 1982. Sports agt. Ft. Worth, 1978-88; entrepreneur Ft. Worth and London, 1986-91; author Equitable Media Svcs., Ft. Worth, 1991—; talk radio show host TalkRadio 570AM/KLIF, Dallas, 1992—; consumer expert Good Morning Tex., WFAA-TV/Ch. 8, Dallas, 1995—; dir. Vanlindon Writing Methods, Sacramento; guest spkr. Author: LIFE AFTER DEBT: The Blueprint For Surviving In America's Credit Society, 1993, BACK OFF! The Definitive Guide To Stopping Collection Agency Harassment, 1994 (#1 nat. bestseller status), Breaking Out of Debtor's Prison, 1995, How To Do Your Own Plastic Surgery, 1995; columnist The Dallas Morning News, 1998—. Bd. dirs. Meml. Soc. of North Tex. Mem. SAG. Libertarian. Avocations: scuba diving, oenophile, motorcycles, travel. E-mail: fd@bendover.com. Fax: 817 441-7188. Home: 6387B Camp Bowie Blvd # 155 Fort Worth TX 76116-5423 Office: c/o Equitable Media Svcs PO Box 9822 Fort Worth TX 76147-2822

DOVER, DEREK JASON, corrections officer; b. Gadsden, Ala., Nov. 9, 1962; s. Orvan Stanley and Kathryn Cynthia (Bonds) D.; m. Jennifer Lynn Phillips, Aug. 21, 1989 (div. Jan. 1991); 1 child, Wade; m. Sheryl Ann Calder, Oct. 26, 1992; stepchildren: Joey, Kelly. AS, Gadsden State C.C., 1992. Security officer Weiser Security Inc., Gadsden, 1983-84, Advance Security Inc., Gadsden, 1984-87; corrections officer Ala. Dept. Corrections, Springville, Ala., 1987—. Mem. Correctional Peace Officers Found. Baptist. Avocations: hiking, swimming. Home: 531 Becky Allen Cir Rainbow City AL 35906-3633 Office: Ala Dept Corrections 1000 Saint Clair Rd Springville AL 35146-5582

DOVEY, BRIAN HUGH, health care products company executive, venture capitalist; b. Cleve., Nov. 12, 1941; s. Hugh Albert and Dorothy (Garde) D.; m. Elizabeth Barrett Hartzell, Aug. 17, 1963; children—Laurel, Kimberly, Christine. A.B., Colgate U., 1963; M.B.A., Harvard U., 1967. Sales mgr. N.Y. Telephone, N.Y.C., 1963-69; dir. planning Howmet Corp., N.Y.C., 1969-70; dir. ops. Howmedica, Inc., Cheshire, Conn., 1970-71; v.p. ops. Survival Tech., Bethesda, Md., 1971-75, pres., 1975-83; pres. surg. products div. Rorer Group Inc., Fort Washington, Pa., 1983-86, exec. v.p., 1985-86; pres. Rorer Group Inc., 1986-88; gen. ptnr. Domain Assocs., 1988—; former dir. Origin Medsys., Inc., Brit. Biotech. Group plc, Health Industry Mfrs. Assn., Washington, Non-Prescription Drug Mfrs. Assn., Virna Pharm., Inc.; former chmn. Athena Neuroscis., ReSound Corp.; bd. dirs. Polar Materials, NABI., Advanced Corneal Systems, Cadent Med. Corp., Vivus, Inc., Trimeris Co., Connetics Corp., Microsurge, Inc., Geron Corp.; pres., bd. dirs. Nat. Venture Capital Assn.; chmn. bd. dirs. Creative BioMolecules; trustee Coriell Inst. for Med. Rsch., 1995—. Inventor syringe assembly. Mem. parents' council James Madison U., Harrisonburg, Va., 1982-88, vice chmn., 1985-86, chmn., 1986-87; trustee Germantown Acad., Fort Washington, 1983—, v.p. 1987—; overseer U. Pa. Sch. Nursing, Phila., 1985—; bd. dirs. Huntington's Disease Soc., 1986-89, chmn. 1988-89, Greater Phila. Economic Devel. Council, 1987-88. Mem. Young Pres.'s Orgn. (exec. com. 1977—, treas. exec. com. 1985-86), Proprietary Assn. (bd. dirs. 1987-88), Nat. Venture Capital Assn. (pres. 1997-98), Phila. Cricket Club, Penllyn Club. Office: Domain Assocs 1 Palmer Sq Princeton NJ 08542-3718*

DOVEY, LAURIE LEE, magazine editor, writer, photographer; b. Johnstown, Pa., July 1, 1954; d. Clayton Cresswell and Adele (Podolka) D.; m. James R. Crisp, Jr., Dec. 29, 1979. Student, U. Denver, 1972-73, U. Fla., 1988. Ptnr. Creative Concepts, Birmingham, Ala., 1988-93; free lance writer, photographer Various Mags., Alpharetta, Ga., 1987—; owner Image Connection, Alpharetta, 1988—; seminar speaker Corps., Assns., U.S., 1991—; pres. Creative Referral Svcs., Alpharetta, Ga., 1992—; media cons. Mfg. Cos., U.S., 1988—; owner, designer Webimages.net, 1998—. Scriptwriter TV show Am. Outdoorsman, 1993-94; equipment editor Golf Illustrated Mag., 1996—; editor-at-large Nat. Com. Pubs., 1996—; contbg. editor: Golf Product News, 1999—; contbr. more than 1000 articles to over 50 mags. in outdoor and golf fields. Mem. Outdoor Writers Assn. Am., (bd. dirs. 1997-98, 3d v.p. 1999—, , 11 awards 1990-96), Golf Writers Assn. Am., Internat. Network of Golf (adv. bd. 1997—, Golf Equipment Reporter of Yr. 1998, Golf. Bus. Reporting award 1999), Southeastern Outdoor Press Assn. (6 awards 1989-91). Avocations: golf, fishing, hunting, camping. E-mail: lldovey@webimages.net. Office: 160 White Pines Dr Alpharetta GA 30004-5657

DOVRING, KARIN ELSA INGEBORG, author, poet, playwright, communication analyst; b. Stenstorp, Sweden, Dec. 5, 1919; came to U.S., 1953, naturalized, 1968; m. Folke Dovring, May 30, 1943. Grad., Coll. Commerce, Gothenburg, Sweden, 1936; MA, Lund (Sweden) U., 1943, PhD, 1951; Phil. Licentiate, Gothenburg U., 1947. Journalist several Swedish daily newspapers and weekly mags., 1940-60; tchr. Swedish colls.; rsch. assoc. of Harold Lasswell Yale U., New Haven, 1953-78; fgn. corr. Swedish newspapers, Italy, Switzerland, France and Germany, 1956-60; freelance writer, journalist, 1960—; represented by Joseph Nicoletti Hollywood, Calif., 1994—; vis. prof. Internat. U., The Vatican, Rome, 1958-60, Gottingen (W.Ger.) U., 1962; lectr. U.S. Army, Peace Corps, Yale U., U. Wis., McGill U., U. Iowa; rsch. assoc. U. Ill., Urbana, 1968-69; invited contbr. Social Sci. Rsch. Coun., 1988; speaker Conf. Law and Policy, Yale U. Law Sch., 1992-93, 99—; adv. coun. Internat. Biographical Ctr., Cambridge, Eng.; interviewee radio and TV programs; writer Ill. Alliance to Prevent Nuclear War, radio, theater; Hollywood songwriter; plays for TV movies. Author: Songs of Zion, 1951, Land Reform as a Propaganda Theme, 3d edit., 1965, Road of Propaganda, 1959, Optional Society, 1972, Frontiers of Communication, 1975, English as Lingua Franca, 1997, (short stories) No Parking This Side of Heaven, 1982, Harold D. Lasswell: His Communication with a Future, 1987, 2d edit., 1988; (novel) Heart in Escrow, 1990; (poems) Faces in a Mirror, 1995, Shadows on a Screen, 1996, Whispers on a Stage, 1996, Voices in A Drama, 1998; contbr. articles to mags.; represented several poetry anthologies. Recipient Swedish Nat. award for short stories Bonniers Pub. House Stockholm, 1951; named to Internat. Poetry Hall of Fame, 1996. Mem. Soc. Jean Jacques Rousseau of Geneva (hon. life), Inst. Freedom of Press (life assoc.). Democrat. Address: 613 W Vermont Ave Urbana IL 61801-4824 Office: care Creative Network Nicoletti Music Co PO Box 2818 Newport Beach CA 92659-0310

DOW, DANIEL GOULD, electrical engineering educator; b. Ann Arbor, Mich., Apr. 26, 1930; s. William Gould and Edna Lois (Sontag) D.; m. Kathleen Mary Bond, June 19, 1954; children—Sarah, Suzanne, Jennifer, Gordon. B.S. in Engring, U. Mich., 1952, M.S., 1953; Ph.D., Stanford U., 1958. Asst. prof. elec. engring. Calif. Inst. Tech., Pasadena, 1958-61; with Varian Assocs., Palo Alto, Calif., 1961-68; prof. U. Wash., Seattle, 1968-95; chmn. dept. elec. engring. U. Wash., 1968-77; assoc. dir. Applied Physics Lab., 1977-79; dir. Washington Energy Research Center, 1979-81; cons. Hughes Aircraft, Malibu, Calif., 1958-61, Varian Assocs., 1968-71, Boeing Co., 1973-74, John Fluke Co., 1979-93; mem. Adv. Group on Electron Devices, Microwave Working Group, 1965-76, Wash. Energy Policy Coun., 1973-74; mem. subpanel on energy rsch. Energy Rsch. Adv. Bd., 1980; mem. panel on measurement svcs. Nat. Acad. Scis. - Nat. Bur. Stds.; bd. dirs. Washington Rsch. Found., 1981-95. Served to lt. USAF, 1953-55. Mem. IEEE. (sr.). Home: 9620 NE 31st St Bellevue WA 98004-1838

DOW, DAVID SONTAG, retired ophthalmologist; b. Ann Arbor, Mich., Feb. 15, 1934; s. William Gould and Edna Lois (Sontag) D.; m. Gail Anita Bade, Feb. 11, 1961; children: Steven Michael, Bonnie Jean, William Herbert, James Patrick. BS with distinction, U. Mich., 1956, MD, 1958, MS in Ophthalmology, 1964. Diplomate Am. Bd. Ophthalmology. Intern Denver Gen. Comm. Hosp., 1958-59; psychiatrist USAF Med. Svc., Wichita Falls, Tex., 1959-61; resident in ophthalmology U. Mich. Med. Ctr., Ann Arbor, 1961-64; pvt. practice ophthalmology Scruggs, Dow, and Kannwischer ptnr., Waco, Tex., 1964-88, Cen. Tex. Eye Clinic, Waco, 1988-97; ret., 1997. Contbg. editor Waco Tribune Herald, 1983—; author pamphlets in field. City coun. mem., mayor, Waco City Coun., 1977-81, 80-81, Woodway City Coun., 1997—; bd. dirs. Waco Symphony Assn., 1970-89, 94—, pres. 1982-83; bd. dirs. Tex. Med. Polit. Action Com., Austin, 1973-82; founding bd. dirs., chmn. Greater Waco Arts Coun., 1986—, chmn. 1992, 94—. Capt. USAF, 1959-61. Mem. Am. Acad. Ophthalmology, Tex. Med. Assn., Waco Striders Club, Ridgewood Country Club, Rotary. Episcopalian. Avocations: politics, musical theater, yard/garden construction, singing. Home: 400 Ivy Ann Ct Waco TX 76712-3629

DOW, MARY ALEXIS, auditor; b. South Amboy, N.J., Feb. 19, 1949; d. Alexander and Elizabeth Anne (Reilly) Pawlowski; m. Russell Alfred Dow, June 19, 1971. BS with honors, U. R.I., 1971. CPA, Oreg. Staff acct. Deloitte & Touche, Boston, 1971-74; sr. acct. Price Waterhouse, Portland, Oreg., 1974-77, mgr., 1977-81, sr. mgr., 1981-84; CFO Copeland Lumber Yards Inc., Portland, 1984-86; ind. cons. in field, 1986-94; elected auditor Metro, Portland, 1995—; bd. dirs. Longview Fibre Co. Contbr. articles to profl. jours. Past bd. dirs., exec. com., treas. Oreg. Mus. Sci. and Industry; past chmn. bd., mem. exec. com. Oreg. Trails chpt. N.W. Regional Blood Svcs. ARC. Mem. AICPA, Pacific N.W. Intergovtl. Audit Forum (exec. com.), Am. Woman's Soc. CPAs, Oreg. Soc. CPAs (bd. dirs.), Fin. Execs. Inst. (exec. com., past pres. Portland chpt., western area v.p.), City Club (bd. govs.), Multnomah Athletic Club (trustee). Roman Catholic. Office: Office of Auditor Metro 600 NE Grand Ave Portland OR 97232-2736

DOW, PETER ANTHONY, advertising agency executive; b. Detroit, Oct. 7, 1933; s. Douglas and Mary Louise (Murray) D.; m. Jane Ann Ottaway, Mar. 21, 1959; children—Jennifer Dow Murphy, Peter Kinnersley, Thomas Anthony. B.A., U. Mich., 1955. Account exec. Campbell-Ewald Co., Detroit, 1958-66, exec. v.p., 1979-82, pres., 1982-93, vice chmn., 1993-95, ret., 1995; account supr. Young & Rubicam, Detroit, 1966-68; advt. dir. Chrysler Corp., Detroit, 1968-77, dir. mktg., 1977-79; bd. dirs. MascoTech., Inc., Comtrad Industries, Inc., The Stroh Brewery Co., The Stroh Cos., Inc. Trustee emeritus Lawrenceville Sch., N.J.; bd. dirs. Boys and Girls Clubs, Detroit, pres. 1989-90. Served to lt. (j.g.) USNR, 1955-58. Mem. Mich. Advt. Industry Alliance (past pres.), Grosse Pointe Club, Detroit Athletic Club, Adcraft Club (past pres.), Country Club Detroit, Old Club. Republican. Presbyterian.

DOW, PHILIP DONOVAN, poet, educator; b. June 4, 1937. BA, MA, San Francisco State Coll.; PhD, SUNY, Buffalo. Prof. SUNY, Binghamton, La. State U., Baton Rouge, St. Mary's Coll., Moraga, Calif., 1992—; poet in residence Reed Coll., Portland, Oreg., Carnegie-Mellon U., Pitts. Author: Paying Back the Sea; editor: 19 New American Poets. Nat. Endowment Arts fellow in poetry. Address: 2193 Ethel Porter Dr Napa CA 94558

DOW, RONALD F., librarian; b. Deadwood, S.D., Jan. 26, 1949; s. Fay Ellsworth and Aldeen Faye (Decker) D.; m. Susan White, Apr. 24, 1982; children: Wesley E., Eleanor W. BA, Augustana Col., 1971; MLS, Syracuse U., 1972; PhD, Penn. State U., 1997. Asst. reference librarian Hamilton Col., Clinton, N.Y., 1972-76; asst. bus. and engring. librarian Dartmouth Col., Hanover, N.H., 1976-80; dir. grad. bus. adminstrn. libr. N.Y.U., 1980-83; first v.p. & dir. libraries Shearson Lehman Am. Express, N.Y.C., 1983-90; assoc. dean of libraries Penn. State U., U. Park, 1990-96; dean River Campus Libararies U. Rochester (N.Y.), 1996—. Editorial bd. mem. U. Rochester Press, J. Acad. Librarianship. Contbr. articles to profl. jours. Dir. Writers & Books, Rochester, N.Y., 1997—, BOA Edits., Ltd., Rochester, N.Y., 1998—. Mem. ALA, Am. Assn. Higher Edn. Office: U Rochester Rush Rhees Library Rochester NY 14627

DOW, WILLIAM GOULD, electrical engineer, educator; b. Faribault, Minn., Sept. 30, 1895; s. James Jabez and Myra Amelia (Brown) D.; m. Edna Lois Sontag., Oct. 24, 1924 (dec. Feb. 1963); children—Daniel Gould, David Sontag; m. Katherine Bird Keene, Apr. 2, 1968 (dec. May 1997); stepchildren—John S. Keene, Margaret Keene Hannan, Karen Keene Day. BS, U. Minn., 1916, EE, 1917; MSE, U. Mich., 1929; DSc (hon.), U. Colo., 1980. Registered profl. engr., Mich. Diversified engring. and bus. experience, 1917-26; faculty, dept. elec. engring. U. Mich., Ann Arbor, 1926-65; prof. elec. engring. U. Mich., 1945-65, chmn. dept. elec. engring., 1958-64, prof. emeritus, 1966—; sr. rsch. geophysicist Space Physics Rsch. Lab., 1966-71; electronics cons. Nat. Bur. Standards, 1945-55; research staff Radio Research Lab., Harvard, 1943-45, assignment, U.K., winter 1944-45; sci. adv. com. Harry Diamond Labs., 1953-64; bus. mgr. Lang. Studies Abroad, Spain, summers, 1965-74; Mem. vacuum tube devel. com. NDRC, World War II; (European vacuum tube research survey), 1953; mem. rocket and satellite research panel, 1946-60; U.S. tech. panel on rocketry IGY, 1956-59; made world tour for space research and engring. edn. survey, 1969-70; Charter mem. bd. trustees Environmental Research Inst. Mich., 1972-90, trustee emeritus, 1990—. Author: Fundamentals of Engineering Electronics, 1937, rev. 1952, Very High Frequency Techniques (co-author), 2 vols, 1947; contr. articles to profl. jours.; patentee trochoidal nuclear fusion system. Lt. C.E. U.S. Army, WWI. Recipient medal, award in elec. engring. edn. IEEE, 1963. Fellow IEEE (bd. editors 1941-54), Engring. Soc. Detroit, AAAS; mem. AAUP, Am. Phys. Soc., Am. Inst. Aeros. and Astronautics, Am. Geophys. Union, Nat., Mich. socs. profl. engrs., Am. Astronautical Soc., N.Y. Acad. Scis., Am. Soc. Engring. Edn., Am. Welding Soc., Nat. Electronics Conf. (dir. 1949-52, chmn. bd. 1951), Masons, Cosmos Club, Sigma Xi, Tau Beta Pi, Eta Kappa Nu. Episcopalian. Home: 400 Ivy Ann Ct Waco TX 76712-3629 *It has been my hope and prayer that I might always: Base decisions for action on my own judgements rather than on opinions of others; Live primarily in a world of people, rather than a world of dollars or of scientific or man-made laws; Always listen for the whistling of the winds of change, and so ever pursue the need to learn new skills of mind and hand, to keep up with the pace of change-for nothing is eternal but change-except that there remains eternal, ever, awareness of beauty, as in things seen and heard, and in graciousness of mind and spirit.*

DOWBEN, ROBERT MORRIS, physician, scientist; b. Phila., Apr. 9, 1927; s. Morris and Zena D.; m. Carla Lurie, June 20, 1950; children—Peter Arnold, Jonathan Stuart, Susan Laurie. AB, Haverford Coll., 1946; MS, U. Chgo., 1947, MD, 1949. Intern U. Chgo. Clinics, 1949-50; research fellow U. Oslo, 1950-51; fellow Johns Hopkins Hosp., 1951-52; resident in medicine U. Pa. Hosp., 1952-53; instr. medicine U. Pa. and dir. radiosotope unit VA Hosp., Phila., 1953-55; asst. prof. medicine Northwestern U. Med. Sch., 1957-62; asso. prof. biology M.I.T., 1962-68; lectr. medicine Harvard U. Med. Sch., 1962-68; prof. med. sci. Brown U., 1968-72; prof. biochemistry U. Bergen, Norway, 1972; prof. physiology and neurology, dir. grad. program in biophysics U. Tex. Health Sci. Center, Dallas, 1972-88; prof. neurology U. Tex. Health Sci. Ctr., Dallas, 1988-93; dir. Med. Cell Biology Lab. Baylor Rsch. Inst., Dallas, 1987-93; prof. physiology Brown U., Providence, R.I., 1993—; cons. neurologist Children's Hosp., Scottish Rite Hosp., Presbyn. Hosp., Baylor Hosp, all Dallas, 1972-93; mem. corp. Haverford (Pa.) Coll., 1979—, Marine Biol. Lab., Woods Hole, Mass., 1964-79; trustee Mt. Desert Island Biol. Lab., 1994-98; ; advt. com. to the pres., Haverford Coll., 1997—; bd. dirs. Greenhill Sch., Dallas, 1974-77. Author: Biol. Membranes, 1969, General Physiology, 1971, Cell Biology, 1972, also numerous articles; editor: Cell and Muscle Motility. Served to capt. M.C. USAF, 1955-57. Lalor fellow; recipient Disting. Service award Assn. Neuromuscular Diseases, 1964, Disting. Service award Alumni Assn. U. Chgo., 1980. Mem. Am. Physiol. Soc., Am. Soc. Biol. Chemists, Am. Chem. Soc., Soc. Exptl. Biology and Medicine, Biophys. Soc., Soc. Clin. Investigation, Central Soc. Clin. Research, Mass. Med. Soc., So. Med. Soc., Dallas County Med. Soc., Tex. Med. Assn., Biochem. Soc. London, Faraday Soc. (London), Phi Beta Kappa, Sigma Xi. Mem. Soc. of Friends. Office: Brown U Physiology Dept PO Box G-B3 Providence RI 02912-9107

DOWD, BARRY, athletic director; m. Janice Dowd. BEd, East Tex. State U., 1960; MEd, U. North Tex. Coach basketball Dallas Ind. Sch., U. Tex. Arlington; asst. coach basketball U. Tex.; coach basketball, athletic dir. East Tenn. State U.; sr. assoc. athletic dir. Okla. State U.; ind. contractor Mktg. and Advt. Co., Calif.; athletic dir. Ark. State U., State University, 1996—. Mem. Nat. Assn. Basketball Coaches (bd. dirs.), Nat. Assn. Coll. Dirs. Athletics. Office: Ark State Univ PO Box 1000 State University AR 72467-1000*

DOWD, DAVID D., JR., federal judge; b. Cleve., Jan. 31, 1929; m. Joyce; children—Cindy, David, Doug, Mark. B.A., Coll. Wooster, 1951; J.D., U. Mich., 1954. Ptnr. Dowd & Dowd, Massillon, Ohio, 1954-55, prtnr., 1957-75; asst. pros. atty. Stark County, 1961-67, pros. atty., 1967-75; judge Ohio 5th Dist. Ct. Appeals, 1975-80, Ohio Supreme Ct., 1980-81; ptnr. Black, McCuskey, Souers & Arbaugh, Canton, Ohio, 1981-82; judge U.S. Dist. Ct. (no. dist.) Ohio, 1982—, now sr. judge, 1996—. Office: US Dist Ct 2 S Main St Akron OH 44308*

DOWD, EDWARD L., JR., prosecutor; s. Edward L. Dowd; m. Jill Goessling; 3 children. JD with distinction, St. Mary's Univ. With Dowd, Oates & Dowd; from asst. atty. to chief narcotics sect. U.S. Atty.'s Office, 1979-84; pvt. practice, 1984-93; atty. ea. judicial dist. U.S. Dept. Justice, St. Louis, 1993—; regional dir. south central region Pres.'s Organized Crime Drug Enforcement Task Force. Office: US Attys Office 401 US Court & Custom House 1114 Market St Saint Louis MO 63101-2043

DOWD, FRANCES CONNELLY, librarian; b. Newburyport, Mass., Dec. 9, 1918; d. Martin Francis and Nelle Magdalen (Quinn) Connelly; m. James Reynolds Dowd, June 7, 1941 (dec. June 1944); children: James Reynolds Jr., Thomas Henry III. AB, Wellesley Coll., 1941; MLS, Columbia U., 1955. Cataloger Phillips Acad. Libr., Andover, Mass., 1955-57; asst. libr. Wheelock Coll. Libr., Boston, 1957-59; head of circulation U. R.I., Kingston, 1959-62; head libr. Ins. Libr., Boston, 1962-66; head bus. & sci. dept. Providence (R.I.) Pub. Libr., 1966-70; reference libr. Boston U. Libr., 1970-74; head libr. Mass. Horticulture Soc., Boston, 1974-79; reference libr. Haverhill (Mass.) Pub. Libr., 1979-89, Endicott Coll. Libr., Beverly, Mass., 1989—. Editor: Whittier, 1992. pres. Whittier Home Assn., Amesbury, Mass., 1989—; treas. Macy-Colby House, 1979; sec. Amesbury Carriage Mus., Amesbury, 1982—; reunion chmn. Wellesley Coll., 1971, 86. Mem. ALA, Abenaqui Country Club, Wellesley Coll. Club. Republican. Avocations: historic houses and gardens, travel, golf, gardening. Home: 3 Hillside Ave Amesbury MA 01913-2213

DOWD, JAMES PATRICK, bookseller, writer; b. Chgo., Apr. 26, 1937; s. James Patrick and Mary Margaret (Healy) D.; m. Frances Marie Allevato, Aug. 4, 1962; children: Mary Frances, Daniel James, Matthew Joseph. Student, Wright Jr. Coll., 1956-58, Harper Coll., 1984, Elgin C.C., 1986; AS, Elgin C.C., 1988. With Spraying Sys. Co., Wheaton, Ill., 1958-78; owner operator Dowd's Bok Shoppe, St. Charles, Ill., 1978-80; tech. specialist Fermi Nat. Accelerator Lab., Batavia, Ill., 1980-86; task order adminstr. Fermi Nat. Accelerator Lab., Batavia, 1986-88, fabrication specialist, 1986-92; ret., 1992; mem. SSC task force, 1984-88, Elgin (Ill.) C.C., 1986-88; hist. cons. Potawatomi Indian Statue Com., St. Charles; cons. midwest ethnohistory. Author: Built Like a Bear, 1979, Custer Lives, 1983, The Potawatomi-A Native American Legacy, 1988, Stories of the Sacred Fire People, 1995, Shabni-His Lands, His Descendants: A Historical Profile and an Opinion, 1995, Introduction: The Narratives of De Calves, John Van Delure and Captain James Van Leason/Apocryphal Accounts of Travel, 1996, Thunders Speak, 1999, The Story of a French Homestead in the Old Northwest, 1999; editor: Life of Black Hawk, 1974; contbr.: Images of the Mystic Truth, 1981, Some Misconceptions of Custer and the Battle of the Little Big Horn, 1986, On Becoming and Being a Neshnabe, 1988, Alien, 1988, Great Poets of the Western World, 1989, All Same...All Same..., 1989, Footsteps Along the Fox, 1989, Native American Paul Revere, 1990, Wabansi, 1992, The Potawatomi-Thoughts on the Culture and Mainstream Assimilation, 1992, Memories of Ballindine, County Mayo, Ireland, 1993, Native American Woodland Culture, 1993. With U.S. Army, 1961-63. Mem. Chgo. Corral of Westerners (assoc. editor 1990-92). Roman Catholic. Avocations: collector of scarce and rare western Americana, Northern Ill. Field Archaeology. Home: 38w281 Toms Trail Dr Saint Charles IL 60175-6037

DOWD, JANICE LEE, foreign language educator; b. N.Y.C., Jan. 6, 1948; d. Edward H. and Mary A. (Vanek) D. BA, Marietta (Ohio) Coll., 1969; MA, Columbia U., 1971, MEd, 1979, EdD, 1984. Cons. tchr. Teaneck (N.J.) Bd. Edn., 1970—; adj. asst. prof. Queens Coll., CUNY, 1984-94, Columbia U., N.Y.C., spring 1988, 93—; N.J. alternate route prof., 1990—; asst. prof. MA TESOL program in China, Changsha, 1986, Shanghai, 1987; SAT program adminstr. Teaneck H.S., 1978-83, yearbook sponsor, 1975-79, newspaper sponsor, 1984-92, co-chair Global/Multicultural Mgmt. Team, 1992-95. Contbr. articles to profl. jours. Mem. program com. PEO, Teaneck, 1966—. Fellow Rockefeller Found., 1988. Mem. Am. Assn. Tchrs. of French, Tchrs. English to Speakers Other Langs., N.Y. State Tchrs. English to Speakers Other Langs., N.J. Tchrs. English to Speakers Other Langs., Am. Assn. Applied Linguists, Am. Coun. Tchrs. Fgn. Langs., Fgn. Lang. Educators N.J., Second Lang. Acquisition Circle N.Y., Nat. Assn. of Dept. Heads and Suprs. of Fgn. Langs. Home: 56 Boulevard New Milford NJ 07646-1602 Office: Teaneck High Sch 100 Elizabeth Ave Teaneck NJ 07666-4798

DOWD, JOHN MAGUIRE, lawyer; b. Brockton, Mass., Nov. 2, 1941; s. Paul L. and Mary (Maguire) D.; m. Carole L. Folts, June 12, 1965; children: Thomas P., Anne M., Sarah E., Michael T., Daniel M. AB cum laude, St. Bernard Coll., Cullman, Ala., 1963; JD, Emory U., 1965. Bar: D.C. 1967, U.S. Dist. Ct. (so. dist.) Ga. 1987, U.S. Supreme Ct. 1970. Trial atty. Tax div. U.S. Dept. Justice, Washington, 1969-72; chief strike force 18 Criminal div. U.S. Dept. Justice, Washington, 1972-78; ptnr. Whitman & Ransom, Washington, 1978-84, Heron, Burchette, Ruckert & Rothwell, Washington, 1984-90, Akin, Gump, Strauss, Hauer & Feld, L.L.P., Washington, 1990—; arbitrator Internat. C. of C., Internat. Ct. Arbitration, 1994—; spl. counsel Commr. of Baseball, 1989-92. Trustee Flint Hill Sch., Oakton, Va. Capt. USMC, 1965-69. Mem. ABA, D.C. Bar Assn., Edward Bennett Williams Inn of Ct. (master). Avocations: golf, swimming, walking, reading, teaching. Office: Akin Gump Strauss Hauer & Feld Ste 400 1333 New Hampshire Ave NW Washington DC 20036-1564

DOWD, JOHN P., III, academic administrator; b. Bennettsville, S.C., Apr. 17, 1967; s. J.P. Dowd Jr. and Lulu Barry (Gibson) Webster; m. Kimberly Sue Littlefield, Dec. 31, 1994. BA in History, Winthrop U., 1989; MEd in Student Pers., U. S.C., 1993. Grad. asst. U. S.C., Columbia, 1991-93; assoc. v.p. for devel. Limestone Coll., Gaffney, S.C., 1993-94; v.p. for devel. Meth. Coll., Fayetteville, N.C., 1994—. Mem. bd. advs. St. Anne's Cath. Sch., Fayetteville, 1997-99; bd. dirs. Rape Crisis Vols., Fayetteville, 1997-98; mem. adminstrv. bd. Haymount United Meth. Ch., Fayetteville, 1996—. Mem. Cape Fear Kiwanis (bd. dirs. 1995-96). Office: Meth Coll 5400 Ramsey St Fayetteville NC 28311-1420

DOWD, KARL EDMUND, priest; b. Nashua, N.H., May 3, 1934; s. Karl Edmund Sr. and Edna Louise (Burque) D. BS, Coll. of Holy Cross, 1956; BTh, U. Ottawa, Ont., Can., 1958, Licentiate in Sacred Theology, 1960; MEd, Rivier Coll., 1964. Ordained priest Roman Cath. Ch., 1960. Tchr. Bishop Bradley High Sch., Manchester, N.H., 1960-62; tchr., athletic dir. St. Thomas Aquinas High Sch., Dover, N.H., 1962-68; adminstr. St. Mary's, Rollinsford, N.H., 1967; assoc. pastor St. Bernard's Parish, Keene, N.H., 1968-69, St. Joseph's Parish, Nashua, 1969-71, Immaculate Heart of Mary, Concord, N.H., 1971-75; pastor St. Joseph's Ch., Salem, N.H., 1975-86; dean Salem Deanery, 1980-86; pastor St. Christopher Ch., Nashua, 1986—; asst. dir. diocesan camps, Fatima and Bernadette, N.H., 1960-62, diocesan dir., 1971-90; mem. New Eng. regional com. Nat. Liturgical Conf., 1961—; adv. diocesan marriage tribunal Diocese of Manchester, 1975—, diocesan consultor, 1980-86; bd. dirs. Nashua Pastoral Care Ctr., 1969—, pres., 1999—. Chaplain Nashua coun. KC, 1970-76, State Prior Columbian Squires, 1973-76; Salem divsn. chaplain Ct. Holy Name, Cath. Daus. Am., 1977-80, state chaplain, 1989—; bd. dirs., exec. com. Concord Mental Health Clinic, 1972-75; chmn. interfaith svc. com. N.H. Hosp., Concord, 1974-75; past pres., bd. dirs., pres. Salemhaven, Inc.; bd. dirs., pres. Silverthorne, Inc., 1992-94; pres. Salem Life Care Found., Inc., 1992-96; clk., bd. dirs. Marklin Candle Design. Named knight of the Holy Sepulchre, 1986; recipient Noyes medal, 1952. Mem. Am. Camping Assn. (nat. bd. dirs., past pres. and bd. dirs. New Eng. sect., regional chair 1986-90, chair ethics com. 1990-92, 96-99), N.H. Camp Dirs. Assn. (bd. dirs. 1971—, pres. 1974-78), U.S. Cath. Conf. (com. on camping 1972-76). Home: 15 Denise St PO Box 3810 Nashua NH 03061-3810 Office: St Christopher Ch 62 Manchester St Nashua NH 03060-6201

DOWD, MAUREEN, columnist; b. Washington, Jan. 14, 1952. BA in English, Catholic U., 1973. From editl. asst. to feature writer The Washington Star, 1974-81; from corr. to writer Time mag., 1981-83; metro reporter N.Y. Times, 1983-86, D.C. reporter, 1986-95, opinion-editl. columnist, 1995—. Office: care NY Times 1627 I St NW Washington DC 20006-4007*

DOWD, MORGAN DANIEL, political science educator; b. Boston, Feb. 21, 1933; s. Joseph Francis and Marion Caroline (Calcari) D.; m. Dianne May Robichaud, Aug. 29, 1959; children: Megan Eileen, Sean Morgan, Colin Martin, Blaine Christopher, Roarke Terence. B.A. cum laude, St. Michael's Coll., 1955; J.D., Catholic U. Am., 1958; M.A., U. Mass., 1962, Ph.D., 1964. Instr. U. Maine, 1959-60, U. Mass., 1960-61; asst. prof. polit. sci. SUNY-Fredonia, 1963-67, assoc. prof., 1967-76, prof., 1976—, dean grad. studies and research, 1969-78, dean faculty for natural and social scis., 1978-84, joint prof. bus. and polit. sci., 1984-99, dist. svc. prof., 1995-99, ret., 1999; cons. Mid. States Assn. Colls. and Univs., 1977—; project dir. USIA grant, Albania, 1992-94, 95-96. Contbr. articles to law jours., 1956-78; co-editor: World Dictionary of Environmental Research Centers, 2d edit., 1974. Bd. dirs. com. Health Systems Agy. Western N.Y., 1986-87, mem. exec. com.; regional member N.Y. state commn. Bicentennial of Constn., 1987; convocation speaker West Chester U. Pa., 1991. Recipient Pres.'s Medallion award, West Chester U. Pa., 1991, Extraordinary Svc. to Commn. on Higher Edn. U. Rochester, 1994. Mem. Columbia U. Seminar on History of Legal and Polit. Theory, Torch Club, Delta Epsilon Sigma, Pi Sigma Alpha, Delta Theta Phi, Phi Eta Sigma. Democrat. Roman Catholic.

DOWD, PETER JEROME, public relations executive; b. Bklyn., Oct. 5, 1942; s. Jerome Ambrose and Mary Agnes (Young) D.; m. Brenda Badura, Nov. 25, 1972; 1 child, Kelly Ann. A.B., Fordham U., 1964. Reporter UPI, N.Y.C., 1964-66; account exec. Hill and Knowlton, N.Y.C., 1966-71; v.p. Hill and Knowlton, 1971-74; sr. v.p., mgr. Hill and Knowlton (Los Angeles office), 1974-78, mng. dir. Western region, 1978-80, exec. v.p., 1980; ptnr. Haley, Kiss & Dowd, Inc., Los Angeles, 1980-83; group v.p. Am. Med. Internat., 1983-88; v.p. pub. rels. Texaco Inc., White Plains, N.Y., 1989-96; sr. v.p. corp. affairs Fidelity Investments, Boston, 1996-99; pub. affairs cons., 1999—; instr. U. So. Calif., Calif. State U., Fullerton. Bd. dirs. Cath. Big Bros., Nature Conservancy (Lower Hudson chpt.). Mem. Pub. Rels. Soc. Am., Alan Page Soc., Town Hall West (v.p., dir.), Westchester County Assn. (bd. dirs.), Nature Conservancy (bd. dirs. Lower Hudson chpt.), U.S. Mil. Acad. Pub. Affairs (adv. com.). Republican. Roman Catholic. Club: Aspetuck Valley Country Club. Office: Fidelity Investments 82 Devonshire St Boston MA 02109-3614

DOWD, SANDRA K., state legislator; b. New Market, Tenn., Aug. 21, 1950; m. John Dowd; 2 children. N.H. state rep. Dist. 13, 1990-98; mem. com. small bus., consumer affairs and econ. devel. N.H. Ho. of Reps., mem. legis. adminstrn., exec. dept. and adminstrv. coms., mem. fin. com., 1998; owner Profl. Image Dry Cleaners and Laundry Ctr., Derry, Londonderry, Manchester, N.H.; pres. D&K Family Enterprises Corp., 1990—. Sec. Derry Rep. Town Com.; mem. Rep. Network to Elect Women; vice chmn. Dem. State Rep. Del. Mem. DAV (life), N.H. Fedn. Rep. Women, Nat. Fedn. Rep. Women, Greater Derry C. of C. Address: NH House of Reps PO Box 1596 Derry NH 03038-6596*

DOWDA, WILLIAM F., internist; b. Cobb County, Ga.. MD, Emory U., 1949. Intern Peter Bent Brigham Hosp., Boston, 1949-50; resident Barnes Hosp., 1950-51, 52-54; staff Piedmont Hosp., 1953-76; clin. assoc. prof. medicine Emory U., 1962-76; pvt. practice internal medicine, 1976—; pathology fellow, mem. staff Grady Meml. Hosp. Lt. med. corps USNR, 1950-52. Mem. ACP, AMA, Inst. Medicine-NAS, Soc. Med. Adminstrs. Address: 490 Peachtree St NE Ste 129B Atlanta GA 30308-3136*

DOWDELL, MICHAEL FRANCIS, critical care and anesthesia nurse practitioner; b. Cleve., June 5, 1949; s. Harry William and Dorothy May (McGivney) D.; 1 child, Michael Patrick. BSN, Ohio State U., 1975; MA in Counseling, Nat. U., San Diego, 1981; MSN, Calif. State U., Long Beach, 1991; diploma in nursing anesthesia, Kaiser Sch. Anesthesia, L.A., 1991; postgrad., Case Western Res. U., 1996—. CCRN, CRNA, ARNP; cert. ACLS instr; cert. community coll. instr., Calif. Enlisted USN, 1968, commd. ensign, 1974, advanced through grades to lt. comdr., 1984, ret., 1988; resident nurse anesthesist Kaiser Sch. Anesthesia for Nurses, 1989-91; staff nurse anesthetist Kaiser Hosp., Panorama City, Calif., 1991-92, HCA Med. Ctr., Largo, Fla., 1992-93, Meml. Mission Hosp., Asheville, N.C., 1993-97; vis. lectr. dept. anesthesia Makerere U., Kampala Uganda, 1995. Decorated Navy Achievement medal. Mem. AACN, NRA, VFW, Am. Assn. Nurse Anesthetists, Assn. Mil. Surgeons U.S., Ret. Officers Assn., Fleet Res. Assn., Am. Legion, Nat. Muzzle-Loading Rifle Assn., North-South Skirmish Assn. Republican. Avocations: fishing, shooting sports, travel. Home and Office: 1466 Sanderling Dr Englewood FL 34224-4720

DOWDEN, CARROLL VINCENT, publishing company executive; b. Louisville, Apr. 9, 1933; s. Charles Merrill and Regina Celestine (Popham) D.; m. Eleanor Therese Dion, Nov. 24, 1956; children: Mark Vincent, Laura Anne, Amy Alexandra, Beth Regina. A.B., U. Notre Dame, 1955; M.S. in Journalism, Columbia U., 1960. Asst. financial editor Louisville Times, 1955-56; asso. editor Ind. U. News Bur., Bloomington, 1956-57; asst. financial editor Courier-Jour., Louisville, 1957-63; with Med. Econs. Co., Oradell, N.J., 1963-84; gen. mgr. Drug Tropics mag., 1972-73; pub. Med. Econs. mag., 1973-77, exec. v.p. co., 1976-77, pres., 1977-84; pres. Next Pub. Co., N.Y.C., 1979-81; chmn. Washington legal com. Am. Bus. Press, 1979-85, 92-95, dir., 1985, 91—, vice chmn., 1995-96, chmn., 1996-97; dir. Bus. Publs. Audit Circulation, Inc., 1981-85, v.p., 1984-85; v.p. Internat. Thomson Orgn., Inc., 1985-86; group v.p. Cahners Pub. Co., N.Y.C., 1986-88; founder, pres. Dowden Pub. Co., Montvale, N.J., 1988—. Trustee Pascack Valley Hosp., Westwood, N.J., 1976-83, v.p. bd., 1978-80. Served to capt. U.S. Army, 1956, 61-62. Pulitzer traveling fellow Columbia U., 1960-61. Mem. Soc. Profl. Journalists. Club: Hackensack Golf (Oradell), Union League (N.Y.C.), Phila. Country (Gladwyne, Pa.). Home: 13 Cameron Rd Saddle River NJ 07458-2935

DOWDEN, CRAIG PHILLIPS, human resources executive; b. Cleve., Dec. 11, 1947; s. Edmund Van Dyke and Margaret (Phillips) D.; m. Jennie Riffe, June 4, 1970; children: Brett, Travis. BS in Indsl. Mgmt., Purdue U., 1970, MS Indsl. Rels., 1972. Adminstr. union rels. GE Silicones, Waterford, N.Y., 1972-73; compensation specialist GE Maj. Appliance, Columbia, Md., 1973-74; union rels. specialist GE Appliance Components, Ft. Wayne, Ind., 1974-75; mgr. rels. GE Mining Products, Houston, 1975-77; mgr. personnel practices GE Carboloy Systems, Warren, Mich., 1977-79, mgr. union rels., 1979-84; dir. employee rels. OMI Internat. Corp., Warren, 1984-87; mgr. employee rels. GE Carboloy Systems, Warren, 1987; dir. human resources Carboloy Inc., Warren, 1987-90; v.p. human resources Thrall Car Mfg. Co., Chicago Heights, Ill., 1990-91, v.p. adminstrn., 1991-97, exec. v.p. adminstrn., 1997—. Past pres. Calumet coun. Boy Scouts Am. Mem. Soc. for Human Resource Mgmt. Avocations: computer political pilot, personal computing. Home: 1330 Tamarack Dr Munster IN 46321-4218 Office: Thrall Car Mfg Co 2521 State St Chicago Heights IL 60411-4300

DOWDEN, G. BLAIR, academic administrator; b. May 11, 1952; s. George D.; m. Chris Decker; children: Beau, Marli. BA, Wheaton Coll., 1974; MA, Ball State U., 1978, EdD, 1981. From admissions counselor to asst. to pres., asst. prof. Taylor U., Upland, Ind., 1974-84; v.p. devel. Houghton (N.Y.) Coll., 1984-91; pres. Huntington (Ind.) Coll., 1991—; coun. of reference mem. Ft. Wayne (Ind.) Christian Sch., 1996—; bd. dirs. Ind. Coll. Ind. Found., Indpls., Ind. Colls. Ind., Norwest Adv. Bank. Author: Presidents: Effective Fundraising, Leadership, 1990, 96, Development, Winning Strategies for Fundraising Success, 1993. Active College Park United Brethren Ch. Mem. Am. Assn. for Higher Edn., Christian Mgmt. Assn., Christian Stewardship Assn. (bd. dirs. 1990-93), Nat. Assn. Evangelicals. Avocation: running. Office: Huntington Coll 2303 College Ave Huntington IN 46750-1237

DOWDEN, THOMAS CLARK, telecommunication executive; b. Ridgetop, Tenn., May 6, 1935; s. James Robert and Anna Mary (Hunter) D.; m. Wendy Ellen Vereen, Jan. 27, 1962; children: Anna V. Dowden Tschetter, Constance H. Cobbs, John T. BA in Journalism, U. Ga., 1962, MA in Polit. Sci., 1963. Account exec. Corinthian Broadcasting, Houston, 1963-65; v.p., sec. Cox Cable Comm., Atlanta, 1965-76; owner, CEO Dowden Comm., Atlanta, 1977—; mem. bd. dirs. Ga. Dept. Industry, Trade and Tourism, 1994-97; bd. dirs., chmn. George Foster Peabody Radio-TV-Cable awards, 1991-93. Organizer Cable TV's Role in 1976 Presdl. Election, Atlanta, 1975-76; trustee Atlanta Boy Choir, 1982-93. Mem. Nat. Cable TV Assn., Cherokee Town and Country Club, Wade Hampton Golf Club (Cashiers, N.C.), Royal St. George's Golf Club (Sandwich, Kent, Eng.). U.S. Sr. Golf Assn. Republican. Episcopalian. Avocations: golf, photography, traveling. Home: PO Box 2645 Cashiers NC 28717-2645 Office: Dowden Communications 650 Blackberry Ln Clarkesville GA 30523

DOWDEN, WILLIAM, councilman. City councilman City of Indpls. Republican. Home: 5826 Common Cir Indianapolis IN 46220-5399 Office: City-County Coun Office 200 E Washington St Ste 241 Indianapolis IN 46204-3310*

DOWDEY, BENJAMIN CHARLES, physician; b. Birmingham, Ala., Apr. 19, 1948; s. Ivan Charles and Benna Jean (Jones) D.; m. Susan Lee Wildsmith, May 26, 1979; 1 child, Amy Elizabeth. BA with distinction, U. Va., 1969; MD, U. Ala., Birmingham, 1973. Diplomate Nat. Bd. Med. Examiners, Am. Bd. Internal Medicine, Am. Bd. Emergency Medicine. Emergency medicine physician, 1976—. Named Ala. Amateur Golfer of Yr., Dixie sect. PGA, 1987. Fellow Am. Coll. Emergency Physicians, 1996; mem. AMA, S.A.R., Ala. Golf Assn. (bd. dirs. 1980—, pres. 1993-94), U.S. Golf Assn. (mem. com. 1981—). Avocations: golf, guitar, genealogy. Home: 3636 Westbury Rd Birmingham AL 35223-1533

DOWDLE, PATRICK DENNIS, lawyer; b. Denver, Dec. 8, 1948; s. William Robert and Helen (Schraeder) D.; m. Eleanor Pryor, Mar. 8, 1975; children: Jeffery William, Andrew Peter. BA, Cornell Coll., Mt. Vernon, Iowa, 1971; JD, Boston U., 1975. Bar: Colo. 1975, U.S. Dist. Ct. Colo. 1975, U.S. Ct. Appeals (10th cir.) 1976, U.S. Supreme Ct. 1978. Acad. dir. in Japan Sch. Internat. Tng., Putney, Vt., 1974; assoc. Decker & Miller, Denver, 1975-77; ptnr. Miller, Makkai & Dowdle, Denver, 1977—; designated counsel criminal appeals Colo. Atty. Gens. Office, Denver, 1980-81; guardian ad litem Adams County Dist. Ct., Brighton, Colo., 1980-83; affiliated counsel ACLU, Denver, 1980—. Mem. Colo. Bar Assn., Denver Bar Assn. (various coms.), Porsche Club of Am. Avocations: scuba diving, photography, wine making, travel, skiing. Home: 3254 Tabor Ct Wheat Ridge CO 80033-5367 Office: Miller Makkai & Dowdle 2325 W 72nd Ave Denver CO 80221-3101

DOWDY, FREDELLA MAE, secondary school educator; b. Granby, Mo., Feb. 2, 1943; d. Arthur Clem and Helen Margaret (Davis) Rinehart; m. David Sherman Dowdy, Aug. 31, 1962; children: Ingrid Cara, Eric Davis. BS in Edn. summa cum laude, Cen. State Coll., Edmond, Okla., 1964; MEd, Cen. State U., Edmond, 1975. Cert. tchr., Okla. Tchr. Hayes County High Sch., Hayes Center, Nebr., 1964-65; sec. Masonic Homes of Okla., Guthrie, 1965-66, 68-73; tchr. Guthrie Pub. Schs., 1966-68, 73—, chmn. dept. bus., 1987-89, 90—, chmn. bus./vocat. dept., 1989-90. Swim instr. aide Logan County Red Cross, Guthrie, 1982-88; accompanist children's choir First So. Bapt. Ch., Guthrie, 1980-83; brownie leader Redlands council Girl Scouts Am., 1977-79. Mem. NEA, Okla. Edn. Assn., Guthrie Asn. Classroom Tchrs. (sec. 1975-76), Cen. State U. Alumni Assn., Okla. Found. for Excellence. Republican. Baptist. Avocations: reading mysteries, sewing, crochet, fitness walking, travel. Home: 1119 Pin Oak Dr Guthrie OK 73044-2017 Office: Guthrie High Sch 200 Crooks Dr Guthrie OK 73044-3927

DOWDY, LINDA KATHERINE, psychiatric and geriatric nurse; b. Jonesboro, Ark., Aug. 15, 1943; d. Eugene Joe and N. Katherine (Pierce) Riegler; m. Luther Joe Dowdy, Aug. 15, 1983; children: Wendy E., Kenneth E. and Katherine H. Garrison. Diploma, St. John's Sch. Nursing, Springfield, Mo., 1974; student, So. Meth. U., Drury Coll., S.W. Mo. State U. Cert. gerontol. nurse. Institutional adv. nurse Div. Aging Div. of Health, State of Mo., Springfield, 1979-83; dir. nursing Greene County Nursing and Health Ctr., Springfield, 1983-85; dir. community health svcs. ARC, Springfield, 1985-88; staff sr. adult psychiat. unit. St. John's Regional Health Ctr., Springfield, 1988-92, staff nurse psychiat. ICU, 1988-95; unit coord. Mercy Villa St. Johns Regional Health Ctr., Springfield, 1995-97; support nurse St. Johns Hospice, Springfield, 1997-98, ret., 1998; profl. practice com. St. John's Regional Health Ctr., 1992-94, sys. rev. com., 1994-95; promoter and breeder of Registered Mo. Foxtrotting Horses, Luther Dowdy Farms, Rogersville, Mo. Chmn. staying healthy after 50 com. Sr. Outreach Program, St. John's Regional Health Ctr., Springfield, Mo. Recipient Health Edn. award Am. Cancer Soc., 1987. Mem. Mo. League of Nursing. Home: 4786 S Farm Road 213 Rogersville MO 65742-9267

DOWELL, ANTHONY JAMES, SR., ballet dancer; b. London, Feb. 16, 1943; s. Arthur Henry and Catherine Ethel D. Studied with, June Hampshire; student, Royal Ballet Sch. Dancer Covent Garden Opera Ballet, 1960; dancer Royal Ballet, 1961-78, prin. dancer, 1966—, asst. to dir., 1984-85, assoc. dir., 1985-86, artistic dir., 1986—; producer Swan Lake for Royal Ballet, 1987; guest artist Am. Ballet Theatre, N.Y.C., 1977-79. Created: dance roles in ballets The Dream, 1964, Monotones, 1965, Jazz Calendar, 1968, Shadowplay, 1967, Enigma Variations, 1968, Meditation, 1971, Anastasia, 1971, Triad, 1972, Pavane, 1973, Manon, 1974, Four Schumann Pieces, 1975, A Month in the Country, 1976, Contre Dances, 1979, Winter Dreams, 1991; appeared in: film Valentino; guest artist: Nat. Ballet Can., 1979, 81. Knight comdr., 1995, Order Brit. Empire, 1973; Recipient award Dance mag., 1972. Office: Royal Ballet Royal Opera House, Covent Garden, London WC2E 9DD, England

DOWELL, EARL HUGH, university dean, aerospace and mechanical engineering educator; b. Macomb, Ill., Nov. 16, 1937; s. Earl S. and Edna Bernice (Dean) D.; children: Marla Lorraine, Janice Lynelle, Michael Hugh. B.S., U. Ill., 1959; S.M., Mass. Inst. Tech., 1961, Sc.D., 1964. Rsch. engr. Boeing Co., 1962-63; rsch. asst. MIT, 1963-64, rsch. engr., 1964, asst. prof., 1964-65; asst. prof. aerospace and mech. engring. Princeton U., 1964-68, assoc. prof., 1968-72, prof., 1972-83, assoc. chmn., 1975-77, acting chmn., 1979; dean Sch. Engring. Duke U., Durham, N.C., 1983—; cons. to industry and govt.; mem. sci. adv. bd. USAF; mem. bd. visitors Office of Naval Rsch. Author: Aeroelasticity of Plates and Shells, 1974, A Modern Course in Aeroelasticity, 1978, 3rd edit., 1995, Nonlinear Studies in Aeroelasticity, 1988; assoc. editor: AIAA Jour., 1969-72, Jour. Sound and Vibration, 1988—, Jour. Fluids and Structures, 1987—, Jour. Nonlinear Dynamics, 1990—; contbr. articles to profl. jours. Chmn. N.J. Noise Control Council, 1972-76. Named outstanding young alumnus U. Ill. Sch. Aero. and Astronautical Engring., 1973, disting. alumnus, 1975; recipient Alumni Honor award Coll. Engring. U. Ill. Fellow AIAA (Structures, Structural Dynamics and Material award 1980, v.p. publs. 1981-83), ASME, Am. Acad. Mechs. (pres. 1991, Disting. Svc. award 1994); mem. NAE, Acoustical Soc. Am., Am. Helicopter Soc. Home: 847 Inglenook Rd Durham NC 27707-3961 Office: Duke U Sch Engring Durham NC 27706

DOWELL, MICHAEL BRENDAN, chemist; b. N.Y.C., Nov. 18, 1942; s. William Henry and Anne Susan (Cannon) D.; m. Gail Elizabeth Renton, Mar. 16, 1968; children: Rebecca, Margaret. B.S., Fordham U., 1963; Ph.D., Pa. State U., 1967. Physicist U.S. Army Frankford Arsenal, Phila., 1967-69; research scientist Parma Tech. Ctr., Union Carbide Corp., (Ohio), 1969-74, devel. mgr. carbon fiber applications, 1974-76, group leader metals and ceramics research, 1976-80, sr. group leader process research, 1980-82; mgr. market devel. Parma Tech. Ctr., Union Carbide Corp., Ohio, 1982-92, Praxair Advanced Ceramics Inc. (formerly Union Carbide Corp.), Ohio, 1992-93, Advanced Ceramics Corp.(formerly Praxair Advanced Ceramics, Inc.), Cleve., 1993—; mem. U.S. Dept. Commerce Materials Tech. adv. com., 1994—. Contbr. articles to profl. jours. Chmn. 14th Congressional Dist. steering com. Common Cause, 1974-76; officer, trustee Hudson Montessori Assn., 1974-79. Served to capt. ordnance AUS, 1967-69. Mem. Am. Chem. Soc., Am. Phys. Soc., Am. Carbon Soc., U.S. Advanced Ceramics Assn. (bd. dirs. 1988-96), Am. Soc. Metals Internat. (govt. and pub. affairs com. 1989—), Phi Lambda Upsilon. Roman Catholic. Home: 368 N Main St Hudson OH 44236-2246 Office: Advanced Ceramics Corp PO Box 94924 Cleveland OH 44101-4924

DOWELL, RICHARD PATRICK, technology company executive; b. Washington, Apr. 21, 1934; s. Cassius McClellan and Mary Barbara (McHenry) D.; m. Eleanor Craddock Halley, Dec. 23, 1957 (div. Sept. 1973); children: Richard Patrick Jr., Robert Paul, Christopher Lee; m. Sandra Susan Humm, June 16, 1974; children: Ethan Leslie Smith, Allison Smith Temple. BS, U.S. Mil. Acad., 1956; MA, Stanford U., 1961, postgrad., 1962; postgrad., The Am. U., 1971-80; grad., The Nat. War Coll., 1975. Commd. 2d lt. USAF, 1956, advanced through grades to lt. col., 1974, ret., 1976; mgr. The BDM Corp., Fairfax, Va., 1977-79; sr. analyst ANSER Inc., Arlington, Va., 1979-81, div. mgr., 1981-84, v.p., 1984-91, cons., 1991; sr. staff MITRE Corp., Arlington, 1991-92; program dir. The Oakland Corp., Silver Spring, Md., 1992-93; pres., CEO Software Valley Corp., Morgantown, W.Va., 1993-97; chmn., pres. Software Valley Found., 1993-97; pres. Tech. Bus. Svcs., Inc., 1997—; exec. dir., bd. dirs. W.Va. Statewide Health Info. Network, 1995-97. Contr. articles to profl. jours. Pres. Alexandria (Va.) Taxpayer's Alliance, 1983. Decorated Bronze star, Air medal with 13 oak leaf clusters, D.F.C. with one oak leaf cluster. Mem. Nat. War Coll. Alumni Assn., Navy League, Air Force Assn. Republican. Episcopalian. Avocations: running, swimming, squash, bridge. Home: 41 Hasell St Charleston SC 29401-1604

DOWIE, IAN JAMES, management consultant; b. London, Mar. 3, 1938; came to U.S., 1980; s. James George and Ethel (Watker) D.; m. Barbara Eva Page, Jan. 9, 1960 (div. 1991); children: Paul James, David Ian; m. Nancy M. Pollard, 1993. BSEE, A.City & Guilds Inst., U. London, 1958. Registered profl. engr., Ont., Can. Seismic engr. Seismograph Svcs. Ltd., Eng., 1958-61; design engr. GE, Toronto, Ont., 1961-62; v.p., div. dir. IBM Can., Toronto, 1962-80; v.p. field ops. Exxon Office Systems, Stamford, Conn., 1980-82; pres. Aregon Internat. Inc., Stamford, 1983-84; pres. Benchmark East, Westport, Conn., 1985-96, Park City, Utah, 1993-97; pres. Benchmark Pub. Inc., Park City, Utah; chmn. Benchmark Ventures LLC, Park City, Utah, 1997—; pres. Benchmark-Goshawk, Inc., Park City, Utah. Pub. Once A Londoner, 1989, What's Love Got To Do With It?, 1993, From Womb to Tomb, 1994, Remuda Dust, 1994. Chmn. Credit Valley Assn. for Handicapped Children, Toronto, 1972-79. Mem. Shore and Country Club (Norwalk, Conn.), Jeremy Ranch Golf Club (Park City, Utah). Avocations: tennis, travel, skiing, golf. E-mail: benchmark@pcfastnet.com.

DOWIS, LENORE, lawyer; b. N.Y., Nov. 7, 1934; d. Thomas and Julianna (Csitkovits) Esteves; children: Daniel, Lenore, Denise, Jonathan. AAS, Suffolk County Community Coll., 1981; BA, SUNY, Stony Brook, 1983; JD, Touro Coll., 1987. Bar: N.Y. 1988, N.J. 1988, U.S. Dist. Ct. N.J. 1988, U.S. Dist. Ct. (so. and ea. dists.) N.Y. 1992, U.S. Ct. Mil. Appeals 1993, U.S. Ct. Claims 1993, U.S. Ct. Appeals (fed. cir.) 1993, U.S. Supreme Ct. 1993. Tel. operator N.Y. Tel. Co., L.I., 1951-58; real estate sales agt. Gen. Devel. Corp., Hauppauge, N.Y, 1974-75; ptnr., owner Davis Trucking Co., Huntington, N.Y., 1957-67; student law clk. to assoc. judge appellate div. U.S. Supreme Ct. N.Y., Bklyn., 1986; staff atty. Nassau/Suffolk Law Svcs., Bay Shore, N.Y., 1988; pvt. practice, Smithtown, N.Y., 1988—. Mem. ABA, Suffolk County Bar Assn., N.Y. State Bar Assn., Phi Theta Kappa, Alpha Beta Gamma. Republican. Home and Office: 33 Beverly Rd Smithtown NY 11787-5324

DOWLEY, JOEL EDWARD, manufacturing executive, lawyer; b. Jackson, Mich., Apr. 27, 1952; s. William J. and Beth E. (Morell) D.; m. Janelle Smith, Nov. 12, 1983; children: Kara Marie, Alayna Kristine. BA, Spring Arbor Coll., 1974; JD, U. Notre Dame, 1977. Bar: Mich. 1977. Atty. Fraser, Trebilcock, Davis and Foster, P.C., Lansing, Mich., 1977-83; exec. v.p., gen. counsel Dowley Mfg. Inc., Spring Arbor, Mich., 1983-87; chmn., chief exec. officer, 1987—. Pub. mem. Mich. Bd. Psychology, 1978-82, vice chmn., 1980, chmn., 1981-82; pub. mem. ethics com. Am. Assn. Marriage and Family Therapy, 1980; mem. Ingham County Republican Exec. Com., Mich., 1978-84, 3d Dist. Rep. Exec. Com., 1983-85; Rep. candidate for Ingham County commr., 1978, 82; trustee Highfield's, Inc., 1983-89, youth opportunity camp, Onondaga, Mich., 1983-89, sec., 1984-85, pres., 1986-87; trustee BoarsHead Theater, Lansing, 1983-92, treas., 1985-87, vice-chmn., 1987-89, Okemos Edn. Found., 1988-90, treas. 1989-90, Handicapped Children and Adults Found., trustee, 1994—, v.p., 1995-96, pres., 1996-97, treas., 1998-99; mem. elected officials compensation commn. Meridian Twp., Mich., 1989—, elected chmn., 1993—. Mem. Mich. Bar Assn., Ingham County Bar Assn., Spring Arbor Coll. Alumni Assn. (trustee 1979-82, pres. 1981-82, Young Leader award 1983), Hand Tools Inst. (bd. dirs. 1986-89, 90—, sec., treas., 1993-95, v.p., 1995-97, pres., 1997—), East Lansing Trinity Church. Methodist. Home: 1864 Cimarron Dr Okemos MI 48864-3810 Office: Dowley Mfg Inc 7750 King Rd Spring Arbor MI 49283-9777

DOWLEY, JOSEPH KYRAN, lawyer, member congressional staff; b. L.A., Apr. 23, 1946; s. Michael F. and Charlotte (Moore) D.; m. Carol Walsh, Jan. 22, 1972; children: Kristin, Michael, Patricia. BA, Georgetown U., Washington, 1968, JD, 1976. Bar: Va. 1976, D.C. 1980. Adminstrv. asst. to Honorable Dan Rostenkowski U.S. Ho. of Reps., Washington, 1977-81, asst. chief counsel Com. on Ways and Means, 1981-84, chief counsel Com. on Ways and Means, 1985-87; ptnr. Dewey Ballantine, 1987—. 1st lt. U.S. Army, 1969-71. Mem. Bar Assn. Va., Bar Assn. D.C., Georgetown Univ. Alumni Club (pres. 1984-85). Roman Catholic. Office: Dewey Ballantine 1775 Pennsylvania Ave NW Washington DC 20006-4672*

DOWLING, EDWARD THOMAS, economics educator; b. N.Y.C., Oct. 22, 1938; s. Edward Thomas and Mary Helen (Finegan) D. B.A., Berchmans Coll., Philippines, 1962, M.A. in Philosophy, 1963; M.Div., Woodstock Coll., Md., 1969; Ph.D., Cornell U., Ithaca, N.Y., 1973. Asst. prof. econs. Fordham U., Bronx, 1973-79, assoc. prof., 1979-85, prof., 1985—, dean, 1982-86, chmn. dept., 1979-82, 88-94. Author: Development Economics, 1977, Mathematics for Economists, 1980, Calculus for Business, Economics, and the Social Sciences, 1990, Introduction to Mathematical Economics, 1992, Mathematical Methods for Business and Economics, 1993. Mem. Am. Econ. Assn. Office: Fordham U Loyola Hall New York NY 10458-5198

DOWLING, JOHN CLARKSON, educator; b. Strawn, Tex., Nov. 14, 1920; s. Albert Clarkson and Georgia Anna (Turrill) D.; m. Constance Guinevere Ford, Dec. 26, 1949; 1 child, Robert Clarkson. BA, U. Colo., 1941; MA, U. Wis., 1942, PhD, 1950. Instr. Spanish U. Wis., Madison, 1951-53; prof., head fgn. langs. Tex. Tech. U., Lubbock, 1953-63; prof., chmn. Spanish & Portuguese Ind. U., Bloomington, 1963-72; prof., head romance langs. U. Ga., Athens, 1973-79, dean grad. sch., 1979-89, prof. alumni found., 1980-91, prof. emeritus alumni found., 1992—; vis. prof. romance langs. U. Tex., Austin, 1957; vis. prof. Spanish U. Iowa, Iowa City, 1993; interim dean arts & humanities Fla. Atlantic U., Boca Raton, 1995. Author: Saavedra Fajardo, 1957, 2d edit., 1977, Moratin, 1971, Jose Melchor Guomis, 1974; contbr. articles to profl. jours. Mem. exec. com. grad. deans African-Am. Inst., N.Y.C., 1985-92. Lt. (j.g.) USNR, 1942-46; lt. comdr. USNR, 1946-66. Rsch. grantee Am. Philos. Soc., 1971, 74; A.C. Markham Travel fellow, U. Wis., 1950-51, J.S. Guggenheim fellow, 1959-60. Mem. Am. Assn. Tchrs. Spanish & Portuguese, Hispanic Soc. Am. (corr.), Critica Hispanica Diecicocho. Episcopalian. Home: 145 Hancock Ln Athens GA 30605

DOWLING, JOHN ELLIOTT, biology educator; b. Pawtucket, R.I., Aug. 31, 1935; s. Joseph Leo and Ruth W. (Tappan) D.; children by previous marriage: Christopher, Nicholas.; m. Judith Falco, Oct. 18, 1975; 1 dau., Alexandra. AB, Harvard U., 1957, PhD, 1961; MD (hon.), U. Lund (Sweden), 1982. Asst. prof. biology Harvard U., 1961-64, prof., 1971-87, Maria Moors Cabot prof. natural sci., 1987—; assoc. prof. Johns Hopkins Sch. Medicine, 1964-71. Author: The Retina: An Approachable Part of the Brain, 1987, Neurons and Networks: An Introduction to Neuroscience, 1992, Creating Mind: How the Brain Works, 1998; contbr. numerous articles on vision to profl. jours. Recipient ann. award N.E. Ophthal. Soc., 1979, award of merit Retina Research Found., 1981, Prentice medal Am. Acad. Optometry, 1991, Von Sallman prize, 1992. Fellow Am. Acad. Arts and Scis., AAAS; mem. Am. Philos. Soc., Assn. Rsch. in Vision and Ophthalmology (Friedenwald medal 1970), Nat. Acad. Sci., Neurosci. Soc.,

Soc. Gen. Physiologists. Home: 135 Charles St Boston MA 02114-3264 Office: Harvard U Biology Labs Cambridge MA 02138

DOWLING, JOSEPH ALBERT, historian, educator; b. Dalmuir, Scotland, Nov. 10, 1926; came to U.S., 1940, naturalized, 1945; s. Joseph Albert and Maud Drury (Mitchell) D.; m. Sylvia Minkin, June 16, 1956; children—David, Kathryn, Juliet, Marc. AB, Lincoln Meml. U., 1948; MA, NYU, 1951, PhD, 1958. Instr. English and history Shorter Coll., Rome, Ga., 1951-52; instr. cultural heritage Bates Coll., Lewiston, Maine, 1955-58; asst. prof. history Lehigh U., Bethlehem, Pa., 1958-61; assoc. prof. Lehigh U., 1961-67, prof., 1967-74, Disting. prof., 1974-93, chmn. dept., 1984-90. Mem. Citizens Adv. Com. to Upper Milford Zoning Commn., 1970-72, Pa. Humanities Council, 1983-87. Served with U.S. Army, 1945-46. Recipient Lindback award for disting. teaching Lehigh U., 1966, Student award for outstanding teaching, 1967, Stabler award for disting. teaching, 1981; Lehigh Yearbook dedication, 1973; Mellon faculty devel. grantee, 1977; Fulbright lectr. Katholieke U., Leuven, Belgium, 1987. Fellow Royal Soc. for Encouragement of Arts, Mfrs. and Commerce; mem. Orgn. Am. Historians. Democrat. Home: 6591 Corning Rd Zionsville PA 18092 Office: Lehigh U Dept History Maginnes 9 W Packer Ave Bethlehem PA 18015-3082

DOWLING, LONA BUCHANAN, nurse; b. Washington, Feb. 7, 1950; d. Aaron Ernie and Louise Katherine (Willis) Buchanan; m. Frankie Lee Dowling, Sept. 18, 1976; children: David Lee, Allison Lynn. Diploma in nursing Washington Hosp. Ctr., 1971. Staff nurse Prince George Gen. Hosp., Cheverly, Md., 1971-72, asst. head nurse emergency room, 1972-74, head nurse, 1974-75; asst. head nurse emergency room Doctors Hosp., Lanham, Md., 1975-79; staff nurse Ashland Dist. Hosp., Kans., 1979-81; community health nurse, county sch. nurse Comanche County, Coldwater, Kans., 1981-90; staff nurse oper. rm. internship program U. Utah, Salt Lake City, 1990—, asst. nurse mgr. gen. surgery, 1991-94, staff nurse oper. rm., 1994—, charge nurse, 1995—; coord., instr. Laparoscopic Cholecystectomy Course for Nurses, 1991-92, Advanced Laparoscopic Course, 1993. Organizer 1st SADD chpt. in Southwest Kans., 1984; ednl. chmn. Comanche County Cancer Soc., 1984—; ednl. co-chmn. South Central Coalition for Health Services, Kans., 1983-84; CPR instr. ARC, Wichita, Kans., 1982—; bd. dirs. Iroquois Ctr. Human Devel. Mem. Kans. Pub. Health Assn., Kans. Assn. Local Health Depts., Bus. and Profl. Women's Club (corr. sec. 1983). Republican. Clubs: Twin Hills Extension Homemaker Unit, Mothers Advancement Protection. Avocations: photography, needlework, horses, entertaining, fishing. Home: 1930 Bonneview Dr Bountiful UT 84010-4116

DOWLING, PAUL DENNIS, bilingual special education educator; b. Bryan, Tex., Mar. 10, 1963; s. Dennis William and Dorothy Patricia (Abney) D.; m. Ronne Kay Johnstone, July 3, 1987; 1 child, Robert Lee Morris II. BA, U. Tex., 1986, MA, 1988; MA, U. Houston, 1992, EdD, 1999. Cert. tchr., Tex. Behavior intervention expert Houston Schs., 1989-91; learning specialist Goose Creek Schs., Baytown, Tex., 1991-95, bilingual life skills instr., 1995-98; lectr. U. Houston, 1996-99; spl. edn. tchr. Toll Mid. Sch., Glendale, Calif., 1998—; CEO, Coll. Houses Co-ops, Austin, 1986-87; mng. editor TAGS dept. German, U. Tex., Austin, 1983-84. Contbr. articles to newspapers and profl. jours. Pres. Students for Coop. Living, U. Tex., 1985-88; poll watcher Dem. Party, Austin, 1986, 88; bd. rep. Coll. Houses Co-ops, 1986-88; del. Dem. Conv.-Travis County, Austin, 1988. Fellow Phi Delta Kappa; mem. Internat. Reading Assn., Nat. Reading Conf., Nat. Coun. Tchrs. English, World Future Soc., Internat. Soc. Contemporary Legend Rsch., Wissenschaftliche Buchgesellschaft. Avocations: reading, Internet, theater, urban legends, foreign languages.

DOWLING, THOMAS ALLAN, mathematics educator; b. Little Rock, Feb. 19, 1941; s. Charles and Esther (Jensen) D.; m. Nancy Lenthe D.; children: Debra Lynn, David Thomas. B.S., Creighton U., 1962; Ph.D., U. N.C., 1967. Research assoc. U. N.C.-Chapel Hill, 1967-69, asst. prof., 1969-72; assoc. prof. math. Ohio State U., Columbus, 1972-82, prof., 1982—; ops. researcher U.S. Govt., Patrick AFB, Fla., 1963-64; faculty fellow NASA at UCLA, Pasadena, summer, 1968; conf. organizer U. N.C., 1967, 70, Ohio State U., 1978, 82, 88, 92, 94, 98. Editor: Combinatorial Mathematics and its Applications, 1967, 70; contbr. article to profl. jours.; discoverer Dowling lattices. NSF grantee, 1972-79. Mem. AAUP, Am. Math. Soc., Math. Assn. Am., Inst. Combinatorics and Applications. Democrat. Home: 2565 Sandover Rd Columbus OH 43220-4828 Office: Ohio State U Dept Math 231 W 18th Ave Columbus OH 43210-1101

DOWLING, VINCENT JOHN, lawyer; b. N.Y.C., Dec. 20, 1927; s. Victor Hurlin and Joan Agnes (Reardon) D.; m. Jane Cooney, Apr. 16, 1958; children: Vincent John, Jr., Douglas J., S. Colin, Joseph G. B.S., Lehigh U., 1949; J.D., U. Conn., 1957. Bar: Conn. 1957, Mass. 1985, Fla. 1986, U.S. Dist. Ct. Conn. 1958, U.S. Ct. Appeals (2d cir.) 1960, U.S. Ct. Claims 1986. Chief mfg. engr. Veeder-Root, Inc., Hartford, Conn., 1949-58; ptnr. Dowling & Dowling, Hartford, 1958-65; ptnr. Cooney, Scully & Dowling, Hartford, 1965—; lectr. constrn. law. Served to capt. U.S. Army, 1951-53. Mem. ASME, ABA, Conn. Bar Assn. (mem. liaison com. with cts., constrn. law com., aleternat dispute resolution com., chmn. specialization com.), Am. Arbitration Assn., Nat. Panel Constrn. Arbitrators and Mediators, Fed. Bar Assn., Mass. Bar Assn., Fla. Bar Assn., Internat. Bar Assn., Diocesan Attys. Assn., Hartford Golf Club, Hartford Club, John's Island Club (Vero Beach, Fla.), Kappa Alpha Soc. Roman Catholic. Address: 10 Columbus Blvd Hartford CT 06106-1976

DOWNEN, ROBERT LYNN, international affairs analyst and consultant, editor, writer; b. Wichita, Kans., Apr. 18, 1951; s. Lyndall Roy and Ruth Ann Downen; m. Holly Hutchens, Sept. 1, 1980; children: Heather Anna Christine, Lindsey Rose Lynn. *A major interest and influence in his life has been his family, past and present. Robert Downen has researched 400 years of family history, and authored a book on his paternal line, a copy of which is in the Library of Congress. Four Mayflower Pilgrims, ten Revolutionary War patriots, many frontier pioneers, and a great number of ordinary, honest, hardworking Americans are among his ancestors; yet he is proudest of his own immediate family. Mr. Downen believes each generation bears its own responsibility for virtuous and respectable living. "A good name is rather to be chosen than great riches." (Proverbs 22:1).* BA cum laude, Washington U., St. Louis, 1973; MA, George Washington U., Washington, 1975. Legis. asst. to Bob Dole, U.S. Senate, Washington, 1973-79; dir. Pacific stds. Ctr. for Strategic and Internat. Studies/Georgetown U., Washington, 1979-84; dir., spl. projects U.S. State Dept./Asia, Washington, 1984-89; v.p. Neill and Co., Washington, 1989-94; sr. v.p. Jefferson Waterman Internat., Washington, 1994-98; pres. Downen Consulting, 1998—. Author: The Taiwan Pawn, 1979, Tattered China Card, 1983, To Bridge the China Strait, 1984; editor: Multi-System Nations and International Law, 1982, The Emerging Pacific Community, 1984. Mem. adv. group Dole for Pres., Washington, 1996, Reagan for Pres., Washington, 1980. Named Kans. DeMolay of Yr., Order of DeMolay, 1969, DeMolay Legion of Honor award, 1983; recipient Wolcott Scholar award Internat. High Twelve Clubs, Mo., 1974, Hon. Mem. award Sojourners Lodge AF & AM, Panama Canal Zone, 1978. Mem. Masons, Phi Beta Kappa, Sigma Nu. Republican. Baptist. Avocations: photography, genealogy, study of American history and government, travel. Home: 4009 Terrace Dr Annandale VA 22003-1856

DOWNER, ROBERT NELSON, lawyer; b. Newton, Iowa, July 15, 1939; s. Lowell William and Mabel Mary (Hannon) D.; m. Jane Alice Glafka, May 29, 1971; children: Elise Michele, Andrew Nelson. BA, U. Iowa, 1961, JD, 1963. Bar: Iowa 1963, U.S. Dist. Ct. (so. dist.) Iowa 1963, U.S. Dist. Ct. (no. dist.) Iowa 1964, U.S. Supreme Ct. 1995. Assoc. Meardon Law Office, Iowa City, 1963-68; mem. Meardon, Sueppel & Downer PLC and predecessor firms, Iowa City, 1969—; dir., sec. KZIA, Inc., Iowa City, 1975—, Iowa City Tennis & Fitness Ctr., 1987-93; trustee The Oaknoll Found., Iowa City, 1990-98; dir. Christian Retirement Svcs., Inc., Iowa City, 1967-82, Iowa State Bar Found., 1996—. Pres. Greater Iowa City Area C. of C., 1979; bd. trustees Iowa City Pub. Libr., 1971-75, chair, 1973-74; chair adminstrv. bd. First United Meth. Ch., Iowa City, 1985-87; del. Rep. Nat. Conv., New Orleans, 1988; mem. Iowa Supreme Ct. Commn. on Continuing Legal Edn., 1975-83, Task Force on Domestic Abuse, 1993-94; bd. dirs. Iowa City Area Devel. Group, 1993—, chmn., 1996-97. Recipient Excellence in Svc. award Legal Svcs. Corp. Iowa, 1996. Fellow Am. Coll. Trust & Estate Counsel, Am. Bar Found., Iowa State Bar Found.; mem. ABA, Iowa State Bar Assn. (chair probate, property and trust law com. 1988-90, chair probate sect. 1990-93, v.p. 1993-94, pres.-elect 1994-95, pres. 1995-96), Johnson County Bar Assn. (pres. 1976), Rotary Club Iowa City (pres. 1988-89). Republican. Methodist. Home: 2029 Rochester Ct Iowa City IA 52245-3246 Office: Meardon Sueppel Downer & Hayes PLC 122 S Linn St Iowa City IA 52240-1830

DOWNER, WILLIAM JOHN, JR., retired hospital administrator; b. Springfield, Ill., Sept. 29, 1932; s. William J. Sr. and Geraldine (Foster) D.; m. Wanda M. Parson, Oct. 3, 1953; children: William E., Lawrence R. BA, Mich. State U., 1954; M in Hosp. Adminstrn., U. Mich., 1961. Various mgmt. positions Blodgett Meml. Med. Ctr., Grand Rapids, Mich., 1961-74; pres., CEO Blodgett Meml. Med. Ctr., Grand Rapids, 1974-84; pres., chief exec. officer Columbus Hosp., Great Falls, Mont., 1985-95, sr. cons., 1995-96; bd. dirs. First Interstate Bank, Great Falls. Contbr. articles to profl. jours. City commr. City of Gt. Falls, 1996—; hosp. divsn. chmn. United Way Kent County, Grand Rapids, 1969; elder Westminster Presbyn. Ch., Grand Rapids, 1968-85, 1st Presbyn. Ch., Great Falls, 1985—; mem. com. on ministry Glacier Presbytery, 1996—, moderator, 1997; mem. cmty. adv. bd. NW Mont. for Horizon Air, 1990-97; bd. dirs. No. Rockies Easter Seals/Goodwill, 1995—; bd. dirs. Big Sky chpt. ARC, 1986-92, 96-97. Lt. col. AUS, ret. Fellow Am. Coll. Healthcare Execs. (life, regent for Mich. 1978-84, regent for Mont. 1986-89, Regent's award 1996); mem. Am. Hosp. Assn. (life, mem. governing coun. sect. for met. hosps. 1991-94), Mont. Hosp. Assn. (bd. dirs. 1987-90, chmn. 1989), Mich. Hosp. Assn. (bd. dirs. 1973-82, chmn. 1980-81, Homminga award 1982), Great Falls C. of C. (mem. exec. com. 1988, chmn. 1991-92, mil. affairs exec. com. 1995—, vice chmn. 1998, chmn. 1999), Rotary, Phi Kappa Phi, Beta Gamma Sigma. Avocations: Civil War history, golf, travel. Home: 2719 Evergreen Dr Great Falls MT 59404-3635 Office: City of Great Falls Civic Ctr 2 Park Dr S Great Falls MT 59401-3636

DOWNES, GREGORY, architectural organization executive; b. Cambridge, Mass., Mar. 17, 1939; s. Thomas M. and Jean (Gregory) D.; m. Sandra Motley Snow, June 9, 1962; children: Katharine Appleton, Elizabeth Amory. BA cum laude, Harvard U., 1961, MArch, 1965. Registered architect, Mass., Conn., D.C., Maine, N.J., R.I. With The Architects Collaborative, Inc., Cambridge, Mass., 1965-95; prin. Symmes Maini & McKee Assoc., Inc., Cambridge, 1995—; instr. Boston Archtl. Ctr., 1972-73, Harvard Grad. Sch. Design, 1973-76. Contbr. articles to profl. jours. Bd. trustees Capt. Robert Bennet Forbes Mus., 1988-98; bd. dirs. Shirley Eustis Historic House, Roxbury, 1986-94; seminarian Boston Mus. Fine Arts, 1988-90; corporator Mt. Auburn Hosp.; mem. vestry Ch. of Redeemer, Brookline, 1982-85, St. Michaels Ch., Milton, 1988-91. Recipient numerous awards of honor. Mem. AIA, Boston Soc. Architects, Am. Planning Assn., Nat. Assn. Indsl. and Office Parks, Urban Land Inst., Harvard Club of Boston, The Country Club, Harvard Faculty Club. Republican. Episcopalian. Avocations: tennis, squash, skeet, gardening, golf. Home: 203 Adams St Milton MA 02186-4215 Office: Symmes Maini and McKee Assocs Inc 1000 Massachusetts Ave Cambridge MA 02138-5304

DOWNES, RACKSTRAW, artist; b. Pembury, Kent, Eng., Nov. 8, 1939; came to U.S., 1961; s Henry Alfred and Rosa Kathleen (Rackstraw) D. BA, Cambridge U., 1961; MFA, Yale U., 1964. Asst. prof. U. Pa., Phila., 1967-78; mem.faculty Skowhegan Sch., Maine, 1975; mem. faculty N.Y. Studio Sch., N.Y.C., 1980-82; editor Fairfield Porter: Art in Its Own Terms, 1979; bd. govs. Skowhegan Sch. Painting and Sculpture, 1981-95. Exhibited one man shows, Kornblee Gallery, N.Y.C., 1972-82, Hirschl & Adler Modern, N.Y.C., 1982-94, Marlborough Galleries, N.Y.C., London, Madrid, 1996—; group shows, San Antonio Mus., 1981, Pa. Acad., Phila., 1981, Carnegie Internat., Pitts., 1983, Whitney Biennial, N.Y.C., 1981; represented permanent collections, Mus. Modern Art, N.Y.C., Houston Mus. Fine Arts, Whitney Mus. Am. Art, N.Y.C., Hirschorn Mus., Washington, Pa. Acad. Fine Art, Met. Mus. Art, N.Y.C., Phila. Mus. Art, Carnegie Inst., Pitts., Corcoran Gallery Art, Smithsonian Mus., Washington, Ludwig Mus., Cologne. Ingram Merrill fellow, 1974; grantee Nat. Endowment for Arts, 1980; recipient Creative Artist's Pub. Svc. award State of N.Y., 1978, Nat. Acad. Arts and Scis. award, 1989; Guggenheim fellow, 1998. Mem. Am. Acad. Arts and Letters.

DOWNES, WILLIAM F., judge; b. 1946. BA, U. North Tex., 1968; JD, U. Houston, 1974. Ptnr. Clark and Downes, Green River, Wyo., 1976-78; mem. Brown & Drew, Casper, Wyo., 1978-94; dist. judge U.S. Dist. Ct. Wyo., Casper, Wyo., 1994—. Capt. USMC, 1968-71. Mem. Wyo. State Bar, Natrona County Bar Assn., Casper Petroleum Club, Wyo. Athletic Club. Office: US Dist Ct 111 S Wolcott St Rm 210 Casper WY 82601-2534*

DOWNEY, ARTHUR HAROLD, JR., lawyer, mediator; b. N.Y.C., Nov. 21, 1938; s. Arthur Harold Sr. and Charlotte (Bailey) D.; m. Gwen Vanden Berg, May 28, 1960; children: Anne Leigh, Neal Arthur, Drew Thomas. BA, Cen. Coll., Pella, Iowa, 1960; LLB, Cornell U., 1963. Bar: Colo. 1963, Wyo. 1991, U.S. Dist. Ct. Colo. 1963, U.S. Dist. Ct. Wyo. 1993, U.S. Ct. Appeals (10th cir.) 1963; diplomage Am. Bd. Forensic Examiners. From assoc. to ptnr. Weller, Friedrich, Ward & Andrew, Denver, 1963-82; ptnr., chief exec. officer Downey Law Firm P.C., Denver, 1982—; trustee panel Colo. Hosp. Assn., 1988-93; del. Nat. Congress Hosp. Trustees, Am. Hosp. Assn., 1988-93. Contbr. articles to profl. jours. Vice moderator Presbytery of Denver, 1972; past pres. Columbine Village Homeowners Assn., Trails End Homeowners Assn., Upper Village Homeowners Assn., Powderhorn Condominium Homeowners Assn., Breckenridge, Colo.; chmn bd. trustees Bethesda Psychealth Sys., Inc., 1990-93. Fellow Internat. Soc. Barristers; mem. ABA, Colo. Bar Assn., Denver Bar Assn., Wyo. Bar Assn., Def. Rsch. Inst. (disting. svc. award), Nat. Inst. Trial Advocacy (teaching faculty, team leader 1973—), Colo. Def. Lawyers Assn. (pres. 1977-78), Am. Coll. Legal Medicine (assoc. in law), Nat. Bd. Trial Advocacy (cert.), Am. Arbitration Assn. Republican. Mem. Reformed Ch. Am. Avocations: photography, woodworking, skiing. Office: Downey Law Firm PC 6655 W Jewell Ave Ste 106 Lakewood CO 80232-7108*

DOWNEY, ARTHUR THOMAS, III, lawyer; b. N.Y.C., Aug. 17, 1937; s. Arthur T. and Beatrice (Fortune) D.; m. Mary S. Downey; children: Thomas, Allison, Paul; stepchildren: Christopher, Sarah, Matthew. BA, St. Vincent, 1959; LLB, Villanova U., 1962; LLM, Georgetown U., 1963. Bar: D.C. 1964. Atty. U.S. Dept. State, Washington and Berlin, 1964-69; prof. staff The Nat. Security Coun., The White House, Washington, 1969-72; assoc. Morgan. Lewis & Bockius, Washington, 1972-75; dep. asst. sec. U.S. Dept. Commerce, Washington, 1975-77; ptnr. Sutherland, Ashill & Brennan, Washington, 1977-90; shareholder Johnson & Gibbs, 1990-92; v.p. Baker Hughes Inc., Washington, 1992—; adj. prof. Georgetown U. Law Sch., Washington, 1978-90. Co-author: Freedom from Federal Establishment, 1964. Mem. UN Assn. of USA (bd. govs. 1985-90), ABA (vice chmn. sec. internat. law 1984). Office: Baker Hughes Inc 816 Connecticut Ave NW Fl 2 Washington DC 20006-2705

DOWNEY, DEBORAH ANN, systems specialist; b. Xenia, Ohio, July 22, 1958; d. Nathan Vernon and Patricia Jaunita (Ward) D. Assoc. in Applied Sci., Sinclair C.C., 1981, student, 1986-91; BA, Capital U., 1994. Jr. programmer, project mgr. Cole-Layer-Trumble Co., Dayton, Ohio, 1981-82; sr. programmer, analyst, project leader Systems Architects Inc., Dayton, 1982-84, Systems and Applied Sci. Corp. (now Computer Sci. Corp.), Dayton, 1984; analyst Unisys, Dayton, 1984-87; systems programmer Computer Sci. Corp., Fairborn, Ohio, 1987—; cons. computer software M&S Garage/Body Shop, Beavercreek, Ohio, 1986-87. Mem. NAFE, Am. Motorcyclist Assn., Sinclair C. C. Alumni Assn., Cherokee Nation Okla., Cherokee Nat. Hist. Soc. Democrat. Mem. United Ch. of Christ. Avocations: motorcycles, miniatures, sports, needlework.

DOWNEY, GARY NEIL, marine corps officer; b. Rochester, N.Y., Nov. 3, 1957; s. Arnold Blaine and Barbara Ann (Quiggle) D. Assoc., Va. Coastal Cmty., Woodbridge, Va., 1978. Commd. USMC, advanced through grades to cwo-5, 1998—; security guard USMC, Casablanca, Morocco, 1980-86; pers. officer USMC, Camp Lejeune, N.C., 1986-89, Hqrs. USMC, Washington, 1989-94; course developer Marine Corps Inst., Washington, 1994-97; pers. officer Basic Sch., Quantico, Va., 1997—. Author: (corr. courses) Supply Chiefs Guidebooks, 1994, Basic Pay Entitlements, 1995, Sassy Computer Classes, 1996. Scoutmaster Boy Scouts Am., 1978-94. Decorated Purple Heart, Meritorious Svc. medal. Mem. Internat. Soc. Performance Instrs. Democrat. Roman Catholic. Avocation: computers. Home: 2030 6th St S Arlington VA 22204-1905 Office: Basic Sch 11101 Lejeune Blvd Quantico VA 22134

DOWNEY, JAMES ERWIN, government official; b. Melita, Man., Can., Aug. 10, 1942; s. Wallace Archibald and Mabel Elizabeth (Bambridge) D.; m. Linda Rowene Johnson, July 27, 1968; 1 child, Ryan James. Agr. Diploma, U. Man., 1964; Auctioneer, Western Coll. Auctioneering, Billings, Mont., 1972. Minister agr. Govt. of Man., Winnipeg, 1977-81, mem. govt. opposition, 1982-88, minister no. affairs, 1988-93, dep. premier, 1989—, minister energy and mines and rural devel., 1989-93, minister industry, trade and tourism, 1993—. Recipient Pres.'s medal U. Man., 1964. Home: PO Box 636, Melita, MB Canada R0M 1L0 Office: Industry Trade and Tourism, 358-450 Broadway Ave, Winnipeg, MB Canada R3C 0V8

DOWNEY, JOHN ALEXANDER, physician, educator; b. Sept. 16, 1930. BSc in Medicine, U. Man., MD with honors, 1954; PhD, Oxford U., 1962. Diplomate Am. Bd. Phys. Medicine and Rehab. Intern Vancouver Gen. Hosp., B.C., Can., 1953-54; resident phys. medicine and rehab. Columbia Presbyn. Med. Ctr., N.Y.C., 1954-56, resident, 1957-58; asst. resident internal medicine Peter Bent Brigham Hosp., Boston, 1956-57; asst. to med. dir., cons. phys. medicine Blythedale Children's Hosp., Valhalla, N.Y., 1957-59; rsch. assoc. Columbia U., 1958-59; vis. fellow Presbyn. Hosp., N.Y.C., 1958-59; sr. resident internal medicine Peter Bent Brigham Hosp., 1959-60; vis. worker Med. Rsch. Coun. Group for Body Temperature Control, Oxford, Eng., 1960-62; assc. prof. rehab. medicine Columbia U. Coll. Physicians ans Surgeons, 1962-64, assoc. prof., 1964-67, prof., 1967-74, Simon Baruch prof., 1974—, chair dept. rehab. medicine, 1974-90, asst. prof. medicine, 1963-64; asst. attending Presbyn. Hosp., N.Y.C., 1962-64, assoc. attending, 1964-68, attending, 1968—, dir. rehab. medicine svc., 1974-90; vis. prof. dept. human physiology and pharmacology U. Adelaide, Australia, 1969. Author: Stroke: Two to Recover, 1969; co-editor: Physiological Basis of Rehabilitation Medicine, 1971, 2d edit., 1994, The Child with Disabling Illness: Principles of Rehabilitation, 1974, 2d edit., 1982, Bereavement of Physical Disability: Recommitment to Life, Health and Function, 1982; editl. bd. Benneman's Practice of Pediatrics, 1974; contbr. articles to profl. jours.; films: Rehabilitation: A Patient's Perspective, 1973, I Had a Stroke, 1978, Physiatry: A Physician's Perspective, 1981. Fellow Royal Coll. Physicians (Can.); mem. AMA, APA, NAS, AAAS, Am. Congress Rehab. Medicine, Am. Acad. Phys. Medicine and Rehab., Am. Rheumatism Assn., N.Y. Rheumatism Assn., N.Y. Acad. Scis., N.Y. Acad. Medicine, N.Y. Soc. Phys. Medicine and Rehab., Med. Soc. N.Y. State, New York County Med. Soc., Internat. Rehab. Medicine Assn. Office: Columbia U Dept Rehab Medicine 630 W 168th St Dept Rehab New York NY 10032-3795*

DOWNEY, JOHN HAROLD, publishing executive; b. Yonkers, N.Y., July 30, 1956; s. John Joseph and Lydia (Lopetz) D.; m. Joanne Patricia Collins, Aug. 2, 1980; children: Gregory John, Sean Collins. BA, Manhattan Coll., 1978; postgrad., NYU, 1981-83. Dir. circulation Backpacker Mag., Bedford Hills, N.Y., 1978; tchr. English/history Ives Sch. Lincoln Hall, Lincolndale, N.Y., 1978-81; v.p. publishing and dir. Editorial Oceana Ednl. Communications, Dobbs Ferry, N.Y., 1981-88; pres. Flashback/Video, Inc., Dobbs Ferry, N.Y., 1987-88; freelance graphic artist Wynter Graphics, Croton, N.Y., 1985-93; dir. spl. needs divsn. Globe Book Co., Simon and Schuster Sch. Group, Englewood Cliffs, N.J., 1988-90; dir. editl. svc. Globe Book Co., 1989-91, v.p., dir. internat. seminars divsn., 1991—. Author: Safe and Sound Children's Safety Primer, 1988, Aware Bears: Drive Safe, 1996; mng. editor: Software in Print, 1985, USME: Market Directory, 1985; editor: The Aware Bears Childrens' Personal Safety Series, 1987—. Coach AYSO. Mem. Nat. Eagle Scout Assn., Coun. for Exceptional Children, Am. Assn. Law Librs. (Washington chpt.). Avocations: reading, writing, music, sports, camping. Office: Oceana Group 75 Main St Dobbs Ferry NY 10522-1632

DOWNEY, JOHN WILHAM, composer, pianist, conductor, educator; b. Chgo., Oct. 5, 1927; s. James Bernard and Augustina (Haas) D.; m. Irusha Czuszakivna; children: Lida, Marc. MusB, DePaul U., 1949; MusM, Chgo. Mus. Coll., 1951; Docteur es Lettres (PhD), U. Paris-Sorbonne, 1957; Prix de Composition (scholar), Paris Conservatory, 1956. Assoc. prof. Chgo. City Coll., 1958-64; prof. music U. Wis., Milw., 1964-86, disting. prof., 1986—, now prof. emeritus; lectr. music theory De Paul U., Chgo., 1960-64, Roosevelt U., Chgo., 1961. Author: La Musique Populaire dans l'Oeuvre de Bela Bartok, 1966; composer Eastlake Terrace (piano solo), 1959 (recorded by Master Musician's Collectif, 1998), Chant to Michelangelo, 1959, Edges (piano solo, 1960), Pyramids (piano solo, 1961), Portrait No. 1 (piano solo, 1980), Gasparo Records, Jingalodeon for Orchestra, 1968, recorded with Cala Records, 1991, Harp Concerto, 1968 (recorded by Master Musician's Collectif 1998), Cello Sonata, CRI label, 1968, Symphonic Modules, 1972, Agort, woodwind quintet, recorded with Orion label, 1973, Gasparo Records, 1989, Adagio Lyrico: 2 pianos, 1953, What If? (composition for mixed choir, solo timpany and brass octet), 1973, Octet for Winds, 1954, A Dolphin, voice and chamber ensemble, 1974, recorded with Orion Label, 1974, Gasparo Records, 1989, Lydian Suite, 1975, Gasparo Records, Cala Records, 1998, String Quartet II, 1975, Gasparo Records, 1976, Crescendo (for large percussion ensemble), 1977, High Clouds and Soft Rain (for mixed flute choir), 1977, The Edge of Space (Fantasy for Bassoon and Orch.), 1977, CD recorded with Chandos Records, 1989, Silhouette (solo Doublebass), 1980, Qu'en Avez-vous Fait? (for voice and piano), 1984, CD recording for Gasparo Records, 1995, Prayer for string trio, 1984, Piano Trio, 1984, Declamations for Large Orch., 1985, recorded with Cala Records, 1991, Discourse for Oboe with String Orch. and Harpsichord, 1986, recorded with Cala Records, 1991, Recombinance for Doublebass and Piano, 1987, Concerto for Doublebass and Orch., 1987, recorded with Cala Records, 1991, Suite of Psalms for a cappella mixed choir, 1988, Fanfare For Freedom for symphonic winds, 1990, Call for Freedom for symphonic winds, 1991, Yad Vashem-An Impression (piano solo), 1991, Memories (piano solo) 1991, Ode to Freedom, for symphony orchestra, 1992, Symphony No. 1, 1993, Rough Road (guitar and flute), 1994, Angel Talk (for eight cellos), 1995, Rememberance-The Swing Set, Reminder-Hungry Squirrel, Reaffirmation-Red Rose, 1995, Song Suite (high voice and piano), 1995, CD recorded by VAI Recordings, 1997, Ghosts (for 12 violins), 1995, Soliloquy (for solo English Horn, recorded for Cala Records) 1997, For Those Who Suffered (for chamber orch.), 1996, recorded on CD by Master Musicians Collective, 1998, Irish Sonata (for violin and piano) 1998, also electronic and computer music; resident artist, MacDowell Colony, summers 1971, 75-77, 82-83, 92, 94, falls 1978, 85, Millay Colony, summer 1991; rec. artist (album) John Downey Plays John Downey, 1987; 5 orchestral works recorded by the London Symphony Orch.: Jingalodeon, Declamations, Concerto for Double Bass and Orch., Discourse for Oboe, Harpsichord and String Orch., The Edge of Space. Decorated Chevalier de l'Ordre des Arts et des Lettres, France, 1980; scholar Fulbright France, 1952-54, winter, 1979, 80, Fulbright Australia, summer, 1987, French Govt., 1954-55; teaching fellow, 1955-56; German Govt. teaching fellow, 1956-57; Copley Found. grantee, 1956-57, 57-58; recipient awards U. Wis., 1971, 73, 75, 77, 79, 83, 87, 93, 95, Ford Found., 1976, Ctr. for L.Am. Studies of the U. Wis.-Milw. award, 1988, NEA, 1977, 83, 94, Moebius award, 1985, New Music for Young Ensembles award, 1986, Walter Heinrichsen award Am. Acad. and Inst. Arts and Letters, 1990, Meet the Composer awards, 1988, 90, 92, 93; named Music Citizen of Yr. Civic Music Assn. of Milw., 1980, Musician of the Yr. Milw Sentinel, 1993; Wis. Arts Bd. Composition fellow, 1991. Mem. Am. Soc. Univ. Composers, Am. Music Ctr., ASCAP (awards 1974—), Am. Fedn. Musicians, Wis. Contemporary Music Forum (founder, chmn. 1970—), Soc. of Composers, Ctr. 20th Century Studies, De Paul U. Alumni Assn. (Disting. Alumni award 1969), Phi Kappa Phi, Delta Omicron (nat. patron), Mu Phi Alpha (Disting. Musician award 1987, other awards 1974-86), Sigma Alpha Iota (Extraordinary Mus. Achievement award Milw. Alumnae chpt. 1986). Avocations: jogging, bicycling. Office: U Wis Sch Fine Arts Music PO Box 413 Milwaukee WI 53201-0413 *Although styles change and vary with place and time, an artist's sincerity of purpose, depth of feeling, and intellectual finesse are values permeating most works of art regardless of time and fashion.*

DOWNEY, MICHAEL PETER, public television executive; b. Springfield, Mass., Apr. 14, 1942; s. Mortimer Leo and Elizabeth Gertrude (Carlin) D.; m. Claudia West Allyn, Sept. 30, 1978 (div. Jan. 1996); children: Sarah Carlin, Caitlin Stanford. B.S. in Broadcasting, Boston U., 1964. TV dir. Sta. WGBH, Boston, 1965-66, producer, dir., 1966-69, ops. mgr., 1969-76; dir. ops. Pub. Broadcasting Svc., Washington, 1977-79, sr. v.p. program adminstrn. and info., 1979-85, sr. v.p. program support and devel., 1985—, sr. v.p. program bus. affairs, 1987-91; dir. Pub. Service Satellite Consortium, 1980-83. Bd. dirs. Kaiser-Permanente of Mid-Atlantic States, 1980-83; Boston's Fourth of July, Inc., 1976—: chmn. Va. Youth Soccer Assn. State Championship. Served with USMCR, 1962. Recipient NET award for Excellence as TV dir., 1968. *

DOWNEY, MORTIMER LEO, III, transportation executive; b. Springfield, Mass., Aug. 9, 1936; s. Mortimer L. and Elizabeth (Carlin) D.; m. Joyce Vander Meyden, Oct. 21, 1961; children: Stephen Michael, Christopher Sean. BA, Yale U., 1958; MPA, NYU, 1966; grad. Advanced Mgmt. Program, Harvard U., 1988. Various positions Port Authority, N.Y. and N.J., 1958-75; supr. rail pub. services Port Authority, 1973-75; budget analyst Ho. of Reps., 1975-76; dep. undersec. Dept. Transp., Washington, 1977; asst. sec. Dept. Transp., 1977-81; asst. exec. dir. N.Y. Met. Transp. Authority, N.Y.C., 1981-83, dep. exec. dir., 1983-85, chief fin. officer, 1985-86; exec. dir., chief fin. officer N.Y. Met. Transp. Authority, 1986-93; dep. sec., COO Dept. Transp., Washington, 1993—; bd. dirs. Nat. Rail Passenger Corp. (AMTRAK), Pa. Sta. Redevel. Corp. Fellow Nat. Acad. Pub. Adminstrn.; mem. Am. Soc. Pub. Adminstrn., Yale Club (N.Y.), Yale Sailing Club, Pi Sigma Alpha. Democrat. Roman Catholic. Home: 10205 Martinhoe Dr Vienna VA 22181-5368 Office: Dept of Transp Office Sec 400 7th St SW Washington DC 20590-0003

DOWNEY, ROBERT, JR., actor; b. N.Y.C., Apr. 4, 1965; s. Robert Downey and Elsie Ford; m. Deborah Falconer; 1 child, Indio. Appeared in plays American Passion, 1983, Alms for the Middle Class, 1983, Fraternity, 1984; TV series Saturday Night Live, 1985-86; TV miniseries Mussolini: The Untold Story, 1985; films include Pound, 1970, Greaser's Palace, 1972, Up the Academy, 1980, Baby It's You, 1983, Firstborn, 1984, To Live and Die in L.A., 1985, Tuff Turf, 1985, Weird Science, 1985, America, 1986, Back to School, 1986, Less Than Zero, 1987, The Pick-Up Artist, 1987, Johnny Be Good, 1988, Rented Lips, 1988, 1969, 1988, True Believer, 1989, Chances Are, 1989, That's Adequate, 1990, Air America, 1990, Too Much Sun, 1991, Soapdish, 1991, Chaplin, 1992 (Acad. award nomination best actor), Heart and Souls, 1993, Short Cuts, 1993, The Last Party, 1993, Natural Born Killers, 1994, Only You, 1994, Restoration, 1994, Hail Caesar, 1994, Richard III, 1995, Home for the Holidays, 1995, Danger Zone, 1996, One Night, 1997, Hugo Pool, 1997, The Gingerbread Man, 1997. Office: Creative Artists Agy 9830 Wilshire Blvd Beverly Hills CA 90212

DOWNEY, ROMA, actress; b. Northern Ireland, United Kingdom, May 6, 1963; m. David Anspaugh, 1995 (div. 1998); 1 child, Reilly Marie. BA in Fine Arts, Brighton Art Coll., England, 1983; diploma, London Drama Studio, 1985. Actress CBS Television, L.A. Appeared in Irelands Abbey Theatre, U.S. tour The Playboy of the Western World, 1991; on Broadway in The Circle; Off Broadway in Love's Labour's Lost, Tamara, Arms and the Man; television includes A Woman Named Jackie, Touched by an Angel, Borrowed Hearts, A Child is Missing; appeared in films including Monday After the Miracle, Devlin. Nominee Helen Hayes Best Actress award, 1991, Emmy award, 1997, 98, Golden Globe award, 1997-98; recipient TV Guide award for favorite actress in a drama, 1999.

DOWNIE, LEONARD, JR., newspaper editor, author; b. Cleve., May 1, 1942; s. Leonard and Pearl Martha (Evenheimer) D.; m. Barbara Lindsey, July 15, 1960 (div. 1971); children: David Leonard, Scott Leonard; m. Geraldine Rebach, Aug. 15, 1971 (div. 1997); children: Joshua Mark, Sarah Elizabeth; m. Janice Galin, Sept. 12. 1997. B.A., Ohio State U., 1964, M.A., 1965, LLD (hon.), 1993. Reporter, editor Washington Post, 1964-74, met. editor, 1974-79, London corr., 1979-82, nat. editor, 1982-84, mng. editor, 1984-91, exec. editor, 1991—; bd. dirs. L.A. Times-Washington Post News Svc., 1991—, Internat. Herald Tribune, 1996—. Author: Justice Denied, 1971, Mortgage on America, 1974, The New Muckrackers, 1976. Trustee Georgetown Day Sch., 1988-93. Recipient Gavel award ABA, 1967, Front Page 1st pl. award for newswriting Washington-Balt. Newspaper Guild, 1967, 68, award John Hancock Ins. Co., 1969; Alicia Patterson Found. fellow, 1971-72. Mem. Am. Soc. Newspaper Editors. Office: Washington Post Co 1150 15th St NW Washington DC 20071-0002

DOWNING, BARBARA KAY, principal; b. Lafayette, Ind., Dec. 3, 1951; d. William Julius and Wilma Gladys (Kephart) Wood; m. David Loraine Downing, Nov. 26, 1971; children: Brian Douglas, Andrew David. BS, Ball State U., 1973, MA, 1978, EdS, 1990. Lic. ednl. adminstr., tchr., Ind. Tchr. Anderson (Ind.) Cmty. Sch., 1973-86, dir. student svcs., 1990-94; asst. prin. Madison Hts. H.S., Anderson, 1986-90; prin. Yorktown (Ind.) Mid. Sch., 1994—; bd. dirs. adv. bd. for tech. edn. Ball State U., Muncie, Ind. Editor: Anderson Community Schools, 1992 (Merit award Nat. Sch. Publ. and Pub. Rels. Assn. 1992). Bd. dirs. Big Bros./Big Sisters, Anderson, 1990-94, Anderson Area Crime Stoppers, 1990-94, Prosecutors Operation Resolve, Anderson, 1990-94; active Mayors Commn. Domestic Violence, Anderson, 1992-94. Recipient Met Life/NASSP Ind. Princ. of the Year, 1998. Mem. ASCD, Nat Assn. Secondary Sch. Prin., Ind. Assn. Sch. Prin. (Mid. Sch. Prin. of Yr. 1997), Ind. Prin. Assn. (bd. dirs. acad. competitions 1996—), Ind. Mid. Level Educators Assn. (regional chair 1996-98), Kiwanis, Phi Delta Kappa (2nd v.p. Ball State U. chpt. 1999—). United Methodist. Avocations: reading, fishing, golfing. Home: 909 S Birmingham Rd Yorktown IN 47396-9376 Office: Yorktown Mid Sch 8820 W Smith St Yorktown IN 47396-1332

DOWNING, CYNTHIA HURST, therapist, addiction and abuse specialist; b. Fort Wayne, Ind., Sept. 10, 1942; d. James Dickson Hurst and Bernadette (Dygert) Lawyer; m. James S. Downing, Sept. 9, 1961 (div. 1979); children: David, Elizabeth, Jeffrey. BA in Psychology, Ursuline Coll., 1980; MA in Human Svcs., John Carroll U., 1982; PhD, Saybrook Inst., 1991. Lic. profl. counselor, Ohio; cert. chm. dependency counselor III-E, Ohio; nat. cert. addiction counselor II, master addiciton counselor. Counselor United Meth. Alcohol and Chem. Counseling, Berea, Ohio, 1980-82; clin. dir. Earthrise Recovery Svcs., Inc., Chagrin Falls, Ohio, 1982—; clin. dir. chem. dependency Brentwood Hosp., Cleve., 1985; program coord. for recovery svcs. U. Hosp. & Health Sys.: Laurelwood Hosp. & Counseling Ctrs., 1998—; coord. case study, instr. Ctr. Applied Scis. Corp. Nat. Relapse Prevention Cert. Sch., Chgo., 1988-98. Author: Triad: The Evolution of Treatment for Chemical Dependency, 1989; mem. editorial adv. bd. Behavioral Health Mgmt. mag., 1991—; contbr. articles to profl. jours. Mem. Nat. Assn. Alcoholism and Drug Abuse Counselors, Nat. Assn. Relapse Prevention Specialists (charter), Assn. Humanistic Psychology, Internat. Soc. for the Study of Dissociation. Office: Earthrise Recovery Svcs Inc 25 W Summit St Chagrin Falls OH 44022-2724

DOWNING, DAVID CHARLES, minister; b. South Gate, Calif., June 24, 1938; s. Kenneth Oliver and Edna Yesobel (Casaday) D.; m. Tommye Catherine Tew, July 11, 1959 (dec. Dec. 11, 1985); children: Sheri Lynn, Teresa Kay, Carla Jeane, Michael David. BA, N.W. Christian Coll., 1961; B in Divinity, Tex. Christian U., 1966, M in Theology, 1973; DMin, San Francisco Theol. Sem., 1987. Ordained to ministry Christian Ch., 1961. Min. Marcola (Oreg.) Ch. of Christ, 1958-59; assoc. min. First Christian Ch., Lebanon, Oreg., 1960-63; min. First Christian Ch., Ranger, Tex., 1963-65, Knox City, Tex., 1966-68, Fredonia, Kans., 1968-74; min. Ctrl. Christian Ch., Huntington, Ind., 1974-77; regional min., pres. Christian Ch. Greater Kansas City, Mo., 1978-94; sr. minister Univ. Christian Ch. (Disciples of Christ), San Diego, 1994—; trustee Phillips Grad. Sem., Enid, Okla., 1988-94; bd. dirs. Ch. Fin. Coun., Indpls., Midwest Career Devel. Svc., Chgo.; v.p. bd. dirs. Midwest Christian Counseling Ctr., Kansas City. Author: A Contrast and Comparison of Pastoral Counseling in Rural and Urban Christian Churches, 1972, A Design for Enabling Urban Congregations to Cope with Their Fear of Displacement When Faced with Communities in Transition, 1987. Pres. Kansas City Interfaith Peace Alliance, 1980-82. Democrat. Avocations: swimming, camping, fishing, water skiing, collecting chalices. Home: 4325 Caminito De La Escena San Diego CA 92108-4201 Office: Univ Christian Ch (Disciples of Christ) 3900 Cleveland Ave San Diego CA 92103-3403

DOWNING, JAMES CHRISTIE, lawyer; b. Los Angeles, Dec. 17, 1924; s. Dorman Perkins and Merle Grace (Christie) D.; m. Betty Griggs, Dec. 23, 1949; children: Colleen, James, Kimberly, Kelly, Kathleen. BS, U. Calif., 1949; LLB, U. Calif.-San Francisco, 1952. Bar: Calif. 1953, U.S. Dist. Ct. (no. dist.) Calif. 1953, U.S. Dist. Ct. (ea. dist.) Calif. 1975, U.S. Ct. Appeals (9th dir.) 1953. Assoc. Walkup, Downing, Shelby, Bastian, Melodia, Kelly & O'Reilly, and predecessors, San Francisco, 1954-59, ptnr., 1959-70, exec. v.p., 1970-84; ptnr. Downing & Downing, 1985—; lectr. Calif. Continuing Edn. of Bar Program. Served in AC, U.S. Army, 1943-45. Decorated Air medal with 5 oak leaf clusters. Fellow Am. Coll. Trial Lawyers; mem. ABA, State Bar Calif., Bar Assn. San Francisco (vice chmn. trial practice com. 1970), San Francisco Trial Lawyers Assn. (pres. 1972), Am. Bd. Trial Advs. (nat. exec. com. 1970-73, nat. sec. 1971, nat. chmn. membership 1972-73, 76-77, nat. pres. 1974, pres. San Francisco chpt. 1974, Calif. Trial Lawyer of Yr. 1978), Internat. Soc. Barristers, Internat. Acad. Trial Lawyers, Trader Brown Soc. Republican. Office: Downing & Downing PO Box 398 Middletown CA 95461-0398

DOWNING, JOAN FORMAN, editor; b. Mpls., Nov. 16, 1934; d. W. Chandler and Marie A. (Forster) Forman; children: Timothy Alan, Julie Marie Downing Giesen, Christopher Alan. BA, U. Wis., 1956. Editorial asst. Sci. Research Assocs., Chgo., 1960-61; asst. editor Sci. Research Assocs., 1961-63, Childrens Press, Chgo., 1963-66; assoc. editor Childrens Press, 1966-68, mng. editor, 1968-78, editor-in-chief, 1978-81, sr. editor, 1981-95; propr. Downing Pub. Svcs., Evanston, Ill., 1995—; dir. Chgo. Book Clinic, 1973-75, publicity chmn., 1973-74. Author: (with Eugene Baker) Workers Long Ago, 1968, Baseball Is Our Game, 1982, Junior CB Picture Dictionary, 1978; project editor: 15 vol. Young People's Story of Our Heritage, 1966 (Graphic Arts Council of Chgo. award), 20 vol. People of Destiny (Chgo. Book Clinic award 1967-68), 20 vol. Enchantment of South and Central America, 1968-70, 36 vol. Open Door Books, 1968, 42 vol. Enchantment of Africa, 1972-78, Hobbies for Everyone: Collecting Toy Trains, 1979 (Graphic Arts award Printing Industries Am.), (multi-vol.) World at War, 1980-87, (52 vol.) America the Beautiful, 1987-91, (52 vol.) From Sea to Shining Sea, 1991-95, (multi-vol.) Rookie Read-About Science, 1994-97, (multi-vol.) Cities of the World, 1995—, (multi-vol.) Encyclopedia of First Ladies, 1997—. Election judge, Cook County (Ill.), 1974—. Mem. Authors Guild, Authors League Am., Alpha Phi. Democrat. Home and Office: 2414 Brown Ave Evanston IL 60201-2526

DOWNING, JOHN HENRY, columnist, journalist; b. Toronto, Ont., Can., June 10, 1936; s. John H. and Lena (Hoogstad) D.; m. Mary A. Horvat, July 8, 1961; children: John Henry III, Brett, Mark. BAA, Ryerson Polytech., 1958; postgrad., U. Toronto, 1972. Editor White Horse Star, Yukon, 1957; reporter Toronto Telegram, 1958-63, asst. city editor, city editor, asst. mng. editor, 1964-71; polit. columnist Toronto Sun, 1971-84, assoc. editor, 1980-84, editor, 1985-97, columnist, 1997—. Co-author: Mayor of all the People, Member for St. Patrick; contbr. chpts., articles to books. Adv. com. Humber Coll.; bd. dirs. Runnymede Hosp., Toronto; life dir. Toronto Outdoor Art Show; life mem. Metro Conservation Authority, Toronto, 1970—; v.p. Can. Nat. Exhbn.; gov. Exhbn. Pl. Recipient 8 column awards Metro Police Assn., 1975—, Priory award St. John's Ambulance, 1983, Svc. medal City of Toronto Coun., 1991, Centennial medal Gov. Gen. of Can., 1993. Mem. Toronto Press Club (past pres.). Baptist. Avocations: swimming, fishing, reading. Office: The Toronto Sun, 333 King St E, Toronto, ON Canada M5A 3X5

DOWNING, KATHRYN M., publishing executive, lawyer; b. Portland, Oregon, Mar. 24, 1953. BA in Econs., Lewis and Clark Coll., 1973; JD, Stanford U., 1979. Various positions Mead Data Ctrl., 1981-90, sr. dir. legal info. pub., 1988; pres., COO Electronic Pub. divsn. Thomson Profl. Pub., 1990-93; pres., CEO Lawyers Coop. Pub. divsn. Thomson Legal Pub., 1993-95, Mathew Bender, 1995-97; pres., CEO Mosby Matthew Bender unit, sr. v.p. Times Mirror, N.Y.C., 1997-98, vice pres., 1996-97, sr. v.p., 1997-98, exec. v.p., 1998-; pres., ceo. Los Angeles Times, Los Angeles, 1998-99, pres., ceo., publisher, 1999-. Mem. bd. visitors Sch. Law Stanford U., trustee Friends of Law Libr. Mem. Am. Assn. Pubs. (bd. dirs.), Am. Inns of Ct. (past pub. trustee), Stanford Law Sch. Bd. of Visitors (mem.), Friends of the Law Lib. of Congress (bd. mem.), Los Angeles Chamber of Commerce, Newspaper Assoc. of Amer., UCLA Anderson Sch. of Bus. (bd of visitors), Times Mirror Found., Jim Murray Mem. Found., Los Angeles Times Fund (pres.). Fax: 908-771-8736. *

DOWNING, M. SCOTT, budget systems analyst; b. Enid, Okla., Aug. 20, 1942; s. Kenneth F. and Maurine (Melvin) D.; m. Ina M. Herrington, June 16, 1963; 1 child, Cynthia Ann. BA, Phillips U., 1963; MA, U. Okla., 1966. Cert. data processor Inst. for Cert. of Computer Profls.; cert. disaster recovery planner Disaster Recovery Inst. Internat.; cert. govt. fin. mgr. Assn. Govt. Accts.; cert. office automation profl.; cert. quality anlyst - Baldridge Stds., Quality Assurance Inst.; cert. quality examiner Baldridge standards Quality Assurance Inst. Instr. Am. history U. Md., Zama, Japan, 1967-69; budget analyst U.S. Bur. of Census, Washington, 1966-67, 69-70, U.S. Food and Nutrition Svc., Washington, 1970-73; budget systems analyst U.S. Dept. of State, Washington, 1973-74; chief, budget execution Fed. Energy Adminstrn., Washington, 1974-77; sr. budget analyst U.S. Dept. of Energy, Washington, 1977-80; contbg. fin. editor Exec. Publs., Washington, 1972-80; mgmt. analyst Gen. Svcs. Adminstrn., Washington, 1980-81, budget systems analyst, 1981-97; bus. mgr. Sew Classy Assocs., Alexandria, Va.; guest instr. Civil Svc. Commn., Washington, 1974, Fed. Regional Couns., 1974-77, Exec. Seminar Ctr., Oak Ridge, Tenn., 1975, Internat. APL Conf., Heidelberg, 1982. Author: (books) The TVA and the Courts, 1966, Dollars and Sense, 1975. Sgt. U.S. Army, 1967-69, PTO. Methodist.

DOWNING, MARGARET MARY, newspaper editor; b. Altoona, Pa., June 3, 1952; d. Irvine William and Iva Ann (Regan) D.; m. Gary Beaver; children: Ian Downing-Beaver, Timothy Downing-Beaver, Abby Downing-Beaver. BA magna cum laude, Tex. Christian U., 1974. Reporting intern Corpus Christi Caller Times, 1973; reporter, bur. chief Beaumont (Tex.) Enterprise & Jour., 1974-76, Dallas Times Herald, 1976-80; reporter, asst. city editor, asst. bus. & met. editor Houston Post, 1980-93, mng. editor, 1993; mng. editor Jackson (Miss.) Clarion-Ledger, 1993-97; editor-in-chief The Houston Press, 1998—; jurist Pulitzer Prize Awards, 1992, 93; bd. dirs. News Media Credit Union, 1993, Santa's Helpers, 1992-93. Respite foster parent vol. Harris County Children's Protective Svcs., 1993; chmn. landscape com. Windsor Hills Homeowners Assn.; active PTA Madison Sta. Elem., 1993-98; coach South Madison County Soccer Orgn., 1997-98; runners club YMCA, 1994, activities adv. bd. 1994, youth soccer and t-ball coach; coach Quail Valley Soccer Assn. Mem. AP Mng. Editor's Assn. (2d v.p. La./Miss. chpt. 1995-96, 1st v.p. 1996—, pres. 1997-98), Soc. Profl. Journalists, Press Club of Houston (pres. 1984, bd. dirs. 1982-85), Nat. Youth Sports Assn. (cert. coach), Quota Club (bd. dirs. 1996-97), Leadership Jackson (bd. dirs. 1996-98). Episcopalian. Home: 3215 Breckenridge Ct Missouri City TX 77459-4907 Office: The Houston Press 1621 Milam St Ste 100 Houston TX 77002-8017

DOWNING, ROBERT ALLAN, lawyer; b. Kenosha, Wis., Jan. 6, 1929; s. Leo Vertin and Mayme C. (Kennedy) D.; m. JoAnn C. Cramton, Apr. 14, 1951 (div. Sept. 1977); children: Robert A., Kevin C., Tracey Downing Clark, Gregory E.; m. Joan Govan, Oct. 29, 1977; 1 child, Charles E. Reiter III. B.S., U. Wis., 1950, J.D., 1956. Bar: Wis. 1956, Ill. 1956, U.S. Supreme Ct. 1965. Assoc. Sidley & Austin, Chgo., 1956-64, ptnr., 1964-94, counsel, 1994-97; counsel Ruff, Weidenaar & Reidy, Ltd., Chgo., 1997—. Trustee, former pres. Episcopal Charities and Cmty. Svcs., Chgo. Diocese. Served to lt. USN, 1950-53, Korea. Fellow Am. Coll. Trial Lawyers; mem. ABA, Soc. Trial Lawyers, Ill. Bar Assn., Chgo. Bar Assn., Wis. Bar Assn., 7th Cir. Bar Assn., Union League Club, Law Club, Legal Club, MidDay Club, Westmoreland Country Club. Republican. Episcopalian. Office: Ruff Weidenaar & Reidy 222 N Lasalle St Ste 1525 Chicago IL 60601

DOWNS, ANTHONY, urban economist, real estate consultant; b. Evanston, Ill., Nov. 21, 1930; s. James Chesterfield and Florence Glassbrook (Finn) D.; m. Katherine Watson, Apr. 7, 1956; children: Katherine, Christine, Tony, Paul, Carol. BA, Carleton Coll., 1952; MA, Stanford U., 1956, PhD, 1956. With Real Estate Rsch. Corp., Chgo., 1959-77; chmn. bd. dirs. Real Estate Rsch. Corp., 1973-77; asst. prof. econs. and polit. sci. U. Chgo., 1959-62; econ. cons. Rand Corp., Santa Monica, Calif., 1963-65; sr. fellow Brookings Instn., Washington, 1977—; bd. dirs. Urban Inst., Manpower Demonstration Rsch. Corp., 1975-80, Pittway Corp., NAACP Legal and Ednl. Def. Fund., Inc., Mass. Mutual Life Ins. Co., Bedford Property Investors, NHP Found., Inc., Gen. Growth Properties, Inc., Essex Property Trust, Inc., Penton Media, Inc.; mem. Nat. Commn. on Urban Problems, 1967-68, Adv. Commn. on Regulatory Barriers to Affordable Housing, 1990-91; mem. adv. bd. Inst. for Rsch. on Poverty, 1970-78; bd. dirs. Rush Presbyn. St Luke's Med. Ctr., Chgo., 1970-77. Author: An Economic Theory of Democracy, 1957, Inside Bureaucracy, 1967, Urban Problems and Prospects, 1970, 2d edit., 1976, Opening Up the Suburbs, 1973, Federal Housing Subsidies, 1973, Racism in America, 1970, Neighborhoods and Urban Development, 1981, Rental Housing in the 1980s, 1983, The Revolution in Real Estate Finance, 1985, Stuck in Traffic, 1992, New Visions for Metropolitan America, 1994, A Re-Evaluation of Residential Rent Control, 1996, Political Theory and Public Choice, 1998, Urban Affairs and Urban Policy, 1998; co-author: Urban Decline and the Future of the American Cities, 1982; co-editor: Do Housing Allowances Work, 1981, Energy Costs, Urban Development, and Housing, 1984. Served with USNR, 1956-59. Mem. Am. Econ. Assn., Am. Soc. Real Estate Counselors, Nat. Acad. Arts and Scis., Urban Land Inst. (bd. dirs.), Anglo Am. Real Property Inst., Phi Beta Kappa, Lambda Alpha. Democrat. Roman Catholic. Home: 8483 Portland Pl Mc Lean VA 22102-1730 Office: 1775 Massachusetts Ave NW Washington DC 20036-2188

DOWNS, DAVID ERSKINE, television executive; b. Leiden, The Netherlands, May 4, 1955; s. Richard Erskine and Julie (Van Oldenborgh) D.; m. Alexis Leland Chapin, Oct. 21, 1978; children: Ashley, Taylor. BA in Am. history, Amherst Coll., 1977. Dir. sports info. Amherst (Mass.) Coll., 1977-78; Olympics rschr. ABC Sports, N.Y.C., 1978-80, assoc. prodr., 1980-82, mgr., 1982-86, dir., 1986-88, v.p. programming, 1988-94, sr. v.p. programming, 1994-98; sr. v.p. ops. and devel. ABC TV Network, N.Y.C., 1998—. Office: ABC Television Network 77 W 66th St New York NY 10023-6298

DOWNS, DAVID RUTHERFORD, minister; b. Birmingham, Ala., Nov. 5, 1957; s. Glen and Beatrice (Roy) D.; m. Laurie Ann Smith, June 20, 1980; children: David, Purity, Carissa, Promise, Jehu. BA cum laude, William Jennings Bryan Coll.; ThM magna cum laude, Dallas Theol. Sem., 1989, postgrad., 1991—. Lic. to ministry So. Bapt. Conv., 1975; ordained to ministry Bible Ch., 1990. Min. youth/music Grace Community Ch., Largo, Fl., 1975-83; assoc. pastor Redeemer Bible Ch., Ft. Worth, 1986-89; pastor Westminster Bible Ch., Henderson, Tex., 1989-92; founding paster Cornerstone Ch., Orlando, Fla., 1992—; ch. planter Conservative Bapt. Home Mission Soc., 1992—. Author: Power Evangelism Exposed, 1988; co-author: God's View of Sex, 1991. Mem. South East Conservative Bapt. Assn. (v.p. 1994—). Office: Cornerstone Ch 2333 Donegan Pl Orlando FL 32826-4305 *Like the story of the Good Samaritan there are three ways to treat people: Beat 'em up, pass 'em up, or help 'em up. I like the last one.*

DOWNS, DONALD ALEXANDER, JR., political scientist, educator; b. Toronto, Ont., Can., Dec. 2, 1948; s. Donald Alexander and Mary Jane (Dutton) D.; m. Susan Yeager, Jan. 30, 1971; children: Jacqueline Marie, Alexander Donald. BS, Cornell U., 1971; MS, U. Ill., 1974; PhD, U. Calif., Berkeley, 1983. Vis. lectr. U. Mich., Ann Arbor, 1981; lectr., then asst. prof. U. Notre Dame, Ind., 1981-85; asst. prof. to full prof. polit. sci. U. Wis., Madison, 1985—, Hawkins prof., 1999—; bd. dirs. J&D Communications, Chralottesville, Va.; lectr. various univs. and other groups, 1985—; sec. Faculty Com. for Acad. Freedom and Rights, Madison, Wis. Author: Nazis in Skokie: Freedom Community and the First Amendment, 1985 (Anisfield Wolf award 1986), The New Politics of Pornography, 1989 (Gladys Kammerer award 1990), More Than Victims: Battered Women, Syndrome Society and the Law, 1996, Cornell '69: Liberalism and the Crisis of the American University, 1999; contbr. articles on free speech to various publs.; commentator Wis. Pub. Radio, 1986—, other radio stas., 1985—. Recipient Alumnus Achievement award Wayland Acad., 1992, Disting. Tchg. award U. Wis., 1989. Mem. Am. Polit. Sci. Assn., So. Poverty Law Ctr., Amnesty Internat. Avocations: coaching basketball, playing basketball, literature, politics, business. Home: 1102 Chapel Hill Rd Madison WI 53711-3102 Office: Univ Wis 110 North Hall Madison WI 53706

DOWNS, FLOYD L., mathematics educator; b. Winchester, Mass., Jan. 21, 1931; s. Floyd L. and Emma M. (Noyes) D.; m. Elizabeth Lenci, Dec. 29, 1955; children: Karla C., John N. AB, Harvard U., 1952; MA, Columbia U., 1955. Lic. math. tchr. Math. tchr. East High Sch., Denver, 1955-60, Kent (Conn.) Sch., 1960-62, Newton High Sch., Newtonville, Mass., 1962-63; math. tchr., dept. chair Hillsdale High Sch., San Mateo, Calif., 1964-89; lectr. Ariz. State U., Tempe, 1988—; math. scis. adv. com. The Coll. Bd., N.Y., 1979-85; mem. U.S. nat. com. 2d Internat. Math. Study, 1979-86; Golden state math. com. Calif. State Dept. Edn., Sacramento, 1985-91; exec. dir. Ariz. Math. Coalition, 1991-96. Co-author: Geometry, 1964, 91. With U.S. Army, 1952-54, Korea. Mem. Nat. Coun. Tchrs. Math., Nat. Coun. Suprs. Math., Math. Assn. Am., Calif. Math. Coun., Ariz. Assn. Tchrs. Math., Phi Delta Kappa. Home: 16751 E Ashbrook Dr Fountain Hills AZ 85268-2802 Office: Ariz State U Math Dept Tempe AZ 85287-1804

DOWNS, HARTLEY H., III, chemist; b. Ridgewood, N.J., Oct. 21, 1949; s. Hartley Harrison and Jennie Mae (Smith) D.; m. Cindy Marie Millen, June 19, 1976; children: Kathryn Marie, Jennifer Anne, Susanna Jayne. BS, Grove City Coll., 1971; MS, Indiana U. of Pa., 1973; PhD, W. Va. U., 1978; postgrad., U. Colo., 1976-77. Postdoctoral rsch. assoc. chemistry dept. U. So. Calif., L.A., 1977-78; staff chemist corp. rsch. labs. Exxon Rsch. and Engring. Co., Linden, N.J., 1978-81, Houston, 1981-83, Annandale, N.J., 1983-86; rsch. scientist, surface chemistry and corrosion sci. group supr. Baker Performance Chems., Houston, 1986-91, rsch. mgr., 1991-92, tech. dir., 1992-97; tech. dir. Baker Petrolite, Houston, 1997—. Contbr. articles to profl. jours., chpt. to book; patentee in field. Recipient Award for Grad. Rsch., Sigma Xi, 1973, Union Carbide award W.Va. U., 1975, Stan Gillman award U. Colo., 1977, Tech. Merit award Baker-Hughes, 1989, 91, 93. Mem. Am. Chem. Soc., Soc. Petroleum Engrs., Offshore Operators Com. (task force on environ. sci.), NACE Internat. (chmn. task force on oil industry biocides 1996—, symposium chmn. mineral scale deposit control in oilfield ops. 1994, 98, chmn. corrosion/94 and corrosion/98 symposia), Phi Lambda Upsilon. Presbyterian. Office: Baker Petrolite PO Box 27714 Houston TX 77227-7714

DOWNS, HUGH MALCOLM, radio and television broadcaster; b. Akron, Ohio, Feb. 14, 1921; s. Milton Howard and Edith (Hick) D.; m. Ruth Shaheen, Feb. 20, 1944; children—Hugh Raymond, Deirdre Lynn. Student, Bluffton (Ohio) Coll., 1938-39, Wayne State U., 1940-41, Columbia, 1955-56. Staff announcer radio sta. WLOK, Lima, Ohio, 1939; program dir. WLOK, 1939-40; staff announcer radio sta. WWJ, Detroit, 1940-42, NBC, Chgo., 1943-54; co-host 20/20 ABC News; spl. cons. UN on refugee problems Middle East, 1961-64; cons. Center for Study Democratic Instns.; chmn. bd. Raylin Prodns., Inc., 1960—. Free-lance radio and TV broadcaster, 1954—; programs include Home Show, 1954-57, Sid Caesar's Hour, 1956-57, Concentration, 1958-68, Jack Paar show Tonight, 1957-62; host: programs include Today Show, 1962-72, TV Mag. of Air 20/20, 1979—, ABC; PBS daily series Over Easy; author: Fifty to Forever, 1994. Chmn. bd. govs. Nat. Space Soc.; chmn. U.S. com. for UNICEF. Office: care 20/20 ABC News 147 Columbus Ave New York NY 10023-5900*

DOWNS, JON FRANKLIN, drama educator, director; b. Bartow, Fla., Sept. 15, 1938; s. Clarence Curtis and Frankie (Morgan) D. Student, Ga. State Coll., 1956-58; BFA, U. Ga., 1960, MFA, 1969. Drama dir. Ga. Perimeter Coll. (formerly DeKalb Coll.), Clarkston, 1969-99. Dir., author The Beastly Purple Forest (marionettes) U. Ga., 1968, Dracula: A Horrible Musical, DeKalb Coll., 1971; dir. A Streetcar Named Desire, DeKalb, 1974, Brigadoon, DeKalb, 1981, West Side Story, 1983, Amadeus, 1984, Noises Off, 1986, The Three Musketeers, 1988, A Midsummer Night's Dream, 1990, A Little Night Music, 1991, Hamlet, 1993, over 200 others; actor Wedding in Japan, N.Y.C., 1960, Dark at the Top of the Stairs, N.Y.C. and on tour, 1961, A Life in the Theatre, DeKalb Coll., 1981, numerous others; designer Sweeney Todd, DeKalb Coll., 1970, Romulus, 1971, Grass Harp, 1972, many others; writer, dir. plays Tokalitta, Gold!, The Vigil; on tour of Ga. summers 1973-76; author: The Illusionist, 1979, Rapunzel, 1997; film reviewer; Southernflair Mag., 1994—. Grantee arts sect. Ga Dept. Planning and Budget, 1973, 74, State Bicentennial Commn., 1975, Nat. Bicentennial Commn., 1975. Mem. Southeastern Theater Conf. (state rep. 1971-73), Ga. Theater Conf. (exec. bd. 1970-73, 79-82). Home: 1124 Forrest Blvd Decatur GA 30030-4736

DOWNS, KATHLEEN ANNE, healthcare consultant; b. Toledo, Sept. 20, 1951; d. Keith Landis and Cecelia Josephine (Wood) Babcock; m. Michael Brian Thomas, July 17, 1971 (dec. Oct. 1973); m. David Michael Downs, Aug. 8, 1981. Student, San Diego Mesa Coll., 1968-70; BS, Union Inst., 1989. Cert. med. staff coordinator, provider credentialing specialist, profl. healthcare quality. Sec. Travelodge Internat., Inc., El Cajon, Calif., 1970-73; intermediate stenographer City of El Cajon, 1973-77; adminstrv. asst. MacLellan & Assocs., El Cajon, 1977-78; sr. sec. WESTEC Services, Inc., San Diego, 1978; adminstrv. sec. El Cajon Valley Hosp., 1978-80; asst. med. staff Grossmont Dist. Hosp., La Mesa, Calif., 1980-83, coord. med. staff, 1983-87, mgr., 1987-94; mgr. med. staff Sharp Meml. Hosp., San Diego, 1994; dir. med. staff svcs. Sharp HealthCare, San Diego, 1994-96, sr. specialist med. staff svcs., 1996; dir. med. staff svcs. Alvarado Hosp. Med. Ctr. and San Diego Rehab. Inst., San Diego, 1996—; tchr. The Vogel Inst., San Diego, 1986; mem. med. staff svcs. adv. com. San Diego C.C. Dist.; adj. faculty Union Inst., 1991-96, Chemeketa C.C., 1991-95; credentials verification orgn. surveyor Nat. Com. Quality Assurance, Washington, 1996—. Mem. Nat. Assn. Med. Staff Svcs. (edn. coun. 1989-93, faculty 1990—, chmn. 1991-93, bd. dirs. 1991-93, editl. bd. Over View 1993-96), Calif. Assn. Med. Staff Svcs. (treas. San Diego chpt. 1984-86, pres. 1986-87, sec. 1999—). Avocations: organic gardening, boating, gourmet cooking, yoga, reading, fitness walking. Office: Alvarado Hosp Med Ctr 6655 Alvarado Rd San Diego CA 92120-5208

DOWNS, MICHAEL PATRICK, retired marine corps officer; b. Oak Bluffs, Mass., Feb. 8, 1940; s. Charles Edward and Margaret Mary (Hickey) D.; m. Martha Leigh Puller, Feb. 15, 1969; children: Michael Patrick Jr., Lewis Burwell. BS, Coll. Holy Cross, Worcester, Mass., 1961; MS, U. So. Calif., 1982; grad., Amphibious Warfare Sch., Quantico, Va., 1967; grad. with honors, U.S. Army Command and Gen. Staff Coll., 1975; grad., Nat. War Coll., 1979; postgrad. program for sr. execs., J.F.K. Sch. Govt., Cambridge, Mass., 1988. Commd. 2d lt. USMC, 1961, advanced through grades to brig. gen., 1987; comdr. Co. F, 2d Bn., 5th Marines, Republic of Vietnam, 1967-68; exec. officer Bn. Landing Team 1/9, Okinawa, Japan, 1975-76; plans officer Allied Forces Cen. Europe, Brunssum, The Netherlands, 1979-82; regtl. comdr. 27th Marines, Twentynine Palms, Calif., 1984-86; dir. facilities and svcs. Hdqrs. USMC, Washington, 1987-89; comdg. gen. 6th Marine Expeditionary Brigade, Camp Lejeune, N.C., 1989-90, Marine Corps Base, Camp Lejeune, 1990-92. Decorated D.S.M., Silver Star, Purple Heart, Vietnamese Gallantry Cross with palm (Republic of Vietnam), Def. Meritorious Svc. medal. Life mem. VFW, Marine Corps Assn., 1st Marine Div. Assn., Nat. War Coll. Assn. Roman Catholic. Avocations: golf, spectator sports. Home: 1811 Edgehill Dr Alexandria VA 22307-1122

DOWNS, THOMAS EDWARD, IV, lawyer; b. South Amboy, N.J., Sept. 27, 1950; s. Thomas Edward III and Theresa Mary (Jaje) D.; m. Marie Popik, Oct. 6, 1979; children: Thomas Edward V, Lauren Ann. BA, St. Peter's Coll., 1972; JD, Seton Hall U., 1975. Bar: N.J. 1975, U.S. Dist. Ct. N.J. 1975, U.S. Dist. Cts. (so. and ea. dists.) N.Y. 1981. Law clk. to presiding judges Middlesex County, N.J., 1975; assoc. Irving Tabman, Old Bridge, N.J., 1975-76; ptnr. Tabman, Downs & McDonnell, Old Bridge, 1976-77, Tabman & Downs, Old Bridge, 1978-82; pvt. practice Old Bridge, 1982—; South Amboy Mcpl. pros., 1977—, Sayreville Mcpl. pros., 1987-90, 94—. Sec. South Amboy Shade Tree com., 1974; co-chmn. South Amboy Blood Bank; pres. South Amboy Young Dem. Orgn.; dep. chmn. Sayreville Dem. Orgn., 1992—. Mem. Assn. Trial Lawyers Am., N.J. State Trial Lawyers Assn., Middlesex County Bar Assn., N.J. State Bar Assn., Lions (pres. South Amboy chpt. 1984). Roman Catholic. Home: 26 Carter Pl Sayreville PO Box Parlin NJ 08859 Office: PO Box 498 Old Bridge NJ 08857-0498

DOWNS, THOMAS K., lawyer; b. New Albany, Ind., Jan. 10, 1949. BA, Ind. U., 1977, JD magna cum laude, 1980. Bar: Ind. 1980. Mem. Ice Miller Donadio & Ryan, Indpls. Exec. editor Ind. Law Jour., 1979-80; contbr. articles to profl. jours. Pres. Ind. Assn. Cities and Towns Found., 1994—; mem. Lt. Gov.'s Jobs Coun. Fellow Am. Coll. Bond Counsel (founding mem., chmn. govt. rels. com., co-chmn. bond buyer midwest pub. fin. conf. 1998); mem. Nat. Assn. Bond Lawyers (steering com. 1985-86, 90, 92, chmn. bond banks workshop 1985-86, tax increment workshop 1989, panelist various workshops, faculty fundamentals mcpl. bond law, opinions and profl. responsibility 1989-90, chair Ann. Washington Conf. 1996), Ind. Continuing Legal Edn. Forum (chmn. mcpl. law seminars 1984-92, practical impact tax reform act of 1986, panelist mcpl. utility fin. 1988, pub. law 10 1991), Ind. Mcpl. Lawyers Assn., Inc. (bd. dirs. 1983—), Order of Coif. Office: Ice Miller Donadio & Ryan Box 82001 1 American Sq Indianapolis IN 46282-0001

DOWS, DAVID ALAN, chemistry educator; b. San Francisco, July 25, 1928; s. Samuel Randall and Rita M. (Bowers) D.; m. Wena Hunt Waldner, July 29, 1950; children—Janet Louise, Carol Marie, Joyce Ellen. B.S., U. Calif. at Berkeley, 1952, Ph.D., 1954. Instr. chemistry Cornell U., 1954-56; instr. U. So. Calif., Los Angeles, 1956-57; asst. prof. U. So. Calif., 1957-59, assoc. prof., 1959-63, prof. chemistry, 1963—, chmn. dept., 1966-72; NATO prof., 1970. Contbr. articles profl. jours. NSF fellow, 1962-63. Mem. Am. Chem. Soc., Am. Phys. Soc., Phi Beta Kappa. Office: U So Calif Dept Chemistry University Park Los Angeles CA 90089-0482

DOWTY, ALAN KENT, political scientist, educator; b. Greenville, Ohio, Jan. 15, 1940; s. Paul Willard and Ethel Lovella (Harbaugh) D.; m. Nancy Ellen Gordon, Sept. 8, 1961 (div. 1972); children: Merav Aurli, Tamar Eliea, Gidon Yair; m. Gail Gaynell Schupack, Jan. 1, 1973; children: Rachel Miriam, Rafael Jonathan. BA, Shimer Coll., 1959; MA, U. Chgo., 1960, PhD, 1963. Lectr. Hebrew U., Jerusalem, 1965-72, sr. lectr., 1972-75; assoc. prof. U. Notre Dame, Ind., 1975-78, prof. polit. sci., 1978—; exec. dir. Leonard Davis Inst., Jerusalem, 1972-74; editl. bd. Middle East Rev., N.Y.C., 1977-90; project dir. Twentieth Century Fund, N.Y.C., 1983-85; reporter experts meeting Internat. Inst. Human Rights, Strasbourg, France, 1989. Author: The Limits of American Isolation, 1971, Middle East Crisis, 1984 (Quincy Wright award 1985), The Arab-Israel Conflict (with others), 1984, Closed Borders, 1987, The Jewish State, 1998; book reviewer Jerusalem Post, 1964-75; contbr. numerous articles to topical pubs. Exec. com. Am. Profs. for Peace in Mid. East, 1976-90; witness U.S. Senate Fgn. Rels. Com., Washington, 1976; nat. adv. com. Union of Couns. for Soviet Jews, Washington, 1980-91. Woodrow Wilson fellow, 1959-60; Rothschild fellow Hebrew U., 1963-64; resident fellow Adlai Stevenson Inst., Chgo., 1971-72; recipient Charles W. Ramsdell award So. Hist. Assn., 1966; grantee Twentieth Century Fund, N.Y.C., 1983. Mem. Am. Polit. Sci. Assn., Internat. Inst. Strategic Studies, Internat. Polit. Sci. Assn., Internat. Studies Assn. (exec. com. 1977-79), Assn. Israel Studies. Jewish. Avocations: travel, Jewish studies. Office: U Notre Dame 313 Hesburgh Ctr Notre Dame IN 46556-5677

DOX, IDA, author, medical illustrator; b. Honduras, Central America, July 8, 1927; came to U.S. 1947; d. John and Catherine (Headman) D.; m. B. John Melloni; children: H. Paul, June L., Peter J., Roy G. BFA, Newcomb Coll., New Orleans, 1950; MS, Johns Hopkins U., 1954; PhD, U. Md., 1990. Med. illustrator Georgetown U. Med. Ctr., Washington, 1954-69; med. illustrator select com. on assassinations of J.F. Kennedy and Martin Luther King, Jr. of U.S. Ho. of Reps, Washington, 1978-79; med. illustrator/author Bethesda, Md., 1969—. Author: Melloni's Illustrated Medical Dictionary, 1979 (Best Med. Book award 1979), Diccionario Medico Illustrado de Melloni, 1983, The Harper Collins Illustrated Medical Dictionary, 1993, Melloni's Illustrated Review of Human Anatomy, 1988 (award of excellence 1989), Attorney's Illustrated Medical Dictionary, 1995, Melloni's Student Atlas of Human Anatomy, 1997, Melloni's Illustrated Dictionary of Obstetrics and Gynecology, 1999; contbr. articles to profl. jours. Recipient L.S. Neill prize, Newcomb Coll., 1949, E. Woodward Meml. prize, 1950, Indsl. Graphics Internat. award, 1977. Address: 9308 Renshaw Dr Bethesda MD 20817-2228

DOYLE, ANTHONY PETER, lawyer; b. Washington, July 13, 1953; s. Francis X. and Anna (Klekotka) D.; m. Maria H. Duda, Aug. 13, 1977; children: Jeffrey Anthony, Joseph Edward, Natalie Maria, Andrew Michael. AA, Berkshire Community Coll., Pittsfield, Mass., 1972-75; BS magna cum laude, Worcester State Coll., 1977; JD, Western New Eng. Coll., 1980. Bar: Mass. 1980; U.S. Dist. Ct. Mass. 1981; U.S. Ct. Appeals (1st cir.) 1981, U.S. Supreme Ct. 1999. Pvt. practice Pittsfield, 1980-84; ptnr. Doyle & Cormier, Pittsfield, 1985-88, Barry, Doyle & Cormier, Pittsfield, 1989, Barry & Doyle, Pittsfield, 1989—. Pres. Hospice of Cen. Berkshire, Pittsfield, 1988-90; v.p. HospiceCare of the Berkshires, Pittsfield, 1990-92, pres. 1992—; bd. dirs. Dalton (Mass.) Youth Ctr., 1986-89, Community Recreation Assn., Dalton, 1989-95; exec. com. Appalachian Trails Dist. Boy Scouts Am., Dalton, 1989-96; mem. Zoning Bd. Appeals, Dalton, 1995—, chmn., 1997—, Dalton Coun. Aging, 1997—. Recipient commendation Western Mass. Pro Bono Referral Svc., 1983-87. Mem. Mass. Bar Assn., Berkshire Bar Assn. (exec. com. 1989-91, v.p. 1997—). Roman Catholic. Avocations: skiing, tennis. Home: 108 Barton Hill Rd Dalton MA 01226-2005 Office: Barry & Doyle 8 Bank Row Ste 2 Pittsfield MA 01201-6224

DOYLE, BILLY HERMAN, film specialist, writer; b. Kyrock, Ky., Oct. 17, 1932; s. Hardin and Bessie (Gross) D. BS, Western State U., Bowling Green, Ky., 1955; postgrad., U. Louisville, 1961-65. Elem. sch. tchr. Louisville, 1955-85. Author: Ultimate Directory of Silent Performers, 1995; contbr. articles to popular publs. Republican. Home: 10008 Bentford Dr Louisville KY 40272-2853

DOYLE, DELORES MARIE, elementary education educator; b. Madison, S.D., July 24, 1939; d. Martin N. and Pearl M. (Anderson) Berkelo; m. Patrick J. Doyle; children: Kathleen, Shawn, Tamara, Timothy. AS, Dakota State Coll., Madison, 1959; BS, Mid. Tenn. State U., 1966, MEd, 1968, EdS, 1975; PhD, Peabody/Vanderbilt U., 1980. Cert. career ladder III tchr. Tchr. 4th grade Meriden-Cleghorn Schs., Meriden, Iowa, 1960-62; tchr. 1st grade Hanover (Ill.) Sch., 1963-66; tchr. 2d grade Hobgood Sch., Murfreesboro, Tenn., 1969-70; tchr. 1st grade Reeves-Rogers Sch., Murfreesboro, 1972-80, tchr. 2d grade, 1981-97, prin., 1997—; summer sch. dir. Murfreesboro City Schs., 1986-89; lead project tutor Reeves-Rogers Sch., 1987-90; cooperating tchr. Mid. Tenn. State U. Student Tchrs., Murfreesboro, 1972-97. Bd. dirs. Grace Luth. Ch., Murfreesboro, 1991-93, mem. choir, 1975—; active Edn. 2000 Com. Murfreesboro C. of C., 1993, task force on edn. Mid. Tenn. State U., 1992-93; trustee Mid. Tenn. State U. Found., 1995—. Named Career Ladder III Tchr., Dept. Edn., Nashville, 1984; recipient Tenn. Tch. of Yr. award State Dept. Edn., Nashville, 1992, Murfreesboro City Tchr. of Yr. award Murfreesboro City Schs., 1991, Mid-Cumberland Dist. Tchr. of Yr. award Dist. Dept. Edn., 1991, Trailblazer award 1995; Creative Tchg. grantee State Dept. Edn., 1992, 93. Mem. NEA, Nat. State Tchr. of Yr. Orgn., Tenn. Edn. Assn. (Disting. Classroom Tchr. award 1991), Murfreesboro Edn. Assn. (pres. 1981-82), Delta Kappa Gamma (2d v.p.), Kappa Delta Pi. Democrat. Avocations: bridge, travel, reading, bicycling. Home: 1710 Sutton Pl Murfreesboro TN 37129-6513 Office: Reeves-Rogers Sch 1807 Greenland Dr Murfreesboro TN 37130-3199

DOYLE, DON HARRISON, history educator; b. Long Beach, Calif., Feb. 23, 1946; s. Leo W. and Barbara (Ferron) D.; divorced, 1989; children: Caroline, Kelly. BA, U. Calif., Davis, 1967; PhD, Northwestern U., 1973. Asst. prof. U. Mich., Dearborn, 1971-74; asst. prof. Vanderbilt U., Nashville, 1974-79, assoc. prof., 1979-86, prof., 1986—, chmn. dept. history, 1987-90; Fulbright sr. lectr. in am. studies U. Rome, 1991; Fulbright sr. lectr. in Am. history U. Genoa, Italy, 1995; vis. prof. history U. Leeds, Eng., 1997-98. Author: Social Order of a Frontier Community, 1978, Nashville in the New South, 1985, Nashville Since the 1920s, 1985, New Men, New Cities, New South, 1990, The South as an American Problem, 1995. Mem. Orgn. Am. Historians, So. Hist. Assn., Am. Hist. Assn., Tenn. Hist. Soc. (pres. 1987-90). Office: Vanderbilt U Dept History PO Box 1738 Nashville TN 37235*

DOYLE, ESTHER PIAZZA, critical care nurse, educator; b. Birmingham, Ala., Apr. 8, 1952; d. Vincent and Dorothy Virginia (Danforth) Piazza; m. James Patrick Doyle III, Sept. 14, 1974. ADN, Jefferson State Coll., Birmingham, 1976; BSN magna cum laude, Spalding U., Louisville, 1988. RN, Ky. Post-op cardiac care Cleve. Clinic Ohio, 1976-77; level I trauma staff nurse surg. ICU Hermann Hosp.-U. Tex., Houston, 1977-79; SICU level I trauma, MICU, burn unit profl. nurse recruiter, trauma clin. coord., utilization rev. coord. Humana-U. Louisville, 1979-90; ICU and CCU nurse, phone triage Presbyn. Hosp., Charlotte, N.C., 1991—; conducted trauma awareness seminars. Author: Family Guide to Critical Care. Bd. dirs., sec.-treas. Neighborhood Assn. Mem. Internat. Honor Soc. Nursing, Sigma Theta Tau. Home: 6016 Mallard Grove Rd Charlotte NC 28269-1389

DOYLE, EUGENIE FLERI, pediatric cardiologist, educator; b. Bklyn., Oct. 19, 1921; d. Paul Charles and Antoinette (Giovannetti) Fleri; m. Joseph Anthony Doyle, Aug. 19, 1944; children: Christopher, Stephen, Eugenie, Jane Marie, Richard. BS, Marymount Coll., Tarrytown, N.Y., 1943, DSc (hon.), 1993; MD, Johns Hopkins U., 1946; DSc (hon.), Coll. New Rochelle, 1975. Intern in pediatrics Johns Hopkins Hosp., Balt., 1946-47; pediatric resident Bellevue Hosp., N.Y.C., 1947-49; fellow pediatric cardiology NYU Med. Ctr., 1949-53, dir. pediatric cardiology, 1958-93; asst. prof. pediatrics NYU Sch. Medicine, 1953-58, assoc. prof., 1959-70, prof., 1970-92, prof. emerita, 1993—; mem. cardiac adv. com. N.Y. State Health Dept., 1983-92; dir. Vis. Nurse Svc., N.Y.C., 1984—. Editor: Pediatric Cardiology, 1985; contbr. articles to profl. jours. Trustee Marymount Coll., 1983-91, vice chair bd., 1988-91. Mem. Am. Acad. Pediatrics, Am. Pediatric Soc., Am. Coll. Cardiology, Am. Heart Assn., N.Y. Heart Assn. (bd. dirs. 1977-84, pres. 1979-81), Cosmopolitan Club. Roman Catholic. Avocations: gardening, travel, ballet. Home: 32 Washington Sq W New York NY 10011-9156 Office: NYU Med Ctr 550 1st Ave New York NY 10016-6481

DOYLE, FREDERICK JOSEPH, retired government research scientist; b. Oak Park, Ill., Apr. 3, 1920; s. John Frederick and Mary Elizabeth (Meyers) D.; m. Mary Blaskovich, June 18, 1955; children: Frederick J., Margaret, Mary Ellen, George. BCE, Syracuse U., 1951; postgrad., Internat. Tng. Ctr. Aerial Sur, Delft, The Netherlands, 1952; D in English (hon.), Tech. U., Hannover, Germany, 1976; DSc (hon.), Ohio STate U., 1986, U. Bordeaux, France, 1987; D in Tech., Royal Tech. U., Sweden, 1987. Assoc. prof. geodetic sci. Ohio State U., 1952-60, chmn. dept., 1959-60; chief scientist Raytheon Autometric Co., Alexandria, Va., 1960-69; sci. advisor nat. mapping divsn. U.S. Geol. Survey, Reston, Va., 1969-89; dir. earth resources observation sys. program U.S. Geol. Survey, Reston, 1978-80; ret., 1989; geodesy cartography adv. com. nat. Acad. Scis., 1967-69; chmn. Apollo orbital Sci. photo team NASA, 1969-73, planetary cartography com., 1974-95; exec. com. divsn. earth sci. NRC, 1973-76. With C.E., AUS, 1943-48, PTO. Recipient Meritorious Svc. award Dept. Interior, 1977, Disting. Svc. medal, 1981, Silver medal City of Paris, 1978; Fulbright fellow Internat. Tng. Ctr. Aerial Survey, 1952, Internat. Tng. Ctr. fellow, 1986. Fellow AAAS; mem. NAE, Internat. Soc. Photogrammetry Remote Sensing (hon.), Am. Congress Surveying Mapping, Am. Geophys. Union, Am. Soc. Photogrammetry (hon., pres. 1969-70, contbg. author, editor publs., Fairchild Photogrammetric award 1968, Alan Gordon award 1985). Home: 1591 Forest Villa Ln Mc Lean VA 22101-4132

DOYLE, GERARD FRANCIS, lawyer; b. Needham, Mass., Oct. 25, 1942; s. John Patrick and Catherine Mary (Lawler) D.; BS in Indsl. Adminstrn., Yale U., 1966; JD, Georgetown U., 1972; m. Paula Marie Dervay, May 14, 1983; children: Laura Dervay, Meredith Lawler, Philip John. Bar: D.C. 1973, U.S. Dist. Ct. D.C. 1973, U.S. Ct. Fed. Claims 1976, U.S. Ct. Appeals (fed. cir.), 1982, U.S. Supreme Ct. 1982. Group head for operating submarine reactors and reactor tech. Div. Naval Reactors, AEC, Washington, 1970-72; atty. firm Morgan, Lewis & Bockius, Washington, 1972-76; legal counsel Am. Nuclear Energy Council, Washington, 1975-76; ptnr. Cotten, Day & Doyle, Washington, 1976-87; ptnr. Doyle & Savit, Doyle, Simmons & Bachman, and Doyle & Bachman, Washington, 1987—; legal counsel Assn. Fed. Data Peripheral Suppliers, Washington, 1979; dir. M Internat., Inc.; author and lectr. in field. Columnist Federal Computer Week, 1989. With USN, 1966-71. Recipient Outstanding Young Man of Year award, 1976. Mem. ABA (mem. coun. publ. contract law sect. 1989-92), D.C. Bar Assn., Fed. Bar Assn., Am. Arbitration Assn. (panel arbitrators), Nat. Contract Mgmt. Assn. Republican. Roman Catholic. Clubs: Met. (Washington), Yale, Washington Golf and Country. Home: 901 Whann Ave Mc Lean VA 22101-1570 Office: Doyle & Bachman 4245 N Fairfax Dr Arlington VA 22203

DOYLE, GILLIAN, actress; b. Maidenhead, Berkshire, Eng.; came to U.S., 1977; d. John Joseph and Joan (Walker) D. BA in Theatre magna cum laude, Am. U., Washington, 1981. Appeared in (off Broadway mus.) Ernest in Love, N.Y.C., 1980, (plays) No Exit, Washington, 1985, Fefu and Her Friends, 1985, The Winters Tale, 1987, A Christmas Carol, 1987, Erpingham Camp, 1989, Turn of the Screw, 1989, Season's Greetings, 1986, Terra Nova, 1987, Mountain, 1990, Old Favorites, 1991, What the Butler Saw, 1993, Fawlty Towers, 1994, Last of the Red Hot Lovers, 1995, The Musical Comedy Murders of 1940, 1996, Move Over Mrs. Markham, 1997, Declarations: Love Letters of the Great Romantics, 1998; (film) Chances Are, 1989, Born Yesterday, 1993, North, 1993, Decade of Love, 1994, Wild Bill, 1994, The Tie That Binds, 1995, Independence Day, 1996; (TV) Ancient Prophecies III, 1995, Friends, 1995, The Martin Short Show, 1995, Days of Our Lives, 1996, Love's Deadly Triangle: The Texas Cadet Murder, 1996, General Hospital, 1997; (music video) Johnny Sportcoat and the Casuals, 1987; (comml.) United Way, 1988. Mem. SAG, AFTRA, Actors Equity Assn., Phi Kappa Phi. Democrat. Roman Catholic. Avocations: equestrienne, golf, swimming, music, philosophy, scuba diving (cert.).

DOYLE, IRENE ELIZABETH, electronic sales executive, nurse; b. West Point, Iowa, Oct. 5, 1920; d. Joseph Deidrich and Mary Adelaide (Groene) Schulte; m. William Joseph Doyle, Feb. 3, 1956. RN, Mercy Hosp., 1941. Courier nurse Santa Fe R.R., Chgo., 1947-50; indsl. nurse Montgomery Ward, Chgo., 1950-54; rep. Hornblower & Weeks, Chgo., 1954-56; v.p. William J. Doyle Co., Chgo., 1956-80, Ormond Beach, Fla., 1980-88. Served with M.C., U.S. Army, 1942-46. Mem. Electronic Reps. Assn. Republican. Roman Catholic. Club: Oceanside Country (Ormond Beach).

DOYLE, JAMES ALOYSIUS, retired association executive; b. Pitts., Mar. 20, 1921; s. James A. and Anna Sophia (Holthaus) D.; m. Ethel Miriam Clancey, Oct. 3, 1943; children: John Kevin, Elizabeth Marie, Brian James, Peter Joseph, Thomas More Patrick. BA, Queens Coll., N.Y.C., 1943. Editor, promotion mgr., circulation dir. Howes Pub. Co., Inc., N.Y.C., 1946-58; publicity chmn. Am. Assn. Textile Chemists and Colorists, 1955-58; exec. sec., dir. Cath. Press Assn. U.S. and Can., 1958-88. Columnist Cath. N.Y.; co-author: (with Brian Doyle) Two Voices, 1996; winner The Christopher award, 1997, Cath. Press Assn. Book award 1997. Master sgt. AUS, 1944-46, PTO; 1st lt. 1951-52, ETO. Decorated Knight St. Gregory the Great (by Pope John Paul II); named Alumnus of Yr., Queens Coll., CCNY, 1984, one of 100 Alumni Stars at Queens Coll. 60th Anniversary, 1998; recipient St. Francis de Sales award Cath. Press Assn., 1988. Mem. Internat. Cath. Union of Press (hon., coun.), Alumni Assn. Queens Coll. (1st pres. 1946-47, bd. dir. 1947-50, 77-80). Home: 25 Gregory Ave Merrick NY 11566-4244

DOYLE, JAMES E(DWARD), state attorney general; b. Washington, Nov. 23, 1945; s. James E. and Ruth (Bachhuber) D.; m. Jessica Laird, Dec. 21, 1966; children: Augustus, Gabriel. Student, Stanford U., 1963-66; AB in History, U. Wis., 1967; JD cum laude, Harvard U., 1972. Bar: Ariz. 1973, Wis. 1975, U.S. Dist. Ct. N.Mex. 1973, U.S. Dist. Ct. Ariz. 1973, U.S. Dist. Ct. Utah 1973, U.S. Dist. Ct. (we. dist.) Wis. 1975, U.S. Dist. Ct. (ea. dist.) Wis. 1976, U.S. Ct. Appeals (10th cir.) 1974, U.S. Ct. Appeals (7th cir.) 1985, U.S. Supreme Ct. 1989. Vol. Peace Corps, Tunisia, 1967-69; atty. DNA Legal Svcs., Chinle, Ariz., 1972-75; ptnr. Jacobs & Doyle, Madison, Wis., 1975-77; dist. atty. Dane County, Madison, 1977-83; ptnr. Doyle & Ritz, Madison, 1983-90; of counsel Lawton & Cates, Madison, 1990-91; atty. gen. State of Wis., Madison, 1991—. Mem. ABA, Wis. Bar Assn. (bd. dirs. criminal law sect. 1988), 7th Cir. Bar Assn. (chair criminal law sect. 1988-89). Democrat. Roman Catholic. Office: Office Atty Gen Dept Justice 123 W Washington Ave Rm 117 Madison WI 53707-7857*

DOYLE, JAMES LEONARD, bishop; b. Chatham, Ont., Can., June 20, 1929; s. Herbert Lawrence and Mary Josephine (Ennett) D. B.A., U. Western Ont., 1950; D.D., St. Peters Sem., London, 1954. Ordained priest Roman Catholic Ch., 1954. Then consecrated bishop; asso. rector St. Peter's Cathedral, London, Ont., 1954-60; rector St. Peter's Cathedral, 1974-76; pastor Sacred Heart Ch., Windsor, Ont., 1960-66; prin. Brennan High Sch., Windsor, 1966-68; pastor Holy Name Ch., Windsor, 1968-74; bishop of Peterborough Ont., 1976—. Address: 350 Hunter St W Box 175, Peterborough, ON Canada K9J 6Y8*

DOYLE, JAMES STEPHEN, publishing company executive, journalist; b. Boston, June 18, 1935; m. Ann Broderick Grady, Dec. 28, 1960; children: Katherine, Rebecca. BS in English, Boston Coll., 1956; MS in Journalism, Columbia U., 1961. Reporter Worcester (Mass.) Telegram, 1956-57; reporter, bur. chief Boston Globe, 1961-69; reporter Washington Star, 1969-73; spl. asst. U.S. Dept. Justice, Washington, 1973-75; corr., dep. bur. chief Newsweek Mag., Washington, 1976-83; v.p., editor, sr. advisor Army Times Pub. Co., Washington, 1983-98. Author: Not Above the Law, 1977; contbr. numerous articles to popular mags. Pres. Merrimack Park Citizen's Assn., Bethesda, Md., 1967; founding mem. Reporters Com./Free Press, Washington, 1969; bd. advisors Pew Ctr. for Civic Journalism, Project for Excellence in Journalism, Com. Concerned Journalists, Coun. on Fgn. Rels. Lt. (j.g.) USN, 1957-60. Co-recipient Pulitzer prize for Disting. Pub. Svc., 1966; Nieman fellow Harvard U., 1965. Roman Catholic. Avocations: birding, hiking. Home: 6401 Tone Dr Bethesda MD 20817-5815 Office: 426 C St NE Washington DC 20002

DOYLE, JENNIFER, surgical educator, scholar; b. Milw., Aug. 23, 1952; d. Sylvester Edward and Ethel Anna (Axmann) D. BA, Mt. Mary Coll., 1974; MA, U. Wis., Milw., 1979; postgrad., Brown U., 1979-84. Grad. tchg. asst. U. Wis., 1977-79; fellow Brown U., Providence, 1979-80, grad. teaching asst., 1981-84; adj. instr. Bryant Coll., Smithfield, R.I., 1985; adj. instr. history R.I. Coll., Providence, 1986-90; residency coord. dept. family medicine Brown U., Providence, 1986-87, edn. coord. dept. surgery, 1987-90; assoc. surgery Harvard Med. Sch., Boston, 1990-92, lectr. in surgery, 1992—; asst. dir. surg. edn. Deaconess Hosp., Boston, 1990-96; dir. ednl. devel. and evaluation Beth Israel Deaconess Med. Ctr., Boston, 1996—. Dem. committeeman, Wauwatosa, Wis., 1976-78; mem. Big Sisters of R.I., Providence, 1980-88; co-organizer Providence Freeze Coalition, 1982. Recipient Charles Edison Meml. fellowship, 1974, Lucetta Bissell Meml. fellowship, 1978, univ. fellowship Brown U., 1979, Wayland Collegium fellowship Brown U., 1988. Mem. Am. Ednl. Rsch. Assn., Assn. Am. Med. Colls., Assn. Surg. Edn., Assn. Program Dirs. in Surgery (assoc.), Assn. of Women Surgeons (assoc.), Assn. for Study of Med. Edn. (U.K.), Generalists in Med. Edn., Am. Evaluation Assn., AAUW, Mass. Consort. on Faculty Devel. Home: 219 Willow St West Roxbury MA 02132-1326 Office: Beth Israel Deaconess Med Ctr Dept Surgery 110 Francis St Ste 3A Boston MA 02215-5501

DOYLE, JILL J., elementary school principal. Prin. George P Way Elem. Sch., Bloomfield Hills, Mich., 1987—. Recipient Elem. Sch. Recognition award U.S. Dept. Edn., 1989-90. Office: George P Way Elem Sch 765 W Long Lake Rd Bloomfield Hills MI 48302-1552*

DOYLE, JOHN LAURENCE, manufacturing company executive; b. Whitestone, Devon, Eng., Sept. 7, 1931; came to U.S., 1953; s. John Edgcumbe and Grace Vera (Burd) D.; m. Judith Anne Nannizzi, Apr. 24, 1965; children: Jeffrey Michael, Peter John. B.S., Stanford U., 1956, M.S., 1959. Gen. mgr. AMD Hewlett Packard, Palo Alto, Calif., 1969-70; v.p., gen. mgr. Aerotherm, Sunnyvale, Calif., 1970-72; dir. corp. devel. Hewlett Packard, Palo Alto, 1972-76, v.p. pers., 1976-81, v.p. R & D, 1981-84, exec. v.p., 1984-91, ret., 1991; bd. dirs. Analog Devices, Du Pont Photomasks, Xilnix, San Jose, Calif. Chmn. bd. C.I.S. Adv. Com., Stanford, 1980-84; bd. dirs. Urban Coalition, 1978-84; cabinet Calif. Poly. Inst., San Luis Obispo, 1980—. RAF, 1951-53. *

DOYLE, JOHN LAWRENCE, artist; b. Chgo., Mar. 14, 1939; s. John W. and Cecelia M. (Tarkowski) D.; children: Lynn, Sean, Morgan. BA, Sch. of Art Inst. Chgo., 1962; MA, No. Ill. U., 1967. Tchr. art Forest View High Sch., Arlington Heights, Ill., 1962-72; Bd. dirs. Toe River Arts Coun., Yancey Libr., Amy Regional Libr. Sys., Yancey History Assn., Yancey Evening Sch. Program, Steering Com., Yancey Mus./Visitor Ctr. Project. One-man shows of prints and/or paintings include: Denver Natural History Mus., Natural Am. Indian Mus., Spokane, Wash., Allen Galleries, Milw., U. N.D., U. S.D., Black Gallery, Taos, N.Mex., Vanderbilt U., Nashville, Tenn., Johns Hopkins U., Balt., Jockey Club Gallery, Miami, Fla., New West Whitney Gallery Western Art, Cody, Wyo., Harvard Med. Library, Lesch Gallery, Mpls., Clev. Clinic, Mayo Clinic, MGM Grand, Las Vegas, Yale U. Hosp., Now and Then Gallery, N.Y.C., Fine Print Unltd., Miami, Grand Gallery, Nev., Galerie Une, Puerto Vallarta, Mex., Welnetz Studio, Wis., Gallery G, Wichita, all 1981; group shows, latest being: U. Miami,

Fla., Tex. Tech U., Amarillo and Lubbock, U. Iowa Hosp. and Clinic, Loma Linda U., Calif., Art Resources, Denver, Hayden Hayes Gallery, Colorado Springs, Colo., Southwestern Gallery, Dallas, Nat. Library of Medicine, Bethesda, Md., Cornell Med. Coll., N.Y.C., Columbia U., N.Y.C., U. Kans., Harvard Law Library, Denver Nat. Hist. Mus., William Mitchell Law Sch., Mpls., United Bank of Austin, Tex., others, 1982-85, Inter Art, Nice, France, Loyola U. Sch. Law, New Orleans, Fine Arts Ltd., Miami, U. Dubuque, Iowa, Art Expo Los Angeles, Art Expo N.Y., Degan Bella Gallery, San Antonio, U. Ariz., Tempe, Midwest Mus. Am. Art, Ind., 1986, U. Ill., Chgo., 1987, R. Volid Gallery, Chgo., 1987, Royce Gallery, Denver, 1987, Denver Mus. Nat. History, 1987, No. Ill. U., DeKalb, 1987, Art Expo, N.Y.C., 1987, U. Ill. Chgo., 1988, R. Volip Gallery, Chgo., 1988, Ramses II Denver Mus., N.H., 1988, Royce Gallery, Denver, 1988, Hayden-Hayes Gallery, Colorado Springs, 1988, World Trade Ctr., Mpls.-St. Paul, 1988, Bergren Gallery, Rockford, Ill., 1988, Red Carpet Gallery, Minn., 1988, Yancey County Hist. Mus., N.C., 1988, Minn. World Trade Ctr., St. Paul, 1989, U. Ill., Champaign, 1989, U. Wis., Madison, 1989, Jean Stephen Gallery, Mpls., 1989, New West Cont. Art, Buffalo Bill Hist. Ctr., Cody, Wyo., 1990, White Thunder World Gallery, Milw., 1990, D. Ehrlein Gallery, Milw., 1990, Bank One, Milw., 1990, White Hart Gallery, Steamboat Springs, Colo., 1991, Suzanne Brown Gallery, Scottsdale, Ariz., 1991, Midwest Mus. Am. Art, Elkhart, Ind., 1991, Scripps Meml. Hosp. Schaetzel Ctr., La Jolla, Calif., 1991, Suzanne Brown Gallery, Scottsdale, Ariz., 1992, Walker Art Ctr., Asheville, N.C., 1992; represented in permanent collections: Library of Congress, Washington, Art Inst. Chgo., Indpls., Mus. Art, Carnegie Inst., Pitts., Norton Gallery of Art, West Palm Beach, Fla., Birmingham (Ala.) Mus. Art, Canton (Ohio) Art Inst., Columbus Mus. Fine Art, Columbus, Ohio, Fort Lauderdale (Fla.) Mus. Art, Miss. Art Mus., Whitney Gallery Western Art, Jackson, Nat. Gallery of Art, Washington, U. Mich., Ann Arbor, Savannah (Ga.) Coll. Art and Design, Scripps Meml. Hosp., La Jolla. Bd. dirs. Family Violence Coalition Yancey County Vol. Coop, Toe River Arts Coun., Yancey Libr., Amy Regional Libr.; pres. Yancey History Assn.; sec., treas. Mus. Visitor Ctr. Project. Recipient Hon. Mention Internat. Printmakers, 1971; George Brown Travelling fellow, 1962. Address: PO Box 715 Burnsville NC 28714-0715

DOYLE, JOHN ROBERT, lawyer; b. Chgo., May 12, 1950; s. Frank Edward and Dorothy (Bolton) D.; m. Kathleen Julius, June 14, 1974; children: Melissa, Maureen. BA magna cum laude, St. Louis U., 1971; JD summa cum laude, DePaul U., 1976. Bar: Ill. 1976, U.S. Dist. Ct. 1976, U.S. Dist. Ct. (no. dist.) Ill. 1982, Ill. Trial Bar 1982, U.S. Ct. Appeals (7th cir.) 1982. Ptnr. McDermott, Will & Emery, Chgo., 1976—. Mem. ABA, Chgo. Bar Assn. (jud. investigative hearing panel 1986-88), Phi Beta Kappa. Office: McDermott Will & Emery 227 W Monroe St Ste 3100 Chicago IL 60606-5096

DOYLE, JOSEPH ANTHONY, retired lawyer; b. N.Y.C., June 13, 1920; s. Joseph A. and Jane (Donahue) D.; m. Eugenie A. Fleri, Aug. 19, 1944; children: Christopher, Stephen, Eugenie, Jane, Richard. BS, Georgetown U., 1941; LLB, Columbia U., 1947. Bar: N.Y. 1948, U.S. Dist. Ct. (so. and ea. dists.) N.Y. 1950, U.S. Ct. Appeals (2d cir.) 1949. Assoc. Shearman & Sterling, N.Y.C., 1947-57, ptnr., 1957-79, 81-97; asst. sec. for manpower, res. affairs and logistics USN, Washington, 1979-81; bd. dirs. Roxbury (Conn.) Land Trust, Inc., The Fuji Bank and Trust Co. Bd. dirs. USO of Met. N.Y., 1982-90. Lt. USNR, 1941-45. Decorated Navy Cross, D.F.C. with 3 gold stars, Air medal with 7 gold stars; recipient Disting. Pub. Service award Sec. of Navy, 1980. Mem. Met. Club (Washington). Democrat. Roman Catholic. Home: 32 Washington Sq W New York NY 10011-9156

DOYLE, JOSEPH FRANCIS, III, art educator; b. Boston, Jan. 20, 1960; s. Joseph Francis Jr. and Ellen Mary (Hayes) D.; m. Ginger Leigh Davis, Dec. 18, 1993. BFA, Tex. Tech U., 1983, M of Edn., 1990. Coord. elem. art Round Rock (Tex.) Ind. Sch. Dist., 1983-84; art educator Ctrl. High Sch., San Angelo, Tex., 1985-86; art educator, art dept. chmn. Aldine Jr. High Sch., Houston, 1986-92; art educator MacArthur Sr. High, Houston, 1992-99; art educator, dist. dir. arts program Aldine Ind. Sch. Dist., Houston, 1999—; tchr. night high sch. continuing edn. Aldine Ind. Sch. Dist., 1988, chmn. dist. youth art month, sponsor nat. jr. art honor soc., 1989-91, chmn. textbook selection com. elem. art, 1989, chmn. textbook selection com. sr. high art, 1995, mem. dist. tchr. of yr. selection com., 1992-93; insvc. trainer Tex. Arts Coun., Austin, 1991-93; presenter in field. Exhibited in group show Tex. Art Edn. Assn., 1988, 89, Tex. Trends Art Edn., 1989, Nat. Art Edn. Assn., 1990. vol. graphic arts Tex. Spl. Olympics, Houston, 1988-90. Recipient Vol. in People award Sta. K-Lite-FM, 1990; named Houston Post Tchr. of Week, 1992; Disting. Alumnus award Texas Tech. U., 1992. Mem. Nat. Art Edn. Assn. (nat. conv. evaluator jr. high concerns, 1988, Western Region Art Educator of Yr., 1992, Nat. Jr. Art Hon. Soc. Sponcer of the Year, 1993), Tex. Art Edn. Assn. (v.p. youth arts month 1993-95, long range task force com., region VI rep., chmn. reps., insvc. presenter 1985-92, Rising Sun award 1983, Excellence in Art award 1990, Outstanding Art Educator jr. high/mid. sch. divsn. 1991, v.p. youth art month 1992-94, state treas. 1995-98), North Houston Art Edn. Assn. (pres. 1989-92). Roman Catholic. Avocations: swimming, martial arts, music. Home: 1402 Plumwood Dr Houston TX 77014-2668

DOYLE, JOSEPH THEOBALD, physician, educator; b. Providence, June 11, 1918; s. Joseph Donald and Gertrude Harriet (Theobald) D.; m. Elizabeth Thompson, Dec. 26, 1944 (dec.); children: Shelagh Thompson, Michael Kedian; m. Joan Gleason Mastrianni, Dec. 30, 1976. A.B., Harvard U., 1939, M.D., 1943. Successively intern, asst. resident, chief resident in medicine Harvard Med. Service, Boston City Hosp., 1943-44, 47-49; Whitehead fellow in physiology, asst. in medicine and physiology Emory U. Med. Sch., 1950-52; assoc. in medicine Duke U. Med. Sch., 1952; mem. faculty Albany (N.Y.) Med. Coll., 1952—, prof. medicine, 1961—, head div. cardiology, 1961-84, dir. cardiovascular health center, 1952-90, head pvt. diagnostic clinic, 1957-82; cons. Albany VA Med. Center, 1962-1991. Author papers in field. Served as 1st lt. M.C. AUS, 1944-45. Fellow A.C.P., Am. Coll. Cardiology; mem. AMA, Am. Heart Assn. (chmn. council epidemiology 1969-71), Assn. Univ. Cardiologists, N.Y. Heart Assembly (pres. 1968-69), Med. Soc. County of Albany (pres. 1971-72). Presbyterian. Clubs: Ft. Orange, Schuyler Meadows. Home: 17 Lenox Ave Albany NY 12203-2005 Office: Albany Med Coll Albany NY 12208

DOYLE, JUDITH STOVALL, real estate executive, retired; b. Dothan, Ala., Apr. 19, 1940; d. E.H. and Justine (Knowles) Stovall; m. John P. Doyle Jr., Aug. 22, 1964; children: John Patrick III, Michael D., Julie A. Boedicker. BS, Miss. State Coll. for Women, 1961. Tchr. math. Jr. H.S., Gulfport, Miss., 1961-62; asst. dir. dept. pub. rels. SUNY-Buffalo, 1962-64; tchr. math. Jr. H.S., Alexandria, Va., 1964-65, Auburn, N.Y., 1970-71; real estate agent Mosher Real Estate, Auburn, 1972-80, Doyle Real Estate, Auburn, 1991—. Active, past pres. Mercy Aux., Auburn; chairperson Owasco County Bd. Assessment Rev., N.Y., 1976-98; v.p. Sacred Heart Parish Coun., Auburn, 1985-89; bd. dirs. Unity House, Auburn, 1985-87, Cayuga County chpt. ARC, 1998—; mem. membership com. YMCA, Auburn. Mem. Ancient Order Hibernians (charter mem. ladies aux. John F. Kennedy divsn.). Democrat.

DOYLE, JUSTIN EMMETT, lawyer, government official; b. Rochester, N.Y., Aug. 12, 1935; s. Emmett L. and Marion E. (Holihan) D.; m. Deborah Shea, Aug. 26, 1961; children: Christine, Clare, Thomas. BA with honors, U. Rochester, 1957; LLB, Cornell U., 1962. Bar: Calif. 1963, N.Y. 1964. Assoc. Gibson, Dunn & Crutcher, Los Angeles, 1962-64, Harris, Beach, et al, Rochester, N.Y., 1964-68; assoc. Nixon, Hargrave, Devans & Doyle, Rochester, 1968-73, ptnr., 1974-92; atty. U.S. Fgn. Svc., Agy. Internat. Devel., Washington, 1992-93; legal adv. USAID, Cairo, 1993-97; sr. regional legal adv. USAID Regional Ctr. for So. Africa, 1998—. Contbr. tax articles to profl jours.; speaker in field. Served to lt. (j.g.) USN, 1957-59. Recipient Citation for Service Nat. Gov.'s Assn., 1986. Mem. ABA, N.Y. Bar Assn., Calif. Bar Assn., Order of Coif. Republican. Roman Catholic. Club: Tennis of Rochester (Pittsford, N.Y.). Avocations: tennis, skiing, investments, reading. Office: USAID Regional Ctr for So Africa USAID/Botswana Dept State Washington DC 20521-2170

DOYLE, JUSTIN P, lawyer; b. Rochester, N.Y., Oct. 26, 1948; s. Justin Joseph and Jane Martha (Kreag) D.; m. Mary Beth Doyle; children: Mary, Joe. BA, Dartmouth Coll., 1970; JD, Cornell U., 1974. Bar: N.Y. 1974. From assoc. to ptnr. Nixon, Hargrave, Devans & Doyle, Rochester, 1974-99; ptnr. Nixon Peabody LLP (formerly Nixon, Hargrave, Devans & Doyle), Rochester, 1999—. Mem. N.Y. Bar Assn., Monroe County Bar Assn. Home: 252 Overbrook Rd Rochester NY 14618-3648 Office: Nixon Peabody LLP Clinton Sq PO Box 1051 Rochester NY 14603-1051

DOYLE, L. F. BOKER, retired trust company executive; b. N.Y.C., Apr. 23, 1931; Luke Cantwell and Rita (Boker) D.; m. Susanna Stone, Jan. 31, 1959; children: Katharine, Nancy, Victoria, Jessica. BA, Yale U., 1953; postgrad., NYU, 1956-63. 1st v.p., dir., mgr. capital mgmt. dept. Smith Barney & Co., N.Y.C., 1956-74; exec. v.p. Fiduciary Trust Co. Internat., N.Y.C., 1974-83, pres., 1983-94, chmn. exec. com., 1994-96, also dir., 1978-96, cons., 1996; dir. U.S. LIfe Ins. Co., 1996-97. Trustee Margaret Sanger Rsch. Bur., N.Y.C., 1962-68, N.Y.C. Sch. Vol. Program, 1979-90, New Sch. for Social Rsch., N.Y.C., 1983-91, Taconic Found., N.Y.C., 1989—, Hudson River Found., 1997—; trustee, sec. Am. Mus. Natural History, N.Y.C., 1968—; bd. dirs. Cultural Instns. Retirement Sys., N.Y.C., 1971-96, chmn. bd., 1980-96; trustee Nature Cons., N.Y. State, 1990—, chmn., 1993-96; trustee Frick Collection, N.Y.C., 1990, treas., 1992—. 1st lt. USMC, 1953-55. Mem. Century Assn., Anglers Club N.Y. (pres. 1976-77). Avocations: fishing, birding, natural history, conservation, antiques. Home: 315 W 106th St New York NY 10025-3445 Office: Fiduciary Trust Co Internat 2 World Trade Ctr New York NY 10048

DOYLE, LLOYD ALLEN, III, minister; b. Atlanta, Apr. 13, 1962; s. Lloyd Allen Jr. and Betty Glen (Barksdale) D.; m. Mary Clare Golson, May 21, 1988; children: Elizabeth Eileen, Lloyd Allen. BBA, Lambuth Coll., 1984; MDiv, Vanderbilt U., 1988; DMin, Wesley Theol. Sem., 1998. Ordained deacon United Meth. Ch., 1987; elder, 1990. Intern, asst. pastor Tulip St. United Meth. Ch., Nashville, 1986-87; intern chaplain VA Med. Ctr., Nashville, 1987-88; min. Evangelism First United Meth. Ch., Murray, Ky., 1988-90; pastor Cowell's Chapel and Shiloh Ch., Camden, Tenn., 1990-95; pastor First United Meth. Ch., Newbern, Tenn., 1995-99, Waverly, Tenn., 1999—. vice-chair Newbern Emergency Aid Assn., 1995-99; chair Memphis Conf. Comms., 1993-99. Blakemore Trust fellow, 1987-88; Magee Christian Found. grantee, Lake Junaluska, N.C., 1987-88; named one of Outstanding Young Men of Am., Montgomery, Ala., 1990. Mem. Am. Assn. Christian Counselors (charter mem. 1997), Omicron Phi Tau, Kappa Sigma (treas. 1982-84). Office: First United Meth Ch PO Box 247 115 W Main St Waverly TN 37185

DOYLE, MATHIAS FRANCIS, university president, political scientist, educator; b. Malone, N.Y., Nov. 18, 1933; s. Francis J. and Madeline L. (Donnelly) D. B.A., Siena Coll., 1955; M.A., Cath. U. Am., 1965; Ph.D., U. Notre Dame, 1968; diploma, Pres.' Assn. of Am. Mgmt. Assn.; Inst. Edn. Mgmt., Harvard U. Lectr. St. Francis Coll., Rye Beach, N.H., 1963-65; assoc. prof. polit. sci. Siena Coll., Loudonville, N.Y., 1968-75; pres. St. Bonaventure (N.Y.) U., 1975-90, also trustee., prof. polit. sci., 1992—; Adminstr.'s fellow AID, Washington, 1990-92; trustee Commn. on Ind. Colls. and Univs. Contbr. articles periodicals. Trustee Siena Coll. Arthur Schmidt fellow, 1966-68. Mem. Am., Northeastern polit. sci. assns., Pi Gamma Mu, Delta Epsilon Sigma. Roman Catholic. Home: The Friary Saint Bonaventure NY 14778 Office: Saint Bonaventure U Polit Sci Dept Saint Bonaventure NY 14778 *A lifetime spent in education and ministry has taught me how true it is that it is better to give then to receive.*

DOYLE, MICHAEL ANTHONY, lawyer; b. Atlanta, Nov. 4, 1937; s. James Alexander and Wilma (Summersgill) D.; children: John, David, Peter; m. Bernice H. Winter, Nov. 12, 1977. BA, Yale U., 1959, LLB, 1962. Bar: Ga. 1961, D.C. 1967, U.S. Dist. Ct. D.C. 1967, U.S. Dist. Ct. (no. dist.) Ga. 1962, U.S. Ct. Appeals (5th cir.) 1962, U.S. Ct. Appeals (11th cir.) 1982, U.S. Ct. Appeals (D.C. cir.) 1968, U.S. Supreme Ct. 1972, U.S. Ct. Appeals (4th cir.) 1985. Assoc. Alston, Miller & Gaines, Atlanta, 1962-67; ptnr. Alston & Bird, and predecessor, Atlanta, 1967—. Bd. dirs. Atlanta Legal Aid Soc., 1969-84, pres., 1975-76; bd. dirs. Ga. Legal Services Program; mem. Leadership Atlanta, 1974. Served to lt. USNR, 1964-69. Mem. ABA, State Bar Ga., Atlanta Lawyers Club, Master, Bleckley Inn of Court, Assn. Yale Alumni, Yale Law Sch. Assn. (nat. v.p. 1982-85, mem. exec. com. 1978-85, chmn. planning com. 1988-90, pres. 1991-92, chmn. exec. com. 1992-94). Roman Catholic. Clubs: Piedmont Driving, Commerce, Yale of Ga. (pres. 1982-84), Yale of N.Y. Office: Alston & Bird 4200 One Atlantic Ctr 1201 W Peachtree St NW Atlanta GA 30309-3424

DOYLE, MICHAEL F., congressman; b. Swissvale, Pa., Aug. 5, 1953; s. Michael Sr. and Rosemarie (Fusco) D.; m. Susan Erlandson; children: Mike Jr., David, Kevin, Alexandra. BS, Pa. State U., 1975. Exec. dir. Turtle Creek (Pa.) Valley Citizens Union, 1977-79; chief of staff State Sen. Frank Pecora, Harrisburg, Pa., 1979-94; co-founder Eastgate Ins. Agy., Pitts., 1983-94; rep. U.S. House of Reps., Washington, 1995—; mem. sci. com., mem. vets. affairs com.; coun. mem. Swissvale (Pa.) Borough Coun., 1977-81. Active Lions Club, Leadership Pitts., Italian Sons & Daughters of Am. Mem. Nat. Dem. Club. Roman Catholic. Avocations: golf, Italian cooking, piano. Office: US House Reps 133 Cannon House Bldg Washington DC 20515*

DOYLE, MICHAEL JOSEPH, mining executive; b. Eveleth, Minn., Nov. 15, 1928; s. Matthew James and Lucile (McNany) D.; m. Virginia Ethel Britt, Aug. 22, 1953; children: Patricia, Matthew, Michael, Mary Anne, Thomas, Molly, Peter, Robert. BA, U. Minn., Duluth, 1952; JD, U. Minn., Mpls., 1958. Bar: Minn., U.S. Supreme Ct. Labor counsel Pickands Mather & Co., Duluth, 1959-64; asst. dir. labor Hanna Mining Co., Cleve., 1964-69, dir. environ. affairs, 1970-74, dir. govt. affairs, 1975-85; dep. dir. Ariz. Dept. Environ. Quality, Phoenix, 1987-90; pres. Nev. Mining Assn., Reno, 1990—; bus. cons. Doyle & Assocs., Chagrin Falls, 1985-87; Ariz. rep. mine waste task force EPA, Denver, 1988-90. Mem. Nev. Natural Resource Adv. Bd., Carson City, 1993—; mem. bus. and mining schs. adv. bd. U. Nev., Reno, 1992—; Nev. rep. Grand Canyon Visibility Transport Commn., Denver, 1993-96. Mem. Carlton Club (Washington). Avocations: family activities, golf. Home: 11735 E Chama Rd Scottsdale AZ 85255-5908

DOYLE, MICHAEL PATRICK, food microbiologist, educator, administrator; b. Madison, Wis., Oct. 3, 1949; s. Donald Vincent and Evelyn (Bauer) D.; m. Annette Marie Ripple, Dec. 27, 1971; children: Michael Patrick, Patrick Matthew, Kristen Anne. BS in Bacteriology, U. Wis., 1973, MS in Food Microbiology, 1975, PhD in Food Microbiology, 1977. Sr. project leader Ralston Purina Co., St. Louis, 1977-80; asst. prof. U. Wis., Madison, 1980-84, assoc. prof., 1984-88, prof., 1988-91; prof., dir. U. Ga., Griffin, 1991—; dept. head U. Ga., Athens, 1993—; Regents prof. Bd. Regents Ga. U. Sys., 1997—; mem. food and nutrition bd. Inst. Medicine, NAS, 1991-97, com. to ensure safe food from prodn. to consumption, 1998; mem. nat. adv. com. on microbiol. criteria for foods USDA, Washington, 1988-90, 94—; trustee Internat. Life Scis. Inst.-N.Am., Washington, 1992—, sci. advisor, 1987-96; mem. Internat. Commn. on Microbiol. Specifications for Foods, 1989—; Wis. disting. prof. bd. regents U. Wis., Madison, 1988-91; James M. Craig meml. lectr. Oreg. State U., Corvallis, 1990; sci. lectr. Am. Soc. Microbiology Found., 1991-93; Peter J. Shields lectr. U. Calif., Davis, 1993 G. Malcolm Trout vis. scholar Mich. State U., Lansing, 1994; mem. sci. adv. coun. The Refrigeration Rsch. and Edn. Found., 1997—; York Disting. lectr. Auburn U., 1999. Editor: Food Microbiology: Fundamentals and Frontiers, 1997, Foodborne Bacterial Pathogens, 1989; contbr. articles to Applied and Environ. Microbiology, Jour. Food Protection, Internat. Jour. Food Microbiology, Jour. Clin. Microbiology. Recipient Am. Agrl. Econs. Assn. award for profl. excellence, 1992, Silver Plow Honor award for Exceptional Svc. USDA, 1998. Fellow Internat. Assn. Milk, Food and Environ. Sanitarians, Inst. of Food Technologists, Am. Acad. Microbiology; mem. Internat. Assn. Milk, Food and Environ. Sanitarians (pres. 1992-93, Norbert F. Sherman article excellence award 1993), Am. Soc. for Microbiology (chmn. food microbiology divsn. 1987-89, P.R. Edwards award for outstanding career achievements 1994), Inst. Food Technologists (Fred. W. Tanner lectr. 1986, sci. lectr. 1987-90, Samuel Cate Prescott award for rsch. 1987, Nicholas Appert award for preeminence in and contbns. to field of food tech. 1996), Phi Kappa Phi, Gamma Sigma Delta. Roman Catholic. Achievements include patent for monoclonal antibody to enterohemorrhagic E. coli; development of methods to control and detect foodborne pathogens. Office: U Ga Ctr Food Safety Quality Enhancement Ga Expt Sta 1109 Experiment St Griffin GA 30223

DOYLE, MICHAEL W., think-tank executive. PhD, Harvard U. Prof. Politics and Internat. Affairs Woodrow Wilson Sch. Pub. and Internat. Affairs, Princeton U., Princeton, N.J.; dir. Ctr. of Internat. Studies Woodrow Wilson Sch. Pub. and Internat. Affairs, Princeton U.; mem. adv. coms. UN High Commr. for Refugees, Lessons Learned Unit, UN Dept. Peacekeeping Ops. Author: Empires: UN Peacekeeping in Cambodia and Ways of War and Peace; co-author: Alternatives to Monetary Disorder; co-editor: Escalation and Intervention, Keeping the Peace and Peacemaking and Peacekeeping for the Next Century. Office: Woodrow Wilson Sch Princeton U Princeton NJ 08544-1013*

DOYLE, NORMAN E., member of Canadian parliament; b. Avondale, Nfld., Can., Nov. 11, 1945; m. Isabelle Hannifan, 1968; children: Dion, Randy. Cert. proficiency in broadcasting, Toronto, 1971. Constrn. worker Nfld./N.Y., 1974-71; broadcaster CFLW-Radio, Wabush, Labrador, Nfld., 1971-73; pvt. businessman Avondale, Nfld., 1973-79; mem. Ho. of Assembly for Harbour Main-Bell Island Can., 1979-93; ret., 1993; M.P. for St. John's East Ho. of Commons, Can., 1997—; parliamentary asst. to Premier A. Brian Peckford, 1981-82; min. responsible for comm., 1982-84, min. mcpl. affairs, 1984-87, min. transp., 1987-89, min. of labor, 1989, opposition party whip, 1989-93, opposition critic health & environment and lands, 1989-93; dep. PC Party whip, 1997; party critic for citizenship and immigration, 1997. Fax: (613) 992-2178. E-mail: doylen@parl.gc.ca. Office: House of Commons, Rm 212, Confederation Bldg, Ottawa, ON Canada K1A 0A6*

DOYLE, O'BRIEN JOHN, JR., emergency medical services consultant, lobbyist, writer; b. Detroit, July 31, 1950; s. O'Brien John Doyle Sr.; m. Sue Ann Woulf, Sept. 6, 1980; children: Catherine Ann, Colleen Elizabeth. Student, Mich. State U., 1970-72; paramedic cert., Vo-Tech. Coll., St. Paul, 1980-81; BA in Human Svcs., Metro State U., St. Paul, 1986. Exec. asst. Mich. Legislature, Lansing, 1972-77; com. aide Ill. Gen. Assembly, Chgo., 1977-79; spl. asst. Gov. Minn., St. Paul, 1979-82; ops. dir. Divine Redeemer Ambulance, South St. Paul, Minn., 1982-84; mktg. dir. Health One Transp., St. Paul, 1984-86; pres. Doyle Consulting, Apple Valley, Minn., 1986—; gen. ptnr., sec. Great Plains EMS, Inc., 1996—; legis. cons. Health Span Transp., Mpls., 1986—, Minn. Ambulance Assn., Mpls., 1986, 91-92, Minn. Hosp. Assn., Mpls., 1991, Mayo Med. Ctr., 1995—, Minn. Air Med. Coun., 1995—, Minn. chpt. Am. Coll. of Emergency Physicians, 1996—; candidate for state senate, 1988; chair Minn. EMS Adv. Task force, 1989; instr. Inver Hills C.C., South St. Paul, Minn.; lectr. U. St. Thomas, Mpls. Contbg. editor Trade Jours, 1992—; pub. Capitol Update, 1986—, Rule Promulgation in Michigan, 1973; EMS contbr. to Fed. EMS Efficiency Act, 1993-95; columnist Jour. Emergency Med. Svcs. Adv. 916 Vocat. Coll., White Bear Lake, Minn., 1989—; state chair Young Republican League of Minn., 1981. Mem. Citizens League, Osman Shrine, Scottish Rite. Roman Catholic. Avocations: archaeology, scuba diving. Home and Office: 12893 Floral Ave Apple Valley MN 55124-7971

DOYLE, PATRICK JOHN, otolaryngologist; b. Moose Jaw, Sask., Can., Nov. 17, 1926; s. William E. and Bertha L. (Fisher) D.; m. Irene Strilchuk, May 21, 1949; children: Sharon, Patrick, Robert, Barbara, Joseph, Kathleen. B.Sc., U. Alta., 1947, M.D., 1949. Diplomate Am. Bd. Otolaryngology (bd. dirs., v.p. 1986-88, pres. 1988-90). Intern U. B.C. Hosp., 1949-50; resident in medicine and pediatrics, 1950-51; resident in otolaryngology U. Oreg. Hosp., 1958-61; asst. prof., then assoc. prof. U. Oreg. Med. Sch., 1965-70; mem. faculty U. B.C. Med. Sch., 1963—, prof. otolaryngology, 1972-91, prof. otolaryngology emeritus, 1992—, head dept., 1972-91, program dir. residency tng. program, 1972-91; head div. otolaryngology St. Paul's Hosp., mem. numerous nat. med. coms. Author numerous articles in field; mem. editorial bds. profl. jours. Fellow Royal Coll. Surgeons Can., Am. Laryngol., Rhinol. and Otol. Soc. (v.p. western sect. 1988, pres. 1994), Am. Laryngol. Soc., Am. Acad. Otolaryngology-Head and Neck Surgery (v.p. 1984, bd. dirs. 1985-87), Am. Otol. Soc.; mem. Can. Soc. Otolaryngology-Head and Neck Surgery (pres. 1987), Pacific Coast Oto-Ophthal. Soc. (pres. 1977), Soc. Univ. Otolaryngologists, U. Oreg. Otolaryngology Alumni Assn. (pres. 1968-70), Am. Otological Soc., Centurion Club, Tinnitus Rsch. Found. Roman Catholic. Office: 150-809 W 41st Ave, Vancouver, BC Canada V5Z 2N6

DOYLE, PATRICK LEE, retired insurance company executive; b. Pitts., July 17, 1929; s. Lee Patrick and Anne Louise (Stattmilller) D.; m. Ann Marie Yuhasz, Apr. 26, 1952; children: Robert Christopher, Patrick Brian, David Alan. BA, Ohio State U., 1951. CPCU, Am. Inst. Property Casualty Underwriters CLU Assoc. in Risk Mgmt., Ins. Inst. Am. Life reins. mgr. Nationwide Ins. Cos., Columbus, Ohio, 1965-70, asst. to pres., 1970-79, v.p., adminstrv. asst. to pres., 1980-81, v.p. human resources, 1981-82, v.p. Office Gen. Chmn., 1982-94; instr. Ohio State U., Columbus, 1969-82, Franklin U., Columbus, 1973-82; mem. exam. com. CPCU, Am. Inst. for Property and Liability Underwriters, Phila., 1969-94; trustee Griffith Found. for Ins. Edn., Columbus, 1975—. Bd. dirs. Cath. Social Svcs., Columbus, 1981-87, St. Stephen's Cmty. House, 1989-94; trustee Kinder Key, 1973—. Mem. Ins. Inst. Am., Soc. CPCU (ednl. dir. 1965-72, Outstanding Educator award), Soc. CLU, Soc. Ins. Research (dir. 1976-79), Gamma Iota Sigma. Republican. Roman Catholic. Home: 2334 Cob Tail Way Blacklick OH 43004-9569

DOYLE, PAUL FRANCIS, lawyer; b. N.Y.C., Sept. 3, 1946; s. Paul Francis and Rita Lilian (Mulcahy) D.; m. Margaret Mary Sullivan, Aug. 23, 1969; children: Karen, Lynn. BA in English, Holy Cross Coll., 1968; JD cum laude, NYU, 1973. Bar: Mass. 1973, N.Y. 1975, U.S. Dist. Ct. (so. and ea. dists.) N.Y. 1975, U.S. Ct. Appeals (2d and 3d cirs.) 1975, U.S. Supreme Ct. 1991, U.S. Dist. Ct. Mass. 1992, U.S. Dist. Ct. (no. dist.) N.Y. 1995. Law clk. Superior Ct. Commonwealth of Mass., Boston, 1973-74; assoc. Kelley, Drye & Warren, N.Y.C., 1974-82, ptnr., 1983—; instr. Nat. Inst. of Trial Advocacy, 1994-95. Assoc. editor Ann. Survey Am. Law, 1972-73. Mem. Planning Bd., Croton-on-Hudson, N.Y., 1989-92; mem. pres.'s coun. Holy Cross Coll. With U.S. Army, 1968-70, Vietnam. Mem. Am. Inns of Ct., Order of Coif. Roman Catholic. Office: Kelley Drye & Warren 101 Park Ave New York NY 10178-0002

DOYLE, REBECCA CARLISLE, state agency administrator; m. Ken Doyle; children: Eric, Ben. BS, U. Ill., 1975, MS, 1977. Pvt. practice Ill.; dir. Ill. Agriculture Dept., Springfield, 1991—. Mem. Internat. Agriculture Mgmt. Assn., Nat. Assn. State Depts. Agriculture (officer), Mid-Am. Internat. Agri-Trade Council (officer), Women Execs. State Govt. Office: Illinois Dept Agriculture State Fairgrounds PO Box 19281 Springfield IL 62794-9281

DOYLE, RICHARD HENRY, IV, lawyer; b. Elgin, Ill., Aug. 8, 1949; s. Richard Henry and Shirley Marian (Ohms) D.; m. Debbie Kay Cahalan, Aug. 2, 1975; children: John Richard, Kerry Jane. BA, Drake U., 1971, JD, 1976. Bar: Iowa 1976, U.S. Dist. Ct. (no. and so. dists.) Iowa 1977, U.S. Ct. Appeals (8th cir.) 1977, U.S. Supreme Ct. 1986. Asst. atty. gen. Iowa Dept. Justice, Des Moines, 1976-77; assoc. Lawyer, Lawyer & Jackson, Des Moines, 1977-79; assoc. Law Offices of Verne Lawyer & Assocs., Des Moines, 1979-93, Reavely, Shinkle, Bauer, Scism, Reavely & Doyle, Des Moines, 1993, Michael J. Galligan Law Firm, P.C., Des Moines, 1994-96. Contbr. articles to profl. jours. With U.S. Army, 1971-73. Fellow Iowa Acad. Trial Lawyers; mem. ABA, ATLA, Iowa Trial Lawyers Assn., Iowa Bar Assn., Iowa State Bar Assn., Polk County Bar Assn., SAR (registrar Iowa 1983-94, v.p. 1994-97, chancellor 1997-99), Order of the Founders and Patriots of Am., Phi Alpha Delta (chpt. pres. 1975). Home: 532 Waterbury Cir Des Moines IA 50312-1316 Office: Galligan Tully Doyle & Reid PC The Plaza 300 Walnut St Ste 5 Des Moines IA 50309-2239

DOYLE, RICHARD JAMES, retired Canadian senator, former editor; b. Toronto, Ont., Can., Mar. 10, 1923; s. James Andrew and Lillian Gibson (Hilts) D.; m. Florence Chanda, Jan. 27, 1952; children: Kathleen Judith, Sean Gibson. City editor Chatham (Ont.) Daily News, 1940-51; mem. staff Globe and Mail, Toronto, 1951—; mng. editor Globe and Mail, 1959-63, editor, 1963-78, editor-in-chief, 1978-83, editor emeritus, 1983-85; mem. Can. Senate, Ottawa, Ont., 1985—; Dir. Michener Found. Author: Royal Story, 1952, Hurly-Burly: A Time at the Globe, 1990. Served with RCAF, World War II. Named to Canadian News Hall of Fame, 1990. Office: Senate of Can, Senate Rm 568-S, Ottawa, ON Canada K1A 0A4*

DOYLE, TOM, sculptor, retired educator; b. Jerry City, Ohio, May 23, 1928; s. John Thomas and Kathleen (Solether) D.; m. Natalie N. Burdette (div. 1957); m. Eva Hesse (dec. 1970); m. Jane Miller. Student, Miami U., Oxford, Ohio, 1948-50; BFA, Ohio State U., 1952, MFA, 1953. Sculptor N.Y.C., to date; artist-in-residence La Napoule Art Found., France, 1989. One-man shows include Dwan Gallery, N.Y.C., 1966, 67, 55 Mercer Gallery, N.Y.C., 1972, 74, 76, Picker Art Gallery, Colgate U., Hamilton, N.Y., 1976, Sculpture Now, Inc., N.Y.C., 1978, The Sculpture Ctr., N.Y.C., 1988, Bill Bace Gallery, N.Y.C., 1991, 93-94, Long House Found., East Hampton, N.Y., 1995, Mattatuck Mus., Waterbury, Conn., 1996, Kouros Gallery, N.Y.C., 1999; exhibited in group shows at Whitney Mus., N.Y.C., 1967, Los Angeles County Mus., 1967, Taft Mus., Cin., 1974, Indpls. Mus. Art, 1974. Recipient commendation GSA, Fairbanks, Alaska, 1980, Jimmy Ernst Lifetime Art Achievement award AAAL, 1994, Ohioana Career award for Lifetime Achievement, 1996; Guggenheim fellow, 1982, Nat. Endowment for the Arts fellow, 1990-91; rsch. grantee CUNY, 1989-90. Mem. Am. Abstract Artists.

DOYLE, WENDELL E., retired band director, educator; b. Higbee, Mo., July 8, 1940; s. Travis E. and Hattie Erma (Webb) D.; m. Julia Ann Vail, June 23, 1963; children: Dora Michelle, Michael E., Melissa Kae. BS in Edn., Northeast Mo. State U., 1962; MEd in Music, U. Mo., 1967. Cert. lifetime tchr., Mo. Band dir. Braymer (Mo.) C-4, 1962-68, Brookfield (Mo.) R-3, 1968-72, Platte County (Mo.) R-III, 1972-92; ret., 1992; exchange tchr. Platte County R-III Schs., Warwickshire, Eng., 1984. Pres. Barry Heights Homes Assn., 1986—; minister of music Park Bapt. Ch., Brookfield, 1968-72, Northgate Bapt. Ch., Kansas City, 1972-85. Mem. Mo. State Tchrs. Assn. (pres. Greater Kans. City dist. 1978), Music Educators Nat. Conf., Mo. Music Educators Assn., Mo. Bandmasters Assn. (sec.), Phi Delta Kappa, Phi Beta Mu (pres. 1990-91, Outstanding Band Dir. award Lambda chpt., 1993), Mo. Bardmasters Assn. (Hall of Fame 1997), Rotary (sec., treas. Braymer, Mo. 1966-68). Democrat. Lodge: Rotary (sec. treas. Braymer, Mo., 1966-68). Avocations: fishing, reading, golfing, travel. Home: 2330 NW Powderhorn Dr Kansas City MO 64154-1311

DOYLE, WILLIAM JAY, II, business consultant; b. Cin., Nov. 7, 1928; s. William Jay and Blanche (Gross) D.; m. Joan Lucas, July 23, 1949; children: David L., William Jay, III, Daniel L. *Father William Jay Doyle was a well-known heating and ventilating design engineer who held numerous pivotal patents in the early HVAC field including the inventor of The Coloric Pipeless Furnace, early clothes dryer and pioneering casting technology. His early research on smoke pollution was acclaimed at the Chicago World Exposition in 1933. He was apprenticed to a pattern maker after the third grade and supplemented this with two decades of engineering education. This resulted in certificates in mechanical, metallurgical and chemical engineering. Son David Lawrence Doyle, BS 1972, Miami University, JD Emory 1975, MBA Chicago 1981 is a well-known Chicago litigator.* BS, Miami U., Oxford, Ohio, 1949; postgrad., U. Cin., 1950-51, Xavier U., 1953-54, Case Western Res. U., 1959-60. Sales rep. Diebold, Inc., Cin., 1949-52, asst. br. mgr., 1953-57, asst. regional mgr., 1957-62, regional mgr., 1962-74; founder, pres. CEO Ctrl. Bus. Group, Cin., 1974-89, chmn., 1989-95, ret., 1995; mem. area contractor's coun. Spacesaver Corp., 1985-89; speaker on bus systems, security concepts. Developer new concepts in tng., cash and securities handling, mobile and mechanized storage and filing. Mem. Armstrong Chapel, Methodist ch., Indian Hill, Ohio. Mem. Bus. Systems and Sales Mgmt. Assn. (nat. bd. dirs. 1977-79, 81-85, pres. 1981-83, 84-85), Inst. of Mgmt. Accts., Ivy Hills Country Club, Masons, Shriners. Republican. Home: 1110 Roseate Ct Bradenton FL 34209-7364

DOYLE, WILLIAM LYNN, fundraising consultant; b. Lanette, Ala., Feb. 1, 1941; s. Leon Hurston and Olla Belle (DeMoss) D.; m. Helen Ruth Reedy, June 16, 1960; children: Dondi Karen, Jay Allen. BA, U. Ark., 1970; grad., Nat. Planned Giving Inst., Memphis, 1990, Exec. Leadership Inst., Indpls., 1991. Owner pvt. bus., Little Rock, Ark., 1962-76; regional dir. March of Dimes, Little Rock, 1976-82; sr. cons. CSB, Inc., Dallas, 1982-88; pres. Holston Valley Heath Care Found., Kingsport, Tenn., 1988-93; exec. dir. Candler Hosp. Found., Savannah, Ga., 1994-96, Diabetes Trust Fund, Inc., 1996-97; mng. ptnr. Am. Fund Raising Inst., 1997—; lectr., seminars Am. Fund Raising Inst., Estate Planning Coun., NSFRE; served on many bds. for seniors, children, various disadvantaged. Publ. Fundraising 101, 1993, Fund Raising Idea, 1995, over 100 how-to booklets; contbr. articles to profl. jours. Past pres. North Hills Jaycees, Pulaski County Young Reps., Mountain Empire Nat. Soc. Fund Raising Execs.; mem. Tri-Cities Estate Planning Coun.; bd. dirs. Roller-Russ Home for the Handicapped; coord. Campaign for Children's Advocacy Ctr., Mt. Region Speech and Hearing. With USAF, 1958-62. Named Outstanding Local Pres. Ark. Jaycees, Sherwood, 1976; Paul Harris Harris fellow Rotary Internat. Mem. Assn. Healthcare Philanthropy (1st place awards 1989-91). Republican. Roman Catholic. Avocations: writing, flying, speaking, organizing fund raising events. Office: Am Fund Raising Inst 7004 Comanche Dr North Little Rock AR 72116-4410

DOYLE, WILLIAM STOWELL, venture capitalist; b. Lowell, Mich., Aug. 14, 1944; s. William Stowell and Eunice Jane D.; m. Permele Elliott Frischkorn, Jan. 7, 1978; children: William Elliott, Permele Crawford. AB, Duke U., 1966. Copywriter Wallace-Blakeslee, Grand Rapids, Mich., 1966-68; dir. mktg. Wolverine Worldwide, Rockford, Mich., 1971-73; v.p., dir. mktg. Chase Manhattan Bank, N.Y.C., also London, Hong Kong, 1973-76, 79-82; pres. Doyle Graf Mabley, 1982-89, Ecomarine Inc., N.Y.C., 1989-92, Strategen, N.Y.C., 1992-95; pres., CEO Taishan Holdings Inc., 1995—; chmn. Taishan Pharms Ltd., Beijing, 1997—, PhytoMedica Pharms. Inc., 1999—. Contbr. articles to profl. jours. Dep. commr. State of N.Y. Dept. Commerce, Albany, 1976-79; bd. dirs. Naturade Inc., L.A., Nat. Meals-on-Wheels Found., Washington; assoc. bd. dirs. Julliard Sch., N.Y.C. With USAF, 1968-69; 1st lt. U.S. Army, 1969-71. Mem. Internat. Inst. Strategic Studies (London), Racquet and Tennis Club (N.Y.C.), Union Club (N.Y.C.). Anglican. Office: 885 3rd Ave Ste 2900 New York NY 10022-4834

DOYLE, WILLIAM THOMAS, retired newspaper editor; b. Oakland, Calif., May 22, 1925; s. Albert Norman and Catherine (Stein) D.; m. Claire Louise Wogan, Sept. 1, 1946 (dec. Nov. 10, 1984); children: Patrick, Lawrence, Brian, Carrie; m. Mary M. Doren, May 3, 1986. B.Journalism, U. Nev., 1950. Reporter Richmond (Calif.) Independent, 1950-53; reporter Oakland Tribune, 1953-62, asst. state editor, 1962-64, telegraph editor, 1964-67, fin. editor, 1967-79; editor San Francisco Bus. Jour., 1979-81; news dir. Fireman's Fund Ins. Cos., Novato, Calif., 1981-84; mng. editor West County Times, Pinole, Calif., 1984-88. Mem. editorial adv. bd.: Catholic Voice. Pres. Richmond Jr. C. of C., 1957-58; bd. dirs. Cath. Social Svc. Contra Costa County, Calif., 1959-62, Bay Area Coop. Edn. Clearing House, 1977-88, Contra Costa Coll. Found., 1984-88, Richmond Unified Edn. Fund, 1984, Am. Cancer Soc.—West Contra Costa, 1986-96; mem. Richmond Schs. Citizens Adv. Com., 1969; pastoral coun. St. David's Cath. Ch., Richmond, 1994—. With USAAF, 1943-45. Recipient award for best financial sect. daily newspaper Calif., Calif. Newspaper Pubs. Assn., 1968, 70, 72, 74, Knowland award for outstanding performance, 1972, Gen. Excellence award Nat. Newspaper Assn., 1987, Outstanding Editorial Writing award Suburban Newspapers Assn., 1989, 90, 1st Place award for editorial writing Nat. Newspaper Assn., 1992; Hughes fellow Rutgers U., 1969. Mem. Soc. Am. Bus. Writers, Marine Exchange San Francisco Bay Area, Sigma Delta Chi. Clubs: Contra Costa (Calif.); Press (Best News Story award 1965) (pres. 1956), Serra of West Contra Costa. Home: 2727 Del Monte Ave El Cerrito CA 94530-1507 Office: West County Times 4301 Lakeside Dr Richmond CA 94806-5281

DOYLE-KIMBALL, MARY, freelance writer, editor; b. Chgo., June 17, 1954; d. Warren J. and Violet M. (Stohl) Doyle; m. David Kimball, Dec. 1, 1979; children: Elizabeth, Henry. BSBA, Georgetown U., 1976. Editor, writer WTOP Radio, Washington, 1976-80; freelance columnist Miami (Fla.) Herald, 1984-96; 1st editor Fla. Design Mag., 1990-95; freelance writer, 1990—; exec. dir. Nat. Assn. Real Estate Editors, Boca Raton, Fla., 1995—. Contbr. to L.A. Times, San Diego Union Tribune, Chgo. Sun Times, San Francisco Examiner, The Oregonian, Seattle Times, Builder Mag. Address: 1003 NW 6th Ter Boca Raton FL 33486-3455

DOYNO, VICTOR ANTHONY, literature educator; b. Chgo., July 12, 1937; s. Victor A. and Sally B. (Finnegan) D.; m. Ellen Joyce Kuchar, Aug. 22, 1959; children: David, Kenneth, Anna. BA, Miami U. of Ohio, 1959; MA, Harvard U., 1960; PhD, U. Ind., 1966. Instr. Rutgers U., New Brunswick, N.J., 1963-64, Princeton U., 1964-65; prof. SUNY, Buffalo, 1966—. Editor: Mark Twain: American Skeptic, 1985, Adventures of Huck Finn, 1996, Random House Huck, 1996, Oxford Huck, 1998; author: Writing Huck Finn, 1992. Recipient Gov.'s award N.Y. Gov. Cuomo, 3 tchg. awards. Office: English Dept SUNY at Buffalo 306 Clemens Buffalo NY 14260

DOZIER, DAVID CHARLES, JR., marketing public relations and advertising executive; b. Santa Fe, Dec. 4, 1938; s. David Charles Sr. and Zelma (Martin) D.; m. Dianne Flusche, June 1, 1960; children: Deborah, Mary Rebecca, Michael, Constance. BA, U. Dallas, 1960. Editor sports Tex. Catholic, Dallas, 1960-70, gen. sales mgr., 1964-70; dir. classified advt. Dallas Times Herald, 1970-74; pres., chmn. DBG&H Unltd. Inc., Dallas, 1974-88; chmn. Dozier Co., Dallas, 1989—; innovator, ptnr. Navi Pesanda Indian Blanket Creations, 1992. Author: A Compendium of Endurance, 1989. Mem. Am. Indian, Santa Clara Pueblo Tribe, N.Mex.; cert. athletic trainer Downtown YMCA, 1990-99. Recipient Disting. Svc. award Pres. U.S. and HUD, 1984. Republican. Roman Catholic. Avocation: completed over 110 marathons. Home: 7102 Wabash Cir Dallas TX 75214-3532 Office: 2021 Farrington Dallas TX 75207

DOZIER, JAMES LEE, former army officer; b. Arcadia, Fla., Apr. 10, 1931; s. Joseph B. and Leota (Caruthers) D.; m. Judith I. Stimpson, June 30, 1956; children—Cheryl Lyn, Scott Lee. B.S., U.S. Mil. Acad., 1956; M.S. in Aerospace Engring., U. Ariz., 1964. Commd. 2d lt. U.S. Army, 1956, advanced through grades to maj. gen., 1984; comdr. 1st Squadron, 1st Cav., 1st Armored Div. U.S. Army, Germany, 1971-73; staff officer Office of Dep. Chief of Staff for Research, Devel. and Acquisition U.S. Army, Washington, 1974-76, also mil. asst. to asst. sec. of army, 1974-76; comdr. 2d Brigade, 2d Armored div. U.S. Army, Fort Hood, Tex., 1976-78, chief of staff 2d Armored div., 1978-79, chief of staff III Corps and Ft. Hood, 1979-80; dep. chief of staff logistics and adminstrn. Allied Land Forces So. Europe U.S. Army, Verona, Italy, 1980-82; asst. comdt. Armor Sch. U.S. Army, Ft. Knox, Ky., 1982-83; dep. comdg. gen. III Corps and Fort Hood U.S. Army, Fort Hood, Tex., 1983-85; ret. U.S. Army, 1985; pres. Golden Grove Mgmt. Corp., Arcadia, Fla., 1985-87, Suncoast Media Group, Venice, Fla., 1987; gen. mgr. David C. Brown Enterprises, 1988-93; owner JCS Group, Ft. Myers, 1993—; lectr., condr. seminars on kidnapping experience. Contbg. author: Winter of Fire, 1990; contbr. articles to mil. jours. Decorated Silver Star, Legion of Merit, Bronze Star with V device and 2 oak leaf clusters, Air medals, Purple Heart. Avocations: fishing; boating; gardening; woodworking.

DOZIER, NANCY KERNS, retired geriatrics nurse; b. Akron, Ohio, May 31, 1930; d. Guy F. and Alma Jane (Good) Kerns; 1 child, Frederick A. Dietz. AAA, Prince George C.C., 1972; student, Catonsville (Md.) Coll., 1976, Catonsville (Md.) Coll., 1978. RN, Ohio, Fla., Md.; cert. in basic and advanced coronary care. Med.-surg., orthopedic staff nurse Childrens Hosp., Balt., 1973-74; nurse med. surg. flr. Bon Secours Hosp., Balt., 1974-76; staff nurse Md. State Maximum Security Penal Inst., Jessup, 1977-78, Bonifay (Fla.) Nursing Home, 1985-86; staff float nurse UpJohn Health Care Svcs. U. Md. Hosp. Balt., 1979-81; charge, treatment nurse Monticello (Fla.) Nursing Home, 1983; supr. Estes Nursing Home (Beverly Enterprises), Tallahassee, 1984; with Campbellton-Graceville Hosp., 1984-85, Sun City (Fla.) Med. Ctr. Hosp., 1986; supr. Ponce De Leon Care Ctr., St. Augustine, Fla., 1987-88; charge nurse Graceville (Fla.) Hosp., 1984; charge, patients care plans nurse U. Nursing Care Ctr., Gainesville, Fla., 1988-90.

DRABBLE, MARGARET, writer; b. Sheffield, England, June 5, 1939; d. John Frederick and Kathleen Marie (Bloor) D.; m. Clive Swift, June 27, 1960 (div. 1975); children: Adam, Rebecca, Joseph; m. Michael Holroyd, 1982. BA with honors, Newnham Coll., Cambridge, 1960; DLitt (hon.), U. Sheffield, 1976, U. Manchester, 1987, U. Keele, 1988, U. Bradford, 1988, U. East Anglia, 1994, U. York, 1995. Author: (novels) A Summer Bird-Cage, 1963, The Garrick Year, 1964, The Millstone, 1965 (John Llewelyn Rhys Meml. award 1966), Jerusalem the Golden, 1967 (James Tait Black Meml. book prize 1968), The Waterfall, 1969, The Needle's Eye, 1972 (Yorkshire Post Book of Yr. award 1972), The Realms of Gold, 1975, The Ice Age, 1977, The Middle Ground, 1980 (ALA notable book citation 1981), The Radiant Way, 1987, A Natural Curiosity, 1989, Gates of Ivory, 1991, The Witch of Exmoor, 1996, Angus Wilson: A Biography, 1995; (short stories) Hassan's Tower, 1966, The Reunion, 1968, The Gifts of War, 1970; (nonfiction) Arnold Bennett, A Biography, 1974, For Queen and Country: Britain in the Victorian Age, 1978, A Writer's Britain, 1979; (play) Bird of Paradise, 1969; (screenplays) Laura, 1964, Isadora, 1968, Thank You All Very Much, 1969; (criticism) Wordsworth, 1966; editor: Jane Austen, Lady Susan, The Watsons, and Sanditon, 1975, The Genius of Thomas Hardy, 1976, Oxford Companion to English Literature, 1985, The Concise Oxford Companion to English Literature, 1987, Angus Wilson a Biography, 1995. Recipient E.M. Forster award Natl. Inst. and Am. Acad. of Arts and Letters, 1973. Office: care Peters Fraser & Dunlop, S/Chambers Chelsea Harbor Lots Rd, London SW10-0XF, England

DRABEK, DOUG (DOUGLAS DEAN DRABEK), baseball player; b. Victoria, Tex., July 25, 1962; m. Kristy Drabek; children: Justin, Kyle. Student, U. Houston. Baseball player Chgo. White Sox, 1983-84, 97, N.Y. Yankees, 1984-86, Pitts. Pirates, 1986-92, Houston Astros, 1992-96, Balt. Orioles, 1997-98. Active in community relations. Winner Cy Young award Baseball Writers' Assn. Am., 1990; named Nat. League Pitcher of Yr., Sporting News, 1990; named to Nat. League All-Star Team, 1994, Sporting News Nat. League All-Star Team, 1990. *

DRABINSKY, GARTH HOWARD, entertainment company executive; b. Toronto, Ont., Can., Oct. 27, 1949; s. Philip and Ethel (Waldman) D.; m. Pearl Kaplan, June 22, 1971; children: Alicia, Marc. LLB, U. Toronto, 1973; LLD, U. B.C., 1995; DLitt, York U., 1995. Chmn. Livent Inc., Toronto, 1989-98; ptnr. Drabinsky and Friedland Galleries; bd. dirs. Mt. Sinai Hosp., Hollinger Inc.; mem. adv. bd. Ctr. for Rsch. in Neurodegenerative Diseases U. Toronto. Author: Motion Pictures and the Arts in Canada: The Business and the Law, 1976; co-author: (autobiography) Closer to the Sun; prod. The Phantom of the Opera, Toronto, 1988—, Kiss of the Spider Woman, Joseph and the Amazing Technicolor Dreamcoat, Show Boat, Sunset Boulevard, Aspects of Love, The Music of Andrew Lloyd Webber in Concert, Ragtime, The Musical; prodr. Parade and Fosse, A Celebration in Song and Dance. Founder United Way, The Tomorrow Fund, 1995, Downtown Place Com., Vancouver, 1995, B'nai B'rith Internat. Garth H. Drabinsky Lecture Series, 1989. Officer Order of Can., 1995; recipient Chetwynd award for entrepreneurial achievement Can. Film and TV Assn., 1986, award for mktg. excellence Am. Mktg. Assn., 1986, lifetime achievement award Can. Calif. C. of C., 1987, Vanier award for outstanding contbn. to bus. of filmaking in Can. award Air Can., 1987, ShoWest award Nat. Assn. Theatre Owners, 1988, Arts and Letters award Can. Club N.Y., 1994; named Renaissance Man of Film, Montreal World Film Festival, 1987, Tourism Man of Yr., Tourism Industry Assn., Can., 1994; hon. fellow Ryerson Poly. Inst., 1987, York U. Faculty Fine Arts, Toronto. Mem. Acad. Motion Picture Arts and Scis., Acad. Can. Cinema and TV, Can. Picture Pioneers, Can. Tourism Commn., Founder's Coun. of the Can. Film Ctr., Variety Club Ont. Office: 113 DuPont St Ste 101, Toronto, ON Canada M5R 1V4

DRABISKA, FRANK JOHN, priest, parochial school educator; b. Ellwood, Pa., Oct. 7, 1950; s. Martin and Eugenia (Galat) D. BA in Philosophy, Duquesne U., 1972; MDiv, St. Francis Coll., 1976; MS in Edn., Duquesne U., 1996. Ordained priest Roman Cath. Ch., 1976. Pastor Diocese of Pitts., 1976—, master catechist, 1982—. Roman Catholic. Home and Office: 7446 Mcclure Ave Pittsburgh PA 15218-2339

DRABKIN, CATHERINE LENORE, painter, educator; b. New Haven, Dec. 4, 1959; d. Irving Leo and Lenore Hannah (Hirshfeld) D. Student, Amherst Coll., 1978; BFA, Md. Inst. Coll. Art, Balt., 1982; MFA, Queens Coll./SUNY, 1985. Adj. lectr. Queens Coll./SUNY, 1987; vis. asst. prof. Dartmouth Coll., Hanover, N.H., 1990, 92, 93; instr. Penland (N.C.) Sch. Crafts, 1994; vis. asst. prof. U. nebr., Omaha, 1994; adj. prof. So. Conn. State U., New Haven, 1995-96; instr., coord. fine art, coord. founds. Del. Coll. Art and Design, Wilmington, 1997—; lectr. Spokane Falls C.C., Spokane, 1997, Buffalo State Coll., 1995; vis. artist St. Mary's Coll. Md., St. Mary's City, 1995. Exhibited paintings in solo shows at Marlboro (Vt.) Coll., 1994, Albright Knox Art Gallery, Buffalo, 1995, Kraushaar Galleries, N.Y.C., 1995, 98, Lorinda Knight Gallery, Spokane, 1997. MacDowell Colony fellow, 1991, Vt. Studio Ctr. fellow, 1993, Va. Ctr. for Creative Art fellow, 1996. Mem. Coll. Art Assn. Office: care Kraushaar Galleries 724 5th Ave New York NY 10019-4106

DRABKIN, MURRAY, lawyer; b. N.Y.C., Aug. 3, 1928; s. Max Drabkin and Minnie (Masin) Weiner; m. Mary Elizabeth Hooper, Nov. 27, 1971. AB, Hamilton Coll., 1950; LLB, Harvard U., 1953. Bar: D.C. 1953, U.S. Ct. Appeals (D.C. cir.) 1954, N.Y. 1966, U.S. Supreme Ct. 1972. Counsel com. on judiciary U.S. Ho. of Reps., Washington, 1957-66; spl. asst. to mayor City of N.Y., 1966-68; pvt. practice N.Y.C. and Washington, 1968-82; ptnr. Cadwalader, Wickersham & Taft, Washington, 1983-92; ret., 1992; ptnr. Hopkins & Sutter, Washington, 1992—; dir. Conn. State Revenue Task Force, 1969-71; mem. adv. com. FRS, Washington, 1970-71, D.C. Tax Revision Com., 1976-77; lectr. law George Washington U., Washington, 1978-80. Contbr. articles to profl. jours. Served with USN, 1953-57, to lt. commdr. USNR. Mem. D.C. Bar Assn., Assn. Bar City N.Y. (com. on mcpl. affairs 1989-92), N.Y. County Lawyers Assn. (chmn. com. on bankruptcy 1987-88), Nat. Bankruptcy Conf. (chmn. com. on R.R. reorgn. 1984—, chmn. com. on bankruptcy crimes 1994-98), Cosmos Club, Harvard Club of N.Y.C., Harvard Club of Washington (bd. dirs. 1996-98), Chesapeake Bay Bermuda 40 Assn., Phi Beta Kappa, Delta Sigma Rho. Office: Hopkins & Sutter 888 16th St NW Ste 600 Washington DC 20006-4135

DRACH, JOHN CHARLES, scientist, educator; b. Cin., Sept. 25, 1939; s. Charles Louis and Edrie B. (Braun) D.; m. Elda Jean Flamm, June 20, 1964; children: Laura J., Diane E. BS in Pharmacy, U. Cin., 1961, MS in Pharm. Chemistry, 1963, PhD in Biochemistry, 1966. From assoc. rsch. scientist to rsch. scientist Parke, Davis and Co., Ann Arbor, Mich., 1966-70; asst. prof. U. Mich. Dental Sch., Ann Arbor, 1970-74; assoc. prof. U. Mich., Ann Arbor, 1974-80, prof., 1980—; assoc. prof. medicinal chemistry U. Mich. Coll. Pharmacy, Ann Arbor, 1978-80; prof. U. Mich., Ann Arbor, 1980—; chmn. dept. oral biology U. Mich. Dental Sch., Ann Arbor, 1985-87, chmn. dept. biologic and materials scis., 1987-95; vis. prof. divsn. virology Burroughs Wellcome Co., Research Triangle Park, N.C., 1994; cons. Adria Labs., Am. Inst. Chem., Am. Pharm. Assn., AMA, Chartwell, Kimberly-Clark, 1976-83. Author: Clinical Pharmacology, 1986; contbr. numerous articles and revs. to profl. jours.; mem. editorial bd. Elsevier Sci. Pubs., 1984—, Antiviral Chemistry & Chemotherapy, 1996—; patentee antiviral drugs. NSF summer fellow, 1963; NIH grad. fellow, 1964-66; NIH grantee, 1970—. Mem. AAAS, Am. Assn. Dental Rsch., Am. Assn. Dental Schs. (pres. oral biology sect. 1990-91), Am. Assn. Oral Biology, Am. Chem. Soc., Am. Soc. Microbiology (mem. editorial bd. 1982-91), Internat. Soc. Antiviral Rsch. (archivist 1992—, chair awards com. 1998—), Sigma Xi, Rho Chi, Omicron Kappa Upsilon. Avocations: jogging, skiing, sailing. Home: 1372 Barrister Rd Ann Arbor MI 48105-2875 Office: U Mich 1011 N University Ave Ann Arbor MI 48109-1078

DRACHLER, STEPHEN EDWARD, press secretary; b. Bainbridge, N.Y., Aug. 2, 1950; s. Ronald Walter Sr. and Dorothy Eleanor (Terry) D.; m. Michelle Lynn Bryce, June 13, 1980; 1 child, Stephanie Lynn. AAS in Journalism, SUNY, Morrisville, 1972. Reporter, bur. chief Ottaway Newspapers, Washington, Harrisburg, Pa., 1975-79; press sec. to Rep. Allen Ertel, U.S. Ho. of Reps., Washington, 1979-80; reporter Reading (Pa.) Times, 1980-81; local news editor The Pocono Record, Stroudsburg, Pa., 1981-85; bur. chief The Morning Call, Allentown, Pa., 1985-90; exec. asst. United Meth. Coun. of Bishops, Washington, 1980-91; dir. comms. Cen. Pa. Conf. United Meth. Ch., Harrisburg, 1991-95; press sec. Pa. Ho. of Reps., Harrisburg, 1995—; bd. dirs. United Meth. Pub. House, Nashville, 1992—; pres. Pa. Legis. Corrs. Assn., Harrisburg, 1988-89; v.p. South Cen. Pa. Radio/TV Ministries, Harrisburg, 1991-95. Contbr. articles to profl. jours. Del. gen. conf. United Meth. Chs., Louisville, Denver, 1992, 96, chmn. comms. com. Cen. Pa. Conf., 1988-91; staff Ridge for Gov. Com., Harrisburg, 1994; chmn. blue ribbon com. Harrisburg Religious Coalition, 1996. Recipient award of excellence Pan Meth. Coalition, Washington, 1992. Home: 3751 Montour St Harrisburg PA 17111-1934 Office: Pa Ho of Reps Rm 110 Main Capitol Harrisburg PA 17120

DRACHMAN, DANIEL BRUCE, neurologist; b. N.Y.C., July 18, 1932; s. Julian Moses and Emily (Deitchman) D.; m. Jephta Piatigorsky, Aug. 28, 1960; children: Jonathan Gregor, Evan Bernard, Eric Edouard. A.B. summa cum laude (N.Y. State scholar), Columbia Coll., 1952; M.D. (N.Y. State Med. scholar), NYU, 1956. Intern in internal medicine Beth Israel Hosp., Boston, 1956-57; asst. resident in neurology Harvard neurol. unit Boston City Hosp., 1957-58, resident in neurology, 1958-59; resident in neuropathology Harvard neurol. unit. and Mallory Inst. Pathology, 1959-60; teaching fellow in neurology Harvard U., 1957-60; clin. assoc. Nat. Inst. Neurol. Diseases and Blindness, NIH, Bethesda, Md., 1960-62, research asso. lab. neuroanat. scis., 1962-63; clin. instr. Georgetown U., 1961-63; asst. prof. neurology Tufts U., 1963-69; assoc. prof. Johns Hopkins U., 1969-73, prof., 1974—; prof. neurosci. Johns Hopkins U., Balt., 1980—; attending neurologist Johns Hopkins Hosp.; adv. bd. Multiple Sclerosis Soc., 1981-85; pres. med. adv. bd. Myasthenia Gravis Found.; adv. bd. Familial Dysautonomia Found.; bd. sci. councillors Nat. Inst. Neurol. and Communicative Disorders and Stroke, NIH, 1985-90; med. adv. com. Muscular Dystrophy Assn., 1994—. Clarinetist.; author publs. on myasthenia gravis, muscular atrophy, muscular dystrophy, clubfoot, devel. disorders, neurology, amyotrohic/ateralsclerosis, chamber music; mem. editl. bd. Muscle and Nerve jour., Exptl. Neurology, Autoimmunity. Served with USPHS, 1960-63. Recipient Founders' Day award NYU, 1956, Jacob Javits award, 1986, Berson Disting. Alumnus award NYU Sch. Medicine, 1999; NIH grantee, 1963—, Muscular Dystrophy Assn. grantee, 1969—. Fellow Am. Acad. Neurology, N.Y. Acad. Scis.; mem. AAAS, Internat. Soc. Devel. Biology, Balt. Neurol. Soc., Phi Beta Kappa, Alpha Omega Alpha. E-mail: dandrac@aol.com. Office: Johns Hopkins U Sch Medicine Dept Neurology 600 N Wolfe St Baltimore MD 21287-7905

DRACHMAN, DAVID ALEXANDER, neurologist; b. N.Y.C., July 18, 1932; s. Julian Moses and Emily Drachman; m. Eleanor Betsy Derby, Nov. 26, 1959; children: Laura Jeanne, Jessica Gail, Douglas Emmet. AB with highest honors, Columbia U., 1952; MD, NYU, 1956. Diplomate: Am. Bd. Psychiatry and Neurology. Intern Duke U. Med. Center, 1956-57; resident in neurology Mass. Gen. Hosp., Boston, 1957-60; clin. assoc. NIH, 1960-63; clin. instr. neurology Georgetown U. Med. Sch., 1961-63; mem. faculty Northwestern U. Med. Sch., 1963-77, dir. neurology clinics, 1963-77, prof. neurology, 1971-77, assoc. chmn. dept., 1972-75; attending physician Passavant Meml. Hosp., Chgo., 1964-72, Northwestern Meml. Hosp., 1972-77; prof. neurology, chmn. dept. U. Mass. Med. Center, 1977—; attending physician U. Mass. Med. Center, St. Vincent Hosp., Worcester; mem. med. adv. bd. Chgo. Multiple Sclerosis Soc., 1971-77, Mass. Multiple Sclerosis Soc., 1979-87; mem. FDA adv. panel on control and peripheral nerve system drugs, 1996—; mem. working group on presdl. disability, 1994-96. Mem. editorial bd. Neurobiology of Aging, 1979-93, Neurology, Archives of Neurology, 1979-91, Jour. of Geriatric Psychiatry and Neurology, Jour. of Rehab. and Health; contbr. articles to med. jours. Fellow Am. Acad. Neurology; mem. AAAS, Am. Neurol. Assn. (hon. mem., pres. 1994-95), Alzheimer's Disease Assn. (chmn. sci. adv. bd. 1986-90, trustee), Am. Neurootology Soc., Assn. Univ. Profs. Neurology, Assn. Rsch. Nervous and Mental Diseases, Mass. Assn. Neurology, N.Y. Acad. Scis., Boston Soc. Psychiatry and Neurology (pres. 1980-81), Phi Beta Kappa, Sigma Xi, Alpha Omega Alpha. Home: 111 Barretts Mill Rd Concord MA 01742-5519 Office: U Mass Med Ctr Dept Neurology 55 Lake Ave N Worcester MA 01655-0002

DRACHNIK, CATHERINE MELDYN, art therapist, artist, counselor; b. Kansas City, Mo., June 7, 1924; d. Gerald Willis and Edith (Gray) Weston; m. Joseph Brennan Drachnik, Oct. 6, 1946; children: Denise Elaine, Kenneth John. BS, U. Md., 1945; MA, Calif. State U., Sacramento, 1975. Lic. family and child counselor; registered art therapist. Art therapist Vincent Hall Retirement Home, McLean, Va., Fairfax Mental Health Day Treatment Ctr.,

McLean, Arlington (Va.) Mental Health Day Treatment Ctr., 1971-72, Hope for Retarded, San Jose, Calif., Sequoia Hosp., Redwood City, Calif., 1972-73; supervising tchr. adult edn. Sacramento Soc. Blind, 1975-77; ptnr. Sacramento Divsn. Mediation Svcs., 1981-82; instr. Calif. State U., Sacramento, 1975-82, 92-93, Coll. Notre Dame, Belmont, Calif., 1975-96; art therapist, mental health counselor Psych West Counseling Ctr. (formerly Eskaton Am. River Mental Health Clinic), Carmichael, Calif., 1975-93; instr. Sacramento City Coll., 1997—; instr. U. Utah, Salt Lake City, 1988-92; lectr. in field. Author: Interpreting Metaphors in Children's Drawings, 1995; one-woman shows include Vacaville (Calif.) Art Gallery, 1995, Dublier Gallery, Sacramento, 1997, Thistle Dew Gallery, Sacramento, 1998; exhibited in group shows Art of Calif. Mag., 1993, Calif. State Fair, Sacramento, 1995, 97, 98, Haggin Art Mus., Stockton, Calif. 1994, 95, 96, 97, 98, Watercolor West, Brea, Calif., 1998, West Valley Art Mus., Phoenix. Active charitable orgns. Mem. Am. Art Therapy Assn. (hon. life, pres. 1987-89), No. Calif. Art Therapy Assn. (hon. life), No. Calif. Arts, Inc., Nat. Art Edn. Assn., Am. Assn. Marriage and Family Therapists, Kappa Kappa Gamma Alumnae Assn. (pres. Sacramento Valley chpt. 1991-92), Alpha Psi Omega, Omicron Nu. Republican. Avocations: swimming, golf, theater. Home and Office: 4124 American River Dr Sacramento CA 95864-6025

DRACKER, ROBERT ALBERT, physician; b. Queens, N.Y., July 28, 1956; s. Albert Donald and Lee (Patruno) D.; m. Maria Elizabeth DiRubbo Dracker; children: Maria Lynn, Robert, Michael. BA in Biology, N.Y.U., 1978; MD, SUNY Health Sci. Ctr., 1982; MS in Health Svcs. Mgmt., New Sch. for Social Rsch., N.Y.C., 1995. Intern dept. pediat. SUNY Health Sci. Ctr., Syracuse, 1982-83, resident dept. pediat., 1983-85, fellow in pediatric hematology and oncology, 1985-87, fellow in blood banking and transfusion medicine, 1987-88, rsch. asst. prof. dept. pathology, 1988-89, dir. transfusion medicine dept. pathology, 1989-93; attending physician ARC, 1994—; pvt. practice, North Syracuse, N.Y., 1988—; med. dir. and founder Infusacare Med. Svcs., P.C., N. Area Pediat., P.C.; rsch. scientist I Masonic Med. Rsch. Lab., Utica, N.Y., 1989—; med. dir. MetraHealth Ctrl. N.Y., 1995-97; assoc. med. dir. POMCO, Syracuse, 1994-97; med. dir. Viacord Inc., Boston, 1998—; med. advisor, reviewer Ctrl. N.Y. Blue Cross/Blue Shield, Health Svcs. Adminstrn.; chmn. Ctr. N.Y. Divsn. Review Island Peer Review Orgn., 1988-90; physician reviewer N.Y. State Office of Med. Misconduct; physician reviewer for dispute resolution, Empire State Med. Scientific and Edn. Found.; consulting physician Jowonio Sch., 1983-85, Devillo Sloan Sch. for Handicapped, 1983-85, Walsh Med. Facility, N.Y. State Dept. Corrections, 1991-97; Neonatal Transport Physician, 1983-86. Contbr. numerous abstracts, letters, presentations, articles to profl. jours. Recipient AMA Physicians' Recognition award 1989-92, 92-95, 95-98, N.Y.U. Alumni award, The Dr. Charipper award, Pediatric Resident Teaching award; grantee Nat. Heart, Lung and Blood Inst, 1984-89, 88-90, Cutter Divsn.of Miles Labs., 1988-89, 90- 91, Pathology Med. Svc. Group SUNY Health Sci. Ctr., 1991-92, Hendricks Fund SUNY Health Sci. Ctr. at Syracuse, 1992. Mem. ARC, AMA, Ctrl. N.Y. AIDS Profl. Group, Vis. Nurse Assn. Ctrl. N.Y., N.Y. State Dept. Health, Ctrl. N.Y. Hosp. Assn., Just For Babies, St. Joseph's Hosp. and Health Ctr., Cmty. Gen. Hosp., Crouse Irving Meml. Hosp., Patients' Choice, Am. Assn. Blood Banks, Am. Acad. Pediatrics, Blood Bank Assn. N.Y. State, Am. Soc. for Apheresis, Med. Soc. N.Y. State, Onodaga County Med. Soc., Onondaga County Pediatric Soc., Internat. Soc. of Hematotherapy and Graft Engring., Am. Soc. for Blood and Marrow Transplantation, Am. Acad. Pediatrics. Roman Catholic. Avocations: reading, woodworking, research and development, coaching baseball, photography.

DRAEGER, KENNETH W., high technology company executive; b. Wyandotte, Mich., July 30, 1940; s. Wilfred Draeger and Marjorie (Rapp) Draeger Fair; m. Carol Ann Ahola, Sept. 7, 1963; children: Kimberley, Tracey. BS, Western Mich. U., 1962; MBA, Wayne State U., 1967. Analyst fin. staff Fort Motor Co., Dearborn, Mich., 1964-69; exec. v.p. Cyphernetics Corp., Ann Arbor, Mich., 1969-76; pres. ADP Network sVc. Div., Ann Arbor, Mich., 1976-81; group v.p. Informatics Gen. Corp., Franklin Lakes, N.J., 1981-84; chmn., chief exec. officer, pres. Compute Corp. of Am., Cambridge, Mass., 1984-86; chief exec. officer, pres. Autographix, Waltham, Mass., 1986-88; pres. Agfa Compugraphic, Wilmington, Mass., 1988-92; chmn., CEO, bd. dirs. DecisionOne Corp., Frazer, Pa., 1992-98, chmn., 1992-98; ret. DecisionOne Corp., Frazer, 1998; bd. dirs. Galileo Electro-Optics Corp., Sturbridge, Mass. Home: 41238 N 109th Pl Scottsdale AZ 85262-3223

DRAEGER, WAYNE HAROLD, manufacturing company executive; b. Watertown, Wis., July 5, 1946; s. Harold A. and Dorothy L. (Wendt) D.; m. Bonnie Eileen Wendt, June 22, 1968; children: Eric Christopher, Kyle Douglas. B.A., Lawrence U., 1968; M.B.A., Dartmouth Coll., 1970. Fin. planning dir. Cummins Engine Co., Columbus, Ind., 1974-76, asst. controller, 1976-78, dir. 10 litre program, 1978-79, exec. dir. fin. adminstrn., 1979-81, v.p. fin. adminstrn., 1981-82, v.p. internat. affiliates, 1982-84, v.p. fin. adminstrn., 1984-97; CFO Cummins Metropower, Bronx, N.Y., 1997—. Served to 1st lt. USAF, 1970-72. Office: 890 Zenega Ave Bronx NY 10473

DRAELOS, ZOE DIANA, dermatologist, consultant; b. Milw., Oct. 13, 1958; d. Dimitri Basil and Lorene June (Legan) Kececioglu; m. Michael Draelos, June 14, 1980; children: Mark, Matthew. BSME, U. Ariz., 1979, MD, 1983. Diplomate Am. Bd. Dermatology. Physician in solo dermatology practice, High Point, N.C., 1988—; cons., owner Dermatology Cons. Svcs., High Point, 1990—. Author: Cosmetics in Dermatology, 1995. Rhodes scholar, Oxford, Eng., 1979. Office: Zoe Diana Draelos MD PA 115B Gatewood Ave High Point NC 27262-4944

DRAFKE, MICHAEL WALTER, business educator, consultant; b. Joliet, Ill., Mar. 23, 1954; s. Raymond and Jeanette (Reich) D.; m. Kathleen Elizabeth Little, Nov. 9, 1985; children: Adam Michael, Erik Michael, Alex Michael. AA, Coll. of DuPage, Glen Ellyn, Ill., 1974; BS, U. Nev., Las Vegas, 1976; MS, Nat. Coll. Edn., Evanston, Ill., 1983; EdD, No. Ill. U., 1998. Registered radiography technologist. Chief radiologic technologist Ivinson Meml. Hos., Laramie, Wyo., 1976; clin. instr. in radiography Sherman Hosp., Elgin, Ill., 1977-79; instr. radiography Coll. of DuPage, Glen Ellyn, Ill., 1979-83, dir. radiography program, 1983-90, prof. bus., mktg. and mgmt., 1990—, rsch. design specialist innovation incubator, 1996—, co-dir. innovation incubator, 1997—; continuing edn. lectr. Ill. Hosp. Assn., Naperville, 1986-90; cons. Mosby-Time-Mirror Pubs., St. Louis, 1990-95, F.A. Davis Pubs., Phila., 1988—, Irwin Pubs., Homewood, Ill., 1992—, Austin Press, Flossmoor, Ill., 1993-95; mktg cons., 1990—. Author: National Radiography Certification Exam 4, 1986, Trauma and Mobile Radiography, 1990—, Working in Healthcare, 1994—, (with Stan Kossen) The Human Side of Organizations, 7th edit., 1997; editor Ill. State Soc. Radiol. Technologists Jour., 1989-96; contbr. articles to profl. jours. IBM Computer grantee League for Innovation, 1988; recipient Outstanding Tchrs. award Ill. C.C. Trustees Assn., 1989, Teaching/Learning Excellence award Ill. C.C. Bd., 1993, Connections 2000 award Ill. State Bd. of Edn., 1996, bright Idea award Ill. Coun. C.C. Adminstrs., 1997. Mem. NEA, Am. Mgmt. Assn., Nat. Bus. Educators Assn., Authors Guild, Am. Mktg. Assn., Ill. State Soc. Radiol. Technologists, Phi Kappa Phi. Avocations: home restoration, woodworking, architecture, photography, paleo-anthropology. Home: 18 Evergreen Pl Lemont IL 60439-3838 Office: Coll of DuPage 425 22nd St Glen Ellyn IL 60137-6784

DRAFT, HOWARD CRAIG, advertising executive; m. Elvy L. Leake; children: Andrew, Anna, Margaret. BA in Philosophy and Art History, Ripon Coll., 1974. With Draft Worldwide, Chgo., 1978—; gen. mgr. Draft Worldwide, N.Y., 1982; pres. Draft Worldwide, 1986, chmn., CEO, 1988; mem. adv. coun. Response TV; bd. mem. Direct Mktg. Assn. Ednl. Found.; spkr. in field. Active Pedia. AIDS Chgo., Herbert G. Birch Svcs.; bd. mem. Chgo. Old Town Sch. Folk Music; trustee Ripon Coll. Named one of 100 Best and Brightest, Advt. Age, one of The Best, The Brightest, The Most Powerful, Target Mktg., Direct Marketer of the Yr., Chgo. Assn. Direct Mktg., 1999. Office: Draft Worldwide 633 N Saint Clair St Chicago IL 60611-3234

DRAGHI, RAYMOND AMADEA, retired postal worker; b. Maple Grove Ohio, Mar. 22, 1927; s. Madea and Emma Maria (Poletti) D.; married, June 14, 1974; children: Michael Joseph, Mary Ann. Degree in bus adminstrn., Bliss Bus. Coll., 1949; degree in acctg., Office Tng. Sch., 1955. Rate clk., then mail clk. U.S. Post Office, Columbus, Ohio, 1957-91; pvt. investigator Columbus, 1958—. Contbr. poems to profl. publs. (Editors Choice awards 1994-96); song writer for Rainbow Records, 1992, Hilltop Records, 1994. With U.S. Army, 1945-46; sgt. USMC, 1950-51. Named to Internat. Poetry Hall of Fame, 1997. Republican. Roman Catholic. Avocations: nature trails, wild life, forest and meadow beauty, wild flowers, trees and shrubs. Home: 704 Robinwood Ave Columbus OH 43213-1759

DRAGO, JOSEPH ROSARIO, urologist, educator; b. Jersey City, N.J., Oct. 28, 1947; m. Diane Lavacca; children: Andrea, Daniella, Denise. BS, U. Ill., 1968, MD, 1972. Diplomate Nat. Bd. Med. Examiners, Am. Bd. Urology; cert. Yag Laser, laparoscopic surgery. Intern in gen. surgery Pa. State U. Milton S. Hershey Med. Ctr., 1972-73, resident in urology, 1973-77, instr. urology, 1976-77; asst. prof. urology, dir. urology oncology U. Calif., Davis, 1977-79; asst. prof. urology, dir. urology oncology Milton S. Hershey (Pa.) Med. Ctr., 1979-80, assoc. prof. to prof. of surgery, dir. urologic oncology, 1980-85; assoc. staff Children's Hosp., Columbus, Ohio, 1985—; interim chief of staff elect, prof., dir. urologic oncology Ohio State U. Arthur G. James Cancer Hosp., Columbus, Ohio, 1990-92; with Easton Warren Urology, Easton, Pa., 1992-95; pvt. practice Washington, N.J., 1995—; editorial bd. In Vivo Jour.;advisor Internat. Urologic Svcs., Inc., 1987; cons. for various coms.; visiting professorship at over 30 univs. and hosps. Author 12 book chpts.; reviewer various profl. jours., 1979—; contbr. articles to profl. jours. Recipient various rsch. grants, 1978-81. Fellow Internat. Coll. Surgeons in Urology; mem. AMA, Am. Coll. Surgeons, Am. Fertility Soc., Am. Inst. Ultrasound in Medicine, Am. Soc. Andrology, Am. Urologic Assn., Assn. Academic Surgery, Assn. Surgical Edn., Hershey Surgical Soc. (sec.-treas. 1983-85), Pa. Med. Soc., Phila. Urologic Soc. and many more. Home: 3295 Beaufort Dr Bethlehem PA 18017-1955 Office: 10 Brass Castle Rd Washington NJ 07882-4327 also: 224 Roseberry St Phillipsburg NJ 08865-1632

DRAGON, WILLIAM, JR., footwear and apparel company executive; b. Lynn, Mass., Dec. 1, 1942; s. William and Anne (Stavru) D.; m. Suzanne Gail Behlmer, Feb. 24, 1968; children: Todd Christopher, Heather Anne, Paige Katherine (dec.). B.S. in Engring. Mgmt., Norwich U., Northfield, Vt., 1964; M.S. in Mgmt. Scis., Rensselaer Poly. Inst., Troy, N.Y., 1965. With mfg., sales and mktg. staff Gen. Electric Co., Mass. and Ky., 1967-73; dir. product planning and design Samsonite div. Beatrice Corp., Denver, 1973-75, dir. mktg. Samsonite div., 1975-78; v.p. mktg. and sales Buxton div. Beatrice Corp., Springfield, Mass., 1978-81; gen. mgr. Johnston & Murphy Div. Genesco Inc., Nashville, 1981-85, exec. v.p., pres. U.S. Footwear Group, 1985-88, also dir.; v.p. Reebok Internat. Ltd., 1989-92; pres. Avia Group Internat. Inc., Portland, Oreg., 1989-92, Promotion Products Inc., Portland, 1992-94; dir. Deja, Inc., Portland, 1993-94; exec. v.p. DEJA Inc., Portland, 1994-95; pres. Pacific Trail divsn. London Fog Industries, 1995—; dean's adv. coun. Oreg. State U., 1994—. Bd. dirs. Nashville Youth Hockey League, 1983-85, Two/Ten Charity Found., 1988-92; vice chmn. Nashville United Way, 1985; mem. men's adv. bd. Cumberland Valley coun. Girl Scouts U.S., 1985-86; mem. adminstrv. bd. Brentwood United Meth. Ch., 1986. 1st lt. U.S. Army, 1965-67, Vietnam. Decorated Bronze Star medal. Recipient Superior Achievement Recognition award Genesco Inc., 1984. Presbyterian.

DRAGONWAGON, CRESCENT (ELLEN ZOLOTOW), writer; b. N.Y.C., Nov. 25, 1952; d. Maurice and Charlotte (Shapiro) Zolotow; m. Mark Parsons, Mar. 20, 1969 (div. 1973); m. Ned Shank, Oct. 1978. owner, operator, Dairy Hollow House, Eureka Spgs., Ark., 1981-99; writing seminars, NY Philadelphia Phoenix, San francisco, co-founder, Writer's Colony at Dairy Hollow, 1999—, lectr./seminar leader, Fearless Writing Wkshps., owner, operator Dairy Hollow House, Eureka Springs, Ark., 1981-98; spokesperson Calif. Almond Bd., 1993; chef du jour TVFN, 1996, Good Morning Amer., 1992. Author: (adult fiction) The Year It Rained, 1985 (N.Y. Times 100 Notable Books of 1985); (children's books) Rainy Day Together, 1970, Strawberry Dress Escape, 1975, Wind Rose, 1976, When Light Turns Into Night, 1977, Will It Be Okay?, 1977, Your Owl Friend, 1977, If You Call My Name, 1981, (with Paul Zindel) To Take a Dare, 1982, Katie in the Morning, 1983, I Hate My Brother Harry, 1983, Coconut, 1984, Jemima Remembers, 1984 (Nat. Coun. Tchrs. English Choice award 1985), Always, Always, 1984 (Parents' Choice Literary Honor 1984, Social Scis. Book of Yr.), Half a Moon and One Whole Star, 1986 (Coretta Scott King Recognition for 1986-87), Diana, Maybe, 1987, Alligator Arrived with Apples, 1987, Dear Miss Moshki, 1988, Margaret Ziegler Is Horse-Crazy, 1988, I Hate My Sister Maggie, 1989, This Is the Bread I Baked for Ned, 1989, The Itch Book, 1990, Homeplace, 1990 (Golden Kite award Soc. Children's Book Writers), Winter Holding Spring, 1990, Alligators and Others All Year Long, 1993, Annie Flies the Birthday Bike, 1993, Brass Button, 1997, Bat in the Dining Room, 1997; (nonfiction) Dairy Hollow House Cookbook, 1986 (World of Cookbooks Best Regional award 1986, L.A. Times 10 Best 1986), Dairy Hollow House Soup and Bread Cookbook (nominated for Julia Child and James Beard awards), 1992; contbr. book revs., articles to mags., newspapers including N.Y. Times, Cosmopolitan, Los Angeles, Lear's, Fine Cooking, Mode, Bon Appetit. Recipient Porter Fund award for writing, Ark., 1991, Women on the Move award, Wyndam, 1997, 1st prize profl. category Newman's Own Recipe Contest, 1997; Ossabaw Found. fellow, 1982, Ragdale Found. fellow, 1990. Mem. Authors Guild, Internat. Assn. Culinary Profls. (judge IACP/Julia Child Cookbook Awards 1997), So. Food Writers' Alliance (Judge James Beard award 1999), Soc. Children's Book Writers, Words, Ark. Lit. Soc., Eureka Group. Avocations: gardening, cooking, reading, restoration of older buildings, canoeing. Home: Rt 4 Box 7 1 Frisco St Eureka Springs AR 72632-3032

DRAGO-SEVERSON, ELEANOR ELIZABETH, developmental psychologist, educator, researcher; b. N.Y.C., Nov. 25, 1961; d. Rosario Philip and Betty Louise (Brisgal) Drago; m. David Irving Severson, Dec. 30, 1989. BA summa cum laude, L.I. U., 1986; EdM, Harvard U., 1989, EdD, 1996. Cert. biology, chemistry tchr., N.Y. Math. tchr. Palm Beach (Fla.) Acad., 1986-87; high sch. math. tchr., basketball coach Hackley Sch., Tarrytown, N.Y., 1987-88; biology tchr., dir. human devel. Palm Beach Day Sch., 1990-91, dir. human devel., 1990-91; tchg. fellow Harvard U., Cambridge, Mass., 1993-96, assoc. in edn. Grad. Sch. Edn., 1996—, postdoctoral fellow Sch. Edn., 1997—, instr., rsch. assoc. Sch. Edn., 1998—, lectr. edn. Grad. Sch. Edn., 1998—; co-dir. J.V. Mara C.Y.O. Sports Camp, Putnam Valley, N.Y., summer 1987; lectr. in edn. Harvard Grad. Sch. of Edn., 1998—. Mem. colloquium com. Harvard U., Cambridge, Mass., 1991-92, chair, 1992, mentor to incoming grad. students, 1992-96. Joseph Klingenstein fellow, 1987, tchg. fellow, 1993-96; doctoral fellow, 1994-96. Mem. ASCD, APA, AAUW, Am. Ednl. Rsch. Assn., Soc. for Rsch. in Adult Devel., Nat. Staff Devel. Coun., Phi Delta Kappa. Home: 39 Kirkland St Apt 403 Cambridge MA 02138-2072

DRAGOUMIS, PAUL, electric utility company executive; b. N.Y.C., Sept. 19, 1934; s. Andrew and Theologie (Pavlou) D.; m. Maria William, Sept. 15, 1957; children—Ann Marie Murtlow, Andrew Paul. BSEE, Poly. Inst. Bklyn., 1956; MS in Nuclear Engring., Internat. Sch. Nuclear Sci. and Engring., Argonne, Ill., 1959; MA in Philosophy, Georgetown U., 1986. Asst. v.p. Am. Electric Power Co., N.Y.C., 1956-70; gen. mgr. corp. exec. staff Allis Chalmers Corp., W. Allis, Wis., 1970-71; v.p. nuclear projects and fossil fuel supply group Potomac Electric Power Co., Washington, 1971-75, v.p. policy, 1976-78, sr. v.p., mem. exec. policy com., 1978-89, exec. v.p., 1989-95; dir. nuclear affairs USFEA, Washington, 1975-76; exec. dir. Pres. Ford's Energy Resources Coun., 1975-76; mem. mgmt. com. PJM Interconnection, 1980-95. Chmn. emeritus Concert Soc. at Md.; trustee, mem. exec. com. The Washington Opera, 1980—, pres., 1990-94; trustee, mem. exec. com. Greater Washington Rsch. Ctr., 1978-97. Named U.S. Outstanding Young Elec. Engr. Eta Kappa Nu, 1964, Outstanding Young Man of Am. Jaycees, 1966; recipient award for meritorious service USFEA, 1976. Mem. Univ. Club (Washington). Republican. Greek Orthodox. Avocation: sailing. Office: Paul Dragoumis Assocs Inc PO Box 5 Cabin John MD 20818-0005

DRAGT, ALEXANDER JAMES, physicist; b. Lafayette, Ind., Apr. 7, 1936; s. Gerrit and Beulah (Westra) D.; m. Lavonne Ann Wolters, Nov. 28, 1957; children: Alison Ann, Alexander James, William David. A.B., Calvin Coll., 1958; Ph.D. in Physics (NSF fellow), U. Calif., Berkeley, 1964. Sr. scientist Lockheed Missiles & Space Corp., Palo Alto, Calif., 1961-62; staff scientist Aerospace Corp., Los Angeles, 1963; mem. Inst. Advanced Study, Princeton, N.J., 1963-65; asst. prof. physics U. Md., 1965-68, assoc. prof., 1968-74, prof., 1974—, chmn. dept. physics and astronomy, 1975-78; mem. vis. staff Los Alamos Sci. Lab., 1978-79, cons., 1979—vis. prof. Tex. A&M U., 1984; mem. vis. staff Tex Accelerator Ctr., 1984; guest scientist Lawrence Berkeley Lab., 1985, cons., 1985—. Fellow Am. Phys. Soc.; Mem. Am. Geophys. Union, AAAS, Am. Math. Soc. Mem. Christian Reformed Ch. Research in theoretical physics, applied math. Office: U Md Dept Physics College Park MD 20742

DRAGUN, JAMES, soil chemist; b. Detroit, July 29, 1949; s. Henry George and Stella (Kubilus) D.; children: Nathan, Heather. BS, Wayne State U., 1971; MS, Pa. State U., 1975, PhD, 1977. Soil chemist U.S. EPA, Washington, 1978-82, Kennedy/Jenks, San Francisco, 1982-84, E. C. Jordan, Southfield, Mich., 1984-87, Stalwart Environ., Auburn Hills, Mich., 1987-88; soil chemist, pres. Dragun Corp., Farmington Hills, Mich., 1988—; prof. Wayne State U., Detroit, U. Mass., Amherst. Author: The Soil Chemistry of Hazardous Materials, 1988, 2d edit., 1998, Elements in North American Soils, 1991, 2nd edit., 1999, Natural Chemicals in Sediments, 1996; editor-in-chief Sci. Jour.; contbr. over 70 articles to profl. publs. Recipient Disting. Svc. award U.S. EPA, 1980, Disting. Svc. award Liquid Indsl. Control and Waste Mgmt. Assn., 1990. Mem. Sigma Xi, Phi Kappa Phi. Office: Dragun Corp 30445 Northwestern Hwy Ste 260 Farmington Hills MI 48334

DRAHMANN, BROTHER THEODORE, religious order official; b. Perham, Minn., June 7, 1926; s. Vincent Henry Drahmann and Louise Cecile Speiser. BS in History, St. Mary's Coll., Winona, Wis., 1949, DEd (hon.), 1981; M in Social and Indsl. Relations, Loyola U., Chgo., 1956; degree in edn. adminstrn., Coll. St. Thomas, St. Paul, 1974. Joined Cath. order Bros. of the Christian Schs. Tchr. De La Salle High Sch., Chgo., 1949-56, prin., 1956-62; counselor St. Mary's Coll., 1963-66; prin. Cretin High Sch., St. Paul, 1966-70; supr. schs. Christian Bros., St. Paul, 1970-72; supt. schs. Archdiocese of St. Paul/Mpls., 1972-78; dir. grad. studies Coll. St. Thomas, 1978-80; pres. Christian Bros. U., Memphis, 1980-93; dir. edn. Christian Bros. Conf., Landover, Md., 1993-98; prof. edn. St. Mary's U. of Minn., Mpls., Minn., 1998—; mem. U.S. Cath. Conf. Com. on Edn., Washington, 1993—; mem. adv. com. Coun. Am. Pvt. Edn., Washington, 1993-98; mem. Chief Adminstrs. of Cath. Edn., 1993—; exec. dir. Lasallian Assn. of Univs. and Colls., 1993-98. Author: (manual) Catholic School Principal-Outline for Action, 1980, rev. 1989, (brochure) Governance & Administration in Catholic Schools, 1985. Trustee St. Mary's Coll., 1972-81, Lewis U., Romeoville, Ill., 1982-93, Coll. Santa Fe, 1995—, De La Salle Inst., 1995—. Named Disting. Grad. Coll. St. Thomas, 1984, Oustanding Tennessean Gov. of Tenn., Nashville, 1988, Most Influential Cath. Educator for Past 25 Yrs., Today's Cath. Tchr. jour., 1997. Mem. Nat. Cath. Ednl. Assn. (Outstanding Educator of Yr. award 1985, bd. dirs. 1986-94), Assn. Cath. Colls. and Univs. (bd. dirs. 1985-94), NCCJ (chmn. bd. Memphis chpt. 1980-93, Humanitarian award 1990), Econ. Club of Memphis (bd. dirs. 1988-93), Rotary (bd. dirs. Memphis club 1984-89, pres. 1987-88), KC, Mil. and Hospitaller Order St. Lazarus Jerusalem (knight comdr. 1991—, Martyrs of Memphis award 1994), Pi Gamma Mu, Alpha Kappa Delta, Delta Epsilon Sigma. Avocations: reading, jogging, cycling, swimming. Office: St Marys Univ Minn 2500 Park Ave South Minneapolis MN 55404

DRAIN, ALBERT STERLING, business management consultant; b. Decatur, Tex., July 5, 1925; s. Albert S. and Bessie (Burk) D.; m. Mauvaline Joyce Beam, Apr. 18, 1946; children: Ronald Dale, Deborah Kay Drain Crawford. Student, Bellville (Ill.) Jr. Coll., Tex. Christian U., Iowa U., Milsaps Coll., Pittsburg (Kans.) Coll. With Armour & Co., 1945-79; regional mgr. Armour & Co., Pitts., 1966-67; mgr. pork div. Armour & Co., Chgo., 1967-68, fresh meats div. mgr., 1968-69; corporate v.p. Armour & Co., 1968-75, exec. v.p., 1971-73, group v.p. food marketing div., 1973-75; pres. Armour Foods, 1975-79; also dir.; exec. v.p. for Iowa Beef Processors Inc., Dakota City, Nebr., 1979-80; group v.p. Greyhound Corp., Phoenix, 1977—; pres. Sterling Mktg. Inc. (ind. bus. cons. to meat industry), Phoenix, 1980-91; pvt. practice mgmt. cons. meat packing Phoenix, 1991-94; pvt. practice Al Drain Mgmt. Cons., Phoenix, 1994—. Served with USNR, 1943-45. Mem. Am. Soc. Agrl. Cons., Masons, Shriners. Baptist. Home and Office: 24 E San Miguel Ave Phoenix AZ 85012-1337

DRAKE, ALBERT ESTERN, retired statistics educator, farming administrator; b. Stamping Ground, Ky., June 12, 1927; s. John L and Dullia Zena (Humphrey) D.; m. Katherine Ashby, June 22, 1952; children: Alan Sanford, Paul Steven, Jane, Philip David. Student, Georgetown Coll., 1946-47; BS, U. Ky., 1950, MS, 1951; PhD, U. Ill., 1958; postgrad., N.C. State U., 1959, 63, U. Fla., 1960. Rsch. asst. U. Ill., 1953-55, rsch. assoc., 1955-59; assoc. prof., assoc. biometrician Auburn U., 1959-62, prof., biometrician, 1962-63; dir. computer ctr. W.Va. U., 1963-65, acting coord. stats., 1965-66; prof. stats. U. Ala., 1966-92, coord. quantitative methods, 1966-72, acting head stats and mgmt. sci., 1981, interim assoc. dean undergrad. programs Coll. of Commerce and Bus. Adminstrn., 1988-90, assoc. dean undergrad. programs Coll. of Commerce and Bus. Adminstrn., 1990-92; prof. emeritus, 1992—; part-time mgr. farming enterprise and rock quarry Georgetown, Ky., 1992—; cons. in field. Contbr. articles to profl. jours., papers to profl. meetings. Bd. dirs. Little League, Auburn, 1961-63; active local council Boy Scouts Am., 1962-63, 66-67. Served with USMC, 1945-46. NSF grantee, 1959, 60, 63; Venture Fund grantee, 1975, 76, 81; inducted to Coll. Commerce & Bus. Adminstrn. U. Ala. Hall of Fame, 1998. Mem. Biometrics Soc., Am. Statis. Assn. (pres. Ala. chpt. 1972), Decision Scis. Inst. (sec. 1973-74, coun. 1969-72, 75-77, mem. editorial bd. 1969-72), Am. Agrl. Econs. Assn. Democrat. Home: 3319 Firethorn Dr Tuscaloosa AL 35405-5456

DRAKE, BARBARA RUTH, writer; b. N.Y.C., Apr. 7, 1961; d. John Raymond and Ann Lucille D.; m. Jorge Alberto Vera DuBois, Jan. 6, 1996; 1 child, Samuel John Vera. Student, U. Hartford, 1979-81, U. Hartford, 1984. Editor Music Alive Mag., Portchester, N.Y., 1986-91; lectr. U. Miami (Fla.) Writing Ctr., 1994-97; staff writer Miami Book Fair Internat., 1994, 95, 97; leader writing workshops Miami Beach (Fla.) Sr. Ctr., 1997-98. Author: Destination Guatemala, 1996; author short stories. Fellow Fontainebleau (France) Ecole des Arts Ams., 1982; grantee Fla. Dept. State Div. Cultural Affairs, 1997-98. Avocations: reading, dancing, cooking. E-mail: BDrake8112@aol.com.

DRAKE, CHARLES WHITNEY, physicist; b. South Portland, Maine, Mar. 8, 1926; s. Charles Whitney and Katharine Gabrielle (O'Neill) D.; m. Ellen Tan, June 15, 1952; children—Judith Ellen, Robert Charles, Linda Ann. B.S., U. Maine, 1950; M.A., Conn. Wesleyan U., 1952; Ph.D., Yale U., 1958. Scientist Westinghouse Atomic Power Div., 1952-53; instr. Yale U., New Haven, 1957-60; asst. prof. Yale U., 1960-66, rsch. assoc., 1966-69; assoc. prof. Oreg. State U., 1966-74; prof., 1974-93, prof. emeritus, 1993—, chmn. dept. physics, 1976-84; vis. prof. Oxford U. Clarendon Lab. and St. Peter's Coll., 1972-73, U. Tuebingen (W.Ger.), 1982. Contbr. articles to profl. jours. Served with USNR, 1944-46. Recipient various fellowships and grants. Mem. Am. Phys. Soc., Am. Assn. Physics Tchrs., Sigma Xi, Tau Beta Pi, Sigma Pi Sigma. Office: Oreg State U Dept Physics Corvallis OR 97331

DRAKE, DAVID LEE, electronics engineer; b. Campton, Ky., Mar. 15, 1960; s. Dudley and Sarah Ellen (Combs) D.; m. Bitha Mae Turner, June 10, 1983; children: Thomas Shelton, Rachel Leann. AAS, Morehead State U., 1981, BS, 1983. Electronics lab. technician Morehead (Ky.) State U., 1979-81; quality control technician Computer Peripherals, Campton, 1981; robotics rsch. engr. Morehead State U., 1981-83; personal computer test technician Campton Electronics, 1984-86; chief engr. Automation Svcs., Lexington, Ky., 1986—. Contbr. articles to profl. jours. Mem. IEEE, Sigma Tau Epsilon (parliamentarian 1982-83). Democrat. Home: PO Box 533 Campton KY 41301-0533 Office: Automation Svcs Inc 2549 Richmond Rd Ste 400 Lexington KY 40509-1595

DRAKE, DIANA ASHLEY, financial planner; b. Poughkeepsie, N.Y., Apr. 28, 1937; d. Albert Jackson and Jane Ashley (Ketchum) D.; m. José Akel Abizaid, Dec. 2, 1956 (div. Nov. 1979); children: Cynthia A. Rush, Allison J. Abizaid, Linda A. Wiener, Carol Lynn Abizaid, Amanda Jo Abizaid, Richard A. Abizaid; m. Sherrill Cleland, Sept. 3, 1988; stepchildren: Ann Cleland Feldmeier, Douglas S. Cleland, Sarah Cleland Allen, Scott C. Cleland. Student, Cornell U., 1955-56, Am. U. of Beirut, Lebanon, 1956-57; BS in Psychology cum laude, Vassar Coll., 1980; CFP, Inst. Fin. Planners,

Denver, 1986. CFP. Divorce mediator Fin. Planning Corp. of Va., McLean, 1983-86; investment advisor Cert. Fin. Svc., McLean, 1986; ptnr. Koelz Drake Advisors, Falls Church, Va., 1987-89; pres. Drake Fin. Svcs., Falls Church, 1986-98; exec. distbr. Nikken health and wellness products, prin. Magnetic Living, 1998—; sec., mem. Bd. Equalization, Falls Church, 1992-94. Contbr. articles to various mags. Elder Falls Church Presbyn. Ch., 1993-96, chair Christian Edn. Com., 1996, planned giving com. 1997-99, revision com. 1997; co-chmn. 100 yrs. aquatics YMCA, New Orleans, 1986. Recipient Disting. Svc. award for 25 Yrs. svcs. Nat. YMCA, 1986. Mem. AAUW, NAFE, DAR, No. Va. Inst. Cert. Fin. Planners (bd. dirs. facilities, sec. 1994-97), Inst. CFPs, Cornell Club of Washington (mem. investment and audit com. 1990-99), Delta Gamma, Zonta (cmty. svc. coord., dir. Arlington club 1992—), Vassar Club of Washington, The Tysons Club. Republican. Avocations: swimming, bridge, writing, photography, travel. Home and Office: 416 Park Ave Falls Church VA 22046-3304

DRAKE, DONALD CHARLES, journalist; b. N.Y.C., Jan. 12, 1935; s. Albert E. and Gloria (Walters) D.; 1 child, Valerie; m. Molly Hindman; 1 step-child, Jennifer. Student, NYU, 1953-56. Copy boy New York Herald Tribune, 1954-55; reporter Patent Trader, Mt. Kisco, N.Y., 1956-57, New Haven Register, 1957-58, Newsday, Garden City, N.Y., 1958-65; med. writer Phila. Inquirer, 1966-93; narrative editor, 1993—. Author: Medical School, 1978, (plays) Words, Saintly Mother, Clear and Present Danger, Final Edition, The Last Appointment, Love Knot, The Passage, Aria. Recipient Russell L. Cecil Writing award Arthritis Found., 1968, John S. Packard award Pa. Tb. and Health Soc., 1968, Howard W. Blakeslee awards Am. Heart Assn., 1969, 76, 81, Walter J. Donaldson awards Pa. Med. Soc., 1970, 71, Keystone Press awards, 1974-81, 83, 84, 87, 88, 90, 93 Claude Bernard award Nat. Soc. for Med. Research, 1978, AP Mng. Editors award Pa., 1978, 81, 84, 93, Robert F. Kennedy Journalism award, 1982, Morse award Am. Psychiat. Assn., 1982, Gen. Motors Cancer Rsch. Found. prize, 1990, others. Mem. Nat. Assn. Sci. Writers, Dramatists Guild. Office: Phila Inquirer 400 N Broad St Philadelphia PA 19130-4099 *Journalism would serve a greater good if it sought the truth instead of just the facts, but that's a lot harder to do.*

DRAKE, DOUGLAS CRAIG, university official; b. July 22, 1946. BA, Mich. State U., 1968, MA, 1969, postgrad., 1969-72. Analyst Mich. Dept. Treasury, 1972-74; rsch. analyst House Majority Policy Staff, 1974-78; dir. house majority policy staff Mich. Ho. of Reps., Lansing, 1978-82, dir. house taxation com. staff, 1982-85; dir. Office Edn., Mich. Dept. Mgmt. and Budget, Lansing, 1985-98; assoc. dir. State Policy Ctr., Wayne State U., Lansing, 1998—. Home: 5743 Bear Creek Dr Lansing MI 48917

DRAKE, ELISABETH MERTZ, chemical engineer; b. N.Y.C., Dec. 20, 1936; d. John and Ruth (Johnson) Mertz; m. Alvin William Drake, July 31, 1957 (div. 1984); 1 child, Alan Lee. SB in Chem. Engring., MIT, 1958, ScD in Chem. Engring., 1966. Registered profl. engr., Mass. Staff engr. Arthur D. Little Inc., Cambridge, Mass., 1958-64, sr. staff, 1966-76, mgr. risk analysis, 1977-82, v.p. tech. risk mgmt., 1980-82, 86-89, cons., 1990-94; assoc. dir. new tech. MIT Energy Lab., 1990—, dir., 1994-95; lectr. U. Calif., Berkeley, 1971; vis. prof. MIT, Cambridge, 1973-74; chmn. chem. engring. dept. Northeastern U., Boston, 1982-86; corp. mgr. MIT, 1981-86; mem. tech. pipeline safety stds. com. U.S. Dept. Transp., 1980-85; mem. mng. bd. Ctr. for Chem. Process Safety, 1988-90; vice chair com. on rev. and evaluation on army chem. stockpile disposal program NRC, 1993-98. Contbr. articles to profl. jours.; inventor fractionation method and apparatus, 1972. Fellow AIChE (bd. dirs. 1987-90); mem. AAAS, NAE, Am. Chem. Soc., Sigma Xi. Home: 30F Inman St Cambridge MA 02139-2411

DRAKE, EMILY E., nurse; b. Washington, Nov. 21, 1962; d. Charles J. and Harriet L. (Jung) Eiwen; m. Edward L. Drake, Sept. 27, 1986; children: Amelie, Richard. BSN, U. Va., 1985, MSN, 1993. RN; cert. Internat. Bd. Cert. Lactation Cons. Primary nurse U. Va. Health Scis. Ctr., Charlottesville, 1985-89, clinician 3, 1989-92, clinician 4, 1992-94; gen. faculty U. Va., Charlottesville, 1994—; reviewer Jour. of Obstetrics-Neonatal Nursing, Washington, 1996-98; test item writer Nat. Cert. Corp., Chgo., 1993-94. Author: Discharge Teaching Topics Q-sort, 1997. Mem. Assn. of Women's Health, Obstet. and Neonatal Nurses, Nat. Assn. and Neonatal Nurses, Sigma Theta Tau (chpt. pres. 1998). Home: 8 Driver Ln Palmyra VA 22963-2517 Office: U Va Sch Nursing McLeod Hall Charlottesville VA 22903-3395

DRAKE, ERVIN MAURICE, composer, author; b. N.Y.C., Apr. 3, 1919; s. Max and Pearl Edith (Cohen) D.; m. Ada Sax, May 28, 1947 (dec. Mar. 1975); children: Linda Shifra, Betsy Jennifer; m. Edith Bein Berman, Nov. 19, 1982. B of Social Sci., CCNY, 1940; studies with Tibor Serly, Jacob Druckman; Mus D (hon.), Five Towns Coll., 1998. Composer popular songs including I Believe, 1998, It Was a Very Good Year, 1999, Tico Tico, Perdido, Al Di Là, A Room Without Windows, Good Morning Heartache, 1999, Come to the Mardi Gras, The Rickety Rickshaw Man, Across the Wide Missouri, My Friend, Father of Girls, Quando Quando Quando, Sonata, Made for Each Other, Cherry, One God, Now That I Have Everything, Just For Today, There Are No Restricted Signs in Heaven, Marilyn; composer, lyricist: What Makes Sammy Run?, 1965; composer music, lyrics and libretto for Her First Roman, 1968, Her First Roman 25th Anniversary Cast Album, 1993; composer music and lyrics Leslie Uggams CD Painted Mem'ries, 1995, From John Gabriel With Love CD, 1997; lyricist, co-librettist, composer music Florence of Arabia, 1985; composer music lyrics and co-librettist Songs in Sophisticated Ladies 1983-84, Shades of Harlem, 1985 and Lady Day, 1987; writer, composer and/or producer TV programs including: To

DRAKE, FRANK DONALD, radio astronomer, educator; b. Chgo., May 28, 1930; s. Richard Carvel and Winifred (Thompson) D.; m. Elizabeth Bell, Mar. 7, 1953 (div. 1977); children: Stephen, Richard, Paul; m. Amahl Zekin Shakhashiri, Mar. 4, 1978; children: Nadia, Leila. B in Engring. Physics, Cornell U., 1952; MA in Astronomy, Harvard U., 1956, PhD in Astronomy, 1958. Astronomer Nat. Radio Astron. Obs., Green Bank, W.Va., 1958-63; sect. chief Jet Propulsion Lab., Pasadena, Calif., 1963-64; prof. Cornell U., Ithaca, N.Y., 1964-84; dir. Nat. Astron. and Ionospace Ctr., Ithaca, 1971-81; dean natural sci. dept. U. Calif., Santa Cruz, 1984-88, prof. astronomy, 1984-95, prof. emeritus, 1995—; pres. SETI Inst., Aptos, Calif., 1984—. Author: Intelligent Life in Space, 1962, Murmurs of Earth, 1978, Is Anyone Out There, The Scientific Search for Extraterrestrial Intelligence, 1992. Lt. USN, 1947-55. Fellow AAAS, Am. Acad. Arts and Scis.; mem. NAS, Internat. Astron. Union (chmn. U.S. nat. com.), Astron. Soc. Pacific (pres. 1988-90), Seti Inst. (pres. 1984—), Explorers Club. Avocation: jewelry making. Home: SETI Inst PO Box 789 Aptos CA 95001 Office: Univ of Calif Dept Astronomy/Astrophysics Santa Cruz CA 95064

DRAKE, GEORGE ALBERT, college president, historian; b. Springfield, Mo., Feb. 25, 1934; s. George Bryant and Alberta (Stimson) D.; m. Susan Martha Ratcliff, June 25, 1960; children: Christopher George, Cynthia May, Melanie Susan. AB, Grinnell Coll., 1956; Fulbright scholar, U. Paris, 1956-57; AB (Rhodes scholar), Oxford U., 1959, MA, 1963; BD, U. Chgo., 1962, MA, 1963, PhD (Rockefeller fellow), 1965; LLD (hon.), Colo. Coll., 1980, Ripon Coll., 1982; LHD (hon.), Ill. Coll., 1985, Ursinus Coll., 1988, Doane Coll., 1995. Instr. history Grinnell Coll., Iowa, 1960-61, pres., 1979-91, prof., 1979—, trustee, prof., 1991—; asst. prof., assoc. prof., prof. history Colo. Coll., Colorado Springs, 1964-79, acting dean of Coll., 1967-68, dean, 1969-73. Trustee Grinnell Coll., 1970-79, Penrose Hosp., 1976-79, 80-84, Grinnell Gen. Hosp., 1980-86; mem. Doane Coll. Bd. Trustees, 1995—, Iowa Peace Inst. Bd., 1994—, chair, 1996—; vol. U.S. Peace Corps, Lesotho, 1991-93; commr. N. Ctrl. Assn. Colls. and Schs., 1998—. NEH fellow, 1974. Mem. Am. Hist. Assn., Am. Ch. History Soc., Nat. Coll. Athletic Assn. (pres. commn. 1984-89), Nat. Merit Scholarship Corp.

DRAKE, GLENDON FRANK, writer; b. Jackson County, Ohio, Mar. 24, 1933; s. Frank H. D. and Margaret C. Andrews; m. Jane Winiker, June 3, 1955; children: Glendon James, Julie Drake-Barraclough, David Bentley. AB in Classics, Miami U., Oxford, Ohio, 1955; MA, Okla. State U., 1959; PhD, U. Mich., 1973. Prof. English linguistics San Diego State U., 1969-74, chmn. dept. linguistics, 1974-79; dean coll. arts & scis. U. Mich., Flint, 1979-81; v.p.acad. affairs Calif. State U., Long Beach, 1981-85; chancellor U. Colo., Denver, 1985-88; pres. Walden U., Mpls., 1990-95; mem. adv. staff Agy. Inernat. Devel., Washington, 1958-62. Author: The Role of Prescriptivism im American Linguistics, Learning in Two Languages The Ideology of the Application of Linguistics Knowledge, 1990; co-author: (chpt.) The Electronic Classroom A Practical Philosophy for the Electronic Classroom, 1999; contbr. articles to profl. jours. Participant Deutscher Akaemischer Austanschdienst, 1984; panelist projects linguistics NEH, Washington, 1990; co-founder Colo. Inst. Hispanic Econ. & Ednl. Devel., Denver, 1987-88. With U.S. Army, 1955-57. Travel grantee Ford Found., 1978; vis. fellow U. Bradford, England, 1980. Fellow Am. Assn. State Colls. & Univs. (sr.). Avocation: swimming. Home and Office: 161 Valencia Way Windsor CA 95492

DRAKE, GORDON WILLIAM FREDERIC, physics educator; b. Regina, Sask., Can., Aug. 20, 1943; s. Thomas Courtney and Alma Marion (Smith) D.; m. Judith Davies, Nov. 17, 1967 (div. 1983); children: Susan Mylo, Peter Courtney; m. Mary Louise Monaghan, Aug. 30, 1986. B.Sc., McGill U., Montreal, Que., 1964; M.Sc., U. Western Ont., London, 1965; Ph.D., York U., Toronto, Ont., Can., 1967. Postdoctoral fellow Smithsonian Astrophys. Obs., Cambridge, Mass., 1967-69; prof. U. Windsor, Ont., Can., 1969—. Contbr. articles to jours. in field, chpts. to textbooks; divisional assoc. editor Phys. Rev. Letters, 1985—; assoc. editor Can. Jour. Physics, 1987—; mem. editorial bd. Phys. Rev. A, 1991—. Recipient Herzberg medal Can. Assn. Physicists, Steacie prize Steacie Found., 1981, Gold medal for achievement in physics Can. Assn. Physicists; Alfred P. Sloan Found. fellow, 1973; Killiam Found. fellow, 1990. Fellow Inst. Physics (U.K.), Am. Phys. Soc., Royal Soc. Can. Home: 3499 Rankin Ave, Windsor, ON Canada N9E 3P4 Office: U of Windsor, Dept of Physics, Windsor, ON Canada N9B 3P4

DRAKE, HUDSON BILLINGS, aerospace and electronics company executive; b. L.A., Mar. 3, 1935; s. Hudson C. and Blossom (Billings) D.; m. Joan M. Johnson, Feb. 9, 1957 (dec. 1997); children: Howard Billings, Paul Marvin. BA in Econs., UCLA, 1957, postgrad., 1990; MBA, Pepperdine U., 1976. Mgr. Autonetics div. Rockwell Inc., Anaheim, Calif., 1958-68; exec. dir. Pres.'s Commn. White House Fellows, Washington, 1969-70; dep. under sec. U.S. Dept. Commerce, Washington, 1970-72; v.p., gen. mgr. Teledyne Ryan Electronics, San Diego, 1972-80, pres., 1980-84; pres., group exec. Teledyne Ryan Aero., San Diego, 1984-88; v.p., group exec. Teledyne Inc., L.A., 1987-88, sr. v.p., group exec., 1988-89, sr. v.p., pres. aerospace and electronics segment, 1989-96; v.p., pres. aerospace and electronics segment Allegheny Teledyne Inc., L.A., 1996-97; ltd. ptnr. Carlisle Enterprises, La Jolla, Calif., 1997—; dir. Parex Inc., Washington, 1997—; mem. Def. Procurement Adv. Com. on Trade, Washington, 1988-93. Contbr. articles to profl. jours. Trustee Children's Hosp., San Diego, 1981-86, chmn. rsch. corp., 1983-86; mem. Pres.'s Coun. San Diego (Calif.) State U., 1984-90; mem. bd. overseers U. Calif., San Diego, 1985-88; mem. vestry, St. James by the Sea, LaJolla, Calif. With USNR, 1953-61. Recipient Exec. of Yr. award Nat. Mgmt. Assn., 1995; named silver knight of mgmt. Nat. Mgmt. Assn., 1975, gold knight of mgmt., 1986; San Diego Bd. Suprs resolution, 1988; White House fellow, 1968. Mem. IEEE, AIAA, Navy League (life), Inst. Navigation, San Diego C. of C. (bd. dirs.), La Jolla Country Club. Republican. Episcopalian. Avocation: golf, sports cars. Home: 1205 Coast Blvd Unit E La Jolla CA 92037-3636 Office: Carlisle Enterprises 7777 Fay Ave Ste 200 La Jolla CA 92037-4390

DRAKE, JAMES, sculptor; b. Lubbock, Tex., Sept. 12, 1946. BFA with honors, Art Ctr. Coll. Design, 1969, MFA, 1970. instr. life drawing Art Ctr. Coll. Design, L.A., 1969-70, U. Tex., El Paso. Solo shows include Contemporary Art Mus., Houston, 1983, New Orleans Mus. Art, 1983, La Jolla Mus. Contemporary Art, 1989, Corcoran Gallery Art, 1990; exhibited works at Amarillo (Tex.) Art Ctr., 1981. Office: care Adair Margo Gallery 415 E Yandell Dr Ste 10-b El Paso TX 79902-5222*

DRAKE, JAMES ALFRED, higher education administrator; b. Columbus, Ohio, Mar. 28, 1944; s. James Watts and Ruth Ann (Riley) D.; m. Mildred Ann Armstrong-Cabrera, Mar. 21, 1970 (div. Dec.. 1980); m. Magali Garriga Drake, Mar. 3, 1995; stepchildren: Magali (Balado) Feller, Kristie Balado. AB, Ohio Dominican Coll., 1967; PhD, Ohio State U., 1973. Cert. tchr., Ohio. Asst. prof. Ithaca (N.Y.) Coll., 1971-73, chmn. dept. edn., 1973-75, dir. televised studies, 1975-79; asst. provost, dean U. Tampa, Fla., 1979-84; v.p., dean U. Findlay, Ohio, 1984-87; rsch. cons., ptnr. The Travis Group, Inc., Columbus, 1987-88; exec. dir., CEO Greenville (S.C.) Univ. Ctr., 1988-94; campus exec. officer U. Ctrl. Fla., Cocoa, 1994—. Author: Rosa Ponselle: Centenary Biography, 1997, Richard Tucker: A Biography, 1984 (Nat. Book Clubs award 1984), Ponselle: A Singer's Life, 1982 (Nat. Book Clubs award 1982), Popular Culture and Am. Life, 1980, Teaching and Critical Thinking, 1976. Chmn. bd. dirs. United Way of Brevard County, Cocoa, 1998—, reg. campaign dir., 1997; v.p. bd. dirs. Jr. Achievement East Ctrl. Fla., Cocoa Beach, 1997-98; v.p. bd. dirs. Brevard Cultural Alliance, Melbourne, Fla., 1997-98; bd. dirs. Brevard Schs. Found., Melbourne, 1995—, Nat. Space Club Fla., Cape Canaveral, 1995-97, Wuesthoff Hosp. Sys., 1998—; bd. advisors Brevard C.C., Cocoa, 1995—, Greenville Tech. Coll., 1988-94. Philosoph of Edn. Soc. fellow, Chgo., 1979. Mem. Civilian-Mil. Alliance. Home: 100 Riverside Dr A802 Cocoa FL 32922 Office: Univ of Central Florida Brevard Campus 1519 Clearlake Rd Cocoa FL 32922-6598

DRAKE, JOHN WARREN, aviation consultant; b. Chgo., July 5, 1930; s. Robert Warren and Winifred Elizabeth (Bramhall) D.; m. Miriam Anna Engleman, Dec. 19, 1960 (div. Dec. 1985); 1 child, Robert Warren. B.S., Rensselaer Poly. Inst., 1952; M.B.A., Harvard U., 1954, D.B.A., 1972. Research asso. Aero. Research Found., Cambridge, Mass., 1956-57; prin. United Research, Inc., Cambridge, 1957-61; v.p. Systems Analysis and Research Corp., Cambridge, 1961-69; prof. emeritus, air transp. area Sch. Aeros. and Astronautics, Sch. Engring., Purdue U., 1972-92, mem. president's council; cons. in field; mem. Transp. Research Bd. NRC. Author: The Administration of Transportation Modeling Projects, 1973. Served with U.S. Army, 1954-56. Mem. Inst. Mgmt. Sci., Air Transp. Research Internat. Forum (council), AIAA, Soc. Automotive Engrs. Club: University (Washington). Home and Office: 3909 Somerset Pl West Lafayette IN 47906-8855

DRAKE, LAURA, director, performer; b. Eureka, Calif., Mar. 1, 1949; d. Stephen Drake and Laura Anne (Filingerie) Morel. BA in Interdisciplinary Creative Arts, San Francisco State U., 1973; MFA in Dramatic Prodn., U. Tex., 1985. Dir., coord. Austin (Tex.) Theatre Artists' Collective, 1984-85; artistic dir. Creatrix Prodns., New Orleans, 1985-89; asst. prof. theatre U. Southwestern La., Lafayette, 1987-91; appt. artist, spare/changes artistic resident Atlantic Ctr. for Arts, 1990; artistic dir. Gabriella Rosetti Prodns., N.Y.C., 1992—; founder, gen. ptnr. Designer's Edge Studio, N.Y.C., 1993—; adj. asst. prof. performing arts, guest dir. CUNY, 1993—. Writer, performer (performance art): Duck/Blind, 1990, Stages: Aphro-Diaspora, 1990 (NEA Inter-Arts award 1990); dir./producer Interdisciplinary Performance Festival, 1988-91 (Lafayette, La.). Morton Brown Rsch. fellow U. Tex., Austin, 1981, 82; recipient Partnership award Acadiana Arts Coun., 1988-91, Inter-Arts award Nat. Endowment for the Arts, 1990, New Performance award La. Div. of the Arts, 1990. Mem. Artists' Alliance (Lafayette, program com. 1989-91, bd. dirs.), Festival Internat. de Louisiane (bd. dirs. 1989-91), Phi Kappa Phi, Alpha Psi Omega. Home and Studio: 1691 3rd Ave Apt 3A New York NY 10128-2113

DRAKE, LUCIUS CHARLES, JR., school administrator, university consultant, educator; b. Tacloban, The Philippines, June 29, 1946; s. Lucius Charles and Victoria (Badiles) D. BA, Fisk U., 1968; EdM, Temple U., 1970; EdD, U. No. Colo., 1995. Cert. sch. adminstr.; cert. guidance counselor. Math. tchr. Sch. Dist. of Phila., 1968-70, Gary (Ind.) City Schs., 1970-72, Dept. Defense Dependents Sch., Fed. Republic Germany and Okinawa, 1972-77; elemtary tchr. Dept. Defense Dependents Sch., Philippines, 1977-79; guidance counselor Dept. Defense Dependents Sch., Japan and Korea, 1979-83; asst. prin. Dept. Defense Dependents Sch., Seoul and Taegu, Korea, 1983-86; univ. cons. U. No. Colo., 1988-89; employment counselor Ft. Collins, Colo., 1989-90; asst. prin. Misawa, Japan, 1990-91, Philippines, 1991-92; sch. adminstr. Okinawa, 1992-93; instr./asst. prof. U. No. Colo., 1994-96; math tchr. Loveland, Colo., 1996-97; asst. prof. Midland Luth. Coll., 1997-98; dir. clin. svcs. Met. State Coll. Denver, 1998—; chmn. math dept. Sayre Jr. High Sch., Phila., 1969-70; math. curriculum rev. com., Dept. Defense Dependents Schs., Karlsruhe, Fed. Republic Germany, 1972-73; dir. Far East Basketball Tourney, Taegu, Korea, 1984-86; mem. regional mgmt. council, Dept. Defense Dependents Schs., Okinawa, 1985-86. Chairperson human rels. commn. Ft. Collins City Coun., 1990. Recipient Disting. Educator award IDEA Acad. Fellows, Denver, 1985. Fellow Am. Bd. Master Educators (disting.); mem. ASCD, Assn. Am. Sch. Adminstrs., Nat. Assn. Secondary Sch. Prins., Nat. Assn. Elem. Sch. Prins., Internat. Educator's Inst., Phi Delta Kappa, Alpha Phi Alpha (edn. sec. Seoul chpt. 1984-85). Democrat. Baptist. Avocations: weight tng., travel, chess, basketball, karate. Home: 3318 B Hickok Dr Fort Collins CO 80526 Office: Met State Coll 1006 11th St Denver CO 80204

DRAKE, MIRIAM ANNA, librarian, educator; b. Boston, Dec. 20, 1936; d. Max Frederick and Beatrice Celia (Mitnick) Engleman; m. John Warren Drake, Dec. 19, 1960 (div. Dec. 1985); 1 child, Robert Warren. BS, Simmons Coll., Boston, 1958, MLS, 1971; postgrad., Harvard U., 1959-60; LHD (hon.), Ind. U., 1994; DLS (hon.), Simmons Coll., 1997. Assoc. United Rsch., Cambridge, Mass., 1958-61; with mktg. svcs. Kenyon & Eckhardt, Boston, 1963-65; cons. Boston, 1965-72; head rsch. unit libraries Purdue U., West Lafayette, Ind., 1972-76, asst. dir. libraries, prof. library sci., 1976-84; dean, dir. libraries, prof. Ga. Inst. Tech., Atlanta, 1984—; trustee Online Computer Libr. Ctr., Inc., 1978-84, chair, 1980-83; trustee Corp. for Rsch. and Edn. Networking, 1991-94, U.S. Depository Libr. Coun., 1991-94. Author: User Fees: A Practical Perspective, 1981; co-author: (with James Matarazzo) Information for Management, 1994; mem. editl. bd. Coll. and Rsch. Librs. Jour., 1985-90, Librs. and Microcomputers Jour., 1983—, Sci. and Tech. Librs., 1989—, Database, 1989-97; contbr. chpts. to books, articles to profl. jours. Recipient Alumni Achievement award Simmons Coll. Sch. Libr. and Info. Sci., 1985, Kent Meckler Media award U. Pitts., 1994. Mem. ALA (councilor at large 1985-89, Hugh Atkinson Meml. award 1992), Am. Mgmt. Assn., Am. Soc. Info. Sci., Spl. Librs. Assn. (pres.-elect 1992-93, pres. 1993-94, H.W. Wilson award 1983). Office: Ga Inst Tech Lib Info Ctr Atlanta GA 30332

DRAKE, OWEN BURTCH WINTERS, association administrator; b. N.Y.C., May 22, 1941; s. Owen Burtch Winters and Louise Harrison (Gwynn) D.; m. Joan Draper, Dec. 15, 1961 (div. July 1975); children: Burtch Winters, Frederic Malcolm; m. Deborah Edmonson, Jan. 8, 1977; children: Kelley Keresey, Colin Edmonson. Student, U. Va., 1958-61. Sr. v.p., mgmt. supr. Dancer, Fitzgerald & Sample Inc., N.Y.C., 1961-78; pres., gen. mgr. Dancer, Fitzgerald & Sample Inc., San Francisco, 1981-84; dir. European area Life Savers Inc., London, 1978-80; sr. v.p., group mgmt. supr. Foote, Cone & Belding, N.Y.C., 1981, exec. v.p., gen. mgr., 1985-86; pres. FCB/Leber Katz Ptnrs., N.Y.C., 1986-87; pres. European area Foote, Cone & Belding, London, 1987-89; exec. v.p., chief oper. officer Am. Assn. Advt. Agys., N.Y.C., 1989-94, pres., CEO, 1994—; Bd. dirs. Advt. Coun., 1994—, Nat. Advt. Rev. Coun., 1994—, Advt. Ednl. Found., 1994—, AAAA Found. Inc., 1997—. Bd. dirs. San Francisco Zool. Soc., 1983-84, Partnership for Drug Free Am., 1994—. With USMCR, 1958-67. Recipient Effie award Am. Advt. Fedn., 1977. Clubs: Racquet and Tennis (N.Y.C.); Rockaway Hunting (Cedarhurst, N.Y.); Lawrence Beach (Atlantic Beach, N.Y.); Coral Beach (Bermuda). Office: Am Assn Advt Agys 405 Lexington Ave New York NY 10174-0002*

DRAKE, PATRICIA EVELYN, psychologist; b. Lewiston, Maine, Feb. 9, 1946; d. Lewis and Anita (Bilodeau) D.; m. Colin Matthew Fuller, May 13, 1973 (div. Aug. 1983); children: R. Matthew, Meaghan Merry. Diploma, St. Mary's Sch. Nursing, 1967; BS, U. Nev., 1985; MA, Calif. Sch. Profl. Psychology, 1987, PhD, 1989. RN. Nurse Maine Med. Ctr., Portland, 1967-73, U. Calif. Sacramento Med. Ctr., 1973-78, Ben Taub Hosp., Houston, 1978-79; psychology intern Shasta County Mental Health Ctr., Redding, Calif., 1988-89, clin. psychologist, 1989-91, tng. dir., chief psychology, 1991—; psychologist pvt. practice, Redding, Calif., 1991—. Mem. AAUW, APA, Calif. Psychol. Assn., Shasta-Cascade Psychol. Assn., Phi Kappa Phi. Democrat. Roman Catholic. Avocations: swimming, cross-country skiing, crafts. Office: Shasta County Mental Health 2640 Breslauer Way Redding CA 96001-4246

DRAKE, RICHARD FRANCIS, state senator; b. Muscatine, Iowa, Sept. 28, 1927; s. Frank and Gladys (Young) D.; student Iowa State U.; BS, U.S. Naval Acad., 1950; m. Shirley Jean Henke; children: Cheryll Dee, Ricky Lee. Commd. ensign U.S. Navy, advanced through grades to lt. comdr., 1954; capt. minesweeper U.S.S. Crow; farmer, mgr., 1954—; mem. Iowa Senate, 1968—. Chmn. Young Republican Orgn. Iowa, 1954-56; adminstrv. asst. Muscatine County Rep. Com., 1956-57, chmn., 1958-66; 1st dist. chmn. Rep. party, 1966-72; chmn. Nat. Task Force Rail Line Abandonment and Curtailment; chmn. states and rail problems Midwestern Council State Govts., 1978-79. Named One of Ten Outstanding Legislators of Yr. Nat. Rep. Lesislators Assn. Mem. Farm Bur., Masons, Elks, Order Eastern Star. Lutheran. Office: State Senate State Capitol Des Moines IA 50319*

DRAKE, RICHARD PAUL, physicist, educator; b. Washington, Oct. 25, 1954; s. Hugh Hess and Florence Jean (Steele) D.; m. Joyce Elaine Penner, Aug. 30, 1980; children: Katherine Anne, David Alexander. BA in Philosophy and Physics magna cum laude, Vanderbilt U., 1975; PhD in Physics, Johns Hopkins U., 1979. Physicist Lawrence Livermore (Calif.) Lab., 1979-89; assoc. prof. dept. applied sci. U. Calif., Davis, 1989-91, prof., 1991-93; dir. Plasma Physics Rsch. Inst. Lawrence Livermore Nat. Lab., 1990-96; vis. prof. U. Mich., Ann Arbor, 1996-98, prof. space sci., dir. Space Physics Rsch. Lab., 1998—; ski instr. Squaw Valley (Calif.) USA, 1985-92; chair Anomalous Absorption Conf., Tahoe City, Calif., 1987; referee NSF, Nature, Phys. Rev. Letters, other jours. Contbr. over 130 articles to sci. publs. Mem. Fellow Am. Phys. Soc.; mem. AAAS, Am. Geophys. Union, Am. Astron. Soc., Am. Vacuum Soc., Optical Sci. Am., Phi Beta Kappa. Achievements include fundamental experiments and theory on waves, instabilities, and turbulence in plasmas; laboratory astrophysics; time-dependent systems. Home: 3204 W Dobson Pl Ann Arbor MI 48105-2580 Office: U Mich Campus 2455 Hayward St Ann Arbor MI 48109-2143

DRAKE, ROBERT ALAN, state legislator, animal nutritionist, mayor; b. Canton, S.D., July 6, 1957; s. Theodore Francis and LaRayne Margaret (Hoffman) D.; m. Pamela Sue Wiechmann, 1977; children: R. Ryan, Kimberly Margaret, Kendra Kay. BS, S.D. State U., 1979, MS, 1981. Animal nutritionist McFleeg Feeds, Bowdle, S.D., 1981—; mayor City of Bowdle, 1988-96; mem. S.D. Ho. of Reps., Pierre, 1995-96, S.D. Senate, 1997—. Supr. Edmunds County Conservation Dist., 1984-96; chmn. N.E. Coun. Govts., Aberdeen, S.D., 1992-93; pres. Bowdle Cmty. Club, 1985-86, Bowdle Devel. Corp., 1985-89. Republican.

DRAKE, RODMAN LELAND, investment company executive, consultant; b. Terre Haute, Ind., Feb. 2, 1943; s. Leland Rodman and Helen Virginia (Frederick) D.; m. Lenir Leme-Lambert, Sept. 26, 1975 (div. 1998); children: Stephan Rodman, Philip Lambert; m. Jacqueline B. Weld, Dec. 18, 1998. BA, Yale U., 1965; MBA, Harvard U., 1969. Assoc. Cresap, McCormick & Paget, Inc., N.Y.C., 1969-70, Monterrey, Mexico, 1971-72; mng. ptnr. Cresap, McCormick & Paget, Inc., São Paulo, Brazil, 1972-77; v.p., bd. dirs. Cresap, McCormick & Paget, Inc., N.Y.C., 1977-81, mng. dir., CEO, 1981-90; pres. Mandrake Group, Inc., N.Y.C., 1993-97; pres., dir. Continuation Investments N.V., N.Y.C., 1997—; bd. dirs. Parsons Brinckerhoff Inc., Alliance Group Svcs., Inc., Excelsior Funds (sponsored by U.S. Trust), Hyperion Total Return Fund, Hyperion 1999 Term Trust, Hyperion 2002 Term Trust, Hyperion 2005 Opportunity Term Trust; co-chmn. KMR Power Corp., 1993-96; former mem. adv. bd. Argentina Pvt. Equity Fund L.P. and Garantia L.P., Brazil, Alex Brown & Sons, Inc., Mueller Industries. Bd. dirs. Planned Parenthood Internat. With U.S. Army, 1965-67. Mem. Waccabuc Golf Club, Yale Club (N.Y.C., sec. Yale U. class of 1965, 1980-85), Waccabuc Club (N.Y.).

DRAKE, STEPHEN DOUGLAS, clinical psychologist, health facility administrator; b. Iola, Kans., Sept. 8, 1947; s. Harry Francis and Emojean (Price) D.; m. Rebecca Gonzalez. June 1, 1968; 1 child, Michael Paul. BA, U. Tex., 1970; PhD, U. North Tex., 1987. Diplomate Am. Bd. Forensic Examienrs; lic. psychologist. Mental health worker Austin (Tex.) State Hosp., 1970-73; claims rep. Social Security Adminstrn., Galveston, Tex., 1974-77; ops. supr. Social Security Adminstrn., Dallas, 1977-79, staff asst., 1979-80; clin. psychologist Terrell (Tex.) State Hosp., 1987-89, Austin (Tex.) State Hosp., 1989-90; program dir. Austin State Hosp., 1990-92; cons. Tex. Rehab. Commn., 1992-98, chief mental med. cons., 1998—. Contbr. articles to profl. jours. Vice-Chmn. bd. dirs. Galveston (Tex.) Island Mental

Health/Mental Retardation Ctr., 1977; v.p. Grad. Assn. Students in Psychology U. North Tex., 1984, grad. rep. exec. com., 1984. Mem. APA, AAAS, Tex. Psychol. Assn., Assn. Advancement Behavior Therapy, Mensa, Phi Kappa Phi. Avocations: Tae Kwon Do, weightlifting, Eastern philosophy, foreign languages, travel. Office: Tex Rehab Commn 6102 E Oltorf St Austin TX 78741

DRAKE, SYLVIE (JURRAS DRAKE), theater critic; b. Alexandria, Egypt, Dec. 18, 1930; came to U.S., 1949, naturalized, 1952; d. Robert and Simonette (Barda) Franco; m. Kenneth K. Drake, Apr. 29, 1952 (div. Dec. 1972); children—Jessica, Robert I.; m. Ty Jurras, June 16, 1973. M. Theater Arts, Pasadena Playhouse, 1969. Free-lance TV writer, 1962-68; theater critic Canyon Crier, L.A., 1968-72; theater critic, columnist L.A. Times, 1971-91, theater critic, 1991-93, theatre critc emeritus, 1993—; lit. dir. Denver Ctr. Theatre Co., 1985; free lance travel writer, book reviewer, pres. L.A. Drama Critics Circle, 1979-81; mem. Pulitzer Prize Drama Jury, 1994; adv. bd. Nat. Arts Journalism Program, 1994-97. Dir. media rels. and publs. Denver Ctr. for the Performing Arts, 1994—; artistic assoc. for spl. projects Denver Ctr. Theatre Co., 1994—. Mem. Am. Theater Critics Assn. Office: Denver Ctr for Performing Arts 1245 Champa St Denver CO 80204-2104

DRAKE, VAUGHN PARIS, JR., electrical engineer, retired telephone company executive; b. Winchester, Ky., Nov. 6, 1918; s. Vaughn Paris and Margaret Turney (Willis) D.; student U. Ky., 1936-41; m. Lina Louise Wilson, May 5, 1946; 1 son, Samuel Willis. With Gen. Telephone Co. Ky., Lexington, 1945-81, asst. engr., 1945-50, field engr., 1950-54, dist. engr., 1954-56, div. engr., 1956-57, depreciation engr., 1957-62, gen. valuation and cost engr., 1962-81. Mem. profl. adv. bd. Zoning Commn., Lexington and Fayette County (Ky.), 1955-57. Served with AUS, 1941-45 (comm. chief, combat engr. group). Decorated Pearl Harbor Commemorative medal, 1991. Registered profl. engr., Ky. Mem. IEEE (sr., chmn. Lexington sect. 1956-57), NSPE, Ky. Soc. Profl. Engrs. (pres. Bluegrass chpt. 1961-62, chmn. engrs. in industry sect. 1967-68, Outstanding Engr. in Industry award 1979), Ind. Telephone Pioneer Assn. (life), Ky. Hist. Soc. Author: (manual) Conduit Engineering for Telephone Engineers, 1958. Home and Office: 633 Portland Dr Lexington KY 40503-2161

DRAKE, W. HOMER, JR., federal judge; b. 1932. AB, Mercer U., 1954, LLB, 1956. Law clk. to Hon. Lewis R. Morgan U.S. Dist. Ct. Ga., 1961-64; ptnr. Swift, Currie, McGhee & Hiers, 1976-79; judge U.S. Bankruptcy Ct., 1964-76; chief judge U.S. Bankruyptcy Ct., 1968-76; bankruptcy judge U.S. Bankruptcy Ct. (no. dist.) Ga., 1979—; adj. prof. U. Ga. Law Sch., 1971-72, Emory U. Law Sch., Atlanta, 1973-75. Author: Bankruptcy Practice for the General Practitioner, 1995; co-author: Chapter 13 Practice & Procedure, 1983, Chapter 11 Reorganizations, 2d edit., 1998. 1st lt. JAGC, U.S. Army, 1956-59. Recipient David W. Pollard achievement award Atlanta Bar Assn., 1994. Fellow Am. Coll. Bankruptcy; mem. Southeastern Bankruptcy Law Inst. (founder, Walter Homer Drake Professorship of Bankruptcy Law established at Walter F. George Sch. Law 1996), Nat. Conf. Bankruptcy Judges (pres. 1972-73). Address: PO Box 1408 Newnan GA 30264-1408 Office: US Courthouse 18 Greenville St Newnan GA 30263-2602

DRAKE, WILLIAM FRANK, JR., lawyer; b. St. Louis, Mar. 29, 1932; s. William Frank and Beatrice Drake; m. Martha Minohr Mockbee. BA, Principia Coll., 1954; LLB, Yale U., 1957. Bar: Pa. 1958. Practice Phila., 1958-68, 84—; mem. firm Montgomery, McCracken, Walker & Rhoads, 1958-68, 87-96, of counsel, 1984-87, 96—; sr. v.p., gen. counsel Alco Std. Corp., 1968-79, 96-98, sr. v.p. adminstrn., 1979-83; chmn., CEO Alco Health Svcs. Corp., 1983-84, vice chmn., 1984-98, also bd. dirs.; vice chmn., gen. counsel Alco Standard Corp. (now Ikon Office Solutions Inc.), 1996-98. Trustee Peoples Light & Theatre Co., Malvern, Pa. With U.S. Army, 1957-58. Mem. ABA, Pa. Bar Assn., Phila. Bar Assn., Union League (Phila.), Roaring Fork Club (Basalt, Colo.), Wilmington (Del.) Country Club, First Troop, Phila. City Calvary. Office: Montgomery McCracken Walker & Rhoads 123 S Broad St Fl 24 Philadelphia PA 19109-1099

DRAKEMAN, DONALD LEE, biotechnology company executive, lawyer; b. Camden, N.J., Oct. 21, 1953; s. Fred J. and Jean (Faucett) D.; m. Lisa Natale Drakeman, Aug. 23, 1975; children: Cynthia, Amy. AB magna cum laude, Dartmouth Coll., 1975; JD, Columbia U., 1979; MA, Princeton U., 1984, PhD, 1988. Bar: N.J. 1979, U.S. Dist. Ct. N.J. 1979, N.Y. 1980, U.S. Supreme Ct. 1984. Assoc. Milbank, Tweed, Hadley & McCloy, N.Y.C., 1979-82; gen. counsel Essex Chem. Corp., Clifton, N.J., 1982-89, v.p., 1987-89; pres. Essex Med. Products, Clifton, 1988-89; pres., CEO Medarex, Inc., Annandale, N.J., 1987—; adj. prof. polit. sci. Montclair (N.J.) State Coll., 1984; rsch. cons. Lilly Found., Inc., 1989-90; lectr. dept. politics Princeton U., 1990-93, 95—; bd. dirs. Immuno-Designed Molecules, Paris; bd. mem. Biotech. Industry Orgn. Author: Church-State Constitutional Issues, 1990; co-editor Church and State in American History, 1986; contbr. articles to profl. jours. Chmn. Montclair Bd. Adjustment, 1984; bd. trustees, chair Biotechnology Coun. N.J.; trustee U. of Charleston, 1999—. Harlan Fiske Stone scholar, Columbia U., 1976-79. Mem. ABA, AAAS, Assn. Bar City N.Y., Nat. Coun. Chs. (religious liberty com.), Am. Arbitration Assn. (arbitrator), Princeton Alumni Coun., John Maclean Soc., Princeton Club, Yale Club. Home: 49 Rolling Hill Rd Skillman NJ 08558-2319 Office: Medarex Inc 1545 Us Highway 22 Annandale NJ 08801-3059

DRAKEMAN, LISA N., biotechnology company executive; b. Boston, Oct. 30, 1953; d. Paul and Josephine (Covino) Natale; m. Donald L. Drakeman, Aug. 23, 1975; children: Cynthia Leigh Drakeman, Amy Elizabeth Drakeman. BA, Mt. Holyoke Coll., 1975; MA, Rutgers U., 1983, Princeton U., 1986; PhD, Princeton U., 1988. Chair, v. chair Monclair (N.J.) Redevelopment Agy., 1981-84; vis. scholar Dartmouth Coll., 1988-89; lectr. Princeton U., 1989-92; asst. dir. Alumni Coun. of Princeton U., 1991; dir. administrn. Medarex, Inc., Princeton, N.J., 1991-94; v.p. adminstrn. Medarex, Inc., 1994-96, v.p., 1996-98, sr. v.p., head bus. devel., 1998—; CEO Genmab A/S, 1999—; faculty fellow Grad. Coll. Princeton U., 1991-93, mem. adv. coun. dept. religion, 1996—; bd. dirs. Medarex Europe, B.V., GenPharm. Internat., Inc. Biopharm. adv. coun. Tech. Coun. Greater Phila., 1993-96; Gov.'s Biopharm. Task Force N.J. Econ. Master Plan Commn., Trenton, 1994-95; biotech. adv. com. The Franklin Inst., Phila., 1994-96; commr. Prosperity N.J., 1995—. Garden State Graduate Fellow State of N.J., 1981-85. Mem. Soc. for Advancement of Women's Health Rsch. (steering com., corp. adv. coun. 1994-97), Biotech. Industry Orgn. (chair nat. capital formation task force 1995-98, Advocate of Yr. award 1995), Biotech. Coun. N.J. (v.p. 1996—, Outstanding Industry Woman of Yr. 1996). Home: 49 Rolling Hill Rd Skillman NJ 08558-2319 Office: Medarex, Inc. 1545 Us Highway 22 Annandale NJ 08801-3059

DRAKES, DUAN ANTHONY, surgeon; b. Christ Ch., Barbados, Mar. 1, 1949; s. Mitchinson and Enid Drakes; m. Sept. 28, 1974; children: Steven Paul, Candice Andrea, Michael Marshall. BSc with hons., CUNY, 1976; MD, Howard U., 1979; mgmt. cert., Johns Hopkins U., 1999. Diplomate Am. Bd. Surgery, Am. Bd. Thoracic Surgery. Pvt. practice surgery Washington, D.C., 1986—; chief cardio-thoracic surgery, D.C. Gen. Hosp., Washington, 1989-92; chief cardiac surgery Howard U. Hosp. 1995. Pres. Christian Home and Family Assn., Md., 1999-2001, Internmed. Investment Group, Md., 1999—; bd. dirs. Health and Temperance Dept., Hyattsville, Md., 1999-2001. Fellow ACS (assoc.); mem. Soc. Thoracic Surgeons. Avocations: skiing, sailing, tennis, swimming, fitness. E-mail: d 3350@ewls.con. Home: 7003 Southwall Ter Hyattsville MD 20782 Office: 106 Irving St NW Washington DC 20010

DRAKULICH, MARTHA, arts educator; b. Wiesbaden, Germany, Feb. 11, 1931; d. Hans and Martha (Minor) Zwinkau; m. Mike Drakulich, Mar. 1953; 1 child, Starley. BA, Von Teuffel, Wiesbaden. Tchr. Phoenix Parks and Recreation and Librs., Phoenix, Glendale (Ariz.) Community Coll. Contbr. articles to profl. jours. Founder, pres. U. Ariz. Coop. Extension Homemaker's Club. Home: 16640 N 34th Dr Phoenix AZ 85053-2914

DRANCHAK, LAWRENCE JOHN, retired mechanical engineer; b. Scranton, Pa., Sept. 1, 1929; s. John J. and Rose (Barron) D.; m. Leota Mae Zimmerman, Aug. 14, 1954; children: Diana Rose, John Lawrence. BSME, Ind. Inst. Tech., 1956, DME, 1994. Ohio master gardener. Quality control technician Wright Aero. Corp., Woodridge, N.J., 1945; weaver L&M Weaving Corp., Scranton, 1947-50; automotive engr. Ford Motor Co., Dearborn, Mich., 1956-94; ret., 1994. Inventor automobile door magnetic weatherstrip. Cub scout advisor Boy Scouts Am., Taylor, Mich., 1963-68; adult advisor CAP, Dearborn, 1970-79; advisor Jr. Achievement, 1975-76. With U.S. Army, 1950-52, N.G., 1947-50. Mem. Soc. Automotive Engrs., Am. Legion, VFW. Republican. Roman Catholic. Avocations: gardening, feline husbandry, radio control model aircraft, computers, old automobile and truck rebuilding. Home: 21810 Rd E PO Box 165 Continental OH 45831

DRANE, WALTER HARDING, publishing executive, business consultant; b. Clarksville, Tenn., Feb. 18, 1915; s. William McClure and Mary Stacker (Luckett) D.; m. Maud Carson Tucker, Aug. 30, 1941; children—Eleanor Drane Christensen, Roberta Luckett, Walter Harding, Beverley Drane Coughlin. AB, U. of South, 1935; postgrad. in bus, Case-Western Res. U., 1936-38. Pres. Banks-Baldwin Law Pub. Co., Cleve., 1960-78, chmn., 1978-93, also bd. dirs.; founder, pres. Walter H. Drane Co., Cleve., 1955-60, chmn., 1960-75; pvt. bus. cons. Author, editor: Journals of William Minor Lile, 2 vols., 1987-88, Ancestors-Growing Up-and Other Things, 1992. Bd. dirs. Univ. Circle br. YMCA, Cleve., 1958-69, Christian Residences Found., 1979-85; mem. adv. com. St. Lukes Hosp., Cleve., 1981—; pres. Cleve. Sr. Council, 1986-87. Served with USN, 1940-45. Episcopalian. Home: 12546 Cedar Rd Apt 3 Cleveland Heights OH 44106

DRANITZKE, RICHARD J., surgeon; b. L.I., N.Y., 1940. MD, Columbia U., 1966. Diplomate Am. Bd. Surgery, Am. Bd. Thoracic Surgery. Intern Columbia-Presbyn. Hosp., N.Y.C., 1966-67; resident in surgery Bellevue Hosp. Ctr., N.Y.C., 1969-73; resident in cardiothoracic surgery Albany Med. Ctr., 1973-75; dir. surgery and chief thoracic and vascular surgery St. Charles Hosp., Port Jefferson, N.Y., 1991—; chief thoracic and vascular surgery St. Charles and J.T. Mather Meml. Hosp., 1985—; chief vascular surgery Brookhaven Meml. Hosp. Med. Ctr., 1985—; clin. instr. dept. surgery Stony Brook U. Hosp., 1994—. Mem. ACP, ACS, AMA, Soc. Thoracic Surgeons. Office: 635 Belle Terre Rd Port Jefferson NY 11777 also: 286 Sills Rd Patchogue NY 11772

DRANSITE, BRIAN ROBERT, electrical engineer; b. Glen Cove, N.Y., Oct. 26, 1964; s. Robert Stanley and Jane Theresa (Reidy) D. AS in Engring. Sci. magna cum laude, Nassau C.C., Garden City, N.Y., 1984; BSEE, Rensselaer Poly. Inst., 1986; MBA in Mgmt., Hofstra U., 1995. Offset printer Plainview (N.Y.)-Old Bethpage Cen. Sch. Dist., 1980-84; project engr. Knogo Corp. (Sentry Technologies), Hauppauge, N.Y., 1987-91; sr. electronic design engr. Ultre divsn. Linotype-Hell, Melville, N.Y., 1991-96; product mgr. Symbol Technologies, Holtsville, N.Y., 1996—. Mem. IEEE, MBA Assn. Hofstra U. (v.p. fin. 1994-95), Planetary Soc., Rensselaer Assn. Divers (equipment mgr. 1986-87), Phi Theta Kappa. Avocations: astronomy, numismatic research, photography, scuba diving, boating.

DRAPALIK, BETTY RUTH, civic worker, artist; b. Cicero, Ill., July 4, 1932; d. Henry William and Jennie Margaret (Robbins) Degen; m. Joseph James Drapalik, Oct. 30, 1951; children: Betty Jennifer Drapalik Coryell, Joseph Henry. Grad. high sch., Cicero. Sec., clk. Gt. Lakes (Ill.) Naval Base, until 1982; sect. to asst. dir. Arden Shore Boys' Home, Lake Bluff, Ill., 1984-87. Group exhbns. include Anderson Art Ctr., Kenosha, Wis., 1994-99, Dellora A. Norris Cultural Arts Ctr., St. Charles, Ill., 1998, 99, Women's Works, Old Courthouse Art Ctr., Woodstock, Ill., 1994, 95, Cmty. Gallery of Art, Coll. of Lake County, Grayslake, Ill., 1993, 94, 96, 97, 98, 99, David Adler Cultural Ctr., Libertyville, Ill., 1994, 97, 98, 99, Lake County Mus. Wauconda, Ill., 1996, 97, 98, 99, Wauconda Pub. Libr., 19, Kenosha Pub. Mus., 1998 (award of excellence 1998), Layson Gallery, Waukegan, Ill., 1993, Spotlight Gallery, Kenosha, Wis., 1998, Monne's Gallery, Kenosha, 1998, Waukegan Visual Arts Ctr., 1998, Hardy Gallery, Ephraim, Wis., 1996, 97, 98 (Purchase award 1998), Hawthorne Hollow Art Festival, Kenosha, Wis., 1997, 98, Deer Path Art League Festival, Lake Forest, Ill., 1997, 99, Lake County Art League (1st pl. watercolor Fine Arts Festival at North Point Marina, Winthrop Harbor, Ill., 1996, 2nd pl. watercolor 1997, 98, pub. rels. chair 1997, 98, 99, Best of Show Fall Membership Show 1996, 97, Award of Merit watercolor 1998, award of Excellence Spring Membership Show, 1999), Truman State U., Kirksville, Mo., 1997, Red River Watercolor Soc. juried show Moorhead (Minn.) State U., 1997, Kenosha Art Assn. and Lake County Art League Combined Art Event, 1997 (Best of Show 1997), Zion (Ill.) Zion Chamber Orch. Concert and Art Contest, 1998 (Best of Show, 1st Pl.), N.W. N.Mex. Arts Coun., Farmington, 1997; two-person shows include Jack Benny Ctr. for the Arts, Waukegan, 1996, 98; one-woman shows include Jack Benny Ctr. for the Arts, 1995, Wauconda Area Pub. Libr., 1999. Former leader and mem. pub. rels. com. Girl Scouts U.S. Recipient purchase award Coll. of Lake County, Grayslake, Ill., 1994, numerous other courtesy awards; featured in Art Mag., 1997. Mem. Lake County Art League (resource person, pres., various bd. positions), Lakes Region Watercolor Guild (rec. sec., co-program chair, exhibit chairperson), Midwest Watercolor Soc., Deerpath Art League, Red River Watercolor Soc., Kenosha Art Assn., N.W. Area Arts Coun., Bloomin' Artists, Internat. Starcraft Camper Club (Ill. chpt. sec./treas. 1975). Evangelical. Avocations: watercolor, photography, camping, gardening, hiking. Home and Studio: 2018 W Grove Ave Waukegan IL 60085-1607

DRAPEAU, PHILLIP DAVID, banking executive; b. Rochester, N.H., July 28, 1938; s. Henry Philip Drapeau and Barbara Rosalee (Tufts) Munroe; children from previous marriage: David, Sandra, Jeffrey, Scott; m. Sandra A. Ruel, Apr. 14, 1978; children: Jennifer, Denise. BS, U. N.H., 1961; diploma mgmt., Ohio State U., 1965; diploma grad. banking, Fairfield U., 1981. Teller Rochester Savings Bank and Trust Co., 1961-63, mortgage officer, 1963-65, asst. treas., 1965-68, v.p., treas., 1968-72, exec. v.p., 1972-81, pres., 1981-82; pres. BankEast Savings Bank and Trust, Rochester, 1982-88; pres., CEO BankEast Mortgage Corp., Manchester, N.H., 1989-92; CEO Siwooganock Bank, Lancaster, N.H., 1993—; past pres., bd. dirs. Indsl. Devel. Com.; past pres. Greater Rochester Devel. Corp. Bd. dirs., treas., Rochester Boys Club, 1972-77; bd. dirs. Rochester Vis. Nurses Assn., 1976-78, N.H. Bus. Devel. Corp., Rochester Econ. Devel. Commn., Gafney Home for Aged; mem. Rochester Citizens Avd. Com.; trustee Noyes Fund; mem. Col. Towne Investment Com. Recipient Man and Boy award Rochester Boys Club, 1977. Mem. Am. Inst. Banking (past pres.), N.H. Bankers Assn., Strafford City Bd. Realtors, Rochester C. of C. (bd. dirs.). Lodges: Rotary, Elks. Avocations: fishing, boating, gardening, travel. Office: Siwooganock Bank Main St Lancaster NH 03584

DRAPER, CHARLES WILLIAM, religious studies educator; b. Jacksonville, Tex., May 25, 1947; s. James Thomas and Lois Jeanne (Keeling) D.; m. Retta Lynn Wymer, June 7, 1969; children: Rachelle Lynn, Charles David. BA, Baylor U., 1968; MDiv, Southwestern Bapt. Theol. Sem., 1971; DMin, Luther Rice Sem., 1981; postgrad., New Orleans Bapt. Theol. Sem. Adj. prof. Wayland Bapt. U., Plainview, Tex., 1990-92, New Orleans Bapt. Theol. Sem., 1993-96; asst. prof. Christian studies North Greenville Coll., Tigerville, S.C., 1996-98; asst. prof. Bibl. studies James P. Boyce Coll. Bible, divsn. So. Bapt. Theol. Sem., Louisville, 1998—. Editor, contbr. Holman Bible Dictionary, 1998; contbr. articles to profl. jours. Mem. Am. Acad. Religion, Soc. Bibl. Lit., N.Am. Patristic Soc., Nat. Assn. Bapt. Prof. Religion, Evang. Theol. Soc. Republican. Avocations: scuba diving, Civil War history. Office: So Bapt Theol Sem 2825 Lexington Rd Louisville KY 40280-0001

DRAPER, DANIEL CLAY, lawyer; b. Boston, June 7, 1920; s. John W. and Lulu H. (Clay) D.; m. Marcia Humphreys, Nov. 25, 1989. BA, W.Va. U., 1940, MA, 1941; LLB, Harvard U., 1947. Assoc. Kelly, Drye & Warren, N.Y.C., 1947-55; ptnr. Cadwalader, Wickersham & Taft, N.Y.C., 1962-91, ret.; bd. dirs. Union Devel., Montclair, N.J.; adj. prof. history Bloomfield Coll., 1991. Contbr. articles to profl. jours. Mgr. campaign Montclair's Cmty. Com. Candidates, 1964; trustee Montclair Art Mus., 1966-71, Bloomfield Coll., 1974-81, 87-95. With USN, 1942-46. Decorated Bronze Star, European Service Ribbon (3 stars). Mem. N.Y. State Bar Assn. (chmn. banking com. 1981-85), N.Y. County Lawyers Assn. (sec. 1979-81, pres. 1984-87, chmn. banking com. 1968-78, housing and urban affairs and real property coms., chmn. investment com.), St. George Soc., Harvard Club, N.Y.C. Episcopalian. Home: 14 Houston Rd Little Falls NJ 07424-2406

DRAPER, EDGAR, psychiatrist; b. St. Louis, Feb. 5, 1926; s. Neal McLain and Florence Mabel (Meyers) D.; m. Norma Jane Alexander, Mar. 16, 1949; children: Sue Draper Masteller, Anne Draper Klevay, Neal Edgar. AB, Washington U., 1946; BD, Garrett Biblical Inst., 1949; MD, Washington U. Med. Sch., 1953; grad., Inst. for Psychoanalysis, Chgo., 1966. Diplomate Am. Bd. Psychiatry and Neurology. Intern Washington U. Svc. City Hosp., St. Louis, 1953-54; resident in psychiatry U. Cin., 1954-55, 57-59; sr. asst. surgeon USPHS, Ft. Worth, 1955-57; from instr. to assoc. prof. U. Chgo., 1959-68; co-dir. psychiat. outpatient dept., prof. psychiatry U. Mich., Ann Arbor, 1968, dir. psychiat. resident edn., 1968-74, prof. postgrad edn., 1970-75; prof., chmn. dept. psychiatry U. Miss. Med. Ctr., Jackson, 1975-93; prof. psychiatry U. Miss., Jackson, 1993-94; prof. emeritus, 1994—; cons. in field. Contbr. numerous articles to profl. jours. Bd. dirs. Friends Libr. Named Vis. scholar U. Chgo., 1987, Fellow Soc. for Sci. Study of Religion, 1987, Man of Month Pastoral Psychology, 1970; recipient Physicians Recognition award, 1982-85, Cert. Appreciation Mental Health Assn. Hinds County, 1983, Plaque of Commendation Chgo. Acad. Religion and Mental Health, 1966-67. Fellow Am. Psychiat. Assn. (life), Am. Coll. Psychiatry (life), Am. Soc. Psychoanalytic Physicians, Soc. for Sci. Study of Religion (life), Am. Coll. Psychoanalysts (life, program chmn.), So. Psychiat. Assn. (parlimentarian 1980—); mem. Miss. Psychiat. Assn. (past pres.), Miss. State Med. Soc., Mich. Psychiat. Soc., Washtenaw County Med. Soc., Mich. State Med. Soc., So. Psychiat. Assn., Mich. Psychoanalytic Soc., Mental Health Assn. (bd. dirs. Jackson).

DRAPER, E(RNEST) LINN, JR., electric utility executive; b. Houston, Feb. 6, 1942; s. Ernest Linn and Marcia L. (Saylor) D.; m. Mary Deborah Doyle, June 9, 1962; children: Susan Elizabeth, Robert Linn, Barbara Ann, David Doyle. Student, Williams Coll., 1960-62; BAChemE, Rice U., 1964, BSChemE, 1965; PhD in Nuclear Engring., Cornell U., 1970. Asst. prof. nuclear engring. U. Tex., Austin, 1969-72, assoc. prof., 1972-79; tech. asst. to CEO Gulf States Utilities Co., Beaumont, Tex., 1979, v.p. nuclear tech., 1980-81, sr. v.p. engring. tech. services, 1981-82, sr. v.p. external affairs, 1982-84, sr. v.p. external affairs and prodn., 1984-85, exec. v.p. external affairs and prodn., 1985-86, vice chmn., 1985-87, COO, 1986, pres., CEO, 1986-92, chmn. bd. dirs., 1987-92; pres. AEPCo., Inc.; pres., COO Am. Electric Power Svc. Corp., Columbus, Ohio, 1992-93; chmn., pres., CEO Am. Electric Power Co. and Svc. Corp., Columbus, 1993—; mem. adv. panel on alternative means of financing and mng. radioactive waste mgmt. U.S. Dept. Energy, 1984-85; bd. dirs. Cellnet Data Sys. Inc., Borden Chems. and Plastics. Fellow NSF, 1965-66, AEC, 1967-68. Mem. NAE, Am. Nuclear Soc. (pres. 1984-85), Nuclear Energy Inst. (chmn. 1993-95), Edison Electric Inst. (chmn. 1996-97). Office: Am Electric Power Inc 1 Riverside Plz Columbus OH 43215-2355

DRAPER, GERALD LINDEN, lawyer; b. Oberlin, Ohio, July 14, 1941; s. Earl Linden and Mary Antoinette (Colotto) D.; m. Barbara Jean Winter, Aug. 26, 1960; children: Melissa Leigh Price, Stephen Edward Draper. BA, Muskingum Coll., 1963; JD, Northwestern U., 1966. Bar: Ohio, 1966, U.S. Dist. Ct. (so. dist.) Ohio, 1966, U.S. Ct. Appeals (6th cir.), 1975, U.S. Supreme Ct., 1980. Ptnr. Bricker & Eckler, Columbus, Ohio, 1966-88, Thompson, Hine & Flory, Columbus, 1989-95, Draper, Hollenbaugh, Briscoe, Yashko & Carmany, Columbus, 1996—. Trustee, past pres. Wesley Glen Retirement Ctr., Columbus, 1979-95; trustee Muskingum Coll., New Concord, Ohio, 1988-92, 93—, vice chair, 1994—; trustee, pres. Wesley Ridge Retirement Ctr., 1995—. Fellow Am. Coll. Trial Lawyers, Am. Bd. Trial Advocates; mem. ABA (Ho. of Dels.), Ohio State Bar Assn. (pres. 1990-91), Ohio State Bar Found. (trustee 1992-97), Columbus Bar Assn. (pres. 1982-83, Bar Svc. medal 1998), Columbus Bar Found. (pres. 1984-86), Nat. Conf. of Bar Found. (trustee 1987-90, 91-94), Ohio Continuing Legal Edn. Inst. (trustee 1992-98, chair 1997-98), Ohio Assn. Hosp. Attys., Def. Rsch. Inst. Avocations: travel, golf, photography. Office: Draper Hollenbaugh Briscoe Yashko and Carmany LPA 175 S 3rd St Ste 1250 Columbus OH 43215-5199

DRAPER, JAMES DAVID, art museum curator; b. Lebanon, Mo., Mar. 6, 1943; s. John Hilton and Hazel (Berg) D. BA, U. Mo., 1965; MA, NYU, 1967, PhD, 1984. Curatorial asst. Met. Mus. Art, N.Y.C., 1969, various positions, 1969-84, dept. curator, 1984—, Henry R. Kravis curator, 1995—; fellow J. Paul Getty Mus., Malibu, Calif. Author: Bertoldo di Giovanni, Sculptor of the Medici Household, 1992; co-author: (exhbn. catalogue) Augustin Pajou, Royal Sculptor, 1998; editor: (rev. critical edit.) The Italian Bronze Statuettes of the Renaissance (W. von Bode), 1980. Episcopalian. Office: Met Mus Art 1000 5th Ave New York NY 10028-0113

DRAPER, JAMES THOMAS, JR. (JIMMY DRAPER), clergyman; b. Hartford, Ark., Oct. 10, 1935; s. James T.Draper; m. Carol Ann Floyd, 1956; children: Randy, Bailey, Terri. BA, Baylor U., 1957; BD, Southwestern Bapt. Theol. Sem., MDiv; DD (hon.), Howard Payne U., Brownwood, Tex.; DHum (hon.), Dallas Bapt. Coll.; DD (hon.), Campbell U., Buies Creek, N.C. Ordained to ministry Bapt. Ch. Pastor Steep Hollow Bapt. Ch., Bryan, Tex., Iredell (Tex.) Bapt. Ch., Temple Bapt. Ch., Tyler, Tex., Univ. park Bapt. Ch., San Antonio, Red Bridge Bapt. Ch., Kansas City, Mo., First So. Bapt. Ch., Del City, Okla.; assoc. pastor First Bapt. Ch., Dallas; pastor First Bapt. Ch., Euless, Tex.; pres. Life Way Christian Resources of the So. Bapt. Convention, 1991—; mem. adminstrv. com. Bapt. Gen. Conv., Tex., mem. exec. bd., mem. missions funding com., mem. exec. dir. search com.; pres. So. Bapt. Conv. (1982-84), So. Baptist Conv. Pastors Conf., 1979-80; trustee So. Bapt. Conv. Annuity Bd., 1974-82, Baylor U., Waco, Tex., 1974-83, Southwestern Bapt. Theol. Sem., 1984-91; preacher numerous convs., confs. Author 22 books; contbr. articles to religious jours. Office: Life Way Christian Resource Office of So Bapt Convention Office of the Pres 127 9th Ave S Nashville TN 37203-3802

DRAPER, JAMES WILSON, lawyer; b. Detroit, Dec. 26, 1926; s. Kenneth Draper and Dorothy (Wilson) Barker; m. Alice Patricia Sullivan, May 16, 1953; children: Catherine Draper Clain, Julie Draper Fazekas, James P., Martha Draper Grossman. BA, U. Mich., 1949, JD, 1951. Bar: Mich. 1951, U.S. Dist. Ct. (so. dist.) Mich. 1951, U.S. Ct. Appeals (6th cir.) 1951. Assoc. Dykema, Jones & Wheat and successor firms, Detroit, 1951-61; ptnr. Dykema Gossett, and predecessor firms, Detroit, 1961—; past chmn. real property law sect. council State Bar Mich. Served with USN, 1944-46. Fellow Am. Coll. Real Estate Lawyers; mem. Mich. State Bar (past chmn. real property law sect., land title stds. com.), Detroit Club, Country Club Detroit (Grosse Point Farms, Mich.). Republican. Presbyterian. Home: 113 Merriweather Rd Grosse Pointe MI 48236-3622 Office: Dykema Gossett 400 Renaissance Ctr Ste 3800 Detroit MI 48243-1668

DRAPER, RICHARD NELSON, banker; b. Washington, July 29, 1959; s. Theron N. and Patricia A. (Rawson) D.; m. Laurel A. Halversen, June 22, 1985; children: R. Nathan, Natalie N., T. Cole. BS in Fin., Brigham Young U., 1985; MBA with honors, U. Utah, 1989. Loan officer First Security Bank of Utah, Salt Lake City, 1985-88; sr. cons. Ernst & Young, Salt Lake City, 1989-91; supervised loans mgr. First Nat. Bank of Layton, Utah, 1991-97, mgr. constrn. dept., 1993-97; area constrn. mgr. First Security Bank, Ogden, Utah, 1997-98; northern Utah constrn. mgr. Washington Mutual Bank, Ogden, Utah, 1998—; pvt. practice cons., fin., real estate advisor, Wasatch Front, Utah, 1994—. Mem. No. Wasatch Home Builder Assn. (chmn. Table Top fund raisers 1996-97), Beta Gamma Sigma. Republican. Mem. LDS Ch. Avocations: skiing, hiking, golf, tennis. Office: Washington Mutual Bank 4185 South Harrison Blvd Ogden UT 84403

DRAPER, SHARON M., educator, author. BA summa cum laude, Pepperdine U., 1970; MA summa cum laude, Miami U., 1973. Cert. Nat. Bd. Profl. Tchg. Stds. Mem. faculty Walnut Hills (Ohio) H.S., 1978—; spkr., presenter in field; bd. dirs. Nat. Bd. Profl. Tchg. Stds. Author: Tears of a Tiger (Best Book for Young Adults, King Genesis award ALA), Lost in the tunnel of Time, Ziggy and the Black Dinosaurs, also short stories (Ebony mag. 1st prize 1991). Recipient Excellence in Tchg. award Nat. Coun. Negro Women, 1998, Gov.'s Ednl. Leadership award Gov. of Ohio, 1998, honors Miss. Coun. Tchrs., Cin. City Coun., Ohio State Ho. of Reps., Cin. Bd. Edn.; named Ohio Tchr. of the Yr., 1997, Nat. Tchr. of the Yr., 1997. Mem. Am. Fedn. Tchrs., Ohio Fedn. Tchrs., Cin. Fedn. Tchrs., Nat. Coun. Tchrs. English, Internat. Reading Assn., Delta Kappa Gamma, Phi Delta Kappa. Office: Walnut Hills JSHS 3250 Victory Pkwy Cincinnati OH 45207-1457

DRAPER, STEPHEN ELLIOT, lawyer, engineer; b. Columbus, Ga., Mar. 17, 1942; s. Philip Henry and Ethel Illges (Woodruff) D.; m. Lucy Leila Hargrett, June 20, 1970; 1 child, Jessie Roxanne. BS, U.S. Mil. Acad., 1964; MBA, C.W. Post/L.I. U., 1976; JD, Ga. State U., 1992; MSCE, PhD, Ga. Inst. Tech., 1971, 81. Registered profl. engr., Ga., Fla. Commd. 2d. lt. U.S. Army, 1964, advanced through grades to col., retired, 1984; forensic engr. Atlanta, 1984-86; pres. and tech. dir. Draper Engring. Rsch., Atlanta, 1986-93, The Draper Group, Atlanta, 1993—. Contbr. articles to profl. jours. Bd. dirs. J.W. & E.I. Woodruff Found., Columbus, Ga., 1991—, Met. Boys Club, Columbus, 1981-84; mem. long-range planning com. Atlanta Area Coun., Boys Scouts Am., 1972; trustee the Foxcroft Sch., Middleburg, Va., 1994; bd. visitors U. Ga. Libr., 1997—; mem. svc. acad. selection bd. U.S. Senate, 1998—. Decorated Gallantry Cross with Silver Star, Legion of Merit, Bronze Star (2), Soldier's medal, Purple Heart (3), Air medal (2), Army Commendation medal (4), others; recipient Am. Jurisprudence award Ga. State U., 1992, Spl. Actions award Women's Equity Action League, 1976. Mem. ABA, ASCE, NSPE, Am. Water Resources Assn., Nat. Acad. Forensic Engrs., Capital City Club, Commerce Club, Sea Island Beach Club. Avocations: travel, history, sports, phys. fitness. Office: The Draper Group 1401 Peachtree St NE Ste 500 Atlanta GA 30309-3000

DRAPER, VERDEN ROLLAND, accountant; b. St. Louis, Feb. 23, 1916; s. Neal McLain and Florence (Meyers) D.; m. Eileen Ogden, Aug. 18, 1940; children: Mallen, Eileen Ann, Cynthia, Patti, Verden. B.S., Washington U., St. Louis, 1938. With Price Waterhouse & Co. (C.P.A.s), St. Louis, 1938-51, Tulsa, 1951-55, Pitts., 1955-60, Buffalo, 1960—; mem. faculty Washington U., St. Louis U., U. Tulsa. Author: (with Robert H. Irving) Accounting Practices in the Petroleum Industry, 1958; contbr. articles profl. publs. Former pres. Better Bus. Bur. Western N.Y. Served with USNR, World War II. Mem. Am. Inst. C.P.A.s Mo., Okla., Pa., N.Y. State socs. C.P.A.s, Am. Accounting Assn., Buffalo Area C. of C. (treas., dir.), Beta Gamma Sigma, Omicron Delta Kappa, Delta Sigma Pi (Alumnae award 1938), Alpha Kappa Psi (hon.), Theta Xi. Presbyterian. Clubs: Buffalo Country (past treas., gov.), Buffalo. Home: Bears Paw Country Club 721 Wildwood Ln Naples FL 34105-3215 Office: 3600 Marine Midland Ctr Buffalo NY 14203-2836

DRAPER, WILLIAM HENRY, III, business executive; b. White Plains, N.Y., Jan. 1, 1928; s. William Henry and Katherine (Baum) D.; m. Phyllis Culbertson, June 13, 1953; children: Rebecca, Polly, Timothy. BA, Yale U., 1950; MBA, Harvard U., 1954; LLD (hon.), Southeastern U., 1985; MA (hon.), Yale U., 1991. With Inland Steel Co., Chgo., 1954-59, Draper, Gaither & Anderson, Palo Alto, Calif., 1959-62; pres. Draper & Johnson Investment Co., Palo Alto, 1962-65; founder, gen. ptnr. Sutter Hill Ventures, Palo Alto, 1965-81; pres., chmn. U.S. Export-Import Bank, Washington, 1981-86; adminstr., CEO, UN Devel. Programme, 1986-93; mng. dir. Draper Internat., San Francisco, 1994—; bd. dirs. numerous cos. Chmn. bd. Am. Conservatory Theatre, 1980-81, bd. dirs., 1977-81; bd. dirs. Population Crisis Com., 1976-81, Atlantic Coun., 1989—, World Rehab. Fund, 1988-92, Ctr. for Econ. Policy Rsch., Stanford U., 1988, Internat. Inst. Edn., 1989—; vice chmn. Population Action Internat., 1993—; mem. adv. bd. Stanford Grad. Sch. Bus. Adminstrn., 1980-86; nat. co-chmn. fin. com. George Bush for Pres., 1980; bd. dirs., former chmn. Rep. Alliance.; trustee Yale U., 1991-98, George Bush Libr. Found., 1993—. With U.S. Army, 1946-48, 51-52. Recipient Alumni Achievement award Harvard Bus. Sch., 1982, Medal of Honor Ellis Island, 1992; named one of the U.S.'s 50 New Corp. Elite, Bus. Week mag., 1985. Mem. Coun. on Fgn. Rels., Overseas Devel. Coun., Pacific Union Club, Bohemian Club, Met. Club, Chevy Chase Club, River Club. Home: 91 Tallwood Ct Atherton CA 94027-6431 Office: Draper Internat 50 California St Ste 2925 San Francisco CA 94111-4726

DRASKOCZY, PAUL R., psychiatrist; b. Stari Becej, Yugoslavia, Mar. 4, 1926; s. Edward and Maria (Szekely) D.; widowed. MD, Med. U. Szeged, 1951. Diplomate Am. Bd. Psychiatry & Neurology. Asst. prof. pharmacology Med. U. Szeged, Hungary, 1951-56; instr., asst. prof. pharmacology Harvard Med. Sch., Boston, 1958-72; resident in psychiatry Boston City Hosp., 1972-75; staff psychiatrist Solomon Mental Health Ctr., Lowell, Mass., 1975-76, VA Hosp., Bedford, Mass., 1976-97; assoc. prof. psychiatry Boston U., 1977—; pvt. practice, Weston, Mass., 1975—. Contbr. numerous articles to profl. jours. in pharmacology and psychopharmacology. Mem. Am. Psychiat. Assn., Am. Soc. Pharmacology & Exptl. Therapies. Home: 726 Wellesley St Weston MA 02493-1000

DRASLER, GREGORY JOHN, artist; b. Waukegan, Ill., June 7, 1952; s. John W. and Patricia A. Drasler; m. Nancy B. Davidson, June 15, 1985. BFA, U. Ill., 1980, MFA, 1983. One person shows include Marianne Deson Gallery, Chgo., 1988, R. C. Erpf Gallery, N.Y., 1986, 87, 88, Shea & Beker Gallery, N.Y., 1990, Ctr. for Contemporary Art, Chgo., 1990, Queens Mus., Bulova Ctr., N.Y., 1994; exhibited in group shows New Mus. Contemporary Art, N.Y.C., 1983, 87, 92, Germans Van Eck Gallery, N.Y., 1984, John Berggruen Gallery, San Francisco, 1985, Jack Tilton Gallery, N.Y.C., 1986, Wellesley (Mass.) Coll. Mus., 1986, Robeson Ctr. Gallery, Rutgers U., Newark, 1987, Ben Shahn Galleries, William Patterson Coll., Wayne, N.J., 1988, Three Rivers Arts Festival, Carnegie Mus. Art, Pitts., 1989, U. Art Mus., SUNY, Binghamton, N.Y., 1989, Artist Space, N.Y.C., 1990, Flint (Mich.) Inst. Arts, Philharm. Ctr. for Arts, Knoxville Mus. Art, 1991-92, Flint Inst. Arts, 1993; represented in permanent collections Dow Jones Inc., N.Y.C., Krannert Art Mus., Champaign, Ill., Samuel Lindenbaum, Fisher Bros., U. Ill., Champaign, John W. Heckenger, Barbara Toll, Emily Landau, Henry Luce III Found., Sawyer Miller Group, N.Y.C.; featured in Flint Inst. Arts Cat., Art Press, 1991, Chgo. Tribune, 1990, Art in Am. mag., 1987, 90, N.Y. Times newspaper, 1987, 88, 91, The Independent Press newspaper, 1991, Ben Shahn Gallery cat., 1988, SUNY Binghamton U. Art Mus. cat., Carnegie Mus. Art cat., Artist Space cat., 1990,. Mary C. MacLellan fellow, 1980; MacDowell Colony Residence fellow, 1986; art fellow N.Y. Found of Arts, 1991; Nat. Endowment of Arts fellow, 1993; Djerassi Resident Artist Program fellow, 1996.

DRASNER, FRED, newspaper publishing executive. Pres., CEO U.S. News and World Report, N.Y.C., 1985-99; chief exec. officer, co-pub. N.Y. Daily News, N.Y.C., 1993-99; chmn., CEO, COO Applied Graphics Techs., 1999—. Office: New York Daily News 450 W 33rd St New York NY 10001*

DRAUGHON, DEBORAH, writer; b. Atlanta, Apr. 23, 1949; d. Kerney Lee and Doris Aline (Snyder) Draughon; m. George Douglas Hosea, 1964 (div. 1981); children: Michael Douglas, David George; m. Marvin Charles Hirsh, June 21, 1984 (div. 1996). AA in Bus. Adminstrn., Gainesville Coll., 1988; BA in Internat. Affairs cum laude, Kennesaw State Coll., 1991. Freelance writer, 1991—. Mem. Concerned Women for Am., Washington, 1991; instr. Am. Red Cross, Atlanta, 1991. Mem. Internat. Club, Blue Key, Golden Key. Republican. Avocations: traveling, gardening, piano. Home: 5180 Arbor View Way Sugar Hill GA 30518-6958

DRAWZ, JOHN ENGLUND, lawyer; b. Duluth, Minn., Aug. 19, 1942; s. Siegfried W. and Vivian M. (Englund) D.; m. Jean Ann Leininger, June 13, 1964; children: Paul Englund, Matthew John. BA, Macalester Coll., 1964; JD, U. Minn., 1967. Bar: Minn. 1967, U.S. Dist. Ct. Minn. 1969, U.S. Dist. Ct. N.D. 1994, U.S. Supreme Ct. 1995. Spl. asst. atty. gen. Office of the Minn. Atty. Gen., St. Paul, 1967-70; ptnr. LeFevere, Lefler, Kennedy, O'Brien & Drawz, Mpls., 1970-89, Messerli & Kramer, Mpls., 1989-91, Fredrikson & Byron, P.A., Mpls., 1991—. 1st lt. Minn. Air N.G., 1966-72. Mem. ABA, Minn. Bar Assn., Hennepin County Bar Assn. Avocations: golf, fishing, ice hockey. Home: 3317 Skycroft Cir St Anthony Village MN 55418-1716 Office: Fredrikson & Byron PA 1100 International Ctr 900 2nd Ave S Minneapolis MN 55402-3314*

DRAY, DWIGHT LEROY, retired school system administrator; b. Carrollton, Ohio, Apr. 15, 1918; s. William Andrew and Florence Emma Dray; m. Nellie Pauline Clark, Jan. 29, 1941 (dec. 1981); children: Mark Stanley, Paula Louise Dray Claypool; m. Eva Mae King, July 17, 1982. BA, Mount Union Coll., Alliance, Ohio, 1957; MA, U. Toledo, Ohio, 1964; postgrad., U. Akron, Ohio. Investigator Ohio Dept. Liquor Control, Columbus, 1946-48; carpenter Kintz Constrn. Co., Alliance, Ohio, 1948-50; clerk Penn R.R., Canton, Ohio, 1950-56; tchr. Perkins local schs., Sandusky, Ohio, 1956-63; elem., jr. high prin. Mapleton Local Schs., Ashland, Ohio, 1963-70; dir. schs. Mene Grande Oil Co., Caracus, Venezuela, 1970-71; supt. schs. Madison Consolidated local schs., Lore City, Ohio, 1971-75; curriculum coord. Guernsey Co. schs., Cambridge, Ohio, 1975-84. Contbr. articles to profl. jours. Councilman Cambridge City Coun., 1979-80, 91-95; pres. Cambridge Rotary Found., 1988-93; pres. Guernsey County Scholarship Found., 1990-93; chmn. fin. com. Boy Scouts Am., Zanesville, 1989-90; pres. Cambridge Area Beautification Coun., 1995-97, Cambridge Area Sign Commn., 1991-97. With U.S. Army, 1942. Named Educator of Yr. Phi Delta Kappa, Zanesville, 1983; Ford Found. scholar Western Carolina U., 1971; Paul Harris fellow Rotary Internat., Evansville, Ind., 1989. Mem. Am. Legion (commander 1960-61), Disabled Am. Vets (life), Phi Delta Kappa, Rotary (pres. 1983-84), Masons. Republican. Protestant. Home: 925 Avon Dr Cambridge OH 43725-2123

DRAY, MARK S., lawyer; b. Alliance, Ohio, Feb. 8, 1943; s. Dwight Leroy and N. Pauline (Clark) D.; m. Jonadell Pascoe, June 5, 1965; children: Melisa Louise, Justin Clark. BA, Mount Union Coll., Alliance, Ohio, 1965; JD, Coll. of William and Mary, 1968, M Law and Taxation, 1969. Bar: Va. 1968, U.S. Dist. Ct. (ea. dist.) Va. 1970, U.S. Tax Court 1971. Tax sr. Price Waterhouse, Washington, 1969-70; assoc. Hunton & Williams, Richmond, Va., 1970-77; ptnr. Hunton & Williams, Richmond, 1977—; adv. coun. William and Mary Tax Conf., 1980-88; mem. So. Employee Benefits Conf., 1974—; trustee So. Fed. Tax Inst., 1989—, chair, 1997. Contbr. articles to profl. jours.; speaker in field. Fellow Am. Coll. Tax Counsel; mem. ABA (com. on employee benefits 1975—, chmn. 1989-90, joint com. on employee benefits 1988-91, chmn. 1990-91), Va. Bar Assn., Richmond Bar Assn., Country Club Va., Order of Coif, Blue Key. Episcopalian. Avocation: golf. Office: Hunton & Williams Riverfront Plz East Tower PO Box 1535 Richmond VA 23218-1535

DRAY, WILLIAM HERBERT, philosophy educator; b. Montreal, June 23, 1921; s. William John and Florence Edith (Jones) D.; m. Doris Kathleen Best, Sept. 18, 1943; children: Christopher Reid, Jane Elizabeth. B.A. in History, U. Toronto, 1949; B.A. in Philosophy, Politics and Econs., Oxford U., 1951, M.A., 1955, D.Phil., 1956; LLD (hon.), Trent U., 1987. Lectr. U. Toronto, 1953-55, asst. prof., asso. prof., 1956-63, prof., 1963-68; prof. Trent U., 1968-76, chmn. dept. philosophy, 1968-73; prof. philosophy U. Ottawa, Ont., 1976-85, emeritus, 1986—. Author: Laws and Explanation in History, 1957, Philosophy of History, 1964, 2d edit., 1993, Perspectives on History, 1980, On History and Philosophers of History, 1989, History as Re-enactment, 1995; editor: Philosophical Analysis and History, 1966; co-editor: Substance and Form in History, 1981, Philosophie de l'histoire et la Pratique historienne d'aujourd'hui, 1982, The Principles of History, 1999. Served with RCAF, 1941-46, air navigator Can. W. Indies, U.K., Southeast Asia, RCAF, active reserve, 1956-66. Am. Council Learned Socs. fellow, 1960-61; Can. Council fellow, 1971-72, 78-79; Killam research fellow, 1980-81; Nat. Humanities Ctr. fellow, 1983-84; recipient Can. Council Molson prize, 1986. Fellow Royal Soc. Can. Home: 818-32 Clarissa Dr, Richmond Hill, ON Canada L4C 9R7 Office: Dept Philosophy, Univ of Ottawa, Ottawa, ON Canada K1N 6N5

DRAYTON, CAREY M., police administrator; b. New Orleans, Apr. 12, 1961; s. Washington Howard Drayton. BGS, U. South La., Lafayette, 1985; student, FBI Acad. Asst. dir. pub. safety U. South La., 1986-89; police officer George Washington U., Washington, 1989-90; dir. pub. safety U. Oreg., Eugene, 1990-95; chief of police The Fla. State U., Tallahassee, 1995—. Mem. Internat. Assn. Campus Law Enforcement Adminstrn. (chair comm. com.), Big Bend Basketball Assn. (pres.), Big Bend Football Assn. Office: Fla State U Police Dept 830 West Jefferson St Tallahassee FL 32306-4215

DRAYTON, JOHN N., publishing executive; b. Adelaide, Australia, Mar. 6, 1944; m. Carol L. Pederson, 1972; 5 children. BA, Brigham Young U., 1969. Missionary Ch. of Jesus Christ of Latter-day Saints, Ctrl. Brit. Mission, 1963-65; mng. editor Brigham Young Univ. Press, Provo, Utah, 1972-80; asst. dir., editor-in-chief U. Okla. Press, Norman, 1981-97, dir., 1998—. Office: U Okla Press 1005 Asp Ave Norman OK 73019-6050*

DRAYTON, WILLIAM, lawyer, social entrepreneur, management consultant; b. N.Y.C., June 15, 1943; s. William A. and Joan (Bergere) D. BA, Harvard, 1965; MA, Oxford (Eng.) U., 1967; JD, Yale, 1970. Bar: N.Y. 1971, D.C. 1976. Cons. McKinsey and Co., Inc., N.Y.C., 1970-77, of counsel, 1981—; vis. assoc. prof. law Stanford, 1975-76; lectr. John F. Kennedy Sch. of Govt., Harvard; also dir. Harvard Regulatory and Mgmt. Group, 1976-77; cons. White House Domestic Council, 1977; asst. adminstr. for planning and mgmt. EPA, 1977-81; pres. Environ. Safety, Washington, 1981-89, chair, 1989—; pres., founder Ashoka: Innovators for the Pub., Arlington, Va., 1980—; nat. staff mem. Hubert H. Humphrey Presdl. Campaign, Washington, 1968; dir. Corp. for Fiscal Policy, 1971-75; founder, chmn. Yale Legis. Svcs.; mem. adv. coun. Carnegie Commn. Sci., Tech. and Govt., 1990-96. Contbr. articles to mgmt., devel. and legal jours. Pres. Ams. in India for McGovern, 1972; mem. Carter-Mondale Policy Planning, 1976, Carter-Mondale Govt. Reorgn. Transition Group, 1976-77; dep. dir. for issues Mondale-Ferraro campaign, 1984; mem. energy and environment com. Dem. nat. Com., 1982-86; bd. dirs. Oxfam Am., 1985-89; bd. dirs. Appropriate Tech. Internat., 1988-97, chmn. bd. dirs., 1989-97; trustee Black Rock Forest (formerly Harvard Forest), N.Y.; chmn. bd. dirs. Youth Venture, 1994—; founder, chair Get Am. Working!, 1997—; pres. Save EPA, Washington, 1981-83. Recipient Ann. award for Entrepreneurial Excellence Yale U. Sch. Mgmt., 1987, Nat. Pub. Svc. award Nat. Acad. Pub. Adminstrn. and Am. Soc. for Pub. Adminstrn., 1995; Henry fellow, 1965-67, MacArthur Prize fellow, 1984-89. Mem. AAAS (com. on sci. pub. policy 1973-76), Assn. Bar City N.Y., Friends of India Soc. (chmn. 1974-75), Coun. Fgn. Rels., Nat. Acad. Pub. Adminstrn., Am. Acad. Arts and Scis., Asia Soc. (contemporary affairs com. 1987—), India Internat. Ctr. (New Delhi), Yale Club N.Y., Phi Beta Kappa. Home: 1200 N Nash St Arlington VA 22209-3616 Office: 1700 N Moore St Ste 1920 Arlington VA 22209-1916

DRAZIN, LISA, real estate and corporate investment banker, financial consultant; b. Washington, Nov. 26, 1953; d. Sidney and Bernice Ann (Jeweler) D. AB with honors, Wellesley Coll., 1976; MBA, George Washington U., 1980. Chartered fin. analyst. Securities analyst Geico, Inc., Chevy Chase, Md., 1982; mng. prin. Jefferson Securities Ltd., Bethesda, Md., 1983; chmn., CEO Drazin & Co., Inc., Bethesda, 1983-89, Drazin Properties, Inc., Bethesda, 1985-89, Drazin Securities, Inc., Bethesda, 1985-88, Woodmont Asset Mgmt. Inc., 1989—; affiliate Montgomery County Bd. Realtors; real estate investment banker Restructuring Fed. Deposit Ins. Corp. Founder Ivy Connection, Washington, 1982; bd. dirs. Friends of Tel Aviv U., actine planning com. Jewish Nat. Fund; mem. Nat. Truste for Historic Preservation, UJA Fedn. of Greater Washington (young leadership divsn., Ruth Heritage Forum), Am. Friends Hebrew U., Nat. Kidney Found. Fellow Wexner Heritage Found., Friends for Life Benefit, Whitman Walker Clinic, Spiritual Ctr. Am., Assn. for Investment Mgmt. and Rsch., Turnaround Mgmt. Assn.; mem. Nat. Assn. Realtors, Comml. Investment Real Estate Coun., Relators Nat. Mktg. Inst., Wash. Soc. Investment Analysts, Inc., Wellesley Club (interns coord., recent grads. rep. 1981-84, Washington), Ben Gurion Club, Beta Gamma Sigma. Office: Woodmont Asset Mgmt Inc 6403 Kirby Rd Bethesda MD 20817-5523

DRAZNIN, JULES NATHAN, journalism and public relations educator, consultant; b. Chgo., May 14, 1923; s. Charles G. and Goldie (Malach) D.; m. Shirley Bernstein, Apr. 9, 1950; children: Dean, Jody, Michael. Student, Wright City Coll., Chgo., 1941; BA in Journalism, Calif. State U., Northridge, 1978, MA in Higher Edn., 1984. Various journalism positions City News Bur., Chgo. Am., Chgo., 1941; promotions and publicity Balaban & Katz Theaters, Chgo., 1942-43; asst. dir pub. rels. Combined Jewish Appeal, Chgo., 1944; prin. J.N. Draznin Assocs., Chgo., 1945-50; account supr. Olian & Bronner Advt. Agy., Chgo., 1951-53; dir. advt. Chgo. Defender, Robert S. Abbott Pub. Co., 1953-55; freelance cons. Chgo., 1955-60; v.p. pub. rels. Harshe-Rotman, Chgo., 1956; pub. rels. dir. Abel and Lamensdorf Properties, Chgo., 1960-62; editor-in-chief, assoc. pub. Indsl. News Bender Publs., Calif., 1962-64; labor editor, spl. features writer Valley News and Green Sheet, Calif., 1964; ind. ins. agt. Calif., 1965-74; tch. pub. rels. UCLA and Calif. State U., L.A.; prof. journalism and pub. rels. L.A. Trade Tech. Coll., 1975-95, chmn. lang. arts dept., 1984-90; ret., 1995; prof. journalism and pub. rels. L.A. City Coll., L.A. Pierce Coll., L.A. Southwest Coll., East L.A. Coll., L.A. Mission Coll.; guest lectr. Calif. State U., Northridge. Coord. Mass Media AARP/Vote Vols., 1996—; apptd. state legis. com. AARP, 1998—. Mem. Assn. for Edn. in Journalism and Mass Comm., Soc. Profl. Journalists. Avocations: golf, classical music, travel. *Until I retired from teaching journalism, I was a voyeuristic/activist. Now I'm a participating activist without journalistic "objectivity", working for the benefit of aged people.*

DR. DRE (ANDRE YOUNG), rapper, record producer; b. L.A.. Cofounder Ruthless Records, 1987. Albums include (with N.W.A.) Straight Outta Compton, 1989, 100 Miles and Runnin', 1990 (EP) Efil4zaggin, 1991, (solo) The Chronic, 1993 (Grammy award Best Pop Solo for "Let Me Ride" 1994); prodr. Snoop Doggy Dog's album "Doggy Style", 1993, U Can't Cee Me and California Love singles, 1996; prodr. soundtrack albums Above the Rim, 1994, Murder Was the Case, 1994. Office: care Interscope Records 10900 Wilshire Blvd Fl 12 Los Angeles CA 90024-6501 also: Aftermath Entertainment 15060 Ventura Blvd Ste 225 Sherman Oaks CA 91403-2487*

DREBEN, RAYA SPIEGEL, judge; b. Vienna, Austria, Dec. 3, 1927; came to U.S., 1928, naturalized, 1936; d. Shalom and Rose (Goldschmiedt) Spiegel; children: Elizabeth, Jonathan. A.B. magna cum laude, Radcliffe Coll., 1949; LL.B. cum laude, Harvard U., 1954. Bar: Mass. 1957, U.S. Supreme Ct. 1960. Law clk. to Judge Bailey Aldrich, U.S. Dist. Ct. for Mass., 1954-55; Bigelow fellow and instr. U. Chgo. Law Sch., 1955-56; asso. Firm Palmer & Dodge, Boston, 1964-71; partner Firm Palmer & Dodge, 1971-79; assoc. justice Mass. Appeals Ct., Boston, 1979—; lectr. in copyright Harvard U. Law Sch., 1973-76; mem. adv. com. on copyright registration and deposit Libr. of Congress, 1993. Trustee Radcliffe Coll., 1981-89. Recipient 1st prize Nathan Burkan competition Harvard U. Law Sch., 1954, nat. winner, 1954. Mem. ABA (chmn. com. on authors 1977-79), Am. Law Inst. (adv. on restatement, property-donative transactions), Am. Bar Found., Copyright Soc. U.S.A. (trustee 1973-76, editorial bd. bull. 1974-85), Jud. Inst. Mass. Judiciary (chmn. adv. com. 1988-96). Office: Appeals Ct Pemberton Sq Boston MA 02108-1701

DREBSKY, DENNIS JAY, lawyer; b. N.Y.C., Sept. 28, 1946; s. Benjamin and Ronnie (Penso) D.; m. Norma Louise Linschitz, Aug. 16, 1970; children: Richard Michael, Joshua William Evan. BBA magna cum laude, CCNY, 1967; JD, Cornell U., 1970. Bar: N.Y. 1971, U.S. Dist. Ct. (so. dist.) N.Y. 1972, U.S. Ct. Appeals (2d cir.) 1971, U.S. Ct. Appeals (5th cir.) 1980, U.S. Ct. Appeals (9th cir.) 1982, U.S. Ct. Appeals (1st cir.) 1981, U.S. Ct. Appeals (10th cir.) 1984, U.S. Ct. Appeals (4th cir.) 1986, U.S. Ct. Appeals (D.C. cir.) 1998. Assoc. Skadden, Arps, Slate, Meagher & Flom, N.Y.C., 1970-77, ptnr., 1978-91; ptnr. Rogers & Wells, 1991—; trustee Community Law Offices, N.Y.C., 1980—. Mem. Assn. of Bar of City of N.Y. (mem. com. on corp. reorgn. 1985—). Jewish. Avocations: reading, jogging, theater. Home: 7 Glen Hill Ct Dix Hills NY 11746-4819 Office: Rogers & Wells 200 Park Ave Fl 8E New York NY 10166-0800

DREBUS, JOHN RICHARD, financial consultant; b. Madison, Wis., Feb. 11, 1951; s. Richard William and Hazel Mae (Redford) D.; m. Pamela Kay Peffito, Jan. 5, 1974; children: Bethea Lynn, Scott Bryan, Cynthia Ann. BA in Zoology, Ind. U., 1973; MS in Mgmt., Purdue U., 1983; Honor Grad., Command & Gen. Staff Coll., 1991. Commd. 2d lt. U.S. Army, 1973, advanced through grades to lt. col., 1994; armor officer U.S. Army, Baumholder, Germany, 1973-77; armor officer, capt. U.S. Army, Fort Knox, Ky., 1977-81; mfg. assoc. Am. Can Co., Hammond, Ind., 1983-84; project mgr. The System Works, Marietta, Ga., 1984-87; bus. rels. specialist Electronic Data Systems, Warren, Mich., 1988-91; supr. Electronic Data Systems, Ypsilanti, Mich., 1991-93; systems engr. Electronic Data Systems, Troy, Mich., 1993-98; sr. cons. Price Waterhouse Coopers LLP, Southfield, Mich., 1998—; project officer Army Force Modernization Team, Fort Knox, 1979-80. Contbr. articles to profl. jours. Dir. sch. bd. Faith Luth. Sch., Marietta, Ga., 1986-88; treas. ann. fund drive St. John Luth. Sch., Rochester, 1992-95; bd. mem. Boy Scout Troop 188, Rochester Hills, Mich., 1993-95. Lt. col. USAR, 1995—, Office of Army Artificial Intelligence, Pentagon. Recipient Disting. Mil. Grad award U.S. Army, 1973, Army Commendation medal, 1977, Army Parachute Badge, 1973. Mem. Computer Soc. of IEEE, N.Y. Acad. Sci., U.S. Army Armor Assn., Assn. of U.S. Army, Mensa. Lutheran. Avocations: classical piano, entomology, fencing, back packing. Home: 1631 Ridgecrest Rochester Hls MI 48306-3159 Office: Price Waterhouse Coopers LLP 40 Oak Hollow Ste 155 Southfield MI 48034

DREBUS, RICHARD WILLIAM, pharmaceutical company executive; b. Oshkosh, Wis., Mar. 30, 1924; s. William and Frieda (Schmidt) D.; m. Hazel Redford, June 7, 1947; children—William R., John R., Kathryn L. Belin. BS, U. Wis., 1947, MS, 1949, PhD, 1952. Tcr. Madison East H.S., 1947-48; Bus. trainee Marathon Paper Corp., Menasha, Wis., 1951-52; tng. mgr. Ansul Corp., Marinette, Wis., 1952-55; asst. to v.p. Ansul Corp., 1955-58, marketing mgr., 1958-60; dir. personnel devel. Mead Johnson & Co., Evansville, Ind., 1960-65; v.p. corporate planning Mead Johnson & Co., 1965-66, internat. pres., 1966-68; v.p. internat. div. Bristol-Myers Co. (merger Mead Johnson & Co. with Bristol-Myers Co.), N.Y.C., 1968-77, sr. v.p., 1977-78, v.p. parent co., 1978-85, sr. v.p. pharm. research and devel. div., 1985-89, ret., 1989. Past bd. dirs. Jr. Achievement S.E. Conn., Meriden Silver Mus.; past bd. dirs. Meriden-Wallingford United Way, chmn. fund raising drive, 1988-89; trustee emeritus Quinnipiac Coll. Served with AUS, 1943-45. Decorated Combat Inf. Badge, Purple Heart, Bronze Star. Mem. APA, N.Y. Acad. Scis., U. Wis. Bascom Hill Soc., Oshkosh Country Club, North Shore Country Club, Phi Delta Kappa. Home: 3720 Pau Ko Tuk Ln Oshkosh WI 54901-7332

DRECHNEY, MICHAELENE, secondary education educator; b. Chgo.; d. Bill and Pearl (Krupocki) D. BS, Loyola U., Chgo., 1968, MA, 1976. Cert. tchr., Ill., Ohio. Tchr. adult edn. Wright Coll., Chgo., 1983-84; tchr. English, Gordon Tech. High Sch., Chgo., 1977-84; tchr. sci. St. Francis Xavier Sch., Wilmette, Ill., 1973-76; tchr. sci., dir. art St. Monica Sch., Chgo., 1977-93; tchr. Thorp Scholastic Acad., Chgo., 1993—. Grantee Edn. System of People's Republic of China, Woodrow Wilson Found., 1989, Nat. Sci. Tchr.'s Assn., NSF, 1990, NSF, Inst. for Chem. Edn., 1991, Project W.I.Z.E., 1995; recipient presdl. award Assn. Sci. Tchrs., Project Lava award 1998. Mem. ASCD, Nat. Sci. Tchrs. Assn. (cert.), Argon Chemistry Tchrs., Nat. Middle Level Sci. Tchrs., Coun. for Elem. Sci. Internat., Nat. Sci. Suprs. Assn., Ill. Sci. Tchrs. Assn. Home: 6550 W Belmont Ave Chicago IL 60634-3995 Office: 6024 W Warwick Ave Chicago IL 60634-2554

DRECHSEL, ROBERT EDWARD, journalism educator; b. Fergus Falls, Minn., Aug. 7, 1949. BA, U. Minn., 1971, MA, 1976, PhD, 1980. Reporter, city editor Daily Jour., Fergus Falls, 1971-74; instr. dept. journalism S.D. State U., Brookings, 1976-77; asst. prof. dept. tech. journalism Colo. State U., Fort Collins, 1979-83; from asst. prof. to assoc. prof. Sch. Journalism and Mass Comm. U. Wis., Madison, 1983-91; prof. U. Wis., Madison, 1991—, dir. Sch. Journalism and Mass Comm., 1991-98. Author: News Making in the Trial Courts, 1983; contbr. articles to profl. jours. Mem. Assn. Edn. Journalism and Mass Comm. (Krieghbaum Outstanding Achievement Rsch., Teaching & Pub. Svc. award 1989), Am. Judicature Soc., Wis. Freedom Info. Coun., Internat. Comm. Assn. Office: U Wis Sch Journalism & Mass Comm 821 University Ave Madison WI 53706-1412

DRECKMAN, BRUCE, umpire; b. Marcus, Iowa, Aug. 7, 1970. Former umpire Appalachian League, Midwest League, Carolina League, So. League, Internat. League, Am. Assn.; umpire maj. league baseball Nat. League, N.Y.C., 1998—; with Umpires Union, Phila. Office: Nat League 350 Park Ave New York NY 10022 also: Umpires Union 1735 Market St Philadelphia PA 19103

DREES, STEPHEN DANIEL, financial services executive, strategy, marketing and product development executive; b. Livingston, N.J., Mar. 11, 1961; s. Daniel Stevenson and Lois Jean (Litzebauer) D.; m. Sandra Lee Van Dusen, Sept. 28, 1985; children: Madeleine Danielle, Meredith Olivia. BA, Bloomsburg U., 1983; MS, U. Pa., 1989; cert., Nat. Sch. Bank Card Mgmt., 1991; Cert. in Strategic Alliances, U. Pa., 1992. Mktg. mgr. Mfrs. Hanover Corp., Phila., 1986-88; asst. v.p. Mellon Bank Corp., Pitts., 1988-90; v.p. MasterCard Internat., Inc., N.Y.C., 1990-93; fin. svcs. cons. Boston, 1993-97; v.p. GE Capital, Cin., 1997—; mem. faculty MasterCard U., 1990-93, chmn. Credit Card Mktg. conf., 1995. Contbr. articles to profl. jours. Mem.

Am. Mktg. Assn., Am. Bankers Assn., The Penn Club, Zeta Psi. Roman Catholic. Office: 5300 Kings Island Dr Mason OH 45040-2353

DREHER, DARRELL L., lawyer; b. Coshocton, Ohio, Dec. 16, 1944. BA, Ohio State U., 1966; JD, George Washington U., 1973. Bar: Ohio 1974. Ptnr. Dreher Langer & Tomkies L.L.P., Columbus, Ohio; founding mem., bd. regents Am. Coll. Consumer Fin. Svcs. Lawyers; sec., mem. governing com. of Conf. on Consumer Fin. Law. Mem. Order of Coif. Office: Dreher Langer & Tomkies LLP 2250 Huntington Ctr Columbus OH 43215

DREHER, NANCY C., federal judge; b. 1942. BA, U. Wis., 1964, JD, 1967. Bar: Minn. 1967, U.S. Dist. Ct. Minn. 1969, U.S. Ct. Appeals (8th cir.) 1969, U.S. Supreme Ct. 1981. Law clk. to chief justice Calif. Supreme Ct., San Francisco, 1967-68; assoc. Leonard, Street & Deinard, 1968-72, ptnr., 1973-88; bankruptcy judge U.S. Bankruptcy Ct., Mpls., 1988—. Recipient Pres. Award for Profl. Excellence, Minn. State Bar Assn., 1985. Office: US Bankruptcy Ct Towle Bldg 300 S 4th St Ste 301 Minneapolis MN 55415-2255

DREHER, NICHOLAS C., lawyer; b. Michigan City, Ind., Nov. 15, 1948. AB magna cum laude, Harvard U., 1970; JD, Stanford U., 1973. Bar: Hawaii 1973. Ptnr. Cades Schutte Fleming & Wright, Honolulu, 1980—, chmn. of fin. and real estate dept., 1991—; vice-chmn. local rules com. U.S. Bankruptcy Ct. Mem. ABA (mem. com. foreclosure and related remedies sect. real property, probate and trust law 1991—), Am. Bankruptcy Inst. (chmn. Hawaii membership com. 1989—, mem. adv. com. bankruptcy rules 1990—), Hawaii State Bar Assn. (v.p. bankruptcy law sect. 1990-91, pres. 1991—, bd. dirs. 1990—). Office: Cades Schutte Fleming & Wright PO Box 939 1000 Bishop St Ste 1400 15th Fl Honolulu HI 96808

DREHOFF, DIANE WYBLE, electrical engineer, marketing manager; b. Amarillo, Tex., Oct. 11, 1950; d. James Stanley and Barbara Luella (Park) Wyble; m. John James Drehoff III, June 25, 1977; children: John, Brian, David. BSEE, Stanford U., 1972. Mktg. rep. Westinghouse, Jefferson City, Mo., 1972-74; sales engr. Westinghouse, Balt., 1974-75; Congl. fellow IEEE, Washington, 1976; govt. rep. Westinghouse, Washington, 1977-80; mktg. staff mgr. Westinghouse, Phila., 1980-81, regional mktg. mgr., 1981-82; regional mktg. mgr. Westinghouse, Orlando, Fla., 1982-84, projects mgr., 1986-89, sales staff mgr., 1989-91, total quality dir., 1991-95, mktg. mgr. power generation svc., 1995—. Contbr. tech. papers to profl. jours. Sun. sch. tchr. Community Alliance Ch., Orlando, 1989-93; participant Leadership Orlando C. of C., 1991-92. Recipient IEEE Congl. fellowship IEEE, 1976, Quality Achievement award Westinghouse, 1985, Corp. Controllers award Westinghouse, 1991. Mem. IEEE (spectrum editorial bd. 1980-81, Congl. fellows selection 1983, long-range planning com. 1989), Am. Soc. for Quality Control, IEEE/Power Engrng. Soc. Avocations: crafts, golf, sailing, water skiing. Office: Westinghouse Electric Corp The Quadrangle 4400 N Alafaya Trl Orlando FL 32826-2399

DREIBELBIS, ELLEN ROBERTS, artist; b. Cleve., Dec. 18, 1946; d. Stanly Vincent and Lylian (Geller) Roberts; m. Walter William Dreibelbis, Nov. 29, 1970 (dec. Feb. 1987). BA in Art Edn., Ohio State U., 1970. Reference asst. Cleveland Heights (Ohio) Pub. Libr., 1971-74; asst. collection devel., interlibr. loan State Libr. Ohio, Columbus, 1974-78; libr. technician U.S. Forest Svc., Berkeley, Calif., 1979-88; tech. info. specialist U.S. Forest Svc., Albany, Calif., 1988-93; artist, illustrator Citibank, Stamford, Conn., 1993-94. One person shows include Montclair Art Festival, Montclair, Village, Calif., 1999, Rouge Gallery, San Francisco, 1997, Strybing Arboreteum, San Francisco, 1995, Tantrums, Santa Rosa, Calif., 1991, Potrero Hill Pub. Libr., San Francisco, 1990; exhibited at group shows at Ashtabula (Ohio) Arts Ctr., 1975, East Bay Open Studio, Oakland, Calif., 1990-93, Stanford U., Palo Alto, Calif., 1985, San Francisco Women Artist's Gallery, 1987, Am. Mus. Quilts, San Jose, Calif., 1987, Met. Mus., Miami, Fla., 1988, ArtWork Gallery, San Francisco, 1995, 96, Rainbow Gallery, Wemme, Oreg., 1978, Green Apple Books, Cleve., 1980, Southern Exposure Gallery, San Francisco, 1986, 87, 88, 89, 90, 91, Bay Area Textile Designers Christmas Show, Oakland, 1986, Fort Mason Art Ctr., San Francisco, 1986, 87, 88, 89, 90, Pro Arts Gallery, Oakland, 1991, 92, 93, O'Brien's Art Emporium, Scottsdale, Ariz., 1996, Somar Gallery, San Francisco, 1996, Bridge Gallery, San Francisco, 1997; rep. in permanent collections at Citibank, N.Y.C., Mr. and Mrs. Stanley Roberts, Cleve., Dr. and Mrs. Henry Channan, Sanibel Island, Fla., Mr. Paul McClain, San Francisco, Mr. Eli Giladi, Tel Aviv, Israel, Dr. Timothy F. Whiteside, N.Y.C., Dr. Don F. Fenn, Oakland; prin. works include Citibank, N.A. and Citicorp Mortgage, Inc., 1993-94, Rod Enterprises, Pasadena, Calif., 1995, USDA Forest Svc., Albany, 1994, Cricket Mag., Peru, Ill., Internal Heritage Tradition, San Francisco, 1997, Cosco Publs., Singapore, 1997, Celebration of Fine Arts, San Francisco, 1998, Strybing Aboretum, San Francisco, CA, 1998; illustrated for books Learning From Our Mothers, 1998, On Mothers Lap, a Teacher's Guide, Perfection Learning (cover illus.), 1998, illustrated cover 25th Anniversary and holiday issue Cricket Magazine, 1998; creator, marketer Native Peoples Series, giclee prints of watercolors of Native Americans, South Americans and Asians. Mem. Am. Acad. Women Artists, Soc. Children Book Writers and Illustrators. Avocations: walking, reading. Address: Suite 5 454 9th Ave San Francisco CA 94118-2943

DREIER, DAVID TIMOTHY, congressman; b. Kansas City, Mo., July 5, 1952; s. H. Edward and Joyce (Yeomans) D. BA cum laude, Claremont McKenna Coll., 1975; MA in Am. Govt., Claremont Grad. Sch., 1976. Dir. corp. rels. Claremont McKenna Coll., 1975-78; dir. mktg. and govt. rels. Indsl. Hydro, San Dimas, Calif., 1978-80; mem. 97th-105th Congresses (now 106th Congress) from 33rd (now 28th) Calif. dist., 1985-97; v.p. Dreier Devel. Co., Kansas City, Mo., 1985—; vice chmn. rules com., 1995-99, chmn., 1999—; chmn. rules of the house subcom.; bd. dirs. Internat. Rep. Inst.; mem. spkrs. steering com. Recipient Golden Bulldog award Watchdogs of the Treasury, 1981-99, Taxpayers Friends award Nat. Taxpayers Union, 1981-99, Clean Air Champion award Sierra Club, 1988. Office: US House of Reps 237 Cannon HOB Washington DC 20515-0528

DREIFUS, CLAUDIA, journalist; b. N.Y.C., Nov. 24, 1944; d. Henry and Marianne (Willdorff) D. BS in Dramatic Arts, NYU, 1966. Assoc. vis. prof. dept. journalism NYU, 1975, instr. mag. writing Sch. Continuing Edn., 1979; lectr. non-fiction writing YWCA N.Y., 1979-84; represented by Gelfman-Schnieder Lit. Agy., Author's Unltd. Lecture Agy.; Disting. vis. prof. grad. English creative writing program CCNY, 1994-98; fellow World Policy Inst., New Sch. for Social Rsch., N.Y., 1997—. Editor: Seizing Our Bodies: The Politics of Women's Health, 1978; author: Interview, 1997; contbr. chpts. to textbooks, anthologies; commentator health and sci. City Edition and Spl. Edition programs Sta. WNET-TV, 1979-80, guest host local issues Live Wire program, 1991; interviewer Sunday mag. L.I. Newsday, 1976-81, Books sect. N.Y. Post, 1990, Playboy mag., 1981—; sci. interviewer N.Y. Times, Sci. Times; contbr. articles to various publs., including N.Y. Times, N.Y. Times Sunday Mag., Premiere, Town and Country, Atlantic, Entertainment Weekly, Modern Maturity, Dial, Progressive, Penthouse, Redbook, Reader's Digest, McCall's, Glamour; writer on politics of TV, TV Guide, 1991—. Recipient award of Merit for Svc. to Women, YWCA N.Y., 1976, Simon Rockower award for Disting. Commentary, Am. Jewish Press Assn., 1988, Am. Values award Cmty. Action Assn., 1996. Am. Soc. Journalists and Authors (Outstanding Article award 1987), PEN. Office: care NY Times 229 W 43rd St Fl 8 New York NY 10036-3913

DREIKAUSEN, MARGRET, artist; b. Cologne, Germany, Jan. 9, 1937; came to U.S., 1961; d. Wilhelm and Anna Maria (Rapp) D. AAS, Fashion Inst. Tech., 1968; BA, CUNY, 1975, MA, 1978. Assoc. prof. U. Conn., Storrs, 1978-79; instr. Fashion Inst. Tech., N.Y.C., 1980, Parsons Sch. Design, N.Y.C., 1979—; dir. LIC Artists, Inc., 1987-95, founder, bd. dirs., pres., 1990—; fashion designer IGS, Istanbul, Turkey, 1970, various mfrs., N.Y.C., 1963-78. Artist numerous group and one-person exhibitions, U.S., Germany; author: Aerial Perception, 1985; contbg. author: Essays on Creativity & Science, 1986. Mem. Coll. Art Assn. Avocations: traveling, swimming, hiking. Home: 141 E 62nd St New York NY 10021-7606 Studio: LIC Artlofts 37-06 36th St Long Island City NY 11101-1630

DREILINGER, CHARLES LEWIS (CHIPS DREILINGER), dean; b. Bklyn., Feb. 19, 1945; s. Samuel Leonard and Harriet Karen (Kaplan) D.; m. Anna Douglas, Mar. 21, 1966; children: Sean Eric, Daniel Ethan, Seth Aaron. BA, Antioch Coll., 1967; MA, Claremont Grad. Sch., 1968. Assoc. for program devel. Union Experimenting Colls. and Univs., Yellow Springs, Ohio, 1968-70; asst. dean, assoc. dean Antioch Coll., Yellow Springs, 1970-73; assoc. dean, acting dean Hobart Coll., Geneva, N.Y., 1973-79; dean John Muir Coll. U. Calif.-San Diego, La Jolla, 1979—. Democrat. Avocation: horticulture. Office: U Calif San Diego J Muir Coll Office of the Dean La Jolla CA 92093*

DREIMANIS, ALEKSIS, emeritus geology educator; b. Valmiera, Latvia, Aug. 13, 1914; s. Peteris and Marta Eleonora (Leitis) D.; m. Anita Kana, Apr. 18, 1942; children: Mara Dreimanis Love, Aija Dreimanis Downing. Mag. rer. nat., U. Latvia, 1938; D.Sc. (hon.), U. Waterloo, Ont., Can., 1969, U. Western Ont., 1980; D Geography (hon.), U. Latvia, 1991, Habilitation, 1942. Asst. to pvt. docent U. Latvia, 1937-44; mil. geologist Latvian Legion, 1944-45; assoc. prof. geology Baltic U., Hamburg and Pinneberg, Germany, 1946-48; mem. faculty U. Western Ont., London, Can., 1948—; prof. geology U. Western Ont., 1964-80, prof. emeritus, 1980—; pres. Commn. on Genesis and Lithology of Quaternary Deposits, Internat. Union Quaternary Research, 1973-87; cons. in field. Assoc. editor Geosci. Can., 1976-78, Quaternary Sci. Revs., 1981-87, Tech. Rev. (in Latvian), 1978—, Geology Proc. Estonian Acad. Scis., 1991-97; contbr. articles to profl. jours. Recipient Centennial medal (Can.); Queen Elizabeth II 25th Anniversary medal; Centennial medal Geol. Survey of Finland, U. Helsinki medal; Albrecht Penck medal, teaching award Ont. Confedn. Univ. Faculty Assns., 1978. Fellow Royal Soc. Can. (Disting.), Geol. Assn. Can. (Logan medal 1978), Geol. Soc. Am. (Disting. Career award Quaternary geology and geomorphology divsn. 1987); mem. Swedish Geol. Soc. (hon. corr. mem.), Can. Quaternary Assn. (W.A. Johnston medal 1989), Am. Quaternary Assn. (pres. 1981-83), Assn. Advancement Baltic Studies, Quaternary Rsch. Assn., Internat. Union for Quaternary Rsch. (hon.), Latvian Nat. Fedn. Can. (chmn. coun. 1953-71, hon. mem.), Latvian Acad. Scis. (fgn. hon.), Latvian Cultural Found. (exec. com. 1973-77), London Latvian Soc. (pres. 1948—), Fraternity Lidums (pres. 1935-36, editor newsletter 1969—), Geol. Soc. Finland (hon. corr. mem.), Latvian Am. Assn. Univ. Profs. and Scientists (pres. 1983-85), Geog. Assn. Latvia (hon.), Assn. Latvian Geologists (hon.), Baltic Rsch. Inst. (hon. corr. mem.), Estonian Geol. Soc. Home: 287 Neville Dr, London, ON Canada N6G 1C2 Office: U Western Ont, Dept Earth Scis, London, ON Canada N6A 5B7

DREISBACH, JOHN GUSTAVE, investment banker; b. Paterson, N.J., Apr. 24, 1939; s. Gustave John and Rose Catherine (Koehler) D.; m. Janice Lynn Petitjean; children: John Gustave Jr., Christopher Erik. BA, NYU, 1963. With Dreyfus & Co., 1959-62, Shields & Co., Inc., 1965-68, Model, Roland & Co., Inc., N.Y.C., 1968-72, F. Eberstadt & Co., Inc., N.Y.C., 1972-74; v.p. Bessemer Trust Co., 1974-78; pres. Cmty. Housing Capital, Inc., 1978-80; chmn., pres. John G. Dreisbach, Inc., Santa Fe, 1980—, JDG Housing Corp., 1982—, JGD Mgmt. Corp., 1996—; gen. ptnr. numerous real estate ltd. partnerships; bd. dirs., pres. The Santa Fe Investment Conf., 1986—; assoc. Sta. KNME-TV. Mem. Santa Fe Cmty. Devel. Commn. With USAFR, 1964. Mem. Internat. Assn. for Fin. Planning, Nat. Assn. Securities Dealers, Inc., NYU Alumni Assn., N.Mex. First, Friends of Vieilles Maisons Francaises Inc., Mensa, Santa Fe C. of C., Augustan Soc., St. Bartholomew's Cmty. Club, Essex Club, Hartford Club, Amigos del Alcalde Club. Republican. Episcopalian. Avocations: travel, art, archdesign appreciation, classical music, Shotokan karate (1st Dan). Fax: 505-989-7381. Home: La Genvrie, 49140 Jarze France Office: 369 Montezuma Ave Santa Fe NM 87501-2626

DREIZEN, ALISON M., lawyer; b. Bklyn., Sept. 14, 1952; d. Nathan Dreizen and Florence (Morgenstern) Barth. BA, Cornell U., 1974; JD, Harvard U., 1977. Assoc. White & Case, N.Y.C., 1977-85, ptnr., 1985-93, 95—; ptnr. White & Case, Moscow, 1993-95. Office: White & Case Bldg Ll 1155 Avenue Of The Americas New York NY 10036-2787*

DRENNAN, HARRY JOSEPH, minister; b. Dallas, Jan. 29, 1933; s. Harry Brown and Ora (Ware) D.; m. Elva Phyllis Rice, Dec. 13, 1952; children: Brian Joseph, Kathryn Phyllis, Paul David. BS, U. Houston, 1957; ThM, ThD, Internat. Sem., 1986; DRE, Northgate Grad. Sch., 1987; EdD, Cornerstone U. and Sem., Jerusalem, 1990; PhD in Psychology, Emmanual Bapt. U., 1991; PhD in Marriage and Family Therapy, Evang. Theol. Sem., 1992. Lic. pastoral counselor, Christian counselor, temperament therapist. Assoc. pastor Evangelistic Temple, Houston, 1971-87; dir. Teen Challenge Ministry, Houston, 1972-79, 700 Club Ministry, Houston, 1973-79, Today's World Ministry Counseling Ctr., Houston, 1976-80; pres. Cornerstone Sem. and Univ., Jerusalem, Israel, 1986—, Hawaii, 1988—. Author: Man's Relationship to Spirit, 1987, Pheumatology, 1988, Hermenutics, 1989, A Study of the Pentateuch, 1990, Pastoral Counseling, 1992, Pre-Marital Counseling, 1992; (O.T. survey) Plus, 1991. With USN, 1952-56, Korea. Recipient Man-of-the-Yr. award, Ford Motor Co., Phila., 1965. Mem. Nat. Christian Counselor Assn. (pres., bd. dirs. 1989—), World Ministry Fellowship Counseling (dir. 1989—), World Ministry Fellowship Counseling (dir. 1990—), Cornerstone Ministririal Assn. (pres. 1988—), Tex. Christian Counselors Assn. (pres. 1993—). Home: 14619 Moss Creek Dr Cypress TX 77429-2233 Office: Journey in Truth Ministries 14619 Moss Creek Dr Cypress TX 77429-2233

DRENNAN, JERRY M., military officer. BS in Engring. Mgmt., USAF Acad., 1972; MBA, U. Mo., 1976; grad., Squadron Officer Sch., 1976, Armed Forces Staff Coll., 1984, Air War Coll., 1989; program for execs., Carnegie-Mellon U., 1995. Commd. 2d lt. USAF, 1972, advanced through grades to brigadier gen., 1997; missile ops. staff officer Air Staff tng. program Dep. Chief Staff for Ops., Hdqs. USAF, Washington, 1977-78, ground-launched cruise missile plans officer, 1980-82, asst. exec. officer, 1982-84; ops. officer 564th Strategic Missile Squadron, Malmstrom AFB, Mont., 1984-85; comdr. 12th Strategic Missile Squadron, Malmstrom AFB, 1985-86; dep. base comdr. 341st Combat Support Group, Malmstrom AFB, 1986-87; dep. comdr. for ops., vice comdr. 487th Tactical Missile Wing, Comiso Air Sta., Italy, 1989-91; comdr. 842d Combat Support Group, Grand Forks AFB, N.D., 1991-92, 321st Missile Wing, Grand Forks AFB, 1992-93; asst. dir. nuclear ops. Hdqs. Def. Nuclear Agy., Alexandria, Va., 1993-95; dep. dir. plans, dir. logistics Hdqs. Air Force Space command, Peterson AFB, Colo., 1995-96; commandant Air Command and Staff Coll., Maxwell AFB, Ala., 1996-98; comdr. 21st Space Wing, Peterson AFB, 1998—. Decorated Def. Superior Svc. medal, Legion of Merit, Meritorious Svc. medal with 5 oak leaf clusters. Office: Ste 205 21 SWICC 775 Loring Ave Peterson AFB CO 80914-1290

DRENNAN, MICHAEL ELDON, banker; b. Yakima, Wash., June 24, 1946; s. George Eldon and Jane (Nilsson) D.; m. Alice Marie Seabolt, May 13, 1972; children: Brian, David. BS in Fin., U. Oreg., 1968; grad., Pacific Coast Banking Sch. U. Wash., 1981. Ops. officer First State Bank, Aloha, Oreg., 1972-73; ops., loan officer First State Bank, Portland, Oreg., 1973-74; asst. mgr. First State Bank, Milwaukie, Oreg., 1974-76; asst. v.p. Citizens Bank, Corvallis, Oreg., 1976-80, v.p., 1980-81; pres., chief exec. officer Bank of Corvallis, 1981-87; v.p. dist. mgr. U.S. Bank, Corvallis, Oreg., 1987; sr. v.p. market area mgr. U.S. Bank, Bend, Oreg., 1988-94; sr. v.p., dist. mgr. U.S. Bank, Eugene, Oreg., 1994-98; v.p. bus. banking Liberty Fed. Bank, 1998—; bd. dirs. Cascades W. Fin. Svcs. Bd. dirs. United Way Benton County, 1984-88; trustee Good Samaritan Hosp. Found., 1984-88; bd. dirs. Jr. Achievement of Benton County, 1983-85, treas, 1984-85, mem. exec. bd., 1984-85; mem. budget comm. Corvallis Sch. Dist., 1987; bd. dirs. Benton County Family YMCA, 1978-80, sec. 1979, mem. fin. com., 1978-80, mem. pers. com., 1979, active sustaining membership dr.; bd. dirs. Cmty. Club, 1978-83, pres., 1978, treas., 1979-80; active Corvallis Ambs., 1976-88; mem. mgmt. com. Corvallis Conf. and Visitors Bur., 1982-85; fund raising chmn. Com. City Improvement Levy, 1980; mem. exec. com. Pack 17 Boy Scouts Am., 1984-87, treas., 1984-87; mem. adv. bd. Ctrl. Oreg. Econ. Devel. Corp., 1988-90, bd. dirs., exec. bd., treas., 1991-93, v.p., 1993, pres., 1994; bd. dirs. Regional Arts Coun. of Ctrl. Oreg., treas., 1989-92; bd. dirs. Ctrl. Oreg. Air Svc. Task Force, 1989-94, chmn. airline rels. com., 1990; mem. Bend Bus. Assistance Team, 1989-90, United Way Deschutes County, chmn. loaned exec. recruitment, 1992; mem. planning com. St. Charles Med. Ctr. Found., 1993, dir. adminstrn. capital fund drive, 1993; mem. adv. bd. Deschutes County Fair, 1993-94; bd. dirs. Birth to Three, Eugene, 1994—, treas., 1995-96, pres.-elect., 1996-97, pres. 1997-98; bd. dirs. Lane Arts Coun., 1995-98, treas. exec. bd., 1996-98; bd. dirs. Conv. and Visitors Assn. Lane County, 1995-, treas. 1998; bd. dirs. Eugene-Springfield Metro Partnership, 1995-99; chmn. maj. firms campaign cabinet United Way of Lane County, 1996-97; bd. dirs. Oreg. Bach Festival, 1999—. Lt. USN, 1968-71. Named Jr. First Citizen, Corvallis, 1980. Mem. Bend C. of C. (chmn. mem. dir. task force 1988, chmn. mem. svcs. coun. 1989, chmn. chamber forums com. 1990, Outstanding Leadership award 1989), Corvallis C. of C. (v.p. fin. 1980-83, pres. 1985-86, chmn. bd. dirs. 1986-87, Econ. Devel. award 1978, Chmn. of Bd. award 1979, George award 1980-81, Devel. award 1983), Am. Inst. Banking (cert.), Rotary (bd. dirs. Corvallis club 1981-87, Bend 1988-94, Eugene, 1994—), Eugene Execs. Assn., Chi Phi, Alpha Kappa Psi, Beta Gamma Sigma. Home: 2574 W 28th Ave Eugene OR 97405-1456 Office: Liberty Bank 899 Pearl St Eugene OR 97401

DRENNAN, ROBERT D., archeology educator, researcher; b. Lexington, Ky., Oct. 15, 1947; s. Robert M. and Ruth (Dickerson) D.; m. Jeanne Ferrary, May 3, 1974; 1 child, Margaret. BA in Art and Archeology, Princeton U., 1969; MA in Anthropology, U. Mich., 1970, PhD in Anthropology, 1975. Curator R.S. Peabody Found. Archeology, Andover, Mass., 1974-77; asst. prof. dept. anthropology U. Pitts., 1977-81, assoc. prof. dept. anthropology, 1981-87, prof. dept. anthropology, 1987—, chair dept. anthropology, 1996-99, faculty assoc. Ctr. Latin Am. Studies, 1977—, interim dir. Ctr. Latin Am. Studies, 1992-93, dir. Latin Am. Archeology Publs., 1988—; assoc. rsch. scientist Mus. Anthropology U. Mich., Ann Arbor, 1976-80; adj. prof. dept. anthropology U. Nacional Colombia, Bogotá, 1988-89; vis. prof. dept. anthropology U. Los Andes, Bogotá, 1983—; rsch. assoc. sect. anthropology Carnegie Mus. Natural History, Pitts., 1978—; organizer, participant in archeol. meetings, confs.; presenter, rschr. in field. Author: Statistics for Archeologists: A Commonsense Approach, 1996; contbr. numerous articles to profl. jours. Fellow AAAS; mem. Am. Anthropol. Assn. (exec. com. archeology sect., program editor 1986-88), Soc. Am. Archeology (mem. editl. adv. com. Lat. Am. Antiquity 1989-93, mem. editl. bd. 1996—; chair task force Lat. Am. 1993-95; mem. com. on Ams. 1997—, chair 1995-97). Office: U Pittsburgh Dept Anthropology Pittsburgh PA 15260

DRENNEN, WILLIAM MILLER, JR., cultural administrator, film executive, producer, director, mineral resource executive; b. Charleston, W.Va., Nov. 5, 1942; s. William Miller and Margaret (Morton) D.; m. Sarah Polk Wilson, Nov. 27, 1969; children: Zachary Polk, Samuel Boyd. BArch., Yale U., 1964; postgrad., George Washington U., 1977, U. Charleston, 1978, W.Va. Grad. Coll., 1989-92; MA in Humanities, W.Va. Grad. Coll., 1993. Freelance writer, film maker, 1967-69; v.p. Communication Corps, Inc., Washington, 1969-79; pres. Briar Mountain Coal and Coke Co., Charleston, 1980-89; founder, pres. Max Media, Inc., Charleston, 1984-89; commr. culture and history State of W.Va., 1989-97, freelance writer, prodr., cons., 1997—; instr. history W.Va. State Coll., 1997-98; mng. gen. ptnr. C&D Enterprises, 1981—; past pres. Cox Morton Co., 1980-89; past pres., founder W.Va. Internat. Film Festival, Charleston, 1986-89. Cameraman (film) Evolving Environment, 1972 (Cine Golden Eagle award); editor (film) River of Life, 1975 (U.S. Film Festival award); patentee computerized optical system. Founder, pres. W.Va. Youth Soccer Assn., 1979-84; bd. dirs. Sunrise Mus., charleston, 1983-86, Renaissance Com., Charleston, 1984-89; trustee U. Charleston, 1985-89; founder W.Va. Assn. Mus., 1990; v.p., sec. W.Va. History Film Project, Inc., 1991-97. Served in USN, 1964-67. Decorated Bronze Star; recipient 2 Cine Eagle awards, cert. Excellence for documentary film work, award Hist. Landmarks Commn. Kanawha County, Tele award, 1997. Mem. Film Arts Guild W.Va. (pres. 1981-87), Cosmos Club, Charleston Rotary, Cress Creek Golf & Country Club. Democrat. Episcopalian. Avocations: tennis, squash, skiing, mountain biking, jogging.

DRENNON-GALA, DONNEY THOMAS, correctional treatment specialist, sociologist; b. Rochester, N.Y., Dec. 20, 1953; s. Donney Lamar and Anna Marie Drennon; m. Katy Rodriguez Gala, May 10, 1980; stepchildren: William G. Bosch, Stephen Bosch, S. Anita Bosch. AAS, Monroe C.C., Rochester, 1974; BS, Rochester Inst. Tech., 1978; MA, U. Ctrl. Okla., 1982; MS in Edn., U. Rochester, 1988, PhD, 1994. Correctional treatment specialist Fed. Bus. Prisons, U.S. Dept. Justice, Chattanooga, 1989—; asst. prof. U. N.C., Fayetteville (N.C.) State U., 1995-97; owner, cons., sociologist practitionr Drennon-Gala & Assocs., Chattanooga, 1995—; mem. bd. Chattanooga Area Law Enforcement Commn., 1991—. Author: Delinquency and High School Dropouts: Reconsidering Social Correlates, 1995; assoc. editor Free Inquiry in Creative Sociology, 1993—. Bd. dirs. Friends of Moccasin Bend Nat. Park, Chattanooga, 1997—. Sgt. USAF, 1976-80. Mem. Am. Sociol. Assn., Am. Soc. Criminology, Am. Correctional Assn. (profl. III), Acad. Criminal Justice Scis., Pachyderm Club, Masons (master), Alpha Phi Sigma, Kappa Delta Pi, Pi Gamma Mu. Avocation: writing. E-mail:ddrennon@bop.gov.

DRENZ, CHARLES FRANCIS, retired army officer; b. Erie, Pa., Aug. 12, 1930; s. Frank and Rose Marie (Cummings) DiRienzo; m. Lillian P. Martin, Jan. 14, 1961; children: Susan Frances, Michael Stuart, Sandra Jeanne. BS, Gannon U., 1953; MS, Fla. Inst. Tech., 1973; postgrad., U. Pitts., 1980; grad., Command and Gen. Staff Coll., Air War Coll. Commd. officer U.S. Army, advanced through grades to maj. gen., project mgr. Cobra Attack helicopter, 1974-77; comdr. Corpus Christi (Tex.) Army Depot, 1977-79; program mgr. UH-60 Black Hawk, U.S. Army Devel. and Readiness Command, St. Louis, 1979-80; comdr. Def. Contract Adminstrn. Services, N.Y.C., 1980-81; dep. dir. Hdqrs. Def. Logistics Agy., Cameron Sta., Alexandria, Va., 1981-83; program mgr. Advanced Attack Helicopter, St. Louis, 1983-86; commanding gen. U.S. Army Test and Evaluation Command, Aberdeen Proving Ground, Md., 1986-88; ret., 1988; pres. FDEI Corp., 1988—; chmn. OTI Inc., 1990-98; cons., 1989—; mem. sci. bd. U.S. Army, 1996—. Decorated Def. Superior Svc. award Legion of Merit with 2 clusters, Bronze Star, Air medal with 8 clusters; recipient Disting. Alumni award Gannon U., Disting. Svc. medal U.S. Army. Mem. Assn. U.S. Army, Am. Aviation Assn. Am. (pres. 1991-93), Am. Helicopter Soc., Nat. Contract Mgmt. Assn., Internat. Test and Evaluation Assn., Ret. Officers Assn., The Mil. Coalition. Office: 5855 Midnight Pass Rd Sarasota FL 34242

DREPAUL, LORIS OMESH, infectious diseases physician; b. Georgetown, Guyana, Feb. 6, 1960; s. Frank Eric and Iris (Masihdas) D.; BA (honors in Philosophy), BS, Phi Beta Kappa, Scholars' Program grad. Bklyn. Coll., CUNY, 1985; MD, NYU, 1989; BS, Phi Beta Kappa Scholar's Prog., Brooklyn Coll., CUNY, 1985; MD, NYU, 1989. Diplomate Am. Bd. Internal Medicine. Intern St. Luke's Hosp., N.Y.C., 1989-90, resident in internal medicine, 1990-91; resident in internal medicine Booth Meml. Hosp., Queens, N.Y., 1991-92; fellow in infectious diseases Mt. Sinai Hosp./VA Med. Ctr., Bronx, N.Y., 1992-94; attending in infectious diseases Mary Immaculate Hosp., Queens, N.Y., 1995-96; faculty, attending in infectious diseases Highland Hosp., Rochester, N.Y., 1997-98; med. dir. Cmty. Health Network, Inc., Rochester, N.Y., 1997-98. Mem. AMA, ACP, Med. Soc. State N.Y. Established HIV/AIDS Bilingual Primary Care OUtreach Program at Bridge Plaza Rehabilitation Clinic, Queens, NY, 1995-96. E-mail: Drepaul@pol.net. Office: Cmty Health Network 758 South Ave Rochester NY 14620 Address: 952 E 214th St Bronx NY 10469-1114

DRESBACH, MARY LOUISE, state educational administrator; b. St. Paul, Feb. 17, 1950; d. Ernest Joseph and Kathryn Marion (Lauer) Mathes; m. David Philip Dresbach, Nov. 29, 1980. BA, Coll. St. Catherine, 1972; postgrad., U. St. Thomas, 1979-80; MA, Coll. of St. Catherine, 1995. Tchr. St. Paul Pub. Schs., 1974-78; dir. human resources and agy. svcs. Minn. Higher Edn. Svcs. Office, St. Paul, 1978—; speaker Minn. Quality Conf., 1994, chair, 1996. Contbg. author Leading Edge Newsletter. Mem. AAUW, Am. Bus. Womens Assn. (sec. 1979-80), Nat. Assn. Exec. Women, Am. Soc. for Quality, Mpls. Inst. Arts, Met. Mus. Art, Dakota County Leadership Initiative, Minn. Ctr. for Women in Govt., Minn. Coun. Mgrs. (chair), Citizens League-Minn., Phi Beta Kappa, Pi Gamma Mu.

DRESCH, STEPHEN PAUL, economist, state legislator; b. East St. Louis, Ill., Dec. 12, 1943; s. Lester Wilson Reuben and Leonore Marie (Steege) D.; m. Linda Carol Ness, May 18, 1963; children: Soren K., Stephanie Elizabeth, Phaedra Augusta, Karl Friedrick Johannes. AB Philosophy, Miami U., Oxford, Ohio, 1963; MPhil Econ., NSF fellow, Yale U., 1966, PhD, 1970. Mem. faculty dept. econs. Miami U., Oxford, Ohio, 1963-64; mem. Yale U., New Haven, Conn., 1966-67, South Conn. State Coll., New Haven, 1968-69, Rutgers U., New Brunswick, N.J., 1970; researcher Nat. Bur. Econ.

Research, N.Y.C. and New Haven, 1969-77; cons. in residence Ford Found., N.Y.C., 1970-72; dir. research in econs. of higher edn. Yale U., 1972-75, chmn. Inst. for Demographic and Econ. Studies, 1975—; dean, prof. econs. and bus. Sch. Bus. and Engring. Adminstrn., Mich. Technol. U., 1985-90; rsch. scholar Internat. Inst. Applied Systems Analysis, Austria, 1983-85; vis. scholar Inst. Econs. and Forecasting of Sci. and Technol. Progress, USSR Acad. of Scis., 1988; mem. from 110th dist. Mich. Ho. of Reps., Lansing, 1990-92. Author: Substituting a Value Added Tax for the Corporate Income Tax, 1977, Occupational Earnings, 1967-81, 86, The Economics of Foreign Students, 1987; contbr. articles to profl. jours. Bd. advisors MacKinac Ctr. for Pub. Policy Rsch., Rep. Liberty Caucus. Mem. AAAS, ACLU, Am. Econ. Assn., Fedn. of Am. Scientists, Assn. for Pub. Policy Analysis and Mgmt., Am. Statis. Assn., Sigma Xi. Republican. Home: 318 Cooper Ave Hancock MI 49930-2112

DRESCHER, FRAN, actress; b. Flushing, N.Y., Sept. 30, 1957; d. Mort and Sylvia D.; m. Peter Marc Jacobson, 1978. Co-creator, writer, prodr., actress in TV series The Nanny; appeared in feature films: Saturday Night Fever, American Hot Wax (Five-Minute Oscar award Esquire mag.), This Is Spinal Tap, Cadillac Man, Serious Money, Dr. Detroit, Gorp, Jack, 1996, Car 54, Where Are You:, 1996, The Beautician and the Beast, 1997; starred in TV series Princesses, What's Alan Watching?, WIOU, (TV film) Terror in the Towers; guest appearances on TV programs Civil Wars, Alf, Night Court, Nine to Five, Fame, The Tracy Ullman Show. Office: care CBS Television City 7800 Beverly Blvd Los Angeles CA 90036-2112 also: Gersh Agy Inc 232 N Canon Dr Beverly Hills CA 90210-5302*

DRESCHER, JACK, psychoanalyst, psychiatrist; b. N.Y.C., Aug. 28, 1951; s. Mayer and Dora (Gajer) D. BA, Bklyn. Coll., 1972; MD, U. Mich., 1980. Diplomate Am. Bd. Psychiatry & Neurology. Internship in psychiatry St. Vincent's Med. Ctr., N.Y.C., 1980-81; residency in psychiatry SUNY Downstate, Bklyn., 1981-83, chief resident in psychiatry, 1983-84, clin. instr. psychiatry, 1984-87, clin. asst. prof. psychiatry, 1987—; dir. affective disorder clinic Downstate Med. Hygiene Assn., Bklyn., 1989-93; pvt. practice N.Y.C., 1985—; assoc. med. dir. HIV svc. William A. White Psychoanalytic Inst., N.Y.C., 1993-97. Author: Psychoanalytic Therapy and the Gay Man, 1998; editor-in-chief Jour. Gay and Lesbian Psychotherapy; contbr. chpts. to books and articles to profl. jours. Founding mem. Network Profl. Orgns., N.Y.C., 1985. Fellow Am. Acad. Psychoanalysis (trustee 1997—), Am. Psychiat. Assn. (sec. N.Y. br., fellowship award 1995); mem. AMA, Group for Advancement of Psychiatry (chair human sexuality com.), William A. White Psychoanalytic Soc. (editor newsletter), Am. Coll. Psychiatrists. Avocations: theater, opera, foreign travel, speaking Italian. Office: 440 W 24th St Apt 1A New York NY 10011-1350

DRESCHER, JOHN WEBB, lawyer; b. Norfolk, Va., May 13, 1948; s. Otto Charles and Anne Best (Webb) D.; m. Dale McKeithan Moore, June 13, 1970; 1 child, Ryan. BA, Hampden-Sydney Coll., 1970; JD, U. Richmond, 1973. Bar: Va. 1973, U.S. Supreme Ct. 1980, U.S. Ct. Appeals (4th cir.) 1985, U.S. Dist. Ct. (ea. dist.) Va. 1976. Assoc. Brydges, Hammers & Hudgins, Virginia Beach, 1973-74; asst. atty. Office of Commonwealth Atty., Virginia Beach, 1974-75; assoc. Pickett, Spain & Lyle, P.C., Virginia Beach, 1976-78; ptnr. Pickett, Lyle , Siegel, Drescher & Croshaw P.C., Virginia Beach, 1979-87, Breit, Drescher & Breit, P.C., Norfolk, 1988—. Pres. Hampden-Sydney Alumni Assn., Tidewater, Va., 1970—. Named among best lawyers in Am. Naifch & Smith, 1995—. Fellow Am. Bd. Trial Advocates; mem. ATLA, Va. Trial Lawyers Assn. (bd. govs. 1990—), Nat. Assn. Criminal Def. Lawyers, Am. Inns Ct., Norfolk-Portsmouth Bar Assn., U. Richmond Law Sch. Alumni Assn., Va. Beach Bar Assn. (pres. 1990). Democrat. Episcopal. Avocations: physical fitness, golf. Home: 925 Holladay Pt Virginia Bch VA 23451-3912 Office: Breit Drescher & Breit 1000 Dominion Twr 999 Waterside Dr Ste 1000 Norfolk VA 23510-3304

DRESCHER, JUDITH ALTMAN, library director; b. Greensburg, Pa., July 6, 1946; d. Joseph Grier and Sarah Margaret (Hewitt) Altman; m. Robert A. Drescher, Aug. 10, 1968 (div. 1980); m. David G. Lindstrom, Jan. 10, 1981. AB, Grove City Coll., 1968; MLS, U. Pitts., 1971. Tchr. Hempfield Sch. Dist., Greensburg, 1968-71; children's libr. Cin. Pub. Libr., 1971-72; br. mgr. Cin. Pub. LIbrary, 1972-74; dir. Rolling Meadows (Ill.) Pub. Libr., 1974-79, Champaign (Ill.) Pub. Libr., 1979-85, Memphis/Shelby County Pub. Libr. and Info. Ctr., 1985—; cons. Providence Assocs., Dallas, 1986-94; Tenn. del. White House Conf. on Librs. and Info. Svcs. Task Force, 1991-92; mem. Tenn. Sec. of State's Commn. on Tech. and Resource Sharing, 1991, 93, steering com. Tenn. Info. and Infrastructure, 1994-97, nat. adv. panel for assessment of role of sch. and pub. librs. U.S. Dept. Edn., 1995-98. Mem. Rhodes Coll. Commn. on 21st Century, Memphis, 1986-88, presdl. adv. com. Rhodes Coll., 1992—; mem. Leadership Memphis, 1987—, selection com., 1992-96; mem. Memphis Arts Coun., 1989-94; bd. dirs. Literacy Coun., 1986-91, Memphis NCCJ, 1989-93, Memphis Grants Info. Ctr., 1992-97, sec., 1993-95; bd. dirs. Memphis Literacy Found., 1988-92, v.p., 1989-90; bd. dirs. Goals for Memphis, 1988-93, chair edn. com., 1989-91, chair nominating com., 1992; bd. dirs. U. Memphis Soc., 1998—; mem. exec. adv. bd. Children's Mus., 1988-94, exec. adv. coun. U. Memphis, 1989-99; mem. allocations subcom. United Way, 1989-91, allocations com. Memphis Arts Coun., 100 for the Arts, 1989-91, Libr. Self-study Com. U. Memphis; pres. adv. coun. Lemoyne Coll. Recipient Govt. Leader award U. Ill. YWCA, 1981; Communicator of Yr. award Pub. Rels. Soc. of Am., 1992. Mem. ALA (chmn. intellectual freedom com. 1986-87, coun. 1992-99), Tenn. Libr. Assn., Memphis Libr. Coun., Pub. Libr. Assn. (v.p., pres. 1994-95), Rotary (bd. dirs. 1992-94, sec. 1993-94, chair mem. devel. com. 1994-95), U. of Memphis Soc. (bd. dirs. 1998—), Beta Phi Mu. Home: 1505 Vance Ave Memphis TN 38104-3810 Office: Memphis Shelby County Pub Libr & Info Ctr 1850 Peabody Ave Memphis TN 38104-4021

DRESCHER, KATHLEEN EBBEN, lawyer; b. Kaukauna, Wis., May 17, 1963; d. Willard Peter and Helen Mary (Joyce) Ebben; m. Park Morris Drescher, Aug. 12, 1989; children: John Park, William Morris. BA, Lawrence U., 1985; JD, Washington U. St. Louis, 1989. Bar: Mo. 1989, Wis. 1992. Assoc. Popkin & Stern, St. Louis, 1989-90; ptnr. Drescher & Drescher, St. Louis, 1990-92; shareholder Drescher & Drescher, S.C., Appleton, Wis., 1992—. Pres. bd. dirs. Emergency Shelters, Appleton, 1992—; bd. dirs. Child Care Resource and Referral, Appleton. Mem. ABA, Wis. Bar Assn., Mo. Bar Assn., Outagamie County Bar Assn. Avocation: tennis. Home: 14 Lamplighter Ct Appleton WI 54914-6519 Office: Drescher & Drescher SC 100 W Lawrence St Fl 3D Appleton WI 54911-5773

DRESCHER, PARK MORRIS, lawyer; b. St. Louis, Apr. 20, 1963; s. John Morris and Katherine (White) D.; m. Kathleen Ebben, Aug. 12, 1989; children: John Park, William Morris. BA, Lawrence U., 1985; JD, St. Louis U., 1988. Bar: Mo., 1989, Wis., 1992, U.S. Ct. of Appeals (8th cir.), 1989. Assoc. Biggs & Hensley, P.C., St. Louis, 1988-90; ptnr. Drescher & Drescher, S.C., Appleton, Wis., 1990—. Trustee The Mari Taniguchi Found., Appleton, 1997—; mem. small bus. sect. Appleton Area C. of C., 1997. Mem. ABA, Wis. Bar Assn., Mo. Bar Assn., Outagamie County Bar Assn. Avocation: tennis. Office: Drescher & Drescher SC 100 W Lawrence St Appleton WI 54911-5773

DRESCHER, SEYMOUR, history educator, writer; b. N.Y.C., Feb. 20, 1934; s. Sidney and Eva Rita (Levine) D.; m. Ruth Lieberman, June 19, 1955; children: Michael, Jonathan, Karen. BA, CCNY, 1955; MS, U. Wis., 1956, PhD, 1960. Instr. history Harvard U., 1960-62; asst. prof. U. Pitts., 1962-65, assoc. prof., 1965-69, prof., 1969-86, Univ. prof., 1986—, chmn., 1980-83; acad. dean. semester-at-sea, 1998; vis. disting. prof. CUNY, 1987; Roger T. Anstey Meml. lectr., Canterbury, Eng., 1984; bd. advisors Slavery and Abolition, 1985—; George A. Miller lectr., 1987, Pa. Commonwealth Speakers Program, 1989-91, rsch. fellow Univ. Ctr. Internat. Studies, Pitts., 1992; C-SPAN adv. com., Tocqueville. Author: Toqueville and England, 1964, Dilemmas of Democracy, 1968, Econocide, 1977, Capitalism and Antislavery, 1986, From Slavery to Freedom, 1999; co-author: The Abolition of Slavery and the Aftermath of Emancipation in Brazil, 1988; editor Jour. Contemporary History, 1991-99; editor: Tocqueville and Beaumont on Social Reform, 1968, Anti-Slavery, Religion and Reform, 1980, Political Symbolism in Modern Europe, 1982, The Meaning of Freedom, 1992, A Historical Guide to World Slavery, 1998; contbr.: Fifty Years Later: Antislavery, Capitalism and Modernity in the Dutch Orbit, 1995, Is the Holocaust Unique?, 1996; creator film: Confrontation, Paris, 1968, 70. Recipient Pres.'s Rsch. award U. Pitts., 1992; Fulbright scholar, 1957-58; NEH fellow, 1973-74, Guggenheim Found. fellow, 1977-78, Resident fellow Bellagio Ctr. for Scholars, 1980, 90, Woodrow Wilson fellow, 1983-84, sec. European program Wilson Ctr., 1984-85. Mem. Am. Hist. Assn., Hist. Soc., Soc. for French Hist. Studies (v.p. 1978-79), N.Am. Conf. on Brit. Studies, Dutch Royal Inst. Linguistics and Anthropology, Fulbright Assn., Commn. Tocqueville (France). Home: 5550 Pocusset St Pittsburgh PA 15217-1913 Office: U Pitts Dept History Pittsburgh PA 15260

DRESCHHOFF, GISELA AUGUSTE MARIE, physicist, educator; b. Moenchengladbach, Germany, Sept. 13, 1938; came to U.S., 1967, naturalized, 1976; d. Gustav Julius and Hildegard Friederike (Krug) D. Ph.D., Tech. U. Braunschweig (Ger.), 1972. Staff scientist Fed. Inst. Physics and Tech. Ger., 1965-67; research assoc. Kans. Geol. Survey, Lawrence, 1971-72; vis. asst. prof. physics U. Kans., 1972-74; dep. dir. radiation physics lab. Space Tech. Ctr., 1972-78, assoc. dir., 1979-84, co-dir., 1984-86, dir., 1996—; sr. sci. geology U. Kans., 1991, adj. assoc. prof. physics and astronomy, 1992; assoc. program mgr. NSF, Washington, 1978-79. Patentee identification markings for gemstones and method of making selective conductive regions in diamond layers. Named to Women's Hall of Fame, U. Kans., 1978; recipient Antarctic Service medal U.S.A., 1979; recipient NASA Group Achievement award, 1983. Fellow Explorers Club; mem. AAAS, Am. Phys. Soc., Am. Geophys. Union, Am. Polar Soc. (v.p.), Antarctican Soc., Sigma Xi. Home: 2908 W 19th St Lawrence KS 66047-2301 Office: Space Tech Ctr 2291 Irving Hill Rd Lawrence KS 66044-7541

DRESHER, PAUL JOSEPH, composer, music educator, performer; b. L.A., Jan. 8, 1951; s. Melvin J. and Martha (Whitaker) D.; m. Robin Naomi Kirck, Mar. 8, 1986; 1 child, Cole Kirck Dresher. MusB, U. Calif., Berkeley, 1977; MA in Composition, U. Calif., La Jolla, 1979. Prof. music Cornish Inst. Arts, Seattle, 1980-83; artistic dir. Paul Dresher Ensemble, Berkeley, 1984—; cons. Nat. Endowment for the Arts, Calif. Arts Coun., 1982-94, Rockefeller Found. Composer: (opera) Slow Fire, 1987, Power Failure, 1989, (music theater) Pioneer, 1989, (orchestral work) Reaction, 1984, (chamber orch.) Cornucopia, 1990, (dances) Shelf Life, 1987, Age of Unrest, 1991, The Gates, 1993, Outawak, 1997, (trio) Double Ikat, 1989, (chamber) Din of Iniquity, 1994, (solo piano) Blue Diamonds, 1995, Violin Concerto (chamber), 1996-97, Elapsed Time (for violin and piano), 1998; works presented by numerous symphonic and other orchs. including N.Y. Philharm. Munich State Opera, London Internat. Festival of Theatre; recordings on New Albion, Lovely, Starkland and New World labels. Bd. dirs. New Langton Arts Orgn., San Francisco, 1984-97, Am. Music Ctr., 1994—. Recipient numerous grants NEA, 1979-97; Fulbright grantee, 1984; Goddard Lieberson fellow, 1982. Mem. Broadcast Music, Inc., Am. Music Ctr., Opera America, Chamber Music America. E-mail: pauldresher@compuserve.com. Home and Office: 51 Avenida Dr Berkeley CA 94708-2145

DRESSEL, BARRY, museum administrator; b. Washington, Jan. 10, 1947; s. August and Uldena (Williams) D.; m. Judith Herdt Riley, 1984; children: Jason, Nicholas Eliot. BA, East Carolina U., 1969, MA, 1972. Asst. curator Hist. Soc. Del., Wilmington, 1975-76; asst. dir. Balt. City Life Mus., 1976-85; dir. City of Detroit Hist. Dept., 1985-89, Berkshire Mus., Pittsfield, Mass., 1989-93; pvt. practice mus. cons., 1993-96; dir. Turks and Caicos (Brit. West Indies) Nat. Mus., 1996-98. Bd. dirs. Walter P. Chrysler Hist. Mus., Auburn Hills, Mich., 1998—; trustee Mus. African Am. Hist., Detroit, 1987-89; founder, chair Consortium of New England Cmty. Mus., 1993-95. Fellow in history East Carolina U., 1969-70, 71-72, U. Del., 1975. Mem. Am. Assn. Mus., Am. Assn. State and Local History. Avocation: sailing.

DRESSEL, HENRY FRANCIS, lawyer; b. Bklyn., Apr. 11, 1914; s. Henry Philip and Ernestine (Delmar) D.; m. Rose Marie Valentine, Nov. 24, 1937; 1 child, Diana (Mrs. Anthony P. Fradella). AB, Washington Square Coll., NYU, 1943, JD, 1949. Bar: N.Y. 1949. Assco. corp. law firm Chadbourne, Stanchfield & Levy (and its successors), N.Y.C., 1933-43; pvt. practice law N.Y.C., 1950-86; ptnr. Dressel & Altman, P.C.; of counsel Berger & Steingut, 1986-93. Lt. USNR, 1943-46. Named hon. col. Okla., 1958, Okie, 1969. Mem. N.Y. State Bar Assn., Assn. Bar City of N.Y., N.Y. County Lawyers, Am. Judicature Soc., Justinian Soc., Internat. Footprint Assn., Phi Delta Phi. Democrat. Episcopalian. Home: 42 Clubhouse Ln Marlboro NJ 07746-1712 Office: Dressel & Hatab PC 18 E 50th St New York NY 10022-6817

DRESSEL, IRENE EMMA RINGWALD, alcoholism and family therapist; b. Enderlin, N.D., Oct. 26, 1926; d. Albert William and Emma Anna Magdelena (Trapp) Ringwald; m. Clarence Irvin Dressel, Jr., Mar. 13, 1946 (div. Nov. 1972); 1 son, Keith Alan. Student pub. schs., Casselton, N.D. Cert. Master addiction counselor, N.D.; cert. chem. dependency counselor, Minn. Alcoholism counseling trainee Heartview Found., Mandan, N.D., 1974-75, family therapy intern, 1975-76, family counselor, 1976-77, supr. family mems. program, 1978; designer, supr. family program The Meadows, Wickenburg, Ariz., 1978-79; treatment programs cons., dir. consultation dept. Johnson Inst., Mpls., 1979-81; designer, assoc. dir. chem. dependency unit Presbyn. Hosp., Oklahoma City, 1981-83; designer, supr. adolescent program United Recovery Ctr., Grand Forks, N.D., 1983-85; dir. Irene Dressel Counseling, Grand Forks, 1985-89; designer, program dir. the Dressel Ctr., Fargo, N.D., 1989-90, ret., 1990; FDR/DIR Your Level Best, 1996. Republican. Lutheran.

DRESSEL, MARGARET JANE, artist, art educator; b. Brookline, Mass., Aug. 25, 1949; d. Chauncey Lovett Megargle and Esther Laura Field; m. Richard Dressel; children: Bethany, Keith. Student, Moore Coll. Art, 1967-68, Nat. Acad. Art, 1985-86; assoc. in Occupl. Studies, Pratt Inst., 1985. Owner, artist Peggy Dressel Studio, Oakland, N.J., 1990—; graphic designer Intra Design Inc., Ramsey, N.J., 1990-94; illustrator, asst. Jacqui Morgan Studio, N.Y.C., 1990-96; painting instr. Ramsey Adult Sch., 1996—, Art Ctr. No. N.J., New Milford, 1999—; founder Pastel Plus, N.J., pres., 1997-99; mem. Blackwell St. Ctr. Arts; chmn. CAA Nat. Juried Exhbns., Ridgewood, N.J., 1993, 94, 95. One-woman shows include St. Peter's Ch., N.Y.C., 1992, Blackwell St. Gallery , Dover, N.J., 1994, Lena DiGangi Gallery, West Paterson, N.J., 1994, Ringwood Manor W. Wing Gallery, N.J. State Pk., 1994, ADP, Inc. Gallery, Roseland, N.J., 1995, Dow Jones & Co., S. Brunswick, N.J., 1994, 96; N.Y. Theol. Sem., N.Y.C., 1998, The Interch. Ctr., N.Y.C., 1998; represented in numerous juried exhbns. and pvt. collections; illustrator mags., books, brochures, ads, posters; featured artist poster and calendar N.J. Fine Artist Collection, 1998. Recording sec. Oakland Libr. Bd., 1979-80, pres., 1980-82. Recipient Purchase award Degas Pastel Soc., 1992, Merit award Degas Pastel Soc., 1992, Cynthia Goodgal Meml., Ridgewood Art Inst., Nat. Bergen Mus., 1997, others; named Best in Show, Inserria Corp., 1992. Mem. Cmty. Arts Assn. (pres. 1994-96), Southea. Pastel Soc. (signature mem.), Oreg. Pastel Soc. (signature mem.), Am. Artist Profl. League. Democrat. Methodist. Avocations: art, music, traveling, gardening. Home: 11 Rockaway Ave Oakland NJ 07436 Office: Peggy Dressel Studio 11 Rockaway Ave Oakland NJ 07436

DRESSELHAUS, MILDRED SPIEWAK, physics and engineering educator; b. Bklyn., Nov. 11, 1930; d. Meyer and Ethel (Teichteil) Spiewak; m. Gene F. Dresselhaus, May 25, 1958; children: Marianne Dresselhaus Cooper, Carl Eric, Paul David, Eliot Michael. BA, Hunter Coll., 1951, DSc (hon.), 1982; Fulbright fellow, Cambridge (Eng.) U., 1951-52; MA, Radcliffe Coll., 1953; PhD in Physics, U. Chgo., 1958; D Engring. (hon.), Worcester Poly. Inst., 1976; DSc (hon.), Smith Coll., 1980, N.J. Inst. Tech., 1984; Doctorat Honoris Causa, U. Catholique de Louvain, 1988; DSc (hon.), Rutgers U., 1989, U. Conn., 1992, U. Mass., Boston, 1992, Princeton U., 1992; DEngring, Colo. Sch. of Mines, 1993; D (hon.), Technion, Israel Inst. Tech., Haifa, 1994; dr honoris causa, Johannes Kepler U., Linz, Austria, 1993; DSc (hon.), Harvard U., 1995, Ohio State U., 1998; Doctorate (hon.), U. Paris, Sorbonne, 1999. NSF postdoctoral fellow Cornell U., 1958-60; mem. staff Lincoln Lab., MIT, Lexington, 1960-67; prof. elec. engring. MIT, Cambridge, 1967—, assoc. dept. head elec. engring., 1972-74, Abby Rockefeller Mauze chair, 1973-85, dir. Ctr. for Materials Sci. and Engring., 1977-83, prof. physics, 1983—, Inst. prof., 1985—; vis. prof. dept. physics U. Campinas, Brazil, summer 1971, Technion, Israel Inst. Tech., Haifa, 1972, 90, Nihon and Aoyama Gakuin Univs., Tokyo, 1973, IVIC, Caracas, Venezuela, 1977; vis. prof. dept. elec. engring. U. Calif., Berkeley, 1985; Graffin lectr. Am. Carbon Soc., 1982; chmn. steering com. on evaluation panels Nat. Bur. Stds., 1978-83; mem. Energy Rsch. Adv. Bd., 1984-90; bd. dirs. Rogers Corp. Contbr. articles to profl. jours. Bd. govs. Argonne Nat. Lab., 1986-89, Weizmann Inst., Reoohot, Israel, 1999—; mem. governing bd NRC, 1984-87, 89-90, 92-96; trustee Calif. Inst. of Tech., 1993—; overseer Harvard U., 1997—. Recipient Alumnae medal Radcliffe Coll., 1973, Killian Faculty Achievement award 1986-87, Nat. Medal of Sci., 1990, Sigri Great Lakes Carbon award, 1997, Profl. Achievement award, 1998; named to Hunter Coll. Hall of Fame, 1972, Women in Tech. Internat. Hall of Fame award, 1998. Fellow IEEE, AAAS (bd. dirs. 1985-89, pres.-elect 1996, pres. 1997, chair bd. dirs. 1998), Am. Phys. Soc. (pres. 1984), Am. Acad. Arts and Scis.; mem. Nat. Acad. Engring. (coun. 1981-87), Soc. Women Engrs. (Achievement award 1977), Nat. Acad. Scis. (coun. 1987-90, 92-96, chmn. engring. sect. 1987-90, chmn. class III 1990-93, treas. 1992-96), Brazilian Acad. Sci. (corr.), The Engring. Acad. Japan (fgn. asoc. 1993—), Am. Philos. Soc., 1995. Office: MIT Rm 13-3005 Dept Elec Engring Cambridge MA 02139

DRESSER, KAREN KERNS, state agency administrator; b. Urbana, Ohio, June 14, 1944; d. Edmund Howard and Kathryn Louise (Strapp) Kerns; m. David I. Dresser, Mar. 20, 1980 (dec. Feb. 1994). BA, Barat Coll., 1966; MA, Am. U., 1969. Mgmt. intern/program officer HUD, Washington, 1968-71; various positions Nat. League of Cities, Washington, 1971-82; v.p. Nat. Ctr. for Housing Mgmt., Washington, 1982-83; program dir. Ohio Dept. Devel., Columbus, 1983-84, asst. dep. dir., 1990—; exec. dir. Ohio Housing Fin. Agy., Columbus, 1984-88; pres. Nat. Affordable Housing Trust, Columbus, 1988-90; treas. Devore-Dresser Devel., Columbus, 1986—. Author: City Council Training Series, 1975-76. Advisor, hon. trustee Ohio Cmty. Devel. Fin. Fund, Columbus, 1991—; bd. dirs. Coun. of State Housing Agys., Washington, 1986-88, Nat. Low-Income Housing Coalition, Washington, 1989-90; vol. German Village Soc., 1986—. Roman Catholic. Avocations: gardening, politics, travel, literacy tutoring. Home: 791 Mohawk St Columbus OH 43206-2112 Office: Ohio Dept Devel 77 S High St Columbus OH 43215-6108

DRESSLER, BRENDA JOYCE, health educator, consultant, book and film reviewer; b. N.Y.C., Jan. 30, 1943; d. Herbert and Betty (Kirshner) Dressler; m. Irving Kaufman, Dec. 30, 1961 (div. Dec. 1979); 1 child, Joshua Ari. BA, CCNY, 1964; MA, CUNY, 1969; PhD, NYU, 1986. Cert. health edn. specialist. CHES educator sex and health N.Y.C. Bd. Edn., 1964-75, 1979—; educator sex and health Sex Info. and Edn. Coun. U.S., N.Y.C., 1985-86; adj. asst. prof. health edn. N.Y. Inst. Tech., Hofstra U., 1995—; prof. tchr. edn. N.Y. Inst. Tech., 1997—; health cons., 1996—; cons. PTA and curriculum adv. com. Steinway Jr. High Sch., N.Y.C., 1985-87, Bayside High Sch., 1987-90; regional coord. and cons. on family living, Queens, 1990—; comprehensive health coord. high sch. HIV/AIDS Edn., Queens, 1991—; adj. instr. C.W. Post, N.Y. Inst. Tech., 1992—; cons. UFT Tchrs. Ctr. Consortium. Columnist: Women Mean Business; contbr. numerous articles to profl. jours.; curriculum writer HIV/AIDS Edn. K-6; writer instrnl. tng. design on HIV/AIDS; tchr. tng. design HIV/AIDS Edn. 7-9; health counselor, instr. Bayside H.S., HIV/AIDS team leader; adj. instr. NYIT, CW POST. Awards chair Sophe, 1996—. Mem. Am. Bd. Sexology, Soc. Phys. and Health Edn., Kappa Delta Pi. Avocations: physical fitness training, piano, traveling, cycling, ping pong. Home and Office: 16241 Powells Cove Blvd Whitestone NY 11357-1449

DRESSLER, DAVID CHARLES, retired aerospace company executive; b. Cleve., June 21, 1928; s. Walter Carl and Beatrice (Albin) D.; m. Dorothea Walker, Dec. 22, 1950; children: David Charles, Bradley, Christopher. B.A., Yale U., 1950; grad., Advanced Mgmt. Program, Harvard Bus. Sch., 1973. With Armstrong Cork Co., 1950-51; with Martin Marietta Corp., 1953-92, pres. Master Builders div., 1977-80, pres. Martin Marietta Chem. Co., 1979-81, corp. v.p., 1979-83, sr. corp. v.p., 1983-92; pres. Master Builders Co. Ltd., Toronto, 1977-81, Martin Marietta Aluminum, 1982-85; chmn. bd. Internat. Light Metals, 1985-91; pres. Martin Marietta Materials, Bethesda, Md., 1985-91; chmn. bd. Martin Marietta Ordnance Systems, 1985-87; chmn. corp. com. Corcoran Mus. Art, 1992; bd. dirs. Bowles Fluidics. Served to capt. USMCR, 1951-53. Mem. Congl. Country Club (Washington) (mem. bd. govs. 1990-96), Harvard Bus. Sch. Club (pres. Washington club 1983, chmn. bd. dirs. 1984), Country Club (Cleve.), Sawgrass Country Club (Ponte Vedra), Phi Beta Kappa. Episcopalian.

DRESSLER, ROBERT A., lawyer; b. Fort Lauderdale, Fla., Aug. 20, 1945; s. R. Philip and Elisabeth (Anthony) D.; chidlren: James Philip, Kathryn S. AB cum laude, Dartmouth Coll., 1967; JD cum laude, Harvard U., 1973. Bar: Mass. 1973, Fla. 1974, D.C. 1980, U.S. Dist. Ct. (so. dist.) Fla., U.S. Dist. Ct. Mass., U.S. Ct. Appeals (1st cir.), U.S. Ct. Appeals (5th cir.), U.S. Supreme Ct. Assoc. Goodwin, Proctor & Hoar, Boston, 1973-75; ptnr. Dressler & Dressler, Ft. Lauderdale, 1975-82; mayor City of Ft. Lauderdale, 1982-86; pvt. practice law Ft. Lauderdale, 1982—. Vice chmn. Broward Tng. and Employment Adminstrn., 1982-86; bd. dirs. Broward County League of Cities, 1985-86; nat. committeeman Fla. Fedn. Young Reps., 1981-83; bd. regents State Univ. System, 1987-93; mem. bd. govs. Nova Law Sch., 1988; mem. Estate Planning Coun. Broward County; adv. com. Fla. Atlantic U., Broward, 1989—; exec. com. Tchr. Edn. Alliance, 1991—; chmn. Seflin Free-Net Adv. Bd., 1994-97. Capt. USMC, 1969-72. Named Person of Yr. Fla. Atlantic U., 1993. Mem. ABA, Greater Ft. Lauderdale C.of C. (bd. govs. 1982-89), Broward County Bar Assn., Fla. Bar Assn., D.C. Bar Assn., Vietnam Vets. Am., Rotary Internat., Tower Forum (bd. govs. 1983-86), Phi Beta Kappa. Presbyterian. Avocations: jogging, scuba diving, hiking. Home: 1608 NE 6th St Fort Lauderdale FL 33304-2976 Office: PO Box 2425 Fort Lauderdale FL 33303-2425

DRESSNER, HOWARD ROY, foundation executive, lawyer; b. N.Y.C., Feb. 14, 1919; s. Sol and Anna (Gross) D.; m. Sonia Segoda, Apr. 6, 1942; 1 son, Robert. B.S., N.Y. U., 1940; LL.B., Columbia U., 1948. With N.Y. U., 1948-64; successively instr. pub. speaking, asst. prof. pub. speaking, asst. v.p. devel.; dir. Albert Gallatin Assos., 1956-65; asst. to v.p. domestic programs Ford Found., 1964-67, sec. found., 1967-71, sec., gen. counsel found., 1971-76, v.p., gen. counsel, sec. found., 1976-84; counsel Shereff, Friedman, Hoffman & Goodman, 1984-90; pres. N.Y. Nonprofit Com., 1984-91. Author: Essays in Bewilderment, 1998; co-author: Business Writing. Candidate for N.Y. State Assembly, 1966; active Nonprofit Com., 1984—. Served to maj. AUS, World War II. Decorated Bronze Star medal. Home: 6 Peter Cooper Rd New York NY 10010-6701

DRESSNER, PAUL ROBERT, outside sales and customer service representative; b. Chester, Pa., Feb. 1, 1955; s. Robert Lodge and Mary Louise (Rutt) D.; m. Donna Ellen Smith, June 1, 1980 (div. Feb. 1990); children: Robert Warren, Christopher Ryan. BS in Hotel and Restaurant Mgmt., U. Wis., Stout, 1977. Asst. mgr. Morrisons Cafeteria, Columbia, S.C., 1977-79, Florence, S.C., 1979-80, Wilmington, N.C., 1980-83; night mgr. ARA Svcs., Greensboro, N.C., 1983-84; food svc. dir. ARA Svcs., Sewanee, Tenn., 1984-86, Americus, Ga., 1986, Frankfort, Ky., 1987, Cleveland, Tenn., 1987-88, Wilmington, N.C., 1988-89; mgr. Dressner's Village Cafe, St. Simons Island, Ga., 1989-90; customer svc. rep., svc. mgr. Island Automotive, St. Simons Island, 1990-95; outside salesman Brooks Auto Parts, Brunswick, Ga., 1995—. Active Coastal Symphony Ga. Named one of Outstanding Young Men of Am., 1985. Avocations: restoring trucks, playing trombone. Home: PO Box 24206 Saint Simons GA 31522

DREW, AUBREY JAY, accountant; b. Dayton, Ky., Aug. 25, 1919; s. Leslie Franklin and Fay (White) D.; children: Michael Wayne, Susan Elaine Drew Kibbe. B in bus. adminstrn., Univ. Cin., 1947. CPA, Tex. 2d lt. to Col. artillery U.S. Army Reserve, San Antonio, Dallas, Tex., 1948-79; asst. store mgr. F.W. Woolworth Co., Cincinnati, Ohio, 1938-42; aerial gunner U.S. Army Air Corps., 1942-45; spl. agt. criminal investigation Criminal Investigation Divsn. IRS, San Antonio, Dallas, Tex., 1948-75; v.p. fin. Tex. Womens Univ., Denton, Tex., 1975-78; investigator Tex. State Atty. Gen., Austin, Tex., 1977-93. Home: 7100 Darcus Cv Austin TX 78759-3721

DREW, BERNARD ALGER, writer; b. West Stewartstown, N.H., Jan. 16, 1950; s. Warren Alger and Jennie Roberta (Rose) D.; m. Donna Marie Archambault, July 16, 1977; children: Jessie, Darcie. BA, Northeastern U., 1973. Asst. editor Mart Mag., Pittsfield, Mass., 1973-75; pub. rels. coord. Berkshire Learning Ctr., Pittsfield, 1975-76; freelance writer, 1976-80; reporter, editor Berkshire Courier, Great Barrington, Mass., 1980-96; freelance writer, editor Great Barrington, 1996—. Author: Hopalong Cassidy, 1991,

100 Most Popular Young Adult Authors, 1996, Great Barrington: Great Town * Great History, 1999, A Berkshire Photo Album, 1999; copy editor Lakeville Jour. Pres. Great Barrington Hist. Soc., 1982-84; pres. Berkshire County Hist. Soc., Pittsfield, 1986-88; chmn. Great Barrington Hist. Dist. Commn., 1989-98; vol. Housatonic Riverwalk, Great Barrington, 1993—. Mem. Soc. Indsl. Archaeology, Great Barrington Land Conservancy. Congregational. Avocations: collecting autographs, hiking, photography. Home: 24 Gilmore Ave Great Barrington MA 01230-1438

DREW, CLIFFORD JAMES, university administrator, special education and educational psychology educator; b. Eugene, Oreg., Mar. 9, 1943; s. Albert C. and Violet M. (Caskey) D. B.S. magna cum laude, Eastern Oreg. Coll., 1965; M.Ed., U.Ill., 1966; Ph.D. with honors, U. Oreg., 1968. Asst. prof. edn. Kent (Ohio) State U., 1968-69; asst. prof. dir. research and spl. edn. U. Tex., Austin, 1969-71; assoc. prof. spl. edn. U. Utah, Salt Lake City, 1971-76; prof. U. Utah, 1977—; asst. dean Grad. Sch. Edn., 1974-77, assoc. dean, 1977-79, 89-95, prof. spl. edn. and ednl. psychology, 1979—, coord. instrnl. tech., acad. v.p.'s office, 1995-97, assoc. acad. v.p., 1997—; cons. HEW, 1969—; Bd. dirs. Far West Lab. Ednl. Research and Devel., San Francisco, 1974-80; mem. exec. bd. Salt Lake County Assn. Retarded Children, 1971-72; mem. adv. com. Mental Retardation Counseling Service, Tex. Dept. Mental Health Mental Retardation, 1969-70. Author: (with P. Chinn and D. Logan) Mental Retardation: A Life Cycle Approach, 2d edit., 1979, Introduction to Designing Research and Evaluation, 2d edit., 1980, (with M. Hardman and H. Bluhm) Mental Retardation: Social and Educational Perspectives, 1977, (with D. Gelfand and W. Jenson) Understanding Children's Behavior Disorders, 1982, 3d edit., 1997, (with M. HArdman and D. Logan) Mental Retardation: A Life Cycle Approach, 4th edit., 1988, 5th edit., 1992, 6th edit., 1996, (with M. Hardman) Mental Retardation: A Life Cycle Approach, 7th edit., 2000, Designing and Conducting Behavioral Research, 1985, (with M. Hardman and W. Egan) Human Exceptionality: Society, School and Family, 1984, 6th edit., 1999, (with B. Wampold) Theory and Application of Statistics, 1990, (with M. Hardman and A. Hart) Designing and Conducting Research: Inquiry in Education and Social Science, 1996; numerous articles in field. NDEA fellow, 1965-66; U.S. Office Edn. fellow, 1966-68. Fellow Am. Assn. Mental Retardation; mem. Am. Psychol. Assn., Am. Ednl. Rsch. Assn. Office: U Utah Acad VPs Office 201 Presidents Cir Rm 205 Salt Lake City UT 84112-8902

DREW, DONALD ALLEN, mathematical sciences educator; b. Margaretville, N.Y., Sept. 11, 1945; s. Howard Charles and Marjorie Belle (Liddle) D.; m. Margaret Esther Miller, June 4, 1966; children—Elizabeth Margaret, Stacey Lynn. BS in Math., Rensselaer Poly. Inst., 1967, MS, 1969, PhD, 1970. Instr. MIT, Cambridge, 1970-71; asst. prof. NYU, 1971-73; asst. prof. math. Rensselaer Poly. Inst., Troy, N.Y., 1973-79, assoc. prof., 1979-83, prof., 1983-94, Ricketts prof., 1995—; cons. Battelle, Richland, Wash., 1975-77, Chevron, 1996; mathematician U.S. Army Rsch. Office, Research Triangle Park, N.C., 1980-81; vis. assoc. prof. U. Wis.-Madison, 1981; summer faculty Sandia Nat. Labs., Albuquerque, 1984; vis. prof. theoretical and applied mechanics Math. Scis. Inst., Cornell U., 1988-89; assoc. dir. Ctr. Multiphase Rsch., 1987-94, dir., 1994-96; vis. faculty Centro Atomico, Bariloche, Argentina, 1997, Southampton (Eng.) U., 1997; vis. scientist Los Alamos (N.Mex.) Nat. Labs., 1997. Contbr. articles to profl. jours. Pres. Faculty Senate, 1993-94. Mem. Soc. Indsl. and Applied Mathematics (mem. edn. com. 1977-80), Soc. Engring. Sci., Soc. Natural Philosophy, Sigma Xi. Republican. Home: 10 Eaton Rd Troy NY 12180-3603 Office: Rensselaer Poly Inst Dept Math Scis Troy NY 12180*

DREW, ELIZABETH, television commentator, journalist, author; b. Cin., Nov. 16, 1935; d. William J. and Estelle (Jacobs) Brenner; m. J. Patterson Drew, Apr. 11, 1964 (dec. 1970); m. David Webster, Sept. 26, 1981. B.A., Wellesley Coll., 1957; LHD, Hood Coll., 1976, Yale U., 1976, Trinity Coll., 1978, Reed Coll., 1979, Williams Coll., 1981, Georgetown U., 1981, George Washington U., 1994. Writer editor Congl. Quar., 1959-64; free lance writer, 1964-67; Washington editor Atlantic Monthly, 1967-73; host TV interview program Thirty Minutes With, 1971-73; commentator TV program Agronsky and Company, 1973-93; commentator syndicated TV program Inside Washington, 1973-92; Washington corr. New Yorker Mag., 1973-92; commentator Monitor Radio, 1992—. Author: Washington Journal, 1975, American Journal, 1977, Senator, 1979, Portrait of an Election, 1981, Politics and Money, 1983, Campaign Journal, 1985, Election Journal, 1989, On the Edge: The Clinton Presidency, 1994, Showdown: The Struggle Between the Gingrich Congress and the Clinton White House, 1996, Whatever It Takes: The Real Struggle for Political Power in America, 1997, The Corruption of American Politics, 1999; contbg. Washington Post; contbg. author various mags. and jours. Recipient award for excellence Soc. Mag. Writers, 1971, Wellesley Alumnae Achievement award, 1973, DuPont award, 1973, Mo. medal, 1979, Sidney Hillman award, 1983, Ambassador of Honor award Books Across the Sea, 1984, Literary Lion award N.Y. Pub. Library, 1985, Edward Weintal prize, 1988. Home & Office: 3000 Woodland Dr NW Washington DC 20008-3543

DREW, ELIZABETH HEINEMAN, publishing executive; b. Evanston, Ill., Aug. 26, 1940; d. Ben Harlow and Marion Elizabeth (Heineman) D. BA, U. Wis., 1961. With Doubleday & Co., Inc., N.Y.C., 1961-84, prodn. asst., 1961-63, personal asst. to editor in chief, 1963-66, adminstrv. asst. to editor in chief, 1966-69, editorial asst. to editor in chief, 1969-71, assoc. editor, 1971-74, editor, 1974-77, sr. editor, 1977-79, exec. editor, editorial dir., 1979-84; v.p., sr. editor William Morrow and Co., N.Y.C., 1984-92; v.p., pub. Lisa Drew Books/Macmillan Pub. Co., N.Y.C., 1993-94; v.p. pub. Lisa Drew Books/Charles Scribner's Sons, N.Y.C., 1994—; tchr. NYU Sch. Continuing Edn., 1981-82. Bd. dirs. Barbara Bush Found. Family Literacy, 1995—. Mem. PEN (N.Y. chpt.), Women's Media Group (treas. 1982-84, pres. 1985-86), Nat. Press Club (Washington), Assn. Am. Pubs. (internat. freedom to pub. com. 1978—, chmn. 1990-93, freedom to read com. 1988—, chmn. 1994-98), Century Assn. (N.Y.), First City Club (Savannah, Ga.). Democrat. Episcopalian.

DREW, FRASER BRAGG ROBERT, English language educator; b. Randolph, Vt., June 23, 1913; s. George Albie and Hazel (Fraser) D. AB magna cum laude, U. Vt., 1933; MA, Duke U., 1935; PhD, U. Buffalo, 1952. Instr. Latin, Green Mt. Coll., Poultney, Vt., 1936-39; grad. asst. English, Syracuse U., 1939-41; instr. English, Buffalo State Coll., 1945-47, asst. prof., 1947-52; prof. SUNY-Buffalo, 1952-73, Disting. Teaching prof., 1973-83. Author: John Masefield's England, 1973; contbr. articles to profl. jours. Chmn. St. Patrick Scholarship Fund, Buffalo, 1969-79. Grantee SUNY Research Found., 1960, 67; St. Patrick's scholar, 1967; recipient Disting. Alumnus award U. Vt., 1968, Irishman of Yr. award United Irish Socs. Western N.Y., 1970. Mem. Irish Am. Cultural Inst., Am. Com. Irish Studies, Acad. Am. Poets, Housman Soc., John Masefield Soc., Ira Allen Soc., Wilbur Soc., Boulder Soc., Hemingway Soc., Robinson Jeffers Tor House Found., Friends of Duke U. Chapel, Duke U. Heritage Soc., Friends of Hemingway Collection, John F. Kennedy Lib., Friends of Bailey/Howe Libr., Lambda Iota, Phi Beta Kappa. Home: 101 Portside Buffalo NY 14202-4356

DREW, JODY LYNNE, secondary education educator; b. L.A., Apr. 12, 1959; d. Marvin Wayne and Patricia Ann (Dozier) D. BA in English, Whitworth Coll., 1981; MA in English, U. Washington, 1990. Cert. tchr., Wash. Tchr. Eastside Catholic H.S., Bellevue, Wash., 1982-87, B.E.S.T. Alternative Sch., Kirkland, Wash., 1987-88, White River H.S., Buckley, Wash., 1989-92; tchr. Issaquah (Wash.) H.S., 1992-96, restructuring chair, 1992; tchr. Roosevelt H.S., Seattle, 1996—. commr. Seattle women's commn. City of Seattle, 1998-99; Officer precinct com. Wash. State Dem. Com., Seattle, 1988-95, mem. McDonnell Project, U. Wash. Mem. ASCD, Nat. Coun. Tchrs. English, Wash. Edn. Assn. (pulse rep. 1992), Issaquah Edn. Assn. (bldg. rep. 1992-96, exec. bd. mem., 1994-96, sr. project coord., 1996), So. Poverty Law Ctr. (tchg. project, leadership conf.). Democrat. Avocations: cycling, rock climbing, Spanish language and literature, AIDS prevention education. Office: Roosevelt HS 1410 NE 66th St Seattle WA 98115-6744

DREW, K, financial advisor, management consultant; b. Freeport, N.Y.; d. Harry P. and Kathleen (Isdal) Barton; children: Karen, Donna. BA, U. Ga., 1960; postgrad., U. Ill., 1961. Dir. YWCA, Corpus Christi, Tex., 1969-72, Dwoskin Nat. Wallcovering Co., Atlanta, 1974-76; dep. asst. fin. presdl. campaign, 1976-77; dir. fin. Presdl. Inaugural, Washington, 1976; dep. adv. for small bus. SBA, Washington, 1977-80, asst. to adminstr., 1980-82; v.p. Alpha Systems, Inc., Washington and Athens, Greece, 1980-85; human resource cons. MBA Mgmt., Inc., McLean, Va., 1982-84; bus. cons. Drew Cons., McLean, 1984—; cons. assoc. Walling, June & Assocs., Old Town Alexandria, Va., 1986-89; fin. advisor The Family Extended, Washington, 1990—; bus. rep. Nikken, Inc., Washington, 1996, KareMor Internat., Inc., Washington, 1996; cons. The B.O.W.L. Group, Washington, 1996—; fin. advisor SAKA, Inc., Merrifield, Va., 1991—, Warrenton, Va., 1991-92, DeLeoand Assocs., McLean, Va., 1991-92; fin. dir. Disting. Environments, Reston, Va., 1992-94. State rep. poverty program and suicide prevention bds. Corpus Christi Bus. Coun., 1969-71; bd. dirs. YWCA, Washington, 1983-85; head speaker's bur. Fairfax Symphony, 1979-85, mem. exec. devel. com., 1979-86; mem. Mental Health Exec. Bd. dirs., Washington, 1983-88; deacon Nat. Presbyn. Ch., Washington, 1988-90; asst. to exec. dir. T. Monk Found., Jazz Sch., Duke U., 1987-89; event dir. Easter Seal Soc., 1990-91; mem. Youth for Tomorrow devel. com. Joe Gibbs Charities, Washington, 1990-98; presdl. campaign team captain Va. and Ga. Inaugural Com., 1993; Ga. Ball host, Washington, 1993; host Presdl. Inaugural Gala, Washington, 1993; In Kind Svc. to White House Advance Office of Pres., 1993—; cons. advisor Battered Spouses & Their Children, Washington, 1995—; campa pres. team, 1996; pres. inaugural host, Washington, D.C., 1996; fin. mgr. Internat. Fellowship Family Extended, Washington, 1993-98; fin., mkgt. adv., mem. new bowl group Urban Prayer Breakfast, Washington, 1997—; job cons. Homeless Bd. and Symposium, Washington, 1997-98; pres. bd. dirs. WAR Against Broken Hearts, Atlanta, 1998—. Mem. Nat. League Am. Pen Women (v.p., pres. Washington Capital chpt. 1987-89, nat. bd. dirs. 1987-90, nat. roster chmn. 1989—), Bus. and Profl. Women Washington, Nat. Platform Assn., Alpha Gamma Delta. Office: 8350 Greensboro Dr Ste 1-121 Mc Lean VA 22102-3533

DREW, KATHERINE FISCHER, history educator; b. Houston, Sept. 24, 1923; d. Herbert Herman and Martha (Holloway) Fischer; m. Ronald Farinton Drew, July 27, 1951. BA, Rice Inst., 1944, MA, 1945; PhD, Cornell U., 1950. Asst. history Cornell U., 1948-50; instr. history Rice U., 1946-48, mem. faculty, 1950—, prof. history, 1964—, Harris Masterson, Jr. prof. history, 1983-85, Lynette S. Autrey prof. history, 1985-96, prof. emeritus, 1996—, chmn. dept. history, 1970-80; editor Rice U. (Rice U. Studies), 1967-81, acting dean humanities and social scis., 1973, acting chmn. dept. art and art history, 1996-98. Author: The Burgundian Code, 1949, Studies in Lombard Institutions, 1956, The Lombard Laws, 1973, Law and Society in Early Medieval Europe, 1988, The Laws of the Salian Franks, 1991, also articles; editor: Perspective in Medieval History, 1963, The Barbarian Invasions, 1970; mem. bd. editors Am. Hist. Assn. Guide to Hist. Lit., 1987-94; contbr.: Life and Thought in the Middle Ages, 1967. Guggenheim fellow, 1959; Fulbright scholar, 1965; NEH Sr. fellow, 1974-75. Fellow Mediaeval Acad. Am. (coun. 1974-77, 2d v.p. to pres. 1985-87, del. to Am. Coun. Learned Socs. 1977-81); mem. Am. Hist. Assn. (coun. 1983-86), Am. Soc. Legal History, So. Hist. Assn. (vice chair, chair European sect. 1986-88, exec. com. 1989-91), Phi Beta Kappa. Home: 509 Buckingham Dr Houston TX 77024-5804 Office: Rice U Dept History MS 42 PO Box 1892 Houston TX 77251-1892

DREW, NANCY MCLAURIN SHANNON, counselor, consultant; b. Meridian, Miss., Apr. 29, 1934; d Julian Caldwell and Emma Katherine (Sanders) Shannon; m. Thomas Champion III, Feb. 11, 1956; children: Thomas Champion IV, Julian C. Shannon. BA, Furman U., 1956; MEd, N.C. State U., 1968. Cert. sch. counselor; cert. supr. curriculum and instrn., N.C. Rsch. asst. N.C. State U., Raleigh, 1957-59; tchr. English Raleigh City Schs., 1959-60; dir. guidance program Millbrook Sr. High/Wake County Schs., Raleigh, 1969-77; guidance chmn. Daniels Middle Sch./Wake County Schs., Raleigh, 1977-84, guidance info. specialist, 1984-85; guidance supr. Wake County Pub. Schs., Raleigh, 1985-88; coord. model dropout prevention program Wake County Pub. Sch./State Dept. Pub. Inst., Raleigh, 1985-88; counseling chmn. Garner Middle Sch., Raleigh, 1988-96; presenter, cons. 1st and 2d Nat. Dropout Prevention Confs., Winston-Salem, N.C., 1986-87, Raleigh, 1986-88, N.C. Sch. Counselors Conf., Raleigh, 1986-88, Am. Pers. and Guidance Assn., 1976, N.C. Mid. Sch. Assn., 1987-88; presenter career workshops ParentScope 1996, speakers' staff ParentScope 1995-96. Contbr. articles to profl. jours. Vice chmn. bd. trustees Crossnore (N.C.) Sch., 1977—; mem. adv. bd. Tamassee DAR Sch., 1994—; sec., bd. dirs. Wake Teen Med. Svcs., Raleigh, 1978-88, Garner Edn. Found., 1991-95; mem. Wake County Bus. and Edn. Leadership Coun., 1992-96. Named Outstanding Sr. Citizen, Raleigh Jaycees, 1999. Mem. AACD, NEA, DAR (area rep. spkrs. staff N.C. 1995-98, chmn. state DAR sch. com. 1985-88, state editor DAR News 1989-91, 94-97, chpt. regent 1992-95, nat. house com. 1992-94, nat. vice chmn. spl. svcs., state officer 1989-91, dir. dist. VI N.C. State DAR, N.C. Outstanding Jr. Mem. 1970, nat. vice chmn. membership 1996-98), N.C. Edn. Assn., Am. Sch. Counselors Assn., N.C. Sch. Counselors Assn., Phi Delta Kappa, Delta Kappa Gamma (pres. chpt. 1985-88, state chmn. 1991-93, state com. chmn. 1994-96). Democrat. Methodist. Home: 6000 Winthrop Dr Raleigh NC 27612-2142

DREW, PAUL, entrepreneur; b. Detroit, Mar. 10, 1935; s. Harry and Elizabeth (Schneider) Schlachman; m. Dove Ann Austin, Sept. 9, 1961. BA, Wayne State U., Detroit, 1957. Disc jockey Port Huron, Mich. and Atlanta, 1955-67; program dir. Sta. WQXI, Atlanta, 1966-67, Sta. CKLW, Detroit, 1967-68; program cons. Storer Broadcasting Co., Phila., 1968-69; program dir. RKO Radio stas. in, Detroit, San Francisco, Washington and L.A., 1970-73; v.p. programming RKO Radio stas., 1973-77; pres. Paul Drew Enterprises, L.A., 1977—; dir. USIA-Radio Marti, 1984-85; pres. USA Japan Co., 1985—, The Mobotron Corp., Hollywood, Calif., 1988—, Fuzzmug Corp., 1991—, 2151 Corp., 1991—; personal mgr. Pink Lady, outside Japan, 1978; ptnr. Teacup-Teaspoon Music Pub. Co., 1978; chmn. Billboard Internat. Programming Conf., 1976; commr. Calif. Motion Picture Coun., 1979-85. Del. Dem. Nat. Conv., 1976; mem. Dem. Nat. Com., Calif. Dem. Com., Dem. Nat. Fin. Council. Named DeeJay of Year Sixteen Mag., 1965; Program Dir. of Year Bill Gavin Report, 1967; recipient Superior Achievement award RKO Radio, 1973; also numerous gold records for contbs. toward million selling records. Mem. NARAS, Am. Advt. Fedn., Am. Film Inst., Hollywood Radio and TV Soc., L.A. World Affairs Coun., Town Hall Calif., Japan Am. Soc., Variety, Friars, Frat. of Friends, Music Ctr. Home: 2151 N Hobart Blvd Los Angeles CA 90027-1002 Office: Sunset-Gower Studios 4151 Prospect Ave Los Angeles CA 90027-4524 *Don't make the same mistake once.*

DREW, PHILIP GARFIELD, consultant engineering company executive; b. Dedham, Mass., Jan. 25, 1932; s. Garfield Albee and Katherine Marion (Dowling) D.; m. Anne Spengler, June 10, 1961 (div. 1972); children: Katherine, Philip Garfield; m. Patrice Anne Prall, May 20, 1978 (div. 1998); children: Evlyn Albee, Charles Prescott. BS, Carnegie-Mellon U., 1954; MS, Harvard U., 1959, PhD, 1964. Registered profl. engr., Mass. Staff Arthur D. Little, Inc., Cambridge, Mass., 1964-81; pres. Drew Cons., Inc., Carlisle, Mass., 1981—, Concord (Mass.) Cons. Group, 1996-97, 99—. Contbg. editor: Diagnostic Imaging, 1982—; assoc. sci. editor: Test and Measurement World, 1984-86; contbr. articles to profl. jours. Chmn. bd. overseers Bustins Island Village Corp., Freeport, Maine, 1981-84; pres. Savoyard Light Opera Co., 1988-90, Brown Bag Opera, 1993—. Served to 1st lt. AUS, 1954-58. Mem. IEEE, Soc. Photo-Optical Instrumentation Engrs., Soc. Computer Applications in Radiology (chmn. 1996), Harvard Club of Boston. Republican. Home: 101 Bedford Rd Carlisle MA 01741-1817 Office: The Concord Cons Group Inc 30 Monument Sq Concord MA 01742-1858

DREW, SHARON LEE, sociologist; b. L.A., Aug. 11, 1946; d. Hal Bernard and Helen Elizabeth (Hammond) D.; children: Keith, Charmagne. BA, Calif. State U., Long Beach, 1983; postgrad., Calif. State U., Dominguez Hills, 1988—. Clerical support Compton (Calif.) Unified Sch. Dist., 1967-78; case worker L.A. County Dept. Pub. Social Svcs., 1978—. Den mother Boy Scouts Am., Compton, 1971-72; employee vol. Dominguez Sr. H.S., Compton, 1972-73; project coord. Calif. Tomorrow's Parent Edn. Leadership Devel. Project, 1990; mem. L.A. Caregiver's Network, 1993-94; vol. Calif. State U., Dominguez Hill's Older Adult Ctr., 1994. Recipient cert. Calif. Tomorrow-Parent Edn. Leadership Devel. Project, 1990. Mem. Am. Statis. Assn. (So. Calif. chpt.), Internat. Soc. Exploration of Tchg. Alternatives, Calif. Sociol. Assn. (1st gov. at large grad. student 1990-91), Dominguez Hills Gerontology Assn. (chairperson 1990-91), Sociology of Edn. Assn., Alpha Kappa Delta (Xi chpt. treas. 1992-95). Home: 927 N Chester Ave Compton CA 90221

DREW, STEPHEN WALKER, chemical engineer; b. Tulsa, Aug. 7, 1945. BS, U. Ill., 1967, MS, 1969; PhD, MIT, 1974. From asst. prof. to assoc. prof. chem. engring. Va. Polytech Inst. & State U., 1974-80; Sr. dir. biochem. engring. Merck & Co. Inc., Rahway, N.J., 1980-87; exec. dir. tech. ops. Merck & Co. Inc., Whitehouse, NJ, 1987-89, v.p. engring. and tech, 1989-93; v.p. vaccine operations Merck & Co. Inc., West Point, PA, 1993-94, v.p. vaccine tech. and engring., 1994-97; dist. sr. scientist Merck & Co. Inc., Rahway, NJ, 1997—. Fellow Am. Inst. Med. and Biol. Engring.; mem. AIChE, Am. Chem. Soc. (indsl. liaison bd.), Nat. Acad. Engring., Am. Soc. Microbiology, Am. Soc. Biol. Sci., Sigma Xi. Achievements include biological and engineering technology for bulk chemical manufacture, processing safety testing systems, scientific engineering and support of vaccine manufacturing operations, processing development to increase manufacturing productivity and performance, support of new product introductions, processing design/scopes for all new vaccine manufacturing facilities worldwide. E-mail: stephenúdrew@merck.com. Office: Merck & Co Inc PO Box 2000-RY84-11 Rahway NJ 07065

DREW, WALTER HARLOW, retired paper industry executive; b. Chgo., Feb. 23, 1935; s. Ben Harlow and Marion Elizabeth (Heineman) D.; m. Gracia Ward McKenzie, June 27, 1959; children: Jeffrey, Martha. BS, U. Wis., 1957. With Kimberly-Clark Corp., 1959-88, exec. v.p., 1985-88; pres., CEO Menasha Corp., 1989-92; chmn. Theda-Clark Hosp., 1992-93; bd. dirs. Fox Citier Bank, Schneider Nat. Inc., U. Wis. Found. Chmn. bd. visitors Bus. Sch., U. Wis., Madison, 1992-93. Lt. USNR, 1957-63. Republican. Episcopalian. Club: North Shore Golf (Menasha, Wis.) (pres. 1983-85).

DREWRY, DON NEAL, fire protection engineer; b. Chgo., Oct. 6, 1949; s. Ruben Neal and Vlasta A. (Waleck) D.; m. Patricia Ann English, Mar. 8, 1975; children: Neal Thomas, Michelle Lynn. BA, Govs. State U., 1978; BS in Engring., U. Hartford, 1984; MS in Fire Protection Engring., Worcester Polytech. Inst., 1986. Mfg. engring./NC programmer Bloomer-Fisk, Chgo., 1974-75; inspector, supr. Hartford Steam Boiler, Chgo., 1975-78; asst. mgr. quality assurance svc. Hartford Steam Boiler Inspection and Ins. Co., 1978-80, project engr., 1980-81, rsch. engr., 1982-84, fire protection cons., 1984-87; regional mgmt. property engr. Hartford Steam Boiler Inspection and Ins. Co., Basking Ridge, N.J., 1987-92, regional manage ins. engr., 1992-94; br. mgr., property program mgr. power generation HSB Profl. Loss Control, Basking Ridge, 1994-97, v.p. industry svcs., 1997-99, v.p. loss control svcs., 1999—; com. fire protection task force Edison Elec. Inst., Washington, 1995. With USN, 1970-74. Mem. ASME, Soc. Fire Protection Engrs., Nat. Fire Protection Assn. (com. NFPA-850 1985—), Nat. Bd. of Boiler and Pressure Vessel Inspectors. Home: 1401 Sycamore Ave Easton PA 18040-8106 Office: HSB Profl Loss Control 188 Mount Airy Rd Basking Ridge NJ 07920-2021

DREWRY, ELIZABETH, newspaper publishing executive. V.p. employee, labor and pub. affairs Newsday, Melville, N.Y., until 1997; sr. v.p. human resources L.A. Times, 1997—. Office: LA Times The Times Mirror Co Times Mirror Sq Los Angeles CA 90053*

DREWRY, JOE SAMUEL JR., design engineer; b. Boykins, Va., Feb. 16, 1921; s. Joe Samuel and Lucy Lavern (Moore) D.; m. Ann Hunter Crutchfield, Oct. 5, 1946 (div. July 1947); m. Virginia Daniel Pearson, June 12, 1948; children: Christopher Morris, Martha Kay. BS, Va. Mil. Inst., 1942. Profl. engr., multiple states. From engr. to asst. chief engr. Va.-Carolina Chem. Corp., Richmond, Va., 1946-62; chief engr. Armour Agrl. Chem. Corp., Atlanta, 1962-66; v.p. engring. Kiernan-Gregory Corp., Atlanta, St. Louis, 1966-82; pres. Drewry & Assocs., Inc., Atlanta, 1982—; dir. Fertilizer Industry Roundtable, Balt., 1962-92; bd. dirs. Tri-State Plant Food Corp., Dothan, Ala. Vol. Boy Scouts Am., Atlanta, 1948—; vol. staff Atlanta Olympic Com., 1996; pres. PTA, Atlanta, 1985-87. Col. U.S. Army, 1942-73, ETO, ret. Decorated Legion of Merit, Bronze Star medal, Purple Heart medal; recipient Bishop's award of merit United Methodist Ch., Atlanta, 1989. Mem. Am. Soc. Civil Engrs. Avocations: golf, music, computer operations, travel. Home and Office: 6640 Williamson Dr NE Atlanta GA 30328-3342

DREWRY, MARCIA ANN, physician; b. St. Louis, Feb. 15, 1951; d. Owen and Annie Vernell (Smith) Palmer; m. Norman T. Drewry, Sept. 18, 1970 (dec. May 1978); 1 child, Tammy Robbins; m. David W. Worsdell Jr., Dec. 7, 1991. AS with honors, Forest Park Coll., 1989; DO, Kirksville Coll. Osteo. Med., 1993. Diplomate Nat. Bd. Osteo. Med. Examiners. Intern Riverside Hosp., Wichita, 1993-94, resident, 1994; med. transcriptionist Malcolm Bliss Mental Health, St. Louis, 1970-78; asst. adminstr. radiology Incarnate Word Hosp., St. Louis, 1977-79; grant writer molecular virolgoy St. Louis (Mo.) U., 1977-79; med. transcriptionist Neurosurg. Assocs., Inc., St. Louis, 1979-87, Stat Transcription, St. Louis, 1987-88, PRN Transcription, St. Louis, 1988-90; physician Anthony (Kans.) Primary Care Ctr., 1994-96; chief of staff Harper County Hosp. Dist. #6, 1995-96; family practice physician Kiowa (Kans.) Hosp. and Clinic, 1997—; dir. credentials, emergency dept. and med. records Anthony (Kans.) Primary Care Ctr., 1995-96. Capt. Operation Safe St., St. Louis, 1985-89; choir mem. Dover Place Christian Ch., St. Louis, 1986-93; mem. Careers for Homemakers, St. Louis, 1987-89. Mem. Am. Coll. Osteo. Family Physicians, Am. Acad. Osteopathy, Am. Osteo. Assn., Kans. Assn. Osteo. Medicine, Bus. and Profl. Women, Beta Sigma Phi, Phi Theta Kappa (pres. 1988-89), Alpha Phi Omega (sec. 1990-91), Theta Psi (promotions asst. 1990-91). Avocations: family activities, cats, travel, singing. Home: 509 S 6th St Kiowa KS 67070-1804 Office: Kiowa Clin 220 S 8th St Kiowa KS 67070-1631

DREWS, JÜRGEN, pharmaceutical researcher; b. Berlin, Aug. 16, 1933; came to U.S., 1991; s. Walter and Charlotte (Schneider) D.; m. Helga Eberlein, July 24, 1963; children: Ulrike, Karoline, Bettina. MD, Free U. Berlin, 1959; Professorship, U. Heidelberg, Fed. Republic of Germany, 1973. Head chemotherapy Sandoz Rsch. Inst., Vienna, Austria, 1976-79, head of inst., 1979-82; head internat. pharm. rsch. and devel. Sandoz, Ltd., Basel, Switzerland, 1982-85; dir. pharm. rsch. F. Hoffmann-La Roche Ltd., Basel, 1985-86, chmn. rsch. bd., mem. exec. com., 1986-90; pres. internat. rsch. and devel., mem. exec. com. Hoffmann-La Roche Inc., Nutley, N.J., 1991-95; pres. global rsch., mem. exec. com. Hoffmann-La Roche Inc., Nutley, 1996-97; chmn. Internat. Biomedicine Mgmt. Ptnrs., Basel, Switzerland, 1998—; prof. medicine U. Heidelberg, 1973—; mem. sci. adv. bd. (jour.) Infection, München, Fed. Republic of Germany, 1973—, Drug News & Perspectives, Barcelona, Spain, 1988—, Klinische Pharmakologie, München, 1989—; bd. dirs. Genentech, Inc., South San Francisco, 1990-97, Protein Design Labs., Mountain View, Calif., MorphoSys GmbH, Munich; bd. dirs., internat. bd. advisors Basel Inst. Immunology, 1986-97; mem. dean's coun. Yale U. Sch. Medicine, 1993—, chmn. sci. panel inter-company collaboration for AIDS drug devel., 1993-96, chmn. bd. participants inter-company collaboration for AIDS drug devel., 1996-97; mem. adv. com. Mass. Gen. Hosp., Boston, 1994-98; chmn. steering com. Sr. Adv. Group Biotech., 1994-96; chmn. bd. mgmt. EuropaBio, 1997-98. Author: Chemotherapie: Grundlagen und Perspektiver, 1979, Immunpharmakologie, Grundlagen und Perspektiven, 1986, Immunopharmacology, Principles and Perspectives, 1990, In Quest of Tomorrow's Medicines, 1999; editor: (with others) Topics in Infectious Diseases, vol. 1, 1975, vol. 2, 1977; also over 250 articles.

DREWS, ROBERT CARREL, retired physician; b. St. Louis, Sept. 9, 1930; s. Leslie C. and Sarah (Carrel) D.; m. Lorene Ruth Loewenguth, June 2, 1951; children: Pamela, Belinda, Carl, Jeanmarie. AB, Washington U., St. Louis, 1952, MD, 1955. Diplomate Am. Bd. Ophthalmology. Intern, St. Luke's Hosp., St. Louis, 1955-56; resident ophthalmology Washington U., St. Louis, 1956-58, chief resident, 1958-59, practice medicine specializing in ophthalmology, St. Louis, 1961-97; lectr. ophthalmology Washington U. Sch. Medicine, 1956-66, asst. prof. clin. ophthalmology, 1966-74, assoc. prof., 1974-79, prof., 1979-1998, prof. emeritus 1998; asst. ophthalmologist to med. staff Barnes Hosp. Group, St. Louis, 1961—; mem. attending staff Bethesda Gen. Hosp., St. Louis, 1958—; mem. staff St. Luke's Hosp., St. Louis, 1971-97, mem. emeritus, 1997—; mem. courtesy staff St. Mary's Hosp., St. Louis, 1961-97, mem. emeritus, 1997—; cons. Faith Hosp., St. Louis, 1961-91; cons. Frisco Employees Hosp., St. Louis, 1961-68; attending ophthalmologist St. Louis Childrens Hosp., 1961-80; attending staff ophthalmologist St. Louis County Hosp., 1972-85; supervising ophthalmologist div. welfare, State Mo.,

1963-81; bd. dirs. St. Louis Soc. Blind, 1961—, sec., 1966-67, v.p., 1967-68, pres., 1968-70, 84-85; cons. Spl. Sch. Dist. St. Louis County, Mo., 1967-80; cons. Nat. Eye Inst. Program Staff, Cataract Panel, The Nat. Plan for Vision Research, 1983; mem. Am. Bd. Ophthalmology, 1985-93; pres. Highlights of Ophthalmology, Inc., 1990—. Mem. editl. bds. Ophthalmology, 1984-98, Pakistan Jour. Ophthalmology, 1984-98. Trustee Washington U., 1984-92. Fellow Royal Coll. Ophthalmologists; mem. St. Louis Soc. Blind, St. Louis Med. Soc., Mo. State Med. Assn., AMA, St. Louis Ophthalmol. Soc., Assn. Research in Ophthalmology, So. Med. Assn., Mo. Ophthalmol. Soc., Contact Lens Assn. Ophthalmologists, Pan-Am. Assn. Ophthalmology, Am. Intra-Ocular Implant Soc., Internat. Intraocular Implant Club, Am. Ophthalmol. Soc., Internat. Ophthalmic Microsurgery Study Group, others. Republican. Lutheran. Club: Washington Univ. Faculty. Avocation: Photography. Office: 211 N Meramec Ave Saint Louis MO 63105-3745

DREXEL, BARON JEROME, lawyer; b. Miami Beach, Fla., Sept. 3, 1954; s. Gustave L. and Dorris J. (Haas) D. AA, U. Fla., 1973; BA, U. Calif. Berkeley, 1979; MA in Econs., U. Miami, 1983, JD cum laude, 1985. Bar: Fla. 1985, Calif. 1987, U.S. Ct. Appeals (9th cir.) 1987, U.S. Ct. Appeals (11th cir.) 1989, U.S. dist. Ct. (no. dist.) Calif. 1986, U.S. Dist. Ct. (ctrl. dist.) Calif. 1987, U.S. Dist. Ct. (so. dist.) Calif. 1988. Survey crew mem. U.S. Forest Svc., Hayfork, Calif., 1979; sales rep. real estate Allen Morris Co., Miami, Fla., 1981-82; assoc. Shutts & Bowen, Miami, 1985-88, Lasky, Haas, Cohler & Munter, San Francisco, 1988-89, Aiken, Kramer & Cummings, Oakland, Calif., 1989-92, Bostwick & Tehin, San Francisco, 1992-95; pvt. practice Oakland, 1995—. Recipient J.B. Spence award U. Miami Law Rev. Mem. Order of Coif. Co-trial couns. for $15.4 million verdict. Avocations: computers, travel, photography, chess, writing poetry. Office: 312 Lee St # 1 Oakland CA 94610-4356

DREXEL, JOHN FREDERICK, poet, writer, editor; b. Stamford, Conn., Aug. 25, 1954; s. Frederick Paul and Jacqueline (Mulock) D.; m. Maureen Bischoff, May 13, 1989. BA, U. Conn., 1976; MA, Leeds (Eng.) U., 1979. Staff writer, editor Visual Edn. Corp., Princeton, N.J., 1984-88; gen. editor Ency. of the 20th Century Facts on File, Inc., N.Y.C., 1989-91; devel. editor Trade Reference Books Oxford U. Press, N.Y.C., 1991-93; dir. Poetry in Britain writing workshops, U.K., 1997—. Author: various poems. Amy Lowell Poetry travelling scholar Amy Lowell Trust, 1993-94; Hawthornden fellow Hawthornden Castle Internat. Retreat for Writers, 1996. Mem. Acad. Am. Poets, Assn. Lit. Scholars and Critics, W.B. Yeats Soc. N.Y. Mem. Anglo-Catholic Ch. Avocations: walking, cricket, real ale, travel, classical record collecting. Home: 42 Edgewood Rd Glen Ridge NJ 07028-2305

DREXEL, PETER GEORGE, computer science educator; b. N.Y.C., Sept. 27, 1945; s. George Drexel and Margaret (Vogl) Metzner; m. Kathryn Ahern Drexel, Aug. 12, 1972; children: Josef, Katherine, Peter. AAS in Elec. Tech., Hudson Valley C.C., Troy, N.Y., 1966; BS in Engring., Rochester Inst. Tech., 1969; MS in Engring., Rochester Inst. of Technology, 1980; PhD in Engring., U. N.H., 1993. Mgr. Moose Mt. Lodge, Athol, N.Y., 1970-72; engr. Electronic Automation Systems, Grand Island, N.Y., 1972-74; assoc. engr. IBM Corp., Essex Junction, Vt., 1974-88; assoc. prof. Plymouth (N.H.) State Coll., 1988—, chair computer sci., 1998—; reviewer Addison-Wesley, Menlo Park, Calif., 1992—; cons. Drexel Assocs., Plymouth, 1995—; AP Computer Sci. Reader, 1996—; summer faculty fellowship program NASA, 1998-99. Contbr. articles to profl. jours. Lab. Software grantee Microsoft Corp., 1995—; Devel. grant Plymouth State Coll., 1988—, Whiting Found., 1997. Mem. IEEE (sr.), IEEE Computer Soc., ACM, Soc. for Computer Simulation. Roman Catholic. Avocations: amateur radio, photography, cinema. E-mail: peter.drexel@plymouth.edu. Office: Plymouth State Coll Computer Sci Dept Memorial Hall Plymouth NH 03264

DREXLER, CLYDE, retired professional basketball player; b. New Orleans, June 22, 1962. Student, U. Houston, 1980-83. Basketball player Portland Trailblazers, 1983-94, Houston Rockets, 1994-98; mem. U.S. Olympic Basketball Team (received Gold medal), 1992. Mem. NBA All-Star Team, 1986, 88-93; mem. all-NBA first team, 1992; mem. All-NBA second team, 1988, 91; mem. All-NBA third team, 1990.

DREXLER, FRED, insurance executive; b. Oakland, Calif., Nov. 17, 1915; s. Frederic I. and Jessie (Day) D.; m. Martha Jane Cunningham, Dec. 26, 1936 (dec. June 1987); children: Kenneth, Roger Cunningham, Martha Drexler Lynn. A.B., U. Redlands, 1936; J.D., Golden Gate U., 1947, LL.D., 1971. Bar: Calif. 1947. Editor Mill Valley (Calif.) Record, 1936-42; employee relations Marinship Corp., 1942-45; office mgr. Bechtel Corp., 1945-46; asst. to pres. Indsl. Indemnity Co., San Francisco, 1946-48; asst. sec. Indsl. Indemnity Co., 1948-51, sec., 1951-56, sr. v.p., sec., 1956-67, exec. v.p., sec., 1967-68, pres., 1968-70, chmn. bd., chief exec. officer, 1970-76, chmn. exec. com., 1976-78, dir., 1957-86; dir. Crum & Forster, 1970-83, Montgomery St. Income Securities, Inc. (dir. 1977, chmn. bd. 1988-91); mem. Calif. Workmen's Compensation Study Commn., 1963-65; founder Calif. Workers Compensation Inst., 1964, pres., 1971-74, honoree testimonial dinner, 1985; pres. Pacific Ins. and Surety Conf., 1967-68. Pres. Marin (Calif.) United Fund, 1956; exec. bd. Marin coun. Boy Scouts Am., 1948-69, adv. bd., 1970—, mem. nat. exec. bd., 1973-87; trustee Marin Country Day Sch., 1960-62, United Bay Area Crusade, 1955-73; trustee Golden Gate U., 1957—, chmn. bd., 1968-70; bd. dirs. San Francisco Bay Area Coun., 1972-76, Buck Ctr. Rsch. in Aging, 1989—; trustee Pacific Presbyn. Med. Ctr., 1974-91; chmn. bd. Inst. Philos. Rsch., 1978-95, trustee, 1973-95; trustee World Affairs Coun. No. Calif., 1973-79, Calif. Pacific Med. Ctr., 1991—. Recipient Silver Beaver, Silver Antelope awards Boy Scouts Am. Mem. Calif. Bar Assn. Baptist. Clubs: Bankers (San Francisco) (pres. 1976-78), Bohemian (San Francisco), Pacific Union (San Francisco); California (Los Angeles). Home: 1 Myrtle Ave Mill Valley CA 94941-1023 Office: 275 Battery St San Francisco CA 94111-3305

DREXLER, JOANNE LEE, art appraiser; b. Washington, Mar. 21, 1944; d. Elias J. and Beatrice Charlotte (Goldberg) D.; m. James R. Cohen, May 31, 1965; children: Terri I., Brett F. Student, Louvre, Paris, 1963-64; BA, Tufts U., 1965; Diamond and Pearl Cert., GIA, N.Y.C., 1974. Tchr. of French Stuyvesant H.S., N.Y.C., 1965-66; decorator, art cons. Joanne Cohen Interiors, Mamaroneck, N.Y., 1967-69; assoc. prof. Hofstra U., L.I., N.Y., 1979-80; pres. Esquire Appraisals, N.Y.C. and Larchmont, N.Y., 1969—; TV appearances include CNN, Sept. 1991; cons., lectr. in field; art judge various contests, art dealer. Organizer, curator N.C. in N.Y. art show Nat. Arts Club, 1993, African Am. art show Nat. Arts Club, 1994; weekly columnist Gannett chain newspapers, 1980-86. Mem. Am. Soc. Appraisers (sr.; v.p. Hudson Valley White Plains chpt. 1989, bd. dirs. 1997, pres. White Plains chpt. 1997-98), Appraisers' Assn. Am. (cert.), Nat. Arts Club N.Y. (exhbn. com.). Avocations: travel, swimming, horseback riding. Home: 23 Trudy Ln Bedford NY 10506-1337 Office: Esquire Appraisals Inc 630 1st Ave New York NY 10016-3700

DREXLER, MARY SANFORD, financial executive; b. Pontiac, Mich., Apr. 19, 1954; d. Arthur H. and Kathryn S. (Sherda) Sanford; m. Brian Day, 1975 (div. 1978); m. York Drexler, 1980. BS, Ea. Mich. U., Ypsilanti, 1976, MA, 1979; postgrad., Walsh Coll., Troy, Mich., 1983. CPA, Mich. Spl. edn. tchr. Oakland Schs., Pontiac, Mich., 1976-83; staff auditor Coopers & Lybrand, Det., 1983-84; sr. auditor Coopers & Lybrand, Det., Mich., 1984-86; asst. contr. Webasto Sunroofs Inc., Rochester Hills, 1986-88; contr. Inalfa Roof Systems, U.S.A., Farmington Hills, Mich., 1988—; v.p. fin., controller Inalfa Roof Sys., Farmington Hills, Mich., 1992-96; CFO, exec. v.p. Inalfa Roof Sys., Farmington Hills, 1997—; bd. dirs. Coun. for Exceptional Children, Oakland County 1976--83. Bd. Dirs. Neighborhood Civic Assn., Troy, 1986—. Mem. Inst. Mgmt. Accts., Oakland County, Mich. Assn. CPA Mich., Forest Lake Country Club. Avocations: photography, painting, golf, swimming. Office: Inalfa Roof Systems USA 1370 Pacific Dr Auburn Hills MI 48326-1569

DREXLER, MICHAEL DAVID, advertising agency executive; b. N.Y.C., Nov. 2, 1938; s. Benn and Evelyn (Goldfarb) D.; m. Nancy Karen Drexler, Apr. 5, 1981 (div.); children: Staci Ann, Denise Susan, Lauren Michele, Benjamin Alex. BS, L.I. U., 1959. Media asst. Ogilvy and Mather Inc., N.Y.C., 1960-62, media planner, buyer, 1963-66, v.p. assoc. media dir., 1967-69, sr. v.p., media dir., 1970-74; exec. v.p., media dir. Doyle Dane Bernbach, N.Y.C., 1974-86; exec. v.p., worldwide media dir. Bozell, Jacobs, Kenyon and Eckhardt, N.Y.C., 1986—; vice-chmn. Audit Bur. Circulation, Schaumburg, Ill., 1980-86. Author: (with others) Marketing in an Electronic Age, 1985; contbr. articles to profl. pubs. Mem. Am. Assn. of Advt. Agencies (media council), Media Dirs. Council (bd. dirs., pres. 1980-81), Advt. Research Found. (co-chmn. TV Audience Measurement Com. 1980-81), Internat. Radio and TV Soc. (bd. dirs. 1980-85), Audit Bur. of Circulations (vice chmn. 1982-86). Avocations: photography, tennis. OFFICE: BOZELL 40 W 23rd St New York NY 10010-5215

DREXLER, NORA LEE, retired educator, writer, illustrator; b. Bellefonte, Pa., Nov. 17, 1947; d. Bengt Gerdis and Leanore Francis (Bates) Bjalme; m. Raymond George Drexler, June 27, 1970; 1 child, Michelle Ann. BA of Sci., Villa Maria Coll., 1969; MEd, Gannon U., 1974. Tchr. gifted and talented Millcreek Sch. Dist., Erie, Pa., 1969-99; ret., 1999; founder, nat. program dir. KIDCO (Kids Interacting Drug-Free Coalition); computer tech. facilitator World Confs. and Ednl. workshops; governing bd. Pennsylvanians Against Underage Drinking; presenter AMA, Parents Resource Inst. for Drug Edn., 2d Comty. Anti Drug Coalition of Am. Recipient 1st Pl. Nat. award for outstanding coalition 1997, Comty. Anti Drug Coalitions of Am., 1997, 1st. Pl. Nat. award Nat. Commn. Against Drunk Driving, 1997, DUI Leadership award, citations Pa. Ho. of Reps. and Pa. Senate. Mem. NEA, Pa. Edn. Assn. Millcreek Edn. Assn. Democrat. Roman Catholic. Avocations: writing, drawing, pet dog. Home: 5639 Mill St Erie PA 16509-2923

DREXLER, RICHARD ALLAN, manufacturing company executive; b. Chgo., May 14, 1947; s. Lloyd A. and Evelyn Violet (Kovaloff) D.; m. Clare F. Stunkel, Aug. 24, 1990; children by previous marriage: Dan Lloyd, Jason Ian. BS, Northwestern U., 1968, MBA, 1969. Staff v.p. Allied Products Corp., Chgo., 1971-75, sr. v.p. adminstrn., 1975-79, exec. v.p., COO, CFO, 1979-82, pres., COO, 1982-86, pres., CEO, 1986-93, chmn., pres., CEO, 1993—. Office: Allied Products Corp 10 S Riverside Plz Ste 400 Chicago IL 60606-3708*

DREXLER, RUDY MATTHEW, JR., professional law enforcement dog trainer; b. Elkhart, Ind., Jan. 16, 1941; s. Rudy Matthew Sr. and Elaine Irene (Hardman) D.; m. Patricia Ann Overmyer, Apr. 4, 1981; children: Scott M., Tina S. Thode. Student, Purdue U., 1960-63. V.p. Custom Booth Mfg. Corp., Elkhart, Ind., 1962-80; pres. Orchard Kennels, Elkhart, Ind., 1964-79; pres., treas. Rudy Drexler's Sch. for Dogs, Inc., Elkhart, Ind., 1980—; lectr. civic orgns.; instr. U. Del. Continuing Edn., Wilmington, 1978. Named to Honorable Order of Ky. Colonels, 1989; named hon. dep. Middlesex County Sheriff's Dept., New Brunswick, N.J., 1984, Daviess County Sheriff's Dept., Owensboro, Ky., 1988, Fairfield County Sheriff's Dept., Lancaster, Ohio, 1982. Mem. Midwest Police K-9 Assn. (founder 1984, tng. dir. 1984-87), Am. Soc. Law Enforcement Trainers (charter mem.), Internat. Narcotics Enforcement Officers Assn. (assoc. mem.), Can. Police K-9 Assn. (assoc. mem.), Nat. Police Res. Officers Assn. (hon. mem.), Moose. Office: Rudy Drexler's Sch for Dogs 50947 County Road 7 Elkhart IN 46514-8853

DREYER, ALEC GILBERT, independent power producer; b. Murphysboro, Ill., Mar. 15, 1958; s. Gilbert Dean and Norma Mae (Cluster) D.; m. Sheri L. Snider, July 26, 1980; children: Hillary Christine, Ahren Grant. BA in Polit. Sci. and Acctg., U. Ill., 1980; MBA with honors, Washington U., 1987. CPA, Ill., Mo. Staff acct. Price Waterhouse, St. Louis, 1980-82, sr. acct., 1982-85, mgr., 1985-88, sr. mgr., 1988-92; contr. Ill. Power Co., Decatur, 1992-94, treas., contr., 1994-95; sr. v.p., 1999—; pres. Illinova Generating Co., Decatur, 1995—; sr. v.p. Illinova Corp., Decatur, 1999—. Asst. treas. Com. To Expand Cervantes Conv. Ctr., St. Louis, 1987-88; mem. Citizens Adv. Coun., Edwardsville, Ill., 1990-91; chmn. pers. svcs. divsn. United Way Macon County, Ill., 1994, bd. dirs., 1995—, co-chmn. campaign drive, 1995, chmn. campaign drive, 1996, vice chmn. bd. dirs., 1997-98, chmn. bd. dirs., 1999—. Mem. AICPAs, Ill. Soc. CPAs, Phi Beta Kappa, Beta Gamma Sigma. Republican. Mem. First Christian Ch. Avocations: golf, computing, in-line skating, reading. Home: 976 Stevens Creek Cir Forsyth IL 62535-9622 Office: Illinova Generating Co 2828 N Monroe St Forsyth IL 62535-3269

DREYFUS, LEE SHERMAN, international speaker; b. Milw., June 20, 1926; s. Woods Orlow and Clare (Bluett) D.; m. Joyce Mae Unke, Apr. 5, 1947; children: Susan Dreyfus Fosdick, Lee S. Jr. BA, U. Wis., 1949, MA, 1952, PhD, 1957; LLD (hon.), Lakeland Coll., Wis., 1978; LHD (hon.), Blackbourne Coll., Ill., 1984; LCD (hon.), Marian Coll., Wis., 1985; LLD (hon.), Hangyang U., Seoul, Korea, 1982. Assoc. prof., gen. mgr. Radio WDET Wayne State U., Detroit, 1952-62; prof., gen. mgr. WHA-TV U. Wis., Madison, 1962-67; chancellor U. Wis., Stevens Point, 1967-79; gov. State of Wis., Madison, 1979-83; pres., COO Sentry Ins. Corp., Stevens Point, 1983-84; pres. L.S.D. Inc., Waukesha, Wis., 1985—; internat. spkr. Washington Spkrs. Bur., Alexandria, Va., 1988—; chief of mission U.S. AID, Vietnam, 1967-74; bd. dirs. Am.-Can. Great Lakes Commn., Washington, 1979-83, Marcus Corp., Assoc. Bank Corp., Nat. Telemedia, Inc.; del. Am. Assn. State Coll. and Univ., China, Taiwan, Poland, 1973-76. Radio child actor regular weekly drama broadcasts Sta. WISN Milw., 1933-44; creator world's 1st intercontinental video classroom, U.S. to France, 1965. Regent U. Wis., Madison, 1990-96; trustee Emerson Coll., Boston, 1988-91; co-chmn. Wis. Sesquicentennial, Madison, 1996—; presdl. del. to Benin, Africa, 1991; spl. del. State Dept. Acad. Mission to Cyprus, 1983; chmn. Wis. Cable TV Commn., Madison, 1972; mem. Wis. Land Stewardship Commn., 1998, Wis. Humanities Commn., 1998. With USNR, 1944-46; comdr.-in-chief Wis. N.G., 1979-83. Recipient Dist. Pub. Svc. medal Dept. Def., 1982, Pres.'s Gold medal U.S. Army, 1984; named Man of the Yr., Kappa Sigma, 1980; named to Hall of Fame, DeMolay Internat., 1991. Mem. Nat. Inst. Former Govs. (sec. 1990-94), Am. Legion (life), VFW (life), Masons (33 deg.), Shriner. Republican. Episcopalian. Avocations: charitable fund raising, reading, civic projects, politics. Home: 3159 Madison St Waukesha WI 53188-4409 Office: PO Box 1776 Waukesha WI 53187-1776

DREYFUS, SUSAN KAHN, elementary education educator; b. Atlanta, Dec. 8, 1946; d. Truman Frederick and Gloria Charlotte (Shefsky) Kahn; children: Diane, Wendy, David. BS, U. Memphis, 1970; M in Adminstrn., Trevecca Nazarene Coll., 1991. Tchr. Montrose (Ark.) Acad., 1976-77, Memphis City Schs., 1986—; founder Circuit Playhouse, Inc., Memphis, 1969; leader The Creative Cir., Overland Park, Kans., 1982-84. V.p. Dem. Women of Memphis, 1993-94, exec. com., 1991-93; vol. Hadassah, Memphis, 1981—, Memphis Polit. Caucus, 1991—; treas. Memphis Women's Leadership Forum, 1998—; vol. Memphis Race for the Cure. Mem. NEA, Tenn. Edn. Assn., Memphis Edn. Assn., ASCD, Tchrs. English, Memphis Assn. Tchrs. Maths., Nat. Reading Assn. Jewish. Avocations: needlework, stamp collecting, fitness training. Home: 1453 Poplar Ridge Memphis TN 38120 Office: Goodlett Elem Sch 3001 S Goodlett St Memphis TN 38118-2900

DREYFUSS, ERIC MARTIN, allergist; b. Bad Homburg, Germany, July 11, 1930; came to U.S., 1934; s. Walter and Hedwig (Herz) D.; m. Sandra Dale Gasul, June 16, 1957; children: Peter, Lisa. AB, Cornell U., 1953; MD, Chgo. Med. Sch., 1957. Diplomat Am. Bd. Allergy and Immunology. Intern Beth Israel Hosp., N.Y.C., 1957-58; resident in pediats. SUNY, Syracuse, 1958-60; fellow in allergy Rochester, N.Y., 1962-64; allergist Allergy Assocs. Rochester, 1964—; asst. clin. prof. U. Rochester Sch. Medicine and Dentistry, 1970—. Capt. U.S. Army, 1960-62. Fellow Am. Acad. Allergy and Immunology, Am. Coll. Allergists, Am. Acad. Pediatrics. Office: Allergy Assocs Rochester 300 Goodman St S Rochester NY 14607-3105

DREYFUSS, JOEL PHILIPPE, magazine editor; b. Port-Au-Prince, Haiti, Sept. 17, 1945; came to U.S., 1950; s. Roger E. and Anne-Marie (Timothée) D.; m. Veronica Pollard, Oct. 4, 1980; 1 child, Justin. BBS, CUNY, 1971. Reporter N.Y. Post, N.Y.C., 1971-73, Washington Post, 1973-76; freelance writer various mags., San Francisco, 1976-79; exec. editor Black Enterprise, N.Y.C., 1980-82; N.Y. bur. chief USA Today, Arlington, Va., 1982-83; assoc. editor Fortune Mag., N.Y.C., 1983-91; editor PC Mag., N.Y.C., 1991-93, Informationweek, Manhasset, N.Y., 1995-96; sr. editor Fortune Mag., N.Y.C., 1997—. Co-author: The Bakke Case, 1979. Mem. Coun. Fgn. Rels., N.Y.C., 1986—. Mem. Am. Soc. Mag. Editors (bd. mem. 1995-96), Nat. Assn. Black Journalists (founding mem.). Avocations: playing bass and guitar.

DREYFUSS, JOHN ALAN, health facility administrator; b. N.Y.C., Dec. 1, 1933; s. Henry and Doris (Marks) D.; m. Katharine Elizabeth Rich, June 28, 1958; children: Karen Elizabeth, James Henry, Kimberly Anne, Katharine Marks. BS in Biology, Boston U., 1959. Tchr. schs. in Montclair, Pebble Beach and Los Olivos, Calif., 1959-63; reporter, editor San Luis Obispo (Calif.) Telegram Tribune, 1963-64; advt. salesman Ventura County (Calif.) Star-Free Press, 1964-66; gen. assignment writer L.A. Times, 1966-69, 73-75, higher edn. writer, 1969-72, environment writer, 1972-73, architecture and design critic, 1975-84, feature writer View sect., 1984-87, graphics editor View sect., 1987-89, asst. to assoc. editor, 1989-93; v.p., CFO, sec. J. Dreyfuss & Assocs., Santa Monica, Calif., 1993-94; newswriter Sta. KTLA-TV, L.A., 1994-95; pub. info. officer Jonsson Comprehensive Cancer Ctr./UCLA, 1995-96, dir. for comm., 1996-98, dir. for planning and comm., 1998—. With U.S. Army, 1953-55. Office: UCLA Jonsson Comprehensive Cancer Ctr 8-684 Factor Bldg Los Angeles CA 90095-1781

DREYFUSS, PATRICIA, chemist, researcher; b. Reading, Pa., Apr. 28, 1932; d. Edmund T. and Anna J. (Oberc) Gajewski; m. M. Peter Dreyfuss, Jan. 30, 1954; children: David Daniel, Simeon Karl. BS Chemistry, U. Rochester, 1954; PhD, U. Akron, 1964. Postdoctoral fellow U. Liverpool (Eng.), 1963-65; rsch. chemist B.F. Goodrich, Brecksville, Ohio, 1965-71; rsch. assoc. Case Western Res. U., Cleve., 1971-73, sr. rsch. assoc., 1973-74; rsch. assoc. Inst. Polymers Sci., U. Akron, Ohio, 1974-84; sr. rsch. scientist, rsch. prof. Mich. Molecular Inst., Midland, 1984-90; vis. rsch. fellow U. Bristol, 1972; cons. in field, 1974—; vis. prof. Polish Acad. Scis., Poland, 1974; adj. prof. Cen. Mich. U., Mt. Pleasant, Mich. Tech U., Houghton, 1986-92, Mich. Molecular Inst., Midland, 1990-92. Author: Poly (Tetrahydrofuran), 1982; contbr. numerous articles to profl. jours.; co-author books. Flutist West Suburban Philharm. Orch., Lakewood, Ohio, 1969-75, Midland (Mich.) Cmty. Orch., 1990-97; Explorer advisor Explorer post 2069 Boy Scouts Am., Akron, 1975-81; sec., bd. dirs. Adhesion Soc., 1976-88; treas. LWV, 1959-60; mem. ensemble Blessed Sacrament Ch., Midland; occasional flute soloist. Centennial scholar U. Rochester, 1950-54; Sohio fellow U. Akron, 1960, NSF Coop. Grad. fellow, 1961-63, Internat. fellow AAUW, 1964-65, NIH Spl. fellow, 1972-73. Mem. Am. Chem. Soc. (cen. region mtg. chmn. 1984-90, loc. sec. chmn., vice chmn., sec. and bd. dirs. Akron chpt. 1974-84, bd. dirs. Midland chpt. 1985-89, Outstanding Leadership Performance award 1981, Disting. Svc. award Akron chpt. 1985), AAUW (bd. dirs. Akron chpt.). Achievements include 4 patents in field. Home: 3980 N Old Pine Trl Midland MI 48642-8891

DREYFUSS, RICHARD STEPHAN, actor; b. N.Y.C., Oct. 29, 1947; s. Norman and Gerry Dreyfuss; m. Jeramie Dreyfuss, 1983; children: Emily, Benjamin, Harry. Student, San Fernando Valley State Coll., 1965-67. Motion picture appearances include American Graffiti, 1972, Dillinger, 1973, The Apprenticeship of Duddy Kravitz, 1974, Jaws, 1975, Inserts, 1975, Close Encounters of the Third Kind, 1976, The Goodbye Girl, 1977, The Competition, 1980, Whose Life Is It Anyway?, 1981, Down and Out in Beverly Hills, 1986, Stand By Me, 1986, Tin Men, 1987, Stakeout, 1987, Nuts, 1987, Moon Over Parador, 1988, Let It Ride, 1989, Always, 1989, Postcards from the Edge 1990, What About Bob?, 1991, Once Around, 1991, Rosencrantz and Guildenstern Are Dead, 1991, Lost in Yonkers, 1993, Another Stakeout, 1993, Silent Fall, 1994, Mr. Holland's Opus, 1995 (Acad. award nominee for best actor 1996), The American President, 1995, Mad Dog Time, 1996, James and the Giant Peach, 1996, Night Falls on Manhattan, 1997, The Call of the Wild, 1997; theatrical appearances include: Julius Caesar, 1978, Othello, 1979, Total Abandon, 1983, Death and the Maiden, 1992; actor, producer: The Big Fix, 1978; actor, TV film: Two For The Money, 1972, Victory at Entebbe, 1976; TV movie, Oliver Twist, 1997; host TV series The Class of the 20th Century, 1991. Participant civil rights marches, lobbying for amnesty bills. Served alt. mil. duty Los Angeles County Gen. Hosp., 1969-71. Recipient Golden Globe award, 1978; Academy award as best actor in The Goodbye Girl, 1978. Mem. ACLU, Screen Actors Guild, Equity Assn., AFTRA, Motion Picture Acad. Arts and Scis. Office: William Morris Agy 151 S El Camino Dr Beverly Hills CA 90212

DREZ, DAVID JACOB, JR., orthopedic surgeon, educator; b. Lake Charles, La., Aug. 21, 1938; s. David Jacob and Hester Adele (Bingham) D.; m. Judith Diane Wolfe, June 5, 1963; children: Susan Drez Joseph, Catherine Ann Self, David Jacob III. BS, Tulane U., 1959, MD, 1963. Diplomate Am. Bd. Surgery, Am. Bd. Orthopaedic Surgery. Intern Charity Hosp., New Orleans, 1963-64, resident in gen. surgery, 1964-68, resident in orthopaedic surgery, 1968-71; resident Scottish Rite Hosp., Atlanta, 1969, USPHS Hosp., New Orleans, 1970; pvt. practice Orthopaedic Assocs., Lake Charles, 1971-82; pvt. practice Orthopaedic and Sports Injury Clinic Knee and Sports Medicine Ctr., Lake Charles, 1982-94; pvt. practice Ctr. for Orthopaedics, Lake Charles, 1994—; staff Lake Charles Meml. Hosp., 1973—, bd. trustees, 1973, 80-82, sec.-treas., 1977, pres., 1981, chief surgery, 1984, 85; med. staff dept. orthopaedics Children's Hosp., New Orleans, 1988; La. state chmn. Orthopaedic Rsch. and Edn. Found., 1987, 90-92; network of orthopedic surgeons U.S. Gymnastics Fedn., 1988—; physician U.S. Soccer Assn., 1988—; examiner Am. Bd. Orthopaedic Surgery, 1989, 91, 92, bd. dirs.; vis. prof. numerous hosps. and univs.; speaker in field. Author: (with R. D'Ambrosia) Prevention and Treatment of Running Injuries, 1982, Prevention and Treatment of Running Injuries, 2d edit., 1989, (with D.W. Jackson) The Anterior Cruciate Deficient Knee-New Concepts in Ligament Repair, 1986, Orthopaedic Sports Medicine: Principles and Practice , 1994 (with Jesse DeLee); author 8 chpts. in books; editor Am. Jour. Sports Medicine, 1988—, Jour. Orthopaedic Techniques, 1993—; co-editor Operative Techniques in Sports Medicine jour., 1993—; mem. editorial bd. Orthopaedics, 1983—, Arthroscopy, 1984-89, Sports Medicine News, 1989—; author 5 video tapes, audio tape; mem. adv. bd. Clin. Update, Sports Medicine, 1983—, Clin. Orthopaedics and Related Rsch., 1987-93; con. rev. bd. Jour. Bone and Joint Surgeons, 1989—; contbr. over 35 articles to profl. jours. Team orthopaedist athletic dept. McNeese State U., Lake Charles, 1974—, pres. 100 Club, 1979; co-dir. Runner's Clinic, La. State U. Sch. Medicine, New Orleans, 1978-81; chief physician NAAU Boxing Championship, Lake Charles, 1979; mem. Gov.'s Coun. on Phys. Fitness and Sports, 1981; bd. dirs. Lake Area Runners, 1989-92. Maj. La. N.G., 1963-71. Named to La. Athletic Trainers Assn. Hall of Fame, 1989, McNeese State U. Hall of Honors, 1990. Mem. Acad. Orthopaedic Soc., Am. Acad. Orthopaedic Surgeons, Am. Acad. Sports Physicians, Am. Coll. Sports Medicine, Am. Coll. Surgeons, Am. Orthopaedic Assn., Am. Orthopaedic Foot Soc., Am. Orthopaedic Foot and Ankle Soc., Am. Orthopaedic Soc. Sports Medicine, Arthroscopy Assn. N.Am., Assn. Bone and Joint Surgeons, Assn. Sports Medicine Fellowship Dirs., Mid. Am. Orthopaedic Assn., Assn. Arthritic Hip and Knee Surgery, Australian-Am. Orthopaedic Soc., Calcasieu Parish Med. Soc., Clin. Orthopaedic Soc., European Soc. Knee Surgery and Arthroscopy, Herodicus Sports Medicine Soc. (past sec., v.p., pres.), Internat. Arthroscopy Assn., Internat. Soc. Knee, La. Orthopaedic Assn. (pres. 1992), La. State Med. Assn., Oscar Creech Surg. Soc., Orthopaedic Rsch. Soc., Soc. Internat. Chirurgie Orthopedique Traumatologie, Soc. Internat. Recherche Orthopedique Tramatologie. Avocations: reading, jogging, traveling, family activities. Office: Ctr for Orthopaedics 3rd Fl 1717 Oak Park Blvd Lake Charles LA 70601-8990

DRIBIN, MICHAEL A., lawyer; b. 1951. BA, Northwestern U., 1972; JD, Loyola U., Chgo., 1975; LLM in Taxation, U. Miami, 1979. Bar: Ill. 1975, Fla. 1975. Mem. Broad and Cassel, Miami, Fla. Fellow Am. Coll. Trust and Estate Counsel; mem. Fla. Bar (bd. cert. estate planning and probate lawyer bd. legal specialization and edn.). Office: Broad and Cassel 201 S Biscayne Blvd Ste 3000 Miami FL 33131-4399

DRIBUS, JOHN ROBERT, geologist; b. Cleve., May 15, 1953; s. John and Virginia (Keenan) D.; m. Virginia M. Faris, Aug. 16, 1975; children: John, Benjamin, Anna, Marian, Stephanie. BS in Geology, Kent (Ohio) State U., 1975, MS in Geology, 1977. Uranium geologist Bendix Corp., Atlanta, 1976-78; lead Uranium geologist Bendix Corp., Casper, Wyo., 1978-79; Uranium geologist Mobil Nuclear Fuels, Corpus Christi, Tex., 1979-81; petroleum geologist Mobil Oil Corp., New Orleans, 1981-83, exploration supr., 1983-85, exploitation supr., 1985-87; prodn. geology supr. Mobil Oil Producing, New Orleans, 1987-93, sr. geologist, 1993-97, project mgr., 1997-98, deep water exploration supr., 1998—; seven habits trainer Mobil, New Orleans, 1994-96, Myers-Briggs analyst, 1995-97, mng. personal growth trainer, 1992-96, master recruiter, 1989-97. Vol. prison chaplain Orleans Parish Prison, New Orleans, 1994-95; camp spkr. St. Tammany Pride, Covington, La., 1996-97, bd. dirs., 1997; chapel spkr. Northlake Christian Sch., Covington, 1995-97. Mem. Am. Assn. Petroleum Geologists, New Orleans Geol. Soc., Assn. Psychol. Type, Oilfield Christian Fellowship. Avocations: bible study/teaching, reading, youth sports coaching, chess. Home: 185

Whisperwood Blvd Slidell LA 70458-1125 Office: Mobil Oil Corp 1250 Poydras St New Orleans LA 70113-1804

DRICKAMER, HARRY GEORGE, retired chemistry educator; b. Cleve., Nov. 19, 1918; s. George Henry and Louise (Strempel) D.; m. Mae Elizabeth McFillen, Oct. 28, 1942; children: Lee Charles, Lynn Louise, Lowell Kurt, Margaret Ann, Priscilla. B.S., U. Mich., 1941, M.S., 1942, Ph.D., 1946; Dr. Chem. Scis. (hon.), Russian Acad. Sci., 1994. Chem. engr. Pan Am. Refining Corp., 1942-46; asst. prof. U. Ill. at Urbana, 1946-49, assoc. prof., 1949-53, prof. chemistry, chem. engring. and physics, 1953-90, prof. emeritus, 1990—; Pitzer lectureship U. Calif., Berkeley, 1997. Recipient Bendix award, 1968, P.W. Bridgman award Internat. Assn. High Pressure Sci. and Tech., 1977; Michelson-Morley award Case Western Res. U., 1978, John Scott award City of Phila., 1984, Alexander von Humboldt award W.Ger., 1986, Robert A. Welch prize Welch Found., 1987, Disting. Profl. Achievement award U. Mich. Alumni Assn., Elliot Cresson medal Franklin Inst., 1988, Nat. Medal of Sci., 1989; Guggenheim fellow, 1952. Fellow Am. Acad. Arts and Scis., Am. Philos. Soc., Am. Phys. Soc. (Buckley Solid State Physics award 1967), Am. Geophys. Union; mem. NAS, NAE, Am. Chem. Soc. (Ipatieff prize 1956, Langmuir award in chem. physics 1974, Debye award in phys. chemistry 1987), Am. Inst. Chemists (Chem. Pioneers award 1983, Gold medal 1996), Am. Inst. Chem. Engrs. (Colburn award 1947, Alpha Chi Sigma award 1967, Walker award 1972, W.K. Lewis award 1986), Faraday divsn. Royal Soc. Chemistry (London), Am. Philos. Soc., Ctr. for Advanced Studies. Home: 304 E Pennsylvania Ave Urbana IL 61801-5129

DRICKAMER, LEE CHARLES, zoology educator; b. Ann Arbor, Mich., May 25, 1946; s. Harry George and Mae Elizabeth (McFillen) D. BA, Oberlin Coll., 1967; PhD, Mich. State U., 1998; postgrad., Northern Ariz. U., 1998—. Asst. prof., assoc. prof. prof. biology Williams Coll., Williamstown, Mass., 1972-87; prof., chmn. zoology So. Ill. U., Carbondale, 1987-91. Author: Animal Behavior, 1982, 86, 91, 96, Postal History of Western Massachusetts, 1982, Fort Lyon to Harpers Ferry, 1986, Behavioral Ecology, 1986, Mammology, 1999; editor: Animal Behaviour Jour., 1988-91. Rsch. grantee NIMH, 1973-74, NIH, 1975-86, NSF, 1986-89, 96—. Mem. Am. Soc. Mammologists, Internat. Soc. Devel. Psychobiology, Internat. Coun. Ethologists (vice sec. 1982-91, sec. gen. 1991-95), Animal Behavior Soc. (program officer 1983-86, pres. sequence 1993-97), Brit. Ecol. Soc. Home: 9475 N Lunar Dr Flagstaff AZ 86004-3116 Office: Dept Biol Sci No Ariz U Life Sci Ii Flagstaff AZ 86011

DRIEHUYS, LEONARDUS BASTIAAN, conductor; b. The Hague, The Netherlands, Mar. 25, 1932; s. Bastiaan Leonardus and Maria Magdalena Driehuys-Bruinsma; m. Henrica Postma, Nov. 19, 1960; children—Nicolette, Bastiaan. Hon. degrees in oboe and piano, Royal Conservatory of Music, The Hague. Prin. oboe Netherlands Opera, Amsterdam, 1952-59; condr. Netherlands Opera, 1959-65, Nederlandse Omroepstichting, 1965—; music dir. Het Gelders Orkest, Arnhem, 1970-74, Charlotte (N.C.) Symphony, 1977-93. Served in Dutch Army. Recipient Fock medal for oboe playing. Club: Rotary (Charlotte). Home: 1016 Churchhill St Davidson NC 28036-9098 Office: Joanne Rile Artists Mgmt Noble Plz Ste 212801 Jenkintown PA 19046-1611*

DRIGGERS, EDWARD ROSEMOND, city administrator; b. Lancaster, S.C., Jan. 6, 1961; s. W.J. and Billie Faye (Moore) D.; m. Christy J. Bigham, July 27, 1985; children: Kathryn Olivia, Mary Moore. AS in Bus. Administrn., U. S.C., Lancaster, 1981; BA in Pub. Rels., U. S.C., Columbia, 1983; MBA, Winthrop U., 1992. Area rep. Am. Cancer Soc., Rock Hill, S.C., 1983-86; sr. area rep. Am. Cancer Soc., Spartanburg, S.C., 1986-88; prodn. mgr. Carolina Tank Corp., Chester, S.C., 1988-96; city adminstr. City of Chester, S.C., 1996—. City councilman City of Chester, 1993-96. Mem. Chester C. of C. (bd. dirs.), Chester Downtown Devel. Assn., Chester Arts Coun., Chester Rotary Club (pres. 1996-97). Avocation: reading. Office: City of Chester 100 W End St Chester SC 29706-1819

DRIGGERS, L. ELEY, clinical metaphysicist; b. Eufaula, Ala., Aug. 24. AA, San Jacinto Coll.-North, 1977; BS, U. Indpls., 1993; doctorate in metaphysics (hon.), Universal Life Ch., 1992. Cert. therapist; ordained to ministry Universal Life Ch. Photographic artist, 1971—; clin. metaphysicist, dir. Inst. Study and Advancement of the Philosophy of Clin. Metaphysics and Sci. Bio-Energetics, 1992—. Author: Introduction to the Philosophy of Clinical Metaphysics and the Science of Bio-Energetics, 1992. Mem., vol. Vols. in Public Schs., Houston, 1977; mem. career adv. panel North Shore Middle Sch., Houston, 1984; del., panel of profls. Dept. of Human Svcs. State of Ind., Indpls., 1990; legis. aid to state rep. State of Tex., 1982; mem. adv. panel Ind. Health Care Campaign, Indpls., 1994. Recipient 1st place Keatin award Ind. Press Assn., 1992. Mem. Internat. Assn. of Counselors and Therapists (life cert.).

DRIGGS, CHARLES MULFORD, lawyer; b. East Cleveland, Ohio, Jan. 26, 1924; s. Karl Holcomb and Lila Vandeveer (Wilson) D.; children: Ruth, Rachel, Carrie, Karl H., Charles M.; m. Ann Eileen Zargari, Oct. 25, 1991. BS, Yale U., 1947, JD, 1950. Bar: Ohio 1951. Assoc. Squire, Sanders & Dempsey, Cleve., 1950-64, ptnr., 1964-88, of counsel, 1988-91; pvt. practice civil law Cleve., 1991-95; ptnr. Driggs, Lucas, Brubaker & Hogg Co., LPA, Mentor, Ohio, 1995—. Pres. Bratenahl (Ohio) Sch. Bd., 1958-62; mem. adv. coun. Cleve. Ctr. for Theol. Edn., 1978—. Mem. ABA, Ohio Bar Assn., Lake County Bar Assn., Cleve. Bar Assn., Greater Cleve. Growth Assn., Cleve. Law Libr. Assn. (trustee 1977-91), Ct. Nisi Prius, Citizens League Greater Cleve., Geauga County Bar Assn., Phi Delta Phi, Tau Beta Pi, Phi Gamma Delta. Home: 151 Southbridge Ln Painesville OH 44077-1377 Office: Old Village Hall 8383 Mentor Ave Ste 201 Mentor OH 44060-5756 *Any success I may have achieved I attribute to my continuing attempt to live and conduct my affairs in a manner that my family and friends may later reflect upon with pride.*

DRIGGS, MARGARET, educator; b. Kansas City, Kans., June 30, 1909; d. William Foster and Lillian Edith (Landers) Brazier; m. J.W. Quarrier, Nov. 26, 1933 (div. July 1945); children: John Chilton, Philip Harrington, Camille Elizabeth; m. Howard R. Driggs, Sept. 26, 1948 (dec.). AB, U. Kans., 1930; postgrad. Hofstra Coll., 1960, Grad. Sch. Libr. Sci., Pratt Inst., 1964-65. Contbr. Kansas City Star and Johnson County (Kans.) Herald, 1930-33; editor Am. Trails Series, filmstrips; nat. dir. pub. rels. Am. Pioneer Trails Assn., 1948; chmn. pub. rels. NYU Faculty Women's Club, 1950-54; nat. 1st v.p. Assn. Parents and Friends Kings Point, 1957-58; judge Nat. Svc. Acad. Debate Tournament, 1956; hostess Kings Point Congl. Com., 1957; mem. Nat. Coun. Coll. Publs. Advisers, 1958; adminstrv. asst. to sec., dir. pub. rels. Hofstra Coll., 1956-61, staff adviser Nexus (yearbook), 1961; mem. faculty Westover Sch., Middlebury, Conn., 1964-65; dir. devel. pub. relations, asst. to dean Cathedral Sch. of St. Mary, Garden City, N.Y., 1965, also yearbook adviser; installed Duchess of Richelieu collection St. Mary's Libr., 1973; co-chmn. guides N.J. Gov.'s Mansion Morven, 1975-82; chmn. docents N.J. Hist. Soc. at Morven, Princeton, 1982-86; curator Driggs Collection of Americana. Represented in the Native North Am. Women Exhbn., Skillman Libr., Lafayette Coll., 1992. Mem. women's coun. Hofstra Coll., 1959-60; mem. U.S. Com. for UN Children's Fund, 1957; mem. Friends of Princeton U. Libr., 1975, Friends of the Winston Churchill Meml. and Lib., Westminster Coll., 1989; mem. Princeton Med. Ctr. Aux.; chair civilian hostesses 15th Ann. U.S. Army Mus. Conf., Princeton, 1986, Salute to Hall of Fame Ceremony the Voice of Am. broadcast Gould Meml. Libr., NYU, 1953; mem. Am. Farm Trust, 1992; mem. Denver Pub. Lib. Friends Found. Recipient Disting. Service citation Am. Pioneer Trails Assn., 1943, Columbia Scholastic Press Assn. medal, 1970, pin for vol. work in Princeton, 1976, French-Am. Alliance medal, cert. and hist. house tile award N.J. Hist. Soc., 1984; Margaret Brazier Driggs Collection of Americana established at U. Kans., 1953, at Hofstra Coll., 1961; advisor on placement donors' collections; Mem. Denver Pub. Lib. Friends Fdn., Colo. Hist. Soc., Governor's Mansion Guides, ALA, Internat. Platform Assn., Assn. Coll. and Rsch. Librs., Hist. Soc. Princeton, Nat. Trust Hist. Preservation, Smithsonian Associates, Nat. Parks and Cons. Assn., Women's Bd. of N.J. Hist. Soc., Met. Mus. Art, Women's Coll. Club Princeton, Amiga of Orgn. of Am. States, NYU Faculty Club (hon. life), Libr. of Congress (charter assoc. 1994), Present Day Club (Princeton), Gold Medal Club (pin and citation for achievement 1930-1980, Kans.), Learned Club, Pi Delta Epsilon (grand councilman 1960-61). Editor: New Light on Old Glory, 1950, Pitch Pine Tales, 1951, Nick Wilson, 1951, George, The Handcart Boy, 1952, The Old West Speaks, 1956, When Grandfather Was a Boy and Western Cowkid, 1957 (all by Howard R. Driggs); contbg. editor Nat. Assn. Ind. Schs. Archives, Harvard, 1965; editor and photographer Vive Rochambeau, Vive Washington. Home: 2943 W 116th Pl Apt 107 Denver CO 80234-2519

DRIMMER, BERNARD E., research physicist; b. N.Y.C., July 31, 1917; s. David and Rebecca (Kupferschmidt) D.; m. Mary E. Bauckman Edwards, Sept. 3, 1966 (div. Sept. 1984); m. Anne R. Yumkas Gordon, Dec. 1, 1993. BS in Chemistry, CCNY, 1938. Clerical positions, 1938-41; analytical chemist Washington Navy Yard, Washington, 1941-42, U.S. Bur. Mines, College Park, Md., 1942-44; gaseous diffusion engr. Columbia U., N.Y.C., 1944, Carbide & Carbon Corp., Oak Ridge, Tenn., 1944-46; explosives rsch. physicist U.S. Naval Ordnance Lab., Indian Head & White Oak, Md., 1946-50; project engr. explosives U.S. Army Office of Chief of Ordnance, Washington, 1950-52; prodn. engr. U.S. Atomic Energy Com., Washington, 1952-53; Brussels rep. USN Ordnance Tech. Office, Brussels, 1953-56; explosives rsch. br. head U.S. Naval Ordnance Lab., White Oak, Md., 1956-63; rsch. dir. explosives and propellants USN Bur. Naval Weapons, Washington, 1963-66; rsch. dir. explosives, propellants and batteries U.S. Naval Ordnance Sys. Command, Washington and Arlington, Va., 1966-74; pvt. practice cons. explosives and rockets various corps., Arlington & Silver Spring, Va., Md., 1974-79; explosives engr. VSE Corp., Alexandria, Va., 1979-90; cons. explosives VSE Corp., Arlington, 1990—. Author: (5 vols.) Navy Bank of Explosives Data, 1983; contbr. articles to profl. jours.; patentee in field. Mem. AAAS, Washington Philos. Soc., Nat. Geographic Soc., Sigma Xi. Home: 5341 Bodega Pl Delray Beach FL 33484-6665

DRINAN, ROBERT FREDERICK, lawyer, former congressman, educator, clergyman; b. Boston, Nov. 15, 1920; s. James Joseph and Ann Mary (Flanagan) D. A.B., Boston Coll., 1942, M.A., 1947; LL.B., Georgetown U., 1949, LL.M., 1950; Th.D., Gregorian U., Rome, 1954; study, Florence, Italy, 1954-55; LL.D. (hon.), Worcester State Coll., 1970, L.I. U., 1970, R.I. Coll., 1971, St. Joseph's Coll., Phila., 1975, Syracuse U., 1977, Villanova U., 1977, Framingham (Mass.) State Coll., 1978, U. Santa Clara, 1980, Kenyon Coll., 1981, Lowell U., 1981, U. Bridgeport, 1981, Loyola U., Chgo., 1981, Gonzaga U., 1981, Curry Coll., 1982, De Paul U., 1984, U. San Diego, 1984, Mt. St. Mary Coll., 1985, Hebrew Coll., 1987, Notre Dame Coll., Manchester, N.H., 1989, Walsh Coll., Ohio, 1990, Georgetown U., 1991. Bar: D.C. 1950, Mass. 1956, U.S. Supreme Ct. 1955; ordained priest Roman Cath. Ch., 1953. Asst. dean Boston Coll. Law Sch., 1955-56, dean, 1956-70; vis. prof. U. Tex. Law Sch., 1966-67; mem. 92d-96th Congresses from 4th Mass. dist.; mem. jud. com., govt. ops. com., house select com. on aging, chmn. subcom. on criminal justice; columnist Nat. Cath. Reporter, 1980; prof., Sch. of Law Georgetown U., Washington, 1980—; chmn. adv. com. Mass. U.S. Civil Rights, 1962-70; mem. vis. com. Div. Sch., Harvard U., 1975-78; bd. dirs. Bread for the World; founder Nat. Interreligious Task Force on Soviet Jewry.; mem. exec. com. Assn. Am. Law Schs.; vis. lectr. Oxford U., England, 1988. Author: Religion, the Courts and Public Policy, 1963, Democracy, Dissent and Disorder, 1969, Vietnam and Armageddon, 1970, Honor the Promise, America's Commitment to Israel, 1977, Beyond the Nuclear Freeze, 1983. Editor: The Right To Be Educated, 1968, God and Caesar on the Potomac, 1985, Cry of the Oppressed: The History and Hope of the Human Rights Revolution, 1987, Stories from the America Soul, 1990, The Fractured Dream, 1991; editor in chief Family Law Quar., 1967-70; contbr. editor: nat. Cath. weekly America, 1958-70. Contbr. articles to jours. of opinion. Pres. Ams. for Dem. Action, 1981-84. Fellow Am. Acad. Arts and Scis.; mem. ABA (chmn. sect. individual rights and responsibilities 1990-91, bd. dels. 1993-96, chmn. standing com. professionalism 1996—), NCCJ (nat. trustee), Am. Law Inst., Common Cause (nat. governing bd. 1984-87, 96-99), Mass. Bar Assn. (v.p. 1961), Boston Bar Assn. Office: Georgetown U Law Ctr 600 New Jersey Ave NW Washington DC 20001-2022

DRINGENBURG, DUANE CLINTON, social services executive; b. Covington, Ky., Apr. 29, 1948; s. Irvin Clinton and Betty Lee (Lockwood) D. BS in Edn., Ea. Ky. U., 1970, MA in Edn., 1976. Tchr., coach varsity football Dayton (Ky.) Pub. Schs., 1970-75; tchr., grad. asst. Ea. Ky. U., Richmond, 1975-76; tchr., coach varsity football George Rogers Clark H.S., Winchester, Ky., 1976-84; med. sales rep. Wendt Bristol/Foster Med., Columbus, Ohio, 1984-91, Crocker Fels Co., Cin., 1991-92; prin. asst. dept. med. svcs. State of Ky., Frankfort, 1992-93, dep. commr. dept. social svcs., 1993-94, prin. asst. cabinet for human resources, 1994-96, divsn. dir. dept. Medicaid Svcs., 1996—. Mem. Centrist Group, Ky., 1997. Mem. Ky. Coaches Assn. Democrat. Lutheran. Avocations: hunting, fishing, farming. Office: Dept Medicaid Svcs 275 E Main St Frankfort KY 40621-0001

DRINKARD, D(ONALD) DWIGHT, SR., sports event director; b. Kansas City, Mo., Mar. 15, 1948; s. Donald and Helen C. (Polson) D.; m. Margaret (Peggy) M. Thweatt, Sept. 17, 1977; children: Donald D. Drinkard, Jr., Kathryn C. Drinkard. BA, Vanderbilt U., 1970; MBA, Ga. State U., 1973. Mktg. dir. Bruce Hardwood Floors, Memphis, 1973-77; v.p. Puckett & Assocs. Advt., Memphis, 1977-79; mktg. dir. Data Comm. Corp., Memphis, 1979-82, RCA Cylix Comm. Network, Memphis, 1982-86; tournament dir. FedEx St. Jude Classic, Memphis, 1986—; pres., bd. dirs. PGA Tour Tournaments Assn., Ponte Vedra, Fla., 1997-99. Bd. dirs. Kidney Found. Western Tenn., 1976-84; grad. Leadership Memphis, 1983. Memphis U. Sch. Alumni Assn. (pres. 1996), Memphis Country Club. Presbyn. Home: 521 S Goodlett St Memphis TN 38117-3600

DRINKO, JOHN DEAVER, lawyer; b. St. Marys, W.Va., June 17, 1921; s. Emery J. and Hazel (White) D.; m. Elizabeth Gibson, May 14, 1946; children: Elizabeth Lee Sullivan, Diana Lynn Martin, John Randall, Jay Deaver. AB, Marshall U., 1942; JD, Ohio State U., 1944; postgrad., U. Tex. Sch. Law, 1944; LLD (hon.), Marshall U., 1980, Ohio State U., 1986, John Carroll U., 1987, Capital U., 1988, Cleve. State U., 1990; DHL (hon.), David N. Myers Coll., 1990, U. N.H., 1992, Baldwin-Wallace Coll., 1993, Ursuline Coll., 1994, Notre Dame Coll., 1997, U. Rio Grande, 1999. Bar: Ohio 1945, D.C 1946, U.S. Dist. Ct. (no. dist.) Ohio 1958. Assoc. Baker & Hostetler, Cleve., 1945-55, ptnr., 1955-69, mng. ptnr., from 1969, sr. adviser to mng. com.; chmn. bd. Cleve. Inst. Electronics Inc., Double D Ranch Inc., Ohio; bd. dirs. Cloyes Gear and Products Inc., McGean-Rohco Worldwide Inc., Orvis Co. Inc., Preformed Line Products Inc., The Standard Products Co. Trustee Elizabeth G. and John D. Drinko Charitable Found., Orvis-Perkins Found., Thomas F. Peterson Found., Mellen Found., The Cloyes-Myers Found., Marshall U. Found.; founder Consortium of Multiple Sclerosis Ctrs., Mellen Conf. on Acute and Critical Care Nursing, Case Western Res. U. Disting. fellow Cleve. Clinc Found., 1991; Ohio State Law Sch. Bldg. named in his honor, 1995, libr. at Marshall U. named in his honor, 1997; inducted into Bus. Hall of Fame, Marshall Univ., 1996. Mem. ABA, Am. Jud. Assn., Bar Assn. Greater Cleve., Greater Cleve. Growth Assn., Ohio State Bar Assn., Jud. Conf. 8th Jud. Dist. (life), Soc. Benchers, Case Western Res. U. Law Sch. Assn., Cleve. Play House, Cleve. Civil War Round-table, Mayfield Country Club, Union Club, The Club at Soc. Ctr., O'Donnell Golf Club, Order of Coif, 33o Scottish Rite Mason, Knight Templar, York Rite, Euclid Blue Lodge No. 599 (Jesters, Shrine, Grotto). Republican. Presbyterian. Home: 4891 Middledale Rd Cleveland OH 44124-2522 also: 1245 Otono Dr Palm Springs CA 92264-8445 Office: Baker & Hostetler 3200 Nat City Ctr 1900 E 9th St Ste 3200 Cleveland OH 44114-3475

DRINKWATER, PETER L., airport executive; m. Joanne Drinkwater; children: Adam, Nathan.; B in Psychology, M in Bus. and Pub. Adminstrn. Airport mgr. Ontario Internat. Airport, 1998—. Active Boy Scouts Am. With USAF. Mem. Exptl. Aircraft Assn. Avocation: licensed pilot. Office: Ontario Internat Airport Terminal Bldg Rm 200 Ontario CA 91761

DRINNAN, ALAN JOHN, oral pathologist; b. Bristol, Eng., Apr. 6, 1932; came to U.S., 1962, naturalized, 1970; s. Leslie Cyril and Doris May (Porter) D.; m. Marguerite G. Bondolfi, Apr. 4, 1956; children: Michael James, Julia Mary. B.D.S., Bristol U., 1954, M.B.Ch.B., 1962; D.D.S., SUNY, 1964. Tutor oral surgery Bristol U., Eng., 1957-58; asst. prof. SUNY-Buffalo, 1964-68, assoc. prof., 1968-71, prof. dept. oral medicine, chmn., 1971-94; disting. prof., 1994—. Contbr. articles to numerous publs. Served to capt. Royal Army Dental Corps Brit. Army, 1955-57. Fulbright sr. scholar U. Melbourne, Australia, 1981. Mem. ADA, Am. Acad. Oral Pathology (pres.), Internat. Assn. Dental Research, Internat. Assn. Oral Pathologists (pres.). Home: 66 Chestnut Hill Ln Buffalo NY 14221-1702 Office: SUNY Squire Dental Sch Rm 342 Buffalo NY 14214

DRINNON, JANIS BOLTON, artist, poet, author, volunteer; b. Pineville, Ky., July 28, 1922; d. Clyde Herman and Violet Ethiele (Hendrickson) Bolton; m. Kenneth Cleveland Drinnon, June 13, 1948; 1 child, Dena Daryl. *The Bolton and Hendrickson families were old established families of Pineville, Kentucky and Harrogate, Tennessee. Janis and her husband, Kenneth, were married at the First Baptist Church in Middlesboro, Kentucky in 1948. Kenneth received his BSEE University Tennessee 1950. Daughter, Dena, BA University Tennessee, MEd Carson-Newman College, is a school teacher. Her husband David E. Foulk, is a newsman with WNOX radio, Knoxville, Tennessee. Grandchildren, Bethany Erah Foulk and Jonathan David Foulk are students at East Tennessee State University. Jonathan received a music scholarship. Julia Elizabeth Foulk is a student at Seymour Middle School. Ms. Drinnon believes family is important and must always come first.* Grad. high sch., Middlesboro, Ky., 1943; student, Lincoln Meml. U., Harrogate, Tenn., 1947-48; commercial art cert., Art Instrn. Sch., Mpls., 1968; student, Newspaper Inst. Am. Author: In HIS Care: A Book of Inspirational Poetry, 1998. Organizer, prodr., dir. religious plays drama dept. Alice Bell Bapt. Ch., Knoxville, Tenn.; mem. New Hopewell Baptist Ch., Knoxville. Recepient Editors Choice award The Nat. Libr. of Poetry; Named to the Internat. Poetry Hall of Fame in 1996. Mem. Internat. Soc. Poets (disting. mem., nom. poet of the year 1995,96,97). Republican. Avocations: arts, crafts, oil painting, composing poetry. Home: 7434 Hodges Ferry Rd Knoxville TN 37920-8136

DRINNON, RICHARD, history educator; b. Portland, Oreg., Jan. 4, 1925; s. John Henry and Emma (Tweed) D.; m. Anna Maria Faulise, Oct. 20, 1945; children: Donna Elizabeth, Jon Tweed. B.A. summa cum laude, Willamette U., 1950; M.A., U. Minn., 1951, Ph.D., 1957. Instr. humanities U. Minn., 1952-53, social sci., 1955-57; instr. Am. history U. Calif., 1957-58, asst. prof., 1958-61; Bruern fellow in Am. studies U. Leeds, 1961-63; faculty research fellow Social Sci. Research Council, 1963-64; assoc. prof. history Hobart and William Smith Colls., 1964-66; chmn. dept. history Bucknell U., 1966-74, prof. history, 1974-87, prof. emeritus, 1987—; vis. prof. U. Paris, 1975. Author: Rebel in Paradise: a Biography of Emma Goldman, 1961, White Savage: The Case of John Dunn Hunter, 1972, Facing West: The Metaphysics of Indian-Hating and Empire-Building, 1980, 90, 97, Keeper of Concentration Camps: Dillon S. Myer and American Racism, 1987; co-editor: Nowhere at Home: Letters from Exile of Emma Goldman and Alexander Berkman, 1974; contbr. articles and revs. to profl. jours. and mags. Served with USNR, 1942-46. NEH sr. fellow, 1980-81. Office: PO Box 1001 Port Orford OR 97465-1001

DRISCOLL, CHARLES FRANCIS, financial services company executive, investment adviser; b. Dubuque, Iowa, July 8, 1943; s. Francis Clarence and Grace Ellen (Shanahan) D.; m. Marie Kathleen McGowan, Aug. 19, 1967; children: Sean, Erin. BA in Econs., Loras Coll., 1968. CLU; registered investment advisor; accredited estate planner. Sr. account mgr. NCR Corp., Davenport, Iowa, 1968-74, St. Louis, 1974-76; fin. planner Mass. Mut. Life Ins. Co., St. Louis, 1976—; pres. Driscoll and Assocs., St. Louis, 1989—; equity sales coord. MML Investor Svcs., Inc., St. Louis, 1983-88. Chmn. Edgewood Program Alumni Recovery Fund, St. John's Mercy Hosp., St. Louis, 1988-90. Mem. Nat. Assn. Life Underwriters, Am. Soc. CLU and ChFC, Estate Planning Coun. St. Lo. Republican. Roman Catholic. Avocations: golf, fishing, hunting, reading, travel. Home: 2324 Manor Lake Ct Chesterfield MO 63017-7817 Office: 100 N Broadway Ste 1810 Saint Louis MO 63102-2709

DRISCOLL, CHARLES FREDERICK, physics educator; b. Tucson, Feb. 28, 1950; s. John Raymond Gozzi and Barbara Jean (Hamilton) Driscoll; m. Susan C. Bain, Dec. 30, 1972; children: Thomas A., Robert A. BA in Physics summa cum laude, Cornell U., 1969; MS, U. Calif. San Diego, La Jolla, 1972, PhD, 1976. Staff scientist Gen. Atomics, San Diego, 1969; rsch. asst. U. Calif. San Diego, La Jolla, 1971-76, rsch. physicist, sr. lectr., 1976-96, prof. physics, 1996—, assoc. dir. Inst. for Pure and Applied Scis., 1998—; cons. Sci. Applications, Inc., 1980-81; staff physicist, cons. Molecular Biosystems, Inc., 1981-82. Editor: Non-Neutral Plasma Physics, 1988; contbr. numerous articles to sci. jours. Fellow NSF, 1969-71. Fellow Am. Phys. Soc. (Excellence in Plasma Physics Rsch. award 1991); mem. AAAS, Math. Assn. Am., Phi Beta Kappa. Achievements include development of quantitative analysis of magnetic targeting of microspheres in capillaries, experiments and theory on magnetized electron plasmas, new camera-diagnosed electron plasma apparatus, new laser-diagnosed ion plasma apparatus for in-situ transport measurements; establishment of magnetic containment characteristics of unneutralized plasmas; measurement of collisional transport of heat and particles to thermal equilibrium; observation of new 2D fluid instability and relaxation of 2D turbulence to vortex crystal states. E-mail: fdriscoll@ucsd.edu. Office: U Calif San Diego Dept Physics 0319 9500 Gilman Dr La Jolla CA 92093-0319

DRISCOLL, DAVID LEE, chiropractor; b. Storm Lake, Iowa, Aug. 3, 1954; s. Glenn Francis and Jeannine Ann (Layer) D.; m. Joan Marie Valle, Sept. 8, 1973; children: Jennifer Marie, Matthew Bryan. D Chiropractic, Logan Coll. Chiropractic, Chesterfield, Mo., 1978. Pvt. practice Colorado Springs, 1978—. Fellow Internat. Biocranial Acad. (assoc. instr., edn1. dir.), Internat. Acad. Clin. Acupuncture; mem. Am. Chiropractic Assn., Colo. Chiropractic Assn., El Paso County Chiropractic Assn., Internat. Biocranial Acad. (edn1. dir.). Republican. Roman Catholic. Avocations: volleyball, golf, reading. Home: 813 Crown Ridge Dr Colorado Springs CO 80904-1731 Office: Driscoll Chiropractic 1819 W Colorado Ave Colorado Springs CO 80904-3836

DRISCOLL, EDWARD CARROLL, construction management firm executive; b. Phila., Dec. 25, 1929; s. Leon Francis and Helen (Carroll) D.; m. Nancy Bell, Sept. 22, 1951; children—Edward Carroll Jr., David B., Susan H. A.B., U. Pa., 1951. Estimator L.F. Driscoll Co., Phila., 1954-67, sec., 1967-69; pres. L.F. Driscoll Co., Bala Cynwyd, Pa., 1969-75, chief exec. officer, chmn. bd., 1975—; bd. dirs. Provident Nat. Bank, Phila., Library Co., Phila., Nat. Bldg. Mus., Washington. Trustee Thomas Jefferson U., 1974—, chmn. bd. trustees, 1984-90; trustee Childrens' Heart Hosp., 1976-81; mem. adv. coun. Wills Eye Hosp., 1979—, bd. dirs., 1979-83; bd. dirs. Internat. House, 1978-89; mem. adv. bd., bd. dirs. U. Pa. Ctr. for Study of Aging, 1983—. Served to lt. USN, 1951-54. Mem. Gen. Bldg. Contractors' Assn. (bd. dirs. 1972-85), Chief Exec.'s Orgn., Phila. Pres.' Orgn., Young Pres.' Orgn., Phila. Club, Phila. Cricket Club, Union League Club (Phila.), Sunnybrook Golf Club (Plymouth Meeting, Pa.). Roman Catholic. Office: LF Driscoll Co 9 Presidential Blvd Bala Cynwyd PA 19004-1003

DRISCOLL, GARRETT BATES, retired telecommunications executive; b. Terre Haute, Ind., July 10, 1932; s. James Edgar and Lorraine Emma (Simmons) D.; m. Suzanne Keder O'Reilly, Apr. 30, 1960 (div. Sept. 1984); children: Garrett Edward, Lorraine Elizabeth Driscoll Veltri; m. Ivy Juanita Bryant, Sept. 24, 1985 (div. Aug. 1995); children: Jennifer Louise, Caroline Margaret; m. Janice Patterson Buckalew, Oct. 25, 1996. AA, Broward C.C., Ft. Lauderdale, Fla., 1973; BA, Fla. Atlantic U., Boca Raton, 1979. Tech. supr. TRT Telecom. Corp., Ft. Lauderdale, 1972-80; asst. mgr. N.Y. ops. TRT Telecom. Corp., N.Y.C., 1980-82; asst. v.p. telecom. 1st Am. Bank, Lake Worth, Fla., 1983-86; dir. telecom. R&D John Alden Sys. Co., Miami, Fla., 1986-97; advisor Jan Gar, Inc., Lake Wales, Fla., 1997—; lectr. U. Miami, 1988-97. *Graduated Greenville (Ohio) High School, 1950. Worked from the age of six. By twelve, he provided all his own clothing, those required by ill father and helped with the household. Entered military at 18, retiring at 39. Saw duty worldwide, including the Pentagon and 13.5 months in Vietnam, where he was injured. Obtained BA at 47. Only sibling is a Who's Who in American Law biographee. Personal hero is his son who gave his life fighting the drug scourge. Attributes success to God's grace and gift of an ability to make new technology work in a practical environment. Tries to learn each day.* With USAF, 1951-71. Lutheran. Avocations: reading, woodworking, exercise.

DRISCOLL, GENEVIEVE BOSSON (JEANNE BOSSON DRISCOLL), management and organization development consultant; b. Pitts., Mar. 26, 1937; d. George August and Emma Haling Bleichner; m. John Edwin Bosson, June 17, 1959; 1 child, Matthew Edwin; m. Frederick Driscoll, Oct.

7, 1972; stepchildren: Jennifer Locke, Cynthia Hall, Molly Davis, Julie Ann. BS cum laude, Fla. State U., 1959; postgrad., Nat. Tng. Labs., 1970. Planning asst. Ctr. Planning and Innovation, Dept. Edn. State of N.Y., 1967-71; planning cons. So. Tier Regional Office for Ednl. Planning, Elmira, N.Y., 1971-72; tng. dir. Neusteters, Inc., Denver, 1973-74; orgn. devel. specialist CONNECT, Inc., N.Y.C., 1975-77; cons. Robert H. Schaffer & Assocs., Stamford, Conn., 1977-80; ptnr. Driscoll Cons. Group, Williamstown, Mass., 1980—; sales tng. mgr. Sheaffer Eaton, Pittsfield, Mass., 1983, mgr. human resources and orgn. devel., 1983-88; dir. human resources Canyon Ranch, Berkshires, 1989-95; dir. The Learning Inst., Bennington, Vt., 1997-99; ret., 1999. Office: 24 Lee Ter Williamstown MA 01267-2039

DRISCOLL, JAMES S., entrepreneurial strategist; b. Boston, Apr. 8, 1966; s. James A. and Edna L. (Rust) Driscoll. BA, Stanford (Calif.) U., 1988; MA, Harvard U., 1995, postgrad., 1995—. Assoc. cons. Braxton Assocs., Boston, 1988-90; mgr. Deloitte & Touche, Moscow, 1990-92; ptnr. IMA Consulting, Boston, 1992-94; dir. consulting Cambridge (Mass.) Interactive Internet Pub., 1994-95; sr. cons. Denneen and Co., Boston, 1997—, of counsel, 1996—. Founder, editor Techne: Jour. Tech., Stanford, 1987-88, Release Mag., Stanford, 1988. Mellon fellow Andrew J. Mellon Found., Princeton, N.J., 1994. Mem. MLA, Am. Conf. Irish Studies, Cumann na Gaeilge im Boston, Soc. for Crit. Exch. Office: 401 Commonwealth Ave Boston MA 02215-2317

DRISCOLL, JOHN J., city manager. BS in Psychology, Seattle U., MA in Bus. Adminstrn. Various positions Mayor's Office, Seattle; gen. mgr. Pers. Dept. City of L.A., 1978-92, exec. dir. Dept. Airports, 1992—. Mem. Am. Assn. Airport Execs., Airports Coun. Internat. N.Am. (govt. affairs com.), Internat. Air Cargo Assn. (trustee). Office: LA Dept Airports PO Box 92216 Los Angeles CA 90009-2216*

DRISCOLL, JOSEPH FRANCIS, real estate executive; b. Louisville, Apr. 23, 1943; s. Francis Xavier and Elizabeth (Brisse) D.; m. Joann Heskamp, Dec. 27, 1967 (dec. Apr. 1979); 1 child, Michael; m. Margaret Rebecca Thomas, Sept. 24, 1982. BA in Edn., Bellarmine Coll., Louisville, 1965. Lic. real estate salesperson, Tenn.; cert. tchr., Tenn. Real estate agt. Baker Harwell, Joel Riggs Better Homes & Gardens, Nashville, 1984-89, Beck & Beck Real Estate, Nashville, 1989-91, Folk-Jordan Better Homes & Gardens, Nashville, 1991—; cons. Sovran Bank/Ctrl. South, Nashville, 1991-92; citizen mem. bd. Regions Bank. Editor, author: Joe's Notes, 1993-95. Candidate U.S. Congress from 5th Dist. Tenn., 1987-88; candidate Mayor of Nashville, 1991; pres. Snap Housing, South Nashville Action People, 1986-92; mem. Low-income Housing Forum, 1986-98; tchr. Holy Rosary Ch., 1992-93. Served with U.S. Army, 1967-69, Vietnam. Decorated Purple Heart. Mem. Nat. Bd. Realtors, Donelson-Hermitage Chamber (bd. dirs. 1987-88). Democrat. Roman Catholic. Avocations: reading, sports, praying. Home: 811 Redwood Dr Nashville TN 37220-1810 Office: Folk-Jordan Better Homes 486 Bell Rd Nashville TN 37217-3837

DRISCOLL, KATHLEEN J, writer, research analyst; b. Boston, MA, May 3, 1946; d. Frederick S. and Catherine T. McNamara D., one child, Catherine. Columnist, journalist The Patriot Ledger, Quincy, MA, 1979-84; editor The Pembroke Mariner, Pembroke, MA, 1984-86; acting pub., columnist South Shore News, Rockland, MA, 1986-94; columnist The Milton Times, Milton, MA, 1995—. author, poetry, Dirty Woman's Rag, 1992, columns, features, NEPA, NFPW, Mass Media Women, etc. vice pres., Natl. Org. for Women/MA, Mass., 1987-89. Mem., Natl. Writer's Union. Office: PO Box 80 Hanover MA 02339

DRISCOLL, LEE FRANCIS, JR., corporate director, lawyer; b. Phila., July 27, 1926; s. Leon F. and Helen (Carroll) D.; m. Phoebe Albert, Dec. 30, 1959; children—Lee Francis III, Patrick McGill, Phoebe Driscoll Fisher, Helen Louise. AB, U. Pa., 1949, LLB, 1953. Bar: Pa. 1954. Dir. ARAMARK Corp., Independence Blue Cross. Pres. Phila. United Way, 1980-82; Dem. candidate for U.S. Congress, 1962. Served with AUS, 1944-46, 50-51. Decorated Bronze Star. Mem. Union League (Phila.), Phila. Club. Roman Catholic. Home: 720 Swedesford Rd Ambler PA 19002-1926 Office: The Aramark Tower 30th Fl 1101 Market St Philadelphia PA 19107-2934

DRISCOLL, MICHAEL P., bishop; b. Long Beach, Calif., Aug. 8, 1939. Student, St. John's Sem., Camarillo, Calif.; MSW, U. So. Calif., 1975. Ordained priest Roman Cath. Ch., 1965, titular bishop of Massita. Aux. bishop Orange, Calif., 1990-99; bishop Boise, Idaho, 1999—. Office: Diocese of Boise 303 Federal Way Boise ID 83705*

DRISCOLL, MICHAEL STEPHAN, priest, liturgy and theology educator; b. Butte, Mont., May 11, 1951; s. Robert Stephen and Mary Catherine (Silver) D. STB, Gregorian U., Rome, 1976; STL, Sant Anselmo, Rome, 1981; STD, Institut Catholique, Paris, 1986; PhD, Sorbonne/Paris IV, 1986. Ordained priest Roman Cath. Ch., 1977. Asst. prof. theology Carroll Coll., Helena, Mont., 1986-93, assoc. prof., 1993-94; vis. asst. prof. U. Notre Dame, Ind., 1994-95, asst. prof. theology, 1995—, Tisch asst. prof., 1998—. Author: Alcuin et la pénitence à l'époque carolingienne, 1999. Mem. N.Am. Acad. Liturgy (group convenor), Societas Liturgica (group convenor), Rotary Club. Avocations: choral music, foreign travel, skiing, gourmet cooking. Office: U Notre Dame Dept Theology Notre Dame IN 46556

DRISCOLL, RAY F., city official; b. June 5, 1935; m. Donna; two children. BA, St. Vincent Coll. Mgr. Houston Assn. Credit, 1976-85; mem. Mayor's Land Use Strategy Com., Houston, 1990; city councilman dist. F Houston, 1994—; pres. Creditors' Rights Mgmt., Inc. Mem. Am. Soc. Assn. Execs., Comml. Law League Am. Office: Houston City Coun PO Box 1562 Houston TX 77251-1562*

DRISCOLL, RICHARD STARK, land use planner; b. Denver, Sept. 16, 1928; s. Myron William and Edith Helene (Stark) D.; m. Joyce Lynn Yarbrough, Jan. 9, 1954; children: Vicki Lynn Driscoll Kiefe, Kelly Sue. BS, Colo. A&M, 1951; MS, Colo. State U., 1957; PhD, Oreg. State U., 1962. Range scientist USDA Forest Svc., Portland, Oreg., 1952-56; rsch. project leader USDA Forest Svc., Portland, 1956-62, Washington, 1962-65, Ft. Collins, Colo., 1965-77; R & D program mgr. USDA Forest Svc., Ft. Collins, 1977-83; cons. FMA Internat., Inc., Gardnerville, Nev., 1983-91; land-use expert UN-FAO, Rome, 1983-89; land use cons. Fust (Föderung von Umweltstudien), Achenkirch/Tyrol, Austria, 1993. Author, editor: Photo Interpretation for Ranges and Range Management, 1997; contbg. author Range Resources: Inventory, Evaluation, Monitoring, 1975; contbr. articles to profl. jours. Dist. chmn. Bend (Oreg.) area Boy Scouts Am., 1962, com. chair troop 26, Ft. Collins, Colo., 1989; mem., chair various coms. Westminster Presbyn. Ch. and Timnath Presbyn. Ch., Ft. Collins, 1972—; mem. and moderator com. on ministry Plains and Peaks Presbytery Presbyn. Ch. U.S.A., 1991-99. Recipient presdl. citation for meritorious svc. Am. Soc. Photogrammetry and Remote Sensing, 1978, 86. Mem. Am. Inst. Biol. Scis., Soc. Range Mgmt. (chair, com. mem., Outstanding Achievement award 1983), Nat. Assn. Ret. Fed. Employees (chpt. pres. 1993-95, mem. and chair various coms. 1988-99, fed. v.p. for dist. IV), Xi Sigma Pi, Beta Beta Beta, Sigma Xi. Achievements include research on use of remote sensing technology for rangeland inventory and classification, range management planning and management, ecological land classification for land use planning in the U.S., and land evaluation, planning and management in the tropics and central Europe. Home and Office: 2217 Sheffield Dr Fort Collins CO 80526-1640

DRISKELL, LUCILE G., artist; b. N.Y.C., Dec. 20, 1924; d. Charles Albert and Clarice Dorothy (Jung) Gall; m. Richard O. Driskell, Sept. 4, 1946; children: Douglas G., Donald A., David O. AA, Finch Coll., 1945; student, La Jolla Art Ctr., Calif., 1956-63, Fratelli Da Prato Foundry, Pietra Santa, Italy, 1973-78, Art Students League, N.Y.C., 1984-88. Artist San Diego, Calif., 1950-63, Cin., 1963-67, Aspen, Colo., 1967-72, Greve in Chianti, Italy, 1972-79, Wellsboro, Pa., 1979—, Phila., 1985—; artist, consignor Environment Gallery, N.Y.C., 1968-84, Rodger Lapelle Gallery, Phila., 1984—, Agora Gallery, N.Y., 1993—. *Throughout her professional art career of over 30 years, Lucile has ignored subject matter such as current affairs and social messages to emphasize purity of form, response to light, and appeal to the mystical. Her use of non-objective abstract art allows complete freedom for expression and also for viewing. Lucile Driskell has had wide experience from direct carving in wood and stone to the creation of models for casting in bronze, stainless steel and aluminum. To express her art in color she creates woodblock prints as well as wall reliefs that combine sculpture and painting.* Artist sculptures, 1960—, wall reliefs, 1988—, prints, 1956—. Recipient Purchase awards Bell Atlantic, Phila., 1991, Core States Bank, Wilmington, Del., 1996, Exxon, N.Y.C., 1978, Macy's, Washington, 1989. Mem. Internat. Sculpture Ctr., Washington Sculpture Group, Art Students League (life). Avocations: hiking, photography, travel. Home: RD 6 Box 78 Wellsboro PA 16901

DRISKILL, CHARLES DWAYNE, agriculture educator, researcher; b. Benton, Ky., Mar. 27, 1954; s. Charles Ausburn and Winetta June (Johnson) D.; m. Jami Jo Hay, 1991. BS, Murray (Ky.) State U., 1976, MS, 1978; EdD, Okla. State U., 1983. Instr. Spoon River Coll., Macomb, Ill., 1979-80, Western Ill. U., Macomb, 1978-80; grad. instr. Okla. State U., Stillwater, 1981-83; asst. prof. agrl. Murray State U., 1984—; cons. Hardy, Terrell and Boswell, Paducah, Ky., 1985; researcher, reviewer Van Nostrand Reinhold Book Co., N.Y.C., 1989-90, Profl. Devel. Seminar, Kansas City, Mo., 1989; developer, condr. mechanics contest at regional, state and nat. level FFA. Jour. referee Jour. Agrl. Mechanization, 1986-89; reviewer Applied Engring. in Agrl., 1991; editor procs. Agr. Mechanization Profl. Devel. Seminar. Murray State U. campaign chairperson United Way; mem. com. Ky. Rural Safety and Health Coun.; trustee Paradise Cemetery Com., Grand Rivers, Ky., 1988-90; instr. electricity class 4-H Orgn., Calloway County, Ky., 1987-90. Recipient Outstanding Tchr. award Coll. of Industry and Tech., Achievement award Briggs and Stratton, 1988, others; named one of Outstanding Young Men of Am., 1989. Mem. Am. Soc. Agrl. Engrs., So. Assn. Agrl. Scientists, Nat. Intercoll. Rodeo Assn., Murray State Alumni Assn. (life), Murray State Agrl. Alumni (life). Democrat. Methodist. Avocations: old car restoration, motorcycles, biking, water skiing, hiking. Home: 476 Applewood Rd Murray KY 42071-7227 Office: Murray State U Dept Agrl Murray KY 42071

DRISKILL, JAMES LAWRENCE, minister; b. Rustburg, Va., Aug. 18, 1920; s. Elijah Hudson and Annie Pharr (Carwile) D.; m. Ethel Lillian Cassel, May 28, 1949; children: Edward Lawrence, Mary Lillian. BA, Pa. State U., 1946; BD, San Francisco Theol. Sem., 1949; ThM, Princeton Sem., 1957; S.T.D., San Francisco Theol. Sem., 1969. Ordained minister in Presbyn. Ch., 1949. Missionary Presbyn. Ch. USA, Japan, 1949-72; stated supply pastor Madison Square Presbyn. Ch., San Antonio, 1973; minister Highland Presbyn. Ch., Maryville, Tenn., 1973-82; supply pastor of Japanese-Am. chs. Presbyn. Ch. USA, Long Beach, Calif., Hollywood, Calif., Altadena, Calif., 1984—; vis. prof. religion dept. Trinity U., 1972-73. Author: Adventures in Senior Living, 1997, Christmas Stories from Around the World, 1997, Worldwide Mission Stories for Young People, 1996, Cross-Cultural Marriages and the Church, 1995, Mission Stories from Around the World, 1994, Japan Diary, 1993, Mission Adventures in Many Lands, 1992; contbr. articles to profl. jours. Mem. Sierra Club, Calif., 1988—; trustee Osaka (Japan) Girls Sch., 1952-65, Seikyo Gakuen Christian Sch., Japan, 1953-92. With USN, 1943-46. Mem. Am. Acad. Religion, Presbyn. Writers Guild. Democrat. Home and Office: 1420 Santo Domingo Ave Duarte CA 91010-2698 *Experience has taught me that, ultimately, the meaning and value of a person's life is determined by the quality of one's personal relationships, especially by the quality of one's relationship to God.*

DRIVER, JOE L., state legislator, insurance agent; b. Rockwall, Tex., Sept. 29, 1946; s. Marshall Laguin and Alice Elizabeth (Patillo) D.; m. S. DeAnne Browning, Nov. 20, 1993; stepchildren: Eric Browning, Lynsey Browning. BBA, U. North Tex., 1971; grad., Garland Citizen's Police Acad., 1993. With Steak & Ale Restauants, Dallas, 1971-73; law instr. Garland (Tex.) Ind. Sch. Dist., 1972; mgr. Marshall Driver Ins., Garland, 1972-73; trainee State Farm Ins. Cos., Dallas, 1973-75, mem. regional advt. bd., 1978-82; owner, agt. Joe Driver Ins.-State Farm, Garland, Tex., 1975—; mem. Tex. Ho. of Reps., 1993—, mem. energy resources com., 1993-95, 97—, mem. ins. com., 1993-97, mem. pub. safety com., 1995—, vice chmn. pub. safety com., 1997-99, chmn. select com. constitutional revision Tex. constitution, 1999—. Pres. Christian Singles Unltd., Garland, 1979; bd. dirs. First United Meth. Ch., Garland, 1979-81, Garland Econ. and Devel. Authority, 1986, Garland Crimestoppers, 1985-88, 93—, Am. Heart Assn., 1991-93; bd. dirs. New Beginning Family and Violence Prevention Ctr., 1988-91, v.p., 1990-91; chmn. SITE Found. of Garland, Inc., 1991-92; mem. bd. mgmt. Garland YMCA, 1983-85; fundraising chmn. YWCA, 1992; mem. long-range planning com. City of Garland, 1986-88; mem. devel. coun. Baylor Med. Ctr., Garland, 1991—; mem. Downtown Citizen Rev. Com., 1991-92; active Tex. Conservative Coalition, 1993—, Rep. Caucus Tex. Ho. of Reps., 1993—. Recipient Human Relations award Dale Carnegie Cos., 1978. Mem. Nat. Assn. Life Underwriters (Nat. Quality award 1978-83, 86-92), Dallas Assn. Life Underwriters, Garland C. of C. (bd. dirs. 1983-87, chmn. 1986, corp. coun. 1988-90), Rowlett C. of C., Sachse C. of C., Tex. Dist. Exch. Clubs (dist. dir. 1984, Outstanding Dist. Dir. award 1985, Pres.'s award 1986), Noon Exch. Club Garland (bd. dirs. 1982-86, 90-91, pres. 1983, 90, Outstanding Svc. award 1986-87), Leadership Garland Alumni Assn. (bd. dirs. 1990-91), U. North Tex. Alumni Assn., Republican Forum, Lambda Chi Alpha (pres. 1971). Avocations: golf, weight training. Office: 201 S Glenbrook Dr Garland TX 75040-6227

DRIVER, LARRY C., medical educator. BA, Austin Coll., 1976; MD, U. Tex., San Antonio, 1980. Diplomate Am. Bd. Anesthesiology. Surg. intern U. Tex. Health Sci. Ctr., San Antonio, 1980-81; anethesiology resident U. Colo. Health Sci. Ctr., Denver, 1982-84; staff anesthesiologist Angelo Cmty. Hosp., San Angelo, Tex., 1984-92, Shannon Med. Ctr., San Angelo, 1992-98; assoc. med. dir. Family Hospice, San Angelo, 1997-98; clin. fellow U. Tex. M.D. Anderson Cancer Ctr., Houston, 1998-99, assoc. prof. pain mgmt. and palliative care, 1999—; vis. clin. fellow Baylor Coll. Medicine, Houston, 1998-99; vis. rsch. fellow Kennedy Inst. Ethics, Georgetown U., Washington, 1999. Editor: Interventional Pain Management, 1999; contbr. chpt. to book. Active Austin Coll. Pres. Coun., Austin Coll. Alumni Assn. Bd. Dirs., 1993-99; founder Hard Hats for Little Heads, Tex., 1994—, AEIOU Group, San Angelo, 1995-96; concept originator Battleship Tex. Resolution, Tex. Legis., 1995. Recipient Recognition award NAACP, San Angelo, 1994, Hard Hats for Little Heads Bicycle Safety Proclamation, San Angelo City Coun., 1998. Mem. AMA, Internat. Order St. Luke the Physician, Internat. Assn. for the Study Pain, Am. Soc. Anesthesiologists, Am. Pain Soc., Am. Acad. Hospice and Palliative Medicine, Christian Med. and Dental Soc., Tex. Med. Assn. (Aesculapius award 1995, Golden Apple award for svc. in disease prevention and health promotion 1995), Tex. Soc. Anesthesiologists, N.Y. Acad. Sci., Tex. Acad. Sci., Beta Beta Beta, Psi Chi. Office: U Tex MD Anderson Cancer Ctr Box 42 1515 Holcombe Blvd Houston TX 77030

DRIVER, LOTTIE ELIZABETH, librarian; b. Newport News, Va., Dec. 6, 1918; d. James W. and Lottie (Williams) D. Student, Averett Coll., 1936-37; B.S., Mary Washington Coll. of U. Va., 1939; A.B.L.S., Coll. William and Mary, 1944. Band instr. Hampton (Va.) Sch. System, 1939-41; asst. librarian Newport News Pub. Library, 1941-47, librarian, 1947-69; asst. dir. Newport News Pub. Library System, 1969, dir., 1977-81; author book rev. column in Daily Press; library news reporter radio sta. WGH, 1959. Author articles for library supply house. Active United Fund. Recipient Community Service certificate Kiwanis Clubs Newport News, 1970; named Outstanding City Employee, 1970. Mem. ALA, Southeastern, Va. library assns., AAUW, P.E.O., DAR, Phi Theta Kappa, Alpha Phi Sigma. Baptist.

DRIVER, MARTHA WESTCOTT, English language educator, writer, researcher; b. N.Y.C., Oct. 24; d. Albert Westcott and Martha Louise (Miller) D. BA, Vassar Coll., 1974; MA, U. Pa., 1975, PhD, 1980. Lectr. English Vassar Coll., N.Y.C., 1980-81; from asst. prof. to assoc. prof. Pace U., N.Y.C., 1981-95, prof. English, 1995—, dir. honors program, 1998—; cons. N.Y. Pub. Libr., 1984; seminar participant Folger Inst., Folger Shakespeare Libr., 1994. Editor: Jour. of The Early Book Society, 1998; guest editor: Film & History: The Middle Ages, 1998; contbr. articles to profl. jours. Vestry mem. Ch. of the Incarnation, N.Y.C., 1995-99; mem., lectr. St. John the Divine, N.Y.C., 1995. Rsch. tools grantee NEH, 1995, travel grantee Am. Coun. Learned Socs., 1995; fellow Houghton Libr. Harvard U., 1996-97. Mem. Early Book Soc. (chair 1988—), Coll. Art Assn., Medieval Acad. Am., Modern Humanities Rsch. Assn. (U.K.), Medieval Club of N.Y. (conf. coord. 1989-94. pres. 1987-89), Internat. Ctr. Medieval Art, Internat. Arthurian Soc., Medieval Feminist Art History Project, New Chaucer Soc. Episcopalian. Avocations: dancing, museums, theater, concerts. Office: Pace U English Dept 41 Park Row New York NY 10038-1508

DRIVER, MINNIE, actress; b. London, England, United Kingdom, Jan. 31, 1971. Actress (films) Circle of Friends, 1995, GoldenEye, 1995, Baggage, 1996, Sleepers, 1996, Big Night, 1996, Grosse Pointe Blank, 1997, Mononoke Hime, 1997, Good Will Hunting, 1997, The Governess, 1998, At Sachem Farm, 1998, Hard Rain, 1998, Slow Burn, 1999, An Ideal Husband, 1999, Tarzan, 1999, South Park: Bigger, Longer and Uncut, 1999; TV appearances include God on the Rocks, 1990, That Sunday, 1994, Cruel Train, 1995, (TV mini-series) Mr. Wroe's Virgins, 1993, The Politician's Wife, 1995; prodr. At Sachem Farm, 1998; TV guest appearances include Lovejoy, 1986, Casualty, 1986, Murder Most Horrid, 1991, Peak Practice, 1993, The Day Today, 1994, Knowing Me, Knowing You with Alan Partridge, 1994. Fax: 310-205-0879. Office: care Wolf Kasteler 132 S Rodeo Dr Ste 300 Beverly Hills CA 90212*

DRIVER, SHARON HUMPHREYS, marketing executive; b. Staten Island, N.Y., Jan. 5, 1949; d. William Edward and Gloria (McCrave) Humphreys; m. William Weston Driver, Jr., June 3, 1972; children: Christopher John, Andrea Nicole. BA, Manhattanville Coll., Purchase, N.Y., 1970; MA, Coll. New Rochelle, N.Y., 1973. Lic. tchr., N.Y. Tchr. Somers (N.Y.) Ctrl. Sch. Dist., 1970-76, Ossining (N.Y.) Village Recreation Dept., 1983-87; media coord./bookkeeper Equation Comm., White Plains, N.Y., 1986-89; media dir. Sims Freeman O'Brien, Elmsford, N.Y., 1989-90; project dir. Rsch. Advantage, Hawthorne, N.Y., 1990-92; asst. v.p. Merson/Greener Assocs., Tarrytown, N.Y., 1992-94; pres. Decision Drivers, Briarcliff, 1994—. Sec. tng. liason, Jr. League, Westchester-on-Hudson, 1982-88; sustainer, trainer-facilitator, Jr. League, Tarrytown, 1988-96; past pres. St. Theresa's Parish Coun., Briarcliff Manor, N.Y.; sec. bd. dirs. Ossining Open Door Health Clinic, 1985-89. Mem. NAFE, Am. Mktg. Assn., Women in Comm., Qualitative Rsch. Cons. Assn., Sleepy Hollow Toastmasters (charter, sec. exec. com.), Ad Club of Westchester. Roman Catholic. Avocations: boating, hiking. Home: 197 Macy Rd Briarcliff Manor NY 10510-1017

DRIVER, TOM FAW, theologian, writer, justice/peace advocate; b. Johnson City, Tenn., May 31, 1925; s. Leslie Rowles and Sarah (Broyles) D.; m. Anne L. Barstow, June 7, 1952; children: Katharine Anne, Paul Barstow, Susannah Ambrose. A.B., Duke U., 1950; M.Div., Union Theol. Sem., 1953; Ph.D., Columbia U., 1957; D.Litt., Denison U., 1970. Ordained to ministry United Meth. Ch., 1951. Dir. youth work Riverside Ch., N.Y.C., 1955-56; faculty Union Theol. Sem., N.Y.C., 1956-93; Paul J. Tillich prof. theology and culture Union Theol. Sem., 1973-93, emeritus, 1993—; drama critic Christian Century, 1956-62, Sta. WBAI-FM, 1960-61, The Reporter, 1963-64; vis. assoc. prof. English Columbia U., 1964-65; vis. assoc. prof. religion Barnard Coll., 1965-66, Fordham U., 1967; cons. humanities and arts Coll. Old Westbury (N.Y.), 1970; William Evans vis. prof. religion U. Otago, N.Z., 1976; vis. prof. religion Vassar Coll., 1978, Montclair State Coll., 1981; vis. prof. English lit. Doshisha U., Kyoto, Japan, 1983. Author: libretto for oratorio The Invisible Fire, 1957; The Sense of History in Greek and Shakespearean Drama, 1960, Jean Genet, 1966, Romantic Quest and Modern Query: A History of The Modern Theater, 1970, Patterns of Grace: Human Experience as Word of God, 1977, Christ in a Changing World: Toward an Ethical Christology, 1981, The Magic of Ritual: Our Need for Liberating Rites that Transform Our Lives and Our Communities, 1991, Liberating Rites: Understanding the Transformative Power of Ritual, 1997; editor: (with Robert Pack) Poems of Doubt and Belief, 1964; also articles. Bd. dirs. dept. worship and arts Nat. Council Chs., 1958- 63, Found. for Arts, Religion and Culture, 1963-67. Served with AUS, 1943-46. Kent fellow, 1953; Guggenheim fellow, 1962-63. Mem. ACLU, Am. Acad. Religion, New Haven Theol. Group, Soc. Values in Higher Edn., Dem. Socialists of Am., Witness for Peace, Phi Beta Kappa, Omicron Delta Kappa. Home: 501 W 123rd St Apt 14G New York NY 10027-5010*

DRIVER, WALTER W., JR., lawyer; b. El Paso, Tex., Apr. 10, 1945; s. Walter Williamson and Carolyn Bonds (Mayfield) D.; m. Bettie Townsend Willerson, Dec. 27, 1970; children: Eleanor, Anna, Walter III. AB, Stanford U., 1967; JD, U. Tex., 1970. Bar: Ga. 1970. Ptnr. King & Spalding, Atlanta, 1976—, chmn. policy com., 1992-94, 98—. Gen. counsel, mem. exec. com. Children's Mus. Atlanta, 1990-95, U.S. Golf Assn.; bd. dirs. Ctrl. Atlanta Progress, 1993—; chair Celebration of Life Cancer Soc., 1993. Mem. ABA, State Bar Ga., Ga. State Golf Assn. (gen. coun., exec. com. 1988-97), Atlanta Bar Assn., Piedmont Driving Club, Peachtree Golf Club (bd. dirs.), Pine Valley Golf Club, Seminole Golf Club. Office: King & Spalding 191 Peachtree St SW Atlanta GA 30303-3637

DRIVER, WILLIAM RAYMOND, JR., banker; b. Germantown, Pa., Nov. 1907; s. William R. and Mary (Swift) D.; m. Charlotte I. Noyes, Apr. 9, 1937 (dec. July 1986); children: Sarah J. Midgette, William R. III, Dorothy Q., Mary S., Emily Driver Moore; m. Phoebe W. Barnes, Feb. 21, 1987; stepchildren: Phoebe Caner, J. Lea Iselin, Charles B. Barnes, Cornelia B. Barnes. AB, Harvard, 1929, MBA, 1933; MusD (hon.), New England Conservatory Music, 1981. With Colo. Nat. Bank, 1930-31, Central Hanover Bank & Trust Co., N.Y.C., 1933-34; sec-treas. 2 divs. Am. Pulp & Paper Assn., 1934-36; asst. cashier Bank of Manhattan Co., 1938-43, asst. v.p., 1943-46, v.p., 1946; v.p. Chase Manhattan Bank, 1955-60; ptnr. Brown Bros. Harriman & Co., 1961-96, ltd. ptnr., 1996—. Hon. trustee New Eng. Conservatory Music; life trustee Mus. of Sci.; life trustee corporator Northeastern U. Mem. Harvard Club (N.Y.C. chpt.), The Country Club. Episcopalian. Home: Fox Hill Village 10 Longwood Dr Apt 462 Westwood MA 02090-1146 Office: Brown Bros Harriman & Co 59 Wall St New York NY 10128

DRIZIN, JULIE, news service executive. BA in Comm., U. Pa., 1985. News dir. Pacifica Network News, Washington, 1993-96, bur. chief, 1996-98; producer Democracy Now, 1996-98; prodr. "Justice Talking" Am. Pub. Policy Ctr., Washington, 1999—. Office: Am Pub Policy Ctr Univ of Penn 320 Nat Press Bldg Washington DC 20045*

DRNEVICH, VINCENT PAUL, civil engineering educator; b. Wilkinsburg, Pa., Aug. 6, 1940; s. Louis B. and Mary (Kutcel) D.; m. Roxanne M. Hosier, Aug. 20, 1966; children: Paul, Julie, Jenny, Marisa. BSCE, U. Notre Dame, 1962, MSCE, 1964; PhD, U. Mich., 1967. Registered profl. engr., Ky., Ind. Asst. prof. civil engring. U. Ky., Lexington, 1967-73, assoc. prof., 1973-78, prof., 1978-91; chmn. civil engring., 1980-84; acting dean engring. U. Ky., Lexington, 1989-90; prof., head Sch. Civil Engring. Purdue U., West Lafayette, Ind., 1991—; dir. joint hwy. rsch. project Purdue U., 1991-95; pres. Soil Dynamics, Instruments, Inc., West Lafayette, 1974—. Inventor in field. Fellow ASCE (chmn. dept. heads coun. exec. com. 1996—, vice chmn. com. on edn.-practitioner interface, 1994-98, Norman medal 1973, Huber Rsch. prize 1980), ASTM (exec. com., tech. editor Geotech. Testing Jour. 1985-89, C.A. Hogentogler award 1979, Merit award 1993, Woodland Shockley award 1996); mem. NSPE, Am. Soc. Engring. Edn. (sec./treas. civil engring. divsn. 1995-98), Transp. Rsch. Bd., Earthquake Engring. Rsch. Inst., Ind. Soc. Profl. Engrs. (pres. A.A. Potter chpt.), Chi Epsilon (Harold T. Larson award 1985, James M. Robbins award 1989). Roman Catholic. Avocations: golf, fishing. Office: Purdue U 1284 Civil Engineering West Lafayette IN 47907-1284*

DROBAC, NIKOLA (NICK DROBAC), educator; b. Rochester, Pa., Feb. 11, 1953; s. Stevan Sr. and Madeline Mildred (Resanovich) D. AS, C.C. of Beaver County, 1975; BS, U. Pitts., 1977; MS, U. So. Calif., 1986. Sr. loss control cons. Fireman's Fund Ins. Cos., Fairfax, Va, 1977-87; risk mgmt. coord. Carnegie-Mellon U., Pitts., 1988-89; ins. mgr. Gen. Nutrition, Inc., Pitts., 1989-90; pers. cons. Tricon Tech., Pitts., 1990-92; lectr. bus. dept. C.C. Beaver County, Monaca, Pa., 1992-93; intermittent intake interviewer unemployment compensation Commonwealth Pa. Dept. Labor & Industry Beaver Cty. Job Ctr., 1992-96; instr. C.C. of Allegheny County, 1994-95; tchr. South Garrett County H.S., Oakland, Md., 1995—, head tennis coach, 1997, head golf coach, 1995-96; adj. instr. bus./computer applications Garrett C.C., McHenry, Md., 1996—. Del. Rep. Presdl. Conv., Washtenaw County, Mich., 1980; vol. basketball coach Carnegie-Mellon U., Pitts., 1988-89; vol. football coach and scout Aliquippa (Pa.) H.S., 1991-92; mem. choir St. Elijah Serbian Orthodex. Ch. Mem. Masons (Monaca Ctr.), Am. Serbian Eastern Rite Brothers (3d v.p.), Shriners. Serbian Orthodox. Avocations:

computers, golf, photography, church choir. Home: 1616 Tyler St Aliquippa PA 15001-2036

DROBENA, THOMAS JOHN, minister, educator; b. Chgo., Aug. 23, 1934; s. Thomas and Suzanne (Durec) D.; m. Wilma S. Kucharek, Dec. 27, 1980; children: Thomas Samuel, Joshua Michael. BA, Valparaiso U., 1964; ThB, Concordia Theol. Sem., 1961, MDiv, 1974; MA, Hebrew U., Jerusalem, 1968; PhD, Calif. Grad. Sch. Theology, 1975; STM, Luth. Theol. Sem., 1986; DSc (hon.), London U. Ordained to ministry Evang. Luth. Ch. in Am., 1962. English pastor Redeemer Luth. Ch., Jerusalem, 1967-68; prin. St. Mark's Luth. Ch., Bklyn., 1968-69; pastor Ascension Luth. Ch., Binghamton, N.Y., 1969-78, Holy Emmanuel, Mahoney City, Pa., 1981-86; pastor St. John, St. Clair, Pa., 1981-86, Nanticoke, Pa., 1981-86; co-pastor Holy Trinity Luth. Ch., Torrington, Conn., 1986—; adj. prof. SUNY, Binghamton, 1975-77; chairperson Global Missions, Evang. Luth. Ch. in Am., Chgo., 1985—; v.p., treas. Slavic Heritage Inst., Torrington, 1965—. Co-author: Heritage of the Slavs, 1976; editor The Zion, 1995—, Slovo, 1998—; contbr. articles to profl. jours. Chaplain Civil Air Patrol USAFA, 1964—; bd. dirs. ARC, 1986—; pres. Crimestoppers, 1988—, New Eng. Hist. Soc., 1990—; co-chair internat. rels. com. ELCA-Slovak Zion Synod, 1995. Grantee U.S. State Dept., Jerusalem, 1967-68, U. Ill. Russian and East European Ctr., Urbana, 1980—. Fellow Istituto Slovacco; mem. Am. Assn. for the Advancement of Slavic Studies, Am. Assn. of Tchrs. of Slavic and East European Langs., Czechoslovak Soc. for the Arts and Scis., New Eng. Luth. Hist. Soc. (pres. 1990—, editor Jour. New Eng. Luth. Hist. Soc. 1995—). Office: Slavic Heritage Inst PO Box 1003 Torrington CT 06790-1003

DROBIS, DAVID R., public relations company executive. Formerly pres., COO Ketchum Pub. Rels., N.Y.C., sr. ptnr. and CEO, 1992—; public relations company executive. Formerly pres., chief operating officer Ketchum Pub. Relations, N.Y.C.; sr. ptnr., 1992—. Office: Ketchum Pub Rels Worldwide 292 Madison Ave New York NY 10017-6307*

DROESSLER, EARL GEORGE, geophysicist educator; b. Dubuque, Iowa, Jan. 14, 1920; married; 5 children. AB, Loras College, Dubuque, Iowa, 1942, ScD (hon.), 1958; MS in Meteorology, U.S. Naval Postgraduate Sch, Annapolis, Md., 1944. Meteorologist Office of Naval Rsch., 1956-50, head geophys. br., 1950; exec. sec. coord. com. gen. sci. Office of Asst. Sec. Def. for R&D, 1954-58; program dir. atmospheric sci. NSF, 1958-1966; prof. atmospheric sci. SUNY, Albany, 1966-1971; prof. geoscis. N.C. State U., 1971-79, prof. emeritus geosciences, 1979—; dir. univ. affairs Nat. Oceanic & Atmospheric Adminstrn., 1979-83; asst. sec. natural resources N.C. Dept. Natural Resources & Cmty. Devel., 1983-85; former head atmospheric scis. divsn. NSF; mem. Adv. Com. Weather Control, 1953-57, U.S. Nat. Com. Internat. Geophys. Year, 1955-64, N.C. Commn. Sci. & Tech., 1971-79; bd. govs. Rsch. Triangle Inst., N.C., 1973-79, exec. com., 1975-79. Fellow Am. Geophys. Union (Waldo E. Smith medal 1993), Am. Meteorol. Soc. (pres. 1983, Charles Franklin Brooks medal 1976, Cleveland Abbe award 1992). Home: 1305 Glen Eden Dr Raleigh NC 27612-4750 Office: NC State U Dept Marine and Atmospheric Scis Raleigh NC 27650

DROKE, EDNA FAYE, elementary school educator, retired; b. Sylvester, Tex., Dec. 4, 1932; d. Ira Selle and Faye Emily (Seckinger) Tucker; m. Louis Albert Droke, June 2, 1951; children: Sherman Ray, Lyndon Allen, Lona Faye Droke Cheairs. BEd, Tarleton State U., Stephenville, Tex., 1983. Cert. ESL and 3d-8th lang. arts tchr., Tex. Tchr. ESL in 3d-8th grades Wingate (Tex.) Ind. Sch. Dist., 1983-86; tchr. 2d grade and ESL Collidge (Tex.) Ind. Sch. Dist., 1986-88; tchr. 4th grade and ESL Peaster (Tex.) Ind. Sch. Dist., 1988-89; tchr. Chpt. I in 1st-6th grades, ESL in K-12th grades Ranger (Tex.) Ind. Sch. Dist., 1989-96, tchr. E.S.L. 3d grade, reading recovery tchr., 1996-98, ret., 1998. Mem. ASCD, Kappa Delta Pi, Alpha Chi. Baptist. Avocations: reading, quilting, knitting, playing piano, painting. Home: PO Box 44 Comanche TX 76442-0044

DROLSHAGEN, LEO FRANCIS, III, radiologist, physician; b. Detroit, June 9, 1956; s. Leo Francis Jr. and Janet Marie (Phillppart) D.; m. Barbara Sharon Ritchie, June 29, 1979; children: Leo VI, Colin, Eric, Helena. BA English magna cum laude, U. Detroit, 1977; MD, Wayne State U., 1981; postgrad., Armed Forces Inst. of Pathology, Washington, 1985. Diplomate Am. Bd. Radiology, Nat. Bd. Med. Examiners; lic. Tenn., Mich., Ark. Resident in radiology Henry Ford Hosp., Detroit, 1981-85; fellow Vanderbilt U. Hosp. Sch. of Medicine, Nashville, Tenn., 1985-86; radiologist Radiologist P.A., Ft Smith, Ark., 1986—; med. dir., magnectic resonance imaging St. Edward Mercy Med. Ctr., Ft Smith, 1986-90; chief, dept. radiology St. Edward Mercy Med. Ctr., 1988-91, vice chief of med. staff elect, 1991-92; v.p. Radiologist P.A., Ft. Smith, 1991-97, pres., 1997—; chief of staff St. Edward Mercy Med. Ctr., 1992—; clinical asst. prof. of Magnetic Resonance Imaging U. Ark., St. Edward Mercy Med. Ctr. Author: (with others) Magnetic Resonance Imaging of the Normal and Abnormal Female Pelvis, 1986, The Pelvis, 1986, Critical Diagnostic Pathways in Radiology, 1987; contbr. articles to profl. jours. Recipient Tchr. of the Year in Sonography award Vanderbilt U. Med. Ctr., 1985-86, Howard Walsh Meml. award U. Detroit, 1977. Mem. AMA, Am. Coll. Radiology, Radiologic Soc. N.Am., Am. Inst. Ultrasound in Medicine, Am. Coll. Radiology, Soc. Magnetic Resonance Imaging in Medicine, Sebastian County Med. Soc., Mensa, Ft. Smith C. of C., Ducks Unlimited, Bonsai Club. Avocations: volleyball, racquetball, piano, swimming. Home: 8223 Cleburne Ct Fort Smith AR 72903-4362 Office: Radiologist PA PO Box 3887 1501 S Waldron Rd Ste 109 Fort Smith AR 72903-2568 also: St Edward Mercy Med Hosp Dept Radiology Fort Smith AR 72903

DROMISKY, STAN, Canadian government official; b. Thunder Bay, Can.. PhD, U. Fla. Mem. Parliament, Ottawa, Ont., Can., 1993—. Office: Ho of Commons, Rm 423 W Block, Ottawa, ON Canada K1A 0A6*

DRONEBURG, NANCY MARIE, geriatrics nurse; b. Frederick, Md., Jan. 29, 1953; d. John G. and Marie K. (Stone) D. AA, St. Phillip's Coll., San Antonio, 1979; BSN, U. Tex., San Antonio, 1983. RN, Tex.; cert. geriatrics, med./surg. Staff nurse Audie L. Murphy VA Hosp., San Antonio, 1983—. With U.S. Army, 1972-79. Home: 513 Mesquite St Converse TX 78109-1313

DRONET, VIRGIE MAE, educational technology educator; b. Kaplan, La., Mar. 17, 1941; d. Percy Joseph and Zula Mae (Harrington) D.; B.S., U. Southwestern La., 1963, M.Ed., 1970; Ed.S., McNeese State U., 1976; Ed.D., E. Tex. State U., 1979. Tchr. sci.-math., Lake Arthur, La., 1962-89; asst. instr. Center Ednl. Media and Tech., E. Tex. State U., 1977-78; with photog. prodn. lab., 1977-78; ; tchr. physics, chemistry, biology, lgebra, computer scis. Lake Arthur High Sch. 1962-88; prof. McNeese State U., 1998—; vis. lectr. McNeese State U., 1982-88; mem. Internat. Scholarship Com., 1980-82; chmn. Internat. Rsch. Com., 1982-84; chmn. Internat. Nom. Com., 1992; mem. Internat. Leadership Devel. Com., 1992-94, Internat. Constitution com., 1996-98. Delta Kappa Gamma scholar, 1973, 77; NSF grantee, 1967; La. grantee, 1990, 96. Mem. NEA, Assn. Ednl. Communications and Tech., Nat. Council Tchrs. Math., Assn. Supervision and Curriculum Devel., La. Assn. Educators, La. Assn. Ednl. Communications and Tech., La. Assn. Supervision and Curriculum Devel., Jefferson Davis Assn. Educators, Catholic Daus. Am., Delta Kappa Gamma (participant leadership seminar Baylor U. 1982), Phi Delta Kappa, Kappa Delta Pi, Kappa Mu Epsilon, Alpha Omega, Delta Kappa Gamma (state pres. 1989-91). Democrat. Author articles in field; editor La. Deltion, 1981-87. Home: PO Box 674 Lake Arthur LA 70549-0674 Office: McNeese State U Coll Edn PO Box 91815 Lake Charles LA 70609-1815

DRONEY, CHRISTOPHER F., judge; b. June 22, 1954; m. Elizabeth Kelly, Oct. 13, 1979; children: Sarah Elizabeth, Emily Christine, Katherine Fitzgerald. BA, Coll. Holy Cross, 1976; JD, U. Conn., 1979. Ptnr. Reid & Riege, P.C., Hartford, Conn., 1983-93; U.S. atty. for dist. of Conn. U.S. Dept. Justice, New Haven, 1993-97; judge U.S. Dist. Ct., Conn., 1997—. Notes and comments editor Conn. Law Rev., 1978-79. mem. U.S. atty. gen. adv. com., 1996-97. Office: 450 Main St Hartford CT 06103-3022

DROOYAN, JOHN NEAL, visual artist, photographer, fine artist; b. Glendale, Ariz., Sept. 29, 1952; s. Irving and Gertrude (Sommers) D. BS in Biology, Stanford U., 1974; MFA in Photography, San Francisco Art Inst., 1988. Photographer, asst. editor Dellen Pub. Co., San Francisco, 1978-84; freelance photographer San Francisco and L.A., 1984—; photographer Unifed Photog. Industries, Galion, Ohio, 1996—, Event Photography Internat., Miami, Fla., 1996—; tchr. color photography A.S.U.C. Studio, U. Calif., Berkeley, 1982-86, San Francisco Art Inst., 1987-90. Solo exhbns. include Union Gallery/U. Calif., Davis, San Jose State U. Union Gallery, San Francisco Mus. Modern Rental Gallery, Sierra Arts Found., Reno, Nev., Brand Art Gallery, Glendale, Calif.; exhibited in grop shows at Spectrum Gallery, San Francisco, Ventura Coll. New Media Gallery, Downey Mus. Art, numerous others. Recipient Gold award for mixed-media art Art of Calif. Mag., 1992. Mem. L.A. Ctr. for Exhbns., Santa Monica Mus. Art, Richmond Art Ctr., Mus. Contemporary Art, L.A. Artcore.

DROPKIN, ALLEN HODES, lawyer; b. Chgo., Oct. 26, 1930; s. Nathan I. and Zelda (Hodes) D.; m. Corrine S. Rose, Aug. 22, 1954; children: Ruth, David, Zachary, Noah. AB, U. Chgo., 1948, JD, 1951. Bar: Ill. 1951, D.C. 1956. Assoc. Arvey, Hodes & Mantynband, Chgo., 1951-54, 57-61; asst. states atty. Cook County, Ill., 1954-56; spl. counsel subcom. on housing, banking/currency com. U.S. Ho. of Reps., Washington, 1956; ptnr. Arvey, Hodes, Costello & Burman, Chgo., 1961-91, Fishman & Merrick PC, Chgo., 1992-98; pvt. practice Chgo., 1998—. Pres. Bd. Jewish Edn., Chgo., 1975-78, Midwest Region United Synagogue Am., 1981-84; dir. Jewish Cmty. Ctrs., Chgo., 1972-76. Avocation: community svc. Home: 1340 N Astor St Chicago IL 60610-2171 Office: 100 N La Salle St Ste 1710 Chicago IL 60602-2407

DROPKIN, MARY JO, nursing researcher, educator; b. Newark, Apr. 9, 1948; d. John Kirwan and Janet Rose Harris; m. Lloyd R. Dropkin, Dec. 2, 1972. BSN, Cornell U., 1971; MSN, U. Nebr., Omaha, 1978; PhD, NYU, 1995. RN, N.Y. Nursing rsch. assoc., staff nurse Meml. Sloan Kettering Cancer Ctr., N.Y.C., nurse clinician; asst. prof. Coll. Nursing Rutgers U., Newark. Contrb. articles to profl. jours. Mem. ANA, Oncology Nursing Soc., Soc. Otorhinolaryngology and Head and Neck Nurses. Home: 81 Irving Pl Apt 10D New York NY 10003-2215

DROUGHT, JAMES HENRY, healthcare business owner, exercise physiologist; b. Aurora, Ill., Mar. 29, 1957; s. James William and Lorna Beryl (Carlson) D. Student, U.S. Mil. Acad., 1975-77; BS in Phys. Edn., Rutgers U., 1980; MS in Clin. Exercise Physiology, Northeastern U., 1995. Comm. coord. Lake Placid (N.Y.) Olympic Organizing Com., 1980-81; dir. Rainmaker Prodns., Boston, 1982-85; health promotion mgr. City of Boston, 1986-87; owner Personal Trainers Strength & Conditioning Consulting, Boston, 1987—; cons. City of Boston, 1988-89, State of Mass., Boston, 1988-89, Lotus Devel. Corp., Cambridge, Mass., 1990-91; mem. (C.O.R.P.S.) nat. bd. Reebok Internat., Ltd., Stoughton, Mass., 1992-96; articles cons. SHAPE mag., 1995—. Exec. editor Conditioning Instr., 1991-93; contbr. articles to profl. jours.; author Ask the Experts Column, Boston Globe, 1990-92. Exec. com. Boston vs. Montreal Fitness Challenge, City of Boston, 1989. Mem. Am. Coll. Sports Medicine, Am. Coun. on Exercise, Nat. Strength and Conditioning Assn. (Mass. state dir. 1992-98, nat. bd. dirs. 1998—, task analysis com. 1992—, nat. conf. com. 1993-95, chmn. personal trainer com. 1991, exam devel. com., 1994—, exec. coun., state dirs. com. 1997—, Challenge Scholarship 1993, State Dir.'s award 1995, Agy. Appreciation award 1995, exec. coun. state dir.'s com. 1997—). Avocations: screenwriting, playwriting, weight training, Boston Marathon running. Home and Office: Kenmore Station PO Box 15601 Boston MA 02215-0011

DROUILHET, PAUL RAYMOND, JR., science laboratory director, electrical engineer; b. San Pedro, Calif., Mar. 11, 1933; s. Paul R. and Elizabeth (Moffatt) D.; m. Betty Bratton; children: Ann, Stephen, Susan. BS, MS in Elec. Engring., MIT, 1955, EE, 1957. Various positions MIT Lincoln Lab., Lexington, 1959-81, div. head, 1981-85, asst. dir., 1985-93; fed. aviation adminstr. Chi Sci. for GPS/CNS, 1994-95, spl. asst. to dir. aviation rsch., 1996; cons. to dir. MIT Lincoln Lab., 1997—. Contbr. articles to profl. jours.; patentee in field. 1st lt. USAF, 1957-59. Fellow IEEE. Avocations: tennis, sailing, travel. Office: MIT Lincoln Lab 244 Wood St Lexington MA 02421-6426

DROUKAS, ANN HANTIS, management executive; b. Boston, Aug. 27, 1923; d. Charles George and Paula (Kanaris) Hantis; m. Peter Droukas Jr., Sept. 28, 1941; children: P. Ronald, Paulette D., Roger C. Grad. high sch., Roxbury, Mass. With Droukas Cut Sole, Inc., Brockton, Mass., 1947—, pres., treas., 1985—; with DBA Drew Leather, Brockton, 1985-89; pres., treas. DBA Campello Tanning, Brockton, 1985-98; mgr. quality control Cape Cod Needleworkers, Brockton, Maine, 1998—. Contbr. to translater textbooks from Spanish and Greek to English. Mem. adv. bd. Lincoln Trust; past adult participant Boy Scouts Am., Girl Scouts U.S.; active Two-Ten Nat. Found., Brockton Art Mus. 1st woman in U.S. to own and operate a cowhide tannery. Mem. Nat. Fedn. Ind. Bus., Assn. Industries Mass., Greek Ladies Philophotos Soc. (past. treas.), Brockton Hist. Soc., Nat. Trust for Historic Preservation, U.S. C. of C., New England Tanners Club, Shoe and Leather Club Cin., Rainbow Mothers Club, Order Ea. Star, Ten Times One Club (past pres.). Avocations: traveling, yachting, writing, reading, automobile collector.

DROULLARD, STEVEN MAURICE, jewelry company executive; b. Pampa, Tex., June 28, 1951; s. Maurice Erskin and Betty (Bonnett) D.; m. Alessia Passalacqua, Dec. 31, 1978. Grad. gemology, Gemological Inst Am., Santa Monica, Calif., 1985. Lic. broadcaster, 1972; lic. securities dealer. Asst. to pres. Standard Coal Co., San Francisco, 1976-78; pres. Adamas Gem Services, Kailua-kona, Hawaii, 1978-82; v.p. Intergem, Inc., Denver, 1982-85, pres., 1985-87, also bd. dirs.; pres., chmn. bd. GMA Inc., 1988—; pres. Steven Maurice Internat. Jewelry, 1993—; broker, mem. exec. rsch. com. Joseph Charles & Assocs., Inc., 1995-99; sr. investment adv. Schneider Securities, Inc., 1999—; cons. Wells Comms., Denver, 1984—, William Randolph Hearst II, 1997—; strategic planning cons. White & Case, 1997—; mem. bd. advisors Colo. Computing Mag., Boulder, 1985—; chmn. Exec. Jewelry Buyers Club, 1988—. Contbr. articles to mags.; also cons. The Great American Sapphire, 1985. Named Bus. Assoc. of Yr. Am. Bus. Women Assoc., 1981. Mem. Gemological Inst. Am. Alumni Assn. (charter, pres. Colo. chpt. 1987—), Accredited Gemologists Assn., Am. Gem Trade Assn., Gem Mcht. Assocs. (pres. 1986), Kailua-Kona C. of C. (v.p. 1981), Cherry Creek C. of C. (bd. dir. 1995-97), Y2K preparedness dir., Nipomo, Calif. Avocations: gem faceting, mineral collecting, hiking, skiing. E-mail: SmauriceD@aol.com.

DROVDLIC, FRED G., community planner; b. Salem, Ohio, Mar. 21, 1969; s. George James and Marjorie Ann (Marks) D.; m. Jody Ann Drovdlic. M of Urban and Regional Planning, U. Pitts., 1996. Grad. asst. U. Pitts., 1994-96; cmty. planner Richard C. Sutter & Assocs., Hollidaysburg and Pitts., 1996—. Author Huntingdon County Comprehensive Plan, 1997, Millcreek Twp. Comprehensive Plan, 1997, Rice's Landing Comprehensive Plan, 1997, Apollo Borough Comprehensive Plan, 1997, Kiskiminentas Twp., 1998-99, Meyersdale Borough, 1998-99, Crawford County Comprehensive Plan, 1998-99, Centerville Region Comprehensive Plan, 1998-99, Donegal Region Comprehensive Plan, 1998-99, Dale Borough Comprehensive Plan, 1998-99, Armstrong County Regional Plan, 1998-99. Mem. AICPA, Am. Planning Assn., Pa. Planning Assn., Pitt Alumni Assn. Democrat. Lutheran. Avocations: golf, racquetball, skiing, computer design and repair. Fax: (724) 457-2863. E-mail: rcspgh@nb.net. Home: 115 Bon Highland Dr Moon Township PA 15108 Office: Richard C Sutter & Assocs PO Box 12303 Pittsburgh PA 15223

DROWN, EUGENE ARDENT, federal agency administrator; b. Ellenburg, N.Y., Apr. 25, 1915; s. Frank Arthur and Jessie Kate D.; BS, Utah State U., 1938; postgrad. Mont. State U., 1939-40; PhD in Pub. Adminstrn., U. Beverly Hills, 1979; m. Florence Marian Munroe, Mar. 5, 1938; children: Linda Harriett Oneto, Margaret Ruth Lunn. Park ranger Nat. Park Svc., Yosemite Nat. Park, 1940-47; forest ranger U.S. Forest Svc., Calif. Region, 1948-56; forest mgr. and devel. specialist U.S. Bur. Land Mgmt., Calif., 1956—; forest engring. cons., 1970—; R&D coord. U.S. Army at U. Calif., Davis., 1961-65. Mem. adv. bd. Sierra Coll., Rocklin, Calif., 1962—; active Boy Scouts Am.; instr. ARC, 1954—. With AUS, 1941-45. Decorated Bronze Star, Silver Star; registered profl. engr., profl. land surveyor, profl. forester, Calif. Recipient Nat. Svc. medal ARC, 1964. Mem. Nat. Soc. Profl. Engrs., Soc. Am. Foresters, Am. Inst. Biol. Scientists, Ecol. Soc. Am., Res. Officers Assn. U.S., NRA, Internat. Rescue and First Aid Assn., Internat. Platform Assn., Bulldog Sentinels of Superior Calif., Masons, Shriners. Methodist. Home: 5624 Bonniemae Way Sacramento CA 95824-1402

DROWOTA, FRANK F., III, state supreme court justice; b. Williamsburg, Ky., July 7, 1938; married; 2 children. B.A., Vanderbilt U., 1960, J.D., 1965. Bar: Tenn. 1965, U.S. Dist. Ct. Tenn. 1965. Sole practice, 1965-70; chancellor Tenn. Chancery Ct. Div. 7, 1970-74; judge Tenn. Ct. Appeals, Middle Tenn. Div., 1974-80; assoc. justice Tenn. Supreme Ct., Nashville, 1980-89, chief justice, 1989-93, assoc. justice, 1993—. Served with USN, 1960-62. Office: Tenn Supreme Ct 318 Supreme Ct Bldg 401 7th Ave N Nashville TN 37219-1406*

DROZD, LEON FRANK, JR., lawyer; b. Victoria, Tex., Sept. 11, 1948; s. Leon Frank and Dorothy Lucille (Smith) D.; BBA, Tex. A&M U., 1971; J.D., U. Denver, 1979. Bar: Colo., Calif., U.S. Dist. Ct. Colo. U.S. Dist. Ct. (no. dist.) Calif., U.S. Ct. Appeals (9th and 10th cirs.). Legis. asst. U.S. Ho. of Reps., also Dem. Caucus, Washington, 1971-74, chief clk. com. on sci. and tech., 1974-75; asst. to dean for devel. Coll. Law, U. Denver, 1975-79; v.p. Braddock Publs., Inc., Washington, 1975-79; land and legal counsel Chevron Shale Oil Co., Chevron Resources Co., 1980-87, ins. div., 1987-88; sr. counsel Chevron Corp. Law Dept. 1987—, Chevron Overseas Petroleum and White Nile Petroleum Co. Ltd. (Sudan), 1983, Colo. elector Anderson/Lucey Nat. Unity Campaign, 1980. Mem. ABA, Colo. Bar. Assn., San Francisco Bar Assn., Fed. Bar Assn., Am. Trial Lawyers Assn., Denver C. of C. (steering com. 1981-82). Office: Chevron Corp Law Dept PO Box 7141 555 Market St San Francisco CA 94105-2870

DROZDECK, STEVEN RICHARD, management consultant; b. N.Y.C., Apr. 23, 1951; s. Frank S. and Jane (Dzingelewski) D.Student, Poly. Inst. Bklyn., 1969-70; BS cum laude in Fin., N.Y. Inst. Tech., 1973. Cert. master practitioner, 1985, trainer of neuro linguistic programming, 1987. Pres., Unltd. Leadership Potential, S.I., N.Y., 1973-74; account exec. Merrill Lynch, Pierce, Fenner & Smith, Bklyn., 1974-78, S.I., 1978-80, sr. sales trainer, N.Y.C., 1980—, adminstrv. mgr. tng. sch., 1983—, asst. v.p., 1984—; affiliate Ea. Neuro Linguistic Programming Inst., 1984—, market and sales cons., 1986, mgr. of fin. cons. profl. devel., 1987, mem. devel. team The Art of Friendly Persuasion, 1984-89; affiliate Comm. Tech., 1989—; affiliate of Lingues-Tech., 1990—; founder, pres. Tng. Groups, Inc., 1990-91, exec. v.p. Fin. Forum, mng.dir. Drozdeck & Gretz Assocs.; pres. SD Mktg. Groups; co-dir. Drozdeck & Gretz Assocs., 1997. Co-author: Empowering Innovative People, 1991, Consultative Selling Techniques for Financial Professionals, 1990, The Effective Manager, 1991, What They Don't Teach You in Sales 101, 1991, The Broker's Edge, 1994, Professional Selling: A Consultative Approach, 1995, Managing Your Business for Success, 1998, The Money Managers Universe, 1998. Mem. Internat. Assn. Fin. Planners, Nat. Soc. Registered Reps. (charter), N.Y. Stockbrokers Club, N.Y. Stock Exch. Qualifications Com. for Gen. Securities Exam., Nat. Assn. Securities Dealers Qualifications Com. Home and office: 494 River Heights Blvd Logan UT 84321-5664

DROZDIS, LORI, medical/surgical nurse; b. Peckville, Pa., Mar. 17, 1967; d. Charles J. and Jean Marie (Zorechak) Vagnarelli. BS, Wilkes U., Wilkes-Barre, Pa., 1989. RN, Pa.; cert. med.-surg. nurse. Charge nurse mgr. Mercy Hosp., Scranton, Pa. Home: 6 River St Archbald PA 18403-2310

DROZDZIEL, MARION JOHN, aeronautical engineer; b. Dunkirk, N.Y., Dec. 21, 1924; s. Steven and Veronica (Wilk) D.; m. Rita L. Korwek, Aug. 30, 1952; 1 child, Eric A. BS in Aero. Engring., Tri State U., 1947, BSME, 1948; postgrad., Ohio State U., 1948, Niagara U., 1949-51, U. Buffalo, 1951-52. Stress analyst Curtiss Wright Corp., Columbus, Ohio, 1948; project engr. weight analysis Bell Aerospace Textron, Buffalo, 1949-52, stress analyst, 1952-60, asst. supr. stress analysis, 1960-64, chief stress analysis propulsion, 1964-79, chief engr. stress and weights, 1979-84, staff scientist, 1984-85, cons. structures and fractures mechanics, 1985—; mem. Am. Aerospace Materials Del. to USSR, 1989, Am. Aerospace Industries Del. to People's Republic China, 1991, Am. Aerospace Materials Del. to Czechoslovakia and Commonwealth Ind. States, 1992. Del. Internat. Citizens Ambassador Prog.; active Buffalo Fine Arts Acad., N.Y. Acad. Scis., Disabled Am. Vets. With U.S. Army, 1944-47. Recipient cert. of achievement NASA-Apollo, 1972; cert. commendation U.K. NATO program, 1982. Mem. AAAS, AIAA (Mem. Chmn.'s award 1998-90, 92-93), Soc. Reliability Engrs. (bd. dirs. 1998), U.S. Naval Inst., Am. Space Found., Nat. Conservancy, Nat. Audubon Soc., Am. Acad. Polit. and Social Sci., Acad. Polit. Sci., Union Concerned Scientists, Air Force Assn., Nat. Space Soc., Soc. Allied Weight Engrs., Planetary Soc., Am. Mgmt. Assn., Bibl. Archeology Soc., Archeol. Inst. Am., Cousteau Soc., Smithsonian Assocs., Buffalo Audubon Soc., Bell Mgmt. Club, Natural History Mus., Internat. Hypersonic Rsch., Disabled Am. Vets, Kosciuszko Found., Exch. Club of Tonawandas (sec. 1996-98, bd. dirs.), Nat. Exch. Club. Republican. Roman Catholic. Achievements include development of criteria and methods of structural analysis extending analyses into the plastic and creep ranges for titanium and columbium rocket nozzle extensions; of criteria and methods of structural analysis for extendable rocket nozzle extensions, including rapid nozzle deployment involving plasticity; of methods of structural analysis for low strength, high ductility steels, aluminums, and teflons as positive expulsion devices for zero gravity application in propellant tanks including bellows, reversing heads, rolling diaphragms devices and collapsing or folding concepts; structural analysis on "X" series of aircraft, on Mercury, Gemini, and Apollo spacecraft reaction control and propulsion systems; structural and weight analysis of programs involving rocket engines, propulsion systems, aircraft, air cushion vehicles, surface-effect ships, laser systems avionics, airborne and ground antennae, Army tanks and fighting vehicles. Home and Office: 152 Linwood Ave Tonawanda NY 14150-4020

DRUCK, KALMAN BRESCHEL, public relations counselor; b. Scranton, Pa., Dec. 6, 1914; s. Jacob L. and Mabelle (Breschel) D.; m. Pearl Spiro, Nov. 26, 1936; children: Ellen Druck Mirtz, Nancy Druck Brassem. B.S. in Journalism, magna cum laude, Syracuse U., 1936. With Hearst Enterprises, 1936-39, Carl Byoir & Assos., 1939-59; pres., vice chmn. Harshe-Rotman & Druck, Inc., N.Y.C., 1960-81; prin. Kalman B. Druck, Inc., 1981—; supr. courses pub. rels. Baruch Sch. Bus., CCNY, 1939-55; mem. adv. com. schs. communications Syracuse U., Boston U.; adj. prof. Grad. Sch. Communication, Fairfield (Conn.) U., 1987-88. Pub. Public Relations Career Guide, Impact of High Technology on Public Relations. Bd. dirs. Union Am. Hebrew Congregations, 1956-71, N.Y. Fedn. Jewish Philanthropies, 1957-72, Am. Jewish Com., 1979-87; hon. bd. dirs. Palm Beach Civic Assn.; v.p. Palm Beach Com. for Good Govt.; past chmn. civilian pub. affairs adv. com. U.S. Mil. Acad., West Point, N.Y. Recipient Disting. Alumnus Centennial medal Syracuse U., 1970. Mem. Pub. Rels. Soc. Am. (pres. N.Y. chpt. 1953-55, nat. chmn. 1972, chmn. com. on profl. devel. 1979-80, trustee Found. for Pub. Rels. Rsch. and Edn. 1981-86, Gold Anvil award 1966, named Pub. Rels. Profl. of Yr. 1966). Home: 1208 Devonshire Way Palm Beach Gardens FL 33418

DRUCKENMILLER, ROBERT THOMPSON, public relations executive; b. Bethlehem, Pa., Mar. 15, 1942. BA in Econs., Colgate U., 1964; MBA, U. Pa., 1966. Account rep. J. Walter Thompson, N.Y.C., 1966-71; advt. dir. Peace Corps/Action, Washington, 1971-72; media dir. Henry J. Kaufman, Washington, 1972-73; ptnr. Porter/Novelli, N.Y.C., 1973-80, sr. v.p., 1980-86, exec. v.p., gen. mgr. D.C. bd., 1986-92, pres., 1992-97, CEO, 1997—. Office: Porter Novelli 220 E 42d St Fl 5 New York NY 10017-6708

DRUCKER, ALAN STEVEN, mechanical engineer; b. Boston, Apr. 22, 1948; s. Eugene Elias and Corrine Ruth (Mintzer) D.; m. Patricia Ellen Sori, Aug. 10, 1974; children: Aaron, Zachary. BS, Cornell U., 1970. Jr. devel. engr. Carrier, Syracuse, N.Y., 1972-78, sr. devel. engr., 1978-82, program mgr., 1982-85, staff engr., 1985-94, sr. staff engr., 1994—. Inventor, patentee in field. Democrat. Jewish. Avocations: diving, scuba, gardening, tennis. Office: Carrier Corp Carrier Pkwy Syracuse NY 13221

DRUCKER, BARRY JULES, environmental health specialist; b. St. Louis, Dec. 29, 1940; s. Morris Josef and Geraldine Drucker; m. Sandra Leta Lew, June 10, 1968; 1 child, Marlon. BA, So. Ill. U., 1969; MA, Webster U., 1976; MPH, St. Louis U., 1992. Registered sanitarian.; cert. profl. environ.

health specialist. Chemist St. Louis City Health Dept., 1970-76; sr. research technician Washington U. Sch. Medicine, St. Louis, 1976-77; sanitarian Mo. Dept. Mental Health, St. Louis, 1977-79; sanitarian, supr. Mo. Dept. Health, St. Louis, 1979-82; program mgr. St. Louis County Health Dept., Clayton, Mo., 1982—; assoc. dir. Mo. Restaurant Assn., St. Louis, 1982—; mem. Mo. Food Adv. coun., Jefferson City, 1982—, St. Louis County Restaurant com., 1982; vice chmn. Mo. Bd. Certification for Sanitarians, Jefferson City, 1987-89, 90-91, mem., 1986-91; adj. faculty St. Louis U., 1992—; mem. Mo. State Milk Bd., Jefferson City, 1995—; mem. adv. bd. Sch. Pub. Health St. Louis U., 1996—. Peer reviewer Jour. of Environ. Health, 1985—; contbr. articles to profl. jours. With USAF, 1960-64. Mem. Mo. Environ. Health Assn. (pres. 1985-86, publ. awards 1986, 87, 88, 93, Sanitarian of Yr. 1987), St. Louis Area Pub. Health Assn. (pres. 1986-87, mem.-at-large 1992—), Mo. Pub. Health Assn. (bd. dirs. 1986-87, pub. award 1988, 93), Nat. Environ. Health Assn. (bd. dirs. 1984-86, Cert. of Merit 1987, Jour. Editor's award 1994). Avocations: antique advertising. Home: 19250 River Ridge Ln Wildwood MO 63005-3818 Office: St Louis County Health Dept 111 S Meramec Ave Saint Louis MO 63105-1711

DRUCKER, DANIEL CHARLES, engineer, educator; b. N.Y.C., June 3, 1918; s. Moses Abraham and Henrietta (Weinstein) D.; m. Ann Bodin, Aug. 19, 1939; children: R. David, Mady Drucker Upham. BS, Columbia U., 1937, MCE, 1938, PhD, 1940; D Engring. (hon.), Lehigh U., 1976; DSc in Tech. (hon.), Technion, Israel Inst. Tech., 1983; DSc (hon.), Brown U., 1984, Northwestern U., 1985, U. Ill., 1992. Instr. Cornell U., 1940-43; supr. Armour Rsch. Found., Chgo., 1943-45; asst. prof. Ill. Inst. Tech., 1946-47; assoc. prof. Brown U., Providence, 1947-50, prof., 1950-64, L. Herbert Ballou Univ. prof., 1964-68, chmn. div. engring., 1953-59, chmn. phys. scis. coun., 1960-63; dean Coll. Engring. U. Ill., Urbana, 1968-84; grad. rsch. prof. engring. scis. U. Fla., Gainesville, 1984-94, prof. emeritus, 1994—; Marburg lectr. ASTM, 1966; mem., past chmn. U.S. Nat. Com. on Theoretical and Applied Mechanics; past chmn. adv. com. for engring. NSF; mem. Nat. Sci. Bd., 1988-94; hon. chmn. 3d SESA Internat. Congress on Exptl. Mechanics; rsch. in stress-strain rels., finite plasticity, stability, fracture and flow on macroscale and microscale. Author: Introduction to Mechanics of Deformable Solids, 1967; contbr. chpts. to tech. books, papers to mech. and sci. jours. Recipient Gustave Trasenster medal U. Liège, Belgium, 1979, Thomas Egleston medal Columbia U. Sch. Engring and Applied Sci., 1978, John Fritz medal Founder Engring. Socs., 1985, Nat. Medal of Sci., 1988, ASME medal, 1992; Guggenheim fellow, 1960-61; NATO Sr. Sci. fellow, 1968; Fulbright Travel grantee, 1968. Fellow AAAS (past chmn. sect. engring., past mem. coun.), AIAA (assoc.), ASME (hon. mem., chmn. applied mechanics div. 1963-64, v.p. policy bd. communications 1969-71, pres. 1973-74, Timoshenko medal 1983, Thurston lectr. 1986, Disting. lectr. 1987-89, Daniel C. Drucker medal established 1997), ASCE (von Karman medal 1966, past pres. New Eng. coun., past pres. Providence sect., past chmn. exec. com. engring mechanics div.), Am. Acad. Mechanics (past pres.), Am. Acad. Arts and Scis. (past mem. membership com.); mem. NSPE, Ill. Soc. Profl. Engrs. (hon.), Soc. Exptl. Stress Analysis (hon.; past pres., W.M. Murray lectr. 1967, M.M. Frocht award 1971), Am. Technion Soc. (past pres. So. N.E. chpt.), Soc. Rheology, Am. Soc. Engring. Edn. (charter fellow mem., past 1st v.p., past chmn. engring. coll. coun., dir., pres. 1981-82, Lamme award 1967, Disting. Educator, Mechanics div. 1985, named to Hall of Fame 1993), NAE (mem. com. on pub. engring. policy 1972-75, chmn. membership policy com. 1982-85), Soc. Engring. Sci. (William Prager medal 1982), Polish Acad. Scis. (fgn. mem.), Internat. Union Theoretical and Applied Mechanics (treas. 1972-80, pres. 1980-84, v.p. 1984-88, personal mem. Gen. Assembly 1988—), Internat. Coun. Sci. Unions (past mem. gen. com.), Sigma Xi (past pres. Brown U. chpt.), Phi Kappa Phi (past pres. U. Fla. chpt.), Tau Beta Pi, Pi Tau Sigma, Chi Epsilon, Sigma Tau. Office: U Fla 231 Aerospace Engring Bldg Gainesville FL 32611-6250

DRUCKER, JACQUELIN F., lawyer, arbitrator, mediator, educator, author; b. Celina, Ohio, Oct. 15, 1954; d. Jack Burton and Dorothea (Eckenstein) Davis; m. John H. Drucker, Sept. 8, 1990. BA with distinction and honors, Ohio State U., 1977, JD with honors, 1981. Bar: Ohio 1981, N.Y. 1992, U.S. Supreme Ct. 1989. Legis. asst. Speaker of Ohio Ho. of Reps., Columbus, 1974-78; rsch. asst. United Auto Workers, Columbus, 1978-81; labor atty. Porter, Wright, Morris & Arthur, Columbus, 1981-84; gen. counsel Ohio Employment Rels. Bd., Columbus, 1984-86, exec. dir., 1986-88, vice chmn., 1988-90; pvt. practice arbitration and mediation N.Y.C. and Ohio, 1990—; dir. labor mgmt. programs sch. indsl. and labor rels. Cornell U., 1994-97; dir. programs for neutrals Cornell U. Sch. of Indsl. and Labor Rels., 1996—; dep. dir. for ednl. svcs. Cornell/PERC Inst. on Conflict Resolution, 1998—; counsel to Gov.'s Task Force on Collective Bargaining, Columbus, 1983-84; adj. prof. labor law Franklin U., Columbus, 1988-89; mem. panel of arbitrators Fed. Mediation and Conciliation Svc., Am. Arbitration Assn., Employment ADR Roster of Neutrals of Am. Arbitration Assn., N.Y. State Employment Rels. Bd.; mem. roster of neutrals N.Y.C. Office of Collective Bargaining; mem. panel V.I. Pub. Employment Rels. Bd., N.J. Pub. Employment Rels. Commn., N.Y. Pub. Employment Rels. Bd.; mem. permanent arbitration panel United Mine Workers and Bituminous Coal Operators Assn., Am. Postal Workers Union, U.S. Postal Svc., Off-Track Betting Corp. and Local 32E, State of N.Y. and Pub. Employees Fedn., State of N.Y. and Civil Svc. Employees Assn., Consolidated Edison and Utility Workers Local 1-2, U. Cin. and Dist. 925, State of N.Y. and Civil Svc. Employees Assn., State of N.Y. and Pub. Employees Fedn.; cons. labor mgmt. cooperation, 1996—; lectr., spkr. in field. Author: Collective Bargaining Law in Ohio, 1993; editor L.I. Indsl. Rels. Quar.; contbg. editor Pub. Sector Law and Employment Law supplement, 1995, Pub. Sector Labor and Employment Law, 2d edit.; assoc. editor Discipline and Discharge in Arbitration, 1998; contbg. editor: Public Sector Labor and Employment Law, 2nd edit., 1998; contbr. numerous articles to profl. jours. Mem. ABA (labor and employment law sect., dispute resolution sect.), Nat. Acad. Arbitrators, Ohio State Bar Assn., Assn. of Bar of City of N.Y., N.Y. State Bar Assn. (labor and employment law sect. sec.-elect, sec. 1997-98, co-chair ADR in employment com. 1998—), N.Y. County Lawyers Assn. (labor rels. com., co-chair), Nassau County Bar Assn., Suffolk County Bar Assn., Indsl. Rels. Rsch. Assn. (N.Y. chpt., Cleve. chpt., L.I. chpt.), Soc. Fed. Labor Rels. Profls. Jewish. Office: 432 E 58th St # 2 New York NY 10022-2331

DRUCKER, MARK LEWIS, public administration educator, consultant; b. Sept. 30, 1947; s. Harry and Helen Drucker; children: Michael, Hilary. BA, Columbia U., 1969; MBA, Harvard U., 1971. Asst. prof. urban affairs and policy analysis New Sch. for Social Rsch., N.Y.C., 1971-75; exec. dir. Coun. of Univ. Insts. for Urban Affairs, N.Y.C., 1974-75; vis. asst. prof. urban affairs St. Louis U., 1975-76; Pew fellow in health policy Boston U., 1988-90; assoc. prof. pub. adminstrn. and policy analysis So. Ill. U., Edwardsville, 1976—, dir. policy analysis grad. program, 1979-88; cons. East-West Gateway Coordinating Coun., St. Louis, 1998, Springfield (Ill.) Housing Authority, 1995, Urban Inst., Washington, 1995, William M. Mercer, Inc., Chgo., 1991-92. Author: Urban Decisionmaking, 1981; contbr. articles to profl. jours. Pres. Housing Solutions, Inc., St. Louis, 1993-95; chair planning bd. Confluence St. Louis, 1987-88; pres. bd. dirs. Satellite Sch., 1984-85; 1st v.p. Greater St. Louis Health Sys. Agy, 1981-82; mem. Children's Summit, 1998-99; mem. St. Louis 2004 Healthcare Cmty. Action Team, 1996-98. Pew Meml. Trusts fellow, 1988-90; Mortgage Bankers Assn. faculty fellow, 1982-84. Mem. Am. Jewish Congress (v.p. midwest chpt. 1996-99), Mo. Pub. Health Assn. (pres. St. Louis chpt. 1996-97, bd. dirs. 1996-97). Jewish. Avocations: reviewing mysteries, community affairs, film, theater, baseball. Email: mdrucke@siue.edu. Home: 18 S Kingshighway Apt 14R Saint Louis MO 63108 Office: So Ill U Edwardsville Dept Pub Adminstrn Alumni Hall Rm 3128 Edwardsville IL 62026-1457

DRUCKER, MORT, commercial artist; b. Bklyn., Mar. 22, 1929; s. Edward and Sarah (Spielvogel) D.; m. Barbara Hellerman, Aug. 28, 1948; children: Laurie Drucker Bachner, Melanie Drucker Amsterdam. Student public schs.; DFA (hon.), Art Inst. Boston, 1995. Staff artist Nat. Periodicals, N.Y.C., 1948-50; freelance artist, 1951—; contbg. artist Mad mag., 1956—. Covers for Time mag; also nat. advt. agencies, TV commls. and movie posters; author: (with Paul Laikin) JFK Coloring Book, 1961, Mort Drucker's Showstoppers, 1985, (with Laikin) Ollie North Coloring Book, 1987, (David Duncan with Mort Drucker) Familiar Faces: The Art of Mort Drucker, 1988, (with Laikin) Farewell Tribute to Ronald Reagan Coloring Book, 1988, (with Lee J. Ames) Draw Fifty Famous Caricatures, 1990; illustrator: Whitefish Will Rides Again!, 1994, Tomatoes from Mars, 1996; co-author: (with Jerry Dumas) "Benchley" comic strip, 1984-86. Recipient cert. merit Art Dirs. Club N.Y., 1968, San Francisco Soc. Communicating Arts award of excellence, 1973, Cert. Merit Soc. Ill. 1991, Gold award, 1980, Booth Newspaper award of excellence Advertising Club of New York, 1981, Andy award Art Directors Show for Consumer Advertising, 1983, Showtime award Rochester Soc. Communicating Arts, 1983, Internat. Comic award Barcelona, Spain, 1985, Best in Spl. Features award Nat. Cartoonist Soc., 1986, 87, 88, 89, Reuben award outstanding cartoonist of the year, 1987, Best Cartoonist award Nat. Cartoonist Soc., 1988, Merit cert. Soc. Ill., 1991, Ink Pot award, 1996. Mem. Graphic Artists Guild, Soc. Illustrators. Time covers in Nat. Portrait Gallery, Smithsonian Instn. Office: care Mad Mag 1700 Broadway New York NY 10019-5905*

DRUCKER, PETER FERDINAND, writer, consultant, educator; b. Vienna, Austria, Nov. 19, 1909; came to U.S., 1937, naturalized, 1943; s. Adolph Bertram and Caroline D.; m. Doris Schmitz, Jan. 16, 1937; children: Kathleen Romola, J. Vincent, Cecily Anne, Joan Agatha. Grad., Gymnasium, Vienna, 1927; LLD, U. Frankfurt, 1931; 25 hon. doctorates. Economist London Banking House, 1933-37; Am. adviser for Brit. banks, Am. corr. Brit. newspapers, 1937-42; cons. maj. bus. corps. U.S., 1940—; prof. philosophy, politics Bennington Coll., 1942-49; prof. mgmt. NYU, 1950-72, chmn. mgmt. area, 1957-62; Clarke prof. social sci. Claremont Grad. Sch. (Calif.), 1971—; prof. dept. art Pomona Coll., Calif., 1979-85. Author: The End of Economic Man, 1939, new edit. 1993, The Future of Industrial Man, 1941, new edit. 1994, Concept of the Corporation, 1946, new edit., 1993, The New Society, 1950, new edit., 1992, Practice of Management, 1954, new edit., 1992, America's Next Twenty Years, 1957, The Landmarks of Tomorrow, 1959, new edit., 1996, Managing for Results, 1964, new edit., 1996, The Effective Executive, 1966, new edit., 1996, The Age of Discontinuity, 1969, new edit., 1992, Technology; Management and Society, 1970, Men, Ideas and Politics, 1971, Management: Tasks, Responsibilities, Practices, 1974, new edit., 1992, The Unseen Revolution: How Pension Fund Socialism Came to America, 1976, new edit. (new title: The Pension Fund Revolution), 1995, People and Performance, 1977, Management, An Overview, 1978, Adventures of a Bystander, 1979, new. edit., 1998, Managing in Turbulent Times, 1980, new edit., 1992, Toward the Next Economics and Other Essays, 1981, (essays) The Changing World of the Executive, 1982, Innovation and Entrepreneurship, 1985, new edit., 1996, The Frontiers of Management, 1986, 6th edit., 1999, The New Realities, 1989, Managing the Non-Profit Organization, 1990, (essays) Managing for the Future, 1992, (essays) The Ecological Vision, 1992, Post Capitalist Society, 1993, (essays) Managing in a Time of Great Change, 1995, 6th edit., 1999, Drucker on Asia: A Dialogue With Isao Nagauchi, 1997, Peter Drucker on the Profession of Management, 1998, Management Challenges for the 21st Century, 1999; (fiction) The Last of All Possible Worlds, 1982, The Temptation to Do Good, 1984; co-author: The Song of the Brush: Japanese painting, 1979; producer: movie series The Effective Executive, 1969, Managing Discontinuity, 1971, The Manager and the Organization, 1977, Managing for Tomorrow, 1981; producer 25 audiocassette series The Non-Profit Drucker, 1988. Recipient gold medal Internat. U. Social Studies, Rome, 1957; Wallace Clark Internat. Mgmt. medal, 1963; Taylor Key Soc. for Advancement Mgmt., 1967; Presdl. citation NYU, 1969; CIOS Internat. Mgmt. gold medal, 1972; Chancellor's medal Internat. Acad. Mgmt., 1987. Fellow AAAS (council), Internat., Am., Irish Acads. Mgmt., Brit. Inst. Mgmt. (hon.), Am. Acad. Arts and Scis.; mem. Soc. for History Tech. (pres. 1965-66), Nat. Acad. Pub. Adminstrn. (hon.), Peter F. Drucker Found. Non Profit Mgmt. (hon. chmn).

DRUCKER, STEPHEN, magazine editor-in-chief. Grad., Vassar Coll.; postgrad., Columbia U. Contbg. editor and exec. editor Travel & Leisure; features dir. HG Mag.; editor The New York Times "Home" section; creator New York Times "Sunday Styles" sect.; sr. editor Vogue, Self Mag.; editor Martha Stewart Living, N.Y.C., editor-in-chief, 1997—; sr. v.p. Martha Stewart Living Omnimedia, N.Y.C.; Editor-in-Chief Martha Stewart Living, 1998—. Office: Martha Stewart Living 20 W 43rd St Fl D24 New York NY 10036-7400*

DRUCKREY, INGE HEIDE, graphic designer, educator; b. Berlin, Germany, Feb. 6, 1940; came to U.S., 1966; d. Hermann Carl Paul and Annemarie Erna Elisabeth (Eick) D.; m. Edward Rolf Tufte. Diploma in graphic design, Allgemeine Gewerbeschule, Basel, Switzerland, 1965. Designer Studio Halpern, Zurich, 1965-66; design instr. Kansas City (Mo.) Art Inst., 1966-68, Werkkunstschule Krefeld, Germany, 1968-71; asst. prof. Phila. Coll. Art, 1971-73; asst. prof. Yale U., New Haven, Conn., 1973-79, assoc. prof., 1979-82, sr. lectr., 1982-83, vis. prof., 1983-84, sr. design critic, 1984—; design cons. Graphics Press, 1982—; part-time faculty RISD, Providence, 1987-94; adj. prof. U. of the Arts, Phila., 1995—. Exhibited in group shows at Gewerbe Mus., Basel, 1983, Walker Art Ctr., Mpls., 1985, Moore Coll. Art, R.I. Sch. Design, Va. Commonwealth U., 1986, Mus. Modern Art, N.Y.C., 1988, U. Arts, Phila., 1989, Herb Lubalin Study Ctr., Cooper Union, N.Y., 1989, Walker Art Ctr., Mpls., IBM Gallery Sci. and Art, N.Y., Phoenix Art Mus., Butler's Wharf, London, 1989, Rockefeller Arts Ctr. Gallery, SUNY, Fredonia, 1992; works in numerous publs. and mus. exhbn. catalogs. Grantee Ford Found., 1979-80. Avocations: horseback riding, hiking. Office: U of the Arts Graphic Design Dept 333 S Broad St Philadelphia PA 19102

DRUDGE, MATT, journalist; b. 1967. Grad., h.s. Founder, editor The Drudge Report website, 1996—; host TV show Drudge, 1998—. Address: PO Box 1171 Hollywood CA 90028*

DRUEHL, LOUIS DIX, biology educator; b. San Francisco, Oct. 9, 1936; naturalized Can. citizen, 1974; s. Louis Dix and Charlotte (Primrose) D.; m. Jo Ann Reeve, Aug. 17, 1967 (div. 1974); m. Rae Kristanne Randolph, Aug. 11, 1983. BSc, Wash. State U., 1958; MSc, U. Wash., 1962; PhD, U. B.C., Vancouver, B.C., 1966. Rsch. advisor Brazil Navy, Cabo Frio, 1975-77; cons. biomass program GE, Catalina, Calif., 1981-83; from asst. prof. to assoc. prof. Simon Fraser U., Burnaby, B.C., 1966-88, prof. biology, 1988—, dir. Inst. Aquaculture Rsch., 1988-90; assoc. dir. Bamfield (B.C.) Marine Sta., 1992-96; rsch. assoc. Inst. Algae Rsch. U. Hokkaido, 1972-73; pres. Can. Kelp Resources Ltd., Bamfield, 1982—. Mem. editorial bd. European Jour. Phycology, 1993-96; contbr. over 50 articles to profl. jours. Recipient Provasoli best paper award Jour. Phycology, 1988, Luigi Provasoli award, 1990, Phycological Soc. Am. Mem. Western Soc. Naturalists (pres. 1988). Avocation: writing poetry. Home: 4 Port Desire, Bamfield, BC Canada V0R 1B0 Office: Bamfield Marine Sta, Bamfield, BC Canada V0R 1B0

DRUGAN, CORNELIUS BERNARD, school administrator, psychologist, musician; b. Youngstown, Ohio, July 23, 1946; s. Francis Edward and Erminia (Costarella) D.; m. Kathleen Anne Cowhard, Aug. 17, 1968; children: Jonelle Kathryn, Noelle Marie. BS, Heidelberg Coll., 1968; AM, John Carroll U., 1970; PhD, Walden U., 1980. Cert. supt.; lic. psychologist. Tchr. Warrensville City Schs., Warrenville Heights, Ohio, 1968-72; intern psychologist Garfield Heights (Ohio) City Schs., 1972-73; psychologist Belmont (Ohio) County Schs., 1973-80; supr. Union Local Schs., Belmont, 1980-83, pupil personnel dir., 1983-87; adminstr. Streetsboro (Ohio) City Schs., 1987—; tchr. Warrenville Heights Recreation Dept., 1968-72, Southgate Music, Maple Heights, Ohio, 1970-73; instr. Cleve. State U., 1970-72; advisor Belmont County Career Ctr., St. Clairsville, Ohio, 1980-86. Organist St. Peter of the Fields Ch., Rootstown, Ohio, 1989—. First place piano competition Portage Music Tchr. Assn., Ravenna, Ohio, 1964. Mem. Am. Guild Organists, Buckeye Assn. Sch. Adminstrs., Jaycees (Jaycee of Month, St. Clairsville, Ohio chpt. 1975), Ohio Assn. Secondary Sch. Adminstrs., K.C. (council 5173), Phi Delta Kappa. Avocations: part-time profl. musician, guitar and amplifier building/collecting. Home: 3138 Robin Dr Ravenna OH 44266-9548 Office: Streetsboro Mid Sch 1951 Annalane Dr Streetsboro OH 44241-1730

DRULINER, MARCIA MARIE, education educator; b. Dec. 18, 1946. M in Secondary Edn., U. Nebr., 1974; PhD, Marquette U., 1992. Assoc. prof. edn. Concordia Coll., Bronxville, N.Y., 1993-95; asst. prof. edn. Northwestern Coll., Orange City, Iowa, 1998—. Home: 305 Zuider Zee Dr SE Orange City IA 51041

DRULLINGER, LEONA PEARL BLAIR, obstetrics nurse; b. Norton, Kans., Aug. 10, 1962; d. Floyd Allen and Frances Marie (Redfield) Blair; m. Richard Lee Drullinger, Aug. 2, 1981; children: Richard Jr., Charity, Kelsy, Brandon. AD in Practical Nursing, Colby (Kans.) C.C., 1985; ADN, Garden City (Kans.) C.C., 1987. RN; cert. BLS, ACLS, neonatal advanced life support, inpatient obstetrics. LPN, Citizens Med. Ctr., Colby, Kans., 1985-86, Nursing Home, Lakin, Kans., 1986-87; RN labor and delivery staff nurse St. Catherine's Hosp., Garden City, Kans., 1987-88; acting head nurse VA Med. Ctr., Lincoln, Nebr., 1988-90; telemetry nurse Bryan Meml. Hosp., Lincoln, 1990-92; relief staff nurse Nurse Finders, Omaha, 1990-92; contract charge obstetric nurse Hunter Med. Inc., Offutt AFB Hosp., Bellvue, Nebr., 1992-94, Med. Nat. Inc., Offutt AFB Hosp., Bellvue, Nebr., 1994-96; staff nurse Brodstone Meml. Nuckolls County Hosp., Superior, Nebr., 1996-97, Cambridge (Nebr.) Meml. Hosp., 1997-98; staff relife nurse Olston-KQC Staffing, 1996—; dir. nursing svc. Good Samaritan Ctr., Arapahoe, Nebr., 1998—. Republican. Avocations: reading, crocheting, camping, cooking, sewing. Home: 304 Holborn PO Box 43 Danbury NE 69026-0007

DRUM, ALICE, college administrator; b. Gettysburg, Pa., June 22, 1935; d. David Wentz and Charlotte Rebecca (Kinzey) McDannell; m. D. Richard Guise, June 15, 1957 (div. Aug. 1975); children: Gregory, Brent, Richard, Robert, Clay; m. Ray Kenneth Drum, Mar. 2, 1979; 1 child, Trevor. BA magna cum laude, Wilson Coll., 1957; PhD, Am. U., 1976. Adj. prof. gen. studies Antioch U., Columbia, Md., 1976-78; adj. asst. prof. English Gettysburg (Pa.) Coll., 1977-80; lectr. in gen. studies Georgetown U., Washington, 1980-81; lectr. in gen. honors U. Md., College Park, 1980-83; asst. prof. English Hood Coll., Frederick, Md., 1981-85, coord. writing program, 1981-83, assoc. dean acad. affairs, 1983-85; dean of frehmen Franklin and Marshall Coll., Lancaster, Pa., 1985-88, v.p., 1988—; team mem. Mid. States Accreditation Assn., 1989-91; cons. in field. Co-author: Funding A College Education, 1996; contbr. chpts. to books, articles and book revs. to profl. jours. Chair Lancaster County DA Commn., Lancaster, 1990-91; mem. Lancaster County Commn. on Youth Violence, Lancaster, 1990-91. Mellon grantee, 1979, Davison Foreman fellow, 1975-76. Mem. MLA, N.E. MLA, Am. Assn. Higher Edn., Assn. Am. Colls., Eastern Assn. Coll. Deans (pres. 1988-89), Coll. English Assn., Phi Beta Kappa (pres. chpt. 1990-91), Phi Kappa Phi. Democrat. Episcopalian. Avocations: hiking, reading, visiting art museums. Office: Franklin & Marshall Coll Lancaster PA 17604-3003

DRUM, JOAN MARIE MCFARLAND, federal agency administrator; b. Waseca, Minn., Mar. 31, 1932; d. Leo Joseph and Bergette (Anderson) McFarland; m. William Merritt Drum, June 13, 1954; children: Melissa, Eric. BA in Journalism, U. Minn., 1962; MEd, Coll. William and Mary, 1975, postgrad., 1984-85. Govt. ofcl. fgn. claims br. Social Security Adminstrn., Balt., 1962-64; freelance writer Polyndrum Publs., Newport News, Va., 1967-73; tchr. Newport News (Va.) Pub. Schs., 1975-79; writer, cons. Drum Enterprises, Williamsburg, Va., 1980-82; developer, trainer communicative skills U.S. Army Transp. Sch., Ft. Eustis, Va., 1982-86; govt. ofcl. test assistance div. U.S. Army Tng. Ctr., Ft. Eustis, 1986, course devel. coord. distributed tng. office, 1992; adj. faculty English dept. St. Leo Area Coll., Ft. Eustis, 1975-78; del. Communicative Skills Conf., Ft. Leavenworth, Kans., 1983; mem. Army Self-Devel. Test Task Force, 1991-92; task force mem. U.S. Army Tng. FAA; program developer multi-media electronic delivery prototype; tech. tng. facility trainer. Author: Ghosts of Fort Monroe, 1972, Travel for Children in Tidewater, 1974, Galaxy of Ghosts, 1992, Hampton's Haunted Houses, 1998, How to Feed a Ghost, 1998; editor: army newsletter for families, 1968-73, Social Services Resource Reference, 1970; contbr. articles to profl. jours. Chmn. Girl Scouts U.S., Tokyo, 1964-66, Army Cmty. Svc., Ft. Monroe, Va., 1967-68; chmn. publicity Hist. Home Tours, Ft. Monroe, 1971-73; chmn. adv. bd. James City County Social Svcs., 1989-95, chmn. adult svcs., 1989-90; mem. James City County Leadership Devel. Program Bd. Recipient numerous civic awards including North Shore Cmty. Svc. award, Hialeah, Hawaii, 1966, Home Bur. Svc. award, 1975, Svc. award Girl Scouts U.S., Tokyo, 1965, Comdrs. achievement award for civilian svc., 1995. Mem. N Va. Writers Club, Kappa Delta Pi. Home: 9 Bray Wood Rd Williamsburg VA 23185-5504

DRUMM, DAVID GARY, lawyer; b. Dallas, Oct. 1, 1955; s. Gary Thomas and Janet (Skiles) D.; m. Ann McDonald, Aug. 7, 1982; children: Colin Andrew, Kelly Aileen. BA, U. Tex., 1977; LLB, So. Meth. U., 1980. Bar: Tex. 1980, U.S. Dist. Ct. (no. dist.) Tex., 1980. Assoc. Carrington, Coleman, Sloman and Blumenthal L.L.P., Dallas, 1980-86, ptnr., 1987—. Home: 4340 Valley Ridge Rd Dallas TX 75220-1928 Office: Carrington Coleman Sloman and Blumenthal LLP 200 Crescent Ct Ste 1500 Dallas TX 75201-1848*

DRUMMER, DONALD RAYMOND, financial services executive; b. Binghamton, N.Y., Oct. 10, 1941; s. Donald Joseph and Louise Frances (Campbell) D.; AS, Broome C.C., 1962; BS, U. Colo., 1972; MBA, Regis U., 1981; m. Rita Kovac, May 22, 1965; children: Shelley Rita, Adam Donn. With, Lincoln First Bank, Binghamton, N.Y., 1962-69; asst. comptr. Adams & Horne, Denver, 1969; with Colo. State Bank, Denver, 1969-87, v.p., 1972-81, comptr., 1972-87, sr. v.p., 1981-87; sr. v.p., CFO Wyo. Nat. Bancorp. (formerly Affiliated Bank Corp. of Wyo.), Casper, 1987-91; v.p., contr. Crop Hail Mgmt., Kalispell, Mont., 1991-92, sr. v.p., CFO, 1992; treas. Rural Cmty. Ins, 1992; sr. v.p., CFO Wyo. Nat. Bank, Casper, Cheyenne, 1987-91; bd. dirs. Wyo. Nat. Bank, Lovell and Kemmerer, 1987-88; corp. sec. Wyo. Nat. Bancorp. (formerly Affiliated Bank Corp. of Wyo.), 1987-91; sr. v.p. finance Am. Nat. Bank, Cheyenne, 1993-95; v.p. Cmty. First Bancorp, Inc., 1994-95, cons. 95—; bd. dirs. Wheatland Ins. Agency, 1989-91; CFO, exec. com. Am. Bankers Assn., 1989-91; adj. faculty Regis U., mem. grad. edn. task force, 1986-87. Editor: Chronicle, 1980-81. Bd. dirs. Girl's Club of Casper, 1988. Mem. Inst. Mgmt. Accts. (dir. 1975-79, v.p. 1977-79), Am. Acctg. Assn., Am. Taxation Assn., Denver Sertoma Club (past pres.), City Club (v.p., dir. 1979-83). Office: 16422 Jefferson St Omaha NE 68135-6364

DRUMMOND, DOROTHY WEITZ, geography education consultant, educator, author; b. San Diego, Dec. 19, 1928; d. Frederick W. and Dora (Weidenhofer) Weitz; m. Robert R. Drummond, Sept. 5, 1953 (dec. June 1982); children: Kathleen, Gael, Martha. AB, Valparaiso U., 1949; MA, Northwestern U., 1951. Cert. tchr., Ind. Social studies tchr. Woodrow Wilson Jr. High Sch., Oxnard, Calif., 1949-50; editorial asst. Am. Geog. Soc., N.Y.C., 1951-53; substitute tchr. Vigo County Sch. Corp., Terre Haute, Ind., 1960-67; social studies tchr. Ind. State U. Lab. Sch., Terre Haute, 1963-64; geog. edn. cons., author, workshop presenter, Terre Haute, 1953—; adj. asst. prof. geography Saint Mary-of-the-Woods (Ind.) Coll., 1967—, Ind. State U., Terre Haute, 1990—; dir. project GEO, Ind. State U., 1992-96; cons. McGraw-Hill, Scott-Foresman, Agy. for Instrnl. Tech., Hudson Inst.; grant developer GIS for the Twenty-First Century, Ind. State u., 1996—. Author: The World Today, 3d edit., 1971, People on Earth, 3d edit., 1988, World Geography, 1989; contbr. numerous articles to profl. jours. Bd. dirs. Mental Health Assn. Wabash Valley, Terre Haute, 1984-93, Coun. on Domestic Abuse, Terre Haute, 1987-92, 97—, United Ministries Ctr., Terre Haute, 1991-94; organizer, leader ednl. tours to China, 1986, 88, 98, Australia, 1993, 96, 97, 99. Fulbright scholar, Burma, 1957-58; grantee Geography Educators Network Ind., 1988-96, Ind. Commn. Higher Edn., 1990, 92, 94, 96, NSF, 1993, 95, 96, 97, U.S. Dept. Edn., 1992-96. Mem. Ind. Coun. Social Studies, Geography Educators Network Ind. (bd. dirs.), Nat. Coun. Geog. Edn. (pres. 1990), Nat. Coun. Social Studies, Nat. Sci. Tchrs. Assn., Assn. Am. Geographers. Office: Ind State U Dept Geog Geol and Anthro Terre Haute IN 47809

DRUMMOND, GARRY N., mining company executive; married. B.S., U. Ala. Chmn. bd., dir. Drummond Coal Co., Inc., 1956—; chmn. bd., dir. Ala.-By-Products Corp., Birmingham, 1977-80. Office: Drummond Co Inc PO Box 10246 Birmingham AL 35202-0246 also: Drummond Co Inc 530 Beacon Pkwy W Birmingham AL 35209-3196*

DRUMMOND, GERARD KASPER, lawyer, retired minerals company executive; b. N.Y.C., Oct. 9, 1937; s. John Landells and Margaret Louise (Kasper) D.; m. Donna J. Mason, Sept. 14, 1957 (div. 1976); children: Alexander, Jane, Edmund; m. Sandra Hamilton, Aug. 31, 1985. B.S., Cornell U., 1959, LL.B. with distinction, 1963. Bar: Oreg. 1963. Assoc. Davies, Biggs, Strayer, Stoel & Boley, Portland, Oreg., 1963-64; assoc., ptnr. Rives, Bonyhadi, Drummond & Smith, Portland, 1964-77; pres. Nerco, Inc., Portland, from 1977-87, chmn. bd. dirs., 1987-93; mem. corp. policy group PacifiCorp, 1979-93, exec. v.p., 1987-93, also bd. dirs.; bd. dirs. Willamette Industries Inc., 1991—; of counsel Stoel Rives, Portland, 1993-98. Pres., bd. dirs. Tri-County Met. Transit Dist., Portland, 1974-85; Oreg. Investment Coun., 1987-98, chmn., 1990-98; bd. dirs. Oreg. Bus. Coun., 1987—; trustee

Reed Coll., 1982—; bd. dirs. Oreg. Symphony, 1987-93, pres., 1990-92; cmty. bd. dirs. Providence Hosp., 1986-95, chmn., 1993; mem. adv. coun. Cornell U. Law Sch., 1991-95; bd. dirs. Oreg. Shakespeare Festival Assn., 1992-98, Oreg. chpt. Nature Conservancy, 1992-93, Oreg. Symphony Found., 1996—; chmn. bd. dirs. N.W. Bus. Commn. for Arts, 1992-94. 1st lt. USAR, 1959-67. Mem. ABA, Oreg. Bar Assn., Am. Mining Congress (bd. dirs. 1986-92), Arlington Club, Univ. Club. Home: 28815 S Needy Rd Canby OR 97013-9570

DRUMMOND, GILLIAN M., home furnishing company executive; b. Apr. 3, 1943; came to U.S., 1951; d. Bernard Gilbert and Margaret (Soot Hutcheson) D. Student, U. Geneva, Switzerland, 1961-62; certificate, N.Y. Sch. Interior Design, 1965; student, Harvard U., 1996. Cert. Interior Designer. Asst. designer B. Altman and Co., N.Y.C., 1966-68; interior designer Tate & Hall, N.Y.C., 1968-72; pvt. practice N.Y.C., 1972-75, 82-85; mgr. customer rels. Marcel Dekker Inc., N.Y.C., 1975-78; exec. dir. S.M. Hexter, N.Y.C., 1978-80, East Coast Winfield Design Assocs., N.Y.C., 1980-82; prin., owner Gillian Drummond Inc., Wilmington, N.C., 1985-90, 94—, Gillian Drummond Interiors, Greenwich, Conn., 1991-93, The Drummond Group, Greenwich, Conn., 1991-93, Interior Design & Home Furnishings Cons., Greenwich, 1994—. Published in Showcase of Interior Design, 1993, 97, Interior Designers Showcase of Colors, 1994, House Beautiful Home Remodeling & Decorating, 1997. Candidate N.Y. Congress, 1974; bd. dirs. Arts Coun. Lower Cape Fear, 1985-87; program chmn. St. Thomas Celebration of Arts, 1985; active Nat. Trust Hist. Preservation, Hist. Wilmington Found., 1984-90. Mem. Decorative Fabrics Assn. (membership chmn. 1982-84)m Nat. Home Fashions League, Decorative Arts Assn., Nat. Assn. Female Execs., Bruce Mus., Greenwich Antiques Soc. Home: 46 Lexington Ave Greenwich CT 06830-5739 Office: Greenwood Garden Edn Ctr 46 Lexington Ave Greenwich CT 06830-5739

DRUMMOND, HAROLD DEAN, education educator; b. Bettsville, Ohio, June 8, 1916; s. Ray W. and Velma T. D.; m. Erma Catherine Street, Aug. 30, 1939 (dec. Aug. 1986); 1 child, Harold Evan; m. E. Josephine (Stanley) Raths, Nov. 23, 1988. Student, Westminster Coll., 1933-35; AB, Colo. State Coll. Edn., 1937, MA, 1940; EdD, Stanford U., 1948. Prin., tchr. White Deer (Tex.) Ind. Sch. Dist., 1938-42; prof. elem. edn. George Peabody Coll. for Tchrs., Nashville, 1947-60; acting prof. tchr. edn. assigned to U. Philippines, Stanford (Calif.) U., 1954-55; prof. elem. edn. U. N.Mex., Albuquerque, 1960-79, emeritus prof., 1979—; adv. bd. Childcraft, 1957-60, 67-80. Author: (with Charles R. Spain and John I. Goodlad) Educational Leadership and the Elementary School Principal, 1956; Our World Today series, A Journey Through Many Lands, Journeys Through the Americas, The Eastern Hemisphere, The Western Hemisphere, 1960-83. Lt. USNR, 1942-45, PTO. Laureate mem. Kappa Delta Pi, 1984; laureate counselor, 1984-88, 89-90. Mem. editl. rev. panel, The Ednl. Forum, 1997—, ASCD (pres. 1964-65), NEA, Nat. Assn. Elem. Sch. Prins., Nat. Coun. Social Studies, Nat. Coun. Geog. Edn., Nat. Soc. Study Edn., Profs. Curriculum. Home: 536 Graceland Dr SE Albuquerque NM 87108-3333

DRUMMOND, JAMES EVERMAN, defense technology transfer consultant, former army officer; b. Stillwater, Okla., July 13, 1932; s. Garrett Bartlett and Frances Elizabeth (Rigdon) D.; m. Helen Wesley Hillman, Dec. 29, 1958; children—James Everman, Sarah Elizabeth. BS, U.S. Mil. Acad., 1955; MS, U. Ariz., 1962; postgrad., Army War Coll., 1975; MA, Central Mich. U., 1982. Commd. 2d lt. U.S. Army, 1955, advanced through grades to maj. gen., served in Europe, Vietnam, Korea, comdr. III Corps Arty., 1979-81, dep. dir. Material Systems Analysis Activity, 1981-82; comdr. TCATA Ft. Hood, Tex., 1983-86; comdr. OTEA Falls Ch., Va., 1986-88; v.p. BDM Corp, Norfolk, Va., 1988-90; pvt. practice cons., 1990-92; v.p. Coe-Truman Tech. Inc., Hampton, Va., 1992-96; asst. prof. U.S. Mil. Acad., 1962-65. Decorated D.S.M., Legion of Merit with 2 oak leaf clusters, Bronze Star, Air medal, others. Mem. Assn. U.S. Army, Soc. Am. Mil. Engrs., Mil. Order World Wars, Assn. Grads. U.S. Mil. Acad., Internat. Test and Evaluation Assn., Co. of Mil. Historians, Sigma Alpha Epsilon, Masons, Kiwanis. Presbyterian. Home: 173 Loch Cir Hampton VA 23669-5525

DRUMMOND, JERE A., telecommunications company executive. Pres., CEO BellSouth Comm. Group, Atlanta. Office: BellSouth Comm Group Ste 2010 1155 W Peachtree St NE Atlanta GA 30309-3610*

DRUMMOND, LACREDA RENEE, journalist; b. Washington, Nov. 6, 1966; d. Percy Eugene and Rosa (Ross) D. BS in Journalism, U. Md., 1988. Wire editor WMUC AM 65/FM 88 Radio Stas., College Park, Md., 1986-87; TV prodn. asst. Strong Points, Hollywood, Md., 1986-87; TV producer The Quill Report, College Park, 1987; chyron operator Maryland Coaches' Corner, College Park, 1987-88; staff writer Diamondback newspaper, College Park, 1987-88; TV field reporter, tech. dir. Tuesday Weekly, Hollywood, Md., 1988; freelance sound tech. Image TV Co., Washington, 1993—; TV prodn. asst. USO World Headquarters, Washington, 1993; on-line asst. editor Henninger Video, Arlington, Va., 1997; assoc. prodr. WJLA-TV, Washington, 1997—. Mem. Soc. Profl. Journalists, (chpt. pres. 186-87). Home: 5491 Bluecoat Ln Columbia MD 21045-2227

DRUMMOND, MARSHALL EDWARD, business educator, university administrator; b. Stanford, Calif., Sept. 14, 1941; s. Kirk Isaac and Fern Venice (McDeritt) D. BS, San Jose State U., 1964, MBA, 1969; EdD, U. San Francisco, 1979. Adj. prof. bus. and edn. U. San Francisco, 1975-81; adj. prof. bus. and info. systems San Francisco State U., 1981-82; prof. MIS, Ea. Wash. U., Cheney, 1985—, exec. dir. info. resources, 1988, assoc. v.p. adminstrv. svcs., chief info. officer, 1988-89, v.p. adminstrv. svcs., 1989-90, exec. v.p., 1990, pres., 1990-98; chancellor L.A. C.C. Dist., 1999—; cons. Sch. Bus., Harvard Coll., U. Ariz. Contbg. editor Diebold Series; contbr. articles to profl. jours. Democrat. Avocations: running, water sports. Office: LA C C Dist 770 Wilshire Blvd Los Angeles CA 90017*

DRUMMOND, PATRICA FERGUSON, secondary education educator; b. Buckhannon, W.Va., Dec. 24, 1941; d. Robert Lewis and Alma Ruth (Miles) Ferguson; m. Fredrick Lane Drummond, Aug. 21, 1965. BA, U. Charleston, 1964; MA, Marshal U., 1971. Tchr. Kanawha County Schs., Charleston, W.Va., 1964-89, South Charleston, W.Va., 1989—. Grantee Greater Kanawha Valley Found., 1993. Avocations: running, crafts, autocrossing. Home: 1601 Kirklee Rd Charleston WV 25314-2426 Office: South Charleston High Sch 1 Eagle Way S Charleston WV 25309-2014

DRUMMOND, ROBERT KENDIG, lawyer; b. Phila., Feb. 9, 1939; s. Winslow Shaw and Dorothy (Moore) D.; m. Carol Young, Sept. 3, 1960; children: Anne Elizabeth, Robert Young D. BA, Coll. Wooster, 1961; JD, Duke U., 1964. Bar: Wis. 1964. Assoc. Foley & Lardner, Milw., 1964-71, ptnr., 1971—; bd. dirs. Bandag Inc., Muscatine, Iowa, Custom Heat Treat Inc., Iron Mountain, Mich. Presbyterian. Office: Foley & Lardner Firstar Ctr 777 E Wisconsin Ave Ste 3800 Milwaukee WI 53202-5367*

DRUMMOND, WINSLOW, lawyer; b. Phila., Jan. 29, 1933; s. Winslow Shaw and Dorothy (Moore) D.; m. Katherine Pace, June 18, 1983; children: Judith L., Kathryn W., Winslow Shaw II. AB, Coll. of Wooster, Ohio, 1954; LLB, Duke U., 1957. Bar: Ark. 1957, U.S. Dist. Ct. Ark. 1957, U.S. Ct. Appeals (8th cir.) 1958, U.S. Supreme Ct. 1992; diplomate Am. Bd. Trial Advs. Mem. firm Wright, Lindsey & Jennings, Little Rock, 1957-82, ptnr., 1962-82; ptnr. McMath, Vehik, Drummond, Harrison & Ledbetter, Little Rock, 1982—; mem. faculty Coll. Advocacy, Hastings Coll. Law, 1974-89, Nat. Inst. Trial Advocacy, 1979-92; chmn. com. on jury instrns. Ark. Supreme Ct., 1980-89. Co-author: Arkansas Model Jury Instructions-Civil, 1965, 3d edit., 1989. Pres., bd. dirs. Urban League Greater Little Rock; bd. dirs. Little Rock Sch. Dist; trustee U. Ozarks, 1991—. With U.S. Army, 1957-58. Fellow Am. Coll. Trial Lawyers, Ark. Bar Found., Am. Inns. of Ct. Found., ABOTA Found.; mem. ABA, ATLA, Ark. Bar Assn. (past chmn. exec. com., ho. of dels.), Pulaski County Bar Assn., Am. Judicature Soc., Ark. Trial Lawyers Assn. (pres. 1985-86), Am. Inn of Ct. (master of the bench), Order of Coif, Phi Alpha Theta. Democrat. Presbyterian. Home: 1 Tree Tops Ln Little Rock AR 72202-1676 Office: McMath Vehik Drummond Harrison & Ledbetter 711 W 3rd St Little Rock AR 72201-2201

DRUMMOND BORG, LESLEY MARGARET, clinical geneticist; b. Wellington, New Zealand, Oct. 26, 1948; came to U.S., 1986; d. Grant Allen and Yolanda Drummond; m. Kenneth Irvin Borg; children: Marc, Kyle. MBChB, Otago Med. Sch., New Zealand, 1971, MD, 1983; BSc, Auckland U., New Zealand, 1976. Diplomate Am. Bd. Pediatrics, Am. Bd. Med. Genetics; cert. clin. geneticist. Fellow in clin. genetics U. Auckland Med. Sch., 1974-77, med. geneticist, 1977-79; pediatric resident Hosp. Sick Children, Toronto, Ont., Can., 1980-82; gen. practitioner ARAMCO, Saudi Arabia, 1983-86; sr. fellow med. genetics U. Wash., Seattle, 1986-88; clin. geneticist Genetic Screening and Counseling Svc., Denton, Tex., 1988-95; dir., genetics divsn. Tex. Dept. of Health, Austin, Tex., 1995—; clin. asst. prof. Tex. A&M U., College Station, 1991—; cons. staff Odessa (Tex.) Women's Children's Hosp., 1991-96, Cook/Ft. Worth Children's Med. Ctr., 1991—. Contbr. articles to profl. jours. Fellow Am. Acad. Pediatrics, Am. Coll. Med. Genetics (founder); mem. AMA, Am. Soc. Human Genetics. Avocations: jogging, swimming, hiking. Office: Tex Dept of Health Div Genetic Screening/Case Mgr 1100 W 49th St Austin TX 78756-3160

DRURY, CHARLES LOUIS, JR., hotel executive; b. Cape Girardeau, Mo., Nov. 4, 1955; s. Charles Louis Sr. and Shirley Jean (Luebbers) D.; m. Michelle Marguerite Swenson, Apr. 28, 1979; children: Charles L. III, Thomas Michael. BSBA, St. John's U., Collegeville, Minn., 1978. Gen. mgr. Drury Inns, Inc., St. Louis, 1978-79, regional mgr., 1979-81, v.p. ops., 1981-85, pres., 1985—, chief exec. officer, 1988—, also bd. dirs.; bd. dirs. Drury Industries, Inc., Cape Girardeau, Drury Displays, Inc., St. Louis, Druco, Inc., St. Louis; mem. exec. bd. Enterprise Bank, St. Louis, 1989—. Bd. dirs. Dismas House of St. Louis, 1987—, Cardinal Glennon Children's Hosp. Devel. Bd. Mem. Pres. Assn., Am. Mgmt. Assn. Roman Catholic. Office: Drury Inns Inc 10801 Pear Tree Ln Saint Ann MO 63074-1450*

DRURY, COLIN GORDON, engineering educator, consultant; b. Skegness, Eng., June 4, 1941; came to U.S. 1972, naturalized U.S. citizen; s. Cecil and Mary (Lomas) D.; m. Margaret Catherine Jackson, Aug. 11, 1962; children: Catherine E., Philip M. B.Sc. in Physics, U. Sheffield, Eng., 1962; Ph.D. in Ergonomics, U. Birmingham, U.K., 1968. Research engr. MIRA, Nuneaton, U.K., 1959-62; lectr. in indsl. engring. U. Birmingham, 1968-69; mng. ergonomics Pilkington Glass Co., St. Helens, Eng., 1969-72; vis. asst. prof. U. Mass., Amherst, 1967-68; prof. indsl. engring. SUNY-Buffalo, 1972—, exec. dir. The Ctr. Indsl. Effectiveness, 1987-92; cons. IBM, 1980—, AT&T, 1980—, Levi Strauss, 1984—, Gen. Motors Corp., 1985—, VF, 1991—, Ryder, 1991—. Author, editor: Safety in Manual Materials Handling, 1978. Editor: Human Reliability in Quality Control, 1975. Contbr. over 100 articles to profl. jours. Fellow Human Factors and Ergonomics Soc. (Fitts award 1992), Ergonomics Soc. (Bartlett Medal 1980), Inst. Indsl. Engrs. Office: SUNY 342 Bell Hall Buffalo NY 14260-0106

DRURY, DAVID J., insurance company executive. Chmn., CEO The Prin. Fin. Group, Des Moines. Office: The Principal Financial Grp 711 High St Des Moines IA 50392-0001*

DRURY, JAMES ANTHONY BARTHOLOMEW, psychiatrist, psychoanalyst; b. Elizabeth, N.J., Sept. 20, 1964; s. James Michael and Teresa Carmel (Morris) D. AS, Essex County Coll., 1984; BS, Rutgers U., 1987; DO, N.Y. Coll., 1993. Diplomate Am. Bd. Osteopathy, Am. Bd. Forensic Examiners, Am. Bd. Forensic Medicine, Am. Bd. Psychol. Specialties, Am. Osteo. Assn., Am. Acad. of Justice Through Sci. (founding fellow). Nursing supr. Saddle Brook (N.J.) Hosp., 1987-89; scholar USPHS, Old Westbury, N.Y., 1989-93; psychiatrist VA, East Orange, N.J., 1993—; asst. clin. instr., child/adolescent fellow divsn. child psychiatry East Carolina U. Sch. Medicine, Greenville, N.C. Mem. Mil. Order of the Golden Chain, Religious and Mil. Order of the Knights of the Holy Sepulchre of Jerusalem. Mem. AMA, Am. Psychiat. Assn., N.J. Psychiat. Assn., Am. Osteo. Assn., Internation Soc. Police Surgeons, N.J. Med. Assn., Am. Coll. Neuropsychiatrists, N.C. Med. Soc., N.C. Psychiat. Assn., N.C. Osteo. Assn., KC (4th degree 1989, med. officer 1989—), Assn. Military Osteopathic Physicians and Surgeons. Republican. Roman Catholic. Avocations: collectibles, community service. E-mail: jimdrury@prodigy.net. Office: East Carolina U Sch Medicine Divsn Child Psychiatry Greenville NC 27858

DRURY, KENNETH CLAYTON, biological scientist; b. Madera, Calif., Mar. 27, 1945; s. Carma and Alice (Zollinger) D.; m. Sandra Rosemary hanlon, Apr. 28, 1972; children: Allison Hanlon, Vanessa Laura. BA, Westmont Coll., 1967; PhD, U. Geneva, Switzerland, 1979. Cert. in andrology and embryology high complexity lab. dir. Am. Bd. Bioanalysts. NIH fellow U. Calif., Berkeley, 1979-82; rsch. scientist Codon Corp., South San Francisco, Calif., 1982-84; sr. scientist Microgenics Corp., Concord, Calif., 1984-86; dir. U. Louisville, 1986-92, In Vitro Fertilization and Gamete Physiology Labs. U. Fla., 1992—. Contbr. articles to profl. jours. 1st Lt. U.S. Army, 1969-72, Vietnam. Mem. Am. Fertility Soc., Am. Coll. Reproductive Biology, Am. Soc. Reproductive Medicine. Achievements include first investigator to directly implicate phosphorylation in mechanism of action of maturation promoting factor; one of first investigators to obtain a human live birth after ultra rapid freezing of embryos; successfully performed preimplantation genetic diagnosis to eliminate inherited genetic disease in pregnancy. Office: U Fla Dept Ob-Gyn Divsn Reprod Endocrinology PO Box 100294 Gainesville FL 32610-0294

DRURY, LEONARD LEROY, retired oil company executive; b. Gillespie, Ill., Nov. 5, 1928; s. Roy August and Regina Loretta (Finnegan) D.; m. Myra Lee Klunk, June 30, 1951; 1 child, Marilyn Jo Drury Chandler. BS in Indsl. Mgmt., St. Louis U., 1950; MBA in Mgmt., U. Houston, 1957. Mgr. systems program info. and computer services Shell Oil Co., N.Y.C., 1966-68; mgr. data processing info. and computer services Shell Oil Co., Menlo Park, Calif., 1968, mgr. acctg. info. and computer services, 1968-69; mgr. MTM bus. systems div. info. and computer services Shell Oil Co., N.Y.C. and Houston, 1969-71; mgr. planning Shell Oil Co., Houston, 1971-73, mgr. planning and tech. info. and computer services, 1973-75, asst. treas. fin., 1975-77, gen. mgr. info. and computer services, 1977-80; liaison Shell Ctr. London Shell Oil Co., 1980-81; gen. mgr. products fin. Shell Oil Co., Houston, 1981-83, v.p. purchasing and adminstrv. services, 1983-86, v.p. info. and computer services, 1986-89, ret., 1989. Mem. United Way, Houston, 1982-89; bd. dirs. South Main Ctr. Assn., Houston, 1986-89. Mem. Fin. Execs. Inst., Am. Petroleum Inst., West Houston Assn. (bd. dirs. 1984-88), Houston Bus. Council (pres. 1985-86), Lakeside Country Club, Sigma Iota Epsilon. Roman Catholic. Home: 11711 Flintwood Dr Houston TX 77024-5110

DRUTZ, DAVID JULES, biotechnology executive; b. Knoxville, Tenn., Apr. 20, 1938; s. Abe Morris and Lillian (Billig) D.; m. Lydia Anne Hall, June 28, 1962; children: Gretchen, Adam, Gregory, Jonathan. BA, U. Louisville, 1958, MD, 1962. Cert. Am. Bd. Internal Medicine. Intern Louisville Gen. Hosp., 1962-63; resident Vanderbilt U. Hosp., 1963-65; infectious disease fellow Vanderbilt U. Med. Ctr., 1965-67; chief infectious diseases San Francisco Gen. Hosp., 1969-74; asst. prof. medicine U. Calif., San Francisco, 1969-74; chief infectious diseases U. Tex. Health Sci. Ctr., San Antonio, 1974-86, prof. medicine and microbiology, 1974-86, founder, dir. Ctr. for Cell Regulation, 1984-86; v.p. SmithKline & French Labs., King of Prussia, Pa., 1986-90; v.p. Daiichi Pharm. Corp., Ft. Lee, N.J., 1990-94, bd. dirs.; pres., CEO, dir. Sennes Drug Innovations, Inc., Houston, 1994-95, Inspire Pharms. Inc., Durham, N.C., 1995-99; pres. Pacific Biopharma Assocs., Chapel Hill, N.C., 1999—; clin. prof. medicine Seton Hall U. Sch. Grad. Med. Edn., Newark, 1990—, U. Pa. Sch. Medicine, Phila., 1986-90, adj. prof. medicine and microbiology Temple U. Med. Sch., Phila., 1986-90; adj. prof. microbiology Coll. Medicine Baylor U., Houston, 1995—. Editor: Systemic Fungal Infections, 1988-89; contbr. articles and abstracts to profl. jours.; assoc. editor Jour. Infectious Diseases, 1983-88, editorial bd., 1988-91; editorial bd. Am. Rev. Respiratory Diseases, 1979-84, Am. Jour. of the Med. Scis., 1983-91. Chmn. sci. adv. bd. Leonard Wood Memnl., 1984-87. Lt. comdr. USNR, 1967-69, Taiwan, Vietnam. Rsch. grantee NIAID, VA, NSF, 1970-86. Fellow Am. Coll. Physicians, Infectious Diseases Soc. Am. (councillor 1986-88); mem. Am. Soc. for Clin. Investigation, Western Soc. for Clin. Investigation, So. Soc. for Clin. Rsch., Am. Soc. for Microbiology, AMA, Alpha Omega Alpha. Avocations: swimming, skiing, biking. Office: Pacific Biopharma Assocs PO Box 3616 Chapel Hill NC 27515-3616

DRUTZ, JAN EDWIN, pediatrics educator; b. Louisville, Jan. 8, 1942; s. Abe Morris and Lillian (Billig) D.; m. Anne Edwina Sussman, June 7, 1965; children: Jeffrey Benjamin, Lisa Michele, Dana Nicole. BA, U. Louisville, 1964, MD, 1968. Pvt. practice Houston, 1973-87; intern, then resident Baylor Coll. Medicine, Houston, 1968-71, clin. asst. prof., 1973-77, clin. assoc. prof., 1977-87, assoc. prof. clin. pediat., 1987-95, dir. pediat. continuity clinic, 1987—, assoc. prof. pediat., 1995—; pres. med. staff Tex. Children's Hosp., 1995. Maj. U.S. Army, 1971-73. Mem. AMA, Harris County Med. Soc., Tex. Pediat. Soc. (adv. com., mem. student preceptorship program 1995—), Houston Pediat. Soc. (sec. 1984-85, pres. 1988-89), Ambulatory Pediat. Assn. (chmn. continuity clinic spl. interest group 1990-95, edn. com. 1993—). Office: Baylor Coll Medicine Dept Pediatrics 1 Baylor Plz Houston TX 77030-3411

DRUZINSKY, EDWARD, musician; b. St. Louis, June 16, 1924; s. Louis Paul and NEttie (Dorn) D.; m. Dorothy Ruth Siegel, Mar. 3, 1953; children: Robert, Michael, Paul. Student, Curtis Inst. Music, 1940-42, Washington U., St. Louis, 1942-44, NYU, 1946-48. Prin. harpist Pitts. Symphony, 1948-52, Detroit Symphony, 1952-57, Chgo. Symphony, 1957-97; prof. harp Carnegie Tech., Pitts., 1948-52, U. Mich., Ann Arbor, 1954-57, Northwestern U., Evanston, Ill., 1963-78; artists rep., cons. Lyon & HEaly, Chgo., 1978-89. Sgt. U.S. Army, 1944-46.

DRVOTA, MOJMIR, cinema educator, author; b. Prague, Czechoslovakia, Jan. 13, 1923; came to U.S., 1958, naturalized, 1963; s. Jan and Zdenka (Krejcikova) D.; m. Jana Kratochvilova, May 18, 1957; 1 child, Monica. Student, Charles U., 1945-48; PhD, Palacky U., 1953; MS, Columbia U., 1961. Stage dir. state theaters Czechoslovakia, 1952-56; libr. Bklyn. Pub. Libr., 1958-62; asst. prof. dramatic arts Columbia U., N.Y.C., 1962-69; assoc. prof. cinema NYU, N.Y.C., 1969-72; prof. cinema Ohio State U., Columbus, 1972-92, prof. emeritus, 1992—. Script writer Czechoslovak State Film, Prague, 1948-52; author: Short Stories, 1946, Boarding House for Artists, 1947, Solitaire, 1974, Triptych, 1980, Solitaire, Triptych in Czech, 1993; The Constituents of Film Theory, 1973, in Czech, 1994. Mem. Univ. Film Assn., AAUP, Phi Kappa Phi. Home: 4605 Winterset Dr Columbus OH 43220-8109 *Everything I stood for was defeated, everything I longed for remained unfulfilled, everything I loved passed beyond reach. In the chasm thus rent I captured a glimpse of what is real and what only is, of what is an act of becoming and what is a mere activity. Henceforth, I made it my task to share in the linking effort of those individuals who communicate in the services of reality: the reality screened by objects into which we are situated.*

DRYCE, H. DAVID, accountant, consultant; b. Bronx, N.Y., Feb. 18, 1930; s. Theodore and Ruth Dryspiel; m. Norma Stein, June 12, 1955; children: Mimi, Arthur, Debra. BA, Yeshiva U., 1952; postgrad., Isaac Elchanan Theol. Sem., N.Y.C., 1955; MBA, CUNY, 1959. CPA, N.Y. 1st lt. U.S. Army, 1955-57, capt., 1957-64; sr. acct. various firms, L.I., N.Y., 1959-63; prin. H. David Dryce, CPA, Old Bethpage, N.Y., 1963-85; exec. officer CHB Inc., Buffalo, N.Y., 1985—; instr. SUNY, Farmingdale, 1966-68; cons. Video Art Prodns. Inc., Palm Harbor, Fla., 1986—. Author: Inventory Verification-Extent of Observation and Acceptable Limitations, 1959; contbr. articles to profl. publs. V.p. United Coun. Civil Assns., Oyster Bay, N.Y., 1966-67, Old Bethpage Civic Assn., 1966-67; pres. Metro Region Men's Clubs, N.Y.C., 1970-71; bd. dirs., treas. Reggie Lewis Found. Mem. AICPA, N.Y. State Soc. CPAs (chmn. mgmt. svcs. com. Nassau County chpt. 1967-69). Home and Office: 4692 Sweetmeadow Cir Sarasota FL 34238-4333

DRYDEN, JOHN CLIFFORD, radio syndicator; b. Balt., May 28, 1951; s. Clifford Edgerton and Mildred Ann (Wise) D.; m. Lorraine Merriken; children: Luke Merriken, Clifford, Andrea. BA in Radio, TV, Film, U. Md., 1974. Writer, producer satirical radio program The Daily Feed, 1981—; pub. (CDs and cassette tapes) Rush to Judgement, 1995, List of Prisoners, 1994, Your Fine, 1993, Trickle to a Halt, 1992, The Domestic Issue, 1991, This S&L Aberrant, 1990, A Capital Decade, 1989, Reagan's Greatest Hits, 1988, The Best of Max Import, 1996, No Controlling Legal Authority, 1997, Executive Timber, 1998. Mem. Nat. Press Club. Democrat. Office: DC Audio 1783 Lanier Pl NW Washington DC 20009-2119

DRYDEN, KEN, sports team executive; b. Etobicoke, Ont., Can.; m. Lynda Dryden; children: Sarah, Michael. Grad., Cornell U.; JD, McGill U.; LLD (hon.), U. Windsor, U. B.C., York U., Toronto. Goaltender Montreal Canadiens, 1971-79; pres., gen. mgr. Toronto Maple Leafs, 1997—; v.p. Maple Leaf Gardens Ltd., 1997—; colour commentator ABC-TV at 1980, 84, 88 Olympic Winter Games. Author: The Game, Home Game, The Moved and the Shaken: The Story of One Man's Life, In School. Initiator Ken Dryden Scholarships; Ont. Youth Commr., 1984-86. Winner Conn Smythe Trophy as Most Valuable Player in playoffs of Stanley Cup, 1971, Calder Trophy, 1971-72, Vezina Trophy (5); inductee Hockey Hall of Fame, 1983. Office: c/o Toronto Maple Leafs, 60 Carlton St, Toronto, ON Canada M5B 1L1*

DRYDEN, MARY ELIZABETH, law librarian, writer, actress; b. Chgo., Oct. 18, 1952; d. James Heard and Hazel Anne (Potts) Rule; m. Ian Dryden, Nov. 22, 1975 (div. 1990); m. Stephen Quadros, Sept. 12, 1992 (div. 1996). Student, U. London, 1969, Bath U., 1970; BA, Scripps Coll., 1971; postgrad. U. Edinburgh, 1971-74. Head libr. Hahn, Cazier & Leff, San Diego, 1980, Fredman, Silverberg & Lewis, San Diego, 1980-83, Riordan & McKinzie, L.A., 1983—; freelance photog. model, 1973—. Theatrical appearances include Antony and Cleopatra, McOwen Theatre, London, 1984, Table Manners, L.A., 1985, Julius Caesar, L.A., 1986, Witness for the Prosecution, L.A., 1987, Come and Go, L.A., 1988, The Actor's Nightmare, L.A., 1989, The Dresser, L.A., 1989, Absent Friends, Long Beach, Calif., 1990, Run For Your Wife!, Long Beach, 1991, The Hollow, Long Beach, 1992, Cock and Bull Story, Fountainhead Theatre, Hollywood, 1993, Towards Zero, Long Beach, 1993, Angel Street, L.A., 1994, Bedroom Farce, L.A., 1995, Postmortem, Westchester Playhouse, L.A., A Weekend with Sam Beckett, San Quentin Drama Workshop, L.A., 1997, Deathtrap, Palos Verdes Players, 1998; (film) Private Collections, 1989, Eye Opener, 1992, A Situation, 1994, Porn Queens of the Seventies, 1994, The Nutty Professor, 1996, The Sophia Replacement, 1996; also music videos and TV Commls.; book critic L.A. Times; contbr. articles to newspapers. Mem. ABA, Brit. Equity, So. Calif. Soc. Law Librs., Brit. Assn. Film and Television Arts, Screen Actor's Guild, Mensa, Phi Beta Kappa. Avocations: photography, wine, architecture, fine art, languages. Office: Riordan & McKinzie 300 S Grand Ave Ste 2900 Los Angeles CA 90071-3139

DRYDEN, ROBERT D., engineering educator; b. Mt. Vernon, Ill., Feb. 12, 1942; s. Ted Allen Richardson and Cleo Marie (Shepherd) Richardson; m. Ruby Jean Dickey, Sept. 3, 1960; children: Julie Ann Dryden, Robert D. AS, No. Okla. Coll., 1965; BS in Indsl. Engring. and Mgmt., Okla. State U., 1967, MS in Indsl. Engring. and Mgmt., 1968; PhD, Tex. Tech U., 1973. Registered profl. engr., Oreg. Asst. prof. indsl. engring. U. Tex., Arlington, 1968-72, asst. prof., then assoc. prof. indsl. engring., 1973-77; part-time instr. Tex. Tech U., Lubbock, 1972-73; prof., chair indsl. engring. dept. Wichita (Kans.) State U., 1977-79; prof., head dept. indsl. and sys. engring. Va. Poly. Inst. and State U., Blacksburg, 1979-95; dean engring. and applied sci. Portland (Oreg.) State U., 1995—; vice chancellor Statewide Oreg. Coll. Engring./Computer Sci. Oreg. U. System, 1998—; mem. Pres.' Commn. on Employment of People with Disabilities, Washington, 1988-94. Contbr. articles to profl. publs., chpts. to book; author monograph in field. With USAR. Recipient Centennial cert. Am. Soc. Engring. Edn., 1993. Fellow Inst. Indsl. Engrs. (group v.p. tech. ops. 1990-92, sec. coun. of fellows 1989, Albert G. Holzman Disting. Educator 1993); mem. Internat. Conf. on Prodn. Rsch. (bd. dirs. 1993—), Internat. Assn. Mgmt. of Tech. (internat. adv. com. 1992—), Alpha Pi Mu (exec. dir. 1984—). Avocations: racquetball, fishing, jogging, home workshop. Office: Portland State U Dean Engring Applied Sci PO Box 751 Portland OR 97207-0751

DRYDEN, ROBERT EUGENE, lawyer; b. Chanute, Kans., Aug. 20, 1927; s. Calvin William and Mary Alfreda (Foley) D.; m. Jetta Rae Burger, Dec. 19, 1953; children: Lynn Marie, Thomas Calvin. AA, City Coll., San Francisco, 1947; BS, U. San Francisco, 1951, JD, 1954. Bar: Calif. 1955; diplomate Am. Bd. Trial Advocates (pres. San Francisco chpt. 1997). Assoc. Barfield, Dryden & Ruane (and predecessor firm), San Francisco, 1954-60, jr. ptnr., 1960-65, gen. ptnr., 1965-89; sr. ptnr. Dryden, Margoles, Schimaneck, Kelly & Wait, San Francisco, 1989—; lectr. continuing edn. of the bar, 1971-77; evaluator U.S. Dist. Ct. (no. dist.) Calif. Early Neutral Evaluation Program; master atty. San Francisco Am. Inn of Ct. Mem. bd. counsellors U. San Francisco, 1993—. With USMCR, 1945-46. Fellow Am.

Coll. Trial Lawyers, Am. Bar Found., Internat. Acad. Trial Lawyers; mem. ABA, San Francisco Bar Assn., Assn. Def. Counsel (bd. dirs. 1968-71), Def. Rsch. Inst., Internat. Assn. Ins. Counsel, Fedn. Ins. Counsel, Am. Arbitration Assn., U. San Francisco Law Soc. (mem. exec. com. 1970-72), U. San Francisco Alumni Assn. (mem. bd. govs. 1977), Phi Alpha Delta. Home: 1320 Lasuen Dr Millbrae CA 94030-2846 Office: Dryden Margoles Schimaneck Kelly & Wait 1 California St Ste 2600 San Francisco CA 94111-5432

DRYE, WILLIAM JAMES, business owner; b. Phila., Aug. 27, 1939; s. William James and Louvenia (Spearman) D.; 1 child, William Bradley. Cert. in acctg., U. Pa., 1966, BBA, 1968. Cert. energy reduction specialist. Clk. U. Pa., Phila., 1957-60, acct., 1960-63, asst. to treas., 1966-67, asst. to bus. mgr., 1967-68, acting comptroller, 1974, asst. comptroller, 1968-81, assoc. comptroller, 1981-83; pres. Delaware Valley Energy Conservation, Phila., 1983—. Mem. Springfield Twp. Town Watch, 1987. Served with U.S. Army, 1963-65. Mem. Am. Mgmt. Assn., Nat. Energy Specialist Assn. (performance award 1987). Avocations: sports, travel, cooking. Home and Office: 1211 Meadow Dr Blue Bell PA 19422-3302

DRYER, DOUGLAS POOLE, retired philosophy educator; b. Toronto, Ont., Can., Nov. 27, 1915; s. William Poole and Mabel Elizabeth (McLeod) D.; m. Pegeen Synge, Mar. 22, 1946; children: Dagny, Matthew, Moira; m. Ellice Baird, May 29, 1965; 1 stepdau., Eleanor. A.B. magna cum laude, Harvard U., 1936, A.M., 1939, Ph.D., 1980. Instr. Union Coll., Schenectady, 1939-41; asst. Harvard Coll., 1943-45; lectr. Tufts Coll., 1944-45; lectr. philosophy U. Toronto, 1945-48, asst. prof., 1948-59, assoc. prof., 1959-63, prof., 1963-81, prof. emeritus, 1981—. Author: Kant's Solution for Verification in Metaphysics, 1966, Introduction to J.S. Mill, Essays on Ethics, Religion and Society, 1969. Fellow Royal Soc. Can.; mem. Am. Philos. Assn., Can. Philos. Assn. Clubs: Alpine of Can, Royal Scottish Country Dancing Soc. Home: 61 Lonsdale Rd, Toronto, ON Canada M4V 1W4

DRYER, MURRAY, physicist; b. Bridgeport, Conn., Nov. 4, 1925; s. Sol and Sarah (Shapiro) D.; m. Geraldine Gray Goodsell, May 12, 1955; children: Steven Michael, Lisa Dryer Travis. Student, U. Conn., 1943-44; B.S., Stanford U., 1949, M.S., 1950; Ph.D., Tel-Aviv U., 1971. Research asst. NACA-NASA Ames Research Ctr., Calif., 1949; aero. research scientist NACA-NASA Lewis Research Ctr., Cleve., 1950-59; assoc. research scientist Martin Marietta Corp., Denver, 1959-65; chief interplanetary physics Space Environ. Lab., NOAA Environ. Research Labs., Boulder, Colo., 1965-94, guest worker emeritus, 1994—; sr. scientist Coop. Inst. for Rsch. in Environ. Scis., U. Colo., Boulder, 1994-96, Exploration Physics Internat., Inc., 1996—; lectr. dept. aerospace engrng. scis. U. Colo., 1963-76, dept. astrogeophysics, 1978; vis. assoc. prof. dept. mech. engrng. Colo. State U., 1966-67; mem. com. solar terrestrial rsch. NAS, 1976-80, 84-91, com. geophys. data NAS, 1987-93. Author: (with others) Solar-Terrestrial Physics in the 1980's, 1981; editor: (with others) Solar Observations and Predictions of Solar Activity, 1972, Exploration of the Outer Solar System, 1976, Solar and Interplanetary Dynamics, 1980, Advances in Solar Connection wirh Interplanetary Phenomena, 1998; spl. issue editor Space Sci. Revs., 1976; contbr. articles to profl. jours. With U.S. Navy, 1944-46. Mem. Am. Phys. Soc., Am. Geophys. Union, AAAS, Sci. Com. Solar-Terrestrial Physics, Internat. Astron. Union, Com. Space Research, AIAA (Space Sci. award 1975), Sigma Xi. Office: Space Environment Ctr NOAA-ERL Mail Code R-E-SE Boulder CO 80303-3328

DRYJA, THADDEUS P., opthalmologist, educator; b. Cleve.. MD, Yale U., 1976. Prof. opthalmology Harvard Med. Sch. Mem. Nat. Acad. Sci. Home: 243 Charles St Boston MA 02114-3002 Office: Harvard Med. Sch. 1350 Mass Ave Cambridge MA 02138-3846*

DRYMALSKI, RAYMOND HIBNER, lawyer, banker; b. Chgo., June 1, 1936; s. Raymond P. and Alice H. (Hibner) D.; m. Sarah Fickes, Apr. 1, 1967; children: Robert, Paige. B.A., Georgetown U., 1958; J.D., U. Mich.-Ann Arbor, 1961. Bar: Ill. 1962. Lawyer, Chgo. Title & Trust Co., 1963-65; asst. sec., atty. No. Trust Co., Chgo., 1965-68; ptnr. Boodell, Sears, Giambalvo & Crowley, Chgo., 1968-87; ptnr. Bell Boyd & Lloyd, Chgo., 1987—. Bd. dirs. Northwestern Meml. Hosp., 1978—, Northwestern Meml. Corp., 1987—, vice-chmn., sec. 1998—; coun. govs. Northwestern Healthcare Network, 1990—, bd. dirs., 1999—; bd. dirs. Lincoln Park Zool. Soc., 1972—, pres. 1980-84; bd. dirs., officer The Offield Family Found., 1990—. Mem. ABA, Econ. Club (Chgo.). Roman Catholic. Contbr. articles to profl. jours. Home: 443 W Eugenie St Chicago IL 60614-5674 Office: Bell Boyd & Lloyd 70 W Madison St Ste 3200 Chicago IL 60602-4244

DRYMON, DAVID E., investigative consultant, background investigator; b. Dover, N.J., Nov. 30, 1944; s. Eldon S. and Virginia D. Drymon; m. Madelina A. Licciardiello, Sept. 9, 1969; children: Derek, Jennifer. BS, Tusculum Coll., 1966. Tchr. Elkton (Md.) Elem. Sch., 1966-67; estate adminstr. Bankers Trust Co., N.Y.C., 1970-71; spl. agt. IRS, Newark, 1972-98; investigative cons. Wharton, N.J., 1998—; expert witness money laundering IRS and U.S. Dist. Cts. N.J. and (so. dist.) N.J., 1995-97. Sgt. U.S. Army, 1967-70. Mem. Fed. Agts. Assn. (local 121), Fed. Law Enforcement Officers Assn. Avocations: golf, oil painting.

D'SOUZA, ALAN S., tax consultant, real estate agent, pianist, writer; b. Calcutta, India, Jan. 11, 1954; came to U.S., 1967; s. Anthony C. and Irene E. (Azavedo) D'S.; m. Mary Ann Conanan, Aug. 6, 1985; children: Angela Bernadette, Anna Maria. BS in Physics, N.E. Mo. State U., 1974; postgrad. in Bus. Adminstrn., U. New Orleans, 1985; diploma in Real Estate, Bob Brooks Sch. of Real Estate, Baton Rouge, 1996. Bus. and estate cons. Hinsdale-Oakbrook (Ill.) Assoc., 1979-82; pianist Marriott Hotels, Lake of the Ozarks and Canal St., New Orleans, 1982-84; revenue officer IRS, Baton Rouge, 1985-89; tax cons., pianist, writer Baton Rouge, 1989—; vol. income tax assistance IRS, Baton Rouge, 1985—. Author: (series) Latin Jazz, 1995-96; author customer svc. manual Beckley Cardy Co., 1974-79; author: (with others) DSK Favorites: Our Best Home Cooking, 1996; featured performer, pianist (Smithsonian event) Beyond Category: The Musical Genius of Duke Ellington, 1996; contbr. articles to profl. jours. Mem. Soc. Profl. Journalists, Acad. Polit. Sci., Jazz Soc. Baton Rouge (founding bd. dirs. 1990—, author newsletter 1992-96, editl. advisor newsletter 1995—), Baton Rouge C. of C. (founding mem. internat. trade coun. 1990—), Smithsonian Instn., Libr. of Congress Assocs. (assoc.). Democrat. Roman Catholic. Avocations: reading, music, writing, soccer, tennis, travel. Home: 15728 Council Ave Baton Rouge LA 70817-5503 Office: Coldwell Banker MacKey Co 4111 S Sherwood Forest Blvd Baton Rouge LA 70816-4369

DU, DING-ZHU, mathematician, educator; b. Qigihaer, China, May 21, 1948; s. Jin-Gao and Ai-Hua (Xu) D.; m. Shu-Mei Li, Jan. 20, 1953; 1 child, Hong-Wei. MS, Chinese Acad. Scis., Beijing, 1982; PhD, U. Calif., Santa Barbara, 1985. Asst. prof. Inst. of Applied Math., Beijing, 1981-82; postdoctoral Math. Scis. Rsch. Inst., Berkeley, Calif., 1985-86; asst. prof. MIT, Cambridge, 1986-87; prof. Inst. of Applied Math., Beijing, 1987-90; rsch. assoc. Princeton (N.J.) U., 1990; prof. U. Minn., Mpls., 1991—. Author: Convergence Theory of Feasible Direction Methods; editor: Gradient Projection Methods in Linear and Nonlinear Programming, 1988, Combinatorics, Computing and Complexity, 1989; contbr. over 95 articles to profl. jours. Mem. Am. Math. Soc. Achievements include proof of Derman, Leiberman and Ross' conjecture on optimal consecutive-2-out-of-n system in 1982, proving Gilbert and Pollak's conjecture on Steiner ratio; solution to open problem on Rosen's method in nonlinear optimization; research on oneway function in complexity theory. Office: U Minn Computer Sci Dept Minneapolis MN 55455

DUANE, THOMAS K., councilman; b. Jan. 30, 1955. Student, Lehigh U. Mem. tenant adv. com. Gov. Cuomo; Manhattan cmty. coord. Comptr. Elizabeth Holtzman, N.Y.C., 1990-91; city councilman Dist. 3 N.Y.C. Coun., 1992-99; state senator Dist. 27 N.Y. State, N.Y.C., 1999—; mem. land use, parks, recreation and cultural affairs, spl. events and gen. welfare coms., chair subcom. pvt. uses of pub. space, N.Y.C. Coun. Former spokesman Tenant Unity Coalition; bd. dirs. Women's Interart Ctr.; mem. adv. bd. Bayview Women's Correctional Facility; former mem. policy adv. com. Manhattan Plaza and Clinton Planning Coun.; bd. dirs. Times Square Hotel and Prince George Hotel; mem. HIV Planning Coun.; past pres. Chelsea Water Park Assn. Mem. NOW, Nat. Abortion and Reproductive Rights Action League, Chelsea for Choice (founder), Chelsea Gay Assn., Chelsea Reform Dem. Club, Gay and Lesbian Ind. Dem. Office: 275 7th Ave Fl 12 New York NY 10001-6708*

DUARTE, CRISTOBAL G., nephrologist, educator; b. Concepción, Paraguay, July 17, 1929; s. Cristobal Duarte and Emilia Miltos; m. Norma Aquino, 1984. BS, Colegio de San José Asuncion, 1947; MD, Nat. U. Asunción, 1953. Intern De Goesbriand Meml. Hosp., Burlington, Vt., 1956; resident in medicine Carney Hosp. and St. Elizabeth's Hosp., Boston, 1956-58; fellow in medicine Lahey Clinc, Boston, 1959; fellow hypertension and renal medicine Hahnemann Hosp., Phila., 1960; assoc. in medicine U. Vt. Coll. Medicine, 1962-65; clin. investigator VA, 1966-68, staff physician, 1968-73; dir. Renal Function Lab., Mayo Clinic and Found., Rochester, Minn., 1973-77; asst. prof. lab. medicine Mayo Med. Sch., 1973-77; commd. lt. col. U.S. Army, 1977-84; assoc. prof. medicine and physiology Uniformed Svcs. U. Health Scis., Bethesda, Md., 1977-84, attending in medicine Walter Reed Army Med. Ctr., Washington, 1977-84; chief nephrology svc. Bay Pines VA Med. Ctr., 1984-87; assoc. prof. medicine U. South Fla., Tampa, 1984-87; med. officer cardio-renal drug products FDA, Rockville, Md., 1987—. Editor: Renal Function Tests, 1980; contbr. articles to profl. jours., chpts. to books. Recipient cert. of accomplishment VA, 1969; physician's recognition award AMA, 1993—; Cordell Hull Found. fellow, 1958-59. Fellow Am. Coll. Nutrition; mem. Nat. Kidney Found., Am. Fedn. Clin. Rsch., Am. Physiol. Soc., Am. Soc. Pharmacology and Exptl. Therapeutics, Midwest Salt and Water Club, Am. Soc. for Clin. Rsch., Inter-Am. Soc. Hypertension, Internat. Soc. Nephrology, Central Soc. for Clin. Rsch., Am. Soc. Nephrology, Sigma Xi. Roman Catholic. Current Work: Radiocontrast-induced renal failure. Subspecialty: Nephrology.

DUARTE, EDUARDO ADOLFO, nursing home administrator; b. Buenos Aires, Argentina, Jan. 29, 1932; came to U.S., 1979; a. Luis and Clementina (Quevedo) D.; m. Beatrice Herrerea, Dec. 12, 1959; children: Claudia B., Luis Eduardo, Gladys Maria, Manuel H., Alicia Nancy. Indsl. engrng., U. Buenos Aires, Argentina, 1959; chem. engrng., U. Sao Paulo, Brazil, 1975; MBA, So. Ill. U., Edwardsville, 1985; nursing home adminstrn., St. Philip's Coll., San Antonio, Tex., 1993. Prodn. mgr. Atomic Energy Commn., Buenos Aires, Argentina, 1953-59; maintenance mgr. Colombia Ceramic Co., Bogota, Colombia, 1960=65; plant mgr. Celanese Mexicana, Toluca, Mex., 1965-69; dir. chem. divsn. Natarazzo Industries, São Paulo, Brazil, 1969-71; gen. mgr. Colombian Ceramic Co., Bogota, 1971-72; indsl. dir. Carbomafra, Curitiba, Brazil, 1972-77; indsl. mgr. Cibran, Niteroi, Brazil, 1978; installation mgr. A. Proudfoot Co., Chgo., 1979-81; gen. mgr. A.E.A.. GE Affiliate, Del Rio, Tex., 1981-93; adminstr. Tex. Health Enterprises, Del Rio, Tex., 1993-95, Living Ctrs. of Am., Laredo, Tex., 1995-98, Sunny Brook Health Care Ctr., Corpus Christi, 1999—. Author: (book) Preventive Maintenance, 1963. V.p. Internat. Good Neighbor, Acuna, Mex., 1988-90, Del Rio, Tex., 1991-95; bd. dirs. United Way, Del Rio, Tex., 1989-93, Boys and Girls Club, Del Rio, 1990-93. Mem. KC (grand knight 1995-96, 3d, 4th degrees 1999), Rotary Club (bd. dirs. 1999). Roman Catholic. Avocations: golf, painting, music, reading. Home: 6607 Brixton Ct Laredo TX 78041-5941 Office: Sunny Brook Health Care Ctr 3050 Sunnybrook Rd Corpus Christi TX 78415-1748

DUARTE, FRANCISCO JAVIER, physicist, researcher; b. Santiago, Chile, Sept. 1, 1954; came to U.S., 1983; s. Luis Enrique and Ruth Virginia (Valenzuela) D. BA with honors, Macquarie U., Sydney, Australia, 1978, PhD in Physics, 1982. Postdoctoral fellow U. NSW, Sydney, 1981-82, Macquarie U., Sydney, 1982-83; asst. prof. physics U. Ala., University, 1983-85; sr. rsch. physicist Eastman Kodak Co., Rochester, N.Y., 1985—; analyst U.S. Army (MICOM) Redstone Arsenal, Ala., 1985-97. Author, co-editor: Dye Laser Principles, 1990; author, editor: High Power Dye Lasers, 1991, Tunable Laser Applications , 1995, Tunable Lasers Handbook, 1995; editor: Selected Papers on Dye Lasers; contbr. more than 100 aricles to profl. jours. Fellow Australian Inst. Physics, 1987, Optical Soc. Am., 1993, recipient Engineering Excellence Award, Optical Soc. Am., 1995; recipient Commonwealth postgrad. rsch. award Govt. of Australia, 1979. Achievements include theoretical and experimental contributions to the physics and technology of narrow-linewidth dispersive tunable laser oscillators and interferometric instrumentation; author of generalized multiple-prism dispersion theory; inventions in the fields of optics and lasers. Home: 112 Applegrove Dr Rochester NY 14612-2804

DUARTE, PATRICIA M., real estate and insurance broker; b. Truro, Mass., Feb. 23, 1938; d. Antone Jr. and Marjorie (Beckley) Duarte. Grad. H.S., Provincetown, Mass. Lic. ins. and real estate broker; constrn. supt. Sec. various ins. agys., Amherst, Mass., 1957-60; ins. and real estate agt. Duarte Ins. & Real Estate, Truro, 1960-66, owner, prin. agt., 1966-78; ins. risk mgr. J.L. Marshall & Sons, Inc., Pawtucket, R.I., 1979-92; owner, mgr. Patricia-Duarte Real Estate, Rockport, Maine, 1988-97; restorer antique homes New Eng., Mass., 1979—. Mem., sec. Truro Planning Bd., 1965-72, chmn., 1974-78; mem. exec. com. Cape Cod Planning and Econ. Devel. Com., 1971-76; mem. Reelect Brawn for Senate Com., Camden, Maine, 1988; mem. Rockport Planning Bd., 1991-94, Rockport Comprehensive Plan Implementation Com., 1991-94; co-chmn. Rockport Capital Improvement Com., 1991-96; bd. dirs. Cape Cod chpt. Am. Heart Assn., 1963-70; mem. Opera House Commn., 1992-94. Mem. Penobscot Bay Bd. Realtors, Profl. Ins. Agts. New Eng. (bd. dirs. 1974-76), Gen. Fedn. Women's Clubs (2d v.p. Camden chpt. 1989), Hist. Preservation Assn. St. Thomas (arts coun. 1998-99, bd. dirs. 1998). Republican. Roman Catholic. Avocations: gourmet cooking, travel, photography, architectural and interior design. Address: Cowpet Bay East 6400 Tracy Way Saint Thomas VI 00802-1015

DUAX, WILLIAM LEO, biological researcher; b. Chgo., Apr. 18, 1939; s. William Joseph and Alice B. (Joyce) D.; m. Caroline Townsend Dowell, May 6, 1966; children: Julia, Sarah, William, Stephen. BA, St. Ambrose Coll., 1961; PhD, U. Iowa, 1967. Postdoctoral research fellow Ohio U., Athens, 1967-68; rsch. assoc. Hauptman-Woodward Med. Rsch. Inst. (formerly Med. Found.), Buffalo, 1968-69; head crystallography dept. Med. Found. Buffalo, 1969-70, head molecular biophysics dept., 1970-88, assoc. dir. research, 1983-88, research dir., 1988-93, exec v.p. rsch., 1993—, v.p., 1998—; adj. assoc. prof. Medicinal Chemistry Dept. SUNY, Buffalo, 1973—, assoc. research prof. Dept. Biochemistry, 1981—; dir. distbn. Cambridge Database in U.S., Buffalo, 1983—; lectr. various internat. confs. Editor: Atlas of Steroid Structure Vol. I, 1975, Vol. II, 1984, Molecular Structure and Biological Activity, 1982, Molecular Structure and Biological Activity of Steriods, 1992, Internat. Union of Crystallography Newsletter, 1993—. Mem. Am. Field Service, Amherst, N.Y. Served with USAR, 1961-67. Fulbright scholar Coun. for Internat. Exchange, 1987; grantee NIH, 1971—; recipient Spl. Merit award Inst. Arthritis and Metabolic Diseases NIH, 1987—, Disting. Alumni award, St. Ambrose Coll., 1983, Clin. Ligand Assay Soc. Disting. Scientist award, 1994. Mem. AAAS, Am. Crystallographic Assn. (v.p. 1985, pres. 1986, exec. officer 1988—), Am. Chem. Soc., Am. Cancer Soc., Biophys. Soc., Endocrine Soc., Peptide Soc., Protein Soc., Internat. Union Crystallography (charter mem., sec. com. on small molecules 1984—), Am. Inst. Physics (bd. govs. 1987-94, exec. com. 1992), Coun. Sci. Soc. Pres. (govt. and pub. affairs com. 1987), Saturn Club (Buffalo). Democrat. Roman Catholic. Office: Hauptman-Woodward Med Rsch Inst Inc 73 High St Buffalo NY 14203-1149

DUBACK, STEVEN RAHR, lawyer; b. Washington, Sept. 4, 1944; s. Paul Hewitt and Natalie (Rahr) D.; children: David, Peter, Andrew. BA, Princeton U., 1966; JD, U. Mich., 1969. Bar: Wis. 1969, U.S. Dist. Ct. (ea. dist.) Wis. 1969, U.S. Ct. Claims 1969, U.S. Tax Ct. 1969. Ptnr. Quarles & Brady, Milw., 1969—; bd. dirs. Oshkosh (Wis.) B'Gosh, Inc., Commerce Indsl. Chems., Inc., Arnold Co., Brady Fin. Co. Pres., dir. Ctr. for the Deaf and Hard of Hearing; bd. dirs., v.p. Milw. Estate Planning Coun., 1988—. Mem. Estate Counselors Forum, Town Club, Milw. Athletic Club, Wis. State and Local Tax Club, Am. Soc. Corp. Secs., Order of Coif, Phi Beta Kappa. Avocations: golf, tennis. Office: Quarles & Brady 411 E Wisconsin Ave Ste 2550 Milwaukee WI 53202-4497

DU BAIN, MYRON, foundation administrator; b. Cleve., June 3, 1923; s. Edward D. and Elaine (Byrne) Du B.; m. Alice Elaine Hilliker, Sept. 30, 1944; children—Cynthia Lynn, Donald Aldous. BA, U. Calif., Berkeley, 1946; grad. exec. program, Stanford U., 1967. Pres., chief exec. officer Fireman's Fund Ins. Cos., 1974-75, chmn., pres., chief exec. officer, 1975-81; chmn., pres., chief exec. officer Fireman's Fund Corp., 1981-82; vice chmn. bd. Am. Express Corp., 1977-82; pres., chief exec. officer, dir. Amfac, Inc., San Francisco, 1983-85; chmn. bd. dirs. SRI Internat., Menlo Park, Calif., 1985-89; also bd. dirs. SRI Internat., 1989-98; bd. dirs. SRI Internat., Menlo Park, Calif., Transamerica Corp., Wells Fargo Bank, SCIOS, Inc. Contbg. author: Property and Casualty Handbook, 1960, The Practical Lawyer, 1962. Bd. dirs. San Francisco Opera; past bd. dirs., past chmn. Invest-In-Am., Inc.; chmn. bd. dirs. James Irvine Found., 1989-96; sr. mem. Conf. Bd. With USNR, 1943-46, 50-52; bd. advisors U. Calif., Berkeley. Mem. Bohemian Club, Pacific Union Club, Calif. Tennis Club, Lagunitas Country Club, Villa Taverna Club. Republican. Episcopalian. Office: 160 Sansome Ste 1700 San Francisco CA 94104-3703*

DUBE, BEATRICE DOROTHY, psychologist; b. Wellesley, Mass., May 20, 1918; d. Charles C. and Rosa (Malaguti) Zoletti; m. Richard Louis Dube, Mar. 17, 1947; children: Jacqueline A., Jonathan, Stephen. BA in Psychology, Boston U., 1949, MA in Psychology, 1950; CAGS, Assumption Coll., 1975; EdD in Clin.-Devel. Psychology, Boston U., 1985. Lic. psychologist, health svc. provider, Mass., sch. psychologist; cert. adult edn. tchr. Sr. supervising psychologist Metrowest Youth Guidance, Framingham, Mass., 1966—; researcher in field; cons. Accept collaborative, Framingham, 1979—, preschool progs., Sherborn, Sudbury, Hopkington, Ashland and Natick, Mass., 1975-78; cons. psychologist Brook Farm, Needham, Mass., 1962-65. Prog. developer Metrowest Youth Guidance Parent Tng. Prog., 1977—. Mem. com. YMCA, Boston, 1940-43; active Friends of Mass. Correctional Instn., Framingham, 1956-61, widows' group liaison, Wellesley, Mass., 1985—; asst. adminstr. New Beginnings Group, 1987—; rsch. asst. for revision of Leiter Internat. Test, Stoelting County. Named Metrowest Woman of Yr., YWCA, 1986; recipient citations Dept. Mental Health, Gov. Michael Dukakis, Mass., 1984, others. Mem. APA, Mass. Psychol. Assn., Nat. Register Health Svc. Providers, Mass. Psychologist. Roman Catholic. Avocations: sports, music, arts, travel. Home: 55 Atwood St Wellesley MA 02482-6061 Office: Metrowest Youth Guidance 88 Lincoln St Framingham MA 01702-6354

DUBÉ, LAWRENCE EDWARD, JR., lawyer; b. Chgo., Sept. 25, 1948; s. Lawrence Edward and Rosemary Nora (Cooney) D.; m. Paula Ann Goodgal, Jan. 10, 1982; 1 child, Charles Bernard. BA in Polit. Sci. cum laude, Knox Coll., 1970; JD with distinction, U. Iowa, 1973. Bar: Ill. 1973, Md. 1982, Pa. 1982, D.C. 1983, U.S. Supreme Ct., 1987. Field atty. NLRB, Chgo., 1973-80, supr. atty., 1980-81; sole practice Balt., 1981-85; assoc. Grove, Jaskiewicz, Gilliam & Cobert, Washington, 1985-87; ptnr. Dubé & Goodgal, P.C., Balt., 1987—. Author: Management on Trial-The Law of Wrongful Discharge, 1987, New Employment Issues: How to Shield your Business from Costly Lawsuits, 1988, Employment References and the Law, 1989; co-author: The Maryland Employer's Guide to Labor and Employment Law, 1984. Mem. Am. Arbitration Assn. (arbitrator), Nat. Assn. Securities Dealers (arbitrator). Home: 622 W University Pky Baltimore MD 21210-2908 Office: Dubé & Goodgal PC 2400 Boston St Ste 407 Baltimore MD 21224

DUBÉ, RICHARD LAWRENCE, landscape specialist, consultant; b. Portland, Maine, Mar. 25, 1950; s. Clarence Everett and Nancy Ann (Rowles) D.; m. Mary Louise Roberts, Sept. 7, 1974. AS in Forestry, Hocking Tech. Coll., 1973, AS in Recreation and Wildlife, 1975. Cert. landscape profl., Maine; cert. profl. landscape designer, cert. conflict mgmt. Interpretive naturalist Ohio Dept. Natural Resources, 1975-78; asst. mgr. Treeland, Portland, 1979-83; landscape designer Lucas Tree Experts, Portland, 1983-86, mgr. landscaping, 1986-88, mgr. landscape and tree depts., 1988-94; pres. Environ. Info. and Design, Inc., Gorham, Maine, 1994—; speaker Celandine Info. Svc., Buxton, Maine, 1987—. Host: (TV show) Backyard Maine, 1992; author: (book) Natural Pattern forms, 1996; co-author: (book) Landscaping Makes Cents, 1997, Natural Stonescapes-the Art, Craft of Stone Placement, 1999. V.p. Japan-Am. Soc. of Maine, Portland, 1989-90; seat on the Nat. Urban and Cmty. Forestry Adv. Coun., USDA; bd. dirs. China-Am. Friendship Assn. of Maine, 1991, Columbia Green, 1998; founder, exec. dir. A Yr. of Peace, 1990. Mem. Maine Landscape and Nursery Assn. (v.p. 1996-97), Maine Arborists Assn. (pres. 1994-96), CAD Inst. (bd. advs.), Ecol. Landscape Assn., Am. Soc. Landscape Architects, New Eng. Hort. Resource Network (bd. dirs.), Nat. Arborist Assn. (chmn. environment issues com.), Assn. Profl. Landscape Designers (bd. dirs. 1997). Avocations: international market and political analysis, writing music, scuba diving, black & White Photography. Office: Environ Info and Design Inc 1651 Calks Ferry Rd Lexington SC 29072-8649

DUBE, ROBERT L., federal judge. Magistrate judge U.S. Dist. Ct. (so. dist.) Fla., Miami, 1996—. Office: 300 NE 1st Ave Ste 236 Miami FL 33132-2135

DUBERG, JOHN EDWARD, retired aeronautical engineer, educator; b. N.Y.C., Nov. 30, 1917; s. Charles Augustus and Mary (Blake) D.; m. Mary Louise Andrews, June 11, 1943; children—Mary Jane, John Andrews. B.S. in Engring, Manhattan Coll., 1938; M.S., Va. Poly. Inst., 1940; Ph.D., U. Ill., 1948; grad., Fed. Exec. Inst., 1971. Engr. Cauldwell-Wingate Builders, N.Y.C., 1938-39; rsch. asst. U. Ill., 1940-43; rsch. engr. NASA, 1943-46; chief structures Langley Labs. NASA, Hampton, Va., 1948-56; mem. staff Langley Rsch. Ctr. NASA, 1959-79, assoc. dir. Langley Rsch. Ctr., 1968-79; rsch. engr. Standard Oil Co. Ind., 1946-48; with Ford Aeros., Glendale, Calif., 1956-57; mem. faculty U. Ill., 1957-59; rsch. prof. aeros. George Washington U., 1979-87; dir. Joint Inst. Advanced Flight Scis., 1971-79; mem. materials adv. bd. Nat. Acad. Sci., 1950; mem. subcom. profl. and sci. manpower Dept. Labor, 1971; mem. indsl. adv. com. U. Va., 1978-80; pres.'s adv. coun. Christopher Newport Coll., 1973-76, vice chmn., 1976; dir. Newport News Savs. Bank, 1966-92. Contbr. articles to profl. jours., chpts. to books. Trustee United Way Va., Peninsula, 1963-82; chmn. Hampton Roads Chpt. ARC, 1984-86. Fellow AIAA (DeFlorez award 1977), AAAS; mem. Va. Acad. Scis., N.Y. Acad. Scis., Am. Soc. Engring. Edn. (dir.), Engrs. Club Va. Peninsula (pres. 1955), Soc. Engring. Scis. (dir.), James River Country Club, Rotary (pres. Newport News chpt. 1967-68). Episcopalian. Home: 4 Museum Dr Newport News VA 23601-3621 Office: GWU/JIAFS NASA Langley Rsch Ctr M/S 269 Hampton VA 23665

DUBERMAN, MARTIN, historian; b. N.Y.C., Aug. 6, 1930; s. Joseph M. and Josephine (Bauml) D. BA, Yale U., 1952; MA, Harvard U., 1953, PhD, 1957. Teaching fellow Harvard U., 1955-57; instr. history Yale U., 1957-61; Morse fellow, 1961-62; bicentennial preceptor, asst. prof. Princeton U., 1962-65, assoc. prof., 1965-67, prof., 1967-71; Distinguished prof. Lehman Coll., City U. N.Y., 1971—; founder Ctr. for Lesbian and Gay Studies, Grad. Ctr. CUNY, 1991, dir., 1986-96. Author: Charles Frances Adams, 1907-1886, 1961 (Bancroft prize 1962), In White America (Vernon Rice award 1963-64), James Russell Lowell, 1967 (finalist Nat. Book award 1966), The Uncompleted Past, 1969, Black Mountain: An Exploration in Community, 1972, About Time: Exploring the Gay Past, 1986, rev. edit., 1991, Paul Robeson, 1989, Cures: A Gay Man's Odyssey, 1991, Stonewall, 1993, Midlife Queer, 1996; editor, contbr.: Antislavery Vanguard, 1965, Hidden From History: Reclaiming the Gay and Lesbian Past, 1989, A Queer World, 1997, Queer Representations, 1997; contbr.: (plays) Metaphors in Collision Course, 1968, The Memory Bank, 1970, The Recorder (in the Best Short Plays of 1970), 1971, The Colonial Dudes (in the Best Short Plays of 1972), 1973, Male Armor (Selected Plays 1968-74), 1975, Visions of Kerouac, 1977, Mother Earth: An Epic Drama of Emma Goldman's Life, 1991. Mem. Am. Hist. Assn., Nat. Gay and Lesbian Task Force, ACLU (bd. dirs. N.Y. chpt. 1982-88), Phi Beta Kappa. Address: 475 W 22nd St New York NY 10011-2549

DUBERSTEIN, CONRAD B., federal judge; b. N.Y.C., Oct. 22, 1915; s. Alex N. and Esther (Drucks) D.; m. Anne Saggio, May 11, 1928; 1 dau., Elysa Rice. Student Bklyn. Coll., 1934-38; LL.B., St. John's U., 1941; LLD (hon.), 1990. Bar: N.Y. 1942, U.S. Dist. Ct. (ea. dist.) N.Y. 1945, U.S. Dist. Ct. (so. dist.) N.Y. 1949, U.S. Dist. Ct. (no. dist.) N.Y. 1963; Supreme Ct. , 1960, U.S. Ct. Appeals (2d cir.) 1966. Ptnr., Schwartz, Rudin & Duberstein, Bklyn., 1954-60, Schwartz & Duberstein, Bklyn., 1960-70; ptnr. Otterbourg, Steindler, Houston & Rosen, P.C., N.Y.C., 1970-80, sr. atty. insolvency dept.; bankruptcy judge U.S. Dist. Ct. (ea. dist.) N.Y., N.Y.C., 1981—, chief judge, 1984—. Pres., Levittown (N.Y.) Republican Club, 1960-61; pres. St.

John's U. Coun. Served with AUS, 1943-45; ETO. Decorated Purple Heart, Bronze Star medal. Fellow Am. Bar Found., Am. Bankruptcy Inst.; mem. ABA, Fed. Bar Council, Comml. Law League, Nat. Conf. Bankruptcy Judges, Am. Coll. Bankruptcy, N.Y. State Bar Assn., Bklyn. Bar Assn., Am. Legion, Jewish War Vets., Mil. Order of Purple Heart, Hist. Soc. Supreme Ct., DAV, B'nai B'rith. Author: A Broad View of the New Bankruptcy Code, 1979; contbg. author: Bankruptcy Reform Act Manual, Bankruptcy Practice and Strategy. Home: 96 Schermerhorn St Brooklyn NY 11201-5039 Office: US Dist Ct 75 Clinton St Rm 313 Brooklyn NY 11201-4201

DUBERSTEIN, JOEL LAWRENCE, physician; b. Bklyn., Jan. 8, 1937; m. Judith Schwartz; children: Laura, Amy. AB, Princeton U., 1957; MD, Columbia U., 1961. Diplomate Am. Bd. Internal Medicine, Am. Bd. Pulmonary Diseases. Intern Mt. Sinai Hosp., N.Y.C., 1961-62, rsch. fellow in medicine, 1962, 65, asst. med. resident, 1963, chief med. resident, 1964, clin. asst., rsch. fellow, 1965-67; asst. chief medicine, chief pulmonary diseases Morrisania Hosp., Montefiore-Morrisania Affiliation, Bronx, N.Y., 1969-71; attending physician dept. medicine Overlook Hosp., Summit, N.J., 1971—, chmn. pulmonary sect., ICU com., med. dir. ICU, 1985-97, divsn. chief pulmonary disease dept. internal medicine; assoc. clin. prof. medicine Columbia U., 1998—; assoc. vis. physician Morrisania City Hosp., Bronx, 1969-71; mem. staff Morristown Meml. Hosp., 1972—, med. co-dir. respiratory svcs., 1977-82; attending phsician dept. medicine St. Barnabas Med. Ctr., Livingston, N.J., 1971-89, past chmn. pulmonary sect.; mem. staff Newark Beth Israel Med. Ctr., 1971-82; spkr. in field; mem. Essex County Med. Soc. TB Control. Contbr. articles to profl. jours. Maj. U.S. Army, 1967-69. Recipient Recognition award Soc. N.J.'s Physicians. Fellow ACP, Am. Coll. Chest Physicians; mem. AMA (Physician's Recognition award), N.J. Med. Soc., Essex Thoracic Soc., N.J. Acad. Medicine. Office: 315 E Northfield Rd Ste 1D Livingston NJ 07039-4800

DUBES, MICHAEL JOHN, insurance company executive; b. Dubuque, Iowa, Oct. 19, 1942; s. Wilmar C. and Cleo (Lenz) D.; m. Glenda Ra. Ackerlund, July 31, 1965; children: Scot (dec.), Heather. BS, Iowa State U., 1966; MS, Am. Coll., Bryn Mawr, Pa., 1981; postgrad., Harvard U., 1987, 90, LIMRA Strategies Inst., 1990. CLU, LLIF; cert. fin. planner; chartered fin. cons. Agt. Northwestern Nat. Life Ins. Co., Des Moines, Iowa, 1967-68, staff asst., Mpls., 1968-70, tng. mgr., St. Paul, 1970-72, supt. agys., Mpls., 1972-73, asst. mgr., Des Moines, 1973-78, br. mgr., 1978-83, regional mgr., 1983-84, 2d v.p. individual ins. sales, Mpls., 1984-85, v.p. indiv. ins. sales, 1985-87, sr. v.p. individual ins., 1987—; exec. v.p. Northwestern Nat. Life Ins. Sales Co., Mpls., 1984-85, pres., 1985-87; vice chmn., CEO Washington Square Securities, Inc., Mpls., 1984-87; chmn. Washington Sq. Securities, Mpls., 1987—; bd. dirs. Mpls., NWNL Found., Washington Sq. Securities Inc., Relia Star Lite, Corp. Coun. of the Arts; mem. NWNL cos. Enterprise Coun., mgmt. com.; bd. dirs. Northern Life Ins. Co. (a Relia Star co.), Seattle, CEO, pres. Amb. Iowa State U.; bd. dirs. Seattle C. of C., 1995—, Seattle Corp. Coun. of the Arts, 1995, Ind. Colls. of Wash., 1995. With USAR, 1967. Recipient Gene Helton award Des Moines Life Underwriters, 1982. Mem. Nat. Assn. Life Underwriters (bd. dirs. 1983-84), Am. Soc. CLUs, Life Ins. Mktg. and Rsch. Assn. (exec. devel. com. 1985-91, ops. com. 1989—, bd. dirs. 1991-93, chmn. membership com.), Agy. Officer Round Table (meeting chmn. 1994), Gen. Agts. and Mgrs. Assn. (pres. 1983-84), Cert. Fin. Planners, MBA Ins. Mgmt. Adv., U. St. Thomas, Ind. Colls. Wash. (bd. dirs.), Met. Breakfast Club (bd. dirs. 1988-94), Interlachen Country Club (bd. govs.), Desert Mountain Country Club, Rainier Club, Amb. Club (Iowa State U.), Variety Club of Iowa (bd. dirs. 1983-84), Sahalee Country Club, Harvard Bus. Sch. Club Minn., Mpls. Club, Boys and Girls Club Mpls. (bd. dirs., exec. com., devel. com.), Rotary (Paul Harris fellow 1988, bd. dirs.), Seattle C. of C. (bd. dirs.). Home: 3529 264th Ave SE Issaquah WA 98029-9138 Office: Northern Life Ins Co 1110 3rd Ave Ste 810 Seattle WA 98101-2930

DUBESA, ELAINE J., biotechnology company executive; b. Alton, Ill., July 26, 1943; m. Michael Dubesa, Oct. 28, 1967. BS in Med. Tech., Loyola U., New Orleans, 1966. Rsch. assoc. pesticides project U. Hawaii, Honolulu, 1968-69; field rep., pesticides project La. State U., New Orleans, 1970-71; lab. supr. Beaufort (S.C.) County Meml. Hosp., 1971-72; asst. supr. hematology Mayo Clinic, Rochester, Minn., 1973-75; edn. coord. Sherman Hosp., Elgin, Ill., 1975-78; sect. chief PCL (now Corning Clin. Labs.), Portland, Oreg., 1978-80; quality control supr. PCL-RIA, Inc., Portland, 1980-82; quality control mgr. Am. Bioclinical Inc., Portland, 1982-87; quality assurance mgr., regulatory affairs mgr. Epitope, Inc., Beaverton, Oreg., 1987-91, v.p. regulatory affairs, 1991-95, v.p. govt. affairs, 1995-97. Active Troutdale (Oreg.) Hist. Soc. Mem. Am. Soc. Quality Control, Regulatory Affairs Profl. Soc., Am. Soc. Clinical Pathologists, Beta Epsilon Upsilon. Avocations: hiking, gardening.

DUBESHTER, BRENT, physician; b. N.Y.C., Nov. 6, 1952; s. Frank S. and Eleanor DuBeshter; m. Roberta S. Saraceno, June 28, 1982; children: Tyler, Paige, Kayle, Hilary. BA, Franklin & Marshall Coll., 1974; MD, U. Va., 1978. Diplomate Am. Bd. Ob-Gyn. Instr. ob-gyn. Harvard U. Sch. Medicine, Boston, 1984-86; asst. prof. ob-gyn. U. Rochester (N.Y.) Sch. Medicine, 1986-89, dir. gynecol. oncology, 1996—; med. dir. ChemoRx Corp., Brookline, Mass., 1996—. Mem. Soc. Gynecol. Oncologists (edn. and exhibits com. 1996—), Genesee Valley Club (sports com. 1996—). Avocations: squash, skiing, SCUBA diving, driving instructor. Office: Gynecol Oncology Assocs 125 Lattimore Rd Rochester NY 14620-4159

DUBIA, JOHN AUSTIN, army executive; b. Dayton, Ohio, July 17, 1943; s. Gilbert Proctor and Mary Gertrude (McHugh) D.; m. Maureen Virginia McDonough, June 10, 1967; children: John Austin, Michael, Christopher. Student, Georgetown U., 1961-62; BS, U.S. Mil. Acad., 1966; MBA, U. S.D., 1972. Commd. 2d lt. U.S. Army, 1966, advanced through grades to lt. maj. gen., 1995—; comdr. div. arty. 1st Armored Div., Nurnberg, Germany, 1988-90; exec. to the comdr.-in-chief U.S. Army Europe, Heidelberg, Germany, 1990; exec. sec. for sec. of def. Immediate Office of Sec. of Def., Washington, 1990-92; dir. officer pers. mgmt. U.S. Army Pers. Command, Alexandria, Va., 1992-93; comdg. gen. U.S. Army Field Arty. Sch. and Ctr., Ft. Sill, Okla., 1993-95; dir. army staff Pentagon, Washington, 1995—. Decorated Legion of Merit (3), Bronze Star medal (3); recipient Def. Disting. Svc. medal, 1992. Mem. Assn. U.S. Army (life), Lawton C. of C. and Industry. Roman Catholic. Office: Dir Army Staff 202 Army Pentagon Washington DC 20310-0202*

DUBIN, ARTHUR DETMERS, architect; b. Chgo., Mar. 14, 1923; s. Henry and Anne (Green) D.; m. Lois Amtman, Mar. 10, 1951 (dec. Sept. 1980); children: Peter Arthur, Polly Louise (Mrs. Scott Pollak); m. Phyllis Vollen Burman, Nov. 27, 1981; stepchildren: Garry Arthur, Jill Meredyth, David Yale, Eric Vollen. Student, Lake Forest Coll., 1943-44; B.Arch., U. Mich., 1949. Architect, partner Dubin & Dubin (architects and engrs.), Chgo., 1950-65, Dubin, Dubin & Black (architects and engrs.), 1965-66, Dubin, Dubin, Black & Moutoussamy, 1966-78, Dubin, Dubin & Moutoussamy, 1978-93; v.p. DDBM, Inc. (constrn. mgmt. cons.), 1975-85; v.p., dir. 7337 South Shore Dr. Corp., 1958-81, 7345 South Shore Dr. Corp., 1962-86; mem. adv. bd. Amtrak, 1972-95; gen. ptnr. 340 Wellington Assocs., 1962-73; spkr. at confs., U.S. and France; hon. rsch. assoc. Smithsonian Instn., 1975; tech. cons. Paramount Pictures, 1991. Author: Some Classic Trains, 1964, More Classic Trains, 1974; author-editor, for N.Am., The Great Trains, 1973; Contbr. articles to mags., Archtl. works include, govtl. bldgs., rail transit stas. and transp. facilities, mil. installations, banks, indsl. plants, schs. and colls., hosps., housing and urban renewal planning. Chmn. Civic Beautification Com., Highland Park, Ill., 1965-74; mem. Bicentennial Commn. Highland Park, 1974-76, Ill. Commn. on High Speed Rail Transit, 1966-68, Met. Housing and Planning Coun. Chgo., Nat. Coun. Archtl. Registration Bds., 1971—; life mem., friend Art Inst. Chgo.; trustee NORTRAN, Des Plaines, Ill., 1980-91, George Krambles Transit Scholarship Fund, 1985—, John W. Barriger III Nat. R.R. Libr., St. Louis, 1989—. With inf. U.S. Army, 1943-46. Decorated Bronze Star with cluster, Purple Heart; recipient award Gen. Svcs. Adminstrn. for U.S. Custom House, Chgo., 1993. Mem. AIA (emeritus), Am. Pub. Transit Assn., Railway and Locomotive Hist. Soc. (bd. dirs. 1960-93, hon. life dir. 1993), Train Collectors Assn., Steamship Hist. Soc. Am., Cliff Dwellers Club (emeritus, bd. dirs. 1972-75), Builders Club (pres. 1970-71, bd. dirs. 1970-80), Arts Club (Chgo.). Home: 229 Park Ave Highland Park IL 60035-2523

DUBIN, CHARLES LEONARD, lawyer; b. Hamilton, Ont., Can., Apr. 4, 1921; s. Harry and Ethel D.; m. Anne Ruth, Dec. 2, 1951. B.A., U. Toronto, Ont., 1941; LL.B., Osgoode Hall Law Sch., 1944. Bar: Ont. 1944, appointed Queen's Counsel 1952. Practiced in Toronto, 1945-73; judge Ont. Supreme Ct. Appeal, Toronto, 1973—; chief justice Ont. Ct. Appeal, Toronto, 1990-96; counsel Tory Tory Des Lauriers & Binnington Barristers, Toronto, 1996—; Royal Commr. to inquire into air safety in Can., 1979; Royal Commr. to inquire into use of drugs and banned practices in athletics, 1988; lectr. Osgoode Hall Law Sch., 1945-48. Mem. York Club, Toronto Hunt Club, Toronto Club. Home: 619 Avenue Rd Apt 1702, Toronto, ON Canada M4V 2K6 Office: Tory Tory Des Lauriers & Binnington Barristers, Ste 3000 Toronto Domin Ctr, PO Box 270, Toronto, ON Canada M5K 1N2

DUBIN, HOWARD VICTOR, dermatologist; b. N.Y.C., Mar. 28, 1938; s. Meyer and Blanche D.; m. Patricia Sue Tucker, June 10, 1962; children—Douglas Scott, Kathryn Sue, David Andrew, Michael Stonier. A.B., Columbia U., 1958, M.D., 1962. Diplomate: Am. Bd. Dermatology, Am. Bd. Internal Medicine. Intern U. Mich., 1962-63, resident in internal medicine, 1963-64, resident in dermatology, 1968-70, asst. prof., 1970-72, asso. prof., 1972-75, clin. asso. prof., 1975-77, clin. prof., 1977—; resident in internal medicine Columbia-Presbyn. Med. Center, N.Y.C., 1966-68; practice medicine specializing in dermatology, Ann Arbor, Mich., 1970—. Contbr. articles to profl. jours. Trustee Greenhills Sch., Ann Arbor, 1979-87, pres. bd. trustees, 1981-84. Served with U.S. Army, 1964-66. Fellow ACP; mem. Am. Acad. Dermatology, Am. Dermatol. Assn., Soc. Investigative Dermatology, Dermatology Found. (mem. exec. com. 1987—, sec.-treas. 1988-91, pres. 1991—), Mich. Dermatol. Soc. (pres. 1985-87), AMA, Mich. Med. Soc., Washtenaw County Med. Soc., Sigma Xi. Club: Rotary. Office: 3250 Plymouth Rd Ann Arbor MI 48105-2592

DUBIN, JAMES MICHAEL, lawyer; b. N.Y.C., Aug. 20, 1946; s. Benjamin and Irene (Wasserman) D.; m. Susan Hope Schraub, Mar. 15, 1981; children: Alexander Philip, Elizabeth Joy. BA, U. Pa., 1968; JD, Columbia U., 1974. Bar: N.Y. 1975, D.C. 1984, U.S. Dist. Ct. (so. and ea. dist.) N.Y. 1975, U.S. Ct. Appeals (2d cir.) 1975. Assoc. Paul, Weiss, Rifkind, Wharton & Garrison, N.Y.C., 1974-82, ptnr. 1982—, chmn. corp. dept., 1995—; bd. dirs. FOJP Svc. Corp., 1988—, Conair Corp., 1995—, Carnival Corp., 1995—. Bd. editors Columbia Law Rev., 1973-74. Bd. dirs. YM-YWHA of Mid-Westchester, Scarsdale, N.Y., 1983-86, chmn. budget and fin. com., 1984-85; bd. dirs., exec. com. Nat. Found. Advancement in Arts, 1991—, vice chmn., 1994—; trustee Solomon Schechter Sch. Westchester, 1991—, vice-chmn. 1997—, chmn. ann. fund, 1993-96, chmn. devel. com., 1994-97, v.p., sec., 1996-97; bd. dirs. Jewish Guild for the Blind, 1989—, exec. com., 1991—, sec., 1992-94, chmn., 1995—, chmn. 75th Anniversary Gala Benefit Jour.; bd. trustee Jewish Cmty. Ctr. of Harrison, 1994-97, bd. edn., 1987-90; chmn. Cable Oversight Com., Harrison, N.Y., 1983-85. With U.S. Army, 1969-71. Mem. ABA, Assn. of Bar of City of N.Y., Am. Arbitration Assn. (comml. panel arbitrators 1989—), Sunningdale Country Club (bd. govs. 1989—, v.p. 1992—), The Dukes Golf Club, Colony Club, Phi Delta Phi. Office: Paul Weiss Rifkind Wharton & Garrison Ste 3700 1285 Avenue of The Americas New York NY 10019-6064

DUBIN, JOSEPH WILLIAM, union representative; b. Middletown, Conn., Apr. 7, 1948; s. Emanuel Saul and Hazel (Brenner) D.; m. Brenda Charlotte Ellen Clark, June 27, 1976; children: Brian Joseph Finnegan, Darren Clark Finnegan, Evan Jared. BA, U. Conn., 1970; postgrad., U. Mass., 1970-73. Rsch. asst. U. Conn. Health Ctr., Farmington, 1973-81; organizer Am. Fedn. Tchrs., Hartford, Conn., 1981-82; field rep. Conn. Fedn. Ednl. and Profl. Employees, Rocky Hill, 1982—, interest arbitrator, 1990—; vice-chmn. Fedn. Nurses and Health Profls. Nat. Steering Com., Washington, 1980-81; v.p. Greater Hartford Labor Coun., AFL-CIO, 1982-84, del., 1980—. Contbr. articles to profl. jours. Mem. Boy Scouts Am., 1979—, com. chmn. troop 355, Newington, Conn., 1980-95, mem. advancement com. Nutmeg dist., 1994—. Recipient Dist. award of Merit Long Rivers Coun. Boy Scouts Am., 1992, Spl. Recognition award Univ. Health Profls., 1990, George Meany award AFL-CIO, 1981. Mem. ACLU, Am. Chem. Soc. (student affiliate chmn. 1969-70), Indsl. Rels. Rsch. Assn. (steering com. 1994—), U. Conn. Health Ctr. Profl. Employees Assn. (pres. 1980-81), Staff Union of Conn. (sec.-treas. 1982-87), Nat. Trust Hist. Preservation, Conn. Trust Hist. Preservation, Newington Hist. Soc. and Trust, Inc., Nat. Audubon Soc., Nat. Wildlife Fedn., World Wildlife Fedn., The Wilderness Soc., Smithsonian Instn. Nat. Assn., Friends of Lucy Robbins Welles Libr., Legis. Electoral Action Program, Peoples Med. Soc., Conn. Citizens Action Group, Libr. of Congress Assn., Conn. Trust for Hist. Preservation. Avocations: photography, cooking. Home: 57 Kirkham Pl Newington CT 06111-2408 Office: Conn Fedn Ednl and Profl Employees 35 Marshall Rd Rocky Hill CT 06067-1400

DUBIN, LEONARD, lawyer; b. Trenton, N.J., July 30, 1934; s. Isadore and Selma (Lotman) D.; m. Marlene B. Bronstein, July 12, 1962; children: Elisa K., David I., Michael B. BS, Temple U., 1956, LLB, 1961. Bar: Pa. 1962. Law clk. Ct. Common Pleas, Phila., 1961-62; assoc. Blank Rome Comisky & McCauley, L.L.P., Phila., 1962-69, ptnr., 1969—. Contbr. articles to profl. jours. Bd. dirs. Juvenile Diabetes Found., 1974-95. 1st lt. U.S. Army, 1956-58. Fellow Am. Bar Found., Pa. Bar Found., Am. Coll. Trial Lawyers, Am. Acad. Matrimonial Lawyers; mem. ABA (ho. of dels. 1988-96), Pa. Bar Assn. (house of dels. 1977—, bd. govs. 1981-84, v.p. 1987-88, pres.-elect 1988-89, pres. 1989-90, chair family law sect. 1991-92), Phila. Bar Assn. (bd. govs. 1975-77). Republican. Jewish. Office: Blank Rome Comisky et al One Logan Sq Philadelphia PA 19103

DUBIN, MARK WILLIAM, educator, neuroscientist; b. N.Y.C., Aug. 30, 1942; s. Sidney Stanley and Dorothy (Cirinsky) D.; m. Alma Hermine Heller, June 27, 1964; children: Lila Rachel, Miriam Rebecca. AB in Biophysics, Amherst Coll., 1964; PhD in Biophysics, Johns Hopkins U., 1969. Research fellow Australian Nat. U., Canberra, 1969-71; asst. prof. dept. molecular, cellular and devel. biology U. Colo., Boulder, 1971-77, assoc. prof., 1977-82, prof., 1982—, chmn. dept., 1983-87, assoc. vice chancellor for acad. affairs, 1988-97, chief info. officer, 1996-97, faculty fellow info. tech. svcs., 1997-98; sci. cons. Wills Found., 1981-91; cons., mem. bd. sci. advisors Columbine Venture Fund, Denver, 1984-94, Photometrics, Tucson, 1987-89; owner MWm Crafts, 1996—; mem. acad. adv. bd. higher edn. Apple Computing, 1997-98. Contbr. articles to profl. jours. Bd. dirs. Congregation Har Ha-Shem, Boulder, 1976-80, pres., 1978, 79, Cmty. Access TV of Boulder, 1996-97. Grantee NIH-Nat. Eye Inst., 1972-90, NSF, 1976-83, March of Dimes Found., 1982-83; Fight for Sight fellow Australian Nat. U., 1969-71. Mem. AAAS, AAHE, AAUP, Assn. Rsch. in Vision and Ophthalmology (sec. chmn. 1981), Soc. Neurosci., Sigma Xi. Democrat. Jewish. Avocation: woodworking. Home: 1010 Grape Ave Boulder CO 80304-2129 Office: Univ Colo Dept Molecular Cellular Biology PO Box 347 Boulder CO 80309-0347

DUBIN, STEPHEN VICTOR, lawyer, holding company executive; b. Bklyn., June 17, 1938; s. Herman E. and Rhoda (Fogel) D.; m. Paula L. Dubin, June 28, 1959; children: Jeffrey D., Michelle L. BA, CUNY, 1961; JD, Boston U., 1961. Bar: N.Y. 1961, Ill. 1975, Pa. 1984, U.S. Dist. Ct. (so. and ea. dists.) N.Y. 1966, U.S. Dist. Ct. (no. dist.) Ill. 1975, U.S. Ct. Appeals (2d cir.) 1975, U.S. Supreme Ct. 1970, U.S. Dist. Ct. (ea. dist.) Pa. 1993, U.S. Ct. Appeals (3d cir.) 1993. Assoc. Kronish, Lieb, Weiner & Hellman, N.Y.C., 1965-67; counsel corp. sec Seligman & Latz, N.Y.C., 1967-72; gen. atty. Montgomery Ward & Co., Inc., N.Y.C., 1972-75; regional counsel, asst. sec. Montgomery Ward & Co., Inc., Chgo., 1975-78; gen. counsel, sr. v.p., sec. dir. CSS Industries, Inc., Phila., 1978—; lectr. consumer law Am. Mgmt. Assn., 1974, 79, 81, Practicing Law Inst., 1982, 88. Nassau County Dem. committeeman, 1967-75, mem. county jud. screening com., 1972-75, del. Nat. Dem. Issues Conv., 1974; pres. Phila. chpt. Am. Jewish Com., 1995-97, chmn. 1997-99, nat bd. govs., 1997—. Capt. JAGC AUS, 1961-65. Mem. ABA, N.Y. State Bar Assn., Pa. Bar Assn., Ill. Bar Assn., Chgo. Bar Assn., Phila. Bar Assn., Bar Assn. Nassau County, N.Y. County Lawyers Assn., Am. Soc. Corp. Secs., Masons (master 1982). Office: CSS Industries Inc 1845 Walnut St Philadelphia PA 19103-4708

DUBINA, JOEL FREDRICK, federal judge; b. 1947. BS, U. Ala., 1970; JD, Cumberland Sch. Law, 1973. Pvt. practice law Jones, Murray, Stewart & Yarbrough, 1974-83; law clk. to presiding judge U.S. Dist. Ct. (mid. dist.) Ala., Montgomery, 1973-74, U.S. magistrate, 1983-86, U.S. Dist. judge, 1986-90; judge U.S. Ct. Appeals (11th cir.), 1990—. Mem. FBA (pres. Montgomery chpt. 1982-83), Nat. Coun. U.S. Magistrate Judges, Fed. Judges Assn. (bd. dirs.), Supreme Ct. Hist. Soc., Ala. State Bar Assn., 11th Cir. Hist. Soc., Montgomery County Bar Assn. (chmn. Law Day com. 1975, constrn. and bylaws com. 1977-80, grievance com. 1981-83), Cumberland Sch. Law Alumni Assn., Lions, Am. Inn of Cts. (pres. Montgomery chpt. 1993-94), Phi Delta Phi. Office: US Cir Ct Appeals 11th Cir PO Box 867 Montgomery AL 36101-0867

DUBLIN, STEPHEN LOUIS, secondary school educator, singer, musician; b. L.A., Aug. 17, 1948; s. Thomas Newton and Carole Louise Dublin. BM, Chapman U., 1970; M in Sch. Adminstrn., U. LaVerne, 1988. Vocal music and English tchr. Leland Stanford Jr. H.S., 1973-74; vocal music and gen. music tchr. Walter B. Hill Jr. H.S., 1974-77, 80-88, Woodrow Wilson H.S., 1977-80; govt. and econs. tchr., mem. various sch. coms., mentor tchr., chmn. history dept. Robert A. Millikan H.S., Long Beach, Calif., 1988—. Mem. campaign com. Harriet Williams Bd. Edn., Long Beach, 1988, 90; Calif. tchr. liason Senate Ralph Dells, Long Beach, 1988-92. Scholar Champman U., 1966-70, Bougess White scholar, 1998; named Tchr. of Yr. Millikan H.S., 1993; nominee Tchr. of Yr., League of Calif. High Schs., 1999; named 1 of 5 most popular tchrs., sr. class Millikan H.S., 1999, Most Inspirational Tchr., 1998, tchr. who influenced 2 students most in their lives, 1999. Mem. Calif. Assn. Econs. (charter), Social Studies Coun., Choral Conductors Guild, So. Calif. Vocal Assn., Constnl. Rights Found. (premier tchr.), Phi Delta Kappa. Avocations: singing, conducting. Home: 4045 E 3d St #112 Long Beach CA 90814

DUBLIN, THOMAS DAVID, retired physician; b. N.Y.C., Jan. 18, 1912; s. Louis I. and Augusta (Salik) D.; m. Christina Macdonald Carlyle, June 3, 1939 (dec. Sept. 1997); children: Sarah Carlyle Dublin Slenczka, Barbara Dublin Van Cleve. A.B., Dartmouth Coll., 1932; M.D., Harvard U., 1936; M.P.H., Johns Hopkins U., 1940, Dr.P.H., 1941. Diplomate Nat Bd. Med. Examiners, Am. Bd. Preventive Medicine (dir. 1961-71, vice. chmn. for gen. preventive medicine 1965-71). Intern 2d Harvard med. service Boston City Hosp., 1936-38; asst. resident physician Hosp. Rockefeller Inst. for Med. Research, N.Y.C., 1938-39; epidemiologist-in-tng. N.Y. State Dept. Health, 1939-40, asst. dist. health officer, 1940, epidemiologist, 1941-42; instr. preventive medicine Johns Hopkins U. Med. Sch., 1940-41; instr. preventive medicine and public health Albany Med. Coll., 1942; lectr. epidemiology DeLamar Inst. Pub. Health, Coll. Physicians and Surgeons, Columbia U., 1942-45; assoc. prof., 1942-43; prof., exec. officer dept. preventive medicine/cmty. health L.I. Coll. Medicine, Bklyn., 1943-48; epidemiologist Kingston Ave. Hosp., Bklyn., 1943-48; exec. dir. Nat. Health Council, 1948-53; med. cons. Nat. Found. for Infantile Paralysis, 1953-55; med. dir. USPHS, 1955-76, Community Services Programs, Office of Dir., NIH, Bethesda, Md., 1955-60; chief epidemiology and biometry br. Nat. Inst. Arthritis and Metabolic Diseases, Bethesda, 1960-66; research adviser, health service Office Tech. Coop. and Research, AID, 1966-68; dir. Office Health Manpower, HEW, 1968-70; program planning officer Bur. Health Manpower, Health Resources Adminstrn., 1970-72, spl. asst. dep. dir. bur., 1972-76; cons. health manpower supply and edn., 1976-78; cons. div. med. edn. AMA and Coordinating Council on Med. Edn., 1976-78; cons. research and devel. Ednl. Commn. for Fgn. Med. Grads., 1978-86; mem. expert adv. panel pub. health adminstrn. WHO, 1954-80; mem. Nat. Adv. Com. Epidemiology and Biometry, 1956-60; chmn. com. on cert. Am. Bd. Med. Specialists, 1972-77. Contbr. articles on internat. health and health manpower to profl. publs. Fellow Am. Pub. Health Assn. (governing council 1954-60, chmn. research policy com. 1957-60), Am. Coll. Preventive Medicine (regent 1973-76), N.Y. Acad. Medicine; mem. AMA, AAAS, Am. Epidemiol. Soc., Assn. Tchrs. Preventive Medicine (sec. 1944-48), Internat. Epidemiol. Assn., Delta Omega. Home: 2949 Garfield Ter NW Washington DC 20008-3507

DUBLIN, THOMAS LOUIS, history educator; b. Norwalk, Conn., Dec. 1, 1946; s. Amos and Louise (Goldschmidt) D.; m. Penny Houston, June 22, 1968 (div. May 1985): children: Sascha, Sonya; m. Kathryn Kish Sklar, Apr. 30, 1988. BA, Harvard U., 1968; PhD, Columbia U., 1975. Prof. history U. Calif.-San Diego, La Jolla, 1976-88, SUNY-Binghamton, Vestal, 1988—. Author: Women at Work, 1979, Farm to Factory, 1981, Transforming Women's Work, 1994, Becoming American, Becoming Ethnic, 1996, When the Mines Closed, 1998; mem. editl. bd. Gender and History, 1993—. Recipient Merle Curti prize Orgn. Am. Historians, 1980, Bancroft prize. Mem. Soc. Am. Historians. E-mail: tdublin@binghamton.edu. Home: RR 1 Box 3088 Brackney PA 18812-9801 Office: SUNY-Binghamton History Dept Binghamton NY 13902

DUBLIS, RAYMOND ANTHONY, insurance executive; b. N.Y.C., Jan. 28, 1957; s. Felix Edward and Jean Lucy (Imprescia) D.; m. Jamie Ann Nicolella, Nov. 16, 1980 (div. Sept. 1989); children: James, Jeana, Matthew; m. Lorraine Schutz, Sept. 13, 1991. Student, Bklyn. Coll. Sales agt. Prudential Inc., Bronx, N.Y., 1982-83, sales mgr., 1983-90; pres. Ray Dublis Ins. Svcs., Bronx, N.Y., 1990-91; pres., CEO Omega Internat. Ins. Brokerage Inc., Southampton, N.Y., 1991—; mem. adv. bd. Bus. Outreach Ctr., N.Y., 1993-96; ins. advisor Rockland County Bar Assn., 1993—, Bronx C. of C., 1993-95, Hunt's Point Market, Bronx, 1993-95, Dental Lab. Assn. of N.Y. State, 1991-97, Kingsbridge Riverdale Van Courtland Devel. Corp., 1993-94, Ins. Adv. Inc. Village Southampton, 1994—; spkr. on health ins. Contbr. articles to profl. jours. Organist Southampton United Meth. Ch.; mem. N.Y. Blood Svc. Gallon Club, 1993—; bd. dirs. Dunes Assn., Southampton, 1994-97, treas. Fountain of Youth Day Care Ctr., 1995-98; pres. soc. com., bd. dirs. bldg. commn., bd. dirs. property commn. Southampton United Meth. Ch., 1998—. Republican. United Methodist. Avocation: music. Home: 9 Meadowgrass Ln Southampton NY 11968-3048 Office: Omega Internat Ins Brokerage Inc 28 Hill St Southampton NY 11968-5317

DUBNER, DANIEL WILLIAM, pediatrician; b. Newark, Apr. 18, 1947; s. Nathan M. and Sara K. (Kuskin) D.; m. Janet Lee, Oct. 5, 1975; children: Sarah, Jeffrey, Emily. BS, Rutgers U., 1969; MD, U. Pa., 1973. Intern, resident Childrens Hosp. Phila., 1973-76; pediatrician Med. Assoc., Chelmsford, Mass., 1978-88, Greater Lowell (Mass.) Pediatrics, 1988—. Author: The Pediatricians' Best Baby Planner for the First Year of Life, 1994. Behavioral Pediatrics fellow U. Wash., Seattle, 1976-77, genetic counseling and birth defect edn. fellow Tufts U., Boston, 1977-78. Fellow Am. Acad. Pediatrics; mem. Mass. Med. Soc. Avocations: running, skiing, travel. Office: Greater Lowell Pediatrics 33 Bartlett St Ste 306 Lowell MA 01852-1398

DUBNER, RONALD, neurobiologist, educator; b. N.Y.C., Oct. 12, 1934; s. Louis and Matilda (Fox) D.; m. Mary Ann Pollack, June 22, 1958; children: Susan R., Andrew D., Julia P. BA, Columbia U., 1955, DDS, 1958; PhD, U. Mich., 1964; Doctorate (hon.), U. Montreal, 1997. Intern USPHS Hosp., Balt., 1958-59; staff dentist Clin. Center, NIH, Bethesda, Md., 1959-61; research scientist Nat. Inst. Dental Research, NIH, 1961-68, chief neural mechanisms sect., 1968-73, chief neurobiology and anesthesiology br., 1973-95; prof., chmn. dept. oral and craniofacial biol. scis. U. Md. at Balt. Dental Sch., Balt., 1995—; vis. scientist dept. anatomy Univ. Coll., London, 1970-71; vis. assoc. prof. Howard U., 1968-80. Co-author: Oral Facial Sensory and Motor Mechanisms, 1971, The Neural Basis of Oral and Facial Function, 1978, Oral-Facial Sensory and Motor Functions, 1981, Current Topics in Pain Research and Therapy, 1983, Advances in Pain Research and Therapy, vol. 9, 1985, vol. 21, 1995, Pain Research and Clinical Management, vol. 3, 1988; mem. edit. bd. Jour. Pain, 1975—, chief editor in Americas, 1990—, Jour. Neurosci., 1980-87, Somatosensory Rsch., 1982-89, Brain Rsch., 1993—, Jour. Dental Rsch., 1995—; contbr. articles to profl. jours., chpts. in books. Recipient Meritorious service medal USPHS, 1975; Birnberg Research Columbia U., 1981; Carl A. Schlack award Assn. Mil. Surgeons U.S., 1985, Second Ann. award for disting. achievement in pain rsch. Bistol-Myers Co., 1989; named J.H. Wolstencroft Meml. lectr. Brit. Brain Research Assn., 1988; Disting. svc. medal USPHS, 1990. Mem. Internat. Assn. Study of Pain (coun. 1975-81, v.p. 1981-87, treas. 1989-93, J. J. Bonica Disting. Lectr. 1996), Soc. Neurosci., Internat. Assn. Dental Research (pres. Neurosci. Group 1977), Am. Physiol. Soc., Am. Assn. Anatomists, AAAS, Am. Pain Soc. (dir. 1980-82, pres. 1987, F.W.L. Keer award lectureship 1992), Omicron Kappa Upsilon. Office: U Md Dental Sch Dept OCBS 666 W Baltimore St Dept Ocbs Baltimore MD 21201-1510*

DUBNICK, BERNARD, retired pharmaceutical company administrator; b. Bklyn., May 29, 1928; s. Jacob Joseph and Lena Bella (Slotkoff) D.; m. Maxine Audrey France, Aug. 31, 1952 (dec. Mar 1963); children: Joshua,

Jeffrey Robert; m. Selma Lydia Blumenthal, July 3, 1966. BS, CCNY, 1949; PhD, U. Ill., 1953. Scientist Warner-Lambert, Morris Plains, N.J., 1953-55, sr. scientist, 1955-62, sr. rsch. assoc., 1962-72, dept. head pharmacodynamics, 1972-77; dir. biochem. pharmacology Warner Lambert/Parke Davis, Ann Arbor, Mich., 1977; dir. CV-CNS rsch. sect. med. rsch. divsn. Am. Cyanamid Co., Pearl River, N.Y., 1977-94, ret., 1994; founder, v.p. Theragem, Inc., Old Tappan, 1994—; chair Biochem. Pharmacology Disc Group, N.Y.C., 1973-74. Author: (with others) Immunopharmacology, 1975, Search for New Drugs, 1978; chpt. co-editor: Psychopharmacology, Third Generation of Progress, 1987. Bd. dirs. Family Svc. West Essex, Essex County, N.J., 1972-73, pres., 1974-75; mem. Family Orgn. Mid-Bergen Mental Health Ctr., Paramus, N.J., 1983. Fellow AAAS, N.Y. Acad. Scis. (chair biochem. sect. 1974-75); mem. Am. Soc. Pharmacology & Exptl. Therapeutics (pharmacology in industry subcom. 1978-80), Am. Chem. Soc. (treas. North Jersey sect. 1960-62). Democrat. Jewish. Home: 129 Lakeview Dr Old Tappan NJ 07675-7071

DUBOFF, SCOTT M., lawyer; b. Chgo., June 19, 1947. BA, U. Wis., 1969, JD cum laude, 1973. Bar: Wis. 1973, D.C. 1975. Atty. office of gen. counsel Fed. Power Commn., 1973-75, atty. office of solicitor, 1975-77; ptnr. Wright & Talisman. Mem. ABA (mem. natural resources sect.), D.C. Bar (mem. environ., energy and natural resources divsn. 1983—). Office: Wright & Talisman 1200 G St NW Ste 600 Washington DC 20005-3838*

DUBOFSKY, JEAN EBERHART, lawyer, retired state supreme court justice; b. 1942; B.A., Stanford U., 1964; LL.B., Harvard U., 1967; m. Frank N. Dubofsky; children: Joshua, Matthew. Admitted to Colo. bar, 1967; legis. asst. to U.S. Senator Walter F. Mondale, 1967-69; atty. Colo. Rural Legal Services, Boulder, 1969-72, Legal Aid Soc. Met. Denver, 1972-73; ptnr. Kelly, Dubofsky, Haglund & Garnsey, Denver, 1973-75; dep. atty. gen. Colo., 1975-77; counsel Kelly, Haglund, Garnsey & Kahn, 1977-79, 88-90, Jean E. Dubofsky, P.C., Boulder, Colo., 1991—; justice Colo. Supreme Ct., Denver, 1979-87; vis. prof. U. Colo. Law Sch., Boulder, 1987-88. Office: 1000 Rose Hill Dr Boulder CO 80302-7148

DUBOIS, ALAN BEEKMAN, art museum curator; b. Forest Glen, N.Y., Dec. 14, 1935; s. Raymond Van Orden and Florence (Beekman) DuB.; m. Joan Edna Burger, Apr. 25, 1959; children: Dean, Ronald, Douglas, Jonathan. BS in Art Edn., SUNY-New Paltz, 1958; MFA in Photography and Related Arts, Ind. U., 1966. Dir. Washington County Mus. Fine Arts, Hagerstown, Md, 1964-66; asst. dir. Mus. Fine Arts, St. Petersburg, Fla., 1966-84, Orlando (Fla.) Mus. Art, 1984-89; curator decorative arts Ark. Arts Ctr., Little Rock, 1989—. Nat. Endowment Arts fellow, 1972, 75. Mem. Nat. Art Edn. Assn., Coll. Art Assn., Am. Assn. Mus. Office: Ark Arts Ctr PO Box 2137 Little Rock AR 72203-2137

DUBOIS, ARTHUR BROOKS, physiologist, educator; b. N.Y.C., Nov. 21, 1923; s. Eugene Floyd and Rebeckah (Rutter) DuB.; m. Roberdeau Callery, June 21, 1950; children: Anne R., Brooks, James E.F. Student, Harvard U., 1941-43; M.D., Cornell U., 1946. Intern in medicine N.Y. Hosp., 1946-47; med. research fellow U. Rochester, 1949-51; asst. resident Peter Bent Brigham Hosp., Boston, 1951-52; asst. prof. to prof. physiology and medicine U. Pa., 1952-74; prof. epidemiology and physiology Yale U., 1974—; dir. John B. Pierce Found. Lab., 1974-88. Author: The Lung, 3d ed. 1986, Body Plethysmography, 1969; contbr. articles to profl. jours. Served with USNR, 1947-49. Recipient Rsch. Career award NIH, 1963-74; Edward Livingston Trudeau medal Am. Lung Assn., 1989. Mem. Am. Physiol. Soc., Am. Soc. Clin. Investigation, Assn. Am. Physicians, Undersea Med. Soc. Democrat. Clubs: Harvard, Cosmos. Home: 370 Livingston St New Haven CT 06511-1336 Office: 290 Congress Ave New Haven CT 06519-1403

DUBOIS, CINDY A., guidance counselor; b. Biddeford, Maine, Aug. 14, 1958; d. Arthur E. and Phyllis L. Dubois. BA in Psychology, Regis Coll., 1980, MA in Spl. Edn., 1983; MA in Counseling Psychology, Tufts U., 1989. Cert. guidance counselor, sch. psychologist, moderate spl. needs tchr., social studies tchr. Spl. edn. tchr. Burlington (Mass.) H.S., 1983-87; spl. edn. tchr. Marshall Simonds Middle Sch., Burlington, 1989-91, guidance counselor, 1991—. Summer camp vol. Burlington (Mass.) Recreation Dept., 1974-75; vol. counselor Burlington (Mass.) Cmty. Life Ctr., 1988-89; religious edn. tchr. St. Malachy's Parish, Burlington, 1994-97. Mem. Nat. Assn. Sch. Psychologists, Mass. Assn. Sch. Psychologists. Roman Catholic. Home: 23 Daniel Dr Burlington MA 01803-2701 Office: Marshall Simonds Middle Sch 114 Winn St Burlington MA 01803-2701

DU BOIS, CLARENCE HAZEL, JR., clergy member; b. Springfield, Ga., Nov. 24, 1929; s. Clarence Hazel and Nettie Lou (Hendry) D.; m. Phyllis June Prior, Sept. 4, 1949; children: Sidney, Hazel, Patricia, Philip. Student, Ga. Tchrs. Coll., 1946-47; degree in Div., New England Sch. Theology, 1950; BA, Berkshire Christian Coll., 1987. Ordained minister of Gospel, 1950. Pres. Ga. Advent Christian Conf., Swainsboro, 1951-55, Pocahontas A.C. Conf., Tazewell, Va., 1964-68, Appalachian Region, Charleston, W.Va., 1966-74, Cen. Region, Ft. Worth, Tex., 1993-95; mem. exec. coun. A.C. Gen. Conf. Advent Christian Denomination, Charlotte, N.C., 1966-74, 93-95; pres. Prairie States A.C. Conf., Chgo., 1983-91; pastor Advent Christian Ch., Mendota, Ill., 1979-96; interim pastor Advent Christian Ch., Friendship, Maine, 1996—. Author: (book) Workbook on Bible Doctrines, 1953. Bd. dirs. Mendota Food Pantry, 1993-96, Mendota Area Sr. Svcs., 1994-96; pres. Washington A.C. Campground Assn., 1996. Named Alumnus of the Yr. Bershire Christian Coll., 1970-71. Mem. Mendota Area Ministerial Assn. (sec. 1988-91), Mendota Union Ch. Pastors (chmn. 1985-90, 93-95). Mem. Advent Christian Ch. Avocation: photography. Home: 7 School St Friendship ME 04547-4418

DUBOIS, JAN ELY, federal judge; b. Phila., Jan. 17, 1931; s. M. Norman and Syd (Stern) DuB.; m. Ruth Harberg, Aug. 19, 1956; children: Marc Norman, Jon Stuart, Peter Andrew, Pamela Sue. BS, U. Pa., 1952; LLB, Yale U., 1957. Law clk. civil div. U.S. Dept. of Justice, Washington, 1956; law clk. to Hon. Harry E. Kalodner Phila., 1957-58; atty. White and Williams, Phila., 1958-64, ptnr., 1964-88; judge U.S. Dist. Ct. (ea. dist.) Pa., Phila., 1988—. Trustee Phila. Bar Found., 1981-89, pres. 1987; trustee Reform Congregation Keneseth Israel, Elkins Park, Pa., pres., 1985-87. 1st lt. U.S. Army, 1952-54, cpt. U.S.A.R., ret. Recipient John Currier Gallagher prize Yale U., 1957. Mem. ABA, Pa. Bar Assn., Phila. Bar Assn. (chmn. medico-legal com. 1981), Yale Law Sch. Assn. of Phila. (past pres.), Yale Club. Office: US Dist Ct 12613 US Courthouse 601 Market St Philadelphia PA 19106-1713

DUBOIS, JEAN HALL, writer; b. Denver, Jan. 4, 1926; d. Forest R. and Meyrtle (Aker) Hall; m. Edward N. Dubois, Aug. 21, 1947; children: Christine Bourne, Katherine Reed, William E. BA in Liberal Arts, U. Wyo., 1947; MA in English, Pa. State U., 1963. Author: Galaxy of Stars, 1976, Patchwork Quilting in Wool, 1978, Silent Stones, 1992, Same Sweet Yellow, 1994; designer, webmaster Under Running Laughter, 1998. Mem. Haiku Soc. Am. (co-editor anthology 1995). Avocations: quilting, fabric art. E-mail: sweetyellow@juno.com. Home: PO Box 1430 Golden CO 80402

DUBOIS, KAREN YORK, secondary school educator; b. Clayton, Ga., Aug. 30, 1947; d. James Carlton and Mary Jo (May) York; divorced; 1 child, James Frederick. AA, Webber Coll., Babson Park, Fla., 1967; BSBA, Brenau Coll., Gainesville, Ga., 1985; MEd, No. Ga. Coll., Dahlonega, 1992. Exec. sec. Bowles & Tillinghast, Inc., Atlanta, 1969-73; office mgr. Physicians Ratchford McDaniel, Atlanta, 1974-75; sales and office mgr. John P. Dillard Realty, Dillard, Ga., 1980-83; with sales dept. Ed West Realty, Clayton, 1983-84; assoc. broker Sheffield Realty, Clayton, 1984-86, ERA-Linda Durrence Realty, Dillard, Ga., 1986—; tchr. bus. edn. Rabun County High Sch., Tiger, Ga., 1986—; co-sponsor varsity cheerleaders Rabun County High Sch., 1990-91, sponsor jr. varsity cheerleaders, 1990-91, prin.'s adv. com., 1990-91, handbook com., 1990-91, attendance com., 1989-90; advisor DECA - Assn. of Mktg. Students; coord. Coop. Bus. Edn. program. Mem. Future Bus. Leaders Assn. (advisor 1986—), Ga. Bus. Edn. Assn., Profl. Assn. Ga. Educators, Nat. Assn. Realtors, Rabun County Bd. Realtors, Nat. Bus. Edn. Assn. Democrat. Methodist. Avocations: reading, art collecting, travel. E-mail: Kayd@rabun.net. Home: PO Box 594 Clayton GA 30525-0594 Office: Rabun County High Sch RR 1 Tiger GA 30576-9801

DUBOIS, MARK BENJAMIN, utility executive; b. Peoria, Ill., Sept. 27, 1955; s. Benjamin John and Marjorie Abigail (Black) DuB.; m. Jeri Rene Simmons, May 24, 1975; 1 child, Benjamin Robert. BS with high distinction, U. Ariz., 1977; MA, U. Kans., 1981. Rsch. asst. State Biol. Survey Kans., Lawrence, 1978-81; systems programmer Cen. Ill. Light Co., Peoria, 1982-84, operating software supr., 1984-85, gen. supr. data processing ops. sect., 1985-88, gen. supr. applications systems sect., 1988-90, security adminstr. staff info. systems, 1990-91, gen. supr. data processing ops. sect., 1991-93, staff info. system planning admin., 1993-95, sr. market rsch. adminstr., 1995-97, team leader Internet Enhancement Project, 1997-98, sr. bus. cons., 1998-99; sr. cons., Heartland Information Tech. Svcs., 1999—; part-time instr. nat. sci. and computer literacy Midstate Coll., 1987—, Internet literacy web page design Ill. Ctrl. Coll., 1998—; rsch. affiliate Ill. Nat. Hist. Survey, Urbana, Ill., 1988—; cons. identifier, Ctr. for Insect Identification, Lansing, Mich., 1988-98. Bd. dirs. Spl. People Encounter Christ, Peoria, 1982-83, Midstate Coll., Peoria, Ill., 1999—; bd. pres. Sun Found., Washburn, Ill., 1998—; treas. Religious Edn. Activities for Cmty. Handicapped, Lawrence, 1978-81; cons. Jr. Achievement, 1987-88; mem. sch. bd. Father Sweeney Sch. for Academically Gifted, 1989-91; chmn. Utility Info. Systems Exchange, 1991-92; amb. Lakeview Mus. Arts Scis., 1992-95, guest curator, 1993-95; editl. bd. Chpt. of Nature Conservancy, 1997—. Mem. AAAS, Data Processing Mgmt. Assn., Internat. Union for Study Social Insects, Am. Entomol. Soc., Am. Inst. Biol. Scis., Mid-Am. Paleontol. Soc., Cen. States Entomol. Soc., Kans. Acad. Sci., N.Y. Entomol. Soc., Animal Behavior Soc., Cambridge Entomological Club, Soc. Systematic Zoology, Sigma Xi, Phi Kappa Phi, Alpha Zeta, Gamma Sigma Delta (agrl. honoraries). Contbr. articles on entomology and personal computer software to profl. jours. E-mail: mbdubois@gateway.net. Home: 116 Burton St Washington IL 61571-2509 Office: Heartland Info Tech Svcs 300 Liberty St Peoria IL 61602-1404

DUBOIS, NANCY Q., elementary school educator; b. St. Petersburg, Fla., June 6, 1960; d. Thomas Malcolm and Barbara Jean (Leitner) Quehl; m. Donald F. Dubois, Nov. 27, 1981; children: Jacquelyn Nicole, Justin Jared. BA, U. South Fla., Tampa, 1983; MEd, U. Fla., 1993; Mid-Mgmt. Cert., Schreiner Coll., 1999. Cert. tchr., Fla., N.Mex., Tex. Tchr. St. Patricks Sch., Fayetteville, N.C., 1984-85, The Most Holy Name Sch., Gulfport, Fla., 1985-88, Kirtland Elem. Sch., Albuquerque, 1988-91; field advisor Coll. Edn., U. Fla., Gainesville, 1991-93; 4th grade tchr. Schulze Elem. Sch., San Antonio, 1993-97; tchr. Bellaire Elem. Sch., San Antonio, 1997—; USI peer tchr., 1997—. Named Tchr. of Yr., Bellaire Elem. Sch., 1998-99. Mem. ASCD, Internat. Reading Assn., Fla. Coun. Tchrs. of Math., Kappa Delta Pi. Republican. Roman Catholic. Avocations: reading, cross-stitch, swimming.

DU BOIS, PAUL ZINKHAN, library director; b. Ravenna, Ohio, Jan. 5, 1936; s. John Harold and Marie Eggleston (Miller) DuB.; m. Carol Ann Johnson, Aug. 15, 1959; children: Megan, Christopher. B.A., Hiram Coll., 1959; M.A. (Crawford scholar), Kent State U., 1960; M.A., Western Res. U., 1962, Ph.D., 1968. Library coordinator Mentor (Ohio) Pub. Sch. System, 1963-64; head librarian N.Y. State Hist. Assn., Cooperstown, 1964-69; asst. dir. Kent State U., 1969-72; dir. library, prof. media communications sci. Trenton (N.J.) State Coll., 1972-91; dean libr. svcs. Winthrop U., Rock Hill, S.C., 1991—; v.p. DuBois Book Store, Inc., Kent, 1969-85; mem. adv. coun. Princeton U. Libr., 1985-89; cons. N.Y. State Coun. on Arts, Nat. Am. Studies Faculty, NEH, Adirondack Mus., Hist. Gainesville, Bucks County Hist. Soc., Inst. Mus. Svcs., N.J. and Pa. Coms. on Humanities, Mid. States Assn. and others; cons. antiquarian books; pres. N.J. Coun. State Coll. and Univ. Librs., 1975-76; mem. N.J. Acad. Libr. Standards Task Force, 1983; mem. adv. bd. N.J. Musto Commn., 1979-80; mem. exec. bd. N.J. Acad. Libr. Network, 1985-91, S.C. Libr. Dirs. Forum, 1993—, Metrolina Libr. Assn., 1992-94; chair S.C. Coun. Librs., 1993-94. Editor: Librarians' Choice, 1972-81, Paul Leicester Ford, An American Man of Letters, 1977, co-editor Reading and the Art of Librarianship, 1986; contbr. articles and revs. to profl. jours. Pres. Pennsbury Scholarship Found., 1986-88; pres. Episc. Faculty Conf., 1986—. Recipient Hugo Alpers award Kent State U., 1960; fellow Seminar for Hist. Adminstrs., Colonial Williamsburg, 1963. Mem. Manuscript Soc., Nat. Assn. Scholars, Nat. Trust Historic Preservation, Beta Phi Mu, Phi Alpha Theta. Episcopalian. Club: Trenton Torch (pres. 1975-76). Home: 1805 Paces River Ave Apt 3-102 Rock Hill SC 29732-1775 Office: Winthrop U Dean Libr Svcs Oakland Ave Rock Hill SC 29733

DUBOIS, RUTH HARBERG, human service agency executive; b. Phila., Apr. 8, 1933; d. Sidney and Lenore (Abramson) Harberg; m. Jan E. DuBois, Aug. 9, 1956; children: Marc, Jon, Peter, Pamela. AB, Mt. Holyoke Coll., 1955. Prin. cons. N.Y. State Heroin and Alcohol Abuse Study, 1981; mem. Pa. Gov.'s Coun. on Drug and Alcohol Abuse, 1977-80; tech. asst. Nat. Inst. Drug Abuse/Pyramid Project, 1978-85; co-dir. DuBois and Rosenwald Associates, 1982-87; with Children's Rsch. and Edn. Inst., 1984-87; exec. dir. Corp. Alliance for Drug Edn., Phila., 1987—; mem. com. on substance abuse The Mayor's Commn. on Health in the Eighties, Phila., 1983; tech. asst. Pa. Dept. Health, Office of Drug and Alcohol Program, 1981-85; rsch. asst. in cancer and endocrinology Yale U. Sch. of Medicine and Thomas Jefferson U., 1955-59. Contbr. articles to profl. jours. Mem. numerous bds. including chmn. bd. dirs. Albert Einstein Med. Ctr., Phila. Citizens for Children and Youth, Montgomery County Mental Health, 1982-85; bd. dirs. Abraxas Found., Inc., Pitts., 1981-97; adv. coun. dept. pub. health Phila. Prevention Partnership, 1992-95; mem. Mayor's Pvt. Sector Task Force on Mgmt. and Productivity/Dept. Human Svcs. Study, Phila., 1992-93, others. Office: Alliance for Drug Edn Corp NBC 10 Bldg City Ave and Monument Rd Bala Cynwyd PA 19004

DU BOIS, TIM, recording industry executive; b. 1948. MS in Acctg., Okla. State U. Former sr. fin. analyst Fed. Res. Bank, Dallas; pres. Arista/Nashville, 1989—. Hit songs include: Love in the First Degree, When I Call Your Name, She Got the Goldmine (I Got the Shaft). Office: Arista Records 1400 18th Ave S Nashville TN 37212*

DU BOIS, WILLIAM, JR., retired public relations professional; b. Hartford City, Ind., Mar. 19, 1933; s. William LeRoy DuBois and Manan Martha Cline; m. Treva Marileen Boise, Apr. 2, 1955; children: Janice Lea and Janelle Lyn (twins), Teresa Ann, Steven Dean. BS in Secondary Edn., Ball State U., 1961, MA in Journalism and Polit. Sci., 1984. Reporter, sportswriter News-Times, Hartford City, 1952-53, 55-56; reporter, sports editor, editor Comml. Rev., Portland, Ind., 1959-60; editor The Graphic, Portland, 1959-60; reporter, copy editor, city editor Muncie (Ind.) Star, 1960-65, mng. editor, 1967-74; info. dir. Ind. C. of C., Indpls., 1965-67; adv. Gov. Otis R. Bowen, exec. asst. to state ch. comm. dir. Ind. Rep. Party, Indpls., 1974-76; exec. asst. to Gov. Bowen State of Ind., Indpls., 1977-80, exec. asst. to Gov. Orr, 1981-83; speechwriter Van P. Smith Ontario Corp., Muncie, 1983-84; exec. dir. State Student Assistance Commn. Ind., 1985-87; pres. Ind. Colls. and Univs. of Ind. Inc., 1987-91; exec. asst. for pub. rels. Ivy Tech. State Coll., Indpls., 1992-98; ret., 1998. Author: Ontario Corporation—A History, 1982, Pyromet, 1983, Descendants and Family of William Cline (1746-1853), Soldier of the American Revolution and American Pioneer, 1990. Mem., bd. dirs., mgmt. com. Ind. Higher Edn. Telecomms. Sys.; mem. exec. com. Midwest Partnership of Ind. Colls.; bd. dirs., publicity chair United Way Delaware County. Named Hon. Jaycee, Muncie Jaycees, 1972; recipient award for advocacy, leadership and sensitivity to problems of the mentally ill Ind. Dept. Mental Health, 1983, award for dedicated svc. to fin. aid profession Ind. Student Fin. Aid Assn., 1987, award for profl. dedication to state student fin. aid programs State Student Assistance Commn. Ind., 1987. Mem. Soc. Profl. Journalists (founding mem. and 1st pres. Ind. East chpt.), Nat. Assn. Ind. Colls. and Univs., State Assn. Execs. Coun., State-Nat. Info. Network (bd. dirs.), Ind. Hist. Soc., Huguenot Hist. Soc., DuBois Family Assn., Ball State U. Alumni Coun., Ball State U. Journalism Alumni Assn. (bd. dirs.), Muncie-Del. County C. of C. (bd. dirs., exec. com.), Indpls. Press Club (bd. dirs.). Avocations: genealogy, Indiana history, art. Home: 430 Shady Ln Greenwood IN 46142

DU BOISE, KIM REES, artist, photographer, art educator; b. Hattiesburg, Miss., Apr. 7, 1953; d. Samernie and Margaret J. (Mitchell) R.; divorced; children: Timothy L., M. Ashley (dec.). BA, U. So. Miss., 1986, M of Art Edn., 1988; postgrad., U. Ala., 1994-95. Art tchr. grades 7-12 Columbia (Miss.) Acad., 1975-76; with prodn./ad design Columbian-Progress/Sunday Mirror (News), Columbia, 1980-81; with advt. design/prodn. Washington Parish ERA-Leader (newspaper), Franklinton, La., 1981; art tchr. grades kindergarten-12 Hattiesburg Prep. Sch., 1984-85; instr. art Pearl River C.C., Poplarville, Miss., 1987-94; artist/photographer Dogwood Studios, 1988-97, Photo Arts Studio, 1997—; adj. instr. U. So. Miss., 1996-97, 98—; festival coord. Very Spl. Arts Festival, SE Dist., Poplarville, Miss., 1989-94; art show juror Lamar County Home Extension Art Show, Lumberton, Miss., 1988; fine art juror Pearl River County Fair Competition, Poplarville, 1989; juror Picayune PTA Competition and Annual Art Competition-Picayune Meml. High Sch., 1990; participant regional round-Table on discipline based art edn. Getty Ctr. for Edn. in Arts, Tulsa, 1988. Sculptor Ann. Student Juried Exhibit, 1986; artist, weaver fine crafts (tapestry) Ann. Student Juried Exhibit, 1986, Ann. Bi-State Competition, 1986, 96; group exhbn. MSC/JCAIA Art Exhbn., 1991, Miss. Cmty. Jr. Coll. Art, 1991-92, Art by Art Tchrs. MAEA, 1992; mixed media/photography Ann. Juried Art Student League Exhibit, 1995, photography Black Warrior 10 Exhibit, U. N.Mex., 1995, others. Chmn. troop 21 Dixie Com. Boy Scouts Am., Hattiesburg, 1989-93; mem. Miss. Jaycettes/Marion County Jaycettes, Columbia, 1976-84, U.S. Jaycee Women, 1976-84. Named one of Outstanding Young Women of Am., 1981-84, First Lady #83 (Life Mem.) Miss. Jaycettes, 1982, Winner Speak-Up Competition, Miss. Jaycettes, 1981. Mem. Miss. Art Edn. Assn., Nat. Art Edn. Assn., New Orleans Mus. of Art (assoc.), So. Miss. Art Assn., Nat. Mus. of Women in the Arts (charter), Am. Crafts Coun., Nature Conservancy, U. So. Miss. Alumni Assn., Walter Anderson Mus. Art, Kappa Delta Pi. Episcopalian. Avocations: camping, fishing, reading, cooking.

DUBOSE, CHARLES WILSON, lawyer; b. Sumter, S.C., Mar. 2, 1949; s. Frank Elsivan and Fannie Louise (Wilson) DuB.; m. Patricia Holman Rayle, Dec. 5, 1987; children: Charles Wilson Jr., Margaret Louise Rayle, Frank Elsivan IV. AB magna cum laude, Harvard U., 1971; JD, U. Va., 1974. Bar: Ga. 1974, U.S. Dist. Ct. (no. dist.) Ga. 1974, U.S. Ct. Appeals (5th cir.) 1976, U.S. Ct. Appeals (4th cir.) 1978, U.S. Supreme Ct. 1979, U.S. Ct. Appeals (11th cir.) 1981, U.S. Dist. Ct. (mid. dist.) Ga. 1982, S.C. 1992. Assoc. Kutak, Rock & Huie and predecessor firms, Atlanta, 1974-79; ptnr. Kutak, Rock & Huie, Atlanta, 1979-84; of counsel Griffin, Cochrane & Marshall, P.C., Atlanta, 1985-86, ptnr., 1986-89, mng. ptnr., 1989-92; ptnr. Schnader, Harrison, Segal & Lewis, Atlanta, 1992—; Atlanta mng. ptnr. Schnader, Harrison, Segal & Lewis, 1995—. Elder Peachtree Presbyn. Ch., Atlanta; mem. adv. bd. Atlanta's Table, 1991—, vice chmn., 1994, chmn., 1995; exec. vice chmn. Atlanta Billy Graham Crusade. Mem. ABA, Am. Law Inst., State Bar Ga. (bd. govs. 1998—, chair ind. def. com. 1997—), Atlanta Bar Assn. (bd. dirs. 1992—, sec. 1993-94, v.p., pres.-elect 1994-95, pres. 1995-96, bd. dirs. litigation sect. 1988-94, chmn. litigation sect. 1992-93), The South Carolina Bar, Lawyers Com. for Civil Rights Under Law (Atlanta steering com.), Atlanta Bar Found. (bd. dirs. 1995-96), Atlanta Vol. Lawyers Found. (bd. dirs. 1995-96), Inst. Continuing Legal Edn. in Ga. (bd. trustees 1995-96), Am. Arbitration Assn. (comml. arbitration panel, constrn. industry arbitration panel), Associated Builders and Contractors of Ga. (chair Olympic task force, legal rights com.), Lawyers Club of Atlanta. Avocations: photography, piano, architecture, historic preservation. Home: 1050 East Ave Madison GA 30650-1467 Office: Schnader Harrison et al 303 Peachtree St NE Ste 2800 Atlanta GA 30308-3263

DUBOSE, ELIZABETH (BETTYE DUBOSE), community health nurse; b. Ozark, Ala., Nov. 11, 1930; d. Samuel D. and Mattie Victoria (Harrell) Preston; m. Charles Raymond Hudson, July 31, 1949; 1 child, Julianne Schenker Adams; m. Frederick William Schenker, Jr., Dec. 15, 1962; m. John Calvin DuBose, July 15, 1978. ADN, Columbus State U., 1973, BSN, 1977. Lab tech. II Ala. Bureau of Labs., Dothan, Ala., 1951-62; student nurse CCU St. Francis Hosp., Columbus, Ga., 1972-73; charge nurse The Med. Ctr., Columbus, 1973-75, infection control nurse, 1975-78; charge nurse The Bradley Ctr., Columbus, Ga., 1974-78; clin. instr. nursing Columbus State U., 1977-78; dir. nursing Oakview Manor Nursing Home, Ozark, Ala., 1979-84; patient care coord. Wiregrass Home Health Agy., 13 Counties in SE Ala., 1984-86; home health coord. Ala. Pub. Health Dept., Abbeville, Ala., 1986-90; home health nurse Dale Co. Health Dept., Ozark, Ala., 1990—; libr. com. mem. The Medical Ctr., Columbus, Ga., 1974-77; chmn. adv bd. Oakview Manor, Ozark, 1980-84. Mem. adv. bd. Henry Co. Health Dept., Abbeville, 1986-88, chmn. adv. bd., 1988-90. Republican. Protestant. Avocations: sewing, knitting, sunday sch. tchr., grandmother. Home: RR 1 Box 68 Ariton AL 36311-9718 Office: Ala State Health Dept Dale Co Ala Home Health Andrews Ave Ozark AL 36360

DUBOSE, FRANCIS MARQUIS, clergyman; b. Elba, Ala., Feb. 27, 1922; s. Hansford Arthur and Mayde Frances (Owen) DuB.; BA cum laude, Baylor U., 1947; MA, U. Houston, 1958; BD, Southwestern Bapt. Sem., 1957, ThD, 1961; postgrad. Oxford (Eng.) U., 1972; m. Dorothy Anne Sessums, Aug. 28, 1940; children: Elizabeth Anne Parnell, Frances Jeannine Huffman, Jonathan Michael, Celia Danielle. Pastor Bapt. chs., Tex., Ark., 1939-61; supt. missions. So. Bapt. Conv., Detroit, 1961-66; prof. missions Golden Gate Bapt. Sem., 1966—, dir. World Mission Ctr., 1979—, sr. prof., 1992; lectr., cons. in 115 cities outside U.S., 1969-82; v.p. Conf. City Mission Supts., So. Bapt. Conv., 1964-66; trustee Mich. Bapt. Inst., 1963-66; mem. San Francisco Inter-Faith Task Force on Homelessness. Mem. Internat. Assn. Mission Study, Am. Soc. Missiology, Assn. Mission Profs. Co-editor: The Mission of the Church in the Racially Changing Community, 1969; author: How Churches Grow in an Urban World, 1978, Classics of Christian Missions, 1979, God Who Sends: A Fresh Quest for Biblical Mission, 1983, Home Cell Groups and House Churches, 1987, Mystic on Main Street, 1994; contbr. to Toward Creative Urban Strategy; Vol. III Ency. of So. Baptists, also articles to profl. jours. Home: 2 Carpenter Ct San Francisco CA 94124-4429 Office: Golden Gate Bapt Sem Mill Valley CA 94941

DUBOSE, JAMES DAULTON, dentist; b. Turbeville, S.C., July 14, 1938; s. Robert Alvin and Olive (Dennis) DuB.; B.S., U. S.C., 1961; D.M.D., U. Louisville, 1965; m. Kathy Elizabeth Johnson, Mar. 14, 1974; children—Olive Elizabeth, Dixie Dawn. Practice dentistry, Bishopville, S.C., 1965-70, Aiken, S.C., 1970-72, Manning, S.C., 1972—; staff mem. Clarendon Meml. Hosp., Manning; pres. D.M.D. Enterprises; owner Bluff Plantation, Colleton County, S.C.; v.p. R.A. DuBose, Inc.; pres. Best Western Inn, Three D. Inc., Santee, S.C. Chmn. Heart Fund, Lee County, S.C., 1966; trustee, deacon Summerton Bapt. Ch., Clarendon Hall Sch. Mem. ADA, Am. Soc. Dentistry for Children, Augusta Dental Soc., Pee-Dee Dist. Dental Soc., Delta Sigma Delta. Baptist. Clubs: Century (Columbia, S.C.); Sertoma (Aiken, S.C.); Lions (Summerton, S.C.). Home: 215 Cooper Dr Santee SC 29142-9319 Office: Mill And Hospital St Manning SC 29102

DUBOVSKY, EVA VITKOVA, nuclear medicine physician, educator; b. Prague, Czechoslovakia, 1933. MD, Charles U. Faculty Medicine, Prague, Czech Republic, 1957. Diplomate Am. Bd. Nuclear Medicine. Intern U. Hosp., Charles U., Prague, 1956-57, chief resident, 1961-63, fellow divsn. endocrinology & metabolism, 1963-65; rsch. fellow divsn. endocrinology U. Ala., Birmingham, 1968-70; clin. assoc. VA Med. Ctr., Birmingham, 1970-72; dir. nuc. medicine U. Ala. Hosp., Birmingham; from instr. to prof. U. Ala., Birmingham, 1954—; vis. prof. U. Cin., 1987, Cleve. CLinic, 1987, VA Med. Ctr., Portland, Oreg.,1988, Columbia Coll. Physicians & Surgeons, 1989, Dartmouth Med. Ctr., 1989, William Beaumont Hosp., 1992, 94, Charles U., 1994, Baptist Med. Ctr. Okla., 1994, U. Louisville, 1994. Editor: Nuclear Medicine Technology Continuing Education Review, 1976, 2d edit., 1981; co-editor: Nuclear Medicine in Clinical Urology and Nephrology, 1985, Atlas of Nuclear Medicine and Imaging; contbr. chpts. to books and articles to profl. jours. Mem. AMA, Am. Coll. Nuclear Physicians, Soc. Nuclear Medicine, Soc. Uroradiology. Office: U Ala Hosp Divsn Nuc Medicine 619 19th St S Birmingham AL 35233-0001

DUBOW, ARTHUR MYRON, investor, lawyer; b. Chgo., Sept. 18, 1933; s. David and Matilda (Polster) D.; m. Isabella Goodrich Breckinridge, Mar. 2, 1962 (div. Dec. 1983); children: Charles Stewart, Alexandra Breckinridge; m. Barbara J. Shattuck, Dec. 27, 1986. AB, Harvard U., 1954, LLB, 1957. Bar: N.Y. 1962. Assoc. firm Webster Sheffield Fleischmann Hitchcock & Chrystie, N.Y.C., 1960-64; v.p., dir. Back Bay-Orient Enterprises, Inc., Boston, 1965-68; pres. Back Bay-Orient Enterprises, Inc., 1968-76; pres., dir. Bayorient Holding Corp., Boston, 1969-76; pres. Korea Capital Corp., N.Y.C., 1968-76, Fortune Capital Ltd., Boston, 1979-84; pres., dir. Boston Co. Energy Advisers, 1981-85; chmn. Instl. Shareholder Svcs., 1989-91; pres. Fourth Estate, Inc., 1990-96; bd. dirs. Sulpetro Can. Ltd., Calgary, Alta.,

1966-76, Dallas, 1973-76, chmn. exec. com., 1974-76; bd. dir. Castle Convertible Fund, Inc., Spectra Fund, Inc., Alger Funds, Coolidge Investment Corp., Herald Prodns., Inc.; fellow Ctr. for Internat. Affairs Harvard U., 1976-77. Mem. mgmt. com. Parenting mag., 1986-90. Mem. vis. com. dept. visual and environ. studies, dept. East Asian langs. and civilizations Ctr. for Sci. and Internat. Affairs, Harvard U., 1971-87; bd. dirs. Inst. Ednl. Leadership, 1982-89, Sabre Found., 1980-96, Thomas Jefferson Forum, 1986-92; chmn. bd. dirs. Potomac Assocs., Inc., Washington, 1975-95; mem. nat. adv. com. on accreditation and instl. eligibility U.S. Dept. Edn., 1982-86; co-chmn. New Am. Filmmakers' Series, Whitney Mus. Am. Art, N.Y.C., 1970-76; mem. adv. bd. Sch. Advanced Internat. Studies, 1980-88; trustee Arthur Dubow Found. With U.S. Army, 1957-59. Clubs: Harvard of N.Y. and Somerset; Tavern (Boston). Home (summer): PO Box 969 Wainscott NY 11975-0969 also (winter): PO Box 840 Patagonia AZ 85624-0840 *Increased urbanization and the concomitant phenomenon of growth in the size of business and government bureaucracy has caused a "me/they" attitude or alienation of the individual in America. We must inculcate a sense of civic and social responsibility, improve our educational system and protect our environment in order to create national prosperity and purposefulness.*

DUBOWSKY, STEVEN, mechanical engineering educator; b. N.Y.C., Jan. 14, 1942. B.M.E., Rensselaer Poly. Inst., 1963; M.S., Columbia U., 1964, Sc.D., 1971. Registered profl. engr., Calif. Engr. Am. Electric Power Service Corp., N.Y.C., 1962; engr. Electric Bd. div. Gen. Dynamics Corp., Groton, Conn., 1963; sr. engr. Optical Tech. div. Perkin Elmer Corp., Wilton, Conn., 1964-71; lectr. adj. Rensselaer Poly. Inst. Hartford Grad. Ctr., East Windsor Hill, Conn., 1970-71; asst. prof. mechanics and structures dept. UCLA, 1971-75, assoc. prof., 1975-80, prof., 1980-82; prof. dept. mech. engring. MIT, Cambridge, 1982—; mem. vis. faculty engring. dept. Cambridge U., Eng., 1977-78; vis. scholar Queen's Coll., Cambridge, 1977-78; vis. prof. engring. div. Calif. Inst. Tech., 1988-89; cons. in field. Contbr. numerous articles to profl. jours. Recipient best paper award 11th Mechanisms Conf., 1971, Tech. Conf., Washington, 1982. Fellow ASME (chmn. mechanisms com. 1978-80, gen. com. design engring. disvn. 1979—, exec. com. 1983-88, best paper award dynamic systems and control divsn. 1979); mem. IEEE (sr. mem.), U.S. Coun. for Theory of Machines and Mechanisms, Robotics Internat. of Soc. Mfg. Engrs. (sr.), Sigma Xi, Tau Beta Pi. Office: MIT 3-469A 77 Massachusetts Ave Cambridge MA 02139-4307

DUBRIN, ANDREW JOHN, behavioral sciences, management educator, author; b. N.Y.C., Mar. 3, 1935; s. Albert Edward and Louise Theresa (Walsh) D.; m. Drew, Douglas, Melanie. A.B., Hunter Coll., 1956; M.S., Purdue U., 1957; Ph.D., Mich. State U., 1960. Diplomate: Am. Bd. Profl. Psychology; cert. psychologist N.Y. state. Psychologist Data Systems div. IBM, Kingston, N.Y., 1962-63; teaching asst., part-time instr. Purdue U., West Lafayette, Ind., 1956-57; psychol. cons. Clark, Cooper, Field & Wohl, N.Y.C., 1963-64; psychol. cons. Rohrer, Hibler & Replogle, N.Y.C., 1964-70, ptnr., 1964-70; assoc. prof. Rochester (N.Y.) Inst. Tech., 1970-72, prof. behavioral sci., 1972—, dept. head mgmt., 1982-84, prof. mgmt., 1984—; mem. N.Y. State Bd. Psychology, 1979—; cons. lectr. in field. Author: The Practice of Managerial Psychology, 1972, Women in Transition, 1972, The Singles Game, 1973, Fundamentals of Organization Behavior: An Applied Perspective, 1974, Survival in the Sexist Jungle, 1974, The New Husbands and How to Become One, 1976, Casebook of Organizational Behavior, 1979, Human Relations: A Job Oriented Approach, 1978, 5th edit., 1992, Fundamentals of Organizational Behavior: An Applied Perspective, 2d edit., 1978, Winning at Office Politics, 1979, Contemporary Applied Management, 1982, 4th edit., 1994, Essentials of Management, 1986, 4th edit., 1997, The Last Straw, 1987, Human Relations for Career and Personal Success, 3d edit., 1992, 4th edit., 1996, 5th edit., 1999, Management and Organization, 1989, 2d edit., 1992, Effective Business Psychology, 1980, 4th edit., 1994, 5th edit., 1999, Winning Office Politics: DuBrin's Guide for the '90s, 1990, Bouncing Back: How to Overcome Adversity in the Workplace, 1992, Your Own Worst Enemy: How to Prevent Career Self-Sabotage, 1992, Stand Out! 330 Ways to Gain the Edge with Superiors, Subordinates, Co-workers, and Customers, 1993, Getting It Done: The Transforming Power of Self-Discipline, 1995, The Reengineering Survival Guide, 1995, The Breakthrough Team Player, 1995, Leadership: Research Findings, Practice and Skill, 1995, 98, Human Relations: Job-Oriented Interpersonal Skills, Fundamentals of Organizational Behavior, The 10-Min. Guide to Effective Leadership, Personal Magnetism, 1997, Complete Idiot's Guide to Leadership, 1998, Looking Around Corners, 1999. Served to capt. U.S. Army, 1960-62. Mem. Am. Psychol. Assn., Am. Mgmt. Assn., Acad. of Mgmt. Home: 2100 Clover St Rochester NY 14618-3209 Office: Rochester Inst Tech Coll Bus Rochester NY 14623-0887

DUBROCK, CALVIN WILLIAM, wildlife program administrator; b. New Castle, Pa., Dec. 6, 1953; s. Calvin Leroy and Janet Marie (Pittaway) DuB.; m. Cynthia Allay, Sept. 7, 1974; children: Joshua Michael, Justin Graham. BS with high honors, Mich. State U., 1977; MS, Va. Poly. Inst., 1980; postgrad., Pa. State U., 1993-94. Survey statistician US Dept. Energy, Energy Info. Adminstrn., Washington, 1979-80; rsch. ecologist U.S. Dept. Interior, Fish and Wildlife Svc., Kearneysville, W.Va., 1980-82; wildlife biometrician State Pa., Game Commn., Harrisburg, 1982-85, wildlife planning chief, 1985-87, wildlife rsch. chief, 1987-91, wildlife mgmt. dir., 1991—; mem. adj. faculty Lord Fairfax C.C., Middletown, Va., 1982; mem. pesticide adv. bd. State of Pa., 1991-95; coord. com. mem. Pa. State U. Coop. Fish and Wildlife Rsch. Unit, 1991—. Contbr. articles to sci. and profl. jours. Program coord., coach Bible quiz team Evang. Free Ch. of Hershey, Pa., 1995—, mem. sr. h.s. youth staff, 1995—. With U.S. Army, 1972-75. Mem. Internat. Assn. Fish and Wildlife Agys., Orgn. Wildlife Planners (reg. dir. Northeast region 1990-93), Wildlife Soc. (pres. Pa. chpt. 1985-87), Northeast Wildlife Adminstrs. Assn. (chmn. 1993-97), Phi Kappa Phi, Phi Sigma, Gamma Sigma Delta. Avocations: golf, skiing, racquetball, hunting, running. Office: State Pa Office Game Commn 2001 Elmerton Ave Harrisburg PA 17110-9762

DUBROFF, HENRY ALLEN, newspaper editor; b. Neptune, N.J., Nov. 28, 1950; s. Sol and Gilda (Burdman) D.; married, 1980 (div. 1986). AB in History and Lit., Lafayette Coll., 1972; MS in Journalism, Columbia U., 1982. Staff writer Dept. Health and Human Svcs., Washington, 1972-73; tchr. English Holyoke (Mass.) St. Sch., 1974-78; employment & tng. program mgr. Knoxville (Tenn.)-Knox CY Community Action, 1978-81; bus. writer, columnist Springfield (Mass.) Newspapers, 1982-85; bus. writer, columnist The Denver Post, 1985-88, bus. editor, 1988-95; editor Denver Bus. Jour., 1995—; contbg. writer CFO Mag., Boston, 1985-90. Contbr. articles to N.Y. Times, 1982-89. Vol. Russian Resettlement Program Jewish Family & Children's Svcs., Denver, 1989-90. Recipient N.Y. Fin. Writers Assn. scholarship, 1982, Morton Margolin prize U. Denver, 1988, Bus. Story of Yr. award AP, 1989, Gen. Excellence award Am. City Bus. Jour., 1996, 97, Human Svc. award Am. Jewish Com., 1999. Mem. Soc. Am. Bus. Editors and Writers (past pres., Best in Bus. award 1995, 96, 98). Avocations: photography, writing, golf. Office: Denver Bus Jour 1700 Broadway Ste 515 Denver CO 80290-1700

DUBROFF, SUSANNE, poet, former social worker; b. Berlin, Dec. 30, 1930; came to U.S., 1936; d. Aba and Frances Taub; m. Paul Dubroff, June 15, 1956 (div. 1981); children: Julie Anne Gallant, Martin, Joseph. AB, Boston U., 1952; M in Social Svcs., Simmons Coll. Sch. Social Work, 1957; postgrad, U. Mass., 1987. Lic. ind. clin. social worker. Social worker dept. child psychiatry Children's Hosp., Boston; Judge Baker Guidance Ctr., Boston; ind. clin. social worker West Roz Park Mental Health Ctr., Perkins Sch. for the Blind, Watertown, Mass., 1958-91; free-lance poet and translator poetry; instr. poetry study North Shore C.C., Beverly, Mass., 1995-98. Author: A Flower on a Volcano, 1981, You and I, 1994; contbr. anthologies, univ. press jours., others. Fellow Va. Ctr. for Creative Arts, 1998, Harwthornden Castle Internat. Retreat for Writers, Scotland, 1997. Mem. Acad. of Am. Poets, New Eng. Poetry Club. Avocatiaons: music, theater, fine arts.

DUBROVSKY, BEN, communications executive; b. Neptune, N.J., June 30, 1961; s. Jack and Gertrude (Wishnick) D. BS in Engring., Tufts U., 1983; MS, Harvard U., 1986; postgrad., MIT, 1990-91. Assoc. programmer IBM, Endicott, N.Y., 1983-84; tech. cons., staff engr. Bolt Beranek & Newman, Cambridge, Mass., 1986-90; dir. multimedia computing Chedd-Angier, Watertown, Mass., 1990-92; instr. Ctr. for Creative Imaging, Camden, Maine, 1992-95; ptnr. Tarragon Interactive, Watertown, Mass., 1995-96; owner Focal Plane Comm., Brookline, Mass., 1992—; ptnr. ReadyAbout Interactive, Boston, 1997—; mem. adv. bd. CoSA, Providence, 1991-94; mem. curriculum adv. panel Ctr. for Creative Imaging, Camden, 1994-95. Author (monthly column), contbg. editor Digital Video Mag., 1996-97; co-author: Creating and Designing Multimedia with Director, 1997. Recipient Silver medal ednl. category N.Y. Film Festivals, 1992, Gold medal N.Y. Film Festivals, 1992, Gold Cindy awards, 1992. Democrat. Jewish. Avocations: photography, community theater. Home and Office: 619 Washington St Brookline MA 02446-4563

DUBROVSKY, ROMAN, engineering educator; b. Moscow, May 14, 1934; s. Izrael and Utta (Frimmer) D.; m. Luiza Dubrovsky, Jan. 28, 1974; 1 child, Larisa. BS, Mech. Inst., Melitopol, 1957, MS, 1959; PhD, Polytech. U., Moscow, 1972. Process engr. Machine Mfg. Plant, Zaporoghe, Ukraine, 1959-64; head of rsch. dept. Machine Mfg. Plant, Moscow, 1973-80; rsch. engr. Car Mfg. Plant, Zaporoghe, 1964-69; prof. N.J. Inst. Tech., Newark, 1983—; cons. Zil Plant, Moscow, 1972-79. Contbr. articles to profl. jours. Vice-pres. Engring./Scientific Soc. fo New Americans, N.Y., 1985-89. Rsch. grantee State Commn. on Sci. and Tech., Trenton, 1989. Mem. Am. Soc. for Metals. Republican. Avocations: downhill skiing, tennis. Home: Apt B 701 4525 H Hudson Pkwy Bronx NY 10471 Office: NJ Inst Tech 200 Central Ave Newark NJ 07103-3918

DUBROW, HEATHER, English educator; b. San Antonio, Mar. 5, 1945; d. Hilliard and Helen (Volk) D.; m. Ian Ousby, June 21, 1969 (div. Dec. 1979). BA summa cum laude, Harvard/Radcliffe, 1966; PhD, Harvard U., 1972. Asst. prof. U. Mass., Boston, 1972-73; Leverhulme vis. fellowship U. Kent, Canterbury, Eng., 1973-74; lectr. U. Sussex, Brighton, Eng., 1974-75; from vis. asst. prof. to asst. prof. U. Md., College Park, 1975-80; from assoc. to prof. Carleton Coll., Northfield, Minn., 1980-90; from prof. to John Bascom prof. and Tighe-Evans prof. U. Wis., Madison, 1990—; external rev. team Oberlin Coll., Bryn Mawr Coll. Author: Genre, 1982, Captive Victors, 1987, A Happier Eden, 1990, Echoes of Desire, 1995, Transformation and Repetition, 1997, Shakespeare and Domestic Loss, 1999; contbr. articles to profl. jours. Recipient Captain Jonathan Fay award Radcliffe Coll., 1966; sr. fellow Nat. Endowment for the Humanities, 1987-88, Hon. fellow AAUW, 1979-80. Mem. MLA (mem. editl. bd., exec. coun. 1996—), Milton Soc. of Am. (exec. com. 1997—), Spenser Soc., Phi Beta Kappa. Democrat. Avocations: architecture, art, cooking. Office: U Wis Dept of English 600 N Park St Madison WI 53706-1403

DUBROW, MARSHA ANN, high technology company executive, composer; b. Newark, Dec. 27, 1948; d. Leo and Rose (Haberman) Dubrow; m. Daniel Leon Chaykin, Jan. 17, 1970 (div. 1985); 1 child, Alexander; m. David Lorin Rosenberg, July 3, 1988; 1 step-child, Oliver. BA cum laude, U. Pa., 1970; MA, NYU, 1975; MFA, Princeton U., 1977, postgrad., 1977-78, 81-82; postgrad., Tufts U., 1987, Am. Women's Econ. Devel. Corp. Inst., 1987-88, Leadership Am., 1988, Leadership N.J., 1990, Leadership Inst. for Workforce Devel., 1993. Prodn. coord. Children's TV Workshop, N.Y.C., 1970-73; instr. Princeton U., N.J., 1976-78; mgr. mktg. communications, ops., human resources AT&T/Techs., Inc., Morristown, N.J., 1978-80; dir. mktg. and ops. Acadia Communications, N.Y.C., 1980-83; dir. planning and mktg. Access Methods, Inc., N.Y.C., 1984-85; mng. dir. Marsha Dubrow Assocs., Upper Montclair, N.J., 1981—; pres., CEO Technolog, Inc., Upper Montclair, N.J., 1985—. Life mem. bus. and profl. group Nat. Coun. Jewish Women, Essex County, N.J., 1983—, Hadassah; mentor U.S. Sml. Bus. Adminstrn., Office of Women Bus. Ownership, Washington, 1989—. Recipient Theodore Presser award U. Pa., 1970; fellow Tisch Sch. Arts, 1993-94; named William C. Langley fellow NYU, 1974, Princeton U. fellow, 1976-78, Josephine de Karman fellow Aerojet-Gen. Corp., 1981, Composer's fellow in Opera-Musical Theatre N.J. State Coun. Arts, 1990, Folk Arts fellow N.J. State Coun. Arts, 1996-98. Mem. NAFE, Internat. Women's Forum (bd. dirs.), Am. Women Entrepreneurs, Am. Mgmt. Assn., Dramatists Guild, Leadership Am. Assn., N.J. Bus. Higher Edn. Forum, N.J. Women's Forum (bd. dirs., pres.), Dramatists Guild, Princeton U. Assn. Princeton Grad. Alumni (governing bd.). Home: 34 Marion Rd Montclair NJ 07043-1932 Office: Technolog Inc 5 Upper Montclair Plz Montclair NJ 07043-1319

DUBROW-EICHEL, STEVE KENNETH, psychologist; b. N.Y.C., Oct. 6, 1954; s. Harry and Edith (Gruenberger) Eichel; 1 child, Jennifer Eichel Dubrow. BA, Columbia U., 1976; MS, U. Pa., 1977, PhD, 1989. Diplomate Am. Bd. Med. Psychotherapy, Am. Acad. Pain Mgmt.; cert. psychotherapist, Pa. Psychologist Irving Schwartz Inst., Phila., 1980-86; clin. supr. child and family svcs. Camcare Cmty. Mental Health Ctr., Camden, N.J., 1986-88; dir. ct. svcs. Steininger Ctr., Cherry Hill, N.J., 1988-89; clin. dir. St. Francis Homes for Boys, Bensalem, Pa., 1989-94; psychologist Verree Psychology Group, Phila., 1994—; adj. prof. Chestnut Hill Coll., Phila., 1997—, Pa. State U., Abington, 1995—; cons. St. Francis Homes for Boys, Bensalem, 1994—. Co-author: Intensive Outpatient Treatment of Sex & Love Addiction, 1993; contbr. articles to profl. jours. adv. bd. Am. Family Found., Bonita Springs, Fla., 1992—; psychosocial com. Sons and Daus. of Holocaust Survivors, Phila., 1985-92. Recipient John G. Clark award Am. Family Found., 1990, Profl. Svc. award Am. Mental Health Counselors Assn., 1984-85. Fellow Pa. Psychol. Assn., Internat. Acad. Behavioral Medicine, Counseling and Psychotherapy; mem. Am. Soc. Clin. Hypnosis (cert.), Am. Acad. Psychotherapists, Am. Coll. Forensic Examiners, Am. Psychol. Assn., Greater Phila. Soc. Clin. Hypnosis (gov. bd., pres. 1998—). Democrat. Jewish. Avocation: poetry. Home: 600 Red Lion Rd Apt V-1 Philadelphia PA 19115-1225 Office: Verree Psychology Group 9877 Verree Rd Philadelphia PA 19115-1927

DUBS, PATRICK CHRISTIAN, publisher; b. Paris, Jan. 18, 1947; came to U.S., 1978; s. Robert and Anne Marie D.; m. Catherine Claude Henry, Feb. 4, 1970; children—Vanessa, Olivier. Diplome de droit et scie. economiques, U. Paris, 1967. With Brit. European Airways, Paris, 1969; export dir. Hachette S.A., Paris, 1970-78; pres. Hachette Inc., N.Y.C., 1978—, Regents Pub. Co., Inc., N.Y.C., 1980—; chmn. bd. Arista Corp., Concord, Calif.; mng. dir. Hachette Edition et Diffusion Francophones, 1987-91, 1991—; pres. France-Edition, Paris, 1991-95; mng. dir. Groupe Hatier Internat., Paris, 1995—; bd. advs. M.A. in Pub. program Pace U., 1985. Mem. Am. Assn. Pubs., French-Am. C. of C. (councillor N.Y. chpt.). Roman Catholic. Club: Manursing Island (Rye). Office: 31 Rue de Fleurus, 75006 Paris France

DUBUC, CARROLL EDWARD, lawyer; b. Burlington, Vt., May 6, 1933; s. Jerome Joachim and Rose (Bessette) D.; m. Mary Jane Lowe, Aug. 3, 1963; children: Andrew, Steven, Matthew. *Carroll Dubuc's son, Steven, is an environmental lawyer with a major Washington,D.C. law firm. Andrew is in the drywall construction business in Washington, Virginia, Maryland and London. Matthew sells computer technology equipment to the Department of Defense.* BS in Acctg., Cornell U., 1955; LLB, Boston Coll., 1962; postgrad., NYU, 1963-64. Bar: N.Y. 1963, U.S. Dist. Ct. (so. and ea. dists.) N.Y. 1964, U.S. Ct. Appeals (2d cir.) 1965, U.S. Supreme Ct. 1970, D.C. 1972, U.S. Ct. Appeals (D.C. cir.) 1972, U.S. Dist. Ct. D.C. 1973, U.S. Ct. Claims 1975, U.S. Ct. Appeals (4th cir.) 1977, U.S. Ct. Appeals (7th cir.) 1984, U.S. Ct. Appeals (9th cir.) 1985, U.S. Ct. Appeals (5th cir.) 1986, U.S. Ct. Appeals (fed. cir.) 1988, U.S. Ct. Internat. Trade 1988, U.S. Ct. Appeals (6th cir.) 1989, Va. 1999; cert. ct. mediator 1998. Assoc. Haight, Gardner, Poor & Havens, N.Y.C., 1962-70, ptnr., 1970-75; resident ptnr. Finley Kumble Wagner Heine Underberg Manley Myerson & Casey, Washington, 1983-87, Lacalt, Washington, Perito & Dubuc, Washington, 1988-90; Washington, Perito & Dubuc Lacalt, Washington, Perito & Dubuc, 1990-91; ptnr. Graham & James, 1991-95, of counsel, 1996-98; of counsel Cohen Gettings & Dunham, 1998—. *Carroll Dubuc has over 35 years of responsible experience as a trial lawyer and counselor to major U.S. and international airlines and their insurers. She is now acting as a mediator/arbitrator in similar technical multi-party protracted disputes. Also, mediator for mediating employment, product liability, aviation, insurance international claims, partnership bankruptcy and unfair competition matters.* Capt. AC USN, 1954-59. Mem. AIAA, ABA (chmn. aviation and space law com. 1985-86, subcom. aviation ins., subcom. internat. practice 1985-87, vice chmn. alternative resolution com., mktg. legal svcs. com. 1991-92, vice chmn. ins. com. 1982-84), N.Y. State Bar Assn. (past chmn. aviation law com.), D.C. Bar Assn., Va. Bar Assn., Assn. of Bar of City of N.Y. (aeroav. com.), Fed. Cir. Bar Assn., 5th Fed. Cir. Bar Assn., Fed. Bar Coun., Nat. Transp. Safety Bd. Bar Assn., Maritime Law Assn. U.S., Naval Aviation Command (vice comdr.), Internat. Assn. Def. Counsel (chmn. alterngte dispute resolution sec., aviation transp. 1996—), Helicopter Assn. Internat., Transp. Lawyers Assn., Assn. Trial Lawyers Am., Def. Assn. N.Y., Boston Coll. Law Sch. Alumni (pres. Washington chpt. 1992-96), Assn. Transp. Practitioners, Internat. Soc. Air Safety Investigators, Soc. Sr. Aerospace Execs., Internat. Aviation Club, Washington chpt Aero Club, Nat. Aerunautic Assn., French-Am. C. of C., N.Y. Athletic Club, Cornell Club, Wings Club, Congrl. Country Club, Sigma Chi.

DUBUC, DEBORAH JO, special education educator; b. Manhattan, Kans., Feb. 7, 1957; d. Philip Louis and Elouise Ann (Vanderbilt) Humbargar; m. Gary Gerard Dubuc, May 31, 1975 (div. July 1976); 1 child, Devin Anthony. BS Edn. and Psychology magna cum laude, Marymount Coll. Kans., Salina, 1981; MS in Spl. Edn., Kans. State U., 1990. Cert. regular and spl. edn.-learning disabilities tchr. Tchr. 3rd grade Unified Sch. Dist. 475, Geary County Schs., Ft. Riley, Junction City, Kans., 1981-87; self-contained learning disabilities tchr. Unified Sch. Dist. 475, Geary County Schs., Junction City, 1987-88; mem. English, reading, math. and sci. task force Unified Sch. Dist. 475, Geary County Schs., Ft. Riley, Junction City, 1986-88; learning disabilities itinerant tchr. United Sch. Dist. 305, Salina (Kans.) Pub. Schs., 1989-95, spl. edn. resource tchr. K-12, 1995-97, interrelated spl. edn. instr., 1997—; realtor Broker's Realty, Salina, Kans., 1995—; univ. supr. on honorarium Kans. State U., 1991; Homebound spl. edn. instr. Unified Sch. Dist. #239, 1992. Co-curriculum guides math., sci., English, reading, 1986-88; contbr. articles to Take Heart spl. edn. monthly, 1988-89. Chairperson Orgns. Com., Salina, 1979-81; scout leader Girl Scouts U.S., Salina, 1980-81; asst. leader Cub Scouts, Boy Scouts Am., Manhattan, Kans., 1985-86, comm. officer, 1986-87; mem. choir First Nazarene Ch., Salina, 1989-92; chairperson Custer Hill Social Com., Ft. Riley, 1986-87; mem. Salina Area Transition Coun., 1990-97. Mem. Coun. for Exceptional Children (rep. 1988-89, 94-95), Kans. Nat. Ednl. Assn. (alt. del. 1998—), Internat. Reading Assn., Junction City Edn. Assn. (mem. pub. rels. com. 1981, elected mem. profl. devel. com. United Sch. Dist. 305 term 1991-92, 92-93), Assn. Ctrl. Colls. of Kans. (univ. supr. 1991, 93, 94, spl. edn. instr. 1993), Learning Disabilities Assn., Alpha Chi. Avocations: gourmet cooking, travel, vocal music, recreational swimming, writing. Home: 232 E Minneapolis Ave Salina KS 67401-6027 Office: Cen Kans Coop in Edn 3023 Canterbury Dr Salina KS 67401-8038

DUBUC, MARY ELLEN, educational administrator; b. N.Y.C. July 20, 1950; d. Patrick Joseph and Catherine (McKenna) Reynolds; BA cum laude (scholar), Marymount Manhattan Coll., 1972; MA, Columbia U., 1973; cert. advanced grad. studies R.I. Coll., 1985; m. Leo Dennis Dubuc Jr., Sept. 9, 1978; children: Brian Robert, Kimberly Ann. Spl. edn. tchr. Cardinal Cushing Sch., Hanover, Mass., 1973-76, Ferncliff Manor Sch., Yonkers, N.Y., 1976-77; program coordinator Bronx Devel. Services, 1977-78; dir. edn. R.I. Assn. Retarded, Woonsocket, 1978-84, spl. edn. cons., 1984-92; qualified med. retardation profl. Seacliff, Inc., Cumberland, R.I., 1988-91; tchr. BICO Collaborative Program, North Attleboro, Mass., 1989; acting exec. dir. Seacliff, Inc., 1991-93; dir. quality assurance Avatar, Inc., 1992; dir. specialized svcs. The ARC of No. R.I., Woonsocket, 1992-99, asst. adminstr. habilitative svcs., 1999—. Fed. trainee, 1971, 72. Mem. North Smithfield PTA, 1986—; ednl. evaluator No. R.I. Collaborative, 1992. Recipient FrankBerchman award for Profl. of Yr., ARC of No. R.I. Mem. Assn. Severely Handicapped, R.I. Assn. Retarded Citizens, NAFE, R.I. Assn. Adult and Continuing Edn. (v.p. pub. rels. 1986-89, corr. sec. 1991-93), Alpha Chi. Democrat. Roman Catholic. Office: The ARC of No RI 80 Fabien St Woonsocket RI 02895-6277

DUBUC, SERGE, mathematics educator; b. Montreal, Que., Can., Apr. 16, 1939; s. Romuald and Fernande (Desmarchais) D.; m. Pierrette Valois, June 3, 1962; children: Benoit, Martin, Jacinthe. B.Sc. in Math., U. Montreal, 1962, M.Sc. in Math., 1963; Ph.D. in Math, Cornell U., 1966. Asst. prof. math. U. Montreal, 1966-71, assoc. prof., 1973-76, prof., 1976-97, prof. emeritus, 1998—; assoc. prof. U. Sherbrooke, Que., Can., 1971-73. Author: Géométrie Plane, 1971, Problèmes d'Optimisation en Calcul des Probabilités, 1978; editor-in-chief: Annales de Sciences Mathematiques du Quebec, 1975-79, mng. editor, 1979-82; co-editor: Fractal Geometry and Analysis, 1991, Spline Functions and the Theory of Wavelets, 1999. Ford Co. fellow, 1968-69; Can. Arts Council Killam fellow, 1975-76. Mem. Association Mathematique du Que. Roman Catholic. Office: Univ of Montreal, Dept Math et Stats, Montreal, PQ Canada H3C 3J7

DU BUSKE, LAWRENCE M., immunologist, allergist, rheumotologist; b. Jersey City, Oct. 16, 1954. BS, Northwestern U., 1976, MD, 1978. Diplomate Am. Bd. Allergy and Immunology, Am. Bd. Internal Medicine, Am. Bd. Rheumatology. Dir. Allergy and Arthritis Family Treatment Ctr., Gardner, Mass., 1984—, Immunology Rsch. Inst. New England, Fitchburg, Mass., 1990—; clin. instr. Harvard Med. Sch., Boston, 1984—; cons. Brigham and Women's Hosp., Boston, 1984—, co-dir. allergy fellow training program , 1994-98; cons. Schering Plough, Kenilworth, N.J., 1994-99, Hoechst Marion Roussel Pharms., Kansas City, Kans, 1995-97, Upjohn Pharms., Mich., 1997; adv. bd. Hycor Biomedical, Garden Grove, Calif., 1985-97, cons., 1995-97. Contbg. Editor Asthma & Allergy Proceedings, 1994-99, Jour. Allergy & Clin. Immunology Supplement, 1996-97, Internal Jour. Immune Rehab., 1998—; contbg. author Exercise Induced Allergy Syndromes. Fellow ACP, ACR, ACAAI, Am. Acad. Asthma, Allergy and Immunology (chmn. practice and therapeutics com. 1996-99, chmn. practice stds. coun. 1999—). Avocations: tennis, piano, jazz. Office: Immunology Rsch Inst New Eng 358 Elm St Gardner MA 01440-3926

DUCAR, TRACY, soccer player; b. Lawrence, Mass., June 18, 1973; m. Chris Ducar, 1997. BS in Biology, U. N.C., 1995. mem. U.S. Nat. Women's Soccer Team, 1996—, including Nike Victory Tour, 1997, U.S. Women's Cup, 1997. Named Team Most Valuable Player, U. N.C., 1995. Mem. Phi Beta Kappa. Office: US Soccer Fedn 1801-1811 S Prairie Ave Chicago IL 60616*

DUCATMAN, ALAN MARC, physician; b. Plainfield, N.J., July 19, 1950; s. Fred Paul and Shirley (Buchman) D.; m. Barbara Steinmetz, June 18, 1978; children: Joseph, David, Samuel. BA, Columbia U., N.Y.C., 1972; MSc, CUNY, 1974; MD, Wayne State U., Detroit, 1978. Resident, fellow Mayo Clinic, Rochester, Minn., 1979-82; dir. occupational health Columbia Park Med., Mpls., 1982-83; dir. Environ. Med. Svcs. MIT, 1986-92; prof., dir. Inst. Occupational and Environ. Health W.Va. U., Morgantown, 1992-97, chair dept. cmty. medicine, 1996—; adj. assoc. prof. Boston U. Sch. Medicine, 1990-92, U. Miss. Sch. Medicine, 1991—; adj. prof. medicine U. S.C., 1994; trustee Am. Bd. Preventive Medicine, 1994—. Contbr. articles to profl. jours. Cmdr. USNR, 1983-86. Fellow ACP, Am. Coll. Occup. and Environ. Medicine (chmn. toxicology com. 1987-92, Adolph G. Kammer Merit Authorship award 1993, Harriet Hardy award 1997). Office: Inst Occupl & Environ Health WVa U/Sch Medicine Morgantown WV 26506-9190

DUCE, ROBERT ARTHUR, atmospheric chemist, university administrator; b. Midland, Ont., Can., Apr. 9, 1935; s. Leonard Arthur and Irma Harriet (Gynn) D.; m. Mary Elizabeth Untz, June 8, 1968; children: Patricia Jean, David Robert. BA cum laude, Baylor U., 1957; postgrad., U. Colo., 1954; PhD in Inorganic and Nuclear Chemistry, MIT, 1964. Teaching asst. dept. chemistry MIT, Cambridge, Mass., 1961-62, rsch. asst. in geochemistry, 1962-63, USPHS predoctoral fellow in air pollution, 1963-64, rsch. assoc. dept. geology and geophysics, 1964-65; from asst. prof. to assoc. prof. chemistry U. Hawaii, Honolulu, 1965-70; assoc. prof. oceanography U. R.I., Kingston, 1970-73, prof. oceanography, 1973-91, dir. Ctr. for Atmospheric Chemistry Studies, 1981-91, dean Grad. Sch. Oceanography, vice provost marine affairs, 1987-91; prof. oceanography and meteorology Tex. A&M U., College Station, 1991—, dean coll. geosciences and maritime studies, 1991-97; vis. prof. Inst. Marine Scis., U. Tex., Pt. Aransas, summer 1975; vis. scientist aeronomy lab. NOAA Environ. Rsch. Labs., Boulder, Colo., 1977; collaborateur etranger CFR/Nat. Ctr. Sci. Rsch., Gif-sur-Yvette, France, 1976-77; William Evans vis. prof. chemistry U. Otago, Dunedin, New Zealand, 1983; participant disting. lecture series in USSR, U.S.-USSR Joint Working Group on Effects of Marine Pollution, 1974; mem. bd. atmospheric scis. and climate NAS/NRC, 1982-86, 89-93, mem. com. atmospheric chemistry, 1987-90, chmn. com. haze in nat. pks. and wilderness areas, 1990-

93; chair NAS/NRC Panel on Global Tropospheric Chemistry, 1982-85; sr. vis. fellow Nat. Environ. Rsch. Coun., Gt. Britain, 1984; bd. govs. Joint Oceanographic Insts., 1987-97, vice chair, 1990-91, Consortium for Oceanographic Rsch. and Edn., 1994-97, vice chair, 1994-96; trustee Univ. Corp. Atmospheric Rsch., 1986-93, sec., 1987-90, mem. exec. com., 1987-90, mem. budget and program com., 1987-88, mem. pers. com., 1990-93; mem. exec. com. Ocean Drilling Program, 1987-97; mem. exec. com. Nat. Assn. State Univs. and Land Grant Colls. Bd. Oceans and Atmospheres, 1993-97; mem. adv. com. geosciences NSF, 1994-97; pres. Internat. Assn. of Meteorogy and Atmosphere Scis., 1995—; vis. pro. environ. scis. U. E. Anglia, Eng., 1997-98. Contbr. articles to profl. jours. Capt. USAF, 1957-61. Fellow AAAS (chmn.-elect sect. atmospheric and hydrospheric scis. 1986-87, chmn. sect. atmospheric and hydrospheric scis. 1987-88, mem. coun. 1990-93), Am. Meteorol. Soc. (mem. coun. 1988-91), Am. Geophys. Union; mem. The Oceanography Soc. (pres.-elect 1994-96, pres. 1996-98), Am. Chem. Soc. (sec.-treas. Hawaiian sect. 1967, chmn.-elect Hawaiian sect. 1969), Geochem. Soc., Am. Geol. Inst., Sigma Xi, Alpha Chi. Avocations: travel, collecting single malt scotch. Home: 4708 Scrimshaw Ln College Station TX 77845-9399 Office: Tex A&M U Coll Geosciences Maritime Studies Dept Oceanography College Station TX 77843

DUCEMAN, MARK EUGENE, county zoning administrator, planner; b. Shamokin, Pa., Oct. 23, 1960; s. John Albert and Margaret Mary (Deeben) D. AS in Mech. Engring., Pa. State U., 1980, BS in Urban Planning, 1983. Asst. planner, engr. Northumberland County Planning Dept., Sunbury, Pa., 1983; planner Pa. Dept. Tranps., Harrisburg, 1984-86; real estate svcs. Shamokin Enterprises, Inc., Albany, N.Y., 1987; pres. Jambion Devels, Inc., Toronto, Ont., Can., 1988-89; owner, mgr., exec. Ben & Jerry's Homemade Ice Cream Franchise, Toronto, 1987-89; assoc. planner Lord Fairfax Planning Dist. Commn., Front Royal, Va., 1989-95; planner cmty. devel. dept. Town of Herndon, 1995-97; zoning adminstr./planner Planning and Zoning dept. County of Shenandoah, Va., 1997—. Mem. Am. Inst. Cert. Planners (cert.), Am. Planning Assn., Potomac Appalachian Trail Club. Democrat. Methodist. Avocations: flying, hiking, swimming, kayaking. Home: PO Box 480 Front Royal VA 22630-0480 Office: Shenandoah County Govt Planning & Zoning Dept 118 Court St Woodstock VA 22664

DUCHIN, PETER OELRICHS, musician; b. N.Y.C., July 28, 1937; s. Edwin Frank and Marjorie (Oelrichs) D.; m. Cheray Zauderer, June 22, 1964 (div. 1982); children: Jason Edwin, Courtnay Oelrichs, Colin Zauderer; m. Brooke Hayward, Dec. 24, 1985. BAU, Yale U., 1958; student polit. scis. and music conservatory, Paris, 1957. Pres. Peter Duchin Orchs., 1963—. Bd. dirs. Chamber Music Soc., Lincoln Ctr., Ballet Theater Found., Citizens Com. for N.Y.C., Inc., N.Y. Found. for the Arts, World Policy Inst., Nat. Jazz Svc. Orgn.; mem. adv. bd. Congl. Arts Caucus Ednl. Program, Planned Parenthood, Musicians Emergency Fund. Mem. Am. Ctr. (bd. dirs.), N.Y. State Coun. on Arts. Clubs: Yale (N.Y.C.); Racquet and Tennis, Century Assn. Office: Peter Duchin Orchs Inc 305 Madison Ave Rm 1526 New York NY 10017-6213

DUCHON, ROSEANN MARIE, business owner, consultant; b. Cleve., Jan. 16, 1950; d. Steve and Mary (Bobak) Gaydos; m. Ronald Joseph Duchon, Oct. 11, 1969 (div. 1994); children: Michelle, Teresa, Megan, Kevin, Jason. Student, Kent (Ohio) State U., 1983-84. Sec. ETC, Inc., Cleve., 1968-69; sec., model Bobbie Brooks, Inc., Cleve., 1969-71; instr. childbirth edn. Childbirth Edn. Assn. Cleve., 1971-83; office mgr. 3690 Corp./Devel. Systems, Beachwood, Ohio, 1984-85, Park Pl. Bus. Services, Hudson, Ohio, 1985-86; owner Hudson Secretarial Services, 1986, Exec. Office Services, Hudson, 1987—, Hudson Telephone Answering Services, Hudson, 1988—; pres. R.M. Duchon, Inc., 1991, Western Reserve Staffing Svcs., 1992—. Chmn. Hudson League for Service, 1980-82; active Better Bus. Bur., 1989-90. Recipient Excellence in Competition award Internat. Model and Talent Assn., 1999. Mem. Hudson Bus. and Profl. Women (nominating com. 1985-86, pres. 1986-87, region mem. chmn., Ohio state membership chair 1993-94), Hudson C. of C., Nat. Assn. Secretarial Svcs., Nat. Fedn. Indep. Bus., Women's Network. Roman Catholic. Office: Exec Office Svcs PO Box 541 Hudson OH 44236-0541

DUCHOSSOIS, RICHARD LOUIS, manufacturing executive, racetrack executive; b. Chgo., Oct. 7, 1921; s. Alphonse Christopher and Erna (Hessler) D.; widower; children: Craig J., Dayle, R. Bruce, Kimberly. Student, Washington & Lee U. Chmn. bd. dirs. Duchossois Industries, Inc., Elmhurst, Ill., chmn., CEO; chmn., dir. Chamberlain Tech. Cos.; chmn. Arlington Internat. Racecourse, Ltd., Arlington Heights, Ill.; chmn. Transp. Corp. Am., Chamberlain Consu.er Products, Duchossois Communications Co.; bd. dirs. Hill 'n Dale Farm. Served with U.S. Army, 1942-46, ETO. Decorated Purple Heart, Bronze Star. Mem. Chief Execs. Orgn., Economic Club, Execs. Club (bd. dirs.), Jockey Club N.Y.C. Republican. Methodist. Office: Duchossois Industries Inc 845 N Larch Ave Elmhurst IL 60126-1196*

DUCHOVNY, DAVID, actor; b. Aug. 7, 1960; s. Amram and Meg Duchovny; m. Tea Lioni May 6, 1997. Student Yale U.; grad., Princeton U. Appeared in TV series as Jake in Red Shoe Diaries, Showtime, 1992, as Fox Mulder in The X-Files, Fox, 1993—, in Larry Sanders Show, HBO, 1996; also appeared as Dennis Denise in Twin Peaks; appeared in TV movies Baby Snatcher, 1992, The Red Shoe Diaries, 1992; movie appearances Working Girl, 1988, New Year's Day, 1989, Bad Influence, 1990, Julia Has Two Lovers, 1991, The Rapture, 1991, Don't Tell Mom the Babysitter's Dead, 1991, Venice/Venice, 1992, Ruby, 1992, Chaplin, 1992, Beethoven, 1992, Kalifornia, 1993, also appeared in The Real World; TV guest appearances include Frasier, 1993, The Simpsons, 1989, The Larry Sanders Show, 1992, Dr. Katz, Professional Therapist, 1995, numerous others. Recipient Golden Globe for best actor in drama series, 1996. Office: The X-Files Production, 110-555 Brooks Bank Ave, Bldg 10, North Vancouver, BC Canada V7J-3S5 Office: 20th Century Fox Film Corp PO Box 900 Beverly Hills CA 90213*

DUCK, PATRICIA MARY, librarian; b. Bklyn., Jan. 22, 1951; d. Warren James and Virginia Susan (Noonan) Johnson; m. John Jacob Duck, Feb. 2, 1973; children: Michael, Jennifer, Matthew. BA, George Washington U., 1974; MLS, U. Pitts., 1980, PhD in Libr. Sci., 1992. Libr., serials cataloger U. Pitts., 1980-84, libr., coord., 1984-85, libr., project supr., 1985-86; dir. libr. U. Pitts. Greensburg, 1986—; facilitator region 10 Gov.'s Conf. Libr. and Info. Svcs., Pitts., 1990. Contbr. articles to profl. jours. Leader troop 47 Girl Scouts U.S., 1990-91; trustee Penn Area Libr., Level Green, Pa., 1989-91. Mem. ALA, Beta Phi Mu. Avocations: art, vol. youth activities. Office: U Pitts Greensburg Campus 1150 Mount Pleasant Rd Greensburg PA 15601-5860

DUCK, STEVE WEATHERILL, communications educator; b. Keynsham, Somerset, Engl., Jan. 4, 1946; s. Kenneth W. and Joan (Stickler) D.; m. Sandra Mariela Allen (div. 1987); children: Christina Louise, James Edward; m. Joanna Margaret Lawson, Dec. 30, 1987; children: Benjamin Lawson-Duck, Gabriel Lawson-Duck. PhD, Sheffield U., Eng., 1971; MA, Oxford U., Eng., 1972. Lectr. Glasgow (Scotland) U., 1970-73; lectr. Lancaster U., Eng., 1973-78, sr. lectr., 1978-85; prof. U. Iowa, Iowa City, 1986—; chair dept. comm. studies, 1994-98; founder Internat. Confs. on Personal Relationships, Internat. Network Personal Relationships. Author: Relating to Others, 1999, Understanding Relationships, 1991, Human Relationships, 3rd edit., 1992; editor: Handbook of Personal Relationships, 1988, 2d edit., 1997, Meaningful Relationships, 1994; co-editor: Studying Interpersonal Interaction, 1991; editor Jour. Social and Personal Relationships, 1984-98. Fellow APA, Am. Psychol. Soc., Interpersonal Comm. Assn. Office: U Iowa Dept Comm Studies 105B CSB Iowa City IA 52242

DUCKER, BRUCE, novelist, lawyer; b. N.Y.C., Aug. 10, 1938; s. Allen and Lillian Ducker; m. Jaren Jones, Sept. 1, 1962; children: Foster, Penelope, John. AB, Dartmouth Coll., 1960; MA, Columbia U., 1963, LLB, 1964. Bar: Colo. 1964, U.S. Dist. Ct. Colo. 1964, U.S. Ct. Appeals (10th cir.) 1964. Gen. counsel Great Western United Corp., Denver, 1972-73; pres., chmn. bd. dirs. Great Western Cities Inc., Denver, 1974-75; pres. Ducker, Montgomery & Lewis P.C., Denver, 1979-97. Author: (novels) Rule by Proxy, 1976, Failure at the Mission Trust, 1986, Bankroll, 1989, Marital Assets, 1993, Lead Us Not Into Penn Station, 1994; contbr. articles, poetry and short stories to lit. jours. Former trustee Legal Aid Found. of Colo., Denver Symphony Assn., Kent Denver Country Day Sch. Mem. ABA, P.E.N., Colo. Bar Assn., Denver Bar Assn., Authors' Guild, Poetry Soc. Am., Denver Club, Cactus Club. Office: Ducker Montgomery & Lewis PC 1560 Broadway Ste 1500 Denver CO 80202-5151

DUCKETT, BERNADINE JOHNAL, retired elementary principal; b. Flint, Mich., Aug. 7, 1939; d. John and Bernice (Robinson) Edwards; m. Ellis Duckett Jr., Apr. 15, 1963; children: Bruce Devlon, Janeen Jae; 1 stepchild, Ellis III; m. Charles Teaberry (div. June 1960). BS in Edn., Ctrl. Mich. U., 1962; MA in Ednl. Adminstrn., U. Mich., 1966; Reading Specialist, Mich. State U., 1970; postgrad., Flint (Mich.) C.C., 1989-92. Cert. elem. tchr., Mich. Classroom tchr. Dort Elem. Sch., Flint, 1959-65; reading tchr. Dort & Dewey Elem. Sch., Flint, 1965-67; instrnl. specialist Doyle and Dewey Elem. Sch., Flint, 1967-71; asst. prin. Dewey, Merrill & Cook Elem. Sch., Flint, 1971-74; prin. Garfield & Elem. M.L. King, Flint, 1974-96; ret., 1996; presenter, mem. Internat. Ednl. Symposium, Rome, 1988-92, Flint Schs. Employee of Month Program, 1985-92. Author: Diet on the Lighter Side, 1988, My Grandparents Said Go 4 It, 1989; author joint books: Bicentennial Sch. Cookbook, 1976, Tapestry, 1988, URA Winner, 1994; contbr. articles to mags. and newspapers. Fundraiser Walk-a-Thons, United Negro Coll. Fund, Children's Miracle, Flint, 1991, Crim Race for Spl. Children, Flint, 1989-99, Riverbend Striders, Flint, 1993—; mem., presenter Consortium to Prevent Child Abuse, 1990; vol. St. Joseph Hosp. Aux., Flint, 1990-98; mem. Greater Flint Afro-Am. Sports Hall of Fame, 1992—; mem. com. Aiding Hard of Hearing, Quota Club Internat., Flint, 1994-99. Recipient Outstanding Educator plaque NAACP, Flint Intern Plaque, 1986, Flint OBE Pioneer Plaque, 1993, Ednl. Contbns. as Family award, 1993, Walker medal Leukemia Soc., 1996; grantee Flint Cmty. Schs., 1990-93. Mem. Nat. Assn. Elem. Sch. Prins. (dir. founds. 1992-96, cons., student discipline Focus Group on Ethnic Minorities 1981, 92, 94, Outstanding Svc. Plaque 1993), Nat. Assn. Media Women (sec. Flint chpt. 1989-92, Media Woman of Yr. 1990), Mich. Assn. Elem. and Mid. Sch. Prins. (chairperson awards, mem. conf. planning and summer camp com., treas., membership chair, del., presenter 1977-92, certs. 1985, 87, 91, plaque 1990), Nat. Alliance Black Sch. Educators (presenter 1993), Internat. Platform Assn., Flint Assn. Elem. Prins. (sec., election chair, social chair 1980-96), Global Network of Schs., U. Mich. Alumni Assn., Nat. Leukemia Soc. (Alaskan marathon walker, medalist 1996). Avocations: speed walking, writing poetry, reading, flower gardening. Home: 3720 Circle Dr Flint MI 48507-1879

DUCKWORTH, GUY, musician, pianist, educator; b. L.A., Dec. 19, 1923; s. Glenn M. and Laura (Lysle) D.; m. Ballerina Maria Farra, May 23, 1948. BA, UCLA, 1951; MusM, Columbia U., 1953, PhD, 1969. Piano soloist Metro Goldwyn Mayer Studios, 1936-41, Warner Bros. Studios, 1936-41, Sta. KFI, L.A., 1938, Sta. KNX, L.A., 1939, Sta. KHJ, L.A., 1940; artist Columbia Artists, 1942-49; asst. prof. music. U. Minn., Mpls., 1955-60, assoc. prof., 1960-62; prof. piano, fellow Northwestern U., Evanston, Ill., 1962-70; chmn. dept. preparatory piano Northwestern U., 1962-70; prof. music U. Colo., Boulder, 1970-88; prof. emeritus U. Colo., 1988, originator, coordinator masters and doctoral programs in mus. arts; piano concert tours in U.S., Can., Mexico, 1947-49; condr. various music festivals, U.S., 1956—; dir. Walker Art Children's Concerts, Mpls., 1957-62; nat. piano chmn. Music Educators Nat. Conf., 1965-71; vis. lectr., scholar 96 univs., colls. and conservatories, U.S. and Can., 1964—; cons. to Ill. State Dept. Program Devel. for Gifted Children, 1968-69; vis. prof. U. Colo., 1988-90. Television series "A New Dimension in Piano Instruction", 1959, rec. Natl. award from Natl. Edn. Television, creator/performer. Author: Keyboard Explorer, 1963, Keyboard Discoverer, 1963, Keyboard Builder, 1964, Keyboard Musician, 1964, Keyboard Performer, 1966, Keyboard Musicianship, 1970, Guy Duckworth Piano Library, 1974, Guy Duckworth Musicianship Series, 1975, Keyboard Musician: The Symmetrical Keyboard, 2 vols., 1987-88, Keyboard Musician: The Symmetrical Keyboard, 1988, rev. edit., 1990; contbr. to over 6 books, 23 articles on pedagogy of music to various jours.; producer, performer video tapes on piano teaching; producer, writer (film) The Person First: A Different Kind of Teaching, 1984. Nominator Irving S. Gilmore Internat. Keyboard Festival, Gilmore Artist and Young Artist Awards. With U.S. Army, 1943-46. Recipient All-Univ. Teaching award for excellence, U. Colo., 1981, Pedagogy Honors award Nat. Conf. Piano Pedagogy, Chgo., 1994; named Pioneer Pedagogue Nat. Corp. Piano Pedagogy, Princeton U. Retrospective, 1992. Mem. Music Tchrs. Nat. Assn., Colo. State Music Tchrs. Assn., Coll. Music Soc., Music Educators Nat. Conf., Music Teachers Assn. Calif., Phi Mu Alpha, Pi Kappa Lambda. Home: 6522 Ambrosia Dr Apt 5108 San Diego CA 92124-3136 Office: U Colo Coll of Music Boulder CO 80302

DUCKWORTH, MARVIN E., lawyer, educator; b. Aug. 16, 1942; s. Marvin E. and Maryann Duckworth; children: Matthew, Brian, Jennifer, Jeffrey. BS in Indsl. Engring., Iowa State U., 1964; JD, Drake U., 1968. Bar: Iowa 1968, U.S. Dist. Ct. (no. and so. dists.) Iowa 1969. Assoc. Davis, Huebner, Johnson & Burt, Des Moines, 1968-70; asst. prof. Drake U., 1970-71, lectr. law, 1971-85, assoc. dean clin. programs, 1986—; shareholder Hopkins & Huebner, P.C., Des Moines, 1971—; spkr. in field. Pres. Drake Law Bd. Counselors, 1991-92, Drake Law Endowment Trust, 1995-96. Named Alumnus of Yr. Drake Law Sch., 1997. Fellow Iowa Bar Found.; mem. ABA (chmn. workers compensation and employers liability law 1986-87, vice hmn. toxic and hazardous substances and environ. law com. 1989-93), Iowa Bar Assn. (pres. young lawyers sect. 1977-78, Merit award 1982, chair workers compensation sect. 1992-93), Def. Rsch. Inst., Fedn. Ins. and Corp. Counsel (workers compensation com.), Iowa Assn. Workers Compensation Lawyers (pres. 1988-89), Iowa Acad. Trial Lawyers, Order of Coif. Office: 2700 Grand Ave Ste 111 Des Moines IA 50312-5215

DUCKWORTH, TARA ANN, insurance company executive; b. Seattle, June 7, 1956; d. Leonard Douglas and Audrey Lee (Limbeck) Hill; m. Mark L. Duckworth, May 16, 1981; children: Harrison Lee III, Andrew James, Kathryn Anne. AAS, Highline C.C., Seattle, 1976. From acctg. clk. to info. sys. supr. SAFECO Ins. Co., Seattle, 1977-90, rate sys. mgr., 1990-94; sys. mgr. SAFECO Mut. Funds, SAFECO Credit, PNMR, Seattle, 1994-97, mktg. comm. and incentives, quality assurance mgr., 1997-98, dir. comml. lines sys., 1998—; mem. tech adv. com. for the computer info. svcs. program North Seattle Community Coll., 1984-96, chairperson tech. adv. com., 1988-90. Mem. Star Lake Improvement Club, 1988-94; mem. fellowship com. St. Lukes Luth. Ch., 1986—; mem. Boy Scouts Am., 1996—. Mem. NAFE, Nat. Assn. for Ins. Women, Soc. for State Filers, Nat. PTA. Office: SAFECO Ins Co SAFECO Plz Seattle WA 98185

DUCKWORTH, WINSTON HOWARD, retired ceramic engineer; b. Greenfield, Ohio, Oct. 15, 1918; s. Benton Raymond and Carrie Lois (Schrock) D.; m. Clara Elizabeth Ayres, Dec. 15, 1941; children—Winston (dec.), Christopher. BChemE, Ohio State U., 1940, MS, 1941. Registered profl. engr., Ohio. With Battelle Meml. Inst., Columbus, Ohio, 1946-94; research engr. Battelle Meml. Inst., 1946-48, asst. chief ceramic research, 1948-52, chief ceramic research, 1952-66, fellow, 1966—; dir. Battelle Meml. Inst. (Def. Ceramic Info. Center), 1967-71, mem. research council, 1979-85; Mem. Engrs. Joint Council, 1968-78, trustee, 1975-77. Author: Engineering Properties of Ceramics; also numerous articles. With AUS, 1941-46; lt. col. USAF; Ret. Fellow Am. Ceramic Soc. (Cramer award 1974, trustee 1968-74, v.p. 1976, disting. life mem. 1985); mem. Nat. Inst. Ceramic Engrs. (pres. 1964, trustee 1963-74, permanent sec. 1978—, Greaves-Walker award 1987), Can. Ceramic Soc., AAAS, Ohio Acad. Sci., Keramos, Sigma Xi. Home: 63 Brevoort Rd Columbus OH 43214-3823

DUCLOW, DONALD FRANCIS, philosophy educator, researcher; b. Chgo., Jan. 11, 1946; s. Francis Harold Duclow and Josephine Theresa (Schutzenhofer) Duclow-Baudler; m. Geraldine Anne Hodzima, July 11, 1970. BA, DePaul U., 1968, MA, 1969; MA, Bryn Mawr Coll., 1972, PhD, 1974. Asst. prof. philosophy Gwynedd-Mercy Coll., Gwynedd Valley, Pa., 1974-79, assoc. prof. philosophy, 1979-89, prof. philosophy, 1989—; vis. prof. Fordham U., Bronx, N.Y., 1978. Contbr. articles to profl. jours.; mem. editl. bd. Listening, 1981-89. Mellon fellow in the Humanities, U. Pa., Phila., 1980-81, sr. fellow Inst. Advanced Study Religion, Divinity Sch., U. Chgo., 1998; grantee NEH, 1987, 93. Mem. AAUP (pres. Gwynedd-Mercy chpt. 1996-97), Am. Acad. Religion, Medieval Acad. Am., Am. Cusanus Soc. (sec. 1985—), German Cusanus Soc. (adv. bd. 1993—), Amnesty Internat., Common Cause. Episcopalian. Office: Gwynedd-Mercy Coll Dept Philosophy Gwynedd Valley PA 19437

DUCLOW, GERALDINE, historian, theatre and film librarian; b. Chgo., Sept. 20, 1946; d. Steve and Irene (Halat) Hodzima; m. Donald F. Duclow, July 11, 1970. BA in English magna cum laude, DePaul U., 1968; MLS, Rosary Coll. (now Dominican U.), 1969. Reference libr. Chgo. Pub. Libr., 1969-70; reference libr. Free Libr. Phila., 1970-71, head theatre collection, 1972—; coord. conf. Preservation Mgmt. for Performing Arts Collections, 1982; cons. Lubin Film Co. exhibit at Nat. Mus. Am.-Jewish History, 1984; cons. and speaker in field. Contbr. articles to profl. jours. Mem. Am. Soc. for Theatre Rsch., Spl. Libr. Assn., Theatre Libr. Assn. (mem. exec. bd. 1980-95, pres. 1995—), Theatre Assn. Pa. Avocation: art. Office: Free Libr Phila 1901 Vine St Philadelphia PA 19103-1189*

DUCRAN, CLAUDETTE DELORIS, bank officer; b. Trinityville, St. Thomas, Jamaica, July 23, 1941; came to U.S., 1962; d. Wellesley Provan and Hilda Maude (Beckford) DuC. Student, Corcoran Sch. Art, Washington, 1967; cert. of diploma, USDA Grad. Sch., Washington, 1972; student, Harvard U., 1976; BBA, George Washington U., 1982; postgrad., Columbia U., 1987. Adminstrv. asst. World Bank, Washington, 1964-75, fin. asst., 1975-85, ops. asst., 1985-88, disbursement asst., 1988-94, disbursement analyst, 1994-96; mem. adv. com. Very Spl. Arts Kennedy Ctr., Washington, 1990-93, Hands Across Hemisphere Craft Ctr., Washington, 1991; founder, pres. Let's Learn by Reading, Jamaica, 1990—. Author: Exhibitors Guidelines, 1989, 2d edit., 1990. Bd. dirs. Craft Ctr., Washington, 1991—; panelist Career Week George Washington U., Washington, 1991, Women's Ctr., McLean, Va., 1991; founder, pres. The Claudette D. Ducran Found., Inc., Kingston, Jamaica, W.I., 1995—, The Eureka Alliance, Inc., Washington, 1995—. Recipient 1st prize Writer's League, Washington, 1967, Internat. Order of Merit, 1994; named Internat. Woman of Yr., 1993-94. Mem. World Affairs Coun., Soc. for Internat. Devel., The World Bank Art Soc. (v.p. 1986-88, pres. 1988-93), UN Assn./Nat. Capital Assn., 1818 Soc., Jamaica C. of C. (hon. Washington rep. 1997-98). Avocations: performing and visual arts, children, travel, working with handicapped, international development. Home: The Brighton 2123 California St NW Apt B1 Washington DC 20008-1804

DUDA, JOHN LARRY, chemical engineering educator; b. Donora, Pa., May 11, 1936; s. John Jr. and Nellie (Tihanski) D.; m. Margaret K. Barbalich, Jan. 27, 1962; children: John Eric, David Andrew, Paul Laurence, Laura Margaret. BSChE Case Inst. Tech., Cleve., 1958; MSChE U. Del., 1961, PhD in Chem. Engring., 1963. Chem. engr. Dow Chem. Co., Midland, Mich., 1963-64, rsch. engr., 1964-69, sr. rsch. engr., 1969-71; assoc. prof. chem. engring. Pa. State U., University Park, 1971-75, prof. chem. engring., 1975—, also head, chem. engring. dept., 1983—. Contbr. articles to profl. jours. Fellow AIChE (co-recipient William H. Walker award 1981, Charles Stine award 1989, dir. materials divsn. 1990—, mem. coun. 1996—, dir. nat. 1996—); mem. Am. Chem. Soc., Am. Soc. Engring. Edn. (Lectureship award 1989, Nat. Acad. Engring., W.K. Lewis award 1994), Soc. Petroleum Engrs., Soc. Plastics Engrs., Soc. Tribol. and Lubr. Engrs. Home: 602 Holmes St State College PA 16803-3619 Office: Pa State U Dept Chem Engring 160 Fenske Lab University Park PA 16802-4400

DUDASH, KAREN SHREFFLER, community health nurse; b. Melrose Park, Ill., Mar. 15, 1947; d. Keith Donald and E. Ruth (Kraemer) Shreffler; m. Joseph F. Dudash, Feb. 23, 1985; 1 child, Ryan Matthew. BS in Nursing, Northeast Mo. U., 1970. Staff nurse gastro-intensive ICU Hines (Ill.) VA Hosp., 1970; staff/charge nurse Story County Hosp., Nevada, Iowa, 1972-73; sch. nurse Lenox (Iowa) Community Sch. System, 1971-72; staff/charge nurse med.-surg. Mercy Hosp., Cedar Rapids, Iowa, 1973-85; Staff/charge nurse oncology med.-surg. Franklin Square Hosp., Balt., 1985-86; home health nurse Balt. County Health Dept., Balt., 1987—, Johns Hopkins Home Health, 1993—. Mem. Assn. for Home Care, Inc. (rep.), Northeast Mo. U. Alumni Assn.

DUDASH, LINDA CHRISTINE, insurance executive; b. Pitts.; d. Andrew Daniel and Lillian (Reynolds) D. BA in English, Point Park Coll., 1969. Tech. writer Am. Insts. for Rsch., Pitts., 1968-69; claim svc. rep. Reliance Ins. Co., Pitts., 1969-70, claim rep., 1970-71; claim mgr. Reliance Ins. Co., Jacksonville, Fla., 1971-73, Harrisburg, Pa., 1973-80, Chgo., 1980-86; H.O. sr. claim supr. Zurich Ins. Co., Schaumburg, Ill., 1986-88; asst. v.p., mgr. liability claims Zurich-Am. Ins., Schaumburg, Ill., 1988-91, asst. v.p., mgr. claims continuous improvement, 1991-92, v.p. dir. field ops., 1992-95; v.p. claims Casualty Ins. Co., divsn. Fremont Compensation Ins. Co., Chgo., 1995-97; sr. v.p. Fremont Compensation Ins. Group, Chgo., 1997—. Office: Freemont Compensation Ins Group 321 N Clark St Chicago IL 60610-4714

DUDDEN, ARTHUR POWER, historian, educator; b. Cleve., Oct. 26, 1921; s. Arthur Clifford and Kathleen (Bray) D.; m. Adrianne Churchill Onderdonk, June 5, 1965; 1 child, Alexis Dudden Eastwood; children by previous marriage: Kathleen Dudden Rowlands, Candace L. Dudden (Schweitzer). A.B., Wayne State U., 1942; A.M., U. Mich., 1947, Ph.D., 1950. Faculty Bryn Mawr Coll., 1950—, prof. history, 1965-92, Fairbank prof. humanities, 1989-92, Katharine E. McBride prof. history, 1992-95, 98-99; instr. CCNY, summer 1950; vis. asst. prof. Am. civilization U. Pa., 1953-54, ednl. coord. spl. program Am. civilization, 1956, mem. faculty Inst. Humanistic Studies for Execs., 1953-59, vis. assoc. prof. history, summers, 1958, 62-65, vis. prof. history, 1965-68; vis. assoc. prof. Princeton (N.J.) U., 1958-59, Haverford Coll., 1962-63; vis. prof. Trinity Coll., summer 1965; cons. Peace Corps, 1962-66; mem. Bicentennial Com. on Internat. Confs. of Americanists, 1973-76; pres. Fulbright Assn. of Alumni, 1976-80, exec. dir., 1980-84; cons. Nat. Archives, 1993-95; adj. prof. history Lehigh U., 1993-95. Author: Teachers Manual to the American Republic, vols. I and II, 1959, 60, 70, Understanding the American Republic, vols. I and II, 1961, 70, Objective Tests, The American Republic, 1962, The Assault of Laughter, 1962, The United States of America: A Syllabus of American Studies, 2 vols, 1963, The Instructor's Guide to the United States, 3d edit, 1972, The Student's Guide to the United States, 2d edit, 1967, Joseph Fels and the Single Tax Movement, 1971, Pardon Us, Mr. President!, 1975, The Fulbright Experience, 1946-1986, 1987, American Humor, 1987, The American Pacific, 1992, paperback edit., 1993; editor: Woodrow Wilson and the World of Today, 1957, The Logbook of the Captain's Clerk, 1995; compiler: International Directory of Specialists in American Studies, 1975; contbr. Ency. Am. Social History, 1993, Ency. U.S. Fgn. Rels., 1997. Served with USNR, 1942-45. Sr. Fulbright scholar Denmark, 1959-60 and West Europe, 1992. Mem. Fellows Am. Studies (sec.-treas. 1957-59, pres. 1960-61), Am. Studies Assn. (treas. 1968, 72, exec. sec. 1969-72, Bode-Pearson prize 1991), Am. Hist. Assn., Orgn. Am. Historians (local arrangements chmn. Phila. 1969), Hist. Soc. of Pa. (bd. trustees 1993—). Home: 829 Old Gulph Rd Bryn Mawr PA 19010-2910

DUDDLES, CHARLES WELLER, food company executive; b. Cadillac, Mich., Mar. 31, 1940; s. Dwight Irving and Bertha (Taylor) D.; m. Judith Marie Robinson, June 23, 1962; children: Paul, Steven, Lisa. B.S., Ferris State U., 1961. C.P.A. Mich., Mo. Audit mgr. Price Waterhouse & Co., Battle Creek, Mich., 1961-72; mgr. gen. acctg. Ralston Purina Co., St. Louis, 1973-77, dir. spl. acctg. services, 1977-79; v.p., controller Foodmaker, Inc., San Diego, 1979-81, sr. v.p. fin. and adminstrn., chief fin. officer, 1981-87, sr. v.p., chief fin. officer, 1988, exec. v.p., chief fin. officer, chief adminstrv. officer, dir., 1988—. Mem. Fin. Execs. Inst., Nat. Assn. Accts., Am. Inst. C.P.A.s. Republican. Presbyterian. Lodge: Rotary (San Diego). Office: Foodmaker Inc 9330 Balboa Ave San Diego CA 92123-1598*

DUDEK, HENRY THOMAS, management consultant; b. Queens, N.Y., Dec. 29, 1929; s. Wojciech and Magdalena (Swiader) D.; m. Olga Waranitsky, June 14, 1953; children: Kathryn, Nancy, Linda, Andrew, Henryk. BBA, CCNY, 1955. Acctg. mgr. A.D.T. Co., N.Y.C., 1948-54; asst. controller Dancer Fitzgerald Sample, Inc., N.Y.C., 1955-60; chief fin. officer Wunderman Ricotta & Kline, Inc., N.Y.C., 1961-69, Van Brunt & Co., N.Y.C., 1970; controller, stockholder Compton Advt., Inc., N.Y.C., 1971; pres., chief exec. officer Henry T. Dudek & Assocs., Inc., Floral Park, N.Y., 1972—; frequent speaker on finance and advt. Mem. Advt. Agy. Fin. Mgmt. Assn. (bd. dirs.). Roman Catholic. Home: 90 Beech St Floral Park NY 11001-3103 Office: PO Box 478 Floral Park NY 11002-0478

DUDEK, RICHARD ALBERT, engineering educator; b. Clarkson, Nebr., Sept. 3, 1926; s. Emil E. and Jennie (Indra) D.; m. Helen M. Staver, Dec. 19, 1954; children: Richard Emil, Rustin Max. B.S. in Mech. Engring., U.

Nebr., 1950; M.S. in Indsl. Engring., U. Iowa, 1951, Ph.D., 1956. Plant indsl. engr. Fairmont Foods Co., Sioux City, Iowa, 1951-52; div. indsl. engr. Fairmont Foods Co., Omaha, 1952-53; research asst. U. Iowa, 1953-54; asst. prof. mech. engring. U. Nebr., 1954-56; research assoc. Sch. of Health Professions, also asso. prof. indsl. engring. U. Pitts., 1956-58; prof., head dept. indsl. engring. Tex. Tech U., Lubbock, 1958-86; dir. Ctr. of Biotech. and Human Performance, 1969-74, P.W. Horn prof., 1970-92, P.W. Horn prof. emeritus, 1992—; tech. cons. industry, instns., religious orgns., hosps., 1951—; instr. TV courses; dir. Found. Internat. Rsch. and Devel., Lubbock, 1960-65, MASET, Inc., Lubbock, 1974-85, Jay Bee Mfg. Inc., Tyler, Tex., 1984-86, Cellular Tech., Inc., Lubbock, 1984-88, Rowden Gas Inc., Lubbock, 1986-92, Sone Energy, Inc., Dallas, 1988-94. Mem. editl. bd. Engring. Costs and Prodn. Econs., 1980-94; contbr. articles to profl. jours. Bd. dirs. South Plains chpt. Muscular Dystrophy Assn. Am., 1966-76, campaign chmn., 1968. Recipient Faculty Recognition award, 1978, Disting. Scientist award Achievement Rewards for Coll. Scientists, 1984, award of Excellence Halliburton Edn. Found., 1987; named South Plains Engr. of Yr. Tex. Soc. Profl. Engrs., 1986. Fellow Am. Inst. Indsl. Engrs. (pres. Great Plains chpt. 1960-61, chmn. nat. student chpt. 1961-63, ECPD guidance rep. 1965-68, research com. 1967-69, regional v.p. 1969-71, Appreciation award 1970, spl. service award 1971); mem. Council Indsl. Engring. Acad. Dept. Heads (asst. sec. 1980, sec. 1981-82, vice chmn. 1982-83, chmn. 1983-84), Am. Soc. Engring. Edn. (editor indsl. engring. div. 1965-66, sec. indsl. engring. div. 1966-67, vice chmn. 1967-68, chmn. 1968-69, chmn. planning com. of council of tech. divs. 1970-71, sec. council 1972-73), Inst. Mgmt. Sci., ASME, Human Factors Soc., Tech. Assessment Soc., Sigma Xi (pres. Tex. Tech. chpt. 1971-72), Tex. Tech. Acad. Indsl. Engrs., Phi Kappa Phi (chpt. pres. 1967), Pi Mu Epsilon, Pi Tau Sigma, Alpha Pi Mu, Tau Beta Pi, Phi Beta Delta. Home: 3707 46th St Lubbock TX 79413-3446

DUDERSTADT, JAMES JOHNSON, academic administrator, engineering educator; b. Ft. Madison, Iowa, Dec. 5, 1942; s. Mack Henry and Katharine Sydney (Johnson) D.; m. Anne Marie, June 24, 1964; children: Susan Kay, Katharine Anne. B in Engring. with highest honors, Yale U., 1964; MS in Engring. Sci. Calif. Inst. Tech., 1965, PhD in Engring. Sci. and Physics, 1967. Asst. prof. nuclear engring. U. Mich., 1969-72, assoc. prof., 1972-76, prof., 1976-81; dean U. Mich. (Coll. Engring.), 1981-86; provost, v.p. acad. affairs U. Mich., 1986-88, pres. univ., 1988-96, pres. emeritus, prof. sci. engring., 1996—; dir. Millennium Project, 1996—. AEC fellow, 1964-68; recipient E. O. Lawrence award U.S. Dept. Energy, 1986, Nat. medal of Tech., 1991; named Nat. Engr. of Yr., NSPE, 1991. Fellow Am. Nuclear Soc. (Mark Mills award 1968, Arthur Holly Compton award 1985); mem. NAE (coun.), Am. Phys. Soc., Nat. Sci. Bd. (chair 1991-94), Am. Acad. Arts & Scis., Sigma Xi, Tau Beta Pi, Phi Beta Kappa. Office: Millennium Project 2001 Media Union Ann Arbor MI 48109

DUDICK, MICHAEL JOSEPH, retired bishop; b. St. Clair, Pa., Feb. 24, 1917; s. John and Mary (Jurick) D. BA, Ill. Benedictine Coll., Lisle, 1943; postgrad., St. Procopius Sem., Lisle, 1943-45; HHD (hon.), Kings Coll., 1987; DD (hon.), Scranton U., 1989. Ordained priest Roman Cath. Ch., 1945. Vice chancellor Exarchate of Pitts., 1946-55; chancellor Diocese of Passaic, N.J., 1963-68; bishop Diocese of Passaic, 1968-96; ret., 1996; mem. N.J. Coalition of Religious Leaders; cons. ecumenical and interreligious com. Nat. Conf. Cath. Bishops, 1986-96. Bd. regents Seton Hall U., 1986-96. *

DUDICS-DEAN, SUSAN ELAINE, interior designer; b. Perth Amboy, N.J., Oct. 22, 1950; d. Theodore W. and Joyce M. (Ryals) D.; m. Rick Dean, Apr. 30, 1989; 1 child, Merissa Joyce. BS in Sociology, W.Va. U., 1972; postgrad. Rutgers U., 1975-78, U. Calif., Irvine, 1979-81, Can. Coll., 1981-89. Programmer Prudential Life, Newark, 1972-73; sr. systems analyst Johnson & Johnson, New Brunswick, N.J., 1973-78, Sperry Univac, Irvine, Calif., 1978-80; sr. systems analyst, project leader Robert A. McNeil, San Mateo, Calif., 1981-83; dist. design dir. TransDesigns, Woodstock, Ga., 1982-93; prin. Celestial Designs, 1980—. lectr., speaker in the field of interior design, sales and Feng Shui, 1986—. Contbr. articles to profl. jours.; writer Drapery and Window Coverings, Design Lines, Window Fashions mag., Designer Lines; guest (TV shows) House Doctor, Marketplace Sta. KGO-TV. High sch. mentor Directions, San Francisco, 1985-95. Mem. Women Entreprenuers (membership com., treas. 1983-87), Cen. N.J. Alumni Assn. Delta Gamma (assoc. sec., founder, pres.), Hagerstown C. of C., Nat. Assn. of Profl. Saleswomen, Am. Soc. Interior Designers (allied mem. 1989-92), Profl. Bus. Women's Assn., Delta Gamma. Recipient awards TransDesigns, Woodstock, Ga., 1984-87, 89-91, MoonRise Galleries, 1994-99. Avocations: skiing, sewing, scuba diving, ballet, handcrafts.

DUDLEY, ANNE, composer. Performer's diploma, Kings Coll., MusB, MusM. Film scores include Disorderlies, 1987, Hiding Out, 1987, Buster, 1988, Silence Like Glass, 1989, The Mighty Quinn, 1989, Say Anything, 1989, The Misadventures of Mr. Wilt, 1990, The Crying Game, 1992, The Hollow Reed, 1996, The Full Monty, 1997, American History X, 1998, Pushing Tin, 1999, In My Father's House, 1999; solo album Ancient and Modern, 1995, The Seduction of Claude Debussy, 1999. Office: Air Edel/Karen Elliott, 18 Rodmarton St, London W1H 3FW, England

DUDLEY, BROOKE FITZHUGH, educational consultant; b. East Orange, N.J., Oct. 22, 1942; s. Benjamin William and Jean (Peeples) D.; AB in Econs., Colgate U., 1966; m. Elizabeth Slater; 1 child, Catherine Sanford. Sales mgr. De La Rue Instruments, Phila., 1968-71; comml. banker Bankers Trust Co., N.Y.C., 1966-68, Provident Nat. Bank, Phila., 1972-74; dir. admissions/fin. aid St. Stephen's Episc. Sch., Austin, Tex., 1974-78; exec. dir. U. Tex. Law Sch. Found., Austin, 1978-85; ednl. cons., 1982—; founding ptnr. The Edn. Group Southwest, Inc., 1989-92; exec. dir. San Antonio Art Inst., 1992-93. Chmn. bd. trustees Austin Evaluation Ctr.; trustee Austin Repertory Theater; chmn. bd. dirs. All Saints Episc. Day Sch., Austin; Bishop's com. St. Michael's and All Angels Episcopal Ch.; bd. dirs. Symphony Sq., Austin Child Guidance and Evaluation Ctr.; advisory trustee Winston Sch., San Antonio; Republican campaign mgr., N.Y.C., 1966-68. Served with U.S. Army, 1962-64. Mem. Ind. Ednl. Cons. Assn. Found. (chmn. bd. trustees), Hill Sch. Alumni Assn. (mem. exec. com. 1968-71), Edna Gladney Austin Aux. (past pres.). Episcopalian. Office: 359 E Hildebrand Ave San Antonio TX 78212-2412

DUDLEY, DELORES INGRAM, secondary education educator, poet, writer; b. Portsmouth, Va., Oct. 9, 1948. BA in English, Norfolk State U., 1971, MA in Comm., 1990; postgrad., U. Va., 1981-84, Old Dominion U., Va. State Coll., U. S.C. Tchr. English Ctrl. Jr. High Sch., Charlotte, Va., 1972-78, Cradock High Sch., Portsmouth, 1982-92; tchr. English and pub. speaking Manor High Sch., Portsmouth, 1992-94; columnist Citizens Press, 1985-87; faculty corr., columnist Portsmouth Times, 1992; guest columnist Va. Pilot Ledger-Star Newspaper. Author: A Collection of Poems, 1993. Dir. Bapt. Tng. Union, 3d Bapt. Ch., 1995—, past ch. activities include sec. youth assembly, 1st v.p. youth assembly, pres. youth assembly, mem. sr. choir, tchr. vacation bible sch., dir. vacation bible sch., co-dir. vacation bible sch., adult city-wide summer missionary, dir. tng. union; vol. Salvation Army, Feed the Hungry Program. Recipient Va. Gov.'s Physical Fitness award, 1989, Apple for Tchr. award Alpha Chi chpt. Iota Phi Lambda, 1997; higher edn. fellow State Coun. Mem. NEA, Nat. Assn. Tchrs. English, AAUW (sec. Portsmouth br.), Portsmouth Edn. Assn., Southeastern Va. Arts Assn. (contbr. articles to monthly newsletter), Internat. Platform Assn. Avocations: writing, aerobics, walking, reading, chess. Home: 907 Tazewell St Portsmouth VA 23701-3229

DUDLEY, DON, broadcast journalist, communications consultant; b. Beaufort, N.C., Oct. 18, 1961; s. Donnie L. and Sara Parkin (Brooks) D. BS in Broadcast Journalism, Boston U., 1984. Reporter, bur. chief Sta. WCSH-TV, Portland, Maine, 1984-85, Stas. WBTW-TV/WSPA-TV, Columbia, S.C., 1985-93; anchor, reporter Sta. WSPA-TV, Spartanburg, S.C., 1993-94; prodr., reporter News Channel 8, Washington, 1994-96; sr. prodr. programming NET Polit. News Talk Network, Washington, 1996-97; news dir., corr. Network USA Aviation News, Washington, 1997—; adj. prof. U. Md. Author: The Dynamic Action Diet: Discover Your Diet Personality, 1994. Bd. dirs. Dynamic Concepts, Inc., Spartanburg, 1993-95, The Agy. for Internat. Understanding, Spartanburg, 1993-95, Piedmont chpt. ARC, Spartanburg, 1993, co-chmn. cmty. rels. bd., 1992-93; hon. chmn. Mobil Meals Found., Greenville-Spartanburg, 1993; master of ceremonies Miss S.C. Pageant, Greenville, 1993-94. Recipient Vol. award ARC, Spartanburg, 1993, Spot News Coverage 1st pl. award Maine Assn. Broadcasters, Portland, 1985, Pub. Svc. award Carolina Power Squadron, Greenville, 1993. Mem. NATAS, Soc. Profl. Journalists (bd. dirs. DC Pro chpt. 1997-98, v.p. 1998-99, pres. 1999—), Nat. Press Club, Radio-TV News Dirs. Assn., Washington Corrs. Assn., Nat. Press club. Episcopalian. Home: 1200 N Veitch St Arlington VA 22201-5818 Office: Network USA 7315 Wisconsin Ave Bethesda MD 20814-3202

DUDLEY, DURAND STOWELL, librarian; b. Cleve., Feb. 28, 1926; s. George Stowell and Corinne Elizabeth (Durand) D.; m. Dorothy Woolworth, July 3, 1954; children: Jane Elizabeth, Deborah Anne. BA, Oberlin Coll., 1948; MLS, Case Western Res. U., 1950. Librarian, Marietta (O.) Coll. Library, 1953-55, Akron (O.) Pub. Library, 1955-60; librarian Marathon Oil Co., Findlay, O., 1960-74, sr. law librarian, 1974-86; supr. tech. services dept. Findlay-Hancock County Pub. Library, Findlay, 1986-88. Mem. Spl. Libraries Assn. Presbyterian (deacon). Home: 807 Red Maple Ct Bluffton OH 45817-8551

DUDLEY, EDWARD JAMES, retired news manager; b. Fairport, N.Y., Mar. 31, 1914; s. Raymond Lockwood and Edith Dennis Dudley; m. Frances Joy MacIntire, May 13, 1944; 1 child, Sara Dudley Harris. BS in Journalism, Syracuse U., 1935. News reporter Jour. America, Rochester, N.Y., 1935-37; news, feature writer Dem. Chronicle, Rochester, 1937-41; pub. rels. rep. Am. Locomotive Co., Schenectady, N.Y., 1946-47; asst. mgr. pub. rels. Am. Can Co., N.Y.C., 1947-55; staff writer Carl Byoir & Assoc., N.Y.C., 1955-59; mgr. news/info. RCA Govt. and Comml. Systems Divsn., Cherry Hill, N.J., 1959-80; owner The Editl. Svcs. Group, Moorestown, N.J., 1983—. Editor Cooper Hosp. Found., 1983-87. Mem. Hawthorne (N.Y.) Sch. Bd., 1955-57. Maj. U.S. Army, 1941-46. Mem. Soc. of Profl. Journalists, Sigma Phi Epsilon. Democrat. Presbyterian. Avocations: reading, walking, photography. Home: 23 S Shirley Ave Moorestown NJ 08057

DUDLEY, ELLEN REVIE, writer, editor, publisher; b. Harvard, Mass.; d. Richard E. and Barbara Teed Dudley; m. Anthony Gordon; 1 child, Laura Spinney. BA, Norwich U.; MFA, Warren Wilson Coll., 1992. Co-owner Constrn. Alchemy, Marlboro, Vt., 1986—; editor, pub. The Marlboro Rev., 1995—. Author: (book of poetry) Slow Burn, 1997. Vol. Morningside Emergency Shelter, Brattleboro, Vt.; bd. dirs. Windham Solid Waste Mgmt. Dist., Battleboro, 1987-93; mem. Ka'u Gallery Coop., Na'alehu, Hawaii, 1997—. Fellow Vt. Arts Coun., 1993, fellow Vt. Art Studio, 1995. Mem. Acad. Am. Poets, Poetry Soc. Am., New Eng. Poetry Club. Avocation: lieder singing. E-mail: dudley@sover.net. Office: The Marlboro Rev PO Box 243 N Pond Rd Marlboro VT 05344

DUDLEY, GEORGE AUSTIN, architect, planning consultant, educator; b. Pitts., Dec. 24, 1914; s. Samuel William and Mabel Eva (Allen) D.; children: George Bergin, Sally Jean, John Phillips, Samuel William III. B.A., Yale U., 1936, B.F.A. in Arch, 1938, M.F.A. in City Planning, 1940. With Office Coordinator of Inter-Am. Affairs, 1941-45; dir. research Conn. Post War Planning Bd., 1944-45; with archtl. firm Harrison & Abramovitz, N.Y.C., 1945-48, 59-60; sec. internat. bd. design UN Hdqrs., 1945-46; pres. IBEC Housing Corp., 1948-59; cons. Internat. Devel. Adv. Bd., 1951; dir. N.Y. State Office Regional Devel.; also sec. Planning Coordination Bd. of Gov. Rockefeller, 1960-62; trustee N.Y. State U. Constrn. Fund; planning coordinator N.Y. State New South Mall Capital, 1962-65; dean Sch. Architecture, Rensselaer Poly. Inst., 1962-65; founding dean Sch. Architecture and Urban Planning, U. Calif. at Los Angeles, 1965-68; chmn. N.Y. State Pure Waters Authority, 1967-70; pres. N.Y. State Environ. Facilities Corp., 1970-72; chmn., chief exec. officer N.Y. State Council on Architecture, 1967-75; sr. cons. and phys. planning officer Kuwait Inst. Sci. Research, 1977-80; cons. master planning Saudi Arabian Nat. Center Sci. and Tech., Riyadh, 1980-84, Amanat Al-Asima, Baghdad, Iraq, 1980-85; advisor master planning King Abdulaziz U., Jeddah, Saudi Arabia, 1986-88; cons. achitect plannner Hotel des Artists, N.Y.C.; lectr. USIS/ICA, Brazil, Venezuela, Trinidad, Honduras, Mexico, India, Singapore, Malaysia, Indonesia, S. Korea, Hong Kong, Japan; mem. U.S. del. UN Conf. Human Settlement, Vancouver, 1976. Author: A Workshop for Peace/Designing the United Nations Headquarters, Architectural History Foundation, 1994; co-author: The Case for Regional Planning, 1947; contbg. editor: Architecture Plus. Trustee Inst. Architecture and Urban Studies, 1968-78; bd. dirs. AIA Found.; mem. overseers vis. com. Harvard Grad. Sch. Design, 1974-79; chmn. Yale Council Com. for Architecture and Art, 1970-75; cons. Rensselaerville (N.Y.) Inst., 1991—. Fellow AIA; mem. Nat. Acad. Design (assoc.). Home: Hickory Hill Rensselaerville NY 12147 also: 1 W 67th St New York NY 10023-6200

DUDLEY, GEORGE ELLSWORTH, lawyer; b. Earlington, Ky., July 14, 1922; s. Ralph Emerson and Camille (Lackey) D.; m. Barbara J. Muir, June 28, 1950 (dec. Feb. 1995); children: Bruce K., Camille Dudley McNutt, Nancy S., Elizabeth Dudley Stephens. BS in Commerce, U. Ky., 1947; JD, U. Mich., 1950. Bar: Ky. 1950, D.C. 1951, U.S. Dist. Ct. (we. dist.) Ky. 1962, U.S. Ct. Appeals (6th cir.) 1987. Assoc. Gordon, Gordon & Moore, Madisonville, Ky., 1950-51; pvt. practice law Louisville, 1952-59; ptnr. Brown, Ardery, Todd & Dudley, Louisville, 1959-72; ptnr. Brown, Todd & Heyburn, Louisville, 1972-92, of counsel, 1992—, mem. mgmt. com., 1972-90, chmn., 1989-90. Pres. Ky. Easter Seal Soc., Louisville, 1971-72; treas. Ky. Dem. Party, Frankfort, 1971-74; bd. dirs. Alliant Adult Health Svcs., Louisville, 1976—; 1st v.p. Nat. Easter Seal Soc., Chgo., 1981. Capt. inf. U.S. Army, 1943-46, ETO; capt. JAGC, U.S. Army, 1951-52. Mem. ABA, Ky. Bar Assn., Louisville Bar Assn., U.S. 6th Cir. Jud. Conf. (life), Harmony Landing Country Club (pres. 1978-79), Tavern Club, Barristers Soc., Omicron Delta Kappa. Presbyterian. Avocations: golf, tennis, travel, sports spectator. Home: 1905 Crossgate Ln Louisville KY 40222-6405 Office: Brown Todd & Heyburn 3200 Providian Louisville KY 40202

DUDLEY, JOHN HENRY, JR., lawyer; b. Lansing, Mich., June 22, 1941; s. John Henry and Elizabeth (Dean) D.; m. Elizabeth Merrill Casgrain, Dec. 27, 1975; 1 child, John. BA, Denison U., 1963; LLB, Stanford U., 1966; MA, U. Mich., 1968. Bar: Mich. 1968, U.S. Ct. Appeals (6th cir.) 1972, U.S. Ct. Appeals (2d cir.) 1987. Assoc. Devine & Devine, Ann Arbor, Mich., 1968-69; ptnr. Butzel Long, Detroit, 1969—; adj. prof. law sch. U. Detroit, 1991. Chair, bd. dirs. Ann Arbor YMCA, 1997-99. Fellow Mich. State Bar Found.; mem. ABA (litig. sect.), Mich. State Bar Assn. (rep. assembly 1974-77), Mich. Bd. Psychology, Detroit Bar Assn. (vol. lawyers com. 1989—), Washtenaw County Bar Assn. Office: Butzel Long 150 W Jefferson Ave Fl 9th Detroit MI 48226-4430*

DUDLEY, JOSEPH MICHAEL, English educator; b. Youngstown, Ohio, Oct. 20, 1962; s. Joseph and Phyllis Ann (Lengenfelter) D. BA, Kent State U., 1986, MA, 1990. Instr. Kent State U., 1991; instr. Kent State U., Warren, Ohio, 1993—, English coord. Skill Ctr., 1993, English coord. AEP, 1994, acad. advisor, 1995-97, program assoc. TRI, 1995-98; web master Skill Ctr. Kent State U., Warren, 1994—, web master spl. programs, 1998; web master Summer Stock '98, Warren, 1998. Contbr. articles to profl. jours. Recipient FACE Project award Trumbull County Family Svcs., 1991. Mem. HTML Writers' Guild. Avocations: wrtiting web pages, vegetarian, cooking, reading science fiction. Office: Kent State U Trumbull Campus 4314 Mahoning Ave NW Warren OH 44483-1998

DUDLEY, PERRY, JR., wireless communications administrator; b. New Haven, June 5, 1928; s. Perry and Ella (Leach) D.; m. June Ungar, Feb. 13, 1993; children: Bruce Lawrence, Virginia Barbara (from previous marriage). BSEE, Purdue U., 1952; MBA, U. Santa Clara, 1966. Sales engr. Reliance Elec. Co., Cleve. and L.A., 1952-60, GTE Sylvania, Burlingame, Calif., 1960-65; sr. applications engr. Varian Assocs., Palo Alto, Calif., 1965-68; product mgr. Ampex Corp., Redwood City, Calif., 1968-70; program mgr. Genesys Sys., Inc., 1972-73; indsl. real estate broker, salesman, 1974-80; program mgr. Dalmo Victor Ops., Bell Aerospace Divsn., Textron, 1980-85; mktg. and program mgr. Loral Data Sys., San Diego, 1986-88; mgmt. cons. San Diego, 1989-94; real estate agent Prudential Atlanta Realty, 1995-96; program mgr. EMS Scis., Norcross, Ga., 1996-97; plan owner GTE Wireless, 1997—; instr. mktg. and mgmt. San Francisco State U., 1982, West Coast U., 1990-94. Pres. Young Rep. Club, Pasadena, Calif., 1959; precinct capt. Menlo Park (Calif.) Rep. Com., 1961-72; elder Presbyn. Ch. With USN, 1946-48. Mem. Nat. Assn. of Mgmt., Assn. of Old Crows, North Fulton County Rep. Club, Purdue Alumni Club (pres. 1959), Mensa, Phi Gamma Delta. Avocations: sailing, cruising. Home: 1030 Taylor Knoll Close Roswell GA 30076-1100 Office: GTE PO Box 7700 600 Embassy Row Atlanta GA 30301

DUDLEY, RICHARD MANSFIELD, mathematician, educator; b. East Cleveland, Ohio, July 28, 1938; s. Winston Mansfield and Charlotte Mae (Wheaton) D.; m. Elizabeth Allen Martin, June 3, 1978. A.B., Harvard U., 1959; Ph.D., Princeton U., 1962. Asst. prof. math. U. Calif., Berkeley, 1963-66; asso. prof. MIT, 1967-72, prof., 1972—. Editor: White Mountain Guide, 1979, Annals of Probability, 1979-81. Alfred P. Sloan Found. fellow, 1966-68, Guggenheim Found. fellow, 1991. Fellow AAAS, Am. Statis. Assn., Inst. Math. Stats.; mem. APHA, Am. Math. Soc., Bernoulli Soc., Internat. Statis. Inst. Democrat. Home: 92 Lewis St Newton MA 02458-1840 Office: MIT 77 Massachusetts Ave Rm 2-245 Cambridge MA 02139-4307

DUDLEY, RICK, professional hockey coach; b. Jan. 31, 1949. Player Am. Hockey League, Internat. Hockey League, World Hockey Assn., Cleve., Cin., 1969-79; player Buffalo Sabres, NHL, 1979-80, head coach, 1989-96; player Winnipeg (Man., Can.) Jets, NHL, 1981; coach Atlantic Coast Hockey League, Internat. Hockey League, Am. Hockey League, 1982-89; v.p., gen mgr Ottawa Senators, 96-. Office: Ottawa Senators, 1000 Palladium Dr, Kanata, ON Canada K2V 1A5*

DUDLEY, WILLIAM SHELDON, historian; b. Bklyn., July 14, 1936; s. William Henry and Dorothy (Lawson) D.; m. Julia Bartel, Aug. 21, 1965 (dec.); children: Jennifer Bee, Mary Megan. BA, Williams Coll., 1958; MA, Columbia U., 1966, PhD, 1972. History tchr. Poly. Prep. County Day Sch., Bklyn., 1963-66; asst. prof. History So. Meth. U., Dallas, 1970-77; supervisory historian Naval Hist. Ctr., Washington, 1977-82, head early history br., 1982-90, sr. historian, 1990-95, dir., sr. exec. svc., 1995—. Editor: Naval War of 1812, vol. 1, 1985, vol. 2, 1992. Pres. Bach Meistersingers, Annapolis, 1985-87. Lt. USNR, 1959-63. Recipient Samuel Eliot Morison award USS Constitution Mus., 1993. Mem. Am. Revolution Roundtable (pres. 1987), Soc. History in the Fed. Govt. (Thomas Jefferson prize 1993), Md. Hist. Soc. (maritime com. 1994—), N.Am. Soc. Oceanic History (pres. 1999—). Avocations: sailing, gardening, choral music. Home: 1003 Old Bay Ridge Rd Annapolis MD 21403-4228 Office: Naval Hist Ctr 901 M St SE Washington DC 20374-0001

DUDMAN, RICHARD BEEBE, communications company executive, journalist; b. Centerville, Iowa, May 3, 1918; s. Virgil Ernest and Wilma (Beebe) D.; m. Helen Sloane, Mar. 14, 1946; children: Iris Janet Sloane, Martha Tod. BA, Stanford U., 1940; LLD (hon.), U. Mo., St. Louis, 1979. Reporter, photographer Oroville (Calif.) Mercury-Register, 1937; reporter Denver Post, 1945-49; reporter St. Louis Post-Dispatch, 1949-53, Washington corr., 1954-68, bur. chief, 1969-81; chmn. bd., treas. Dudman Communications Corp., Ellsworth, Maine, 1981-92, chmn. emeritus, 1992-99; mem. adv. com. Nieman Found. for Journalism, 1977-81; trustee South-North News Svc., 1985-95, pres., 1987-90, mng. editor, 1987-95; cons. to Washington Bur., 1997. Author: Men of the Far Right, 1962, 40 Days with the Enemy, 1971, also articles. Trustee Washington Journalism Ctr., 1974-92, Inst. Current World Affairs, 1983-89, 95-98; bd. dirs. Downeast Family YMCA, Ellsworth, 1987-91; pub. mem. Maine Lobster Promotion Coun., 1991—. With USNR, 1942-45. Recipient award Asia Overseas Press Club, 1972, Edward Weintal award, 1979, Mo. medal U. Mo., 1981, Gold Polk Career award, 1993; Nieman fellow Harvard U., 1953-54, Knight Internat. Press fellow, South Africa, 1994, 96. Mem. Nat. Assn. Broadcasters (First Amendment com. 1985-89). Club: Gridiron (Washington). Lodge: Rotary. Avocations: sailing, boat building. Office: Dudman Communications Corp PO Box 1129 68 State St Ellsworth ME 04605-1924

DUDRICK, STANLEY JOHN, surgeon, scientist, educator; b. Nanticoke, Pa., Apr. 9, 1935; s. Stanley Francis and Stephania Mary (Jachimczak) D.; m. Theresa M. Keen, June 14, 1958; children: Susan Marie, Paul Stanley, Carolyn Mary, Stanley Jonathan, Holly Anne, Anne Theresa. B.S. cum laude, Franklin and Marshall Coll., 1957; M.D., U. Pa., 1961. Diplomate Am. Bd. Surgery. Intern Hosp. of U. Pa., Phila., 1961-62, resident in gen. surgery, 1962-67; acad. practice specializing in surgery Phila., 1967-72, 88-90; pvt. practice specializing in surgery Houston, 1972-88, 90-94; chief surg. svcs. Hermann Hosp., Houston, 1972-80, surgeon in chief, dir. Ctr. Cardiovascular Disease, dir. nutritional support svcs., dir. Nutritional Sci. Ctr., 1990-94; prof. surgery U. Tex. Med. Sch., Houston, 1972-82, clin. prof. surgery, 1982-95, chmn. dept. surgery, 1972-80; cons. in surgery M.D. Anderson Hosp. and Tumor Inst., 1973-88, clin. prof. surgery, cons. to pres., 1982-88; sr. cons. surgery and medicine Tex. Inst. for Rehab. and Rsch., 1974-88; mem. Anatomical Bd., State of Tex., 1973-78; examiner Am. Bd. Surgery, 1974-78, bd. dirs., 1978-84, sr. mem. 1984—, also mem. and chmn. various coms.; chmn. sci. adv. com. Tex. Med. Ctr. Libr., 1974; mem. food and nutrition bd. NRC-Nat. Acad. Scis., 1973-75; mem. sci. adv. com. Nat. Found. for Ileitis and Colitis; mem. surgery, anesthesia and trauma study sect. NIH, 1982-86; chmn. dept. surgery Pa. Hosp., Phila., 1988-90, surgeon in chief, 1988-91, hon. surgery staff, 1991—; clin. prof. surgery U. Pa., 1988-93; assoc. chmn. dept. surgery, 1994—, dir. surgery program, 1994—, assoc. chmn, dept. surg., 1994—, dir. Med. Edn., 1995—, St. Mary's Hosp., Waterbury, Conn., 1994—; clin. prof. surgery, Yale, New Haven, Conn., 1995—; adj. prof. surgery Quinippiac U., 1996—. Editor: Manual of Surgical Nutrition, 1975, Manual of Preoperative and Postoperative Care, 1983, Current Strategies in Surgical Nutrition, 1991, Practical Handbook of Nutrition in Clinical Practice, 1994, Surgical Nutrition: Strategies in Critically Ill Patients, 1995; assoc. editor Nutrition in Medicine, 1975—; editorial bd. Annals of Surgery, 1975—, Infusion, 1978—, Nutrition and Cancer, 1980—, Nutrition Support Services, 1980-86, Jour. Clin. Surgery, 1980-83, Nutrition Research, 1981—, Intermed. Communications Nursing Services, 1981—, Postgraduate General Surgery, 1992—; others; contbr. chpts. to books, articles to profl. jours.; inventor of new technique of intravenous feeding and anti-cholesterol therapy. Bd. dirs. Found. for Children, Houston, Harris County unit Am. Cancer Soc., Phila. chpt., 1988-90; trustee Franklin and Marshall Coll., 1985—, mem. student life and trusteeship coms., 1986—, mem. overseers bd., 1986—, exec. com. 1986—, alumni programs and devel. com., 1991—, pres. regional adv. coun., 1992—, vice chmn. 1994—, John Marshall Soc., 1993—. Decorated knight Order St. John of Jerusalem Knights Hopitalier; recipient VA citation for significant contbn. to med. care, 1970; Mead Johnson award for rsch. in hosp. pharmacy, 1972; Seale Harris medal So. Med. Assn., 1973; AMA-Brookdale award in medicine, 1975; Great Texan award Nat. Found. Ileitis and Colitis, 1975; Modern Medicine award, 1977; Disting. Alumnus citation Franklin and Marshall Coll., 1980; WHO, Houston, 1980; Stinchfield award Am. Acad. Orthopedic Surgery, 1981; Bernstein award Med. Soc. State of N.Y., 1986, Alumni Svc. award U. Pa. Med. Sch., 1996; numerous others. Fellow ACS (vice chmn. pre and post operative com. 1975, gov. 1979-85, com. on med. motion pictures 1981-90, SESAP com. 1990-94, co-chmn. multiple choice com. 1993-94, mem. Conn. chpt.), Philippine Coll. Surgeons (hon.), Coll. Medicine and Surgery of Costa Rica (hon.), Am. Coll. Nutrition (Grace A. Goldsmith award 1982); mem. AMA (council on food and nutrition 1971-76, exec. com. 1975-76, council on sci. affairs 1976-81, Goldberger award in clin. nutrition 1970), AAAS, AAUP, Am. Surg. Assn. (Flance-Karl award 1997), Am. Acad. Pediatrics (hon., Ladd medal 1988), Am. Pediatric Surg. Assn. (hon.), Am. Soc. Nutritional Support Services (bd. dirs. 1982-87, pres. 1984, Outstanding Humanitarian award 1984) Soc. Univ. Surgeons (exec. council 1974-78), Assn. for Acad. Surgery (founders group), Internat. Soc. Surg., Internat. Fedn. Surg. Colls., Internat. Soc. Parenteral Nutrition (exec. council 1975—, pres. 1978-81), Internat. Fedn. Surgery Soc., So. Med. Assn. (chmn. surgery sect. 1984-85), Houston Gastroent. Soc., Houston Surg. Soc., Tex. Surg. Soc., Tex. Med. Assn. (com. nutrition and food resources), Tex. Med. Found., Harris County Med. Soc., New Haven (Conn.) County Med. Soc., Conn. Soc. Am. Bd. Surgeons, New England Surg. Soc., Am. Radium Soc., Am. Soc. Clin. Oncology, Am. Soc. Parenteral and Enteral Nutrition (pres. 1977, bd. advs. 1978—, chmn. bd. advisers 1978, Vars award 1982, Rhoads lectr. 1985, Dudrick Rsch. Scholar award named in his honor), Penn. Nutritionists Soc. (pres. 1985), Am. Gastroent. Assn., Soc. Surg. Oncology, James Ewing Soc., Ravdin-Rhoads Surg. Assn., Excelsior Surg. Soc. (Edward D. Churchill lectr. 1981), Soc. Laparoendoscopic Surgery, Soc. Surg. Chairmen, So. Surg. Assn., Southwestern Surg. Congress, Southeastern Surg. Congress, Surg. Biology Club II, Surg. Infection Soc. (chmn. membership com. 1987-90), Western Surg. Soc., Halsted Soc., Allen O. Whipple Surg. Soc., Am. Inst. Nutrition, Soc. Clin. Surgery, Am. Soc. Clin. Investigation, Soc. for Surgery of Alimentary Tract, Am. Trauma Soc. (founders group), Am. Assn. for Surgery of Trauma, Soc. Clin. Surgery, Am. Soc. Clin.

Nutrition, Fedn. Am. Soc. Exp. Biology, Am. Burn Assn., John Marshall Soc., Coll. Physicians Phila., Phila. Acad. Surgeons, George Hermann Soc., Union League Phila., Med. Club Phila., Franklin Club Phila., Houston Doctors Club (gov. 1973-76), Nat. Alumni Coun. U. Pa. Med. Sch. (chmn. 1994—), Conn. United for Rsch. Excellence (bd. dirs. 1995—), Cosmos Club, Athenaeum, The Penn Club (charter), Phi Beta Kappa, Phi Beta Kappa Assocs., Sigma Xi, Alpha Omega Alpha. (sec.-treas. Houston chpt. 1982-83),. Home: 3050 Locke Ln Houston TX 77019-6202 Office: St Mary's Hosp Dept Surgery 56 Franklin St Dept Surgery Waterbury CT 06706-1238*

DUDROW, PETER WARREN, human resources executive, consultant; b. Bath, Maine, Oct. 13, 1935; s. Daniel Edward and Barbara Joan (Lemen) D.; m. Jewell Gloria Glover, Mar. 31, 1955 (div. Apr. 1975); children: Rebecca, Michelle, Laura, Leah, William; m. Nancy Carol Chirdon, Apr. 1, 1978 (div. May 1988). BSBA in Pers. Mgmt., La. State U., 1960; MBA, Wayne State U., 1964. Pers. mgmt. Chrysler Corp., Highland Park, Mich., 1960-66; sr. cons. A. T. Kearny & Co., Inc., Chgo., 1966-72; dir. compensation and benefits Northwest Industries, Chgo., 1972-75; cons. Dept. Def., Washington, 1975-78; mgr. exec. compensation and pers. practices Peat, Marwick, Mitchell & Co., N.Y.C., 1978-81; v.p. Mgmt. Consulting Divsn. Alexander and Alexander, Greenwich, Conn., 1981-83; prin. Human Resource Assocs. Am., Denville, N.J., 1983—. Contbr. articles to profl. jours. Mem. Dist. 57 Pub. Sch. Bd., Mount Prospect, Ill., 1970-73; bd. dirs., chmn. pers. com. Somerset Coun. Alcoholism and Drug Abuse, Somerville, N.J., 1992-95; bd. dirs., steering com. YMCA, local ch. Career Forum, Bernardsville, N.J., 1991-95; past chmn. bd. dirs. Encompass, the Music Theater, 1979-81. Col. U.S. Army, ret., 1955-95. Mem. Free Masons, Sojourners. Republican. Presbyterian. Avocations: golf, squash, bridge, nature hiking. Home: 68 Franklin Rd Denville NJ 07834-1557

DUDT, CHARMAZEL, classics educator; b. Allahabad, India, Aug. 30, 1940; came to U.S., 1964; d. Roger C. and Mary L. D. BA, Allahabad U., India, 1959, MA in English, 1961; PhD in English, Tex. Tech. U., 1971. Asst. prof. West Tex. A&M U., Canton, 1970-78, assoc. prof., 1978-84, 84—, head English dept., 1988-97, prof. Shakespeare studies, 1997—; sec. Coun. Humanities, Austom,. 1998—; mem. bias rev. com. TASP, Austin, 1997—; trustee U. of the South, Sewanee, Tenn., 1996—. Mem. Modern Lang. Assn., South Ctrl. Modern Lang. Assn., Calif. Coll. Tchrs. English, Conf. Christianity & Lit. Democrat. Episcopalian. Avocations: reading, photography, travel. Office: WTAMU English Dept Box 908 Canyon TX 79016

DUDUKOVIC, MILORAD P., chemical engineering educator, consultant; b. Beograd, Yugoslavia, Mar. 25, 1944; came to U.S., 1968; s. Predrag R. and Melita Maria Dudukovic; m. Judith Ann Reiff, Dec. 27, 1969; children: Aleksandra Anne, Nicole Maria. BS in Engring., U. Beograd, 1967; M.S., Ill. Inst. Tech., 1970, PhD, 1972. Rsch. engr. Process Design Inst., Beograd, 1967-68; instr. Ill. Inst. Tech., Chgo., 1970-72; asst. prof. Ohio U., Athens, 1972-74; assoc. prof. Washington U., St. Louis, 1974-80, prof., dir., 1980—, Laura and William Jens prof. environ. engr., 1993—, chmn., dept. chem. engring., 1998—; cons. in field. Assoc. editor: Ind and Engineering Chemistry Research, 1991—; contbr. articles to profl. jours. Recipient Burlington Northern Found. Teaching award, 1986, Nat. Catalyst award Chem. Mfrs. Assn., 1988, St. Louis award ACS, 1995; 2 NASA certs. of recognition and citations; Fulbright scholar Inst. for Higher Edn., 1968. Fellow Am. Inst. Chem. Engrs. (R.H. Wilhelm award, 1994); mem. Am. Chem. Soc., Am. Assn. Engring. Edn., AAAS, Sigma Xi. Club: Century (St. Louis). Avocations: hiking, swimming, travel. Achievements include pioneering work on trickle bed reactors, bubble columns; research in Czochralski crystal growth, novel experimental techniques for multiphase reactors; environmentally benign processing. Office: Washington U Dept Chem Engring Campus Box 1198 One Brookings Dr Saint Louis MO 63130-4899

DUDYCHA, ANNE ELIZABETH, retired special education educator; b. Rockford, Ill., Aug. 15, 1934; d. O. Garfield and Agnes Marie (Anderson) Beckstrand; m. W. Johnson, 1956 (div. Nov. 1978); children: Carole, Deanna, Sheila; m. Lee Dudycha, Feb. 1993. BA, Carthage Coll., 1956; MEd, U. Minn., 1982. Cert. tchr., emotional/behavioral disorders, dir. spl. edn., learning disabilities. Tchr., English Edn. Han. Jr. H.S., Lancaster, Pa., 1956-57; home bound. Hopkins and St. Louis Park (Minn.) Sch. Dists., 1971; tchr., spl. edn., adolescent therapy program Golden Valley (Minn.) Health Ctr., 1972-77, tchr., spl. edn., 1977-80, 82-85; tchr., spl. edn., emotional and behavioral disorders Robbinsdale (Minn.) Jr. H.S., 1977-79; tchr., spl. edn., emotional and behavioral disorders Sandburg Mid. Sch., Golden Valley, 1979-93, spl. edn. adminstrv. liaison, 1990-92, behavior specialist, cons., 1992-93, dist. spl. edn. coord., 1993-96; ret., 1996; lectr. Carthage Coll., Kenosha, Wis., 1996—; program com. mem. Devel. Severely Emotionally Disordered, Robbinsdale, 1985-86, 90-96; com. mem. Program and Curriculum for Implementation of Mid. Sch., Robbinsdale, 1986-87. Mem. design com. Holy Nativity Luth. Ch., New Hope, Minn., 1987-90, co-chmn. fund drive, 1987, mem. coun., 1988-93, pers. com., 1985-96, mem. choir, 1970-96. Mem. Minn. Educators Emotionally Disordered (profl. growth chmn. 1982-83), Minn. Coun. Children-Behavioral Disorders (pres. 1987-88, advocacy com. 1989-96), Minn. Assn. Mid. Level Edn. (bd. dirs. 1991-94), Phi Kappa Phi. Avocations: concerts, plays, reading, walking, hand work.

DUDZIAK, DONALD JOHN, nuclear engineer, educator; b. Alden, N.Y., Jan. 6, 1935; s. Joseph and Josephine Mary (Ratajczak) D.; m. Judith Ann Staib, Aug. 22, 1959; children: Alan Joseph, Matthew John, Karin Marie. BS in Marine Engring., U.S. Mcht. Marine Acad., 1956; MS in Radiation Biology/Radiol. Physics, U. Rochester, 1957; PhD in Applied Math., U. Pitts., 1963. Registered profl. engr., Calif. Commd. ensign USN, 1956, advanced through grades to capt.; sr. engr. Bettis Atomic Power Lab., Pitts., 1957-65; staff mem. U. Calif.-Los Alamos (N.Mex.) Nat. Lab., 1965-68, 69-74, assoc. and alt. group leader, 1974-78, group leader, 1978-81, dep. group leader, sect. leader, 1982-88, lab. fellow, 1988—; ret. USN, 1995; prof., head dept. nuclear engring. N.C. State U., Raleigh, 1990—; pres. Pinorealosa Corp, 1989-90; vis. prof. U. Va., Charlottesville, 1968-69; adj. prof. U. N.Mex., 1966, Kans. State U., 1989-90; guest scientist Swiss Fed. Inst. Reactor Rsch., Wuerenlingen, 1981-82; mem. lab. microfusion facility steering com. U.S. Dept. Energy, 1986-90, inertial confinement fusion adv. com., 1992-96; vice chair accelerator prodn. of tritium rev. panel Los Alamos Nat. Lab., 1995-98; chmn. fusion tech. working group Neutronics, Brookhaven, N.Y., 1975; mem. Nat. Nuc. Accrediting Bd., Nat. Acad. Nuc. Tng., 1998—; cons. nuclear power schs. USN, 1962-65; cons. Oak Ridge Nat. Lab., 1993-96, TSI Rsch. Co., 1992—, U.S. Nuc. Regulatory Commn., 1997, Am. Coun. on Edn., 1995—, Duke U., 1997-98. Editor: Reactor Principles, 1964, Radiation Shielding, 1964, Progress in Nuclear Energy, 1992—; contbr. editor Fusion Tech., 1987—; contbr. articles to profl. publs. Vice-chair Los Alamos County Planning and Zoning Commn., 1969-74. Fellow Am. Nuclear Soc. (divsn. chair 1972-73, 77-78, 92-93, gen. chair fusion energy divsn. nat. meeting 1994); mem. Am. Soc. Engring. Edn., U.S. Naval Inst., Los Alamos Sunrise Kiwanis (treas. 1987-89), Sigma Xi. Office: NC State Univ Dept Nuclear Engring PO Box 7909 Raleigh NC 27695

DUDZIAK, MARY LOUISE, law educator, lecturer; b. Oakland, Calif., June 15, 1956; d. Walter F. Dudziak and Barbara Ann Campbell; 1 child, Alicia Ammerman. AB in Sociology with highest honors, U. Calif., Berkeley, 1978; JD, Yale Law Sch., 1984; MA, MPhil in Am. Studies, Yale U., 1986, PhD in Am. Studies, 1992. Adminstrv. asst. to dep. dir. Ctr. Ind. Living, Berkeley, 1978-80; law clk., nat. legal staff ACLU, N.Y.C., 1983; law clk. Judge Sam J. Ervin, III Fourth Cir. Ct. Appeals, Morganton, N.C., 1984-85; assoc. prof. coll. law U. Iowa, Iowa City, 1986-90, prof. coll. law, 1990-98; vis. prof. U. So. Calif., 1997-98, prof. U. So. Calif., 1998—; mem. faculty senate task force on faculty devel. U. Iowa, 1989-90, mem. faculty welfare com., 1990-92, mem. faculty senate task force on faculty spouses and ptnrs., 1991-92, mem. presdl. lecture com., 1992-95; v.p. rsch. adv. com. in social scis., 1992-94; presenter in field. Contbr. articles to profl. jours. Bd. dirs. Iowa Civil Liberties Union, 1987-88; chairperson office svcs. for persons with disabilities program rev. com., U. Iowa, 1987-88, law sch. ombudsperson, 1991. Charlotte W. Newcombe Doctoral Dissertation fellow Woodrow Wilson Fellowship Found., 1985-86; Old Gold fellow U. Iowa, 1987, 88, 89, Moody Grant Lydon Baines Johnson Fdn., 1998, Theodore C. Sorenson Fell., JFK Libr. Fdn., 1997; travel grantee Eisenhower World Affairs Inst., 1993; recipient Scholars Devel. award Harry S. Truman Libr. Inst., 1990. Mem. Am. Soc. Legal History (mem. com. on documentary preservation 1988—, mem. program com. for 1988 conf., mem. exec. com., bd. dirs. 1990-92, 95-97, chairperson program com. 1993, mem. nominating com. 1999—), Am. Hist. Assn. (Littleton-Griswold rsch. grantee 1987), Am. Studies Assn. (mem. nominating com. 1999—), Assn. Am. Law Schs. (sec.-treas. legal history sect. 1987, vice chairperson 1988, chairperson 1989), Law and Soc. Assn. (mem. Hurst prize com. 1992), Orgn. Am. Historians, Soc. Am. Law Tchrs., Soc. for Historians Am. Fgn. Rels. Democrat. Office: U So Calif Law Sch Los Angeles CA 90089

DUDZIK, CAROL JOANNE, lawyer, art educator; b. Evergreen Park, Ill., Nov. 28, 1950; d. Thomas Michael and Geraldyne Blake; m. Terrence L. Dudzik, June 24, 1972. BA, Western Ill. U., 1972, MA, 1975; MA, U. Ill., 1981; JD, John Marshall Law Sch., Chgo., 1987. Bar: Ill. Cert. tchr., Ill. Tchr. North Palos Sch. Dist. #117, Hickory Hills, Ill., 1973—; pvt. practice Western Springs, Ill., 1987—; Instr., workshop presenter Moraine Valley C.C., Palos Hills, Ill., 1982-90; atty. Ill. Edn. Assn. Legal Svcs., Chgo., 1988. Murals include Spirit of '76, 1976, Loch Ness, 1980, Animal Kingdom, 1987, Dorn, 1993; art editor: (literary jour.) Pendemonium, 1990—; designer: (rubber stamp catalog) Zoo Stamps, 1992-96. Mem. People for Ethical Treatment of Animals, 1973—, Planned Parenthood, 1973—, Humane Soc. & Animal Protection Inst., 1975. Recipient 10-yr. svc. award St. Patricia Ch., Hickory Hills, 1988. Mem. Chgo. Bar Assn., Ill. Stoneware & Pottery, North Palos Edn. Assn. (chief negotiator 1980—, membership chair), Ill. Edn. Assn., Conrady Sch. Artists (sponsor 1995—). Avocations: painting, jewelry, collecting, travel.

DUE, DANFORD ROYCE, lawyer; b. Louisville, Sept. 28, 1948; s. Victor T. and Betty (Duffy) D.; m. Susan L. Landrum, Aug. 14, 1971; children: Stephen L., Michael R. BA, Vanderbilt U., 1970; JD cum laude, Ind. U., 1973. Bar: Ind. 1973, U.S. Dist. Ct. (so. dist.) Ind. 1973, U.S. Dist. Ct. (no. dist.) Ind. 1980, U.S. Ct. Appeals (7th cir.) 1986. Assoc. Stewart, Irwin, Gilliom, Fuller & Meyer, Indpls., 1973-79, ptnr., 1979-84; ptnr. Stewart, Due, Doyle & Pugh, Indpls., 1984—. Contbg. author (Continuing Legal Edn. series) Uninsured/Underinsured Motorist Coverage in Indiana, 1988, The Wrongful Death Case in Indiana, 1989, Sucessful Handling of Wrongful Death Cases: The Experts Share Their Secrets, 1998. Bd. mgrs. Baxter YMCA, Indpls., 1983—. Mem. ABA, Def. Rsch. Inst., Ind. State Bar Assn., Ind. Def. Lawyers Assn., Johnson County Bar Assn. Avocations: golf, reading, mountain hiking, fishing. Home: 524 Ho Hum Ct Greenwood IN 46142 Office: Stewart Due Miller & Pugh 55 Monument Circle 900 Circle Tower Indianapolis IN 46204

DUE, JAMES M., pharmacist; b. Racine, Wis., May 9, 1944; s. Stanley Walter and Gertrude (Brix) D.; m. Colleen R., May 4, 1974; children: Matthew M., Maria M., Joshua J. BS in Pharmacy, U. Wis., 1967; MS in Pharmacy Adminstrn., U. Minn., 1975. Registered pharmacist. Asst. mgr. Walgreen's, Kenosha, Wis., 1968-71; staff pharmacist VA Hosp., Milw., 1971-73; resident registered pharmacist VA Hosp., Mpls., 1973-75; supervisory pharmacist VA Hosp., Palo Alto, Calif., 1975-77; dir. pharmacy VA Hosp., Tomah, Wis., 1977—. Mem. Am. Soc. Hosp. Pharmacists, Alpha Chi Rho, Rho Chi. Avocation: collecting sports cards. Home: RR 2 Box 22-b Camp Douglas WI 54618-9802 Office: VA Med Ctr 500 E Veterans St Tomah WI 54660-3105

DUE, JEAN MARGARET, agricultural economist, educator; b. Peterborough, Ont., Can., Sept. 19, 1921; d. Allan B. and Katherine Jean (Calder) Mann; m. John F. Due, Aug. 18, 1950; children—Allan Malcolm, Kevin John Burritt. B.Com., U. Toronto, 1946; M.S., U. Ill., 1950, Ph.D., 1953. Economist Dept. Agr., Ottawa, Ont., 1946-49; research asso. in home econs. U. Ill., 1959-61, vis. prof., 1965-70, prof. dept. agr. econs., 1970-90. Contbr. articles to profl. jours. Mem. African Studies Assn., Am. Econ. Assn., Am. Agrl. Econs. Assn., Internat. Assn. Agrl. Econs., Assn. Women Internat. Devel. Home: 1208 Clark Lindsey Village 101 W Windsor Rd Urbana IL 61802-6663 Office: Univ Illinois 305MH 1301 W Gregory Dr Urbana IL 61801-3608

DUE, JOHN FITZGERALD, economist, educator emeritus; b. Hayward, Cal., July 11, 1915; s. Jackson Angelo and Emmarene (Hurd) D.; m. Margaret Jean Mann, Aug. 18, 1950; children: Nancy, Allan, Kevin. A.B., U. Calif.-Berkeley, 1935, Ph.D., 1939; A.M., George Washington U., 1936. Instr. U. Utah, 1939-42, asst. prof., 1945-48; economist Treasury Dept., 1942; faculty U. Ill., 1948-86, prof. econs., 1951-86, prof. emeritus, 1986—, chmn. dept. econs., 1963-67, 71-72; acting dean Coll. Commerce U. Ill., 1976, 85-86. Author: Taxation and Economic Development in Tropical Africa, 1963, Indirect Taxation in Developing Economies, 2d edit., 1988; co-author: Sales Taxation: State and Local Structure and Operation, 1983; rev., 1994, The Electric Interurban Railway in America, 1960, Rails to The Ochoco Country-The City of Prineville Railway, 1968, Government Finance, 7th edit, 1981, Rails to the Mid Columbia Wheatlands, 1979, Roads and Rails South from the Columbia, 1991. Served with USMCR, 1942-45. Mem. Am. Econ. Assn., Nat. Tax Assn., Phi Beta Kappa. Home: 101 W Windsor Rd Apt 1208 Urbana IL 61802-6663 Office: Univ Ill Com W 1206 S 6th St Champaign IL 61820-6915

DUECKER, ROBERT SHELDON, retired bishop; b. Medina County, Ohio, Sept. 4, 1926; s. Howard LaVerne and Sarah Faye (Simpson) D.; m. Marjorie Louise Clouse, June 13, 1948; children: Philip Lee, Christine Cay Duecker Isle. B in Religion, AB, Indiana Wesleyan U., 1948; BD, MS, Christian Theol. Sem., Indpls., 1952, DD (hon.), 1969; D in Pub. Svc. (hon.), Kendall Coll., 1996. Ordained to ministry United Meth. Ch., 1952. Pastor Dyer (Ind.) United Meth. Ch., 1952-54; sr. pastor Gethsemane United Meth. Ch., Muncie, Ind., 1954-62, Grace United Meth. Ch., Hartford City, Ind., 1962-65, 1st United Meth. Ch., Warsaw, Ind., 1965-70, Simpson United Meth. Ch., Ft. Wayne, Ind., 1970-72; dir. No. Ind. Conf. Coun. Ministries United Meth. Ch., Marion, 1973-77; dist. supt. No. Ind. Conf. United Meth. Ch., Ft. Wayne, 1977-82; sr. pastor High St. United Meth. Ch., Muncie, 1982-88; bishop Chgo. area United Meth. Ch., 1988-96; ret., 1996; instr. Christian Theol. Sem., Indpls., 1998; trustee United Theol. Sem., Dayton, Ohio, 1985-88, Kendall Coll., Evanston, Ill., 1988-96, North Ctrl. Coll., Naperville, Ill., 1988-96, Garrett Theol. Sem., Evanston, 1988-96; mem. gen. bd. publ. United Meth. Ch., 1988-92, gen. bd. higher edn. and ministry, 1992-96, univ. senate, 1992-96; mem. adv. coun. Ams. United for Separation of Ch. and State; instr. Christian Theol. Sem., Indpls., 1998. Author: Tensions in the Connection, 1982; also monographs. Mem. Kosciusko County Health Planning Coun., Warsaw, Ind., 1968-70; bd. dirs. Goodwill Industries, Ft. Wayne, Muncie, 1977-88; former pres. Del. County Mental Health Assn., Muncie. Named Sagamore of the Wabash Gov. of Ind., 1988. Mem. Coun. of Religious Leaders of Met. Chgo. (pres. 1996—), Coun. Bishops United Meth. Ch., North Ctrl. Jurisdiction Coll. Bishops, Kiwanis, Rotary, Theta Phi. Avocations: stamp collecting, golf.

DUELL, DANIEL PAUL, artistic director, choreographer, lecturer; b. Rochester, N.Y., Aug. 17, 1952; s. Seth Joseph and Ellen Catharine (Newton) D. Diploma, Profl. Children's Sch., N.Y.C., 1970; scholarship student, Sch. Am. Ballet, 1969-72. Mem., N.Y.C. Ballet, 1972-87, soloist, 1977-79, prin. dancer, 1979-87; choreographer in repertoire of Ballet Hispanico, N.Y., Dayton Ballet, Ballet Chgo.; mem. edn. dept., N.Y.C. Ballet; now artistic dir., choreographer Sch. Ballet Chgo. Mem. Sch. Am. Ballet Assn., Dance/USA, Chgo. Dance Coalition. Office: Ballet Chgo 185 N Wabash Ave Ste 2300 Chicago IL 60601-3622*

DUEMLING, ROBERT WERNER, diplomat, museum director; b. Ann Arbor, Mich., Feb. 8, 1929; s. Werner William and Anne (Lindemulder) D.; m. Louisa duPont Copeland, May 15, 1982. B.A., Yale U., 1950, M.A., 1953; student, Cambridge U., Eng., 1950-51. Joined fgn. service Dept. State, Washington, 1957, with, 1957-60, 66-70; with Am. embassy, Rome, 1960-63, Kuala Lumpur, 1963-65, Tokyo, 1970-74; U.S. consul Kuching, Malaysia, 1965-66; exec. asst. to dep. sec. state Dept. State, Washington, 1974-76; dep. chief of mission with rank of minister Am. embassy, Ottawa, Ont., Can., 1976-80; chief Fgn. Contingents, Multinat. Force and Observers, Sinai, 1981-82; U.S. ambassador to Suriname, to Paramaribo, 1982-84; dir. Nicaraguan Humanitarian Assistance Office, Dept. State, 1985-87; pres., dir. Nat. Bldg. Mus., Washington, 1987-94. Trustee Washington Tennis Found., Cafritz Found., Nat. Gallery of Art, Washington nat. Monument Assn. Served in U.S. Navy, 1953-57. Henry fellow, 1950-51, Washington Coll. sr. fellow; decorated Order of the Palm (Suriname). Fellow Royal Soc. for Arts (U.K.); mem. Washington Inst. Fgn. Affairs, Met. Club, Century Assn., Alibi Club. Home: 2950 University Ter NW Washington DC 20016-3461

DUERINCK, LOUIS T., retired railroad executive, attorney; b. Chgo., Aug. 1, 1929; s. Aloys L. and Thais E. (De Backer) D.; m. Patricia A. Bird, June 27, 1953; children: Louis M., Kathleen M. Lutgen, Kevin F., Mark V., Lynn P. Dressel, Brian T., Paul S. Student, U. Notre Dame, 1947-48; JD, DePaul U., Chgo., 1952. Bar: Ill. 1952. Commerce atty. N.Y. Cen. R.R., Chgo., 1955-65; gen. atty. Nat. Ry. Labor Conf., Chgo., 1967-68; with C&NW Ry. Co., Chgo., 1965-67, 68-89; sr. v.p. law and real estate C&NW Transp. Co., 1979-83, sr. v.p. traffic, 1983-88, sr. v.p., 1988-89, also bd. dirs. Served with AUS, 1952-55. Mem. ABA, Transp. Practitioners Assn., Ill. Bar Assn., Tower Club (Chgo.), Glen Oak Country Club, Wyndemere Country Club (Naples). Roman Catholic. Home and Office: 718 Midwest Club Pky Oak Brook IL 60523-2531

DUERKSEN, GEORGE LOUIS, music educator, music therapist; b. St. Joseph, Mo., Oct. 29, 1934; s. George Herbert and Louise May (Dalke) D.; m. Patricia Gay Beers, June 3, 1961; children—Mark Jeffrey, Joseph Scott, Cynthia Elizabeth. Student, Tabor Coll, 1951-52; BMusEdn, U. Kans., 1955, MMusEdn, 1956, PhD, 1967. Cert. music edn., Kans., Mo.; bd. cert. music therapist, Nat. Certification Bd. for Music Therapy (CBMT). Tchr. music Tonganoxie High Sch., Kans., 1955-56, Stafford Jr. and Sr. High Sch., Kans., 1959-60, Labette County High Sch., Altamont, Kans., 1960-62, Shawnee Mission (Kans.) North High Sch., 1962-63; asst. prof., dir. psychology of music lab. Mich. State U., East Lansing, 1965-69; prof., chmn. dept. art and music edn. and music therapy U. Kans., Lawrence, 1969-93, dir. Singing Jayhawks, 1979-83; prof., dir. music edn. and music therapy divsn. U. Kans., Lawrence, 1993—; assoc. dir. Kans. North Ctrl. Assn. Colls. and Schs., 1992—; cons., vis. prof. U. Hawaii, Honolulu, summer 1978; cons., vis. prof. U. Melbourne, Australia, summer 1981; cons., lectr. N.Z. Soc. for Music Therapy, Wellington, 1983, Ctr. for Contemporary Music Rsch., Athens, 1991, U. Thessaloniki, Greece, 1993, Korean Assn. for Music Therapy, 1994, 97, Sook Myung U., Seoul, 1997; cons. functional music applications, 1967—, Deakin U., Geelong, Victoria, Australia, 1990. Author: (monograph) Teaching Instrumental Music, 1973; Music for Exceptional Children, 1981; contbr. articles to profl. jours. Fulbright scholar Inst. for Internat. Edn., Australia, 1956-57; U.Kans. fellow, Lawrence, 1963-64; U.S. Office Edn. grantee, 1966-67, 73-75, 78-81. Mem. AAAS, Music Educators Nat. Conf., Am. Music Therapy Assn., Music Edn. Rsch. Coun. (chmn. 1980-82), Brit. Soc. for Music Therapy, Coun. for Rsch. in Music Edn., Pi Kappa Lambda, Phi Mu Alpha, Phi Delta Kappa. Avocations: photography; boating; travel. Office: U Kans Music Edn/Music Therapy Div 311 Bailey Hall Lawrence KS 66044-7503

DUERR, DAVID, civil engineer; b. Newark, July 4, 1953; s. Warren August and Dorothy (Lanzillo) D.; m. Roberta Kay Apolant, Oct. 12, 1991. B of Engring., Pratt Inst., 1975; MS, U. Houston, 1985. Registered profl. engr. Project engr. Hoffman Internat., Pt. Newark, N.J., 1974-76; chief engr. Williams Crane & Rigging, Richmond, Va., 1976-79; sr. structural engr. Hudson Engring. Corp., Houston, 1980-86; pres. 2DM Assocs., Inc., Houston, 1986—; frequent lectr. constrn. industry seminars. Contbr. tech. papers to profl. jours. Mem. ASCE, ASME (mem. B30.20 design task group), Am. Cons. Engrs. Coun., Soc. Automotive Engrs., Soc. Naval Archs. and Marine Engrs., Specialized Carriers and Rigging Assn. (crane and rigging group safety com.). Achievements include research in the design of pinned connections and development of standards for the design of mobile industrial gantries. Avocations: music, theater, travel, martial arts. Home: 8439 Hunters Creek Dr Houston TX 77024-3204 Office: 2DM Assocs Inc 7322 Southwest Fwy Houston TX 77074-2010

DUERR, DIANNE MARIE, physical education educator, professional sports medicine consultant; b. Buffalo, July 14, 1945; d. Robert John and Aileen Louise (Scherer) D. *Ms. Duerr's paternal great-grandparents, William Duerr and Charles J. and Charlotte Clune Gunning, descended from German and Irish immigrants. Her maternal great-grandparents, Jerome and Louise Witzel Scherer and John and Anna Meidel Brown, descended from Swiss and German immigrants who founded a fine jewelry store in 1903 in Buffalo, New York. Her father, Robert J. Duerr, served as an administrator in the Buffalo City Schools and contributed to the development of School #84. Her mother, Aileen L. Duerr, maintained the Duerr household and contributed to the activities of the children.* BS in Health and Phys. Edn., SUNY, Brockport, 1967; cert., SUNY, Oswego, 1982; postgrad., Canisius Coll., 1970-71. Cert. tchr., N.Y. Tchr. North Syracuse (N.Y.) Sch. Dist., 1967—; tchr. dept. orthopedic surgery SUNY Health Sci. Ctr. at Syracuse, 1982—; creator Inst. for Sports Medicine and Human Performance SUNY Health Sci. Ctr., Syracuse, 1988; coord. scholastic sports injury reporting system project SUNY, 1985-98; mem. com. on scholastic sports-related injuries NIH Inst. Arthritis, Musculoskeletal and Skin Diseases, 1993-96. *Ms. Duerr is an educator and a facilities development creator/coordinator with 18 years experience in the design, development, funding and construction of models for relevant health care research, education and patient care. She recently completed a $65 million project at the SUNY Health Science Center at Syracuse known as the Institute for Human Performance. She is responsible for the concept, design, program coordination and funding of the facility. Gwathmey Siegel Architects for the State University Construction Fund designed the Institute. The Institute for Human Performance is dedicated to the study of the human potential.* Author: SSIRS Pilot Study Report, 1987, SSIRS Fall Study Report, 1988, SHASIRS Report, 1991; creator Scholastic Sports Injury Reporting System, 1985, Scholastic Head and Spine Injury Reporting System, 1989. Co-chmn. sports medicine USA Amateur Athletic Union, Nat. Jr. Olympic Games, Syracuse, 1987; vol. sports medicine N.Y. State Sr. Games, 1990-95, sports medicine coord., 1990-95, U.S. Roller Skating Nat. Championships, 1995, N.Y. State Womens Lacrosse Championships, 1995; mem. com. sports injury surveillance Ctrs. for Disease Control, 1995; cons. N.Y. Sci., Tech. and Soc. Edn. Project, 1995; sports medicine coord. for U.S. Nat. Precision Ice Skating Championships, 1997, Youth Basketball of Am., Northeast Regional Tournament, 1999. Mem. AAUW, AAHPERD (N.Y. State chpt. pres. exercise sci. and sports medicine sect.), Am. Coll. Sports Medicine, United Univ. Profs., Women's Sports Fedn., Am. Fedn. Tchrs., N.Y. United Tchrs., North Syracuse Tchrs. Assn., Phi Kappa Phi. Avocations: swimming, cycling, ice skating, reading, photography. Home: 418 Buffington Rd Syracuse NY 13224-2208 Office: SUNY 4400 University Hosp 750 E Adams St Syracuse NY 13210-2399

DUERR, HERMAN GEORGE, retired publishing executive; b. Nagold, Germany, June 24, 1931; came to U.S., 1949, naturalized, 1975; s. Adolf Gustav and Wilhelmine Dorothea (Walz) Durr; m. Shirley Yvonne Jones, June 29, 1957; children: Suzanne, Steffan, Krista. B.F.A., Wayne State U., 1958. Publs. designer Ceco Communications Inc., Warren, Mich., 1958-60; art dir. Am. Youth mag., 1960-67; art dir. Friends mag., 1967-86, exec. editor, 1978-87; v.p. Lintas/CECO Communications, Inc., 1981-91; dir. mktg. prodn. Ceco Pub. Co., 1987-91; publ. cons. Harrison, Mich., 1991—; adj. faculty mem. Mid Mich. C.C., 1991—. Served with U.S. Army, 1952-55.

DUESBERG, PETER HEINZ HERMANN, molecular biology educator; b. Münster, Germany, Dec. 2, 1936; s. Richard and Hilde Maria (Saettele) D.; children: Nicola, Sibyl, Susi, Max; m. Sigrid Sachs, 1994. Grad., U. Würzburg, 1958, U. Basel, Switzerland, 1959; diploma in chemistry, U. Munich, Fed. Republic Germany, 1961; PhD in Chemistry, U. Frankfurt, Fed. Republic Germany, 1963. Postdoctoral fellow Max-Planck Inst. Virus Research, Tübingen, Fed. Republic Germany, 1963; asst. research virologist Virus Lab., U. Calif., Berkeley, 1964-66, postdoctoral fellow, 1966-68, asst. prof. in residence, asst. research biochemist, dept. molecular biology, 1968-70; asst. prof. molecular biology U. Calif., Berkeley, 1970-71, assoc. prof., 1971-73, prof., 1973—. Recipient Merck award, 1969, Calif. Scientist of Yr. award, 1971, 1st Ann. Am. Med. Ctr. Oncology award, 1981, Outstanding Investigator award NIH, 1985, Fogarty Scholar-in-Residence award NIH, Bethesda, Md., 1986-87, Johann-Georg-Zimmermann prize, 1988. Mem. Nat. Acad. Scis. Office: U Calif Dept Molecular-Cell Biology Stanley Hall Berkeley CA 94720

DUESENBERG, RICHARD WILLIAM, lawyer; b. St. Louis, Dec. 10, 1930; s. (John August) Hugo and Edna Marie (Warmann) D.; m. Phyllis

Evelyn Buehner, Aug. 7, 1955; children: Karen, Daryl, Mark, David. BA, Valparaiso U., 1951, JD, 1953; LLM, Yale U., 1956. Bar: Mo. 1953. Prof. law NYU, N.Y.C., 1956-62; dir. law ctr. publs., 1960-62; sr. atty. Monsanto Co., St. Louis, 1963-70, asst. gen. counsel, asst. sec., 1975-77, sr. v.p., sec., gen. counsel, 1977-96; dir. law Monsanto Textiles Co., St. Louis, 1971-75; corp. sec. Fisher Controls Co., Marshalltown, Iowa, 1969-71, Olympia Industries, Spartanburg, S.C., 1974-75; vis. prof. law U. Mo., 1970-71; faculty Banking Sch. South, La. State U., 1967-83; vis. scholar Cambridge U., England, 1996; vis. prof. law St. Louis U., 1997-98. Author: (with Lawrence P. King) Sales and Bulk Transfers Under the Uniform Commercial Code, 2 vols, 1966, rev., 1984, New York Law of Contracts, 3 vols, 1964, Missouri Forms and Practice Under the Uniform Commercial Code, 2 vols, 1966; editor: Ann. Survey of Am. Law, NYU, 1961-62; mem. bd. contbg. editors and advisors: Corp. Law Rev, 1977-86; contbr. articles to law revs., jours. Mem. lawyers adv. coun. NAM, Washington, 1980, Adminstrv. Conf. U.S., 1980-86, legal adv. com. N.Y. Stock Exch., 1983-87, corp. law dept. adv. coun. Practising Law Inst., 1982; bd. dirs. Bach Soc., St. Louis, 1985-86, pres., 1973-77; bd. dirs. Valparaiso U., 1977—, chmn. bd. visitors law sch., 1966—, Luth. Charities Assn., 1984-87, vice chmn., 1986-87; bd. dirs. Luth. Med. Ctr., St. Louis, 1973-82, vice chmn., 1975-80; bd. dirs. Nat. Jud. Coll., 1984-90, St. Louis Symphony, 1988—, Opera Theatre St. Louis, 1988—, Luth. Brotherhood, Mpls., 1992—, Liberty Fund, Inc., Indpls., 1997—. Served with U.S. Army, 1953-55. Named Disting. Alumnus Valparaiso U., 1976. Fellow Am. Bar Found.; mem. ABA (chmn. com. uniform comml. code 1976-79, coun. sect. corp., banking and bus. law 1979-83, sec. 1983-84, chmn. 1986-87), Mo. Bar Assn., Am. Law Inst., Mont Pelerin Soc., Nat. Jud. Coll. (bd. dirs. 1984-90), Order of Coif, Bach Soc., Am. Soc. Corp. Sec. (bd. chmn. 1987-88), Assn. Gen. Coun., Am. Arbitration Assn., St. Louis Club. Home: 1 Indian Creek Ln Saint Louis MO 63131-3333

DUESENBERG, ROBERT H., lawyer; b. St. Louis, Dec. 10, 1930; s. Hugo John August and Edna Marie (Warmann) D.; m. Lorraine Freda Hall, July 23, 1938; children: Lynda Renee, Kirsten Lynn, John Robert. BA, Valparaiso (Ind.) U., 1951, LLB, 1953; LLM, Harvard U., 1956. Bar: Mo. 1953, U.S. Supreme Ct. 1981, Va. 1993. Pvt. practice St. Louis, 1956-58; atty. Wabash R.R. Co., St. Louis, 1958-65, Norfolk & Western Ry. Co., St. Louis, 1962-65; atty., assoc. gen. counsel Pet Inc., St. Louis, 1965-77, v.p., assoc. gen. counsel, 1977-80, v.p., gen. counsel, 1980-83; v.p., gen. counsel Gen. Dynamics Corp., Falls Church, Va., 1984-91, sr. v.p. and gen. counsel, 1991-93; ret., 1993; bd. dirs. VisionAire Corp., St. Louis, Valparaiso (Ind.) U. Contbr. numerous articles to profl. jours. Sec., treas., legal advisor Am. Kantorei, St. Louis, 1970-75; mem. Coun. on World Affairs, St. Louis, 1975—, Mo. Coordinating Bd. for Higher Edn., Jefferson City, 1976-83, chmn., 1978-81; mem. pres.'s coun. Valparaiso (Ind.) U., 1979—, bd. dirs., 1995—; bd. dirs. Higher Edn. Loan Authority, 1982-84; mem. adv. bd. Northwestern U. Corp. Counsel Ctr., 1988—, chmn. adv. bd., 1992; bd. dirs. Opera Theatre of St. Louis, 1988—. Cpl. U.S. Army, 1953-55. Recipient Disting. Alumnus award Valparaiso U., 1982. Mem. ABA, Va. Bar Assn., Mo. Bar Assn., St. Louis Bar Assn. (chmn. antitrust com. 1971-73, v.p. bus. law sect. 1972-73, chmn. 1973-74), Am. Law Inst., Gen. Counsels Assn., Machine and Allied Products Inst. (legal counsel 1986—), Am. Corp. Counsel Assn., S.W. Legal Found. (adv. bd.), Aerospace Industry Assn. (legal com. 1981-88), Bach Soc. of St. Louis (bd. dirs.). Republican. Lutheran. Home: 10171 Castlewood Ln Oakton VA 22124-3027 Office: Gen Dynamics Corp 3190 Fairview Park Dr Ste 1 Falls Church VA 22042-4523

DUFAULT, PETER KANE, writer, musician; b. Newark, N.J., Apr. 22, 1923; s. Roland Hubert and Christine Joyce (Kane) D.; children: Tadea (dec.), Scott, Mark, Ethan. BA, Harvard, 1947. Freelance writer New Yorker, New Republic, Atlantic, Harper's, others, Hillsdale, N.Y., 1947—; poetry readings recitals, Smith Coll., 1970's, Vassar Coll., 1996, Dartmouth, 1980's, William Coll., 1970's. Author numerous poems; author: Angel of Accidence, 1953, For Some Stringed Instrument, 1957, On Balance, 1979, New Things Come Into the World, 1993. Congressional candidate N.Y. State Liberal Party, 1968. With USAF, 1944-45, ETO. E-mail: http://www.Taconic.net/duFault. Home: 56 Hickory Hill Rd RR 2 Hillsdale NY 12529-9802

DUFF, BRIAN BARNETT, federal judge; b. Dallas, Sept. 15, 1930; s. Paul Harrington and Frances Ellen (FitzGerald) D.; m. Florence Ann Buckley, Nov. 27, 1953; children: F. Ellen, Brian Barnett Jr., Roderick FitzGerald, Kevin Buckley, Daniel Harrington. AB in English, U. Notre Dame, 1953, postgrad., 1997—; JD, DePaul U., Chgo., 1962. Bar: Ill. 1962, Mass. 1962, U.S. Dist. Ct. (no. dist.) Ill. 1962, U.S. Supreme Ct. 1968. Mgmt. trainee, multiple line underwriter Continental Casualty Co., Chgo., 1956-60; mgmt. cons. Booz, Allen and Hamilton, Chgo., 1960-62; asst. to chief exec. officer Bankers Life and Casualty Co., Chgo., 1962-67; atty. Sloan & Bragiel, Chgo., 1965-68; exec. v.p., gen. counsel R.H. Gore Co., Chgo., 1968-69; atty. Brian B. Duff & Assocs., Chgo., 1969-76; judge Cir. Ct. Cook County Ill., Chgo., 1976-85; judge U.S. Dist. Ct. (no. dist.) Ill., Chgo., 1985—, now sr. judge; rep. Ill. Gen. Assembly, Springfield, 1971-76; chmn. House Judiciary Com., 1973-74, minority whip, 1975-76; vis. com. Coll. Law U Chgo., 1977-79; lectr. Law Sch. Loyola U., 1978-79; adj. prof. John Marshall Law Sch., 1985-90, DePaul U. Sch. Law, 1990. Served to lt (j.g.) USN, 1953-56. Mem. ABA, Chgo. Bar Assn., Fed. Judges Assn., Am. Judicature Soc., Nat. Lawyers Club, Inc., (hon.), Legal Club Chgo. (hon.), Law Club, Ill. State Bar Assn. Roman Catholic. Avocations: fishing, reading, travel, writing. Office: US Dist Ct 219 S Dearborn St Chicago IL 60604-1702*

DUFF, DONALD JAMES, religious organization administrator; b. Addis Ababa, Ethiopia, Mar. 22, 1938; came to U.S., 1953; s. Clarence Walker and Dorothea Louisa (Kuehner) D.; m. Margaret Louisa Graham, Jan. 29, 1966; children: Robert Joel, Jennifer Beth, Sarah Ruth. AB, Calvin Coll., 1960; BD, Westminster Theol. Sem., Phila., 1964. Ordained to ministry Orthodox Presbyn. Ch., 1968. Tchr. Bible Timothy Christian High Sch., Elmhurst, Ill., 1966-69; pastor Bethel Orthodox Presbyn. Ch., Grand Junction, Colo., 1971-78, Bonita (Calif.) Orthodox Presbyn. Ch., 1978-80, Convent of Grace Orthodox Presbyn. Ch., Oxnard, Calif., 1981-92; stated clk. gen. assembly Orthodox Presbyn. Ch., Willow Grove, Pa., 1992—; sec. N.Am. Presbyn. and Reformed Coun., 1992—. Home: 23 E Benezet St Philadelphia PA 19118-3515 Office: Orthodox Presbyn Ch Box P Willow Grove PA 19090-0920

DUFF, DORIS EILEEN (SHULL), critical care nurse; b. Va., Feb. 23, 1960; d. Harley Ray and Eloise (Whitmer) Shull; m. William DeLaney Duff, Feb. 1, 1992; children: William D. II, Emma R. BS in Gen. Sci., Radford (Va.) U., 1983; diploma in nursing, Roanoke (Va.) Meml. Hosps., 1985. RN, Va.; cert. emergency nurse. Med.-surg. nurse Roanoke Meml. Hosp., 1985-87, nurse emergency-trauma dept., 1987—; mem. Emergency Nurses Cancel Alchohol Related Emergencies (ENCARE). Mem. Emergency Nurses Assn., Roanoke Meml. Hosps. Sch. Nursing Alumni Assn. (mem. hosp. ethics com.). Office: Roanoke Meml Hosp Belleview at Jefferson Sts Roanoke VA 24033

DUFF, JAMES GEORGE, retired financial services executive; b. Pittsburg, Kans., Jan. 27, 1938; s. James George and Camilla (Vinardi) D.; m. Linda Louise Beeman, June 24, 1961 (div.); children: Michele, Mark, Melissa; m. Beverly L. Pool, Nov. 16, 1984. BS with distinction, U. Kans., 1960, MBA, 1961. With Ford Motor Co., Dearborn, Mich., 1962-97; various positions fin. staff Ford Motor Co., 1962-71; dir. product, profit, price, warranty Ford of Europe, 1972-74; controller Ford Div., 1974-76, controller car ops., 1976, controller car product devel., 1976-80; exec. v.p. Ford Motor Credit Co., 1980-88, bd. dirs.; pres., COO U.S. Leasing Internat. Inc. (now USL Capital), San Francisco, 1988-89, pres., CEO, 1990-91; chmn., CEO USL Capital, San Francisco, 1991-97, also bd. dirs.; bd. dirs. Preferred Income Mgmt. Fund; mem. Conf. Bd., 1990-97. Mem. adv. bd. U. Kans. Sch. Bus., 1980-98; bd. dirs. Bay Area Coun., 1990-97; trustee San Francisco Mus. Modern Art, 1990-97; chmn. bus. devel. unit Detroit United Fund, 1980-85, chmn. edn. and local govt. unit Detroit United Fund, 1986-88. Sunray Mid-Continent scholar, Bankers scholar, to 1960. Mem. San Francisco C. of C. (bd. dirs. 1990-91). Home: 6325 N Yucca Rd Paradise Valley AZ 85253-4294

DUFF, JAMES HENRY, museum director, environmental administrator; b. Pitts., Oct. 11, 1943; s. James Sylvester and Virginia (Henry) D.; m. Sally Kathryn Tredwell, Sept. 14, 1963; children: Abigail Margaret, Jessica Lauren. BA, Washington and Jefferson Coll., 1965; MA, U. Mass., 1970. Teaching asst. U. Mass., Amherst, 1965-66; dir. Mus. of Hudson Highlands, Cornwall-on-Hudson, N.Y., 1966-73, Brandywine River Mus., Chadds Ford, Pa., 1973—; exec. dir. Brandywine Conservancy, Chadds Ford, 1976—; cons. N.Y. State Coun. on Arts, 1970-72; panel mem. Pa. Coun. on Arts, 1976-79, 83-85; mem. adv. coun. Nat. Mus. Act, 1982-85; mem. Nat. Mus. Svcs. Bd., 1986-95. Author: The Western World of N. C. Wyeth, 1980, Landscapes, Still Lifes and Portraits by N. C. Wyeth, 1982, An American Vision, 1987; contbr. articles on mus. programs to profl. jours. Trustee Wyeth Endowment for Am. Art, 1986-95, Am. Arts Alliance, 1995-96. With U.S. Army, 1967-69. Mem. Mid-Atlantic Assn. Mus. (pres. 1983-85, The Katherine Coffey award 1992), Assn. Art Mus. Dirs. (trustee 1993-98, v.p. 1995-96, pres. 1996-97), Am. Assn. Mus. (trustee 1983-88). Home: PO Box 297 Chadds Ford PA 19317-0297 Office: Brandywine River Mus Brandywine Conservancy PO Box 141 Chadds Ford PA 19317-0141

DUFF, JOHN BERNARD, college president, former city official; b. Orange, N.J., July 1, 1931; s. John Bernard and Mary Evelyn (Cunningham) D.; m. Helen Mezzanotti, Oct. 8, 1955 (div.); children: Michael, Maureen, Patricia, John, Robert, Emily Anne; m. Estelle M. Shanley, July, 1991. B.S., Fordham U., 1953; M.A., Seton Hall U., 1958; Ph.D., Columbia U., 1964; DHL (hon.), Seton Hall U., 1976, Northeastern U., 1982, Emerson Coll., 1983, Lincoln Coll., 1993. Sales rep. Remington-Rand Corp., 1955-57, dist. mgr., 1957-60; mem. faculty Seton Hall U., 1960-70, prof. history, 1968-70, acad. v.p., 1970-71, exec. v.p., acad. v.p., 1971-72, provost, acad. v.p., 1972-76; pres. U. Lowell, Mass., 1976-81; chancellor of higher edn. State of Mass., 1981-86; commr. Chgo. Pub. Libr. System, 1986-92; pres. Columbia Coll., Chgo., 1992—; mem. Gov.'s Commn. to Study Capital Punishment, 1972-73; chmn. bd. dirs. Mass. Corp. Ednl. Telecommunications, 1983—; dir. Mass. Tech. Park Corp. Author: The Irish in the United States, 1971, also articles.; Editor: (with others) The Structure of American History, 1970, (with P.M. Mitchell) The Nat Turner Rebellion: The Historical Event and the Modern Controversy, 1971, (with L. Greene) Slavery: Its Origin and Legacy, 1975. Dem. candidate to U.S. Congress, 1968; mem. State Bd. Edn., 1981-86; chmn. Livingston Town Dem. Com., 1972-76; bd. dirs. Merrimack Regional Theatre, 1981-84, Mass. Higher Edn. Assistance Corp., 1981-86, Chgo. Metro History Fair ; trustee Essex County Coll., 1966-70, Mass. Community Coll. System., St. John's Prep. Sch., Danvers, Mass.; chmn. Lowell Hist. Preservation Commn., 1979-86; mem. adv. bd. Wang Inst., 1979-81; mem. bd. visitors Emerson Coll., 1986-90; pres. Nat. Coun. of Heads of Public Higher Edn. Systems; mem. nat. adv. com. on accreditation and indsl. eligibility U.S. Dept. Edn., 1981-82; mem. Ill. Lit. Coun., 1986-92, adv. com. Ill. State Libr., 1986-92; chmn. Fedn. Ind. Ill. Colls. and Univs., 1996—. With U.S. Army, 1953-55. Mem. Fedn. Ind. Coll. and Univ. Ill. (sec., treas.). Club: K.C.

DUFF, JOHN EWING, sculptor; b. Lafayette, Ind., Dec. 2, 1943; s. John Ewing and Ruth (Miller) D. B.F.A., San Francisco Art Inst., 1967. One man shows include: Margo Leavin Gallery, L.A., 1981, Blum-Helman Gallery, N.Y.C., 1985-90, L.A., 1987, 91, San Jose (Calif.) Mus. Art, 1991, Gallery 57, Madrid, 1992, Salama Caro Gallery, London, 1992, David McKee Gallery, 1995, JohnsonCounty C.C. Gallery Art, 1995, Knodler Gallery, N.Y.C., 1997, Hill Gallery, Birmingham, Mich., 1999, Brantley Gallery, Scottsdale, Ariz., 1999; two-person show at Hill Gallery, Birmingham, Mich., 1996; group exhbns. include Whitney Mus., N.Y.C., 1969, 81, David Whitney Gallery, N.Y.C., 1970, 71, Irving Blum Gallery, L.A., 1972, John Bernard Meyers Gallery, N.Y.C., 1972, 73, Willard Gallery, N.Y.C., 1975-78, Whitney Mus. Equitable Ctr., 1987, The Edward R. Broida Collection, Orlando Mus. of Art, 1998; represented in public collections Kaiser Wilhelm Mus., Krefeld, Fed. Republic Germany, Mus. Modern Art, N.Y.C., Walker Art Ctr., Mpls., Met. Mus. Art, N.Y.c., Solomon R. Guggenheim Mus., N.Y.C., L.A. Mus. Contemporary Art, Mus. Contemporary Art, Chgo. Recipient Theodoren award Guggenheim Mus., 1977, award Am. Acad. and Inst. Arts and Letters, 1981, John Simon Guggenheim fellowship, 1979-80, Brandeis U. Creative Arts award Citation in Sculpture, 1987. Home and Office: 7 Doyers St New York NY 10013-5112

DUFF, MICHAEL JAMES, physicist; b. Manchester, Jan. 28, 1949; s. Edward and Elizabeth (Kaylor) D.; m. Lesley Yearling, 1984; children: Jessica, Matthew. BS, Queen Mary Coll., U. London, 1969; PhD, Imperial Coll., U. London, 1972. Postdoctoral fellow in theoretical physics Internat. Ctr. Theoretical Physics, Trieste, Italy, Oxford (Eng.) U., U. London, Brandeis U., Waltham, Mass., 1972-79; faculty mem. Imperial Coll., 1979-88; sr. physicist CERN, Geneva, 1984-87; prof. physics Tex. A&M U., College Station, 1988-92, Disting. prof. physics, 1992-99; Oskar Klein prof. physics U. Mich., Ann Arbor, 1999—. Contbr. articles to profl. jours. Fellow Am. Phys. Soc. Avocations: scuba diving, golfing. Home: 846 Arboretum Dr Saline MI 48176 Office: U Mich Dept Physics Ann Arbor MI

DUFF, STEVEN BARRON, cardiovascular surgeon; b. Jan. 15, 1955. BS, Miami U., Oxford Ohio, 1977; MD, U. Cin., 1981. Cardiovasc. and thoracic surgeon Cardiovasuclar Assocs., Columbus, Ohio, 1988—; chief of cardiac surgery Riverside Meth. Hosp., Columbus, Ohio, 1997—. Office: Ste 2070 3555 Olentangy River Rd Columbus OH 43214-3935

DUFF, WILLIAM GRIERSON, electrical engineer; b. Alexandria, Va., Dec. 16, 1936; s. Johnnie Douglas and Annetta Osceola (Rind) D.; BEE, George Washington U., 1959, postgrad., 1959-72; MS, Syracuse U., 1969; DSc in Elec. Engring., Clayton U., 1977; m. Sandra K. Via, June 25, 1983; children: Warren David, Valerie Lynn, Dawn Elizabeth, Deborah Arleen, Kelly Juanita. Chief engr. systems engring. div. Computer Scis. Corp., Springfield, Va., 1959—; asst. prof. Capitol Inst. Tech., Greenbelt, Md., 1972—; instr. Interference Control Technologies, Don White Cons., Inc., Gainesville, Va. Counselor, Meth. Sr. High Youth Group, 1965-73. Recipient Good Citizenship award DAR, 1955; Math. award George Washington High Sch., Alexandria, 1955. Fellow IEEE (pres. EMC Soc., assoc. editor group newsletter 1970—); mem. AIEE (Best Paper award 1961), George Washington U. Engring. Alumni Assn. (pres. 1963-64, Engring. Alumni Svc. award 1980), Springfield Golf and Country Club, Occoquan Water Ski Club (pres. 1976), Sigma Tau, Theta Tau. Author: EMI Handbook, vol. 5, EMI Prediction and Analysis Techniques, 1972; Mobile Communications, 1976, Fundamentals of EMC, 1988, EMC in Telecommunications, 1988; contbr. articles to profl. jours. Home: 7601 S Valley Dr Fairfax VA 22039-2965 Office: Computer Scis Corp 5501 Backlick Rd Ste 300 Springfield VA 22151-3940

DUFF, WILLIAM LEROY, JR., university dean emeritus, business educator; b. Oakland, Calif., Sept. 14, 1938; s. William Leroy and Edna Francis (Gunderson) D.; m. Arline M. Wight, Sept. 1, 1962; children—Susan M., William Leroy III. B.A., Calif. State U., San Francisco, 1963, postgrad., 1963-64; M.S.Sc., Nat. Econs. Inst., U. Stockholm, 1965; Ph.D., UCLA, 1969. Research assoc. C.F. Kettering Found., 1967-69; asst. JOBS program Nat. Alliance Businessmen, 1969-70; prof. U. No. Colo., Greeley, 1970—, dir. Sch. Bus., Bur Bus. and Pub. Research, 1972-75, dean Coll. Bus. Adminstrn., 1984—, interim v.p. acad. affairs, 1987; chmn. faculty senate U. No. Colo., 1981-82; on leave as UN adviser to Govt. of Swaziland, 1975-77; cons. in field. Contbr. articles to profl. jours. Mem. Greeley Planning Commn., 1972-75, chmn., 1974-75; trustee U. No. Colo., 1983; mem. Greeley Water and Sewer Bd. With U.S. Army, 1958-60. Mem. Greeley Rotary Club (bd. dirs.), Greeley Area C. of C. (bd. dirs.). Home: 1614 Lakeside Dr Greeley CO 80631-5343 Office: U No Colo Coll Bus Adminstrn Kepner Greeley CO 80639

DUFF-BLOOM, GALE, marketing executive. Pres. mktg. and co. comm. JC Penney Co., Inc., Plano, Tex., 1996—. Office: JC Penney Co Inc 6501 Legacy Dr Plano TX 75024-3698*

DUFFEY, GEORGE HENRY, physics educator; b. Manchester, Iowa, Dec. 24, 1920; s. Henry Alfred and Marion Ella (Barr) D.; m. Helen Susie Hooper, Sept. 17, 1945; children: Ann Elizabeth, James Roy, Mary Kay. BA, Cornell Coll., 1942; PhD, Princeton (N.J.) U., 1945. Asst. prof. chemistry S.D. State Coll., Brookings, 1945-49, assoc. prof. chemistry, 1949-55, prof. chemistry, 1955-58; prof. chemistry physics U. Miss., Oxford, Miss., 1958-59; prof. physics S.D. State U., Brookings, 1959—; vis. prof. physics U. Western Australia, Perth, 1977. Author: Physical Chemistry, 1962, Theoretical Physics, 1980, A Development of Quantum Mechanics, 1984, Quantum States and Processes, 1992, Applied Group Theory, 1992, Modern Physical Chemistry, 1999; editor: Poems from the 1830s by a Poor Son of Ireland, 1977; contbr. articles to profl. jours. including Jour. Chem. Physics, Phys. Rev., Jour. Phys. Chemistry, Founds. of Physics and Jour. Chem. Edn. Recipient Excellence in Teaching award Western Elec. Fund, 1971-72. Mem. AAAS, Am. Phys. Soc., Am. Chem. Soc., Societa Italiana di Fisica, Philosophy of Sci. Assn. Baptist. Home: 628 11th Ave Brookings SD 57006-1526 Office: SD State U Dept Physics Brookings SD 57007-0395

DUFFEY, JOSEPH DANIEL, educational administrator; b. Huntington, W.Va., July 1, 1932; s. Joseph I. and Ruth (Wilson) D.; m. Anne Wexler, 1974; children: Michael and David Duffey, Danny and David Wexler. BA, Marshall U., Huntington, 1954; STM, Yale U., 1963; BD, Andover Newton Theol. Sch., 1958; PhD, Hartford Sem. Found., 1969; LHD, CUNY, 1978, U. Cin., 1978, U. Mass., 1991; LittD, Dickinson Coll., Pa., 1978, Centre Coll., Ky., 1977, Gonzaga U., Wash., 1980, Monmouth Coll., 1980, CCNY; LLD, Amherst Coll., Bethany Coll., Austin Coll., Ritsumaneu U., Kyoto, Japan, 1993; LittD, Alderson-Broadus Coll., Adelphi U., Central Fla. Asst. prof. Hartford (Conn.) Sem., 1960-63; assoc. prof. and dir. Center for Urban Studies, 1965-70; fellow Harvard U. Kennedy Sch. Govt., 1971; adj. prof. and fellow Calhoun Coll., Yale U., 1971-73; exec. officer AAUP, 1974-77; asst. sec. for edn. and cultural affairs Dept. State, 1977; chmn. NEH, 1978-81; chancellor U. Mass., Amherst, 1982—, pres., 1990-91; pres. Am. U., Washington, 1991-93; dir. U.S. Info. Agy., Washington, 1993-98; sr. exec., chmn. internat. univ. project Sylvan Learning Sys., Washington, 1999—; mem. U.S. del. 20th and 21st Gen Confs., UNESCO, 1978, 80; mem. exec. com. Nat. Council on Competitiveness Govt. and Industry Univ. Panel, Nat. Acad. Scis.; bd. dirs. Bay Bank of Springfield (Mass.). Contbr. numerous articles to profl. jours. Bd. dirs. Woodrow Wilson Internat. Ctr. for Scholars, East-West Ctr., Western Mass. Area Devel. Corp., Jewish Theol. Sem. Libr., Springfield Symphony. Decorated Order of Leopold IV (Belgium); recipient Tree of Life award Nat. Jewish Fund, 1987; Rockefeller scholar, 1966-68. Mem. Coun. Fgn. Rels., Century Assn., Cosmos Club. Office: Sylvan Learning Sys Apt 311 2801 New Mexico Ave NW Washington DC 20007

DUFFEY, LEE, communications company executive. BA, U. Ga. Pres. Duffey Comms., Inc., 1984—. Officer, mem. exec. com. Buckhead Coalition, Atlanta, 1985. Office: Ste 600 11 Piedmont Ctr Atlanta GA 30305

DUFFEY, WILLIAM SIMON, JR., lawyer; b. Phila., May 9, 1952; s. William Simon and Elinor (Daniluk) D.; m. Betsy Byars, Dec. 17, 1977; children: Charles, Scott. BA in English, honors, Drake U., 1973; JD cum laude, U. S.C., 1977. Bar: S.C. 1977, Ga. 1982, U.S. Dist. Ct. (no., mid. and so. dists.) Ga. 1982, U.S. Ct. Appeals (llth cir.) 1983, U.S. Supreme Ct., 1992. Atty. Nexson, Pruet, Jacobs & Pollard, Columbia, S.C., 1977-78, King & Spalding, Atlanta, 1982-94; dep. ind. counsel Office of the Ind. Counsel, Little Rock, 1994-95; ptnr. King & Spalding, Atlanta, 1995—. Articles editor S.C. Lawyer, 1990-94. Pres. Pine Hills Civic Assn., Atlanta, 1984-88; trustee Drake U.; mem. Atlanta Task Force Neighborhood Buyouts, 1986, Ga. Rep. Found., Leadership Atlanta; chmn. bd. dirs. Ga. Wilderness Inst., 1992—; mem. Peachtree Rd. Race Com., 1993—, chmn. Ga. Good Govt. Com.; chmn. bd. advisors Coverdell Leadership Inst., 1995—. Mem. Altanta Bar Assn. (chmn. alt. dispute resolution com. 1984-88), Lawyers Club, Atlanta Track Club (gen. counsel 1993—), Nat. Practitioners Advisory Coun. The Fed. Soc. Republican. Avocation: running. Home: 4825 Franklin Pond NE Atlanta GA 30342-2765 Office: King & Spalding 191 Peachtree St NE Atlanta GA 30303-1740

DUFFIE, JOHN ATWATER, chemical engineer, educator; b. White Plains, N.Y., Mar. 31, 1925; s. Archibald Duncan and Lulie Adele (Atwater) D.; m. Patricia Ellerton, Nov. 22, 1947; children—Neil A., Judith A. Duffie Schwarzmeier, Susan L. Duffie Buse. B.Ch.E., Rensselaer Poly. Inst., 1945, M.Ch.E., 1948; Ph.D., U. Wis., 1951. Registered profl. engr., Wis. Instr. chem. engring. Rensselaer Poly. Inst., 1946-49; research asst. U. Wis., 1949-51; research engr. DuPont Co., 1951; sci. liaison officer Office Naval Research, 1952-53; mem. faculty dept. chem. engring. U. Wis.-Madison, 1954—, prof., 1957-88, prof. emeritus, 1988—, dir. solar energy lab., 1956-88; Fulbright scholar U. Queensland, Australia, 1964; sr. Fulbright-Hays scholar Commonwealth Sci. and Indsl. Research Orgn., Australia, 1977; hon. sr. research fellow U. Birmingham, 1984. Author: (with W.A. Beckman) Solar Energy Thermal Processes, 1974, Solar Engineering of Thermal Processes, 1980, 2d edit., 1991; (with W.A. Beckman, S.A. Klein) Solar Heating Design, 1977. Served with USN, 1943-46, 52-53. Fellow Am. Inst. Chem. Engrs.; mem. Internat. Solar Energy Soc. (past pres., Charles G. Abbott award Am. sect. 1976, editor Solar Energy jour. 1985-93, Farrington Daniels award 1987). Home: 5710 Dorsett Dr Madison WI 53711-3404 Office: Univ Wis 1500 Johnson Dr Madison WI 53706-1609

DUFFIE, VIRGIL WHATLEY, JR., state agency administrator; b. Greenwood, S.C., Sept. 10, 1935; s. Virgil Whatley and Lorena (Ouzts) D.; m. Mary Hartzog, Oct. 6, 1962; children: Rebecca Louise, Mary Page, Virgil W. III. BA, U. S.C., 1957, JD, 1959. Bar: S.C. 1959. Trust officer Bankers Trust S.C., Columbia, 1959-67, sr. trust officer, 1967-70, sr. v.p., 1970-73, exec. v.p., 1973-84, 1st exec. v.p., 1984-86; sr.v.p., trust officer NCNB S.C., Columbia, 1986; sr. v.p. Interstate Securities Corp., Columbia, 1987-88; dir. spl. gifts U. S.C., Columbia, 1988-89; apptd. commr. S.C. Dept. Labor, Columbia, 1989-94, appt. dir. labor, licencing and regulations, 1994-95, dept. dir. labor, licensing and regulations, 1995—; bd. dirs. Index-Pub. Co., Greenwood, Stier Supply Co., Columbia, George W. Park Seed Co., Greenwood. Bd. dirs. Palmetto Boys State, Charleston, S.C., 1954-74; chmn. bd. Carolina Children's Home, Columbia, 1976; sec. bd. dirs. Richland Meml. Hosp., Columbia, 1970-73. Mem. ABA, S.C. Bar Assn., S.C. Bankers Assn. Home: 34 Quinine Hl Columbia SC 29204-3414 Office: SC Dept Labor PO Box 11329 Columbia SC 29211-1329

DUFFIELD, THOMAS ANDREW, art director, production designer; b. Grosse Pointe, Mich., Sept. 8, 1951; s. Thomas A. Sr. and Grace A. (Schaefer) D. BArch, Calif. State Poly. U., San Luis Obispo, 1976. Set designer Universal Studios, L.A., 1976-79; freelance designer L.A., 1979-84, 87—; asst. art dir. Michael Landon Prodns., Culver City, Calif., 1984-86; art dir. Warner Bros., Burbank, Calif., 1986-87; prodn. designer Touchstone Pictures, L.A., 1993—. Prodn. designer: (films) Ed Wood, 1994; art dir.: (films) The Lost Boys, 1987, The Accidental Tourist, 1988, Beetlejuice, 1988, Ghostbusters II, 1989, Joe Versus the Volcano, 1990, Edward Scissorhands, 1990, Batman Returns, 1992, Grand Canyon, 1991, Wolf, 1994, A Little Princess, 1995, The Bird Cage, 1996, Men In Black, 1996, Primary Colors, 1997, Wild, Wild West, 1998, What Planet are You From, 2000. Mem. SAG, Acad. Motion Picture Arts and Scis., Internat. Alliance Theatrical Stage Employees. Avocations: art, sports, photography, sports cars, investments. Home: 17031 Lisette St Granada Hills CA 91344-1435 Office: care Soc Motion Picture Art Dirs 11365 Ventura Blvd Studio City CA 91604-3148

DUFFIELD-MYERS, ARLENE ANNA, elementary education educator; b. Camden, N.J., Nov. 3, 1936; d. Herbert and Hilda (Hurst) Duffield; m. Benjamin Frank Myers, July 15, 1959 (dec. 1984); children: Benjamin Frank Jr., Janet Lorraine Bennett. BA cum laude, Glassboro State Coll., 1973, MA summa cum laude, 1976; postgrad., Rutgers U., 1980-81, Rowan U., 1983-88. Cert. prin./supr., student personnel svcs., elem. educator. Tchr. 3rd grade Woodbury (N.J.) Pub. Schs., 1974-84, tchr. 5th grade, 1984—, elem. enrichment tchr., 1990-91, chair site-based com., 1994-96; advisor N.J. Math. Computer Sci. Instrl. Improvement Program, Rowan U., 1988-90, adj. faculty, 1990-92; grad. degree com. Antioch U., Yellow Springs, Ohio, 1989-92. Author: The Effects of Token Payment Upon Standardized Achievement Test Scores, 1988-89, Teaching Time to Developmentally Delayed Children, 1980, Drug and Alcohol Addiction Prevention for Primary Grades, 1979. Resource mem. N.J. Supreme Ct. Jud. Conf., 1990; mem. N.J. Gov.'s Coun. on Alcoholism and Drug Abuse, 1991-97, 2d vice chmn., 1992-94, chmn. alliance com., 1993; chmn. state edn. com. N.J. Gov.'s Coun., 1991, 2d vice-chmn., 1993, 94. Recipient Outstanding Vocat. award, Rotary, 1993, Rowan Summer Inst. award for Dedication to Children of N.J., 1993; named Gloucester County Women of Yr., 1993. Mem. ASCD, NEA, N.J. Edn. Assn., Woodbury Edn. Assn. (pres. 1979-81, v.p. 1984-85), Rotary (mem. community involvement com. 1990, dir. youth svcs. 1992-93, mem. dist. vocations com. 1993, chair dist. 4-way test com. 1994, mem. dist. interact com. 1994). Avocations: reading, writing, international travel. Home: 5 Bittersweet Pl Mount Laurel NJ 08056 Office: Woodbury Pub Schs Jackson St Woodbury NJ 08096

DUFFNER, LEE R., ophthalmologist; b. Milw., June 3, 1936; m. Alvina Bross, Aug. 31, 1957; children—Fay, Rachel, Tamar. B.S. in Engring., Purdue U., 1957; M.S. in Physiology, Marquette U., 1961; M.D., Med. Coll. Wis., 1962. Diplomate Am. Bd. Ophthalmology. Intern, Stanford U., 1962-63; resident U. Miami, Fla., 1966-69; practice medicine specializing in ophthalmology, Hollywood, Fla., 1969—; clin. prof. ophthalmology U. Miami Sch. Medicine, 1969—; dir. Am. Bd. Ophthalmology, 1995—. Pres. town council Town of Golden Beach, Fla., 1983-95. Served to capt. USAF, 1963-66. Fellow Am. Acad. Ophthalmology, ACS; mem. Miami Ophthal. Soc. (pres. 1983-84). Jewish. Avocation: racewalking. Home: 185 Ocean Blvd Golden Beach FL 33160-2208 Office: 2740 Hollywood Blvd Hollywood FL 33020-4826

DUFFY, ANDREW ENDA, language educator; b. Roscommon, Ireland, Nov. 30, 1960; came to U.S., 1981; s. Andrew and Mary (McDermott) D.; m. Maurizia Boscagli, July 23, 1988. BEd, Nat. U. Ireland, Dublin, 1981; MA, Rutgers U., 1984; PhD, Harvard U., 1990. Asst. prof. Reed Coll., Portland, Oreg., 1990-91, Wesleyan U., Middletown, Conn., 1991-93; faculty fellow Humanities Ctr., 1993; Asst. prof. U. Calif., Santa Barbara, 1993-95, assoc. prof., 1995—. Author: The Subaltern Ulysses, 1994; contbr. articles to literary jours., short stories to Irish publs. Whiting fellow Whiting Found., 1989. Mem. Am. Conf. in Irish Studies, MLA, James Joyce Found. Avocations: modernist architecture. Office: U Calif English South Hall Santa Barbara CA 93106

DUFFY, BRIAN FRANCIS, immunologist, educator; b. St. Louis, June 20, 1959; s. Francis G. and Eithne (Neville) B.; m. Katharine Tibbs, May 18, 1984. BS in Microbiology, Pub. Health, Mich. State U., 1981; MA in Biotech., Washington U., St. Louis, 1991. Cert. histocompatibility specialist Am. Bd. Histocompatibility and Immunogenetics. Rsch. technician ARC, St. Louis, 1981-87; rsch. devel. technologist Barnes Hosp., St. Louis, 1987-89; technologist specialist Barnes-Jewish Hosp., St. Louis, 1990—; cons. Washington U. Sch. Medicine, St. Louis, 1991—. Contbr. articles to Jour. Immunol. Methods, Transfusion, Transplantation, Transplantation Proceedings, Hybridoma, Jour. Immunology, Human Immunology. Mem. Am. Soc. Histocompatibility Immunogenetics (lab. inspector 1988—, mem. exam. com. 1989—, chmn. regional edn. com. 1992—), N.Y. Acad. Sci. Achievements include patent for method of ultra-violet irradiation of platelets that are transfusable, non-immunogenic and functional.

DUFFY, DENNIS M., federal agency administrator; m. Roberta Lenart. Grad., Edinboro U. of Pa., 1970; MPA, U. Pa., 1981. With VA Vets. Benefits Adminstrn.; with regional office VA Vets. Benefits Adminstrn., Pitts.; dir. congl. rels., conl. rels. officer VA, dep. asst. sec. for congl. affairs; asst. sec. for policy and planning Dept. VA Affairs. With U.S. Army, Vietnam. Office: Dept Vets Affairs Policy & Planning 810 Vermont Ave NW Washington DC 20420-0001

DUFFY, EARL GAVIN, hotel executive; b. Boston, Oct. 11, 1926; s. William Emmett and Mary Irene (Costello) D.; m. Bernice Rose MacMaster, Feb. 14, 1948; children—Earl Gavin, Joan Irene, Mark Charles, Neil William, Lynn Anne. Student public schs., Boston. In various hotel positions Boston, 1941-52; sales mgr. Somerset Hotel, Boston, 1952-56; eastern sales mgr. Hotel Corp. Am., Boston, 1956-59; asst. nat. sales mgr. Hotel Corp. Am., 1959-61, nat. sales mgr., 1961-64; v.p., gen. mgr. Hotel America, Houston, 1964-67, Hartford, Conn., 1967-69; v.p., gen. mgr. Royal Sonesta Hotel, New Orleans, 1969-71, Soneta Beach Hotel, Key Biscayne, Fla., 1971-76, Boston Park Plaza Hotel, 1977-80; pres. Earl G. Duffy & Assos., 1981—; guest lectr. Cornell U., 1961, U. Houston, 1965, Wash. State U., 1966, Fla. Internat. U., 1971-76; pres. Greater Hartford Conv. and Visitor's Bur., 1969. Chmn. div. bus. and industry Harris County (Tex.) March of Dimes, 1964-67; pres. New Orleans Jazz Festival, 1970-71. Served with USN, 1943-46. Recipient Golden Host award Wash. State U., 1964. Mem. Skal Club, Am. Hotel and Motel Assn., Hotel Sales Mgmt. Assn. Internat., Greater Boston Hotel and Motor Inn Assn., Mass. Hotel and Motel Assn., New Eng. Innkeepers Assn., Boston Exec. Club. Roman Catholic. Club: Rotary. Home and Office: 345 W Enid Dr Key Biscayne FL 33149-2005 *There is no question in my mind that anyone who wants to "make it" in America can do so.*

DUFFY, FRANCIS J., public relations executive; b. Jan. 28, 1942. BS, Boston Coll., 1963; MBA, Columbia U., N.Y.C., 1965. V.p. TWA, N.Y.C., 1968-74; pres. Pucheck Internat., N.Y.C., 1976-85; chmn. Grace Properties, East Hampton, N.Y., 1989-98, Protocol Ltd., East Hampton, N.Y., 1998—. E-mail: fjduffy@msn.com. Address: 50 Egypt Close East Hampton NY 11937-2625

DUFFY, HENRY J., museum curator, consultant; b. San Antonio, Dec. 25, 1952; s. Philip E. and Natalie W. (Willman) D. BA in Art with honors, Drew U., 1975; MA in Art History, Williams Coll./Clark Art Inst., Williamstown, Mass., 1977; postgrad., Rutgers U. Grad. asst. dept. Am. decorative arts Met. Mus. Art, N.Y.C., 1987; registrar The Hermitage/State of N.J., Hohokus, 1989; curator Lyndhurst Nat. Trust for Hist. Preservation, 1990-95; dir. Glebe House Mus. and Gertrude Jekyll Garden, Woodbury, Conn., 1996-97; curator Saint-Gaudens Nat. Hist. Site, Cornish, N.H., 1997—; adj. asst. prof. art history Marymount Coll., 1984—; guest lectr., guest curator Katonah Mus., Scarsdale Hist. Soc., others; mus. cons., 1995—. Appearance on "America's Castles, Arts & Entertainment TV, 1994, ESPN Sports Network, others. Fellow Rutgers. Mem. Victorian Soc., Am. Assn. Museums. Office: Saint-Gaudens Nat Hist Site RR 3 Box 73 Cornish NH 03745-9704

DUFFY, IRENE KAREN, artist; b. Chgo., Mar. 10, 1942; d. Andrew Earl and Irene Margaret Kane (Barthley) James; m. James Ora Duffy, Jan. 24, 1963 (div. Oct. 20, 1993); children: Dawn Ann, James Sean, Maureen Marie. BA, Wash. State U., 1985, MFA, 1989. Juried invitational exhbns. include Gallery X "Out of the Box", Art Inst. Chgo., 1995, Wash. State U./U. Ill., 1994, Virginia Inn, Seattle, 1993, Chase Gallery, Spokane, 1992, Union Gallery, Pullman, 1991, Acad. Arts, Riga, Latvia, 1990, Galeria 5, Caracas, Venezuela, 1989; collections include Johanna Bur. for the Handicapped, Chgo., Gordon Gilkey Collection, Portland Art Mus., Modern Art Gallery, Leningrad, Russia, Neill Pub. Libr. Bd. dirs. Pullman/Moscow Regional Airport, 1981-84. Recipient Civic Appreciation award City of Pullman (Mayor Pete Butkus), 1984. Mem. Palouse Folklore Soc., Lions Club Internat. Avocations: skiing, folk dancing, flying, travel, gardening. Home: PO Box 215 Palouse WA 99161-0215 Studio: Artspace 114 E 525 Church PO Box 247 Palouse WA 99161-0247

DUFFY, JAMES DESMOND, neopsychiatrist, palliative care physician; b. Liverpool, Eng.; s. Desmond Joseph and Josie Margaret Duffy; married, Oct. 27, 1984; children: Sarah, Mark, Andrew. B Medicine B Surgery, U. Rhodesia, Salisbury, 1979. Diplomate Am. Bd. Psychiatry and Neurology, Am. Bd. Hospice and Palliative Care Medicine. Intern U. Rhodesia, 1980, resident in internal medicine, 1981; resident in internal medicine U. Witwatersrand, Johannesburg, South Africa, 1982; resident in psychiatry Brown U., Providence, 1985-88, fellow in neuropsychiatry, 1989-90, asst. prof., 1990-92; fellow in neuropsychiatry Harvard U., Boston, 1988-89, Med. Coll. Pa./Hahneman, Pitts., 1992-95; assoc. prof. U. Conn., Farmington, 1995—; dir. psychiat. cons. svcs. Hartford (Conn.) Hosp./Inst. of Living, 1998—; dir. Huntington's disease program U. Conn. Med. Sch., Farmington, 1998—. Editor: Educational Text on Psychiatry, 2d edit., 1988; contbr. over 50 articles to profl. jours. Chmn. Conn. Coalition to Improve End-Of-Life Care, Meriden, 1998—. Robert Wood Johnson grantee, 1999. Mem. Am. Neuropsychiat. Assn. (chmn. rsch. com. 1997-99). Buddhist. Home: 11 Cricket Ln Avon CT 06001 Office: CB 401 Hartford Hosp Hartford CT 06102

DUFFY, JAMES FRANCIS, III, lawyer; b. Providence, Jan. 28, 1956; s. James Francis Jr. and Eileen (Barry) D. BA, U. R.I., 1978; JD, Harvard U., 1981. Bar: Mass. 1981, U.S. Dist. Ct. Mass. 1982. Assoc. Peabody & Brown, Boston, 1981-89, ptnr., 1989—. Mem. ABA, Boston Bar Assn. (real estate steering com. 1991-93, chmn. equity fin. com. of real estate sect. 1991-93), Mass. Bar Assn. E-mail: jduffy@peabodybrown.com. Home: 17 Jackson Rd Somerville MA 02145-2908 Office: Peabody & Brown Fl 11 101 Federal St Boston MA 02110-1832

DUFFY, JAMES HENRY, writer, former lawyer; b. Lowville, N.Y., Feb. 3, 1934; s. William Christopher and Phyllis Catherine (Rofinot) D.; m. Martha McDowell, May 25, 1968 (dec. 1997). AB, Princeton U., 1956; LLB, Harvard U., 1959. Bar: N.Y. 1960. Assoc. Cravath, Swaine & Moore, N.Y.C., 1959-67, ptnr., 1968-88; bd. dirs. Grove/Atlantic Monthly Press, Albanian-Am. Enterprise Fund, Am. Bank of Albania. Author: Domestic Affairs: American Programs and Priorities, 1979, (under pseudonym Haughton Murphy) Murder for Lunch, 1986, Murder Takes a Partner, 1987, Murders and Acquisitions, 1988, Murder Keeps a Secret, 1989, Murder Times Two, 1990, Murder Saves Face, 1991, A Very Venetian Murder, 1992. Mem. Mayor's Commn. Cultural Affairs, 1981-91; bd. dirs. Nat. Corp. Fund for Dance, Inc., 1981-88, Sch. Am. Ballet, Commonweal Mag., Alliance for the Arts, N.Y.C. Mem. Assn. of Bar of City of N.Y., Coun. Fgn. Rels., Mystery Writers Am. (bd. dirs. 1986-92, treas. 1992), Authors Guild (mem. coun. 1993—), Crime Writers Assn. (U.K.), Century Assn. Democrat. Roman Catholic. Address: 116 E 68th St New York NY 10021-5905

DUFFY, JAMES JOSEPH, engineer; b. Pawhuska, Okla., Aug. 28, 1917; s. James Leo and Margretta Marsden (Wittlinger) D.; m. Edna Jean Laramie, Aug. 15, 1953; children: Paul Edward, Donald Lawrence. BSME, Rice U., 1941; MS in Auto Engring., Chrysler Inst., 1948. Registered profl. engr., Mich. Jr. petroleum engr. Humble Oil and Refining Co., Houston, 1941-42; engine devel. engr. Chrysler Corp., Detroit, 1948-52, resident engr., 1952-54; auto transmission engr. Ford Motor Co., Dearborn, Mich., 1954-59, steering design engr., 1962-65, adv. steering design engr., 1965-90, tech. specialist advanced steering, 1990-95 (ret.); valve design engr. AiRsch., Phoenix, 1959-62. Patentee in field. 1st lt. USAF, 1943-45, SW Pacific. Recipient Disting. Inventor award Intellectual Property Owners, 1988. Mem. Soc. Automobile Engrs., Tau Beta Pi, Sigma Xi. Republican. Lutheran. Avocation: golf. Home: 35594 Orangelawn St Livonia MI 48150-2539

DUFFY, JAMES PATRICK, writer; b. N.Y.C., July 13, 1941; s. Michael J. and Dorothy Veronica (Somerville) D.; m. Kathleen Mary Gallagher, Sept. 21, 1985; children: Alexandra, Olivia. Author: Hitler Slept Late, 1991, Target Hitler, 1992, Czars, 1995, Lincoln's Admiral, 1997, The Assassination of John F. Kennedy, 1992. With USN, 1968-72. Roman Catholic. Fax: 732-767-0371. Home: 496 Grove Ave Edison NJ 08820-3647

DUFFY, JOHN CHARLES, psychiatric educator; b. Cleve., June 19, 1934; s. John Joseph and Hannah (McIllwee) D.; m. Francoise C. Antonini; children: Charles, Robert, John. Grad., Boston Coll., 1956; MD, N.Y. Med. Coll., 1960. Intern Henry Ford Hosp., Detroit, 1960-61; resident Mayo Clinic, Rochester, Minn., 1963-67; exec. dir. Tucson Child Guidance Ctr., 1971-74; commd. med. officer USPHS, 1974; prof., assoc. chmn. Uniformed Svcs. U. Sch. Medicine, Bethesda, Md., 1974-81; assoc. commr. health affairs FDA, cons. Surgeon Gen., Rockville, Md., 1981-88; asst. surgeon gen. USPHS, 1983-92, chief physician officer, 1983-88; dir. C. Everett Koop Inst. Dartmouth Coll., Hanover, N.H., 1992-94; prof. psychiatry Uniformed Svcs. U. Sch. Medicine, Bethesda, 1981-94, clin. prof., 1994—; surveyor Joint Commn. on Accreditation of Healthcare Orgns., 1998—. Author: Psychiatric Morbidity of Physicians, 1964, Psychiatric Issues in the Lives of Physicians, 1966, Child Psychiatry, 1972, 86, Psychiatric Reviews, 1976; founding editor-in-chief Child Psychiatry and Human Devel., 1970-83; editor: Ship's Medical Chest, 1984; editor-in-chief Mil. Medicine; mem. editl. bd. MD mag., 1976-90. Recipient OutstandingSvc. medal Bd. Regents Uniformed Svcs. U., 1981, Surgeon Gen.'s medallion. Fellow Am. Psychiat. Assn. (life), Aerospace Med. Assn. (assoc.; Longacre medal); mem. Assn. Mil. Surgeons U.S., Sigma Xi. Roman Catholic. Office: 8723 Oakthorpe Dr Charlotte NC 28277-0416

DUFFY, JOHN FITZGERALD, law educator; b. Pittsfield, Mass., Nov. 22, 1963; s. Thomas Francis and Noreen (Brett) D.; m. Anne Sprightley Ryan, July 3, 1998; 1 child, Clara Trinity. AB in Physics cum laude, Harvard Coll., 1985; JD cum laude, U. Chgo., 1989. Bar: Pa. 1991, D.C. 1994, U.S. Patent and Trademark Office 1996. Law clk. to Hon. Stephen Williams U.S. Ct. of Appeals for the D.C. Cir., Washington, 1989-90; atty. advisor Office of Legal Counsel, U.S. Dept. Justice, Washington, 1990-92; law clk. to Hon. Antonin Scalia U.S. Supreme Ct., Washington, 1992-93; assoc. Covington & Burling, Washington, 1993-96; asst. prof. law Cardozo Law Sch., Yeshiva U., N.Y.C., 1996—. Avocation: distance running. Office: Cardozo Sch Law 55 5th Ave Fl 10 New York NY 10003-4391

DUFFY, JOHN JOSEPH, retired academic administrator, history educator; b. Charleston, S.C., Apr. 25, 1931; s. John Joseph and Mary (McMahon) D.; m. Marcia Fletcher Tinkham, Aug. 15, 1959; children: Katharine, John Joseph, Eleanor. BA in History, Coll. Charleston, 1952; MA in History, U. S.C., 1955, PhD in History, 1963. Dir. U. S.C., Beaufort, 1959-66; assoc. prof. history U. S.C., Columbia, 1964-98, acad. coord. Coll. Gen. Studies, 1966-67, asst. provost regional campuses, 1967-68, assoc. provost regional campuses, 1968-72, assoc. v.p. regional campuses, 1972-77, system v.p. univ. campuses and continuing edn., 1977-88, chancellor univ. campuses and continuing edn., 1988-91; vice provost for regional campuses and continuing edn., 1991-92; vice provost, exec. dean regional campuses/continuing edn. U. S.C., Columbia, 1992-98; ret., 1998. Author: (radio script) Secession Convention of 1860, 1960; (pamphlet) A Short History of Beaufort County, 1975, also articles. Dist. chmn. Midlands coun. Boy Scouts Am., 1969-71; sustaining mem. S.C. Dem. Party. Recipient Disting. Svc. award Garnet and Black of U. S.C., 1969, Outstanding Edn. Profl. award S.C. Assn. Higher Continuing Edn., 1983, Disting. Svc. award Ednl. Found. U. S.C., 1989; named Young Man of Yr. Jaycees, Beaufort County, S.C., 1964. Mem. So. History Assn., S.C. History Assn., Nat. Univ. Continuing Edn. Assn. (chair region III 1980-82), Nat. Assn. State Univs. and Land Grant Colls., Rotary, Phi Beta Kappa. Roman Catholic. Avocations: reading, music.

DUFFY, JOHN LEWIS, retired Latin, English and reading educator; b. Whittemore, Iowa, Oct. 6, 1934; s. Lewis A. and Dorothy (Bestenlehner) D.; m. Anne O'Brien, July 19, 1958; children: Jane, Paul, Sarah, Steven. BA, Loras Coll., Dubuque, Iowa, 1956; MS Ed, Creighton U., 1961; student, U. Minn., summer 1967. Jr. and sr. H.S. tchr., coach Presentation Acad., Whittemore, Iowa, 1957-58; H.S. tchr. Clear Lake (Iowa) Cmty. Schs., 1958-61; teaching asst. U. Iowa, Iowa City, 1961-62; tchr. Latin Larkin H.S., Elgin, Ill., 1962-96; students' coun. advisor Larkin H.S., Elgin, 1965-71; chmn. English and fgn. langs. Larkin H.S., Elgin, Ill., 1969-77; chmn. English and reading divsn. Larkin H.S., Elgin, 1977-96; tchr. prep. courses for ACT, PSAT and SAT Elgin YWCA and Larkin H.S., Elgin, 1977-96. Summer chef's asst. The Frugal Gourmet, WTTW-TV, Chgo., 1983. Bd. trustees Elgin C.C., 1975—, chmn., 1980-81, 85-87, 97-99, vice-chmn., 1981-84, 94-95; bd. dirs. Elgin Area Cath. Social Svcs., 1981-90, pres., 1986-88; mem. St. Laurence Parish Bd., 1974-79, Edn. Commn., 1972-79, chmn. Edn. Commn., 1974-79; state advisor Iowa Jr. Classical League, 1960-61. Named Kane County Disting. Educator of Yr., 1982, Outstanding Young Men in Am., 1970; recipient Outstanding Young Educator award Elgin Jaycees, 1969. Mem. Assn. C.C. Trustees (chmn. ctrl. region nominating com. 1981-82, sgt.-at-arms ann. conv. 1982, mem. com. on internat. rels. 1983-84, chmn. future directions com. 1984-86, chmn. ctrl. region 1987-88, fed. rels. commn. 1985-93, vice-chmn. fed. rels. commn. 1987-88, chmn. fed. rels. commn. 1988-89, chmn. ctrl. region nominating com. 1992-93, Ctrl. Region Trustee of Yr. award 1991, bd. dirs. 1983-89), Am. Assn. C.C. (bd. dirs. 1990-93), Ill. C.C. Trustees Assn. (chmn. fed. rels. com. 1982-87, bd. rep. 1986-95, 97-99, exec. com. 1981-84, 98-2000), Ill. Edn. Assn. (chmn. ad hoc com. on tchr. tenure 1972-73, state legis. chmn. 1972-73, legis., chmn. northeastern divsn. 1968-71), Elgin Tchrs. Assn. (welfare chmn. and chief negotiator 1963-65, pres. 1966-67), Elgin Assn. Sch. Adminstrs., Am. Classical League, Ill. Classical League, Nat. Coun. Tchrs. English, Ill. Coun. Tchrs. English, Am. Assn. Cmty. and Jr. Colls. Fax: 847-429-0408. Home: 192 Kathleen Dr Elgin IL 60123-5914

DUFFY, KEVIN THOMAS, federal judge; b. N.Y.C., Jan. 10, 1933; s. Patrick John and Mary (McGarrell) D.; m. Irene Krumeich, Nov. 9, 1957; children: Kevin Thomas, Irene Moira, Gavin Edward, Patrick Giles. AB, Fordham Coll., 1954, LLB, 1958. Bar: N.Y. 1958. Clk. to chief circuit judge N.Y.C., 1955-58; asst. chief criminal div. U.S. Atty.'s Office, N.Y.C., 1958-61; assoc. Whitman, Ransom & Coulson, N.Y.C., 1961-66; ptnr. Gordon & Gordon, N.Y.C., 1966-69; regional adminstr. SEC, N.Y.C., 1969-72; judge U.S. Dist. Ct. (so. dist.), N.Y., 1972—; adj. prof. securities law Bklyn. Law Sch., 1975-80; prof. trial advocacy NYU, 1982-84, Pace Law Sch., 1984-85, Fordham Law Sch., 1993—. Author: Cross-Examination of Witnesses: The Litigator's Puzzle, 1990, Impeachment of Witnesses, 1990. Recipient Achievement in Law award Fordham Coll. Alumni Assn., 1976, Alumni Gold medal Fordham Law Sch., 1984, Kupferman's award Laymen's Nat. Bible Assn., 1992, Disting. Pub. Svc. award N.Y. County Lawyers' Assn., Lifetime Achievement award SEC, 1995. Mem. ABA, Am. Bar Assn., N.Y. State County Bar Assn., Westchester County Bar Assn., Assn. of Bar of City of N.Y., Fed. Bar Council (trustee 1970-72), Fordham Law Sch. Alumni Assn. (trustee 1969—, v.p.). Clubs: Merchants (N.Y.C.). Office: US Dist Ct US Courthouse 40 Foley Sq New York NY 10007-1502*

DUFFY, LAWRENCE KEVIN, biochemist, educator; b. Bklyn., Feb. 1, 1948; s. Michael and Anne (Browne) D.; m. Geraldine Antoinette Sheridan, Nov. 10, 1972; children: Anne Marie, Kevin Michael, Ryan Sheridan. *Wife Geraldine is president of Fairbanks Board of Realtors and a member of the board of directors for the Alaska BOR; daughter Anne Marie received her MFA from Pratt Institute in Brooklyn, New York, in 1999; son Kevin hosts a show on the radio station, KSUA.* BS, Fordham U., 1969; MS, U. Alaska, 1972, PhD, 1977. Teaching asst. dept. chemistry U. Alaska, 1969-71, rsch. asst. Inst. Arctic Biology, 1974-77; postdoctoral fellow Boston U., 1977-78, Roche Inst. Molecular Biology, 1978-80; rsch. asst. prof. U. Tex. Med. Br., Galveston, 1980-82; asst. prof. neurology (biol. chemistry) Med. Sch. Harvard U., Boston, Mass., 1982-87, adv. biochemistry instr. Med. Sch., 1983-87; instr. gen. and organic chemistry Roxbury Community Coll., Boston, 1984-87; prof. chemistry and biochem. U. Alaska, Fairbanks, 1992—, head dept. chemistry and biochemistry, 1994—; coord. program biochemistry and molecular biology for summer undergrad. rsch., 1987-96, pres.-elect U. Ak., Fairbanks, faculty senate. Mem. editl. bd. Sci. of Total Environ. Pres., bd. dirs. Alzheimer Disease Assn. of Alaska, 1994-95; mem. instnl. rev. bd. Fairbanks Meml. Hosp., 1990; sci. adv. bd. Am. Fedn. Aging Rsch. (AFAR); mem. Am. Soc. Circumpolar Health Bd. Lt. USNR, 1971-73. NSF trainee, 1971; J.W. McLaughlin fellow, 1981; W.F. Milton scholar, 1983; recipient Alzheimers Disease and Related Disorders Assoc. Faculty Scholar award, 1987; Carol Fiest Outstanding Advisor award, 1994, 97, Nat. Inst. Deafness & Commn. Disorders, NIH Cert. of Merit for mentoring, 1996, North Star Bough Sch. Dist. Svc. award, 1998. Fellow Am. Inst. Chemists (cert. profl. chemist, mem. editl. bd. Sci. of the Total Environment 1999); mem. Am. Soc. Neurochemists, Am. Soc. Biol. Chemists, N.Y. Acad. Sci., Am. Chem. Soc. (Analytical Chemistry award 1969), Internat. Soc. Toxinologists, Am. Soc. Circumpolar Health (bd. dirs.), Sigma Xi (pres. 1991 Alaska club, regional nominating com.), Soc. Environ. Toxicologists Chemists (SETAC), Phi Lambda Upsilon. Roman Catholic. Office: U Alaska Fairbanks Inst Arctic Biology Fairbanks AK 99775

DUFFY, MARTIN EDWARD, management consultant, economist; b. Fall River, Mass., May 24, 1940; s. Arthur Louis and Edna Marie (Cunneen) D.; m. Irene Patricia Daley, Aug. 24, 1968 (div. Jan. 1980); 1 child, Kathryn; m. Priscilla Claire Stieff, May 14, 1988; 1 child, Brianna. BS in History, BSEE, Tufts U., 1963; MBA, U. Pa., 1967. Asst. dean U. Pa., 1967-71; asst. dir. Fels Ctr., U. Pa., 1971-73; v.p. Data Resources, Lexington, Mass., 1975-84; v.p., gen. mgr. MRCA Info. Svcs., Cambridge, 1984-86; pres. The Perseus Group/RCG, Boston, 1986—; co-founder All Seasons Investments GGC, 1999—; planning com. White Ho. Conf. on Aging, Washington, 1981; cons. La in 2001, Baton Rouge, 1982; lectr. in field; adj. prof. mgmt. Emmanuel Coll.; conf. leader Presdl. Summit for Am.'s Future, 1997. Author: The Elderly in Future Economy, 1981. Lt. USN, 1963-65. Mem. Am. Econs. Assn., Nat. Assn. Forensic Economists, Cambridge Sports Union, Tufts U. Alumni Assn. (pres. 1985, exec. com. 1982-87, mem. coun. 1978—), Nat. Bus. Travelers Assn. (bd. dirs. ednl. com. 1988-93). Roman Catholic. Avocations: running marathons, mountain climbing, biking. *A career is an unfolding process, like the gradual opening of an exotic design, demanding only our presence, attention and determination to do well.*

DUFFY, MARTIN PATRICK, lawyer; b. Louisville, Feb. 2, 1942; s. Martin Joseph and Elsie (Shrader) D.; m. Virginia Schoo, Mar. 20, 1970; children: Timothy Brian, Kathleen Kelly. AB in English, U. Notre Dame, 1964; JD, U. Louisville, 1975. Bar: Ky. 1975, U.S. Tax Ct. 1980. Ptnr. Olson, Baker, Henriksen & Duffy, Louisville, 1978-79, Wyatt, Tarrant & Combs, Louisville, 1979--. Bd. dirs. Bellarmine Coll. Overseers, Louisville, 1974-80; trustee St. Mary & Elizabeth Hosp., Louisville, 1980-86, chmn. bd. 1982-85. With U.S. Army, 1964-65, 68-69. Mem. ABA, Ky. Bar Assn., Louisville Bar Assn. Democrat. Roman Catholic. Avocations: running, golf. Office: Wyatt Tarrant & Combs 2700 Citizens Plz Louisville KY 40202

DUFFY, MARY KATHLEEN, neonatal nurse; b. Oak Park, Ill., Aug. 10, 1949; d. William F. and Mary F. (Lang) D. ADN, Triton Coll., River Grove, Ill., 1976; BSN with honors, Ill. Benedictine Coll., Lisle, 1986. Staff nurse gen. med./surg. unit MacNeal Hosp., Berwyn, Ill., 1976-80, staff nurse, level II nursery, 1980-86; staff nurse, neonatal intermediate intensive care nursery DeKalb Gen. Hosp., Decatur, Ga., 1986-87; staff nurse level II nursery MacNeal Hosp., Berwyn, 1987-88; staff nurse neonatal intensive care nursery Good Samaritan Hosp., Downers Grove, Ill., 1988—. Mem. Nat. Assn. Neonatal Nurses, Sigma Theta Tau.

DUFFY, PATRICK, broadcast executive. V.p., gen. mgr. Sta. KRTH-FM, L.A. Office: Sta KRTH-FM 5901 Venice Blvd Los Angeles CA 90034-1708*

DUFFY, PATRICK MICHAEL, judge, federal. BA, The Citadel, 1965; JD, U. S.C., 1968. Bar: S.C., U.S. Dist. Ct. S.C., U.S. Claims Ct., U.S. Ct. Internat. Trade, U.S. Tax Ct., U.S. Ct. Appeals (4th cir.), U.S. Supreme Ct. Asst. county atty. Charleston (S.C.) County, 1973-74; ptnr. Hollings & Hawkins; prin. McNair Law Firm; fed. judge U.S. Dist. Ct., Charleston, 1995—. With U.S. Army, 1969-71. Mem. ABA, Def. Rsch. Inst., Am. Bd. Trial Advocates (Charleston chpt. pres. 1991, rep. 1988-91), S.C. Bar Assn., S.C. Def. Lawyers Assn., Charleston County Bar Assn. Fax: 803 727-4771. Office: US Dist Ct PO Box 835 Charleston SC 29402-0835*

DUFFY, PATRICK SEAN, television production executive; b. Long Beach, Calif., Sept. 16, 1964; s. Thomas Peter Duffy and Maureen Lucille (McNerney) Habel. BA in Econs., U. Calif., San Diego, 1986. Asst. to v.p. and gen. mgr. Kaiser Devel. Co., Carlsbad, Calif., 1986; treasury adminstrn. specialist Imperial Corp. Am., San Diego, 1986-87; v.p. Market Profiles San Diego, 1987-93; owner, mgr. Cmty. Info. Systems, San Diego, 1992-93; corp. mktg. rsch. mgr. INCO Homes Corp., Upland, Calif., 1993-94; pub. The New Home Report, 1994-96; project mgr. digital studies divsn. Sony Pictures Entertainment, 1996-98, LMNO Prodns., 1998—. Contbr. articles to profl. publs. Bd. dirs., treas. San Diego Uptown Cmty. Planning Com., 1991-93; bd. dirs. ReVisions Resources, 19916; mem. host com. AIDS Found. San Diego, 1993; grad. L.E.A.D. San Diego, 1994; event chair AMFAR, 1999—; mem nat. steering com. Gore 2000. Mem. Constrn. Industry Fedn. San Diego (alt. mem. polit. policies com. 1993, mem., co-chmn. fund raising subcom. 1993), Bldg. Industry Assn. San Diego (mem., column editor real estate fin. com. 1990-91, planning retreat com. 1992, co-chmn. SAM awards com. 1993), Toastmasters (v.p. pub. rels. 1992, chmn. exec. com. 1997—, event vol. AIDS walk 1996—). Avocations: piano, writing, volunteer activities, fundraising events. Address: 940 Hancock Ave Apt 1 Los Angeles CA 90069-4015

DUFFY, ROBERT ALOYSIUS, aeronautical engineer; b. Buck Run, Pa., Sept. 9, 1921; s. Joseph Albert and Jane Veronica (Archer) D.; m. Elizabeth Reed Orr, Aug. 19, 1945 (dec.); children: Michael Gordon, Barclay Robert (dec.), Marian Orr (dec.), Judith Elizabeth Parsons, Patricia Archer; m. Jenifer Williams Pickett, Nov. 28, 1992. B.S. in Aero. Engring., Ga. Inst. Tech., 1951. Commd. 2d lt. U.S. Army, 1942; commd. U.S. Air Force, advanced through grades to brig. gen., 1967; service in C.Z., Morocco, Algeria, Tunisia, Sicily, Italy, Vietnam; vice comdr. USAF Space and Missile Systems Orgn., L.A., 1970-71; ret., 1971; v.p., dir. Draper Lab. div. MIT, Cambridge, Mass., 1971-73; pres., chief exec. officer Charles Stark Draper Lab., Inc., 1973-87, dir., 1973-91, dir. emeritus, 1991—. Contbr. articles to profl. jours. Decorated Disting. Svc. medal, Legion of Merit; recipient

Thomas D. White award Nat. Geog. Soc., 1970; named to Ga. Tech. Engring. Hall of Fame, 1994. Fellow AIAA; mem. NAE, Internat. Acad. Astronautics, Inst. Navigation (Thurlow award 1964, pres. 1976-77), Air Force Assn., Tau Beta Pi. Home: 27300 Hickory Blvd Bonita Springs FL 34134-8407 Office: Charles Stark Draper Lab 555 Technology Sq Cambridge MA 02139-3539

DUFFY, ROBERT JOHN, police chief; b. Rochester, N.Y., Aug. 21, 1954; s. Cornelius Leo and Catherine Elaine Duffy; married; children: Erin, Shannon. AAS, Monroe C.C., 1988; BS, Rochester Inst. Tech., 1993; MA, Syracuse U., 1998. Police officer Rochester Police Dept., 1976-85, police sgt., 1985-89, police lt., 1989-92, police capt., 1992, dep. chief, 1992-98, police chief, 1998—. Mem. adv. bd. Boys/Girls Club, Rochester, 1992-98, Families/Friends of Murdered Children, Rochester, 1992—, Urban League Rochester, 1998—, ARC, Rochester, 1998—. Mem. Internat. Assn. of Chiefs of Police, Am. Soc. Pub. Adminstrs., Pub. Exec. Rsch. Forum, Rochester Rotary. Avocations: running, weight training, reading. E-mail: rjd-401@msn.com. Home: 164 Croydon Rd Rochester NY 14610 Office: Rochester Police Dept 150 S Plymouth Ave Rochester NY 14614

DUFFY, WILLIAM EDWARD, JR., retired education educator; b. Fostoria, Ohio, Aug. 30, 1931; s. William Edward and Margaret Louise (Drew) D.; B.S., Wayne State U., 1958, M.Ed., 1960; Ph.D., Northwestern U., 1967; m. Sally King Wolfe, Nov. 21, 1958 (div. 1978). Tchr. social studies Detroit pub. schs., 1957-61; instr. Northwestern U., Evanston, Ill., 1961-65; asst. prof. edn. U. Iowa, Iowa City, 1965-70, assoc. prof., 1970-94, coordinator Soc. Found. Edn. program, 1978-93, chmn. div. founds., postsecondary edn., 1981-88; ret., 1994; lectr. in field. Served with USAF, 1951-54. Fellow John Dewey Soc., Philosophy of Edn. Soc.; mem. Am. Ednl. Research Assn., History of Edn. Soc., Am. Ednl. Studies Assn. Editorial bd. Ednl. Philosophy Theory, 1969-71; contbr. book revs. and articles to profl. publs. Home: 376 Samoa Pl Iowa City IA 52246-3632

DUFNER, EDWARD JOSEPH, business newswriter; b. Reading, Pa., May 26, 1960; s. Edward J. Sr. and Marcia (Keiser) D.; m. Connie Elizabeth Pryzant, July 29, 1984; children: Elena Miriam, Adam Joseph. BS in Journalism, Northwestern U., 1982. Reporter, asst. regional editor Abilene (Tex.) Reporter-News, 1982-83; news editor Arlington (Tex.) Daily News, 1983, editor, 1984; copy editor The Dallas Morning News, 1984-86, asst. nat. editor, 1986-89, nat. editor, 1990-91, 93-95, polit. editor, 1992, 96, bus. editor, 1997—. Bd. trustees Temple Emanu-El, Dallas, 1996—. Jewish. Avocations: running, youth sports, historical reading. Office: The Dallas Morning News Comms Ctr PO Box 655237 Dallas TX 75265-5237*

DUFNER, MAX, retired German language educator; b. Davos-Platz, Switzerland, June 17, 1920; came to U.S., 1926, naturalized, 1952; s. William and Béatrice Philomène (Collin) D.; m. Marguerite Little, Aug. 30, 1951; children: Margaret Beatrice, Christina Marie, Thomas William. A.A., Grand Rapids Jr. Coll., 1940; A.B., U. Mo., 1942; M.A., U. Ill., 1947, Ph.D., 1951. Instr. German U. Ky., Lexington, 1947, U. Ill., Urbana, 1951-52; instr. German U. Mich., Ann Arbor, 1952-56; asst. prof. German U. Mich., 1956-61, assoc. prof. German, 1961-69; prof. German U. Ariz., Tucson, 1969-87; head dept. U. Ariz., 1969-77; resident dir. Wayne State U. Jr. Year Program, Freiburg, Germany, 1962-63. Editor: (with V.C. Hubbs) German Essays: Vol. I, Aufklärung, Vol. II, Goethe, Vol. III, Schiller, Vol. IV, Romanticism, 1964; translator: C.M. Wieland. History of the Abderites, with Introduction and Annotations by Max Dufner, 1993. Served with AUS, 1942-46. Mem. MLA, AAUP, Lessing Soc., Goethe Soc. N.Am., Am. Soc. 18th Century Studies, Phi Beta Kappa, Phi Kappa Phi, Delta Phi Alpha. Home: 8440 E Kent Pl Tucson AZ 85710-4220

DUFOE, WILLIAM STEWART, lawyer; b. Tallahassee, Oct. 24, 1950; s. Fabbian George and Marion Elizabeth (Rogers) D.; m. Judy Karen Rawls, July 31, 1980; 1 child, James Robert. BS, Fla. State U., 1972, JD, 1977; MS, U. So. Calif., L.A., 1975. Bar: Fla. 1978, U.S. Supreme Ct. 1987, U.S. Ct. Appeals (11th cir.) 1988, U.S. Dist. Ct. (middle dist.) Fla. 1978; cert. cir. court mediator, Fla. Assoc. Holland & Knight, Bartow, Fla., 1978-85; ptnr. Holland & Knight, Lakeland, Fla., 1985—; arbitrator 10th Jud. Cir. Fee Arbitration Com., 1990-92. 1st lt. U.S. Army, 1972-75. Mem. Polk County Trial Lawyers Assn., Lakeland Bar Assn., Willson Am. Inn of Ct. (master), Lakeland C. of C. (Leadership Lakeland program 1988-89), Order of the Coif, Rotary. Democrat. Methodist. Avocation: music. Office: Holland & Knight PO Box 32092 Lakeland FL 33802-2092*

DUFOUR, JEAN-MARIE, economics researcher, educator; b. Montreal, Que., Can., Dec. 27, 1949; s. Jean-Marie Dessureault and Bella Dufour. BA, U. Montreal, 1969; BSc in Math., McGill U., Montreal, 1971; MSc in Stats., U. Montreal, 1973; MA in Econs., Concordia U., 1974, U. Chgo., 1978; PhD in Econs., U. Chgo., 1979. Lectr. stats. U. Que., Trois-Rivières, 1972-73; prof. math. Coll. Édouard-Montpetit, Montreal, 1973-75; rsch. assoc. Inst. Applied Econ. Rsch. Concordia U., 1978-79; lectr. econs. U. Montreal, 1978-79; mem. rsch. staff ctr. recherche en développement économique, 1979-85; sr. mem. rsch. staff, dir. rsch. program in econometrics and macroecons. ctr. de recherche et développement en économique U. Montreal, 1985-90, asst. prof., 1979-83, assoc. prof., 1983-88, prof., 1988—, dir. ctr. recherche et développment en économique, 1988-95, 97—, chmn. dept. econs., 1995-97; vis. scholar MIT, 1980, Queen's U., 1986, CEPREMAP, Paris, 1986, U. Libre de Bruxelles, 1988, 89, 90, 91, 93, Ecole Nat. des Stats. et l'Adminstrn. Economique, Paris, 1990, 91, 93, 95, U. Scis. Sociales de Toulouse, France, 1992, 94, Humboldt U. Berlin, 1994; cons. Econ. Coun. Can., 1981, Office de Planification et Devel. economique du Que., 1982, Royal Commn. Econ. Union and Devel. prospects for Can., 1983-84; invited prof. U. de Toulouse I, 1983, U. Pa., 1992, U. Lausanne, 1995; rsch. fellow Ctr. Ops. Rsch. and Econometrics U. Cath. de Louvain, 1985-86; bd. dirs. Soc. Can. de Sci. Economique, 1984-87; Benjamin Meaker chair, U. Bristol, 1993; lectr. in field. Assoc. editor Econometrica, 1996—, Jour. Econometrics, 1994—, Empirical Econs., 1994—, Econometric Theory, 1991-93, Econometric Reviews, 1991-96, Annales d'Économie et de Statistique, 1990—, Cahiers de Centre d'Études de Recherche Opérationnelle, 1989—, Can. Jour. Econs., 1984-88; guest editor Jour. Econometrics, 1992-93, Empirical Econs., 1993—; contbr. 70 articles to profl. jours. Recipient Excellence in Rsch. award Soc. Can. de Sci. Économique, 1988, Leave fellowship Social Scis. and Humanities Rsch. Coun. Can., 1985-86, Doctoral fellowship Can. Coun., 1975-78, Doctoral fellowship Govt. Que., 1975-78, Scholarship, U. Montreal, 1971-72; rsch. grantee Ministry Edn. Que., 1979-80, 80-81, 81-82, Social Scis. and Humanities Rsch. Coun. Can., 1980-81, 83, 83-85, 87-89, 89-91, 91-94, 94-97, 97—, U. Montreal 1979-80, Econ. Coun. Can., 1981, Govt. Que., 1982-83, 83-84, 84-85, 85-86, 86-87, 87-90, 90-93, 96-96, 96—, Royal Commn. on Econ. Union and Devel. Prospects per Can., 1983-84, Natural Scis. and Engring. Rsch. Coun. Can., 1983-86, 87-90, 89-91, 91-94, 94-97, 97—, Govt. Que. and Communauté française de Belgique, 1989-90, Govt. Que. and Govt. France, 1990-92, Can. Internat. Devel. Agy., 1991-93; Killam fellow Can. Coun. for Arts, 1998—. Fellow Royal Soc. Can., Econometric Soc.; mem. Am. Econ. Assn., Am. Statis. Assn., Can. Econs. Assn. (spl. prize outstanding rsch. 1994), Statis. Soc. Can. (rsch. com. 1988—), Can. Econometric Study Group Bd., Internat. Statis. Inst., Econometric Soc., Inst. Mathematical Stats., Société canadienne de sci. économique (bd. dirs. 1984-87, pres. elect, 1998—). Home: 1060 Ave Bernard Apt 8, Outremont, PQ Canada H2V 1V2 Office: U Montreal C R D E, Case Postale 6128, Montreal, PQ Canada H3C 3J7

DUFOUR, RICHARD JOSEPH, district attorney; b. Milw., Aug. 3, 1956; s Robert Alfred and Claire Lorraine (Gamache) D.; m. Shelley Sue Freitag, Oct. 1, 1983; 1 child, Genevieve Claire. BA cum laude, Marquette U., 1978, JD, 1981. Bar: Wis., U.S. Dist. Ct. Wis. Assoc. Rudolph, Kubasta, Rathjen & Murach, Wautoma, Wis., 1981-85; ptnr. Kubasta, Rathjen, Murach, Dufour & Bickford, Wautoma, 1985-90; dist. atty. Marquette County, Wis., Montello, 1990—; cons. Dept. of Justice, Madison, 1992—; com. mem. Statewide Prosecutor Edn. and Tng. Bd. Wis. Dist. Atty.'s Assn., Info. Tech. Com., Madison, 1995—. Bd. dirs. Waushara Industries, Wautoma, 1985-91, United Cerebral Palsy, Winnebagoland, Oshkosh, Wis., 1991—, Madison, 1995—, Marquette County Hist. Soc., Westfield, Wis., 1996. Recipient Am. Jurisprudence award Lawyer's Coop. Pub., 1979, Lawyer's Coop. Pub., 1981. Mem. Rotary Club of Montello (pres. 1994-95), Phi Alpha Theta. Republican. Roman Catholic. Avocations: golf, computers, skiing, working with youth. Home: PO Box 54 494 S Lake St Montello WI 53949 Office: Marquette County Dist Attys Office PO Box 396 77 W Park St Montello WI 53949-9366

DUFOUR, VAL (ALBERT VALERY DUFOUR), actor; b. New Orleans, Feb. 5, 1927; s. Albert Valery and Cleotile (Brouillette) D. B.A., La. State U., 1949; M.A., Cath. U. Am., 1952. Appeared in: Broadway plays High Button Shoes, 1950, Mister Roberts, 1951, The Grass Harp, 1952, South Pacific, 1953, Media, 1953, Abe's Irish Rose, 1954; appeared in: films The Lonely Night, 1952, The Undead, 1957, Ben Hur, 1957, King of Kings, 1957, Land of Plenty, 1960, She-God, 1961; appears in role of John Wyatt: television series Search for Tomorrow, 1972— (Recipient Emmy award 1977). Roman Catholic. Office: CBS 51 W 52nd St New York NY 10019-6119 *I live only for my art, which is sad.*

DUFRESNE, ARMAND FREDERICK, management and engineering consultant; b. Manila, Aug. 10, 1917; s. Ernest Faustine and Maude (McClellan) DuF.; m. Theo Rutledge Schaefer, Aug. 24, 1940 (dec. Oct. 1986); children: Lorna DuFresne Turnier, Peter, m. Lois Burrell Klosterman, Feb. 21, 1987. BS, Calif. Inst. Tech., 1938. Dir. quality control, chief product engr. Consol. Electrodynamics Corp., Pasadena, Calif., 1945-61; pres., dir. DUPACO, Inc., Arcadia, Calif., 1961-68; v.p., dir. ORMCO Corp., Glendora, Calif., 1966-68; mgmt., engring. cons., Duarte and Cambria, Calif., 1968—; dir., v.p., sec. Tavis Corp., Mariposa, Calif., 1968-79; dir. Denram Corp., Monrovia, Calif., 1968-70, interim pres., 1970; dir., chmn. bd. RCV Corp., El Monte, Calif., 1968-70; owner DUFCO, Cambria, 1971-82; pres. DUFCO Electronics, Inc., Cambria, Calif., 1982-86, chmn. bd. 1982-92; pres. Freedom Designs, Inc., Simi Valley, Calif., 1982-86, chmn. bd. dirs., 1982-97; owner DuFresne Consulting, 1992—; chmn. bd., pres. DUMEDCO,Inc., 1993-95. Patentee in field. Bd. dirs. Arcadia Bus. Assn., 1965-69; bd. dirs. Cambria Community Services Dist., 1976, pres., 1977-80; mem., chmn. San Luis Obispo County Airport Land Use Commn., 1972-75. Served to capt. Signal Corps, AUS, 1942-45. Decorated Bronze Star. Mem. Instrument Soc. Am. (life), Arcadia (dir. 1965-69), Cambria (dir. 1974-75) C. of C., Tau Beta Pi. Home: 901 Iva Ct Cambria CA 93428-2913

DUGAN, CHARLES FRANCIS, II, lawyer; b. Ann Arbor, Mich., Aug. 8, 1939; s. Charles F. and Mary (Minton) D.; m. Janice C. Prior, June 11, 1961; children: Heather, Stephanie, Suzanne, Kathleen. B.A., Miami U., Oxford, Ohio, 1960; J.D., U. Mich., 1963. Bar: Ohio 1963. Assoc., Vorys, Sater, Seymour & Pease, Columbus, Ohio, 1963-69, ptnr., 1970-91 ; bd. dirs., sec. Buckeye Fin. Corp., 88 Fund, Inc., Ohio Inst. Fin., Columbus, 1974-90, TEAM Am. Corp., 1992—; co-chmn. enforcement adv. com. Ohio Securities div., Columbus, 1980-91; lectr. in field. Contbr. articles to profl. jours. Trustee, sec. Nat. Ch. Residences of Worthington, 1972—; pres. Seal of Ohio council Girl Scouts Am., 1976-79.; music dir. Berlin Presbyn. Ch., Del. County, Ohio, 1987—. Mem. Columbus Bar Assn. (securities law com.), Ohio State Bar Assn. (corp. law com.), ABA (fed. regulation of securities com.). Home and Office: 10747 Campden Lakes Blvd Dublin OH 43016-9527

DUGAN, EDWARD FRANCIS, investment banker; b. Jersey City, July 3, 1934; s. Edward F. and Anna V. Dugan; m. June D. Hulings, June 28, 1958 (div. 1981); children: Jamie, Edward, Kirsten; m. Susan Blackstock, June 2, 1984; 1 child, Kelley Nicole. B.S., St. Peter's Coll., Jersey City, 1958; M.B.A., NYU, 1961. With Smith Barney & Co., N.Y.C., 1961-75; pres. Warburg Paribas Becker, Inc., N.Y.C., 1975-78; mng. dir. Paine Webber Inc., N.Y.C., 1978-90; pres. Dugan Assocs. Inc., N.Y.C., 1991—; bd. dirs. SFX Entertainment, Inc. Served as officer USAR, 1959-61. Club: Bond (N.Y.C.). Office: 14 E 90th St Fl 7 New York NY 10128-0671

DUGAN, JOHN F., lawyer; b. Phila., May 25, 1935; s. Albert C. and Helen Josephine (Pritchard) D.; m. Colette Gregory, Jan. 18, 1987. AB, U. Pa., 1956, LLD, 1960. Bar: Pa. 1961, U.S. Ct. Appeals (3d cir.) 1961, Va. 1966, U.S. Supreme Ct. 1967. Assoc. Obermayer Rebmann Maxwell & Hippel, Phila., 1960-66; of counsel Reynolds Metals Co., Richmond, Va., 1966-69, Pennwalt Corp., Phila., 1969-71; ptnr. Berkman Ruslander, Pitts., 1971-85, Kirkpatrick & Lockhart, Pitts., 1985—; labor rels. law rep. mgmt., Kirkpatrick & Lockhart. Mem. Pitts. Field Club, Duquesne Club, Order of the Coif, Phi Beta Kappa. Republican. Office: Kirkpatrick & Lockhart 1500 Oliver Building Pittsburgh PA 15222-2312

DUGAN, JOHN LESLIE, JR., foundation executive; b. Phila., Nov. 6, 1921; s. John Leslie and Ellen May (Reid) D.; m. Barbara McClelland Day, Dec. 21, 1946; children: Barbara Nicholas, Geoffrey McClelland, Sara Ellen. B.S., Swarthmore Coll., 1943; postgrad., Harvard U., 1947-48; M.B.A., U. Pa., 1950. Instr. Swarthmore Coll., 1946-47, U. Pa., 1948-50; cons. Booz, Allen and Hamilton, 1951-55; asst. to pres. Grace Nat. Bank, N.Y.C., 1955-58; treas. Underwood Corp., N.Y.C., 1958-60; v.p. fin. Chicopee div. Johnson & Johnson, New Brunswick, N.J., 1960-75; dir., adminstr. Robert Wood Johnson Found., Princeton, N.J., 1975-77; exec. v.p. Am. Diabetes Assn., Inc., N.Y.C., 1977-80; exec. dir. Fin. Analysts Fedn., N.Y.C., 1981-84; pres. The Greenwall Found., N.Y.C., 1981-90; founder, pres. Buck Hill Conservation Found., 1992-97, trustee, 1992-99; adj. prof. mgmt. St. Peter's Coll., 1975-81. Committeeman Millburn Twp., N.J., 1975-79, commr. fin. and welfare, 1976-79; vestryman, warden, lay reader Christ Ch. in Short Hills, N.J. Served to lt. comdr. USNR, 1943-46. Mem. Tau Beta Pi. Republican. Clubs: Baltusrol Golf, Short Hills, Ozone, Buck Hill Golf. Home: PO Box 851 New Vernon NJ 07976-0851

DUGAN, MICHAEL JOSEPH, former air force officer, health agency executive; b. Albany, N.Y., Feb. 22, 1937; s. D. Joseph and Dorothy M. (Krebs) D.; m. Grace A. Robinson, Aug. 9, 1958; children: Colleen, Erin, Mike, Sean, Kathleen, Kevin. BS, U.S. Mil. Acad., 1958; MBA, U.Colo., 1972. Commd. officer USAF, 1958, advanced through grades to gen.; comdr.-in-chief U.S. Air Forces Europe, 1989-90; comdr. Allied Air Forces Cen. Europe, 1989-90; chief of staff USAF, 1990, ret., 1991; lectr. in strategic studies Johns Hopkins U., Washington, 1991-92; pres., CEO Nat. Multiple Sclerosis Soc., N.Y.C., 1992—. Decorated D.S.M., Silver Star, Legion of Merit, D.F.C., Purple Heart; Knight's Cross (Germany). Home: 10 Old Jackson Ave Hastings Hdsn NY 10706-3203 Office: NMSS 733 3rd Ave New York NY 10017-3204

DUGAN, PATRICK RAYMOND, microbiologist, university dean; b. Syracuse, N.Y., Dec. 14, 1931; s. Francis Patrick and Joan Irma (Clause) D.; m. Patricia Ann Murray, Sept. 22, 1956; children: Susan Eileen, Craig Patrick, Wendy Shawn, Carolyn Paige. B.S., Syracuse U., 1956, M.S., 1959, Ph.D., 1964. Asso. research scientist Syracuse U. Research Corp., 1956-63; mem. faculty Ohio State U., Columbus, 1964—, asso. prof., 1968-70, prof., chmn. dept. microbiology, 1970-73; acting dean Ohio State U. (Coll. Biol. Scis.), 1978-79, dean, 1979-85; prin. scientist EG&G Idaho Nat. Engring. and Environ. Lab., Idaho Falls, 1987-91, sci. and engring. fellow, 1991-94, dir. Ctr. for Bioprocessing Tech., 1987-94; ret., cons., 1994—. Author: Biochemical Ecology of Water Pollution, 1972. Trustee, Columbus Zool. Assn. and Zoo, 1982-87. Fellow Am. Acad. Microbiology; mem. AAAS, Am. Soc. Microbiology (Ohio pres. 1968-70), Soc. Indsl. Microbiology, Am. Chem. Soc.

DUGAN, ROBERT PERRY, JR., minister, religious organization administrator; b. Morristown, N.J., Jan. 19, 1932; s. Robert P. and Marion Frances (Sahrbeck) D.; m. Marilyn I. Wertz, Aug. 8, 1953; children: Robert Perry III, Cheryl. AB, Wheaton Coll., 1953; MDiv, Fuller Theol. Sem., 1956; DD, Denver Conservative Bapt. Sem., 1985; LHD, Geneva Coll., 1985; LLD, Roberts Wesleyan Coll., 1990. Ordained to ministry Conservative Bapt. Assn. Am. 1957. Postgrad. teaching fellow in Hebrew Fuller Theol. Sem., 1954-57; minister of youth ch. Bloomfield, N.J., 1957-58; pastor Rochester, N.H., 1959-63, Elmhurst, Ill., 1963-69; pastor Trinity Baptist Ch., Wheat Ridge, Colo., 1970-75; chaplain Senate of State of Colo., 1974-75; pres. Conservative Baptist Assn. Am., 1973-76; v.p. Rockmont Coll., Lakewood, Colo., 1976-78; dir. Office of Pub. Affairs, Nat. Assn. Evangelicals, Washington, 1978-96; v.p. governmental affairs Nat. Assn. Evangelicals, Washington, 1996-98; bd. dirs. Denver Sem., chmn., 1998—; Staley disting. Christian scholar lectr., 1973, 82, 84, 86, 88, 94; participant Internat. Congress on World Evangelism, Lausanne, Switzerland, 1974. Author: Winning the New Civil War: Recapturing America's Values, 1991, Stand and Be Counted: A Washington Insider Tells How to Preserve America's Liberties for You and Your Children, 1995; editor monthly newsletter NAE Washington Insight, 1979-97. Candidate for U.S. Congress, 1976; mem. ethics adv. bd. USIA, 1982-84; bd. dirs. Justice Fellowship, 1983-91, Transformation Internat., 1987-91; bd. trustees Williamsburg Charter Found., 1988-89. Home: 1712 Paisley Blue Ct Vienna VA 22182-2326 Office: Nat Assn Evangelicals Ofc for Govt Affairs 1023 15th St NW Washington DC 20005-2602

DUGGAN, CAROL COOK, research director; b. Dillon, S.C., May 25, 1946; d. Pierce Embree and Lillian Watkins (Eller) Cook; m. Kevin Duggan, Dec. 29, 1973. BA, Columbia Coll., 1968; MS, U. Ky., 1970. Reference asst. Richland County Pub. Libr., Columbia, S.C., 1968-69, asst. to dir., 1970, chief adult svcs., 1971-82; dir. Maris Rsch., Columbia, 1982—; lectr., mem. Friends of Richland County Pub. Libr., 1977—, Greater Columbia (S.C.) Literacy Coun., 1973—; mem. worship com. Washington St. United Meth. Ch., Columbia, 1985-86, mem. staff-parish relations com., 1986-91, mem. history and archives com., 1988—, mem. adminstrv. bd., 1992-97, chair staff-parish relations com., 1993, trustee 1995-98; mem. exec. bd. United Meth. Women 1983—, treas. unit 7, 1989-91, pres. unit 5, 1992-97, treas., 1998—. Author: A History of the City of Forest Acres, S.C., 1998. Recipient Sternheimer award, 1968; treas. Friends S.C. Librs., 1995—. Mem. ALA (councilor 1980-82, chmn. state membership com. 1979-83), S.C. Libr. Assn. (sec. 1976, exec. bd. 1976, 78-82), S.C. Pub. Libr. Assn. (pres. 1980-81), Columbia Coll. Alumnae Assn. Coun. (spl. events com. 1996—), Beta Phi Mu. Methodist. Club: PEO (pres. 1983-85, chmn. amendments and recommendations com. 1983-85, historian 1986-87, 90-92, treas. State conv., 1987-88, v.p. 1998-99). Home: 2101 Woodmere Dr Columbia SC 29204-4341

DUGGAN, DENNIS MICHAEL, newspaper editor; b. Detroit, Oct. 12, 1927; s. Michael and Anne (Judge) D.; divorced; 1 child, Nancy Ellen. A.B., Wayne U., Detroit, 1952. Wall St. columnist N.Y. Herald Tribune, 1960-61; asst. real estate editor N.Y. Times, 1961-62; fin. writer N.Y. Daily News, 1967; sr. editor, N.Y. bur. chief Newsday, 1973-83; columnist, 1983—. Recipient Meyer Berger award for disting. reporting Columbia U. Grad. Sch. Journalism, 1987; co-recipient Pulitzer prize for local news and reporting N.Y. Newsday, 1991. Mem. Inner Circle, Soc. Silurians (winner Peter Kihss award for disting. reporting), Dutch Treat Club. Home: 235 W 11th St New York NY 10014-2277 Office: 780 3rd Ave New York NY 10017-2024

DUGGAN, EDWARD MARTIN, secondary education educator; b. Tacoma, Sept. 23, 1953; s. John and Catherine Patricia (Fitzgerald) D.; children: Rory Emmett, Orlaith Catherine Mary. BS in Psychology, U. Wash., 1979, BA in Zoology, 1979, BS in Botany, 1980, MEd in Sci. Edn., 1982. Cert. tchr., Wash., police commr., Wash., EMT. Sci. tchr. Federal Way (Wash.) Pub. Schs., 1982—; track coach Federal Way (Wash.) Pub. Schs., Wash., 1996; gymnastics coach Tacoma Pub. Schs., 1982-84, track coach, 1982-88, cross country coach, 1983-88; police officer Ruston (Wash.) Police Dept., 1996—. Mem. NSTA, Audubon Soc., Nat. Wildlife Fedn. Roman Catholic. Avocations: skiing, sailing, scuba diving, science, biking. Home: 2729 SW 349th Pl Federal Way WA 98023-3090

DUGGAN, ERVIN S., federal agency administrator; b. Atlanta, June 30, 1939; s. James Henry Jr. and Lillian (Benbow) E.; m. Julia L. Prather, May 20, 1972; children: Edward Ervin, Laurens Paul. BA, Davidson Coll., 1961; student, U. de Montpelier, France, 1961-62. Reporter Washington Post, 1964-65; staff asst. to the Pres The White House, 1965-69; dir. spl. projects, history and art Smithsonian Inst., 1969-71; spl. asst. to Sen. Adlai E. Stevenson Ill., 1971-77; with Depts. of State and HEW, 1977-81; pres. Ervin S. Duggan Assoc., 1981-90; commr. FCC, Washington, 1990-94; pres., CEO PBS, Alexandria, Va., 1994—. Author: Against All Enemies, 1977; contbr. articles to profl. jours. Former nat. chmn. Presbyns. for Democracy and Religious Freedom; elder Chevy Chase Presbyn. Ch., Washington. 1st Lt. U.S. Army, 1962-64. Decorated Army Commedation medal. Mem. Kenwood Golf and Country Club. Office: Public Broadcasting Service 1320 Braddock Pl Alexandria VA 22314-1649*

DUGGAN, JOHN PETER, lawyer; b. Newark, June 28, 1946; s. Patrick Joseph and Mary Ellen (Gallagher) D.; m. Bernadine Ann Lehman, Oct. 24, 1976; children: Erin, Sean, Mary Kate. BA, Montclair State U., 1968; JD with honors, Rutgers U., 1973. Bar: N.J. 1973, U.S. Dist. Ct. N.J. 1973, U.S. Supreme Ct. 1982, U.S. Ct. Appeals (3d cir.) 1988. Asst. prosecutor Middlesex County Prosecutor's Office, New Brunswick, N.J., 1973-78; assoc. Francis H. Wolff, P.A., Red Bank, N.J., 1978-80; ptnr. Wolff, Helies & Duggan, P.A., Red Bank, 1980—. Mem. ABA, N.J. Def. Assn., N.J. Bar Assn., Monmouth County Bar Assn. (chmn. civil practice com. 1990-91, 92-93, 96-97, 97—, sec. 1997—). Office: Wolff Helies & Duggan PA 188 E Bergen Pl Red Bank NJ 07701-2161

DUGGAN, JOSEPH PATRICK, public affairs executive; b. St. Louis, July 5, 1955; s. Martin Lawler and Mary Margaret (Mae) D.; m. Juanita Sheryl donaghey, Oct. 29, 1983 (div. July 1996); children: James Joseph Lawler, Edward Scott Wilson. BA in Classics magna cum laude, U. Dallas, 1976. Editl. writer The Greensboro (N.C.) Record, 1977-79; asst. editor editl. page Richmond (Va.) Times-Dispatch, 1979-81; spl. asst. to ambassadors Jeane Kirkpatrick & Edward Rowny U.S. Dept. of State, Washington, 1981-85, 86-91; speechwriter to Pres. The White House, Washington, 1991-92; budget & econ. policy advisor Office of U.S. Rep. Christopher Cox, Washington, 1993-94; comm. & policy dir. U.S. Senate Commerce Com., Washington, 1994-95; v.p., dir. media rels. Powell Tate, Washington, 1995-98; sr. v.p. The DCS Group, Washington, 1998—; bd. vis. Gerogetown U. Inst. Polit. Journalism, Washington, 1985, Inst. Comparative Polit. & Econ., 1983-84. Founder, chmn. Washington Cath. Forum, 1985; comm. advisor Rep. Nat. Conv., San Diego, 1996. Mem. U.S. Senat Press Secs. Assn., Cosmos Club. Roman Catholic. Home: 3632 Jenifer St NW Washington DC 20015 Office: The DCS Group 410 1st St SE Washington DC 20003

DUGGAN, KEVIN CHARLES, city manager; b. N.Y.C., May 25, 1950; s. Joseph Raymond and Doris Margaret (McCue) D.; m. M. Roberta Walker, Oct. 27, 1973; children: Julie Rebecca, Andrew Kevin. BA in Polit. Sci., San Jose State U., 1972, MPA, 1974. Adminstrv. intern City of Mountain View, Calif., 1971-72; city mgr. City of Mountain View, 1990—; adminstrv. intern City of Campbell, Calif., 1972-73; adminstrv. asst. City of Campbell, 1973-76, asst. city mgr., 1976-84, city mgr., 1984-90; polit. sci. lectr. San Jose State U., 1988. Author: (with others) Partnerships in Local Governance--Effective Council-Managers Relations, 1989; contbr. articles to profl. jours. Bd. dirs. State Bd. Fire Svcs., Sacramento, Calif., 1990-98, League Calif. Cities, Sacramento, 1991-96; mem. pres.'s adv. com. Foothill C.C., Los Altos Hills, Calif., 1996—; mem. pub. adminstrn. program adv. San Jose State U., 1994-97. Mem. ASPA (exec. bd. dirs. Santa Clara Valley chpt. 1993-94), Santa Clara County/City Mgrs. Assn. (pres. 1988). Democrat. Roman Catholic. Avocations: backpacking, furniture refinishing. Home: 1309 Brookdale Ave Mountain View CA 94040 Office: City of Mountain View 500 Castro St Mountain View CA 94041

DUGGAN, PATRICK JAMES, federal judge; b. 1933. BS in Econs., Xavier U., 1955; LLB, U. Detroit, 1958. Pvt. practice law Brashear, Duggan & Tangora, 1959-76; judge Wayne County Cir. Ct., 1977-86, U.S. Dist. Ct. (ea. dist.) Mich., Detroit, 1987—; adj. prof. Madonna U., Livonia, Mich., 1975-93. Chmn. Livonia Family YMCA, 1970-71; mem. bd. trustees Madonna U., 1970-79. Mem. Mich. Jaycees (pres. 1967-68). Office: US Dist Ct 251 Theodore Levin US Courthouse 231 W Lafayette Blvd Detroit MI 48226-2702*

DUGGER, JOE E., accountant; b. Tulsa. BS in Acctg., Okla. State U., 1978. CPA, Okla. Sr. audit mgr. Arthur Andersen & Co., Tulsa, 1979-90; contr. Liberty Glass Co., Sapulpa, Okla., 1990-94; controller Sammons Distbn. Inc., Dallas, 1994-97, v.p., CFO, 1997—. Bd. dirs., past chmn. Consumer Credit Counseling United Way Agy., Tulsa, 1984-96. Mem. AICPA's, Okla. Soc. CPA's, Fin. Execs. Inst. Office: Sammons Distbn Inc 3010 Lbj Fwy Ste 800 Dallas TX 75234-2707

DUGONI, ARTHUR A., orthodontics educator, university dean; b. San Francisco, June 29, 1925; s. Arthur B. and Lina Marie (Bianco) D.; m. Katherine Agnes Grou, Feb. 5, 1949; children: Steven, Michael, Russell, Mary, Diane, Arthur, James. DDS, Coll. Physicians and Surgeons, San Francisco, 1948; MSD, U. Wash., 1963; BS, Gonzaga U., 1986; DHL honoris causa, U. Detroit, 1997. Diplomate Am. Bd. Orthodontics (bd. dirs., pres. 1979-86). Clin. instr. operative dentistry Coll. Physicians and Surgeons, San Francisco, 1951-55, asst. clin. prof. operative dentistry, 1955-60, asst. clin. prof. orthodontics, 1963-64, chair dept. orthodontics, 1963-67; assoc. prof. orthodontics U. Pacific, San Francisco, 1966-77, prof., 1977—, dean sch. dentistry, 1978—; chair coun. deans Am. Assn. Dental Schs., Washington, 1985; active Pew Commn. for the Health Professions, 1993-96. Recipient award San Mateo County Dental Soc., 1971, Disting. Svc. award Pacific Coast Soc. Orthodontists, 1976, Disting. Practitioner award Nat. Acads. Practice Press Club, 1987, Hinman medallion, 1989, medallion of distinction U. Pacific, 1989, Orthodontic Edn. and Rsch. Found. disting. merit award, 1993, Albert H. Ketcham award Am. Bd. Orthodontics, 1994, Chmn.'s award Am. Dental Trade Assn., 1994, Dr. Irving E. Gruber award, 1997, List of Honor of FDI World Dental Fedn., 1998; named Person of Yr., South San Francisco, 1960, Alumnus of Yr., U. Pacific Sch. Dentistry, 1983, U. Wash., 1984, U. San Francisco, 1988, Gonzaga U., 1992, Gold medal Pierre Fauchard Acad., 1996. Fellow Am. Coll. Dentists, Internat. Coll. Dentists, Pierre Fauchard Acad., Acad. Dentistry Internat., Acad. Gen. Dentistry (hon. fellow 1992); mem. ADA (trustee 1984-87, treas. 1987-88, pres. 1988-89, Pres.'s citation 1994, Disting. Svc. award 1995), Fedn. Dentaire Internat. (councilor 1989-92, treas. 1992-98), Am. Assn. Dental Schs. (pres. 1995), Calif. Dental Assn. (pres. 1982-83), Concordia-Argonaut Club, Peninsula golf and Country Club, Omicron Kappa Upsilon, Tau Kappa Omega, Xi Psi Phi. Republican. Roman Catholic. Avocation: golf. Office: U of Pacific 2155 Webster St San Francisco CA 94115-2333

DUGUID, DOROTHY ANN RAMSEYER, artist; b. Bloomington, Ill., Nov. 8, 1924; d. Roy Arthur and Ruth Frances (Bodell) Ramseyer; m. James Mitchell Duguid, mar. 31, 1947; children: John Robinson, Robert Mitchell, Carol D. Hootman, Barbara P. Ungs. Student, U. Ill., Champaign, Coe Coll. Cert. tchr. Tchr. Jr. High Sch., San Antonio, Tex., Albuquerque; tchr. Urbana (Ill.) Jr. High; substitute tchr. Bloomington H.S. Mem. McLean County Weavers Guild, Bloomington - Normal Artists Guild, PEO, Margaret Fuller Club, Epsilon chpt. Kappa Kappa Gamma. Republican. Presbyterian. Avocation: piano.

DUGUNDJI, JOHN, aeronautical engineer; b. N.Y.C., Oct. 25, 1925; s. Basile and Rosa (Finale) D.; m. Wraye Polkey, July 25, 1965; children: Elenna Rose, Elisa Anthe. B.A.E., N.Y. U., 1944; M.S. in Aero. Engring, M.I.T., 1948, Sc.D. in Aero. Engring, 1951. Research engr. Grumman Aircraft Co., Bethpage, N.Y., 1948-49; dynamics engr. Republic Aviation Corp., Farmingdale, N.Y., 1951-56; research asso. M.I.T., 1956-57, asst. prof. aero. engring., 1957-62, asso. prof., 1962-70, prof., 1970-93, sr. lectr., 1993-99. Served with USN, 1944-46. Mem. AIAA, Sigma Xi, Tau Beta Pi. Greek Orthodox. Home: 39 Albert Ave Belmont MA 02478-4203 Office: MIT Dept Aeros & Astronautics Cambridge MA 02139

DUHAMEL, PIERRE ALBERT, English language professional; b. Putnam, Conn., Feb. 6, 1920; s. Albert and Rose (Comeau) D.; m. Helen L. Stowell, Sept. 4, 1943; 1 dau., Mary Elizabeth. A.B., Holy Cross Coll., 1941; M.A., Boston Coll., 1942; Ph.D., U. Wis., 1945. Prof. U. Chgo., 1945-49; prof. English Boston Coll., 1949-90, Philomatheia prof., 1954-90, prof. emeritus, 1991-99; vis. prof. U. Wis., 1947, 49; lit. editor Boston Herald Am., 1965-82; mem. Pulitzer Prize Jury, 1967-74, Nat. Book Awards Jury, 1973-74, Am. Book Awards, 1980, 81; Nat. Endowment for Humanities lectr. Boston Pub. Libr., 1976; mem. adv. bd. Assumption Coll., 1958-70. Moderator: TV program I've Been Reading, 1956-63; Author: Essays in American Catholic Tradition, 1960, Rhetoric, 1962, Persuasive Prose, 1963, Principles of Rhetoric, 1964, Literature: Form and Function, 1965, After Strange Fruit, 1980, also weekly columns, essays, book revs. Mem. AAUP (chpt. pres. 1949-56), Shakespeare Soc., Nat. Conf. Tchrs. English. Home: Saddle Ridge Rd Dover MA 02030 Office: Boston Coll Chestnut Hill MA 02167

DUHAMEL, RONALD J., Canadian government official. Sec. state, sci., R&D and Western Econ. Devel. Govt. of Can., Ottawa, Ont., Can. Office: Sci and Rsch Devel, 235 Queen St, Ottawa, ON Canada K1A 0H5

DUHE, JOHN MALCOLM, JR., judge; b. Iberia Parish, La., Apr. 7, 1933; s. J. Malcolm and Rita (Arnandez) D.; children: Kim Duhe Holleman, Jeanne Duhe Sinitier, Edward M., M. Bofill. Student Washington and Lee U., 1951-53, BBA, Tulane U., 1955, LLB, 1957. Atty. Helm, Simon, Caffery & Duhe, New Iberia, La., 1957-78; dist. judge State of La., New Iberia, 1979-84; judge U.S. Dist. Ct. (we. dist.) La., Lafayette, 1984-88; cir. judge, U.S. Ct. Appeals (5th cir.), Lafayette, 1988-99, sr. judge, 1999—. Assoc. editor Tulane Law Rev., 1956, editor-in-chief, 1967. Mem. Order Coif, Omicron delta Kappa, Kappa Delta Phi. Office: US Ct Appeals 556 Jefferson St Ste 200 Lafayette LA 70501-6945*

DUHIG, SUSAN C., English language and literature educator; b. Atlanta, June 27, 1963; d. James Joseph and Kay Elizabeth (Hudgins) D. BA in English lit. summa cum laude, Emory U., 1985; MA in English lit., Cornell U., 1990, PhD in English lit., 1994. Rsch. asst. Cornell U., Ithaca, N.Y., 1987-93, lectr., 1993-94, prof. English lang. and lit., 1994—; presenter in field. Harry S. Truman scholar, 1983, Robert T. Jones scholar, 1985-86; Sage fellow, 1986-87, Mellon fellow, 1991-92. Mem. MLA, N.Am. Soc. Study for Romanticism, Tchrs. for Dem. Culture, Marxist Lit. Group, Phi Beta Kappa. Office: Cornell U English Dept Goldwin Smith Hall Ithaca NY 14853

DUHL, LEONARD, psychiatrist, educator; b. N.Y.C., May 24, 1926; s. Louis and Rose (Josefsberg) D.; m. Lisa Shippee; children: Pamela, Nina, David, Susan, Aurora. BA, Columbia U., 1945; MD, Albany Med. Coll., 1948, postgrad., 1956-64. Diplomate Am. Bd. Psychiatry and Neurology (examiner 1977, 85). With USPHS, 1951-53, 54-72, med. dir., 1954-72; fellow Menninger Sch. Psychiatry Menninger Sch. Psychiatry, Winter VA Hosp., Topeka, 1949-51, resident psychiatry, 1953-54; asst. health officer Contra Costa County (Calif.) Health Dept., 1951-53; with USPHS, 1949-51, 53-54; psychiatrist profl. svcs. br., chief office planning NIMH, 1954-66; spl. asst. to sec. HUD, 1966-68; cons. Peace Corps, 1961-68; assoc. psychiatry George Washington Med. Sch., 1961-63, asst. clin. prof., 1963-68, assoc. prof., 1966-68; prof. public health Sch. Pub. Health U. Calif., Berkeley, 1968—; prof. city planning Coll. Environ. Design U. Calif., Berkeley, 1968-92; dir. dual degree program in health and med. scis. U. Calif., Berkeley, 1971-77; clin. prof. psychiatry U. Calif., San Francisco, 1969—; pvt. practice psychiatry Berkeley; sr. assoc. Youth Policy Inst., Washington; mem. sci. adv. coun. Calif. Legis., 1970-73, sr. cons. Assembly Office of Rsch., 1981-85; cons. Health Cities Program, Environ. Health, WHO, UNICEF, ICDC, Florence, Global Forum of Parliamentarians and Spititual Leaders, 1989-90, Ctr. for Fgn. Journalists, 1987-90, Am. Hosp. Assn. Health Rsch. and Edn. Trust, 1995—. Author: Approaches to Research in Mental Retardation, 1959, The Urban Condition, 1963, (with R.L. Leopold) Mental Health and Urban Social Policy, 1969, Health Planning and Social Change, 1986, Social Entrepreneurship of Change, 1990, 1995, Health and the City, 1993; bd. editors Jour. Community Psychology, 1974, Jour. Cmty. Mental Health, 1974—, Jour. Mental Health Consultation and Edn., 1978—, Jour. Prevention, 1978—, Nat. Civic Rev., 1991—; contbr. articles to tech. lit. Trustee Robert F. Kennedy Found., 1971-83; bd. dirs. Citizens Policy Ctr., San Francisco, 1975-85, New World Alliance, 1980-84, Calif. Inst. for Integral Studies, 1991-95, Ptnrs. for Dem. Change, 1990—; chair First Internat. Healthy Cities Conf., San Francisco, 1993; exec. trustee Nat. Inst. for Citizen Participation and Negotiation, 1988-90; trustee Menninger Found., Topeka, 1994—, bd. dirs., 1995—; bd. dirs. Louis August Jonas Found. (Camp Rising Sun), 1990—, Ctr. for Transcultural Studies, 1996—; exec. dir. Internat. Healthy Cities Found., 1993—. Recipient World Health Day award for Healthy Cities, WHO, 1996, Health Cities award for Coalition of Healthier Cities and Cmtys., 1999. Fellow Am. Psychiat. Assn. (life), Am. Coll. Psychiatry (life), No. Calif. Psychiat. Soc. (life), Group for Advancement in Psychiatry (chmn. com. preventive psychiatry 1962-66). Home: 639 Cragmont Ave Berkeley CA 94708-1329 Office: U Calif Sch Pub Health 410 Warren Hall Berkeley CA 94720

DUHL, MICHAEL FOSTER, lawyer; b. Chgo., July 12, 1944; s. Samuel Harold and Gertrude (Crodgen) D.; m. Judith Ann Currie, Jan. 30, 1970; children: Emilie Ann, Benjamin Currie. BBA, U. Mich., 1966; JD magna cum laude, Harvard U., 1969. Bar: Ill. 1969; CPA, Ill. Law clk. to presiding justice Ill. Supreme Ct., Chgo., 1969-70; assoc. Hopkins & Sutter, Chgo., 1971-75, ptnr., 1976-96; prin. Deloitte & Touche, L.L.P., Chgo., 1997—. Bd. editors Harvard Law Rev., 1967-69. Treas. Winnetka (Ill.) Pub. Libr. Dist. Bd., 1980-85; bd. dirs. Winnetka Hist. Soc., 1990-94, Winnetka Landmark Preservation Commn., 1992-96; bd. trustees Village of Winnetka, 1996—. Mem. ABA, Univ. Club Chgo. Jewish. Office: Deloitte & Touche LLP 2 Prudential Plz 180 N Stetson Ave Fl 19 Chicago IL 60601-6779*

DUHME, CAROL MCCARTHY, civic worker; b. St. Louis, Apr. 13, 1917; d. Eugene Ross and Louise (Roblee) McCarthy; m. Sheldon Ware, June 12, 1941 (dec. 1944); 1 child, David; m. H. Richard Duhme, Jr., Apr. 9, 1947; children: Benton (dec.), Ann, Warren (dec.). AB, Vassar Coll., 1939. Tchr. elem. sch., 1939-41, 42-44; moderator St. Louis Assn. Congl. Chs., 1952; dir. Christian edn. First Congl. Ch., St. Louis, 1959-62, trustee, 1964-66, mem. ch. coun., 1974-75, 84-85, 87-89, bd. deaconesses, 1978-81, bd. deacons, 1982-85, 92-95; chmn. bd. Christian Edn., 1987-88; former bd. dirs. Community Music Schs., St. Louis, Community Sch., Ch. Women United, John Burroughs Sch., St. Louis Bicentennial Women's Com., St. Louis Jr. League; pres. St. Louis Vassar Club; pres. bd. dirs. YWCA, St. Louis, 1973-76, chmn. ann. fund, 1989-90; bd. dirs. North Side Team Ministry, 1968-84, Chautauqua (N.Y.) Instn., 1971-79, mem. adv. coun. to bd., 1987—; adv. coun. Mo. Bapt. Hosp., 1973-89; exec. com. bd. dirs. Eden Theol. Sem., 1981-95, presdl. search com. 1986-87, 92-93, v.p. bd. dirs., 1991, chmn. 150th Anniversary com., 1996—; sec. bd. dirs. UN Assn., St. Louis, 1976-84, coun. of advisors, 1993—, nat. coun. 1995—; mem. nat. coun. UN-USA, 1995—; pres. bd. dirs. Family and Children's Svc. Greater St. Louis, 1977-79; mem. chancellor's long-range planning com. Washington U., 1980-81, mem. Nat. Coun., Sch. Social Work, 1987—; chmn. Benton Roblee Duhme Scholarship Fund; trustee Joseph H. and Florence A. Roblee Found., St. Louis, 1984—, pres., 1984-90, bd. dirs.; chmn. Chautaugua Bell Tower Scholarship Fund, 1961—; bd. dirs. Nat. Inland Waterways Libr., St. Louis Merc. Libr. Mem. corp. assembly Blue Cross Hosp. Svc. of Mo., 1978-86. Recipient Mary Alice Messerley award for volunteerism Health and Welfare Coun. St. Louis, 1971; Vol. of Yr. award, YWCA, 1976; Woman of Achievement award St. Louis Globe Democrat, 1980; Outstanding Lay Woman nomination Mo. United Ch. of Christ, 1991; Outstanding Alumna award John Burroughs Sch., 1992. Home: 8 Edgewood Rd Saint Louis MO 63124-1817

DUHME, H(ERMAN) RICHARD, JR., sculptor, educator; b. St. Louis, May 31, 1914; s. Herman Richard and Ruth Frances (Leggat) D.; m. Carol Louise McCarthy, Apr. 9, 1947; children: David W., Benton Roblee (dec. 1971), Ann Duhme Welker, Warren L. (dec. 1990). Student, Pa. Acad. Fine Arts, 1932-38, U. Pa., 1934, Am. Sch. Classical Studies, Athens, Greece, 1951; B.F.A., Washington U., St. Louis, 1953. Prof. sculpture Washington U., St. Louis, 1947-82, prof. emeritus, 1982—; head sculpture dept. Chautauqua Instn. Summer Sch., 1953-85, Syracuse U. Chautauqua Center, 1953-69. Numerous sculpture commns. including St. Martin and the Beggar, Episcopal Cathedral, Erie, Pa., Lion Cub Fountain, Mycenae, Greece, Bears, Washington U., St. Louis, Busts, John Horan, Merck Chem. Co., Rahway, N.J., George Kassabaum, St. Louis, Dr. Koici Iwadare, Tokyo, Dr. William H. Danforth, St. Louis, others. Served with USAAF, 1942-46. Decorated Bronze Stars; designed medals Shepherd's award Nat. Coun. Chs., Mo. Sesquicentennial, Chatutauqua Centennial, Dr. Evarts A Graham medal, Christi Vivit medal Concordia Sem., others. Fellow Nat. Sculpture Soc.; mem. Allied Artists Am., Lauderdale Yacht Club, Town Club (Jamestown, N.Y.), St. Louis Country Club, Univ. Club. Home: 8 Edgewood Rd Saint Louis MO 63124-1817 Office: Sculpture Dept Washington U Saint Louis MO 63130 *I feel that an artist's life and work is of no importance unless it touches those around him and gives pleasure, help, or increased knowledge and enrichment in so doing. I have tried to remember this in creating my sculpture and in my contacts with my students.*

DUHNKE, ROBERT EMMET, JR., retired aerospace engineer; b. Manitowoc, Wis., Jan. 28, 1935; s. Robert Emmet and Vivian Dorothy (Abel) D.; m. Patricia R. Ebben, 1956 (div. 1972); children: Kim Marie, Lori Ann, Dawn Diane, Robert III, Mary Lynn; m. Judy Anne Lind, Feb. 14, 1978. BS in Aero. Engring., Purdue U., 1957. Assoc. engr. Convair/Aerodyns. Group, Pomona, Calif., 1957-58; assoc. engr., instr. Boeing Co., Seattle, 1964-66, instr. maintenance tng., 1972-83, navigation sys. analyst, 1983-90, sr. specialist engr., instr. comml. maintenance tng. ctr., 1990-95; flight navigator Flying Tigers, San Francisco, 1966-68; salesman various real estate and ins. cos., Seattle, 1968-72; shuttler Hertz, Seattle, 1996-97; reservation sales agt. Alaska Airlines, Phoenix, 1997—; contract aerospace engr. Superior Design Co., Inc., Kirkland, Wash., 1996—. Author poems in English, German, French and Spanish. Sponsor World Vision, Pasadena, Calif.; mem. Citizens Against Govt. Waste. Capt. USAF, 1958-64. Recipient Hon. Freedom Fighter award Afghan Mercy Fund, 1987. Mem. Inst. Navigation, Air Force Assn. Avocations: sailing, fishing, biking, German, Spanish and French language studies. Home: 1219 30th St NE Auburn WA 98002-2471 also: 30 W Carter Dr Apt 19-206 Tempe AZ 85282-7712

DUHON, DAVID LESTER, business educator, management consultant; b. Crowley, La., Oct. 21, 1948; s. J. Lester and Winona Faye Duhon; m. Roxanne Istre, Jan. 25, 1970; children: Jonathan, Leah, Sarah. BS in Bus., U. Southwestern La., 1970; MBA, La. State U., 1975, PhD in Mgmt., 1981. Instr. mgmt. La. State U., Baton Rouge, 1978-80; from asst. prof. to assoc. prof. U. Southwestern La., Lafayette, 1980-88, petroleum land mgmt. coord., 1981-88; from asst. prof. to assoc. prof. U. So. Miss., Hattiesburg, 1988—, dir. external rels. Coll. Bus., 1995—; cons. Jaws Offshore, Lafayette, 1984-88, Continuing Edn. U. So. Miss., Hattiesburg, 1988—, Miss. Personnel Bd., Jackson, 1990—, Pine Belt Mental Health, hattiesburg, 1992-98; interim chair divsn. bus. U. S. Miss. - Gulf Coast, Long Beach, 1996-97; vis. lectr. Ecole Superieure de Commerce, Fontainbleu, France, 1997, 98. Contbr. articles to profl. jours. Chair fin. com. Ch. of the Nazarene, Hattiesburg, 1992-99, chair lay retreat com., Jackson, 1994-96; pres. faculty senate, U. So. Miss., Hattiesburg, 1997-98, co-chair United Way campaign, 1998-99. Summer Instrn. grantee U. So. Miss., 1992, 95. Fellow E./W. Centre-Honolulu; mem. Area Devel. Partnership, Acad. Mgmt., Allied Acads., So. Mgmt. Assn. Republican. Avocations: reading, traveling, hunting, fishing. E-mail: duhon@cba.edu. Home: 2264 Old Hwy 24 Hattiesburg MS 39402

DUIGAN, JOHN, film director; b. Hartley Wintney, Hampshire, Eng., June 19, 1949. MA in Philosophy, U. Melbourne, Australia, 1973. Faculty U. Melbourne, Latrobe U. Dir., writer exptl. short: The Firm Man, 1974; novels include: Badge, Players, Room to Move; dir., writer (films) The Trespassers, 1976, Mouth to Mouth, 1978, Winter of our Dreams, 1981 (Australian Writers Guild award), Far East, 1983, One Night Stand, 1984, Room to Move, 1985, The Year My Voice Broke (Australian Acad. Awards for best dir. and best screenplay, Australian Writers Guild best screenplay), Flirting, 1990, Sirens (also actor), 1994; dir.: (films) Dimboola, 1979, Wide Sargasso Sea, 1993, The Journey of August King, The Leading Man, 1996, Lawn Dogs, 1997, Molly, 1999; co-dir. TV mini-series Vietnam, (film) Fragments of War: The Story of Damien Parer, co-writer: Australian Penguin TV Awd., best dir., Byron Kennedy Awd. for contribution to Australian Cinema.

DUING, EDNA IRENE, women's health nurse, nurse educator; b. Crystal City, Mo., July 11, 1959; d. Edwin Fred Duing and Ann Marie (Duro) Ems; m. James Roger Davis, June 19, 1982; children: April Ann Rena Duing-Davis, Sarah Elizabeth Duing-Davis, Kenneth Alexander Duing-Davis. BA in History, S.E. Mo. State U., 1981, BSN, 1994; ADN, Jefferson Coll., 1989. RN, Mo.; cert. obstetric nurse, ACLS, pediat. ACLS. Ob/gyn staff nurse Jefferson Meml. Hosp., Crystal City, 1989-95; obstet. nursing instr. St. Louis Coll. Health Careers, 1995; home care nurse Washington County Meml. Hosp. Home Health Agy., Potosi, Mo., 1996—; 1st aid, CPR instr. ARC, 1987—, flood shelter nurse, Festus and Crystal City, Mo., 1993. 1st lt. USAF, 1982-86. Mem. Mo. Perinatal Assn., La Leche League Internat., Amvets, Order of Ea. Star. Mem. Christian Ch. (Disciples of Christ). Avocations: swimming, camping, scuba diving, travel, horseback riding. Home: Rt 1 Box 1837 Cadet MO 63630 Office: Washington County Meml Hosp Home Health Agy 300 Health Way Dr Potosi MO 63664-1420

DUITMAN, LOIS ROBINSON, artist, writer; b. Green Bay, Wis.; m. Rock Duitman; children: Christine M. Bomgardner, Brian R. Plog. Student, Art Student's League, N.Y., Women's U. of The Philippines, Manila, Baylor U., Waco, TX, Orange Coast Coll., Saddleback Coll., CA. Chief copywriter J.C. Penney's, L.A.; asst. editor Calif. Girl Mag., L.A.; tchr. art workshop Pepperdine U., Calif. One woman shows include Palm Harbor, Fla., Spearfish State Teachers' Coll., S. Dak., Roswell Art Mus., State Art Mus. of Santa Fe, Hawaii, 1984, Clearwater, Jacksonville, Dunedin, Sarasota, 1991-97, St. Petersburg, Fla., Rio Rancho (N.Mex.) Country Club, 1997; exhibited in group shows at State Art Mus. of Santa Fe, (award), Natl. Art Gallery of The Philippines, Manila, Jehinger Art Gallery, Bombay, Roswell Art Mus., State Art Mus., Santa Fe, N.Mex., numerous others, India, Mex.; painted in Spain, Portugal, France, Aden, Jamaica, The Bahamas, Africa, P.R., Germany, Singapore, Mozambique, others. Mem. Internat. Soc. Marine Painters, N.Mex. Watercolor Soc., N. Mex. Art League, N. Mex., West Mesa Woman's Club. Avocations: skiing, tennis, swimming, biking, bowling. Home: 64 Parkside Rd SE Rio Rancho NM 87124-3983

DUJACK, STEPHEN RAYMOND, editor; b. N.Y.C., Apr. 7, 1953; s. Raymond Leon and Inge (Wassermann) D. BA, Princeton U., 1976. Assoc. editor Princeton (N.J.) Alumni Weekly, 1976-80; graphic artist Forte, Inc., Alexandria, Va., 1980-81; editor Fgn. Svc. Jour., dir. comms. Am. Fgn. Svc. Assn., Washington, 1981-88; dir. comms. Worldwatch Inst., Washington, 1988-90, Environ. Law Inst., Washington, 1990—; lectr. George Washington U., Washington, 1983-88. Editor: The Environ.. Forum, 1990—; contbr. articles on pub. policy to The Washington Post, The New Republic, The Christian Sci. Monitor, Gannett Syndicate, L.A. Times Syndicate. Recipient Allen Furniss award Daily Princetonian, Princeton, 1976; Best Feature Article, Soc. Nat. Assn. Publs., 1983, Best Spl Issue, 1983, Most Improved Mag., 1992, Best Ann. Report, 1994, 96, 1st pl. Master's Divsn., S.W. Airlines Biathlon Series, 1994. Office: Environ Law Inst 1616 P St NW Ste 200 Washington DC 20036-1423 *Honor is the central principle of a moral life.*

DUJARDIN, RICHARD CHARLES, journalist; b. Queens, N.Y., Dec. 20, 1944; s. Julien Camille and Veronica (Venesoen) D.; m. Rosemarie Catherine Levesque, Jan. 20, 1947; children: Julianne, Peter, Philip, Joelle, Jean-Paul, Jeffrey. BA in Comm. Arts, Fordham U., 1966. Reporter Providence Jour.-Bulletin, 1966-68, 71-75, bureau mgr., 1975-77, religion writer, 1977—. V.p. Action for Franco-Ams. in N.E., 1991-93, dir., 1986-94; dist. pres. Union St. Jean Baptiste, 1990-94. Lt. (j.g.) USN, 1968-71. Recipient Wilbur award Religious Pub. Rels. Coun., 1986, 91, 95. Mem. Religion Newswriters Assn. (treas. 1989-90, v.p. 1990-94, pres. 1994-96, Supple Meml. award 1986, Templeton Reporter of Yr. award 1991). Roman Catholic. Home: 129 Hillside Ave Providence RI 02906-2900 Office: Providence Jour-Bulletin 75 Fountain St Providence RI 02902-0050

DUJON, DIANE MARIE, director, activist; b. Boston, Dec. 29, 1946; d. Alfred and Agnes C. (Hall) White; 1 child, Lisa M. Dujon. BA, U. Mass., 1983, MS, 1996. Asst. dir. assessment Coll. Pub. and Cmty. Svc. U. Mass., Boston, 1984-93, co-dir. assessment Coll. Pub. and Cmty. Svc., 1993-97, dir. independent learning Coll. Pub. and Cmty. Svc., 1997—. Co-editor: For Crying Out Loud: Women's Poverty in U.S., 1996 (Myers Ctr. for the Study of Human Rights in N.Am. Outstanding Book award 1997); prodr. (radio documentary) Workfare: Anatomy of a Policy, 1982 (Alice award 1982), Nat. Commn. on Working Women. V.p. Survivors, Inc., Boston, 1986—. Recipient Earl Douglas award City Mission Soc., 1987; named Unsung Heroine Rosie's Place, 1997. Mem. Nat. Welfare Rights Union, Mass. AFL-CIO (mem. exec. women's com. 1997), U. Mass. Profl. Staff Union (bd. mem. chpt. Svc. Employees Internat. Union, Local 509). Baptist. Office: U Mass/Boston 100 Morrissey Blvd Boston MA 02125-3300

DUKE, ANTHONY DREXEL, sociologist, educator, philanthropist; b. N.Y.C., July 28, 1918; s. Angier Buchanan and Cordelia (Biddle) D.; children by previous marriage: Anthony D. Jr., Nicholas R., Cordelia Duke Jung, Josephine Duke Brown, December Duke McSherry, John O., Douglas D.; m. Maria Luly de Lourdes Alcebo, Sept. 27, 1975; children: Lulita C., Washington A., James B. Student, Princeton U., 1941; DHL (hon.), Adelphi Coll., 1957, L.I. U., 1988, Drexel U., 1991. With Import Export Co., 1946-50; prin. A.D. Duke Realty, Inc., 1955-65; chmn. bd. dirs., pres., founder Boys Harbor Inc., 1937—. Trustee Big Brother Movement, 1951-63; past trustee Henry St. Settlement, N.Y.C.; del. Internat. Conf. Pvt. Sector Initiatives, 1986; hon. commr. Manhattan Borough Projects, 1954-57, Civic Affairs and Pub. Events, N.Y.C.; mem. N.Y.C. Youth Bd., 1955-58; rep. Internat. Rescue Com., Vietnam War, Meriel refugee crisis Cuba, 1983; active Save the Children, Pomfret Sch., Duke U., U.S. Naval Acad. Lt. comdr. USNR, 1941-46, PTO, ATO, ETO. Decorated Bronze Star. Recipient Town and Country Most Generous Am. award 1988, Save the Children award, 1977; Presdl. citation for pvt. sector commendation, 1986, Citation for Promotion of Human Welfare Commonwealth of Mass., 1987. Mem. Bodman and Achelis Found., Nat. Com. on Am. Fgn. Policy, Maidstone Club (former gov.), Piping Rock (former gov.), River Club, Racquet and Tennis Club, Beaver Dam Club. Home: PO Box 177 East Hampton NY 11937-0177 Office: Boys Harbor Inc 1 E 104th St New York NY 10029-4495

DUKE, BILL, film director, actor; b. Poughkeepsie, N.Y., Feb. 26, 1943. Student, Boston U., NYU Sch. Arts. Actor (pictures): Car Wash, American Gigolo, Commando, Predator, No Man's Land, Action Jackson, Bird on a Wire, Street of No Return, Menace II Society, (TV) Love is Not Enough, Sgt. Matiovich Vs the U.S. Air Force, (series) Palmerstown U.S.A.; dir. (films): Johnnie Mae Gison: FBI, 1986, A Rage in Harlem, 1991, Deep Cover, 1992, The Cemetery Club, 1993, Sister Act II, 1993, (series) A Man Called Hawk, Cagney & Lacey, Hill Street Blues, Miami Vice, Dallas, (spls.) The Killing Floor, A Raisin in the Sun, The Meeting. Recipient Best Young Dir. award for short The Hero, Am. Film Inst. (Gold award Houston Film Festival). Mem. Am. Film Inst. (bd. dirs.).

DUKE, CHARLES BRYAN, research and development manufacturing executive, physics educator; b. Richmond, Va., Mar. 13, 1938; s, Charles Joseph Jr. and Virginia (Welton) D.; m. Ann Evans, July 1, 1961; children: Amy Dickerson, Emily Elizabeth. BS in Math., Duke U., 1959; PhD in Physics, Princeton U., 1963. Staff corp. rsch. GE, Schenectady, N.Y., 1963-69, cons., 1969-72; prof. of physics U. Ill., Urbana, 1969-72; mgr., sr. fellow Xerox Corp., Webster, N.Y., 1972-88; dep. dir., chief scientist Battelle Pacific Northwest Div., Richland, Wash., 1988-89; sr. rsch. fellow Xerox Corp., Webster, N.Y., 1989-96, v.p., sr. rsch. fellow, 1996—; bd. govs. Am. Inst. Physics, N.Y.C., 1976-82, 84-87; adj. prof. physics, U. Rochester (N.Y.), 1972-88; affiliate prof. physics, U. Wash., Seattle, 1988-89; gen. chmn. Phys. Electronics Conf., 1997—. Author: Tunneling in Solids, 1969, Surface Science: The First Thirty Years, 1994, Color Systems Integration, 1998; editor-in-chief Jour. Materials Rsch., 1985-86, Surface Sci., 1992—; contbr. over 350 articles to profl. jours. Named one of 1000 Most Cited Scientists, Inst. for Sci. Info., 1981. Fellow IEEE, Am. Phys. Soc. (councillor 1995-98, exec. bd. 1997-98), Am. Vacuum Soc. (hon. mem., bd. dirs. 1973-76, 78-80, pres. 1979, M.W. Welch award in vacuum sci. and tech. 1977); mem. NAE, Materials Rsch. Soc. (councillor 1988-90, 95-97, treas. 1991-92). Office: Xerox Wilson Ctr for R & T 800 Phillips Rd # 114-38D Webster NY 14580-9720

DUKE, CHARLES RICHARD, academic dean; b. West Stewartstown, N.H., July 6, 1940; s. George Tunicliffe and Evelyn Agnes (Murray) D.; m. Leona Ruth Hubbard, June 1, 1983. BE, Plymouth (N.H.) State Coll., 1962; MA, Middlebury (Vt.) Coll., 1968; PhD, Duke U., 1972. Tchr. English, head dept. Sunapee (N.H.) High Sch., 1962-68; prof. English Plymouth State Coll., 1968-78, Murray (Ky.) State U., 1978-84; prof., head dept. secondary edn. Utah State U., Logan, 1984-89; dean Coll. Edn. and Human Svcs. Clarion (Pa.) U., 1989-94; dean Coll. Edn. Appalachian State U., Boone, N.C., 1995—; dir. West Ky. Writing Project, 1980-84; co-dir. Utah Writing Project, 1984-89, Clarion U. Student Literacy Corps, 1990-94. Author: Creative Dramatics and English Teaching, 1974, Writing Through Sequence, 1983, Strategies for Teaching, 1987; contbr. articles to profl. jours.; editor: Exercise Exchange, 1979—, Poets Perspectives, 1992. Am. Studies fellow Coe Found., 1964; recipient Alumni Outstanding Svc. award Plymouth State Coll., 1977. Mem. ASCD, Internat. Reading Assn., Nat. Coun. Tchrs. English, Am. Assn. Colls. Tchr. Edn., Assn. Tchr. Educators, Phi Delta Kappa. Office: Appalachian State U PO Box 32038 Boone NC 28608-2038

DUKE, DONALD NORMAN, publisher; b. L.A., Apr. 1, 1929; s. Roger V. and Mabel (Weineger) D. BA in Ednl. Psychology, Colo. Coll., 1951. Comml. photographer Colorado Springs, Colo., 1951-53; pub. rels. Gen. Petroleum, L.A., 1954-55; agt. Gen. S.S. Corp., Ltd., 1956-57; asst. mgr. retail advt., sales promotion Mobil Oil Co., 1958-63; pub. Golden West Books, Alhambra, Calif., 1964—; dir. Pacific R.R. Publs., Inc., Athletic Press; pub. relations cons. Santa Fe Ry., 1960-70. Author: The Pacific Electric: A History of Southern California Railroading, 1958, Southern Pacific Steam Locomotives, 1962, Santa Fe...Steel Rails to California, 1963, Night Train, 1961, American Narrow Gauge, 1978, RDC: the Budd Rail Diesel Car, 1989, The Brown Derby, 1990, Camp Cajon, 1991, Fred Harvey: Civilizer of the American West, 1994, editor: Water Trails West, 1977, Branding Iron, 1988-91, Santa Fe...The Railroad Gateway to the American West, Vol. 1, 1995, Vol. 2, 1997, Incline Railways of Los Angeles and Southern California, 1998, Electric Railroads of San Francisco Bay, Vols. 1 and 2, 1999. Recipient Spur award for Trails of the Iron Horse Western Writers Am., 1975. Mem. Ry. and Locomotive Hist. Soc. (dir. 1944-98), Western History Assn., Newcomen Soc., Lexington Group of Transp. History, Western Writers Am., P.E.N. Internat. (v.p. 1975-77), Authors Guild Am., Book Pubs. Assn. So. Calif. (dir. 1968-77), Cal. Writers Guild (dir. 1976-77), Calif. Book Pubs. Assn. (dir. 1976-77), Westerners Internat. (hon., editor Branding Iron 1971-80, 88-91), Hist. Soc. So. Calif. (dir. 1972-75), Henry E./Arabella Huntington Soc., Kappa Sigma (lit. editor Caduceus 1968-80). Home: PO Box 80250 San Marino CA 91118-8250 Office: Golden West Books 525 N Electric Ave Alhambra CA 91801-2032

DUKE, ELLEN KAY, community activist, trainer; b. Indpls., June 7, 1952; d. Richard Thomas and Ruby Mae (Wright) D. Student Chapman Coll., Orange, Calif., 1972; BS in Pub. Affairs, Ind. U.-Bloomington, 1975; postgrad. Portland State U., 1980-81; MPA Calif. State U., 1998. Cert. playground safety specialist/inspector. Cert. Dale Carnegie Pub. Speaking Instr., 1987-93; News reporter, Salem Statesman, Corvallis, Oreg., 1976-78; com. adminstr. Oreg. State Legislature, Salem, 1979-80; pub. involvement coord. Met. Regional Svc. Dist., Portland, 1981-82; account mgr. Thunder & Visions, Portland, 1982-83; project asst. Amdahl Corp., Sunnyvale, Calif., 1983-84; spl. project coord. Computerland Corp., Hayward, Calif., 1984-89; prodr., lead facilitator Sage, Inc., Walnut Creek, Calif., 1982—; loan broker Capital Trust Mortgage, Campbell, Calif., 1994—; pub. rels. dir. local YMCA. Co-author: (ednl. film) Communication Skills, 1975. Chairperson Corvallis Budget Commn., Oreg., 1978; commr. Hayward Library, Calif., 1985—, Alameda County Consumer Affairs, Oakland, 1985; rep. Nat. Democratic Conv., N.Y.C., 1982. Named Able Toastmaster Toastmasters Internat., 1981; grad. Leadership Oakland, 1991. Mem. NAFE, ASTD, Pub. Rels. Soc. Am., Sierra Club (San Francisco). Office: We Build Playgrounds 1997 1st Ave Walnut Creek CA 94596-2540

DUKE, GARY JAMES, electronics executive; b. Norman, Ark., Aug. 3, 1947; s. Arley Matthew and Evelyn Ethia (Cogburn) D.; m. Evonne Pearson, Oct. 7, 1966; children: Arlon Matthew, Anton Lee, Angela Michelle. Student, U. Ark., Little Rock, 1969-70. With Diebold Inc., 1970—; dist. mgr. Diebold Inc., San Antonio, 1974-75, Charleston, W.Va., 1975-76; area tech. specialist Diebold Inc., Little Rock, 1976; tech. mgr. south cen. area Diebold Inc., Memphis, 1977-87; tech. mgr. southwestern area Diebold Inc., Dallas, 1988; tech. mgr. so. div. Diebold Inc., Atlanta, 1988-90; customer svc. mgr. Diebold Inc., Memphis, 1990—; mem. gen. adv. coun. State Tech. Inst. at Memphis, 1984-86; mem. Tenn. Gov.'s Task Force, 1984; v.p.-employer Tenn. Coll. Placement Assn., 1985. Contbr. articles to various publs. Brotherhood dir. 1st Bapt. Ch., Collierville, Tenn., 1985-88, Shelby Bapt. Assn., Memphis, 1987-88; v.p. Bapt. Men, Tenn. Bapt. Brotherood, 1987-88. Sgt. USMC, 1965-69. Recipient honor award Armed Forces Communications and Electronics Assn., 1966, Exceptional Svc. award State Tech. Inst. at Memphis, 1985. Avocations: computers, data communications. Home: 1213 Greenview Rd Collierville TN 38017-1161 Office: Diebold Inc 3895 Vantech Dr Ste 9 Memphis TN 38115-5938

DUKE, GEORGE WESLEY, financial executive; b. Nashville, Dec. 27, 1953; s. Harold Wesley and Justine Hope (Perry) D.; m. Lucy Neale; children: Elizabeth, Margaret, Hope. BBA, Coll. William and Mary, 1976; M Taxation, Va. Commonwealth U., 1981; MBA, Darden Sch., 1983; MEd, Vanderbilt U., 1989; M of Liberal Arts, Johns Hopkins U., 1992. CPA, Va. Acct. KPMG Peat Marwick, Richmond, Va., 1976-81; v.p. Jacques-Miller, Nashville, 1983-86; sr. v.p. Alex Brown Kleinwort Benson, Balt., 1986-94; prin. LaSalle Ptnrs. (formerly Alex Brown Kleinwort Benson), Balt., 1994-99, Jones Lang LaSalle, Inc. (formerly LaSalle Ptnrs.), Balt., 1999—. Mem. AICPA, Pension Real Estate Assn., Ctr. Club, Darden Sch. Alumni Assn. (past pres. alumni bd.). Office: Jones Lang LaSalle Inc 100 E Pratt St Baltimore MD 21202-1009

DUKE, MICHAEL B., aerospace scientist; b. L.A., Dec. 1, 1935; s. Leon and Eva (Siegel) D.; m. Julia Elizabeth Bartram, 1958 (div. 1966); children: Lisa, Stuart; m. Mary Carolyn Creamer, July 17, 1967; children: Kenneth, Donna. BS Geology, Calif. Inst. Tech., 1957, MS Geochemistry, 1961, PhD Geochemistry, 1963. Rsch. scientist U.S. Geol. Survey, Washington, 1963-70; lunar sample curator NASA, Houston, 1970-77, chief solar system exploration div., 1977-90, dep. for sci., moon/Mars exploration, 1990-95; sr. project coord. Lunar & Planetary Inst., Houston, 1995—; adv. manned space exploration. Organizer: Lunar Bases Symposia, 1984-88; contbr. articles to profl. jours. Adult leader Boy Scouts Am. Houston, 1980-90. Recipient Nininger Meteorite award, 1963, Presdl. Meritorious award, 1988. Fellow AIAA (Space Sci. award 1991), AAAS, Meteoritical Soc.; mem. Internat. Acad. Astronautics, Geol. Soc. Washington (D.C.). Office: Lunar & Planetary Inst Houston TX 77058

DUKE, PATTY (ANNA MARIE DUKE), actress; b. N.Y.C., Dec. 14, 1946; d. John P. and Frances (McMahon) Duke; m. John Astin, 1973 (div. 1985); children: Sean, Mackenzie; m. Michael Pierce, March 15, 1986. Grad., Quintano's School for Young Profls. Pres. SAG, 1985-88, lectr. Am. Film Inst., 1988. TV appearances include Armstrong Circle Theatre, 1955, The SS Andrea Doria, The Prince and the Pauper, 1957, Wuthering Heights, 1958, U.S. Steel Hour, 1959, Meet Me in St. Louis, 1959, Swiss Family Robinson, 1958, The Power and the Glory, 1961, All's Fair, 1981-82; (series) The Brighter Day, 1957, Kitty Foyle, 1958, Patty Duke Show, 1963-66, It Takes Two, 1982-1983, Hail to the Chief, 1985, Karen's Song, 1987; (TV films) The Big Heist, 1957, My Sweet Charlie, 1970 (Emmy award 1970), Two on a Bench, If Tomorrow Comes, 1971, She Waits, Deadly Harvest, 1972, Nightmare, 1972, Look What's Happened to Rosemary's Baby, 1976, Fire!, 1976, Rosetti and Ryan: Men Who Love Women, Curse of the Black Widow, Killer on Board, The Storyteller, 1977, Having Babies III, Captain and the Kings, 1977 (Emmy award 1977), A Family Upside Down, 1978, Women in White, Hanging By A Thread, Before and After, The Miracle Worker, 1979 (Emmy award 1980), The Women's Room, Mom, The Wolfman and Me, The Babysitter, 1980, Violation of Sarah McDavid, Please, Don't Hit Me Mom, 1981, Something So Right 1982, September Gun, 1983, Best Kept Secrets, 1984, George Washington: The Forging of a Nation, 1984, A Time To Triumph, 1986, Fight for Life, 1987, Perry Mason: The Case of the Avenging Angel, Fatal Judgement, 1988, Everybody's Baby: The Rescue of Jessica McClure, Amityville: The Evil Escapes, 1989, Call Me Anna, 1990, Always Remember I Love You, 1990, Absolute Strangers, 1991, Last Wish, 1992, Grave Secrets: The Legacy of Hilltop Drive, 1992, A Killer Among Friends, 1992, A Family of Strangers, 1993, Cries From the Heart, 1994, One Woman's Courage, 1994, When the Vows Break, 1995, To Face Her Past, 1996, Race Against Time: The Search for Sarah, 1996, The Disappearing Act, 1997, A Christmas Memory, 1997; (theatre) The Miracle Worker, 1959-61, Isle of Children, 1962; motion picture appearances in I'll Cry Tomorrow, 1955, The Goddess, 1958, Happy Anniversary, The 4-D Man, 1959, The Miracle Worker, 1962 (Acad. award as best supporting actress 1962), Billie, 1965, Valley of the Dolls, 1967, Me, Natalie, 1969 (Golden Globe award as best actress 1970), The Swarm, 1978, Something Special, 1987, Prelude to a Kiss, 1992; co-author Surviving Sexual Assault, 1983, Call Me Anna, 1987, A Brilliant Madness: Living with Manic-Depressive Illness, 1992. Nat. corp. council Muscular Dystrophy Assns. Am. Recipient Emmy Awards, 1964, 69, 76, 79. Mem. AFTRA. Office: William Morris Agy 151 S El Camino Dr Beverly Hills CA 90212-2775*

DUKE, PAUL ROBERT, lawyer; b. Phila., Mar. 1, 1929; s. Robert James and Sara Mary (Dougherty) D.; m. Cecilia Mary McCann, Aug. 8, 1953; children: Paul R. Jr., Michael C., Thomas J., Kathleen M., Kevin E., Robert James III, Mary Beth, John P. AB magna cum laude, St. Joseph's U., 1950; LLB cum laude, U. Pa., 1953. Bar: Pa. 1954, D.C. 1976. Law clk. to presiding justice Pa. Supreme Ct., 1955-56; asst. solicitor Pa. R.R., Phila., 1956-59, asst. gen. solicitor, 1959-65; asst. gen. counsel Pa. Cen. Transp. Co., Phila., 1965-71, gen. reorgn. counsel, 1971-73, gen. counsel, 1973-75, v.p. law, 1975-76; ptnr. Covington & Burling, Washington, 1976—. Mem. Del. County Rep. Exec. Com., Pa., 1960-64; Del. County Home Rule Study Commn., 1973-76. Served to 1st lt. Med. Service Corps., AUS, 1953-55. Mem. D.C. Bar Assn., Phila. Bar Assn. Roman Catholic. Home: 4300 Sunflower Dr Rockville MD 20853-1464 Office: Covington & Burling 1201 Pennsylvania Ave NW PO Box 7566 Washington DC 20044-7566

DUKE, PHYLLIS LOUISE KELLOGG HENRY, school administrator, management consultant; b. Mason City, Iowa, May 3, 1932; d. Wilbur Rhode and Dorothy Margaret (Bauer) Kellogg; children—Curtis Dean Henry, Catherine Rose Henry Jones, David Russell Henry. A.A. in Elem. Teaching, U. No. Iowa, 1953; B.A. Calif. State U.-Los Angeles, 1963, M.A., 1968. Cert. elem. tchr., cert. reading specialist, sch. adminstrn. credential. Tchr., Arlington pub. schs., Iowa, 1951-52, St. Louis Park pub. schs., Minn., 1953-55; tchr., supr. ABC Sch. Dist., Cerritos, Calif., 1963-69; cons. in reading State Dept. of Calif., Sacramento, 1969-70; cons. in edn. Orange County Dept. Edn., Santa Ana, Calif., 1970-75; sch. adminstr. Oakwood Acad., Long Beach, Calif., 1975—; chmn. bd. dirs. New City Bank, Orange, Calif.; cons. in field. Author: Song of Sounds, 1969; (with others) Beginnings for Christian Schools, 1976. Conf. coordinator State Dept. Edn., Calif., Sacramento, Santa Barbara, 1970 (Outstanding Leadership award 1974-75). Mem. Nat. Ind. Pvt. Sch. (v.p. 1982-83, dir. seminars 1983), Pre-Sch. Assn. Calif. (legis. chair 1978-84), Reading Specialists Calif. (pres. 1970-73). Republican. Avocations: skiing; scuba diving; painting; photography; travel. Home: 1208 S Lemon Ave Walnut CA 91789-4822 Office: Oakwood Acad 2951 N Long Beach Blvd Long Beach CA 90806-1532

DUKE, ROBERT DOMINICK, mining executive, lawyer; b. Goshen, N.Y., Oct. 14, 1928; s. Robert DeWitt and Elma Christina (Dominick) D.; m. Jeannette Parham, Apr. 24, 1954; children: Katherine Campbell, Robert Dominick, Peter Benjamin DeWitt, Lois Christina. B.A., Va. Mil. Inst., 1947; LL.B., Yale U., 1950; M.B.A., U. Pa., 1952. Bar: N.Y. 1950, Conn. 1989. With Cravath, Swaine & Moore, N.Y.C., 1951-52, 54-64, Freeport-McMoRan Inc. and predecessors, N.Y.C., 1964-84; gen. counsel Freeport-McMoRan Inc. and predecessors, 1970-84, sr. v.p., 1973-84; sr. v.p., gen. counsel The Pittston Co., Stamford, Conn., 1984-93, sr. counsel, 1993—, also bd. dirs., 1991-93. Served as 1st lt. JAGC, U.S. Army, 1952-54. Mem. ABA, Assn. Bar City N.Y., Yale Club (N.Y.C.), Sky Club (N.Y.C.), Wilton Riding Club, Silvermine Golf Club, Silver Spring Golf Club. Presbyterian. Home: 67 Ridgefield Rd Wilton CT 06897-3006 Office: care Brinks Inc Ste 4600 60 E 42nd St New York NY 10165

DUKE, STEPHEN OSCAR, physiologist, researcher, educator; b. Battle Creek, Mich., Oct. 9, 1944; s. Oscar and Azalee Rosa (Tallant) D.; m. Barbara Alice Rowe, June 2, 1967 (div. Dec. 1993); children: Gregory Ivan, Robin Anne. BS, Henderson State U., 1966; MS, U. Ark., 1969; PhD, Duke U., 1975. Plant physiologist So. Weed Sci. Lab., USDA, Stoneville, Miss., 1975-84, rsch. leader, 1984-87, lab. dir., 1987-96; rsch. leader USDA, Oxford, Miss., 1996—; adj. prof. Miss. State U., Starkville, 1978—, U. Miss., Oxford, 1996—. Co-author: Physiology of Herbicide Action, 1993; editor: Weed Physiology, 2 vols., 1985, Pest Control with Enhanced Environmental Safety, 1993, Porphyric Pesticides, 1994, Herbicide Resistant Crops, 1995; contbr. articles to profl. jours. Head referee Greenville Youth Soccer Assn. (Miss.), 1982-96; soccer coach Washington Sch., Greenville, 1986-88. Served to 1st lt. U.S. Army, 1968-70, Vietnam. Decorated Bronze Star; recipient Edminster award USDA, 1986, Disting. Alumnus award Henderson State U., 1989, CIBA-GEIGY/Weed Sci. Soc. Am. award CIBA-GEIGY Corp., 1990. Fellow AAAS, Weed Sci. Soc. Am. (assoc. editor 1978-83, pres. 1996, Outstanding Young Scientist award 1984, Outstanding Article award 1984, Rsch. award 1990); mem. Internat. Weed Sci. Soc. (v.p. 1999—), Am. Soc. Plant Physiology (chmn. so. sect. 1985-86), Coun. for Agrl. Sci. and Tech. (bd. dirs. 1993-94), Am. Chem. Soc., So. Weed Soc. (pres. 1995, disting. svc. award 1998). Avocations: gardening, writing. Home: 9 Private Rd 3078 Oxford MS 38655

DUKE, STEVEN BARRY, law educator; b. Mesa, Ariz., July 31, 1934; s. Alton and Elaine (Altman) D.; m. Janet Truax, 1956; children: Glenn, Warren, Alison, Sally; m. Margaret Munson, 1984; children: Jennifer, Lauren. B.S., Ariz. State U., 1956; J.D., U. Ariz., 1959; LL.M., Yale U., 1961. Bar: Ariz. 1959. Law clk. to Supreme Ct. Justice Douglas, 1959; grad. fellow Yale Law Sch., 1960, mem. faculty, 1961—, prof. law, 1966—, Law of Sci. and Tech. prof., 1982—; vis. prof. U. Calif.-Berkeley, 1965, Hastings Coll. Law, 1981, Ariz. State U., 1986; Bd. dirs. New Haven Legal Assistance Assn., 1968-70; cons. Commn. to Revise Fed. Criminal Code; mem. Conn. Commn. on Medicolegal Investigations, 1976—; bd. visitiors Fordham U. Law Sch., 1986—. Author: (with A. Gross) America's Longest War: Rethinking Our Tragic Crusade Against Drugs, 1993; editor-in-chief Ariz. Law Rev.; contbr. articles to profl. jours. Mem. Woodbridge (Conn.) Bd. Edn., 1970-72; mem. Woodbridge Democratic Town Com., 1967-72. Mem. Nat. Assn. Criminal Def. Lawyers, Am. Trial Lawyers, ACLU, Phi Kappa Phi, Alpha Tau Omega. Home: 250 Grandview Ave Hamden CT 06514-3028 Office: Yale Law Sch PO Box 208215 New Haven CT 06520-8215

DUKE DE LEONEDES OF SPAIN SICILY GREECE, HIS ROYAL HIGHNESS See SANCHEZ, LEONEDES MONARRIZE WORTHINGTON

DUKELOW, SAMUEL GRIFFITH, engineering consultant; b. Hutchinson, Kans., Aug. 26, 1917; s. Elmer R. and Jeannette H. (Clapham) D.; m. Evelyn C. Ellsworth, May 22, 1941; 1 child, William T. BSME, Kans. State U., 1941. From cadet engr. to mgr. power generation mktg. Bailey Controls Co., Wickliffe, Ohio, 1941-80; engrng. cons. Hutchinson, Kans., 1980—; taught more than 100 seminars on boiler control in U.S., Can., Saudi Arabia, United Arab Emirates and Ireland. Author: Control of Boilers, 1986, 2d edit., 1991, Improving Boiler Efficiency, 1980, 2d edit., 1985; author software; contbr. articles to profl. jours. Recipient Albert Sperry award, 1979, medal for Disting. Achievement, 1991. Fellow Internat. Soc. Measurement and Control; mem. ASME (life). Republican. Presbyterian. Achievements include patents for heat flow meter and evaporator control system; design and implementation of first power plant performance computer in 1956. Avocations: photography, baking, gardening, writing, mapmaking. Home: 304 Kisiwa Pkwy Hutchinson KS 67502-4459

DUKE-MASTERS, VELMA REGINA, pediatrics and psychiatric-mental health nurse; b. Bklyn., Nov. 28, 1936; d. Juliano and Elise (Lewis) Duke; m. Howard E. Masters, May 26, 1962; children: Wendy C., Howard C. AAS in Nursing, N.Y.C. Community Coll., Bklyn., 1973; BS, St. Joseph's Coll., Bklyn., 1981. RN, N.Y. Staff nurse emergency room St. John's Hosp., Bklyn., 1979-82; charge nurse psychiat.-mental health unit Regent Hosp., N.Y.C., 1980-90; nurse Kingsboro Mental Health Ctr., Bklyn., 1994—; Staff Kirby Francis Inst., 1990-94. Office: Kingsboro Mental Health Ctr 681 Clarkson Ave Brooklyn NY 11213

DUKES, FRANK RONALD, career military, collections investigator; b. Oct. 29, 1949. BA in Social Sci., Fordham U., 1972; BSc in Bus. Mgmt., Saint Francis U., 1978; MSc in Bus. Adminstrn., U. Notre Dame, 1985. Supr. investigator City of N.Y. Dept. Finance, Bklyn., 1973—. Major USAR, 1972—. Home: 358 Webster Ave # 2 Brooklyn NY 11230-1407

DUKES, JACK RICHARD, history educator; b. Indpls., Jan. 21, 1941; s. Richard Eugene and Kathleen (Cox) D.; m. Joanne Petty, June 15, 1963; children: Gregory Scott, Richard Aaron. BA, Beloit Coll., 1963; MA, No. Ill. U., 1965; PhD, U. Ill., 1970. Asst. prof. Macalester Coll., St. Paul, 1969-70; asst. prof. Carroll Coll., Waukesha, Wis., 1970-75, assoc. prof., 1975-83, prof. 1983—, chmn. dept. history, 1971-96, dir. Russian Area Studies program, 1972-75; vis. assoc. prof. U. Calif., Santa Barbara, 1980-81; Scholar-Diplomat U.S. Dept. State, 1977; mem. exec. comm. Wis. Inst. for the Study of War, Peace and Global Cooperation, 1988-92. NEH fellow SUNY, Albany, 1974; U. Ill. assoc. in Russian history, 1977; NEH fellow in residence, U. Calif., Santa Barbara, 1977-78, St. Petersburg, Russia, 1992; fellow U. Calif. Inst. for Global Conflict and Cooperation, 1989; recipient Benjamin F. Richardson Excellence in Teaching, Rsch. and Ednl. Innovation Faculty award, 1991, Disting. Svc. citation Beloit Coll., 1993, Beloit Coll., 1998, Cmty. Svc. award Carroll Coll., 1998; named Hon. Citizen, City of Kokshetau, Kazakhstan, 1995. Mem. Am. Hist. Assn., Am. Assn. for Advancement Slavic Studies, Conf. Group Study Central European History, Soc. History Am. Fgn. Rels., German Studies Assn., Waukesha Sister Assn. (pres. 1989-91, exec. dir. 1991-99). Author: (with Joachim Remak) Another Germany: A Reconsideration of the Imperial Era, 1988; contbr. articles to profl. jours. Home: 114 W Laflin Ave Waukesha WI 53186-6230 Office: Carroll Coll Dept History Waukesha WI 53186

DUKES, REBECCA WEATHERS (BECKY DUKES), musician, singer, songwriter; b. Durham, N.C., Nov. 21, 1934; d. Elmer Dewey Weathers and Martha Rebecca (Kimbrough) Weathers-Hall; m. Charles Aubrey Dukes Jr., Dec. 20, 1955; children: Aurelia Ann, Charles Weathers, David Lloyd. BA, Duke U., 1956. Lic. elem. sch. tchr. Tchr. Durham City Schs., 1956-57; sec. USMC, Arlington, Va., 1957-58; tchr. Arlington County Schs., 1958-59; office mgr. Dukes and Kooken, Landover, Md., 1976; musical performer Washington and various locations, Va., Md., 1982—. Vocal student Todd Duncan; pianist, vocalist Back Alley Restaurant Lounge, 1982, various hotels, lounges, 1982—; original program, A Life Cycle in Song, presented throughout mid-Atlantic states and Washington; full operatic solo recital, 1983; featured performer benefit for Nat. Symphony Orch., P.G. Philharm. Orch., 1999; performer Capital Ctr., Cole Field House, George Washington U., Smith Ctr.; operatic solo concert with pianist Glenn Sales, 1985; benefit appearance U. Md. Concert Series, 1986-87; composer over 100 original songs including Between the Lovin' and the Leavin', Covers of My Mind, Gentle Thoughts (lead song Nat. Capitol Area Composers Series), Headin' Home Again, I Would Like to Be Reborn, Miss You, Tears, You Played a Part in My Life, Christmas Memories, Mood Rhapsody, Let Freedom Ring; songwriter, vocalist (album releases-12 songs) Alive, 1992, Rainbow, 1994, Borrow The Sun, 1995, Almost Country, 1999; author: (poems) Pottery, Canyons and Connections, Let the Trees of the Forest Rustle with Praise; contbr. poems to A Question of Balance, 1992, Treasured Poems of America, 1993, Distinguished Poets of 1994. Pres. Nat. Capitol Law League, Washington, 1976-77; pres. women's group, deacon, elder Riverdale Presbyn. Ch., Hyattsville, Md., 1968-94, elder, 1994; chmn. event honoring wives of Supreme Ct. justices, 1981; bd. dirs., women's com. Nat. Symphony, 1980—, bd. dirs.; chmn. awards event Marian Anderson Internat. Vocal Arts Competition, 1991, 95; bd. dirs. Md. Coll. Art and Design, 1996—, WC/Nat. Symphony Orch., 1999. Recipient Friend of Yr. award Md. Summer Inst. for Creative and Performing Arts, U. Md., 1986, award for Vol. Svcs., Duke U., 1992, Hon. Mention award For the Children of the World Billboard mag., 1996; named Hon. trustee Prince George's (Md.) Arts Coun., 1984—, one of Women of Outstanding Achievement, Prince George's County, 1994. Mem. ASCAP (Popular Music award 1994-97), Nat. Acad. Recording Arts and Scis., Nashville Songwriters Assn. Internat., Songwriters Assn. Washington, William Preston Few Assn. of Duke U. (pres. couns., exec. bd. of ann. fund), Internat. Platform Assn., Pres.'s Club of U. Md., Univ. Club, Founders Club of Duke U. Republican. Home and Office: 7111 Pony Trail Ln Hyattsville MD 20782-1031

DUKKIPATI, RAO VENKATESWARA, engineering educator, researcher, scientist; b. Bhyravapatnam, India, Jan. 20, 1945; came to U.S., 1971; s. Nagabhushanam and Annapurnamma (Vallurupalli) D.; m. Sudha R. Tummala, May 28, 1969; 1 child, Ravi. BS in Mech. Engrng., Sri Venkateswara U., Tirupathi, India, 1966; MS, Andhra U., Waltair, India, 1969; MScE, U. N.B., Can., 1971; PhD, Okla. State U., 1973. Registered profl. engr., Ont. Structures analyst Pratt & Whitney Aircraft, Montreal, 1973-78; sr. rsch. officer NRC, Ottawa, Ont., Can., 1978-95; sr. rsch. engr. U. Windsor, Ont., 1976; vis. prof. U. Toledo, Ohio, 1997—; adj. prof. Concordia U., Montreal, 1978—, U. Western Ont., London, 1988-94. Co-author: Dynamics of Railway Vehicle Systems, 1984, Computer-Aided Simulation in Railway Dynamics, 1988, Mechanism and Machine Theory, 1992, Computer-Aided Analysis and Design, 1997. Recipient Disting. Engr. award TANA-N.Am., 1985, B. Roth award Applied Mechanisms and Robotics, 1997. Fellow ASME, Can. Soc. for Mech. Engrs.; mem. Soc. Automotive Engrs. Hindu. Avocations: swimming, philosophy, social service. Home: 2711 Wyldewood St, Gloucester, ON Canada K1T 2S1 Office: U Toledo Mime Dept Toledo OH 43606

DULA, BRETT M., retired military officer; b. Upland, Calif., June 30, 1942; s. Mason Aurelius and Phyllis Grace (Jennings) D.; m. Terri Ann Van Epps, Apr. 30, 1972; children: Jennings, Mason, Lindsey. BS, USAF Acad., 1964; MA, Pepperdine U., 1976; grad., Armed Forces Staff Coll., 1978, Nat. War Coll., Washington, 1985. Commd. 2d lt. USAF, 1964, advanced through grades to maj. gen., 1991; co-pilot 19th Bombardment Wing USAF, Homestead AFB, Fla.; with 23d Tactical Air Support Squadron USAF, Nakhon Phanom Royal Thai AFB, Thailand, 1967-68; forward air controller 20th Tactical Air Support Squadron USAF, Da Nang Air Base, South Vietnam, 1968; aircraft comdr., instr. pilot 2d Bombardment Wing USAF, Barksdale AFB, La., 1969-71, aide-de-camp to 2d air force comdr., 1971; aide, asst. exec. officer to chief of staff Supreme Hdqs. Allied Powers Europe USAF, Mons, Belgium, 1972-74; flight comdr., asst. ops. officer, wing exec. officer 27th Tactical Fighter Wing USAF, Cannon AFB, N.Mex., 1974-77; action officer Directorate of Aeronautical Requirements Office of Dep. Chief of Staff for Plans, Hdqs. SAC USAF, Offutt AFB, Nebr., chief air vehicles and advanced devel. divsns.; squadron comdr. FB-111A USAF, Plattsburgh AFB, N.Y., 1980-82; comdr. 416th Bombardment Wing USAF, Griffiss AFB, N.Y., 1985-87; comdr. 2d Bombardment Wing USAF, Barksdale AFB, 1987-88; SAC inspector gen. USAF, Offutt AFB, 1988-89; dep. dir., then dir. legis. liaison Office of Sec. Air Force USAF, Washington, 1989-91; vice comdr. 8th Air Force USAF, Barksdale AFB, 1991-92; comdr. 2d Air Force USAF, Beale AFB, Calif., 1992-93; dep. dir. ctrl. imagery office USAF, Vienna, Va., 1993-95; dep. inspector gen. USAF, Washington, 1995, vice comm. air combat command, to comdr., 1995-98, 98—. Decorated D.S.M., Legion of Merit, D.F.C. with oak leaf cluster, Air medal with 18 oak leaf clusters, Air Force Commendation medal. Mem. Air Force Assn., Soc. Daedalians. Avocations: sports car restoration, hunting, fishing. *

DULA, ROSA LUCILE NOELL, retired secondary education educator; b. Hillsborough, N.C., May 18, 1914; d. Frederick Young and Mary Rebecca (Lloyd) Noell; m. Thomas Hershaw Dula (dec.); children: Thomas Hunter, Harry Sutton, Frederick Lloyd (dec.). BA, East Carolina U., 1934; MEd, Duke U., 1951. English, history and algebra I tchr. Hillsborough High Sch., 1935-36; English and history tchr. Aberdeen (N.C.) High Sch., 1937, Hillsborough High Sch., 1937-40, Garner (N.C.) High Sch., 1942-43; tchr. Caldwell High Sch., Rougemont, N.C., 1943-44, Elon College (N.C.) High Sch., 1944-45; English and history tchr. Aycock High Sch., Cedar Grove, N.C., 1945-48; English Tchr. Burlington (N.C.) High Sch., 1948-51; English, speech and advanced composition tchr. Walter Williams High Sch., Burlington, 1951-74; speech events coach Burlington High Sch., Williams High Sch., 1948-74; mem. com. readers N.C. English Tchrs., 1960-84. Author: Pelican Guide to Hillsborough, 1979, rev. edit., 1989, Morsels for Miscellaneous Moments, 1986; contbr. prose, fiction, poems to lit. publs. Editor newsletter St. Matthew's Episcopal Ch., Hillsborough, 1983, lay reader, 1982-85, 95—, 1st woman lay reader 1981; judge local speech events; speaker to schs., civic and religious groups; v.p. Orange County Retired Sch. Pers., 1994-96. Recipient Commendations for high sch. Voice of Democracy participation VFW, 1959-61, Degree of Distinction, Nat. Forensic League, 1957, Honor plaques Freedom's Found. Valley Forge, 1969-72, Extraordinary Woman of N.C. award Lady Stetson div. City, 1987, light verse awards Idaho Writers League, 1988, N.C. Poetry Soc., 1989, Valley Forge Tchrs. award, 1974; Nat. Coun. Tchrs. of English grantee English Inst., Duke U., summer 1962, Purdue Speech Workshop, summer, 1969. Mem. Am. Assn. Ret. Persons, Acad. Am. Poets, N.C. Poetry Soc., Hillsborough Hist. Soc., N.C. Ret. Tchrs. Assn., Orange County Rep. Sch. Pers. (v.p. 1994—), Am. Legion Aux., Nat. Soc. of the DAR (cert. award outstanding achievement in history 1997), Nat. Soc. of the SAR (Bronze good citizenship medal, cert. in recognition of notable svcs.), Kappa Delta Pi. Democrat. Avocations: communications, area cultural events, protecting and preserving environment and human and animal rights. Home: PO Box 222 Hillsborough NC 27278-0222

DU LAC, LOIS ARLINE, writer; b. Cleve., July 17, 1920; d. Carl Walter and T. Henrietta Stein; m. Leo Joseph Du Lac, Apr. 20, 1941; children:

Arline Du Lac Gerard, Linda Du Lac Jennings, Glen, Carl, Ralph. BA cum laude, UCLA, 1942, MA, 1962; JD, Western State U., Fullerton, Calif., 1982. Tchr. Cornelia Connelly H.S., Anaheim, Calif., 1962-63, Montebello (Calif.) Sch. Dist., 1963, Excelsior/Norwalk (Calif.) Sch. Dist., 1963-64, Garden Grove (Calif.) Unified Sch. Dist., 1964-69. Creative editor, contbg. author: Constitutional Law, 1981; contbg. author: Murder California Style, 1987, Mord in Kalifornie, 1988. Vol. law clk. Cmty. Law Ctr., Santa Ana, Calif., 1982. Mem. Mystery Writers Am. (contbg. author Edgar Ann. 1990, 92), Cath. Press. Assn., Phi Beta Kappa, Alpha Mu Gamma. Avocations: singing, reading, gardening, interior decorating, arranging flowers. Office: PO Box 403301 Hesperia CA 92340-3301

DULACK, DAVID DONALD, retired city inspector; b. Watertown, N.Y., Oct. 1, 1931; s. William and Vivian (Laforty) D.; m. Mary F. Kennedy, Nov. 12, 1952; children: Kathy, James. Grad. H.S., Watertown. Cert. fire inspector, housing inspector, N.J. County comdr. Am. Legion, Hudson County, N.J., 1977-78; city inspector Bldg. Dept., City of Union City, N.J., 1982-98; ret., 1998. Committeeman Dem. Orgn., Union City, 1987-97. Cpl. U.S. Army, 1949-52, Korea. Recipient Union City svc. award Kiwanis Hudson Dispach, Hudson County, Union City, 1985. Mem. Am. Legion (post comdr.). Home: 1610 Kennedy Blvd Union City NJ 07087-1912

DULAINE, PIERRE, ballroom dancer. Ballroom dancer Eng.; became ptnr. to Yvonne Marceau, 1976; founder Am. Ballroom Theatre, N.Y.C., 1984—; guest tchr. Sch. Am. Ballet, N.Y.C., The Juilliard Sch., N.Y.C. Appearances include Smithsonian Inst., Washington, JFK Ctr. Performing Arts, Washington, White House, 1992, (Broadway and London show) Grand Hotel, 1989-92; toured with Yvonne Marceau and Am. Ballroom Theatre numerous internat. locations. Recipient Brit. Theatrical Arts Championships 4 times, Spl. Astaire award, Dance Educator awards, Outstanding Achievement in Dance award Nat. Dance Coun. Am., 1992, Dance Mag. award, 1993. Office: Am Ballroom Theatre 305 E 24th St Apt 7T New York NY 10010-4024

DULAN, HAROLD ANDREW, former insurance company executive, educator; b. Bridgeton, N.J., June 28, 1911; s. Thomas Francis and Mamie (Corson) D.; m. Bess Gunn, May 31, 1946; children: Susan Matilda Dulan Hall, Kathleen Dulan Alexander, Elizabeth Ann Dulan Sexton. B.B.A., U. Tex., 1936, M.B.A., 1937, Ph.D., 1945; postgrad., Harvard, summer 1955, U. Chgo., Beloit, Wis., 1956, 63. C.P.A., Tex., Ark. Mem. faculty Tex. A&M Coll., 1938-42; pub. accountant Dallas, 1941-46; financial economist Fed. Res. Bank, Dallas, 1944-46; faculty Dallas Coll., So. Meth. U., 1945; pres., investment counsellor Harold A. Dulan Inc., Fayetteville, 1938—; prof., former head dept. finance U. Ark., Fayetteville, 1946-82; co-founder Participating Annuity Life Ins. Co., Fayetteville, 1954; chmn. investment com., v.p., pres., chmn. bd. Participating Annuity Life Ins. Co., 1954-68; financial cons. Argentine bus. concern, Buenos Aires, summer 1953; lectr., moderator Southwestern Bell Telephone Co. Mgmt. Seminars, Galveston, Tex., 1956-58, Hot Springs, Ark., 1958; conferee Conf. Savs. and Residential Financing Savs. and Loan League, Chgo., 1958; mem. Financial Analysts Fedn. European Econ. Conf. Tour, 1964; dir. First Ark. Devel. Finance Corp.; fellow N.Y. Fin. Dist., 1950; mem. chancellor's council U. Tex.; mem. Ark. Econ. Devel. Study Commn., 1975-76; condr. econ. study of capital formation, Australia, Orient, 1971, of high level inflation, Brazil, Argentina, Chile, 1975, of econ. growth and monetary aspects of Circum-Pacific capital formation in Singapore, Indonesia and Malaysia, 1980; mem. citizens ambassador program securities mgmt. delegation to People's Republic of China, summer 1987. Contbr. articles to profl. jours. Commr. Tex. Centennial Statehood, 1946; commr., vice chmn. Gov.'s Commn. Status of Women for Ark., 1964-65; mem. securities mgmt. del. Citizen Ambassador Program, People's Republic China, 1987. Mem. Am. Inst. C.P.A.'s, Am. Inst. Chartered Financial Analysts (past mem. council examiners), Nat. Assn. Bus. Economists, N.Y. Soc. Security Analysts, Am. Finance Assn., Southwestern Social Sci. Assn. (past pres. finance sect.), Ark. Soc. C.P.A.'s, Fayetteville C. of C., Beta Gamma Sigma, Beta Alpha Psi, Sigma Iota Epsilon. Methodist. Clubs: Fayetteville Country. Lodge: Rotary. Home: 1500 Clark St Fayetteville AR 72701-3710 Office: Harold A Dulan Inc 414 W Ila St Fayetteville AR 72701-3317

DULANEY, WILLIAM MARVIN, history educator, curator; b. Troy, Ala., July 21, 1950; s. Willie Frank and Pauline Dulaney; m. Carol Ann Simmons, June 6, 1973; 1 child, Malik Hashim. BA, Ctrl. State U., 1972; MA, Ohio State U., 1974, PhD, 1984. Career counselor Wittenberg U., Springfield, Ohio, 1978-81; intercultural affairs advisor Tex. Christian U., Fort Worth, 1981-83; asst. dir. U. Tex., Arlington, 1983-85, asst. prof., 1986—; asst. prof. St. Olaf Coll., Northfield, Minn., 1985-86; dir. Avery Rsch. Ctr., Charleston, S.C., 1994—; dir. African-Am. studies program Coll. of Charleston, 1994—, chmn. history dept., 1999—; curator of history African-Am. Mus., Dallas, Tex., 1986—; exec. dir. African-Am. Rsch. Assocs., Dallas, 1992—; dir. Avery Rsch. Ctr. Coll. Charleston, 1994—. Author: Black Police in America, 1996; editor: Essays on American Civil Rights, 1993. Chmn. bd. dirs. Our Brothers' Keeper NDUGU, Dallas, 1993—. Recipient Carter G. Woodson award African Am. Cultural Ctr., Dallas, 1989, Urban League svc. award Urban League Young Adult Coun., 1991. Mem. Assn. Study of Afro-Am. Life and History, Orgn. Am. Historians, So. Conf. Afro-Am. Studies (v.p.), Tex. State Hist. Assn. Avocations: raquetball, reading, computer programming. Office: Avery Rsch Ctr 125 Bull St Charleston SC 29424*

DULANY, ELIZABETH GJELSNESS, university press administrator; b. Charleston, S.C., Mar. 11, 1931; d. Rudolph Hjalmar and Ruth Elizabeth (Weaver) Gjelsness; m. Donelson Edwin Dulany, Mar. 19, 1955; 1 son, Christopher Daniel. BA, Bryn Mawr Coll., 1952. Editor, R.R. Bowker Co., 1948-52; med. editor U. Mich. Hosp., Ann Arbor, 1953-54; editorial asst. E.P. Dutton & Co., N.Y.C., 1954-55; editorial asst. U. Ill. Press, Champaign, 1956-59, asst. editor, 1959-67, assoc. editor, 1967-72, mng. editor, 1972-90, asst. dir., 1983-90, assoc. dir., 1990—. Democrat. Episcopalian. Home: 73 Greencroft Dr Champaign IL 61821-5112 Office: U Ill Press 1325 S Oak St Champaign IL 61820-6903

DULANY, WILLIAM BEVARD, lawyer; b. Sykesville, Md., Sept. 4, 1927; s. William Washington and Helen Marie (Bevard) D.; m. Anna Winifred Spencer, Aug. 16, 1952; children: William Bryant, Thomas Patrick, Anne French. AB, Western Md. Coll., 1950; postgrad., U. Mich. Law Sch., 1950-51; JD, U. Md., 1953; LLD (hon.), Western Md. Coll., 1989. Bar: Md. 1953, U.S. Dist. Ct. Md. 1954, U.S. Supreme Ct. 1990. Assoc. Baldwin, Jarman & Norris, Balt., 1953-59; sr. ptnr. Dulany & Leahy LLP, Westminster, Md., 1959—; mem. character com. Md. Ct. Appeals, Annapolis, 1974-93; chmn. bd. dirs. Mu. Fire Ins. Carroll County, Westminster; chmn. bd. dirs. Mason-Dixon Bancshares, Inc., Westminster and Carroll County Bank & Trust Co., Westminster, Md. Mem. Md. Ho. of Dels., Annapolis, 1962-66, Md. Constl. Conv., Annapolis, 1967-68, Md. Regional Planning Coun., 1964-66; chmn. Md. Fair Campaign Practices Commn., 1975-78; chmn. adv. com. Carroll County C.C., 1976; trustee Western Md. Coll., Westminster, 1976—; bd. dirs. nat. office Am. Heart Assn., Dallas, 1982-89, chmn., 1987-88; bd. dirs. Episcopal Ministries to Aging, Inc., Fairhaven, 1982—, chmn., 1986—; former commr. Md. Human Rels. Commn.; vice chmn. Md. Spl. Com. on Gen. Equality, 1989-91; trustee Md. Hist. Soc., 1991—; past pres. Hist. Soc. Carroll County; former mem. Vestry Ascension Episc. Ch. Named one of Outstanding Young Men of Am., Westminster chpt. Jaycees, 1961, Alumnus of Yr., Western Md. Coll., 1986; recipient Outstanding Citizen award Westminster chpt. Rotary, 1985. Fellow Md. Bar Found. (pres. 1986-88, bd. dirs.); mem. ABA, Md. Bar Assn. (v.p. 1970-71), Carroll County Bar Assn. (pres. 1966-67), Am. Judicature Soc., Am. Bar Found., Bachelor's Cotillon Club (Balt.), Phi Alpha Delta. Avocations: travel, vol. work in non-profit orgns. Home: 1167 Old Taneytown Rd Westminster MD 21158-3605 Office: Dulany & Leahy LLP PO Box 1125 127 E Main St Westminster MD 21157-5012

DULAUX, RUSSELL FREDERICK, lawyer; b. West New York, N.J., Dec. 30, 1918; s. Frederick and Theresa A. (Noble) L.; m. Ann deFriedberg, Aug. 22, 1962 (dec.); m. Eva DeLuca, Dec. 24, 1985. Student, Drake's Bus. Sch., 1937; Student, Pace Inst., 1938-40, Fordham U., 1946-48; LLB summa cum laude, N.Y. Law Sch., 1950; postgrad., Pace Coll., 1951, Columbia U., 1955. Bar: N.Y. 1951, U.S. Dist. Ct. (so. dist.) N.Y. 1951, U.S. Ct. Appeals (2d cir.) 1951, U.S. Ct. Claims 1952, U.S. Tax Ct. 1952, U.S. Dist. Ct. (ea. dist.) N.Y. 1953, U.S. Ct. Customs and Patent Appeals 1963, U.S. Ct. Mil. Appeals 1963, U.S. Supreme Ct. 1963. Mem. staff N.Y. State Dept. Law, Richmond County Investigations, 1951-54, N.Y. State Exec. Dept. Office of Commr. of Investigations, 1954-57; comptroller-counsel Odyssey Productions, Inc., 1957-59; ptnr. Ryan, Murray & Laux, N.Y.C., 1951-61, Ryan & Laux, N.Y.C., 1961; pvt. practice N.Y.C., 1961—. Served with AUS, 1940-46; capt. JAG, vet. corps. of arty. State of N.Y., 1975-92, maj., 1992—; spl. agt. counter intelligence corps and security intelligence corps; col. U.S. Army. Recipient Eloy Alfaro Grand Cross Republic of Panama, Cert. of World Leadership for Leadership and Achievement, 1987, Cert. of Merit for Disting Achievement, 1984, Cert. for Internt. Contemporary Achievement for Outstanding Contbr. to Soc., 1984, Disting. Leadership award for Contbns. to the Legal Profession, Award of Merit for Outstanding Profl. and Pub. Svc., Guglielmo Marconi Bronze award, 1987; inducted Hall of Fame for Contbn. to Legal Profession. Mem. NATAS, Bronx County Bar Assn. (Townsend Wandell Gold medal), Met. Opera Guild, Internat. Platform Assn., VFW (adjutant Floyd Gibbons Post 500, Cert. of Recognition and Appreciation Polit. Action Com. 1990, Cert. of Svc. on Pres. Rehab. Com. Vets. sect.), Order of Lafayette, Sons Union Vets. Civil War, Soc. Am. Wars, Nat. Sojourners, Heroes of '76, Navy League, St. Andrews Soc. N.Y., St. George Soc. N.Y., Soc. Friendly Sons St. Patrick, English Speaking Union, Asia Soc., China Inst. Am., Army and Navy Union USA, Am. Legion (past post comdr. admen's post 209), Mid Manhattan C. of C., Res. Officers Assn. U.S. (col.), Humanity Against Hatred, Delta Theta Phi, Lambs Club, Knights Hospitaller of St. John of Jerusalem, Grand St. Boys' Club, Soldiers' Club, Sailors' and Airmen's Club, Order Ea. Star, Masons (past comdr. N.Y. Masonic War Vets), Shriners, Knights of Malta, Knights of St. George, Sovereign Mil. Order of Temple of Jerusalem. Office: FDR Station PO Box 477 New York NY 10150

DULBECCO, RENATO, biologist, educator; b. Catanzaro, Italy, Feb. 22, 1914; came to U.S., 1947, naturalized, 1953; s. Leonardo and Maria (Virdia) D.; m. Gulseppina Salvo, June 1, 1940 (div. 1963); children: Peter Leonard (dec.), Maria Vittoria; m. Maureen Rutherford Muir; 1 child, Fiona Linsey. M.D., U. Torino, Italy, 1936; D.Sc. (hon.), Yale U., 1968, Vrije Universiteit, Brussels, 1978; LL.D., U. Glasgow, Scotland, 1970. Asst. U. Torino, 1940-47; research asso. Ind. U., 1947-49; sr. research fellow Calif. Inst. Tech., 1949-52, asso. prof., then prof. biology, 1952-63; sr. fellow Salk Inst. Biol. Studies, San Diego, 1963-71; asst. dir. research Imperial Cancer Research Fund, London, 1971-74; dep. dir. research Imperial Cancer Research Fund, 1974-77; disting. research prof. Salk Inst., La Jolla, Calif., 1977—, pres., 1989-92; pres. emeritus Salk Inst., La Jolla, 1993—; prof. pathology and medicine U. Calif. at San Diego Med. Sch., La Jolla, 1977-81, mem. Cancer Ctr.; with Nat. Rsch. Coun. Milan; vis. prof. Royal Soc. G.B., 1963-64, Leeuwenhoek lectr., 1974; Clowes Meml. lectr. Atlantic City, 1961; Harvey lectr. Harvey Soc., 1967; Dunham lectr. Harvard U., 1972; 11th Marjory Stephenson Meml. lectr., London, 1973, Harden lectr., Wye, Eng., 1973, Am. Soc. for Microbiology lectr., L.A., 1979; mem. Calif. Cancr Adv. Coun., 1963-67; mem. vis. com. Case Western Res. Sch. Medicine; adv. bd. Roche Inst., 1968-71, Inst. Immunology, Basel, Switzerland, others; esperto Italian Nat. Rsch. Coun.; trustee Am.-Italian Fedn. for Cancer Rsch.; mem. bd. dirs. Scientific Counselors Dept. Etiology NCI; cons. Nat. Rsch. Coun. ESPERTO, 1994—. Trustee La Jolla Country Day Sch., Am.-Italian Fedn. for Cancer Rsch.; bd. mem. sci. counselors dept. etiology Nat. Cancer Inst. Recipient John Scott award City Phila., 1958, Kimball award Conf. Pub. Health Lab. Dirs., 1959, Albert and Mary Lasker Basic Med. Rsch. award, 1964, Howard Taylor Ricketts award, 1965, Paul Ehrlich-Ludwig Darmstaedter prize, 1967, Horwitz prize Columbia U., 1973, (with David Baltimore and Howard Martin Temin) Nobel prize in medicine, 1975, Targa d'oro Villa San Giovanni, 1978, Mandel Gold medal Czechoslovak Acad. Scis., 1982, Via de Condotti prize, 1990, Cavaliere di Gran Croce Italian Rep., 1991, Natale Di Roma prize, 1993, Columbus prize, 1993; named Man of Yr., London, 1975, Italian Am. of Yr., San Diego County, 1978; hon. citizen City of Imperia (Italy), 1983, City of Arezzo, City of Sommariva Perno, City of Catanzaro, City of Torino; Guggenheim and Fulbright fellow, 1957-58; decorated grand ufficiale Italian Republic, 1981; hon. founder Hebrew U., 1981. Mem. NAS (Selman A. Waksman award 1974, com. on human rights), Am. Assn. Cancer Rsch., Internat. Physicians for Prevention Nuclear War, Am. Philos. Assn., Academia Nazionale del Lincei (fgn.), Academia Ligure di Scienze e Lettre (hon.), Royal Soc. (fgn.), Fedn. Am. Scientists, Am. Acad. Arts and Scis., Comitato di Collaborazione Culturale (hon. mem.), Alpha Omega Alpha. Home: 7525 Hillside Dr La Jolla CA 92037-3941 Office: CNR-ITBA, Via Ampere 56, Milan Italy also: Salk Inst PO Box 85800 San Diego CA 92188-5800

DULIN, MAURINE STUART, volunteer; b. Lonerock, Iowa, Feb. 16, 1919; d. Frank Meagher and Fern Adrienne (Wetzel) Stuart; m. William Carter Dulin, Oct. 5, 1940; children: Jacquelyn Dulin Wilson, Patricia F., Stuart M. AB in Polit. Sci./Econs., The Coll. of William and Mary, 1939. Coll. cons. Woodward and Lothrop, Washington, 1939-40; adminstr. asst. Sightler and Cox, Washington, 1942-43; acctg. dept. asst. The Am. U., Washington, 1964-69; corp. sec. Bittinger and Dulin, Arlington, Va., 1949-73; ptnr. 41 Limited Partnership, Bethesda, Md., 1979—, Montrose-270 Ltd. Partnership, Bethesda, 1979—. Mem. Rock Creek Womens Rep. Club, Bethesda, 1951-57; sgt.-at-arms Montgomery County Fed. of Rep. Women, Bethesda, 1952-53, State Fedn. of Womens Rep. Club, 1953-54; charter mem., com. chmn. Nat. Mus. of Women in the Arts; mem. Women's Bd.Cathedral Choral Soc. 1975—, com. chmn., 1988-90; mem. Women's Bd. George Washington U. Hosp., 1970—, Save Our Seminary at Forest Glen, Md., 1989—. Mem. The Town Club (pres. 1958-59), Pi Beta Phi (nat. com. chmn. 1971-75, province officer 1967-71). Episcopalian. Home: 5612 Grove St Chevy Chase MD 20815-3421

DULIN, THOMAS N., lawyer; b. Albany, N.Y., May 26, 1949; s. Joseph Paul and Mary Carol (Keane) D.; m. Pamela Lee Kendall, May 14, 1983; 1 children: Chelsea K., Danielle Y. Boshea, Amanda L. Boshea, Thomas M. Boshea. BA, Siena Coll., 1972; JD, Western New England U., 1976. Bar: N.Y. 1977, U.S. Dist. Ct. (no. dist.) N.Y. 1977, U.S. Supreme Ct. 1984. Asst. dist. atty. Albany County, 1977-81; assoc. McCarthy & Evanick, Albany, 1981-83; sole practice Albany, 1983-88; sr. ptnr. Dulin, Harris & Bixby, Albany, 1988-92; ptnr. Gerstenzang, Weiner & Gerstenzang, Albany, 1992-93, The Dulin Law Firm, Albany, 1993—; staff atty. Albany County Pub. Defender's Office, 1983—. Bd. dirs. Big Bros. and Sisters of Albany County, Inc., 1983-92, pres., bd. dirs. , 1988-90. Mem. ABA, N.Y. State Bar Assn. (lectr. criminal justice sect.), Nat. Assn. Criminal Def. Lawyers, N.Y. State Assn. Criminal Def. Lawyers, Capital Dist. Trial Lawyers Assn., Albany County Bar Assn., Assn. Trial Lawyers Am., N.Y. State Trial Lawyers Assn. Democrat. Avocations: skiing, golfing, swimming. Home: 2 Country Rdg Schenectady NY 12304-2531 Office: 4 Tower Pl Exec Park Tower Albany NY 12203

DULING, EDWARD BURGER, music education educator; b. Coshocton, Ohio, Dec. 6, 1954; s. Edwin Tracy and Mary Helen (Burger) D. MusB, Capital U., 1977; MA, Ohio State U., 1987, PhD, 1992. Cert. elem. tchr., music tchr., supr., Ohio. Tchr. music, English Cedar Cliff Local Schs., Cedarville, Ohio, 1984-89; grad. teaching assoc. Ohio State U., Columbus, Ohio, 1989-91; lectr. music edn. Ohio State U., Newark, Ohio, 1991-93; asst. prof. Morehead (Ky.) State U., 1993-94; co-dir. Southeast Inst. Edn. in Music, Chattanooga, Tenn., 1994-95; tchr. gen. music Chattanooga (Tenn.) City Schs., 1995-96; asst. prof. Bowling Green (Ohio) U., 1996—; facilitator Southeast Inst. for Edn. in Music, Chattanooga, 1996, discipline-based expert, New Orleans, 1997, 98, 99; presenter in field; church organist 24 yrs., tubist, trombonist. Contbr. article and book revs. to profl. jours. Recipient Outstanding Faculty Svc. award ProMusica of Coll. of Musical Arts, Bowling Green State U., 1996-97, Disting. Faculty award Phi Mu Alpha Sinfonia, 1997-98, Dean's award, 1999. Mem. Ohio Music Edn. Assn., Tubists Universal Brotherhood Assn., Internat. Trombone Assn., Music Educators Nat. Conf., Phi Mu Alpha Sinfonia Frat. (chpt. advisor 1996—). United Methodist. Avocations: art pottery, gardening, collecting sheetmusic and memorabilia. Office: Bowling Green State U Moore Musical Arts Ctr Bowling Green OH 43403

DULL, WILLIAM MARTIN, engineering executive; b. Buchanan, Mich., June 24, 1924; s. Curtis Frank and Daisy Julia (Sharp) D.; m. Margaret Ann McMillan, Apr. 10, 1976; children: Richard William, Beverly Ann, William McMillan. BSME, U. Mich., 1945. Registered profl. engr., Mich. Dir. tech. staff Detroit Edison, 1951-66, asst. gen. supt. cen. plants, 1966-70, gen. supt. underground lines, 1970-71, mgr. employee relations, 1971-74, mgr. orgn. planning and devel., 1974-89; pres. Charleston Engring. Cons., 1990—; chmn. Charleston Engrs. Joint Coun., 1991—, chmn. 1993-94. Bd. dirs. World Med. Relief, Detroit, 1971-90, chmn., 1988-90; bd. dirs. Jr. Achivement, Southeastern Mich., 1971-90; trustee Detroit Sci. Ctr., Inc., 1979-85. Served to lt. (s.g.) USN, 1942-51, PTO. Recipient Gold Leadership award Jr. Achievement, 1985. Fellow Engring. Soc. Detroit (pres. 1970-71, Disting. Svc. 1980, life); mem. ASHRAE (pres. 1964-65, Outstanding Engr. award 1965, life), ASME (life), IEEE (chmn. nat. conf. 1971), NSPE (life), Architects, Engrs., Surveyors Registration Coun. (chmn. 1968-69), Mich. Soc. Profl. Engrs. (bd. dirs. 1973-75, Disting. Engr. 1980), S.C. Soc. Profl. Engrs. (bd. dirs. 1994-95), Charleston Engrs. Joint Coun. (chmn. 1994-95), U. Mich. Alumni Assn. (v.p., bd. dirs. 1964-71, Disting. Svc. award 1970), Charleston Navy League (v.p., bd. dirs. 1993—). Republican. Methodist. Club: Detroit Yacht.

DULLEA, CHARLES W., university chancellor emeritus, priest. Joined S.J., ordained priest Roman Catholic Ch. Chancellor emeritus U. San Francisco. Office: U San Francisco Xavier Hall 650 Parker Ave San Francisco CA 94118-4267

DULLES, AVERY, priest, theologian; b. Auburn, N.Y., Aug. 24, 1918; s. John Foster and Janet Pomeroy (Avery) D. AB, Harvard U., 1940, postgrad. in law, 1940-41; PhL, Woodstock Coll., 1951, STL, 1957; STD, Pontifical Gregorian U., Rome, 1960; LLD, St. Joseph's Coll., Phila., 1969, Iona Coll., New Rochelle, N.Y., 1980; LHD, Georgetown U., 1977, Creighton U., 1983, Seton Hall U., 1989, Stonehill Coll., 1990, Loyola U., Chgo., 1990, Christ the King Seminary, East Aurora, N.Y., 1994, U. Mass., Boston, 1998; ThD, U. Detroit, 1978, U. Dayton, 1992; DD, St. Anselm Coll., Manchester, N.H., 1981, Jesuit Sch. Theology, Berkeley, Calif., 1984, Protestant Episcopal Theol. Sem., Alexandria, Va., 1986, Carthage Coll., Kenosha, Wis., 1991, Nashotah House, Nashotah, Wis., 1996; STD (hon.), Providence Coll., 1991; Litt.D., Fordham U., 1996. Joined S.J., Roman Cath. Ch., 1946, ordained priest, 1956. Instr. philosophy Fordham U., 1951-53, vis. lectr., 1970, Laurence J. McGinley prof. religion and society, 1988—; mem. faculty Woodstock Coll., N.Y.C., 1960-74; prof. theology Woodstock Coll., 1969-74, Cath. U. Am., Washington, 1974-88; Gasson prof. theology Boston Coll., 1981-82; prof. emeritus Cath. U. Am., Washington, 1988—; vis. lectr. Weston Coll., 1971, Union Theol. Sem., 1971-74, Princeton Theol. Sem., 1972, Pontifical Gregorian U., 1973, 90, 93, Episcopal Theol. Sem., 1975, Luth. Sem. Pa., 1978; Martin C. D'Arcy lectr. Campion Hall, Oxford (Eng.) U., 1983; vis. John A. O'Brien prof. theology Notre Dame U., 1985; vis. prof. theology Cath. U. of Leuven, 1992; vis. prof. religious studies Yale U., New Haven, 1996; fellow Woodrow Wilson Internat. Ctr. for Scholars, 1977; mem. Commn. on Christian Unity, Archdiocese of Balt., 1962-70, Cath. Bishops' Adv. Coun., 1969-75; consultor to Papal Secretariat for Dialogue with Non-Believers, 1966-73, mem. U.S.A. Luth.-Cath. Dialogue, 1972-92; cons. to com. on doctrine Nat. Conf. Cath. Bishops, 1991—; mem. Internat. Theol. Com., 1992-97; mem. Luth.-Roman Cath. Coord. Com., 1994-96. Author: Princeps Concordiae, 1941, A Testimonial to Grace, 1946, (with others) Introductory Metaphysics, 1955, Apologetics and the Biblical Christ, 1963, The Dimensions of the Church, 1967, Revelation and the Quest for Unity, 1968, Revelation Theology: A History, 1969, (with others) Spirit, Faith and Church, 1970, The Survival of Dogma, 1971 (Christopher award 1972), A History of Apologetics, 1971, Models of the Church, 1974, 2d rev. edit., 1987, Church Membership as a Catholic and Ecumenical Problem, 1974, The Resilient Church, 1977, A Church to Believe In, 1982, Models of Revelation, 1983, 2d rev. edit., 1992, (with Patrick Granfield) The Church: A Bibliography, 1985, The Reshaping of Catholicism, 1988, The Craft of Theology, 1992, expanded edit., 1995 (Best Book in Theology Cath. Press Assn. 1993), The Assurance of Things Hoped For, 1994, A Testimonial to Grace and Reflections on a Theological Journey, 1996, The Priestly Office, 1997, (with Patrick Granfield) The Theology of the Church; Bibliography, 1999; assoc. editor for ecumenism Concilium, 1963-70, adv. editl. bd., 1970-92; adv. editl. bd. Midstream: An Ecumenical Jour., 1974—; mem. editl. bd. Logos: A Jour. of Cath. Thought and Culture, 1997—; contbr. column to Theology for Today, America, 1967-68; contbg. editor New Oxford Rev., 1990—; cons. Theology Digest, 1985—; mem. adv. coun. Pro Ecclesia, 1991—; contbr. articles to theol. publs. Bd. dirs. Georgetown U., 1966-68, Woodstock Theol. Center, 1974-79; trustee Fordham U., 1969-72, St. Mary's Sem. and Univ., Balt., 1992-98; acad. council Irish Sch. Ecumenics, 1971-78. Served to lt. USNR, 1942-46. Decorated Croix de Guerre, France; scholar-in-residence St. Joseph's Sem., Dunwoodie, N.Y., 1996; recipient Cardinal Spellman award for distinguished achievement in theology, 1970, Religious Edn. Forum award Nat. Cath. Edn. Assn., 1988, Campion award Cath. Book Club, N.Y., 1989, F. Sadlier Dinger award, 1994, Choate Alumni Seal prize Choate Rosemary Hall, 1995. Mem. Cath. Theol. Soc. Am. (bd. dirs. 1970-72, 74-77, v.p. 1974-75, pres. 1975-76), Am. Theol. Soc. (v.p. 1977-78, pres. 1978-79), Cath. Commn. on Intellectual and Cultural Affairs (exec. com. 1991-94), Phi Beta Kappa. Office: Fordham U Keating 322 Bronx NY 10458

DULLES, JOHN WATSON FOSTER, history educator; b. Auburn, N.Y., May 20, 1913; s. John Foster and Janet Pomeroy (Avery) D.; m. Eleanor Foster Ritter, June 15, 1940; children: Edith, John, Ellen, Avery. AB, Princeton U., 1935; MBA, Harvard U., 1937; BS in Metall. Engring., U. Ariz., 1943, Metall. Engr., 1951. Clk. The Bank of N.Y., N.Y.C., 1937-38; miner Callahan Zinc-Lead Co., Patagonia, Ariz., 1938-41; head ore dept., smelter operator Cia Minera de Peñoles, S.A., Monterrey, Mex., 1943-49; head comml. divsn. Cia Minera de Pañoles, S.A., Monterrey, Mex., 1949-51, asst. gen. mgr., 1951-59, exec. v.p., 1959; v.p. Cia de Mineracão Novalimense, Belo Horizonte, Brazil, 1959-62; prof. history U. Ariz., Tucson, 1966-91; univ. prof. L.Am. studies U. Tex., Austin, 1962—; advisor to U.S. delegation to OAS Conf., Vina Del Mar, Chile, 1967; cons. U.S. Dept. State, Bur. Intelligence and Rsch., 1968-72. Author: Yesterday in Mexico, 1961, Vargas of Brazil, 1967, Unrest in Brazil, 1970, Anarchists and Communists in Brazil, 1973, Castello Branco: The Making of a Brazilian President, 1978, President Castello Branco, 1980, Brazilian Communism, 1935-1945, 1983, The São Paulo Law School, 1986, Carlos Lacerda: Brazilian crusader, Vol. 1, 1991, Vol. 2, 1996. Recipient Achievement medal U. Ariz., 1960, Ptnrs. of the Alliance Medal, Brazilian Govt., 1966. Fellow Calif. Inst. Internat. Studies; mem. The Am. Soc. of the Most Venerable Order of the Hosp. of St. John of Jeruslaem (knight), Am. Hist. Assn., Tex. Inst. of Letters, Theta Tau (Alumni Hall of Fame), Inst. History and Geography Brasil. Avocation: tennis. Office: Univ of Texas at Austin PO Box 7934 Austin TX 78713-7934

DULUDE, RICHARD, glass manufacturing company executive; b. Dunbarton, N.H., Apr. 20, 1933; s. Joseph Phillip and Anna (Lenz) D.; m. Jean Anne MacDonald, Sept. 11, 1954; children: Jeffrey, Jonathan, Joel. BME, Syracuse U., 1954; postgrad., MIT, 1969. With Allis Chalmers Mfg. Co., Milw., 1954-55; with Corning (N.Y.) Glass Works, 1957—, v.p., gen. mgr. tech. products divsn., 1972-75, v.p., gen. mgr. European ops., 1975-78, pres., 1978-80; pres. Corning Europe Inc., 1980-83, sr. v.p., dir. mktg. and bus. devel., 1980-83; pres. Telecommmunications and Elect. group Corning (N.Y.) Glass Works, 1983-85, group pres., 1985-90, vice-chmn., 1990-93, chmn., chief exec. officer Corning Europe, 1987-89, also bd. dirs.; mem. exec. com., bd. dirs. Corning Inc., 1983-93; bd. dirs. N.H. Lang. Mgmt., Inc., Raychem. Corp., Ambac Corp., HCIA, Welch-Allyn, DuVoice Corp., Landec; mem. Brit. N.Am. Com. Patentee combination space lighting, heating and ventilation fixture. Past bd. dirs. Corning YMCA, Better Vision Inst., N.Y.C., Am. Sch., Paris, Clarkson U., Am. Hosp., Am. C. of C., Paris, Grumman Corp., Dow-Corning, Siecor, Siecor GmBH, OF Ltd.; trustee Syracuse U. 1st lt. AUS, 1955-57. Mem. Optical Soc. Am., Illuminating Engring. Soc., Nat. Ski Patrol System, Nat. Planning Assn. (Brit. N.Am. Com.), Travellers Club (Paris), Univ. Club (N.Y.C.). Home: PO Box 102 Georges Mills NH 03751

DUMA, RICHARD JOSEPH, microbiologist, physician, pathologist, researcher, educator; b. Bethlehem, Pa., Apr. 2, 1933; s. Joseph Anthony and Helen Veronica (Bartek) D.; m. Mary Alyce Fridley, Apr. 18, 1957; 1 child, Scott. BA, Va. Poly. Inst., 1955; MD, U. Va., 1959; PhD, Va. Commonwealth U.-Med. Coll. Va., 1978. Diplomate Am. Bd. Internal Medicine. Intern, then resident in medicine U. Ala. Med. Center, Birmingham, 1959-60, 62-65; research fellow Harvard U. Med. Sch.-Mass. Gen. Hosp., 1965-67; mem. faculty Med. Coll. Va., Richmond, 1967-91; chmn. div. infectious diseases Med. Coll. Va., 1974-92, prof. medicine and pathology, 1975-92, prof. microbiology, 1977-92; mem. U. S. Pharmacopeia Adv. Panel on Hosp. Practices, 1971-82, chmn. subcom. rsch., 1976-82, clin. prof. medicine and infectious diseases Med. Coll. Richmond, 1992—; exec. dir. Nat. Found. for Infectious Diseases, 1991-94, v.p. bd. dirs., 1973-75, pres., 1975-91; chmn. Nat. Coalition for Adult Immunization, 1988-94; didr. infectious diseases Halifax Med. Ctr., Daytona Beach, Fla., 1995—. Served with M.C. USNR, 1960-62. Fellow ACP, Infectious Disease Soc. Am., Royal Soc. Tropical Medicine and Hygiene, Am. Soc. Tropical Medicine and Hygiene, Am. Soc. Rickettsiology, Fla. Infectious Disease Soc. (pres. 1997—); mem. AAAS, Am. Fedn. Clin. Rsch., Am. Soc. Microbiology, Va. Soc. Microbiology, Am. Soc. Internal Medicine, Va. Soc. Internal Medicine, Richmond Soc. Internal Medicine, So. Soc. Clin. Investigation, Am. Thoracic Soc., Royal Soc. Medicine, Med. Soc. Va., Richmond Acad. Medicine, Acad. of Medicine, Washington, Med. Assn. Fla., Volusia Med. Soc., Sigma Xi, Tau Beta Pi. Home: 407 Long Cove Rd Ormond Beach FL 32174-9241 Office: Halifax Medical Ctr PO Box 2830 303 N Clyde Morris Blvd Daytona Beach FL 32114-2700

DUMAINE, R. PIERRE, bishop; b. Aug. 2, 1931. Student, St. Joseph Coll., Mountain View, Calif., 1945-51, St. Patrick Sem., Menlo Park, Calif., 1951-57; PhD, Cath. U. Am., 1962. Ordained priest Roman Cath. Ch., 1957. Asst. pastor Immaculate Heart Ch., Belmont, Calif., 1957-58; mem. faculty dept. edn. Cath. U. Am., Belmont, Calif., 1961-63; tchr. Serra High Sch., San Mateo, Calif., 1963-65; asst. supt. Cath. schs. Archdiocese of San Francisco, 1965-74, supt., 1974-78; ordained bishop, 1978; bishop of San Jose Santa Clara, Calif., 1981—; dir. Archdiocesan Ednl. TV Ctr., Menlo Park, Calif., 1968-81. Mem. Pres.'s Nat. Adv. Council on Edn. of Disadvantaged Children, 1970-72. Bd. dirs. Cath. TV Network, 1968-81, pres. 1975-77; bd. dirs. Pub. Svc. Satellite Consortium, 1975-81. Mem. Nat. Cath. Edn. Assn., Assn. Cath. Broadcasters and Allied Communicators, Internat. Inst. Communications, Assn. Calif. Sch. Adminstrs. Office: Diocese of San Jose 900 Lafayette St Ste 301 Santa Clara CA 95050-4966*

DUMARS, JOE, III, retired professional basketball player; b. Shreveport, La., May 24, 1963; m. Debbie Nelson, 1989; 1 child, Jordan. Grad. in bus. mgmt., McNeese State U., 1985. With Detroit Pistons, 1985-99; mem. NBA Championship team, 1989, 90, Dream Team II, 1994. Named Most Valuable Player NBA finals, 1989; Mem. NBA All-Star team, 1990-93; mem. NBA All-Defensive first team, 1989-90, 92, 93, second team, 1991, 93; mem. NBA All-Rookie team, 1986; mem. All-NBA third team, 1990, 91; mem. Sporting News NCAA All-America second team, 1985; named to Dream Team II, 1994; recipient Citizenship award, 1994. Office: Detroit Pistons 2 Championship Dr Auburn Hills MI 48326-1753*

DUMAS, JEFFREY MACK, lawyer; b. Corpus Christi, Tex., Sept. 29, 1945; s. Glenn Irven and Virginia (Jones) D.; m. Penny Mary Walter, June 5, 1971; children: Todd Glenn, Rebecca Hope. BS, U.S. Naval Acad., 1968; MSEE, Stanford U., 1969; JD, Harvard U., 1978. Bar: Wash. 1979, U.S. Ct. Appeals (9th cir.) 1979, Mont. 1981, Calif. 1983, U.S. Supreme Ct. 1984, U.S. Patent and Trademark Office 1990, Colo. 1995; registered profl. engr., Colo., Wash., Mont., Calif. Fellow UN, N.Y.C., 1978; corp. counsel Boeing Co., Seattle, 1978-80; atty. McClelland Law Office, Missoula, Mont., 1980-82; gen. counsel Briton-Lee, Inc., Los Gatos, Calif., 1982-83; sr. counsel Nat. Semicondr. Corp., Singapore, 1983-87; gen. counsel, sec. Cypress Semicondr. Corp., Santa Clara, Calif., 1987-91; assoc. gen. counsel Silicon Graphics, Inc., Santa Clara, 1991-95; v.p., gen. counsel, sec. Symbios Logic, Inc., Ft. Collins, Colo., 1995-98; corp. v.p., gen. counsel, sec. Storage Tech. Corp., Boulder, Colo., 1998—. Author: (with Richard Gowan) Signals and Systems, 1975; contbr. articles to profl. jours. Chmn. Common Cause, Mont., 1982, Vietnam Vets. of Mont., 1982; chmn. Pikes Peak chpt. Sierra Club, 1975, treas. Cascade chpt., Seattle, 1980. With USN, 1968-75, aviator S.E. Asia, 1970-73. Decorated D.F.C., Air Medal with bronze star; recipient George Washington medal Freedoms Found., 1975. Mem. IEEE, AIAA, Coun. Fgn. Rels., U.S. Naval Inst., Navy League, Sigma Xi. Address: 1297 Blackbird Ct Boulder CO 80303

DUMAS, RHETAUGH ETHELDRA GRAVES, university official; b. Natchez, Miss., Nov. 26, 1928; d. Rhetaugh Graves and Josephine (Clemmons) Graves Bell; m. A.W. Dumas, Jr., Dec. 25, 1950; 1 child, Adrienne. BS in Nursing, Dillard U., 1951; MS in Psychiat. Nursing, Yale U., 1961; PhD in Social Psychology, Union Grad. Sch., Union for Experimenting Colls. and Univs., Cinn., 1975; also various other courses; D Pub. Svc. (hon.), Simmons Coll., 1976, U. Cin., 1981; LHD (hon.), Yale U., 1989; LLD (hon.), Dillard U., 1990; LHD (hon.), U. San Diego, 1993, Georgetown U., 1996; DPub. Svc., Fla. Internat. U., Miami, 1996; DSc (hon.), Ind. U., Gary, 1996; JD (hon.), Bethune-Cookman Coll., 1997, DSc (hon.), 1997; JD (hon.), U. Mass, 1997; LHD (hon.), U. Mass, 1997. Instr. Dillard U., 1957-59, 61; research asst., instr. Sch. Nursing Yale U., 1962-65, from asst. prof. nursing to assoc. prof., 1965-72, chmn. dept. psychiat. nursing, 1972; dir. nursing Conn. Mental Health Ctr., Yale-New Haven Med. Ctr., 1966-72; chief psychiat. nursing edn. br. Div. Manpower and Tng. Programs, NIMH, Rockville, Md., 1972-76; dep. dir. Div. Manpower and Tng. Programs NIMH, 1976-79, dep. dir. alcohol, drug abuse and mental health adminstrn., 1979-81; dean, prof. U. Mich. Sch. Nursing, 1981-94; vice provost health affairs U. Mich., 1994-97, Lucille Cole prof. sch. nursing, 1994—, vice provost emerita, 1997—, dean emerita, 1997—; dir. Group Rels. Confs. in Tavistock Model; cons., speaker, panelist in field; fellow Helen Hadley Hall, Yale U., 1972, Branford Coll., 1972; dir. Community Health Care Ctr. Plan, New Haven, 1969-72; mem. U.S. Assessment Team, cons. to Fed. Ministry Health, Nigeria, 1982; mem. adv. com. Health Policy Agenda for the Am. People, AMA, 1983-86; cons. NIH Task Force on Nursing Rsch., 1984; mem. Nat. Commn. on Unemployment and Mental Health, Nat. Mental Health Assn., 1984-85; mem. com. to plan maj. study of nat. long-term care policy Inst. Medicine, 1985; mem. adv. com. to dir. NIH, 1986-87; mem. Sec.'s Nat. Commn. on Future Structure of VA Health Care System, 1990-91; mem. coun. on grad. med. edn. Nat. Adv. Coun. on Nurse Edn. and Practice Workgroup on Primary Care Workforce Projection, Divsn. Nursing, 1994; mem. com. to rev. breast cancer rsch. program U.S. Army Med. Rsch. and Material Command, Inst. of Medicine, 1996-97; mem. Pres.'s Nat. Bioethics Adv. Commn., 1996—. Author profl. monographs; contbr. over 40 articles to profl. publs.; mem. editorial bd. Community Mental Health Rev., 1977-79, Jour. Personality and Social Systems, 1978-81, Advances in Psychiat. Mental Health Nursing, 1981. Bd. dirs. Afro Am. Ctr., Yale U., 1968-72; mem. New Haven Bd. Edn., 1968-71, New Haven City Demonstrations Agy., 1968-70, Human Rels. Coun. New Haven, 1961-63, Nat. Neural Circuitry Database Com., Inst. Medicine, Nat. Acad. Scis., mem. bd. scientific advisors, 1985—; mem. commn. on future structure of vets. health care U.S. Dept. Vets. Affairs, 1990; mem. Pres. Clinton's Nat. Bioethics Adv. Commn., 1996—. Named Disting. Alumna, Dillard U., 1966; recipient various awards, including cert. Honor NAACP, 1970, Disting. Alumnae award Yale U. Sch. Nursing, 1976, award for outstanding achievement and service in field mental health D.C. chpt. Assn. Black Psychologists, 1980, Pres. 21st Century award The Nat. Women's Hall of Fame, 1994. Fellow A.K. Rice Inst., Am. Coll. Mental Health Adminstrs. (founding), Am. Acad. Nursing (charter, pres. 1987-89); mem. Inst. Medicine NAS, Am. Nurses Assn., Nat. Black Nurses Assn., Am. Assn. Colls. Nursing (govtl. affairs com. 1990-93), Am. Pub. Health Assn., Nat. League Nursing (pres. 1997—), Sigma Theta Tau Internat. (mentor award 1989), Delta Sigma Theta. Office: U Mich 400 N Ingalls St Rm 4320 Ann Arbor MI 48109-2003*

DUMKE, MELVIN PHILIP, dentist; b. Sleepy Eye, Minn., Jan. 23, 1920; s. Herman Gustav and Else Ida (Battig) D.; D.D.S., U. Minn., 1943; m. Phyllis Lorraine Steuck, June 25, 1950; children: Pamela, Bruce, Shari. Practice dentistry, Sleepy Eye, 1946-50, Morgan, Minn., 1950-66, Mankato, Minn., 1966—. Lectr. dental assts. Mankato State Coll., 1967-69. Mem. Town Council, Morgan, 1960-65. Bd. control Martin Luther Acad., New Ulm, Minn., 1965-79; bd. dirs. The Luth. Home, Belle Plaine, Minn., 1981-96, Orgn. Wis. Luth. Svcs.; pres. Luth. Congregation, 1970, 86-87. Served to capt., Dental Corps, AUS, 1943-46. Fellow Royal Soc. Health, Internat. Coll. Dentists, Am. Coll. Dentists, Pierre Fouchard Acad.; mem. ADA (ho. of dels. 1977-87), Minn. Dental Assn. (chmn. peer rev. com. 1973-79, mem. ho. of dels. 1978-89, pres. 1983-84, guest of honor 1993), So. Dist. Dental Soc. (exec. coun., trustee 1988-89, Guest of Honor 1986), South Cen. Dental Study Club (pres. 1970), Fedn. Dentaire Internationale, U. Minn. Alumni Assn., V.F.W. (recipient Distinguished Service award 1966, comdr. 1965), Am. Legion, Lions (pres. 1965, 74, zone chmn. 1975, Melvin Jones fellow 1999), Mankato Golf Club, U. Minn. Sch. Dentistry Century Club, Psi Omega. Home: 364 Carol Ct Mankato MN 56003-3300 Office: 430 S Broad St Mankato MN 56001-3703

DUMMETT, CLIFTON ORRIN, dentist, educator; b. Georgetown, British Guiana, May 20, 1919; came to U.S., 1936; s. Alexander Adolphus and Eglantine Annabella (Johnson) D.; m. Lois Maxine Doyle, Mar. 6, 1943; 1 child, Clifton Orrin Jr. BS in Psychology, Roosevelt U., Chgo., 1941; DDS, Northwestern U., 1941, M.Sc.D., 1942, D.Sc. (hon.), 1976; M.P.H., U. Mich., 1947; Sc.D. (hon.), U. Pa., 1978. Diplomate Am. Bd. Periodontology, Am. Bd. Oral Medicine. Dean, and prof. periodontology Meharry Med. Coll., Nashville, 1945-49; chief dental service VA Hosp., Tuskegee, Ala., 1949-65, assoc. chief staff for research and edn., 1958-65; chief dental service VA Hosp., Chgo., 1965-66; dental dir., dir. ctr. Watts Health Ctr., Los Angeles, 1966-69; assoc. dean, chmn. dept. community dentistry Sch. Dentistry, U. So. Calif., L.A., 1969-75, prof., 1969-89, prof. emeritus, 1989-96, disting. emeritus prof., 1997—; adj. prof. Northwestern U. Dental Sch., 1989; vis. prof., cons. Sch. Vet. Medicine, Tuskegee Inst., 1962-65; vis. prof. Meharry Med. Coll., 1989—; trustee Am. Fund Dental Health, Chgo., 1968-78; chmn. devel. component rev. panel Calif. Regional Med. Programs, L.A., 1975-77; mem. Pres.'s Com. on Nat. Health Ins., 1977. Author: Community Dentistry, 1974, Afro-Americans in Dentistry: Sequence and Consequence of Events, 1977, Charles Edwin Bentley, 1982, Dental Education of Meharry Medical College: Origin and Odyssey, 1992, Culture and Education in Dentistry at Northwestern University, 1993; (editorial) Nor Yet the Last, 1962 (W.J. Gies award 1963), The Hillenbrand Era, 1986; editor Nat. Dental Assn., 1953-75; contbr. over 300 papers and articles to profl. jours., chpts. to books. Chmn. adv. bd. Econ. and Youth Opportunity Agy. Project Head Start, Tuskegee, Ala, 1964-65; mem. spl. health adv. com. Calif. Bd. Edn., Los Angeles, 1972-74; mem. Los Angeles regional hearing planning council, President's Com. on Health Edn., Los Angeles, 1973-74. Served to lt. col. USAF, 1955-58. Recipient Alumni award of Merit Northwestern U., 1971, Fones Gold medal Conn. Dental Assn., 1976, Pierre Fauchard Gold medal Pierre Fauchard Acad., 1980; named to U. So. Calif. Dental Hall of Fame, 1997. Fellow Internat. Coll. Dentists, Am. Coll. Dentists (Wm. J. Gies award 1992), Am. Pub. Health Assn. (John W. Knutson Disting. Svc. award 1992), Am. Pub. Health Assn. (v.p. for U.S., 1995-96), AAAS (chmn. dental sect. 1975-76, 87-88), Am. Acad. History of Dentistry (pres. 1982-83, Hayden and Harris award 1987); mem. ADA (hon.), Internat. Assn. Dental Rsch. (pres. 1969-70), Assn. Mil. Surgeons U.S. (life), Am. Assn. Dental Editors (editor 1963-72, pres. 1974-75, Disting. Svc. medal 1976), Nat. Acads. Practice (Disting. Practitioner 1987), Inst. Medicine Nat. Acad. Sci. (sr. mem.), Sigma Xi. Sigma Pi Phi, Alpha Phi Alpha, Omicron Kappa Upsilon (pres., founder Nashville chpt. 1947-49), Delta Omega. Democrat. Episcopalian. Avocations: music; politics; track. Home: 5344 Highlight Pl Los Angeles CA 90016-5119 Office: U So Calif Sch Dentistry PO Box 77006 Los Angeles CA 90007-0006

DUMOND, ROBERT WILFRED, mental health consultant, lay pastoral worker; b. Lawrence, Mass., Nov. 1, 1952; s. Wilfred Albert and Claire Marie (Dumas) D.; m. Doris Ann Cocchiaro, May 1, 1976; children: Amy Marie, Matthew Christian, Claire Elizabeth. BA in Psychology, U. Mass., 1974; MA in Counseling Psychology, Assumption Coll., Worcester, Mass., 1982. Lic. cert. social worker, Mass.; lic. mental health counselor, Mass.; cert. rape investigator, Mass.; lic. clin. mental health counselor, N.H.; lic. marriage and family therapist, Mass.; lic. rehab. counselor, Mass.; cert. justice of peace, N.H., 1988—; nat. cert. counselor Am. Acad. Cert. Clin. Mental Health Counselors; cert. trainer prison fellowship, 1998—. Child care counselor St. Anne's Home, Inc., Methuen, Mass., 1971-74; dir. region IV The Key Program, Inc. (formerly Cmty. Advancement Program), Lawrence, 1974-79; dir. victim/witness assistance program Commonwealth of Mass., Essex County Dist. Atty's Office, Lawrence, 1979-83, Haverhill, 1983-87; mem. continuing edn. faculty Franklin Pierce Coll., Salem, N.H., 1984—; prin. psychologist Commonwealth of Mass. Dept. Correction, Concord, 1987-91; mental health clinician EMSA Correctional Care, Inc., various cities, Mass., 1992-94; mental health adminstr. Correctional Med. Svcs., Inc., Gardner, Mass., 1994-95; vol. mental health cons., educator Roman Cath. Diocese of Manchester, N.H., 1997—, State of N.H., Concord, 1997—; pastoral/correctional liaison Roman Cath. Diocese of Manchester and State of N.H. Dept. of Corrections, 1997—; v.p., bd. dirs. C'ESTA, Inc., Manchester, 1995—; cons. Safer Soc. Program and Press, Orwell, Vt., 1992-94, Fed. Emergency Mgmt. Agy., Boston, 1991-92; mem., provider Dept. Mental Health, Cmty. Mental Health and Retardation Area Bd., Lawrence, 1981-83; cons., faculty mem. Nat. Coun. on Crime and Delinquency, Hackensack, N.J., 1980-82; cons. City of Hartford, Conn., 1976; gov.'s appointee N.H. State Rehab. Coun., Concord, 1998—; mem. N.H. HIV Prevention Cmty. Planning Group, Concord, 1998—; sr. lectr. divsn. Grad. and Profl. Studies Franklin Pierce Coll., N.H., 1998—. Contbr. articles to profl. jours. and tng. manuals; contbg. author manuals, resource handbooks, ednl. audiotapes. Pastoral care vol. St. Joseph's Hosp., Nashua, N.H., 1997—; bd. dirs. Lazarus Ho. Ministries, Inc., Lawrence, 1986-89, Family Svcs. Assn. Greater Lawrence, Inc., 1982-84, Mental Health and Retardation Svcs., Inc., Lawrence, 1981-83, N.H. Brain Injury Assn., 1997—; mem. human rights com. Area Agy. for Developmental Disability, Nashua, 1997—; disability rights advocate U. N.H. Inst. Disabilities, Concord, 1997—; mem. steering com. Citizens for Discipline in the Schs., Hudson, N.H., 1995-97; participant, panelist, profl. expert various confs., commns., and pub. hearings, in areas of juvenile justice, prison sexual assault, prison conditions, child abuse, and violent crime; mem. No. Essex (N.H.) Com. Against Sexual Assault, 1985-87, co-chair, 1986-87; pres. Mass. Dept. Social Svcs. Area Bd. #12, 1980-81; mem. Mass. Office for Children Statewide Adv. Coun., 1975-77; pres. Greater Lawrence Coun. for Children, 1975-76; vol. coord. prison ministries Roman Cath. Diocese Manchester, N.H., 1998—. Recipient Beyond Excellence Recognition award, Commr. Mass. Dept. Correction, Boston, 1990, Liberty Bell award for Outstanding Cmty. Svc., Lawrence Bar Assn., 1976. Mem. APA (assoc. mem., chair symposium 103rd conf. and session 98th conf. 1990), Nat. Assn. Cath. Chaplains (student mem.), Acad. Criminal Justice Scis. (roundtable convenor 1995, workshop panelist 1992), Am. Acad. Psychiatric Svcs. to Children (presenter 36th and 37th Ann. Confs., 1985, 86), Nat. Orgn. Victim Assistance (presenter Ann. Conf. 1981, nominated to U.S. Dept. Justice Symposium 1984), The Perspectives Network, Inc., New England Assn. Child Care (presenter 1975 spring and fall meetings), New Hampshire Brain Injury Assn., Knights of Columbus (coun. 5162, coun. recorder, officer 1998-99, 4th degree mem., youth dir. 1997—, Knight of Yr. 1997). Roman Catholic. Avocations: playing guitar, Biblical archeology, antiquarian books, on-line computing, writing. E-mail: rwdumond@aol.com. Home: 27 Baker St Hudson NH 03051-3606

DUMONT, ALLAN ELIOT, retired physician, educator; b. N.Y.C., Oct. 8, 1924; m. Joan Auerbach, Oct. 1, 1949; children: Mark E., James A., David H. BA, Hobart Coll., 1945; MD, NYU, 1948. Diplomate Am. Bd. Surgery. Intern Bellevue Hosp., N.Y.C., 1948-49, resident, 1949-51, 53-54, chief resident, 1954-55; instr. surgery NYU, 1955-59, asst. attending surgeon Univ. Hosp., asst. vis. surgeon 3d and 4th surg. divs. Bellevue, 1955-60, asst. prof. surgery, 1959-62, assoc. vis. surgeon 3d and 4th surg. div. Bellvue, 1961-65; attending surgeon Manhattan VA Hosp., N.Y.C., 1958-67, cons. surgeon, 1967-90; assoc. attending surgeon Univ. Hosp. NYU, 1961-68, attending surgeon, 1968-90, assoc. prof. surgery, 1962-68, prof. surgery, 1968-73, Jules Leonard Whitehill prof. surgery, 1973-90, prof. emeritus, 1990—; clin. prof. surgery U. Conn. Sch. Medicine, 1991; career scientist N.Y.C. Health Research Council, 1959-62; univ. senate NYU, 1966-69; vis. surgeon Bellevue Hosp., 1965-90, assoc. dir. surg. service, 1975-90; cons. surgeon St. Francis Hosp., Hartford, 1990—. Editor: Lymphology. 1974-84. Served to lt (j.g.) USN, 1951-53. Recipient Research Career Devel. award USPHS, 1961-71, Purkinje medal, Czechoslovakia, 1977. Mem. Am. Coll. Surgeons, New Eng. Surg. Soc., Harvey Soc., N.Y. Surg. Soc. (pres. 1987-88), Am. Physiol. Soc., Soc. for Exptl. Biology and Medicine, Soc. Univ. Surgeons, Soc. for Surgery Alimentary Tract, Internat. Soc. Lymphology (pres. 1979-83), Transplantation Soc., Am. Surg. Assn.

DUMONT, EDWARD ABDO, architect, interior designer; b. Bklyn., July 4, 1961. AA, Miami Dade Community Coll.; BArch, U. Fla., 1984. Designer Paul, Paul and Madrid Architects, Houston, 1984-87; project mgr. William Crosskey and Assocs. Architects, Hartford, Conn., 1987-89, Brand Allen Architects, Houston, 1989-98, Gensler-Houston, 1998-99; with Gotsdiner Archs., Houston, 1999—. Mem. Rice Design Alliance, Tex. Soc. Interior Designers, Mus. Fine Arts Houston, U. Fla. Nat. Alumni Assn. Avocations: art, photography, furniture design. Home: 4412 Effie St Bellaire TX 77401-5617 Office: Gotsdiner Archs Ste 200 5712 Valverde Houston TX 77057

DUMONT, JAMES KELTON, JR., actor, producer; b. Chgo., Aug. 12, 1965; s. James Kelton and Judith Katherine (Johnson) DuM.; m. Wendell Faith Hall, Dec. 14, 1968. Student, Boston U., 1983-85. Pres., CEO DuMont Entertainment Group, Hollywood, Calif., 1994—; mem. Ensemble Studio Theatre, N.Y.C., 1989—; co-artistic dir. Ensemble Studio Theatre-The L.A. Project, 1994-96; producer Winterfests 1994-96—, First Look L.A., 1996. Appeared in Broadway play Six Degrees of Separation, 1990-93, (off-Broadway play) Tony & Tina's Wedding, 1989-90; films Speed, 1993, Combination Platter, 1993, Bombshell, 1996, The Peacemaker, 1996, Primary Colors, 1996, Erasable You, 1997, In Quiet Night, 1997, Bellyfruit, 1998; television series NYPD Blue, 1995, Lois & Clark, 1996, Chgo. Sons, 1996, Track Takes on 1995, Fallen Angels, 1995, The Client, 1995, Sweet Justice, 1995, Can't Hurry Love, 1995, Arliss, 1998; producer, actor: (film) The Confession, 1996. Democrat. Buddhist. Avocations: writing prose and short stories, plays and screenplays. Office: Ensemble Studio Theatre 137 N Larchmont Blvd # 134 Los Angeles CA 90004-3704

DU MONT, NICOLAS, psychiatrist, educator; b. San Juan, P.R., Dec. 22, 1954; s. Joseph Henri and Isabel (Solano) Du M. Postgrad. adult psychiatry, Columbia U., 1990; MD, U. P.R., 1986; postgrad. child, adolescent psychiatry, Columbia U., 1992, postgrad. pub. cmty. psychiatry, 1993. Assoc. prof. Polytech. U., San Juan, 1984-88, InterAm. U., San Juan, P.R., 1986-87; med. dir. Holistic Med. Ctr., N.Y.C., 1993-94; asst. prof. Albert Einstein Coll. of Medicine, N.Y.C., 1991-96, Mt. Sinai Sch. of Medicine, N.Y.C., 1993-96, Columbia Physicians and Surgeons Coll. Medicine, N.Y.C., 1997—; asst. physician Elmhurst Med. Ctr., N.Y.C., 1993-94, Mt. Sinai Med. Ctr., N.Y.C., 1993-96; v.p., CEO Engring. Med. Support, Inc., N.Y.C., 1992—; asst. prof. Columbia Physicians and Surgeons Coll. Medicine, N.Y.C., 1997—; attending physician Westchester Jewish Med. Svcs., Hartsdale, N.Y., 1990-95, Montefiore Med. Ctr., N.Y.C., 1991-96, Albert Einstein Coll. Medicine, 1991-96, Puerto Rican Family Inst., 1994—; asst. attending physician and med. dir. Tavares Hispanic Mental Health Clin. at Columbia Presbyn. Med. Ctr., 1997—. Assoc. editor: Jour. Pagan Studies (N.Y. edit.), 1990—. Officer Am. Soc. for Minority Advocacy, N.Y.C., 1991—. Vis. fellow N.Y. State Psychiat. Inst., 1992-93. E-mail: info@dumont.org. Office: Engring Med Support Inc Ste 8F 200 W 70th St New York NY 10023-4326

DUMONT, VIRGINIA PETERSON, educator, writer; b. Salt Lake City, Jan. 19, 1918; d. Frederick L. and Florence Julia (Carpenter) Peterson; B.A. with honors in English, Mills Coll., 1938; postgrad. (grad. scholar), Bryn Mawr Coll., 1938-39, (spl. fellow), 1939-40; m. R. Peaslee DuMont, Aug. 5, 1940; children—Virginia Patricia DuMont Kelly, Peaslee Frederick, Jayne Louise DuMont Mack, Julia Blanche DuMont Rivin, Peter Bruce, Lorna Elizabeth DuMont Shinkle, Edward Carroll. Home tchr. Piedmont (Calif.) High Sch., 1970-73; pvt. tutor in English and reading skills, 1970-90. Mem. adv. com. on ednl. philosophy Piedmont Unified Sch. Dist., 1967-68; mem. Piedmont bd. Am. Field Service, 1965-69. Mem. Mills Coll. Alumnae Assn. (chmn. continuing ednl. pilot study 1957-59, nat. gov. 1958-59, dir. Phila. br. 1939, pres. Washington br. 1946-47, pres. Oakland, Calif. br. 1969-70, v.p. program 1983-84), Calif. Writers Club, LWV (v.p. Piedmont 1978-83), Oakland Mus. Calif., Phi Beta Kappa. Contbr. poetry and articles to profl. books; editorial bd. Mills Coll. Alumnae Quar., 1978-87. Address: 100 Bay Pl Apt 1601 Oakland CA 94610-4447

DUMOULIN, DIANA CRISTAUDO, marketing professional; b. Washington, Jan. 5, 1939; d. Emanuel A. and Angela E. (Cogliano) Cristaudo; m. Philip DuMoulin, May 30, 1964; children: Joanmarie Patricia, John Philip. MA, U. Wis., 1967; BA, Rosary Coll., 1961. Project mgr. IDC Cons. Group, Framingham, Mass., 1982-84; sr. market analyst Cullinet, Inc., Westwood, Mass., 1984-86; prof. assoc. Ledgeway Group, Lexington, Mass., 1987-89; prin. Customer Mktg. Specialist, Brookline, Mass., 1989-93; pres. Customer Solutions Internat., Phoenix, 1994—; adj. faculty Ulster Count Community Coll., Stone Ridge, N.Y., 1967-74, Mass. Bay Community Coll., Wellesley Hills, Mass., 1983; lectr. Boston Coll., Chestnut Hill, Mass., 1976. Author: Ourselves in the Garden, 1998; contbr. articles to profl. jours. Pres. LWV, Kingston, N.Y., 1973-74. Recipient Svc. to Young Adults award 70001 Career Assn., 1977, Honorable Mention award Writers Digest Writing Competition, 1996, 98; faculty fellow U. Wis., 1964-66. Mem. Am. Field Svc. Mgrs. Internat. (software support spl. interest group, chmn. minuteman chpt. 1991-92), Nat. Assn. Women Bus. Owners, Ariz. Book Pubs. Assn. Office: Customer Solutions Internat 8441 N 1st Dr Phoenix AZ 85021-5515

DUMOVICH, LORETTA, real estate and transportation company executive; b. Kansas City, Kans., Sept. 29, 1930; d. Michael Nicholas and Frances Barbara (Horvat) D. Student public schs., Kansas City. Lic. real estate broker, Kans., Mo. Corp. sec., dir. Riss Internat. Corp., 1950-86, Riss Intermodal Corp., 1969-86, World Leasing Corp., 1969-86; pres., dir. Columbia Properties, Inc., 1969-86; v.p., dir. Republic Industries, 1969-86; corp. sec., dir. Comml. Equipment Co. Inc., Charlotte, N.C., 1980-93; v.p., corp. sec. Commonwealth Gen. Ins. Co., Kansas City, Mo., 1986-93, Heart of Am. Fire & Casualty Co., Kansas City, 1986-93. Mem. Kansas City (Mo.) Real Estate Bd., Bldg. Owners and Mgrs. Assn. of Kansas City (Mo.), Terminal Properties Exchange (founding mem.), Am. Royal Assn. (gov.). Office: 215 W Pershing Rd Kansas City MO 64108-4317

DUMVILLE, JOHN P., historic site director; b. Hanover, N.H., Feb. 17, 1950. BA, U. Vt., 1972, MA, 1976. Tchr. Turnbridge (Vt.) Sch. Sys., 1974-75; arch. historian State of Vt., 1976-79; dir. Vt. State Historic Sites, Montpelier, 1979—. Selectboard Town of Royalton, Vt., 1994—. Office: Historic Preservation Nat Life Bldg Drawer 20 Montpelier VT 05620-0501

DUMYCH, DANIEL MARTIN, historian; b. Niagara Falls, N.Y., Nov. 10, 1956; s. John and Ann (Lysack) D.; 1 child, Ian Martin. BA, SUNY, Buffalo, 1979, MS, 1981. Freelance writer, hist. cons.; local history specialist Niagara Falls Pub. Libr., 1995—; historian Tesla Meml. Soc., Inc., Lackawanna, N.Y., 1988-91; bd. dirs. Niagara County Hist. Soc., 1994-95; vice chmn. N.Y. State Archives Week Com., 1994-95; adv. com. Documentary Heritage Program, Buffalo, 1997—. Author: The Canadian Niagara Power Company: 100 Years, 1992, A Monument of Light, 1993, Images of America: Niagara Falls, 1996, Ninety Years of Light, 1997, Niagara Falls, Vol. I, 1996, Vol. II, 1998. Mem. Am. Assn. State and Local History, Old Fort Niagara Assn., Inc., Lundy's Lan Hist. Soc., Soc. Indsl. Archaeology, N.Y. State Hist. Assn. Avocations: gardening, walking, reading. E-mail: dumych@sprynet.com. Home: Apt 8 12 Rockne Rd Kenmore NY 14223-3167

DUN, DAVID W., museum director; b. Exerton, Pa., Nov. 22, 1953. BA, Gettysburg Coll., 1975; postgrad., U. Del., 1980-83, U. Colo., 1990. Intern Hist. Soc. York County, Pa., 1975, preparator, 1975-76, acting curator, 1976-77; exec. dir. Packwood House Mus., Lewisburg, Pa., 1977-90; mus. and hist. site adminstr. Somerset (Pa.) Hist. Ctr., 1990-97; dir. R.R. Mus. of Pa., Strasburg, 1997—. Project dir. Survey of Vernacular Arch. of Somerset County, Somerset Hist. Ctr., 1995, Clocks of the Susquehanna Valley, Packwood House Mus., 1990; mem. Lancaster County Heritage Tourism Com., The Strasburg Mktg. Group. Recipient S.K. Stevens award for excellence in Pa. history, 1995. Mem. Am. Assn. Mus., Pa. Fedn. Mus. and Hist. Orgns. (bd. dirs. 1983-94, Award of Merit 1990, 95), Assn. Rwy. Mus., Am. Assn. State and Local History (award of merit 1995), Mid-Atlantic Assn. Mus., Nat. Rwy. Hist. Soc. Office: Railroad Museum of Pa PO Box 15 Strasburg PA 17579-0015*

DUNAEVSKY, VALERY, mechanical engineer, researcher; b. USSR, Dec. 25, 1942; came to U.S., 1979, naturalized, 1985; s. Victor and Alla (Shmulian) D.; m. Ada Shalyt; 1 child, Victoria. MSME, Riga (Latvia) Tech. U., 1965, PhD in Tribology, 1975. Sr. technol./test engr. Diesel Engine Plant, Riga, 1969-76; sr. designer Diesel Locomotive Plant, Riga, 1977-79; sr. staff engr. Westinghouse Air Brake Co., Wilmerding, Pa., 1980-87; tribology group leader Copeland Corp., Sidney, Ohio, 1988-92; group leader compressor engring. Allied Signal/Truck Brake Sys. Co., Elyria, Ohio, 1993—. Editor translation: Handbook of Friction Units of Machines, 1987, Accuracy of Metal-Cutting Tools, 1988; co-author: CRC/STLE Tribology Data Handbook, 1997; contbr. articles to Jour. Tribology, Tribology Trans, SAE Papers. Mem. ASME, Soc. Tribologists and Lubrication Engrs. E-mail: val.dunaevsky@alliedsignal.com. Home: 20110 Lorain Rd Bldg 3213

Fairview Park OH 44126-3481 Office: Allied Signal/Truck Brake Sys Co 901 Cleveland St Elyria OH 44035-4109

DUNAGAN, GWENDOLYN ANN, special education educator; b. Youngstown, Ohio, Sept. 27, 1941; d. Charles Jefferson and Emma Juanita (Alexander) Hicks; m. Willie Miles, 1966; 1 child, Byron Keith Miles; m. Kenneth Robert Dunagan, July 1, 1972. BS in Edn., Youngstown U., Ohio, 1963; postgrad., Ashland U., 1986-89. Cert. elem. tchr., Ohio, learning disabilities tchr., Ohio, tchr. to severe behavior disorder, Ohio. Elem. tchr. Youngstown Bd. Edn., 1963-67, 1968-72; adminstr., tchr. Free Kindergarten Assn., Youngstown, 1967-68; liaison home-sch. Alliance (Ohio) Bd. Edn., 1972-86, tchr. disadvantaged pupils, 1986-89, intervention tchr. learning disabilities, 1989-90, tchr. specific learning disabilities, 1990-94, tchr. spl. edn., 1990-96; contestant, winner TV show Price is Right; group leader Youngstown Detention Ctr. Contbr. articles to profl. mags., area newspapers. Pres. Domestic Violence Shelter, Alliance, 1990-92, hon. mem., 1992—; pres. John Slimack Homeless Shelter, Alliance, 1989-93; pres., founder Cmty. Civic Com., Alliance, 1987—; treas. Altrusic Civic Club, Alliance, 1988-91; mem. choir Holy Temple Ch. God in Christ, Alliance, 1972—, mem. usher bd. dirs., fin. sec., sec. Sunday sch., 1989—; chair Alliance Area Desert Storm Celebration, 1991; mem. Family Counseling Ctr., YWCA, Dr. King Birthday Celebration Com.; mem. Dr. Martin Luther King Jr. Steering Com., 1995; tchr. Prayer and Bible Band, 1990—; adv. bd. Salvation Army, 1994—; parade marshal Dr. M.L. King Jr. Hist. Parade, 1998; mem. Union of Missions. Honored for community svc. Stark County Community Action Agy., 1990. Mem. NAFE, AAUW, Alliance Edn. Assn. (Dowling scholarship com.), NAACP (2d v.p. 1990-93), McKinley Reading Assn., Quota Club, Alpha Kappa Alpha. Avocations: writing poetry, collecting poetry and readings, collecting antique plates, gospel music, scrabble. Home: 1115 S Seneca Ave Alliance OH 44601-4068

DUNAGAN, WALTER BENTON, lawyer, educator; b. Midland, Tex., Dec. 11, 1937; s. Clinton McCormick and Allie Mae (Stout) D.; m. Tera Childress, Feb. 1, 1969; children: Elysha, Sandi. BA, U. Tex., 1963, JD, 1965, postgrad., 1965-68. Bar: Tex. 1965, Fla. 1970, U.S. Dist. Ct. (mid. dist.) Fla. 1971, U.S. Ct. Appeals (11th cir.) 1982. Corp. atty. Gulf Oil, New Orleans, 1968-69, Getty Oil Co., L.A., 1969—, Westinghouse/Econocar, Internat., Daytona Beach, Fla., 1969-72; assoc. Becks & Becks, Daytona Beach, 1973-75; prin. Walter B. Dunagan, Daytona Beach, 1975—; cons. Bermuda Villas Motel, Daytona Beach, Buccanneer Motel, Daytona Beach, Pelican Cove West Homeowners Assn., Edgewater, Fla. Organizer Interfaith Coffee House, New Orleans; tchr., song leader various chs.; chief Indian guide/princess program YMCA, Daytona Beach; bd. dirs. Legal Aid, Daytona Beach. Lance cpl. USMC. Mem. Volusia County Bar Assn., Lawyers Title Guaranty Fund, Phi Delta Phi. Avocations: reading, languages. Home: 714 Egret Ct Edgewater FL 32141 Address: 1141 S Ridgewood Ave Daytona Beach FL 32114-6149

DUNAHOO, CHARLES, religious publisher, religious organization administrator, consultant, human resource director. Coord. Christian Education and Publications of the Presbyterian Ch. in Am., Atlanta. Office: Presbyn Ch Am 1852 Century Pl NE Atlanta GA 30345-4305*

DUNATHAN, HARMON CRAIG, college dean; b. Celina, Ohio, July 25, 1932; s. Harry V. and Mildred B. (Greek) D.; m. Katy Mary Dragati, Mar. 15, 1956 (div. July 1990); children: Christine, Susan, Amy, Andrea; m. Mary Frances Pitts, Sept. 29, 1990. B.A., Ohio Wesleyan U., 1954; M.S., Yale U., 1956, Ph.D., 1958. Mem. faculty Haverford (Pa.) Coll., 1957-75, assoc. prof. chemistry, 1964-70, prof., 1970-75; provost, dean faculty Hobart and William Smith Colls., Geneva, N.Y., 1975-84; acting pres. Hobart and William Smith Colls., 1978-79; dean faculty Hampshire Coll., 1984-87; dean acad. affairs Rhodes Coll., Memphis, 1987-93; prof. chemistry, dir. rsch. and sponsored programs LeMoyne-Owen Coll., Memphis, 1993-95, prof. chemistry, interim v.p. instl. advancement, 1996-97, prof. chemistry, spl. asst. to pres., 1997—. Home: 2014 Hallwood Dr Memphis TN 38107-4703

DUNAVANT, WILLIAM BUCHANAN, JR., textiles executive; b. Memphis, Dec. 19, 1936; s. William Buchanan Sr. and Dorothy (Knight) D.; m. Lillian Dobson (div. May 1975); children: Elizabeth Cornel Dunavant Adams, Dorothy Dobson Dunavant Fisher, William Buchanan III, John Dobson, Buchanan Dobson; m. Ann Querbes (div. Apr. 1989); children: Woodson Querbes, Forrest Buchanan. Student, Vanderbilt U.; BBA, Memphis State U.; HHD (hon.), Rhodes Coll. Jr. ptnr. T.J. White & Co. (now W.B. Dunavant & Co.), Memphis, 1952-56, ptnr., 1956-60; chmn. bd. dirs., chief exec. officer Dunavant Enterprises, Memphis, 1957—; bd. dirs. Nat. Bank of Commerce, Promus, Ptnrs., Inc., Browning Ferris Industries, Inc.; mem. Nat. Adv. Com. on Cotton Mktg. King of Memphis Cotton Carnival, 1973. Chickasaw Coun. Scout Ctr. named in his honor Boy Scouts Am., 1983; recipient Outstanding Community Salesman of the Yr. award Sales and Mktg. Execs. of Memphis, 1980, Spirit of Life award NCCJ, 1984, Outstanding Citizen of the Yr. award Civitan Club, 1984, Master of Free Enterprise award Jr. Achievement, 1984, Humanitarian of the Yr. award Rhodes Coll., 1984, Disting. Alumnus award McCallie Sch., 1986, Alumnus of the Yr. award Memphis State U., 1989. Mem. N.Y. Cotton Exch. (bd. mgrs.), Cotton Coun. Internat. (past bd. dirs.), Nat. Cotton Coun. (chmn. bd. dirs., past pres. and bd. dirs.), Am. Cotton Shippers Assn. (past pres. and bd. dirs.), New Orleans Commodity Exch. (past bd. dirs.), Memphis Cotton Exch. (past bd. dirs.), Southern Cotton Assn. (past pres. and bd. dirs.), Am. Cotton Exporters Assn. (bd. dirs.). Presbyterian. Avocations: tennis, hunting, golf. Office: Dunavant Enterprises Inc PO Box 443 Memphis TN 38101-0443*

DUNAWAY, CAROLYN BENNETT, retired sociology educator; b. Atlanta, Mar. 3, 1943; d. Clarence Rhodes and Gay (McKenzie) Bennett; m. William Preston Dunaway, Aug. 26, 1967; 1 child, Robert Bennett Dunaway. BS, Auburn U., 1966, EdD, 1983; MA, U. Ala., Tuscaloosa, 1967. Instr. sociology Jefferson State C.C., Birmingham, Ala., 1967-69; prof. Auburn U., Montgomery, Ala., 1970-71; prof. sociology and gerontology dept. Jacksonville (Ala.) State U., 1971-95; student counselor Jacksonville State U., Ala., 1971—. Contbd. articles to profl. jours. Cons., trainer Calhoun County Hospice Anniston, Ala., 1983—; presenter Calhoun County Gerontology, Anniston, 1985—; officer Jacksonville Book Club, Ala., 1984; officer, tchr. St Luke's Episcopal Ch., Jacksonville, 1993. Recipient 100 Most Outstanding Women Alumna award Auburn U., 1991, U. Rsch. award Jacksonville State U., 1989. Mem. Ala.-Miss. Sociol. Assn. (v.p. 1975-76, ciology Club,Inter-Se Study Club, Ala. Fedn. Womens Club (dist. sect.), Phi Kappa Phi, Kappa Delta Pi, Delta Delta Delta, Phi Delta Kappa. Democrat. Episcopalian. Avocations: flower arranging, gardening, reading. Home: 902 11th St NE Jacksonville AL 36265-1230

DUNAWAY, (DOROTHY) FAYE, actress; b. Bascom, Fla., Jan. 14, 1941; d. John and Grace D.; m. Peter Wolf, Aug. 7, 1974 (div.); m. Terrence O'Neill; 1 son. Student, U. Fla., Boston U. Appearences include as original mem. Lincoln Ctr. Repertory Co., N.Y.C., off-Broadway in Hogan's Goat; also in (play) Curse of the Aching Heart, 1982; motion picture appearences include Bonnie in motion picture Bonnie and Clyde, 1967, Hurry Sundown, 1967, Puzzle of a Downfall Child, The Happening, 1967, The Thomas Crown Affair, 1968, A Place For Lovers, 1969, Little Big Man, 1970, Doc, 1971, La Maison Sous les Arbres, 1971, The Getaway, 1972, Oklahoma Crude, 1973, The Three Musketeers, 1973, Chinatown, 1974, The Towering Inferno, 1974, The Four Muscateers, 1975, Three Days of the Condor, 1975, Network, 1976 (Acad. award for Best Actress), The Voyage of the Damned, 1976, The Eyes of Laura Mars, 1978, The Champ, 1979, The First Deadly Sin, 1980, Mommie Dearest, 1981, The Wicked Lady, 1982, Ordeal by Innocence, 1985, Supergirl, 1984, Barfly, 1987, Burning Secret, 1988, La Partita, 1988, Midnight Crossing, 1988, The Gamble, 1989, In a Moonlight Night, 1989, Wait Until Spring, Bandini, 1989, The Handmaid's Tale, 1990, Three Weeks in Jerusalem, 1990, Scorchers, 1990, Arrowtooth Waltz, 1991, Double Edge, 1992, The Temp, 1993, Point of No Return, 1993, Even Cowgirls Get the Blues, 1994, Don Juan DeMarco, 1995, En brazos de la mujer madura, 1996, The Chamber, 1996, Albino Alligator, 1996, Dunston Checks In, 1996, Twilight of the Golds, 1997, Drunks, 1997, Fanny Hill, 1998 Love Lies Bleeding, 1999, The Yards, 1999, Joan of Arc, 1999; TV movies: After the Fall, 1974, The Disappearance of Aimee, 1976, Evita Peron, 1981, 13 at Dinner, 1985, Beverly Hills Madame, 1986, Casanova, 1987, Cold Sassy Tree, 1989, Silhouette, 1990 (co-exec. prodr.), Columbo: It's All in the Game (Emmy award for Guest Actress in Drama 1994), Mother Love, 1995, A Family Divided, 1995, The People Next Door, 1996, Rebecca, 1997, Gia, 1998 ; TV miniseries: Ellis Island, 1984, Christopher Columbus, 1985; TV series: It Had To Be You, 1993, A Will of Their Own, 1998. Recipient Most Promising Newcomer Award Brit. Film Acad., 1968. Address: c/o ICM 8942 Wilshire Blvd Beverly Hills CA 90211-1934*

DUNAWAY, MARGARET ANN (MAGGIE DUNAWAY), state agency consultant; b. Fresno, Calif., Feb. 10, 1943; d. Joseph John and Anna Frances (Dice) Cumero; children from previous marriage: Christian Anthony Freitag, Erika Lynn Bullard; m. Michael Earl Babcoke, Oct. 6, 1990; 1 stepchild, Jason Ethan Babcoke. Student, U. Calif., Davis, 1960-62, U. Calif., Berkeley, 1962-63. Supr. Gov's Office, Sacramento, 1969-72; office mgr. State Health and Welfare Agy., Sacramento, 1972-73; analyst regulations devel. Calif. State Depts. Health and Social Svcs., Sacramento, 1974-84, cons. adult and children's svcs., 1984-90, rep. adult svcs., 1984-90, with food drive com., 1987-88, rep. ind. living program com., 1989-90; community program specialist Calif. State Dept. Devel. Svcs., Sacramento, 1990—; project coord. SDSS study L.A. County Children's Svcs. Caseload, 1989-90; primary cons. SDDS study Family Home Agy. Program, 1998—. Active Southpark Homeowner's Assn., Sacramento, 1974-78; presenter Adult Svcs. Ann. Asilomar Conf., 1987; coord., presenter 1st ann. Adult Family Home Conf., L.A., 1999. Office: Calif Dept Devel Svcs 1600 9th St Ste 320 Sacramento CA 95814-6414

DUNAWAY, SAMANTHA JO, secondary school educator; b. Cin., Apr. 28, 1971; d. Joseph A. and Patricia A. (Lindsley) D.; m. Mark A. Gillespie, dec. 31, 1993. BS, Morehead (Ky.) State U., 1993. Substitute tchr. Kodiak Island (Alaska) Borough Sch. Dist., 1993-94, spl. edn. tchr.'s aide, 1994, spl. edn. tchr., 1994-95; libr. A. Holmes Johnson Meml. Libr., Kodiak, 1994-95; receptionist/sec.. Kodiak Island Borough Mental Health Ctr., 1995; tchr. Kenny Lake Sch., Copper Center, Alaska, 1995-96; tchr. Nome (Alaska) Pub. Schs., 1996—, chmn. dept. English, 1996—. Author book rev. col.: Life and Lit in Bering strait Record, 1996-97; author essays and poetry. Choir mem. Nome Cmty. Chorus, 1998-99, Kodiak Cmty. Chorus, 1993-94; flutist Cmty. Band, Kodiak, 1993-95. Mem. Nome Edn. assn. (publicity officer 1996—), Nome Reading Cir., Phi Kappa Phi, Kappa Delta Pi. Democrat. Unitarian Universalist. Avocations: reading, writing, hiking, singing, playing flute. Home: PO Box 1822 Nome AK 99762-1822 Office: Nome-Beltz High School PO Box 131 Nome AK 99762-0131

DUNBAR, BRUCE STEPHEN, photographer, gallery administrator; b. Stratford, Conn., Aug. 12, 1967. BA, Boston U., 1989. Gallery mgr. Silvermine Guild Arts Ctr., New Canaan, Conn., 1995—; photography instr. Silvermine Sch. Art, 1998—; freelance photographer, Stratford, Conn., 1996—. Contbr. photographs to Greenwich Mag., Metroline.

DUNBAR, DAVID WESLEY, bank executive; b. New Haven, June 23, 1952; s. Carl Owen and Ann Harris (Peck) D; m. Cynthia Susan Minnick, Mar. 8, 1980. BS in Fin., Acctg., Fla. State U., 1974; Cert. Comml. Lender in Comml. Lending and Fin., U. Okla., 1977; cert. in banking and fin., La. State U., 1982. Legis. analyst Fla. State Ho. of Reps., Tallahassee, 1973-74; mgmt. trainee S.E. Banking Corp., Miami, 1975; asst. v.p. S.E. Bank of St. Petersburg (Fla.), 1976; v.p. S.E. Bank of Pinellas, Largo, Fla., 1977-80; v.p. regional S.E. Banking Corp., Tampa, Fla., 1980-81; pres., CEO Republic Bank, Clearwater, Fla., 1981-88, 91-93; pres. Dunbar Corp., Palm Harbor, Fla., 1989-91; exec. v.p., bd. dirs. Peoples State Bank, New Port Richey, Fla., 1993-95; chmn., CEO, founder Peoples Bank, Palm Harbor, Fla., 1995—; chmn. Fla. Bankpac Fla. Bankers Assn., Tallahassee, 1985-87. Treas. Morton Plant-Mease Hosp. Found., Clearwater, 1986-88, 94-96; mem. Donald Roebling Soc., dress circle Performing Arts Ctr. Theater; bd. dirs. Retarded Citizens Found., Clearwater, 1982-90, 98—, Pinellas County Edn. Found., Largo, 1986-92, Pinellas County Arts Coun., 1985-86; gov.'s appointee as commr. to Taxation and Budget Reform Commn. State of Fla., 1990—; trustee Morton Plant-Mease Hosp., 1997—, Morton Plant Mease Health Care, 1997—, North Bay Hosp., 1998—, New Port Richey, Fla.; gov. apptd. commr. Fla. Elections Commn., 1998—, dir. CNL Health Care Properties Inc., 1998—. Named one of Outstanding Young Men of Am., U.S. Jaycees, 1980, Fla. Advance Team Mem., U.S. White House, 1980. Mem. Fla. State U. Found. (Pres.'s Club), Weston Innisbrook Resort, Cypress Run Country Club. Avocations: golfing, sport fishing. Office: Peoples Bank 32845 Us Highway 19 N Palm Harbor FL 34684-3140

DUNBAR, IAN FRASER, veterinarian, animal behaviorist; b. Hemel Hempstead, Eng., Apr. 15, 1947; came to U.S., 1971; s. Kenneth James Dunbar and Betty May Stanbridge; m. Mimi Whei Ping Lou, May 1, 1979 (div. Dec. 1989); 1 child, Jamie Lu. BSc, U. London, 1967, B in Vet. Medicine, 1971; PhD, U. Calif., Berkeley, 1974; DHC (hon.), Sch Agr., Høng, Denmark, 1996. Rsch. assoc. U. Calif., Berkeley, 1971—; dir. Sirius Puppy Tng., Berkeley, 1981—; dir., CEO Ctr. for Applied Animal Behavior, Berkeley, 1986—, James & Kenneth Pubs., Berkeley, 1986—; cons. San Francisco SPCA, 1985-86, Nabisco, N.J., 1998—; cons. editor Howell Book House, N.Y., 1998—. Author: Dog Behavior, 1987, How to Teach a New Dog Old Tricks, 1996; author, host video: Sirius Puppy Training, 1987; host TV series Dogs With Dunbar, 1991-97. Recipient 4 Maxwell awards Dog Writers Assn. Am. Mem. Royal Coll. Vet. Surgeons, Calif. Vet. Med. Assn., Sierra Vet. Med. Assn., Assn. Pet Dog Trainers (founder, hon. life), Am. Vet. Soc. of Animal Behavior, Can. Assn. Profl. Pet Dog Trainers (hon. life). Avocations: gardening, reading, skiing. Office: James & Kenneth Pubs 2140 Shattuck Ave # 2406 Berkeley CA 94704

DUNBAR, LESLIE WALLACE, writer, consultant; b. Lewisburg, W.Va., Jan. 27, 1921; s. Marion Leslie and Minnie Lee (Crickenberger) D.; m. Peggy Rawls, July 5, 1942; children: Linda Dunbar Kravitz, Anthony Paul; 1 foster child, Nha Van. M.A., Cornell U., 1946, Ph.D., 1948. Asst. prof. polit. sci. Emory U., Atlanta, 1948-51; chief community affairs Savannah River plant AEC, Aiken, S.C., 1951-54; asst. prof. polit. sci. Mt. Holyoke Coll., 1955-58; dir. research So. Regional Council, Atlanta, 1958-61; exec. dir. So. Regional Council, 1961-65; exec. dir., sec. Field Found., N.Y.C., 1965-80; vis. prof. polit. sci. U. Ariz., 1981; cons. Fund for Peace, Nat. Urban League, 1981-84; sr. project assoc. social welfare policy, 1985-87, Ford Found.; guardian ad litem State of N.C., 1993—. Author: A Republic of Equals, 1966, The Common Interest, 1988, Reclaiming Liberalism, 1990; co-author, editor: Minority Report, 1984; book rev. editor So. Changes, 1989-93. Pres. Nation Inst., 1980-84, bd. dirs., 1980-86; bd. dirs. Village of Pelham (N.Y.) Library Bd., 1980-84, pres., 1982-84; bd. dirs. Children's Found., 1980-86, pres., 1982-84; bd. dirs. Franklin and Eleanor Roosevelt Inst., 1987—, v.p., 1987-92; bd. dirs. Eleanor Roosevelt Inst., 1976-87, Field Found., 1978-80, Minority Rights Group, N.Y.C., 1980-85, Ctr. Nat. Security Studies, 1980-87, Amnesty Internat./U.S.A., 1984-86, Winston Found. for World Peace, 1985-98, Voter Edn. Project, 1987-90, N.C. Coun. Chs., 1991-93, Ruth Mott Fund, 1988—, chair, 1992-94, Windcall Resident Program (selection com.), 1990-94, Southeastern Efforts Developing Sustainable Staples, Inc. (SEEDS), 1998—; deacon Watts St. Bapt. Ch., Durham, 1998—. Guggenheim fellow, 1954-55; United Negro Coll. Fund scholar-at-large, 1984-85. Fellow So. Regional Coun. (life). Home: 10 Whitburn Pl Durham NC 27705-5586

DUNBAR, MABLE CLEONE, counselor education, family; b. May 3, 1953; d. Byron Anderson and Ellen Elizabeth (Lynch) Douglas; m. Colin A. Dunbar, Aug. 13, 1972; children: Elrene Dunbar Perez, Elizabeth, Colin II. BA in Secondary Edn., West Indes Coll., Mandeville, Jamaica, West Indies, 1975; MA in Edn. and Counseling Psychology, Andrews U., 1990; PhD in Family Mediation, La Salle U., Mandeville, La., 1995. Lic. prof. counselor, Mich. Sec. Bermuda Conf. of S.DA, Bermuda, 1983-85; tchr. secondary sch. Bermuda Inst., 1986-88; dir. childrens' ministries Bermuda Conf. of S.DA, Bermuda, 1988; grad. asst. Andrews U., Berrien Springs, Mich., 1988-90; parent educator St. Joseph Med. Ctr., South Bend, Ind., 1989-90; exec. dir., counselor Safe Shelter, Inc., Benton Harbor, Mich., 1990-97; CEO, pres. Women In Renewal, Inc., Niles, Mich., 1997—. Founder Shelter Program for Christian Women in Crisis. Named Woman of Yr., Assn. of Adventist Women, Boston, 1997. Mem. Optimist Club. Seventh Day Adventist. Avocations: gardening, music, reading, walking, people. Home: 4756 Greenfield Dr Berrien Springs MI 49103-9554 Office: Women In Renewal Inc PO Box 102 Berrien Center MI 49102

DUNBAR, MARY ASMUNDSON, communications executive, investor and public relations consultant; b. Sacramento, Calif., Feb. 6, 1942; d. Vigfus Samundur and Aline Mary (McGrath) Asmundson; m. Robert Copeland Dunbar, June 21, 1969; children: Geoffrey Townsend, William Asmundson. BA in English Lit., Smith Coll., 1964; MA in Communications, Stanford, 1967; MBA in Fin., Case Western Res. U., 1985. Cert. pub. rels. profl. Tchr. Peace Corps, Cameroun, Africa, 1964-66; writer, editor Ednl. Devel. Corp., Palo Alto, Calif., 1967-68, Addison-Wesley, Menlo Park, Calif., 1969-70; free lance writer, editor various, Cleve., 1970-85; account exec. Edward Howard & Co., Cleve., 1985-87; account exec. Dix & Eaton, Inc., Cleve., 1987-89, sr. account exec., 1990-92, v.p., 1992-96, sr. v.p., 1997—. Author publs. in field. Trustee Cleve. Coun. World Affairs, 1994—. Smith Coll. scholar, Northampton, Mass., 1960-64; fellowship Stanford Univ., Palo Alto, Calif., 1967; recipient Internat. Assn. Bus. Comm. award, 1987, Women in Comm. award, 1987, Arthur Page award, 1990. Mem. Smith Coll. Club Cleve., Pub. Rels. Soc. Am. (Silver Anvil award 1997), Nat. Investor Rels. Inst. (pres. Cleve.-No. Ohio chpt.), Cleve. Soc. Security Analysts, Cleve. Com. Fgn. Rels. Republican. Episcopalian. Avocations: jogging, music. Home: 2880 Fairfax Rd Cleveland OH 44118-4014 Office: Dix & Eaton Inc 1301 E 9th St Ste 1300 Cleveland OH 44114-1820

DUNBAR, PATRICIA LYNN, new product development consultant; b. St. Louis, Feb. 11, 1953; d. William R. and Beryl Ione Noland (Ferrand) D.; m. Michael R. Jeffrey, Oct. 2, 1950. BS, Northwestern U., 1973, MFA, 1975. With NBC-TV, Chgo., 1975-79; regional sales/mktg. mgr. HBO, Chgo., 1979-81; sr. product mgr. Bank of Am., San Francisco, 1981-82, v.p., 1982-84; v.p. electronic commerce GMAC, 1999—; Internet/Intranet strategic and mktg. planning cons. prodr. and cons., 1984—; bd. dirs. Sci. and Tech. Enrichment Program, 1982—, pres., 1993-94; exec. prodr. Oracle Ann. Report on CD-ROM, 1994. Patentee child's chair. Mem. Interactive Svcs. Assn., Women in Cable (1st pres. Chgo. chpt. 1981), Jr. League Seattle. Episcopalian.

DUNBAR, PRESCOTT NELSON, investment company executive; b. New Orleans, Feb. 22, 1942; s. Lewis D. Prescott and Eleanor (Nelson) D.; BA, U. of South, 1964; MA, La. State U., 1967; MA (Ford fellow), Harvard U., 1969; m. Sarah W. Blodgett, Feb. 10, 1969; children: P. Hayden, Lander G. Financier, New Orleans. Trustee, New Orleans Mus. Art, 1974-93, 97-2000, 1st. v.p., 1979, treas., 1978, chmn. of accessions, 1977, 1998, 1999, sec., 1982, 86, 2d v.p, 1984, 85; pres. of fellows, 1993, 96, 97, trustee New Orleans Ballet, 1983-87, English Speaking Union New Orleans, 1986—, Friends of French Market, 1984, pres. 1985, U. of the South, 1989-91; bd. dirs. Save Our Cemeteries, 1975-86, Anglo-Am. Mus. Friends, 1985, La. Soc. Prevention of Cruelty to Animals, 1981-84, Friends of Stage Harbor Waterways, 1982—. Mem. La. Hist. Soc., Friends of Cabildo, Friends of Winterthur, Provincetown Art Assn., Am. Assn. Mus. Trustees, Royal Order of Soc. St. George, Stage Harbor Yacht Club, Chatham Beach and Tennis Club, Harvard Club of N.Y., New Orleans Country Club, Internat. House Club, Internat. Dendrology Soc. Republican. Episcopalian. Author: History of the New Orleans Museum of Art: The First 75 Years, 1990. Home and Office: 2423 Prytania St New Orleans LA 70130-5807

DUNBAR, R. ALLAN, college administrator, clergyman; b. Calgary, Alta., Can., Nov. 24, 1939; s. Marvel Dale and Marie Alma (Gonyea) D.; m. Judy Ann Johnson, Sept. 10, 1960; children: Daren Kirk, Jill Dione. BTh, Alta. Bible Coll., Calgary, 1961; MA, Lincoln (Ill.) Christian Sem., 1968; DDiv, Pacific Christian Coll., Fullerton, Calif., 1996. Ordained to ministry Christian Ch., 1961. Sr. min. Hanna (Alta.) Ch. of Christ, 1961-64; assoc. min. Southside Christian Ch., Hammond, Ind., 1964-68; sr. min. First Christian Ch., Florence, Oreg., 1968-73; sr. pastor Bow Valley Christian Ch., Calgary, 1973-95; dir., host TV ministry To You. . .With Love, Calgary, 1973-95; pres. Puget Sound Christian Coll., Edmonds, Wash., 1995—; pres. N.Am. Christian Conv., Louisville, 1989; founding pres. Western Can. Christian Conv., Calgary, 1992-93. Recipient Shalom award State of Israel, 1987, Outstanding Svc. award Lincoln Christian Coll., 1990. Mem. Rotary Club (pres. 1972). Avocations: woodworking, photography, sports. Office: Puget Sound Christian Coll 410 4th Ave N Edmonds WA 98020-3171

DUNCALF, DERYCK, retired anesthesiologist; b. York, Eng., Nov. 14, 1926; came to U.S., 1956; s. Hubert Claude and Anne Elizabeth D.; m. Mira Novakovic, July 23, 1978; children: Richard Michael, Tamara, Sharon. MB, ChB, U. Leeds, 1950. Diplomate Am. Bd. Anesthesiology. Resident in anesthesia St. James Hosp. and Gen. Infirmary, Leeds, 1950-54, Cardiff Royal Infirmary, Wales, 1954-56; fellow faculty anaesthetists Royal Coll. Physicians and Surgeons, 1954; fellow in anesthesiology Mercy Hosp., Pitts., 1956-57, Montreal Children's Hosp., Que., Can., 1958-59; staff anesthesiologist Kings County Hosp., Bklyn., 1959-62; staff anesthesiologist Montefiore Med. Ctr., Bronx, 1962-97, chmn. dept. anesthesiology, 1975-85; prof. anesthesiology Albert Einstein Coll. Medicine, Bronx, 1971-97, vice-chmn. dept. anesthesiology, 1985-94, emeritus prof., 1997—; cons. Wyckoff Heights Hosp., Bklyn., 1966-85. Author: (with D.H. Rhodes) Anesthesia in Clinic Ophthalmolgy, 1963; contbr. articles to profl. jours. Fellow Am. Coll. Anesthesiologists; mem. Am. Soc. Anesthesiologists, N.Y. State Soc. Anesthesiologists, Pan Am. Med. Assn. (diplomate and hon. life mem. sect. anesthesiology), N.Y. Acad. Medicine, Assn. Univ Anesthetists, Ecuatoriano de Anesthesiologia (hon.). Home: 33 Ferncliff Rd Cos Cob CT 06807-1206

DUNCAN, A. BAKER, investment banker; b. Waco, Tex., Dec. 29, 1927; s. A. Baker and Frances (Higginbotham) D.; m. Sally P. Witt, Jan. 31, 1953; children: Addison Baker III, Richard Witt, Andrew Prescott. Grad., Woodberry Forest (Va.) Sch., 1945; B.A., Yale, 1949; M.A., U. Tex., 1952. Master Hill Sch., Pottstown, Pa., 1949-51; partner Rotan Mosle & Co. (investment bankers), Houston, 1953-61; headmaster Woodberry Forest Sch., 1962-70; sr. v.p., dir. Rotan Mosle Inc., 1970-78; chmn. Duncan-Smith Co., 1978—. Bd. dirs. Trinity U., S.W. Rsch. Inst.; gov. emeritus Tex. Mil. Inst. Mem. Chi Psi. Democrat. Episcopalian. Home: 610 Garraty Rd San Antonio TX 78209-6149 Office: East Travis Bldg 311 3rd St San Antonio TX 78205-1907

DUNCAN, CAROL GREENE, art historian, educator; b. Chgo., Nov. 10, 1936. AB, U. Chgo., 1958, AM, 1960; PhD, Columbia U., 1968. Prof. art history Ramapo Coll. N.J., Mahwah, 1972—; vis. prof. U. Queensland, Brisbane, Australia, 1985, UCLA, 1974, U. Calif., San Diego, 1976, U. Pitts., 1994, Fla. State U., 1999. Author: Aesthetics of Power, 1993, Civilizing Rituals, 1995.

DUNCAN, CHARLES LEE, food products company executive; b. Waynesboro, Tenn., Oct. 10, 1939; s. Grady E. and D. Pearl (Dotson) D.; m. Barbara C. Woodburne, June 21, 1967; children: Stuart L., Andrew R., Amy L. BS, U. Tenn., Martin, 1961; MS, La. State U., 1963; PhD, U. Wis., 1967. Postdoctoral fellow dept. nutrition sci. U. Wis., Madison, 1966-68, asst. prof. Food Rsch. Inst. and dept. bacteriology, 1968-72, assoc. prof., 1972-76, prof., 1976-77; dir. food safety and nutrition Campbell Soup Co., Camden, N.J., 1977-79, v.p. food sci. and tech., 1979-81; v.p. R & D Hershey (Pa.) Foods Corp., 1981—; postdoctoral fellow dept. microbiology U. Wash., Seattle, 1975. Contbr. numerous articles to sci. jours. Recipient Rsch. Career Devel. award NIH, 1974-79. Mem. Am. Soc. Microbiology, Internat. Life Scis. Inst. (treas.), Inst. Food Technologists (mem. rsch. com. 1986-89), AAAS. Republican. Mem. Ch. of Christ. Avocation: orchid growing. Office: Hershey Foods Corp 1025 Reese Ave Hershey PA 17033-2272*

DUNCAN, CHARLES TIGNOR, lawyer; b. Washington, Oct. 31, 1924; s. Robert Todd and Nancy Gladys (Jackson) D.; m. Dorothy Adelena Thrasher, July 31, 1947 (dec. Dec. 1972); 1 child, Charles Todd; m. Pamela Jo Thurber, Aug. 10, 1996. BA, Dartmouth Coll., 1947, LLD (hon.), 1986; JD, Harvard U., 1950. Bar: N.Y. 1951, D.C. 1953, U.S. Supreme Ct. 1954, Md. 1955. Assoc. Rosenman, Goldmark, Colin & Kaye, N.Y.C., 1950-53; partner Reeves, Robinson & Duncan, Washington, 1953-60; prin. asst. U.S. atty. Washington, 1961-65; gen. counsel U.S. Equal Employment Opportunity Commn., Washington, 1965-66; corp. counsel D.C., 1966-70; acting dir. pub. safety, 1969; partner Epstein, Friedman, Duncan & Medalie, Washington, 1970-74; dean, prof. law Sch. Law Howard U., 1974-78; ptnr. Peabody, Lambert & Meyers, Washington, 1978-84, Reid & Priest, Washington, 1984-90; sr. counsel Reid & Priest, 1990-94; mem. Iran-U.S. Claims Tribunal, The Hague, The Netherlands, 1994—. Trustee Northfield Mt. Hermon Sch., 1980-90, chmn. 1987-90; trustee NAACP Legal Def. and Edn.

Fund. With USNR, 1944-46. Recipient Distinguished Service award D.C. Bar, 1974. Fellow Am. Bar Found. (life); mem. ABA, Nat. Bar Assn., D.C. Bar Unified (Pub. Service award 1974, pres. 1973-74), Phi Beta Kappa, Alpha Phi Alpha, Sigma Pi Phi, Delta Theta Phi. Democrat. Lodge: Masons (32 deg.). Active participant in preparation and presentation of sch. desegregation cases before U.S. Supreme Ct., 1953-55. Home: 1362 Myrtle Ave Annapolis MD 21403-4952

DUNCAN, CHARLES WILLIAM, JR., investor, former government official; b. Houston, Sept. 9, 1926; s. Charles William and Mary Lillian (House) D.; m. Thetis Anne Smith, June 10, 1957; children: Charles William III, Mary Anne. BSChemE, Rice U., 1947; postgrad. mgmt., U. Tex., 1948-49. Roustabout, chem. engr. Humble Oil & Refining Co., 1947; with Duncan Foods Co., Houston, 1948-64; adminstrv. v.p. Duncan Foods Co., 1957-58, pres., chmn. adv. bd., 1958-64; pres. Coca-Cola Co. Food Div., Houston, 1964-67; chmn. Coca-Cola Europe, 1967-70; exec. v.p. Coca-Cola Co., Atlanta, 1970-71; pres. Coca-Cola Co., 1971-74; chmn. bd., dir. Rotan Mosle Fin. Corp., Houston, 1974-77; dep. sec. Dept. Def., Washington, 1977-79; sec. Dept. Energy, Washington, 1979-81; bd. dirs. Am. Express, United Techs. Inc., Newfield Exploration Co.,; dir. Welch Found. Trustee emeritus, immediate past chmn. Rice U. With USAAF, 1944-46. Mem. Coun. Fgn. Rels., Houston Country Club, River Oaks Country Club, Allegro Club, Sigma Alpha Epsilon, Sigma Iota Epsilon. Methodist. Home: 9 Briarwood Ct Houston TX 77019-5801 Office: 600 Travis St Ste 6100 Houston TX 77002-3007

DUNCAN, CHERYL L., critical care/cardiac catherization nurse; b. Fayette County, Ky., Apr. 26, 1960; d. Thomas Jr. and Nadine (Johnson) Dabney; m. Anthony W. Duncan, Aug. 30, 1986; children: Anthony Thomas, Ashley Jadine. BSN, Ea. Ky. U., Richmond, 1983. RN, Ky., Tex.; cert. BCLS, CPR instr. Nurse level I critical care unit Meth. Hosp., Houston, 1984-85, 86-87, asst. head nurse 3-11 shift coronary care unity, 1987-89, staff nurse level II cardiac catherization lab., 1989—; clin. level I nurse St. Joseph Hosp., Lexingotn, Ky., 1983-84, 85-86. Mem. ANA, AACN, Am. Heart Assn., N.Am. Soc. Pacing and Electrophysiology, Networks for Health Awareness, Soc. Critical Care Medicine, Sigma Theta Tau. Home: 7919 Candle Ln Houston TX 77071-2010

DUNCAN, CONSTANCE CATHARINE, psychologist, educator, researcher; b. Watertown, Wis., Nov. 2, 1948; d. Howard Burton and Mary Elizabeth (Fagan) Duncan; m. Allan Franklin Mirsky, July 4, 1986. BA, Northwestern U., 1970; AM, U. Ill., 1973, PhD, 1978. Sr. rsch. analyst Adolf Meyer Mental Health Ctr., Decatur, Ill., 1971-73; asst. in rsch. and tchg. dept. psychology U. Ill., Champaign, 1974-78; NIMH postdoctoral fellow in neuroscis. Stanford U. Sch. Medicine, Palo Alto, Calif., 1978-81; rsch. psychologist VA Med. Ctr., Palo Alto, 1978-81; sr. staff fellow Lab. Psychology and Psychopathology, NIMH, 1981-88; chief unit on psychophysiology NIMH, Bethesda, Md., 1982-89, rsch. psychologist, 1988-89, rsch. specialist, 1989-93; pvt. practice Bethesda, Md., 1981—; adj. assoc. prof. Johns Hopkins Sch. Hygiene and Pub. Health, Balt., 1987—; guest rschr. Lab. of Psychology and Psychopathology NIMH, 1993-97, Lab. of Brain and Cognition, 1997—; rsch. assoc. prof. Uniformed Svcs. U. Health Scis., 1993—; mem. assembly of scientists coun. NIMH/NINCDS, 1982-84. Assoc. editor Psychophysiology, 1987-91; cons. editor numerous sci. jours.; contbr. articles to profl. jours., chpts. to books. Found. assoc. Nat. Women's Econ. Alliance; mem. NIMH/NINCDS Assembly of Scientists Coun., 1982-84. Recipient Nat. Rsch. Svc. award, NIMH, 1978-81, Golden Anniversary Scholarship award, AAUW, 1974; NIMH fellow, 1970-74. Fellow APA, Am. Psychol. Soc.; mem. Soc. for Psychophysiol. Rsch. (dir. 1982-85, Disting. Sci. award for early career contbn. 1980, chmn. awards com. 1981-84, chmn. conv. com. 1983-87, mem. conv. com., 1996-99, chmn. program com. 1987, mem. Blue Ribbon panel on State of the Soc. in the Yr. 2000, 1990-93, chmn. enhancement com., 1992-93, chmn. early career award com. 1994-96, sec.-treas. 1996—), Soc. for Rsch. in Psychopathology (dir. 1986-88, membership com. 1987-88), Soc. for Neurosci., Internat. Neuropsychol. Soc., Am. Psychopathol. Assn., Mortar Bd., Shi-Ai, Sigma Xi, Phi Kappa Phi, Alpha Lambda Delta, Pi Mu Epsilon, Phi Beta Kappa. Achievements include electrophysiological and neuropsychological research on normal and disordered attention and cognition. Office: Uniformed Svcs U Hlth Scis Dept Psychiatry 4301 Jones Bridge Rd Bethesda MD 20814-4712

DUNCAN, DALE A., publishing executive. BA in Journalism, Cen. Mich. U., 1976; student, Am. Press Inst., 1980, 83, 86, Northwestern U., 1996. Reporter Belleville (Ill.) News-Dem. and Oakland Press, Pontiac, Mich., 1976-80; exec. editor, city editor Times Leader, Wilkes-Barre, Pa., 1980-86, pres., pub., 1986-94; pres., pub. Oakland Press, Pontiac, 1995-97; v.p. ABC Pub. Group, 1995-97; pres., gen. mgr. Indpls. Newspapers, Inc., 1998—. Bd. chmn. Salvation Army; dir. F. M. Kirby Ctr. for Performing Arts; bd. dirs. United Way Oakland County; adv. bd. Clinton Valley coun. Boy Scouts Am.; mem. ch. and soc. task force St. Paul's United Meth. Ch.; co-chair minority journalism fundraising com. Cen. Mich. U. Recipient 3 nat. journalism awards Scripps-Howard, 4 Pa. state awards for editl. writing, Disting. Citizen award Penn Mountains coun. Boy Scouts Am., 1995. Mem. Pa. Newspaper Pub.'s Assn. (bd. dirs., chmn. diversity com.), C. of C. Fax: (317) 633-9331. Office: Indpls Newspapers Inc 307 N Pennsylvania St Indianapolis IN 46204-1899

DUNCAN, DAN L., gas company executive. CEO Enterprise Products, Houston. Office: Enterprise Products PO Box 4324 Houston TX 77092*

DUNCAN, DEBORAH L., bank executive. Sr. v.p. corp. treas. Chase Manhattan, N.Y.C. Office: Chase Manhattan One Chase Manhattan Plz New York NY 10081*

DUNCAN, DONALD PENDLETON, retired forestry educator; b. Joliet, Ill., Feb. 24, 1916; s. Kenneth Whitney and Nettie (Pendleton) D.; m. Dymer Mercein Benzie, July 6, 1956; children: Kenneth Houlton, Nancy Susan, Debra Mercein. Student, North Park U., 1934-35, Mich. Coll. Mining and Tech., summer 1935; BS in Forestry, U. Mich., 1937, MS in Zoology, 1939; PhD, U. Minn., 1951. Shelter belt asst. U.S. Forest Svc., Meade, Kans., 1939-40; jr. forester U.S. Forest Svc., Harrison, Ark. and Brooklyn, Miss., 1940-41; instr. Kans. State U., Manhattan, 1941-42, extension forester, 1946-47; instr. Army U., Florence, Italy, 1945; from instr. to prof. U. Minn., St. Paul, 1947-59, prof., 1959-65, asst. dir. Sch. Forestry, 1964-65; dir. Sch. Forestry, Fisheries and Wildlife, U. Mo., Columbia, 1965-85; forester Coop. Rsch.-Sci. and Edn. Adminstrn., USDA, Washington, 1980-81; cons. Minn. Natural Resources Coun., 1961-63, Coop. State Rsch. Svc., 1969-84, Fgn. Area Fellowship Program, 1969, 70, Coun. Grad. Schs., 1970, Ohio State U., 1975, Duke U., 1975, U. Ky., 1976, U. Fla., 1979, TVA, 1979, U. Ark., 1980, U. Tenn., 1984, U.S. Forestry Edn. Assessment, 1986-88, Mo. Conservation Fedn., 1989-93; vis. scientist NSF, 1965, 68, 69, 72; mem. Nat. Coop. Forestry Rsch. Adv. Bd., 1967-74; mem. exec. bd. Assn. State Coll. and U. Forestry Rsch. Orgns., 1967-68, v.p., 1975-76,pres. 1977-78; chmn. Coun. Forestry Sch. Exec., 1970-71, Com. on Forestry Accreditation, 1970-74; mem. forestry del. to China, 1980. Dist. chmn. Boy Scouts Am., 1969-71; elder, trustee Presbyn. Ch. With AUS, 1942-45. Decorated Bronze Star, Purple Heart; recipient Disting. Alumnus award U. Mich., 1987. Fellow AAAS, Soc. Am. Foresters (past sect. chmn. and sec.-treas., chmn. recreation and edn. divs., chmn. com. on accreditation, com. on ednl. policies, Karkhagne award for disting. svc. 1985); mem. Am. Forestry Assn., Forest History Soc. (past bd. dirs.), Mo. Acad. Sci., Mo. Conservation Fedn. (v.p. forestry com. 1990-94, Conservationist of Yr. award 1985), Audubon Soc. (past chpt. chmn.), Kiwanis, Sigma Xi, Gamma Alpha, Xi Sigma Pi, Phi Sigma, Gamma Sigma Delta (Disting. Adminstrn. award 1975). Achievements include research in forest ecology, forest influences, outdoor recreation, forestry education. Home: 221 W Brandon Rd Columbia MO 65203-3574 *If other commitments permit, when opportunities arise to assume important responsibilities, assume them—but stay consistently within your limitations. Importance is measured by the magnitude of the contribution to other people. The importance of any particular responsibility changes over time and the good judgment to distinguish at any given time between the important and the less important is paramount.*

DUNCAN, DONALD WILLIAM, lawyer; b. Baldwin, Md., May 18, 1932; s. William Rush and Mary Alice (MacBlane) D.; children: David, Lisa. A.A., U. Balt., 1956, J.D., 1960. Bar: Md. 1960, Fla. 1992; cert. family law, County Ct. mediator. Asso. Haynie & McFerrin, C.P.A., Balt., 1956-61; controller H.C. Weiskettel Co., Balt., 1961-62; v.p., counsel, sec., Balt. Aircoil Co., Inc., 1962-87. Served with USAF, 1951-55. Mem. AICPA, Md. Bar Assn., Fla. Bar. Republican. Presbyterian.

DUNCAN, DORIS GOTTSCHALK, information systems educator; b. Seattle, Nov. 19, 1944; d. Raymond Robert and Marian (Onstad) D.; m. Robert George Gottschalk, Sept. 12, 1971 (div. Dec. 1983). BA, U. Wash., Seattle, 1967, MBA, 1968; PhD, Golden Gate U., 1978. Cert. data processor, systems profl., computer profl., data educator. Comm. cons. Pacific N.W. Bell Tel. Co., Seattle, 1968-71; mktg. supr. AT&T, San Francisco, 1971-73; sr. cons., project leader Quantum Sci. Corp., Palo Alto, Calif., 1973-75; dir. co. analysis program Input Inc., Palo Alto, 1975-76; lectr. acctg. and info. systems Calif. State U., Hayward, 1976-78, assoc. prof., 1978-85, prof., 1985—, coord. computer info. sys., 1994—; dir. info. sci. dept. Golden Gate U., San Francisco, 1982-83, mem. info. systems adv. bd., 1983-85; cons. pvt. cos., 1975—; vis. prof. U. Wash., Seattle, 1997-98; spkr. profl. groups and confs. Author: Computers and Remote Computing Services, 1983; contbr. articles to profl. jours.; mem. editl. rev. bd. Jour. Info. Systems Edn., 1992—. Loaned exec. United Good Neighbors, Seattle, 1969; nat. com. woman bd. dirs. Young Reps., Wash., 1970-71; advisor Jr. Achievement, San Francisco, 1971-72; mem. nat. bd. Inst. for Certification of Computer Profls. Edn. Found., 1990-93; bd. dirs. Computer Repair Svcs., 1992-94. Named Computer Educator of Yr., Internat. Assn. Computer Info. Systems, 1997. Mem. Data Processing Mgmt. Assn. (Meritorious Svc. award, Bronze award 1984, Silver award 1986, Gold award 1988, Emerald award 1992, Diamond award 1994, Double Diamond award 1999, Nat. grantee, 1984, dir. edn. chmn. San Francisco chpt. 1984-85, sec. and v.p. 1985, pres. 1986, assn. dir. 1987, by-laws chmn. 1987, chair awards com. 1992-95, nat. bd. dirs. spl. interest group in edn. 1985-87), Am. Inst. Decision Scis., Western Assn. Schs. and Colls. (accreditation evaluation team 1984-85), Assn. Computing Machinery, Jr. Club of Seattle (Beautiful Home award Foster City 1994, 95, winner Tournament of Christmas Lights 1996), Bus. Honor Soc., Beta Gamma Sigma. Subspecialties: Information systems (information science). Current work: curriculum development, professionalism in data processing field, professional certification, industry standards, computer literacy and user education, system analysis and design, design of data bases and data banks. Office: Calif State U Sch of Bus and Econs Hayward CA 94542

DUNCAN, ED EUGENE, lawyer; b. Gary, Ind., Dec. 10, 1948; s. Attwood and Freddie Leon (Ballard) D.; m. Patricia Louise Revado, Sept. 8, 1973 (div.); children: Kristin, Anika, Gregory. BA, Oberlin Coll., 1970; JD, Northwestern U., 1974. Bar: Ohio 1974, U.S. Dist. Ct. (no. dist.) Ohio 1977, U.S. Supreme Ct. 1977. Assoc. Arter & Hadden, Cleve., 1974-82, ptnr., 1982—. Bd. mem. Glenville br. YMCA, Cleve., 1979—, Ohio Bd. of Bldg. Standards, Columbus, 1986-89; trustee Legal Aid Soc., Cleve., 1990-91. Mem. Ohio Bar Assn., Cleve. Bar Assn., Minority Ptnrs. in Majority Corp. Law Firms, Internat. Assn. Def. Counsel. Avocations: writing, reading. Home: 935 Roland Rd Cleveland OH 44124-1033 Office: Arter & Hadden 925 Euclid Ave Ste 1100 Cleveland OH 44115-1475

DUNCAN, ELIZABETH CHARLOTTE, marriage and family therapist, educational therapist, educator; b. L.A., Mar. 10, 1919; d. Frederick John de St. Vrain and Nellie Mae (Goucher) Schwankovsky; m. William McConnell Duncan, Oct. 12, 1941 (div. 1949); 1 child, Susan Elizabeth Duncan St. Vrain. BA, Calif. U., Long Beach, 1953; MA, UCLA, 1962; PhD, Internat. Coll., 1984. Cert. marriage and family therapist; cert. clin. psychopathologist. Wash. Dir. gifted program Palos Verdes Sch. Dist., Calif., 1958-64; TV tchr., participant ednl. films L.A. County, 1961-64; dir. U. So. Calif. Presch., L.A., 1965-69, Abraham Maslow rsch. assoc., 1962-69; pvt. practice family counselor, Malibu and Ventura, Calif., Eastsound, Wash., 1979—, also, Seattle, pvt. practice in psychotherapy, West Seattle, 1994—; pub. spkr., lectr. comm.; cons. in field; psychotherapist Mentor Program Eastsound, 1992; bd. dirs. Children's Program North Sound Regional Support Network, 1992; resident psychologist for film series Something Personal, 1987—; mem. Rsch. Inst. of Scripps Clinic, La Jolla, Calif.; charter mem. Inst. Behav. Med., Santa Barbara, Calif.; TV performer: (documentary) The Other Side, 1985. Creator: Persephone's Child, 1988. Active Chryalis Ctr., L.A., 1984-86, Ventura County Mental Health Adv. Bd., Calif., 1985-86, United Way, L.A., 1985-92; mem. Menninger Found. San Juan County, Wash., 1992; adv. bd. North Sound Regional Support Network, 1992, Amb's People to People, San Juan County Network, 1998—. Recipient Emmy award for best documentary Am. TV Arts and Scis., 1976, Child Adv. of Yr. Calif. Mental Health Adv. Bd., 1987. Mem. AACD (Disting. Svc. award 1990), Transpersonal Psychol. Assn., Calif. State Orgn. Gifted Edn. (sec. 1962-64), Internat. Platform Assn., Am. Assn. for Marriages and Family Therapy. Democrat. Avocations: swimming, plays, concerts, boating, political issues, especially women and child abuse. *It takes a great deal of courage to live life at the highest we know. It doesn't take courage to do something we're not afraid to do—only the things we fear. But, our sense of who we are is greatly influenced and strengthened by being courageous.*

DUNCAN, FRANCES MURPHY, retired special education educator; b. Utica, N.Y., June 23, 1920; d. Edward Simon and Elizabeth Myers (Stack) Murphy; m. Lee C. Duncan, June 23, 1947 (div. June 1969); children: Lee C., Edward M., Paul H., Elizabeth B., Nancy R., Richard L. BA, Columbia U., 1942; MEd, Auburn U., 1963, EdD, 1969. Head sci. dept. Arnold Jr. H.S., Columbus, Ga., 1960-63; tchr. physiology, Spanish, Jordan H.S., Columbus, 1963-64; tchr. spl. edn. mentally retarded Muscogee County Sch. System, Columbus, 1964-65; instr. spl. edn. Auburn (Ala.) U., 1966-69; assoc. dir. Douglas Sch. for Learning Disabilities, Columbus, 1969-70; prof. edn. and spl. edn. Columbus Coll., 1970-85; ret., 1985. Past dir. Columbus Devel. Ctr. Past sec. exec. bd. Muscular Dystrophy Assn., 1968-70; 73-74; mem. Gov.'s Commn. on Disabled Georgians; past trustee Listening Eyes Sch. for Deaf; past mem. Mayor's Com. on Handicapped; mem. team for evaluation and placement of exceptional children Columbus Pub. Schs. Fellow Am. Assn. Mental Retardation; mem. AAUP, AAUW (pres. 1973-75, div. rec. sec. 1975—), Council Exceptional Children (legis. chmn. 1973-74), Psi Chi, Phi Delta Kappa. Roman Catholic. Home: 1811 Alta Vista Dr Columbus GA 31907-3210

DUNCAN, FRANCIS, historian, government official; b. Oak Park, Ill., July 12, 1922; s. Fred B. and Olive (Whitney) D.; m. Frances M. Mergus, Aug. 16, 1947; children: Evan, April. BA, Ohio Wesleyan U., 1944; MA, U. Chgo., 1947, PhD, 1954. Instr. history Wayne State U., Detroit, 1947-50; civilian employee Office of Intelligence, USAF, Washington, 1950-57; analyst Office of Controller, AEC, Washington, 1957-62, asst. historian, 1962-74; asso. historian div. naval reactors ERDA, 1974-77; historian div. naval reactors Dept. Energy, 1977-86, cons. hist. divsn., 1986-96. Author: Rickover and the Nuclear Navy, the Discipline of Technology, 1990, (with Richard G. Hewlett) Atomic shield, 1969, Nuclear Navy 1946-62, 1974; author articles in naval history. Served with USNR, 1943-46. Recipient David D. Lloyd Prize in History 1970, Theodore and Franklin D. Roosevelt Naval History Prize, 1991. Mem. AAAS, U.S. Naval Inst., Soc. for History in the Fed. Govt., Naval Submarine League, Naval Hist. Found., Nat. Coun. on Pub. History. Home: 9209 Ewing Dr Bethesda MD 20817-3313

DUNCAN, GLORIA CELESTINE, elementary educator; b. Columbia, S.C., May 31, 1944; d. John DuBois and Fannie Ruby Batiste; m. (div. Dec. 1975); 1 child, Jason Ira. AA, City Coll. San Francisco, 1965; BA, U. Bridgeport, 1968; MA, U. San Francisco, 1984. Presenter Calif. State Dept., Long Beach, 1990; mentor tchr. Alum Rock Sch. Dist., San Jose, 1990-94, educator, 1972—; adv. bd. San Jose Writing Project, 1993-96; assoc. dir. San Jose State U., 1993-96. Mem. youth adv. bd. Am. Cancer Soc., Santa Clara County, 1995—, vol., 1985—; mem. edn. com. Kids Voting U.S.A., Silicon Valley, 1994—; sr. warden St. Philip's Episcopal Ch., San Jose, Calif., 1988. Mem. Informal Computer Using Educators (membership co-chair, adv. bd. mem.), Delta Kappa Gamma (co-pres. 1996, pres. Gamma Psi chpt. 1998—), Phi Delta Kappa (Stanford chpt. historian 1995-96, treas. 1996—), Beta Pi Sigma (Soror of Yr. 1996). Avocations: travel, reading, sewing, knitting, playing tennis. Office: Mildred Goss Elem Sch 2475 Van Winkle Ln San Jose CA 95116-3758

DUNCAN, GRIFF, opera company executive; b. Morselton, Ark., Mar. 25, 1933. BA, Chico State Coll., 1957. Co-founder Contra Costa Music Theatre, Walnut Creek, Calif., 1961—; co-founder, gen. mgr. Fullerton (Calif.) Civic Light Opera Co., 1971—. Producer more than 100 Broadway musicals. Recipient Best Prodn. award Critic's Choice, 1995, Bus. of Yr. award Fullerton C. of C., 1983, Founder's award, 1997. Mem. Nat. Alliance Music Theatre Producers. Office: Fullerton Civic Light Opera Co 218 W Commonwealth Ave Fullerton CA 92832-1880*

DUNCAN, JAMES RICHARD, systems administrator; b. Little Rock, June 3, 1948; s. James Richard and Mary (Bond) D. BA in Geography, U. Calif., Berkeley, 1969; postgrad. in mass comms., Denver U., 1970. Contract engr. San Jose, Calif., 1972-90; engring. mgr. Nationwide Comms., San Jose, Calif., 1985-90; corp. engr. Kool Comms., San Jose, Calif., 1990-95; network adminstr. United Broadcasting, San Jose, 1995-96; v.p. info. systems Taxwright, Inc., 1996-98; cons. Ohlone C.C., Fremont, Calif., 1990—; chief designer Okay Multimedia, 1998—. Mem. Am. Coun. for Arts, Ariel Dance Co., Santa Clara Ballet. Avocations: LINUX, internat. folk dance, ballet performance, ice skating. E-mail: JIM@OKAY.com.

DUNCAN, JENNINGS LIGON, minister; b. Greenville, S.C., Nov. 29, 1960; s. Jennings Ligon and Shirley Anne (Ledford) D.; m. Marjorie Anne Harley, Jan. 25, 1992; 1 child, Sarah Kennedy. BA, Furman U., 1983; MDiv, Covenant Theol. Sem., St. Louis, 1986, MA, 1987; PhD, U. Edinburgh, 1995. Ordained Presbyn. minister, 1990. Asst. pastor Trinity Presbyn. Ch., Jackson, Miss., 1990-95; prof. theology Reformed Theol. Sem., Jackson, 1990-96; sr. minister First Presbyn. Ch., Jackson, 1996—; interim pastor 1st Presbyn. Ch., Yazoo City, Miss., 1993; editl. dir. Reformed Acad. Press, Greenville, S.C., 1993—; adj. prof. Reformed Theol. Sem., 1996—. Author: The Westminster Assembly: A Guide To Basic Bibliography, 1993; editor, author: A Short History of the Westminster Assembly, 1993; editor: Method for Prayer, 1994; contbr. articles to profl. publs. Bd. dirs. Belhaven Coll., Jackson, 1998—; adv. bd. Values Investing Forum, Jackson, 1997—, Kindness Found., Hattiesburg, Miss., 1997—. Fellow Ctr. Advancement Paleo-Orthodoxy, Carl F.H. Henry Inst. for Evang. Engagement; mem. Scottish Evang. Theology Soc., Rutherford House Fellowship, N.Am. Patristic Soc., Evang. Theol. Soc., S.C. Hist. Soc. Presbyn. Avocations: reading, music, chess, basketball, tennis. Office: 1st Presbyn Ch 1390 N State St Jackson MS 39202

DUNCAN, JOHN DEAN, JR., lawyer; b. Detroit, Nov. 25, 1950; s. John Dean Duncan and Ann Marie (Bruton) Bridges; m. Vickie Renee Olafson, May 10, 1986; children: Katherine Lund, John Dean III. Student, USAF Acad., 1969-71; BA, Cath. U., 1973, JD, 1976; MPA, Harvard U., 1991. Bar: U.S. Ct. Appeals Md. 1976, U.S. Ct. Appeals D.C. 1978, U.S. Supreme Ct. 1980. Law clk. to presiding justice 6th Jud. Ct., Rockville, Md., 1976-77; sr. asst. state's atty. Montgomery County, Rockville, 1977-81; sr. trial atty. pub. integrity sect., criminal div. Dept. Justice, Washington, 1981-87; chief counsel to Inspector Gen. Dept. State, Washington, 1987-98, sr. seminar, 1998—; career mem. Sr. Exec. Svc. U.S., 1987—. Mem. admissions com. J.F. Kennedy Sch. of Govt., Harvard U., Cambridge, Mass., 1991; bar liaison Law Related Edn. Project of Md., 1979-80; alumni rep. nat. phonethon Cath. U., Washington, 1980. Named one of Outstanding Young Men Am., 1980. Mem. D.C. Bar Assn., Mountgomery County Bar Assn. (editor manual on local practice and procedure 1980), Nat. Dist. Attys. Assn., Aircraft Owners and Pilots Assn. Avocations: flying, alpine skiing, squash, sports car driving, jogging. Office: Dept State Nat Sec Council The White House Washington DC 20520-0001

DUNCAN, JOHN J., JR., congressman; b. Lebanon, Tenn., July 21, 1947; m. Lynn Hawkins; children: Tara, Whitney, John J. III, Zane. BS, U. Tenn., 1969; JD, George Washington U., 1973. Pvt. practice Knoxville, Tenn., 1973-81; state trial judge, 1981-88; mem. 100th-106th Congresses from 2nd Tenn. dist., Washington, 1988—; mem. pub. works and transp. com., chmn. aviation subcom., mem. natural resources com. Bd. dirs. or past bd. dirs. ARC, YWCA, Sunshine Ctr. for Mentally Retarded, Beck Black Heritage Ctr., Knoxville Union Rescue Mission, St. Citizens Home Aid Svc., Knoxville Girls Club, others; active elder Eastminster Presbyn. Ch. Capt. U.S. N.G. and Res. Mem. Am. Legion, Elks, Sertoma Club, 40&8, Masons, Shriners. Office: US Ho of Reps 2400 Rayburn House Office Bldg Washington DC 20515-4202

DUNCAN, JOHN M., Canadian government official; b. Winnipeg, Can., Dec. 19, 1948. Degree in forestry, U. B.C. Mem. Parliament, Ottawa, Ont., Can., 1993—. Office: Ho of Commons, Rm 249 180 Wellington St, Ottawa, ON Canada K1A 0A6*

DUNCAN, JOHN PATRICK CAVANAUGH, lawyer; b. Kalamazoo, Mich., Jan. 25, 1949; s. James H. and Colleen Patricia (Cloney) D.; children: Sarah Eleln, James Patrick Cloney. BA cum laude, Yale U., 1970; JD, U. Chgo., 1974. Bar: Ill. 1974, U.S. Dist. Ct. (no. dist.) Ill. 1974, U.S. Ct. Appeals (7th cir.) 1975, U.S. Supreme Ct. 1979. Assoc. firm Holleb & Coff, Chgo., 1974-79; mem., 1979-87; ptnr. Jones, Day, Reavis & Pogue, Chgo., 1987—; leader banking and investment practice area, 1996—; adj. prof. IIT Chgo.-Kent Coll. Law Fin. Svcs. LLM Program, 1988—; mem. Fulbright Vis. Scholar Adv. Bd., 1995-98; mem. Chgo. com. Chgo. Coun. on Fgn. Rels., 1998—. Contbr. articles to profl. jours. Fellow NSF, 1970. Fellow Ill. Bar Found.; mem. ABA (bus. and banking sect., chmn. securities activities banks subcom. 1995-98, privacy task force 1998—), Chgo. Bar Assn. (chmn., fin. insts. coms. 1985-86), Ill. Bankers Assn. (legal affairs com. 1986-87), Yale U. Club (Chgo.). Home: 3814 N Paulina St Chicago IL 60613-2716 Office: Jones Day Reavis & Pogue 77 W Wacker Dr Ste 3500 Chicago IL 60601-1692

DUNCAN, JOSEPH WAYMAN, business economist; b. Cambridge, Ohio, Dec. 2, 1936; s. George Wendall and Elizabeth (Fuller) D.; m. Janice Elaine Gouveia, Aug. 19, 1961; children: Jeffrey Wayman, James Wendall. B.S. in Mech. Engring, Case Inst. Tech., 1958; M.B.A., Harvard U., 1960; Ph.D., Ohio State U., 1970. Economist Battelle Meml. Inst., Columbus, Ohio, 1961-68; coordinator urban affairs Battelle Meml. Inst., 1969-73; dep. asst. sec. for econ. policy Dept. Commerce, Washington, 1968-69; dep. assoc. dir. Office Mgmt. and Budget, Washington, 1974-78; dir. Office Fed. Statis. Policy and Standards, Dept. Commerce, Washington, 1978-81; asst. adminstr. for statis. policy Office of Info. and Regulatory Affairs, Office of Mgmt. and Budget, Washington, 1981; corp. economist and chief statistician Dun & Bradstreet Corp., 1982-96, corp. officer, 1986-96, v.p., 1989; chmn. Micro Mite, Inc., 1996—; chmn. coordination bd. OAS Com. on Improvement of Nat. Statis., 1975-79; U.S. rep. UN Statis. Commn., 1974-81, chmn. 1981. Author: Statistics for the 21st Century, 1993, 2d edit. 1995; contbr. articles to profl. jours. Fellow Am. Statis. Assn., Nat. Assn. Bus. Economists (pres. 1992-93, editor stat. corner, bus. econs. 1986-95); mem. NAS (math. sci. edn. bd. 1989-92), Nat. Economists Club (pres. 1979, chmn. 1980), Conf. Bus. Economists (elected), Internat. Statis. Inst. (v.p. 1991-93), Internat. Assn. Ofcl. Stats. (v.p. 1987-91), Forecasters Club N.Y. (pres. 1986-87), Cosmos (Washington). Home: 909 Holoma Dr Vero Beach FL 32963-3405

DUNCAN, LARRY EDWARD, councilman; b. Davenport, Iowa, Feb. 17, 1946; m. Susan Marie (Shorey) Duncan, 1967. BA, Drake U., 1968; MLA, So. Meth. U., 1978. Computer cons., 1967—; councilman Dist. 4 City of Dallas, 1991—. With U.S. Army, 1968-70. Decorated Bronze Star. Home: 5415 Banting Way Dallas TX 75227-1410 Office: 1500 Marilla St Rm 5fn Dallas TX 75201-6300

DUNCAN, LELAND RAY, retired mission administrator; b. Bee Branch, Ark., Nov. 9, 1929; s. Enoch R. and Julia C. (Lane) D.; m. M. Ruth Tindall, May 28, 1952; children: Wallace L., Gregory A. BA, Oakland City U., 1962; postgrad., So. Theol. Sem., 1966-67; DD, Oakland City U., 1974. Owner, oper. Twin City Radio & TV, North Little Rock, Ark., 1956-59; pastor Gen. Bapt. Chs., Ind., Ark., Ky. & Mo., 1959-71; exec. dir. Gen. Bapt. Home Missions, Poplar Bluff, Mo., 1972-97, pres., until 1997; ret., 1997; chmn. com. to revise Gen. Bapt. Statements of Faith, 1968-71; founder Gen. Bapt. Investment Fund, Popular Bluff, 1974, pres., 1974—; chmn. nominating com. N.Am. Bapt. Fellowship, Washington, 1978, chmn. cons. on ch. planting, 1979; mem. Connect Mo., Jefferson City, 1994. Mem. Poplar BLuff PTA, 1969-73; pres. Poplar BLuff Min.'s Assn., 1971. With

7th infantry divns. U.S. Army, 1951-52, Korea. Mem. Am. Legion, Am. Woodcarvers Assn. Avocations: wood carving, gardening, walking, reading. Home: 3643 Mclane Dr Poplar Bluff MO 63901-8752

DUNCAN, MARGARET CAROLINE, physician; b. Salt Lake City, June 9, 1930; d. Donald and Margaret Aileen (Eberts) D.; m. N. Paul Arceneaux, Dec. 26, 1958; children—David Paul, Eleanor Anne, Stephen Louis, Andre. B.A., U. Tex., 1952, M.D., 1955. Intern Kings County Hosp., Seattle, 1955-56; resident in pediatrics John Sealy Hosp., Galveston, Tex., 1956-58; resident in neurology Charity Hosp., New Orleans, 1958-60; fellow child neurology Johns Hopkins Hosp., 1960-61; mem. faculty La. State U. Med. Center, New Orleans, 1961—; prof. neurology and pediatrics La. State U. Med. Center, 1973—. Chmn. La. Com. Epilespy and Cerebral Palsy, 1976-79. Fellow Am. Acad. Neurology, Am. Acad. Pediatrics; mem. Child Neurology Soc., Profs. Child Neurology, Alpha Omega Alpha. Episcopalian. Office: 1542 Tulane Ave New Orleans LA 70112-2825

DUNCAN, MARK, government official. BME, Royal Mil. Coll., 1968; Diploma of Pub. Adminstrn., Dalhousie U., 1975; MA in Pub. Adminstrn., Carleton U., 1981. Comml. pilot, 1974; registered profl. engr., Ont. Supt. airport sys. Transport Can., Ottawa, Ont., 1975-78; dep. airport gen. mgr., mgr. ops. Lester B.Pearson Airport Transport Can., Toronto, 1978-87; regional dir. gen. Airports Group Transport Can., Vancouver, B.C., 1987-96; regional dir. gen. Pacific Region Transport Can., Vancouver, 1996—; chmn. Pacific Coun. of Sr. Fed. Ofcls., 1994-95. Account exec. United Way; mem. Vancouver Bd. of Trade. Recipient Achievement award Internat. N.W. Aviation Coun., 1995. Home: 3116 Duchess Ave, North Vancouver, BC Canada V7K 3B6 Office: Dept Transport Pacific Reg, 800 Burrard St PO Box 620, Vancouver, BC Canada V6Z 2J8

DUNCAN, MAURICE GREER, accountant, consultant; b. Marshall, Mo., July 16, 1928; s. Carl I. and Marguerite (Greer) D.; m. Sara Bangert, Aug. 29, 1959; children: Nancy L., Guerry M., Barbara D. BSBA, U. Okla., 1950. CPA, Okla. Staff acct. Amoco Corp., Houston, 1951-52; staff acct. B.W. Vetter & Co., CPAs, Tulsa, 1953-58, ptnr., 1959-73; ptnr. Hurdman & Cranston, CPAs, Tulsa, 1974-79; mng. ptnr. Main Hurdman, CPAs, Tulsa, 1979-87; ptnr. KPMG Peat Marwick, CPAs, Tulsa, 1987-88; cons. Maurice G. Duncan, CPA, Tulsa, 1988—; mem. Tulsa Estate Planning Forum, 1978-88, pres. 1981. With USNR, 1950-59. Mem. AICPAs, Okla. Soc. CPAs, Tulsa Execs. Assn. (pres. 1985), Kiwanis. Republican. Methodist. Home and Office: 4325 E 87th St Tulsa OK 74137-2726

DUNCAN, NORA KATHRYN, lawyer; b. Chgo., Feb. 23, 1946; d. Robert Ferrie and Elise Grace (Walker) D. BA in Sociology, MacMurray Coll., 1968; JD, La. State U., 1973; LLM in Internat. and Comparative Law, George Washington U., 1979. Bar: La. 1973, U.S. Dist. Ct. (mid. dist.) La. 1974, U.S. Supreme Ct. 1978, D.C. 1979, U.S. Dist. Ct. (we. dist.) La. 1981, U.S. Ct. Appeals (5th and 11th cirs.) 1981. Staff atty. La. Dept. of Justice, Baton Rouge, 1973-76; contract counsel lands and natural resource La. Dept. of Justice, Washington, 1976-78; staff atty. La. Dept. of Justice, Shreveport, 1980; assoc. Cady & Thompson, Shreveport, 1981-82; ptnr. Cady, Thompson & Duncan, Shreveport, 1983; pvt. practice Shreveport, 1984-86, 87-88; ptnr. Walker, Tooke, Perlman & Lyons, Shreveport, 1986; atty. U.S. Immigration and Naturalization Service Dept. Justice, Oakdale, La., 1988-92, ret., 1992; instr., dir. paralegal studies program Draughon Bus. Coll., 1987. Atty., speech writer Gahagan for U.S. Senate, Augusta, 1978; bd. dirs. Better Bus. Bur., Shreveport, 1985-86; lit. tutor and trainer Allen Parish Libraries Adult Literacy Program; pres. Oakdale-Elizabeth Branch Friends of the Library, 1994-96; founder, 1st pres. Reading Edn. for Adult Devel.-READ, 1997—. Paul Harris fellow Rotary Found., 1981. Mem. Toastmasters Internat. (area 11 gov. 1986-87, area 18 gov. 1994-95, pres. local chpt. 1986, 88, 94, named dist. 68 Gov. of Yr. 1987, dist. 25 Govt. of the Yr. 1995), Rotary (dist. 6290 group study exch. team leader 1997), Rotarian of the Yr. 1994-95, sec. 1995-96). Republican.

DUNCAN, PEARL ROSE, writer, poet; b. Feb. 24, 1947. BA, Bryn Mawr Coll., 1969; MPhil, Newton Coll., 1972. Author: poems, short stories; contbr. Essence mag., New York mag. Home: PO Box 1274 Church St New York NY 10008-1274

DUNCAN, POPE ALEXANDER, college administrator; b. Glasgow, Ky., Sept. 8, 1920; s. Pope Alexander and Mabel (Roberts) D.; m. Margaret Flexer, June 30, 1943; children—Mary Margaret Jones, Annie Laurie Kelly, Katherine Maxwell. B.S., U. Ga., 1940, M.S., 1941; Th.M., So. Bapt. Theol. Sem., 1944, Ph.D., 1947; postgrad., U. Zurich, 1960-61; LLD (hon.), Rollins Coll., 1987; LittD (hon.), Limestone Coll., 1987; LLD (hon.), Stetson U., 1987; EdD (hon.), Alderson-Broaddus Coll., 1994; LLD (hon.), William Jewell Coll., 1999. Instr. physics U. Ga., 1940-41; fellow So. Bapt. Theol. Sem., 1944-45; dir. religious activities Mercer U., 1945-46, Roberts prof. ch. history, 1948-49; prof. religion Stetson U., 1946-48, 49-53; prof. ch. history Southeastern Bapt. Theol. Sem., 1953-63; dean Brunswick Coll., 1964; pres. South Ga. Coll., Douglas, 1964-68; v.p. Ga. So. U., Statesboro, 1968-71, pres., 1971-77; pres. Stetson U., DeLand, Fla., 1977-87, chancellor, 1987—. Author: Our Baptist Story, 1958, The Pilgrimage of Christianity, 1965, Hanserd Knollys, 1965. Pres. Wake Forest Civic Club, 1959-60, Ga. Assn. Colls., 1968-69; pres. Coastal Empire council Boy Scouts Am., 1973-74; chmn. council of presidents So. Consortium for Internat. Edn., Inc., 1974-75; mem. commn. on colls. So. Assn. Colls. and Schs., 1978-82; bd. dirs. Fla. Endowment for Humanities, 1978; chmn. pres.'s council Ind. Colls. and Univs. Fla., 1982-84 ; chmn. Fla. Ind. Colls. Fund, 1980-81; mem. exec. com. So. Univ. Conf., 1981-85. Mem. Am. Hist. Assn., Am. Soc. Ch. History, Douglas Coffee County C. of C. (dir. 1966-68), DeLand (Fla.) C. of C. (dir. 1978-81), Nat. Assn. Ind. Colls. and Univs. (dir. 1979-83), Fla. Assn. Colls. and Univs. (bd. dirs. 1978-85, v.p. 1981-82, pres. 1982-83, Disting. Service award 1987), Nat. Collegiate Athletic Assn. (pres.'s commn. 1985-87), Assn. So. Bapt. Colls. and Schs. (pres. 1980-81), Assn. Ch. Related Colls. and Univs. of the South (pres. 1984-85), Phi Beta Kappa, Omicron Delta Kappa, Phi Kappa Phi, Phi Delta Kappa, Kappa Delta Pi, Pi Mu Epsilon, Phi Eta Sigma, Sigma Phi Sigma. Democrat. Baptist. Lodge: Rotary (dir. 1965-66, 70-72, pres. 1967-68). Office: Stetson U Office of the Chancellor Deland FL 32720

DUNCAN, RICHARD LEO, communications educator; b. Plymouth, Ill., Dec. 7, 1936; s. Gilbert Leo and Vera Viola (Payne) D.; m. Mary Rose Hackett, Dec. 16, 1962 (div. Nov. 1981); m. Eva Elena Hargis, Mar. 26, 1994; 1 child, Sean Mackenzie; stepchildren: Danielle M. Adams, Joshua M. Adams. BA in Chemistry, Knox Coll., 1958; MDiv, Pacific Sch. Religion, 1969; postgrad., San Diego C.C., 1977-81. Ordained United Ch. of Christ, 1970. Min. youth and edn. Kensington Cmty. Ch., San Diego, 1969-74; campus min. Calif. State U., Long Beach, 1975-77; exec. dir. Religious Media Ministry-United Ch. of Christ, San Diego, 1977-88; pastor media ministry Shiloh Ch.-United Ch. of Christ, Dayton, Ohio, 1988-94; faculty, dir. Comm. Ctr. United Theol. Sem., Dayton, 1994—; prodr. KGTV (ABC), San Diego, 1977-88; host, prodr. KFMB-TV (CBS), San Diego, 1978-88; v.p., bd. dirs. ECUMEDIA-Coun. of Chs., L.A., 1980-88, interim exec., 1982; bd. dirs. NATAS, San Diego, 1987-88. Mem. editl. com.: You Own More Than Your TV Set, 1983. Mem. adv. bd. Congressman Jim Bates, San Diego and Washington, 1984, Calif. Assemblywoman Lucy Killea, San Diego and Sacramento, 1984. Capt. U.S. Army, 1960-68. Recipient Gabrial Cert. of Merit, U.S. Cath. Conf./UNDA, 1978, Emmy awards NATAS, San Diego, 1980, 84, Award of Merit, Religious Pub. Rels. Coun., 1983, Merit award Internat. TV Assn., San Diego, 1985. Mem. Nat. Assn. for Better Broadcasting (bd. dirs. 1981—), Internat. TV Assn., N.Am./World Assn. Christian Communicators (mem. nat. steering com. 1995-97), Telecom. Consumer Coalition, United Ch. of Christ Conf.-Ohio/SONKA Assn. Democrat. Avocations: snow skiing, whitewater rafting, skydiving, camping, glass blowing, stained glass art. Office: United Theol Sem 1810 Harvard Blvd Dayton OH 45406-4539

DUNCAN, RICHARD RAY, history educator; b. Cin., Aug. 30, 1931; s. Ray Howard and Emma (Swing) D. BA, Ohio U., 1954, MA, 1955; PhD, Ohio State U., 1963. Instr. Kent State U., 1961-64; asst. prof. U. Richmond, Va., 1964-67; prof. Georgetown U., Washington, 1967--;; vis. assoc. prof. Ohio State U., Columbus, summer 1971; chmn. bd. dirs. Duncan Bros. Tire Co., Winchester, Va. Author: Lee's Endangered Left, 1998; editor: Alexander Neil and the Last Valley Campaign, 1996, Maryland Historical Magazine, 1967-74; compiler: Theses and Dissertations on Virginia History, 1986; contbr. articles to profl. jours. Episcopalian. Home: 6101 Edsall Rd Apt 1802 Alexandria VA 22304 Office: Georgetown U History Dept Washington DC 20057-1035

DUNCAN, ROBERT BANNERMAN, strategy and organizations educator; b. Milw., July 4, 1942; s. Robert Lynn and Irene (Hoenig) D.; m. Susan Jean Phillips, June 12, 1965; children: Stephanie Olcott, Christopher Robert. BA, Ind. U., 1964, MA, 1966; PhD, Yale U., 1971. Asst. prof. Northwestern U. Kellogg Grad. Sch. Mgmt., Evanston, Ill., 1970-73, assoc. prof. orgn. behavior, 1973-76, prof., 1976, Earl Dean Howard prof. orgn. behavior, 1980-83, J.L. Kellogg disting. prof. strategy and orgns., 1983-86, 92—, J. Allen disting. prof. strategy and orgns., 1986-89; Richard L. Thomas prof. leadership orgnl. change Northwestern U., Evanston, 1996—; assoc. dean acad. affairs Northwestern U. Kellogg Grad. Sch. Mgmt., Evanston, Ill., 1975-76, 80-82, 84-86; provost, chief acad. affairs Northwestern U., Evanston, 1987-92. Co-author: Innovations and Organizations, 1973, Strategies for Planned Change, 1977; also numerous articles in profl. jours. Fellow Acad. Mgmt. (chair nat. program 1980-81, pres. 1983-84). Avocation: sailing. Office: Northwestern U Grad Sch Mgmt Leverone Hall Evanston IL 60208-2011

DUNCAN, ROBERT CLIFTON, retired government official; b. Jonesville, Va., Nov. 21, 1923; s. Robley Evans and Selva (Cooney) D.; m. Rosemary Fleming, Mar. 19, 1949; children: Melissa, Babette Duncan Wilson, Robert, Scott. B.S., U.S. Naval Acad., 1945, U.S. Naval Postgrad. Sch., 1953; S.M., MIT, 1954, Sc.D., 1960. Commd. ensign USN, 1945, advanced through grades to comdr., naval aviator fighters and heavy attack aircraft; chief space programs br., chief naval ops. Washington, 1960-61, staff asst., dir. def. research and engring., 1961-64; ret., 1965; chief guidance and control div. Manned Spacecraft Ctr., NASA, Houston, 1964-67; asst. dir. Electronics Research Ctr., NASA, Cambridge, Mass., 1967-68; v.p. Polaroid Corp., Cambridge, 1968-85; dir. Def. Advanced Research Projects Agy., Washington, 1985-88; asst. sec. def. for research and tech. U.S. Dept. Def., Arlington, Va., 1986-87; dir. def. research and engring. The Pentagon, Washington, 1987-89, dir. operational test and evaluation, 1989-93; v.p. Hicks & Assocs. Inc., McLean, Va., 1993—; dir. Charles Stark Draper Lab., Cambridge, 1974-85. Author: Dynamics of Atmospheric Entry, 1962; contbr. articles to profl. jours. Dist. chmn. Norumbega council Boy Scouts Am., Weston, Mass., 1969-72, exec. bd., Waban, Mass., 1969-85; mem. indsl. and profl. adv. council Pa. State U., 1973-78; deacon Trinitarian Congregation Ch., Wayland, Mass., 1981-85; trustee Forsyth Dental Ctr., Boston, 1967-85; pres. Polaroid Found., Cambridge, 1978-82. Decorated Legion of Merit; recipient Hayes award Inst. Navigation, Exceptional Svc. medal NASA, 1968, Silver Beaver and Disting. Eagle Scout award Boy Scouts Am., 1984, Disting. Pub. Svc. medal Dept. Def., 1987, 89, 93. Mem. Nat. Acad. Engring. Republican. Avocations: backpacking; hiking; camping. Home: 5109 Yuma St NW Washington DC 20016-4336 Office: Hicks & Assocs Inc 1710 Goodridge Dr Ste 1300 Mc Lean VA 22102-3701

DUNCAN, ROBERT MICHAEL, banker, lawyer, Republican national committeeman; b. Oneida, Tenn., Apr. 14, 1951; s. Robert C. and Barbara (Taylor) D.; m. Joanne Kirk, June 3, 1972; children: Robert Michael. BA, Cumberland Coll., 1971; JD, U. Ky., 1974; postgrad., U. Wis., 1977-80; LLD (hon.), Cumberland Coll., 1990; owner pres. mgmt. program, Harvard U., 1990. Cert. lener-bus. banking, 1994. V.p. Inez (Ky.) Deposit Bank, 1974-77, exec. v.p., 1977-81, chmn., 1981—; chmn. Community Holding Co., Inez, 1983—; with First Nat. Bank, Louisa, Ky., 1984—; dir. Cin. Br. of Cleve. Fed. Res. Bank, 1987-90; chmn. Morehead State U., 1985-86; trustee, chmn. Alice Lloyd Coll., Pippa Passes, Ky., 1978—, acting pres., 1993-94; ptnr. Kirk Ins. Agy., 1978—; mem. class XX Pres.'s Commn. on Exec. Exchange assigned to White House Office Pub. Liaison as asst. dir.; dir. Christian Appalachian Project, 1995—. Del. Rep. Nat. Conv., 1972, 76, 92, 96; nat. committeeman for Ky., Rep. Nat. Com., vice chmn. so. region, 1992—, exec. com., 1996; chmn. Ky. Rep. Com., 1995; trustee Highlands Regional Med. Ctr., 1977—; active Govt. Rels. Coun., White House Conf. on Small Bus., 1995; chmn. Govs. Scholars, 1995—, bd. dirs. 1996—; chmn. East Ky. Corp., 1996, vice chmn. Ctr. Econ. Devel.; chmn. Bunning for U.S. Senate campaign, 1998. Named Cumberland Coll. Outstanding Alumnus, 1976, Outstanding Young Man, Ky. Jaycees, 1982; U. Ky. fellow, 1978, White House fellow finalist, 1989; recipient Cmty. Leadership award McConnell Scholars U. Louisville. Mem. Am. Bankers Assn., Ky. Bankers Assn. (pres. 1985-86, dir.), ABA, Ky. Bar Assn., Ky. C. of C. (dir.), Kiwanis (lt. gov. 1983-84). Baptist. Home: PO Box 331 Inez KY 41224-0331 Office: PO Box 365 Inez KY 41224-0365

DUNCAN, RONNY RUSH, agriculturist, turf researcher, consultant; b. Hereford, Tex., May 21, 1946; s. George Wesley and Nancy Marie (Olson) D.; m. Nancy Elizabeth Douglass, June 10, 1971; children: Cady Meyer, Drew Wesley, Carey Elizabeth. BS, Tex. Tech. U., 1969; MS, Tex. A&M U., 1974, PhD, 1977. Grad. rsch. asst. Tex. A&M U., College Station, 1969, 73-77; asst. prof. U. Ga., Griffin, 1977-82, assoc. prof., 1982-88, prof., 1988—; cons. environ. stress problems on recreational/landscape turf; specialist in salt-affected soils, effluent or ocean water irrigation, paspalum turfgrass. Co-author: Salt Affected Environments—Assessment and Management, 1998, Seashore Paspalum-The Environmental Turfgrass; editor: Crops As Enhancers of Nutrient Use, 1990; editor Sorghum Newsletter, 1990-95. Sgt. USAF, 1969-73. Mem. Am. Soc. Agronomy, Crop Sci. Soc. Am., Internat. Turfgrass Soc., Turfgrass Breeders Assn., Coun. for Agr., Sci. and Tech., Sports Turf Mgrs. Assn., Golf Course Supts. Assn. Am., Turfgrass Prodrs. Internat., Gamma Sigma Delta, Sigma Xi. Democrat. Baptist. Achievements include development of environmentally friendly turfgrasses with low fertilizer and pesticide requirements, which grow with recycled or ocean water; specialist in breeding and stress physiology of grasses including turfgrasses. E-mail: texas2ga@bellsouth.net. Office: U Ga 1109 Experiment St Griffin GA 30223-1797

DUNCAN, STEPHEN MACK, lawyer; b. Oklahoma City, Mar. 28, 1941; s. Marion Claude and Helen Colleen (Stone) D.; m. Luella S. Rinehart, Mar. 13, 1965 (dec. Aug. 1996); children: Kelly Lue, Paige Anne. BS, U.S. Naval Acad., 1963; AM in Govt., Dartmouth Coll., 1969; JD, U. Colo., 1971. Bar: Colo. 1972, U.S. Dist. Ct. Colo. 1972, U.S. Ct. Appeals (10th cir.) 1972, U.S. Ct. Mil. Appeals 1973, U.S. Supreme Ct. 1975, Va. 1993, D.C. 1996. Asst. U.S. atty. U.S. Attys. Office, Denver, 1972-73; pvt. practice Denver, 1973-82; ptnr. Hopper, Kanouff, Smith, Peryam, Terry and Duncan, Denver, 1982-87; asst. sec. of def. for res. affairs Dept. Def., Washington, 1987-93, coord. for drug enforcement policy and support, 1989-93; counsel Mays & Valentine, McLean, Va., 1993-99; pres., CEO SCCI, Frederick, Md, 1999—; mem. faculty U. Va. Trial Adv. Inst., Charlottesville, 1986—, Nat. Inst. Trial Adv., Boulder, Colo., 1981; mem. adv. bd. RAND Drug Policy Rsch. Ctr. Author: Citizen Warriors: America's National Guard and Reserve Forces and the Politics of National Security, 1997, A Woman of Noble Character, 1999; contbr. articles to profl. jours. Nominee for atty. gen. Colo., 1978; elder Presbyn. ch.; pres. U.S. Naval Acad. Class of 1963, 1998—. Lt. USN, 1963-69; capt. USNR, 1969—. Decorated Cross of Gallantry, Republic of Vietnam; recipient medal and 2 awards for Disting. Pub. Svc., Dept. Def., 1989, 93, William J. Brennan Advocacy award U. Va. Sch. Law, 1992; adj. fellow Ctr. for Strategic and Internat. Studies, disting. fellow Inst. Nat. Strategic Studies, Nat. Defense U. Fellow Internat. Soc. Barristers; mem. ABA (adv. com. of standing com. on law and nat. security), Colo. Bar Assn. (vice chmn. litigation coun. 1984-85, mem. bd. govs. 1979-81), Denver Bar Assn. (mem. bd. trustees 1984-87), Res. Officers Assn., U.S. Naval Inst., Army-Navy Club. Republican. Avocations: hiking, cross-country skiing, sculling. Office: SCCI 3 Hillcrest Dr Ste A-201 Frederick MD 21703-6116 *What counts most is not celebrity status, wealth, personal popularity, or even doing the "thing" right; rather, the permanent reward is in having the courage and integrity to do the "right" thing and the wisdom to apply in daily life, the aspiration of our nation's motto: "In God We Trust".*

DUNCAN, STEPHEN ROBERT, elementary education educator; b. Lancaster, Pa., June 23, 1950; s. Robert L. Duncan and Joan L. (McLaughlin) Turns; m. Deborah R. Jakubik, June 30, 1973; children: Rhiannon Alissa, Teague Stephen. BS in Edn., California U. of Pa., 1972; MEd, Coll. N.J., 1977, postgrad. Cert. elem. tchr., sch. program specialist, Pa. 5th grade tchr. Council Rock Sch. Dist., Richboro, Pa., 1972-83, 85-90, 2d grade tchr., 1983-85, math. and computer specialist, 1990—, staff computer instr., 1982—. Chmn. Newtown (Pa.) Twp. Youth Aid Panel, 1987-97. Recipient Outstanding Svc. award Bucks County Juvenile Cts., 1991. Mem. NEA, Nat. Coun. Tchrs. Math., Pa. State Edn. Assn., Coun. Rock Edn. Assn. Avocations: golf, tennis, computers. E-mail: sduncan@cynet.net. Office: Newtown Elem Sch 1 Wrights Rd Newtown PA 18940-1336

DUNCAN, THOMAS WEBB, magazine publishing executive; b. Rhinebeck, N.Y., Nov. 3, 1946; s. J. Webb and Hazel Mary (Smith) D.; m. Robin Eloise Walker, Oct. 27, 1985. BA in English, Wake Forest U., 1968. Reporter, asst. city editor Poughkeepsie (N.Y.) Jour., 1968-72; mng. editor Dutchess Suburban Newspapers, Hyde Park, N.Y., 1973-74; editor-in-chief Taconic Press, Millbrook, N.Y., 1974-76; assoc. editor McGraw-Hill Inc., N.Y.C., 1976-79; sr. editor, regional mgr. McGraw-Hill Inc., San Francisco, 1979-88; v.p., editor-in-chief FM Bus. Publs., N.Y.C., 1989-91; editor-in-chief, assoc. pub. Intertec Pub. Corp., Stamford, Conn., 1992-96; pub. Primedia Intertec, Stanford, Ct., 1996—. Editor Fleet Owner Mag., 1983 (ABP award 1983, Folio award 1996, 98). Mem. Civil War Trust, Friends of the Nat. Parks at Gettysburg, Mus. of the Confederacy, Nat. Rep. Com., Washington, 1995. With USANG, 1968-74. Mem. Am. Trucking Assn., Western Hwy. Inst., Assn. for the Preservation of Civil War Sites. Republican. Presbyterian. Avocation: Civil War studies. Address: Intertec Pub Corp 11 Riverbend Dr S PO Box 4211 Stamford CT 06907-0211

DUNCAN, TIM, professional basketball player; b. Apr. 25, 1976. Center San Antonio Spurs, 1997—. Recipient Naismith award, 1996, Wooden award NCAA, 1996;. Mem. San Antonio Spurs, NBA Champions, 1999. Office: 100 Montana St San Antonio TX 78203-1033*

DUNCANSON, HARRY RICHARD, accountant, financial executive; b. San Diego, Mar. 10, 1947; s. Howard Milton Duncanson and Claire Marie (Ouellette) Wolfert; m. Carole Lynn Brame; children: Lisa, Sheree, Amber, Shannon. Student, Miami (Fla.) Dade Jr. Coll., 1967; BBA, U. Miami, 1972. CPA, Fla. Asst. shortage contr. Burdine's Dept. Stores, Miami, 1967-68; contr. Dukane Press, Inc., Hollywood, Fla., 1968-71; staff acct. Stanley Cohen and Co., CPA, North Miami Beach, Fla., 1972; v.p. fin. Dynacolor Graphics, Inc., Miami, 1973—; ptnr. Duncanson & Sheinfeld P.A., CPAs, Hollywood, 1990—; cons. in field; arbitrator Am. Arbitration Assn., Miami, 1982—; del. White House Conf. on Small Bus., Washington, 1986. Mem. Broward Rep. Exec. Com., Ft. Lauderdale, 1981-96; chmn. adv. com. acctg. and bus. Miami-Dade Cmty. Coll., 1984-87; treas. Fla. Fedn. Young Reps., 1986-87; del. gov.'s conf. on Small Bus., 1988; mem. bd. commrs. South Broward Hosp. Dist.; apptd. by Gov. to Bd. of Coms., So. Broward Hosp. Dist., 1988, 92, 96, vice chmn., 1988-89, chmn., 1989-91, 97-99; bd. dirs. Broward Ambulatory Ctr., 1991-95, Hollywood Econ. Growth Corp., 1994-97; guardian Nat. Fedn. Ind. Bus. of Fla., 1987—; mem. Broward County Alcohol, Drug Abuse and Mental Health Coun.; mem. So. Broward unit Am. Cancer Soc., 1989-91. Mem. AICPAs, Fla. Soc. CPAs (bd. dirs. Dade County chpt. 1981-83), Hollywood C. of C. (bd. dirs. 1991—, pres. 1994, Inaugural Presdl. award 1995, Cmty. Svc. award 1996), Rotary (treas. Miami-Norland chpt. 1986-88, Hollywood Cmty. Svc. award 1996), Beta Alpha Psi. Roman Catholic. Office: 1182 NW 159th Dr Miami FL 33169-5808 also: 2131 Hollywood Blvd Ste 507 Hollywood FL 33020-6753

DUNCOMBE, RAYNOR LOCKWOOD, astronomer; b. Bronxville, N.Y., Mar. 3, 1917; s. Frederic Howe and Mabel Louise (Taylor) D.; m. Julena Theodora Steinheider, Jan. 29, 1948; 1 son, Raynor B. B.A., Wesleyan U., Middletown, Conn., 1940; M.A., State U. Iowa, 1941; Ph.D., Yale U., 1956. Astronomer U.S. Naval Obs., Washington, 1942-62; dir. Nautical Almanac Office, 1963-75; prof. aerospace sci. U. Tex., Austin, 1976—; research assoc. Yale U. Obs., 1948-49; lectr. dynamical astronomy U. Md., 1963, Yale Summer Inst., 1959-70, Office Naval Research Summer Inst. in Orbital Mechanics, 1971, NATO Advanced Study Inst., 1972; cons. orbital mechanics Projects Vanguard, Mercury, Gemini, Apollo, USN Space Surveillance System; mem. NASA space scis. steering com., NASA research adv. panel in applied math., 1967; adviser Internat. Com. on Weights and Measures, Internat. Radio Consultative Com., Internat. Telecommunications Union; mem. NAS-NRC astronomy survey com., 1970-72, Hubble Space Telescope Astrometry Team, 1976—. Author: Motion of Venus, 1958, Coordinates of Ceres, Pallas, Juno and Vesta, 1969; editor: (with V.G. Szebehely) Methods in Celestial Mechanics, 1966, Dynamics of the Solar System, 1979; (with D. Dvorak and P.J. Message) The Stability of Planetary Systems, 1984; assoc. editor: Fundamentals of Cosmic Physics, 1971; exec. editor: Celestial Mechanics, 1977-85; contbr. articles to profl. jours. Fellow Royal Astron. Soc., AAAS (sect. chmn.); assoc. fellow AIAA; mem. Internat. Astron. Union (pres. com. on ephemerides), Minor Planet 3368 named Duncombe, 1988), Am. Astron. Soc. (chmn. div. dynamical astronomy 1970), Inst. Navigation (councillor 1960-64, v.p. 1964-66, pres. 1966-67, Superior Achievement award 1967, Hays award 1975), ASME (sponsor applied mechanics div. 1968-70), Internat. Assn. Insts. Nav. (v.p.), Assn. Computing Machinery, Sigma Xi. Home: 1804 Vance Cir Austin TX 78701-1035 Office: U Tex Dept Aerospace Engring Austin TX 78712

DUNDAS, PHILIP BLAIR, JR., lawyer; b. Middletown, Conn., Apr. 29, 1948; s. Philip Blair and Madolyn Margaret Dundas; m. Elizabeth Anne Adorno, Aug. 9, 1969; children: Philip Blair III, Chapman P. BA, Wesleyan U., Conn., 1970; JD, Washington and Lee U., 1973. Bar: N.Y. 1974. Assoc. Shearman & Sterling, N.Y.C., 1973-81, ptnr., 1981—, ptnr. in charge of Abu Dhabi, United Arab Emirates Office, 1981—. Mem. ABA, Internat. Bar Assn., N.Y. State Bar Assn., Assn. Bar City N.Y., Union Internationale des Avocats, Clinton Country Club. Home: 288 Old Kelsey Point Rd Westbrook CT 06498-2132

DUNDES, ALAN, writer, folklorist, educator; b. N.Y.C., Sept. 8, 1934; s. Maurice and Helen (Rothschild) D.; m. Carolyn M. Browne, Sept. 8, 1958; children: Alison, Lauren, David. BA, Yale U., 1955, M.A.T., 1958; PhD, Ind. U., 1962. Instr. English U. Kans., 1962-63; asst. prof. anthropology U. Calif., Berkeley, 1963-65, assoc. prof., 1965-68, prof. anthropology and folklore, 1968—. Author: The Morphology of North American Indian Folktales, 1964, Analytic Essays in Folklore, 1975, Essays in Folkloristics, 1978, Interpreting Folklore, 1980, Life is Like a Chicken Coop Ladder: A Portrait of German Culture Through Folklore, 1984, Cracking Jokes: Studies of Sick Humor Cycles and Stereotypes, 1987, Parsing Through Customs: Essays by a Freudian Folklorist, 1987, Folklore Matters, 1989 From Game to War and Other Psychoanalytic Essays on Folklore, 1997, Two Tales of Crow and Sparrow: A Freudian Folkloristic Essay on Caste and Untouchability, 1997, Holy Writ as Oral Lit: The Bible as Folklore, 1999; co-author: La Terra in Piazza: An Interpretation of the Palio of Siena, 1975, Urban Folklore from the Paperwork Empire, 1975, The Art of Mixing Metaphors: A Folkloristic Interpretation of the Netherlandish Proverbs of Pieter Bruegel the Elder, 1981, First Prize: Fifteen Years! An Annotated Collection of Romanian Political Jokes, 1985, When You're Up to Your Ass in Alligators: More Urban Folklore from the Paperwork Empire, 1987, Never Try to Teach a Pig to Sing: Still More Urban Folklore from the Paperwork Empire, 1991, Sometimes The Dragon Wins: Yet More Urban Folklore from the Paperwork Empire, 1996; editor: The Study of Folklore, 1965, Every Man His Way: Readings in Cultural Anthropology, 1968, Mother Wit from the Laughing Barrel: Readings in the Interpretation of Afro-American Folklore, 1972, Varia Folklorica, 1978, The Evil Eye: A Folklore Casebook, 1981, Cinderella: A Folklore Casebook, 1982, Sacred Narrative: Readings in the Theory of Myth, 1984, The Flood Myth, 1988, Little Red Riding Hood: A Casebook, 1989, The Blood Libel Legend: A Casebook in Anti-Semitic Folklore, 1991, The Cockfight: A Casebook, 1994, The Walled-Up Wife: A Casebook, 1996, The Vampire: A Casebook, 1998; co-editor: The Wisdom of Many: Essays on the Proverb, 1981, Oedipus: A Folklore Casebook, 1983, The Wandering Jew: Essays in The Interpretation of a Christian Legend, 1986, Folk Law: Essays in the Theory and Practice of Lex Non Scripta, 1994; compiler: Folklore Theses and Dissertations in the United States, 1976; contbr. articles to Ency. Britannica, Worldbook Ency., The Book of Knowledge, various profl. jours. With USNR, 1955-57. Recipient Chgo. Folklore 2d prize 1962, 1st prize 1976, Pitrè Prize, Sigillo d'oro, 1993; Guggenheim fellow, 1966-67, NEH sr. fellow, 1972-74. Mem. Am. Folklore Soc. (pres. 1980), Fellows of the Am. Folklore Soc. (pres.) Calif. Folklore Soc., Internat. Soc. Folk Narrative Rsch. Home: 1590 La Vereda Rd Berkeley CA 94708-2036 Office: U Calif Dept Anthropology 201 Kroeber Hall Berkeley CA 94720 *As a psychoanalytic folklorist, my profes-*

sional goals are to make sense of nonsense, find a rationale for the irrational, and seek to make the unconscious conscious.

DUNDON, MARGO ELAINE, museum director; b. Cleve., July 3, 1950; d. Elmer Edward and Ruth Ann (Dreger) Buckeye. BS in Communications cum laude, Ohio U., 1972; postgrad. in Mus. Studies, U. Okla, 1987. Mem. gen. staff Grout Mus. History and Sci., Waterloo, Iowa, 1974-75; coordinator edn. Grout Mus. History and Sci., Waterloo, 1976-78, co-dir., 1979-87, dir., 1988-90; exec. dir. Mus. Sci. and History, Jacksonville, Fla., 1990—. Chairperson Waterloo Hist. Preservation Commn., 1987-88; cultural com. Visitors and Conv. Bur., Waterloo, 1988-90, My Waterloo Days, 1982, 93; mem. Jacksonville Women's Network, Non-Profit Execs. Round Table, 1990-95; bd. dirs. Resource Plus, Waterloo-Cedar Falls, Iowa, 1986-88; mem. Jacksonville C. of C., 1990—; bd. dirs. CJI; bd. dirs. Girls Inc. of Jacksonville, 1994-95, LaVilla Cultural & Heritage Assocs., 1998—. Am. Law Inst.-ABA scholar, 1979, 86; recipient Mayor's Vol. Performance award, Waterloo, 1983, Vol. award Gov. of Iowa, 1990. Mem. Am. Assn. Mus. (site surveyor mus. assessment program 1982—, site examiner mus. accreditation commn. 1987—, regional councilor 1988-90), Midwest Mus. Conf. (pres. 1988-90), S.E. Mus. Conf., Fla. Assn. Mus. (pres. 1995-96), Fla. Attractions Assn. (bd. dirs. 1997-98), Iowa Mus. Assn. (pres. 1984-86), Rotary, Quota Club (pres. 1982). Avocations: snorkeling, scuba diving, travelling, gardening. Office: Mus Sci & History 1025 Museum Cir Jacksonville FL 32207-9006 *Share your life with a cat. When life is cold and hard edged, a cat is warm and soft. Cats do not fawn over our successes or judge us lacking for our failures. Cats remind us of the importance of life's simple gifts: a good meal, a warm nap, a relaxing bath, and an interesting bird at the window. For balance, there is nothing like living with a cat.*

DUNE, STEVE CHARLES, lawyer; b. Vithkuqi, Korca, Albania, June 15, 1931; s. Costa Pappas and Evanthia (Vangel) D.; m. Irene Duff Boudreau, Sept. 4, 1955; children: Michelle Dune Hopper, Christopher Michael. AB, Clark U., 1953; JD, NYU, 1956. Bar: N.Y. 1957. Law clk. U.S. Ct. Appeals 1st Cir., 1956-57; from assoc. to ptnr. Cadwalader, Wickersham & Taft, N.Y.C., 1957-95; counsel Albanian-Am. Enterprise Fund, 1995-96. Trustee Clark U., Worcester, Mass., 1974-86, 93-97, hon. trustee, 1997—, vice-chmn. bd. dirs., 1980-84, chmn. bd. dirs., 1984-86, chmn. presdl. search com., 1983-84, mem. pres.'s coun., 1987-90; dir. Albanian Children Fund, 1998—, chmn. Albanian-Am. C. of C., 1995-96. Root-Tilden scholar, 1953-56. Mem. ABA (internat. law and practice sect.), N.Y. State Bar Assn., Assn. Bar City N.Y. (com. on Ea. European affairs 1992-95, admiralty com. 1976-79, 87-90), Maritime Law Assn. U.S. (marine fin. com. 1980-95), Internat. Bar Assn. (bus. and law sect. Ea. European Forum), India House, Phi Beta Kappa. Home and Office: PO Box 456 98 Barrett Hill Rd Brooklyn CT 06234-0456 *Commitment, determination and perseverance are a person's best allies in solving any problem, meeting any challenge or realizing upon any opportunity of life.*

DUNEA, GEORGE, nephrologist, educator; b. Craiova, Rumania, June 1, 1933; came to U.S., 1964; s. Charles L. and Gerda (Low) D.; m. Mary Mills Barr, 1969; 1 dau., Melanie; stepchildren—Mary Louise, John Barr. M.D., U. Sydney, Australia, 1957. Diplomate Am. Bd. Internal Medicine, Am. Bd. Nephrology. Intern Royal North Shore Hosp., Sydney, 1958-59; resident in internal medicine Australia and Eng., 1959-63; fellow in nephrology Cleve. Clinic, Presbyn.-St. Luke's Hosp., Chgo., 1964-66; practice internal medicine specializing in nephrology Chgo., 1972—; attending physician Cook County Hosp., Chgo., 1966—, dir. dept. nephrology-hypertension, 1969—; prof. medicine U. Ill., Chgo., 1986—; exec. dir. Hektuen Inst. of Med. Rsch., 1991—; vis. prof. medicine Rush Med. Sch., Chgo., 1976—. Contbr. chpts. to books, articles to profl. publs. Fellow A.C.P., Royal Coll. Physicians (London, Edinburgh); mem. AMA, Am. Soc. Nephrology, Brit. Med. Assn., Soc. Med. History. Home: 222 E Chestnut St Chicago IL 60611-2360 Office: 1835 W Harrison St Chicago IL 60612-3701

DUNFEE, THOMAS WYLIE, law educator; b. Huntington, W.Va., Nov. 15, 1941; s. Wylie Ray and Chloe Edith (Wylie) D.; m. Dorothy Jane Taylor, Aug. 26, 1967; children: John Wylie, Jennifer Sue, Shannon Elizabeth. AB, Marshall U., 1963; JD, NYU, 1966, LLM, 1969. Instr. N.Y. Inst. Tech., 1965-68; asst. prof. Ill. State U., Normal, 1968-70; asst. prof. Ohio State U., Columbus, 1970-72, assoc. prof., 1972-74; assoc. prof. legal studies Wharton Sch., U. Pa., Phila., 1974-79, prof., 1979—, Kolodny prof. social responsibility, 1982—, chmn. dept. legal studies, 1980-84, 87-91, dir. Wharton ethics program, 1995-96, dir. Zicklin Ctr. for Bus. Ethics Rsch., 1997—; vis. prof. U. Fla., 1989, U. Newcastle, Australia, 1981, 85, Georgetown U., 1994; cons. United Way of Am., McGraw-Hill, Nynex, Citibank, GM, Honda, SmithKline & Beecham, AT&T. Author: Business and Its Legal Environment, 1992, Modern Business Law, 1996; editor: Business Ethics: Japan and the Global Economy, 1993, (with Thomas Donaldson) Ethics in Business and Economics, 2 vols., 1997, Ties That Bind: A Social Contracts Approach to Business Ethics, 1999; editor-in-chief Am. Bus. Law Jour., 1976-79; contbr. articles to profl. jours. Grantee Exxon Found., 1985-86, Kemper Found., 1993. Mem. Acad. Legal Studies in Bus. (pres. 1989-90, Disting. Sr. Faculty award for Excellence 1991), Soc. Bus. Ethics (pres. 1995-96). Home: 517 Arthur Dr Cherry Hill NJ 08003-3005

DUNFORD, DAVID JOSEPH, foreign service officer, ambassador; b. Glen Ridge, N.J., Feb. 24, 1943; s. Thomas Joseph and Katherine Celeste (Jahn) D.; m. Sandra Corbett Mitchell, Dec. 18, 1965; children: Gregory, Kristina. BS in Engring., MIT, 1964; MA in Polit. Sci., Stanford U., 1965, MA in Econs., 1976. Jr. officer Am. Embassy, Quito, Ecuador, 1967-68; econ.-commercial officer Am. Embassy, Helsinki, Finland, 1969-72; dir. planning and econ. analysis staff Dept. State, Washington, 1977-79, dir. Office of Devel. Fin., 1979-80; dep. asst. U.S. trade rep. Office of U.S. Trade Rep., Washington, 1980-81; minister-counselor for econ. affairs Am. Embassy, Cairo, 1981-84; dir. Egyptian affairs Dept. State, Washington, 1984-87; dep. chief of mission Am. Embassy, Riyadh, Saudi Arabia, 1988-92; amb. to Oman, Am. Embassy, Muscat, 1992-95; ret. from fgn. svc., 1995; adj. prof. dept. polit. sci. U. Ariz., 1995—; coord. transition team Menabank, Cairo, 1997-98; adj. prof. Am. Grad. Sch. Internat. Mgmt., 1998—. Recipient Presdl. Meritorious Svc. awards, 1991, 92, Disting. Citizen award U. Ariz. Alumni Assn., 1994. Mem. Am. Fgn. Svc. Assn. (Christian A. Herter award 1991). Avocations: tennis, biking, hiking, writing fiction, photography.

DUNGAN, GLORIA KRONBECK, critical care nurse; b. Little Falls, Minn., July 4, 1938; d. Hans Emil and Marie (Hahn) Kronbeck; divorced; 1 child, Kirk. Diploma, Abbott Hosp. Sch. Nursing, Mpls., 1958; BS in Nursing, U. Alaska, 1978. CCRN. Nurse at hosps. Mpls., Anchorage, 1958-63; staff nurse, charge nurse Narrabri (Australia) Hosp., 1963-64; night supr., staff nurse, charge nurse Providence Hosp., Anchorage, 1964-65; night supr., staff nurse Anchorage Community Hosp., 1966-67, Greater Juneau Borough Hosp., Juneau, Alaska, 1968-69; asst. head nurse nights intensive care unit Providence Hosp., Anchorage, 1970-77; staff nurse Alaska Nurses Registry, Anchorage, 1977-78; from nurse mgr. to staff nurse intensive care unit Providence Hosp., Anchorage, 1978-83; staff nurse intensive care unit King Fahd Mil. Hosp., Jeddah, Saudi Arabia, 1983-84; staff nurse intensive care Providence Hosp., Anchorage, 1984-90; staff nurse critical care Am. Critical Care Svcs., Anchorage, 1990-92, Humana Hosp. Alaska, Anchorage, 1992, Alaska Native Med. Ctr., 1992—. Mem. Am. Assn. Critical Care Nurses (pres. Anchorage chpt. 1980-81, presenter ednl. programs), Sigma Theta Tau.

DUNGAN, JOHN RUSSELL, JR. (TITULAR VISCOUNT DUNGAN OF CLANE AND HEREDITARY PRINCE OF ARA), anesthesiologist; b. Boston, Dec. 12, 1953; s. John Russell and Nancy Pauline (Beaton) D.; m. Nancy Elizabeth Perkins, July 12, 1986 (div. 1997); children: Elizabeth Adelaide, Thayer Warren, Eleanor Grace Appleton. *John (Sr.) is, in Celtic succession, the hereditary chief of his name: Ó Donnacháin (Ua Donnagáin) and would be the 61st Prince of Ara (Ard rí Aradh), in Tipperary, a tribe dispersed in 1318. In Anglo-Irish succession he is by right the 11th Earl of Lymerick, the 11th Viscount Dungan of Clane and Baron Dungan of Castletown, and the 14th baronet and knight. These honors were forfeited in 1691 and restored in 1698, but they have not been much known since settling in New York at that time. As heir, John (Jr.) has the courtesy title of viscount. The heads of the family were also lords of the manors of Castletown in New York and Ireland, lords of the manor of Martha's Vineyard, and commanders of the Military Order of the Knights of Leinster (the Clanna Baoisgne).* AB magna cum laude, Harvard Coll., 1977; EdM, Harvard U., 1978; DDS, Baylor U., 1984; MD cum laude, Creighton U., 1989. Diplomate Am. Bd. Anesthesiology (dir. 1989-92, 97—, v.p. 1997—), Am. Acad. Pain Mgmt. Instr. anesthesiology Boston U. Sch. Medicine, 1986-89; attending staff anesthesiologist, residency instr. Boston City Hosp., 1986-89; anesthesiologist, chief Tobey Hosp., Wareham, Mass., 1989-91; chief of anesthesia Mary Lanning Hosp., Hastings, Nebr., 1991—; chief of surgery Mary Lanning Hosp., Hastings, 1995; pres. Hastings Anesthesiology Assocs., 1992—; chmn. pharmacy and therapeutics, 1993-94, 96—. Author: The Kings of the Picts and Dál Riads, 1976, The Beatons, 1976, Angus Macdonald, 1977; contbr. articles to profl. jours. Rschr. nat. trust Restoration of Celbridge Chapel and Cemetery, Kildare, Ireland, 1995. John Eliot Scholar, 1967; Nat. Merit scholar, 1971; Internat. fellow English-Speaking Union, 1971-72; Harvard Coll. scholar, 1975-77, John Harvard scholar, 1976; head and comdr. Mil. Order Knights of Leinster; hereditary Knight of the Golden Chain (Ireland); named to Honorable Order of Ky. Cols. Mem. Am. Soc. Anesthesiologists, English-Speaking Union U.S., Nebr. Soc. Anesthesiologists, N.Y. Biog. and Geneal. Soc., N.Y. Irish History Roundtable, N.Eng. Historic Geneal. Soc., United Empire Loyalists Assn. (Can.), Phi Beta Kappa, Cum Laude Soc. (Tabor chpt.), Hasty Pudding Inst. 1770, Harvard Club of Nebr., Old Tonbridgian Soc., The Wild Geese, Clan Dungan (acting chief and pres. 1998—). Republican. Episcopalian. Avocations: Medieval and Jacobean British history research, family history. Home: Heartwell Park 923 N Elm Ave Hastings NE 68901-4021 Office: Hastings Anesthesiology 608 W 6th St Hastings NE 68901-5124

DUNGAN, PAUL BARNES, director city-county health department; b. Wellsville, N.Y., Jan. 15, 1944. BS in Chem., U. Syracuse, 1965; DVM, Cornell U., 1969; MPH, U. Minn., 1980. Pub. health officer USAF, Tinker AFB, 1989-96; dir. City County Health Dept., Okla. City, Okla., 1994—. Mem. Okla. Pub. Health Assn. (pres.-elect), Ctrl. Okla. Integrated Network System (bd. dirs.). Office: City County Health Dept 921 NE 23d Oklahoma City OK 73105*

DUNGAN, WILLIAM JOSEPH, JR., insurance broker, economics educator; b. New London, Conn., Mar. 19, 1956; s. William Joseph and Alpha (Combs) D.; m. Janet Dudek, May 28, 1983. BS in Biology, Old Dominion U., 1978, postgrad. in Econs., 1978-80; postgrad., U. Pa., 1984-85, Coll. for Fin. Planners, 1983-84; MS in Fin. Svcs., Am. Coll., 1988, MS in Mgmt., 1990. CLU; chartered fin. cons., cert. fund. specialist,. Rep. Prudential Ins. Co., Norfolk, Va., 1979-80; assoc. Russ Gills and Assocs., Virginia Beach, Va., 1980-88; instr. Tidewater C.C., Virginia Beach, Va., 1979-86; v.p. life and employee benefits Henderson & Phillips Inc., Norfolk, Va., 1988—; founding prin. First Fin. Resources, 1987—; instr. employee benefits and econs. Inst. Mgmt., Old Dominion U., 1988—, chmn. cert. employee benefit specialists adv. bd. Bd. dirs. Epilepsy Assn. Va.; trustee Old Dominion U. Ednl. Found., 1991—; v.p. Epilepsy Assn. of Va. Mem. Internat. Assn. Fin. Planning (pres. Hampton Rds. chpt.), Nat. Assn. Life Underwriters, Assn. for Advanced Life Underwriting, Inst. Cert. Fin. Planners, Inst. Cert. Employee Benefits Specialists, Am. Soc. CLUs, Norfolk Assn. Life Underwriters (bd. dirs.), Monarch Bus. Soc., Old Dominion Univ.'s Ins. and Fin. Svcs. Ctr., Epilepsy Assn. Va. (bd. dirs.), Million Dollar Round Table. Republican. Avocations: tennis, travel, reading. Home: 4201 Mercedes Ct Virginia Beach VA 23455-5649 Office: Henderson & Phillips Inc 235 E Plume St Norfolk VA 23510-1755

DUNGY, TONY, professional sports team executive; b. Jackson, Mich., Oct. 6, 1955. Def. asst. Pitts. Steelers, 1981-83, def. back coach, 1982-83, def. coord., 1984-88; def. backs coach Kansas City Chiefs, 1989-91; def. coord. Minn. Vikings, 1992-95; head coach Tampa Bay (Fla.) Buccaneers, 1996—. Mem. Super Bowl Championship Team, 1978. Office: Tampa Bay Buccaneers One Buccaneer Pl Tampa FL 33607*

DUNHAM, ANNE, educational institute director. Exec. dir. Youth Sci. Inst., L.A., 1995—. Office: Youth Sci Inst 296 Garden Hill Dr Los Gatos CA 95032-7669

DUNHAM, BARBARA JEAN, administrator; b. Brockton, Mass., May 30, 1948; d. Colin Laird Manzer and Beatrice May (Anderson) Manzer-Sweetman; m. Carroll James Dunham, Aug. 6, 1989; children: Richard Howard Cicchetti Jr., Derek Colin Cicchetti. BS, Bridgewater State Coll., 1977; MEd, Bridgewater State U., 1982, CAGS Computers in Edn., 1986; EdD in Ednl. Leadership, Nova Southeastern U., 1998. Reading specialist Sharon (Mass.) High Sch., 1978-90; dir. tech. Sharon Schs., 1984-98, tchr. computer applications/programming, 1985-95; owner, cons. BJC Software, Sharon, 1980—; instr. Bridgewater (Mass.) State Coll., 1987. Author: (software) Teacher Student Vocabulary, 1982. Horace Man grantee, Mass. Dept. Edn., Sharon, 1988,'89. Mem. ASCD, Internat. Soc. Tech. in Edn., Mass. Tchrs. Assn., Sharon Tchrs. Assn., Mass. Computer-Using Educators, Boston Computer Soc. Avocations: computer-related activities, horses, animals, swimming, motorcycling. Home: 13 High Plain St Sharon MA 02067-1042 Office: Sharon Schs 181 Pond St Sharon MA 02067-2000

DUNHAM, BENJAMIN STARR, editor, arts administrator; b. N.Y.C., Sept. 19, 1944; s. George Roscoe and Portia Elizabeth (Playfair) D.; m. Wendy H. Rolfe-Dunham, Apr. 12, 1986; children: Samuel Edward Rolfe. BA, Harvard U., 1966; postgrad., Boston U., 1970, Cath. U., 1971-73. Asst. editor Music Educators Jour., Washington, 1967-70; editor Symphony News, Vienna, 1971-78; exec. dir. Chamber Music Am., N.Y.C., 1978-82, Am. Symphony Orchestra, N.Y.C., 1982-84; exec. v.p. Nat. Music Council, N.Y.C., 1984-90; editor Am. Recorder, 1990—; cons. to TV, fundraising and mktg. in chamber music, pubs. and rsch.; cons. on period instrument orch. program Andrew W. Mellon Found., 1989-91; lectr. in field; mem. music faculty Trinity Coll., Washington, 1973-75; pvt. tchr. recorder, 1971-78; MusiCo-op, Wareham, Mass., 1986-92, Cranberry Concerts, 1993—. Contbr. numerous articles on chamber music, symphony orch. and the performing arts; prin. recorder performer Handel Festival Orch., Washington, 1977-78; mem. The Washington Consort, 1973-78. Mem. Wareham Arts and Humanities Coun., 1986-90, chmn., 1992-94; mem. Hist. Dist. Commn., Wareham, 1986-97; bd. dirs. Marion Art Ctr., 1996-99; mem. Sippican Elem. Sch. Coun., 1998—. Named Arts Adminstr. of Yr. Arts Mgmt. mag., N.Y.C., 1981. Mem. Early Music Am. (bd. dirs. 1988-92, 93-99, treas. 1993-95), Nat. Guild Cmty. Schs. Art (trustee 1982-87), Am. Recorder Soc. (bd. dirs. 1984-89).

DUNHAM, CHARLOTTE ANN, English language educator; b. Centralia, Ill., Apr. 23, 1943; d. Raymond Arthur and Helen Rose (Phillips) Richardson; m. Roger Kyle Dunham, Jan. 2, 1965; children: Craig Mitchell, Jamie Ann Kelley, Jill Suzanne Kunzeman. BS in Edn., So. Ill. U., 1965. Tchr. English Brownstown (Ill.) H.S., 1965-67, Effingham (Ill.) H.S., 1968-70, Griggsville (Ill.) Jr. High, 1981-88, Griggsville-Perry H.S., 1988—. Home: RR 1 New Salem IL 62357-9801 Office: Griggsville-Perry H S Stanford & Liberty Griggsville IL 62340

DUNHAM, CHRISTOPHER SCOTT, librarian; b. Balt., Mar. 12, 1964; s. Curtis Lee and Susan Ingrid (Meyer) D.; m. Colleen Marie Davis, Nov. 16, 1997. BA, Rutgers U., 1986, MLS, 1994. Dist. exec. Boy Scouts of Am., Denville, N.J., 1987-91; trips dir. Citta Scout Reservation at Brookville, Barnegat, N.J., 1991, aquatics dir., asst. camp dir., 1992; info. supr. Rutgers U., New Brunswick, N.J., 1992-94, reference libr., 1993-95; reference libr. Sussex County C.C., Newton, N.J., 1993-97, Montclair State U., Upper Montclair, N.J., 1994-95; electronic resources libr. Passaic County C.C., Paterson, N.J., 1995-97; reference libr. Fairfield (Conn.) U., 1997—. Mem. ALA, Rutgers U. Sch. Comm. Info. and Libr. Studies Alumni Assn. (exec. com. 1995-99), N.J. Recreation and Park Assn. (conf. com. 1992-98), N.J. Forest Fire Svc. (sect. sec. 1992—). Avocations: travel, outdoor adventure, theatre, aquatics, music. Office: Fairfield Univ/Nyselius Lib 1073 No Benson Rd Fairfield CT 06430-5195

DUNHAM, CORYDON BUSNELL, lawyer, broadcasting executive; b. Yonkers, N.Y., Nov. 14, 1927; s. Corydon Busnell and Marion (Howe) D.; m. Janet Burke, Oct. 29, 1966; children: Corydon B. III, Christopher B. B.A., Bowdoin Coll., 1948; LL.B., Harvard U., 1951. Bar: N.Y. 1951, D.C. 1990. Assoc. Cahill, Gordon & Reindel, N.Y.C., 1951-65, counsel, 1990—; asst. gen. atty. NBC Inc., N.Y.C., 1965-68, v.p., gen. counsel, 1971-76, exec. v.p., gen. counsel, 1976-89, exec. v.p., sr. counsel to pres., 1989-90; guest scholar Woodrow Wilson Internat. Ctr. for Scholars, 1995. Author: Fighting for the First Amendment, Staunton of CBS vs. Congress and the Nixon White House, 1997. Served to 2d lt. Arty AUS, 1944-46, Japan. Mem. Am. Arbitration Assn. (dir.), Nat. Acad. TV Arts and Scis. (legal com. chair N.Y. chpt.), Harvard Club. Office: Cahill Gordon & Reindel 80 Pine St Fl 17 New York NY 10005-1790*

DUNHAM, JOAN ROBERTS, administrative assistant; b. Dayton, Ohio, Jan. 25, 1933; d. Harold Hathaway and Lydia Roberts Dunham. BA, U. Colo., 1954; postgrad., U. Pa., 1959-65, U. Chgo., 1971-72. Office clk. Daniels R. Fisher Stores, Denver, 1954-56; clk., stenographer Dept. of State, Madras, India, 1957-59; clk., stenographer, analyst Dept. of State, Washington, 1966-69; clk. admissions office Temple Buell Coll., Denver, 1968-78; typist, adminstrv. clk. State of Colo., Denver, 1987—. Fgn. lang. fellow U.S. Dept. Health, Edn. and Welfare, U. Pa., 1961-62. Republican. Christian Scientist. Home: Apt 1308 901 Sherman St Denver CO 80203-2923 Office: State Dept Regulatory Agys Ste 550 1580 Logan St Denver CO 80203-1941

DUNHAM, MICHAEL HERMAN, human services executive; b. Dayton, Ohio, Mar. 30, 1951; s. Robert Fredrick and Marjory Katherine (Fortune) D.; m. Nancy Lynn Cross, July 2, 1977; children: Lisa Yandow Olson, A. Richard Yandow. Student, Kent State U., 1970-72, U. Vt., 1975-77; BA in sociology, U. Wis., 1980. Rsch. assoc. U. Wis., Madison, 1977-84; dir. managed care Univ. Health Care, Inc., Madison, 1984-86; dir. fiscal affairs Health & Hosps. Corp., N.Y.C., 1986-88; CEO Total Health HMO, Inc., N.Y.C., 1988-89; pres., CEO Practice Mgmt., Inc., Madison, 1989-92, Cmty. Care Mgmt., Inc., Madison, 1992—; faculty mem. CASSP Inst., Georgetown U., Washington, 1992-96. Contbr. chpts. to books, articles to profl. jours. Mental health Interagy. Coun. State Wis., Madison, 1992-94, grad. med. edn. rev. commn., 1986, cert. need adv. com., 1984-86. Mem. N.Y. State HMO Coun. (exec. bd. 1988), Wis. Assn. Family & Children's Agys. Home: Kennedy Manor 504 1 Langdon St Madison WI 53703 Office: Cmty Care Mgmt Inc 16 N Carroll St Ste 640 Madison WI 53703-2756

DUNHAM, PHILIP BIGELOW, biology educator, physiologist; b. Columbus, Ohio, Apr. 26, 1937; s. T. Chadbourne and Margaret (Bigelow) D.; m. Gudrun Bjarnarson, Mar. 9, 1985. B.A., Swarthmore Coll., 1958; Ph.D., U. Chgo., 1962. USPHS postdoctoral fellow Carlsberg Found., Copenhagen, 1962-63; asst. prof. zoology Syracuse U., 1963-67, assoc. prof., 1967-71, prof. biology, 1971—; rsch. prof. pharm. SUNY Health Sci. Ctr., Syracuse, 1990—; vis. assoc. prof. physiology Yale U. Sch. Medicine, 1968-70, vis. prof., 1986; vis. prof. medicine U. N.C., 1993-94; vis. scientist physiol. lab. Cambridge (Eng.) U., 1979, August Krogh Inst., Copenhagen, 1985-87; vis. prof. biochemistry U. Copenhagen, 1994; vis. honors examiner Swarthmore Coll., 1966-67, 74-76, mem. alumni coun., 1971-73; mem. exec. com. bd. trustees Marine Biol. Lab., Woods Hole, Mass., 1972-76; mem. physiology study sect. NIH, 1986-89; mem. review panel Am. Heart Assn., 1994-97, co-chair, 1995, 97. Assoc. editor Am. Jour. Physiology, 1984-87; contbr. over 100 rsch. publs. in field. Rsch. grantee NSF, 1963-65, NIH, 1965—, MERIT grantee NIH, 1996-2004; recipient Chancellor's Citation for Exceptional Acad. Excellence, Syracuse U., 1994-95. Mem. Soc. Gen. Physiologists (council 1967-69), Am. Physiol. Soc., Biophys. Soc. Home: 6402 Terese Ter Jamesville NY 13078-9430 Office: Syracuse U 130 College Pl Syracuse NY 13210-2819

DUNHAM, REBECCA BETTY BERES, school administrator; b. Cleve., Aug. 30, 1948; d. Michael Charles and Veda Mary (Vardian) Beres; m. William Grant Dunham, Mar. 15, 1969; children: Heidi Rebecca, Aaron William, Amanda Elisabeth (dec.), Meredith Lynne. BA, Kent State U., 1977. Rschr. Phillips Exeter (N.H.) Acad., 1977-84, dir. found. support, 1984-88, assoc. dir. capital giving, 1988-93; assoc. dir. alumni and alumnae affairs and devel. Groton (Mass.) Sch., 1993-95, dir. alumni and alumnae affairs and devel., 1995—; pres., v.p. Richie McFarland Children's Ctr., Exeter, 1981-89; spkr., mem. Gov. Coun. Volunteerism, Concord, N.H., 1985-86; chair, vice-chair Partnership Philanthropy, N.H., Maine, Vt., 1990-91. Trustee Mary Bartlett Meml. Libr., Brentwood, N.H., 1992-93; vol. Swasey Ctrl. Sch., Brentwood, 1978-85; bd. dirs., sec. bd., Montessori Sch. Creative Learning, North Hampton, 1976-78; active Friday Forum, 1996—, Women in Devel., 1997—, Greater Lowell Cmty. Found., 1998—. Mem. Coun. Advancement and Support Edn., Coun. N.H. Fund Raising (pres. bd. 1989-92), Planned Giving Group New Eng., Assn. Ind. Schs. New Eng. (devel. com., evaluation team 1997), Aisa Soc., N.Y. Hist. Soc. Avocations: historic preservation, perennial gardens, quilting, fishing.

DUNHAM, STEPHEN SAMPSON, lawyer; b. Bloomington, Ind., Oct. 19, 1945; s. Allison and Anne Campbell (Toll) D.; m. Victoria Baldwin Cass, May 24, 1969; children: Sarah W., Isaac P. BA, Princeton U., 1966; JD, Yale U., 1969. Bar: Calif. 1970, U.S. Dist. Ct. (no. dist.) Calif. 1972, U.S. Ct. Appeals (9th cir.) 1972, U.S. Dist. Ct. (cen. dist.) Calif. 1973, U.S. Supreme Ct. 1978, Minn. 1979, U.S. Dist. Ct. Minn. 1982, U.S. Ct. Appeals (8th cir.) 1983, Colo. 1988, U.S. Ct. Appeals (10th cir.) 1990. Law clk to Judge Stanley A. Weigel U.S. Dist. Ct. Calif., San Francisco, 1969-70; acting prof. law U. Calif., Davis, 1970-71; vis. assoc. prof. law Nat. Chengchi U., Taipei, 1971-72; assoc. Morrison & Foerster, San Francisco, 1972-76, ptnr., 1976-79; ptnr. Morrison & Foerster, Denver, 1988—; assoc. prof. law U. Minn., Mpls., 1979-82, gen. counsel, 1982-85, v.p., gen. counsel, 1985-88; instr. Nat. Inst. Trial Advocacy, Boulder, Colo., 1980, 83, Harvard U. Law Sch., Cambridge, Mass., 1985. Mem. Calif. State Bar (chair com. on legal svcs. 1978), Nat. Assn. Coll. and Univ. Attys. (bd. dirs. 1986-88), Colo. Lawyers Com. (bd. dirs. 1989—). Home: 650 Emerson St Denver CO 80218-3217 Office: Morrison & Foerster 5200 Republic Plaza 370 17th St Denver CO 80202-5638*

DUNHAM, WOLCOTT BALESTIER, JR., lawyer; b. N.Y.C., Sept. 14, 1943; s. Wolcott Balestier and Isabel Caroline (Bosworth) D.; m. Joan Scott Findlay, Jan. 26, 1974; children: Mary Findlay, James Wolcott. AB magna cum laude, Harvard U., 1965, LLB cum laude, 1968. Bar: N.Y. 1969. Vol. VISTA, 1968-69; assoc. Debevoise & Plimpton and predecessor Debevoise, Plimpton, Lyons & Gates, N.Y.C., 1969-76, ptnr., 1977—; exec. dir. N.Y. State Exec. Adv. Commn. on Ins. Industry Regulatory Reform, 1982. Co-author: Insurance M&A, 1997—; contbr. articles to profl. jours.; gen. editor and chpt. author, New York Insurance Law, 1991, and ann. supplements. Treas., trustee Fund for Astrophys. Rsch., N.Y.C., 1970—, sec., 1970-84, pres., 1984—; bd. dirs. UN Assn., N.Y.C., 1973-79, vice chmn., 1975-79, adv. coun., 1992—; vestry mem. St. James Ch., N.Y.C., 1987-93, clk., 1988-93, jr. warden, 1993-94, sr. warden, 1994-95, chancellor, 1994—; bd. dirs. Neighborhood Coalition for Shelter, Inc., 1983—; pres., bd. dirs. East Side Cmty. Ctr., Inc., 1988—; bd. dirs. Dutchess Land Conservancy, 1996—; bd. mgrs. Shekomeko Valley Farm Assn., LLC, 1996—. Fellow Am. Coll. Investment Counsel; mem. ABA (chmn. com. on ins. sect. adminstrv. law 1979-83), Assn. Bar City N.Y. (com. on ins. 1981-87, chmn. com. 1984-87), Union Internationale des Avocats, Am. Soc. Internat. Law, Harvard Law Sch. Assn. N.Y.C. (dir. 1978-81). Episcopalian. Office: Debevoise & Plimpton 875 3rd Ave Fl 23 New York NY 10022-6256

DUNHILL, ROBERT W., advertising direct mail executive; b. L.A., Sept. 28, 1929; s. Herbert G. and Irma (Meyer) Odza; m. Joan Scheer, Dec. 19, 1952; children: Andrew, Candy, Cindy. BS, Adelphi Coll., 1952; MBA, NYU, 1954. Prin. Dunhill Internat. List Co., Inc., N.Y.C., 1952—; pres., chmn. Dunhill Internat. List Co., Inc., 1975—. With USNR, 1955-57. Mem. Chgo. Assn. of Direct Mktg., Widener U. Alumni Assn., Direct Mktg. Assn., Fla. Direct Mktg. Assn. (chmn.). Republican. Home: 5820 Harrington Way Boca Raton FL 33496-2511 Office: Dunhill Internat List Co 1951 NW 19th St Boca Raton FL 33431-7363

DUNIGAN, DENNIS WAYNE, real estate executive; b. Cin., Apr. 28, 1952; s. Park George and Hazel Edna (Hines) D. AA, U. Cin., 1974, BBA, 1975. Salesman Comey and Shepherd, Inc., Cin., 1978-79; property mgr. Dunigan Properties, Cin., 1980—; assoc. T.J. Carter Realty, Cin., 1984—. Contbr. articles to profl. jours. Chmn. trans. com. Reagan for Pres. Cin., 1980--; active Cin. Hist. Soc., Mus. of Nat. Hist., 1987--, Cin. Zoo, 1987--, Contemporary Arts Ctr., Cin., 1988--, The Taft Mus., 1988--; contbg. mem. Cin. Art Mus., 1987--. Mem. Supreme Ct. Hist. Soc. (contbg.), U. Cin. Alumni Assn., Ohio Assn. Realtors, Cin. Bd. Realtors, Nat. Baseball Hall of Fame and Mus., Greater Cin. Tennis Assn., U.S. Tennis Assn., U.S. Golf Assn., PGA Tour Ptnrs., UCats Club, Silver Bearcats. Republican. Avocations:

golf, tennis, reading, stamp and coin collecting, baseball, football. Home: 6022 St Regis Dr Cincinnati OH 45236-4218

DUNIGAN, PAUL FRANCIS XAVIER, JR., federal agency administrator; b. Richland, Wash., June 22, 1948; s. Paul Frances Xavier Sr. and Eva Lucille (Reckley) D.; m. Elizabeth Anne Henricks, Apr. 8, 1978; children: Katherine Anne, Theresa Anne. BS in Biology, Gonzaga U., 1970; MS in Environ. Sci., Washington State U., 1973. Tech. program mgr. ERDA, AEC, Richland, 1972-75; environ. biologist U.S. Dept. Energy, ERDA, Richland, 1975-81; waste mgmt. engr. U.S. Dept. Energy Waste Mgmt., Richland, 1981-84; civilian program mgr. Surplus Facilities Mgmt. Program U.S. Dept. Energy, Richland, 1984-87, environ. biologist, 1987—; also compliance officer Nat. Environ. Policy Act; leader Nat. Environ. Policy Act team and adminstr. Hanford Fed. Facility Agreement, Dept. of Energy, 1995-96, leader Nat. Environ. Policy Act compliance team, 1996-98, leader Nat. Environ. Policy Act and natural resources team, 1998—. Contbr. articles to profl. jours. Mem. AAAS, Water Pollution Control Fedn., Pacific Northwest Pollution Control Fedn. Roman Catholic. E-mail: paulúfújrúdunigan@rl.gov. Home: 1612 Judson Ave Richland WA 99352-2944 Office: US Dept Energy PO Box 550 Richland WA 99352-0550

DUNION, CELESTE MOGAB, consultant, township official; b. Atlantic City, Mar. 6, 1932; d. Cyril Joseph and Lavina Edna (Bolen) Mogab; m. John Joseph Dunion, May 8, 1954 (dec. Apr. 1978); children: Dana, John, Robert, Denise. Tech. degree, Am. Acad. Dramatic Arts, N.Y.C., 1951; grad. advanced govt. fin. inst., Georgetown U., 1986. Cert. govt. fin. mgr.; lic. notary pub., Pa. Asst. to bus. mgr. Rose Tree Media Sch. Dist., Media, Pa., 1969-78; dir. fin., tax collector, treas. Twp. of Middletown, Glen Riddle, Pa., 1978-98; profl. model, N.Y.C., Phila., Atlantic City; mem. Christy Modeling Agy., Phila. Models Guild, Atlantic City Models Guild, Atlantic City Press Bur.; cons. in fin. mgmt. peer-to-peer program Pa. Dept. Cmty. Affairs, Harrisburg, 1988-96; treas., bd. dirs. Pa. Mcpl. Investment Program, 1990-98. Past sec. Wyncroft Civic Assn.; former committeewoman Middletown Twp. Recipient Dedicated Pumper award Lenni Fire Co., 1983, President's award Lima Fire Co., 1985, Outstanding Leadership award Pa. East Govt. Fin. Officers Assn., 1986, Cmty. Svc. award Middletown Fire Co., 1996. Mem. Govt. Fin. Officers Assn. (Pa. rep., nat. cash mgmt. com., women's fin. network, Mid-Atlantic rep.), Assn. Govt. Accts., Pa. Govt. Fin. Officers Assn. (past pres., sec., Southeast bd.), MidAtlantic Govt. Fin. Officers Assn. (Pa. rep., mem. legis. com.), Women's Fin. Officers Network (chmn. membership), Delaware County Tax Collectors Assn. (v.p. 1984-85, pres. 1986), Pa. Tax Collectors Assn., Pa. Assn. Notaries. Republican. Roman Catholic. Avocations: silk flower arranging, tap dancing, country and western dancing, writing poetry, cooking. cmdcgfm@bellatlantic.net. Office: CMD/CGFM 8 S Bryn Mawr Pl Media PA 19063-5338

DUNIPACE, IAN DOUGLAS, lawyer; b. Tucson, Dec. 18, 1939; s. William Smith and Esther Morvyth (McGeorge) D.; m. Janet Mae Dailey, June 9, 1963; children: Kenneth Mark, Leslie Amanda. BA magna cum laude, U. Ariz., 1961, JD cum laude, 1966 Bar: Ariz. 1966, U.S. Supreme Ct. 1972, Nev. 1994, Colo., 1996. Reporter, critic Long Branch (N.J.) Daily Record, 1963; assoc. firm Jennings, Strouss, Salmon & Trask, Phoenix, 1966-69; assoc. Jennings, Strouss & Salmon, PLC, Phoenix, 1969-70, ptnr., 1971-93, mem., 1993—, chmn. comml. practice dept., 1998—. Reporter Phoenix Forward Edn. Com., 1969-70; mem. Phoenix Arts Commn., 1990-93, chmn., 1992-93; bd. mgmt. Downtown Phoenix YMCA, 1973-80, chmn., 1977-78; bd. dirs. Phoenix Met. YMCA, 1976-87, 88—, chmn., 1984-85; bd. mgmt. Paradise Valley YMCA, 1979-82, chmn., 1980-81; bd. mgmt. Scottsdale/Paradise Valley YMCA, 1983, mem. legal affairs com. Pacific Region YMCA, 1978-81; chmn. YMCA Ariz. State Youth and Govt. Com., 1989-95; bd. dirs. The Schoolhouse Found., 1990-96, pres., 1990-94, Kids Voting, 1990-94, Beaver Valley Improvement Assn., 1977-79, Pi Kappa Alpha Holding Corp., 1968-72, The Heard Mus. 1993-94, Ariz. Bar Found., 1996—, treas. 1998-99, v.p., 1999—; trustee Paradise Valley Unified Sch. Dist. Employee Benefit Trust, 1980-93, chmn., 1987-93, Sch. Theology, Claremont, Calif., 1994—; trustee First Meth. Found. of Phoenix, 1984-93; mem. Greater Paradise Valley Cmty. Coun., 1985-87; bd. dirs. Heard Mus. Coun., 1990-95, pres. 1993-94; mem. Ariz. Venture Capital Conf. Planning Com., 1994—, mem. exec. com., 1997—, vice chmn., 1999—; mem. Assn. for Corp. Growth, 1995-96, Ariz. Bus. Leadership Assn., 1996—; bd. visitors U. Ariz. Law Coll., 1996—. Capt. AUS, 1961-63. Mem. State Bar Ariz. (securities regulation sect. 1970—, chmn., 1991-92, mem. com. unauthorized practice of law 1972-84, chmn. 1975-83, mem. bus. law sect. 1981—, chmn., 1984-85), State Bar Nev., State Bar Colo., Am., Fed. (pres. Ariz. chpt. 1980-81), Maricopa County Bar Assns. (bd. dirs. Corp. Coun. Divsn. 1996—), Ariz. Zool. Soc., U. Ariz. Law Coll. Assn. (bd. dirs. 1983-90, pres. 1985-86, bd. visitors 1996—), Smithsonian Assn., U. Ariz. Alumni Assn. (bd. dirs. 1985-86), Phi Beta Kappa, Phi Kappa Phi, Phi Delta Phi, Phi Alpha Theta, Sigma Delta Pi, Phi Eta Sigma, Pi Kappa Alpha (nat. counsel 1968-72). Democrat. Methodist (mem. met. Phoenix commn. 1968-71, lay leader 1975-78, trustee 1979-81, pres. 1981; mem. Pacific S.W. ann. conf. 1969-79, lawyer commn. 1980-85, chancellor Desert S.W. ann. conf. 1985—). Clubs: Arizona, Renaissance, Orange Tree. Lodges: Masons, Kiwanis (pres. Phoenix 1984-85, disting. lt. gov. 1986-87, SW dist. cmty. svc. chmn. 1987-88, dist. activity com. coord. 1988-89, dist. laws and regulation chmn. 1989-90, 92-93, 95-96, asst. to dist. gov. for club svcs. 1990-91, field dir. 1991-92, dist. conv. chmn., 1993-94, pub. rels. chmn. 1996-98, mem. internat. com. on Project 39, 1988-89, internat. com. On to Anaheim 1990-91, internat. com. on leadership tng. and devel. 1991-92, 93-94, trustee SW dist. found. 1987-92, 1st v.p. 1990-92). Comments editor Ariz. Law Rev., 1965-66. Home: 4147 E Desert Cove Ave Phoenix AZ 85028-3514 Office: Jennings Strouss & Salmon PLC 2 N Central Ave Fl 14 Phoenix AZ 85004-2393

DUNITZ, JACK DAVID, retired chemistry educator, researcher; b. Glasgow, Scotland, Mar. 29, 1923; s. William and Mildred (Gossman) D.; m. Barbara Steuer, Aug. 11, 1953; children: Marguerite, Julia. BS, Glasgow U., 1944, PhD, 1947, DSc (hon.), 1999; DSc (hon.), Technion Haifa, 1990; PhD (hon.), Weizmann Inst., 1992. Rsch. fellow Oxford U., 1946-48, 51-53, Calif. Inst. Tech., Pasadena, 1948-51, 53-54; vis. scientist NIH, Bethesda, Md., 1954-55; sr. rsch. fellow Royal Instn., London, 1956-57; prof. chem. crystallography Swiss Fed. Inst. Tech., Zurich, 1957-90; ret., 1990. Author: X-Ray Analysis and the Structure of Organic Molecules, 1979, (with others) Reflections on Symmetry...in Chemistry and Elsewhere, 1993, (with others) Structure Correlation, 1994; contbr. articles to profl. jours. Recipient Havinga medal U. Leiden, Netherlands, 1980, Paracelsus prize Swiss Chem. Soc., 1986, Bijvoet medal U. Utrecht, 1989, Aminoff prize Swedish Royal Acad., 1990; Churchill Coll. Overseas fellow, 1968. Fellow AAAS, Royal Soc. London, Academia Europaea; mem. NAS (fgn. assoc.), Am. Acad. Arts and Scis. (fgn. hon.), Am. Philos. Soc. (fgn.), Deutsche Akademie Leopoldina, Am. Chem. Soc. (Cope scholar 1997), Brit. Chem. Soc., Am. Crystallographic Assn. (Buerger award 1991), Brit. Crystallographic Assn., Swiss Crystallographic Soc. (hon.), Royal Netherlands Acad. Sci. (fgn.), European Acad. Scis. and Ats. Home: 77 Obere Heslibach Str, Küsnacht 8700, Switzerland Office: ETH-Zentrum, 16 Universitatstrasse, Zurich Switzerland

DUNIVENT, JOHN THOMAS, artist, educator; b. Moberly, Mo., Apr. 24, 1928; s. Everett B. and Bertha (Goetze) D. Student, St. Louis U., 1946-47; BFA, Washington U., St. Louis, 1951; postgrad., Berkshire Music Ctr., Lenox, Mass., 1951; MA, N.Mex. Highlands U., 1957. Asst. prof. drama dept. Fontbonne Coll., St. Louis, 1967-71; lectr. photography and society U. Mo., St. Louis, 1984, 90; lectr. history of photography Washington U. Sch. Fine Arts, St. Louis, 1987; art instr. Parkway Sch. Dist., St. Louis County, Mo., 1960-67, 71-94; vis. prof. art edn. U. Maine, Portland, summers 1971, 72. Illustrator (ink drawings, book) Amerind: Gestural Communication for the Speechless, 1978, (photographs, book) St. Louis Currents, 1986; painter ann. midyear show Butler Inst. Am. Art, Youngstown, Ohio, 1981; solo exhibit of photographs Ctr. for Met. Studies, U. Mo., St. Louis, 1988. Panel mem. master tchr. symposium U. Kans. Sch. Fine Arts, Lawrence, 1985; bd. dirs. Young Audiences, Inc., St. Louis, 1968-74, 80-83. Spl. agt. Counter Intelligence Corps, U.S. Army, 1952-54. Recipient award for pastel painting Chautauqua (N.Y.) Inst., 1959. Avocation: collecting photographs. Home and Office: 607 Forest Ct Saint Louis MO 63105-2759

DUNKELBERG, LEE, journalist; b. Ft. Worth, Jan. 25, 1995; s. Stephen B. and Jane West D.; m. Clare Campbell, May 27, 1995. BA in Comm., Journalism, U. Tex., Arlington, 1975. Reporter Dallas Morning News, 1974-76; press aide U.S. Congress, Washington, 1976-77; reporter Victoria (Tex.) Adv., 1977-79, Sta. KRLD-AM, Dallas, 1979-81; capital corr. Austin, Tex., 1987-94; reporter Sta. KIII-TV, Corpus Christi, Tex., 1987-91, Sta. KSAT-TV, San Antonio, 1991-97; exec. prodr. Dunkelberg Prodns., San Antonio, 1997—. Prodr., writer, narrator (documentary) USS Lexington: Always Ready!, 1997 (Telly award 1998). Methodist. Avocations: photography, fishing, gardening, collecting hats and telephones. Fax: 210-344-3394. E-mail: LeeúDunkenberg@hotmail.com. Office: Dunkelberg Prodns 210 Glentower Dr San Antonio TX 78213-1913

DUNKELBERGER, STEVE WALTER, journalist; b. Hunnington, W.Va., Dec. 5, 1971; s. James Walter and Connie (Preuss) D. BA, Western Wash. U., 1994. Various editl. positions Klipsun Mag., Bellingham, Wash., 1992-94; news reporter Lakewood (Wash.) Jour., 1994—; mem. adv. bd. McNiel Island (Wash.) Prison, 1996—. Mem. Ft. Steil Mus., Lakewood, 1996—. Democrat.

DUNKELMAN, LORETTA, artist; b. Paterson, N.J., June 29, 1937; d. Samuel and Rae (Gutkin) D. BA, Rutgers U., 1958; MA, Hunter Coll., 1966. Lectr. Hunter Coll., N.Y.C., 1966-67; vis. artist U. Cin., 1974; asst. prof. U. R.I., Kingston, 1974-75, Cornell U., Ithaca, N.Y., 1977-80; vis. artist Ohio State U., Columbus, 1984; asst. prof. Va. Commonwealth Univ., Richmond, 1986-88; vis. artist The Sch. of the Art Inst. of Chgo., 1990; vis. prof. art U. Calif., Berkeley, 1993-94; One woman shows include A.I.R. Gallery, N.Y., 1973-74, 78, 81, 83, 87, Douglass Coll., New Brunswick, 1973, U. Cin., 1974, U. R.I., Kingston, 1975, 1708 E. Main Gallery, Richmond, 1987; exhibited in group shows at Whitney Mus. Am. Art, N.Y., 1973, N.Y. Cultural Ctr., N.Y., 1973, Newark Mus., 1973, Cranbrook Acad. Art Mus., Bloomfield Hills, Mich., 1974, Grand Rapids (Mich.) Art Mus., 1974, Johnson Mus., Cornell U., Ithaca, N.Y., 1977, Inst. Art and Urban Resources, Pub. Sch. 1, N.Y.C., 1978, McIntosh/Drysdale Gallery, Washington, 1980, Douglass Coll., Rutgers U., New Brunswick, 1981, Kulturhuset, Stockholm and Lunds Konsthall, Sweden, 1981-82, Picker Art Gallery, Colgate U., Hamilton, N.Y., 1983, Hopkins Hall Gallery, The Ohio State U., 1984, Kenkeleba Gallery, N.Y., 1985, A.I.R. Gallery, 1985, 91, Bernice Steinbaum Gallery, N.Y., 1986, Anderson Gallery, Va. Commonwealth U., Richmond, Va., 1987, Rabbet Gallery, New Brunswick, N.J., 1989, Michael Walls Gallery, 1989, 148 Duane St., N.Y.C., 1992, Contemporary Art Inst., N.Y.C., 1994, Mason Gross Sch. of the Arts Galleries, Rutgers U., New Brunswick, N.J., 1996, A.I.R. Gallery, N.Y.C., 1997, Kingsborough C.C., Bklyn., 1998; represented in permanent collections Bellevue Med. Ctr., N.Y.C., The Chase Manhattan Bank, N.Y.C., City Univ. Grad. Ctr., N.Y.C., The Picker Art Gallery, Dana Art Ctr., Colgate U., Hamilton, N.Y., U. Cin., Gene Swenson Collection, U. Kansas Art Mus., Lawrence, Bristol-Myers, Squibb, Lawrenceville, N.J., Hunter Coll., N.Y.C. CAPS fellow N.Y. State Coun. Arts, 1975; Visual artist fellow Nat. Endowment for the Arts, 1975, 82, 93, AAUW fellow, 1976-77, Artist fellow N.Y. Found. for the Arts, 1991; grantee Adolph & Esther Gottlieb Found., 1991. Home and Office: 151 Canal St New York NY 10002-5033

DUNKIS, PATRICIA B., school system administrator. Prin. C.R. Streams Elem. Sch., Upper St. Clair, Pa., 1982—; dir. elem. edn. Upper St. Clair Sch. Dist. Recipient Elem. Sch. Recognition award U.S. Dept. Edn., 1989-90. Office: 1820 Mclaughlin Run Rd Upper Saint Clair PA 15241

DUNKLAU, RUPERT LOUIS, personal investments consultant; b. Arlington, Nebr., May 19, 1927; s. Louis Z. and Amelia S. (Gnuse) D.; m. Ruth Eggert, June 4, 1950; children: Paul, Janet. B.S., U. Nebr., 1950; Litt.D. (hon.), Concordia Coll., St. Paul, 1982; LL.D. (hon.), Midland Luth. Coll., Fremont, Nebr., 1985. Exec. v.p. Valmont Industries, Inc., Valley, Nebr., 1950-73; dir. Fremont Nat. Bank, Nebr., 1968—. Bd. dirs. Midland Lutheran Coll., Community Chest, Meml. Hosp. Dodge County, Fremont, Luth. Ch.-Mo. Synod, St. Louis, Concordia Pub. House, Valparaiso (Ind.) U. Served with USNR, 1945. Republican. Club: Rotarian. Home: 2146 Phelps Ave Fremont NE 68025-4522 Office: PO Box 1558 Fremont NE 68026-1558

DUNKLE, KEITH ALLEN, military officer; b. Waverly, Mo., Feb. 2, 1958; s. Elden Thomas Dunkle and Margaret Alice Petet; m. Brenda Ann Dulle, Oct. 8, 1994. BS, BA, Cen. Mo. State U., 1990. Commd. 2d lt. U.S. Army, 1990, advanced through grades to capt., 1999; security officer nuclear weapons detachment 558th U.S. Field Arty., Perivolaki, Greece, 1991-92; field arty. officer 41st Field Arty. Regiment, Ft. Stewart, Ga., 1992-95; spl. forces operational detachment "A" comdr. 7th Spl. Forces Group, Ft. Bragg, N.C., 1996—. Avocations: chess, reading, outdoor sports. E-mail: kaddunk@worldnet.att.net. Home: 39 Prestige Dr Cameron NC 28326 Office: B Co 2d Bn 7th SFG (A) Fort Bragg NC 28307

DUNKLE, LISA MARIE, clinical research executive; b. Ann Arbor, Mich., Oct. 31, 1946; d. Robert Henry and Dorothy Rose (Heagstedt) D.; m. Richard James Scheffler, Dec. 28, 1972; children: Richard James Scheffler III, Margaret Dorothy Scheffler. AB, Wellesley Coll., 1968; MD, Johns Hopkins U., 1972. Diplomate Nat. Bd. Med. Examiners, Am. Bd. Pediat., Am. Bd. Pediat. Infectious Diseases, Pediat. Infectious Disease Soc. Intern Washington U., St. Louis, 1972-73, resident in pediat., 1973-74, fellow infectious diseases, 1974-76; asst. prof. pediat. St. Louis U., 1976-79, assoc. prof. pediat., 1979-85, assoc. prof. microbiology, 1979-85, prof. pediat., 1985-89; dir. pediat. infectious diseases, 1976-89; dir. infectious diseases lab. Cardinal Glennon Hosp., St. Louis, 1976-89; dir. infectious control program, 1976-89; dir. antiviral clin. rsch. Bristol-Myers Squibb, Wallingford, Conn., 1989-95, exec. dir. HIV clin. rsch., 1995-97, exec. dir. antiviral clin. rsch., 1997—. Mem. editorial bd. Pediatric Infectious Disease Jour., 1989-92; contbr. articles to profl. jours. Fundraiser Wellesley (Mass.) Coll., 1975-88, 97-99, The Forsyth Sch., St. Louis, 1988-89. Scholar Johns Hopkins U., 1972; Rsch. grantee Cystic Fibrosis Found., 1984. Fellow Infectious Disease Soc. Am.; mem. Soc. for Pediatric Rsch., Midwest Soc. for Pediatric Rsch. (sec. 1983-88, pres. 1989-90), Interscience Conf. on Antimicrobial Agts. and Chemotherapy (program com. 1992-96). Republican. Episcopalian. Achievements include identification of plasmid-mediated gene responsible for surface adhesion of S. aureus; direction of clinical development and FDA and European Medicines Evaluation Agy. approval of ZERIT. Office: Bristol Myers Squibb 5 Research Pky Wallingford CT 06492-1927

DUNKLY, JAMES WARREN, theological librarian; b. Alexandria, La., Aug. 1, 1942; s. James Warren and Frances Estelle (Jones) D.; m. Nancy Rose; children: Margaret Rose, Michael Benjamin. BA, Tex. Christian U., 1963; diploma in Theology, Oxford U., Eng., 1964; MA, Vanderbilt U., 1968, PhD, 1982. Grad. fellow, tutor Episcopal Theol. Sch., Cambridge, Mass., 1969-71; libr. Nashotah (Wis.) House, 1975-83; dir. librs. Episcopal Div. Sch., Weston Sch. Theology, Cambridge, 1983-92; libr. Sch. Theology U. of the South, Sewanee, Tenn., 1993—; assoc. libr. U. of the South, Sewanee, 1995—; instr. Inst. Christian Studies, Milw., 1975-83, Wis. asst. editor N.T. Abstracts, 1971-72, mng. editor, 1972-75; mem. corp. for Anglican Theol. Rev., 1976-95, asst. editor for N.T., 1976-84, editor, 1984-88; mem. bd. Sewanee Theol. Rev., 1994—; contbr. articles to profl. jours. Conant Fund grantee, Episcopal Ch., 1981-82; Henry fellow, Oxford U., 1963-64, Vanderbilt U. teaching fellow, 1967-69, Rockefeller doctoral fellow, 1969-70; Vanderbilt U. scholar, 1966-67. Mem. Soc. Bibl. Lit., Cath. Bibl. Assn., Am. Theol. Libr. Assn. (publs. com. 1977-83, bd. dirs. 1980-83, task force on structure, 1981, index bd. 1985-89, exec. com. index and preservation bds. 1988-89, v.p. 1989-90, pres. 1990-92), Anglican Assn. Biblical Scholars. Home: PO Box 3206 Sewanee TN 37375-3206 Office: U of the South du Pont Libr Sewanee TN 37383-1000

DUNLAP, CONNIE, librarian; b. Lansing, Mich., Sept. 9, 1924; d. Frederick Arthur and Laura May (Robinson) Robson; m. Robert Bruce Dunlap, Aug. 9, 1947. AB, U. Mich., 1946, AM in Libr. Sci., 1952. Head acquisitions dept., then head grad. library U. Mich. Libr., 1961-75, dep. assoc. dir., 1972-75; univ. libr. Duke U., 1975-80; cons., 1981—. Contbr. articles to publs. in field, chpts. in books. Forewoman Grand Jury U.S. Dist. Ct. 13th Dist. Mich., 1967-68; bd. dirs. U. Mich. Libr. Friends, v.p., 1997—; treas. Ann Arbor Hist. Found., 1998—. Recipient Disting. Alumnus award U. Mich. Sch Libr. Sci., 1977. Mem. ALA (mem. coun. 1974-83, mem. exec. bd. 1978-83, pres. resources and tech. svcs. divsn. 1972-73), AAUP, Assn. Coll. and Rsch. Librs. (pres. 1976-77), Assn. Rsch. Librs. (bd. dirs. 1976-80, pres. 1979-80). Address: 1570 Westfield Ave Ann Arbor MI 48103-5740

DUNLAP, CONNIE SUE ZIMMERMAN, real estate professional; b. Defiance, Ohio, Mar. 3, 1952; d. John Eldon and Loisann (May) Zimmerman; m. Joseph Richard Dunlap, Dec. 20, 1972; children: Brad, Todd, Eric. Student, MacMurray Coll., 1970-71, Ohio State U., 1973; BA, Wayne State U., 1989. Grad. Realtor Inst.; cert. residential specialist, 1991. Dental hygienist Dr. A. Lamar Byrd, San Diego, 1973-75; realtor, assoc. broker Champion & Baer, Inc., Grosse Pointe, Mich., 1986-95, Bolton-Johnston Assocs., Grosse Pointe Farms, Mich., 1995—; mem. Grosse Pointe Bd. Realtors, Macomb Bd. Realtors. Mem. Jr. League of Detroit, 1981—. Nat. Merit scholar Mature and Returning Women Wayne State U., Detroit, 1985-89. Mem. Phi Beta Kappa, Kappa Alpha Theta. Republican. Presbyterian. Home: 544 University Pl Grosse Pointe MI 48230-1640 Office: Bolton-Johnston Assocs 18332 Mack Ave Grosse Pointe MI 48236-3219

DUNLAP, DAVID HOUSTON, judge; b. Columbia, Mo., Apr. 24, 1947; s. James Vardeman and Cynthia May (Roby) D.; m. Dana Sue Coburn, Apr. 23, 1982. BA, Southwest Mo. State U., 1969, MA, 1971; JD, U. Mo., 1975. Assoc. Campbell, Morgan & G, Kansas City, Mo., 1975-82; editor Mo. Law Tape, Inc., Kansas City, 1982-86; judge Howell County Cir. Ct. (37th cir.), West Plains, Mo., 1986—; cons. appellate law, Mo., 1982-86; profl. judge USA Nat. Debate tournament, 1972, 73. Author, editor: (audio tapes) Legal Ednl., 1974-86; author: The Adult Abuse Act: Theory vs. Practice, 1996; contbr. articles to profl. publs. Speaker Mo. Right-to-Work Com., Kansas City, 1978; bd. dirs. St. Francis' Farm, West Plains, Mo., 1986-90; mem. Mo. Task Force on Gender and Justice, 1990-93. Am. Forensic Assn. grantee, 1971. Mem. Mo. Bar Assn., Mo. Judicial Conf., Ozark Gastronomic Soc. (bd. dirs. 1983—). Avocations: gastronomy, horticulture. Home: 1611 Luna Dr West Plains MO 65775-4220 Office: Howell County Cir Ct Assoc Div Howell County Courthouse West Plains MO 65775

DUNLAP, DONALD KELDER, rental company executive; b. Johnson City, N.Y., Nov. 30, 1964; s. Leslie David and Eunice Krom Dunlap; m. Anna Elizabeth Beaty, Aug. 18, 1985; 1 child, Donald Kelder Jr. MusB, Mars Hill Coll., 1985; MBA, Winthrop U., 1994. Co-mgr. Winner's Corp., Asheville, N.C., 1985-87; supr. Meml. Mission Hosp., Asheville, 1987; asst. mgr. Rose's Stores, Inc., Hendersonville, N.C., 1988-89; sr. asst. mgr. Rose's Stores, Inc., Brevard, N.C., 1989-90; sta. mgr. The Hertz Corp., Charlotte, N.C., 1990-95; pool fleet mgr. The Hertz Corp., Atlanta, 1995-98, region yield mgr., 1998—. Mem. South Metro Concert Band (treas. 1996-97, chmn. 1997-98). Avocations: music, literature, computers. Home: 722 Monticello Ln Mcdonough GA 30253-7910 Office: The Hertz Corp SE Region 4751 Best Rd Ste 400 Atlanta GA 30337-5611

DUNLAP, ELLEN S., library administrator; b. Nashville, Oct. 12, 1951; d. Arthur Wallace and Elizabeth (Majors) Smith; m. Arthur H. Dunlap, Jr., Dec. 27, 1972 (dec. 1977); m. Frank Armstrong, May 11, 1979; 1 child, Libbie Sarah. BA, U. Tex., Austin, 1972, MLS, 1974. Rsch. assoc. Humanities Rsch. Ctr. U. Tex., Austin, 1973-76, rsch. libr., 1976-83; exec. dir. Rosenbach Mus. and Library, Phila., 1983-92; pres. Am. Antiquarian Soc., Worcester, Mass., 1992—; bd. dirs. Rsch. Librs. Group, Inc., Mountain View, Calif.; dir. 18th Century Short Title Catalogue/N.Am., 1992—; corporator Alliance for Edn., Worcester, Mass., 1993—. Mem. acad. affairs com. Winterthur Mus., 1995—; bd. dirs. Book Arts Press, U. Va., 1994—, Mass. Found. for Humanities, 1996—; dir. Worcester Mcpl. Rsch. Bur., 1993—; mem. fin. com. Town of West Boylston, Mass., 1997—; corporator Greater Worcester Cmty. Found., 1997—. Mem. Am. Antiquarian Soc., Colonial Soc. Mass., Grolier Club (N.Y.C.), Worcester Club. Office: Am Antiquarian Soc 185 Salisbury St Worcester MA 01609-1636

DUNLAP, F. THOMAS, JR., lawyer, electronics company executive; b. Pitts., Feb. 7, 1951; s. Francis Thomas and Margaret (Hubert) D.; m. Kathy Dunlap; children: Bridgette, Katie. B.S.E.E., U. Cin., 1974; J.D., U. Santa Clara, Calif., 1979. Bar: Calif., 1979, U.S. Dist. Ct. (no. dist.) Calif. 1979. Mgr. engring. Intel Corp, Santa Clara, Calif., 1974-78, adminstr. tech. exchange, 1978-80, European counsel, 1980-81, sr. atty., 1981-83, gen. counsel, sec., 1983-87, v.p., gen. counsel, sec., 1987—. drafter, lobbyist Semiconductor Chip Protection Act, 1984. Republican. Roman Catholic. Avocation: jogging. Office: Intel Corp Ste 4 2200 Mission College Blvd Santa Clara CA 95054-1549*

DUNLAP, HALLOWELL, data processing executive; b. Lancaster, Pa., Apr. 1, 1948; s. Lawrence Hallowell and Elizabeth Metcalfe (Suter) D.; m. Hanna-Aurelia Hipp, Dec. 21, 1984; 1 child, Jed Christopher Peck. BA, New Coll., Sarasota, Fla., 1969; MA, Dartmouth Coll., 1974; cert. postgrad. study, U. Cambridge, U.K., 1975. Self-employed investor London, 1975-83; pres. Dunlap and Kerst Inc., Lancaster, 1983-87, Nova Computer Svcs., Inc., Lancaster, 1987—. Pres. Lawrence H. and Elizabeth S. Dunlap Found., 1998—. With U.S. Army, 1970-72. Woodrow Wilson fellow, 1969. Mem. Cambridge U. Chem. Soc. (life). Avocations: hot air ballooning, amateur radio, private railroad car owner. Home: 241 W Chestnut St Lancaster PA 17603-3546

DUNLAP, JAMES ELVIE, school superintendent, educator; b. Longview, Tex., Jan. 25, 1947; s. Elvie Hallmark and Annie Mae (Pitts) D.;m. Linda Sue Sample, June 6, 1969; children: Merridythe Brette, Jeffrey Wayne. BS, Stephen F. Austin State Coll., 1969, MEd, 1976; postgrad., Tex. A&M U., 1981-82. Cert. profl. supt., Tex. Tchr. Ctrl. Ind. Sch. Dist., Pollok, Tex., 1969-71; tchr. Diboll (Tex.) Ind. Sch. Dist., 1971-78, prin., 1979-81, bus. mgr., 1981-85, supt. schs., 1985-91; supt. schs. Beckville (Tex.) Ind. Sch. Dist., 1991-94, Hallsville (Tex.) Ind. Sch. Dist., 1994—. Pres. Diboll Booster Club, 1985-86; bd. dirs. Beckville Cmty. Devel. Found., 1992-94. Recipient Disting. Svc. award Tex. Vocat. Agrl. Tchrs. Assn. Tex., 1987-91. Mem. Tex. PTA Assn. (life), Lions (pres. Diboll chpt. 1987; prse. Beckville chpt. 1993), Masons (sr. deacon 1979, jr. warden 1980, sec. 1978). Democrat. Baptist. Avocations: jogging, gardening, fishing, target shoooting. E-mail: jdunlap@hisd.com. Office: Hallsville Ind Sch Dist Walnut & Green St Hallsville TX 75650

DUNLAP, JAMES RILEY, SR., former financial executive, credit manager; b. Portland, Oreg., May 21, 1925; s. William Gates and Laura (Riley) D.; m. Betty Towe; children: James R. Jr., Brian Jay, William David. BSBA, U. Oreg., 1950; postgrad., Portland State Coll., 1963-65. Sales rep. Hyster Co., Portland, 1950-61; br. asst. mgr. Reynolds Metals Co., Portland, 1961-71; corp. credit mgr. Burns Bros. Inc., Portland, 1971-79, sec.-treas., 1979-89. Contbr. articles on credit and fin. mgmt. to profl. jours. With USAAF, 1943-46. Melvin Jones fellow. Mem. Nat. Assn. Credit Mgmt. (past pres., bd. dirs.), Internat. Assn. Credit Mgmt. (past pres., bd. dirs., Disting. Svc. award 1985, Herb Barnes Meml. award 1987), Portland Retail Credit Assn. (past pres., bd. dirs.), Oreg. State Cons. Credit Assn. (past pres., lifetime bd. dirs.), Portland Jaycees, Oreg. Motor Supply Credit Assn. (past pres., bd. dirs.), Consumer Counseling Svc. Oreg. (exec. com. 1979-89), Am. Contract Bridge League (past pres. Portland chpt., gold life master), Lions (past pres. host club), Masons (life), Elks, Delta Tau Delta Alumni Assn. (past pres.). Avocations: philately, bridge.

DUNLAP, JOHN DANIEL, III, association administrator; b. Cass City, Mich., Feb. 5, 1959; s. John Daniel Dunlap Jr. and Karen Louise (Matthews) Kleba; m. Jane Margaret Austin, June 6, 1981; children: John IV, Kathryn, Claire. BA in Polit. Sci., U. Redlands, 1981; M of Pub. Policy in Environ. Policy, Claremont Grad. Sch., 1982. Planner, policy analyst Computer Transp. Svc., Inc., L.A., 1981-83; planner, program mgr. South Coast Air Quality Mgmt. Dist., El Monte, Calif., 1983-89, pub. advisor, 1989-93; chief dep. dir. Dept. Toxic Substances Control, Sacramento, 1993-94; chair Calif. Air Resources Bd., Sacramento, 1994-98; ceo, pres. Calif. Restaurant Assn., 1998—. Mem. staff to Congressman Jerry Lewis, Redlands, 1980; chmn. troop com. Boy Scouts Am., Alta Loma and Auburn, Calif., 1994—; chmn. Environ. Mgmt. Com., Rancho Cucamonga, Calif., 1990-94; mem. alumni coun. Claremont Grad. Sch., 1992-96; mem. adv. coun. Chaffey C.C., 1992-96. Recipient Alumni Career Achievement award U. Redlands, 1995. Republican. Mem. LDS Ch. Avocations: scouts, canoeing, hiking. Office: Calif Restaurant Assn. 980 9th Ste Ste 1480 Sacramento CA 95814

DUNLAP, KATHLEEN JANE, public relations executive; b. Roanoke, Va., Jan. 1, 1946; d. James Grantham and Kathleen Meredith (Haggerty) D. AB in English, Greensboro (N.C.) Coll., 1967; grad. pub. procedures, Radcliffe Coll., 1970; MA in Mass Comm. Rsch./Journalism, U. N.C., 1971. Tchr.

Dept. Edn., Va., 1968-70; asst. dir. devel. Washington and Lee U., Lexington, Va., 1970-73; dir. devel., instr. So. Sem. Jr. Coll., Buena Vista, Va., 1973-74; admissions rep. Art Inst. of Ft. Lauderdale, 1974-78; pres. Dunlap Assocs., Seattle, 1979-94; prin. Skinner Dunlap and Stevens Internat., LLC, 1994—; dir. pub. rels. Exploration Cruise Lines, Seattle, 1985-88, Soc. Expeditions, Seattle, 1989-90; mgr. pub. rels. Windstar Cruises, Inc., 1991-94. Writer video script, 1983 (Bronze medal Internat. Film & TV Festival of N.Y. 1984); editor Outlet, 1982-84 (Pacesetter award Internat. Assn. Bus. Communicators 1982-84), Live Wires, 1984—. Mem. pub. rels. com. Seattle Women's Commn., 1984. Recipient Golden Bell award Hospitality Sales Mktg. Internat. Assn., 1995. Mem. Pub. Rels. Soc. Am. (chair travel and tourism sect. 1991, 92, bd. dirs. 1997—, Totem award Puget Sound chpt. 1995, 98, APEX '98 Award of Excellence), Travel Industry Assn. Am. (press and pub. rels. com. 1989-91), Soc. Am. Travel Writers, Sound of Baskerville (Seattle), DAR (Va. Frontier chpt., editor Silver Anniversary Yearbook Francis Broward chpt. 1976), Va. Soc. Colonial Dames of 17th Century, Magna Carta. Office: 959 Thorn Hill Rd Lexington VA 24450

DUNLAP, PATRICIA C., state legislator; b. Rochester, N.H., Nov. 6, 1926. Grad. h.s. N.H. state rep.; mem. comm., small bus., consumer affairs, econ. devel. coms. N.H. Ho. of Reps.; ward clk., Rochester, N.Y., 1991-92, supr. checklist, 1992; bank customer rels. rep., 1990. Treas. Gafney Home for Aged Mgmt. Bd., 1992—; asst. treas. 1st Ch. Congl. Mem. DAR (asst. treas. Mary Torr chpt. 1992—). Office: NH House of Reps 107 N Main St Concord NH 03301-4951

DUNLAP, RICHARD DONOVAN, artistic director; b. Pomona, Calif., Jan. 30, 1923; s. James Lavern and Elizabeth (Eason) D. BA, Yale U., 1945, MFA, 1948. Dir., producer Acad. Award Show, ABC, Hollywood, Calif., 1960-71; TV dir. The Young and the Restless CBS, Hollywood, 1972-80; TV dir. As the World Turns CBS, N.Y.C., 1982-85; artistic dir. Berkshire Theatre Festival, Stockbridge, Mass., 1988-92; cons. Telemundo, San Juan, P.R., 1985-86. Dir. (TV) The Young and the Restless (Emmy Best Dir. of Daytime Drama 1974-75, 77-78. Lt. (j.g.) USN, 1943-46, PTO. Roman Catholic.

DUNLAP, RICHARD FRANK, school system administrator; b. Chester, Pa., July 13, 1936; s. Maurice Edwin and Christine (Mingis) D.; m. Annis Glenn, June 13, 1959; children: Richard Frank, Jr., Gwenn Lynn. BS in Secondary Edn., West Chester State Coll., 1958; MEd in Elem. Edn., Temple U., 1966, postgrad., 1970. Cert. secondary tchr. social studies/geography, elem. edn./adminstrn., Pa. Elem. prin. Glenwood Sch., Media, Pa., 1992; prin. Indian Lane Elem. Sch., Media, 1992—. Recipient award Four Chaplains Ch., Phila., 1972, Rose Tree Media Svc. award Rose Tree Media Schs., 1973. Mem. Delaware County Prins., Pa. Assn. Supervision and Curriculum Devel., ASCD, Nat. Assn. Elem. Sch. Prins. (award for Sch. of Excellence 1990), Pa. Assn. Elem. Sch. Prins. Avocations: reading, travel, photography. Office: Indian Lane Elem Sch 309 S Old Middletown Rd Media PA 19063-4798*

DUNLAP, RILEY EUGENE, sociologist; b. Wynne, Ark., Oct. 25, 1943; s. Riley W. Dunlap Jr. and F. Eugenia (Jones) Anderson; m. Lonnie Jean Brown, Aug. 20, 1966; children: Sara Jean, Christopher Eugene. MS, U. Oreg., 1969, PhD, 1973. From asst. prof. to prof. sociology Wash. State U., Pullman, 1972-85, 85-96, Boeing Disting. prof. environ. sociology, 1996—; mem. socioeconomic peer review panel Office of Exploratory Rsch., U.S. EPA, 1991; mem. panel on aesthetic attributes in water resources planning NRC/Nat. Acad. Scis., 1982; Gallup fellow in environment George H. Gallup Internat. Inst., 1992—. Editor, author: (jour. symposium) Am. Behavioral Scientist, 1980, Internat. Sociology, 1998; editor book: American Environmentalism: The U.S. Environmental Movement, 1970-90, 92, Pub. Reactions to Nuclear Waste, 1993. Mem. AAAS (rural sociol. soc. rep. to sect. K 1986-89), Internat. Sociol. Assn. (pres., rsch. com. on environ. and soc. 1994-98), Am. Sociol. Assn. (chmn. sect. on environ. sociology 1981-83, disting. contbn. award 1986), Rural Sociol. Soc. (chmn. natural resources rsch. group 1978-79, award of merit 1985), Soc. for Study of Social Problems (chmn. environ. problems divsn. 1973-75). Achievements include being credited as co-founder of field of environmental sociology. Fax: (509) 335-2125. E-mail: dunlap@wsu.edu. Office: Washington State Univ Dept Sociology Pullman WA 99164-4020

DUNLAP, WALLACE HART, pediatrician; b. Wichita, Kans., Oct. 16, 1935; s. Fred Everett and Ermalea (Hart) D.; m. Judith Nell Gardner, Aug. 29, 1963 (div. 1974); children: Susan Margaret, John Gardner; m. Jane Stokley Davis, July 3, 1984; stepchildren: Hugh Wilson Raetzsch, Susan Stokely Raetzsch Copeland. BA in Zoology, Kans. U., 1957, MD, 1961. Intern U. Okla. Med. Ctr., Oklahoma City, 1961-62, resident in pediat., 1962-63; resident in pediat. Children's Med. Ctr., Dallas, 1963-64; pvt. practice Baton Rouge, 1966—. Bd. dirs. Baton Rouge Area Found., 1994—. Capt. U.S. Army Med. Corps, 1964-66. Fellow Am. Acad. Pediat. (pres. La. chpt. 1974-80, D.W. Van Gelder MD Disting. Svc. award 1994); mem. AMA (alt. del. 1997—), La. State Med. Soc. (chmn. coun. legis. 1984-93, bd. dirs. 1984-92, sec., treas. 1996—, bd. govs. 1966—, bd. dirs. MD Health Shares 1997—, patient's choice HMO pres. 1996—), La. Med. Polit. Action Com. (chmn. 1994—). Presbyterian. Avocations: bichon frise show dogs, computers, bicycling, genealogy. Office: The Pediatric Clinic 888 Tara Blvd Ste F Baton Rouge LA 70806-7895

DUNLAP, WILLIAM CRAWFORD, physicist; b. Denver, July 21, 1918; s. William Crawford and Helen (Kiester) D.; m. Ellen Hebrew, Mar. 22, 1940; 1 dau., Nancy. B.S., U. N.M., 1938; Ph.D., U. Calif. at Berkeley, 1943. Asst. physicist Dept. Agr., 1942-45; research asso., research lab. Gen. Electric Co., 1945-55, cons. physicist electronics lab., 1955-56; supr. solid state research, research lab. Bendix Corp., 1956-58; dir. solid state electronic research Raytheon Co., 1958-64; asst. dir. electronic components research Electronics Research Center, NASA, Cambridge, Mass., 1964-68; dir. research Electronics Research Center, NASA, 1968-70; sci. adviser to dir. U.S. Transp. Systems Center, Cambridge, 1970-75; pres. W.C. Dunlap & Co., 1975—. Author: An Introduction to Semiconductors, 1957; editor-in-chief Solid State Electronics, 1959-94. Fellow IEEE (dir. 1966-68, dir. region I 1966-68), Am. Phys. Soc., AIAA (assoc.). Spl. research transistor prodn. techniques in alloying, diffusion, epitaxy. Home: 126 Prince St Newton MA 02465-2604

DUNLAP, WILLIAM DEWAYNE, JR., advertising agency executive; b. Austin, Minn., Apr. 8, 1938; s. William D. and Evelyn (Hummel) D.; m. Lois Mary Apple, Sept. 23, 1961; children: Kristin, Leslie, Brenda. B.A., Carleton Coll., 1960. Brand mgr. soap Procter & Gamble, Cin., 1960-69; asst. postmaster gen. U.S. Postal Svc., Washington, 1970-75, chmn. postmaster gen.'s customer coun., 1971-75, chmn. stamp adv. coun., 1972-75; pres. MCA Advt., Westport, Conn., 1976-81; chmn. Campbell-Mithun Esty, Mpls., 1981—. Bd. dirs. Operation Smile Internat. Lutheran. Home: 951 Springhill Rd Wayzata MN 55391-9553 Office: Campbell-Mithun-ESTY 222 S 9th St 26th Fl Minneapolis MN 55402-3803*

DUNLEAVY, JANET FRANK EGLESON, English language educator; b. N.Y.C., Dec. 16, 1928; d. Christian Joseph and Evelyn Vivienne (Aaron) Frank; m. James D. Egleson (div. 1962); m. Gareth W. Dunleavy; children: Karen, Gweneth, Stephen. BA, Hunter Coll., 1951; MA, NYU, 1962, PhD, 1966. Editor, writer, 1951-64; lectr. English Hunter Coll., 1964-66; asst. prof. English SUNY, Stony Brook, 1966-70; master Benedict Coll., 1969-70; asst. prof. U. Wis., Milw., 1970-71, assoc. prof., 1971-76, prof. English, 1976-89, prof. English and comparative lit., 1989-93; prof. emeritus, 1993—; sr. Fulbright lectr. Tel Aviv U., 1986. Author: Daddies, 1954, Davy Crockett and the Indians, 1955, Happy Days, 1955, (with James D. Egleson) Parents Without Partners, 1961, Design for Writing, 1970, George Moore: The Artist's Vision, the Storyteller's Art, 1973, (with Gareth W. Dunleavy) The O'Conor Papers, 1977, Douglas Hyde: A Maker of Modern Ireland, 1991; editor: Castle Richmond (Anthony Trollope), 1981, George Moore in Perspective, 1983, (with Dunleavy) Selected Plays of Douglas Hyde, 1991, Classics of Joyce Criticism, 1991, (with Melvin J. Friedman and Michael Patrick Gillespie) Joycean Occasions, 1991. Named to Hunter Coll. Hall of Fame, 1978; Am. Council Learned Socs. grantee, 1971, Am.-Irish Found. grantee, 1973-74; Am. Philos. Soc. grantee, 1980; Guggenheim fellow, 1983-84, Camargo Found. fellow, 1984-85, 88-89. Mem. MLA, Am. Com. for Irish Studies (editor Newsletter 1971-78), Internat. Assn. for Study Anglo-Irish Lit., James Joyce Found. Home: Riverwoods C112 7 Riverwoods Dr Exeter NH 03833-4374

DUNLEAVY, KRISTIE LYN, direct marketing and advertising executive; b. Washington, July 21, 1957; d. James Elliot and Betty Jean (Heflin) D. V.p. Direct Answer, Inc., Oxon Hill, Md. Mem. Direct Mktg. Assn. Washington (bd. dirs. 1990-93, vol. of Yr. award 1988, Gold MAXI award 1989), Fulfillment Mgmt. Assn., Newsletter Pubs. Assn. Roman Catholic. Avocations: genealogy, Virginia history, photography. Home: 2842 Dover Ln Falls Church VA 22042-2842 Office: Direct Answer Inc 6424 Bock Rd Oxon Hill MD 20745-3001

DUNLEAVY, MICHAEL JOSEPH, professional basketball coach; b. Brooklyn, NY, Mar. 21, 1954; m. Emily Dunleavy; children: Michael, William Baker, James. Ed., Univ. S.C. Player Phila. 76ers, NBA, 1976-77; former player-coach Carolina Lightning, All-Am. Basketball Alliance; player Houston Rockets, NBA, 1978-83, San Antonio Spurs, NBA, 1982; player Milw. Bucks, 1984, asst. coach, to 1990; head coach L.A. Lakers, 1990-92; head coach Milw. Bucks, 1992-93, gen. mgr., v.p. basketball ops., 1993-96; head coach Portland (Oreg.) Trailblazers, 1997—. Office: Portland Trailblazers One Center Ct Ste 200 Portland OR 97227*

DUNLOP, DAVID JOHN, geophysics educator, researcher; b. Toronto, Ont., Can., Jan. 30, 1941; s. Harry John Ewart and Mary Scott (Burkholder) D.; children: Lisa Karen, Jennifer Michelle; m. Özden Özdemir, June 2, 1987. BASc, U. Toronto, 1963, MA, 1964, PhD, 1968. Postdoctoral studies U. Tokyo, 1968-69; rsch. fellow Université de Paris VI, 1969-70; asst. prof. U. Toronto, 1970-73, assoc. prof., 1973-78, prof., 1978—; vis. scientist NASA Johnson Space Ctr., Houston, 1972; sr. vis. scientist CSIRO, Sydney, Australia, 1992; assoc. prof. U. Montpellier, France, 1997. Editor: Origin of Thermomagnetism, 1977; assoc. editor Can. Jour. Earth Scis., 1983-94; co-author: Rock Magnetism Fundamentals and Frontiers, 1997. Killam Found. fellow, Can. Coun., 1983-85, USSR Acad. Scis. fellow, 1988, Sr. Rsch. fellow Tokyo Inst. Tech., 1988-89, DAAD rsch. fellow Munich, 1990; sr. rsch. fellow Kyoto (Japan) U., 1997; recipient Louis Néel medal European Geophys. Soc., 1999. Fellow Royal Soc. Can., Am. Geophys. Union (sect. pres. 1992-94), Geol. Assn. Can. (councillor 1985-87); mem. Can. Geophys. Union (pres. 1985-87; Tuzo Wilson medal 1999). Avocations: canoeing, hiking, lepidoptera, photography, restoring old houses. Office: U Toronto, Dept Physics, Toronto, ON Canada M5S 1A7

DUNLOP, EDWARD ARTHUR, computer company executive; b. Wilmington, Del., Jan. 22, 1951; s. Edward C. and Eleanor (Smith) D.; m. Gladys Englehart, July 21, 1984; 1 child, Elizabeth. BS, U. Del., 1978, postgrad., 1978-79. Rsch. asst., cons. U. Del., Newark, 1972-78; pres. Technology Logistics, Newark, 1978-85, West Chester, Pa., 1989—; asst. to v.p. Continental Ins. Co., Neptune, N.J., 1985-88; sr. project mgr., asst. to vice chmn. Roy F. Weston Inc., West Chester, 1988-89; voting mem. Nat. Standards com. on Local and Metro. Area Networks, 1994—. Mem. Coun. on Environ Control State of Del., 1975-81. Univ. fellow bus. and govt. ethics U. Del., 1983-85. Mem. IEEE, IEEE Computer Soc., Assn. for Computing Machinery, Ea. Tech. Coun. Office: Technology Logistics 1265 Estate Dr West Chester PA 19380-1258

DUNLOP, FRED HURSTON, lawyer; b. Clarksville, Tenn., May 3, 1946; s. William Barrett and Nelle Major (Hurston) D.; m. Jacqueline Rae Thompson, Aug. 17, 1968; children: Holt McKinney, Lindsay Barrett. BA, Vanderbilt U., 1968, JD, 1971. Bar: Tenn. 1971, Tex. 1972; comml. mediator, arbitration cert. Internat. Ctrs. Arbitration. Assoc. Baker & Botts LLP, Houston, 1972-78; ptnr. Baker & Botts, Houston, 1979—. 1st lt. U.S. Army, 1971-72. Fellow Tex. Bar Found.; mem. ABA, Am. Coll. Real Estate Attys., State Bar Tex., Houston Bar Assn., Houston Real Estate Lawyers Coun., Coll. of State Bar of Tex. Avocations: golf, hunting, skiing. Home: 5609 Tupper Lake Dr Houston TX 77056-1628 Office: Baker & Botts LLP 1 Shell Pla 910 Louisiana St Ste 3100 Houston TX 77002-4916

DUNLOP, GEORGE RODGERS, retired surgeon; b. St. Peter, Minn., Mar. 31, 1906; s. George Crawford and Pearl (Rodgers) D.; m. Barbara Wallace, Apr. 3, 1939; children: Susan Dunlop Roberts, Madora Howell. B.S., U. Cin., 1927; M.D., Harvard U., 1931. Diplomate Am. Bd. Surgery. Intern Cin. Gen. Hosp., 1931-32; asst. resident in surgery N.Y. Hosp.-Cornell Med. Ctr., 1932-35; resident in surgery Worcester (Mass.) City Hosp., 1935-36; practice medicine specializing in surgery, 1935-82; sr. surgeon, past chief surgery Worcester Meml. Hosp.; prof. surgery emeritus U. Mass. Med. Sch.; dir., past chmn. Mass. Blue Shield; bd. dirs., past chmn. bd. Nat. Assn. Blue Shield Plans; past dir. Med. Indemnity Am.; bd. commrs. Joint Commn. Accreditation Hosps., chmn. bd. coms.; mem. Pres.'s Commn. for Study of Ethical Problems in Medicine and Biomed. and Behavioral Rsch. Bd. dirs. Meml. Hosp. Found.; bd. dirs., past chmn. Mass. divsn. Am. Cancer Soc., also, Worcester Found. Exptl. Biology; bd. dirs. U. Mass. Med. Sch. Found., Meml. Health Care Found.; past bd. dirs. Bancroft Sch., Worcester Boys' Club, Cmty. Chest. Served to lt. comdr. M.C. USNR, 1942-45. Fellow ACS (past pres.), Royal Australasian Coll. Surgeons (hon.); mem. AMA, New Eng. Surg. Soc. (past pres.), New Eng. Cancer Soc., Northwestern Med. Soc. (past pres.), Am. Surg. Assn., Boston Surg. Soc., Soc. Surgery Alimentary Tract (founder), Pan Am. Med. Assn. Club: Worcester. Home: 54 Massachusetts Ave Worcester MA 01602-2139 Office: 340 Main St Ste 356 Worcester MA 01608-1606

DUNLOP, JOHN BARRETT, foreign language educator, research institution scholar; b. Boston, Sept. 10, 1942; s. John Thomas and Dorothy Emily (Webb) D.; m. Olga Verhovskoy, Sept. 12, 1965; children—Maria, John, Olga, Catherine. B.A., Harvard Coll., 1964; M.A., Yale U., 1965, Ph.D., 1973. Prof. Russian Oberlin Coll., Ohio, 1970-83, chmn. dept. German and Russian, 1976-82; sr. fellow Hoover Instn., Stanford U., Calif., 1983—, assoc. dir., 1983-87; mem. Soviet Union in the Eighties Project, CSIS, Georgetown U., 1982-83; mem. Eastern Great Lakes regional selection com. Mellon Fellowships in Humanities, 1982-83, applicant evaluations com. Woodrow Wilson Internat. Ctr. for Scholars, 1989-93; exec. coun. Midwest Slavic Conf., 1977-79; mem. editl. bd. Russian Archives Preservation Project, 1992—; mem. rsch. coun. Internat. Forum Democratic Studies Nat. Endowment for Democracy, 1994—; mem. exec. com. Assn. Study of Nationalities, 1994-97, mem. adv. com., 1997—; mem. steering com. Ctr. Russian and East European Studies Stanford U., 1995-97; mem. overseers' com. Vis. to Kathryn W. and Shelby Cullom Davis Ctr. for Russian Studies, Harvard U., 1997—; disting. vis. U. Alta., 1995. Author: Staretz Amvrosy, 1972, 2d edit. 1975; The New Russian Revolutionaries, 1976; The Faces of Contemporary Russian Nationalism, 1983, The New Russian Nationalism, 1985, The Rise of Russia and the Fall of the Soviet Empire, 1993, 2d edit. 1995, Russia Confronts Chechunya, 1998; co-editor: Aleksandr Solzhenitsyn, 1973, 2d edit, 1975; Solzhenitsyn in Exile, 1985. Recipient Edward Chandler Cumming prize Harvard Coll., 1964; Woodrow Wilson fellow, 1965, Younger Humanist fellow, 1974-75, Hoover Instn. nat. fellow, 1978-79, Olin vis. sr. Fellow Radio Liberty, Munich, 1991-92; rsch. scholar Kennan Inst., 1987. Mem. Am. Assn. for Advancement of Slavic Studies, Western Slavic Assn. Eastern Orthodox. Office: Stanford U Hoover Instn Stanford CA 94305

DUNLOP, JOHN THOMAS, economics educator, former secretary of labor; b. Placerville, Calif., July 5, 1914; s. John W. and Antonia (Forni) D.; m. Dorothy Webb, July 6, 1937; children: John Barrett, Beverly Claire, Thomas Frederick. AB, U. Calif., 1935, PhD, 1939; LLD, U. Chgo., 1968, U. Pa., 1976, Harvard U., 1987. Acting instr. Stanford U., 1936-37; instr. Harvard U., 1938-45, assoc. prof. econs., 1945-50, prof. econs., 1950-85, Lamont U. prof., 1970-85, dean faculty arts and scis., 1970-73; Served as vice chmn. Boston Regional War Labor Bd., 1944-45; chmn. Nat. Joint Bd. for Settlement of Jurisdictional Disputes in bldg. and constrn. industry, 1948-57; cons. Office Econ. Stabilization, 1945-47, NLRB, 1948-52, Atomic Energy Labor Panel, 1948-53; mem. bd. inquiry Bituminous Coal Industry, 1950; pub. mem. ESB, 1950-52; mem. Emergency Bds. 109, 130, 167; mem. Presdl. R.R. Commn., 1960-62, Missile Sites Labor Commn., 1961-67, Pres.'s EEOC, 1964-65; impartial chmn. Constrn. Industry Joint Conf., 1959-68; dir. Cost of Living Coun., 1973-74; sec. labor, 1975-76; chmn. Pay Adv. Com., 1979-80, Social Security Coun., 1989-91; chmn. Future Worker/Mgmt. Rels. Com., 1993-95. Author: Wage Determination under Trade Unions, 1944, Collective Bargaining: Principles and Cases, 1949, 2d edit., 1953, Industrial Relations Systems, 1958, 2d edit., 1993, (with D.C. Bok) Labor and the American Community, 1970, The Lessons of Wage and Price Controls, 1977, Business and Public Policy, 1980, Dispute Resolution: Negotiation and Consensus Building, 1984, The Management of Labor Unions, 1990, (with A.M. Zack) Mediation and Arbitration of Employment Disputes, 1997; editor Wertheim Series in Industrial Relations, 1945—. Named to Nat. Housing Hall of Fame; recipient Murray, Meany, Green award AFL-CIO, 1987. Mem. Am. Acad. Arts and Scis., Am. Philos. Soc., Inst. Medicine (life), Nat. Acad. Arbitrators, Nat. Acad. Human Resources. Home: 509 Pleasant St Belmont MA 02478-3238 Office: Harvard U 208 Littauer Ctr Cambridge MA 02138

DUNLOP, MICHAEL, broadcast executive; b. Pontiac, Mich., Nov. 11, 1946. Student, Wayne State U. Exec. v.p. Sta WKBD-TV, Southfield, Mich., 1998—. Office: Sta WKBD-TV 26905 W 11 Mile Rd Southfield MI 48034-2292*

DUNMAN, LEONARD JOE, III, trucking company executive; b. Louisville, June 8, 1952; s. Leonard Joe Jr. and Betty (Moody) D.; m. Carol Ann Heckel, Aug. 10, 1974 (div. Sept. 1990); children: Leonard Joe IV, Jacob Martin, Kathryn Elaine; m. Bridgette Denise Posante, Sept. 10, 1994; 1 child, Logan Tyler Dunman; 1 stepchild, Jordan Scott Hinton. BS in Bus., Murray State U., 1974. Supr. Philip Morris USA, Louisville, 1974-75, Boone Box Co., Louisville, 1975-77; mgr. sales Atlas Concrete Co., Louisville, 1977-81, East & Westbrook Concrete Constrn., Buckner, Ky., 1981-82; mgr. Mercer Transp. Co., Louisville, 1982—; v.p. Bridgette Dunman Svcs. LLP., La Grange, KY, 1994—; instr., Nat. Safety Coun., Indpls., 1984-89; expert witness on trucking matters, various law firms in Louisville area, 1986-87. Pres. Crescent Hill Community Coun., Louisville, 1987-89; v.p. Louisville Inter-Neighborhood Coalition, 1988-90; pres. Peterson-Dumesnil Found., Louisville, 1989-90, sec., 1992-93; asst. cub pack leader Louisville area Boy Scouts Am., 1988-90; bd. dirs. Jefferson County Pub. Schs., 1990—; chmn. Crescent Hill Libr. Task Force, 1990-91; mem. strategic planning and fin. com. Louisville-Jefferson County Met. Sewer Dist., 1992—; bd. dirs. Shippingport Centre Bus. Assn., 1998—. Mem. Am. Mgmt. Assn., Internat. Facility Mgmt. Assn. Democrat. Avocations: photography, camping, home remodeling, motorcycling, model railroading. Home: 3626 Echo Valley Cir La Grange KY 40031-9680 Office: Mercer Transp Co PO Box 35610 Louisville KY 40232-5610

DUNMEYER, SARAH LOUISE FISHER, retired health care consultant; b. Ft. Wayne, Ind., Apr. 13, 1935; d. Frederick Law and Jeanette Blose (Stults) Fisher; m. Herbert W. Dunmeyer, Sept. 9, 1967; children: Jodi, Lisa. BS, U. Mich., 1957; MS, Temple U., 1966; EdD, U. San Francisco, 1983. Lic. clin. lab. technologist, Calif. Instr. med. tech. U. Vt., Burlington, 1966-67; instr. med. tech. Northeastern U., Boston, 1967-68, instr. lab. asst. program, 1968-70; educator, coord. sch. med. tech. Children's Hosp., San Francisco, 1970-73; dir. continuing edn. program Pacific Presbyn. Med. Ctr., San Francisco, 1974-82; project mgr., cons. Peabody Mktg. Decisions, San Francisco, 1983-87; sr. rsch. assoc. Inst. for Health and Aging, U. Calif., San Francisco, 1986-89; rsch. analyst student acad. svcs. U. Calif., San Francisco, 1991-94; external cons. Health Care Consulting Svcs., San Francisco, 1986-97; clin. lab. technologist Kaiser Hosp., San Francisco, 1989-99, ret., 1999; seminar presenter Am. Assn. Blood Banks, San Francisco, 1976, Am. Soc. Clin. Pathologists, Miami Beach, Fla., 1977, Ann. Meeting of Am. Soc. Med. Technology, Atlanta, 1977; site surveyor Nat. Accrediting Agy. for Clin. Lab. Scis., Chgo., 1974-80. Contbr. articles to profl. jours.

DUNMIRE, WILLIAM WERDEN, author, photographer; b. Alameda, Calif., Feb. 24, 1930; s. Samuel P. Dunmire and Margaret L. (Dickinson) D.; m. Marjorie S. Schoder, June 14, 1954 (div. 1972); children: Glenn E., Peter P.; m. Evangeline L. Blinn, Oct. 17, 1972. BA, U. Calif., 1954, MA, 1957. Chief park naturalist Nat. Park Svc., Badlands Nat. Monument, S.D., 1961-63, Isle Royale Nat. Park, Mich., 1963-66, Yellowstone Nat. Park, Wyo., 1968-72; chief interpretation Nat. Park Svc., Washington, 1973-77; supt. Coulee Dam NRA, Washington, 1977-81, Carlsbad Caverns/Guadalupe Mountains Nat. Parks, N.Mex., 1981-85; N.Mex. pub. lands coord. The Nature Conservancy, Santa Fe, 1985-92; curatorial assoc. Mus. Southwestern Biology, U. N.Mex., 1992—; adj. naturalist N.M. Museum of Natural History & Sci., 1997—; assoc. in biology U. N.Mex., 1998. Co-author: Wild Plants of the Pueblo Province, 1995, Wild Plants and Native Peoples of the Four Corners, 1997; author more than 60 tech. and popular booklets and articles. Bd. dirs. United Way, Carlsbad, 1981-84, div. chmn., 1983-84. Served to cpl. U.S. Army, 1954-56. Recipient Meritorious Svc. award U.S. Dept. Interior, 1973. Mem. Sierra Club, Wilderness Soc. Home: 12 Camino A Las Estrellas Placitas NM 87043-8804

DUNN, ANN-MARGARET, pediatrics nurse; d. Joseph and Theresa (LaGuardia) D. BSN, Coll. New Rochelle (N.Y.), 1988; MS, Columbia U., 1992. RN. Cert. pediatric nurse practitioner. Student nurse extern NYU Med. Ctr., 1987-88, staff nurse, 1988-92; pediatric nurse practitioner N.Y. Presbyterian Hosp., N.Y.C., 1992—; clin. faculty for pediatric nurse practitioner students Columbia U. Sch. Nursing, 1997—; clin. assoc. faculty Hunter-Bellvue Sch. Nursing, 1997—; mem. AIDS adv. com. Post-Masters Cert. Program in HIV/AIDS Nursing, Coll. New Rochelle, 1996-97; dir. AIDS program tng., nursing cons. Cath. Guardian Soc., N.Y.C., 1993-98; co-investigator Pediatric AIDS Clin. Trials Group, Pharm. Sponsored Clin. Trials for children with HIV infection. Contbr. articles to profl. jours.; lectr. in field. Participant Immunization Day programs Cornell U. Med. Coll., 1993-94; participant Will Rogers Found. quarterly tuberculosis screening for impoverished children and adults N.Y. Presbyn. Hosp., chair cmty. adv. bd. Pediatric AIDS Clin. Trial Group, 1997-98, mem. nutrition working group, 1997—. Recipient XI Internat. Conf. on AIDS scholarship, Vancouver, B.C., 1996. Fellow Nat. Assn. Pediatric Nurse Practitioners; mem. Sigma Theta Tau. Roman Catholic. Home: 2533 Pearsall Ave Bronx NY 10469-5351

DUNN, ARNOLD SAMUEL, biochemistry educator; b. Rochester, N.Y., Jan. 31, 1929; s. Alexander and Dora (Cohen) D.; m. Doris Ruth Frankel, Sept. 14, 1952; children: Jonathan Alexander, David Hillel. B.S., George Washington U., 1950; Ph.D., U. Pa., 1955; LHD (hon.), Hebrew Union Coll., 1995. Research assoc. Michael Reese Hosp. Research Inst., Chgo., 1955-56; asst. prof. NYU Sch. Medicine, N.Y.C., 1956-62; vis. prof. Weizmann Inst. Sci., Rehovot, Israel, 1972-73, 83-84, Hebrew U., Jerusalem, 1972-73; prof. molecular biology U. So. Calif., Los Angeles, 1962—; dir. molecular biology U. So. Calif., L.A., 1982-90, assoc. dean, 1990-92; vis. fellow history sci. Princeton U., 1993. Contbr. articles to profl. jours.; mem. editorial bd.: Am. Jour. Physiology, 1979—, Analytical Biochemistry, 1980—. Recipient award for Teaching Excellence U. So. Calif., 1969; recipient award for Research Excellence U. So. Calif., 1972, Raubenheimer award U. So. Calif., 1981; UPSHS fellow, 1972, 83; Meyerhoff fellow Weizmann Inst. Sci., 1983. MEm. Am. Physiol. Soc., Am. Soc. Biol. Chemists, Endocrine Soc., Phi Beta Kappa, Sigma Xi, Phi Kappa Phi, Golden Key. Office: U So Calif University Park Los Angeles CA 90089

DUNN, BERNARD DANIEL, former naval officer, consultant; b. Providence, Feb. 10, 1934; s. Alexander Gerard and Mary Alice (Fitzpatrick) D.; m. Hilda Hughes Tunney, Jan. 4, 1958; children: Bernard Daniel Jr., Brian Lindsay, Mary Catherine, J. Alexander. BS in Econs., Villanova U., 1956; MBA in Transp., Mich. State U., 1971. Commd. ensign USN, 1956, advanced through grades to capt.; asst. supply officer USS Rushmore, Norfolk, Va., 1957-58; asst. material divsn. officer, stock control divsn. officer Sub Base New London, Groton, Conn., 1958-61; material and fiscal divsn. supt. Ship Repair Facility, Guam, 1961-63; nuclear weapons material divsn. officer Naval Supply Ctr., Oakland, Calif., 1963-64; supply ops. officer Nuc. Weapons Supply Annex, Oakland, Calif., 1964-65; commn. supply officer USS Fox, 1965-68; project officer Naval Supply Sys. Command, Washington, 1968-70; asst. for sea transp. Office Chief Naval Ops., Washington, 1971-73; sr. mem. Mobile Tng. Team, Bogota, Colombia, 1973; dir. warehousing, chief transp. officer Def. Depot, Tracy, Calif., 1973-76; dep. project mgr., Navy rep. Joint Container Steering Group Office of Sec. of Def., Washington, 1976-77; dir. transp. field ops. divsn. Naval Supply Sys. Command, Washington, 1977-78; head transp. mgmt. and policy br. Office Chief Naval Ops., Washington, 1978-83; comptr./dir. supply Naval Edn. and Tng. Command, Newport, R.I., 1983-85; A-76 program officer Mil. Sealift Command, Washington, 1985; acting dir./chief staff commn. on Merchant

Marine and Def., Alexandria, Va., 1985-88; bd. dirs., corp. sec. Greenwich Ctr., Inc., East Greenwich, R.I., 1988—; cons., Alexandria, 1988-91; chief program analyst Resource Cons., Inc., Vienna, Va., 1991-94, sr. supply specialist, 97-98. Life mem. East Greenwich (R.I.) Fire Dept., 1953—. Decorated Def. Meritorious Svc. medal, Meritorious Svc. medal, Joint Svc. Commendation medal with oak leaf cluster, Navy Meritorious Unit commendation, Air Force Outstanding Unit award, Humanitarian medal, Nat. Def. Svc. medal, Vietnam Svc. medal with one bronze star, Rep. of Vietnam Campaign medal. Mem. U.S. Naval Inst., Nat. Def. Transp. Assn. (pres. San Joaquin chpt. 1974-75), USCG Acad. Found., East Greenwich Vets. fireman Assn., Ret. Officers Assn., Washington Area Supply Corps Assn., Naval Submarine League, USS Rushmore Assn. (founder and charter mem., assoc. treas.). Roman Catholic. Avocations: stamp collecting, ice hockey, running, volunteer fireman, golf. Home: 5817 Shalott Ct Alexandria VA 22310-1427

DUNN, BRUCE SIDNEY, materials science educator; b. Chgo., Apr. 22, 1948; s. George Bernard and Goldye Rosalyn (Opper) D.; m. Wendy Joan Rader, June 7, 1970; 1 child, Julianne. BS in Ceramic Engring., Rutgers U., 1970; MS in Materials Sci., UCLA, 1972, PhD in Materials Sci., 1974. Staff scientist GE, Schenectady, N.Y., 1976-80; assoc. prof. materials sci. UCLA, 1981-85, prof., 1985—; cons. to numerous corps.; invited prof. U. Paris, 1986, 91, 92, 93, 98. Contbr. articles to profl. jours. Fulbright fellow, 1985-86. Fellow Am. Ceramic Soc.; mem. Electrochem. Soc., Materials Rsch. Soc. Achievements include patents in field. Office: UCLA Dept Materials Scis and Engring 6532 Boelter Hall Los Angeles CA 90095-1595

DUNN, CHARLES ANTHONY, family physician; b. Phila., June 17, 1937; s. Charles Anthony Dunn and Mary M. (Millos) Sackett; m. Kathryn Deyo, Sept. 9, 1962; children: Holly, Kim, Charles W. MD, U. Miami, 1962. Diplomate Am. Bd. Family Practice. Intern Duval Med. Ctr., Jacksonville, Fla., 1962-63, family physician in pvt. practice, 1965—; sec. med. staff, chief dept. family medicine Duval Med. Ctr., 1985-87, v.p. med. staff, 1988-90, chmn. quality assurance com., 1988-89, med. dir. skilled nursing care unit, 1989—, pres. med. staff, 1990-93, chmn. exec. com., 1990-93, chmn. credentials com. 1990-95, 96-98, ; Doctors' Hosp., Coral Gables, Fla., mem. coord. com. nat. high blood pressure edn. program NIH, Washington, 1986-90. Bd. dirs. John T. McDonald Found., 1993—; vice-chmn. bd. dirs. Metro-Dade Transit 2020 Coalition, 1994—. Capt. U.S. Army Med. Corps, 1963-65. Recipient Disting. Alumnus award U. Miami, Sch. of Med., 1997. Mem. AMA (del. 1994—), Fla. Acad. Family Physicians (pres. 1979-80, Fla. Family Physician of Yr. 1990), Fla. Med. Assn. (del. 1968—, coun. splty. medicine 1982-87, co-chmn. 1990, PRO com. 1983-92), Dade County Med. Assn. (pres., chmn. bd. dirs. 1982-83, chmn. pub. rels. com. 1993, chmn. ethics com. 1998—), Am. Acad. Family Physicians (del. 1981-88), Nat. Assn. Railroad Passengers (bd. dirs.), Nat. Railway Hist. Soc. (pres. Miami chpt.), Alpha Omega Alpha. Iron Arrow, Roman Catholic. Avocation: railroad passenger advocacy. Home: 1131 Catalonia Ave Coral Gables FL 33134-6304 Office: 4950 S Le Jeune Rd Ste A Coral Gables FL 33146-2231

DUNN, CHARLES DEWITT, academic administrator; b. Magnolia, Ark., Dec. 2, 1945; s. Charles Edward and Nora Lucille (Bailey) D.; m. Donna Jane Parsons, Apr. 9, 1966; children: Aimee, James, Joseph, Mary Elizabeth. BA, So. Ark. U., 1967; MA, North Tex. State U., 1970; PhD, So. Ill. U., 1973; cert. inst. edni. mgmt., Harvard U.; 1991. Instr. polit. sci. U. Ark., Monticello, 1969-72, asst. prof., 1972-75; assoc. prof. U. Ctrl. Ark., Conway, 1975-80, prof., 1980—, chmn. dept. polit. sci., 1976-82, dir. govt. rels., 1982-86; pres. Henderson State U., Arkadelphia, Ark., 1986—. Chmn. Commn. for Ark.'s Future, 1989-93; chmn. Ark. Higher Edn. Coun., 1992-96; chmn. fin. com. Ark. Cmty. Found. Bd. Dirs. Mem. Am. Polit. Sci. Assn., Am. Assn. State Coll. and Univs., NCAA (pres.'s commn. 1996-97, mem. pres.' coun. 1997—), Ark. Polit. Sci. Assn. (pres. 1976-77), Conway C. of C. (bd. dirs. 1984-85, v.p. 1985-86), Arkadelphia C. of C. (bd. dirs. 1987-91), Rotary. Methodist. Office: Henderson State U PO Box 7532 1100 Henderson St Arkadelphia AR 71999-0001*

DUNN, CHARLES WILLIAM, Celtic languages and literature educator, author; b. Arbuthnott, Scotland, Nov. 30, 1915; came to U.S., 1928, naturalized, 1961; s. Peter Alexander and Alberta Mary Margaret (Freeman) D.; m. Patricia Campbell, June 21, 1941 (dec. 1973); children: Deirdre, Peter Arthur; m. Elaine Birnbaum, Oct. 25, 1974; 1 son, Alexander Joseph. B.A. with honors, McMaster U., 1938; A.M., Harvard, 1939, Ph.D., 1948; LL.D. (hon.), St. Francis Xavier U., 1983. Asst. in English Harvard, 1939-40, tutor, 1940-41; instr. humanities Stephens Coll., 1941-42; instr. English Cornell U., 1943-46; instr. then assoc. prof. English Univ. Coll., U. Toronto, 1946-56; prof. English N.Y. U., 1956-63; prof. Celtic langs. and lits., chmn. dept. Harvard U., 1963-84, emeritus prof., 1984—, master of Quincy House, 1966-81, Margaret Brooks Robinson prof. Celtic langs. and lits., 1967-84; Taft lectr. U. Cin., 1956. Author: Highland Settler: A Portrait of the Scottish Gael in Nova Scotia, 1953, corrected reprint, 1968, rev. edit., 1991, The Foundling and the Werwolf: A Study of Guillaume de Palerne, 1960 (Chgo. Folklore prize 1960), (with Morton W. Bloomfield) The Role of the Poet in Early Societies, 1989; editor: A Chaucer Reader, 1952, History of the Kings of Britain (Geoffrey of Monmouth), 1958, Chronicles (Froissart), 1961, Romance of the Rose, 1962, Lays of Courtly Love, 1963, (with Edward Byrnes) Middle English Literature, 1973, rev. edit., 1990; contbr. articles, revs. to profl. jours. Dexter fellow N.S., summer 1941; Rockefeller fellow N.S., 1942-43; Nuffield fellow Dublin, Edinburgh and Aberystwyth, 1954-55; Guggenheim fellow Scotland, Wales and Brittany, 1962-63; recipient Canada award Fedn. Gaelic Socs., 1955. Fellow Am. Acad. Arts and Scis., Soc. Antiquaries of Scotland; mem. MLA, Medieval Acad. Am., Early English Text. Soc., Scottish Text Soc., Royal Scottish Country Dance Soc., St. Andrews Soc. N.Y., Mass. Hist. Soc. (resident), Comunn Gaidhealach (Scotland), Scots' Charitable Soc. Boston, Commanderie de Bordeaux Boston (Maitre), Tavern Club, Somerset Club, Odd Volumes Club, Phi Beta Kappa (hon). Home: 25 Longfellow Rd Cambridge MA 02138-4737

DUNN, CRAIG ANDREW, entertainer, conductor, composer, educator; b. Point Pleasant, N.J., Nov. 11, 1947; s. Andrew Robert and Ruth Agnes (Schott) D.; m. Crystal Lynn Kesler, May 26, 1970. MusB, U. Cin., 1972; MusM, Ohio U., 1973; EdD, Nova Southeastern U., 1996. Cert. tchr., Fla. Dir. bands Greenville (S.C.) Sr. H.S., 1973-74, Bayonne (N.J.) H.S., 1974-75; studio instr. Buddy Rogers Music Studios, Inc., Cin., 1975-78; music specialist, music dir. Diocese of St. Petersburg, Fla., 1979-88; music specialist Sch. Dist. of Hillsborough County, Tampa, Fla., 1988—; performing artist, entertainer, 1972—; mem. adv. bd. Am. Youth Symphony Band and Chorus, Pitts., 1980-85, artistic advisor, coach, 1980, 83, 85. Pub. composer popular and religious music. Mem. Music Educators Nat. Conf., Fla. Music Educators Assn., Nat. Acad. Songwriters. Avocations: orchestrating, writing, reading. Home: 11800 4th St E Isle of Capri Treasure Island FL 33706

DUNN, DAVID E., university dean; b. Dallas, Oct. 13, 1935; s. Nelson E. and Lemoine (Kellett) Dunn Neal; m. Gretchen Yost, Jan. 24, 1958 (dec. 1987); children: Dusty, Peter; m. Sarah Sue Holmes, Dec. 25, 1990. B.S. in Geology, So. Meth. U., 1957, M.S., 1959; Ph.D., U. Tex., 1964. Cert. profl. geologist. Instr. geology U. Tex., Austin, 1960-61; asst. prof. geology Tex. Tech. Inst., Lubbock, 1962-63; asst. prof. geology U. N.C., Chapel Hill, 1963-66, assoc. prof., 1967-73, prof., 1973-79; dean coll. sci. U. New Orleans, 1979-84; dean Sch. Natural Sci. and Math. U. Tex.-Dallas, 1984-97; cons. various legal firms, N.C., 1967-79, Pennzoil, Houston, 1980-87, Amoco, Houston, 1982-89. Oryx. 1991-92; chmn. La. Univs. Marine Consortium, Baton Rouge, 1981-83; chmn. bd. dirs. Drilling, Observation and Sampling of Earth's Continental Crust Inc. 1991-93; chmn. steering com. VIIth Internat. Symposium on Continental Sci. Drilling, 1994. Co-author: A Characterization of Faults in the Appalachian Foldbelt, 1980; contbr. chpt. to book, articles to sci. jours. Fund-raiser numerous candidates, Chapel Hill, 1969-75. Fellow Geol. Soc. Am. (chmn. structure and tectonics div. 1983, councilor 1985-87, 92—, treas. 1992—); mem. AAAS, Am. Geophys. Union, Am. Inst. Profl. Geologists, Carolina Geol. Soc. (chmn. 1968-69). Home: 6 Crown Pl Richardson TX 75080-1603 Office: Univ of Tex at Dallas Dept Geoscis PO Box 688 Richardson TX 75083-0688

DUNN, DAVID JOSEPH, financial executive; b. Bklyn., July 30, 1930; s. David Joseph and Rose Marie (McLaughlon) D.; m. Marilyn Percaccia, June 1955 (div.); children: Susan, Steven, Linda; m. Marilyn Bell, Apr. 1994. BS, U.S. Naval Acad., 1955; MBA, Harvard U., 1961. Investment banker G.H. Walker & Co., N.Y.C., 1961-62; ptnr. J.H. Whitney & Co., N.Y.C., 1962-70; mng. ptnr. Idanta Ptnrs., San Diego, 1971—; chmn. bd. Iomega Corp., Ogden, Utah, Munchkin Bottling, Inc., Van Nuys, Calif.; bd. dirs. Visionary Design Systems, Inc., Sunnyvale, Calif., Boxer/Cross, Menlo Park, Calif. With USMC, 1950-51, 55-59. Mem. Univ. Club (N.Y.C.), San Diego Yacht Club, LaJolla Country Club. Office: Idanta Ptnrs 4660 La Jolla Village Dr San Diego CA 92122-4601

DUNN, DEBORAH DECHELLIS, special education educator; b. Plainfield, N.J., Jan. 16, 1960; d. Anthony and Joan Dora (Brown) DeChellis; m. Paul Michael Dunn, May 13, 1989; children: Joseph Daniel, Brian Jacob. BS in Elem. Spl. Edn., U. Hartford, 1982. Spl. edn. tchr. Hartford (Conn.) Pub. Schs., 1982-83, East Hartford (Conn.) Pub. Schs., 1983-84; individual retirement account ops. supr. Conn. Nat. Bank, Hartford, 1984-87; individual retirement account adminstr. Glastonbury (Conn.) Bank & Trust, 1987, mgr. fin. mgmt. svc. ops., 1987-91; asst. treas., FMS adminstr. Glastonbury (Conn.) Bank & Trust Co., 1988-94, investment rep., trust adminstr., asst. treas.; fin. cons. Mktg. One Inc., 1994-95, Dime Securities N.Y., Inc., 1995-96; tchr. of handicapped, 1996—; investment cons., 1994; ind. edn. cons. Democrat. Methodist. Avocations: reading, cooking, needlework, racquetball, softball.

DUNN, DELMER DELANO, political science educator; b. Sentinel, Okla., Oct. 31, 1941; s. Robert Patrick and Mildred Marion (Morris) D.; m. Ann Gregg Swinford, May 15, 1971; children—John Swinford, Kielly McKee. B.A., Okla. State U., 1963; M.S., U. Wis., 1964, Ph.D., 1967. Asst. prof. polit. sci. U. Ga., Athens, 1967-71, assoc. prof., 1971-77, prof., 1977-82, Regents prof., 1982—, dir. Inst. Govt., 1973-82, acting head dept. polit. sci., 1987-88, assoc. v.p. acad. affairs, 1988-91; rsch. assoc. The Brookings Instn., Washington, 1969-70; vis. fellow dept. polit. sci. faculty of arts The Australian Nat. U., Canberra, 1992. Author: Public Officials and the Press, 1969, Financing Presidential Campaigns, 1972, Politics and Adminstration at the Top: Lessons from Down Under, 1997 (Charles Levine Book award for best book in pub. policy and adminstrn. 1998); mem. editl. bd. Social Sci. quar., 1988-94; contrbr. articles to profl. jours. Trustee Leadership Ga., 1976-82; pres. Clarke/Oconee unit Am. Cancer Soc., 1981-82, chmn., 1982-83. Mem. AAAS, Am. Polit. Sci. Assn. (Congl. fellow, 1968-69), So. Polit. Sci. Assn., Nat. Assn. Schs. of Pub. Affairs and Adminstrn. (pres. 1987-88), Am. Soc. Pub. Adminstrn., Pi Alpha Alpha (nat. pres. 1983-85). Presbyterian. Office: Univ Ga Dept Polit Sci Athens GA 30602

DUNN, DENNIS STEVEN, artist, illustrator; b. San Diego, Apr. 30, 1951; s. Dean Stanley and Phyllis Marie (Pratt) D.; m. Donna Rae Krogh, Dec. 29, 1973; 1 child, Claire Estelle. BA with distinction, San Diego State U., 1973. Master printer, intaglio Orr's Gallery, San Diego, 1973-74, instr. intaglio, 1974; graphic artist NARF/North Island Naval Air Sta., Coronado, Calif., 1974-76; illustrator NETSCPAC/Naval Tng. Ctr., San Diego, 1976-81, Fleet Combat Tng. Ctr., Point Loma, Calif., 1981-82, FASO Det/Miramar Naval Air Sta., San Diego, 1982-86, DTRA/Kirtland AFB, Albuquerque, 1986—; life drawing instr. U. N.Mex., Albuquerque, 1986-87. Group exhibits include Traveling Exhbn. to Turkey and Greece, 1975, San Diego Print Club, 1984, Spectrum Gallery, San Diego, 1986, Stables Art Gallery, Taos, N.Mex., 1986, The Wedge Gallery, Rochester, N.Y., 1988, Print Club of Albany, N.Y., 1989, Clary Minor Gallery, Buffalo, 1990, U. Anchorage, 1990, Bradley U., Peoria, Ill., 1991, Artlink Gallery, Ft. Wayne, Ind., 1991, Garret Gallery, St. Louis, 1993; works included in various mags. Recipient Letter of Commendation USN, 1985. Mem. Albuquerque United Artists (bd. dirs. 1987-88), SIGGRAPH. Avocations: writing short stories, playing and performing Renaissance music. Home: 6209 Arvilla Ave NE Albuquerque NM 87110-2651

DUNN, DONALD JACK, law librarian, law educator, dean, lawyer; b. Tyler, Tex., Nov. 9, 1945; s. Loren Jack and Clara Inez (Milam) D.; m. Cheryl Jean Sims, Nov. 24, 1967; 1 child, Kevin. BA., U. Tex.-Austin, 1969, MLS, 1972; JD, Western New Eng. Coll., 1983. Asst. to law libr. U. Tex., 1969-72, supervising libr. Criminal Justice Reference Libr., 1972-73; law libr., prof. law Western New Eng. Coll., Springfield, Mass., 1973-96, interim dean, 1996-98, dean, 1998—. Editor: Immigration and Nationality Law Rev., vols. 3-7, 1979-84, (with Jacobstein and Mersky) Fundamentals of Legal Research, 7th edit., 1998. Bd. dirs. Pioneer Valley chpt. ARC. Mem. ALA, ABA (chair law librs. com. 1988-92), Am. Assn. Law Librs. (chair acad. law librs. spl. interest sect. 1989-90), Spl. Libr. Assn., Law Librs. New Eng. (pres. 1982-83). Democrat. Episcopalian. Office: Western New Eng Coll Sch Law 1215 Wilbraham Rd Springfield MA 01119-2612

DUNN, DOUGLAS MURRAY, university dean. BS in Physics, Ga. Inst. Tech., 1964, MS in Indsl. Mgmt., 1965; PhD in Bus., U. Mich., 1970. Prof. indsnl. adminstrn. and stats. Carnegie Mellon U., Pitts., dean, CEO Grad. Sch. Indsl. Adminstrn.; bd. dirs. Universal Stainless & Alloy Products, Inc., InnovationWorks, RIDC. Contbr. articles to profl. jours., chpt. to book. Bd. trustees Fisk U., 1990—; bd. dirs. Boy Scouts Am., Pitts. Mem. Am. Statis. Assn. (bd. dirs. 1978-85), Greater Pitts. C. of C. (bd. dirs. 1996—). E-mail: dmdunn@andrew.cmu.edu. Office: Grad Sch Indsl Adminstrn Carnegie Mellon U Schenley Park Pittsburgh PA 15213

DUNN, EDWARD THOMAS, JR., lawyer, educator; b. L.A., Dec. 7, 1954; s. Edward Thomas and Beverly Jean (Dixon) D.; m. Marcy Jean McNeely, Nov. 5, 1977; children: Charles Jason Thomas, Laura Brianna, Kaeli Carissa Michele, Edward Thomas IV. BA, Biola U., 1977; postgrad., U. Calif., Irvine, 1980-81; JD, Southwestern U., 1984. Bar: Calif. 1985, U.S. Dist. Ct. (cen. dist.) Calif. 1985, U.S. Dist. Ct. (ea., no. and so. dists.) Calif. 1986, U.S. Ct. Appeals (9th cir.) 1985, U.S. Supreme Ct. 1989. Mem. minority staff com. on rules Ho. of Reps., Washington, 1976-77; asst. v.p., br. mgr. Downey Savs. & Loan Assn., Rolling Hills Estates, Calif., 1977-80; sr. atty. Calif. Ct. Appeal, Santa Ana, 1989, 97—; assoc. prof. law Orange County U., Newport Beach, 1990-94; pros. Orange County Dist. Atty. Office, Santa Ana, 1985-97; adj. prof. law Western State U., Fullerton, Calif., 1991—, Whittier Law Sch., 1997—. Bd. dirs. Whittier Christian H.S., La Habra, Calif., 1995—; assoc. mem. ctrl. com. Orange County Calif. Rep. Orgn., 1997-99; candidate Orange County Superior Ct. Judge, 1996; mem. First Evang. Free Ch. of Fullerton, 1964—, elder, 1995-99. Named Atty. of Yr. Constnl. Rights Found., 1988, Vol. of Yr. Calif. Rep. Orgn., 1997. Mem. Orange County Bar Assn. (ethics com. 1992-96, Cert. of Recognition 1995, appellate com. 1992-95), Orange County Attys. Assn. (bd. dirs. 1993-94), Calif. Family Support coun. (appellate com. 1975-95). Calif. Dist. Attys. Assn. (appellate com. 1987-96), Calif. State Bar (cert. specialist in criminal law). Avocations: keyboards, writer, musical arranger, sailing. Office: Calif Ct Appeal 4th Dist Divsn 3 925 N Spurgeon St Santa Ana CA 92701-3700

DUNN, ERAINA BURKE, non-profit organization administrator, city official; b. Oct. 4, 1945; d. Marion H. and Lolita D. (Ward) Moore; m. James Dunn, July 23, 1981; children: Kyle T. (dec.), Jamison L. BA, Wilberforce U., 1968. Programmer, analyst Blue Cross/Blue Shield, Chgo., 1968-74; membership cons. Blue Cross Assn., 1975; pers., benefits specialist Kimberly-Clark Corp., Atlanta, 1976-78; sch. dist. coord. Dist. 147, Harvey, Ill., 1980-88. Active comty.-based edn., tng. workshops, voter registration, mgmt. tng., crime prevention, adult literacy, effective parenting, environ. justice, 1971-88; coord. Tchr. Corps. Project, Comty. Coun., 1980—; exec. dir. The Human Action Comty. Orgn., 1989—; comty. liaison for Met. Drug Enforcement Group of Cook County, 1993-96; dir. human svcs. and devel. City of Harvey, 1995, dir. health and human svcs. dept., 1999; vol. After Sch. Tutorial Program, 1981—, United Family Found., 1981—, South Area Literacy Coun., South Suburban Act-So, West Harvey Block Captains, South Suburban Citizen Patrol, 1994; chairperson PAC, 1983-88; v.p. human action comty. orgn. Minority Women's Devel.; chairperson adminstrv. coun. Wesley Meml. United Meth. Ch., 1987; chair Harvey Area Youth Devel. Task Force, 1990, 97; mem. adv. bd. YWCA, 1990, Policy Rsch. Action Group, Loyola U., 1993-94; petitioner Chgo. Cumulative Risk Initiative, 1996; mem. steering com., founding mem. Healthcare Without Harm campaign, 1996—; mem. State's Atty.'s African Am. Adv. Cook County, 1997, Congressman Jesse Jackson Jr.'s Environ. Adv. Com., 1998. Recipient Outstanding Vol. Svc. award B.U.I.L.D., 1971, Outstanding Comty. Svc. award Dist. 147, 1981, Vol. After Sch. Tutorial Program award, 1981, Image award Fred Hampton Found., 1994, Heart of Gold citation United Way, 1990, Concerned Citizens for a Better Comty. Dedication for Outstanding Svc. to African Am. Comty. award, 1998; fellow Leadership in Primary Care, U. Ill. Sch. Nursing/Sch. Medicine, 1992-93. Mem. Nat. Comty. Edn. Assn., Ill. Comty. Edn. Assn., Delta Sigma Theta. Missionary Baptist. Home: 14746 Leavitt Ave Harvey IL 60426-1522 Office: HACO PO Box 1703 Harvey IL 60426-7703

DUNN, FLOYD, biophysicist, bioengineer, educator; b. Kansas City, Mo., Apr. 14, 1924; s. Louis and Ida (Leibtag) D.; m. Elsa Tanya Levine, June 11, 1950; children: Andrea Susan, Louis Brook. Student, Kansas City Jr. Coll., 1941-42, Tex. A&M U., 1943; BS, U. Ill., Urbana, 1949, MS, 1951, PhD, 1956. Rsch. assoc. elec. engring. U. Ill., Urbana, 1954-57; rsch. asst. prof. elec. engring. U. Ill., 1957-61, assoc. prof. elec. engring. and biophysics, 1961-65, prof., 1965—, prof. elec. engring., biophysics and bioengring., 1972-95; faculty mem. Beckman Inst. for Advanced Sci. and Tech., prof. emeritus, 1995—; dir. bioacoustics rsch. lab. U. Ill., 1976-95, chmn. bioengring. faculty, 1978-82; vis. prof. dept. microbiology U. Coll., Cardiff, Wales, 1968-69; vis. sr. scientist Inst. Cancer Research, Sutton, Surrey, Eng., 1975-76, 82-83, 90; vis. prof. Inst. Chest Diseases and Cancer, Tohoku U., Sendai, Japan, 1982, 89-90, U. Nanjing, Nanjing, People's Republic of China, 1983; mem. radiation study sect. NIH, 1976-81; adj. prof. radiation oncology U. Ariz., Tucson, 1996—; steering com. NSF Workshop on Interaction of Ultrasound and Biol. Tissues, 1971-72; chmn. WHO working group on health aspects of exposure to ultrasound radiation, London, 1976; mem. FDA tech.-elec. products radiation stds. com. 1974-76, NIH bioengring., radiation and diagnostic radiology study sects., 1970-81; faculty mem. Beckman Inst. Advanced Sci. and Tech.; adj. prof. radiation oncology U. Ariz., Tucson, 1996—; adv. bd. Ency. Applied Physics, 1981—. Mem. editl. bd. Jour. Acoustical Soc. Am., Ultrasound in Medicine and Biology, Ultrasonics, Handbook of Acoustics, and Encyclopedia of Applied Physics, 1981—, Am. Inst. of Physics Series in Modern Acoustics and Signal Processing, 1990-97; contbr. articles on biophys. acoustics to profl. jours. Trustee Hensley Twp., Ill., 1980-81. With AUS, 1943-46. NIH Spl. Rsch. fellow, 1968-69, Am. Cancer Soc.-Eleanor Roosevelt-Internat. Cancer fellow, 1975-76, 82-83, Fulbright fellow, 1982-83, Japan Soc. for Promotion of Sci. fellow, 1982, 1996, Fogarty Internat. fellow, 1990; recipient U. Ill. Sr. Scholar award, 1988, medal Spl. Merit Acoustical Soc. Japan, 1988, AIUM/WFUMB History Med. Ultrasound Pioneer award, 1988. Fellow AAAS, IEEE (Engring. Medicine and Biology Soc. Career Achievement award 1995, Edison medal 1996), Internat. Acad. Med. Biol. Engring., Am. Inst. Med. Biol. Engring., Acoustical Soc. Am. (assoc. editor Jour., pres. 1985-86, Silver medal 1989, Gold medal 1998), Am. Inst. Ultrasound in Medicine (William J. Fry Meml. award 1984, Joseph H. Holmes Basic Sci. Pioneer award 1990), Inst. Acoustics (U.K.); mem. NAS, NAE, Am. Inst. Physics (mem. editl. bd. series in modern acoustics and signal processing 1990-97, publs. policy com. 1992—), Biophys. Soc., Japan soc. Ultrasound in Medicine (hon.), Nat. Coun. Radiation Protection & Measurement, Rochester Soc. Biomed. Ultrasound (hon.), Sigma Xi, Sigma Tau, Eta Kappa Nu, Tau Beta Pi, Pi Mu Epsilon, Phi Sigma, Phi Sigma Phi. Home: 2631 E Avenida De Maria Tucson AZ 85718-3081 Office: U Ill Bioacoustics Rsch Lab Beckman Institute Urbana IL 61801-2918 *Excellent, dedicated and understanding teachers, bright and energetic students, and a single-mindedness to see a problem to solution are the ingredients for a modest success.*

DUNN, FLOYD EMRYL, psychiatrist, neurologist, consultant; b. Wilkes-Barre, Pa., Apr. 25, 1910; s. Adrian Anson and Frances Amanda (Culver) D.; m. Wilda Kathryn Lauer, Aug. 14, 1943; children: Kathryn Alice (dec.), Deborah Lee. Student, Temple U., 1929-32; DO, Phila. Coll. Osteo. Medicine, 1936. Diplomate Am. Osteo. Bd. Neurology and Psychiatry. Resident in neurology, psychiatry Still-Hildreth Hosp., 1941-45, staff psychiatrist, 1945-49; chmn. divsn. neurology, psychiatry Kirksville Coll. Osteo. Medicine, 1945-48, Kansas City Coll. Osteo. Medicine, U. Health Scis., Mo., 1949-68; mem. staff VA Hosp., Knoxville, Iowa, 1968-76, chief psychiatry svc., 1970-76; clin. prof. neurology, psychiatry Coll. Osteo. Medicine, Des Moines, 1970-74; mem. Nat. Bd. Examiners for Osteo. Physicians and Surgeons, 1965-74, Excellence award, 1974; cons. neurology, psychiatry, Chgo., 1974-96; cons., examiner sect. of disability determinations Mo. Dept. Elem. and Secondary Edn., Jefferson City, 1985-96. Author: (monograph) History of the American College of Neuropsychiatrists, 1984; contbr. articles to profl. jours. Mem. Iowa Adv. Coun. on Mental Health Ctrs., Des Moines, 1972-78, Cen. Regional Adv. Coun. for Comprehensive Psychiat. Svcs., Columbia, Mo., 1978-86. Fellow Am. Coll. Neuropsychiatrists (life, sec.-treas. 1948-52, pres. 1954-55, 63-64, Disting. Svc. award 1967, Disting. Fellow award 1984, 1st Fellows' Lecture Honoree 1989), Am. Assn. on Mental Deficiency; mem. AMA (life), Am. Osteo. Assn. (life, editl. cons. publs. 1958-95, del. 1960-69, pres.'s adv. coun. 1973), Am. Coll. Neuropsychiatrists (life), Am. Osteopathic Assn. (life, cons. examiner of neurology and psychiatry residency tng. programs 1988-91), Mo. Assn. Osteo. Physicians and Surgeons (hon. life, del. 1958-69, v.p. 1969-70), Lions (pres. Gravois Mills, Mo. chpt. 1984-85, sec. 1985-88, del. to internat. conv. 1985, 86, 87), Masons (32d degree), Abou Ben Adhem Temple, Elks (life), Alpha Phi Omega, Phi Sigma Gamma (pres. grand coun. 1952-53, coun. sec.-treas. 1953-59, editor Speculum 1959-65, 95—, Meritorious Svc. award 1965, 87-91, exec. sec.-treas. grand coun. 1980-95). Republican. Methodist. Avocations: photography, travel, journalism. Home: 30171 Millcreek Loop Gravois Mills MO 65037-4118

DUNN, FRANK M. (FRANCIS MICHAEL DUNN), banker; b. Sigourney, Iowa, Feb. 27, 1933; s. John Michael and Marie Catherine (Strohman) D.; m. Maryann Lee Peiffer, Aug. 18, 1956; children: Katrina, Theresa, Michael, Nancy, Kelly, Patrick. Student, U. Denver, 1957-66, U. Colo., Denver, 1959-66; grad., So. U. Ill. Grad. Sch. Banking, Carbondale, 1973; BA in Bus. Adminstrn., Columbia State U., 1996, MBA, 1997. Ordained deacon Roman Cath. Ch., 1992. Real estate broker, mortgage banker, ins. broker Denver, 1956-66; exec. v.p., dir. E. Dubuque (Ill.) Savs. Bank, 1967-76; cons. in banking E. Dubuque, 1976-80; v.p., dir. Tri-State Bank, E. Dubuque, 1980-84; pres., dir. First Nat. Bank, Glidden, Iowa, 1984-86; v.p., dir. and br. mgr. Swea City State Bank/Graettinger (Iowa) Bank Office, 1986-93; CEO, dir. Iowa Fin. Cons. Ltd., Estherville, 1993—; mgr., owner, broker Iowa Realty, Estherville, 1994-98. Mem. Joint County Sch. Bd., 1973-76; pres. bd. dirs. Horizons Unltd., 1990-98, Estherville Youth Corp., 1993-98; organizer, developer, pres. Dunlieth Park and Pool, Jo Daviess County, Ill., 1972. Mem. Ill. Bankers Assn. (agr. com. 1968-75), Iowa Bankers Assn. (agr. com. 1985-87), Thunder Hill Country Club (bd. dirs., organizer, treas. 1972-76), Lions (pres., bd. dirs. 1967-76). Office: Iowa Financial Cons 1718 Plymouth Ct Dubuque IA 52003

DUNN, GLENNIS MAE, retired writer, lyricist; b. Montevideo, Minn., Sept. 11, 1938; d. James Arnold and Mabel Helmina (Anderson) Haugernd; m. Edward Henry Roske, Mar. 19, 1956 (div. Mar. 1975); children: Daniel Edward, Deborrah Kay Roske Hawthorne, Judith Ann Roske Rinker, Kristine Jean Roske Harbeson, James William, William Benjamin; m. George Maurice Dunn, Sept. 1, 1984 (dec. Dec. 1992). Grad., Montevideo High Sch. Cert. pvt.-instrument pilot, basic ground flight instr. Comml.-instrument ground instr. Sawyer Aviation, Phoenix, 1976-78; pvt.-instrument pilot West Air Flight Club, Phoenix, 1976—; sales telemarketer Lone Star Performing Arts, 1994—, group sales rep., 1996; entrepreneur, 1996, travel cons., 1997; security pub. adminstrn. officer Star of Tex., Galveston, 1994; flight program specialist Embery Riddle Aero. U., Daytona Beach, Fla., 1980-83; ind. contractor, tour condr. Am. Hawaii Cruises, 1998—. Author: You Never Need to Worry-If You Forget to Grow Up, 1985, Someday Darling, Under My Wings We'll Fly, 1993; author, lyricist (song) A Vet's Song, 1992, My Red, White and Blue, 1993, Little Crystal Town, 1993, Riverwalk Christmas, 1993, Santa Keeps an Eye on Me, 1993, One for the Duck, One for Mother, 1993, Texas Auction at the Wheel, 1993, Love your Irish Blue Eyes, 1994. Named to Tex. Hall of Fame, 1996. Mem. Nat. FAA Pilot Assn. (radio operator), Internat. Platform Assn., Am. Legion Aux., Fraternal Order Eagles Aux. Republican. Avocations: swimming, writing, golf, jogging, singing. Home and Office: PO Box 1643 12 Seadrift Dr Crystal Beach TX 77650

DUNN, GLORIA JEAN, artist; b. Detroit, Apr. 21, 1927; d. Donald Stanton and Etta Florence (Barber) Hopkins; m. Eugene Oliver Dunn, Dec. 28, 1944; children: Michael Eugene, Patricia Ann. Student, Wayne County C.C., Taylor, Mich., 1987-90. Instr. arts and crafts YWCA, Wyandotte, Mich., 1963-86; instr. painting and calligraphy, adult edn. Lincoln Park (Mich.) Sch. Sys., 1982-90; owner, mgr. Pen, Brush and Anvil Studio, Southgate, Mich., 1975-95, Gloria Hopkins Dunn Studio of Fine Art, Wyandotte,

1995—; represented by Swann Gallery, Detroit, Craig Gallery, Ferndale, Mich., Front Street Gallery, Monroe, Mich.; mem. adv. bd. Wyandotte St. Art Fair, 1962—, organizer, co-chair, 1962-81. One-woman shows include Taylor (Mich.) Cmty. Libr., Southgate (Mich.) City Hall, Swann Gallery, Detroit, Taylor (Mich.) City Hall, Trenton (Mich.) City Hall. Mem. Southgate Cultural Commn., 1974-82, 91—. Recipient Cmty. Svc. award City of Southgate, 1978, Hon. Tribute, City of Wyandotte, 1982, 20 Yrs. Dedication to Art award City of Wyandotte, 1991. Mem. Acanthus Art Soc. Wyandotte (pres. 1994—), Downriver Arts and Crafts Guild (exhibit chair 1995, 96, 97), Art Ambience (historian 1993—, bd. dirs.), Nat. Assn. Fine Arts. Avocations: swimming, photography, gardening, riding. Office: 2930 Biddle St Wyandotte MI 48192-5214

DUNN, H. STEWART, JR., lawyer; b. Pitts., July 9, 1929; s. H. Stewart and Marie (Galvin) D.; m. Martha J. Hoovler (dec. Sept. 1975); children—Christopher T., Anthony S., Timothy P.; m. Loti Kennedy, Aug. 3, 1978. A.B., Yale U., 1951; LL.B. magna cum laude, Harvard U., 1954. Bar: D.C. 1954, U.S. Supreme Ct. 1960. Assoc. firm Ivins, Phillips & Barker, Washington, 1957-61; partner Ivins, Phillips & Barker, 1962—; bd. dirs. Wilmington Trust Co.; adj. prof. Georgetown U. Law Ctr.; mem. U.S. Com. Selection Jud. Officers, 1977-79, chmn., 1979-81; lectr. Harvard Law Sch., 1986. Bd. editors: Harvard Law Rev, 1953-54. Fellow Am. Bar Found., Am. Coll. Trust and Estate Counsel; mem. ABA (vice chmn. sect. taxation 1970-73), Coll. Tax Counsel, Am. Law Inst. Office: 1700 Pennsylvania Ave NW Washington DC 20006-4704

DUNN, HERBERT IRVIN, lawyer; b. Balt., July 19, 1946; s. Albert M. and Hilda F. (Winakur) D.; m. Marsha Edith Greenfield, Apr. 1, 1979; children: Marla Phyllis, Jonathan Howard. BS with high honors, U. Md., 1969, JD, 1971. Bar: Md. 1971, D.C. 1971, U.S. Ct. Claims 1972, U.S. Tax Ct. 1972, U.S. Dist. Ct. D.C. 1971, U.S. Ct. Appeals (D.C. cir.) 1971, U.S. Supreme Ct. 1975. Atty.-adviser Office of Gen. Counsel U.S. Gen. Acctg. Office, Washington, 1971-83, sr. atty., 1983—. Served with USAR, 1968-74. Mem. FBA (treas. younger lawyers divsn. 1977-79, nat. coun. 1978-79, 91—, Capitol Hill chpt. exec. coun. 1975-83, v.p. 1990-91, pres.-elect 1991-92, pres. 1992-93, v.p. D.C. cir. 1994—), Md. Bar Assn., Northwest Br. Citizens Assn. (sec. 1988-95, 1st v.p. 1995-99), Omicron Delta Epsilon. Office: 441 G St NW Washington DC 20548-0001

DUNN, HORTON, JR., organic chemist; b. Coleman, Tex., Sept. 3, 1929; s. Horton and Lora Dean (Bryant) D. BA summa cum laude, Hardin-Simmons U., 1951; MS, Case Western Res. U., 1975, PhD, 1979. Instr. chemistry Hardin-Simmons U., 1951; ONR fellow Ohio State U., Columbus, 1951-52; teaching fellow in chemistry Purdue U., Lafayette, Ind., 1952-53; rsch. chemist Lubrizol Corp., Cleve., 1953-70, dir. tech. info. ctr., 1970-79, supr. rsch. divsn., 1980-98; cons. in chemistry, 1998—; chmn. bd., bus. mgr. Isotopics, Cleve., 1964-67, editor, 1961-63. Contbr. articles to profl. jours.; patentee in field. Treas. Cleve. Cir. Decorative Arts Trust, 1990-91, 93—, v.p., 1992-93; active Cleve. Art Assn., Cleve. Mus. of Art, Rock and Roll Hall of Fame, Mus. Founders Club.; mem., vol. Great Lakes Sci. Ctr., Cleve. Mus. Natural History; mem. Cleve. Bot. Garden. Fellow Am. Inst. Chemists; mem. AAAS, SAR (life), Am. Chem. Soc. (treas. Cleve. chpt. 1968-70, chmn. 1987, bd. dirs. 1990—), Am. Soc. for Info. Sci. (chpt. pres. 1973-74), Royal Soc. Chemistry (life), Soc. Tribologists and Lubrication Engrs., Nat. Coun. Met. Opera, Royal Oak Soc. (life), Cleve. Tech. Soc. Coun. (treas. 1987), Cleve. Art Assn., Univ. Club, Cleve. Club, Cleve. Play House Club, Rock and Roll Hall of Fam Mus. Founders Club (charter). Fax: 216-541-6431. Home and Office: One Bratenahl Pl #103 Bratenahl OH 44108

DUNN, JAMES BERNARD, mining company executive, state legislator; b. Lead, S.D, June 27, 1927; s. William Bernard and Lucy Marie (Mullen) D.; m. Elizabeth Ann Lanham, Sept. 5, 1955; children: Susan, Thomas, Mary Elizabeth, Kathleen. BS in Bus. Adminstrn. and Econ., Black Hills State U., 1962. Heavy equipment mechanic Homestake Mining Co., Lead, 1947-62, asst. dir. pub. relations, 1962-78, dir. pub. affairs, 1978; mem. S.D. Ho. Reps., Pierre, 1971-72; mem. S.D. State Senate, Pierre, 1973—, asst. majority leader, 1989-92, asst. minority leader, 1993-94, asst. majority leader, 1995—; exec. com. Nat. Conf. State Legislatures, 1979-81, 93-95, Coun. State Govt., 1983—; chmn. Midwestern Conf. Coun. of State Govts., 1984; bd. dirs. S.D. Blue Shield, S.D. Automobile Assn. Editor: Homestake Gold Mine 1876-1976, 1976, Bulldog Mountain Silver Mine, 1978. Bd. dirs. S.D. State Hist. Soc., Pierre,. 1971—; chmn. bd. trustees Adams Mus., Deadwood, S.D., 1962—. With U.S. Army, 1945-47. Republican. Roman Catholic. Avocations: hunting, fishing, hiking, historical research. Home: 619 Ridge Rd Lead SD 57754-1144 Office: State Senate State Capitol Pierre SD 57501

DUNN, JAMES JOSEPH, magazine publisher; b. N.Y.C., July 22, 1920; s. James A. and Mary A. (Kelly) D.; m. Elinor M. Hargesheimer, Aug. 30, 1943; children—Patricia Ann, Kevin James, Gregory John, Sean David, Christopher Kelly. B.B.A., Manhattan Coll., 1941. With McCall Corp., 1946-50; with Time, Inc., 1950-66; advt. dir. Life mag., N.Y.C., 1961-66; pub., v.p. Forbes, Inc., 1966-88, vice chmn., 1989-92, cons., 1992—. Lt. comdr. USNR, 1941-46. Clubs: Laurel Valley, Jupiter Hills, Everglades. Home: 631 Turtle Beach Rd No Palm Beach FL 33408-3438 Office: Forbes 60 5th Ave New York NY 10011-8882

DUNN, JAMES MILTON, religious organization adminstrator; b. Ft. Worth, Tex., June 17, 1932; s. William Thomas and Edith (Campbell) Dunn; m. Marilyn McNeely, Dec. 19, 1958. BA, Tex. Wesleyan Coll., 1953; BD, Southwestern Bapt. Theol. Sem., 1957, ThD, 1966, PhD, 1978; LLD, Alderson-Broaddus Coll., William Jewell Coll., Linfield Coll. Ordained to ministry So. Bapt. Conv. and Am. Bapt. Ch. in U.S.A., 1955. Assoc. pastor First Bapt. Ch., Weatherford, Tex., 1955-57; pastor Emmanuel Bapt. Ch., Weatherford, 1957-61; religion instr., campus minister W. Tex. State U., Canyon, 1961-66; dir. christian life commn. Bapt. Gen. Conv. Tex., Dallas, 1967-80; exec. dir. Bapt. Joint Com. on Pub. Affairs, Washington, 1981—; sec. bd. Ams. United for Separation Ch. & State, Silver Spring, Md., 1978-88; bd. dirs. Bread for the World, Washington, pres., 1987; chmn. ethics commn. Bapt. World Alliance, McLean, Va., 1975-80; bd. dirs. Ch.'s Ctr. for Theology and Pub. Policy, Washington, 1993—; vis. prof. Wake Forest Div. Sch. Editor, co-author: Politics a Guidebook for Christians, 1970, Endangered Species, 1976; co-author: An Approach to Christian Ethics, 1979, Teacher Renewal, 1987; author: (with others) Equal Separation, 1990, The Fundamentalist Phenomenon, 1990. Sec. Anti-Crime Coun. Tex., Dallas, 1968-80; founding mem. Dallas Dem. Forum, 1976-80; mem. Fair Campaign Practices Com., Dallas, 1972-76, Gov.'s Juvenile Coun., State of Tex., Austin, 1976-77. Recipient Disting. Svc. award Christian Life Commn. of So. Bapt. Conv., 1979, Moore-Bowman Award of Excellence, Tex. Coun. on Family Relations, 1979, Disting. Svc. award Chs. Ctr. for Theology and Pub. Policy, 1993, T.B. Maston Christian Ethics award, 1995, Abner V. McCall Religious Liberty award Baylor U., 1998, Disting. Svc. award Christian Life Commn. Bapt. Gen. Conv. Tex., 1998. Mem. Soc. for the Sci. Study of Religion. Avocation: music. Office: Baptist Joint Com 200 Maryland Ave NE Ste 302 Washington DC 20002-5797 *All freedom is rooted in our being made in the image of God and is one aspect of the two-sided coin of freedom and responsibility. The two go together inextricably.*

DUNN, JAMES RANDOLPH, corporate executive; b. Newport News, Va., June 23, 1948; s. Joseph Thomas Jr. and Nancy C. (Hall) D.; m. Muriel Word, Mar. 17, 1978; children: Emily Muriel, Allison Margaret. BSBA in Acctg., Old Dominion U., 1970; postgrad., Fairleigh Dickinson U., 1973. CPA, Tex., Md. Operational auditing Exxon Co. U.S.A., Md., N.J. and Houston, 1970-82; v.p., CFO Modern Furniture Rentals, Houston, 1982-84; sr. v.p., CFO Tex. Pipe and Supply Co., Inc., Houston, 1984—; pub. acctg. James R. Dunn, CPA, Houston, 1980-82; spkr. in field. Mgr. Little League Baseball, Md. Sgt. USMCR, 1970-76. Recipient Life Flight Man of Yr. award Hermann Hosp., Houston, 1994. Mem. AICPA, Tex. Soc. CPA (Houston chpt.), Md. Assn. CPA, Alpha Kappa Psi (life, chaplain), Am. Legion. Republican. Episcopalian. Avocations: tennis, gardening, collecting, golf, speaking to students on perseverance and motivation. Home: 6921 Cutten Pkwy Houston TX 77069-1790 Office: Tex Pipe and Supply Co Inc 2330 Holmes Rd Houston TX 77051-1014

DUNN, JANE GRACE, retired educator; b. Roxas City, Philippines, Jan. 5, 1935; came to U.S., 1959; d. Gonzalo Cristobal and Iluminada (Menez) Fernandez; m. William King Dunn, Mar. 1, 1960; children: Ann Marie, Francis Jules, William Henry. BS in Edn., Santo Tomas U., Manila, 1956; grad., Northeast Mo. State U., 1960; MA in Lit., Webster U., 1974. Tchr. high sch. English Palawan High Sch., Puerto Princesa, Philippines, 1956-59, St. John Bapt. Coll. Prep. High Sch., St. Louis, 1966-98; dept. head St. John's High Sch., St. Louis, 1978-96. Mem. Nat. Coun. Tchrs. English. Roman Catholic. Home: 5623 Oleatha Ave Saint Louis MO 63139-1503

DUNN, JEFFREY EDWARD, neurologist; b. Shaker Heights, Ohio, Nov. 27, 1960; s. John Kenneth and Mary Margaret (O'Neill) D.; m. Sandra Lee Judy, Feb. 3, 1990; children: Caitlin Irene, Bronwyn Leigh, Colin John Donald. BA in French Lit., Haverford (Pa.) Coll., 1983; MD, Temple U., 1989. Diplomate Am. Bd. Psychiatry and Neurology. Molecular immunologist Fox Chase Cancer Ctr., Phila., 1984-85; intern Ea. Va. Grad. Sch., Norfolk, 1989-90; resident in neurology U. Wash., Seattle, 1990-93; attending physician Neurol. Assocs. of Wash., Bellevue, 1993—; clin. asst. prof. neurology U. Wash., Seattle, 1993—; founder, med. dir. Overlake Multiple Sclerosis Ctr., Bellevue, Wash., 1996—. *Jeff maintains a private neurological practice on Seattle's east side. He is the founder and present medical director of the Overlake Multiple Sclerosis Center, and a clinical assistant professor in neurology at the University of Washington.* Guest physician TV: MS Update, Denver, 1994, ALS Update, Seattle, 1995. Recipient Cert. of Excellence in MS Rx, Prodigy Online Com., 1995; named to Outstanding Young Men of Am., 1996. Mem. Am. Acad. Neurology, Am. Neurol. Assn., World Congress Neurology, North Pacific Soc. of Psychiatry and Neurology. Avocations: golf, skiing, camping, outdoor recreation. Office: Neurol Assocs of Wash 13107 121st Way NE Kirkland WA 98034

DUNN, JENNIFER BLACKBURN, congresswoman; b. Seattle, Wash., July 29, 1941; d. John Charles and Helen (Gorton) Blackburn; div.; children: Bryant, Reagan. Student, U. Wash., 1960-62; BA, Stanford U., 1963. Former chmn. Rep. Party State of Wash.; now mem. 103rd Congress (now 106th Congress) from 8th Wash. dist., Washington, D.C., 1993—; mem. house oversight com., mem. Ways and Means Com. Del. Rep. Nat. Conv., 1980, 84, 88; presdl. apptd. adv. coun. Historic Preservation; presdl. apptd. adv. coun. volunteerism SBA. Mem. Gamma Phi Beta. Office: US House of Reps 432 Cannon Bldg Washington DC 20515-4708*

DUNN, JIM EDWARD, sales executive; b. Ft. Belvoir, Va., Feb. 22, 1948; s. James Edward and Alice Jane (Dunlap) D.; m. Karen Lorraine Dunn (div. Nov. 1974); m. Mary Margaret McElroy; children: Dana Leigh, Erica Ann. Student, Southwestern State Coll., Weatherford, Okla., 1966-67, U. Md., 1969-70, Abilene Christian Coll., 1970-71; BS, West Tex. State U., 1975. Warehouse asst., deliveryman Bamco, Inc., Amarillo, Tex., 1971-73; inside sales Bamco, Inc., Amarillo, 1973-75, purchasing agt., 1975-77, outside sales, 1977-82, br. mgr., 1982-85; dist. mgr. Kaman Bearing & Supply Co., Amarillo, 1985—; ptnr. KDS Sales. ISR Filtration, 1990—; sales coord. Johnson Filtration Products, Inc., Amarillo, 1991-93, sales mgr., 1993—. Served to sgt. USAF, 1967-71, Vietnam. Waukika High Sch. scholar, 1966. Mem. Am. Bus. Clubs, S.W. Football Officials Assn. (Amarillo chpt. rec. 1994-97, divsn. # 2 rep. 1997-98), Panhandle Purchasing Assn. (chmn. membership 1975-81, bd. dirs. 1981-83, v.p. 1983-84, Curtis Barrett award 1982). Republican. Clubs: Pioneer Gun (Claude, Tex.), Amarillo S.W. Optimist. Lodges: Shriners, 1330 San Jacinto, Masons. Avocations: golf, fishing, water and snow skiing, softball, football. Home: 6610 Drexel Rd Amarillo TX 79109-6917

DUNN, JOHN CLINTON, writer, editor, organization executive; b. Little Rock, Mar. 12, 1942; s. Eugene William and Clara Ava (Samuel) D.; m. Wanda Padgett, Aug. 29, 1970; children: Jonathan Victor, Gene Stephen, Samuel Padgett. Student, U. Ala., 1961-64; BA in English, Columbus (Ga.) State U., 1974. Reporter, city editor, state editor The Columbus Enquirer, 1967-75; dir. pub. rels. LaGrange (Ga.) Coll., 1975-78; editor News/Daily of Clayton County, Jonesboro, Ga., 1978-80; asst. exec. dir. Ga. Tech. Alumni Assn., Atlanta, 1980—. Editor Ga. Tech. Alumni Mag., Tech. Topics alumni newspaper. With U.S. Army, 1964-67. Avocations: gardening, tennis, reading, travel. Home: 9450 Brown Rd Jonesboro GA 30238-5962 Office: Georgia Tech Alumni Assn 225 North Ave NW Atlanta GA 30332-0002

DUNN, JOHN FRANCIS, lawyer, state representative; b. Logansport, Ind., Dec. 24, 1936; s. John Francis and Bertha (Newman) D.; m. Barbara Burke, Feb. 10, 1962; children: John F. III, Robert E., William M., Nancy L. BS in Chem. Engring., U. Notre Dame, 1958, JD, 1961. Bar: Ill. 1961, Ind. 1961, U.S. Dist. Ct. (so. dist.) Ill. 1961, U.S. Ct. Appeals (4th cir.) 1962. Atty. Standard Oil Ind. (now Amoco), Chgo., 1961-64; assoc. Morey and Dunn, Attys., Decatur, Ill., 1964-74; ptnr. Dunn and Fichter, Attys., Decatur, Ill., 1975-85; pvt. practice Decatur, Ill., 1986—. State rep. Ill. Gen. Assembly, Springfield, 1974-94, asst. majority leader; city councilman City of Decatur, 1971-74. Democrat. Roman Catholic. Avocations: bicycling, jogging. Office: 330 Millikin Ct Decatur IL 62523-1399

DUNN, JOHN RAYMOND, JR., stockbroker; b. Pittsfield, Mass., Aug. 24, 1937; s. John Raymond and Margaret Mary (Coyne) D.; 1 child, John Raymond III. AB, Boston Coll., 1960. Ins. agt. John Hancock Ins. Co., Boston, 1964-67; dist. mgr. Nat. Life Ins. Co., Montpelier, Vt., 1967-74; gen. agt. United Life & Accident Ins. Co., Concord, N.H., 1974—; stockbroker, regional mgr. Cornerstone Fin. Svcs., Inc., Boston, 1974-80; stockbroker, br. mgr. Weinrich, Zitzman, Whitehead Fin. Svcs., Inc., St. Louis, 1980—; pres. Dunn Assocs., Amherst, Mass., 1965—; br. mgr. Jefferson Pilot Securities Corp., 1998—; field adv. mem. Pres. Adv. Coun. CFS-Div. Weinrich, Zitzman, Whitehead, Inc., 1982—; named to gen. agts. adv. com. Chubb Life Am./Chubb Securities Corp., 1988-89; dist. mgr. Chubb Securities Leaders' Club; lectr. in field. Author seminar: Let's Make Money; freelance writer Investment Dealer Digest, 1980; film prodr. Ernest Hemingway documentary. Mem. Rep. Town Com., Amherst, Mass., 1980—; dir. Parents and Tchrs. for Social Responsibility, Moretown, Vt., 1982-85. Mem. White Mountain Club (Club award 1984-92), Summit Club, Life U.S.A. Club, Chmns. Club., Pres. Club. Roman Catholic. Fax: 413-253-9356.

DUNN, JON MICHAEL, philosophy educator; b. Ft. Wayne, Ind., June 19, 1941; s. Jon Hardin and Philomena Elizabeth (Lauer) D.; m. Sarah Jane Hutchison, Aug. 8, 1964; children—Jon William, Jennifer Anne. A.B., Oberlin Coll., 1963; Ph.D., U. Pitts., 1966. Asst. prof. philosophy Wayne State U., Detroit, 1966-69; vis. asst. prof. philosophy Yale U., New Haven, 1968-69; assoc. prof. philosophy Ind. U., Bloomington, 1969-76, prof., 1976—, Oscar Ewing prof. philosophy, 1989—, chmn. dept. philosophy, 1980-84, 94-97, adj. prof. computer sci., 1987-89, prof., 1989—, assoc. dean Coll. Arts and Scis., 1988-91, exec. assoc. dean, 1991-93, dir. informatics, 1999—; vis. fellow Inst. Advanced Studies, Australian Nat. U., Canberra, 1975-76; sr. visitor Math. Inst., U. Oxford, Eng., 1978; faculties vis. scholar U. Melbourne, Australia, 1983; fellow Ind. U. Inst. for Advanced Study, 1984; sr. visitor Ctr. for Philosophy of Sci., U. Pitts., Nov. 1984; adj. prof. U. Mass., Amherst, spring 1985. Contbg. author: Entailment, Vol. I, 1975, co-author Vol. II, 1992; editor: (with A. Gupta) Truth of Consequences: Essays in Honor of Nuel Belnap, 1990, (with G. Epstein) Modern Uses of Multiple-Valued Logic, 1975; editor Jour. Symbolic Logic, 1982-87; chief editor Jour. Philos. Logic, 1987-95; mem. editl. bds. Jour. Philos. Logic, 1979-87, Nous, 1968—, Studia Logica, 1978—, Jour. Non-Classical Logic, 1985-91. Am. Council Learned Socs. fellow, 1984-85; NSF prin. investigator, 1969-74; Fulbright-Hays research sr. scholar, 1974. Mem. Assn. Symbolic Logic (exec. com. 1978-81, council 1982—), Soc. Exact Philosophy (treas. 1982-84, v.p. 1986-88, pres. 1988-90), Am. Philos. Assn. (com. research and publs. 1985-88). Office: Ind U Dept Philosophy Sycamore Hall # 026 Bloomington IN 47405

DUNN, JUDITH LOUISE, secondary school educator; b. L.A., Jan. 6, 1945; d. Arthur B. and Lillian M. (Eyrich) D. BA, U. Calif., Santa Barbara, 1966; MA Edn., Pepperdine U., 1978; postgrad., U. Calif., Santa Barbara, 1967. Cert. secondary tchr., adminstr., Calif; cert. lay speaker United Meth. Ch. English tchr. Santa Maria (Calif.) Joint Union High Sch. Dist., mentor tchr., chmn. dept. English, 1991-94, lead tchr. Am. Lit.; mem. adv. coun. Student Age Parenting and Infant Devel. Program; dist. tchr. rep. Impact II Adv. Coun., 1992-94; dist. rep. Ctrl. Coast Literacy Coun.; mem. schoolwide assessment team, del. tchrs. of English of People to People Citizen Amb. Program visitation to Gt. Britain, 1995; mem. Sch. Site Coun., Steering Com. for Accreditation. Assoc. lay leader Santa Barbara dist. Calif.-Pacific Annual Conf., 1986-89, United Meth. Ch., bd. Higher Edn. and Campus Ministry, 1982-90; English tchr. del. citizen amb. program People to People to Gt. Britain, 1995. Fellow South Coast Writing Project; Disseminator grantee, 1988, 89, 91, 97, Adaptor grantee, 1991, 92. Mem. CTA, NEA, Nat. Coun. Tchrs. English, Local Faculty Assn. (profl. rels. chair 1986-88), Delta Kappa Gamma (past pres. Eta Lambda chpt.). Office: Santa Maria High Sch 901 S Broadway Santa Maria CA 93454-6613

DUNN, KENNETH RALPH, insurance company executive; b. Paterson, N.J., Apr. 9, 1958; s. Ralph and Florence Louise (May) D.; m. Martha Jean Davis, Sept. 6, 1980; children: Laura Jean, Jonathan Ralph, David Allan. BS, Messiah Coll., 1980. Cert. in gen. ins.; lic. resident property and liability ins. agt., N.C. From external auditor to br. bond mgr. Selective Ins. Co. Am., Branchville, N.J., 1980-95; corp. bond mgr. Aegis Security Ins. Co., Harrisburg, Pa., 1995—. Author: Messiah College Baseball Encyclopedia, 1991. Treas., deacon, softball coach, youth leader Newton (N.J.) 1st Bapt. Ch., 1980-84; ordained deacon, chmn. pastoral search com., recreation dir., chm. tng. dir., softball coach Calvary Bapt. Ch., Belair, Md., 1984-90; chmn. personnel com., ordained deacon, body life coord., softball coach, recreation dir., Covenant Bapt. Ch., Charlotte, N.C., 1990-95; sec., pres. Sussex County Softball League, Newton, 1982-84; adv. bd. Messiah Coll. Falcon Club, 1994; active Rep. Nat. Com., 1994—. Mem. Mid-Atlantic Surety Assn. (by-law com. 1987, sec. 1988, treas. 1989), Messiah Coll. Baseball Assn. (founder, pres./sec. 1989, sec. 1990, newsletter editor 1989-94, pres. 1994), Soc. Am. Baseball Rsch., Carolinas Surety Underwriters Assn. (treas. 1992, sec. 1993, v.p. 1994, pres. 1995), Ala. Surety Assn., Surety Assn. Atlanta, Geneal. Rsch. Soc. Northeastern Pa. Republican. Baptist. Avocations: coin collecting, baseball card collecting, athletics, ch. choir mem. Home: 14316 Blue Granite Rd Pineville NC 28134-8312 Office: Aegis Security Ins Co 2407 Park Dr # 200 Harrisburg PA 17110-9303

DUNN, LEO JAMES, obstetrician, gynecologist, educator; b. Trenton, N.J., May 23, 1931; s. Augustine Leo and Molly (McDaid) D.; m. Betty Beatrice Buchanan, Aug. 28, 1954; children: Laurie, Cary. AB, Hofstra U., 1952; MD, Columbia U., 1956. Diplomate: Am. Bd. Ob-Gyn., Am. Bd. Gyn. Oncology. Intern Cin. Gen. Hosp., 1956-57; resident Sloane Hosp for Women, Columbia-Presbyn. Med. Ctr., 1957-62; asst. prof. ob-gyn U. Iowa Coll. Medicine, Iowa City, 1962-65, assoc. prof. ob-gyn, 1965-67; prof., former chmn. dept. Med. Coll. Va., Richmond, 1967—, interim dean, chmn. of dept. Ob-Gyn., 1983-85; pres Am. bd. med. specialties, 1998—; bd. dirs. Am. Bd. Ob-Gyn, 1975—, pres., 1982—; mem. Nat. Bd. Med. Examiners, 1979-83. Recipient Silver medal as disting. alumnus Columbia U. Coll. Physicians and Surgeons, 1967; Markle scholar, 1963. Fellow Am. Coll. Ob-Gyn (dist. v.p. 1976-78); mem. Soc. Gynecol. Oncology (chmn. program com., v.p.), Am. Assn. Ob-Gyn (council 1975-79, pres. found. 1980-82, trustee 1975-82), Va. Ob-Gyn Soc. (pres. 1981-82), Phi Beta Kappa. Office: Med Coll Va MCD Station PO Box 980034 Richmond VA 23298-0034*

DUNN, LORETTA LYNN, lawyer; b. Owensboro, Ky, Dec. 3, 1955; d. John Edwin and Arnetta Mae (Trunnell) D.; m. Herbert S. Lunenfeld, Oct. 18, 1985; 1 child, Jack W. BA, U. Ky., 1976, JD, 1979; LLM, Georgetown U., 1983. Bar: Ky. 1979, D.C. 1984. Staff atty. U.S. Senate Com. Commerce, Sci. and Transp., Washington, 1979-86, minority counsel, 1982-86, sr. trade counsel, 1987-93; asst. sec. for legis. and intergovernmental affairs Dept. Commerce, 1993-95; v.p. govt. affairs Hughes Electronics, Arlington, Va., 1995—. named Order of Coif. Mem. D.C. Bar Assn., Ky. Bar Assn., Washington Internat. Trade Assn., Women Internat. Trade, Trade Policy Forum, Phi Beta Kappa. Office: Hughes Electronics 1530 Wilson Blvd Ste 1000 Arlington VA 22209*

DUNN, M. CATHERINE, college administrator, educator; b. Chgo., Mar. 26, 1934; d. John and Catherine (Donovan) Dunn. BA, Ariz. State U., 1968, MA, 1970, PhD, 1977. Cert. tchr., Iowa, Ariz. Tchr. St. Mathew Sch., Phoenix, 1956-60; tchr. St. Vincent Sch., Chg., 1960-68; asst. prin. Carroll Sch., Lincoln, Ill., 1970-73; mem. faculty Clarke Coll., Dubuque, Iowa, 1973-79, v.p. devel., 1979-84, pres., 1984—; bd. dirs. Am. Trust Bank, Dubuque, 1989—; cons. in field. Bd. dirs. Internat. Student Leadership, Notre Dame, Ind., 1975—, Med. Assocs. HMO, Dubuque, 1980—, Jr. Achievement, 1982—; mem. Iowa Dept. Transp. Commn., Ames, 1989—. Named One of Ten Outstanding Leaders in Dubuque Telegraph Herald newspaper, 1987, 88, 89. Mem. Am. Coun. Edn., Coun. Ind. Colls. (bd. dirs.), Am. Assn. Cath. Colls., Iowa Assn. Coll. Pres. (bd. dirs. 1984—), Ariz. State Alumni Assn., Dubuque C. of C. (mem. coun. 1973—, bd. dirs. 1986—, Outstanding Civic Leader award 1974, Civic Svc. award 1993), Coun. Advancement and Support Edn. (bd. dirs.), Phi Delta Kappa, Pi Lambda Theta. Avocations: cooking; music; walking; traveling. Home: 2350 Clarke Crest Dr Dubuque IA 52001-3125 Office: Clarke Coll 1550 Clarke Dr Dubuque IA 52001-3117*

DUNN, MARGARET ANN, religious studies educator, administrator, minister; b. Marshall, Mich., Nov. 18, 1953; d. Lee Donald and Hazel Lucille (Boehmer) D. BS cum laude, Alma Coll., 1975; MDiv, Asbury Theol. Sem., 1983; MA, Ball State U., 1989; EdD, U. Houston, 1995. Lic. minister Ch. of God (Anderson, Ind.), 1989, ordained, 1996. Tchr. Lydia Patterson Inst., El Paso, Tex., 1976-79; campus affiliate InterVarsity Christian Fellowship, Richmond, Ky., 1980-81; tchg. asst. Asbury Theol. Sem., Wilmore, Ky., 1981-83; tchr. Southwood Christian Acad., Indpls., 1984-85, Liberty Christian Sch., Anderson, 1985-86; libr. clk. Anderson Sch. Theology, 1986-88; prof. religious studies, registrar, dir. admissions Bay Ridge Christian Coll., Kendleton, Tex., 1988-98, registrar, 1993-95; tchr. Acad. of Clear Lake, Houston, 1998—; vis. lectr. Asbury Theol. Sem., 1983; min. Christian edn. Rosenberg (Tex.) 1st Ch. God, 1991-92, coord. women in ministry-mission Ch. of God, Anderson, Ind., 1992-94; dir. student ministries Bay Ridge Christian Coll., 1992-93, 94-96, v.p. acad. affairs, 1996-98; mem. Sunday Sch. TEAM Bd. of Christian Edn., Ch. of God, 1993—; mem. Christian Edn. bd. Pargate Cmty. Ch., Pasadena, Tex.; adj. prof. U. Houston, Victoria, Tex., 1995-96, 97. Co-author: Framework of Our Faith, 1983. Chmn. Christian edn. com. S.E. Tex. Ministerial Assembly, mem. credentials com., 1996, vice chmn., 1997—; mem. planning bd. Internat. Wesleyan Holiness Clergy Women Confs., 1996—. Mem. Women in Ministry and Mission, Gamma Delta Alpha, Omicron Delta Kappa. Avocations: reading, embroidering, spectator sports, travel.

DUNN, MARGARET M., general surgeon; b. Freeport, N.Y., Sept. 8, 1954; d. Howard James and Evelyn Ann (Madden) D.; m. William Anthony Spohn, July 4, 1982; children: Christopher, Marie. BS, Pa. State U., 1974; MD, Jefferson Med. Coll., 1977. Diplomate Am. Bd. Surgery. Resident in surgery Montefiore Hosp., Bronx, N.Y., 1977-82; prof. surgery Wright Sch. Medicine, Dayton, Ohio, 1982—. Fellow Am. Coll. Surgeons; mem. Assn. Women Surgeons, Am. Med. Women's Assn., Ctrl. Surg. Assn., Soc. Surgery of Alimentary Tract. Office: Wright State Dept Surgery 1 Wyoming St Dayton OH 45409-2722

DUNN, MARVIN IRVIN, physician; b. Topeka, Dec. 21, 1927; s. Louis and Ida (Leibtag) D.; m. Maureen Cohen, Mar. 10, 1956 (dec. Nov. 1988); children: Jonathan Louis, Marilyn Paulette. B.A., U. Kans., 1950, M.D., 1954. Intern USPHS, San Francisco, 1954-55; resident U. Kans., 1955-58, fellow, 1958-59, instr. medicine, 1958-60, assoc. in medicine, 1960-62, asst. prof. medicine, 1962-65, assoc. prof., 1965-70, prof., 1970—, Franklin E. Murphy Disting. prof., 1978—, dir. Cardiovascular Lab., head sect. Cardiovascular Disease Med. Center, 1963-92, dean Sch. of Medicine, 1979-84; cons. USAF, 1971-95; spl. cons. to fed. air surgeon of FAA, 1990—. Author: Home Study Course: Difficult EKG Diagnosis, 1969, Translator Deductive and Polyparametric Electrocardiography, 1970; (with others) Clinical Vectorcardiography and Electrocardiography, 2d edit., 1977, Clinical Electrocardiography, 8th edit., 1989; editor in chief Cardiovascular Perspectives, 1985-89; mem. editl. bd. Am. Jour. Cardiology, 1970-75, Catheterization and Cardiovascular Diagnosis, 1980-87, AMA Archives Internal Medicine, 1984-94, Jour. Am. Coll. Cardiology, 1983-89, Biomedicine and Pharmacotherapy, 1985-90, Am. Jour. Noninvasive Cardiology, 1985-89, Chest, 1984-89, 94—, Practical Cardiology, 1980-88, Heart and Lung, 1986-88, Bd.-Advanced in Therapy, 1992, Slovak Jour. Noninvasive Cardiology, 1993, Griffith Resource Libr., 1980-90, Am. Heart Jour., Jour. Acoustical Soc. Bd. dirs. Hebrew Acad. Jewish Geriatric and Convalescent Center, Beth Shalom Synagogue. Served with AUS, 1946-47. Recipient Alumnus of

Yr. award U. Kansas Sch. Medicine, 1987, silver medal U. Socrates, Thessaloniki, Greece, 1992. Master Am. Coll. Chest Physicians (mem. bd. regents, pres. 1988-89, gov. State of Kans.); fellow ACP (Laureate award 1990), Am. Coll. Cardiology (trustee), Am. Heart Assn., Royal Acad. Medicine (Ireland), Royal Coll. Physicians (Valencia, Spain); mem. Am. Physicians Fellowship (dir.), Univ. Cardiologists, Alpha Omega Alpha, Phi Chi. Home: 3205 Tomahawk Rd Mission Hills KS 66208-1861 Office: U Kans Hosp 3901 Rainbow Blvd Kansas City KS 66160-0001 *My small modicum of success was achieved by hard work, dedication to a single goal, and an application of total energy in achieving this goal. Open-mindedness, imaginativeness, and fair play have helped to make the road easier.*

DUNN, MARY JARRATT, public relations executive; b. Clifton Forge, Va., Oct. 29, 1942; d. Robert Bell and Mary Louise (Wood) J. B.A., Mary Baldwin Coll., Staunton, Va., 1964; cert. bus., Katharine Gibbs Sch., Boston, 1965. Staff asst. com. on agr. U.S. Ho. of Reps., 1975-81; asst. sec. food and consumer services Dept. Agr., 1981-85; v.p. Wampler & Assocs. Inc., Washington, 1985-86; pres. Jarratt & Assocs., Inc., Washington, 1986-90. Editor various legis. reports. Republican. Episcopalian. Home: The Pines 510 Wiley Dr Charlottesville VA 22903-4647

DUNN, MARY MAPLES, library director; b. Sturgeon Bay, Wis., Apr. 6, 1931; d. Frederic Arthur and Eva (Moore) Maples; m. Richard S. Dunn, Sept. 3, 1960; children—Rebecca Cofrin, Cecilia Elizabeth. BA, Coll. William and Mary, 1954, LHD (hon.), 1989; MA, Bryn Mawr Coll., 1956, PhD, 1959; LLD (hon.), Marietta Coll., 1987, Amherst Coll., 1987, Brown U., 1989; LittD (hon.), Lafayette Coll., 1988, Haverford Coll., 1991; LHD (hon.), Transylvania U., 1991, U. Pa., 1995, Mt. Holyok Coll., 1996, Smith Coll., 1998, U. Mass., 1998. Faculty Bryn Mawr Coll., 1958-85, prof. history, 1974-85; acting dean Undergrad. Coll. Bryn Mawr (Pa.) Coll., 1978-79, dean, 1980-85; pres. Smith Coll., Northampton, Mass., 1985-95; Carl and Lily Pforzheimer Found. dir. Arthur and Elizabeth Libr. Radcliffe Coll., 1995—. Author: William Penn: Politics and Conscience, 1967; editor: Political Essay on the Kingdom of New Spain (Alexander von Humboldt), 1972, rev., 1988, (with Richard S. Dunn) Papers of William Penn, vols. I-IV, 1979-87. Trustee The Clark Sch. for the Deaf, 1988-95, Acad. Mus., 1985-95, Hist. Deerfield, Inc., 1986—, Bingham Fund for Teaching Excellence at Transylvania U., 1987—, John Carter Brown Libr., 1994—, NOW/Legal Def. and Edn. Fund., 1996. Recipient Disting. Tchg. award Lindbeck Found., 1969; Fellow Inst. Advanced Study Princeton U., 1974. Mem. Berkshire Conf. Women Historians (pres. 1973-75), Coordinating Com. Women Hist. Profession (pres. 1975-77), Am. Hist. Assn., Inst. Early Am. History and Culture (chmn. adv. council 1977-80), Mass. Hist. Soc., Phi Beta Kappa. Office: Schlesinger Libr 10 Garden St Cambridge MA 02138-3630

DUNN, MICHAEL J., dean. Dean Med. Coll. Wis., Milw. Office: Med Coll Wis 8701 Watertown Plank Rd Milwaukee WI 53226-3548*

DUNN, MICHAEL M., military officer. BS in Astrodynamics, USAF Acad., 1972; grad., Squadron Officer Sch., 1976; MS in Sys. Mgmt., U. So. Calif., 1981; grad., Air Command and Staff Coll., 1983; nat. security mgmt. course, 1984; grad., Air War Coll., 1986. Commd. 2d lt. USAF, 1972, advanced through grades to brigadier gen., 1996; action officer Air Staff tng. program, sec. Air Force legis. liaison, Washington, 1978-79; instr. pilot, chief of tactics, R&D Interceptor Weapons Sch., Tyndall AFB, Fla., 1979-82; F-15 pilot, chief plans, programs, spl. projects 18th Tactical Fighter Wing, Kadena Air Base, Japan, 1983-85; F-15 pilot, dir. fighter ops. Hdqs. 5th Air Force, Yokota Air Base, Japan, 1983-85; div. chief Pacific East divsn., dir. plans, dep. chief staff Hdqs. USAF, Washington, 1989-90, dep. asst. dir. Joint Nat. Security Coun. Matters, 1991, exec. asst. to dep. chief of staff, plans and ops., 1991-92; comdr. 1st Ops. Group 1st Fighter Wing, Langley AFB, Va., 1992-93; divsn. chief strategy, resources, legis. affairs divsn. Hdqs. U.S. European Command, Stuttgart, Germany, 1993-94; exec. officer to dep. comdr. in chief U.S. European Command, Stuttgart, Germany, 1994-95; sr. mil. fellow Coun. on Fgn. Rels., N.Y.C., 1995-96; sr. mil. asst. to dep. sec. of def. The Pentagon, Washington, 1996-97; dir. plans and programs Hdqs. Pacific Air Forces, Hickam AFB, Hawaii, 1997—. Decorated Def. Disting. Svc. medal, Def. Superior Svc. medal, Meritorious Svc. medal with 3 oak leaf clusters. Office: HQ PACAF/XP Ste F214 25 E St Hickman A F B HI 96853-5417

DUNN, MICHAEL V., federal agency administrator; m. Brook Dunn; 4 children. Acting under sec. rural econ. and comty. devel. USDA, Washington, 1994-95, asst. sec. agr. for mktg. and regulatory programs, 1995-98; undersec. for mktg. and regulation program USDA, 1998—; housing dir., adminstr. City of Keokuk, Iowa; chair Iowa State's City Devel. Bd.; former commr. Iowa Devel. Commn.; staff specialist farm credit and rural devel. Senate Com. Agriculture, Nutrition and Forestry; v.p. Nat. Farmers Union, Washington; Midwest dir. Farmers Home Adminstrn., 1977-81, adminstr., 1993-94. *

DUNN, MIGNON, mezzo-soprano; b. Memphis, June 17, 1931; d. Dudley and Nancy Christine (Lundee) D.; m. Kurt Klippstatter, July 1972. Studies with Karin Branzell; MusD (hon.), Southwestern Coll., 1975; studies with Armen Boyajian, studies with Mrs. Hardesty Johnson. Recorded with Heritage, Angel, Deutsche Grammophon, Serato, EMI; faculty Am. Inst. Mus. Studies, Graz, Austria, Music Club Am., N.C., Internat. Vocal Arts Inst., Fla., Israel, Manhattan Sch. Music, U. Ill., Urbana. Debut at Town Hall with Little Orch. Soc., 1954, debut in New Orleans as Carmen, 1955; debut at N.Y.C. Opera as Carmen, 1956; debut with Met. Opera in Boris Godunov, 1958, debut Arena diVerona, Italy, 1970, Covent Garden, Eng., 1973, Teatro Colon, 1964, Vienna, 1973, LaScala, Milan, 1986; appeared with maj. opera cos. throughout Europe, U.S., Can., Mex., and S.Am.,including, Paris Opera, Vienna State Opera, Hamburg State Opera, Berlin, Helsinki, Budapest, Monte Carlo, Arena d'Orange; numerous roles including Judith in Bartok's Bluebeard's Castle, Azucena in Verdi's Il Trovatore, Amneris in Aida, Dalila in Saint Saens's Samson et Dalila, Carmen in Bizet's Carmen, Kostelnicka in Janacek's Jenufa, Marina in Boris Godunov, Herodias in Strauss' Salome, Jerzi Baba in Janacek's Rusalka; also entire Wagnerian, Straussian and Verdian repertoire of mezzo-soprano roles; recitalist; soloist with major orchs. in Europe, U.S., Can., Mex.; appeared at Spoleto Festival, Charleston, S.C., 1987-88, Spoleto, Italy; recs. include Rigoletto, Mother of Us All, Salome, Verdi Requiem. Recipient Beethoven prize Memphis, Exptl. Opera Theatre Am. award, 1955, N.Y. Singing Tchrs. award 1984, Hall of Fame Vocal Arts Acad. award, Phila., 1986. Office: Joel E Bloch Artists Mgmt 12 Cornelia St Apt 5C New York NY 10014-5653*

DUNN, MOIRA C., golf professional; b. Utica, N.Y., Aug. 3, 1971. Winner N.Y. State Jr. Girls Championship title, 1989, N.Y. State Women's Amateur Championship titles, 1992-94, Women's Western Amateur Championship, 1992; runner-up Doherty Championship, 1993; named second team collegiate All-Am., Fla. Internat. U., 1993-94, Acad. All-Am., 1993; tied for 7th Fieldcrest Cannon Classic, 1995, tied for 11th at State Farm Rail Classic, 1995, 14th PING-AT&T Wireless Svcs. LPGA Golf Championship, 1995, tied for 23rd Safeway LPGA Golf Championship, 1996, tied for 36th at PING Welch's Championship in Boston, 1996. Avocations: sports, music, reading. Office: c/l Ladnes Profl Golf Assn 100 International Golf Dr Daytona Beach FL 32124-1082*

DUNN, M(ORRIS) DOUGLAS, lawyer; b. Ionia, Mich., Nov. 1, 1944; s. Morris Frederick and Lola Adella (Gee) D.; m. Jill Lynn Fasbender, July 22, 1967; children: Brooks, Gillian, Joshua. BS in Mech. Engring., U. Mich., 1967; JD, Vanderbilt U., 1970. Bar: 1971, U.S. Dist. Ct. (so. dist.) N.Y. 1972, U.S. Ct. Appeals (2d cir.) 1973, U.S. Supreme Ct. 1978. Assoc. Winthrop Stimson, Putnam & Roberts, N.Y.C., 1970-78, ptnr. 1978-84; sr. v.p., mng. dir. Shearson Lehman Bros. Inc., N.Y.C., 1984-85; ptnr. Milbank, Tweed, Hadley & McCloy, N.Y.C., 1985—. Contbr. articles to profl. jours. Fellow Am. Bar Found., ABA (fed. regulation of securities com. bus. law sect. mem. 1981—, chair pub. utility, comms. and transp. law sect. 1997-98, bd. govs. 1998—); mem. Assn. Bar City N.Y. (chmn. nuclear tech. and law com. 1976-77), Internat. Bar Assn. (com. chmn. 1990-94), Alumni Bd. Vanderbilt U. Law Sch. (1987-90), Down Town (N.Y.C.), Canoe Brook Country Club (Summit, N.J.), Park Ave. Club (Florham Park, N.J.). Office: Milbank Tweed Hadley & McCloy 1 Chase Manhattan Plz Fl 47 New York NY 10005-1413

DUNN, NORMAN SAMUEL, plastics and textiles company executive; b. Woonsocket, R.I., Sept. 17, 1921; s. Israel M. and Ida (Mayerson) D.; m. Mildred M. Michaels, Aug. 31, 1975; 1 son, by previous marriage, Jeffrey Mark. Ph.B. cum laude, Providence Coll., 1942. Purchasing agt. Uniroyal Inc., Conn., 1942-48; pres. Emerson Textile Co., Chelsea, Mass., 1948-64; exec. v.p., treas. Chelsea Industries Inc., 1948-84, officer, bd. dirs., 1948—; chmn. bd. Am. Shacks Inc., 1982—; dir. NFA Corp. Trustee Combined Jewish Philanthropies; overseer Beth Israel/Deaconess Hosp., Boston; past chmn. 330 Beacon St. Condominium Trust; hon. trustee The Rehab. Ctr. for the Aged, Boston. Mem. Two Ten Nat. Found. Clubs: Belmont Country (Mass.); Rockrimmon Country (Stamford, Conn.). Home: 330 Beacon St Boston MA 02116-1153 also: Bayberry Way Pound Ridge NY 10576 Office: PO Box 505807 181 Spencer Ave Chelsea MA 02150-3000

DUNN, PARKER SOUTHERLAND, retired chemical company consultant; b. Portsmouth, Ohio, Aug. 25, 1910; s. Joseph Sidney and Florence (Bowen) D.; m. Mayde Smith, July 15, 1939 (dec. May 1996); children: Joseph Smith, Dwight James. B.Chem. Engring., Ohio State U., 1930; M.S., MIT, 1931. Tech. asst. Mead Corp., Chillicothe, Ohio, 1930-32; foreman Columbia Southern Corp., Barberton, Ohio, 1932-33; asst. plant supt. Columbia Southern Corp., Corpus Christi, Tex., 1934-38; tech. dir. Columbia Southern Corp., 1938-41; research dir. Potash Co. Am., Carlsbad, N.Mex., 1941-46; resident mgr. Potash Co. Am., 1946-51; asst. v.p. Am. Potash & Chem. Corp., Trona, Calif., 1951-52; v.p. Am. Potash & Chem. Corp., Trona, 1952-55, Los Angeles, 1955-63; dir. Am. Potash & Chem. Corp., 1958-71, pres., 1963-69, chmn. bd., 1969-71; v.p. Kerr McGee Corp., 1968-73, cons., 1975-90; v.p. Kerr McGee Nuclear Corp., 1974-75; v.p., dir. Am. Lithium Chems. Co., 1959-64, San Antonio Chem. Co., 1957-75. Recipient Benjamin Garver Lamme engring. medal Ohio State U., 1966. Mem. Am. Inst. Chem. Engrs., AIME. Anglican. Home: 14901 N Pennsylvania Ave Oklahoma City OK 73134-6072

DUNN, PATRICIA ANN, school system administrator, English language educator; b. Englewood, N.J., Mar. 17, 1942; d. Thomas Joseph and Rosanna Valerie (Cummings) D.; m. James Edward Egan, 1963 (div. 1974); 1 child, Deirdre Tracy. BA in English Edn., William Paterson U., 1963, MA in Communication Arts, 1974; postgrad., Montclair (N.J.) State U., 1986—. Cert. tchr., N.J., N.Y.; cert. prin., supr., N.J. Tchr. English, Intermediate Sch. Dist. 218, Bklyn., 1965-66, tchr. English and humanities, 1966-67, co-chmn. dept. humanities, 1967-68; tchr. English Midland Park (N.J.) Schs., 1969-91, staff devel. coord., 1987—, dir. curriculum, instrn., staff devel., 1991—; coord. bus. workshops Women in Bus., 1983, Stress, 1983. Editor N.J. Staff Devel. Coun. Newsletter, 1988-91, 96—; contbr. articles to profl. publs. Co-founder, coord. Ministry for Separated and Divorced Caths., Montclair, 1983-86. Recipient N.J. Woman of Distinction award World of People. Mem. ASCD, AAUW, N.J. Prins. and Suprs. Assn., Nat. Staff Devel. Coun., N.J. Staff Devel. Coun. (co-founder, dir. 1991-94, pres. 1995-96, trustee 1997—, editor Exchange 1996—), N.J. Ctr. for Achievement of Sch. Excellence (co-chair), N.J. Coalition Essential Schs. (del. to Nat. Congress 1996—), Nat. Coun. Tchrs. English, Le Terrace Club (Nutley, N.J.), Midland Park Adminstrs. and Suprs. Assn. (pres. 1996—). Democrat. Roman Catholic. Avocations: dance, reading. Office: Midland Park High Sch 250 Prospect St Midland Park NJ 07432-1398

DUNN, PATRICIA C., social work educator; b. Gastonia, N.C., Jan. 27, 1938; d. Thomas S. and Hazel (Twitty) Crawford; m. Ernest F. Dunn, Sept. 8, 1962; children: Celeste, Amina. BA, Va. Union U., 1960; MSW, Mich. State U., 1967; EdD, Rutgers U., 1985. Social worker Ingham County (Mich.) Dept. Social Svc., Lansing, 1963-65; clin. social worker Family Svc. Agy., Lansing, 1967-69; dir. acad. found. Livingston Coll., New Brunswick, N.J., 1969-71; asst., then assoc. prof., dir. continuing edn. program Sch. Social Work, Rutgers U., New Brunswick, N.J., 1989—, assoc. dean, 1993-94; cons. in field. Chmn. cmty. task force for sch. reform, Plainfield (N.J.) Bd. Edn., 1995-99. Mem. Nat. Assn. Social Workers (sect. alcohol, tobacco and other drugs, chmn. ACSW exam. rev. bd. 1997-99, chmn. task force for ATOD cert.). Democrat. Congregationalist. Avocations: reading, bead making, photography, travel. Office: Rutgers U Sch Social Work 536 George St New Brunswick NJ 08901-1167

DUNN, RANDALL L., federal judge. Apptd. bankruptcy judge U.S. Dist. Ct. Oreg., 1998. Office: Rm 700 1001 SW 5th Ave Ste 700 Portland OR 97204-1141

DUNN, RANDY EDWIN, lawyer; b. Hutchinson, Kans., Oct. 8, 1954; s. Roy Edwin and Joan Irene (Farney) D.; m. Michelle Renee Sandwith, Dec. 18, 1976 (div. Aug. 1979); 1 child, Brandi Dawn Sandwith; m. Rosalind O'Nita Heiman, Dec. 22, 1990. BA magna cum laude, Wichita State U., 1977; JD, U. Colo., 1983. Bar: Colo. 1983, U.S. Dist. Ct. Colo. 1986. Store and sales mgr. Pop Shoppe, Inc., Wichita, Kans., 1976-77; sales rep. Lifesavers, Inc., Wichita, 1977-80; asst. mgr. Quik Trip, Inc., Wichita, 1980; assoc. McIntyre & Varallo, P.C., Greeley, Colo., 1983-85; pvt. practice law Denver, 1985-87; ptnr. Dean & Dunn, P.C., Denver, 1987-89; assoc. Lau & Choi, P.C., Denver, 1989-90, Baker & Hostetler, Denver, 1991, Hopper & Kanouff, P.C., Denver, 1991-95; pvt. practice law Denver, 1995—. Mem. ABA, Colo. Bar Assn., Denver Bar Assn., Masons. Democrat. Office: Clanahan Tanner Downing and Knowlton PC 730 17th St Ste 500 Denver CO 80202-3580

DUNN, RICHARD JOSEPH, retired investment counselor; b. Chgo., Apr. 5, 1924; s. Richard Joseph and Margaret Mary (Jennett) D.; AB, Yale U., 1948; LLB, Harvard U., 1951; MBA, Stanford U., 1956; m. Marygrace Calhoun, Oct. 13, 1951; children: Richard, Marianne, Anthony, Gregory, Noelle. Admitted to Tex. bar, 1952; mem. firm Carrington, Gowan, Johnson & Walker, Dallas, 1951-54; investment counselor Scudder, Stevens & Clark, San Francisco, 1956-84, v.p., 1965-77, sr. v.p., 1977-84, gen. ptnr., 1974-84; ret. Served with AUS, 1943-46. Decorated Combat Infantry Badge, Bronze Star, Purple Heart; Knight of the Sovereign Mil. Hospitaller Order of St. John of Jerusalem of Rhodes and of Malta, Western Assn., 1978—, chancellor 1987-93, pres. 1993—, knight of obedience, 1990, comdr. Cross of Merit, 1989, Grand Cross The Sacred Mil. Constantinian Order of St. George, 1995; recipient Assumpta award Archdiocese of San Francisco, 1996. Roman Catholic. Home: 530 Junipero Serra Blvd San Francisco CA 94127-2727

DUNN, ROBERT ELBERT, education consultant, principal; b. Newark, May 26, 1928; s. George Elbert and Ruth Marie (Barker) D.; m. Gladys Annette Bovino, June 28, 1958. BA, Bates Coll., 1950; MA, U. Conn., 1951, PhD, 1955; spl. cert., U. Birmingham, Eng., 1952. Tchr. of sociology Hall H.S., West Hartford, Conn., 1952-54, guidance counselor, 1953-55, asst. prin., 1955-57, vice prin., 1957-62, prin., 1962-90; dept. head West Hartford Schs., 1953-54; dep. headmaster, ednl. cons. Seoul (Korea) Internat. Schs., 1990-95. YM-YWCA Bd. YMCA, West Hartford, 1965-85; chmn. sch. and cmty. orgns., 1965-85. Rotary Found. fellow, 1951-52, Whitehead fellowship Harvard U., 1970-71, Paul Harris fellow Rotary Internat., 1993; recipient Noah Webster award C. of C., 1989, Prin. of Yr. State of Conn., 1989-90. Mem. West Hartford Rotary Club (hon.). Congregationalist. Avocation: travel. Home: 37 Ranger Ln West Hartford CT 06117-3040

DUNN, ROBERT SIGLER, engineering executive; b. Cin., Aug. 13, 1926; s. John W. and Mirian S. (Sigler) D.; m. Barbara A. Rigdon, June 26, 1949; children: Anne Dunn Stockman, John R., Mark A. BSME, BSEE, Purdue U., 1949. With Collins Radio Co., Cedar Rapids, Iowa, 1949-72; regional v.p., gen. mgr. Collins Radio Co., Cedar Rapids; v.p. ops. King Radio Corp., Olathe, Kans., 1973-91; also bd. dirs. King Radio Corp., Olathe; pvt. cons., 1991—; Mem. Iowa State Bd. Engring. Examiners, 1969-72. Bd. dirs., v.p. Olathe Comm. Hosp., 1982-90; mem. bd. trustees, past chmn. Olathe Health Sys.; chmn. bd. trustees Miami County Med. Ctr.; mem. bd. advisors Kans. U. Sch. Engring., 1979—. Mem. IEEE, NSPE, Am Soc. Quality, Rotary, Pi Tau Sigma, Eta Kappa Nu, Tau Beta Pi. Home and Office: 15320 Melrose Pl Overland Park KS 66221-9556

DUNN, RONALD HOLLAND, civil engineer, management executive, consultant; b. Balt., Sept. 15, 1937; s. Delmas Joseph and Edna Grace (Holland) D.; m. Verona Lucille Lambert, Aug. 17, 1958; children: Ronald H., Jr. (dec.), David R., Brian W. BS in Engring., Johns Hopkins U., 1969. Registered profl. engr., Va., D.C.; diplomate forensic engring. Field engr. Balt. & Ohio R.R., Balt., 1958-66; chief engr. yards, shops, trackwork DeLeuw, Cather & Co., Washington, 1966-73; mgr. engring. support Parsons-Brinckerhoff-Tudor-Bechtel, Atlanta, 1973-76; dir. railroad engring. Morrison-Knudsen Co., Inc., Boise, Idaho, 1976-78; v.p. Parsons-Brinckerhoff-Centec, Inc., McLean, Va., 1978-83; v.p., area mgr., tech. dir. railway engring., profl. assoc. Parsons Brinckerhoff Quade & Douglas, Inc., McLean and Pitts., 1983-84; dir. transp. engring. R.L. Banks & Assocs., Inc., Fairfax, Va., 1984-91, Williamsburg, Va., 1991—; insp., rail transit facilities, Europe, 1980, 82, 84, China and Hong Kong, 1985; involved in engring. of 18 railroads and 17 rail transit systems throughout N.Am., in over 40 states, Washington D.C. and 6 provinces; guest Japan Railway Civil Engring. Assn., 1972, French Nat. Railroads and Paris Transport Authority, 1988; mem. adv. com. track engrs. U.S. Dept. Transp., 1968-71. Chmn. Cub Scout Pack, Boy Scouts Am., 1972-73, committeeman, 1973-75, troop committeeman, 1979-85. Fellow ASCE, Inst. Transp. Engrs., Nat. Acad. Forensic Engrs.; mem. NSPE, NAS (mem. select panel), Arbitration Assn., Am. Mgmt. Assn., Am. Rlwy. Engring. Assn. (life), Am. Pub. Transit Assn., Soc. Am. Mil. Engrs., Roadmasters and Maintenance of Way Assn. Am., Am. Rlwy. Bridge and Bldg. Assn., Constrn. Specifications Inst., Transp. Rsch. Bd., Nat. Assn. R.R. Safety Cons. and Investigators, Can. Soc. Civil Engring., Va. Soc. Profl. Engrs., Can. Urban Transit Assn., Rlwy. Tie Assn., Inst. Rapid Transit, Phi Kappa Sigma. Methodist. Office: PO Box 3106 Williamsburg VA 23187-3106

DUNN, ROY J., landscape architect; b. Camden, N.J., July 23, 1946; s. John S. and Almira G. (Dott) D. BS, Rutgers U., 1968. Registered landscape arch., N.J., Pa. Landscape architect Edward R. Bachtle, ASLA, Wilmington, Del., 1968-70, Land Design, Inc., Cherry Hill, N.J., 1970-76, Robert Kraeger, Inc., Horsham, Pa., 1976-77, Taylor, Wiseman & Taylor, Mt. Laurel, N.J., 1977-85; prin. Roy Dunn & Assocs., Inc., Medford, N.J., 1985—; chmn., mem. Unified Nat. Exam. Com., Syracuse, N.Y., 1978-81, N.J. Bd. Landscape Archs., Newark, 1984-93. Trustee Rutgers U., 1989-95, chair bldgs. and grounds com., 1994-95; bd. dirs. Landscape Arch. Found., Washington, 1991-92. Named Outstanding Alumni of Yr., Cook Coll. Landscape Architecture Dept., 1990; recipient Dean's Svc. award, Cook Coll., 1996, Meritorious Svc. award Rutgers U, 1997. Fellow Am. Soc. Landscape Archs. (trustee 1978-85, nominating com. 1988-89, chair ann. meeting program 1991, Pres. medal 1992, N.J. Chpt. Svc. award 1986). Cook Coll. Agr. and Environ. Scis. Alumni Assn. (bd. dirs. 1984—, pres. 1988-89). Office: Roy Dunn & Assocs 200 Woodland Ave Medford NJ 08055-3460

DUNN, SHANNON, olympic athlete; b. Steamboat Springs, Colo., Nov. 26, 1972. Olympic athlete specializing in snowboarding halfpipe. Winner 1998 Bronze Medal for snowboarding halfpipe, Nagano, 4th in World Championships, 1997, 1st place, World Cup, 1996, 5th, 1995, numerous other awards. Achievements include becoming one of the dominant halfpipe competitors in the world; key athlete in the progression of women's snowboarding. Office: c/o US Ski and Snowboarding Assn PO Box 100 Park City UT 84060-0100*

DUNN, SUZANNE LYNNE, media company executive; b. Evanston, Ill., Sept. 2, 1962; d. William Leo and Roberta Elaine (Johnston) D. BS in Fin., Pa. State U., 1984; MBA in Bus. Policy and Fin., U. Chgo., 1990. Sr. cons. Andersen Cons., Washington and London, 1986-88, A.T. Kearney Inc., Chgo. and Amsterdam, The Netherlands, 1989-91; v.p. devel., exec. dir. Zelos Digital Learning, San Francisco, 1992-96; sr. prodr. Ifusion Com, San Francisco, 1996-97; dir. content partnerships Network Computer Inc., Redwood Shores, Calif., 1997-99; dir. advanced products Directv, El Segundo, Calif., 1999—. Named to Top 100 Multimedia Prodrs., Multimedia Prodr. mag., 1995. Mem. Multimedia Devel. Group, Internat. Interactive Comms. Soc. (Best of Show and Gold awards 1995).

DUNN, WALTER SCOTT, JR., writer, former museum director, consultant; b. Detroit, Apr. 5, 1928; s. Walter Scott and Minnie (Van Lahr) D.; m. Jean Wendeberg, July 11, 1959. B.A., U. Durham, Eng., 1951; M.A., Wayne State U., 1953; Ph.D., U. Wis., 1971. Curator indsl. history Detroit Hist. Mus., 1952-56; chief curator State Hist. Soc. Wis., Madison, 1956-63; mus. cons., 1962—; dir. Buffalo and Erie County Hist. Soc., 1963-78, Des Moines Ctr. Sci. and Industry, 1978-84, Nat. Mus. Transport, St. Louis, 1984-86, Dog Mus., St. Louis, 1987-89. Author: Western Commerce, 1760-1774, 1971, Second Front Now, 1943, 80, Hitler's Nemesis: The Red Army, 1994, The Soviet Economy and the Red Army 1930-1945, 1995, Kursk: Hitler's Gamble, 1943, 1997, Frontier Profit and Loss, 1760-1764, 1998, Views of America: Walworth County, 1998; host several Pub. TV series on mil. history, Madison, Wis. and Buffalo, 1959-78. Served with AUS, 1946-47. Mem. Walworth County Hist. Soc. (pres. 1996). Home: N6539 Peck Station Rd Elkhorn WI 53121-3246 *Human progress can be achieved only through constant questioning of the past and innovative action to solve the problems of the future.*

DUNN, WARREN HOWARD, retired lawyer, brewery executive; b. Omaha, Sept. 25, 1934; s. John Ralph and Frances (Liddell) D.; m. Nancy Ann Nolan, July 2, 1955; children—Kathleen, Erin, Theresa, Maureen. B.S. in Bus. Adminstrn, Creighton U., Omaha, 1956, J.D., 1958. Bar: Nebr. 1958, Wis. 1967. Claims adjuster U.S. Fidelity & Guarantee Co., Omaha, 1958-59; spl. agt. FBI, 1959-66; with Miller Brewing Co., Milw., 1966-94, v.p., gen. counsel, 1973-84, sr. v.p. adminstrn., 1984-90, exec. v.p., 1990-91, pres., CEO, 1991-92, chmn., CEO, 1992-93; ret., 1994. Mem. ABA, Wis. Bar Assn., Nebr. Bar Assn.

DUNN, WENDELL EARL, III, business educator; b. Boca Raton, Fla., Aug. 20, 1945; s. Wendell Earl Jr. and Lillian Dunn; m. Kathleen Ann Riley, Mar. 29, 1981; 1 child, Elissa Brooks. BA, Johns Hopkins U., 1966; MBA, U. So. Calif., 1973; PhD, U. Mich., 1981. Cert. EMT, N.J.; registered mine mgr., Queensland, Australia. Asst. to dir. pers. Johns Hopkins U., Balt., 1967-68; pilot project mgr. Chlorine Tech. Ltd., Sydney, Australia, 1968-71; securities analyst Alex Brown & Sons, Balt., 1973-74; lectr. bus. adminstrn. U. Mich., Ann Arbor, 1977-80; asst. prof. bus. adminstrn. Coll. of William and Mary, Williamsburg, Va., 1980-81; prin. W.E. Dunn & Assocs., Phila., 1981-91; assoc. dir. Sol C. Snider Entrepreneurial Ctr., 1991-94, acad. dir., 1995-96; prof. bus. adminstrn. Colgate Darden Grad. Sch. Bus. Adminstrn., U. Va., Charlottesville, 1996—, exec. dir. Batten Ctr. Entrepreneurial Leadership, 1996—; legis. asst. Sen. Paul W. Fannin, 1974; sr. lectr. mgmt. Wharton Sch. U. Pa., Phila., 1981-82, lectr., 1984-88, adj. assoc. prof., 1989-93, adj. prof. mgmt., 1993-96, adv. bd. Sol C. Snider Entrepreneurial Ctr., course head Entrepreneurship and New Venture Initiation, 1986-92, faculty Wharton Exec. MBA Program, 1988-96, entrepreneurship curriculum coord., 1991-94, acad. dir. entrepreneurship programs, 1993-96; faculty Aresty Inst. Exec. Edn., 1990-96; adj. asst. prof. fine and performing arts mgmt. Columbia U., N.Y.C., 1983-84; adj. assoc. prof. emergency medicine The George Washington U., Washington, 1994-96; mem. planning com. U.S. Dept. Commerce Nat. Innovation Workshops, N.J., 1986, leader, N.Y.C., 1987; spl. advisor Hopkins/Nanjing program Sch. Advanced Internat. Studies, Johns Hopkins U., Washington, 1987-89; mgmt. cons., exec. edn. AT&T, DuPont, GM, IBM, Steel Svc. Ctr. Inst., Digital Equipment, SmithKline Beecham, ASEA Brown Boveri; guest lectr. Inst. Rlwy. Engrs. and Russian Acad. Scis., St. Petersburg, Russia, 1992; judge Moot Corp. Internat. Bus. Plan Competition, Austin, Tex., 1993; keynote spkr. Tex. Entrepreneurial Forum, Austin, 1993; investment adv. com. Benjamin Franklin Tech. Ctr. Southeastern Pa., 1993-94; compensated spokesman AT&T 800-line Svc. media tour, 1993; bd. dirs., exec. com. U. Va. Patent Found., 1997—; adv. bd. Virginia Gateway, 1998—. Mem. editl. bd. Jour. of Bus. Venturing, 1987-92, 99—; contbr. articles to profl. jours. Active Luth. Student Found., Ann Arbor, 1978-80; trustee Internat. Peace Policy rsch. Inst., 1989-94; founding trustee Consortium for MBA Enterprise Corps, 1991-93, mem. exec. com., 1992-93; cons. Bus. Vols. for Arts, Phila., 1982-83; active Luth. Retirement Homes, Phila., 1983-84; mem. Haddonfield (N.J.) Ambulance Assn., 1990-96, EMS squad co-capt., 1992; mem. task force on EMS response Camden County N.J. Ambulance Assn., 1993-95. Robert Rodkey Found. fellow, 1974. Mem. Acad. Mgmt., Am. Soc. Inventors (life, bd. dirs. 1984-87, pres. 1985-86), U.S. Distance Learning Assn., Assn. Univ. Tech. Mgrs., Licensing Execs. Soc. U.S. and Can., Corinthian Yacht Club Phila., Greencroft Club, Beta Gamma Sigma, Phi Kappa Phi. Avocations: flying, sailing, gardening. Home: PO Box 4313 Charlottesville VA 22905-4313 Office: Darden Grad Sch Bus Adminstrn U Va PO Box 6550 Charlottesville VA 22906-6550

DUNN, WILLIAM BRUNA, III, journalist; b. Streator, Ill., Jan. 26, 1947; s. William Bruna and Mary Elizabeth (Allgaier) D.; m. Sandra Lee Ann Klein, Aug. 23, 1969; 1 child, William IV. B.S. in Journalism, U. Fla., 1969. Reporter Orlando (Fla.) Sentinel, 1967-69, mag. editor, 1970-80, dep. mng. editor, 1979-81, mng. editor, 1981-91, assoc. mng. editor, designer, 1991—. Author: Kidding Around, 1973; editor: SHAQ! That Magical Rookie Season, 1993; editor: Martin Andersen: Editor, Publisher, Galley Boy, 1996. Recipient Silver Gavel award ABA, 1974; Gold and Silver medal Soc. Newspaper Design, 1984. Mem. Nat. Press Photographers Assn., Fla. Soc. Newspaper Editors, Soc. Profl. Journalists (past pres. Cen. Fla. chpt.). Roman Catholic. Home: 4 E Vanderbilt St Orlando FL 32804-5925 Office: Sentinel Communications Co 633 N Orange Ave Orlando FL 32801-1300

DUNNAVANT, TRACY LYNN, planning administrator; b. Ft. Lee, Va., Aug. 12, 1966; d. Robert Henry and Janet Sue (Fulkerson) Schneider; m. James H. Dunnavant, June 7, 1997; 1 child, James Phillip. BA, Ky. Wesleyan Coll., 1988; MPA, Western Ky. U., 1990. Intern Sen. Wendell Ford, Owenboro, Ky., 1988, City of Bowling Green, Ky., 1990; spl. projects coord. City of Villa Rica, Ga., 1990-96; planning & zoning adminstr. City of Carrollton, Ga., 1996—; sec. Carrollton Planning Commn., 1996—; bd. dirs. Carrollton Main St., 1996—; bd. dirs. Carroll County C. of C., 1994—; sec./treas. Villa Rica Downtown Devel. Auth., 1992—. Republican. Baptist. Avocation: tennis. Office: City of Carrollton 315 Bradley St Carrollton GA 30117-3219

DUNNE, DESMA, medical/surgical nurse; b. N.Y.C., Dec. 10, 1955; d. Louis and Mary (Genè) Tahan; children: Robert, Ryan. AAS, N.Y. Tech. Coll., Bklyn., 1981; BSN, Coll. S.I., 1989; MSN, Wagner Coll., 1993. Cert. med.-surg., geriatrics nurse, clin. nurse specialist; cert. emergency med. technician. Dir. nursing svcs. N.Y. Multi-Care, S.I., 1988-90; nurse Luth. Med. Ctr., Bklyn., 1981—; clin. nurse specialist St. Elizabeth's Hosp., Elizabeth, N.J., 1994—; ind. nurse cons. Mem. ANA, Am. Assn. Diabetes Educators, N.Y. State Nurses Assn., Oncology Nurses Assn., S.I. Coll. Nursing Honor Soc. (founding mem.), Tau Phi Sigma, Sigma Theta Tau. Home: 91 Charleston Ave Staten Island NY 10309-1655

DUNNE, DIANE C., marketing executive; b. Milw.; d. Francis and Ruth Borman Cantine; 1 child, Dana Philip. BS, Marquette U.; MBA, NYU, 1985. Mgr. advt. NBC, N.Y.C., 1975-77; dir. mktg. CBS, N.Y.C., 1977-80; dir. funding Bloomingdale's, N.Y.C., 1980—; dir. 750 Park Ave. Corp., N.Y.C., 1985—; dir. Women's Econ. Round Table, 1988—; v.p. events, bd. dirs. The Oxford U. Alumni Assn. N.Y., 1993—. Author: Guidelines to Advertising All News Radio, 1976, Guidelines for Catalogue Copywriters, 1985; asst. editor Am. Cancer Soc., Gourmet Guide for Busy People by Famous People, 1985, The International Directory of Distinguished Leadership; contbr. articles to profl. jours. Mem. Am. Cancer soc., N.Y.C., 1980—; chair Feed the Homeless com. St. James Ch., N.Y.C., 1984-87; mem. pastoral and cmty. ministry com. St. James Altar Guild. Mem. Fashion Group (co-chair regional com.), Women's Econ. Roundtable (bd. dirs. 1988), NYU Exec. MBA Assn. Episcopalian. Avocations: opera, jogging, skiing, rollerblading. Home: 750 Park Ave New York NY 10021-4252 Office: Bloomingdales 770 Lexington Ave New York NY 10021-8165

DUNNE, GERARD FRANCIS, lawyer; b. Huntington, N.Y., Aug. 23, 1947; s. Frank and Adele A. (Malerba) D.; m. Judith Ellen Gordon, Dec. 5, 1976; 1 child, Heather Chelsey. B in Engring., Manhattan Coll., 1969; JD, U. Balt., 1974. Bar: D.C. 1974, N.Y. 1974, U.S. Patent Office, U.S. Dist. Ct. (ea. and so. dists.) N.Y. 1976, U.S. Ct. Appeals (fed. cir.) 1982, U.S. Ct. Appeals (2d and 8th cirs.) 1985, U.S. Supreme Ct. 1987. Examiner patents U.S. Patent Office, Washington, 1969-74; assoc. Law Offices of Albert C. Johnston P.C., N.Y.C., 1974-76; assoc. Wyatt, Gerber, Burke & Badie, N.Y.C., 1976-82, ptnr., 1982-94. Mem. ABA, Assn. of Bar of City of N.Y., Fed. Bar Council, Am. Intellectual Property Law Assn. Home: 89-04 63rd Ave Flushing NY 11374-2815 Office: 156 5th Ave Ste 1223 New York NY 10010-7002

DUNNE, GRIFFIN, actor, producer; b. June 8, 1955; s. Dominick and Ellen (Griffin) D.; m. Carey Lowell. Student, Neighborhood Playhouse. Actor: (stage prodns.) Marie and Bruce, 1980, Coming Attractions, 1982, Hooters, 1984, Search & Destroy, 1991, (films) The Other Side of the Mountain, 1975, The Fan, 1981, An American Werewolf in London, 1981, Cold Feet, 1983, Almost You, 1984, Johnny Dangerously, 1984, Who's That Girl?, 1987, Amazon Women on the Moon, 1987, The Big Blue, 1988, Me and Him, 1989, My Girl, 1991, Straight Talk, 1992, Big Girls Don't Cry...They Get Even, 1992, The Pickle, 1993, Naked in New York, 1994, I Like it Like That, 1994, Quiz Show, 1994, Search & Destroy, 1995, (TV movie) The Wall, 1980; actor, prodr.: (films) Head Over Heels, 1979, After Hours, 1985, Once Around, 1991; prodr.: (films) Baby It's You, 1983, Running on Empty, 1988, White Palace, 1990; prodr. short action film: Duke of Groove, 1995 (Acad. award nominee for best live short action film 1996). Mem. Actors' Equity Assn., Screen Actors Guild, AFTRA. Office: care UTA 9560 Wilshire Blvd Fl 5 Beverly Hills CA 90212-2401*

DUNNE, JAMES ROBERT, academic administrator, management consultant, business educator; b. Cleve., July 8, 1929; s. Carroll Joseph and Wilma Agnes (Sutmore) D.; m. Nancy Anne McSween, Oct. 28, 1952; children: James Jr., Stephen. BA, Albion Coll., 1951; MA, SUNY, Albany, 1964, PhD, 1972. Sect. mgr. news bur. GE, Schenectady, N.Y., 1955-63; asst. to chancelor SUNY, Albany, 1963-68; dir. pub. affairs N.Y. State Office Gen. Svcs., Albany, 1968-73; v.p. mktg. N.Y. State Higher Edn. Assistance Corp., Albany, 1973-76; exec. on loan N.Y. State U.S. Office Edn., 1976-78; pres. J.R. Dunne, Inc., Orlando, Fla., 1978-94; program mgr. Eagle Tech., Inc., Orlando, 1983-85; asst. prof. mgmt., acad. program chmn. Fla. Inst. Tech., Orlando, 1985-89; sr. mgmt. analyst Star Mountain, Inc., 1989-90; regional dir. Webster U., Orlando, Fla., 1990-98; spl. asst. devel. to exec. v.p. Webster U., Orlando, 1998—; adj. prof. Schenectady C.C., 1968-76, SUNY, Brockport, 1970-72; adj. instr. Valencia C.C., Orlando, 1980-94, Fla. So. Coll., Orlando, 1980-81, Brevard C.C., Titusville, Fla., 1979-80, Columbia Coll., Orlando, 1980-94; mem. nat. faculty Nova U., Ft. Lauderdale, Fla., 1980-91; acad. assoc. Atlantic Coun., 1982—; advisor doctoral dissertation Nova U., 1988-98; cons. Am. Schs. Corp., 1998—. With USN, 1952-55, capt. USNR, 1985, ret. 1989. Paul Harris fellow, 1989. Mem. Rotary (chmn. dist. youth exch. 1981-91, mem. Paul Harris Sch. com. 1988-99, Rotarian of Yr. Altamonte Springs chpt. 1981, 83, 85). Republican. Roman Catholic. Avocations: golf, travel. Home: 6400 Flotilla Dr Unite 31 Holmes Beach FL 34217

DUNNE, JOHN GREGORY, author; b. Hartford,, Conn., May 25, 1932; s. Richard Edwin and Dorothy (Burns) D.; m. Joan Didion, Jan. 30, 1964; 1 child, Quintana Roo. A.B., Princeton U., 1954. Writer, editor Time mag., N.Y.C. Columnist: New West, Saturday Evening Post, 1967-69, Esquire, 1976-77, 1986-87; author: books, including: Delano: The Story of the California Grape Strike, 1967, The Studio, 1969, Vegas: A Memoir of a Dark Season, 1974, True Confessions, 1977, Quintana and Friends, 1978, Dutch Shea, Jr., 1982, The Red White and Blue, 1987, Harp, 1989, Crooning, 1990, Playland, 1994, Monster: Living Off the Big Screen, 1997; (with Joan Didion) screenplay Panic in Needle Park, 1971, Play It As It Lays, 1973, A Star is Born, 1976, True Confessions, 1981, Hills Like White Elephants, 1991, Broken Trust, 1995, Up Close & Personal, 1996; contbr. articles to mags., including New Yorker, New York Rev. Served with U.S. Army, 1954-56. Office: Janklow & Nesbit Assocs 598 Madison Ave New York NY 10022-1614*

DUNNE, JOHN RICHARD, lawyer; b. Garden City, N.Y., Jan. 28, 1930; s. Frank and Virginia (Heckman) D.; m. Denise Maher, June 21, 1958; children: Joanne, Peter, Timothy, Hilary. AB, Georgetown U., 1951; LLB, Yale U., 1954. Bar: N.Y. 1955, D.C. 1993, U.S. Dist. Ct. (ea. and so. dists.) N.Y. 1956, U.S. Ct. Appeals (2d, 9th, 10th and 11th cirs.), U.S. Supreme Ct. 1960. Assoc. Milbank Tweed Hope & Hadley, N.Y.C., 1954-56; chief law asst. Nassau County Ct., Mineola, N.Y., 1957-62; law sec. Supreme Ct. State of N.Y., 1963-65, state senator, 1966-89; chmn. various N.Y. State Senate coms., also dep. majority leader, 1987-88; ptnr. Colleran, O'Hara, Kennedy, Lilly & Dunne P.C., Garden City, N.Y., 1966-79, Rivkin, Radler, Dunne & Bayh, Uniondale, N.Y., 1979-90; asst. atty. gen. civil rights U.S. Dept. Justice, Washington, 1990-93; counsel Whiteman, Osterman, Hanna, Albany, N.Y., 1994—. Roman Catholic. Home: PO Box 270 Spencertown NY 12165-0270*

DUNNE, KEVIN JOSEPH, lawyer; b. Pitts., Sept. 22, 1941; s. Matthew S. and Marjorie (Whelan) D.; m. Heather Wright Dunne, Sept. 27, 1963; children: Erin, Kevin Jr., Patrick, Sean. BA, U. Conn., 1963; JD, Georgetown U., 1966. Bar: Calif. 1967, U.S. Dist. Ct. (no. dist.) Calif., 1967, U.S. Dist. Ct. (ea. dist.) Calif. 1969, U.S. Dist. Ct. (ctrl. dist.) Calif. 1971, U.S. Ct. Appeals (9th cir.) 1971. Assoc. Sedgwick, Detert, Moran & Arnold, San Francisco, 1968-75, ptnr., 1975—; adj. prof. U. San Francisco Sch. Law, 1980-86; bd. editorial advisors Bender's Drug Product Liability Reporter, 1988-92. Author: Dunne on Depositions, 1995; editor Defense Counsel Training Manual, 1989; contbr. articles to profl. jours. Capt. U.S. Army, 1966-68, Vietnam. Recipient Bronze Star, Army Commendation medal; recipient Exceptional Performance award Def. Rsch. Inst., 1988. Fellow Internat. Acad. Trial Lawyers, Am. Coll. Trial Lawyers; mem. No. Calif. Assn. Def. Counsel (pres. 1987-88), Internat. Assn. Def. Counsel (pres. elect 1994-95), Am. Bd. Trial Advocates. Roman Catholic. Avocation: golf. Office: Sedgwick Detert Moran & Arnold 1 Embarcadero Ctr Ste 1600 San Francisco CA 94111-3716

DUNNE, MATTHEW BAILEY, state legislator; b. New Haven, Conn., Nov. 20, 1969; s. John Bailey and Faith Leah (Weinstein) D. BA with honors, Brown U. State rep. Vt. Ho. of Reps., 1993—; dir. mktg. Logic Assn., 1997—; vice chmn. transp. com. Vt. Ho. of Reps., 1997-99, chair state house advisor com., 1995-99; account exec. Pierce & Thibodeau, 1994-97; asst. majority leader Vt. Ho. of Reps., 1999—; bd. dirs. State Infrastructure Bank. Contbg. reporter: Chaote-Rose Mary Hall Alumni Mag. Trustee Vt. Arts Coun., 1992—, Vt. Film Commn., 1996—; bd. overseers Dartmouth Hitchcock Med. Ctr., 1996—; dir. pub. rels. Glory Days of RR Festival, 1993-94. Address: RR 1 Box 186 Hartland VT 05048

DUNNE, NANCY ANNE, retired social services administrator; b. Ionia, Mich., Aug. 5, 1929; d. Warner Kingsley and Hazel Fern (Alliason) McSween; m. James Robert, Oct. 28, 1952; children: James Robert Jr., Stephen Michael. BA, Albion (Mich.) Coll., 1951. Tchr. Oakdale Elem., Grand Rapids, Mich., 1951-53, Lakeside Sch., East Grand Rapids, Mich., 1953; clk. Office of Naval Rsch., Washington, 1954-55; dir. pub. rels. Diocesan Office Health and Social Svcs., Albany, N.Y., 1971-74; dir. vol. action dept. Coun. of Human Resources, Schenectady, N.Y., 1974-76; pers. asst. Am. Soc. Assn. Execs., Walshington, 1977-78; adminstrv. asst. N.Y. Soc. Cons. Engrs., N.Y.C., 1978-79, Assessment Designs, Inc., Orlando, Fla., 1980-82; adminstrv. asst. Catholic Social Svcs., Orlando, Fla., 1982-84, ret., 1984. Only female mem. N.Y. State Comm. Cultural Resources, Albany, 1970-73; bd. dirs. Coalition for the Homeless, Orlando, 1983-87. Mem. Jr. League of Schenectady (Vol. of Yr. award 1965-66), Schenectady Symphony Orch. (pres. 1969-70), Ladies of Charity (pres. Albany chpt. 1970-72, pres. Orlando chpt. 1984-86, nat. pres. 1990-94, v.p. internat. 1990-94, bd. dirs. 1994—). Roman Catholic. Avocations: reading, traveling, golfing, bridge, entertaining friends. Home: 102 Hickory Dr Longwood FL 32779-2420

DUNNE, PETER BENJAMIN, university administrator; b. N.Y.C., Oct. 16, 1933; s. Finley Peter Jr. and Evelyn (Johnson) D.; m. Faith Weber, Nov. 30, 1963; children: Sarah, Andrew. BA, Harvard U., 1955; MD, Columbia U., 1960. Diplomate Nat. Bd. of Med. Examiners, Am. Bd. of Psychiatry and Neurology. Clin. asst. prof. neurology U. So. Calif., L.A., 1967-68, 70-71; assoc. prof. neurology U. Vt. Med. Ctr., Burlington, 1971-73; assoc. prof. neurology U. South Fla., Tampa, 1973-77, clin. assoc. prof., 1977-83, 83-92; chief neurology James Haley VA Hosp., Tampa, 1973-77; pvt. practice Tampa, 1997-91; assoc. prof. U. South Fla., Tampa, 1992—, interim chmn., 1998—; attending neurologist Tampa Gen. Hosp., 1992—; chief multiple sclerosis clinic Tampa Gen. Hosp. and U. South Fla., 1992—. Bd. dirs. Master Chorale, Tampa, 1981-96; chmn. United Way Hillsborough County Med. Soc., Tampa, 1990. Lt. col. U.S. Army, 1968-70. Nat. scholarship Harvard Coll., 1951. Fellow Am. Acad. of Neurology; mem. AMA, Soc. of Clin. Neurologists, Hillsborough County Med. Assn., Fla. Med. Assn., Gulf Coast Multiple Sclerosis Soc. (med. adv. bd., chmn.), Nat. Multiple Sclerosis Soc. (med. adv. bd. 1988—, physicians adv. coun.), Fox Club, Hasty Pudding Inst. of 1776. Avocations: running, tennis, classical music, languages. E-mail: pdunne@coml.med.usf.edn. Home: 921 North Riverhills Dr Temple Terrace FL 33617 Office: Univ of South Fla Dept Neurology 12901 Bruce B Downs Blvd Tampa FL 33612

DUNNE, THOMAS, geology educator; b. Prestbury, U.K., Apr. 21, 1943; came to U.S., 1964; s. Thomas and Monica Mary (Whitter) D. BA with honors, Cambridge (Eng.) U., 1964; PhD, Johns Hopkins U., 1969. Research assoc. USDA-Agrl. Research Service, Danville, Vt., 1966-68; research hydrologist U.S. Geol. Survey, Washington, 1969; asst. prof. McGill U., Montreal, Que., Can., 1969-73; from asst. prof. to prof. U. Wash., Seattle, 1973-95, chmn. dept., 1984-89; prof. sch. environ. scis. & mgmt. U. Calif., Santa Barbara, 1995—; vis. prof. U. Nairobi, Kenya, 1969-71; cons. in field, 1970—. Author (with L.B. Leopold) Water in Environmental Planning; (with L.M. Reid) Rapid Evaluation of Sediment Budgets, 1996. Fulbright scholar 1984; grantee NSF, NASA, Rockefeller Found., 1969—; named to NAS, 1988, Guggenheim fellow, 1989-90. Fellow Am. Geophys. Union (Robert E. Horton award 1987), Am. Acad. Arts and Scis., Calif. Acad. Scis.; mem. AAAS, NAS (G.K. Warren prize in Fluviatile Geology 1998), Geol. Soc. Am., Sigma Xi. Office: U Calif Donald Bren Sch Environ Scis & Mgmt 4670 Physical Sciences N Santa Barbara CA 93106

DUNNEL, LESLIE B., conductor. Degree clarinet performance, U. Rochester, 1978; MA in Music Theory/Musicology, Queen's Coll., 1979; D of Musical Arts, U. Cin., 1982. Assoc. to asst. condr. Detroit Symphony Orch., 1987—; music dir. Symphony Nova Scotia, Dearborn Symphony Orch.; prin. condr. Harlem Festival Orch.; music dir. Detroit Symphony Civic Orch.; prin. guest condr. Dance Theatre of Harlem, N.Y.C.; guest condr. internat. tours including S.Am., Eng., Gala Performance for Diana, Princess of Wales, Scotland, Austria's Salzburg Festival, Denmark's Tivoli Festival, Soviet Union, South Africa, also Atlanta, Chgo, Cin., Dallas, Indpls., N.Mex., Pitts., San Diego, San Antonio, San Francisco, Canton, Colorado Springs, Columbus, Shreveport, Windsor Symphony Orch., Minn. and Louisville Orch., Denver and Ohio Chamber Orchs., N.Y.C. Ballet, Mich. Opera Theatre, State Ballet of Mo., South Africa's Opera, Ballet of the Performing Arts Transvaal, Symphony Orch. of Madrid, Lisbon, 1994, N.Y. Philharmonic, Royal Ballet in Covent Garden, London, Birmingham Royal Ballet, Cleve. Orch., Savannah Symphony, Nat. Symphony Orch. Johannesburg, Nat. Philharmonic, Camerata, St. Petersburg, 1997; bd. dirs. Am. Music Ctr., N.Y.C. Recipient Prize winner Arturo Toscanini Internat. Conducting Competition, 1986, First Man of Yr., Spirit of Detroit award Zeta Phi Beta, 1988, James Weldon Johnson award NAACP, 1991, Disting. Achievement award Detroit br. NAACP, 1992, Disting. Young Alumnus award U. Cin.; condr. Detroit Symphony Orch. in spl. performance for President Bill Clinton. Mem. Am. Soc. of Composers, Authors and Publishers. Office: Symphony Nova Scotia, Parklane Ste 301, Halifax, NS Canada B3J 3R4

DUNNELL, ROBERT CHESTER, archaeologist, educator; b. Wheeling, W.Va., Dec. 4, 1942; s. Arthur and Kathryn (McCarter) D.; m. Mary Jewett Davidson, June 4, 1966. BA, U. Ky., 1964; PhD (Woodrow Wilson fellow/Univ. fellow), Yale U., 1967. Asst. prof. anthropology U. Wash., Seattle, 1967-71; assoc. prof. U. Wash., 1971-74, prof., 1974-97; prof. emeritus, 1998—; chmn. dept. anthropology U. Wash., 1973-85; prin. investigator Nat. Park Service contracts, U.S. Army Corps Engrs. contracts; adj. curator N.Am. archaeology Burke Meml. Wash. State Mus., 1971-97; mem. sci. com. Wash. Archaeol. Research Center, 1975-79; adj. prof. Quaternary Research Center, 1976—; mem. coun. from Anthropology to Quaternary Rsch. Ctr. Adn. Coun., 1976-79; curatorial affiliate in anthropology Peabody Mus. Naturay History, Yale U., 1985—; mem. nat. adv. coun. Desert Rsch. Inst., 1987-89; adj. prof. U. Tenn., 1997—, Miss. State U., 1997—. Mem. editorial bd.: Advances in Archaeological Theory and Method, 1977-87, Studies in Archaeol. Method and Theory, 1987—, Jour. Field Archaeology, 1985—. Fellow AAAS; mem. Soc. for Am. Archaeology (rep. to sect. H exec. bd. of AAAS 1988-90), Assn. Field Archaeology (pres. 1985-88), Sigma Xi. Office: 21 Pruett Rd Natchez MS 39120-9427

DUNNER, DAVID LOUIS, medicine educator; b. Bklyn., May 27, 1940; s. Edward and Reichel (Connor) D.; m. Peggy Jane Zolbert, Dec. 27, 1964; children: Laura Louise, Jonathan Michael. AA, George Washington U., 1960; MD, Washington U., St. Louis, 1965. Diplomate Am. Bd. Psychiatry and Neurology. Intern Phila. Gen. Hosp., 1965-66; resident in psychiatry Barnes Renard Hosp. of Washington U., St. Louis, 1966-69; research psychiatrist N.Y. State Psychiat. Inst., N.Y.C., 1971-79; from asst. prof. to assoc. prof. clin. psychiatry Columbia U., N.Y.C., 1972-79; chief psychiatry Harborview Med. Ctr., Seattle, 1979-89, dir. outpatient psychiatry, 1989-97; prof. psychiatry and behavioral scis. U. Wash., Seattle, 1979—, vice chmn. clin. svcs., 1989-97; dir. Ctr. for Anxiety & Depression, 1997—; cons. Found. for Depression and Manic Depression, N.Y.C., 1974—. Editor-in-chief Comprehensive Psychiatry, 1997—; contbr. articles to profl. jours. Served to lt. comdr. USPHS, 1969-71. Fellow Am. Psychiat. Assn., Am. Psychopathol. Assn. (pres. 1986), Am. Coll. Neuropsychopharmacology, West Coast Coll. Biol. Psychiatry (charter, pres. 1987); mem. Psychiat. Research Soc. (pres. 1984). Office: Ctr for Anxiety and Depression Ste 306C 4225 Roosevelt Way NE Seattle WA 98105-6099

DUNNER, DONALD ROBERT, lawyer; b. Bklyn., 1931; s. Edward Dunner and Mollie Friedman; m. Jenny Sue Dailey, 1957; children: Jennifer D. Weaver, Lisa A. BSChemE, Purdue U., 1953; JD, Georgetown U., 1958. Bar: D.C. 1958, U.S. Supreme Ct. 1963, U.S. Ct. Appeals (fed. cir.) 1982. Patent examiner U.S. Patent & Trademark Office, Washington, 1955-56; law clk. U.S. Ct. Customs and Patent Appeals, Washington, 1956-58; assoc. Strauch, Nolan & Neale, Washington, 1958-60; assoc., ptnr. Diggins & Le Blanc, Washington, 1960-62; ptnr. Lane, Aitken, Dunner & Ziems, Washington, 1962-78; of counsel Finnegan, Henderson, Farabow & Garrett, Washington, 1978-79; ptnr. Finnegan, Henderson, Farabow, Garrett & Dunner, Washington, 1979—; mem. Pres. Adv. Com. on Indsl. Innovation, 1978-79; professorial lectr. in law George Washington Law Ctr., 1969-82; adj. prof. Washington Coll. of Law, Am. U., 1992—. Co-author: Patent Law Perspectives, 1970-89, Court Review of Patent Office Decisions: CCPA, 1973, Court of Appeals for the Federal Circuit: Practice and Procedure, 1985. Chmn. Fed. Cir. Adv. Com., 1982-92; mem. adv. commn. on Patent Law Reform, 1991-92. With U.S. Army, 1953-55. Recipient Best Article of Yr. award Patent Office Soc., 1980, award Patent Resources Group, 1980. Fellow Am. Coll. Trial Lawyers; mem. ABA (chair intellectual property law sect. 1995-96), Am. Intellectual Property Law Assn. (pres. 1979-80), D.C. Bar Assn. (chmn. patent, trademark and copyright law sect. 1964-65), D.C. Bar (chair patent, trademark and copyright law sect. 1976-77), Fed. Cir. Bar Assn. (bd. dirs. 1999—), Am. Inn of Ct. (pres. Giles S. Rich Inn 1994-95), Cosmos Club. Avocations: tennis, skiing, sailing. Office: Finnegan Henderson Farabow 1300 I St NW Washington DC 20005-3315

DUNNETT, DENNIS GEORGE, state official; b. Auburn, Calif., Aug. 5, 1939; s. George DeHaven and Elizabeth Grace (Sullivan) D. AA in Elec. Engring., Sierra Coll., 1959; AB in Econs., Sacramento State Coll., 1966. Engring. technician State of Calif., Marysville, 1961-62; data processing technician State of Calif., Sacramento, 1962-67, EDP programmer and analyst, 1967-74, staff services mgr. and contract adminstr., 1974-76, hardware acquisition mgr., 1976-86, support services br. mgr., information security officer, 1986-90, chief Office Security and Operational Recovery, 1990-92, spl. projects mgr., 1992-93, customer support ctr. mgr., 1994, procurement mgr., 1994-97, chief bur. adminstrn., 1997—. Mem. AARP, IEEE Computer Soc., Assn. Info. Tech. Profls., Assn. Inst. Cert. of Computers Profls. (certs.), Calif. Assn. Mgrs. and Suprs., Fine Arts Mus. of San Francisco, Crocker Art Mus. Home: 729 Blackmer Cir Sacramento CA 95825-4704 Office: Teale Data Ctr 2005 Evergreen St Sacramento CA 95815-3831

DUNNIGAN, BRIAN LEIGH, military historian, curator; b. Detroit, July 11, 1949; s. James Patrick and Dorothy Jane (McKay) D.; m. Carol Lynn Fredriksen, Sept. 21, 1974 (div. Oct. 1988); m. Candice Maria Cain, Apr. 22, 1989; children: James Cain, Claire Beausom. BA in History, U. Mich., 1971, MA in History, 1973; MA in History and Museum Studies, Cooperstown Grad. Programs, 1979. Curator Mackinac Island (Mich.) State Park Commn., 1971-74; mng. dir. Historic Fort Wayne, Ind., 1974-79; exec. dir. Old Fort Niagara Assn., Youngstown, N.Y., 1979-96; curator of maps William L. Clements Libr. U. Mich., Ann Arbor, 1996—. Author: History and Guide to Old Fort Niagara, 1985, Siege-1759, 1986, rev. edit., 1996, Glorious Old Relic, 1987, Forts Within A Fort, 1989, Old Fort Niagara in Four Centuries, 1991; editor: Pouchot's Memoirs on the Late War in North America, 1994, Niagara, 1796, 1996. Fellow Co. Mil. Historians. Home: 402 W Chicago Blvd Tecumseh MI 49286-1308 Office: William L Clements Libr 909 S University Ave Ann Arbor MI 48109-1190

DUNNIGAN, MARY ANN, former educational administrator; b. St. Maries, Idaho, Sept. 7, 1915; d. William Henry and Mary Ellen (Kelly) D.; BA, Holy Names Coll., Spokane, 1942; MA, Gonzaga U., Spokane, 1957; postgrad. U. Idaho, UCLA. Tchr. rural schs. Bonner County, 1936-41, elem. schs., 1941, 45-59, high sch., 1942, 45, coordinator elem. edn., 1959-78; prin. kindergarten Sch. Dist. 271, Coeur d'Alene, Idaho, 1978-81; tchr. extension classes U. Idaho; curriculum chmn. Gov.'s Conf. on Edn.; adv. council Head Start. Mem. adv. coun. Coun. for Aging; mem. N. Idaho Mus., Community Council, Community Concerts, Community Theater, N. Idaho Booster Club, Mayor's Com. on Handicapped; mem. task force and diocesan bd. Cath. Edn. of Idaho, 1969-74; mem. Coeur d'Alene U.S. Constn. Bicentennial Com., 1986-91. Bd. dirs. Coeur d'Alene Tchrs. Credit Union, 1958-87, pres., treas., 1976-89; hist. chmn. Coeur d'Alene Centennial, 1986-89, chmn. hist. com., 1988, mem. state centennial com. for Koetenai county, 1990; parliamentarian Idaho Coun. Catholic Women State Conv., 1993, Idaho Cath. Daus. of Am. State Conv., 1994, sterring com. New Holy Famliy Cath. Sch. in Koatenai County Idaho, 1994, Parliomentation fo Idaho Coun. of Cath. Women, 1992. Named Citizen of Yr. N. Idaho Coll., 1974, Idaho Cath. Dau. of Year, 1968, Educator of Yr. Koatenai County Women's Forum, 1998; named to Idaho Retired Tchr.'s Hall of Fame, 1987; recipient Hon. Alumnus award N. Idaho Coll., 1987, Nat. Community Svc. award AARP/NRTA, 1989. Mem. Idaho Edn. Assn., NEA, Idaho Ret. Tchrs. Assn. (state chmn. pre-retirement 1985-92), Kootenai County Ret. Tchrs. Assn. (pres. 1983-87), Delta Kappa Gamma (charter, past pres Zeta chpt 1947-92; recipient Silver Bell award for 50 years, 1997). Club: Cath. Daus. Am. (state regent 1956-62, recipient 50 Year Pin, 1997). Home: 720 N 9th St Coeur D Alene ID 83814-4259

DUNNIGAN, T. KEVIN, electrical and electronics manufacturing company executive; b. Montreal, Que., Can., Jan. 31, 1938; s. John George and Olive Mary (Brophy) D.; m. Beverley Alice Laramee, Apr. 11, 1960 (div. June 1980); children: David, Kathleen; m. Leah Anne Merlo. BA in Commerce, Loyola U., 1971. With Can. Elec. Distbg. Co., prior to 1962; salesman No. Telecom, Montreal, 1956-60; purchasing agt. Black-MacDonald, Montreal, 1960-62; salesman Thomas & Betts Corp., Iberville, Que., 1962-67, v.p. sales, 1967-70, pres., 1970-73; div. pres. Thomas & Betts Corp., Bridgewater, N.J., 1974-78, corp. exec. v.p. electronics, 1978-80, pres., 1980—, chief oper. officer, 1980-85, chief exec. officer, 1985-97, chmn. bd., 1992—; bd. dirs. C.R. Bard Inc. Office: Thomas & Betts Corp 8155 T&B Blvd Memphis TN 38125

DUNNING, DAVID MICHAEL, history educator; b. Buffalo, Feb. 18, 1945; s. Francis S. and Marion P. Dunning; m. Judith A. Dunning. BA, Occidental Coll., 1966; PhD, U. Ill., 1995. Instr. Honolulu (Hawaii) C.C., 1988-91; assoc. faculty Seattle Ctrl. C.C., 1991-93, Mohave C.C., Lake Hausu City, Ariz., 1993-96, West Shore C.C., Ludington, Mich., 1996-97, Grand Valley State U., Allendale, Mich., 1997; asst. prof. history U. Alaska Southeast, Ketchikan, Alaska, 1997—. Adv. bd. Tongass Hist. Mus., Ketchikan, 1998—; bd. dirs. Ketchikan Hist. Com., 1998—; bd. dirs., treas. Hist. Ketchikan, 1998—; apptd. mem. Kaneohe Bay Task Force, Kaneohe, 1990-91; del., platform com. Dem. Party State Conv., Honolulu, 1990; dist. 3 rep., vice chair Kahuluu Neighbor Bd. #29, Kahaluu, 1987-91. Wilson grantee U. Alaska S.E., 1998, Ketchikan Centennial Planning grantee Alaska Humanities Forum, 1998; postdoctoral fellowship Lilly Found., 1996. Mem. Tongass Hist. Soc. (v.p. 1999—), Mining History Assn., Gastineau Channel Hist. Soc., Alaska History Soc., Am. Hist. Assn. Home: 1715 Second Ave #1 Ketchikan AK 99901 Office: U Alaska SE 2600 7th Ave Ketchikan AK 99901

DUNNING, DEBBE, actress; b. Burbank, Calif., July 11, 1966. Actress in films including: Dangerous Curves, 1988, The Misery Brothers, 1995, Leprechaun 4: In Space, 1996; actress in TV series Home Improvement, 1993—; TV guest appearances include: Baywatch, 1989, Who's the Boss?, 1984, Married...with Children, 1987, Vinnie & Bobby, 1992, Silk Stalkings, 1991, Tales from the Crypt, 1989, Burke's Law, 1994, American Gladiators, 1989, Boy Meets World, 1993. Office: Wind Dancer Prodn Group Prodn Bldg 3rd Flr 500 S Buena Vista Burbank CA 91521-2215*

DUNNING, JOHN, university volleyball coach; m. Julie Chiappe, Nov. 6, 1950; children: Lisa, Lauren. BA in Math. and Econs., San Deigo State U., 1973. Volleyball, tchr. Fremont H.S., 1973-84; head volleyball coach U. of the Pacific, Stockton, Calif., 1986—; coach North squad U.S. Olympic Festival, 1995; NCAA divsn. I rep. to AVCA bd. dirs., mem. divsn. I All-Am. selection com. Named Nat Coach of Yr. Volleyball Monthly, 1985, Prep Coach of Yr. Calif. Coaches Assn., 1980. Mem. Am. Volleyball Coaches Assn. (pres. 1993-94),. Office: Univ of the Pacific Dept Athletics 3601 Pacific Ave Stockton CA 95211-0197

DUNNING, KENNETH OWEN, mental health counselor; b. Portland, Oreg., June 26, 1950; s. David Dale and Ellen Natalie (Ecklund) D.; m. Virginia Evens, Dec. 10, 1970 (div. 1977); m. Yang Ja Ju, Dec. 10, 1979 (div. July 1987); 1 child, David Kee-Young Samuel; m. Riitta Hannele Ylinen, Dec. 12, 1988; children: Hanna Emilia, Tomas Mikael. Assoc. Gen. Studies, Centralia (Wash.) C.C., 1976; BA, Eastern Wash. State Coll., Cheney, 1977; MS, Western Oreg. State Coll., Monmouth, 1989. Cert. mental health counselor, Wash.; nat. cert counselor. Counselor J Bar D Boy's Ranch, Ione, Wash., 1983-84; child care worker Secret Harbor Sch., Anacortes, Wash., 1988-90; therapist Skagit Mental Health, Mt. Vernon, Wash., 1989-95; team leader Cath. Cmty. Svcs., Bellingham, Wash., 1995-96; pvt. practice Mt. Vernon, Wash., 1995—; mem. adv. bd. Fetal Alcohol Syndrome Family Resource Inst., Lynnwood, Wash., 1993—. Collaborator: (directory) Residential Child Care in America, 1990. Named Very Important Prevention Person, Skagit County Substance Abuse Coalition, 1995. Mem. ACA. Avocation: music.

DUNNING, STEPHEN (ARTHUR S. DUNNING, JR.), writer, consultant, retired English educator; b. Duluth, Minn., Oct. 31, 1924; s. Arthur Stephenson and Julia (Hunter) D.; m. Florence Jane Danielson, Sept. 2, 1950; children: Steven, Elizabeth, Julia, Sarah. BA, Carleton Coll., 1949; MA, U. Minn., 1951; PhD, Fla. State U., 1959. Tchr. English high schs., St. Paul, Los Alamos, N.Mex., Tallahassee, 1951-59; asst. prof. Duke U., Durham, N.C., 1959-62; assoc. prof. Northwestern U., Evanston, Ill., 1962-64; assoc. prof., then prof. U. Mich., Ann Arbor, 1964-87; writer, cons., 1987—; James Hill disting. vis. prof. U. Minn., 1991; vis. prof. Columbia U., N.Y.C., 1996-97; condr. workshops in 48 states, 1965—. Author: (poetry) Good Words, 1991, (fiction) Hunter's Park, 1996, (with William Stafford) Getting the Knack, 1992; co-editor: (poetry collection) Reflections on a Gift of Watermelon Pickle..., 1995. With AC, U.S. Army, 1943-45. Recipient Alumni Achievement award Carleton Coll., 1978; recipient James B. Hall fiction award, 1986, World's Best Short Short Story award, 1990, syndicated fiction awards NEA, 1986-91; high sch. tchr. fellow Ford Found., N.Mex., Calif., 1952-53; creative artist grantee Mich. Coun. for Arts, 1983, 89, 93. Mem. Conf. on English and Edn. (nat. chmn. 1970-72), Nat. Coun. Tchrs. English (pres. 1974-75), Mich. Coun. Tchrs. English (pres. 1968-69), Charles C. Fries award 1979). E-mail: dunnings@umich.edu. Home: 517 Oswego St Ann Arbor MI 48104

DUNNING, STEVEN, painter; b. Herkimer, N.Y., Aug. 13, 1957; s. Francis R. and Angela (Cushman) D. BA, SUNY, Oneonta, 1989; MFA, U. Cin., 1992. Painting and video exhbns. include Artcite, Windsor, Ont., Can., 19916, Paint Creek Ctr. for the Arts, Rochester, Mich., 1996, TW Wood Gallery and Arts Ctr., Montpelier, Vt., 1996, The Collective Ctr. for the Arts, Jackson, Mich., 1995, Pyramid Arts Ctr., Rochester, 1995, Sage Jr. Coll., Albany, N.Y., 1994, Upper Catskill Cmty. Coun. of the Arts, Oneonta, N.Y., 1994, U. Vt., Burlington, 1994, Castleton State Coll., Vt., 1994, N. BIAS Gallery, Bennington, Vt., 1993, Kent State U., Ohio, 1993; Elvis and Marilyn exhbns. include Tenn. State Mus., Nashville, 1996, Columbus Mus. of Art, Ohio, 1996, Philbrook Mus. of Art, Tulsa, 1996, Portland Mus. of Art, 1996, others; group shows include: In Situ Gallery, Cin., 1993, Semantics Gallery, Cin., 1992, SUNY, Oneonta, 1992, N.E. Mo. State U., Kirksville, 1996, Lulu Gallery, Albany, N.Y., 1995, Austin Peay State U., Clarksville, Tenn., 1994, others; work collected in The DeCordova Mus. Corp. Program, Lincoln, Mass., Dennis Barrie, Cleve., Nicholas Chaparos, Cin., others. Recipient scholarship U. Cin., 1990-92, SUNY Oneonta, 1988; grantee SUNY Rsch. Found., 1988. Home: 5777 Main St Manchester Center VT 05255

DUNNING, THOM H., JR., environmental molecular science executive. BS in Chemistry, U. Mo., Rolla, 1965; PhD in Chem. Physics, Calif. Inst. Tech., 1970. Rsch. fellow, instr. Calif. Inst. Tech.; staff mem. Los Alamos Nat. Lab., 1973-78; sr. scientist Argonne Nat. Lab., 1978-89, group leader theoretical and computational chemistry group, 1978-89, head chem. dynamics program, 1978-89; assoc. dir. for theory, modeling and stimulation Pacific Northwest Nat. Lab., 1989-94, dir. Environ. Molecular Scis. Lab., 1994—; mem. chemistry adv. com. NSF; mem. exec. com. Energy Rsch. Supercomputer Users Group; mem. policy bd. Concurrent Supercomputing Consortium; mem. CRF adv. com. Sandia Nat. Lab., DOE's Coun. on Chem. Scis., NRC's Chem. Scis. Roundtable; affiliate prof. U. Wash., 1990—; adj. prof. Wash. State U., 1990—. Series editor Advances in Molecular Electronic Structure, 1987—; topical editor Computer Physics Comm.; contbr. articles to profl. jours. Recipient E.O. Lawrence award DOE, 1996, Ernest Orlando Lawrence Meml. award, 1996; Woodrow Wilson fellow, 1965-66, NSF fellow, 1966-69, postdoctoral fellow Battelle Meml. Inst., 1970. Fellow AAAS, Am. Phys. Soc.; mem. Am. Chem. Soc. Office: Battelle Pacific NW Labs Environ Molecular Scis Lab Richland WA 99352*

DUNNING, THOMAS E., newspaper editor; b. Lamasco, Ky., Nov. 2, 1944; s. Floyd Bowman and Tylene Elizabeth (Garrett) D.; m. Judy Davis, Feb. 28, 1981; children: Thomas Matthew, William Davis. BA, U. Evansville, 1967. Sportwriter Evansville (Ind.) Press, 1962-67; city editor The Evansville Courier, 1970-76; Sunday editor The Knoxville (Tenn.) News-Sentinal, 1976-77; asst. mng. editor The Cin. Post, 1977-81, mng. editor, 1981-85; asst. mng. editor Scripps Howard News Svc., 1985-87; dep. mng. editor news Cin. Enquirer, 1987-90, mng. editor, 1990-93, night mng. editor, 1993-95; mng. editor Boston Bus. Jour., 1996-97; news editor The Patroit Ledger, Quincy, Mass., 1997—. Bd. dirs. The Mental Health Assn., Cin., 1982, Leadership Cin., 1982-84; trustee Family Svcs. Cin. With USCG, 1967-70. Mem. AP Mng. Editors, Am. Soc. Newspaper Editors, Soc. Profl. Journalists, Nat. Press Club. Episcopalian. Office: The Quincy Patriot Ledger 400 Crown Colony Dr PO Box 9159 Quincy MA 02269-9159

DUNPHY, EDWARD JAMES, crop science extension specialist; b. Frederick, Md., Nov. 14, 1940; s. Edward John and Marie W. (Barlow) D.; m. Judith Kay Mitchell, Aug. 18, 1962; children: Kevin James, Brian Patrick, Cory Edward. MS, U. Ill., 1964; PhD, Iowa State U., 1972. Rsch. asst. U. Ill., Urbana, 1962-64; agronomist Dunphy's Feed & Fertilizer, Sullivan, Ill., 1964-66; rsch. asst. Iowa State U., Ames, 1969-72; crop prodn. specialist Iowa State U., Des Moines, 1972-75; extension specialist soybeans N.C. State U., Raleigh, 1975—, prof. crop sci., 1986—; instr. soybean prodn. N.C., 1975—; mem. N.C. Land Use Value Adv. Bd., Raleigh, 1987—. Author 4 computer programs; contbr. numerous articles to profl. jours. Cubmaster Boy Scouts Am., Raleigh, 1976-81, troop com. chair, 1979-98; officer Athens Dr. Band Boosters, Raleigh, 1983-90. Sgt. U.S. Army, 1966-69. Recipient Meritorious Svc. award N.C. Soybean Producers. Mem. Am. Soc. Agronomy (com. chair, fellow), Crop and Soil Sci. Socs. Am., Am. Soybean Assn. (mem. S.Am. soybean mission), Coun. for Agrl. Sci. and Tech., Alpha Zeta, Epsilon Sigma Phi, Gamma Sigma Delta, Phi Eta Sigma, Phi Kappa Phi, Sigma Xi. Achievements include rsch. on soybean varieties, production, management and economics. Home: 1329 Swallow Dr Raleigh NC 27606-2414 Office: NC State U Box 7620 Raleigh NC 27695

DUNPHY, JERRY RAYMOND, television news anchor, lyric writer; b. Milw., June 9, 1921; s. Raymond Huston and Hazel Lillian (Lusty) D.; m. Mary Gertrude Dunphy, Jan. 28, 1944 (div. Sept. 1978); children: Jerry Raymond, Karen, Linda, Thomas, Megan; m. Michelle Stride, June 23, 1979 (div. 1982); m. Sandra Joann Dunphy, Jan. 27, 1985; 1 child, Erin. BA in Journalism, U. Wis., 1948; postgrad., Northwestern U., 1948. Sportscaster WHA Radio, Madison, Wis., 1947-48; announcer, newscaster WIBU/WCCF-FM Radio, Madison, 1948; announcer, newscaster, sales KOAT Radio, Albuquerque, 1948; news dir., reporter KSTT Radio, Davenport, Iowa, 1948-50, gen. mgr., 1952-53; news dir., reporter WTVH-TV, Peoria, Ill., 1953-54, KEDD-TV, Wichita, 1954-55; news dir. WXIX-TV, Milw., 1955-57; staff announcer, sportscaster, newscaster WBBM-TV, Chgo., 1957-60; news anchor, reporter KNXT-TV, L.A., 1960-75, KABC-TV, L.A., 1975-89, KCAL-TV-Disney, L.A., 1989-94, KCBS-TV, L.A., 1994-97, KCAL-TV, L.A., 1997—. Writer lyrics for songs Cowboy's Christmas, 1991, Saturday Night Special, 1992, From the Desert to the Sea, 1993, others. Mem., chief Vikings Charities/Muscular Dystrophy, 1966—; mem. Marine Toys for Tots, 1970s-80s. Capt. USAF, 1942-45, Guam. Decorated D.F.C., Air medal with clusters; recipient 11 Golden Mike awards, 1961-93, 6 Emmy awards, Golden Bell award Portals House, 1973; honoree City of Hope, L.A., 1996. Mem. AFTRA, SAG, L.A. Press Club (pres.). Roman Catholic. Home: 23364 Park Colombo Calabasas CA 91302

DUNPHY, MAUREEN ANN, educator; b. Springfield, Mass., Feb. 25, 1949; d. Donald J. and Mary C. (Tabb) Milbier; m. Terrence Michael Dunphy. BS in Edn., Westfield State Coll., 1971, MEd, 1975, Cert. Advanced Grad. Study, 1988; cert. paralegal, 1996. Tchr. Thornton Burgess Intermediate Sch., Hampden, Mass., 1971-75; reading specialist, reading dept. head West Springfield Jr. High Sch., 1975—; acting asst. prin. W. Springfield Jr. High Sch., 1989; cons. Nat. Evaluations Systems, Amherst, Mass. Mem. Long Range Bldg. Needs Com., Westfield, 1986-87. Mem. Pioneer Valley Reading Coun. (pres. 1977-79), Mass. Reading Assn. (dir. 1977-81), West Springfield Edn. Assn. (negotiations sec.), Mass. Tchrs. Assn., Hampden County Tchrs. Assn. Home: 282 Steiger Dr Westfield MA 01085-4934 Office: West Springfield Middle Sch 32 Middle School Dr West Springfield MA 01089-2724

DUNSIRE, P(ETER) KENNETH, insurance company executive; b. Spearhill, Man., Can., Mar. 1, 1932; came to U.S., 1969; s. Robert Anderson and Margaret (Kinnear) D.; m. Lily Martha Bell (div. Nov. 1971); children: Robert K., Barbara L. Dunsire Belanger; m. Stephanie Alice Mooradian. Student, U. B.C., Can., 1949-50, U. Alta., Can., 1955-56. V.p. Avco Fin. Services, Newport Beach, Calif., 1961-71; exec. v.p. Carte Blanche, Los Angeles, 1971-74, pres., 1974-78; chmn. Am. Benefit Plan Adminstrn., Los Angeles, 1978-80; exec. v.p. Paul Revere Life Ins. Co., Worcester, Mass., 1980-84; exec. v.p. Lincoln Nat. Life Ins. Co., Ft. Wayne, Ind., 1984-86, also bd. dirs.; exec. v.p. Lincoln Nat. Corp., Ft. Wayne, Ind., 1986-95, ret., 1995; bd. dirs. Ft. Wayne Med. Soc. Found., Ft. Wayne C. of C. Found., Nat. Auto & Truck Mus.; chmn. Cannon Lincoln Plc., London, 1984-90, chmn. bd., 1992-95. Chmn. bd. Sta. WFWA-TV, Ft. Wayne, 1985-91, Auburn Cord Duesenberg Mus., Ind., 1986—, Ft. Wayne Civic Theater, 1985-86. Mem. Ft. Wayne C. of C. (vice-chmn. 1989-91, chmn. 1991-92). Republican. Avocation: automobile collecting. Home: 8140 Auburn Rd Fort Wayne IN 46825-3016 also: 24906 Danamaple Dana Point CA 92629-1148

DUNSKY, MENAHEM, retired advertising agency executive, communications consultant, painter; b. Montreal, Que., Can., July 5, 1930; s. Shimson D. and Esther Dunsky; children: Ron Abraham, Ilan Isaac, Dan David Gil. Teaching diploma, Jewish Tchrs. Sem., Montreal, 1948; B.A., Concordia U., Montreal, 1952; M.A., NYU, 1954; diploma, Parsons Sch. Design, 1956. Tchr. Jewish People's Schs., Montreal, 1948-52; asst. art dir. L.W. Frohlich Advt., N.Y.C., 1956-58; creative dir. Gordon, Lewinson Advt., Tel Aviv, 1958-59; lectr. art history Saidye Bronfman Cultural Centre, Montreal, 1960-63; founder, pres. Dunsky Advt. Ltd., Westmount, Que., Can., 1960-87; cons. Govt. of Man., Winnipeg, 1970-77, Govt. of Sask., Regina, 1971-82, Govt. of B.C., Victoria, 1972-75; panelist pub. symposium Politics and the Media, 1980. Published Jewish Iconography, 1961; paintings exhibited at Jewish Pub. Libr., Montreal, 1962. Chmn. bd. Saidye Bronfman Cultural Centre, 1969-70; officer Jewish People's Sch. System, Montreal, 1982-85; chmn. edn. com. Bialik High Sch., Montreal, 1981-85, chmn. personnel com., 1983-85; exec. mem. YM/YWHA, Montreal, 1969-71; chmn. nat. edn. com. Can. Zionist Fedn., 1984-88; mem. nat. exec. com., 1985-88; bd. dirs. Jewish Edn. Coun., 1986-88; chmn. pub. rels. com. Can. Ben Gurion Centennial Celebration, 1986-87. Mem. Trans Can. Advt. Agy. Network-Toronto (founding mem.), Trans. Can. Advt. Agy. Network-Toronto (bd. dir. 1962-87), Trans Can. Advt. Agy. Network-Toronto (pres. 1965), Inst. Can. Advt.-Toronto (dir. 1972-75), Inst. Can. Advt. (chmn. profl. com. 1974-75), Advt. Agy. Coun. Que. (founding mem., exec. com. 1969-75). Jewish. Home: 406 Chemin Du Lac des Chats, Saint Sauveur, PQ Canada J0R 1R1 *The extent to which one manages to meld the pursuit of one's career interests with considerations of a broader social and cultural nature has always served me as a principal concern. As well, I have kept career considerations from diminishing the time and quality of attention which family and self deserve and require.*

DUNSON, DIANE ELAINE, elementary education educator, computer specialist; b. Gadsden, Ala., Jan. 3, 1944; d. William Edward and Adele Helen (Plasman) Frantz; m. Palmer Wayne Dunson, Dec. 18, 1998. BS, Jacksonville (Ala.) State U., 1965; MEd, Ga. State U., 1972; cert. 6th yr. specialist in adminstrn., Troy State U., 1996. Cert. adminstr., supr., tchr. math, Ala., Ga. Actuarial clk. Life Ins. Co. Ala., Gadsden, 1965-66; tchr. Trinity Pvt. Sch., Columbus, Ga., 1968-69, Phenix City (Ala.) Sch. Sys., 1969-71; tchr. mid. grades Post Dependent Schs., Ft. Benning, Ga., 1970-82, chair dept. math., 1973-85, coord. curriculum, 1980-84, instr. staff devel., 1985—, tchr. math. grade 7, 1991-96, tchr. math. grade 8, 1996—, edn. technologist, 1997—; chairperson negotiation contract com. Post Dependent Schs., Ft. Benning, Ga., 1993—, mediation trainer, 1994, mem. salary negotiations team, 1993—, faculty rep., 1992—; owner computer bus., 1984-85; active Tchr. in Space Program NASA, 1985; sch. sys. rep. to survey Rand Corp., 1987; pres. Fla. Instrnl. Computing Conf. for Computer Using Educators, 1988, North Cook Ednl. Svc. Ctr., St. Charles, Ill., 1990, Ga. Tech. Conf., Columbus; liaison Nat. Coun. Tchrs. Math. and Chattahoochee Coun. Tchrs. Math., 1996; mem. joint stds. com. Dept. Def. Edn. Activity, 1998—. Contbr. to curriculum guide, 1969, vignette to text book. Sec. PTA, 1979-80, Columbus Cmty. Concerts, 1983; usher Springer Theater, Columbus, 1984. Mem. ASCD, NEA (del. 1998—), Nat. Coun. Tchrs. Math. (guest spkr. 1979, 70, contact person 1996), Profl. Assn. Ga. Educators, Ga. Coun. Tchrs. of Math., Benning Edn. Assn. (sec. 1973-77, v.p. 1992—), Fed. Edn. Assn. Methodist. Avocations: bridge, travel, shopping. Home: 4151 Anglin Rd Apt 19A Columbus GA 31907-8144

DUNST, KIRSTEN, actress; b. Point Pleasant, NJ, Apr. 30, 1982; d. Klaus and Inez Dunst. Appeared in films Bonfire of the Vanities, 1990, High Strung, 1991, Greedy, 1994, Interview with the Vanpire, 1994, Little Women, 1994, Jumanji, 1995; appeared on TV in Storytime, 1994, Darkness before Dawn, 1993, Saturday Night Live, others. Recipient Golden Globe Award nomination for best supporting actres, 1995. Office: care Iris Burton Agy PO Box 15306 Beverly Hills CA 90209-1306

DUNST, LAURENCE DAVID, advertising executive; b. N.Y.C., Feb. 21, 1941; s. Philip R. and Mae (Fruchthendler) D.; m. Diane Gordon, Dec. 22, 1962; children: Lee Gordon, Melissa Susan. B.A., Syracuse U., 1961. Advt. copywriter R.H. Macy & Co., 1961-63; with Daniel & Charles, N.Y.C., from 1963; pres. Laurence, Charles, Free & Lawson, Inc., N.Y.C., 1969-86, chmn., 1986-91, pres., CEO, 1991-95; chmn, CEO Gotham Inc., N.Y.C., 1995—. Mem. Young Pres.'s Orgn. Home: 1172 Park Ave New York NY 10128-1216 Office: Gotham Inc 100 5th Ave New York NY 10011-6903*

DUNSTAN, LARRY KENNETH, insurance company executive; b. Payson, Utah, May 26, 1948; s. Kenneth Leroy Dunstan and Verna Matilda (Carter) Taylor; m. Betty K. Limb, Sept. 23, 1966 (div. June 1975); children: Tamara, Thane; m. Jacqueline Lee Darron, Oct. 7, 1975; children: Tessa, Matthew, Bennett, Spencer, Adam. CLU, CPCU, chartered fin. cons., registered health underwriter, life underwriter tng. council fellow. Mgr. Diamond Bar Inn Ranch, Jackson, Mont., 1972-73; agt. Prudential Ins. Co., Missoula, Mont., 1973-77; devel. mgr. Prudential Ins. Co., Billings, Mont., 1977-78; div. mgr. Prudential Ins. Co., Gt. Falls, Mont., 1978-83; pres. Multi-Tech Ins. Services, Inc., West Linn, Oreg., 1983—; agy. mgr. Beneficial Life Ins. Co., Portland, Oreg., 1983-88. Mem. planning commn. City of West Linn, Oreg., 1985-87; mem. bishopric Ch. Jesus Christ of Latter Day Sts., West Linn, 1984-86, exec. sec. Lake Oswego Oreg. Stake, 1987-89; scouting coord. Boy Scouts Am., West Linn, 1984-86, scoutmaster various troops; pres. West Linn Youth Basketball Assn., 1991-97, West Linn/Wilsonville Youth Track Club, 1993-96. Named Eagle Scout Boy Scouts Am., 1965, recipient Heroism award 1965. Fellow Life Underwriter Tng. Coun. (bd. dirs. local chpt. 1980-81); mem. Gen. Agts. and Mgrs. Assn. (bd. dirs. local chpt. 1981-82), Am. Soc. CLU (pres. local chpt. 1982-83). Republican. Avocations: sports, stamp collecting, hunting, gardening, photography. Home: 19443 Wilderness Dr West Linn OR 97068-2005 Office: Multi-Tech Ins Svcs 19125 Willamette Dr West Linn OR 97068-2019

DUNSTON, LEIGH EVERETT, lawyer; b. N.Y.C., Mar. 12, 1944; s. George Everett and Florence (Lamb) D.; m. Pamela Tomlinson, July 3, 1972. BS, St. Joseph's U., Phila., 1966; JD, Georgetown U., Washington, 1970; LLD, Northwood Inst., West Palm Beach, Fla., 1991. Bar: Fla. 1970, U.S. Ct. Appeals (5th and 11th cirs.) 1981, U.S. Dist. Ct. (so. dist.) Fla. 1982, U.S. Dist. Ct. (mid. dist.) Fla. 1987, Fla. Supreme Ct. 1971. In-house counsel John D. MacArthur, West Palm Beach, Fla., 1970-72; assoc. Gunster, Yoakley & Stewart, West Palm Beach, 1972-77, ptnr., 1977—; chmn. Jud. Nominating Com., Palm Beach County, 1982, Jud. Recruiting Com., Palm Beach County, 1984-85. Contbr. articles to profl. jours. Bd. dirs., past chmn. Econ. Coun. Palm Beach County; bd. dirs. W. Palm Beach, 1990—; chmn. bd. dirs. Fla. Atlantic U. Found., Boca Raton, 1990—; bd. trustees, bd. govs. Northwood U., W. Palm Beach. Mem. ABA, Assn. Trial Lawyers Am., Am. Inns of Ct. LIV (master of bench 1988—), Fla. Bar, Acad. Fla. Trial Lawyers, Palm Beach County Bar Assn. Avocations: running, hiking, reading, travel. Office: 777 S Flagler Dr Ste 500E West Palm Beach FL 33401-6194*

DUNSTON, SHAWON DONNELL, professional baseball player; b. Bklyn., Mar. 21, 1963. Grad. high sch., N.Y.C. Shortstop Chgo. Cubs, 1985-97, Pitts. Pirates, 1997, Cleve. Indians, 1998-99; outfield St. Louis Cardinals, 1999—. Named to Nat. League All-Star Team, 1988, 90, "The Sporting News" Nat. League All-Star Team, 1989. Achievements include Nat. League East Divsn. Champions, 1989. Office: St Louis Cardinals Busch Stadium 250 Stadium Plz Saint Louis MO 63102*

DUNTEMAN, GEORGE HENRY, psychologist; b. Little Falls, N.Y., Sept. 10, 1935; s. George Henry and Bertha Ernestine (Bollman) D.; m. Rosarie Ann Brandfino, Apr. 20, 1963; children: George Eric, Elizabeth Ann. BA, St. Lawrence U., 1957; MS, Iowa State U., 1959; Ph.D., La. State U., 1962. Grad. research asst. La. State U., Baton Rouge, 1959-62; asst. prof. U. Rochester Coll. Bus. Adminstrn., N.Y., 1962-63; research psychologist U.S. Army Personnel Research Office, Washington, 1963-64; assoc. prof. U. Fla., Gainesville, 1964-67; research project dir. Ednl. Testing Service, Princeton, N.J., 1967-69; chief scientist Research Triangle Inst., Research Triangle Park, N.C., 1969—; vis. prof. mgmt. Babcock Sch. Mgmt., Wake Forest U., 1987-88. Author: Introduction to Linear Models, 1984, Introduction to Multivariate Analysis, 1984, Principal Components Analysis, 1989; author, contbg. author numerous presentations, articles to profl. jours., policy reports to govt. agys. Recipient Profl. Devel. award Research Triangle Inst., 1977. Mem. Sigma Xi, Psi Chi, Sigma Alpha Epsilon. Home: 332 Wesley Dr Chapel Hill NC 27516-1523 Office: Rsch Triangle Inst PO Box 12194 Rtp NC 27709-2194

DUNTLEY, LINDA KATHLEEN DAY, network executive, artist, educator, author, educator, researcher; b. Corona, Calif., Aug. 5, 1955; d. Donald Elmes and Leah Doris (Staudte) Day; m. Mark Andrew Duntley Jr., June 1978 (div. Dec. 1986). BA, San Francisco U., 1980, MA in Home Econs., 1982. cert. tchr., Calif. Regional supervising mgr. Western Empire, Seattle, 1973-76; artist Wash., Calif., 1973—; model/talent/art judge Calif., 1978—; substitute tchr. Marin County Pub. Schs., Calif., 1980-82; doctor of dress, color doctor Profl. Image Color, 1982—; corp. instr. BFAS, 1983-88; TV speaker Public TV, Santa Barbara, Calif., 1990; documentary movie speaker Faces in the Fire, Santa Barbara, Calif., 1991; pres., network exec. Profl. Image Color, Santa Barbara, Calif., 1982—; orgn. facilitator, image enhancer color and dress ann. conv. Assn. Coll. Profs. Clothing and Textiles, 1982—; juror Marin Soc. of Artists, Kent, Calif., 1979-82; dir., organizer Animal/Life Enhancement Resource Kingdom; crown exec. Infinity Internat. Author, rschr., pub.: (book) Color of Dress as it Relates to First Impressions of Personality Traits, 1982—; spkr. (documentary) Faces in the Fire (Emmy, Diamond award); contbr. articles to profl. jours. Recipient LifeRich Pioneer Exec. Mentor award. Mem. Order Internat. Fellowship, Noble Order Internat. Fellows, Pi Lambda Theta. Avocations: classical dance, dyeing and weaving fabric art, gardening, world travel, swimming. Fax: 805-964-8585. Home and Office: Profl Image PO Box 2422 Santa Barbara CA 93120-2422 Office: 2015 State St Santa Barbara CA 93105-3553

DUNTON, GARY C., insurance company executive. In sr. positions Aetna Life & Casualty Co., 1980s; pres. Family and Bus. Ins. Group, USF&G Ins., 1997—; with MBIA, 1997—; pres., CEO MBIA Inc., 1999—, also bd. dirs. Office: MBIA Ins Inc 113 King St Armonk NY 10504*

DUNTON, JAMES RAYNOR, publisher; b. Wilmington, Del., June 17, 1955; s. Guthrie Raynor III and Jane (Hill) D. BA, U. Va., 1977; MBA, Boston U., 1981. Editor Quorum Books, Westport, Conn., 1984-87; sr. editor Praeger Pubs., N.Y.C., 1987-91, editor-in-chief, 1991-94; pub. acad. and trade Greenwood Pub. Group, Westport, 1994-96; dir. pubs. Ctr. for Strategic and Internat. Studies, Washington, 1996—. Mem. Va. Club of N.Y. Home: 1520 16th St NW Apt 704 Washington DC 20036-1448 Office: Ctr for Strategic and Internat Studies 1800 K St NW Washington DC 20006-2202

DUNTON-DOWNER, LESLIE LINAM, writer; b. Washington, Mar. 2, 1961; d. Ronald Kaye Dunton and Elizabeth Earle (Downer) Simpson; m. Ashley Everett Rountree; 1 child, Jordan Tucker Rountree. AB, Harvard Coll., 1983; AM, PhD, Harvard U., 1992. Tchg. fellow Harvard Coll., Cambridge, Mass., 1986-92; lectr. Harvard U., Cambridge, Mass., 1992-93; jr. fellow Harvard Soc. Fellows, Cambridge, Mass., 1993-96; founding editor Harvard Review, Cambridge, 1984-86; vis. lectr. Tufts U., Medford, Mass., 1988-89. Author (opera libretto) Ligeia, 1994 (Internat. Orpheus prize 1994), (opera libretto) Conquering the Fury of Oblivion, 1995, (opera libretto) Belladonna, 1999; performer (theater) Addresses for Life, 1997; contbr. articles to books and profl. jours. Recipient Sheldon fellowship Harvard U., 1988-89, Rsch. grant Am. Coun. Learned Socs., Eng., 1994, Bellagio Ctr. award Rockefeller Found., Italy, 1997, Ind. Scholar grant Nat. Endowment for the Humanities, 1998-99. Mem. ASCAP, MLA, Phi Beta Kappa.

DUNTZ, DAVID W., career officer; b. Hudson, N.Y., July 2, 1947; s. Henry Siepel and Alyce May (Fraleigh) D.; m. Frances Ann Allen, Apr. 13, 1991; 1 child, Mark. BS, SUNY, Buffalo, 1970; MS, U. So. Calif., 1981. Cert. program mgmt. level 3, USAF; cert. flight instr., FAA, cert. air transport pilot. Commd. 2d lt. USAF, Fla., 1970; advanced through grades to col. USAF, 1996; comdr., FTD 314, ATC McCoy AFB, Fla., 1970-72; program mgr., satellite attack warning sys., SMC L.A. AFB, 1978-80, dep. dir. spl. activities, SMC, 1980-83; dir. ACM dual source, ASC Wright Patterson (Ohio) AFB, 1987-88; program dir., 60K loader, WR-ALC Robins (Ga.) AFB, 1989-94, comdr., Joint Stars SATAF, ESC, 1994-95, RFPSO chief advisor, WR-ALC, 1995-96; pilot Aviance Internat. Inc., Macon, Ga., 1997—. Avocation: flying. Home: 115 Pheasant Ridge Dr Warner Robins GA 31088-6563

DUNWODY, EUGENE COX, architect; b. Macon, Ga., July 19, 1933; s. William Elliott and Mary Bennet (Cox) D.; m. Susan Howe Foxworth, June 15, 1957; children: Susan, Eugene Jr., George, Mary Bennet. BS, Ga. Tech., 1955, BArch, 1956. Registered architect, Ga., Fla. V.p., treas. W. Elliott Dunwody Jr., Macon, 1959-69; pres. Dunwody and Co., Macon, 1969-81, Dunwody, Beeland and Henderson Architects Inc., Macon, 1981-97, Dunwody, Beeland, Azar, Walsh, and Matthews, Architects Inc., Macon, 1997—. Pres. Rotary, Macon, 1974, City Coun., Macon, 1975-87, C. of C., Macon, 1977; dir. Ga. Mcpl. Assn., Atlanta, 1982-83, Nat. League Cities, Washington, 1985-87; chmn. Macon-Bibb County Indsl. Authority, 1992-93, 99, Macon Econ. Devel. Commn., 1992-93, 99; deacon Presbyn. Ch. Named Community leader of Yr. Robins Air Logistics Ctr., Warner Robins, Ga., 1987; recipient Motie Wiggins award for Outstanding elected ofcl. Ga. Mcpl.

Assn., Atlanta, 1987. Fellow AIA; mem. Middle Ga. chpt. AIA (pres. 1993), Ga. Assn. AIA (dir. 1992-93). Democrat. Presbyterian. Avocations: golf, piano, choir. Office: Dunwody Beeland Azar et al 484 Mulberry St Ste 220 Macon GA 31201-7922

DUNWOODY, KENNETH REED, magazine and book editor; b. Washington, Iowa, Oct. 1, 1953; s. Kenneth W. and Marilyn Jane (Green) D.; m. Patricia P. Seale, July 7, 1990. B.S. in Journalism with honors, U. Ill., 1976. Sports announcer Sta. WPGU, Champaign, Ill., 1972-75; sports editor Free Press Newspaper Group, Carpentersville, Ill., 1976-79, Daily Crystal Lake Herald, Ill., 1979-82; mag. editor Fur-Fish-Game mag. A.R. Harding Pub. Co., Columbus, Ohio, 1982-86, art dir., 1982-86; mag. editor Game & Fish Pub., Marietta, Ga., 1986-88, editorial dir., 1989—. Contbr. articles to mags. Recipient Journalist of Yr. award Free Press Newspapers, 1977, 79, Sports Photography award Ill. Press Assn., 1978, Best Sports Writing award UPI, Ill. Press Assn., 1979, 80, Best Sports Column award UPI, 1979, 80, 81. Mem. Outdoor Writers Assn. Am. Avocations: photography; writing; fishing; baseball. Home: 2381 N Forest Dr Marietta GA 30062-6553 Office: Game & Fish Pub 2250 New Market Pkwy SE Ste 110 Marietta GA 30067-9394

DUNWORTH, JOHN, retired college president; b. L.A., Jan. 6, 1924; s. Charles William and Alice (Morris) D.; m. Lavona Anita Walden, July 7, 1956. BA, U. Calif.-Berkeley, 1949, MA, 1953; EdD, U. So. Calif., 1959. Cons. spl. edn. San Diego County pub. schs., 1949-51; speech therapist Walnut Creek (Calif.) Sch. Dist., 1952-54; tchr., vice prin., then prin. Torrance (Calif.) Unified Sch. Dist., 1954-59; asst. supt. Lawndale (Calif.) Sch. Dist., 1959-62; supt. schs. Beaumont (Calif.) Unified Sch. Dist., 1962-64; supt. dependents schs. Dept. Def., Pacific and Far East, 1964-66; dean Tchrs. Coll., Ball State U., Muncie, Ind., 1966-73; pres. George Peabody Coll. for Tchrs., Nashville, 1974-79; dean Coll. Edn., U. West Fla., Pensacola, 1979-82; supt. Santa Ana (Calif.) Unified Sch. Dist., 1982-85; Jones disting. univ. prof. Emporia (Kans.) State U., 1987-89; interim dean Sch. Edn., Calif. State U., San Bernardino, 1990-91; prin. Munson (Fla.) Elem. Sch., 1997-98; lectr. U. Redlands, 1963, U. Hawaii, 1965, U. So. Calif., 1968; del. World Conf. on Edn., Switzerland, 1975; commr. Ind. Sch. Fund Commn., 1969-73. Author: (with E. Stoops) Classroom Discipline, 1958, (with T. Drysdale) Millions of People, 1965, Kindergarten Overseas, 1967, (with L. Dunworth and E. Stoops) (bimonthly periodical) Discipline, 1962-93. Bd. dirs. Am. Coun. on Edn., 1974-75, Nashville Symphony, 1975-79, Pensacola Symphony, 1992-97, Tenn. Coun. Econ. Edn., 1976-79, Aerospace Edn. Found., 1981-83; pres. Beaumont C. of C., 1963-64. With U.S. Maritime Svc., 1943-46. Recipient svc. award L.A. Community Chest, 1961, Am. Educator medal Freedoms Found., Valley Forge, 1960, Outstanding Pub. Svc. medal U.S. Sec. Def., 1976, Nat. Leadership award George Washington U., 1979, Outstanding Ret. Sch. Adminstr. award Phi Delta Kappa N.W. Fla., 1998, Outstanding Older Worker for Santa Rosa County award N.W. Fla. Agy. on Aging, 1999. Mem. Ind. Assn. Colls. for Tchr. Edn. (pres. 1970-71), Am. Assn. Sch. Adminstrs., Council Ednl. Facility Planners (dir. 1969-72), So. Assn. Colls. and Schs. (commn. on colls.), Am. Assn. Colls. for Tchr. Edn. (pres. 1975-76). Episcopalian.

DUNYE, CHERYL, artist, film maker; b. Phila.. BA, Temple U.; MFA, Rutgers U. part-time instr. dept. media studies Pitzer Coll., Calif. Film maker (short film) Greetings from Africa, 1994, (video) The Potluck and the Passion; dir., creator (film) The Watermelon Woman; contbr. articles to profl. jours. Recipient MARMAF Pa. Major Artists award, 1993; grantee Astrea Found., 1992, Frameline, 1992, Nat. Endowment of the Arts, 1995; fellow Rugers U., 1990, 91, Art Matters, Inc., 1992. Office: c/o Media Studies Pitzer Coll Scott Hall North Rm 4 1050 N Mills Ave Claremont CA 91711-6101*

DUONG, THIEU, anesthesiologist; b. Hanoi, Vietnam, June 21, 1936; came to U.S., 1975; s. Phan T. and Thao T. (Pham) D.; m. Diep T. Nguyen; children: Anh T., Vi T., Mai T. MD, Saigon Med. Sch., 1962; MPH, Tulane U. Sch. Pub. Health, 1971. Diplomate Am. Bd. Anesthesiology. Intern Framingham (Mass.) Union Hosp., 1977-78; resident, fellow in anesthesiology Brigham and Women's Hosp., Boston, 1980-83; attending physician Cen. Hosp., Hue, Vietnam, 1966-67; chief Provincial Health Dept., Dalat, Vietnam, 1967-70; chmn. dept pub. health tng. Nat. Inst. Pub. Health, Saigon, Vietnam, 1971-75; anesthesiologist Boston U. Med. Ctr. Hosp., 1983—, assoc. clin. prof. in anesthesiology; sole proprietor AnesMED, Anesthesia Mgmt. Edn. and Design, Sharon, Mass. Contbr. articles to profl. jours. Mem. Mass. Soc. Anesthesiologists, Soc. Cardiovascular Anesthesia, Am. Coll. Physician Execs., Soc. Edn. in Anesthesia. Mem. Am. Soc. Anesthesiologists. Roman Catholic. Avocations: management, education and design in anesthesia. Home: 18 Forge Rd Sharon MA 02067-2881 Office: Boston Med Ctr One Boston Med Ctr Pl Boston MA 02118

DUPEY, MICHELE MARY, communications specialist; b. Bronx, N.Y., Feb. 26, 1953; d. William B. and Sandra Nancy (Raia) D.; m. Daniel Michael Gieser, July 14, 1980 (div. May 1991). BA, Montclair State Coll., 1975; cert. in Copywriting. NYU, 1988. Sec. DDB Needham Worldwide Inc. Advt. (formerly Doyle Dane Bernbach Advt. Co.) N.Y.C., 1985-88; asst. pub. info. officer Hudson County (N.J.) Bd. Chosen Freeholders, 1988—. Creator ann. Hudson County women's history month program; In-house planning chair 150th anniversary celebration of Hudson County; freelance copywriter Jersey City, 1988—; spkr. in field; ind. distbr. Km/Matol Bot. Internat. Comm. Gay Games IV, N.Y.C., 1991-94; planning com., pub. rels. Hudson County Am. Heritage Festival, 1994, 95 (winner gov.'s award for best new cultural and heritage event 1995); program producer, pub. rels. 1996 Olympic Torch Relay Hudson County, 1996; developer Hudson County Adv. Commn. on Women; developer seminars, prodr. video What is a Freeholder?; fellow Leadership N.J., 1995. Contbr. articles to profl. pubs. Mem. Internat. Platform Assn. Democrat. Roman Catholic. Home: 206 Washington St Apt 3A Jersey City NJ 07302-4566

DUPIES, DONALD ALBERT, retired civil engineer; b. Waukegan, Ill., Apr. 17, 1934; s. Renie Bernard and Catherine Marie (Dowe) D.; m. Margaret T. McKibbin, Sept. 29, 1962; children: Mark, Patrick, Peggy, Colleen. BCE, Marquette U., 1957. Registered profl. engr., Wis., Ill., Ohio, Mich., N.D., S.D., Minn., Mass. With Howard, Needles, Tammen & Bergendoff, Milw., 1959—, office engr., 1969-71, engr. in charge, 1971-74, assoc., 1974-79, cons. engr., ptnr., 1980-95; pres. Great Lakes divsn. HNTB Corp., ret., 1995. Bd. dirs. Centurions of St. Joseph Hosp., Milw., 1971-76; cubmaster Milw. County coun. Boy Scouts Am., 1973-75; mem. bd. Appeals, Town of Delafield, Wis., 1996—. Served with C.E. U.S. Army, 1957-59. Mem. ASCE (nat. dir. 1982-85), Wis. Assn. Mfg. and Commerce, Wis. Council for Transp. Info., Engrs. and Scientists of Milw., Inst. Transp. Engrs., Am. Mgmt. Assn., Internat. Bridge, Tunnel and Turnpike Assn., Bicentennial Engring., Sci. and Tech. Exposition and Conf. Council, Am. Pub. Works Assn., Water Pollution Control Fedn., Transp. Research Bd., Soc. Am. Mil. Engrs., Marquette U. Engring. Alumni Assn. (dir. Milw. 1976-83), Tau Beta Pi, Chi Epsilon. Roman Catholic. Home: W283 N 3917 Yorkshire Trace Pewaukee WI 53072-3307

DUPILL, MICHAEL JOSEPH, tax accountant; b. Boston, Mar. 6, 1971; s. Bertrand M. and Mildred M. (Sheehan) D. BSBA, Stonehill Coll., 1993; MS in Taxation, Northeastern U., 1995. CPA; cert. mgmt. acct. Tax acct. Deloitte & Touche, Boston, 1993—. Eucharistic min., mem. pastoral coun. St. Ann's Ch., Quincy, Mass. Mem. AICPA (Elijah Watt Sells award 1994), Inst. Mgmt. Acctg., Mass. Soc. CPAs (Bronze medal 1994), Delta Mu Delta, Lambda Epsilon Sigma, Beta Gamma Sigma. Republican. Roman Catholic. Avocations: swimming, tennis, skiing, baseball, basketball. Home: 945 Quincy Shore Dr Quincy MA 02170-3532 Office: Deloitte & Touche 125 Summer St Ste 2000 Boston MA 02110-1623

DUPLANTIER, ADRIAN GUY, federal judge; b. New Orleans, Mar. 5, 1929; s. F. Robert and Amelie (Rivet) D.; m. Sally Thomas, July 15, 1951; children: Adrian G., David L., Thomas, Jeanne M., Louise M., John C. J.D. cum laude, Loyola U., New Orleans, 1949; LLM, U. Va., 1988. Bar: La. 1950, U.S. Supreme Ct. 1954. Pvt. practice law New Orleans, 1950-74; judge Civil Dist. Ct. Parish of Orleans, 1974-78; judge U.S. Dist. Ct., New Orleans, 1978-94, sr. judge, 1994—; part-time prof. code of civil procedure Loyola U., 1951—, lectr. dental jurisprudence, 1960-67, lectr. English dept., 1948-50, chmn. law sch. vis. com., 1995-97; mem. La. State Senate, 1960-74; 1st asst. dist. atty. New Orleans, 1954-56; mem. Jud. Conf. of U.S. Bankruptcy Rules Adv. Com., 1994-96, chmn. 1997—. Editorial bd.: Loyola Law Rev, 1947-48; editor-in-chief, 1948-49. Del. Democratic Nat. Conv., 1964; pres. Associated Cath. Charities New Orleans, Social Welfare Planning Council Greater New Orleans; mem. adv. bd. St. Mary's Dominican Coll., 1970-71, Ursuline Acad., 1968-73, Mt. Carmel Acad., 1965-69; chmn. pres.'s adv. council Jesuit High Sch., 1979—, Boys Hope, 1980—; active Assn. Retarded Children. Recipient Meritorious award New Orleans Assn. Retarded Children, 1965; Gov.'s Cert. of Merit, 1970. Mem. ABA (award 1960), La. Bar Assn., New Orleans Bar Assn., Jud. Conf. of U.S., Order of Coif, Alpha Sigma Nu. Office: US Dist Ct C-205 US Courthouse 500 Camp St New Orleans LA 70130-3313

DUPONT, COLYER LEE, television and film producer, video and film distributing company executive; b. Golden, Colo., Oct. 23, 1957; s. Alfred Lee and Frances Dudley (Smith) D. BA, More U., 1980. Advt. mgr. Magical Blend mag., San Francisco, 1981-83; owner, mgr. Newave Co., San Francisco, 1983; mktg. dir. Venture Rsch., Inc., San Francisco, 1983-84; assoc. producer Left Coast Prodns., San Francisco, 1984-86; owner, mgr. Cinemagic Prodns., San Francisco, 1986—. Writer, producer, dir. TV spl. Computer Magic, 1987; videoworks exhibited Mus. Modern Art, N.Y.C., Nat. Mus. Natural History, Smithsonian Inst., Washington, N.Y. Hall of Sci., Corona, Fine Arts Mus. L.I., Hempstead, N.Y.; inventor belt-attached carrier. Recipient Chris award 34th Columbus (Ohio) Internat. Film and Video Festival, 1986, Silver medal Internat. Film and TV Festival N.Y., 1986, Joey award of merit Profl. Media Network, 1986, Golden Eagle award Coun. for Internat. Non-theatrical Events, 1987, Gold Electra award Birmingham (Ala.) Internat. Edn. Film Fetival, 1987, Silver plaque Chgo. Internat. Film Festival, 1987. Mem. Bay Area Video Coalition, Ind. Film-makers No. Calif. (founder), Film Arts Found., Visual Communicators Calif., San Francisco Advt. Club (Excellence award 1987). Avocations: art, scuba diving, travel. Office: Cinemagic Prodns 537 Jones St Ste 898 San Francisco CA 94102-2007

DUPONT, HERBERT LANCASHIRE, medical educator, researcher; b. Toledo, Nov. 12, 1938; s. Robert L. and Martha (Lancashire) DuP.; m. Margaret Wright, June 9, 1963; children: Denise Lorraine, Andrew Wright. BA, Ohio Wesleyan U., 1961; MD, Emory U., 1965. Diplomate Am. Bd. Internal Medicine. Resident U. Minn. Med. Ctr., Mpls., 1965-67; officer epidemic intelligence service CDC Atlanta, infectious disease fellow U. Md. Sch. Medicine, Balt., 1967-69; faculty, prof., dir. Ctr. for Infectious Diseases U. Tex., Houston, 1973-94, prof. Sch. Pub. Health, 1975—, prof. medicine M.D. Anderson Cancer Ctr., 1988—, Mary W. Kelsey prof. med. sci., 1988—, interim chmn. dept. internal medicine, 1987-89; chief internal medicine svc. and Baylor Coll. Medicine, H. Irving Schweppe chair in internal medicine St. Luke's Episcopal Hosp., Houston, 1995—; adj. prof. medicine and microbiology Baylor Coll. Medicine, Houston, 1977—; prin. investigator rsch. grants U.S. NIH, 1975-97; mem. vaccines and related biologic products adv. com. U.S. FDA, 1989-93; sci. adv. com. Inst. Medicine, Nat. Acad. Scis., 1989-94; bd. sci. counselors Nat. Ctr. for Infectious Diseases, Ctrs. for Disease Control, 1992-96; mem. standing sci. adv. com. Thrasher Rsch. Fund, 1993-96. Author: various medical books; assoc. editor Am. Jour. of Epidemiology, 1978-81, Jour. of Infectious Diseases, 1983-88; editorial bd.: Clinical Infectious Diseases, 1990-95, Infectious Diseases in Clinical Practice, 1992—; contbr. articles to profl. jours. Served to lt. comdr. USPHS, 1967-69. Fellow ACP; mem. Am. Soc. Clin. Investigation, Infectious Diseases Soc. Am. (counselor 1978-81, sec. 1982-87, pres. 1989-90), Nat. Found. Infectious Diseases (bd. dirs. 1981—, v.p. 1994-97, pres. 1997-99), Am. Clin. and Climatol. Assn., Am. Epidemiology Soc., Assn. Am. Physicians, U.S.-Mex. Found. Sci. and Tech. (com. chair health 1994—), Internat. Soc. Travel Medicine (pres. 1991-93), Alpha Omega Alpha. Republican. Methodist. Home: 1111 Hermann Dr Apt 19F Houston TX 77004-6931 Office: Saint Luke's Episcopal Hosp # MC 1-164 6720 Bertner St Houston TX 77030-2697

DU PONT, PIERRE SAMUEL, IV, lawyer, former governor of Delaware; b. Wilmington, Del., Jan. 22, 1935; s. Pierre Samuel and Jane (Holcomb) du P.; m. Elise Ravenel Wood, 1957; children: Elise, Pierre, Benjamin, Eleuthere. Grad., Phillips Exeter Acad., 1952; B.S. M.E., Princeton U., 1956; LL.B., Harvard U., 1963. Bar: Del. 1964. Mem. staff Photo Products Dept., E.I. duPont Co.; mem. Del. Ho. of Reps., 1968-70; mem.-at-large 92d to 94th congresses from Del., Washington; gov. State of Del., State of Del., 1977-85; mem. Richards, Layton and Finger, Wilmington, 1985—. Served with USNR, 1957-60. Republican. Office: Richards Layton and Finger 1 Rodney Sq Wilmington DE 19801-3305

DUPONT, RALPH PAUL, lawyer, educator; b. Fall River, Mass., May 21, 1929; s. Michael William and Gertrude (Murphy) D.; children: Ellen O'Neill, Antonia Chafee, William Albert. AB cum laude with highest honors in Am. Civilization, Brown U., 1951; JD cum laude, Harvard U., 1956. Bar: Conn. 1956, U.S. Supreme Ct. 1967; diplomate Nat. Bd. Trial Advocacy; cert. civil trial specialist, Conn. Assoc. Davies, Hardy & Schenck, N.Y.C., 1956-57; ptnr. Copp & Dupont, New London, Conn., 1957-60; mem. Suisman, Shapiro & Wool, New London, 1961-63; ptnr. Dupont & Dupont (and successor firms), New London, 1963-91; of counsel Durant, Nichols, Houston, Mitchell & Sheahan, Bridgeport, Conn., 1992-97; ptnr. Dupont and Radlauer LLP, New London, Conn., 1997—; instr. Am. history and bus. law Mitchell Coll., New London, 1955, 57-58, trustee, 1991-94; instr. bus. law U. New Haven, 1998; vis. prof. Northeastern U. Sch. Law, 1977-78; vis. prof. law Bridgeport Law Sch. Quinnipiac Coll., 1991-92, We. New Eng. Coll. Law, 1992-94; lectr.-on-law U. Conn. Sch. Law, 1980-86; mem. exec. bd., adj. prof. Quinnipiac Coll. Sch. Law, Hamden, Conn., 1994-96; trustee Anne S.K. Brown Mil. Collection, Brown U., 1988-94, presiding trustee, 1990-92; mem. Conn. Legal Svcs. Adv. Coun., 1980-82; pres. Conn. Acad. Cert. Trial Lawyers, 1998—. Author: Litigation in 1 Attorney's Desk Library, 1994, Dupont On Connecticut Civil Practice, 1998. Mem. bd. edn. New London, Conn., 1959-61; Dem. candidate for Conn. Senate, 1960; trustee U.S. Atlantic Tuna Tournament, 1984-85, pres. 1988-90. Lt. (j.g.) USNR, 1951-53. Named Outstanding Young Man of Yr. Conn. Jr. C. of C., 1960; recipient Disting. Svc. award Greater New London Jr. C. of C., 1960. Fellow Am. Coll. Trust and Estate Counsel; mem. ATLA, ABA, FBA, Conn. Bar Assn., Conn. Bar Found. (bd. dirs. 1975-79), Internat. Acad. Trust and Estate Law, Harvard U. Law Sch. Assn., Harvard Club, Delta Sigma Rho, Kappa Sigma. Roman Catholic. Home: PO Box 710 New London CT 06320-0710 Office: Dupont and Radlauer LLP PO Box 710 165 State St New London CT 06320-6304

DUPONT, TODD F., mathematics and computer science educator; b. Houston, Aug. 29, 1942; s. T.F. and Nan G. D.; m. Judy Smith, Aug. 20, 1964; children: Michelle, Todd K. BA, Rice U., 1963, PhD, 1968. Research mathematician Esso Prodn. Research, Houston, 1968; instr. U. Chgo., 1968-69, asst. prof., 1969-72, assoc. prof., 1972-75, prof. math., 1975—, prof. computer sci., 1985—, chmn. computer sci., 1994-97; prin., officer, past bd. dirs. DREM (formerly Dupont-Rachford Engring. Math. Co.), Houston, 1969-92; prin. tech. adv. Stoner Assocs., Inc., 1992—. Past assoc. editor: Math. of Computation, SIAM Jour., others; contbr. articles to profl. jours. Fellow AAAS; mem. Am. Math. Soc., Soc. Indsl. and Applied Math., Assn. Computing Machinery. Home: 1335 E Park Pl Chicago IL 60637-1767 Office: Univ Chgo Dept Computer Sci 1100 E 58th St Chicago IL 60637-1588

DUPONT, WILLIAM DUDLEY, biostatistician, educator; b. Montreal, Que., Can., Nov. 6, 1946; came to U.S., 1971; s. Charles Thomas and Jean (White) Dupont; m. Susan Miller McChesney, July 20, 1974; children: Charles Thomas, Peter William. BSc, McGill U., 1969, MSc, 1971; PhD, Johns Hopkins U., 1976. Lectr. U. Md., Balt., 1976-77; asst. prof. biostats. Vanderbilt U. Sch. Medicine, Nashville, 1977-85, assoc. prof., 1986-92, prof., 1992—, dir. divsn. biostats., 1989—. Nat. Cancer Inst. grantee, 1980—. Mem. AAAS, Am. Statis. Assn., Biometric Soc., Soc. Clin. Trials, Soc. Epidemiol. Rsch. Office: Vanderbilt U Med Sch Dept of Preventive Medicine A-1124 Med Ctr N Nashville TN 37232-2637*

DUPRE, JUDITH ANN NEIL, real estate agent, interior decorator; b. Houma, La., May 7, 1945; d. Herbert Joseph and Doris Mae (LeBouef) Neil; m. Michael Anthony Dupre, Jan. 7, 1962 (div. Aug. 1987); children: Arienne Danielle, Travis Lance. BA in Psychology, S.E. Okla. State U., 1982. Lic. life and health agt., real estate. Fin. mgr., supr. Gen. Fin. Loan Co., La., Colo., 1960-69; exec. sec. Progressive Bank & Trust Co., Houma, La., 1973-74; health coord. Spring Cypress Cultural & Recreation Ctr., 1974-75; bus. mgr., buyer June Morris Boutique, Ardmore, Okla., 1978-79; actress, model David Payne Agy., Dallas, 1985—; real estate agt. Vonnie Cobb Inc. Realtors, Sugar Land, Tex., 1986-91, Raymond Jepta Daniel, Jr., 1991—; nat. mktg. asst. North American Mortgage Co. (subs. MONY Mut. N.Y.), Houston, 1987-88; managed care coord. Sanus N.Y. Life, Inc., 1988-89; mgr. PPO Am. Health Network, 1989—; dir. bus. devel. and case mgmt. Houston Back Injury Ctr., 1989; dir. admissions and bus. devel. The Transitional Learning Cmty., Galveston, Tex., 1990-92; founder, owner, pres. Paradigm Health Care, 1993—, Alternative Info. Mgmt., Inc.; exec. dir. Rehab. Svcs. Network, Inc.; workers compensation cons. ETHIX S.E.; owner, pres. Summit Internat. Cons., Charlotte, N.C., Houston, 1991—, Ams. With Disabilities Act, Charlotte, 1991; peer reviewer ADA, Washington, 1991; exec. dir. Rehab. Svcs. Network, Inc., 1997—; founder, pres. JD Enterprises Internat., Inc., 1994—; adminstr. Ea. Carolina Med. Assn., Florence, S.C., 1995—, Coastal Physicians Orgn., LLC, Conway, S.C., 1995—, dir. mktg. med. billing dept.; chief network officer, v.p. Best Doctor's in Am., Inc., 1997-98; spkr. in field. Author: The Networks Are Coming; contbr. articles to profl. jours. Active Strake Jesuit-Mothers' Club, Houston, 1985-87, St. Agnes Acad. Womens Club, Houston, 1985-87, Ft. Bend Republican Women, Sugar Land, 1985-86, Charlotte Philharm., 1994—, mem. CAST, 1994—; chair Texans War on Drugs, Sugar Land, 1985-86; bd. dirs. dist. 6 MUD, Sugar Land, 1986-92; youth tchr., St. Anne's. Mem. Cath. Daus. of the Americas, Nat. Assn. Realtors, Tex. Assn. Realtors, Bal Harbour Homeowners Assn., Assn. Profl. Mortgage Women, Lake Wylie Homeowners Assn., Sweetwater Ladies Golf Assn., Sweetwater Country Club, Assn. River Hills Country Club, Palmetto Shores Assn., Ladies Assn., Alpha Chi. Roman Catholic. Avocations: tennis, golf, fishing, boating, dancing. Home: 106 Timberlake Dr Florence SC 29501-9309

DUPRÉ, LOUIS, retired philosopher, educator; b. Veerle, Belgium; came to U.S., 1958, naturalized, 1966; s. Clement and Francisca (Verlinden) D. PhD, U. Louvain, Belgium; PhD (hon.), Loyola Coll., 1989, Sacred Heart U., 1992, Georgetown U., 1996, Siena Coll., 1997. From asst. prof. to prof. philosophy Georgetown U., Washington, 1959-73; T. Lawrason Riggs prof. philosophy of religion Yale U., New Haven, 1973-98. Author: Kierkegaard as Theologian (also in Dutch), 1963, The Philosophical Foundations of Marxism, 1966, Dutch edit., 1970, Korean edit., 1982, The Other Dimension, 1972, French edit., 1977, Chinese edit., 1986, Polish edit., 1990, Dutch edit., 1991, Korean edit., 1995, Spanish edit., 1999, Transcendent Selfhood, 1976, Dutch edit., 1981, Marx's Social Critique of Culture, 1983, The Common Life, 1984, Polish edit., 1994, Passage to Modernity, 1993, Metaphysics and Culture, 1994, Religious Mystery and Rational Reflection, 1997; editor: Faith and Reflection, 1968; co-editor: Light from Light, 1987; contbr. articles to profl. jours. Recipient Phi Beta Kappa medal as Tchr. of Yr. at Yale U., 1996, Aquinas medal, Am. Cath. Philos. Assn., 1997. Mem. Am. Cath. Philos. Assn. (pres. 1971), Hegel Soc. Am. (pres. 1972-73), Am. Acad. Arts and Scis., Belgian Acad. Letters, Arts, & Scis. Roman Catholic. Home: 67 N Racebrook Rd Woodbridge CT 06525-1407 Office: 320 Temple St New Haven CT 06511-6601

DUPRE, THOMAS L., bishop; b. Holyoke, Mass., Nov. 10, 1933. Student, Sem. of Philosophy, Montreal, Que. Can., Grand Sem., Montreal; postgrad., Cath. U. Am.; GED, 1967. Ordained priest Roman Cath. Ch., 1959. Former Defender of the Bond and Pro-Synodal judge Diocese of Springfield, Mass., chancellor, 1977-94, titular bishop of Hodelm, aux. bishop, 1990-95, adminstr., 1994-95, bishop, 1995—. Office: Chancery Office 76 Elliot St Springfield MA 01105-1714 also: PO Box 1730 Springfield MA 01101-1730*

DUPREE, STANLEY M., lawyer; b. Thomaston, Ga., Sept. 7, 1946. BA, Stanford U., 1971; JD, U. Calif., 1974. Bar: CAlif. 1974. Instr. U. Calif., 1976-82; law clerk, acting ct. commr. San Francisco Superior Ct., 1974-76; ptnr. Schultz & Dupree, San Francisco, Dupree & Colvin. Mem. ABA, State Bar Calif., Bar Assn. San Francisco. Office: Dupree & Colvin 1 Sansome St San Francisco CA 94104-4448

DUPREE, THOMAS ANDREW, forester, state official; b. Cambridge, Mass., Jan. 18, 1950; s. Glenn Stewart and Elvira (Pacifici) D.; m. Sandra Ann Becker, Aug. 31, 1975; 1 child, Steven. BS in Forestry, U. Mass., 1972. Svc. forester R.I. Div. Forest Environ., Hope Valley, 1974-76, sr. forester, 1976-78, prin. forester, 1978-86; chief R.I. Div. Forest Environ., Scituate, 1986—; chmn. R.I. Tree Farm Com., 1976-78; chmn. Arcadia Mgmt. Coun., 1981-86. Bd. mem. USS Mass. Meml. Com., Fall River, 1987—; vice chmn. Northea. Forest Fire Protection Commn., 1988-89, chmn., 1990-92; pres. So. New England Forest Consortium, Inc., 1990—; mem. forest productivity working group N.E. Govs.' and Ea. Can. Premiers, 1986-91; bd. dirs. R.I. Urban and Cmty. Forestry Coun., Inc., 1993—, R.I. Resource Conservation and Devel. Area, Inc., 1996—; coach Coventry Basketball Assn., 1994—, sec., 1997-98. Mem. Soc. Am. Foresters (vice chmn. 1987, sec.-treas. 1986, chmn. Yankee divsn. 1988), Am. Forestry Assn., Nat. Assn. State Foresters (exec. com. 1992-93, chmn. forest health com. 1992-96, bd. dirs. found. 1995—, chmn. stats. com. 1998—, v.p. found. 1998—), New Eng. Soc. Am. Foresters (exec. com. 1982-90), N.E. Area Assn. State Foresters (sec.-treas. 1990, v.p. 1991, pres. 1992, chmn. R.I. rural lands coalition 1997—), R.I. Fire Chiefs Assn. Avocations: golf, hiking, hunting, fishing, coaching basketball. Home: 20 Gentry Farm Rd Coventry RI 02816-6952 Office: RI Div Forest Environ 1037 Hartford Pike North Scituate RI 02857-1030

DUPRIEST, DOUGLAS MILLHOLLEN, lawyer; b. Ft. Riley, Kans., Dec. 28, 1951; s. Robert White and Barbara Nadine (Millhollen) DuP. AB in Philosophy with high honors, Oberlin Coll., 1974; JD, U. Oreg., 1977. Bar: Oreg. 1977, U.S. Dist. Ct. Oreg. 1977, U.S. Ct. Appeals (9th cir.) 1977. Assoc. Coons & Anderson and predecessors, Eugene, Oreg., 1977-81, Hutchinson, Harrell et al, 1981; ptnr. Hutchinson, Anderson, Cox, Coons & DuPriest and predecessors, 1982—; adj. prof. sch. law U. Oreg., 1986; mem. task forces Wetlands Mgmt., 1988-89, 92-93. Author: (with others) Land Use, 1982, Administrative Law, 1985; contbg. editor Real Estate & Land Use Digest, 1983-86; articles editor, mng. bd. mem. U. Oreg. Law Rev., 1976-77. Bd. dirs. Home Health Agy., Eugene, 1977-79, pres., 1978-79; bd. dirs. Oreg. Environ. Coun., Portland, 1979-84, pres., 1980-81; mem. Lane Econ. Com., 1989-91; chair voters pamphlet com. Eugene City Club, 1993. Recipient Disting. Svc. award Oreg. Environ. Coun., 1988. Mem. Oreg. Bar Assn. (exec. com. real estate and land use sect. 1978-81). Home: 225 Dartmoor Dr Eugene OR 97401-6620 Office: Hutchinson Anderson Cox Coons & DuPriest 777 High St Ste 200 Eugene OR 97401-2750

DUPUIS, KATERI THERESA, elementary education educator; b. Menominee, Mich., Dec. 1, 1941; d. Edmund Bruno and Emelie Josephine (Archambault) D. BA, Cardinal Stritch Coll., 1964; MS, Lesley Coll., 1989. Cert. elem. tchr. 4-8, Wis. Tchr. grade 5 St. Michael's Indian Sch., St. Michael, N.D., 1964-65; tchr. grades 4, 6 and 8 Cudahy (Wis.) Pub. Schs., 1965-99; ret., 1999. Mem. French Can./Acadian Genealogists of Wis. (treas. 1992-93), Cudahy Edn. Assn. (pres., v.p., sec., negotiator, com. chair 1967-82). Avocations: genealogy, photography, computers, Tiffany glass work. Home: 2414 N 56th St Milwaukee WI 53210-2230 : Cudahy Middle Sch 5530 S Barland Cudahy WI 53110

DUPUIS, ROBERT SIMEON, sales executive; b. Palmer, Mass., Aug. 31, 1941; s. Bertrand Leonard and Hanora Theresa (Crean) D.; m. Dianne Cecile Gibouleau, Aug. 20, 1960; children: Kathleen, Corinne, Lynn, Robert. Student, Springfield Tech. C.C. Laborer Springfield (Mass.) Foundry, 1959-60; warehouse forklift operator Ludlow (Mass.) Industries, 1960-62; machinists, mechanic Tambrands, Inc., Palmer, Mass., 1962-64; apprentice toolmaker Pratt & Whitney Aircraft, East Hartford, Conn., 1964-66; toolmaker Target Tool Co., Three Rivers, Mass., 1966-68; tool and die maker Brookfield Machine Corp., West Brookfield, Mass., 1968-75, Prodn. Tool & Die, Springfield, 1975-77; tool and die engr. Vogform Tool & Die, West Springfield, 1977-85; regional mgr. Dayton (Ohio) Progress Corp., 1985—; cons., speaker Worcester (Mass.) Poly. Inst., 1991—. Chmn., vice chair Palmer (Mass.) Sch. Com., 1977—; sec. Three River Prudential Fire Dept. Com., 1978-80; chmn., subcom. Palmer Fin. Com., 1971-77; mem. Palmer Libr. Com., 1988-90. Mem. SME (sr., speaker), Precision Metal Forming Assn. (tech. cons., speaker 1985—), Three Rivers C. of C. Roman Catholic. Avocations: deep sea fishing, scuba diving, hiking, biking, golf, boating. Home and Office: Dayton Progress Corp 322 Flynt St Palmer MA 01069-1657

DUPUIS, RUSSELL DEAN, electrical engineer, research scientist; b. Kankakee, Ill., July 9, 1947; s. Rudolph William and Evelyn Marie (Hoevet) D.; m. Dana Elizabeth Gammage, Nov. 19, 1973; 1 child, Elizabeth Anne. BSEE, U. Ill., 1970, MSEE, 1971, PhD in Elec. Engring., 1973. Mem. tech. staff Tex. Instruments Corp., Dallas, 1973-74, Rockwell Internat. Corp., Anaheim, Calif., 1975-79; mem. tech. staff AT&T Bell Labs., Murray Hill, N.J., 1979-85, disting. tech. staff mem., 1985-89; prof. and Judson S. Swearingen Regents Chair in Engring. Dept. Elec. and Computer Engring U. Tex., Austin, 1989—. Contbr. articles to profl. jours. Recipient Disting. MTS award AT&T-Bell Labs., 1985, Nat. Acad. Engring, 1989, Young Scientist award GaAs Symposium, 1986, Disting. Alumnus award U. Ill., 1987. Fellow IEEE (Morris Liebmann award 1985); mem. Lasers and Electro-Optics Soc. of IEEE (bd. govs. 1989, tech. achievement award 1995), Am. Phys. Soc., Electrochem. Soc., Electronics Materials Com., Optical Soc. Am. Avocation: genealogy. Office: U Tex Microelectronics Rsch Ctr PRC-MER1.606/R9900 Austin TX 78712-1100

DUPUIS, VICTOR LIONEL, retired curriculum and instruction educator; b. Chgo., Oct. 30, 1934; s. Edward G. and LaVerne Ann (Brown) D.; m. Mary Jean Miles, Aug. 11, 1956; children: Mary Catherine, Victor Edward, Elizabeth Ann. B.S., Northwestern U., 1956; M.A., Am. U., 1961; Ph.D., Purdue U., 1965. Tchr. jr. high sch. Arlington, Va., 1956-61; tchr. Klondike Sch. Dist., West Lafayette, Ind., 1961-63; curriculum dir. Klondike Sch. Dist., 1962-63; grad. instr. Purdue U., West Lafayette, 1963-65, 1963-65; asst. prof. No. Ill. U., DeKalb, 1965-67; asst. prof. Pa. State U., University Park, 1967-70, assoc. prof. curriculum, 1970-74, prof. edn. curriculum and instruction, 1974-92, Waterbury prof. secondary edn., 1990-92, chmn. curriculum and supervision, 1971-92, prof. emeritus curriculum and instrn., 1992—; CEO Dupuis Assocs.; cons. to various pvt. and public schs., state depts. edn. Native Am. programs. Author: (with others) Introduction to the Foundations of American Education, 1966, Introductory Readings in the Foundation of American Education, 1966, Resource Booklet and Overhead Transparency Masters for the Foundations of American Education, 1966, An Introduction to the Foundations of American Education, 1969, 11th edit., 1998, Foundation of American Education: Readings, 1969, 6th edit., 1985, Resource Booklet: Foundations of American Education, 11th edit., 1998, Issues in Education, 1991. Chmn. Patton Twp. (Pa.) Park Bd., 1969-70, Patton Twp. Planning Commn., 1971-73; Democratic precinct committeeman Patton Twp., 1971-76, chmn., twp. supr., 1973-92. Served to 2d lt. inf. U.S. Army, 1957-59. Mem. ASCD, Am. Ednl. Rsch. Assn., Nat. Staff Devel. Coun., Pa. Assn. for Supervision and Curriculum Devel., Phi Delta Kappa. Home: 3203 Buffalo Run Rd Bellefonte PA 16823-9027 Office: Pa State U Coll Edn University Park PA 16802

DUQUE, RICARDO GERMAN, analytical chemist; b. Panama City, Panama, Nov. 14, 1970; came to U.S., 1988; s. Gabriel E. and Hilda Teresa (Soto) D. BS in Biochemistry, UCLA, 1993; MS in X-Ray Crystallography, Calif. State U., Northridge, 1998. Lab. asst. Inst. Geophysics and Planetary Physics, UCLA, 1991-94, Jerry Lewis Neuromuscular Rsch. Ctr., UCLA, 1993-94; tchg. asst. Calif. State U., Northridge, 1993-98; high sch. sci. tchr. Bridges Acad., L.A., 1996-97; analytical chemist Micropolis, L.A., 1996-97; head media engr. chem. integration Maxtor Corp., Milpitas, Calif., 1998—. Mem. ACS, UCLA Assn. Chemists and Biochemists, UCLA Alumni Assn., Sigma Xi Sci. Rsch. Soc. (Donald Bianchi award 1996). Home: 6730 Ruffner Ave Van Nuys CA 91406-5641 Office: 510 Cottonwood Dr Milpitas CA 95035

DUQUES, RIC, information services executive. Chmn., CEO First Data Corp., Atlanta. Office: First Data Corp Ste 1400 5660 New Northside Dr Atlanta GA 30328*

DUQUESNAY, ANN, actress, singer. Appeared in Broadway plays including Jelly's Last Jam, The Wiz, Blues in the Night; appeared in off-Broadway plays including Spunk; appeared in other plays including Ma Rainey's Black Bottom, House of Flowers, Porgy and Bess, The Outcast, Lady Day, Black Nativity, Bubbling Brown Sugar, Betsey Brown; appeared on TV shows including PBS' Reading Rainbow, Another World; co-lyricist, co-composer cast album Bring in Da Noise, Bring in Da Funk, 1997 (Grammy nominee). Recipient AUDELCO, San Francisco's Bay Area Theatre Critics Circle award, Best Supporting Actress in a Musical Tony award Bring in Da Noise, Bring in Da Funk, 1996. Address: Ascap One Lincoln Plz New York NY 10023*

DUQUETTE, DANIEL F., professional baseball team executive. V.p. of player personnel, gen. mgr. Montreal Expos, 1991-94; exec. v.p., gen. mgr. Boston Red Sox, 1994—. Office: Boston Red Sox 4 Yawkey Way Boston MA 02215-3496*

DUQUETTE, DAVID JOSEPH, materials science and engineering educator; b. Springfield, Mass., Nov. 4, 1939; s. Joseph Albert and Jeannette Marie (Bernier) D.; m. JoAnn Nazarko, July 31, 1982; children: David Joseph Jr., Peter James. BS, USCG Acad., 1961; PhD, MIT, 1968. Commd. officer USCG, 1961, advanced through grades to lt., 1965; rsch. asst. MIT, Cambridge, Mass., 1965-68; sr. rsch. assoc. Adv. Materials R&D Lab. Pratt & Whitney, Middletown, Conn., 1968-70; faculty mem. Rensselaer Poly. Inst., Troy, N.Y., 1970—; vis. prof. Imperial Coll. of Sci. & Tech., U. London, 1973; vis. sr. scientist Max Planck Institut fur Eisenforschung, Dusseldorf, 1983-84; mem. panel on material performance 5 NAS/NAE, Washington, 1980—, NASA Space Processing Rev. Com., Huntsville, Ala., 1978-83. Contbr. 160 articles to tech. jours. Mem. North Colonie Bd. of Edn., 1974-79, Albany County Airport Adv. Com., 1976-79. Recipient Excellence award ALCOA Found., 1978, 79, Humboldt prize Alexander von Humboldt Found., 1983, Willis Rodney Whitney award Nat. Assn. of Corr. Eng., Tex., 1990, Centennial scholar Case Inst. of Tech., Cleve., 1980, fellow ASM Internat., Metals Park, Ohio, 1986. Fellow Nat. Assn. Corosion Engrs. Internat.; mem. Alpha Sigma Mu (hon.). Avocations: skiing, sailing. Office: Rensselaer Poly Inst Materians Sci and Engring Dept Troy NY 12180

DUQUETTE, DIANA MARIE, company official; b. Plattsburgh, N.Y., May 21, 1952; d. Clarence Elmer and Ruth Virginia (O'Connell) Duquette; 1 child, Marcelle Lynn. A in Humanities, Clinton C.C., Plattsburgh, N.Y., 1972; BS in Gen. Bus., SUNY, Albany, 1997. Pers. asst. Georgia-Pacific Corp., Plattsburgh, 1973-85, asst. prodn. control mgr., 1985-87; allocation and inventory control mgr. Georgia-Pacific Corp., Atlanta, 1987-90, customer svc. mgr., 1990-93, nat. customer svc. mgr., 1993-95, logistics svcs. mgr., 1995-96, supply chain mgr., 1996-97; asst. gen. mgr. Weyerhaeuser Corp., Atlanta, 1997-98; gen. mgr. Weyerhaeuser Corp., Council Bluff, Iowa, 1998—. Active Christian Action Ministry Program. Mem. Metro Omaha Builders Assn. Home: 116 Bonham Cir Council Bluffs IA 51503-4976 Office: Weyerhaeuser Corp 3308 S 11th St Council Bluffs IA 51501-8006

DUQUETTE, JEAN-PIERRE, French language and literature educator; b. Valleyfield, Que., Can., June 27, 1939; s. J.-Armand and Marguerite (Besner) D. BA, Université de Montréal, Can., 1960, L ès L, 1963; Doctorat 3e cycle, Paris X, France, 1969. Asst. prof. French McGill U., Montréal, 1969-73, assoc. prof. French, 1973-83, prof. French, 1983—. Author: Flaubert, 1972, Germaine Guèvremont, 1973, Fernand Leduc, 1980, Colette, 1984, L'Espace du regard, 1994. Named to Académie des Lettres du Que., 1982. Mem. Internat. PEN Que., McGill U. Faculty Club. Office: McGill U Dept of French Lang, 3460 McTavish St, Montreal, PQ Canada H3A 1X9

DUR, PHILIP ALPHONSE, automotive executive, retired naval officer; b. Bethesda, Md., June 22, 1944; s. Philip Francis and Elena (Delgado) D.; m. Kathleen Mary Donovan, June 6, 1966; children: Courtney Morris, Philip Ralston. BA, U. Notre Dame, 1965, AM, 1966; MPA, Harvard U., 1973, PhD, 1976. Commd. ensign USN, 1965, advanced through grades to rear adm., 1991; strategic planner Office of the Chief Naval Ops. USN, Washington, 1977-79, mil. asst. Office of Sec. Def., 1979-80, dir. polit. mil. affairs Nat. Sec. Coun., 1982-84, exec. asst. Chief Naval Ops. plans, policy, ops., 1984-86, exec. asst. sec. of navy, 1988-89; commanding officer USS Comte De Grasse USN, Norfolk, Va., 1980-82, commanding officer USS Yorktown, 1986-88, 91-93; U.S. def. attache Am. embassy Paris, 1989-91; comdr. Cruiser Destroyer Group Eight, 1991-93; dir. strategy and policy Office of the Chief Naval Ops., Washington, 1993-95; retired USN, 1995; v.p. Tenneco Inc., Houston, 1995-96; exec. v.p. Walker-Gillet Europe, Edenkoben, Germany, 1996-97; v.p. worldwide bus. devel. & strategy Tenneco, Inc., Lake Forest, IL, 1997—. Scoutmaster Boy Scouts Am., Gaeta, Italy, 1967. Decorated Def. Disting. Svc. medal, Navy Disting. Svc. medal, Def. Superior Svc. medal, Legion of Merit; comdr. Ordre Nat. du Merite (France). Mem. U.S. Naval Inst., Cercle de l'Union Interalliee, Surface Navy Assn., Marine Acad. (France), Nat. Eagle Scouts Assn., Notre Dame Alumni Club, Army-Navy Club, Harvard Club (Washington). Avocations: history, golf, foreign languages. Office: Tenneco Automotive 500 N Field Dr Lake Forest IL 60045-2595

DUR, PHILIP FRANCIS, political scientist, educator, retired foreign service officer; b. St. Louis, June 30, 1914; s. Alphonse and Sarah (Ralston) D.; m. Elena Delgado, June 30, 1942; children: Elena (Mrs. Philip A. Morris), Philip, Stansbury, Carmen (Mrs. Norman B. Conley, Jr.), Jacqueline (Mrs. James Chase Sheppard), John. A.B., Harvard U., 1935, Ph.D., 1941; postgrad., Fgn. Service Inst., 1961. Consul, pub. affairs officer Lyon, France, 1948-51; chief Office Pub. Affairs, Office U.S. High Commr. for Germany, Bonn, 1951-52; consul, exec. officer Bremen, Germany, 1952-53; comml. controls officer Mil. Security Bd., Coblenz, Germany, 1953-54; consul Colon, Panama, 1954-55, Yokohama, Japan, 1955-58; pub. affairs adviser Dept. State, 1958-61; consul Nagoya, Japan, 1961-65; Jefferson Caffery prof. polit. sci. U. Southwestern La., Lafayette, 1965-84; prof. emeritus U. Southwestern La., 1984—, faculty senate, 1969-84; adviser Council for Devel. of French in La., 1968—; mem. U. Southwestern La. Found., 1969-71; pres. France-Amerique de la Louisiane Acadienne, 1970-72; resident dir. La. Consortium Colls. and Univs., Montpellier, France, 1976-77; organizer, exchange prof. La. Ctr. for Studies, U. Paul Valéry, Montpellier. Served to lt. comdr. USNR, 1942-46. Decorated Acad. Palms (France); recipient Nat. Medal of Honor, DAR, 1983, 1st prize French poetry Deep South Writers Conf., 1995. Mem. Am. Fgn. Service Assn., La. Historical Assn., Phi Beta Kappa. Home: 517 Woodvale Ave Lafayette LA 70503-3435 *After a fairly long (84 years), somewhat productive (6 children), and definitely tranquil (49 years of marriage to the same woman) life, I look back on the whole process with a touch of nostalgia. I wish I could start all over again, but I'm not sure what I would change. There is a design in this web of fortuity. Which thread could be cut without unraveling the whole? In daily shuttle we weave a pattern beyond our devising. But if we know what we mean we can accept what we do. George Washington put it more simply: "Let us raise a standard to which the wise and honest can repair. The event is in the hand of God."*

DURAN, MICHAEL CARL, bank executive; b. Colorado Springs, Colo., Aug. 27, 1953; s. Lawrence Herman and Jacqueline Carol (Ward) D. BS magna cum laude, Ariz. State U., 1980. With Valley Nat. Bank (name now Bank One, Ariz., N.A.), Phoenix, 1976—; corp. credit trainee Bank One Ariz. (formerly Valley Nat. Bank Ariz.), Phoenix, 1984-85; comml. loan officer Valley Nat. Bank Ariz. (name now Bank One Ariz.), Phoenix, 1985-86; br. mgr., asst. v.p. Valley Nat. Bank Ariz. (name now Bankone, Ariz.), Phoenix, 1986-90, comml. banking officer, asst. v.p., 1990-93, credit mgr., v.p., 1993—; cons. various schs. and orgns., 1986—; incorporator Avondale Neighborhood Housing Svcs., 1988. Mem. Cen. Bus. Dist. Revitalization Com., Avondale, Ariz., 1987-88, Ad-Hoc Econ. Devel. Com., 1988; coord. Avondale Litter Lifters, 1987-88; vol. United Way, Phoenix, 1984; bd. dirs. Jr. Achievement, Yuma, Ariz., 1989-91, vol., Phoenix, 1993—; yokefellow 1st So. Bapt. Ch. of Yuma, 1990-91; treas. Desert View Bapt. Ch., Gilbert, Ariz., 1998—. Recipient Outstanding Community Svc. award City of Avondale, 1988. Mem. Robert Morris Assocs., Ariz. State U. Alumni Assn. (life), Toastmasters, Kiwanis (local bd. dirs. 1986-88), Beta Gamma Sigma, Phi Kappa Phi, Phi Theta Kappa, Sigma Iota Epsilon. Democrat. Baptist. Avocations: art, photography, hiking, jogging. Home: 925 N Quartz St Gilbert AZ 85234-3661

DURANT, FREDERICK CLARK, III, aerospace history and space art consultant; b. Ardmore, Pa., Dec. 31, 1916; s. Frederick Clark, Jr. and Cornelia Allen (Howel) D.; m. Carolyn Griscom Jones, Oct. 4, 1947 (dec.); children: Derek C. (dec.), Carolyn M., William C. (dec.), Stephen H. BSChemE, Lehigh U., 1939; postgrad., Phila. Mus. Sch. Indsl. Arts, 1946-47. Registered profl. engr., D.C., Mass. Engr. E.I. duPont de Nemours & Co., Inc., 1939-41; rocket engr. Bell Aircraft Corp., 1947-48; dir. engring. Naval Air Rocket Test Sta., 1948-51; cons. Washington, 1952-53; mem. sr. staff Arthur D. Little, Inc., 1954-57; dir. Maynard Ordnance Test Sta., 1954-55; exec. asst. to dir. Avco-Everett Rsch. Lab., 1957-59; dir. pub. and govt. rels., rsch. and advanced devel. divsn. Avco Corp., Wilmington, Mass., 1959-61; sr. rep. Bell Aerosys., Washington, 1961-64; asst. dir. and head astronautics dept. Nat. Air and Space Mus., Smithsonian Instn., Washington, 1964-80; cons., 1980—; dir. Nat. Space Soc., Washington, 1982-88; conservator Bonestell Space Art and Space Art Internat.; dir. Arthur C. Clarke Found. U.S. Inc.; cons. space mus. Nippon Steel Corp., Japan, 1989—; participant ann. congresses Internat. Astron. Fedn., 1951—, pres., 1953-56; mem. organizing com. Project Orbiter, 1954; cons. Astro Assocs., Space Art Internat. Author: First Steps toward Space, 1975, Worlds Beyond: The Art of Chesley Bonestell, 1983; Contbg. editor Missiles and Rockets, 1956-58; contbr. to Ency. Brit., 1958-96, Funk & Wagnalls Year Book; contbr. space terms to Am. Heritage Dictionary. Comdr. as naval aviator USNR, 1941-46,48-52. Recipient spl. medal L'Assn. Pour l'Encouragement de l'Aeronautique et de l'Astronautique, 1963, Charles A. Lindbergh award Smithsonian Instn., 1976, hon. 6 Dan Karate-Do, Japan, 1978, Rathbone Alumni Achievement award Lehigh U., 1989. Fellow Am. Astronautical Soc., AIAA, Am. Rocket Soc. (pres. 1953); mem. Internat. Acad. Astronautics (co-chmn. history com. 1981-89), Nat. Space Club (gov. 1961), Nat. Space Club (Disting. Svc. award 1982), hon. fellow or mem. numerous fgn. rocket and space flight socs., Cosmos Club. Home and Office: 2440 Springmoor Cir Raleigh NC 27615

DURANT, GRAHAM JOHN, medicinal chemist, drug researcher; b. Newport, Gwent, U.K., Mar. 14, 1934; came to U.S., 1987; s. Edgar Counsell and Florence (Pocock) D.; m. Rosemary Margaret Towle, Apr. 14, 1962; children: Julian Clive, Adrian Charles. BSc in Chemistry with honors, U. Birmingham, U.K., 1955, PhD, 1958; postdoctoral study, State U. Iowa, Iowa City, 1958-59. Sr. rsch. officer Smith Kline & French Rsch., Welwyn Garden City, Hertfordshire, U.K., 1960-75, head dept. medicinal chemistry, 1975-85, head rsch. adminstrn., 1985-86; Disting. prof. medicinal chemistry Coll. Pharmacy, U. Toledo, Ohio, 1987-92, dir. Ctr. for Drug Design and Devel., 1987-92; sr. dir. chemistry Cambridge (Mass.) Neurosci., Inc., 1992—. Contbr. articles to profl. jours.; co-holder over 100 patents. Trustee Inventure Place, Akron, Ohio, 1990—. Inducted into Nat. Inventors Hall of Fame, 1990. Fellow Royal Soc. Chemistry (Medicinal Chemistry award 1983, mem. fine chemicals group com. 1985-87); mem. Am. Chem. Soc., Soc. for Medicines Rsch. (U.K.), Pharm. Soc. (U.K.). Avocations: genealogy, travel. Home: 4 Bow St Wellesley Hls MA 02481-3304 Home: 5 Wingfield Thurlestone, Kingsbridge Devon TQ7 3TE, United Kingdom Office: Cambridge Neurosci Inc 1 Kendall Sq Bldg 700 Cambridge MA 02139-1562

DURANT, JOHN RIDGEWAY, physician; b. Ann Arbor, Mich., July 29, 1930; s. Thomas Morton and Jean Margaret (deVries) D.; m. Mary Sue Avery Dillon, Jan. 13, 1990; children by previous marriage: Christine Joy, Thomas Arthur, Michele Grace, Jennifer Margaret. B.A., Swarthmore (Pa.) Coll., 1952; MD, Temple U., Phila., 1956; hon. degree, U. Ala., 1993. Diplomate: Am. Bd. Internal Medicine. Intern, then jr. asst. resident in medicine Hartford (Conn.) Hosp., 1956-58; resident in medicine Temple U. Med. Center, 1960-62; spl. fellow med. neoplasia Meml. Hosp. for Cancer and Allied Diseases, N.Y.C., 1962-63; Am. Cancer Soc. advanced clin. fellow Temple U. Health Scis. Center, 1964-67, instr., then asst. prof. medicine, 1963-67; clin. assoc. chemotherapy Moss Rehab. Hosp., Phila., 1964-67; research assoc. Fels Research Inst., Phila., 1965-67; mem. faculty U. Ala. Med. Center, Birmingham, 1968-82; prof. medicine, dir. comprehensive cancer center U. Ala. Med. Center, 1970-82, prof. radiation oncology, 1978-82, chmn. Southeastern coop. cancer study group at univ., 1975-82, Disting. faculty lectr., 1980; pres. Fox Chase Cancer Ctr., Phila., 1982-88; sr. v.p. health affairs and dir. med. ctr. U. Ala., Birmingham, 1988-95; exec. v.p. Am. Soc. Clin. Oncology, Alexandria, Va., 1995—; chmn. coop. group exec. com. Nat. Cancer Inst., NIH, 1977-82, chmn. coop. group chairmen, 1979-82; cons. VA Hosp., Tuskegee, Ala., 1970-82; exec. com. Birmingham chpt. ARC, 1972-77; mem. Nat. Cancer Adv. Bd., 1986-92. Mem. editorial bd. Cancer Clin. Trials, 1979-82, assoc. editor, 1982—; editorial bd. Med. and Pediatric Oncology News, 1975-90; assoc. editor Cancer, 1984-92; contbr. numerous articles to med. jours. Served as officer M.C. USNR, 1958-60. Recipient Oncologist of Yr. award So. Oncology Assn., 1999; named Temple U. Med. Sch. Alumnus Yr., 1982. Fellow ACP, Coll. Physicians Phila.; mem. Am. Cancer Soc. (vice chmn. advanced clin. fellowship com. 1974-76, 85-87, mem. instl. rsch. grant com. 1979-82, pres. Ala. divsn. 1973-75, 77-79, mem. blue ribbon com. to rev. nat. rsch. program 1994-95), Am. Assn. Cancer Rsch., Am. Radium Soc. (pres. 1984), Am. Bd. Int. Med. Oncology (subcom. 1979-85, chmn. 1983-85), Assn. Am. Cancer Insts. (dir. 1978—, pres. 1982-83), Assn. Cmty. Cancer Ctrs. (dir. 1979-81), Am. Soc. Clin. Oncology (chmn. pub. rels. com. 1976-79, bd. dirs. 1979-82, 84-87, pres. 1985-86, Spl. Recognition award 1999), others. Methodist.

DURANT, MARC, lawyer; b. N.Y.C., Jan. 17, 1947; s. Sidney Irwin and Estelle (Haas) D.; m. Karen Rose Baker, June 9, 1968 (div. 1975); children: Lauren, Elyssa; m. Rita Mary Tatar, Dec. 31, 1979; children: David, Alexander. BS, Cornell U., 1968; JD, Harvard U., 1968-71. Bar: Pa. 1972, U.S. Dist. Ct. (ea. dist.) Pa. 1972, U.S. Supreme Ct. 1980, U.S. Ct. Appeals (3d cir.) 1981, N.Y. 1991. Law clk. U.S. Dist. Ct., Wilmington, Del., 1971-72; assoc. Schnader, Harrison, Segal & Lewis, Phila., 1972-75; asst. U.S. Atty. U.S. Dept. Justice, Phila., 1975-77; dep. chief criminal divsn.v. U.S. Atty.'s Office, Phila., 1977-81; ptnr. Durant and Durant, Phila., 1981—. Mem. ABA, FBA, Nat. Assn. Criminal Def. Lawyers, Pa. Bar Assn., Phila. Bar Assn. Office: Durant & Durant 325 Chestnut St Philadelphia PA 19106-2611

DURANT, PENNY LYNNE RAIFE, author, educator; b. Albuquerque, May 22, 1951; d. John Carl and Patricia Fay (Bremermann) Raife; m. Omar Duane Durant, Jan. 2, 1971; children: Geoffrey Alan (dec.), Adam Omar. Student, Lawrence U., Appleton, Wis., 1969-70; BS, U. N.Mex., 1973, MA, 1980. Mem. adv. bd. Soc. Children's Book Writers and Illustrators/N.Mex., Albuquerque, 1996—. Author: Make a Splash!, 1991, Prizewinning Science Fair Projects, 1991, When Heroes Die, 1993 (Lambda Lit. award 1993, 1st prize juvenile novel Nat. League Am. Pen Women 1993, award of excellence N.Mex. Press Women 1993), Bubblemania!, 1995, Exploring the World of Plants, 1995, Exploring the World of Animals, 1995, More Prizewinning Science Fair Projects, 1998; works put to music, performed include We Are One, Aki's Story, Mayhem and Malarkey; conbr. articles to Parents Mag., Durango Mag., Working Parents, The Luth. Sec. bd. dirs. Albuquerque Children's Theatre, 1995—. Mem. Nat. League Am. Pen Women (v.p. Albuquerque br. 1990, sec. 1996, state letters chair 1996), S.W. Writers Workshop, Soc. Children's Book Writers and Illustrators (mem. adv. bd. N.Mex. chpt. 1997—). Democrat. Lutheran. Home: 305 Quincy St NE Albuquerque NM 87108-1344

DURAWA, DANIEL T., state commissioner; b. Buffalo, N.Y., Sept. 11, 1944. Commr. City of Buffalo, 1994—. Mem. Niagra Frontier Parks, Recreation, Buffalo Olmsed Parks Conservancy. Office: City of Buffalo Human Svcs Parks Recreation Delaware Labor Ctr 17 Meadowview Pl Buffalo NY 14214-2646*

DURAY, JOHN ROBERT, physicist; b. East Chicago, Ind., Jan. 28, 1940; s. John S. and Margaret A. D.; m. Elizabeth A. Meyer, Nov. 19, 1966; children: Sam, Vince, Mike. BS, Benedictine U., 1962; PhD, U. Notre Dame, 1968. Postdoctoral fellow Ohio State Univ., Columbus, 1968-70; instr. Princeton (N.J.) Univ., 1970-75; asst. prof. Ind. Univ. N.W., Gary, 1975; mgr. subsurface sys. Bendix Field Engring., Grand Junction, Colo., 1975-86; mgr. tech. programs Rust Geotech, Grand Junction, 1986-96; prin. scientist Sensible Environ. Solutions, Grand Junction, 1996—. Chmn. bd. dirs. Holy Family Edn. Found. Mem. Am. Phys. Soc., Sigma Xi. Fax: (970) 256-0108. E-mail: jrd@gj.net, ses@wic.net. Home: 2137 Banff Ct Grand Junction CO 81503-1032 Office: Sensible Environ Solutions 454 Main St Ste 1 Grand Junction CO 81501-2512

DURBIN, ENOCH JOB, aeronautical engineering educator; b. N.Y.C., Sept. 6, 1922; s. David and Ida (Deutsch) D.; m. Marilyn Lehman, Sept. 15, 1945; 3 children. B.S., CCNY, 1943; M.S., Rensselaer Poly. Inst., 1947. Rsch. scientist NACA, Langley, Va., 1947-51; sr. mem. tech. staff Am. Aviation, Downey, Calif., 1951-54; prof. aero-mech. sci. Princeton U., 1957—, sr. rsch. assoc., 1954-57, dir. instrumentation and control lab., 1954—; founder, dir. Ctr. Alt. Fueling of Combustion Engines, U. B.C., 1980-82; chmn. steering com. Nat. Ctr. Alt. Transp. Fuels, 1989—; founder, dir. Entrepreneural Ctr. Princeton U., 1993—; cons. European and U.S. auto industry. Author: Methane-fuel for the Future, 1982; gen. editor, contbg. author: Flight Test Manual, 1964; patentee in field including natural gas storage system and traveling spark ignition system. Mem. Princeton Borough Council, 1965-68; pres. Unitarian Ch. Princeton, 1975-77. Served with U.S. Army, 1943-46. Fellow AAAS, Instrument Soc. Am.; mem. Internat. Symposium on Automotive Tech. and Automation, Sigma Xi. Home: 246 Western Way Princeton NJ 08540-5306 Office: Princeton U Dept Mech and Aerospace Engring Engring Quadrangle Princeton NJ 08544

DURBIN, RICHARD JOSEPH, senator; b. East St. Louis, Ill., Nov. 21, 1944; s. William and Ann D.; m. Loretta Schaefer, June 24, 1967; children: Christine, Paul, Jennifer. B.S. in Econs., Georgetown U., 1966, J.D., 1969. Bar: Ill. 1969. Chief legal counsel Lt. Gov. Paul Simon of Ill., 1969; mem. staff minority leader Ill. Senate, 1972-77, parliamentarian, 1969-77; practice law, 1969—; assoc. prof. med. humanities So. Ill. U., 1978—; mem. 98th-104th Congresses from 20th Dist. Ill., 1983-97; U.S. senator from Ill., 1997—, mem. Judiciary com., govtl. affairs com., budget com.; mem. appropriations com., subcoms. on agriculture, rural devel. and related agys., def., legis. br., and D.C. (ranking mem.), 1999—; mem. budget com.; mem. govt. affairs com. subcom. on oversight of govt. mgmt., restructuring and the D.C., 1999—, and permanent subcom. on investigations, 1997—; mem. select com. on ethics, 1999—; asst. Dem. fl. leader. Campaign worker Sen. Paul Douglas of Ill., 1966; staff Office Ill. Dept. Bus. and Econ. Devel., Washington; candidate for Ill. Lt. Gov., 1978; staff alt. Pres.'s State Planning Council, 1980; advisor Am. Council Young Polit. Leaders, 1981; mem. YMCA Ann. Membership Roundup, YMCA Bldg. Drive, Pony World Series; bd. dirs. Cath. Charities, United Way of Springfield, Old Capitol Art Fair, Springfield Youth Soccer; mem. Sch. Dist. 1986 Referendum Com., Springfield NAACP. Democrat. Roman Catholic. Office: US Senate 364 Russell Sen Office Bldg Washington DC 20510-1302*

DURBIN, RICHARD LOUIS, SR., healthcare administration consultant; b. Millersport, Ohio, Aug. 28, 1928; s. Clark Babe and Mabel (Bushee) D.; m. Carolyn Bohrer, Mar. 18, 1955; children: Richard Louis, Margot Jane, Melissa Bushee. BA, Ohio State U., 1949; MBA, U. Chgo., 1956; MPA, U. Ariz., 1969; postgrad., Pace Coll., 1973; MPH, U. Tex. Sch. Pub. Health, 1992, postgrad, 1999—. Registered sanitarian; cert. govt. fin. mgr., Assn. Govt. Accts., 1996. Research chemist Battelle Meml. Inst., Columbus, Ohio, 1949-50; sales rep. Am. Cyanamid Co., N.Y.C., 1953-54; adminstrv. asst. Lancaster (Ohio)-Fairfield Hosp., 1954; with Bus. Devel. Outreach Helath, Austin, 1995—; asst. adminstr. City of Memphis Hosps., 1956-58, assoc. adminstr., 1958-60; dir. outpatient and profl. services Presbyn.-St. Luke's Hosp., Chgo., 1960-61; assoc. dir. grad. program in hosp. adminstrn., faculty U. Chgo. Grad. Sch. Bus., 1961-62; exec. sec. Am. Assn. Univ. Programs in Hosp. Adminstrn., 1960-62; assoc. prof. bus. adminstrn. Temple U., 1967-69, prof. mgmt., 1969-70, founder, dir. grad. program in health care adminstrn., 1967-70, exec. dir., 1966-70; exec. dir. Lubbock (Tex.) County Dist. Hosp., 1970-71; v.p. Coll. Medicine and Dentistry N.J., 1971-75; also v.p. Acad. Health Center; asst. prof. N.J. Med. Sch., 1973-75; pres., chief exec. officer Harris County Hosp. Dist., Houston, 1975-89; asst. regional dir., Region #6 Tex. State Dept. Health, 1989-92; adminstr. Tex. Alcoholic Beverage Commn., Austin, 1992-93; pres., CEO Durbin Internat., San Marcos, Tex., 1993—; health dir. Cameron County Health Dept., San Benito, Tex., 1995—; cons. in field, pres. D&H Enterprises, Durbin Internat.; project dir., chief planner, exec. dir. Newark Comprehensive Health Plan, 1974; cons. div. hosp. and med. facilities HEW, 1967—, mem. design adv. group, mem. nat. rev. com., cons. expt. health systems, 1971-73; cons. Nat. Commn. on Productivity, U.S. Bur. Prisons, 1968—; mem. Hosp. Devel., Inc., N.J. Gov.'s Correctional Health Svc. Investigations Com.; mem. adv. bd. Comprenetics, Inc., 1967—; mem. steering com. Tucson Hosp. and Health Planning Commn., 1962—, Assoc. Hosp. Svcs. Ariz., 1963-64; treas. Ariz. League Nursing, 1963-64; adj. assoc. prof. Tex. Woman's U.; mem. coordinating coun. Tex. Health and Human Svcs., 1986—; mem. appraisal rev.

bd. Travis Ctrl. Appraisal Dist., 1994—; dir. bus. devel. Outreach Health Svcs., 1995—; adj. assoc. prof. U. Tex. Sch. Pub. Health, 1996; mem. med. adv. com. Tex. Workman's Compensation Commn. Author: A Statistical Methodology of Evaluating a Medical Staff, 1961, New Ideas and Concepts in Outpatient Management, 1963, (with others) Ivory Tower to Workshop, 1964, Ambulatory Care Development, 1966, (with W.H. Springall) Organization and Administration of Health Care, 2d edit, 1974, (with Springall, P. High) Manual for Hospital Program and Performance Budgeting at the Operating Level, 1968, (with G. Connor) Design of a City-Wide HMO, 1974; cons. editor: Hosp. Topics; editor: The Forum, What's Going On: Hospital Topics; mem. editorial adv. bd. Physician Weekly, editorial adv. com. Who's Who in America - 45th Edit.; contbr. articles to profl. jours. Mem. Phila. Crime Commn., 1967—; bd. dirs. Ariz. Blue Cross, Mexic-Arte Mus., 1994—; mem. Tex. Indigent Care Task Force; chmn. Harris County Jail com., 1987-88; chmn. Health Services com. AIDS panel. Served to lt. USNR, 1945-46, 50-53. Recipient Editorial award Hosp. Mgmt. mag., 1961, 63, 65; Cert. of Merit Gov. Ariz., 1967, 68; Silver medal (Debakey) award Baylor Coll. of Medicine, 1986. Fellow Am. Coll. Hosp. Adminstrs.; mem. Nat. Assn. Pub. Hosps. (dir.), Am. Chem. Soc., Nat. Assn. Clinic Mgrs., Am. Hosp. Assn. (council pub. hosps.), Pa. Hosp. Assn., Tex. Hosp. Assn. (bd. dirs., mem. exec. com. 1987-88), Nat. Assn. Pub. Hosps. (founder), So. Ariz. Hosp. Council (pres. 1963), Am. Criminology Soc., Am. Soc. Pub. Adminstrn., Am. Inst. Mgmt., Internat. Hosp. Fedn., Am. Mgmt. Assn. (Excellence award 1968), Am. Coll. Healthcare Assn. (chmn. book award com. 1983, membership com. 1986), AAUP, U. Tex. Faculty Ctr., U. Tex. Recreational Sports (life), Am. Coll. Managed Care Adminstrs., Tex. Pub. Health Assn., Tucson Press Club (life), Quadrangle (U. Chgo.) Club, Buckeye Lake Yacht Club, Columbian Yacht Club (Chgo.), Headliners Club (Austin, Tex.), Hillcrest Country Club, Houston Yacht Club, Army-Navy Capitol Hill Club (Washington), Pa. Soc. Club, Rotary, Houston C. of C. (health com.), Sigma Xi, Sigma Alpha Epsilon. Presbyterian (deacon). E-mail: dickd@ORHS.com. Home: 505 W 7th St Apt 319 Austin TX 78701-2836 Office: 1114 Lost Creek Blvd Austin TX 78746-6300

DURBIN, RICHARD LOUIS, JR., lawyer; b. Gary, Ind., Dec. 23, 1955; s. Richard Louis and Carolyn Martha (Bohrer) D.; m. Diana Cabaza Durbin, June 2, 1979; children: Louis Eloy, Laura Elena. Student, Rutgers U., 1973-75; BA, U. Chgo., 1977; JD, U. Tex., 1980. Bar: Tex. 1980. Law clk. to presiding judge U.S. Dist. Ct. (we. dist.) Tex., San Antonio, 1980-82; assoc. Susman, Godfrey & McGowan, Houston, 1982-83; asst. U.S. atty. Organized Crime Drug Enforcement Task Force U.S. Atty.'s Office (we. dist.), San Antonio, 1983-88, chief criminal sect., 1988-90, 98—, chief narcotics sect., 1990-92, chief appellate sect., 1992-98; chief Organized Crime Drug Enforcement Task Force U.S. Atty.'s Office (we. dist.), 1997-98; adj. prof. law St. Mary's U. Sch. of Law, 1995—; instr. U.S. Atty. Gen. Adv. Inst., Washington, 1987-99. Editor Tex. U. Law Rev., 1979-80. Interviewer U. Chgo. Alumni Schs. Com., San Antonio, 1984-97. Recipient Dir.'s award Tex. Dept. Pub. Safety, Austin, 1985. Mem. Tex. State Bar, Coll. State Bar Tex., Order of Coif, Phi Beta Kappa. Office: US Attys Office 601 NW Loop 410 Ste 600 San Antonio TX 78216-5512

DURBIN, ROBERT CAIN, retired hotel executive; b. Rushville, Ind., Dec. 24, 1931; s. Leo and Mary Inez (Cain) D.; m. Ruth Ann MacMahon, Feb. 1, 1969; children: Robert Cain, Bridget Ruth, Timothy Leo, Patrick Joseph, William Michael. BS magna cum laude, Xavier U., Cin., 1954. With Durbin Hotel, Rushville, Ind., 1949-54; mgr. Clifty Inn, Madison, Ind., 1957-61; resident mgr. Pioneer Hotel, Tucson, 1961-62; exec. v.p. Del E. Webb Hotels, Las Vegas, Nev., 1962-70; exec. v.p., dir. ops. ITT Sheraton Corp. Am., Boston, 1970-80; exec. v.p. Heritage Travel Inc., Cambridge, Mass., 1980-89; pres. Corp. Svcs. Internat., Cambridge, 1980-89; prin. Robert Durbin Cos., Inc., 1989-90; gen. mgr. Indpls. Marriott, 1990-99. 1st Lt. Fin. Corps U.S. Army, 1954-56. Mem. Am. Hotel and Motel Assn. Home: 7821 Holly Creek Ln Indianapolis IN 46240-2824

DURCHSLAG, STEPHEN P., lawyer; b. Chgo., May 20, 1940; s. Milton Lewis and Elizabeth (Potovsky) D.; m. Ruth Florence Mayer, Nov. 21, 1976; children: Rachel Beth, Danielle Leah. BS, U. Wis., 1963; LLB, Harvard U., 1966. Bar: Ill. 1966. Assoc. Sidley & Austin, Chgo., 1966-89; ptnr. Winston & Strawn, Chgo., 1989—. Contbr. articles to numerous publs. Bd. dirs. Anshe Emet, Chgo., 1983—; bd. trustees Nathan Cummings Found., 1996—. Mem. ABA (AAF legal com.), Promotion Mktg. Assn. (bd. dirs.), Am. Standard Club, East Bank Club. Jewish. Avocations: skiing, running, tennis, rare books. Office: Winston & Strawn 35 W Wacker Dr Ste 4200 Chicago IL 60601-1695

DUREK, DOROTHY MARY, retired English language educator; b. Pitts., Jan. 23, 1926; d. Joseph Adam and Helen Barbara (Ondich) D. BS in Edn., Youngstown State U., 1962; MS in Edn., Westminster Coll., 1969. Cert. English tchr., Ohio, comprehensive English cert., Pa. Tchr. English Brookfield (Ohio) Schs., 1962-64, Sharon (Pa.) City Schs., 1964-88; mem., pres. Coll. Club Sharon, 1993-94. Charter mem., bd. dirs. LWV Mercer County, Pa., 1993-97; mem. docent Butler Inst. Am. Art, Youngstown, 1988—; mem. Shenango Valley Women's Interfaith Coun., Jewish-Christian Dialogue Group, Sharon, Youngstown Symphony Soc., Youngstown Opera Guild; charter mem. Mus. Women's Art, Washington, Nat. Mus. of the Am. Indian, Washington; mem., bd. dirs. Christian Assocs. Shenango Valley. Mem. NEA, Pa. State Educators Assn., Sharon Tchrs. Assn., Cath. Collegiate Assn., Sharon Lifelong Learning Coun. (bd. dirs. 1995), Read and Discuss Group. Roman Catholic. Home: 1726 Ashton Ave Sharpsville PA 16150-1028

DURELL, JACK, psychiatrist; b. N.Y.C., July 5, 1928; s. Sam and Helen (Schwartzman) D.; m. Viviane M. diGioja, May 19, 1955. BA summa cum laude, Harvard U., 1949; MD cum laude, Yale U., 1953. Rsch. biochemist NIMH, Bethesda, Md., 1954-57; chief, sect. of psychiatry NIMH, 1963-67; v.p. med. affairs, clin. dir. The Psychiat. Inst., Washington, 1967-72; pres., med. dir. The Psychiat. Inst., 1972-78; assoc. dir. sci. Nat. Inst. Drug Abuse, Rockville, Md., 1979-86; med. dir. clin. affairs div. Ea. Va. Med. Authority, Norfolk, 1986-87; chmn. dept. psychiatry Mercy Cath. Med. Ctr., Phila., 1987-92; prof. psychiatry U. Pa., Phila., 1987—; exec. dir. Treatment Rsch. Inst., 1992—; pres. Delta Metrics, 1994—; pres. The Psychiat. Inst. Found., Washington, 1973-78; trustee Phila. Mental Health Care Connection, 1987-89. Editor: The Changing Clinical Picture of Schizophrenia, 1977; asst. editor-in-chief Jour. Psychiat. Rsch., 1966-82, mem. editorial bd., 1982—; contbr. to numerous med. publs. With USPHS, 1953-86. Fellow Am. Psychiat. Assn.; mem. Am. Acad. Psychiatrists in Alcoholism and Addictions (sec.-treas. 1985—), Am. Psychopathological Assn., Am. Coll. Neuropsychopharmacology.

DUREN, MICHAEL, cardiologist; b. Galveston, Tex., Nov. 16, 1939; s. Norman and Edwina M. Duren; m. Esther Louise Lutzweiler, July 27, 1979; children: Tracy Norman, Lara Michelle; stepchildren: Royce, Jennifer, Timothy Bane. BA, U. Tex., 1962; MD, U. Tex. Med. Br., 1966. Diplomate Am. Bd. Internal Medicine. Intern Meth. Hosp. Dallas, 1966-67; resident in internal medicine Meth. Hosp. of Dallas, 1969-70, 71-72; fellow in cardiology Cardiopulmonary Inst. Meth. Hosp. Dallas-Tex. and Southwestern Med. Sch., 1970-71; pvt. practice Baylor Med. Ctr., Garland, Tex., 1972—, chief of medicine, 1990—, chief of ICU, 1990-93, chief of cardiology, 1990-94, med. advisor cardiac rehab. program, 1989—; bd. dirs. Cardiovascular Ctr. of Excellence, Humana Med. City Hosp., Dallas, Med. City Hosp. Dallas. Mem. adv. bd. to editors: Am. Jour. Sports Medicine; contbr. articles to med. jours. Bd. dirs. Health Occupations Students Am. program Garland Ind. Sch. Dist.; bd. dirs. Garland Civic Theater. Capt. M.C., USAF, 1967-69. Fellow ACP, Am. Coll. Sports Medicine (speakers bur.); mem. Am. Coll. Cardiology, Am. Soc. Echocardiography, Am. Soc. Internal Medicine, Am. Heart Assn. (bd. dirs., speakers bur.), Am. Profl. Practice Assn., Tex. Med. Assn., Dallas County Med. Soc. Avocations: fitness, chess, reading, civil war history. Home: 540 Buckingham Rd Apt 517 Richardson TX 75081-5663 Office: 700 Walter Reed Blvd Ste 206 Garland TX 75042-5743

DUREN, STEPHEN D., artist; b. Fairfield, Calif., Apr. 8, 1948; s. Donald and Ruth Lenore (Alley) D.; m. Maureen Jo Dozeman, Nov. 11, 1972 (div. Aug. 1986); children: Adelle Meadow, Havalah Rose; m. Victoria S. Peabody, Aug. 25, 1995; 1 child, Lindsey McNeil. Diploma, Def. Info. Sch., Indpls., 1970; BFA, San Francisco Art Inst., 1974; MA, Calif. State U., Sacramento, 1977. Asst. prof. Kendall Coll. Art and Design, Grand Rapids, Mich., 1979-84; artist-in-residence Oxvow Art Camp, Saugatuck, Mich., 1984, Niangua Colony, Mo., 1986, Ucross Found., Wyo., 1988, Shoreline Arts Project, Muskegon, Mich., 1989; adj. artist William James Coll., Allendale, Mich., 1978, Muskegon C.C., 1978, Grand Valley State U., Allendale, Mich., 1984, 86. One-person shows include Grand Rapids Art Mus., 1994, Dennos Mus. Ctr., Traverse City, Mich., 1995, Midland Art Ctr., Mich., 1995, Krasl Art Ctr., St. Joseph, Mich., 1995. Spkr. Grand Valley State U., Allendale, 1981, Muskegon Mus. of Art, 1984, Acquinas Coll., Grand Rapids, 1992, Grand Rapids Art Mus., 1994. With USN, 1968-72. Recipient Best of Show Mich. Found./Arts, Battle Creek Art Ctr., Mich., 1984, 88, 1st prize Grand Rapids Arts Coun., 1986, CAA Drawing award Nat. Exhibit, Am. Art, Chautauqua, N.Y., 1987. Avocations: black and white photography, gardening. Home: 6087 100th St SE Caledonia MI 49316-9431

DURFEE, HAROLD ALLEN, philosophy educator; b. Bennington, Vt., May 21, 1920; s. Lynn Stanton and Ethel (Foster) D.; m. Doris Graver, Aug. 10, 1944; children: Peter Allen, Gary Robert. Ph.B., U. Vt., 1941; B.D., Yale U., 1944; Ph.D., Columbia U., 1951; postgrad., Harvard U., 1954-55, Oxford U., 1968-69, 76. Ordained to ministry Presbyn. Ch., 1944; chmn. dept. philosophy Park Coll., Parkville, Mo., 1946-55; assoc. prof. philosophy Am. U., Washington, 1955-57; chmn. dept. philosophy and religion Am. U., 1957-73, William Frazer McDowell prof. philosophy, 1957-90, William Frazer McDowell prof. philosophy emeritus, 1990—; faculty Forum on Psychiatry and Humanities, Washington Sch. Psychiatry, 1979-80; dir. seminar contemporary European philosophy, 1963; exchange prof. Cath. U. Am., 1972; pres. Mo. Philos. Assn., 1953-54. Author: (with Harold E. Davis) The Teaching of Philosophy in Universities of the United States, 1965, Foundational Reflections: Studies in Contemporary Philosophy, 1987; editor: Analytic Philosophy and Phenomenology, 1976; co-editor, contbr.: Explanation: New Directions in Philosophy, 1973, Phenomenology and Beyond: The Self and Its Language, 1989; assoc. editor, contbr. Psychiatry and The Humanities, Vol. II, Thought, Consciousness and Reality, 1977, Vol. V, Kierkegaard's Truth: The Disclosure of the Self, 1981; chmn. editorial bd. Am. U. Publs. in Philosophy, 1973-88; editor Am. Univ. Publications in Philosophy, 1989—. Trustee Washington Consortium of Univs., 1970-90. Recipient Scholar/Tchr. of Yr. award Am. U., 1985, Outstanding Service award Am. U., 1987; Fund for Advancement Edn. fellow, 1954-55. Mem. Am. Philos. Assn., Metaphys. Soc. Am., Am. Acad. Religion, Internat. Soc. Metaphysics, Internat. Phenomenological Research Soc., AAUP, Washington Philosophy Club (pres. 1961-62), Kappa Sigma, Phi Kappa Phi. Home: Hilton Head Plantation 71 Dolphin Head Dr Hilton Head Island SC 29926-1920 Office: Am U 4400 Massachusetts Ave NW Washington DC 20016-8003

DURGIN, FRANK HERMAN, II, aeronautical engineer; b. Exeter, N.H., Aug. 24, 1926; s. John Frank and Eudora Bissette (Gallant) D.; m. Marianne Hamilton, June 15, 1953; children: John, Jane, Laura, Sally, Frank. SB, MIT, 1948, SM, 1954, cert. engr., 1957. Rsch. engr. Naval Supersonic Lab. MIT, Cambridge, Mass., 1948-61, sr. scientist Aeroelastic Lab., 1961-69, assoc. dir. Wright Bros. Wind Tunnel, 1969-91; pvt. cons., Belmont, Mass., 1991—. Contbr. articles to profl. publs. Mem. Town Meeting, 1963-96; mem. Ran Sch. Com., Belmont, 1966; active Waverly Congl. Ch., 1960—. With U.S. Army, 1946-47. Mem. AIAA, NSPE, ASCE (chmn. manual of practice for wind tunnel testing of bldg. and structures 1981-86, chmn. manual update 1991-97). Achievements include research in solving major engineering problems at John Hancock Bldg., Boston, Sears Tower, Chgo., Coll. Life Ins. Co. Hdqrs., Indpls. Home: 19 Payson Rd Belmont MA 02478-2720

DURGIN, SCOTT BENJAMIN, radio frequency engineer, physics educator; b. Lewiston, Maine, July 9, 1966; s. Walter Brian and Mae Susan (Fenner) D.; m. Lisa Marie Haskell, Sept. 3, 1988; children: Lindsay Rebecca, Brittany Mae. AA, Ea. Nazarene Coll., Boston, 1990; BSEE, U. Maine, Orono, 1993, BS in Physics, 1993. Rsch. asst. high power microwave comm. The Mitre Corp., Lexington, Mass., 1989-90; engring. tech. high frequency analog/digital circuitry Integrated Tech. Corp., Tempe, Ariz, 1990-92; product design and devel. engr. radio frequency components Passive Power Products, Gray, Maine, 1993—; contr., acct. Kornerstone Kindergarten, Auburn, Maine, 1995—; tchr. physics Ctrl. Maine Tech. Coll., Auburn, 1997—; engring. sales mgr. Passive Power Products, 1997—; CFO, bus. mgr. Korderstone Kindergarten & Preesch., Auburn, 1997—. Sunday sch. tchr. Ch. of the Nazarene, Phoenix, Ariz., 1991-92. Mem. IEEE, Giga Soc., Glia Soc., One-in-a-Thousand Soc., Top-One-Percent Soc., Triple Nine Soc., Triple Nine Soc., One-in-a-Thousand Soc., Pi Mu Epsilon. Libertarian. Avocations: antique collector, amateur historian, biking, hiking, student of freemasonry. Home: 89 Sunset Ave Auburn ME 04210-4127 Office: Passive Power Products PO Box 1176 97 Shaker Rd Gray ME 04039-7701

DURHAM, BARBARA, state supreme court justice; b. 1942. BSBA, Georgetown U.; JD, Stanford U. Bar: Wash. 1968. Former judge Wash. Superior Ct., King County; judge Wash. Ct. Appeals; assoc. justice Wash. Supreme Ct., 1985—, chief justice, 1995-99, justice, 1999—. Office: Wash Supreme Ct Temple of Justice PO Box 40929 Olympia WA 98504-0929

DURHAM, BETTY BETHEA, therapist; b. S.C., Jan. 27, 1933; d. Liston Fenton and Rosalie (Bracey) Bethea; m. John Lewis Cottrell, June 8, 1952 (div. June 1972); children: John Lewis Jr., Gregory Bethea; m. John I. Durham, Apr. 29, 1988. BS, Pembroke State U., 1974; MSW, U. Ga., 1981. Psycho-social specialist Dublinaire Nursing Care, Dublin, Ga., 1979-80; med. social worker C. Vinson V.A. Med. Ctr., Dublin, 1982-86; therapist Raleigh (N.C.) Employee's Assistance Program, 1987-88; pastoral counselor Greenwich (Conn.) Bapt. Ch., 1988-94; therapist Big Island, Va., 1995—; marriage and family counselor Bapt. Ch., Greenwich, 1988-94; supr. grad. studies U. Ga., Fla. State U., Dublin, 1982-86. Editor Hospital Social Svc. manuals, 1982-86. Mem. Laurens County Ga. Mental Health Bd., 1975-76, Ga. Grand Jury and Gov. Com. on Drug Abuse, 1977; survey and coord. of nursing home svcs., 52 counties in Ga., 1982-86. Recipient Citation for Developing Nursing Home Fund Drive Nat. Heart Assn., 1979, Hands and Heart award VA, 1984. Mem. AAUW, Nat. Mus. of Women in the Arts (tour leader Europe and Mid. East 1988—). Mem. United Meth. Ch. Avocations: needlepoint, painting, horticulture, reading the classics. Home: 1509 Tolley Meadow Rd Big Island VA 24526-2977

DURHAM, CAROLYN RICHARDSON, foreign language and literature educator; b. Bklyn., Jan. 13, 1947; d. Herbert Nathaniel and Fannie Elaine (Franklin) Richardson; m. Edward Cassell Durham; children: Diana Kristine, Dara Marie. BA, Drew U., Madison, N.J., 1968; MA, Rutgers U., 1972, PhD, 1987. Rsch. analyst Equitable Life Assurance Soc., N.Y.C., 1968-69; instr. Hampton (Va.) U., 1972-76, asst. prof. fgn. lang. and lit., 1976-91, coordinator modern fgn. lang., 1981-91; assoc. prof. Tex. Christian U., Ft. Worth, 1991—; cons. Archdiocese of N.Y. Schs., N.Y.C., 1982, U.S. Dept. Edn., 1992, 95, NEH, 1992. Author, co-editor, translator: Finally Us: Contemporary Black Brazilian Women Writers, 1995; contbr. articles to profl. jours. Bd. dirs. Adv. Bd. on Black Adoptions, Va., 1983-85; interpreter ARC, Yorktown, Va., 1981—; del. nominating conv. Dem. Party, 1984, 86. Ford Found. fellow, 1990; Fulbright-Hays awardee, 1989; NEH seminar award, 1989; Russell fellow, 1972; recipient Cert. of Recognition, State of Va., 1984, TCU Rsch. award 1991, 94, 96, 97, 98, TCU Edn. in a Global Soc. award 1993, 97. Mem. MLA, Afro-Latin Am. Rsch. Assn., Am. Coun. on Tchg. and Fgn. Lang., Am. Assn. Tchrs. Spanish and Portuguese, Coll. Lang. Assn., South Ctrl. MLA, Assn. Acad. Programs in Latin Am. and the Caribbean, Feministas Unidas, Phi Sigma Iota, Sigma Delta Pi. Democrat. AME Zion Ch. Office: Tex Christian U Dept Spanish and Latin American Studies Fort Worth TX 76129

DURHAM, CHRISTINE MEADERS, state supreme court justice; b. L.A., Aug. 3, 1945; d. William Anderson and Louise (Christensen) Meaders; m. George Homer Durham II, Dec. 29, 1966; children: Jennifer, Meghan, Troy, Melinda, Isaac. A.B., Wellesley Coll., 1967; J.D., Duke U., 1971. Bar: N.C. 1971, Utah 1974. Sole practice law Durham, N.C., 1971-73; instr. legal medicine Duke U., Durham, 1971-73; adj. prof. law Brigham Young U., Provo, Utah, 1973-78; ptnr. Johnson, Durham & Moxley, Salt Lake City, 1974-78; judge Utah Dist. Ct., 1978-82; assoc. justice Utah Supreme Ct., 1982—. Pres. Women Judges Fund for Justice, 1987-88. Fellow Am. Bar Found.; mem. ABA (edn. com. appellate judges' conf.), Nat. Assn. Women Judges (pres. 1986-87), Utah Bar Assn., Am. Law Inst. (coun. mem.), Nat. Ctr. State Courts (bd. dirs.). Home: 1702 Yale Ave Salt Lake City UT 84108-1836 Office: Utah Supreme Ct PO Box 140210 Salt Lake City UT 84114-0210

DURHAM, FLOYD WESLEY, JR., economist, educator; b. Yuma, Ariz., Feb. 9, 1930; s. Floyd Wesley and Inez (Irvin) D.; BA, North Tex. State U., 1951, MA, 1952; PhD, U. Okla., 1963; m. Patricia Keehan, May 24, 1973; children—Mark Kipling, Ronald Chappell. Claimsman, Liberty Mutual Ins. Co., Boston and Ft. Worth, 1955-58; mem. faculty dept. econs. Tex. Christian U., Ft. Worth, 1960—, prof., 1971—; cons., 1964—. Pres., Suicide Prevention Tarrant County, 1968-69. Bd. dirs. Ft. Worth Literacy Council, 1963-70, Cen. Tax Authority, Parker County, Tex. Served with AUS, 1953-55. Danforth Found. grantee, 1969-70. Mem. AAUP, Am. So. Econ. Assns., Southwestern and Western Social Sci. Assns., Western Writers Am., Beta Gamma Sigma, Omicron Delta Epsilon, Lambda Chi Alpha. Author: A Pilot Methodological Study to Determine Dibilitating Conditions, 1967; The Trinity River Paradox; Flood and Famine, 1976. Contbr. articles to profl. jours. Home: 6025 Wrigley Way Fort Worth TX 76133-3535

DURHAM, HARRY BLAINE, III, lawyer; b. Denver, Sept. 16, 1946; s. Harry Blaine and Mary Frances (Oliver) D.; m. Lynda L. Durham, Aug. 4, 1973; children: Christopher B., Laurel A. BA cum laude, Colo. Coll., 1969; JD, U. Colo., 1973. Bar: Wyo. 1973, U.S. Tax Ct. 1974, U.S. Ct. Appeals (10th cir.) 1976. Assoc. Brown, Drew, Apostolos, Massey & Sullivan, Casper, Wyo., 1973-77; ptnr. Brown & Drew, Casper, Wyo., 1977—. Articles editor U. Colo. Law Rev., 1972-73. Bd. dirs. Casper Symphony Assn. 1974-88, v.p. 1979-82, pres. 1983-87; bd. dirs. Natrona County United Way, 1974-76, pres., 1975-76; mem. City of Casper Parks and Recreation Commn., 1985-94, vice chmn., 1987-94; Rep. precinct committeeman, 1999—. Named Permanent Class Pres., Class of 1969, Colo. coll., Nat. alumni coun. Colo. Coll.; recipient State Heroes award SGMA, 1997. Mem. ABA, Wyo. Bar Assn., Natrona County Bar Assn., Nat. Assn. Railroad Trial Counsel, Phi Beta Kappa, Casper Amateur Hockey Club (bd. dirs. 1970-77, sec. 1974-77), Wyo. Amateur Hockey Assn. (bd. dirs., sec. 1974-85, pres. 1985-88). Republican. Home: 3101 Hawthorne Ave Casper WY 82604-4975 Office: 123 W 1st St Ste 800 Casper WY 82601-2486

DURHAM, HARVEY RALPH, academic administrator. BS, Wake Forest U., 1959; MA, U. Ga., 1962, PhD in Math., 1965. Asst. prof. math. Appalachian State U., Boone, N.C., 1965-67, assoc. prof., chair dept. math., 1967-71, prof. math., 1971-74, assoc. dean faculty, 1971-74, assoc. vice chancellor for acad. affairs, 1974-79, acting vice chancellor for acad. affairs, 1979-80, vice chancellor for acad. affairs, 1980-89, provost, vice chancellor for acad. affairs, 1989—. Office: Appalachian State U Office of Acad Affairs Boone NC 28608*

DURHAM, J(AMES) MICHAEL, retail executive; b. Louisville, Oct. 2, 1945; s. James Alton and Mary E. (Agustus) D.; m. Linda R. Hastings, June 5, 1965 (div. July 1983); m. Germaine Myra Judd, Jan. 26, 1987; children: Cassandra, Jason, Jamie. BA in English, U. Ky., 1968. English tchr. Clark County High Sch., Winchester, Ky., 1969-70; sales rep. Mass. Mutual Ins. Co., Lexington, Ky., 1970-71, Lorillard Tobacco Co., Lexington, 1972-79; owner/mgr. Durham Sales, Louisville, Lexington, 1979-85; owner/pres. Chesapeake Sport Shop, Balt., 1985—, Stadium Sports, Balt., 1991—. Mem. Nat. Sporting Goods Assn., Harbor Place Mchts. Assn. (pres. 1993-98), Balt. Tour Assn., Balt. C. of C. Avocations: golf, reading fiction. Office: The Sport Shop 201 E Pratt St Baltimore MD 21202-1039

DURHAM, JAMES MICHAEL, SR., marketing consultant; b. Shreveport, La., May 27, 1937; s. Judson Burney and Edith Eloise (Whittington) D.; m. Constance Manuela Alvarez, June 4, 1960; children: Jennifer Paige Esperanza Kessler, James Michael Jr., Christopher Jon, David Bradley, Matthew Craig. BS in Math., Centenary Coll. of La., 1959; MSME, N.Mex. State U., 1963; MS in Sys. Mgmt., U. So. Calif., 1981; MBA, Mich. State U., 1988. Commd. 2d lt. U.S. Army, 1959, advanced through grades to col., 1979, mgmt. analyst Army Office Chief of Staff, 1972-74; command and staff positions 3d Infantry Div. U.S. Army, Wurzburg, Germany, 1974-77; student U.S. Army War Coll., Carlisle Barracks, Pa., 1977-78; product mgr. U.S. Army Tank-Automotive Materiel Readiness Command, Warren, Mich., 1978-80; commander Mainz Army Depot, Mainz, Germany, 1980-83; exec. officer to deputy commanding gen. U.S. Army Devel. and Readiness Command, Alexandria, Va., 1983; program mgr., tactical vehicles U.S. Army Tank-Automotive Command, Warren, Mich., 1984-86; ret. U.S. Army Tank Automotive Command, Warren, Mich., 1986; dir. tank automotive programs Cypress Internat., Troy, Mich., 1986-89; v.p. govt. business Cummins Engine Co., Inc., Columbus, Ind., 1989-92, v.p. govt. products, 1992-95, ret., 1995; pres. Cummins Mil. Sys. Co., Inc., Columbus, 1992-93, JD Interests Inc., Farnham, Va., 1995—. Chmn. Bartholomew County Solid Waste Mgmt. Dist. Citizens Adv. Com., 1991-95, Bartholomew County Solid Waste Mgmt. Authority, 1993-95, Bartholomew County Landfill Site Selection Com., 1993; co-chmn. Project Water, Columbus, 1990-95; chmn. bd. dirs. Am. Youth Activities Assn., Mainz, Germany, 1980-83, pres. Am. Youth Activities Assn., Kitzingen, Germany, 1975-77; bd. dirs. Indpls. Mus. Art-Columbus Gallery, 1995; chmn. devel. com. Richmond County (Va.) Habitat for Humanity, 1996—, bd. dirs., 1997—, v.p., 1998, pres., 1999; trustee Assn. for the Preservation of Va. Antiquities, 1999. Decorated Legion of Merit with oak leaf cluster, Bronze Star, Vietnam campaign medal with 60 device, Vietnamese Cross of Gallantry with palm. Mem. ASME, Nat. Def. Indsl. Assn. (exec. bd. tank and automotive sys. divsn. 1991—, steering com. combat vehicle sys. divsn. 1988—, chmn. 1991-95, steering com. tactical vehicle sys. sect. 1986-95), Assn. U.S. Army, Soc. Mfg. Engrs., Soc. Automotive Engrs., Ret. Officers Assn. (sec. Potomac chpt. 1997-98, dir. 1999—, mem. No. Neck chpt.), U.S. Army Ordnance Corps Assn., Armor Assn., Pi Kappa Alpha. Republican. Avocation: reading. Home: 2494 Simonson Rd Farnham VA 22460-2212

DURHAM, JO ANN FANNING, artist; b. Sulphur Springs, Tex., May 31, 1935; d. William Jeffress and Merle Jo (Barrett) Fanning; m. William E. Durham; children: William, John Lee (dec.). BS, Tex. A&M U., 1956; postgrad., U. Tex., Austin, 1953-55, Tex. Woman's U., Denton, Tex., 1953-55; docteur honoris causa in arts, 1994. *Jo Ann has had her paintings published in many publications including: Red Triangles in Creative Watercolor by Mary Ann Beckwith, 1996, which has also been on the cover and inside page for Rockport Publisher's Catalogue, 1996-97; Notion, International Women Artists, 1997; Photon Field I, Manhattan Arts, 1997; and Photon Field V, Spectrum Variations, Island Magic, Indian Rock, 1994,95, 98. Jo Ann first learned about art from her grandmother, Callie Jeffress Fanning Smith, who has a Picture Frame Quilt on display at the FDR Museum in Hyde Park, NY, in the Eleanor Roosevelt Room. Jo Ann is the president of International Society of Experimental Arts.* Exhibited in group shows at: Galerie Jean Lammelin, Paris, 1991, Salon D'Automne Grand Palais, Paris, 1992,93, Vanderbilt Museum, Long Island VIU, N.Y., 1995, Lever House, VIU, N.Y., 1995, Pen and Brush Club, 1995,96, VIU, N.Y., 1996, Templeton, Fort Worth Artists and Co., Fort Worth, 1996, Sumner Art Museum, Washington, 1996, Belgium Grand Prix, De Paadestallen Van Het Park Van Enghien, Belgium, 1996, Soc. Internat. Des Beaux Arts, Paris, 1996,97, Southwestern Watercolor Soc., D-Art, Dallas, 1996,97, Anthology Art Gallery, Lebanon, 1997, Longboat Key Art Ctr., North Texas Health Sci. Ctr., 1997, Atrium Gallery, Fort Worth, 1998, Laura Knott Gallery, Bradford Coll., Mass., 1998, Lee Scarfone Gallery, U. Tampa, Fla., 1998, Fort Mason, San Francisco, 1998. Recipient Gold medal Belgium Grand Prix, 1993. Mem. Soc. of Watercolor Artists (signature mem.), Internat. Soc. of Exptl. Artists (signature mem.; pres. 1998), Soc. of Layerists in Multimedia, Allied Artists, Tex. Fine Arts Assn. (past pres., regional dir., exec. bd.), D Art, Dallas Women's Caucus for the Arts, Dallas Artists Rsch. and Exhbn., Southwestern Watercolor Soc., Tex. Visual Artists Assn., Fort Worth Woman's Club Art Dept., Templeton Art Ctr., Nat. League of Am. Pen Women, Contemporary Art Ctr., Christians in the Visual Arts, Nat. coll. Soc. Fax: 817-737-6520. Home: 4300 Plantation Dr Fort Worth TX 76116-7607

DURHAM, JOHN I., retired religious studies educator; b. Bucyrus, Ohio, May 29, 1933; s. John Isaac and Lula Frances (Jackson) D.; m. Betty Ann Bethea, Apr. 29, 1988; children: Gwynne, Jeremy. BA magna cum laude, Wake Forest U., 1955; BD, Southeastern Sem., Wake Forest, 1959, THM,

1961; DPhil, U. Oxford, Eng., 1963. Pastor Sharon & Dobson's Chs., Chinquapin, N.C., 1955-61; acting instr., Latin Meredith Coll., Raleigh, N.C., 1955-56; prof. Hebrew and Old Testament Studies Southeastern Sem., Wake Forest, N.C., 1963-88; pastor Greenwich (Conn.) Bapt. Ch., 1988-94; mem. Gov.'s Commn. on Art and Religion, N.C., Raleigh, 1977-81; lectr. in Bibl. studies Regent's Park Coll., Oxford, 1981; Albritton lectr. Wake Forest U., Winston-Salem, N.C., 1987; lectr. art and architecture Europe and the Middle East tours. Cons. editor: Broadman Bible Commentary, Nashville, 1967-72; author: (books) Psalms Commentary, 1970, Commentary on Exodus, 1987, Understanding the Basic Themes of Exodus, 1991; contbg. author: Oxford Companion to the Bible, 1993; co-editorProclamation and Presence, 1970. Grantee Am. Assn. of Theol. Schs., 1969-70; Sabbatical scholar Fgn. Mission Bd., Rüschlikon, Switzerland, 1976-77, others. Avocations: classical music, gardening. Home: 1509 Tolley Meadow Rd Big Island VA 24526-2977

DURHAM, MICHAEL JONATHAN, information technology company executive; b. N.Y.C., Jan. 19, 1951; s. Walter Allen and Joyce D. (Packham) D.; m. Marilyn James Marr, May 19, 1984; children: Michael Allen, Elizabeth Marr. BA in Econs., U. Rochester, 1973; MBA in Fin., Cornell U., 1977. Asst. v.p. Bank Julius Bar & Co., N.Y.C., 1978-79; sr. analyst fin. planning Am. Airlines, Ft. Worth, 1979-80, mgr. corp. fin., 1980-82, dir. corp. fin., 1982-84, asst. treas. corp. fin., 1984-85, v.p. corp. devel., 1985-87, v.p. fin. and planning, 1987-89, CFO, 1989-95, sr. v.p. fin., CFO, 1989—; pres., CEO The SABRE Group, Dallas, 1996—; Exec. bd. Edwin L. Cox Sch. Bus., 1992; trustee, vis. com. William E. Simon Sch. Grad. Sch. Bus. Adminstrn., 1994-95; bd. dirs. The SABRE Group Holdings, Inc. Bd. dirs. Zale Lipshy U. Hosp., 1991—, Dallas Opera, 1992—; trustees coun. U. Rochester, 1992—. Mem. Las Colinas Sports Club. Republican. Episcopalian. Avocations: bridge, tennis, golf. Office: The SABRE Group PO Box 619615 MD 4319 Dallas TX 75261-9615

DURHAM, ORMONDE GEORGE, III, manufacturing executive; b. Glen Ridge, N.J., Oct. 22, 1946; s. Ormonde and Dolores (Cannon) D.; m. Jeanette Louise Randall, June 26, 1971; 1 child, Ormonde Ethan. BS in Engring., Stevens Inst. Tech., 1971; postgrad., Vassar Coll., 1972-73. Engr. IBM, 1971-77, mktg., 1978-84; v.p. High Tech. Solutions, N.Y., 1985; pres., CEO Opto Generic Devices, Van Hornesville, N.Y., 1986—. Patentee in field; contbr. articles to profl. jours. Recipient N.Y. State Tech. award, 1994, Nat. Innovation award Data Automation/DSN Monitor, 1995; rsch. grantee N.Y. State Rsch. Devel. Authority, 1994. Mem. Audi Quattro Club. Home: 111 Hoke Rd Jordanville NY 13361-2017 Office: Opto Generic Devices PO Box OGD Pumpkin Hook Rd Van Hornesville NY 13475

DURHAM, ROBERT DONALD, JR., state supreme court justice; b. Lynwood, Calif., May 10, 1947; s. Robert Donald Durham and Rosemary Constance (Brennan) McKelvey; m. Linda Jo Rollins, Aug. 29, 1970; children: Melissa Brennan, Amy Elizabeth. BA, Whittier Coll., 1969; JD, U. Santa Clara, 1972; LLM in the Judicial Process, U. Va., 1998. Bar: Oreg. 1972, Calif. 1973, U.S. Dist. Ct. Oreg. 1974, U.S. Ct. Appeals (9th cir.) 1980, U.S. Supreme Ct. 1987. Law clk. Oreg. Supreme Ct., Salem, 1972-74; ptnr. Bennett & Durham, Portland, Oreg., 1974-91; assoc. judge Oreg. Ct. Appeals, Salem, 1991-94; assoc. justice Oreg. Supreme Ct., Salem, 1994—; mem. adv. com. to Joint Interim Judiciary Com., 1984-86; chair Oreg. Commn. on Adminstrv. Hearings, 1988-89; faculty Nat. Jud. Coll., Reno, Nev., 1992; mem. Case Disposition Benchmarks Com., 1992-93, Coun. on Ct. Procedures, 1992-93, 95—; mem. Oreg. Rules of Appellate Procedure Com., 1998—. Mem. ACLU Lawyer's Com., Eugene and Portland, Oreg., 1978-91. Recipient award for civil rights litigation ACLU of Oreg., 1988, Ed Elliott Human Rights award Oreg. Edn. Assn., Portland, 1990. Mem. Am. Acad. Appellate Lawyers (ninth cir. screening com. 1991—, rules com. 1994, cochair appellate cts. liaison com. 1994), Oreg. Appellate Judges Assn. (pres. 1996-97), Oreg. State Bar (chair labor law sect. 1983-84, adminstrv. law com. govt. law sect. 1986), Calif. State Bar, Willamette Valley Inns of Ct. (master of bench, team leader 1994-98). Office: Oreg Supreme Ct 1163 State St Salem OR 97310-1331

DURHAM, THENA MONTS, microbiologist, researcher, management executive; b. Bradenton, Fla., July 10, 1945; d. Turner Monts and Silverrene (Taylor) M.; m. Millard Durham, Aug. 30, 1969; children—Bryce Vincent-Barnard, Brittanie Yvonne. B.S., Fisk U., 1966; M.S. Purdue U., 1968. Research microbiologist Ctrs. for Disease Control, Atlanta, Ga., 1968-86, assoc. dir. for programs Nat. Ctr. for Prevention Svcs., 1988-95; program analyst Ctr. for Health Promotion and Edn., Office of the Dir., 1986-88; dir. exec. secretariat Ctr. Disease Control and Prevention, Atlanta, 1995—; cons. FDA. Mem. NAACP, Neighborhood Planning Unit. Recipient Superior performance award Ctrs. for Disease Control and Prevention, 1972, 85, 86, 87, 88, 89, 90, 91, 92 and 93, numerous deptl. and spl. act awards. Mem. Sci. Research Soc., AAAS, Am. Soc. Microbiologists, CDC Assn. of Exec. Women (founder, co-chair), Women in Sci. and Engring., Sigma Xi. Democrat. Author numerous tech. papers; contbr. articles to profl. jours.

DURHAM, WARREN JOHN, television and radio producer; b. Spokane, Wash., Jan. 20, 1925; s. John J. and Esther Marion (Smith) D.; m. Lucy Maye Fleming, Apr. 8, 1950; children: James and Deborah (twins), Anne. BA, Wash. State U., 1949. Owner Sta. KLOQ, Yakima, Wash., 1956-62, Sta. KWIQ, Moses Lake, Wash., 1958-61, Sta. KDNC-AM-FM, Spokane, Wash., 1962-67, Cable Channel 9 TV, Spokane, 1977-81; host Nostalgia Cruises, 1990—; celebrity host Home Shopping Network, 1995—. Host, founder (nat. TV show) Big Band Days; play-by-play announcer, disc jockey, packager, producer numerous nat. TV shows 1939—; exec. prodr. Belle of the White Star, 1996; prodr. (nat. touring prodn.) A Night to Remember; host nat. radio show Big Band Classics, 1997. Lt. (j.g.) USN, 1943-57, World War II. Home and Office: 901 W Rolland Ave Spokane WA 99218-2633

DURICKO, ERMA O., stage director, educator; b. Scranton, Pa., Sept. 3; d. Daniel and Nellie (Consagra) Fricchione; m. Allen John Duricko, June 28, 1969; children: Jeffrey Allen, Marissa Danielle. BA, Ariz. State U., 1969, MA, 1973. High sch. tchr. Phoenix, 1970-74; artistic dir. White Birch Theatre, Dalton, Pa., 1975-78; theatre arts dir. Tiffany Falls Performance Ctr., Pa., 1975-78; resident dir. women's project Ampitheatre Actors, N.Y.C., 1980-81; freelance dir.; founder, artistic dir. 4-Tenn Prodns., 1996—; mem. adj. faculty U. Scranton, 1977-78, guest artist-in-residence, 1993—; dir. Nat. Theatre Summer Inst., N.Y., 1988, 90; speaker at issue ceremony for Tennessee Williams postal stamp; asst. dir. Long Wharf Theatre, Conn.; prodn. "Robbers" by Lyle Kesseer. Dir. (Tennessee Williams festivals) Lady of Larkspur Lotion, New Orleans, 1991, Reflections of His Soul, Miss., 1993; dir., guest artist Camino Real, 1994; guest artist Strider; conceiver, dir. Tennessee and His Women, N.Y.C.; asst. dir. to Marshall Mason, Robbers, Long Wharf Theatre, Conn., 1995; appearing as Blanche in Streetcar, 1997; mem. The Lab, N.Y.C., 1997—; dir. Readings of Plays by M. O'Brien, N.Y.C., 1996; dir. For All Day Sucker, N.Y.C. Mem. exec. coun. North Pocono PTA, Moscow, Pa., 1985-94; dist. cultural arts dir. Pa. PTA, 1989-94; bd. dirs. Community Concerts Assn., Scranton, 1982-84; mem. The Lab in N.Y.C. M. Cervantes grantee Stage Dirs./Choreographers Found., 1990, Moscow Cultural Arts grantee, 1991, 92. Mem. Am. Theatre Wing, Soc. Stage Dirs./Choreographers. Avocations: Tang Soo Doo karate (black belt). Home: Lake Watawga Gouldsboro PA 18424

DURIG, JAMES ROBERT, college dean; b. Washington, Pa., Apr. 30, 1935; s. and Roberta Wilda Mounts; m. Kathryn Marlene Sprowls, Sept. 1, 1955; children: Douglas Tybor, Bryan Robert, Stacey Ann. B.A., Washington and Jefferson Coll., 1958, D.Sc. (hon.), 1979; Ph.D., M.I.T., 1962. Asst. prof. chemistry U. S.C., Columbia, 1962-65; asso. prof. U. S.C., 1965-68, prof., 1968-93, Ednl. Found. prof. chemistry, 1970-73, dean Coll. Sci. and Math., 1973-93; dean Coll. Arts & Scis. U. Mo., Kans. City, 1993—. Editor: Vibrational Spectra and Structure, 22 vols., 1972—, Jour. Raman Spectroscopy, 1979-94; mem. editl. bd. Jour. Molecular Structure, 1972—; contbr. articles to profl. jours. Served with Chem. Corps U.S. Army, 1963-64. Recipient Russell award U.S.C., 1968; Alexander von Humboldt Sr. Scientist award W. Ger., 1976; award Spectroscopy Soc. of Pitts., 1981; U. S.C. Ednl. Found. award, 1984. Mem. Am. Chem. Soc. (So. Chemist award Memphis sect. 1976, Charles A. Stone award S.E. Piedmont sect. 1975), Am. Phys. Soc., Soc. for Applied Spectroscopy (Pitts. award 1981), Coblentz Soc. (mem. governing bd. 1972-76, pres. 1974-76, award for outstanding research in molecular spectroscopy 1970), Internat. Union Pure and Applied Chemistry (chmn. sub-commn. on infrared and Raman spectroscopy 1975-95, mem. commn. molecular spectra and structure 1978-89, sec. 1981-83, chmn. 1983-89), Blue Key Soc., Phi Beta Kappa (pres. Alpha chpt. S.C. 1970), Sigma Xi, Phi Lambda Upsilon. Presbyterian. Home: 1213 W 64th Ter Kansas City MO 64113-1516 Office: Univ Mo 306 Scofield Hall Kansas City MO 64110 *Everything has a lighthearted side which is sometimes difficult to recognize. Never lose your sense of humor.**

DURIZCH, MARY LOU, radiology educator; b. Sayre, Pa., July 1, 1939; d. Ralph Elwood and Mary Louise (Inman) Goble; m. Frank Durizch, July 7, 1956 (div. Sept. 1960); children: Terry Ann, John Alex; m. Jesse Littleton III, Mar. 25, 1995. Radiologic Technologist, Robert Packer Hosp., Sayre, Pa., 1960-63; AS, Mansfield (Pa.) U., 1975; BS, Springhill Coll., Mobile, Ala., 1980; MBA, U. South Ala., Mobile, 1986. Cert. radiologic technologist. Staff radiologic technologist Robert Packer Hosp. and Guthrie Clinic, Sayre, 1963-64, dir. tomographic tech., 1964-77, co-chief radiologic technologist, 1974-77; tech. clin. and rsch. asst. dept. radiology U. South Ala. Coll. Medicine, Mobile, 1977-82, lectr., 1983-92, instr., 1992-93, asst. prof., 1994—; cons., radiographic equipment developer, presenter, exhibitor; mem. admissions com. Sch. Radiologic Tech., U. South Ala., Mobile, 1981—, Robert Packer Hosp. Sch. Radiologic Tech., Sayre, 1974-77; radiology rep. to med. staff quality assurance com., 1991—. Mem. editl. bd. Applied Radiology, 1988-89; contbg. author: Learning the Principles of Tomography: A Programmed Learning Workbook, 1975; author: Technical Aspects of Tomography, 1977, Traumex-TRX5: Quick Reference Instruction Manual, 1987, (with J. T. Littleton and W.C. Lim) Chest Atlas: Radiographically Correlated Thin-Section Anatomy in Five Planes, 1994; editor: (with J.T. Littleton) Sectional Imaging Methods: A Comparison, 1983; contbr. articles to profl. jours. Bd. dirs. Eichold-Heustis Med. Mus., Mobile, 1990. Mem. Am. Soc. Radiologic Technologists, Ala. Soc. Radiologic Technologists (program com. chmn. 38th ann. meeting 1985), Acad. Health Svcs. Mktg. of Am. Mktg. Assn. Methodist. Avocation: photography. Office: U South Ala Med Ctr 2451 Fillingim St Mobile AL 36617-2238

DURKEE, JACKSON LELAND, civil engineer; b. Tatanagar, India, Sept. 20, 1922; s. E. Leland and Bernice J. (Jackson) D.; m. Marian H. Carty, Feb. 20, 1943; children: Janice D. Parry, Judith D. Burton, Christine D. Simpson. BSCE, Worcester Poly. Inst., 1943, CE, 1951; MCE, Cornell U., 1947. Registered profl. engr., Calif., Conn., N.Y., Pa.; chartered engr., U.K. Designer Douglas Aircraft Co., 1943-44; various engring. positions Fabricated Steel Constrn. div. Bethlehem Steel Corp., 1947-65, chief bridge engr., 1965-76; vis. prof. structural engring. Cornell U., 1976; ptnr. Modjeski and Masters, cons. engrs., Harrisburg, Pa., 1977-78; cons. structural engr. Bethlehem, Pa., 1978—; mem. numerous tech. and profl. coms. Contbr. articles on bridge structural analysis, rsch., design, constrn., contracting, innovation and history to profl. jours.; originator, dir. devel. of shop-fabricated parallel-wire-strand method for constrn. of suspension bridge cables and pipe-assembly anchorage method and plastic-type weather protection sys. for such cables. Served to lt. USNR, 1944-46, PTO. Recipient constrn. industry citation Engring. News-Record, 1968. Fellow ASCE (Ernest E. Howard award 1982, hon. mem. 1996), Instn. Civil Engrs. (U.K.), Instn. Structural Engrs. (U.K.); mem. NSPE, Am. Ry. Engring. Assn., Am. Arbitration Assn., Am. Welding Soc., Structural Stability Rsch. Coun., Internat. Assn. for Bridge & Structural Engring., Nat. Acad. Engring. (cited for origination and devel. of innovations in fabrication and erection engring. of longspan bridges). Republican. Mem. Moravian Ch. Clubs: Silver Creek Country (Hellertown, Pa.); Cosmos (Washington); St. Andrews Golf, New Golf (St. Andrews, Scotland). Home and Office: 217 Pine Top Trl Bethlehem PA 18017-1729

DURKEE, JOE WORTHINGTON, JR., nuclear engineer; b. Albuquerque, Mar. 10, 1956; s. Joe Worthington Sr. and Hallie Mae (Payne) D. BS, Tex. A&M U., 1978, ME, 1981, PhD, 1983. Staff mem. Los Alamos (N.Mex.) Nat. Lab., 1983-95; asst. prof. radiology U. Tex. Southwestern Med. Sch., Dallas, 1995—; rsch. proposal reviewer LANL, 1986-87, Dept. Energy/ER Nuc. Engr. Proposal Rev. Panel, 1988-94. Invited rsch. paper reviewer Jour. Nuclear Tech., 1987, Jour. Biomech. Engr., 1991; contbr. articles to Jour. Physics in Medicine and Biology, Progress in Nuclear Energy, Annuals Nuclear Energy, Jour. Nuclear Tech. Mem. Am. Nuclear Soc. (admissions com. 1986—, chair 1990—), Tex. A&M Former Student Assn., Nat. Space Soc., N.Y. Acad. Sci. Achievements include development of Sn and Monte Carlo reactor physics design calculations for a number of thermal and fast nuclear reactor designs, of mathematical models depicting heat transport in the human body; notation of bifurcating behavior of multiregion bioheat and neutron diffusion equations and development of techniques to solve and computationally evaluate these expressions; research in space-time neutron diffusion and fission-product convective diffusion, reactor physics calculations in support of the LANL Omega West Reactor reconfiguration to product radioisotopes for medical applications; design of medical imaging devices. Office: Univ of Texas Southwestern Medical Ctr 5323 Harry Hines Blvd Dallas TX 75235-7208

DURKEE, WILLIAM ROBERT, retired physician; b. Kansas City, Mo., Apr. 12, 1923; s. Dwight and Bessie Deane (Williams) D.; m. Billie Maxine Schreiner, Sept. 19, 1946; m. Jeanne Elizabeth Wells, June 7, 1975; children—Bruce William, Ellen Jeanne. A.A., Kansas City Jr. Coll., 1941; student, U. Chgo., 1941-42; M.D., U. Kans., 1945. Diplomate Am. Bd. Internal Medicine. Intern U. Kans. Med. Ctr., Kansas City, 1945-46, resident, 1948-51; practice medicine specializing in internal medicine Manhattan, Kans., 1951-91; ptnr. Ball Meml. Clinic, 1951-76, Drs. Durkee and Boese, 1976-91; med. dir. Kans. Farm Bur. Life Ins. Co., Manhattan, 1963-91; ret., 1991; mem. staff Mercy Health Ctr.; trustee Meml. Hosp., Manhattan, Kans. Bd. dirs. Friends of McCain, 1988-95, Sunset Zoo Wildlife Conservation Trust, Manhattan, 1995—, pres., 1998; mem. adv. bd. Friends of Libr., Kans. State U., 1993—. Capt. U.S. Army, 1943-48. Fellow ACP, Am. Coll. Cardiology (assoc.); mem. AMA, Riley County Med. Soc., Kans. Med. Soc., Am. Soc. Internal Medicine, Manhattan C. of C., Pres.'s Club Kans. State U., Manhattan Country Club, Rotary. Republican. Methodist. Home: 440 Oakdale Dr Manhattan KS 66502-3736

DURKIN, DOROTHY ANGELA, university official; b. Glen Cove, N.Y., June 23, 1945; d. Frank Vincent and Rose Marie Durkin; 1 child, David Francis. BA, SUNY, Stony Brook, 1968; MA, NYU, 1974. Adminstrv. asst. SUNY, Stony Brook, 1965-67; prodn. editor Holt, Rhinehart & Winston, Inc., Stony Brook, 1967-69; editor Hill & Wang Pub., Inc., N.Y.C., 1969-70; asst. dir. pub. info. NYU Sch. Continuing Edn., N.Y.C., 1970-72; assoc. dean pub. affairs and student svcs. Sch. Continuing Edn. NYU, N.Y.C., 1983—; cons. N.Y.C. Ctr. for Lifelong Learning, 1974; producer TV series Continuum, Sta. WNYC, 1974. Editor: NSF student mag., 1961. Recipient Merit award Andy Advt., 1972, Art Dirs. Club, 1980, Soc. Illustrators, 1980, Big Apple award N.Y. Radio Broadcasters Assn., 1985, Admissions Mktg. Report awards, 1987-88, 98, Catalog Age awards, 1988, 93. Mem. Univ. Continuing Edn. Assn. (chair info. svcs. 1980-81, nat. award chair, chair mktg. adv. com. 1989-98, group leader Learn From Success series 1989-90, bd. dirs. 1991-93, membership com. 1994-95, mktg. conf. planning com. 1993-99, presenter, Bronze, Silver and Gold medals 1978, 81-98, Internat. Leadership in Continuing Edn. award 1999), Am. Coll. Pub. Rels. Assn. (nat. award 1973), Coun. for Advancement and Support of Edn. (awards 1982-83, 85-87, 89-90, 92-94), Women in Comms. (job chair), Pub. Rels. Soc. Am. (Am. demographics adv. bd. 1989-90), Direct Mktg. Assn. (Echo Leadership award 1987, 88), Internat. Direct Mktg. Assn., SUNY Alumni Assn. (bd. dirs.), The College Bd. (speaker, cons.), Learning Resources Network. Office: NYU Sch Continuing Edn 7 E 12th St Fl 11 New York NY 10003-4475

DURKIN, RAYMOND J., federal judge. Bar: Pa. Magistrate judge for mid. dist. Pa., U.S. Magistrate Ct, Wilkes-Barre. Office: US Magistrate Ct 205 Fed Bldg 197 S Main St Wilkes Barre PA 18701-1500

DURLAND, JACK RAYMOND, lawyer; b. Taylor, Tex., Sept. 21, 1916; s. Den D. and Percy (Langrill) D.; m. June Kathryn Cain, Feb. 5, 1937; children: Jack Raymond, Diane Elizabeth. LLB, U. Okla., 1941. Bar: Okla. 1941. Spl. agt. FBI, 1942-46; sole law practice Oklahoma City, 1946-50; asst. to pres. Cain's Coffee Co., Oklahoma City, 1950-52, pres., 1952-82; pres. Gallery at Nichols Hills Inc., Oklahoma City, 1982-87; Chmn. bd. Nat. Coffee Assn., 1961-62. Bd. dirs. Met. YMCA, Oklahoma City. Mem. ABA, Okla. Bar Assn., World Pres. Orgn. Home: 1620 Queenstown Rd Oklahoma City OK 73116-5523

DURN, RAYMOND JOSEPH, lawyer; b. Cleve., Nov. 28, 1925; s. Joseph Frank and Mary (Spenko) D.; m. Emmy Reboly, June 5, 1954; children: David, Sarah, Tamara. B.A., Harvard U., 1950, LL.B., 1953. Bar: Ohio 1953, U.S. Dist. Ct. Ohio 1954, U.S. Ct. Appeals 6th cir. 1974. Assoc. Jones, Day, Reavis & Pogue, Cleve., 1953-60, ptnr., 1960-89; acting gen. counsel Univ. Hosps., Cleve., 1989-91, sr. counsel, 1991-93. Trustee Cleve. Neighborhood Health Svcs., Inc., 1969-93, pres., 1987-89; trustee Chester Twp., Ohio, 1972-75; mem. Chester Twp. Bd. Zoning Appeals, 1969-72, Chester Twp. Zoning Commn., 1985-91. Served with USAAF, 1944-46. Mem. Ohio Bar Assn., Cleve. Bar Assn. Democrat. Unitarian. Home: 13088 W Geauga Trl Chesterland OH 44026-2830*

DURNBAUGH, DONALD FLOYD, church history educator, researcher; b. Detroit, Nov. 16, 1927; s. Floyd Devon and Ruth Elsie (Tombaugh) D.; m. Hedwig Therese Raschka, July 10, 1952; children: Paul D., Christopher S., Renate E. BA, Manchester Coll., Ind., 1949, LHD (hon.), 1980; MA, U. Mich., 1953; PhD, U. Pa., 1960. Dir. program Brethren Svc. Commn., Austria, 1953-56; asst. prof. history Juniata Coll., Huntingdon, Pa., 1958-62, J. Omar Good disting. prof. evang. christianity, 1988-89, archivist, 1992—; assoc. prof. ch. history Bethany Theol. Sem., Oak Brook, Ill., 1962-69, prof. ch. history, 1970-88; Carl W. Zeigler prof. religion and history Elizabethtown (Pa.) Coll., 1989-93; dir. in Europe Brethren Colls. Abroad, France, Germany, 1964-65; cons. Brethren Hist. Com., Elgin, Ill., 1982—; moderator Ch. of the Brethren, 1985-86. Author: European Origins of the Brethren, 1958, 4th edit., 1986, The Brethren in Colonial America, 1967, 3rd edit., 1996, Guide to Research in Brethren History, 1968, The Believers' Church: The History and Character of Radical Protestantism, 1968, 2nd edit., 1985, Every Need Supplied: Mutual Aid and Christian Community in the Free Churches, 1525-1675, 1974, Pragmatic Prophet: The Life of M.R. Zigler, 1989, Brethren Beginnings: The Origin of the Church of the Brethren in Early Eighteenth-Century Europe, 1992, Fruit of the Vine: A History of the Brethren, 1708-1995, 1997; editor: Die Kirche der Brueder: Vergangenheit und Gegenwart, 1971, The Church of the Brethren: Past and Present, 1971, To Serve the Present Age: The Brethren Service Story, 1975, On Earth Peace: Discussion on War/Peace Issues Between Friends, Mennonites, Brethren and European Churches, 1935-1975, 1978, Church of the Brethren: Yesterday and Today, 1986; editor-in-chief The Brethren Ency., Inc., 1978-84; contbr. articles, book revs. to scholarly jours., periodicals. Alternative svc. as conscientious objector, 1953-56. U. Pa. Scholar, 1956-57, fellow, 1957-58; NEH sr. fellow, 1976-77; fellow Assn. Theol. Schs., 1986-87; recipient Alumni award Manchester Coll., 1978. Fellow Young Ctr. for Study of Anabaptist and Pietist Groups; assoc. Inst. of Mennonite Studies; mem. Am. Soc. Ch. History, Brethren Jour. Assn., Soc. German Am. Studies, Communal Studies Assn., Pa. German Soc. Mem. Ch. of the Brethren. Home: PO Box 484 James Creek PA 16657-0484 Office: Juniata Coll PO Box 948 Huntingdon PA 16652-0948

DURNEY, MICHAEL CAVALIER, lawyer; b. Piedmont, Calif., May 20, 1943; s. James Joseph and Camille (Cavalier) D.; m. Ann E. Belanger, Nov. 27, 1971; 1 child, Christine Cavalier. BA, U. Calif., Berkeley, 1965; JD, U. Calif.-Hastings Coll. of Law, 1968. Bar: Calif. 1969, D.C. 1972, U.S. Supreme Ct. 1972. Trial atty. Tax div. Dept. Justice, Washington, 1968-72, dep. asst. atty. gen. Tax div., acting asst. atty. gen., 1986-88; assoc. Hamel and Park, Washington, 1972-78, ptnr., 1978-86; ptnr. Myerson, Kuhn & Sterrett, Washington, 1988-89, Law Offices of Michael C. Durney, Washington, 1990—. Chmn. bd. trustees St. Patrick's Episcopal Day Sch., Washington, 1989-92. Mem. ABA (tax and litigation sects.), Fed. Bar Assn. (chmn. tax sect. 1982-84), Calif. Bar Assn., D.C. Bar Assn. Republican. Episcopalian. Clubs: Metropolitan (Washington), Burning Tree. Avocation: golf. Home: 6732 Selkirk Dr Bethesda MD 20817-4955 Office: 1072 Thomas Jefferson St NW Washington DC 20007-3832

DURNIL, GORDON KAY, lawyer, diplomat, arbitrator, political party official; b. Indpls., Feb. 20, 1936; s. J. Ray and E. Merle Durnil; m. Lynda L. Powell, Mar. 1, 1963; children—Guy S., Cynthia L. B.S., Ind. U., 1960, J.D., 1965. Bar: Ind. 1965. Sales rep. Franklin Life Ins. Co., 1956, Moore Bus. Forms, Inc., 1960; sole practice, Indpls., 1965—; profl. arbitrator, mediator, Indpls., 1993—; active Republican Party, 1960—, publicity com. Marion County com. (Ind.), 1966-67, campaign coordinating com., mem. campaign coordinating com. Ind. State Com., 1968-80, mem. congressional coordinating com., 1973-74, campaign dir., 1978, state chmn., 1981-89; campaign mgr. for numerous candidates; mem. Exec. Council Rep. Nat. Com., 1985-89; chmn. Midwestern Rep. State Chmn. Assn., 1988-89, Ind. del. chmn., del. to 1984 and 1988 Rep. Nat. Conv.; nominated by the Pres. and confirmed by U.S. Senate U.S. chmn. Internat. Joint Commn. U.S. and Can., 1989—; head of del. U.N. Conf. on Environment and Devel., Rio de Janeiro, 1992; v.p. Ind. Ornamental Iron Works, Inc., 1960-65; dep. prosecutor Marion County (Ind.), 1965-66; legal counsel Ind. Fedn. Young Republicans, 1965-68; spl. asst. Office of Bus. Service U.S. Dept. Commerce, 1971. Pres. Emmerich Manual High Sch. Alumni Assn., 1968; justice of peace Washington Twp. (Ind.), 1967-70; bd. dirs. Our House, Inc. (Ind. Ronald McDonald House); chmn. Marion County Election Bd., 1978-81. Served with U.S. Army; Korea. Mem. Ind. Bar Assn., Am. Assn. Polit. Cons., Soc. Profls. in Dispute Resolution. Presbyterian. Author: The Making of a Conservative Environmentalist, 1995, Is America Beyond Reform?, 1997, Soft Money, 1998; editor: The Marion County Republican Reporter, 1966-71. Office: Internat Joint Commn 1250 23rd St NW Ste 100 Washington DC 20037-1100

DURNIN, RICHARD GERRY, education educator; b. Haverhill, Mass., Mar. 9, 1920; s. William Edward and Ethel (Millett) D. BS, Columbia U., 1947; MEd, Harvard U., 1950; postgrad. summers, U. Nottingham, 1950, U. Oxford, 1956; EdD, U. Pa., 1968. Tchr. pub. schs., N.J., Mass., 1946-49; instr. State Coll. at Fitchburg (Mass.), 1949-51; dir. Antioch Sch., Yellow Springs, Ohio, 1951-52; asst. prof. SUNY, Buffalo, 1952-58; vis. lectr. edn. Tufts U., spring 1957; dir. Smith Coll. Day Sch., 1958-59; asst. prof. edn. Rutgers U., 1959-65; prof. social and hist. founds. of edn. CCNY, 1965-90, prof. emeritus, 1990—; instr. U. Nev., U. N.H., Coll. William and Mary, Johns Hopkins U., summers 1951-68. *Mr. Durnin has served in the profession of education at all levels, as a teacher, headmaster and professor, for forty-four years. He is a product of time and is doubtful he would be in harmony with today's classes and schools.* Author: American Education: A Guide to Information Sources, 1982; contbr. articles to profl. jours. Bd. dirs. Internat. Social Svc.-WAIF; mem. nat. coun. Travelers Aid Internat. Social Svc., 1972-77, Middlesex County (N.J.) Cultural and Heritage Commn., 1976-95; mem. adv. commn. Mercer County (N.J.) C.C., 1980-87; trustee Proprietary House Assn., N.J., 1977-97; mem. adv. com. The Old Barracks, Trenton, N.J., 1982-88, trustee, 1992-98; Rep. committeman Middlesex County (N.J.), 1992—. 1st lt. USAAF, 1942-46. Mem. SAR, History of Edn. Soc., New Brunswick (pres. 1969-71), N.Y., N.J., Nat. Hist. Socs., Soc. War of 1812, Jamestowne Soc., Essex Inst., Soc. Mayflower Descendents, Soc. Colonial Wars, Joyce Kilmer Centennial Commn. (v.p. 1986—), English-Speaking Union (pres. New Brunswick br. 1991-93), St. George Soc. N.Y., Colonial Order Acorn, Kappa Delta Pi, Phi Delta Kappa. Episcopalian. Home: 50 Chester Cir New Brunswick NJ 08901-1526

DURNING, CHARLES, actor; b. Highland Falls, N.Y., Feb. 28, 1923; m. Carol Durning (div.); children: Michele, Douglas, Jeanine; m. Mary Ann Amelio, 1974. Former boxer, cab driver, waiter, ironworker, constrn. worker, elevator operator. Profl. theatre debut with nat. co. of The Andersonville Trial, 1960; since 1962 has appeared in Measure for Measure, King John, Chronicles of Henry IV, N.Y. Shakespeare Festival; stage appearances include That Championship Season (Drama Desk award 1972), Boom Boom Room, Child Buyer, Drat! The Cat!, Lemon Sky, Comedy of Errors, Au Pair Man, Knock Knock, Cat on a Hot Tin Roof, 1990, (Antoinette Perry award, 1990), others; movie appearances include Harvey Middleman, Fireman, 1965, Stiletto, 1969, I Walk the Line, 1970, Hi, mom!, 1970, Pursuit of Happiness, 1971, Dealing, 1972, Deadhead Miles, 1972, The Sting, 1973, Sisters, 1973, Front Page, 1974, Hindenburg, 1975, Dog Day Afternoon, 1975, Harry & Walter go to New York, 1976, Breakheart Pass, 1976, An Enemy of the People, 1977, Twilights' Last Gleaming, 1977, Choirboys, 1977, Tilt, 1978, Greek Tycoon, 1978, The Fury, 1978, When A

Stranger Calls, 1979, Starting Over, 1979, North Dallas 40, 1979, Muppet Movie, 1979, Die Laughing, 1980, Final Countdown, 1980, True Confessions, 1981, Sharky's Machine, 1981, Working, 1982, Tootsie, 1982, Best Little Whorehouse in Texas, 1982, To Be or Not To Be, 1983, Two of a Kind, 1983, Mass Appeal, 1984, Hadley's Rebellion, 1984, Stick, 1985, Stand Alone, 1985, Man with One Red Shoe, 1985, Tough Guys, 1986, Big Trouble, 1986, Solar Babies, 1986, Where The River Runs Black, 1986, Rosary Murders, 1987, Tigers' Tale, 1987, Far North, 1988, Dick Tracy, 1990, V.I. Warshawski, 1991, Brenda Starr, 1992, The Music of Chance, 1993, The Hudsucker Proxy, 1994, I.Q., 1994, Home for the Holidays, 1995, The Grass Harp, 1995, Spy Hard, 1996, One Fine Day, 1996, Shelter, 1997, Secret Life of Algernon, 1997, Justice, 1998, Jerry & Tom, 1998, Hi-Life, 1998, State and Maine, 1999, Hunt for the Devil, 1999; appeared in TV films including The Trial of Chaplain Jensen, The Connection, Switch (Emmy nomination), Mrs. Santa Claus, 1996; TV series The Cop and the Kid, Captains and the Kings, Evening Shade, 1990-94, A Woman of Independent Means, 1995 (miniseries); other TV appearances include The Queen of the Stardust Ballroom, High Chapparral, The Defenders, Madigan, All in the Family, Attica, Studs Lonigan, Death of a Salesman, 1985, mini series Kennedys of Mass. (Golden Globe award). Served with U.S. Army. Decorated Purple Heart, Silver Star. *

DUROCHER, FRANCES ANTOINETTE, physician, educator; b. Woonsocket, R.I., Mar. 11, 1943; d. Armand D. and Teresa (Leverone) DuRocher. BA with honors, Trinity coll., 1964; MS, Brown U., 1966; postgrad., Woman's Med. Coll., 1970. Med. resident Phila. VA Hosp. and Med. Coll. Pa., 1971-73; assoc. in internal med. Guthrie Clinic Ltd., Sayre, Pa., 1973-79, Annandale (Va.) Group Health Assocs., 1979-87; assoc. chair internal med. Annandale Group Health Assoc., 1986-87; pvt. practice, Fairfax, Va., 1987—; clin. asst. prof. med. and health svcs. George Washington U. Med. Sch., Washington, 1994—. Bd. dirs. Fairways of Penderbrook Homeowners Assn., 1993—, sec., 1995-96, pres., 1996—. Mem. AMA, ACP-Am. Soc. Internal Medicine, Am. Med. Women's Assn. (exec. bd. br. I, 1985-91, pres. 1987-88), Med. Soc. Va., Fairfax County Med. Soc. Avocations: reading, traveling. Office: 9926 Main St Fairfax VA 22031-3901

DU ROCHER, JAMES HOWARD, lawyer; b. Racine, Wis., Aug. 4, 1945; s. Howard James and Frances Ann (Rasmussen) Du R.; m. Rosalyn Ann, Sept. 2, 1972; children: Jessica Lynn, James Howard, Emily Rosalyn. Student U.S. Mil. Acad., 1963-65, Ripon Coll., 1965-66; JD, U. Wis., 1969. Bar: Wis. Assoc. Stewart, Peyton, Crawford & Josten, Racine, 1969-78; pres. Du Rocher, Murphy, Murphy & Schroeder, S.C., Racine, 1978-96, Du Rocher Law Offices, S.C., 1996—; bd. dirs., Careers Industries, Inc., pres., 1988-89. Bd. dirs. Racine Area United Way, 1973-79, v.p., 1977-79; chmn. Park Trails Dist. Boy Scouts Am., 1979-82; bd. dirs. Careers for Retarded Adults, Inc., 1982, pres., 1983, 90; bd. dirs. A-Center of Racine, Inc., 1978-85, pres., 1985; bd. dirs. Careers Industries Support Found., Inc., 1993—; deacon Atonement Luth. Ch., Racine, 1978-81; mem. adv. bd. Children's Svc. Soc. Wis. Capt. JAGC, U.S. Army, 1969-73. Decorated Bronze Star. Mem. State Bar Wis., Mason, Rotary (pres. Racine-West club 1998—). Home: 5531 Whirlaway Ln Racine WI 53402-1865 Office: 827 Main St PO Box 1406 Racine WI 53401-1406

DURONI, CHARLES EUGENE, retired lawyer, food products executive; b. McCune, Kans., Apr. 9, 1933; s. Charley S. and Dorothy M. D.; m. Charlene D. White, Feb. 18, 1978; children: Renee, Ashley, Michele, Lance. B.S., U. Kans., 1955; LL.B., U. Wis., 1962. Bar: Wis. 1962, Pa. 1979, U.S. Supreme Ct. 1979, U.S. Dist. Ct. (mid. dist.) Pa. 1980, U.S. Ct. Appeals (3d cir.) 1982. Staff atty. FTC, 1962-64; staff counsel Rockwell Internat. Co., Pitts., 1964-68; sr. atty. H.J. Heinz Co., Pitts., 1968-77; sr. assoc. counsel, asst. gen. counsel Hershey (Pa.) Foods Corp., 1977-79, v.p., gen. counsel, 1979-93; ret., 1993; bd. dirs. U.S. Trademark Assn., 1972-76; trustee Food & Drug Law Inst. Served with USAF, 1955-59. Mem. ABA (com. corp. law depts., com. corp. counsel), Wis. Bar Assn., Pa. Bar Assn., Lancaster County Bar Assn., Am. Law Inst., Atlantic Legal Found., The Bus. Roundtable (lawyers steering com.), Cen. Pa. Corp. Lawyers Group, Grocery Mfrs. Am. (legal com.), Sigma Chi, Phi Delta Phi, Met. Club (N.Y.C.). Home: 928 Forest Rd Lancaster PA 17601-2203 *Of the highest importance in the legal and business world is the exercise of imaginative good judgment consistently exercised with a sensitivity to others.*

DUROSE, RICHARD ARTHUR, lawyer; b. Cleve., Nov. 6, 1937; s. Arthur H. and Helen G. (Doran) DuR.; m. Nancy Ann Hunter, Aug. 9, 1959; children: Steven A., Carolyn M., Douglas H. AA, Graceland Coll., 1957; BA, Ohio State U., 1959, JD, 1962. Bar: Ohio 1962, Fla. 1988. Atty., ptnr. Foley & Lardner, Orlando, 1990—. Contbr. articles to profl. jours. Mem. ABA, Fla. Bar Assn., Ohio Bar Assn., Def. Rsch. Inst., Quest, Inc. (pres. 1993-94),Isleworth Country Club. Democrat. Avocations: tennis, golf. Office: Foley & Lardner 111 N Orange Ave Ste 1800 Orlando FL 32801-2386

DUROSE, STANLEY CHARLES, JR., insurance executive; b. Joliet, Mont., Oct. 26, 1923; s. Stanley Charles and Wilhelmena Amelia (Zwicky) DuR.; m. Lorraine Homan, May 27, 1977. B.S., U. Wis., 1948. Various positions Wis. Dept. Ins., Madison, 1948-65; dep. commr. ins. State of Wis., Madison, 1965-69, commr. ins., 1969-75; v.p. govt. relations Cuna Mut. Ins., Madison, 1976-80; sr. v.p. adminstrn., Cumis Ins. Soc., 1980-86, sr. v.p. reinsurance, 1986-88; dep. commr. of Ins., State of Wis., 1989-91; ret., 1991. Contbr. articles to profl. publs. Served with USAF, 1943-45 and 1951-52. Mem. Casualty Actuarial Soc., Am. Acad. Actuaries. Home: 201 Durose Ter Madison WI 53705-3322

DURR, EISENHOWER, protective services official; b. Magee, Miss., Aug. 21, 1948. BS, Jackson State U., 1973. Supervisor sch. safety Bd. of Edn., Bklyn., 1974-75; corrections officer Bur. of Prisons, N.Y.C., 1976-78; insp. Law Enforcement Tng. Acad., Glynco, Ga., 1983-87; supr. U.S. Marshall Svc., St. Louis, 1987-88; chief dep. U.S. Marshall Svc., Jackson, Miss., 1988-94; U.S. Marshal, So. Dist. Miss., Jackson, 1994—. With U.S. mil., Korea, 1967-70. Office: U.S. Marshall Svc James O Eastland Fed Court 245 E Capitol St Rm 305 Jackson MS 39201-2409*

DURR, ROBERT JOSEPH, construction firm executive, mechanical engineer; b. N.Y.C., June 25, 1932; s. Otto and Veronica U. (Quinlan) D.; m. Julia Loretta, Apr. 16, 1955; children—Kathryn A., Robert J. Jr., Kenneth A., Jennifer L. B.B.A., Iona Coll., 1954; Cert. in Mech. Engring., NYU, 1957. Mem. staff Courter & Co., Inc., N.Y.C., 1955-60, mgr., 1960-71, v.p., 1971-81; pres. Courter & Co., Inc., Secaucus, NJ, 1981-85; pres. Durr Mech. Constrn., Inc., N.Y.C., 1986-98, chmn., 1998—; chmn. Nat. Joint Steamfitter Apprenticeship Com., Washington, 1980-84; trustees Nat. Cert. Pipe Welding Bur., Washington, 1983—. Recipient Recognition award Nat. Cert. Pipe Welding Bur., 1980. Mem. Subcontractors Trade Assn., Mech. Contractors Assn. Am. (bd. dirs. 1989—, mem. exec. bd. 1993, pres. 1996), Mech. Contractors Assn. N.Y. (bd. dirs., pres. 1976-82, Appreciation award 1982), N.Y. Bldg. Congress (bd. govs. 1978-84), Bldg. Trade Employers Assn. N.Y. (Greater N.y. welding chpt. 1975-88, chmn. 1979-88), Upper Montclair (N.J.) Country Club. Roman Catholic. Avocations: golf; swimming; sailing.

DURRANI, SAJJAD HAIDAR, retired space communications engineer; b. Jalalpur, Pakistan, Aug. 27, 1928; came to U.S., 1959, naturalized, 1966; s. Inayat Ullah and Hameedah Khanum D.; m. Brita Katarina Yasmin Portin, May 21, 1959; children: Zarina, Amina, Arif. B.A., Govt. Coll. Lahore, Pakistan, 1946; B.Sc. in Elec. Engring. with honors, Engring. Coll. Lahore, 1949; M.Sc.Tech., Coll. Tech., Manchester, Eng., 1953; Sc.D., U. N.Mex., 1962. Lectr., asst. prof. Engring. Coll., Lahore, 1949-59; instr., research assoc. U. N.Mex., Albuquerque, 1959-62; sr. engr. Gen. Electric Co., Lynchburg, Va., 1962-64; prof., chmn. dept. elec. engring. Engring. U. Lahore, 1964-65; assoc. prof. Kans. State U., Manhattan, 1965-66; sr. engr. RCA Space Center, Hightstown, N.J., 1966-68; staff scientist, br. mgr. COMSAT Labs., Clarksburg, Md., 1968-73; sr. scientist Ops. Research, Inc., Silver Spring, Md., 1973-74; sr. engr. NASA-Goddard Space Flight Center, Greenbelt, Md., 1974-79; mgr. for system planning, tracking and data relay satellite system NASA-GSFC, 1981-84; mgr. research and planning NASA Communications Div., 1984-88; chief communications scientist NASA Hdqrs., Washington, 1979-81, program mgr., Advanced Systems Office, 1988-92; consulting engr. Computer Scis. Corp., Beltsville and Seabrook, Md., 1992-98; ret., 1998; vis. prof. U. Md., 1972; adj. prof. George Washington U., 1980-82, 86, 87, rsch. prof., 1993-97; mem. Engring. Manpower Commn., Am. Assn. Engring. Socs., 1981; cons. Aerospace Inst., Space and Upper Atmosphere Rsch. Commn., Pakistan, UN Devel. Program, 1999. Mem. editorial bd.: COMSAT Tech. Rev., 1972, IEEE Spectrum, 1975-78, IEEE Procs., 1988-92. Pres. Muslim Cmty. Ctr., Silver Spring, Md., 1976-82, trustee, 1989-94, 95—, chmn., 1998—. Recipient spl. achievement award NASA, 1977, 78, 90. Fellow AIAA (assoc.), IEEE (gov. aerospace and electronic sys. soc. 1977-93, 97—, pres. 1982-83, Citation of Honor U.S. Activities Bd., 1980, Outstanding Mem. Region 2 1982, dir. Divsn. IX 1984, 85, mem. publs. bd. 1986, 87, 91, 92, bd. dirs. nat. telesys. conf. 1991-94, meritorious achievement in continuing edn. award 1994, Ambassador award/Computer Scis. Corp., 1996).

DURRANT, DAN MARTIN, lawyer; b. Franklin, Idaho, Apr. 24, 1933; s. Thomas Henry and Norma (Shaffer) D.; m. Joyce Wadsworth, June 1, 1956; children: Shari Lynn Durrant Anderson, Victoria Leigh Durrant Farnworth, Lisa Joyce Durrant King, Cynthia Dyan Durrant Jensen, Daniel Wadsworth. JD, U. Utah, 1965. Bar: Ariz. 1965, U.S. Dist. Ct. Ariz. 1965, U.S. Ct. Claims 1991, U.S. Ct. Appeals (9th cir.) 1973, U.S. Supreme Ct. 1970, Nev. 1992, U.S. Dist. Ct. Nev. 1992, Utah 1994, U.S. Dist. Ct. Utah 1994. Assoc. Kramer, Roche, Burch & Streich, Phoenix, 1965-71; ptnr. Streich, Lang, Weeks & Cardon, Phoenix, 1971-90; ptnr. Streich Lang, Phoenix, 1990—, also bd. dirs. Contbr. articles to profl. jours. Mem. State Bar Ariz. (chmn. various coms.), Maricopa County Bar Assn. (chmn. jud. salary com. 1988), Def. Rsch. Inst. (environ. com.), Abota, Order of Coif. Republican. Mem. LDS Ch. Office: Two North Central Ave Phoenix AZ 85004-2391

DURRANT, GEOFFREY HUGH, retired English language educator; b. Pilsley, Eng., July 27, 1913; s. John and Charlotte (Atkinson) D.; m. Barbara Joan Altson, June 2, 1942; children—John Guy, Catherine Jane. B.A., Cambridge (Eng.) U., 1932-35; diploma in edn., London U., 1935-36; student, Tuebingen (W. Ger.) U., 1937-39. Prof., English U. Natal, South Africa, 1945-60; head dept. English U. Natal; prof. U. Man., Winnipeg, Can., 1961-66; now prof. emeritus U. B.C., Vancouver, Can.; master tchr. U. B.C., 1973. Author: William Wordsworth, 1969, Wordsworth and the Great System, 1970. Served with South African Armed Forces, 1940-44. Carnegie fellow, 1960; Killam sr. fellow, 1976. Fellow Royal Soc. Can.; mem. Assn. Can. Univ. Tchrs. English. Anglican. Home: 3994 W 34th Ave, Vancouver, BC Canada V6N 2L5

DURRENBERGER, WILLIAM JOHN, retired army general, educator, investor; b. Wadena, Minn., Mar. 15, 1917; s. John George and Mary Angela (Weibeler) D.; m. Alma Mary Pagliai, Jan. 3, 1947; children: William John, Robert Scott, Philip Michael. Student, U. Minn., 1935-40, Brit. Coll. Mil. Sci., 1943; B.S., U. Md., 1951; M.B.A., Syracuse U., 1954; grad., Indsl. Coll. Armed Forces, 1960. Commd. 2d lt. U.S. Army, 1939, advanced through grades to maj. gen., 1968; chief logistics plan div. (UN Command), Korea, 1960-61; dep. comdr. Ordnance Weapons Command Illinois, 1962; comdg. officer Springfield (Mass.) Armory, 1963-65; comdg. gen. Army Tank Automotive Center Warren, Mich., 1965-66; comdg. gen. U.S. Army Weapons Command Rock Island, Ill., 1966-68; dep. chief of staff Logistics; acting chief staff U.S. Army, Pacific, 1968-70; ret., 1970; dir. Des Moines/Polk County (Iowa) Met. Criminal Justice Center, 1971-73; asst. v.p. ednl. services Drake U., 1971-81; profl. asso. Mitchell & Mitchell Economists, 1979-82. Author over 100 tech. intelligence reports on Brit. and German combat vehicles and weapons, 1943-46. Decorated D.S.M. with oak leaf cluster, Bronze Star, Army Commendation medal with oak leaf cluster. Mem. Assn. U.S. Army, Cath. League Religious and Civil Rights, Am. Legion, VFW (nat. aide-de-camp to comdr.-in-chief, 1986), KC, DAV, Ret. Officers Assn. Roman Catholic. Home: 2708 Lynner Dr Des Moines IA 50310-5835

DURRETT, JAMES FRAZER, JR., lawyer; b. Atlanta, Mar. 23, 1931; s. James Frazer and Cora Frazer (Morton) D.; m. Lucretia McPherson, June 9, 1956; children: James Frazer III, William McPherson, Lucretia Heston Miller, Thomas Ratcliffe. AB, Emory U., 1952; postgrad., Princeton U., 1952-53; LLB cum laude, Harvard U., 1956. Bar: Ga. 1955. Ptnr. Alston & Bird (and predecessor firm), Atlanta, 1956-97, retired, 1997; adj. prof. Emory U. Law Sch., 1961-77. Trustee Student Aid Found., The Howard Sch. Mem. Am. Law Inst. (adv. estate and gift tax project, restatement, second. property, Fed. Income Tax project), Capital City Club, Harvard Club (Atlanta). Presbyterian. Home: 3483 Ridgewood Rd NW Atlanta GA 30327-2417 Office: Alston & Bird 1 Atlantic Ctr 1201 W Peachtree St NW Ste 4200 Atlanta GA 30309-3424

D'URSO, JOSEPH PAUL, interior designer; b. Newark, Apr. 8, 1943; s. Dominick and Rose (Maffiore) D'U. BFA, Pratt Inst., 1965. Pres., sole designer D'Urso Design Inc., N.Y.C., 1967—. Major projects include 4 showrooms Calvin Klein, Esprit store, Washington, Esprit store and showroom, Los Angeles, furniture collection Knoll Internat. Fellow Royal Coll. Art, London, 1967, Manchester (Eng.) Poly., 1969; named to Interior Design Hall of Fame Interior Design mag., 1986; recipient Prix Di Rome, Am. Acad. Rome, 1987. Avocations: collecting books, antiques, travel. Home and Office: PO Box 1154 Water Mill NY 11976-1154

DURST, CAROL GOLDSMITH, educator; b. Bklyn., Mar. 1, 1952; d. Hyman and Florence (Weisblatt) Goldsmith; m. Marvin Ira Durst, June 18, 1972 (div. Sept. 1977); m. Leslie Mark Wertheim, Apr. 1, 1984; 1 child, William David. BA, Hamilton Kirkland Coll., 1973; MA, Columbia U., 1974. Career counselor Hofstra U., Hempstead, N.Y., 1974-75, Ocean County C.C., Toms River, N.J., 1975-76; rsch. assoc. Catalyst, N.Y.C., 1975-77; coord. displaced homemakers program N.Y. State Dept. Labor, N.Y.C., 1977-79; dir. N.Y. restaurant sch. New Sch. Social Rsch., N.Y.C., 1979-83; pres., owner New Am. Catering Corp., N.Y.C., 1983-98; tchr., career counselor Peter Kump's N.Y. Cooking Sch., N.Y.C., 1988-98; lectr. food studies dept. NYU, 1997—. Author: I Knew You Were Coming So I Baked a Cake, 1997. Mem. AAUW, N.Y. Women's Culinary Alliance (new mem. chair 1995-96), Internat. Assn. Culinary Profls., Women Chefs and Restaurateurs (job bank com. 1995—), Internat. Test Garden Soc., Older Women's League, Nat. Mus. Women in the Arts. Avocations: fine arts, piano, opera, ice skating. Home and office: 210 W 70th St New York NY 10023-4304

DURST, GARY MICHAEL, management trainer, speaker; b. Mt. Clemens, Mich., May 21, 1945; s. Carl William and Rosaline Rita (Constance) D.; m. Margaret Ellen O'Reilly, Sept. 2, 1966, (div. May 1977); children: Gregory, John, David. BA, Oakland U., 1966; MA, Mich. St. U., E. Lansing, 1968; PhD., Loyola U., 1972. Tchr. Avondale Pub. Sch., Auburn Hieghts, Mich., 1966-68; counselor/adminstr. U. of Ill. Med. Cntr., Chicago, 1968-69; assoc. dean of students Elmhurst Coll, Ill., 1969-72; v.p. Great Western Learning Systems, Denver; pres. Training Systems, Inc., Evanston, Ill., 1974--. Author: Napkin Notes: On the Art of Living 1979, Management By Responsibility, 1982, Responsibility: The South African Imperative, 1997. Named Prominent Training Professional- McMilan Co. 1986. Mem. ASTD. Avocations: swimming, hiking, collecting antiques and mechanical musical instruments. Office: Tng Systems Inc PO Box 788 Evanston IL 60204-0788

DURST, ROBERTA J., accountant, healthcare consultant; b. Ft. Benning, Ga., Aug. 10, 1964; d. Joseph S. and Marian J. (Arndt) T.; m. James A. Durst, Sept. 7, 1985; children: Debra A., James W. AS in Acctg., Lakeland C.C., Mentor, Ohio, 1993; BS in Acctg., Lake Erie Coll., Painesville, Ohio, 1995. CPA, Ohio. Staff acct. Howard, Wershbale & Co., Beachwood, Ohio, 1995-96, sr. acct., 1996-97; supr. Picker, Mayfield, Ohio, 1997—. Mem. Ohio Soc. CPAs.

DURSUM, BRIAN A., museum curator, art educator. BA in History, La Salle Coll., 1970; MA in East Asian History and Culture, U. Pitts., 1974. Instr. English Taiwan Normal U., Taipei, 1971-73; clk. Otto G. Richter Libr., U. Miami, Coral Gables, Fla., 1973, account clk., 1974-75; teaching asst. in history U. Pitts., 1973-74; account clk. Lowe Art Mus., U. Miami, Coral Gables, 1975-76, asst. to dir., 1976-82, acting chief adminstr., 1978, curator Oriental art, 1978—, registrar, 1982-90, acting dir., 1989-90, dir., 1990—; lectr. art dept., dir., chief curator U. Miami, 1992—; rschr. in field. Contbr. articles to profl. jours. Grantee Southeast Banking Corp., 1979, Wilder Found., 1979, 80, Ryder Sys., Inc., 1981, 83, Sun Glass Hut, Inc., 1989, Stiefel Labs., Inc., 1989, Federated Dept. Stores, Inc., 1989, 90, 92, MegaBank, Inc., 1989, Alma Jennings Found., 1989, 90, Manny and Ruthy Cohen Found., 1992. Mem. Am. Assn. Muss., Assn. Art Mus. Dirs., Phi Alpha Theta. Home: 1249 Mariana Ave Coral Gables FL 33134-2360 Office: 1301 Stanford Dr Miami FL 33146-2005*

DURYEE, DAVID ANTHONY, management consultant; b. Tacoma, Wash., July 29, 1938; s. Schuyler L. and Edna R. (Muzzy) D.; m. Anne Getchell Peterson, Nov. 26, 1966; children: Tracy Anne, Tricia Marie. BA in Bus., U. Wash., 1961, MBA, 1969; diploma, Pacific Coast Banking Schs., Seattle, 1973. Cert. fin. planner. Lending officer Seattle 1st Nat. Bank, 1964-68, v.p., trust officer, 1970-80; cons., chmn. Mgmt. Adv. Svcs., Inc., Seattle, 1980-93; mng. prin. Moss Adams Adv. Svcs., Moss Adams LLP, 1994—; bd. dirs. Lafromboise Newspapers, Inc., Seattle; lectr. in field; expert witness Wash., N.Y., Md., Calif., Mass., Ind., Fla. Author: The Business Owners Guide to Achieving Financial Success, 1994; contbr. articles to profl. jours. Capt. U.S. Army, 1962-64. Mem. Am. Soc. Appraisers, Internat. Assn. Fin. Planners, Inst. for Cert. Planners, Inst. Bus. Appraisers (speaker), Am. Bankers Assn., Nat. Retail Jewelers, Nat. Moving and Storage assn., Pacific N.W. Bankers Assn., Internat. Assn. for Fin. Planning, Estate Planning Coun. Seattle, Washington Bar Assn., Wash. State Trial Lawyers Assn., Wash. State Automobile Dealers Assn., Ky./Mo. Auto Dealers Assn., Motor Dealers Assn. B.C., Nat. Office Products Assn., Mayflower Warehousemen's Assn., Can. Movers Assn., Fedn. of Automobile Dealer Assns. of Can., Seattle Tennis Club, Seattle Yacht Club, Rotary. Avocations: tennis, boatin, skiing. Home: 3305 E John St Seattle WA 98112-4938 Office: Moss Adams Adv Svcs 1001 4th Ave Ste 2700 Seattle WA 98154-1101

DURYEE, HAROLD TAYLOR, insurance executive; b. Willoughby, Ohio, Feb. 11, 1930; s. Gerald Fancher and Margaret Grace (Taylor) D.; m. Phyllis Annette Painter, June 18, 1966. AB, Kenyon Coll., 1951. Field rep. Mahoning Valley Coun., Boy Scouts Am., Youngstown, Ohio, 1951-56; mgr. claims svcs. Nationwide Ins. Cos., Canton, 1956-65; legis. and field dir. Ohio Rep. Party, Columbus, 1965-70, exec. dir., 1970-77, cons., 1980-81; dep. adminstr. Ohio Bur. Workers' Compensation, Columbus, 1977-84; exec. dep. adminstr. Fed. Ins. Adminstrn., Washington, 1984-86; adminstr. fed. ins. Fed. Emergency Mgmt. Agy., Washington, 1986-90; dir. Ohio Dept. Ins., 1991-99; Trustee, exec. com. Griffith Found. for Ins. Edn.; mem. Ohio Elections Commn., 1980-84. Vice chmn. North Canton City Planning Commn., 1958-67; precinct committeeman Stark County Cen. Com., 1958-72; organizer North Canton Rep. Com., 1958, chmn., 1960-72; sec. North Canton Area Devel. Com., 1959-64; chmn. North Canton City Charter Commn., 1960; campaign mgr. U.S. Rep. Frank T. Bow, 1962, Oliver P. Bolton for U.S. Congress, 1964, Clarence J. Brown, Jr. for U.S. Congress, 1965; state chmn. Ohio League Young Rep. Clubs, 1962-63; nat. vice chmn. Young Rep. Nat. Fedn., 1963-65; former chmn. bd. trustees Nat. Assn. Ins. Commrs. Edn. and Rsch. Found.; former trustee ASFPM Edn. and Rsch. Found. Recipient Disting. Svc. award Jaycees, 1961, Civic Affairs award Rotary, 1964, Meritorious Svc. award Fed. Emergency Mgmt. Agy., 1989, Disting. Civilian Svc. medal, Fed. Emergency Mgmt. Agy., 1990. Mem. Nat. Assn. Ins. Commrs. (mem. exec. com. 1992-95, 98), Acad. Polit. Sci. Episcopalian. Avocation: genealogy. Home: 925 City Park Ave Columbus OH 43206-2511

DUSAN, MAKAVEJEV, film director, film producer; b. Belgrade, Yugoslavia, Oct. 13, 1932; m. Bojana Marijan, 1964. Grad. psychology, Belgrade U., 1955; student, Acad. Theater, Radio, Film, TV, Belgrade. Filmmaker Kino-Club, 1955-58, Zagreb Films, 1958, Avala Films, 1961. Dir., prodr. (shorts and documentaries) Jatagan Mala, 1953, The Seal, 1955, anthony's Broken Mirror, 1957, Don't Believe in Monuments, 1958, Beekeepers Scrapbook, 1958, Damned Holiday, 1958, Colors are Dreaming, 1958, What is a Woerkers' Coun., 1959, One Potato, Two Potato..., 1961, Smile 61, 1961, Educational Fairy Tale, 1961, Parade, 1962, Down with the Fences, 1962, Miss Yugoslavia 62, 1962, Film about the Book, 1962, New Domestic Animal, 1964, (feature films) Man is Not a Bird, 1966, Love Affair, 1967, Switchboard Operator, 1967, An Affair of the Heart, 1967, Innocnece Unprotected, 1968, W.R.: Mysteries of the Organism, 1971, Sweet Movie, 1974, Montenegro, 1981, The Coca-Cola Kid, 1985, For a Night of Love, 1988, Manifesto, 1989, Gorilla Bathes at Noon, 1993; author: A Kiss for Komradess Slogan, 1964, Innocence Unproteted, 1968, WR: Mysteries of the Organism, 1972; contbr. articles to profl. jours. With Yugoslavian Mil., 1959-60. Ford Found. grantee.

DUSANENKO, THEODORE ROBERT, retired educator, county official; b. Bronx, N.Y., Jan. 28, 1942; 010s. Teddy B. and Harriet T. Dusanenko; m. Jean Jenks, Apr. 24, 1983 (div. Mar. 1985); m. Dolores A. James, Aug. 31, 1986; children: Debra Garvey, Roger L. James. BS, SUNY, Albany, 1964, MS, 1967. Cert. secondary math. tchr., N.Y. Tchr. math. Clarkstown North H.S., New City, N.Y., 1964-80, 82-83, 85-96, wrestling coach, 1964-73; ret., 1996; legislator Rockland County, New City, 1979-85, 89—; salesman Ddolores A. James Real Estate, Piermont, N.Y., 1986—. Mem. New City Vol. Ambulance Corps, 1964-76, Rockland County Rep. Com., 1964—, O'Grady Brown Scholarship Com., 1981—; supr. Town of Clarkstown, New City, 1980-85, councilman, 1992-95; mem. Hudson River Valley Econ. Devel. Comm.; mem. region III N.Y. State Fish and Wildlife Bd.; initiator Clarkstown Youth Ct., 1981—. Mem. Elks. Roman Catholic. Avocations: gardening, grandparenting. Home: 462 Storms Rd Valley Cottage NY 10989-1213 Office: Dolores A James Real Estate 540 Piermont Ave Piermont NY 10968-1035

DUSANIC, DONALD GABRIEL, parasitology educator, microbiologist; b. Chgo., Dec. 15, 1934; s. Gabriel John and Harriet (Rojewski) D.; m. Roberta Leona Drost (dec. Feb. 1970); children: Donald, Robert; m. Jane Mitchell Haw, June 11, 1971; children: Belinda Conrad, Karla Conrad, Allan Conrad. BS, U. Chgo., 1957, MS, 1959, PhD, 1963. Instr. U. Chgo., 1963-64; asst. prof. U. Kans., Lawrence, 1964-68, assoc. prof., 1968-71, prof., 1971-72; prof. parasitology Ind. State U., Terre Haute, 1972-95, dir. Interdisciplinary Ctr. for Cell Products and Techs., 1987-95; prof. emeritus, 1995—; vis. prof. U. Philippines Sch. Medicine, Manila, 1964, Nat. Taiwan U. Sch. Medicine, Taipei, 1971, Nat. Sun Yat-sen U., Kaohsiung, Taiwan, 1991; adj. prof. Ind. U. Sch. Medicine, Terre Haute, 1982-95. Contbr. numerous articles on biochemistry and immunology of schistosomes, nematodes, amebae, and trypanosomes to sci. jours., chpts. to books. Recipient rsch. and creativity award Ind. State, 1982, Coll. Arts and Scis. Disting. Prof. award, 1990; rsch. grantee NIH, NSF, Office Naval Rsch. Mem. Am. Soc. Parasitologists, Am. Soc. Tropical Medicine and Hygiene, Am. Soc. Protozoologists, Am. Assn. Immunologists, N.Y. Acad. Scis., Sigma Xi. Home: 5726 E Cougar Dr Terre Haute IN 47802-8533 Office: Ind State U Dept Life Scis Terre Haute IN 47809

DUSANSKY, RICHARD, economist, educator; b. Bklyn., Dec. 23, 1942; s. Abraham and Mary (Strawitz) D.; m. Abigail November, July 3, 1965; children: Eric, Deborah. BA cum laude, Bklyn. Coll., 1964; PhD in Econs., Brown U., 1969. Asst. prof. econs. SUNY, Stony Brook, 1968-72, assoc. prof, 1972-74, prof., 1974-84, dir. Econ. Rsch. Bur., 1977-82; prof., head dept. econs. U. Ga., 1984-89; Powell Centennial prof. dept. econs. U. Tex., Austin, 1989-91, Richard Gonzalez Regents Chair prof. econs., 1991—, chmn., 1989-97, 98—; vis. scholar dept. econs. U. Calif., Berkeley, 1973, 78, 96; vis. prof. dept. econs. U. Wis., Madison, 1974-75. Contbr. articles on econs. to profl. jours. Ford Found. fellow, 1967-18. Mem. Am. Econs. Assn., Econometric Soc. Office: U Tex Dept Econ Austin TX 78712

DUSARD, JAY, photographer; b. St. Louis, Feb. 18, 1937; s. Justin Rime and Dorothy Mildred (May) D.; m. Katherine Elizabeth Kraetz, Oct. 9, 1965. BArch, U. Fla., 1961. Cowboy, Slaughter Ranch, Douglas, Ariz., 1963; designer, draftsman Ellery C. Green, Architect, Tucson, 1964; cartographic draftsman water resources divsn. U.S. Geol. Survey, Tucson, 1965-66; designer, lithographer Northland Press, Flagstaff, Ariz., 1966-68; asst. prof. light graphics Prescott (Ariz.) Coll., 1968-75; engring. tech. VA, Prescott, 1975-81; freelance photographer Prescott, 1981—, Cochise County, Ariz.; cons. Malpai Borderlands Group, Douglas, 1994-98; quarter horse breeder J Bar D Quarter Horses, Douglas, 1998—; amateur jazz musician. Author, photographer: The North American Cowboy: A Portrait, 1983, Open Country, 1994 (Third Place award Photography Book of Yr. Competition, 1994); photographer: La Frontera: the United States Border with Mexico, 1986 (Four Corners Book award, 1988), Beyond the Rangeland Conflict: Toward a West That Works, 1995 (Pulitzer Prize nominee, 1996). Mem. bd. advisors Ctr. for Photographic Art, Carmel, Calif.; adv. bd. Ctrl.

Ariz. Land Trust; mem. Malpai Borderlands Group, Ariz.-N. Mex. Jaguar Conservation Team. With U.S. Army, 1961-63. County of Dade Archs. travelling scholar, 1960; photography fellow Guggenheim Meml. Found., 1981. Avocations: horsemanship. Home and Office: 5261 N Stewart Ranch Rd Douglas AZ 85607-6289 Mailing: PO Box 3923 Douglas AZ 85608-3923

DUSCHA, JULIUS CARL, journalist; b. St. Paul, Nov. 4, 1924; s. Julius William and Anna (Perlowski) D.; m. Priscilla Ann McBride, Aug. 17, 1946 (dec. Sept. 1992); children: Fred C., Steve D., Suzanne, Sally Jean; m. Suzanne Van Den Heurk, June 21, 1997. Student, U. Minn., 1943-47; AB, Am. U., 1951; postgrad., Harvard Coll., 1955-56. Reporter St. Paul Pioneer Press, 1943-47; publicist Dem. Nat. Com., 1948, 52; writer Labor's League for Polit. Edn., AFL, 1949-52, Internat. Assn. Machinist, 1952-53; editorial writer Lindsay-Schaub Newspapers, Ill., 1954-58; nat. affairs reporter Washington Post, 1958-66; assoc. dir. profl. journalism fellowships program Stanford (Calif.) U., 1966-68; dir. Washington Journalism Ctr., 1968-90; columnist, freelance journalist, West Coast corr. Presstime mag., San Francisco, 1990—; contbg. editor News Inc., San Francisco, 1998—. Author: Taxpayer's Hayride: The Farm Problem from the New Deal to the Billie Sol Estes Case, 1964, Arms, Money and Politics, 1965, The Campus Press, 1973; editor: Defense Conversion Advisory; contbr. articles to mags., including Washingtonian, N.Y. Times Mag., Changing Times. Recipient award for distinguished Washington corr. Sigma Delta Chi, 1961. Mem. Cosmos Club (Washington), Kappa Sigma. Home: 2200 Pacific Ave Apt 7D San Francisco CA 94115-1412

DUSCHA, LLOYD ARTHUR, engineering executive; b. Foley, Minn., Mar. 18, 1925; s. Michael Frederick and Augusta Johanna (Leyk) D.; m. Edris Jeanette Finden, , Mar. 20, 1948; children: Mary L. Jalenak, Kevin J., Karen L. Goldrich. BCE, U. Minn., 1945. Registered civil engr., registered structural engr. Civil engr. Garrison dist. U.S. Army C.E., Bismarck, N.D., 1946-50; structural engr. Garrison dist. C.E., Riverdale, N.D., 1950-59; chief engring. br. ballistic missile constrn. office (Atlas) Corps Engrs., Omaha, Lincoln, Nebr., 1959-62; chief engring. br. ballistic missile constrn. office (Minuteman) C.E., Grand Forks, Minot, N.D., 1962-66; chief engring. divsn. Phila. dist. C.E., Phila., 1966-71; chief engring. divsn. Missouri River divsn. C.E., Omaha, 1971-79; chief engring. divsn., civil works directorate C.E., Washington, 1979-83, dep. dir. engring. and constrn. directorate, corps hdqrs., 1983-89; cons. to pvt. sector and pub. orgn. domestic-fgn. clients, 1990—; with AECOM Tech. Corp., Washington, 1990—; chmn. com. on dam safety Internat. Commn. Large Dams, 1982-88; pres. U.S. Nat. Com. on Large Dams, 1983-84; vice chmn. U.S. Nat. Com. Tunneling Tech., 1993-95; mem. Nat. Rsch. Coun. Bd. on Intrastructure and Constructed Environ., 1995-98. Contbr. articles to profl. jours. Comdr. USNR. Recipient Wheeler medal Soc. Am. Military Engrs., 1975, Outstanding Achievement award U. Minn. Regents, 1988, Pub. Servant of Yr. award Am. Cons. Engrs. Coun., 1990; NAE fellow, 1987. Fellow ASCE (Pres.'s medal 1989), NSPE (chpt. pres. 1977-79), Soc. Am. Mil. Engrs.; mem. Tau Beta Pi, Chi Epsilon. Home and Office: 11802 Grey Birch Pl Reston VA 20191-4223

DUSENBERRY, PHILIP BERNARD, advertising executive; b. Bklyn., Apr. 28, 1936; s. Harry Augustus and Margaret Maria (Shaw) D. Student, Emory and Henry Coll., 1955. Copywriter Batten, Barton, Durstine & Osborne, Inc., N.Y.C., 1962-65, creative supr., 1965-67, v.p., 1967-69, assoc. creative dir., sr. v.p., dir., 1977-78, creative dir., 1978-80, exec. creative dir., exec. v.p., mem. exec. com., 1980-86, later vice chmn., exec. creative dir.; vice chmn. BBDO Worldwide, 1986—, also bd. dirs.; chmn. bd. BBDO N.Y.; owner Dusenberry-Ruriani-Kornhauser, N.Y.C., 1969-73, Clyne-Dusenberry, 1973-76. Author: (motion picture) (with Larry Spiegel) Hail to the Chief, 1973, (screenplay, with Roger Towne) The Natural, 1975, (with Norman Cohen) August Strangers, 1977. Served with USNG, 1960-61. Office: BBDO Worldwide Inc 1285 Avenue Of The Americas New York NY 10019-6028*

DUSENBERY, WALTER CONDIT, sculptor; b. Alameda, Calif., Sept. 21, 1939; s. Walter A. and Allegra V. (McIlrath) D.; m. Irene McManus, Jan. 25, 1986. Student, San Francisco Art Inst., 1961; M.F.A., Calif. Coll. Arts and Crafts, Oakland, 1969. Instr. U. Calif. Extension-San Francisco, 1967-69; vis. sculptor Grad. Sch. Design-Harvard U., Cambridge, Mass., 1979—; dir. Stone divsn. Johnson Atelier, 1996—. Exhibitor one-man shows, Laumeir Internat. Sculpture Park, St. Louis, 1983, Va. Commonwealth U., Richmond, 1983, Harvard U. Grad. Sch. Design, 1982, Nassau County Mus. Fine Art, Roslyn, N.Y., 1981, Hamilton Gallery Contemporary Art, N.Y.C., 1978, 80, Fendrick Gallery, Washington, 1986, 88; represented in permanent collections, Carnegie Inst., Pitts., Columbus (Ohio) Mus. Art, Commune of Glostrup, Denmark, Solomon R. Guggenheim Mus., N.Y.C., Huntington (W. Va.) Galleries, Met. Mus. Art, N.Y.C., San Francisco Mus. Modern Art, U. N.Mex. Mus., Albuquerque, Jerusalem Found, Israel, City of Portland Oreg., U. No. Iowa, Cedar Falls, Rainier Bank, Seattle; author: The Story of the Bed, 1970. Recipient Meml. prize Augustus St. Gaudens Found.; fellow Creative Artists Program Svc., N.Y.C., 1980, Nat. Endowment for Arts, 1980. Home: 109 Cemetery Rd Fly Creek NY 13337-9703

DU SHANE, JAMES WILLIAM, physician, educator; b. Madison, Ind., Apr. 17, 1912; s. Donald and Harriette Graham (McLell) DuS.; m. Mary Margaret Hill, May 7, 1939; children: Mary Margaret, James Anderson. A.B., DePauw U., 1933; M.D., Yale U., 1937. Diplomate Am. Bd. Pediatrics (chmn. sub-bd. cardiology 1961-66). Intern Yale-New Haven Hosp., 1937-38, resident in pediatrics, 1938-39; resident Children's Meml. Hosp., Chgo., 1939-42; pvt. practice pediatrics Evanston, Ill., 1942-44; instr. Northwestern U. Med. Sch., 1942-44; mem. staff Mayo Clinic, Rochester, Minn., 1946—; head sect. pediatrics Mayo Clinic, 1957-69, mem. bd. govs., 1961-73; prof. pediatrics Mayo Found., U. Minn., 1960—. Contbr. articles to med. jours. Trustee Mayo Found., 1967-73. Served to lt. USNR, 1944-46. Mem. AMA, Am. Acad. Pediatrics (founding chmn. cardiology sect. 1958), Am. Coll. Chest Physicians, Am. Pediatric Soc., Am. Heart Assn. (chmn. council rheumatic fever and congenital heart disease 1960-62), Alpha Omega Alpha, Phi Kappa Psi. Home: 211 2nd St NW Rochester MN 55901-2807 Office: Mayo Clinic Rochester MN 55905

DUSOLD, LAURENCE RICHARD, chemist, computer specialist; b. Chgo., Nov. 15, 1944; s. Henry E. and Colette M. Dusold; m. Karen A. Marsh, Aug. 29, 1970; children: Amy, Lauren, Patricia, Amanda. BS in Chemistry, Purdue U., 1966; MS, U. N.C., 1969; postgrad., Wayne State U., 1969-71. Rsch. chemist, residue analysis and methods investigation br. Bur. Foods FDA, Washington, 1971-75, chemist, computer specialist, div. chemistry and physics, 1975-81, sr. chemist, computer specialist, div. of chemistry and physics, 1981-86, chief telecomms. and sci. computer support, 1986—; mem. faculty, evening divsn. U. Md., 1973—; mem. fed. engring. planning group Dept. HHS, 1990-95. Mem. editl. bd. Sci. Computing and Automation, 1990-98; contbr. articles to profl. jours., chpts. to books. Mem. AAUP, Am. Chem. Soc., Internet Soc., IEEE, IEEE Computer Soc., Assn. Computing Machinery (chmn. SIGAPL, D.C. chpt. 1978-91, vice chmn. Potomac chpt. 1993-96), Greater Washington Fed. Agy. APL Users Group (co-chmn. 1977-87), Alpha Chi Sigma, Phi Lambda Upsilon. Republican. Roman Catholic. Office: FDA 200 C St SW Washington DC 20204-0001

DUSSAULT, JEAN H., endocrinologist, medical educator; b. Que., Apr. 6, 1941. BA, U. Montreal, 1960; MD, Laval U., 1965; MSc, U. Toronto, 1969. Intern Hosp. Enfant-Jesus, 1964-65, chief resident, 1965-67; Med. Rsch. Coun. Can. sr. rschr. in endocrinology U. Toronto/Wellesley Hosp., 1967-69, UCLA Sch. Medicine/Harbor Gen. Hosp., 1969-71; from asst. prof. to assoc. prof. Laval U. Sch. Medicine, Quebec City, 1971-81, prof. medicine, 1981—; dir. rsch. unit ontogenesis and molecular genetics Ctrl. Hosp./Laval U., 1986-96. Recipient Ross award Am. Acad. Pediatrics, 1976, Manning award Can. Assn. Endocrinology and Metabolism/Can. Diabetes Assn., 1987. Fellow Royal Coll. Physicians (Can.); mem. Am. Thyroid Assn., Can. Med. Assn., Am. Fedn. Clin. Rsch., Endocrine Soc., Can. Soc. Clin. Rsch., Can. Soc. Endocrinology and Metabolism, Soc. Pediatric Rsch., N.Y. Acad. Sci. Office: Unit of Rsch Human Genetics, 2705 boulevard Laurier, Sainte Foy, PQ Canada G1V 4G2

DUSSAULT, NICHOLAS F., educator; b. Conover, Wis., Sept. 7, 1948; s. Francis L. and Mary Agnes Dussault; m. Carol H. Kettenhoven, Sept. 4, 1971; children: William F., Christine C. BA, U. Wis., Milw., 1971, PhD, 1980; MA, No. Ill. U., 1974. Coord. rsch. and evaluation Sheboygan (Wis.) Area Sch. Dist., 1980—; co-founder Wis. Assessment Consortium, 1990—. Bd. dirs. Sheboygan Area United Way, 1994—. Named Adminstr. of Yr., Wis. State Reading Assn., 1997. Home: 2734 N 30th St Sheboygan WI 53083 Office: Sheboygan Area Sch Dist 830 Virginia Ave Sheboygan WI 53281

DUSSEAULT, C. DEAN, lawyer; b. Boston, Mar. 22, 1938; s. Chester H. and Barbara E. (McMullin) D.; m. Gail S. Roberts, July 1, 1961; children: Karen Dusseault Monroe, Christopher D. BA, Yale U., 1959; JD, Harvard U., 1962. Bar: Mass. 1962, U.S. Dist. Ct. (Mass.) 1962, U.S. Ct. Appeals (1st cir.) 1965. Atty. Office of Gen. Counsel to Sec. of Air Force, Washington, 1962-65; assoc. Ropes & Gray, Boston, 1965-73, ptnr., 1973—. Chancellor, Cathedral Ch. of St. Paul, Boston; dir. Yale Club of Boston; chmn. Yale Alumni Schs. Com. for Eastern Mass. Mem. ABA, Mass. Bar Assn., Boston Bar Assn., Yale Club Boston, Soc. St. John the Evangelist (assoc.). Episcopalian. Republican. Avocations: music, sports. Home: 16 Edgemoor Rd Belmont MA 02478-3918 Office: Ropes & Gray 1 International Pl Boston MA 02110-2602

DUSSMAN, JUDITH ANN, publishing executive; b. Chgo., Aug. 23, 1947; d. Thomas Raymond and Dorothy M. (Stalzer) D.; div. 1985; children: John Thomas, Douglas Jude, Luke Price, Katherine Cannon. BA, Northwestern U., 1969; postgrad., Fordham U., 1974; JD, Loyola U., 1975. Bar: Ill. 1993, U.S. Dist. Ct. (no. dist.) Ill. 1993. Advt. sales mgmt. Chgo. Sun Times, Daily News, 1970-77, New York Trib, 1977-78, New York Times, Golf Digest, Tennis, 1979-81; assoc. pub. Ofcl. Airline Guides mag. div. Dun & Bradstreet, Oak Brook, Ill., 1981-83; pub. New Connections mag. Dun & Bradstreet, N.Y.C., 1984; circulation dir. Ofcl. Airlines Guide, Oak Brook, Ill., 1985-87; chief exec. officer, gen. mgr. Wordright Enterprises Inc., Evanston, Ill., 1987-89. Contbg. editor: (book) Where The Fun Is, 1968; footnote editor: (book) Re-issue Of The Impending Crisis Of The South, 1969. Bd. dirs., chmn. legal com. Kemeys Cove Condo., Scarborough, N.Y., 1976-80; mem. Friends Brookfield Zoo; pres. parents' coun. Ill. Math. and Sci. Acad., 1992—; vol. atty Office of Pub. Guardian, Cook County. Mem. MENSA, Am. Electronics Assn., Midwest Chpt. Speakers Com., Chgo. Assn. Direct Mktg., Am. Soc. Travel Agts. Educators Forum, Ill. Bar Assn., DuPage Bar Assn., Chgo. Bar Assn., Direct Mktg. Assn., Women in Mgmt., Advt. Women N.Y., Loyuola Law Alumni, Northwestern U. Alumni Assn., Cross Country Flying Club, DuPage County Bar Assn., Chgo. Coun. Lawyers, DuPage Assn. Women Lawyers, Ill. Bar Assn., Zonta, Chi. Omega. Roman Catholic. Club: Sales and Mktg. Exec. N.Y. Avocations: flying, travel, hiking, running, pets. Home: 46 S Madison St Hinsdale IL 60521-3236 Office: Dussman and Assocs Hinsdale IL 60521 *Personal philosophy: Do your best.*

DUSTAN, HARRIET PEARSON, former physician, educator; b. Craftsbury, Vt., Sept. 16, 1920; d. William Lyon and Helen Gordon (Paterson) D. BS, U. Vt., 1942, MD, 1944, DSc (hon.), 1977; DSc (hon.), Med. Coll. Wis., 1986. Diplomate Am. Bd. Internal Medicine. Intern Mary Fletcher Hosp. U. Vt., Burlington, 1944-45; asst. resident medicine Royal Victoria Hosp., Montreal, Que., Can., 1945-46; asst. prof. Coll. Medicine U. Vt., 1946-48; rsch. fellow Cleve. Clinic, 1948-51, mem. staff rsch. dir., 1951-77, asst. dir., 1971-77; prof. medicine Sch. Medicine U. Ala., Birmingham, 1977-90; VA disting. physician Birmingham VA Med. Ctr., 1987-90; emeritus prof. medicine Sch. Medicine U. Ala., Birmingham, 1990—; mem. adv. coun. Nat. Heart, Blood, Lung Inst., Bethesda, Md., 1972-76; bd. regents Am. Coll. Physicians, Phila., 1979-84; mem. Am. Bd. Internal Medicine, Phila., 1973-79. Recipient Sci. Achievement award AMA, 1988. Fellow Am. Heart Assn. (pres. 1976-77, Lifetime Achievement award 1991); mem. Am. Coll. Physicians (master, John Phillips Meml. award 1994), Assn. Am. Physicians, Inst. Medicine. Avocations: history, cooking. Home: 34 Lang Dr Essex Junction VT 05452-3379

DUTCHER, JAMES MARSHALL, English language educator; b. Rochester, N.Y., Jan. 28, 1956; s. Henry Redman D. Jr. and Cecile Genhart Sarra; m. Jennifer Mary Dobson, June 30, 1979; children: Lindsay Jane, Katherine Sarah. A-level certs., The Mill, Sussex, Eng., 1974; BA, Hobart & William Smith Coll., 1978; MA, U. Mass., 1982, PhD, 1993. Instr. U. Mass., Amherst, 1979-84; prof. English Holyoke (Mass.) C.C., 1984—, dir. honors program, 1993—; staff mem., mem. adv. coun. Mass. Ctr. for Renaissance Studies, Amherst, 1987—; dir. writing ctr., St. Hyacinth Coll. and Sem., Granby, Mass., 1992-96; adviser Alpha Xi Omega chpt. Phi Theta Kappa, Holyoke, 1989—; cons. U. Plymouth, Eng., 1990—; mem. seminar Folger Shakespeare Inst., Washington, 1998; mem. NSF, Chautauqua, San Francisco, 1996. Editor, co-author: (book) Belchertown Historical Coloring Book, 1994; editor: (jour.) Mass. Studies in English, 1980-85; contbr. articles to profl. jours. Mem. h.s. coun. Belchertown (Mass.) H.S., 1994—; exec. bd. dirs. Belchertown PTO, 1988-97; exec. com. Commonwealth honors program, 1999—. Mem. MLA, Nat. Collegiate Honors Coun., Five-Coll. Faculty Seminar on the Renaissance. Democrat. Avocations: sailing, skiing, mountaineering, rock climbing. E-mail: jdutcher@hcc.mass.edu. Office: Holyoke C C Honors Program 303 Homestead Ave Holyoke MA 01040

DUTCHER, JANICE JEAN PHILLIPS, oncologist; b. Bend, Oreg., Nov. 10, 1950; d. Charles Glen and MayBelle (Fluit) Phillips; m. John Dutcher, Sept. 8, 1971 (div. 1980). BA with honors, U. Utah, 1971; MD, U. Calif., Davis, 1975. Diplomate Am. Bd. Internal Medicine, Am. Bd. Med. Oncology. Intern Rush-Presbyn. St. Luke's Hosp., Chgo., 1975-76, resident, 1976-78; clin. assoc. Balt. Cancer Rsch., Nat. Cancer Inst., 1978-81, sr. investigator, 1981-82; asst. prof. U. Md., Balt., 1982; asst. prof. Albert Einstein Coll. Medicine, N.Y.C., 1983-86, assoc. prof., 1986-92, prof., 1992-98; course co-dir. Advances in Cancer Treatment Rsch. Albert Einstein Coll. Medicine, Manhattan, 1984-96; prof. medicine N.Y. Med. Coll., 1998—; assoc. dir. for clin. affairs Comprehensive Cancer Ctr., Our Lady of Mercy Med. Ctr., 1998—; chmn. biol. response mod. com. Ea. Coop. Oncology Group, Madison, Wis., 1989-95, mem. exec. com., 1995-97, chair renal subcom., 1998—; mem. data safety com. Nat. Heart Lung Blood Inst., Bethesda, Md., 1990-95; mem. biologic response modifier study sect. Nat. Cancer Inst., Bethesda, 1988, 90, 94, 96; mem. NIH Consensus Panel on Early Melanoma, 1992; mem. FDA Oncology Drug Adv. Bd., 1995-99, chair FDA-ODAC, 1996-99, NCI subcom. D for program project rev., 1995-98, mem. subsplty. med. oncology bd. Am. Bd. Internal Medicine, 1997—; mem. NCI subcom. A for Cancer Ctrs., 1998—. Editor: Handbook of Hematology/Oncology Emergencies, 1987, Modern Transfusion Therapy, 1990; sect. editor: Neoplastic Diseases of the Blood, 3d edit., 1996; mem. editl. bd. Jour. Immunotherapy, Med. Oncology, Jour. Clin. Oncology, Jour. Clin. Pharm.; contbr. articles to Blood, Leukemia, Jour. Clin. Oncology. Recipient Beecham award in Hematology So. Blood Club, 1983, Henry C. Moses Clin. Rsch. award Montefiore Med. Ctr., 1989, Outstanding Alumnus award U. Calif., Davis, 1989; named Outstanding Young Investigator Ea. Coop. Oncology Group, 1993; recipient numerous grants. Fellow ACP; mem. Am. Soc. Clin. Oncology (program com. 1988, 97, nominating com. 1999—), Am. Assn. Cancer Rsch. (faculty workshop clin. trials methodology 1996, 97, 98, 99, internat. trials workshop 1999), Am. Soc. Hematology, Soc. for Biol. Therapy, Am. Radium Soc. (chair Jane Way com. 1995-96, exec. com. 1997—), Phi Beta Kappa (Presdl. scholar 1968), Alpha Lambda Delta, Phi Kappa Phi, Alpha Omega Alpha. Achievements include findings related to management of alloimmunization to platelet transfusions, intensive maintenance of patients with acute leukemia, studies of new biologic response modifiers as antitumor drugs, management of renal cell cancer and breast cancer, study and treatment with biologic antitumor agents. Address: Our Lady of Mercy Medical Cen Comprehensive Cancer Cen 600 E 233rd St Bronx NY 10466-2604

DUTILE, ROBERT ARTHUR, management consultant; b. Stoneham, Mass., Dec. 26, 1959; s. Robert Arthur and Mary-Helene (Revane) D.; m. Ellen R. Ahearn, June 9, 1995. BS, Boston Coll., 1981. Cons. Monchik-Weber, Boston, 1981-83, Gately, Glew & Co., Wellesley, Mass., 1983-84; dir. MIS Reebok Internat., Ltd., Stoughton, Mass., 1984-91; sr. cons. Grant Thornton, LLP, Boston, 1992, mgr., 1992-95, sr. mgr., 1995-97, prin., 1997—. Author: The Benchmarking Course, 1993. Mem. Am. Soc. Quality Control, Am. Mgmt. Assn., Am. Prodn. & Inventory Control Soc., Am. Mountain Guides Assn., Am. Alpine Club (life), Two/Ten Found. (life.). Avocations: writing, rock climbing, mountaineering, golf. Office: Grant Thornton, LLP 98 N Washington St Ste 400 Boston MA 02114-1907

DUTKA, LINDA SEMROW, psychiatric and addictions nurse; b. New Britain, Conn., Nov. 10, 1948; d. Walter J. and Mary Helen (MacPherson) Semrow; m. David L. Dutka, Sept. 12, 1970; children: Matthew, Keith, Michael Paul. Diploma RN, Joseph Lawrence Sch. Nursing, New London, Conn., 1970; BA summa cum laude, Eastern Conn. State U., 1985; MSN, U. Conn., 1990. Cert. biofeedback therapist Glastonbury (Conn.) Health Assocs., Counseling Affiliates, Inc., Farmington, Conn., Stress Medicine, Inc., Hartford, Conn., 1982-87; psychiat. nurse Manchester (Conn.) Meml. Hosp., 1987-90; nurse coord. Blue Ridge Ctr., Bloomfield, Conn., 1990; addictions nurse therapist edn. & rsch. U. Conn. Health Ctr., Farmington, 1991-94; immunization coord. East Hartford (Conn.) Health Dept., 1995-97, cmty. health edn. coord., 1995—. Mem. ANA, CNA, New Eng. Biofeedback Soc., Assn. for Applied Psychophysiology & Biofeedback, Sigma Theta Tau. Home: 188 Northfield Rd Coventry CT 06238-1423 Office: E Hartford Health Dept 740 Main St East Hartford CT 06108

DUTKO, MICHAEL EDWARD, lawyer; b. Memphis, Jan. 18, 1954; s. Edward James and Norma Dean (Sparks) D.; m. Bettie Ballowe, Mar. 14, 1981; children: Michael, Christina, Ashley. BA, Biscayne Coll., 1978; JD, Nova U., 1984. Police officer, detective Ft. Lauderdale (Fla.) Police Dept., 1976-81; pros., asst. state atty. Broward State Atty.'s Office, Ft. Lauderdale, 1984-86; assoc. Kay & Bogenschutz, P.A., Ft. Lauderdale, 1986-90; ptnr. Kay, Bogenschutz & Dutko, Ft. Lauderdale, 1990-92, Bogenschutz & Dutko, P.A., Ft. Lauderdale, 1992—. Mem. Broward Assn. Criminal Def. Lawyers. Democrat. Roman Catholic. Avocations: golf, boxing, motorcycles. Office: Bogenschutz & Dutko PA 600 S Andrews Ave Ste 500 Fort Lauderdale FL 33301-2851

DUTOIT, CHARLES, conductor; b. Lausanne, Switzerland, Oct. 7, 1936. Studied at, Conservatory of Lausanne, Acad. Music, Geneva, Academia Musicale Chigiana, Siena, Conservatory Benedetto Marcello, Venice, Italy; attended session in conducting, Berkshire Music Center, Tanglewood, Mass.; DMus (hon.), McGill U., Montreal U., Laval U. Prin. condr. NHK Symphony Orch., N.Y.C., 1996, Montreal Symphony Orch. Formerly violinist with Lausanne Chamber Orch.; debut as condr. with Bern Symphony Orch., Switzerland, 1963; condr. and asst. music dir., Bern Symphony Orch., 1964, later music dir.; condr. and artistic dir., Radio-Zurich Orch., Switzerland, 1967; also guest condr. Vienna Opera; mus. dir. Nat. Symphony Orch. of Mex., Orch. Nat. de France, 1991—; apptd. chief condr. Goteborg Orch., Sweden, 1975; music dir., condr., Montreal Symphony Orch., 1977—; prin. guest condr. Minn. Orch., 1982-85; prin. condr., artistic dir. Phila. Orch., 1990-91; artistic dir., prin. condr. summer festivals Phila. Orch., at Mann Ctr. for Performing Arts, Saratoga Performing Arts Ctr.; prin. condr. NHK Symphony Orch., Tokyo, 1996; guest condr. all major orchs., S.Am., Europe, Japan, Australia, U.S., Can. and Israel, rec., Deutsche Gramophon, Erato, CBS, Decca/London, Philips, EMI; with Bavarian Radio Symphony, Boston Symphony Orch., Montreal Symphony Orch., L.A. Philharm., many London orchs., others. Recipient Canadian Music Coun. medal, 1988. Office: KM Artits LTD 40 W 57th St New York NY 10019-4001 Office: Orchestre Symphonique de Montreal, Orch Symph de Montreal, 260 de Maisonneuve Blvd W, Montreal, PQ Canada H2X 1Y9*

DUTRO, JOHN THOMAS, JR., geologist, paleontologist; b. Columbus, Ohio, May 20, 1923; s. John Thomas and Dorothy Durstine (Smith) D.; m. Nancy Ann Pence, Jan. 2, 1948; children: Sarah Dutro Cormier, Christopher, Susan Dutro Hultman. BA, Oberlin Coll., 1948; MS, Yale U., 1950, PhD, 1953; DSc, Denison U., 1993. Geologist, U.S. Geol. Survey, 1948-94, chief paleontology and stratigraphy br., 1962-68, mem. geologic names com., 1962-83; ret., 1994; emeritus vol. U.S. Geol. Survey, 1994—; rsch. assoc. Smithsonian Instn., 1962—; vis. lectr. Am. U., 1957-59, George Washington U., 1962-63; mem. geology panel Bd. Civil Svc. Examiners, 1958-65; dir., field trip chmn. 9th Internat. Carboniferous Congress, 1979. Active area PTA, 1959-69, Boy Scouts Am., 1963-66, Fairlington Players, 1965-75. With USAAF, 1943-46. Recipient Meritorious Svc. award U.S. Dept. Interior, 1983, Disting. Svc. award, 1996; Sterling fellow, 1949. Fellow AAAS (sec. sect. E 1981-85, Pacific divsn. pres. 1996-97), Arctic Inst. N.Am., Geol. Soc. London, Geol. Soc. Am. (assoc. editor 1974-82); mem. Am. Geol. Inst. (vis. geoscientist 1961-67, bd. dirs., sec.-treas. 1965-71), Paleontol. Soc. (tech. editor 1991), Paleontol. Assn., Paleontol. Rsch. Inst. (trustee 1986—, v.p. 1990-91, pres. 1992-94), Internat. Paleontol. Assn., Paleontol. Soc. Washington (pres. 1955-56), Geol. Soc. Washington (sec. 1959-60, pres. 1978), Assn. Earth Sci. Editors (pres. 1989-90), Am. Polar Soc., Alaska Geol. Soc., Sigma Xi, Pick and Hammer Club, Cosmos Club, Yale Club (Washington). Democrat. Research and publs. on brachiopoda, Paleozoic biostratigraphy and biogeography of Arctic regions and western hemisphere and history of paleontology. Home: 5173 Fulton St NW Washington DC 20016-3448 Office: US Nat Mus Natural History Washington DC 20560-0137

DUTSON, THAYNE R., university dean; b. Idaho Falls, Oct. 3, 1942; s. Rollo and Thelma (Fugal) D.; m. Joyce Cook, Dec. 19, 1962 (div. 1980); 1 child, Bradley; m. Margaret McCallum, June 30, 1989; children: Taylor, Alexandra. BS, Utah State U., 1966; MS, Mich. State U., 1969, PhD, 1971. Postdoctoral fellow U. Nottingham, Sutton Bonnington, Eng., 1971-72; prof. Tex. A&M U., College Station, 1972-83; dept. head Mich. State U., East Lansing, Mich., 1983-87; dir. agrl. exptl. sta. Oreg. State U., Corvallis, 1987-93, dean, dir. Coll. Agrl. Sci., 1993—. Editor: Advances in Meat Research (11 vols.) 1985-97; contbr. articles to profl. jours. Scoutmaster Boy Scouts Am., Mich., 1966-71. Fellow Inst. Food Technologists; mem. Am. Meat Sci. Assn. (bd. dirs. 1979-81, Disting. Rsch. award 1985), Am. Soc. Animal Sci. (Meat Rsch. award 1981), Coun. for Agr. Sci. and Tech. (pres. 1988), Phi Kappa Phi, Sigma Xi. Avocations: skiing, running, exercise, golf.

DUTTA, PARITOSH CHANDRA, immunologist. MD, Prince Wales Med. Coll., Patna U., India. Intern Queen Elizabeth Hosp., Montreal, 1960-61; resident in immunology Queen Mary VA Hosp., Montreal, 1961-62, Montreal Gen. Hosp., 1962-63; resident Kingston Gen. Hosp., 1964-65; fellow in allergy Montreal Gen. Hosp., 1963-64; staff mem. internal medicine for allergy and immunology Richardson Med. Ctr., Dallas; pvt. practice. Mem. Am. Acad. Allergy and Immunology, Am. Coll. Allergy and Immunology, Royal Coll. Physicians. Office: 4222 Trinity Mills Rd Ste 1 Dallas TX 75287-7603

DUTTON, CLARENCE BENJAMIN, lawyer; b. Pitts., May 31, 1917; s. Clarence Benjamin and Lillian (King) D.; m. Marian Jane Stevens, June 21, 1941; children: Victoria Lynn Dutton Sheehan, Barbara King Dutton Morgan. BS with distinction, Ind. U., 1938, JD with high distinction, 1940, LLD, 1970. Bar: Ind. 1940. Instr. bus. law Ind. U. Sch. Bus., 1940-41; atty. E.I. duPont de Nemours & Co., Inc., Wilmington, Del., 1941-43; asst. prof. law Ind. U. Sch. Law, 1946-47; pvt. practice, Indpls., 1947—; bd. dirs. Sarkes Tarzian, Inc.; mem. Ind. Jud. Study Commn., 1965-74; regional adv. group Ind. U. Sch. Medicine, 1966-75; mem., sec. Ind. Civil Code Study Commn., 1967-73; mem. Ind. Commn. on Uniform State Laws, 1970—, chmn., 1980-91, life mem., 1991. Author: (bus. law sect.) Chemical Business Handbook, 1954; contbr. articles to profl. jours. Bd. dirs. Found. Ind. U. Sch. Bus., Found. Econ. and Bus. Studies; mem. bd. visitors Ind. U. Sch. Law, 1971—, chmn., 1974-75; bd. dirs. Soc. for Advanced Study, Ind. U., 1984-95, pres., 1985-87; mem. Acad. Alumni Fellows, Ind. U. Sch. Law, 1988. Comdr. USNR, 1943-45. Recipient Ind. Bar Found. 50-Yr. award, 1992, Ind. U. Disting. Alumni Svc. award, 1995. Mem. ABA (ho. of dels. 1960-62, state del. 1967-72, bd. govs. 1971-74, chmn. gen. practice sect. 1971-72), Ind. State Bar Assn. (bd. mgrs. 1957-63, pres. 1961-62), Indpls. Bar Assn. (v.p. 1957), Ind. Soc. Chgo., Lawyers Club (pres. 1959-60), Indpls. Country Club (pres. 1955), Columbia Club, Woodstock Club, Wilderness Country Club (Naples, Fla., dir. 1991-94). Republican. Presbyterian. Home: 1402 W 52d St Indianapolis IN 46228-2317

DUTTON, DIANA CHERYL, lawyer; b. Sherman, Tex., June 27, 1944; d. Roy G. and Monett (Smith) D.; m. Anthony R. Grindl, July 8, 1974; children: Christopher, Bellamy. BS, Georgetown U., 1967; JD, U. Tex., 1971. Bar: Tex. 1971. Regional counsel U.S. EPA, Dallas, 1975-79, dir. enforcement div., 1979-81; ptnr., head firm-wide environ. sect., mem. Dallas practice com. Akin, Gump, Strauss, Hauer & Feld, L.L.P., Dallas, 1981—. Mem. ABA, Tex. Bar Assn. (chmn. environ. and natural resources law sect. 1985-86), Dallas Bar Assn. (chmn. environ. law sect. 1984). Episcopalian.

Office: Akin Gump Strauss Hauer & Feld LLP 1700 Pacific Ave Ste 4100 Dallas TX 75201-4675

DUTTON, FRANK ELROY, data processing executive; b. Warren, Ohio, Nov. 16, 1946; s. Robert Wade and Ann Victoria (Sessions) D.; m. Nancy June Gephart, Nov. 6, 1965 (div. 1981); children: Cynthia, Frank, Robert; m. Margaret Elizabeth Sessions, Dec. 16, 1981 (div. Dec. 1987); m. Paula Kay Gately, Feb. 14, 1992 (div. Sept. 1994). With sales dept. Zylco Cutlery Rena Ware Distrs., Warren, 1964-68; advt. salesman Directory Dept. Ohio Bell Telephone Co., Cuyahoga Falls, 1968-69; pvt. practice residential constrn. Warren and Hammond (La.), 1970-74; technician J. Ray McDermott & Co., New Orleans, 1974-83, McDermott Internat., Antwerp, Belgium, 1975, McDermott SE Asia, Singapore, 1981-83; owner Computer Time, Inc., Hammond, 1983-85; mgr. tech. services Industry Programs, Inc., Houston, 1985-86; owner Affordable Automation, Houston, 1987-89; program, analyst The Phillips Group, Stafford, Tex., 1989-92; owner software and hardware integrator IHMS Software Support, Hemphill, Tex., 1992—; owner computer software, internet web site design hosting Fred Software, Hemphill, 1998—; cons. in computer communications Southmark Industries, Houston, 1986-87, Crown Broadcasting, Hammond, La., 1987-89, Bee-Line Delivery Svc., Houston, 1986-89. Author, designer various computer games, utility software programs, computer software for radio stas., computer software for retail furniture stores, Turbo Pascal Toolbox, 1988 (award of disting. tech. communication 1989, award of excellence Internat. Soc. Tech. Communication 1989), French transl., 1988, Portuguese trans., 1990, French trans., 1990; contbr. articles to profl. jours. Served with USAR, 1966-72. Mem. Am. Mensa Soc. Avocation: astrology. Home and Office: HC 52 Box 842 Hemphill TX 75948-9625

DUTTON, JOHN ALTNOW, meteorologist, educator; b. Detroit, Sept. 11, 1936; s. Carl Evans and Velma (Altnow) D.; m. Frances Elizabeth Andrews, Jan. 13, 1962; children—Christopher Evan, John Andrews, Jan Frederik. B.S., U. Wis., 1958; M.S., 1959, Ph.D., 1962. Mem. faculty Pa. State U., University Park, 1965—; assoc. prof. meteorology Pa. State U., 1968-71, prof., 1971—, head dept. meteorology, 1981-86, dean Coll. Earth and Mineral Scis., 1986—; expert aero. system div. USAF, 1965-71; vis. scientist Riso Rsch. Establishment, Roskilde, Denmark, 1971-72, summer 1975, 78-79; vis. prof. Tech. U., Denmark, 1978-79; v.p. UCAR Found., 1986-87, pres., 1987-95, chmn. bd. dirs., 1995—. Author: The Ceaseless Wind: An Introduction to the Theory of Atmospheric Motion, 1976, 2d edit., 1986 (reprinted as Dynamics of Atmospheric Motion, 1995), (with H.A. Panofsky) Atmospheric Turbulence: Models and Methods for Engineering Applications, 1984; assoc. editor: Meteorol. Monographs, 1973-79, editor, 1979-84; contbr. articles to profl. jours. Trustee Univ. Corp. for Atmospheric Rsch., 1974-81, sec., 1977, treas., 1978-79, vice-chmn., 1980-84, chmn. unidata steering com., 1982-86, chmn. unidata policy com., 1986-88; chmn. long-range planning com. NSF-Univ. Corp. for Atmospheric Rsch., 1986-87; mem. bd. atmospheric scis. and climate NRC, 1982-83, 88-97, chmn. bd., 1989-97, mem. internat. space yr. planning com., 1986-89, panel of experts on earth sci. and tech. Internat. Space Yr. in 1992, 1989-92, space sci. bd. com. on earth scis., 1987-89, mem. space studies bd., 1989-93, chmn. task group priorities space rsch. of space studies bd., 1989-94, mem. nat. weather svc. modernization com., 1989-95; mem. Nat. Aviation Weather Svcs. Com., 1994-95; mem. com. long-term retention sci. and tech. records of fed. govt., 1993-95; ex-officio mem. Com. on Global Change Rsch., 1995—; mem. space and earth scis. adv. com. NASA, 1982-86, earth system sci. com., 1983-87, ctr. sci. assessment team, 1986-88. With USAF, 1962-65. Fellow AAAS (steering group sect. atmospheric and hydrospheric scis.), Am. Meteorol. Soc. (councillor 1986-88, chmn. publs. commn. 1984-85); mem. Math. Assn. Am., Soc. Indsl. and Applied Math., Sigma Xi, Phi Kappa Phi, Theta Delta Chi. Home: 240 Mount Pleasant Dr Boalsburg PA 16827 Office: 116 Deike Bldg University Park PA 16802-2710

DUTTON, KAREN VANDER WALL, critical care nurse; b. Hammond, Ind., June 17, 1942; d. Peter R. and Gertrude (De Jong) VanderWall; m. Ronald E. Dutton, Dec. 21, 1963; children: David Brian, Katherine Louise. RN, Chgo. Wesley Meml. Hosp., 1963; student, Calif. State U., L.A., 1967-69. RN, Ill., Wyo.; ACLS cert.; cert. trauma nursing core course instr., flight nurse advanced trauma life support provider; cert. flight RN; CEN; cert. emergency nurse pediat. course instr. Staff nurse Chgo. Wesley Meml. Hosp., 1963; head nurse in-svc. edn., staff nurse ICU/CCU St. Francis Hosp., Lynwood, Calif., 1964-75; staff nurse emergency rm. and ICU/CCU Wyo. Med. Ctr., Casper, 1977-86, interim clin. dir. emergency rm., 1992-93; chief flight nurse Wyo. Life Flight, Casper, 1986-92, emergency/life flight staff nurse, 1993—. Mem. Emergency Nurses Assn. (govs. state emergency med. svcs. adv. com.), Nat. Flight Nurses Assn.

DUTTON, PAULINE MAE, fine arts librarian; b. Detroit, July 15; d. Thoralf Andreas and Esther Ruth (Clyde) Tandberg; 1 child, Nancy Katherine; B.A. in Art, Calif. State U., Fullerton, 1967; M.S. in Library Sci., U. So. Calif., 1971; m. Richard Hawkins Dutton, June 21, 1969. Elem. tchr., Anaheim, Calif., 1967-68, Corona, Calif., 1968-69; fine arts librarian Pasadena (Calif.) Public Library, 1971-80; art cons., researcher, 1981—. Mem. Pasadena Librarians Assn. (sec. 1978, treas. 1979-80), Calif. Library Assn., Calif. Soc. Librarians, Art Librarians N.Am., Nat. Assn. Female Execs., Am. Film Inst., Am. Entrepreneurs Assn., Gilbert and Sullivan Soc., Alpha Sigma Phi. Club: Toastmistress (local pres. 1974). Office: Altadena Libr Dist 600 E Mariposa St Altadena CA 91001

DUTTON, PETER LESLIE, biochemist, educator; b. Ashton-Under-Lyne, Lancashire, U.K., Mar. 12, 1941; came to U.S., 1968; s. Arthur Bramwell and Mary (Drake) D.; mn. Julia R. Dwyer, July 19, 1965; children: Michael, Sara, Simon. BSc in Chemistry with honors, U. Wales, 1963, PhD in Biochemistry, 1967. Postdoctoral fellow with W. Charles Evans U. Wales, U.K., 1967; postdoctoral fellow Johnson Rsch. Found., U. Pa., Phila., 1968, asst. prof., 1971-75; assoc. prof. dept. biochemistry and biophysics U. Pa., Phila., 1976-80, prof. dept. biochemistry and biophysics, 1981—, acting chmn. dept., 1993-94, chmn. dept., 1994—, dir. Johnson Rsch. Found., 1991—; vis. prof. Imperial Coll., London, 1994, Univ. Coll., London, 1995. Author: Frontiers of Biological Energetics: From Electrons to Tissues, 1978, Protein Structure: Molecular and Electronic Reactivity, 1987; patentee in field; mem. editorial bd. Archives of Biochemistry, 1976-79; editor FEBS Letters, 1981-89; mng. editor Bioenergetics Revs. Sect. Biochimica et Biophysica Acta, 1981-96, Biochimica et Biophysica Acta, 1989-96. Mem. NIH adv. com. Molecular and Cellular Biophysics Study Sect., 1986-90; reserve mem. NIH Adv. Coms., 1990-94. Fellow Royal Soc. London. Office: Johnson Rsch Found B501 Richards Bldg Philadelphia PA 19104-6089

DUTTON, ROBERT W., electrical engineer. Dir. rsch. ctr. integrated systems Stanford (Calif. U.), 1991—. Mem. Nat. Acad. Engring. Office: Stanford U CISX 333 Stanford CA 94305-4075*

DUTTON, STEPHEN JAMES, lawyer; b. Chgo., Sept. 20, 1942; S. James H. and Marjorie C. (Smith) D.; m. Ellen W. Lee; children: Patrick, Mark. BS, Ill. Inst. Tech., 1965; JD, Ind. U., 1969. Bar: Ind. 1969, U.S. Dist. Ct. (so. dist.) Ind. 1969, U.S. Ct. Appeals (7th cir.) 1972, U.S. Ct. Appeals (D.C. cir.) 1980, U.S. Supreme Ct. 1978. With McHale, Cook & Welch, P.C., Indpls., 1969-86, Dutton & Overman, P.C., 1986-91, Dutton & Bailey, P.C., 1991-94, Locke, Reynolds, Boyd & Weisell, 1994-99, Leagre, Chandler & Millard, LLP, Indpls., 1999—; mem. Com. on Law of Cyberspace Bus. Law Sect. Mem. ABA. Home: 3705 Spring Hollow Rd Indianapolis IN 46208-4169 Address: 201 N Illinois St Ste 1000 Indianapolis IN 46204-4227

DUUS, GORDON COCHRAN, lawyer; b. Ridley Park, Pa., Oct. 17, 1954; s. Frank Martin and Shirley (Cochran) D.; m. Mary Ellen Moses, Nov. 9, 1985; children: Alexander, Hannah, Julianne. BA magna cum laude, U. Pa., 1977; JD with honors, George Washington U., 1981. Bar: D.C. 1981, N.J. 1982, Calif. 1987, U.S. Dist. Ct. N.J. 1982, U.S. Supreme Ct. 1989. Assoc. Previti, Todd, Gemmel, Fitzgerald & Nugent, Linwood, N.J., 1982-87; ptnr., chmn. environ. law dept. Margolis, Chase, Kosicki, Aboyoun & Hartman, Verona, N.J., 1987-90, Cole, Schotz, Meisel, Forman & Leonard, Hackensack, N.J., 1990—; mem. faculty Cook Coll. of Rutgers U., New Brunswick, N.J., 1991-99, Nat. Bus. Insts., Saddlebrook, N.J., 1992, Govt. Inst., Atlantic City, 1995; spkr. in field. Contbr. articles to profl. jours. Mem. ABA, N.J. Bar Assn., Bergen County Bar Assn. Office: Cole Schotz Meisel Forman & Leonard 25 Main St Hackensack NJ 07601-7015

DUUS, PETER, history educator; b. Wilmington, Del., Dec. 27, 1933; s. Hans Christian and Mary Anita (Pennypacker) D.; m. Masayo Umezawa, Nov. 25, 1964; 1 child, Erik. AB magna cum laude, Harvard U., 1955, PhD, 1965; MA, U. Mich., 1959. Asst. prof. history Washington U., St. Louis, 1964-66, Harvard U., Cambridge, Mass., 1966-70; assoc. prof. history Claremont (Calif.) Grad. Sch., 1970-73; assoc. prof. history Stanford (Calif.) U., 1973-78, prof., 1978—. Author: Party Rivalry and Political Change in Taishó Japan, 1968, Feudalism in Japan, 1969, The Rise of Modern Japan, 1976, The Cambridge History of Japan, Vol. 6: The Twentieth Century, 1989, The Japanese Informal Empire in China, 1989, The Abacus and the Sword: The Japanese Penetration of Korea, 1995, The Japanese Discovery of America, 1996, Modern Japan, 1997. Exec. sec. Inter-Univ. for Japanese Lang. Studies, Tokyo, 1974-90; bd. dirs. Com. for Internat. Exchange of Scholars, Washington, 1987-91. Served with U.S. Army, 1955-57. NEH sr. fellow, 1972-73, Japan Found. postdoctoral fellow, 1976-77, Fulbright rsch. fellow, 1981-82, 94-95, Japan Found. rsch. fellow, 1986-87. Fellow AAAS, mem. Assn. for Asian Studies (bd. dirs. 1972-75, nominating com. 1983, v.p. 1999—), Am. Hist. Assn. (bd. editors 1984-87). Avocations: squash, gardening, travel. Home: 818 Esplanada Way Palo Alto CA 94305-1015 Office: Stanford U Dept of History Stanford CA 94305

DUVA, LOU, boxing promoter, manager; b. N.Y.C., May 28, 1922; children. Former boxer, former bail bondsman; promoter Main Events, Totowa, N.Y., 1978—; past pres. Teamster Local 286. Named. Mgr. of Yr. Boxing Writers Assn. Am., 1985, Trainer of Yr. World Boxing Assn., 1987, 97; named to Internat. Boxing Hall of Fame, Canastota, N.Y., 1998. Achievements include the traning of 11 world champions: Joey Giardello, 1963, Johnny Bumphus, 1984, Rocky Lockrikdge, 1984, Livingstone Bramble, 1984, Mike McCallum, 1984, Evander Holyfield, 1986, Mark Breland, 1987, Vinnie Paziena, 1987, Pernell Whitaker, 1989, Darrin Van Horne, 1989, John-John Molina, 1989; corner-man over 70 world title fights including Michael Moorer, Arturo Gatti, Junior Jones. Fax: 973-389-9080. E-mail: www.mainevents.com. *

DUVAL, ALBERT FRANK, paper company executive; b. Holyoke, Mass., Oct. 31, 1920; s. Albert Frank and Lena (Potvin) D.; m. Mary Tague, Apr. 12, 1947; children: Denise, Richard, Nanette, Robert, Carolyn, Michele, Kathleen. B.A., Amherst Coll., 1943. Mgr. Calif. div. U.S. Envelope Co., 1946-52, sales mgr., 1952-55, v.p. sales, 1955-60, pres., 1960; v.p. Hammermill Paper Co., Erie, Pa., 1960-69; sr. v.p. Hammermill Paper Co., 1969, pres., 1970—, chief exec. officer, 1971-85, chmn., 1983-85. Trustee Mercyhurst Coll.; trustee St. Vincent's Hosp., chmn., 1976. Served with USAAF, 1944-46, ETO. Mem. Envelope Mfrs. Assn. (pres. 1963-65), Am. Paper Inst. (chmn. 1976). Club: Kahkwa (Erie) (pres. 1969—). Home: 3220 Georgian Ct Erie PA 16506-1116

DUVAL, DANIEL WEBSTER, manufacturing company executive; b. Cin., May 27, 1936; s. Harry A. and Wilda (Webster) V.; m. Sue Ann Howard, July 20, 1962; children: Laurie Ann, Paula Lee, Christopher Webster. BA, U. Cin., 1960. V.p. staff elec. products div. Midland-Ross, Cleve., 1976-78; group v.p. Midland-Ross, 1979-81, exec. v.p., 1981-83, pres., chief operating officer, 1983-86; pres., chief exec. officer Robbins & Myers Inc., Dayton, Ohio, 1986-98, also bd. dirs., vice-chmn. bd., 1999—; bd. dirs. Arrow Electronics, Nat. City Bank, Cleve., Danis Cos., Inc., Dayton, Gosiger, Inc., Dayton, ABC-Naco, Inc., Downers Grove, Ill., Allied Products, Chgo. Patentee container coupling mechanism. Bd. trustees Wright State U., Wright State U. Found.; pres. Civitan Found., Ariz., 1973-74, Dayton Ballet Assn., 1990-93; participant Leadership Cleve.; mem. Area Progress Coun.; bd. mem. U.S. Air and Trade Show. Mem. Dayton Racquet Club. Republican. Roman Catholic. Home: 1160 Ridgeway Rd Dayton OH 45419-3031 Office: Robbins & Myers Inc 1400 Kettering Tower Dayton OH 45423-1400

DUVAL, DAVID ROBERT, golfer; b. Jacksonville, Fla., Nov. 9, 1971. Student, Ga. Tech. Profl. golfer, 1993—; mem. Walker Cup team, 1991, Presidents Cup team, 1996. Winner Nike Wichita Open, 1993, Nike Tour Championship, 1993, Michelob Championship at Kingsmill, 1997, Walt Disney World/Oldsmobile Classic, 1997, The Tour Championship, 1997, Tucson Chrysler Classic, 1998, Shell Houston Open, 1998, NEC World Series of Golf, 1998, Michelob Championship at Kingsmill, 1998, Mercedes Championship, 1999, Bob Hope Chrysler Classic, 1999, The Players Championship, 1999, Bell South Classic, 1999; recipient Dave Williams award, 1993, Jasper award, Jacksonville, 1996; named Collegiate Player of Yr., 1993. Avocations: reading, fly fishing, surfing, skiing, baseball. Office: PGA of Am Box 109601 100 Ave of Champions Palm Beach Gardens FL 33410*

DUVAL, MICHAEL RAOUL, investment banker; b. San Francisco, July 18, 1938; s. Richard and Sylvia Raoul-Duval. A.B., Georgetown U., 1961; J.D., U. Calif., San Francisco, 1967. Bar: Calif. 1967, U.S. Supreme Ct. 1971. Atty. U.S. Dept. Transp., Washington, 1967-70; staff asst. to Pres., asso. dir. Domestic Council, spl. counsel to Pres., Washington, 1970-77; various exec. positions Mead Corp., Dayton, Ohio, 1977-84; mng. dir. First Boston Corp., N.Y.C., 1984-90; ltd. ptnr. Anthem Ptnrs., L.P., N.Y.C., 1990-92; chmn. Michael Duval & Assocs., Ltd., Santa Fe, 1994—; bd. dirs. British Aerospace Holdings, Inc. Mem. Def. Policy Bd., 1989-94, SEC's Emerging Markets Adv. Com., 1989, Nat. Commn. on Fin. Instn. Reform, Recovery and Enforcement, Washington. Capt. USMC, 1960-64. Mem. N.Y. Council Fgn. Relations. Republican. Roman Catholic.

DUVAL, ROBERT, leasing company executive; b. Bronx, N.Y., June 23, 1937; s. Jack Leon and Cornelia (Gerry) D.; m. Harriet Elin, June 4, 1960; children: Stacey R., Jennifer E. BS., Cornell U., 1959; LL.B., St. Johns U., 1967. Bar: N.Y. 1968, Pa. 1976, U.S. Supreme Ct. 1971. Assoc. firm Hart & Hume, N.Y.C., 1967-69, Kelley, Drye & Warren, N.Y.C., 1969-72, Gates & Laber, N.Y.C., 1972-75; mem. law dept. Westinghouse Electric Corp., Pitts., 1976-78; gen. counsel, sec. Pitts.-Des Moines Co., Pitts., 1978-87; v.p., sec., gen. counsel Wheeling-Pitts. Steel Corp., 1987-92; legal affairs cons. Pitts., 1992—; pres. Ardco Leasing Svc., 1993—. Served with U.S. Army, 1961. Mem. N.Y. Bar Assn., Am. Arbitration Assn. (arbitrator). Home: 1350 Old Meadow Rd Pittsburgh PA 15241-3426 Office: PO Box 12962 Pittsburgh PA 15241*

DUVAL, STANWOOD RICHARDSON, JR., judge; b. New Orleans, Feb. 8, 1942; m. Deborah Barnes, Jan. 20, 1979. BA, La. State U., 1964, LLB, 1966. Ptnr. Duval, Funderburk, Sundbery & Lovell, 1966-94; dist. judge U.S. Dist. Ct. (ea. dist.), La., 1994—. Mem. City of Houma Charter Commn., 1975, vice chmn. Charter Commn., 1980-81, Terrebonne Port Commn., 1987-88. Mem. ABA, Am. Trial Lawyers Assn., La. State Bar Assn., Terrebonne Parish Bar Assn., La. Trial Lawyers Assn. (bd.. gov. 1976-77), Whiskey Pass Silver King Assn., Houma-Terrebonne Jaycees. Avocations: traveling, scuba diving, hunting, fishing, performing arts. Office: U S Dist Ct Ea Dist 500 Camp St Rm C-368 New Orleans LA 70130-3313*

DUVAL-CARRIÉ, EDOUARD, artist; b. Haiti, 1954. Student, Ecole Nat. Superieure des Beaux Arts, Paris, 1988-89; BA, U. Loyola Montreal, 1978; student, McGill U., U. Montreal. resident Arts Internat.--Fondation Claude Monet, Giverny, France, 1998. One-man shows include Art Ctr., Port-au-Prince, Haiti, 1980, Franz Bader Gallery, Washington, 1982, Paul Waggoner Gallery, Chgo., 1983, Anderson Gallery, Va. Commonwealth U., Richmond, Va., 1986, Brent Gallery, Houston, 1987, Nicole Gallery, Chgo., 1987, Malraux Gallery, L.A., 1991, Armand Gallery, Paris, 1991, Mus. de Arte Contemporaneo de Monterrey, Mex., 1992, Porter Randall Gallery, San Diego, Calif., 1994, Lakaye Gallery, L.A., 1994, 98, Galeria Fernando Quintana, Bogota, Columbia, 1994, Gutierez Fine Arts, Miami Beach, Fla., 1994, Musée du Coll. St. Pierre, Port-au-Prince, 1996, Polk Mus. Art, Lakeland, Fla., 1997, Quintana Gallery, Miami, 1997, David Beitzel Gallery, Project Room, N.Y.C., 1997; group shows at Southeastern Ctr. Contemporary Art, Winston-Salem, N.C., 1997, Palacio del Segundo Cabo, Havana, Cuba, 1997, Mus. African Am. Art, Tampa, Fla., 1998, Internat. Arts Club, Chgo., 1973, Ramscale Gallery, N.Y.C., 1998, Taller Boricua Gallery, Julia de Burgos Cultural Ctr., N.Y.C., 1998, numerous others; represented in pub. collections; cover illustrator Imagen mag., 1995, Cantos to Blood and Honey, 1997, numerous others; contbr. articles to profl. jours. Fellow S. Fla. Cultural Consortium Visual Art, 1995; fellow So. Arts Fedn. Visual Art, 1996.

DUVALL, BERNICE BETTUM, artist, exhibit coordinator, jewelry designer; b. Washington, Mar. 17, 1948; d. William A. and Bergny (Farovig) Bettum; m. Donald Dunn Duvall, Oct. 5, 1968; children: Gregory Thomas, Peter Brian. Grad. high sch., Washington, 1966; art edn. pvt. study, 1970-74. Artist watercolor, acrylic, needlework design Chevy Chase, Md., 1972—; exhibit coord. Discovery Channel, Learning Channel, Discovery Comms., Inc., Bethesda, N.Y.C., 1993—, Your Choice TV, Bethesda, Md., 1995-97; with pub. rels. and publicity Town Ctr. Gallery, Rockville, Md., 1986-89; banner designer St. Paul's Luth. Ch., Washington, 1985—; sch. art project coord. Am. Speech-Lang.-Hearing Assn., Rockville, Md., 1998-99. Exhbns. include Capricorn Gallery, Bethesda, 1982, Westmoreland Mus. Art, Greensburg, Pa., 1982, 87, Hull Gallery, Washington, 1983, 85, Butler Inst. Am. Art, Youngstown, Ohio, 1983, DeLand (Fla.) Mus., 1984, Springfield (Mo.) Art Mus., 1988, 95, 98, Newberry Gallery, Pa., 1989, Broadway Gallery, Va., 1989, Watergate Gallery, Washington, 1990, Fine Art Mus. of South, Mobile, Ala., 1990, Images Internat. Gallery, Bethesda, 1991, 92, 93, So. Watercolor Soc., 1993, 99, Charles Sumner Sch. Mus., Washington, 1994, Sugar & Frichtl Gallery, Kensington, Md., 1994, Univ. Club, Washington, 1995, NIH, Bethesda, 1995, Margaret Smith Gallery, Ellicott City, Md., 1995, Univ. Club Washington, 1995, Office Gov. State of Md., Balt., 1996, Md. State House, Annapolis, 1996, Fine Arts Invitational, Oxford, Md., 1996, 97, 99, Hughes Network Sys., Germantown, Md., 1996, Arlington County Sch. Bd., Arlington, Va., 1997, Delaplaine Visual Art Ctr., Frederick, Md., 1998, Mt. St. Mary's Coll., Emmittsburg, Md., 1998, Howard County Pub. Sch. Adminstrn. Gallery, Ellicott City, Md., 1999 (one-person show), Wash. County Mus. Art, Hagerstown, Md., 1999 (group exhbt), others; juried exhbns. include Internat. Artists in Watercolor, London, 1981; prin. works represented in many pub. and pvt. collections including Montgomery County Contemporary Art Acquisitions, New Eng. Life Ins. Co., Pelavin Assocs., Inc., Capricorn Gallery, Univ. Club Washington; contbr. articles to Am. Artist, Watercolor, The Artist mag. Vol. artist Nat. Zoo, Washington, 1985-91; art judge Art in Schs., Parks, Pub. Places, Montgomery County, Md., 1988-90; speaker various pub. schs., Montgomery County, 1988, 92. Recipient Award of High Commendation Internat. Artists in Water Colors, 1981, Arthur Alexander award So. Water Color Soc., 1981, Award of Merit Md. Fedn. Art, 1980, Liquitex award Adirondacks Am. Watercolorists, 1989, Bendann Gallery award Balt. Water Color Soc., 1990, Washington Water Color Assn. award, 1993, Patron's award Watercolor U.S.A., 1995, First Place award Fed. Reserve, 1995. Mem. Pa. Watercolor Soc., Art League (bd. dirs. 1982-86), Washington Water Color Assn. (bd. dirs. 1986-87, award 1993), Town Ctr. Gallery (bd. dirs. 1986-89), Potomac Valley Watercolorists (bd. dirs. 1993—), Artists Equity, Arts Coun. Montgomery County, So. Watercolor Soc. (co-chmn. ann. juried exhibit 1993), Balt. Watercolor Soc., Strathmore Arts Found., Women's Club Chevy Chase. Lutheran. Avocations: gardening, horseback riding, needlework. Home and Studio: 3414 Taylor St Chevy Chase MD 20815-4024

DUVALL, CATHLEEN ELAINE, elementary school educator, consultant; b. Port Hueneme, Calif., Apr. 19, 1954; d. Joseph Manuel and Mary Kathryn (Gerweck) Morris; m. Edward Mehl Duvall, Aug. 16, 1980; children: Nicolette Mareen, Rebecca Lauren. BS, Longwood Coll., 1976; MEd, Va. Commonwealth U., 1980; postgrad., U. St. Thomas, 1989-92. Cert. reading specialist, supr., early childhood tchr., gifted specialist, elem. tchr., writing project trainer, Tex. Classroom tchr. Chesterfield (Va.) County Pub. Schs., 1976-80; classroom tchr. Alief (Tex.) Ind. Sch. Dist., 1980-82, reading specialist, 1982-85, gifted specialist, 1985-86, social studies specialist, 1985-90; English lang. arts coord. Fort Bend Ind. Sch. Dist., Sugar Land, Tex., 1990—; instr. U. Houston/Victoria; cons. Port Nueces Groves Ind. Sch. Dist., LaMarque Ind. Sch. Dist., Northside Ind. Sch. Dist., Alief Ind. Sch. Dist., Tex., Ctrl. Daulphin Sch. Dist., Pa. Mem. Internat. Reading Assn., Tex. State Reading Assn., Greater Houston Area Reading Coun. (bd. dirs. 1991—, pres. 1997), Nat. Coun. Tchrs. English, Tex. Coun. Tchrs. English (Outstanding Elem. English Lang. Arts Educator award 1996-97), West Houston Area Coun. Tchrs. English (bd. dirs. 1991—, pres. 1995-97), Assn. Tex. Profl. Educators (pres. region IV 1990-93, Christa McAuliffe Tchg. Excellence award 1988). Republican. Avocations: reading, gardening, cooking, traveling. Office: Fort Bend Ind Sch Dist 16431 Lexington Blvd Sugar Land TX 77479-2308

DUVALL, CHARLES PATTON, internist, oncologist; b. Evanston, Ill., June 16, 1936; s. Charles Fleming and Edith (Osgood) D.; m. Nancy Ash, June 21, 1958; children: Lawrence Charles, Stephen Rogers, Douglas Patton, Lauren Lynne. AB, Cornell U., 1958; MD, U. Rochester, N.Y., 1962. Diplomate Am. Bd. Internal Medicine, Am. Bd. Med. Oncology. Intern Yale New Haven Med. Ctr., 1962-63; resident in internal medicine U. Rochester, 1963-64; clin. assoc. Nat. Cancer Inst., NIH, Bethesda, Md., 1964-66; resident in medicine Georgetown U. Hosp., Washington, 1966-67, USPHS spl. fellow in hematology, 1967-68; physician Foxhall Internists, Washington, 1978—; clin. prof. medicine Georgetown U. Hosp., Washington, 1968—; vice chmn. dept. medicine Sibley Hosp., Washington, 1987-90, chmn., 1990-91; mem. emeritus staff Washington Hosp. Ctr., 1988—. Contbr. articles to profl. jours. Elder Bradley Hills Presbyn. Ch., Bethesda, 1974-77; mem. prof. edn. com. Am. Cancer Soc., D.C. chpt., 1978-79; chmn. bd. Blue Cross Blue Shield Nat. Capital area, Washington, 1986-94, Group Hospitalization Med. Svcs., Inc., Washington, 1986-94; vice chmn., bd. trustees Vols. in Medicine Inst., Hilton Head, S.C. Lt. comdr. USPHS, 1964-66. Recipient 5 Yr. Svc. award Am. Cancer Soc., 1978. Fellow ACP (Outpatient Tchg. award 1998); mem. Am. Soc. Internal Medicine (DC chpt. pres. 1977, pres. rsch. found. 1987-88, pres.-elect 1988-89, pres. 1989-90, speaker ho. of dels. 1991-95, chmn. federated coun. internal medicine 1989-90, Spl. Recognition award 1979-2000), AMA (del. 1988-93, coun. on legislation 1991-2000, coun. on legislation vice chmn. 1995-96, chmn. 1996-97), Spltys. and Svcs. Soc. (pres. 1990-91, sect. coun. IM), Coun. Internal Medicine (chmn. sect. 1987-88), Osler Soc. D.C. (pres. 1978-79), Clin. Pathologic Soc. (pres. 1995-96), Congl. Country Club, Country Club of Hilton Head (S.C.), Bear Creek Club, Alpha Omega Alpha, Sigma Chi. Republican. Presbyterian. Avocations: golf, skiing, photography. Home: 4924 Sentinel Dr # 302 Bethesda MD 20816 Office: Foxhall Internists 3301 New Mexico Ave NW Ste 331 Washington DC 20016-3600

DUVALL, JACK, television executive, fund raiser, speechwriter; b. San Diego, July 10, 1946; s. John William and Margaret (Clark) DuV. AB cum laude, Colgate U., 1968. Mgmt. cons. Ohio Bell, Cleve., 1969; spl. agt. Air Force Office of Spl. Investigations, 1969-72; compliance officer Price Commn. U.S., Washington, 1972-73; chief industry compliance br. Cost Living Council, Exec. Office Pres. U.S., Washington, 1973-74; dir. pub. affairs Nat. Soybean Processors Assn., Hearing Industries Assn., Nat. Assn. Child Devel. Edn., and Food Protein Council, Washington, 1975-80; dir. corp. relations U. Chgo., 1980-85; v.p. program resources WETA TV/Radio, Washington, 1985-89; prin. Mars Hill, Alexandria, Va., 1989—; cons. Albert Einstein Peace Prize Found., Chgo., 1983-84; advisor-cons. Mil. Reform Inst., Washington, 1984-87, Sta. KCET-TV, 1989-91, Sta. WTVS-TV, 1990-92, The Learning Channel, 1990-92, Vision Interfaith Satellite Network, 1990-95, Jefferson Energy Found., 1990-91, Nat. Found. for People with Disabilities, 1990-91, Compass Films, Ltd., 1990-91, NOVA Child Devel. Ctrs., 1989-90, Hr Prodns., 1991-92, Nat. Park Trust, 1992, Lifetime Med. TV., 1991-92, Boston Ballet, 1992-93, Maritime Heritage Prints Video, 1992-93, Mind Ext. U., 1992-93, Jefferson Ctr. New Dem. Processes, 1993, Brit. Consulate Gen. L.A., 1990-95, Sta. WLIW-TV, 1992-93, Sta. WBGU-TV, 1992-93, Com. on Constitutional Sys., 1990-94, Colonial Williamsburg Fd., 1993-94, Christian Sci. Monitor, 1994, Nat. Video Comms., 1994-95, TCI, Inc., 1995-96, Md. Pub. TV, 1995-96, Turner Broadcasting Sys., 1995-96, S.C. Ednl. TV, 1996-98, First Ch. of Christ Scientist, 1996-97, Hedrick Smith Prodns., 1995-98, Advanced Network & Svcs., Inc., 1997-98, White House Writers Group, 1998, Walker Prodns., 1998; coord. Working Group on Ednl. Tech. and Programing, 1992-93. Author: (with others) Historical Working Papers of the Economic Stabilization Program, 1975; co-author: Victory Without Violence, 2000; exec. prodr. TV series Economic life, 1993, Learning About Democracy, 1993, Victory Without Violence, 1998—; contbr. poems and articles to various publs. Speechwriter Sen. Adlai Stevenson Ill. gov. campaign, 1982; Ill. spokesman Sen. Gary Hart pres. campaign, 1983-84; mem. Nat. Dem. Platform Com., Washington, 1984, Social Services Adv. Bd., Alexandria, 1986-87, mem. bd. advisors Ctr. for A New Democracy,

Washington, 1985-87; issues, speech advisor presdl. campaign Gov. Michael S. Dukakis, 1987-88; mem., bd. dirs. Arlington Inst., 1991—; pres. 5th Ch. of Christ Scientist, Washington, 1997-98. Capt. USAF, 1969-72. Mem. Delta Sigma Rho, Phi Beta Kappa, Phi Alpha Theta. Office: Mars Hill PO Box 707 Alexandria VA 22313-0707

DUVALL, LORRAINE, recreation center owner; b. Hamilton, Ohio, Jan. 31, 1925; d. Saul and Martha Jane (Huff) Baker; m. Ray DuVall, June 12, 1951; children: Sharon DuVall Keese, Deborah D. Velchoff, Steve, Annette. BA, U. Cin., 1951; MA, Tex. A&I U., 1963; postgrad. Miami U., Oxford, Ohio, 1958, U. Toledo, 1959, U. Tex.-Austin, 1968. Elem. tchr. Larkmoor, Lorain, Ohio, 1956-60; tchr. math. Incarnate Word High Sch., Corpus Christi, 1964-70; owner, instr. Aerobic Fitness, Corpus Christi, 1973-93; owner, coach Corpus Christi Marlin Swim Team, 1972—; mgr. Corpus Christi Country Club Pool, 1973-88; pres., mgr. Club Estates Pool Chems., Corpus Christi, 1980-89, Club Estates Recreation, Corpus Christi, 1977—. Vol. psychiat. ward Meml. Hosp., Corpus Christi, 1966-70, U.S. Swimming Club Devel., 1993-97; harpist First Bapt. Ch. Orch., 1995—; adminstrv. vice-chair South Tex. Swimming, 1996—; liaison to U.S. Swimming Club Devel. Com., 1995; bd. dirs. vol. YWCA, Corpus Christi, 1970-77; water safety trainer ARC, Corpus Christi, 1975-82; CPR instr. Am. Heart Assn., Corpus Christi, 1980-84; vol. children's choir dir. St. John Methodist Ch., Corpus Christi, 1966-78, Asbury United Meth. Ch., 1980-93; vol. harpist 1st Bapt. Ch., 1995—. NSF grantee U. Tex.-Austin, 1968. Mem. Am. Swim Coaches Assn., Am. Harp Soc. Avocations: music, swimming, tennis, skiing, backpacking. Home: 6709 Pintail Dr Corpus Christi TX 78413-2337 Office: 4902 Snowgoose Dr Corpus Christi TX 78413-2328

DUVALL, PATRICIA ARLENE, secondary education educator; b. Pitts., June 27, 1950; d. William Richard and Willene Alberta (Goode) Addison; 1 child, Tiyonda Aikee. B.A. in Math., Carnegie-Mellon U., 1972; M.Ed., U. Pitts., 1981. Long distance telephone operator AT&T, Pitts., summers 1968-71; switchboard operator Union Nat. Bank, Pitts., summers 1972; math tchr. Allegheny Intermediate Unit, Pitts., summers, 1978-79; math skills program Chatham Coll., Pitts., 1983—; tchr. math Pitts. Bd. Pub. Edn., 1972—; math instr. Kids and Teens coll. program Community Coll. Allegheny County, summer 1986, 87; tennis coach Allegheny High Sch., Pitts., 1979-81. Mem. U.S. Tennis Assn., Am. Alliance for Health, Phys. Edn., Recreation and Dance, Women's Tennis Assn., Nat. Coun. Tchrs. Math. Jehovah's Witness. Avocations: stamp collecting, tennis, reading, collecting comic books, home computers.

DUVALL, RICK, education educator; b. Bowling Green, Ky., Jan. 30, 1965. BA, U. Ky., 1987; MA, U. S.C., 1992, PhD, 1997. Cert. tchr., S.C. Tchr. English Ctrl. Comprehensive Sch., Grantham, Eng., 1987; tchr. 6th grade S.A. Hull Middle Sch., Jacksonville, Fla., 1988-89; tchr. 5th grade Joseph Keels Elem., Columbia, S.C., 1989; tchr. 5th grade Horrell Hill Elem. Sch., Hopkins, S.C., 1990-91, tchr. spl. edn., 1991-93, curriculum resources coord., 1993-94, with multi-age class, 1994-95; tchr. in residence U. S.C., 1995-96; upper grade tchr. Ctr. for Inquiry, 1996-98; asst. prof. elem. and mid. grades edn. Western Carolina U., 1998—; counselor Gwynn Valley Camp, Brevard, N.C., 1987-95; trainer The Wright Group, Bothell, Wash., 1992—; instr. U. S.C., S.C. State Dept. Edn., Columbia, 1992-97; mem. writing team S.C. English Lang. Arts Curriculum Framework, S.C. Nat. Goals document Putting Children and Families First, Lt. Govs. Action Coun. for Youth, 1993-94. Author: Building Character and Community in the Classroom, 1997. Youth advisor Eastminster Presbyn. Ch., Columbia, 1989-97; vol. Habitat for Humanity, 1990—. Named Sallie Mae Tchr. of Yr., 1988, Richland I Dist. Tchr. of Yr., 1992-93, S.C. Sci. Educator of Yr., 1994; grantee S.C. Dept. Edn., 1990-91, BellSouth, Columbia, 1992-93. Mem. NEA, Nat. Coun. Tchrs. English, Nat. Coun. Tchrs. Math., Nat. Sci. Tchrs. Assn., Internat. Reading Assn., S.C. Tchrs. Forum (leadership coun.), Richland I Tchrs. Forum (chmn.), Whole Lang. Umbrella, S.C. Bus. Edn. Partnership. Avocations: camping, skiing, rafting, tennis, reading. Home: PO Box 2463 Cullowhee NC 28723-2463

DUVALL, ROBERT, actor; b. San Diego, Calif., Jan. 5, 1931; s. William Howard Duvall; m. Gail Youngs, m. Sharon Brophy, May 1, 1991. Grad., Principia Coll., Ill.; student, Neighborhood Playhouse, N.Y. Film appearances include To Kill a Mockingbird, 1963, Captain Newman, M.D, 1964,The Chase, 1965, Countdown, 1968, The Detective, 1968, Bullitt, 1968, True Grit, 1969, The Rain People, 1969, M*A*S*H, 1970, The Revolutionary, 1970, THX-1138,1971, Lawman, 1971, The Godfather, 1972 (N.Y. Film Critics award for best supporting actor 1972, Acad. award nominee for best supporting actor), Tomorrow, 1972, The Great Northfield, Minnesota Raid, 1972, Joe Kidd, 1972, Lady Ice, 1973, Badge 373, 1973, The Outfit, 1974, The Conversation, 1974, The Godfather Part II, 1974, Breakout, 1975, The Killer Elite, 1975, Network, 1976, The Seven Per Cent Solution, 1976, The Eagle Has Landed, 1977, The Greatest, 1977, The Betsy, 1978,Apocalypse Now, 1979 (Acad. award nominee for best supporting actor), The GreatSantini, 1980 (Academy award nominee for best actor 1981), True Confessions, 1981, The Pursuit of D.B. Cooper, 1981, Tender Mercies, 1983 (Academy award for best actor 1984), The Stone Boy, 1984, The Natural, 1984, The Lightship, 1986, Let's Get Harry, 1986, Belizaire the Cajun, 1986, Colors, 1988, Convicts, Roots in a Parched Ground, The Handmaid's Tale, 1990, A Show of Force, 1990, Days of Thunder,1990, Rambling Rose, 1991, Newsies, 1992, Falling Down, 1993, Geronimo, 1993, Wrestling Ernest Hemingway, 1993, The Paper, 1994, The Stars Fell on Henrietta, 1995, The Scarlet Letter, 1995, Sling Blade, 1996, Phenomenon, 1996, A Family Thing, 1996, Gingerbread Man, 1997, The Apostle, 1997 (nominated Oscar for Best Actor), Deep Impact, 1998; TV movies include Fame is the Name of the Game, 1966, The Terry Fox Story, 1983, Stalin, HBO, 1992 (Emmy nomination, Lead actor -Miniseries, 1993); plays including A View from the Bridge, 1965 (Obie award), Wait Until Dark, 1966, American Buffalo, 1977; TV miniseries include Ike, 1979, Lonesome Dove, 1989; dir.: film We're Not the Jet Set; actor, dir. film: Angelo My Love, 1983; rec. artist: Triad Records. Recipient Golden Globe award, Brit. Acad. award, Nat. Assn. Theatre Owners award. Office: William Morris Agy 151 El Camino Dr Beverly Hills CA 90212-2775*

DUVENHAGE, IAN, head tennis coach; b. Kuruman, South Africa, Jan. 10, 1959; m. Taryn Jones, May 8, 1982. BA in Fin., U. Miami, 1980, MBA, 1983. Asst. tennis profl. Tokeneke Beach Club, Darien, Conn., 1980-82; head women's coach U. Miami, 1982-88; head tennis profl. Innes Arden Gold Club, Old Greenwich, Conn., 1984-86; head coach U. Fla., Gainesville, 1989—. Ranked top 300 world tennis players, top 200 doubles ranking. Office: U Fla Athletic Dept PO Box 14485 Gainesville FL 32604-2485*

DUVERNOY, WOLF F.C., cardiologist; b. Stuttgart, Germany, Apr. 16, 1935; came to U.S., 1960; s. Friedrich Ludwig and Hedwig Luise (Elben) D.; m. Eva Sibylle Hummel, Feb. 27, 1960; children: Christian L., Claire S. Abitur, Wilhelms Gymnasium, Stuttgart, 1954; MD, U. Tubingen, Germany, 1959. Diplomate Am. Bd. Internal Medicine, Am. Bd. Cardiovascular Disease. Intern Flower Hosp., Toledo, 1960-61; resident in internal medicine Henry Ford Hosp., Detroit, 1962-65, resident in cardiology, 1965-66, staff cardiologist, 1969-75, dir. EKG Lab., 1973-75; chief sect. cardiology Providence Hosp., Southfield, Mich., 1984—, pres. med. staff, 1985-86; ptnr. pvt. practice Southfield; clin. prof. internal medicine Wayne State U., Detroit, 1994—. Contbr. articles to profl. publs. Mem. tech. adv. panel Greater Detroit Area Health Coun., 1993—; mem. profl. edn. com. Mich. Heart Assn., Detroit; pres. Detroit Heart Club, 1984. Maj. U.S. Army, 1966-69. Fellow ACP, Am. Coll. Cardiology (gov. Mich. 1993-96, pres. Mich. chpt. 1993-96), Am. Coll. Chest Physicians, Am. Heart Assn. Address: 22250 Providence Dr Southfield MI 48075-4825

DUVICK, DONALD NELSON, plant breeder; b. Sandwich, Ill., Dec. 18, 1924; s. Nelson Daniel and Florence Henrietta (Appel) D.; m. Selma Elizabeth Nelson, Sept. 10, 1950; children: Daniel, Jonathan, Randa. BS, U. Ill., 1948; PhD, Washington U., St. Louis, 1951. With Pioneer Hi-Bred Internat., Inc., Johnston, Iowa, 1951-90, corn breeding coordinator Ea. and So. div., 1965-71, dir. corn breeding dept., 1971-75, dir. plant breeding div., 1975-85, v.p. research, 1985-86, sr. v.p. research, 1986-90; co. dir. Pioneer Hi-Bred Internat., Inc., 1982-90; affiliate prof. Iowa State U., 1990—; chmn. nat. plant genetic resources bd. USDA, 1990-91, vice-chmn. nat. genetic resources adv. com., 1992-93; trustee Internat. Ctr. for Maize and Wheat Improvement, 1988-94, trustee Internat. Rice Rsch. Inst., 1996-98; lectr. in field. Assoc. editor: Plant Physiology Jour., 1977-78; contbr. articles on genetics and plant breeding, devel. anatomy and cytology, cytoplasmic inheritance, quantititive genetics and biodeversity. Pres. Johnston Consol. Sch. Bd., 1965-67. Served with AUS, 1943-46. Pioneer Hi-Bred fellow U. London, 1968; Disting. fellow Iowa Acad. Sci. Fellow AAAS, Crop Sci. Soc. Am. (pres. 1986), Am. Soc. Agronomy (pres. 1992), Iowa Acad. Sci.; mem. N.Y. Acad. Sci., Coun. Agrl. Sci. and Tech. (bd. dirs. 1987-90), The Nature COnservancy (chair bd. trustees Iowa chpt. 1994). Democrat. Mem. United Ch. Christ. Achievements include identification of intra cellular site of zein storage in maize endosperm; research in maize cytoplasmic male sterility, in plant breeding's effects on crop plant genetic diversity, in changes in productivity of hybrid maize since 1930. Office: 6837 NW Beaver Dr Johnston IA 50131-1245 *Love science and humanity with equal fervor. Pursue knowledge for its own sake but also seek to apply it to useful ends.*

DUVICK, RANDA JANE, French language educator; b. Des Moines, Mar. 21, 1956; d. Donald N. and Selma N. Duvick; m. David Paul Grosnick, June 6, 1992. BA, Luther Coll., 1978; MA, U. Chgo., 1980, PhD, 1988. Instr. French Concordia Coll., Moorehead, Minn., 1985-86; assoc. prof. French Valparaiso (Ind.) U., 1986—, chmn. internat. econs. and cultural affairs program, 1995—. Fulbright fellow, 1978-79, Govt. of France fellow, 1982-83, Alliance Française N.Y. fellow, 1982-83. Mem. MLA, Am. Assn. Tchrs. French, N.W. Ind.-am. Assn. Tchrs French (v.p. 1998—), 19th Century French Studies Colloquium. Mem. United Ch. Christ. Home: 702 Hastings Ter Valparaiso IN 46383 Office: Valparaiso U 116 Meier Hall Valparaiso IN 46383

DUVIN, ROBERT PHILLIP, lawyer; b. Evansville, Ind., May 18, 1937; s. Louis and Henrietta (Hamburg) D.; m. Darlene Chmiel, Aug. 23, 1961; children: Scott A., Marc A., Louis A. BA with honors, Ind. U., 1958, JD with highest honors, 1961; LLM with highest honors, Columbia U., 1963. Bar: Ohio 1964. Since practiced in Cleve.; pres. Duvin, Cahn & Hutton, 1972—; lectr. law schs.; labor adviser corps., cities and hosps. Contbr. to books and legal jours.; bd. editors: Ind. Law Jour., 1961, Columbia Law Rev., 1963. Served with AUS, 1961-62. Mem. Am., Fed., Ohio, Cleve. bar assns. Jewish. Clubs: Cleve. Racquet, Beechmont Country, Soc., Canterbury Golf Club. Home: 2775 S Park Blvd Cleveland OH 44120-1669 Office: Duvin Cahn & Hutton Erieview Tower 1301 E 9th St Ste 2000 Cleveland OH 44114-1886

DUVIVIER, KATHARINE KEYES, lawyer, educator; b. Alton, Ill., Jan. 1, 1953; d. Edward Keyes and Marjorie (Attebery) DuV.; m. James Wesley Perl, Mar. 30, 1985 (div. Aug. 1997); 2 children: Alice Katharine Perl, Emmett Edward Perl. BA in Geology and English cum laude, Williams Coll., 1975; JD, U. Denver, 1982. Bar: Colo. 1982, U.S. Dist. Ct. Colo. 1982, U.S. Ct. Appeals (10th cir.) 1982. Intern-curator Hudson River Mus., Yonkers, N.Y., 1975; geologist French Am. Metals Corp., Lakewood, Colo., 1976-79; assoc. Sherman & Howard, Denver, 1982-84, Arnold & Porter, Denver, 1984-87; atty. Office of City Atty., Denver, 1987-90; sr. instr. sch. law Univ. Colo., 1990—; chair Appellate Practice Subcommittee. Contbr. articles to profl. jours. Mem. Denver Botanic Garden, 1981-88; vol. Outdoor Colo., Denver, 1985-87, 1998—. Mem. ABA (vice chmn. subcom. 1985-91), Colo. Bar Assn., Boulder Bar Assn., Boulder Women's Bar Assn. (pres. 1991-93), Alliance Profl. Women (bd. dirs. 1985-90, pres. 1988-89), Work and Family Consortium (bd. dirs. 1988-90), St. Ives, William Coll. Alumni Assn. (co-pres. Colo. chpt. 1984-86), Phi Beta Kappa. Avocations: geology, hiking, skiing, dancing, swimming. Home: 4761 Mckinley Dr Boulder CO 80303-1142 Office: U Colo Sch Law PO Box 401 Boulder CO 80303

DUVO, MECHELLE LOUISE, oil company executive, consultant; b. East Stroudsburg, Pa., Apr. 25, 1962; d. Nicholas and Arlene Birdie (Mack) D. AS, Lehigh County Community Coll., 1982. Rehab. counselor Phoenix Project, Bakersfield, Calif., 1982-84; nat. sales mgr. Olympia Advt., L.A., 1984-85; oil exploration cons. Cimmaron Mgmt., Nashville, 1985-86; exec. sec. Pueblo Resources Corp., Bowling Green, Ky., 1986-87; nat. oil cons. El Toro, Inc., Bowling Green, 1986-87; founder, pres. and CEO Majestic Mgmt. Corp., Glasgow, Ky., 1987—; nat. oil cons. Impact Oil, Inc., Glasgow, 1987—; lease procurator El Toro, Inc., 1986-87; spkr. Nat. Investment Seminars, 1994—. Editor, pub.: (newsletter) The Majestic Field Copy, 1994—. Fundraiser Am. Cancer Soc., L.A., 1984-85; vol. Humane Soc., Nashville, 1985-86, Humane Soc., Bowling Green, 1986-87; counselor Salvation Army, Bakersfield, 1982-84. Mem. NAFE (exec. program), Internat. Platform Assn., Ky. Oil & Gas Assn. Avocations: house plants, gardening, music, gourmet cooking. Home and Office: Majestic Mgmt Corp 1202 S Green St Glasgow KY 42141-2014

DUXBURY, THOMAS CARL, planetary scientist; b. Fort Wayne, Ind., Dec. 8, 1941; s. John Lawrence and Justine Agnus (Jaron) D.; m. Natalia Duxbury, Nov. 8, 1990; 1 child from previous marriage, Brett Harding Duxbury. BSEE, Purdue U., 1965, MSEE, 1966. Planetary scientist Jet Propulsion Lab., Pasadena, Calif., 1966—. Co-author: Television Investigations of Phobos, 1994. Recipient Sci. Achievement medal NASA, Washington, 1972, Space Mission Svc. medal Russian Lavochkin Assn., The Hague, The Netherlands, 1991, Burka award Inst. of Navigation, 1973, Achievement awards NASA, 1980, 82. Mem. Am. Geophysical Union, 1978—, Am. Astronomical Soc., 1980—, Russian Assn. for Space Sci. & Tech., 1993—. Achievements include prodn. of first map of another planet's moon, 1972; discovery of the Groove Network on Phobos (Mars moon), 1978; co-discovery of the Rings of Jupiter, 1979, of the Jupiter Lightning, 1979; selection by NASA/Soviet Union to participate in the Soviet PHOBOS Mission to Mars, 1988-89, Dept. Def. (DOD) Clementing Sci. Team for Lunar Exploration, 1992-94, Russian Mars 1994-96 Mission Sci. Team, 1992-97, project dir. NASA STARDUST Mission, 1996—, participating scientist Mars Global Surveyor Mission, 1996—, USAF/NASA Sci. Defination Team Deputy Leader, 1997-98, interdisciplinary scientist on European Space Agy. Mars Express Mission, 1999—. Office: Jet Propulsion Lab 4800 Oak Grove Dr # 301-429 Pasadena CA 91109-8001

DUYCK, KATHLEEN MARIE, poet, musician, retired social worker; b. Portland, Oreg., July 21, 1933; d. Anthony Joseph Dwyer and Edna Elisabeth Hayes; m. Robert Duyck, Feb. 3, 1962; children: Mary Kay Boeyen, Robert Patrick, Anthony Joseph. BS, Oreg. State U., 1954; MSW, U. Wash., 1956. Cert. NASW, Oreg. Adoption worker Cath. Svcs., Portland, 1956-61, Cath. Welfare, San Antonio, 1962; musician Tucson Symphony, 1963-65; prin. cellist Phoenix (Ariz.) Coll. Orch., 1968-78, Scottsdale (Ariz.) Symphony, 1974-80; poet, 1993—. Author: (poetry cassettes) Visions, 1993 (Contemporary Series Poet 1993), Visions II, 1996 (Contemporary Series Poet 1996); contbr. to 10 Nat. Libr. of Poetry Anthologies. Rep. worker Maricopa County Reps., Phoenix, 1974; mem. Scottsdale Cultural Coun.; NASW bd. Cath. Charities Rep., Portland, 1959-61. Recipient Golden Poet award World of Poetry, 1991, 92, Editor's Choice awards Nat. Libr. Poetry, 1993—, Sec. gift Phoenix Exec. Bd., 1976. Recognition award Archbishop Howard, 1961, 5-Yr. Kathleen Duyck award Cello Congress V, 1996. Mem. Internat. Poetry Hall Fame, Ariz. Cello Soc., Nat. Libr. Poetry, Internat. Soc. Poets, Phoenix Symphony Guild (exec. bd. 1970-80). Republican. Roman Catholic. Avocations: pianist, photography, poetry, artistic collections, attending concerts. Home: 4545 E Palomino Rd Phoenix AZ 85018-1719

DUZEY, ROBERT LINDSEY, lawyer; b. Long Beach, Calif., Nov. 15, 1960; s. Donald Bohdan and Noreen (Rosen) D.; m. Susan Misook Yoon, Mar. 14, 1987; children: Dylan Grey, Zenon Drake. BA, U. Calif., Irvine, 1984; JD, Western State U., Fullerton, Calif., 1994. Bar: Calif. 1994, U.S. Dist. Ct. (so., ctrl., ea. and no. dists.) Calif., U.S. Ct. Appeals (9th cir.). Claims rep., mgr. Farmers Ins. Group, Santa Ana, Calif., 1985-89; risk mgr. Dollar Rent A Car, Irvine, 1989-93; law clk. Callahan, McCune & Willis, Tustin, Calif., 1994-96; atty. Madigan, Evans & Boyer, Costa Mesa, Calif., 1996-98, Law Offices of Robert Lindsey Duzey, Costa Mesa, 1998—. Recipient Am. Jurisprudence award, 1993. Mem. ATLA, ABA, Orange County Bar Assn., Fed. Bar Assn., Risk and Ins. Mgmt. Soc. (bd. dirs. 1991-93), Orange County Barristers, Orange County Trial Lawyers Assn., Def. Rsch. Inst., Assn. So. Calif. Def. Counsel, Am. Inns of Ct., Peter M. Elliot Inn, L.A. County Bar Assn., Long Beach Bar Assn., Delta Theta Phi. Avocations: golf, gardening, skiing, cigars. Fax: (562) 862-7721. E-mail: RDuzey@aol.com. Office: Law Offices Robert Lindsey Duzey 9900 Lakewood Blvd Ste 250 Downey CA 90240

DÜZGÜNES, NEJAT A., biophysicist, microbiologist; b. N.Y.C., Feb. 28, 1950; s. Orhan and Zeliha Duzgunes. BS, Mid. East Tech. U., Ankara, Turkey, 1972; PhD, SUNY, Buffalo, 1978. Postdoctoral fellow U. Calif., San Francisco, 1978-81, asst. rsch. biochemist, 1981-87, asst. adj. prof., 1985-87, assoc. rsch. biochemist, 1987-91, assoc. adj. prof., 1987-97; assoc. prof., chmn. dept. microbiology U. Pacific, San Francisco, 1990-95, prof., chmn. dept. microbiology, 1995—; vis. prof. dept. biophysics Kyoto (Japan) U., 1988. Editor: Membrane Fusion in Fertilization, Cellular Transport and Viral Infection, 1988, Mechanisms and Specificity of HIV Entry into Host Cells, 1991, Membrane Fusion Techniques, Methods in Enzymology, Vols. 220 & 221, 1993; co-editor Trafficking of Intracellular Membranes, 1995. Vol. AFS Internat. Intercultural Programs, N.Y.C., 1969-86. Co-recipient Orgn. award U.S.-Japan Binat. Seminar on Membrane Fusion, NSF, 1992; Japan Soc. Promotion of Sci. fellow, 1988; grantee Am. Heart Assn., 1983-87, Calif. Univ. Wide AIDS Rsch. Program, 1986-90, 92-93, NIAID/NIH, 1988-97. Mem. Am. Soc. Cell Biology, Am. Soc. Microbiology, Internat. Soc. Antiviral Rsch., Am. Assn. Dental Schs., Am. Assn. Dental Rsch., Biophys. Soc., Am. Soc. Virology. Office: U Pacific Dept Microbiology 2155 Webster St San Francisco CA 94115-2333

DVOICHENKO-MARKOV, DEMETRIUS, history educator; b. Saloniki, Greece, July 10, 1921; came to U.S., 1942, naturalized, 1943; s. Vladimir and Eufrosina M. (de Markov) Dvoichenko de Kovalevski; baccalaureate, German Ev. Lyceum, Rumania, 1941; Cert. U. Basel, Switzerland, 1948, Wiedeman Bus. Acad., 1948; AB, UCLA, 1950; MA, Columbia U., 1951; m. Inna Moore, July 18, 1952; children: Vlad, Laria. Libr. Spanish legation Bucharest Kingdom Romania, 1940-41; translator, research analyst U.S. War Dept., OCCWC, Nuremberg, Germany, 1946-47; research analyst Dept. Def., Washington, 1952-53; asst. field dir. ARC, Alexanderia, Va., 1954-56; tchr. German and Spanish, Wakefield High Sch., Arlington, Va., 1956-57; instr. Russian and social sci., Monmouth Coll., W. Long Branch, N.J., 1957-61, asst. prof., 1961-81, assoc. prof., 1981-92, prof. emeritus, 1992—; instr. Russian lang., Western Civilization I and II, Geography S.W. Asia Ft. Monmouth, N.J., 1959-63, 83; lectr. history and geography Newark State Coll., 1964-69; lectr. history Trenton (N.J.) State Coll., 1985, War Crimes Then and Now; tchr., lectr. Brookdale C.C., Lincroft, N.J., 1994; instr. Sr. Citizens Activities Network, Eatontown, N.J., 1994-95; presenter in field. Mem. Gov.'s Commn. on Eastern European and Captive Nation History, State of N.J., 1985-89. Served with U.S. Army, 1942-45. Am. Council of Learned Socs. travel grantee, 1971; recipient Dimitrie Cantemir medal, Rumanian Nat. Acad. Scis., 1975, Bronze Serban Canatacuzino medal Internat. Cultural Assn. Rumanain Ethnicity, Vienna, Austria, 1983, Faculty Assn. Donald C. Warnke award for disting. svc. Monmouth Coll., 1992. Mem. Am. Hist. Assn., Assn. Am. Geographers, UCLA Alumni Assn., Am. Assn. Advancement of Salvic Studies, Assn. Study of the Nationalities (USSR and Eastern Europe), Am. Assn. SE European Studies, AAUP, U.S. Commn. on Mil. History, N.J. Commn. on Eastern European and Captive Nation History, Am.-Romanian Acad. Arts and Scis., Acad. People of Sci. from Romania, N.J. Ednl. Assn., Soc. Romanian Studies, Knights Malta, Delta Tau Kappa, Phi Alpha Theta, Gamma Theta Upsilon. Mem. Eastern Orthodox. Ch. Contb. articles and revs. to profl. jours. Home: 359 Lowden Ct Apt 68 Long Branch NJ 07740-6310 Office: Monmouth U West Long Branch NJ 07764

DVORAK, ALLEN DALE, radiologist; b. Dodge, Nebr., Mar. 13, 1943; s. Rudolph Charles and Mildred B. (Misek) D.; m. Carol Ann Cockson, July 22, 1967; children: Kristin Ann, Andrea Marie, Ryan Allen. Grad., Creighton Coll. Arts and Scis., Omaha, Nebr., 1961-64; MD, Creighton Sch. Medicine, Omaha, Nebr., 1969. Intern Creighton Meml. St. Joseph Hosp., Omaha, 1969-70; resident Ind. U. Med. Ctr., Indpls., 1970-73; asst. prof. radiology Creighton U. Sch. Medicine, Omaha, 1973-83; mng. ptnr., 1987—; diagnostic radiologist Nebr.-Iowa Radiology Cons., Papillion, Nebr., 1983—; staff radiologist Midlands Cmty. Hosp., Papillion, 1983—; med. staff exec. bd. Nebr. State Bd. Health, 1997—, sec.-treas. 1999. Author: (chpt.) Ultrasound, 1981; contbr. articles to profl. jours. Chmn. Midlands Area Health Adv. cuon., State of Nebr., 1982-86; trustee Duchesne Acad., 1988-91, Boys Town Nat. Coun. Friends, 1989—; bd. dirs. Safety and health Coun. of Greater Omaha, 1990-91; mem. Gov.'s Blue Ribbon Coalition to Study Health Care in Nebr., 1991-98; mem. Creighton Med. Sch. Alumni Adv. Bd., 1993—, pres., 1998—. Fellow Am Coll. Radiology; mem. AMA (alt. del. 1992—, del. 1999—), Nebr. Radiol. Soc. (pres. 1980-81), Omaha Midwest Clin. Soc. (pres. 1982), Nebr. Assn. Nuclear Physicians (pres. 1976-78, del. 1984—), Met. Omaha Med. Soc. (exec. com. 1980—, pres. 1990), Nebr. Med. Assn. (del. 1986—, pres. 1997-98), Regency Lake and Tennis Club (bd. dirs. 1981-85, chmn. bd. 1983-85), Happy Hollow Country Club. Avocations: tennis, boating. Home: 9733 Brentwood Rd Omaha NE 68114-4970 Office: Nebr-Iowa Radiology Cons Mng Ptnr 401 E Gold Coast Rd Ste 102 Papillion NE 68046-4194

DVORAK, CLARENCE ALLEN, microbiologist; b. Cedar Rapids, Iowa, July 6, 1942; s. Clarence Louis and Lily Ann (Duda) D. BS, Iowa State U., 1969. Microbiologist Penford Products Co., Cedar Rapids, 1969—, analytical chemist, 1970-81, sci. photographer. Mem. AAAS, TAPPI, Am. Soc. Microbiology, Soc. Indsl. Microbiology. Home: 119 18th St SW Cedar Rapids IA 52404-1759

DVORAK, GEORGE J., mechanics and materials engineering educator; came to U.S., 1964; Degree in Civil Engring., Czech Technol. U., Prague, 1956, DSc (hon.), 1997; C.Sc., Czechoslovak Acad. Sci., Prague, 1964; PhD, Brown U., 1968. Rsch. assoc. divsn. engring. Brown U., 1964-67; with civil engring. and biomedical engring. dept. Duke U., Durham, N.C., 1967-79; prof., chmn. civil engring., prof. materials sci. U. Utah, Salt Lake City, 1979-84; prof., chmn. dept. civil and environ. engring. Rensselaer Poly. Inst., Troy, N.Y., 1986—, prof. mech. engring., aero. engring. and mechanics, chmn. civil and environ. engring., William Howard Hart prof. mechanics; sr. vis. fellow Brit. sci. rsch. coun. Cambridge U., Eng.; vis. fellow Clare Hall, Cambridge, 1975-76; vis. prof. Politecnico di Milano, Milan, Italy; with inst. ctr. composite materials and structures Rensselaer Poly. Inst., dir. univ. rsch. initiative Dept. Def. Assoc. editor Internat. Jour. Plasticity, 1984—, Mech. Composite Mater Structures, 1993—, Jour. Applied Mechanics, 1989-95, Applied Mechanics Revs., 1989-95. Recipient Citations for Accomplishment of Spl. Merit, Army Rsch. Office, 1977, 79; Fulbright fellow Tech. U. Denmark, 1995, Brown Engring. Alumni medal Brown U., 1999. Fellow ASME (founding chmn. com. composite materials applied mechanics divsn., Arpard L. Nadai award 1992), ASCE, Am. Acad. Mechanics, Soc. Engring. Sci. (William Prager medal in mechanics of solids 1994), Nat. Acad. Engring. Achievements include research in mechanics, physics of solids, micromechanics of heterogeneous media, mechanical behavior of composite materials. Office: Dept Mech & Aero Engring and Mechanics Jonsson Engring Ctr 5003 Rensselaer Polytech Inst Troy NY 12180

DVORAK, HAROLD F., pathologist, educator, scientist; b. Milw., June 20, 1937; s. Harold J. and Laura (Fisher) D.; m. Ann Marie Tompkins, June 13, 1962; children: John, Laura, Jane. AB, Princeton U., 1958; MD, Harvard U., 1963. Diplomate: Am. Bd. Pathology. Practice medicine specializing in pathology Boston; asst. prof. pathology Harvard Med. Sch., Boston, assoc. prof., prof., Mallinckrodt prof. pathology, 1979—; mem. staff Mass. Gen. Hosp., asst. pathologist, 1969-75, assoc. pathologist, 1975-78, head immunopathology unit, 1976-80; chief dept. pathology Beth Israel Hosp., Boston, 1979-96, Beth Israel Deaconess Med. Ctr., Boston, 1996—; mem. study sect. pathology B NIH, 1978-82, Am. Cancer Soc., N.Y.C., 1982-86; chmn. merit rev. bd. immunology VA, Washington, 1982-84. Served to lt. comdr. USPHS, 1965-67. Mem. Am. Assn. Immunologists, Am. Soc. Investigative Pathology (v.p. 1996, pres.-elect), Internat. Acad. Pathology, Pluto Club, Collegium Internat. Allergologicum, Phi Beta Kappa, Sigma Xi, Alpha Omega Alpha. Office: Beth Israel Deaconess Med Ctr 330 Brookline Ave Boston MA 02215-5400*

DVORAK, ROGER GRAN, health facility executive; b. St. Paul, Aug. 30, 1934; s. William Anthony and Evelyn Carolyn (Gran) D.; m. Gail Ann Peterson, Dec. 30, 1960; children: Karen, Mark. BBA, U. Minn., 1955, MHA, 1957. Asst. adminstr. Glenwood Hills Hosp., Mpls., 1958-61; asst. hosp. adminstrv. svcs. dir. Phila. Gen. Hosp., 1961-65; asst. dir. Presbyn. U.

Pa. Med. Ctr., Phila., 1965-67, assoc. dir., 1967-72; adminstr. Symmes Hosp., Arlington, Mass., 1972-78; exec. dir. Lawrence Hosp., Bronxville, N.Y., 1978-86, pres., 1986—; Bd. dirs. Hosp. Underwriters Mutual, Latham, N.Y., No. Met. Hosp. Assn., Newburgh, N.Y., Hosp. Assn. N.Y. State, Albany; mem. bd. advisors Habitat for Humanity Northeast. Adv. bd. The Counseling Ctr. of Southern Westchester; mem. session of Hitchcock Presbyn. Ch., Scarsdale, N.Y. 1st Lt. Med. Svcs. Corp., 1957-66. Fellow Am. Coll. Healthcare Execs. Presbyterian. Avocations: painting, running, music. Home: 11 Rolling Ridge Rd White Plains NY 10605-4526 Office: Lawrence Hospital 55 Palmer Ave Bronxville NY 10708-3491

DVORETZKY, ISRAEL, dermatologist; b. Jerusalem, June 4, 1944; came to U.S., 1976; s. Itzak and Zippora (Levit) D.; m. Ayala Chenstochovsky, Oct. 11, 1970; 1 child, Shay. MD, Tel Aviv U., 1971. Intern Meir Kfar-Saba Hosp., Tel-Aviv, Israel, 1971-72; resident in dermatology Chaim Sheba Med. Ctr., Tel-Aviv, 1973-76; 2d resident in dermatology Yale New Haven Hosp., 1976-78; vis. assoc. At. Cancer Inst. NIH, Bethesda, Md., 1978-82; asst. clin. prof. dermatology Yale U. Sch. Medicine, New Haven, 1982-88, assoc. clin. prof., 1988-97, clin. prof. dermatology, 1997—; pvt. practice Ansonia, Conn., 1982—. Author: Chemistry and Biology of Interferon, 1982; contbr. articles to profl. jours.; patentee in wart therapy. Fellow Am. Acad. Dermatology, Soc. Dermatol. Surgery, Soc. Pediat. Dermatology, Soc. Internat. Dermatology, Soc. Investigative Dermatology; mem. New Eng. Dermatol. Soc. Avocations: classical music, jazz, international music, reading, writing. Office: 22 Westfield Ave Ansonia CT 06401-1158

DVORKIN, LOUIS, neuropsychologist; b. Phila., July 24, 1951; s. Benjamin and Eleanor (Braverman) D.; m. Jori Harriet Potiker, May 30, 1977 (div. July 1980); m. Gail Myra Apple, Oct. 18, 1987; children: Lauren, Adam, Elyse. BA in Psychology, Am. U., 1972; MA in Psychology, Wayne State U., 1978, PhD in Psychology, 1980; postgrad. in aging psychology, U. Mich., 1977. Lic. psychologist, Mich. Staff psychologist Rehab. Inst., Detroit, 1980-83; dir. neuropsychology Wyandotte (Mich.) Hosp. and Med. Ctr., 1983-87; pres. Louis Dvorkin PhD & Assocs., West Bloomfield, Mich., 1988—; cons. in neuropsychology Ctr. for Forensic Psychiatry, Ann Arbor; mem. adj. med. staff Crittenton Hosp., Rochester, Mich., 1992—; mem. med. staff Pontiac (Mich.) Osteopathic Hosp., 1990—, Sinai Hosp., Detroit, 1990—; mem. adj. mem. staff Rehab. Inst., 1980—. Fellow Adminstrn. on Aging, 1979, Wayne State U., 1975-76. Mem. APA, Mich. Psychol. Assn. (ethics com. 1994—), Internat. Neuropsychol. Soc., Nat. Acad. Neuropsychology, Am. Bd. Forensic Examiners, Psi Chi. Jewish. Avocations: tennis, skiing, golf, travel. Home: 4948 Lakebluff Ct West Bloomfield MI 48323-2426 Office: Louis Dvorkin PhD & Assocs 6016 W Maple Rd Ste 701 West Bloomfield MI 48322-4411

DVORKIN, RONALD ALAN, emergency physician; b. N.Y.C., May 1, 1945. BS in Chemistry, U. Rochester, 1966; MD, SUNY, Syracuse, 1970. Assoc. dir., dept. emergency medicine Lawrence Hosp., Bronxville, N.Y., 1982-87; assoc. dir., dept. emergency City Hosp. Ctr., Elmhurst, N.Y., 1987-88; chmn., dept. emergency svcs. St. John's Episcopal Hosp., Smithtown, N.Y., 1988—; asst. prof. medicine Mt. Sinai Sch. Medicine, 1988; asst. clin. prof. emergency medicine, SUNY, Stony Brook, 1990. Fellow Am. Coll. Emergency Physicians; mem. N.Y. Acad. Scis., Soc. for Acad. Emergency Medicine. Office: St John's Episcopal Hosp Rte 25A Smithtown NY 11787*

DWAN, DENNIS EDWIN, broadcast executive, photographer; b. St. Joseph, Mich., Oct. 6, 1958; s. Edwin O. and Elizabeth L. (Miller) D.; m. Tami L. Nixon, Oct. 13, 1984; children: Megan, Kaitlyn. BA, Mich. State U., 1981. Photographer Sta. WJIM-TV, Lansing, Mich., 1981-83, Sta. KAYU, Spokane, Wash., 1984-86, Sta. KREM-TV, Spokane, 1984-87; ops. mgr. Sta. KOMO-TV, Seattle, 1987—. Mem. Nat. Press Photographers Assn. *

DWEK, CYRIL S., banker; b. Kobe, Japan, Nov. 9, 1936; s. Nessim S. and Alice (Stambouli) D.; children: Nevil, Alicia. B.S., Wharton Sch., U. Pa., 1958. With Trade Devel. Bank, Geneva, Switzerland, 1962-65; with Republic Nat. Bank of N.Y., 1966—, dir., 1967—, exec. v.p., 1973—, vice chmn., 1983—; dir. Republic N.Y. Corp., 1974—, vice chmn., 1983—; chmn. Republic Nat. Bank, France; vice chmn. Republic Nat. Bank, Mexico. Mem. Brazilian Am. C. of C. (v.p., adv. bd.), The Spanish Inst. (dir.), Racing Club de France (Paris). Office: Rep NY Corp 452 5th Ave 9 Floor New York NY 10018-2706

DWELLEY, MARILYN JOAN, artist; b. Taunton, Mass., Mar. 4, 1937; d. Walter Stanley and Mary Mildred Wonchoba; m. Norman W. Dwelley, Sept. 1, 1957; 1 child, Frank Roy. BS, Wash. State Tchrs. Coll., 1961; MEd, U. Maine, 1974. Tchr. Union 52, China, Maine, 1957-70; founder Maine Open Juried Art Show, Waterville, 1989. Author, illustrator 3 field guides for trees and flowers, 1973-77. Recipient more than 200 art awards. Mem. Waterville Area Art Soc. (founder, officer), Bangor Art Soc. (pres., treas.), Josselyn Botanical Soc. (treas.). Republican. Baptist. Avocations: naturalist, braiding rugs, gardening. Home: Box 41 China Neck Rd China ME 04926

DWIGGINS, CLAUDIUS WILLIAM, JR., chemist; b. Amity, Ark., May 11, 1933; s. Claudius William and Lillian (Scott) D. BS, U. Ark., 1954, MS, 1956, PhD, 1958. With U.S. Dept. of Energy Bartlesville Tech. Ctr., Okla., 1958-83, chemist, 1958-60, project leader surface physics project, 1960-65, project leader petroleum composition rsch. project, 1965-80, supervisory rsch. chemist, thermodynamics divsn., 1980-83; sr. chemist Nat. Inst. Petroleum and Energy Rsch., 1983-84, cons., 1984—. Contbr. articles to profl. jours. Am. Oil Co. fellow, Coulter-Jones scholar. Mem. Am. Chem. Soc., N.Y. Acad. Scis., AAAS, Am. Crystallographic Assn., Am. Inst. Physics, Sigma Xi (sec. 1966-67), Alpha Chi Sigma, Delta Sigma Phi (treas. 1952). Home: 1211 S Keeler Ave Bartlesville OK 74003-4756

DWIGHT, DONALD RATHBUN, newspaper publisher, corporate communications executive; b. Holyoke, Mass., Mar. 26, 1931; s. William and Dorothy Elizabeth (Rathbun) D.; m. Susan Newton Russell, Aug. 9, 1952 (div. Aug. 1982); children: Dorothy Campbell, Laura Newton, Eleanor Addison, Arthur Ryan, Stuart Russell.; m. Nancy John Sinnott, Dec. 18, 1982; children: Christopher Sinnott, Helen Rathbun. AB, Princeton U., 1953; DSc (hon.), U. Mass., Lowell, 1974. Reporter, asst. to pub. Holyoke (Mass.) Transcript-Telegram, 1955-63, assoc. pub., 1966-69; assoc. commr. Mass. Dept. Pub. Works, Boston, 1963-66; commr. adminstrn. Commonwealth Mass., Boston, 1969-70, lt. gov., 1971-75; assoc. pub., v.p. Mpls. Star and Tribune, 1975-76, pub., sr. v.p., 1976-81; pres., pub. Star & Tribune Newspapers, Mpls., 1981-82; exec. v.p., dir. Cowles Media Co., 1981-82; chmn. Newspapers of New Eng., Inc., 1982-98; assoc. The Prospect Group, N.Y.C., 1983-88; chmn., mng. ptnr. Clark, Dwight & Assocs., Inc., 1988-90; pres. Dwight Ptnrs., Inc., Lyme, N.H., 1988—; v.p. Wood River Capital Corp., 1984-88; exec. v.p. Entretech Inc., 1988-90; trustee Eaton Vance Mut. Funds, Boston, 1986—, The Royce Funds, N.Y.C., 1998—. Mem. Town Meeting, South Hadley, Mass., 1957-69; bd. dirs. Mpls. Soc. Fine Arts, 1976-82; trustee Twin Cities Pub. TV, 1976-82; chmn. bd. Guthrie Theater Found., 1978-81; v.p., dir. Nat. Corp. Theatre Fund, 1985-88; dir. Joint Action in Cmty. Svc., Washington, 1989-92, Lyme (N.H.) Found., Inc., 1994-98; trustee Trust Funds, Lyme, N.H., 1997—; mem. vestry St. Thomas Episcopal Ch., Hanover, N.H. 1st lt. USMCR, 1953-55. Mem. Newspaper Assn. of Am., Princeton Club, Knickerbocker Club N.Y.C., Round Hill Club Greenwich, Hillsboro Club Fla. Republican. Episcopalian. Home and Office: 16 Clover Mill Ln Lyme NH 03768-3301

DWIGHT, HARVEY ALPHEUS, retired small business owner; b. Albany, N.Y., Apr. 21, 1928; s. Harvey Alpheus and Tessa Blanche (Gellert) D.; m. Helen Jean Fowler, Apr. 20, 1951 (dec. Sept. 1992); children: Diana, Lesley, Jessie, Harvey. Grad. high sch., Albany, N.Y., 1947. Lic. master plumber, N.Y. Owner Dwight Heating Supply Co., Rensselaer, N.Y., 1943-93; pvt. practice mech. cons., 1993—. With Army N.G., 1949-58. Mem. Albany Lic. Plumbers (v.p. 1985-86). Avocations: hunting, fishing, flying, gardening.

DWIGHT, REGINALD KENNETH See JOHN, ELTON HERCULES

DWIGHT, WILLIAM, JR., former newspaper executive, restaurateur; b. Holyoke, Mass., June 19, 1929; s. William and Dorothy (Rathbun) D.; m. Maria Melon Burgee, Sept. 25, 1954 (div. 1982); children: William H., Leslie R., Valle E., Timothy M. (dec.), Ryan H.; m. Julie Eastwood, Feb. 19, 1983. AB, Princeton U., 1951. With Hartford (Conn.) Courant, 1953-55; reporter Holyoke Transcript-Telegram, 1955-57, asst. to pub., 1957-58, 61-66, assoc. pub., 1966-75, editor, 1968-82, pub., 1976-82; adminstrv. asst. to Rep. Silvio O. Conte U.S. Ho. of Reps., Washington, 1959-60; owner, mgr. Golden Lemon, Holyoke, 1982-89; dist. aide U.S. Rep. John Olver, 1991—; v.p. Newspapers of New Eng.; bd. dirs. Greenfield (Mass.) Recorder-Gazette; pres. New Eng. Daily Newspapers Assn., 1974-76. Co-chmn. Total Community Devel., 1966-67; pres. Holyoke Street Sch., 1972-82; treas. Geriatric Authority of Holyoke; v.p., bd. dirs. Mt. Tom coun. Boy Scouts Am., 1955-60; bd. dirs. YMCA, Vis. Nurse Assn., Pioneer Valley Assn., Mental Health Clinic; v.p. New Eng. Farm Workers Coun., Springfield, Mass., 1980—. Capt. USMCR, 1951-53, Korea. Recipient Citizenship award Holyoke St. Patrick's Com., 1988. Mem. Am. Newspaper Pubs. Assn., Holyoke C. of C. (past pres., Young Man of Yr. award 1963), Rotary, Sigma Delta Chi. Republican. Episcopalian. Avocations: reading, travel. Home: 30 Cleveland St Holyoke MA 01040-2600

DWINELL, ANN JONES, special education educator; b. Lowell, Mass., Oct. 28, 1934; d. George Hubert and Bridget Jones; m. Roland A. Dwinell, Dec. 23, 1956; children: Theresa, Joseph, Richard, John. BA, Framingham State Coll., 1972; MEd, Lesley Coll., 1974; PhD, Boston Coll., 1991. Cert. Eng. tchr., moderate spl. needs instr., Mass., adminstr., supt., spl. edn. adminstr., R.I. Spl. edn. tchr., adminstr. Marlborough (Mass.) Pub. Sch., 1972-78; core chairperson Malden (Mass.) Pub. Schs., 1978-80, spl. edn. specialist, 1980—. Contbr. articles to profl. jours. Mem. NEA, Mass. Tchrs. Assn. (rep. 1983-85, liaison 1987—), Phi Delta Kappa. Roman Catholic. Avocations: dancing, music, boating, reading.

DWON, LARRY, retired electrical engineer, educator, consultant; b. N.Y.C., May 2, 1913; s. Lucas and Mary (Woytowich) Dzwonczyk; m. Mary Jean Skala, Feb. 14, 1941; children: Lawrence A. Dwon, Roger R. Dzwonczyk. D in Electrical Engring., Cornell U., 1935; MBA, NYU, 1954. Registered profl. engr., N.Y., N.C. Engr. Diehl Mfg. Co., Elizabethport, N.J., 1935-37, Holophane Lighting, Inc., Newark, Ohio, 1937-38; mem. tech. staff Office Sci. and Rsch. Devel. Harvard Radio Rsch. Lab., Bell Telephone Labs., N.Y.C., 1942-45; engr. Am. Electric Power Svc. Corp., N.Y.C., 1938-45, sr. engr., 1945-52, operating sponsor (reporting to operating exec. v.p.), 1952-55, adminstrv. asst. to exec. v.p. ops., 1955-57, mgr. engring. manpower, 1957-78; cons., cons. instr. N.C. State U., Raleigh, 1978—, N.C. State U. Coll. Engring., 1979—; self-employed cons., Apex, N.C., 1978—. Author: History of Eta Kappa Nu, 1976; contbr. over 200 tech. and profl. papers to many profl. jours. Recipient Plummer lecture medal Am. Welding Soc., 1975, Disting. Svc. award Power Engring. Edn. Com., 1977, spl. citation Edison Electric Inst., 1977, Disting. Svc. award, 1978, others. Fellow IEEE (chmn. various coms. from 1969, U.S. Activities Bd. award 1982, Centennial medal 1984, Lit. Contbns. award 1988); mem. Am. Assn. Concerned Engrs. (bd. dirs.), Cornell Engring. Soc., Eta Kappa Nu (v.p. 1958, pres. 1959, emminent mem. 1984, Disting. Svc. award 1976). Avocations: classical music, writing, speaking. Home and Office: PO Box 216 West Kill NY 12492-0216

DWORAK, MARCIA LYNN, library director, library building consultant; b. L.A., Mar. 31, 1939; d. John T. and Mary E. (Evans) Gilbert; children: James J. Zielinski, Susan L. Zielinski Driscoll; m. Robert J. Dworak, Nov. 22, 1974. BA in History, Calif. State U., Fullerton, 1972, MLS, 1973; MA in Adminstrn., Sangamon State U., 1979. Libr. Calif. State U., Fullerton, 1972-74; asst. prof. Sangamon State U., Springfield, Ill., 1974-78; dir. libr. Coll. Atlantic, Bar Harbor, Maine, 1978—; adv. bd. N.E. Document Conservation Ctr., Andover, Mass., 1989-94, Maine Libr. Commn., Augusta, 1980-90. Co-author: Financial Management Handbook for Libraries, 1986; contbr. articles to profl. jours. Sec.-treas. Mt. Desert Dem. Com., Northeast Harbor, Maine, 1990-92; chmn. bd. trustees Mt. Desert Island Hosp., Bar Harbor, 1990—. Mem. Maine Libr. Assn. (chair Maine Acad. and Rsch. libr. 1988, chair standing adv. com. continuing edn. 1983, Outstanding Libr. award 1994), New Eng. Assn. Schs. and Colls. (evaluator 1993—), Phi Kappa Phi, Phi Alpha Theta. Home: 89 Bartletts Landing Rd Mount Desert ME 04660-6011 Office: Coll of the Atlantic 109 Eden St Bar Harbor ME 04609-1105*

DWORETZKY, JOSEPH ANTHONY, lawyer, city official; b. N.Y.C., Sept. 17, 1951; s. Lawrence H. and Grace W. (Jackson) D.; m. Amy L. Banse; children: Lydia Light, Adam Eliot. BA with distinction, Purdue U., 1972; JD summa cum laude, Villanova U., 1977. Bar: Pa. 1977, D.C. 1978. Law clk. to judge U.S. Ct. Appeals 2d Cir., N.Y.C., 1977-78; assoc. Drinker Biddle & Reath, Phila., 1978-84, ptnr., 1984-93, mng. ptnr., 1992-93; chmn. corp. group law dept. City of Phila., 1993, city solicitor, 1994-96; shareholder Hangley Aronchick Segal & Pudlin, 1997—; adj. prof. Rutgers U. Sch. Law, Camden, 1986-93. V.p., bd. dirs. Phila. Vol. Lawyers for Arts, 1981-84, Phila. Bd. Pensions, 1994-96, Phila. Indsl. Devel. Corp., 1994-96, Phila. Theatre Co., 1998—; sec.-treas., bd. dirs. Consumer Bankruptcy Assistance Project, 1992—, Acad. for Law, Pub. Adminstrn. and Criminal Justice, 1995-98. Fellow Am. Coll. Bankruptcy; mem. ABA, Pa. Bar Assn., Phila. Bar Assn., Order of Coif, Phi Beta Kappa. E-mail: jad@hangley.com. Home: 7801 Huron St Philadelphia PA 19118-4218

DWORETZKY, MURRAY, physician, educator; b. N.Y.C., Aug. 18, 1917; s. Samuel and Frieda (Newhoff) D.; m. Barbara Ratner, June 11, 1943; children: Thomas Alan, Joan Mara. B.A., U. Pa., 1938; M.D., SUNY, Coll. Medicine, N.Y.C., 1942; M.S. in Medicine, U. Minn., 1950. Diplomate: Am. Bd. Internal Medicine (examiner allergy subbd. 1967-71), Am. Bd. Allergy and Immunology (founding mem., dir. 1971-74), Pan Am. Med. Assn. Intern City Hosp., N.Y.C., 1942-43; asst. resident pathology City Hosp., 1943, fellow in pathology, 1946-47; resident pathology U. Chgo., 1947-48; fellow in medicine Mayo Found., Rochester, Minn., 1948-50; practice medicine, specializing in internal medicine, allergy and clin. immunology N.Y.C., 1951—; asst. physician N.Y. Hosp., 1951, physician, 1951-56, asst. attending physician, 1956-61, assoc. attending, 1961-66, attending physician, 1966—, physician-in-charge Allergy Clinic, 1961-88; asst. in medicine Cornell U. Med. Coll., 1951-52, instr. medicine, 1952-56, clin. asst. prof., 1956-61, clin. asst. prof. pub. health, 1957-62, clin. assoc. prof. medicine, 1961-66, dir. tng. program div. allergy and immunology, 1961-88, clin. prof. medicine, 1966—; attending physician Manhattan Eye, Ear and Throat Hosp., 1953-62; Med. dir.-at-large Asthma-Allergy Found. Am., 1963-64, bd. dirs., 1964-78, mem. exec. com., 1964-77; founding mem. bd. dirs. Am. Bd. Allergy and Immunology, 1971-74; examiner sub-bd. allergy Am. Bd. Internal Medicine, 1967-71. Contbr. articles to profl. jours. Served to capt., M.C. AUS, 1943-46. Recipient Frank L. Babbott M.D. Meml. award Alumni Assn. Coll. Med. SUNY, 1992. Fellow Am. Acad. Allergy and Immunology (past pres. 1968; Disting. Service award 1989), N.Y. Acad. Medicine, ACP; mem. N.Y. County Med. Soc., N.Y. Allergy Soc. (past pres., exec. com. 1958-94, tchg. day dedicated in his honor 1995), Soc. Exptl. Biology and Medicine, Harvey Soc., Am. Fedn. Clin. Research, AMA (chmn. allergy sect. council 1974-77, mem. residency rev. com. for allergy and immunology 1980-85), Am. Assn. Immunologists, Sigma Xi. Home: 21 E 87th St New York NY 10128-0506 Office: 115 E 61st St New York NY 10021-8183

DWORIN, MICKI (MAXINE), automobile dealership executive; widowed; children: Judy, Diane. V.p. Dworin Chevrolet, Inc., East Harford, Conn., 1955-83, Dworin Auto Leasing; pres. Eastern Auto Ins., Conn. Chevrolet Dealers Assn., Tarrytown Zone Dealer Coun., Atlantic Coast Region Dealer Coun., Boulevard, Inc. Sec. BBB, Hartford, Conn.; vol. coord. Vol. Broward, 1998-99, Children's Diagnostic and Treatment Ctr., 1996-98, Am. Cancer Soc., 1994-96, Kids in Distress, 1991-95; hon. trustee Hartford Coll. for Women; sec., bd. govs. Point of Am. Condominium; coord. Trinity Coll.; bd. dirs. Combined Health Appeals; chmn. King David Soc., 1995—. Mem. Advt. Assn. Grtr. Hartford. Fax: (954) 522-6770. E-mail: volbrow@safari.net. Office: 1300 S Andrews Ave Ft Lauderdale FL 33316

DWORKIN, GARY STEVEN, insurance company executive; b. N.Y.C., July 7, 1947; s. Irving Milton and Grace Wilhelmina (Korn) D.; student Hofstra U., 1965-68, N.Y. U., 1969-71; m. Linda Lee Fuchs, Aug. 28, 1970; children: Robert Benjamin, Alexandra Tenille. Sales mgr. Chatham Blankets, N.Y.C., 1968-70; ins. agt. Travelers Ins. Co., Hartford, Conn., 1970-74; broker Dworkin Assos., Rochester, N.H., 1974-76; pres. Dworkin Assos., Inc. (DAI), Rochester, 1976—. Registered health underwriter; chartered life underwriter. Mem. Nat. Assn. Life Underwriters, Life Inc., Lifemark Assocs. Inc., Home Office Life Underwriters Assn., reg. principal, bd. dirs. Lifemark Securities Corp., N.H. Assn. Life Underwriters, Life, Inc., Southeastern N.H. Assn. Life Underwriters, New Eng. Forum, Nat., Nat. Assn. Health Underwriters, Am. Risk and Ins. Assn., Risk Appraisal Forum, Nat. Assn. Ind. Life Brokerage Agys. (charter). Republican. Office: PO Box 2000 Rochester NH 03866-2000

DWORKIN, HOWARD JERRY, nuclear physician, educator; b. Bklyn., Oct. 29, 1932; s. Joseph Henry and Mollie M. (Hodas) D.; m. Gina Gora; children: Rhonda Fran, Steven Irving, Paul J., Edward Joshua. BSChemE, Worcester Poly. Inst., 1955; MD, Albany Med. Coll., 1959; MS in Radiation Biology, U. Mich., 1965. Diplomate Am. Bd. Internal Medicine, Am. Bd. Nuclear Medicine. Intern Albany Hosp., N.Y., 1959-60; resident Rochester Gen. Hosp., N.Y., 1960-62; resident U. Mich. Hosps., 1962-65, asst. coord. nuclear medicine unit, 1963-66, instr., 1965-66; asst. prof. medicine U. Toronto, Ont., Can., 1966, assoc. prof., 1967; head dept. nuclear medicine Princess Margaret Hosp., Toronto, 1967; head nuclear medicine sect., radiology Nat. Naval Med. Ctr., Bethesda, Md., 1967-69; dir. sch. nuclear medicine tech. William Beaumont Hosp., Royal Oak, Mich., 1969—, chief dept. nuclear medicine, 1969—, dir. nuclear medicine resident tng. program, 1970—, chmn. CME com., 1993—; clin. asst. prof. dept. medicine Wayne State U. Med. Sch., Detroit, 1970—; asst. clin. prof. dept. radiology Mich. State U., East Lansing, 1976—; clin. prof. med. physics Ctr. for Health Scis., Oakland U., Rochester, Mich., 1977—; mem. Am. Bd. Nuclear Medicine, 1979—, treas., 1982-84. Author: (with N. Aspin and R.G. Baker) Clinical Use of Isotopes in the Physics of Radiology, 1969, Part Two, Clinical Prodedures in Radioisotope Laboratory Procedures, 1969; contbr. articles and chpts. to med. jours. and texts; patentee radioactive labeled protein material process and apparatus. Served with USN, 1967-69. Fellow ACP; mem. AMA, Accrediation Coun. for Continuing Med. Edn. (chmn. 1998), Soc. Nuclear Medicine (trustee 1973-81, v.p. 1982, pres. 1986-87), Am. Fedn. Clin. Rsch., Am. Thyroid Assn., Endocrine Soc., Am. Coll. Nuclear Physicians (sec. 1974-75, pres. 1978-79). Office: William Beaumont Hosp Dept Nuclear Medicine Royal Oak MI 48073

DWORKIN, IRMA-THERESA, school system administrator, researcher, educator; b. Busk, Galacia, Poland, May 1, 1942; d. Moses E. and Hedwig (Rappaport) Auerbach; m. Sidney Leonard Dworkin, Aug. 19, 1975 (dec. June 1984); children: Marc Elazar, Meyer Charles, Rebecca Joy. BS in Edn., CCNY, 1964, MS in Ednl. Psychology, 1966, cert. in clin. sch. psychology, 1968; EdD in Reading and Human Devel., Harvard U., 1971. Cert. tchr.; cert. reading cons.; cert. sch. psychologist; cert. sch. adminstr. Tchr. N.Y.C. Pub. Schs., 1964-66; rsch. asst., lectr. Bd. Higher Edn., N.Y.C., 1966-69; lectr., prof. Haifa (Israel) U., 1971-74; lectr., sr. investigator CUNY, N.Y.C., 1974-76; adminstr., evaluator, proposal and grant writer Bridgeport (Conn.) Pub. Schs., 1984—; asst. Edn. Clinic CCNY, 1964-66; endowed prof. chair Kunin-Lunenfeld Found., Haifa U., 1973. Contbr. articles to profl. jours. Bd. dirs. Jewish Bd. Edn., Bridgeport, Jewish Fedn. Greater Bridgeport, chairperson Holocaust edn. com., 1986-89, sec., 1996; mem., sec. Rep. Town Com., Bridgeport, 1992—; vol. Cmty. Closet, Bridgeport, 1991-98. Grolier fellow Harvard U., 1969-71. Mem. Conn. Testing Network (newsletter editor), Conn. Assn. Sch. Psychologists, Bridgeport Coun. Adminstrs. and Suprs. (editor, exec. bd. dirs. 1992-98, continuing edn. units mgr. 1993-98, v.p. 1994-98), Conn. Fedn. Sch. Adminstrs. (sec. 1997—, newsletter editor, website editor 1997—). Avocations: reading, physical fitness, painting, writing. Office: Bridgeport Pub Schs 45 Lyon Ter Bridgeport CT 06604-4023

DWORKIN, MARTIN, microbiologist, educator; b. N.Y.C., Dec. 3, 1927; s. Hyman Bernard and Pauline (Herstein) D.; m. Nomi Rees Buda, Feb. 2, 1957; children—Jessica Sarah, Hanna Beth. B.A., Ind. U., 1951; Ph.D. (NSF predoctoral fellow), U. Tex., Austin, 1955. NIH research fellow U. Calif., Berkeley, 1955-57; vis. prof. U. Calif., summers 1958-60; asst. prof. microbiology Ind. U. Med. Sch., 1957-61, assoc. prof., 1961-62; assoc. prof. U. Minn., 1962-69, dir. MD/PhD tng. program, 1990-97, prof., 1969—; vis. prof. U. Wash., summer 1965, Stanford U., 1978-79; vis. scholar Oxford (Eng.) U., 1970-71; Found. for Microbiology lectr., 1973-74, 76-77, 81-82; Sackler scholar Tel Aviv U., 1992. Author: Developmental Biology of the Bacteria, 1985, Microbial Cell-Cell Interactions, 1991; contbr. numerous articles, revs. to profl. publs.; mem. editorial bd. Jour. Bacteriology, 1967-74, 86-88, Ann. Revs. Microbiology, 1975-79, The Prokaryotes, 2d edit. Alt. del. Democratic Nat. Conv., 1968; mem. Minn. Dem. Farm Labor Central Com., 1969-70. Served with U.S. Army, 1946-48. Recipient Career Devel. award NIH, 1963-68, 68-73; John Simon Guggenheim fellow, 1978-79. Fellow Am. Acad. Arts and Scis.; mem. Am. Soc. Microbiology (vice chmn. div. gen. microbiology 1977-78, chmn. 1978-79, div. councillor 1980-82), Soc. Gen. Microbiology (Eng.). Home: 2123 Hoyt Ave W Saint Paul MN 55108-1314 Office: U Minn Dept Microbiology Minneapolis MN 55455

DWORKIN, PAUL HOWARD, pediatrician; b. Paterson, N.J., Oct. 22, 1947; s. Bernard and Ruth (Steinhauer) D.; m. Sheila Ann Maher, Oct. 7, 1979; children: Molly Maher, Eamon Timothy. AB, Rutgers U., 1969; MD, Johns Hopkins U., 1973. Diplomate Am. Bd. Pediatrics. Pediatric registrar Paddington Green Children's Hosp./St. Mary's Med. Sch., London, 1976; resident in pediatrics Children's Hosp., Boston, 1973-75, fellow in ambulatory pediatrics, 1976-78; asst. prof. pediatrics W.Va. U. Sch. Medicine, Morgantown, 1978-81; prof./asso. chair pediats., head div. gen. peds., asst. dean U. Conn. Sch. Medicine, Farmington, 1981-98, prof./chair pediats., 1998—; dir., chair pediats. St. Francis Hosp. and Med. Ctr., Hartford, Conn., 1992—; prof., chair pediats. U. Conn. Sch. Medicine, Farmington, 1998—; physician-in-chief Conn. Children's Med. Ctr., Hartford, 1998—. Author: Learning and Behavior Problems of Schoolchildren, 1985; editor: Pediatrics: National Medical Series for Independent Study, 1987, 3d edit., 1996; editor Jour. Devel. & Behavioral Pediats., 1996—; editl. bd. Pediats., Ambulatory Child Health, Current Pediatrics, 1991—. Vol. Salvation Army Shelter Pediat. Clinic, Hartford, 1991—. Fellow Am. Acad. Pediats. (chair com. on scientific mtgs. 1994-98); mem. Ambulatory Pediat. Assn., Soc. Devel. and Behavioral Pediats. Office: Conn Children's Med Ctr 282 Washington St Hartford CT 06106-1860

DWORKIN, SAMUEL FRANKLIN, dentist, psychologist; b. Freedom, Ohio, Sept. 26, 1933; s. Louis and Minnie (Katz) D.; m. Mona Mae Moskowitz, Dec. 23, 1956; children: Adam, Ted. B.S., CCNY, 1954; D.D.S., NYU, 1958, Ph.D., 1969. Practice dentistry N.Y.C., 1959-65; Nat. Inst. Dental Research spl. fellow, 1965-69; asst. prof. dept. preventive dentistry and community health NYU Coll. Dentistry, 1969-70; assoc. prof. div. preventive dentistry, dir. office of edn. and behavioral research Columbia U. Sch. Dental and Oral Surgery, 1970-74; prof. oral surgery, assoc. dean acad. affairs U. Wash. Sch. Dentistry, Seattle, 1974-77; prof. psychiatry and behavioral sci. U. Wash. Sch. Medicine, 1977—; prof. oral medicine, 1977—; dir. psychophysiologic liaison clinic dept. psychiatry and behavioral sci. U. Wash. Sch. Medicine, 1978-89, Washington dental svc. disting. prof. dentistry, 1999—; clin. dir. Regional Clin. Dental Rsch. Ctr., U. Wash.; cons. NIH, ADA, Am. Dental Hygiene Assn.; mem. behavioral medicine study sect. NIH, 1985-90. Cons. editor Jour. Dental Edn., 1976—, Jour. Dental Rsch., 1976—, Pain, 1984—, Clin. Jour. Pain, 1989—, Psychosomatic Medicine, 1989—; guest editor Jour. Preventive Dentistry, 1977, Jour. ADA, Pain; contbr. articles to profl. jours. Co-founder, pres. League of Parents of Hearing Impaired Infants, N.Y.C., 1966-70; v.p. N.Y. State Parents of Hearing Impaired Children, 1970-74; adv. coun. Lexington Sch. of Deaf, N.Y.C., 1970-74; bd. dirs. Seattle Pro-Musica, 1977, v.p., 1978-81, treas., 1991-98, pres. 1995-98, pres. emeritus, 1999. Grantee NIH, 1979-99. Fellow Internat. Assn. for Study of Pain, Am. Pain Soc.; mem. ADA (coun. dental health edn., coun. nat. bd. exams. 1974-79), AAAS, APA, Am. Assn. Dental Schs., Behavioral Scientists in Dental Rsch. (pres. 1975, 90), Internat. Assn. for Dental Rsch. (Disting. Scientist award behavior and health svcs. rsch.), Internat. Soc. Clin. and Exptl. Hypnosis, Behavioral Scis. Group (Disting. Rschr. award), Behavioral and Health Svcs. Rsch. Group (pres. 1990-91). Office: U Wash Dept Psychiatry Seattle WA 98195

DWORSKI, SYLVIA, modern languages educator; b. New Haven, Conn., Apr. 10, 1915; d. Louis and Ida (Miller) D. BA with highest honors, Conn. Coll. for Women, 1935; MA with distinction, Yale U., 1937, PhD, 1941; cert., U. Paris, 1939. Instr. Spanish New Haven State Tchrs. Evening Coll., 1941-44; tchr. French, Spanish and English East Haven (Conn.) H.S., 1942-44; instr. Romance langs. Sweet Briar (Va.) Coll., 1944-46, St. Helena Ext.

Coll. William and Mary, Norfolk, Va., 1946-48; asst. prof. French Wilkes Coll., Wilkes-Barre, Pa., 1948-54, assoc. prof. modern langs., 1954-63; assoc. prof. modern langs. St. Mary's Coll., Notre Dame, Ind., 1963-64, co-chmn. dept. modern langs., 1963-65, prof. modern langs., 1964-80, chmn. dept. French, 1965-67, prof. emeritus modern langs., 1980—; vis. faculty mem. grad. sch. langs. U. Notre Dame, summers 1967, 68. Grantee Spanish Lang. Inst. U. Mex., summer 1944; vis. fellow Romance langs. Yale U., New Haven, 1941-42, French Traveling fellow Yale U., 1938-39; Winthrop scholar Conn. Coll., 1934. Mem. AAUP (St. Mary's Coll. chpt. founding mem. 1965, sec.-treas. 1965-66, 78-79, exec. bd. 1979-80), Am. Assn. Tchrs. French (hon. life mem.), Gray Panthers (exec. bd. 1988-96), Phi Beta Kappa. Jewish. Avocations: reading, music, opera, theatre, movies. Home: 70 Byron Pl New Haven CT 06515-2406

DWORSKY, DANIEL LEONARD, architect; b. Mpls., Oct. 4, 1927; s. Lewis and Ida (Fineberg) D.; m. Sylvia Ann Taylor, Aug. 10, 1957; children: Douglas, Laurie, Nancy. B.Arch., U. Mich., 1950. Practice architecture as Dworsky Assocs., Los Angeles, 1953—; design critic, lectr. arch. U. So. Calif., U. Mich., UCLA, 1983-84; chmn. archtl. rev. panel Fed. Res. Bank. Recipient Design citation Progressive Arch. mag. 1967, Gov. Calif. award 1966, 3 Los Angeles Grand Prix awards So. Calif. AIA and City of Los Angeles 1967; prin. works include Angelus Plaza Elderly Housing, Los Angeles, 1981, Ontario (Calif.) City Hall, 1980, CBS Exec. Office Bldg, North Hollywood, Calif., 1970, U. Calif. at Los Angeles Stadium, 1969, Fed. Res. Bank Bldg., Los Angeles, 1987, U. Mich. Crisler Arena at Ann Arbor, 1966, Dominguez Hills State U. Theatre, 1977, Ventura County Govt. Center, 1979, Northrop Electronics Hdqrs., Los Angeles, 1983, Hewlett-Packard Region Office, North Hollywood, 1984, Los Angeles County Mcpl. Cts. Bldg., 1985, Tom Bradley Internat. Terminal L.A. Airport, 1984, City Tower, City Orange Calif., 1988, The Met. Apt. L.A., 1989, Fed. Office Bldg., Long Beach, Calif., 1992. Fellow AIA (more than 80 awards including 20 awards Calif. chpts., Nat. Honor award 1974, 68-69, Firm award Calif. chpt. 1985, L.A. Gold Medal award 1994). Home: 9225 Nightingale Dr Los Angeles CA 90069-1117 Office: Dworsky Assocs 3530 Wilshire Blvd Ste 1000 Los Angeles CA 90010-2341

DWOSKIN, JOSEPH Y., pediatric urologist; b. Chgo., July 14, 1935; divorced. BS, Springfield Coll., Mass., 1961; MD, Jefferson Med. Coll., 1965. Diplomate Am. Bd. Urology. Clin. asst. prof. urology SUNY, Buffalo, 1970-74; asst. attending physician pediatric urology Children's Hosp., Buffalo, 1970-78; asst. prof. Buffalo (N.Y.) Gen. Hosp., 1970—; clin. asst. prof. SUNY, Buffalo, 1974—; acting chief urology dept. Children's Hosp., Buffalo, 1978-83, attending physician pediatric urology, 1978—, chief urology, 1983-84; attending physician Mercy Hosp., Buffalo, 1986—, chief urology dept., 1989—. Contbr. articles to profl. jours. Fellow Am. Acad. Pediatrics, ACS; mem. AMA, Am. Urol. Assn., Soc. Pediatric Urology. Office: 313 Elmwood Ave Buffalo NY 14222-2203

DWOYER, DOUGLAS LEON, engineering executive; b. Elizabeth, N.J., Feb. 1, 1942; s. Charles Francis and Adolpha (Kwiatkowski) D.; m. Nancy Lester Dalton; children: Diana Ruth, Emily Rose. BS in Aerospace Engring., Va. Poly. Inst. and State U., 1964, MS in Aerospace Engring., 1967, PhD in Aerospace Engring., 1975. Rsch. engr. United Techs. Rsch. Ctr., East Hartford, Conn., 1973-75; asst. prof. aerospace engring. Va. Poly. Inst. and State U., Blacksburg, 1975-77; rsch. engr. NASA Langley Rsch. Ctr., Hampton, Va., 1977-81, head computational methods br., 1981-87, dir. hypersonic tech. office, 1987-89, chief fluid mechanics divsn., 1989-93, dir. for rsch. and tech., 1993—; dir. rsch. & tech. group NASA Hdqrs., Washington, summer 1993; professorial lectr. mech. engring. George Washington U., Hampton, 1978-93. Editor: Theoretical Approaches to Turbulence, 1985, Finite Elements, 1986, Stability of Time Dependent and Spatially Varying Flows, 1987, 11th International Conference on Numerical Methods in Fluid Dynamics, 1989; contbr. numerous articles to profl. publs. Mem. Gloucester (Va.) Village Planning Com., 1991. Capt. USAF, 1968-73. Fellow AIAA. Avocation: woodworking. Home: PO Box 613 Gloucester VA 23061-0613 Office: NASA Langley Rsch Ctr MS 103 Hampton VA 23681-0001*

DWYER, CHARLES BREEN, arbitrage and Eurobond specialist; b. Lawrence, Mass., Sept. 25, 1952; s. Joseph Justin and Gertrude Caroline (Breen) D. Student, Cambridge (Eng.) U., 1972; AB in English Lit. cum laude, Georgetown U., 1973; postgrad., U. Geneva, 1974. Asst. to consul Australian Consulate, Geneva, 1975-78; pres. Commd. Cleaning Co., Andover, Mass., 1979-84, CBD Assocs., Andover, 1985—; chmn. Major's Bay Devel. Corp., Cayman Islands, 1987—; Bd. dirs. SBS N.Am. Author: The Senator's Son, 1978. Mem. SAR, Pioneer Inst., Internat. Soc. Financiers (cert.), Royal Over-Seas League, Georgetown Clubs Boston and London, Chemists' Club N.Y., Royal Overseas League (London). Roman Catholic. Avocations: competitive swimming, skiing, tennis, sailing.

DWYER, DARRELL JAMES, financial executive; b. Vermillion, S.D., Nov. 27, 1946; s. Michael Leroy and Faye Awilda (Hansen) D.; m. Helen K. Howard, 1989; 1 child, Sean Patrick. BS, Mankato State U., 1977; MBA, U. Calif., Berkeley, 1978. CPA; Cert. Mgmt. Acct., Internal Auditor; cert. data processor. Acct. Touche Ross & Co., Salem, Oreg., 1978-79; cons. Arthur, Persons Co., Salem, 1980-82; v.p. fin. Evergreen Internat. Airlines Inc, McMinnville, Oreg., 1982-87; chief fin. officer The Erickson Group Ltd., Medford, Oreg., 1987-89; sr. v.p., corp. sec. Evergreen Internat. Aviation, Inc., McMinnville, Oreg., 1989-90; pres., chief exec. officer The Dwyer Co., Sacramento, Calif., 1990—. Calif. State scholar; recipient award of merit Evergreen Internat. Aviation, McMinnville, Oreg., 1984. Mem. AICPA, Calif. Soc. CPA, Inst. Cert. Mgmt. Accts. Republican. Episcopalian. Avocations: skiing, tennis, travel. Office: The Dwyer Co 3900 Rocklin Rd Rocklin CA 95677-2708

DWYER, DENNIS D., information technology executive; b. Oak Park, Ill., July 19, 1943; s. John J. and Jessie M. Dwyer; m. Carolyn R. Schultz, Apr. 29, 1967; children: David, Julianne. Various positions Harris Bank, Chgo., 1967-83, mgr. info. tech. planning, 1983-86, v.p. tech. facilitation, 1986—; resolutions chmn. Cooperating Users of Burroughs Equipment, Detroit, 1978-82; cons. Unisys mainframe computers. Pres. Hunting Ridge Homeowners Assn., 1983-85; mem. Palatine Plan Commn., 1984—, chmn., 1989—. Recipient Tom Grier award for Excellence Unisys Users Group, 1988. Home: 1032 Raven Ln Palatine IL 60067-6649 Office: Harris Bank PO Box 755 Chicago IL 60690-0755

DWYER, DORIS DAWN, adult education educator; b. Cin., Feb. 19, 1948; d. James Daniel and Marjorie Elaine (Fisher) D. ABin Social Sci., Ea. Ky. U., 1970, MA in History, 1971; PhD, Miami U., Oxford, Ohio, 1979. Instr. social sci. Ea. Ky. U., Richmond, 1971-74; doctoral fellow Miami U., Oxford, 1974-78; asst. prof. social sci. Coll. Ganado (Ariz.), 1979-80; prof. history Western Nev. C.C., Fallon, 1980—; bd. dirs. Nev. Humanities Com., Reno, 1983-89, mem. chautauqua performance, Nev. and Calif., 1994—. Author: A Century of City-Building, 1983. Mem. World History Assn., Western History Assn., Nev. Hist. Soc., Nev. Women's History Project; mem. women's archives bd. Reno Libr., U. Nev., 1995—; vice-chmn. bd. dirs. Nev. State Mus. and History, Carson City, 1994—; bd. dirs. Nev. Hist. Preservation, Carson City, 1990-94; chmn. bd. trustees Churchill County Libr., Fallon, Nev., 1989-96. Named Cmty. Woman of the Yr. Fallon Bus. and Profl. Women, 1992. Democrat. Roman Catholic. Avocations: travel, walking. Office: Western Nev C C 160 Campus Way Fallon NV 89406-2661

DWYER, GERALD PAUL, JR., economist, educator; b. Pittsfield, Mass., July 9, 1947; s. Gerald Paul and Mary Frances (Weir) D.; m. Katherine Marie Lepiane, Jan. 15, 1966; children: Tamara K., Gerald P. III, Angela M., Michael J.L., Terence F. BBA, U. Wash., 1969; MA in Econs., U. Tenn., 1973; PhD in Econs., U. Chgo., 1979. Economist Fed. Res. Bank, St. Louis, 1972-74, Chgo., 1976-77; asst. prof. Tex. A&M U., College Station, 1977-81; asst. prof. Emory U., Atlanta, 1981-84, sr. rsch. assoc. Law and Econ. Ctr., 1982-84; assoc. prof. U. Houston, 1984-89; prof. Clemson (S.C.) U., 1989-99, acting head dept. econ., 1992-93; asst. v.p. Fed. Res. Bank Atlanta, 1997-98, v.p., 1998—; vis. scholar Fed. Res. Bank, St. Louis, 1987-89, Atlanta, 1982-84, 94-97, Fed. Reserve Bank of Mpls., 1995; cons. FTC, Washington, 1983-84, Arthur Bros., Corpus Christi, Tex., 1980-81, Amerigas, Houston, 1985, Western Container Corp., 1987, Metrica, Inc., Bryan, Tex., 1989-93; vis. fin. economist Commodity Futures Trading Commn., Washington, 1990. Contbr. articles to profl. jours. NSF trainee U. Tenn., 1970-72; Weaver fellow Intercollegiate Studies Inst., 1974-75, Earhart Found. fellow, 1975-77; rsch. grantee NSF, Earhart Found. Mem. Am. Econ. Assn., Am. Stats. Assn., Econometric Soc., Econ. Hist. Assn., We. Econ. Assn., So. Econ. Assn., Beta Gamma Sigma, Phi Kappa Phi. Avocation: computers.

DWYER, JIM, reporter, columnist; b. N.Y.C., Mar. 4, 1957; s. Philip and Mary (Molloy) Dwyer; m. Catherine Muir Dwyer; 2 children. BS, Fordham Coll., 1979; MS, Columbia U., 1980. Reporter Hudson Dispatch, Union City, N.J., 1980-82, Elizabeth (N.J.) Jour., 1982, Bergen Record, Hackensack, N.J., 1983-84; reporter, columnist N.Y. Newsday, N.Y.C., 1984-95; columnist N.Y. Daily News, 1995—. Author: Subway Lives, 1991, (with others) Journalism Collection of Best Newspaper Writing, 1991, Two Seconds Under the World, 1994. Recipient Outstanding Column award Nat. Headliners Soc., 1987, 88, Meyer Berger prize Columbia U., 1988, Writing award Am. Soc. Newspaper Editors, commentary, 1991, Pulitzer Prize for commentary, 1995. Mem. Graphic Communications Internat. Union. Roman Catholic. Office: Daily News 450 W 33rd St Fl 3 New York NY 10001-2681*

DWYER, JOHN CHARLES, lawyer; b. San Francisco, Mar. 26, 1962; s. Richard Thomas and Dorothy (Blake) D. BS, U. Calif., Berkeley, 1984; JD, Harvard U., 1988. Bar: Calif. 1988, U.S. Dist. Ct. (no. dist.) Calif. 1988, U.S. Ct. Appeals (9th cir.) 1988. Assoc. Jackson, Tufts, Cole & Black, San Francisco, 1989-93; dep. assoc. atty. gen. U.S. Dept. Justice, Washington, 1993—. Democrat. Roman Catholic. Office: US Dept Justice 10th and Constitution NW Washington DC 20530*

DWYER, JOHN JAMES, mechanical engineer; b. Jersey City, Mar. 1, 1928; s. John J. and Margaret (Casey) D.; m. Joan Catherine Hyde, June 26, 1954 (div. Jan. 1984); children: William J., Kathleen M., Barbara A.; m. JoAnna Mary Kuta, Feb. 4, 1989 (dec. July 5, 1994). BS, N.J. Inst. Tech., 1957; MBA, Lehigh U., 1972. Registered profl. engr., Pa., Tex. Machinery engr. Air Products and Chems., Inc., Allentown, Pa., 1957-63, mgr. machinery engring., 1963-83; cons. Houston, 1983-97. Sgt. U.S. Army, 1950-52, Korea. Mem. ASME (mem. performance test code for centrifugal compressors com. 1975-98), NSPE, Tex. Soc. Profl. Engrs. Roman Catholic. Home: 800 Hausman Rd Apt 276 Allentown PA 18104-8493

DWYER, JOHN M., mathematician, statistician, computer scientist; b. Ann Arbor, Mich., June 8, 1937; s. Paul Sumner and Florence Baylis (Brown) D.; children: Anne Louise, Laura Beth. BA, U. Mich., 1959, MS, 1965; PhD, Tex A&M U., 1971. Asst. prof. stats. U. Wyo., Laramie, 1962-66; asst. prof. math. U. Detroit, 1969-73, assoc. prof. math., 1974—, chair, 1974-77, interim chair, 1989-91; vis. assoc. prof. dept. mgmt. and mktg. Northern Mich. U., Marquette, 1983-84; dir. rsch. Detroit Inst. Abuse Rsch. and Tng., 1973-74; cons. Detroit Tax Assessor's Office, 1971; expert witness Focus: HOPE, Detroit, 1981-86; panelist "Ask the Professor" radio show U. Detroit, 1977-83. Mem. AAAS, Math. Assn. Am., Am. Statis. Assn., Union of Concerned Scientists, Computer Profls. for Social Responsibility (co-founder Mich. Chpt. 1997, chair 1998). E-mail address: dwyerjm@unmercy.edu. Office: U Detroit Mercy Dept Math and Computer Sci P O Box 19900 Detroit MI 48219-0900

DWYER, LAURAINE THERESA, ambulatory care administrator, rehabilitation nurse; b. Detroit, Feb. 29, 1948; d. Thomas Z. and Mary Alice (Parker) D. BSN, Ariz. State U., 1970, MS in Nursing, 1976; cert. nursing practitioner, Calif. State U., Long Beach, 1979. Cert. rehab. nurse. Staff and charge nurse Good Samaritan Hosp., Phoenix, 1970-75; staff nurse in neurology VA Med. Ctr., Phoenix, 1976-77, spinal cord injury nurse practitioner, 1980-85; rehab. clin. nurse specialist, 1977-85; assoc. chief nursing svc. spinal cord injury unit and ambulatory care VA Med. Ctr., San Diego, 1985-91, assoc. chief nursing svcs., ambulatory care, 1991-97, dir. ambulatory care svcs., 1997—. Mem. editorial adv. bd. Rehab. Mgmt., 1992-94. Chair logistics commn. 17th Ann. Nat. Vets. Wheelchair Games, 1997. Named Nurse of Yr., Dist. 18 Ariz. Nurses Assn., 1982. Mem. Assn. Rehab. Nurses (pres. Ariz. chpt. 1979-81, treas. San Diego chpt. 1990-94), Am. Assn. Spinal Cord Injury Nurses (bd. dirs. 1991-94, chmn. editl. bd. 1988-94, co-editor 1983-86, Disting. Svc. award 1994), Am. Acad. Ambulatory Care Nursing (sec. San Diego chpt. 1993-97, chair VA spl. interest group 1995-97). Sigma Theta Tau. Home: 8719 Ginger Snap Ln San Diego CA 92129-3715

DWYER, RALPH DANIEL, JR., lawyer; b. New Orleans, Apr. 23, 1924; s. Ralph Daniel Sr. and Carolyn (Nolting) D.; m. Gwendolyn Betpouey, Feb. 12, 1955; children: Ralph, Bridget Mary, Frederick Henry, Patrick Rees, John Betpouey, Timothy Paul, Kathleen Mary, Mary Megan, Pegeen Mary. BS in Econs., Loyola U., New Orleans, 1943; Japanese area and lang. program, U. Chgo., U. Mich., 1943-45; JD, Loyola U., New Orleans, 1950; grad., Army War Coll., 1976. Bar: La. 1950. Law clk. to judges Civil Dist. Ct., Parish Orleans, 1950-51; pvt. practice, New Orleans, 1950—. Mem. La. Civil Service League, 1968—, bd. govs., 1984—; past pres. Japanese Soc. New Orleans. Served to col. AUS, La. N.G., 1978, ret. Decorated Order of Sacred Treasure (Japan), Order of Medallion of St. Louis, Archdiocese of New Orleans, 1982; recipient Monte M. Lemann award La. Civil Svc. League, 1982, 84, La. Disting. Svc. medal 1978. Mem. La. State Bar Assn. (com. on law reform 1971-82, ho. of dels. 1975-77), New Orleans Bar Assn. (3d v.p. 1968-69), St. Thomas More Cath. Lawyers Assn. (pres. 1968-70). Democrat. Roman Catholic. Avocations: reading, family, fly-fishing. Home and Office: 1622 Cadiz St New Orleans LA 70115-4816

DWYER, WILLIAM L., federal judge; b. Olympia, Wash., Mar. 26, 1929; s. William E. and Ila (Williams) D.; m. Vasiliki Asimakopulos, Oct. 5, 1952; children: Joanna, Anthony, Charles. BS in Law, U. Wash., 1951; JD, NYU, 1953; LLD (hon.), Gonzaga U., 1994. Bar: Wash. 1953, U.S. Ct. Appeals (9th cir.) 1959, U.S. Supreme Ct. 1968. Law clk. Supreme Ct. Wash., Olympia, 1957; ptnr. Culp, Dwyer, Guterson & Grader, Seattle, 1957-87; judge U.S. Dist. Ct. (we. dist.) Wash., Seattle, 1987—; now sr. judge U.S. Dist. Ct. (we. dist.) Wash. Author: The Goldmark Case, 1984 (Gavel award ABA 1985, Gov.'s award Wash. 1985). 1st lt. U.S. Army, 1953-56. Recipient Outstanding Svc. award U. Wash. Law Rev., 1985, Helen Geisness disting. Svc. award Seattle-King County Bar Assn., 1985, Disting. Alumnus award U. Wash. Sch. of Law, 1994, W.G. Magnuson award King County Mcpl. League, 1994, Judge of Yr. Wash. State Trial Lawyers, 1994, Outstanding Jurist award Am. Bd. Trial Advocates, Washington, 1998, William L. Dwyer Outstanding Jurist Award, King County Bar Assn., 1998. Fellow Am. Coll. Trial Lawyers, Am. Bar Found., Hon. Order of Coif; mem. ABA, Inter-Am. Bar Assn., Am. Judicature Soc., Supreme Ct. Hist. Soc., 9th Cir. Hist. Assn. Office: US Dist Ct 502 US Courthouse Seattle WA 98104-1189*

DWYRE, WILLIAM PATRICK, journalist, public speaker; b. Sheboygan, Wis., Apr. 7, 1944; s. George Leo and Mary Veronica (O'Brien) D.; m. Jill Ethlyn Jarvis, July 30, 1966; children—Amy, Patrick. B.A., U. Notre Dame, Ind. Sports copy editor Des Moines Register, 1966-68; sports writer, asst. sports editor, sports editor Milw. Jour., 1968-81; asst. sports editor, sports editor Los Angeles Times, 1981—; speaker Mark Reede's Sportstars, Los Angeles, 1986; columnist Referee Mag., 1977—; voting mem., bd. dirs. Amateur Athletic Found. Nat. Sports Hall of Fame, 1981—. Bd. dirs. Honda-Brockerick Cup Women's Collegiate Athlete of Yr.; treas. Casa Colina Hosp. Rehab., Pomona. Named Sportswriter of Yr., Wis. Nat. Sportscasters, Sportswriters Assn., 1980; Nat. Editor of Yr., Nat. Press Found., 1985; recipient award for Sustained Excellence by Individual, L.A. Times, 1985, Red Smith award AP sports Editors, 1996, Powerade Sport Story of Yr. award Nat. Sportswriter and Sportwriters Assn., 1999. Mem. Assoc. Press Sports Editors (pres. 1989), Nat. Baseball, Pro Basketball and Football Writers Assn. Club: Milw. Pen and Mike. Avocation: tennis. Office: Los Angeles Times Times Mirror Sq Los Angeles CA 90012

DYAL, WILLIAM M., JR., federal agency administrator; b. Austin, Tex., May 13, 1928; s. William M. and Midlred Eleanor (Taylor) D.; m. Edith Colvin, May 6, 1950; children: Kathy Lynn Dyal Schwab, Deborah Irene Dyal DeMeo, Maria Lisa Dyal Reese. AB, Baylor U., 1949; ThM, So. Theol. Sem., 1953. With Fgn. Mission Bd., Costa Rica, Guatemala and Argentina, 1953-62; dir. orgn. Christian Life Commn., 1962-66; dir. Peace Corps, Colombia, 1966-69; regional dir. Peace Corps, N. Africa, Near East and S. Asia, 1969-71; pres. Inter-Am. Found., Rosslyn, Va., 1971-80; advisor to pres. Ford Found., N.Y.C., 1980-81; pres. Am. Field Service Internat./Intercultural Programs, N.Y.C., 1981-86; pres. St. John's Coll., Annapolis, Md., 1986-90, ret., 1990; dir. Peace Corps, Panama, 1995-97; retired. Author: It's Worth Your Life, 1967, Un Desafio al Discipulado, 1970, also articles. Recipient Santander Gold medal Colombia, 1968. Home: 611 Fauquier St Fredericksburg VA 22401-3745

DY-ANG, ANITA C., pediatrician; b. Cavite, The Philippines, Feb. 21, 1943; came to U.S., 1970; m. Raymundo Ang., May 1, 1977; children: Aileen Ang, Audrey Ang. MD, U. East Ramon Magsaysay, Quezon City, Philippines, 1967. Diplomate Am. Bd. Pediatrics. Pediat. resident Tulane U. Charity Hosp. New Orleans, 1973; pvt. practice Warsaw, N.Y.; mem. attending staff Wyoming County Cmty. Hosp. Mem. Wyoming County Med. Soc. Office: 78 N Main St Warsaw NY 14569-1329

DYBECK, ALFRED CHARLES, labor arbitrator; b. Camden, Del., Nov. 16, 1928; s. George L. and Freda (Alexander) D.; m. Leah Anne Pestell, June 28, 1952; 1 son, Alfred Arthur. Student, Emmanuel Missionary Coll., 1946-49; B.A., George Washington U., 1955, J.D., 1958. Bar: Va. 1958. Field atty. NLRB, Pitts., 1958-63, supervising atty., 1963-65; asst. regional atty. NLRB, Milw., 1965; assoc. chmn. bd. arbitration United Steelworkers Am. and; U.S. Steel Corp., Pitts., 1965-78; chmn. bd. arbitration U.S. Steel Corp., 1979-96; exec. sec. Nat. Acad. Arbitrators, 1971-77, pres., 1989-90. Served with AUS, 1951-53. Mem. Order Coif. Home: 1235 Cardinal Dr Pittsburgh PA 15243-1207 Office: 2101 Greentree Rd Pittsburgh PA 15220-1400

DYBEK, STUART, English educator, writer; b. Chgo., Apr. 10, 1942; s. Stanley and Adeline (Sala) S.; m. Caren Bassett, Feb. 7, 1967; children: Anne, Nicholas. BS, Loyola U., Chgo., 1964, MA, 1967; MFA, U. Iowa, 1973. Tchr. U.S. V.I. Sch., St. Thomas, 1968-70, U. Iowa, Iowa City, 1970-73; prof. English Western Mich. U., Kalamazoo, 1973—; vis. prof. creative writing Princeton (N.J.) U., 1991, U. Calif., Irvine, 1995, U. Iowa, 1998. Author: (poetry) Brass Knuckles, 1979; (fiction) Childhood and Other Neighborhoods, 1980, The Coast of Chicago, 1990. Guggenheim fellow, 1982; recipient Whiting Writers award, 1985, O. Henry first prize, 1985, Acad. award in fiction Am. Acad. Arts and Letters, 1994, PEN/Malamud award, 1995, Lannan Lit. prize, 1998. Mem. PEN. Home: 320 Monroe St Kalamazoo MI 49006-4436 Office: Western Michigan U Dept English Kalamazoo MI 49008 also: care Amanda Urban Intl Creative Mgt 40 W 57th St New York NY 10019-4001

DYBMAN, NICK NISON, poet; b. Tientsin, China, Dec. 23, 1945; Came to U.S., 1950; s. Gregory and Alla D. BA, Queens Coll., 1972. Pres. Aleza Records, Forest Hills, N.Y., 1989. Avocation: drawing. Home: 66-36 Yellowstone Blvd Forest Hills NY 11375-2514

DYBOWSKI, DOUGLAS EUGENE, education educator, economist; b. Wiesbaden Air Base, Germany, Dec. 7, 1946; s. Eugene L. and Margaret Alma (Hart) D.; m. Deborah Jane Dalpiaz, Dec. 27, 1986; children: Noelle C., Eric W. BA in Govt. and Politics, U. Md., College Park, 1969; grad. edn. econ., Trinity U., San Antonio, 1971; Calif. teaching credential, Calif. State U., San Bernardino, 1975; AS in Computer Sci., San Bernardino Valley Coll., 1982. Stockman J.C. Penny Co., 1965; advtg. asst. Sears & Roebuck, Washington, D.C., 1966; air conditioning and heating asst. J&W Contractors, McLean, Va., 1967; legis. aide to hon. Michael Feighan, U.S. Congress, Washington, 1969; asst. mgr. Mr M Food Store, San Antonio, Tex., 1970-71; econ. Bur. Labor Statistics Dept. Labor, Dallas, 1971-73; fine jewelry salesman May Co., San Bernardino, Calif., 1974-78; tchr. Rialto and San Bernardino Sch. Dists., 1973-85; realtor Gallery of Homes, San Bernardino, Calif., 1979; tchr. Diocese of San Bernardino, Calif., 1985-87; instr. computer sci. San Bernardino Valley Coll., Calif., 1983-84; tchr. Colton (Calif.) Joint Unified Sch. Dist., 1987—; art ctr. San Bernardino, Calif., 1989-95; cons. Rickert's Art Ctr. Artist (painting) San Bernardino County Mus., 1994, Riverside (Calif.) City Mus., 1997. Recipient Lounsbury Svc. award San Bernardino Valley Coll., 1982. Mem. Sigma Chi. Republican, Presbyterian. Avocations: art collecting, painting, gourmet cooking, letter writing, gardening. Office: Colton Joint Unified Sch Dist 1212 Valencia Dr Colton CA 92324-1798

DYCHE, DAVID BENNETT, JR., retired management consultant; b. Port Chester, N.Y., July 23, 1932; s. David B. and Julia H. D.; m. Mary J. Moorman, Apr. 28, 1956; children—David B. III, Williard H. AB, Dartmouth Coll., 1954; MBA, U. Pa., 1958. Chartered fin. analyst. With J.P. Morgan & Co., and Morgan Guaranty Trust Co., N.Y.C., 1958-81; dir. fin. industries Arthur D. Little, Inc., 1981-98. Bd. dirs. Gasparilla Island Water Assn. Served with U.S. Army, 1954-56. Mem. Assn. Investment Mgmt. Rsch., N.Y. Soc. Security Analysts. Home: Box 502 Boca Grande FL 33921-0502

DYCHE, KATHIE LOUISE, secondary school educator; b. Waynoka, Okla., Sept. 8, 1949; d. Loren Neil and Bessie Louise (Wait) Callaway; m. Steven Lee Dyche, July 5, 1969; children: Cherilyn Nettie, Bradley Callaway. BA in Edn. in Art, Northwestern Okla. State U., 1972; postgrad., Southwestern Okla. State U., 1975, 78, Phillips U., 1981, 83-85; MEd, U. Cen. Okla., 1993. Cert. art; Am. history and democracy tchr., Okla. Tchr. art Fairview (Okla.) Pub. Schs., 1973-81, cons., 1973-76; asst. to handicapped Glenwood Elem. Sch., Enid, Okla., 1982-83; reading and math. asst. Longfellow Jr. High Sch., Enid, 1983-84; tchr. art Emerson Jr. High Sch., Enid, 1984—; freelance artist Gaslight Theater, Okla. Small Bus. Devel. Ctr., also others; represented by Galery of Fine Arts, Enid, Okla. Exhibited in group shows Amarillo (Tex.) Artists' Studio, 1975, Kallistos Invitational Show, 1985, Dean Lively Gallery, Edmond, Okla., Art Educators as Artists exhibit Philbrook, Tulsa, 1994, 96, Oklahoma Fall Arts Inst. Capitol Exhibit, Oklahoma City State Capitol, 1997. Pres., v.p., sec., historian, reporter Gamma Mother's Club, Fairview, 1973-80; co-chmn. Fairview Show of Arts, 1979, 80; art vol. Glenlwood Elem. Sch., 1981-82; pres., historian, parlimentarian Delta Child Study Club, Enid, 1981-84. Recipient Okla. Fall Arts Inst. Honor award, 1992, 94, 95, 96, 97, 98, 99; Northwestern Okla. State U. scholar, 1968. Mem. NEA, Nat. Art Edn. Assn., Okla. Art Edn. Assn., Okla. Edn. Assn., Cardinal Key, Kappa Delta Pi, Delta Kappa Gamma (sec. 1986-88, scholar 1993; 2d v.p. 1994-96), Phi Delta Kappa (historian 1995-96, v.p. 1998—). Episcopalian. Avocations: drawing, painting, designing clothes, reading, crafts. Office: Emerson Jr High Sch 700 W Elm Ave Enid OK 73701-3000

DYCK, ANDREW ROY, philologist, educator; b. Chgo., May 24, 1947; s. Roy H. and Elizabeth (Beck) D.; m. Janis Mieko Fukuhara, Aug. 20, 1978. BA, U. Wisc., 1969; PhD, U. Chgo., 1975. Sessional lectr. U. Alta., Edmonton, Can., 1975-76; asst. prof. U. Minn., Mpls., 1977-78; vis. asst. prof. Classics UCLA, 1976-77, asst. prof., 1978-82, assoc. prof., 1982-87, prof., 1987—, chmn. dept. classics, 1988-91; mem. Inst. for Advanced Study, Princeton, 1991-92; vis. fellow All Souls Coll., Oxford, 1998, Clare Hall, Cambridge, 1999. Author: A Commentary on Cicero, De Officiis, 1996; editor: Epimerismi Homerici, 2 vols., 1983, 95, Essays on Euripides and George of Pisidia and on Helidorus and Achilles Tatius (Michael Psellus), 1986. Alexander von Humboldt-Stiftung fellow, Bonn, Fed. Republic of Germany, 1980-89; NEH fellow, 1991-92; vis. fellow All Souls, Oxford, 1998; vis. fellow Clare Hall, Cambridge, 1999. Mem. Am. Philol. Assn., Calif. Classical Assn., U.S. Nat. Com. on Byzantine Studies. Office: UCLA Classics Dept 405 Hilgard Ave Los Angeles CA 90095-9000

DYCK, ARTHUR JAMES, ethicist, educator; b. Saskatoon, Sask., Can., Apr. 27, 1932; s. Jacob Peter and Mary (Zacharias) D.; m. Sylvia Willms, Sept. 2, 1952; children—Sandra Lynn and Cynthia Ann (twins). B.A., Tabor Coll., 1953; M.A., U. Kans., 1958, U. Kans., 1959; Ph.D., Harvard, 1966. Research asst. psychology U. Kans., 1957-60; spl. lectr. philosophy U. Sask., 1964-65; asst. prof. social ethics Harvard Div. Sch., 1965-69; Mary B. Saltonstall prof. population ethics Harvard Sch. Pub. Health, 1969—, Co-dir. Kennedy Interfaculty Program in Med. Ethics, 1971—, mem. Ctr. for Population Studies and Div. Sch. Faculty, 1965—. Author: On Human Care: An Introduction to Ethics, 1977, Rethinking Rights and Responsibilities: The Moral Bonds of Community, 1994; editor: (with S.J. Reiser, W.J. Curran) Ethics in Medicine, 1977; assoc. editor: Jour. Religious Ethics; mem. editorial bd. Linacre Quar.; contbr. articles to profl. jours. Mem. Am. Soc. Christian Ethics, The Hastings Ctr., Soc. European Culture, Am. Pub. Health Assn., N.Am. Soc. for Social Philosophy, Phi Beta Kappa. Congregationalist.

Home: RR 1 Box 236A Alton NH 03809-9738 Office: 45 Francis Ave Cambridge MA 02138-1911 *I do not measure success apart from what moral principles require of me. To do my chosen scholarly work honestly, fairly, enthusiastically, and in ways that contribute, however modestly, to learning, knowledge and social justice is success. The most important measures of success are the increase of love for others and for the divine power that makes the moral life possible on earth. This is true in my family as well as in my vocation.*

DYCK, PETER, neurosurgeon; b. Neuhalbstadt, Russia, June 16, 1935; came to the U.S., 1962; s. Peter Dueck and Margaret Derksen; m. Barbara Ann Keenan, 1959 (div. 1964); children: Deborah Nailon, Carrie Froese; m. Carole Jean Cassetto, Oct. 30, 1964; children: Christopher, Michelle. MD, U. B.C., Vancouver, Can., 1961. Rotating intern Youngstown, Ohio, 1961-62; neurosurg. resident U. So. Calif., L.A. County Med. Ctr., 1962-64; pvt. practice Calif., 1962—; clin. prof. neurosurgery U. So. Calif., L.A. Editor: 2 books, 1984, 89; contbr. chpts. to books and articles to profl. jours. Elder First Hollywood Presbyn. Ch. Fellow ACS; mem. AMA, Internat. Soc. for Study of the Lumbar Spine, Royal Coll. Medicine, Western Neurosurg. Soc., Congress Neurol. Surgeons, Calif. Assn. Neurol. Surgeons, Calif. Assn. Neurol. Surgeons (pres. 1997-98), Calif. Med. Assn., L.A. County Med. Assn. Republican. Avocations: golf, reading, poetry, fishing. Home: 484 Starlight Crest Dr La Cañada CA 91011 Office: Univ So Calif Ste 130 2750 Washington Blvd Pasadena CA 91107

DYCK, WESLEY JAMES, personnel director; b. Winnipeg, Can., July 28, 1965; s. Peter Henry and Esther Elizabeth (Affleck) D.; m. Deanna Dale Vater, June 9, 1990; 1 child, Jenneth Lee. BA in History, Pensacola Christian Coll., 1991, BS in Acctg., 1992. Staff acct. The Heritage Found., Washington, 1992-95, pers. dir., 1995—. Precinct chmn. Fairfax County Rep. Party, 1995—; fin. sec. Engleside Bapt. Ch., 1994-98, deacon, 1998—. Mem. Worthington Woods Homeowner's Assn. (pres. 1995-97). Office: The Heritage Found 214 Massachusetts Ave NE Washington DC 20002-4958

DYCKMAN, THOMAS RICHARD, accounting educator; b. Detroit, Feb. 25, 1932; s. Clovis E. and Wildarene A. (Andrus) D.; m. Alice Ann Pletta, Nov. 14, 1955; children: Daniel, James, Linda, David. B.A., U. Mich., 1954, M.B.A., 1955, Ph.D., 1961. Asst. prof. acctg. U. Calif., Berkeley, 1961-64; assoc. prof. Cornell U., Ithaca, N.Y., 1964-68, prof., 1968—, Ann Whitney Olin prof. bus., 1978—, assoc. dean Johnson Grad. Sch. Mgmt., 1985-95, acting dean, 1996-97, acting v.p. for info. tech., 1998-99; cons. Fin. Acctg. Standards Bd., IBM, GTE, SNET. Author: Topics in Cost Accounting and Decisions, 1963, Statistical Decision Theory, 1968, Algebra and Calculus for Business, 1975, Managerial Cost Accounting, 1971, 2d edit., 1976, Fundamental Statistics for Business and Economics, 1977, Efficient Capital Markets, 1975, 2d edit., 1986, Cases in Financial Accounting, 1987, 3d edit., 1989, Cost Accounting: Concepts and Managerial Applications, 1990, 2d edit., 1994, Intermediate Accounting, rev. edit., 1992, 4th edit., 1998. Mem. adv. com. Fin. Acctg. Standards Bd., 1984-88, Fin. Acctg. Found., 1990-93. With USNR, 1955-58. Recipient Gold medal award AICPA, 1968, 76. Mem. Am. Acctg. Assn. (pres. 1981-82, dir. rsch. 1976-78, Outstanding Acctg. Educator award 1987). E-mail: trdz@cornell.edu. Home: 135 Eastlake Rd Ithaca NY 14850-9700 Office: Cornell U Sage Hall Ithaca NY 14853

DYDEK, MALGORZATA, professional basketball player; b. Poland, Apr. 28, 1974. Center Poznan Olympia, 1992-94; center France, 1994-96, Spain, 1996-98; center Utah Starzz, Salt Lake City, 1998—; mem. Polish Nat. Team. Avocations: billiards, reading, videos, movies. Office: Utah Starzz 301 W South Temple Salt Lake City UT 84101*

DYE, BRADFORD JOHNSON, JR., lawyer, former state official; b. Tallahatchie County, Miss., Dec. 20, 1933; married; 3 children. BBA, LLB, U. Miss. Bar: Miss. 1959. Practiced law Grenada, Miss., 1959-61, later in Jackson, Miss.; mem. Miss. Ho. of Reps., 1960-64, Miss. Senate, 1964-68; dir. Agrl. and Indsl. Bd., 1968-71; treas. State of Miss., 1972-76; lt. gov. State of Miss., 1980-92; ptnr. Pyle, Dreher, Mills & Dye PA, 1992—; bd. dirs. Fed. Home Loan Bank, Dallas; southeastern adv. bd. Alexander Proudfoot Productivity Mgmt. Co.; formerly served with U.S. Senate Judiciary Com. Staff; pres. Jackson Fed. Savs. Assn., 1976-79; charter pres. Bus. Sch. Alumni Assn. Univ. of Miss. Charter v.p. Grenada Jaycees; former mem. adv. bd. Miss. State U. Sch. Bus. and Industry; bd. dirs. Jr. Achievement; active state heart fund drive, ARC, United Way, Cancer Drive, YMCA Youth Sports; del. Dem. Nat. Conv., 1980, 84. Mem. U. Miss. Bus. Alumni Assn. (charter pres.), Masons, Shriners, Pi Kappa Alpha. Methodist. Office: Pyle Dreher Mills & Dye 779 Avery Blvd # 200 Ridgeland MS 39157-5218*

DYE, ELAINE GIBSON, home health nurse; b. Talladega, Ala., Aug. 23, 1944; d. John Lewis and Eunice (Vickers) Gibson; divorced; 1 child, Steven Dean Herring. Diploma, Sylacauga Hosp. Sch. Nursing, 1983. RN, Ala. ICU staff nurse Sylacauga (Ala.) Hosp., 1983-85; field staff nurse ABC Home Health Svcs., Talladega, 1985-88, quality appraisal coord., 1990-91, coord. adminstrn., 1991—; emergency rm. staff nurse Coosa Valley Med. Ctr., Sylacauga, 1988-89, Cooper Green Hosp., Birmingham, Ala., 1989-90; adminstr. Sylacauga (Ala.) Agy. of ABC Home Health Svcs., Inc., 1991—. Mem. Sylacauga C. of C., Bus. and Profl. Women (Sylacauga chpt.). Episcopalian. Avocations: reading, swimming, crafts. Office: First Am Home Care 401 W 3rd St Sylacauga AL 35150-1916

DYE, H. MICHAEL, marketing executive; b. Parkersburg, W.Va., Jan. 21, 1941; s. Max D. and Pauline (Gygax) D.; m. Carolyn A. Moore, Apr. 30, 1964; children: M. Andrew, Elizabeth Anne. BA in Econs., U. Charleston, 1966; MPA in Polit. Adminstrn., Fla. State U., 1978. Spl. asst. Nat. Govs. Conf., Washington, 1970-73; state-fed. programs coord. Fla. Dept. Transp., Tallahassee, 1973-76; regional mgr. Tallahassee office Post, Buckley, Schuh & Jernigan, Inc., 1976-83, v.p., dir. mktg., 1983-88, sr. v.p., dir. mktg., 1988-90, exec. v.p., dir. administrv. svcs., 1989-90; pres. Post, Buckley, Schuh & Jernigan, Inc., Miami, Miami, 1990—; pres., CEO Post, Buckley, Schuh & Jernigan, Inc., Miami, 1990—; adv. bd. NationsBank South Fla., 1998—. Trustee Fla. State U. Found., 1994—; mem. adv. bd. St. Thomas U., Miami, Enterprise Fla. Inc., Internat. Trade Econ. Devel, Orange Bowl Com., 1996—; mem. United Way Cabinet, 1998—; exec. com. Floridians for Better Transp. Mem. Pres., Fla. C. of C. (bd. dirs. 1989—, chmn. 1991-92), Greater Miami C. of C. (bd. govs., bd. trustees 1993—). Avocations: tennis, travel. Office: PBSJ Corporation 2001 NW 107th Ave Miami FL 33172-2507*

DYE, HENRY C., public relations firm executive. BA, U. Tenn., 1963. Ptnr. Dye, Van Mol & Lawrence Pub. Rels., 1980—. Office: 209 7th Ave N Nashville TN 37219

DYE, JAMES LOUIS, chemistry educator; b. Soudan, Minn., July 18, 1927; s. Ray Ashley and Hildur Ameda (Limstrom) D.; m. Angeline Rosalie Medure, June 10, 1948; children: Roberta Rae, Thomas Anthony, Brenda Lee. AA, Virginia (Minn.) Jr. Coll., 1948; BA, Gustavus Adolphus Coll., 1949; PhD, Iowa State U., 1953; DSc (hon.), No. Mich. U., 1992. Rsch. assoc. Iowa State U., Ames, 1953; asst. prof. chemistry Mich. State U., East Lansing, 1953-60, assoc. prof., 1960-63, prof., 1963-94, chmn. dept. chemistry, 1986-90, prof. emeritus, 1994—; vis. scientist Ohio State U., Columbus, 1968-69; cons. AT&T Bell Labs., Murray Hill, N.J., 1982-83. Author: Thermodynamics and Equilibrium, 1978; contbr. over 200 articles to profl. jours. With U.S. Army, 1945-46. NSF fellow, 1961-62, Guggenheim fellow, 1975-76, 90-91, Fulbright scholar, 1975-76; recipient Disting. Alumni award Gustavus Adolphus Coll., 1969. Fellow AAAS; mem. NAS, Am. Acad. Arts and Scis., Am. Chem. Soc. (Inorganic Chemistry award 1997), Am. Inst. Chemists (Chem. Pioneer award 1990), Am. Phys. Soc., Materials Rsch. Soc., Phi Kappa Phi, Sigma Xi (rsch. awards 1968, 87), Golden Key (teaching award 1986). Lutheran. Avocations: fishing, golf. Home: 2698 Roseland Ave East Lansing MI 48823-3847 Office: Mich State Univ Dept Of Chemistry East Lansing MI 48824

DYE, JOHN, actor; b. Amory, Miss., Jan. 31, 1963. Films include Making the Grade, 1984, Modern Girls, 1986, Campus Man, 1987, Mother, Mother, 1989, Best of the Best, 1989, The Perfect Weapon, 1991, Sioux City, 1994; T.V. series include Tour of Duty, 1989-90, Jack's Place, 1992, Hotel Malibu, 1994, Touched by an Angel, 1994—; also T.V. guest appearances. Office: c/o William Morris Agy 151 El Camino Dr Beverly Hills CA 90212

DYE, NANCY SCHROM, academic administrator, history educator; b. Columbia, Mo., Mar. 11, 1947; d. Ned Stuart and Florence Andrea Elizabeth (Ahrens) Schrom; m. Griffith R. Dye, Aug. 21, 1972; children: Molly, Michael. AB, Vassar Coll., 1969; MA, U. Wis., 1971, PhD, 1974. Asst. prof. U. Ky., Lexington, 1974-80, assoc. prof., 1980-88, prof., 1988, assoc. dean arts and scis., 1984-88; dean faculty Vassar Coll., Poughkeepsie, N.Y., 1988-92; acting pres. Vassar Coll., 1992-94; pres. Oberlin Coll., Oberlin, Ohio, 1994—. Author: As Equals And As Sisters, 1981; contbr. articles to profl. jours. Mem. Coun. of Colls. of Arts and Scis. (bd. dirs. 1989—). Office: Oberlin Coll 70 N Professor St Oberlin OH 44074-1019*

DYE, ROBERT HARRIS, retired manufacturing company executive; b. N.Y.C., Feb. 22, 1918; s. Abatha Agusta and Julia (Harris) D.; m. Tereseua Vergine, May 13, 1950; 1 child, Leslie Julie. BSEE, Purdue U., 1942. Engr. Gen. Elec. Co., Schenectady, 1942-43, 46-47; field engr. Gen. Elec. Co., Key West, Fla., 1947-49; prog. mgr. Gen. Elec. Co., Schenectady, 1949-53; divsn. chief guidance and control Dept. of Navy, Newport, R.I., 1953-56; sect. mgr. Gen. Precision Co., Little Falls, N.J., 1956-60; prog. mgr. Gen. Precision Co./Singer, Little Falls, 1960-87; ret. Lt. USN, 1942-46. Mem. IEEE, Submarine Vet. WWII, NRA, Am. Legion. Republican. Achievements include development of procedures for mine field penetration by submarine. Avocation: woodworking.

DYE, SHARON ELIZABETH HERNDON, speech pathologist; b. Springfield, Mo., June 14, 1952; d. Leonard Leroy and Virginia Louise (Kennard) Herndon; divorced children: Brian Keith Dye, Johnathan Paul Dye, Christopher Shawn Dye. BS, Marquette U., 1973, MS, 1975. Speech pathologist Milw. Pub. Schs., 1976-98; head start speech pathologist Peace Action Milwaukee-Milwaukee, Inc., Milwaukee, 1998—; head start itinerant speech pathologist, Wisconsin Speech Language Hearing Assn., 1998-99, North Divn. High School PTA, 1998—, Exceptional Edn. Com. Mem. Author: (poetry) Wind Riders, 1996; guest host area cable TV program MATA. Vol. House of Correction, Franklin, Wis., 1993, glaucoma screenings, 1995, 96; mem. Jobs for Peace, 1994, 95; past mem. Progressive Milw., Jamie's Club Theatre, featured poet, 1999—. Mem. Nat. Assn. Black Speech, Lang. and Hearing, Milw. Tchrs. Edn. Assn. (parent tchr. cmty. partnerships com.), Marquette U. Alumni Assn., Eta Phi Beta. Baptist. Avocation: writing inspirational songs and poetry.

DYE, STUART S., lawyer; b. Ogden, Utah, 1939. BS cum laude, U. Utah, 1961; LLB, U.Va., 1967. Bar: Va. 1967, D.C. 1967. Sec. Navy staff deep submergence systems rev. group Office of Legis. Affairs, 1963-64; spl. asst. on law of the sea matters internat. law divsn. Office of Judge Advocate Gen., 1965-66; ptnr. Holland & Knight, Washington; adv. bd. Latin Am. Law and Bus. Report, 1994—. Mem. editl. bd. Va. Jour. Internat. Law, 1966-67; contbg. editor Oil and Gas Regulations Analyst, 1976-82. Lt. comdr. USNR. Mem. ABA (natural resources law sect., adminstrv. law sect.), Maritime Law Assn. U.S., Maritime Adminstrv. Bar Assn., U.S.-Mex. C. of C. (bd. dirs. 1988—, sec., exec. com., pres. Mid-Atlantic chpt. 1994-97, chmn. transp. task force), Phi Alpha Delta. Office: Holland & Knight 2100 Pennsylvania Ave NW Washington DC 20037-3295

DYE, THOMAS ROY, political science educator; b. Pitts., Dec. 16, 1935; s. James Clair and Marguerite Ann (Dewan) D.; m. Joan Grace Wohleber, June 29, 1957; children: Roy Thomas, Cheryl Price. BA, Pa. State U., 1957, MA, 1959; PhD, U. Pa., 1961. Asst. prof. polit. sci. U. Wis., Madison, 1962-63; asso. prof., head dept. polit. sci. U. Ga., Athens, 1963-68; prof., chmn. dept. govt. Fla. State U., Tallahassee, 1968-72; dir. policy scis. Fla. State U., 1978-91, McKenzie prof. govt., 1991-98; pres. Lincoln Ctr. for Pub. Svc., 1998—; vis. prof. polit. studies Bar Ilan U., Israel, 1972, U. Ariz., 1976. Author: Politics, Economics and the Public, 1966, Politics in States and Communities, 1969, 9th edit., 1997, The Irony of Democracy, 1970, 11th edit., 1999, The Politics of Equality, 1971, Understanding Public Policy, 1972, 9th edit., 1998, Power and Society, 1975, 8th edit., 1998, Who's Running America, 1976, Policy Analysis, 1976, Who's Running America-The Carter Years, 1979, Determinants of Public Policy, 1980, Who's Running America-The Reagan Years, 1983, Politics in the Media Age, 1983, 4th edit., 1992, Who's Running America-The Conservative Years, 1986, Power Elites and Organizations, 1987, Who's Running America-The Bush Era, 1990, American Federalism: Competition Among Governments, 1990, Politics in America, 1994, 3d edit., 1999, Who's Running America-The Clinton Years, 1994, Politics in Florida, 1998. Served to 1st lt. USAF, 1961-62. Mem. Am. Polit. Sci. Assn. (sec. 1969-72), So. Polit. Sci. Assn. (v.p. 1974-75, pres. 1976-77), Phi Beta Kappa, Omicron Delta Kappa. Home: 1057 Del Haven Dr Delray Beach FL 33483-6528 Office: 1801 S Federal Hwy Ste 311 Delray Beach FL 33483-3335

DYE, WILLIAM ELLSWORTH, lawyer; b. Detroit, Oct. 15, 1926; s. Edward Ellsworth and Elizabeth (Esther Bloom) D.; m. Joy Ann Kuehneman, Apr. 28, 1956 (div.); children: Constance, Elizabeth, William. BA, U. Wis., 1948, LLB, 1951. Bar: Wis., 1951. Assoc. John F. Thompson, Racine, Wis., 1951-75; ptnr. Heft, Dye, Paulson & Nichols, Racine, 1975-87; ptnr. Foley, Dye, Foley and Tollaksen, S.C., Racine, 1987-92, Coates, Dye, Foley & Shannon, S.C., Racine, 1993-98, Dye, Foley, Krohn & Shannon, S.C., Racine, 1998—; instr. U. Wis. Law Sch., 1970-71. Bd. Visitors U. Wis., 1982-85. With U.S. Army, 1946-47. Mem. ABA, State Bar Wis. (bd. govs. 1972-78), Racine County Bar Assn. (pres. 1985-86). Republican. Episcopalian. Clubs: Racine Country, U. Milw., Somerset of Racine. Home: 111 11th St Racine WI 53403-1966 Office: Dye Foley Krohn & Shannon 1300 S Green Bay Rd Racine WI 53406-4469

DYEN, ISIDORE, linguistic scientist, educator; b. Phila., Aug. 16, 1913; s. Jacob and Dena (Bryzell) D.; m. Edith Brenner, June 11, 1939 (dec. 1976); children—Doris Jane, Mark Ross. B.A., U. Pa., 1933, M.A., 1934, Ph.D. in Indo-European Linguistics, 1939; postgrad. Slavic, Columbia, 1938-39, Yale, 1939-40. Faculty Yale U., 1942-84, prof. Malayan langs., 1957-58, prof. Malayopolynesian and comparative linguistics, 1958-73, prof. comparative linguistics and Austronesian langs., 1973-84, prof. emeritus, 1984—, dir. grad. studies Indic and Far Eastern langs. and lit., 1960-62, Indic and Southeast Asia, 1960-66, dir. grad. studies linguistics, 1966-68; adj. prof. linguistics U. Hawaii, 1985-89; linguist Coordinated Investigation Micronesian Anthropology, Truk, 1947, Sci. Investigation Micronesia, Yap, 1949; vis. prof. U. Padjadjaran, Bandung, 1960-61, U. Auckland, summer 1969, Australian Nat. U., fall 1971, U. Philippines, spring 1972, Inst. Study of Langs. and Cultures of Asia and Africa, Tokyo U. for Fgn. Langs., 1982-83; coordinator linguistics sect. 10th Pacific Sci. Congress, Honolulu, 1961; asso. prof. U. Chgo. and Linguistic Soc. Am. Summer Inst., 1955; prof. U. Mich. and Linguistic Soc. Am. Summer Inst., 1957; dir. SE Asia Linguistics Program, 28th Internat. Congress Orientalists, Canberra, 1971; organizing com. Conf. Genetic Lexicostatistics, New Haven, 1971; organizer 1st Eastern Conf. Austronesian Linguistics, New Haven, 1973; adv. com. 1st Internat. Conf. Comparative Austronesian Linguistics, Honolulu, 1974; mem. adv. bd. Oceanic Linguistics. Author: Spoken Malay, 2 vols., 1945, The Proto-Malayo-Polynesian Laryngeals, 1953, A Lexicostatistical Classification of the Austronesian Languages, 1965, A Sketch of Trukese Grammar, 1965, A Descriptive Indonesian Grammar, 1967, Beginning Indonesian, 4 vols., 1967, Lexicostatistics in Genetic Linguistics: Proc. of Yale Conf., 1973, (with David Aberle) Lexical Reconstruction: The Case of the Athapaskan Kinship System, 1974, Linguistic Subgrouping and Lexicostatistics, 1975, (with Guy Jucquois) Lexicostatistics in Genetic Linguistics II, 1976, (with Joseph B. Kruskal and Paul Black) An Indoeuropean Classification: A Lexicostatistical Experiment, 1992. Research fellow Slavic Am. Council Learned Socs., 1938-40; Guggenheim fellow, 1949, 64; Tri-Instl. Pacific Program grantee, 1956-57; NSF grantee, 1960-77. Mem. Linguistic Soc. Am., Am. Oriental Soc. (v.p. 1965-66), Am. Anthrop. Assn., Current Anthropology, Société de Linguistique de Paris, Koninklijk Instituut voor Taal-, Land-, en Volkenkunde, New Haven Oriental Club (pres. 1963-64, 74-76). Office: Univ Hawaii-Manoa Dept Linguistics Honolulu HI 96822 also: Yale U Dept Linguistics Hall of Grad Studies New Haven CT 06520 *My aim has been to further linguistic science, particularly in comparative linguistics, by research in both Austronesian and Indoeuropean languages. In large part my work has been devoted to combining traditional and mathematico-statistical methods to improve subgrouping procedures. The different interlocking roles of theory, hypothesis, and methodology have been kept to the fore throughout. I hope my research will develop strong evidence regarding the Austronesian homeland.*

DYER, ARLENE THELMA, retail company owner; b. Chgo., Oct. 23, 1942; d. Samuel Leo Sr. and Thelma Arlene (Israel) Lewis; m. Don Engle Dyer, July 3, 1965 (div. 1970); 1 child, Artel Terren. Cert. in mgmt. effectiveness, U. So. Calif., 1987. Community resource rep. Calif. State Employment Devel. Dept., Los Angeles, 1975-76, spl. projects rep., 1976; employment services rep. Culver City, Calif., 1977; contract writer L.A., 1976-80, employment program rep., 1980—; pres. Yabba and Co., L.A., 1981-83; pres., designer, cons. Spiritual Ties Custom Neckwear, L.A., 1985—; pres. Dyer Custom Shirts, Blouses and Suits, Beverly Hills, Calif., 1988—; founder self-evaluation seminar; pres. MYSELF, Inc., 1998. Author: Who Are You and What Are You All About?, 1994, Escaping to the Workplace, 1996, I Got the Job!. . .Now What?, 1998, You Got the Job?...Now What?, 1999; exhibited in fashion shows, Calif., 1984—; radio personality, 1995. Vol. Big Sister Gwen Bolden Found., L.A., 1986, Juvenile Hall, 1996; mem. Operation PUSH, Chgo., 1983, Mahogany Cowgirls & Co.; program chair Black Advs. in State Svc., 1987—; leader Girl Scouts U.S., L.A., 1982, L.A. Urban League; spirit team leader Calif. Special Olympics; mem. Big Sisters of L.A. Recipient IRWIN award, 1998. Mem. NAACP (Beverly Hills-Hollywood chpt.), Nat. Alliance Homebased Businesswomen (v.p., program chair 1987), Nat. Assn. Female Execs., Calif. State Employees Assn., L.A. C. of C., Kiwanis Club, U. So. Calif. Alumni Assn., L.A. Urban League, Black Women's Forum. Democrat. Club: 92d St Block. Avocations: traveling, reading, bicycling, roller skating.

DYER, CHARLES RICHARD, law librarian, law educator; b. Richmond Heights, Mo., Aug. 20, 1947; s. Helmuth Kinner and Sue Anne (Stone) D.; m. Cecelia Ann Duncan, Dec. 20, 1969 (div. June 1982); m. Roberta Sharlyn Monroe, June 2, 1984; 1 child, Christina L. Floyd. BA, U. Tex., 1969; MA, Northwestern U., 1971; JD, U. Tex., 1974, MLS, 1975. Bar: Tex. 1974. Assoc. law libr., asst. prof. law St. Louis U., 1975-77; law libr., assoc. prof. U. Mo., Kansas City, 1977-87; dir. librs. San Diego County Pub. Law Libr., 1987—; cons. in field. Editor Law Libr. Jour., 1972-74. Mem. Am. Assn. Law Librs., Mid-Am. Assn. Law Librs (sec.-treas. 1976-78), Southwestern Assn. Law Librs. (v.p. 1981-82, pres. 1982-83), So. Calif. Assn. Law Librs. (mem. exec. bd. 1991-93), Coun. Calif. County Law Librs. (pres. 1998—). Democrat. Unitarian. Home: 2323 Montclair St San Diego CA 92104-5344 Office: San Diego County Pub Law Library 1105 Front St San Diego CA 92101-3904

DYER, CROMWELL ADAIR, JR., lawyer, international organization official; b. St. Louis, Sept. 9, 1932; came to Netherlands, 1973; s. Adair and Tompie Leora (Giles) D.; m. Margaret Copeland Peickert, June 12, 1958 (div. Aug. 1976); children: Gretchen, Jack, Julie, Stephen; m. Susan Aynesworth, Aug. 20, 1977; stepchildren: Carol Godso, Amanda McDonough, Donne Brown. B.A., U. Tex.-Austin, 1954, J.D., 1961; LL.M., Harvard U., 1971. Bar: Tex. 1961, U.S. Dist. Ct. (no. dist.) Tex. 1965, U.S. Ct. Apls. (5th cir.) 1965, U.S. Dist. Ct. (ea. dist.) Tex. 1966, U.S. Ct. Apls. (11th cir.), 1982. Law clk. FTC, Washington, 1960; assoc. Branscomb, Gary, Thomasson & Hall, Corpus Christi, 1961-62; staff atty. So. Union Gas Co., Dallas, 1962-64; assoc. Dedman & May, Dallas, 1964-65, White, McElroy & White, Dallas, 1965-67; sole practice, Dallas, 1967-73; sec. Hague Conf. on Pvt. Internat. Law, The Hague, The Netherlands, 1973-78, 1st sec., 1978-93, dep. sec. gen., 1993-97; observer or cons. to intergovernmental orgns., 1976-97; conductor seminars. Author articles in field; co-author: (with Hans van Loon) Report on Trusts and Analogous Institutions, 1982. Served to lt. (j.g.) U.S. Navy, 1954-57. Mem. jury for award of Diploma in Internat. Law, Hague Acad., 1980, 84, 85, 86, 87, 91, 94, 95, 96, dir. studies, 1985, course on Unfair Competition in Private International Law, 1988; lectr. Asser Coll. Europe, 1992-96, U. Calif. Davis Sch. of Law, 1996, Brigitte M. Bodenheimer Meml. Lecture on the Family, UC Davis (Calif.) Law Sch., 1996. Mem. ABA, ATLA, Internat. Bar Assn., Inter-Pacific Bar Assn., Am. Soc. Internat. Law, Inter-Am. Bar Assn., Am. Fgn. Law Assn., Dutch Eisenhower Exchange Fellowship Selection Com., 1994, Travis County Bar Assn., Dallas Bar Assn., Internat. Soc. Family Law, Assn. Louis Chatin pour la d'efense des droits de l'enfant (Paris). Club: Club du jeudi (pres. 1983-85) (The Hague). Fax: 512-231-9498. E-mail: adyer@jump.net. Office: 9130 Jollyville Rd Ste 250 Austin TX 78759-7473

DYER, DORIS ANNE, nurse; b. Washington, Jan. 14, 1944; d. William Edward and Helen Gertrude (Smith) Swain; m. Robert Francis Dyer, Jr., June 27, 1970; children: Robert Francis, William Edward, Anne-Marie Helen Sallie, Scott Robertson McGavin. RN cum laude, Sibley Nursing Sch., Washington, 1964; BS, Am. U., 1966, MEd, 1969. Mem. staff emergency medicine dept. George Washington U. Hosp., 1960-69, emergency specialist protective svcs. clinic, 1967-70, adminstr. asst. to dir. clinic, 1970-78; nurse cons., 1987—. Author: Say Ah, 1971; also articles. Patron Sibley Meml. Hosp. Chapel, 1992. Trinity Coll. scholar, 1960; Lucy Webb Hayes scholar, 1964; recipient Martha Washington award Md. Soc. SAR, 1977, Community Leaders award, 1979, Washington medal, 1984, Disting. Women of Washington award 1987; decorated Comdr. Order of St. Lazarus, 1984, medal of Merit, 1989; created dame Order of Sovereign Mil. Order, 1980, dame comdr., 1992; named Dame Grand Cross, 1984, Dame Grand Officier, 1992. Mem. Am. Nurses Assn., D.C. Nurses Assns., Am. Acad. Ambulatory Nursing Adminstrs., Washington Med.-Surg. Soc. Aux. (pres.), Am. U. Grads. Assn., DAR, Washington Assembly, Washington Club, Annapolis Yacht Club, Kenwood Golf and Country Club. Address: 5608 Albia Rd Bethesda MD 20816-3303

DYER, FREDERICK CHARLES, writer, consultant; b. St. Louis, Feb. 17, 1918; s. George Leo and Katherine Mary (Dobson) D.; m. Lucrecia E. Herrera-Ibarguen, 1946; children: John R., Michael G., Lisa M. Dyer Fitzpatrick. B.A., Holy Cross Coll., 1938; M.B.A., Dartmouth Coll., 1948. Ednl. writer, editor tng. publs. Bur. Naval Personnel, 1948-58, asst. for spl. projects, leadership staff, 1958-64; spl. asst. to Undersec. Navy U.S. Navy, 1964-66; asst. for spl. projects Office Civilian Manpower Mgmt., Dept. Navy, 1966-68; dir. program analysis div. Navy Publs. and Printing Service, Washington, 1968-74; profl. lectr. George Washington U., 1956-60; adj. prof. Drexel Inst. Tech., 1962-67; profl. lectr. Am. U., 1967-73; adv. Ctr. for Applied Research in Apostolate, 1979-85. Author, co-author: Putting Yourself Over in Business, 1957, Executive's Guide to Handling People, 1958, Executive's Guide to Effective Speaking and Writing, 1962, Blueprint for Executive Success, 1964, Bureaucracy vs. Creativity, 1965, rev. edit., 1969, How to Make Decisions About People, 1966, The Petty Officer's Guide, 6 edits., 1952-66, The Enjoyment of Management, 1971, 82; contbr. more than 70 articles to profl. jours.; contbg. editor The Pope Speaks mag., 1954-64, Wall St. Rev. of Books, 1977-82. Mem. Town Council Somerset, Md., 1962-64; chmn. U.S. Civil Service Task Force on Mgmt. Edn. for Computers, 1965-66. Served with USNR, 1943-46; PTO; Navy Dept., 1948-52; ret. comdr., 1961. Mem. Authors Guild, Authors League Am., Columbia Country Club (Chevy Chase, Md.), Cosmos Club (Washington, fin. and hist. coms.), Nat. Press Club (Washington, libr. com.), Army and Navy Club (Washington). Home and Office: 4509 Cumberland Ave Bethesda MD 20815-5459*

DYER, GERALDINE A. (GERI A. DYER), artist, poet; b. Bklyn., Nov. 4, 1921; d. Edward and Chattie (Holmes) Bingham; m. Ralph Dyer, Oct. 1956. Student, N.Y. Phoenix Sch. Design, N.Y.C., 1946-48; pvt. studies in voice with Julia Gille, 1947-50. Reader poetry Bklyn. Poetry Cir., Moroccan Star, Bklyn., 1994; artist, poet; b. Bklyn., Nov. 4, 1921; d. Edward and Chattie (Holmes) Bingham; basRalph Dyer, Oct. 1956. Student, N.Y. Phoenix Sch. Design, N.Y.C., 1946-48, Bklyn. Mus. Art Sch., 1959, Bklyn. Coll., 1939; pvt. studies in voice with Julia Gille, 1947-50; reader poetry Bklyn. Poetry Circle, Bklyn., Moroccan Star, Bklyn., 1994. Commd. U.S. Army, 1941, ret. exec. USCG, 1979. One-woman art shows include Henry Hicks Gallery, N.Y.C., 1978-79, 81, Womanart Gallery, N.Y.C., 1980, Keane Mason Gallery, N.Y.C., 1981, Esta Robinson Gallery, N.Y.C., 1983, Bklyn. Heights Br. Libr., Bklyn., 1986-89, St. Mary Star of the Sea, Bklyn., 1993; exhibited at numerous group shows; represented in permanent collection Samuel Schulman Inst., Bklyn.; author poetry in collections. Recipient numerous awards including Art Horizons Internat. Art Competition, 1988, Alma E. Wright Meml. poetry award, 1989, 90, BPC Critics Poetry award,

1991, 94, Editor's Choice award Nat. Libr. of Poetry, 1994, 95, 1st prize Meml. Contest Bklyn. Poetry Cir.; named Internat. Woman of Yr., 1991-92. Mem. Poetry Soc. Am., Bklyn. Mus., Mus. Modern Art. One-woman art shows include Henry Hicks Gallery, N.Y.C., 1978-79, 81, Womanart Gallery, N.Y.C., 1980, Keane Mason Gallery, N.Y.C., 1981, Esta Robinson Gallery, N.Y.C., 1983, Brooklyn Heights Br. Libr., Bklyn., 1986-89, St. Mary Star of the Sea, Bklyn., 1993; exhibited in numerous group shows; represented in permanent collection Samuel Schulman Inst., Bklyn.; contbr. to poetry collections. Commd. U.S. Army, 1941, ret. exec. USCG, 1979. Recipient numerous awards, including Art Horizons Internat. Art Competition, 1988, Alma E. Wright Meml. poetry award, 1989, 90, BPC Critics Poetry award, 1991, 94, Editor's Choice award Nat. Libr. Poetry, 1994, 95, 1st prize Meml. Contest Bklyn. Poetry Cir.; named Internat. Woman of Yr., 1991-92. Mem. Poetry Soc. Am., Bklyn. Mus., Poets Ho.

DYER, IRA, ocean engineering educator, consultant; b. N.Y.C., June 14, 1925; s. Charles and Frieda (Griffman) D.; m. Betty Ruth Schanberg, Sept. 4, 1949; children: Samuel S., Debora J. SB, MIT, 1949, SM, 1951, PhD, 1954. V.p. Bolt Beranek & Newwman Inc., Cambridge, Mass., 1951-70; prof. ocean engring. MIT, Cambridge, 1971-89, Weber Shaughness prof., 1989-96, head dept., 1971-81, dir. MIT Sea Grant program, 1973-75, Robert Bruce Wallace lectr., 1982-83, emeritus prof., 1996—; vis. fellow Cambridge (Eng.) U., 1979-80; cons. Oasis Inc., Lexington, Mass., 1988—; advisor U.S. Dept. Def., Washington, 1988—, Am. Inst. Physics, N.Y.C., 1988-91. Contbr. over 100 articles to sci. jours. With USAAF, 1944-45. Recipient Meritorious Pub. Svc. award USCG, 1979. Fellow AAAS, IEEE (disting. tech. award 1982), Acoustical Soc. Am. (pres. 1986-87, Lindsay award 1960, gold medal 1996); mem. NAE, Marblehead Yacht Club, Blue Water Sailing Club. Avocation: sailing.

DYER, JAMES MASON, JR., investment company executive; b. Corsicana, Tex., Sept. 22, 1928; s. James Mason Sr. and Tabby (Jackson) D.; m. Lorelle Wright, Dec. 29, 1954; children: James Mason IV, Diane Dyer Campbell. BBA, U. Tex., 1950. V.p. J. M. Dyer Co., Corsicana, 1954-77, pres., 1978-87; nmg. ptnr. J.M. Dyer Co., Corsicana, 1987—; pres. The Piccolo Co., Corsicana, 1988—. 1st lt. U.S. Army, 1952-54, ETO. Episcopalian. Office: JM Dyer Co PO Box 620 Corsicana TX 75151-0620

DYER, JOHN MARTIN, lawyer, marketing educator; b. St. Louis, Feb. 27, 1920; s. George L. and Katharine (Dobson) D.; m. Emily Ramsay Young, Aug. 9, 1947; children: Katherine, Susan, Patricia Ann, Theresa, Carolyn. A.B., St. Louis U., 1941; M.B.A., U. Pa., 1953; J.D., U. Miami, Fla., 1967. Bar: Fla. 1951, U.S. Supreme Ct. 1966. Practiced in Miami, 1951—; assoc. prof. mktg. U. Miami, 1958-59, prof., 1969—, acting chmn. dept. mktg., 1968-69, chmn. mktg. dept., 1982-84; adj. prof. Fla. Atlantic U., Boca Raton, 1995, St. Thomas U., Miami, Fla., 1996—; speaker, cons. in field; dir. Atlas Sewing Ctrs. Inc., 1960; vis. prof. U. Del., 1969, 70, Disting. vis. prof., 1969; lectr. Universidad Nacional, Leon, Nicaragua, 1959; Disting. vis. prof. San Francisco State U., summer 1975; mem. adv. bd. Internat. Bank of Miami, 1971-75; dir. U.S. Govt. Securities Fund, Inc., Fla. Mut. Ins. Co.; mem. Fla. Dist. Export Council, 1971, 73-75, 76-77, 81-99; dir. subcom. for Latin Am. U.S. Senate Interstate and Fgn. Commerce Com. Staff, 1960; mem. Southeastern World Trade Group, U.S. Dept. Commerce, 1957; trustee Ctr. for Internat. Bus., Dallas, 1976—; ednl. cons. Nat. Assn. Credit Mgmt., S. Fla., 1977; editor conf. reports, program dir. various internat. trade seminars; dir. Rayne Internat., Inc., Pinnacle Fund, Fla.; editorial cons. Internat. Round Table Journal, 1988; bd. dirs. Internat. Mktg. Inst. Sports, 1988; appointed by U.S. Sec. Commerce to Fla. Dist. Export Coun., 1992; bd. dirs. Destination Sun Airways, Starwood Furniture Mfr., Inc., 1994; adj. prof. Fla. Atlantic U., 1991, Thomas U., Miami. Contbg. author: Marketing in Latin America, 1960; author: United States-Latin American Trade and Financial Relations, 1961, (with F. C. Dyer) Export Financing, 1963, Bureaucracy vs. Creativity: The Dilemma of Modern Leadership, 1965, The Enjoyment of Management, 1971, Guidelines to Operating in Latin America, 1970, International Finance Law and Marketing, 1976, 4th edit., 1980; contbr. (with F. C. Dyer) articles, revs. to profl. jours.; cons. editor: (with F. C. Dyer) Industria Turistica, 1972—; contbg. editor: (with F. C. Dyer) Wall Street Rev. of Books; cons. editor: Internat. Round Table Jour. 1986—. Spkr. platform com. Nat. Rep. Conv., 1968; mem. Fla. dist. export coun. U.S. Dept. Commerce/U.S. sec. of Commerce; bd. dirs. Goodwill Industries, Inc., Miami, 1977—, mem. adv. bd., 1978—, Destination Sun Airlines, 1992—; mem. internat. trade com. City of Miami; hon. advisor World Trade Coun. Palm Beach County, 1982. Named hon. vice consul Govt. Guatamala, 1959; recipient Phi Sigma Phi award for achievement in fgn. commerce Propeller Club U.S., 1954, Forum on Finance award Am. Securities Assn., 1954, N.Y. Stock Exchange Faculty fellow, 1954, Bus. Week plaque U. Miami, 1972, Iron Arrow award Arrow U., 1970, cert. of appreciation student chpt. Alpha Kappa Phi, 1971, First Pres's. award Am. Grad. Sch. Internat. Mgmt., 1975, Gold Key City of Coral Gables, Fla., Met.-Dade County cert. of appreciation, 1980, Internat. Mktg. award Fla. Exporters and Importers Assn, 1983, Dyer Internat. Scholarship award U. Miami, 1989, Internat. award Ill. Defense Coun., 1994; Hall of Fame award World Trade Ctr., Miami, 1996. Mem. Acad. Mktg. Scis., Am. Inst. Fgn. Trade (assoc.), Fed. Bar Assn., Fla. Bar Assn., Am. Fgn. Law Assn., Assn. Edn. Internat. Bus., Acad. Mktg. Sci., Nat. Airlines Three Coast Club, Internat. Exec. Svc. Corps, Am. Arbitration Assn., Fla. Internat. Devel. Adv. Coun., Fla. Coun. Internat. Devel. (hon.), Caribbean C. of C. (bd. dirs. 1991-92, 92-93, sr. dir. strategy group 1991), Coral Gables Country Club, Beta Gamma Sigma, Lambda Chi Alpha, Alpha Kappa Psi, Phi Alpha Delta. Home: 7701 SW 52nd Ct Miami FL 33143-5923

DYER, JOSEPH EDWARD, company executive; b. Vinalharen, Maine, Dec. 7, 1924; s. Leslie and Hazel Mae (Rogers) Brown; m. Sarahj L. Rae, June 8, 1958 (div.); children: Deborah, Diana, Deedee. BA, U. Maine, 1958. Mgr. Blue Cross & Blue Shield, 1958-62; exec. v.p. Romer Tissu Mills, 1962-70, U.S. Industries, 1970-75, Skybel Industries, 1975-80, Linweave Fine Papers, Inc., 1980-89; ret.; cons. Enfield, Conn., 1990—. Home: 73 Park Ave # 1 Enfield CT 06082-2931

DYER, JOSEPH WENDELL, career officer; b. Murphy, N.C., Mar. 2, 1947; s. Joseph Wendell Sr. and Margaret (Kale) D.; m. Melda F. Goldfinch, Mar. 29, 1969. BSChemE, N.C. State U., Raleigh, 1969; MS in Fin. Mgmt., Naval Post Grad. Sch., Monterey, Calif., 1981. Commd. ensign USN, 1969, advanced through grades to rear admiral, 1997; pilot USN, Patuxent River, Md., 1976-80; sys. integrator USN, China Lake, Calif., 1982-84; Commanding Officer Plant Rep. Office USN, Melbourne, Australia, 1984-87; dep. program mgr. F/A-18 program USN, Washington, 1988-90, AX airplane chief engr., 1990-91, exec. asst. to comdr. naval air sys. command, 1991-92; chief test pilot USN, Patuxent, Md., 1992-93; mgr. F/A 18 program USN, Washington, 1993-97; comdr. Naval Air Warfare Ctr., Aircraft Divsn., 1997—; asst. comdr. for rsch. and engring. Naval Air Sys. Command, 1997—. Contbr. articles to profl. jours. Recipient Acquisition Excellence award U.S. Dept. Def. Assoc. fellow: Soc. Exptl. Test Pilots; mem. Assn. of Old Crows. Avocations: sailing. Home: 110 Harvard St Alexandria VA 22314-2713

DYER, L. KEITH, entertainment company producer; b. Deland, Fla., May 9, 1963; s. Leslie Jay and Helen Frieda (Brock) D. MusB, Fla. So. Coll., 1987; postgrad., Fla. State U., 1987-89. Tech. dir. Lake Junaluska (N.C.) Assembly, 1984-89; music mgr. Up With People, Denver, 1989-91, show mgr., 1991-92; stage technician Disney-MGM Studios, Lake Buena Vista, Fla., 1992-93; prodn. coord. Walt Disney Entertainment, Lake Buena Vista, 1993-94, prodn. mgr., 1994—, writer, music prodr., 1995—; show prodn. cons. Up With People, Denver, 1996. Mem. Order of Omega, Pi Kappa Lambda, Omicron Delta Kappa, Lambda Chi Alpha (grad. scholar 1987, High Alpha 1986-87, sr. leader 1987). Methodist. Avocations: travel, computers, films, reading.

DYER, MARSHA JEAN, critical care nurse; b. Brockton, Mass., Mar. 13, 1964; d. Kenneth J. and Janice M. (Maver) D. BSN, Fitchburg (Mass.) State Coll., 1986. CCRN; cert. ACLS instr. Staff and charge nurse ICU, instr. ICU Goddard Meml. Hosp., Stoughton, Mass., 1986—; ICU nurse Good Samaritan Med. Ctr., Stoughton, 1986—. Mem. AACCN. Home: 63 Lincoln St North Easton MA 02356-1733

DYER, MICHAEL GEORGE, educator in computer science; b. Washington, Nov. 30, 1948. BA, Dartmouth Coll., 1970; MS, U. Kans., 1978; PhD, Yale U., 1982. Sr. rsch. scientist Cognitive Systems, Inc., New Haven, Conn., 1983; asst. prof. computer sci. UCLA, 1983-86, assoc. prof., 1986-92, prof., 1992—. Author: In-Depth Understanding, 1993; mem. editl. bd. Internat. Jour. Expert Sys., 1987—, Knowledge-Based Sys., 1988—, Connection Sci., 1989—, Applied Intelligence, 1991—, Artificial Life, 1993—. Office: UCLA Computer Sci Dept 4532 Boelter Hall Los Angeles CA 90095

DYER, PAUL D., municipal official; b. Houston, Nov. 11, 1947. BS, Tex. Tech. U., 1971. Consulting engr. Dallas, 1970-74; dir. of facilities Dallas Ind. Sch. Dist., 1974-82; supt. planning & engring. Park & Recreation Dept. City of Dallas, 1982-86, asst. dir. design & devel. Park & Recreation Dept., 1987-92, interim dir. Dallas Zoo, 1991-92, dir. Park & Recreation Dept., 1992—. Recipient Engring. Acad. award. Mem. Nat. Recreation & Park Assn., Tex. Recreation & Park Soc., Tex. Tech. Acad. Engrs., Urban Recreation & Park Alliance (co-chair 1995-96). Office: Park & Recreation Dept City Hall Rm 6F N 1500 Marilla St Dallas TX 75201-6300*

DYER, PHILIP E., insurance company executive; b. Salem, Oreg., Feb. 10, 1953; s. William Connell Jr. and Clara Belle (Burnside) D.; m. Carolyn J. Pierce, Mar. 11, 1978; children: Pierce, Peyton. BS, Oreg. State U., 1976; grad., U.S. Army Command and Gen. Coll., Leavenworth, Kans., 1983. Cert. ins. counselor. Commd. 2d lt. U.S. Army Nat. Guard, 1971, advanced through grades to maj.; account exec. Marsh and McLennan, Inc., Seattle, 1977-80, 85-86; comml. mktg. rep. Indsl. Indemnity, Seattle, 1980-81; regional v.p. Ins. Corp. Am., Houston, 1981-85; pres. Doctor's Agy. Wash., Inc., Seattle, 1987-94; sr. v.p. Wash. Casualty Co., 1994-96; v.p. The Doctors' Co., Seattle, 1996—; cons. Group Health Coop., Seattle, 1987. Pres. Eagle Ridge Homeowners Assn.; rep. 5th Legis. Dist. Wash. Ho. of Reps., Issaquah, chmn. health care com., 1994—; tech. advisor Wash. State Health Care Commn., Olympia, 1990-92; ranking minority mem. Ho. Reps. Health Care Com.; asst. ranking mem. Fin. Inst. Ins. Commn.; mem. legis. com. Liability Reform Coalition, Seattle, 1988—; precinct officer Rep. Com., Issaquah, 1991—; cons., mem. ins. com. Issaquah Sch. Dist., 1992; mem. youth div. staff Re-elect Pres. Ford Commn., Washington; staff researcher Oreg. Legislature; chmn. Health Care Com. Wash. Ho. of Reps.; mem. Wash. Health Policy Bd. Mem. Wash. Health Care Risk Mgmt. Soc. (com. chair 1989-90), Soc. Am. Mil. Engrs., Aircraft Owners and Pilot Assn., Profl. Liability Underwriting Soc. (bd. dirs. 1988-89), Issquah Valley Kiwanis. Republican. Episcopalian. Avocations: snow and water skiing, reading, private piloting. Home: 4127 205th Ave SE Issaquah WA 98029-9600 Office: Doctor's Company 1420 5th Ave Ste 2925 Seattle WA 98101-2320

DYER, RITA FRANCES, medical/surgical and oncology nurse; b. Meridian, Miss., Sept. 14, 1947; d. Jesse E. and Frances A. (Nelson) Hahn; m. Lloyd D. Dyer, Mar. 9, 1985; children: Michelle Lee Belcourt, Michael Thomas Belcourt. Grad., Phillips Bus. Coll., Gulfport, Miss., 1966; lic. practical nurse, No. Mont. Coll., 1976; AS in Nursing, Miss. Gulf Coast Jr. Coll., Gulfport, 1985; student, St. Joseph's Coll., Windham, Maine; BSN, Elmira Coll., 1994. Cert. audiology tester. Staff nurse Gulfport Meml. Hosp., 1985-86; head nurse Coventry (R.I.) Health Ctr., 1987; charge nurse Biloxi (Miss.) Regional Med. Ctr., 1985-86; staff and charge nurse South County Hosp., Wakefield, R.I., 1987-90; staff nurse VA Hosp., Bath, N.Y., 1990—. With USAR Corp. Mem. ANA, N.Y. Nurses Assn.

DYER, SUZETTE MORALES, higher education administrator; b. New Orleans, Oct. 19, 1952; d. A.J. and Josie C. Morales; m. Richard S. Bacon (div. Apr. 1984); children: Scott P. Bacon, Sean R. Bacon. BA, U. Southwestern La., 1973; M Human Rels., U. Okla., 1987. Svc. coord. Ind. Living Project, Norman, Okla., 1971-74; dir. older workers program Okla. State AFL-CIO, Oklahoma City, 1984-87; sr. mediator Client Assistance Program, Oklahoma City, 1987-90; jud. coord., dir. disability svcs. U. Okla., Norman, 1991—; social worker Dept. Human Svcs., Ft. Dodge, Iowa, 1979-81. Vice chair Norman Pub. Transp. Com., 1999; bd. dirs. Total Ind. Living Today, 1984-99. Mem. Okla. Assn. on Higher Edn. and Disability (pres. 1998-99). Democrat. Avocations: pets, camping, travel, writing. E-mail: sdyer@ou.edu. Office: U Okla 900 Asp Ave 370 Norman OK 73019

DYER, V. JEFFREY, principal; b. Richardson, Tex., July 30, 1967; s. Van E. and Deborah L. Dyer; m. Robin Jane, Dec. 16, 1989; 1 child, Drew Jeffrey. BS in Elem. Edn., Henderson St. U., 1989, MS in Elem. Adminstrn., 1995. Elem. tchr. Port Arthur (Tex.) Sch. Dist., 1989-91; mid. sch. tchr. Bryant (Ark.) Sch. Dist., 1991-92, elem. tchr., 1992-96; elem. asst. prin. Alma (Ark.) Sch. Dist., 1996—. Area dir. Ark. Spl. Olympics. Mem. NAESP, ASCD, Ark. Assn. Edn. Adminstrs., Henderson St. Alumni Bd., Saline Co. Henderson Alumni (charter, pres. 1993-95), Sigam Phi Epsilon. Avocations: golf, softball, reading, movies. E-mail: jdyer@alma-aps.wsc.k12.ar.us. Home: 3202 Green Way Alma AR 72921 Office: Alma Sch Dist 1600 Hwy 64 E Alma AR 72921-2299

DYER, WAYNE WALTER, psychologist, author, radio and television personality; b. Detroit, May 10, 1940; s. Melvin L. and Hazel I. (Vollick) D.; m. Marcelene Louise Dyer; children: Tracy, Stephanie, Skye, Sommer, Serena, Sands Jay, Saje Eykis. BS, Wayne State U., 1965, MS in Counseling and Ednl. Psychology, 1966, EdD in Counseling and Psychology, 1970. Tchr. and counselor Pershing H.S., Detroit, 1965-67; instr. counselor edn. Wayne State U., Detroit, summer, 1970, 71, 72, 73; dir. guidance and counseling Mercy H.S., Farmington, Mich., 1967-71; staff cons. and trainer guidance and sch. psychol. personnel Half Hollow Sch. Dist., Huntington, N.Y., 1973-75; staff cons. Drug Info. and Svc. Ctr., N.Y., 1972-74, Herman Kiefer Hosp., Detroit, 1974-75; mem. tchg. faculty North Shore U. Hosp. divsn. Cornell U. Med. Coll., Manhasset, N.Y., 1974-75; pvt. practice counseling and psychotherapy Huntington, N.Y., 1973—; asst. prof. counselor edn. St. John's U., Jamaica, N.Y., 1971-74; assoc. prof., 1974-77. Over 4000 appearances on TV and radio shows and programs including Phil Donohue Show, Tonight Show, Dinah Shore Show, Merv Griffin Show, Mike Douglas Show, Good Morning America, Canada A.M., Oprah Winfrey Show, numerous other talk shows in every state; radio host for: Kathryn Crosby Show, San Francisco, At Your Service program, Sta. KMOX, St. Louis.; Author: (with John Vriend) Counseling Effectively in Groups, 1973, Counseling Techniques That Work, 1974, 2d edit., 1977, Group Counseling for Personal Mastery, 1980, Your Erroneous Zones, 1976 (Literary Guild selection, Psychology Today Book Club selection, also 4 others), Pulling Your Own Strings, 1977, 1978 (Lit. Guild main selection, also 6 others), The Sky's the Limit, 1980 (Lit. Guild selection); novel Gifts from Eykis, 1983, What Do You Really Want for Your Children?, 1985, Happy Holidays, 1986, You'll See It When You Believe It, 1988, Real Magic, 1992, Everyday Wisdom, 1994, Your Sacred Self, 1995, Staying on the Path, 1995, A Promise is a Promise, 1996, Manifest Your Destiny, 1997, Wisdom of the Ages; cassette tape series The Wit & Wisdom of Dr. Wayne W. Dyer, 1977, How To Be a No-Limit Person, 1981, Secrets of the Universe, Choosing Your Own Greatness, What Do You Really Want for Your Children?, Transformation: You'll See It When You Believe It, The Awakened Life, others; contbr. chpts. on counseling to books on psychology, numerous articles on psychology to popular mags. and articles on counseling to profl. jours.; producer tape recordings on counseling techniques; audio cassette program Secrets of the Universe. Served with USN, 1958-62. Named Disting. Alumni of Yr., Wayne State U., 1980; recipient Golden Gavel award Internat. Toastmasters, 1987.

DYER, WILLIAM EARL, JR., retired newspaper editor; b. Kearney, Nebr., May 15, 1927; s. William Earl and Hazel Maud (Hosfelt) D.; m. Betty M. Meisinger, June 26, 1967; children—Lee Michael, Scott William. B.A., U. Nebr., 1949. Reporter, Nebraska City Daily News Press., 1943-44; reporter, copy editor The Lincoln Star (Nebr.), 1948-50, city editor, 1951-60, exec. editor, 1960-92; pres. Nebr. AP Editors, 1964; author: Headline: Starkweather, 1993. Pres., Lincoln Unitarian Ch., 1962-63; state chmn. Nebr. We Shake Hands Indian Project, 1958-60; mem. Nebr. Adv. Com. on Indian Law Enforcement, 1960-62; mem. State Adv. Com. to Welfare Dept., 1970-73, 80-84. Served with AUS, 1945-46. Named Hon. Mem., Omaha Indian Tribe. Mem. Phi Beta Kappa, Sigma Delta Chi. Democrat. Club: Open Forum. Home: 1115 Fall Creek Rd Lincoln NE 68510-4947 Office: Jour-Star Printing Co PO Box 81609 926 P St Lincoln NE 68508-3615

DYER-RAFFLER, JOY ANN, special education diagnostician, educator; b. Stiltner, W.Va., Aug. 10, 1935; d. Ralph William and Hazel (Terry) Dyer; m. John William Raffler, Sr., Jan. 1, 1993; 1 child from a previous marriage, Keith Brian DeArmond. BA, U. N.C., 1969; MEd in Secondary Edn., U. Ariz., 1974, MEd in Spl. Edn., 1976. Cert. spl. edn.-learning disabilities, art edn., spl. edn.-emotionally handicapped. Art educator Tucson Unified Sch. Dist., Tucson, 1970-75, spl. edn. educator, 1975-89, spl. edn. diagnostician, 1989—. Den mother Cub Scouts Am., Raleigh, N.C., 1968-69. Recipient grant Tucson Unified Sch. Dist., 1977. Mem. NEA, CEC, Internat. Reading Assn., Tchrs. Applying Whole Lang., Tucson Edn. Assn., Learning Disabilities Assn., Tucson Tchrs. Applying Whole Lang., Coun. Ednl. Diagnostic Svcs. Avocations: oil painting, snow skiing, bird watching, weight lifting, jogging. Home: 4081 N Kolb Rd Tucson AZ 85750-6127 Office: AJO Svc Ctr 2201 W 44th St Tucson AZ 85713-4575

DYESS, BOBBY DALE, lawyer; b. Waxahachie, Tex., Jan. 27, 1935; s. Robert Olin and Rubie Lee (Odom) D.; m. Janet Lee Hassell, Jan. 30, 1960 (dec. 1973); children: Robert Dale, Jonathan David, Julianna Whitfield; mem. Sharon Erwin Saylor, June 6, 1974. BA, U. N. Tex., Denton, 1956; JD, So. Methodist U., 1959. Bar: Tex. 1959. Since practiced in Dallas; partner firm Elliott, Churchill, Hansen, Dyess & Maxfield, 1965-82, DeHay & Blanchard, 1983-92, Payne & Blanchard, Dallas, 1992—; chmn. bd. Rainbow Sound, Inc., 1975-85. Editor: Bests, Life and Health Ins. Edit., 1973-85. Mem. bd. mgmt. East Dallas YMCA, 1970, 76, campaign chmn., 1976, chmn. bd. mgmt., 1977-79; chief Indian Guides, 1971; chmn. Cub Scout pack com. Boy Scouts Am., 1970; active Dallas Hist. Soc.; mem./sponsor Dallas Mus. Art, Mus. Natural History, Dallas Symphony Orch. Mem. ABA, Tex. Bar Assn., Dallas Bar Assn., Tex. Bar Found., Dallas Bar Found. (charter), Am. Arbitration Assn. (mem. comml. panel 1978—), Am. Counsel Assn. (membership chmn. 1976, bd. dirs. 1977-78, pres. 1979-80, sec.-treas. 1984-87), Hist. Preservation League, Scribes (bd. dirs. 1976), Am. Soc. Legal Writers (pres. 1975), Assn. Atty.-Mediators, Coll. State Bar Tex. (dir. 1996—, chmn. 1999—). Presbyterian. Home: 1600 Little Creek Dr Waxahachie TX 75165-1944 Office: Payne and Blanchard 500 N Tower Plz of America Dallas TX 75201

DYESS, JOSEPH DWIGHT, commercial banker; b. Hattiesburg, Miss., Dec. 18, 1949; s. Lonnie Jr. and Modena (Richardson) D.; m. Kathy Marlene Lee, Feb. 3, 1973; 1 child, Walker Lee. BSBA, Miss. State U., 1972, MS in Econs., 1980; postgrad., La. State U., 1979, U. Okla., 1980. V.p. Merchants and Farmers Bank, Starkville, Miss., 1975-81; fin. cons. Merrill Lynch, Jackson, Miss., 1982-87; cmty. bank pres. Bank of Miss., Starkville, 1987-91; pres. Hattiesburg divsn. Bancorp South, Hattiesburg, Miss., 1991—; chmn. Area Devel. Partnership, Hattiesburg, 1996. Dir. Miss. Econ. Coun., Jackson, 1989-90, Miss. Power Found., Hattiesburg, 1991-94, Hattiesburg Area Edn. Found., S.E. Miss. Cert. Investment Corp.; dir., vice chmn. Forrest County Indsl. Park Commn., 1994—, Pearl River Coll. Workforce Adv. Coun. U. Southern Miss. Found., 1992-95; adv. The U. of So. Miss. Coll. Bus., Hattiesburg, 1992—; chmn. Tourism Commn., Hattiesburg, 1992—; bd. dirs. Salvation Army Southern Miss.; asst. campaign chair United Way S.E. Miss. Named Exec. of Yr. Sales and Mktg. Internat., 1997. Mem. Rotary Internat., Hattiesburg Country Club, Hattiesburg Racquet Club. Episcopalian. E-mail: dwight.dyess@BXS.com. Fax: 601-545-5159. Office: Bank of Miss 100 Hardy St Hattiesburg MS 39401-3819

DYK, TIMOTHY BELCHER, lawyer, educator; b. Boston, Feb. 14, 1937; s. Walter and Ruth (Belcher) D.; m. Inga Shirer, June 18, 1960 (div. 1970); children: Deirdre, Caitlin; m. Sally Katzen, Oct. 31, 1981; 1 child, Abraham Benjamin. AB, Harvard U., 1958, LLB magna cum laude, 1961. Bar: D.C., N.Y. Law clk. to Justices Reed and Burton U.S. Supreme Ct., Washington, 1961-62; law clk. to Chief Justice Earl Warren U.S. Supreme Ct., 1962-63; spl. asst. to asst. atty. gen. U.S. Dept. Justice, Washington, 1963-64; assoc. Wilmer Cutler & Pickering, Washington, 1964-69; ptnr. Wilmer Cutler & Pickering, 1969-90, Jones, Day, Reavis and Pogue, Washington, 1990—; adj. prof. Georgetown U. Law Ctr., Washington, 1983, 86, 89, 91, U. Va. Law Sch., Charlottesville, 1984-85, 87-88, Yale U. Law Sch., 1986-87, 89. Mem. Harvard Law Rev., 1959-61; contbr. articles to profl. jours. Bd. dirs. Farmworker Litigation Support Fund. Democrat. Office: Jones Day Reavis & Pogue 51 Louisiana Ave NW Washington DC 20001-2088

DYKE, CHARLES WILLIAM, retired army officer; b. Covington, Ga., July 28, 1935; s. John William and Chessie Belle (Burke) D.; m. Hedwig Friederike Adam, Dec. 1958 (div. 1979); children: Michael Alexander, Eva Joyce, Charles Martin, Robert William; m. Nancy Jeanne Bearg, June 22, 1980; children—Sarah Claire, Rachel Anne. B.A. in History, U. So. Miss., 1963; M.Mil. Arts and Sci., U.S. Army Command and Gen. Staff Coll., 1967; M.A. in Internat. Relations, George Washington U., 1968; postgrad., U.S. Army War Coll., 1970-71; postgrad. in polit. sci., Shippenburg State Coll., 1970-71. Served as enlisted man U.S. Army, 1954-55, commd. 2d lt., 1955, advanced through grades to lt. gen., 1985; exec. officer 1st Brigade, 101st Airborne Div. U.S. Army, Vietnam, 1968, comdr. 2d Bn., 327th Inf., 1968-69, G1, later G3, 101st Airborne Div., 1969-70; exec. asst. Ops. Directorate J3 Orgn. Joint Chiefs of Staff, Washington, 1971-72; asst. sec. of gen. staff Office Chief of Staff, U.S. Army, Washington, 1972-73; mil. asst., later exec. to sec. of army The Pentagon, Washington, 1973-75; comdr. 1st Brigade, 101st Airborne Div. U.S. Army, Ft. Campbell, Ky., 1975-76; asst. div. comdr. 3d Inf. Div. U.S. Army, W. Ger., 1976; exec. to supreme allied comdr. Europe, Belgium, 1977-78; dir. internat. standardization for NATO, Hdqs. Dept Army, Washington, 1978-79; vice dir. J3, later vice dir. joint staff Orgn. Joint Chiefs of Staff, The Pentagon, Washington, 1979-82; dep. chief staff for ops. U.S. Army, Europe, 1982-83; comdg. gen. 8th Inf. Div (Mechanized) U.S. Army, 1983-85; comdr. U.S. Army Japan/IX Corps, 1985-88, ret., 1988; exec. advisor Aerospace divsn. Mitsubishi Corp., Tokyo, 1988—; pres., CEO Internat. Tech. and Trade Assocs. Inc., Washington, 1989—. Decorated DSM with oak leaf cluster, Silver Star with oak leaf cluster, Def. Superior Service medal, Legion of Merit with 3 oak leaf clusters, Soldiers medal, Bronze Star with V device and 2 oak leaf clusters, Joint Service Commendation medal, Army Commendation medal with 4 oak leaf clusters, Air medal (19), Purple Heart, U.S. Presdl. Unit citation, Joint Chiefs of Staff and Army Gen. Staff indentification badges, others, also various fgn. decorations including Japanese Order of Rising Sun (2d class) with gold and silver stars. Mem. Assn. U.S. Army, 101st Airborn Div. Assn., Army Aviation Assn., Nat. Def. Indsl. Assn., USAF Assn., Armed Forces Comm. and Electronics Assn., Pen and Sword Assn., Nat. Beta Club, Pi Gamma Mu, Phi Alpha Theta. Office: Internat Tech and Trade Assocs Inc 1330 Connecticut Ave NW Ste 210 Washington DC 20036-1726

DYKE, WILLIAM DANIEL, circuit court judge; b. Princeton, Ill., Apr. 25, 1930; s. Alfred Daniel and Vinnie Pauline (Thompson) D.; children: Wade, Sarah, Kathryn. BA, DePauw U., 1952; LLB, U. Wis., 1960. Bar: Wis. 1960. Radio, TV personality WISC Radio and TV, Madison, Wis., 1956-61; atty. Mistele & Smith, Jefferson, Wis., 1960-63; asst. to lt. gov. State of Wis., Madison, 1963-65; pvt. practice Madison, 1963-69, 73-78; mayor City of Madison, 1969-73; atty. Johnson & Kranz, Darlington, Wis., 1978-80; pvt. practice Mineral Point, Wis., 1980-96; cir. ct. judge State of Wis., Dodgeville, 1997; cons. U.S. Dept. of Transp., Sec. of State, HUD, Washington, 1970-74. Author, editor books; artist-illustrator paintings, mags.; recording artist audio/video tapes. Candidate for gov. State of Wis., Madison, 1974. With U.S. Army, 1952-55. Named Man of Yr. Res. Officer's Assn. Wis. chpt. 1971. Mem. State Bar of Wis. (bd. govs. 1993-97), Wis. Law Found. (treas. 1992-95), Trial Judges Assn. Avocations: artist, educator, illustrator, recording artist. Office: Iowa County Courthouse 222 N Iowa St Dodgeville WI 53533-1557

DYKEMAN, ALICE MARIE, public relations executive; b. Fremont, Nebr., May 18; d. Cecil Victor and Dorothy Lillian (Sillik) Jansen; divorced; children: David Clair, Cinda Cecille Dykeman Nordgren. Student, Nebr. Wesleyan U., 1949-50, So. Meth. U., 1960-70. Women's editor, feature writer Fremont (Nebr.) Guide and Tribune and Biloxi (Miss.) Daily Herald, 1950-55; adminstrv. asst. to v.p. sales promotion A. Harris & Co., Dallas, 1957-60; account exec. Contact Corp., Dallas, 1960-61; pub. relations dir. Meth. Hosp., Dallas, 1961-72; regional pub. info. officer Small Bus. Adminstrn., Dallas, 1972-74; owner Dykeman Assocs. Inc., Dallas, 1974—; adj. prof. U. Dallas Grad. Sch. Mgmt., Irving, Tex. 1972-78; guest lectr. numerous Univs., and seminars; mem. pub. relations com. Dallas/Ft. Worth Fed. Exec. Bd., 1973, mem. minority bus. oportunity com., 1974; mem. Gov.'s Council on

Small Bus., Tex., 1980-81, 500, Inc., 1982-90; chmn. export council pub. affairs task force U.S. Dept. Commerce, 1980-83. Contbr. articles to bus., health care and pub. rels. jours. Mem. fgn. visitors com. Dallas Council on World Affairs, 1962—, North Tex. Commn., Dallas Pub. Health Bd., 1972-74, Dallas Urban Rehab. Standards Bd., 1981-83, Econ. Devel. Adv. Bd., City of Dallas, 1983-86; pres. Concerned Citizens for Cedar Springs, 1982—; bd. dirs. Oak Lawn Forum, 1983-92; mem. exec. com. Oak Lawn Com., 1983-95. Recipient Matrix award Women in Communications, Dallas, 1968, 88. Fellow Pub. Rels. Soc. Am. (accredited, chmn. S.W. dist. 1971-72, bd. dirs. North Tex. chpt. 1966-72, pres. 1969, assembly del. 1970-73, 91); mem. Internat. Trade Assn. Dallas-Ft. Worth, North Dallas Fr. Forum (pres. 1991), Nat. Assn. Women Bus. Owners, S.W. Venture Forum, North Dallas C. of C. (bd. dirs. 1980-82, chmn. networking skills workshop 1990—), co-founder Breakfast Dallas 1994—, religion comm. coun. 1997—), Press Club Dallas (bd. dirs. 1981-83, headliner 4 times), SMU Mustang Club (bd. dirs. 1996—), also others. United Methodist. Office: Dykeman Assocs Inc 4115 Rawlins St Dallas TX 75219-3661

DYKEMAN, WILMA, writer, lecturer; b. Asheville, N.C., May 20, 1920; d. Willard J. and Bonnie (Cole) Dykeman; m. James R. Stokely Jr., Oct. 12, 1940; children: Dykeman Cole, James R. III. BS inSpeech, Northwestern U., 1940; LittD, Maryville Coll., 1974; LHD, Tenn. Wesleyan Coll., 1978; DHL (hon.), U. N.C., Asheville, 1997. Lectr. English dept. U. Tenn., Knoxville, 1975-95, adj. prof., 1985-95; columnist Knoxville News-Sentinel, 1962—; historian State of Tenn., 1980—; nat. lectr. in field; bd. dirs. First Union Bank. Author 18 books including: The French Broad: A Rivers of America Volume, 1955, The Tall Woman, 1962, Seeds of Southern Change, 1962, The Far Family, 1966, Return the Innocent Earth, 1973; co-author: Neither Black Nor White, 1957, Tennessee: A Bicentennial History, 1976, Tennessee Women: An Infinite Variety, 1993, Explorations, a collection of essays, 1984, others; contbr. articles to nat. mags. and Ency. Brit. Trustee Berea Coll., 1971—, Phelps Stokes Fund, 1981-91, U. N.C.-Asheville, 1985-91; active Friends of Great Smokies Nat. Park. Guggenheim fellow, 1956-57, NEH fellow, 1976-77; recipient Hillman award, 1957, Disting. So. Writers award So. Festival of Books, 1989; N.C. Gold medal for Contbn. to Am. letters, 1985. Mem. PEN, Authors Guild, So. Hist. Assn., Cosmos Club, Phi Beta Kappa, Delta Kappa Gamma. Home: 282 Clifton Heights Rd Newport TN 37821-2402 also: 189 Lynn Cove Rd Asheville NC 28804-1910

DYKERS, CAROL REESE, communications educator; b. Cherry Point, N.C., Nov. 30, 1946; d. Charles Lawrence and Eleanor Zahniser Reese; m. Newton Adnair Collyer, Feb. 4, 1968 (div. Dec. 1979); m. John Reginald Dykers Jr., May 12, 1984. BA, U. North Tex., 1968; MA, U. N.C., 1992, PhD, 1995. Advt. copywriter WBEU AM-FM Radio, Beaufort, S.C., 1968; reporter Longview (Tex.) Daily News, 1968-69; tchr. Beaufort H.S., 1970; reporter Savannah (Ga.) Morning News, 1970-73; hist. planning and pub. rels. dir. Lowcountry Coun. Govts., Yemessee, S.C., 1973; editor Hilton Head news Savannah Morning News, 1973-74; editor Longview (Tex.) Morning Jour., 1974-76; editor, then editl. writer Charlotte (N.C.) Observer, 1976-87; asst. metro editor Greensboro (N.C.) News and Record, 1986-88; asst. prof. comms. Salem Coll., Winston-Salem, N.C., 1995—. Contbr. chpt. to book: Assessing Public Journalism, 1998. Mem. Assn. for Edn. in Journalism and Mass Comm. (rsch. chair civic journalism 1997—), Internat. Comm. Assn. (rsch. paper reader), N.C. Cattlemen's Assn. (past bd. dirs.), Am.-Internat. Charolais Assn., Chatham County Cattlemen's Assn. (past bd. dirs.), Kappa Tau Alpha. Democrat. Episcopalian. Avocations: farming, photography. E-mail:dykers@salem.edu. Home: 1783 Alston Bridge Rd Siler City NC 27344 Office: Salem Coll Main Hall 601 S Church St Winston Salem NC 27108

DYKES, ARCHIE REECE, financial services executive; b. Rogersville, Tenn., Jan. 20, 1931; s. Claude Reed and Rose (Quillen) D.; m. Nancy Jane Haun, May 29, 1953; children: John Reece, Thomas Mack. BS cum laude, East Tenn. State U., 1952, MA, 1956; EdD, U. Tenn., 1959. Prin., Church Hill (Tenn.) High Sch., 1955-58; supt. Greeneville (Tenn.) Schs., 1959-62; prof. edn., dir. U. Tenn. Ctr. for Advanced Grad. Study in Edn., Memphis State U., 1962-66; chancellor U. Tenn. at Martin, 1967-71, at Knoxville, 1971-73; chancellor U. Kans., 1973-80; chmn., pres., chief exec. officer Security Benefit Group of Cos., Topeka, 1980-88; chmn. Capital City Holdings Inc., 1988—; bd. dirs. Whitman Corp., Chgo., Fleming Cos., Inc., Oklahoma City, Hussman Internat., Inc., St. Louis, Midas, Inc., Chgo., The Employment Corp., Nashville; trustee Keene Industries Trust, N.Y.C., Kans. U. Endowment Assn. Author: School Board and Superintendent, 1965, Faculty Participation in Academic Decision Making, 1968. Vice chmn. Commn. on Operation U.S. Senate, 1975-76; mem. Nat. Adv. Coun. Edn. Professions Devel., 1975-76; trustee Truman Libr. Inst., 1973-80, Menninger Found., 1982-88, Nelson Art Gallery, 1973-80, Dole Found., William Allen White Found.; chmn. bd. trustees U. Mid-Am., 1978-79; mem. adv. commn. U.S. Army Command. and Gen. Staff Coll., 1974-79, chmn., 1978-79; mem. consultative bd. regents U. Qatar, 1979-80; mem. bd. regents State of Kans., 1982-86. Ford Found. fellow, 1957-59; Am. Council on Edn. postdoctoral fellow U. Ill., 1966-67; named Outstanding Alumnus, E. Tenn. State U., 1970. Mem. Tenn. Coll. Assn. (pres. 1969-70), Am. Coun. Life Ins. (dir. 1981-86), Nat. Assn. State Univs. and Land Grant Colls. (coun. pres. 1971-80), Newcomen Soc. N.Am., Kans. Assn. Commerce and Industry (dir. 1975-82), Phi Kappa Phi. Home: 506 Belgrave Park Nashville TN 37215-2450

DYKES, JOHN HENRY, JR., retired finance executive; b. Wichita, Kans., July 14, 1934; s. John Henry Sr. and Kathryn (Klotzbach) D.; m. Lucille Beard, May 29, 1958; children: John Henry III, Robert Douglas, Laura Kathryn. BS in Engring. Physics, U. Okla., 1956, BSEE, 1957; MBA with high distinction, Harvard U., 1959. Fin. analyst TRW, Inc., Los Angeles, 1959-62; gen. mgr. TRW, Inc., Mexico City, 1962-65; internat. mgr. TRW, Inc., Chgo., 1965-70; dir. acquisitions Stanray Corp., Chgo., 1970-72, group v.p., 1972-75; pres. SAFT Am., Inc., Valdosta, Ga., 1975-78; v.p., chief fin. officer Engraph Inc., Atlanta, 1978-95; bd. dirs. RPR Enterprises, Inc., Atlanta, Fun Co., Inc., Atlanta; chmn. bd. dirs. Fin. Execs. Rsch. Found. Mem. adv. bd. St. Mary's Hosp., Ogden, 1971-74. Named Exporter of Yr. World Trade Assn., 1972. Mem. Fin. Execs. Inst. (pres. Atlanta chpt. 1990), Ashford Club, Rotary (sec.-treas. 1981-82, 89-90, bd. dirs. 1986, pres. 1991-92). Republican. Episcopalian. Avocation: outdoor sports. Home: 7275 Twin Branch Rd NE Atlanta GA 30328-1745

DYKES, OSBORNE JEFFERSON, III, lawyer; b. L.A., Dec. 3, 1944; s. Osborne J. Jr. and Frances (Fox) D.; m. Ann Dennis, Dec. 29, 1973; children: Barbara Nell, Osborne J. IV. BA, Stanford U., 1966, MA, 1968; JD, U. Tex., 1972. Bar: Tex. 1973, U.S. Supreme Ct. 1977, U.S. Ct. Appeals (5th cir.) 1973, U.S. Ct. Appeals (11th cir.) 1981, U.S. Dist. Ct. (so. dist.) Tex. 1975, U.S. Dist. Ct. (ea. dist.) Tex. 1976, U.S. Dist. Ct. (no. dist.) Tex. 1994. Law clk. to Hon. Homer Thornberry U.S. Ct. Appeals 5th Cir., Austin, Tex., 1972-73; ptnr. Fulbright & Jaworski, Houston, 1973—. Contbr. articles to profl. publs. With U.S. Army, 1969-71. Fellow Am. Bar Found., Tex. Bar Found. (life); mem. ABA (chmn. property ins. law com. 1983-84, tort and ins. practice sect.), Am. Bd. Trial Advs., Tex. Assn. Civil Trial Specialists (pres. 1982-83, bd. dirs. 1984—), Fedn. Ins. and Corp. Counsel. Republican. Episcopalian. Avocations: tennis, bicycling. Home: 5135 Holly Terrace Dr Houston TX 77056-2125 Office: Fulbright & Jaworski 1301 Mckinney St Houston TX 77010-3031

DYKEWICZ, PAUL GREGORY, journalist; b. Flint, Mich., Oct. 31, 1960; s. Richard Alfred and Evelyn Ellen (Ingrody) D. B Gen. Sci., U. Mich., 1982; MA, Mich. State U., 1986. Rschr. Crain Comm., Washington, 1985-86; bus. reporter Balt. Bus. Jour., Bus. Jour. Cos., 1986-89; bus. editor Daily Record, Balt., 1989-92; Washington corr. Jour. Commerce Knight Ridder, Washington, 1992-93; fin. reporter USA Today, N.Y.C., 1994; editor Satellite News Phillips Bus. Info., Potomac, Md., 1994-96, editor Airline Fin. News, asst. mng. editor Aviation Group, 1996-98; sr. analyst Satellite Group, 1998—; spkr. in field. Author: The Secret Tricks of Top Urgent Care Center Operators, 1985. Vol. So Others May Eat, Washington, 1996-97, Our Lady of Mercy, Potomac, 1996-97, Little Flower, Bethesda, Md., 1996-98, Holy Trinity, Washington, 1997, Ritchie Park Elem. Sch., Potomac, 1999. Recipient Cert. of Merit Muscular Dystrophy Assn., 1983, Nat. Editl. award Newsletter Pubs. Assn., 1999, numerous other journalism awards for news stories. Mem. Soc. Satellite Profls. Internat. (chpt. bd. dirs. 1998—), Kappa Tau Alpha. Avocations: running, sports, classical music, travel, volunteering. Office: Phillips Bus Info 1201 Seven Locks Rd Potomac MD 20854-2931

DYKLA, K.H.S. EDWARD GEORGE, retired social services administrator; b. Chgo., Apr. 13, 1933; s. Edward P. and Rose (Jedrzejczyk) D.; m. Loretta Gilski, Aug. 15, 1959; children: Michael, Mark. BA, Benedictine Coll. Tchr. Weber High Sch., Chgo., 1957-74. Chmn. bd. dirs. Polish Mus. Am., Chgo., 1986-98; bd. dirs. St. Joseph's Home, Chgo., 1986-92; trustee Felician Coll., Chgo., 1984-95; adv. bd., bd. govs. St. Mary's Nazareth Hosp., Chgo., 1988; nat. pres. emeritus and amb. Polish Roman Cath. Union Am., Chgo., 1999—; trustee Northeastern Ill. U., 1996—; trustee Pope John Paul II Cultural Ctr., Washington DC, 1997—; adv. bd. Ill. Tollway Commn., 1995—. With U.S. Army, 1953-55. Mem. Polish Am. Congress (treas. 1986-94, v.p. Ill. div. 1974—, nat. dir. 1994-99), Ill. Fraternal Congress (pres. 1984-86). Roman Catholic. Home: 733 Woodbridge Ct LBS Barrington IL 60010-3857

DYKSTRA, CLIFFORD ELLIOT, chemistry educator, researcher; b. Chgo., Oct. 30, 1952; s. Raymond and Vivian (Mishkutz) D.; m. Dana Ruth Stowers, July 29, 1988; children: Connor Thomas, Tracey Lauren. BS in Physics, U. Ill., 1973, BS in Chemistry, 1973; PhD, U. Calif., Berkeley, 1976. Mgmt. trainee Western Electric Co., Chgo., 1972; rsch. asst. U. Calif., Berkeley, 1973-77; asst. prof. chemistry U. Ill., Urbana, 1977-83, assoc. prof. chemistry, 1983-88, prof. chemistry, 1988-90; prof. chemistry Ind. Univ.-Purdue Univ., Indpls., 1990—; assoc. dean of sci., 1992-96; cons. Argonne Nat. Lab., Chgo., 1978-80; mem. editoral bd. Chem. Physics Letters, 1988—, Theoretical Chemistry Accounts, 1997—. Author: Calculation of Structures and Properties of Molecules, 1988, Quantum Chemistry and Molecular Spectroscopy, 1992, Physical Chemistry—A Modern Introduction, 1997; editor: Jour. Molecular Structure Theochem., 1993—. Beckman Rsch. fellow Ctr. for Advanced Study, 1986, Alfred P. Sloan Found. fellow, 1979. Mem. Phi Beta Kappa. Office: Ind Univ Purdue Univ Indpls Dept Chemistry 402 N Blackford St Indianapolis IN 46202-3217

DYKSTRA, DANIEL JAMES, lawyer, educator; b. Fremont, Mich., Feb. 25, 1916; s. John D. and Elizabeth (Grotemat) D.; m. Lily M. Salay, Aug. 1, 1942; children: Daniel James, Ann Marie. BS, Wis. State U., River Falls, 1938; LLB, U. Wis., 1947, SJD, 1950. Bar: Wis. 1948, Utah 1952. Asst. prof. law Drake U., 1948-49; mem. faculty Coll. Law U. Utah, 1949-66, prof. law, 1952-66, dean, 1954-61, acad. v.p., 1961-63; prof. U. Calif., Davis, 1966—, dean Sch. Law, 1971-74; atty. Office of Price Stabilization, 1952; vis. prof. U. Minn., summer 1950, U. Wis., summers 1957, 58, U. Pa., 1963, Stanford U., 1965-66, Tex. U., 1968, U. Hawaii, 1983, 89, 90, 92, 93; Fulbright prof. U. Melbourne, Australia, 1959; Frederick William Reynolds lectr. U. Utah, 1959. Author: (monograph) Right Most Valued by Civilized Man, 1959. With USNR, 1942-45. Recipient Distinguished Alumnus award Wis. State U., River Falls, 1970. Mem. ABA, Utah Bar Assn., Am. Law Inst., Order of Coif. Home: 44670 Country Club Dr El Macero CA 95618-1045 Office: U Calif Sch Law Davis CA 95616

DYKSTRA, DAVID CHARLES, management executive, accountant, consultant, author, educator; b. Des Moines, July 10, 1941; s. Orville Linden and Ermina (Dunn) D.; children: Suzanne, Karin, David S. BSChemE, U. Calif., Berkeley, 1963; MBA, Harvard U., 1966. CPA, Calif. Corp. contr. Recreation Environs., Newport Beach, Calif., 1970-71, Hydro Conduit Corp., Newport Beach, 1971-78; v.p. fin. and adminstrn. Tree-Sweet Products, Santa Ana, Calif., 1978-80; pres., owner Dykstra Cons., Irvine, Calif., 1980-88; pres. Easy Data Corp., 1981-88; pub. Easy Data Computer Comparisons, 1982-87; sr. mgr. Deloitte & Touche, Costa Mesa, Calif., 1988-90; prof. mgmt. info. systems Nat. U., Irvine, 1984-90; pub. Dykstra's Computer Digest, 1984-90; pres., owner Golden West Pers., Long Beach, 1992-93; exec. v.p. Tegris Corp., Bellevue, Wash., 1994-98; pres., owner Dykstra Cons., Mercer Island, Wash., 1998—. Author: Manager's Guide to Business Computer Terms, 1981, Computers for Profit, 1983; contbr. articles to profl. jours. Chmn. 40th Congl. Dist. Tax Reform Immediately, 1977-80; mem. nat. com. Rep. Com.; vice-chmn. Orange County Calif. Rep. Assembly, 1979-80; bd. dir. Corona Del Mar Rep. Assembly, 1980-94, v.p., 1980-87, pres. 1987-89; mem. Mercer Island Presbyn. Ch., 1998—. Mem. AICPA, Am. Mgmt. Assn., Calif. Soc. CPA's, Data Processing Mgmt. Assn., Am. Prodn. and Inventory Control Soc., Ind. Computer Cons. Assn., Internat. Platform Assn., Data Processing Mgmt. Assn., Orange County C. of C., Newport Beach C. of C., Harvard U. Bus. Sch. Assn. Orange County (bd. dir. 1984-90, v.p 1984-86, 87-88, pres. 1986-87, 91-92, chmn. 1993-94), Harvard U. Bus. Sch. Assn. So. Calif. (bd. dirs. 1986-87, 91-92, v.p. 1992-93), Harvard U. Bus. Sch. Assn. Puget Sound, Town Hall, Mercer Island Presbyterian Ch., 1998—, John Wayne Tennis Club, Lido Sailing Club, Columbia Tower Club, Rotary (bd. dirs. 1984-86). Home and Office: 2805 75th Pl SE Apt 44 Mercer Island WA 98040-2746

DYKSTRA, DENNIS DALE, physiatrist; b. Lakewood, Ohio, Feb. 21, 1950; s. Gerald and Grace Maire (Thomas) D.; m. Mary Louise Kerker, May 16, 1992; children: Dorothy, Perry, Caitlin, Patrick. AB in Zoology summa cum laude, Ohio U., 1972; MD, U. Cin., 1976; PhD, U. Minn., 1988. Diplomate Am. Bd. Pediatrics, Am. Bd. Phys. Medicine and Rehab. Intern/resident Cin. Children's Hosp., 1976-81; instr. U. Minn., Mpls., 1981-88, asst. prof., 1988-92, assoc. prof. phys. medicine/rehab./pediatrics/urol. surgery, 1992—, head dept. phys. medicine/rehab., 1992—; assoc. chief staff for rehab. VA Med. Ctr., Mpls., 1994-97. Author: Krusen's Handbook of Phys. Medicine and Rehabilitation, 1991; contbr. articles to profl. jours. Med. advisor Minn. Spasmodic Torticolits Soc., Duluth, Minn., 1991—. Recipient Phys. Med. and Rehab. Investigator award Phys. Med. and Rehab. Rsch. Found., 1984, 85; Spinal Cord Soc. grantee, 1990. Fellow Am. Acad. Phys. Med. and Rehab. (chair edn. com. 1994—), Am. Acad. Pediatrics, Am. Assn. Electrodiagnostic Medicine. Achievements include 2 patents on method of apparatus for mechanical stimulation of nerves, method and device for pharmacological control of spasticity. Avocations: Karate (Black Belt), classical music. Office: Univ of Minn 420 Delaware St SE Box 297 Mayor Bldg Minneapolis MN 55455

DYKSTRA, EDIE M., human resource director; b. Gary, Ind., Nov. 9, 1954; d. Wayne H. and Edith P. (Christoff) D. BA in History, Ind. U., 1976; MPA in Urban, State, Fed. Gov. and Human Resources, Golden Gate U., 1986. Supr. internal acctg. KPMG Peat Marwick, San Francisco, 1980-87; asst. to dir. fin. City of Oakland, Calif., 1987; compensation and benefits analyst The Harper Group, San Francisco, 1987-89; mgr. internal svcs. Watson Wyatt Worldwide (formerly The Wyatt Co.), San Francisco, 1989-92; mgr. human resources The Wyatt Co., San Francisco, 1992-94, dir. human resources, 1994-95; mgr. human resources Graham & James, San Francisco, 1995-98; dir. human resources Lucas Arts Entertainment Co. LLC, 1998—; adj. faculty U. San Francisco Coll. Profl. Studies/Orgnl Behavior Program. Vol. Raphael House Shelter for Homeless Families, San Francisco, 1988—, vol., crisis counselor Woman Inc., 1988—. Mem. ASTD, Soc. for Human Resource Mgmt., Bay Area Personnel Assn. (pres. 1990-91), Bay Area Orgnl. Devel. Network, No. Calif. Human Resource Coun. (bd. dirs.). Democrat. Office: Lucas Arts Entertainment Co LLC PO Box 10307 San Rafael CA 94912-0307

DYKSTRA, PAUL HOPKINS, lawyer; b. Chgo., July 13, 1943; s. Paul C. and Frances Marie (Hopkins) D. Student, Exeter Coll. Oxford U., Eng., 1964; AB, Princeton U., 1965; LLB, Yale U., 1968. Bar: Ill. 1968, D.C. 1977. Assoc. Gardner, Carton & Douglas, Chgo., 1968-74, ptnr., 1975—, ptnr. Washington office, 1977-79, fin. ptnr., 1985-89, chmn., 1989-95. Contbr. articles to profl. jours. Trustee Chgo. Theatre Group, Inc., 1975—, pres., 1983-85, vice chmn., 1988-92, pres., 1992-97; mem. aux. bd. Art Inst. Chgo., 1973-77, 79-88, exec. com., 1976-77, 82-87; chmn. Orange and Black Club of Princeton Club of Chgo., 1987-90; chmn. maj. gifts Princeton U. Class of 1965, 1982-85; mem. cultural affairs adv. bd. City of Chgo., 1990—, Blue Skies for Kids, Chgo. Cmty. Trust, Chgo. Pub. Libr. Bd., 1991-97, chmn. adminstrv. and fin. com., 1996—. Mem. ABA (fed. and regulation of securities com.), Chgo. Bar Assn. (sec. 1976-77), Chgo. Hist. Soc. (mem. Making History awards com. 1994—), Econ. Club of Chgo. (reception com. 1982-85), Legal Club of Chgo., Law Club Chgo., Racquet Club of Chgo. (bd. govs., vice chmn. membership com. 1980-83), Chgo. Club (bd. dirs., sec. 1996—), Shoreacres, Chgo. Commonwealth Club, The Comml. Club of Chgo., Princeton Club of N.Y., Chgo. Coun. Fgn. Rels. (Chgo. com.). Episcopalian. Avocations: travel, golf, bicycling. Office: Gardner Carton & Douglas 321 N Clark St Ste 3300 Chicago IL 60610-4793

DYKSTRA, ROBERT, retired education educator; b. Vesper, Wis., Feb. 26, 1930; s. John and Anna (Holstein) D.; m. Lou Ann Conselman, Oct. 6, 1956; children: S. Kim, Paul, Randall. BS in Elem. Edn., U. Wis., River Falls, 1957; MA in Ednl. Psychology, U. Minn., 1959, PhD in Ednl. Psychology, 1962. Cert. elem. edn. Elem. tchr. Cedar Grove (Wis.) Pub. Sch., 1954-55; asst. prof. U. Minn., Mpls., 1962-64, assoc. prof., 1965-69, prof., 1970-73, chair dept. curriculum and instrn., 1974-85, prof., 1986-93, ret., 1993. Co-author: Teaching Reading, 1974, Language Arts: Teaching and Learning Effective Use of Language, 1988; contbr. articles to profl. jours. With U.S. Army, 1952-54. Recipient Disting. Alumnus award U. Wis./River Falls, 1998; elected to Reading Hall of Fame, 1996; U.S. Office Edn. rsch. grantee, 1963, 65. Mem. Nat. Coun. Tchrs. of English (mem. exec. com. 1969-71), Nat. Conf. on Rsch. in English (pres. 1984-85), Twin City Area Reading Coun. (pres. 1990-91), Internat. Reading Assn. (mem. pub. com. 1975-77), Nat. Reading Conf. (mem. pub. com. 1978-80). Lutheran. Avocations: barbershop quartet singing, reading, golf. Home: 1998 16th St NW Saint Paul MN 55112-5555

DYKSTRA, RONALD JOSEPH, military officer; b. Savannah, Ga., Mar. 17, 1960; s. Joseph Henry and Barbara Eden (Holm) D.; m. Michele Marie Maestaz, Dec. 27, 1984; children: Grant Michael, Nathan Taylor. BS in Engring., U.S. Mil. Acad., 1982. Commd. 2d lt. U.S. Army, 1982, advanced through grades to major, 1988, various positions, 1983-86; asst. ops. officer 2nd brigade, 4th infantry divsn. U.S. Army, Colorado Springs, 1986-88; co. comdr. A co./1-82 cavalry U.S. ARNG, Fallon, Nev., 1988-90; officer HQ STARC, chief mobilization readiness br. U.S. ARNG, 1990-95, bn. exec. officer 422 big bn., 1995-96, bn. comdr., 1996-97; sig bn. IT program mgmt. office GTE, 1997—. Cubmaster pack 100 Pinenut dist. Nev. area coun. Boy Scouts Am., 1992-97; admissions rep. U.S. Mil. Acad., 1991-94; mem. U.S. Acads. Selection Bd., 1991-93; rep. Vucanovich's Def. Adv. Bd., 1992-94. Mem. Nat. Guard Assn. U.S. (life), K.C. Home: 1136 Trailwood Dr Hurst TX 76053-4318 Office: GTE 919 Hidden Ridge Irving TX 76053

DYKSTRA, VERGIL HOMER, retired academic administrator; b. Harrison, S.D., Feb. 1, 1925; s. Broer Doekeles and Nellie (Schippers) D.; m. Shirley Margaret Leslie, June 9, 1949 (div. July 1978); children: Leslie Fran, Lynne Meredith, Craig David, Kevin Scott; m. Wanda Rappaport, Feb. 10, 1980 (div. Apr. 1987). BA summa cum laude, Hope Coll., 1949; MA, U. Wis., 1950, PhD, 1953. Instr. philosophy U. Cin., 1953-54; instr. U. Oreg., 1954-56, asst. prof., 1957-60, assoc. prof., 1960-61; vis. lectr. U. Wis., 1956-57; postdoctoral fellow U. Mich., 1961-62; assoc. dean Harpur Coll., 1962-64; dean adminstrn. SUNY, Binghamton, 1964-65, v.p. adminstrn., 1965-69, prof. philosophy, 1969-73; pres. George Mason U., Fairfax, Va., 1973-77; ednl. cons., 1977-78; adminstrv. v.p. Montgomery Coll., Rockville, Md., 1978-89, ret., 1989. Contbr. articles to profl. jours. With USNR, 1943-46. Home: 5225 Pooks Hill Rd Bethesda MD 20814-2052

DYKSTRA, WILLIAM DWIGHT, business executive, consultant; b. Grand Rapids, Mich., June 15, 1927; s. John Albert and Irene (Stable Kamp) D.; m. Ann McGuiness, Nov. 2, 1957 (dec. 1988); children: William Hugh, Mary Irene. AB, Hope Coll., 1949; MBA, Ind. U., 1951. Asst. mgr. Ply-Curves, Inc., 1950; originator magnesium metal furniture, 1951; pres. Dwight Corp., 1952-56, W.D. Dykstra Group, Grand Rapids, 1956—; pres. Burton L. Norton Co., 1990, Tie Life Care, Inc.; bd. dirs. Sheldon Co., Orchard Machine Co., Equine World, Inc. Author: Management and the 4th Estate, New Profits for Management. George F. Baker Scholar selector; elder Dutch Ref. Ch. Recipient Outstanding Furniture Merit award, 1955, Vehicle Color Design award, 1967, P.I.A. Graphic award, 1971, Am. Advt. Fedn. award, 1971, 73, 76, Disting. Entrepreneur Alumnus award Ind. U., 1983. Mem. Am. Econs. Assn., Am. Inst. Graphic Arts (Packaging award 1965, 67), Acad. Polit. Sci., Am. Mktg. Assn. (Mktg. Man of Yr. 1981), Engring. Soc. of Detroit, Soc. Packaging and Handling Engrs., Rotary, Phi Kappa Psi, Pi Kappa Delta. Republican. Home: 1145 Edison Ave NW Grand Rapids MI 49504-3919 Office: Old Tallmadge Grange Hall 01845 W Leonard St Grand Rapids MI 49544

DYKSTRA LYNCH, MARY ELIZABETH, library and information science educator; b. Philadelphia, Pa., May 21, 1939; arrived in Canada, 1964; d. Edward and Marietta R. (Kuiper) Heerema; m. Michael F. Lynch, Aug. 12, 1995; children from previous marriage: Mark Edward, Jeffrey Garth. BA, Calvin Coll., 1960; MLS, Dalhousie U., Halifax, N.S., 1970; PhD, Sheffield (Eng.) U., 1986. Head cataloguer Dalhousie U. Libr., 1970-74; asst. prof. Sch. Libr. Svc. Dalhousie U., 1974-78, assoc. prof., 1978-82, assoc. prof. Sch. Libr. and Info. Studies, 1983-86, prof., 1987-97, prof. emeritus, 1997—; sr. audiovisual libr. Nat. Film Bd. of Can., Montreal, 1982-83, cons. 1977-83; cons. Coun. Mins. Edn., Toronto, Ont., 1984-85, art history info. program J. Paul Getty Trust, Williamstown, Mass., 1988-94; mem. adv. bd. Sch. Health Records Sci., Halifax Infirmary, 1984-97, Libr. Technician Programme, Kings Regional Vocat. Sch., N.S., 1987-90; mem. Can. Commn. on Cataloguing, 1986-94; mem. working group on stds. for subject access Nat. Archives of Can., 1987-93; mem. Can. Adv. Com. for Internat. Orgn. for Standardization, Tech. Commn., Info. and Documentation, 1991—; mem. nat. info. highway adv. coun. of Can., 1994-95, 96-97; rsch. officer U. Sheffield (Eng.), 1996-97. Author: Access to Film Information, 1977, Precis: A Primer, 1985; editor 2 books, several film catalogues; editl. bd. Film Canadiana, 1982-84, Cataloging and Classification Quar., 1980-86, Expert Sys. for Info. Mgmt., 1990-93, Libr. and Info. Sci. Rsch., 1992-96; series editor, occasional papers Sch. Libr. and Info. Studies Dalhousie U., 1986-94; contbr. articles to profl. jours. Pres. Citadel North Neighbourhood Assn., Halifax, 1988; bd. dirs. CANARIE (Canadian Network for Advancement of Rsch., Industry & Edn.), 1996-98, internat. consultants com. World Info. and Comm. Report, UNESCO, Paris, 1998—. Rsch. grantee Dalhousie U., 1976, 80, 90, 96, Social Scis. and Humanities Rsch. Coun., Ottawa, 1987-90. Mem. Can. Libr. Assn. (rep. Can. com. on cataloguing 1986-94), Can. Assn. for Info. Sci., Am. Soc. for Info. Sci., Nova Knowledge, Can. Classification Rsch. Group, Indexing and Abstracting Soc. Can. (founding exec. mem. 1977-78, regional dir. 1980-82), Internat. Soc. for Knowledge Orgn. Office: Dalhousie Univ, Sch Libr & Info Studies, Halifax, NS Canada B3H 4H8

DYLAN, BOB (ROBERT ALLEN ZIMMERMAN), singer, composer; b. Duluth, Minn., May 24, 1941. Student, U. Minn., 1960; self-taught on guitar, piano, autoharp, harmonica; Mus.D. (hon.), Princeton U., 1970. Performer numerous tours and concerts, 1960—. Albums include Bob Dylan, The Free Wheelin' Bob Dylan, The Times They Are a Changin', Another Side of Bob Dylan, Bringing It All Back Home, Highway 61 Revisited, Blonde on Blonde, John Wesley Harding, Nashville Skyline, Self Portrait, New Morning, Desire, Infidels, Empire Burlesque, Dylan, Planet Waves, (with The Band) Before the Flood, 1986, Hard Rain, Blood on the Tracks, (with The Band) The Basement Tapes, Street Legal, Slow Train Coming, Knocked Out Loaded, 1986, (5 record set) Biograph, 1960—, Down In The Groove, 1988, (with Traveling Wilburys) Traveling Wilburys, 1988, (with Grateful Dead) Dylan and the Dead, 1989, Oh Mercy, 1989, Under The Red Sky, 1990, (with Traveling Wilburys) Vol. 3, 1990 (Grammy award), The Bootleg Series, 1961, 1990, Good as I Been to You, 1992, World Gone Wrong, 1993, Unplugged, 1995, Time Out of Mind (Grammy award 1998); film appearances include Don't Look Back, Renaldo and Clara, Eat the Document, Pat Garrett and Billy the Kid, Concert for Bangla Desh, Hearts of Fire, 1987; composer numerous songs including Blowin' in the Wind, Like a Rolling Stone, Lay, Lady, Lay, Subterranean Homesick Blues, Forever Young, Gotta Serve Somebody, Don't Think Twice, It's Alright, A Hard Rain's A-Gonna Fall, The Times They are A-Changin', Just Like a Woman, I'll Be Your Baby Tonight, I Shall Be Released, Mr. Tambourine Man, Simple Twist of Fate, Paths of Victory, others; author numerous publs. including Tarantula, 1966, 71, Writings and Drawings by Bob Dylan, 1973, The Songs of Bob Dylan from 1966-1975, 1976, Lyrics, 1985, Drawn Blank, 1994; interactive CD-ROM: Highway 61 Revisited, 1995. Inducted into Rock and Roll Hall of Fame, 1988; Grammy nomination (Best Rock Duo or Group Performance, 1994) for "My Back Pages" (with Roger McGuinn, Tom Petty, Neil Young, Eric Clapton, and George Harrison). Devised and popularized folk-rock. Office: Columbia Records 550 Madison Ave New York NY 10022-3211*

DYLEWSKI, GARY R., military officer; b. Erie, Pa., Nov. 22, 1952; m. Lynne Rousey; 2 children: Christopher, Matthew. BA in Biology, Kent State U., 1974; M in Mgmt., Troy State U., 1980; grad., Squadron Officer Sch., 1985, Air Command and Staff Coll., 1993, Air War Coll., 1993. Commd. 2d lt. USAF, 1975, advanced through grades to col., 1993; squadron weapons officer, flight examiner, instr. 425th Tactical Fighter Tng. Squadron, Williams AFB, Ariz., 1980-85; assignments officer, rated force mgr. for dep. chief staff Pers., Hdqs., Tactical Air Command, Langley AFB, Va., 1985-88; Air Force aide to Pres. Reagan The Pentagon, Washington, 1988-89; dir. tng. 21st Tactical Fighter Wing, Elmendorf AFB, Alaska, 1989-90; ops. officer 43d Tactical Fighter Squadron, Elmendorf AFB, 1990-91; comdr. 90th Tactical Fighter Squadron, Elmendorf AFB, 1991-92; joint dir. for ops. Alaskan Air Command, Elmendorf AFB, 1993-95; comdr. 33d Fighter Wing, Eglin AFB, Fla., 1996-97, 1st Fighter Wing, Langley AFB, 1997—. Decorated Def. Superior Svc. medal, Meritorious Svc. medal with 3 oak leaf clusters. Office: 1 FW/CC Ste 200 159 Sweeney Blvd Langley AFB VA 23665-2292

DYM, CLIVE LIONEL, engineering educator; b. Leeds, Eng., July 15, 1942; came to U.S., 1949, naturalized, 1954; s. Isaac and Anna (Hochmann) D.; children: Jordana, Miriam; m. Joan Dym, June 28, 1998. BCE, Cooper Union, 1962; MS, Poly. Inst. Bklyn., 1964; PhD, Stanford U., 1967. Asst. prof. SUNY, Buffalo, 1966-69; assoc. profl. lectr. George Washington U., Washington, 1969; research staff Inst. Def. Analyses, Arlington, Va., 1969-70; assoc. prof. Carnegie-Mellon U., Pitts., 1970-74; vis. assoc. prof. TECHNION, Israel, 1971; sr. scientist Bolt Beranek and Newman, Inc., Cambridge, Mass., 1974-77; prof. U. Mass., Amherst, 1977-91, head dept. civil engring., 1977-85; Fletcher Jones prof. engring. design, dir. Ctr. Design Edn. Harvey Mudd Coll., Claremont, Calif., 1991—; vis. sr. rsch. fellow Inst. Sound and Vibration Rsch., U. Southampton, Eng., 1973; vis. scientist Xerox PARC, 1983-84; vis. prof. civil engring. Stanford U., 1983-84, Carnegie Mellon U., 1990; Eshbach vis. prof. Northwestern U., 1997-98; cons. Bell Aerospace Co., 1967-69, Dravo Corp., 1970-71, Salem Corp., 1972, Gen. Analytics Inc., 1972, ORI, Inc., 1979, BBN Inc., 1979, Avco, 1981-83, 85-86, TASC, 1985-86, D.H. Brown Assocs., 1991, Johnson Controls, 1996; vice chmn. adv. bd. Amerinex Artificial Intelligence, 1986-88. Author: (with I.H. Shames) Solid Mechanics: A Variational Approach, 1973, Introduction to the Theory of Shells, rev. edit. 1990, Stability Theory and Its Applications to Structural Mechanics, 1974, (with E.S. Ivey) Principles of Mathematical Modeling, 1980, (with I.H. Shames) Energy and Finite Element Methods in Structural Mechanics, 1985, (with R.E. Levitt) Knowledge-Based Systems in Engineering, 1990, Engineering Design: A Synthesis of Views, 1994, Structural Modeling and Analysis, 1997, (with P. Little) Engineering Design: A Project-Based Introduction, 1999; editor: (with A. Kalnins) Vibration: Beams, Plates, and Shells, 1977, Applications of Knowledge-Based Systems to Engineering Analysis and Design, 1985, Computing Futures in Engineering Design, 1997, Artificial Intelligence for Engring. Design Analysis and Mfg., 1986-96; contbr. articles and tech. reports to profl. publs. NATO sr. fellow in sci., 1973. Fellow Acoustical Soc. Am., ASME, ASCE (Walter L. Huber research prize 1980); mem. Am. Assn. for Artificial Intelligence, Computer Soc. of IEEE, ASEE (Western Electric Fund award 1983). Jewish. Office: Harvey Mudd Coll Engring Dept 301 E 12th St Claremont CA 91711-5901

DYM, MARTIN, medical educator; b. Montreal, Que., Can., Oct. 19, 1941; came to U.S., 1969; married; 3 children. BSc, Sir George Williams U., Montreal, 1964; MSc, McGill U., Montreal, 1966, PhD, 1969. Postdoc. fellow Harvard Med. Sch., Boston, 1970, instr., 1972-73, asst. prof., 1973-77, assoc. prof., 1977-81; prof., chmn. dept. cell biology Georgetown U. Sch. Medicine, Washington, 1981—; dir. med. gross anatomy, Georgetown U. Sch. Medicine, Washington, 1982-88, 95—; mem. reproductive biology study section NIH, 1988-92, mem. various other study sections, site visitor, grant reviewer; grant reviewer NSF, Med. Rsch. Coun. Can., others; presenter in field; vis. cons. Rsch. Inst. Family Planning, Beijing, 1991. Mem editl. bd. Micron, Anatomical Record, 1978—, Jour. Andrology, 1981-86, Biology of Reproduction, 1990—; manuscript reviewer various scientific jours; contbr. over 200 articles to profl. publs., chpts. to books. Grantee Population Coun., 1973-75, NSF, 1979-80, Office Naval Rsch., 1984-85, Mellon Found., 1982-86, 86-89, 90-93, NIH, 1971-92, 92-95, 92-96, others; fellow Rockefeller Found., 1973. Mem. Endocrine Soc., Am. Soc. Cell Biology, Am. Assn. Anatomists, Soc. Study Reproduction, Am. Soc. Andrology (exec. coun. 1979-83, chmn. publ. com. 1981-85, program. chmn. ann. meeting 1993), Peripatetic Club. Office: Med-Dent 3900 Reservoir Rd NW Rm SW 209 Washington DC 20057*

DYMALLY, MERVYN MALCOLM, retired congressman, international business executive; b. Cedros, Trinidad, W.I., May 12, 1926; s. Hamid A. and Andreid S. (Richardson) D.; m. Alice M. Gueno; children: Mark, Lynn. BA in Edn., Calif. State U., 1954; MA in Govt., Calif. State U., Sacramento, 1970; PhD in Human Behavior, U.S. Internat. U., 1978; JD (hon.), Lincoln U., Sacramento, 1975; LLD (hon., U. W. L.A., 1970, Calif. Coll. Law, L.A., City U., L.A., 1976, Fla. Meml. Coll., 1987, Lincoln U., San Francisco, 1984; HLD (hon.), Shaw U., N.C., 1981; PHD (hon.), Calif. Western. U., 1982. Cert. elem., secondary and exceptional children tchr. Tchr. L.A. City Schs., 1955-61; coord. Calif. Disaster Office, 1961-62; mem. Calif. Assembly, 1962-66, Calif. Senate, 1967-74; lt. gov. Calif., 1975-79; mem. 97th-102nd Congresses from 31st Calif. dist., 1981-92; pres. Dymally Internat. Group Inc., Inglewood, Calif., 1992—; mem. Com. on Fgn. Affairs and its subcoms. on Internat. Ops., chmn. subcom. on Africa, 1989-92; mem. Com. on D.C. and chmn. subcom. on judiciary and edn., 1981-92; chmn. Congl. Task Force on Minority Set Asides, 1987-92; chmn. Senate Majority Caucus, Senate Select Com. on Children and Youth; chmn. Senate coms. on mil. and vets. affairs, social welfare, elections and reapportionment, subcom. on med. edn. and health needs; chmn. joint coms. on legal equality for women, on revision of election code; chmn. assembly com. on indsl. rels.; current mem. Congl. Hispanic Caucus, Congl. Caucus Women's Issues, Congl. Human Rights Caucus, Congl. Black Caucus and chmn. of its task force on Caribbean; chmn. Caribbean Action Lobby, Caribbean Am. Rsch. Inst.; founder Congl. Inst. for Space, Sci. and Tech., chmn. adv. bd.; past chmn. Calif. Commn. Econ. Devel., Commn. of Califs. (U.S., Baja Calif., Calif. Sur, Mex.); past vice chmn., Nat. Conf. Lt. Govs.; former Gov.'s designee U.S. Border States Commn.; past mem. State Lands Commn., others; lectr. Claremont (Calif.) Grad. Sch., Golden Gate U., Sacramento, Pepperdine U., L.A., Pomona (Calif.) Coll., U. Calif., Davis, Irvine, Whittier (Calif.) Coll., Shaw U., Raleigh, N.C.; Disting. prof. Ctrl. State U. Author: The Black Politician-His Struggle for Power, 1971; co-auhtor: (with Dr. Jeffrey Elliot) Fidel Castro: Nothing Can Stop the Course of History, 1986, also articles; former editor:The Black Politician (quar.). Mem. L.A. County Water Appeals bd.; chmn. Grace Home for Waiting Children, Inglewood, 1995—. Recipient numerous awards including Chaconia Gold medal Govt. Trinidad and Tobago, Adam Clayton Powell award Congl. Black Caucus, Dr. Solomon P. Fuller award Black Psychiatrists of Am., others from Golden State Med. Assn., United Tchrs. L.A., Bd. Suprs. L.A., L.A. City Coun., various univs., colls., orgns. Mem. AAUP, NAACP, Am. Acad. Polit. Sci., Am. Polit. Sci. Assn., Am. Acad. Polit. and Social Sci., ACLU, Urban League, Phi Kappa Phi, Kappa Alpha Psi. Office: Dymally Internat Group Inc 222 W Florence Ave Inglewood CA 90301-1310

DYMICKY, MICHAEL, retired chemist; b. Synewidsko Wyzhne, Urkraine, Oct. 1, 1920; came to U.S., 1949; s. Mykola and Eva (Andrushkiw) D.; m. Olga Zhmurko, Jan. 22, 1943; children: Lida Dymicky Pakula, Oksana Dymicky Matla. Degree in chem. tech., Chem. Tech. Polytechnic, Lwiw, 1943; BS, U. Innsbruck, Austria, 1947, Doctorandum, 1949; PhD, Temple U., 1960. Chemist Am. Sugar Refining Co., Phila., 1949-52; rsch. chemist U. Pa. Med. Sch., Phila., 1952-53, Wyeth Inst. Med. Rsch., Radnor, Pa., 1953-56, 59-62; rsch. chemist Agr. Rsch. Svc. USDA, Phila., 1956-59, 66-89; assoc. prof. Kutztown (Pa.) U., 1962-65; gen. sec. Internat. Student Svcs., Innsbruck, 1947-49. Author: Servant of God Metropolitan Andrei Sheptyts'kyi, 1996; contbr. articles to profl. jours.; patentee in amino acid derivatives and anticlostridial agts. Mem. adv. bd. and chmn. pub. rels. com. Menor Jr. Coll. Jenkintown, Pa., 1976-82. Recipient Citation of Merit DAV, 1970, Chem. Abstract Svc., 1971, USDA, 1989; Inventor's award U.S. Dept. Commerce, 1987. Mem. Am. Chem. Soc. (student adviser 1963-65), Shevchenko Sci. Soc. (coun. 1968—). Avocations: swimming, volleyball, making perfumes. Home: 9653 Dungan Rd Philadelphia PA 19115-3221

DYMOND, LEWIS WANDELL, lawyer, mediator, educator; b. Lansing, Mich., June 28, 1920; s. Lewis Wandell and Irene (Parker) D.; m. Betty Louise Blood, Sept. 6, 1942; children: Lewis W., Jean Ann; m. Joann Surrey, Sept. 3, 1966; 1 son, Steven Henry. J.D. cum laude, U. Miami, 1956. Bar: Fla. 1957; cert. ct. mediator, Fla. With Nat. Airlines, Inc., Miami, Fla., 1938-62; mechanic, agt., sta. mgr., flight dispatcher, ops. mgr., pilot, v.p. ops., maintenance and engring. Nat. Airlines, Inc., 1955-62; pres., chief exec. officer, dir. Frontier Airlines, 1962-79; adj. prof. Sch. Bus. U. Miami, Coral Gables, Fla. Mem. U. Miami Alumni Club, Union League, Surf Club, Masons, Shriners, Phi Kappa Phi, Phi Alpha Delta. Home and Office: 6 E Belleview Way Greenwood Village CO 80121-1408

DYNES, ROBERT C., academic administrator; b. London, Ont., Can.. B of Math. & Physics, U. Western Ont.; M of Physics, McMaster U., D of Phys. Rsch. scientist, dept. head, dir. chem. phys. rsch. AT&T Bell Labs., 1968-90; prof. U. Calif., San Diego, 1991-95, sr. vice chancellor, 1995—, Chancellor. Recipient Fritz London award Low Temp. Physics, 1990. Fellow Am. Phys. Soc., Can. Inst. Advanced Rsch.; mem. Nat. Acad. Scis., Am. Acad. Arts & Scis. Office: U Calif 9500 Gilman Dr La Jolla CA 92093-5003*

DYNKIN, EUGENE B., mathematics educator; b. Leningrad, USSR, May 11, 1924; came to U.S., 1977, naturalized, 1983; s. Boris and Rebecca (Sheindlin) D.; m. Irene Pakshver, June 2, 1959; 1 child, Olga. B.A., Moscow U., 1945, Ph.D., 1948, D.Sc., 1951; D Honors Causa, U. Pierre and Marie Curie, Paris, 1997. Asst. prof. Moscow U., 1948-49, assoc. prof., 1949-54, prof., 1954-68; sr. research scholar Central Inst. Math. Econ. Acad. of Sci., Moscow, 1968-76; prof. math. Cornell U., Ithaca, N.Y., 1977—. Author: Theory of Markov Processes, 1960, Mathematical Conversations, 1963, Markov Processes, 1965, mathematical problems, 1969, Markov Processes-Theorems and Problems, 1969, Controlled Markov Processes, 1979, Markov Processes and Related Problems of Analysis, 1982, An Introduction to Branching Measure-Valued Processes, 1994, Biography and Bibliography in the Dynkin Festschrift, Markov Processes and Their Applications, Mark I. Freidlin, Ed, Birkhauser, 1994. Fellow AAAS, Inst. Math. Stats.; mem. Moscow Math. Soc. (hon., prize 1951), Nat. Acad. Scis., Am. Math. Soc. (Leroy P. Steele prize 1993), Bernoulli Soc. Math. Stats. and Probability. Home: 107 Lake St Ithaca NY 14850-3855 Office: Cornell U Dept Math White Hall Ithaca NY 14853

DYREGROV, MICHAEL See BAKER, JOHN STEVENSON

DYRENFURTH, MICHAEL JOHN, vocational technical and industrial technology educator, consultant; b. Schlitz, Fed. Republic Germany, June 16, 1946; came to U.S., 1970; m. Mary Belle Gullekson, June, 1967; children: Walter John, Michelle Lee, Grant Michael. EdB, U. Alta., Can., 1968, MEd, 1970; PhD, Bowling Green (Ohio) State U., 1973. Cert. tchr., Alta. Tchr. indsl. arts pub. schs., Alta., 1967-69; asst. prof., chmn. dept. indsl. edn. Valley City (N.D.) State Coll., 1972-75; assoc. prof. indsl. edn. Montclair (N.J.) State Coll., 1975-78; prof. tech. and industry, practical arts, vocat. tech. edn. U. Mo., Columbia, 1978-98; prof., grad. coord. dept. indsl. edn. and tech. Iowa State U., Ames, 1998—; pres. Applied Expertise Assocs.; dep. chair World Coun. Assns. Tech. Edn. Contbr. articles to profl. jours. Mem. Internat. Tech. Edn. Assn. (Outstanding Young Leader award 1985), Internat. Vocat. Edn. and Tng. Assn., Am. Vocat. Assn. (Svc. award 1983, IAD Profl. Leadership award 1986), Coun. Tech. Tchr. Edn., Nat. Assn. Indsl. and Tech. Tchr. Edn. (pres.), Indsl. Tech. Edn. Assn. Mo., Mo. Vocat. Assn. (Outstanding Svc. award 1985), Phi Delta Kappa, Kappa Delta Phi, Epsilon Pi Tau (Laureate Citation 1996). Office: Iowa State U Dept Indsl Edn and Tech Rm 118 Indsl Edn II Ames IA 50011-3130

DYRSTAD, JOANELL M., former lieutenant governor, consultant; b. St. James, Minn., Oct. 15, 1942; d. Arnold A. and Ruth (Berlin) Sletta; m. Marvin Dyrstad, 1965; children: Troy, Anika. BA, Gustavus Adolphus Coll., St. Peter, Minn., 1964; MA, Hamline U., 1996. Mayor City of Red Wing, Minn., 1985-90; lt. gov. State of Minn., 1991-94; now independent bus. & govt. consultant; ptnr. Corner Drugstore, Red Wing, 1968—; v.p. League Minn. Cities, 1990-91, Minn. Mayors Assn., 1989-90; mem. Nat. Conf. Lt. Gov.'s, 1991-94, chair, 1993-94. Trustee Gustavus Adolphus Coll., 1989-98, U. Minn. Found., 1993—; dir. corp. bd. Fairview Health Sys. Mem. AAUW (Citizen of yr. award 1985), LWV.

DYRUD, AMOS OLIVER, minister, educator; b. Newfolden, Minn., June 6, 1915; s. Petter Andrew and Marie (Hanson) D.; m. Ovidie Marie Evenson, June 15, 1948; children: Peter, Naomi, Rebecca, Samuel. BA, Augsburg Coll., 1949; postgrad. in Christian Theology, Luth. Free Ch. Theol. Sem., 1949; cert., L'Alliance Francaise, Paris, 1950. Ordained to ministry Free Luth. Ch., 1949. Pastor, missionary Luth. Free Ch., and Am. Luth. Ch., Madagascar, 1949-69; instr. Assn. Free Luth. Congregations Schs., Mpls., 1969—, dean theol. sem., 1971-81; chmn. World Missions Com., Assn. Free Luth. Congregations, 1982-88. With USN, 1943. Home: 4509 Jersey Ave N Minneapolis MN 55428-5139

DYRUD, JARL EDVARD, psychiatrist; b. Maddock, N.D., Oct. 20, 1921; s. Jens Bernard and Lena Bertina (Engebretson) D.; m. Rose Hildreth Bullard, Aug. 22, 1952; children: Jarl Edvard, Anne Hildreth, Christine Maria. A.B., Concordia Coll., 1942; M.D., Johns Hopkins U., 1945. Intern Johns Hopkins U., Balt., 1945-46; resident in psychiatry Chestnut Lodge, Rockville, Md., 1949-51; resident, USPHS fellow Spring Grove State Hosp., 1952-53; mem. psychiat. staff Chestnut Lodge, 1951-52, 53-56, dir. research, 1967-68; research asso., prin. investigator Inst. Behavioral Research, 1963-68; asso. prof. psychiatry U. Chgo., 1968-71, prof., 1971-92, prof. emeritus, 1993—; assoc. dean faculty U. Chgo. (div. biol. scis.), 1978-81; bd. dirs. Chestnut Lodge Research Inst. Contbr. articles to profl. jours. Served with USNR, 1946-48. John Nuveen lectr. Div. Sch., U. Chgo., 1978. Fellow Am. Psychiat. Assn. (life); mem. Ill. Psychiat. Soc., Chgo. Psychoanalytic Soc., Am. Psychoanalytic Assn. (life), Internat. Psychoanalytic Assn. (life), Sigma Xi. Republican. Episcopalian. Home: 5728 S Woodlawn Ave Chicago IL 60637-1634 Office: 5841 S Maryland Ave Chicago IL 60637-1463 also: 8 S Michigan Ave Chicago IL 60603-3357

DYSART, BENJAMIN CLAY, III, environmental consultant, conservationist, engineer; b. Columbia, Tenn., Feb. 12, 1940; s. Benjamin Clay and Kathryne Virginia (Thompson) D.; m. Nancy Elizabeth McDonald, Dec. 28, 1991. BE, Vanderbilt U., 1961, MS in San. Engring., 1964; PhD in Civil Engring., Ga. Inst. Tech., 1969. Staff engr. Union Carbide Corp., 1961-62, 64-65; from asst. prof. to prof. Clemson U., 1968-90, McQueen Quattlebaum prof. engring., 1982-83, dir. S.C. Water Resources Rsch. Inst., 1968-75, dir. water resources engring. grad. program, 1972-75, adj. prof., 1990-93; facility devel. mgr. Chem. Waste Mgmt., Inc., Marietta, Ga., 1990-91; regional facility devel. mgr. Chem. Waste Mgmt., Inc., Memphis, 1991; dir. project planning and integration Waste Mgmt., Inc., Washington, 1991-92; pres. Dysart & Assocs., Inc., Atlanta, 1992—; sci. advisor Office Sec. of Army, Washington, 1975-76; mem. EPA Sci. Adv. Bd., from 1983; sr. fellow The Conservation Found., 1985—; mem. adv. coun. Electric Power Rsch. Inst., 1989-95; mem., chief of engrs. environ. adv. bd. U.S. Army Corps Engrs., 1988-92; mem. Glacier Nat. Park Sci. Coun., Nat. Park Svc., 1988-91; mem. S.C. Gov.'s Wetlands Forum, 1989-90; sec. appointee Outer Continental Shelf Adv. Bd. and OCS Sci. Com. Dept. Interior, 1979-82; mem. S.C. Environ. Quality Control Adv. Com., 1980-90, chmn., 1980-81; mem. Sci. Panel to Rev. Interagy. Rsch. on Impact of Oil Pollution NOAA, Dept. Commerce, 1980; mem. Nuclear Energy Ctr. Environ. Task Force Dept. Energy-So. States Energy Bd., 1978-81; mem. Nonpoint Source Pollutant Task Force EPA, 1979-80; mem. civil works adv. com. Office Sec. Army-Young Pres.'s Orgn., 1975-76; mem. S.C. Heritage Adv. Bd., 1974-76; cons. on strategic environ. mgmt., corp. environ. leadership programs and stakeholder involvement matters to industry and govt. agys. Editor: (with Marion Clawson) Managing Public Lands in the Public Interest, 1988, Public Interest in the Use of Private Lands, 1989; contbr. articles on math. modeling in water quality and environ. mgmt. and pub. involvement to profl. jours.; author numerous profl. papers, reports. Trustee Rene Dubos Ctr. for Human Environs., 1985-94, vice chmn., mem. exec. com., 1988-94; bd. visitors Kanuga Episcopal Conf. Ctr., 1988—. Recipient Tribute of Appreciation for Disting. Svc. EPA, 1981, 86, McQueen Quattlebaum Engring. Faculty Achievement award Clemson U., 1982, Order of Palmetto Gov. S.C., 1984; named Hon. Ky. Col., 1976. Mem. ASCE, Trout Unltd. (trustee 1990-94), Nat. Wildlife Fedn. (bd. dirs. 1974-90, v.p. 1978-83, pres., chmn. bd. dirs. 1983-85), Assn. Environ. Engring. Profs. (bd. dirs. 1978-83, pres., chmn. bd. dirs. 1981-82), Water Environ. Fedn. (hon., bd. dirs. Rsch. Found. 1989-91), S.C. Wildlife Fedn. (bd. dirs. 1969—, pres., chmn. bd. dirs. 1973-74, S.C. Wildlife Conservationist Yr.), The Ga. Conservancy (bd. trustees 1994-97), Cosmos Club (Washington), Sigma Xi, Tau Beta Pi, Phi Kappa Phi, Chi Epsilon, Omega Rho, Sigma Nu. Episcopalian. Office: Dysart & Associates Inc 224 Broadland Ct NW Atlanta GA 30342-3601

DYSART, DIANA MARIE, women's health nurse, medical/surgical nurse; b. Kans. City, Mo., July 9, 1957; d. M. Earle and Evelyn I. (Mishler) Zeiler; married; 1 child, Daniel. ASN cum laude, State Fair Community Coll., 1987; BSN cum laude, Southwest Mo. State U., 1989. RN, Mo., Kans. Mm. Phi Theta Kappa, Phi Kappa Phi, Sigma Theta Tau. Home: PO Box 242 Osceola MO 64776-0242

DYSART, JOHN, historic site administrator; b. Asheville, N.C., Aug. 9, 1955. BA, U. N.C., Raleigh, 1977. Site mgr. Ft. Dobbs (N.C.) Hist. Site, 1978-79, Reed Gold Mine State Hist. Site, Stanfield, N.C., 1979—. Mem. Soc. Mining Engrings. Office: Reed Gold Mine State Historic Site 9621 Reed Mine Rd Stanfield NC 28163-9673*

DYSART, RICHARD A., actor; b. Brighton, Mass., Mar. 30, 1929; m. Kathryn Jacobi. BS, Emerson Coll., 1956, MS, 1983, LLD (hon.), 1988; PhD (hon.), U. Maine, 1992. Appeared off Broadway in Our Town, Six Characters in Search of an Author; on Broadway in A Man for All Seasons, The Little Foxes, A Place Without Doors, That Championship Season, Another Part of the Forest; (feature films) Petulia, The Lost Man, The Sporting Club, The Hospital, The Terminal Man, The Day of the Locust, The Hindenberg, Prophecy, Meteor, Being There, An Enemy of the People, The Thing, The Falcon and the Snowman, Mask, Pale Rider, Wall Street, Back to the Future Part III, Hard Rain; (TV movies) The Autobiography of Miss Jane Pittman, It Happened One Christmas, First You Cry, Bogie, The Ordeal of Dr. Mudd, Churchill and the Generals (BBC), Sandburg's Lincoln, People Vs. Jean Harris, Bitter Harvest, Last Day of Patton, Malice in Wonderland, Day One, Truman; (series) L.A. Law, 1986-94 (Supporting Actor TV-Series Emmy award 1992); (PBS spl.) Concealed Enemies; (mini-series) War and Remembrance. Trustee Gallaudet U., Washington, Gould Acad., Maine; founding mem. Am. Conservatory Theatre, San Francisco; active Native Am. Rights Fund. Mem. Am. Judicature Soc. (bd. dirs.), Beverly Hills Bar Assn., Better Hearing Inst.

DYSINGER, PAUL WILLIAM, physician, educator, health consultant; b. Burns, Tenn., May 24, 1927; s. Paul Clair and Mary Edith (Martin) D.; m. Yvonne Minchin, May 11, 1958; children: Edwin, Wayne, John, Janelle. B.A., So. Missionary Coll., 1951; M.D., Coll. Med. Evangelists, 1955; M.P.H., Harvard, 1962. Diplomate Nat. Bd. Med. Examiners, Am. Bd. Preventive Medicine. Intern Washington, 1955-56; sr. asst. surgeon USPHS; with Blackfeet Indians in Mont., Navajos of Ariz., 1956-58; physician, med. adviser Am. embassy, PhnomPenh, Cambodia, 1958-60; rsch. assoc. dept. preventive medicine Loma Linda (Calif.) U. (formerly Coll. Med. Evangelists), 1960-62, dir. field sta. Western Tanganyika, 1962-64, adminstrv. asst. div. pub. health, 1964-67, asst. to dean, chmn. dept. tropical health Sch. Pub. Health, 1967-69, asst. dean for acad. affairs and internat. health Sch. Pub. Health, 1969-71, assoc. dean for acad. affairs, 1971-79, dir. preventive med. residency Sch. of Medicine, 1983-88; pres. Devel. Svc. Internat., Williamsport, Tenn., Tenn., 1992—; med. cons. dept. Vocat. Rehab., Riverside, Calif., 1964-88; mother and child health cons. Ministry of Health, Tanzania, 1978-80; med. dir. Village Health Program, Punjab, Pakistan, 1980-81, tchr., cons., S.Am. and Caribbean, 1981-83; chief preventive medicine Pettis Meml. VA Hosp., Loma Linda, 1986-88; sr. health advisor Adventist Devel. and Relief Agy., 1988-92; country dir. ADRA, Yemen, 1998-99. Contbr. articles to med. publs. WHO fellow, Somalia, Ethiopia, India, Nepal and Burma, 1969. Fellow Royal Soc. Tropical Medicine and Hygiene, Am. Pub. Health Assn., Am. Coll. Preventive Medicine, Internat. Health Soc. (pres.); mem. AMA, Nat. Council for Internat. Health, Adventist Internat. Med. Soc. (pres. 1983-84), Delta Omega (nat. pres. 1977-78). Adventist. Home and Office: 684 Dry Prong Rd PO Box 210 Williamsport TN 38487-0210

DYSON, ALLAN JUDGE, librarian; b. Lawrence, Mass., Mar. 28, 1942; s. Raymond Magan and Hilda D.; m. Susan Cooper, 1987; 1 child, Brenna Ruth. BA in Govt., Harvard U., 1964; MSLS, Simmons Coll., 1968. Asst. to dir. Columbia U. Librs., N.Y.C., 1968-71; head Moffitt Undergrad. Libr. U. Calif., Berkeley, 1971-79; univ. libr. U. Calif., Santa Cruz, 1979—. Editor Coll. and Rsch. Librs. News, 1973-74; chmn. editl. bd. Choice mag., 1978-80, Am. Librs., 1986-89. CFO Cabrillo (Calif.) Music Festival, 1985-86; chmn. No. Calif. Regional Libr. Bd., 1986-88, 94-98, U. Calif. Librs. Group, 1998—. Lt. U.S. Army, 1964-66. Decorated Army Commendation medal; Coun. on Libr. Resources fellow, 1973-74. Mem. ALA, ACLU, Assn. Coll. and Rsch. Librs., Librs. Assn. U. Calif. (pres. 1976), Sierra Club. Home: 110 Rollingwoods Dr Santa Cruz CA 95060-1030 Office: U Calif McHenry Libr Santa Cruz CA 95064

DYSON, ESTHER, publisher, editor; b. Zurich, Switzerland, July 14, 1951; d. Freeman John and Verena Esther (Huber) D. B.A., Harvard U. Reporter Forbes Mag., N.Y.C., 1974-77, columnist 1987—; v.p. New Court Securities, N.Y.C., 1977-80, Oppenheimer & Co., N.Y.C., 1980-82; pres., owner EDventure Holdings, N.Y.C., 1982—; pub., editor Computer Industry Daily, N.Y.C., 1985; editor, pub. Release 1.0, 1982—; moderator ann. Personal Computer Forum. ; mem. Esquire Register, 1985. Contbr. articles to profl. jours. Mem. Women's Forum N.Y., Assn. Data Processing Service Orgns., Software Pubs. Assn. Avocation: swimming. Office: EDventure Holdings 104 5th Ave Fl 20 New York NY 10011-6987*

DYSON, FREEMAN JOHN, physicist; b. Crowthorne, Eng., Dec. 15, 1923; s. George and Mildred Lucy (Atkey) D.; m. Verena Haefeli-Huber, Aug. 11, 1950 (div. 1958); children—Esther, George; m. Imme Jung, Nov. 21, 1958; children—Dorothy, Emily, Mia, Rebecca. B.A., Cambridge U., 1945. Operations research RAF Bomber Command, 1943-45; fellow Trinity Coll., Cambridge U., Eng., 1946-49; Commonwealth fellow Cornell U., Princeton, 1947-49; prof. physics Cornell U., 1951-53; prof. Inst. Advanced Study, Princeton, 1953-94; prof. emeritus, 1994—. Author: Disturbing the Universe, 1979, Weapons and Hope, 1984, Origins of Life, 1986, Infinite in all Directions, 1988, From Eros to Gaia, 1992, Imagined Worlds, 1997. Recipient Enrico Fermi award U.S. Dept. of Energy, 1995. Fellow Royal Soc. London; mem. NAS, Am. Phys. Soc. Home: 105 Battle Road Cir Princeton NJ 08540-4904

DYSON, MARV, broadcast executive. Pres. Sta. WGCI-AM, Chgo. Office: WGCI Radio 332 S Michigan Ave Ste 600 Chicago IL 60604-4392*

DYSON, ROBERT HARRIS, museum director emeritus, archaeologist, educator; b. York, Pa., Aug. 2, 1927; s. Robert and Harriet Myrtle (Duck) D. *Great grandfather John Dyson (1828-1902) came to Pennsylvania in 1840 from Huddersfield, Yorkshire, England. A methodist minister, he married Mary Elizabeth Wilson (1836-1915) at Elkdale, Chester County, Pennsylvania in 1856. Son Charles Wilson Dyson (1861-1930), later a Rear Admiral in the US Navy, married Lillie Harris (1869-1944), daughter of engineer Robert Lewis Harris (1837-1889), US Navy and had four children. Son Robert Harris Dyson (1903-1991), my father, married Harriet Duck (1907-1981) whose family came to Trunbull County, Ohio in 1872 from Shepton Mallet, Somerset-shire, England.* AB, Harvard U., 1950, PhD, 1966; AM (hon.), U. Pa., 1971. Asst. curator, asst. prof. U. Pa. Mus., Phila., 1955-62, assoc. curator, assoc. prof., 1962-67, curator, prof., 1967-95; curator, prof. emeritus, 1995—; dean faculty arts and scis. U. Pa., Phila., 1979-82; dir. mus. U. Pa. Mus., Phila., 1982-94; dir. emeritus, 1995—; field dir. Iran expdn. U. Pa. Mus., Phila., 1956-77. Hon. trustee Am. Inst. Iranian Studies, 1975-78, 79—, pres., 1968, 87-89; mem. Archaeological Inst. Am., pres., 1979-81; mem. Brit. Sch. Archaeology Iraq, Brit. Inst. of Persian Studies. Decorated chevalier de l'Ordre des Artes et des Lettres (France); Order Houmouyan 4th rank (Iran). Mem. Soc. Fellows Harvard U., Am. Philos. Soc., Deutschen Archäologischen Inst., Inst. Italiano per il Medio ed Estremo Oriente. E-mail: robertd@sas.upenn.edu. Office: U Pa Mus Archaeology & Anthropology 33rd & Spruce Sts Philadelphia PA 19104

DYSON, WILLIAM R., state legislator, educator; b. Waycross, Ga., July 12, 1940; s. Edward James Jr. and Lula Lorene (William) D.; m. Rebecca Johnson, 1964; children: Sonia, Wilfred, Erick, Michael. BA, Morris Coll., 1962; postgrad., NYU, 1963-66, Howard U., 1970; MA, So. Conn. State U., 1976, diploma, 1981. Alderman New Haven, Conn., 1976; mem. Dist. 94 Conn. Ho. of Reps., 1977—, asst. minority leader, mem. edn. com., chmn. appropriations com., mem. gov.'s child care study com.; tchr. Blackshear, Ga., 1967, Douglas, Ga., 1968-69, New Haven, Conn., 1970—. Mem. NEA, Conn. Edn. Assn., New Haven Edn. Assn., Masons. Address: 196 Mansfield St New Haven CT 06511-3539

DYWAN, JEFFERY JOSEPH, judge; b. Hammond, Ind., Apr. 26, 1949; s. Joseph Michael and Florence Marie (Buda) D.; m. Jacque Ann Shulmistras, June 20, 1971; children: Dina, Abigail, Kathryn. BS in Indsl. Engring., Purdue U., 1971; JD, Valparaiso U., 1974. Bar: Ind. 1974, U.S. Dist. Ct. (no. and so. dists.) Ind. 1974, U.S. Ct. Appeals (7th cir.) 1975, Ill. 1984, U.S. Dist. Ct. (no. dist.) Ill. 1986. Assoc. Breclaw & Dywan, Griffith, Ind., 1974-77; sole practice Griffith, 1977-81; dep. prosecuting atty. Lake County, Crown Point, Ind., 1978-80, pub. defender, 1981-83; assoc. Chudom & Meyer, Schererville, Ind., 1981-89; ptnr. O'Drobinak, Dywan & Austgen, Crown Point, 1989-91; judge Lake Superior Ct., Hammond, Ind., 1991-98; chief judge Lake Superior Ct., Hammond, 1998—; instr. Calumet Coll., Hammond, Ind., 1974-76, Ind. Vocat. and Tech. Coll., Gary, Ind., 1978-79. Mem. Ind. State Bar Assn., Lake County Bar Assn., Am. Judicature Soc., KC. Roman Catholic. Office: Lake Superior Ct 232 Russell St Hammond IN 46320-1814

DYYON, FRAZIER MARIO (LEROY FRAZIER), artist; b. Fort Myers, Fla., May 2, 1946; s. Sallie Frazier. Lectr., Westside Community Ctr., N.Y.C., 1971, Case Western Res. U., 1983. Group exhbns. include Cleve. Top Artists, Intown Club, Cleve., 1969, Art Inst. Akron, 1969-70, Mus. Modern Art, N.Y.C., 1970, Whitney Mus. Ann., 1972, Mus. Contemporary Hispanic Art, 1985; one-man show at Case Western Res. U., 1983; represented in permanent collections Mus. Modern Art, N.Y.C., Whitney Mus. Am. Art, N.Y.C., Case Western Res. U., Larry Aldrich Mus., Conn., various pvt. collections. Printmaker's Workshop scholar, 1982. Roman Catholic. Address: 155 W 73rd St New York NY 10023-2921 *Success is a love for your work. This may be too broad. Let me put a fine point on it. How to be successful really? In all your deeds, and in your dreams, try to make God smile. So, throw your vanity out the window and get to work. Be as the common tern, on the move.*

DZEDA, BRUCE MICHAEL, history educator; b. Cleve., June 11, 1948; s. Joseph and Hattie D.; m. Christine Joanne Dedon. BS, Kent State U., 1970, MA, 1979. Tchr. Project Head Start, San Francisco, 1971; tchr. emotionally disturbed High Meadows Sch., Hamden, Conn., 1971-73; tchr. history Beachwood (Ohio) H.S., 1973-77, Monticello Jr. H.S., Cleve., 1977-79, Cleveland Heights (Ohio) H.S., 1979-80, Theodore Roosevelt H.S., Kent, Ohio, 1980—. Co-author: Cleveland Heights High School 1901-1966, 1966. Mem. Kent Edn. Assn., Phi Alpha Theta. Home: 422 Park Ave Kent OH 44240-2228

DZIEDUSZKO, JANUSZ WLADYSLAW, electrical engineer; b. Jaslo, Poland, Aug. 25, 1939; came to U.S., 1966; s. Wladyslaw and Waleria (Pankiewicz) D.; m. Lucyna Janina Ryba, Apr. 15, 1963; 1 child, Philip. MSEE, Acad. Mining and Metallurgy, Cracow, Poland, 1962. Sr. systems engr. Westinghouse Electric, Pitts., 1967-79, 86-90; mgr. hardware devel. BBC Brown Boveri, Pitts., 1979-84; mgr. power line comm. GE, Malvern, Pa., 1984-85; mgr. product devel. ABB Power Transmission & Distbn. Co., Coral Springs, Fla., 1990—. Contbr. papers to profl. confs. Mem. choir St. Andrews Roman Catholic Ch., Coral Springs, 1989—. Mem. IEEE. Democrat. Achievements include 3 patents in digital data communication and data acquisition; significant contribution in data communication and microprocessor product design for electrical power industry. Avocations: classical music, bicycling, chess. Home: 5412 Pine Dr Raleigh NC 27606-9589 Office: ABB Power Transmission & Distbn Co 4300 Coral Ridge Dr Coral Springs FL 33065-7699

DZIEWANOWSKA, ZOFIA ELIZABETH, neuropsychiatrist, pharmaceutical executive, researcher, educator; b. Warsaw, Poland, Nov. 17, 1939; came to U.S., 1972; d. Stanislaw Kazimierz Dziewanowski and Zofia Danuta (Mieczkowska) Rudowska; m. Krzysztof A. Kunert, Sept. 1, 1961 (div. 1971); 1 child, Martin. MD, U. Warsaw, 1963; PhD, Polish Acad. Sci., 1970. MD recert. U.K., 1972, U.S., 1973. Asst. prof. of psychiatry U. Warsaw Med. Sch., 1969-71; sr. house officer St. George's Hosp., U. London, 1971-72; assoc. dir. Merck Sharp & Dohme, Rahway, N.J., 1972-76; vis. assoc. physician Rockefeller U. Hosp., N.Y.C., 1975-76; adj. asst. prof. of psychiatry Cornell U. Med. Ctr., N.Y.C., 1978—; v.p., global med. dir. Hoffmann-La Roche, Inc., Nutley, N.J., 1976-94; sr. v.p. and dir. global med. affairs Genta Inc., San Diego, 1994-97; sr. v.p. drug devel. and regulatory Cypros Pharms. Corp., Carlsbad, Calif., 1997—; lectr. in field U.S. and internat. confs. Contbr. articles to profl. publs. Bd. dirs Royal Soc. Medicine Found.; mem. alumni coun. Cornell U. Med. Ctr. Recipient TWIN Honoree award for Outstanding Women in Mgmt., Ridgewood (N.J.) YWCA, 1984. Mem. AMA, AAAS, Am. Soc. Pharmacology and Therapeutics, Am. Coll. Neuropsychopharmacology, N.Y. Acad. Scis., PhRMA. (vice chmn. steering com. med. sect., chmn. internat. med. affairs com., head biotech. working group), Royal Soc. Medicine (U.K.), Drug Info. Assn. (Woman of Yr. award 1994), Am. Assn. Pharm. Physicians. Roman Catholic. Achievements include original research on the role of the nervous system in the regulation of respiratory functions, research and development and therapeutic uses of many new drugs, pharmaceutical medicine and biotechnology; molecular biology derived as well as conventional products including antisense, interferon efficacy in cancer, virology and AIDS and drugs useful in cardiovascular, immunological, neuropsychiatric, infectious diseases, and others; impact of different cultures on medical practices and clinical research; drug evaluation and development management strategies of pharmaceutical industries; treatments against cardiac and brain ischemia, cytoprotection; speaker in field. Office: Cypros Pharms Corp 2714 Loker Ave W Carlsbad CA 92008-6603

DZIEWONSKI, ADAM MARIAN, earth science educator; b. Lwow, Poland, Nov. 15, 1936; came to U.S., 1965; s. Jan Roman and Jadwiga (Smulikowska) D.; m. Sybil W. McDonald, Nov. 15, 1967. M.S., U. Warsaw, Poland, 1960; D.Tech. Sci., Acad. Mines and Metallurgy, Cracow, Poland, 1965; M.S. (hon.), Harvard U., 1976. Research assoc. S.W. Ctr. Advancement Studies, Richardson, Tex., 1965-69; asst. prof. U. Tex.-Dallas, 1969-72; assoc. prof. geology Harvard U., Cambridge, Mass., 1972-76, prof. geology, 1976-94; Frank B. Baird, Jr. prof. of sci. Harvard U., 1994—; chmn. dept. Harvard U., Cambridge, Mass., 1982-86; Disting. Fairchild scholar Calif. Inst. Tech., Pasadena, 1983-84; chmn. panel movement measurements NAS, 1979-81; chmn. bd. trustees Assn. Rsch. Inst. for Seismology, 1983-84, mem. exec. com., 1984-86. Contbr. articles to profl. jours. NSF grantee, 1969-95; Guggenheim fellow, 1994-95. Fellow Am. Geophys. Union, Am. Acad. Arts and Scis.; mem. NAS, Seismol. Soc. Am., Soc. Exploration Geophysicists. Roman Catholic. Office: Harvard U Dept Earth And Planetary Scis 20 Oxford St Cambridge MA 02138-2902*

DZIORDZ, WALTER MICHAEL, priest; b. New Bedford, Mass., Oct. 20, 1951; s. Michael Raphael and Jane (Szczepanik) D. BA, U. Mass., 1977; MDiv, Washington Theol. Union, Silver Spring, Md., 1984; cert., Salem Inst., 1988; postgrad., Oblate Sch. Theology. Joined Soc. Marians, Roman Cath. Ch.; ordained priest; cert. in reality therapy. Asst. pastor St. Joseph's Cath. Ch., Pittsfield, Mass., 1984-85; pastor Our Lady of Grace Cath. Ch., Greensboro, N.C., 1988—; dir. vocation Marian Fathers-Province of St. Stanislaus Kostka, Stockbridge, Mass., 1986-87; dir. of resident/non resident candidates Marian Fathers Scholasticate, Washington, 1987-88, councilor 1st house, 1987-88; superior local house Marian Community for Our Lady of Grace Parish, Greensboro, 1988—; 3d provincial councilor Congregation of Marians, Stockbridge, Mass., 1989—; del. provincial chpt. Marian Province of St. Stanislaus Kostka, Stockbridge, 1984, 90, elected provincial superior, 1993; chaplain pilgrimage Marian Helpers Ctr., Stockbridge, 1990. Sgt. U.S. Army, 1970-73; N.G., 1973-74. Mem. Washington Theol. Union Alumni Assn., KC (chaplain Greensboro chpt. 1988—, cert. appreciation 1989, 90). Republican. Home: 201 S Chapman St Greensboro NC 27403-1611 Office: Our Lady of Grace Cath Ch 2205 W Market St Greensboro NC 27403-1515

DZIUBA, HENRY FRANK, university official; b. Detroit, Feb. 16, 1918; s. Frank and Anna (Jarzynka) D.; m. Stella Madeline Walush, May 28, 1948; children—Kenneth John, Denise Susan. D.D.S., U. Detroit, 1942. With U. Detroit Sch. Dentistry, 1945—, prof. prosthetics, 1962-91, prof. emeritus, cons., 1991—, coord. clinics, 1962-63, asst. dean, 1962-66, dean, 1967, assoc. dean clin. affairs, 1977-92; ret., 1992. Recipient inter-prof. award Advocates, 1967, Prestigious Tower award, 1976; named Alumnus of Yr. U. Detroit, 1975. Fellow Am. Coll. Dentistry, Internat. Coll. Dentistry ; mem. ADA, Am. Prosthodontic Soc., Detroit Dist. Dental Soc., Mich. Dental Assn., Omicron Kappa Upsilon, Psi Omega. Home: 250 Claremont St Dearborn MI 48124-1368

DZIUK, PHILIP JOHN, animal scientist educator; b. Foley, Minn., Mar. 24, 1926; s. Edmund William and Ellen Catherine (Carlin) D.; m. Patricia Rosemary Weber, Sept. 29, 1951; children: Corinne, Constance, Rita, Catherine, Kenneth, Ronald, Carl. BS, U. Minn., 1950, MS, 1952, PhD, 1955. From rsch. asst. to rsch. assoc. U. Minn., Mpls., 1950-55; from asst. prof. to prof. U. Ill., Urbana, 1955-88, prof. emeritus, 1988—; cons. Upjohn, Abbott, Eli Lilly, Am. Cynamid, Schering, Batelle; reviewer of grants NIH, Bethesda, Md., 1982-86, USDA, Beltsville, Md., 1983-89. Contbr. peer reviewed publs. in sci. and profl. jours. With USN, 1945-46. Fellow Lalor Found., 1958, 61, Pig Industry Devel. Authority, Eng., 1961; recipient Achievement in Rsch. award Am. Fertility Soc., 1970, Sr. Scientist award Alexander von Humboldt Found., 1981. Mem. AAAS, KC, Am. Assn. Anatomist, Am. Soc. Animal Scis. (fellow 1987, Rsch. in Physiology award 1971), Soc. Study of Fertility, Soc. Study of Reproduction (dir., pres. 1987-88, Disting. Svc. award 1989), Lions Internat. (pres., sec. 1992-94), Farm House, Sigma Xi, Gamma Alpha, Phi Kappa Phi, Phi Zeta, Gamma Sigma Delta, Alpha Zeta. Avocations: woodworking, gardening, racquetball. Office: U Ill Dept Animal Scis 1207 W Gregory Dr Urbana IL 61801-3838

DZUIBLINSKI, GERARD ARTHUR, theatre educator, artistic director; b. Detroit, Sept. 23, 1954; s. Arthur Harold and Irene (Rogacki) D.; m. Anne Mansfield, Oct. 12, 1991; 1 child, Illyana. BA in Comms. and Learning Environments, Antioch Coll., 1975; MA in Directing, Antioch U., 1991. Ednl. cons. Project Headline, Detroit, 1976; co-dir. Fantasy Theatre, Detroit, 1977-78; artistic dir. Exptl. Performing Arts Assn., Chira Twp., Mich., 1978—; theatre faculty Wayne County C.C., Detroit, 1979-87; children's theatre instr. Marygrove Coll., Detroit, 1982-96; TV acting faculty Detroit Bd. Edn., 1985-87; adj. theatre faculty Henry Ford C.C., Dearborn, Mich., 1987—, tech. dir., 1996—; drama dir. Crestwood H.S., Dearborn Hts., Mich., 1993—; TV acting faculty Casablancas Model and Talent, Sterling Hts., Mich., 1996—; bd. dirs. Treehouse Players, Grosse Pointe, Mich., 1995—. Author: (play) The Lion Roars, 1996; adaptor: (play) A Christmas Carol, 1995; co-author: (handbook) Our New Family: Instructor's Guidebook, 1991, (Cable mini-series) The Gerry the Fool Show, 1986, (mime show) Only Fooling, 1983. Recipient Keystone award Dearborn Press and Guide, 1992. Mem. ASCD, Theatre Comms. Group, Network of Performing and Visual Arts Schs. Home: 5744 Mckinley Rd China MI 48054-4303 Office: Henry Ford CC 5101 Evergreen Rd Dearborn MI 48128-2407

DZUL, PAUL J., physician, medical journal editor; b. Milno, Ukraine, Oct. 14, 1921; came to U.S., 1949; s. John M. and Maria H. (Maibrodsky) D.; m. Irene M. Blichar, May 26, 1951; children: Andrew I., George O. MD, U. Innsbruck, Austria, 1948; Doctor honoris causa, Odessa (Ukraine) Med. U., 1996. Pres. Lakeshore ENT Ctr., St. Clair Shores, Mich., 1966-88; assoc. prof. Wayne State U., Detroit, 1970-87; editor Jour. Ukrainian Med. Assn., Grosse Pointe, Mich., 1967—. Co-author: English-Ukrainian Medical Dictionary, 1996; editor: History of Ukrainian Medicine, 1988, Milennium of Christianity In Ukraine, 1988, History of Ukrainian Medical Association of North America, 1990. Recipient Pro Ecclesia Et Pontifice award Pope John Paul II, 1991; named Ukrainian of Yr., Ukrainian Grads., Detroit, 1973. Mem. World Fedn. Ukrainian Med. Assn. (pres. 1992). Avocation: medical writing. Home: 21 Woodland Shores Dr Grosse Pointe MI 48236-2633

DZURY, STEPHEN DANIEL, insurance company official; b. Plainfield, N.J., Apr. 21, 1971; s. Daniel Stephen and Donna Delores (Huffman) D.; m. Michele Lauren Jost, May 13, 1995; 1 child, Nicolas Daniel. BA in Polit. Sci. cum laude, Temple U., 1994. Analytical chemist asst. Boyle-Midway, Cranford, N.J., 1989-90; maintenance foreman Westfield (N.J.) Bd. of Edn., 1991-93; environ. claim mgr. Travelers Ins., Balt., 1994-96, account exec., 1997-99; complex dir. AIG, N.Y.C., 1999—. Mem. Theta Chi Nat. Frat., Golden Key Nat. Honor Soc. Home: 1410 Rahway Ave Westfield NJ 07090

DZYALOSHINSKII, IGOR EKHIELIEVICH, physicist; b. Moscow, Feb. 1, 1931; s. Ekhiel Moiseevich and Maria Semionovna (Aseeva) D.; m. Elena Aronovna Lebedeva, Dec. 2, 1960; 1 child, Elena. MA in Physics, Moscow State U., 1953; PhD in Physics, Inst. for Phys. Problems, Moscow, 1957, DSc in Physics, 1962. Sr. rschr. Inst. for Phys. Problems, Moscow, 1957-65; head dept. magnetism Landau Inst. for Theoretical Physics, Moscow, 1965-91; prof. physics U. Calif., Irvine, 1992—. Author: Methods of Quantum Field, Theory in Statistical Physics (in Russian, English, Japanese and Chinese), 1962, 3d edit., 1975. Decorated Order of Red Banner of Labour, Order of Honor, Medal of Vet. of Labour, Govt. of Russia; recipient State prize Govt. USSR, 1984. Fellow Am. Phys. Soc.; mem. Russian Acad. Scis. (Lomonosov prize 1962, Landau prize 1989), Am. Acad. Art and Scis. (hon. fgn. mem.). Achievements include research in theory of weak ferromagnetism; theory of van der Waals forces in condensed media; theory of one-dimensional metals. Avocation: history. Office: Univ Calif Dept Physics Irvine CA 92697

EACHO, ESTHER MACLIVELY, special education educator; b. Springfield, Mass., Feb. 28, 1943; d. Charles James and Mary Eileen (May) MacL.; m. Robert Lee Eacho, Sept. 11, 1971; 1 child, Carla Eileen. BS in Edn., Westfield (Mass.) State Coll., 1964; MA in Edn., Am. Internat. Coll., 1969; M in Learning Disabilities, Am. U., 1990; postgrad., Harvard U., 1998. Cert. tchr., Va., Md., Conn. Classroom tchr. Conn., Md., 1964-71; pres. Eileen-Lee Assocs., McLean, Va., 1979-83; v.p. ops. Fabulous Foodstuffs, Ltd., Alexandria, Va., 1983-89; dir. of learning disabilities program Seton Cts., Falls Church, Va., 1989-92; learning disabilities specialist Fairfax County Pub. Schs., Va., 1992—; edn. specialist, cons. Va., 1998—; bd. dirs. Gourm-E-Co Imports, Sterling, Va. V.p., sec. Jr. Woman's Club, McLean, 1972-79. Mem. ASCD, ASTD, CEC. Avocations: reading, travel, cooking, creative design.

EACHUS, JOSEPH J(ACKSON), computer scientist, consultant; b. Anderson, Ind., Nov. 5, 1911; s. Lewis and Irene (Rogers) E.; m. Ruth Porter, 1938 (div. 1946); children: Alan C., W. James; m. O. Barbara Abernethy, 1947. AB, Miami U., Oxford, Ohio, 1983; MA, Syracuse U., 1936; PhD, U. Ill., 1939. Instr. Purdue U., West Lafayette, Ind., 1939-42; civil servant Dept. Defense, Washington, 1946-55; scientist Honeywell EDP, Waltham, Mass., 1955-76; cons. Cambridge, Mass., 1977-78; engr. Raytheon Co., Sudbury, &, 1979-80; cons. Sarasota, Fla., 1980—. Contbr. articles to profl. jours.; patentee in field. Lt. comdr. USNR, 1942-46, ETO. Fellow IEEE, AAAS; mem. Am. Math. Soc. (emeritus), Assn. Computing Machinery (mem. nat. coun. 1960-62). Home: 4935 Stevens Dr Sarasota FL 34234-3756 Office: Eachus EDP Cons 4935 Stevens Dr Sarasota FL 34234-3756

EADDY, PAULA JOHNSON, women's health nurse; b. Raleigh, N.C., June 9, 1965; d. Jack R. and Alice Faye (Paul) Johnson; m. Joseph Marion Eaddy III, June 3, 1995; 1 child, Steven. Student, East Carolina U., Greenville, 1983-85; AAS, Ctrl. Carolina C.C., Sanford, 1987; AAS in Nursing, Wake Tech. C.C., Raleigh, 1990. RN, N.C.; BLS; cert. neonatal resusitation; cert. maternal newborn nursing, AAP neonatal resusitation instr. Vet. med. technician N.C. State U., Raleigh, 1987-88; nurse technician II Wake Med. Ctr., Raleigh, 1988-90, maternal/child staff nurse II, staff nurse III, 1990—. Presbyterian. Avocations: reading, music, raising Abyssinian cats. Office: 3000 New Bern Ave Raleigh NC 27610-1215

EADE, GEORGE JAMES, retired air force officer, research executive, defense consultant; b. Lockney, Tex., Oct. 27, 1921; s. George William and Isabel Theresa (Barnd) E.; m. Colette Eliane Cachelin, May 18, 1946 (dec. 1994); children: George Walter, Helen Marie-Louise (Mrs. Jean Oesch), Anne Catherine Eade Berry, Christine Colette, Dominique Frances. Commd. 2d lt. USAAF, 1942; advanced through grades to gen. USAF; pilot 37 combat missions in Europe World War II, 1942-46; pilot, squadron comdr., B-52 wing comdr.; airborne emergency action officer, sr. staff officer Strategic Air Command, Nat. Strategic Target Planning Staff, 1947-70; dep. chief of staff plans and ops. Hdqrs. USAF, Washington, La., 1971-72; commdr.-in-chief U.S. Forces Europe, 1972-75; ret., 1975. Pres. Catholic Edn. Assn., Omaha, 1968-70. Decorated DSM with two oak leaf clusters, Legion of Merit, DFC, Air medal with five oak leaf clusters, Air Force Commendation medal with two oak leaf clusters; Order of Merit (France). Home: 1131 Sunnyside Dr Healdsburg CA 95448-3536 *Establish some general goals and lay plans to reach them. Neither be capricious nor struggle doggedly toward a goal no longer of interest. Above all follow your own plan, not what someone plans for you. The ultimate objective is to make a contribution to mankind and be happy in the process of so doing. Putting the two together is to discover the art of living.*

EADES, J. A., electron microscopist, physicist, consultant; b. Ashbourne, Eng., Dec. 27, 1939. BA, Cambridge (Eng.) U., 1962, PhD in Physics, 1967. Prof. physics U. Chile, Santiago, 1967-73, U. Bristol, Eng., 1974-81, U. Ill., Champaign-Urbana, 1981-97, Lehigh U., Bethlehem, Pa., 1997—; cons. in electron diffraction and crystallography. Mem. Am. Phys. Soc., Micros. Soc. Am. E-mail: jae5@lehigh.edu. Office: Dept Materials Sci & Engring Lehigh U 5 E Packer Ave Bethlehem PA 18015-3102

EADES, JAMES BEVERLY, JR., aeronautical engineer; b. Bluefield, W.Va., July 22, 1923; s. James Beverly and Harriet Beulah (Smith) E.; m. Sara M. Porterfield, Dec. 20, 1950; children: Sara Leslie, Beverly Anne, James Christian. Student, Bluefield Coll., 1940-42; B.S. in Aero. Engring., Va. Poly. Inst., 1944, M.S. in Applied Mechanics, 1949, Ph.D., 1958. Registered profl. engr., Va., W.Va. Asst. prof. aero. engring. Va. Poly. Inst., Blacksburg, 1947-50, asst. prof., research assoc. aero. engring., 1953-58, prof. aero. engring., 1958-60, 60-67, head aerospace engring., 1961-67; aero. research scientist NACA, Langley Research Center, Langley Field, Va., 1958, 59, Naval Ordnance Lab., Silver Spring, Md., 1960, 63-69; research assoc. NAS, Goddard Space Flight Center, NASA, Greenbelt, Md., 1967-69; sr. scientist Analytical Mechanics Assocs., Inc., Seabrook, Md., 1969-77; sr. staff scientist Bus. and Technol. Systems, Inc., Seabrook, 1977-79, prin. scientist, 1979-81; v.p., prin. scientist Engring. and Sci. Assocs., Inc., Rockville, Md., 1981-93; cons., sr. scientist Analytical Mechanics Assocs., Inc., Hampton, Va., 1990-94; dir. Conf. Lunar Explorations, 1962. Asst. exec. editor: Celestial Mechanics Jour., 1969-75. Served to lt. USNR, World War II, 1951-53, Korea; comdr. Ret. Res. Assoc. fellow AIAA (chmn. Blue Ridge sect. 1964, profl. edn. com. 1969-75); mem. Celestial Mechanics Inst. (v.p.), Am. Astronautics Soc., Va. Acad. Sci. (sec. engring. sect. 1961, chmn. sect. 1962, mem. council, chmn. space sci. and tech. sect. 1968), Sigma Xi, Sigma Gamma Tau, Tau Beta Pi. Club: Mason. Home: 1603 Peacock Ln Silver Spring MD 20904-1427

EADIE, CHARLES D., city planner, consultant, writer; b. Redlands, Calif., Feb. 20, 1952. BA with honors, U. Calif., Santa Cruz, 1974; MJ, U. Calif., Berkeley, 1981; postgrad., U. Tex., 1982-85. Cons. Charles Eadie Consulting, Santa Cruz, Calif., 1979-82, 93—; assoc. planner City of Santa Cruz, 1975-79; asst. instr. U. Tex., Austin, 1983-85; lectr. U. Calif., Santa Cruz, 1986-87; project mgr./assoc. planner City of Santa Cruz, 1987-91; asst. cmty. devel. dir./prin. planner City of Watsonville, Calif., 1991-99; dir. campus and cmty. planning U. Calif., Santa Cruz, 1999—; cons., advisor, lectr. Fed. Emergency Mgmt. Agy.-Nat. Emergency Tng. Ctr., Emmitsburg, Md., Calif. Specialized Tng. Inst., San Luis Obispo, 1992—; advisor Nat. Earthquake Hazard Reduction Program, Disaster Resistant Communities Program Activity, Com. on Sci. and Tech. Policy-U.S. Ho. of Reps., Washington, 1994-95, 96-97. Author, editor (tng. course) Recovery From Disaster, 1998; reviewer numerous publs. Pres., bd. dirs. Cultural Coun. Santa Cruz County, 1990-95; v.p. bd. dirs. Pajaro Valley Performing Arts Assn., Watsonville, 1995—; co-chair 5th and 6th U.S./Japan workshops on urban earthquake hazard reduction Earthquake Engring. Rsch. Inst., Inst. Social Safety, Pasadena, Calif. and Kobe, Japan, 1997, 99. Recipient Hearst Prize for investigative reporting U. Calif. Berkeley Honors Soc., 1981, Patterson fellowship U. Tex., 1982-85. Mem. ASPA, Am. Planning Assn. (Cert. of Appreciation 1994, 95, 96), Earthquake Engring. Rsch. Inst. (chair com.), Assn. Environ. Profls., Phi Kappa Phi. E-mail: ceadie@worldnet.att.net. FAX: 831-7286173. Home: 724 Escalona Dr Santa Cruz CA 95060 Office: City of Watsonville PO Box 50,000 Watsonville CA 95077-5000

EADIE, JOHN WILLIAM, history educator; b. Ft. Smith, Ark., Dec. 18, 1935; s. William Robert and Helen (Montgomery) B.; m. Joan Holt, Aug. 18, 1957; children: Robin, Christopher. B.A. with honors, U. Ark., 1957; M.A., U. Chgo., 1959; Ph.D., Univ. Coll., London, 1962. Asst. prof. Ripon Coll., Wis., 1962-63; asst. prof. history U. Mich., Ann Arbor, 1963-67, assoc. prof., 1967-73, prof., 1973-86, assoc. chmn. dept. history, 1970-71, humanities-arts advisor Office V.p. for Research, 1974-86, assoc. dean Rackham Sch. Grad. Studies, 1984-86; prof. history, dean Coll. Arts and Letters Mich. St. U., East Lansing, 1986-97, sr. advisor to Provost, 1997—; dir. Consortium for Inter-Instnl. Collaboration in African and L.Am. Studies, 1989—, chmn. liberal arts and scis. dean, 1991-94. Author: The Breviarium of Festus: A critical-Edition with Historical Commentary, 1967, The Conversion of Constantine, 1971, (with others) Western Civilization, 1975; editor: Classical traditions in Early America, 1976; co-editor The Craft of the Ancient Historian, 1985. Chmn. Mich. Council for Humanities, E. Lansing, Mich., 1977-80, Mich. Alliance for Conservation Cultural Heritage, 1988-90. Marshall scholar Brit. Marshall Commn. Univ. Coll., London, 1960-62; recipient Disting. Service award Mich. Council Humanities, 1980. Mem. Am. Hist. Assn., Assn. Ancient Historians, Soc. Promotion Roman Studies, Archaeol Inst. Am. Democrat. Presbyterian. Office: Mich State U 752 Wells Hall East Lansing MI 48824-1027

EADIE, MARGARET L., educational and career consultant. BA, Miami U., Oxford, Ohio; MA, Chapman U., Orange, Calif.; Advanced MEd, U. So. Calif. Master tchr. Tustin (Calif.) H.S.; lectr., continuing edn. program coord. Calif. State U., Fullerton; edn. and career cons. Pacific Grove, Calif. Recipient 2 Panhellenic awards. Mem. APA, Nat. Comm. Assn., Hon. Assn. of Women in Edn., Delta Delta Delta (nat. networking cons., alumnae chpt. pres.), Philanthropic and Edn. Orgn. (chpt. pres.), Orton Dyslexia Soc. Office: 1000 Sage Pl Pacific Grove CA 93950-5007

EADS, GEORGE CURTIS, economic consultant; b. Clarkesville, Tex., Aug. 20, 1942; s. Delbert Curtis and Eliza Mae (Hicks) E.; m. Margaret Helen Hall, Nov. 17, 1973; children: Geoffrey Thomas, Katherine Elizabeth. BA, U. Colo., 1964; MA, Yale U., 1965; MPhil, 1967; PhD, Yale U., 1968. Asst. prof. econs. Harvard U., Cambridge, Mass., 1968-69, Princeton U., 1969-71; spl. asst. antitrust div. Dept. Justice, Washington, 1971-72; assoc. prof. George Washington U., Washington, 1972-74; asst. dir. Council Wage and Price Stability, Washington, 1974-75; exec. dir. Nat. Commn. Supplies and Shortages, Washington, 1975-77; economist, research program dir. Rand Corp., Santa Monica, Calif., 1977-79, 81; mem. Pres.'s Council Advisors, Washington, 1979-81; prof. Sch. Pub. Affairs, U. Md., College Park, 1981-85; dean Sch. Pub. Affairs Sch. Pub. Affairs, U. Md., 1985-86; v.p., chief economist GM, 1986-95; v.p. Charles River Assoc., Washington, Charles River Assocs., Washington, 1995—. Author: The Local Service Airline Experiment, 1972, Relief or Reform? Reagan's Regulatory Strategies, 1984. Mem. Am. Econ. Assn. Democrat. Home: 3718 Harrison St NW Washington DC 20015-1816 Office: Charles River Assoc 600 13th St NW Ste 700 Washington DC 20005-3094

EADS, ORA WILBERT, clergyman, church official; b. Mill Spring, Mo., Jan. 2, 1914; s. John Harrison and Effie Ellen (Borders) E.; m. Mary Ivaree Cochran, Mar. 25, 1944; children—Ora Wilbert, Wayne B., Carol Vernice, Janet Karen and Janice Inez (twins). J.D., John Marshall Law Sch., Atlanta, 1940, LL.M., 1941; postgrad., Sch. Theology, St. Lawrence U., Canton, N.Y., 1947-48. Bar: Ga. bar 1940. Practiced in Atlanta, 1940-46; ordained to ministry Christian Congregation, Inc., 1946; parish minister Sampson County, N.C., 1948-52; evangelist Charlotte, N.C., 1952-61; gen. supt. Christian Congregation, Inc., 1961—. Author numerous books of poetry, 1967—. Office: Christian Congregation Inc 804 W Hemlock St La Follette TN 37766-3947 *A high school teacher asked her class, "What is our purpose on earth? Why are we here?" We students didn't know the answer. I now believe, some 65 years later, that the highest responsibility of any individual is to achieve his best potential.*

EADS, RONALD PRESTON, management consultant; b. Greensboro, N.C., Oct. 17, 1948; s. Wayne Oather and Marcella (Tatarski) E.; m. Gail Senn, Feb. 8, 1975; children: Tanya, Michael, Shannon, Kevin. BBA, Roanoke Coll., 1970. Mgmt. trainee GE, Salem, Va., 1970-71; dept. mgr. Mauney Hosiery, Kings Mountain, N.C., 1971-72; v.p. Eads Mgmt. Devel. Assocs., Gastonia, N.C., 1972-82; pres. Eads Mgmt. Devel. Assocs., 1982—. Co-author: Let's Plan Management Together, 1983. Deacon, First Presbyn. Ch., Gastonia, 1986-88, elder, 1990—. Republican. Avocations: basketball, ballroom dancing. Home: 3548 Gardner Park Dr Gastonia NC 28054-4946 Office: Eads Mgmt Devel Assocs 3017 Redbud Dr Gastonia NC 28056-8441

EADY, CAROL MURPHY (MRS. KARL ERNEST EADY), retired medical association administrator; b. Cleve., Dec. 3, 1918; d. Alfred John and Beatrice B. (Winternitz) Murphy; m. Karl Ernest Eady, July 7, 1945. Diploma, St. Luke's Hosp. Sch. Nursing, Cleve., 1940; B.S. magna cum laude, Baldwin-Wallace Coll., 1943; M.S. in Adminstrn. in Schs. of Nursing, Western Res. U. (now Case Western Res. U.), 1955. Dir. edn. Elyria (Ohio) Meml. Hosp. Sch. Nursing, 1952-57; dir. nursing edn. Mt. Sinai Hosp. Sch. Nursing, Cleve., 1957-62, Michael Reese Hosp. Sch. Nursing, Chgo., 1962-73; coordinator of nursing component Area Health Edn. System, U. Ill., Chgo., 1973-77; asst. dir. dept. health manpower AMA, Chgo., 1977-81, dir. office of related health professions, 1981-83; ret., 1983; Vice pres. Chgo. Video Nursing, 1966-68; mem. project grants rev. com. Nurse Tng. Act USPHS, 1966-70. Recipient Alumni Merit award Baldwin-Wallace Coll., 1993. Recipient Alumni Merit award St. Luke's Hosp. Sch. Nursing, Cleve., 1994. Fellow Inst. Medicine Chgo.; mem. AMA (life), Nat. League Nursing (vice chmn. bd. rev. for diploma programs in nursing 1964-68, 3d v.p. 1969-71, pres. 1973-75, Disting. Svc. to Nursing award 1983), Ill. League Nursing (pres. 1978-82). Republican. Lutheran. Home: 57 Asbury Ln Elyria OH 44035-0801

EAGAN, CATHERINE BERNICE, financial executive; b. N.Y.C., Jan. 14, 1954; d. Edward James Doyle Davis and Adele Helen (Dixon) Cartey; m. Jay Victor Eagan. BA, Simmons Coll., 1975; EdM, Harvard U., 1978, Harvard U., 1983; DDS, U. Mich., 1983. Program cons. United Community Svcs. Met., Detroit; comml. credit analyst Nat. Bank Detroit Comml. Lending Div., 1980-82; dir. comml. devel. Detroit Econ. Growth Corp., 1982-93; v.p. Mich. Nat. Bank, Bloomfield Hills, 1993-98; CFO Eagan Orthodontics, P.C., Southfield, Mich., 1998—; pres. CDC Consulting, Southfield, Mich., 1985—. Author: Neighborhood Economic Development Strategies, 1989. Mem. exec. com. Joy of Jesus; mem. fin. planning United Way Southeastern Mich., mem. allocations com.; dir. pers. com. Women's Econ. Club, Detroit; chmn., life mem. Comml. Real Estate Women, Troy, Mich., 1990—, Bus. Role Model/Detroit Pub. Schs., 1987-93; mem. exec. com. Ctrl. Bus. Dist. Assn. Mem. Harvard Club Eastern Mich. Avocations: swimming, golf, reading, writing, exercise. Office: Eagan Orthodontics PC 17600 W 12 Mile Rd Ste 4 Southfield MI 48076-1911

EAGAN, CLAIRE VERONICA, magistrate judge; b. Bronx, N.Y., Oct. 9, 1950; d. Joseph Thomas and Margaret (Lynch) E.; m. M. Stephen Barrett, Aug. 25, 1978 (div. 1984); m. Anthony J. Loretti, Jr., Feb. 13, 1988. Student, U. Fribourg, Switzerland, 1970-71; BA, Trinity Coll., Washington, 1972; postgrad., U. Paris, 1972-73; JD, Fordham U., 1976. Bar: N.Y. 1977, Okla. 1977, U.S. Dist. Ct. (no. dist.) Okla. 1977, U.S. Ct. Appeals (10th cir.) 1978, U.S. Supreme Ct. 1980, U.S. Dist. Ct. (we. dist.) Okla. 1981, U.S. Ct. Appeals (5th cir.) 1982, U.S. Dist. Ct. (ea. dist.) Okla. 1988, U.S. Ct. Appeals (Fed. cir.) 1990. Mem. Hall, Estill, Hardwick, Gable, Golden & Nelson, Tulsa, 1978-98, shareholder, 1981-98, also bd. dirs., exec. com.; magistrate judge U.S. Dist. Ct. (no. dist.) Okla., Tulsa, 1998—. Editor Fordham Law Rev., 1975-76. Bd. dirs. Cath. Charities, Tulsa, 1983-98, Cystic Fibrosis Found., Tulsa, 1982-84; mem. Jr. League Tulsa, Inc., 1983—; trustee Gannon U., Erie, Pa., 1995-98; bd. dirs. Okla. Sinfonia, Tulsa, 1982-86; adj. settlement judge, Tulsa County, 1990-97. Fellow Am. Bar Found.; mem. Tulsa County Bar Assn., 10th Cir. Jud. Conf., Am. Inns of Ct. (chpt. pres. 1999—). Republican. Roman Catholic. Office: US Dist Ct No Dist Okla 333 W 4th St Ste 411 Tulsa OK 74103-3819

EAGAN, ROBERT T., oncologist; b. Bridgeport, Conn., June 13, 1943; s. Robert Thomas and Mary Louise (Petrucelli) E.; m. Mary Beth Hrivnock, June 12, 1965. BS, Fairfield U., 1964; MD, Albany Med. Coll., 1968. Diplomate Am. Bd. Internal Medicine. Intern, resident in medicine Mary Imogene Bassett Hosp., Cooperstown, N.Y., 1968-70; sr. resident in medicine U. Vt., Burlington, 1970-71; fellow in oncology Dartmouth-Hitchcock Med. Ctr., Hanover, N.H., 1971-73; cons. med. oncologist Mayo Clinic, Rochester, Minn., 1973-94; med. dir. St. Joseph Hosp. Cancer Ctr., Orange, Calif., 1994—; prof. oncology Mayo Med. Sch., Rochester, 1983-94; pres. Litebulb, Inc., Santa Ana, Calif., 1996—; cons. Lifestyles for Living, Orange, Calif., 1997—. Grantee Guenther Found., 1997, Nat. Cancer Inst., 1977-82. Mem. Am. Assn. Cancer Rsch., Am. Soc. Clin. Oncology, Assn. Cancer Execs., So. Calif. Assn. Clin. Oncology. Office: St Joseph Hosp Regional Cancer Ctr 1100 W Stewart Dr Orange CA 92868-3849*

EAGAN, SHERMAN G., producer, communications executive; b. Peoria, Ill., Feb. 12, 1942; s. Joseph K. and Gracia (Sherman) E.; m. Paige Mannelly, Aug. 13, 1966; children: S. Joseph, Shannon Colleen. BA, U. N.Mex., 1967; postgrad., Northwestern U., 1967-68. Mgr. sales adminstrn. NBC-TV, Chgo., 1967-68; copywriter, producer D'Arcy Advt., St. Louis, 1968-69, Ad Com div. Quaker Oats, Chgo., 1969-71; writer CBS TV, Chgo., 1971-75; producer CBS News, N.Y.C., 1975-79; producer, dir. CBS Sports, N.Y.C., 1979-84; pres. Conn. Yankee Internat., Darien, 1984—; cons. Tokyo Broadcasting Co., 1976-84. Producer, dir. U.S. Open Tennis, 1980-90, Daytona: Drama, Danger, Dedication, 1991; producer, dir. Daytona 500, 1992, producer, 1994; dir., writer Battle of the NASCAR Legends, CBS, 1991; dir. Internat. Emmy Presentation, 1989, supervising producer The Winners, 1991; exec. producer IBM TV, 1993, 94; producer NFL Sunday, Fox Sports, 1995-98; editor: Aerodynamic Trading, 1995. Recipient Emmy award NATAS, 1984, 86, Telly award, 1995, 96, 97, 98, Exec. Prodr. and Dir. Entrepreneur of Yr. awards CNBC, 1996, 97, field producer Fox Superbowl Sunday, 1997, 99. Mem. Dirs. Guild Am. Office: Conn Yankee Internat Inc 9 Mott Ave Ste 107 Norwalk CT 06850-3359

EAGAN, WILLIAM LEON, lawyer; b. Tampa, Fla., Feb. 10, 1928; s. John Robert and Margaret (Williams) E.; m. Marjorie Young, Mar. 6, 1949; children—Barbara Anne, Rebecca Elizabeth, Laurel Lea. Student U. Tampa, 1959, LL.B., U. Fla., 1961. Bar: Fla. 1961, U.S. Dist. Ct. (mid. dist.) Fla. 1959, U.S. Dist. Ct. (so. dist.) Fla. 1962, U.S. Ct. Appeals (5th cir.) 1972; bd. cert. civil trial lawyer, Fla. Assoc. Dexter, Conlee & Bissell, Sarasota, Fla., 1961-62; ptnr., v.p. Arnold, Matheny & Eagan, P.A., Orlando, 1962—; mem. Fla. Bar Ninth Circuit Grievance Com., 1982-84; mediator Family Law Mediation Program. Articles editor U. Fla. Law Rev., 1961. Chmn. bd. trustees First Baptist Ch. Winter Park, Fla., 1970-72, chmn. bd. deacons, 1967-69; active Indsl. Devel. Commn. Mid-Fla., Orlando, 1979-84. Served to seaman 2d class USN, 1945-46. Mem. Acad. Fla. Trial Lawyers, Am. Trial Lawyers Assn., Lawyers Title Guaranty Assn., Orange County Bar Assn. (exec. council), Order of Coif, Phi Alpha Delta, Phi Kappa Phi. Republican. Baptist and Methodist. Clubs: University, Citrus (Orlando). Office: Arnold Matheny & Eagan PA 801 N Magnolia Ave Ste 201 Orlando FL 32803-3842

EAGAR, STEPHEN WADE, television news anchor, reporter; b. Lompoc, Calif., Sept. 5, 1962; s. David Melvin and Judith Lynn (Chippendale) E.; m. Michele Lisa Salmon, Sept. 18, 1985; children: Camden Clarke, Kelsey Nicole, Kyle David. Student, Utah Tech. Coll., 1980-82; BA, Brigham Young U., 1987. Profl. baseball player Detroit Tigers, 1984-86; news anchor/reporter Sta. KYMA-TV, Yuma, Ariz., 1987-89, Sta. KVBC-TV, Las Vegas, Nev., 1989-91, Sta. KSL-TV, Salt Lake City, 1991-95, Sta. KDFW-TV, Dallas, 1995—. Mem. adv. bd. Easter Seal Soc., Plano, Tex., 1996—, Caring for Children, Collin County, Tex., 1996—. Recipient Best Newscast, Best Series Reporting award Ariz. Assoc. Press, Yuma, 1988; Best TV Spot News Story award Utah Broadcasters Assn., Salt Lake City, 1992, 93; Emmy nominee news anchor, 1997. Mem. NATAS, Profl. Baseball Players Alumni Assn., Soc. of Profl. Journalists (chpt. pres. 1987, Best TV Spot News Story 1992), Radio & TV News Dirs. Assn. (Edward R. Murrow regional award Best News Series 1995). Mem. LDS Ch. Office: KDFW-TV 400 N Griffin St Dallas TX 75202-1996

EAGAR, THOMAS WADDY, metallurgist, educator; b. Chattanooga, Jan. 9, 1950; s. Harry Douglas Sr. and Emily Clarkson (Thompson) E.; m. Pamela Dozier Garrett, Apr. 17, 1973; children: Matthew, Rebekah, Linda, Karen, James, Anna, Thomas. BS in Metallurgy, MIT, 1972, ScD in Metallurgy, 1975, postgrad., 1988; postgrad., Lehigh U., 1975-76. Registered profl. engr., Mass. Rsch. engr. Homer Rsch. Labs. Bethlehem (Pa.) Steel Corp., 1974-76; asst. prof. materials engring. MIT, Cambridge, 1976-80, assoc. prof., 1980-87, prof., 1987—, acting dept. head, 1989, Richard P. Simmons prof. materials engring., 1990-93, Posco prof. materials engring., 1993-99, dir. materials Processing Ctr., 1990-93, dir. mfg. program, 1993-95; dept. head, 1995—; liaison Scientist U.S. Office Naval Rsch., Tokyo, 1984-85; dir. metall. engring. Simpson, Gumpertz and Heger, Inc., 1994; adv. bd. Edison Welding Inst., Columbus, Ohio, 1989-95; unit mfg. process rsch. com. Nat. Rsch. Coun., Washington, 1990-94; tech. rev. bd. U.S. Army Rsch. Labs., 1993-95; cons. metallurgy and metall. failure analysis, 1976—; presenter and lectr. in field. Mem. adv. and tech. rev. bds. Materials Tech.; key reader Welding Jour.; contbr. over 165 articles to tech. publs.; patentee method of resistance welding, non-hygroscopic welding flux binders, large diameter stud and method and apparatus for welding same, laser instrument, age-hardenable sterling silver, emissivity independent multi-wavelength pyrometry, silver alloys of exceptional and reversilbe hardness. Named Internat. Jr. Civitan of Yr., 1968; Dennison K. Bullens scholar, 1969-71, Foundry Edn. Fund scholar, 1970-71; grad. fellow NSF, 1972-74, Creativity Ext. award, 1988-90. Fellow Am. Soc. Metals (Henry Marion Howe medal 1992), Am. Welding Soc. (hon., Adams meml. fellow award 1979-83, Warren F. Savage award 1990, 96, Williams Sparagen award 1991, 94, Comfort A. Adams lectr., 1992, Charles H. Jennings Meml. medal 1983, 91, William Irrgang award 1993); mem. AIME (metallurgy and metals prize Boston sect. 1972, Champion H. Mathewson Gold medal 1987, Henry Krumb lectr. 1987), Nat. Acad. Engring., AAAS, ASTM, ASME, Am. Ceramic Soc., Materials Rsch. Soc., Soc. Automotive Engrs., Soc. Mfg. Engrs., Welding Rsch. Coun. Internat. Inst. Welding (Am. coun. Houdremont lectr. 1990), Japan Welding Soc., Tau Beta Pi (bd. dirs. New England dist. 1977-80, advisor MIT chpt., disting. svc. award 1980), Phi Lambda Epsilon. Mem. LDS Ch. Office: MIT 77 Massachusetts Ave Rm 8-309 Cambridge MA 02139-4307

EAGER, GEORGE SIDNEY, JR., electrical engineer, business executive; b. Balt., Sept. 5, 1915; s. George S. and Ada Elizabeth (Heinz) E.; m. Ruth Duff, Oct. 13, 1945; children: Robert W., John W., George S. III. BEE, Johns Hopkins U., 1936, PhD in Engring., 1941. Rsch. supr., asst. dir., assoc. dir. to dir. rsch. Gen. Cable Corp., Edison, N.J., 1945-80; pres. GRJ Cons. Svcs. Inc., Upper Monclair, N.J., 1980—. Contbr. numerous articles to profl. jours. Author 35 patents elec. wires and cables. Lt. col. Signal Corps, U.S. Army, 1941-45, ETO. Fellow IEEE, Montclair Golf Club. Republican. Congregationalist. Home: 14 Bellegrove Dr Montclair NJ 07043-2527

EAGER, WILLIAM EARL, information systems corporation executive; b. Trenton, N.J., Dec. 22, 1946; s. Earl V. and Dorothy E. (Bowen) E.; m. Janice M. Kudlak, July 12, 1969; 1 child, Jason C. BA, Lycoming Coll., 1968; MBA, Gannon U., 1977; postgrad., Kent State U., 1984—. Cert. data processing. Systems supr. Gen. Electric Co., Erie, Pa., 1969-72; sr. cons. Touche Ross & Co., Detroit, 1972-74; mgmt. infor. systems dir. Limbach, Inc., Pitts., 1974-81; dir. systmes GenCorp, Inc., Akron, Ohio, 1981-87; sr. v.p. First Bancorp of Ohio, Akron, 1987-90, pres., CEO FBOH Svcs. Divsn., exec. v.p., 1991-94; sr. v.p. and CIO Cmty. Mut. Ins. Co., Cin., 1994-95; sr. ptnr. and E-bus. practice mgr. Computer Scis. Corp. Consulting, Boston, 1996—. Contbg. editor: Corp. Computing mag., 1992-93;. Home: 3420 Ivy Hills Blvd Cincinnati OH 45244-2569

EAGLE, JACK, commercial actor, comedian; b. N.Y.C., Jan. 15, 1926; s. Henry Eagle and Ida Mershon; children: Nikki, Jobbi, Ian; m. Susan M. Mohney, July 31, 1988 (div.). Trumpet player Muggsy Spanier, Georgie Auld, Henry Jerome, Boyd Raeburn, 1943-55; comedian Eagle & Man, 1955-65; solo comedian and comml actor., 1965—; comml. actor, goodwill ambassador Xerox, 1975—. Comml. actor for numerous cos. including Xerox's "Broth Dominic" (Clio award 1976), Fleischman Margarine's "Mr. Cholesterol:, Carefree Chewing Gum's "Colombus's 1st Mate", Gillette's "The Perfect Face", N.Y. State Lottery "The Maize"; appeared in films New York Crossing, 1996, Step-Mom, 1997, Isn't She Great, 1998. Recipient Man of Yr. award Quick Print mag., Mr. Printing Week award Printing Industries. Mem. AFTRA, AGVA, Screen Actors Guild, Am. Fedn. Musicians. Avocations: drawing, collecting things.

EAGLES, SIDNEY SMITH, JR., judge; b. Asheville, N.C., Aug. 5, 1939; s. Sidney Smith Sr. and Mildred Truman (Brite) E.; m. Rachel Phillips, May 22, 1965; children: Virginia Brite, Margaret Phillips. BA, Wake Forest U., 1961, JD, 1964. Bar: N.C. 1964. Revisor Gen. Statutes Commn., Raleigh, N.C., 1967-70; asst. atty. gen. legis. drafting service Office Atty. Gen. N.C., Raleigh, 1970-74, dep. atty. gen. spl. prosecution divsn., 1974-76; counsel to speaker N.C. State Legislature, Raleigh, 1976-80; ptnr. Eagles Hafer & Hall, Raleigh, 1977-82; judge N.C. Ct. Appeals, Raleigh, 1983—, chief judge, 1998—; adj. prof. Campbell U. Sch. Law, 1977—; chmn. N.C. Jud. Stds. Commn., 1994-96; mem. faculty Appellate Judges Sch. Law Sch. NYU, N.Y.C., 1993—. Co-author: North Carolina Criminal Procedure Forms, 1975, 3d edit., 1989; contbr. articles to profl. jours. V.p. Raleigh Jaycees, 1972-73; mem. Senatorial Dist. Dem. Com., 1979-81; bd. dirs. Wake County (N.C.) Symphony Soc., 1980-81, Women's Aid of Wake County, 1978—; bd. elders, bd. deacons, trustee, tchr. Sunday sch. Hillyer Meml. Christian Ch., 1980—, chmn bd., 1989; bd. visitors Wake Forest U. Sch. Law; trustee and vice chair Barton Coll. Served to capt. USAF, 1964-67; col., ret. 1991. Named Disting. Law Alumnus, Wake Forest U., 1981; N.C. Justice Found. fellow, 1972. Mem. ABA (chmn. appellate judges conf. 1993-94, mem. appellate jud. edn. com. 1994—, ho. of dels. 1992—), Am. Law Inst. (uniform laws conf. 1968-83, 92—), N.C. Bar Assn. (v.p. 1989-90), Wake county Bar Assn. (chmn. exec. com. 1975), N.C. State Bar, Execs. Club (pres. 1985), Kiwanis (disting. pres. Raleigh 1986-87, disting. lt. gov. 1995, Kiwanian of Yr. award 1989), Phi Delta Phi, Phi Alpha Delta (James Iredell award 1990). Avocations: politics, reading. Office: NC Ct of Appeals PO Box 888 Raleigh NC 27602-0888

EAGLES, STUART ERNEST, business executive; b. Saint John, N.B., Can., July 29, 1929; s. Ernest Lyle and Evelyn Gertrude (Feltmate) E.; m. Margaret Anne Gulliver, Sept. 30, 1952; children: James Stuart, Patricia Anne, Mark Edward. B.Sc., Acadia U., 1949, D.C.L. (hon.), 1992. Pres. Aegean Devel. Inc., Toronto, 1988—; bd. dirs. AGF Trust Co., AGF Mgmt. Ltd., Hardit Corp., OPB Realty (Mgmt.) Inc., Gibbons-Daley Found.; past trustee, dir. Internat. Coun. Shopping Ctrs.; past pres. and dir. Can. Inst. Pub. Real Estate Cos. Gov. Jr. Achievement Can. Mem. Nat. Club (past pres.), Can. Club, Empire Club. Home: 24 Garfield Ave, Toronto, ON Canada M4T 1E7

EAGLESON, PETER STURGES, hydrologist, educator; b. Phila., Feb. 27, 1928; s. William Boal and Helen (Sturges) E.; m. Marguerite Anne Partridge, May 28, 1949 (div.); children: Helen Marie, Peter Sturges, Jeffrey Partridge; m. Beverly Grossmann Rich, Dec. 27, 1974. B.S. in Civil Engring, Lehigh U., 1949, M.S., 1952; Sc.D., MIT, 1956; D of Engring. (hon.), Lehigh U., 1998. Jr. engr. George B. Mebus (cons. engr.), Glenside, Pa., 1950-51; teaching asst. Lehigh U., 1951-52; research asst. Mass. Inst. Tech., 1952-54; mem. faculty MIT, 1954-93, prof. civil engring., 1965-93, head dept. civil engring., 1970-75, emeritus prof. civil and environ. engring., 1993—; vis. asso. Calif. Inst. Tech., 1975-76; Fulbright sr. research scholar Commonwealth Sci. and Indsl. Research Orgn., Canberra, Australia, 1966-67. Author: (with others) Estuary and Coastline Hydrodynamics, 1966, Dynamic Hydrology, 1970. Served to 2d lt. C.E. AUS, 1949-50. Recipient Desmond Fitzgerald medal, 1959, Clemens Herschel prize, 1965 both Boston Soc. Civil Engrs., rsch. prize ASCE, 1963, William Bowie medal Am. Geophysical Union, 1994, Stockholm Water prize Stockholm Water Found., 1997. Fellow AAAS, Am. Meteorol. Soc., Am. Geophys. Union (Robert E. Horton award 1979, Robert E. Horton medal 1988, pres. 1986-88, William Bowie medal 1994), Internat. Assn. Hydrological Scis. (Internat. Hydrology prize 1991); mem. NAE, European Geophys. Soc. (John Dalton medal 1999). Office: MIT Dept Civil & Environ Engring Room 48-335 Cambridge MA 02139

EAGLESON, WILLIAM BOAL, JR., banker; b. Phila., Dec. 10, 1925; s. William Boal and Helen (Sturges) E.; m. Catherine West McLean, May 28, 1960; children: Elizabeth E. Mackie, John McLean. BS, Lehigh U., 1949, LLD, 1983; MBA, U. Pa., 1951. With Fed. Res. Bank Phila., 1949-51; investment officer Girard Bank, Phila., 1951-61, v.p., 1961, exec. v.p., 1967; pres., dir. Girard Co., Girard Bank, 1970-80, chmn. bd., 1974-85; chmn. bd. Mellon Bank Corp., 1983-85, chmn. emeritus, 1985—; chmn. bd. Grant St Nat. Bank, 1988-95; mem. pres.'s adv. coun. The Gen. Theol. Sem.; former mem. adv. bd. Yamaichi Internat. Am.; bd. dirs., chmn. exec. com. Gen. Accident Ins. Co.; advisor Tokai Bank Ltd.; hon. consul gen. Japan in Phila., 1991—. Mem. Phila. City Planning Commn., 1970-74; mem. U.S. Treas. Govt. Borrowing Com., 1976-80, Fed. Adv. Council, 1978-80; bd. dirs. Nat. Alliance of Bus.; chmn. Gov.'s State Job Tng. Council, 1983-84; chmn. Pvt. Industry Council Phila., 1978-83; trustee Acad. Natural Scis., Phila., 1967-75; trustee, chmn. fin. com. Lehigh U.; bd. dirs. Phila. Orch. Assn.; vice chmn. World Affairs Council of Phila.; mem. adv. council East Asian studies Princeton U. With USNR, 1944-46. Mem. Am. Philos. Soc. (chmn. fin. com.), Phila. Club, Gulph Mills Golf Club, Rolling Rock Club, Phi Beta Kappa. Episcopalian. Home: 1241 Denbigh Ln Radnor PA 19087-4646

EAGLET, ROBERT DANTON, electrical engineer, aerospace consultant, retired military officer; b. Cleve., Mar. 2, 1934; s. Albert Rudy and Dorothy Margaret (Beamer) E.; m. Sally Perry; children: Suzanne Carolyn, Allison Leigh, Kevin Robert. BSEE, U. Ariz., 1962; MSEE, U. So. Calif., 1968, PhD in Elec. Engring., 1970. Commd. 2d lt. USAF, 1956, advanced through grades to maj. gen., 1986, forward air contr. in Vietnam, 1965-66; div. chief classified program space div. USAF, L.A., 1966-68; chief strategic def. div. hdqrs. USAF, Washington, 1970-74, mil. asst. to dep. undersec. def., 1974-75; dep. gen. mgr. NATO airborne early warning program Brussels, 1975-79; dep. chief of staff systems devel. planning command USAF, Andrews AFB, Md., 1979-84; dep. comdr. armament div. USAF, Eglin AFB, Fla., 1984-86; dir. F-16 multinat. fighter program USAF, Wright Patterson AFB, Ohio, 1986-89; dep. asst. sec. of air force Pentagon, Washington, 1989-91; ret. USAF, 1991; pres. Eaglet Internat. Assocs., McLean, Va., 1992—. Decorated Disting. Svc. medal with oak leaf cluster, Legion of Merit with oak leaf cluster, Silver star, Disting. Flying Cross with oak leaf cluster, Bronze star with Valor device, Air medal with 24 oak leaf clusters, Purple Heart; named Outstanding Alumnus U. So. Calif. Mem. Air Force Assn., Armed Forces Comm.-Electronics Assn., Nat. Def. Indsl. Assn. (v.p., tech. svcs. bd.), Assn. Old Crows, Assn. U.S. Army, Navy League, Blegian-Am. Assn. (bd. dirs.), French Am. Assn. Republican. Avocation: wind surfing.

EAGLSTEIN, WILLIAM HOWARD, dermatologist, educator; b. Kansas City, Mo., Mar. 27, 1940; s. Max A. and Mildred (Bernstein) E.; m. Janet Strickland, Aug. 23, 1979. M.D., U. Mo., 1965. Intern Kings County (N.Y.) Hosp., 1965-66; resident U. Miami, 1966-69, prof. dermatology, 1971-80; prof., chmn. dept. dermatology U. Pitts., 1980-86; chmn. dept. dermatology U. Miami, Fla., 1986—; chmn. dermatologic adv. com. FDA, 1983-85; mem. nat. adv. bd. for arthritis, musculoskeletal and skin diseases HHS. Author: Office Techniques for Diagnosing Skin Diseases, 1978, 86, Leg and Foot Ulcers: A Clinician's Guide, 1994; assoc. editor Jour. Dermatology and Related Allergies, 1978-80. Served with USN, 1969-71. Robert Wood Johnson Health Policy fellow Inst. Medicine, 1986-87. Fellow Am. Bd. Dermatology; mem. AMA, Am. Acad. Dermatology (bd. dirs.), Soc. Investigative Dermatology (bd. dirs.), Am. Dermatol. Assn., Wound Healing Soc. (founding bd. dirs.), Assn. Profl. Dermatology (bd. dirs., officer). Jewish. Home: 29 E San Marino Dr Miami FL 33139-1101 Office: U Miami Dept Dermatology PO Box 16250 Miami FL 33101-6250

EAKELEY, DOUGLAS SCOTT, lawyer; b. Morristown, N.J., Mar. 2, 1946; m. Priscilla Van Tassel, June 2, 1973. BA, Yale U., 1968, JD, 1972; MA in Jurisprudence, Oxford U., Eng., 1970. Bar: N.Y. 1973, U.S. Ct. Appeals (2nd cir.) 1974, N.J. 1978, U.S. Ct. Appeals (3rd cir.) 1980, U.S. Supreme Ct. 1981. Law clk. to judge Harold R. Tyler, Jr. U.S. Dist. Ct. (so. dist.) N.Y., N.Y.C., 1972-73; assoc. Debevoise, Plimpton, N.Y.C., 1973-80; ptnr. Riker, Danzig, Scherer, Hyland & Perretti, Newark and Morristown, N.J., 1980-90, 91-94; first asst. atty. gen. State of N.J., 1990-91; ptnr. Lowenstein Sandler, PC, Roseland, N.J., 1994—; chmn. Legal Svcs. N.J., North Brunswick, 1981-90, Legal Svcs. Corp., Washington, 1993—; pres. Legal Svc. Found. Essex County, Newark, 1981-90; chmn. N.J. Sentencing Policy Study Commn., 1992-93; trustee Practising Law Inst., N.Y.C., 1994—; trustee Boys and Girls Clubs of Newark, N.J., 1993—. Chmn. bd. editors N.J. Law Jour., 1984-90. Trustee N.J. Network Found., 1994—, N.J. Inst. for Social Justice, 1996—; pres. N.J. Shakespeare Festival, Madison, 1982-86. Rhodes scholar Oxford U., 1968. Fellow Am. Bar Found.; mem. ABA (John Minor Wisdom award for professionalism and pub. svc., litigation sect. 1997), N.J. Bar Assn., Essex County Bar Assn., Fed. Bar Assn. N.J. (v.p. 1983-90), Urban League of Essex County (trustee 1987-88), Assn. Am. Rhodes Scholars (bd. dirs. 1995—), Phi Beta Kappa. Democrat. Office: Lowenstein Sandler PC 65 Livingston Ave Ste 9 Roseland NJ 07068-1725

EAKER, IRA, publishing executive; b. N.Y.C., Jan. 14, 1922; s. Samuel and Hannah (Conner) E.; m. Lee Ann Eisenberg, Nov. 24, 1946; children—Sherry Ellen, Dean Ross. Grad. bus. sch. in advt., CCNY, 1948. Advt. sales rep. John Morris Chanin Orgn., N.Y.C., 1946-48; advt. mgr. Show Bus. Weekly, N.Y.C., 1948-60; founder, pub., advt. dir. Back Stage Publs., N.Y.C., 1960-89. Served with F.A. AUS, 1943-46, ETO. Mem. Woodmont Country Club (Tamarac, Fla.). Democrat. Jewish. Avocations: golf, music, travel, personal mgmt.

EAKER, SHERRY ELLEN, entertainment newspaper editor; b. N.Y.C., Nov. 30, 1949; d. Ira and Lee (Eisenberg) E. BA, Queens Coll., 1971, MS, 1976. Tchr. art, English N.Y.C. Bd. Edn., 1971-76; editor-in-chief Back Stage, The Performing Arts Weekly, N.Y.C., 1977—. Editor, compiler: Handbook for Performing Artists: The How-to and Who-to-Contact Reference for Actors, Singers, Dancers, 1989, rev., 1991, 95. Mem. Drama Desk (sec. 1984-87, v.p. 1987-91), Am. Theatre Critics Assn., Nat. Theatre Conf. (trustee), League Profl. Theatre Women, N.Y. Coalition Profl. Women in Arts and Media (spl. adv.), advisory coun. Inst. of Outdoor Drama, Manhattan Assn. Cabarets. Avocations: theatre, cabaret. Office: Back Stage Publs 1515 Broadway New York NY 10036-8901

EAKIN, RICHARD RONALD, academic administrator, mathematics educator; b. New Castle, Pa., Aug. 6, 1938; s. Everett Glenn and Mildred May (Hammerschmidt) E.; m. Jo Ann McGeehan, Aug. 23, 1960; children: Matthew Glenn, Maridy Lynn. AB in Math., Geneva Coll., Beaver Falls, Pa., 1960; MA in Math., Washington State U., 1962, PhD in Math., 1964. Asst. prof. math. Bowling Green (Ohio) State U., 1964-68, assoc. prof. math., 1968-87, asst. dean grad. sch., 1969-72, vice-provost student affairs, 1972-80, vice-provost instl. planning, 1979-80, exec. vice-provost budgeting and planning, 1980-83, v.p. budgeting and planning, 1983-87; chancellor, prof. math. East Carolina U., Greenville, N.C., 1987—. Editor revs. and evaluations sect. (jour.) The Math. Tchr., 1968-70. V.p. and mem. bd. dirs. Nat. Hemophilia Found., N.Y.C., 1983-84, chmn. bd., v.p. adminstrn. and fin., 1984-87. NDEA fellow Wash. State U., Pullman, 1960-63, NSF fellow, 1963-64. Mem. Math. Assn. Am., So. Assn. Colls. and Schs. (commn. on colls.), Sigma Xi, Phi Kappa Phi, Omicron Delta Kappa. Office: East Carolina U Office of Chancellor Greenville NC 27858

EAKLE, ARLENE HASLAM, genealogist; b. Salt Lake City, July 19, 1936; d. Thomas E. and Margaret (Mitchell) Haslam; m. Alma D. Eakle, Jr., Feb. 8, 1957; children: JoAnn, Richard, Linda, John. ADN, Weber State U.; MA in English history, U. Utah, PhD of English history. Author: (with Linda Brinkerhoff) Family History for Fun and Profit-The Research Process, 1997, Genealogy in Land Records, 1998, (with Johni Cerny) The Source: A Guidebook for American Genealogy, 1984, Ancestry's Guide to Research, 1985; editor: Research News, Immigration Digest; editor: Virginia Notebooks, N.Y. Rsch. Fellow Utah Geneal. Assn., 1987; recipient Award of Merit Fedn. Geneal. Soc., 1984. Mem. Am. Family Records Assn. (bd. dirs.), Assn. Profl. Genealogists (pres. 1980-82, Grahame Thomas Smallwood Jr. Award of Merit 1984), Md. Geneal. Soc., Utah Geneal. Assn., West Fla. Geneal. Soc. Office: Genealogical Inst PO Box 129 Tremonton UT 84337-0129

EAKMAN, MARK, chemist; b. Sharon, Pa., Apr. 23, 1958; s. Carl Leroy and Freida (Diacoganis) E. BS, Pa. State U., 1980. Chemist Clark Oil & Chem., Cleve., 1981-90, quality mgr., 1990-92; tech. svc. engr. Houghton Internat., Valley Forge, Pa., 1992-93; chem. mgmt. tech. svc. engr. Fuchs Lubricants, Harvey, Ill., 1994-95, chem. mgmt. site mgr., 1995—. Mem. Soc. Tribologists & Lubrication Engrs., Pa. State U. Alumni Assn. (Cleve. chpt. pres.), Order of Ahepa (chpt. 480 pres. 1984-86). Democrat. Greek Orthodox. Avocations: numismatics, gourmet cooking, reading, music. Office: Fuchs CMS PO Box 42008 Cleveland OH 44142-0008

EALES, JOHN GEOFFREY, zoology educator; b. Wolverhampton, Staffordshire, Eng., Sept. 9, 1937; arrived in Can., 1959; s. John Gordon Robinson and Marion Mabel Eva (Phipps) E.; m. Sachiko Tabata, May 25, 1963; children: David, Carol. BA, Oxford U., Eng., 1959; MSc, U. B.C., Can., 1961, PhD, 1963. Asst. prof. U. N.B., Can., 1963-67; asst. prof. U. Man., Winnipeg, Can., 1967-69, assoc. prof., 1969-73, prof., 1973-89, assoc. dean grad. studies, 1979-80, Disting. Univ. prof., 1989—; mem. grant coms. NSERC, 1980—. Mem. editorial bd. Gen. and Comparative Endocrinology, 1974—; editor-in-chief Can. Jour. Zoology, NRC, Ottawa, 1989-94; contbr. articles to profl. jours. Killam Rsch. fellow Can. Coun., 1989-91; NSERC grantee, 1964—. Fellow Royal Soc. Can.; mem. Can. Soc. Zoologists (Fry medal 1998), Am. Soc. Zoologists. Avocations: running, reading, fly fishing, cottage building. Home: 75 Fordham Bay, Winnipeg, MB Canada R3T 3B8 Office: U Man, Dept Zoology, Winnipeg, MB Canada R3T 2N2

EALY, CARLETON CATO, investment banker; b. Little Rock, Ark., Jan. 14, 1957; s. Carleton Clarence and Ruby Florence (Cato) E.; m. Kerry Katherine Kelly, Mar. 22, 1986. BA in Econs., Yale U., 1979; MS in Mgmt., MIT, 1983. Assoc. pub. fin. Paine Webber, Inc., N.Y., 1983-84, assoc. mortgage fin., 1984-86, v.p. mergers and acquisitions, 1986—. Republican. Club: Yale (N.Y.C.). Office: Paine Webber Inc Rm 623 1285 Avenue Of The Americas Fl Sconc New York NY 10019-6096

EALY, JONATHAN BRUCE, lawyer; b. L.A., Apr. 20, 1960; s. Donald Rae and Cynthia Howland (Pike) E. AB cum laude, Harvard U., 1982; JD, Duke U., 1985. Bar: Alaska 1986, U.S. Ct. Appeals (9th cir.) 1986. Clk. judge Karen Hunt Alaska Superior Ct., Anchorage, 1985-86; assoc. Taylor & Hintz, Anchorage, 1986-89, Heller, Ehrman, White & McAuliffe, Anchorage, 1989-93; gen. counsel Borisovich Internat., Inc., Anchorage, 1993—; of counsel Partnow, Sharrock & Tindall, Anchorage, 1995—; bd. dirs. Borealis Brewing Co.; prin. Na'au, Inc., 1998—. Author: Third Story, 1998. Pres. Anchorage Youth Ct., 1993-94, legal advisor, 1989-92; bd. dirs. Kids Voting Alaska, Anchorage, 1993. Mem. Anchorage Bar Assn. (pres. 1994, v.p. 1993, pres. young lawyers sect. 1988-90). Office: 510 L St Ste 500 Anchorage AK 99501-1956

EAMES, JOHN HEAGAN, etcher; b. Lowell, Mass., July 19, 1900; s. Albert Melvin and Amanda Kneeland (Matthews) E.; m. Muriel MacMicken, May 17, 1924; 1 child, Consuelo. A.B., Harvard, 1922; student, Royal Coll. Art, London, 1933, 35, 37; pupil of, Malcolm Osborne, Robert Austin. Engaged in archtl. work N.Y.C., 1923-31. Artist, Eng. and France, 1931-39, N.Y.C., 1939—; exhibited drawings, etchings Royal Acad., London, 1935, 37, 40, N.Y. World's Fair, 1939, Internat. Print Exhbn., Art Inst. Chgo., 1939, Biennial Exhbn., Venice, Italy, 1940, Met. Mus., 1942, 52, Carnegie Inst., 1945, N.A.D. Exhbn. Contemporary Am. Drawings, 1945, 46, Bklyn. Mus. 1950, Albany (N.Y.) Inst. History and Art, 1949, Albright Art Gallery, Buffalo, 1950, Sweat Meml. Art Mus., Portland Maine, 1952, 53, 54, Am. Acad. Arts and Letters, 1953, Smithsonian Instn. Traveling Exhbn. Am. Drawings, 1954, Soc. Am. Graphic Artists Exch. Exhbn., Eng., 1954, Maine State Art Biennial, 1979-81, 84; ann. exhibitor, N.A.D., Soc. Am. Graphic Artists; represented permanent collection Libr. of Congress, Met. Mus. Art, Bates Coll., Maine, Ashmolean Mus., Oxford, Eng.; also pvt. collections; retrospective exhbn. Bates Coll., Maine, 1992. Served with U.S. Army, 1918. Recipient Kate W. Arms Meml. prize for best miniature etching Soc. Am. Graphic Artists, 1952, 54, 57, John Taylor Arms prize for etching, 1953; Henry B. Shope prize, etching, 1957; Purchase prize Albany Inst. Art, 1957, 69. Academician N.A.D.; sr. fellow Royal Soc. Painters-Etchers; mem. Soc. Am. Graphic Artists. Address: PO Box 222 Boothbay Harbor ME 04538-0222

EARHART, EILEEN MAGIE, retired child and family life educator; b. Hamilton, Ohio, Oct. 21, 1928; d. Andrew J. and Martha (Waldorf) Magie; m. Paul G. Earhart; children: Anthony G., Bruce P., Daniel T. B.S., Miami U., Oxford, Ohio, 1950; M.A. in Adminstrn. and Ednl. Services, Mich. State U., 1962, Ph.D. in Edn., 1969; H.H.D. (hon.), Miami U., Oxford, Ohio, 1980. Tchr. home econs. W. Alexandria (Ohio) Schs., 1950-51; elementary tchr. Waterford Twp. Schs., Pontiac, Mich., 1958-65; reading specialist Waterford Twp. Schs., 1965-67; prof., chmn. family and child ecology dept. Mich. State U., East Lansing, 1968-84; prof., head dept. home and family life Fla. State U., Tallahassee, 1984-89; ret., 1989. Author: Attention and Classification Training Curriculum; co-editor spl. issue of Family Relations, 1984; contbr. chpts. to profl. jours., books. Mem. adv. bd. Lansing Com. on Children's TV, Family/Sch./Cmty. Partnership Project, Tallahassee; bd. dirs. Women's Resource Ctr., Grand Rapids, Mich., Wesley Found., Fla. State U., 1989-98; mem. campus ministries bd. Fla. A&M U., 1995-98; mem. Mich. Gov.'s Task Force on Youth. Mem. Nat. Coun. Family Rels. (pres. Assn. of Couns. 1987-88, bd. dirs. 1986-88, chair nat. meeting local arrangements 1992), Fla. Coun. Family Rels. (pres. elect 1985-86, pres. 1986-87), Nat. Assn. Edn. Young Children, Assn. Childhood Edn. Internat., Am. Home Econs. Assn. (named AHEA leader at 75th Ann. of Assn. 1984), Internat. Fedn. Home Econs., Mich. Home Econs. Assn. (pres. 1980-82), Fla. Home Econs. Assn. (chmn. scholarship com. 1986-88, dist. chmn. 1990-91, chmn. nominating com. 1991-92, co-chair ann. meeting 1995), Ednl. Rsch. Assn., Killearn United Meth. Ch., United Meth. Women (cir. chair 1993-97, pres. 1994), Phi Kappa Phi (pres. Fla State U. chpt. 1988-89), Delta Kappa Gamma, Omicron Nu, others. Summer: 744 Cannon Trl Franklin NC 28734-7999 Home: 744 Cannon Trl Franklin NC 28734-7999*

EARHART, LUCIE BETHEA, volunteer, former secondary school educator; b. Atlanta, July 17, 1954; d. Rufus Hagood and Jacqueline (Harrington) Bethea; m. Philip Charles Earhart, Nov. 27, 1976; 1 child, Carolyn Frances. BA, U. of South, 1976; MEd, U. New Orleans, 1989. Asst. actuary Waters-Parkerson, New Orleans, 1976-80, Franklin H. Jones & Co., Inc., New Orleans, 1980-81; tchr. math. Jefferson Parish Sch. Bd., Metairie, La., 1984, St. Martin's Episcopal Sch., Metairie, 1984-85, Crescent City Bapt. Sch., Metairie, 1987-90, Calcasien Parish Sch. System, Lake Charles, La., 1990-94. Bd. dirs. Lake Charles Symphony. Mem. Jane Austen Soc., Jr. League of Lake Charles. Republican. Episcopalian. Avocations: reading, needlework. Home: 5001 W St Charles St Lake Charles LA 70605-6754

EARL, ANTHONY SCULLY, former governor of Wisconsin, lawyer; b. Lansing, Mich., Apr. 12, 1936; s. Russell K. and Ethlynne Julia (Scully) E.; children: Julia, Anne, Mary, Catherine. B.S., Mich. State U.; J.D., U. Chgo. Bar: Wis., Minn. Asst. dist. atty. Marathon County, Wausau, Wis., 1965-66; city atty. City of Wausau, 1966-69; mem. Wis. Assembly, Madison, 1969-74; mem. firm Crooks, Low & Earl, 1969-74; sec. Wis. Dept. Adminstrn., Madison, 1974-75, Dept. Nat. Resources, Madison, 1975-80; v.p. firm Foley & Lardner, Madison, 1980-82; gov. State of Wis., Madison, 1983-87; ptnr. Quarles and Brady, Madison, 1987—. Served as lt. USN, 1962-65. Democrat. Roman Catholic. Office: Quarles & Brady 1 S Pinckney St PO Box 2113 Madison WI 53701-2113

EARL, LEWIS HAROLD, economics and management consultant, lawyer; b. Guthrie, Tex., Dec. 17, 1918; s. Henry W. and Ruth (O'Neal) E.; m. Patricia Miller, Mar. 5, 1943 (dec. 1973); children: William Lee, Patricia Lewise, Robert Charles, James Michael; m. Meade Randolph Loomis, July 1, 1977 (div. 1979); m. Maxine Durrett Marks, Jan. 31, 1981. *Lewis Earl's father Henry W. Earl (1881-1973) and mother Ruth O'Neal Earl (1888-1977) were public school teachers in one and two teacher rural schools in four or five West Texas counties from 1916-1946. As strict disciplinarians, they insisted that their students be prepared with basic reading and math skills for advancement and that their four children be models for their classrooms. Lewis's son, William Lee Earl, earned a BS from Beloit in 1967 and a PhD from the University of California at Berkeley in 1975. William works on energy research at Los Alamos Laboratory in New Mexico. Lewis also has a daughter, Patricia Lewise Earl, who earned her BS from Lawrence in 1969 and her PhD from the University of Iowa in 1975. She is currently a researcher in genetics and biology at NIH in Bethesda, Maryland.* B.A., Tex. Technol. Coll., 1939; student, U. Tex., 1939-40, Am. U., 1941-42, George Washington U., 1942-62; J.D., Georgetown U., 1950. Bar: D.C. 1950, U.S. Supreme Ct. 1972, Tex. 1983. With Bur. Labor Statistics, Dept. Labor, 1940-42, 46-54; industry, commodity economist NPA Dept. Commerce, 1951-53; productivity specialist, economist, program analyst, asst. program officer U.S. Tech. Cooperation Program in Brazil, 1953-57; program officer U.S. Tech. Cooperation Program, Argentina, 1957-59, El Salvador, 1959-61; internat. relations officer AID, Washington, 1961-63; chief internat. research Office Manpower Automation and Tng., U.S. Dept. Labor, Washington, 1963-65; chief Fgn. manpower program staff Office Manpower Policy, Evaluation and Research, Dept. Labor, 1965-70; U.S. del. 8th meeting Am. mem. states ILO, 1966, U.S. del. to chem. industries com., 1969; tech. dir. Seminar for Ministry Labor Tng. Coordinators, OAS, Mexico City, 1970; asst. dir. for program devel. Ctr. for Human Resources U. Houston, 1970-75; manpower planning officer Gulf Coast CAMPS Secretariat, Mayor's Office, City of Houston, 1970-74; cons. Tex. Gov.'s Office Policy Coordination, Austin, 1974; asso. dir. human resources program, instr. econs. U. Mo.-Columbia, 1975-78; expert cons. Human Resources Devel., Bur. Internat. Labor Affairs, U.S. Dept. Labor and UN Devel. Program for Egypt, 1978-80; staff adv. Am. Productivity Center, Houston, 1980; expert cons. UN Indsl. Devel. Orgn., Cairo, Egypt, 1981; lectr. Coll. Bus. Adminstrn. Tex. Tech U., 1982-83; mgr. Post C. of C., 1984-87. Sec.-treas. Post Econ. Devel. Corp., 1984-90; bd. dirs. Tex. Common Cause, 1987—, legis. liaison, 1991, 93; mem. Lubbock-Garza County Pvt. Industry Coun., 1986-92, Friends of the Libr., Tex. Tech. U., Tex. Indsl. Devel. Coun.; chmn. Garza County Dem. Com., 1986-87, 91—; bd. dirs. Tex. Alliance for Edn. and the Arts, 1991-97, Maxine Durrett Earl Charitable Found. Lt. (j.g.) USNR, 1942-46, lt. comdr. USNR ret. Mem. ASTD, VFW, Am. Statis. Assn., Am. Acad. Polit. and Social Soc., Acad. Polit. Sci., Houston Pers. Assn., South Plains Cmty. Action Assn., Soc. Internat. Devel., Nat. Planning Assn., Indsl. Rels. Rsch. Assn., Nat. Economist Club, Garza County Trail Blazers (pres. 1994-97), Rotary, Lions, Alpha Chi, Omicron Delta Epsilon, Pi Sigma Alpha, Sigma Iota Epsilon. Methodist. Home: 1929 Stoney Brook Houston TX 77063-1809 Office: 601 W Main St Post TX 79356-3123 *I believe that individuals will make the right decisions if they have full and adequate information and facts, and therefore, I have sought to find the truth that will make men free.*

EARLE, ARTHUR PERCIVAL, textile company executive, airport executive; b. Montreal, Que., Can., Apr. 23, 1922; s. Arthur Percival and Bernadette (Gosselin) E.; m. Muriel Elizabeth Vining, June 1, 1946; children: Arthur Percival, Richard John, Janet Elizabeth. BEE, McGill U., Montreal, 1949; MMP, Harvard U., 1957. Registered profl. engr., Que., Ont. With Shawinigan Water & Power Co., 1949-63, asst. mgr. prodn. and plant; with Dominion Textile Inc., Montreal, 1963-90, chief engr., then group v.p. subs., 1970-78, sr. v.p. ops. svcs., 1978-87, sr. v.p., 1987-88, cons. corp. affairs, 1988-90; bd. dirs. Stella Jones Inc., chmn., 1993; bd. dirs. Shermag Inc.; past pres. Lana Knit Ltd., Fireside Fabrics Ltd., Fiber-World Ltd., Elpee Yarns Ltd., Jaro Ltd., Esmond Mills Mtd.; past chmn. Pemans Ltd., Foresbec Inc., 1988-93; chmn. Aeroport de Montreal, 1989-96, bd. dirs., 1989-96, pres., 1989-90. Bd. dirs. Ecole de Technologie Superieure, U. Que., 1978-85, mem. exec. com., 1981-85; pres. Montreal Bd. Trade, 1980-81, chmn. bd. dirs., 1981-82; pres., exec. com. Phoenix Found., 1985-89; bd. dirs. Lakeshore Gen. Hosp., Pointe Claire, Que., 1987-94, vice chmn., 1989-94; chmn., Les Mercuriades Bus. Awards, 1985; chmn., bd. dirs. Aeroport De Montreal, 1989-96, pres., 1989-90; founding chmn. Can. Airports Coun., 1990-93, bd. dirs., 1990-96; chmn., pres. La Societe De Promotion Des Aeroport De Montréal, 1987-96; hon. chmn. bd. Phoenix Ctr., 1991-96. With RCAF, 1941-45. Recipient Award of Distinction Concordia U., 1989, 125th Anniversary of Can. Commemorative medal, 1992; mem. Order of Can., 1997. Fellow Engring. Inst. Can. (hon. treas. 1986-88, sr. v.p. 1988-89, pres. 1989-90); mem. IEEE (past sect. chmn.), Order Engrs. Que., Assn. Profl. Engrs. Ont., Am. Textile Managerial Engring. Soc., Que. C. of C. (pres. 1983-84, chmn., 1984-85), Royal Montreal Golf Club, Thistle Curling Club (pres. 1974-75), Mt. Stephen Club, Montreal Thistle Curling Club. Anglican.

EARLE, CLIFFORD JOHN, JR., mathematician; b. Racine, Wis., Nov. 3, 1935; s. Clifford John and Anne Elizabeth (Griffith) E.; m. Elizabeth Joan Deutsch, Dec. 27, 1960; children—Rebecca Ann, Susan Deborah. B.A., Swarthmore Coll., 1957; M.A., Harvard U., 1958, Ph.D., 1962. Instr. Harvard U., 1962-63, vis. lectr., 1968-69; mem. Inst. for Advanced Study, Princeton, N.J., 1963-65, 81; asst. prof. Cornell U., Ithaca, N.Y., 1965-66; assoc. prof. Cornell U., 1966-69, prof., 1969—, chmn. dept. math., 1976-79; vis. prof. U. Warwick, 1967; vis. lectr. Inst. Mittag-Leffler, 1972; mem. geometric function theory program, Math. Scis. Rsch. Inst., Berkeley, Calif., 1986. Assoc. editor Duke Math. Jour., 1973-79; contbr. articles to math. rsch. jours. John Simon Guggenheim Meml. fellow, 1974-75. Mem. Am. Math. Soc. (editor Proc. 1989-97, mng. editor 1997—). Home: 314 Elmwood Ave Ithaca NY 14850-4812 Office: Cornell U Dept Math Ithaca NY 14853-4201

EARLE, DAVID PRINCE, JR., physician, educator; b. Englewood, N.J., May 23, 1910; s. David Prince and Paula (Benner) E.; m. Elizabeth Temple Ingraham, June 27, 1936 (dec. Dec. 1998); children—David Prince III, Paul Winthrop, Kevin Campbell, Charles Benner. A.B., Princeton, 1933; M.D., Columbia, 1937, Sc.D. in Medicine, 1942. Intern St. Luke's Hosp., N.Y.C., 1937-39; resident Columbia Univ. Research Service, Goldwater Meml. Hosp., N.Y.C., 1939-41; research assoc. NYU Service, N.Y.C., 1939-41, dir., 1947-48; asst. prof. medicine, then assoc. prof. NYU Coll. Medicine, 1943-54; prof. Northwestern U. Med. Sch., Chgo., 1954-78, prof. emeritus, 1978—, chmn. med. dept., 1965-73; chmn. dept. research Chgo. Wesley Meml. Hosp., 1960-69, attending physician, 1969-73; attending physician Bellevue Hosp., N.Y.C., 1948-54, Passavant Meml. Hosp., Chgo., 1954-73; attending physician Northwestern Meml. Hosp., Chgo., 1973-78, sr. attending physician, 1978-87, emeritus physician, 1987—; sec. clin. testing panel, bd. coordination antimalarial studies NRC, 1943-45; mem. medicine test com. Nat. Bd. Med. Examiners, 1956-60, chmn., 1960; mem. cardiovascular study sect. NIH, 1958-61, mem. diabetes and metabolism tng. com., 1964-67, chmn., 1966-67, chmn. urology tng. com., 1967-68, mem. nat. adv. arthritis and metabolic diseases council, 1970-73, mem. artificial kidney and chronic uremia rev. com., 1970-75; mem. ad hoc group clin. and preclin. pharmacology Walter Reed Army Inst. Research, 1967-76, chmn., 1976; mem. sci. adv. bd. Nat. Kidney Found., 1965-68, Ill. Kidney Found., 1966-84, chmn., 1969-70, chmn. nat. med. adv. council, 1969-70; mem. malaria commn. Armed Forces Epidemiological Bd., 1966-73; chmn. Internat. Com. Nomenclature and Nosology of Renal Disease. Author articles, chpts. in books in field.; editor Jour. Chronic Diseases, 1966-81, editor emeritus, 1981—; mem. editorial bd. Clin. Pharmacology and Therapeutics, 1967-73; mem. adv. bd. Internat. Dictionary Medicine and Biology, 1976-88; mem. editorial bd. Cardiovascular Medicine, 1976-79, Cardiovascular Revs., 1980-87. Fellow AAAS, ACP (master, rep. residency rev. com. internal medicine 1961-65); mem. Am. Heart Assn. (dir. 1962-65, chmn. council circulation 1963-65), Ill. Heart Assn., Chgo. Heart Assn. (dir.) (1966-69), Central Soc. Clin. Research (pres. 1964-65), Am. Soc. Clin. Investigation (editorial com. 1952-57), Assn. Am. Physicians, Am. Clin. and Climatological Assn. (councilor 1970-73, 78-81, pres. 1978), AMA, Chgo. Soc. Internal Medicine (pres. 1967-68), Am. Soc. Nephrology (founding mem.), Internat. Soc. Nephrology (exec. com. 1975-84), Assn. Former Chairmen of Medicine (pres. 1980), Alpha Omega Alpha. Club: Indian Hill (Winnetka, Ill.). Office: 764 Locust St Winnetka IL 60093-1822

EARLE, ELIZABETH DEUTSCH, biology educator; b. Vienna, Austria, Oct. 6, 1937; came to U.S., 1939; d. George F. and Sabina (Edel) Deutsch; m. Clifford J. Earle, Jr., Dec. 27, 1960; children: Rebecca A., Susan D. BA, Swarthmore Coll., 1959; MA, Radcliffe Coll., 1960; PhD, Harvard U., 1964. Rsch. fellow biology Harvard U., Cambridge, Mass., 1968-69; rsch. assoc. floriculture Cornell U., Ithaca, N.Y., 1970-74; rsch. assoc. plant breeding Cornell U., Ithaca, 1975-78, sr. rsch. assoc. plant breeding, 1978-79, assoc. prof. plant breeding, 1979-86, prof. plant breeding, 1986—; vis. scholar biology Stanford (Calif.) U., 1986, chmn. plant breeding, 1993—; mem. NSF Review Panel, Washington, 1979-82, USDA Review Panel, Washington, 1983-85; dir. Plant Tissue Culture Facility, Cornell U., Ithaca, 1983-89; cons. on internat. biotech. issues. Editor Plant Cell Reports, 1986—. Recipient predoctoral fellowship NSF, 1959-63, postdoctoral fellowship NIH, 1964-65; grantee NSF, USDA, Dept. Energy, Industry, 1978—. Mem. Internat. Assn. Plant Tissue Culture, Am. Soc. Plant Physiologists, Internat. Assn. for Plant Molecular Biology, Crucifer Genetics Coop., Sigma Xi, Phi Beta Kappa. Achievements include development of procedures for tissue culture and genetic manipulation of maize, sorghum, brassica, tomato, potato; development of improved cytoplasmic male-sterile lines of brassica vegetables. Office: Cornell U Dept Plant Breeding 252 Emerson Hall Ithaca NY 14853-1901

EARLE, JEAN BUIST, computer company executive; b. Newton, N.J., Oct. 5, 1951; d. Richardson and Jean (Mackerly) Buist; m. Terry Dean Earle, Mar. 4, 1989; children: Morgan, Abigail. AB, Cornell U., 1973; MEd, Coll. William and Mary, 1974; MBA, U. Pa., 1987. Mgr. The Korman Corp., Jenkintown, Pa., 1975-77; v.p. ops. Community Assn. Mgmt. Co., Havertown, Pa., 1977-78; adminstrv. asst. Albert Einstein Med. Ctr., Phila., 1978-83; assoc. adminstr. Meml. Hosp. Burlington County, Mt. Holly, N.J., 1983-87; v.p. Overlook Hosp., Summit, N.J., 1987-95; exec. dir. Summit (N.J.) Child Care Ctrs., Inc., 1995-96; owner, ptnr. Computer Edn. Inst., Warren, N.J., 1996—. Chmn. Kirby Ctr. YMCA Family Coun., 1996-98. Fellow Am. Coll. Healthcare Execs; mem. Am. Hosp. Assn., Assn. for Health Svcs. Rsch., U. Pa. Wharton Sch. Alumni Assn., Cornell Club (trustee Family Link of Union and Essex counties 1994-96, past pres.), Ctr. for Enabling Tech. (bd. trustees 1997—). Home: 31 Broadview Ter Chatham NJ 07928-1826 Office: Washington Sq 104 Town Center Dr Warren NJ 07059-5692

EARLE, MARY MARGARET, marketing executive; b. Newberry, Mich., June 26, 1947; d. William Loren and Naida Theresa (Ward) E. Student, St. Mary's Coll., Notre Dame, Ind., 1965-67. Cert. employment cons. Receptionist Western Girl World, San Francisco, 1968-69; receptionist, sec. Advanced Memory Systems, Sunnyvale, Calif., 1969-71; career cons. Qualified Personnel, Madison, Wis., 1972-75; VIP asst. Summit Sports Arena Grand Open, Houston, 1975, S. Petroleum Gp/OTC, Houston, 1976, Astrodomain Assn., Houston, 1976-77; bus. mgr. Mobile Colo TV Prodn., Houston, 1977-80; broadcast bus. affairs dir. G.D.L. & W. Adv., Houston, 1980-90; broadcast talent cons. Willis, Tex., 1990-93; mktg. cons., pvt. practice Marquette, Mich., 1993-95; pres. IXL Creative-Mktg. Excellence, Marquette, Mich., 1996—; modeling judge Page Parks Sch. Modeling, Houston, 1988-91; cons. industry/union rels. AFTRA/SAG, Houston, 1985-92. Houston mem. Fashion Group, 1989-90; sec. Bluebell Estates Assn., Willis, 1991, pres. 1992; pub. rels. vol. Women's Ctr. seminars, Houston, 1984-85. Named Disting. Salesman of Yr. Sales and Mktg. Execs., Madison, 1973, 74. Mem. Adminstrv. Mgmt. Soc. (cons. ofcl. panel 1974), Pers. Adminstrs. Soc., Am. Assn. Advt. Agys. (so. broadcast policy com.), Lake Superior Art Assn. (bd. dirs. 1996—). Avocations: sculling, jazzercise, raising dogs. Home and Office: 612 County Road 480 Marquette MI 49855-9411

EARLE, PATRICIA NELSON, artist; b. West Point, N.Y., Dec. 18, 1942; d. Wilton Haynsworth and Patricia Ann (Nelson) Earle; m. James Edward Lipscomb III, 1970 (div. 1998); 1 child, Drayton Earle. AA, Mt. Vernon Coll., 1963; BS, Furman U., 1986. Exhibited in solo shows at Furman U., Greenville, S.C., 1993, Barnes and Noble, Greenville, 1997, Cafo Ristretto, Greenville, 1997; group exhbns. include Taos (N.Mex.) Art Assocs., 1994, Carolina/Ga. Blood Ctr., Greenville, 1998, Art in the Park, Greenville, 1996, 97, others; represented in pub. collections including Liberty Life Corp., N.Y.C., Carolina First Bank, Greenville, Summit Nat. Bank, Greenville, Erskine (S.C.) Coll., numerous pvt. collections. Mem. Upstate Visual Arts, Jr. League of Greenville. Democrat. Episcopalian. Avocation: travel. Home: 622 Mcdaniel Ave Greenville SC 29605-2830

EARLE, RALPH, II, lawyer; b. Bryn Mawr, Pa., Sept. 26, 1928; s. George Howard and Huberta (Potter) E.; m. Eleanor Forbes Owens, Nov. 29, 1952 (div. 1985); children: Eleanor F., Ralph III, Duncan O., Amanda W., Caroline E.; m. Julie von Sternberg Collins, May 23, 1986. AB, Harvard U., 1950, LLB, 1955. Bar: Mass. 1955, Pa. 1957, D.C. 1980. Law clk. U.S. Dist. Ct., 1955-56; assoc., then ptnr. Morgan, Lewis & Bockius, Phila., 1956-68, 72-73; prin. dep. asst. sec. internat. security affairs U.S. Dept. Def., Washington, 1968-69; def. advisor U.S. mission to NATO, 1969-72; rep. to SALT II U.S. Arms Control/Disarmament Agy. (ACDA), 1973-77, ambassdor, alt. chmn. U.S. del, 1977-78, chmn., 1978-80, spl. rep. for arms control and disarmament negotiations, 1977-80, dir., 1980-81; assoc. Ctr. for Fgn. Policy Devel., Brown U., Providence, 1981-82; ptnr. Earle and Greene & Co., Stamford, Conn., 1982-83, Baker & Daniels, Washington, 1983-86; nat. policy dir. Lawyers Alliance for World Security, Washington, 1987-90, chmn., bd. dirs., 1990-94; dep. dir. Arms Control & Disarmament Agy., Washington, 1994-99; vis. prof. Ind. U. Law Sch., 1994. Served with AUS, 1950-52. Mem. Am. Law Inst., Coun. Fgn. Rels., Internat. Inst. Strategic Studies, Phila. Club, Met. Club (Washington), Harvard Club (pres. Phila. club 1967-68), Brook Club (N.Y.C.), Rockaway Hunting Club (L.I.), Lawrence Beach (L.I.) Club. Office: Ste 305 1901 Pennsylvania Ave NW Washington DC 20006

EARLE, SYLVIA ALICE, research biologist, oceanographer; b. Gibbstown, N.J., Aug. 30, 1935; d. Lewis Reade and Alice Freas (Richie) E. BS, Fla. State U., 1955; MA, Duke U., 1956, PhD, 1966, PhD (hon.), 1993; PhD (hon.), Monterey Inst. Internat. Studies, 1990, Ball State U., 1991, George Washington U., 1992; U. R.I., 1996, Plymouth State Coll., 1996; DSc (hon.), Ripon Coll., 1994, U. Conn., 1994. Resident dir. Cape Haze Marine Lab., Sarasota, Fla., 1966-67; research scholar Radcliffe Inst., 1967-69; research fellow Farlow Herbarium, Harvard U., 1967-75, researcher, 1975—; research assoc. in botany Natural History Mus. Los Angeles County, 1970-75; research biologist, curator Calif. Acad. Scis., San Francisco, from 1976; research assoc. U. Calif., Berkeley, 1969-75; fellow in botany Natural History Mus., 1989—; chief scientist U.S. NOAA, Washington, 1990-92, advisor to the adminstr., 1992-93; founder, pres., CEO, bd. dirs. Deep Ocean Engrs., Inc., Oakland, Calif., 1981-90; founder, chmn., CEO Deep Ocean Exploration and Rsch., Oakland, 1992—, bd. dirs., 1992—; advisor SeaWeb, 1996—; bd. dirs. Dresser Industries, Oryx Energy, Inc.; explorer-in-residence Nat. Geog., 1998; dir., Natl. Geographic Sustainable Seas Expedition, 1998—. Author: Exploring the Deep Frontier, 1980, Sea Change, 1995; editor: Scientific Results of the Tektite II Project, 1972-75; contbr. 100 articles to profl. jours. Trustee World Wildlife Fund U.S., 1976-82, mem. coun., 1984—; trustee World Wildlife Fund Internat., 1979-81, mem. coun., 1981-95; trustee Charles A. Lindbergh Fund, pres., 1990-95; trustee Ctr. Marine Conservation, 1992—, Perry Found., chmn., 1993-95; mem. coun. Internat. Union for Conservation of Nature, 1979-81; corp. mem. Woods Hole Oceanographic Inst., trustee, 1996—; mem. Nat. Adv. Com. on Oceans and Atmosphere, 1980-94. Recipient Conservation Svc. award U.S. Dept. Interior, 1970, Boston Sea Rovers award, 1972, 79, Nogi award Underwater Soc. Am., 1976, Conservation Svc. award Calif. Acad. Sci., 1979, Order of Golden Ark Prince Netherlands, 1980, David B. Stone medal New Eng. Aquarium, 1989, Gold medal Soc. Women Geographers, medal Radcliffe Coll., 1990, Pacon Internat. award, 1992, Dirs. award Natural Resources Coun. Am., 1992, Washburn award Boston Mus. Sci., 1995, Charles A. and Ann Morrow Lindbergh award, 1996, Julius Stratton Leadership award, 1997, Kilby award, 1997, Bal de la Mar Found. Sea Keeper award, 1997, Sea Space Environment award, 1997; Environmental Global Zoo Awd., 1998; U.S. Environmental Hew Awd., 1998; named Woman of Yr. L.A. Times, 1970, Scientist of Yr., Calif. Mus. Sci. and Industry, 1981. Fellow AAAS, Marine Tech. Soc. (Compass award 1997), Calif. Acad. Scis., Calif. Acad. Sci., Explorers Club (hon., bd. dirs. 1989-94, Lowell Thomas award 1980, Explorers medal 1996); mem. Internat. Phycological Soc. (sec. 1974-80), Phycological Soc. Am., Am. Soc. Ichthyologists and Herpetologists, Am. Inst. Biol. Scis., Brit. Phycological Soc., Ecol. Soc. Am., Internat. Soc. Plant Taxonomists. Home and Office: 12812 Skyline Blvd Oakland CA 94619-3125*

EARLE, TIMOTHY KEESE, anthropology educator; b. New Bedford, Mass., Aug. 10, 1946; s. Osborne and Eleanor (Clark) E.; m. Eliza Howe, June 14, 1969; children: Caroline, Hester. BA summa cum laude, Harvard U., 1969; MA, U. Mich., 1971, PhD, 1973. Rsch. archaeologist Bishop Mus., Honolulu, 1971-72; prof. anthropology UCLA, 1973-95, dir. Inst. of Archaeology, 1987-92; prof. anthropology Northwestern U., Evanston, Ill., 1995—, chair dept., 1995—. Author: How Chiefs Come to Power, 1997; co-author: Evolution of Human Society, 1987; editor: Exchange Systems in Prehistory, 1977, Contexts for Prehistoric Exchange, 1982, Chiefdoms, 1991.

Mem. Am. Anthrop. Assn. (pres. archaeology divsn. 1995-97), Soc. Am. Archaeology, Soc. Econ. Anthrop., Phi Beta Kappa.

EARLE, VICTOR MONTAGNE, III, lawyer; b. N.Y.C., June 13, 1933; s. Victor Montagne and Marian Jeanette (Litonius) E.; m. Lois MacKennan, Dec. 28, 1955 (div. Jan. 1980); children: Jane Stewart, Susan Elizabeth, Anne McCallum; m. Karen Peterson Howard, Aug. 24, 1985. AB, Williams Coll., 1954; LLB, Columbia U., 1959. Bar: N.Y. 1960, U.S. Supreme Ct. 1963. Law clk. to Hon. Leonard Moore, U.S. Ct. Appeals (2nd cir.), 1959-60; assoc. Cravath, Swaine & Moore, N.Y.C., 1960-68; gen. counsel KPMG Peat Marwick, N.Y.C., 1968-86, Peat, Marwick Internat., 1978-86; ptnr. Cahill, Gordon & Reindel, N.Y.C., 1986-89; sr. v.p., gen. counsel Minet North Am., N.Y.C., 1989-93; gen. counsel KWELM Cos. and KWELM Holdings Ltd., N.Y.C., London, 1993-98, sr. counsel, 1998—; lectr. constl. and corp. law issues, U.S. and abroad. Contbr. articles to profl. jours. and popular mags. With U.S. Army, 1954-56. Recipient Constitutional Law prize Columbia U. Mem. ABA, N.Y. State Bar Assn., Internat. Bar Assn., Assn. of Bar of City of N.Y. (judiciary com. 1983-86), Am. Law Inst., Lawyers Com. Civil Rights under Law (trustee), Legal Aid Soc. (bd. dirs. 1980-86), Fund for Modern Cts. (bd. dirs.), Columbia U. Alumni Assn. (bd. dirs. 1982-87). Office: 599 Lexington Ave Ste 1803 New York NY 10022-6030*

EARLES, PAT, city administrator; b. Nov. 5, 1938. AA, Paducah C.C. Spl. programs summer supervisor City of Paducah, Ky.; phys. edn. instr. City Bd. Edn., Paducah; supervisor arts & spl. programs Parks Dept., Paducah. Home: 525 Joe Clifton Paducah KY 42001

EARLEY, KATHLEEN SANDERS, municipal official; b. Ortonville, Minn., Jan. 14, 1946; d. Robert E. and Shirley C. (Stansfield) Sanders; m. Jack L. Earley; children: Michael, Ralph. BA in English, Carroll Coll., Waukesha, Wis., 1975; student, Wright State U., 1974-75, 78-79; postgrad., Ariz. State U., 1985, 90. In accounts receivable Pickett Industries, Inc., Santa Barbara, Calif., 1969-71; in customer svc. Vernay Labs. Inc., Yellow Springs, Ohio, 1972-76; contracts adminstr. Western Gear, Flight Systems, Jamestown, N.D., 1977-78; adminstrv. asst. City of Fairborn, Ohio, 1978-79; new student coord. DeVry Inst. Tech., Phoenix, 1979-80; adminstrv. asst. City of Mesa, Ariz., 1980-90; asst. to city mgr. City of Big Bear Lake, Calif., 1990-92; budget & mgmt. analyst Coconino County, Flagstaff, Ariz., 1992-94; adminstrv. asst. Lockwood Greene Engrs., Cin., 1994-96; city/twp. adminstr. Fairfield Twp./City of Indian Springs, Ohio, 1996—; mem. staff Big Bear Lake Film Commn., 1990-92. Editor: Earley Stop Smoking Plan, 1987, Earley Approach to Hatha Yoga, 1988, Earley's Customer Service, 1988; author: (poetry) Into the Night, 1967. Chair bd. dirs. Mesa Leadership Tng. and Devel. Alumni Assn., 1985; chair com. Mesa Cmty. Coun., 1986; mem. Cmty. Coun., Pleasant Ridge, Ohio, 1996, Greater Hamilton Safety Coun., 1997—; mem. Hamilton-Fairfield Symphony Chorale. Mem. Internat. City/County Mgmt. Assn., League of Calif. Cities, Mcpl. Mgmt. Assts. So. Calif., Ariz. Mcpl. Mgmt. Assts. (sec. 1983), Calif. Assn. Pub. Info. Ofcls., Pub. Risk Mgmt. Assn., Gov. Fin. Officers Assn., Mesa Red Tape Toastmasters (charter mem., adminstrv. v.p. 1987, pres. 1989, 1st Place Area Speech Contest 1990), Ohio Twp. Assn. Avocations: aerobics, yoga, hiking, travel, t'ai chi. E-mail: kearley@fairfieldtwp.org. Home: 5881 Mindy Dr Indian Spgs OH 45011-2209 Office: Fairfield Twp 6032 Morris Rd Indian Spgs OH 45011-5118

EARLEY, LAURENCE ELLIOTT, medical educator; b. Ahoskie, N.C., Jan. 23, 1931; s. Frank Claxton and Eleanor (Dilday) E.; m. Joanne Frances Sinclair, Sept. 5, 1953; children: Laurence Elliott Jr., Peter Hunter. BS, U. N.C., 1953, MD, 1956; MA (hon.), U. Pa., 1978. Diplomate Am. Bd. Internal Medicine (chmn. 1987-88). Asst. prof. Harvard Med. Sch., Boston, 1967-68; assoc. prof. U. Calif. Sch. Medicine, San Francisco, 1968-69, prof., 1969-73, chief of nephrology, 1968-73; prof., chmn. dept. medicine U. Tex. Health Sci. Ctr., San Antonio, 1973-77; chmn. dept. medicine, Frank Wister Thomas Prof. U. Pa., Phila., 1977-90, chmn. dept. phys. medicine & rehab., 1987-90, Francis C. Wood prof., 1983-95, sr. assoc. dean., 1992-95; clin. prof. medicine U. N.C., Chapel Hill, 1995—; mem. study sect. NIH, Bethesda, Md., 1969-77. Editor: Diseases of The Kidney; contbr. articles on Kidney desease and physiology to profl. jours. Chmn. sci. adv. bd. Nat. Kidney Found., N.Y.C., 1973-74. Sr. asst. surgeon USPHS, 1959-61. Recipient Kaiser award U. Calif. San Francisco, 1972, Disting. Svc. award U. N.C., 1976. Master ACP; mem. Assn. Profs. Medicine (pres. 1983-84), Am. Soc. for Clin. Investigation (pres. 1975-76), Am. Soc. Nephrology (pres. 1977-78), Inst. Medicine, Assn. Am. Physicians (pres. 1988-89), Phi Beta Kappa, Alpha Omega Alpha. Avocations: photography, woodwork. Home: 209 Huntington Dr Chapel Hill NC 27514-2419

EARLEY, MARK LAWRENCE, state attorney general; b. Norfolk, Va., July 26, 1954; s. Whitmel Franklin and Ann Harris Earley; m. Cynthia Ellen Breithaupt, June 5, 1982; children: Rachel, Justin, Mark, Jr., Mary Catherine, Franklin Edward, Anne Harris. BA in Religion, Coll. William and Mary, 1976, JD, 1982. Bar: Va. Ptnr. Tavss, Fletcher, Earley and King, P.C., Norfolk, 1982-97; senator Senate of Va., 1987-97; atty. gen. Commonwealth of Va., 1998—; Senate Rep. Whip, 1993; mem. privileges and elections com. Va. State Senate, 1993—, cts. justice com., 1988—, local govt. com., 1988—, rehab. and social svcs. com., 1988—; chmn. local govt. charter subcom. Va. State Senate, 1992—; mem. Gov.'s Commn. Parole Abolition and Sentencing Reform, 1994, Gov.'s Commn. Champion Schs., 1994, State Water Commn., 1994, Commn. Preservation of Capitol, 1994, Adv. Commn. Welfare Reform, 1994, Commn. Youth's Juvenile Detention Task Force, 1994, Commn. Sentencing and Parole Policies and the Need to Establish Truth in Sentencing, 1993—, Quadrennial Review Panel for Child Support Guidelines, 1994, Poverty Commn., 1992-93, Chowan River Commn., 1988—, Commn. Youth's Task Force, 1992-94; mem. environ. quality and natural resources com. So. Legis. Conf., 1994; mem. family ct. pilot project com. Supreme Ct. Va., 1989-93. Del. Rep. Nat. Conv., 1988, 92, mem. platform com., 1992; founding mem. Rep. Leadership Network; hon. chmn. Va. chpt. United Negro Coll. Fund, 1990; mem. Atlantic Shores Bapt. Ch.; mem. Chesapeake Cmty. Svcs. Bd., 1985-87; mem. Chesapeake Cmty. Corrections Resources Bd., 1985-87, vice-chmn., 1986-87; mem. Leadership Hampton Roads, 1990; bd. dirs. Comprehensive Health Investment Project, 1994, Va. CARES, Inc., 1993—, Tidewater Legal Aid, 1993—; Chesapeake bd. dirs. Commerce Bank, 1993—. Recipient Environ. award Port Folio Mag., 1990, Appreciation award Va. Crime Prevention Assn., Outstanding Alumnus and Disting. Pub. Svc. award Presdl. Classroom for Young Ams., 1994; Henry Toll fellow Coun. State Govts., 1994. Mem. Am. Trial Lawyers Assn., Nat. Rep. Legislators Assn. (bd. dirs. 1990-97; Legislator of Yr. award 1997), Va. State Bar, Va. Bar Assn., Va. Trial Lawyers Assn., Chesapeake Bar Assn., Norfolk-Portsmouth Bar Assn., Tidewater Pro Bono Program, Rotary Club, Great Bridge Sertoma Club. Office: Office of Atty Gen 900 E Main St Richmond VA 23219-3513 also: PO Box 36347 Richmond VA 23235-8007*

EARLL, JERRY MILLER, internist, educator; b. Hawarden, Iowa, Aug. 15, 1928; s. Harry Ezra and Magdalene Anna (Miller) E.; m. Faith Anne Allbaugh, Sept. 14, 1956; children: Leslie Anne, Nikki Lee, Holly Magdalene. B.S., U. Nebr., 1950; M.D., U. Iowa, 1958; postgrad., U. Calif., 1965-66. Diplomate: Am. Bd. Internal Medicine, Am. Bd. Endocrinology, Am. Bd. Nuclear Medicine, Am. Bd. Geriatrics. Commd. 2d lt. U.S. Army, 1951, advanced through grades to col., 1972; intern Letterman Gen. Hosp., San Francisco, 1958; resident in internal medicine Letterman Gen. Hosp., 1959-62; chief endocrinology and metabolism William Beaumont Gen. Hosp., El Paso, 1963-65, Tripler Gen. Hosp., Honolulu, 1965-69, Walter Reed Army Inst. Research and Walter Reed Army Hosp., Washington, 1969-76; chief dept. medicine Walter Reed Army Hosp., 1976-79; cons. endocrinology Office Surgeon Gen.; asso. prof. medicine U. Hawaii, 1967-69; clin. prof. medicine Georgetown U., 1976-79; prof. medicine, vice chmn. dept. medicine Uniformed Services Univ. Health Scis., Washington, 1977-79; prof. and chief divsn. internal medicine Georgetown U., Washington, 1979-94; dir. geriatrics svc. Georgetown U. and Hosp., Washington, 1993—; med. dir. to v.p. med. affairs Washington Home, 1996, 97—. Decorated Legion of Merit, Army Commendation medal, Meritorious Service medal. Fellow ACP; mem. Am. Fedn. Clin. Rsch., Am. Diabetes Assn., Endocrine Soc., N.Y. Diabetes Assn., Assn. Mil. Surgeons, Acad. Medicine of Washington (Regional Laureate award of Am. Coll. of Physicians). Research and publs. on pituitary and thyroid physiology. Home: 8529 Brickyard Rd Potomac MD 20854-4834 Office: Georgetown U Hosp 3800 Reservoir Rd NW Washington DC 20007-2113

EARLOUGHER, ROBERT CHARLES, SR., petroleum engineer; b. Kans., May 6, 1914; s. Harry Walter and Annetta (Partridge) E.; m. Jeanne D. Storer, Oct. 6, 1937; children: Robert Charles, Jr., Janet Earlougher Craven, Anne Earlougher O'Connell. Grad., Colo. Sch. Mines, 1936. Registered profl. engr., Calif., Okla., Tex., Kans. Supr. core lab. The Sloan and Zook Co., Bradford, Pa., 1936-38; co-owner, cons. Geologic Standards Co., Tulsa, 1938-45; owner, cons. Earlougher Engring., Tulsa, 1945-73; chmn., cons. Godsey-Earlougher, Inc., Tulsa, 1973-76, Petroleum Cons. div. Williams Bros. Engring. Co., Tulsa, 1976-88, Reactivated Earlougher Engring., Inc., Tulsa, 1988. Patentee in field. Mem. AIME (hon., Anthony F. Lucas Gold medal 1980), Am. Petroleum Inst. (chmn. mid-continent dist. 1961-62, citation for service 1964), Ind. Petroleum Assn. Am. (bd. dirs. 9 yrs.), Interstate Oil Compact Commn. (oil recovery com. 1947-96), Soc. Petroleum Engrs. (disting. svc. award 1973, disting. mem. award 1983, hon. mem. 1985, enhanced oil recovery pioneer 1992), Soc. Petroleum Evaluation Engrs. (hon. life award 1993), Summit Club, Petroleum Club, Southern Hills Country Club (Tulsa), Masons, Tau Beta Pi. Republican. Episcopalian. Home: 2135 E 48th Pl Tulsa OK 74105-8764 Office: Ste 15 2250 E 49th St Tulsa OK 74105-8773

EARLS, FELTON, child psychiatrist. Intern in pediats. Metro. Hosp., N.Y.C.; prof. child psychiatry Harvard Med. Sch., Boston, 1978—; prof. human behavior & devel. Harvard Sch. Pub. Health, Boston, 1978—; adj. prof. Rockefeller U.; prin. investigator Project Human Devel., Chgo.; Fellow AAAS; mem. Am. Psychiat. Assn. (disting. psychiatrist award, Blanche F. Ittleson award, Am. Acad. Pediats. (Dale Richmond award), NAS Inst. Medicine. Office: Harvard Sch Pub Health Dept Maternal & Child Health Kresge 313 677 Huntington Ave Boston MA 02115-6096

EARLS, IRENE ANNE, art history educator; d. William Thomas and Constance Ellen (Yanalavage) O'Connor; m. Walter Edward Earls, June 21, 1958. BA, U. Miami, Coral Gables, Fla., 1959; MA, U. Colo., 1968; PhD, U. Ga., 1975. Tchr. advanced placement history of art, English lang. and composition Orlando (Fla.) Pub. Schs.; prof. classics dept. U. Fla., Gainesville, 1994—. Author: Book Renaissance Art, 1987, Napoléon III l'Architecte et l'Urbaniste de Paris, 1991, Baroque Art, 1997; contbr. articles to profl. jours. Named Tchr. of Yr., 1987-88, Nat. Honor Soc. Tchr. of Yr., 1987-88, also others. Mem. Western Soc. French History (officer of program com.), Soc. for French Hist. Studies, Consortium on Revolutionary Europe. Avocation: writing. Office: 1625 Beulah Rd Winter Garden FL 34787-4407

EARLS, KEVIN GERARD, insurance company executive; b. N.Y.C., Mar. 24, 1952; s. Kevin Gerard and Geraldine Earls; m. Juliet Posner, Jan. 21, 1989; children: Tara, Sean. BS, Fordham U., 1974; MS, Columbia U., 1980. ChFC, CLU. Sales rep. Phoenix Home Life, N.Y.C., 1982-85, sales supr., 1985-87, asst. gen. mgr., 1987-90, assoc. gen. mgr., 1990-98; pres. Kevin G. Earls & Assocs., 1990—; sr. v.p. fin. svcs. The Am. Phoenix Corp., N.Y.C., 1998—; lectr. N.Y. Med. Coll. Contbg. author, illustrator: New Techniques in Rehabilitation, 1982. Mem. Am. Soc. Fin. Svcs. Profls., U.S. Judo Assn., U.S. Judo Fedn., Gen. Agts. and Mgrs. Assn. (bd. dirs. N.Y.C.), NALU, Am. Soc. CLU and ChFC, U.S. Judo Inc., N.Y. Athletic Club (judo chmn. 1980—), Douglaston Club. Avocations: judo, art, reading. Office: The Am Phoenix Corp 1211 Ave of AmericasFl 27 New York NY 10036-8701

EARLY, AMES S., healthcare system executive; b. Allison, Iowa, Apr. 18, 1937; s. W.C. and F. Eva Early; m. Beryl J. Early; 1 child, Barbara. BA, Drake U., 1959; MHA, U. Iowa, 1961. Adminstrv. resident, adminstrv. asst. U. Minn. Hosp., Mpls., 1961-67; exec. dir. Mary Francis Skiff Meml. Hosp., Newton, Iowa, 1967-68; asst. adminstr. Mercy Hosp., Miami, Fla., 1968-76; pres. Scripps Meml. Hosp., La Jolla, Calif., 1976-91; exec. v.p., COO Scripps Instns. Medicine and Sci., ScrippsHealth, 1991-93; pres., CEO Scripps Health, San Diego, 1994-98, vice chmn., CEO, 1999—. Pres. So. Fla. Hosp. Assn., 1974-75, bd. dirs., 1971-76; bd. dirs. Fla. Hosp. Assn., 1974-76, Comprehensive Health Planning of So. Fla., 1974-76, Nat. Coun. Cmty. Hosp., 1974—, Hosp. Coun. San Diego and Imperial Counties, 1978-86, Calif. Polit. Action Com., 1979-85, Calif. Health Decisions, 1994—, Catholic Healthcare West (bd. mem. 1996—), San Diego Econ. Devel. (bd. mem. 1990—), Blue Cross/Hosp. Adv. Com., 1982, Vol. Hosp. Am. West, 1986-91, San Diego Hospice (bd. mem. 1997—); mem. peer rev. panel Fla. Blue Cross Assn., 1975-76; trustee Calif. Assn. Hosp. and Health Sys., 1984-92, mem. exec. com., 1984-90, mem. legis. com., 1985, mem. hosp. med. staff bylaws com., 1985-86, treas., 1987, chmn., 1989; mem. Healthcare Forum. Recipient Headline of Yr. in Healthcare San Diego Press Club, 1987. Mem. Am. Coll. Healthcare Execs., Am. Hosp. Assn., Am. Assn. Hosp. Planning. Office: Scripps Health 4275 Campus Point Ct San Diego CA 92121-1513

EARLY, BERT HYLTON, lawyer, legal search consultant; b. Kimball, W.Va., July 17, 1922; s. Robert Terry and Sue Keister (Hylton) E.; m. Elizabeth Henry, June 24, 1950; children—Bert Hylton, Robert Christian, Mark Randolph, Philip Henry, Peter St. Clair. Student, Marshall U., 1940-42; A.B., Duke U., 1946; J.D., Harvard U., 1949. Bar: W.Va. 1949, Ill. 1963, Fla. 1981. Assoc. Fitzpatrick, Marshall, Huddleston & Bolen, Huntington, W.Va., 1949-57; asst. counsel Island Creek Coal Co., Huntington, W.Va., 1957-60, assoc. gen. counsel, 1960-62; dep. exec. dir. ABA, Chgo., 1962-64, exec. dir., 1964-81; sr. v.p. Wells Internat., Chgo., 1981-83, pres., 1983-85; pres. Bert H. Early Assocs. Inc., Chgo., 1985-94, Early Cochran & Olson, Chgo., 1994-98; of counsel Early Cochran & Olson, 1998—; dir. Am. Bar Found., Chgo., 1993-95; instr. Marshall U., Huntington, W.Va., 1950-53; cons. and lectr. in field. Bd. dirs. Morris Meml. Hosp. for Crippled Children, 1954-60, Huntington Pub. Libr., 1951-60, W.Va. Tax Inst., 1961-62, Huntington Mus. Art, 1961-62; mem. W.Va. Jud. Coun., 1960-62, Huntington City Coun., 1961-62; bd. dirs. Cmty. Renewal Soc., Chgo., 1965-76, United Charities Chgo., 1972-80, Hinsdale (Ill.) Hosp. Found., 1987-93, Internat. Bar Assn. Found., 1987-89; bd. dirs. Am. Bar Endowment, 1983-95, sec., 1987-89, treas., 1989-91, v.p., 1991-93, pres., 1993-95, dir. emeritus, 1995—; mem. vis. com. U. Chgo. Law Sch., 1975-78; trustee Davis and Elkins Coll., 1960-63; mem. Hinsdale Plan Commn., 1982-85. 1st lt. AC, U.S. Army, 1943-45. Fellow Am. Bar Found., Ill. Bar Found. (charter); mem. ABA (ho. of dels. 1958-59, 84-93, chmn. young lawyers divsn. 1957-58, Disting. Svc. award young lawyers divsn. 1983), Am. Law Inst. (life), Internat. Bar Assn. (asst. sec. gen. 1967-82), Nat. Legal Aid and Defender Assn., Legal Aid Soc. Chgo., Am. Judicature Soc. (bd. dirs. 1981-84), Fla. Bar, W.Va. Bar Assn., Chgo. Bar Assn. Presbyterian. Office: Early Cochran & Olson Inc 401 N Michigan Ave Ste 515 Chicago IL 60611-4280

EARLY, DELOREESE PATRICIA See REESE, DELLA

EARLY, GERALD, writer; b. Phila., Apr. 21, 1952; s. Henry Early and Florence (Fernandez) Oglesby; m. Ida Haynes, 1977; children: Linnet, Rosalind. BA cum laude, U. Pa., 1974; MA, Cornell U., 1980, PhD, 1982. Instr. Wash. U., St. Louis, 1982, asst. prof. black studies, 1982-84, asst. prof. English and African and Afro-American studies, 1984-88, assoc. prof. English and African and Afro-American studies, 1988-91; prof. English and African and Afro-American Studies Wash. U., 1991—, Merle Kling prof. modern letters, 1996—; mem. W. E. B. Du Bois Award Com., Wash. U., 1982; chmn. Toussaint L'Overture Award Com., Wash. U., 1983-84; African and Afro-American Studies Program rep., Univ. Coll. Coun., Wash. U., 1984-85; mem. Affirmative Action Com., Wash. U., 1984-85, 87-88, 88-89; mem. exec. com. Wash. U. English Dept., 1987-88, mem. undergrad. com., 1988-89; chmn. undergrad. honors program in English, Wash. U., 1988-89; assoc. prof. English and Afro-American studies, writer-in-residence Randolph-Macon Coll., 1990; script adviser (TV series) The Mississippi, Warner Bros. Comms., 1983, cons. Ken Burns' Baseball, 1994. Author: Tuxedo Junction: Essays on American Culture, 1990, The Culture of Bruising: Essays on Literature, Prizefighting, and Modern American Culture, 1991 (Nat. Book Critics Circle award in criticism 1994), One Nation Under a Groove: Motown and American Culture, 1994, Daughters: On Family and Fatherhood, 1994, How the War in the Streets Is Won: Poems of a Black American's Journey into Himself, 1995; editor: The Selected Writings of Countee Cullen, 1991, My Soul's High Song, 1991, Lure and Loathing: Essays on Race, Identity, and the Ambivalence of Assimilation, 1993; contbr. to periodicals including N.Y. Times Book Rev., Kenyon Rev., Antioch Rev., Black American Lit. Forum, American Poetry Rev., Antaeus, Obdidian II; spkr. in field. Cornell U. grad. fellow, 1977, 81, summer fellow, 1978-80; Josephine de Karman grad. fellow, 1981; Wash. U. summer rsch. fellow, 1984; U. Kans. minority postdoctoral fellow, 1985-87; Mo. Com. for Humanities grantee, 1983; recipient Creative Writing award Coun. of Creative and Performing Arts, 1978, Dissertation Rsch. award Cornell U., 1980, Whiting Found. Writer's award, 1988, General Electric Found. award for younger writers Coordinating Coun. Lit. Mags., 1988. Mem. Am. Studies Assn., MLA. Office: Wash Univ Old McMillan Bldg Rm 226 1 Brookings Dr Saint Louis MO 63130-4862*

EARLY, GREGG STEVEN, executive editor; b. Alexandria, Va., Sept. 11, 1963; s. Harry Alvin and Ruth Seder Early; m. Rocio Gonzalez Early, Nov. 26, 1990 (div. July 1998); m. Debra Lee Holtzclaw, Oct. 4, 1998; children: Megan, Maggie. BA, James Madison U. Proofreader Michie Co., Charlottesville, Va., 1985-87; staff writer Computech Pub., Falls Church, Va., 1987-88; editor Nat. PTA, Chgo., 1988-90; staff writer Kelly Comms., Charlottesville, Va., 1990-91; assoc. editor Am. Banker Newsletters, Bethesda, Md., 1991; mng. exec. editor KCI Comms., McLean, Va., 1991—; moderator pub. TV show, 1990-95. Author: (play) Bartleby Meets the Glurons, 1985, Tripwine Territory, 1987; contbr. poems and short stories to publs. Mem. PTA, Alexandria, 1998-99. Recipient Newsletter Pubs. Found. award for editl. excellence in newsletter journalism, 1994, 95, 96, 98, 99. Mem. Nat. Press Club, BMW Car Club of Am. Buddhist. Avocations: golf, hiking, rock climbing, cooking. E-mail: gearly@kci-com.com. Office: KCI Comms 1750 Old Meadow Rd Ste 300 Mc Lean VA 22102

EARLY, JACK JONES, foundation executive; b. Corbin, Ky., Apr. 12, 1925; s. Joseph M. and Lela (Jones) E.; m. Nancye Bruce Whaley, June 1, 1952; children: Lela Katherine, Judith Ann, Laura Hattie. A.B., Union Coll., Barbourville, Ky., 1948; M.A., U. Ky., 1953, Ed.D. (So. scholar 1955-56), 1956; B.D., Coll. of Bible, Lexington, Ky., 1956; D.D., Wesley Coll., Grand Forks, N.D., 1961; LL.D., Parsons Coll., 1962, Iowa Wesleyan Coll., 1972; Litt.D., Dakota Wesleyan U., 1969; L.H.D., Union Coll., Barbourville, Ky., 1979; D.Adminstrn., Cumberland Coll., 1981. Ordained to ministry Methodist Ch., 1954; pastor Rockhold Circuit, Ky., 1943-44, Craig's Chapel and Laurel Circuit, London, Ky., 1944-47, Trinity Ch., Oak Ridge, summer 1945, Hindman Ch., Ky., 1947-52; dean of men Hindman Settlement Sch., 1948-51; assoc. pastor Park Ch., Lexington, Ky., 1952-54; asst. to pres., dean Athens Coll., Ala., 1954- 55; v.p., dean of coll. Iowa Wesleyan Coll., Mount Pleasant, 1956-58; pres. Dakota Wesleyan U., 1958-69, Pfeiffer Coll., Misenheimer, N.C., 1969-71; exec. dir. Am. Bankers Assn., Washington, 1971-73; pres. Limestone Coll., Gaffney, S.C., 1973-79; exec. dir. edn. Combined Ins. Co. Am., Chgo., 1979-82, v.p., exec. dir. edn. and communications, 1982-84; pres. Ky. Ind. Coll. Fund, Louisville, 1984-93, pres. emeritus, 1993—; dir. edn., con. Napoleon Hill Found., Northbrook, Ill., 1997—; pres. W. Clement Stone PMA Communications, Inc., Chgo., 1987—. Active Boy Scouts Am.; mem. pres. adv. coun. North Pk. Coll.; mem. Felician adv. bd. Felician Coll.; mem. Ky. Ho. of Reps., 1952-54; bd. dirs. S.D. Found. Pvt. Colls., S.D. Meth. Found., Nat. Coun. on Youth Leadership, Ctr. for Citizenship Edn., YMCA, Motivational Inst., Mid-Am. chpt. ARC, 1980—, W. Clement and Jessie V. Stone Found., Northbrook Symphony Orch., Ky. Mountain Laurel Festival, 1990—, Internat. Coun. on Edn. for Teaching, 1990—; chmn. bd. Religious Heritage Am., 1989-92, Internat. Leadership Network, 1991—. Recipient Spoke award Mitchell Jr. C. of C., 1959, Disting. Svc. award, 1960, Disting. Svc. award S.D. Jr. C. of C., 1960, Gaffney Jaycees, 1979, Chief Iron Eyes Cody medal of Peace, 1987, Outstanding Kentuckian award O'Tucks, 1990; named Outstanding Former Kentuckian, 1963; hon. fellow Wroxton Coll., Oxfordshire, Eng.; named to Disting. Alumni Hall of Fame, U. Ky., 1965. Mem. Am. Soc. Assn. Execs., Louisville C. of C., Blue Key, Masons (33d degree, chaplain Valley of Louisville chpt. 1990—), Rotary (pres. Louisville 1992-93, dist. 6710 gov. 1996—), Ky. Soc. Sons of the Am. Revolution (pres. 1998—), Soc. War of 1812 in the Commonwealth of Ky. (pres. 1997—), Huguenot Soc. of Ky. (pres. 1999—), Huguenot Soc.-Soc. of Manakin (Ky. br. pres. 1999—), Gen. for Pub. Rels.-Gen. Soc. of the War of 1812 (v.p. 1998—), Del. State Soc. of Cin., Nat. Sojourners Camp #134, Heroes of '76 (E.B. Jones Camp), Kappa Delta Pi, Phi Delta Kappa (bd. dirs. Northwestern U. chpt. 1980—), Kappa Phi Kappa, Alpha Psi Omega, Theta Phi, Pi Tau Chi. Republican. Home and Office: 9002 Hurstwood Ct Louisville KY 40222-5716

EARLY, JAMES H., JR., lawyer; b. Henderson, N.C., May 6, 1939; s. James Howard and Nettie Anna (Hicks) E.; m. Ida Patricia Robinson; children: James H. III, Anna Elizabeth, Mary Elizabeth. AA, Mars Hill Coll., 1960; BA, Wake Forest U., 1962, LLB, 1964, JD, 1970. Bar: N.C. 1964, U.S. Dist. Ct. (mid. dist.) N.C. 1970, U.S. Ct. Appeals (4th cir.) 1995; cert. mediator Superior Cts. of N.C., 1992. Pvt. practice Winston-Salem, 1964—; mediator Adminstrv. Office of the Cts. of N.C., 1992—; mediator Am. Arbitration Assn., 1992—. Contbr. articles to profl. jours. With U.S. Army, 1957. Chmn. fundraising Cub Scouts/Boy Scouts Am., Little League, Pop Warner, Indian Guides, March of Dimes, others. With U.S. Army. Mem. ABA, ATLA, N.C. Bar Assn. (chmn. continuing legal edn. subcom., mem. effectiveness and quality of life com., moderator skills course com.), , Forsyth County Bar Assn. (sec. 1970-71), N.C. Acad. Trial Lawyers, Phi Alpha Delta (alumni advisor 1969-84, Outstanding Alumnus award 1967), Kiwanis (pres. 1989-90, 91-92), Masons. Baptist. Avocations: hunting, fishing, walking horses, bird dogs, racing. Home: 519A S Salisbury St Mocksville NC 27028 Office: 1320 Westgate Center Dr Winston Salem NC 27103-2933

EARLY, JAMES MICHAEL, electronics research consultant; b. Syracuse, N.Y., July 25, 1922; s. Frank J. and Rhoda Gray Early; m. Mary Agnes Valentine, Dec. 28, 1948; children: Mary Beth Early Dehler, Kathleen, Joan Early Farrell, Rhoda Early Alexander, Maureen Early Mathews, Rosemary Early North, James, Margot Early Staton. B.S., N.Y. Coll. Forestry, Syracuse, N.Y., 1943; M.S., Ohio State U., 1948, Ph.D., 1951. Instr., research assoc. Ohio State U., Columbus, 1946-51; dir. lab. Bell Telephone Labs., Murray Hill, N.J., 1951-64, Allentown, Pa., 1964-69; dir. research and devel. Fairchild Semicondr. Corp., Palo Alto, Calif., 1969-83, sci. advisor, 1983-86; research cons., 1987—. Contbr. over 20 papers to profl. jours. Served with U.S. Army, 1943-45. Fellow AAAS, IEEE (numerous coms., John Fritz Medal bd. of award); mem. IEEE Electron Device Soc. (J.J. Ebers award 1979), Am. Phys. Soc., Internat. Platform Assn. Roman Catholic. Achievements include 14 patents; discovery of Space Charge Layer Widening effect (now called Early effect); invention of the high frequency bipolar transistor and intrinsic barrier transistor; developer of Telstar solar cells and transistors, of sealed junction beam lead integrated circuits; design theory of bipolar transistors; definition of fundamental speed-power limits in junction devices; first commercial use of ion implanter in semiconductor devices; first use of buried channel charge coupled devices, of traveling wave charge-coupled detectors, of high speed ECL and advanced CMOS; procurement of first practical commercial electron beam machine for maskmaking; proposing fastest bipolar circuit. Home and Office: 708 Holly Oak Dr Palo Alto CA 94303-4142 *Each experiment is inexact. Each theory has an assumption. Each miracle is doubted. Each person is free. Faith is a gift. Our lives tell our philosophies. Happiness is a habit. Proverbs are mostly true. Noble spirits are everywhere. Love and sacrifice give example and opportunity. Malice is rare. Ignorance and indifference make problems.*

EARLY, JUDITH K., social services director; b. Evansville, Ind., 1954; d. Forrest M. and Dorothea E. Early. BA, Brescia Coll., 1976; MS, So. Ill. U., 1985, RhD, 1991. Cert. vocat. evaluator. Work activity supr. So. Ind. Rehab. Svcs., Inc., Boonville, 1976-78; vocat. evaluator Evansville Assn. for Retarded Citizens, 1978-85; vocat. evaulator Evaluation and Developmental Ctr., Carbondale, Ill., 1985-88; grad. asst., program evaluator So. Ill. U., Carbondale, 1988-90, rsch. and teaching asst., 1990-91; exec. dir. Albion Fellow Bacon Ctr., Evansville, Ind., 1991-93; family svcs. dir. Goodwill Family Ctr., Evansville, 1993-95, program evaluation dir., 1995-96, dir., 1996—. Contbr. articles to profl. publs. Bd. dirs. So. Ill. Ctr. for Ind. Living, Carbondale, 1990-91; bd. dirs., youth worker 1st United Meth. Ch., Carbondale, 1989-91; v.p. Altrusa of Evansville, 1993-94; bd. dirs. Youth as Resources, 1995—; chmn. Transitional Svcs., Inc., Human Rights Com., 1992—. Mem. ACA, AAUW, Nat. Rehab. Assn. (accessibility site surveyor 1990—), Vocat. Evaluation and Work Adjustment Assn. (chmn. student affairs com. 1988-90, Student Lit. award 1987), Ill. Rehab. Assn. (bd. dirs. 1989-91), Ill. Vocat. Evaluation and Work Adjustment Assn. (chmn. mem. 1989-91, pres. 1991—, Disting. Svc. award 1989), Am. Assn. Mental Retardation, Assn. Retarded Citizens, Kiwanis (sec. North Park chpt. 1993-

94). Avocations: needlepoint, gardening, photography, cooking. Office: Goodwill Family Ctr 1351 W Buena Vista Rd Evansville IN 47710-3338

EARLY, WILLIAM JAMES, education educator; b. Holyoke, Mass., Mar. 22, 1921; s. John J. and Mary Leah (LaPointe) E.; m. Clare Patricia Milacki, June 8, 1946; children: Patricia, John, Kathleen, Marilyn. B.S., U. Toledo, 1946; M.A., U. Mich., 1949; Ph.D., Mich. State U., 1963. Tchr. social studies and English Bedford High Sch., Temperance, Mich., 1946-54; supt. schs. Deerfield (Mich.) Pub. Schs., 1954-57, Fenton (Mich.) Area Pub. Schs., 1957-63, Rochester (Mich.) Community Schs., 1963-66, Flint (Mich.) Community Schs., 1966-73, West Irondequoit Cen. Sch. Dist., Rochester, N.Y., 1973-82; prof. edn. Corpus Christi (Tex.) State U., 1983-94, Tex. A&M U., Corpus Christi, 1994—; cons. HEW Vocat. Dept.; mem. faculty Nat. Acad. for Sch. Execs. Decorated Silver Star, Purple Heart. Mem. Nat. Sch. Pub. Relations Assn., Am. Assn. Sch. Adminstrs. (past chmn. fed. policy and legis. com.), Phi Delta Kappa. Clubs: Kiwanis (Frankfort, Mich.), Crystal Downs Golf (Frankfort, Mich.); Pharoahs Country (Corpus Christi). Home: 4600 Ocean Dr Corpus Christi TX 78412-2589 Home: 113 S Shore E Frankfort MI 49635-9540 Office: 6300 Ocean Dr Corpus Christi TX 78412-5503

EARLY, WILLIAM TRACY, journalist; b. Scurry County, Tex., Feb. 20, 1934; s. Willis Worley Jr. and Lillian Marian (Walton) E. BA, Baylor U., 1954; BDiv, Southeastern Bapt. Sem., 1958; ThD, Union Theol. Sem., 1963. Ordained minister So. Bapt. Conv, 1957. Pastor Urbanna (Va.) Bapt. Ch., 1964-68; editl. asst. World Coun. Chs., N.Y.C., 1968-69; freelance journalist N.Y.C., 1969—. Author: Simply Sharing, 1980. 1st lt., chaplain U.S. Army, 1957-59. Democrat. Home: 102 W 80th St Apt 31 New York NY 10024

EARNER, WILLIAM ANTHONY, JR., naval officer; b. Pitts., Nov. 2, 1941; s. William Anthony and Marie Veronica (Ward) E.; m. Jennifer Elizabeth Laurence, Dec. 11, 1971; children: William Andrew, John Laurence. BS, U.S. Naval Acad., 1963; MS, U.S. Naval Postgrad. Sch., 1969; DBA, Harvard U., 1973. Commd. ensign USN, 1963, advanced through grades to vice adm., 1994; 1st lt. USS Blue USN, Yokosuka, Japan, 1963-65; weapons officer USS Black USN, San Diego, 1965-67; ops. officer River Sect. 534 USN, Vietnam, 1967-68; weapons officer USS Dale USN, Mayport, Fla., 1973-75, exec. officer USS Luce, 1975-77; prof. Naval War Coll. USN, Newport, R.I., 1977-78, fellow strategic studies group, 1987-88; with Office Chief Naval Ops. USN, Washington, 1978-81; comdg. officer USS Deyo USN, 1981-83; mil. asst. to dir. NET assesment Office of Sec. Def. USN, Washington, 1983-85, comptr. naval air systems, 1988-90; comdr. Destroyer Squadron Four USN, Charleston, S.C., 1985-87; comdr. naval Surface Group Mid-Pacific USN, Pearl Harbor, Hawaii, 1990-92; budget officer Dept. Navy, 1992-94, dep. chief naval ops. (logistics), 1994-96; exec. v.p. Navy Fed. Credit Union Dept. Navy, Merrifield, Va., 1996-97, sr. exec. v.p. Navy Fed. Credit Union, 1998—; instr. Harvard Grad. Sch. Edn., Cambridge, Mass., 1972-73; adj. prof. Bryant Coll., Smithfield, R.I., 1977-78; sr. exec. v.p. UP Navy Fed. Credit Union, 1998—. Decorated D.S.M., Legion of Merit, Bronze Star with V device. Mem. U.S. Naval Inst., Am. Soc. Mil. Comptrs., Credit Union Exec. Soc., U.S. Naval Acad. Alumni Assn. Avocations: running, gardening. Office: Navy Fed Credit Union PO Box 3000 Merrifield VA 22119-3000

EARNHARDT, (RALPH) DALE, professional race car driver; b. Concord, N.C., Apr. 29, 1951; s. Ralph Lee and Martha King (Coleman) E.; m. Teresa Dianne Houston, Nov. 14, 1982; children: Taylor Nicole, Ralph Dale Jr., Kelley King, Kerry Dale. Lic. race car driver Automobile Competition Commn. for U.S.; lic. gold driver Nat. Assn. Stock Car Auto Racing. Late model sportsman driver Nat. Assn. Stock Car Auto Racing, 1974-85; Busch Grand Nat. driver, 1986—, Winston Cup Grand Nat. driver, 1979—, Winston Cup driver, 1986—; participant Internat. Race of Champions, 1980, 84, 87-94, champion, 1990. Hon. mem. Chgo. Boys Club, 1981-94; dir. youth svcs. Stonewall Jackson Sch., 1979. Named Grand Nat. Rookie of Yr., Nat. Assn. Stock Car Auto Racing, 1979, Winston Cup Grand Nat. Champion, 1980, 86, 87, 90, 91, 93, finalist as Pro Athlete of Yr., Carolinas Charlotte Athletic Club, 1980, 87, Carolinas Pro Athlete Yr., Carolinas Charlotte Athletic Club, 1986, Nat. Motorsports Press Assn. Driver of Yr., 1986, 87, 89, 90; winner Copenhagen All Pro Team Driver of Yr., 1987, 89, 90, 91, 93, finalist, 1986, 88; Am. Motorsports Driver of Yr., 1987, 90, Auto Racer of Yr. Acad. Sports Writers & Broadcasters, 1992; top dollar winner in Am. motorsports; winner numerous auto races including 62 Winston Cup wins, 5 Busch Clash wins, 22 Busch Grand Nat. wins, 4 Internat. Race of Champions (IROC) wins, 3 The Winston (All Star) wins, Transouth 500, 1993, 94, Coca Cola 500, 1993, Budweiser 500, 1993, Miller Genuine Draft 500, 1993, Die Hard 500, 1993, 99, Ford City 500, 1994, Daytona 500, 1998; inducted N.C. Sports Hall of Fame, 1994; recipient N.C. State Order of Long Leaf Pine award. Address: care NASCAR PO Box 2875 Daytona Beach FL 32120-2875 *Positive attitude and steadfast goals.**

EARNHARDT, DALE, JR., professional race car driver; b. Concord, N.C., Oct. 10, 1974. Co-owner, NASCAR Winston Cup Series No. 3 ACDelco-sponsored Chevrolet, 1998—; 13th-place finish NASCAR Busch Series event, Myrtle Beach, S.C. Avocations: water sports, computers. Office: Dale Earnhardt Inc 1675 Coddle Creek Hwy Mooresville NC 28115-8245*

EARNHARDT, HAL J., III, automotive executive. CEO, pres. Earnhardt's Motor Cos., Gilbert, Ariz., 1986. Office: Earnhardt's Motor Cos 1301 N Arizona Ave Gilbert AZ 85233-1600*

EARWOOD, BARBARA TIRRELL, artist; b. Quincy, Mass., July 18, 1920; d. Irving John and Vernice Estelle (Carraway) Tirrell; m. Armer Fred Earwood, May 30, 1942; children: Elsie E. Belk, Melinda Earwood Crain, Edward A. Student, Angelo State U., 1968-69; grad., Washington Sch. Art, 1974, North Light Art Sch., 1989; postgrad., Robert E. Wood Sch., 1978-80. 4th v.p. San Angelo (Tex.) Art Club, 1973-74; pres. Big Country Art Assn., Abilene, Tex.; pres. Region XVII Tex. Fine Arts Assn.; bd. dirs. West Tex. Art Guild, Sonora, 1992-95; tchr. Barbara Earwood Art Sch., Sonora, 1970-93; rancher family ranch; sec., treas. Am. Plains Artist, 1999. Permanent exhbts. include First Nat. Bank Sonora, Sutton County Libr.; artist Girl Scouts Am. pamphlet. Leader Girl Scouts Am., Sonora, 1952-53. Recipient State citation Tex. Fine Arts Assn., 1972, 76, Purchase prize, 1975, Best of Show award San Angelo Stock Show, 1973. Mem. Tex. Watercolor Soc. (signature mem., Purple Sage, Russell Rogers Purchase award for transparent watercolor 1974), Southwestern Watercolor Soc. (signature), San Antonio Watercolor Group (signature), Am. Plains Artists (signature). Episcopalian. Avocations: music, swimming, walking, stamp collecting. Home: PO Box 1604 Hwy 277 S Sonora TX 76950

EASLEY, CHRISTA BIRGIT, nurse, researcher; b. Berlin, Apr. 30, 1941; came to U.S., 1966; d. Albert and Marianne (Uhlmann) Baldauf; m. Loyd Allen Easley, Oct. 23, 1964 (widowed Dec. 1993). Degree in nursing, Pawlow Coll. of Nursing, Aue, Fed. Republic of Germany, 1959; BS, NYU, Albany, 1978; MBA, Cen. Mich. U., 1979; EDS, Ctrl. Mo. U., 1983; PhD, Kensington U., Glensdale, Calif., 1983. With placement sect. Sembach, A.B., Fed. Republic of Germany, 1972-73, suggestion program mgr., 1973-74; adminstrv. clk. Lajes Field, A.B., Terceira, Acores, Portugal, 1975-78, incentive awards and suggestion program mgr., 1978-79; intern Cen. Mo. State U., Warrensburg, 1980-81; instr. in bus. overseas campus Cen. Tex. Coll./Yokota, A.B., Japan, 1983; instr. Tokyo Ctr. for Lang. and Culture, 1981-83; tchr. dept. of def. Yokota Dept. of Def., Yokota AFB, Japan, 1981-84; tax examiner IRS, Austin, Tex., 1984-86; sr. clin. rsch. coord. HealthQuest Rsch., Austin, 1987-96; v.p. Austin Clin. Rsch., 1996—. Treas. Am. Sch. System PTA, Acores, 1978-79; precinct chmn. Austin Rep. Com., 1988-96. Mem. Am. Acad. Allergy & Immunology, Am. Assn. Translators, AAUW, Sigma Tau Delta. Methodist. Avocations: rock hunting, flower gardens. Home: 12422 Deer Trak Austin TX 78727-5746 Office: Austin Clin Rsch Inc 12885 Research Blvd # 109 Austin TX 78750-3220

EASLEY, DAVID, economics educator; b. Lexington, Ky., Nov. 3, 1952; s. Alan Eugene and Jean (Ogden) E.; m. Maureen O'Hara, July 13, 1977; children: Megan, Casey. BA, U. Ky., 1974; PhD, Northwestern U., 1979. Asst. prof. econs. Cornell U., Ithaca, N.Y., 1979-84, assoc. prof., 1984-88, prof., 1988—, chmn. econs. dept., 1988-93, Henry Scarborough prof. econs., 1996—, dir. Ctr. for Analytical Econs., 1996—; vis. prof. Calif. Inst. Tech., Pasadena, 1985-86; Overseas fellow Churchill Coll., Cambridge U., 1993-94. Contbr. articles to profl. jours. Recipient numerous grants NSF. Fellow Econometric Soc. Office: Cornell U Dept Econ Uris Hall Ithaca NY 14853

EASLEY, GEORGE WASHINGTON, construction executive; b. Williamson, W.Va., Mar. 14, 1933; s. George Washington and Isabel Ritchie (Saville) E.; children: Bridget Bland, Kathy Clark, Saville Woodson, Marie Alexis, Isabell Roxanne, George Washington, Laura Dean, Dorothy Elizabeth, Isabel Louiza; m. Bettyrae Fedje Hanner, Sept. 15, 1990. Student, U. Richmond, 1952-56. Registered profl. engr., Calif. Hwy. engr. Va. Dept. Hwys., Richmond, 1956-62; dep. city mgr. City of Anchorage, 1962-68; prin. assoc. Wilbur Smith & Assocs., L.A., 1969-70; commr. pub. works State of Alaska, Juneau, 1971-74; exec. v.p. Burgess Internat. Constrn. Co., Anchorage, 1974, pres., 1975; pres., chmn. bd. George W. Easley Co., Anchorage, 1976-86, also bd. dirs.; pres. Alaska Aggregate Corp., Fairbanks Sand & Gravel Co., Anchorage, 1986-90; constrn. mgr. Alaska Pipeline Svc. Co., 1990-96; ind. cons., 1996—; CEO Eklutna, Inc., 1997—; bd. dirs. Totem Ocean Ocean Trailer Express, Inc. Recipient commendations City of Anchorage, 1966, Greater Anchorage, Inc., 1969, Ketchikan C. of C., 1973, Alaska State Legis., 1974, Gov. of Alaska, 1974; named one of Outstanding Young Men, Anchorage Jaycees, 1964. Mem. U.S. C. of C., Alaska C. of C. (dir. 1978—, chmn. 1982-83), Anchorage C. of C. (sec.-treas. 1976, v.p. 1977, pres.-elect 1978, pres. 1979-80, dir. 1982-88, Gold Pan award 1969, 77), Hwy. Users Fedn. Alaska (dir. 1972—, treas. 1974—), Orgn. Mgmt. Alaska's Resources (past dir.), Am. Pub. Works Assn., Anchorage Transp. Commn. (past chmn.), Assoc. Gen. Contractors (dir. Alaska chpt. 1978—, chpt. treas. 1980-81, sec. 1981, pres. 1984, nat. com. labor rels., Hard Hat award 1985), Am. Mil. engrs. (v.p. Alaska chpt. 1978), Alaska Trucking Assn. (bd. dirs. 1986-90), Inst. Mcpl. Engrs., Inst. Traffic Engrs., Internat. Orgn. Masters, Mates, and Pilots (hon.), Common Sense for Alaska (past pres.), Commonwealth North (charter), San Francisco Tennis Club, Rotary. Democrat. Presbyterian. Home and Office: 4921 Sportsman Dr Anchorage AK 99502-4193

EASLEY, JUNE ELLEN PRICE, genealogist; b. Chgo., June 7, 1924; d. Fred E. and Bernadette (Mailloux) Price; m. Raymond Dale Easley, Dec. 24, 1945. *Great grandfather, William Price, was born March 22, 1817, in Virginia and married Lavinia Badger in Grant County, Indiana, November, 1889. Lavinia was the daughter of John Badger and his wife, Ann Fuller, granddaughter of Daniel Badger and Hannah Mallot. Grandfather, Oliver Price, and his wife, Minnie Cain, were the parents of Fred E. Price who married Bernadette Mailloux, daughter of Frank Mailloux and Lily La Plante of Bourbonnais, Illinois. June and Raymond Easley had one child, Linda Victoria Easley Haney, born October 28, 1946 and mother of five daughters and twelve grandchildren.* Student, McCormack Sch. Commerce, Englewood Jr. Coll., Chgo. Lic. genealogist Assn. Profl. Genealogists. Statis. clk. Arthur Andersen & Co., Chgo., 1968-74; corr. sec. ICG R.R., Chgo., 1974-86; self-employed genealogist-computers Arlington Heights, Ill., 1986-94, Mountain Home, Ark., 1994—; editor, typist genealogical books, 1996—. Contbr. religion articles to Daily Herald, 1991; editor romance stories, 1990—, genealogy books, 1996—. Sec. Citizens for Clean Water, Mountain Home, Ark., 1996-98. Mem. AARP (sec. 1997-98), DAR (auditor-treas. Chgo. chpt. 1981-82, rec. sec. Chgo. chpt. 1982-88, Mountain Home ROTC 1995-97, publicity chmn. 1996-97), Huguenot Soc., Nat. Soc. R.R. Bus. Women (newsletter editor 1991—), Northwest Suburban Coun. Genealogists (pres. 1988-90, corr. sec. 1990-94), Daus. of War 1812. Republican. Methodist. Avocations: genealogy, writing, antiques, computers, travel. Home and Office: 1601 Franklin Ave Mountain Home AR 72653-2041

EASLEY, LOYCE ANNA, painter; b. Weatherford, Okla., June 28, 1918; d. Thomas Webster and Anna Laura (Sanders) Rogers; m. Mack Easley, Nov. 17, 1939; children: June Elizabeth, Roger. BFA, U. Okla., 1943; postgrad., 1947-49; student, Art Students League, N.Y.C., 1977; postgrad., Santa Fe Inst. Fine Arts, 1985. Tchr. Pub. Sch., Okmulgee, Okla., 1946-47, Hobbs, N.Mex., 1947-49; tchr. painting N.Mex. Jr. Coll., Hobbs, 1965-80; tchr. Art Workshops in N.Mex., Okla., Wyoming. Numerous one-woman shows and group exhbns. in mus., univs. and galleries, including Gov.'s Gallery, Santa Fe, Selected Artists, N.Y.C., Roswell (N.Mex.) Mus., N.Mex. State U., Las Cruces, West Tex. Mus., Tex. Tech U., Lubbock; represented in permanent collections USAF Acad., Colorado Springs, Colo., Roswell Mus., Carlsbad (N.Mex.) Mus., Coll. Santa Fe, N.Mex. Supreme Ct, also other pvt. and pub. collections; featured in S.W. Art and Santa Fe mag., 1981, 82. Named Disting. Former Student, U. Okla. Art Sch., 1963; nominated for Gov.'s award in Art, N.Mex., 1988. Mem. N.Mex. Artists Equity (lifetime mem. 1963). Democrat. Presbyterian. Home: 10909 Country Club St NE Albuquerque NM 87111-6548

EASLEY, MACK, retired state supreme court chief justice; b. Akins, Okla., Oct. 14, 1916; s. John Robert and Mary Ellen (Duggins) E.; m. Loyce Anna Rogers, Nov. 17, 1939; children: June, Roger. Student, Northeastern Okla. State Coll., 1935-39; LL.B., U. Okla., 1947. Bar: N.Mex. 1948. Practiced law Hobbs, 1948-74; asst. dist. atty. Lea County, 1949-50; mem. N.Mex. Ho. of Reps., 1951-52, 55-62, speaker, 1959-60; lt. gov. State of N.Mex., 1963-66; mem. N.Mex. Senate, 1967-70, majority whip, 1969-70; judge 5th Dist. Ct. N.Mex., 1974-76; justice N.Mex. Supreme Ct., 1976-82, chief justice, 1981-82; chmn. N.Mex. Legis. Council, 1960, N.Mex. Jud. Conf., 1978-79, N.Mex. Democratic Conv., 1960, 69, 70, 72; mem. Nat. Dem. Charter Commn., 1973-74; dir. Nat. Lt. Govs. Conf., 1966. Served with USAAF, 1942-46. Mem. ABA., N.Mex. Bar Assn., Lea County Bar Assn. (pres. 1950), N.Mex. Judges Assn. (pres. 1979-80), VFW, Am. Legion. Presbyterian. Club: Lions.

EASLEY, MICHAEL F., state attorney general; b. Rocky Mount, N.C., 1950; m. Mary Pipines; 1 child, Michael F., Jr. BA in Polit. Sci. cum laude, U. N.C., 1972; JD cum laude, N.C. Ctrl. U. Dist. atty. 13th Dist., N.C., 1982-91; pvt. practice Southport, N.C., 1991-93; atty. gen. N.C., 1993—. Contbr. numerous articles in field. Recipient Pub. Svc. award U.S. Dept. Justice, 1984. Pres. N.C. Conf. Dist. Attys.; mem. N.C. Dist. Attys. Assn. (past pres., legis. chmn.). Avocations: hunting, sailing, woodworking. Office: Justice Department/Attorney General PO Box 629 114 West Edenton St Raleigh NC 27602-0629*

EASLEY, PAULINE MARIE, retired elementary school educator; b. Peoria, Ohio, July 8, 1937; d. Ivan Albert and Helen Margaret (Thompson) Barton; m. Homer Eugene Easley, June 21, 1959; children: David Lynn, Sherryl Lynn Easley Frank. BA in Elem. Edn., Aurora (Ill.) Coll., 1959; MAT, Aurora U., 1987; postgrad., No. Ill. U., 1977-80. Cert. tchr., Ill. Tchr. 2d grade Balt. County Sch. System, 1959-60, Frank Hall Elem./West Aurora Dist., 1960-62; tchr. 1st grade Abraham Lincoln Sch., Aurora, 1962-64; substitute tchr. West Aurora Sch. Dist. 129, Aurora, 1964-65, tchr. 2d grade, 1966-73, tchr. learning ctr., 1973-94; ret., 1994; adj. instr. Aurora U., 1987-92. Bd. trustees Advent Christian Ch., Aurora, 1989—; co-pres. Aurora Advent Christian Women's Fellowship, 1987-89; chairperson Aurora Advent Christian Ch. Deaconess, 1970; bd. dirs. at large Women's Home and Fgn. Mission Soc., 1990-95, 96—. Recipient Golden Apple award West Aurora Sch. Dist., 1986. Mem. West Aurora Edn. Assn. (bldg. rep. 1960-62), Women's Home and Fgn. Mission Soc. (pres. bd. dirs. Ctrl. region), Delta Kappa Gamma (2d v.p. Alpha Epsilon chpt. 1992-95, Lambda state orgn. mem. state profl. affairs com. 1993-94, various coms.). Avocations: landscaping, crafts, travel. Home: 1529 Southlawn Pl Aurora IL 60506-5358

EASON, MARCIA JEAN, lawyer; b. Dallas, Aug. 31, 1953; d. John Keller and Sara Marguerite (Prindle) McCarron; m. S. Lee Meredith, Sept. 12, 1981 (div. Oct. 1989); m. David O. Eason, Aug. 21, 1993; stepchildren: Chelsea, Shannon, Valerie. BA magna cum laude, Trinity U., 1975; JD, U. Houston, 1979. Bar: Tex. 1978, U.S. Dist. Ct. (so. dist.) Tex. 1978, U.S. Ct. Appeals (5th cir.) 1979, Tenn. 1985, U.S. Dist. Ct. (ea. dist.) Tenn. 1985, U.S. Supreme Ct. 1985, U.S. Ct. Appeals (6th cir.) 1986, U.S. Ct. Appeals (4th cir.) 1994. Ptnr. Byrnes & Martin, Houston, 1984-85, Miller & Martin, Chattanooga, 1987—. Pres., bd. dirs. Chattanooga's Kids on the Block, 1987-94; bd. dirs. AIM Ctr, Chattanooga, 1993—; campaign chair, attys. divsn. United Way, Chattanooga, 1994, leadership campaign chair, 1998. Mem. ABA, Tenn. Bar Assn., Chattanooga Bar Assn. (com. chair 1985-86), Tenn. Lawyers Assn. for Women (co-chair com. 1994, treas. 1995-97, pres. 1998). Home: 33 Rock Crest Dr Signal Mountain TN 37377-2326 Office: Miller & Martin 832 Georgia Ave Ste 1000 Chattanooga TN 37402-2289

EASON, WILLIAM EVERETTE, JR., lawyer; b. Elizabeth City, N.C., Jan. 20, 1943; s. William Everette and Helen (Mathews) E.; m. Mildred Judith Harris, Aug. 20, 1965; 1 child, Kimberly. AB, Duke U., 1965, JD, 1968. Bar: Ga. 1968. Ptnr. Paul, Hastings, Janofsky & Walker, Atlanta; sr. v.p., gen. counsel, sec. Scientific Atlanta, Inc., 1994—. Bd. dirs. Herty Found., Savannah, Ga., 1984-94, Families First, Atlanta, 1978-88, SciTrek Mus., Atlanta, 1995—; trustee, chmn. exec. com. Woodward Acad., Atlanta, 1987—; pres. North Atlanta Club Area Civic Assn., 1981-82; mem. Leadership Atlanta; gen. counsel Met. Atlanta Olympic Games Authority, 1989—. Mem. Ga. Bar Assn. (chmn. corp. and banking law sect. 1988-89, chmn. corp. counsel sect. 1996-97), Capital City Club, Georgian Club Atlanta (dir. 1987-90). Methodist. Office: Paul Hastings Janofsky & Walker 600 Peachtree St NE Ste 2400 Atlanta GA 30308-2214 also: Sci-Atlanta Inc One Technology Pky S Norcross GA 30092

EASSON, WILLIAM MCALPINE, psychiatrist; b. Evanston, Ill., July 3, 1931; s. Alexander and Anne Meldrum (Watson) E.; m. Gwendolyn Bowen, May 31, 1958; children: Anne, Jane, David, Michael. M.B., Ch.B., U. Aberdeen, Scotland, 1954, M.D., 1967. Fellow in medicine and psychiatry Mayo Clinic, Rochester, Minn., 1956-59; resident in psychiatry U. Sask., 1959-60, instr. psychiatry, 1959-61; fellow in child psychiatry Menninger Clinic, Topeka, 1961-63; staff child psychiatrist Menninger Clinic, 1963-67; prof. psychiatry, chmn. dept. Med. Coll. Ohio, Toledo, 1967-72; prof., dir. div. child and adolescent psychiatry U. Minn. Med. Sch., Mpls., 1972-74; prof. psychiatry La. State U. Med. Ctr., New Orleans, 1974-96, head dept. psychiatry, 1974-82, prof. emeritus, 1996—; vis. prof. psychiatry U. Garyounis Med. Sch., Benghazi, Libya, 1979; prof. grad. studies U. Riyadh, Saudi Arabia; U.S.-USSR health scientist, Moscow and Leningrad. Author: The Severely Disturbed Adolescent, 1969, The Dying Child, 2d edit., 1981, Psychiatry Exam. Rev., 5th edit., 1994, Psychiatry Patient Mgmt. Rev., 1977, (with N. Rock) Psychiatry Splty. Bd. Rev., 1991, The Management of the Severely Disturbed Adolscent, 1996; editor: Jour. Clin. Psychiatry, 1977-80. Carnegie fellow, 1956-58; Anderson fellow, 1956-58; WHO fellow, 1976. Fellow Am. Psychiat. Assn. (life), Royal Coll. Psychiatrists. Home: 5218 Saint Charles Ave New Orleans LA 70115-4943

EAST, DONALD ROBERT, civil engineer; b. Kimberley, South Africa, June 2, 1944; came to U.S., 1985; s. Robert George and Gladys Enid (Macintyre) E.; m. Diana Patricia Ruske, Dec. 21, 1968 (div. Mar. 1993); children: Lisa Ann, Sharon Margaret; m. Miriam B. Thompson, Mar. 16, 1996. BSCE, U. Cape Town, 1969; MSc in Found. Engring., U. Birmingham, England, 1971. Jr. engr. Ninham Shand & Ptnrs., Cape Town, South Africa, 1968-71; mgr. Civilab Ltd., Johannesburg, South Africa, 1972-74; ptnr. Watermeyer, Legge, Piesold & Uhlmann, Johannesburg, 1975-85; pres., CEO Knight Piesold LLC, Denver, 1985—; Contbr. articles to profl. jours. Fellow South Africa Instn. Civil Engrs. (chmn. 1979-85); mem. ASCE, Soc. Mining Engrs. (com. mem. 1988-89). Home: 7902 E Iowa Ave Denver CO 80231-5654 Office: Knight Piesold LLC 1050 17th St Ste 500 Denver CO 80265-0501

EAST, MARK DAVID, physician; b. Baton Rouge, July 22, 1955; s. Charles Ray and Gloria Lee (Fairbanks) E.; m. Cara Elizabeth Sherk; children: Nicole, Sara, Mark, Kyle, Erin. BS in Pharmacy, U. Miss., 1978; DO, U. Health Scis., Kansas City, Mo., 1983. Diplomate Nat. Bd. Examiners, Am. Bd. Internal Medicine. Pharmacist asst. mgr. Sav-On Drugs, Inc., McComb, Miss., 1978-79; intern Normandy Hosps., St. Louis, 1983-84; resident in internal medicine Normandy Osteo. Hosps., St. Louis, 1984-87; fellow in pulmonary, critical care and environ. medicine U. Mo., Columbia, 1987-89; physician pulmonary, critical care, internal medicine Tri-County Pulmonary Medicine, St. Peters, Mo., 1989-90, Lake Internal Med. Specialists, Osage Beach, Mo., 1990—; med. dir. ICU and cardiopulmonary dept. Lake of the Ozarks Gen. Hosp., Osage Beach, 1990—; chmn. dept. medicine Lake Ozarks Gen. Hosp., 1991-96, 98—, chmn. infection control and pharmacy & therapeutics com., 1991—; vice chief of staff Lake of the Ozarks Gen. Hosp., 1996-98; treas., bd. dirs. Mid-Mo. Med. Care. Asst. scoutmaster 14th World Scout Jamboree, Boy Scouts Am., Lillehammer, Norway, 1975, patrol leader 13th World Jamboree, Fuminamiya City, Japan, 1971, staff mem. 8th Nat. Scout Jamboree, Moraine State Park, Pa., 1973. Mem. AMA, Am. Osteo. Assn., Am. Thoracic Soc., Mo. Assn. Osteo. Physicians, Sigma Sigma Phi, Phi Delta Chi. Republican. Methodist. Avocations: photography, swimming, boating, jet skiing. Office: Lake Internal Medicine Specialists 54 Hospital Dr Ste 205 Osage Beach MO 65065-3050

EAST, MAURICE ALDEN, political scientist, educator; b. Trinidad, Colo., Feb. 21, 1941; s. Maurice Leland and Irene Rose (Pedri) E.; m. Jessie Elizabeth Like, June 11, 1963 (div.); 1 child: Barrett David; m. Robyn Crossley, Dec. 27, 1997. BA, Colgate U., 1963; MA, Princeton U., 1967, PhD, 1970. Asst. prof. grad. sch. internat. studies U. Denver, 1967-72; assoc. prof. to prof. dept. polit. sci. U. Ky., Lexington, 1972-83; sr. fellow Strategic Concepts Devel. Ctr. Dept. Def., Washington, 1984-85; dean Elliott Sch. Internat. Affairs George Washington U., Washington, 1985-94, prof. internat. affairs, 1994—; vis. lectr. Makerere U., Kampala, Uganda, 1971-72; vis. prof. U. Oslo, 1978-79, Victoria U., Wellington, New Zealand, 1994-95; adv. pub. opinion Dept. State, 1970-73; cons. Norwegian Fgn. Ministry, 1978-82. Co-author: Why Nations Act, 1978; co-editor: Analysis of International Politics, 1972. Bd. dirs. Atlantic Coun., 1993—. Woodrow Wilson Found. fellow, Princeton, N.J., 1963, Irwin Found. fellow, Homewood, Ill., 1966-67; Fulbright research scholar, U. Oslo, 1978-79. Mem. UN Assn. (exec. bd. capital area divsn. 1985-93), Coun. Fgn. Rels., Internat. Studies Assn. (exec. bd. 1977-78, nat. conv. chmn. 1982, pres. Washington divsn. 1987, nat. pres. 1991-92), Phi Beta Kappa. Avocations: squash, tennis, bicycling. Home: 442 N Park Dr Arlington VA 22203-2344 Office: George Washington Univ Elliott Sch Internat A Washington DC 20052-0564

EASTAUGH, ROBERT L., state supreme court justice; b. Seattle, Nov. 12, 1943. BA, Yale U., 1965; JD, U. Mich., 1968. Bar: Alaska 1968. Asst. atty. gen. State of Alaska, 1968-69, asst. dist. atty., 1969-72; lawyer Delaney, Wiles, Hayes, Reitman & Brubaker, Inc., 1972-94; assoc. justice Alaska Supreme Ct., 1994—. Office: Alaska Supreme Court 303 K St Anchorage AK 99501-2013*

EASTBURN, RICHARD A., consulting firm executive; b. West Chester, Pa., Jan. 16, 1934; s. Louis W. and Alma S. (Shellin) E.; m. Heidi Fritz, June 15, 1963 (dec. 1991); children: Karin J., R. Marc; m. Carol Mc Devitt, Oct. 24, 1993. BA, Shelton Coll., 1956; MST, N.Y. Theol. Sem., 1959; MEd, Temple U., 1970; MBA, Columbia U., 1979. Ordained to ministry Am. Bapt. Conv., 1959. Minister Laurelton, N.J., 1959-61; dir. adult programs Ctrl. YMCA, Phila., 1961-65; dir. Opportunities Industrialization Ctr., Phila., 1965-67; mgr. tng. and devel. Missile & Surface Radar divsn. RCA, Moorestown, N.J., 1967-68, mgr. mgmt. devel. govt. and comml. sys. sector, 1969-71, dir. mgmt. devel., 1969-71; group mgr. personnel for internat. field mktg. & svc. Digital Equipment, Maynard, Mass., 1971-75; corp. dir. orgn. and productivity devel. Am. Standard, Inc., N.Y.C., 1975-79; corp. dir. mgmt. devel. edn. and staffing TRW, Inc., Cleve., 1979-86; founder Premium Life Care Retirement Cmty., Hudson, Ohio, 1988; sr. v.p. Strategic Mgmt. Group of Phila., 1986-88; exec. dir. mfg. Studies Bd. NAS, 1989-90; pres. Mgmt. Ops. Solutions, Chagrin Falls, 1990—; chmn. The Exec. Com. of Cleve., 1988—. Prodr., moderator Ask the Clergy Sta. WIP, Phila., 1965-67. Bd. dirs., bd. advisors Travaco Mgmt. Sys., Wellsboro (Ohio) Foundry, Camet Corp., Johnson Industries, exec. program adv. bd. U. Ind., Burlington County (N.J.) Cmty. Com., 1967-69; pres. Rehab. Am., Inc., 1991-93. Recipient Disting. Cmty. Svc. award Shelton Coll. Alumni, 1956; Dedicated Svc. award Phila. March of Progress, 1967. Mem. Am. Soc. Tng. and Devel. (dir. 1979-80), Chagrin Valley C. of C., Cleve. Advanced Mfg. Program, Ops. Mgmt. Assn., Soc. Mfg. Engrs., Wembley Swim and Tennis Club, A & A Sportsman Club. Mem. United Ch. Christ. Home and Office: 612 Magnolia Ln Chagrin Falls OH 44023-2529

EASTER, STEPHEN SHERMAN, JR., biology educator; b. New Orleans, Feb. 12, 1938; s. Stephen Sherman and Myrtle Olivia (Bekkedahl) E.; m. Janine Eliane Piot, June 4, 1963; children—Michele, Kim. BS, Yale U., 1960; postgrad., Harvard U., 1961; PhD, Johns Hopkins U., 1966. Postdoctoral fellow Cambridge U., Eng., 1967; postdoctoral U. Calif., Berkeley, 1968-69; asst. prof. biology U. Mich., Ann Arbor, 1970-74, assoc. prof., 1974-78, prof., 1978—, assoc. chmn., 1992-93, mem. Coll. Lit., Sci. and the Arts exec. com., 1993-96, dir. neurosci. program, 1984-88, Mathew Alpern Collegiate prof., 1998—; vis. prof. U. Murcia, Spain, 1997, Ecole Normale Supérieure, Paris, 1997. Editor Vision Rsch., 1978-85, Jour. Neurosci., 1989-95, Visual Neurosci., 1990-92, Investigative Ophthalmology and Visual Sci., 1992-97, Jour. Comparative Neurology, 1994-98. Recipient Sokol award, 1998. Mem. Soc. Neurosci., Assn. Rsch. in Vision and Ophthalmology, Internat. Brain Rsch. Orgn., Soc. for Devel. Biology. Office: U Mich Dept Biology 3113 Natural Sci Bldg Ann Arbor MI 48109-1048

EASTER, WAYNE ARNOLD, Parliament member; b. Charlottetown, PEI, Can., 1949. B.Agr., N.S. Agrl. Coll., 1970; LLD (hon.), U. PEI, 1988. Pres. Canadian Natl. Farmers Union, 1982-93; mem. parliament Malpeaue, PEI, 1993—; parliamentary sec. Min. of Fisheries and Oceans, Ottawa, Ont., 1997—. Recipient Can. 125 medal, 1992. Office: House of Commons, Rm 732 Confedn Bldg, Ottawa, ON Canada K1A 0A6*

EASTERBROOK, FRANK HOOVER, federal judge; b. Buffalo, Sept. 3, 1948; s. George Edmund and Vimy (Hoover) E. B.A., Swarthmore Coll., 1970; J.D., U. Chgo., 1973. Bar: D.C. Law clk. to judge U.S. Ct. Appeals, Boston, 1973-74; asst. to solicitor gen. U.S. Dept. Justice, Washington, 1974-77, dep. solicitor gen. of U.S., 1978-79; asst. prof. law U. Chgo., 1978-81, prof. law, 1981-84, Lee & Brena Freeman prof., 1984-85; prin. employee Lexecon Inc., Chgo., 1980-85; sr. lectr. U. Chgo., 1985—; judge U.S. Ct. Appeals (7th cir.), Chgo., 1985—; mem. adv. com. on tender offers SEC, Washington, 1983. Author: (with Richard A. Posner) Antitrust, 1981, (with Daniel R. Fischel) The Economic Structure of Corporate Law, 1991; editor Jour. Law and Econs., Chgo., 1982-91; contbr. articles to profl. jours. Trustee James Madison Meml. Fellowship Found., 1988—. Recipient Prize for Disting. scholarship Emory U., Atlanta, 1981. Mem. AAAS, Am. Law Inst., Mont Pelerin Soc., Order of Coif, Phi Beta Kappa. Office: US Ct Appeals Everett McKinley Dirksen Fed Bldg 219 S Dearborn St Rm 2746 Chicago IL 60604-1702*

EASTERBROOK, JAMES ARTHUR, psychology educator; b. East Baudette, Minn., Apr. 10, 1923; s. William James and Bertha Lillian (Amorde) E.; m. Margaret Pamela Edith Evans, Nov. 19, 1944; children: Christine, Anthony, Pamela, Laurence, Margaret. B.A. with honors, Queen's U., Kingston, Ont., Can., 1949, M.A. (J. McBeth Milligan fellow), 1954; Ph.D., U. London, 1963. Mem. Canadian Def. Research Sci. Service, Churchill, Man., Edmonton, Alta., Halifax, N.S., 1950-57; research psychologist Burden Neurol. Inst., Bristol, Eng., 1959-61; mem. faculty medicine U. Alta. at Edmonton, 1961-67; prof. psychology U. N.B. at Fredericton, 1967-88, prof. emeritus, 1990—; mem. N.B. Bd. Examiners in Psychology, 1973-79, chmn., 1978-79. Served with RCAF, 1941-45. Mem. Brit. Psychol. Soc. (life), Coll. Psychologists New Brunswick (life). Home: 749 Charters Settlement Rd, Charters Settlement, NB Canada E3C 1V8

EASTERDAY, BERNARD CARLYLE, veterinary medicine educator; b. Hillsdale, Mich., Sept. 16, 1929; s. Harley B. and Alberta M. Easterday. D.V.M., Mich. State U., 1952; M.S., U. Wis., 1958, Ph.D., 1961. Diplomate Am. Coll. Veterinary Microbiologists. Pvt. practice veterinary medicine Hillsdale, Mich., 1952; veterinarian U.S. Dept. Def., Frederick, Md., 1955-61; assoc. prof., then prof. veterinary sci. U. Wis., Madison, 1961-94, prof. emeritus, 1994—, dean Sch. Vet. Medicine, 1979-94, dean emeritus, prof emeritus Sch. Vet. Medicine, 1994—; mem., chmn. com. animal health Nat. Acad. Sci.-NRC, Washington, 1980-83, mem. com. on sci. basis meat and poultry inspection program, 1984-85; mem. tech. adv. com. Binat. Agrl. Research and Devel., Bet-Degan, Israel, 1982-84; mem. expert adv. panel on zoonoses WHO, Geneva, 1978-94; mem. tech. adv. com. on avian influenza USDA, 1983-85; mem. sec. USDA adv. com. on fgn. animal and poultry diseases, 1991-96. 1st lt. V.C., U.S. Army, 1952-54. Recipient Disting. Alumnus award Coll. Vet. Medicine, Mich. State U., 1975; named Wis. Veterinarian of Yr., Wis. Vet. Med. Assn., 1979. Mem. AVMA, Am. Assn. Vet. Med. Colls. (pres. 1975), Am. Assn. Avian Pathologists. Office: U Wisconsin-Madison Sch Vet Medicine 2015 Linden Dr W Madison WI 53706-1100*

EASTERLING, CHARLES ARMO, lawyer; b. Hamilton, Tex., July 22, 1920; s. William Hamby and Jennie (Arilla) E.; m. Irene A. Easterling, Apr. 25, 1943; children: Charles David, Danny Karl, Jan Easterling Petty. BBA, Baylor U., 1951, LLB, 1951, JD 1969. Bar: Tex. 1950, U.S. Supreme Ct. 1954. Sr. asst. city atty. City of Houston, 1952-64; sole practice, Houston, 1964-70; city atty. Pasadena (Tex.), 1970-82; of counsel Easterling and Easterling, Houston, 1982—; instr. So. Tex. Coll. Law, 1954-69. Served to lt. col. (ret.) USAFR. Mem. Houston-Harris County Bar Assn., Phi Alpha Delta. Democrat. Methodist. Clubs: Masons (33d deg.; insp. gen. hon.), Shriners, Jesters, Arabia Temple Shrine (past potentate), Red Cross Constantine (past sovereign).

EASTERLING, EDDIE JEAN, publisher; b. Norton, Va., Jan. 18, 1955; s. William Delmar Easterling and Betty Jean (Jordan) Whitaker; children: Jonathan, Micah, Emily. BS, Bluefield Coll., 1996. With USPS, Roanoke, Va., 1979—; owner Avenel Pub., Roanoke, 1995—. Author, photographer: In Search of A Golden Vault, 1995; camerman, co-producer short film Dare to Care, 1977. Mem. Beale Cypher Assn. Avocations: treasure hunting, stained glass art, travel. Home: PO Box 7773 Roanoke VA 24019-0773 Office: Avenel Pub PO Box 7773 Roanoke VA 24019-0773

EASTERLING, KATHY, school system administrator. Prin. Hillrise Elem. Sch., Las Cruces, N.Mex., 1987-93; dir. spl. edn. Las Cruces Sch. Dist. Recipient Elem. Sch. Recognition award U.S. Dept. Edn., 1989-90. Office: Las Cruces Sch Dist 505 S Main St Ste 249 Las Cruces NM 88001-1243*

EASTERLING, WILLIAM EWART, JR., obstetrician, gynecologist; b. Raleigh, N.C., Nov. 8, 1930; s. William Ewart and Hannah Montgomery E.; m. Mary Ellyn Royer, June 7, 1952; children—William E. III, David R., John Wyatt, Robert Bryan, Jeffrey T. A.B., Duke U., 1952; M.D., U. N.C., 1956. Intern N.C. Meml. Hosp., 1956-57, resident in ob-gyn, 1957-61; instr. ob-gyn U. N.C. Sch. Medicine, 1960-61, asst. prof., 1964-67, assoc. prof., 1967-72, prof., 1972—, asst. dean, 1974-76, assoc. dean, 1976-77, vice dean, 1977-81, assoc. dean clin. affairs, 1981-89; assoc. dean continuing med. edn. and alumni affairs U. N.C. Sch. Medicine, Chapel Hill, 1989—; chief staff U. N.C. Hosp., Chapel Hill, 1974-89; mem. Council on Resident Edn. in Obgyn, 1972-80, chmn., 1978-80. Contbr. chpts. to textbooks; contbr. articles to profl. jours. Bd. dirs. Episcopal Home for Aging, Carol Woods Retirement Community, N.C. div. Am. Cancer Soc., chmn., 1976-77, pres., 1977-78. Capt. M.C. USAF, 1961-63; USPHS traniee 1963-64. Mem. ACOG, Am. Assn. Obstetricians and Gynecologists, Assn. Profs. in Gynecology and Obstetrics, Endocrine Soc., Soc. Gynecol. Investigation, Assn. Am. Med. Colls. (group on faculty practice, chair 1989-90, adminstrn. bd. 1992-95, steering com. interim chair, CME sect. 1996-97, group on edn. affairs), Coun. Acad. Socs., Soc. Med. Coll. Dirs. Continuing Med. Edn. (bd. dirs., pres. 1996-97). Home: 304 Nottingham Dr Chapel Hill NC 27514-6574 Office: U NC Sch Medicine Dept Ob-Gyn 4027 Old Clinic Bldg Chapel Hill NC 27599

EASTERLY, DAVID EUGENE, communications executive; b. Denison, Tex., June 26, 1942; s. Claud Eugene and Ruth Eleanor (Davis) E.; children: Jennifer, Greg, Anne. BA in Polit. Sci., Austin Coll., 1965. Reporter Denison (Tex.) Herald, 1964-66; reporter, news editor San Angelo (Tex.) Standard-Times, 1967-68; asst. mng. editor Austin (Tex.) Am.-Statesman, 1968-70; pres. Dayton (Ohio) Newspapers, Inc., 1977-81, Atlanta Jour. and Constn., from 1982; former pres. Cox Newspapers; pres., COO Cox Enterprises, 1994—. Mem. AP, So. Newspaper Pubs. Assn. (bd. dirs.), Newspaper Assn. Am. Office: Cox Enterprises 1400 Lake Hearn Dr NE Atlanta GA 30319-1418*

EASTERLY, SUSAN, music and humanities educator; b. St. Petersburg, Fla., Feb. 2, 1963; d. Kenneth Rudolph and Adeline Betty (Martin) E.; life ptnr. Sylvia Kay Fisher, Feb. 14, 1983; 1 child, Elise Dolores Easterly Fisher. AA, U. South Fla., 1983, BA, 1985, MusM, 1987; BA, Regents Coll., Albany, 1990; MA, Calif. State U., Dominguez Hills, 1991. Pvt. piano tchr., 1980—; gen.-vocal music tchr. Prince George's County Pub. Schs., Beltsville, Md., 1996-97; adj. instr. Hillsborough C.C., Tampa, Fla., 1988-89, Polk C.C., Lakeland, Fla., 1989, Pasco-Hernando C.C., Brooksville and New Port Richey, Fla., 1989-93, Miami-Dade C.C., 1994, Strattford Coll., Falls Church, Va., 1999—; piano tchr. Performer's Music Inst., Miami, Fla., 1994-95, Travelling Tchrs., Inc., Silver Spring, Md., 1995-96; accompanist Harmonic Dissidents, Tampa, 1993; pianist River Grove United Meth. Ch., 1987-88, Classical Ballet Ctr. of Tampa, 1988-89, Dove Ensemble, Tampa, 1991-92, Met. Cmty. Ch., Tampa, 1990-93, others; accompanist, mem. prodn. com. Crescendo-The Tampa Bay Womyn's Chorus, 1991-93. Contbr. articles to profl. publs. Recipient State Cmty. Svc. award Fla. State Music Tchrs.' Assn., 1981, Cmty. Svc. award, 1981, acad. scholarship Kiwanis Club of Seminole, 1981-82, talent grant U. S. Fla., 1982-85, others. Mem. AAUW, Coll. Music Soc., Cultural Alliance Greater Washington, Triangle Artists Group. Democrat. Unitarian Universalist. Avocations: visiting museums, concerts, plays, travel, reading.

EASTERSON, SAM, artist; b. Hartford, Jan. 24, 1972. BFA, 1994; MS, U. Minn. instr. Art Inst. Minn., 1998—. Exhibited in group shows at New Mus., N.Y.C., 1998, Sanburg Inst., Amsterdam, Holland, 1998, others; guest artist Mass. Coll. Art, Boston, 1995, Grinnell Coll., Iowa, 1997. Recipient Book prize R.I. Sch. Design, 1990.

EASTHAM, ALAN WALTER, JR., foreign service officer, lawyer; b. Dumas, Ark., Oct. 16, 1951; s. Alan Walter and Ruth E. (Clayton) E.; m. Carolyn Laux, Aug. 2, 1974; children: Mark A., Michael S.G. B.A., Hendrix Coll., Ark., 1973; J.D. cum laude, Georgetown U., 1982. Bar: D.C. 1982. Mgr. KDDA-AM Radio, Dumas, Ark., 1973-74; vice consul Am. Embassy, Kathmandu, Nepal, 1975-78; info. officer Dept. State, Washington, 1978-80; staff mem. office for combatting terrorism Dept. State, 1980-82, desk officer Sri Lanka and Maldives, 1982-83, polit. officer for India, 1983-84; prin. officer Am. consulate, Peshawar, Pakistan, 1984-87; spl. asst. to under sec. polit. affairs Dept. State, 1987-89; counselor Am. Embassy, Nairobi, Kenya, 1989-92, Kinshasa, Zaire, 1992-94; consul gen. Bordeaux, France, 1994-95; counselor Am. Embassy, New Delhi, India, 1995-97; dep. chief of mission Am. Embassy, Islamabad, Pakistan, 1997-99; dep. asst. sec. of state for South Asian affairs Dept. of State, Washington, 1999—. Methodist. Office: SA Room 6254 NS Dept of State Washington DC 20520-6258

EASTHAM, DENNIS MICHAEL, advertising executive; b. Jacksonville, Ill., Dec. 18, 1946; s. Glenn R. and Ona M. (Camerer) E.; m. Dianne C. L. Watts; children: Susie, Brian, Brad. BA in Fin., U. Ill., 1968; MBA, U. Santa Clara, 1972. Asst. v.p. Crocker Bank, San Francisco, 1976-79; v.p. T & E Card div. Citicorp, L.A., 1979-81; exec. v.p. Barry Blau and Ptnrs. Inc., L.A., N.Y.C. and Chgo., 1981-87; pres. Barry Blau and Ptnrs. Inc., Chgo., 1987—; bd. dirs. Barry Blau and Ptnrs. Inc., Fairfield, Conn., 1985—. Mem. Direct Mktg. Assn. Home: 21835 Vernon Ridge Dr Mundelein IL 60060-5316 Office: Barry Blau & Ptnrs Inc 875 N Michigan Ave Ste 2800 Chicago IL 60611-1898

EASTHAM, JOHN D., business executive. Profl. Degree, Burnley Sch., Seattle, 1967. Mng. ptnr. EMB Ptnrs., Seattle, 1994—. Recipient Clio awards, 1986, Effie, Am. Mktg. Assn., 1991, Totem awards Pub. Rels. Soc. Am., 1982. Office: EMB Ptnrs 1520 4th Ave Ste 600 Seattle WA 98101

EASTHAM, THOMAS, foundation administrator; b. Attelboro, Mass., Aug. 21, 1923; s. John M. and Margaret (Marsden) E.; m. Berenice J. Hirsch, Oct. 12, 1946; children: Scott Thomas, Todd Robert. Student English, Northwestern U., 1946-52. With Chgo. American, 1945-56, asst. Sunday editor, 1953-54, feature writer, 1954-56; news editor San Francisco Call Bull., 1956-62, exec. editor, 1962-65; exec. editor, then D.C. bur. chief San Francisco Examiner, 1965-82; dir. pub. info,press sec. to mayor of San Francisco, 1982-88; v.p., western dir. William Randolph Hearst Founds., 1988—. Active Nat. Trust Historic Preservation; mem. Pres.'s Roundtable, U. San Francisco. Pulitzer prize nominee, 1955. Mem. Am. Soc. Newspaper Editors, Inter-Am. Press Assn., Am., Internat. press insts., White House Corrs. Assn., Nat. Press Club, Ind. Sector, Coun. on Foundations, Commonwealth Club, Sigma Delta Chi. Home: 1473 Bernal Ave Burlingame CA 94010-5559 Office: Hearst Found 90 New Montgomery St Ste 1212 San Francisco CA 94105-4596

EASTIN, DELAINE ANDREE, state agency administrator; b. San Diego, Aug. 20, 1947; d. Daniel Howard and Dorothy Barbara (Robert) Eastin; m. John Stuart Saunders, Sept. 17, 1972. BA in Polit. Sci., U. Calif., Davis, 1969; MA in Polit. Sci., U. Calif., Santa Barbara, 1971. Instr. Calif. Community Colls., various locations, 1971-79; acctg. mgr. Pacific Bell, San Francisco, 1979-84; corp. planner Pacific Telesis Group, San Francisco, 1984-86; assemblywoman Calif. State Legis., Sacramento, 1986-95; supt. of public instruction Calif. Edn. Dept., Sacramento, 1995—. Bd. dirs. CEWAER, Sacramento, 1988—; commr. Commn. on Status of Women, Sacramento, 1990—; mem. coun. City of Union City, Calif., 1980-86; chair Alameda County Libr. Commn., Hayward, Calif., 1981-86; planning commr. City of Union City, 1976-80; mem., pres. Alameda County Solid Waste Mgmt. Authority, Oakland, Calif., 1980-86. Named Outstanding Pub. Ofcl. Calif. Tchrs. Assn., 1988, Cert. of Appreciation Calif. Assn. for Edn. of Young Children, 1988-92, Legislator of the Yr. Calif. Media Libr. Educators, 1991, Calif. Sch. Bd. Assn., 1991, Ednl. Excellence award Calif. Assn. Counseling and Devel., 1992. Mem. Am. Bus. Women's Assn. (Outstanding Bus. Woman 1988), The Internat. Alliance (21st Century award 1990), World Affairs Coun., Commonwealth Club. Democrat. Avocations: photography, hiking, reading, theater. Home: 2140 Springwater Dr Fremont CA 94539-5956

EASTIN, KEITH E., lawyer; b. Lorain, Ohio, Jan. 16, 1940; s. Keith Ernest and Jane E. (Heimer) E. A.B., U. Cin., 1963, M.B.A., 1964; J.D., U. Chgo., 1967. Bar: Ill. 1967, Tex. 1974, Calif. 1975, U.S. Supreme Ct. 1975, D.C. 1983. Atty. Vedder, Price, Kaufman & Kammholz, Chgo., 1967-73; v.p., sec., gen. counsel Nat. Convenience Stores, Inc., Houston, 1973-79; ptnr. Payne, Eastin & Widmer, Houston, 1977-83; dep. under sec. U.S. Dept. Interior, 1983-86; prin. dep. asst. sec. USN, 1986-88; ptnr. Hopkins & Sutter, Washington, 1989-91; sr. v.p. Guy F. Atkinson Co., San Francisco, 1991-92; dir. environ. svcs. Deloitte & Touche, Washington, 1992—; sr. v.p., gen. counsel Guy F. Atkinson Co., 1991-92; dir. Nat. Money Orders Inc., Feast & Co., Inc., Kempco Petroleum Co., Bertman Drilling Co., Pacific Options, Inc., Del Rey Food Svcs., Inc., Stratford Feedyards, Inc., Deloitte & Touche, 1993-98, Pricewaterhouse Coopers, 1998—; prin. Westec Environ., Inc., Reno, 1993—. Bd. dirs. Theatre Under the Stars, Houston, Statue of Liberty-Ellis Island Found.; mem. exec. com. Harris County Republican Party, 1976-83. Mem. ABA, Ill. Bar Assn., Tex. Bar Assn., D.C. Bar Assn., State Bar Calif., Knights Templar, Beta Gamma Sigma, Phi Delta Phi, Beta Theta Pi. Clubs: University (Houston); Capitol Hill (Washington). Home and Office: Unit F 101 Westheimer Houston TX 77006

EASTLAND, LARRY L., entertainment and theme park development executive; b. Nampa, Idaho, Mar. 16, 1943; s. Fred and Edla Jennett (Homer) E.; m. Beverly Ann Caulder, Jan. 19, 1971; children: Christopher, Rebekah, Justin, Ashley. BA, Brigham Young U., 1967; AM, U. So. Calif., 1973, PhD, 1976. Rsch. asst. in fgn. policy U.S. Senator Len B. Jordan, Washington, 1969-71; staff asst. Gerald R. Ford/The White House, Washington, 1974-77; pres. Lea Mgmt. Corp., Conn., Va., Idaho, 1977—; dir. ops. Summit of Industrialzed Nations, 1982-83; pres. Medtex Corp., Salt Lake City, 1994-96; chmn. bd. Northwest Parks LLC, Boise, Idaho, 1996—. Author: Harvesting Dollars, 1993. Bd. dirs. World Sports Humanitarian Hall of Fame, Boise, 1996—, Unruh Inst. Politics/U. So. Calif., 1978-92; mem. Pres.'s Dist. Export Coun., Boise, 1988-94; U.S. del. World Tourism Orgn., Sofia, Bulgaria, 1985; candidate for Gov., State of Idaho, 1994; chmn. Idahoans for Competitive Govt., 1991-92; fin. chair Idaho Rep. Party, Boise, 1989-90; mem. nat. fin. com. Bush-Quayle, 1992. Capt. USMCR, 1967-73, Vietnam. Decorated Bronze Star with V. Mormon. Avocations: teaching, music, writing, golf. Email: swj@micron.net. Office: Northwest Parks LLC PO Box 2696 Boise ID 83701

EASTMAN, CAROLINE MERRIAM, computer science educator; b. Columbus, Ohio, Dec. 25, 1946; d. Robert Merriam and Kathryn Parmelee (Benedict) E.; m. Robin Michael Carter, Mar. 31, 1968. AB magna cum laude, Radcliffe Coll., 1968; MS in Computer Sci., U. N.C., 1974, PhD in Computer Sci., 1977. Asst. prof. dept. math. and computer sci. Fla. State U., Tallahassee, 1977-82; asst. prof. dept. computer sci. and engring. So. Meth. U., Dallas, 1982-84, assoc. prof., 1984-85; program dir. NSF, Washington, 1984-85; assoc. prof. dept. computer sci. U. S.C., Columbia, 1986-91, prof., 1991—. Contbr. articles to profl. jours. Rsch. grantee NSF, Fla. State U., 1980-82, So. Meth. U., 1982-84, Air Force Office Sci. Rsch., Fla. State U., 1981-82. Mem. AAAS (nominating com. sec. 1987-90, mem.-at-large sect. 1993-97, sect. chair 1998-99), Assn. Computing Machinery (v.p. N.W. Fla. chpt. 1978-79), Assn. Women in Computing (bd. dirs.-at-large 1979-83), Am. Soc. Info. Sci. Office: Dept Computer Sci Univ of South Carolina Columbia SC 29208-0001

EASTMAN, DEAN ERIC, science research executive; b. Oxford, Wis., Jan. 20, 1940; m. Ella Mae Staley. BSEE, MIT, 1962, MSEE, 1963, PhDEE, 1965. Rsch. staff IBM T.J. Watson Rsch. Ctr., Yorktown Heights, N.Y., 1963-71, mgr. photoemission and surface physics group, 1971-81, mgr. lithography packaging and compound semicondr. tech., 1981-82, dir. Advanced Packaging Tech. Lab., 1983-85, rsch. v.p. system tech. and sci., 1986-94; dir. product devel. IBM Systems Tech. Div., Danbury, Conn., 1985-86; dir. hardware devel. reengring. IBM Corp., Armonk, N.Y., 1994-96; dir. Argonne Nat. Lab., 1996-98; prof. physics U. Chgo., 1998—. Contbr. over 180 articles to profl. jours. Recipient Oliver E. Buckley prize, 1980; IBM Corp. fellow, 1974. Fellow Am. Phys. Soc.; mem. NAS, NAE, Am. Acad. Arts and Scis. Office: University of Chicago RI 231 5640 S Ellis Ave Chicago IL 60637-1433

EASTMAN, DONALD, church officer; b. Sheboygan, Wis., Feb. 1, 1941. Student, Cen. Bible Coll., 1966. Ordained minister Assemblies of God. Pastor Assemblies of God, Wis., 1966-72; ofcl. Am. Lung Assn., Iowa, 1972-75; pastor MCC congregations UFMCC, Des Moines and Dallas, 1978-86; 2d vice moderator, treas. UFMCC. Activist civil and human rights of gays and lesbians; lobbyist repeal of state sodomy laws, Iowa; speaker Tex. State Bd. of Health; bd. dirs. AIDS Nat. Interfaith Network, 1988-90, founding mem., first chairperson. Office: UFMCC 2d Fl 8704 Santa Monica Blvd West Hollywood CA 90069-4548*

EASTMAN, DONNA KELLY, composer, music educator; b. Denver, Sept. 26, 1945; d. Donald Lewis and Frances Marie (Smith) Kelly; m. John Bernard Eastman, July 1, 1973; children: Jonathan Kelly, James Alan; stepchildren: Barbara Kathleen, Sally Toye. B Music Edn., U. Colo., 1967; MA, U. Md., 1973, D in Mus. Arts, 1992. Pvt. studio tchr., coach, 1960—; choral dir. Dept. Def. Overseas Schs., Okinawa, Japan, 1970-72; dir. Choraleers Choral Ensemble, Stuttgart, Germany, 1974-76, Bangkok (Thailand) Music Soc. Ensemble and Madrigal Singers, 1982-84; instr. in music No. Va. C.C., Alexandria, 1986-89; creator, pianist, vocalist Am. Music Programs for U.S. Mission, Thailand, 1981-84; vis. asst. prof. Ill. Wesleyan U., Bloomington, 1994; vis. composer Sweet Briar (Va.) Coll., 1998. Composer choral, orchestral, opera, vocal/instrumental solo and chamber, and electronic works; recs. include Soc. of Composers, Inc. Series, Contemporary Am. Flute Music-Capstone Recs., Living Artist Recs.; rec. series Contemporary American Eclectic Music for Piano; contbr. to jours. Fellow Charles Ives Ctr. for Am. Music, 1990, 93, Ragdale Found., 1991, Va. Ctr. for Creative Arts, 1991-99; recipient 6 Internat. Composition awards Composers' Guild, 1991—, Internat. Piano Composition award Roodeport Internat. Eisteddfod, South Africa, 1991, Glad-Robinson-Youse Composition award Nat. Fedn. Music Clubs, 1992, Internat. Choral Composition award Florilège Vocal de Tours, France, 1995, Keyboard award Delius Composition Competition, 1997, Margaret Fairbank Jory Copying Assistance award Am. Music Ctr., 1999. Mem. Soc. for Electro-Acoustic Music in the U.S., International Alliance for Women in Music, Soc. of Composers, Inc., Nat. Mus. Women in Arts (charter), Broadcast Music, Inc., Am. Composers Forum, Southeastern Composer's League, Friday Morning Music Club Washington, Phi Kappa Phi, Pi Kappa Lambda, Sigma Alpha Iota. Avocations: travel, handicrafts, photography. Home: 6812 Dina Leigh Ct Springfield VA 22153-1019

EASTMAN, FRANCESCA MARLENE, volunteer, art historian; b. Jamaica Plain, Mass., Jan. 26, 1952; d. Therald Carlton and Martha Jane (Welch) E.; m. Edward Charles Goodstein, Aug. 27, 1989. AB in Art History, Manhattanville Coll., 1972; MA in Art History, Clark Art Inst./Williams Coll., 1974; postgrad., Stanford U., 1976-80. Intern Mus. of Fine Arts, Boston, summers 1971-73; lectr. in art Regis Coll., Weston, Mass., 1974-76; sr. house assoc. Stanford (Calif.) U., 1977-80, tchg. fellow, 1978-79; student svcs. intern Menlo Coll., Atherton, Calif., 1980-81; now freelance editor. Bd. sec. Trinity Episcopal Sch., Menlo Park, Calif., 1992-96, bd. chair, 1996-98; adv. bd., chair Trinity Sch., 1998—; trustee David B. and Edward C. Goodstein Found., L.A., 1995—; vol. scholarship com. Peninsula Cmty. Found., San Mateo, Calif., 1995—; grad. Leadership Redwood City, Calif., 1995—; arts commr., co-chair Town of Atherton, Calif., 1996—, 75th ann. com. leadership coun., 1998; mem. steering com., chair edn. com. Peninsula Episcopal H.S. Project, Foster City, Calif., 1996—. Mem. Cornell Club (N.Y.C.), Williams Club (N.Y.C.), Pacific Athletic Club. Democrat. Roman Catholic. Avocations: art collecting, piano.

EASTMAN, JOHN RICHARD, retired manufacturing company executive; b. Ottawa, Ohio, Sept. 28, 1917; s. Herbert Parrett and Marie (Brown) E.; m. Hope Ruth, June 12, 1943; 1 child, Janet Ruth. B.A., Ohio State U., Columbus, 1939, LL.B., 1941. Bar: Ohio 1941. With firm Eastman, Stichter, Smith & Bergman, Toledo, 1941-42, 46-75; ptnr. Eastman, Stichter, Smith & Bergman, 1950-75; sr. v.p., gen. counsel Sheller-Globe Corp., Toledo, 1975-77; pres. Sheller-Globe Corp., 1977-82, vice chmn., 1982-86; lectr. Coll. Law, U. Toledo, 1954-55. Bd. dirs. United Way, 1978-82, 84-87. Served with USNR, 1942-46. Decorated Purple Heart. Mem. ABA., Ohio Bar Assn., Lucas County Bar Assn. (pres. 1960), Toledo Bar Assn. (exec. com. 1963-69), Am. Judicature Soc., Internat. Assn. Ins. Counsel, Am. Coll. Trial Lawyers, Toledo C. of C. (chmn. 1985-86). Clubs: Toledo, Toledo Country, Belmont Country. Home: 29607 Gleneagles Rd Perrysburg OH 43551-3516

EASTMAN, LESTER FUESS, electrical engineer, educator; b. Utica, N.Y., May 21, 1928; s. Howard Socrates and Mayme Lois (Fuess) E.; m. Anne Marie Gardner, Dec. 22, 1948; children: David Joel, Daniel Gardner, Laurie Suzanne. BEE, Cornell U., 1953, MS, 1955, PhD, 1957. Instr. Cornell U., Ithaca, N.Y., 1954-56; asst. prof. Cornell U., 1957-60, assoc. prof., 1960-66, prof. elec. engring., 1966-84; John L. Given Found. Chair prof. elec. engring., 1985—, founder, dir. joint services electronics program and research lab., 1977-87; founding mem. Nat. Rsch. and Resource Facility for Submicron Structures, 1977—; laborator Chalmers Tech. U., Gothenburg, Sweden, 1960-61; mem. tech. staff RCA Rsch. Lab., 1964-65; founder, pres. Cayuga Assoc., Ithaca, 1971-72; mem. tech. staff MIT, Lincoln Lab., Lexington, Mass., 1978-79; dir. Cornell Rsch. Found., 1974-86; mem. U.S. Adv. Group Election Devices, 1978-85, 86-88; vis. scientist IBM Watson Rsch. Lab., 1985-86; founder, chmn. bd. dirs. N.E. Semicondr., Inc., 1987-93; cons. to industry. Guest editor IEEE transactions, 1967, 78; Contbr. articles to profl. jours. Served with USN, 1946-48. Recipient Welker medal and award Internat. Symposium Gallium Arsenide and Related Compounds, 1991, Aldert Van Der Ziel award, 1995; Sperry Gyroscope fellow, 1953-54, GE fellow, 1956-57, Humboldt Sr. fellow, 1994—. Fellow IEEE (Grad. Educator award 1999); mem. NAE, Electromagnetics Acad., Sigma Xi, Eta Kappa Nu, Tau Beta Pi, Phi Kappa Phi. Presbyterian. Patentee in field. Home: 61 Burdick Hill Rd Ithaca NY 14850-9760 Office: Cornell U 425 Phillips Hall Ithaca NY 14853-5401 *As a professor, I believe that my life contribution is through giving many students the opportunity to reach their full potential in the highest technology available.*

EASTMAN, THOMAS GEORGE, investment management executive; b. L.A., July 28, 1946; s. George Lockwood and Louisa (Forrester) E.; m. Terry Beckley, Aug. 20, 1972; children: Timothy, David. AB, Stanford U., 1968; MBA, Harvard U., 1970. Analyst Systech Fin. Corp., Walnut Creek, Calif., 1971-72; v.p. for acquisitions Coldwell Banker, L.A., 1972-79; sr. v.p. The Boston Co. Real Estate Counsel, Boston, 1979-81; exec. dir., co-chmn. Aldrich, Eastman & Waltch, Boston, 1981-96; founder Forrester Capital LLC, Boston, 1997—; bd. dirs. Bedford Property Investors, Inc. Mem. Urban Land Inst., The Counsellors of Real Estate, Nat. Assn. Real Estate Investment Mgrs. (past chmn.). Office: Forrester Capital LLC 31 Milk St Ste 901 Boston MA 02109

EASTMAN, WILFRED W., retired surgeon; b. Takoma Park, Md., Feb. 12, 1915; s. Willie Walter (King) E.; m. Mary Elizabeth Hyatt, July 15, 1937;

children: Nancy Ann Marter, Sally Jo Walther, Wilfred W. Jr., Lana Lee Plum, Tana Lee Plauger. Student, Columbia Union Coll.; MD, Loma Linda U., 1940. Diplomate Am. Bd. Surgery. Intern Montgomery Hosp., Norristown, Pa., 1939-40; resident in surgery Gallinger Mcpl.-George Washington U., 1946-49; mem. staff Mayers Meml. Hosp., Fall River Mills, Calif.; ret. Gallinger Hosp. George Washington U., D.C., 1949-69; surgeon Borneo, 1970, D.C., 1970-80; ret., 1993; chief of staff Washington Adventist Hosp., Takoma Park; mem. staff Sibley Hosp., Dr.'s Hosp., Leland Meml. Hosp., Hanley Hosp., Children's Hosp., Mayers Meml. Hosp. Vol. surgeon Mission Hosp., Bangkok, and Thailand, 1969, Singapore, 1970. Lt. col. U.S. Army, WWII. Fellow ACS; mem. AMA, Alumni Assn. Columbia Union Coll. (pres.), Alumni Assn. Loma Linda Med. Sch. (pres.), Rotary (pres. Silver Spring chpt.).

EASTON, CHARLES CLEMENT, JR., corporate executive; b. Allentown, Pa., July 14, 1930; s. Charles Clement and Harriet Ida (Williamson) E.; m. Priscilla Emma Herbert, Dec. 26, 1954; children: Joanne, Charles III, June, Jennifer. BS in Econs., Wharton Sch., 1952; MBA, Harvard U., 1956. CFP. Asst. to treas. Inmont Corp., N.Y.C., 1956-62, asst. treas., 1962-67, treas., 1967-80; treas. Inmount Div./United Technologies, Clifton, N.J., 1980-84; dir. fin. planning Coatings and Inks Div./BASF Corp., Clifton, 1984-88; sr. rep. Excel Comms., Inc., Boca Raton, Fla. and Short Hills, N.J., 1995—. Trustee, bd. dirs. Comm. Agys. Corp., Newark, N.J., 1989—. 1st lt. USAF, 1952-54, Korea. Mem. Wyo. Club of Millburn, N.J., Racquets Club of Boca Raton, Alpha Chi Rho. Republican. Congregationalist. Avocations: tennis, bridge.

EASTON, GLENN HANSON, JR., management and insurance consultant, federal official, naval officer; b. N.Y.C., Mar. 11; s. Glenn Herman and Cornelia Blanchard (Hanson) E.; m. Jeanne Milhall, June 15, 1944; children: Jeanne, Glenn Hanson III, Michelle, Carol. Assoc. in Bus. Adminstrn., U. Pa., 1949, B.A. in Econs., 1950; M.B.A., NYU, 1959. USCG lic. as 3d asst. engr. steam vessels of any horsepower, as 3d mate of steam and motor vessels of any gross tons upon the waters of oceans; CLU. Various positions to asst. traffic mgr. Keystone Shipping Co., Phila., 1940-54, Phila. Jr. C. of C., 1946-54; various positions to mgr. transp. econs. div. Standard-Vacuum Oil Co., White Plains, N.Y., 1954-59; various positions to cons. to pres. S.R. Guggenheim Found., N.Y.C., 1959-84; pres. Glenn Easton & Assocs. (mgmt. and ins. cons.), Port Chester, N.Y., 1970—; emeritus spl. agent Northwestern Mutual Life Ins. Co., 1974—; polit. appointee U.S. Dept. Labor, Washington, 1982-88; emeritus spl. agt. Northwestern Mut. Life Ins. Co., 1974—; assoc. prof. mgmt. L.I. U., Brookville, N.Y., 1971-72. *Commander Easton graduated from Morse High School in Bath, Maine with honors andas senior class president. Commander Easton began his military career as a machine gunner with the 240th coast artillery headed for an appointment to West Point. Later he switched to the U.S. Navy. While on sea duty in the pacific, Commander Easton participated in the Leyte, Luzon, Iwo Jima and Okinawa campaigns. As a political appointee during the Reagan administration, Commander Easton served as Special Assistant to the wage and hour administrator in the U.S. Department of Labor.* Rep. candidate for congressman, N.Y., 1972, 74, 80; pres. local Rep. Club, 1973-74; mem. Westchester County Rep. Com., 1972-83; Rep., Conservative and Ind. candidate for supr. Town of Rye, N.Y., 1973, 75, 79, 81, Rep. Candidate for councilman, 1977; vice chmn. Ind. Conservative Caucus, Westchester, 1977-83; exec. v.p. bd. trustees N.Y.-Phoenix Schs. Design, 1968-74; Eagle Scout with 4 Silver Palms. With Maine N.G., 1936-38; served to comdr. USN, 1938-40, 43-46, 50-54, 70, PTO, ret., 1979. Mem. Soc. Naval Archs. and Marine Engrs. (life, Golden award), Navy Athletic Assn., Sr. Execs. Assn., Fed. Exec. Inst., Ret. Officers' Assn., C. of C., Am. Mgmt. Assn., Naval Res. Assn. (life, v.p. Westchester chpt.), Militia Assn. N.Y. (life), Westchester Organ Soc. (v.p.), Met. Organ Soc. Va., No. Va. Ragtime Soc., Am. Theatre Organ Soc., U.S. Capitol Hist. Soc., The Conservative Network (life), Am. Legion, Masons, Shriners, Kiwanis, Elks, Pi Gamma Mu, Sigma Kappa Phi, Phi Delta Theta (Golden Legionnaire). Avocations: swimming, reading, music, archery, numismatics. Home: 1385 Old Quincy Ln Reston VA 20194-1309 Office: 1537 Inlet Ct Reston VA 20190-4423 *Much hard work, a desire for knowledge, great integrity, persistence, enthusiasm, determination, and some vision are essential ingredients in the success formula. In addition, successful leaders must never shrink from responsibility! While it helps to be lucky, to have friends in the right places, or to be in the right place at the right time, it is more important in a man's quest for success to deal honestly and fairly with one's fellowman in order that when material success is achieved peace of mind and happiness come with it.*

EASTON, JILL JOHANNA, state official; b. Nassua County, N.Y., June 6, 1949; d. E. Paul and Thelma R. Easton. BA, U. So. Miss., 1971, MPA, 1986. Mgr. classified advt. Thibodeaux (La.) Daily Comet, 1971-73; on-air personality Sta. WNAT, Natchez, Miss., 1973-74; classified sales rep. Natchez Democrat, 1974; co-owner House of Pisces Pet Shop, Vidalia, La., 1974-75; employment interviewer Miss. Employment Svc., Gulfport, 1976-80; pub. relations rep. Miss. Dept. Health, Gulfport, 1980-83, health program rep., 1983—; pres. J & K Ltd. Columnist Advertiser News, Hattiesburg, Miss., Fishing Along the Gulf Coast; contbg. writer Today in Miss. Instr., trainer CPR First Aid. Mem. Divers Alert Network, Miss. Archaeology Assn. (bd. dirs.), So. Miss. Hist. and Geneal. Soc., S.E. Outdoor Press Assn. (bd. dirs.), Rotary. Lutheran. Avocations: scuba diving, painting, field archaeology. Home: 206 Kuyrkendall Pl Long Beach MS 39560-3308 Office: Harrison County Health Dept PO Drawer T 4521 Old Pass Rd Gulfport MS 39501-2578

EASTON, J(OHN) DONALD, neurologist, educator; b. Saskatoon, Sask., Can., Apr. 1, 1938; s. John and Winnifred J. (Small) E.; m. Carol Anne May, 1959 (div. 1984); children: Erin, John, Murray; m. K. Von Gunten, May 19, 1985; children: Andrew, Alexander. BS in Zoology, Wash. State U., 1960; MD, U. Wash., 1964. Cert. Am. Bd. Psychiatry and Neurology (examiner, dir. 1984-92). From asst. to assoc. prof. U. Calif., San Diego, 1970-73; from assoc. prof. to prof. So. Ill. U. Sch. Medicine, Springfield, 1974-77; prof., chair neurology dept. U. Mo. Sch. Medicine, Columbia, 1977-82, U. Tex. Health Sci. Ctr., San Antonio, 1982-86, Brown U. Sch. Medicine, Providence, 1986—; pres. Neurology Found., Inc., Providence, 1990—. Author med. books; editor med. jours. Fellow Am. Heart Assn. Stroke Coun., 1971—, chmn., 1991-93, vol., Providence, 1986—. With USN, 1968-70. Fellow Am. Acad. Neurology; mem. Am. Neurol. Assn., Alpha Omega Alpha, Phi Beta Kappa. Presbyterian. Avocations: travel, computers, sports. Home: 7 Seaview Ave Jamestown RI 02835-1644 Office: RI Hosp Brown U 110 Lockwood St Providence RI 02903-4801

EASTON, JOHN JAY, JR., lawyer; b. San Francisco, June 16, 1943; s. John Jay and Julia (Crawford) E.; m. Donna Cecilia Ringger Startzel, May 4, 1996. B.S., U. Colo., 1964; J.D., Georgetown U., 1970. Bar: Va. 1970, Vt. 1971. Mktg. rep. Gen. Dynamics Corp., Washington, 1968-70; assoc. Paterson, Gibson, Noble & Brownell, Montpelier, Vt., 1970-72; ptnr. Davison & Easton, Stowe, Vt., 1972-75; asst. atty. gen., chief consumer protection Office Vt. Atty. Gen., 1975-78; dir. div. rate setting Vt. Agy. Human Services, 1978-80; atty. gen. State of Vt., 1981-85; pvt. practice, Burlington, Vt., 1985-86; v.p. Syn-Cronamics, Inc., Englewood Cliffs, N.J., 1986-87, Miller, Eggleston & Rosenberg, Ltd., 1987-89; asst. sec. Internat. Affairs and Energy Emergencies Dept. Energy, Washington, 1989-91, gen. counsel, 1991-92, asst. sec. Domestic and Internat. Energy Policy, 1992-93; sole practice, 1993-94; v.p. internat. programs Edison Elec. Inst., 1994—; mem. product safety adv. council U.S. Consumer Product Safety Com., 1977-79. Mem. Vt. Natural Resources Coun., 1976-89; Rep. nominee for gov. of Vt., 1984. Served to capt. USAF, 1964-68. Mem. ABA (ho. of dels. 1979-84), Vt. Bar Assn. (del. 1980-84, chmn. coms. 1974-78, bd. mgrs. 1973-75), Am. Legion, VFW. Republican. Roman Catholic. Home: 5310 Saint Albans Way Baltimore MD 21212-3305 Office: Edison Elec Inst 701 Pennsylvania Ave NW Washington DC 20004-2608

EASTON, MICHELLE, foundation executive; b. Phila., Aug. 12, 1950; d. Glenn H. Jr. and Jeanne (Mulhall) Easton; m. Ron Robinson, Sept. 14, 1974; children: Ronald Jr., Daniel, Thomas. AA, BA, Briarcliff Coll., 1972; JD, Am. U., Washington, 1980. Bar: Va. 1981. Asst. to exec. dir. Young Ams. for Freedom, Sterling, Va., 1973-78; asst. to dir. pub. rels. Nat. Right to Work Com., Springfield, Va., 1978; legal asst. Nat. Right to Work Legal Def. Found., 1979; transition team mem. Office of Pres.-Elect, Equal Employment Opportunity Commn., Washington, 1980-81; atty. U.S. Dept. Justice, Washington, 1981; spl. asst. to gen. counsel U.S. Dept. Edn., Washington, 1981-83; pvt. vol. orgns. liaison officer, Africa Bur. Agy. for Internat. Devel., 1984; dir. Missing Children's Program Office of Juvenile Justice and Delinquency Prevention, U.S. Dept. Justice, 1985-87; dir. intergovtl. affairs U.S. Dept. Edn., Washington, 1987-88, dep. under sec. for intergovtl. and interagy. affairs, 1988-91; dir. Office Pvt. Edn., Washington, 1991-93; pres. Clare Boothe Luce Policy Inst., 1993—. Apptd. by Gov. Allen to Va. State Bd. Edn., Richmond, 1994-98, bd. pres. 1996; bd. dirs. The Family Found., Richmond, Va., 1998. Mem. The Phila. Soc. (trustee 1998). Republican. Episcopalian.

EASTON, ROBERT MORRELL, JR., optometric physician; b. Miami, Fla., Sept. 23, 1954; s. Robert Morrell Easton Sr. and Joan (Saxon) Faust; m. Gloria Rocio Flores, Mar. 19, 1983; children: Robert Morrell Easton III, Linda Easton. AA, Broward Community Coll., 1974; BS in Chemistry, U. Cen. Fla., 1977; OD, U. Houston, 1982. Bd. cert. Optometric physician, Fla. Extern Bascom Palmer Eye Inst., Miami; pvt. practice Ft. Lauderdale, 1982—. Recipient Up & Comer's award for Health Care South Fla. Mag., 1993; named One of Top Optometrists in U.S., 20/20 mag., 1991. Fellow Am. Acad. Optometry; mem. Fla. Optometric Assn. (pres. 1993-94), Am. Optometric Assn. (state rep. 1987-95, polit. action, profl. rels. com. 1994-95, bd. dirs., treas. AOA-PAC 1994—), Fla. Pub. Health Assn. (charter, chmn. vision care sect. 1992-93), Broward County Optometric Assn. (past pres., Optometrist of Yr. 1985), Tower Forum (v.p. 1994-95, treas. 1999—), East Oakland Park Blvd. Bus. Assn. (charter pres. 1998—), Leadership Broward Alumni Assn., Rotary (bd. dirs. Ft. Lauderdale 1986-89, svc. award 1989),. Republican. Presbyterian. Avocations: physical fitness, hunting, fishing, surfing, martial arts. Office: 2708 E Oakland Park Blvd Fort Lauderdale FL 33306-1605

EASTON, SHEENA, rock vocalist; b. Bellshill, Scotland, Apr. 27, 1959; m. Tim Delarm, July 28, 1997; children: Jake, Skylar. Grad., Royal Scottish Acad. Music and Drama, 1979. Albums include Take My Time, 1981, You Could Have Been with Me, 1981, Madness, Money and Music, 1982, Best Kept Secret, 1983, A Private Heaven, 1984, The Lover in Me, 1988, Greatest Hits, 1989, My Cherie, 1994, (with Luis Miguel) Me Gustas Tal Como Eres (Grammy award for Mexican-Am. performance 1984), No Strings, 1993; TV appearances include Miami Vice, 1987, Body Bags, The Highlander, The Adventure of Brisco County Jr., Outer Limits, 1996; Broadway appearances: Man of La Mancha, 1992, Grease; voiceovers for All Dogs Go to Heaven, T.V. Road Rovers. Recipient Grammy award for best new artist, 1981. Office: Harriet Wasserman Mgmt 18122 Hatteras St Tarzana CA 91356

EASTUP, LAVONDA JO, writer, poet, songwriter; b. Valdasta, Tex., Aug. 29, 1931; d. Ira Albert and Maxine Lottie (Box) Greer; m. Admah C. Eastup, Jr., Dec. 12, 1948 (div. Oct. 1985); children: Lana Kay, Reggie Dale, Allen Ray, Debra Darlene. Grad. h.s. Author: Two Wheels to Glory--The Gentle Giant, 1982, Silver Teardrops and Golden Manna, Great Poems of the Western World, 1990, (with others) The World of Poetry Anthology, 1991, Who's Who in Poetry, Vol. III, 1991, Gold and Silver Poems, 1992, Poems that Will Live Forever, 1993, Great Poems of Our Time, 1993, Our World's Favorite Poems, Who's Who in Poetry, 1993, Outstanding Poets of 1994; contbr. poetry to books, including: On the Threshold of a Dream, Vol. 3, 1992, Selected Works of Our World's Best Poets, 4 poems made into songs and released by Rainbow Records, 1991, 92. Recipient numerous awards and plaques for poetry. Mem. Little Black Book Poetry Soc. of Hunt County, Tex., Internat. Soc. Poets (hon.). Republican. Baptist. Avocations: gardening, raising cats and flowers.

EASTWOOD, CLINT, actor, director, former mayor; b. San Francisco, May 31, 1930; m. Dina Ruiz. Student, Oakland Tech. High Sch.; attended, Los Angeles City Coll. Worked as lumberjack in Oreg. before being drafted into the Army; formed Malpaso Prodns., 1969. Starred in TV series Rawhide, 1959-1966. Motion pictures include: (actor) Revenge of the Creature, 1955, Francis in the Navy, 1955, Lady Godiva, 1955, Tarantula, 1955, Never Say Goodbye, 1956, The First Travelling Saleslady, 1956, Star in the Dust, 1956, Escapade in Japan, 1957, Ambush at the Cimmaron Pass, 1958, Lafayette Escadrille, 1958, A Fistful of Dollars, 1964, For a Few Dollars More, 1965, The Good The Bad and The Ugly, 1966, The Witches, 1967, Hang 'Em High, 1968, Coogan's Bluff, 1968, Where Eagles Dare, 1969, Paint Your Wagon, 1969, Two Mules for Sister Sara, 1970, Kelly's Heroes,1970, The Beguiled, 1971, Dirty Harry, 1972, Joe Kidd, 1972, Magnum Force, 1973, Thunderbolt and Lightfoot, 1974, The Enforcer, 1976, Every Which Way But Loose, 1978, Escape from Alcatraz, 1979, Any Which Way You Can, 1980, City Heat, 1984, Pink Cadillac, 1989, In the Line of Fire, 1993; (dir.) Breezy, 1973, (dir., actor) Play Misty For Me, 1971, High Plains Drifter, 1973, The Eiger Sanction, 1975, The Outlaw Josey Wales, 1976, The Gauntlet, 1977, Bronco Billy, 1980, The Rookie, 1990, A Perfect World, 1994, Absolute Power, 1996; (actor, prod.) Tightrope, 1984, The Dead Pool, 1988; (dir., prod.) Bird, 1988, Midnight in the Garden of Good and Evil, 1997; (dir., actor, producer) Firefox, 1982, Honky Tonk Man, 1982, Sudden Impact, 1983, Pale Rider, 1985, Heartbreak Ridge, 1986, White Hunter, Black Heart, 1990, Unforgiven, 1992 (Academy Award Best Director, Best Picture), The Bridges of Madison County, 1995, Absolute Power, 1997, True Crime, 1998; (exec. producer) Thelonious Monk-Straight, No Chaser, 1989, The Stars Fell on Henrietta, 1995; singer (Midnight soundtrack album) Ac.cent.uate the Positive, 1997, (with Randy Travis) Smokin' the Hive; documentaries include Don't Pave Main St., 1994, Eastwood After Hours: A Night of Jazz. Mem. Nat. Coun. Arts, 1973. *

EASTWOOD, D(ANA) ALAN, author, publisher, consultant; b. Poughkeepsie, N.Y., June 1, 1947; s. Donald Edward and Edith Margaret (Davis) E.; m. Cynthia Carol Allen, Jan. 1, 1984; children: Athena Yvonne, Ashlee Lyn, Alysa Bryhn. Diploma, Am. Inst. Banking, Washington, 1980; diploma with highest honors, Paralegal Inst., Phoenix, 1983. Proprietor Eastwood Studio, Hyde Park, N.Y., 1965-70; credit rep. Bankers Trust of Hudson Valley, N.A., Poughkeepsie, 1970-73; installment loan supr. Poughkeepsie Savs. Bank, 1973-75, installment loan mgr., 1975-78, consumer loan officer, 1978-79, compliance officer, 1979-87, compliance officer, data security adminstr., 1987-89; compliance, community reinvestment act and loan rev. officer, 1989-91; pres. Modern Bus. Advisors of the Mid-Hudson, 1991-97; editor/pub. Blue Knight Enterprises, 1997—; pres., chmn. bd. Consumer Credit Assn., Mid-Hudson Valley, Poughkeepsie, 1973-75; 1st v.p. Consumer Credit Group N.Y. State, N.Y.C., 1978-79; v.p. dist. 2 Internat. Consumer Credit Assn., N.Y. and N.J., 1978-79; mem. consumer credit com. Savs. Banks Assn. N.Y. State, N.Y.C., 1982-85; mem. supervisory com. Hudson Valley Fed. Credit Union, 1994-96. Author: Gravity Park, 1978, UFOmetry, 1997, Blue Rainbows, 1997, The Thirteenth Sign, 1999; editor The Right Banker, 1979-82; also painter of modern acrylic artworks. Consumer edn. adv. com. Dutchess County Coop. Extension Assn., Millbrook, N.Y., 1975-77. Recipient Award for Outstanding Leadership Consumer Credit Assn. Mid-Hudson Valley, Poughkeepsie, 1974, John C. Corliss Meml. award, 1977, Dedicated Service award Consumer Credit Group N.Y. State, N.Y.C., 1979. Fellow Soc. Cert. Credit Execs.; mem. Internat. Assn. for New Sci. Home and Office: 7 Carriage House Ct Hyde Park NY 12538-1505

EASTWOOD, DELYLE, chemist; b. Upper Darby, Pa., Nov. 19, 1932; d. Earl Vivian and Thelma Bernice Eastwood. MS in Phys. Chemistry, U. Chgo., 1955, PhD in Phys. Chemistry, 1964; MS in Mgmt. Sci., Rensselaer Poly. Inst., 1982. Postdoctoral rsch. fellow Harvard U., Cambridge, Mass., 1964-66; rsch. assoc. U. Wash., Seattle, 1966-69, Northeastern U., Boston, 1970-71; sr. scientist Baird Atomic Corp., Bedford, Mass., 1971-72; project chemist Bendix Rsch. Ctr., Southfield, Mich., 1972-73; rsch. chemist USCG Rsch. and Devel. Ctr., Groton, Conn., 1974-81; sr. staff scientist Brookhaven Nat. Lab., Upton, N.Y., 1981-83; Nat. Superfund design ctr. chemist U.S. Army Corps Engrs., Omaha, 1983-88; sr. staff scientist Lockheed Environ. Sys. and Tech. Co., Las Vegas, Nev., 1988-95; consulting scientist, 1996; sr. rsch. assoc. dept. engring. physics Air Force Inst. Tech., Wright-Patterson AFB, Ohio, 1996—; adj. prof. physics U. Nev., Las Vegas, 1990-99. Editor books in field; contbr. articles to profl. pubs., chpts. to books. Recipient Silver medal for Meritorious Svc. U.S. Dept. Transp., 1978. Fellow ASTM (chmn. subcom E13, exec. bd. 1983—, chmn. task force D19 1974—, E-13 Award of Merit, 1996, D-19 Stds. Devel. award 1991); mem. Soc. Applied Spectroscopy (chmn. Nev. chpt. 1988-90), Assn. Women in Sci. (facilitator, nat. contact So. Nev. chpt. 1989-94), Am. Chem. Soc., Am. Phys. Soc., Soc. of Photo Optical Instrumentation Engrs. Office: Air Force Inst Tech Dept Engring Physics 2950 P St Wright Patterson AFB OH 45433

EASTWOOD, JAMES W., naval officer; b. Phila., Sept. 12, 1945. Degree in civil engring., Villanova U., 1968. Commd. ensign USN, advanced through grades to rear adm.; dep. commdr. 2d fleet USNR, 1997—; pres. Granary Assocs., Phila., 1988—; with Granary Assocs., Phila. Office: Granary Assocs 411 N 20th St Philadelphia PA 19130-3846*

EASTWOOD, SUSAN, medical scientific editor; b. Glens Falls, N.Y., Jan. 2, 1943; d. John J. and Della Eastwood; m. Raymond A. Berry. BA, U. Colo., 1964. Diplomate Bd. Editors in Life Scis. Adminstr. rsch. assoc. Depts. Psychol., Psychiat., Stanford (Calif.) U., 1965-68; prin., tchr. Colegio Capitan Correa, Arecibo, P.R., 1968-70; sr. editor dept. lab. medicine U. Calif., San Francisco, 1971-77, prin. analyst sci. publs. dept. neurol. surgery and Neurosurgical Rsch. Ctrs., 1977—; cons. March of Dimes Calif. Birth Defects Monitoring Program, Emeryville, 1988—; mem. QUOROM, CONSORT, coord., Asilomar Working Group on recommendations for reporting clinical trials, 1993-99; chair, coun. Biology Editors task forces for strategic planning, 1996-98, acad. networks, 1998—; co-chair, Liaison Task Force on Biomed. Authorship. Collaborating editor: Current Neurosurgical Practice, 1984-91, Brain tumor biology and therapy, 1984; editor: Brain Tumors: A Guide, 1992; author: Guidelines on Research Data and Manuscripts, 1989; author and editor: Biomedical Research Papers - A Guide, 1998. Recipient Pres. award Am. Med. Writers Assn., Bethesda, Md., 1989, Chancellors Outstanding Achievement award U. Calif., San Francisco, 1989, 94, Cert. of award Nat. Brain Tumor Found., 1992, Am. Soc. Journalists and Authors, 1992. Fellow Am. Med. Writers Assn.; mem. AAAS, European Assn. Sci. Editors, Internat. Fedn. Sci. Editors, N.Y. Acad. Scis., Coun. Biology Editors (v.p. 1995-96, pres. 1996-97). Office: U Calif Dept Neurosurgery M-779 Box 0112 505 Parnassus Ave San Francisco CA 94122-2722

EASUM, DONALD BOYD, consultant, educator, former institute executive, diplomat; b. Ind., Aug. 27, 1923; m. Augusta Pentecost (dec.). BA, U. Wis., 1947; MPA, Princeton U., 1950, MA, 1950, PhD, 1953. Tchr., 1947-48, newspaper reporter, 1949; independent rsch. London, 1950-51, Buenos Aires, 1951-52; with U.S. Dept. of State, 1953-79; pers. officer Washington, 1953-54; econ.-labor officer Nicaragua, 1955-57; cons., econ. officer Indonesia, 1957-59; exec. secretariat Washington, 1959-61; exec. sec. ICA, 1961, AID, 1962-63; polit. officer Senegal, Gambia, Port Guinea, 1963-66; counsellor, dep. chief mission Niger, 1966-68; sr. sem. in fgn. policy Fgn. Svc. Inst., Washington, 1968-69, staff dir. interdepartmental group for Latin Am., 1969-71; amb. E. and P. to Upper Volta, 1971-74, asst. sec. state for African affairs, 1974-75, amb. to Nigeria,, 1975-79; pres. African-Am. Inst., N.Y.C., 1980-88; lectr. Princeton (N.J.) U., 1991; dir. World Space Found., Washington. Trustee The Rothko Chapel, Houston, Am. Sch. in Tangier; dir. Renewable Energy for African Devel., Washington, Friends of Boys Town South Africa; v.p. Global Bus. Access, Ltd., Washington; mem. Corp. Coun. for Africa, Washington. Woodrow Wilson Nat. fellow, 1988-90, Paul Harris fellow Rotary Internat., 1995, Stimson fellow Yale U., 1999. Address: 801 W End Ave Apt 3A New York NY 10025-5361

EATENSON, ERVIN THEODORE, retired librarian; b. Apr. 18, 1924. BS in Journalism, So. Meth. U., 1946; MS, Columbia U., 1955. Optometry libr. Columbia U., N.Y.C., 1952-55; sci. libr. San Jose (Calif.) State U., 1955-62; adult coord., libr. for collection enrichment Dallas Pub. Libr., 1962-86; editor, info. cons. Dallas, 1986—. Editor: 6th Floor: John F. Kennedy and the Memory of a Nation, Dallas, 1989. Mem. Am. Libr. Assn., Tex. Libr. Assn., Soc. Profl. Journalists., PEN (v.p. 1995—). Home: # 12D 3701 Turtle Creek Blvd Dallas TX 75219

EATON, ALLEN OBER, lawyer; b. Waterford, N.Y., May 28, 1910; s. Arthur Chester and Ethel (Obear) E.; m. Marjorie Eisenwinter, Sept. 8, 1934; 1 child, Barbara Eaton Neilson. B.S., U. Vt., 1932; LL.B., Harvard, 1935. Bar: Mass. 1935. Practiced in Boston, 1935—; with Ropes & Gray (and predecessor firm), 1935—, partner, 1944-83, of counsel, 1983—. Trustee U. Vt., 1970-76, chmn. bd. trustees, 1975-76. Mem. ABA, Mass. Bar Assn., Boston Bar Assn., Sigma Phi. Congregationalist. Home: Brookhaven at Lexington 1010 Waltham St Apt 408A Lexington MA 02421-8064

EATON, ALVIN RALPH, aeronautical and systems engineer, research and development administrator; b. Toledo, Ohio, Mar. 13, 1920; s. Alvin Ralph and Katherine (Hasel) E.; AB in Physics (Miller scholar), Oberlin Coll., 1941; MS in Aeronautical Engring. Calif. Inst. Tech., 1943; m. Kathleen Steiner, Aug. 15, 1942 (div.); children: Eric Lloyd, Alan Ralph; m. Ellen Griffiths Phillips, Oct. 3, 1970. Rsch. asst. Calif. Inst. Tech., 1941-44; engr. So. Calif. Co-op Wind Tunnel, Pasadena, 1944-45; with The Johns Hopkins U. Applied Physics Lab., Silver Spring, Md., 1945-75, Laurel, Md., 1975—, mem. prin. profl. staff, 1950—, supr. aerodynamics, dynamics and guidance analysis groups, 1949-54, program supr. supersonic missile and weapon system programs, 1954-64, supr. missile systems div., 1964-73, faculty evening coll. grad. sch. 1973-75, supr. fleet systems dept. 1973-83, asst. dir. for tactical systems Applied Physics Lab. 1973-79, asst. dir., 1979-86, assoc. dir., 1986-89, sr. fellow, dir. spl. programs, 1989—, mem. Johns Hopkins U. adv. bd. for Applied Physics Lab, 1963, 69-70, 73-89. Chmn. Def. Sci. Bd. Task Force, 1977-78, mem. task forces 1979-83; cons. to under sec. def. for rsch. and engring., 1977-83, chmn. and mem. special NATO and U.S. task forces 1977-92, mem. under sec. def. high energy laser rev. group, 1981-83, mem. under sec. def. durability of electronic countermeasures rev. group, 1983-86; mem. Navy planning and steering adv. Group for Surface Ship Security, 1979-82, chmn. and mem. subgroups 1979-82; cons. to Asst. Sec. of Army for research, devel. and acquisition, 1969-74, 80-86, chmn., Asst. Sec. of Army ind. rev. panel for patriot air def. system, 1980-86; mem. Army Sci. Bd., 1980-86, 89-95; chmn. panel on adv. syst. test, 1980-81; dep. chmn. summer studies on sci. and engring. pers. and future devel. goals, 1982-83 , mem. subgroup on ballistic missile def., 1984-86, 89; chmn. atmospheric scis. lab. effectiveness rev., 1985, chmn. panel on electromagnetic/electrothermal gun tech. devel., 1989-92; chmn. subgroup on Army tactical space systems, 1991-92; mem. rsch. and new initiatives issue group, 1991-95; mem. ad hoc study group on space systems and airland ops., 1992; mem. summer study on future army missile programs, 1993; mem. ad hoc study group missile tech. shelf life, 1994; chmn., asst. sec. army rsch., devel. and acquisition ind. rev. panel for anti-tactical missile programs, 1986—; chmn. high attitude theater missile def. sensor panel Army Strategic Def. Command, 1992-93; dep. chmn., exec. bd. Air Armaments Systems Div. of the Am. Def. Preparedness Assn., 1984-90 (life mem.). Trustee Howard County (Md.) Gen. Hosp., 1977-85, chmn. fin. com., treas. 1979-81, vice-chmn., 1981-83, chmn., 1983-85, chmn. Community Rels. Coun., 1988-94. Mem. editorial bd. Jour. Def. Rsch., 1988-92, Johns Hopkins APL Tech. Digest, 1995—. Recipient Meritorious Pub. Svc. award USN, 1957, Disting. Pub. Svc. award, 1975, Gov. Md. citation for leadership of Howard County (Md.) Gen. Hosp. Cmty. Rels. Coun., 1994, Patriotic Civilian Svc. award U.S. Army, 1995, Disting. Alumni award Morrison R. Waite High Sch., Toledo, Ohio, 1995. Mem. Balt. Coun. on Fgn. Affairs, Rotary, Phi Beta Kappa, Sigma Xi. Methodist. Clubs: Cosmos (Washington); Rolling Road Golf (Balt.); Hilton Head Country, Oyster Reef Golf (Hilton Head Island, S.C.). Inventor in field; contbr. articles to profl. jours. Home: 6701 Surrey Ln Clarksville MD 21029-1605 Office: Johns Hopkins Rd Laurel MD 20723-6099

EATON, BERRIEN CLARK, retired lawyer, author; b. Chgo., Feb. 12, 1919; s. Berrien Clark and Gladys (Hambleton) E.; m. Donna K. Prestwood (dec. Mar. 1991); children: Theodore Hambleton, Ann Berrien, Cody M. Prestwood. Student, Williams Coll., 1936-38; BS, U. Va., 1940, LLB, 1948, JD, 1970. Bar: Mich. 1948, Ariz. 1969, Ga. 1971. Pvt. practice law Detroit, 1948-69, Phoenix, 1969-94; ret., 1994; assoc. Miller, Canfield, Paddock & Stone, 1948-58, pntr., 1958-69; ptnr. Leibsohn, Eaton, Gooding & Romley, P.C., 1971-79, Gray, Plant, Mooty, Mooty & Bennett, Phoenix, 1979-80, Eaton, Lieberman & Dodge Ltd. and successors, 1981-94; instr. Wayne State U. Law Sch., 1954-69; prof. U. Ga. Law Sch., 1970-71; lectr. at law Ariz. State U. Coll. Law, 1970-71. Author: Professional Corporations and Associations, 7 vols., 1970, updated twice annually; co-author: tax newsletter VEBA Report, 1984-87; mem. editorial bd. jour. Estate Planning; notes editor Va. Law Rev.; contbr. articles to profl. jours. Capt. field arty. AUS, PTO, 1941-46. Decorated Bronze Star. Fellow Am. Coll. Trust and Estate Counsel, Am. Coll. Tax Counsel (regent 1980-86); mem. ABA (real property, probate and trust sect., past chmn. 3 tax sect. coms., mentor tax sect., com.

chmn. sr. lawyers sect.), AAUP, Mich. Bar Assn. (past chmn. tax sect.), Ariz. Bar Assn. (past chmn. tax sect.), Ga. Bar Assn., Newcomen Soc. N.Am., Order of Coif, Raven Soc., Waweatoning Club (Mich.), Kappa Alpha. Episcopalian. Home and Office: 2935 N 18th Pl Apt 200 Phoenix AZ 85016-7729

EATON, CURTIS HOWARTH, academic administrator, banker, lawyer; b. Twin Falls, Idaho, Sept. 3, 1945; s. Curtis Turner and Wilma (Howarth) E.; m. Mardo Ohlsson, Aug. 2, 1969; 1 child, Dylan Alexander. B.A., Stanford U., 1969; M.P.A., Johns Hopkins U., 1971; J.D., U. Idaho, 1974. Bar: Idaho 1974. Atty., Idaho Atty. Gen.'s Office, Boise, 1974-76, Stephan, Slavin, Eaton, Twin Falls, 1976-82; exec. v.p. Twin Falls Bank & Trust, 1982-84, area pres., 1984—, also bd. dirs.; v.p., bd. dirs. 1st Security Bank at Idaho, pres., 1992—; bd. dirs. San Francisco Fed. Res., Salt Lake City. Bd. dirs. United Way of Magic Valley, 1978—, Sr. Citizens, 1978-82, mem., Idaho State Bd. of Edn., 1993—, now pres.; Twin Falls C. of C., 1983—; trustee YFCA, 1981—; pres. Coll. So. Idaho Found., 1986-88. Mem. Idaho Bar Assn., Assn. Trial Lawyers Am.*

EATON, EDGAR EUGENE, retird educator, writer; b. Kline, Colo., Nov. 9, 1934; s. Randy Biggs Eaton and Merle Lamar (Behrmann) Mathews; m. Clayta Bernice Hathaway, Dec. 3, 1954; children: Steven, Elizabeth, Robert, Jennifer. BS, Ricks Coll., 1956; MA, U. Wash., 1964, So. Ill. U., 1970. Reporter Standard-Jour., Rexburg, Idaho, 1956; sports editor Evening Observer, LaGrande, Oreg., 1956, Post-Register, Idaho Falls, Idaho, 1957; tchr. Sugar-Salem H.S., Sugar City, Idaho, 1957-59, Centralia (Wash.) Coll., 1960-65, Green River C.C., Auburn, Wash., 1965-97; reporter, editor Valley Daily News, Kent, Wash., summers 1965-85. Author: Linemen Don't Score Touchdowns, 1984, Strike Two, 1994; playwright (one-act plays) Kissing Bandit Plus Four, 1996, (three-act play) Ginny, Kate, and Lady Di. Chair Auburn Planning Commn., 1996-98. Mormon. Avocations: cartooning, speaking to churches and civic groups. Home: 1313 F St SE Auburn WA 98002-6750 Office: Green River CC 12401 SE 320th St Auburn WA 98092-3622

EATON, GARETH RICHARD, chemistry educator, university dean; b. Lockport, N.Y., Nov. 3, 1940; s. Mark Dutcher and Ruth Emma (Ruston) E.; m. Sandra Shaw, Mar. 29, 1969. BA, Harvard U., 1962; PhD, MIT, 1972. Asst. prof. chemistry U. Denver, 1972-76, assoc. prof., 1976-80, prof., 1980-97, dean natural scis., 1984-88, vice provost for rsch., 1988-89, John Evans prof., 1997—; organizer Internat. Electron-Paramagnetic Resonance Symposium. Author, editor 3 books; mem. editorial bd. 4 jours.; contbr. articles to profl. jours. Lt. USN, 1962-67. Mem. AAAS, Am. Chem. Soc., Royal Soc. Chemistry (London), Internat. Soc. Magnetic Resonance, Soc. Applied Spectroscopy, Am. Phys. Soc., Internat. Electron Paramagnetic Resonance Soc. Office: U Denver Dept Chem/Biochem Denver CO 80208

EATON, GORDON PRYOR, geologist; b. Dayton, Ohio, Mar. 9, 1929; s. Colman and Dorothy (Pryor) E.; m. Virginia Anne Gregory, June 12, 1951; children: Gretchen Maria, Gregory Mathieu. BA, Wesleyan U., 1951; MS, Calif. Inst. Tech., 1953, PhD, 1957. From instr. geology to asst. prof. Wesleyan U., Middletown, Conn., 1955-59; from asst. prof. to assoc. prof. U. Calif., Riverside, 1959-67, chmn. dept. geol. sci., 1965-67; with U.S. Geol. Survey, 1963-65, 67-81, 94-97; dep. chief Office Geochemistry and Geophysics, Washington, 1972-74; project chief geothermal geophysics Office Geochemistry Geophysics, Denver, 1974-76; scientist-in-charge Hawaiian Volcano Obs., 1976-78; assoc. chief geologist Reston, Va., 1978-81; dean Tex. A&M U. Coll. Geoscis., 1981-83; provost, v.p. acad. affairs Tex. A&M U., 1983-86; pres. Iowa State U., Ames, 1986-90; dir. Lamont-Doherty Earth Obs. Columbia U., Palisades, N.Y., 1990-94, U.S. Geol. Survey, Reston, Va., 1994-97; prin. Pac NW, SeaMountain Country, Colo., Tex., Wash., W.Va., 1997—; mem. Commn. on Internat. Edn., Am. Coun. Edn.; mem. coun. advisors World Food Prize; mem. bd. earth scis. and resources; ocean studies bd., and com. on formation of nat. biol. survey NRC, also mem. geophysics study com.; bd. dirs. Midwest Resources, Inc., Bankers Trust; mem., chair adv. com. U.S. Army Command and Gen. Staff Coll.; adv. bd. Sandia Nat. Lab. Geoscis. & Environ. Ctr.; adv. bd. Ohio State U. Ctr. Mapping. Mem. editl. bd. Jour. Volcanology and Geothermal Rsch., 1976-78; contbr. articles to profl. jours. Trustee Wesleyan U.; pres., bd. dirs. Iowa 4-H Found., 1986-90; mem. U.S. del. sci. & tech. com. Gore-Chernomyrdin Commn., 1996-97; adv. bd. Sch. Earth Sci. Stanford U. Standard Oil fellow Calif. Inst. Tech., 1953; NSF grantee, 1955-59. Fellow Geol. Soc. Am., AAAS. E-mail: geaton@whidbey.net. Home: 709 Snowberry Ln Coupeville WA 98239 Office: SeaMountain Country 705 N Snowberry Ln Ste O Coupeville WA 98239

EATON, HENRY FELIX, public relations executive; b. Cleve., Nov. 30, 1925; s. Henry F. and Stella (Simon) E.; m. Barbara Feder, Aug. 28, 1950; children: Deborah, Richard, David, Susan. B.A., U. Chgo., 1947. Asst. advt. mgr. Kromex Corp., Cleve., 1947-48; editor Material Handling mag., Cleve., 1948-52; chmn. Dix & Eaton, Inc., Cleve., 1952—. Vice chmn. bd. trustees Playhouse Sq. Found., Mus. Arts Assn., Cleve. With AUS, 1944-46. Mem. Pub. Rels. Soc. Am. (counselors sect.), Nat. Investor Rels. Inst., Union Club, Pepper Pike Club, Cleve. Racquet Club, Oakwood Country Club. Home: 23690 Letchworth Rd Cleveland OH 44122-4110 Office: Dix & Eaton Inc 1301 E 9th St Ste 1300 Cleveland OH 44114-1820

EATON, HENRY TAFT, forest products executive, consultant; b. N.Y.C., Aug. 29, 1918; s. Henry Taft and Ina (Kissel) E.; m. Gladys Foote, June 12, 1938 (dec.); children: Penelope (dec.), Wendy Remick; m. Phyllis Elaine Thompson, Oct. 13, 1989; stepchildren: Vaile Thompson, Danny Thompson, Terry Thompson, Theresa Rose. Student, Harvard U., 1941. Pres. Eaton-Young Lumber Co., Eugene, Oreg., 1948-68, Henry Eaton & Co., Eugene, 1969-78; owner Henry Eaton & Co., 1979—; pres. Veneer Products Singapore-U.S.A. div., Eugene, 1969-74; v.p. Persis Corp, Honolulu, 1977-79; cons. Bunnings Bros. Pty. Ly., Perth, West Australia, 1982-90, Persis Corp., 1980-92, Renyed Inc., Que., 1998—. Author: (tech. manual) Tropical Hardwood Plywood, 1972; inventor The Time Wheel. Chmn. Eugene Airport Commn., 1960-67; comdr. CAP, Eugene, 1964-66; mem. mktg. adv. coun. U. Oreg., Eugene, 1965-67. 1st lt. inf. U.S. Army, World War II, ETO. Decorated Purple Heart. Mem. Feranandina Beach CAP Squadron, Golf Club Amelia Island, South Cowichan Law Tennis Club, Yakima (Wash.) Tennis Club. Republican. Avocations: flying, golf, tennis, skiing. Home and Office: 4441 Captains Way Fernandina Beach FL 32034-4351

EATON, JAMES COLEMAN, music educator, therapist; b. Frederick, Md., Nov. 18, 1949; s. Henry and Ethelene (Harper) E.; m. Sooki Ja Russin, Aug. 25, 1989. B Music Edn. and Music Therapy, Shenandoah U., 1979; MA in Spl. Edn., Hood Coll., 1984; MS in Music Edn., Towson State U., 1993. Cert. tchr., music and spl. edn. tchr., music therapist, Md. Music instr., therapist Daytona Beach (Fla.) C.C., 1980-81; music therapist Henryton (Md.) Ctr. for Mental Retardation, 1981-84; elem. music tchr., therapist Prince Georges County Pub. Schs., Upper Marlboro, Md., 1984-99. Arranger music books: Memories in Melodies, 1981, Songs for Special Occasions, 1981, Happy Holidays Song Book, 1982. With USN, 1969-71, Vietnam. Mem. Music Educators Nat. Conf. (registered music educator), Coun. for Exceptional Children, Am. Music Therapy Assn. Avocation: ballroom dancing. Home: 11109 Luttrell Ln Silver Spring MD 20902-3556

EATON, JERRY, television executive; b. L.A., June 13, 1945. BS in Biology, Trinity Coll. V.p., gen. mgr. KYW, Phila., KPIX-TV, San Francisco, 1997—. Office: KPIX-TV 855 Battery St San Francisco CA 94111-1597*

EATON, JOE OSCAR, federal judge; b. Monticello, Fla., Apr. 2, 1920; s. Robert Lewis and Mamie (Gireadeau) E. AB, Presbyn. Coll., 1941, LLD (hon.), 1979; LLB, U. Fla., 1948. Pvt. practice law Miami, Fla., 1948-51, 55-59; asst. state atty. Dade County, Fla., 1953; circuit judge Miami, 1954-55, 59-67; mem. Fla. Senate, 1956-59; mem. law firm Eaton & Achor, Miami, 1955-58, Sams, Anderson, Eaton & Alper, Miami, 1958-59; judge U.S. Dist. Ct. (so. dist.) Fla., 1967-83, chief judge, from 1983, now sr. judge; Instr. law U. Miami Coll. Law, 1954-56. Served with USAAF, 1941-45; Served with USAF, 1951-52. Decorated D.F.C., Air medal. Methodist. Club: Kiwanian.

EATON, JOHN C., composer, educator; b. Bryn Mawr, Pa., Mar. 30, 1935; s. Harold C. and Fannie E. (Geer) E.; m. Nelda E. Nelson, May 31, 1973; children: Elizabeth Estela, Julian R.P. AB, Princeton U., N.J., 1957, MFA, 1959. Performing artist Columbia Artists, N.Y.C., 1961-65; prof. music Ind. U., Bloomington, 1970—, U. Chgo., 1991—; composer-in-residence Am. Acad., Rome, Italy, 1975-76; lectr. Salzburg Seminar in Am. Studies, Austria, 1976; honored guest Soviet Composers Soc., 1977. Composer numerous operas, most recently: Myshkin, 1972 (Peabody award 1972), Danton and Robespierre, 1978, The Cry of Clytaemnestra, 1980, The Tempest, 1985 (Santa Fe Commn.), The Reverend Jim Jones, 1988, Peer Gynt, 1989, Let's Get This Show on the Road, 1993, Don Quixote, 1994, Golk, 1995, Travelling with Gulliver, 1997, Antigone, 1999, numerous chamber orchs. and elec. comps.; featured in numerous articles in profl. jours. Recipient Prix de Rome, Am. Acad., Rome, 1959-62; citation Am. Inst. Arts and Letters, 1972; plaque Ind. Arts Council, 1975; MacArthur award, 1990; Guggenheim fellow, 1962, 65. Has been called the most interesting opera composer writing in America today. Office: U Chgo Dept Music Chicago IL 60637

EATON, JOHN MONROE, neurologist, educator; b. New Haven, Sept. 23, 1934; s. Monroe Davis and Laura Mitchell E.; m. Mary Elizabeth Beale, June 20, 1959; children: John, Virginia, Michelle. BA, Stanford U., 1956; MD, Harvard U., 1960. Diplomate Am. Bd. Neurology. Neurologist Neurology Med. Assn., San Mateo, Calif., 1967-86; clin. prof. Stanford (Calif.) U., 1968-86; prof. U. Nev., Reno, 1986—. Founding mem. Truckee (Calif.) Donner Land Trust, 1990; v.p. Mountain Arts Preservation Found., Truckee, 1988-91. Capt. U.S. Army, 1961-62. Fellow Am. Acad. Neurology; mem. AAAS, Soc. Neurologists, Sierra Arts Network, Alpha Omega Alpha. Avocations: painting, hiking, cross country skiing, photography, bicycling. E-mail: jme703@aol.com. Home: Box 808 Truckee CA 96160 Office: VA Hosp 1000 Locust St Reno NV 89520

EATON, JOSEPH W., sociology educator; b. Nuremburg, Germany, Sept. 28, 1919; s. Jacob and Flora (Wechsler) E.; m. Helen Goodman, June 8, 1947; children: David, Seth, Debra, Jonathan. BS, Cornell U., 1940; PhD, Columbia U., 1948. Faculty Wayne State U., Detroit, 1947-56; lectr., then vis. prof. Sch. Social Welfare, U. Calif. at Los Angeles, 1956-60; prof. social work research U. Pitts., 1960-70, dir. advanced program, 1966-69, prof. sociology in pub. health and social work research, 1970-73; prof. sociology in pub. health and social work research Sch. Pub. and Internat. Affairs, 1974—, prof., later dir. program in econ. and social devel.; Russell Sage Found. vis. prof. Western Res. U. (Med. Sch.), 1958-59; project dir. Conf. on Social Welfare Consequences of Migration and Residential Movement, 1969; dir. instn. bldg. program Interuniv. Rsch. Consortium, 1966-71; curriculum cons., later dir. social work and social adminstrn. program U. Haifa, Israel, 1970-74 USIA cons., lectr., Africa, 1979, Sweden, Fed. Republic Germany, 1982, 86, Romania, 1982, Abu Dhabi, Pakistan, Egypt, Sudan, Israel, 1986, Nepal, Pakistan, Egypt, Ethiopia, Iraq, 1988, Yugoslavia, USSR, 1989; Fulbright lectr. and cons., 1979, Nat. Acad. Scis. guest scholar in Poland and German Dem. Republic, 1980; co-dir. Jordan River Basin Water Resources Devel., U.S. Inst. Peace, 1992—; co-investigator search for inherited causes of schizophrenia in a genetically isolated cmty., 1997—; co-prin. investigator A Pub. Policy-Oriented Audit of Title Ins., 1999—. Author: (with Saul M. Katz) Research Guide on Cooperative Group Farming, 1942, Exploring Tomorrow's Agriculture, 1943, (with Albert Mayer) Man's Capacity to Reproduce, 1954, (with Robert J. Weil) Culture and Mental Disorders, 1955, (with Kenneth Polk) Measuring Delinquency, 1961, Stone Walls Not a Prison Make: The Anatomy of Planned Adminstrative Change, 1962, Prisons in Israel, 1964, (with Michael Chen) Influencing the Youth Culture: A Study of Youth Organization in Israel, 1970, The Rurban Village, 1980, Can Business Save South Africa, 1980, Card Carrying Americans: Security, Privacy and the National ID Card Controversy, 1986, (with Yuri Lvov) Capitalist Communism, 1991; also contbr. chpts. to books, articles to profl. jours.; editor: Institution Building and Development, 1972. Mem. cable svc. adv. com. City of Pitts. City Coun., 1994—, chmn. cable communications adv. com., 1996—. With AUS, 1941-46. Faculty Research fellow Social Sci. Research Council, 1962. Mem. Nat. Assn. Social Workers (chmn. research council 1968-71), Internat. Assn. Social Psychiatry (mem. council 1969-72), Am. Soc. for Pub. Adminstrn. Home: 5844 Beacon St Pittsburgh PA 15217-2004

EATON, LARRY RALPH, lawyer; b. Quincy, Ill., Aug. 18, 1944; s. Roscoe Ralph and Velma Marie (Beckett) E.; m. Janet Claire Rosen, Oct. 28, 1978. B.A., Western Ill. U., 1965; J.D., U. Mich., 1968. Bar: Ill. 1968, U.S. Dist. Ct. (no. dist.) Ill. 1976, U.S. Supreme Ct. 1978, U.S. Ct. Appeals (D.C. cir.) 1984, U.S. Ct. Appeals (7th cir.) 1989. U.S. Peace Corps vol. Instr. law U. Liberia Sch. Law, Monrovia, 1968-70; lawyer Forest Park Found., Peoria Heights, Ill., 1970-71; asst. atty. gen. State of Ill., Springfield, 1971-75; ptnr. Peterson & Ross and predecessor firms, Chgo., 1975-94; founder Blatt, Hammesfahr & Eaton, Chgo., 1994—; instr. environ. law Quincy Coll., Ill., 1973-75; mem. Ill. Indsl. Pollution Control Financing Authority, 1979; bd. dirs. Near North Montessori Sch., 1989-95, vice chair 1992-95. Contbg. writer Chgo. Daily Law Bull., 1975-77; field editor Pollution Engring., 1976. Fellow Ill. Bar Found. (charter); mem. ABA (environ. ins. litigation task force 1990—), Atticus Finch Inn of Ct., Ill. Bar Assn. (chmn. environ. control law sect. 1976-77, mem. coun. 1973-77, 1990-94, editor sect. newsletter 1972-77, mem. assembly 1980-86, 89-92), Chgo. Bar Assn. (environ law sect. 1990—), Bar Assn. for 7th Jud. Cir., Law Club Chgo.

EATON, LEONARD JAMES, JR., aerospace executive; b. N.Y.C., Sept. 18, 1934; s. Leonard James and Alice Edna (Leach) E.; m. Patricia Pride, Nov. 30, 1957; children: Leslie, Pamela, Alexander. B.A., Cornell U., 1956; postgrad., Harvard, 1971. With First Nat. City Bank, N.Y.C., 1956-71; exec. v.p. Bank of Okla. N.A. (formerly Nat. Bank of Tulsa), 1972-73, pres., 1973-78, chmn. bd., chief exec. officer, 1978-91, also dir.; dir. fin. The Nordam Group, 1993—; chmn. bd., chief exec. officer dir. BancOkla. Corp.; cons. in field. Bd. trustees Meadville/Lombard Theol. Sch. affiliated with U. Chgo.; regent Okla. State Regents for Higher Edn.; dir. Okla. chpt. The Nature Conservancy, corp. fin. The Nordam Group, Inc.; mem. adv. coun. Harry Ransom Humanities Rsch. Ctr. U. Tex. at Austin. Mem. Met. Tulsa C. of C. (bd. dirs.). Office: Nordam Group PO Box 3365 Tulsa OK 74101-3365*

EATON, LEONARD KIMBALL, retired architecture educator; b. Mpls., Feb. 3, 1922; s. Leo Kimball and Elizabeth (Barber) E.; m. Ann Valentine White, Dec. 24, 1979; children—Mark. R., Elisabeth K. B.A., Williams Coll., 1943; M.A., Harvard U., 1948, Ph.D., 1951. Mem. faculty U. Mich., Ann Arbor, 1950-89, prof. architecture, 1963-89. Author: New England Hospitals, 1790-1833, 1956, Landscape Artist in America, 1964, Two Chicago Architects and Their Clients, 1969, American Architecture Comes of Age, 1972, Gateway Cities and Other Essays, 1989, also numerous articles, revs.; book rev. editor Jour. Soc. Archtl. Historians, 1967-69. Democratic candidate for coun., City of Ann Arbor, 1957. With AUS, World War II, MTO. Decorated Bronze Star; recipient Finlandia award Finlandia Soc. Met. N.Y., 1965; Ford Found. faculty fellow, 1954-55. Mem. Soc. Archtl. Historians (bd. dirs. 1957-58), Phi Beta Kappa. Club: Army-Navy (Washington). Home: PO Box 300 Otter Rock OR 97369-0300

EATON, MERRILL THOMAS, psychiatrist, educator; b. Howard County, Ind., June 25, 1920; s. Merrill Thomas and Dorothy (Whiteman) E.; m. Louise Foster, Dec. 23, 1942; children: Deirdre Ann, Thomas Anthony, David Foster. AB, Ind. U., Bloomington, 1941, MD, 1944. Diplomate: Am. Bd. Psychiatry. Intern St. Elizabeth's Hosp., Washington, 1944-45; resident Sheppard and Enoch Pratt Hosp., Towson, Md., 1948-49; pvt. practice medicine specializing in psychiatry Kansas City, Kans., 1949-60, Omaha, 1960—; dir. Nebr. Psychiat. Inst., 1968-85; assoc. in psychiatry Kans. U. Sch. Medicine, 1949-50, asst. prof., 1951-54, assoc. prof., 1954-60; assoc. prof. psychiatry U. Nebr. Coll. Medicine, 1960-63, prof., 1963-88, prof. emeritus, 1989—, chmn. dept. psychiatry, 1968-85; psychiatrist Immanuel Mental Health Ctr., 1986-88; pvt. practice cons. Omaha, 1989—. Author: Psychiatry, 1967, 5th edit., 1985, (with David Kentsmith) Treating Sexual Problems in Medical Practice, 1979. Served to capt. U.S. Army, 1945-47. Fellow ACP, Am. Psychiat. Assn.; mem. Group for Advancement Psychiatry (chmn. com. on mental health services 1970-73, chmn. publ. bd. 1976-83, cons. pub. bd. 1983—, bd. dirs. 1984-86), Nebr. Med. Assn., Nebr. Psychiat. Soc. (pres. 1973-75).

EATON, MICHAEL WILLIAM, lawyer, educator; b. Dallas, July 28, 1958; s. Charles H. and Helen Gilbough (Miller) E. BS in Polit. Sci., So. Meth. U., 1980, JD, 1984; postgrad., U. Tex., Dallas, 1997—. Bar: Tex. 1984, U.S. Dist. Ct. (no. dist.) Tex. 1985, U.S. Ct. Appeals (5th cir.) 1986, U.S. Supreme Ct. 1988. Asst. gen. counsel Kirby Oil Co., Inc., Dallas, 1984-85; ptnr. Leonard & Eaton, Dallas, 1985-86; assoc. Page & Addison, P.C., Dallas, 1986-87; pvt. practice Dallas, 1987—; pres. San Jacinto Investments Group, 1992—; lectr. in econs. El Centro (Tex.) Coll., 1995—; lectr. in constl. law U. Tex., Dallas, 1996—; founder, dir. Tex. Jury Rsch. Inst., 1996—; founding ptnr. Affordable Housing Solutions, 1998—. Co-author: Expert Witnesses in The Courtroom, 1996; reviewer Am. Jour. of Polit. Sci., 1994—. Vol. Texans for Bush/Quayle, Dallas, 1988; del. John Connolly for Pres. Campaign, Dallas, New Orleans, 1980; north Tex. youth coord. William P. Clements for Gov. Campaign, Dallas, Ft. Worth, Denton, 1978; So. Meth. U. re-election chmn. John Tower for U.S. Senate Campaign, Dallas, 1978. Mem. Nat. Audubon Soc., Nature Conservancy, State Bar Tex., Tex. Young Lawyers Assn., Dallas Assn. Young Lawyers, Assn. Trial Lawyers Am., Lawyers Concerned for Lawyers (officer Dallas Lawyers Concerned Lawyers 1996-97, 1997—), Smithsonian Instn. Nat. Arbor Day Found., Phi Alpha Delta, Ancient Order of Hibernians (pres. 1998—). Republican. Roman Catholic. Avocations: golf, gourmet cooking, travel. Office: 4151 Belt Line Rd Ste 124 Dallas TX 75244-2323 also: 704 Oakwood Tower 3626 N Hall St Dallas TX 75219-5107

EATON, NANCY RUTH LINTON, librarian, university dean; b. Berkeley, Calif., May 2, 1943; d. Don Thomas and Lena Ruth (McClellan) Linton; m. Edward Arthur Eaton III, June 19, 1965 (div. 1980). AB, Stanford U., 1965; MLS, U. Tex., 1968. postgrad., 1969. From cataloger to asst. to dir. U. Tex. Libr., Austin, 1968-74; automation libr. SUNY, Stony Brook, 1974-76; head tech. svcs. Atlanta Pub. Libr., 1976-82; dir. libr. U. Vt., Burlington, 1982-89; dean libr. svcs. Iowa State U., Ames, 1989-97; dean univ. librs. Pa. State U., University Park, Pa., 1997—; bd. dirs. Ctr. for Rsch. Librs., 1988-92, chair, 1989-90; del. user's coun., mem. exec. com. Online Computer Libr. Ctr., Inc., Dublin, Ohio, 1980-82, 86-88, trustee, 1987—, chair bd. trustees 1992-96; mgr. Nat. Agrl. Text Digitalizing Project, 1986-92; bd. dirs. New Eng. Libr. Network, 1987-89. Co-author: Optical Information Systems: Implementation Issues for Libraries, 1988.; co-editor: A Cataloging Sampler, 1971, Book Selection Policies in American Libraries, 1972; contbr. articles to profl. jours. U.S. Office of Edn. post-master's fellow, 1969; Dept. Edn. Title II-C grantee, 1985, 87-88, Title II-D grantee, 1992-96. Mem. ALA, AAUW, Libr. and Info. Tech. Assn. (pres. 1984-85, bd. dirs. 1980-86), Assn. Rsch. Librs. (bd. dirs. 1994-97). Democrat. Avocations: tennis, walking. Home: 441 Homan Ave State College PA 16801-6337 Office: Pa State Univ E510 Paterno Libr University Park PA 16802

EATON, RICHARD GILLETTE, surgeon, educator; b. Forty Fort, Pa., Dec. 3, 1929; s. Walter L. and Ruth (Shaw) E.; B.A., Franklin and Marshall Coll., 1951; M.D., U. Pa., 1955; m. Du Ree Hunter, June 13, 1954; children: Bradford (dec.), Holly, Hillary. Intern U. Pa. Grad. Hosp., 1956; gen. surg. resident Peter Bent Brigham Hosp., Boston, 1957; orthopedic resident Children's Hosp. Med. Center, Mass. Gen. Hosp. and Peter Bent Brigham Hosp., Boston, 1959-62; hand surgery fellow J.W. Littler, Roosevelt Hosp., N.Y.C., 1962, now attending orthopedic surgery and reconstrn., chief hand surgery service; prof. clin. orthop. surgery Columbia Coll. Physicians and Surgeons, N.Y.C. Ruling elder Huguenot Presbyn. Ch., Pelham, N.Y. Capt., M.C., U.S. Army, 1957-59. NIH fellow, 1963-64. Diplomate Am. Bd. Orthopedic Surgeons. Mem. Am. Acad. Orthopedic Surgery, Am. Orthopaedic Assn., Am. Soc. Surgery of Hand, A.C.S., Interurban Orthopedic Club, N.Y. Acad. Medicine, J.W. Littler Soc., N.Y. Soc. Surgery of Hand. Author: Joint Injuries of the Hand, 1971; also articles. Home: 640 Ely Ave Pelham NY 10803-2402 Office: St Luke's-Roosevelt Hosp CV Starr Hand Ctr 1000 10th Ave New York NY 10019-1192

EATON, ROBERT JAMES, automotive company executive; b. Buena Vista, Colo., Feb. 13, 1940; s. Eugene Hiram and Mildred Inez (Stokes) E.; m. Cornelia Cae Drake, June 28, 1964; children: Scott C., Matthew D. BSME, U. Kans., 1963. Exec. engr. engring. staff GM, Warren, Mich., 1974-75, chief engr. small family car project Chevrolet div., 1975-76, chief engr. car programs engring. staff, 1976-79; asst. chief Oldsmobile div. GM, Lansing, Mich., 1979-82, dir. reliability, 1982; v.p. advanced product and mfg. engring. staff GM, Lansing, Detroit, 1982-86; v.p. and group exec. Tech. Staffs Group GM, 1986-88; pres. GM Europe, Zurich, Switzerland, 1988-92; vice chmn., COO, Chrysler Corp., Auburn Hills, Mich., 1992-93, chmn., CEO, pres., from 1993; chmn. Daimler Chrysler Corp., Auburn Hills, Mich.; chmn. bd. dirs. SAAB Automobile; bd. dirs. Internat. Paper Co. Mem. indsl. adv. coun. Coll. Engring., Stanford U., 1986—, U. Mich.; chmn. indsl. adv. group Stanford Inst. for Mfg. and Automation, 1984-86; bd. chmn. Met. Ctr. for High Tech., 1982-88; chmn. Detroit Renaissance; dir. United Way of Southeastern Mich., Econ. Alliance for Mich., Detroit Symphony Orch., Mich. Leaders Health Care Group. Chevalier du Tastevin, 1989—. Fellow Soc. Automotive Engrs. (chmn. tech. bd. 1986-87, fin. com. 1985—, chmn. Engring. Expo), Engring. Soc. Detroit (co-chmn. membership com. 1986-87, bd. dirs.); mem. NAE, Am. Automobile Mfrs. Assn. (chmn., dir.), Indsl. Tech. Inst. (bd. dirs. 1982-85), Electronic Data Systems (bd. dirs. 1984-89), Group Lotus (bd. dirs.), Bus. Coun., Bus. Roundtable, U.S./Japan Bus. Coun., Pres.'s Adv. Com. on Trade Policy & Negotiations. Office: Daimler Chrysler Corp 1000 Chrysler Dr Auburn Hills MI 48326-2766*

EATON, SABRINA CATHERINE ELIZABETH, journalist; b. N.Y.C., Mar. 5, 1965; d. Barton Denis and Anne Elizabeth (Schaeffer) Eaton; 1 child, Isaac Nicholas Rodgers-Eaton. BA, U. Pa., 1985. Correspondent The Record, Hackensack, N.J., 1985-87; reporter Daily Record, Morristown, N.J., 1987-88; Washington correspondent States News Svc., Washington, 1988-90; metro reporter The Plain Dealer, Cleve., 1990-94; Washington correspondent The Plain Dealer, Washington, 1994—. Mem. DAR, Nat. Press Club, Nat. Lesbian and Gay Journalists Assn., Investigative Reporters and Editors. Episcopalian. Office: The Plain Dealer Wash Bur 930 National Press Building Washington DC 20045-1901

EATON, STEPHANIE, state legislator; b. Littleton, N.H., July 22, 1936. BA, Middlebury Coll., 1958, MA, 1967; JD, Franklin Pierce Law Ctr., 1990. N.H. state rep.; mem. pub. works and hwys. com. N.H. Ho. of Reps.; cartographer; mem. sci. & tech. com. N.H. Ho. of Reps. Mem. Glenwood Cemetery Com., 1990-94; trustee Littleton Trust Funds, 1992-94. Mem. LWV, Profile Women's Club. Address: 243 Pleasant St Littleton NH 03561-4917*

EAVES, ALLEN CHARLES EDWARD, hematologist, medical agency administrator; b. Ottawa, Ont., Can., Feb. 19, 1941; s. Charles Albert and Margaret Vernon (Smith) E.; m. Connie Jean Halperin, July 1, 1975; children—Neil, Rene, David, Sara. BSc, Acadia U., Wolfville, N.S., Can., 1962; MSc, Dalhousie U., Halifax, N.S., 1964, MD, 1969; PhD, U. Toronto, Ont., Can., 1974. Intern Dalhousie U., Halifax, N.S., Can., 1968-69; resident in internal medicine Sunnybrook Hosp., Toronto, 1974-75, Vancouver Gen. Hosp., 1975-79; dir. Terry Fox Lab., Cancer Control Agy. B.C., Vancouver, Can., 1980—; asst. prof. medicine U. B.C., 1979-83, assoc. prof., 1983-88, head div. hematology, 1985—, prof., 1988—; pres. StemCell Technologies, Inc., Vancouver, 1993—. Treas. Found. for Accreditation of Hematopoetic Cell Therapy, 1995—. Fellow Royal Coll. Physicians (Can.), ACP; mem. Internat. Soc. Hematotherapy and Graft Engring. (pres. 1995-97), Am. Soc. Blood and Marrow Transplantation (pres. elect 1998-99, pres. 1999—). Home: 2705 W 31st Ave, Vancouver, BC Canada V6L 1Z9 Office: Terry Fox Lab Cancer Rsch, 601 W 10th Ave, Vancouver, BC Canada V5Z 1L3

EAVES, ARTHUR JOSEPH, English literature educator; b. Phila., May 17, 1942; s. Charles Arthur and Helen Pollick Eaves. BA, Columbia U., 1965; MA, PhD, U. Notre Dame, 1973. Instr. U. Notre Dame, South Bend, Ind., 1973-75, U. Akron, Ohio, 1978; prof. Austin Peay State U., Clarksville, Tenn., 1979—. Home: 350 Hickory Hts Clarksville TN 37040-3938 Office: Austin Peay State U Box 4487 Clarksville TN 37044

EAVES, DOROTHY ANN GREENE, music educator; b. Pinson, Ala., Feb. 27, 1938; d. Albert Anderson Greene and Dorothy Elizabeth McCool; m. Richard Glen Eaves, June 19, 1959; 1 child, Lisa Michelle Eaves Stooksbury. MusB magna cum laude, Miss. State Coll. for Women, 1959; student, Peabody Coll., 1959, U. Ala., 1960-65; MEd, Auburn U., 1970. Tchr. piano and organ Clarke Coll., Newton, Miss., 1959-62; min. of music Bay Springs (Miss.) Bapt. Ch., 1960-62; ind. piano tchr. Clinton, Miss., Tuscaloosa and

Auburn, Ala., 1963-86; adj. tchr. music edn. Auburn U., 1971-72; adj. tchr. piano and ch. music Miss. Coll., Clinton, 1984-89; pianist Woodville Heights Bapt. Ch., Jackson, Miss., 1985-86; music accompanist Auburn U., 1968-70; piano competition judge, recitalist, Ala., Miss., La., 1970—; instr. piano and music history Hinds C.C., Raymond, 1986—. Mem. faculty Miss. Piano Camp, Raymond, 1988, 90, 95—. Faculty devel. grantee Hinds C.C., Raymond, 1995, 98. Mem. Music Tchrs. Nat. Assn. Republican. Baptist. Avocations: travel, reading, walking, church projects. Home: 5 Pheasant Run Clinton MS 39056-3538

EAVES, GEORGE NEWTON, lecturer, consultant, research administrator; b. Athens, Tenn., Mar. 12, 1935; s. Felmont Farrell and Margaret Isobel (Dobson) E. BA, U. Chattanooga, 1957; MS, U. Tenn., 1959; PhD, Wayne State U., 1962. Postdoctoral fellow Bryn Mawr Coll., Pa., 1963-65; postdoctoral fellow, guest investigator The Rockefeller U., N.Y.C., 1970-71; exec. sec. molecular biology study sect. NIH, Bethesda, Md., 1967-73; exec. sect. Nat. Heart and Lung Adv. Coun., NIH, Bethesda, 1973-74; assoc. staff dir. Pres.'s Biomed. Rsch. Panel, Washington, 1974-76; dep. dir. Divsn. Blood Diseases and Resources, NIH, Bethesda, 1976-83, dep. dir. Divsn. of Stroke and Trauma, 1983-94; lectr. on tech. writing, grant applications and peer rev.; bd. dirs. Cyclotec Med. Industries, Inc.; asst. prof. Washington & Jefferson Coll., 1991-92. Cons. editor Procs. NAS, 1973-76; mem. editl. bd. Grants Mag., 1978-81, Nonprofit Mgmt. and Fin., 1981—; contbr. articles to tech. jours. and chpts. to sci. books. Mem. adv. coun. Park and Tree Commn., City of Savannah, 1994—. Recipient Citation for Profl. Achievement, McDonnell Douglas Corp., 1968, NIH Dir.'s award, 1976, 86, Sustained High Quality Performance award NIH, 1970, 74, 79, Spl. Achievement award HHS, 1989, Spl. Recognition award Pub. Health Svc., 1990. Mem. Sigma Xi. Republican. Anglican. Avocation: church organist. Home: 100 W Gordon St Savannah GA 31401

EAVES, MORRIS EMERY, English language educator; b. Monroe, La., May 12, 1944; s. Archie Harmon and Mary Louise (Morris) E.; m. Georgia Ann Butler, Dec. 24, 1963; children: Obadiah, Dashiell. BA, L.I. U., 1966; PhD, Tulane U., 1972. Asst. prof. English U. N.Mex., Albuquerque, 1970-74, assoc. prof. English, 1974-82, prof. English, 1982-86; prof. English U. Rochester, N.Y., 1986—, chmn. dept., 1988—; Presdl. prof. U. N.Mex., 1985-86. Author: William Blake's Theory of Art, 1982, The Counter-Arts Conspiracy: Art and Industry in the Age of Blake, 1992; editor: Romantic Texts, Romantic Times, 1982, Romanticism and Contemporary Criticism, 1986, William Blake: The Early Illuminated Books, 1993; editor: Blake/An Illustrated Quar., 1970—; co-editor: William Blake Archive, 1995—. Nat. Humanities Ctr. fellow Research Triangle Park, N.C., 1984-85; Guggenheim fellow, 1997. Mem. MLA (William Riley Parker prize, 1977-78). Democrat. Office: U Rochester Dept English Arts & Scis River Campus Rochester NY 14627

EAVES, RICHARD GLEN, history educator, dean; b. Louisville, Miss., Nov. 20, 1932; s. James Tildon and Lillian Lee (Haggard) E.; m. Dorothy Ann Greene, June 19, 1959; 1 child, Lisa Michelle Eaves Stooksbury. BS, Miss. State U., 1953, MA, 1960; MA, George Peabody Coll., Nashville, 1956; PhD, U. Ala., 1970. Instr., dean of men Clarke Coll., Newton, Miss., 1958-62; asst. prof. history Birmingham (Ala.) So. Coll., 1962-63; from asst. to assoc. prof. history Auburn (Ala.) U., 1966-82; prof. history Miss. Coll., Clinton, 1982—, dean arts and scis., 1982-98. Author: Henry VIII's Scottish Diplomacy, 1513-1524, 1971, Henry VIII and James V's Regency, 1524-1528, 1987. Mem. exec. com. Ala. Rep. Party, 1972-82. With U.S. Army, 1953-55, Korea and Japan. Assoc. Danforth Found., 1971. Mem. Rotary, Phi Alpha Theta (pres. 1964-65), Omicron Delta Kappa, Pi Tau Chi, Phi Eta Sigma. Baptist. Avocations: travel, tennis. Home: 5 Pheasant Run Clinton MS 39056 Office: Miss Coll PO Box 4006 Clinton MS 39058

EAVES, SALLY ANN, logistics director, research administrator; b. Salt Lake City, Feb. 25, 1945; d. Frank C. and Magdalene (Buller) Winslow; m. Stephen Douglas Eaves, Apr. 27, 1974; children: Trevor Bernard, Lindsay Douglas, Christian Francis. BA in English, Gonzaga U., 1967; postgrad., Utah State U., 1980, U. So. Calif., 1985. Individual mobilization asst. to dir. of logistics U.S. Forces Korea, 1983-87; individual mobilization asst. to chief of transp., dir. distbn., dir. commodities Ogden (Utah) Air Logistics Ctr., 1987-93; individual mobilization asst. to dir. logistics N.Am. Aerospace Def. Command and U.S. Space Command, Peterson AFB, Colo., 1993-95; mobilization asst. to commdr. Okla. Air Logistics Ctr., Oklahoma City, 1995-98; mobilization asst. to dir. logistics Air Combat Command, Langley AFB, Va., 1998—; v.p. N.W. Rsch. Inst., Las Vegas, 1996—. V.p., bd. dirs. The Pond Homeowners Assn., Arvada, Colo., 1992-95; ednl./comty. vol. Jeffco Pub. Schs., 1992-95; ch. vol. Spirit of Christ Cath. Ch., Arvada, 1989—; career devel. counselor Adams County Sch. Dist. 50, Westminster, Colo., 1989—. Brig. gen. USAFR, 1967—. Decorated Def. Meritorious Svc. medal, Meritorious Svc. medal. Mem. Nat. Def. Transp. Assn., Soc. Logistics Engrs., Air Force Assn., Res. Officers Assn. (v.p. Okla. chpt. 1996-97). Home: 8708 Independence Way Arvada CO 80005-1247

EAVES, SANDRA AUSTRA, social worker; b. Chgo., Aug. 30, 1960; m. Gerald Eaves, Oct. 7, 1989. BA, Northwestern U., 1982; MSW, Loyola U., Chgo., 1984. Social worker Chgo. Pub. Schs., 1982-83, Cook County Hosp., Chgo., 1983-84; pvt. practice Dr. Harry A. Croft & Assoc., PA, San Antonio, 1990-98, New Braunfels, Tex., 1992—; social worker VA, San Antonio, 1984-91. Mem. NASW, Tex. Soc. for Clin. Social Work, Coun. Nephrology Social Workers. Lutheran. Avocations: sports, pottery, classical piano.

EAVES, STEPHEN DOUGLAS, educator, vocational administrator; b. Honolulu, Aug. 30, 1944; s. Alfred Aldee and Phyllis Clarissa (Esty) E.; m. Sally Ann Winslow, Apr. 27, 1974; children: Trevor Bernard, Lindsay Douglas, Christian Francis. BA in Polit. Sci., U. Hawaii, 1967; MS in Bus. Mgmt., U. Ark., 1974; PhD in Edn. Adminstrn., Colo. State U., 1997. Cert. secondary tchr., prin., vocat. dir., post secondary bus. tchr., Colo. Commd. 2d lt. USAF, 1967, advanced through grades to lt. col., ret., 1989; aerospace sci. tchr. Adams County Sch. Dist. 50, Westminster, Colo., 1989-94, vocat. dir./asst. prin., 1994—; cons. Dept. of Edn., Colo., 1993—. Eucharistic min. Spirit of Christ Cath. Ch., Arvada, Colo., 1989—. Decorated Silver Star, DFC, Air medals, Commendation medals, Air Force Achievement medal; named Outstanding Tchr. Focus on Excellence Program, 1992, Outstanding Nat. Aerospace Sci. Tchr., 1994. Mem. ASCD, Coun. for Exceptional Children, Am. Vocat. Assn., Colo. Vocat. Assn., Colo. Assn. Vocat. Adminstrs., Colo. Assn. Sch. Execs., Am. Nat. Rose Soc., Royal Nat. Rose Soc., Lions (sec. Adams Centennial chpt. 1991-92, Lion of Yr. 1992), Elks, Phi Delta Kappa, Omicron Tau Delta. Avocations: snow skiing, rose gardening. Home: 8708 Independence Way Arvada CO 80005-1247 Office: Career Enrichment Park 7300 Lowell Blvd Westminster CO 80030-4821

EBACHER, ROGER, archbishop; b. Amos, Que., Can., Oct. 6, 1936. Ordained priest Roman Cath. Ch., 1961; ordained bishop of Diocese of Baie-Comeau, Que., 1979; chevalier de Colomb de 4e degré, 1983; apptd. bishop Diocese of Gatineau-Hull, Que., 1988, archbishop, 1990—. Address: 180 Mont-Bleu, Hull, PQ Canada J8Z 3J5

EBASHI, SETSURO, scientist, educator; b. Tokyo, Aug. 31, 1922; s. Haruyoshi and Hisaji (Watanabe) E.; m. Fumiko Takeda, May 20, 1956. MD, U. Tokyo, 1944; PhD, 1954. Prof. pharmacology U. Tokyo, 1959-83, prof. biophysics, 1971-83, prof. emeritus, 1983Ō; prof. Nat. Inst. Physiol. Sci., Okazaki, Japan, 1983-86, dir.-gen., 1985-91, prof. Grad. U. Advanced Studies, 1988-91, prof. emeritus, 1993Ō; pres. Okazaki Nat. Rsch. Inst., 1991-93; vis. prof. U. Calif., San Francisco, 1963, Harvard U., Cambridge, Mass., 1974; pres. Internat. Union for Pure and Applied Biophysics, 1978-81, Internat. Union Pharmacology, 1990-94. Decorated Grand Cordon of Order of the Sacred Treasure Japanese Govt., 1995; recipient Asahi prize Asahi Newspaper Pub. Co., Tokyo, 1968, Imperial prize Japan Acad., 1972, Order of Cultural Merit, Japanese Govt., 1975, Peter Harris award Internat. Soc. Heart Rsch., 1986. Mem. NAS, Am. Physiol. Soc. (hon.), Am. Soc. Biochemistry and Molecular Biology, Am. Acad. Arts and Scis., Royal Soc. (London), Deutsche Akademie Leopoldina, Academie Royale de Medecine de Belgique, Accademia Nationale dei Lincei, Academia Europaea. Fax: 81-564-52-3719. E-mail: ebashi@nips.ac.jp. Home: 17-503 Nagaizumi Myodaiji, Okazaki 444 0864, Japan

EBAUGH, DAVID PAUL, minister, school system administrator; b. Indpls., June 22, 1930; s. Paul Edward and Gladys Rachael (Ruddick) E.; m. Betty LeTourneau, Apr. 9, 1950; children—Michael, Marcellene, Diane, Rosalie. Tool and test equipment engr. IBM, Lexington, Ky., 1956-62; sr. indsl. engr. Goodyear Aerospace Corp., Akron, 1962-64; supr. mfg. methods engrng. AMP, Inc., Harrisburg, Pa., 1965-67; ordained to ministry Ind. Assembly of God Ch., 1968; founder, pres. David Ebaugh Bible Sch., Harrisburg, 1968—; pastor Ch. of Revelation, 1982—. Served with USN, 1947-52. Mem. IEEE (profl. diploma 1959), Soc. Am. Value Engrs., Am. Inst. Indsl. Engrs., Am. Soc. Tool and Mfg. Engrs. Clubs: Christian Businessmen's Com. (pres. Lexington chpt. 1960), Full Gospel Businessmen's Com. (pres. Harrisburg chpt. 1967). Author, pub.: Key to Revelation, 1969, Key to Priesthood, 1970, Third Salvation, 1972, Keys to Marriage Divorce and Remarriage, 1973, Free to Live, 1976, My Daddy and Me, 1980, Daniel's 70 Weeks, 1986, David's Tabernacle Now, 1993, Faith Hope and Love, 1994, Circumcise My What?, 1995, El Elyon Now, Names of God, 1997; pub. Monarch Monthly. Home and Office: 102 Park Ter Harrisburg PA 17111-1667 *Bible study indicates that a group of people will not die; but the changes in human personality that are prerequisite to enter that group are enormous. My life experiences and study indicate that immortality is a goal worth pursuing.*

EBAUGH, HELEN ROSE, sociology educator, researcher; b. San Angelo, Tex., June 21, 1942; d. Arnold and Agnes (Halfman) Fuchs; m. Albert L. Ebaugh, Aug. 3, 1975; children: Sarah, Stephen. BA, Our Lady of Lake U., 1966; MA, U. Tex., 1968; PhD, Columbia U., 1975. Asst. prof., dept. sociology U. Houston, 1973-79, assoc. prof., 1979-89, chmn. dept., 1985-87, prof., 1993—. Author: Out of the Cloister, 1977, Becoming an Ex, 1988, Women in the Vanishing Cloister, 1993. Mem. Am. Sociol. Assn. Office: U of Houston 4800 Calhoun Rd Houston TX 77004-2610

EBB, FRED, lyricist, librettist; b. N.Y.C., Apr. 8, 1936; s. Harry and Anna Evelyn (Gritz) E. B.A., NYU, 1955; M.A. in English Lit., Columbia U., 1957; Hon. Degree in Theatre Arts, Emerson U., 1975. lectr. in field. Lyricist: musicals Flora, The Red Menace, 1963, Cabaret, 1965, Zorba, 1966, The Happy Time, 1968, (also co-author book) 70, Girls, 70, 1971, (also book with Bob Fosse) Chicago, 1974, The Act, 1977, Woman of the Year, 1981, The Rink, 1983, Kiss of the Spider Woman, 1990 (Best Lyrics Tony Award 1993, Drama Critics Circle award 1993, Drama Desk award 1993), And The World Goes Round, 1991, Chicago (revival), 1996, Steel Pier, 1997; TV shows Liza with a Z, 1967, Ole Blue Eyes is Back, 1972, Gypsy in My Soul, 1976, Goldie and Liza Together, 1980, Baryshnikov on Broadway, 1980, Liza at Radio City Music Hall (Best Music and Lyrics Emmy award 1993), 1992; motion pictures Cabaret, 1970, Funny Lady, 1973, Lucky Lady, 1976, New York, New York, 1977, Stepping Out, 1991. Recipient Tony award League N.Y. Theatres and Prodrs., 1967, 81, 93, Drama Desk award N.Y. Drama Critics Circle, 1967, 68, Outer Circle award Orgn. Writers on Theatre, 1968, 69, George Foster Peabody award Grady Sch. Journalism, U. Ga., 1972, Drama Critics Circle award, 1967, Image award NAACP, 1973, Ace award Standing Room Only—Liza in London, Achievement award B'nai B'rith, 1978, Christopher award Cath. Soc., 1976, George Abbott award Stage Dirs. and Choreographers Found., 1996, Helen Hayes award, 1999; named to Songwriters Hall of Fame, 1983, Theatre Hall of Fame, 1991, NYU Musical Theatre Hall of Fame, 1996, Winner Outer Circle Critics Circle, 1990; honoree Kennedy Ctr., 1998. Mem. Dramatists Guild, Equity, Nat. Acad. TV Arts and Scis. (Emmy award 1972, 75, 76, 93), Am. Guild Authors and Composers, Acad. Motion Picture Arts and Scis.

EBBELS, BRUCE JEFFERY, physician, health facility administrator; b. N.Y.C., Dec. 26, 1924; s. Walter Jeffery and Mildred Christiana (Bruce) E.; m. Shirley Marie Cooley, July 3, 1950; children: Bruce Jeffery Jr., Cynthia, Stephanie, Leslie, David. Student, Colgate U., 1943-44; MD, N.Y. Med. Coll., 1948. Intern Hurley Med. Ctr., Flint, Mich., 1948-49; resident in internal medicine VA Hosp., Richmond, Va., 1951-54; pvt. practice gastroenterology and internal medicine Watertown, N.Y., 1954-90; med. dir. N.Y. Air Brake Co., Watertown, 1992-94; med. coord. VA Clinic, Watertown, N.Y., 1994-97; mem. med. com. Cmty. Ctr. for Alcoholism, Watertown, N.Y., 1992—; staff Genesis Healthcare, Watertown, N.Y., 1998—; chief medicine Mercy Hosp., Watertown, N.Y., 1975-78, House of the Good Samaritan Hosp., Watertown, 1978-83, pres. med. staff, 1978; cons. in internal medicine E.J. Noble Hosp., 1960-88, Lewis County Gen. Hosp., 1960-88, Carthage Area Hosp., 1966-88; cons. in field. Contbr. chpt. to book. Pres. Jefferson County Assn. for Mental Health, Watertown, 1969-70; bd. trustees Watertown (N.Y.) Savs. Bank, 1971—; bd. vestry Trinity Ch., Watertown, 1972-78. Capt. USNR, 1979—. Recipient John Philips Rice Svc. award Jefferson County Assn. for Mental Health, Watertown, 1970, Disting. Svc. award Jefferson County divsn. Am. Heart Assn. Fellow ACP (life), Am. Coll. Gastroenterology (sr.); mem. AMA (life), Med. Soc. State N.Y. (life), Med. Soc. Jefferson County (life; pres. 1979-80), Staplin Creek Soc. (past pres.). Republican. Episcopalian. Avocations: aquatic sports, scuba diving, writing, lecturing. Home and Office: 283 Thompson Blvd Watertown NY 13601-4123

EBBEN, JAMES ADRIAN, college president. V.p. planning/resource allocation Siena Heights Coll., Adrian, Mich., 1986-87; pres. Edgewood Coll., Madison, Wis., 1987—. Office: Edgewood Coll Office of Pres 855 Woodrow St Madison WI 53711-1958*

EBBERS, BERNARD J., communications executive. BA in Phys. Edn., Miss. Coll. Pres., CEO WorldCom, 1985-98; pres., CEO, chmn. MCI WorldCom, Jackson, Miss., 1998—. Office: care MCI WorldCom Inc 515 E Amite St Jackson MS 39201-2702*

EBBERS, LARRY HAROLD, education educator; b. Rockwell, Iowa, June 17, 1941; s. Harold Theodore and Gertrude Elanor (Robeoltmann) E.; m. Barbara Ellen Smith, June 17, 1962; children: Lori Ann, Kimberly Jo. BS, Iowa State U., 1962, MS, 1968, PhD, 1971. Vocat. agrl. instr. Iowa Falls (Iowa) Sch., 1962-63, Spencer (Iowa) Schs., 1963-65; asst. dir. residences Iowa State U., Ames, 1965-72, asst. prof., 1972-75, assoc. prof., 1975-80, prof. edn., 1981—, dept. chair, prof. studies in edn., 1983-93; asst. to dean Coll. Edn., 1972-76, asst. dean, 1976-83; assoc. dean, 1996—. Contbr. articles to profl. jours. Bd. dirs. Ames Parks and Recreation Commn., 1983-86, Iowa State U. Meml. Union, 1989-94; pres. Ctrl. Iowa Regional Substance Abuse Ctr., Ames, 1984-85, Meeker Sch. PTO, Ames, 1975-76; mem. task force on campus ministry Am. Luth. Ch., Des Moines, 1979-84. Recipient Outstanding Young Alumnus award, 1976, Outstanding Acad. Adv. award, 1977, Human Rels. award Human Rels. Commn., 1984, Human rels. award Student Affairs Divsn., 1985, Outstanding Faculty Citation award, 1991, Cardinal Key Leadership Hon., 1995, Golden Key Honor Soc., 1996, Pres.'s Disting. Svc. award, 1999, all from Iowa State U.; Rotary Found. fellow, Brazil, 1977. Mem. Nat. Assn. Student Pers. Adminstrs. (dir. rsch. and program devel. 1979-81, chmn. Am. Coun. on Edn. Inst. 1984-86, editor jour. 1981-84, pres. 1987-88, v.p. Found. 1989-92, Disting. Svc. award 1990, Fred Turner award 1991, nat. conf. program chair 1992), Assn. Study of Higher Edn. (Robert Shaffer award for academic excellence as a grad. faculty mem. 1996), Kiwanis (Ames pres. 1977-78), Phi Delta Kappa, Phi Kappa Phi (pres. 1977-79, centennial medalist 1997). Lutheran. Avocations: athletics, spectator sports, jogging, mng. family farm. Home: 220 24th St Ames IA 50010-4832 Office: Iowa State U E262 N Lagomarcino Hall Ames IA 50011

EBBERT, ARTHUR, JR., retired university dean; b. Wheeling, W.Va., Aug. 25, 1922; s. Arthur and Margaret (Henning) E. B.A., U. Va., 1944, M.D., 1946; M.A. (hon.), Yale U., 1971. Intern, then asst. resident in internal medicine U. Va. Hosp., 1946-51, resident in med. service, 1951-52; instr. internal medicine, asst. to dean U. Va. Med. Sch., 1952-53; mem. faculty Yale U. Med. Sch., 1953-88, prof. clin. medicine, 1971-78, prof. medicine, 1978-88, prof. emeritus of medicine, 1988—, dep. dean, 1974-87. Editor: Yale Medicine, 1966-86. Served as officer M.C. AUS, 1947-49. Mem. Conn. Med. Soc., New Haven County Med. Assn., Beumont Med. Club, Alpha Omega Alpha.

EBBITT, JAMES ROGER, government official; b. Hudson, Mich., July 18, 1947. BBA, Cleary Coll., 1970. Cert. fraud examiner; cert. govt. fin. mgr. Auditor office of inspector gen. U.S. Dept. Agr., Chgo., 1970-76; supervisory auditor U.S. Dept. Agr., San Francisco, 1976-80; auditor food stamp program U.S. Dept. Agr., Washington, 1980-82; regional inspector gen. U.S. Dept. Agr., San Francisco, 1982-87; asst. inspector gen. for audit U.S. Dept. Agr., Washington, 1987—; chair adv. bd. U.S. Dept. Agr. Grad. Sch., Govt. Auditors Tng. Inst.; past chair Fed. Audit Exec. Coun.; mem. audit com. Inter-Am. Inst. for Coop. on Agriculture. Mem. Assn. Govt. Accts., Inst. Internal Auditors, Assn. Cert. Fraud Examiners. Office: Dept of Agrl Audit Dept 14th & Independence Ave SW Washington DC 20250

EBBS, GEORGE HEBERLING, JR., university executive; b. Sewickley, Pa., Sept. 20, 1942; s. George Heberling and Mae Isabelle (Miller) E.; m. Agnes Rak, 1989; children: Stacey Kirsten, Cynthia Lynn, George Heberling III, Alexandra Christine. BS in Engring., Purdue U., 1964; MBA, U. Wash., 1966; PhD in Bus., Columbia U., 1970. Sr. engr. Boeing Co., Seattle, 1966; assoc. Booz Allen & Hamilton, N.Y.C., 1969-72, sr. v.p., 1974-86; v.p. Fry Cons., N.Y.C., 1973; chmn., pres. The Canaan Group, Park City, Utah, 1986-98; pres. Embry-Riddle Aeronautical U., Daytona Beach, Fla., 1998—; adj. prof. Columbia U., N.Y.C., 1978-80; mem. internat. adv. bd. FLS Aerospace; bd. dirs. The Canaan Group, Pinnacle Bank. Trustee Utah Opera; bd. dirs. Fla. Internat. Festival. Bronfman fellow, Columbia U., N.Y.C., 1967; Purdue Old Master. Fellow Royal Aeronautical Soc.; mem. Met. Opera Club, Wings Club, Iron Key, Oceanside Country Club, Prestwick Country Club, Omicron Delta Kappa, Beta Gamma Sigma. Presbyterian. Office: Embry-Riddle Aeronautical U 600 S Clyde Morris Blvd Daytona Beach FL 32114-3966

EBEL, DAVID M., federal judge; b. 1940. BA, Northwestern U., 1962; JD, U. Mich., 1965. Law clk. assoc. justice Byron White U.S. Supreme Ct., 1965-66; pvt. practice Davis, Graham & Stubbs, Denver, 1966-88; judge U.S. Ct. Appeals (10th cir.), Denver, 1988—; adj. prof. law U. Denver Law Sch., 1987-89; sr. lectr. fellow Duke U. Sch. Law, 1992-94. Mem. Am. Coll. Trial Lawyers, Colo. Bar Assn. (v.p. 1982), Jud. Conf. U.S. (com. on codes of conduct 1991-98, co-chair 10th cir. gender bias task force 1994—). Office: US Ct Appeals 1823 Stout St Rm 109L Denver CO 80257-1823

EBELING, ARTHUR WILLIAM, mechanical engineer; b. Beloit, Wis., Aug. 31, 1926; s. Ernst E. and Ida (Lindeman) E.; m. Nancy M. Raes, July 9, 1951 (dec. Sept. 1989); children: Bertha, Mary, August. BSME, Rose Poly. Inst., Terre Haute, Ind., 1951. Area foreman Koppers Chem., Kobuta, Pa., 1951-53; field engr. Am. Bridge, Ambridge, Pa., 1953-61; engr. Griffin Wheel, Chgo., 1961-64; project engr. Armsted Rsch. Lab., Bensenville, Ill., 1964-69; dist. salesmgr. Beardley & Piper, Chgo., 1969; project engr. Kawecki Berylco, Reading, Pa., 1969-80; Midwest dir. ASME, Mt. Prospect, Ill., 1980-98; retired, 1998; speaker in field. Mem. citizens adv. bd. Wilson H.S., Reading, 1978. Sgt. USAF, 1944-47. Fellow ASME (sect. officer Reading 1977-80); mem. Ky. Cols. Achievements include patents in steel industry. Avocation: NASCAR Championship racing. Home: 1074 Crimson Dr Wheeling IL 60090-5536

EBELL, C(ECIL) WALTER, lawyer; b. Baker, Oreg., June 26, 1947; s. Cecil John and Sylvia Jean (Malone) E.; m. Dianna Rae Gentry, June 2, 1980; children: Anne, Erik, Michael. BS, Oreg. State U., 1970; MS, U. No. Colo., 1973; JD, Lewis and Clark Coll., 1977. Bar: Oreg. 1977, Alaska 1978, U.S. Ct. Appeals (9th cir.) 1981, U.S. Supreme Ct. 1985, Wash. 1990. Pvt. practice Portland, Oreg., 1977-78; ptnr. Hartig, Rhodes, Norman & Mahoney, Anchorage, 1978-84, Jamin, Ebell, Bolger & Gentry, Kodiak, Alaska, 1984-97, Jamin, Ebell, Schmitt & Mason, Seattle, 1997—. Press sec., Clay Myers for Gov. campaign, Oreg., 1974. Capt. USMC, 1970-73. Mem. ABA, Assn. Trial Lawyers Am., Rotary. Democrat. Avocations: photography, fishing, skiing. Office: Jamin Ebell Schmitt Mason 300 Mutual Life Bldg 605 1st Ave Seattle WA 98104-2207

EBER, KEVIN, science writer; b. Cleve., Aug. 14, 1958; s. Julius Louis and Winifred Ann (Hanf) E. BSChemE, Case Western Res. U., 1980; MA in Journalism, U. Colo., Boulder, 1990. Engr. Westinghouse Naval Reactors Facility/Idaho Nat. Engring Lab., Idaho Falls, 1980-82, Northeast Utilities, Berlin, Conn., 1982-87; tech. writer Stoller Corp., Boulder, 1988-89; sci. writer Brookhaven Nat. Lab., Upton, N.Y., 1989; journalism intern Boulder Daily Camera, 1990; sci. writer Nat. Renewable Energy Lab., Golden, Colo., 1991—. Asst. editor: Advances in Solar Energy, vol. 7, 1992; author, project leader various publs. on energy sources; writer, editor (e-mail newsletter) Energy Efficiency and Renewable Energy Network News. Mem. Nat. Assn. Sci. Writers. Avocations: hiking, biking, backpacking, skiing, rollerblading. Office: Nat Renewable Energy Lab 1617 Cole Blvd Golden CO 80401-3305

EBER, LORENZ, aeronautical engineer, civil engineer, inventor; b. Bad Oldesloh, Germany, Jan. 30, 1963; came to U.S., 1980; s. Gerhard Clemens and Ursula (Eberhart) E.; m. Paula Susette Holmes, June 9, 1985; children: Anya C., Yvonne R. Student, Columbia U., 1981-83; BSCE, Northwestern U., 1986; postgrad., U. Tunis, Tunisia, 1986-87, U. Wash., 1996—. Registered profl. engr., Wash. Coop. engr. Harza Engring. Co., Chgo., 1985-86; civil engr. Howard Needles Tammen & Bergendoff, Chgo., 1988-90; project design engr. Andersen Bjornstad Kane Jacobs Inc., Seattle, 1990-93; owner, pres. Inventexx Co., 1993-97; engr. Boeing Aircraft Co., 1997—; enging. vol. Navajo Indian Tribe, Window Rock, Ariz., 1984; product devel. cons. Ingenieur Büro Eber, Steinburg, Germany, 1983. Pres. Winslow Park Condominiums, Bainbridge Island, Wash., 1990-92; v.p. Northwestern Outing Club, Evanston, Ill., 1984-86. Recipient Boeing fellowship, 1996. Mem. AIAA, ASCE (treas. 1984-86), Inst. Transp. Engrs. Achievements include patent for surveying field book cover; invention of mechanical cable drum lifter, air cushion highway cleaning machine, novel airplane wing structure, boundary layer airplane controls. Home: 12106 Heron St NE Bainbridge Is WA 98110-1236

EBERBACH, STEVEN JOHN, consumer electronics company executive; b. Ann Arbor, Mich., Apr. 30, 1943; s. Robert Ottmar and Marie (Eichelberger) E.; m. Mary Jean Head, Oct. 15, 1983; children: Amy Elizabeth, Michael James, Amanda Claire, Kathryn Louise. BSEE, MIT, 1965; MBA, U. Mich., 1967. Engr. U. Mich. Space Physics Research Lab., Ann Arbor, 1967-73; founder, owner, engr., pres. and chmn. DCM Corp., Ann Arbor, 1974—. Inventor in field of loudspeaker design, 1979—. Mem. IEEE, Audio Engring. Soc., Foresight Inst. (sr. assoc.), Mac Technics Club. Avocations: sailing, photography, cross country skiing, computer sci. and programming. Home: 4455 E Loch Alpine Dr Ann Arbor MI 48103-9422 Office: DCM Corp 670 Airport Blvd Ann Arbor MI 48108-1681

EBERHARD, WILLIAM THOMAS, architect; b. St. Louis, Apr. 11, 1952; s. George Walter and Bettie Alma (Seilkop) E.; m. Cynthia Ann Hardy, Aug. 20, 1977 (div. 1981); m. Linda W. Bayer, Dec. 5, 1986; children: Elena Lynn, Alysse Marie. BArch, U. Cin., 1976; postgrad. Archtl. Assn., London, 1974. Registered arch. Ohio, Mich., Pa., Fla., D.C., Ill., Mo. V.p. Visnapuu & Assocs. Inc., Cleve., 1972-82; prin.-in-charge Oliver Design Group, Cleve., 1983—; v.p., prin.-in-charge Grubb & Ellis, Cleve., Detroit, Pitts., 1989-90, Grubb & Ellis Nat. Accounts Team, 1987-90. Author: Public Interiors, 1986, 2nd edit., 1996, Professional Office Design, 1988, Docket, 1988, Facility Design & Managment, 1990, 91, Interior Design, 1992, Contract Design, 1995, Architecture Record Lighting, 1996, Facility Management Journal, 1996; contbr. articles to profl. jours. Profl. team leader Inst. Urban Design, Cleve., 1983; mem. evangelism com. First Bapt. Ch. of Greater Cleve., 1990—. Recipient Best Comml. Interior Design Project award NAIOP, 1991-96, Best Office Interior Design Project award, 1992, Best Renovation Project, 1995, Design award Nat. Inst. Bus., 1992, 93, Best Comml. Space, 1993, NAIOP Design award Best Pub. Space, 1993, Best Comml. Interior Design, 1994, 95, 96, 97, Best Renovation Project, 1995, 1st. Pl. award Build Ohio Competition, 1992, AIA, 1993, Cleve. Chpt. Design award AIA, 1993, 94, Ohio Area Design awards AIA, 1994-95, Internat. Int. Design awards, 1992, 94, 95, Best of Show, First Place Large Corp. Category, Details Category, Award of Merit Details Category, Award of Merit Retail Category IIDA Regional Design Awards Program, 1998. Mem. AIA (chpt. sec. 1982-84, 2 Design awards, 1993, 1 Design award, 1994), Internat. Facility Mgrs. Assn., Cleve. Art Assn., Nat. Trust for Hist. Preservation, Inst. Urban Design, Am. Soc. Interior Designers (assoc.), Seminotic Soc. Am. (founding), Design Forum of Cleve. (founding 1990—, pres. 1991—), Club Soc. Ctr. (founding), Cleve. Design Task Force (founding pres. 1996—), Shaker Heights Country Club (house com., design com.), Union Club of Cleve. Avocations: drawing, photography, tennis, snowmobiling, golf. Home: 2867 Torrington Rd Shaker Hts OH 44122-2555

Office: Oliver Design Group One Park Pla 1111 Chester Ave Cleveland OH 44114-3516

EBERHARDT, DANIEL HUGO, lawyer; b. Milw., Feb. 19, 1938; s. Erwin M. and Hazel M. (Daley) E.; m. Josephine E. Jeka, Sept. 10, 1960; children: Daniel Hugo Jr., Mark John. BS, Colo. State U., 1962; JD, Marquette U., 1968. Bar: Wis. 1968, U.S. Dist. Ct. (ea. dist.) Wis. 1968. Assoc. Morrissy, Morrissy, Sweet & Race, Elkhorn, Wis., 1968-70; ptnr. Sweet & Eberhardt, Elkhorn, 1970-76; sole practice Elkhorn, 1976—; commr. Walworth County Cir. Cts., 1975—. Served to 1st lt. U.S. Army, 1962-65, AUS. Mem. ABA, Wis. Bar Assn., Assn. Trial Lawyers Am.; Walworth County Bar Assn. (sec., treas. 1983-85, v.p. 1985-86, pres. 1986-87), VFW (comdr. 1980-81). Republican. Roman Catholic. Lodge: Rotary (pres. 1980-81). Home: N6601 Peck Station Rd Elkhorn WI 53121-3247 Office: 18 S Broad St PO Box 258 Elkhorn WI 53121-0258

EBERHARDT, GRETCHEN ANN, lawyer, hearing officer; b. Denver, Feb. 9, 1964; d. Robert Schuler and Lusetta Mary (Bush) E. BA in Sociology, U. Colo., 1986; JD, Whittier Coll., 1991. Bar: Colo. 1992, U.S. Ct. Appeals (10th cir.) 1992. Flight attendant Continental Airlines, Denver, 1987-88; due process hearing officer Colo. Dept. Edn., Denver, 1991—; ptnr. Eberhardt & Eberhardt, Littleton, Colo., 1991—; spkr. estate planning seminars AARP, Denver, 1996; phone-in cons. Law Line 9—Legal Questions, Channel 9, Sta. KUSA, Denver, 1994—. Vol., supr. Rocky Mountain PBS, Denver, 1993—; chmn. Arapahoe County Young Reps., Aurora, Colo., 1992-97; chmn. 26th Rep. Senatorial Dist., Arapahoe County and Jefferson County, 1997-99. Mem. Colo. Bar Assn., Arapahoe County Bar Assn. Republican. Roman Catholic. Avocations: traveling, skiing, swimming, reading, hiking. Office: Eberhardt & Eberhardt 8441 W Bowles Ave Ste 210 Littleton CO 80123-9501

EBERHART, RALPH E., general United States Air Force. BS in Polit. Sci., USAF Acad., 1968; grad., Squadron Officer Sch., 1973, Air Command and Staff Coll., 1974; MS in Polit. Sci., Troy State U., 1977; postgrad. studies, Nat. War Coll., Ft. Lesley J. McNair, Washington, 1987. Commd. 2d lt. USAF, 1968, advanced through grades to gen., 1997; forward air controller Tactical Air Support Squadron USAF, Plieka Air Base, S. Viet Nam, 1970; from instr. pilot to squadron hdqrs. comdr. 71st Flying Tng. Wing Air Tng. Command USAF, Vance AFB, Okla., 1970-74; flight commdr., instr. pilot 525th Tactical Fighter Squadron USAFs in Europe, Bitburg Air Base, Germany, 1975-77; instr. pilot. flight examiner, asst. chief evaluation 50th Tactical Fighter Wing, Hahn Air Base, Germany, 1977-78; action officer, chief exec. com. Air Force Budget team Hdqs. USAF, Washington, 1979-80; aide to comdr.-in-chief, comdr. Air Forces Ctrl. Europe USAF, Ramstein AFB, Germany, 1980-82; comdr. 10th tactical fighter squadron, asst. dep. comdr. ops. 50th tactical fighter wing USAF in Europe, Hahn Air Base, Germany; exec. officer to Air Force chief of staff Hdqs. USAF, Washington, 1984-86; vice comdr. to comdr. 363d tactical fighter wing Tactical Air Command USAF, Shaw AFB, S.C., 1987-90; dep. chief of staff, plans and ops. Hdqs. USAF, Washington, 1995-96; cmdr. U.S. Forces Japan, cmdr. 5th Air Force USAF, Yokota Air Base, Japan, 1996-97; vice chief of staff Hdqs. USAF, Washington, 1997—. Numerous decorations include: Legion of Merit with Oak Leaf cluster, Disting. Flying Cross, Air medal with 11 Oak Leaf clusters, Vietnam Svc. medal with 3 svc. stars, Humanitarian Svc. medal with svc. star, Republic of Vietnam Gallantry Cross with Palm, Republic of Vietnam Campaign medal, The Grand Cordon of the Order of the Sacred Treasure, Japan, and many others. Mem. Coun. of Fgn. Rels. Office: Sec Air Force Office Pub Affairs 1690 Air Force Pentagon Washington DC 20330

EBERL, JAMES J., consultant; b. Dunkirk, N.Y.; s. George Mathias Eberl and Florence Eberl Stedler; m. Donna Davis, July 18, 1954 (dec. Sept. 1991); m. Margaret Elizabeth Shill, June 3, 1994. BA, U. Buffalo, 1938, PhD, 1941; AMP, Harvard U., 1955. Asst. prof. chemistry U. Del., Newark, 1941-42; mgr. rsch. Hercules Inc., Wilmington, Del., 1942-43; sr. fellow Mellon Inst. Ind. Rsch., Pitts., 1943-44; dir. spl. products rsch. Johnson & Johnson, New Brunswick, N.J., 1944-48; v.p. rsch. Scott Paper Co., Phila., 1948-70; pres., CEO Newbold, Inc., Phila., 1970-72; cons. Eberl Cons., Moylon, Pa., 1972—; pres. Empire Paper Rsch., Syracuse, N.Y., 1965-71; chmn. Phila. Rsch. Mgrs. Group, 1960-70. Contbr. articles to profl. jours.; patentee over patents in chemistry, med. and chem. processing. Trustee Franklin Inst., phila., 1961—; trustee, chmn. rsch. fund Phila. Gen. Hosp., 1963-76; mem. adv. coun. Pa. State Tech. Assistance Program, Harrisburg, 1965-71. Mem. Am. Chem. Soc., N.Y. Acad. Scis., Sigma Xi. Republican. Roman Catholic. Avocations: photography, gardening. Home and Office: 2179 Graystone Dr Sumter SC 29150-2372

EBERL, JAMES JOSEPH, physical chemist, consultant; b. Dunkirk, N.Y., Oct. 7, 1916; s. George M. and Florece S. (Stedler) E.; m. Donna Davis, July 18, 1996. BA, U. Buffalo, 1938, PhD, 1941; AMP, Harvard U., 1955. Asst. prof. chemistry U. Del., Newark, 1941-42; mgr. rsch. Paper Chem. Divsn. Hercules Inc., Wilmington, Del., 1942-43; sr. fellow Mellon Inst. Indsl. Rsch., Pitts., 1943-44; dir. spl. prodn. rsch. Johnson and Johnson, New Brunswick, N.J., 1944-48; asst. corp. v.p. Scott Paper Co., Chester, Pa., 1948-70; pres., CEO Newbold Inc., Phila., 1970-72; cons. Moylan, Pa., 1972—. Contbr. articles to profl. jours. Trustee The Franklin Inst., Phila., 1960—, mem. sci. and arts com., 1987—; chmn. bd. dirs. rsch. fund Phila. Gen. Hosp., 1963-76; mem. adv. com. Pa. Tech. Assistance program Pa. State U., 1965-71. Receipent Disting. Alumni award, U. Buffalo, 1999. Mem. Am. Chem. Soc., Am. Inst. Chem. Engrs., N.Y. Acad. Scis., Empire State Paper Rsch. Assn. (pres. 1965-71), Sigma Xi (Disting. Alumni award 1999). Achievements include 50 patents for dusting powder for surgical rubber gloves that does not produce abdominal adhesions, single crystal whisker fibers, process for making hard coated plaster of Paris bandages, process for making high strength plaster of Paris, polystyrene foam sheet process, making soybean protein, bleaching process for groundwood pulp; for new chemical sterilization of microbes with epoxides, hemostatic agents for synthetic paper pulp fibrous extenders; process for the manufacture of Viva paper towel. Home: 7 Rose Hill Rd Moylan PA 19065

EBERLE, CHARLES EDWARD, paper and consumer products executive; b. St. Louis, Mar. 20, 1928; s. Charles Edward and Hazel (Williams) E.; m. Nancy Ellen Paddock, Aug. 1, 1953 (div. June 1995); children: Charles Edward, Richard Clay, Julia Lee; m. Denise S. Jackson, Apr. 12, 1997. B.S. in Chem. Engring., Washington U., St. Louis, 1949. Prodn. mgr. Procter & Gamble, St. Louis, 1949-55; plant mgr. Procter & Gamble, Lexington, Ky., 1955-57, St. Louis, 1957-60, Sacramento, 1960-64; mgr. mfg. Procter & Gamble, Cin., 1964-79, v.p. mfg., 1979-84, v.p. engring., 1984-85; pres. CEE Enterprises, Cin., 1985-88, Thomas & Eberle Assocs., Inc., Cin., 1986-88; v.p., James River Europe James River Corp., 1988-90, sr. v.p., group exec., 1990, exec. v.p. consumer products bus., 1990-91; pres. CEE Enterprises, Richmond, 1992—; chmn. exec. com. Richmond area TEC, Midlothian, Va., 1997-98; v.p. corp. devel. Lloyd Assocs., Inc., Richmond, 1999—; mem. mfg. studies bd. NRC/NAS, 1984-89. Vice pres. bd. trustees Children's Hosp. Med. Ctr., Cin., 1975-78; mem. Cin. Council on World Affairs, 1979-89; v.p. Dan Beard coun. Boy Scouts Am., 1982-85. With U.S. Army, 1951-52. Recipient Engring. Alumni Achievement award Washington U., 1977. Mem. Commonwealth Club.

EBERLE, MARY U., state legislator; b. St. Louis, June 6, 1949; m. James T. Graha; 3 children. BA, St. Louis U., 1971; JD, U. Mich., 1976. Mem. Dist. 15 Conn. Ho. of Reps., 1993—; pvt. practice Bloomfield. Mem. Bloomfield (Conn.) Bd. Tax Rev., 1983-85; chmn. Bloomfield Bd. Edn., 1985-91, mem., 1992. Mem. Bloomfield C. of C. Address: 205 Duncaster Rd Bloomfield CT 06002-1140 Office: Legis Office Bldg Rm 3900apitol Hartford CT 06106-1591*

EBERLE, WILLIAM DENMAN, international management consultant; b. Boise, Idaho, June 5, 1923; s. Julius Louis and Clare (Holcomb) E.; m. Jean Cilista Quick, Sept. 20, 1947; children—Jeffrey Louis, William David, Francis Quick, Cilista Clare. B.A., Stanford U., 1945; M.B.A., Harvard U., 1947, JD, 1949; LLB (hon.), Gonzagua U., 1976. Bar: Idaho 1950. Ptrn. firm Richards, Haga & Eberle, Boise, 1950-60; mem. Idaho Ho. of Reps. from Ada County, 1953-61, majority leader, 1957, minority leader, 1959, speaker, 1961; dir. Boise Cascade Corp., 1952-68, v.p., 1961-66; pres., chmn., dir. Am. Standard, Inc., N.Y.C., 1966-71; U.S. trade rep., amb. Washington, 1971-75; exec. dir. Cabinet Council on Internat. Econ. Policy, 1974-75; mem. Pres.'s Econ. Policy Bd., 1974-75; pres., chief exec. officer Motor Vehicle Mfrs. Assn., 1975-77; chmn. Holders Capital Corp., Santa Monica, Calif., 1977—, EBCO Inc., Boise, 1978—, Manchester Assocs. Ltd., Washington, 1977—; bd. dirs. Konover Property Trust, Mitchell Energy and Devel. Corp., Ampco-Pitts. Corp.; of counsel Kaye, Scholer, Fierman, Hays and Handler, N.Y.C.; chmn. Am. Svc. Group, Showscan Entertainment, Inc.; co-chmn. Mid-States Plc. Chmn. Idaho Rep. Fin. Com., 1961-66; mem. nat. Rep. Fin. Com., 1961-66; trustee Stanford U., 1970-80, Com. for Econ. Devel. Lt. USNR, 1944-46. Mem. ABA, Idaho Bar Assn., Coun. Fgn. Rels., Internat. C. of C., Aspen Inst., Future of the World Economy, Univ. Club (N.Y.C.), Met. Club (Washington). Episcopalian. Office: Manchester Assoc PO Box 1425 13 Garland Rd Concord MA 01742-2214

EBERLEIN, PATRICIA JAMES, mathematician, computer scientist, educator; b. Washington, July 15, 1925; d. William Stubbs and Rose Ramsay James; m. Wentzle Ruml, 1944; m. Elroy Wells, 1946; m. William Eberlein, June 23, 1956; children: Patrick, Kathy, Michael, Sarah, Robert, Mary, Kris. B.S., U. Chgo., 1944; Ph.D., Mich. State U., 1955. Asst. prof. Wayne State U., 1955-56; with electronic computer project Inst. for Advanced Study, 1956-57; asst. prof. bus. adminstrn., asst. dir. computer center U. Rochester, 1957-67; assoc. prof. math. and computer sci. SUNY-Buffalo, Amherst, 1967-75; prof. computer sci. SUNY-Buffalo, 1975—, chmn. dept., 1981-84, prof. emerita, 1996—; NSF vis. prof. Cornell U., 1984-85; vis. sr. scientist Argonne Nat. Lab., summer 1988. Treas. Soc. of Friends, Rochester, 1970-76. Mem. IEEE Computer Soc., AAAS (del. to coun. 1992-96), Am. Math. Soc., Assn. Computing Machinery (vis. lectr. 1968-71), Soc. Indsl. and Applied Math. (coun. 1971-77, chmn. vis. lectureship program 1977-80), Assn. Women in Math., Am. Math. Assn. (vis. lectr. 1975-78). Office: SUNY-Buffalo Dept Computer Sci 219 Bell Hall Buffalo NY 14260-0106*

EBERLEY, HELEN-KAY, opera singer, classical record company executive, poet; b. Sterling, Ill., Aug. 3, 1947; d. William Elliott and P. (Conneely) E. MusB, Northwestern U., 1970, MusM, 1971. Chmn., pres. Eberley-Skowronski, Inc., Evanston, Ill., 1973-92; founder H.K.E. Enterprises, 1993—, pres., 1993—; circulation libr. Evanston Pub. Libr., 1995—; artistic coord. Eberley-Skowronski, Inc., 1973-92; founder EB-SKO Prodns., 1976-92, tchr., coach, 1976—; exec. dir., performance cons. E-S Mgmt., 1985-92; featured artist Honors Concert, Northwestern U., 1970, Master Class and guest lectr. various colls. and univs.; host Poetry in Process monthly seminar Barnes & Noble; music lectr. rep. Harvard Club, Chgo.; numerous TV and radio talk show appearances and interviews. Operatic debut in Peter Grimes, Lyric Opera, Chgo., 1974; starred in: Cosi Fan Tutte, Le Nozze Di Figaro, Dido and Aeneas, La Boheme, Faust, Tosca, La Traviata, Falstaff, Don Giovanni, Brigadoon, others; jazz appearances with Duke Ellington, Dave Brubeck and Robert Shaw; performing artist Oglebay Opera Inst., Wheeling, W.Va., 1968, WTTW TV/PBS, Chgo., 1968; solo star in: Continental Bank Concerts, 1981-89, United Airlines-Schubert, Schumann, Brahms, Mendelssohn, Faure, Mozart, Duparc/Wolf, Supersta. WFMT Radio, Chgo., 1982-90; featured artist with North Shore Concert Band, 1989; starring artist South Bend Symphony, 1990, Mo. Symphony Soc., 1990, Milw. Symphony, 1990; spl. guest artist New Studios Gala Sta. WFMT, 1995, West Valley Fine Arts Concert Series, Phoenix, 1999; prodr.-annotator Gentlemen Gypsy, 1978, Strauss and Szymanowski, 1979, One Sonata Each: Franck and Szymanowski, 1982; starring artist-exec. prodr. Separate But Equal, 1976, All Brahms, 1977, Opera Lady, 1978, Eberley Sings Strauss, 1980, Helen-Kay Eberley: American Girl, 1983, Helen-Kay Eberley: Opera Lady II, 1984; performed Am. and Can. nat. anthems for Chgo. Cubs Baseball Team, 1977-83, Chgo. Bears Football, 1977; also starred in numerous concert recital and symphony appearances, Europe, Can., U.S.; author: Angel's Song, 1994, The Magdaleva Poems, 1995, ChapelHeart, 1996, Desert Dancing, 1997. Docent, new mem. tour guide Art Inst. Chgo.; new mem. Tours Guide; spl. events hotline vol. Art Inst. Chgo., Chgo. Christian Indsl. League, St. Joseph's Table of St. Peter's in the Loop, Chgo.; vol., facilitator City Yr. Chgo.-Urban Peace Corps; Chgo. Humanities Festival VIII of Ill. Humanities Coun., Evanston Shelter for Battered Women, Rape Victim Adv., Habitat for Humanity; Midwest Vol. Facilitator 1st Indsl. Realty Trust; mem. Mayor's founding com. Evanston Arts Coun., 1974-75; judge Ice-Skating Competition, Wilmette (Ill.) Park Dist., 1974-77, bd. dirs., 1973-77; bd. dirs. Ctr. for Voice, Chgo., 1994-96; vol. Saints-Usher Corps of Chgo., 1998-99. Recipient Creative and Performing Arts award Ind. Jr. Miss. and South Bend Jr. Miss, 1965, Milton J. Cross award Met. Opera Guild, 1968; prize winner Met. Opera. Nat. Auditions, 1968, 1st pl. prize for The Pond, Chicagoland Poetry Contest, 1997; F.K. Weyerhauser scholar Met. Opera, 1967. Mem. People for Ethical Treatment of Animals, Am. Soc. for Prevention of Cruelty to Animals, Am. Guild Mus. Artists, Internat. Platform Assn., Whale Adoption Project, Amnesty Internat., Environ. Def. Fund, Doris Day Animal Found., Humane Soc., Greenpeace, Physicians Com. for Responsible Medicine, St. Mary's Acad. Alumnae Assn., Delta Gamma. Clubs: St. Mary's Acad. Alumnae Assn., Delta Gamma. Office: HKE Enterprises 1726 Sherman Ave Evanston IL 60201-3713

EBERLIN, RICHARD D., education educator; b. Erie, Pa., Sept. 28, 1947; s. Harry M. and Florence F. (Space) E.; m. Deanna A. Barron, Aug. 7, 1971; children: Richard D., Charles A. BS in Edn., Edinboro State Coll., 1969, MS in Edn., 1973. Tchr. Crawford Cen. Sch. Dist., Meadville, Pa., 1969-76, Millcreek Twp. Sch. Dist., Erie, Pa., 1976—. Bd. dirs. Pa. State Edn. Assn., Harrisburg, 1996—, pres. N.W. region, 1998—; ass t. scoutmaster Boy Scouts of Am., Erie, 1985-96. Office: McDowell HS 3580 W 38th St Erie PA 16506-4021

EBERLY, HARRY LANDIS, retired communications company executive; b. Lancaster, Pa., Nov. 1, 1924; s. Chester Landis and Nola Marie (Clark) E.; m. Marion Ruth Royer, May 26, 1951; children: Jenny Ellen Eberly Holmes, Susan Lynn Eberly Patrick. B.S. in Chem. Engring., Pa. State U., 1945; postgrad., Lehigh U., 1947-48, Franklin and Marshall Coll., 1949. Engr. We. Electric, N.Y.C., 1945-49; mfg. engr. RCA, Lancaster, Pa., 1949-51; product devel. RCA, Harrison, N.J., 1951-64; mgr. mfg. RCA, Somerville, N.J., 1964-66; plant mgr. RCA, Palm Beach Garden, Fla., 1996-68; mgr. purchasing RCA, Palm Beach Gardens, Fla., 1968-72; v.p. Telex Computer Products, Inc., Tulsa, 1972-76, sr. v.p., 1976-77; pres. Communication Products div. Telex Computer Products, Inc., Raleigh, N.C., 1977-83; exec. v.p. Telex Computer Products, Inc., Raleigh, 1983-88; mem. exec. com. Telex Computer Products, Inc., Tulsa, 1984-88, dir., 1982-84; exec. v.p. Memorex Telex Corp., 1988-90; COO, Novatel Comm., Ltd., Calgary, Can., 1991-92. Mem. bd. assocs. Meridith Coll., Raleigh, 1981—, presdl. adv. coun., 1999—; mem. bd. assocs. Barton Coll. Global Focus Program 1988-97; bd. dirs. Wake Tech. Cmty. Coll. Found., Raleigh, 1982-97, chmn., 1990-94; mem. N.C. State U. Engring. Found., Raleigh, 1984-87, exec. com. Edn. and Psychology Found., 1990-95; vice chmn. Triangle East N.C., 1986-90, chmn., 1990-92; bd. dirs., 1988 campaign chmn. United Way Wake County, 1980-89; regional maj., gifts chmn. Campaign for Pa. State, 1986-90; Pa. State Grand Destiny 2000 Campaign, 1997—; bd. dirs., exec. com. Occoneechee Coun. Boy Scouts Am., 1989-95; bd. dirs. Raleigh Little Theatre, 1989-92, 95—; bd. dirs. Raleigh Housing Authority Scholarship Fund, 1993-98. Mem. IEEE (life), Wake County Edn. Found. (bd. dirs. 1990-92), Greater Raleigh C. of C. (bd. dirs. 1979-87), North Ridge Country Club, Masons, Shriners, Delta Gamma Delta. Methodist. Home: 7003 North Ridge Dr Raleigh NC 27615-7036

EBERLY, JOSEPH HENRY, physics educator, consultant; b. Carlisle, Pa., Oct. 19, 1935; s. Norman McKinley and Mary Weigle (Keeny) E.; m. Shirley Warren Smith; children: Rebecca Leas, Virginia Westcott, Lynn Elizabeth. B.S., Pa. State U., 1957; Ph.D., Stanford U., 1962. Prof. physics U. Rochester (N.Y.), 1976-79, prof. physics and optics, 1979—; Andrew Carnegie prof. physics, 1996—; dir. Rochester Theory Ctr. for Optical Sci. and Engring., 1995—; vis. fellow Joint Inst. for Lab. Astrophysics and Nat. Bur. Stds., Boulder, Colo., 1977-78, sci. and engring. rsch. coun. physics dept. London Imperial Coll., 1983; vis. mem. Max-Planck Inst. Quantum Optics, Munich, 1985, 89, 95; adv. editor for physics John Wiley Pubs., N.Y.C., 1975—; cons. U.S. Dept. Energy, 1974—, Battelle Labs., Durham, N.C., 1974-84, Inst. Def. Analyses, 1986-94; mem. physics adv. com. Lawrence Livermore Nat. Lab., 1995-97. Author: Lasers, 1988, Optical Resonance and Two-Level Atoms, 1975; editor: Multiphoton Bibliography, 1970—, Multiphoton Processes, 1978, Optics Express, 1996—. Recipient Alexander von Humboldt award, 1984, Marian Smoluchowski medal, 1987, Charles H. Townes award Optical Soc. Am., 1994, Disting. Alumni award Pa. State Coll. Sci., 1998, Outstanding Sci. Alumni award, 1998. Fellow Optical Soc. Am. (bd. dirs.), Am. Phys. Soc. (chair divsn. laser sci. 1996-97), C.V. Tummer Soc. (founding mem.).

EBERLY, ROBERT EDWARD, oil and gas production company executive; b. Greensboro, Pa., July 14, 1918; s. Orville Sebastian and Ruth Rhoda (Moore) E.; m. Elouise Ross Conn., Sept. 25, 1982; children: Robert E. Jr., Paul O., Mary Katherine Zickefoose, Sue C. O'Brien, Thomas J. Conn, William H. Conn, Robert E. Conn. BA in Chemistry, Pa. State U., 1939; LittD (hon.), Calif. U. Pa., 1991, Waynesburg (Pa.) Coll., 1992; LLD (hon.), Slippery Rock U., 1994; D Pub. Svc. (hon.), Thiel Coll. Chemist Dept. Navy, 1940-45; pres., gen. mgr. Eberly Natural Gas Co., Uniontown, Pa., 1945-86; pres., treas. GNB Corp., Uniontown, Pa., 1969-77, chmn. bd., 1977-85; chmn. bd. Gallatin Nat. Bank, Uniontown, 1977-90, bd. dirs.; chmn. bd. Eberly and Meade, Inc., Uniontown, Pa., 1986; chmn. bd. Eberly and Meade, Inc., 1986—; gen. mgr. Eberly Family Trust, 1983—; sec. treas. Eberly Found., 1963-88, pres., 1988—; chmn. Chalk Hill Gas, Inc., 1986-94, Greystone Resources, Inc., 1986—; pres. Fay-Penn Econ. Devel. Coun., 1991, Greystone Prodn. Co., 1992, Greystone Acquisition Corp., 1992, Greystone Oil and Gas Corp., 1994. Pres. bd. trustees Uniontown Hosp. Assn., 1968-70, trustee emeritus, 1978—; bd. dirs. Penn's Southwest Assn., 1980—, trustee, 1978—; bd. dirs., past pres. Uniontown Indsl. Fund, 1971; nat. chmn. alumni fund Pa. State U., 1972-74, mem. Found. Bd., mem. adv. bd. Fayette Campus Br., nat. treas. Campaign for Pa. State U., 1985-90, treas. Nat. Devel. Coun., 1991—; Penn State U. Libraries feasibility study, 1992-93; past sec. Uniontown Planning and Zoning Commn.; bd. dirs. Laurel Highlands, Inc., 1987—; active Westmoreland/Fayette coun. Boy Scouts Am.; bd. dirs. WQED-TV, 1990-94; chmn. Uniontown YMCA Pool Campaign, 1988-90, Uniontown Hosp. Found. Inc., 1990-91; Hist. Soc. Western Pa. (Blue Ribbon Comm.), 1992—; Honorary Chmn. Fayette County Columbus Quincentennial Celebration, 1992; hon. mem. Uniontown Area YMCA, 1995. Recipient Rockwell Recognition award, 1970, Jerusalem City of Peace award Fayette County Israel Bond Com., 1985, Silver Beaver award Boy Scouts Am., 1987, Eleanor Coldren award ARC-Uniontown Ch., 1993, Sheepskin award for disting. svc. to higher edn. Pa. Assn. Colls. and Univs., 1994, Libr. Citizien of Yr. award Pa. Citizens for Better Librs., 1993, Man of Yr. award B'nai B'rith, 1995; Melvin Jones fellow Lions Club Internat., 1993. Mem. Okla. Oil and Gas Assn., Okla. Ind. Petroleum Assn., Ohio Oil and Gas Assn., W.Va. Oil and Gas Assn., Pa. Oil and Gas Assn., Pa. Geol. Soc., Ind. Petroleum Assn., Greater Uniontown C. of C. (bd. dirs., past pres., named Man of Yr. 1968), Uniontown Country Club (past v.p., bd. dirs.), Rotary (past pres. Uniontown), Masons (past Master, hon. 33 degree), The Pa. Soc., Theta Chi. Office: Eberly & Meade Inc PO Box 2023 Uniontown PA 15401-1623*

EBERLY, WILLIAM SOMERS, financial consultant; b. Toledo, Sept. 25, 1921; s. Somers L. and Clara B. (Valentine) E.; m. Catharine L. Sloan (dec. Nov. 1979); children: Stephen, Michael; m. Elizabeth Eberly, Nov. 28, 1980. BBA, U. Toledo, 1943. Various positions Bklyn. Dodgers Nat. League Baseball team, 1944-52; bus. mgr. Milw. Braves Nat. League Baseball team, 1953-65; promotion mgr. Gladiux Corp., Toledo, 1966; fin. cons., sr. v.p. Salomon Smith Barney, 1967—; spkr. on evolution of big league baseball. Mem. adv. bd. U. Toledo Ctr. for Women, 1982—. Recipient Blue T award U. Toledo, Eli Lilly Pharm. award, 1996, New Deaconess Diabetic Achievement award, 1997. Mem. U. Toledo Alumni Assn. (pres., 1972), Toledo Exch. Club (pres.). Home: 2521 Middlesex Dr Toledo OH 43606-3117

EBERSBERGER, ARTHUR DARRYL, insurance company executive, consultant; b. Balt., June 18, 1946; s. George Henry and Althea May Ebersberger; m. Judith Simison, Nov. 18, 1982; 1 child, Leonard Darryl. BS, Susquehanna U., 1968; MBA, Loyola Coll., Balt., 1985; postgrad., Am. Coll., Bryn Mawr, Pa. CLU, ChFC; mem. Md. Bd. Architects. Owner Ebersberger & Assocs., Inc., Severna Park, Md., 1968—; pres. Ebersberger Consulting Inc., Severna Park, Md., 1986—; pres. Anne Arundel Trade Coun., 1995-96, chmn., 1996-97; mem. Md. Bus. and Econ. Devel. Commn., 1995-99; mem. Md. Bd. Architects, 1993—. *In 1993, Arthur served on the governor's task force on the Standard Benefits Bill for Maryland. In 1994, Arthur chaired the Anne Arundel County Ad Hoc Committee on Adequacy of School Facilities, and in 1998 co-chaired the Anne Arundel County Executive's Committee on Repairing and Preparing our Schools for the 21st Century. Since 1994, he served on the MD-US Olympic Committee.* Pres. Sheltered Workshop of Anne Arundel County, Glen Burnie, Md., 1978; pres., founder Leadership Anne Arundel, Inc., 1993-95, bd. dirs., 1995-96, chmn., immediate past pres., 1995-96, chmn. Exec. Series Program, 1997-99; mem. Anne Arundel County Planning Adv. Bd., 1996-99; chmn. v.p. Md. Conf. on Sml. Bus., 1989-90; grad. Leadership Md., 1993; bd. dirs. Ginger Cover Retirement Cmty, 1994-99, ASPIRE, 1995-99; trustee Anne Arundel Health Sys., Inc., 1997—, Anne Arundel C.C., 1998—. With USNR, 1960-71, Vietnam. Named Small Bus. Advocate of Yr., SBA, 1993. Mem. U.S. Jaycees (adv. bd. 1982, Outstanding Young Man Am. 1980-81, pres. Severna Park br. 1976), Assoc. Builders and Contractors (pres. 1986), Anne Arundel Life Underwriters (pres. 1981, life mem.), Million Dollar Round Table, CLU's (bd. dirs. Balt. chpt. 1981-83), Md. C. of C. (vice chmn. 1998-99, chmn. 1999—), Chesapeake chpt. SCI (pres. 1998—), Profl. Liability Agts. Network (pres. 1985-86, exec. com. 1986-98), Chartwell Golf and Country Club (bd. dirs. 1981-83). Republican. Lutheran. Avocations: golf, fly fishing, hunting, hiking, karate. Home: 51 Boone Trl Severna Park MD 21146-4501 Address: PO Box 959 Severna Park MD 21146-0959

EBERSOL, DICK, television broadcasting executive; b. N.Y.C., 1968. Student, Yale U. Former exec. asst. to Roone Arledge ABC Sports; former sports prodr. ABC Wide World of Sports; dir. weekend late night programming NBC, N.Y.C., 1974-75, v.p. late night programming, 1976-77, v.p. comedy, variety and event programming, 1977-81; co-creator Saturday Night Live, N.Y.C., 1975, exec. prodr., 1981-85; founder No Sleep Prodns., 1983—; pres. NBC Sports, 1989-98; sr. v.p. NBC News, 1989—; chmn. NBC Sports & NBC Olympics, 1998—. Creator: NBC's Friday Night Videos, Saturday Night's Main Event, Later with Bob Costas. Office: NBC Sports 30 Rockefeller Plz Fl 2 New York NY 10112-0036*

EBERSOLE, BRIAN, mayor. BA, U. Tenn.; M in Ednl. Psychology, U. Conn. Tchr., counselor, adminstr. Tacoma Pub. Schs.; adminstr. Tacoma C.C., 1989-91; spkr. Wash. State Ho. of Reps.; state house majority leader; mayor Tacoma, 1995—; chair House Edn. Com., 1985-87; prime sponsor Omnibus Sch. Fin. Reform Act, 1987, Omnibus Drug Bill, 1989. Named Legislator of Yr. (6 consecutive yrs.), Assn. for Vocat. Edn., Legislator of Yr., Wash. State Firefighters Assn. and Wash. State Coun. of Policy Officers. Office: Ste 1200 747 Market St Tacoma WA 98402

EBERSOLE, J. GLENN, JR., engineering, marketing, management and public relations executive; b. Lancaster, Pa., Feb. 8, 1947; s. J. Glenn and Maroe Christine (Stoner) E.; m. Helen Walton, July 11, 1970. Student, Ohio No. U., 1965-67; BSCE, Pa. State U., 1970, M of Engring. Sci., 1973. Registered profl. engr., Pa. Vt., Md., Del., N.J. Rsch. tech. Pa. State U., University Park, 1968-70; civil engring. intern Pa. Dept. Transp., Harrisburg, 1970-71, asst. dist. design liaison engr., 1971, head rsch. & spl. studies Bus. Traffic Engring., 1971-76; asst. chief engr.-traffic Pa. Turnpike Commn., Harrisburg, 1976-78; chief transp. mgr. Huth Engrs., Inc., Lancaster, 1978-81; exec. engr. GCGSB, Clarks Summit, Pa., 1981-82; founder, CEO J.G. Ebersole Asocs., Lancaster, Pa., 1982—, The Renaissance Group TM, Lancaster, Pa., 1983—; part-time lectr. Pa. State U.; bus. agt. former NFL players; profl. mgr. & publicist for artists and authors. Contbr. articles to profl. jours. Ch. sch. tchr., lector, past chmn. brochure com. Ch. of the Apostles, past chmn. faith promiose campaign, past mem. ch. coun., ch. steering com. for long range planning; past chmn. cable TV com.; past chmn. Rapho Twp. Planning Commn.; mem. regional devel. coun. Pa. State U., active Pa. State legis. liaison program; bd. dirs., past pres. bd. trustees Actors Co. Pa.; past co-chmn. Le Cabaret Moulin Rouge Gala; past co-chmn. devel. com. Gt. Gatsby Gala; past chmn. fundraising campaign restortion project Mill Mus.; past trustee, past treas. bd. trustees Lancaster Found. Ednl. Enrichment; asst. sec., bd. dirs. lancaster Indsl. Devel. Authority; past bd. dirs. Lancster Family YWCA, Ctrl. Pa. Friends Jazz; planning commn. Lancaster County, econ. devel. task force, urban issues subcom. Mem. ASCE, NSPE, Am. Mktg. Assn. (dir., past Ctrl. Pa. chpt. pres.), Inst.

Transp. Engrs., Lancaster C. of C. (govt. affairs com., chmn. golf com. 1985-87, long range transp. task force, local affairs com., mem. priority rds. task force, mem. mktg./comm. coun.), Pa. Soc. Profl. Engrs., Pa. Soc., Pa. State Alumni Assn. (regional devel. coun.), Pa. State of Lancaster County (past pres., bd. dirs.), Pa. State Civil & Environ. Engring. Soc. (past pres., bd. dirs.), Pa. State Engring. Soc. (past bd. dirs.), Hershey Country Club, Shriners, Masons (past master Mt. Joy, Pa. club, Royal Order of Jesters, Allentown, Ct.), Phi Eta Sugma, Alpha Sigma Phi. Home and Office: 1305 Wheatland Ave Lancaster PA 17603-4720

EBERSOLE, MARK CHESTER, emeritus college president; b. Hershey, Pa., Nov. 3, 1921; s. Benjamin W.S. and Mary (Patrick) E.; m. Dorothy Baugher, June 26, 1943; children—Philip B., Stephen B. B.S., Elizabethtown (Pa.) Coll., 1943, LL.D., 1969; B.D., Crozer Theol. Sem., 1946; M.A., U. Pa., 1948; Ph.D., Columbia, 1952. UNRRA relief adminstr. Europe, 1946-47; asst. prof. religion and philosophy Elmira Coll., 1952-53; faculty Bucknell U., 1953-69, prof. religion, chmn. dept., chaplain of univ., 1958-61, asst. dean univ., 1961; dean Coll. Arts and Scis., 1961-62, v.p. acad. affairs, 1961-68, univ. provost, 1968-69; project specialist, spl. projects in edn. Ford Found., 1967-69, program adviser, 1969-71; dean Grad. Sch.; assoc. v.p. for acad. affairs Temple U., 1971-77; pres. Elizabethtown (Pa.) Coll., 1977-85, pres. emeritus, 1985—; bd. dirs. Educators Mutual Life Ins. Co.; interim pres. Maryville Coll., 1992-93; ednl. cons., 1987—. Author: Christian Faith and Man's Religion, 1961; editor: Hail to Thee, Okoboji U. A Humor Anthology on Higher Education, 1992; contbr. articles to profl. jours. Trustee Linden Hall Sch., 1992—. J.P. Crozer Found. fellow, 1949-51. Mem. Pa. Soc., Cliosophic Soc. Home: 1166 Country Club Dr Lancaster PA 17601-5206

EBERSOLE, PRISCILLA PIER, mental health nurse, geriatrics nurse; b. Salem, Oreg., Aug. 17, 1928; d. Joseph H. and Miriam E. (Holder) Pierre; m. Raymond V. Ebersole, May 14, 1948; children: Lorraine, Raymond, Randolph, Elisabeth. AA, Coll. San Mateo, 1965; BS, San Francisco State U., 1971; MS, U. Calif., San Francisco, 1973; PhD, Columbia Pacific U., 1986. RN, Calif.; BRN; VSC. Instr. Chabot Coll., Hayward, Calif., 1973, U. So. Calif., L.A., 1977-80; prof. nursing San Francisco State U., 1973-95; vis. prof. Cellar Endowed Chair in Gerontology Case Western Res. U., Cleve. 1988. Editor Geriatric Nursing Jour. Named Alumni of Yr. San Francisco State U., 1987. Mem. ANA, ASA, GSA, AGHE, WIN. Home: 2790 Rollingwood Dr San Bruno CA 94066-2610

EBERSTEIN, ARTHUR, former biomedical engineering educator, researcher; b. Chgo., Apr. 23, 1928; s. Nathan and Sara (Estes) E.; m. Marion Apfel, Aug. 1, 1961; children—Sharon, Laura. B.S., Ill. Inst. Tech., 1950; M.S., U. Ill., 1951; Ph.D., Ohio State U., 1957. Asst. mem. Inst. for Muscle Disease, N.Y.C., 1959-61; sr. scientist Am. Bosch Arma Corp., 1961-63; dir. biomed. engring. Lundy Electronics, Inc., Glen Head, N.Y., 1963-64; prof., dir. research dept. rehab. medicine NYU Med. Ctr, N.Y.C., 1964-96; rsch. coord. dept. rehab. medicine Kingsbrook Jewish Med. Ctr., Bklyn., 1997—. Co-author: Electrodiagnosis of Neuromuscular Disease, 1983. Served with U.S. Army, 1955-57. Fellow NSF, 1958, NIH, 1959. Mem. Am. Physiol. Soc., Biophys. Soc., Biomed. Engring. Soc. Am. Assn. Electrodiagnostic Medicine, Sigma Pi Sigma. Jewish. Avocations: skiing; tennis.

EBERT, DOROTHY ELIZABETH, county clerk; b. Beaver Dam, Wis., Apr. 16, 1941; d. Merlin Herman and Gertrude Elizabeth (Hupke) E. Grad. high sch., Beaver Dam. Sec., receptionist Household Fin. Corp., Beaver Dam, 1958-67; dep. county clk. Dodge County, Juneau, Wis., 1967-82, county clk., 1983—. Past bd. dirs. Dodge County chpt. Am. Cancer Soc. Mem. Wis. County Clks. Assn. (historian 1994-95, treas. 1995-96, sec. 1996-97, v.p. 1997-98, pres. 1998-99). Republican. Lutheran. Avocations: bowling, golf, calligraphy, singing, bell choir. Office: County Clk Office 127 E Oak St Juneau WI 53039-1329

EBERT, DOUGLAS EDMUND, banker; b. Washington, Oct. 21, 1945; s. Edmund Francis and Lathelia Marie (Keesey) E.; m. Linda Sue Weick, June 24, 1994; children: Elizabeth Anne, Leslie Anne, Kevin Edward, Ashley Edward. B.A., Williams Coll., 1968. Asst. sec. Mfrs. Hanover Trust Corp., N.Y.C., 1969-72, asst. v.p., 1972-73, v.p., 1973-76, sr. v.p., dep. gen. mgr., 1976-82, exec. v.p., 1982-85, sr. exec. v.p. investment banking sector, 1985-90; pres., CEO S.E. Bank N.A., Miami, 1990-91, also chmn. bd. dirs., 1990-91; with Lincoln Fin. Corp., Fort Wayne, Ind., 1992-93; pres., COO Mich. Nat. Bank, Farmington Hills, 1993-95; pres., CEO Mich. Nat. Bank, Mich. Nat. Corp., 1995—; pres., chief exec. officer, S.E. Banking Corp., 1990-91, Miami, also bd. dirs.; bd. dirs. HomeSide Internat., Inc., Ind. One Capital Mgmt., Independence One Mortgage Corp., Detroit Renaissance, Detroit Symphony Hall, Detroit Regional C. of C., Detroit Econ. Club; trustee Cranbrook Inst. Sci. Bd. dirs. Cancer Research Ctr. Mem. Com. Econ. Devel., Bankers Assn. Fgn. Trade, U.S. Bus. Council, Bank Adminstrn. Inst., Assn. Res. City Bankers. Avocations: tennis, golf, bicycling, carpentry, reading. Office: Mich Nat Bank 27777 Inkster Rd Farmington Hills MI 48334-5326

EBERT, JAMES DAVID, research biologist, educator; b. Bentleyville, Pa., Dec. 11, 1921; s. Alva Charles and Anna Frances (Brundege) E.; m. Alma Christine Goodwin, Apr. 19, 1946; children—Frances Diane, David Brian, Rebecca Susan. AB, Washington and Jefferson Coll., 1942, ScD, 1969; PhD, Johns Hopkins U., 1950; ScD (hon.), Yale, 1973, Ind. U., 1975, Duke U., 1992; LL.D. (hon.), Moravian Coll., 1979. Jr. instr. biology Johns Hopkins U., 1946-49, Adam T. Bruce fellow biology, 1949-50, hon. prof. biology, 1956-86, hon. prof. embryology Sch. Medicine, 1956-86; instr. biology Mass. Inst. Tech., 1950-51; asst. prof. zoology Ind. U., 1951-54, assoc. prof., 1954-56, Patten vis. prof., 1963; dir. dept. embryology Carnegie Instn. of Washington, 1956-76, pres., 1978-87, trustee, 1987—; prof. biology Johns Hopkins U., 1987—, dir. Chesapeake Bay Inst., 1987-92; vis. scientist med. dept. Brookhaven Nat. Lab., 1953-54; Philips vis. prof. Haverford Coll., 1961; instr. in charge embryology tng. program Marine Biol. Lab., summers 1962-66, trustee, 1964-98, hon. trustee, 1998—, pres., 1970-78, 91-98, dir., 1970-75, 77-78; mem. Commn. on Undergrad. Edn. in Biol. Scis., 1963-66; mem. vis. com. for biol. and phys. scis. Western Res. U., 1964-68; Mem. panels on morphogenesis and biology of neoplasia of com. on growth NRC, 1954-56; mem. adv. panel on genetic and developmental biology NSF, 1955-56, mem. divisional com. for biology and medicine, 1962-66, mem. univ. sci. devel. panel, 1965-70, adv. com. for instl. devel., 1970-72; mem. panel basic biol. rsch. in aging Am. Inst. Biol. Sci., 1957-60; mem. panel on cell biology NIH, USPHS, 1958-62, mem. child health and human devel. tng. com., 1963-66; mem. bd. sci. counselors Nat. Cancer Inst., 1967-71, Nat. Inst. Child Health, 1973-77; mem. Com. on Scholarly Communication with People's Republic of China, 1978-81, chmn., 1989-95; chmn. Nat. Com. on Sci. Edn. Stds. & Assessment, 1992-93, chmn. Com. on Transportation and a Sustainable Environment, Transportation Rsch. Bd., 1995-97; mem. vis. com. to dept. biology Mass. Inst. Tech., 1959-68; mem. vis. com. biology Harvard, 1969-75, Princeton, 1970-76; chmn. bd. sci. overseers Jackson Lab., 1976-80; mem. Inst. Medicine; bd. dirs. Baxter Internat., Transcend Therapeutics, Inc. (formerly known as Free Radical Sci., Inc.). Author: (with others) The Chick Embryo in Biological Research, 1952, Molecular Events in Differentiation Related to Specificity of Cell Type, 1955, Aspects of Synthesis and Order in Growth, 1955, Interacting Systems in Development, 2d edit., 1970, Biology, 1973, Mechanisms of Cell Change, 1979, This Our Golden Age, 1994; mem. editl. bd. (with others) Abstracts of Human Developmental Biology; editor: (with others) Oceanus; contbr. (with others) articles to profl. jours. Trustee Worcester Found. Lt. USNR, 1942-46. Decorated Purple Heart. Felow AAAS (v.p. med. scis. 1964), Am. Acad. Arts and Scis., Internat. Soc. Devel. Biology; mem. NAS (chmn. assembly life scis. 1973-77, v.p. 1981-93, chmn. Govt., Univ. and Industry Rsch. Roundtable 1987-92, chmn. on transp. and a sustainable environment 1994-97), Korean Acad. Sci. and Tech. (hon. fgn. mem.), Am. Philos. Soc., Am. Inst. Biol. Scis. (pres. 1964, President's medal 1972), Am. Soc. Naturalists, Am. Soc. Zoologists (pres. 1970), Soc. Study Growth and Devel. (pres. 1957-58), Phi Beta Kappa, Sigma Xi, Phi Sigma. Home: 4100 N Charles St Baltimore MD 21218-1065 Office: Marine Biol Lab Woods Hole MA 02543

EBERT, ROBERT ALVIN, retired lawyer, retired airline executive; b. Mpls., Oct. 13, 1915; s. Alvin C. and Caroline (Reutelsterz) B.; m. Trudy M. O'Leary, Feb. 8, 1947; children: Kathryn, Richard Friess. Student, U. Minn., 1933-35; J.D. cum laude, St. Paul Coll. Law, 1939. Bar: Minn. 1939, U.S. Supreme Ct. 1976. Practiced in Brainerd, until 1942; with Dept. Justice, 1942-43; with Northwest Airlines, Inc., 1943-76, v.p. personnel, 1960-76; pvt. practice St. Paul, 1976-90, mgmt. cons., 1990—; mgmt. cons. Bd. dirs. Salvation Army, William Mitchell Coll. Law, Svc. Corp. Ret. Execs. Mem. Pool and Yacht Club. Home: 1181 Edgcumbe Rd Apt 1206 Saint Paul MN 55105-2835*

EBERT, ROGER JOSEPH, film critic; b. Urbana, Ill., June 18, 1942; s. Walter H. and Annabel (Stumm) E.; m. Chaz Hammelsmith, July 18, 1992. BS, U. Ill., 1964; postgrad., U. Cape Town, South Africa, 1965, U. Chgo., 1966-67; LHD (hon.), U. Colo., 1993. Editor Daily Illini, 1963-64; pres. U.S. Student Press Assn., 1963-64; staff writer News-Gazette, Champaign-Urbana, Ill., 1958-66; film critic Chgo. Sun-Times, 1967—, US mag., 1978-79, NBC-TV News, Chgo., 1980-83, ABC-TV News, Chgo., 1984—, N.Y. Post, N.Y.C., 1986-88, N.Y. Daily News, 1988-92, Compu Serve, 1991—; pres. Ebert Co., Ltd., 1981—; Microsoft Cinemania, 1994-97; instr. English Chgo. City Coll., 1967-68; lectr. film criticism, fine arts program U. Chgo., 1969—; Kluge fellow U. Va., 1995-96; lectr. film Columbia Coll., Chgo., 1973-74, 77-80; cons. Nat. Endowments for Arts and Humanities, 1972-77; juror film festivals. Co-host (TV shows) Sneak Previews, PBS, 1976-82, At the Movies, syndicated, 1982-86, Siskel & Ebert, syndicated, 1986—; broadcaster: Movie News, ABC Radio, 1982-85; author: An Illini Century, 1967, (screenplay) Beyond the Valley of the Dolls, 1970, Beyond Narrative: The Future of the Feature Film, 1978, A Kiss Is Still a Kiss, 1984, Roger Ebert's Movie Home Companion, 1986-93, Roger Ebert's Video Companion, 1994-98, (with Daniel Curley) The Perfect London Walk, 1986, Two Weeks in the Midday Sun, 1987, Behind the Phantom's Mask, 1993, Ebert's Little Movie Glossary, 1994, Roger Ebert's Book of Film, 1996, Questions for the Movie Answer Man, 1997, Roger Ebert's Movie Yearbook, 1998—, Ebert's Bigger Little Movie Glossary, 1999; co-author: The Future of the Movies, The Computer Insectiary, 1994. Recipient Overseas Press club, 1963, award Chgo. Headline Club, 1963, award Chgo. Newspaper Guild, 1973, Pulitzer prize, 1975, Emmy award, 1979, Peter Lisagor award, 1998; inducted into Chgo. Journalism Hall of Fame, 1997; Rotary fellow, 1965, Kluge fellow in film studies U. Va., 1995-96. Mem. Newspaper Guild, Writers Guild Am. West, Nat. Soc. Film Critics, Acad. TV Arts and Scis., Arts Club of Chgo., Cliff Dwellers, Acad. Club (London), Sigma Delta Chi, Phi Delta Theta. Avocations: drawing, painting, art collecting. Office: Chgo Sun-Times Inc 401 N Wabash Ave Rm 110 Chicago IL 60611-3532

EBERWEIN, BARTON DOUGLAS, construction company executive, consultant; b. Balt., Aug. 19, 1951; s. Bruce George and Thelma Joyce (Cox) E. BS, U. Oreg., 1974, MBA, 1988. Sales mgr. Teleprompter of Oreg., Eugene, 1974-75; pres., owner Oreg. Images, Eugene, 1975-80; mktg. mgr. Clearwater Prodns., Eugene, 1980-82; sales mgr. Western Wood Structures, Portland, Oreg., 1982-84, mktg. coordinator, 1984-85, mktg. dir., 1985-89; dir. bus. devel. Hoffman Constrn. Co., Portland, 1989-93, v.p., 1993—. Bd. dirs. N.W. Youth Corps, Eugene, 1984—, Police Activity League, 1991, Portland Arts and Lectrs., 1994—; vol. bd. dirs. Goodwill, Oreg. Symphony, Portland Inst. for Contemporary Art, 1997—. Mem. AIA (bd. dirs.), Soc. Mktg. Profl. Svcs., Am. Mktg. Assn., Univ. Club, Founders Club, Riverplace Athletic Club. Democrat. Presbyterian. Avocations: rare books, photography, outdoor recreation, architectural preservation. Home: PO Box 391 Portland OR 97207-0391 Office: Hoffman Constrn Co 1300 SW 6th Ave Ste 400 Portland OR 97201-3486

EBERWEIN, GRANVILLE ALLEN, lay minister, civil servant; b. Balt., June 14, 1947; s. Jacob Parker, Jr. and Dorothy Marguerite (Hambury) E.; m. Virginia Maryann Shanklin, Nov. 8, 1970; children: Cynthia Ann, Carrie Ellen. AA, Essex C.C., Balt., 1976; BS, Towson State U., 1980; DD, Charter Ecumunical Ministries, Salvisa, Ky., 1995. Lead computer operator Johns Hopkins U., Balt., 1969-70; computer programmer, analyst Army Corps of Engrs., Balt., 1971-83, computer systems analyst, 1983-85, chief programming, info integration GM13, 1985-92, info systems mgmt. specialst, 1992-96, info. arch. coord., 1996—. Editor: (newsletters) The Outreach, 1981-84, Over and Undertones, 1993-94, PC Tips, 1995-96. Deacon Presbyn. Ch., Louisville, 1984—, mem. nominating com. Presbyn. Ch./Balt. Presbytery, 1990; merit badge counselor Boy Scouts of Am., Balt., 1982—; mem. Heritage Found., Washington, 1995-96; dir., State Guard Benefit Found., Md., 1998—, vice pres. Free State Mill Gun Club, 1998—, hon. dir. Appalachian Lit. Project, Commonwealth of Ky., 1996. With U.S. Army, 1966-68, Vietnam; capt. Md. state guard, first Lt., Civil Air Patrol Pilot. Recipient City of Balt. Radio award 10-10 Net, 1964, cert. appreciation State of Israel/Ministry of Def., Tel Aviv, 1994, State of Md. Commendation Medal, 1998, Pro Dro Et Patria award Boy Scouts Am., 1962, Eagle Scout, 1993. Mem. VFW (life), Data Processing Mgmt. Assn., Md. State guard Assn., State Guard Assn. of U.S. (life), Hartford Flying Club, Downtown Sailing Ctr. (com. mem. 1996—), Phi Alpha Theta. Republican. Avocations: Bible study, sailing, model railroading, amateur radio, historic restorations. Home: 4551 Shanklin Dr White Hall MD 21161-9629 Office: US Army Corps of Engrs 10 S Howard St Baltimore MD 21201-2526

EBERWEIN, JANE DONAHUE, English educator; b. Boston, Sept. 13, 1943; d. Joseph Daniel and Mary Leyden (O'Brien) Donahue; m. Robert T. Eberwein, July 10, 1971. A.B., Emmanuel Coll., 1965; Ph.D., Brown U., 1969. From asst. prof. to prof. English Oakland U., Rochester, Mich., 1969—. Author: Dickinson: Strategies of Limitation, 1985. Editor: Early American Poetry, 1978, An Emily Dickinson Encyclopedia, 1998. Contbr. articles to profl. jours. Mem. MLA, Am. Studies Assn., Mich. Acad. Sci., Arts and Letters, Emily Dickinson Internat. Soc., Phi Beta Kappa. Home: 379 W Frank St Birmingham MI 48009-1412 Office: Dept English Oakland U Rochester MI 48063

EBIE, WILLIAM D., museum director; b. Akron, Ohio, Feb. 7, 1942; s. William P. and Mary Louise (Karam) E.; m. Gwyn Anne Schumacher, Apr. 11, 1968 (div. Jan. 1988); children: Jason William, Alexandra Anne; m. Mary Teresa Hayes, June 10, 1989. BFA, Akron Art Inst., 1964; MFA, Calif. Coll. of Arts and Crafts, 1968. Graphic artist Alameda County Health Dept., Oakland, Calif., 1967-68; instr. painting Fla. A&M U., Tallahassee, 1968-69; instr. photography Lawrence (Kans.) Adult Edn. Program, 1969-70; asst. dir. Roswell (N.Mex.) Mus. & Art Ctr., 1971-87, dir., 1987-98; dir. Millicent Rogers Mus., Taos, N.Mex., 1998—; juror various art exhbns., 1971—; panelist N.Mex. Arts Divsn., Santa Fe, 1983-87; field reviewer Inst. for Mus. Svcs., 1988-90; mem. State Capitol Renovation Art Selection Com., Santa Fe, 1991-92; bd. dirs. State Capitol Found., Santa Fe, 1992—. Chmn. Roswell Cultural Arts Com.; bd. dirs. Roswell Symphony Orch., 1995—. Mem. Am. Assn. of Mus., Mountain Plains Mus. Assn., N.Mex. Assn. of Mus. Democrat. Avocations: photography, carpentry. Office: Millicent Rogers Museum PO Box A Taos NM 87571-0546

EBIEFUNG, ANIEKAN ASUKWO, mathematics educator and researcher; b. Nto Mbadum, Akwaibom State, Nigeria, Nov. 10, 1958; came to U.S., 1985; s. Asukwo Thomas and Florence Asukwo (Udofa) E.; m. Anne Aniekan Ekon, Jan. 2, 1989; children: Ediobong, Uduak. BS in Math. and Statistics with honors, U. Calabar, Nigeria, 1982; MS in Math., Howard U., 1987; PhD in Math. Scis., Clemson U., 1991. Instr. math. Federal U. of tech., Owerri, Nigeria, 1982-83, U. Cross River State, Uyo, Nigeria, 1983-85, U. D.C. Lorton (Va.) Prison Coll. Program, 1987-88, Howard U., Washington, 1985-88; teaching asst. Clemson U., 1988-91; asst. prof. math. U. Tenn., Chattanooga, 1991-96, U.C. found. assoc. prof., 1996—; lectr. in field; ctr. chmn. Tenn. Math. tchrs. Assn. state-wide math contest, U. Tenn., Chattanooga, 1992—. Contbr. articles to profl. jours.; editor NASM Bull., 1980-81. Grantee Ctr. of Excellence for Computer Applications, 1993, scholar, 1995-96, 98-99; grantee Oak Ridge Assoc. Univs., 1993, UC Found., 1993, Tenn. Higher Edn. Commn., 1994-95, 97-99. Mem. Math. Assn. Am., Am. Math. Soc., Ops. Rsch. Soc. Am., Chattanooga Area Math. Tchrs. Assn., Internat. Linear Algebra Soc. Avocations: writing, tennis, reading. Office: Univ of Tenn 615 Mccallie Ave Chattanooga TN 37403-2504

EBIN, LEONARD NED, radiologist, educator, consultant; b. Moscow, Russia, Oct. 20, 1926; arrived in U.S., 1939; s. Emanuel and Helen (Goldin) E.; m. Eva V. Siegel, Nov. 24, 1953; children: Paul, Jane, Susan, Amy. BA, U. Va., 1946, MD, 1951. Diplomate Am. Bd. Radiology, Am. Bd. Internal Medicine, Am. Bd. Nuclear Medicine, Am. Bd. Quality Assurance. Intern Morissanna, Bronx, N.Y., 1951-52; resident Flower Fifth Ave. Hosp., N.Y.C., 1952-55, fellow, 1955-59; asst. instr. radiology N.Y. Med. Coll., Valhalla, N.Y., 1956-57, asst. clin. instr. in radiology, 1957-60, clin. instr. radiology, 1960-66, asst. prof. radiology, 1966-68, asst. clin. prof. radiology, 1968-81, clin. assoc. prof. radiology, 1981-96; asst. roentgenologist Met. Hosp., N.Y.C., 1960-76, assoc. attending radiologist, 1979-94; asst. roentgenologist Coler Meml. Hosp., Roosevelt Island, N.Y., 1960-76, physician-in-charge divsn. nuclear medicine dept. radiology, 1969-87, assoc. attending radiologist, 1976-81, attending radiologist, 1981-82, supervising roentgenologist, 1982-87; asst. attending radiologist Flower Fifth Ave. Hosp., N.Y.C., 1966-78; cons. malpractice panel Queens County, N.Y., 1985-88; cons. radiologist N.Y. Times, 1990-96. Contbr. articles to profl. jours. Fellow Am. Coll. Gastroenterology, N.Y. Acad. Medicine; mem. Am. Coll. Radiology, Am. Coll. Nuclear Physicians (charter), Am. Acad. Legal and Indsl. Medicine, N.Y. State & County Med. Soc., N.Y. Acad. Gastroenterology, N.Y. Roentgen Ray and Radiol. Soc., Radiol. Soc. N.Am. Avocations: impressionistic paintings, opera, football. Office: Ste 475-N 98 Cutter Mill Rd New York NY 11021*

EBISUZAKI, YUKIKO, chemistry educator; b. Mission City, B.C., Can., July 25, 1930; came to U.S., 1957; d. Masuzo and Shige (Kusumoto) E. BS with honors, U. Western Ont., London, Can., 1956, MS, 1957; PhD, Ind. U., 1962. Postdoctoral U. Pa., Phila., 1962-63; faculty rsch. assoc. Ariz. State U., Tempe, 1963-67; acting asst. prof. UCLA, 1967-75; assoc. prof. N.C. State U., Raleigh, 1975—. Contbr. articles to profl. jours. Ont. Rsch. Found. fellow Ont. Rsch. Coun., 1957-60, Gerry fellow Sigma Delta Epsilon, 1977-78. Mem. AAUW, Am. Chem. Soc., Sigma Xi. Office: NC State Univ Dept Chemistry Clb # 8204 Raleigh NC 27695

EBITZ, DAVID MACKINNON, art historian, museum director; b. Hyannis, Mass., Oct. 5, 1947; s. Robert White Creeley and Ann (MacKinnon) Kucera; m. Mary Ann Stankiewicz, Jan. 1, 1983; children: Rebecca Aemilia, Cecilia Charlotte. BA, Williams Coll., 1969; AM, Harvard U., 1973, PhD, 1979. Teaching fellow, then head teaching fellow dept. fine arts Harvard U., Cambridge, Mass., 1975-78; asst. prof., then assoc. prof. dept. art U. Maine, Orono, 1978-87, interim dir. galleries, curator univ. art collection, 1986-87; head dept. edn. and acad. affairs J. Paul Getty Mus., Santa Monica, Calif., 1987-92; dir. John and Mable Ringling Mus. Art, Sarasota, Fla., 1992—; vis. faculty Bangor (Maine) Theol. Sem., 1981; lectr. in field; presenter workshops. Author exbhn. revs., book revs.; contbr. articles to arts publs., exhbn. catalogues. Heritage Found. fellow, 1968. Mem. Assn. Art Mus. Dirs., Coll. Art Assn., Nat. Art Edn. Assn., Am. Assn. Museums (mus. edn. com.), Medieval Acad. Am., Internat. Ctr. Medieval Art, Phi Beta Kappa. Office: John & Mable Ringling Mus of Art 5401 Bay Shore Rd Sarasota FL 34243-2161

EBITZ, ELIZABETH KELLY, lawyer; b. LaPorte, Ind., June 9, 1950; d. Joseph Monahan and Ann Mary (Barrett) Kelly; m. David MacKinnon Ebitz, Jan. 23, 1971 (div. 1981). AB with honors, Smith Coll., 1972; JD cum laude, Boston U., 1975. Bar: Maine 1979, Mass 1975, U.S. Supreme Ct 1982, U.S. Dist. Ct. Mass. 1976, U.S. Dist. Ct. Maine 1979, U.S. Ct. Appeals (1st cir.) 1976. Law clk. Boston Legal Assistance Project, 1973-75; law clk., assoc. Law Offices of John J. Thornton, Boston, 1974-76; ptnr. Ebitz & Zurn, Northampton, Mass., 1976-79; assoc. Gross, Minsky, Mogul & Singal, Bangor, Maine, 1979-80; pres. Elizabeth Kelly Ebitz, P.A., Bangor, 1980-92; pres. Ebitz & Thornton, P.A., 1993—. Pres. Greater Bangor Rape Crisis Bd., 1983-85; bd. dirs. Greater Bangor Area Shelter, 1985-92, 93—, Maine Women's Lobby, 1986-89, No. Maine Bread for the World, 1987-90; bd. dirs. Am. Heart Assn., Maine, 1989—, chair-elect, 1991-93, chair, 1993-95, past chair, 1995-97; mem. various peace, feminist and hunger orgns., Bangor, 1982—. Named Young Career Woman of Hampshire County, Nat. Bus. and Profl. Women, Northampton, 1979. Mem. ABA, Assn. Trial Lawyers Am., Sigma Xi. Democrat. Roman Catholic. Home: 111 Maple St Bangor ME 04401-4031 Office: 15 Columbia St PO Box 641 Bangor ME 04402-0641

EBNER, KURT EWALD, biochemistry educator; b. New Westminster, B.C., Can., Mar. 30, 1931; s. Sebastian Alois and Martha (Gmundner) E.; m. Dorothy Colleen Reader, May 4, 1957; children: Roger, Michael, Colleen, Paul. B.S.A., U. B.C., 1955, M.S.A., 1957; Ph.D., U. Ill., 1960; postdoctoral, U. Reading, Eng., 1960-61, U. Minn., 1961-62. Diplomate Nat. Bd. Med. Examiners. Mem. faculty Okla. State U., Stillwater, 1962-74; prof. biochemistry Okla. State U., 1969-71, Regents prof., 1971-74; chmn. dept. biochemistry U. Kans. Med. Ctr., Kansas City, 1974-94, prof., 1994-98, prof. emeritus, 1998—. Can. Overseas Postdoctoral fellow, 1960; recipient NIH Career Devel. award, 1969, Borden award Am. Chem. Soc., 1969; Okla. State U. Sigma Xi lectr., 1970. Mem. AAAS, Am. Soc. Biol. Chemistry, Coun. Acad. Socs., Sigma Xi, Phi Kappa Phi, Gamma Sigma Delta. Presbyterian (elder). Home: 7210 W 101st Ter Overland Park KS 66212-2520 Office: U Kans Med Ctr Dept Biochem Kansas City KS 66103-7421

EBSWORTH, WILLIAM ROBERT, investment company executive; m. Anandi Pratap. BA, Johns Hopkins U., 1980; MBA, Wharton Sch., 1984. Chartered fin. analyst. Chief investment officer Fidelity Investments, Hong Kong, 1991-97, officer, various fidelity funds, 1994—, dir. of rsch., 1997—; bd. dirs. Stock Exch. Hong Kong Options Clearing House, H.K. Securities Clearing Co., China Securities Investment Trust, Taipei, Taiwan, Thailand Internat. Fund, London; v.p. Fidelity Advisor Korea Fund, N.Y.C., Emerging Asia Fund, N.Y.C. Mem. Boston Security Analysts Soc., Hong Kong Security Analysts Soc., Internat. Soc. Fin. Analysts Soc., Am. Club Hong Kong, China Club, Penn Club (N.Y.C.). Office: Fidelity Investments 82 Devonshire St Boston MA 02109-3614

EBY, CARL PETER, English educator. PhD, U. Calif., Davis, 1995. Lectr. Mich. State U., East Lansing, 1996-98; asst. prof. English U. S.C., Beaufort, 1998—. Author: Hemingway's Fetishism, 1999. Recipient Robert J. Stoller Found. Essay award for Psychoanalytic Rsch., 1996, John F. Kennedy Libr. Hemingway Rsch. Grant, 1996. E-mail: eby@pilot.msu.edu.

EBY, CECIL DEGROTTE, English language educator, writer; b. Charles Town, W.Va., Aug. 1, 1927; s. Cecil and Ellen (Turner) E.; m. Eleonora Arato; children from previous marriage: Clare Virginia, Lillian Turner. AB, Shepherd Coll., 1950; MA, Northwestern U., 1951; PhD, U. Pa., 1958. Instr., then asst. prof. English High Point Coll., 1955-57; asst. prof., then asso. prof. Madison Coll., 1957-60; mem. faculty Washington and Lee U., 1960-65; prof. U. Mich., 1965—; prof. English, chmn. dept. U. Miss., University, 1975-76; Fulbright prof. Am. lit. U. Salamanca, Spain, 1962-63; Fulbright prof. Am. studies U. Valencia, 1967-68; Fulbright prof. Am. lit. U. Budapest, 1981; prof. U. Szeged, 1988-89. Author: Porte Crayon: The Life of David H. Strother, 1960, The Siege of the Alcazar, 1965, (translations in Italian, German, Finnish, Dutch, Portuguese) Between the Bullet and the Lie: American Volunteers in the Spanish Civil War, 1969 (transl. in Spanish), That Disgraceful Affair: The Black Hawk War, 1973, The Road to Armageddon: The Martial Spirit in English Popular Literature, 1987, The War in Hungary: Civilians and Soldiers in World War II, 1998; editor: The Old South Illustrated, 1959, A Virginia Yankee in the Civil War, 1961. Served with USNR, 1945-46. Rackham rsch. grantee, 1967, 71, 77, 79, 90, 93. Episcopalian.

EBY, FRANK SHILLING, retired research scientist; b. Kansas City, Mo., Apr. 6, 1924; s. Frank Shilling and Irene (Trissler) E.; m. Nancy Rea Vinsonhaler, Sept. 2, 1958; children: Elizabeth, Susan, Carl. BS, U. Ill., 1948, MS, 1949, PhD, 1954. Group leader fusion research Lawrence Livermore (Calif.) Nat. Lab., 1954-58, group leader, 1958-66, div. head, 1967-72, sr. scientist, 1978-93; retired, 1993. Inventor classified mil. weaponry. Served to 1st lt. USAAF, 1942-46, PTO. Recipient Intelligence Community Seal medallion, 1992. Mem. AAAS. Avocations: hiking, camping, gardening, music. Home: 3263 Vineyard Ave # 58 Pleasanton CA 94566-6335

EBY, JOHN W., sociology educator; b. Littz, Pa.; s. Wilmer M and Arlene B. E.; m. Joyce R. Rutt, June 29, 1963; children; Carol L., Scott L. BA in Chemistry, Ea. Mennonite Coll., 1962; MS in Devel. Sociology, Cornell U., 1970, PhD in Devel. Sociology, 1972. Dir. voluntary svc. Ea. Mennonite Bd. Missions, Salunga, Pa., 1962-67; prof. sociology, chair sociology dept. Ea. Mennonite Coll., Harrisonburg, Va., 1970-74; sec. relief & svc. Mennonite Bd. Missions, Elkhart, Ind., 1974-79; country rep. Mennonite Ctrl. Com., Akron, Pa., 1979-82; prof. bus. & sociology, chair bus. dept. Ea. Mennonite

Coll., 1982-89; acad. dean Goshen (Ind.) Coll., 1989-94; prof. sociology, dir. svc.-learning, dir. agape Messiah Coll., Grantham, Pa., 1994—; chair Ctr. Indsl. Tng., Silver Springs, Pa., 1999—. Co-author: Business Through the Eyes of Faith, 1990; editor: Service-Learning: Linking Academics and the Community, 1995. Mem. Am. Sociol. Assn., Am. Assn. Higher Edn., Phi Kappa Phi. Office: Messiah Coll Coll Ave Grantham PA 17027

EBY, MARTIN KELLER, JR., construction company executive; b. Wichita Falls, Tex., Apr. 19, 1934; s. Martin and A. Pauline (Kimbell) E.; m. Melodee Stanley, Aug. 20, 1955; children: Stanley, Suzanna, David. B.S. in Civil Engring, Kans. State U., 1956. Registered profl. engr., Kan. With Martin K. Eby Constrn. Co., Inc., Wichita, Kan., 1956—; engr., project mgr., v.p. Martin K. Eby Constrn. Co., Inc., 1956-67, pres., 1967-92, chmn., 1979—; bd. dirs. Intrust Bank in Wichita, Intrust Fin. Corp., SBC Comms. Inc.; mem. engring. adv. coun. Kans. State U., Manhattan, 1970—. Bd. dirs. Kans. Pub. Policy Inst., chmn.; mem. Kans. State U. Coll. of Engring. Hall of Fame, 1989—; chmn. Constrn. Industry Polit. Action Com. of Kans., Topeka, 1978. Mem. ASCE, NSPE, Kans. Engring. Soc., Wichita Profl. Engring. Soc., Chief Execs. Orgn., Beavers (bd. dirs., pres. 1996-97), Moles (hon.). Congregationalist. Home: 624 N Longford Ln Wichita KS 67206-1818 Office: Martin Eby Constrn Co Inc PO Box 1679 610 N Main St Wichita KS 67203-3601

EBY, MICHAEL JOHN, marketing research and technology consultant; b. South Bend, Ind., Aug. 3, 1949; s. Robert T. and Eileen Patricia (Holmes) E.; m. Judith Alyson Gaskell, May 17, 1980; children: Elizabeth, Katherine. Student, Harvey Mudd Coll., 1969-70; BS in Biochemistry with high honors, U. Md., 1972, MS in Chemistry, 1977; postgrad., IMEDE, Lausanne, Switzerland, 1984. Product mgr. LKB Instruments Inc., Rockville, Md., 1976-79; mktg. mgr. LKB-Produkter AB, Bromma, Sweden, 1979-87; strategic planning mgr. Pharmacia LKB Biotech. AB, Bromma, 1987-88; dir. mktg. Am. Bionetics, Hayward, Calif., 1988-89; pres. PhorTech Internat., San Carlos, Calif., 1989—. Author: The Electrophoresis Explosion, 1988, Electrophoresis in the Nineties, 1990, DNA Amplification, 1993, Blotting and Hybridization, 1993, Capillary Electrophoresis, 1993, Global Laboratory Product Usage, 1994, Densitometers and Image Analysis, 1995, Microplate Equipment, 1995, Synthetic Oligonucleotides, 1995, Electrophoretic Gel Media, 1995, Visualization Reagents, 1995, U.S. Laboratory Product Usage, 1996, Cell Biology Reagent Systems, 1996, Centrifugation, 1996, Molecular Biology Reagent Systems, 1997, DNA Sequencing, 1997, DNA Diagnostics, 1997, DNA Amplification in Europe, 1998, Recombinant Protein Expression Systems, 1998, Worldwide Directory of Life Science Distributors, 1998, DNA Sequencing in Europe, 1998, Cytokines and Growth Factors, 1998, Molecular Biology Reagent Systems in the Far East, 1998, HPLC in the Life Sciences, 1998, Cytokines and Growth Factors, 1998, Cell and Tissue Culture, 1998, Monoclonal Antibodies, 1999; contbr. articles to profl. jours. Mem. AAAS, European Soc. Opinion and Mktg. Rsch., Am. Chem. Soc., Am. Soc. Cell Biology, The Electrophoresis Soc., Spirit of LKB Internat. Assn., U. Md. Alumni Assn., Am. Mensa Ltd., Calif. Separation Sci. Soc. Episcopalian. Avocations: astronomy, cheesemaking, photography, travel. Office: PhorTech Internat 238 Crestview Dr San Carlos CA 94070-1503

ECCLES, MATTHEW ALAN, golf course and landscape architect; b. Ft. Dodge, Iowa, Apr. 19, 1956; s. Guy Eldon Jr. and Mary Ellen (Baldwin) E.; m. Debra Kay Sorenson, Mar. 19, 1983; children: Stephanie Ann, Jason Alan. BS in Landscape Architecture, Iowa State U., 1978. Registered landscape architect, Kans., Minn. From project mgr. to dir. golf course design THK Assocs., Inc., Greenwood Village, Colo., 1980-94; pres. Eccles Design Inc., Englewood, Colo., 1994—. Mem. Am. Soc. Landscape Architects, U.S. Golf Assn., Golf Course Supts. Assn. Am., Nat. Golf Found., Nat. Ski Patrol, Tau Sigma Delta. Avocations: golf, skiing, fishing, photography. Home: 8120 S Monaco Cir Englewood CO 80112-3022 Office: Eccles Design Inc 8120 S Monaco Cir Englewood CO 80112-3022

ECCLES, SPENCER FOX, banker; b. Ogden, Utah, Aug. 24, 1934; s. Spencer Stoddard and Hope (Fox) E.; m. Cleone Emily Peterson, July 21, 1958; children: Clista Hope, Lisa Ellen, Katherine Ann, Spencer Peterson. B.S., U. Utah, 1956; M.A., Columbia U., 1959; degree in Bus. (hon.), So. Utah State Coll., 1982; LLB (hon.), Westminster Coll., Salt Lake City, 1986. Trainee First Nat. City Bank, N.Y.C., 1959-60; with First Security Bank of Utah, Salt Lake City, 1960-61, First Security Bank of Idaho, Boise, 1961-70; exec. v.p. First Security Corp. Salt Lake City, 1970-75, pres., 1975-86, chief operating officer, 1980-82, chmn. bd. dirs., chief exec. officer, 1982—; dir. Union Pacific Corp., Anderson Lumber Co., Zions Corp., Merc. Instn.; mem. adv. council U. Utah Bus. Coll. Served to 1st lt. U.S. Army. Recipient Pres.'s Circle award Presdl. Commn., 1984, Minuteman award Utah N.G., 1988; Named Disting. Alumni U. Utah, 1988. Mem. Am. Bankers Assn., Bankers Roundtable, Salt Lake Country Club, Alta Club. Office: 1st Security Corp PO Box 30006 79 S Main 2d Fl Salt Lake City UT 84130

ECHOHAWK, JOHN ERNEST, lawyer; b. Albuquerque, Aug. 11, 1945; s. Ernest V. and Emma Jane (Conrad) E.; m. Kathryn Suzanne Martin, Oct. 23, 1965; children: Christopher, Sarah. BA, U. N.M., 1967, JD, 1970. Bar: Colo. 1972, U.S. Dist. Ct. Colo. 1972, U.S. Appeals (8th cir.) 1976, U.S. Ct. Appeals (9th cir.) 1980. Research assoc. Calif. Indian Legal Services, Escondido, 1970, Native Am. Rights Fund, Berkeley Calif. and Boulder, Colo., 1970-72; dep. dir. Native Am. Rights Fund, Boulder, 1972-73, 1975-77, exec. dir., 1973-75, 1977—; mem. task force Am. Indian Policy Rev. Commn., U.S. Senate, Washington, 1976-77; bd. dirs. Am. Indian Lawyer Tng. Program, Oakland, Calif., 1975—; bd. dirs. Assn. Am. Indian Affairs, 1980—, Nat. Com. Responsive Philanthropy, Washington, 1981—; mem. Clinton Adminstrn. Transition Team for Interior Dept., 1992-93. Presdl. appointee Western Water Policy Rev. Adv. Commn., 1995-97; Ind. Sector, Washington, 1986-92; mem. Natural Resources Def. Coun., N.Y.C., 1988—; bd. dirs. Nat. Ctr. Enterprise Devel., 1988—, Keystone Ctr., 1993—, Environ. and Energy Study Inst., 1994—. Recipient Disting. Service award Ams. For Indian Opportunity, 1982, Pres. Indian Service award Nat. Congress Am. Indians, 1984, Annual Indian Achievement award Indian Council Fire, 1987; named one of most influential attys. Nat. Law Jour., 1988, 91, 94. Mem. Native Am. Bar Assn., Colo. Indian Bar Assn. Democrat. Avocations: fishing, skiing. Home: 4660 Quail Creek Ln Boulder CO 80301-3871 Office: Native Am Rights Fund 1506 Broadway St Boulder CO 80302-6217*

ECHOLS, IVOR TATUM, retired educator, assistant dean; b. Oklahoma City, Dec. 28, 1919; d. Israel E. and Katie (Bingley) Tatum;. AB, U. Kans., 1942; postgrad., U. Nebr., 1945-46; MS in Social Work, Columbia U., 1952; postgrad., U. So. Calif., 1961-62, DSW, 1968. Tchr. social studies h.s. Holdenville, Okla., 1942-43, Geary, Okla., 1943-45; caseworker ARC, Chgo., 1946-47; resident group worker Dosoris House for Teen-Age Girls Cmty. Svcs. Soc., N.Y.C., 1950-51; supr. group work Walnut Grove Ctr. Neighborhood Clubs, Oklahoma City, 1948-51; program dir. Camp Lookout YWCA, Denver, 1951; dir. program svcs. Presbyn. Neighborhood Svcs., Detroit, summer 1960; supr. group work Merrill-Palmer Inst., Detroit, 1951-70; asst. dir. Merrill-Palmer Camp, Dryden, Mich., 1951-59; prof. Sch. Social Work U. Conn., West Hartford, 1970-89, also asst. dean, ret., 1989; del. Inter-Univ. Consortium of Social Devel., Nairobi, Kenya, 1974, Hong Kong, 1980; mem. Conn. adv. com. U.S. Commn. Civil Rights. Mem. ad hoc com. Citizens Concerned with Equal Ednl. Opportunity, Detroit, 1964—; cons. to NFA Conf. Family Camping Washington, 1959, ednl. film Scott Paper Co., Phila., 1963, 64; summer study skills project Presbyn. Ch. Bd. Nat. Missions, Knoxville, Tenn., 1965—; nat. sec. United Neighborhood Ctrs. Am., N.Y.C.; pres. Protestant Cmty. Svcs., Detroit, 1969-70; trustee Conn. Energy Found., 1987-92; commr. Conn. Hist. Commn., 1986-96, ret., 1996. ARC scholar; fellow Nat. Urban League, Porter R. Lee fellow, fellow NIMH; recipient Educator Human Rights award UN Assn., 1987, Sojourner Truth award Detroit chpt. Nat. Assn. Negro Bus. and Profl. Women, 1969, UN Assn. award for Edn. and Women's Rights, 1987, Maria R. Stewart Women's Rights award Conn. Women's Ednl. and Legal Found., 1991, Outstanding Women award U. Conn., 1991, Achievement award Assn. Advancement Soc. Groupwork, 1994, 1st Truth award Capitol C.C. Hartford, 1999; named Conn. Social Worker of Year NASW, 1979; Ivor J. Echols Endowment Fund named in her honor U. Conn. Found., 1990. Mem. Nat. Assn. Colored Women's Clubs (participant White House conf. on Children and Youth 1960), A.M.E. Ministers Wives, Acad. Certified Social Workers (hon.), Nat. Assn. Black Social Workers (honored as founding mem. 1998), Nat. Trust for Hist. Preservation, Delta Sigma Theta. Mem. A.M.E. Ch. Home: 51 Chestnut Dr Windsor CT 06095-1113 Office: U Conn 1798 Asylum Ave Ste 1 West Hartford CT 06117-2699

ECHOLS, JAMES, agricultural products supplier. Pres. Hohenberg Bros. Co., Cordova, 1990—. Office: Hohenberg Bros Co 7101 Goodlett Farms Pkwy Cordova TN 38018-4909*

ECHOLS, M(ARY) EVELYN, travel consultant; b. LaSalle, Ill., Apr. 5, 1915; d. Francis Ira and Mary Irene (Coleman) Bassett; m. David H. Echols, Aug. 31, 1951 (dec.); children: Susan Echols O'Donnell, William. Grad. high. sch., Chgo. Founder Internat. Travel Tng. Courses, Inc., Chgo., 1962—; pres. Evelyn Echols Cons. Ltd., 1998; mem. Pres.'s Conf. on Tourism; mem. Gov. Edgar's Adv. Tourism Bd.; cons. to Paul G. Vallas, supt. Chgo. Pub. Schs. Bd. dirs. Better Bus. Bur., Chgo. Conv. and Tourism Bur.; past pres. Pres. Reagan's Adv. Com. for Women's Bus. Ownership; v.p. United Cerebral Palsy Assn. Named Entrepreneur of Yr. Women Bus. Owners N.Y., 1985, Bus. Woman of Yr. Nat. Assn. Women Bus. Owners, 1985, Crain's Chgo. Bus., 1993; named to Chgo.'s Hall of Fame, 1992. Mem. Chgo. Execs. Club, Acad. TV Arts and Scis., Soc. Am. Travel Agts., Chgo. Network, English Speaking Union, Com. of 200. Home: 200 E Delaware Pl Apt 26E Chicago IL 60611-7702 Office: Echols Internat Travel & Hotel Schs Inc 28 E Jackson Blvd Ste 1800 Chicago IL 60604-2214

ECHOLS, ROBERT L., federal judge; b. 1941. BA, Rhodes Coll., 1962; JD, U. Tenn., 1964. Law clk. to Hon. Marion S. Boyd U.S. Dist. Ct. (we. dist.) Tenn., Nashville, 1965-66; legis. asst. Congressman Dan Kuykendall, 1967-69; ptnr. Baily, Ewing, Dale & Conner, Nashville, 1969-72, Dearborn & Ewing, Nashville, 1972-92; fed. judge U.S. Dist. Ct. (mid. dist.) Tenn., Nashville, 1992—, chief judge, 1998—. With U.S. Army, 1966; col. Tenn. Army N.G., 1969—. Mem. ABA, Am. Bar Found., Am. Coll. Mortgage Attys., Fed. Judges Assn., Tenn. State-Fed. Jud. Coun., Am. Judicature Soc., Tenn. Bar Found., Tenn. Bar Assn., Nashville Bar Assn., Nashville Bar Found., Harry Phillips Am. Inn of Ct., Jud. Br. Com. U.S. Jud. Conf. Office: US Dist Ct 801 Broadway Ste 824 Nashville TN 37203-3868

ECK, DAVID WILSON, minister; b. Pitts., Apr. 7, 1962; s. Herbert Walter Eck and Linda Joan (Pitrusu) Butera. BS in Chemistry, U. Pitts., 1984; MDiv, Luth. Theol. Sem., Gettysburg, Pa., 1988. Ordained to ministry Evang. Luth. Ch. in Am., 1988. Assoc. pastor Mt. Zion Luth. Ch., Conover, N.C., 1988-93; pastor Abiding Savior Luth. Ch., Asheville, N.C., 1993—; mem. young adult com. N.C. Synod, Salisbury, 1989-90, mem. worship and mus. com. N.c. Synod, 1993-95, mem. AIDS Taskforce N.C. Synod, 1992, N.C. Synod Coun., 1995-98; bd. dirs. Coop Christian Ministry, Hickory, N.C., 1989; owner Twelvestring Pub., 1995—; worship and evangelism resource specialist ELCA, 1998—. Mem. editl. adv. bd. Soli Deo Gloria, 1990-97, also contbr. articles, poetry and music; singer, songwriter, music pub. Recipient cert. of achievement Billboard Songwriting Contest, 1990. Democrat. Home: 110 Coleman Ave Asheville NC 28801-1304 Office: Abiding Savior Luth Ch 801 Charlotte Hwy Fairview NC 28730-9782 *Creativity is the lifeblood of the human race. If we fail to dream, to generate new ideas, to look toward the future with great hope and enthusiasm, we will surely perish from the face of the earth.*

ECK, GEORGE GREGORY, lawyer; b. Evanston, Ill., Sept. 3, 1950; s. George F. and Dorothy E. (Frake) E.; m. Margaret K. Gorman, Sept. 1, 1973; children: Jessica Elizabeth, Michele Margaret. BS, No. Ill. U., 1972; JD cum laude, U. Minn., 1977. Bar: Minn. 1977, U.S. Dist. Ct. Minn. 1977, U.S. Ct. Appeals (8th cir.) 1977. Assoc. Dorsey & Whitney, Mpls., 1977-83, ptnr., 1983—. Mem. editorial bd. U. Minn. Law Rev., 1977. With USN, 1972-74. Home: 6413 Mendelssohn Ln Hopkins MN 55343-8424 Office: Dorsey & Whitney 220 S 6th St Ste 2200 Minneapolis MN 55402-1498*

ECK, KENNETH FRANK, pharmacist; b. Alma, Kans., Feb. 4, 1917; s. Clarence Joseph and Rosa Barbara (Noller) E.; m. Ouida Susie Landon, July 2, 1938 (dec. Sept. 1986); children: Alan Grantland, Mark Warren, Dana Landon; m. Lorraine B. Wooster Rubottom, Apr. 14, 1989. BS in Pharmacy summa cum laude, Southwestern Okla. State U., 1950. Ptnr., mgr. Taylor Drug Store, Healdton, Okla., 1950-51, Taylor-Eck Drug Store, Healdton, 1951-59, Johnson-Eck Drug Store, Healdton, 1959-72; pres. Eck Drug Co., Inc., Healdton, 1972-87, cons., relief pharmacist, 1987—; cons., relief pharmacist Eck Drug and Gift, Waurika, Okla., 1987—; affiliate instr. pharmacy Southwestern Okla. State U., Weatherford, 1970-87, mem. dean's adv. com. Sch. of Pharmacy, early 1980's; bd. dirs. med. adv. bd. Dept. Human Svcs. Okla., Oklahoma City, 1990-91. Columnist Healdton Herald, 1996—. Rep. Silver Haired legis. (senator, 1986-88, elected Floor leader), 1982-86, past mem. governing bd. Healdton Mcpl. Hosp.; mem. Okla. Profl. Responsiblity Tribunal of Okla. Bar Assn., 1983-88, vice chief master, 1988; past mem. bd. dirs. Carter County chpt. ARC, Ardmore, Okla.; bd. dirs. Healdton Oil Mus., 1993—, treas., 1997-98; pres. bd. dirs. Okla. Pharmacy Heritage Found., 1994-95; mem. fin. com. Healdton br. Chickasaw Libr., 1993; bd. dirs. Healdton Econ. Devel., 1993-95; deacon Ch. of Christ, 1945—. With USN, 1942-45, PTO. Recipient Achievement award Merck Sharp & Dohme, 1991, Bowl of Hygeia, 1985, outstanding svc. award Okla. Profl. Responsibility Tribunal of Okla. State Bar Assn., citation State of Okla. Ho. of Reps., 1996, 97; named to Hall of Fame, Okla. Pharmacy Heritage Found., 1996; named Outstanding Older Oklahoman, Soda Dist., 1997. Mem. VFW (post comdr. Healdton 1974-78), Okla. Pharm. Assn. (pres. 1990-91, plaque 1991) Healdton C. of C. (bd. dirs. 1975—, pres. 1984-85), So. Okla. Devel. Assn. (coun. area agy. on aging adv. bd. 1987—, 1st v.p. 1994-95, pres. 1995-96), Nat. Assn. Retail Druggists (profl. affairs com. 1990-91), Am. Legion (post comdr. Healdton 1985—), Lions (eye bank bd. 1993-95, coord. campaign first sight 1993-94, pres. Healdton 1994-95), Silvered Haired legis. Alumni (v.p., 1998). Democrat. Avocations: photography, travel, fishing, boating, reading. Home: 1033 E Texas St Healdton OK 73438-3017

ECK, ROBERT EDWIN, physicist; b. Ames, Iowa, Nov. 28, 1938; s. John Clifford and Helen (Behrendt) E.; m. Carolyn Jennie Vodicka, May 11, 1974; children: David Michael, Elizabeth Claire. BA in Physics, Rutgers U., 1960; MS in Physics, U. Pa., 1962, PhD in Physics, 1966; MA in Econs., U. Calif., Santa Barbara, 1973. Sr. rsch. scientist Ford Motor Co., Newport Beach, Calif., 1966-69; project engr. Santa Barbara Rsch. Ctr., Goleta, Calif., 1969-73, asst. mgr. infrared components, 1974-81, mgr. major program, 1982-84, dir. tech., 1985-88, dir./mgr. engring., 1989-95; new bus. devel. mgr. R.G. Hansen & Assocs., Santa Barbara, Calif., 1995-96; program mgr. Optoelectronics-Textron, Petaluma, 1996—. Bd. dirs. Goleta Edn. Found. Mem. Goleta Noontime Rotary Club (pres. 1989-90). Achievements include patents on superconductors, infrared detector testing and magnetoresistor sensors. Office: Optoelectronics-Textron 1309 Dynamic St Petaluma CA 94954-1491

ECKARDT, RICHARD WILLIAM, lawyer; b. St. Charles, Ill., Mar. 8, 1938; s. Frederick William and Mira Helen Louise (Vance) E. BA, Ohio State U., 1959; JD, U. So. Calif., 1966. Bar: Calif. 1967, U.S. Dist. Ct. (no. and ctrl. dists.) Calif. 1967, U.S. Supreme Ct. 1972. Mem. legal staff Pacific Lighting Corp., L.A., 1968-70; assoc. Mitchell and Mitchell, L.A., 1970-71, Sprague and Clements, L.A., 1971-73; pvt. practice L.A., 1973-81, 82-87, 88—; ptnr. Katsky, Ker, Eckardt & Hunt, L.A., 1981-82, Eckardt & Ruonala, L.A., 1987-88; judge pro tem Los Angeles Mcpl. Ct., 1978-85. Mem. ABA, Fed. Bar Assn., L.A. Lawyers for Human Rights (sec. 1979-85, bd. of trustees 1979-85), L.A. County Bar Assn. (legal svcs. for the poor com. 1985-89, del. to state bar conf. 1983—, exec. com. of delegation 1986-89, jud. evaluation com. 1989—, bus. and corp. law sect., real property, taxation, probate and trust law sects., law office mgmt.), Assn. Bus. Trial Lawyers, Calif. Bar Assn., Am. Judicature Soc., L.A. World Affairs Coun., Legion Lex., Univ. Club (L.A.), Phi Alpha Delta. Home: 1155 Nithsdale Rd Pasadena CA 91105-1434 Office: 333 S Grand Ave Los Angeles CA 90071-1504*

ECKART, DENNIS EDWARD, lawyer, former congressman; b. Cleve., Apr. 6, 1950; s. Edward Joseph and Mary Eckart; m. Sandra Jean Pestotnik; 1 son, Edward John. B.S., Xavier U., 1971; LL.B., Cleveland John Marshall Law Sch., 1974. Mem. Ohio Ho. of Reps., 1975-80; chmn. Cuyahoga County del., 1979-80; mem. 97th Congress 22d Ohio dist. and 98th-102nd Congress 11th Ohio dist., 1981-92; ptnr. Winston & Strawn, Washington, 1993-94, Arter & Hadden, Washington, 1994—. Office: Arter & Hadden 1801 K St NW Washington DC 20006-1301 also: 1100 Huntington Bldg 925 Euclid Ave Cleveland OH 44115-1408

ECKAUS, RICHARD SAMUEL, economist, educator; b. Kansas City, Mo., Apr. 30, 1926; s. Julius and Bessie (Finklestein) E.; m. Patricia L. Meaney; 1 child, Susan L. B.S., Iowa State Coll., 1946; M.A., Washington U., St. Louis, 1948; Ph.D., MIT, 1954. Instr., asst. prof., assoc. prof. Brandeis U., 1951-62; rsch. assoc. Ctr. Internat. Studies MIT, Cambridge, 1954-61, from assoc. prof. to prof., 1962—, Ford internat. prof., 1977-96, head dept. econs., 1987-90, prof., 1996—; mem. Bd. Econ. Advisors to Gov. Mass., 1963-65; cons. ADB, OECD, AID, World Bank, govts. of Jamaica, Portugal, Egypt, Sri Lanka, Chile, China, Mexico. Author: (with K. Parikh) Planning for Growth, 1968; editor: (with J. Bhagwati) Foreign Aid, 1970, Development and Planning, 1973, Basic Economics, 1972, Estimating the Returns to Education, 1973, Appropriate Technologies for Developing Countries, 1976; contbr. articles to profl. jours. Served with USNR, 1944-46. Guggenheim and Social Sci. Research Council fellow, 1962; Ford Found. Faculty fellow, 1965; vis.scholar Roxbury C.C., 1996—. Mem. Am. Econ. Assn. Home: 131 Sewall Ave Apt 72 Brookline MA 02446-5336 Office: MIT Dept Econs 50 Memorial Dr Cambridge MA 02142-1347

ECKBERG, E. DANIEL, secondary education educator; b. Mpls., June 13, 1936; s. E.B.L. and Alvina H. (Sunde) E.; m. Mary Alice Banke, Dec. 27, 1962 (dec. Oct. 1982); children: David D. (dec.), Paul A. BA, St. Olaf Coll., 1958; BS, U. Minn., 1962, PhD, 1986. cert. tchr. econs., history, social studies, curriculum coord. K-12. Recording engr. WCAL-Radio, Northfield, Minn., 1954-58; recording engr., film editor TALC Divsn. TV, Radio and Film, St. Paul, Minn., 1958-62; tchr. Hopkins (Minn.) H.S., 1962-97, chmn. social studies dept., 1967-68; instr. Coll. Edn. U. Minn., Mpls., 1964-66; asst. dir. Hopkins (Minn.) Modular Curriculum Project, 1968-70; project dir. Demonstration Evaluation Ctr., Hopkins, 1970-73; coord. instr. svcs. Hopkins H.S., 1970-97; coord. dist. TV Hopkins Sch. Dist., 1982-97; ednl. cons., 1997—; mem. social studies adv. com. Minn. State Bd. Edn., St. Paul, 1966-68; mem. European history and world cultures com. Coll. Entrance Exam. Bd., Princeton, N.J., 1970-81; mem. evaluation teams Nat. Coun. for Accreditation of Tchr. Edn., Va., Colo., Wis., 1974-82; mem. program goals for media arts participation Minn. Sch. and Resource Ctr. of the Arts, 1987; curriculum writer various orgns. Producer: (TV program) All the Difference: Youth Svc. in Minn., 1988, A Gift of Yourself, 1990. Chmn. tng. com. viking coun. Boy Scouts of Am., Mpls., 1960-62, scoutmaster, 1962-74. Recipient Nat. Physics Hon. award Sigma Pi Sigma St. Olaf Coll., 1957, Outstanding Sr. Man award Coll. Edn. U. Minn., 1962, Program of Excellence award Commr. Edn. State of Minn., 1985, Exec. Dept. Commendation award Gov. State of Minn., 1988, 91. Mem. Nat. Coun. Social Studies (nom. com., curriculum com.), Minn. Fedn. Local Cable Programmers, Alliance for Cmty. Media, Phi Kappa Phi Nat. Grad. Student Honor Soc., Phi Delta Kappa. Office: 5211 Kellogg Ave Minneapolis MN 55424-1304

ECKBO, GARRETT, landscape architect, urban designer; b. Cooperstown, N.Y., Nov. 28, 1910; s. Axel and Theodora (Munn) E.; m. Arline Williams, Sept. 17, 1937; children: Marilyn Kweskin, Alison Peper. B.S., U. Calif., Berkeley, 1935; M. Landscape Architecture, Harvard U., 1938; DFA honoris causa, U. N. Mex., 1992. Landscape architect Armstrong Nurseries, Ontario, Calif., 1935-36, Farm Security Adminstrn., U.S. Dept. Agr., San Francisco, 1939-42; pvt. practice landscape architecture San Francisco Bay Area, 1942-46, 65-97, L.A., 1946-65; vis. lectr. landscape architecture U. So. Calif., 1948-56; prof. landscape architecture U. Calif., Berkeley, 1965-78; chmn. dept. landscape architecture U. Calif., 1965-69; ret., 1998. Author: Landscape for Living, 1950, The Art of Home Landscaping, 1956, Urban Landscape Design, 1965, The Landscape We See, 1969, Home Landscape, 1978, Public Landscape, 1978, People in a Landscape, 1998; spl. issue Philosophy of Landscape, Process: Architecture 90 Tokyo Japan, GE MOdern Landscapes for Living, 1997. Recipient numerous awards including; Calif. Gov.'s award for Union Bank Sq. Los Angeles, 1966; AIA citation for excellence in community architecture for Fresno (Calif.) Mall, 1965; Am. Soc. Landscape Architects medal, 1975; merit award for Shelby Farms, Memphis, 1976; spl. award for U. N.Mex., 1978; honor award for Tucson Community Center, 1978; certificate of achievement in publ. and writing Harvard U. Dept. Landscape Architecture, 1976. Fellow Am. Soc. Landscape Architects (Classic award 1997); mem. Internat. Fedn. Landscape Architects, World Soc. for Ekistics. Home and Office: 110 41st St Oakland CA 94611-5250 *My fundamental focus has been on the qualitative nature of relations between people and environment; between construction and open space; between architecture and nature; and between development and conservation. The environmental response of the American people during the last twenty years has exceeded our profession's wildest dreams.*

ECKDAHL, DONALD EDWARD, manufacturing company executive; b. Los Angeles, Apr. 29, 1924; s. Edward Bernhard and Esther Amelia (Nystrom) E.; m. Barbara D. Crease, May 1, 1981; children by previous marriage: Karin, Robert. B.S.E.E., U. So. Calif., 1944, M.S.E.E., 1949. Project engr. Northrop Aircraft Corp., Hawthorne, Calif., 1946-50; founder, v.p. ops. Computer Research Corp., Hawthorne, 1950-53; v.p., gen. mgr. data processing div. NCR Corp., Hawthorne, 1953-70; sr. v.p. engring. and mfg. group NCR Corp., Dayton, Ohio, 1970-81, ret., 1981; sr. v.p. McCray, Shriver, Eckdahl and Assocs., Inc., Los Angeles, 1982-84; pres., chief exec. officer, chmn. bd. Multiflow Computer Inc., Branford, Conn., 1984-90; ptnr. ESA, Madison, Conn., 1990—. Served with USNR, 1943-46. Mem. IEEE, Assn. Computing Machinery. Democrat. Lutheran. Address: 871 E Desert Glen Dr Tucson AZ 85737-8816

ECKEL, GRASON JOHN-ALLEN, lawyer; b. Cambridge, Md., Feb. 2, 1956; s. Allen Wilbert and Marie Kuhn Eckel. BA in Polit. Sci., Pa. State U., 1977; JD, Antioch U., 1981. Bar: Md. 1997, U.S. Dist. Ct. Md. 1997, D.C. 1998. U.S. senate intern criminal law subcom. Sen. Charles Mathias Jr., Washington, 1980; law clk. Cir. Ct. for Balt., 1984-86; legis. asst. Md. Senate, Annapolis, 1989; legal asst. Office of Pub. Defender, Balt., 1990-93; campaign mgr. Pat Smith for Atty. Gen., Balt., 1993-94; victim-witness asst. State's Atty.'s Office, Dorchester County, Md., 1994-95; pres. Eckel Polit. and Legal Assocs., Cambridge, Md., 1994—; broadcaster Sta. WCEM-FM, Cambridge, 1997—. Eastern shore coord. Amnesty Internat., Cambridge, 1997—; bd. dirs. Dorchester County Commn. on Aging, Cambridge, 1997-99; mem. Dem. state cen. com. for Balt., Md. Dem. Party, 1990-94. Mem. D.C. Bar, Md. Bar. Avocation: Pennsylvania State football. E-mail: grasoneckel@webtv.net. Home: 213 Sandy Hill Rd Cambridge MD 21613-1331 Office: Eckel Polit and Legal Assocs 213 Sandy Hill Rd Cambridge MD 21613-1332

ECKEL, JAMES ROBERT, JR., financial planner; b. Morley, Tenn., Nov. 3, 1927; s. James Robert and Jane Scott (Seymour) E. BS magna cum laude, U. Tenn., 1953, MS, 1957; JD, U. West L.A., 1974. CFP; enrolled agt.; registered patent agt. Instr. elec. engring. U. Tenn., 1953-57, U. Wis., 1957-62; sr. engr. Northrop Corp., L.A., 1962-66; staff engr. TRW Systems, L.A., 1966-69; sr. project engr. Hughes Aircraft Co., Culver City, Calif., 1969-89; fin. planner Culver City, 1989—; real estate broker, Calif. With USN, 1946-49. Mem. IEEE, Am. Inst. Aeros. and Astronautics, Am. Soc. for Engring. Edn., Sigma Xi, Kappa Sigma, Omicron Delta Kappa, Phi Kappa Phi, Tau Beta Pi, Eta Kappa Nu, Phi Eta Sigma. Episcopalian. Home and Office: 5104 Copperfield Ln Culver City CA 90230-7501

ECKEL, THOMAS WARNE, secondary education educator, musician; b. Phillipsburg, N.J., Nov. 5, 1962; s. Henry W. Jr. and Marie L. (Curry) E.; m. Nicole A. Frumerie, May 28, 1988 (div. Jan. 1991). Cert., Tech. Career Inst., N.Y.C., 1985; MusB, Berklee Coll. Music, 1991; MA, NYU, 1996. Cert. guidance counselor, N.Y., N.J., Pa., N.Y.C.; cert. music educator Mass., N.Y., Pa., N.J., N.Y.C. Electrician Renaissance Elec., Stewartsville, N.J., 1986-91; tchr. music Morris H.S., Bronx, N.Y., 1992-94; psychotherapist Cath. Charities, Phillipsburg, 1995-97; tchr. music Frederick Douglass Acad., N.Y.C., 1997—; pres. Eckelworks Pub./BMI, N.Y.C., 1990—, Eckelworks Inc., N.Y.C., 1996—. Pianist, singer, songwriter: Thomas Eckel, 1994; artist: (music videos) Alone, 1995, When Will We See, (original music CDs) Thomas Eckel, The Story; composer over 70 popular/rock songs, 1989-96. Mem. Am. Fedn. Musicians, United Fedn. Tchrs. Avocations: hiking, swimming, camping, performing arts, in-line skating. Home: 1825 Riverside Dr Apt 4D New York NY 10034-5360

ECKELMAN, RICHARD JOEL, engineering specialist; b. Bklyn., Mar. 25, 1951; s. Leon and Muriel (Brietbart) E.; m. Janet Louise Fenton, Mar. 21, 1978; children: Christie, Melanie, Erin Leigh. Student, Ariz. State U., 1988—. Sr. engr., group leader nondestructive testing engring. Fluor Corp., Irvine, Calif., 1979-83; sr. engr. nondestructive testing McDonnell Douglas Helicopter Co., Mesa, Ariz., 1983-91; engring. specialist Convair div. Gen. Dynamics, San Diego, 1991-94; sr. tech. specialist McDonnell Douglas Techs., Inc., San Diego, 1994-96; scientist, engr. The Boeing Co., Mesa, Ariz., 1996—. Mem. Am. Soc. Nondestructive Testing (nat. aerospace com. 1987—, sec. Ariz. chpt. 1987-88, treas. 1988—, sect. chmn. 1989—, sect. bd. dirs. 1990-91), Am. Soc. Quality Control, Soc. Mfg. Engrs., Lindbergh Yacht Club. Avocations: racquetball, sailing. Home: 11820 N 111th Pl Scottsdale AZ 85259-3070

ECKENHOFF, EDWARD ALVIN, health care administrator; b. Durham, N.C., Mar. 4, 1943; s. James Edward and Bonnie Lee E.; m. Judi G. Vicich, May 27, 1978. BA, Transylvania U., 1966; MA, U. Ky., 1968; MHA, Washington U., 1974. V.p., adminstr. Rehab. Inst. Chgo., 1976-82; pres., chief exec. officer Nat. Rehab. Hosp., Washington, 1982—; asst. prof. dept. community and family practice Med. Sch., Georgetown U., Washington, 1983-94; v.p. Medlantic Healthcare Group, 1987—; pres. Nat. Rehab. Services Corp., 1987-92; chmn. bd. NASCOTT, IBIS; instr. Med. Sch., Northwestern U., preceptor Grad. Sch. Bus.; mem. Ill. Commn. on Health Assistance Programs; mem. Ill. adv. com., chmn. exec. com. Internat. Yr. of Disabled; surveyor Commn. on Accreditation of Rehab. Facilities, bd. dirs., 1980-82; bd. dirs. Nat. Assn. Rehab. Facilities, 1982-83; mem. com. on accreditation and edn. Am. Phys. Therapy Assn.; mem. Healthcare Rsch. Devel. Inst.; bd. dirs. Am. Med. Rehab. Provider Assn. Contbr. articles to profl. jours. Bd. dirs. Am. Occupl. Therapy Found., Easter Seal Soc., Boy Scouts Am., Chgo. Area Coun., Nat. Area, 1987-87, Operation ABLE Chgo., Access Living of Met. Chgo., Am. Chamber Symphony, Chgo. Named Washingtonian of the Yr., Washingtonian Mag., 1989; recipient Citation for Disting. Svc., AMA, 1990. Fellow Inst. Medicine Chgo., Am. Coll. Hosp. Execs.; mem. Am. Hosp. Assn. (chmn. governing coun. for rehab. hosps. 1985, trustee 1991-93, chmn. policy com. 1993, mem. exec. com. 1993), Am. Congress Rehab. Medicine (chmn. policy and devel. com.), Chgo. Hosp. Coun. (chmn. com. rehab. 1978-82, exec. com. 1983), Healthcare Devel. and Rsch. Inst. Episcopalian. Home: 1658 35th St NW Washington DC 20007-2360 Office: Nat Rehab Hosp 102 Irving St NW Washington DC 20010-2949

ECKER, G. T. DUNLOP, hospital administration executive; b. Charlottesville, Va., June 8, 1940; s. Henry Dunlop and Margaret Louise (Mehring) E.; m. Carolyn Christine Smith, June 24, 1967; children: Charlotte Christine, Franklin Henry Dunlop. BS, Washington & Lee U., 1962; MA, U. Iowa, 1964; JD, Samford U., 1973. Asst. adminstr. Washington Hosp. Ctr., 1966-69, exec. v.p., 1982-85, pres., 1985-90; adminstrv. asst. to assoc. adminstr. U. Ala. Hosps. and Clinics, Brimingham, 1970-73; adminstr. Greater Southeast Community Hosp., Washington, 1973-78, exec. v.p., 1978-79, pres., 1979-82; exec. v.p. Washington Hosp. Ctr., Washington, 1982-85, pres., 1985-90; v.p. domestic provider networks Group Hospitalization and Med. Svcs., Inc., Washington, 1991-93; cons., 1993-94; pres. Loudoun Healthcare, Inc., Leesburg, Va., 1994—. *Mr. Ecker is a Not-for-Profit hospital executive with 35 years' experience in community hospitals and large urban teaching hospitals. He demonstrated success in developing collaborative medical staff relationships and organizational structures. His particular expertise is in "turnaround" operations and new hospital certificate of need acquisition, financing and construction.* Coach Montgomery Soccer, Inc., Bethesda, Md., 1986, 87; chmn. hosp. div. United Way D.C., 1983-85; bd. dirs. Vis. Nurse Assn., Washington, 1974-82. Fellow Am. Coll. Healthcare Execs.; mem. Am. Hosp. Assn., Nat. Health Lawyers Assn., Leadership Washington, D.C. C. of C., Met. Club. Episcopalian. Avocations: woodworking, tennis, golf, gardening. Home: 611 S 32nd St Purcellville VA 20132-3412 Office: Loudoun Healthcare Inc 44045 Riverside Pkwy Leesburg VA 20176-5101

ECKER, HOWARD, lawyer; b. N.Y.C., June 10, 1946; s. David and Sylvia (Goldstein) E.; children: David, Ashley. BA, U. Mich., 1967; JD, NYU, 1971. Bar: Nev. 1973, U.S. Dist. Ct. Nev. 1974, U.S. Ct. Appeals (9th cir.) 1976, U.S. Supreme Ct. 1976. Pub. defender Clark County Pub. Defender's Office, Nev., 1973-77; ptnr. Ecker & Standish, Chtd., Clark County, Nev., 1977—; apptd. settlement judge in appeals Nev. Supreme Ct., 1997—; guest lectr. in field. Mem. Nev. Employee Mgmt. Rels. Bd., Las Vegas, 1990-94. Mem. ATLA, State Bar Nev. (bd. govs. 1984-90), Clark County Bar Assn., Nev. Trial Lawyers Assn. (bd. govs. 1977-89, pres. 1985-86), Nev. Am. Inns of Ct. (barrister 1990-93, master 1993—). Avocations: travel, golf, reading. Office: Ecker & Standish Chtd 300 S 4th St Ste 611 Las Vegas NV 89101-6017

ECKER, PAUL GERARD, physician, educator; b. Cleve., Dec. 28, 1919; s. Enrique Eduardo and Marie Josephine (van Reeth) E.; m. Henriette Juliette Dumas, Nov. 25, 1950; children: Hendrik Michel, Christian Paul. BS, Case Western Res. U., 1942, MD, 1944. Fellow Rockefeller Inst., N.Y.C., 1946-48; teaching fellow Med. Sch. Harvard U., Boston, 1948-49; instr. Columbia-Presbyn. Coll., N.Y.C., 1950-55; asst. prof. psychiatry U. Pa., Phila., 1955-60; chief functional disease svc. Hosp. U. of Pa., Phila., 1957-60; tng. analyst Inst. Phila. Assn. for Psychoanalysis, Phila., 1968—; cons. surgeon gen. USAF, USN, US Army, Washington. Mem. acquisitions com. Phila. Mus. of Art; benefactor Cleve. Mus. Art, Phila. Mus. Art., Mc Darcy Mus. Chgo.; patron Met. Mus., N.Y.C. With USN, 1945-46, 52-54, capt. USNR. Decorated Legion of Merit. Fellow ACP, Am. Coll. Psychiatrists; mem. Am. Psychoanalytic Assn., Century Assn., Soc. Med. Cons. to Armed Forces (past pres.), Phila. Assn. for Psychoanalysis (past pres.), Royal Navy Club London, Sigma Xi. Roman Catholic. Avocations: collector Chinese and Medieval art, flying. Home and Office: 631 St Georges Rd Philadelphia PA 19119-3341

ECKER, PEDER KALOIDES, former judge; b. Sioux City, Iowa, Oct. 21, 1929; s. Peder Kornelius and Amalia Helena (Kaloides) E.; m. Marjorie Mae, Feb. 14, 1990; children: Diane Jankord, Debra Maniaci, Dorothy Ann Dupper, Dawn Nelson, Donna. BS in Polit. Sci., U. S.D., 1954, JD, 1955. Bar: S.D. 1955, Nebr. 1958, U.S. Dist. Ct. S.D. 1960. Ptnr., Dana, Golden, Moore & Rasmussen, Sioux Falls, S.D., 1959-77; judge U.S. Bankruptcy Ct., Sioux Falls, 1969-94, ret., 1994; sole practice, Sioux Falls, 1977-79; U.S. magistrate Dist. S.D., Sioux Falls, 1977-79; founding dir., chmn. bd. Sun Bank of S.D., Sioux Falls, 1974-79; party chmn. Democrat Minnehaha County, 1965-68; state chmn. South Dakota Democratic Party, 1968-69. Served with U.S. Army, 1948-49, to capt. Res., 1962-68. Recipient Achievement award ABA, 1965. Mem. Am. Bankruptcy Inst., 2d Cir.Bar Assn., Nebr. Bar Assn., Nat. Conf. Bankruptcy Judges (past bd. govs.), S.D. Young Lawyers Assn. (past pres.), S.D. Bar Assn. (bd. commrs. 1965-68), Comml. Law League, S.D. Trial Lawyers Assn. Lutheran. Lodges: Masons, El Riad Shrine, El Riad Clowns. Home: 3300 W 33rd St Sioux Falls SD 57105-4219

ECKERSLEY, NORMAN CHADWICK, bank executive; b. Glasgow, Scotland, June 18, 1924; came to U.S., 1969; s. James Norman and Beatrice (Chadwick) E.; m. Rosemary J. Petes, May 23, 1986; 1 child, Anne. D Laws, Strathclyde U., Scotland. With Chartered Bank, London and Manchester, 1947-48; acct. Bombay, 1948-52, Singapore, 1952-54, Sarawak, 1954-56, Pakistan, 1956-58, Calcutta, 1958-59, Hong Kong, 1959-60; asst. mgr. Hamburg, 1960-62; mgr. Calcutta, 1962-67; pres. Chartered Bank London, San Francisco, 1964-74, chmn., ceo, 1974-79; chmn. Std. Chartered Bancorp, 1978-81; dep. chmn. Union Bank, San Francisco and L.A., 1979-82; chmn., ceo The Pacific Bank, San Francisco, 1982-93; chmn. emeritus, 1993; chmn. Diners Club (Asia), 1967-69, Devel. Bank Thailand, 1967-69, Scottish Am. Investment Com., U. Strathclyde Found.; chmn. Balmoral Fin. Corp., 1995—. With RAF, 1940-46. Decorated D.F.C., comdr. Order Brit. Empire. Mem. Overseas Banks Assn. Calif. (chmn. 1972-74), Calif. Coun. Internat. Trade, San Francisco C. of C., World Trade Assn., Royal and Ancient Club, Royal Troon Golf Club (Scotland), World Trade Club, San Francisco Golf Club, Pacific Union Club (San Francisco). Mem. Ch. of Scotland. Home: 265 Casitas Ave San Francisco CA 94127-1603 Office: 333 Pine St # 200 San Francisco CA 94104

ECKERSLEY, RICHARD LAURENCE, accountant; b. Scranton, Pa., July 29, 1948; s. Robert Neal and Helen Elizabeth (Palmer) E.; m. Linda K. Forsythe, Feb. 11, 1967; children: Laura Lynnette, Tristan Dael, Travis Morgan. AB in English, U. Scranton, 1971, MA in History, 1993. CPA, Pa. Staff acct. Acctg. Svc. Assocs., Inc., Scranton, 1967-77; ptnr. Eckersley Acctg. Svc., Scranton, 1977-80; shareholder, pres. Eckersley and Eckersley, P.C., Scranton, 1980-86; ptnr. Eckersley and Ostrowski, LLP, Scranton, 1987—; lectr. acctg. Keystone Jr. Coll., LaPlume, Pa., 1974-76. Asst. treas. The Real Bob Casey Com., Scranton, 1985-96; bd. dirs., officer Family Svc. Lackawanna County, Scranton, 1978-84, Planned Parenthood N.E. Pa., Trexlertown, Pa., 1981-86, 89-93; treas. Casey for Congress Com., 1998—. Mem. AICPA, Pa. Inst. Cert. Pub. Accts. Methodist. Avocations: reading, history, hunting, diving. Home: RR 3 Box 5 Dalton PA 18414-9528 Office: Eckersley and Ostrowski LLP 300 Gerard Bldg Scranton PA 18503

ECKERT, ALLAN WESLEY, writer; b. Buffalo, Jan. 30, 1931; s. Edward Russell and Ruth Rose (Roth) E.; m. Joan Dowling, 1955 (div.1975); children: Joseph Matthew, Julie Anne; m. Gail Greene, 1977 (div. 1978); m. Nancy Dent, 1978. Student, U. Dayton, 1951-52, Ohio State U., 1953-54; PhD (hon.), Bowling Green State U., 1985, Wright State U., 1998. Assoc. editor Nat. Cash Register Co. News, Dayton, 1955-58; reporter, columnist Dayton Jour. Herald, Dayton, 1958-60; free-lance writer, 1960—; cons. LaSalle Extension U., Chgo. Writer over 200 TV scripts for NBC's Wild Kingdom; created courses article and short story writing Writer's Digest; author: The Great Auk, 1963, A Time of Terror, 1965, The Silent Sky, 1965, Wild Season, 1967, The Frontiersmen, 1967, Bayou Backwaters, 1967, The Dreaming Tree, 1967, The Crossbreed, 1968, Blue Jacket, 1968, The King Snake, 1968, Wilderness Empire, 1968, In Search of a Whale, 1969, The Conquerors, 1970, Incident at Hawk's Hill, 1971, The Court-Martial of Daniel Boone, 1973, The Owls of North America, 1973, The HAB Theory, 1976, The Wilderness War, 1978, The Wading Birds of North America, 1979, Savage Journey, 1979, Song of the Wild, 1980, Whattizit?, 1981, Gateway to Empire, 1982, Johnny Logan: Shawnee Spy, 1982, The Dark Green Tunnel, 1983, The Wand, 1984, The Scarlet Mansion, 1985, Earth Treasures, 4 vols., 1987, Twilight of Empire, 1988, A Sorrow in Our Heart: The Life of Tecumseh, 1991, That Dark and Bloody River: Chronicles of the Ohio River Valley, 1995, The World of Opals, 1997, Return to Hawk's Hill, 1998, The Green Conspiracy, 2000, (outdoor drama) Tecumseh!, 1971, (screenplays) Kentucky Pioneers, 1969, The Legend of Koo-Tan, 1971, (playscript) Tecumseh!, 1974; editor: A Treasury of Tips for Writers, 1966; contbr. articles to popular and profl. publs. Trustee Dayton Museum Natural History, 1963-65; Founder, chmn. bd. Lemon Bay Conservancy, Englewood, Fla. Served with USAF, 1948-52. Recipient Ohioana Book award, 1968, Best Book award Friends of Am. Writers, 1968, Emmy award outstanding program achievement Nat. Acad. TV Arts and Scis., 1968-69, Newbury-Caldecott Honor Book award, 1972, George G. Stone/Claremont Colls. Recognition of Merit, 1974, Austrian Juvenile Book of Yr. award, 1976, Americanism award The Daniel Boone Found., 2d Ann. Silver Arrow Humanitarian award Scioto Soc., 1987, Internat. Readers Assn. Tchrs. Choice award, 1999; commd. Ky. Col. by Gov. State of Ky., 1987; finalist Spur award Western Writers Am., 1995; named Writer of Yr., Am. Culture Assn., 1997; nominated 7 times for Pulitzer prize; Allan W. Eckert Collection established at Mugar Meml. Libr., Boston U., 1965, at the Filson Club Hist. Soc., Louisville, Ky., 1993. Mem. Authors Guild, Dayton soc. Natural History (life), Am. Soc. of Gem Cutters, Mazon Greek Project (life). Office: care Virginia Kidd Agy Inc PO Box 278 538 E Harwood St Milford PA 18337

ECKERT, CHARLES ALAN, chemical engineering educator; b. St. Louis, Dec. 13, 1938; s. Clarence Theodore and Mildred Hortense (Potlitzer) E.; children: Carolyn Helen, Theodore James; m. Susan Schneider, 1997. S.B., MIT, 1960, S.M., 1961; Ph.D., U. Calif.-Berkeley, 1964. Postdoctoral fellow CNRS, Paris, 1964-65; asst. prof. U. Ill., Urbana, 1965-69, assoc. prof., 1969-73, prof., 1973-89, head dept. chem. engring., 1980-86; J. Erskine Love prof. engring. Ga. Inst. Tech., Atlanta, 1989—, Inst. prof., 1994; dir. Splty. Separations Ctr., 1991—; cons. numerous cos. Author several books, instructional computer programs. Fellow NATO, 1964, Guggenheim Found., 1971. Fellow AIChE (Allan Colburn award 1973, William H. Walker award 1999); mem. NAE, Internat. Soc. for Advancement of Supercritical Fluids (v.p.) Am. Chem. Soc. (Ipatieff prize 1977, Murphree award 1995), Am. Soc. Engring. Edn. Home: 1053 Saint James Xing NE Atlanta GA 30319-1984 Office: Ga Inst Tech Sch Chem Engring Atlanta GA 30332-0100

ECKERT, RALPH JOHN, insurance company executive; b. Milw., Mar. 12, 1929; s. John C. and Vlasta (Stauber) E.; m. Greta M. Allen, July 11, 1953; children: Maura Eckert Benseler, Peter, Thomas, Karen Eckert Schmidt, Edward. BS, U. Wis., 1951. With Trustmark Life Ins. Co., Lake Forest, Ill., 1954—; chmn. bd., chief exec. officer Benefit Trust Life Ins. Co., Chgo., 1971-91; chmn. bd. of pensions Evang. Luth. Ch. Am., Mpls., 1991-97; chmn. bd. Trustmark Life Ins. Co., Lake Forest, Ill., 1991-97, chmn. emeritus, 1997—; bd. dirs. Prin. Preservation Mutual Funds, 1996—. With AUS, 1951-53. Fellow Soc. Actuaries; mem. Am. Acad. Actuaries, Ill. Life Ins. Coun. (chmn. 1978-79), Ill. Life & Health Ins. Guaranty Assn. (chmn. 1980-81), Health Ins. Assn. Am. (bd. dirs., chmn. 1984-85), Am. Coun. Life Ins. (bd. dirs. 1986-88), Masons. Lutheran. Office: Trustmark Life Ins Co 400 N Field Dr Lake Forest IL 60045-4809

ECKERT, ROGER E(ARL), chemical engineering educator; b. Lakewood, Ohio, Aug. 8, 1926; s. Elmer George and Elsie V. (Schwede) E.; children: Roger Earl, Rhonda Carol, Robyn Claire. B.S., Princeton U., 1948; M.S., U. Ill., 1949, Ph.D., 1951. Process devel. engr., indsl. and biochems. dept. E.I. duPont de Nemours & Co., Inc., Wilmington, Del., 1951-64; math. cons. E.I. duPont de Nemours & Co., Inc., 1956-60, sr. research engr., engring. research lab. and elastomers chems. dept., 1960-64; assoc. prof. Purdue U., West Lafayette, Ind., 1964-73; asst. head Sch. Chem. Engring., 1970-75, prof. chem. engring., 1973—; vis. prof. U. Colo., 1971, U. Wis., 1981; Am. Soc. Engring. Edn.-NASA faculty fellow Case Western Res. U. and Lewis Research Center, 1966-67. Contbr. tech. articles to profl. jours. Served with U.S. Army, 1946-47. Mem. Am. Inst. Chem. Engrs., Phi Beta Kappa, Sigma Xi, Phi Lambda Upsilon, Pi Mu Epsilon, Alpha Chi Sigma. Presbyterian. Home: 153 Indian Rock Dr West Lafayette IN 47906-1255 Office: Sch Chem Engring Purdue U West Lafayette IN 47906

ECKERT, TOM W., artist, educator; b. Apr. 10, 1942. AA, Phoenix Coll., 1963; BFA, Ariz. State U., 1966, MFA, 1971. Prof. art Ariz. State U., Tempe, 1971—. E-mail: tom.eckert@asu.edu.

ECKERT, WILLIAM DEAN, retired educator, artist; b. Coshocton, Ohio, Oct. 10, 1927; s. Charles Alvin and Ethel Nydia (Gonter) E. BA, BFA, Ohio State U., 1950, MA, 1951; PhD, U. Iowa, 1961. Instr. U. Kans., Lawrence, 1951-52, Coll. of Wooster, Ohio, 1953-54, Fla. So. Coll., Lakeland, 1954-57; grad. asst. U. Iowa, Iowa City, 1957-59; assoc. prof. Western Ill. U., Macomb, 1959-65, Union Coll., Schenectady, N.Y., 1965-68; prof. art history, painting Lindenwood Coll., St. Charles, Mo., 1968-91; prof. emeritus Lindenwood Coll., St. Charles, 1991—; juror Albany Art Inst., 1968, An Art Affair, St. Louis, 1989; advisor Assocs. of the Fine Arts, Lindenwood Coll., St. Charles, 1977-91. Works have appeared at Ark. Art Ctr., Little Rock, Evansville Mus. Art, Butler Inst. Am. Art, Youngstown, Ohio, various corp. and pvt. collections. Cpl. U.S. Army Air Corps, 1945-47, PTO. Recipient Lifetime Disting. Svc. award C. of C., St. Charles, 1992. Mem. Asian Art Soc. St. Louis (bd. dirs., publs. chair 1992—), St. Louis Artists' Guild (bd. govs., treas. 1996-97), Art St. Louis, Soc. Archtl. Historians, The Decorative Arts Trust. Democrat. Home: 1302 Musket Holw Saint Charles MO 63303-6131

ECKHARDT, AUGUST GOTTLIEB, law educator; b. Sylvan, Wis., Aug. 8, 1917; s. Levi and Euphemia (Hall) E.; m. Catherine Louise Henderson, June 26, 1942; children—James Henderson, Patricia Kay. Student, Nebr. State U. at Kearney, 1935-37; B.A., U. Wis., 1939, LL.M., 1946, S.J.D., 1951; LL.B., George Washington U., 1942. Bar: D.C. bar 1941, Wis. bar 1946, Ariz. bar 1974. Sole practice Merrill, Wis., 1946-47, 50-52; asst. prof. law George Washington U., 1947-49; prof. law U. Wis.-Madison, 1954-72; prof. law U. Ariz., Tucson, 1972-89, prof. emeritus, 1989—; dir. Continuing Legal Edn. Wis., 1954-58, 63-67; labor arbitrator, 1955-89. Author: Eckhardt's Workbook for Wisconsin Estate Planners, 1961, (with others) revised edit., 1997, supplement, 1999. Served with USNR, 1942-46. Mem. State Bar Ariz. (founder world peace through law sect. 1989). Home: 2002 E 3rd St Tucson AZ 85719-5103

ECKHARDT, CRAIG JON, chemistry educator; b. Rapid City, S.D., June 26, 1940; s. Reuben H and Hilda W. (Craig) E. BA magna cum laude, U. Colo., 1962; MS, Yale U., 1964, PhD, 1967. Asst. prof. chemistry U. Nebr., Lincoln, 1967-72, assoc. prof., 1972-78, prof., 1978—, interim chmn. dept. chemistry, 1986-87, prof. physics, 1988—; cons., mem. adv. panel, condensed matter scis. div. materials research NSF, 1976-79. NIH predoctoral fellow, 1964-67; Yale predoctoral fellow, 1967; John Simon Guggenheim fellow, 1979-80; German Acad. Exchange fellow; Grantee NSF, 1974-84, Dept. Energy, 1979-82, Petroleum Rsch. Fund-Am. Chem. Soc., 1968-72, Rsch. Corp., 1971-74, 3M Corp., 1983-89, Army Rsch. Office, 1989—. Mem. Am. Phys. Soc., Am. Assn. Physics Tchrs., Optical Soc. Am., Am. Chem. Soc., Royal Chemistry Soc., Phi Beta Kappa, Sigma Xi. Office: U Nebr Dept Chemistry Lincoln NE 68588

ECKHART, WALTER, molecular biologist, educator; b. Yonkers, N.Y., May 22, 1938; s. Walter and Jean (Fairnington) E. BS, Yale U., 1960; postgrad., Cambridge U., Eng., 1960-61; PhD, U. Calif.-Berkeley, 1965. Postdoctoral fellow Salk Inst., San Diego, 1965-69, mem., 1970-73, assoc. prof. molecular biology, 1973-79, prof., 1979—; dir. Salk Inst. Cancer Ctr., San Diego, 1976—; adj. prof. U. Calif.-San Diego, 1973—. Contbr. articles on molecular biology and virology to profl. jours. NIH research grantee, 1967—. Mem. AAAS, Am. Assn. Cancer Rsch., Am. Soc. Microbiology, Am. Soc. Virology. Home: 951 Skylark Dr La Jolla CA 92037-7731 Office: Salk Inst Cancer Ctr Salk Inst for Biol Studies PO Box 85800 San Diego CA 92186-5800

ECKL, WILLIAM WRAY, lawyer; b. Florence, Ala., Dec. 2, 1936; s. Louis Arnold and Patricia Barclift (Dowd) E.; m. Mary Lynn McGough, June 29, 1963; children—Eric Dowd, Lynn Lacey. B.A., U. Notre Dame, 1959, LL.B., U. Va., 1962. Bar: Va. 1962, Ala. 1962, Ga. 1964. Law clk. Supreme Ct. of Ala., 1962; ptnr. Gambrell, Harlan, Russell & Moye, Atlanta, 1965-68, Swift, Currie, McGhee & Hiers, Atlanta, 1968-82, Drew, Eckl & Farnham, Atlanta, 1983—. Served to capt. JAGC, USAR, 1962-65. Mem. Def. Research Inst., State Bar of Ga. Roman Catholic. Clubs: Lawyers of Atlanta, Brookwood Hills. Home: 348 Camden Rd NE Atlanta GA 30309-1513 Office: Drew Eckl & Farnham 880 W Peachtree St PO Box 7600 Atlanta GA 30357-0600

ECKLAND, JEFF HOWARD, lawyer; b. Warren, Ohio, Jan. 17, 1957; s. William Howard and Barbara Ann (Hirsch) E.; m. Deborah Pauline Causey, May 27, 1989. BA summa cum laude, U. Minn., 1979; JD, U. Chgo., 1982. Bar: Minn. 1982, U.S. Dist. Ct. Minn. 1982, U.S. Ct. Appeals (8th cir.) 1987, U.S. Ct. Appeals (9th cir.) 1990, U.S. Ct. Appeals (fed. cir.) 1993, U.S. Ct. Fed. Claims 1993 (fed. cir.), U.S. Supreme Ct. 1997. Ptnr. Faegre & Benson, Mpls., 1982—. Mem. ABA, Minn. Bar Assn., Hennepin County Bar Assn., Phi Beta Kappa. Avocations: sailing, tennis. Office: Faegre & Benson LLP 2200 Norwest Ctr 90 S 7th St Ste 2200 Minneapolis MN 55402-3901

ECKLES, SUSAN, management executive; b. St. Louis, Oct. 8, 1939. Dir. Resource Mgmt., Dept. of Defense, Washington, 1998—. Office: Dept of Def Command Control Comm & Intelligence 6000 Defense Pentagon Washington DC 20301-6000

ECKLEY, WILTON EARL, JR., humanities educator; b. Alliance, Ohio, June 25, 1929; s. Wilton Earl and Louise (Bert) E.; m. Grace Ester Williamson, Sept. 12, 1954; children: Douglas, Stephen, Timothy. B.A., Mt. Union Coll., 1952; M.A., Pa. State U., 1955; Ph.D., Case Western Reserve U., 1965; John Hay fellow, Yale U., 1961-62. Chmn. English Euclid (Ohio) Sr. High Sch., 1955-63; dir. tchr. tng. Hollins Coll., 1963-65; prof. English Drake U., 1965-84, chmn. dept. English, 1965-80; head dept. humanities and social scis. Colo. Sch. Mines, 1984-93, dir. honors program, 1989-92; prof. humanities Drake U., 1984—; prof. humanities and internat. studies Colo. Sch. Mines, 1994—; Fulbright prof. Am. lit. U., Ljubljana, Yugoslavia, 1972-73, U. Veliko, Turnovo, Bulgaria, 1981-82; vis. prof. Bilkent U., Ankara, Turkey, 1993-94. Chmn. bd. dirs. Colo. Endowment for the Humanities, 1989-91, chmn. bd. dirs., Colo. Endowment for the Humanities, 1989. Coe fellow Am. Studies, 1957—. Mem. MLA, Circus Hist. Soc., AAUP, Phi Kappa Tau. Home: 636 Ridgeside Dr Golden CO 80401-5757

ECKLIN, ROBERT LUTHER, materials company executive; b. Lancaster, Pa., Sept. 26, 1938; s. Luther Joseph and Ella Frances (Smith) E.; m. Loretta Rohrer Stoner, Sept. 3, 1960; children: Robert Luther, Jr., Suzanne Beth, Kristina Ann, Stephanie Ann. B in Archtl. Engring., Chgo. Tech. Coll., 1961; postgrad., Dartmouth U., 1983, cert., 1984. With Corning Inc., N.Y.C., 1961—; pres. Corning Engring. Corning (N.Y.) Glass Works, 1982-86, corp. v.p. bus. devel., chmn. Corning Engring., 1986-88, sr. v.p., 1988-99, exec. v.p., 1999—; chmn. Maklin Ltd., Stone-on-Trent, Eng., 1983-86; ptnr. Ecklin & Ecklin Investments, Lancaster, 1986—; bd. dirs. Corning, U.S. Precision Lens, Cin., Alfred U. Tech. Resources, Pitts.-Corning Corp.; chmn. bd. dirs. Quanterra, Inc., Denver, Cormetech Inc., Durham, N.C. Chmn. Com. of 50, Corning, 1985—; pres. Univ. Industry Pub. Partnership for Econ. Growth; mem. adv. bd. Chase Manhattan Bank; rsch. adv. bd. N.Y. State U. Mem. U.S. Advanced Ceramics Assn. (bd. dirs.), Corning C. of C., Corning Country Club. Republican. Methodist. Home: 248 Cedar St Corning NY 14830-3128 Office: Corning Inc Houghton Pk Corning NY 14831

ECKLUND, CONSTANCE CRYER, French language educator; b. Chgo., Nov. 20, 1938; d. Gilbert and Electra (Papadopoulos) Cryer; m. Robert Lyons, June 18, 1966 (div. 1974); m. John E. Ecklund, Mar. 22, 1975. BA magna cum laude, Northwestern U., 1960; PhD, Yale U., 1965. Asst. prof. Ind. U., Bloomington, 1964-66; asst. prof. French Southern Conn. State U., New Haven, 1967-70, assoc. prof., 1970-76, prof., 1976—; speaker in field. Contbr. articles to profl. jours. Mem. AAUP, Am. Coun. Teaching Fgn. Langs., Am. Assn. Tchrs. French, Modern Lang. Assn., Phi Beta Kappa. Republican. Avocations: piano, gardening, cooking, travel, graphic art. Home: 27 Cedar Rd Woodbridge CT 06525-1642

ECKLUND, JUDITH LOUISE, academic administrator; b. Baton Rouge, June 14, 1946; d. Norman Carl and Laverne (Borg) E. BA, U. Calif., Davis, 1968; MA, Cornell U., 1971, PhD, 1977. Adminstr. U. Calif., Berkeley, 1971-72, Cornell U., Ithaca, N.Y., 1976-78; adminstr. Tulane U., New Orleans, 1980-90, v.p. devel. & alumni affairs, 1984-87, co-dir. internat. devel. ctr., 1987-90; dir. devel. The Carter Ctr., Atlanta, 1990-92; dir. internat. devel. UCLA, L.A., 1992—; mem. adv. coun. Cornell U., 1991—. Fellow Am. Anthropology Assn.; mem. Assn. Asian Studies. Office: UCLA Devel Office Ste 1400 10920 Wilshire Blvd Los Angeles CA 90024-6502

ECKMAN, DIANNE INGEBORG, critical care nurse; b. Pitts., Aug. 8, 1965; d. Mary M. Moloney Eckman. BS in Nursing, Carlow Coll., Pitts., 1987. Commd. 2d lt. U.S. Army, 1987, advanced through grades to capt., 1993; staff nurse orthopedic surgery Walter Reed Army Med. Ctr., Washington, 1987-90, staff nurse ICU, 1990-91, 92-95; staff nurse surg. ICU Johns Hopkins Hosp., Balt., 1991-92; staff nurse ICU DeWitt Army Cmty. Hosp., Ft. Belvoir, Va., 1995-97; staff nurse United Health Care Optum Nurseline, McLean, Va., 1997-99; supr. United Health Care Optum Nurseline, McLean, 1999—. Mem. Am. Assn. Critical Care Nurses, Sigma Theta Tau. Home: 2210 Montgomery Ave Woodbridge VA 22191-2619 Office: United Health Care Ste 500 8201 Greensboro Pike Mc Lean VA 22101

ECKMAN, FERN MARJA, journalist; b. N.Y.C., Aug. 27; d. Isidor Peter and Zara Nettie (Sloate) Friedman; m. Irving Eckman, June 21, 1957. B.A., N.Y. U., 1957. Reporter N.Y. Post, 1944-78; assigned to UN, 1945-49, 60-65. Author: The Furious Passage of James Baldwin, 1967; contbg. editor Working Mother, 1981-91; feature writer for nat. publs., 1965-90. Recipient George Polk Meml. award for distinguished met. reporting, 1951, 55; Page One award for community service N.Y. Newspaper Guild, 1955, for best feature reporting, 1961; citation for community service Council Puerto Rican and Spanish-Am. Orgns., 1955; Lasker award for med. journalism, 1960; Front Page award for distinguished feature writing, News Women's Club N.Y., 1949, 51, 56, 64; for distinguished series (co-recipient), 1970; Cultural News award Newspaper Reporters Assn., N.Y.C., 1967; Empire State award for excellence in med. reporting, 1968. Mem. Soc. of the Silurians. Home: 749 W End Ave New York NY 10025-6224

ECKSTAT, ARTHUR GENE, consultant; b. N.Y.C., Feb. 11, 1943; s. Maurice and Sophie Rebecca E.; m. Barbara June Tausend, Feb. 1, 1964 (div. July 1986); 1 child, Tony. BSME, Detroit Inst. Tech., 1968; MBA, U. Phoenix, 1985; DBA, Nova Southwestern U., 1999. Test engr. continental Aviation & Engring., Detroit, 1966-68; engring. specialist Allied Signal Aerospace, Phoenix, 1968-98; v.p. tng. & orgn. devel. PBT Personal Bridges to Teamwork, Inc., Phoenix, 1996-98; pres. Global Turbine Specialists, Chandler, Ariz., 1998—. Mem. Nat. Assn. Gender Diversity Trainers, Acad. Mgmt. Avocations: boating, male-female conflict mamagement. Office: Global Turbine Specialists PO Box 130 Chandler AZ 85244-0130

ECKSTEIN, JEROME, philosopher, educator; b. N.Y.C., June 28, 1925; s. Marcus and Blanche (Wohlberg) E.; m. Kathleen Sharon Hoisington; 1 stepchild, Mari O'Donnell Midurski; children: Esther Schwartz, Sandra Bellehsen, Michael. Student, Rabbi Isaac Elchanan Theol. Sem., 1943-45; B.A., Bklyn. Coll., 1949; postgrad., New Sch. Social Research, 1949-50; Ph.D., Columbia U., 1961. Buyer antique silverware Blanche Eckstein Silverware, Bklyn., 1944-53; dir. edn. and youth activities, various Hebrew congregations, 1950-61; lectr. philosophy CCNY, 1955-56, Bklyn. Coll., 1955-60; instr. contemporary civilization and philosophy Columbia U., N.Y.C., 1960-63; asst. prof., then assoc. prof. philosophy, coordinator div. humanities Adelphi Suffolk Coll., Adelphi U., 1963-66; prof. philosophy of edn. SUNY-Albany, 1966-70, also first chmn. Judaic studies, 1970-74, prof. Judaic studies, 1970-97, prof. religious studies, 1990-97, prof. emeritus, 1997—; participant Internat. Philosophy Yr., Brockport, N.Y., 1967, Conf. on Gerontology, U. Minn., 1978; vis. prof. philosophy Bar-Ilan U., Israel, 1978-79. Author: The Platonic Method: An Interpretation of the Dramatic-Philosophic Aspects of the Meno, 1968; The Deathday of Socrates, 1981, Metaphysical Drift: Love and Judaism, 1991; also numerous articles. Fellow in logic CCNY, 1955-56; vis. scholar Va. Commonwealth U., Richmond, 1975; Am. Council Learned Socs. sr. fellow, 1973. Mem. Phi Beta Kappa. Office: SUNY at Albany Dept of Judaic Studies 1400 Washington Ave Dept Of Albany NY 12222-1000

ECKSTEIN, JOHN WILLIAM, physician, educator; b. Central City, Iowa, Nov. 23, 1923; s. John William and Alice (Ellsworth) E.; m. Imogene O'Brien, June 16, 1947; children: John Alan, Charles William, Margaret Ann, Thomas Cody, Steven Gregory. BS, Loras Coll., 1946; MD, U. Iowa, 1950. Asst. prof. internal medicine U. Iowa, Iowa City, 1956-60; assoc. prof. U. Iowa, 1960-65, prof., 1965-92, prof. emeritus, 1993; assoc. dean VA Hosp. affairs, 1969-70, dean coll. medicine, 1970-91, dean emeritus, 1993; chmn. cardiovascular study sect. NIH, 1970-72, Nat. Heart, Lung and Blood Adv. Couhn., 1974-78; mem. VA Manpower Study Group, 1988-92; mem. adv. com. to dir. NIH, 1990-95. Author papers and abstracts. Served with USAAF, 1943-45, U.S. Army Med. Corps., 1950-51. Rockefeller Found. postdoctoral fellow, 1953-54; Am. Heart Assn. Research fellow, 1954-55; Nat. Heart Inst. spl. research fellow, 1955-56; Am. Heart Assn. established investigator, 1958-63; recipient USPHS Research Career award, 1963-70, Disting. Alumni Svc. award U. Iowa, 1994, Disting. Physician Dept. Vets. Affairs, 1995-98; Eckstein Med. Rsch. Bldg. named in his honor, U. Iowa, 1988. Mem. Am. Heart Assn. (v.p. 1969, chmn. coun. on circulation 1969-71, pres. 1978-79), AMA (mem. health policy agenda panel 1982-86, governing coun. sect. on med. schs. 1985-92, mem. study sect. faculty and rsch. 1985-86, alt. del. Ho. of Dels. 1986-90, del 1990-92, Disting. Svc. award 1992), Am. Fedn. Clin. Rsch. (chmn. Midwestern sect. 1965), Ctrl. Soc. Clin. Rsch. (sec.-treas. 1965-70, pres. 1973-74), Am. Soc. Clin. Investigation, Am. Clin. and Climatol. Assn., Assn. Am. Physicians, Assn. Am. Med. Colls. (exec. coun. 1981-82, adminstrv. bd. 1980-82, 85-86), Inst. of Medicine of Nat. Acad. Scis., Assn. Acad. Health Ctrs. (mem. sci. policy study group 1988-93). Home: 1415 William White Blvd Iowa City IA 52245-4443 Office: U Iowa Hosps & Clinics Iowa City IA 52242-1101

ECKSTUT, MICHAEL KAUDER, management consultant; b. Prague, Czechoslovakia, Mar. 13, 1952; came to U.S., 1960; s. Robert and Erika Kauder (Neumann) E.; m. Mary Jane Haymond, May 21, 1978; children: Martina, Robert. BS in Chem. Engring., Rensselaer Poly., 1973, MS in Chem. Engring., 1974; MBA, Harvard U., 1978. Chem. engr. E.I. DuPont de Nemours, Wilmington, Del., 1974-76; assoc. Idanta Ptnrs., La Jolla, Calif., 1978-79; v.p. Booz, Allen & Hamilton, Inc., N.Y.C., 1979-93, A.T. Kearney Inc., N.Y.C., 1993—. Home: 66 Glenbrook Rd Apt 4126 Stamford CT 06902-8406 Office: A T Kearney Inc 153 E 53rd St Fl 27 New York NY 10022-4611

ECONOMAKI, CHRIS CONSTANTINE (CHRISTOPHER ECONOMAKI), publisher, editor; b. Bklyn., Oct. 15, 1920; s. Christopher C. and Gladys Toomey (Burt) E.; m. Alvera H. Tomljanovic, May 29, 1946; children: Christine, Corinne. Student, Drake U. Sales rep. Divco Corp., 1946-49; editor, pub. emeritus Nat. Speed Sport News newspaper; pres. Kay Pub. Co., Harrisburg, N.C., 1949—; Color commentator Wide World of Sports ABC-TV, 1961-83, CBS-TV Sports, 1984-93. Served with AUS, 1942-46, ETO. Recipient Tom Marchese award for dedication to automobile racing, 1972, Henry McLemore award for excellence in broadcast journalism, 1973, Ken Purdy award Internat. Motor Press Assn., 1978, Ray Marquette Meml. award, 1981, Patrick Jacquemart award for service to motorsports, 1983, Dave Fritzlen Meml. award Outstanding Service to Chgo. Lathrop Boys Club, 1984, Walt Ader Meml. award, 1985, 1st Hugh Deery Meml. award for long service to automobile racing, 1985, Excellence award Nat. Assn. for Stock Car Auto Racing, 1990, Presdl. award U.S. Auto Club, 1992, Appreciation award svc. auto racing Charlotte, N.C. Motor Speedway, 1990, Chevy Proud award to Dean Am. Motorsports Journalism, 1990, Achievement award svc. racing Ford Motor Co., 1990, Dean Batchelor award Lifetime Achievement, 1996, Lifetime Media award NASCAR/ESPN, 1998; Economaki Award named in his honor Driver of Yr. Panel, 1991; Amb. Motorsports Time, Cleve., 1992; Lifetime Achievement award named in his honor; named to Stock Car Hall of Fame, Oceanside (Fla.) Rotary Club, 1993, Nat. Sprint Car Hall of Fame, Knoxville, Iowa, 1993, Motorsports Hall of Fame, 1994. Mem. Am. Assn. Auto Racing Writers and Broadcasters (pres. 1969-71), Nat. Motorsports Press Assn., Ea. Motorsports Press Assn., Oceanside Rotary. Home: 9506 Charolais Ln Charlotte NC 28213-3741 Office: PO Box 1210 Harrisburg NC 28075-1210

ECONOMIDES, CHRISTOPHER GEORGE, pathologist; b. Alexandria, Egypt, Dec. 25, 1940; came to U.S., 1967; s. George and Tina E. MD, Alexandria U., 1966. Diplomate Am. Bd. Anatomic Pathology, Am. Bd. Clin. Pathology, Am. Bd. Cytopathology. Intern Alexandria U. Hosps., 1965-66, Balt. City Hosps., 1967-68; resident in anatomic pathology, then chief resident Jackson Meml. Hosp., U. Miami, Fla., 1968-70, resident in clin. pathology, 1970-71, 73-74, resident in ob-gyn., 1971-72, resident in anatomic pathology, 1972-73; pathologist Hialeah (Fla.) Hosp., 1974, chief dept. pathology, 1975—; officer med. bd. Hialeah Hosp., 1975—, chief of staff, chmn. med. bd., 1980, 81, trustee, 1989-95, chmn. governing com., 1996—, mem. numerous coms.; med. and surg. clerkships Alexandria U. Hosp., Victoria Hosp., Scotland, Royal Salop Infirmary, England; mem. family planning program Broward County Health Dept., Fla., 1972-77; mem. courtesy staff North Shore Hosp., Miami, 1975, Palmetto Gen. Hosp., Hialeah, 1979-90; clin. asst. prof. pathology U. Miami, 1980-85; med. dir. SmithKline-Beechman Clin. Labs., 1983-92; bd. dirs. Immunopathology Labs., 1987-92, Ambulatory Ctr. of Hialeah, 1987-95, Dimension Health-PHO, 1993—. Trustee The Hialeah Found., 1989-91, Dade Community Found., 1992-94. Trustee The Hialeah Found., 1989-91, Dade Community Found., 1992—. Recipient Physician Recognition award AMA, 1971—, St. Marks Cross from His Holiness Patriarch Nicholaus I, 1981. Fellow Am. Soc. Clin. Pathologists, Coll. Am. Pathologists, Internat. Coll. Surgeons; mem. Am. Soc. Cytology, Internat. Acad. Pathology, Internat. Acad. Cytology, Fla. Med. Assn., Fla. Soc. Pathologists, South Fla. Soc. Pathology (pres. 1983, 84), Dade County Med. Assn., N.Y. Acad. Sci., Fisher Island Club (charter). Avocation: sailing. Office: Hialeah Hosp 651 E 25th St Hialeah FL 33013-3878

ECONOMOS, NIKKIANN, physical therapist; b. Canton, Ohio, Sept. 25, 1963; d. Anna (Hadjian) Economos; m. Robert D. Jordan, May 2, 1997. BS in Biology, Ind. U., 1985; MS in Phys. Therapy, Boston U., 1988. Lic. phys. therapist, Calif., Mass., Ohio. Staff phys. therapist Spaulding Rehab. Hosp., Boston, 1989-91, acting supr., 1991-92, 95, sr. phys. therapist, 1992-93; travelling phys. therapist Health Providers Inc., Ft. Lauderdale, Fla., 1994; contract phys. therapist Discharge Resource Group, San Francisco, 1995; dir. phys. therapy svcs. SpeechPath Integrated Resources, Dayton, Ohio, 1995-96; mem., owner Lifeskills Phys. Therapy Ltd., Yellow Springs, Ohio, 1996—; guest lectr. Northeastern U., Boston, 1991-93; presenter in field. Mem. faculty Motivaction-Ambassadors Summit, Keene, N.H., 1991; mem. staff Am. Youth Found., 1983-99, conf. dir., 1997—. Mem. Am. Phys. Therapy Assn. Avocations: modern dance, travel, experiential education. Home: 111 S Walnut St Yellow Springs OH 45387 Office: Lifeskills Phys Therapy Ltd PO Box 64 Yellow Springs OH 45387-0064

ECONOMOU-PEASE, BESSIE CARASOULAS, city planner, consultant; b. N.Y.C., Sept. 29, 1933; d. Alexander Stelianos and Maria (Trilivas) Carasoulas; m. Constantine J. Economou, Sept. 10, 1955 (div. May 1966); m. Robert Barnard Pease, Oct. 1, 1976; children: Robert W., Richard B. BA, Barnard Coll., 1955; postgrad., Columbia U., 1955-57, MS in Urban Planning, 1960. Med. researcher Coll. Physicians and Surgeons Columbia U., N.Y.C., 1955-60; planning and renewal cons. Brown & Anthony, Engrs. Planners, N.Y.C., 1960-62; dir. research, edn. ACTION Inc., N.Y.C., 1962-66; exec. asst. to adminstr. N.Y.C. Housing and Devel. Admin., N.Y.C., 1966-69; dep. dir., exec. asst. N.Y. State Urban Devel. Corp., N.Y.C., 1969-73; exec. v.p. Nat. Housing Conf., Washington, 1973-76; prin. Bessie C. Economou Assocs., Pitts., 1976—; dir. ACTION Housing, Inc., Pitts., 1982-88, Nat. Housing Conf., Washington, 1973—, also exec. v.p. 1973-76, Health Systems Agy. Western Pa., Pitts., 1984-87; adj. prof. U. Pitts, 1986—; mem. adv. com. bur. Census Housing, 1977-81. Mem. Am. Inst. Cert. Planners (cert.), Nat. Assn. Housing and Redevel. Officials, Lamda Alpha.

ECONOMUS, PETER CONSTANTINE, judge; s. Constantine G. Economus; m. Marie Misko, June 29, 1968; children: Paula, Kristine, Jennifer. BA, Youngstown (Ohio) State U., 1967; JD, Akron U., 1970. Bar: Ohio, 1971. Ptnr. Economus, Economus & Economus; judge Ct. Common Pleas, Mahoning County, Ohio, 1982-95; U.S. dist. judge No. Dist. Ohio, Youngstown, 1995—; apptd. mentor new judges, vis. judge various Ohio Ct. Appeals. Chmn. Cmty. Corrections Planning Bd., 1987-91; former trustee Ohio Common Please Judges Assn., legis. com.; bd. trustees U. Akron Sch. Law Alumni Assn, 1989-95; mem. com. celebrate bi-centennial U.S. Constn. Youngstown State U.; mem. adv. bd. State Victims, 1986-95. Recipient Outstanding Citizen's award Buckeye Elks Lodge #73, 1988, Pub. Svc. award Cmty. Corrections Assn., 1989, Office Holder of Yr. Truman Johnson Women's Dem. Club, 1990, Gt. Communicator award cmty. svc. Youngstown Hearing & Speech Ctr., 1995, Outstanding Alumni award U. Akron Law Alumni Assn., 1996. Mem. Am. Judges Assn., Mahoning County Bar Assn. Office: US Courthouse 125 Market St Youngstown OH 44503-1780

ECROYD, LAWRENCE GERALD, trade association administrator; b. Montreal, Que., Can., Sept. 14, 1918; s. George Smith and Marie (Guibord) E.; m. Dorothy Gertrude Howson, Dec. 26, 1949; children: Lynn (Mrs. Thomas Egan), Claire (Mrs. Lawrence Northway), Beverly, Bruce. Intermediate cert., U. London, Eng., 1960; M.B.A., Fla. Atlantic U., 1972. B.C. mgr. Can. C. of C., Vancouver, 1946-53; exec. dir. Mitchell Press Ltd., Vancouver, 1953-61; exec. v.p. Travel Industry Assn. Can., Ottawa, Ont., 1961-73; pres. Can. Inst. Plumbing and Heating, Toronto, 1973-84, cons., 1984—. Served to lt. comdr. Royal Can. Navy, 1941-45. Recipient Bota award tourism, 1973. Mem. Am. Soc. Assn. Execs. (Merit award 1971, Cert. Assn. Exec. 1974), Inst. Assn. Execs. (Can.). Home: 1510 Riverside Dr Apt 402, Ottawa, ON Canada K1G 4X5

ECTON, DONNA R., business executive; b. Kansas City, Mo., May 10, 1947; d. Allen Howard and Marguerite (Page) E.; m. Victor H. Maragni, June 16, 1986; children: Mark, Gregory. BA (Durant Scholar), Wellesley Coll., 1969; MBA, Harvard U., 1971. V.p. Chem. Bank, N.Y.C., 1972-79, Citibank, N.A., N.Y.C., 1979-81; pres. MBA Resources, Inc., N.Y.C., 1981-83; v.p. adminstrn., officer Campbell Soup Co., Camden, N.J., 1983-89; chmn. Triangle Mfg. Corp. subs. Campbell Soup Co., Raleigh, N.C., 1984-87; sr. v.p., officer Nutri/System, Inc., Willow Grove, Pa., 1989-91; pres., CEO Van Houten N.Am., Delavan, Wis., 1991-94, Andes Candies Inc., Delavan, 1991-94; chmn., pres., CEO Bus. Mail Express, Inc., Malvern, Penn., 1995-96; COO PETsMART, Inc., Phoenix, 1996-98; chmn., pres., CEO EEI Inc., Phoenix, 1998—; bd. dirs. Barnes Group Inc., Bristol, Conn., Vencor, Inc., Louisville, Ky., H&R Block, Kansas City, Mo.; commencement speaker Pa. State U., 1987. Bd. Overseers Harvard U., 1984-90; mem. Coun. Fgn. Rels., N.Y.C., 1987—; trustee Inst. for Advancement of Health, 1988-92. Named One of 80 Women to Watch in the 80's, Ms. mag., 1980, One of All Time Top 10 of Last Decade, Glamour mag., 1984, One of 50 Women to Watch, Bus. Week mag., 1987, One of 100 Women to Watch, Bus. Month mag., 1989; recipient Wellesley Alumnae Achievement award, 1987; Fred Sheldon Fund fellow, 1971-72. Mem. Harvard Bus. Sch. Assn. (pres. exec. council 1983-84), N.Y.C. Harvard Bus. Sch. Club (pres. 1979-80), Wellesley Coll. Nat. Alumnae Assn. (bd. dirs., 1st v.p.). Avocations: pub. speaking, art, gardening, skiing, reading.

EDBERG, JUDITH FLORENCE, music educator; b. Royal Oak, Mich., Apr. 13, 1933; d. DeWitt and Florence (Machris) Patterson; m. Hugo Charles Edberg; children: Charles Eric, Christine Elisabeth. B Music, Wayne State U., 1954, M Music, 1971. Tchr. Royal Oak Pub. Sch. Sys., 1952-54; pianist, artist tchr. Edberg Music Studio, Royal Oak, 1950-71; prof. music U. Tampa, Fla., 1972—, pre-coll. music program exec. dir., 1981—; pre-concert lectr. Fla. Orchestra, 1990—, mem. edn. com., 1998—; co-dir. Nicaragua Music Edn. Project, 1998—. Pianist recording Piano Works of Clark Eastham, 1987. Mem. governing bd. Tampa Bay Youth Orch., Tampa, 1990—; bd. dirs. Sarasota Music Archives, Tampa, 1995-98. Grantee Dana Found., 1987, 95; named Outstanding Musical Artist, Tampa Bay Chamber Orch., 1996. Mem. Nat. Guild Piano Tchrs. (chmn. Tampa chpt. 1994—, adjudicator 1997—), Fla. Music Tchrs. Assn. Democrat. Avocations: herbalist, couture sewing, photography. Office: U Tampa Music Dept Tampa FL 33606

EDDE, HOWARD JASPER, retired engineering executive; b. Page City, Kans., Dec. 14, 1937; s. Gilbert Herman and Jennie (Foulke) E.; m. Marilyn Ann Scheleen, Sept. 9, 1961; children: Michael, Heather, Sonja. BS, Kans. State U., 1959; MS, U. Kans., 1961; PhD, U. Tex., 1967. Registered profl. engr. Wash., Oreg., Pa., Ariz. Project engr. State of Kans. Dept. Highways, Topeka, 1959-60, Nat. Council Paper Industry for Air and Steam Improvement, Baton Rouge, La., 1961-64; regional engr. Nat. Council Paper Industry for Air and Steam Improvement, Balt., 1967-70; project engr. Roy F. Weston Co., West Chester, Pa., 1966-67; v.p. EKONO OY, Helsinki, Finland, 1970-74; pres. Howard Edde, Inc., Bellevue, Wash., 1974-96; affiliate prof. U. Wash., Seattle, 1972-92; lectr. Johns Hopkins U., Balt., 1967-70; mem. contractor selection com. EPA, 1985—; prof. Seattle U., 1987-89, chmn. civil engring. adv. bd., 1986-90; numerous speaking engagements. Author: (textbooks) Environmental Control for Pulp and Paper Mills, 1984, Environmental Aspects of Pulping Operations and Their Wastewater Implications, 1989; contbr. over 65 articles on energy conservation and environ. control to profl. jours. Fellow ASCE (chmn. Tech. Coun. on Cold Climate Engring. awards coms. 1988-90, various coms.); mem. TAPPI (chmn. wastewater treatment com. 1978-81, process energy use subcom. 1984, Best Paper award-gen. category 1991); Water Environment Fedn. (various coms.), Nat. Sci. and Engring. Rsch. Coun. Can., Am. Bd. Engring. and Tech., Inc. Republican. Lutheran. Avocations: skiing, sailing. Home: 3001 164th Pl NE Bellevue WA 98008-2022*

EDDINS, JAMES WILLIAM, JR., marketing executive; b. Wadesboro, N.C., Dec. 22, 1944; s. James William and Mildred Ruth Eddins; m. Barbara Ann Nelson, Oct. 2, 1965 (div. 1986); 1 child, Christopher; m. Ann Manley McAdams, Sept. 25, 1988; 1 stepchild, Keith. AB, Pfeiffer Coll., 1966; M.Pub. Sch. Adminstrn., Appalachian State U., Boone, N.C., 1968; postgrad., U. N.C., 1969. Prin. Stanly County Bd. Edn., Albemarle, N.C., 1966-70; gen. sales mgr. ITT Continental Baking Co., Tampa, Fla., 1970-75; reg. sales mgr. Sunshine Biscuit Co., Tampa, 1975-81; nat. sales mgr. Beatrice Foods, Bakery div., Augusta, Ga., 1981-83; dir. sales/mktg. Bensons, Inc., Athens, Ga., 1983-86; reg. sales mgr. Sunshine Biscuit Co., Greenville, S.C., 1986-87; dir. sales, nat. accts. Christie-Brown and Co., Burlington, N.C., 1987—; dir., v.p. Atlas Mktg.-Food Broker, Charlotte, N.C., 1996—; cons. in field. Active in past various charitable orgns. Named Outstanding Prin., Stanly County Bd. Edn., 1970. Mem. Biscuit Cracker Distbrs. Assn., Nat. Food Distbrs. Assn. Republican. Methodist. Avocations: tennis, basketball, travel. Home: 3230 Ardmore St Burlington NC 27215-8109 Office: Christie-Brown & Co PO Box 994 Burlington NC 27216-0994

EDDISON, ELIZABETH BOLE, entrepreneur, information specialist; b. Bronxville, N.Y., June 3, 1928; d. Hamilton Biggar and Elizabeth Owsley (Boyle) Bole; m. John Corbin Eddison, Feb. 10, 1951 (dec. Jan. 1993); children: Jonathan B., Elizabeth O., Martha C. AB, Vassar Coll., 1948; MS, Simmons Coll., 1973. Pres., bd. dirs. Lahore (Pakistan)-Am. Sch., 1959-61; chmn. evaluation com. Karachi (Pakistan)-Am. Sch., 1961-63; treas. bd. dirs. La Paz Coop. Sch., Bolivia, 1963-65; v.p. Assn. Am. Fgn. Svc. Women; coord. social svcs. Urban Svc. Corps, Washington Pub. Schs., 1965-69; sec. bd. dirs. Colegio Nueva Granada, Bogota, Colombia, 1969-71; chmn., treas. Warner-Eddison Assocs., Inc., Cambridge, Mass., 1973-88, pres., 1981-88; chmn., v.p. Inmagic Inc., Woburn, Mass., 1984-98; chmn., emeritus v.p., 1998—; mem. steering com. State House Conf. on Small Bus., Mass., 1986-88; mem. bd. advisors Internat. Sch. Info. Mgmt., Irvine, Calif., 1984—; mem. adv. coun. Engring. Info., Inc., N.Y.C., 1989-93; computer applications com. Cary Meml. Libr., Lexington, Mass., 1986; mem. State Adv. Commn. on Librs., Boston, 1993-96. Compiler: Words that Mean Business, 1981; contbr. articles to profl. jours. Mem. adv. com. on internat. and tech. devel. U.S. Dept. State, 1980-83; mem. small bus. com. Mass. Gov.'s Bus. Adv. Coun., 1985-89; co-chmn. Lexington Dem. Town Com., 1990-92; active Mass. Bd. Libr. Commrs., 1990-91; mem. bd. corporators Symmes Hosp., Arlington, Mass., 1992-94; mem. Bd. Selectmen, Lexington, 1993—; mem. adv. bd. Babson Coll. Info. Tech. and Svcs. Divsn., 1996—. Recipient Alumni Achievement award Simmons Coll., 1986, Disclosure Achievement award Libr. Mgmt. Bus. and Fin. div. Spl. Librs. Assn., 1987. Mem. Am. Soc. Info. Scis., Info. Industry Assn. (chmn. emeriti com. 1983-88, small bus. forum 1986-89, entrepreneur award com. 1989-90, co-chmn. publs. com. 1984-87, Entrepreneur award 1989), Assoc. Info. Mgrs. (chmn. publs. com. 1984-86, bd. dirs. 1984-86, Knox award 1988), Spl. Librs. Assn. (chmn. program com. libr. mgmt. divsn. 1984-85, profl. devel. com. 1987-88, chmn.-elect 1988, chmn. 1989-90, bd. dirs. 1991-94, mem. consultation com. 1994-96, chmn. endowment fund program com. 1996-98, chair bylaws com. 1998—), Nat. Info. Stds. Orgn. (bd. dirs. 1994-97), Beta Phi Mu. Democrat. Office: Inmagic Inc 800 W Cummings Park Woburn MA 01801-6372

EDDLEMAN, WILLIAM ROSEMAN, lawyer; b. Shelby, N.C., May 21, 1913; s. William Peter and Nellie Holland (Roseman) E.; 1 child, William Lammers; m. Sarah J. Seawell, Sept. 21, 1985 (dec. Nov. 1989); m. Rubie Dimmette, Dec. 30, 1990. Student, U.N.C., 1930-34, Pace Inst., 1934-35, Am. U., 1935-37; LLB, Gonzaga U., 1939; Licenciado en Derecho, Nat. U. Mex., 1968; D (hon), Mex. Acad. Internat. Law, 1988. Bar: Wash. 1939, U.S. Supreme Ct. 1945, Mexico 1968, Tex. 1962. Mem. firm Eddleman & Wheeler, Seattle, 1946-64, Perez, Verdia, Eddleman, Seattle, 1963-64; with Parker Sch. Internat. Law, Columbia, 1964; with law faculty Nat. U. Mex., 1964-67; ptnr. Bufete-Eddleman, Mex., 1968—; mem. firm Carp & Eddleman, Dallas, 1972-88; sr. ptnr. Eddleman, Clark & Rosen, Dallas, 1989—; del. Internat. Bar Assn. mtg., Mex. 1964; del. Inter-Am. Bar Assn. mtg., Mex., 1944; ABA del. to Inter-Am. Bar Assn., 1984, Academia Mexicana de Derecho Internacional, 1988. Exec. bd. Chief Seattle council Boy Scouts Am., 1959-61. Author: Legal Aspects of LAFTA, 1967, Full Faith and Credit in Federal Systems, 1968, Conflicts-Private International Law, 1969, Legal Aspects Current Latin American Integration and Development, 1979, Latin American Regional Development and Debt, 1985, NAFTA and Beyond, IABA, 1995. Republican dist. leader, King County, Wash., 1949-52, mem. exec. com., 1950-52. Mem. Inter-Am. (chmn. com. legal aspects devel. and integration 1978-81, coun. 1982—), Internat. (charter patron), Am. (nat. chmn. younger lawyers 1948-49, ho. dels. 1949-50, vice chmn. sr. lawyers div. pub. affairs 1986-89, chmn. health maintenance com. 1990-92, chmn. ins. and retirement benefits com. 1991-93, nat. vice chair probate and guardianships 1995—), Wash. (chmn. war readjustment and traffic court coms. 1944-46), Dallas (internat. com. 1974-95), Tex. (internat. sec. 1980—, lawyer referral 1981-87, immigration law 1987-90, rels. with Mex. bars 1990-93), AILA 1994—. Mem. Whitman County Bar Assn. (pres. 1943-44), Fedn. Ins. Counsel (v.p. 1960-61), Am. Soc. Internat. Law, Dallas Internat. Lawyers, Comml. Law League Am. (pres. 1961-62), Nat. Geneal. Soc., Delta Upsilon (pres. publications 1934, Gonzaga sr. gold medal rep. 1938) Selden Soc., SAR (Dallas chpt. pres. 1981, Tex. chancellor 1983, trustee Tex. 1986-87, v.p. S. Ctrl. Dist. 1987-89, pres. Tex. 1985-86, v.p. Western Hemisphere 1989-90, nat. chancellor gen. 1990-92), Am. Law Students Assn. (found. 1948), Epsicopalian (vestryman 1970-72), Odd Fellow (sovereign grand rep. 1954), Lion (dir. 1963-64), NSSAR Minutemen (1992). Home: 7149 Northaven Rd Dallas TX 75230-3601 Office: 4627 N Central Expy Dallas TX 75205-4022 *The rewards of life arise from faith, service and loyalty. The law recognizes justice can only be achieved by strong advocacy and equality.*

EDDY, CHARLES ALAN, chiropractor; b. Kansas City, Mo., Feb. 20, 1948; s. Sam Albert and Ella Louise (Gani) E.; m. Donna Darlene Perry, Oct. 23, 1971. Student, U. Mo., Kansas City, 1967; D in Chiropractic, Cleveland Chiropractic, Kansas City, 1970. Diplomate Nat. Bd. Chiropractic Examiners. Pvt. practice Kansas City, 1970—; peer rev. bd. Blue Cross and Blue Shield, Kansas City, 1972; pres. hon. bd. govs. Bapt. Hosp., Kansas City, 1993-94; cons. Quality Corp., Overland Park, Kans., 1988. Leader, profl. musician Chuck Eddy Band, Kansas City, 1964—; res. officer Kansas City Police Dept., 1970-77, sgt., 1977-82, capt., 1982-94; vice chmn. Citizens Assn., 1995-98, candidate for City Coun., Kansas City, 1995, elected 6th Dist. City Council 1999—; mem. pub. impro vement adv. com. City of Kansas City. Mem. Am. Chiropractic Assn., Mo. State Chriopractic Assn., Mo. Dist. II Chiropractic Assn. (bd. dirs., v.p. 1998—), Cleve. Chiropractic Coll. (trustee 1990, vice chmn. 1992-98), Cleve. Chiropractic Alumni Assn. (v.p. 1995-97, pres. 1997-98, bd. dirs. 1990—, amb.'s soc. 1983—, chmn. 1990-96), Optimist Club of Landing (pres. 1980, lt. gov. Mo. dist. 1982), South Kansas City C. of C. (Sml. Bus. of Yr. award 1998), Am. Lebanon Syrian Men's Club (pres. 1988-91, chmn. bd. 1992), St. Andrews Soc. (drummer in pipe band), DeMolay Legion Hon. (sec. 1988, treas. 1990, vice-dean 1991, dean 1992), Pipes and Drums of Ararat (treas. 1977-90, pres. 1985, dir. 1989, 90), Elks, Shriners (Potentate of Ararat shrine temple 1999, publicity chmn. 1991-92), Royal Order Jesters, Order Quetzalcoatl. Episcopalian. Avocations: photography, guns, stereo and video entertainment. Home: 406 W 109th St Kansas City MO 64114-4910 Office: 8301 State Line Rd # 108 Kansas City MO 64114-2019

EDDY, CHARLES CHRISTOPHER, educator; b. L.A., July 21, 1948; s. Leon Tanner and May Lillian Eddy; m. Nancy Dianne Bottrell, July 5, 1969; 1 child, Katherine Jean. BA in Polit. Sci. magna cum laude, Calif. State U., Hayward, 1973; MA in Edn., U.S. Internat. U., San Diego, 1985. Tchr. Marian Coll., Melbourne, Australia, 1974-75, Martin Elem. Sch., Santa Ana, Calif., 1976-82, MacArthur Intermediate Sch., Santa Ana, Calif., 1982—; fellow SDB Found., Johns Hopkins U., Glendale, Calif., 1990—. With U.S. Army, 1969-72. Recipient Presdl. award for tchg. math. Orange County Maths. Coun., 1988. Mem. NEA. Avocations: tennis, golf, reading. Office: MacArthur Intermediate Sch 600 W Alton Santa Ana CA 92706

EDDY, COLETTE ANN, aerial photography studio owner, photographer; b. Sept. 14, 1950; d. William F. and Jeanne (Valeski) Trump; m. Robert K. Eddy, Aug. 21, 1976 (div. Sept. 1992). AA, St. Petersburg (Fla.) Jr. Coll., 1970; BA, U. South Fla., 1973; MS, Nova U., 1988. Yacht caretaker The Sundowner, St. Petersburg, 1972-73; mgr. Aunt Hattie's Restaurant, St. Petersburg, 1973-79, Johnathan Jones, Inc., St. Petersburg, 1979-80; photographer, sales rep. Smith Aerial Photos, Tampa, Fla., 1980—; owner, aerial photographer Aerial Innovations, Inc., Tampa, 1987—; owner Havanna Connection Inc., Carribean. Mem. Tampa Mus. Art. Mem. Profl. Photographers Am. (30 Merit awards), Fla. Profl. Photographers (20 Merit awards 1987-90), Profl. Aerial Photographers Assn., Tampa C. of C., Emerging Bus. Coun. Republican. Home: 198 Ceylon Ave Tampa FL 33606-3330 Office: Aerial Innovations Inc 1413 S Howard Ave Ste 206 Tampa FL 33606-3176

EDDY, DARLENE MATHIS, poet, educator; b. Elkhart, Ind., Mar. 19, 1937; d. William Eugene and Fern (Paulmer) Mathis; m. Spencer Livingston Eddy, Jr., May 23, 1964 (dec. May 1971). B.A., Goshen Coll., 1959; M.A., Rutgers U., 1961, Ph.D., 1967. Instr., lectr. Douglass Coll. and Rutgers U., 1962-64, 66-67; asst. prof. English Ball State U., Muncie, Ind., 1967-70, assoc. prof., 1971-75, prof., 1975-99, poet-in-residence, 1989-93, prof. emerita, 1999; tchr., cons. numerous creative writing workshops. Author: The Worlds of King Lear, 1968, Leaf Threads, Wind Rhymes, 1985, Weathering, 1991, Portraits, 1992; poetry editor Forum, 1985-89; contbg. editor Snowy Egret, 1988-89; cons. editor Blue Unicorn, 1995—; founding editor The Hedge Row Press, 1995; contbr. articles to English Lang. Notes, Am. Lit., other jours.; contbr. poetry to various publs. Mem. commn. on the status of women in the profession, Nat. coun. of Teachers of English, 1976-79; coord. Women's Studies program, 1976-82. Woodrow Wilson Nat. fellow, 1959-62, Notable Woodrow Wilson fellow, 1991, Rutgers U. grad. honors felllow, 1964-65; recipient numerous rsch., creative teaching and creative arts grants. Mem. MLA, AAUP, DAR (Soc. Mayflower Descendants, Washington), Shakespeare Assn., Nat. League Am. Pen Women. Home: 1409 W Cardinal St Muncie IN 47303-2769 Office: Ball State Univ RB 248 English Muncie IN 47303

EDDY, DAVID LATIMER, banker; b. Simsbury, Conn., July 3, 1936; s. Edward McChesney and Alberta (Messenger) E.; m. Doris Janeczek, Jan. 7, 1958 (div.); children: Craig, Carol, Dianne, Linda, Elizabeth; m. Gaye Margaret Peterson, May 15, 1976; children: Breese, Taryn, Daniel. BS, U. Conn., 1958; MBA, Harvard U., 1960. Asst. mgr. No. Trust Co., Chgo., 1964-68, 2d v.p., 1968-72, v.p., 1972-85, sr. v.p., 1986—; sr. v.p., treas. No. Trust Corp., Chgo., 1986—. Mem. Planning Forum, Fin. Execs. Inst. Congregationalist. Clubs: Harvard (Chgo.), Harvard Grad. Bus. Sch. Office: No Trust Corp 50 S La Salle St Chicago IL 60603-1006

EDDY, DAVID MAXON, health policy and management administrator. BA, Stanford (Calif.) U., 1964, PhD with great distinction, 1978; MD, U. Va., 1968. Intern in gen. surgery Stanford U. Med. Ctr., 1968-69, resident, postdoct. fellow cardiovascular surgery, 1969-71, acting asst. prof., 1976-78; assoc. prof. Dept. Engring.-Econ. Systems, Stanford U., 1978-80, prof., 1980-81; J. Alexander McMahon prof. health policy and mgmt. Duke U., 1986-90, prof. health policy and mgmt., 1990-95; dir. WHO Collaborating Ctr. for Rsch. in Cancer Policy, 1984-95; sr. advisor health policy mgmt. Kaiser Permanente So. Calif. Region, 1991—; columnist Jour. of the AMA, 1990—; spl. govt. employee Hillary Rodham Clinton's Health Care Task Force, 1993; expert adv. panel on cancer WHO, 1981-96; cons. numerous cos., orgns. and assns. Author: A Manual for Assessing Health Practices and Designing Practice Policies, 1992, FAST*PRO: Software for Meta-Analysis by the Confidence Profile Method, 1992, The Synthesis of Statistical Evidence: meta-Analysis by the Confidence Profile Method, 1992, Common Screening Tests, 1991, Screening for Cancer: Theory, Analysis and Design, 1980, (Lanchester Prize, 1981), Clinical Decision Making: From Theory to Practice, 1996; contbr. articles to profl. jours. Recipient Sci. and Technol. Achievement award EPA, 1993, FHP Prize Internat. Soc. of Tech. Assessment in Health Care, 1991, USQA Quality Algorithm award, 1995, Novartis Outcomes Leadership award, 1997, Founders award Am. Coll. Med. Quality, 1998. Mem. Inst. of Medicine, Nat. Acad. Scis.

EDDY, DON, artist; b. Long Beach, Calif., Nov. 4, 1944; s. Myron and Ruth (Chase) Eddy King; m. Nancy Walker, June 12, 1967 (div. 1976); 1 dau., Sarah. B.F.A., U. Hawaii, 1967, M.F.A., 1969. Artist N.Y.C. One man shows include Galerie Petit, Paris, 1973, Nancy Hoffman Gallery, N.Y.C., 1974, 76, 79, 83, 86, 90, 92, 93, 94, 96, 98, Mitch Shaheen Gallery, Cleve., 1994, Molly Barnes Gallery, L.A., 1970, 71, French & Co., N.Y.C., 1971, Huntington (W.Va.) Mus., 1996; exhibited in group shows U.S. and Europe; represented in permanent collections Akron Art Inst., Cleve. Mus. Art, Fogg Art Mus., Harvard U., Utrecht Mus., Belgium, Toledo Mus. Art, Whitney Mus. Am. Art and others.

EDDY, DONALD DAVIS, English language educator; b. Norfolk, Va., Apr. 19, 1929; s. Clarence Ford and Rebekah (Proctor Davis) E.; m. Edith Ann Quattlebaum, Dec. 20, 1954; children: Edith Evelyn, Elizabeth Nelson. B.A., Dartmouth Coll., 1951; MA, PhD, U. Chgo.; M.A. (Munby fellow), Cambridge (Eng.) U., 1978. Prof. English Cornell U., Ithaca, N.Y., 1961-96, head dept. rare books univ. libr., 1968-89, prof. emeritus, 1996—. Works include A Bibliography of John Brown, 1971, Samuel Johnson: Book Reviewer in the Literary Magazine, 1979, Samuel Johnson, LL.D., 1983. Served with USN, 1952-55. Mem. MLA, Bibliog. Soc., Oxford Bibliog. Soc., Cambridge Bibliog. Soc., Bibliog. Soc. Am., Bibliog. Soc. U. Va. Episcopalian. Clubs: Grolier; Athenaeum (London); The Johnsonians. Home: 240 Renwick Dr Ithaca NY 14850-2142

EDDY, ELSBETH MARIE, retired government official, statistician; b. Buffalo, Apr. 8, 1934; d. Willy and Wilhelmine (Hartman) Gnueg; m. Leonard John Eddy, Feb. 5, 1956; children: John, Bruce, Lisa. Student, schs. in Md., Va., N.C.; spl. courses, U.S. Dept. Agriculture Grad. Sch.; cert. in mgmt., Prince Georges Coll., 1976. With fgn. trade div. U.S. Bur. Census, Washington, 1967-90, chief metals and minerals, 1980-90. Recipient Cert. of Appreciation, USAF, 1973. Democrat. Avocations: swimming, gardening, food preservation, oil painting, mineral and gem collecting. Home: 13000 Piscataway Dr Fort Washington MD 20744-6620

EDDY, JOHN JOSEPH, diplomat; b. Lakewood, Ohio, Jan. 8, 1933; s. John Ezekiel and Pauline Edna (Ryan) E.; m. Armonia Badenes, Feb. 14, 1967; children—John Louis, Christopher Robert, William Francis, Isabel Ann (dec.). A.B., Boston Coll., 1960; M.A., Fletcher Sch. of Law and Diplomacy, 1961; student, Nat. Def. U., 1979-80. Joined Fgn. Service, Dept. State, 1966; asst. comml. attache Am. Embassy, Caracas, Venezuela, 1966-69; comml. attache Am. Embassy, San Salvador, El Salvador, 1970-71; first sec., comml. attache Am. Embassy, Bogota, Colombia, 1971-74; counselor for econ. and comml. affairs Am. Embassy, Nairobi, Kenya, 1974-77; dep. chief of mission Am. Embassy, Bridgetown, Barbados, 1977-79; dir. Office Regional Econ. Policy, Bur. Inter-Am. Affairs, Dept. State, 1980-81; consul gen. Am. consulate gen., Dhahran, Saudi Arabia, 1983-87, Am. Consulate Gen., Bombay, 1987-90; sr. spl. asst. to dir. gen. Fgn. Svc., Dept. State, Washington, 1991-92; sr. insp. Dept. State, 1992-94, ret., 1994, cons., 1994—. Served with USAF, 1952-56, Korea. Roman Catholic. Office: Dept State Oig Isp Rm 6817 Washington DC 20520

EDDY, JULIA VERONICA, educator; b. Phila., May 25, 1950; d. Horace Charles and Pearl Marie (Houser) E. BA in Liberal Arts, Rutgers U., 1973; MA in History Edn., SUNY, Stonybrook, 1974, MA in L.Am. History, 1979, postgrad. Cert. secondary tchr. Social studies dir. Community Voyage Sch., Phila., 1976-79; edn. mgr. Project 70001, Phila., 1979-82, Am. Bus. Inst., Phila., 1982-84; vis. lectr. C.C. Phila., 1984-87; mgr. Pvt. Industry Coun., Phila., 1988-92, Tradeswomen of Phila. in Non-Traditional Work, Inc., 1991-93; founder Eddy & Assocs., Phila., 1993—; tchr. tech. studies Sch. Dist. Phila., 1994—; computer specialist cons., 1997—; cons. Jr. Achievement of Am., 1996—, WAWA Teen Parenting, Phila., 1995-96, Top/Win, Inc., Phila., 1991-92, Sch. for Exec. Secs., Newark, 1984, Voyage House, Inc., Phila., 1980; workshop presenter. Editor, contbr: Women in Technology & Trades, 1992; contbg. editor: JTPA/PIC Case Management, 1991; editor: Unions/Apprenticeship in Pennsylvania, 1991. Bd. dirs. New Birth, Inc., Phila., 1993—; founder, pres. Mentor, Phila., 1993—; mem. Doris Day Animal League, Washington, 1989—. Recipient PIC Excellence award Pvt. Industry Coun., 1988, Phila. Sch. Dist. Mentor award, 1998; Samuel Robinson fellowship Lincoln U., 1970. Mem. Tutor Roundtable (treas. 1986), Am. Hist. Assn., Lamba Kappa Mu, Inc. (workshop presenter 1993, Community Svc. award 1993). Democrat. Roman Catholic. Avocations: amateur radio, cats, puzzles. Home: 717 Cobbs Creek Pkwy Philadelphia PA 19143-2210 Office: Eddy & Assocs 717 Cobbs Creek Pkwy Philadelphia PA 19143-2210

EDDY, WILLIAM BAHRET, psychology educator, university dean. BS, Kans. State U., 1955, MS in Indsl. Psychology, 1957; PhD in Indsl. Psychology, Mich. State U., 1963. Lic. orgnl. psychologist, Mo. Asst. prof., assoc. prof. U. Mo., Kansas City, 1962-71, dir., Ctr. for Mgmt. Devel., 1966-69, prof., dir. pub. adminstrn., 1972-77, Helen Kemper prof. adminstrn., 1977-81, assoc. dean, 1981-86, dean and Harzfeld prof. Bloch Sch. Bus. and Pub. Adminstrn., 1986—; bd. dirs. Metcalf Bank; prof., assoc. dir. Fed. Exec. Inst., U.S. Civil Svc. Commn., Charlottesville, Va., 1971-72; lectr. Woodrow Wilson Dept. Govt. and Fgn. Affairs, U.Va., 1972; presenter in field. Author: Public Organization and Development, 1981, The Manager and the Working Group, 1985, others; contbr. articles to profl. jours.; coeditor Adminstr. and Soc., 1980-86. Chmn. nat. bd. trustees Shepherd's Ctrs. of Am., 1991-96; founding bd. dirs., pres. citizens league Kansas City Consensus, 1985-86; pres. bd. Greater Kansas City Mental Health Found., 1987-88. Fellow APA; mem. Gold Key, Psi Chi, Phi Kappa Phi, Beta Gamma Sigma, Delta Sigma Pi, Alpha Tau Omega. Home: 611 E 54th St Kansas City MO 64110-2411 Office: U Missouri Henry Bloch Sch Bus & Pub Adminstrn 5110 Cherry St Kansas City MO 64110-2426

EDEAWO, GALE PAULA, publishing company executive, writer; b. Detroit, Mar. 22, 1946; d. John Bryd Martin and Minerva Lee Dubrey; m. Robert Judkins, Jan. 23, 1965 (div. Jan. 1979); children: Consuella Judkins. AA, L.A. City Coll., 1977; student, Calif. State U., L.A., 1977-78. Telecom. PBXtra Placement, L.A., 1979-98; owner, mgr., writer Sky Publs., Savannah, Ga., 1998—; travel cons. Alwayz Travel, Inglewood, Calif., 1989-92. Peer counselor Rosa Parks Rape Crisis Ctr., L.A., 1990-98; AIDS activist, contbg. writer Project Azuka, Savannah, 1998—; cmty. outreach, spkr. Alzheimer's Assn., L.A., 1996-97; bd. dirs. Alcoholism Ctr. Women, L.A., 1992-94; mem. Ga. Hist. Soc., 1996—. Mem. Am. Legion Women's Aux. (mem. pub. rels. 1986). Democrat. Methodist. Avocations: traveling, writing, cats, reading, researching the South. Fax: 912-961-9076. Office: Sky Publs 12511 Largo Dr Savannah GA 31419

EDEL, ABRAHAM, philosophy educator; b. Pitts., Dec. 6, 1908; s. Simon and Fannie (Malamud) E.; m. May Mandelbaum, Jan. 30, 1934 (dec. May 1964); children: Matthew (dec.), Deborah; m. Elizabeth Flower, May 11, 1973 (dec. June 1995); m. Sima Szaluta, Apr. 20, 1997. BA, McGill U., 1927, MA, 1928; BA, Oxford U., 1930; PhD, Columbia U., 1934. Mem. faculty dept. philosophy CCNY, 1931-73, prof., 1962-73, prof. emeritus, 1973—; Disting. prof. Grad. Sch. CUNY, 1970-73; emeritus City U. N.Y. Grad. Sch., 1973—; research prof. philosophy U. Pa., 1974—; vis. appointments instns. including Columbia U., U. Calif., Berkeley, Swarthmore Coll., U. Pa., Case Western Res. U., SUNY, Downstate Med. Ctr., others. Author: The Theory and Practice of Philosophy, 1946, Ethical Judgement, 1955, 2d edit. with new intro., 1995, Science and the Structure of Ethics, 1961, 2nd edit., 1998, Method in Ethical Theory, 1963, with new intro., 1994, Aristotle, 1967; co-author: (with May Edel) Anthropology and Ethics, 1959, rev. edit., 1971, Analyzing Concepts in Social Science, 1979, Exploring Fact and Value, 1980, Aristotle and His Philosophy, 1982, with new intro., 1996, Interpreting Education, 1985, (with Elizabeth Flower and Finbarr O'Connor) Morality, Philosophy and Practice, 1988, Relating Humanities and Social Thought, 1990, The Struggle for Academic Democracy, 1990, In Search of the Ethical, 1993, (with others) Critique of Applied Ethics, 1994; (with Yervant H. Krikorian) Contemporary Philosophic Problems, 1959; editor: (with May M. Edel) The Chiga of Uganda, 1996. Assoc. Nat. Humanities Ctr., 1978-79; sr. fellow Ctr. for Dewey Studies, 1981-82. Recipient Butler Silver medal Columbia U., 1959; Guggenheim fellow, 1944-45; Grantee, Rockefeller Found., 1952-53, NSF, 1959-60. Mem. Am. Philos. Assn. (v.p. Ea. div. 1972), Metaphys. Soc., Am. Soc. Polit. and Legal Philosophy, Am. Soc. Value Inquiry (pres. 1984), Internat. Assn. Philosophy Law and Social Philosophy (v.p. Am. sect. 1971-73, pres. 1973-75, hon. pres. 1997), Philosophy Edn. Soc., Soc. for Advancement Am. Philosophy.

EDELBAUM, PHILIP R., lawyer; b. Bklyn., June 2, 1936; s. Maurice and Selma (Samuels) E.; m. Corinne Edelbaum, May 29, 1960 (div. Mar. 1974); children: Stacey K. Boretz, Evan Mark. BA, Adelphi U., 1957; LLB, NYU, 1960. Bar: N.Y. 1961, U.S. Dist. Cts. (so. and ea. dists.) N.Y. 1962, U.S. Ct. of Appeals (2d cirs.) 1964, (3d cir.) 1977, U.S. Supreme Ct. 1965. Atty. criminal div. Legal Aid Soc., N.Y.C., 1961-63; pvt. practice N.Y.C., 1963—; faculty Nat. Inst. Trial Advocacy-N.E. Region, Nat. Inst. Trial Advocacy-N.E. Master Advocates, Hempstead, N.Y., 1985—, Cardozo Law Sch. intensive trial advocacy program, 1993—, ABA/USTA Trademark Trial Advocacy Inst., 1993—, Widener U. Sch. Law intensive trial advocacy program, 1995—; faculty trial techniques program Hofstra U. Sch. of Law, Hempstead, 1985—. Chmn. pool feasibility com. Town of Eastchester, N.Y., 1971-72. Mem. Nat. Def. Lawyers Criminal Cases, N.Y. Criminal Bar Assn., N.Y. State Bar Assn., Assn. of Bar of City of N.Y. (com. on criminal cts. op. and budget 1988-92, chmn. com. on criminal advocacy 1995—, mem. coun. criminal justice 1992—, com. to study alts. to incarceration and probation 1993-94, numerous sub-coms. on criminal justice 1988—). Avocations: classical music, bird watching, N.Y. Mets, cooking. Home: 345 E 93rd St New York NY 10128-5515 Office: 100 Church St New York NY 10007-2601

EDELCUP, NORMAN SCOTT, management and financial consultant; b. Chgo., May 8, 1935; s. Irving L. and Pauline (Bolz) E. BS in Bus. Adminstrn, Northwestern U., 1957. C.P.A., Fla., Ill. Sr. accountant Arthur Andersen & Co., Chgo., 1957-62; sec.-treas. Acme Printing Ink Co., Chgo., 1962-65; accountant, asst. to chmn. Commonwealth Edison Co., Chgo., 1965-68; sr. v.p., vice-chmn. bd. Keller Industries, Miami, Fla., 1968-76; v.p., treas. Avatar Holdings (formerly GAC Corp.), 1976-80, exec. v.p., treas., chief fin. officer, dir., mem. exec. com., 1980-83; pres., treas., dir. Avatar Properties Inc. (formerly GAC Properties, Inc.), 1976-83, Avatar Properties Credit (formerly GAC Properties Credit, Inc.), 1976-83; vice chmn., chief operating officer Nat. Banking Corp. Fla., Miami, 1983-84; chmn. treas. Scroll Casual Inc., 1983-84; chmn. Fla. Powder Coatings, Inc., Confidata Corp., 1983-87; chmn., treas. First United Leasing Corp., 1983-86; ptnr. E&H Assocs., 1983-91; chmn. Item Processing Am. Inc., Miami, 1987-98; bd. dirs. Valhi Inc., Baron Asset Fund. Served with AUS, 1958-60. Mem. Am. Inst. CPA's, Fla. Inst. CPA's, Ill. Inst. CPA's, Greater Miami C. of C. (trustee 1979-83). Lodge: Kiwanis. Home: 244 Atlantic Isle Miami FL 33160-4516 Office: Item Processing Am Inc 5190 NW 167th St Ste 300 Hialeah FL 33014-6338

EDELHAUSER, HENRY F., physiologist, ophthalmic researcher, educator; b. Dover, N.J., Sept. 9, 1937; married, 1961; 2 children. BA, Patterson State Coll., 1961; MS, Mich. State U., 1964, PhD in Physiology, 1966. Lab. technician Warner Lambert Pharm. Rsch. Inst., 1962-65; from instr. to prof. physiology and ophthalmology Med. Coll. Wis., 1966-89; prof. ophthalmology, dir. rsch. Emory U., Atlanta, 1989—, dir. grants dept. ophthalmology, 1990; bd. dirs. Am. Fight-for-Sight, Inc., 1975-90; prin. investigator Mt. Desert Island Biol. Lab., 1977; sci. cons. Alcon Labs. Fellow Marquette U., 1966-67; grantee Nat. Eye. Inst., 1969—, Wis. Dept. Nat. Rsch., 1969-71; Olga K. Weiss Rsch. Scholar; named Marjorie and Joseph Heil prof. ophthalmology, 1988, Ferst prof. ophthalmology, 1989. Mem. Assn. Rsch. Vision and Ophthalmology (pres. 1990-91), Am. Physiol. Soc., Am. Acad. Opthalmology (Honor award). Achievements include research in membrane physiology, pathophysiology of eye, fish physiology and eye disease, ocular toxicology, physiological effects of vitrectomy, cellular toxicology and ophthalmic drugs. E-mail: ophthfe@emory.edu. Office: Emory U Dept Ophthalmology Emory Eye Ctr 2600 1365 B Clinton Rd NE Atlanta GA 30322-1013*

EDELHEIT, LEWIS S., research physicist; b. Chgo., Aug. 24, 1942; m. Susan Wershkoff, 1965; children: David, Dena. BS, U. Ill., 1964, MS, 1965, PhD in Physics, 1969. Physicist GE R&D Ctr., Schenectady, N.Y., 1969-76; mgr. Applied Sci. & Diagnostic Imaging Lab. GE Med. Sys., Milw., N.Y., 1976-80; mgr. computed tomography prodn. engring. GE Corp. R&D, Schenectady, N.Y., 1980-82, gen. mgr. dept. engring., 1982-83, gen. mgr. dept. computed tomography programs, 1983-85; pres., CEO Quantum Med. Sys., 1985-91, Schenectady, N.Y., 1985-91; mgr. electronics sys. rsch. ctr. GE Corp. R&D, Schenectady, N.Y., 1991-92; sr. v.p. GE Corp. R&D, Schenectady, 1992—; pres., CEO Quantum Med. Sys., 1985-91. Mem. NAE, Am. Physics Soc., Indsl. Rsch. Inst., Sigma Xi. Achievements include research in medical imaging systems, computerized imaging systems. Office: GE Corp R&D Ctr Bldg K1 Rm 5A1 One Rsch Cir Niskayuna NY 12309*

EDELHERTZ, HELAINE WOLFSON, mathematics educator; b. Queens, N.Y., June 22, 1953; d. David and Sylvia Guttman Wolfson; m. Melvyn Paul, June 6, 1976; children: Allyson Leigh, Dustin Scott. BS, SUNY, Oneonta, 1977; MS, SUNY, New Paltz, 1985. Cert. tchr., N-6, N.Y. Substitute tchr. Roscoe (N.Y.) Cen. Sch., 1978-82; tchr. Yeshiva Sch., South Fallsburg, N.Y., 1982-83; substitute tchr. Middletown (N.Y.) City Sch. Dist., 1984-86, home tchr., 1984-87, math. specialist, 1987-92; with Math Turnkey, Meml. Elem. Sch., Middletown, 1989-93, Excellence and Accountability Program, 1989-92; math. com. Middletown Schs., 1989-95; bldg. com. Study Math. Portfolios, 1992—, instr. math. manipulations. Bd. dirs. Wallkill Farms Homeowner's Assn., 1986-88, budget com., 1992—; asst. summer coord. Roscoe Free Libr., 1983. Mem. Am. Math. Tchrs. N.Y. State, Nat. Coun. Tchrs. Math., Middletown Tchrs. Assn. (sr. bldg. rep. 1992-95, bldg. rep. 1997-99, exec. bd. dirs.). Jewish. Avocations: gardening, sewing, knitting, cooking, dance. Home: 118 Rolling Meadows Rd Middletown NY 10940-2611 Office: Maple Hill Elem Sch 491 County Rte 78 Middletown NY 10940

EDELMAN, ALAN IRWIN, lawyer; b. Poughkeepsie, N.Y., June 14, 1958; s. Edwyn Herman and Shirley Frances (Kandel) E.; m. Erica Joy Schwartz, Aug. 16, 1981; children: Leah Hanit, Avram Natan, Samuel Aaron. BA, Cornell U., 1980; JD, Boston U., 1983. Bar: D.C. 1983, U.S. Dist. Ct. D.C. 1985, U.S. Supreme Ct. 1991. Atty. enforcement div. SEC, Washington, 1983-86, atty. Office of Gen. Counsel, 1986-87; counsel U.S. Senate Permanent Subcom. on Investigations, Washington, 1987-97, U.S. Senate Com. on Govtl. Affairs, 1997—. Edward F. Hennessy scholar Boston U., 1983. Mem. ABA, Fed. Bar Assn. Office: US Senate 326 Dirksen Senate Bldg Washington DC 20510

EDELMAN, ALVIN, lawyer; b. Chgo., Dec. 12, 1916; s. Leon and Sally (Kramer) E.; m. Rose Marie Slossy, Sept. 22, 1940; children: Marilyn Frances Edelman Snyder, Stephen D., Leon F. B.S. in Law, Northwestern U., 1938, J.D., 1940. Bar: Ill. 1940. Practiced in Chgo., 1940—; pres. Edelman & Edelman, Chartered, and predecessors, 1973—; gen. counsel Internat. Coll. Surgeons; lectr. Internat. Mus. Surg. Sci. and Hall of Fame; chmn. wills and gifts com. Medinah Temple of Masonic Shrine, Chgo., 1975-79; pres. Lawyers Shrine Club of Medinah Temple, 1971-73. Contbr. articles to profl. jours. Fellow Am. Coll. Trust and Estate Counsel; mem. ABA, Ill., Chgo. (chmn. grievance com. 1971-72) Bar Assns., Phi Beta Kappa (pres. Chgo. area assn. 1975-85), Phi Beta Kappa Assocs. (bd. dirs. 1985—, nat. v.p. 1986-95, nat. pres. 1996—). Lodges: Elks (past exalted ruler) (Chgo.) Office: 100 W Monroe St Chicago IL 60603-1967

EDELMAN, DANIEL JOSEPH, public relations executive; b. N.Y.C., July 3, 1920; s. Selig and Selma (Pfeiffer) E.; m. Ruth Rozumoff, Sept. 3, 1953; children: Richard, Renee, John. Grad., Columbia U., 1940; MS, 1941. Reporter Poughkeepsie (N.Y.) newspapers, UPI, 1941-42; news writer CBS, 1946-47; staff mem. Edward Gottlieb & Assocs., 1947; pub. rels. dir. Toni Co., Chgo., 1948-52; founder, chmn. 37 offices Daniel J. Edelman, Inc. (Edelman Pub. Rels. Worldwide and P.R. 21), Chgo., 1952—. Mem. Ill. Lottery Control Bd., 1974; mem. comm. com. Boy Scouts Am., Chgo.; chmn. vis. com. U. Chgo. Libr., 1976; bd. dirs. Ill. Children's Home and Aid Soc., Chgo.; chmn. sustaining fellows individual campaign Chgo. Art Inst., 1982; bd. dirs. Lyric Opera Chgo.; mem. Philanthropy Task Force/Chgo. United, 1988; dir. Comm. for Econ. Growth of Israel. With U.S. Army, 1942-46. Recipient Disting. Alumnus award Columbia U., 1988, John Jay award Columbia U., 1990; named Pub. Rels. Profl. of Yr. Pub. Rels. News, 1993, Agy. of Yr. Inside PR Mag., 1993, Lifetime Achievement All-Star Inside PR mag. award, 1998, St. Bonaventure U. Tom Mosser award, 1998; named to Chgo. Bus. Hall of Fame, Jr. Achievement. Fellow Pub. Rels. Soc. Am. (past chmn. counselor sect., 31 Silver Anvil awards, Top Gun Career Achievement award 1998), Young Pres. Orgn. (chmn. Chgo. chpt. 1963), Chief Execs. Orgn., Arthur Page Soc., Chgo. Club, Std. Club, Harmonie Club, Mid-Am. Club, Casino Club, Phi Beta Kappa. Jewish. Home: 1301 N Astor St Chicago IL 60610-2186 Office: Edelman Pub Rels Amoco Bldg 200 E Randolph Dr Chicago IL 60601-6436

EDELMAN, GERALD MAURICE, biochemist, neuroscientist, educator; b. N.Y.C., N.Y., July 1, 1929; s. Edward and Anna (Freedman) E.; m. Maxine Morrison, June 11, 1950; children: Eric, David, Judith. B.S., Ursinus Coll., 1950, Sc.D., 1974; M.D., U. Pa., 1954, D.Sc., 1973; Ph.D., Rockefeller U., 1960; M.D. (hon.), U. Siena, Italy, 1974; DSc (hon.), Gustavus Adolphus Coll., 1975, Williams Coll., 1976; DSc Honoris Causa, U. Paris, 1989; LSc Honoris Causa, U. Cagliari, 1989; DSc, Georgetown U., 1989; DSc Honoris Causa, U. degli Studi di Napoli, 1990, Tulane U., 1991, U. Miami, 1995, Adelphi U., 1995, U. Bologna, 1998. Med. house officer Mass. Gen. Hosp., 1954-55; asst. physician hosp. of Rockefeller U., 1957-60, mem. faculty, 1960-92, assoc. dean grad. studies, 1963-66, prof., 1966-74, Vincent Astor disting. prof., 1974-92; mem. faculty and chmn. dept. neurobiology Scripps Rsch. Inst., La Jolla, Calif., 1992—; mem. biophysics and biophys. chemistry study sect. NIH, 1964-67; mem. Sci. Council, Ctr. for Theoretical Studies, 1970-72; assoc., sci. chmn. Neurosciences Research Program, 1980—, dir. Neuroscis. Inst., 1981—; mem. adv. bd. Basel Inst. Immunology, 1970-77, chmn., 1975-77; non-resident fellow, trustee Salk Inst., 1973-85; bd. overseers Faculty Arts and Scis., U. Pa., 1976-83; trustee, mem. adv. com. Carnegie Inst., Washington, 1980-87; bd. govs. Weizman Inst. Sci., 1971-87, mem. emeritus; researcher structure of antibodies, molecular and devel. biology. Author: Neural Darwinism, 1987, Topobiology, 1988, The Remembered Present, 1989, Bright Air, Brilliant Fire, 1992. Trustee Rockefeller Bros. Fund., 1972-82. Served to capt. M.C. AUS, 1955-57. Recipient Spencer Morris award U. Pa., 1954, Ann. Alumni award Ursinus Coll., 1969, Nobel prize for physiology or medicine, 1972, Albert Einstein Commemorative award Yeshiva U., 1974, Buchman Meml. award Calif. Inst. Tech., 1975, Rabbi Shai Shacknai meml. prize Hebrew U.-Hadassah Med. Sch., Jerusalem, 1977, Regents medal Excellence, N.Y. State, 1984, Hans Neurath prize, U. Washington, 1986, Sesquicentennial Commemorative award Nat. Libr. Medicine, 1986, Cécile and Oskar Vogt award U. Dusseldorf, 1988, Disting. Grad. award U. Pa., 1990, Personnalité de l'année, Paris, 1990, Warren Triennial Prize award Mass. Gen. Hosp., 1992. Fellow AAAS, N.Y. Acad. Scis., N.Y. Acad. Medicine; mem. Am. Philos. Soc., Am. Soc. Biol. Chemists, Am. Assn. Immunologists, Genetics Soc. Am., Harvey Soc. (pres. 1975-76, Am. Chem. Soc., Eli Lilly award biol. chemistry 1965), Am. Acad. Arts and Scis., Nat. Acad. Sci., Am. Soc. Cell Biology, Acad. Scis. of Inst. France (fgn.), Japanese Biochem. Soc. (hon.), Pharm. Soc. Japan (hon.), Soc. Developmental Biology, Council Fgn. Relations, Sigma Xi, Alpha Omega Alpha. Office: Scripps Rsch Inst Dept Neurobiol SBR-14 10550 N Torrey Pines Rd La Jolla CA 92037-1000

EDELMAN, HARRY ROLLINGS, III, engineering and construction company executive; b. Pitts., Aug. 16, 1928; s. Harry Rollings, Jr. and Marian A. (Crooks) E.; m. Nancy Jane McCune, Aug. 26, 1950; children: Lisa E. Turbeville, Harry Rollings IV, John Reed, Amy E. Carrick. B.S., U. Pitts., 1950. CEO, chmn. CCL-X Mgmt. Inc., Pitts., 1993—; chmn. Heyl & Patterson, Inc., Heylpat Techs., Inc., Bridge & Crane Inspection, Inc., ForeTesting Labs., Inc. Author papers in engring., constrn., religion and mgmt. Past bd. dirs. Allegheny Health Edn. and Rsch. Found., Allegheny Gen. Hosp., Allegheny U. Med. Scis.; past pres. Christian Assn. S.W. Pa.; past chmn. Allegheny Neuropsychiat. Inst., Vocat. Rehab. Ctr. Allegheny County, Allegheny Singer Rsch. Inst., Med. Coll. Pa.; chmn. Presbyn. SeniorCare; past chmn. Allegheny U. Hosp. East; past moderator Pitts. Presbytery. With AUS, 1952-54. Recipient Regional Ecumenism award, 1985, Allegheny Disting. Svc. award, 1997. Mem. World Pres.'s Orgn., Duquesne Club, Pitts. Field Club, The Club at Seabrook Island. Office: CCL-X Mgmt Inc PO Box 36 Pittsburgh PA 15230-0036

EDELMAN, HENDRIK, library and information science educator; b. Wageningen, Netherlands, Nov. 27, 1937; came to U.S., 1967; s. Cornelis Hendrik and Johanna (van Werkhoven) E.; m. Antoinette M. Kania; children: Stijn Willem, Mark Bastiaan, Kees Maarten. MLS, George Peabody Coll., 1969. With Martinus Nijhoff (Pubs. & Booksellers), Netherlands, 1958-65, D. Reidel Pub. Co., Netherlands, 1965-67; bibliographer Vanderbilt U., 1967-70; asst. dir. Cornell U. Libraries, Ithaca, N.Y., 1970-78; libr. Rutgers-State U. N.J., New Brunswick, 1979-85, prof. libr. and info. studies, 1985—; chmn. bd. Ctr. Book Rsch., U. Scranton, 1983-88; chmn. bd. Rsch. Libr. Group, Inc., 1982-83; bd. dirs. Book Industry Study Group, 1977-84; USIA/ALA Libr./Book fellow, U. Surinam, 1992-93; editorial mktg. cons. Am. European pubs. (booksellers); acad. libr. cons.; chmn. edn. com. Netherland Am. Found., 1997—. Author: The Dutch Language Press in America, 1986, Libraries and Information Science in the Electronic Age, 1986, A History of Religious Publishing and Bookselling in the United States and Canada, 1640-1985, 1987; contbr. articles, revs. to profl. jours. Mem. ALA, Soc. for Scholarly Pub., Bibliog. Soc. Am., Am. Antiquarian Soc., Grolier Club, Beta Phi Mu. Office: Rutgers U 138 Colton Ave Sayville NY 11782

EDELMAN, ISIDORE SAMUEL, biochemist and medical educator; b. Bklyn., July 24, 1920. Student, Bklyn. Coll., 1937-39; BA, Ind. U., Bloomington, 1941; MD, Ind. U., Indpls., 1944. Resident Montefiore Hosp., Bronx, N.Y., 1947-48; AEC postdoctoral fellow Harvard Med. Sch., 1948-49; research fellow Am. Heart Assn. Brigham Hosp., Boston, 1950-52; asst. prof. medicine U. Calif., San Francisco, 1952-54, assoc. prof. medicine, 1954-60, prof. medicine, 1960-78, assoc. dir. cardiovascular research inst., 1960-69, prof. biophysics, Samuel Neider rsch. prof. medicine, 1967-78; chief med. service San Francisco Gen. Hosp., 1956-58; chmn. dept. biochemistry and molecular biophysics Columbia U., N.Y.C., 1978-88, Robert Wood Johnson Jr. prof. biochemistry, 1978-90, prof. emeritus, 1991-95, dir. Genome Ctr., 1995—; dir. Columbia Genome Ctr., 1995—. Contbr. articles to profl. jours. Served to capt. M.C., U.S. Army, 1945-47. Recipient Homer W. Smith award N.Y. Heart Assn., 1980, Mayo H. Soley medal We. Soc. Clin. Rsch., 1980, Disting. Svc. award Columbia U., 1993; Calif. Inst. Tech. sr. rsch. fellow, 1958-59. Fellow AAAS; mem. NAS, Inst. Medicine, Am. Acad. Arts and Scis., Assn. Am. Physicians, Biophys. Soc., Endocrine Soc. (Eli Lilly Lectureship award 1969, Robert H. Williams Disting. Leadership award 1996), Harvey Soc. (pres. 1989-90), Am. Soc. Biochem. and Molecular Biology. Established investigator Am. Heart Assn., 1952-57. Home: 464 Riverside Dr New York NY 10027-6801*

EDELMAN, JANICE, artist, educator; b. Phila., Apr. 13, 1933; d. Samuel and Anna (Finkelstein) Fishman; 1 child, Susan Helfrich. Degree, Art Inst. Phila., 1956; studied with, Henry Hensche, Provincetown, Mass., 1957, Boris Blai, Phila., 1979-80. Cert. art tchr., Pa. Advt. illustrator John Wanamaker, Phila., 1954-66; advt. art dir. Strawbridge & Clothier, Phila., 1967-76; comml. art instr. Hussian Sch. of Art, Phila., 1976-77; head of art dept. Montgomery County Vocat. Sch., Upper Moreland, Pa., 1978-79; watercolor instr. Woodmere Art Mus., Phila., 1991—; docent Woodmere Art Mus., 1989-91; judge juror Glassboro State Coll., N.J., 1992; bd. dirs. Friends of Moore Coll. of Art, Phila., 1977. Exhibited in group shows at Fashion Group of Phila., 1955, 57, (Fine Arts Gala award 1955, 1st prize 1957), Phila. Club Advt. Women 12 Ann., 1966, 67 (1st prize for layout 1966, for art-layout 1967), 13th Ann., 1974 (1st prize for art-layout 1974, 75), Artist Guild of Delaware Valley 25th Ann., 1975 (Bronze award 1975), Art Dirs. Club of Phila. 39th Ann., 1979 (2 awards for excellence, layout design 1979), Am. Coll., 1985, Phila. Water Color Club 67th Ann., 1985, 70th Ann., 1988, 71st Ann., 1989, 74th Ann., 1992, 75th Ann., 1993 (award of excellence 1988, show chmn. 1992), Watercolor Soc. Ala. 45th Ann., 1986, Oreland Art Ctr. Ann., 1986 (1st prize in watercolor 1986), Artilleries Gallery, 1987, Perkiomen Valley Retirement Cmty., 1987, Charlotte Watercolor Soc., 1987, Woodmere Art Mus. 47th Ann., 1987, 48th Ann., 1988, 49th Ann., 1989, 52nd Ann., 1992, 56th Ann., 1996, Abington Art Ctr. Ann., 1988, Pa. Watercolor Soc. 10th Ann., 1988, 11th Ann., 1989 (Grumbacher award 1988), Salmagundi Club 11th Ann., N.Y., 1988, 16th Ann., 1993 (Merit award 1988), Yellow Spring Art Show, 1989, Art Inst. Phila., 1989, Phila. Art Show, 1989, 90, Balt. Watercolor Soc., 1990, Susquehanna Art Soc. 84th Biennial, 1990, Barn Studio Gallery, 1990, Greater Harrisburg (Pa.) Arts Coun., 1993, Springfield Art League 74th Nat., 1993, Artist Guild Nat., Scottbluff, Nebr., 1993, Batavia (N.Y.) Soc. Artists 9th Nat., 1993, Watercolor Art Soc., Houston, 1994, W.Va. Water Color Soc., 1994, Watercolor West XXVI Ann., Brea, Calif., 1994, Main Line Arts Festival, Haverford, Pa., 1994, Nat. Watercolor Soc., Calif., 1995, Pitts. Watercolor Soc. Ann., Pa., 1995, Bald Eagle Art League Nat., Pa., 1995, North West N.Mex. Arts Coun. (award), 1997; solo show Woodmere Art Mus., Phila., 1997, Phila. Water Color Club 98th juried exhibition, 1998. mem. mus. com. Keneseth Israel Congregation. Mem. Am. Watercolor Soc. (assoc.), Nat. Watercolor Soc. (assoc.), Pa. Watercolor Soc., Phila. Watercolor Soc., Art Dirs. Club Phila. (pres. 1978-80), Phila. Water Color Club (v.p. 1993-94), Rotary Club of Huntingdon Valley. Jewish. Avocations: painting, traveling, reading, creative cooking. Home: 3505 Hale Rd Huntingdon Valley PA 19006-3230

EDELMAN, JOEL, medical center executive; b. Chgo., Mar. 24, 1931; s. Maurice B. and Ethel J. (Newman) E.; m. Beth L. Sommers, July 31, 1955; children: Peter J., Ann Elizabeth, Deborah S. B.A. in Spl. Edn., U. Mich., 1952; J.D., DePaul U., 1960. Bar: Ill. 1961. Program dir. Chgo. Heart Assn., 1955-61; staff atty. Michael Reese Hosp. and Med. Center, Chgo., 1961-70; exec. v.p. Michael Reese Hosp. and Med. Center, 1971-73; dir. Ill. Dept. Pub. Aid, 1973-74; exec. dir. Ill. Legis. Adv. Com. on Pub. Aid, 1974-77; pres. Rose Med. Ctr., Denver, 1979-95; prin., sr. v.p. Frontier Holdings, Inc., Englewood, Colo., 1995—; asst. prof. dept. preventive medicine U. Colo.; U.; dir. office legal affairs Am. Hosp. Assn., 1970. Contbr. articles to profl. jours. Served with AUS, 1955. Mem. Soc. Hosp. Attys. (charter). Home: 3156 S Hills Ct Denver CO 80210-6830

EDELMAN, JUDITH H., architect; b. Bklyn., Sept. 16, 1923; d. Abraham and Frances (Israel) Hochberg; m. Harold Edelman, Dec. 26, 1947; children: Marc, Joshua. Student, Conn. Coll., 1940-41, NYU, 1941-42; BArch, Columbia U., 1946. Designer, drafter Huson Jackson, N.Y.C., 1948-58; Schermerhorn traveling fellow, 1950, pvt. practice architecture, 1958-60; ptnr. Edelman & Salzman, N.Y.C., 1960-79; partner Edelman Partnership (Architects), N.Y.C., 1979—; adj. prof. Sch. Architecture CUNY, 1972-76, vis. lectr. grad. program in environ. psychology, 1977, 77; vis. lectr. Washington U., St. Louis, 1974, U. Oreg., 1974, MIT, 1975, Pa. State U., 1977, Rensselaer Poly. Inst., 1977, Columbia U., 1979; First Claire Watson Forrest Meml. lectr. U. Oreg., U. Calif., Berkeley, U. So. Calif., 1982. Major archtl. works include Restoration of St. Mark's Ch. in the Bowery, N.Y.C., 1970-82, Two Bridges Urban Renewal Area Housing, 1970-96, Jennings Hall Sr. Citizens Housing, Bklyn., 1980, Goddard Riverside Elderly Housing and Cmty. Ctr., N.Y.C., 1983, Columbus Green Apartments, N.Y.C., 1987, Chung Pak Bldg., N.Y.C., 1992. Recipient Bard 1st honor award City Club N.Y., 1969, Bard award of merit, 1975, 82, award for design excellence HUD, 1970, 1st prize Nat. Trust for Hist. Preservation, 1983, award of merit Mcpl. Art Soc. N.Y., 1983, Pub. Svc. award Settlement Housing Fund, 1983, Women of Vision award NOW, 1989, 1st prize for design excellence C. of C., Borough of Queens, N.Y., 1989, Best in Srs.' Housing award Nat. Assn. Home Builders, 1993, Hamilton-Madison House Cmty. Svc. award, 1997. Fellow AIA, dir. N.Y. chpt., chmn. commn. on archtl. edn. 1971-73, chmn. nat. task force on women in architecture 1974-75, v.p. N.Y. chpt. 1975-77, chmn. ethics com. 1975-77, Residential design award 1969, Pioneer in Housing award 1990, N.Y. State Assn. Architects-AIA Honor award 1975); mem. Alliance of Women in Architecture (founding, mem. steering com. 1972-74), Architects for Social Responsibility (mem. exec. com. 1982-85), Columbia Archtl. Alumni Assn. (bd. dirs. 1968-71). Home: 13 Bank St New York NY 10014-5252 Office: Edelman Partnership 434 6th Ave Fl 6 New York NY 10011-8411

EDELMAN, MARIAN WRIGHT (MRS. PETER B. EDELMAN), lawyer; b. Bennettsville, S.C., June 6, 1939; d. Arthur J. and Maggie (Bowen) Wright; m. Peter B. Edelman, July 14, 1968; children: Joshua, Jonah, Ezra. Merrill scholar, Univs. Paris, Geneva, 1958-59; BA, Spelman Coll., 1960; LLB (J.H. Whitney fellow 1960-61), Yale U., 1963, LLD (hon.); LLD (hon.), Smith Coll., 1969, Lowell Tech. U., 1975, Williams Coll., 1978, Columbia U., U. Pa., Amherst Coll., St. Joseph's Coll.; DHL (hon.), Lesley Coll., 1975, Trinity Coll., Washington, Russell Sage Coll., 1978, Syracuse U., Coll. New Rochelle, 1979, Swarthmore Coll., 1980, SUNY Old Westbury, Northeastern U., 1981, Bard Coll., 1982, U. Mass., 1983, Hunter Coll., U. So. Maine, SUNY, Albany, 1984, Columbia U., U. Pa., Yale U., 1985, Rutgers U., Bates Coll., Maryville Coll., Bank St., 1986, Claremont Grad Sch., Lincoln U., Georgetown U., Chgo. Theol. Coll., 1987, Wheaton Coll., Tulane U., Grinnell Coll. Brandeis U., Wheelock Coll., Dartmouth Coll., U. S.C., U. N.C., Grad. Ctr. CUNY, U. Wis. Milw., 1988, Interdenom. Theol. Ctr., Hofstra U., Tufts U., Borough Manhattan Community Coll., Wesleyan U., Calif. State U. L.A., Dillard U., U. Md., U. Miami, 1989, Howard U., Beloit Coll., Queens Coll., Am. U., New Sch. of Social Rsch., Coll. of Notre Dame, DePaul U., 1990, Beaver Coll., Fordham U., Simmons Coll., Hamline U., Clark U., Harvard U., Union Coll., 1991, Tuskegee U., Washington U. St. Louis, Hood Coll., Duke U., Mercy Coll., 1992, Princeton U., U. Ill., Calif. State U. San Francisco, Wittenberg (Ohio) Coll., Shaw U., So. Meth. U., 1993, Brown U., U. Balt., Ea. Conn. State U., U. Notre Dame, 1994. Bar: D.C., Miss., Mass. Staff atty. NAACP Legal Def. and Ednl. Fund, Inc., N.Y.C., 1963-64; dir. NAACP Legal Def. and Ednl. Fund, Inc., Jackson, Miss., 1964-68; Congl. and fed. liaison Poor People's Campaign, summer 1968; partner Washington Research Project of So. Center for Pub. Policy, 1968-73; dir. Harvard U. Center for Law and Edn., 1971-73; pres., founder Children's Def. Fund, 1973—. Author: The Measure of Our Success: A Letter To My Children and Yours, 1992, Families in Peril, 1987. Mem. exec. com. Student Non-Violent Coordinating Com., 1961-63; mem. adv. coun. Martin Luther King Jr. Meml. Libr.; mem. adv. bd. Hampshire Coll.; mem. Presdl. Commn. on Missing in Action, 1977, Presdl. Commn. on Internat. Yr. of Child, 1979, Presdl. Commn. on Agenda for 80's, 1980; bd. dirs. NAACP Legal Def. and Ednl. Fund; trustee Spelman Coll., Carnegie Coun. on Children, 1972-77, Martin Luther King Jr. Meml. Ctr.; mem. Yale U. Corp., 1971-77, Aetna Found., Nat. Commn. on Children, 1989—; bd. dirs. Aetna Life Casualty Found., Citizens for Constitutional Concerns, US. com. UNICEF, Robin Hood Found., Aaron Diamond Found., Nat. Alliance Business, City Lights, Leadership Conf. Civil Rights, Skadden Fellowship Found., Parents as Tchrs. Nat. Ctr., Inc.; U.S. rep. UNICEF; active U.S. Olympic Com. Named one of Outstanding Young Women of Am., 1966; recipient Mademoiselle mag. award, 1965, Louise Waterman Wise award, 1970, Washington of Yr. award, 1979, Whitney M. Young award, 1979, Profl. of Yr. award Black Ent., 1979, Leadership award Nat. Women's Polit. Caucus, 1980, Black Womens Forum award, 1980, medal Columbia Tchrs. Coll., Barnard Coll., 1984, Eliot award Am. Pub. Health Assn., John W. Gardner Leadership award of Ind. Sector, Pub. Svc. Achievement award Common Cause, Compostela award Cathedral St. James, 1987, MacArthur prize fellow, 1985, Albert Schweitzer Humanitarian prize Johns Hopkins U., 1987, Philip Hauge Ahelson award AAAS, 1988, Hubert Humphrey Civil Rights award, AFL-CIO award, 1989, Radcliffe Coll. medal, 1989, Fordham Stein prize, 1989, Gandhi Peace award, 1990, M. Carey Thomas award, Robie award for humanitarianism, Essence award, numerous others; hon. fellow U. Pa. Law Sch. Mem. Phi Beta Kappa (hon.). Address: Children's Def Fund 25 E St NW Washington DC 20001-1522*

EDELMAN, NORMAN HERMAN, medical educator, university dean and official; b. N.Y.C., May 21, 1937; s. Irving H. and Pearl Ruth (Solomon) E.; m. Ida Nadel, June 1959; children: David, Ruth, Deborah. AB, Bklyn. Coll., 1957; MD, NYU, 1961. Diplomate Am. Bd. Internal Medicine, Am. Bd. Pulmonary Diseases. Intern NYU Med. Sch., N.Y.C., 1961-62, resident, 1962-63; rsch. fellow NIH, Balt., 1963-65; vis. fellow Columbia U., Presbyn. Med. Ctr., N.Y.C., 1965-67; rsch. assoc. Michael Reese Med. Ctr., Chgo., 1967-69; asst. prof. medicine U. Pa. Sch. Medicine, Phila., 1969-72; prof. medicine, chief pulmonary medicine Robert Wood Johnson Med. Sch., U. Medicine and Dentistry of N.J., New Brunswick, N.J., 1972-95, dean, 1988-95; prof. medicine and physiology and biophysics SUNY, Stony Brook, 1996—, v.p. health sci. ctr., dean Sch. Medicine, 1996—; cons. for sci. Am. Lung Assn., N.Y.C., 1984—; mem. pulmonary disease adv. com. NIH, 1984-88. Contbr. articles, abstracts to profl. jours., chpts. to med. textbooks; mem. editorial bd. Jour. Applied Physiol., Am. Rev. Respiratory Diseases. Served as surgeon USPHS, 1963-65. Mem. Assn. Am. Physicians, Am. Soc. Clin. Investigation, Am. Thoracic Soc., Am. Physiol. Soc. Office: SUNY 170 Health Scis Ctr Stony Brook NY 11794-8430

EDELMAN, PAUL STERLING, lawyer; b. Bklyn., Jan. 2, 1926; s. Joseph S. and Rose (Kaminsky) E.; m. Rosemary Jacobs, June 15, 1951; children: Peter, Jeffrey. AB, Harvard U., 1946, JD, 1950. Bar: N.Y. 1951, U.S. Dist. Ct. (so. and ea. dists.) N.Y. 1954, U.S. Ct. Appeals (2d cir.) 1965, U.S. Supreme Ct. 1967. Ptnr. Kreindler & Kreindler, N.Y.C., 1953-95, counsel, 1996—; legal advisor Andrea Doria TV show, 1984, QE2 TV show, 1995. Author: Maritime Injury and Death, 1960; editor: Maritime Law Reporter, 1987—, Marine Laws, 1993, 94; columnist N.Y. Law Jour. Served with U.S. Army, 1944-46. Fellow N.Y. Bar Found.; mem. ABA (past chmn. admiralty com., toxic and hazardous substances litigation com., mem. long range planning com. 1982-84, 88—, mem. TIPS council 1984-88, Soviet-Am lawyers conf. Moscow 1987, 94, TIPS lawyers conf. Russia 1993), Maritime Law Assn. (rep. to law of the sea seminar Moscow, 1994), N.Y. State Bar Assn. (INCL award 1980, 90, 93, chmn. INCL sect. 1982-83, editor Ins. Jour. 1973—), Assn. Trial Lawyers Am. (past chmn. admiralty coms.), Maritime Law Assn., World Peace Through Law Ctr., Hudson Valley Tennis Club, Hastings on Hudson (past chmn., planning bd.). Democrat. Jewish. Home: 57 Buena Vista Dr Hastings Hdsn NY 10706-1103 Office: 100 Park Ave New York NY 10017-5516

EDELMAN, PETER BENJAMIN, lawyer; b. Mpls., Jan. 9, 1938; s. Hyman and Miriam Hazel (Lieberman) E.; m. Marian Elizabeth Wright, July 14, 1968; children: Joshua, Jonah, Ezra. A.B., Harvard U., 1958, LL.B., 1961. Bar: N.Y. 1962, D.C. 1979. Law clk. Judge Henry J. Friendly, N.Y.C., 1961-62, Justice Arthur J. Goldberg, Washington, 1962-63; spl. asst. to asst. atty. gen. John Douglas Dept. Justice, Washington, 1963-64; legis. asst. to Sen. Robert F. Kennedy, Washington, 1964-68; assoc. dir. Robert F. Kennedy Meml., Washington, 1969-70; staff dir. Pres.'s Com. on the Future of U. Mass., Boston, 1971; v.p. univ. policy U. Mass., 1972-75; dir. N.Y. State Div. Youth, Albany, 1975-79; ptnr. Foley, Lardner, Hollabaugh & Jacobs, Washington, 1979-82; prof. law Georgetown U. Law Ctr., Washington, 1982-93, 96—, assoc. dean, 1989-92; counselor Sec. of Health and Human Svcs., Washington, 1993-95; asst. sec. for planning and evaluation Dept. of Health and Human Svcs., Washington, 1995-96; lectr. MIT, 1972-75; issues dir. presdl. campaign Senator Edward M. Kennedy, 1980; co-dir. Justice Dept. Transition, 1992-93. Chmn. bd. New World Found., 1982-87; vice chmn. bd. Ctr. for Comty. Change, 1983-87, chmn., 1987-93, bd. dirs., 1996—; mem. exec. com. Washington Lawyers Com. for Civil Rights Under Law, 1981-93, 97—; bd. dirs. Ctr. for Nat. Policy, 1981-93; trustee U. D.C., 1984-90; bd. dirs. Food Rsch. and Action Ctr., 1988-93, Pub. Voice, 1988-93; mem. nat. gov. bd. Common Cause, 1989-93; chmn. bd. Fair Employment Coun. Greater Washington, 1990-93; co-chmn. Americans for Peace Now, 1990-93, bd. dirs., 1997—; bd. dirs. Pub. Welfare Found., 1994-95, 96—, New Israel Fund, 1997—, Ctr. for Law and Social Policy, 1997—, Juvenile Law Ctr., 1997—, Nat. Ctr. for Youth Law, 1997—, Chapin Hall Ctr. for Children, 1997—. With Air N.G., 1963. Ford Found. travel-study grantee, 1968; U.S.-Japan leadership program fellow, 1985; J. Skelly Wright Meml. fellow Yale Law Sch., 1991. Democrat. Jewish. Home: 3208 Newark St NW Washington DC 20008-3345 Office: Georgetown U Law Ctr Washington DC 20001

EDELMAN, RICHARD WINSTON, public relations executive; b. Chicago, Ill., June 15, 1954; s. Daniel J. and Ruth Ann (Rozumoff) E.; m. Rosalind Ann Walrath, May 17, 1986. B.A., Harvard U., 1976, M.B.A., 1978. Mgr. N.Y. office Daniel J. Edelman, Inc., N.Y.C., pres. U.S. opers.; pres., chief oper. officer Daniel J. Edelman, Inc. (now Edelman Worldwide), N.Y.C., 1989-96; CEO Edelman Worldwide, N.Y.C., 1996—, pres., CEO, 1996—; rep. in crisis mgmt. Great Lakes Dredge & Dock Co., Time-Warner, E.F. Hutton, CBS vs. Westmoreland trial, Star-Kist. Bd. dirs. Young Profls. for Gov. Jim Thompson, Chgo., 1978, Young People for Ed Koch, N.Y.C., 1985, Planned Parenthood Fedn. Am., 1980-81, The Jewish Mus.; active polit. campaign Robert Abrams, N.Y. State Attorney Gen. for Senate. Mem. Pub. Relations Soc. Am. (Silver Anvil award 1981). Jewish. Clubs: Harvard, Harmonie (N.Y.C.). Avocations: squash, history. Home: 277 W End Ave Apt 4B New York NY 10023-2608 Office: Edelman Worldwide 1500 Broadway New York NY 10036-4015*

EDELMAN, SAMMIE (SAMM) KAY, theologian, writer; b. Duncan, Okla., Nov. 4, 1948; d. William Kern and Dorothy Byers Edelman; m. Bill R. Pullen, Dec. 2, 1966 (div. Aug. 15, 1973); children: Sherry Dawne Myers, Jon Michael Pullen; life ptnr. Hank Richard, Nov. 29, 1984. BA in Classical Studies, Millsaps Coll., 1989. Pastor MCC Ozarks, Fayetteville, Ark., 1979-83, Springfield (Mo.) MCC, 1983-84; area II coord. Gt. Lakes dist. UFMCC, Dayton, Ohio, 1984-85; pastor Jackson (Miss.) MCC, 1985-89; dir. Ecclesia Docens, Little Rock, 1990—; auditor Bapt. Health, Little Rock, 1991-96; ch. growth advisor Living Rock Ministries, Little Rock, 1990—. Pianist, bd. dirs. Spirit Song, 1992-97; bd. dirs., dir. switchboard AGLTF, Little Rock, 1993-94; pianist Grace Bapt., Scott, Ark., 1995-96; care team leader Regional AIDS Internat. Network, Little Rock, 1995-97. Tchg. fellow Ford Fellowship Found., 1988, 89. Mem. Women's Ctr., League, Phi Beta Kappa. Avocations: music composition and performance, theatre, travel. E-mail: samme@ix.netcom.com. Home: 222 W G Ave North Little Rock AR 72116

EDELMANN, CAROLYN FOOTE, author, poet, editor; b. Toledo, Ohio. Studied with Theodore Weiss, Galway Kinnell, Stanley Plumly, Princeton U. Author: (poetry) Gatherings, 1987, Between the Dark and the Daylight, 1997; appearances include (TV) People are Talking, Phila., (radio) Pub. Radio, Manhattan; poetry readings: Encore Books and Music, Princeton, N.J., Mary Jacobs Libr., Rocky Hill, Beaver Pond Poetry Forum, New Hope, Pa. Recipient William Carlos Williams prize Paterson Pub. Libr., 1977, N.J. Poetry Monthly prize, 1978, Delaware Valley Poets prize, 1992, Press prize, 1997. Mem. Acad. Am. Poets, Nat. League Am. Penwomen, Poetry Soc. Am., N.J. Penwomen, U.S. 1 Poet's Coop., Poets and Writers.

EDELSBERG, SALLY C., physical therapy educator and administrator; b. Rowno, Poland, Aug. 6, 1937; came to U.S., 1949; d. Joseph Luria and and Chana (Bebczuk) Comins; m. Warde C. Pierson, Oct. 8, 1968 (div. 1978); m. Paul Edelsberg, Feb. 2, 1979; 1 child, Tema. BS in Phys. Medicine, U. Wis., 1963; MS, Northwestern U., 1972. Lic. phys. therapist. Staff and supervisory phys. therapist Hines VA Hosp., Maywood, Ill., 1963-67; program dir. Health Careers Council of Ill., Chgo., 1967-70; instr., clin. edn. coordinator Programs in Phys. Therapy, Northwestern U. Med. Sch., Chgo., 1970-73, dir., assoc. prof., 1973—; pres. Phys. Therapy Ltd., Chgo., 1986-95; v.p. World Confedn. Phys. Therapy, 1995—, exec. com., 1991-95. Home: 3500 N Lake Shore Dr Apt 9B Chicago IL 60657-1823*

EDELSBRUNNER, HERBERT, computer scientist, mathematician; b. Graz, Styria, Austria, Mar. 14, 1958; s. Herbert and Berta Edelsbrunner; m. Ping Fu, Nov. 14, 1991; children: Daniel, Xixi. MS in Tech. Math., Tech. U. Graz, 1980, PhD in Tech. Math., 1982. Vertragsassistent Inst. Informationsverarbeitung Tech. U. Graz., 1981-84, Universitätsassistent Inst. Informationsverarbeitung, 1984-85; asst. prof. dept. computer sci. U. Ill., Urbana-Champaign, 1985-87, assoc. prof. dept. computer sci., 1987-90, prof. dept. computer sci., 1990—; lectr. in field. Author: Algorithms in Combinatorial Geometry, 1987. Recipient Alan T. Waterman award NSF, 1991, Univ. Scholar award U. Ill. Found., 1990, Sr. Xerox award, 1989; grantee NSF, 1988-90, 90-92, 92—, Amoco Found. 1985-88. Achievements include research in data structures and algorithms, computational geometry, geometric visualization, discrete geometry, combinatorial topology, scientific computation. Office: Univ of Ill Dept of Computer Sci 1304 W Springfield Ave Urbana IL 61801-2910*

EDELSON, BURTON IRVING, electrical engineer; b. N.Y.C., July 31, 1926; s. Samuel and Margaret (Raff) E.; m. Betty Frances Good, Aug. 30, 1952; children: Stephen, John, Daniel. BS, U.S. Naval Acad., 1947; MS, Yale U., 1954, PhD, 1960; DSci (hon.), Capital Inst. Tech., 1986. Registered profl. engr., Ohio. Ensign USN, 1947, advanced through grades to comdr., 1963, ret., 1967; with Communications Satellite Corp., Washington, 1967-82; assoc. adminstr. NASA, Washington, 1982-87; fellow Fgn. Policy Inst. Johns Hopkins U., Washington, 1987-93; prof. elec. engring. George Washington U., Washington, 1990—. Trustee U.S. Naval Acad. Found., Annapolis, 1986—, Univ. Space Rsch. Assn., 1994—. Decorated Legion of Merit; recipient Howe Rsch. medal Am. Soc. Metals, 1963, Wilbur Cross medal Yale U., 1984, NASA Exceptional Service medal, 1987. Fellow AIAA, AAAS, IEEE. Clubs: Army Navy, Cosmos (Washington); Yale (N.Y.C.). Home: 116 Hesketh St Chevy Chase MD 20815-4223

EDELSON, GILBERT SEYMOUR, lawyer; b. N.Y.C., Sept. 15, 1928; s. Saul and Sarah (Sunshine) E.; m. Jane Barbara Levin, Sept. 6, 1953; children: Martha Jane, Paula Topal, Dorothy Rachel. BS, NYU, 1948; LLB, Columbia U., 1955. Bar: N.Y. 1955, U.S. Dist. Ct. (so. dist.) N.Y. 1959, U.S. Ct. Appeals (2d cir.) 1959, U.S. Dist. Ct. (ea. dist.) N.Y. 1960, U.S. Ct. Appeals (9th cir.) 1995. Assoc. Rosenman Goldmark Colin & Kaye, N.Y.C., 1955-63; ptnr. Rosenman & Colin, N.Y.C., 1963-97, counsel, 1997—; adminstrv. v.p., counsel Art Dealers Assn. Am., N.Y.C., 1985—. Editor Columbia Law Rev., 1955. Bd. dirs. Coll. Art Assn. Am., N.Y.C., 1969-88; sec., trustee Am. Fedn. Arts, N.Y.C., 1984-94; trustee Internat. Found. for Art Rsch., 1986—, N.Y. Studio Sch., 1989—, Archives Am. Art, N.Y.C., 1989—. With U.S. Army, 1950-52, JLC. Mem. ABA, N.Y. Bar Assn., Assn. Bar of N.Y.C. (chmn. com. on art law 1992-95), Columbia U. Law Sch. Alumni Assn. (bd. dirs. 1981-84), Century Assn. Jewish. Avocation: collecting art. Home: 580 W End Ave New York NY 10024-1723 Office: Rosenman & Colin 575 Madison Ave New York NY 10022-2585

EDELSON, MARSHALL, psychiatry educator, psychoanalyst; b. Chgo., May 31, 1928; s. George I. E. and Ida (Bernstein) Riskind; m. Zelda Sarah Toll, Dec. 27, 1952; children: Jonathan Toll, Rebecca Jo, David Jan. Ph.B., U. Chgo., 1946, Ph.D., 1954, M.D., 1955; A.B., Stanford U., 1949; M.A. hon., Yale U., 1976. Diplomate: Nat. Bd. Med. Examiners. Intern Presbyterian Hosp., Chgo., 1955-56; resident in psychiatry Sheppard and Enoch Pratt Hosp., Towson, Md., 1956-59; asst. prof. psychiatry U. Okla., Oklahoma City, 1961-63; staff psychiatrist Austen Riggs Ctr., Stockbridge, Mass., 1964-68; assoc. prof. psychiatry Yale U., New Haven, 1968-76, prof. psychiatry, 1976-97, prof. emeritus, psychiatry, 1998—; dir. research outpatient div. Yale's Conn. Mental Health Ctr., 1983-88; ednl. cons. Western New Eng. Inst. Psychoanalysis, 1973-97. Author: Sociotherapy and Psychotherapy, 1970, Language and Interpretation in Psychoanalysis, 1975, Hypothesis and Evidence in Psychoanalysis, 1984, Psychoanalysis: A Theory in Crisis, 1988, (with David N. Berg) Rediscovering Groups: A Psychoanalyst's Journey Beyond Individaul Psychology, 1999. Served to capt. U.S. Army, 1959-61. Recipient Heinz Hartmann award N.Y. Psychoanalytic Inst., 1973; NIMH Career Tchr. fellow, 1962. Fellow APA (life); mem. AMA, Am. Psychoanalytic Assn. (cert.), Internat. Psychoanalytic Assn., Western New Eng. Inst. Psychoanalysis and Psychoanalytic Soc. Office: Yale U Sch Medicine Dept Psychiatry 25 Park St # 6 New Haven CT 06519-1189

EDELSON, MARY BETH, artist, educator; b. East Chicago, Ind.; d. Albert Melvin and Mary Lou (Young) Johnson; children: Lynn Switzman, Nick. Student, Art Inst. Chgo., 1953-54; BA, DePauw U., 1955; MA, NYU, 1959; DFA (hon.), DePauw U., 1993. Instr. Corcoran Sch. Art, Washington, 1970-75; artist in residence U. Ill., Chgo., 1982, 88, U. Tenn., Knoxville, 1983, Ohio U., Columbus, 1984, Md. Inst. Art, Balt., 1985, Kansas City Art Inst., Mo., 1986, Cleve. Art Inst., 1991, U. Colo., 1993, Clemson U., 1994, McMullen Mus. of Art, Boston Coll., 1997; lectr. at various art gatherings. Solo exhbns. include Nicole Klagsburn Gallery, N.Y.C., 1993, A/C Project Rm., N.Y.C., 1993, Creative Time, N.Y.C., 1994, Nicolai Wallner, Copenhagen, Denmark, 1996, Halle für Kunst, Berlin, 1997, Agency Gallery, London, 1998; group exhbns. include Internat. Feministiche Kunst, Stichting de Appel, Amsterdam, The Netherlands, 1980, Mendel Gallery, Mus. du Que., Phillips Gallery, Can., 1986-88, Corcoran Gallery Art, Washington, 1989, Mus. Modern Art, N.Y.C., 1988-89, Walker Art Ctr., Mpls., 1989, W.P.A., Washington, 1989, A.C. Project Room, N.Y.C., 1991-97, Phillippe Rizzo, Paris, 1992, P.P.O.W., N.Y.C., 1992, Fawbush Gallery, N.Y.C., 1992, Amy Lipton Gallery, N.Y.C., 1992, David Zwirner Gallery, N.Y.C., 1993, Turner/Krail Galleries, L.A., 1993, Mercer Union, Toronto, 1996, The Agency, London, 1995, Lombard/Freid, N.Y.C., 1995, Chaisse Post gallery, Atlanta, 1996, Linda Kirkland Gallery, N.Y.C., 1996, Boston Mus. Art, McMullen, 1997, Magasin Ctr. National D'Art Contemporain, Grenoble, France, 1997, Dorfman Projects, N.Y.C., 1998, Internat. Ctr. Photography, N.Y.C., 1997, Neuberger Mus., Purchase, N.Y., 1999, Nicolai Wallner, Copenhagen, 1999; represented in permanent collections: Walker Art Ctr., Nat. Mus. Am. Art, Washington, Nat. Collection, Washington, Nat. Mus. Women in the Arts, Washington, Guggenheim Mus. Art, N.Y.C., Mus. Contemporary Art, Chgo., Cleveland Inst. Art., 1993, and others; subject of 15-yr. retrospective travelling to numerous art and ednl. instns. throughout U.S., 1988-91; author: Seven Cycles: Public Rituals, 1981, To Dance: Painting with Performance in Mind, 1985, Seven Sites, 1988-90, Shape Shifter: Seven Mediums, 1990; author/photographer: Firsthand, 1993; contbr. articles to profl. jours.; included numerous books. Recipient Visual Arts grant NEA, 1981, Creative Artists Pub. Svc. grant State of N.Y., 1982. Mem. Conf. Women in Visual Arts (founding mem.), Women's Action Coalition, Heresies Mag. Collective (founding mem.). Home: 110 Mercer St New York NY 10012-3865

EDELSTEIN, DAVID NORTHON, federal judge; b. N.Y.C., Feb. 16, 1910; s. Benjamin and Dora (Mancher) E.; m. Florence Koch, Feb. 18, 1940; children: Jonathan H., Jeffrey M. BS, Fordham U., MA, LLB. Bar: N.Y., Ct. Appeals Paris. Practiced in N.Y.C.; atty. claims divsn. U.S. Dept. Justice, 1944; asst. U.S. atty. So. Dist. N.Y., 1945-47, spl. asst. to atty. gen. in charge of lands divsn., 1947-48, asst. atty. gen. in charge customs divsn., 1948-51; judge U.S. Dist. Ct. So. Dist. N.Y., N.Y.C., 1951-94, chief judge, 1971-80, sr. judge, 1994—; former elected mem. Jud. Conf. U.S.; rep. Nat. Conf. Fed. Trial Judges, also mem. exec. and program coms., 1975-86; assisted Pres.'s Temporary Commn. on Employee Loyalty, preparation of report, 1946; mem. legis. com. Attys. Gen. Conf. on Crime, 1950; former mem. steering com. N.Y. Fed. Exec. Bd.; former mem. planning commn. Met. Conf. Chief Judges; founder student litigation tng. program So. Dist. N.Y.; mem. com. courtroom facilities Jud. Adminstrv. Div.; mem. White Plains Courthouse Com., 1983—, mem., former chmn. rules com.; former mem. nat. adv. bd. Ctr. for the Study of the Presidency; former mem. planning and program com. Jud. Conf. (2d cir.), mem. Jud. Adminstrn. Div. Com. to coordinate revision of Code of Jud. Conduct, mem. com. on jury charge simplification; mem. Com. So. Dist. N.Y. Ct. History. Author: The Ethics of Dilatory Motion Practice: Time for Change, 1976; co-author: Jouralist Privilege and the Criminal Defendant, 1979, The Continued Role of the Judiciary in Securities After McMahon, 1988; contbr. articles to Fordham Law Rev., Securities Arbitration, N.Y. Law Jour. Bd. advisors Health Edn. Found.; moderator Jud. Conf. on Legalization of Drugs in U.S.; former hon. mem. Beth Israel Med. Ctr., Interfaith Movement, Internat. Trade Divsn. of Wall St. Synagogue; former participant 23d annual Air War Coll. nat. security forum Chopin Found. Recipient medal of recognition Interfaith Movement, 1964, Humanitarian award N.Y. Philanthropic League, Juristic Excellence award Fed. Bar Coun., The Forum Club, Svc. Beyond Self award Rotary Internat. N.Y. Coun. Explorer Divsn. award, Jud. Recognition award Assn. Bar City N.Y., Greater N.Y. Coun., Explorer's Divsn. award for serving youth, 1979, Dean's medal of recognition Fordham U., 1990, Gold Medal Honor for Achievement award; named to James Monroe H.S. Hall of Fame, Hon. Mem. Crew of USS Franklin D. Roosevelt, Hon. Order of Ky. Cols.; included in Am. Jury Trial Found. A Tribute to Trial by Jury; former fellow Am. Bar Found. Mem. ABA (spl. com. to survey legal needs 1971-77, past chmn. speedy trial planning group, subcom. on planning for Dist. Cts., jud. adminstrn. div. lawyers conf. state and fed. practice com. 1989-90, lawyers conf. civil justice reform initiatives com. 1993—), Nat. Conf. Fed. Trial Judges (liaison to ABA), Fed. Bar Assn. (past pres. Empire chpt., past nat. del., past jud. selection com., past alt. del. ho. of dels), Maritime Lawyers Assn. (jud.), ATLA (hon.), Nat. Lawyers Club (hon.), Fordham Alumni Assn. (bd. dirs.), Lawyers Assn. Textile Industry (1st hon.), Pan Am. Med. Soc. (hon.), Phi Delta Phi (hon.). Office: US Dist Ct US Courthouse Foley Sq New York NY 10007-1501

EDELSTEIN, DAVID SIMEON, historian, educator; b. N.Y.C., Jan. 19, 1913; s. William and Clara (Brener) E.; m. Frances Fisher, June 4, 1939 (dec. Jan. 1990); children: Helen Freedman, Henry, Daniel Louis; m. Gertrude Bernstein, Jan. 5, 1997. BA, CCNY, 1932; MA, Columbia U., 1933, PhD, 1949. Cert. elem. tchr., N.Y. Tchr., adminstr. various schs., N.Y.C., 1934-57; lectr. in-svc. courses Bd. Edn., N.Y.C., 1946-65; lectr. History CCNY, 1947-67; lectr. Edn. U. Colo., 1960, Yeshiva U. Grad. Sch. Edn., 1960-61, Hunter Coll., 1964-65; prof. Edn. Western Conn. State U., Danbury, 1967-83; adj. assoc. prof. History Fordham U., Bronx, N.Y., 1967-70; instr. in-svc. course Stamford (Conn.) Bd. Edn., 1970-71; adj. assoc. prof. History CUNY, 1970-75; adj. prof. History Western Conn. State U., Danbury, 1984-85; lectr. in field. Author: Joel Munsell, Printer and Antiquarian, 1950; author: (with others) M. Stern: editor: Publishers for Mass. Entertainment in the Nineteenth Century, 1980; contbr. biog. sketches Nat. Am. Biography, 1990; contbr. articles to profl. jours. Mem. AAUP, Am. Assn. Sch. Adminstrs., Am. Hist. Assn., Conn. Edn. Assn., Nat. Assn. of Elem. Sch. Prins., N.Y.C. Elem. Sch. Prins. Assn. (life), Nat. Coun. of Local Adminstrs. of Vocat. Edn., Social Studies Coun., Coun. of Chmn. of Acad. Subjects, Nat. Soc. for the Study of Edn., New Eng. Hist. Assn., New Eng. Assn. of Tchr. Educators, Phi Alpha Theta, Phi Delta Kappa. Democrat. Jewish. Home: 118 Rosedale Rd Yonkers NY 10710-3033 Office: Western Conn State U 181 White St Danbury CT 06810-6826

EDELSTEIN, JASON ZELIG, rabbi, psychologist; b. Boston, Jan. 31, 1930; s. Abraham and Anna (Freedman) E.; m. Eva Bamberger, Aug. 3, 1952; children: Philip, Sharon, Joseph. BA in Psychology, U. N.H., 1951, MA in Clin. Psychology, 1953; BHL, Hebrew Union Coll., 1956, MAHL, 1959; DMin, Pitts. Theol. Sem., 1977; DD, Hebrew Union Coll.-Jewish Inst. Religion, 1983. Ordained rabbi, 1958. Rabbi emeritus Temple David, Monroeville, Pa., 1960-95; chaplain VA Med. Ctr., Pitts., 1962-90; lectr. St. Vincent Coll. and St. Vincent Sem., Latrobe, Pa., 1968-95, Seton Hill Coll., Greensburg, Pa., 1981—; nat. coord. Hotline, Cen. Conf. Am. Rabbis, N.Y.C., 1979-95; partial psychol. cons. Sisters of Mercy, Pitts., 1990-92; mem. com. Chesky Inst. on Judaism and Psychotherapy, N.Y.C., 1990-94; assoc. prof. religious studies St. Vincent Coll. and Seminary, 1995. Contbr. articles to profl. pubis. Lt. USN, 1955-60. Mem. Cen. Conf. Am. Rabbis (ex-officio mem. long range planning com. 1990-95, ex-officio mem. rabbi's family com. 1989-95), Am. Psychol. Assn., Viktor Frankl Inst. Logotherapy (diplomate in logotherapy), Nat. Honor Soc. in Psychology. Home: 135 Mayberry Dr Monroeville PA 15146-4721

EDELSTEIN, JOAN ERBACK, physical therapy educator; b. East Orange, N.J., Mar. 28, 1935; d. Frank William and Sadie Edith (Levine) Erback; m. Haskell Edelstein, Jan. 19, 1964; children: David, Benjamin. BS magna cum laude, NYU, 1956, MA, 1958. Lic. phys. therapist, N.Y. Chief phys. therapist children's div. Rusk Inst. (formerly Inst. Phys. Medicine & Rehab.), N.Y.C., 1956-59; instr. U. Wis., Madison, 1959-61; clin. asst., prof., sr. rsch. scientist NYU, N.Y.C., 1961-91; assoc. prof. clin. phys. therapy Columbia U., 1991—, dir. program in phys. therapy, 1992—; organizer and condr. seminars nationwide and worldwide. Author: Prosthetic and Orthotic Educational Aids, 1987; contbr. numerous articles to profl. jours.; mem. editorial bd. Jour. Assn. Children's Prosthetic-Orthotic Clinics, 1983-91, Jour. Rehab. R&D, 1984-94, Archives Phys. Medicine and Rehab., 1991-95. Trustee N.Y. Youth Symphony, N.Y.C., 1986—, Lark Quartet, N.Y.C., 1989-94. Nat. Found. for Infantile Paralysis grantee, 1959. Fellow Internat. Soc. for Prosthetics and Orthotics (sec., treas. 1979-88, vice chmn. 1988-91); mem. Am. Phys. Therapy Assn., Am. Congress of Phys., Medicine and Rehab., N.Y. Acad. Scis., Acad. of Content Experts, Soc. Scholarly Publs., Nat. Flute Assn. (performance health com. 1991—). Home: 340 E 69th St New York NY 10021-5706 Office: Columbia University 710 W 168th St New York NY 10032-2603

EDELSTEIN, MARK GERSON, college president. BA in English, Colby Coll., 1968; MA in English, U. N.H., 1971; PhD in English, SUNY, Stony Brook, 1982. English faculty Palomar C.C., 1976-85; exec. dir. intersegmental coordinating coun. Coll. of Redwoods, 1987-91, v.p. acad. affairs, 1991-96; pres. Diablo Valley Coll., 1996—; pres. acad. senate Calif. C.C.; spkr. in field. Co-author: Inside Writing. Office: Diablo Valley Coll 321 Golf Club Rd Pleasant Hill CA 94523

EDELSTEIN, ROBERT GLENN, magazine editor; b. Bronx, N.Y., May 3, 1960; s. Stanley and Laura (Ressel) E.; m. Loren Ginsberg, Mar. 28, 1993; 1 child, Rachel Ione. BA, SUNY, Albany, 1982. Mng. editor, designer Video Industry Profile, N.Y.C., 1982; editl. asst. Emergency Medicine, N.Y.C., 1982-83; asst. editor Montcalm Pub., N.Y.C., 1983; mng. editor Rave Comms., N.Y.C., 1984-85, editl. dir., 1985-87; freelance writer N.Y.C., 1988-91; mng. editor TVSM, Inc., N.Y.C., 1991-94, exec. editor, 1994—. Vol. tutor Lit. Vols. N.Y.C., 1990-94, 97—. Avocations: reading, origami, writing, guitar. Office: Cable Guide/See 211 6th Ave FL 4 New York NY 10036*

EDELSTEIN, ROSEMARIE, nurse educator, medical-legal consultant; b. Drake, N.D., Mar. 3, 1935; d. Francis Jerome and Myrtle Josephine (Merbach) Hublou; m. Harry George Edelstein, June 22, 1957 (div.); children: Julie, Lori, Lynn, Toni Anne. *William and Wilhelmina (Minnie) Merbach had a ranch farm house in Drake, North Dakota in the late 1890s. Interested in raising cattle, hogs and grains, William, Minnie and four surviving children moved into a town home adjacent to the hospital. William remained mayor through thirteen elections. Martin and Mary (Mame) Hublou met roofing the New Catholic Church in Anamoose, North Dakota. Martin of Belgium-French heritage and Mame, directly from County Claire, Ireland, parented six children. Until the Great Depression, Martin was the local banker, later taking on the John-Deere Implement dealership and grain elevator* BSN, St. Teresa of Avila Coll., Winona, Minn., 1956; MA in Edn., Holy Names Coll., Oakland, Calif., 1977; EdD, U. San Francisco, 1982, postgrad., 1987; postgrad. in pub. health U. Ariz., 1985—; cert. pub. health nurse U. Calif., Berkeley, 1972. Dir., clin. supr. San Francisco Sch. for Health Professions, 1971-74, Rancho Arroyo Sch. of Vocat. Nursing, Sacramento, 1974-75; intensive care nurse Kaiser-Permanente Hosp., San Rafael, Calif., 1976-77; dir. inservice edn. Ross Hosp., Calif., 1977-78; assoc. dir. nursing, nursing edn. St. Francis Meml. Hosp., San Francisco, 1978-85; med.-legal nursing cons., med.-surg. staff nurse met. hosps., San Francisco, 1985-90, St. Luke's Hosp., Duluth, Minn., 1990-91, St. Charles Hosp., New Orleans, 1992, UTMB, Galveston, Tex. 1992-94, staff RN family medicine faculty practice, 1995; med.-surg. nurse St. Anthony of Padua Hosp., Oklahoma City, Okla., 1994-95; medical medicare experience; RN medics and treatments Northgate Conv. Hosp., San Rafael, Calif., 1995—; RN, night charge nurse Creekside Conv. Hosp., Santa Rosa, Calif., 1996; RN, charge nurse medications, treatment and alzheimers unit, Fallon Conv. Ctr., Nev., 1996; RN charge medicare unit White Pine Conv. Ctr., Ely, Nev., 1997; RN emergency room and intensive care, Battle Mountain Gen. Hosp., Nev., 1997; RN supr., charge Medicare-Med. Seaview Care Ctr. Sun Corp., Eureka, Calif., 1997-98; mem. staff Walker Post Manor Oxford, NE Lantis Corp., 1998, RN 1998, The Lincoln Ambassador, 1999; invited mem. People to People Nursing Edn. and Adminstrn., candidate to East Asia, Philosophy, 1985; postgrad. candidate U. Zurich, Switzerland, 1988. Candidate U.S. Senate Inner Circle, 1988, 89. Lt. col. USAR Med. Res. Mem. Calif. Nurses Assn., Am. Heart Assn., Sigma Theta Tau. Roman Catholic. Author: (with Jane F. Lee) Acupuncture Atlas, 1974; The Influence of Motivator and Hygiene Factors in Job Changes by Graduate Registered Nurses, 1977; Effects of Two Educational Methods Upon Retention of Knowledge in Pharmacology, 1981.

EDELSTEIN, TERI J., art history educator, art federation administrator; b. Johnstown, Pa., June 23, 1951; d. Robert Morten and Hulda Lois (Friedhoff) E. BA, U. Pa., 1972, MA, 1977, PhD, 1979; cert., NYU, 1984. Lectr. U. Guelph, Ont., 1977-79; asst. dir. for acad. programs Yale Ctr. Brit. Art, New Haven, Conn., 1979-83; dir. Mt. Holyoke Coll. Art Mus., South Hadley, Mass., 1983-90; dir. Skinner Mus., 1983-90, mem. faculty dept. art, 1983-90; dir. Smart Mus. Art U. Chgo., 1990-92, sr. lectr. dept. art, 1990—; dep. dir. Art Inst. Chgo., 1992-99; bd. dirs. Am. Fedn. Arts; mem. adv. bd. Sculpture Chgo., 1991-96, Mus. Loan Network, Knight and Pew Founds., 1994-96. Office: 1648 E 50th St 6B Chicago IL 60615-6492

EDELSTEIN, TILDEN GERALD, academic administrator, history educator; b. N.Y.C., June 11, 1931; s. Theodore and Nettie (Strusser) E.; m. Rose Ann Stargardter, Nov. 1, 1970; children: Jordan, Russell. BS, U. Wis., 1953; PhD, Johns Hopkins U., 1961. From instr. to assoc. prof. Simmons Coll., Boston, 1957-67; from adj. assoc. prof. to prof. history Rutgers U., New Brunswick, N.J., 1967-89, chmn. history dept., grad. dir., 1974-81, assoc. dean social sci. and humanities, faculty personnel, 1981-84, dean faculty arts and scis., 1984-89; prof. history, provost, acad. v.p. SUNY, Stony Brook, 1989-93, prof. history, provost, exec. v.p. for academic affairs, 1992-94; v.p. for acad. affairs Wayne State U., Detroit, 1995-98, prof. history, 1998—; hist. cons. Columbia Pictures, Hollywood, Calif., 1978-80, NBC, N.Y.C., 1980-89; chair Sponsors Bd. The Thomas A. Edison Papers Project, 1980-89. Author: Strange Enthusiasm, 1970; co-editor: The Black Americans, 1975. Commr. Housing Authority, Highland Park, N.J., 1977-89; Einstein Archives Adv. Com. Hebrew U., 1993-94. Mem. Orgn. Am. Historians. Office: Wayne State U Coll :iberal Arts Dept of History Detroit MI 48202

EDEMEKA, UDO EDEMEKA, surgeon; b. Ndon Eyo, Akwa Ibom, Nigeria, Sept. 11, 1944; came to U.S., 1973; s. Buddie Udo and Dinah Buddie (Ekwere) E.; m. Iboro Udo David Akpan, May 18, 1973; children: Ubong, Dinah, Idara, David, Dennis, Donald. MB and BS, U. Ibadan, Nigeria, 1970; diploma in anesthesia, U. Lagos, 1972. Diplomate Am. Bd. Surgery, Am. Bd. Emergency Physicians. Instr. surgery Downstate Med. Ctr., Bklyn., 1974-80; attending physician Kings County Hosp. Ctr., Bklyn., 1980-91, Meth. Hosp., Bklyn., 1988—. Leverhulme Exchange scholar Lever Bros. U. Coll. Hosp., London, 1969. Fellow N.Y. Acad. Scis., Internat. Coll. Surgeons, Am. Coll. Emergency Physicians. Office: Meth Hosp 506 6th St Brooklyn NY 11215-3645

EDEN, ALVIN NOAM, pediatrician, author; b. Bklyn., Mar. 21, 1926; s. Emanuel M. and Rae (Taran) Edelstein; m. Elaine R. Jaffe, Nov. 20, 1952; children: Robert, Elizabeth. BA, Columbia Coll., 1948; MD, Boston U., 1952. Intern Bellevue Hosp., N.Y.C., 1952-53; resident in pediatrics Univ. Hosp., N.Y.C., 1953-55; pvt. practice specializing in pediatrics Forest Hills, N.Y., 1955—; assoc. clin. prof. pediatrics NYU Sch. Medicine, 1960-84; chmn., dir. dept. pediatrics Wyckoff Heights Med. Ctr., Bklyn., 1959; lectr. SUNY-Downstate Med. Ctr., Bklyn., 1984-86, assoc. clin. prof. pediatrics, 1986-90; assoc. clin. prof. pediatrics Cornell Med. Coll., 1990—. Author: Growing Up Thin, 1975, Handbook for New Parents, 1978, Positive Parenting, 1980, Dr. Eden's Healthy Kids, 1987; contbr. articles to profl. jours.; author text and reference materials. Served to mate 2d class U.S.M., 1944-46. Mem. N.Y. Pediatric Soc. (pres. 1980-81), Queens Pediatric Soc. (pres. 1972-73), N.Y. Acad. Medicine (chmn. pediatric sect. 1985-89), Am. Acad. Pediatrics (chmn. nutrition com. chpt. 2 1985-89). Avocation: tennis. Home: 710 Park Ave New York NY 10021-4944 Office: 10721 Queens Blvd Forest Hills NY 11375-4451

EDEN, BARBARA JANIECE, commercial and residential interior designer; b. Inpls., Oct. 14, 1951; d. Justin January and Marjorie May (Miller) E.; m. Stephen A. Bowman, Oct. 25, 1975; children: Christopher Eden Bowman, Jessica Eden Bowman. BA, Purdue U., 1973. Interior design dir. Bohlen, Meyer, Gibson & Assoc., Indpls., 1973-78; interior designer, sole propr. Barbara Eden Design, Indpls., 1978-85; pres., prin. designer Eden Design Assocs., Inc., Carmel, Ind., 1985-97; prin. Carson Design Assocs. Design/Project Mgmt./ Mktg., Carmel, Ind., 1997—; past mem. accreditation team Found. for Interior Design Edn. Rsch. (FIDER); past mem. adv. bd. Purdue U. Interior Design Dept. Prin. projects include wheelchair accessible bathroom Kohler (Wis.) Design Ctr., United Airlines, Indpls. Maintenance Ctr., regional hdqrs. Hardees Food Systems, Carmel, Ind., Huntington (Ind.) Coll. Libr. & Fine Arts Ctr., Charles Schwab & Co., Inc., Fishers, Ind., Oakwood Inn, Syracuse, Ind., Resort Condominiums, Internat., Carmel, Ind.; also corp., healthcare, schs., univs., librs., elderly residential interior design, space planning. Mem. AIA (assoc.), Internat. Facility Mgrs. Assn., Internat. Interior Design Assn., Illuminating Engring. Soc., Carmel Clay C. of C. (mem. exec. bd., chair edn. com., Small Bus. Person of Yr. 1993). Avocations: hiking, horseback riding, traveling. email: edenbj@carsondesign.co. Office: Carson Design Assocs 11590 N Meridian St Ste 104 Carmel IN 46032-6955

EDEN, BARBARA JEAN, actress; b. Tucson, Arizona, Aug. 23, 1934; d. Harrison Connon and Alice Mary (Franklin) Huffman; 1 child, Matthew Michael Ansara; m. Jon Trusdale Eicholtz, Jan. 5, 1991. Student, San Francisco City Coll., San Francisco Conservatory of Music, Elizabeth Holloway Sch. of Theatre. Pres. Mi-Bar Productions; bd. dirs. Security First Nat. Bank of Chgo. Films include Voyage to the Bottom of the Sea, 1961, Five Weeks in a Balloon, 1962, Wonderful World of the Brothers Grimm, 1963, Seven Faces of Dr. Lao, 1964, Harper Valley PTA, 1978, also The Brass Bottle, Ride the Wild Surf, The New Interns, The Girls in the Office, 1979, Condominium, 1980, Return of the Rebels, 1981, Chattanooga Choo Choo, 1984, A Very Brady Sequel, 1996; TV debut on series West Point, 1956; numerous other TV appearances; starred in TV series I Dream of Jeannie, 1965-69, Harper Valley P.T.A., 1980-82; appeared in several TV movies including The Feminist and the Fuzz, 1971, A Howling in the Woods, 1971, The Woman Hunter, 1972, Guess Who's Sleeping in My Bed, 1973, The Stranger Within, 1974, Let's Switch, 1975, How to Break Up a Happy Divorce, 1976, Stonestreet: Who Killed the Centerfold Model, 1977, The Stepford Children, I Dream of Jeannie: 15 Years Later, Secret Life of Kathy McCormick, 1989, Your Mother Wears Combat Boots, 1989, Brand New Life, 1989, Her Wicked Ways, 1990, Hell Hath No Fury, 1991, I Still Dream of Jeannie, 1991, Visions of Murder, 1993, Eyes of Terror, 1994, Dead Man's Island, 1995; also stage and club appearances. Office: William Morris Agy c/o Gene Schwam 151 S El Camino Dr Beverly Hills CA 90212-2775 *My life has been blessed with good friends, a wonderful family and a productive profession. I hope I have contributed to the world at least a small measure of the joy that has been afforded me.**

EDEN, F(LORENCE) BROWN, artist; b. Jericho Center, Vt., Oct. 10, 1916; d. Arthur Castle and Eva Merita (Lowrey) Brown; m. Edwin Winfield Eden, Sept. 4, 1937; children: Donna Jean, Sandra Elizabeth, Kathy Lynn. Student, U. Fla. Extension, 1955-59, U. Mich., 1963. Art instr. Ann Arbor (Mich.) City Club, 1962-63; tchr., oil painting, printmaking Jacksonville (Fla.) Art Mus., 1963-68. One-woman shows include The Fox Galleries, Atlanta, 1986, Harmon Galleries, Sarasota, 1987, 89-90, 92-93, Gallery Contemporanea St. Augustine, Jacksonville, Artist Assocs. Gallery, Atlanta, 1965-1990, The Hodgell Gallery, Sarasota, 1997-99, The Center, Ponte Vedra, Fla., 1999, Kent Campus Gallery, Jacksonville, Fla., 1999; represented in permenant collections Fed. Res. Bank Atlanta, Bank Am., Coca-Cola Co., So. Bell, Sheraton Corp., AT&T, Trust Co. Ga., Shell Oil, Touche Ross, Cooper and Lybrand, Delta Airlines, 5th Dist. Ct. Appeals Bldg., Daytona Beach, Fla., Edwin and Ruth Kennedy Mus. Am. Art, U. Ohio, Athens; exhibited in group shows at Ala. Nat. Watercolors, Fla., Ga. Nat., Audubon Nat., Painters in Casein and Acrylics Nat., N.Y.C. Mem. Jacksonville Mus. Contemporary Art (chmn. N.E. Fla. 1979-89). Recipient First award Fla. Artist Group, 1971, 79, Fla. Artists, 1969, The Painting award Major Fla. Artists, 1979, numerous other 1st place awards. Mem. Am. Women Artists, Nat. Mus. of Women in the Arts (charter mem.), So. Watercolor Soc., Fla. Watercolor Soc., Ga. Watercolor Soc., Ala. Watercolor Soc., Jacksonville Coalition of Visual Artists, Fla. Artists Jacksonville, Fla. Crown Treasures. Avocation: playing organ. Home and Studio: 5375 Sanders Rd Jacksonville FL 32277-1333

EDEN, JAMES GARY, electrical engineering and physics educator, researcher; b. Washington, Oct. 11, 1950; s. Robert Otis and Joyce (West) E.; m. Carolyn Sue Thomas, June 10, 1972; children: Robert Douglas, Laura Ann, Katherine Joy. BS, U. Md., 1972; MS, U. Ill., 1973, PhD, 1976. Teaching asst. elec. engring. dept. U. Ill., Urbana, Jan.-June 1972, rsch. asst., 1972-75, asst. prof. elec. engring. dept., 1979-81, assoc. prof., 1981-83, prof. elec. engring. dept. and rsch. prof. Coordinated Sci. Lab, 1983—, assoc. dean Grad. Coll., 1994-96, mem. physics grad. rsch. faculty, asst. dean Coll. Engring., 1992-93; postdoctoral rsch. assoc. NRC, Washington, 1975-76; rsch. physicist Naval Rsch. Lab., Washington, 1976-79; assoc. mem. Ctr. for Advanced Study, U. Ill., 1987-88; mem. program com. Conf. on Lasers and Electro-Optics, 1982, 83, 88, 89, 94-97; chmn. Engring. Found. Conf. Ultraviolet Lasers, 1987, co-chair, 1990, 94; program chair ann. meeting IEEE Lasers and Electro-Optics Soc., 1990, conf. chair, 1992; program vice chmn. Interdisciplinary Laser Sci. Conf. V, 1989; program chair ILS V, 1990, conf. chair ILS VII, 1992; mem. adv. bd. Chem. Vapor Deposition, 1995—, CRC Handbook Series Laser Sci. and Tech., 1996—. Author: Photochemical Vapor Deposition, 1992; editor IEEE Jour. Quantum Electronics, 1996—; assoc. editor Photonics Tech. Letters, 1988-94; contbr. numerous articles to profl. jours.; patentee for 12 inventions. Recipient Rsch. Publ. award Naval Rsch. Lab., 1978, Beckman Rsch. award U. Ill., 1988, IBM Rsch. award U. Ill., 1994; James F. Towey U. scholar, U. Ill., 1996-99; recipient IEEE Lasers and Electro-Optics Soc. Disting. Svc. award, 1996. Fellow IEEE, Optical Soc. Am., Am. Phys. Soc.; mem. IEEE Lasers and Electro-Optics Soc. (bd. govs. 1991-93, v.p. for tech. affairs 1993-95, pres. 1998), Sigma Xi, Tau Beta Pi, Eta Kappa Nu, Phi Kappa Phi. Republican. Avocation: amateur radio. Home: 513 Taylor Dr Mahomet IL 61853-9246 Office: U Ill Everitt Lab 1406 W Green St Urbana IL 61801-2918

EDEN, MURRAY, electrical engineer, emeritus educator; b. Bklyn., Aug. 17, 1920; s. Emanuel and Rae (Taran) Edelstein; m. Patricia Warnock, Sept. 16, 1962; stepchildren—Shirley Hartle McDaniel, John W. Hartle; children by previous marriage—Abigail, Susanna, Mark D. BS, CCNY, 1939; MS, U. Md., 1944, PhD, 1951. Physc. chemist Nat. Bur. Standards, 1943-49; biophysicist Nat. Cancer Inst., 1949-53; spl. fellow math. USPHS, Princeton, 1953-55; biophysicist Nat. Heart Inst., 1955-59; prof. elec. engring. MIT, 1959-79, prof. emeritus, 1979—; adj. prof. elec. engring. Johns Hopkins U., 1979-81; guest prof. Ecole Federale Polytechnique de Lausanne (Switzerland), 1983, 87; dir. bioengring. and instrumentation program NIH, 1976-94, scientist emeritus, 1994—; lectr. preventive medicine Harvard Med. Sch., 1960-74, Am. U., 1949-50; adj. prof. environ. health Sch. Pub. Health, Boston U., 1999; cons. for rsch. to dir. gen. WHO, 1963-74. Author: (with David Rutstein) Engineering and Living Systems, 1970; editor: (with Paul Kolers) Recognizing Patterns, 1968, (with Henry S. Eden) Microcomputers in Patient Care, 1981, (with John W. Boretos) Contemporary Biomaterials for Clinical Care, 1983, (with Leonid Yarsolavsky) Fundamentals of Digital Optics, 1996; editor-in-chief: Information and Control, 1961-84; editor: Methods of Information in Medicine, 1961-82; mem. editl. bd.: Med. Rsch. Engring., 1964-80, Internat. Jour. Health Care Tech. Assessment, 1986-92, Real Time Imaging, 1994—; adv. editl. bd.: Linguistic Inquiry, 1970-85. Chmn. U.S. Nat. Com. Engring. in Medicine and Biology, 1967-73. Recipient Med. Soc. medal WHO, 1983, Dirs. award NIH, 1993. Fellow IEEE (chmn. adminstrv. com. group engring. in medicine and biology 1964-66, 87-90, mem. editl. bd. Spectrum 1990-92, mem. press bd. 1993—, mem. publs. adv. bd. 1998, Centennial medal 1984), AAAS, Am. Inst. for Med. Biol. Engring.; mem. Am. Physiol. Soc., Biophys. Soc., Am. Soc. for Engring. Edn., Cosmos Club, Sigma Xi, Tau Beta Pi. Home: 148 University Rd Brookline MA 02445-4546 Office: 148 University Rd Brookline MA 02445-4546

EDEN, NATHAN E., lawyer; b. Key West, Fla., Mar. 24, 1944; s. Delmar M. and Lois (Archer) E.; m. Cindy Pike, Jan. 4, 1964 (div. Mar. 1984); 1 child, Jennifer S. BA, U. Fla., 1966; JD magna cum laude, Stetson U., 1969. Bar: Fla. 1969, U.S. Dist. Ct. (so. and mid. dists.) Fla. 1969, U.S. Ct. Appeals (5th cir.) 1969, U.S. Ct. Appeals (11th cir.) 1982. Assoc. Nelson, Stinnett, Surfus, et al, Sarasota, Fla., 1969; ptnr. Feldman & Eden & predecessors, Key West, 1970-84; sole practice Key West, 1984—; of counsel Lazzara and Paul, P.A., Tampa, 1982—; bd. atty. Utility Bd. of Key West, 1974—; asst. pub. defender State of Fla., Key West, 1970, county solicitor State of Fla., Key West, 1970-72; chief asst. state atty State of Fla., Key West, 1972-74; U.S. magistrate, U.S. Dist. Ct. (so. dist.) Fla., 1974-78. Mem. jud. nominating com. 16th Jud. Cir. State of Fla., 1995, bd. dirs. Hospice Monroe County. Mem. Acad. Trial Lawyers, Fla. Acad. Trial Lawyers, Nat. Assn. Criminal Def. Lawyers, Fla. Bar Assn. (bd. govs. 1976-80), North Am. Hunt Club, NRA. Democrat. Avocations: hunting, softball, jogging, basketball. Office: 417 Eaton St Key West FL 33040-6511 also: Lazzara and Paul PA Ste 2001 606 Madison St Tampa FL 33602-4017

EDENFIELD, BERRY AVANT, federal judge; b. Bulloch County, Ga., Aug. 2, 1934; s. Perry and Vera E.; m. Vida Melvis Bryant, Aug. 3, 1963. B.B.A. U. Ga, 1956, LL.B., 1958. Bar: Ga. 1958. Partner firm Allen, Edenfield, Brown & Wright (and predecessors), Statesboro, Ga., 1958-78; judge U.S. Dist. Ct. (so. dist.) Ga., Savannah, 1978-90, chief judge, 1990-97, judge, 1997—. Mem. Ga. Senate, 1965-66. Office: US Dist Ct PO Box 9865 Savannah GA 31412-0065*

EDENS, BETTY JOYCE, reading recovery educator; b. Hillsboro, Tex., Oct. 20, 1944; d. Edward Alton and Mary Alma (Pendley) Harbin; m. Eugene Cliett Edens, May 29, 1964; children: Michael Eugene, Anne-Marie DeWitt, Kristen Babovec. *Great grandparents were Caleb Hill and Elizabeth White, descendents of first baby born on the Mayflower, Peregrine White, and of Colonel Daniel White. Grandparent Dee Finis Pendley was a part of the Oklahoma land rush, and later became a banker in Paoli, Oklahoma. He married Mary Hill, daughter of Mary Elizabeth Creal and Samuel Almon Hill. While banking in Paoli, Mary and Dee F. were robbed and kidnapped by Sam Shockley in 1937, but were successfully rescued by a rancher near Turner Falls, Oklahoma. Betty's parents, Mary Alma Joyce Pendley and Edward Alton Harbin, met at Oklahoma University in Norman, Oklahoma.* BEd, Ind. U., 1985; MS, Tex. A&M of Commerce, 1995. Cert. elem. tchr., reading tchr., Tex. 1st grade tchr. Monday Primary, Kaufman, Tex., 1986-93; 1st grade tchr. Franklin Elem., Hillsboro, Tex., 1993-96, reading recovery tchr., 1994—. Mem. early literacy com. TSRA, 1998, Susan G. Komen Found. Mem. Reading Recovery Coun. of N.Am., Internat. Reading Assn., Tex. Reading Assn., Monday Rev. Club. Republican. Mem. Ch. of Christ. Avocations: recreational reading, walking, computers.

EDENS, DONALD KEITH, oil company executive; b. Salt Lake City, Aug. 3, 1928; s. Roger Edward and Elsie Vera (Johnson) E.; m. Elizabeth Adele Mays, Dec. 29, 1950; children: Karen Elizabeth, Donald Edward, Douglas Mays. B.S. in Bus. Adminstrn, U. Utah, 1951. With Phillips Petroleum Co., 1953-72; mng. dir. Phillips Petroleum Ltd., London, 1964-68; v.p. Coastal Corp., Houston, 1972-74; pres., chief exec. officer Union Petroleum Corp., Revere, Mass., 1974-78; sr. v.p. Oasis Petroleum Corp.; also, pres. Gulf Coast and Eastern region Oasis Petroleum Corp., Houston, 1979-82; v.p. Barrick Petroleum Corp., Toronto, Ont., Canada, 1983-85, Barrick Petroleum (USA) Inc., Houston, 1983-85; cons. to petroleum industry, 1985—. Served with AUS, 1946-48; Served with USAAF, 1951-53. Recipient

Chmn.'s Cup award Phillips Petroleum Co., 1971. Mem. 25 Yr. Club of Petroleum Industry, UN Assn., Beta Theta Pi. Clubs: Champions Golf, Houston. Lodge: Masons. Home: 6110 Rolling Water Dr Houston TX 77069-2546

EDENS, FRED JOE, petroleum engineer; b. Guymon, Okla., Oct. 3, 1952; s. Bill H. and D. Jeanne (Clifford) E.; m. Becky A. Yost, Oct. 25, 1976; children: Jason, Jarrod. BCE, Okla. State U., 1974. Registered profl. engr., Tex. Civil engr. U.S. Army Corps Engrs., Tulsa, 1975-81; petroleum engr. Amoco Prodn. Co., Liberal, Kans., 1981-84; prodn. foreman Amoco Prodn. Co., Casper, Wyo., 1984-86, facilities engr., 1986-89; mech. engr. Amoco Prodn. Co., Denver, 1989-92; petroleum engr., field foreman Amoco Prodn. Co., Ratliff City, Okla., 1992-98; petroleum engr. BP Amoco Plc., Perryton, Tex., 1998—. Capt. USAF, 1974-85. Mem. Soc. Petroleum Engrs. Republican. Baptist. Home: 2506 Texas St Perryton TX 79070-5731 Office: Crescendo Resources LP PO Box 1005 Perryton TX 79070-1005

EDENS, GARY DENTON, broadcasting executive; b. Asheville, N.C., Jan. 6, 1942; s. James Edwin and Pauline Amanda (New) E.; m. Hannah Suellen Walter, Aug. 21, 1965; children: Ashley Elizabeth, Emily Blair. BS, U. N.C., 1964. Account exec. PAMS Prodns., Dallas, 1965-67; account exec. Sta. WKIX, Raleigh, N.C., 1967-69; gen. mgr. Sta. KOY, Phoenix, 1970-81; sr. v.p. Harte-Hanks Radio, Inc., Phoenix, 1978-81, pres., chief exec. officer, 1981-84; chmn., chief exec. officer Edens Broadcasting, Inc., 1984-95; dir. Gt. Western Bank & Trust Ariz., 1975-86, Citibank Ariz., 1986—, Inter-Tel, Inc., 1994—; chmn. The Hanover Cos., Inc., 1995—. Bd. dirs. Valley Big Bros., 1972-80, Ariz. State U. Found., 1979—, COMPAS, 1979—, Men's Arts Coun., 1975-78. Named One of Three Outstanding Young Men, Phoenix Jaycees, 1973; entrepreneurial fellow U. Ariz., 1989. Mem. Phoenix Execs. Club (pres. 1976), Nat. Radio Broadcasters Assn. (dir. 1981-86), Radio Advt. Bur. (dir. 1981—), Young Pres. Orgn. (chmn. Ariz. chpt. 1989-90), Chief Execs. Orgn., Ariz. Pres. Orgn. Republican. Methodist. Office: 5112 N 40th St Ste 102 Phoenix AZ 85018

EDENS, MYRA JIM, health facility nursing administrator; b. Charlotte, N.C., Nov. 16, 1951; d. James O. and Edna M. (Wright) Mullis; m. Stephen J. Edens; children: Matthew Brandon, Jeremy Michael, Carrie Elizabeth. Diploma, Presbyn. Hosp. Sch. Nursing, Charlotte, 1972; AA, Santa Fe C.C.; BSN, U. Fla., 1984, MSN in Nursing Adminstrn., 1989. RN, Fla., Va., R.I. Pediatric staff nurse N.C. Meml. Hosp., Chapel Hill, 1972-75, Mercy Hosp., Charlotte, 1975-76; staff supplement RN Shands Hosp., U. Fla., Gainesville, 1975-76, RN II neonatal ICU, 1976-77, supr. neonatal ICU I and II, 1977-87, assoc. dir. staffing resources, 1987-89, acting dir. women's haelth, 1988; dir. nursing support svcs. Johnson City (Tenn.) Med. Ctr. Hosp., 1990-91, dir. women's and children's health svcs., 1991-95; dir. pediatric patient care scvs. Hasbro Children's Hosp. at R.I. Hosp., Providence, 1995—; adj. faculty mem. East Tenn. State U., 1991-95. Contbr. articles to profl. jours. Mem. neonatal grant adv. bd. Coll. Nursing, U. Fla., 1986-89; mem. coordinating com. N.E. Tenn. Nursing Rsch. Consortium, 1991. Fla. C.C. scholar, 1981. Mem. Am. Orgn. Nurse Execs., Tenn. Orgn. Nurse Execs. (fin. officer), Tenn. Nurses Assn., Tenn. Hosp. Assn., Presbyn. Hosp. Alumnae Assn., Phi Kappa Phi, Sigma Theta Tau (2d v.p. Epsilon Sigma chpt. 1991, chmn. cmty. schs.). Avocations: antiques, reading, walking. Office: Hasbro Children's Hosp RI Hosp 593 Eddy St Providence RI 02903-4923*

EDER, HOWARD ABRAM, physician; b. Milw., Sept. 23, 1917; s. Samuel and Rebecca (Abram) E.; m. Barbara Straus, July 15, 1954 (dec. Nov. 1997); children—Rebecca, Susan, Michael. A.B., U. Wis., 1938; M.D., Harvard U., 1942, M.P.H., 1945; MD honoris causa, U. Linkoping, Sweden. Intern Peter Bent Brigham Hosp., Boston, 1942-43; asst. resident Peter Bent Brigham Hosp., 1943-44; research fellow in medicine Harvard Med. Sch., 1943-44, research fellow in biochemistry, 1945-46; asst. in medicine, asst. physician Rockefeller U. Hosp., 1946-50; asst. prof. medicine Cornell U. Med. Coll., N.Y.C., 1950-53; mem. staff Nat. Heart Inst., Bethesda, Md., 1953-55; asso. prof. medicine State U. N.Y., Downstate Med. Coll., Bklyn., 1955-57; asso. prof. medicine Albert Einstein Coll. Medicine, 1957-60, prof., 1960-88, prof. emeritus, 1989—; chmn. lipid metabolism adv. com. Nat. Heart, Lung and Blood Inst., 1978-80, mem. bd. sci. counselors, 1986-90, chmn., 1989-90; mem. diabetes and heart disease rev. panel NIH, 1995, 96. Editorial bd.: Am. Jour. Physiology, 1968-71, 79-82, Jour. Lipid Research, 1964—, Am. Jour. Medicine, 1976-80. Mem. Assn. Am. Physicians, Am. Soc. Clin. Investigation, Am. Soc. Biol. Chemists, Am. Physiol. Soc., Am. Heart Assn. (Disting. Accomplishment award 1985, mem. coun. on arteriosclerosis, Spl. Recognition award 1993), Inst. of Medicine NAS, Interurban Clin. Club (pres. 1971-72), Phi Beta Kappa, Alpha Omega Alpha. Home: 4465 Douglas Ave Bronx NY 10471-3525 Office: Albert Einstein Coll Medicine 1300 Morris Park Ave Bronx NY 10461-1926

EDER, RICHARD GRAY, newspaper critic; b. Washington, Aug. 16, 1932; s. George Jackson and Marceline (Gray) E.; m. Esther Garcia Aguirre, Apr. 21, 1955; children: Maria, Ann, Claire, Michael, Luke, Benjamin, James. BA, Harvard U., 1954. Fgn. corr. N.Y. Times, various countries in Europe and Latin Am., 1962-77, 80-82; book critic N.Y. Times, 1999—, theater critic, 1977-79; book critic L.A. Times, 1982-99, L.A. Times and Newsday, 1992-99; vis. lectr. Bard Coll., 1983, Boston U., 1986-87; lectr. MIT, 1997. Ferris Fellow Princeton U., 1984-85, 95-96; recipient Pulitzer prize for criticism, 1987. Mem. Nat. Book Critics Circle (citation for reviewing 1987). Roman Catholic. Office: Los Angeles Times 86 Charles St Boston MA 02114-4630

EDERER, GRACE MARY, clinical laboratory scientist, retired; b. Morton, Minn., June 27, 1919; d. John and Mary (Prosser) Ederer. BA, Coll. of St. Catherine, 1941; M in Public Health, U. Minn., 1962. Staff technologist, chemistry Henry Ford Hosp., Detroit, 1942-44; instr. biol. scis. Coll. of St. Catherine, St. Paul, 1944-45; supr. bacteriology Northwestern Hosp., Mpls., 1945-52; adminstrv. lab. technologist, instr. Clin. Labs., U. Minn. Hosp., Mpls., 1952-63, asst. to dir. of Clin. labs., asst. prof., 1963-67; assoc. prof. dept. lab. medicine and pathology U. Minn., Mpls., 1967-76, prof. lab. med. and pathology, 1976-82, prof. emeritus, 1982—; acting dir. bacteriology, mycology and parasitology Clin. Labs. U. Minn. Hosp., Mpls., 1981-82; cons. microbiology Minn. Mining and Mfg., St. Paul, 1976-80. Co-author: Principles of Biochemical Tests in Diagnostic Microbiology, 1975; contbr. articles to profl. jours. Alternate delegate Rep. Party, Edina, Minn., 1992-96; mem. adult edn. com. Annunciation Parish, Mpls., 1986-92, ch. People to People com., 1993-97; ch. Health com. U. Minn. Retirees, Mpls., 1984-88; fund raiser Coll. of St. Catherine, St. Paul, 1982, 91, 96. Recipient Kimble award Conf. of Public Health Labs., 1985, Coll. of St. Catherine Alumnae award, 1996. Mem. Am. Soc. for Clin. Lab. Scientists (emeritus), Sigma Delta Epsilon, Iota Sigma Pi (life), Alpha Mu Tau. Republican. Roman Catholic. Avocation: harmonica band. Home: Ste 817 7500 York Ave South #817 Minneapolis MN 55435-4758

EDERLE, DOUGLAS RICHARD, investment manager; b. St. Louis, Aug. 10, 1962; s. Richard Joseph and Mary Ellen (Gorman) E.; m. Virginia Foss Mara, June 5, 1988; children: Ryan Douglas, William Gorman, Samuel Mara, Katherine Rose. BS in Acctg. magna cum laude, U. Ill., 1984; JD, Harvard U., 1987. Bar: Tex. 1987, Mass. 1989. Assoc. Hughes & Luce, Dallas, 1987-88; ptnr. Testa, Hurwitz & Thibeault, Boston, 1989-98; sr. v.p., mng. dir. Pell, Rudman Trust Co., N.A., Boston, 1998—. Bd. advisors Project Bug Light, Little Angels Fund; treas. Duxbury Edn. Found. Mem. ABA, Tex. Bar Assn., Mass. Bar Assn., Boston Bar Assn. Roman Catholic. Avocations: golf, basketball, tennis. Home: PO Box 1942 32 Hounds Ditch Ln Duxbury MA 02332-4421 Office: Pell Rudman Trust Co NA 100 Federal St Ste 3700 Boston MA 02110-1823

EDGAR, ALVIS, JR. See OWENS, BUCK

EDGAR, GILBERT HAMMOND, III, business administrator; b. Wilkes-Barre, Pa., Jan. 5, 1947; s. Gilbert Hammond Jr. and Alice (Taylor); children: Gilbert H. IV, Cynthia; m. Angelina Bogert, Nov. 17, 1975. AS in Applied Sci. and Tech., Thomas Edison State Coll., Trenton, N.J., 1987. Cert. comml. pilot. Instr., charter pilot Cherry Ridge Flying Service, Forty Fort, Pa., 1972-75; mktg. rep. SRC Inc., Pittston, Pa., 1975-79; asst. to pres., v.p. mktg. Pocono Airlines, Avoca, Pa., 1979-86; corp. dir. adminstrv. services Patrick Media Group, Inc., Scranton, Penn., 1986-89; gen. mgr. Marquis Art & Frame, Wilkes-Barre, Pa., 1989—. Served with USN, 1965-67, Res., 1967-70. Republican. Avocations: numismatics, photography, computers, astronomy.

EDGAR, HAROLD SIMMONS HULL, legal educator; b. 1942. AB, Harvard U., 1964; LLB, Columbia U., 1967. Bar: N.Y. 1968. Law clk. to judge U.S. Ct. Appeals (D.C. Cir.), 1967-68; asst. prof. law Columbia U., N.Y.C., 1968-73; now Julius Silver prof. law, sci. and tech., and dir. program in law, sci. and tech. Columbia U. Sch. Law, N.Y.C., 1985—; mem. The Hastings Ctr., 1978—, Rapporteur, UNESCO Internat. Com. on Bioethics., 1992-96. Office: Columbia U Law Sch 435 W 116th St New York NY 10027-7201

EDGAR, JAMES MACMILLAN, JR., management consultant; b. N.Y.C., Nov. 7, 1936; s. James Macmillan Edgar and Lilyan (McCann) E.; m. Judith Frances Storey, June 28, 1958; children: Suzanne Lynn, James Macmillan, Gordon Stuart. B in Chem. Engring., Cornell U., 1959, MBA with distinction, 1960. CPA; cert. mgmt. cons. New product rep. E.I. duPont Nemours, Wilmington, Del., 1960-63, mktg. svcs. rep., 1963-64; with Touch Ross & Co., 1964-78; mgr. Touch Ross & Co., Detroit, 1966-68; ptnr. in charge, mgt. svcs. ops. for No. Calif. and Hawaii Touch Ross & Co., San Francisco, 1971-78, ptnr. Western regional mgmt. svcs., 1978; sr. ptnr. Edgar, Dunn & Co., San Francisco, 1978—; bd. dirs. Associated oreg. Industries Svcs. Corp., 1991—. Patentee nonwoven fabrice. Active San Francisco Mayor's Fin. Adv. Com., 1976—, mem. exec. com., 1978—, Blue Ribbon com. for Bus., 1987-88, Alumnae Resources adv. bd., 1986-94, San Francisco Planning and Urban Rsch. Bd., 1986-89, mem. adv. bd., 1989-93, mem. program adv. com., 1996—; mem. alumni exec. coun. Johnson Grad. Sch. Mgmt. Cornell U., Cornell Coun., 1970-73; mem. steering com. Bay Area Coun., 1989-95, mem. program adv. com., 1996—; chmn. San Francisco Libr. Found., 1989-96; bd. dirs. Rosenberg Found., 1995—, Harding Lawson Assoc. Group, 1996—, Golden Gate U., 1997—. Recipient Award of Merit for outstanding pub. svc. City and County of San Francisco, 1978, Honor award for outstanding contbns. to profl. mgmt. Johnson Grad. Sch. Mgmt., Cornell U., 1978. Mem. AICPA, Assn. Corp. Growth (v.p. membership San Francisco chpt. 1979-81, v.p. programs 1981-82, pres. 1982-83, nat. bd. dirs. 1983-86), Calif. Soc. CPAs, Inst. Mgmt. Cons. (regional v.p. 1973-80, bd. dirs. 1975-77, v.p. 1977-80), San Francisco C. of C. (bd. dirs. 1987-89, 91—, mem. exec. com. 1988-89, 91-95, chmn. mktg. San Francisco program 1991-92, membership devel. 1993, chmn. bd. dirs. 1994, dir. emeritus 1995—), Bay Area Coun. (bd. dirs. 1998—), Pacific Union Club, Commonwealth Club of San Francisco, Marin Rod and Gun Club, Tau Beta Pi. Home: 10 Buckeye Way San Rafael CA 94904-2602 Office: Edgar Dunn & Co Inc 847 Sansome St Ste 400 San Francisco CA 94111-1585

EDGAR, JIM, former governor; b. Vinita, Okla., July 22, 1946; m. Brenda Smith; children: Brad, Elizabeth. Grad., Eastern Ill. U., 1968; postgrad., U. Ill., Sangamon State U., 1971-74. Legis. intern pres. pro tem Ill. Senate, 1968; key asst. to speaker ho. Ill. Ho. of Reps., 1972-73; aide to pres. Ill. Senate, 1974, to Ho. minority leader, 1976; mem. Ill. Ho. of Reps., 1977-79; dir. legis. affairs Ill. Gov., 1979-80; sec. state State of Ill., 1981-91; gov. State of Ill., 1991-98; disting. fellow Inst. Govt. and Publs. U. Ill., Urbana, 1999—; co-lead gov. Nat. Gov.'s Assn. Transp. Com., 1995-96; chair Edn. Commn. of States, 1993-94; chair Nat. Gov.'s Assn. Com. on Econ. Devel. and Commerce, 1992-93; pres. Coun. State Govts., 1992-93; chair Gov.'s Ethanol Coalition, 1992-93; chair Nat. Gov.'s Assn. Com. on Econ. Devel. and Tech. Innovation, 1991-92. Precinct committeeman, treas. Coles County Rep. Com., 1974; dir. state svc. Nat. Conf. State Legislatures, 1975, 76; mem. campaign com. Ill. Ho. of Reps.; pres. Nat. Assn. Secs. of State, 1988; exec. com. Coun. State Govts., 1988, v.p. exec. com., 1991, pres., 1992-93; bd. dirs. Nat. Commn. Against Drunk Driving, 1989; chmn. Ill. Literacy Coun., 1989; chmn. Edn. Commn. of the States, 1993-94; chmn. Gov.'s Ethanol Coalition, 1992-93; pres. Bd. Coun. State Govts. Mem. Nat. Govs. Assn. (chmn. econ. devel. and commerce com. 1992-93, strategic planning rev. task force 1991—, past chmn. task force on edn., mem. edn. goals panel, chair com. econ. devel. and technol. innovation 1991-92, edn. commn. of states 1993-94, co-lead gov. transp. com. 1995-96), Coles County Hist. Soc. (pres. 1976-79). Baptist. Office: Office of Gov 207 State House Springfield IL 62706-0001 Office: U Ill Inst Govt and Publ Affairs 1007 W Nevada MC 037 Urbana IL 61801*

EDGAR, JOHN M., lawyer; b. Tex., 1943. BS, U. Kans., 1965; JD with distinction, U. Mo., Kans. City, 1968. Bar: Mo. 1968. Resident mng. ptnr. Bryan Cave LLP, Kans. City, Mo. Mem. Lawyers Assn. Kansas City, Phi Alpha Delta, Order of Bench and Robe. Office: Bryan Cave LLP 3500 1 Kansas City Pl Kansas City MO 64105

EDGAR, R(OBERT) ALLAN, federal judge; b. Munising, Mich., Oct. 6, 1940; s. Robert Richard and Jean Lillian (Hansen) E.; m. Frances Gail Martin, Mar. 30, 1968; children: Amy Elizabeth, Laura Anne. BA, Davidson Coll., 1962; LLB, Duke U., 1965. Bar: Tenn. 1965. From assoc. to ptnr. Miller & Martin, Chattanooga, 1967-85; judge U.S. Dist. Ct. (ea. dist.) Tenn., Chattanooga, 1985—; mem. com. ct. adminstrn. and case mgmt. Jud. Conf. of the U.S. Mem. Tenn. Ho. of Reps., Nashville, 1970-72, Tenn. Wildlife Resources Commn., Nashville, 1979-85. Served to capt. U.S. Army, 1966-67, Vietnam. Decorated Bronze Star, 1967. Mem. Fed. Bar Assn., Chattanooga Bar Assn. Episcopalian. Office: US Dist Ct PO Box 1748 960 Georgia Ave Chattanooga TN 37402-2220

EDGAR, THOMAS FLYNN, chemical engineering educator; b. Bartlesville, Okla., Apr. 17, 1945; s. Maurice Russell and Natalie (Flynn) E.; m. Donna Jean Proffitt, July 15, 1967; children: Rebecca, Jeffrey. B.S. in Chem. Engring., U. Kans., 1967; Ph.D. in Chem. Engring., Princeton U., 1971. Registered profl. engr., Tex. Process engr. Conoco, Balt., 1968-69; prof. chem. engring. U. Tex., Austin, 1971—, chmn. dept., 1985-93, Abell chair, 1991—, assoc. dean engring., 1993-96, assoc v.p. acad. computing, 1996—; prof. chem. engring. U. Calif., Berkeley, 1978; pres. CACHE Corp., Austin, Tex., 1981-84; pres. Am. Automatic Control Coun., Chgo., 1990-91; chair Coun. for Chem. Rsch., Washington, 1992-93. Author: Coal Processing and Pollution Control, 1983; co-author: Real Time Computing, 1982, Optimization of Chemical Processes, 1988, Process Dynamics and Control, 1989; editor: Chemical Process Control, 1981, In Situ (Marcel Dekker), 1977-89; also jours. Recipient Edn. award Am. Automatic Control Coun., 1992. Fellow AIChE (Outstanding Counselor award 1975, Colburn award 1980, Computing in Chem. Engring. award 1995, editl. bd. jour. 1983-85, chmn. cast divsn. 1986, bd. dirs. 1989-92, v.p. 1996, pres. 1997); mem. Am. Soc. Engring. Edn. (Westinghouse award 1988, Meriam-Wiley Disting. Author 1990, Chem. Engring. Divsn. Leadership award 1996), Instrument Soc. Am. (Eckman Edn. award 1993), Am. Chem. Soc., Tau Beta Pi, Phi Lambda Upsilon, Omicron Delta Kappa, Phi Kappa Phi (Joe King award U. Tex. 1989, U. Kans. Disting. Engring. Svc. award 1990). Democrat. Methodist.

EDGAR, WALTER BELLINGRATH, historian; b. Mobile, Ala., Dec. 10, 1943; s. Charles Ernest, Jr. and Amelia Lyon (Moore) E.; m. Elizabeth Giles, Aug. 6, 1966; children: Eliza, Amelia. A.B., Davidson Coll., (N.C.), 1965; M.A., U. S.C., 1967, Ph.D., 1969. From asst. prof. to prof. history U. S.C., Columbia, 1974—, dir. Inst. So. Studies, 1980—, Neuffer prof. so. studies, 1995—. Author: History of Santee Cooper, 1984, South Carolina in the Modern Age, 1992, South Carolina: A History, 1998; co-author: The Governor's Mansion of the Palmetto State, 1979, Columbia: Portrait of a City, 1986; editor: The Letterbook of Robert Pringle, 1972, A Southern Renascence Man: Views of Robert Penn Warren, 1984, South Carolina: The WPA Guide to the Palmetto State, 1988; co-editor: Southern Landscapes, 1996; compiler: The Biographical Directory of the South Carolina House of Representatives: Vol. 1, Session Lists, 1974, Vol. II, The Commons House of Assembly, 1977. Served to capt. U.S. Army, 1969-71; col. Res. Decorated Bronze Star, Legion of Merit; Nat. Hist. Publs. Commn. fellow, 1971-72. Mem. Am. Hist. Assn., Orgn. Am. Historians, So. Hist. Assn., S.C. Hist. Assn. (pres. 1982-83), South Caroliniana Soc. (pres. 1984-87), Blue Key, Omicron Delta Kappa, Phi Alpha Theta. Home: 1731 Hollywood Dr Columbia SC 29205-3215 Office: U SC Inst So Studies Columbia SC 29208

EDGAR, WILLIAM JOHN, philosophy educator; b. Charlottesville, Va., Jan. 20, 1933; s. William John and Frances (Ring) E.; m. Stacey Lynn Walter, June 20, 1962; children: Michael Kent, Stephen Scott, Elizabeth Anne, Chandra Lynn. BA, Cornell U., 1959; M.A., Syracuse U., 1966, Ph.D., 1972. Systems analyst Advanced Electronics Ctr., Ithaca, N.Y., 1959-62, Electronics Lab., Syracuse, N.Y., 1962-65; asst. prof. philosophy SUNY-Geneseo, 1969-74, assoc. prof., 1974-79, disting. teaching prof., chmn. dept., 1979—. Author: Evidence, 1980, The Problem Solver's Guide to Logic, 1983, The Elements of Logic, 1989; contbr. articles to profl. jours. Served to 1st lt. U.S. Army, 1952-56. Recipient Chancellor's award for excellence in teaching, 1974, 76, Excellence award State of N.Y. and UUP, 1991; fellow NDEA Title IV Syracuse U., 1965-68. Mem. Am. Philos. Assn. Home: 5722 Logan Rd RD 1 Mount Morris NY 14510 Office: SUNY Dept Philosophy Geneseo NY 14454

EDGE, JAMES EDWARD, health care administrator; b. Anacortes, Wash., Apr. 29, 1948; s. Edward and Carol Marie (Lian) E.; m. Nellie Ruth Horton, Mar. 21, 1970; children: Elissa Marie, Gina Dawn. BS in Pharmacy, U. Wash., 1971; MPH, U. Hawaii, 1979. Registered pharmacist. Commd. USPHS, 1969—, advanced through grades to capt.; staff pharmacist USPHS Indian Hosp., Albuquerque, 1971-73; chief pharmacy, lab/x-ray S.W. Indian Poly. Inst., Albuquerque, 1972-73, Neah Bay Indian Health Ctr., Wash., 1973-75; svc. unit dir. Neah Bay Svc. Unit, Indian Health Svc., 1975-78, Western Oreg. Service Unit, Indian Health Svc., Salem, 1980—; cons. in field. Active Combined Fed. Campaign, Salem, 1985—. John Quick Pharmacy scholar, U. Wash., 1967, Health Professions scholar, 1969. Mem. APHA, Am. Coll. Healthcare Adminstrs., Am. Acad. Med. Adminstrs., Assn. Mil. Surgeons U.S., Mensa, Res. Officers Assn., Commd. Officer USPHS, Wash. Pharm. Assn., nat. Coun. Svc. Unit Dirs. (chmn. 1986-88). Avocations: running, antique cars, sculling. Office: PHS Indian Health Ctr 3750 Chemawa Rd NE Salem OR 97305-1119

EDGE, JOHN FORREST, banker; b. Iowa City, Iowa, Sept. 7, 1948; s. John G. and Ann E. (Fields) E.; m. Jacqueline M. Stoken; children; Lisa, Alex. BA, U. MO., 1972; MBA, Drake U., 1990. CEO State Savs. Bank, Baxter, Iowa, 1974—; mem. Econ. Devel. Corp., Baxter, 1985-95. Mem. Des Moines Bldg. Bd. Appeal, 1996-97. With U.S. Army, 1971-72. Mem. Des Moines Golf and Country Club. Avocations: golf, reading. Office: State Savs Bank 102 S Main Baxter IA 50028

EDGE, MARIANNE SMITH, business owner; b. Covington, Ky., Feb. 19, 1955; d. Robert Huey and Jeanette Allen (Edwards) Smith; m. John Ralph Edge, Mar. 27, 1982. BS in Dietetics, U. Ky., 1977; MS in Pub. Health, Western Ky. U., 1981. Lic. dietitian, Ky. Licensure Bd. Nutritionists and Dietitians (bd. dirs. 1994—); registered dietitian, Commn. on Dietetic Registration. Cons. dietitian, sr. divsn. dietitian Unicare Health Facilities, Evansville, Ind., 1981-86; owner MSE & Assocs., Owensboro, Ky., 1986—; healthcare mktg. cons. Mena Magic Foods, Indpls., 1986-96, Diamond Criptal Splty. Foods, Boston, 1996—. Co-author: Developing Marketable Skills in Healthcare—The Consultant Dietitian, 1991. Bd. dirs. Owensboro-Daviess County Hosp., 1995—, Owensboro Symphony Orch., 1987-97, area hospice, 1996—. Fellow Am. Dietetic Assn. (bd. dirs. 1997—, chmn. Cons. Dietitians in Healthcare 1988-89); mem. Am. Soc. Parenteral and Enteral Nutrition, Ky. Dietetic Assn. (bd. dirs., com. chairperson, Outstanding Dietitian of Yr. 1995), U. Ky. Nat. Alumni Assn. (pres. 1997-98, Svc. award 1996). Democrat. Methodist. Avocations: volunteering, snow skiing, golf. Home: 516 Ford Ave Owensboro KY 42301-4629 Office: MSE & Assocs 516 Ford Ave Owensboro KY 42301-4629

EDGE, RONALD DOVASTON, physics educator; b. Bolton, Eng., Feb. 3, 1929; came to U.S., 1958, naturalized, 1968; s. James and Mildred (Davies) E.; m. Margaret Skulina, Aug. 14, 1956 (div. 1989); children: Christopher James, Michael Dovaston; m. Gertrude Hansen, Dec. 31, 1992. B.A., Cambridge U., 1950, M.A., 1952, Ph.D., 1956. Research fellow Australian Nat. U., Canberra, 1954-58; asst. then assoc. prof. physics U. S.C., Columbia, 1958-63; prof. U. S.C., 1964-94, disting. prof. emeritus, 1994—; research assoc. Yale U., New Haven, 1963-64; vis. prof. Stanford U., Calif. Tech. Inst., U. Munich, U. Sussex, U. Witwatersrand, U. Aarhus, Oak Ridge Nat. Lab., Los Alamos Nat. Lab.; leader 1st Am. team Internat. Physics Olympiad, 1986. Author: Physics in the Arts, 1973, String and Sticky Tape Experiments, 1978; contbr. articles to profl. jours. Recipient Russell award U. S.C., Guy And Rebecca Forman award tchg. Physics, Vanderbilt U., 1998. Fellow Am. Phys. Soc. (James B. Pegram award 1979), Am. Assn. Physics Tchrs. (apparatus award 1973, v.p. 1995, pres. elect 1996, pres. 1997). Unitarian (past pres. Columbia fellowship). Home: 220 Jadetree Dr Hopkins SC 29061-9347 Office: U SC Physics Dept Columbia SC 29208

EDGE, THOMAS LESLIE, minister; b. Detroit, Dec. 20, 1935; s. Leslie Joseph and Flora Marie (Dirksen) E.; m. Betty Ruth Maxwell, Aug. 22, 1959; children: Elizabeth Anne, Christopher Thomas Gregory, Angela Michelle Marie. BA, Concordia Sem., St. Louis, 1957, MDiv, 1960. Ordained to ministry Luth. Ch.-Mo. Synod, 1960. Founding pastor Luth. Ch. St. Ambrose, Pennsville, N.J., 1960-67; Pastor All Saints Luth. Ch., Charlotte, N.C., 1967-70, Christ the King Luth. Ch., Ringwood, N.J., 1970—; chmn. commn. on worship N.J. Dist. Luth. Ch.-Mo. Synod, 1972-74, mem. bd. adjudication, 1974-78; mem. Luth. Hour Rsch. Com., 1973-80; chaplain Fire Dept., Ringwood, 1970—. Contbr. articles to religious mags. Co-founder Charlotte Citizens for Peace in Viet-Nam, 1967; dir. Ambulance Corps, Ringwood, 1970-84; trustee Luth. Social Ministries of N.J., 1995—; vice chmn. bd. Crane's Mill Life Care Ctr., West Caldwell, N.J., 1996—; 3d v.p. N.J. Dist. Luth. Ch.-Mo. Synod, 1997—. Home: 222 Skylands Rd Ringwood NJ 07456-2905 Office: 50 Erskine Rd Ringwood NJ 07456-2150

EDGECOMB, VIRGINIA, real estate broker; b. Dallas, Mar. 13, 1955; d. Charles Reaves and Jacqueline Lee (Hail) Pate; m. John Robb Edgecomb, Nov. 4, 1978; children: John Robb Jr., Eric Durst, Evan Mail. BS, Southwestern U., Georgetown, Tex., 1978. Cert. tchr., Tex.; lic. realtor, Tex. Real estate broker Keller Williams, Austin, Tex., 1995—. Chmn. Laguna Gloria Fiesta, Austin, Tex., 1992; chmn. Kiker Elem. PTA, Austin, 1992-98; fundraising chair PTA, 1985-98. Mem. Tex. Assn. Realtors, Austin Bd. Realtors, Zeta Tau Alpha Alumni, Austin Woman's Club (arts com.), Austin Symphony League (showhouse 1992-97), Assistance League (ways and means com. 1983-85, award 1984). Republican. Methodist. Home: 5616 Van Winkle Ln Austin TX 78739-1692 Office: Keller Williams Realty Ste 179 3755 S Capital Of Texas Hwy Austin TX 78704-7999

EDGELL, BRADLEY GASKINS, legislative staff member; b. Ann Arbor, Mich., July 17, 1963. BA, U. Mich., 1985. Polit. liaison Dem. Congl. Campaign Com., Washington, 1985-86; sr. legis. asst. U.S. Rep. Claude Harris, Washington, 1987-92; legis. dir. U.S. Rep. Marjorie Margolies-Mezvinsky, Washington, 1993-94, Office Rep. Ken Bentsen, Washington, 1995—. Office: Office US Rep Ken Bentsen 326 Cannon House Office Washington DC 20515-4325*

EDGELL, STEPHEN EDWARD, psychology educator, statistical consultant; b. Inglewood, Calif., June 20, 1947; s. Stephen F. and Evelyn L. (Humborg) E.; m. Donna M. Grassello, Aug. 17, 1974. AA in Math., El Camino Jr. Coll., Gardena, Calif., 1968; AB in Psychology, Calif. State U., Long Beach, 1970; PhD in Math. Psychology, Ind. U., 1974; MA in Math., U. Louisville, 1987. Tchg. and rsch. asst. Ind. U., Bloomington, 1971-72, rsch. asst., computer sys. programmer, 1972, fellow, 1972-73, assoc. instr., 1973-74; asst. prof. psychology U. Louisville, 1974-80, assoc. prof., 1980-85, prof., 1985—, dir. exptl. psychology program, 1983, 88-91; mgr. software devel. Shelton Metrology Lab., Paducah, Ky., summer 1979; cons. on statis. analysis and exptl. design, product design, customer profile analysis, discrimination, computer software sys.; presenter in field at confs. and profl. meetings. Contbr. articles to profl. jours. Fellow NIMH, 1970-71. Mem. Soc. for Judgment and Decision Making (sec.-treas. 1986-89), Soc. for Math. Psychology, Am. Statis. Assn., Psychometric Soc., Psychonomic Soc., Cognitive Sci. Soc., Sigma Xi. Achievements include research on judgment, decision making and choice with emphasis on using mathematical models, artificial neural network models, artificial intelligence and computer simulation of decision making, including Bayesian methods, development of statistical techniques. Home: 10604 Grassy Ct Louisville KY 40241-2011 Office: U Louisville Dept Psychology Louisville KY 40292

EDGEMAN, RICK LEE, statistics educator, consultant; b. Pueblo, Colo., Nov. 28, 1954; s. Howard Curtis and Eunice Marie (Stucker) E.; m. Lisa Anne Allen, Aug. 12, 1978; children: Emily, Grant, Stephen. BS in Exptl.

Psychology, U. So. Colo., 1977; MS in Rsch. and Statis. Methodology, U. No. Colo., 1979; PhD in Stats., U. Wyo., 1983. Lectr. in stats. U. Wyo., Laramie, 1981-83; asst. prof. bus. Bradley U., Peoria, Ill., 1983-85; study design and analysis mgr. Bausch and Lomb, Rochester, N.Y., 1985; asst. prof. stats. Rochester (N.Y.) Inst. Tech., 1985-86; asst. prof. mgmt. sci. U. North Tex., Denton, 1986-88; assoc. prof. computer info. sys. Colo. State U., Ft. Collins, 1988-93, prof. computer info. systems, 1993—, dir. SABER Inst. for Self-Assessment & Bus. Excellence Rsch., 1988—; statis. cons. Eastman-Kodak, Rochester, 1985-86, Mobil Chem., Macedon, N.Y., 1985-86, Hewlett-Packard, Ft. Collins, 1988-89, Colo. Dept. Social Svcs., Denver; vis. prof. quality and innovation, Aarhus Sch. Bus., Denmark, 1997-98; exec. dir. Multinational Alliance for the Advancement of Orgnl. Excellence. Contbr. some 100 articles to profl. jours. Pres. Colo. Citizens for Decency, Ft. Collins, 1989-91; dir. Jesus Video Project Ft. Collins (Colo.), Campus Crusade for Christ, 1993-94. Caterpillar Tractor Co. Rsch. fellow Caterpiller Rsch. Found., Peoria, 1983-84. Mem. IEEE (mem. reliability soc., higher edn. com.), Am. Soc. for Quality Control (editor Quality Progress 1991-94), Am. Statis. Assn. (pres. Rochester N.Y. chpt. 1985-86), Sigma Xi. Republican. Avocations: baseball coaching, poetry writing, public speaking, hiking, religious teaching. Home: 709 Gilgalad Way Fort Collins CO 80526 Office: Computer Info Sys Dept Coll Bus Rockwell Hall Colo State Univ Fort Collins CO 80523

EDGERLY, WILLIAM SKELTON, banker; b. Lewiston, Maine, Feb. 18, 1927; s. Stuart and Florence (Skelton) E.; m. Lois Stiles, June 12, 1948; children: Leonard Stuart, Stephanie Lois. B.S. in Econs. and Engring., MIT, 1949; M.B.A., Harvard U., 1955. With Eastman Kodak Co., 1949-50; with Cabot Corp., Boston, 1952-75, fin. v.p., 1969-75, also dir.; chief exec. officer State St. Boston Corp., 1975-91, chmn., 1992, chmn emeritus, 1993—; chmn. Found. for Partnerships, 1992—; bd. dirs., former chmn. Met. Boston Housing Partnership; bd. dirs. Fed. Res. Bank Boston, Depository Trust Co., N.Y.C., Arkwright-Boston Ins. Co.; mem. MIT Corp. Bd. fellows Harvard Med. Sch.; bd. dirs. Jobs for Mass., former pres.; dir. Boston Pvt. Industry Coun., former chmn.; bd. dirs. Inst. for Fgn. Policy Analysis and Pioneer Inst.; trustee Com. Econ. Devel., The Gen. Hosp. Corp.; former mem. fed. adv. coun. Fed. Res. Bd., Washington. With USNR, 1945-46, 50-52. Mem. MIT Alumni Assn. (pres. 1973-74), Harvard Bus. Sch. Assn., Assn. res. City Bankers, Boston Econ. Club, Somerset Club, Cambridge Boat Club. Office: 124 Mount Auburn St Cambridge MA 02138-5758

EDGERTON, BRADFORD WHEATLY, plastic surgeon; b. Phila., May 8, 1947; s. Milton Thomas and Patricia Jane (Jones) E.; children: Bradford Wheatly Jr., Lauren Harrington; m. Louise Dungan Edgerton; stepchildren: Catherine Kelleher, Robert Kelleher. BA in Chemistry, Vanderbilt U., 1969, MD, 1973. Diplomate Am. Bd. Plastic Surgery, Am. Bd. Hand Surgery. Intern U. Calif., San Francisco, 1973-74; resident U. Va., Charlottesville, 1974-78; resident in plastic surgery Columbia-Presbyn., N.Y., 1979-81; fellow in hand surgery NYU, 1981-82, clin. instr. plastic surgery, 1981-89; ptnr. So. Calif. Permanente Med. Group, L.A., 1989—; assoc. prof. clin. plastic surgery U. So. Calif., L.A., 1989—. v.p., trustee W. Alton Jones Found., Charlottesville, Va., 1978—. Mem. Am. Assn. Hand Surgery, Am. Soc. Plastic and Reconstructive Surgery, Am. Soc. Surgery of Hand, L.A. Tennis Club. Episcopal. Home: 494 S Spalding Dr Beverly Hills CA 90212 Office: 6041 Cadillac Ave Los Angeles CA 90034-1702

EDGERTON, BRENDA EVANS, soup company executive; b. Halifax, Va., June 15, 1949; d. Elmer and Bernice (Chalmers) Evans; children from previous marriage: Lauren, Eric. Student, Pa. State U., 1967-69; BA, Rutgers U., 1970; MBA, Temple U., 1976. Mgr. acctg. Scott Paper Co., Phila., 1976-78; mgr. project fin. Scott Paper Co., 1978-82, mgr. money and banking, 1982-83; dir. fin. Campbell Soup Co., Camden, N.J., 1984-85, asst. treas., 1985-88, dep. treas., 1988-89, v.p., treas., 1989-94, v.p. fin. U.S. soup, 1994-96, v.p. bus. devel., 1996-98; CFO C&S Wholesalers, Bradboro, Vt., 1998—; bd. dirs. Frontier Corp. Office: C&S Wholesalers PO Box 821 Brattleboro VT 05302*

EDGERTON, RICHARD, restaurant and hotel owner; b. Haverford, Pa., May 2, 1911; s. Charles and Ida (Bonner) E.; m. Marie Lytle Page, Oct. 24, 1936; children: Leila, Margaret, Carol. LLD (hon.), Berry Coll., Mt. Berry, Ga. Chmn. Lakeside Inn Properties, Inc., Mt. Dora, Fla., 1935-80; pres. emeritus Twoton Inc.; owner 35 Burger King restaurants, Pa., 1967—; gen. mgr., pres. Buck Hill Falls (Pa.) Co., 1961-65; pres., CEO Eustis Sand Co., Mt. Dora, Fla., 1961—; founding dir. Fla. Service Corp., Tampa; v.p., dir. 1st Nat. Bank, Mt. Dora. Mem. Gov.'s Little Cabinet, Fla. Hotel & Restaurant Commmr., 1955-61. Trustee emeritus Berry Coll.; bd. dirs. Mt. Dora Cmty. Trust Fund; past. mem. Lake County Fla. Indsl. Devel. Commn.; past trustee Lake Sumter Mental Health Ctr. Found.; trustee emeritus Lake Sumter C.C. Served to lt. USNR, 1944-46; ETO. Named to Mid-Fla. Bus. Hall of Fame, 1994. Mem. Am. (dir.), Fla. (hon., past pres.) hotel and motel assns., N.H. Hotel Assn. (past pres.), Newcomen Soc., Welcome Soc., Pa. Soc. Clubs: Mt. Dora Yacht (past commodore, present fleet capt.), Mt. Dora Golf. Lodge: Mt. Dora Kiwanis (past pres.).

EDGERTON, WILLIAM B., foreign language educator; b. Winston-Salem, N.C., Mar. 11, 1914; s. Paul Clifton and Annie Maude (Benbow) E.; m. Jewell Mock Conrad, June 6, 1935; children: Susan, David. B.A., Guilford Coll., 1934; M.A., Haverford Coll., 1935; Ph.D., Columbia U., 1954. Tchr. French, German, Spanish, English in secondary schs. U.S. and France, 1935-39; faculty French and Spanish Guilford Coll., 1939-47; faculty Russian lit. Pa. State U., University Park, 1950-56, U. Mich., Ann Arbor, 1954-55, Columbia U., N.Y.C., 1956-58; prof. Slavic langs. and lits. Ind. U., Bloomington, 1958-83, prof. emeritus, 1983—, chmn. Slavic dept., 1958-65, 69-73, acting dir. Russian and East European Inst., 1981-82; cons. Ford Found., 1952-61; mem. joint com. on Slavic studies Am. Coun. Learned Socs., 1951-62, chmn. 1958-61; vis. rsch. scholar USSR Acad. of Sci., 1963-64, 78, 87, 88, 89, 90, Bulgarian Acad. Scis., 1986, 88. Editor, co-author: Quaker Profiles, 1995; gen. editor: Columbia Dictionary of Modern European Literature, 1980; translator, editor: Satirical Stories of Nikolai Leskov, 1969, Memoirs of Peasant Tolstoyans in Soviet Russia, 1993; editor: Ind. Slavic Studies, III, 1963, Ind. Slavic Studies, IV, 1967, Am. Contributions to the Fifth Internat. Congress of Slavists, 1963; contbr. articles to profl. internat. jours. Bd. dirs. Am. Friends Svc. Com., 1956-59; trustee Guilford Coll., 1969-86; mem. vis. com. for Slavic Studies Harvard U., 1967-77; mem. adv. com. Nat. Humanities Ctr., 1978—; war relief work Am. Friends Svc. Com. Yugoslav refugee camp, Egypt, 1944-45, dir., lectr. internat. student seminars U.S., 1948, 51, Geneva, 1949, Vienna, 1956, Leningrad, 1960; organizing search fgn. child victims Nazis, Germany, 1945-46, Quaker relief work, Poland, 1946, internat. missions Yugoslavia, Greece, 1950, USSR, 1955, Poland, 1957. Recipient Josef Dobrovsky medal Czechoslovak Acad. Sci., 1968; Am. Council Learned Socs. fellow, 1948-50; Guggenheim fellow, 1963-64. Mem. MLA (exec. council 1962-65), Am. Assn. Advancement Slavic Studies (pres. 1961), Am. Com. Slavists (chmn. 1958-78), Internat. Com. Slavists (Am. rep., 1958-78, hon. mem 1978—). Quaker. Home: 1801 E Maxwell Ln Bloomington IN 47401-5208 Office: Ind U Ballantine Hall # 502 Bloomington IN 47405-9999

EDGERTON, WINFIELD DOW, gynecologist; b. Caruthersville, Mo., Nov. 8, 1924; s. Winfield Dow and Anna Kathryn (Hale) E.; m. Rose Marie Cahill, June 24, 1945; 1 child, Winfield Dow. Student, Central Coll., Fayette, Mo., 1942-44; MD, Washington U., St. Louis, 1947. Intern St. Luke's Hosp., St. Louis, 1947-48; resident Chgo. Lying-In Hosp., 1948-49, Free Hosp. for Women, Brookline, Mass., 1951, U.S. Naval Hosp., Chelsea, Mass., 1951-53; practice medicine specializing in obstetrics and gynecology Davenport, Iowa, 1955-87; clin. asst. prof. obstetrics and gynecology U. Iowa Coll. Medicine, 1971-78, clin. assoc. prof., 1979-82, clin. prof., 1982—; mem. staff, med. dir. Maternal Health Ctr. St. Luke's Hosp. (name changed to Genesis Med. Ctr.). Contbr. articles to med. jours. and texts. Served to lt. M.C., USN, 1949-55. Fellow Am. Coll. Obstetricians and Gynecologists (past chmn. Iowa sect.), Royal Soc. Medicine; mem. Central Assn. Obstetricians and Gynecologists, Am. Fertility Soc., Am. Assn. Gynecologic Laparoscopists (past trustee), Gynecologic Laser Soc., AMA, Iowa Med. Soc., Scott County Med. Soc. (past pres.). Republican. Congregationalist. Home: 4 Lombard Ct Davenport IA 52803-2348 Office: Ste 400 Duck Creek Plz Bettendorf IA 52722

EDGETT, WILLIAM MALOY, lawyer, labor arbitrator; b. Balt., Feb. 26, 1927; s. Eugene Albert and Priscilla Ruff (Streett) E.; m. Bronwen Winifred Reese, Nov. 25, 1950. A.A., Towson State Coll., 1949; B.A., U. Md., 1951, J.D., 1959; LL.M., Georgetown U., 1970. Bar: Md. bar 1959. Asst. personnel mgr. Am. Sugar Refining Co., Balt., 1951-55; supr. indsl. relations Westinghouse Electric Co., Balt., 1955-61; sr. labor relations specialist Martin Co., Balt., 1961-64; asst. mgr. indsl. relations Md. Shipbuilding and Drydock Co., Balt., 1964-67; pvt. practice law, 1967—; Asst. prof. Towson State U., 1971-72. Mem. Md. Commn. Nursing, 1974-76; chmn. pub. law bds. Nat. Mediation Bd., 1971—; neutral mem. Nat. R.R. Adjustment Bd., 1971—. Served to staff sgt. USAAF, 1944-46. Mem. ABA. Nat. Acad. Arbitrators, Am. Arbitration Assn., Am., Roster Arbitrators Fed. Mediation and Conciliation Service. Home: 3 Beechmere Ln Cockeysville Hunt Valley MD 21030-1101 Office: PO Box 203 Cockeysville Hunt Valley MD 21030-0203

EDGINGTON, THOMAS S., pathologist, educator, molecular biologist; b. L.A., Feb. 10, 1932. BA in Biol. Scis., Stanford U., 1953, MD, 1957. Diplomate Am. Bd. Pathology, spl. cert. immunopathology. Intern Hosp. Univ. Pa., Phila., 1957-58; resident Ctr. Health Scis. UCLA, 1958-60; sr. postdoctiral fellow immunology Scripps Clinic & Rsch. Found., La Jolla, Calif., 1965-68, assoc. mem. dept. exptl. pathology, 1968-71; founder, head dept. anatomic pathology and lab. medicine Scripps Clinic and Rsch. Found., La Jolla, Calif., 1968-74, prof. depts. immunology and vascular biology, 1971—; asst. prof., surg. pathologist dept. pathology UCLA Sch. Medicine, 1962-65; assoc. adj. prof. pathology U. Calif., San Diego, La Jolla, 1968-75, adj. prof., 1975—; cons. Centocor, 1993-95, Eli Lilly, 1982-85, Becton-Dickinson, 1977-80; founder, bd. dirs. NuVas. Contbr. articles to profl. jours. Recipient Coll. de France medal, 1981, John A. Lynch Molecular Biology award U. Notre Dame, 1992, Rous-Whipple prize Am. Soc. Investigative Pathology, 1995, Disting. Career award Internat. Soc. Thrombosis and Hemostatis, 1995. Fellow AAAS; mem. Fedn. Am. Socs. Exptl. Biology (pres., chmn. bd. 1990-91), Internat. Soc. Thrombosis and Haemostatis, Thrombosis Inst. (bd. sci. govs. 1995—), Inst. of Medicine of NAS. Office: Scripps Rsch Inst 10550 N Torrey Pines Rd La Jolla CA 92037-1000

EDGINTON, CHRISTOPHER R., educator, academic administrator; b. Oak Harbor, Wash., Apr. 12, 1946; s. Clifford James and Ruth May E.; m. Susan Renee Hayes, Mar. 25, 1966; childre: Carole Noelle, David Clifford, Hanna Michelle. AA, Foothill Coll., 1966; BA in Recreation, San Jose State Coll., 1969; MS in Park & Recreation Adminstrn., U. Ill., 1971; PhD in Higher Edn. Mgmt., U. Iowa, 1975. Assoc. prof. sch. phys. edn. Dalhousie U., Halifax, Can., 1977-78; assoc. prof. divsn. recreation & leisure studies North Tex. State U., Denton, 1978-80; prof., head dept. leisure studies & Svcs. U. Oreg., Eugene, 1980-91; prof., dir. sch. health, phys. edn. & leisure U. No. Iowa, Cedar Falls, 1991—; asst. prof. dept. recreation U. Waterloo, Ont., Can., 1975-77; instr. recreation edn. program U. iowa, Iowa City, 1972-77; dir. parks & recreation City of Wooster, Ohio, 1971-72; recreation supr. II Arlington Heights (Ill.) Park Dist., 1970-71. Contbr. articles to profl. jours. Co-chair U. No. iowa United Way Campaign, 1998; mem. Cedar Falls Healthy Com. Action Project, Cedar Falls, 1992-94; bd. dirs. Jr. Achievement Black JHAwk Land, Cedar Falls, Waterloo, 1992-95. Disting. Alumni award San Jose State U., 1998, Disting. Alumni award San Jose State U., 1998; U. No. Iowa scholar, 1994. Fellow Acad. Leisure Scis.; mem. Am. Assn. Leisure & Recreation (pres. 1994-95 Meritorious Svc. award 1990, Hon. award 1995, J.B. Nash scholar 1998)), Nat. Recreation & Park Assn. (Profl. of Yr. 1986), Iowa Park and Recreation Assn., Oreg. Park & Recreation Soc. (v.p. 1985-86), Leisure & Recreation Assn. Korea (hon. life), Hong Kong Recreation & Mgmt. Assn. Avocation: collecting antiquarian books. Home: 1017 Oak Park Blvd Cedar Falls IA 50613 Office: U No Iowa Sch Health Phys Edn Leisure 203 Wellness/Recreation Ctr Cedar Falls IA 50614-0241

EDGINTON, JOHN ARTHUR, lawyer; b. Kingsburg, Calif., July 23, 1935; s. Arthur George and Pochantas Clementina (Ball) E.; m. Jane Ann Simmons, June 25, 1960. AA, U. Calif., Berkeley, 1955, AB in Econs., 1957, JD, 1963. Bar: Calif. 1964, No. Marianas 1969, U.S. Ct. Claims 1969, U.S. Ct. Appeals (9th cir.) 1969, U.S. Supreme Ct. 1969. Assoc. Graham & James, San Francisco, 1964-71, ptnr., 1971-94; ptnr. Dezurick Edginton & Harrington LLP, Emeryville, Calif., 1994-98, Booth Banning LLP, San Francisco, 1998—. Author: Maritime Bankruptcy, 1989; editor-in-chief Maritime Practice and Procedure, vol. 29 Moore's Federal Practice, 1997; contbr. numerous articles to profl. jours. With USN, 1957-60. Disting. U. Calif. alumni Order of Golden Bear. Mem. Maritime Law Assn. (chmn. practice and procedure com. 1991-95, bd. dirs. 1993-96), Swedish-Am. C. of C. (pres. Western Nat. 1988-90, 98—, nat. vice chmn. 1988-90, bd. dirs. 1971—), Sierra Club (nat. outing com. 1964—, chmn. ins. com. 1991—, internat. trips 1992-95). Democrat. Methodist. Avocations: mountaineering, hiking, photography, model railroads. E-mail: jedginton@boothbanning.com. Office: Booth Banning LLP 275 Battery St 27th Fl San Francisco CA 94111

EDGREN, GRETCHEN GRONDAHL, magazine editor; b. Portland, Oreg., Mar. 17, 1931; d. Jack W. and Alice Belle (Wells) Grondahl; m. James McNeese, Oct. 22, 1955 (div. Nov. 1974); children: Amy, Terence James; m. Alvin H. Edgren, Dec. 14, 1984. BJ, U. Oreg., 1952. Staff writer The Oregonian, Portland, 1952-61; editor Sunday mag. The San Juan (P.R.) Star, 1963-65; inventory and info. specialist USAF and U.S. Army Recruiting Command, San Antonio and Chgo., 1965-67; assoc. editor VIP mag. Playboy Clubs, Chgo., 1967-69, mng. editor, 1969-70; assoc. editor Playboy mag., Chgo., 1970-74, sr. editor, 1974-92, contbg. editor, 1992—. Author: The Playboy Book, 1994, The Playmate Book, 1996, Inside the Playboy Mansion, 1998; editor: New Credit Rights for Women, 1976; contbr. articles to mags. Adv. bd. Old Oreg. Alumni mag. U. Oreg., Eugene, 1988-96; pres. bd. dirs. Civic Arts Coun., Oak Park, Ill., 1976-84; bd. dirs. Village Players, Oak Park-River Forest (Ill.) Symphony Assn., Oak Park Concert chorale, 1975-91; mem. Oak Park Cable TV Commn., 1984-86; active Anna Maria Island (Fla.) Cmty. Chorus, 1992—, Anna Maria Island Turtle Watch, 1992—. Mem. Confrerie des Vignerons de St. Vincent Mâcon (maitresse du chpt. 1988-92), Webfoot Soc. U. Oreg., Phi Beta Kappa, Delta Delta Delta. Episcopalian. Avocations: singing, sailing, travel, loggerhead turtle rescue, wines.

EDIGER, MARK D., chemistry educator; b. Newton, Kans., July 26, 1957. BA in Chemistry and Math., Bethel Coll., 1979; PhD in Phys. Chemistry, Stanford U., 1984. Asst. prof. dept. chemistry U. Wis., Madison, 1984-90, assoc. prof., 1990-94, prof. dept. chemistry, 1994—. Grantee Polymers Program, NSF, 1998—, Chemistry Program, 1997—, Am. Chem. Soc., 1996—. Fellow Am. Phys. Soc.; mem. Am. Chem. Soc. Office: Univ Wis Dept Chemistry 1101 University Ave Madison WI 53706-1322

EDIGER, ROBERT IKE, botanist, educator; b. Hutchinson, Kans., Apr. 2, 1937; s. Peter F. and Martha (Friesen) E.; m. Patricia L. Dickerson, Feb. 7, 1981; children: Madeline, Maureen, Alan, Shelly. B.A., Bethel Coll., 1959; M.S., Emporia State U., 1964; Ph.D., Kans. State U., 1967. Tchr. public schs. Ford, Kans., 1959-62, Hays, Kans., 1962-63; teaching and research asst. Kans. State U., 1964-67; asst. prof. dept. biol. scis. Calif. State U., Chico, 1967-71; asso. prof. Calif. State U., 1971-74, prof., 1975—, chmn. dept. biol. scis., 1974-77, dir.Eagle Lake field sta., 1967-73. Mem. Am. Soc. Plant Taxonomists, Orgn. Biol. Field Stas. (pres. 1975), Calif. Bot. Soc., Calif. Native Plant Soc. Methodist. Home: 5359 Royal Oaks Dr Oroville CA 95966-3837 Office: Calif State U Dept Biol Scis Chico CA 95929

EDIGHOFFER-MURRAY, ANNA BARBEL, procurement officer, pharmacist, political scientist; b. Annweiler, Germany, Apr. 9, 1956; came to U.S., 1988; d. Kurt and Irmgard (J.) Edighoffer; m. Peter Ian Murray, Apr. 6, 1996. Diploma in Polit. Sci., Freie Universität Berlin, 1985, Cert. in Internat. and European Law, 1987. Cert. pharmacist asst. Germany. With pharm. bus., until 1977; editl. asst. Der Tagesspiegel, Berlin, 1980-81; rsch. asst. Freie U., Berlin, 1984-86; JPO UN, N.Y.C., 1988-89, procurement, adminstrv. officer, 1989—. Mem. Nat. Assn. Procurement Mgmt., Gewerkschaft Oeffentlicher Transport und Verkeh. Office: UN Procurement Divsn 304 E 45th St Rm FF-251 New York NY 10017-3425

EDIN, CHARLES THOMAS, lawyer; b. Williston, N.D., Mar. 23, 1955; s. Charles Crane and A. Borgni (Skorpen) E.; children: Charles, Taylor Marie. BA summa cum laude, Concordia Coll., 1978; JD with honors, U.N.D., 1983. Bar: N.D. 1984, U.S. Dist. Ct. N.D. 1984, U.S. Ct. Appeals (8th cir.) 1984. With Landman Westex Petroleum Corp., Bismarck, N.D., 1980-82; ptnr. Zuger Kirmis & Smith, Bismarck, 1984-94; pvt. practice Bismarck, 1995—; spl. asst. atty. gen. State of N.D., Bismarck, 1998—. Precinct committeman Rep. Party, Bismarck, 1990. Burtness scholar U. N.D., 1983. Mem. ABA (litigation and natural resources sects.), N.D. Bar Assn. (mineral title stds. com. real property sect.), Burleigh County Bar Assn., Rocky Mountain Mineral Law Found. (N.D. case law reporter Mineral Law Newsletter 1988-96). Lutheran. Office: PO Box 2391 Bismarck ND 58502-2391

EDINGER, LEWIS JOACHIM, political science educator; b. Frankfort, Germany, Feb. 1, 1922; came to U.S., 1936; s. Mark A. and Dora (Meyer) E.; m. Hanni Blumenfeld, Sept. 11, 1950; children: Monica Ruth, Susan Yvonne. A.B., Wabash Coll., 1943; Ph.D., Columbia U., 1951. Instr. NYU, 1947-49; vis. asst. prof. Sweet Briar Coll., 1950-51; vis. lectr. Vassar Coll., 1951-52; vis. asst. prof. U. N.C., 1952-53; assoc. prof. Air War Coll., 1953-57; asst. prof.to prof. Mich. State U., East Lansing, 1957-63; Fulbright prof. Free U. Berlin, 1959-60; prof. Washington U., St. Louis, 1963-67; Fulbright prof. U. Bonn, 1964-65; prof. govt. and mem. Inst. Western Europe, Columbia U., N.Y.C., 1967-92, prof. emeritus, 1992; co-adj. prof. Rutgers U., 1975; disting. Fulbright prof. U. Bonn, Fed. Republic Germany, 1980-81; vis. fellow Nuffield Coll., Oxford U., 1981; vis. prof. U. Bonn, 1988, U. Florence, Italy, 1989. Author or co-author: Germany Rejoins the Powers, 1959, 73, Kurt Schumacher: A Study in Personality and Political Behavior, 1965, France, Germany, and the Western Alliance, 1967, Political Leadership in Industrialized Societies, 1967, 76, Politics in Germany, 1968, Politics in West Germany, 1977, West German Politics, 1986, From Bonn to Berlin: German Politics in Transition, 1998; mem. editorial bd. Comparative Politics; contbr. articles to profl. jours. Ford Found. fellow, 1956-57; Social Sci. Research Council grantee, 1958, 59-63; NSF grantee, 1971-73; Guggenheim Found. fellow, 1973-74. Mem. ACLU, Hemlock Soc. Home: 83 Lefurgy Ave Dobbs Ferry NY 10522-1205 Office: 420 W 118th St New York NY 10027-7213

EDINGTON, ROBERT VAN, university official; b. Burns City, Ind., July 19, 1935; s. Guy Franklin and Nancy (Banks) E.; m. Ann Beach, July 18, 1959; children: Ellen, Russell, Garrett. AA., Vallejo Community Coll., 1955; B.A. in Internat. Relations, San Francisco State Coll., 1957; M.A. in Polit. Sci, U. Wash., 1963; Ph.D. in Polit. Sci., 1968. Student activities advisor Office Dean Students, Sacramento State Coll., 1959-62; chmn. internat. studies James Madison Coll., Mich. State U., East Lansing, 1971-74; assoc. dean Coll. Liberal Arts Idaho State U., Pocatello, 1975-76; dean arts and scis. Idaho State U., 1976-83; acad. v.p. Clarion U. of Pa., 1983-88; provost Cen. Wash. U., Ellensburg, 1988-91; adminstr. Steilacoom, Lynnwood and SeaTac Campus br. Ctrl. Wash. U., Lakewood, Wash., 1992—. Author: The Recruiting and Retention of Students: Handbook for an Experimental Program, 1979, (with R. Foster) Viewing International Relations and World Politics, 1985; contbr. articles to profl. jours. Co-founder Pocatello Forward; mem. State Idaho Profl. Stds. Commn., 1979-83, Mayor's Commn. for Hist. Preservation, 1995—; mem. Preservation and Rev. Bd. NSF fellow, 1967-68; Dept. State Scholar-Diplomat, 1970. Mem. Am. Assn. Univ. Adminstrs., Am. Polit. Sci. Assn., Western Polit. Sci. Assn., Soc. for Coll. and Univ. Planning, Rotary. Republican.

EDIS, GLORIA TOBY, pediatrician; b. N.Y.C., Dec. 6, 1939; d. Murray Alvin and Anna G. (Goldstein) E.; m. Myron Royal Schoenfeld, June 14, 1959; children: Bradley, Glenn, Dawn, Melody. BA, Cornell U., 1960; MD, NYU, 1963. Intern Montefiore Hosp., N.Y.C., 1963-64; pediatric resident Columbia Presbyn. Med. Ctr., N.Y.C., 1966-68; pediatrician Scarsdale (N.Y.) Pediatric Assocs., 1977—; pediatric attending Albert Einstein Med. Coll., Bronx, 1968-70; pediatrician Barsky Med. Group, N.Y.C., 1970-80. Fellow Am. Acad. Pediatrics; mem. AMA, Westchester County Med. Soc., Cornell Alumni Assn. Avocations: hiking, cycling, reading, weight training, theater. Office: Scarsdale Pediatric Assn 2 Overhill Rd Scarsdale NY 10583-5316

EDISEN, CLAYTON BYRON, physician; b. Chgo.; s. Byron Parker and Elsie Elinor (Mielkie) E.; m. Adele Uskali, 1948 (div. 1968); children: Laura, Glenn, Lynn; m. Barbara S., Dec. 1968. PhB, U. Chgo., 1949, MD, 1953. Diplomate Am. Bd. Neurology and Psychiatry. Various positions in field to psychiatrist The Monroe (La.) Area Guidance Ctr., 1956-58, med. dir., psychiatrist, 1957-58; instr. psychiatry Tulane U. Sch. Medicine, New Orleans, 1956-57; staff cons. Children's Bur., New Orleans, 1958-60; staff psychiatrist The Guidance Ctr., New Orleans, 1957-59; staff cons. Crippled Children's Divsn./La. State Dept. Health, 1959; with New Orleans Psychoanalytic Tng. Ctr., 1958-61; pvt. practice New Orleans, 1957—; apptd. in psychiatry De Paul Hosp., New Orleans, 1957—; Adj. full prof. exptl. comms. design, Tulane U., New Orleans, 1973-74; courtesy staff Coliseum Med. Ctr., New Orleans, 1974—; fellow Scientific Coun. of the Internat. Coll. of Angiology, 1972; del. Internat. Congress on Drug Edn., Montreux, Switzerland/World Psychiat. Assn., 1973, others; vis. faculty lectr. Sch. of Social Work, Tulane U., 1958-60; asst. vis. physician Charity Hosp. of La., New Orleans, 1954-56; vis. staff psychiatrist Touro Infirmary, New Orleans, 1958-72; temporary dir. De Paul Hosp., New Orleans, 1960; lectr. to Annual Life Inst., Jewish Fedn. New Orleans, 1961, others; panelist/lectr. in field. Contbr. numerous articles to profl. jours. and publs. Sgt. U.S. Army, 1945-47, ETO. Fellow Am. Geriatric Soc., Interam. Coll. Physicians and Surgeons, Royal Soc. Health/London; mem. AMA (Physicians Recognition awards), Am. Group Psychotherapy Assn., La. Group Psychotherapy Soc. and Inst., La. State Med. Soc. (numerous offices), Orleans Parish Med. Soc., Am. Psychiat. Assn., So. Med. Assn., New Orleans Psychiat. Forum, 2nd Dist. Med. Soc., La. Dist. Br. APA, New Orleans Area Psychiat. Soc., La. Psychiat. Assn., Pan Am. Med. Assn., World Psychiatric Assn., Assn. Am. Physcians and Surgeons, Am. Heart Assn., N.Y. Acad. Scis., Sigma Xi, others. Republican. Avocations: golf, bridge. Office: 2900 Hessmer Ave Metairie LA 70002-5820

EDISON, ALLEN RAY, electrical engineer, educator; b. Plainview, Nebr., Sept. 21, 1926; s. Arthur and Lela (Johnson) E.; m. Betty Jean Broer, Dec. 27, 1949; children—Karl Arthur, Kathryn Johannah. B.S., U. Nebr., 1950, M.S., 1957; D.Sc., U. N.M., 1962. Engr. Silas Mason Co., Burlington, Iowa, 1950-53; instr. U. Nebr., Lincoln, 1953-57; prof. elec. engring. U. Nebr., 1957-89, prof. emeritus, 1989—, chmn. dept. elec. engring., 1964-70. Served with USNR, 1944-46. Mem. I.E.E.E. (past sect. chmn.), Sigma Xi, Sigma Tau, Eta Kappa Nu. Home: 511 S 54th St Lincoln NE 68510-2006

EDISON, BERNARD ALAN, retired retail apparel company executive; b. Atlanta, 1928; s. Irving and Beatrice (Chanin) E.; m. Marilyn S. Wewers, Apr. 26, 1975. B.A., Harvard U., 1949, M.B.A., 1951. With Edison Bros. Stores Inc., St. Louis, 1951—; asst. v.p. Edison Bros. Stores Inc., 1957-58, v.p. leased depts., 1958-67, v.p., asst. treas., 1967-68, pres., 1968-87, chmn. fin. com., 1987-89, dir. emeritus, 1989-96; bd. dirs. Gen. Am. Life Ins. Co., Anheuser-Busch Cos., Inc., Reinsurance Group Am., Inc. Office: Edison Bros Stores Inc 501 N Broadway Saint Louis MO 63102-2102

EDISON, DIANE, artist, educator, administrator; b. Plainfield, N.J., Sept. 3, 1950; d. Anthony Joseph and Davie Wilhelmina (Johnson) E. BFA, Sch. Visual Arts, N.Y.C., 1976; postgrad., Skowhegan Sch. Painting, 1984; MFA, U. Pa., 1986. Asst. prof. Savannah (Ga.) Coll. Art and Design, 1990-92; asst. prof. U. Ga., Athens, 1992-96, assoc. prof., 1997—, assoc. dir. Lamar Dodd Sch. Art, 1997-99; asst. prof. U. Ga. Studies Abroad, Cortona, Italy, 1993, 99; panelist Telfair Acad. Arts and Scis., Savannah, 1992, Ga. Mus. Art, Athens, 1993, Ga. Coun. for Arts, 1993—, Womens Caucus for Arts Nat. Conf., Phila., 1997, Ark. Art Ctr., Little Rock, 1996, Mid-Am. S.E. Coll. Art Assn., 1997; mem. gala com. Kwang Ju (Korea) Biennial Korea, 1997, Geffen Contemporary Mus. Art, L.A., 1997, Grand Arts, Kansas City, 1998. Solo exhbn. Macon Mus. Arts and Scis., 1998; exhbns. include Marymount Manhattan Coll. Gallery, N.Y.C., 1989, Islip (N.Y.) Art Mus. Brookward Hall, 1989, The Bertha and Karl Leubsdorf Art Gallery, N.Y.C, 1990, Cork Gallery Lincoln Ctr., N.Y.C., 1990, Salena Gallery L.I. U., Bklyn., 1990, Savannah Coll. Art and Design, 1990, Rotunda Gallery, Bklyn., 1991, St. Louis Artist Guild, 1992, Frumkin/Adams Gallery, N.Y.C., 1992, 94-95, Ark. Arts Ctr., Little Rock, 1992-96, Ga. Mus. Art, Athens, 1993, Ga. Artist Registry, Atlanta, 1994, Charles More Gallery,

Phila., 1994, U. Mo., Kansas City, 1994, U. Ga., Athens, 1994, Southeastern Ctr. Contemporary Art, Winston-Salem, N.C., 1994, Chattahoochee Valley Art Mus., Lagrange, Ga., 1995, Nexus Contemporary Art Ctr., Atlanta, 1995, George Adams Gallery, N.Y.C., 1995-97, SFA Gallery, Nacogdoches, Tex., 1996, Sawhill Gallery James Madison U., 1997, Tatischeff & Co., Inc., N.Y.C., 1997, Macon Mus. Arts and Scis., 1998, George Adams Gallery, 1998, Grand Arts, Kansas City, 1998, Berman Mus., Collegeville, Pa., 1998-99, Nexus Biennial, 1999; represented in permanent collections at Ark. Arts Ctr., Am. Embassy, Moscow, Agnes Scott Coll., Decatur, Ga., also pvt. collections. Artist grantee Ga. Coun. for Arts, 1993, Nat. Endowment for Arts, 1994, jr. faculty rsch. grantee U. Ga., 1994; Milton Avery Found fellow, N.Y.C., 1995; artist resident Millay Colony for Arts Inc., Austerlitz, N.Y., 1995, Blue Mountain Ctr., Blue Mountain Lake, N.Y., 1996. Mem. AAUP, Coll. Art Assn. Democrat. Episcopalian. Avocation: guitar. Office: U Ga Visual Arts Bldg Jackson St Athens GA 30602

EDLES, GARY JOEL, lawyer; b. N.Y.C., Feb. 27, 1941; s. Allen Irving and Helen (Hurowitz) E.; m. Nadine Cohen, Feb. 15, 1973. BA, Queens Coll., 1962; JD, NYU, 1965; LLM, George Washington U., 1966, DJuridical Sci., 1975. Bar: N.Y. 1966, U.S. Ct. Appeals (D.C. cir.) 1970. Staff atty. Civil Aeronautics Bd., Washington, 1967-75, assoc. gen. coun., 1975-77, dep. gen. coun., 1977-80; dir. office of procs. Interstate Commerce Commn., Washington, 1980-81; adminstrv. appeals judge Nuclear Regulatory Commn., Washington, 1981-87; gen. coun. Administrv. Conf. U.S., Washington, 1987-95; fellow Am. U., 1995; faculty Dept. Justice Legal Edn. Inst., 1982-97; vis. prof. U. Sheffield, Eng., 1994, U. Hull, Eng., 1997—. Co-author: Federal Regulatory Process, 2d edit., 1989; contbr. articles to profl. jours. Mem. ABA, Fed. Bar Assn. (chmn. administrv. law sect. (1989-91). Home: 10 Keldgate, Beverley HU17 8HY, England

EDLICH, RICHARD FRENCH, biomedical engineering educator; b. N.Y.C., Jan. 19, 1939; married, 1961; 3 children. MD, NYU, 1962; PhD, U. Minn., 1973. From instr. to assoc. prof. U. Va. Sch. Medicine, Charlottesville, 1971-76, prof. plastic surgery and biomed. engring., 1976-82, disting. prof. plastic and maxillofacial surgery and biomed. engring., 1983-96, now Raymoon F. Morgan prof. plastic surgery and disting. prof. biomed. engring., 1996—; dir. Emergency Med. Svc. and Burn Ctr., 1974-85; physician tech. adviser Bur. Emergency Svc., HEW, 1974-79; cons. Divsn. Health Manpower and Nat. Ctr. Health Svc. Rsch., 1977-79. Recipient outstanding teaching award U. Va., 1989, Thomas Jefferson award, 1991, outstanding faculty award Commonwealth of Va. Coun. Higher Edn., 1989. Mem. ACS, Soc. Univ. Surgeons, Am. Assn. Surg. Trauma, Am. Burn Assn., Univ. Assn. Emergency Medicine, Am. Soc. Plastic and Reconstructive Surgeons, Soc. of Acad. Emergency Medicine, Coll. Emergency Physicians, Am. Surg. Assn. Research in biology of wound repair and infection. Office: U Va Sch Med PO Box 332 Charlottesville VA 22902-0332

EDLOE, LEONARD LEVI, pharmacist; b. Richmond, Va., July 10, 1947; s. Leonard Lacy and Lucille (Harris) E.; m. Serita V. Hamilton, Jan. 16, 1988; 1 child, Leonard Lenisse. BS in Pharmacy, Howard U., 1970; MDiv, Va. Union U., 1999. Ptnr. Harrington's Pharmacy, Richmond, Va., 1970-72; pres. Leonard L. Edloe Corp., Richmond, 1973—; chmn. bd., chief exec. officer Pharmaceutical Assocs., Inc., Richmond, 1985—; asst. clin. prof. pharmacy Med. Coll. Va./Va. Commonwealth U. Sch. Pharmacy. Bd. dirs. Richmond Renaissance, Richmond Conv. and Visitors Bur., chmn. bd., 1990-91, Va. Retail Mchts; Alcohol and Drug Abuse Prevention and Tng. Svcs.; pres. Churchill Model Cities, 1973, Richmond Urban League, 1975-78; pastor Antioch Bapt. Ch., Susan, Va.; mem. Acute Care Bd. Bon Secour Richmond; mem. adv. bd. of health City of Richmond; v. chmn., mem. Pvt. Enterprise Commn., Commonwealth of Va. Named one of Outstanding Young Men Am. U.S. Jaycees, 1983, Practitioner of Yr. Assn. Black Hosps., 1984, Alumnus of Yr. Howard U. Coll. Pharmacy, 1985, Pharmacist of Yr. Old Dominion Pharmaceutical Assn., 1989. Mem. Am. Pharm. Assn. (trustee), Nat. Pharm. Assn., Am. Assn. Colls. Pharmacy, Va. Pharm. Assn. (Cert. Merit 1982), Richmond Pharm. Assn., Met. Richmond C. of C. (bd. dirs.), Retail Merchants Assn. Great Richmond (bd. dirs., vice chmn. Disting. Retailer of Yr. 1993). Baptist. Home: 7109 Foxbernie Dr Mechanicsvlle VA 23111-5646 Office: 1124 N 25th St Richmond VA 23223-5256

EDLOW, KENNETH LEWIS, securities brokerage official; b. Washington, July 27, 1941; s. Ellis and Leonora (Kraft) E.; m. Mary Glanzrock, Dec. 19, 1970; children: Elizabeth, Brian. BS in Econ., U. Pa., 1963. Stockbroker Ferris & Co., Washington, 1963-69; various positions Bear, Stearns & Co., Inc., N.Y.C., 1969—; corp. sec. Bear Stearns Cos. Inc., 1987—; pres. Monterey Fund, Inc.; v.p., sec. The Edlow Family Fund, Inc. Trustee Congregation Emanu-El, N.Y.C., 1994—. Mem. Am. Numismatic Soc. (trustee 1993—). Jewish. Avocations: fishing, numismatics. Home: 35 E 85th St New York NY 10028-0954 Office: Bear Stearns & Co Inc 245 Park Ave New York NY 10017-2500

EDLUND, TIMOTHY WENDELL, management educator, consultant, researcher; b. Niagara Falls, N.Y., May 28, 1930; s. Sidney Wendell and Mary (Garlichs) E.; m. Patricia Johannsen, June 10, 1952; children: S. Rebecca, Stephen W. BSME, Cornell U., 1952; MS in Engring. Administrn., Case Inst. Tech., 1960; MBA, Boston U., 1984, D of Bus. Adminstrn., 1986. Registered profl. engr., N.Y., Ind., Wis. Facilities engr. Otis Elevator Co., Yonkers, N.Y., 1961-68; sr. assoc. Mfg. Systems, Milw., 1968-70; asst. to mfg. v.p. Perfex Inc., Milw., 1970-72; mgr. mfg. engring. Madison Industries, Smithfield, R.I., 1972-75; chief mfg. engr. Energy Products Divsn. Gulf & Western, Warwick, R.I., 1975-78, Atwood & Morrill, Salem, Mass., 1978-81; vis. asst. prof. U. N.H., Durham, 1985-86; asst. prof. Loyola Coll., Balt., 1986-91; assoc. prof. strategic mgmt. Morgan State U., Balt., 1991—. Contbr. articles to profl. jours. Lt. j.g. USN, 1952-55. Recipient tchg. grant Shriver Ctr. of U. Md., 1996. Mem. N.am. Case Rsch. Assn. (v.p. 1996-97, pres.-elect 1997-98, pres. 1998-99), Acad. Mgmt., Internat. Assn. for Bus. and Soc. (charter), Strategic Mgmt. Soc., The Case Assn. Episcopalian. Avocations: sailing, singing. Home: 16 Coldwater Ct Baltimore MD 21204-2043 Office: Morgan State U 1700 E Cold Spring Ln Baltimore MD 21251-0002

EDMANDS, SUSAN BANKS, consulting company executive; b. New Rochelle, N.Y., Oct. 7, 1944; d. George Dixon and Marian (Lepied) Banks; children: Whatleigh Winthrop, Benjamin Bruce II. BS, Boston U., 1966; cert. in libr. sci., Northeastern U., Boston, 1974. Tchr. project head start Office Econ. Opportunity, Washington, 1966; English tchr. Wattana Sch., Bangkok, 1969-71; market researcher Pauline Rendell Assocs., Somerville, Mass., 1971-72; food info. specialist FIND/SVP Inc., N.Y.C., 1977-80; mgr. tech. and indsl. group Find/SVP, Inc., N.Y.C., 1980-90, dir. consulting svcs. divsn., 1990—. Pres. Packer Collegiate Parents Orgn., Bklyn. Heights, N.Y., 1987-89, trustee, 1987-89. Mem. Soc. Chimie Industrielle (v.p. Am. sect. 1985-93), Chemists Club (trustee 1984-93), Am. Soc. Info. Sci. Avocations: antique collecting and restoration, travel, cooking, bicycling, gardening. Home: 24 Deming Ln Stamford CT 06903-4729 Office: Find/SVP Inc 625 Avenue Of The Americas New York NY 10011-2095

EDMINSTER, WALTER B., protective services official; b. Boone, N.C., Sept. 29, 1945. BA, Appalachian State U., 1970. Agt. U.S. Dept. Treasury, Ill., Ga., 1970-76; spl. agt. U.S. Forest Svc., USDA, 1976-94; U.S. marshal U.S. Marshal Svcs., Asheville, 1994—. Office: Office of US Marshal 100 Otis St Asheville NC 28801-2611*

EDMISTON, GUY S., JR., bishop. Bishop Lower Susquehanna region Evang. Luth. Ch. in Am., Harrisburg, Pa. Office: Evang Luth Ch in Am 900 S Arlington Ave Ste 208 Harrisburg PA 17109-5024*

EDMISTON, MARK MORTON, publishing company executive; b. Yonkers, N.Y., July 9, 1943; s. Marcus Morton and Josephine (Brown) E.; m. Lisa Mary Pustorino, Aug. 28, 1965; children: Ann Kathleen, Laura Mary. BA, Wesleyan U., 1966. Circulation mgr. Life mag., N.Y.C., until 1969; circulation and mktg. dir. Life mag., Tokyo, 1969-70; circulation dir. Saturday Rev., Inc., 1971-73; circulation dir. internat. edits. Newsweek, Inc., 1973-76, pub., 1976-78, pres., 1978-79, corp. exec. v.p., 1979-81, chmn. and pres., 1981-86; pres. TVSM Inc., N.Y.C., 1987-91; exec. v.p. Times Mirror Mag., N.Y.C., 1991-92; co-chmn. The Jordan Edmiston Group Inc., N.Y.C., 1992-98; mng. dir. Admedia Ptnrs., Inc., N.Y.C., 1998—. Founder Civilization: The Mag. of the Libr. of Congress, Univ. Bus. Mag. Trustee emeritus Wesleyan U., Children's Aid Soc., Cmty. Svc. Soc. N.Y. Office: Admedia Ptnrs 444 Madison Ave New York NY 10022

EDMONDO, DOUGLAS BRIAN, marine engineer; b. Plainfield, N.J., Feb. 13, 1960; s. Donald Brian and Sally Ann (Emery) E.; m. Yvonne Janssen, July 11, 1987; children: Brian James, Daniel John. BS, Calif. Maritime Coll., 1982. Lic. pvt. pilot; marine engr. Field engr. Westinghouse Marine, Sunnyvale, Calif., 1982-87, project engr., 1987-88, sr. engr., 1988-89, IPMP site mgr., 1990-92, svc. supr., 1992-95; product support mgr. Applied Materials, Santa Clara, Calif., 1995-98; prin. engr. Northrop Grumman Marine Divsn., Sunnyvale, 1998—. Mem. Soc. Naval Architects and Marine Engrs., Am. Soc. Naval Engrs. Home: 942 Dana Cir Livermore CA 94550-3782

EDMONDS, ANNE CAREY, librarian; b. Penang, Malaysia, Dec. 19, 1924; d. William John and Neil (Carey) E. Student, U. Reading, England, 1942-44; BA, Barnard Coll., 1948; MSLS, Columbia U., 1950; MA, Johns Hopkins U., 1959; postgrad., Western Res. U., 1960-61; LHD, Mount Holyoke Coll., 1994. With War Damage Commn., London, 1944-46; children's asst. Enoch Pratt Free Libr., Balt., 1948-49; reference libr. Sch. Bus. Adminstrn., CCNY, 1950-51; reference libr. then asst. libr. readers' svcs. Goucher Coll., Balt., 1951-60; exchange reference libr. European svcs. libr. BBS, London, 1955; instr. Sch. L.S., Syracuse U., summer 1960; libr. Douglass Coll., Rutgers U., New Brunswick, N.J., 1961-64, instr., summer 1962, fall 1963; libr. Mt. Holyoke Coll., 1964-94; vis. libr. U. North, Turfloop, South Africa, 1976-77; mem. libr. vis. com. Wheaton Coll., Norton, Mass., 1978-92; mem. local systems adv. group Online Computer Libr. Ctr., Inc., 1984-87, mem. adv. com. on coll. and univ. librs., 1988-89. Author: A Mempry Book: Mount Holyoke College, 1834-1987, 1988 (with Gai Carpenter and others) Computing Strategies in Liberal Arts Colleges, 1992. Mem. South Hadley (Mass.) Bicentennial Com., 1975-76; mem. accreditation teams Middle State Assn. Colls. and Secondary Schs., 1963-94, New Eng. Assn. Schs. and Colls., 1986-94; bd. dirs. U.S. Book Exch., 1973-76, 80-83; exec. com. New Eng. libr. Info. Network, 1974-76, 79-85, chmn., 1982-84; mem. Adv. Commn. Historic Deerfield, 1975-81, 86-94. Mem. AAUW (bd. dirs. main chpt. 1998—), ALA, Assn. Coll. Rsch. Librs. (pres. 1970-71, chmn. constn. and bylaws com. New Eng. chpt. 1975-76, pres. New Eng. chpt. 1983-84). E-mail: ACE13@midcoast.com.

EDMONDS, IVY GORDON, writer; b. Frost, Tex., Feb. 15, 1917; s. Ivy Gordon and Delia Louella (Shumate) E.; student pub. schs.; m. Reiko Mimura, July 12, 1956; 1 dau., Annette. Freelance writer; author books including: Solomon In Kimono, 1957; Ooka the Wise, 1961; The Bounty's Boy, 1963; Hollywood RIP, 1963; Joel of the Hanging Gardens, 1966; Trickster Tales, 1966; Taiwan—the Other China, 1971; The Possible Impossibles of Ikkyo The Wise, 1971; The Magic Man, 1972; Mao's Long March, 1973; Motorcycling for Beginners, 1973; Micronesia, 1974; Pakistan, Land of Mystery, Tragedy and Courage, 1974; Automotive Tuneups for Beginners, 1974; Ethiopia, 1975; The Magic Makers, 1976; The Shah of Iran, 1976; Allah's Oil: Mid-East Petroleum, 1976; Second Sight, 1977; Motorcycle Racing for Beginners, 1977; Islam, 1977; Buddhism, 1978; The Mysteries of Troy, 1977; Big U Universal in the Silent Days, 1977; D.D. Home, 1978; Bicycle Motocross, 1979; Hinduism, 1979; Girls Who Talked to Ghosts, 1979; The Magic Brothers, 1979; (with William H. Gebhardt) Broadcasting for Beginners, 1980; (with Reiko Mimura) The Oscar Directors, 1980; The Mysteries of Homer's Greeks, 1981; The Kings of Black Magic, 1981; Funny Car Racing for Beginners, 1982; The Magic Dog, 1982; author textbooks: (with Ronald Gonzales) Understanding Your Car, 1975, Introduction to Welding, 1975; also author pulp and soft cover fiction and nonfiction under names of Gene Cross and Gary Gordon and publishers house names; pub. relations mgr. Northrop Corp., Anaheim, Calif., 1968-79, indsl. editor, Hawthorne, Calif., 1979-86. Served with USAAF, 1940-45, USAF, 1946-63. Decorated D.F.C., Air medals, Bronze Star. Home: 5801 Shirl St Cypress CA 90630-3326

EDMONDS, JAMES PATRICK (JIM EDMONDS), baseball player; b. Fullerton, Calif., June 27, 1970. Grad. H.S., Calif. Outfielder Calif. Angels (now Anaheim Angels), 1993—. Selected to Am. League All-Star Team, 1995. Office: Anaheim Angels 2000 E Gene Autry Way Anaheim CA 92806-6100*

EDMONDS, KENNY See BABYFACE

EDMONDS, MARY PATRICIA, biological sciences educator; b. Racine, Wis., May 7, 1922; d. Millard Samuel and Sarah (Gibbons) E. BA, Milw.-Downer Coll., 1943; MA, Wellesley (Mass.) Coll., 1945; PhD, U. Pa., 1951; DSc (hon.), Lawrence U., 1983. Instr. Wellesley Coll., 1945-46; postdoctoral fellow U. Ill., Urbana, 1950-52, U. Wis., Madison, 1952-55; rsch. assoc. Montefiore Hosp., Pitts., 1955-65; asst. prof. U. Pitts., 1965-71, assoc. prof., 1971-76, prof. emeritus, 1976—; mem. molecular biology study sect. NIH, Bethesda, Md., 1974-78. Contbr. articles to profl. jours. Recipient Woman of Yr. in Sci. award Chatham Coll., 1986; Rsch. Career Devel. award NIH, 1962-71, rsch. grantee, 1962-91. Mem. NAS, Am. Soc. Biol. Chemists, Am. Soc. for Cancer Rsch. Office: U Pitts Dept Biol Sci Pittsburgh PA 15260

EDMONDS, MICHAEL DARNELL, music educator; b. May 19, 1960; s. William Thomas and Virginia (Haskins) E.; m. Janet Denise Wyche. BS, Norfolk State U., 1987. Minister of music Christian Charities Deliverance, Wakefield, Va., 1980-92; sale specialist B.D. Laderberg and Son, Inc., Suffolk, Va., 1989-91; sales specialist T.J. Maxx, Chesapeake, Va., 1991-97; reporter Maxxline for T.J. Maxx, Chesapeake, 1991-98; customer svc. rep. Apac Telesvcs., Newport News, Va., 1998—; music dir. First Calvary Handbell Choir, Norfolk, Va., 1982-83, Norfolk State U. Gospel Choir, 1984-85, Little Gilfield Bapt. Ch. Gospel Choir, Irov, Va., 1988; music min. Full Gospel Ch. of Deliverance, Norfolk, 1986-87; singer with I. Sherman Greene Chorale, Norfolk, 1984-88, Covenant Presbyn. Choir, 1984-85, 87-88, The Brown Delegation of Ivor, 1987-89; mem. Norfolk State U. Concert Choir and Chamber Emsemble, 1983-87; mus. dir. pageant Shiloh Bapt. Ch., Zuni, 1988; founder, dir. Interdenominational Singers, Norfolk, 1984-85, New Horizon Singers of Ivor, 1987-89; choir, vocal coach, tchr. piano Ctr. State Theatre, Norfolk, 1985-87; performer sixth ann. Am. Negro Spiritual Festival; tchg. asst. Jr. Music Program Norfolk State U., 1983-84; sales specialist So. Food Stores, Windsor, Va., 1988-89; tchr. asst. specialist Southampton Sch. Sys., 1987-89; customer svc. rep. T.J. Maxx, Janaf and Norfolk, Va., 1985-87. Editor Chrisitn Charity Newsletter, Wakefield, 1980-90, composer choral gospel arrangements. Mem. Choir of Joy, Suffolk, Va., 1991; mem. Crusade choir St. Mark Ch. of Deliverance, Portsmouth, Va., 1993, sr. sunday sch. asst. tchr., 1991-92, club staff mem., praise and worship leader; mem. nat. nomination com. Outstanding Young Women of Am., 1997, Outstanding Young Med. of Am., 1998. Mem. Music Educators Nat. Conf., Intercollegiate Music Assn. Avocations: photography, computers. Home: 1038 Cherokee Rd Apt H Portsmouth VA 23701-1858 Office: APAC Telesvcs 11008 Warwick Blvd Newport News VA 23601-3216

EDMONDS, RICHARD H., dean. Exec. assoc. dean Albany (N.Y.) Med. Coll. Office: Albany Med Coll 47 New Scotland Ave # A34 Albany NY 12208-3412*

EDMONDS, THOMAS ANDREW, state bar executive director; b. Jackson, Miss., July 5, 1938. B.A., Miss. Coll., 1962; LL.B., Duke U., 1965. Bar: Fla. 1965, Va. 1981. Pvt. practice law Orlando, Fla., 1965-66; assoc. prof. law U. Miss., Oxford, 1966-70; assoc. prof.law Fla. State U., Tallahassee, 1970-74, prof., 1974-77; dean Sch. Law, U. Richmond (Va.), 1977-87, U. Miss. Sch. Law, University, 1987-89; exec. dir. Va. State Bar, Richmond, 1989—; vis. assoc. prof. Duke U., 1968-69; vis. prof. McGeorge Sch. Law of the Univ. of the Pacific, 1975-76. Served with USMC, 1957-60. Office: VA State Bar 707 E Main St Ste 1500 Richmond VA 23219-2800

EDMONDS, THOMAS LEON, lawyer, management consultant; b. Borger, Tex., May 10, 1932; s. Cline Azel and Flora (Love) E.; m. Virginia Marguerite Leon, June 20, 1960; 1 child, Stephanie Lynn. BS in Chem. Engring., Tex. Tech. U., 1953, JD, 1973. Bar: Tex. 1974, U.S. Tax Ct. 1975, U.S. Ct. Appeals (5th cir.) 1975, U.S. Dist. Ct. (no. dist.) Tex. 1976, U.S. Supreme Ct. 1996. Registered profl. engr., Tex. Engr. computers-exec. dept. Phillips Petroleum, Bartlesville, Okla., 1953-67; mktg. specialist Control Data, Dallas, 1967-68; exec. v.p. CUI, Austin, Tex., 1968-70; mgmt. cons. Mcauto, St. Louis, 1970-71; sr. ptnr. Edmonds & Assocs., Borger, 1973—; city atty. City of Borger, 1991—; treas., dir. Ram Biochems., Inc. Bd. dirs., pres. chancellor's coun. Tex. Tech U.; bd. dirs. Can. River Mcpl. Water Authority, Hutchinson County Tex. Hist. Commn., chmn. Mem. Borger Bar Assn. (pres. 1998—), Borger Country Club. Home: 210 Broadmoor St Borger TX 79007-8210 Office: PO Box 985 Borger TX 79008-0985

EDMONDS, THOMAS NELSON, advertising executive; b. Alexandria, Va., Dec. 14, 1943; s. Ralph Goodman Edmonds and Dorothy Bell (Patteson) Colprit; m. Geraldine Bayne, May 6, 1964 (div.); 1 child, Catherine Denise; m. Schuyler Mason Richardson, May 4, 1985; 1 child, Charles Thomas. Student, Richmond Profl. Inst., 1966. Media asst. Cargill, Wilson & Acree, Richmond, Va., 1966-67; v.p., media dir. Robert Kline & Co., Richmond, Va., 1967-70; pres. Edmonds & Green Advt., Inc., Richmond, 1970-74; v.p. Morrison, Williams, Demaine, Alexandria, 1974-79; pres. Edmonds Assocs., Inc., Washington, 1979—; chmn. and founder Multi Media Services Corp., Washington, 1983—. Mem. Am. Assn. Polit Cons. (pres., v.p. 1986—). Republican. Episcopalian. Avocation: antique car restoration. Office: Edmonds Assocs Inc 900 2nd St NE # 110 Washington DC 20002-3557*

EDMONDS, WILLIAM FLEMING, retired engineering and construction company executive; b. Birmingham, Ala., June 11, 1923; s. Henry M. and Mary (Fleming) E.; m. Joan McCoy, Aug. 7, 1953; children: Henry Morris, Bryson Glass. BSCE, Va. Mil. Inst., 1948; DSc (hon.), U. Ala., Birmingham, 1986. Former registered profl. engr., Ala., Ark., Calif., Fla., Ga., Ind., Mich., N.C., Tenn., Va. Project mgr. Rust Engring. & Harbert Constrn., Birmingham, 1953-58; v.p., chief engr. Rust Engring. Co., Birmingham, 1958-66; sr. v.p. Rust Engring. Co., Pitts., 1969-72; pres. Coppee-Rust, Brussels, Belgium, 1967-69; pres., chief exec. officer BE&K Inc., Birmingham, 1972-83, chmn., 1983-89, ret. Pres. bd. dirs. Presbyn. Retirement Homes; former trustee Ala. Symphony, Birmingham, 1982-93, So. Rsch. Inst.; hon. mem. pres.'s coun. U. Ala., Birmingham, 1980-92, pres., 1985, former bd. dirs. Rsch. Found. Capt. U.S. Army, 1943-46, 51-53, ETO, PTO, Korea. Decorated knight Order of Crown (Belgium); named Engr. of Yr., Engring. Coun., Birmingham, 1983, Soc. Profl. Engrs., Montgomery, Ala., 1983, Citizen of Yr., Young Men's Bus. Club Birmingham, 1988; inducted into Ala. Engring. Hall of Fame, 1992, Ala. Acad. Honor, 1991; recipient Disting. Eagle Scout award, 1996. Fellow ASCE, Newcomen Soc.; mem. NSPE. Republican. Presbyterian. Lodges: Rotary, Redstone. Avocations: golf; snow skiing; tennis. Home: 2600 Arlington Ave S Apt 60 Birmingham AL 35205-4160

EDMONDS, WILLIAM L., federal judge; b. 1944. BA, U. Mo., 1966, MA, 1969; JD, U. Iowa, 1978. Ptnr. Carter, Star, Edmonds & Green, 1978-87; bankruptcy judge U.S. Bankruptcy Ct. (no. dist.) Iowa, Sioux City, 1987—, now chief bankruptcy judge. Office: Fed Bldg and US Courthouse 320 6th St Sioux City IA 51101-1245

EDMONDSON, AUSTIN HAROLD, city manager; b. Vincennes, Ind., Sept. 7, 1951; s. Austin Harold Sr. and Anna Louise Edmondson; m. Rebecca Ann Dominy, Aug. 20, 1977; children: Sean A., Amanda C. B in Gen. Studies, U. Nebr., Omaha, 1992, MPA, 1994. Enlisted USAF, 1972, advanced through grades to sr. master sgt.; logistics mgr. USAF, Offutt AFB, Nebr., 1986-92; city adminstr. City of Dakota City, Nebr., 1994-98, City of Morganfield, Ky., 1998—. Mem. Internat. City/County Mgmt. Assn. E-mail: cityadm@dynasty.net. Fax: 502-389-2157. Home: 311 E Waller St Morganfield KY 42437 Office: City of Morganfield 130 E Main St Morganfield KY 42437

EDMONDSON, DAMON WAYNE, financial analyst, consultant; b. Atlanta, Aug. 9, 1972; s. Fred Wayne and Rita Margaret E.; m. Louisa Bowen, June 21, 1997; 1 child, Jeb. BA in History, The Citadel, 1993. Coord. customer svc. ValuJet Airlines, Atlanta, 1994-95, coord. ground security, 1994-97, supr. customer svc., 1995-97; sr. analyst mktg. and pricing AirTran Airlines, Atlanta, 1997; fin. analyst Account Portfolios, Inc., Atlanta, 1997—; alcohol and drug abuse prevention counselor, 1992-93; cons. revenue mgmt. various cos., Atlanta. Organizer blood drive ARC, 1994-96; airport fundraising coord. Empty Stocking Fund, Atlanta, 1994-96; active ASPCA; active Ga. Rep. Party, 1997; patron High Mus. of Art.; mem. Rep. Nat. Com. Recipient Voice of Democracy award of merit VFW. Mem. Nat. Trust for Historic Preservation, Libr. of Congress Assn., Assn. Citadel Men, Pi Sigma Alpha. Avocations: Schutzhunds, Kendo, reading. Home: 175 White Pines Dr Alpharetta GA 30004

EDMONDSON, FRANK KELLEY, astronomer; b. Milw., Aug. 1, 1912; s. Clarence Edward and Marie (Kelley) E.; m. Margaret Russell, Nov. 24, 1934; children: Margaret Jean Olson, Frank K. Jr. *Wife Margaret was the youngest of four children of the eminent astronomer HenryNorris Russel, a genius in the accurate meaning of the word. Margaret was the one who had the closest intellectual rapport with her father, and she showed her inheritance. She had a better mind than Mr. Edmonson, and, he says, this was an important factor in making their marriage of 64 years such a happy one. Margaretdied on January 16, 1999, a month and a day before her 85th birthday.* A.B., Ind. U., 1933, A.M., 1934; Ph.D., Harvard U., 1937. Lawrence fellow Lowell Obs., 1933-34, research asst., 1934-35; Agassiz fellow Harvard Obs., 1935-36, asst., 1936-37; instr. astronomy Ind. U., Bloomington, 1937-40; asst. prof. Ind. U., 1940-45, assoc. prof., 1945-48, prof., 1949-83, prof. emeritus, 1983—, dir. Kirkwood Obs., 1945-78; dir. Goethe Link Obs., 1948-78, chmn. astronomy dept., 1944-78; research assoc. McDonald Obs., 1944-83; Observations of asteroids in cooperation with Internat. Astron. Union's Minor Planet Center; statistical adviser to Prof. Alfred Kinsey for gall wasp and human sex behaviour rsch., 1939-56; program dir. for astronomy NSF, 1956-57; acting dir. Cerro Tololo Inter-Am. Obs., 1966; lectr. astron. socs.; mem. adv. bd. Lowell Obs., 1988—. *Mr. Edmondson was on the teaching faculty of Indiana University for 46 years, and Chairman of the Department of Astronomy for 34 years. His retirement began in 1983, a month before his 71st birthday. It has been a "permanent sabbatical." The Cambridge University Press published his history of the Association of Universities for Research in Astronomy (AURA), xv pages, in 1997. A related paper was published in the November 1998 issue of the Journal for the History of Astronomy.* Author: AURA and its US National Observatories, 1977; contbr. numerous papers to Am., Brit., German astron. jours. Decorated Order of Merit Chile, 1964; recipient Meritorious Pub. Service award NSF, 1983, Disting. Alumni Svc. award Ind. U., 1997; honored with Daniel Kirkwood (1814-95) in Ho. Resolution No. 58 adopted by Ind. 109th Gen. Assembly, First Session, 1995. Fellow AAAS (chmn. sect. D, v.p. 1962); mem. Assn. Univs. Research in Astronomy (v.p. 1957-61, pres. 1962-65, dir. 1957-83, cons./historian 1983—), Can. Astron. Soc., Am. Astron. Soc. (treas. 1954-75), Astron. Soc. Pacific, Internat. Astron. Union (chmn. U.S. nat. com. 1963-64, v.p. commn. minor planets, comets and satellites 1967-70, pres. 1970-73), Ind. Acad. Science, Am. Mus. Natural History (corr. mem.), Explorers Club, Phi Beta Kappa, Sigma Xi. Home: 716 S Woodlawn Ave Bloomington IN 47401-4936 Office: Ind U Dept Astronomy 319 Swain Hall West Bloomington IN 47405-4201 *President Calvin Coolidge was right when he said: "Nothing in the world can take the place of persistence."*

EDMONDSON, FRANK KELLEY, JR., lawyer, legal administrator; b. Newport, R.I., Aug. 27, 1936; s. Frank Kelley Sr. and Margaret (Russell) E.; m. Christiane Semirot, Mar. 5, 1959 (div. Sept. 1969); children: Mylene Anne, Yvonne Marie, Catherine May; m. Elaine Sueko Kaneshiro, Aug. 17, 1970 (div. June 1992); m. Karen Louise Bishop, Feb. 27, 1993 (div. Feb. 1996). BBA, Ind. U., 1958; MBA, So. Ill. U., 1978; JD, U. Puget Sound, 1982. Bar: Wash. 1982, U.S. Dist. Ct. (we. dist.) Wash. 1983. Commd. 2d lt. USAF, 1959, advanced through grades to maj., 1969, ret., 1979; contracts specialist Wash. State Lottery, Olympia, 1982-85, asst. contracts adminstr., 1985-87; contracts officer 1989 Washington Centennial Commn., 1987-90; fin. svc. officer Office of the Adminstr. for the Cts., 1990-92; contracts officer, office of adminstr. for the cts. State of Wash. Supreme Ct., Olympia, 1992—; mem. Seattle U. Sch. Law, Law Alumni Soc. Nat. Coun., 1997—, scholarship com. Wash. State Employees Credit Union, 1995—. Bd. dirs. Friends of Chambers Creek, Tacoma, 1981-90; mem. pro bono panel Puget Sound Legal Assistance Found., Olympia, 1985-90; mock trial program com. Youth and Govt. YMCA, 1994-96. Mem. ABA, Wash. State Bar Assn. (spl. dist. counsel 1993-95), Thurston County Bar Assn., Govt. Lawyers Bar

Assn. (sec. 1985-86, 1st v.p. 1986-87, pres. 1987-89, liaison to Wash. State Bar Assn. 1989-93), Beta Gamma Sigma, Coll. Club. Home: 6600 Miner Dr SW Tumwater WA 98512-7282 Office: State of Wash Supreme Ct Office of Adminstr for Cts PO Box 41170 Olympia WA 98504-1170

EDMONDSON, JAMES HOWARD, former insurance executive, investor; b. Topeka, Kans.; s. Frazor T. and Sally Ann (Anderson) E.; m. Janice Sue Elliott, July 1969 (div. Jan. 1993); children: Frazor T., James H., Robert. BA, Va. Mil. Inst., 1955. Ins. exec. Jim Edmondson & Assocs., Dallas, 1958-91; now in investments. Presbyterian. Avocations: tennis, reading. Home: 7704 Glenshannon Cir Dallas TX 75225

EDMONDSON, JAMES LARRY, federal judge; b. Jasper, Ga., July 14, 1947; s. James George and Betty Ruth (Holcomb) E.; m. Eugenia Dettelbach (div. 1992); children: Kelley Eugenia, Alexandra Lisa. BA, Emory U., 1968; JD, U. Ga., 1971; LLM in Jud. Process, U. Va., 1989. Bar: Ga. 1971. Law clk. to dist. judge U.S. Dist. Ct. (no. dist.) Ga., Gainesville, 1971-73; instr. in trial practice U. Ga. Sch. Law, Athens, 1975-84; assoc. Webb, Fowler, Tanner & Edmondson, Lawrenceville, Ga., 1973-76, ptnr., 1976-81; mem. firm Tennant, Davidson & Edmondson, P.C., Lawrenceville, 1982-86; judge U.S. Ct. Appeals (11th cir.), Atlanta, 1986—; instr. U. Ga. Sch. Law, 1975-84. Contbr. articles to legal jours. Trustee Inst. Continuing Legal Edn., 1980-84. Mem. State Bar Ga. (bd. govs. 1982-86), Gwinnett County Bar Assn. (pres. 1980-81), Fellows Ga. Bar Found. (charter), Old War Horse Lawyers Club, Order of Barristers, Pi Sigma Alpha. Episcopalian. Office: US Ct Appeals 11th Circuit 56 Forsyth St NW Atlanta GA 30303-2205*

EDMONDSON, JOHN RICHARD, lawyer, pharmaceutical manufacturing company executive; b. N.Y.C., Mar. 1, 1927; s. Richard Emil and Josephine (Schroeter) E.; m. Rozanne Hume, Oct. 30, 1954; children: Lisa M., Kate H., Timothy H., Nicholas D., Julia N. A.B., Georgetown U., 1950; LL.B., Columbia U., 1953. Bar: N.Y. 1953. Assoc. atty. Winthrop, Stimson, Putnam & Roberts, N.Y.C., 1953-59; with Bristol-Myers Co., N.Y.C., 1959—; asst. sec. Bristol-Myers Squibb Co., N.Y.C., 1960-69, sec., 1969-74, v.p., 1974-80, gen. counsel, 1977-89, sr. v.p., 1980-92; cons., 1992-94, ret., 1994. Served with AUS, 1945-47. Mem. ABA, Assn. Bar City N.Y., Univ. Club, Lake Waramaug Country Club, Longboat Key Club, Honourable Co. of Edinburgh Golfers. Home: 43 Old Stilson Hill Rd New Milford CT 06776-5413

EDMONDSON, KEITH HENRY, chemical company executive, retired; b. Wheaton, Ill., May 16, 1924; s. Edwin Ray and Mildred Lorraine (Henry) E.; m. Peggy Eleanor Wood, Sept. 22, 1945; children—Robert Earl, Kris E., John David, Keith Clark. B.S., Purdue U., 1948, M.S., 1949. With Upjohn Co., Kalamazoo, Mich., 1949-86; exec. v.p. internat. div. Upjohn Co., 1962-67, v.p., gen. mgr. chem. div., 1967-86; exec. dir. Stryker Ctr., 1986-90; prof. Kalamazoo Coll., 1986-90; dir. Career Devel. Ctr., Kalamazoo Coll., 1990-94; retired, 1994—. Mem. Kalamazoo Bd. Edn., 1958-62, pres., 1962. Served to 1st lt. USAAF, 1942-45. Decorated D.F.C. with oak leaf cluster, Air medal with 6 oak leaf clusters. Mem. Internat. Isocyanate Inst. (pres. 1976), Kalamazoo C. of C. (v.p. 1973), Kalamazoo Mgmt. Assn. (pres. 1957), Am. Inst. Chem. Engrs., Am. Chem. Soc., Tau Beta Pi, Sigma Xi, Phi Lambda Upsilon. Republican. Methodist. Home: 8565 W H Ave Kalamazoo MI 49009-7516 Office: Kalamazoo Coll 1200 Academy St Kalamazoo MI 49006-3268

EDMONDSON, LINDA LOUISE, optometrist; b. Wyandotte, Mich., Dec. 11, 1947; d. Richard Eugene and Mildred Louise (Horste) Weaver; m. William Edmondson II, June 1, 1969. BA, Ohio Wesleyan U., 1969; AM, Ind. U., 1971; BS, Pa. Coll. Optometry, 1975, OD, 1977. Assoc. instr. Ind. U., Bloomington, 1967-72; editor biol. abstracts Biosis Info. Svcs., Phila., 1972-73; pvt. practice pvt. practice, Bluefield, W.Va., 1977-84; prof. Northeastern State U. Coll. Optometry, Tahlequah, Okla., 1984—; referee Jour. of Am. Optometric Assn., 1988—, Optometry and Vision Sci., 1990—. Editor: Eye and Vision Conditions in the American Indian, 1990; contbr. articles to profl. jours. Approved arranger Sweet Adelines Internat.; active Okla. Jubilee Chorus. Mem. Am. Acad. Optometry, Am. Optometric Assn., Okla. Profl. Country Dance Assn., Cherokee County Soc. for Prevention of Cruelty to Animals, Beta Sigma Kappa. Avocation: piano, arranging barbershop music, computer music. Home: PO Box 871 Tahlequah OK 74465-0871 Office: NSU Coll of Optometry Tahlequah OK 74464

EDMONDSON, W(ALLACE) THOMAS, retired limnologist, educator; b. Milw., Apr. 24, 1916; s. Clarence Edward and Marie (Kelley) E.; m. Yvette Hardman, Sept. 26, 1941. BS, Yale U., 1938, PhD, 1942; postgrad., U. Wis., 1938-39; DSc (hon.), U. Wis., Milw., 1987; HHD (hon.), Seattle U., 1996. Research assoc. Am. Mus. Natural History, 1942-43, Woods Hole Oceanographic Instn., 1943-46; lectr. biology Harvard U., Cambridge, Mass., 1946-49; mem. faculty U. Wash., Seattle, 1949—, prof., 1957-86, prof. emeritus, 1986—, Jessie and John Danz lectr., 1987; R.E. Coker Meml. lectr. U. N.C., 1977; Brode lectr. Whitman Coll., 1988. Editor: Freshwater Biology (Ward and Whipple), 2d edit., 1959; contbr. articles to profl. jours. Recipient Einar Naumann August Thienemann medal Internat. Assn. Theoretical and Applied Limnology, 1980, Outstanding Pub. Svc. award U. Wash., Seattle, 1987, commendation State of Wash., 1987; NSF sr. postdoctoral fellow Italy, Eng. and Sweden, 1959-60. Fellow AAAS; mem. NAS (Cottrell award 1973), Am. Soc. Limnology and Oceanography (G. Evelyn Hutchinson medal 1990, celebratory issue of Limnology and Oceanography 1988), Internat. Assn. Limnology, Ecol. Soc. Am. (Eminent Ecologist award 1983), Yale Grad. Sch. Alumni Assn. (Wilbur Lucius Cross medal 1993). Office: U Wash Dept Zoology PO Box 351800 Seattle WA 98195-1800

EDMONDSON, WILLIAM ANDREW, state attorney general; b. Washington, Oct. 12, 1946; m. Linda Larason; children: Mary Elizabeth, Robert Andrew. BA in Speech Edn., Northeastern State U., Tahlequah, Okla., 1968; JD, U. Tulsa, 1978. Mem. Okla. Legislature, 1974-76; intern Office Dist. Atty., Muskogee, Okla., 1978—, asst. dist. atty., 1979, chief prosecutor, 1982—, dist. attorney, 1982-92; pvt. practice atty. Muskogee, 1979-82, Green & Edmondson, 1992-94; atty. gen. State of Okla., 1994—. With U.S. Navy, 1968-72. Named Outstanding Dist. Atty., State of Okla., 1985. Mem. Okla. Bar Assn., Okla. Dist. Attys. Assn. (pres. 1983—). Office: Office Atty Gen 2300 N Lincoln Blvd Rm 112 Oklahoma City OK 73105-4894

EDMONDSON, WILLIAM BROCKWAY, retired foreign service officer; b. St. Joseph, Mo., Feb. 6, 1927; s. Harold and Anna Laura (Sherman) E.; m. Donna Elizabeth Kiechel, Oct. 6, 1951; children: Barbara Elizabeth Edmondson Schneider, Paul William. A.B. with high distinction, U. Nebr., 1950; M.A., Fletcher Sch. Law and Diplomacy, 1951; student African area studies, Northwestern U., 1957-58. Joined U.S. Fgn. Service, 1952; fgn. affairs officer Bur. UN Affairs, State Dept., 1951-52; adviser U.S. delegation 11th session UN Trusteeship Council, 1952; vice consul Dar es Salaam, Tanganyika, 1952-55; 3d sec., then 2d sec. embassy Bern, Switzerland, 1955-57; research analyst, then acting chief W. Africa div. Office Research and Analysis for Africa, State Dept., 1958-61; 2d sec., then 1st sec. and consul, polit. sect. chief Am. embassy, Accra, Ghana, 1961-64; officer charge Ghanaian affairs Bur. African Affairs, State Dept., 1964-65; counselor of embassy, dep. chief of mission Lusaka, Zambia, 1965-68; chargé d'affaires ad interim, 1968-69; assigned Nat. War Coll., 1969-70; dep. dir. African programs Bur. Ednl. and Cultural Affairs, Dept. State, 1970, dir. Office African Programs, 1971-74; minister-counselor, dep. chief mission Am. embassy, Pretoria, South Africa, 1974-76; dep. asst. sec. for African affairs State Dept., 1976-78; ambassador to South Africa Pretoria, 1978-81; sr. fgn. service insp., 1981-82, dep. insp. gen., 1982-86. Served to 1st lt. AUS, 1944-48. Mem. Am. Fgn. Svc. Assn. Diplomatic and Consular Officers Ret. (past pres., hon. life gov.), DACOR Bacon House Found. (past pres., trustee), Phi Beta Kappa. Address: 4900 28th St N Arlington VA 22207-2712 *Persistent hard work, sincerity, broad intellectual curiosity and a strong touch of idealism in striving for a better world are qualities I admire and try to emulate.*

EDMONSTON, WILLIAM EDWARD, JR., publisher, educator; b. Balt., Nov. 20, 1931; s. William Edward and Helen (Mallonee) E.; m. Nellie Jane Kerley, Aug. 3, 1957; children—Kathryn Nell, Rebecca Jane, Owen William. BA, Johns Hopkins U., 1952; MA, U. Ala., 1956; PhD, U. Ky., 1960. Diplomate: Am. Bd. Psychol. Hypnosis. Instr., asst. prof. Washington U., St. Louis, 1960-64; mem. faculty Colgate U., Hamilton, N.Y., 1964-93, dir. neurosci. program, 1972-93, prof. psychology, 1973-93, prof. emeritus, 1993—; chmn. dept. psychology Colgate U., 1971-81; Gast prof. U. Erlanger, Nürnberg, Fed. Republic Germany, 1982; pub. Edmonston Pub., Inc., Hamilton. Author: Hypnosis and Relaxation: Modern Verification of an Old Equation, 1981, The Induction of Hypnosis, 1986, Unfurl the Flags: Remembrances of the American Civil War, 1989; editor: Am. Jour. Clin. Hypnosis, 1968-76; contbr. articles to profl. jours. Served with U.S. Army, 1952-54. Sloan Found. fellow, 1967, 69, Fulbright Found. fellow, 1982, U. Wash. sr. fellow, 1971; recipient Bernard E. Gorton award, 1961, grant USPHS, 1964-65, Prof. of Yr. award CASE N.Y. State, 1988. Mem. Sigma Xi. Home: RR 2 Box 103A Hamilton NY 13346-9522 *By being born to intelligent parents, I started with the genetic potential for success and was reared in a social atmosphere in which hard work, honesty, thrift and accomplishment were highly regarded. I later recognized perseverance, even in the face of apparent failure, and a compulsive attention to (but not an obsession with) details as fundamental to accomplishment. Perseverance is by far the most regnant, for without tenacity one's genetic potential and early social learnings will lie fallow. There is a time for action and a time for reflection. Choosing the appropriate time for each is the secret of happiness and success.*

EDMUND, NORMAN W., educational researcher; b. Feb. 27, 1916. Cert., U. Pa., 1939. Founder, pres. Edmund Sci. Co., Barrington, N.J., 1942-75; ednl. rschr. Ft. Lauderdale, Fla., 1989—. Author: The General Pattern of the Scientific Method. E-mail: nwe@scientificmethod.com. Office: 407 NE 3rd Ave Fort Lauderdale FL 33301-3233

EDMUNDS, CECELIA POWERS, health facility administrator; b. Dinwiddie County, Va., June 6, 1937; d. Charles Hardy and Maude Beatrice (Prosise) Powers; m. Thomas Fitzgerald Edmunds Jr., Apr. 5, 1956; children: Thomas Fitzgerald III, Anne Hardy, William McIlwaine, Cecelia Lynn, John Powers. RN, Johnston-Willis Hosp., Richmond, Va., 1957; BS in Health Sci., Chapman U., 1981; MS in Adminstrn. Health, Ctrl. Mich. U., 1996. RN, Va.; lic. nursing home adminstr., Va., adminstr. preceptor, Va. Staff nurse, head nurse Tucker Psychiat. Hosp., Richmond, 1957-59; pvt. duty nurse Johnston Willis Hosp., Richmond, 1959-65; head nurse Ctrl. State Hosp., Petersburg, Va., 1970-71; head nurse, instr. Petersburg Tng. Ctr., 1971-75; tng. coord., coord. ops., dir. nursing. Southside Va. Tng. Ctr., Petersburg, 1975-94, asst. dir. health svcs., 1994—; chairperson Dept. Mental Health Mental Retardation and Substance Abuse Svcs. Nursing Svcs. Group Commonwealth Va., Richmond, 1993-96. Mem. NAFE, Am. Coll. Health Care Adminstrs., Devel. Disabilities Nurses Assn. (charter). Republican. Presbyterian. Avocations: gardening, aerobics, shopping. Home: 8319 Mckenney Hwy Mc Kenney VA 23872-3435 Office: Southside Va Tng Ctr PO Box 4110 Petersburg VA 23803-0110

EDMUNDS, JANE CLARA, communications consultant; b. Chgo., Mar. 16, 1922; d. John Carson and Clara (Kummerow) Carrigan; m. William T. Dean, Aug. 30, 1947 (div. 1953; dec. July 1984); 1 son, John Charles; Edmund S. Kopacz, Sept. 24, 1955 (div. 1973); children: Christine Ellen, Jan Carson. Student in chemistry and math., Northwestern U. Chemist Mars Inc., Oak Park, Ill., 1942-47; with Cons. Engr. Mag., Maujer Pub. Co., St. Joseph, Mich., 1953-58, 69-74; sr. editor Cons. Engr. Mag. Tech. Pub. Co., Barrington, Ill., 1975-77, exec. editor, 1977-82, editorial dir., 1983-86; asst. editor women's pages rewrite desk News-Palladium, Benton Harbor, Mich., 1967-68; free lance journalist St. Joseph, 1959-68; communications cons. Schaumburg, Ill., 1987—. Chmn. Berrien County (Mich.) Nat. Found. March of Dimes, 1968; mem. campaign com. Rep. Party, 1954. Recipient award Bausch & Lomb, 1940, award Nat. Found. Service, 1969, Silver Hat award Constrn. Writers Assn., 1986, Chmn.'s award Profl. Engrs. in Pvt. Practice div. NSPE, 1987; grantee AID, 1979. Assoc. fellow Soc. Tech. Communication (chmn. St. Joseph chpt. 1972 Disting. Tech. Communication awards); mem. Am. Soc. Bus. Press Editors (past bd. mem.), Constrn. Writers Assn. (past dir.), Smithsonian Instn., Chgo. Art Inst. Assocs., Field Mus. Assocs. Republican. Episcopalian. Office: 1404 Hampton Ln Schaumburg IL 60193-2531

EDMUNDS, (ARTHUR) LOWELL, philology educator; b. Franklin, N.H., Oct. 11, 1938; s. Arthur Lowell and Ruth Harriet (Humphrey) E.; m. Susan Dain Trafton, June 22, 1966; children: Hannah, Leah. AB, Harvard U., 1960, PhD, 1970; MA, U. Calif., Berkeley, 1965. From asst. to assoc. prof. Harvard U., Cambridge, Mass., 1970-78; assoc. prof. Boston Coll., Chestnut Hill, Mass., 1978-83; prof., chmn. dept. Johns Hopkins U., Balt., 1983-88; prof. Rutgers U., 1988—, chmn. dept., 1990-96. Author: Chance and Intelligence in Thucydides, 1975, Oedipus: A Folklore Casebook, 1983, 2d edit., 1995, Oedipus: The Ancient Legend and its Later Analogues, 1985, Approaches to Greek Myth, 1989, From a Sabine Jar: Reading Horace, Odes 1.9, 1991, Myth in Homer: A Handbook, 1992, 2d edit., 1993, Theatrical Space and Historical Place in Sophocles' Oedipus at Colonus, 1996. Mem. Am. Philol. Assn., Assn. Ancient Historians. Avocations: yoga, recorder-playing. E-mail: edmunds@rci.rutgers.edu.

EDMUNDS, NANCY GARLOCK, federal judge; b. Detroit, July 10, 1947; m. William C. Edmunds, 1977. BA cum laude, Cornell U., 1969; MA in Teaching, U. Chgo., 1971; JD summa cum laude, Wayne U., 1976. Bar: Mich. 1976. With Plymouth Canton Public Schools, 1971-73; law clk. Barris, Sott, Denn & Driker, 1973-75; law clk. to Hon. Ralph Freeman U.S. Dist. Ct. (ea. dist.) Mich., 1976-78; ptnr. litigation sect. Dykema Gossett, 1984-92, resident Oakland County, 1986-92; judge U.S. Dist. Ct. (ea. dist.) Mich., 1992—; trustee Hist. Soc. U.S. Dist Ct. (ea. dist.) Mich. Bd. trustees Temple Beth El; mem. bus. and profl. women's divsn., lawyers' divsn. Jewish Welfare Fedn./Allied Jewish Campaign; mem. Saginaw Valley State U. Bd. Control, 1991-92. Mem. ABA, Fed. Judges Assn., Nat. Assn. Women Judges, Federalist Soc., State Bar Mich. (chair U.S. cts. com. 1990-91). Avocations: skiing, reading. Office: US Dist Ct US Courthouse #211 231 W Lafayette Blvd Detroit MI 48226-2702*

EDMUNDS, ROBERT THOMAS, retired surgeon; b. Toledo, Sept. 14, 1924; s. Marion Kenneth and Frances Ethel (McCauley) E.; widowed, 1983; children: Nancy, Priscilla, Elizabeth, Cynthia, Robert. BA, Harvard U., 1947; MD, Columbia U., 1951. Diplomate Am. Bd. Surgery. Intern St. Luke's Hosp., N.Y.C., 1951-52, asst. resident surgery, 1952-55, resident surgery, 1955-56, attending surgeon, 1956-78; clin. prof. surgery Columbia Coll. Physicians and Surgeons, N.Y.C., 1966-78; mini-residency in occupational medicine Inst. Environ. Health U. Cin. Coll Medicine, 1983; med. dir. U.S. Steel Corp., Pitts., 1978-89; ret., 1989; prin. investigator Cen. Oncology Group, Madison, Wis., 1956-70. Contbr. articles to profl. jours. Lt. (j.g.) USNR, 1942-46. Fellow ACS; mem. Union Club. Republican. Congregationalist. Achievements include enhancement of vision in albino children by use of contact lenses with opaque sclerae. Home: Glencrest Glen Hill Rd Danbury CT 06811

EDMUNDSON, CHARLES WAYNE, mechanical engineer, communications executive; b. Fairhope, Ala., July 23, 1942; s. Charles Vogel and Helen Bell (Winberg) E.; m. Linda Louise Lingren, June 13, 1964 (div. 1984); m. Jane Marie Byerlotzer, Apr. 11, 1986; children: Charles Bryan, Elizabeth Courtney, Joseph Michael. BSME, Texas A & M U., 1965. Registered Profl. Engr. Student Engr. Southwestern Bell Telephone Co., Dallas, 1964, staff asst., 1965, asst. engr., 1965, engr., 1967-68; sr. engr. Southwestern Bell Telephone Co., San Antonio, Tex., 1969-71; supr. engr. Southwestern Bell Telephone Co., San Antonio, 1971-73, equipment engr., 1973-76; div. staff supr. Southwestern Bell Telephone Co., St. Louis, 1976-79, div. mgr., 1979-93, dir. strategic sourcing, 1993-96, dir. purchasing & gen. contracting, 1996-97; pres. Facility Svcs. Integration LLC, St. Louis, 1998—; dir. Gateway Metro Credit Union, St. Louis, 1983—; pres. St. Louis Area Constrn. Users Coun., 1988-91. Campaign Chmn. United Way Campaign, Southwestern Bell Telephone Co., St. Louis 1985. Capt. U.S. Army Corps of Engrs. 1966-68, Germany. Named Young Engr. of the Yr. Bexar Chpt., Tex. Soc. of Prof. Engr., San Antonio, 1973-74. Mem. ASME (San Antonio Sec., treas. 1972-73, sec. 1973-74, chmn. 1974-75), Tex. Soc. Profl. Engrs. (dir. 1972-73, sec./treas. State PEI 1975-76), Gateway A&M Club (pres. 1988-89), Tex. A&M Former Students Assn. (nat. rep. 1990-95), Foreman Supr. Club (pres. 1988-89, 93). Republican.

EDRINGTON, SUE ELLEN, critical care nurse; b. Noblesville, Ind., Sept. 14, 1955; d. Donald Mur and Edna Irene (Carraway) E. BS in Secondary Edn., Bob Jones U., 1978, BSN, 1982; MS in Adult Health, Clemson U., 1994. RN, S.C., Ind., Mo.; cert. critical care nurse. Staff nurse ICU, med.-surg. emergency rm. St. Francis Hosp., Greenville, S.C., 1982-95, asst. head nurse ICU, head nurse ICU, acute dialysis, staff devlop. post coronary; spl. projects coord.; CNS Intensive Care Svcs. St. Francis Med. Ctr., Cape Girardeau, Mo., 1995-96; CNS Critical Care Svcs. Piedmont Med. Ctr., Rock Hill, S.C., 1997—. Mem. AACN, Sigma Theta Tau.

EDSALL, DAVID LEONARD, councillor, religious educator; b. Flint, Mich., Jan. 12, 1954; s. Leonard William Edsall and Ruth Mildred (Cooper) Britt. Student, Flint Bible Inst., 1978. Two-way radio installer Blumerick Comm., Flint, 1975-77; hot tar roofer Flint Watercraft, 1977; childcare worker Pied Piper, Flint, 1980; janitor-newspaper asst. The Flint Jour., 1980-83; councillor The Christian Coun., Flint, 1991—. With USN, 1971-74. Mem. Flint Chess Club. Avocations: long distance walking, tennis, bicycling, classic movies, chess. Office: The Christian Coun PO Box 372 Flint MI 48501-0372

EDSALL, JOHN TILESTON, biological chemistry educator; b. Phila., Nov. 3, 1902; s. David Linn and Margaret Harding (Tileston) E.; m. Margaret Dunham, May 1, 1929 (dec. 1987); children—James Lawrence Dunham (dec.), David Tileston, Nicholas Cranford. A.B., Harvard U., 1923, M.D., 1928; postgrad., Cambridge U., Eng., 1924-26; D.Sc. (hon.), U. Chgo., Western Res. U., U. Mich., N.Y. Med. Coll.; D.Phil. (hon.), U. Göteborg, Sweden, 1972. With Harvard U., Cambridge, Mass., 1928—; asst. prof. biol. chemistry Harvard U., 1932-38, assoc. prof., 1938-51, prof., 1951-73, emeritus, 1973—; John Simon Guggenheim Meml. Found. fellow Calif. Inst. Tech., 1940-41, Harvard U., 1954-56; Fulbright lectr. U. Cambridge, 1952, U. Tokyo, 1964; vis. prof. Coll. de France, Paris, 1955; pres. 6th Internat. Congress Biochemistry, N.Y.C., 1964; vis. prof. UCLA, 1977; vis. lectr. Australian Nat. U., Canberra, 1970. Author: (with E.J. Cohn) Proteins, Amino Acids and Peptides, 1943, (with J. Wyman) Biophysical Chemistry, 1958, (with H. Gutfreund) Biothermodynamics, 1983; editor: (with F.M. Richards, C.B. Anfinsen, D.S. Eisenberg and others) Advances in Protein Chemistry, Vols. 1-47, 1944-95, 1995, Jour. Biol. Chemistry, 1958-67; (with D. Bearman) Archival Sources for the History of Biochemistry and Molecular Biology, 1980; chmn. editl. bd. Procs. NAS, 1968-72; chmn. survey of sources The History of Biochemistry and Molecular Biology, 1975-80; contbr. articles to profl. jours. Recipient Passano Found. award, 1966; scholar Fogarty Internat. Ctr. NIH, Bethesda, Md., 1970-71. Mem. Am. Philos. Soc., Nat. Acad. Scis., Am. Chem. Soc. (sec. div. biol. chemistry 1946-48, chmn. 1948-49, Willard Gibbs medal Chgo. sect. 1972), Am. Soc. Biol. Chemists (pres. 1957-58), Am. Acad. Arts and Scis. (rep. on U.S. Nat. Commn. for UNESCO 1950-56), AAAS (mem. com. on sci. freedom and responsibility 1976-82, chmn. 1979-81, Philip Hauge Abelson award 1989), Deutsche Akademie der Naturforscher, European Molecular Biology Orgn. (assoc.), Royal Danish Acad. Scis., Royal Swedish Acad. Scis. Home: 985 Memorial Dr Apt 503 Cambridge MA 02138-5804 Office: Harvard U Dept Molecular & Cellular Biol 7 Divinity Ave Cambridge MA 02138-2019

EDSON, ANDREW STEPHEN, public relations executive; b. N.Y.C., Jan. 8, 1946; s. Herbert and Frances (Bauling) E.; m. Marilyn Borer, July 22, 1972; children: Garrett Matthew, Gregory Todd. BA, Fairleigh Dickinson U., 1967; MA, Memphis State U., 1969. Staff writer Memphis Press-Scimitar, 1968-69; account exec. Harshe-Rotman & Druck, Inc., Memphis, 1969-70, Ruder & Finn, Inc., N.Y.C., 1970-73; asst. dir. corp. pub. relations Anaconda Co., N.Y.C., 1973-74; pub. affairs mgr. Citicorp, N.Y.C., 1974-78; sr. account exec. Padilla & Speer Inc., N.Y.C., 1978-79, v.p., 1979-86, sr. v.p., 1986; sr. v.p. Padilla Speer Beardsley Inc., N.Y.C., 1986-94; pres., COO Anreder and Co., N.Y.C., 1994-96; chmn. Andrew Edson & Assocs., Inc., N.Y.C., 1996—; sr. counselor, corp. and fin. rels. Manning, Selvage & Lee, Inc., N.Y.C., 1996—; adj. asst. prof. NYU, 1983-87; sec., bd. dirs. The Worldcom. Group, Inc., N.Y., 1988-96; bd. dirs. Finch Apt Corp., N.Y.C. Mem. Jericho Pub. Libr. (trustee), The Racquet Club at Old Westbury (L.I.). Republican. Avocations: tennis, skiing, bicycling. Office: Andrew Edson & Assoc 79 Madison Ave Fl 3 New York NY 10016-7802

EDSON, CHARLES LOUIS, lawyer, educator; b. St. Louis, Dec. 14, 1934; s. Harry G. and Mildred (Solomon) E.; m. Susan Kramer, Mar. 29, 1959; children: Richard, Nancy, Margaret. AB, Harvard U., 1956, LLB, 1959. Bar: Mo. 1959, U.S. Supreme Ct. 1966, D.C. 1967. Assoc. Lewis, Rice, Tucker, Allen & Chubb, St. Louis, 1959-65; chief ops. officer Legal Svcs. Program, OEO, Washington, 1966-67; gen. counsel Pres.'s Commn. on Postal Orgn., Washington, 1967-68; chief pub. housing sect. Officer of Gen. Counsel, HUD, Washington, 1968-70; ptnr. Lane and Edson, P.C., Washington, 1970-89, Kelley, Drye & Warren, Washington, 1989-93, Peabody & Brown, Washington, 1993-99, Nixon Peabody, Washington, 1999—; adj. prof. law Georgetown U. Law Sch., Washington, 1970-76; HUD coord. Pres. Carter's Transition Staff, 1976-77. Co-author: A Practical Guide to Low and Moderate Income Housing, 1972, A Leased Housing Primer, 1975, A Section 8 Deskbook, 1976, Guide to Federal Housing Programs, 1982, Secondary Mortgage Market Guide, 1985, HDR Affordable Seniors Housing Handbook, 1986. Councilman Town of Somerset, Md., 1976-78; trustee Md. Hist. Trust, 1995—. With USNR, 1953-61. Alt. White House fellow, 1965. Mem. ABA (chmn. forum com. on affordable housing and comm. devel. 1991-93, chmn. spl. housing and urban devel. 1987-90), Harvard U. Law Sch. Assn. D.C. (pres. 1972-73), Cosmos Club (Washington). Home: 5802 Surrey St Chevy Chase MD 20815-5419 Office: 1255 23rd St NW Ste 800 Washington DC 20037-1125

EDSON, GARY FRANCIS, museum director; b. Bethany, Mo., Sept. 5, 1937; s. Manly Wayne and Delores Rugina (Cox) E.; m. Miriam Denise Zook, Aug. 20, 1980; children: Sean Christian, Suni Mahala. BFA, Kansas City (Mo.) Art Inst., 1960; MFA, Tulane U., 1962. Potter Edson Pottery, San Antonio, 1962-64; recreation supr. Dept. Army, Republic of Korea, 1964-66; vol. Peace Corps, Ecuador, 1966-68; asst. prof. art Northwestern La. U., Natchitoches, 1968-70; prof. art Herron Sch. Art, Indpls., 1970-80; chmn. div. fine art W.Va. U., Morgantown, 1980-84; chmn. dept. art Tex. Tech U., Lubbock, 1984-85, exec. dir. mus., 1985—; cons. Ecuadorian Mus. Assn., 1992, Museo del Barro, Asuncion, Paraguay, 1994; adminstrv. coord. Nat. Coun. Art Adminstrs., 1988-92. Author: Mexican Market Pottery, 1979; co-author: The Handbook for Museums, 1994; author, editor: Museum Studies International, 1994. Mem. W.Va. Art Curriculum Steering Com., 1981-84, W.Va. Study Program for Gifted, 1982-84, Lubbock Cultural Affairs Coun., 1986-90; chmn. Lubbock Tourism Com., 1989-90; pres. Lubbock Lakesite Found., 1990—. Recipient Headliner award Women in Comm., 1991, advancement award Coun. for Advancement and Support Edn., 1991; grantee USIA, Ecuador, 1992, Paraguay, 1994. Mem. Assn. Coll. and Univ. Mus. and Galleries (bd. dirs. 1988—), Internat. Coun. Mus. (U.S. bd.dirs. 1988—), Am. Assn. Mus. (bd. dirs. 1986—, sec. internation com. on mus. tng. 1986-95, chmn. com. on mus. profl. tng. 1990-94, com. on museology 1988—). Office: Museum of Texas Tech University 4th and Indian Ave Lubbock TX 79409-3191

EDSON, HERBERT ROBBINS, retired foundation and hospital executive; b. Upper Darby, Pa., Dec. 26, 1931; s. Merritt Austin and Ethel Winifred (Robbins) E.; m. Constance Anne Lowell, May 20, 1961 (div. Nov. 8, 1967); m. Rose Anne McGowan, July 25, 1970; children: Patricia Anne, David William, Merritt Austin III, Herbert Robbins Jr. BA, Tufts U., 1955; MBA, U. Pa., 1972. Commd. 2d lt. USMC, 1955, advanced through grades to major, 1967, adminstr., mgr., supr. various orgns., 1955-72; controller III Marine Amphibious Force and 3d Marine Div. USMC, Camp Butler, Japan, 1972-73; dir. acctg. Marine Corps Supply Activity USMC, Phila., 1973-75; ret. USMC, 1975; cons. acctg. Ardmore, Pa., 1975-77; CFO Mercy Meml. Hosp. Corp., Monroe, Mich., 1977-92, Mercy Meml. Hosp. Found., Monroe, 1986-92, Monroe Health Ventures Inc., 1986-92, Monroe Community Health Svcs., 1989-92, Byerly Hosp., Hartsville, S.C., 1992-95, Byerly Found., Hartsville, S.C., 1995-97; ret., 1997; assoc. Quorum Health Resources, Inc., Brentwood, Tenn., 1992-95. Co-pres. Custer Elem. Sch. Parent Tchr. Orgn., Monroe, 1985-87; v.p., trustee Christ Evang. Luth. Ch., Monroe, 1981-86; dir. Monroe County C. of C., 1982-84; treas., chmn. Taylor Endowment Fund com. St. Paul's Evang. Luth. Ch., Ardmore, Pa., 1974-76, trustee, chmn. property com., 1976. Decorated Purple Heart, Navy Commendation medal, Combat Action ribbon. Mem. NRA (life), U.S. Naval Inst. (life), Marine Corps Assn. (life), 1st Marine Div. Assn. (life), Edson's Raiders Assn. (hon. life 1st Marine Raider Bn.), Ret. Officers Assn. (life), Am. Assn.

Ret. Persons, Nat. Geog. Soc., Edson Geneal. Assn., Marines Meml. Club, Army and Navy Club. Republican. Lutheran. Home: PO Box 569 Ellenton FL 34222-0569

EDSON, MARGARET, playwright; life ptnr. Linda Merrill. Student, Smith Coll. Tchr. kindergarten Centennial Place Elem. Sch., Atlanta. Author: (play) Wit. Recipient Pulitzer prize for letters, drama and music, 1999. Address: Centennial Place Elem Sch 531 Luckie St NW Atlanta GA 30313

EDSON, MARIAN LOUISE, communications executive; b. Sidney, Mont., Mar. 21, 1940; d. David Ira and Myrtle (Ewing) Drury; m. James Arthur Edson, Oct. 14, 1961; children: Nadine L. Mykins, Jeanine Clare Edson. Student, U. Wash., 1961-62; BS, Mont. State U., 1962; postgrad., SUNY, Binghamton, 1975-76. Cert. tchr. Mont., Wash., N.Y. Lead editor, flight data file Johnson Space Ctr., Houston, 1980-85, coordinator for payload reconfiguration data collection, 1985-86, supr. flight data file, 1986-87; lead technical editor Bell Aerospace/Textron, Buffalo, N.Y., 1987; prodn. mgr. ASYST Software Tech., Rochester, N.Y., 1987-88, publ. mgr., 1988-94; mgr. advanced techs. Ziff-Davis, Rochester, 1997-98; publ. mgr. Raymond Corp., Greene, N.Y., 1994-97, project dir., 1998—; project dir. Raymond Corp., Greene, N.Y., 1994-97. Edn. com. Bay Area League Women Voters, Houston, 1984-85; assoc. Rochester Women's Network, 1987—; founding mem. Macedon (N.Y.) Reading Ctr., 1968—. Fellow Life Office Mgmt. Assn.; mem. AIAA, Soc. Tech. Communicators (pres.), Nat. Mgmt. Assn., Nat. Assn. Purchasing Mgrs., Women in Comm. Inc., Genesee Ornithol. Soc. (newsletter editor), Rochester Acad. Sci. Republican. Avocations: bird watching, horseback riding, hiking, biking, reading. Home: 4 Boulevard Pky Rochester NY 14612-5515

EDSON, PAUL LYNWOOD, quality assurance professional; b. Teaneck, N.J., June 14, 1966; s. Lunwood Michael E. and Corraine Augustina Summo; m. Diane Colgan, Nov. 5, 1994; 1 child, Garrett. BS, Montclair State U., 1989. Investigator U.S. Food & Drug Adminstrn., West Orange, N.J., 1990-93; cons. Hoffman-LaRoche, Nutley, N.J., 1993-96; dir. Johnson & Johnson, New Brunswick, N.J., 1996—. Mem. Am. Soc. Quality, Pareneral Drug Assn. Avocations: gem cutting, golf. Office: Johnson & Johnson 410 George St New Brunswick NJ 08901

EDSON, WAYNE E., retired dentist, consultant; b. Marinette, Wis., July 4, 1947; s. E.J. Edson and Anita (Pearson) Edson Sebero; m. Linda Mary Hullison, Apr. 3, 1971; children: William Earl, Erin Hullison, Thomas John. BS, U. Wis.-Madison/Milw., 1973; DDS, Northwestern U., 1977. Gen. practice dentistry, Winnetka, Ill., 1982-97, ret., 1996 . Pres. Kenilworth United Fund, 1983-84, bd. dirs., 1981-85; com. mem. Kenilworth Baseball, 1978-83; troop leader Boy Scouts Am., Kenilworth, 1994—. . Served with USN, 1965-72. Mem. Chgo. Dental Soc., Ill. State Dental Soc., ADA. Roman Catholic. Avocations: hunting; fishing, curling. Clubs: John Evans of Northwestern U., G.V. Black Soc. of Northwestern U., Kenilworth, Chgo. Curling Club. Home: 624 Exmoor Rd Kenilworth IL 60043-1021

EDSON, WILLIAM ALDEN, electrical engineer; b. Burchard, Nebr., Oct. 30, 1912; s. William Henry and Pearl (Montgomery) E.; m. Saralou Peterson, Aug. 23, 1942; children: Judith Lynne, Margaret Jane, Carolyn Louise. B.S. (Summerfield scholar), U. Kans., 1934, M.S., 1935; D.Sc. (Gordon McKay scholar), Harvard U., 1937. Mem. tech. staff Bell Telephone Labs., Inc., N.Y.C., 1937-41; supr. Bell Telephone Labs., Inc., 1943-45; asst. prof. elec. engring. Ill. Inst. Tech., Chgo., 1941-43; prof. physics Ga. Inst. Tech., Atlanta, 1945-46; prof. elec. engring. Ga. Inst. Tech., 1946-51, dir. sch. elec. engring., 1951-52; vis. prof., research asso. Stanford U., 1952-56, cons. prof., 1956; mgr. Klystron sub-sect. Gen. Electric Microwave Lab., Palo Alto, Calif., 1955-61; v.p., dir. research Electromagnetic Tech. Corp., Palo Alto, 1961-62; pres. Electromagnetic Tech. Corp., 1962-70; sr. scientist Vidar Corp., Mountain View, Calif., 1970—71; asst. dir. Radio Physics Lab., SRI Internat., Menlo Park, Calif., 1971-77; sr. prin. engr. Geosci. and Engring. Ctr., SRI Internat., 1977—; cons. high frequency sect. Nat. Bur. Standards, 1951-64; dir. Western Electronic Show and Conv., 1975-79. Author: (with Robert I. Sarbacher) Hyper and Ultra-High Frequency Engineering, 1943, Vacuum-Tube Oscillators, 1953. Life fellow IEEE (chmn. San Francisco sect. 1963-64, com. standards piezoelectricity 1950-67); mem. Am. Phys. Soc., Sigma Xi, Tau Beta Pi, Sigma Tau, Phi Kappa Phi, Eta Kappa Nu, Pi Mu Epsilon. Home: 23350 Sereno Ct Unit 29 Cupertino CA 95014-6543 Office: SRI Internat 333 Ravenswood Ave Menlo Park CA 94025-3453

EDWARD, JOHN THOMAS, chemist, educator; b. London, Mar. 23, 1919; s. John William and Jessie Christina (Simpson) E. (parents Can. citizens); m. Deirdre Mary Waldron, Mar. 21, 1953; children: John Valentine, Jeremy Bryan, Julian Kevin. B.S., McGill U., Montreal, Que., Can., 1939, Ph.D., 1942; D.Phil., Oxford U., Eng., 1949; M.A., Dublin U., Ireland, 1955; Sc.D., Dublin U., 1971. Postdoctoral fellow Iowa State U., 1942-43; research scientist div. explosives NRC Can., Ottawa, Ont., 1943-45; lectr. U. Man., Can., 1945-46; Imperial Chem. Industries research fellow U. Birmingham, Eng., 1949-52; lectr. Trinity Coll., Dublin U., 1952-56; mem. faculty McGill U., 1956—, asst. prof. chemistry, 1957-61, assoc. prof., 1961-66, prof., 1966—, MacDonald prof. chemistry, 1973—, prof. emeritus, 1986—. Contbr. articles to profl. publs. Fellow AAAS, Royal Soc. Can., Chem. Inst. Can.; mem. Am. Chem. Soc. Home: 51 Chesterfield, Montreal, PQ Canada H3Y 2M4 Office: McGill U Dept Chemistry, 801 Sherbrooke St W, Montreal, PQ Canada H3A 2K6

EDWARD, THOMAS L., federal agency administrator; b. Montgomery, Ala., June 16, 1950. Assoc. adminstr. rsch., demonstration, innovation Dept. Transp., Washington. Office: Dept Transp 400 7th St SW TRI-1 Washington DC 20590-0001

EDWARDS, ADRIAN L., medical educator. MD, Harvard U., 1960. Prof. med. Med. Sch. Cornell U., 1968—. Mem. Inst. Medicine-NAS. Office: 135 E 71st St New York NY 10021-4258*

EDWARDS, ALISYN ARDEN, marriage and family therapist; b. Winfield, Kans., Nov. 8, 1960; d. Warren Dale and Vera Colleen (Edwards) Andreas; m. Brad Edwards, 1991; 1 child, Emlyn Arden. BA, U. Kans., 1982; M Marriage and Family Therapy, Abilene Christian U., 1984. Lic. master's level psychologist; lic. marriage and family therapist. Psychotherapist Mental Health Ctr. East Cen. Kans., Emporia, 1988-90; psychologist Sedgwick County Dept. Mental Health, Wichita, Kans., 1990-92; psychotherapist MCC Behavioral Care, Wichita, 1992-93, R & L Counseling & Referral Svc., Wichita, 1993-94; psychologist El Dorado Correctional Ctr, Eldorado, 1994—; intra-familial sexual abuse treatment team Mental Health Ctr. East Cen. Kans., Emporia, 1988-90. Violinist Mid-Kans. Symphony Orch., Friends U. Community Symphony, 1991-93; mem. Run Wichita team Leukemia Soc. 1995. Mem. Am. Assn. Marriage and Family Therapy (clin.), Kans. Assn. Marriage and Family Therapy. Avocations: sports, music, friends, family, reading. Office: El Dorado Correctional Facility PO Box 311 El Dorado KS 67042-0311

EDWARDS, ANN CONCETTA, human resources manager, writer; b. Bklyn., Feb. 15, 1941; d. Joseph T. and Anna R. Lazzarino; m. Andrew F. Edwards, Jan 14, 1967; children: Alison, Jacqueline. BA, U. S.C., 1961; MA, St. John's U., Jamaica, N.Y., 1963. Cert. sr. profl. human resources. From asst. to mgr. human resources Lab-Volt Sys., Inc., Wall Township, N.J., 1982-97, human resources mgr., 1997—. Writer Shore News, Sea Girt, N.J., 1970-75; cons. Edwards Assocs., Sea Girt, 1975-82. Recipient Govs. Certificate of Achievement award N.J. Sch. to Careers Sys., 1997-98. Mem. Soc. for Human Resource Mgmt. (found. chair 1997—, trustee Garden State coun., dir. 1994—, high tech. net 1998—), Nat. Assn. Female Execs., Jersey Shore Assn. Human Resources (area 1 rep. 1990—). Avocation: writing. Office: Lab Volt Systems Inc PO Box 686 Farmingdale NJ 07727

EDWARDS, ANTHONY, actor; b. Santa Barbara, CA, July 19, 1962. Student, Royal Acad. of Dramatic Art, London, 1980. Films include: Fast Times at Ridgemont High, 1982, Heart Like a Wheel, 1982, Revenge of the Nerds, 1984, The Sure Thing, 1985, Gotcha!, 1985, Top Gun, 1985, Summer Heat, 1987, Revenge of the Nerds II: Nerds in Paradise, 1987, Mr. North, 1988, Miracle Mile, 1989, How I Got Into College, 1989, Hawks, 1989, Downtown, 1990, Pet Sematary II, 1992, The Client, 1994, Us Begins with You, 1998; television movies include: The Killing of Randy Webster, 1981, High School U.S.A., 1983, Going for the Gold: The Bill Johnson Story, 1985, El Diablo, 1990, Hometown Boy Makes Good, 1990, In Cold Blood, 1996; series include: It Takes Two, 1982-83, Northern Exposure, 1992-93, ER, 1994—. *

EDWARDS, ARDIS LAVONNE QUAM, retired elementary education educator; b. Sioux Falls, S.D., July 30, 1930; d. Norman and Dorothy (Cade) Quam; m. Paul Edwards, Apr. 18, 1953 (dec. Sept. 1988); children: Kevin (dec. 1980), Kendall, Erin, Sally, Kristin, Keely. Tchg. credentials, Augustana Luth. Coll., Sioux Falls, 1949; provisional tchg. credentials, San Jose State Coll., 1953, student, 1953-57. Lic. pvt. pilot, FAA. Mgr. The Cottage Restaurant, Sioux Falls, 1943-50; one-room sch. tchr. Whaley Sch., Colman, S.D., 1949-50; one-room sch. tchr. 8 grades East Sioux Sch., Sioux Falls, 1950-51; recreation dir. City of Albany, Calif., 1951-52; first grade tchr. Decoto (Calif.) Sch. Dist., 1952-58; ret., 1958. Author Health Instrn. Unit Study Packet for Tchrs. Bible sch. tchr. East Side Luth. Ch., Sioux Falls, S.D., 1945-51, Sunday sch. tchr., 1945-51; charter mem. Our Savior Luth. Ch., Fremont, Calif., 1964—, mem. choir; Christian Week Day Sch. tchr., 1970, 87, ch. historian, 1986—, other offices; treas. PTA, Hayward, Calif., 1959; pres. Luth. Women's Missionary League, 1976; chmn. OSLC Blood Bank, 1968—; edn. officer, fraternal communicator, respecteen officer Luth. Brotherhood; officer Healthy Cmtys. Healthy Youth; mem. Am. Heart Assn., March of Dimes, Am. Cancer Soc., Arthritis Found., Tri-Cities Assn. Evangs.; room mother, Chadbourne Grammar Sch.; team mother, Fremont Little League. Recipient Spl. Svc. award Girl Scouts U.S., 1971, Arthritis Found., Fremont, 1974-75, Spl. Commendation March Fong Eu, 1954. Mem. NAFE, AARP, Republic Airlines Ret. Pilots Assn., Ret. Airline Pilots Assn., N.W. Airlines Ret. Pilots Assn., Aircraft Owners and Pilots Assn., S.W. Airways Pilots Wives Assn., Concerned Women for Am., World Affairs Coun., Mission Swim Club, Philomathian Lit. Soc., Tri-Cities Assn. Evangelicals. Republican. Avocations: Bible study, grandchildren, flying, history, antiques. *My greatest sense of fulfillment is in being a Christian, wife, mother, teacher and writer...in that order.*

EDWARDS, BENJAMIN FRANKLIN, III, investment banker; b. St. Louis, Oct. 26, 1931; s. Presley William and Virginia (Barker) E.; m. Joan Moberly, June 13, 1953; children: Scott P., Benjamin Franklin IV, Pamela M. Edwards Bunn, Susan B. B.A., Princeton U., 1953. With A.G. Edwards & Sons, Inc., St. Louis, 1956—; pres. A.G. Edwards & Sons, Inc., 1967—, chmn., 1983—, also CEO, 1983—; bd. dirs. Jefferson Bank and Trust Co., Psychol. Assocs., Helig-Meyers, Inc., N.Y. Stock Exch., Washington U., St. Louis Art Mus., Barnes Hosp. Mem. U. Mo., St. Louis, Civic Progress, Arts and Edn. Coun. With USNR, 1953-56. Mem. Investment Bankers Assn. (gov. 1968—), Securities Industry Assn. (gov. 1974-81, chmn. 1980—). Presbyterian. Clubs: Old Warson Country (St. Louis); Bogey. Office: A G Edwards & Sons Inc 1 N Jefferson Ave Saint Louis MO 63103-2205*

EDWARDS, BERT TVEDT, accountant; b. Washington, Aug. 23, 1937; s. Archie Campbell and Geniana (Rasmussen) E.; m. Susan Elizabeth Dye, July 18, 1964; children: Christopher Andrew, Stacey Elizabeth. BA, Wesleyan U., 1959; MBA, Stanford U., 1961. CPA, D.C. With Arthur Andersen LLP, Washington, 1961-69, 70-94, mgr., 1965-69, 70-71, ptnr., 1971-94, ret. ptnr., cons., 1994-98; fin. v.p. Leisure Time Industries, Inc., 1969-70; CFO, asst. sec. U.S. Dept. State, 1998—. Trustee Barker Found., 1968-78, 94-96, treas., 1968-71, 1st v.p., 1971-72, pres., 1972-75; trustee, treas. Population Reference Bur., Inc., 1975-98, vice chmn., 1993-94; bd. dirs. Jr. Achievement Met. Washington, Inc., 1973-87, treas., 1973-74, 2d v.p., 1974-75, 1st v.p., 1975-77, pres., 1977-78, chmn., 1978-80; bd. dirs., treas. Heritage Walk Homes Corp., 1975-80; mem. Spl. Adv. Commn. for Indsl. and Comml. Devel., D.C. City Coun., 1972-74; mem. D.C. Mayor's Commn. on Budget and Fiscal Priorities, 1989-91, 93-95, mem. D.C. Tax Rev. Commn., 1996-98; chmn. JA Nat. Bus. Leadership Conf., 1978; chmn. Metro Washington Boys and Girls Clubs Ann. Congl. Dinner, 1993, dinner com. mem. 1992-98, found. bd., 1995—; treas. Nat. Com. Pub. Employee Pension Syss., 1993-98; bd. dirs., treas. Bethany West Recreation Assn., 1994-98; bd. dirs. D.C. Appleseed Found. Ctr. for Law and Justice, 1995-98, treas., 1998; bd. dirs. Com. for Capital City, 1995-98; mem. cmty. rels. bd. Sta. WAMU, 1994-97. Recipient Outstanding Achievement award Stanford U., 1982, Outstanding Publ. award Soc. Mil. Comptrollers, 1984, Bronze Leadership award Jr. Achievement, 1979, Silver Leadership award, 1981; Victor Royall fellow Stanford U., 1960-61. Mem. AICPA (govt. acctg. and auditing com. 1981-84, 1985-88, 89-92, fed. govt. audit subcom. 1981-84, ad hoc task force univ. audit 1985-87, task force on quality of govt. audits 1986-87, author, editor single audit course 1985-92, 94-96, task force on quality of fed. program audits 1991-94), Greater Washington Soc. CPAs (chmn. membership com. 1973-74, chmn. SEC com. 1974-75, chmn. govt. acctg. com. 1979-81, chmn. rels. with DC govt. com., 1995-98, Lifetime Pub. Svc. award 1997), Assn. Govt. Accts. Edn. and Rsch. Found. (chmn. bd. dirs. 1993-95), Va. Soc. CPAs, Inst. Mgmt. Accts., Am. Acctg. Assn. (vice chair govt. nonprofit sect. 1993-94), Assn. Sch. Bus. Ofcls., Govt. Fin. Officers Assn. (co-chmn. ann. conf. 1987), Md. Pub. Fin. Officers Assn. (bd. dirs. 1992-94), Assn. Govt. Accts. (Andy Barr Lifetime Achievement award 1993), Govt. Fin. Officers Assn. Met. Washington (co-founder, bd. dirs. 1984-91, outstanding svc. award 1993), Met. Washington Bd. Trade, Wesleyan U. Alumni Club Wash. (pres. 1969-71), Univ. Club (mem. bd. admissions 1976-82, chmn. 1980-82, bd. govs. 1982-85). Methodist. Home: 7805 Stable Way Potomac MD 20854-1790 Office: US Dept State 2201 C St NW Rm 7427 Washington DC 20520-7427

EDWARDS, BOB (ROBERT ALAN EDWARDS), radio news anchor; b. Louisville, May 16, 1947; s. Joseph Richard and Loretta Bernardine (Fuchs) E.; m. Sharon Ann Kelly, May 14, 1979; children: Brean, Susannah, Eleanor. B.S. in Commerce, U. Louisville, 1969, D.Pub. Service (hon.), 1985; M.A. in Communication, Am. U., 1972; LHD (hon.), Grinnell Coll., 1991, Spalding U., 1998. News dir., program dir. Sta. WHEL-AM, New Albany, Ind., 1968-69; news anchor Sta. WTOP-AM, Washington, 1972; corr., night editor Mut. Broadcasting System, Washington, 1972-73; assoc. producer Nat. Pub. Radio, Washington, 1974, co-host All Things Considered, 1974-79, host Morning Edit., 1979—. Author: Fridays with Red, 1993. Served in U.S. Army, 1969-71, Korea. Recipient Edward R. Murrow award Corp. for Pub. Broadcasting, 1984, Oral Communication award L.I.U., 1980, Fleur-de-Lis award Louisville Forum, 1985, Unity award in media Lincoln U., Jefferson City, Mo., 1983, Gabriel award Cath. Assn. Broadcasters, 1987, 90, Alumni Recognition award Am. U., 1991, Oak award Ky. Advs. for Higher Edn., 1991, Alumni fellow U. Louisville, 1994, duPont Columbia award, Silver Baton, 1995; named to Esquire Register, Esquire mag., 1986. Mem. AFTRA (nat. v.p. 1988—), Radio-TV Corrs. Assn., Soc. Profl. Journalists, U. Louisville Alumni Assn., St. Xavier H.S. Alumni Assn. Avocations: softball, genealogy, tennis. Office: Nat Pub Radio 635 Massachusetts Ave NW Washington DC 20001-3753

EDWARDS, BRIAN FRANCIS PEREGRINE, science educator; b. Kamloops, B.C., Can., Jan. 4, 1947; m. Lana Lee; children: David, Sarah. BS, U. B.C., 1969; AM, Harvard U., 1971, PhD, 1975. Rsch. assoc. U. Alberta, Edmonton, 1975-77, profl. assoc., 1977-80; asst. prof. to prof. Wayne State U., Detroit, 1980-89, prof., 1989—. Mem. Am. Chem. Soc., Can. Fedn. Biol. Socs., Am. Cystallographic Assn., Biophys. Soc., Am. Soc. Biochemistry and Molecular Biology, Protein Soc. Office: Wayne State U Biochemistry 540 E Canfield St Detroit MI 48201-1928

EDWARDS, CARL ELMO, JR., lawyer; b. Henderson, N.C., July 23, 1941; s. Carl E. and Dorothy (Wade) E.; m. Jeanne F. Antaya; children: Scott M., Glenn M., Jeffrey M. BS in Math., Syracuse U., 1965; MS in Computer Sci., So. Meth. U., 1970, LLM, 1987; JD, U. Denver, 1975; MA in Internat. Mgmt., U. Tex., Dallas, 1992. Bar: Colo. 1975, Iowa 1975, Tex. 1983. Commd. 2d lt. USAF, 1961, advanced through grades to lt. col., 1981; base staff judge adv. San Vito Air Sta., Italy, 1977-79, F.E. Warren AFB, Cheyenne, Wyo., 1979-82; ret., 1983; chief cir. def. counsel San Antonio, 1982-83; assoc. Smith, Underwood & Hunter, Dallas, 1983-84; assoc. gen. counsel Electronic Data Systems Corp., Dallas, 1984-88; v.p. gen. counsel, sec. Elcor Corp., Dallas, 1988-92; exec. v.p., gen. counsel, sec. Lennox Internat., Inc., Dallas, 1992—; bd. dirs. Ky. Elec. Steel; mem. devel. bd. U. Tex., Dallas, 1995—. Mem. ABA, Tex. Bar Assn., Iowa Bar Assn., Colo. Bar Assn., Assn. Trial Lawyers Am. Avocations: jogging, golf. Home: 7510 Vista Ridge Ct Garland TX 75044-2065 Office: 2100 Lake Park Blvd Richardson TX 75080-2254

EDWARDS, CARL NORMAND, lawyer; b. Norwood, Mass., Jan. 22, 1943; s. Wilfred Carl and Cecile Marie-Anne (Pepin) E.; m. Mary Louise Buyse, Jan. 22, 1982. MEd, Suffolk U., 1969; postgrad. Harvard U.; JD, Boston Coll., 1998; PhD, U. So. Calif., 1997. Cons. dept. social relations Harvard, 1966-69, research fellow, 1969-71, lectr. social relations, 1971-72; cons. research psychologist Cambridge Computer Assocs., Mass., 1966—; assoc. clin. prof. psychiatry Tufts U. Sch. Medicine, 1971—, research social psychologist Tufts-New Eng. Med. Center, 1969—; dir. Four Oaks Research Inst., Norfolk, Mass., 1974—; sr. assoc. for policy planning and research Justice Resource Inst., 1971—; field faculty grad. program Goddard Coll., Plainfield, Vt., 1972-82; chmn. bd. dirs. MEDx Systems, Ltd., Dover, Mass., 1985—; chmn. bd. trustees Ctr. for Birth Defects Info. Services, Inc., Dover, 1984—; tchr. seminars; cons. to major corps., govt. agys. and pub. instns. in human dynamics and pub. policy; lectr., thesis adviser, program devel. cons. schs., colls., insts. Contbr. articles to profl. jours., monographs, revs. Mem. USNG, 1963-64. Mem. Am., Mass. psychol. Assns., Soc. for Psychol. Study Social Issues, Peace Research Soc., Nat. Pilots Assn., Nat. Trust for Hist. Preservation, Harvard Club, Appalachian Mt. Club, Norfolk Hunt Club, Blue Ridge Hunt Club. Author: Drug Dependence: Social Regulation and Treatment Alternatives. Contbr. articles to profl. jours., monographs, revs. Home: Four Oaks PO Box 1776 Dover MA 02030-0279

EDWARDS, CAROLYN MULLENAX, public relations executive; b. French Camp, Calif., Dec. 3, 1943; d. Charles Harold and Jessie Jewel Mullenax; m. Helton Pressley (div.); m. Dennis D. Edwards, May 29, 1993. BFA, U. Tulsa, 1967; MEd, Ea. N.Mex. U., 1976. Artist Wessels Agy., Spokane, Wash., 1968-70; pub. rels. dir. Spokane (Wash.) Symphony Soc., 1970-72; advt. coord. Crescent Dept. Store, Spokane, 1972-73; art dir., copywriter Sta. KMTY Radio, Clovis, N.Mex., 1976; news editor Clovis News Jour., Clovis, 1976-77; promotion and art dir. Sta. KENW-TV, Portales, N.Mex., 1977-78; coord. alumni affairs and pubs. Ea. N.Mex. U., Portales, 1978-80; dir. pubs., TV and pub. info. Ea. N.Mex. U., Clovis, 1985-90; dir. mktg. & pub. info. Clovis Community Coll. (formerly Ea. N.Mex. U.-Clovis), 1990-98; producer pub. affairs program Sta. KMCC-TV, Clovis, 1981-84; devel. and pub. info. dir. Mental Health Resources Inc., Portales, N.Mex., 1980-85; asst. dir. alumni affairs Mental Health Resources Inc., Portales, 1998—. Bd. dirs. N.Mex. Outdoor Drama Assn., San Jon, 1986-95, Univ. Symphony League, Clovis, 1984-88. Mem. N.Mex. Press Women (scholarship chair 1994-99, comm. awards 1981-99), Nat. Fedn. Press Women (comm. awards 1984-97), Am. Women in Radio and TV, Clovis C. of C. (bd. dirs. 1984-89), Jr. League (Lubbock, Tex.), Coun. for Advancement and Support Edn. (sec.-editor dist. IV 1990-92, design award 1991, 99), Nat. Coun. for Mktg. and Pub. Rels. (dist. IV award 1989-91, 93-97, nat. award 1993-98), Altrusa Club, Nat. Assn. of Vocational and Tech. Edn. (awards 1995-96), Delta Delta Delta (former dist. alumnae officer, chair Delta century fund, graphics cons.). Republican. Episcopalian. Avocations: reading, classical music, free lance art, volunteer work, dancing. Office: Ea NMex Univ Alumni Affairs Sta #48 Portales NM 88130

EDWARDS, CHARLES, neuroscientist, educator; b. Washington, Sept. 22, 1925; s. James Moses and Lola (Rosenthal) Edlavitch; m. Lois Bender, Aug. 12, 1951; children: Jan, James, Sally, David. AB, Johns Hopkins U., 1945, MA, 1948, PhD, 1953. Found. Infantile Paralysis postdoctoral fellow, asst. lectr. Univ. Coll., London, 1953-55; instr., asst. prof. physiol. optics Johns Hopkins U., Balt., 1955-58; asst. prof. physiology U. Utah, Salt Lake City, 1958-60; assoc. prof. physiology U. Minn., Mpls., 1960-65, prof., 1965-67; prof. biol. scis., dir. neurobiology rsch. ctr. SUNY, Albany, 1967-84, prof. emeritus biol. sci., 1986—; spl. asst. to sci. dir. Nat. Inst. Diabetes and Digestive and Kidney Diseases, NIH, 1984-88; prof. physiology, assoc. dean rsch. and grad. affairs U. South Fla. Coll. Medicine, Tampa, 1988-91; Grass lectr. CIEA del IPN, Mexico City, 1966; vis. prof. Karolinska Inst., 1975, 79, 84; mem. physiology study sect. NIH, 1971-75. Mem. editorial bd. Am. Jour. Physiology, 1967-73, Gen. Physiology Biophysics, 1983-95, Neurosci., 1979-92, Neurosci. Rsch., 1984-94. Mem. ACLU, Md. chpt., 1956-58, Utah chpt., 1959-60; mem. citizen adv. com. Sarasota Bay Nat. Estuary Program, 1994—. Lalor fellow, 1957, Lederle fellow, 1959-60; Nat. Acad. Scis. Czechoslovak Acad. Sci. Exchange fellow, 1980, 82, 84, 87, Japan Soc. Promotion of Sci. fellow, 1981, Naito Found.fellow, 1985; named to Johns Hopkins Univ. Soc. Scholars, 1987. Fellow AAAS; mem. AAUP (mem. coun. 1972-75), Am. Physiol. Soc., Marine Biol. Lab., Biophys. Soc., Physiol. Soc. Japan (hon.), Soc. Gen. Physiology (sec. 1971-73), Neurosci. Soc.

EDWARDS, CHARLES ARCHIBALD, lawyer; b. Lumberton, N.C., Sept. 19, 1945; s. Charles Edwin and Elizabeth Gertrude (Gooden) E.; m. Judy Carol Griffin, Aug. 14, 1966; children: Lee McNeill, Caroline Averitt. AB, Davidson Coll., 1967; JD, U. N.C., 1970. Bar: Ga. 1970, U.S. Supreme Ct. 1974, D.C. 1981, N.C. 1987. Assoc. Connerat, Dunn, Hunter, Houlihan, Maclean & Exley, Savannah, Ga., 1970-71, ptnr., 1972-76; ptnr. Constangy, Brooks & Smith, Atlanta, Ga., 1976-82, Greene, Buckley, Derieux & Jones, Atlanta, 1982-86, Graham & James, Raleigh, N.C., 1986-94, Womble Carlyle Sandridge & Rice, PLLC, Raleigh, 1994—. Author: Georgia Employment Law, 1983; contbr. articles to profl. publs. Mem. N.C. Bar Assn., Fed. Bar Assn., Atlanta Bar Assn. (chmn. labor law sect. 1983-84). Republican. Episcopalian. Office: Womble Carlyle Sandridge & Rice PO Box 831 2100 1st Union Capitol Ctr Raleigh NC 27602

EDWARDS, CHARLES ARTHUR, college administrator; b. Chgo., May 7, 1940; s. Arthur Lewis and Kathleen (McGinnis) E.; children from previous marriage: Valerie Kathleen, Jennifer Anne; m. C. Lynn Kiaer. AB, U. Chgo., 1965. Pres. The Edwards Group, Terre Haute, Ind., 1984-98; v.p. coll. rels. Green Mountain Coll., Poultney, Vt., 1998—. Mem. exec. com. Nat. Alumni Fund Bd., U. Chgo., 1975-77, Conn. Gov.'s Com. on Arts and Tourism, 1973-75; mem. Nat. Alumni Cabinet, U. Chgo., 1969-72; chmn. New Eng. Conf. Devel. Group, Am. Assn. Mus., 1977-78; bd. dirs. Pegasus Players, Chgo., 1988-89; bd. trustees Anne S.K. Brown Mil. Coll., Brown U. Libr., Providence, R.I., 1994—. With U.S. Army, 1958-62. Decorated Officer Order of Polonia Restituta and Cross of Merit 2d Class (London). Mem. Nat. Soc. Fund Raising Execs. (cert., bd. dirs. Chgo. chpt. 1986-89, asst. treas. 1988-89), Art Mus. Devel. Assn. (pres. 1976-77), Ill. St. Andrew Soc. (bd. govs. 1989-95, v.p. 1992-95), Royal Humane Soc. (gov. 1991—), Intelligence Corps Assn. (hon. life), Newport Arty. Co. (hon.), Victory Club (London). Congregationalist. Office: Green Mountain Coll One College Circle Poultney VT 05764

EDWARDS, CHARLES CORNELL, physician, research administrator; b. Overton, Nebr., Sept. 16, 1923; s. Charles Busby and Lillian Margaret (Arendt) E.; m. Sue Cowles Kruidenier, June 24, 1945; children: Timothy, Charles Cornell, Nancy, David. Student, Princeton U., 1941-43; B.A., U. Colo., 1945, M.D., 1948; M.S., U. Minn., 1956; L.L.D. (hon.), Phila. Coll. Pharmacy and Sci.; L.H.D. (hon.), Pa. Coll. Podiatry, U. Colo.; LHD (hon.), U. Colo., 1993. Diplomate: Am. Bd. Surgery. Intern St. Mary's Hosp., Mpls., 1948-49; resident surgery Mayo Found., 1950-56; pvt. practice medicine specializing in surgery Des Moines, 1956-61; mem. surg. staff Georgetown U., Washington, 1961-62; also cons. USPHS; dir. div. socio-econ. activities A.M.A., Chgo., 1963-67; v.p., mng. officer health and sci. affairs Booz, Allen & Hamilton, 1967-69; commr. FDA, Washington, 1969-73; asst. sec. for health HEW, Washington, 1973-75; sr. v.p., dir. Becton, Dickinson & Co., 1975-77; pres. Scripps Clinic and Research Found., La Jolla, Calif., 1977-91; pres., CEO Scripps Insts. Medicine and Sci., La Jolla, 1991-93; bd. dirs. Bergen Brunswig Corp., Molecular Biosys., Inc., No. Trust Bank, IDEC Pharms., Matenir, Inc., Scripps Health Systems; bd. trustees Scripps Insts. Medicine & Sci.; trustee Scripps Rsch. Inst.; bd. regents Nat. Libr. Medicine, 1981-85; mem. Nat. Leadership Commn. on Health Care, 1986—; bd. govs. Hosp. Corp. Am., 1986-89; chmn. bd. dirs. San Diego Hospice. Trustee San Diego Hospice, San Diego YMCA. Lt. M.C. USNR, 1942-46. Recipient Disting. Svc. award U.S. Dept. Health, Edn., Welfare, Disting. Alumnus award Mayo Found., 1986, Humanity award Nat. Conf., 1994. Mem. Inst. Medicine, Am. Hosp. Assn. (hon.), Nat. Acad. Scis., Princeton Club, La Jolla Country Club, La Jolla Beach and Tennis Club. Office: Scripps Rsch Inst 10666 N Torrey Pines Rd La Jolla CA 92037-1027

EDWARDS, CHARLES MUNDY, III, financial consultant; b. N.Y.C., Jan. 30, 1935; s. Charles Mundy Jr. and Nancy Blow (Rawls) E.; m. Janice Elaine

Petty, Oct. 22, 1966; children: Melanie LeMoyne, Meghan Elizabeth Adams. AB, Princeton U., 1957; postgrad., NYU, 1959-63. With Shearson Lehman Bros., Inc., N.Y.C., 1959-85, assoc., asst. v.p., v.p., sr. v.p.; prin. Grumman Hill Assocs., Inc., Westport, Conn., 1985—, also bd. dirs.; bd. dirs. Fast Bar, Inc., Richmond, Va.; cons. Lynch & Mayer, Inc., N.Y.C., 1994. Treas. fund for Ednl. Advancement, Newark, 1985-87, pres., 1988-90, v.p., 1990-97, trustee, 1985—; trustee Family Svc. Assn. of Summit, 1987-91; pres., adminstrv. bd. United Meth. Ch., Summit, 1987-94, trustee, 1990-94; mem. City Planning Bd., Summit, 1989-91; mem. adminstrv. bd. Mt. Bethel United Meth. Ch., Marietta, Ga., 1995—, mem. fin. com., 1995—, chmn. endowment com., 1997—; bd. advisors Thurston Arthritis Rsch. Ctr., Chapel Hill, N.C., 1999— 1st lt. USMCR, 1957-59. Mem. Princeton Quadrangle Club, Beacon Hill Club (pres. 1987-88, v.p. 1986-87, treas. 1985-86), Chattahoochee Plantation Tennis Club. Republican. Methodist. Home: 495 Atlanta Country Club Dr Marietta GA 30067-4684

EDWARDS, CHARLES RICHARD, entomology and pest management educator; b. Lubbock, Tex., Jan. 22, 1945; s. Troy B. and Jeanette E. E.; m. Claudia Frances Henderson, Dec. 21, 1966; children: Cecily Elizabeth, Celeste Elaine. BS, Tex. Tech. U., 1968; MS, Iowa State U., 1970, PhD, 1972. Bd. cert. entomoloist. Prof. Entomology Purdue U., West Lafayette, Ind., 1972—; cons. Consortium for Internat. Crop Protection, Champaign, Ill., 1985—, Food and Agr. Orgn. UN, 1985—. Contbr. articles to profl. jours. Mem. Entomol. Soc. Am. (Ext. Achievement award 1984, award of merit 1985), Royal Entomol. Soc. London, Am. Soc. Agronomy, Sigma Xi, Alpha Zeta, Gamma Sigma Delta. Avocations: running, woodworking. Office: Purdue U 1158 Entomology Hall West Lafayette IN 47907-1158

EDWARDS, CHET, congressman; b. Corpus Christi, Tex., Nov. 24, 1951. BA, Tex. A&M U.; MBA, Harvard U. Legislative and dist. aide to Rep. Teague 1974-77; assoc. Trammell Crow Ptnrs.; pres. Edwards Communications Corp.; state senator, 1983-90; chmn. Tex. Sunset Commn.; mem. 102nd-106th Congresses from 11th Tex. dist., Washington, D.C., 1991—; dem. cheif dep. whip 102nd-103rd Congresses from 11th Tex. dist., Washington, D.C.; mem. appropriations com. 102nd-103rd Congresses from 11th Tex. dist., Washington; mem. Nat. Security Com., ranking min. mem. vets. affrs. subcom. on hosp. and health care. Office: US House of Reps 2459 Rayburn Washington DC 20515-0003*

EDWARDS, CHRISTINE ANNETTE, lawyer, securities firm executive; b. Ft. Monmouth, N.J., Aug. 30, 1952; d. Harry W. Jr. and Elizabeth Power; m. John H. Edwards, Aug. 24, 1974; children: Lindsey, John. BA, U. Md., College Park, 1974; JD with honors, U. Md., Balt., 1983. Bar: Md. 1983, D.C. 1984, Ill 1990. With Sears, Roebuck and Co., Md., 1971-81; sr. paralegal, staff asst. Sears, Roebuck and Co., Washington, 1981-83, atty. govt. affairs, 1983-87; asst. v.p., dir. govt. affairs Dean Witter Fin. Svcs. Group, Washington, 1987-88; v.p., gen. counsel Dean Witter Fin. Svcs. Group, Lincolnshire, Ill., 1988-89, sr. v.p., 1989-91; exec. v.p., sec., chief legal officer Dean Witter Fin. Svcs. Group, N.Y.C., 1991-97; exec. v.p., chief legal officer, corp. sec. Morgan Stanley Dean Witter & Co. (merger Dean Witter Discover & Co. with Morgan Stanley & Co. Inc.), N.Y.C., 1997—; mem. bd. Fin. Svcs. Coun., Washington, 1990—; bd. trustees Nat. Found. for Consumer Credit Counseling Svcs., Silver Spring, Md., 1990-92; mem. Women in Housing and Fin., Washington, 1982—, SAI Letigation Com., 1995—, N.Y. Stock Exchange Legal Adv. Com., 1992-95; bd. dirs. Chgo. Bd. of Options Exchange, SPS Transaction Svcs. Inc.; exec. v.p., chief legal officer, corp. sec. CLO Roundtable, 1995—. Recipient Disting. Mem. award Women in Housing and Fin., Washington, 1988; named 1 of 50 Top Women Lawyers Nat. Law Journal, 1998. Mem. ABA, Securities Industry Assn. (mem. fed. regulation com. 1990—). Office: Morgan Stanley Dean Witter & Co Law Dept 1585 Broadway 38th Flr New York NY 10036-8200*

EDWARDS, CLIFFORD HENRY COAD, law educator; b. Jamalpur, Bihar, India, Nov. 8, 1924; s. George Henry Probyn and Constance Ivy (Coad) E.; m. Kathleen Mary Faber, Jan. 6, 1951; children: Jeanette Marie, John Philip, Michael Hugh, Margaret Susan. LLB with 1st class honors, U. London, 1945. Sr. lectr. Kumasi Coll., Chana, 1956-58; assoc. prof. law U. Man., Winnipeg, 1958-64, prof., dean Sch. Law, 1964-79, dean emeritus, 1986—; pres. Man. Law Reform Commn., 1979—; Queen's coun., 1980. Recipient Stanton Tchg. Award for Excellence, U. Man., 1994. Mem. Soc. Internat. Ministries (chmn. 1984-90), Can. Bar Assn., Man. Bar Assn. (Disting. Svc. award 1995). Baptist. Office: University of Manitoba, Robson Hall, Fort Garry Campus, Winnipeg, MB Canada R3T 2N2

EDWARDS, D. M., retail, wholesale distribution and commercial real estate investment executive; b. Tyler, Tex., Apr. 12, 1953; s. Welby Clell and Davida (Mount) E.; m. Susan Alicia Pappas, 1984 (div. 1986). AA cum laude, Tyler Jr. Coll., 1974; BBA, Baylor U., 1976. Corp. coord. Dillard Dept. Stores, Inc., Ft. Worth, 1976-77; exec. v.p. W.C. Supply Co., Tyler, 1977-83; pres., owner Walker Auto Spring, Inc., Shreveport, La., 1978-88, Edwards & Assocs., Inc., 1984-96; v.p. W.C. Square, Inc., 1976-92; chmn. bd. dirs., CEO Pruitt Co. Inc., Houston, 1988—; chmn. bd., CEO Odessa Spring Brake & Axle, Inc., 1991—, pres., owner Shreveport Spring, Brake & Axle, Inc., 1998—; comml. real estate investor, Shreveport, La., Houston, Odessa, and Tyler Tex; gen. prin. ESE Properties, Tyler, 1991—; mng. gen. ptnr. Heritage Dr. Plz. Office Stes., 1992-95. Mem. planning com. Tyler Heritage Tour, 1982-83; originator Designer Show-Case, Tyler, 1983; founder, chmn. Rose Garden Trust Fund, 1981-87; bd. dirs. Carnegie History Ctr., 1984-85; chmn. merger com. Smith County Hist. Soc. and Carnegie History Ctr. merger, 1993-94; pres. East Tex. Baylor Club, 1986-87, scholarship com. chair, 1997—, Smith County Youth Found., 1986-87, mem., bd. dirs., 1984-91; pres. East Tex. State Fair, 1991-94; bd. assocs. East Tex. Bapt. U., Marshall, 1988—, v.p. bd. assocs., 1990-91, pres. bd. assocs., 1991-93; mem. exec. com. bd. trustees East Tex. Bapt. U., Marshall, 1996—, mem. exec. com., East Texas State Fair, 1990—; V.P. Camp Fannin Assoc., 1992-97; Tyler, 1992—; trustee Timberline Bapt. Camp and Conf. Ctr., 1987-90, treas., 1989-90; mem. Smith County Hist. Commn, 1984-85, 91-94; chmn. stewardship com. First Bapt. Ch. Tyler, 1995-96, mem. fin. com. 1997—. Mem. Tyler Area C. of C., Smith County Hist. Soc. (chmn. bd. govs. 1984-85, 87-88, pres. 1984-85, bd. govs. 1991-94), Hist. Tyler, Inc., Tyler Jaycees (v.p. 1982-83, bd. dir. 1981-85), Nat. Trust for Hist. Preservation, SCV (treas. camp 124, 1979-83). mem. Rotary Club of Tyler, 1997—; mem. brd. of dir., Rotary Club of Tyler, 1998—; Paul Harris fell. of Rotary intl., 1998; Baptist. Clubs: Willow Brook Country (stockholder), Hollytree Country. Home: 3102 Bracken Dr Tyler TX 75701-7844 Office: PO Box 929 Tyler TX 75710-0929 also: Mountwood Ranch RR 17 Box 30 Tyler TX 75704-9817

EDWARDS, DALE LEON, library director; b. Nampa, Idaho; s. Wayne Martin and Thelma Lucile Edwards; m. Julie Ann Rosa, Aug. 19, 1975; children: David, Corey, Stephen, Lisa, Russell. BA, Brigham Young U., 1980, M of Libr. and Info. Sci., 1990. Program dir., announcer Sta. KSUB, Cedar City, Utah, 1977-80; news dir. Sta. KRPX, Price, Utah, 1980-84; news writer Sun Advocate Newspaper, Price, 1984-86; dir. Learning Resource Ctr., Price Libr., Price, 1986-90; dir. libr. svcs. Treasure Valley Community Coll., Ontario, Oreg., 1990—; legis. com. mem. Utah Libr. Assn., Salt Lake City, 1986-90. Recipient Excellence in Reporting award Utah Sch. Bds. Assn., 1985. Mem. ALA, Oreg. Libr. Assn., Oreg. C.C. Libr. Assn. (pres. 1993-94), Oreg. Edn. Assn. (legis. com. 1990—), East Oreg. Libr. Assn. (pres. 1997—), Pacific N.W. Libr. Assn., Treasure Valley Chorale (pres. 1991-93), Beta Phi Mu. Mormon. Avocations: music, dancing, sports. Office: Treasure Valley CC Libr 650 College Blvd Ontario OR 97914-3423

EDWARDS, DANIEL PAUL, lawyer; educator; b. Enid, Okla., Apr. 15, 1940; s. Daniel Paul and Joye Virginia (van Horn) E.; m. Virginia Lee Kidd, Mar. 27, 1976; children: Austin Daniel, David Paul, Anne Marie. BA, U. Okla., 1962; JD, Harvard Law Sch., 1965. Bar: Colo. 1965, Hawaii, 1987, Ariz. 1988. Ptnr., v.p. Cole, Helox, Tolley, Edwards & Keene, P.C., Colorado Springs, 1965-82; sole practice, Colorado Springs, 1983-94; ptnr. Edwards & Sabo, Colorado Springs, 1994—; lectr. law Colo. Coll., 1976-87. Pres. Springs Area Beautiful Assn., 1978. Mem. ABA, Colo., Ariz. and Hawaii Bar Assn., Harvard Law Sch. Assn. Colo. (pres. 1986-87), El Paso Club, Broadmoor Golf Club, Cheyenne Mt. Club, Garden of the Gods Club, Kapalua Tennis Club, Phi Beta Kappa, Phi Delta Theta. Republican. Presbyterian.

EDWARDS, DANIEL WALDEN, lawyer; b. Vancouver, Wash., Aug. 7, 1950; s. Chester W. Edwards and Marilyn E. Russell; m. Joan S. Heller, Oct. 18, 1987; children: Nathaniel, Matthew, Stephen, Alexander. BA in Psychology magna cum laude, Met. State Coll., Denver, 1973, BA in Philosophy, 1974; JD, U. Colo., 1976. Bar: Colo. 1977, U.S. Dist. Ct. Colo. 1977. Dep. pub. defender State of Colo., Denver, 1977-79, Littleton, 1979-81, Pueblo, 1981-86; head office pub. defender State of Colo., Brighton, 1987-89; mem. jud. faculty State of Colo., 1988-91; sole practitioner Denver, 1991-93; magistrate Denver Juvenile Ct., 1993—; instr. sch. of law U. Denver, 1988-91, adj. prof., 1991—, coach appellate advocacy team, 1991—; adv. coun. Colo. Legal Svcs., 1989—; adj. mem. Colo. Supreme Ct. Grievance Com., 1991—. Author: Basic Trial Practice: An Introduction to Persuasive Trial Techniques, 1995. Mem. visual arts com. City Arts III, 1989-90, com. chmn., mem. adv. coun., 1991; bd. dirs. Metropolitan State Coll., Alumni Assn., 1991-92; vol. lectr. CSE Thursday Night Bar Pro Se Divorce Clinic, 1991—. Named Pub. Defender of Yr. Colo. State Pub. Defender's Office, 1985, Outstanding Colo. Criminal Def. Atty., 1989. Mem. ABA, Assn. Trial Lawyers Am., Colo. Bar Assn., Adams County Bar Asss., Denver Bar Assn., Met. State Coll. Alumni Assn. (bd. dirs. 1991—). Home: 2335 Clermont St Denver CO 80207-3134 Office: Denver Juvenile Ct Divsn 6 City and County Bldg Denver CO 80202

EDWARDS, DARREL, psychologist; b. San Francisco, July 9, 1943; s. Darrus and Rose Pearl (Sannar) E.; children: Alexander Hugh, Peter David, James Royce. BS in Psychology and Philosophy, Brigham Young U., 1965, MS in Psychology and Philosophy, 1967, PhD in Clin. Psychology and Philosophy, 1968. Diplomate Am. Bd. Profl. Psychology. Postdoctoral fellow in psycholinguistics Pa. State U., 1969; commd. lt. (j.g.) USN, 1970, advanced through grades to lt. comdr., 1978; dir. psychologist Tri Community Svc. Systems, San Diego, 1973-78; prof. Calif. Sch. Profl. Psychology, San Diego, 1971-78; dir. Grid Rsch., San Diego, 1978-83; pres. The Edwards Assoc., San Diego, 1983—; pres. Strategic Vision, 1987—; cons. strategist for govt. and pvt. sector, U.S., Eng., France, Germany, Italy, Mex., Brazil, Argentina, Russia, Republic of China, Japan, Can., 1978—; established Inst. for Value-Centered Life, 1999. Co-inventor in field; contbr. articles to profl. jours. Cons., researcher U.S., U.K., France, Germany, Hungary, Japan, Brazil, Argentina, Mexico, Colombia, Kenya, Central America, India, Italy, Republic of China, Russia, numerous other countries, 1986—. Mem. Am. Psychol. Assn. Achievements include creation of Values Centered research and consulting procedures, The Inst. for Value Centered Life, Training Value Centered Vision of principles of excellence; total quality measures for the automotive industry; total customer experience measures for 30 product and service categories; Values in America bi-annual survey; four fold principles of motivation; ValueCentered theory, clinical interview, and intervention; quality research in medicine service delivery and outcomes. Office: The Edwards Assocs PO Box 420429 San Diego CA 92142-0429

EDWARDS, DONALD MERVIN, biological systems engineering educator, university dean; b. Tracy, Minn., Apr. 16, 1938; s. Mervin B. and Helen L. (Halstenrud) E.; m. Judith Lee Wilson, Aug. 8, 1964; children: John, Joel, Jeffrey, Mary. B.S., S.D. State U., 1960, M.S., 1961; Ph.D. in Agrl. Engring. Purdue U., 1966. Registered profl. engr. With soil conservation svc. U.S. Dept. Agr., Marshall, Minn., 1957-62; teaching, rsch. asst. S.D. State U. and Purdue U., 1960-66; assoc. prof. agrl. engring. U. Nebr., Lincoln, 1966-71, prof., 1971-80; asst. dean Coll. Engring and Architecture U. Nebr., 1970-73, assoc. dean, dir. Engring Rsch. Ctr., Coll. Engring and Tech., 1973-80, dir. Energy Rsch and Devel. Ctr., 1976-80; prof. and chmn. dept. agrl. engring Mich. State U., East Lansing, 1980-89; prof. biol. systems engring., dean Coll. Agrl. Scis. and Natural Resources U. Nebr., Lincoln, 1989—; mem. Engring. Accreditation Commn. of Accreditation Bd. Engring. and Tech.; collaborator, cons. to numerous industries and agys., 1966—. Contbr. numerous articles on irrigation, water pollution, remote sensing, energy, agrl., natural resources and engring. edn. to profl. jours. Active Boy Scouts Am., Am. Field Svc., 4-H; past bd. dirs. Nat. Safety Coun.; past chmn. bd. dirs. Lincoln Transp. System. Recipient Massey-Furguson award Am. Soc of Agriculture Engineers, 1994, Outstanding Tchr. award U. Nebr. Fellow Am. Soc. Engring. Edn., Am. Soc. Agrl. Engrs.; mem. AAAS, NSPE (nat. bd. dirs., nat. v.p.), Profl. Engrs. Nebr., Mich. Soc. Profl. Engrs., Coun. for Agrl. Sci. and Tech., Farmhouse Club, Sigma Xi, Alpha Gamma Rho, Triangle. Home: 11420 Wenzel Dr Lincoln NE 68527-9484 Office: U Nebr Agrl Hall Rm 103 Lincoln NE 68583

EDWARDS, DORIS PORTER, computer specialist; b. Lambert, Miss., Jan. 18, 1962; d. Willie Morris and Carrie Mae (Tillman) E.; 1 child, Stacy Nicole. AA in Computer Sci., Draughons Coll., Memphis, 1981. Counselor French Riviera Spa, Memphis, 1989-90; pvt. practice, computer application developer Memphis, 1990—; owner, fin. cons., fund locator Developing Processing in Comm., Memphis, 1998—. Developer cosmetic cream. Jehovah's Witness. Avocations: mathematics, reading. Home and Office: 2638 Burns Ave Memphis TN 38114-4913

EDWARDS, DURWOOD, federal judge; b. 1941. JD, South Tex. U., 1973. Pvt. practice, 1974-80; apptd. magistrate judge we. dist. U.S. Dist. Ct. Tex., 1980. Fax: (210) 703-2074. Office: 111 E Broadway St Rm D-218 Del Rio TX 78840-5573

EDWARDS, ELGIN C., federal judge. Magistrate judge for ctrl. Calif., U.S. Magistrate Ct., Santa Ana, 1991—. Office: US Magistrate Ct 34 Civic Center Plz Ste 904 Santa Ana CA 92701-4044

EDWARDS, ELWOOD GENE, mathematician, educator; b. New Bern, N.C., Jan. 5, 1944; s. Calvin and Blanche Ethel (Edwards) E.; m. Lucretia Walker; children: Ronnie, Glenn, Myrei Chrysti. BA, CCNY, 1966; MA, NYU, 1969; MS, Columbia Pacific U., 1982, PhD, 1982; DD (hon.), Am. Bapt. U., 1980. Cert. math. tchr., N.Y. Ins. cons. Met. Life Ins. Co., N.Y.C., 1966-68; tchr. math., math. staff developer, tchr. trainer N.Y.C. Bd. Edn., 1968—; lectr., adj. prof. CUNY, 1969-78; tax preparer Bklyn., 1973—; tutor math., Spanish, English, Bklyn., 1969—. Contbr. articles to profl. jours. V.p. 89th St./Ave. B Block Assn., Bklyn., 1987-89. Mem. AAAS, Soc. for Indsl. and Applied Math., Am. Statis. Assn., The Planetarium Soc., Nat. Coun. Tchrs. Math., Math. Assn. Am., Am. Math. Soc., N.Y. Acad. Sci., Phi Theta Kappa. Democrat. Universalist. Avocations: reading, walking, bowling, golf, creating recreational math puzzles.

EDWARDS, ESTHER G., museum administrator, former record, film and entertainment company executive; b. Oconee, Ga.; d. Berry and Bertha Ida (Fuller) Gordy; m. George H. Edwards, Apr. 12, 1951 (dec.); 1 son (by previous marriage), Robert Berry Bullock. Ed., Howard U., Wayne State U. Sr. v.p., sec., dir. Motown Record Corp., Detroit, 1959-1988; with Jobete Music Pub. Co., Inc., 1959—; sr. v.p., corporate sec. Motown Industries, Hollywood, Calif., 1973-88; founder, chmn., CEO Motown Hist. Mus., Detroit, 1985—; dir. Bank of the Commonwealth, 1972-79. Bd. dirs. Detroit Econ. Growth Corp.; founder, exec. dir. Gordy Found., 1968—; chmn. Wayne County Dem. Women's Com., 1956; Mich. del.-at-large Dem. Nat. Conv., 1960; bd. dirs. Martin Luther King Ctr. for Non-Violent Social Change; former trustee Detroit Inst. Arts; mem. corp. Lawrence Tech. U., Southfield, Mich.; commr. Mich. Hist. Commn., 1989-95. Mem. Greater Detroit C. of C. (treas., exec. bd. 1973-79), Met. Detroit Conv. and Visitor's Bur. (dir.), Econ. Club Detroit (dir.), African Am. Heritage Assn. (founder, chmn.), Alpha Kappa Alpha, Gamma Phi Delta. Office: Motown Hist Mus 2648 W Grand Blvd Detroit MI 48208-1237 *I accredit my accomplishments to keeping an open mind, listening to understand, communicating, accepting responsibility; recognizing opportunities; being responsible, goal oriented and performing to the best of my ability, caring about the welfare and well being of others, especially youth.*

EDWARDS, FRANCIS CHARLES, municipal official; b. Trenton, N.J., July 11, 1947; s. Frank Layton and Jane Marie (Archer) E.; m. Gloria Theresa Gioscio, June 14, 1969; children: Elaine Elizabeth, Denise Michelle. BA in Secondary Edn., Trenton State Coll., 1965-69; MA in Geography, Rutgers U., 1972-74; M in Regional Planning, Pa. State U., 1974-76; M in Pub. Adminstrn., Old Dominion U., 1978-81. Cmty. planner II Pasco County Fla. Planning Dept., Port Richey, 1976-77; city planner II Va. Beach Planning Dept., Va., 1977-81, devel. review coord., 1981-84; dir. planning and zoning Newport (R.I.) Planning Dept., 1984-87; acting mgr. City of Newport, R.I., 1986-87, mgr., 1987-95; mgr. Twp. of Howell, N.J., 1995-97; mcpl. mgr. Twp. of Lakewood, N.J., 1997—. With U.S. Army, 1969-71. Mem. Am. Planning Assn., Am. Inst. Cert. Planners, Am. Soc. Pub. Adminstrn., Internat. City Mgmt. Assn., R.I. City and Town Mgmt. Assn. (pres.), N.J. Mcpl. Mgrs. Assn., Phi Kappa Phi, Pi Alpha Alpha. Avocations: running, weight training. Office: Mcpl Bldg Lakewood NJ 08701

EDWARDS, FRANKLIN R., economist, educator, consultant; b. Palmerton, Pa., May 5, 1937; s. Franklin Richard and Mary Edytha (Morgan) E.; m. Linda Nasif, June 9, 1968; children—Rebecca, Jarett. BA in Econs., Bucknell U., 1958, MA in Econs., 1960; PhD in Econs., Harvard U., 1964; JD, NYU, 1968. Economist Bankers Trust Co., N.Y.C., 1961; economist Fed. Res. Bd., Washington, 1962, 63-64; sr. economist Office of Comptroller of Currency, Washington, 1964-66; asst. prof. Bus. Sch. Columbia U., N.Y.C., 1966-68, assoc. prof. Bus. Sch., 1968-74, prof. Bus. Sch., 1974—, vice dean acad. affairs, 1979-81, dir., prof. Columbia Futures Ctr., 1980—; vis. scholar Am. Enterprise Inst., Washington, 1994-95; vis. prof. Inst. des Sci. Economique, Ctr. Rsch. Interdisciplinaires Droit-Economie, U. Cath., Louvain, Belgium, 1969-70. Assoc. editor Jour. of Futures Markets; editor Jour. Fin. Svcs.; contbr. articles to profl. jours. Mem. adv. bd. Futures Industry Assn. Bd., 1981-88; nominating com. Am. Stock Exchange, 1988-90; mem. bus. conduct com. N.Y. Merc. Exchange, 1989-92. Mem. Am. Econ. Assn., Am. Fin. Assn., Soc. Royale D'Economie Politique Belgique (hon.), Shadow Fin. Regulations Com., Fin. Economists Roundtable. Home: 25 Fairview Rd Scarsdale NY 10583-2137 Office: Columbia U Dept Fin Uris Hall 625 3022 Broadway New York NY 10027-6945

EDWARDS, FRED L., JR., writer consultant; b. Muskogee, Okla., Oct. 3, 1932; s. Fred L. Edwards Sr. and Mary Jane (Stewart) Johnson; m. Wilma Pauline Utter, Nov. 10, 1950; children: Fred Curtis, Jerri Jane. BA in Sociology summa cum laude, Park Coll., 1970; postgrad., U. S. Fla., 1980-82. Enlisted USMC, 1949, advanced through grades to lt. col., 1973, ret., 1979; pres. F.L. Edwards & Co., St. Petersburg, Fla., 1979-87; exec. asst. to pres. EXAMCO Inc., Kenner, La., 1990-92; gen. ptnr. Fred Edwards Writer-Cons., St. Petersburg, 1987-97; free-lance writer, St. Petersburg, 1979-87; writer, cons. Sea Sch., St. Petersburg, 1986-88, Houston Marine Tng. Svcs., Kenner, 1989-90; tech. cons. Sailors' Gazette, St. Petersburg, 1986-88. Author: Sailing as a Second Language, 1988, Charter Your Boat for Profit, 1989, Making Money with Boats, 1996. Bd. dirs. Vol. Action Com., St. Petersburg, 1980; mem. Mayor's Adv. Com., South Pasadena, Fla., 1992-99, City Charter Rev. Com., South Pasadena, 1992-93, City Fin. com., 1996-99. Decorated Legion of Merit, Meritorious Svc. medal; recipient George Washington hon. medal Freedom's Found; named Eagle Scout Boy Scouts Am. Mem. Ret. Officers Assn. (chpt. pres. 1996-97, chmn. legis. affairs v.p. 1998-99, state coun. 1996-99, v.p. state coun. 1989-99), Pinellas County Veterans Liaison Coun. (v.p. 1997-99). Republican. Home and Office: Ste 607 7979 Sailboat Key Blvd S Saint Petersburg FL 33707

EDWARDS, GEOFFREY HARTLEY, newspaper publisher; b. Liverpool, Eng., Mar. 28, 1936; s. James S. and Edith (Ellison) E.; m. Pamela Duncan, Oct. 9, 1965; children: Robert James, Alistair Duncan. HNC Mech. Engring., Merseyside Tech. Coll., Birkenhead. Plant mgr. Inverest Paper Group, Derbyshire, Eng., 1962-65; gen. mgr. Liverpool Web Offset Ltd., 1965-68; asst. gen. mgr. Liverpool Daily Post & Echo, 1968-71, dir., gen. mgr., 1971-77; pub. Jour. Newspapers, Inc., Washington, 1977-91, Army Times, Washington, 1991-93; pub., CEO Current Newspapers, Washington, 1993-94; v.p. Washington Times, 1994—. Bd. dirs. Greter Washington Bd. Trade, Cultural Alliance Greater Washington, pres., 1984-86; mem. kennedy Ctr. Cmty. & Friend Bd., 1987—; campaign chmn. United Way of Nat. Capital Area, 1989, pres., 1998—. Mem. Brit. Newspaper Soc. (coun. 1974-77), Indsl. Rels. Newspaper Soc. (vice chmn. 1974-77).

EDWARDS, GEORGE ALVA, physician, educator; b. Killeen, Tex., Oct. 19, 1916; s. John Clem and Maude May (Lam) E.; m. Winnie Belle Landes, Jan. 23, 1946; children—Karen Leigh, David Glen. B.A., Howard Payne Coll., 1939; postgrad., N. Tex. State Coll., 1946; M.D., U. Tex., Southwestern Med. Sch., 1950. Intern Johns Hopkins Hosp., Balt., 1950-51, resident, 1952-53; resident Duke Hosp., Durham, N.C., 1951-52, Firmin Desloge Hosp., St. Louis, 1953-54; asst. chief med. service VA, St. Louis, 1954-55; chief med. service VA Hosp, McKinney, Tex., 1955-59, Pitts., 1959-66; asst. chief med. service Dallas, 1966-68, chief of staff, 1972-84, assoc. chief staff for extended care, 1984-85; chief med. service Cin., 1968-72; asst. prof. Southwestern Med. Sch., U. Tex., Dallas, 1955-59, assoc. prof., 1966-68, prof. medicine, 1972-86, emeritus prof., 1987—, asst. dean, 1973-84; assoc. prof. U. Pitts., 1959-66; prof. U. Cin., 1968-72. Served with USAAF, 1940-46. Decorated Air medal. Fellow ACP; mem. Alpha Omega Alpha. Baptist. Home: 3630 Granada Ave Dallas TX 75205-2014

EDWARDS, GEORGE KENT, lawyer; b. Ogden, Utah, Oct. 3, 1939; s. George and S. Ruth Edwards; m. Linda E. Brown; children: Scott M., Stacey R., Mark D. B.A., Occidental Coll., 1961; J.D., U. Calif.-Berkeley, 1964. Bar: Calif. 1965, Alaska 1966. Legislative counsel Alaska Legislature, 1964-66; ptnr. law firm Stevens, Savage, Holland, Erwin & Edwards, Anchorage, 1966-67; dep. atty. gen. Alaska, 1967-68, atty. gen., 1968-70; U.S. atty. Dist. Alaska, 1971-77; pvt. practice, 1977-81; shareholder Hartig Rhodes Norman Mahoney & Edwards, Anchorage, 1981—; mem. Nat. Conf. Commrs. Uniform State Laws, 1968-70; chmn. Gov. Alaska Planning Coun. Adminstrn. Criminal Justice, 1968-70; guest lectr. bus. law U. Alaska, 1981-82; guest editorial columnist Anchorage Times, 1982-88. Co-author: Considerations in Buying or Selling a Business in Alaska, 1992. Pres. Greater Anchorage Area Young Reps., 1967; chmn. Carrs Great Alaska Shootout, 1995; pres. bd. dirs. Miss Alask Scholarship Pageant, 1980-84; bd. dirs. Anchorage Crime Stoppers, 1981-85; pres. Common Sense Alaska, 1982-85, 91—; bd. dirs., 1986—. Mem. ABA, Calif. Bar Assn., Alaska Bar Assn., Nat. Assn. Attys. Gen., Nat. Assn. Former U.S. Attys. (bd. dirs., pres.), Anchorage C. of C. (bd. dirs. 1989-96), Rotary (scholarship chair 1993, 95-98), Phi Delta Phi, Sigma Alpha Epsilon (Outstanding Sr. award Calif. Epsilon chpt. 1961). Home: 2113 Duke Dr Anchorage AK 99508-4553 Office: 717 K St Anchorage AK 99501-3330

EDWARDS, GERALD, plastics company executive; b. Chgo., July 13; m. Jada; children: Charlene, Candice Rae, Gerald II. Student, Heidelberg Coll. With Ford Motor Co.; asst. plant mgr., then plant mgr. Detroit Plastic Molding; pres., CEO Engineered Plastic Products, 1987—. Office: Engineered Plastic Products Inc 699 James L Hart Pkwy Ypsilanti MI 48197

EDWARDS, GLENN THOMAS, history educator; b. Portland, Oreg., June 14, 1931; s. Glenn Thomas E. and Marie Ann (Cheska) McMullen; m. Nannette Wilhelmina McAndie, June 15, 1957; children: Randall Thomas, Stephanie Lynn. B.A., Willamette U., 1953; M.A., U. Oreg., 1960, Ph.D., 1963. Asst. prof. San Jose State U., 1962-64; asst. prof. Whitman Coll., Walla Walla, Wash., 1964-68, assoc. prof., 1968-75, prof., 1976—; cons. TV documentary Yakima Valley Mus. on William O. Douglas, Yakima, Wash., 1981-82; trustee Wash. Commn. of Humanities, Olympia, 1980-86. Author: Sowing Good Seeds: The Northwest Suffrage Campaigns of Susan B. Anthony, 1990, The Triumph of Tradition: The Emergence of Whitman College, 1859-1924, 1992; co-editor: Experiences in a Promised Land: Essays on Pacific Northwest History, 1986; contbr. articles to profl. jours. Mem. pub. edn. adv. com. State Supt. of Pub. Instrn., Olympia, 1975-78; mem. bd. trustees Wash. State Hist. Soc., 1983-92. Served with U.S. Army, 1954-56. Grantee Am Philos. Soc., 1971. Mem. Orgn. Am. Historians, Western History Assn., Oreg. Hist. Soc., Washington Hist. Soc. (photography cons. 1980). Congregationalist. Office: Whitman Coll Dept History Walla Walla WA 99362

EDWARDS, HAROLD MORTIMER, mathematics educator; b. Champaign, Ill., Aug. 6, 1936; s. Harold Mortimer and Marian Bell (Scarlett) E.; m. Betty Rollin, Jan. 21, 1979. BA, U. Wis., 1956; MA, Columbia U., 1957; PhD, Harvard U., 1961. Instr. Harvard U., 1961-62; rsch. assoc. Columbia U., 1962-63, asst. prof., 1963-66; asst. prof. N.Y. U., N.Y.C., 1966-69; assoc. prof. N.Y. U., 1969-79, prof. math., 1979—; vis. sr. lectr. Australian Nat. U., 1971. Author: Advanced Calculus, 1969, Riemann's Zeta Function, 1974, Fermat's Last Theorem, 1977, Galois Theory, 1984, Divisor Theory, 1990, Linear Algebra, 1995. Guggenheim fellow, 1981-82. Mem. Am. Math. Soc. (Steele prize 1980), Math. Assn.

Am., N.Y. Acad. Scis. Home: 67 Park Ave New York NY 10016-2557 Office: 251 Mercer St New York NY 10012-1110

EDWARDS, HARRY LAFOY, lawyer; b. Greenville, S.C., July 29, 1936; s. George Belton and Mary Olive (Jones) E.; m. Suzanne Copeland, June 16, 1956; 1 child, Margaret Peden. LLB, U. S.C., 1963, JD, 1970. Bar: S.C. 1963, U.S. dist. Ct. S.C. 1975, U.S. Ct. Apls. (4th cir.) 1974. Assoc. Edwards and Edmunds, Greenville, 1963; v.p., sec., dir. Edwards Co., Inc., Greenville, 1963-65; atty. investment legal dept. Liberty Life Ins. Co., Greenville, 1965-67, asst. sec., asst. v.p., head investment legal dept., 1967-70; asst. sec. Liberty Corp., 1970-75; asst. v.p. Liberty Life Ins. Co., 1970-75; sec. Bent Tree Corp., CEL, Inc., 1970-75; sec., dir. Westchester Mall, Inc., 1970-75; asst. sect. Libco, Inc., Liberty Properties, Inc., 1970-75; pvt. practice, Greenville, 1975—. Editor U. S.C. Law Rev., 1963. Com. mem. Hipp Fund Spl. Edn., Greenville County Sch. System; mem. Boyd C. Hipp II Scholarship Com., Wofford Coll. Spartanburg, S.C.; mem. scholarship com. Liberty Scholars, U. S.C., 1984, 86-99. With USAFR, 1957-64. Mem. ABA, S.C. Bar Assn., Greenville County Bar Assn., Phi Delta Phi, Greenville Lawyers, Poinsett Club (Greenville). Baptist. Home: 106 Ridgeland Dr Greenville SC 29601-3017 Office: PO Box 10350 Greenville SC 29603-0350

EDWARDS, HARRY T., federal judge; b. N.Y.C., Nov. 3, 1940; s. George H. E. and Arline (Ross) Lyle; children: Brent, Michelle. BS, Cornell U., 1962; JD, U. Mich., 1965. Assoc. firm Seyfarth, Shaw, Fairweather & Geraldson, Chgo., 1965-70; prof. law U. Mich., 1970-76, 77-80; vis. prof. law Harvard U., 1975-76, prof., 1976-77; now judge U.S. Ct. Appeals, Washington, 1980—; vis. prof. Free U. Brussels, 1974; dir. AMTRAK, 1977-80, chmn. bd., 1979-80; disting. lectr. law Duke U., 1983-85; lectr. law Georgetown Law Ctr., 1986-87; chief judge U.S. Ct. Appeals (D.C. cir.), Washington, 1994—; adj. prof. law NYU Law Sch., 1990—; lectr. Harvard Law Sch., 1982-88, Mich. Law Sch., 1989—. Mem. Adminstrv. Conf. of U.S., 1976-80. Co-author: Labor Relations Law in the Public Sector, 1975, 79, 85, Lawyer as a Negotiator, 1977, Collective Bargaining and Labor Arbitration, 1979, Higher Education and the Law, 1979. Mem. Nat. Acad. Arbitrators (dir. 1975-80, v.p. 1978-80), Am. Acad. Arts and Scis., Am. Arbitration Assn. (dir. 1979-80), Am. Bar Assn. (sec. sect. labor law 1976-77), Am. Law Inst., Order of Coif. Office: US Ct Appeals 333 Constitution Ave NW Washington DC 20001-2866

EDWARDS, HELEN THOM, physicist; b. Detroit, May 27, 1936; d. Edgar Robertson and Mary (Milner) Thom; m. Donald A. Edwards. BS in Physics, Cornell U., 1957, MA in Physics, 1963, PhD in Physics, 1966. Rsch. assoc. Cornell U., Ithaca, N.Y., 1966-70; assoc. head booster Fermi Nat. Accelerator Lab., Batavia, Ill., 1970-71, staff physicist, M.R., 1971-75, head switchyard extraction group, 1975-78, leader tevatron design group, 1978-79, dep. head saver div., 1980-81, dep. head accelerator div., 1981-86, head accelerator div., 1987-88; head accelerator constrn. div. SSC/URA, Dallas, 1989-90, tech. dir., 1990-91. Recipient Achievement in Accelerator Physics and Tech. U.S. Summer Sch. on Particle Accelerator Prize, 1985, Ernest O. Lawrence award Dept. of Energy, 1986, Nat. Medal Tech., 1989; MacArthur Found. Chgo. fellow, 1988. Fellow Am. Phys. Soc.; mem. NAE.

EDWARDS, HORACE BURTON, former state official, former oil pipeline company executive, management consultant; b. Tuscaloosa, Ala., May 20, 1925; children: Adrienne, Paul, David, Michael; m. Fran M. Allerheiligen, Sept. 3, 1994. BS in Naval Sci., Marquette U., 1947, BSME, 1948; MBA in Fin. Mgmt., Iona Coll., 1972; LDH (hon.), Tex. So. U., 1982; LLD, Stillman Coll., 1984. Registered profl. engr., Wis., Kans. Various engring. positions Allis Chalmers, 1948-52, GM, 1952-56, Conrac, 1956-63, Northrop, 1963-71; with Atlantic Richfield Co., 1967-80; mgr. planning, evaluation Atlantic Richfield Co., N.Y.C., 1976-79; v.p. planning, control Atlantic Richfield Co., L.A., 1979-80; pres., CEO, chmn. bd. dirs. ARCO Pipe Line Co., Independence, Kans., 1980-86; sec. transp. State of Kans., 1987-91; pres. Edwards and Assocs. Inc., Topeka, 1991—; mem. adv. bd. Energy Bur., Strategic Hwy. Rsch. Program. res. Mississippi Valley Conf. State Hwy. and Transp. Ofcls., 1989-90; trustee Kans. Coun. Econ. Edn., Topeka, 1981—, Leadership Independence, 1984-86, Kans. Ind. Coll. Fund, 1985-91, Stillman Coll., Tuscaloosa, Ala., 1985—, Ins. Logopedics, Wichita, Kans., 1985-91. Recipient Marquette U. Dist. Engring. Alumnus award, 1984. Mem. Am. Petroleum Inst., Assn. Oil Pipelines (mem. adv. com.), Am. Assn. Blacks in Energy (bd. dirs.), Kans. C. of C. and Industry (trustee Leadership Kans. 1983, bd. dirs. 1983-91), Kans. Contractors Assn., Assn. Gen. Contractors (assoc.). Office: Edwards & Assocs Inc 106 E 11th St Ste 1450 Kansas City MO 64106-2120 also: Edwards & Assocs Inc King Blvd 1805 N Dr Martin Luther Milwaukee WI 53212-3623*

EDWARDS, HOWARD LEE, retired petroleum company executive, lawyer; b. Baker City, Oreg., June 10, 1931; s. Elmer L. and Bernice (Stringham) E.; m. Carolyn Bagley, Mar. 19, 1954; children: Bryant B., H. McKay, Mitchell L., Paul S. B.S., Brigham Young U., 1955; postgrad., Stanford U., 1955-56, U. Utah, 1956-57; J.D., George Washington U., 1959. Bar: Utah 1959, Colo. 1981, Alaska 1982, Calif. 1987. Legal asst., atty. U.S. Dept. Interior, Washington and Salt Lake City, 1957-61; ptnr. Van Cott, Bagley, Cornwall & McCarthy, Salt Lake City, 1961-68; asst. gen. counsel Anaconda Co., N.Y.C., 1968, asst. to chmn. bd., 1969, v.p., sec., 1970-77; gen. atty. Denver, 1977-82, Anchorage, 1982-83; corp. sec. Atlantic Richfield Co., L.A., 1984-95; ret., 1995; bd. dirs. Dynatronics Corp. Trustee Rocky Mountain Mineral Law Found., 1968-87; mem. nat. adv. coun. Brigham Young U. Sch. Mgmt., 1972-85; mem. nat. adv. coun. Dixie Coll., St. George, Utah, 1987—, chmn., 1994-95; bd. visitors J. Reuben Clark Law Sch., 1980-83; bd. dirs. L.A. region NCCJ, 1987-94, Ettie Lee Homes for Youth, 1989—, Kostopoulos Dream Found., 1997—, Deseret Found.; chmn. cmty. adv. coun. Heart and Lung Rsch. Found.; mem. exec. bd. Verdugo Hills coun. Boy Scouts Am., 1992-95, Verdugo Hills Hosp. Found., 1992-95. Mem. Am. Mining Congress (chmn. pub. lands com. 1970-84, Disting. Svc. award 1983), Coun. on Fgn. Rels., Pacific Coun. on Internat. Policy, Brigham Young U. Alumni Assn. (bd. dirs. 1974-83, pres. 1980-81), Econ. Round Table, Rotary. Republican. Mem. LDS Ch. Home: PO Box 680934 Park City UT 84068-0934*

EDWARDS, IAN KEITH, retired obstetrician, gynecologist; b. Spartanburg, S.C., Mar. 2, 1926; s. James Smiley and Georgina (Waters) E.; m. Glenda Melissa Joselyn, Dec. 27, 1968; children—Darien, Jennifer, Carol, Terry. AB, Duke U., 1949, MD, 1953. Diplomate Am. Bd. Ob-Gyn. Spl. study pediatrics St. Bartholomew's Hosp., London, 1952; resident in ob-gyn Grady Meml. Hosp., Atlanta, 1955-58; chief ob-gyn Valley Forge (Pa.) Army Hosp., 1958-61; practice medicine specializing in ob-gyn Olney, Ill., 1969—; ptnr. Trover Clinic, Madisonville, Ky., 1961-68, Weber Med. Clinic, Olney, 1969-96; dir. dept. ob-gyn Weber Med. Clinic, 1970-74, 78-83, 93-95, Richland Meml. Hosp., 1989-95; chmn. bd. dirs. Weber Med. Clinic, 1983-87, med. dir., 1987-95; ret., 1996; chief staff Hopkins County Hosp., Ky., 1967-68, Richland Meml. Hosp., Olney, 1974-76; clin. instr. ob-gyn. U. Ky. Med. Ctr., Lexington, 1965-68; cons.; vice-chmn. Ill., sec. ACOG, adv. coun. dist. VI, 1990-93. Contbr. articles to med. jours. Citizen amb. Profl. Exchange Program, Moscow and St. Petersberg, Russia, 1992; mem. found. com. Olney Central Coll., long range planning and bldg. com. Served to capt. M.C., U.S. Army, 1954-55; Korea. Fellow ACOG (Ill. sec. dist. VI, vice chmn. 1990-93); mem. AMA, Phila. Obstet. Soc., Ill. Med. Soc., Hopkins County Med. Soc. (pres. 1968), Richland County Med. Soc. (pres. 1974-76), Am. Soc. Colposcopists and Cervical Pathology, Am. Assn. Gynecol. Laparoscopists, So. Ill. Med. Assn., Am. Legion. Democrat. Apostolic. Home: Rte 45 N PO Box 102 Louisville IL 62858-0102

EDWARDS, IRENE ELIZABETH (LIBBY EDWARDS), dermatologist, educator, researcher; b. Winston-Salem, N.C., Mar. 17, 1950; d. Robert Dixon Edwards and Irene Octavia (Temple) Fisher; m. Clayton Samuel Owens, Apr. 19, 1985; 1 child, Sarah Tay. BS magna cum laude, Wake Forest U., 1972; MD, Bowman Gray Sch. Medicine, 1976; postgrad., N.C. Bapt. Hosp., 1979, U. Ariz., 1981, 84. Diplomate Nat. Bd. Med. Examiners, Am. Bd. Internal Medicine, Am. Bd. Pediatrics, Am. Bd. Dermatology. Intern N.C. Bapt. Hosp., Winston-Salem, 1976-78, resident in pediatrics, 1978-79; resident in internal medicine U. Ariz. Health Scis. Ctr., Tucson, 1979-81, resident in dermatology, 1982-84; instr. dermatology U. Ariz. Coll. Medicine, Tucson, 1984-85, asst. prof. dermatology, 1985-90; chief section dermatology Tucson VA Med. Ctr., 1984-90; chief dermatology Carolinas Med. Ctr., Charlotte, N.C., 1990—; clin. assoc. prof. dermatology, clin. rsearcher Wake Forest U., Winston-Salem, 1993—; clin. assoc. prof. dermatology, clin. researcher U. N.C., Chapel Hill, 1993—; nat. lectr. in field. Author: Dermatology in Emergency Care, 1997; co-author: Genital Dermatology, 1994; contbr. chpts. to books, numerous articles to profl. jours. Reynolds scholar, 1969-72. Fellow Am. Acad. Dermatology, Am. Acad. Pediatrics; mem. Soc. Pediatric Dermatology, Internat. Soc. Tropical Dermatology, Soc. Investigative Dermatology, Women's Dermatologic Soc., Internat. Soc. for Study of Vulvovaginal Disease (sec.-gen.), Charlotte Dermatological Soc., Phi Beta Kappa, Alpha Epsilon Delta. Home and office: 2409 Cuthbertson Rd Waxhaw NC 28173-8110

EDWARDS, JACK, former congressman, lawyer; b. Birmingham, Ala., Sept. 20, 1928; s. William Jackson and Sue (Fuhrman) E.; m. Jolane Vander Sys, Jan. 30, 1954; children: Mrs. Richard Weavil, Richard Arnold. BS in Commerce and Bus. Adminstrn., U. Ala., 1952, LLB, 1954. Bar: Ala. 1954, D.C. 1983. Practice Mobile, 1954-64; mem. 89th-98th Congresses from 1st Dist. Ala., 1965-85; mem. com. appropriations; mem. def. and transp. sub-com.; vice chmn. Ho. Rep. Conf.; with Hand Arendall L.L.C., Mobile, Ala., 1985—; bd. dirs. The Southern Co., Holnam Inc., Northrop Grumman Corp., QMS, Inc. Trustee U. Ala. Served with USMC, 1946-48, 50-51. Mem. ABA, Ala. Bar Assn., Mobile Bar Assn. (sec. 1956), Mobile Jr. Bar Assn. (pres. 1957), D.C. Bar Assn., Mobile Area C. of C. (chmn. bd. 1986), Kappa Alpha (pres. 1951-53), Omicron Delta Kappa. Presbyterian. (elder). Office: First Nat Bank Bldg Ste 3000 Mobile AL 36601

EDWARDS, JAMES BENJAMIN, accountant, educator; b. Atlanta, Apr. 27, 1935; s. James T. and Frances L. (McEachern) E.; m. Virginia Ann Reagin, Feb. 21, 1958; children: James Benjamin II, Chad Reagin, Calli Ann, Judy Clair. *Son James B. Edwards, II is a Principal Systems Engineer with Viasoft, Inc. He is an accomplished trumpet player and holds an Associates degree in Computer Science from Midlands Technical College and a BBA degree in Business Administration from the University of South Carolina. Son Chad Reagin Edwards is a CAD program designer with Integraph Corporation. He is an accomplished drummer and holds a degree in Civil Engineering from Clemson University and a Masters degree in Structural Engineering from Carnegie-Mellon University. Daughter Calli Ann Edwards Wilson recently completed a Masters degree in Early Childhood Education at the University of South Carolina. She is an accomplished French Horn player and holds an undergraduate degree in Art from Columbia College. Daughter Judy Clair Edwards holds a Masters degree in Special Education for the Blind from the University of South Carolina and an undergraduate degree in Education from the University of South Carolina. She teaches the blind and creates braille and is an accomplished flute player. Wife Virginia Ann Edwards is the most valuable player of the family. She is the catalyst.* BBA in Fin., U. Ga., 1958, MBA, 1962, PhD in Bus. Adminstrn., 1971. CPA Tenn., Ga., S.C.; cert. mgmt. acct.; cert. internal auditor; cert. in data processing; cert. cost analyst. Contr. Better Maid Dairy Products, Inc., Athens, Ga., 1958-62; staff acct. Max M. Cuba & Co., Atlanta, 1962-63; mng. ptnr. Wilson, Edwards and Swang, accts., Nashville, 1964-66; ptnr. Q.F. Lester & Co., Athens, 1967-68; v.p., chmn. bd. dirs. Gen. Data Svc. Inc., Athens, Ga., 1970-71; internal cons. J.W. Hunt and Co., CPAs, Columbia, 1983-84; v.p. Integrated Cost Mgmt. Systems Inc., Arlington, Tex., 1990-91; instr. David Lipscomb Coll., Nashville, 1963-66; instr. Nashville Ctr. U. Tenn., 1964-66; instr. acctg. U. Ga., Athens, 1966-71; asst. prof. U. S.C., Columbia, S.C., 1971-73, assoc. prof., 1973-77, prof., 1977—, fellow Bus. Partnership Found., 1977-90; William W. Bruner Disting. Faculty fellow U. S.C., Columbia, 1990—; instr. staff tng. program local C.P.A. firms, Nashville, 1963-66. *James B. Edwards is an international management accounting consultant and a professor. Dr. Edwards has published approximately 80 articles in professional publications, receiving eight national awards for his writings. He is the author or coauthor of three books and served as assistant editor of Managerial Planning Magazine for five years. In 1986, he conducted a special study for the National Commission on Fraudulent Financial Reporting, "Expansion of Non-Audit Services and Auditor Independence." He is a contributing author to Evaluating the Performance of International Operations, published in 1989. Dr. Edwards has conducted training and consulting engagements for clients such as IBM Corp., Daimler-Benz Corp., Allied Corp., Wheel Trueing Co., ARAMCO, Smith & Nephew, Inc., Anchor Continental, Inc., NCR Corp., Milliken Research Company, Sonoco Products Company, Blue-Cross/Blue Shield of South Carolina, CMI, several State Societies of CPAs, and the US-SBA.* Editor: (ann. publs. Warren, Gorham & Lamont, Inc.) Emerging Practices in Cost Management and, Activity-Based Mnagment, Handbook of Cost Management for Service Industries, 1997—; contbr. articles on mgmt. acctg. to profl. publs. Coach Little League Baseball, Columbia, 1972-76; bd. dirs. Atlanta Bible Camp, Inc.; bd. dirs. Ga. Christian Found., Inc., pres., 1968-69; bd. dirs. Spring Valley Edn. Found., 1983-93, v.p., 1983-85, treas., 1985-93. Recipient 8 nat. awards for contbns. to acctg. lit. Mem. Am. Acctg. Assn., Am. Inst. CPAs, Inst. Internal Auditors, Planning Execs. Isnt. (asst. editor nat. mag. 1971-77), Am. Inst. Decision Scis. (v.p. Southeastern sect. 1975-76), Inst. Mgmt. Accts. (pres. Columbia chpt. 1973-74, nat. rsch. com. 1974-75, nat. edn. com. 1977-80, 95—, nat. dir. 1975-77, pres. Carolinas coun. 1976, nat. v.p. 1980-81), S.C. Soc. CPAs, S.C. Assn. Acctg. Instrs. (founding pres. 1972-73), Omicron Delta Epsilon, Beta Alpha Psi, Delta Sigma Pi, Sigma Chi. Mem. Ch. of Christ. Clubs: Five Points Optimist of Athens, Spring Valley Band Boosters. Office: c/o U SC Sch Acctg Darla Moore Sch 1705 College St Columbia SC 29208 *James B. Edwards is an international management accounting consultant and a professor. Dr. Edwards has published approximately 80 articles in professional publications, receiving eight national awards for his writings. He is the author or coauthor of three books and served as assistant editor of Managerial Planning Magazine for five years. In 1986, he conducted a special study for the National Commission on Fraudulent Financial Reporting, "Expansion of Non-Audit Services and Auditor Independence." He is a contributing author to Evaluating the Performance of International Operations, published in 1989. Dr. Edwards has conducted training and consulting engagements for clients such as IBM Corp., Daimler-Benz Corp., Allied Corp., Wheel Trueing Co., ARAMCO, Smith & Nephew, Inc., Anchor Continental, Inc., NCR Corp., Milliken Research Company, Sonoco Products Company, Blue-Cross/Blue Shield of South Carolina, CMI, several State Societies of CPAs, and the US-SBA.**

EDWARDS, JAMES BURROWS, university president, oral surgeon; b. Hawthorne, Fla., June 24, 1927; s. O.M. and Bertie R. (Hieronymus) E.; m. Ann Norris Darlington, Sept. 1, 1951; children: James Burrows Jr., Catharine Edwards Wingate. BS, Coll. of Charleston, 1950, LittD, 1975; DMD, U. Louisville, 1955, D Social Sci., 1982; postgrad. advanced correlated clin. scis., U. Pa. Grad. Med. Sch., 1957-58; LittD (hon.), Coll. Charleston, 1975; LLD (hon.), U. S.C., 1975, Bob Jones U., 1976, The Citadel, 1977; HHD (hon.), Francis Marion Coll., 1978, Bapt. Coll. Charleston, 1981; DS (hon.), Erskine Coll., 1982, Georgetown U., 1982; D of Social Sci. (hon.), U. Louisville, 1982; LLD (hon.), Newberry Coll., 1986; others. Diplomate Am. Bd. Oral and Maxillofacial Surgery. Resident in oral surgery Henry Ford Hosp., Detroit, 1958-60; practice dentistry specializing in oral and maxillofacial surgery Charleston, S.C., 1960—; gov. State of S.C., 1975-79; U.S. sec. energy, 1981-82; pres. Med. U. S.C., Charleston, 1982—; bd. dirs. Nat. Data Corp., Atlanta, GS Industries, Inc., Charlotte, N.C.; mem. adv. bd. Norfolk-So. Corp., Va. Past bd. dirs. Coastal Carolina coun. Boy Scouts Am.; past trustee Charleston County Hosp., Greater Charleston YMCA, Coll. Preparatory Sch., Charleston, Baker Meml. Hosp., Charleston; chmn. Charleston County Rep. Party, 1964-69; del. to Nat. Rep. Convs., 1968, 72, 76, 80, 84, 88, 92l chmn. 1st Congl. Dist. Rep. Com., 1970; mem. S.C. State Senate, 1972-74; chmn. subcom. on nuclear energy Nat. Govs. Assn., 1978; chmn. So. Govs. Conf., 1978; founder, charter mem., chmn. bd. dirs. Oral Surgery Polit. Action Com., 1971-73; bd. dirs. Harry Frank Guggenheim Found., N.Y.C., Gaylord and Dorothy Donnelley Found., Chgo. With USNR. Fellow Internat. Coll. Dentists, Am. Coll. Dentists; mem. ADA, S.C. Dental Soc., Coastal Dist. Dental Soc. (past pres.), Chalmers J. Lyons Acad. Oral Surgery, Southeastern Soc. Oral and Maxillofacial Surgeons, Am. Soc. Oral and Maxillofacial Surgeons, Brit. Assn. Oral and Maxillofacial Surgeons, Internat. Soc. Oral and Maxillofacial Surgeons, Fedn. Dentaire Internat., S.C. Soc. Oral and Maxillofacial Surgeons (founder, charter mem., past pres.), Oral Surgery Polit. Action Com. (founder, charter mem., chmn. bd. dirs. 1971-73), Navy League U.S., Am. Hellenic Ednl. Progressive Assn., AHEPA (Plato chpt. # 4), Rotary, Masons, Pi Kappa Phi, Delta Sigma Delta, Omicron Delta Kappa. Office: Med U SC 171 Ashley Ave Charleston SC 29425-0001

EDWARDS, JAMES D., accounting company executive; b. Cleveland, Tenn., Nov. 4, 1943; s. James D. and Elizabeth (Reynolds) E.; m. Sharon E. Bordelon, May 2, 1968; 1 child, David. BS in Acctg., Bob Jones U., 1964. CPA, Ga. From staff acct. to ptnr. Arthur Andersen & Co., Atlanta, 1964-73; mng. ptnr. Atlanta office Arthur Andersen & Co., 1979-87; mng. ptnr. Americas Arthur Andersen & Co., N.Y.C., 1987—. Bd. dirs., exec. com. Atlanta C. of C., 1982-85, Woodruff Arts Ctr., Atlanta, 1986-87; chmn. Cen. Atlanta Progress, 1986-87. Mem. Board Room (N.Y.C.),d The Stanwich Club (Greenwich, Ct.) Atlanta Country Club. Office: Arthur Andersen 1345 Avenue Of The Americas New York NY 10019-5374

EDWARDS, JAMES DALLAS, III, consulting company executive; b. Harriman, Tenn., Aug. 9, 1937; s. James Dallas Jr. and Helen Louise (Milburn) E.; m. Louisa Diane Fultz, July 15, 1961. BBA, U. Tenn., 1959. Customer service supr. Aluminum Co. Am., Alcoa, Tenn., 1964-67; staff product planner Aluminum Co. Am., Pitts., 1967-70, traffic mgr., 1970-74; plant mgr. Soundesign Corp., Santa Claus, Ind., 1974-78; v.p., gen. mgr. Thermwood Corp., Dale, Ind., 1978-81; pres., chief exec. officer Spencer Plastic Products Corp. (name now Spencer Industries), Dale, 1981-92, also bd. dirs.; pres. Edwards & Assocs., Santa Claus, Ind., 1992—. Chmn. bd. dirs. So. Ind. Rehab. Services, Boonville, 1977-82; bd. dirs. Southwest Ind. Pvt. Industry Coun., 1989—, Ind. Small Bus. Coun.; mem. Santa Claus Indsl. Park Bd., Santa Claus, 1978—; pres. Licolnland Econ. Devel. Corp. Named Ind. Small Bus. Person of Yr., 1989, Ind. Entrepeneur of Yr., 1989, recipient Ind. Global Competitiveness award, 1989. Mem. Am. Prodn. and Inventory Control Soc. (bd. dirs. 1970-72), Soc. Plastics Engrs., Soc. Mfg. Engrs., Naval Res. Assn. (pres. 1967-71), SBA (Ind. adv. coun. 1989—), Res. Officers Assn., Ind. C. of C. (dir.), Dale C. of C., Rolling Hills Country Club, Kiwanis, Elks, Optimist. Presbyterian. Avocations: golf, reading. Home: 188 Balthazar Dr Santa Claus IN 47579 Office: PO Box 372 Santa Claus IN 47579-0372

EDWARDS, JAMES EDWIN, lawyer; b. Clarkesville, Ga., July 29, 1914; s. Gus Calloway and Mary Clara (McKinney) E.; m. Frances Lillian Stanley, Nov. 22, 1948; children: Robin Anne Edwards Kaylor, James Christopher, Clare Edwards Weber. Student U. Tex. 1931-33; B.A., George Washington U., 1935, J.D. cum laude, 1946. Bar: Fla. 1938, Va 1987. Practice law, Cocoa, Fla., 1938-42; hearing and exam. officer USCG, 1943-45; div. asst. State Dept., Washington, 1945-50; practice law Ft. Lauderdale, Fla., 1951-55, 59-77; mem. firm Bell, Edwards, Coker, Carlon & Amsden, Ft. Lauderdale, 1956-59; sole practice, Coral Springs, Fla., 1977-81, 84-85; asst. city atty. Fort Lauderdale, 1961, 63-65; mem. firm. Edwards & Leary, Coral Springs, 1981-84; mem. panel Am. Arbitration Assn., 1984—; sole practice, Albemarle County, Va., 1987-88, Charlottesville, Va., 1988—. Author: Myths About Guns, 1978. Commr., Coral Springs, 1970-76, mayor, 1972-74; mem. bd. suprs. Sunshine Water Mgmt. Dist., 1976-80; chmn. Ft. Lauderdale for Eisenhower, 1952; pres. Fla. Conservative Union, Broward County, 1976. Served to lt. USCGR, 1943-45, to lt. col. JAG, USAFR, 1950-68. Recipient 50-Yr. award Fla. Bar, 1988. Mem. SAR, English Speaking Union Club (Charlottesville), The Ret. Officers Assn., Air Force Assn., Rotary. Office: Commonwealth Ctr 300 Preston Ave Ste 312 Charlottesville VA 22902-5044

EDWARDS, JAMES OWEN, engineering and construction company executive; b. McComb, Miss., Sept. 10, 1943; s. James Oscar and Ruth Johanna (Dorshell) E.; m. Janet Anne Katek, June 25, 1966; children: Jennifer, Timothy. BS, Northwestern U., 1965; MBA, Harvard U., 1967. Asst. to pres. East African Rys. & Harbours, Nairobi, Kenya, 1967-70; various positions Office Mgmt. and Budget HEW, Washington, 1970-72; pres. Am. Capital & Rsch., Washington, 1974-87; chmn., chief exec. officer ICF Kaiser Internat., Fairfax, Va., 1984—. Trustee Folger Shakespeare Libr., Marymount U. Avocations: tennis, squash, antiquarian books. Home: 12000 Piney Meetinghouse Rd Potomac MD 20854-1431 Office: ICF Kaiser Internat Inc 9300 Lee Hwy Fairfax VA 22031-1200

EDWARDS, JEROME, lawyer; b. N.Y.C., July 5, 1912; s. Philip and Anna (Hollinger) E.; m. Mildred Kahn, Dec. 7, 1941 (dec.); children: Susan, Bruce (dec.). BS, NYU, 1931, JD, 1933. Bar: N.Y. State 1934, Calif. 1975. Asso. firm T.J. Lesser, 1934-36; pvt. practice N.Y.C., 1936-42; sr. partner Phillips, Nizer, Benjamin, Krim & Ballon, N.Y.C., 1942-64; v.p., gen. counsel 20th Century Fox Film Corp., N.Y.C. and Los Angeles, 1962-77; of counsel Kaplan, Livingston, Goodwin, Berkowitz & Selvin, Beverly Hills, Calif., 1977-81, Musick, Peeler & Garrett, Los Angeles, 1982-83, Phillips, Nizer, Benjamin, Krim & Ballon, Los Angeles, 1985-89. Mem. ABA, Am. Arbitration Assn. (nat. panel), Am. Film Mktg. Assn. (arbitrator panel).

EDWARDS, JESSE EFREM, physician, educator; b. Hyde Park, Mass., July 14, 1911; s. Max and Nellie (Gordon) E.; m. Marjorie Helen Brooks, Nov. 12, 1952; children—Ellen Ann Villa, Brooks Sayre. BS, Tufts Coll., 1932, MD, 1935; DSc (hon.), Georgetown U., 1990. Diplomate Am. Bd. Med. Examiners, Am. Bd. Pathology. Resident Mallory Inst. Pathology, Boston, 1935-36; asst. Mallory Inst. Pathology, 1937-40; intern Albany (N.Y.) Hosp., 1936-37; instr. pathology Boston U., 1938; instr. pathology, bacteriology, surgery Tufts Med. Coll., 1939-40; research fellow Nat. Cancer Inst. USPHS, 1940-42; cons. sect. pathologic anatomy Mayo Clinic, 1946-60; asst. prof. grad. sch. U. Minn., Mpls., 1946-51; asso. prof. U. Minn., 1951-54; prof. pathologic anatomy U. Minn., 1954-60; clin. prof. med. sch., prof. pathology grad. sch. U. Minn., 1960—; chief pathologist United Hosp. (formerly Chas. T. Miller Hosp.), St. Paul, 1960-80; cons. pathologist Hennepin County Hosp., Mpls., 1964—; cons. dept. pathology Mpls. Vets. Hosp., 1966—; cons. pathologist St. Paul Ramsey Hosp., 1967-80; dir. registry of cardiovascular disease United Hosp., St. Paul, 1980-87, sr. cons. registry of cardiovascular disease, 1987—, also sr. cons. Jesse E. Edwards Registry of Cardiovascular Disease, 1987—; pres. World Congress Pediatric Cardiology, 1980; mem. pathology study sect. USPHS, 1957-62; civilian cons. surgeon gen. AUS, 1947-69. Author: Atlas Acquired Diseases of Heart and Great Vessels, 1961, (with T.J. Dry and others) Congenital Anomalies of the Heart and Great Vessels, 1948, (with others) An Atlas of Congenital Anomalies of the Heart and Great Vessels, 1954, (with R.S. Fontana) Congenital Cardiac Disease, 1962, (with J.R. Stewart, O. Kincaid) An Atlas of Vascular Rings and Related Malformations of the Aortic System, 1963, (with C.A. Wagenvoort, D. Heath) Pathology of Pulmonary Vasculature, 1963, (with others) Correlation of Pathologic Anatomy and Angiocardiography, 1965, Coronary Arterial Variations in the Normal Heart and in Congenital Heart Disease, 1975, Coronary Heart Disease, 1976; Editor: (with others) Circulation; Contbr. (with others) articles to profl. jours. Served from capt. to lt. col. M.C. AUS, 1942-46. Recipient Distinguished Tchr. award Minn. Med. Found., 1974; Gold Heart award Am. Heart Assn., 1970; Gifted Tchr. award Am. Coll. Cardiology, 1977. Mem. AMA, Minn. Med. Assn., Soc. Exptl. Biology and Medicine, Am. Heart Assn. (pres. 1967-68), Minn. Heart Assn. (pres. 1962-63), Internat. Acad. Pathology (pres. 1955-56), Am. Assn. Pathologists and Bacteriologists, World Congress Pediat. Cardiology, Coll. Am. Pathologists, Am. Soc. Exptl. Pathology, Sigma Xi, Alpha Omega Alpha. Home: 1565 Edgcumbe Rd Saint Paul MN 55116-2304 Office: United Hosp Saint Paul MN 55102

EDWARDS, JOAN ANNETTE, elementary art educator; b. Dayton, Ohio, Sept. 16, 1945; d. Austin David and Delphine Edwards; children: Allen Stephen Ashcraft, Rhonda Ashcraft Snyder. AA, Enterprise (Ala.) State Jr. Coll., 1982; BFA, Fla. Atlantic U., Boca Raton, 1986; MEd, Columbus (Ga.) State U., 1997. Cert. art educator, Ga. Tchr. art Muscogee County Sch. Dist., Columbus, Ga., 1992—. Exhibited in juried art exhibit at Memphis Arts Festival, 1997, 98, Ctrl. Wyo. Coll., Riverton, 1998, 99. Recipient Silver award Decatur (Ga.) Arts Alliance Visual Arts Exhbn., 1997. Office: Georgetown Elem Sch 954 High Ln Columbus GA 31907-4699

EDWARDS, JOANN LOUISE, human resources executive; b. Lebanon, Pa., June 15, 1955; d. Harold Eugene and Kathryn Faye (Smith) E. AA in Human Svcs. with honors, Harrisburg Area C.C., 1975; BS with honors, Pa. State U., 1981; MA in Indsl. Rels./Human Resources Mgmt., St. Francis Coll., 1994. Residential program worker Pan Am. Corp., Hershey, Pa., 1975-80, residential program supr., 1981-82, intensive behavior shaping supr., 1982-83; program mgr. Devel. Resources, Inc., Harrisburg, Pa., 1983-85, dir. minimum supervision, 1985-86, dir. human resources, 1986-96; dir. human resources Northwestern Human Svcs., Inc. of Ctrl./Western Region, Harrisburg, Pa., 1996—; mem. New Directions for Progress Pers. Com., Harrisburg, 1988-96. Mem. Christian Chs. United Pers. Com., Harrisburg, 1989-90. Mem. Harrisburg Area Pers. Assn. (treas.), Soc. Human Resource Mgmt., Harrisburg Pers. Assn. (v.p.). Methodist. Avocations: theater, classical music, antiques. Office: Northwestern Human Svcs 2209 Forest Hills Dr Ste 21 Harrisburg PA 17112-1095

EDWARDS, JOHN DAVID, investment executive; b. Gallipolis, Ohio, Apr. 14, 1958; s. Vernard David and Virginia Isabelle (Tate) E. Student, Rio Grande Coll., 1976-78. V.p. VD Edwards Ins. Agy., Inc., Pomeroy, Ohio, 1979-85, pres., 1985-86; pres. CLC Ltd. Gold and Silver, Inc., Athens, Ohio, 1987-88; presiding ptnr. NXS Investment Club, Pomeroy, 1988—. Mem. High Frontier, Va., 1987; chmns. advisor U.S. Congl. Adv. Bd., Washington, 1987; charter mem. Ronald Reagan Trust, Washington, 1988; mem. Rep. Presdl. Task Force, Washington, 1988. Recipient Medal of Honor, High Frontier, 1987. Mem. Am. Def. Preparedness Assn. (life), U.S. Naval Inst. (assoc.), Assn. of U.S. Army, Am. Numismatics Assn., Am. Film Inst., Nat. Geog. Soc., Players Club Internat. (charter mem.), Single Action Shooting Soc. Methodist. Avocations: coins, photography, target shooting, reading, Civil War mementos. Home: 100 Union Ave Pomeroy OH 45769-1000

EDWARDS, JOHN DUNCAN, law educator, librarian; b. Louisiana, Mo., Sept. 15, 1953; s. Harold Wenkle and Mary Elizabeth (Duncan) E.; m. Beth Ann Rahm, May 21, 1977; children: Craig, Martha, Brooks. BA, Southeast Mo. State U., 1975; JD, U. Mo., Kansas City, 1977; MALS, U. Mo., Columbia, 1979. Bar: Mo. 1978, U.S. Dist. Ct. (we. dist.) Mo. 1978. Instr. legal research and writing U. Mo., Columbia, 1978; dir. legal research and writing, librarian U. Mo., 1979-80; pub. svcs. librarian Law Sch., U. Okla., Norman, 1980-81; assoc. librarian Law Sch., U. Okla., 1981-84, adj. instr. sch. library sci., 1983-84; prof. law, dir. law library law sch. Drake U., Des Moines, 1984—; adj. instr. Columbia Coll., 1979-80; cons. Cleveland County Bar Assn., 1984. Contbr. articles to profl. jours. Cons. Friends Drake U. Libr., 1985—; coach, mgr. Westminster Softball Team. Des Moines, 1987-94; pres. Crestview Parent-Tchr. Coun., Des Moines, 1988-90; trustee Westminster Presbyn. Ch., Des Moines, 1988-89, treas., 1990, pres., 1991; mem. Clive City Coun., 1995—, mayor pro tem, 1998—; trustee Des Moines Metro Transit Authority, 1996—, chmn. bd. dirs., 1997-98, sec., treas., 1996. Recipient Presdl. award Drake U. Student Bar Assn., 1987; named Outstanding Vol., Crestview Elem. Sch., 1989-90. Mem. Am. Assn. Law Librs. (chmn. awards com. 1987-88, chmn. grants com. 1996-97, chmn. scholarship com. 1998-99), Mid-Am. Assn. Law Librs. (chmn. resource sharing 1986-93, v.p. 1994-95, pres. 1995-96), Mid-Am. Law Sch. Librs., Consortium (pres. 1986-88), Delta Theta Phi, Beta Phi Mu. Avocations: softball, tennis. Office: Drake U Libr Law Sch 27th & Carpenter Sts Des Moines IA 50311

EDWARDS, JOHN R., senator, lawyer; b. Seneca, S.C., June 10, 1953; s. Wallace R. and Catherine Edwards; m. Mary Elizabeth Anania; children: Lucius Wade (dec.), Katherine Elizabeth, Emma. BS with high honors, N.C. State U., 1974; JD with honors, U. N.C., 1977. Bar: N.C. 1977, Tenn. 1978, U.S. Dist. Ct. (ea. dist.) N.C. Assoc. Dearborn & Ewing, Nashville, Tenn., 1978-81; assoc. Tharrington Smith & Hargrove, Raleigh, N.C., 1981-83, ptnr., 1984-92; ptnr. Edwards & Kirby, LLP, Raleigh, 1993-99; U.S. senator from N.C., 1999-. Bd. dirs. Urban Minitries, Raleigh, 1996-97; soccer coach Capital Area Soccer League, Raleigh, 1985-97; v.p. Challenge Soccer League, Raleigh; youth basketball coach YMCA Salvation Army, Raleigh; visonary com. Edenton St. United Meth. Ch. Named Lawyer of Yr. Lawyers Weekly, 1996. Fellow Am. Coll. of Trial Lawyers; mem. Inner Circle of Advocates, Am. Bd. of Trial Advocacy, Chief Justice Susie M. Sharp Inns of Ct. (master), N.C. Acad. of Trial Lawyers (v.p., bd. govs.), N.C. Bar Assn., Tenn. Bar Assn., The Assn. of Trial Lawyers of Am., So. Trial Lawyers Assn., Order of Coif, Phi Kappa Phi. Office: US Senate 825 Hart Senate Office Bldg Washington DC 20510*

EDWARDS, JOHN RALPH, chemist, educator; b. Streator, Ill., Feb. 27, 1937; s. Ralph E. and Ruth M. Edwards; m. Margaret E. Smith, July 15, 1961; children: Peter J., Sharon E., Susan D. BS, Ill. Wesleyan U., 1959; PhD, U. Ill., 1964. NIH postdoctoral fellow Tufts U., Boston, 1964-66; asst. prof. chemistry Villanova (Pa.) U., 1966-73, assoc. prof., 1973-80, prof., 1980—, chmn. dept. chemistry, 1980-90, asst. chmn., 1996—. Contbr. articles to profl. jours. NIH grantee, 1970-76. Mem. Am. Soc. Biochemistry and Molecular Biology, Am. Chem. Soc., U.S. Orienteering Fedn., Sigma Xi, Phi Kappa Phi. Office: Villanova U Dept Chemistry Villanova PA 19085

EDWARDS, JOHN W., school superintendent; b. Schenectady, May 27, 1944; s. William T. and Dorothy (Wells) E. BA, SUNY, New Platz, 1966, MS, 1968, cert. advanced study, 1973; postgrad., NYU. Cert. dist. supt., R.I., N.J., N.Y.; sch. psychologist, N.Y., N.J.; elem. tchr., N.Y. Dir. spl. svcs. Marlboro (N.J.) Bd. Edn., 1980-83; dir. region V. New Milford (N.J.) Bd. Edn., 1983-84; dir. pupil pers. svcs. Middletown (N.J.) Bd. Edn., 1984-88; supt. schs. Bridgehampton (N.Y.) Union Free Sch. Dist., 1990—; supt. Tiverton (R.I.) Sch. Dept., 1988-90. Recipient community svc. resolution N.J. Senate; grad. fellow SUNY. Mem. ASCD, Am. Assn. Sch. Adminstrs. (Nat. Supt.'s Acad. 1988), Nat. Assn. Secondary Sch. Prins., N.Y. ASCD, R.I. ASCD. Home: PO Box 313 Bridgehampton NY 11932-0313 Office: Bridgehampton Sch PO Box 3021 Bridgehampton NY 11932-3021

EDWARDS, KATHRYN A., history educator; b. San Jose, Calif., Apr. 6, 1964; d. Bruce Wellington Edwards and Bonnie Carol Amner. BA in History, Trinity Coll., Ireland, 1986; MA in History, U. Calif., Berkeley, 1988, PhD in History, 1993. Asst. prof. dept. history U. So. Miss., Hattiesburg, 1993-99; Eccles postdoctoral rsch. fellow Tanner Humanities Ctr. U. Utah, 1997-98; asst. prof. dept. history U. S.C., Columbia, 1999—; advisor Students for Progress, 1995-97; mem. humanities lectr. series planning com. Miss. Instns. Higher Learning, 1997; nat. evaluator summer stipend proposals NEH, 1998—; presenter in field. Contbr. articles to profl. jours. Coord. Miss. State Jr. Hist. Soc., 1994-95; mem. Am. Hist. Assn., So. Hist. Assn. (European sect.). Recipient Instrnl. Materials award U. So. Miss., 1994, Summer Stipend, NEH, 1995, Tchg. award U. So. Miss. Honors Students' Assn., 1997; Rsch.-asst. fellow and Dept. History fellow U Calif., Berkeley, 1987-92; Medieval Studies Com. grantee and Humanities Grad. Rsch. grantee, 1987-92; Ctr. Reformation Rsch. Jr. fellow Summer Paleography Inst., 1990; George Lurcy fellow, 1990-91; Faculty Rsch. grantee U. So. Miss., 1994; Gilbert Chinard scholar Inst. Francais de Washington, 1994; NEH at-large grantee, 1995; Bernadotte Schmitt grantee Am. Hist. Assn., 1995. Mem. MLA, Medieval Acad. Am., Renaissance Soc. Am., Frühe Neuzeit Interdisziplinär, Rocky Mountain Medieval and Renaissance Assn., Rocky Mountain MLA, Sixteenth-Century Soc. (mem. com. to assist tchrs. European history in secondary schs. 1994—), Southea. Renaissance Conf., Wc. and So. Assns. Women Historians, Golden Key Nat. Honor Soc. (hon. life mem. 1997), Phi Alpha Theta (Omega Omega br.). Office: U SC Dept History Gambrell Hall Columbia SC 29208

EDWARDS, KATHRYN INEZ, educational technology consultant; b. L.A., Aug. 26, 1947; d. Lloyd and Geraldine E. (Smith) Price; 1 child, Bryan. BA in English, Calif. State U., L.A., 1969, supervision credential, 1974, adminstrn. credential, 1975; MEd in Curriculum, UCLA, 1971; PhD, Claremont Grad. Sch., 1979. Tchr., L.A. Pub. Schs., 1969-78, adv. specially funded programs, 1978-80, advisor librs. and learning-resources program, 1980-81, instructional specialist, 1981-84; cons. instructional media L.A. County Office of Edn., Downey, Calif., 1984-90; coord. ednl. media and tech. Pomona (Calif.) Unified Sch. Dist., 1990-92; cons. edn. tech. Apple Computer, Inc., 1992-96; client mktg. rep. IBM; sales devel. mgr. SUN Microsys., 1999—; cons. Walt Disney Prodns., Alfred Higgins Prodns., others; mem. distance lng. think tank U.S. Office Edn., 1997. Author guides and curriculum kits. Appointed by assembly speaker Willie Brown to Calif. Ednl. Tech. Com., 1990-92, Calif. State Assembly Resolution from Gwen Moore, 1988, Edn. Coun. for Tech. in Learning, 1993-96; mem. spl. com. Cable Access Corp. Cowners, 1991-92. Recipient cert. commendation Senator Diane Watson, 1988; Mabel Wilson Richards scholar, 1968, Calif. Congress Parents and Tchrs. scholar, 1968; UCLA fellow, 1968; named Outstanding Woman of Yr. L.A. Sentinel, 1987. Mem. Nat. Assn. Minority Polit. Women, Internat. Reading Assn. (speaker nat. conv. 1988), L.A. Reading Assn. (pres.), Calif. Assn. Tchrs. of English (conf. del. 1982), Assn. Supervision and Curriculum Devel., Calif. Media and Libr. Educators Assn. (state conf. co-chair 1989, v.p. legal divsn. 1992—), Nat. Assn. Media Women (Media Woman of Yr. 1987), Alpha Kappa Alpha. Democrat. Roman Catholic. Avocations: reading, gardening, travel. Office: IBM Corp 355 S Grand Ave Los Angeles CA 90071-3161

EDWARDS, KENNETH NEIL, chemist, consultant; b. Hollywood, Calif., June 8, 1932; s. Arthur Carl and Ann Vera (Gomez) E.; children: Neil James, Peter Graham, John Evan. BA in Chemistry, Occidental Coll., 1954; MS in Chem. and Metall. Engring., U. Mich., 1955. Prin. chemist Battelle Meml. Inst., Columbus, Ohio, 1955-58; dir. new products rsch. and devel. Dunn-Edwards Corp., L.A., 1958-72; sr. lectr. organic coatings and pigments dept. chem. engring. U. So. Calif., L.A., 1976-80; bd. dirs. Dunn-Edwards Corp., L.A.; cons. Coatings & Plastics Tech., L.A., 1972—. Contbr. articles to sci. jours. Mem. Am. Chem. Soc. (chmn. divisional activities 1988-89, exec. com. divsn. polymeric materials sci. and engring. 1963-96, chair divsn. 1970, mem. devel. adv. com. 1996-99, Disting. Svc. award 1996, chair Disting. Svc. award selection 1997—, chair So. Calif. local sect. 1999), Alpha Chi Sigma (chmn. L.A. profl. chpt. 1962, counselor Pacific dist. 1967-70, grand profl. alchemist nat. v.p. 1970-76, grand master alchemist nat. pres. 1976-78, nat. adv. com. 1978—). Achievements include patents for air-dried polyester coatings and application, for process and apparatus for dispensing liquid colorants into a paint can, fluidic fillers, and for mechanical mixers. Home: Bottle Bay Rd Sagle ID 83860 also: 2926 Graceland Way Glendale CA 91206-1331 Office: Dunn Edwards Corp 1011 S Myrtle Ave Monrovia CA 91016-3426

EDWARDS, KENNETH S., principal. Prin. Silas Deane Middle Sch. Recipient Blue Ribbon Sch. award, 1990-91. Office: Silas Deane Mid Sch 551 Silas Deane Hwy Wethersfield CT 06109-2216*

EDWARDS, KIRK LEWIS, real estate company executive; b. Berkeley, Calif., July 30, 1950; s. Austin Lewis and Betty (Drury) E.; m. Randi Edwards, Feb. 14, 1998; children: Elliott Tyler, Jonathan Bentley. BA in Rhetoric and Pub. Address, U. Wash., Seattle, 1972; postgrad., Shoreline Coll., 1976. Cert. bus. broker. From salesperson to mgr. Rede Realty, Lynnwood, Wash., 1973-77; br. mgr. Century 21/North Homes Realty, Lynnwood, Wash., 1977-79, Snohomish, Wash., 1979-81; pres., owner Century 21/Champion Realty, Everett, Wash., 1981-82, Champion Computers, Walker/Edwards Investments, Everett, 1981-82; br. mgr. Advance Properties, Everett, 1982-87; exec. v.p. Bruch & Vedrich Better Homes & Garden, Everett, 1987-88, dir. career devel., 1988-90; pres., chief exec. officer Century 21/Champion Realty, Everett, 1991-95; pres., CEO KR Bus. Brokers, Bellevue, Wash., 1995—. Named Top Business Broker In Washington Investment Brokers Assn., 1994, 95, 96. Mem. Snohomish County Camano Bd. Realtors (chmn. 1987-88), Snohomish County C. of C., Hidden Harbor Yacht Club, Mill Creek Country Club. Republican. Avocations: travel, water skiing, scuba diving. Office: KR Business Brokers 16301 NE 8th St #223 Bellevue WA 98008

EDWARDS, LARRY DAVID, internist; b. Macomb, Ill., June 20, 1937; s. Richard Marshall and Anna Louise (Hare) Edwards; m. Ann Leanor Will, Mar. 31, 1959; children: Elliott, Sharon, Beth. Pre-Med, U. Ill., 1961, MD, 1965. Diplomate Am. Bd. Internal Medicine, Am. Bd. Infectious Disease, Am. Bd. Geriatric Medicine, Nat. Bd. Med. Examiners, Am. Bd. Med. Mgmt., Am. Coll. Healthcare Execs; cert. physician exec., healthcare exec. Rotating intern USPHS Hosp., Staten Island, N.Y., 1965-66, resident in internal medicine, 1966-68; fellow in infectious diseases Rush-Presbyn.-St. Luke's Med. Ctr., Chgo., 1968-70; instr. dept. internal medicine U. Ill. Coll. Medicine, Chgo., 1968-70; asst. prof. depts. internal medicine, preventive medicine, microbiology Rush Med. Coll., Chgo., 1972-74; assoc. prof. internal medicine U. Ill. Coll. Medicine, Rockford, 1974-80, prof., 1980-81; prof. internal medicine Oral Roberts U. Sch. Medicine, Tulsa, 1981-90; dir. div. infectious diseases Rockford Sch. Medicine, 1974-81, dep. head dept. biomed. scis., 1980-81; prof. internal medicine U. Va., Charlottesville, 1991-92; chief of staff VA Med. Ctr., Salem, Va., 1990-92; assoc. dean for acad. affairs VA, U. Va., Charlottesville, 1991-92; adj. assoc. prof. epidemiology, U. Ill. Sch. Pub. Health, 1977-81; affiliate dept. medicine, Abraham Lincoln Sch. Medicine, U. Ill., Chgo., 1980-81; dir. div. infectious diseases Oral Roberts U., 1981-84; assoc. dean clin. affairs Oral Roberts Sch. Medicine, 1981, 84, vice chmn. dept. internal medicine, 1981-83, chmn., 1983-86, chmn. preventive and internat. medicine, 1987-88, dean, 1984-90, v.p. for health affairs, 1987-90 and chief operating officer City of Faith Med. & Rsch. Ctr., 1989-90; med. dir. Cen. Bapt. Home for Aged, Norridge, Ill., 1968-74, Columbia County Homes, Wyocena, Wis., 1974-80; asst. dir. infectious diseases, hosp. epidemiologist, dir. infectious disease research Rush-Presbyn.-St. Luke's Hosp., Chgo., 1972-74, asst. sci. dept. microbiology, 1970-74; asst. med. dir. Mcpl. Contagious Disease Hosp., Chgo., 1970-74; cons. infectious diseases numerous other hosps. and med. ctrs.; med. dir. City of Faith Hosp., Tulsa, 1984-87, chmn. bd., 1989-90; bd. dirs. City of Faith Clinic, Tulsa, 1985-87; pres. Infectious Diseases Cons. Svcs., Inc., Barnhart, Mo., 1993—. Contbr. numerous articles to med. jours. Advisor resource com. Sch. Health Coalition of N.W. Ill., 1979-81; mem. med. adv. com. State of Ill. Refugee Health Services Program, 1980-81; mem. Ill. health services task force State of Ill. Dept. Pub. Health, 1980-81; mem. infectious disease adv. com. Tulsa City-County Health Dept., 1981-88; mem. physician manpower adv. com. Okla. Bd. Regents, 1984-88; mem. Oral Roberts U. Titan Scholarship Bd., 1985-87; v.p. World-Wide Med. Missions, Oral Roberts Evangelistic Assn., 1986-88, pres. 1989-90; mem. Leadership Roanoke Valley, 1991-92. Served with U.S. Army, 1955-58, with USPHS, 1965-70, lt. col. USAR, 1985, col. 1990-97, ret., 1997. Recipient Smith, Kline and French fellowship for study in Ethiopia, 1964; named Outstanding Faculty Mem. of Yr. Oral Roberts U. Sch. Medicine, 1982-83. Fellow ACP, Infectious Diseases Soc. Am., Am. Coll. Physician Execs., Am. Coll. Healthcare Execs. Avocations: reading, writing.

EDWARDS, LINDA L., elementary education educator. Tchr. Highland Park Elem. Sch., Lewistown, Mont. Named Mont. State Elem. Tchr. of Yr., 1993. Office: Highland Park Elem Sch 1312 7th Ave N Lewistown MT 59457-2112*

EDWARDS, LOUIS WARD, JR., diversified manufacturing company executive; b. Detroit, July 22, 1936; s. Louis Ward and Sally (Tryke) E.; m. Juanita Krause, Dec. 28, 1963; children: Louis Ward III, Preston Stephen, Alisa Macall. B.A., Albion Coll., 1958. Mgr. Price Waterhouse & Co. (C.P.A.'s), Milw., 1958-67; treas. Fuqua Industries, Inc., Atlanta, 1967-72; v.p. Ivy Corp., Atlanta, 1972-83; treas., dir. Fabco-Air, Inc., Gainesville, Fla., 1981—; v.p., dir. Moore-Handley, Inc., Birmingham, 1981—; partner Edwards-Harvey Organ Co., Atlanta.; Bd. dirs. Druid Hills Civic Assn. C.P.A., Wis.; treas., dir. Tru-Die, Inc., Chgo. Mem. Am. Inst. C.P.A.s, Ga. Soc. C.P.A.s, Tax Execs. Inst. (treas. 1971). Republican. Home: 1156 Lullwater Rd NE Atlanta GA 30307-1246 Office: Georgia Pacific Ctr Atlanta GA 30303

EDWARDS, LYDIA JUSTICE, state official; b. Carter County, Ky., July 9, 1937; d. Chead and Velva (Kinney) Justice; m. Frank B. Edwards, 1968; children: Mark, Alexandra, Margot. Student, San Francisco State U. Began career as acct., then Idaho state rep., 1982-86; treas. State of Idaho, 1987-98; legis. asst. to Gov. Hickel, Alaska, 1967; conf. planner Rep. Gov.'s Assn., 1970-73; mem. Rep. Nat. Commn., 1972, del. to nat. conv., 1980. Mem. Rep. Womens Fedn. Congregationalist. Office: State Treas Office PO Box 35 Donnelly ID 83615

EDWARDS, MARGARET H., English as second language instructor; b. Falkirk, Scotland, Jan. 28, 1940; came to U.S., 1967; d. John Hobbs and J. Catherine Muir (Rankine) Erskine; m. W. Peter Edwards, Dec. 24, 1964; 1 child, Gemma Rhiain. Diploma, U. Grenoble, France, 1960, U. Santander, Spain, 1962; BA, U. Durham, Eng., 1961, MA; MA, U. Wash., 1970; grad. diploma in edn., U. Leicester, 1962. Head dept. French Chester-le-Street H.S., England, 1962-64; tchr. English, French, Spanish Maple Ridge Sr. H.S., Haney, B.C., Can., 1964-66; tchg. asst. U. Wash., Seattle, 1968-69; instr. Sullivan lang. sch. Behavioral Rsch. Labs., Palo Alto, Calif., 1970-71; field researcher DIME Project, Denver, 1971-72; instr. French Evergreen State Coll., Olympia, Wash., 1986-91; ESL, French, Spanish instr. No. Thurston H.S., Lacey, Wash., 1976—. Mem. Wash. Assn. Educators of Spkrs. of Other Langs., TESOL (Tchr. of Yr. 1977, Dick Williams award 1998). Avocations: travel, language learning, tennis. Office: No Thurston HS 600 Sleater Kinney Rd NE Lacey WA 98506-5241

EDWARDS, MARGARET MCRAE, college administrator, lawyer; b. Wadesboro, N.C., July 2, 1931; d. Martin Alexander and Margaret Ashe (Redfearn) McRae; m. Sterling J. Edwards, June 30, 1953; children: Martin, Robert, Lee, Elizabeth. BA cum laude, Agnes Scott Coll., 1953; JD cum laude, Cumberland Law Sch., 1979. Bar: N.C. 1979, Ala. 1980, Fla. 1981. Asst. to alumnae dir. Mt. Vernon Coll., Washington, 1961-64; devel. staff S.E. Inst., Chapel Hill, N.C., 1973-75; law clk. U.S. Dist. Ct., Birmingham, 1979-80; atty. Carlton, Fields, Tampa, Fla., 1980-82; pvt. practice Birmingham, 1983-85; dir. planned giving Birmingham-So. Coll., 1985-90, assoc. v.p. for endowment and planned giving, 1991—; cons. Blackbaud Planned Giving Conf., Charleston, S.C., 1991—, Planned Giving, Philanthropic Action Coun., Tampa, 1980-82, Am. Philanthropy Group, Birmingham, 1983-88; prof. bus. law Samford U., Birmingham, 1984. Index editor: Manual for Complex Litigation, 1985. Bd. dirs. Girls Club, Birmingham, 1984-90, Ala. Planned Giving Coun., 1991-94, Ala. divsn. Am. Cancer Soc., co-chair major gifts, 1991—; spkrs. bur. Nat. Com. on Planned Giving; bd. dirs. South Highland Found., 1997—. Recipient Achievement award in Planned Giving, Coun. for Achievement and Support of Edn., 1992, Will/Tax award Young Lawyers Assn., 1979, Estate Planning award Am. Jurisprudence, 1979, Outstanding Fund Raiser award Ala. chpt. Nat. Soc. fund Raising Execs., 1997. Mem. Am. Arbitration Assn. (arbitrator 1985—), Audubon Soc. (bd. dirs., treas. 1996-98), Agnes Scott Alumnae (pres. Birmingham 1967-69, Charleston, S.C. 1954-55). Presbyterian. Home: 4239 Chickamauga Rd Birmingham AL 35213-1811 Office: Birmingham-So Coll Arkadelphia Rd Birmingham AL 35254

EDWARDS, MARK E., healthcare company lawyer; b. Iowa City, Iowa, July 25, 1950. BBA, U. Iowa, 1972; JD, Vanderbilt U., 1975. Assoc. Fisher & Phillips, 1979-86; ptnr. Ford & Harrison, 1986-90; labor counsel Hosp. Corp. Am., 1990-94; chief labor counsel Columbia/HCA Healthcare Corp., Nashville, 1994—. Capt. USAF, 1975-79. Mem. ABA, Ga. Bar Assn., Iowa Bar Assn., Tenn. Bar Assn. Office: Columbia/HCA Healthcare Corp 2501 Park Plz Nashville TN 37203-1512*

EDWARDS, MARK U., JR., college president, history educator, author; b. Oakland, Calif., June 2, 1946; s. Mark U. and Margaret Edwards; m. Linda Johnson, Mar. 1968; 1 child, Teon. BA in Psychology, Stanford U., 1968, MA in History, 1969, PhD in History, 1974. Jr. fellow U. Mich., 1971-74; asst. prof. history Wellesley (Mass.) Coll., 1974-80; asst. prof. Purdue U., West Lafayette, Ind., 1980-83, assoc. prof., 1983-86, prof. history, 1986-87; prof. christianity Harvard U., Cambridge, Mass., 1987-94; pres. St. Olaf Coll., Northfield, Minn., 1994—; founder, v.p. ELK Software Devel. Corp., 1985—; pres. Sixteenth Century Studies Conf., 1987-88; chair continuing com. Internat. Congress for Luther Rsch., 1988-94; bd. dirs. Wittenberg U., 1985—. Author: Luther and the False Brethren, 1975, Luther's Last Battles, 1983, Printing, Propaganda and Martin Luther, 1994; co-author: Luther, A Reformer for Churches, 1983; mem. editl. bd. The Ency. of the Reformation, 1989—. Bd. dirs. Holden Village, 1993-94, 96—. Mem. Am. Norwegian Hist. Assn. Office: St Olaf Coll 1520 Saint Olaf Ave Northfield MN 55057-1574

EDWARDS, MARVIN RAYMOND, investment counselor, economic consultant; b. N.Y.C., June 29, 1921; s. Albert H. and Blanche (Gans) E.; m. Helene C. Sirota, Mar. 20, 1955; children: Jeffrey Randall, Douglas Lee, Carolyn Beth. BS, NYU, 1947. Pres. White Star Sales Corp., Jacksonville, Fla., 1947-58; pres. Edwards & Edwards, Inc., Jacksonville, 1958—. Interviews on investments and the economy have appeared in numerous publs. including Bus. Week, Scrap Age, Miami Herald, Tampa Tribune, The Market Chronicle, others; polit. columnist Folio Weekly, 1996—; subject of interview ABC World News Tonight, 1993, 94. Exec. v.p., bd. dirs. Greater Jacksonville Taxpayers Assn., 1965-71; pres., bd. dirs. Better Schs. Citizens Com, Jacksonville, 1959-65, Community Service Planning Council, Jacksonville, 1955-58; v.p., b.d dirs. Jacksonville Humane Soc., 1953-56, Jacksonville Safety Council, 1948-50; bd. dirs. North East Fla. Kidney Found., Jacksonville, 1971-73. Lt. USAF, 1943-46, ETO. Decorated Air medal; recipient Outspoken Citizen's award Jacksonville Southside Bus. Men's Club, 1993. Mem. Jacksonville Fin. Analysts Soc. (pres., bd. dirs. 1977-78, 87-88), Econ. Roundtable Jacksonville (pres., bd. dirs. 1975-77, 90-91, 95—), Assn. for Investment Mgmt. and Rsch., Nat. Assn. bus. Economists, Nat. Economists Club, Soc. Profl. Journalists, Nat. Press Club of Washington, Vets. of the Office of Strategic Svcs., Mosquito Aircrew Assn. Eng. Home: 1345 Riverbirch Ln Jacksonville FL 32207-7540 Office: Edwards & Edwards Inc PO Box 33 Jacksonville FL 32201-0033

EDWARDS, MAUREEN CRITTENDEN, neonatologist, educator; b. Washington, July 8, 1944; m. George W. Edwards Jr. BS, Marquette U., 1966; MD, George Washington U., 1970, MPH, 1991, specialist in health svcs. adminstrn., 1995. Bd. cert. in pediats. and neonatal-perinatal medicine; recert. pediats. and neonatal-perinatal medicine; lic., D.C., Md. Assoc. neonatologist Children's Nat. Med. Ctr., Washington, 1975-78; dir. newborn svc. George Washington U. Med. Ctr., Washington, 1978—, assoc. prof. pediats. and ob-gyn., 1979—. Office: George Washington U Med Ctr 901 23rd St NW Rm 3246S Washington DC 20037-2327*

EDWARDS, MAYA MICHELLE, secondary education educator; b. Texarkana, Tex., Feb. 22, 1971; d. William Morris and Linda Carolyn (Morrow) E.; 1 child, William Dustin Ellis Stone. BE, East Tex. State, 1992. Cert. tchr., Tex. Gifted and talented educator Redwater (Tex.) Mid. Sch., 1994—; student coun. sponsor Middle Sch., Redwater, 1995-98. Vol. water safety instr. ARC. Bapt. Home: 12 Cardinal Ln Texarkana TX 75501-0221 Office: Redwater Mid Sch PO Box 347 Redwater TX 75573-0347

EDWARDS, MICHAEL GERARD, physician; b. Duluth, Minn., Apr. 27, 1956; s. Charles and Cecelia Edwards; m. Patricia Ann Roedl; children: Matthew, Conor, Anne. BA, U. Notre Dame, 1978; MD, Creighton U., 1982. Resident in radiology SUNY, Buffalo, 1983-86; fellow William Beaumont Hosp., Royal Oak, Mich., 1986-87, staff radiologist, 1987-92; staff radiologist Providence Hosp., Southfield, Mich., 1992—. Address: 20265 Wellesley St Beverly Hills MI 48025-2862

EDWARDS, MICHELLE DENISE, professional basketball player; b. Y, Mar. 6, 1966. Degree in gen. studies, Iowa State U., 1988. Basketball player Faenza, Italy, 1989-90, Pistoia, Italy, 1990-93, Ferrara, Italy, 1993-95, Pavia, Italy, 1995-97; basketball player Cleveland Rockers Women's NBA, Cleve., 1997—. Mem. Olympic Festival Team, 1985; recipient Bronze medal Pan Am. Games, 1991; named MVP Italian League All-Star team, 1997. Office: Cleveland Rockers Gund Arena One Center Ct Cleveland OH 44115*

EDWARDS, N. MURRAY, professional sports team owner. B Commerce, U. Saskatchewan; LLB, U. Toronto. bd. dirs. Can. Natural Resources, Ltd., Foremost Industries, Inc., Rio Alto Exploration, Ltd., Penn West Petroleum Ltd, Ensign Resource Svc. Group, Inc., Cathedral Gold Corp., Magellan Aerospace Corp., Imperial Metals Corp. Pres., CEO Edco Fin. Holdings, Ltd.; co-owner Calgary Flames. Office: Calgary Flames, PO Box 1540 Station M, Calgary, AB Canada T2P 3B9*

EDWARDS, NILOO MARIO, surgeon; b. Sri Lanka, May 11, 1959. MD, Columbia U., 1986. Diplomate Am. Bd. Surgery, Am. Bd. Thoracic Surgery. Intern, then resident Strong Meml. Hosp., Rochester, N.Y., 1986-92; fellow in cardiothoracic surgery Columbia Presbyn. Med. Ctr., N.Y.C., 1994-96; pvt. practice Albany Cardiothoracic Surgery, N.Y.C., 1997—. Office: NY Presbyn Hosp 177 Fort Washington Ave New York NY 10032

EDWARDS, NINIAN MURRY, judge; b. St. Louis, Jan. 11, 1922; s. N. Murry and Mabel E. (Dailey) E.; m. Mary Catherine McKeown, May 12, 1944; children: Katherine S. Edwards Burckhalter, Barbara Edwards Perkins. JD, U. Mo., 1947. Trial lawyer St. Louis area, 1947-65; cir. judge St. Louis County, Clayton, Mo., 1965-66, 70-88, sr. judge, arbitrator, mediator, 1988—. Coun. mem. City of Kirkwood, Mo., atty., 1968-70. Maj. USAFR, 1950-90, ret. Mem. Mo. Bar Assn. (past bd. govs.), Bar Assn. Met. St. Louis, St. Louis County Bar Assn. (Disting. Svc. award 1970), Nat. Coun. Juvenile and Family Ct. Judges (bd. trustees, past sec., treas., v.p., pres. elect 1990, pres. 1991-92), Phi Delta Phi. Democrat.

EDWARDS, PATRICIA ANN, poet; b. Deadwood, S.D., Dec. 16, 1957; d. Leonard James and Rose Ella (Mitchell) Barr; m. Calvin L. Edwards; children: Michael George, Jeanette Ruth, Stephanie Ann. Degree in nutrition, Pa. State U., 1984. Author: Memories for Tomorrow, 1996. Active Run for the Moving Wall and Run for the Wall, Washington; active oral readings/ceremonies for Moving Wall, Meadville, Pa., 1998. Mem. DAV (Silver leader 1994), Internat. Soc. Poets (disting. mem., Poet of Yr. 1997). Avocations: poetry, photography, motorcycling, supporting veterans programs. Home: 323 N Irvine Ave Sharon PA 16146-1320

EDWARDS, PATRICIA BURR, small business owner, counselor, consultant; b. Oakland, Calif., Feb. 19, 1918; d. Myron Carlos and Claire Idelle (Laingor) Burr; m. Jackson Edwards, Nov. 14, 1942; children: Jill Forman-Young, Jan Kurzweil. AB, U. So. Calif., 1939, MSEd, 1981. Prin. Constructive Leisure, L.A., 1968—; spkr. in field; writer, prodr. counseling materials for career, leisure, life planning including computer software, audio cassettes and assessment surveys. Author: You've Got to Find Happiness: It Won't Find You, 1971, Leisure Counseling Techniques: Individual and Group Counseling Step-by-Step, 1975, 3d edit., 1980; (software) Leisure PREF, 1986, Over 50: Needs, Values, Attitudes, 1988, Adapting to Change: The NVAB Program, 1997; contbr. articles to profl. jours., mags. and books. Chmn. L.A. County Foster Families 50th Anniversary, 1962-64, L.A. Jr. League Sustainers, 1964-65, Hollywood Bowl Vols., L.A., 1960-61, Hollywood Bowl Patroness com., 1961—. Mem. Am. Counseling Assn., Calif. Assn. for Counseling and Devel., Nat. Recreation and Park Assn., Assn. for Adult Devel. and Aging, Trojan League, Travellers Aid Soc. L.A., Jr. League L.A., First Century Families of L.A., Delta Gamma. Republican. Episcopalian. Avocations: family activities, singing, dancing, pets, learning.

EDWARDS, PATRICIA K., dean. Dean architecture and urban studies Va. Poly. Inst. and State U., Blacksburg, 1997, prof. urban affairs and planning, 1997—. Office: Va Poly Inst and State U Architecture & Urban Study 201 Architecture Annex Blacksburg VA 24061-0205*

EDWARDS, PATRICK MICHAEL, sales consultant; b. Burbank, Calif., Sept. 20, 1947; s. Kenneth Charles and Thelma Kay (Allen) E. BS, Calif. Poly State U., 1975. Med. salesperson Burroughs Wellcome Co., Research Triangle Park, N.C., 1975-79; profl. cons. G.D. Searle & Co., Chgo., 1979—; bd. dirs. Calif. Poly. Alumni Assn., 1999—. Author photo essay in Ford Times mag., 1989. With USCG, 1968-72. Mem. Assn. of Pharm. Reps. (pres. 1986), Toastmasters Internat. Republican. Avocations: photography, hiking, biking, sailing, scuba diving. Home and Office: 344 N 16th St Grover Beach CA 93433-1850

EDWARDS, PATRICK ROSS, former retail company executive, lawyer, management consultant; b. Montreal, Que., Can., Mar. 17, 1940; came to U.S., 1952; s. Claude Victor and Edith May Peace (Wyatt) E.; m. Gracelyn Regina LaSala, July 2, 1961; children—Pamela Lynn, Jennifer Anne. B.A., Kenyon Coll., 1962; J.D., Columbia U., 1965. Bar: N.Y. 1967. Staff atty. Allied Stores Corp., N.Y.C., 1965-69, asst. to pres., 1970-74, v.p. adminstrn., 1974-83, sr. v.p. ops. and adminstrn., 1983-85; pres., chief operating officer Genovese Drug Stores, Inc., Melville, N.Y., 1985-86; exec. v.p., chief operating officer Am. Trim Products, Inc., 1987-88, pres., chief exec. officer, 1988-89; prin. The Rosse Co., 1990—; sr. v.p. sys. svcs. North Shore--L.I. Jewish Health Sys., 1996—. Trustee Northshore U. Hosp., Manhasset, N.Y., 1984-93, spl. asst. to pres., 1993-96; mem. exec. coun. Inner City Scholarship Fund, N.Y.C., 1983-93; mem. deans adv. coun. SUNY Sch. Bus., Albany, 1984-86; mem. Ea. regional panel Pres.'s Commn. on White House Fellowships, N.Y.C., 1984-86. Mem. Kenyon Coll. Alumni Assn. Roman Catholic. Club: Strathmore Vanderbilt Country (Manhasset).

EDWARDS, PETER, educator, writer; b. Kalgoorlie, Australia; m. Susan Christine Maslowski, Feb. 1, 1985; children: Lance, Michael, Diana, Tania, Dean, Monique. BA, U. West Australia, Perth, 1964, BEd, 1968; MA, U. B.C., Vancouver, Can., 1972, EdD, 1974. Cert. tchr., West Australia, B.C., Va. Tchr. Edn. Dept. West Australia, Perth, 1957-68, Edn. Dept. B.C., Vancouver, 1968-71; lectr. edn. U. B.C., 1974-75; sr. lectr. Monash U., Melbourne, Victoria, Australia, 1976-89; adj. instr. Saginaw (Mich.) Valley State U., 1989-90; assoc. prof. Clarion (Pa.) U. Pa., 1990-92; prof. SUNY, Plattsburgh, 1992-98, Va. Edn. Dept., 1998—; cons. Tchrs.' Resource Ctr., Canberra, Australia, 1976, Aboriginal Affairs, Melbourne, 1977, 80, Commonwealth of Australia, Canberra, 1980-83. Author: Reading Problems, 1981, Edwards Diagnostic Reading Test, 1981, Seven Keys to Successful Study, 1991, 2d edit., 1996, Literacy Techniques, 1995, 2d edit., 1998; (with others) Reading Education, 1981, Special Education, 1981; (simulation game) Successful Negotiation, 1984; (computer program) Reading and Study Skills, 1998; (video) Creative Responses to Reading, 1991, Reading Showcase, 1992; contbr. articles to ednl. publs. Mem. Assn. Tchr. Educators, Internat. Reading Assn., Kappa Delta Phi. Avocations: creative writing, music. Office: Marsteller Mid Sch Manassas VA 20110-4484

EDWARDS, RALPH M., librarian; b. Shelley, Idaho, Apr. 17, 1933; s. Edward William and Maude Estella (Munsee) E.; m. Winifred Wylie, Dec. 25, 1969; children: Dylan, Nathan, Stephen. B.A., U. Wash., 1957, M.Library, 1960; D.L.S., U. Calif.-Berkeley, 1971. Libr. N.Y. Pub. Libr., N.Y.C., 1960-61; catalog libr. U. Ill. Libr., Urbana, 1961-62; br. libr. Multnomah County Libr., Portland, Oreg., 1964-67; asst. prof. Western Mich. U., Kalamazoo, 1970-74; chief of the Central Libr. Dallas Pub. Libr., 1975-81; city librarian Phoenix Pub. Libr., 1981-95, ret., 1996—. Author: Role of the Beginning Librarian in University Libraries, 1975. U. Calif. doctoral fellow, 1967-70; library mgmt. internship Council on Library Resources, 1974-75. Mem. ALA, Pub. Library Assn. Democrat. Home: 2884 Spring Blvd Eugene OR 97403-1662

EDWARDS, RENEE CAMILLE, logistics engineer, public relations professional; b. Falls Church, Va., Aug. 6, 1961; d. Walter Thomas and Elizabeth Ann Holt. BS, George Mason U., Fairfax, 1983; MS, Central Mich. U., Merrifield, 1988; grad. program mgmt. course, Def. Systems Mgmt. Coll., 1990. Cert. contracting officer's rep. Logistics analyst The BDM Corp., McLean, Va., 1983-85; deputy program mgr. COMARCO/IBS, Arlington, Va., 1985-88; logistics mgr., speaker, briefer SWL, Inc., Arlington, Va., 1988-89; mem. profl. staff Def. Systems Mgmt. Coll., Ft. Belvoir, Va., 1989-92; dir. computer-aided acquisition and logistics support tng. and edn. Office Asst. Sec. of Def. Prodn. and Logistics, Falls Church, Va., 1992-93; dir. pub. affairs U.S. Dept. Commerce, Nat. Tech. Info. Svc., Springfield, Va., 1993—; co-chmn. computer aided acquisition Logistics Systems Rsch. Group. Contbr. articles to profl. jours. Bd. dirs. Woodwalk Condominium, Burke, Va., 1987-96, mem. indsl. tech. adv. com., 1997-99. Named Best Speaker Toastmasters, McLean, 1985, Best Evaluator Toastmasters, McLean, 1985; recipient Excellence award Dept. Def., 1993, Outstanding Svc. award Dept. Commerce, 1996. Mem. Soc. of Logistics Engrs. Republican. Avocations: racquetball, cycling, embroidery, guitar. Office: US Dept Commerce NTIS 5285 Port Royal Rd Springfield VA 22161-0001

EDWARDS, RICHARD ALAN, lawyer; b. Portland, Oreg., June 28, 1938; s. Howard A. and Kay E. (Sheldon) E.; m. Renee Rosier, June 18, 1960; children: Teri Edwards Obye, Lisa Edwards Smith, Steve. BS, Oreg. State U., 1960; JD summa cum laude, Willamette U., 1968. Bar: Oreg. 1968, U.S. Dist. Ct. Oreg. 1968, U.S. Ct. Appeals (9th cir.) 1969. Various positions 1st Interstate Bank of Oreg., Portland, 1960-65; assoc. Miller, Nash, Wiener, Hager & Carlsen, Portland, 1968-74, ptnr., 1974—, mng. ptnr., 1991-96. Editor Willamette Law Jour., 1967-68. Mem. ABA (litigation sect. 1972), Oreg. State Bar (chairperson debtor-creditor sect. 1981-82, mem. various coms.). Republican. Presbyterian. Avocation: breeding and racing thoroughbred race horses. Office: Miller Nash Wiener Hager & Carlsen 111 SW 5th Ave Ste 3500 Portland OR 97204-3699

EDWARDS, RICHARD LANSING, lawyer; b. Wilmington, Del., Apr. 16, 1944; s. Robert Wilson Jr. and Eleanor (Inscho) E.; m. Betsey Ann Barney, Aug. 24, 1980; children: Beth, Melissa, Jeffrey, Jason, Karen. BS in Indsl. Engring., Lehigh U., 1966; JD, Northeastern U., 1980. Bar: Mass. 1980, U.S. Dist. Ct. Mass. 1981, U.S. Ct. Appeals (1st cir.) 1983, U.S. Supreme Ct. 1985, U.S. Dist. Ct. Conn. 1998. Lawyer Craig & Macauley, Boston, 1980-83; lawyer, shareholder Campbell, Campbell & Edwards, P.C. (and predecessor firm), Boston, 1983—. Contbr. articles to profl. jours. Capt. USAF, 1966-70. Decorated Bronze star. Mem. ABA (tort and ins. practice and litigation sect. 1984—), Mass. Bar Assn. (civil litigation sect. 1983—), Def. Rsch. Inst. (products liability com., chmn. 1997-99, chmn. duty to warn and labeling subcom. 1985-88, steering com. 1988—), Internat. Assn. of Def. Counsel (chmn. advocacy practice and procedure com. 1993-95), Mass. Def. Lawyers Assn., Soc. of Automotive Engrs., Product Liability Adv. Coun., Boston Bar Assn. Office: Campbell Campbell & Edwards PC One Constitution Plaza Boston MA 02129

EDWARDS, RICHARD LEROY, academic dean, social work educator, non-profit management consultant; b. Rahway, N.J., Aug. 9, 1943; s. Richard Lorraine and Norma (Higley) E.; m. Kathryn Ellen Self, Feb. 16, 1973 (div. July 1980); children: Jeffrey, Julia, Jennifer; m. Mary Agnes Altpeter, July 1, 1984. BA, Augustana Coll., Rock Island, Ill., 1965; MA, U. Chgo., 1967; PhD with distinction, SUNY, Albany, 1986. Social worker Ill. State Psychiat. Inst., Chgo., 1967-70; asst. prof. Augustana Coll., 1970-74; staff assoc. Nat. Assn. Social Workers, Washington, 1974-77; assoc. dir. continuing social work edn. U. Tenn., Knoxville, 1977-80; assoc. prof., assoc. dean SUNY, Albany, 1980-88; prof., dean Mandel Sch. Applied Social Scis. Case Western Res. U., Cleve., 1988-92; dean sch. of social work U. N.C., Chapel Hill, 1992—. Editor: Skills for Effective Human Services Management, 1991; editor-in-chief Ency. of Social Work, 1995; contbr. numerous articles to profl. jours.; chpts. to book. Elected mem. Bd. Edn., Davenport, Iowa, 1972-74; trustee numerous non-profit agy. bds. Recipient Achievement in Edn. award No. Ohio Live Mag., 1991. Mem. Acad. Cert. Social Workers, Nat. Assn. Social Workers (Social Worker of Yr. award N.Y. chpt. 1987, pres. 1989-91), Coun. on Social Work Edn. Unitarian. Avocation: golf. Home: 224 Oxford Hills Dr Chapel Hill NC 27514-2129 Office: U NC Sch of Social Work 301 Pittsboro St Chapel Hill NC 27599*

EDWARDS, ROBERT, professional football player; b. Oct. 2, 1974. U. Ga. Running back New Eng. Patriots, 1998—. Office: New England Patriots 60 Washington St Foxboro MA 02035*

EDWARDS, ROBERT HAZARD, college president; b. London, May 26, 1935; s. Arthur Robinson and Marjorie Hazard (Mayes) E. (father Am. citizen); m. Blythe Morton Bickel, Nov. 5, 1988; children from previous marriage: Elizabeth, Daphne, Nicholas. AB, Princeton U., 1957; BA, Cambridge (Eng.) U., 1959, MA (hon.), 1977; LLB, Harvard U., 1961; LHD (hon.), Carleton Coll., 1986. Bar: Fed. 1961. Fellow Ford Found, Africa, 1961-63; with UN polit. affairs Dept. State, 1963-65, Ford Found., 1965-77; rep. for Pakistan, 1968-72; head Middle East and Africa, 1973-77; pres. Carleton Coll., Northfield, Minn., 1977-86; head social welfare dept. Secretariat of the Aga Khan, Paris, 1986-90; pres. Bowdoin Coll., Brunswick, Maine, 1990—; bd. vis. U. Maine. Mem. Coun. on Fgn. Rels. N.Y.C., Maine Math. and Sci. Alliance (chmn.). Office: Bowdoin Coll Office of President Brunswick ME 04011

EDWARDS, ROBERT NELSON, lawyer; b. Sugar Creek, Pa., May 25, 1946; s. Robert Francis and Kathryn Lucille (Nelson) E.; m. Joyce Mary Olejar, July 14, 1973; 1 child: Suzanne Kathryn. BS cum laude, St. Louis U., 1967; postgrad. St. Mary's U. Sch. Law, San Antonio, 1970-72; J.D., Seton Hall U., 1977. Bar: N.J. 1977, U.S. Dist. Ct. N.J. 1977, U.S. Tax Ct. 1979, N.Y. 1990. Assoc., Frank J. Planer, Hackensack, N.J., 1977-78; assoc. Michael J. Mella, Fair Lawn, N.J., 1978-79; sole practice, Elmwood Park, N.J., 1979-83; corp. atty., asst. nat. mgr. of contracts The Perkin-Elmer Corp., Oceanport, N.J., 1983-85; v.p., gen. counsel, sec. Info. Sci. Inc., Montvale, N.J., 1985-92; v.p., gen. counsel, asst. sec. Fedders Corp., Liberty Corner, N.J., 1992—. Councilman, Borough of Elmwood Park, N.J., 1983-85; commr. Vol. Fire Dept., Elmwood Park, 1983-85. Served to sgt USAF, 1968-72. Recipient Am. Jurisprudence award Bancroft-Whitney Co., St. Mary's U. Sch. Law, 1970, 71; Mgmt. Achievement award The Perkin-Elmer Corp., 1983. Mem. ABA, Computer Law Assn., N.J. Corp. Counsel Assn., Phi Delta Phi, Alpha Eta Rho. Republian. Roman Catholic. Clubs: Rotary (Elmwood Park, v.p. 1982-83), Homeowners Assn. (sec. 1979). Lodge: Elks. Home: 497 Calvin St Washington Tp NJ 07675-4401 Office: 505 Martinsville Rd Liberty Corner NJ 07938

EDWARDS, ROBIN MORSE, lawyer; b. Glens Falls, N.Y., Dec. 9, 1947; d. Daniel and Harriet Morse; m. Richard Charles Edwards, Aug. 30, 1970; children: Michael Alan, Jonathan Philip. BA, Mt. Holyoke Coll., 1969; JD, U. Calif., Berkeley, 1972. Bar: Calif. 1972. Assoc. Donahue, Gallagher, Thomas & Woods, Oakland, Calif., 1972-77, ptnr., 1977-89; ptnr. Sonnenschein, Nath & Rosenthal, San Francisco, 1989—. Mem. ABA, Calif. Bar Assn., Alameda County Bar Assn. (bd. dirs. 1978-84, v.p. 1982, pres. 1983). Jewish. Avocations: skiing, cooking. Office: Sonnenschein Nath Rosenthal 685 Market St Ste 10 San Francisco CA 94105-4200

EDWARDS, ROY ALVIN, physician, psychiatrist, educator; b. Huntington, W.Va., June 23, 1921; s. Roy Alvin and Willie Hazel (Stanley) E.; m. Dorothea Frances Brodtrick, June 16, 1943 (div. Aug. 1973); children: Madalin Ann, Mary Margaret, John Brodtrick; m. Wanda Jean Ferrell, Nov. 30, 1973. BS, Marshall U., 1942; MD, Med. Coll. Va., 1948. Diplomate Am. Bd. Psychiatry and Neurology. Rotating intern Med. Coll. Va. Hosps., Richmond, 1948-49; resident in internal medicine C&O Hosp., Huntington, W.Va., 1949-50; resident in psychiatry Columbus (Ohio) State Hosp., 1950-52, Cleve. Receiving Hosp., 1952-53; supt. Western State Hosp., Hopkinsville, Ky., 1953-56; pvt. practice psychiatry Huntington, 1956-86; mem. med. staff Huntington State Hosp., 1986—, clin. dir., 1986-95; clin. prof. Marshall U. Med. Sch., Huntington, 1986-94; clin. prof. Marshall U. Med. Sch., Huntington, 1986-94; dir. Christian County Mental Health Clinic, Hopkinsville, 1953-56; psychiat. cons. Outwood (Ky.) VA Hosp., 1954-56; mem. courtesy staff St. Mary's Hosp., Huntington, 1956—. Contbr. articles to med. jours. Mem. W.Va. Ho. of Dels., Charleston, 1973-75; mem., chmn. numerous civic orgns., 1957-80. With AUS, 1943-46. Named Ky. Col., 1975. Fellow Am. Psychiat. Assn. (life); mem. AMA, So. Med. Assn., W.Va. Med. Assn., W.Va. Psychiat. Assn. (pres. 1961, 68), Guyam Golf and Country Club. Republican. Methodist. Home: 25 Parkway Dr Huntington WV 25705-2716

EDWARDS, RYAN HAYES, baritone; b. Columbia, S.C.; s. William Munroe and Dorothy LeGrande (Sawyer) Faucett; m. Leila Scelonge; 1 son, Geoffrey C. MusB, U. Tex.; MusM, Tex. Christian U. artistic cons. Marquee Theatre Co., Evanston, Ill., tchr. Internat. Opera Acad., Rome, master tchr. Scholar Julliard Am. Opera Ctr., N.Y.C., debut, N.Y.C. Opera, Hollywood Bowl, N.Y. Philharm., L.A. Philharm., Chgo. Symphony, London Symphony, Boston Symphony, San Francisco Opera Co., Teatro del Liceo, Barcelona, Royal Festival Hall, London, Metropolitan Opera; radio debut, O.R.T.F., Paris; films and recs. include Caterina Cornaro, I Pagliacci, Maid of Orleans, Mahler Symphony No. 8 others; author: The Verdi Baritone: Studies in Development of Dramatic Character. Rockefeller grantee, Nat. Opera Inst. grantee, Edwin H. Mosler Found. grantee, William Mathews Sullivan Mus. Found. grantee. Mem. Nat. Opera Assn. (bd. dirs.), Am. Guild Musical Artists, Actors Equity, Phi Mu Alpha, Lambda Chi Alpha, Pi Kappa Lambda. Winner San Angelo Symphony competition, Nat. Radio Auditions for Acad. Vocal Arts, Phila., Internat. Verdi competition, Busseto, Italy. *I was a totally American trained and prepared artist. Hopefully this fact will be of inspiration to other young American singers who, for too many years, have had to try to impress European smaller companies before becoming worthy to have any sort of career here in their own country. America is finally coming to acknowledge its own native operatic talent.*

EDWARDS, SIR SAMUEL FREDERICK, physicist, educator; b. Swansea, U.K., Feb. 1, 1928; ed. Cambridge U., Harvard U.; D.Sc. (hon.), U. Bath, U. Edinburgh, U. Loughborough, U. Salford, U. Birmingham, 1976, U. Strasbourg, 1986, U. Wales, 1987, U. Sheffield, 1989, U. Dublin, 1991, U. Leeds, U. Swansea, 1994, U. East Anglia, 1995; m. Merriell Bland, 1953; 1 son, 3 daus. Mem. Inst. Advanced Study, Princeton, N.J.; research fellow U. Birmingham; prof. U. Manchester; emeritus Cavendish prof. physics Cavendish Lab., pro vice chancellor Cambridge U., 1992-95; fellow, pres. Gonville and Caius Coll.; vis. prof. U. Calif., San Diego, 1980-81; dir. Lucas Industries, 1981-93; chmn. Sci. Research Council U.K., 1973-77, Def. Sci. Adv. Council, 1977-80; chief sci. advisor U.K. Dept. Energy, 1983-88; program dir. ITP U. Calif., Santa Barbara, 1997. Recipient Sci. pour L'Art prize Louis Vuitton Moet Hennessy, 1993, Boltzmann medal Internat. Union Pure and Applied Physics, 1995. Fellow Royal Soc. (Davy medal 1985), Inst. Physics (Maxwell medal, Guthrie medal), Royal Soc. Chemistry, Inst. Math. (Gold medallist 1986), Am. Phys. Soc. (High Polymer Physics prize), Brit. Assn. Advancement of Sci. (chmn. 1977-82, pres. 1988-89), Brit. Soc. Rheology (Gold medal 1991), French Acad. Scis. (fgn. assoc.), NAS (fgn. assoc.), French Phys. Soc. (hon.), European Phys. Soc. (hon.); mem. Athenaeum Club. Contbr. articles to sci. jours. E-mail: sfe11@phy.cam.ac.uk. Home: 7 Penarth Pl, Cambridge CB3 9LU, England Office: Cavendish Lab, Cambridge CB3 OHE, England

EDWARDS, SAMUEL LEE, religious organization executive; b. Waynesville, N.C., June 18, 1954; s. James Roy and June Elise (Settle) E.; m. Dorinda Kay Waddell, June 9, 1979; children: David Thomas, Rachel Karen. Diploma, Brevard (N.C.) Coll., 1974; BA magna cum laude, Am. U., Washington, 1976; MDiv cum laude, Nashotah (Wis.) House, 1979. Ordained Anglican deacon, 1979, priest, 1980. Curate St. Timothy's Episcopal Ch., Ft. Worth, Tex., 1979-81, rector, 1989-93; vicar St. Laurence Episcopal Ch., Grapevine, Tex., 1980-81; instr. Anglican Sch. Theology, Irving, Tex., 1980-87; theol. cons. Schs. of Spirituality, Dallas, 1981—; curate St. Francis Episcopal Ch., Dallas, 1981-87; vicar St. Patrick's Episcopal Ch., Bowie, Tex., 1987-89, Trinity Episcopal Ch., Henrietta, Tex., 1987-89; exec. dir. Episcopal Synod of Am., Ft. Worth, 1993—; priest/assoc. Cmty. of St. Mary, 1982—. Editl. bd.: The Anglican Service Book, 1990; features editor The Evangelical Catholic, 1985-89; contbr. articles to profl. jours.; contbg. author: The Future of Anglicanism, 1996, Quo Vaditis? The State Churches of Northern Europe, 1996. Mem. Sons of Confederate Vets. (camp chaplain 1993-96), Mil. Order of the Stars and Bars, Soc. of King Charles the Martyr. Republican. Office: Episcopal Synod of America 6300 Ridglea Pl Ste 910 Fort Worth TX 76116-5735*

EDWARDS, SARAH ANNE, radio, cable TV personality, clinical social worker; b. Tulsa, Jan. 7, 1943; d. Clyde Elton and virginia Elizabeth Glandon; m. Paul Robert Edwards, Apr. 24, 1965; 1 son, Jon Scott. BA with distinction, U. Mo., Kansas City, 1965; MSW, U. Kans., 1974. Cmty. rep. OEO, Kans. City Regional Office, 1966-68; social svc./parent involvement and resource specialist Office of Child Devel., HEW, Kansas City, Kans., 1968-73; dir. tng. social svcs. dept., children's rehab. unit U. Affiliated Facility, U. Kans. Med. Ctr., Kansas City, 1975-76; co-dir. Cathexis Inst. S., Glendale, Calif., 1976-77; pvt. practice psychotherapy, tng. and cons. personal and interpersonal, orgnl. behavior, Sierra Madre, Calif., 1973-80; sys. operator CompuServe Info. Svc., 1983—; prodr., co-host radio show Working From Home, on Bus. News Network, 1988—; co-host cable show Working from Home Scripp's Howard Home and Garden Cable TV Network, 1995—; commentator CNBC, 1996—, NPR Marketplace, 1996—. Columnist for Home Office Computing Mag., 1988—, Your Home Office, L.A. Times Syndicate, 1997—, Entrepreneur's Home Office, 1998—; co-author: How to Make Money with Your Personal Computer, 1997, Getting Business to Come to You, 1998, Working From Home, rev. edit., 1994, Secrets of Self-Employment, 1996, Finding Your Perfect Work, 1996, Teaming Up, 1997, Home Businesses You Can Buy, 1997, Cool Careers for Dummies, 1998, Making Money in Cyberspace, 1998. Address: 2624 Teakwood Ct Pine Mountain CA 93222

EDWARDS, STEPHEN ALLEN, lawyer; b. Battle Creek, Mich., July 12, 1953; s. Louis Ward and Elizabeth Yvonne (Stahl) E.; children: Amelia Hatfield, Nathaniel Gordon. BA with high honors, U. Mich., 1975, JD cum laude, 1978. Bar: Wis. 1978, U.S. Dist. Ct. (ea. and we. dists.) Wis. 1978, Mich. 1980, Pa. 1980. Assoc. Godfrey & Kahn S.C., Milw., 1978-80, Pepper, Hamilton & Scheetz, Phila., 1980-82; assoc. Morgan, Lewis & Bockius, Phila., 1982-87, ptnr., 1987-98; ptnr. Kilpatrick Stockton LLP, Altanta, 1998—. Author: Arbitrage, 1990; exec. editor: The Issuer's Guide to Tax-Exempt Finance, 1994, Municipal Leasing, 1999. Mem. ABA (tax sect.), Wis. Bar Assn., Mich. Bar Assn., Phila. Bar Assn., Nat. Assn. Bond Lawyers (chmn. arbitrage seminar 1990, edn. com. 1990-91, bd. dirs. 1991-94, treas. 1994-95), Bond Attys. Workshop (panelist 1984-95, mem. steering com., chmn. arbitrage 1986-87), Pa. Soc. SR (bd. dirs. 1991-94), Phila. Club, Ojibway Club. Republican. Episcopalian. Avocation: cycling. Home: 1156 Lullwater Rd NE Atlanta GA 30307 Office: Kilpatrick Stockton LLP 1100 W Peachtree St NW Ste 2800 Atlanta GA 30309-3609

EDWARDS, STEVEN ALAN, lawyer; b. Louisville, Apr. 3, 1956; s. Herbert Martin and Mary Catherine (Hill) E.; children: Matthew Wilson, Mark Alan. AB, Western Ky. U., 1978; JD, U. Louisville, 1985. Bar: Ky. 1985, U.S. Dist. Ct. (we. dist.) Ky. 1986, U.S. Ct. Appeals (6th cir.) 1993, U.S. Ct. Mil. Appeals. Assoc. Westfall, Talbott & Woods, Louisville, 1985-92, Woodward, Hobson & Fulton, Louisville, 1992-94, Hirn Doheny & Harper, Louisville, 1994-96, Bowles, Rice, McDavid, Graff & Love, Louisville, 1996—. Vol. Arbitrator Better Bus. Bur., Louisville, 1985-90. Capt. USAR, 1988—. Mem. ABA (outreach program nat. pub. svc. conf. 1987, 90), Ky. Bar Assn., Louisville Bar Assn. (sec. young lawyers sect. 1987, exec. com. 1986—, chmn. cmty. svc. com. 1986—, chmn. driving-under-influence edn. com. 1991, treas. 1991, chmn.-elect 1990, bd. dirs. 1993—, chmn. young lawyers sect. 1993—), Delta Theta Phi. Democrat. Lutheran. Avocations: Tae Kwon Do, sports, music, travel. Home: 3308 Gatecreek Rd Louisville KY 40272-2665 Office: Bowles Rice McDavid Graff & Love 633 Starks Bldg 455 S 4th Ave Louisville KY 40202-2593

EDWARDS, SUSAN M., hotel executive; b. Bristol, Eng., Jan. 2, 1953. Student in English lit., 1970. Office mgr. Godfrey Davis Internat., San Francisco, 1970's; dir. sales Karageorgis Cruises, San Francisco, 1980's; regional sales dir., then nat. sales dir. Aston Hotels and Resorts, Hawaii, 1981-91, assoc. v.p., 1981-91; pres. Delfin Hotels & Resorts, Santa Cruz, Calif., 1991—. Avocation: dogs. Office: Delfin Hotels & Resorts 627 Center St Santa Cruz CA 95060

EDWARDS, TERRI MICHELE, special education educator; b. Feb. 17, 1959. AAS in Early Childhood Edn., Parkland Coll., 1979; AAS in Electronics, Pima C.C., Tucson, 1986; BS in Edn., Ea. Ill. U., 1997. Tchr. E. Richland Schs., Olney, Ill., 1997-98, Indpls. Pub. Schs., 1998—. E-mail: terri.edwards4@gte.net. Home: 4815 N Broadway Indianapolis IN 46205

EDWARDS, TONY M., lawyer; b. N.Y.C., Dec. 2, 1950; s. Allan Abraham and Sylvia (Salzman) E.; m. Joan Stabins, June 5, 1976; children: Samuel Jacob, Elliot Joseph. BA magna cum laude, Lehigh U., 1972; JD cum laude, U. Miami, 1975; LLM in Taxation, Georgetown U., 1979. Bar: Fla. 1975, D.C. 1976. Tax advisor Interpretative Div. IRS Office of Chief Counsel, Washington, 1975-79; assoc. Morgan, Lewis & Bockius, Washington, 1980-84; assoc. Morrison & Foerster, Washington, 1984-86, ptnr., 1986-93; v.p., gen. counsel, sec. Nat. Assn. Real Estate Investment Trusts, Washington, 1993—; v.p., 1995-98, sr. v.p. and gen. counsel, 1998—. Contbr. articles to profl. jours. Mem. ABA (taxation sect., real estate com.). Democrat. Jewish. Home: 109 Primrose St Chevy Chase MD 20815-3324 Office: Nat Assn Real Estate Investment Trusts 1875 Eye St NW Ste 600 Washington DC 20006-5413

EDWARDS, VICKI ANN, elementary school assistant principal; b. Fremont, Nebr., Dec. 19, 1947; d. Howard Carl and Donna Marie (Earleywine) Schneider; m. Charles Douglas Edwards, May 27, 1977; 1 child, Janci. BS in Edn., Midland Luth. Coll., Fremont, 1972; MA in Edn., Ariz. State U., 1979, No. Ariz. U., 1986; EdD in Curriculum and Instrn., No. Ariz. U., 1988. Lang. arts tchr. Arlington (Nebr.) Pub. Schs., 1972-76, Glendale (Ariz.) Elem. Sch. Dist., 1977-80; reading specialist Deer Valley Sch. Dist., Phoenix, 1980-92, asst. prin., 1992—. Recipient award of achievement U.S. West Comm., Ariz., 1992. Mem. Internat. Reading Assn., Assn. for Supervision and Curriculum Devel. Nat. Coun. Tchrs. English, Phi Kappa Phi, Phi Delta Kappa. Democrat. Avocations: reading, needlework, music. Home: 2336 W Laurel Ln Phoenix AZ 85029-3423 Office: Mountain Shadows Elem Sch 19602 N 45th Ave Glendale AZ 85308-7339

EDWARDS, VICTOR HENRY, chemical engineer; b. Galveston, Tex., Oct. 17, 1940; s. Philip Lacy and Margaret Ruth (Hopkins) E.; m. Mary Margaret Litzmann, June 10, 1963; children: Henry L., Mary E. BA, Rice U., 1962; PhD in Chem. Engring., U. Calif., Berkeley, 1967. Registered profl. engr., Tex. Asst. prof. chem. engring. Cornell U., Ithaca, N.Y., 1967-73; mgr. adv. tech. U.S. Nat. Sci. Found., Washington, 1971-72; rsch. fellow Merck, Sharp, Dohme Rsch., Rahway, N.J., 1973-76; supr. rsch. engring. United Energy

Resources, Houston, 1976-79; vis. prof. environ. engring. Rice U., Houston, 1979-80; sr. process engr. Fluor Engrs. and Constructors, Houston, 1980-82; southwest editor Plant Services mag., Chgo., 1982-85; project engr. Allstates/BE&K, Inc., Houston, 1984-90, lead process engr., 1990-93, process engring. mgr., 1993-94; prin. engr. process and environ. Allstates/BE&K, Inc., 1994-95; process dir. Kvaerner Engrs. and Constructors, Houston, 1995—; tech. adv. com. Mary Kay O'Connor Process Safety Ctr., Tex. A&M U., 1995—. Contbr. articles to profl. jours. Mem. organizing com. Woodlands (Tex.) Harvest Festival, 1979-86; chmn. industry adv. coun., dept. chem. engring. Prairie View A&M U., 1991-94. Recipient Disting. Svc. award dept. chem. engring. Prairie View A&M U., 1992, 94, Shield of Irenee award for excellence in engring. design E.I. duPont de Nemours & Co., 1994, 98, Environ. Excellence award, 1994, Safety, Health, and Environ. Excellence award, 1996. Fellow AIChE (chmn. Process Plant Safety Symposium 1992, program co-chmn. 1994, exec. position 1 1993, chmn. 1995, South Tex. sect. chmn. 2d internat. plant ops. and design conf. 1997, Churchwell award South Tex. sect. 1981, Disting. Svc. award 1991); mem. AAAS, NSPE, Am. Chem. Soc. (chmn. Ithaca sect. 1969, councilor divsn. biochem. and microbial tech. 1970-77), Engrs. Coun. Houston (councilor 1987-92), N.Y. Acad. Scis. (life mem.), Rice U. Alumni Assn. (class of '62 reunion com. 1982, 87, 92, 97, co-chmn. fundraising drive 1998). Methodist. Avocations: reading, tennis, sailing, golf. Office: Kvaerner Process 7909 Parkwood Circle Dr Houston TX 77036-6565

EDWARDS, WALLACE WINFIELD, retired automotive company executive; b. Pontiac, Mich., May 9, 1922; s. David W. and Ruby M. (Nutting) E.; m. Jean Austin Wolfe, Aug. 24, 1944; children: Ronald W., Gary R., Ann E. B.S. in Mech. Engring, Gen. Motors Inst., 1949; M.B.A., Mich. State U., 1966. With GMC Truck & Coach div. Gen. Motors Corp., Pontiac, Mich., 1940-78; truck service mgr. GMC Truck & Coach div. Gen. Motors Corp., 1961-62, head engine design, 1962-64, dir. reliability, 1964-66, dir. prodn. control and purchasing, 1966-70, dir. engring., 1970-78; dir. Worldwide Truck Project Center, Warren, Mich., 1978-80; gen. dir. Worldwide Truck and Transp. Sys. Center, 1980-81; v.p. G.M.O.D.C., 1980-81; group mgr. small and light truck and van ops. Truck and Bus Group, Gen. Motors Corp., 1981-82, mgr. internat. staff, 1982-84, gen. dir. mil. vehicle ops. Power Products and Def. Group, 1984-86; bd. dirs. Advertel Communications Systems Inc., Ann Arbor, Crystal Mountain Resort, Thompsonville, Mich., 1991—. Past pres., mem. exec. com. Clinton Valley coun. Boy Scouts Am.; trustee Grand Travers Regional Land Conservancy, 1991—, chmn. 1996-98; regent Nat. Eagle Scout Assn. (life). Served with USNR, 1944-46. Mem. Soc. Automotive Engrs., Def. Preparedness Assn., Am. Security Council, U.S. Navy League, Tau Beta Pi, Beta Gamma Sigma. Office: 5089 Crystal Dr Beulah MI 49617-9617

EDWARDS, WARD DENNIS, psychology and industrial engineering educator; b. Morristown, N.J., Apr. 5, 1927; s. Corwin D. and Janet W. (Ferriss) E.; m. Sandra Fraser, Oct. 31, 1998; children: Tara, Page. B.A., Swarthmore Coll., 1947; M.A., Harvard U., 1950, Ph.D., 1952. Instr. Johns Hopkins U., 1951-54; with Pers. and Tng. Rsch. Ctr., USAF, Denver, 1954-56, San Antonio, 1956-58; rsch. psychologist U. Mich., 1958-63, prof. psychology, 1963-73, head Engring. Psychology Lab., 1963-73; assoc. dir. Hwy. Safety Rsch. Inst., 1970-73; prof. psychology and indsl. engring. U. So. Calif., 1973-95, prof. emeritus, 1995—, dir. Social Sci. Rsch. Inst., 1973-93; pres. Wise Decisions, Inc., 1995—; vis. prof. dept. psychiatry UCLA, 1997—; cons. in field. Author: (with J. Robert Newman) Multiattribute Evaluation, 1982, (with D.V. Winterfeldt) Decision Analysis and Behavioral Research, 1986; editor: (with A. Tversky) Decision Making: Selected Readings, 1967; editor: Utility Theories: Measurements and Applications, 1992; contbr. to Ency. Social Scis., 1968. Served with USNR, 1945-46. Recipient Franklin V. Taylor award Soc. Engring. Psychologists, 1978, James McKeen Cattell Fellow award in applied psychology Am. Psychol. Soc., 1995, Disting. Sci. award in applications of psychology APA, 1996. Fellow APA, Decision Scis. Inst.; mem. Western Psychol. Assn., Psychonomic Soc., Soc. Med. Decision Making, Ops. Rsch. Soc. Am. (Frank P. Ramsey medal 1988), Decision Analysis Soc. (pres. 1994-96), Inst. Mgmt. Scis. (pres. Coll. Managerial Problem Solving 1987-88).

EDWARDS, WARREN CHAPPELLE, military career officer; b. Franklin, Va., June 3, 1947; m. Diane Dorsey; 1 child, Joel. BS in English, U. Richmond; MA in Nat. Security, U.S. Naval War Coll.; M in Mil. Arts and Scis., U.S. Army Command & Gen. Coll.; grad., Army Command & Gen. Staff Col., Naval War Coll. Commd. 2nd lt. U.S. Army, advanced through grades to maj. gen., 1998, comdr. 4th Squadron, 7th Cavalry; comdr. 5th Squadron, 17th Cavalry, 2nd Infantry Divsn. U.S. Army, Korea; comdr. 10th Mountain Aviation Brigade, 10th Mountain Divsn. U.S. Army, chief, ops. directorate Office Joint Chiefs; chief of staff U.S. Army Aviation Ctr., Ft. Rucker, Ala.; asst. divsn. comdr. 2nd Infantry Divsn. U.S. Army, Korea; dep. commanding gen. Fifth U.S. Army, 1997—. Decorated Def. Superior Svc. medal, Legion of Merit with 2 oak leaf clusters, Meritorious Svc. medal with oak leaf cluster, 10 air medals, Army Commendation medal. Office: Fifth US Army Fort Lewis WA 98433

EDWARDS, WAYNE FORREST, paper company executive; b. St. Louis, Dec. 30, 1934; s. Forrest M. and Irma (Muecke) E.; m. Cela Ann Williams, June 14, 1958; children: Laura, Sally. BSBA, Washington U., St. Louis, 1957, MBA, 1958; PhD, St. Louis U., 1965. With Crown Zellerbach Corp., San Francisco, 1957—; group controller, containers and packaging Crown Zellerbach Corp., 1973-76; v.p. fin., v.p. for Latin Am. Crown Zellerbach Internat., 1977-82, v.p. subs. and affiliates, 1982-83, v.p. So. Timber and Wood Products, 1983-85, v.p. corp. devel., 1985-86, pres., 1986-87, v.p. corp. devel.; sr. v.p. Gaylord Container Ltd.; v.p. spl. projects James River Corp., 1987; pres. Edwards Assocs., San Mateo, Calif., 1988-90, Austin, Tex., 1990—; instr. MBA Program U. South Fla., 1961-65; bd. dirs. Sell-Thru Svcs. Inc., Fellers, Ginny's, House of Hattan, Binks Sames Corp.; chmn. bd. Sames Corp. Former vice chmn. Pacific Sch. Religion; moderator Congl. Ch. San Mateo. Served with U.S. Army, 1954-56. Office: Edwards Assocs Ste 210A 4210 Spicewood Springs Rd Austin TX 78759-8654

EDWARDS, WILLIAM H., SR., retired hotel corporation executive; b. Muskegon, Mich., May 25, 1917; s. William H. and Ruby A. (Tipson) E.; m. Ruth Ann Nolan, May 16, 1942; children: William H. Jr., Bradley N. Sr. BA, U. Mich., 1939; LLD, Northwood U., Midland, Mich., 1982. Cert. hotel adminstr. V.p., mng. dir. Palmer House Hilton, Chgo., 1966-68; v.p. Chgo. div. Hilton Hotels Corp., Chgo., 1968-70, sr. v.p., 1970-71, exec. v.p. ops., 1971-78; pres. Hilton Hotel div. Hilton Hotels Corp., Beverly Hills, Calif., 1978-89, vice chmn., 1985-89, bd. dirs., mem. exec. com., 1971-89, vice chmn. and dir. emeritus, 1989—; bd. dirs. Conrad Hilton Found., L.A., 1989—; bd. dirs. Travel and Tourism adv. bd. Dept. Commerce, Washington, 1983-88. Trustee Radiol. Soc. N.Am./Rsch. and Edn. Fund, Oak Brook, Ill., 1988-93, treas. 1988-89; trustee, v.p. So. Calif. chpt. Nat. Multiple Sclerosis Soc., 1984—. Recipient Cmty. Svc. award Brandeis U., 1975, Am. Tourism award New Sch. for Social Rsch., 1983, Amb. of Hospitality award Nat. Restaurant Assn. Ednl. Found., 1990, Convention Liaison Coun.-Hall of Leaders award, 1985. Mem. Am. Hotel Motel Assn. (pres. 1986, chmn. 1987), Travel Industry Assn. Am. (nat. chmn. 1982-84, bd. dirs. 1978—), L.A. Country Club. Republican. Roman Catholic. Avocation: golf. Home: 10350 Wilshire Blvd Los Angeles CA 90024-4700

EDWARDS, WILLIAM HAROLD, JR., nursing administrator, consultant; b. Valdosta, Ga., Oct. 24, 1954; s. William Harold Sr. and Mary Joyce (Harvey) E. Diploma, Med. Ctr. Cen. Ga., Macon, 1975; BS in Edn. cum laude, U. Ga., 1980; MS Candidate, Kennedy-Western U., 1991—. RN, cert. in gerontol. nursing; lic. nursing home adminstr. Sr. staff nurse Med. Ctr. Cen. Ga., Macon; utilization reviewer St. Mary's Hosp., Athens, Ga.; asst. adminstr. Grandview Care Ctr., Inc., Athens; sr. exec. v.p., chief med. svcs. officer ABC Home Hlth Svcs., Inc., Brunswick, Ga.; exec. v.p., COO Medshares, Inc., Memphis, 1994—. Mem. Nat. Assn. for Home Care, Nat. Gerontol. Nurses Assn., Am. Orgn. Nurse Execs., Am. Coll. Healthcare Execs., Tenn. Assn. for Home Care, Golden Key, Phi Kappa Phi, Kappa Delta Pi. Office: Medshares Inc 2714 Union Avenue Ext Memphis TN 38112-4402

EDWARDS, WILLIAM HENRY VON, III, United States marshal; b. Birmingham, Ala., June 26, 1945; m. Hedy J. Young, Aug. 5, 1972; 2 children. BS, Tuskegee Inst., 1968; JD, Birmingham Sch. Law, 1995. Various positions U.S. Marshal Svc., 1970-94; U.S. marshal no. dist. Ala. apptd. by Pres. Clinton U.S. Marshal Svc., Birmingham, 1994—. With U.S. Army, 1968-70, Korea. Mem. NOBLE, Alpha Phi Alpha. Baptist. Avocations: scuba, golf.

EDWARDS, WILLIAM JAMES, broadcasting executive; b. Birmingham, Ala., Mar. 30, 1915; s. Perron Austin and Eugenia (Evans) E.; m. Julia M. Stacey, May 15, 1937; children: Julia Beverly, Linda J. Edwards Riley. Student, Birmingham-Southern Coll., 1935-37; LLD (hon.), Saginaw Valley State U., 1994, Northwood U., 1995. Announcer, Sta. WBRC, Birmingham, 1933-34; program dir. Sta. WMBR, Jacksonville, Fla., 1934; announcer Sta. WLW, Cin., 1938; comml. mgr. Storer Broadcasting, Fairmont, W.Va., 1939-42; news commentator Sta. KMTR (now KLAC), Hollywood, Calif., 1944-45; exec. Sta. WIBC, Indpls., 1942-44; founder, pres. Lake Huron Broadcasting Corp., Saginaw, Mich., 1947—; pres. G.C.C. Communications of Houston, Inc., Suncoast Stereo Corp., St. Petersburg, Fla.; (Stas. KRBE-FM & AM, Houston, WQYK, Tampa-St. Petersburg); dir. Design Craftsmen, Inc., Midland, Mich.; Co-chmn. Saginaw chpt. ARC, 1951, gen. fund chmn., 1952. Pres. Saginaw Symphony Orch. Assn., 1954; pres. United Fund Saginaw County, 1960-62, Saginaw Community Chest, 1960-62; chmn. YWCA Adv. com., 1955-68; mem. Saginaw Libr. Commn., 1952-70, Am. Coun. United Funds, 1965-66; bd. of fellows Saginaw Valley State U., 1968-75; trustee Alvin M. Bentley Found., Owosso, Mich., 1969—, Birmingham-So. Coll., Ala., 1989—; pres. Julia M. and William J. Edwards Found.; gen. ptnr. Edwards Family Partnership, chmn. bd. govs., 1994; chmn. bd. govs. Northwood U., West Palm Beach, Fla., 1991—, bd. trustees, Midland, Mich., 1993—. With Armed Forces Radio Svc., USN, 1945-46. Recipient Disting. Svc. award Jaycees, 1951, Outstanding Bus. Leaders award Northwood U., West Palm Beach, Fla., 1991; named Saginaw Man of Yr., 1950. Mem. Birchwood Golf and Country Club, USN League (chpt. dir.), Govs. Club of Palm Beaches, Ballen Isles Country Club, City Club of Palm Beaches, Palm Beach Round Table (bd. dirs. 1994), Masons, Shriners, Rotary (pres. Saginaw club 1959-60). Republican. Methodist. Home: 1275 S Ocean Blvd Palm Beach FL 33480-5008 Office: 840 US Hwy 1 North Palm Beach FL 33408-3830 also: Birchwood Farms Estate 1087 Maple Way Harbor Springs MI 49740-9234

EDWARDS, WILLIAM PEARSON, retail company executive; b. Norwalk, Conn., Sept. 9, 1940; s. Magnus William and Faire Jane (Rindfusz) E.; m. Isabel Gomez, July 13, 1963 (div. June 1986); children: Katherine, Anthony; m. Amei Wallach, Sept. 9, 1989. BA cum laude, Harvard U., 1962; MA, U. Minn., 1966. V.p., merchandise mgr. B. Dalton Bookseller, Mpls., 1968-73, 79-86; v.p. merchandise Paperback Booksmith, Boston, 1973-74; divisional merchandise mgr. Diamond's Dept. Stores, Phoenix, Ariz., 1974-79; dep. dir. Mus. Modern Art, N.Y.C., 1987-89; vice chmn., co-founder The Mus. Co., Fairfield, N.J., 1989—; bd. dirs. The Mus. Co. Bd. dirs. Exit Art, N.Y.C., 1995—, Neighborhood Justice Ctr., St. Paul, 1984-87, The Mus. Co., 1989—. Fulbright scholar, 1967. Avocations: travel, music, woodworking.

EDWARDS, WILLIAM STERLING, III, cardiovascular surgeon; b. Birmingham, Ala., July 23, 1920; s. William Sterling, Jr. and Elizabeth Alabama (Wyman) E.; m. Ann Rohrer Dudley, July 13, 1946; children—Bruce Sterling, Peter Dudley, Katherine Wyman, Benjamin Wyman. B.S., Va. Mil. Inst., 1942; M.D., U. Pa., 1945. Diplomate: Am. Bd. Surgery, Am. Bd. Thoracic Surgery (dir. 1973-79). Intern, then resident in surgery Mass. Gen. Hosp., Boston, 1945-52; from instr. to prof. surgery Med. Coll. Ala., 1952-69; prof., chief div. cardio thoracic surgery U. N.Mex. Med. Sch., Albuquerque, 1969-74; prof., chmn. dept. surgery U. N.Mex. Med. Sch., 1974-87, emeritus prof. surgery, 1987—. Served to capt. M.C. AUS, 1946-48. Fellow A.C.S.; mem. Am. Surg. Assn., Soc. Vascular Surgery (pres. 1970), Internat. Cardiovascular Soc. (pres. N.Am. chpt. 1978), Am. Thoracic Soc., Soc. Thoracic Surgeons, So. Surg. Assn., Western Surg. Assn., Rocky Mountain Vascular Surgery Soc. (pres. 1980), Western Vascular Soc. (pres. 1987). Episcopalian. Devel. 1st prefabricated and corrugated cloth arterial graft for human use. Home: 2312 Hannett Ave NE Albuquerque NM 87106-3709

EDWARDSON, JOHN RICHARD, retired agronomist; b. Kansas City, Mo., Apr. 17, 1923; s. George Edward and Louise Marie (Sundstrom) E.; m. Betty Jo Cook, Aug. 24, 1948 (dec.); children: George, Elizabeth, Sarah; m. Mickie Newbill, Dec. 26, 1969. BS in Agr., Tex. A&M U., 1948, MS in Agronomy, 1949; PhD in Biology, Harvard U., 1954. Asst. agronomist U. Fla., Gainesville, 1953-60, assoc. agronomist, 1960-66, agronomist, 1966-97; ret., 1997. Author: Some Properties of the Potato Virus Y Group, 1974; co-author: Viruses Infecting Legumes, CRC Handbook, 1991; contbr. articles to Am. Jour. Botany, 1966. Staff sgt. U.S. Army, 1943-45, ETO. Fellow AAAS, Am. Phytopathol. Soc. (Ruth Allen award 1992). Democrat. Achievements include research in describing the structure of potyvirus-induced cylindrical inclusions, using cylindrical inclusions for classification of potyviruses, using cylindrical inclusions in diagnosing infections induced by potyviruses. Home: 2721 SW 3rd Pl Gainesville FL 32607-3109

EDWARDS-TATE, LAURIE ELLEN, homecare services company executive, educator; b. San Diego, June 3, 1951; d. Donald Morgan and Doral (Erickson) Hurd; m. William James Tate Jr., Jan. 1, 1995. Student Calif. Poly. State U., 1977; BA, Nat. U., San Diego, 1978; postgrad. U. Calif., San Diego, 1982-84; MS, Chapman Coll., 1986. Founder, owner Am. Med. Claims, La Jolla, 1981-86; pres., founder At Your Home Svcs., San Diego, 1985—, At Your Home Family Care, 1996—; instr. bus. Palomar Coll., Mira Costa Coll., San Diego Community Colls., 1981—; lectr. in field. Mem. golden Triangle Chamber, Rancho Bernardo Chamber, Health Access of San Diego, San Diego Regional Coun. Quality Care, San Diego Coun. on Aging, North County Providers Coun., South Bay Providers Coun., Long Term Care Pub. Interest Ctr. Mem. NAFE, Calif. Assn. Health Svcs. at Home (past bd. dirs., steering com.), Rancho Bernardo C. of C., Nat. U. Alumni Assn. Avocations: photography, travel, exercising. Office: At Your Home Svcs 6540 Lusk BlvdSte C-266 San Diego CA 92121 also: At Your Home Family Care 16466 Bernardo Center Dr San Diego CA 92128-2508

EEKMAN, THOMAS ADAM, Slavic languages educator; b. Middelharnis, Holland, May 20, 1923; came to U.S., 1966; s. Thomas Adam and Anna (de Kruyff) E.; m. Tine de Jong, May 2, 1946; children: Menno, Roeland, Ivo (dec.), Milja. M.A., U. Amsterdam, 1946, Ph.D., 1951. Research asst. Russian Inst., Amsterdam U., 1948-55, lectr. Slavic langs. at univ., 1955-60, asst. prof., 1960-66; vis. prof. UCLA, 1960-61, prof. Slavic langs., 1966-90, chmn. dept., 1968-72; ret., 1990. Author: The Realm of Rime, A Study of Rime in the Poetry of the Slavs, 1974, Thirty Years of Yugoslav Literataure, 1945-75, 1978; editor: Anton Cechov, 1860-1960, (with A. Kadic) Juraj Krizanic (1618-1683) Russophile and Ecumenic Visionary, 1976, (with P. Debreczeny) Chekhov's Art of Writing, 1977, (with H Birnbaum) Fiction and Drama in Eastern Europe, Evolution and Experiment in the Postwar Period, 1980, Calif. Slavic Studies, 1972-92, (with D.S. Worth) Russian Poetics, 1983; Critical Essays on Chekhov, 1989; contbr. articles to profl. jours. Decorated Order Yugoslav Flag, 1964; recipient Martinus Nijhoff prize, 1981. Mem. Am. Assn. Advancement Slavic Studies, Bulgarian Studies Assn., Philol. Assn. Pacific Coast (pres. 1971), N.Am. Soc. Serbian Studies, N.Am. Chekhov Soc. Unitarian Universalist. E-mail: 105477.1637@compuserve.com. Address: 334 Santa Margarita Dr San Rafael CA 94901-1640

EELLS, WILLIAM HASTINGS, retired automobile company executive; b. Princeton, N.J., Mar. 30, 1924; s. Hastings and Amy (Titus) E.; 1 child, Jonathan William. BA, Ohio Wesleyan U., 1946; MA, Ohio State U., 1950; DHL (hon.), Kent State U., 1983 D of Pub. Service, Bowling Green State U., 1983. Asst. to dir. Inst. Practical Politics, Ohio Wesleyan U., 1948-50, dir., 1953-57, instr. dept. polit. sci., 1952-59; instr. polit. sci. Mt. Union Coll., 1950-51; Mem. Ohio Gov.'s Cabinet, 1957-59; coord. Atomic Devel. Activities, State of Ohio, 1957-59; Midwest regional mgr. civic and govtl. affairs Ford Motor Co., Columbus, 1959-87. Mem. Nat. Coun. on Arts, Nat. Endowment for the Arts, 1976-82; chmn. bd. Blue Cross of Northeast Ohio, 1963-72, Blossom Music Ctr., Cleve., 1968-76; chmn. bd. govs. Gov.'s Coun. on Rehab., 1966-68; mem. exec. com. Met. Opera's Nat. Council, 1967-81; pres. Nat. Coun. High Blood Pressure Research, 1974-79; chmn. Ohio Pub. Expenditure Coun., 1981-84, Ohio Adv. Coun. Coll. Prep. Edn., 1981-84, Gov.'s Task Force on State Ops., 1984-85; vice chmn. Ohio Northwest Bicentennial Com., 1986-87; bd. dirs. Am. Heart Assn., 1974-79, Columbus Mus Art, 1982-88, Opera/Columbus, 1984-86, Columbus Ballet, 1985-86, Nat. Coun. French Am. Scholarship Found., 1985-87; trustee Cleve. Orch., 1964—, Hist. Morven Found., Princeton, N.J., 1988-96, Ednl. TV, Cleve., 1965-75, Cleve. Playhouse, 1965-82, Cleve. Ballet, Cleve. Zoo, 1965-76, Ohio Arts Coun., Columbus Symphony, Cleve. Luth. Hosp., 1966-76, Mt. Union Coll., 1984—, Ohio Wesleyan U.,1988—; mem. adv. coun. Meth. Theol. Sem. Trustee Franklin U., 1987—; trustee Columbus Assn. Performing Arts, 1978—, Ohio Found. Independent Colls., 1986—, Grady Meml. Hosp., 1987-94, Riverside Hosp. Found., 1990-96; hon. chmn. Del. Arts Ctr., 1989—; life trustee Fairview Health Cleve., 1980—; trustee, v.p. Oak Grove Cemetery, 1983—; chmn. Ohio Commn. for Son of Heaven Imperial Arts of China, 1988; mem. Ohio Humanities Coun., 1993-95; fellow Morgan Libr., N.Y.C., 1995—; trustee, pres. Delaware County Dist. Libr. Bd., 1994—; mem. Ohio Bicentennial Commn., 1997—; trustee Columbus Zoo Assn., 1998—; mem. Friends Princeton U. Libr., 1997—. Author: (book) Your Ohio Government, 1953 (6 edits.); contbr. numerous articles to profl. jours. Recipient USCG Disting. award, 1965, Silver medal Royal Life Saving Soc., Ohio State U. Devel. award, 1967, award for disting. svc. Am. Heart Assn., 1979, Ohio Arts Coun. award, 1979, Ohio Theatre Alliance award, 1981, Gov. award, 1985, Alumni Achievement award Ohio State U., 1987, Silver medal Japanese Red Cross Soc. Mem. Am. Fedn. Aging Rsch. (bd. dirs. 1994—), SAR, Ohio C. of C. (v.p., chmn., 1963-89, life dir. 1989—, Disting. Svc. award 1991), Ohio Mfrs. Assn. (trustee 1965-88), Ohio Acad. History, Western Reserve Hist. Soc., N.J. Hist. Soc. (trustee 1983-86), Soc. Cin., Princeton Club (N.Y.C.), Columbus Club, Univ. Club Columbus (pres. 1985), Union Club (Cleve.), F Street Club (Washington), Lakes Country Club, Kit Kat Club of Columbus, Pi Sigma Alpha, Pi Gamma Mu, Omicron Delta Kappa, Delta Tau Delta. Republican. Presbyterian. Home: Honeystone 54 Elmwood Dr Delaware OH 43015-1617 *Parents, teachers and friends can do just so much, you have to do the rest. God helps those who help themselves, and being in the right place at the right time does help.*

EFAW, CARY ROSS, manufacturing company executive; b. Waynesburg, Pa., Dec. 26, 1949; s. William C. and Julia M. (Whitfield) E.; m. Kathleen E. Dunkle, July 21, 1973; children: Dawn, Heather, Nathan. BS in Acctg./Econs., Waynesburg Coll., 1975; MBA, Youngstown State U., 1989. CPA, Pa.; cert. mgmt. acct. Sr. acct. Ernst & Young LLP, Pitts., 1975-79; staff acct. Equitable Resources, Pitts., 1979-81; sr. fin. analyst Joy Mfg. Co., Pitts., 1981-82; owner, cons. Efaw Enterprise, Pitts., 1982—; mgr. gen. and cost acctg. Cooper Energy Svcs., Grove City, Pa., 1987-98; ptnr. Ruddy & Assocs. CPAs, Wexford, Pa., 1999—; bd. dirs., advisor 84 Electronics, Houston, Pa., 1980-87; cons. Hodor Assocs., Eighty-Four, Pa., 1979-85, Lindley Enterprise, Washington, Pa., 1981-85. Contbr. articles to profl. jours. Advisor, state rep. Upper St. Clair, Pa., 1981-84; Sunday sch. tchr. Westminster Ch., Upper St. Clair, 1982-85; elder, chmn. long range planning com. Calvin Ch., Zelienople, Pa.; v.p. S.V. Track Boosters; bd. dirs. Grove City Area Fed. Credit Union, 1999. With USMC, 1969-71, Vietnam. Named Competent Toastmaster, 1980. Mem. AICPA, Pa. Inst. CPAs (contrs. conf. com.), Assn. Inst. Mgmt. Accts. (bd. dirs. Pitts. chpt.), Assn. MBA Execs., Am. Legion, VFW, DAV (life), Nat. Assn. Accts. (assoc. dir. 1977-78), Steel Town Corvettes Club (treas. 1977-80), Masons, Alpha Kappa Psi (v.p. Seneca Valley H.S. track & field booster club). Presbyterian. Avocations: auto racing, golf, softball, running, weight lifting. Home: 1 Zelie Dr Zelienople PA 16063-9707 Office: Ruddy & Assocs CPAs PO Box 537 11676 Perry Hwy Ste 1307 Wexford PA 15090

EFFEL, LAURA, lawyer; b. Dallas, May 9, 1945; d. Louis E. and Fay (Lee) Ray; m. Marc J. Patterson, Sept. 19, 1992; 1 child, Stephen. BA, U. Calif., Berkeley, 1971; JD, U. Md., 1975. Bar: N.Y. 1976, U.S. Dist. Ct. (so. and ea. dists.) N.Y. 1976, U.S. Ct. Appeals (2d cir.) 1980, U.S. Supreme Ct. 1980, D.C. 1993, N.C. 1998. Assoc. Burns Jackson Miller Summit & Jacoby, N.Y.C., 1975-78, Pincus Munzer Bizar & D'Alessandro, N.Y.C., 1978-80; v.p., sr. assoc. counsel Chase Manhattan Bank, N.A., N.Y.C., 1980-96; counsel Baker & McKenzie, N.Y.C., 1996-99; gen. counsel Garban Cos., 1999—; bd. dirs. Bklyn. Legal Svcs. Corp. A. Mem. ABA (litigation sect. co-chair com. on midyear and regional meetings 1997-98) , Am. Corp. Counsel Assn. (dir. emeritus, pro bono svc. award 1989), Assn. of Bar of City of N.Y. (com. on lectures and continuing edn. 1991-96, com. on banking law 1997—). Office: Garban 120 Broadway 21st Fl New York NY 10271

EFFINGER, STEVEN CRAIG, state agency administrator; b. Cheverly, Md., Oct. 12, 1956; s. William Davis Roberts and Naomi Mary (Effinger) Guthrie. Grad. h.s., Heathsville, Va. Transp. coord. Rappahannock C.C., Warsaw, Va., 1978-84; office svcs. asst. Public Records-Dept. of Accounts, Richmond, Va., 1985-91; office svcs. specialist Va. Dept. of Transp., Richmond, 1991-96, records mgmt. coord., 1996—. Mem. Va. Assn. of Govt. Archives and Records Adminstrs., Assn. of Records Mgrs. and Adminstrs. Internat., Va. Govtl. Employees Assn. Episcopalian. Avocations: music collecting, LP's, CD's memorabilia. Office: Va Dept of Transp 1401 E Broad St Richmond VA 23219-2000

EFFORD, MICHAEL ROBERT, police administrator, educator; b. L.A., July 22, 1950; s. Robert Victor and Mary (Athens) E.; m. Jolene Lynn Buttner, Mar. 20, 1976 (dec. Jan. 1980); m. Patricia Ann Jones, Feb. 2, 1985; children: Stacy Anne, Ashley Elizabeth. AA in Criminal Justice, Western Nev. Community Coll., 1976; BA in Bus., Calif. Coast U., 1993, MBA, 1996. Trooper Nev. Hwy. Patrol, Las Vegas, 1976-80; law instr. Western Nev. Community Coll., Carson City, 1980-94; adminstrv. lt. Carson City Sheriff's Dept., 1972—, in charge of planning & tng., 1993—; sheriff Carson City, 1980-94; chief of police Sonora (Calif.) Police Dept., 1994—; instr. Reno Police Acad., 1980-94, Nev. Hwy Patrol Acad., Carson City, 1980-94, Nev. Peace Officer Stds. and Tng. Acad. Editor Carson City Sheriff's Supervisory Assn. newsletter, 1989—. Pres. Carson City Labor Coalition, 1992—, planning commr. Regional Planning Commn., Carson City, 1989—; mem. Mainstreet/Redevel. Authority Carson City, 1991-94; mem. Nev. Day com., Carson City, 1985-94, 4th of July com., 1985-94, Gov.'s Ball com., 1985-94; apptd. to criminal justice tech. skills com. Western Nev. C.C., 1994. Sgt. U.S. Army, 1970-73. Recipient Svc. award Carson City Bd. Suprs., 1984, Excellence in Govt. award Tuolumne County C. of C., 1997. Mem. AFL-CIO Police Assn. (pres. 1989—), Kiwanis. Republican. Roman Catholic. Avocations: golf, computers, backpacking, skiing, reading. Home: 100 S Green St Sonora CA 95370-4643

EFFRON, ANDREW S., federal judge; b. 1948. BA, Harvard U., 1970, JD, 1975; student, JAG's Sch. U.S. Army, 1976, 84. Legis. aide to mem. Ho. of Reps., 1970-76; with Office of staff Judge Adv., Ft. McClellan, Ala., 1976-77; atty.-advisor Office of Gen. Counsel, Dept. Def., 1977-87; counsel, gen. counsel and minority counsel Senate Armed Svcs. Com., Washington, 1987-96; judge U.S. Ct. Appeals for the Armed Forces, Washington, 1996—. Office: 450 E St NW Washington DC 20442-0001

EFFRON, DAVID LOUIS, conductor, music director; b. Cin., July 28, 1938; s. Sigmund and Babette Jane (Holstein) E.; children: Michael, Daniel. MusB, U. Mich., 1960; MusM, Ind. U., 1962. Asst. conductor, conductor N.Y.C. Opera, 1964-82; asst. conductor Nat. Ballet, Washington, 1969-70; music dir. Central City (Colo.) Opera, 1972-76; conductor Curtis Inst. Music, Phila., 1970-77; music dir. Eastman Philharm., Eastman Sch., Rochester, N.Y., 1977-98, Youngstown (Ohio) Symphony Orch., 1987-96, Heidelberg (Fed. Republic Germany) Castle Festival, 1980-92, Chautaugua Instn. Music Sch. Festival Orch., 1990-96; artistic dir., prin. conductor Brevard (N.C.) Music Ctr., 1996—; prof. instrumental conducting Ind. U., Bloomington, 1998—. Condr. recs. Schwantner Aftertones, 1983, Schuman Judith, 1984, Benita Valente, 1986, Mahler & Berlioz with Jan deGaetani, 1989. Recipient Grammy award, 1984, Best Contemporary Rec. award Ovation Mag., 1988. Office: Brevard Music Center PO Box 312 Brevard NC 28712-0312

EFFRON, SETH ALAN, editor, journalist; b. July 23, 1952; m. Nancy G. Thomas; children: Rebecca, Eve. BA in Polit. Sci. with honors, U. N.C., 1974. Asst. to editor Fayetteville (N.C.) Times (now Fayetteville Observer-Times), 1974-75, reporter, 1975-77; reporter Tallahassee Dem., 1977-80; reporter Wichita (Kans.) Eagle-Beacon (now Wichita Eagle), 1980-82, 83-85, coord. legis. coverage, 1982; stage govt. and polit. reporter Greensboro (N.C.) News & Record, 1985—; editor, founder the insider, N.C. State Govt. News Svc., Raleigh, 1993-96; exec. editor on-line content Nando Media,

Nando Times, Raleigh, 1996—; NEH summer fellow Williams Coll., 1979; lectr. Freedom Forum Media Studies Ctr., Columbia U., N.Y.C., 1995, Annenberg Washington program Northwestern U., 1995, Ctr. for Pub. TV, U. N.C., N.C. Fellow, U. N.C., 1993, Press Assn., 1994, Inst. for Polit. Leadership, 1994, Salzburg (Austria) Seminar, 1994, Human Svcs. Automation Conf., 1994. Author: 100 Proof Pure Old Jess: Jesse Helms Quoted, 1993, Coachspeak: Triangle ACC Men's Basketball Coaches Quoted, 1995, North Carolina Almanac of Government and Politics 95-96, 1995; contbr. articles to popular publs., including Los Angeles Herald-Examiner, Des Moines Register, Christian Science Monitor. Mem. adv. panel Z. Smith Reynolds Found., 1988-91; mem. area edn. adv. bd. Broughton H.S., 1996—; v.p. Fred A. Olds Elem. Sch. PTA, 1994-95, pres., 1995-96; bd. dirs. Edenton St. United Meth. Ch. Child Devel. Ctr., 1986-88, 93-94. Nieman fellow Harvard U., 1991-92; recipient Cert. of Merit, Am. Acad. Trial Lawyers, 1975, Pub. Svc. award N.C. Press Assn., 1976, various reporting awards, most recently News Enterprise award William Allen White Found., 1985, 2nd pl. awards N.C. Press Assn., 1987, 89, 3rd pl. awards, 1990. Home: 308 Dixie Trl Raleigh NC 27607-7018 Office: Nando Media 127 W Hargett St Ste 406 Raleigh NC 27601-1351

EFIRD, JAMES MICHAEL, theology educator; b. Kannapolis, N.C., May 30, 1932; s. James Rufus and I. Z. (Christy) E.; m. Vivian Lee Poythress, Mar. 7, 1975; 1 child, Whitney Michelle; 1 stepchild, Anthony Kevin Crumpler. AB, Davidson Coll., 1954; MDiv, Louisville Presbyn. Theo. Sem., 1958; PhD, Duke U., 1962. Ordained to ministry Presbyn. Ch., 1958. Asst. prof. Duke Div. Sch., Durham, N.C., 1962-68, assoc. prof., 1958-85, prof., 1985—, dir. acad. affairs, 1971-75; interim min. Glenwood Presbyn. Ch., Greensboro, N.C., 1989-91, Mebane Meml. Presbyn. Ch., Roxboro, N.C., 1991-92, Hillsborough Presbyn. Ch., 1993, Little River Presbyn. Ch., 1995-98, Jonesboro Presbyn. Ch., 1998—. Author: How To Interpret the Bible, 1984, Marriage and Divorce, 1985, End-Times: Rapture, Anti-Christ, and Millennium, 1986, Revelation for Today, 1989, A Grammar For New Testament Greek, 1990. Duke U. scholar, 1958-62. Mem. Soc. Bibl. Lit., Phi Beta Kappa. Home: 6101 Bent Oak Dr Durham NC 27705-9115 Office: Duke Div Sch Durham NC 27708-0967

EFORO, JOHN FRANCIS, financial officer; b. N.Y.C., June 30, 1930; s. John J. and Rose (Lo Trionti) E.; m. Tina Liggio, Dec. 23, 1956; children—Joanne, Carla, John C. B.A. in Econs, CCNY, 1952; postgrad., Am. Inst. Banking, 1953-55. Asst. v.p. ops. Nat. Bank of N.Am., N.Y.C., 1958-69; v.p., comptroller United Mut. Savs. Bank, N.Y.C., 1969-82; officer, dir. Joint Computer Ctr., Inc., N.Y.C., 1974-82; sr. v.p., chief fin. officer State of N.Y. Mortgage Agy., 1982-94, N.Y. State Fin. Agy., 1993-94, N.Y. State Med. Care Facilities Fin. Agy., 1993-94; cons., 1994—. Home: 53 Sprague Rd Scarsdale NY 10583-6239

EFRAT, ISAAC, financial analyst, mathematician; b. Jerusalem, Oct. 27, 1957; came to U.S., 1979; s. Elisha and Nina (Buckshester) E. BS, Hebrew U. Jerusalem, 1979; MS, NYU, 1981, PhD, 1983. C.L.E. Moore instr. MIT, Cambridge, Mass., 1983-85; Joseph Fels Ritt asst. prof. Columbia U., N.Y.C., 1985-90; assoc. prof. U. Md., College Park, 1990-94; fellow Inst. Phys. Sci. & Tech., College Park, Md., 1993; trader L.A.F. Capital Mgmt., N.Y.C., 1993-95; fin. mgr. Renaissance Software, N.Y.C., 1995-96; sr. analyst structured finance Moody's Investor Svcs., N.Y.C., 1996-97, v.p., 1997-98, v.p., sr. credit officer, 1998—; quantitative analyst Bear, Stearns Inc., N.Y.C., 1991-92; mem. Math. Scis. Rsch. Inst., Berkeley, 1986. Author: The Selberg Trace Formula for PSL2(R). NSF fellow, 1986, Sloan Found. fellow, 1987. Mem. Am. Math. Soc. (Centennial fellow 1989). Office: 99 Church St New York NY 10007-2707

EFRON, BRADLEY, mathematics educator; b. St. Paul, May 24, 1938; s. Miles Jack and Esther (Kaufman) E.; m. Gael Guerin, July 1969 (div.); 1 child, Miles James; m. Nancy Troup, June 1986 (div.). BS in Math., Calif. Inst. Tech., 1960; PhD, Stanford U., 1964; DSc (hon.), U. Chgo., 1995; D (hon.), U. Carlos III de Madrid, 1998. Asst. and assoc. prof. stats. Stanford (Calif.) U., 1965-72, chmn. dept. stats., 1976-79, 1991—, chmn. math. scis., 1981—, prof. stats., 1974—, assoc. dean humanities and scis., 1987-90, endowed chair Max H. Stein prof. humanities and scis., 1991-94, chmn. dept. stats., 1991—; statis. cons. Alza Corp., 1971—, Rand Corp., 1962—. Author: Bootstrap Methods, 1979, Biostatistics Casebook, 1980. MacArthur Found. fellow, 1983; named Outstanding Statistician of Yr. Chgo. Statis. Assn., 1981; Wald and Rietz Lectr. Inst. Math. Stats., 1977, 81; recipient Fisher award, Chgo., 1996; recipient Parzen prize for statis. innovation, 1998. Fellow Inst. Math. Stats. (pres. 1987), Am. Statis. Assn. (Wilks medal 1990); mem. NAS, Am. Acad. Arts and Scis., Internat. Statis. Assn. Office: Stanford U Dept Stats Sequoia Hall Stanford CA 94305

EFROS, ELLEN ANN, lawyer; b. N.Y.C., Jan. 18, 1950; d. Edwin David and Judith (Breitman) E.; m. Fritz R. Kahn, June 26, 1983. BA, Case Western Res. U., 1971; MA, St. John's U., 1973; JD, Hofstra U., 1978. Bar: D.C. 1978, N.Y. 1979, Md. 1990, U.S. Ct. Appeals (5th cir.) 1978, U.S. Ct. Appeals (2d, 7th and D.C. cirs.) 1979, U.S. Ct. Appeals (Fed. cir.) 1993, U.S. Dist. Ct. D.C. 1981, U.S. Ct. Claims 1986, U.S. Supreme Ct. 1989. Trial atty. ICC Gen. Counsel, Washington, 1978-79; assoc. Verner & Liipfert, Washington, 1979-81; ptnr. Vorys, Sater, Seymour & Pease, Washington, 1981-97; hearing officer, office dispute resolution NASD Regulation, Inc., Washington, 1997—. Asst. editor Antitrust Law Jour., 1987-90. Mem. ABA (sects. antitrust and litigation), D.C. Bar Assn., N.Y. Bar Assn., Md. Bar Assn. Office: NASD Regulation Inc 1800 K St NW Ste 800 Washington DC 20006-2220

EFROS, LEONID, computer software scientist and developer; b. Balhash, Kazakhstan, USSR, Apr. 16, 1943; came to U.S., 1991; s. Boris and Anna (Taraseiskaya) E.; m. Svetlana Efros; children: Daniel, Olga. MS in Quantum Electronics, Leningrad (Russia) Inst., 1965; PhD in Computer Scis., Acad. Scis. USSR, Novosibirsk/Moscow, 1974. Chief rsch. lab., project leader, rschr. Acad. Scis. USSR, Novosibirsk Academcity, 1965-88; sr. sys. rschr. Acad. Scis., Vilnius, Lithuania, 1988-91; software engr., rschr. & developer NView Corp., Newport News, Va., 1992-93; cons., computer software developer Old Dominion U. Rsch. Found., Norfolk, Va., 1993-94; sr. project and sys. analyst Allied Signal, Inc./Aerospace, Goddard Corporate Pk., Lanham, Md., 1994-97; sr. computer software rschr. and system analyst SpaceTec, Inc., Hampton, Va., 1997-98; beam physics software scientist Thomas Jefferson Nat. Accelerator Facility-Jefferson Lab., Newport News, Va., 1998—. Contbr. articles to profl. jours. Recipient prize Coun. Ministers of USSR, 1983. Mem. N.Y. Acad. Scis. Achievements include research on real-time and large-scale software project design and implementation, software/hardware integration and software technology, parallel programming, network-oriented applications; avocatins: classical music, travel.

EFTEKHARI, NASSER, physiatrist; b. Aug. 15, 1940. MD, U. Tehran, 1965. Diplomate Am. Bd. Phys. Medicine and Rehab. Intern Greater Balt. Med. Ctr., 1967-68; resident in phys. medicine and rehab. Temple U. Sch. Med., Phila., 1968-70, Hahneman Med. U., Phila., 1970-71; rsch. fellow SUNY, Bklyn., 1971-72; chief dept. phys. medicine and rehab. Shafa Rehab. Hosp., Tehran, Iran, 1973-75; dean Coll. of Rehab. Scis., Tehran, 1973-79; phys. med. and rehab. cons. Golestan Clinic, Mehr Hosp., Tehran, 1980-84; staff physician VA Hosp., Miami, Fla., 1985—, Mercy Hosp., 1989—, West Gables Rehab. Hosp., 1989—, Bapt. Health Sys. Hosp. South Fla., Miami, 1996—; chief phys. med. and rehab. svc. VA Hosp., Miami, 1997—; clin. asst. prof. orthopedics, rehab. U. Miami Sch. Med., 1989—. Mem. Fla. Soc. Phys. Medicine and Rehab., AMA, Am. Acad. Phys. Medicine and Rehab., Am. Assn. Electrodiagnostic Medicine. Office: VA Med Ctr PMR-117 1201 NW 16th St Miami FL 33125-1624

EFTIMOFF, ANITA KENDALL, educational consultant; b. Granite City, Ill., May 3, 1927; d. David Harlow and Ollie Lorena (Galloway) Kendall; m. Vasil Eftimoff, June 14, 1959; 1 child, James Kendall. BA, Washington U., St. Louis, 1949; MA, So. Ill. U., Edwardsville, 1978, EdD, 1983. Cert. in multiple gen. edn., spl. edn., Ill. Spl. edn. instr. Community Unit 9, Granite City, 1968-83; ednl. cons. Efti Enterprises, Granite City, 1982—; program dir. At-Risk Presch. Grant, Granite City, 1986—; del. NDEA Conf. Ea. Mich. U., Ypsilanti, 1968, Gifted Edn. Conf. Ill. Office of Edn., Springfield, 1975-77; adminstrv. intern Ill. State Bd. Edn., Springfield, 1981. Editor: Symphony Youth Orch. Newsletter, 1991—, Symphony Vol. Key Notes Newsletter, 1991-93. Bd. dirs. Ill. Gov.'s Adv. Coun. on Women's Affairs, Springfield, Rape Crisis and Sexual Abuse Ctr., So. Ill. U., 1978-82, Family Resource Ctr.; chmn. adopt-a-friend St. Louis Ambs., 1982-84, co-chmn. Vets. Day, 1984-86; chmn. St. Louis Symphony Youth Orch., 1985—, St. Louis Symphony Young Artists Competitions, 1993—; mem. aux. St. Louis Children's Hosp., 1980; v.p. mus. activities St. Louis Symphony Vol. Assn.; bd. pres. Ill. Ctr. for Autism, 1993. At-risk presch. grantee Ill. Bd. Edn., 1986—. Mem. World Coun. for Gifted and Talented Children, Nat. Assn. for Gifted Children, Assn. for the Gifted, Ill. Council for the Gifted, Women's Assn. (bd. dirs. 1961—, pres. 1989-91), St. Louis Symphony Women's Assn., AAUW, Delta Kappa Gamma, Phi Delta Kappa. Lodges: Daus. of Nile, Rotary-Anns. Avocations: performing arts, classical music. Home: 2800 Michigan Ave Granite City IL 62040-3536 Office: At-Risk Presch Program 2300 W 25th St Granite City IL 62040-2025

EGAN, CHARLES JOSEPH, JR., lawyer, greeting card company executive; b. Cambridge, Mass., Aug. 11, 1932; s. Charles Joseph and Alice Claire (Ball) E.; m. Mary Bowersox, Aug. 6, 1955; children: Timothy, Sean, Peter, James. AB, Harvard U., 1954; LLB, Columbia U., 1959. Bar: N.Y. 1960, Mo. 1973. Assoc. Donovan, Leisure, Newton & Irvine, N.Y.C., 1959-62; ptnr. Hall, McNicol, Marett & Hamilton, N.Y.C., 1962-68; v.p., gen. counsel Thomson & McKinnon Securities, N.Y.C., 1969-70, Hallmark Cards, Inc., Kansas City, Mo., 1972—; bd. dirs. Am. Multi Cinema, Inc., Kansas City, Mo. Trustee Notre Dame de Sion Sch., Kansas City, 1973-77, Pembroke Country Day Sch., Kansas City, 1976-82, Kansas City Art Inst., 1995—; bd. dirs. Kansas City YMCA, 1976-80; mem. dean's coun. Columbia Law Sch., 1991—; vice chmn. Harvard Coll. Fund, 1994—. Served to 1st lt. USMC, 1954-56. Mem. Mo. Bar Assn., Kansas City Lawyers Assn., Harvard Alumni Assn. (pres. 1989-90, exec. com. 1987—), Century Assn., Somerset Club, Harvard Club of N.Y., Harvard Club of Kansas City (pres. 1985-87). Roman Catholic. Office: Hallmark Cards Inc 2501 Mcgee St Kansas City MO 64108-2600

EGAN, CORRINE HALPERIN, trade association administrator; b. Providence, Feb. 8, 1936; d. Barney and Rose Ruth (Bilsky) Gordon; m. Leo William Egan, Nov. 28, 1966 (dec.); children: Karen Halperin Shor, Michael Jay, Amy Marlene. BA, Mercyhurst Coll., 1980. Exec. dir. Coun. Vols. Erie County, 1971-78; exec. dir. YWCA, Erie, 1978-81; unit dir. Am. Cancer Soc., Erie, 1982; adj. faculty Mercyhurst Coll., dir. cmty. edn., 1982-84, dir. spl. events, 1984-85; program dir. Northwest Pa. Area Labor Mgmt. Coun., Erie, 1985-86, exec. dir., 1986—. Mem. Pa. Commn. for Women, 1990-96, N.W. Regional Pa. Planning Commn.; trustee Metro Health Ctr.; bd. dirs. Nat. Labor Mgmt. Assn., Pa. Breast Cancer Coalition, 1993—. Home: 3756 Gable Ct Erie PA 16506-4084 Office: NW Pa Area Labor Mgmt Coun 1525 E Lake Rd Erie PA 16511-1088

EGAN, DANIEL FRANCIS, priest; b. N.Y.C., June 18, 1915; s. Thomas J. and Mary (Bierne) E. AB in Philosophy, Cath. U. Am., 1941, MA in Edn., 1945; LHD (hon.), Marist Coll., 1980, Dominican Coll., 1988. Joined Soc. of Atonement, Roman Cath. Ch., 1936, ordained priest, 1945; cert. alcohol/drug abuse counselor. Assigned Negro mission So. U.S., 1947-49; assigned preaching missions Ea. U.S., 1949-59; founder half-way house for female drug addicts Village Haven, N.Y.C., 1963; founder live-in therapeutic community for female addicts New Hope Manor, Barryville, N.Y., 1970-78; program dir. St. Joseph's Rehab. Ctr. for Male Alcoholics, Saranac Lake, N.Y., 1978-79; assigned W.I. missions, Jamaica, 1979-81; dir. Drug Prevention Programs for Children, Youth, Adults, Graymoor, Garrison, N.Y., 1981—, Drug Rehab. and Prevention, Calcutta, India, 1989-92; drug, alcohol counselor St. Christopher's Inn, Graymoor, N.Y., 1992—; mem. White House Conf. on Youth, 1960, White House Conf. on Drugs, 1960; lectr. on drug abuse to various orgns., 1960—; mem. drug task force N.Y. State, 1978-79; pastoral min. Woodycrest AIDS Hosp., N.Y.C., 1994. Contbr. articles to profl. jours.; appearances on nat. and internat. tv on drug issues; subject of: The Junkie Priest (John D. Harris). Recipient Nat. Cath. Good Samaritan award, 1974, Aquinas Humanitarian award Mt. St. Mary Coll., N.Y., 1986, Alumni award Cath. U. Am., 1991, awards from U.S. Army, USN, USMC for pioneering drug programs in armed forces, svc. award Am. Coun. Drug Edn., 1995. Mem. New Eng. Police Women's Assn. (hon., award 1965). Address: Graymoor Garrison NY 10524 *If we had the vision of faith, we would see beneath every behavior - no matter how repulsive - beneath every bodily appearance - no matter how dirty or deformed - a priceless dignity and value that makes all material facts and scientific technologies fade into insignificance!.*

EGAN, DENISE, home health nurse; b. Boston, Dec. 29, 1954; d. Walter A. and Frances Sullivan; children: Colleen, Edward Jr., Jason. Diploma LPN, Boston Pub. Schs. LPN Program, 1976; BSN, Curry Coll., Milton, Mass., 1986; postgrad. in Enterostomal Therapy, Wicks Harrisburg Program, 1997. RN, Mass. Supr. Hyde Park Convalescent Home, Hyde Park, Mass., 1986-88; staff nurse/prenatal nurse Roslindale Med. and Dental Ctr., Roslindale, Mass., 1988-90; pediatric home care nurse STAFF Builders Agy., Boston, 1990, cmty. health nurse, 1991—; asst. dir. nursing Presentation Manor Nursing Home, Brighton, Mass., 1990-91; nurse reviewer divsn. med. assistance Commonwealth of Mass., Brighton, 1999—. Home: 39 Farnum Rd Pembroke MA 02359-3602

EGAN, EDWARD M., bishop; b. Oak Park, Ill., Apr. 2, 1932; s. Thomas J. and Genevieve (Costello) E. PhB, St. Mary of Lake, Mundelein, Ill., 1954; STL, Gregorian U., Rome, 1958; JCD, Gregorian U., 1963. Ordained priest Roman Catholic Ch., 1957. Sec. to Albert Cardinal Meyer Archdiocese of Chgo., 1958-60, sec. to John Cardinal Cody, 1966-68, co-chancellor, 1969-71; faculty Pontifical N.Am. Coll., Vatican City, 1960-65; judge Sacred Roman Rota, Vatican City, 1972-85; aux. bishop, vicar for edn. Archdiocese of N.Y., N.Y.C., 1985-88; bishop of Bridgeport Conn., 1988—; chmn. bd. trustees Sacred Heart U., Fairfield, Conn., 1988—, chmn. bd. Bishop Curtis Homes, Fairfield County, Conn.; mem. adminstrv. bd. U.S. Cath. Conf., 1991-94, 96—; chmn. bd. govs. Pontifical N.Am. Coll., Vatican City, 1991-95; trustee Thomas More Coll., Merrimack, N.H., 1995—; chmn. bd. trustees St. Joseph Med. Ctr., Stamford, Conn., 1988—. Office: 238 Jewett Ave Bridgeport CT 06606-2845

EGAN, FRANK T., writer, editor; b. N.Y.C., May 1, 1933; s. Frank X. and Ann M. (Hatton) E.; m. Helen Birmingham, June 5, 1954; children: Patricia, Thomas, Barbara, Richard, Maureen. Student, Drexel Inst. Tech., 1955-56, N.Y. U., 1956-60. Editor, Mc-Graw-Hill Pub. Co., N.Y.C., 1956-65, Hayden Pub. Co., Rochelle Park, N.J., 1965-71, Cahners Pub. Co., Boston, 1971-76, Hearst Bus. Pub., Garden City, N.Y., 1976—; Author: Ideas for Design, 1970. Served with USN, 1951-55. Home: 10221 Maple Leaf Dr Lawrenceville NJ 08648-1225 Office: Hearst Bus Pub 645 Stewart Ave Garden City NY 11530-4709

EGAN, JOHN FREDERICK, retired electronics executive; b. Council Bluffs, Iowa, Feb. 25, 1935; s. Frederick Emerson and Ruth Pauline (Russell) E.; m. Anne B. Patterson, June 14, 1958; children: John Jr., James Michael. *A fourth-generation Iowan, John Egan grew up with his parents, a brother and sister, and many relatives in Missouri Valley, Iowa where his father practiced law and his grandparents ran a grocery and dry-goods store. He was married for 41 years, and met his bride-to-be from La Grange, Illinois at Grinnell College where she majored in music education. After graduate school, he was assigned as an Air Force officer to a research and development job in Massachusetts. With children born in Concord, Massachusetts, fell in love with New England, and moved permanently to New Hampshire in 1973.* AB in Physics with honors, Grinnell Coll., 1957; MSEE, Northwestern U., 1958, PhD in Elec. Engring., 1961. Tech. dir. computer systems, Electronics Systems div. USAF, Bedford, Mass., 1964-67; sr. staff specialist intelligence Office Dir. Def., Research and Engring., Washington, 1967-71; chief scientist command support Office Chief Naval Ops., Washington, 1971-73; group dir. fed. systems Sanders Assocs., Inc., Nashua, N.H., 1973-77; v.p. Sanders Assoc., Inc., Nashua, N.H., 1977-87; group v.p. Lockheed Corp., 1987-93; corp. v.p. corp. devel. Lockheed Martin Corp., Bethesda, Md., 1993-98; mem. exec. panel Chief Naval Ops., Washington, 1971—; mem. naval studies bd. dirs. NRC, 1990-98. *John Egan has over 37 years of experience in the management of high technology enterprises involving both the public and private sector in defense, aerospace, electronics and information systems. During a 25-year career with Lockheed Martin, he held executive positions in the management of acquisitions, mergers, joint ventures, strategic planning, business development and research and development. He was general manager of profit/loss divisions engaged in development and manufacturing of defense electronics and computer peripherals. For 12 years, he held several key technical positions with the department of defense. He currently serves on several boards and committees of government, industry, and academe.* Dir. alumni fund Grinnell Coll., 1972—; mem. dean's adv. com. Northeastern U. Sch. Engring., 1987-93; trustee Daniel Webster Coll., 1998—. With USAF, 1961-64. Baker scholar, 1953-57; Transp. Ctr. fellow, 1957-61. Mem. IEEE, AIAA, AAAS, Sigma Xi.

EGAN, KEVIN JAMES, lawyer; b. Chgo., June 24, 1950; s. Raymond Basil and Harriet Olene (Landbo) E.; children: Ryan, Daniel. BA, U. Ill., 1972; JD, Northwestern U., 1975. Bar: Ill. 1975, U.S. Dist. Ct. (no. dist.) Ill. 1975, U.S. Ct. Appeals (7th cir.) 1976, U.S. Ct. of Customs and Patent Appeals 1978. Law clk. to judge U.S. Dist. Ct. (no. dist.) Ill., Chgo., 1975-77; assoc. Pattishall, McAuliffe & Hofstetter, Chgo., 1977-78; asst. U.S. atty. No. Dist. of Ill., 1978-82; assoc. Winston & Strawn, Chgo., 1982-84, ptnr., 1984-93; ptnr. Sonnenschein, Nath & Rosenthal, Chgo., 1993-99, Foley & Lardner, Chgo., 1999—. Article editor Jour. Criminal Law and Criminology, 1974-75. Bd. trustees Village of Frankfort, 1991—. Mem. ABA, Chgo. Bar Assn. (com. mem.), Bar Assn. of 7th Cir., Prestwick Country Club (Frankfort, Ill.). Roman Catholic. Avocation: hockey. Home: 904 Huntsmoor Dr Frankfort IL 60423-8747 Office: Foley & Lardner 330 N Wabash Ave Ste 3300 Chicago IL 60611*

EGAN, MICHAEL JOSEPH, retired lawyer, state legislator; b. Savannah, Ga., Aug. 8, 1926; s. Michael Joseph and Elise (Robider) E.; m. Donna Cole, Apr. 14, 1951; children: Moira Elizabeth, Michael Joseph, Donna, Cole, Roby, John Patrick. B.A., Yale U., 1950; LL.B., Harvard U., 1955. Bar: Ga., D.C. Assoc. Sutherland, Asbill & Brennan, Atlanta, 1955-61; ptnr. Sutherland, Asbill & Brennan, 1961-77, 79-97, ret. ptnr., 1998; mem. Ga. Ho. of Reps., 1966-77, minority leader, 1971-77; assoc. atty. gen. U.S. Dept. Justice, Washington, 1977-79; mem. Ga. Senate, 1989—. Served with U.S. Army, 1945-47, 50-52. Mem. ABA, Atlanta Bar Assn., State Bar Ga., Am. Law Inst., Am. Coll. Trust and Estate Counsel. Republican. Roman Catholic. Home: 97 Brighton Rd NE Atlanta GA 30309-1518 Office: Sutherland Asbill & Brennan 999 Peachtree St NE Fl 24 Atlanta GA 30309-3915 also: 1275 Pennsylvania Ave NW Washington DC 20004-2404

EGAN, PATRICIA JANE, former university development director, writer; b. San Francisco, Aug. 7, 1951; d. James Egan; 1 child, Kathryn Michele. AB, U. Calif., Berkeley, 1978; postgrad., N.J. Inst. Tech., 1996—. Cert. fund raising exec. Grants officer The Mus. Modern Art, N.Y.C., 1979-81; assoc. devel. officer grants Whitney Mus. Am. Art, N.Y.C., 1981-84; assoc. dir. devel. Columbia Bus. Sch., Columbia U., N.Y.C., 1984-86; mgr. major gifts New York Bot. Garden, N.Y.C., 1987-88; dir. devel. N.Y.C. Partnership, 1989-91; dir. devel. Cal Performances U. Calif., Berkeley, 1991-92; cons., 1992—; cons. to various cultural and environ. orgns., N.Y., N.J., Calif., 1983—; co-prodr. distance learning course proposal writing N.J. Inst. Tech., 1997—. Prodr., program host including Terpsichore, KUSF-FM, 1978-79. Bd. dirs. Universala Esperanto Asocio/N.Y., 1980-83, Dance Perspectives Found., N.Y.C., 1985—; trustee Riverside Ch., N.Y.C., 1986-87. Fellow Nat. Endowment Arts, 1977. Mem. Soc. for Tech. Comm. (Samuel J. Goodman Meml. award N.Y. Metro chpt. 1998), Women in Comm., Internat. Assn. Bus. Communicators, Esperanto League of N.Am., Jr. League of San Francisco, Order of Ea. Star. Democrat. Avocations: children's photography, ballet, modern dance, martial arts. Office: PO Box 194391 San Francisco CA 94119-4391

EGAN, SHIRLEY ANNE, retired nursing educator; b. Haverill, Mass.; d. Rush B. and Beatrice (Bengle) Willard. Diploma, St. Joseph's Hosp. Sch. Nursing, Nashua, N.H., 1945; B.S. in Nursing Edn., Boston U., 1949, M.S., 1954. Instr. sci. Sturdy Meml. Hosp. Sch. Nursing, Attleboro, Mass., 1949-51; instr. sci. Peter Bent Brigham Hosp. Sch. Nursing, Boston, 1951-53, ednl. dir., 1953-55, assoc. dir. Sch. Nursing, 1955-59, med. surg. coord., 1971-73, assoc. dir. Sch. Nursing, 1973-79, dir., 1979-85; cons. North Country Hosp., Newport, Vt., 1985-86; infection control practitioner, 1986-87; contract instr. Natchitohes Area Tech. Inst., 1988-90, Sabine Valley Tech Inst., 1990-91; coord. quality assurance Evangeline Health Care Ctr., 1991-92, asst. dir. nursing, 1992-93; coord. quality assurance Evangeline Health Care Ctr., Natchitoches, La., 1994-96, retired, 1996; nurse edn. adviser AID (formerly ICA), Karachi, Pakistan, 1959-67; prin. Coll. Nursing, Karachi, 1959-67; dir. Vis. Nurse Service, Nashua, N.H., 1967-70; cons. nursing edn. Pakistan Ministry of Health, Labour and Social Welfare, 1959-67; adviser to editor Pakistan Nursing and Health Rev., 1959-67; exec. bd. Nat. Health Edn. Com., Pakistan; WHO short-term cons. U. W.I., Jamaica, 1970-71; mem. Greater Nashua Health Planning Council. Contbr. articles to profl. publs. Bd. dirs. Matthew Thornton health Ctr., Nashua, Nashua Child Care Ctr.; vol. ombudsman N.H. Council on Aging; mem. Nashua Service League. Served as 1st lt., Army Nurse Corps., 1945-47. Mem. Trained Nurses Assn. Pakistan, Nat. League for Nursing, Assn. for Preservation Hist. Natchitoches, St. Joseph's Sch. Nursing Alumnae Assn., Boston U. Alumnae Assn., Brit. Soc. Health Edn., Cath. Daus. Am. (vice regent ct. Bishop Malloy), Statis. Study Grads. Karachi Coll. Nursing, Sigma Theta Tau. Home: 729 Royal St Natchitoches LA 71457-5716

EGAN, SUSAN CHAN, security analyst; b. Manila, Feb. 11, 1946; came to U.S., 1969; d. Mariano Sui Ming and Rita Patricia (Quejong) Chan; m. Ronald Christopher Egan, Mar. 22, 1971; 1 child, Louisa. BA in Chinese Lang. and Lit., U. Wash., 1970; MBA, Boston U., 1981; MA in Comparative Lit., U. Wash., 1971. Chartered Fin. Analyst. Bus. counselor Local Devel. Corp. of South End, Boston, 1973-74; cons. Boston, 1974-76; dir. edn. and tng. Mass. Dept. Commerce and Devel., Boston, 1976-79, program devel. cons., 1979-81; trust investment officer State St. Bank and Trust Co., Boston, 1981-83, sr. trust investment officer, 1983-86, v.p., 1986-87; v.p. Scudder, Stevens & Clark, L.A., 1987-98; pres. Pacific Trade Winds Co., Santa Barbara, Calif., 1998—. Author: Coping With Utility Bills and Other Enegry Costs, 1971, How to Do Business with the State, 1980, New Business, 1981, A Latterday Confucian, 1987, Hung Yeh Chuan, 1992, An Introduction to Securities Markets, 1997. Mem. Assn. for Investment Mgmt. and Rsch., L.A. Soc. Fin. Analysts. Office: 921 W Campus Ln Santa Barbara CA 93117-4341

EGAN, VINCENT JOSEPH, journalist, newspaper columnist; b. Toronto, Ont., Can., July 23, 1921; s. James Aloysius and Margaret (Ahearn) E.; m. Margaret Mary Maley, Apr. 23, 1962. BA, U. Toronto, 1951; MBA, 1955. Asst. editor Financial Post, Toronto, 1952-61; asst. to pres. Toronto Stock Exch., 1961-62; fin. columnist Globe and Mail, Toronto, 1962-68; fin. editor Toronto Telegram, 1968-71; columnist Thomson Newspapers, 1972-96; freelance travel writer, 1996—. Author: Making Money In The Market, 1955. Served with Royal Can. Navy, 1942-46. Decorated Victory medal; Can. Vol. Service medal. Roman Catholic. Home: 50 Rolph Rd, Toronto, ON Canada M4G 3M6

EGAN, WESLEY WILLIAM, JR., ambassador; b. Madison, Wis., Jan. 21, 1946; s. Wesley William and Ruth (Skeuse) E.; m. Virginia Warren, Aug. 15, 1967; children: Wesley Matthew, Kimberly Katherine. B.A. with honors, U. N.C., 1968. Vice consul Am. Consulate Gen., Durban, South Africa, 1972-74; spl. asst. to sec. state Dept. State Washington, 1974-77; 1st sec. Am. embassy, Portugal, 1977-79; dep. chief mission Am. embassy, Republic Zambia, 1979-82; ambassador to Republic of Guinea-Bissau, 1983-85, Chief of Staff to Dep. Sec. of State, 1985-87; Dep. Chief of Mission Am. Embassy, Lisbon, Portugal, 1987-90, Cairo, Egypt, 1990-93; amb. Hashemite Kingdom of Jordan, 1994-98; dep. insp. gen. Dept. of State, Washington, 1998—. Mem. Am. Fgn. Service Assn.; life mem. U. N.C. Alumni Assn. Episcopalian.

EGBERT, EMERSON CHARLES, retired publisher; b. Los Angeles, Nov. 30, 1924; s. Charles Barnes and Ethel Annette (Feader) E.; m. Kathryn Eleanor Tressel, Apr. 6, 1947; children—Susan Ann, John Charles, James Emerson, Michael Warren, Patricia Ann. Ed., Pasadena Jr. Coll., Woodbury Bus. Coll. Distbn. mgr. Newsstand Distbrs., 1947-49; dist. sales mgr. So. Calif., Pocket Books, Inc., 1949-59, sales mgr. Eastern div., 1959-61, v.p., circulation dir., 1961-71; pres. Pocket Books Distbn. Corp., N.Y.C., 1971-81; sr. v.p. Silhouette Books div. Simon & Schuster, 1981-85, sr. v.p. trade pub.

group, 1985-89; ret., 1989; pres. B/K Book Cons. Svcs. Inc., Rockville Ctr., N.Y., 1990-93, Madison, Conn., 1993-97; ret., 1997. Past dist. commr. Boy Scouts Am.; bd. dirs. 25 Yr. Club; bd. dirs. YMCA, Westbrook, Conn.; mem. vestry com. St. Andrew's Episcopal Ch., Madison. With USNR, 1942-45. Decorated D.F.C., Air Medal with 4 oak leaf clusters. Mem. Ind. Newsstand Circulation Execs. Assn. (past chmn.), Internat. Periodical Distbrs. Am. (chmn.), Bur. Ind. Pubs. and Distbrs. (past chmn. book com.), Anti-Defamation League. Republican. Home: 287 Legend Hill Rd Madison CT 06443-1864

EGBERT, PETER R., ophthalmologist, educator; b. Indpls., Dec. 6, 1941. BA magna cum laude, DePauw U., Greencastle, Ind., 1963; MD, Yale U., 1967. Diplomate Nat. Bd. Med. Examiners, Am. Bd. Ophthalmology. Intern Cleve. Met. Gen. Hosp., 1967-68; resident in ophthalmology Yale U., New Haven, 1968-69, 71-73; acting asst. prof. surgery (ophthalmology Stanford (Calif.) U., 1973-74, dir. Ophthalmic Pathology Lab., 1973—, asst. prof. surgery, 1974-81; acting head divsn. ophthalmology Stanford U. Med. Ctr., 1980-82, assoc. prof. surgery, 1981-88, prof. ophthalmology, 1988—, chmn. dept. ophthalmology, 1992-97; vis. prof. ophthalmology Govt. Hosp., San Pedro Sula, Honduras, 1974, Noor Eye Hosp., Kabul, Afghanistan, 1975, U. West Indies Med. Sch., Kingston, Jamaica, 1976, Princess Marina Hosp. - The Ctrl. Govt. Hosp., Gadorone, Botswana, 1978, Grenfell Regional Health Svcs., St. Anthony, Nfld., 1981, Govt. Hosp., Western Samoa, 1982, Project Orbis, Ismir, Turkey, 1985, Bamako, Mali, 1983, San Jose, Costa Rica, 1986, Port-au-Prince, Haiti, 1987, King Khaled Eye Hosp., Rihayd, Saudi Arabia, 1985, Korle-bu Teaching Hosp., U. Ghana, Accra, 1987, Leicester Royal Infirmary, Eng., 1987, Esperanca Hosp., Santarem, Brazil, 1987, Chinese Med. Sch., Hong Kong, Inst. Ophthalmology, Canton, Peking Med. Coll., Beijing, 1988, Nepal-Trilovan Teaching Hosp., 1990. Recipient Bordon prize DePauw U., 1960. Mem. Am. Acad. Ophthalmology, Am. Assn. Ophthalmic Pathologists, Am. Intra-Ocular Implant Soc., Assn. for Rsch. in Vision and Ophthalmology, Michael Hogan Eye Pathology Soc., No. Calif. Soc. to Prevent Blindness, Peninsula Eye Soc., Verhoeff Ophthalmic Pathology Soc., Alpha Omega Alpha, Phi Beta Kappa. Office: Stanford U Sch Medicine 300 Pasteur Dr Stanford CA 94305-5308*

EGBERT, RICHARD COOK, retired banker; b. N.Y.C., June 23, 1927; s. Lester D. and Beatrice (Cook) E.; m. Anne Merrill Becker, Sept. 11, 1954; children: Allison Huntting (Mrs. Roberts Wyckoff Brokaw III), Anne Merrill (Mrs. Thomas Hamilton Grape), Richard Cook Jr. B.A., Yale U., 1950. With Chase Nat. Bank, 1950-53; with Estabrook & Co., N.Y.C., 1954-68, ptnr., 1963-68; v.p. Spencer Trask & Co., Inc. (and successor cos.), N.Y.C., 1968-79, Bankers Trust Co., N.Y.C., 1979-84; v.p. Hamilton, Johnson & Co., Inc., N.Y.C., 1984-87, ret., 1987; Mem. Blue Hill Troupe, Ltd., N.Y.C., 1951—, pres., 1961-62; v.p., dir. 1030 Fifth Ave. Corp., 1968-72. Trustee, former treas. and chmn. finance com. W. Side Day Nursery, N.Y.C., 1957—; adv. bd. Nat. Choral Council, 1981—. Served with USNR, 1945-46. Mem. Soc. Colonial Wars, Colonial Order of Acorn, St. Nicholas Soc. N.Y., Pilgrims U.S., Chi Phi. Presbyn. (past deacon). Home: 250 Old Church Rd Greenwich CT 06830-4823

EGDAHL, RICHARD HARRISON, surgeon, medical educator, health science administrator; b. Eau Claire, Wis., Dec. 13, 1926; s. Harry I. and Rebecca (Ball) E.; children: Scott, David, Bruce, Julie; m. 2d, Cynthia Taft, Apr. 1983. M.D., Harvard U., 1950; Ph.D., U. Minn., 1957. Intern U. Minn. Hosp., 1950-51, resident, 1956-57; prof. surgery Med. Coll. Va., 1957-64; prof., chmn. surgery Boston U. Med. Ctr., 1964-73, dir., 1973-96; dir. Health Policy Inst., Boston U.; Alexander Graham Bell prof. health care entrepreneurship Boston U.; bd. trustees Pioneer Family of Mut. Funds. Past mem. editl. bd. Am. Jour. Surgery, New Eng. Jour. Medicine. Lt. USNR, 1952-55. Mem. ACS, Soc. Univ. Surgeons (pres. 1970-71), Am. Surg. Assn. (1st v.p. 1980), Boston Surg. Soc. (pres. 1977), Soc. Med. Adminstrs., Endocrine Soc. (CIBA award 1961), Inst. Medicine NAS, Internat. Assn. Endocrine Surgeons (pres. 1981-83), Comml. Club, Brookline Country Club, Algonquin Club, Badminton and Tennis Club, The Registry Resort, Phi Beta Kappa, Alpha Omega Alpha. Home: 333 Commonwealth Ave Apt 23 Boston MA 02115-1931 Office: Boston U Health Policy Inst 53 Bay State Rd Boston MA 02215-2101

EGE, HANS ALSNES, securities company executive; b. Haugesund, Norway, Jan. 31, 1924; came to U.S. 1953; naturalized, 1961; s. Sigvald Svendsen and Hilda Svendsen (Hansen) E.; m. Else Mathea Lindstrom, July 11, 1953; children: Elisabeth, Anne Christine. Bus. degree, Oslo Handelsgymnasium, 1946; student spl. bus. courses, City of London Coll., 1947; MBA, Drexel U., 1950. Analyst Alderson & Sessions, Mgmt. & Mktg. Cons., Phila., 1950-51; exec. asst. to U.S. ambassador to Norway Oslo, 1951-53; asst. to pres., asst. v.p. corp. sec. A.M. Kidder & Co., Inc., N.Y.C., 1953-64; stockbroker Reynolds Securities Inc., N.Y.C., 1964-65; mgr. Ridgewood (N.J.) Office, 1965-71; mgr. and resident officer, 1971-77; resident v.p., mgr. Dean Witter Reynolds, Inc., Ridgewood, 1978-82, v.p. investments, 1983—; trustee, v.p. The Bay Found., N.Y.C., Josephine Bay-Paul & C. Michael Paul Found., N.Y.C. Trustee The Norwegian Seamen's Ch., N.Y.C., Norwegian Immigration Assn., N.Y.C.; mem. Pres.'s Club Drexel U.. Served with Norwegian Underground, 1942-45. Decorated War medal. Mem. Am. Scandinavian Found., Norwegian Am. C. of C., Joe Jefferson Club (pres. 1969-70), Saddle River (N.J.) Club, Norwegian Club (N.Y.C.), Tau Kappa Epsilon. Home: 877 Roslyn Rd Ridgewood NJ 07450-2101 Office: 1200 E Ridgewood Ave Ridgewood NJ 07450-3937

EGELAND, ANDREW M., JR., military officer. BA in Chemistry, U. Va., 1965, JD, 1968; grad., Squadron Officer Sch., 1976; disting. grad., Air Command and Staff Coll., 1978; grad., Air War Coll., 1982, Nat. War Coll., 1984. Bar: U.S. Supreme Ct., U.S. Ct. Fed. Claims, U.S. Tax Ct., U.S. Ct. Mil. Appeals, Va. Supreme Ct. Appeals. Commd. 2d lt. USAF, 1965, advanced through grades to maj. gen., 1996; chief civil law and mil. affairs, staff judge advocate 4756th Combat Support Group, Tyndall AFB, Fla., 1968-72; staff judge advocate Judge Advocate Gen.'s Sch., Maxwell AFB, Ala., 1975-77, 8th Tactical Fighter Wing, Kunsan Air Base, South Korea, 1978-79; chief adminstrv. br. and pers. law br. gen. law divsn. Hdqs. USAF, Washington, 1979-83; dir. civil law Hdqs. U.S. Air Forces in Europe, Ramstein Air Base, West Germany, 1984-86; dep. staff judge advocate Hdqs. 8th Air Force, Barksdale AFB, La., 1988-91; dir. civil law and litigation Air Force Legal Svcs. Agy., Va., 1991-93; dep. judge advocate gen. Hdqs. USAF, Washington, 1993—. Contbr. articles to law revs. and jours. Decorated Legion of Merit with oak leaf cluster, Meritorious Svc. medal with 5 oak leaf clusters. Office: HQ USAF/JA 1420 Air Force Pentagon Washington DC 20330-1420

EGENOLF, ROBERT F., lawyer; b. San Francisco, Jan. 23, 1946; s. John D. and Virginia (Kirkland) Butler; m. Judy Wish, Jan. 23, 1970; children: Cristi Michelle, Jonah Wish. BA, U.S. Internat. U., San Diego, 1970; JD, Calif. Western U., San Diego, 1973; LLM, U. Miami, Fla., 1974. Bar: Calif. 1973, U.S. Tax Ct. 1974. Assoc. Blum & Blum, Oakland, Calif., 1974-75; ptnr. Westwick & Collison, Santa Barbara, Calif., 1976-80, Egenolf & Moore, Santa Barbara, 1980-94; pres., founder Calif. Exchange Corp., Santa Barbara, 1984-90, Santa Barbara Exch. Corp., 1984-90, 97—, First Exch. Corp., Santa Barbara, 1988-90, Amherst Exch. Corp., Santa Barbara, 1989—; instr., lectr. Santa Barbara City Coll., 1987—; lectr. in real estate exch. seminars Lawyers Throughout the U.S., 1987—. Bd. dirs. Tri Counties Devel. Disabilities Bd., Santa Barbara, 1977-78, Child Abuse Listening Mediation, Santa Barbara, 1979-80, Ensemble Theatre Project, Santa Barbara, 1981-83, Santa Barbara City Coll. Theatre Group, 1983-84; trustee Laguna Blanca Sch., 1997—; dir. Am. Inst. Food and Wine, 1991-93, Santa Barbara Wine Auction, 1993-94, Semana Nautica Masters Volleyball Tournament, 1993-97; mem. polit. action com. Planned Parenthood, 1995; mem. fin. devel. steering com. Santa Barbara Contemporary Arts Forum, 1995-96. With USN, 1967-69, PTO. Mem. Calif. Bar Assn. (co-chair joint tax subsect. 1990-95), Santa Barbara Bar Assn. (bd. dirs. 1978, 95—, pres. elect 1999), Barristers Santa Barbara (pres. 1976-77). Avocations: pilot, volleyball. E-mail: egenolf@agenolf.com. Office: Egenolf Assocs LLP 130 E Carrillo St Santa Barbara CA 93101-2111

EGER, DENISE LEESE, rabbi; b. New Kensington, Pa., Mar. 14, 1960; d. Bernard D. and Estelle (Leese) E. BA in Religion, U. So. Calif., 1982; MA in Hebrew Letters, Hebrew Union Coll., L.A., 1985; Rabbi, Hebrew Union Coll., N.Y.C., 1988. Ordained rabbi, 1988. Chaplain Rabbi Beth Chayim Chadashim, L.A., 1988-92; founding rabbi Congregation Kol Ami, West Hollywood, Calif., 1992—. Columnist Edge mag., Lesbian News; contbr. articles to religious publs., chpts. to anthologies. Exec. com. So. Calif. Bd. of Rabbis; cmty. adv. bd. Shanti Found.; treas. Women Rabbinic Network; chair Task Force on Gays and Lesbians in the Rabbinate. Recipient Rainbow Key award City West Hollywood, L.A.C.E. Spirituality award L.A. Gay and Lesbian Ctr. Mem. Cen. Conf. Am. Rabbis, Interfaith Clergy Assn. (past chair gays and lesbians bd.). Avocation: guitar. Office: Congregation Kol Ami 9056 Santa Monica Blvd Ste 100 West Hollywood CA 90069-5545 *I have found that in my work with the lesbian and gay community, as well as persons with AIDS, a unique resourcefulness, wellsprings of spirit and hope, in the face of death and oppression. These are truly inspirational and gifts to be shared with all humanity.*

EGER, JOSEPH, conductor, music director; b. Hartford, Conn., July 9, 1925; s. Abraham and Clara (Ellovich) E. Grad., Curtis Inst., Berkshire Music Center; studied with, Monteux, Stokowski, Steinberg, Lert, Rudolf, Kahne. Faculty Aspen (Colo.) Music Festival, 1952-57, Peabody Conservatory, 1962-65, New Sch., 1971-72; creator Harlem Music Project (published by Schirmer's, Consol. Music Pubs.); condr. seminar Smithsonian Instn., 1979; faculty, dir. internat. concert/seminar Salzburg Seminars, 1980. First horn N.Y. Philharm., L.A. Philharm., Israel Philharm., other major orchs.; solo rec. artist: RCA Victor, (albums) Joseph Eger Retrospective Series, 1978, also for motion picture, TV and radio; French horn soloist world concert tours, 1956; lectr., music dir. Eger Players; founder, condr. Camera Concerti Chamber Orch., 1958, Westside Symphony Orch., 1961, N.Y. Orch. Soc., 1963-73; condr. Midland (Mich.) Symphony, 1962-64, Town Hall series, 1962-63, Carnegie Hall, 1964-71, Philharm. Hall, 1965-72, Athens Festival, young people and teenage concerts, (concert series) UN, 1980, N. Miami Beach Symphony, 1997; guest condr. Royal Philharm., London Philharm, Moscow State Symphony, Lithuania State Symphony, New Philharmonia, Sinfonia of London, Pitts. Symphony Orch., Dallas Symphony, Cin Symphony Orch., Balt. Symphony Orch., Am. Symphony Orch., Vienna Radio Orch., Dessoff Choir, Haifa, Nat. Symphony Costa Rica, Nat. Symphony Cuba, Nat. Symphony South Africa, Nat. Symphony Ireland, Bucharest Philharm. Orch., 1997, Romanian Orch., 1997, others; assoc. condr. to Leopold Stokowski, 1967-70; composer: (recs.) Life mag., 1966, Westminster Record Co., 1967; (film score) Carolina, 1970, Hidden Fears; music dir. Indian Hill, 1967, N.Y. Symphony Premiere Performance, 1968, N.Y. Concertante, Symphony for UN, 1975—, UN Singers, 1975, Bklyn. Heights Symphony, 1978-82, S.W. Fla. Symphony, 1986-90, Champlain Islands Symphony, 1988—; founder, music dir. Symphony of N.Y., Aware, N.Y., 1971-74, Internat. Yoga Symphony, Can. and N.Y., 1973; founder Crossover; apptd. prin. guest condr. Ctrl. Symphony, Beijing, People's Republic of China; contbg. author: UNESCO Cultures; author: (guest editorials) Newsweek mag., 1980, Christian Sci. Monitor, 1981, N.Y. Times, 1982; editor: Citibank AWARE Playbill; exec. producer: (TV film/music video) Ode to Joy, 1988. Chmn. UN Coord. Com. for Nongovtl. Orgns., 1990—. Served to staff sgt. USAAF. Recipient Eleanor Roosevelt Man of Vision award, 1994, N.Y.C. Mayor's award, 1975, Internat. Music Therapist award, 1993. Mem. Nat. Assn. Am. Condrs. and Composers (program chmn. 1965-67), Acad. Ind. Scholars. Home: 170 W End Ave Apt 27L New York NY 10023-5418

EGER, MARILYN RAE, artist; b. Offett AFB, Nebr., Jan. 2, 1953; d. John W. Shaver and Joyce Faye (Carpenter) Shaver (dec.), stepmother Myrle I. MAsoner; m. Darrell W. Masoner, Feb. 28, 1971 (div. Sept. 1977); children: William Matthew, Melissa Rae; m. Gerard J. Eger, Jan. 30, 1982. BA, Calif. State U., Turlock, 1987. Cert. art tchr. 1990, Calif., lang. devel. specialist, 1993. Freelance artist oil painting Gibson Greetings Inc., Cin., 1992-97; tchr. art, A.P. art, advanced art Bear Creek High Sch., Stockton, Calif., chmn. dept. art, 1994-99, mentor tchr., 1998-2000; pvt. art tchr. One-woman shows include Stockton Fine Arts Gallery, 1984-88, Accurate Art Gallery, Sacramento, 1989-90, Sharon Gile Gallery, Isleton, Calif., 1988-91, Le Galerie, Stockton, 1989-91, Masterpiece Gallery, Carmel, Calif., 1991-95, Alan Short Gallery, Stockton, 1991, Lodi Art Ctr., 1997; represented by Iona's Gallery, Stockton, 1995-96, Heart of the Arts Gallery, Stockton, 1996—, C's Floral Gallery, Stockton, 1995-98, Lodi Art Ctr., 1984—, feature artist, 1985—; represented in permanent collections Gulf Oil Chems., Kaiser Permanente, Masterpiece Gallery, U. Calif. Davis Med. Ctr.; prints pub. in Mus. Edits. West. Bd. dirs. Lodi Art Ctr., 1988-91, chmn. 1989. Recipient Award of Excellence Unitarian Fall Art Festival, 1990, Award of Excellence in Oils, 1992, Ben Day Meml. award, 1993, Bank Stockton award and H.M. Haggin Mus., 1989, U.S. Nat. Collegiate Art Merit award, 1988, Lodi 31st Ann., 1st Oils, 1988, Award of Excellence in Pastel Haggin Mus., 1992, 1st Oils and Don Morrell Meml. award CCAL Gallo Show, 1993, Art of Calif. Bronze Discovery award, 1993, 1st pastel Lodi Art Ann., 1995, Hon. mention, 1998, award of merit Haggin Mus., 1997, 3rd in graphics Unitarian Fall Art Festival, 1998, 3rd Graphics award Lodi Art Ann., 1998, numerous others; Mellon grantee, 1994. Mem. Calif. Art Edn. Assn., Stockton Art League, Nat. League Am. Pen. Women, Ctrl. Calif. Art League. Republican. Methodist. Avocations: sculpting, gardening, vineyards, painting, travel. Home: 1295 E Peltier Rd Acampo CA 95220-9652 Office: 1295 1/2 E Peltier Rd Acampo CA 95220-9652

EGERTON, CHARLES PICKFORD, anatomy and physiology educator; b. Toronto, Ont., Can., Mar. 17, 1939; (parents Am. citizens); s. Matthew Davis and Margaret Swain (Pickford) E.; m. Carol Anne Carlson, Dec. 16, 1976; children: Matthew, Andrew, Victoria. BA in Zoology, Duke U., 1962; BS in Medicine, U. Okla., Oklahoma City, 1978; MS in Sci. Edn., U. So. Miss., 1981, PhD in Sci. Edn., 1991, MPH in Health Edn., 1994. Cert. physician asst. Nat. Commn. on Cert. Physician Assts. Commd. 2d lt. USAF, 1962, advanced through grades to maj., 1980, ops. officer, 1962-76; primary care med. officer USAF, Keesler AFB, Miss., 1978-88; ret., 1988; instr. anatomy and physiology Miss. Gulf Coast C.C., Gautier, 1992—; mem. Miss. Health Adv. Coun., Jackson, 1990—; guest lectr. dept. physician asst. studies U. South Ala. Author: Student Study Guide for Anatomy and Physiology; editor: Physician Assistant Handbook, 1995, Principles of Anatomy and Physiology, 9th edit.; contbr. articles to profl. jours. Lectr. Miss. Inst. Drug-Free Sch., Hattiesburg, 1992; lectr. single parent-displaced spouse, Gautier, 1994-97; dir. smoking cessation Keesler AFB Med. Ctr., 1986-88; lay reader St. Luke's Anglican Ch., Gulfport, Miss., 1986-94. Mem. Am. Assn. Anatomists, Am. Acad. Physician Assts., Human Anatomy and Physiology Soc., Miss. Acad. Scis., Miss. Sci. Tchrs. Assn., Phi Delta Kappa, Eta Sigma Gamma. Democrat. Avocation: boating. Home: 6008 E Moreton Pl Ocean Springs MS 39564-2725 Office: Miss Gulf Coast CC PO Box 100 Gautier MS 39553-0100

EGERTSON, THILDA AMANDA, retired librarian and elementary educator; b. Decorah, Iowa, Aug. 26, 1904; d. Ole Lewis Wennes and Caroline Larson; m. Hagbard O. Egertson (dec. 1985); children: Jordan Wennes (dec.), Margarethe Wennes, Paul Wennes, Sylvia Wennes. BA in Psychology, UCLA, 1950; MA in Spl. Edn., Calif. State U., L.A., 1955; postgrad., U. Minn., 1955-56. 5 tchg. credentials, Calif. Legal sec. Will/Nelson Law Firm, Decorah, 1924-27; tchr. spl. edn. L.A. City Schs., 1953-60; tchr. parochial Westchester and North Hollywood Elem., 1950-53; libr. L.A. City Schs., 1960-70, Luth. Bible Coll., L.A. and Anaheim, 1972-94. Contbr. articles to profl. publs. Vol. libr. Theological Coll., S. Africa, Ethiopia, 1963-64, Nigeria, 1966, New Guinea, 1966, Wycliffe Bible Translators, Mexico City, 1973, Union Theol. Sem. Librs., 1973, Am. Luth. Theol. Sem., St. Paul, 1993; tchr. Honolulu, 1967, Sells, Ariz., 1979, Fairbanks, Ala., 1981, Adelaide, Australia, 1994. Thilda Wennes Egertson Libr. named in her honor. Mem. Luth. Ch. Libr. Assn. (nat. pres. 1976, mem. adv. bd., award for orgn. of chpts. and tchg.). Republican. Lutheran. Avocations: writing, reading, knitting, tatting, traveling. Home: 118-K 1571 Golden Rain Rd Seal Beach CA 90740-4911

EGGE, JOEL, clergy member, academic administrator. Pres. Lutheran Brethren Schools of the Church of the Lutheran Brethren of America, Fergus Falls, Minn., Luth. Brethren Schs., Fergus Falls, Minn. Office: Lutheran Brethren Schools Ch of Lutheran Brethren of Am 815 W Vernon Ave Fergus Falls MN 56537-2699*

EGGEN, SVEIN, company executive. Factory worker Aker Verdal, 1974-84, mng. dir., 1984-88; exec. v.p. Aker Offshore, 1988-90; pres. Aker Maritime, 1996—. E-mail: ami@akerusa.com. Fax: 281-588-7599. Office: Aker Maritime Inc Ste 1300 11757 Katy Freeway Houston TX 77079

EGGENBERGER, ANDREW JON, federal agency administrator; b. Harlowton, Mont., May 8, 1938; s. Andrew D. and Gladys E. Eggenberger. BS, Carnegie Mellon U., 1961, PhD, 1967; MS, Ohio State U., 1963. Prof. U. S.C., Columbia, 1967-72; project mgr. D'Appolonia Cons. Engrs., Pitts., 1972-84; program dir. NSF, Washington, 1984-89; vice chmn. Def. Nuclear Facilities Safety Bd., Washington, 1989—; fellow Marshall Space Flight Ctr., Huntsville, Ala., 1969, Lewis Rsch. Ctr., Cleve., 1967, 68; rsch. engr. Boeing Co., Seattle, 1961-63. Recipient Ralph R. Teetor award Soc. Automotive Engrs., 1968. Mem. AIAA, Am. Nuclear Soc., Earthquake Engrng. Rsch. Inst., Sigma Alpha Epsilon. Lutheran. Avocations: auto racing, flying. Office: Def Nuclear Facilities Safety Bd 625 Indiana Ave NW Ste 700 Washington DC 20004-2901

EGGER, ROSCOE LYNN, JR., consultant, former IRS commissioner; b. Jackson, Mich., Sept. 19, 1920; s. Roscoe L. and Harriette L. (Youngs) E.; m. Betty Slattery; children: Gabrielle Egger Shaykin, Antoinette Egger Taylor. BA, Ind. U., 1942; LLB, George Washington U., 1950. With GAO, 1946-48; pvt. practice acctg., 1948-50, pvt. practice law, 1956-81; founder Office of Govt. Svcs., 1956-81; with Office of Govt. Service, Price Waterhouse, 1981-86; commr. IRS, Washington, 1981-86. Mem. Commn. on Adminstrv. Rev. Ho. of Reps.; chmn. bd. Nat. Cathedral Sch. for Girls, 1974-76; chmn. bd. dirs. Wolf Trap Assocs.; bd. dirs. C. of C. U.S.A., 1973-79, Chesapeake Bay Maritime Mus. With U.S. Army, 1943-46. Mem. ABA, AICPA, D.C. Bar Assn. Republican. Episcopalian. Clubs: Met. (Washington), Country Club of Green Valley, Ariz. Home: 363 W Mission Twin Buttes Rd Green Valley AZ 85614-1624

EGGERS, ALFRED JOHN, JR., research corporation executive; b. Omaha, June 24, 1922; s. Alfred John and Golden May (Meyers) E.; m. Elizabeth Ann Hills, Sept. 9, 1950; children—Alfred John III, Philip Norman. B.A., U. Nebr.-Omaha, 1945; M.S., Stanford U., 1951, Ph.D., 1957. Aerospace scientist, asst. dir. NASA Ames Research Ctr., Mountain View, Calif., 1944-64; dep. assoc. adminstr., asst. adminstr. for policy NASA, Washington, 1964-71; Hunsaker prof. MIT, Cambridge, 1969-71; asst. dir. NSF, Washington, 1971-77; dir. Lockheed Research Lab., Palo Alto, Calif., 1977-79; chmn. bd., chief exec. officer RANN, Inc., Palo Alto, Calif., 1979—; mem. sci. adv. bd. USAF, Washington, 1958-72, Aerospace Engring. Bd., NAE, Washington, 1973-77; mem. adv. bd. Solar Energy Rsch. Inst., Golden, Colo., 1985-89; chmn. A.J. Eggers & Co., Atherton, Calif., 1981—. Author: Hypersonic Flow, 1962; contbr. articles to profl. jours.; patentee in field. Vice chmn. Sch. Community Devel. Com., Los Altos Hills, Calif., 1963-64; mem., chmn. troop com. Boy Scouts Am., Arlington, Va., 1968-75; mem. safety com. ARC, Arlington, 1975-77. Served to lt. (j.g.) USN, 1943-46. Recipient Arthur S. Flemming award USJCC, 1956, TOYM award USJCC, 1957, Exceptional Svc. medal NASA, 1971, Disting. Svc. medal NSF, 1975, Disting. Svc. medal Pres. of U.S., 1977, commendation Nat. Sci. Bd., 1977. Fellow AAAS, AIAA (founder, bd. dirs. 1962-66, Sylvanus Albert Reed award 1961), Am. Astron. Soc.; mem. NAE (long-range planning and devel. com. 1983-85), Am. Wind Energy Assn., Washington Golf and Country Club, Sigma Xi, Tau Beta Pi. Republican. Avocations: swimming; golf; skiing. Home: 23 Fair Oaks Ln Atherton CA 94027-3808 Office: RANN Inc 744 San Antonio Rd Ste 26 Palo Alto CA 94303-4624 *Success in life is always burdened by achieving competence and working hard at what you do. Happiness is the unique reward for enjoying what you do.*

EGGERS, GEORGE WILLIAM NORDHOLTZ, JR., anesthesiologist, educator; b. Galveston, Tex., Feb. 22, 1929; s. George William Nordholtz and Edith (Sykes) E.; m. Mary Futrell, Dec. 30, 1955; children: Carol Ann, George William Nordholtz III. BA, Rice U., 1949; MD, U. Tex., 1953. Diplomate Am. Bd. Anesthesiology. Instr. dept. anesthesiology, U. Tex., Galveston, 1956-59, asst. prof., 1959-61; assoc. prof. dept. anesthesiology, U. Mo., Columbia, 1961-67; prof. dept anesthesiology U. Mo., Columbia, 1967—, acting chmn. dept. anesthesiology, 1969, chmn. dept. anesthesiology, 1970-94, prof. emeritus, 1994—; vis. instr. USAF Hosp., Lackland AFB, San Antonio, 1956-61; vis. research prof. dept. anesthesiology Northwestern U. Med. Sch., Chgo., 1968-69; research assoc. Space Sci. Research Ctr., Columbia, 1965-66. Contbr. over 50 articles to profl. jours. Recipient Ashbel Smith Disting. Alumnus award U. Tex., 1993. Mem. Am. Soc. Anesthesiology (bd. dirs. 1979-86, v.p. 1986-88, 1st v.p. 1989, pres.-elect 1990, pres. 1991), Am. Coll. Anesthesiology (bd. govs. 1965-74, chmn. bd. govs. 1973), Soc. Acad. Anesthesiology Chmn. (pres. 1971), Assn. Am. Med. Colls. (adminstrv. bd. council acad. socs. 1976-79), Mo. Soc. Anesthesiologists (pres. 1970), Tex. Gulf Coast Anesthesiology Soc. (v.p. 1960), Boone County Med. Soc. (pres. 1988), Am. Bd. Anesthesiology (assoc. examiner 1968, joint council with Am. Soc. Anesthesiology on in-tng. exams.), Acad. Anesthesiology (pres. 1994, Citation of Merit 1997), Accreditation Council Grad. Med. Edn. (mem. residency rev. com. for anesthesiology 1989-94), Anesthesia Found. (trustee 1993—), Alpha Omega Alpha, Mu Delta, Sigma Xi. Republican. Roman Catholic. Avocations: shooting, hunting, astronomy, magic, photography. Home: 1509 Woodrail Ave Columbia MO 65203-0931 Office: Univ Mo Dept Anesthesiology 1 Hospital Dr Dept Columbia MO 65201-5276

EGGERS, JAMES WESLEY, executive search consultant; b. Des Moines, Feb. 7, 1925; s. Paul William and Opal Imo (Cardiff) E.; m. Marjorie Mardell Freel, Aug. 2, 1947; children: James S., Barbara Bucher, Mark D. Grad., Knoxville High Sch., 1943. Farmer Knoxville, Iowa, 1948-55; sales rep. Iowa Power & Light Co., Des Moines, 1953-60, Cedar Rapids, Iowa, 1960-62; sales exec. Thomas D. Murphy Co., Red Oak, Iowa, 1962-67; pres., owner Eggers Cos., Omaha, 1967—; bd. dirs. Nebr. State Bank, Omaha; owner, mgr. Exec. Realty and Mgmt. Co., Omaha, 1979—. Bd. dirs. local Meth. Ch.; chmn. local dist. George Bush for Pres. campaign, Nebr., 1988; chmn. State of Nebr. Merit Coun., Lincoln, 1979-83; chmn. and mem. various civic bds.; mem. New Methodist Hosp. Found. Mem. Nebr. Assn. Pers. Cons. (pres. 1974-75), Nat. Assn. Pers. Cons. (mem. nat. com. 1979-83, cert.), Omaha C. of C. (bd. dirs. 1980-83), Rotary (bd. dirs. Omaha chpt. 1983—, sgt.-at-arms 1986-90), Masons, Shriners. Republican. Avocations: reading, travel, religious study, walking. Office: Eggers Cons Co Inc Eggers Plz 11272 Elm St Omaha NE 68144-4788

EGGERS, JENNIFER CHRISTINE, management consultant; b. Harrisburg, Pa., Jan. 11, 1972; d. William A. and Cecilia Theresa (Demovich) E. BS in Mktg., Pa. State U., 1994. Security sys. designer Lifesafe Inc., Allentown, Pa., 1991; territory mgr. McNeil Consumer Products, Allentown, 1992; transp. assoc. Air Products and Chems., Allentown, 1993; sr. cons. Arthur Andersen LLP, Roseland, N.J., 1994-98; pres. Empowered Synergy, Hopatcong, N.J., 1998—; grad. asst. Dale Carnegie Tng., Allentown, Elmwood Park, N.J., 1987—. Vol. alumni bd. dirs. Smeal Coll. Bus., State College, Pa.; vo. Lake Hopatcong Hist. Soc., 1993—; walk for the cure team capt. Juvenile Diabetes Found., giralda Farms, N.J., 1995; asst. coord. Corp. Challenge 5K Race, N.Y.C., 1997. Mem. NAFE, Assn. Psychol. Type, Orgnl. Devel. Network, Pa. State Alumni Soc. Avocations: singing, scuba diving, water skiing, guitar. E-mail: esynergy@in.netcom.com.

EGGERS, WALTER FREDERICK, academic administrator; b. Mt. Vernon, N.Y., May 31, 1943; s. Walter F. and Catherine Elaine (Carney) E.; m. Sue Mac Hatcher, Aug. 21, 1967 (div. 1981); m. Kelly Ann Houston, Dec. 26, 1986; children: Walter F. III, Jane Branson, Robert Houston, Sam Houston, Max Brand. AB in English with honors, Duke U., 1964; PhD, U. N.C., 1971. Vis. asst. prof. St. Andrews Coll., Laurinburg, N.C., 1967-68; lectr. U. N.C., Chapel Hill, 1968-69; from asst. prof. to full prof. U. Wyo., Laramie, 1969-89; dean Coll. ARts and Scis. Arts and Scis., Laramie, 1985-89; prof., provost, v.p. acad. affairs U. N.H., Durham, 1989—; commr. Commn. on Higher Edn. New Eng. Assn. Schs. and Colls. Author: (with Sigrid Mayer) Ernst Cassirer: An Annotated Bibliography, 1988; co-editor: Teaching Shakespeare, 1977; contbr. articles to profl. jours. Recipient Teaching award Amoco found., 1975, Program award Assn. Am. Colls., Program award NEH, 1983-85; faculty fellow Sch. of Criticism and Theory U. Calif., Irvine, 1977. Mem. MLA, Am. Assn. Higher Edn., Academic Roundtable. Home and Office: Univ NH Office Academic Affairs Durham NH 03824-4724

EGGERT, ROBERT JOHN, SR., economist; b. Little Rock, Dec. 11, 1913; s. John and Eleanora (Fritz) Lapp; m. Elizabeth Bauer, Nov. 28, 1935 (dec. Dec. 1991); children: Robert John, Richard F., James E.; m. Annamarie Hayes, Mar. 19, 1994. BS, U. Ill., 1935, MS, 1936; candidate in philosophy,

U. Minn., 1938; LHD (hon.), Ariz. State U., 1988. Research analyst Bur. Agrl. Econs., U.S. Dept. Agr., Urbana, Ill., 1935; sec. War Meat Bd., Chgo., 1942-45, prin. marketing specialist, 1943; rsch. analyst U. Ill., 1935-36, U. Minn., 1936-38; asst. prof. econs. Kans. State Coll., 1938-41; asst. dir. mktg. Am. Meat Inst., Chgo., 1941-43; economist, assoc. dir. Am. Meat Inst., 1943-50; mgr. dept. mktg. rsch. Ford div. Ford Motor Co., Dearborn, Mich., 1951-53; mgr. program planning Ford div. Ford Motor Co., 1953-54, mgr. bus. rsch., 1954-57, mgr. mktg. rsch. mktg. staff, 1957-61, mgr. mktg. rsch., 1961-64, mgr. internat. mktg. rsch. mktg. staff, 1964-65, mgr. overseas mktg. rsch. planning, 1965-66, mgr. mktg. rsch. Lincoln-Mercury div., 1966-67; dir. agribus. programs Mich. State U., 1967-68; staff v.p. econ. and mktg. rsch. RCA Corp., N.Y.C., 1968-76; pres., chief economist Eggert Econ. Enterprises, Inc., Sedona, Ariz., 1976—; lectr. mktg. U. Chgo., 1947-49; chmn. Fed. Statistics Users Conf., 1960-61; adj. prof. bus. forecasting No. Ariz., 1976-79; mem. econ. adv. bd. U.S. Dept. Commerce, 1969-71, mem. census adv. com., 1975-78; mem. panel econ. advisers Congl. Budget Office, 1975-76; interim dir. Econ. Outlook Ctr. Coll. Bus. Adminstrn. Ariz. State U., Tempe, 1985-86, cons., 1985—; mem. Econ. Estimates Commn. Ariz., 1979—; apptd. Ariz. Gov.'s Commn. Econ. Devel., 1991—, vice chmn. investment adv. coun. Ariz. State Retirement System, 1993-98; trustee Marcus J. Lawrence Med. Ctr. Found., 1992-96; chmn. market rsch. com. Gov.'s Strategic Partnership for Econ. Devel.; co-chmn. Ariz. Sr. Industries Cluster, 1995-97. Contbr. articles to profl. lit.; founder, editor emeritus: monthly Blue Chip Econ. Indicators, 1976—; exec. editor Ariz. Blue Chip, 1984—, Western Blue Chip Econ. Forecast, 1986—, Blue Chip Job Growth Update, 1990—, Mexico Consensus Econ. Forecast, 1993—. Mem. long range planning com. Ch. of Red Rocks, 1998—. Recipient Econ. Forecast award Chgo. chpt. Am. Statis. Assn., 1950, 60, 68; Seer of Yr. award Harvard Bus. Sch. Indsl. Econs., 1973, Golden Gloves Boxing award, U. Ill., 1935. Fellow Am. Statis. Assn. (chmn. bus. and econ. stats sect. 1957—, pres. Chgo. chpt. 1948-49), Nat. Assn. Bus. Economists (coun. 1969-72); mem. Coun. Internat. Mktg. Rsch. and Planning Dirs. (chmn. 1965-66), Am. Mktg. Assn. (dir., v.p. mktg. mgmt. divsn. 1972-73, nat. pres. 1974-75), Fed. Stats. Users Conf. (chmn. trustees 1960-61), Conf. Bus. Economists (chmn. 1972-74), Am. Quarter Horse Assn. (dir. 1966-73), Ariz. Econ. Roundtable, Am. Econs. Assn., Phoenix Econ. Club (hon.), Ariz. C. of C. (bd. dirs. 1991-95), Alpha Zeta. Republican. E-mail: eee@sedona.net. Office: Eggert Econ Enterprises Inc PO Box 2243 Sedona AZ 86339-2243 *I have always strived to be a person of greater value. My modest success has resulted largely from the manifold contribution of others. For example, my AG teacher, Ralph K. Morray at Lincoln, Ill., obtained a four year scholarsip for me at the University of Illinois in 1931. In fact, the only true measure of my accomplishments will unfold in the future. What the future will be is difficult to foretell, but it always has been a challenge to maximize productivity and to look ahead, and to dream of things that never were and say—why not? My motto is "Aiming for Excellence in Economic Forecasting".*

EGGERT, RUSSELL RAYMOND, lawyer; b. Chgo., July 28, 1948; s. Ralph A. and Alice M. (Nischwitz) E.; m. Patricia Anne Alegre, 1998. AB, U. Ill., 1970, JD, 1973; postgrad., Hague Acad. Internat. Law, The Netherlands, 1972. Bar: Ill. 1973, U.S. Supreme Ct. 1979. Assoc. U. Ill., Champaign, 1973-74; asst. atty. gen. State of Ill., Chgo., 1974-79; assoc. O'Conor, Karaganis & Gail, Chgo., 1979-83; legal counsel to Ill. atty. gen., Chgo., 1983-87; ptnr. Mayer, Brown & Platt, Chgo., 1987—. Contbr. various articles to profl. jours. Mem. ABA. Democrat. Office: Mayer Brown & Platt 190 S La Salle St Ste 3100 Chicago IL 60603-3441

EGGERTSEN, JOHN HALE, lawyer; b. Ann Arbor, Mich., Jan. 7, 1947; s. Claude Andrew and Nita (Wakefield) E.; m. Claire Chenoweth, July 19, 1969 (div. 1987); children: Melissa Anne, Helen Emma; m. Sharon Ingram, June 13, 1987 (div. 1994); children: Alexandria, Andrea; m. Robin Rich, Sept. 23, 1995; 1 child, Brendon Hale. BA, U. Mich., 1968; JD cum laude, U. Toledo, 1974; LLM in Taxation, NYU, 1975. Bar: Ohio 1974, Mich. 1975. Instr. Highland Park (Mich.) Sch. Dist., 1968; claims adjuster State Farm Mutual Ins. Co., Ann Arbor, Mich., 1968-70; ptnr. Honigman Miller Schwartz and Cohn, Detroit, 1975—; adj. prof. Wayne State U. Law Sch., Detroit, 1980-94; active Mich. Employee Benefits Conf., Detroit, 1980—. Contbr. articles to profl. jours. Bd. dirs. Neighborhood Svcs. Orgn., Detroit, 1992—, pres., 1994-97. Rsch. grantee NYU, 1974-75; Gerald Wallace scholar NYU, 1974-75. Mem. ABA (taxation sect., employee benefits com.), State Bar Ohio, State Bar Mich. Democrat. Mem. LDS Ch. Avocations: softball, bowling, reading. Home: 1044 Ferdon Rd Ann Arbor MI 48104-3631 Office: Honigman Miller Schwartz & Cohn 2290 First National Bldg Detroit MI 48226

EGGERTSEN, PAUL FRED, psychiatrist; b. Manti, Utah, Feb. 26, 1925; s. Claude E. and Helen E. (Blackett) E.; m. Maurine Child, Feb. 26, 1945 (div. Apr. 1978); children: Joe Paul, Marline Eggertsen Lesh, Sam Child, Ben Thomas, Ann Eggertsen Caley, Laura Mae Eggertsen Pierson, Alice Eggertsen Sheasley; m. Ann Stevens Airy, June 12, 1978. MD, U. Utah, 1949; cert., Washington Psychoanalytic Inst., 1965. Diplomate Am. Bd. Psychiatry. Commd. 1st lt. USAF, 1950, advanced through grades to col., 1962; intern Fitzsimons Army Hosp.; resident in psychiatry U. Colo. Med. Ctr., 1952-55; flight surgeon, psychiatrist, various assignments; staff psychiatrist, chief of psychiatry Lackland AFB, Andrews AFB, Travis AFB hosps.; USAF chief of psychiatry Office of Surgeon Gen., Washington, 1958-64; rsch. psychiatrist Armed Forces Inst. Pathology, Washington, 1964-65; ret. USAF, 1966; pvt. practice Seattle, 1966-78; regional med. officer, psychiatrist for Europe and USSR region Dept. State, Vienna, Austria, 1979-83; dep. asst. sec. for mental health svcs. Dept. State, Washington, 1983-88, dep. dir. Office Med. Svcs., 1988-90; psychiatrist, cons. Washington, 1991-92; psychiatrist Atascadero (Calif.) State Hosp., 1993-95; pvt. practice, 1996—. Contbr. articles to profl. jours. Home: 789 Pacific St Morro Bay CA 93442-2383

EGGINTON, EVERETT, educational administrator; b. N.Y.C., Apr. 6, 1943; s. Hersey Benner and Mary Florence (Twining) E.; m. Wynn Meagher, Sept. 27, 1986; 1 child from previous marriage, William Everett. BA in Econs., Colgate U., 1965, MA in Social Sci. Edn., 1968; MS in Comparative Edn., Syracuse U., 1971, PhD in Edn., 1974; EdD (hon.), U. Francisco Gavidia, San Salvador, El Salvador, 1990. Asst. prof. U. Louisville, 1974-78, acting dir. Internat. Ctr., 1978-79, assoc. prof., 1978-84, prof. edn., 1984—, dir. L.Am. Ctr., 1986—, chair ednl. founds., 1989—, exec. dir. Internat. Ctr., 1996—; sr. policy analyst U.S. Dept. Health, Washington, 1980-81; pres. Consortium of Ctrl. Am. Univs., 1990-96, sec.-gen., 1991-98; cons. Ministries of Edn., El Salvador and Honduras, 1992—. Contbg. editor U.S. Libr. of Congress, Washington, 1980-88; contbr. revs., articles to profl. publs. and encys. Fulbright/Stanford fellow U. Santiago Compostela Espana, 1977, HEW fellow, 1979-80, Fulbright Rsch./Lectr. award El Salvador, 1999—. Home: 2600 Broadmeade Rd Louisville KY 40205-2208 Office: U Louisville Sch Edn Bldg 338 Louisville KY 40292

EGGLESTON, ALAN EDWARD, musician, opera singer, Boy Scout executive; b. Elkhart, Ind., Feb. 19, 1956; s. Richard Eugene Eggleston And Margaret May (O'Brien) Reid; m. Shannon Eggleston; 4 children. MusB, Ind. U., 1980; MusM, Mich. State U., 1984; D. Music, Ind. U., 1988. Pvt. tchr. Elkhart, 1980, East Lansing, Mich., 1980-90, Fayetteville, Ark., 1990-96; vis. asst. prof. music U. Idaho Lionel Hampton Sch. Music, Moscow, 1989-90; asst. prof. U. Ark., Fayetteville, 1990-96; dist. exec. Boy Scouts Am., Ind., 1996—; profl. mgmt. through Raab Agy., Vienna, Austria. Appeared in Lucia di Lammermoor as Enrico, Houston, 1995; appeared in, dir. La Traviata as Giorgio Germont, U. Ark., 1993, Mikado as Mikado, 1991; appeared in Madame Butterfly as Sharpless, 1993, Beethoven's Ninth Symphony as bass soloist, 1992, Orfeo as Satiro, Ind. U., Bloomington, 1988, in Peter Grimes as Hobson, 1987, Legend of Tsar Saltan, 1987, Marriage of Figaro as Figaro, Mich. State U., 1983, Rigoletto as Monterone, Notre Dame U., 1982, The Tempest, 1986, H.M.S. Pinafore as Dick Deadeye, Michiana Opera Guild, South Bend, Ind., 1985, Merry Widow as Kromov, Dayton Opera Theatre, 1985, Barber of Seville as Don Basilio, 1985, Gianni Schicchi as Schicchi, 1984. Asst. scoutmaster Boy Scouts Am., Elkhart, 1980-85, OA chpt. adviser, 1980-84; choir dir. St. Johns United Meth. Ch., Elkhart, 1984-85. Friends of Music scholar Ind. U., 1988, voice scholar Mich. State U., 1982, 83, Spl. Merit scholar Ind. U., 1974; named one of Outstanding Young Men of Am., 1987. Avocations: swimming, sailing, travel, painting, making folk instruments. Home: 3647 N 600 E Rolling Prairie IN 46371-9623

EGGLESTON, G(EORGE) DUDLEY, management consultant, publisher; b. Buffalo, June 11, 1936; s. George Staub and Betty (Ball) E.; m. Susan Michaels, June 4, 1960 (div. Sept. 1987); children: George Dudley Jr., Michele Blair; m. Linda Stephens, Mar. 31, 1990 (div. Sept. 1996). BE, Vanderbilt U., 1960; MBA, Ga. State U., 1979. Product mgr. Exxon Chem., N.Y.C., 1960-71; real estate agt. Woodward & Assocs., Atlanta, 1971-74; v.p. JFK Land Co., Atlanta, 1974-75; pres. Dudley Eggleston Co., Atlanta, 1975—, Maids Unique, Atlanta, 1976-81, Eggleston Cons. Internat., Atlanta, 1981—; pub. revenue-producing Web site eggcon.com.; v.p. Land Resource Group, 1999—. Pres. Fanwood-Scotch Plains, N.J., Jaycees, 1968. Capt. USMC, 1960-63. Mem. Urban Land Inst., Beta Gamma Sigma. Republican. Episcopalian. Avocations: boating, skiing, tennis.

EGGLETON, ARTHUR C., Canadian government official, member of Parliament; b. Toronto, Ont., Can., Sept. 29, 1943; 1 child, Stephanie. Acct., up to 1969; mem. Toronto City Coun., Met. Toronto Coun., 1969-91, city budget chief, 1973-80; mayor City of Toronto, 1980-91; mem. from York Centre in City of North York Parliament of Can., 1993—, pres. treasury bd., minister for infrastructure, 1993-96; min. international trade Can., 1996-97, min. nat. def., 1997—; mem. Bd. Fedn. Can. Mcpls.; chmn. Internat. Programs Com.; co-chmn. Nat. Action Com. Race Rels., apptd. Minister for Internatl. Trade, 1996, apptd. pres. of treas. bd. and Minister, Infrastructure, 1993, appointed Minister of Natl. Defense, 1997, vice chmn. of cabinet com. on Econ. Policy. Mem. Met. Toronto Police Comm., Bd. Can. Nat. Exhbn. Recipient Civic Award of Merit, City of Toronto, 1992. Mem. York Centre for City of Toronto. Office: M Gen Pearkes Bldg 13N, 101 Colonel By Dr, Ottawa, ON Canada K1A 0K2*

EGGLETON, ELIZABETH, gerontologist, educator; b. Aug. 2, 1938. Cert. advanced studies in gerontology, L.I. U., 1988, MPA, 1990; postgrad., Kennedy-Western U., Cheyenne, Wyo. Mng. dir. Surrogate for Family, Smithtown, N.Y., 1988—; adj. prof. dept. health care and pub. adminstrn. C.W. Post Coll., L.I. U., Brookville, N.Y., 1991—, assoc. dir. Ctr. on Aging, 1996—; project dir. Babylon (N.Y.) Home Sharers, 1988-97.

EGIELSKI, RICHARD, illustrator; b. N.Y.C., July 16, 1952; s. Joseph and Caroline (Rzepny) E.; m. Denise Saldutti, May 8, 1977. Student, Pratt Inst., Bklyn., 1970-71, Parsons Sch. Design, N.Y.C., 1971-74. Illustrator: (children's books) Moonguitars, 1974, The Porcelain Pagoda, 1976, The Letter, the Witch and the Ring, 1976, I Should Worry, I Should Care, 1979, Finders Weepers, 1980, Louis the Fish, 1980, Getting Even, 1982, It Happened in Pinsk, 1983 (Plaque award 1985), Lower! Higher! You're a Liar!, 1984, The Little Father, 1985, Amy's Eyes, 1985, Hey, Al, 1986 (Caldecott medal 1987), Friend's Forever, 1988, Bravo Minski, 1988, The Tub People, 1989, Oh, Brother, 1989, A Telling of Tales: Five Stories, 1990, Christmas in July, 1991, The Lost Sailor, 1992, Ugh, 1992, The Tub Grandfather, 1993, Fire! Fire! Said Mrs. McGuire, 1995, Call Me Ahnighito, 1995, Buz, 1995 (Best Illustrated Book of 1995, N.Y. Times), The Gingerbread Boy, 1997. Recipient Cert. of Merit Soc. of Illustrators, N.Y.C., 1978, 81, 84, 85. Avocation: playing the mandolin. Office: care Farrar Straus & Giroux 19 Union Sq W New York NY 10003-3304*

EGINTON, WARREN WILLIAM, federal judge; b. Bklyn., Feb. 16, 1924. AB, Princeton U., 1948; LLB, Yale U., 1951. Bar: N.Y. 1952, Conn. 1954. Assoc. Davis Polk & Wardwell, N.Y.C., 1951-53; ptnr. Cummings & Lockwood, Stamford, Conn., 1954-79; judge U.S. Dist. Ct., Bridgeport, Conn., 1979—. Mem. ABA, Am. Judicature Soc., Am. Bar Found., Conn. Bar Assn., Fed. Bar Coun., Fed. Bar Assn., Ins. Jud. Adminstrn., Jud. Leadership Devel. Coun., Fgn. Policy Assn. Office: US Dist Ct 915 Lafayette Blvd Ste 335 Bridgeport CT 06604-4765

EGLEE, CHARLES HAMILTON, television and movie writer, producer; b. Boston, Nov. 27, 1951; s. Donald Read and Nancy (Hamilton) E.; m. Madeline Dalton, Feb. 29, 1984; children: Blythe Dalton, Eli Hamilton. BA in English, Yale U., 1974. Teaching asst. Yale U., New Haven, 1976; producer, writer for film Deadly Eyes Warner Bros., L.A., 1982; story editor for TV series St. Elsewhere MTM Prodns., Studio City, Calif., 1984-86; exec. story cons. for TV series Moonlighting ABC Circle Films, L.A., 1986-87, producer for TV series Moonlighting, 1987-89; exec. producer 20th Century Fox TV, 1989-91; writer, co-exec. producer "Civil Wars" Steven Bochco Prodns., 1991-93; writer L.A. Law, 1992; co-creator, exec. producer The Byrds of Paradise (Steven Bochco Prodns.), 1993-94; co-exec. producer N.Y.P.D. Blue (Steven Bochco Prodns.), 1994-95; co-creator, exec. prodr. Murder One (Steven Bochco Prodns.), 1995-97, Total Security (Steven Bochco Prodns.), 1997-98; co-creator, exec. prodr. TV series Dark Angel, 1999—. Story editor (St. Elsewhere episode) Bye George, 1985 (Humanitas prize); co-writer (St. Elsewhere episode) Haunted, 1986 (Emmy nomination, Salute to Excellence Award nominee NAACP 1986), (Moonlighting episode) I Am Curious, Maddie, 1987 (Emmy nomination), N.Y.P.D. Blue, 1994 (Emmy award for best drama), Murder One, 1996 (People's Choice award for best new drama, Emmy nomination, best writing in one hour drama, pilot episode 1996, Golden GLobe nomination 1996, best fgn. drama Brit. Acad. Film and TV, 1996). Nominee Best Drama award Writers Guild Am., 1996. Mem. Acad. TV Arts and Scis., Writers Guild Am., U.S. Power Squadron, Yale U. Alumni Fund, Mory's Assn. (New Haven). Democrat. Avocations: sailing, skiing, Am. art pottery, gardening.

EGLEY, THOMAS ARTHUR, computer services executive, accountant; b. Aberdeen, S.D., June 23, 1945; s. Ralph Joseph and Cora Ellen (Wade) E.; m. Cecelia K. Kuskie, Feb. 22, 1985. BBA, U. Mont., 1967, postgrad., 1973-75. CPA, Mont. Programmer, analyst Comml. Data, Missoula, Mont., 1973-77; data processing mgr. John R. Daily, Inc., Missoula, 1977-78; ptnr. Egley & White CPA's, Missoula, 1978-84, Egley & White Computer Services, Missoula, 1978-85; pres. Able Fin., Inc., Missoula, 1984—, PC Software, Inc., 1987—, E & W Computer Services, Inc., 1983—; lectr., Missoula, 1973—. Bd. dirs. Missoula Children's Theater, 1975-82. Served to sgt. U.S. Army, 1968-71. Mem. Am. Inst. CPAs, Mont. Soc. CPAs, Phi Sigma Kappa Alumni Club (pres. 1973—). Republican. Lutheran. Lodge: Elks. Avocations: fishing, photography, travel. Home and Office: E&W Computer Svcs Inc PO Box 2729 Missoula MT 59806-2729

EGLOFF, FRED ROBERT, manufacturers representative, writer, historian; b. Evanston, Ill., Nov. 30, 1934; s. Edward Gottfried and Pearl Elizabeth (Fischrupp) E.; m. Sharon Lee Geyer, June 30, 1962. BS in Commerce, Loyola U., 1956. Asst. adv. mgr. The Englander Co., Chgo., 1956-57; indsl. film svc. Accurate Cinema Svc., Chgo., 1960-62; indsl. sales The EMF Co., Chgo., 1962-69, Avery Internat., Azusa, Calif., 1969-77, The Stanley Works, Hartford, Conn., 1977-78; mfg. rep. ARTCO, Chgo., 1979—; v.p., bd. dirs. Westerners Internat., Oklahoma City, 1982—, pres. 1997—; cons. ALA, Chgo., 1982—; tchr. New Trier Extension, Wilmette, Ill., 1985—. Author: El Paso Lawman, 1982; editor Westerners Brand Book, 1986-96. Bd. dirs. Wilmette Hist. Soc., 1973-77; hist. cons. Wilmette Hist. Mus., 1978; com. mem. Save the Depot Preservation, Wilmette, 1974; sec. Wilmette Sailing Assn., 1974. Capt. U.S. Army, 1957-59. Recipient Don Russell Meml. award, 1998. Mem. Western History Assn., Western Writers Am., Soc. Midland Authors, Chgo. Corral the Westerners (sheriff 1978-80, sidewinder 1984), Windy City BMW Car Club Am. (pres. 1976, Big Wheel 1972, Founders Recognition award 1997), Vintage Sportscar Club (sec. 1972-80, top competitor award 1970, 97), Nat. Cowboy Hall Fame. Republican. Roman Catholic. Avocations: vintage sports cars, photography, skiing, horseback riding, books. Home: 2035 Greenwood Ave Wilmette IL 60091-1439 Office: ARTCO 2035 Greenwood Ave Wilmette IL 60091-1439

EGNOR, JOANNE MCCLELLAN, psychology educator; b. Williamson, W.Va.; d. Ernest Edward and Thelma Isabel (Chafin) McC.; children: Michael Edward, Sherry Beth, William Mark. BS in Psychology, U. North Fla., 1987; MS in Mental Health Counseling, Nova U., 1992. Adj. prof. psychology and human growth and devel. Fla. C.C., Jacksonville; mem. adv. com. Clay County Health and Human Svcs., Orange Park, Fla., 1996-98; mem. adv. coun. Calvary United Meth., Orange Park, 1996—; presenter in field. Author (booklet) AAD Doesn't ADD UP, 1996; author, pub.: Care and Feeding of the Chronologically Gifted (Older) Brain, 1999; contbr., pub. (monthly newsletter) FCCJ FACC Facts, 1996-98. Mem. DAR (chair Constitution Week Jacksonville chpt. 1999—), Fla. Assn. C.C.'s (rep., sec. Learning Resources Commn. 1998—, pub., editor FCCJ chpt. newsletter 1996-98, 99—, winner career employees commn. writing contest 1997, chair instnl. effectiveness 1999—), Marshall U. Alumni Assn., U. North Fla. Alumni Assn., Nova U. Alumni Assn., Cummer Mus. (Jacksonville), Nat. Soc. DAR (rec. sec. Jacksonville chpt. 1998—, chair Constitution Week 1999—), Sigma Kappa.

EGOLD, THOMAS A., electronics company administrator; b. May 17, 1943. BA in Acctg., Marian Coll., 1965. Mgr. materials RCA ops. Thomson Consumer Electronics, Taiwan, China, 1985-90; mng. dir. Singapore ops. Thomson Consumer Electronics, Singapore, 1991-94; mgr. prodr. rebuild ops. Thomson Consumer Electronics, El Paso, Tex., 1994-97; gen. mgr. N.Am. logistics Thomson Consumer Electronics, Indpls., 1997—. Home: 3004 Greensview Dr Greenwood IN 46143-9573

EGOYAN, ATOM, film director; b. Cairo, July 19, 1960; arrived in Can., 1962; s. Joseph and Shushan (Devletian) E.; m. Arsinee Khanjian; 1 child, Arshile. BA in Internat. Rels. with honours, U. Toronto, Ont., Can., 1982; Phd (hon.), Trinity Coll., U. Toronto and U. Victoria. Dir. Ego Film Arts, Toronto, 1982—; films shown at internat. film festivals of Sydney, Birmingham, Melbourne, Valladolid, Picadilly, Cleve., Berlin, Hong Kong, Locarno, Melbourne, Jerusalem, London, L.A., Miami, Turin, Cairo, Antwerp, Montreal, Uppsala, Ghent, Chgo., Chgo., Sao Paulo, N.Y.C., Edinburgh, San Francisco, Rotterdam, also others. Writer, dir., prodr. (feature films) Next of Kin, 1984 (Gold Ducat award Mannheim Internat. Film Week 1984), Family Viewing, 1987 (Internat. Critics award 1988, Best Feature Film award Uppsala, Priz Alcan, Festival du Nouveau Cinema, Montreal), Speaking Parts, 1989 (best screenplay prize Vancouver Internat. Film Festival), The Adjuster, 1991 (spl. prize of jury Moscow Film Festival, Golden Spike award Valladolid Film Festival), Calendar, 1993 (prix Berlin Internat. Film Festival), Exotica, 1994 (Internat. Film Critics award Cannes Film Festival 1994, Prix de la Critique award for best foreign film 1994, Acad. award nominee), Salome Canadian Opera Co., 1996, Houston Grand Opera, 1997, The Sweet Hereafter, 1997 (Grand Prix, Internat. Critics prize Cannes Film Festival 1997, Acad. award nominee), Elsewhereless, 1998, Dr. Ox's Experiment, 1998, Felicia's Journey, 1999. Recipient numerous awards and nominations for awards. Avocation: classical guitar. Office: Ego Film Arts, 80 Niagara St, Toronto, ON Canada M5V 1C5*

EGUCHI, YASU, artist; b. Japan, Nov. 30, 1938; came to U.S., 1967; s. Chihaku and Kiku (Koga) E.; m. Anita Phillips, Feb. 24, 1968. Student, Horie Art Acad., Japan, 1958-65. Exhibited exhbns., Tokyo Mus. Art, 1963, 66, Santa Barbara Mus. Art, Calif., 1972-74, 85, Everson Mus. Art, Syracuse, N.Y., 1980, Nat. Acad. Design, N.Y.C., 1980—; one-man shows include Austin Gallery, Scottsdale, Ariz., 1968-87, Joy Tash Gallery, Scottsdale, 1989-99, Greystone Galleries, Cambria, Calif., 1969, 70, 72, Copenhagen Galleries, Calif., 1970-78, Charles and Emma Frye Art Mus., Seattle, 1974, 84, 98, Hammer Galleries, N.Y.C., 1977, 79, 81, 93, City of Heidenheim, Germany, 1980, Artique Ltd., Anchorage, 1981—; pub. and pvt. collections, Voith Gmbh, Germany, City of Giengen and City of Heidenheim, Germany, represented, Deer Valley, Utah, Hunter Resources, Santa Barbara, Am. Embassy, Paris, Charles and Emma Frye Art Mus., Seattle, Nat. Acad. Design, N.Y.C.; author: Der Brenz Entlang, 1980; contbr. to jours in field. Active Guide Dogs for the Blind, San Raphael, Calif., 1976; active City of Santa Barbara Arts Council, 1979, The Eye Bank for Sight Restoration, N.Y., 1981, Anchorage Arts Council, 1981, Santa Barbara Mus. Natural History, 1989. Recipient Selective Artist award Yokohama Citizen Gallery, 1965; recipient Artist of Yr. award Santa Barbara Arts Council, 1979, Hon. Citizen award City of Heidenheim, 1980, The Adolph and Clara Obrig prize NAD, 1983, Cert. of Merit NAD, 1985, 87. Home: PO Box 30206 Santa Barbara CA 93130-0206

EHLE, JOHN MARSDEN, JR., writer; b. Asheville, N.C., Dec. 13, 1925; s. John M. and Gladys (Starnes) E.; m. Gail Oliver, Aug. 30, 1952 (div. Apr. 1967); m. Rosemary Harris, Oct. 22, 1967; 1 child, Jennifer Anne. BA, U. N.C., 1949; DFA (hon.), N.C. Sch. Arts, 1981; LHD (hon.), Berea Coll., 1986, U. N.C., Asheville, 1987; DLitt (hon.), U. N.C., Chapel Hill, 1990. Faculty U. N.C., Chapel Hill, 1951-63; spl. asst. to Gov. Terry Sanford, Raleigh, N.C., 1963-64; program officer Ford Found., N.Y.C., 1964-65; spl. cons. Duke U., 1976-80; co-founder N.C. Gov.'s Sch., N.C. Sch. Arts, N.C. Sch. Sci. and Maths. Author: (novels) Move Over, Mountain, 1957, Kingstree Island, 1959, Lion on the Hearth, 1961, The Land Breakers, 1964, The Road, 1967, Time of Drums, 1970, The Journey of August King, 1971, The Changing of the Guard, 1975, The Winter People, 1981, Last One Home, 1983, The Widows Trial, 1989, (biographies) The Free Men, 1965 (Mayflower Soc. cup), The Survivor, 1968, Shepherd of the Streets, 1960, Dr. Frank, Living with Frank Porter Graham, 1993, (non-fiction) The Cheeses and Wines of England and France, with Notes on Irish Whiskey, 1972, Trail of Tears: The Rise and Fall of the Cherokee Nation, 1988; pub. also in several fgn. countries; (screenplay) The Journey of August King, 1996. Active White House Group for Domestic Affairs, 1964-66, Nat. Coun. Humanities, 1966-70; mem. exec. com. Nat. Book Com., N.Y.C., 1972-75, N.C. Sch. Arts Found., Winston-Salem, 1970-75; mem. awards commn. State of N.C., 1982-93, Mary Reynolds Babcock Found., Winston-Salem, 1985-89. With AUS, 1944-46. Recipient Walter Raleigh prize for fiction N.C. Dept. Cultural Affairs, 1964, 67, 70, 75, 84, State of N.C. award for Lit., 1972, Gov.'s award for Disting. Meritorious Svc., 1978, Lillian Smith prize Southern Regional Coun., 1982, Disting. Alumnus award U N.C., Chapel Hill, 1984, Thomas Wolfe Meml. award Western N.C. Hist. Assn., 1984, W.D. Weatherford award Berea Coll., 1985, Caldwell award N.C. Humanities Coun., 1995; named to N.C. Lit. Hall of Fame, 1997. Mem. PEN, Authors League, Century Club (N.Y.C.). Democrat. Methodist. Home: 125 Westview Dr NW Winston Salem NC 27104

EHLEN, MARTIN RICHARD, state agency administrator, management analyst; b. Highland Park, Ill., Dec. 28, 1953; s. Martin Henry and Marilyn Lucille (Tomtingen) E. BA in Polit. Sci., Western Ill. U., 1976; MA in Pub. Adminstrn., Norwich U., 1993. Mktg. and sales exec. Reedy Industries, Inc., Glenview, Ill., 1978-86; owner, CEO San Diego Pub. Rels. and Advt. Co., San Diego, 1986-88; non commd. officer U.S. Army, 1988-91; grad. student Norwich U., Montpelier, Vt., 1992-93; records adminstr. Dept. Hwy. Safety and Motor Vehicle, Fla., 1994-95; sr. mgmt. analyst Dept. Revenue, Fla., 1995—; cons. San Diego Pub. Rels. and Mktg., Calif., Ill., Fla., 1986-88; mem. ASPA Washington, Fla., 1991—, Acad. Polit. Sci., Washington, 1995—. Mem. governing bd. Assoc. Students of Polit. Sci., Western Ill. U., 1974-76. With U.S. Army, 1988-91. Recipient Mil. Commendation, Nat. Def. and Achievement medals, U.S. Army, 1990, 91. Mem. ASPA, Toastmasters Internat. Avocations: golf, power boating, water and snow skiing. Home: 3733 Sutor Ct Tallahassee FL 32311-4071 Office: State of Fla Dept Revenue 4070 Esplanade Way Tallahassee FL 32311-7830

EHLERMAN, PAUL MICHAEL, industrial battery manufacturing company executive; b. Montgomery, Ala., 1938. BBA, U. Notre Dame, 1960. With GE, 1960-65, U.S. Gypsum, Chgo., 1965-68, Northwest, Inc., Chgo., 1968-75, Gen. Battery, Exide Corp., Reading, Pa., 1975-91; vice chrmn., ceo Yuasa, Inc., Reading, 1991—; also bd. dirs. Yuasa Inc., Reading, Pa., Yuasa Corp., Tokyo, Japan; mem. exec. com., bd. dirs. Greater Berks Devl. Fund; bd. dirs. Battery Coun. Internat. Lead Indust. Assoc. Pres., bd. dirs. Civic Ctr., Berks County Mfrs. Assn.; mem. exec. com., fin. chmn. Alvernia Coll.; bd. dirs., chmn. Berks County Conv. Ctr. Authority; bd. dirs. Reading Hosp. & Med. Ctr. Office: Yuasa Inc PO Box 14145 Reading PA 19612-4145

EHLERS, EILEEN SPRATT, family therapist; b. Maynard, Mass., Feb. 28, 1948; d. Cyril J. and Irma A. (Wirkkanen) Spratt; m. Robert K. Ehlers, June 13, 1970; children: Robert (dec.), Edward, Erin, Katherine. BA, Boston Coll., 1970; MEd, Notre Dame Coll., Manchester, N.H., 1992. Social worker Cath. Med. Ctr., Manchester, 1991; grief counselor Hospice, Concord, N.H., 1992; program dir. Am. Cancer Soc., Bedford, N.H., 1992; pvt. practice family therapy Familystrength, Concord, 1993-96; coord. Worldwide Marriage Encounter, 1983-96; coord., supr. Mental Health Ctr. of Greater Manchester, N.H., 1996—; coord. Toward Marriage, Concord; regional dir., clin. supr. Family Strength, 1993-96; mem. Dist. Coun. for N.H. Health Care Reform; supr. Mental Health Ctr. Greater Manchester, 1996—. Mem. Mental Health Counseling Assn., Assn. for Counselor Edn. and Supervision, Internat. Assn. of Marriage and Family Counseling, Nat. Assn. for Family Based Svcs/. Democrat. Roman Catholic. Avocations: reading, cooking, walking. Home: 14 Ardon Dr Hooksett NH 03106-1536 Office: Child and Adolescent Svcs 493 Beech St Manchester NH 03104-4955

EHLERS, KATHRYN HAWES (MRS. JAMES D. GABLER), physician; b. Richmond Hill, N.Y., Aug. 22, 1931; d. Albert and Edna (Hawes) E.; m. James D. Gabler, Dec. 5, 1959; children—Jennifer K., Emily E. A.B., Bryn Mawr Coll., 1953; M.D., Cornell U.; M.D. (Hannah E. Longshore Meml. Med. scholar 1953-57, Elsie Strang L'Esperance scholar 1956-57), 1957. Diplomate: Am. Bd. Pediatrics, Am. Bd. Pediatric Cardiology. Intern N.Y. Hosp., 1957-58, asst. resident pediatrics, 1958-60; fellow in pediatric cardiology Cornell U. Med. Coll., N.Y.C., 1960-64; instr. pediatrics Cornell U. Med. Coll., 1964-66, asst. prof., 1966-70, asso. prof. pediatrics, 1970-75, prof., 1975-96, prof. emeritus, 1996—, vice-chmn. pediat., 1988-96; practice medicine specializing in pediat. cardiology N.Y.C., 1958-96. Contbr. articles to profl. jours. Research trainee N.Y. Heart Assn., 1960-62, Am. Heart Assn., 1962-64. Fellow Am. Coll. Cardiology; mem. N.Y. Heart Assn., Am. Heart Assn., Harvey Soc., Am. Pediatric Soc., Am. Acad. Pediatrics, Alpha Omega Alpha. Home: 1035 Park Ave New York NY 10028-0912 Office: 525 E 68th St New York NY 10021-4873

EHLERS, VERNON JAMES, congressman; b. Pipestone, Minn., Feb. 6, 1934; m. Johanna Meulink, 1958; children: Heidi, Brian, Marla, Todd. Student, Calvin Coll.; AB, U. Calif., Berkeley, 1956, PhD in Physics, 1960. Tchg. asst. U. Calif., Berkeley, 1956-57, rsch. asst., 1957-60, lectr. in physics, 1960-66; prof. physics Calvin Coll., 1966-83; mem. Mich. State Ho. of Reps., 1983-85; mem. Mich. State Senate, 1985-94, pres. pro tem, 1991-94; mem. 103d-106th Congress from 3d Mich. Dist., 1994—; mem. Gov. Milliken's Task Force on Environ. Problems, 1977, Kent County Rep. Exec. Com., Kent County Bd. Commrs., 1975-83, chmn., 1979-82, Mich. Toxic Substance Control Commn., 1982; asst. floor leader Mich. State Ho. of Reps., 1983-85, congrl. com., mem. transp. and infrastructure com., sci. com., edn. and workforce com., house adminstrn. com.; pres. protem Mich. State Senate, 1991-94. Contbr. articles to profl. jours. NATO Rsch. fellow U. Heidelberg, Germany, 1961-62, Sci. Faculty fellow NSF, Joint Insts. for Lab. Astrophysics, U. Colo. 1971-72, fellow Calvin Coll. Ctr. for Christian Scholar, 1977-78. Mem. AAAS, Am. Phys. Soc., Am. Assn. Phys. Tchrs. Mem. Christian Reformed Ch. Home: 1848 Morningside Dr SE Grand Rapids MI 49506-5121 Office: Federal Bldg 110 Michigan St NW Grand Rapids MI 49503-2313 also: Ho of Reps Washington DC 20515-2203

EHLINGER, JANET ANN DOWLING, elementary school educator; b. Des Moines, Mar. 1, 1955; d. Joseph Patrick and Sadie Agnes (Klein) Dowling; m. Steven Mark Ehlinger, July 22, 1989; children: Bridget Ann, Brian Mark. BS, Benedictine Coll., Atchison, Kans., 1977; MEd, U. St. Thomas, Houston, 1985. Cert. tchr., Tex. Tchr. English, sci. Our Lady Mt. Carmel, Houston, 1977-78; tchr. social studies, history, religion St. Michael's Sch., Houston, 1978-82; tchr. social studies and history Kinkaid Sch., Houston, 1982-90; substitute tchr. St. Thomas More Sch., Houston, 1998-99. Active Mus. Fine Arts, Houston, 1992, Children's Mus. of Houston, 1993-96; bd. dirs. St. Cyril of Alexandria Ladies Guild, Houston, 1992; leader Girl Scouts Am., 1996—. Mem. Nat. Coun. Social Studies, Tex. State Hist. Assn., Houston Zool. Soc., Kappa Delta Pi (rep.-at-large Pi Lambda chpt. 1985-86, sec. 1987-89). Avocations: reading, sewing, piano, travel. Home: 6111 Cheena Dr Houston TX 77096-4614

EHLINGER, RALPH JEROME, lawyer; b. Oconto, Wis., Mar. 22, 1941; s. Jerome Nicholas and Margaret Ann (Otradovec) E.; m. Nancy L. McKinley, Dec. 26, 1966 (div. Oct. 1986); children: Nicholas Joseph, Martha Johanna; m. Mary Verstegen, Sept. 25, 1987; children: Autumn V., Andrea V., Jessa V. BA in Philosophy, St. Paul Sem., 1963; JD, Georgetown U., 1968. Bar: Wis. 1968, U.S. Dist. Ct. (ea. dist.) Wis. 1969, U.S. Dist. Ct. (we. dist.) Wis. 1977, U.S. Ct. Appeals (7th cir.) 1983, U.S. Supreme Ct. 1986, D.C. 1988, U.S. Ct. Appeals (4th cir.) 1988. Ptnr. Meissner, Tierney, Ehlinger & Whipp, Milw., 1968-86; pvt. practice Milw., 1986-87; counsel Casson, Harkins & LaPallo, Washington, 1987-88; pres. Ehlinger & Krill, SC, Milw., 1988—; dir. Milw. Bar Assn., 1990-93. Articles editor: The Georgetown Law Jour., 1967-68 (Outstanding Editor 1968); editor-in-chief: The Milwaukee Lawyer, 1982-84. Trustee Wis. Sch. Profl. Psychology, Milw., 1990-93; bd. pres. Grand Ave Club, Milw., 1990-92, Mental Health Assn., Milw., 1992-93; dir. Centro Legal Por Derechos Humanos, 1996—. Mem. ATLA, Am. Judicature Soc., Wis. Acad. Trial Lawyers, Milw. Bar Assn. Found. (pres. 1994-97), Nordic Ski Club (life), Milw. Bar Assn. (Lawyer of Yr. award 1997). Democrat. Roman Catholic. Avocations: instrumental and vocal music, cross-country skiing, backpacking, canoeing, poetry. Office: Ehlinger & Krill SC 316 N Milwaukee St Ste 410 Milwaukee WI 53202-5832

EHMANN, ANTHONY VALENTINE, lawyer; b. Chgo., Sept. 5, 1935; s. Anthony E. and Frances (Verweil) E.; m. Alice A. Avina, Nov. 27, 1959; children: Ann, Thomas, Jerome, Gregory, Rose, Robert. BS, Ariz. State U., 1957; JD, U. Ariz., 1960. Bar: Ariz. 1960, U.S. Tax Ct. 1960, U.S. Sup. Ct. 1968; CPA, Ariz.; cert. tax specialist, trusts and estates specialist. Spl. asst. atty. gen., 1961-68; mem. Ehmann and Hiller, Phoenix, 1969—. Republican dist. chmn. Ariz., 1964; pres. Grand Canyon council Boy Scouts Am., 1987-89, mem. exec. com., 1981—; v.p. western region Boy Scouts Am., 1991—; mem. bd. dirs. Nat. Catholic Com. on Scouting, 1995—. Recipient Silver Beaver award Boy Scouts Am., 1982, Bronze Pelican award Cath. Com. on Scouting, 1981, Silver Antelope award Boy Scouts Am., 1994. Fellow Am. Coll. Trusts & Estate Counsel; mem. State Bar Ariz. (chmn. tax sect. 1968, 69), Central Ariz. Estate Planning Council (pres. 1968, 69). Republican. Roman Catholic. Clubs: KC (grand knight 1964, 65) (Glendale, Ariz.), Serra Internat. (pres. Phoenix club 1992-93, dist. gov. Ariz. 1993-95), Knight of Holy Sepulchre, Knight of Malta. Office: Ehmann & Hiller 2525 E Camelback Rd Ste 720 Phoenix AZ 85016-4229

EHMANN, CARL WILLIAM, consumer products executive, researcher; b. Buffalo, Aug. 30, 1942; s. Christian John and Grayce E. (Packer) E.; m. Elaine Ann O'Gorek, June 22, 1968; children: Elayne Grayce, Karen Beth. BA, SUNY, Buffalo, 1963, MD, 1967. Diplomate Am. Bd. Dermatology. Intern Buffalo Deaconess Hosp., 1967-68; resident U. Wash. Sch. Medicine, Seattle, 1970-72; asst. prof. dermatology SUNY, 1973-75, clin. asst. prof., 1983-87; pvt. practice, Virginia, Minn., 1975-79; dir. clin. rsch. in dermatology Hoffman-LaRoche, Nutley, N.J., 1979-83; v.p. rsch. in dermatology Bristol-Myers & Westwood, Buffalo, 1983-87; v.p. R & D, Johnson & Johnson Baby Products Co., Skillman, N.J., 1987-89; exec. v.p. R & D, Johnson & Johnson Consumer Products Worldwide, Skillman, 1989-92; exec. v.p. R&D R.J. Reynolds Co., Winston-Salem, N.C., 1992-96; pres. Reynolds Techs., Inc., Winston-Salem, 1994-96; bd. dirs., head worldwide R&D Reckitt and Colman, Wayne, N.J., London, 1996—; clin. assoc. prof. dermatology U. Medicine and Dentistry N.J., Piscataway, 1987-92, U. Pa., Phila., 1988-92, Wake Forest U. Bowman Gray Sch. Medicine, Winston-Salem, N.C., 1993-97; clin. asst. prof. skin and cancer NYU, N.Y.C., 1986-89; mem. adv. bd. Touch Rsch. Inst., U. Miami; bd. dirs. rectors Advanced Polymer Sys., Calif., 1993—. Surgeon USPHS, 1968-70. Fellow ACP, Am. Acad. Dermatology, Am. Acad. Med. Dirs., Am. Soc. Clin. Pharmacology and Therapy, N.Y. Acad. Medicine. Lutheran. Office: Reckitt & Coleman, 67 Alma Rd, Windsor Berkshire SL4 3HO, England*

EHNES, JACK, state insurance commissioner. BS, Cornell U., 1973; MA, Vanderbilt U., 1975. Pers. rsch. psychologist State of Tenn., 1981-83; pers. specialist Colo. Dept. Pers., 1983-86, mgmt. analyst, 1986-87; mgr. employee benefits Colo. Dept. Adminstrn. Dept. Pers., Denver, 1987-91; dir. fin. and benefits divsn. Colo. Dept. Pers., Denver, 1991-92; dep. commr. ins. Colo. Divsn. Ins., Denver, 1992-94, commr. of ins., 1994—; chmn. Nat. Assn. Ins. Commr.'s spl. com. on Blue Cross, vice-chair accident and health com.; bd. dirs. Colo. State Employees Credit Union. Trustee Pub. Employees Retirement Assn. Office: Divsn of Ins 1560 Broadway Ste 850 Denver CO 80202-4942

EHNTHOLT, DANIEL JAMES, chemist; b. Manchester, N.H., Sept. 19, 1945; s. Daniel James Dolores (Donohue) E.; m. Eileen Marie Dunne, Aug. 14, 1971; children: Kimberly, Amy, Christopher. BS, Fordham U., 1966; PhD, SUNY, Stony Brook, 1971. Postdoctoral fellow Brandeis U., Waltham, Mass., 1971-72; asst. prof. Boston U., 1972-77, Worcester (Mass.) State Coll., 1977-78; cons. Arthur D. Little, Inc., Cambridge, Mass., 1978-84, unit mgr., 1984-91, v.p., 1991—, also dir. Contbr. articles to profl. jours. Commr. Conservation Commn., Hudson, Mass., 1974-79; mem. Bd. Health, Hudson, 1981-88, 91—, chmn. 1995-98. N.Y. State Regents fellow, 1962-70, German Acad. Exchange fellow Max Planck Inst., Mülheim an der Ruhr, 1974. Mem. ACS (Petroleum Rsch. fellow 1970), Am. Inst. Chemists, Nat. Sci. Tchrs. Assn., Phi Lambda Upsilon. Roman Catholic. Office: Arthur D Little Inc 15 Acorn Park Cambridge MA 02140-2301

EHRE, VICTOR TYNDALL, insurance company executive; b. Boston, July 25, 1913; s. Victor H. and Ethel (Woods) E.; m. Allison DeWolfe, Aug. 20, 1938 (dec. Oct. 1986); children: Victor Tyndall, Donald DeWolfe, Susan Margaret; m. Hanna G. Abbott, Feb. 14, 1987. BS cum laude, Wharton Sch., U. Pa., 1935; HHD, Springfield Coll., 1980. With Travelers Ins. Co., 1935-38, Kemper Orgn., 1938-55; with Buffalo Ins. Co., 1955-64, pres., 1956-64; pres., chief exec. officer Utica Mut. Ins. Co., N.Y., 1964-79; chmn. bd., chief exec. officer Utica Mut. Ins. Co., 1970-84, chmn., 1979-84, also dir.; trustee Adirondack Ry. Corp.; trustee, past chmn. Bus. Council of N.Y. State Ins. Fund; governing com., past chmn. Improved Risk Mutuals. Bd. dirs., dir., adv. bd. State Traffic Council N.Y.; bd. dirs. Central N.Y. Health Systems Agy., Inc., Hospice Care Inc.; dir., past 1st pres. Western N.Y. Traffic Safety Council; bd. dirs. Central N.Y. Community Arts Council, Utica Found.; vice chmn. Concerned Citizens for the Arts; adv. com. Nat. Alliance Businessmen; past chmn. N.Y. State adv. bd. Future Bus. Leaders Am.; past pres. Civic Mus. Soc. Utica; pres. Utica Bus. Opportunities Corp.; founder Operation Sunshine; pres. United Arts Fund of Mohawk Valley; mem. N.Y. Gov.'s Statewide Com. Children and Youth; past chmn. Region II Boy Scouts Am.; also mem. exec. bd. Nat. council; bd. dirs., exec. bd. Land of Oneida council; mem. U. Pa. Alumni Clubs Adv. Council; pres., past chmn. Atlantic Coast Hockey League; chmn. N.Y. Gov.'s Project Rev. Com.; chmn. SUNY Coll. Tech. Found.; trustee SUNY Coll. Tech., Hobart and William Smith Colls. Served to lt. (s.g.) USNR, 1943-46. Recipient Award of Merit Gov. Rockefeller of N.Y., 1965; named Indsl. Man of Year, 1968, Ins. Man of Year, 1971; recipient Rotarian Citizen's award, 1969, Alumni award merit U. Pa., 1977, Presdl. award Nat. Assn. Mut. Ins. Cos., 1979, Kiwanis Meml. award, 1986, Caritas Benigna Est award Sisters of St. Francis, 1985; named Hon. Alumnus, SUNY Coll. Tech., 1986. Mem. Greater Utica C. of C. (dir.), Am. Arbitration Assn. (dir.), U. Pa. Alumni Club Western N.Y. (past pres.), Sadaquada Golf Club, Lake Placid Club, Masons (33d degree, trustee Masonic Hall and Asylum Fund). Episcopalian (warden). Home: Blairstone Forest 120 Groton Dr Amherst NY 14228-2550 also: Rd #1 2104 Willow Point Dr Blossvale NY 13308 Office: PO Box 530 Utica NY 13503-0530 *I think that the thing that has guided me the most through life is the combination of the Cub Scout and Boy Scout mottos of the Boy Scouts of America. "Be prepared and do your best."*

EHREN, CHARLES ALEXANDER, JR., lawyer, educator; b. N.Y.C., Dec. 13, 1932; s. Charles Alexander and Alma Elise (Holmstrom) E.; m. Joan Anne Bansemer, Sept. 4, 1954. AB, Columbia U., 1954, JD, 1956. Bar: N.Y. bar 1956. Asso. firm LeBoeuf, Lamb and Leiby, N.Y.C., 1958-67; Reginald Heber Smith fellow U. Pa. Sch. Law at Legal Aid Soc. of Westchester County (N.Y.), White Plains, 1967-68, dir. soc., 1975-77; dir. curriculum Nat. Inst. Edn. in Law and Poverty, Northwestern U., 1968-70; asso. prof. law U. Denver, 1970-74, prof., 1974-75; dean, prof. Pace U. Sch. Law, 1975-76; vis. scholar Columbia U. Sch. Law, 1976-77; dean Valparaiso U. Sch. Law, 1977-82, prof., 1977-96, prof. emeritus, 1996—; trustee Ind. Continuing Legal Edn. Found., Ind. Bar Found., 1977-82; dir. Westchester Legal Services, 1975-77. Author: (with others) Electricity and the Environment, The Reform of Legal Institutions, 1972. Served with U.S. Army, 1956-58. Mem. Ind. State Bar Assn. (ho. of dels. 1977-82), Assn. Bar City N.Y. (exec. dir. spl. com. on electric power and environment 1971-73), ABA, N.Y. State Bar Assn., Fed. Energy Bar Assn., Soc. Am. Law Tchrs. Democrat. Lutheran. Home: 16 High Point Rd East Hampton NY 11937-1059

EHRENBERG, EDWARD, executive, consultant; b. N.Y.C., Aug. 24, 1930; s. Meyer and Bessie (Purkin) E.; children from previous marriage: Ellen, Roger. BS, NYU, 1956; MBA, U. Pa., 1958. With Ford Motor Co., Dearborn, Mich., 1957-70, Xerox Corp., Rochester, N.Y., 1970-78, Internat. Harvester Co., Chgo., 1978-85, Beatrice Cos., 1985; owner, CEO, Capital Hardware Mfg., Nat. Store Fixtures and Sel-O-Rak Internat., Chgo., 1986-91; exec. v.p. Enzon, Inc., Piscataway, N.J., 1992-94; v.p., gen. mgr. Electrocatalytic, Inc., Union, N.J., 1995, cons., advisor, 1995—. Served with USAF, 1950-54. Home: 76 Sayre Dr Princeton NJ 08540-5814

EHRENBERG, RONALD GORDON, economist, educator; b. N.Y.C., Apr. 20, 1946; s. Seymour and Judith G. E.; m. Randy Ann Birch, June 29, 1967; children: Eric L., Jason H. BA cum laude in Math., SUNY, Binghamton, 1966; MA, PhD, Northwestern U., 1970. Instr. Econs. Northwestern U., Evanston, Ill., 1970; asst. prof. Econs. Loyola U., Chgo., 1970-71, U. Mass., Amherst, 1971-72; assoc. prof. Econs. U. Mass., 1972-75; assoc. prof. Econs., Labor Econs. Cornell U., 1975-77, chmn. Dept. Labor Econs., 1976-81, prof. Econs., Labor Econs., 1977-85; dir. rsch. N.Y. State Sch. Indsl. and Labor Rels., 1979-95; Irving M. Ives prof. Indsl., Labor Rels. and Econs. Cornell U., 1985—, v.p. for acad. programs, planning and budgeting, 1995-98; rsch. assoc. Nat. Bur. Econ. Rsch., 1981—; dir. Cornell Inst. Labor Mktg. Policies, 1990-98, dir. Cornell Higher Edn. Rsch. Inst., 1998—; staff mem. Coun. Econ. Advisors, 1970; cons. to numerous govt. agencies, commns. and ednl. instns. Author: Fringe Benefits and Overtime Behavior: Theory and Econometric Analysis, 1971, The Demand for State and Local Government Employees: An Economic Analysis, 1975, The Regulatory Process and Labor Earnings, 1979, (with R. Smith) Modern Labor Economics: Theory and Public Policy, 1982, 6th edit., 1997, (with others) Economic Challenges in Higher Education, 1991, Labor Markets and Integrating National Economics, 1994, Contemporary Policy Issues in Education, 1995, The American University: National Treasure of Endangered Species, 1997, Gender and Family Issues in the Workplace, 1997; contbr. numerous articles to profl. jours. Rsch. grantee NSF, U.S. Dept. Labor, various pvt. founds.; NDEA fellow, 1969; Woodrow Wilson Nat. Fellowship Found. Dissertation Yr. fellow, 1970. Mem. AAUP, Am. Econ. Assn. (exec. com. 1996-98), Econometric Soc., Indsl. Rels. Rsch. Assn., Am. Edn. Fin. Assn., Assn. for Pub. Policy and Mgmt., Assn. Pot Pub. Policy Analysis and Mgmt. Office: Cornell U 256 Ives Hall Ithaca NY 14853-3901

EHRENFELD, DAVID WILLIAM, biology educator, author; b. N.Y.C., Jan. 15, 1938; s. Irving and Anne (Shapiro) E.; m. Joan Gardner, June 28, 1970; children: Kate, Jane, Jonathan, Samuel. BA, Harvard Coll., 1959; MD, Harvard Med. Sch., 1963; PhD, U. Fla., 1966. From asst. prof. biology to assoc. prof. biology Barnard Coll. Columbia U., N.Y.C., 1967-74; prof. biology Cook Coll. Rutgers U., New Brunswick, N.J., 1974—. Author: Biological Conservation, 1970, The Arrogance of Humanism, 1978, 2d edit., 1981, Beginning Again: People and Nature in the New Millennium, 1993, 95; founder, editor Conservation Biology, 1987-93, consulting editor, 1994—; bd. editors Ecosys. Health, 1994—; columnist mag. Orion, 1989—; contbr. articles to jours. Tech. Rev., Hudson Rev., Animal Behaviour, Sci., others. Trustee E. F. Schumacher Soc., Great Barrington, Mass., 1979—, Caribbean Conservation Corp., Gainesville, Fla., 1980—, Ednl. Found. Am., Westport, Conn., 1987-93, 98—. Fellow AAAS; mem. Ecol. Soc. Am., Internat. Union for the Conservation of Nature, Marine Turtle Specialist Group, Specialist Group on Sustainable Use of Wild Species. Jewish. Home: 44 N 7th Ave Highland Park NJ 08904-2931 Office: Rutgers U PO Box 231 New Brunswick NJ 08903-0231

EHRENFELD, ELLIE (ELVERA EHRENFELD), health science association administrator; b. Phila., Mar. 1, 1942; m. Donald F. Summers. BA cum laude, Brandeis U., 1962; PhD in Biochemistry, U. Fla., 1967; postdoctoral student, Albert Einstein Coll. Medicine, 1967-74. From assoc. prof.to prof. biochemistry and biology U. Utah, 1974-92; dean sch. biol. scis. U. Calif., Irvine, 1992-97; dir. ctr. scientific rev. Dept. Health and Human Svcs., Bethesda, Md., 1997—; mem. various coms. including rsch. adv. panel Walter Reed Army Inst. Rsch., exptl. virology study sect. NIH; mem. bd. sci. counselors Nat. Inst. Allergy and Infectious Diseases; cons. immunopathology lab. Scripps Inst. Med. Rsch. Recipient Bill Joklik Lectureship award Am. Soc. Virology; Nat. Sci. scholar Brandeis U. Office: Rockledge II Bldg 6701 Rockledge Dr Rm 3109 Bethesda MD 20892-7776

EHRENFELD, JOHN ROOS, environmental policy educator; b. Chgo., May 16, 1931; s. Louis and Alice (Roos) E.; m. Myrna A. Goodman (div.); children: Elizabeth, Thomas; m. Ruth M. Rahn Budd. SB in Chem. Engring., MIT, 1953, SCD in Chem. Engring., 1957. Dir. applied rsch. GCA Corp., Bedford, Mass., 1962-67; pres. Walden Rsch. Corp., Cambridge, Mass., 1967-75; v.p. Energy Resources Co., Cambridge, 1975-78; chmn. New Eng. River Basin Commn., Boston, 1978-81; sr. cons. Arthur D. Little, Inc., Cambridge, 1981-85, Abt Assocs., Inc., Cambridge, 1985-86; sr. rsch. assoc. MIT, Cambridge, 1987—; prin. John Ehrenfeld & Assocs., Lexington, Mass., 1986—. Co-editor Jour. Indsl. Ecology, 1996—; mem. editl. adv. bd. Environ. Sci. and Tech. Product, 1996—; editl. bd. Jour. Sustainable Design, 1997—; contbr. articles to profl. publs. Chmn. Town Dem. Com., Acton, Mass., 1960-67, Lincoln, Mass., 1968-72. 1st lt. U.S. Army, 1957-59. Mem. AIChE (Gary Leach award 1995), Am. Chem. Soc. (chmn. divsn.), Air and Wast Mgmt. Assn. Avocation: fly fishing. Home: 29 Percy Rd Lexington MA 02421-5637 Office: MIT 77 Massachusetts Ave Cambridge MA 02139-4307

EHRENFELD, PHYLLIS RHODA, editor, playwright, book reviewer; b. Montreal, Que., Can., Sept. 28, 1932; came to U.S., 1954; d. Carl and Thelma (Azeff) S.; m. Sylvain Ehrenfeld, May 29, 1955; children: David, Temma. BA in Psychology, Sir George Williams Coll., Montreal, 1952; BSW, McGill Sch. of Social Work, Montreal, 1953; postgrad. in lit., Columbia U., 1954-57. Social worker Jewish Family Welfare, Baron de Hirsch Inst., Montreal, 1952-54; tchr., program dir. Jack & Jill Day Care Ctr., Landing, N.J., 1956—; editor-in-chief, sr. editor Am. Anorexia Bulimia Assn. Newsletter, N.Y.C., 1980-93; producing artistic dir. The Superfluous Lover, Ethical Culture Soc. Bergen County, 1996. Playwright five plays; book reviewer No. N.J. NOW Newsletter, 1987-88, New Directions for Women, 1989—; editor: Ethical Culture Review of Books. Publicity chmn. Ethical Culture Soc. of Bergen County, Teaneck, 1987-88; drama coord. Garden State Playwrights, Teaneck, 1989—; tchr. adult edn. programs, libs., svc. groups. Recipient Arnold Gingrich award for Fiction, N.J. State Council on the Arts, 1980-81, nomination for Hodder Fellowship in the Humanities, Princeton (N.J.) U., 1981. Mem. Am. Anorexia Bulimia Assn. (bd. dirs. 1981-89, sec. 1981-87, rec. sec. 1990-91), Inst. for Ethical Edn. (program com.), Ethical Culture Soc. (program chmn. 1992-94, co-chmn. 1997-98). Avocations: hiking, gardening. Home: 276 Grove St Teaneck NJ 07666-3214

EHRENHAFT, PETER DAVID, lawyer; b. Vienna, Austria, Aug. 16, 1933; came to U.S., 1940, naturalized, 1945; s. Bruno B. and Ann J. (Polacek) E.; m. Charlotte Kennedy, May 4, 1958; children: Elizabeth Ann, James Bruno, Daniel Parker. AB with honors, Columbia Coll., 1954; LLB, M Internat. Affairs with honors, Columbia U., 1957. Bar: N.Y. 1958, D.C. 1961. Motions law clk. to U.S. Ct. Appeals (D.C. cir.), 1957-58; sr. law clk. to Chief Justice U.S. Supreme Ct., 1961-62; assoc. Cox, Langford & Brown, Washington, 1962-66, ptnr., 1966-68; ptnr. Fried, Frank, Harris, Shriver & Kampelman, Washington, 1968-77; dep. asst. sec., spl. counsel tariff affairs U.S. Dept. Treasury, Washington, 1977-79; ptnr. Hughes Hubbard & Reed, Washington, 1980-83, Bryan Cave, Washington, 1984-95; shareholder Ablondi, Foster, Sobin & Davidow, P.C., Washington, 1995—; professorial lectr. law George Washington U., 1965-72, U. Pa., 1980-85; mem. faculty Salzburg (Austria) Seminar in Am. Studies Law Session, 1973; mem. Fed. Jud. Ctr. Study Group on Workload of Supreme Ct., 1971-74; mem. adv. com. U.S. Ct. Appeals (fed. cir.), 1992-96; mem. industry sector adv. com. on trade in svcs. Dept. Commerce, 1999—. Contbr. articles and revs., primarily on internat. trade, to law jours.; mem. adv. bd. Jour. Law and Policy in Internat. Bus., 1967—, Patent, Trademark and Copyright Jour., 1970—; mem. editl. bd. Internat. Legal Materials, 1977-87. Pres. bd. trustees Nat. Child Rsch. Ctr., Washington, 1976-77; mem. adv. coun. George Washington U. Med. Ctr., 1990-96. With USAF, 1958-61, with Res., 1962-88; judge Ct. Mil. Rev., 1987-88. Mem. ABA (mem. coun. internat. law sect. 1983-85, 89-97, vice chair 1993-94, Internat. Legal scholar 1994-97, chmn. task force on legal svcs. in Japan 1991-98, liaison to Gen. Agreement on Tariffs and Trade 1992-94, vice chair transnational practice com. 1998—), Am. Law Inst., Am. Soc. Internat. Law, Washington Fgn. Law Soc. (bd. govs. 1982-92, pres. 1986-87). Home: 2510 Virginia Ave NW Washington DC 20037-1904 Office: Ablondi Foster Sobin et al 1150 18th St NW Washington DC 20036-3816

EHRENKRANZ, JOEL S., lawyer; b. Newark, Mar. 25, 1935; s. George J. and Hilda (Schreiber) E.; m. Anne Bick, June 9, 1963; children: Alissa, John, Jeanne. BS in Econs., U. Pa., 1956, MBA, 1957; LLB, NYU, 1961, LLM in Taxation, 1964. Bar: N.Y. 1961; CPA, N.Y. Acct. Peat, Marwick, Mitchell & Co., N.Y.C., 1957-62; sr. ptnr. Ehrenkranz & Ehrenkranz, N.Y.C., 1962—. Trustee, mem. distbn. com. Fedn. Jewish Philanthropies, N.Y.C., 1971-82; trustee, treas. Blythedale Children's Hosp., Valhalla,N.Y., 1966-74, United Jewish Appeal/Fedn. Jewish Philanthropies, N.Y.C., 1979-83, Jewish Communal Fund, 1982-92, pres., 1987-92; trustee Archives Am. Art, 1973, pres., 1984-86; trustee Whitney Mus. Am. Art, 1973—, v.p., 1978-98, pres., 1998—; trustee NYU Law Sch., 1992—; mem. grad. bd. Wharton Sch. U. Pa., 1985—; trustee, vice chmn., mem. exec. com. Mt. Sinai Med. Ctr., N.Y.C., 1987-92, chmn. fin. budget and accts. com. 1992-95; trustee NYU, 1998—. Mem. Century Club (White Plains, N.Y.). Office: 375 Park Ave New York NY 10152-0002 also: Keeler Ln North Salem NY 10560 also: Mayfly Dr Wilson WY 83014

EHRENPREIS, SEYMOUR, pharmacology educator; b. N.Y.C., June 20, 1927; s. William and Ethel (Balk) E.; m. Bella R. Goodman, June 30, 1953; children: Mark, Eli, Ira. B.S., CCNY, 1949; Ph.D., NYU, 1954. Mem. faculty dept. pharmacology Chgo. Med. Sch., prof., 1976—, chmn. pharmacology, 1976-85; prof. emeritus, 1985—; rsch. adj. prof. medicine Chgo. Med. Sch., 1992—; grants reviewer NSF, 1977-83, March of Dimes, 1983; vis. prof. Keio U., Tokyo, 1974, U. Ill. Sch. Medicine, Rockford, 1991—, Showa Med. Sch., Tokyo, 1985. Editor: Neurosciences Research, vols. 1-5, 1967-75, Revs. of Neurosci., vols. 1-3, 1974-77, Methods in Narcotics Research, 1974, Degradation of Endogenous Opoids, 1983; mem. editorial bd. Jour. Medicinal Chemistry, 1969-72, Jour. Clin. Pharmacology, 1991-96. Served with USN, 1945-46. Recipient Meritorious Service award Coll. Pharm. Sci., Columbia U., 1976; recipient Parker award Chgo. Med. Sch., 1981, Vis. Prof. award Japan Soc. Promotion Sci., 1974, cert. of merit for research Showa Med. Sch., 1985. Fellow AAAS, Am. Coll. Clin. Pharmacology (editl. bd. Jour. Clin. Pharmacology 1991—), N.Y. Acad. Sci. (chmn. cholinergic mechanisms conf. 1966), Am. Inst. Chemists; mem. Am. Soc. Hypertension, Soc. Neurosci., Am. Soc. Biol. Chemistry, Am. Soc. Pharmacology and Exptl. Therapeutics, Sigma Xi. Office: Univ Health Sci Chgo Med Sch 3333 Green Bay Rd North Chicago IL 60064-3037

EHRENREICH, HENRY, physicist, educator; b. Frankfurt, Germany, May 11, 1928; came to U.S., 1940, naturalized, 1945; s. Nathan and Frieda (Rosenstein) E.; m. Tema P. Hasnas, Feb. 1, 1953; children: Paul, Beth Herst, Robert. Student, Columbia U., 1950-51; BA, Cornell U., 1950, PhD, 1955; MA (hon.), Harvard U., 1963. Theoretical physicist Gen. Electric Research Lab., Schenectady, N.Y., 1955-63; vis. lectr. Harvard U., 1960-61, Gordon McKay prof. applied physics, 1963-82, Clowes prof. sci., 1982—; vis. prof. Brandeis U., 1969, U. Paris, 1969, U. Pa., 1976; mem. def. scis. rsch. coun. Advanced Rsch. Projects Agy., U.S. Dept. Def., 1972—; sec. solid state commn. Internat. Union Pure and Applied Physics, 1978-81; mem. solar photovoltaic energy adv. com. Dept. Energy, 1980-83; dir. Harvard Materials Rsch. Lab., 1982-90; cons. White House Office Sci. and Tech., 1991. Contbr. articles to profl. jours.; bd. editors Phys. Rev. 1965-67; co-editor: Solid State Physics, 1966—; asst. editor Annals of Phys., 1984—. Trustee Dibner Inst. for History of Sci. and Tech., 1992-98; cons. Wolf Found., 1997—. Fellow AAAS, Am. Acad. Arts and Scis., Am. Phys. Soc. (chmn. div. solid state physics 1969, chmn. study group on solar energy 1977-81, chmn. panel on pub. affairs 1990-91); mem. Phi Beta Kappa, Sigma Xi. Office: Harvard U Divsn Engring and Applied Scis and Physics Dept Cambridge MA 02138

EHRENREICH, JOHN HERMAN, psychologist; b. Phila., Feb. 20, 1943; s. Joseph and Freda (Steinbrook) E.; m. Barbara Alexander, Aug. 16, 1966 (div. June 1981); m. Sharon McQuaide, Feb. 14, 1987; children: Rosa, Benjamin, Alexander. BA, Harvard Coll., 1964; PhD, Rockefeller U., 1969, New Sch. Social Rsch., 1989. Lic. clin. psychologist, Conn., N.Y. Rsch. assoc. Health Policy Adv. Ctr., N.Y.C., 1969-72; sr. psychologist North Ctrl. Bronx Hosp., N.Y.C., 1989-90; prof. psychology Coll. Old Westbury, SUNY, 1972—; pvt. practice Sherman, Conn., 1990—. Author: The Altruistic Imagination, 1985; co-author: Long March, Short Spring, 1969, The American Health Empire, 1971; editor: The Cultural Crisis of Modern Medicine, 1976; contbr. various articles to profl. jours. Mem. APA, PEN,

Nat. Assn. Neuropsychology, Mental Health Workers Without Borders. Office: SUNY Coll at Old Westbury 223 Store Hill Rd Old Westbury NY 11568

EHRENREICH, ROBERT MARC, archaeologist, materials scientist, museum administrator; b. Schenectady, N.Y., May 8, 1960; m. Carmel Rafaella McGill, Apr. 14, 1991; children: Deborah Niamh, Nathan Patrick. AB with honors, Harvard U., 1982; PhD in Archaeology, Oxford U., 1985. Computer database specialist Harvard U. Peabody Mus., 1983, 84-85; postdoctoral rsch. fellow Smithsonian Instn., Washington, 1985-87; sr. program mgr. Nat. Materials Adv. Bd., NRC, Washington, 1987-99; assoc. rsch.prof. George Washington U., Washington, 1994-95; dir. univ. programs divsn. Ctr. for Advanced Holocaust Studies U.S. Holocaust Meml. Mus., Washington, 1999—; rsch. assoc. Smithsonian Instn., 1990-94; archaeometall. expert Roanoke (N.C.) Lost Colony excavations, 1992-96; mem. ASM Internat. Hist. Landmarks award selection com., 1994-96; mem. first Brit. Coun. Archaeol. Acad. Exch. with No. Ireland, 1989; rsch. assoc. Materials Rsch. Lab., U. Ill., 1987. Editor: Archeomaterials, 1991-94; cons. editor Jour. Archaeol. Method and Theory, 1994—; coord. editor JOM, 1994-99; mem. editl. rev. bd. ARD, 1997—; contbr. numerous articles and book revs. to profl. jours.; lectr. in field. Recipient Egyptian Antiquity Orgn. grant to attend 1st Internat. Symposium on the Gt. Sphinx, Cairo, 1992, 3 Meyerstein awards for Oxford U. Archaeology Grad. Students, 1982-85, CETS Sr. Program Mgr. Achievement award Nat. Rsch. Coun., 1998. Fellow Am. Anthropol. Assn.; mem. Am. Rsch. Ctr. in Egypt, Am. Soc. for Materials Internat., Hist. Metallurgy Soc., Soc. for Anthropology of Europe, Soc. for Am. Archaeology, Soc. for Archaeol. Scis. Office: US Holocaust Meml Mus 100 Raoul Wallenberg Pl SW Washington DC 20024-2126

EHRENSTEIN, GERALD, biophysicist; b. N.Y.C., Sept. 27, 1931; s. Irving and Adele (Holzer) E.; m. Deborah Ploscowe, Dec. 17, 1960; children: Ruth, David, Steven. BEE, Cooper Union, 1952; MA, Columbia U., 1958, PhD, 1962. Engr., Arma Corp., N.Y.C., 1952; rsch. physicist, NIH, Bethesda, Md., 1962-75, chief biophysics sect., 1975—. Corp. mem. Marine Biol. labs., Woods Hole, Mass., 1970-86 . Mem. editl. bd. Biophys. Jour., 1980-83; editor Methods of Exptl. Physics-Biophysics, 1982. Lt. (j.g.) USCG, 1952-54. Mem. Biophys. Soc. (mem. program com. 1981-84, 1992-93, coun. mem. 1992-95, mem. pub. policy com. 1991-96), Am. Phys. Soc., Sigma Xi. Avocation: birdwatching. Home: 7502 Nevis Rd Bethesda MD 20817-4742 Office: NIH 9000 Rockville Pike Bethesda MD 20892-0003

EHRENWERTH, DAVID HARRY, lawyer; b. Pitts., Apr. 22, 1947; s. Ben and Beatrice Lee (Schwartz) E.; m. Judith B. Ehrenwerth; children: Justin Reid, Lindsey Royce. BA, U. Pitts., 1969; JD, Harvard U., 1972. Bar: Pa. 1972, U.S. Dist. Ct. (we. dist.) Pa. 1972, U.S. Ct. Appeals (3d cir.) 1976. Asst. atty. gen. Commonwealth of Pa., Pitts., 1972-74; assoc. Kirkpatrick & Lockhart, Pitts., 1974-79, ptnr., 1979—. Pres. Pitts. chpt. Am. Jewish Com., 1988-90, nat. bd. govs., 1991-95, chmn. Pitts. chpt., 1996-98; mem. nat. adv. coun. Fed. Nat. Mortgage Assn., 1984-85; bd. dirs. Pa. Bd. Vocat. Rehab., Harrisburg, 1983-88, United Jewish Fedn., Pitts., 1991-93, Presbyn. U. Hosp., Pitts., 1993-94, Riverview Ctr. for Jewish Srs., 1991-93, U. Pitts. Cancer Inst., 1995—; bd. dirs. Montefiore Hosp., Pitts., 1985-93, treas., 1989, vice chmn., 1990-92, chmn., 1992-93; bd. govs. Pa. Econ. League, Western Region, 1999—. Named Pittsburgher to Watch Pitts. Mag., 1980. Mem. Pa. Bar Assn. (chmn. real estate fin. com. 1985-87), Allegheny County Bar Assn. (chmn. real property sect. 1989), Harvard U. Law Alumni Assn. Western Pa. (pres. 1986-87), Concordia Club, Westmoreland Country Club, Heinz Fifty-Seven Club (chmn. 1974-91), Duquesne Club, Phi Beta Kappa. Republican. Jewish. Avocations: tennis, golf. Home: 413 Windmere Dr Pittsburgh PA 15238-2440 Office: Kirkpatrick & Lockhart 1500 Oliver Building Bldg Pittsburgh PA 15222-2312

EHRET, JOSEPHINE MARY, microbiologist, researcher; b. Roswell, N.Mex., Feb. 26, 1934; d. Edward and Glenna (Memmer) E. BS, U. N.Mex., 1955. Med. technologist U. Colo. Health Scis. Ctr., Denver, 1956-75, rsch. microbiologist, 1975—; rsch. microbiologist Denver Dept. Health and Hosps., 1980—; instr. sch. medicine U. Colo., 1985—. Contbr. articles to profl. publs. Mem. Am. Soc. for Microbiology, Am. Soc. Med. Technologists (cert.), Am. Venereal Disease Assn., Calif. Assn. Continuing Med. Lab. Edn. Democrat. Avocations: reading, birding. Home: 1344 S Eudora St Denver CO 80222-3526 Office: Denver Pub Health Dept 605 Bannock St Denver CO 80204-4505

EHRHORN, RICHARD WILLIAM, electronics company executive; b. Marshalltown, Iowa, Jan. 21, 1934; s. Theodore Raymond and Zelda Elizabeth (Axtell) E.; BSEE, U. Minn., 1955; MSEE, Calif. Inst. Tech., 1958; m. Marilyn Patrick, Aug. 1, 1959; children: Scott Patrick, Kimberlee Dawn. Sr. engr. Gen. Dynamics Corp., Pomona, Calif., 1956-60; sr. rsch. engr. Calif. Inst. Tech. Jet Propulsion Lab., Pasadena, 1960-63; mgr. advanced devel. lab. Electronic Communications Inc., St. Petersburg, Fla., 1963-68; gen. mgr. Signal/One div., 1968-70; chmn. bd. dirs., CEO Ehrhorn Tech. Ops., Inc., Colorado Springs, Colo., 1970-95; vice chmn. ASTeX/ETO, Inc., Colorado Springs, 1996-99; chmn., CEO Alpha/Power, Inc., Longmont, Colo., 1996—. Regent Liberty U., 1995—. Mem. IEEE (sr.), Am. Radio Relay League, Radio Club Am., Quar. Century Wireless Assn. Author: (with others) Principles of Electronic Warfare, 1959; patentee in field. Home and Office: 3040 Sheiks Pl Colorado Springs CO 80904-1138

EHRICH, FREDRIC F., aeronautical engineer; b. N.Y.C., Dec. 17, 1928; s. William and Yetta (Benjamin) E.; m. Joan Collier, Sept. 5, 1955; children: Diane, Elliott, Noami. BS, MIT, 1947, ME, 1949, ScD, 1951; postgrad., Tech. Inst. at Delft, 1947-48. Engr., sr. engr., engring. supr. Aircraft Gas Turbine div. Westinghouse Electric Co., Phila., 1951-55; resident rep. at Rolls Royce Westinghouse Electric Co., Derby, Eng., 1955-56; adv. engr. Westinghouse Electric Co., Kansas City, Mo., 1956-57; aerodynamics engr. aircraft engines GE, Lynn, Mass., 1957-58, mgr. preliminary design, 1958-59, mgr. T64 engine design, 1959-63, mgr. design tech. ops., 1963-69, mgr. tech. and advanced product plans, 1969-82, cons. engr., staff engr., 1982-93; instr. Drexel Inst. Tech., Phila., 1952-53, U. Kans., Kansas City, 1957. Editor: Handbook fo Rotor Dynamics, 1991; assoc. editor Internat. Jour. Turbo and Jet Engines, 1988—; contbr. articles to profl. jours. and encys.; patentee aircraft engine tech. field. Mem. edn. coun. MIT, Cambridge, 1983—. Fellow ASME (chmn. design engring. div. 1972-73, editor Jour. Mech. Design and Vibration 1979-84), AIAA (program chmn. 1988); mem. NAE, Am. Helicopter Soc., Sigma Xi, Tau Beta Pi, Pi Tau Sigma. Jewish. Office: 58 Beacon St Marblehead MA 01945-2622*

EHRLE, RAYMOND ALBERT, retired psychologist and university official; b. Cochecton, N.Y., Mar. 4, 1926; s. Otto Joseph and Ella Ada (Fisher) E.; m. Betty Louise Turner, Aug. 7, 1954; children: John Raymond, Richard Stephen; m. Sally Irene Allen, Dec. 26, 1964. AB, Syracuse U., 1951; MA, George Washington U., 1956; EdD, U. Mo., 1961. Lic. psychologist, Md., D.C. Dir. psychol. counseling Pa. Rehab. Ctr., Johnstown, 1961-63; dir. counseling br. USES, Washington, 1963-64; dir. rehab. counseling tng. U. Md., College Park, 1964-69; dir. manpower projects Teledyne Econ. Devel. Co., Washington, 1969-76; manpower cons., New Carrollton, Md., 1977-83; dir. rsch. support Bus. Sch., George Washington U., Washington, 1983-89; ret., 1989. Author: Biographical Data in Vocational Rehabilitation, 1961, Counseling in the Public Employment Service, 1963, The Kool Aid Kid: A Trilogy, 1989, The Ehrle Family of ISNY and New York, 1991, Inspired By My Muse, 1997, others; editor, founder Jour. Employment Counselors, 1965-69; editor Rehab. Counseling Bull., 1969-71. Sec., newsletter editor German Heritage Soc., Washington, 1991-97. Maj. USAF, 1951-58. Mary E. Switzer fellow Nat. Rehab. Assn., 1976. Mem. APA (sec. divsn. 22 1966-68), APGA (bd. dirs. 1964-66), Am. Rehab. Counseling Assn. (pres. 1972-73), Nat. Employment Counselors Assn. (pres. 1964-65), Ret. Officers Assn. (life), Alpha Tau Omega (alumni pres. Epsilon Phi chpt. 1988-93, newsletter editor 1992—, Outstanding Alumni award 1994). Avocations: finance, genealogy, painting, gardening, reading. Home: 11328 Montgomery Rd Beltsville MD 20705-2937

EHRLICH, AMY, editor, writer; b. N.Y.C., July 24, 1942; d. Max and Doris (Rubenstein) E.; m. Henry A. Ingraham; 1 son, Joss. Student, Bennington Coll., 1960-63, 64-65. Roving editor Family Cir. Mag., N.Y.C., 1975-76; sr. editor Dial Books for Young Readers, N.Y.C., 1977-82, exec. editor, 1982-85; v.p., editor-in-chief Candlewick Press, Cambridge, Mass., 1991-95, editor at large, 1996—. Author: children's book Zeek Silver Moon, 1972 (named Best Book of Yr. 1972), Leo, Zack and Emmie (named booklist reviewers choice Sch. Libr. Jour. 1981), Leo, Zack and Emmie Together Again, The Snow Queen, 1982, The Random House Book of Fairy Tales, others, (novel) Where It Stops, Nobody Knows, 1988 (ALA booklist Best of the Decade 1989, Dorothy Canfield Fisher award), The Story of Hannukah, Leo Zack and Emmie Together Again, Pome and Peel, 1990, The Dark Card, 1991, Lucy's Winter Tale, 1992, Parents in the Pigpen, Pigs in the Tub, 1993 (Best Youth Picture Book award Booklist 1993), Maggie and Silky and Joe, 1994; editor: When I Was Your Age: Original Stories of Growing Up, Vol. 1, 1996, Vol. 2, 1999.

EHRLICH, ANNE HOWLAND, research biologist; b. Des Moines, Nov. 17, 1933; d. Winston Densmore and Virginia Lippincott (Fitzhugh) Howland; m. Paul Ralph Ehrlich, Dec. 18, 1954; 1 child: Lisa Marie Daniel. Student, U. Kans., 1952-55; LLD (hon.), Bethany Coll., 1990. Technician Dept. Entomology U. Kans., Lawrence, 1955; rsch. asst. Dept. Biol. Scis. Stanford (Calif.) U., 1959-72, rsch. assoc., 1972-75, sr. rsch. assoc., 1975—; assoc. dir. Ctr. for Conservation Biology Stanford U., 1987—; bd. dirs. Ctr. for Innovative Diplomacy, Pacific Inst., Rocky Mountain Biol. Lab., Sierra Club, Ploughshares Fund. Author: (with others) Ecoscience: Population, Resources, Environment, 1977, The Golden Door, 1979, Extinction, 1981, Earth, 1987, The Population Explosion, 1990, Healing the Planet, 1991, The Stork and the Plow, 1995, Betrayal of Science and Reason, 1996; editl. bd. Pacific Discovery; contbr. articles to profl. jours. Named to Global 500 Roll of Honour for Environ. Achievement, UN, 1989, UNFP-Sasekawa prize, 1994, Heinz award, 1995, Tyler prize. Fellow Am. Acad. Arts & Scis., Calif. Acad. Scis. (hon.); mem. Am. Humanists Assn. (hon. life, Disting. Svc. 1985, Raymond B. Bragg award 1985), Sierra Club. Avocations: flyfishing, hiking, reading. Home: Pine Hill Stanford CA 94305 Office: Stanford U Dept Biol Scis Stanford CA 94305

EHRLICH, AVA, television executive; b. St. Louis, Aug. 14, 1950; d. Norman and Lillian (Gellman) Ehrlich; m. Barry K. Freedman, Mar. 31, 1979; children: Alexander Zev, Maxwell Samuel. BJ, Northwestern U., 1972, MJ, 1973; MA, Occidental Coll., 1976. Reporter, asst. mng. editor Lerner Newspapers, Chgo., 1974-75; reporter, news editor Sta. KMOX, St. Louis, 1976-79; producer Sta. WXYZ, Detroit, 1979-85; exec. producer Sta. KSDK-TV, St. Louis, 1985—; guest editor Mademoiselle mag., N.Y.C., 1971; freelance writer, coll. prof. Detroit, Chgo., St. Louis, 1987; adj. faculty mem. Washington U., St. Louis, 1994—. Trustee CORO Found., St. Louis, 1976-77, 86—; bd. dirs. Nat. Kidney Found., St. Louis, 1987. Named Outstanding Woman in Broadcasting, Am. Women in Radio & TV, 1983; recipient Journalism award Am. Chiropractic Assn., 1989, AP award Ill. UPI, 1989, Illuminator award AMC Cancer Rsch., 1994, Women in Comms. Nat. award, 1988, Emmy award, 1995; CORO Found. fellow in pub. affairs, 1975-76. Mem. NATAS (com. mem. 1986—, bd. dirs. 1994—), 13 local Emmy awards 1986—), Women in Comms., Inc. (sec. 1978-79, Clarion award 1989, Best in Midwest Feature award 1989), Soc. Profl. Journalists. Democrat. Jewish. Home: 8002 Walinca Ter Saint Louis MO 63105-2565 Office: Sta KSDK-TV 1000 Market St Saint Louis MO 63101-2011

EHRLICH, BERNARD HERBERT, lawyer, association executive; b. Washington, Apr. 3, 1927; s. Samuel Zachary and Elsie (Klein) E.; m. Edna Kraft, June 17, 1951 (div.); children—Vivian Rose, Beverly Denise, Brenda Susan, Lisa Jean. AB, George Washington U., 1946, LLB, 1949, MA, JD, 1950. Bar: D.C. bar 1949. Pvt. practice Washington; gen. counsel numerous corps., industries, 1947-89; mgr., gen. counsel Inst. Indsl. Launderers, Washington, 1947-89; counsel KEX Nat. Assn., 1960-94; counsel Nat. Home Study Coun., 1947-89; mem. adv. panel employee recruitment and job devel. U.S. C. of C., 1967-84; mem. Pres.'s Com. on Employing the Handicapped, 1975—; gen. counsel KEX Nat. Assn., 1960-95; Accrediting Bur. Health Edn. Schs., 1965-92, Commn. Accredited Truck Driving Schs., 1985-92, Nat. Assn. Trade and Tech. Schs., 1968-86. Bd. dirs. Washington B'nai B'rith Hillel Found. With USN, 1943-45. Recipient svc. plaque Am. Inst. Launderers, 1966, svc. plaque Nat. Assn. Trade and Tech. Schs., 1967, svc. plaque Nat. Home Study Coun., 1970, svc. plaque Accrediting Bureau of Health Edn. Schs., 1992, svc. plaque Commn. Accredited Truck Driving Schs., 1992. Mem. ABA, Bar Assn. D.C., Am. Soc. Internat. Law, Am. Hist. Assn., Am. Soc. Assn. Execs., Soc. Am. Travel Writers, Am. Polit. Sci. Assn., Nat. Assn. Trade and Tech. Schs. (hon.), KEX Nat. Assn. (hon.), Inst. Indsl. Launderers (hon.), Am. Forestry Assn. (life), Phi Beta Kappa, Nu Beta Epsilon, Phi Delt Pi. Jewish. Home and Office: 5505 Seminary Rd Apt 1704N Falls Church VA 22041-3541

EHRLICH, CLIFFORD JOHN, hotel executive; b. N.Y.C., Nov. 17, 1938; s. Joseph George and Eugenia Marie (Rybacky) E.; m. Patricia Marie Stankunas, June 20, 1964; children: Susan, Brian, Scott. B.A. in Econs., Brown U., 1960; J.D., Boston Coll., 1965; H.H.D. (hon.), Bethany Coll., 1986. With Monsanto Co., 1960-73; dir. labor relations, then v.p. employee relations Marriott Corp., Washington, 1973-78; sr. v.p. human resources Marriott Internat., 1978-97; chmn. Alexus Internat., 1997—. Chmn. Employment Policy Found., 1995-97. Fellow Nat. Acad. Human Resources; Pers. Roundtable (chmn. 1993-95), Bus. Roundtable (chmn. employee rels. com. 1990-91), Labor Policy Assn. (vice chmn. 1994-97). Club: Congl. Country. Home: 9128 Vendome Dr Bethesda MD 20817-4021 Office: Alexus Internat Ste 480 555 Quince Orchard Rd Gaithersburg MD 20878-1437

EHRLICH, DAVID GORDON, film director, educator; b. Elizabeth, N.J., Oct. 14, 1941; s. Max and Jeannette (Gordon) E.; m. Marcela Josepha Rydlova, July 17, 1975. BA in Govt., Cornell U., 1963; sculpture cert., Madras Sch. Fine Arts, India, 1964; MA in Dramatic Art, U. Calif., Berkeley, 1966; MFA in Film, Columbia U., 1975. Artist-in-residence Vt. Coun. on Arts, Montpelier, Vt., 1978—, N.H. Coun. on Arts, Concord, N.H., 1986—; vis. prof. film studies Dartmouth Coll., Hanover, N.H., 1993—; Lectr. art U. Vt., 1977-82; adj. asst. prof. interdisciplinary arts SUNY, Purchase, 1971-75; instr. animation summer session U. Calif., Berkeley, yearly 1988-93, summer session U. Hawaii, Honolulu, yearly 1991-98, Mongolia Coll. Art, Ulan, Baatar, Mongolia, CAS Sch., Karachi, Pakistan, 1993; mem. adv. bd. ADA Animation Inst., Shanghai, 1988—; vis. prof. film MRDH Coll., Volda, Norway, 1990-91; art therapy cons. Manhattan State Hosp., 1975-76; presenter various internat. confs. and festivals. Author: The Bowel Book, 1981; dir., animator: (animated short films) Vermont Etude, 1977, Robot, 1977, Vermont Etude, No. 2, 1979, Robot Two, 1979, Precious Metal, 1980, Dissipative Dialogues, 1982, Precious Metal Variations, 1983, Point, 1984, Dissipative Fantasies, 1986, Pixel, 1987, Dryads, 1988, Academy Leader Variations, 1987, Animated Self-Portraits, 1989, A Child's Dream, 1990, Dance of Nature, 1991, Genghiz Khan, 1993, Etude, 1994, Interstitial Wavescapes, 1995, Robot Rerun, 1996, Asifa Variations, 1997, Radiant Flux, 1999; mem. editl. bd. Animation Jour., 1991—; contbr. articles to profl. jours.; films in collections at MOMA, Pacific Film Archive, Berlin ASIFA Animation Archive, Tokyo Internat. Animation Libr., Montreal Cinematheque Quebecoise, Moscow Film Archive; film retrospectives include Balt. Film Forum, Cinanima Animation Festival, Portugal, 1990, N.W. Film & Video Study Ctr., 1989, Pacific Film Archives, Shanghai Animation Festival, 1988, Mus. Modern Art, Varna World Animation Festival, Bulgaria, Belgrade Film Inst., Yugoslavia, 1987, Sinking Creek Film Celebration, Vienna Art Acad., 1986, Mus. Moving Image, 1985, Turin (Italy) City Hall, Cakovec Cultural Ctr., Yugoslavia, 1984, SUNY at Plattsburgh, Bradford Coll., 1982, Animators Gallery, N.Y.C., 1982, BVAU Gallery, Boston, Umwelt Galerie, Stuttgart, Germany, 1979. Recipient awards Cannes Film Festival, Chg. Film Festival, San Francisco Film Festival, Am. Film Festival, Krakow Film Festival, Cinanima Film Festival, Houston Film Festival, WorldFest, Charleston Film Festival, Roshd Film Festival, Iran, Murcia Film Festival, Spain; travel grantee Arts Internat., N.Y.C., 1992-93, Am. Film Inst. grantee, 1988, Holographic Film Found grantee, 1978, 83, 84; Fulbright fellow, 1963-64. Mem. Nat. Expressive Therapy Assn. (chair adv. bd. NETA Jour., cert. expressive therapist), Internat. Animation Assn. (exec. bd. 1988—, v.p. 1991—), Soc. Animation Studies (mem. steering com. 1999—), Asian Cinema Studies Soc., Vt. Coun. on Arts (filmmaking grantee 1978, 79, 84, 86, 89, 90, 91), Mongolia Soc., Miagmar Animation Workshop (bd. dirs. 1992—). Avocations: composing music, painting, sculpture, dancing, travel. Office: Dartmouth Coll Film Studies Wilson Hall Hanover NH 03755

EHRLICH, GEORGE EDWARD, rheumatologist, international pharmaceutical consultant; b. Vienna, Austria, July 18, 1928; came to U.S., 1938, naturalized, 1944; s. Edward and Irene (Elling) E.; m. Gail S. Abrams, Mar. 30, 1968; children: Charles Edward, Steven L. Abrams, Rebecca Sayles. AB cum laude, Harvard U., 1948; MB, MD, Chgo. Med. Sch., 1952. Intern Michael Reese Hosp., Chgo., 1952; resident Francis Delafield Hosp., N.Y.C., 1955, Beth Israel Hosp., Boston, 1956, New Eng. Center Hosp., Boston, 1957; fellow rheumatology NIH, Bethesda, Md., 1958, Hosp. for Spl. Surgery, N.Y.C., 1959-61; asst. attending physician Hosp. for Spl. Surgery, 1960-64; spl. fellow Sloan Kettering Inst., 1960-61; instr. medicine Cornell U., 1960-64; dir. Arthritis Center, chief rheumatology Albert Einstein Med. Center and Moss Rehab. Hosp., Phila., 1964-80; asst. prof. medicine Temple U., 1964-67, assoc. prof. medicine, 1967-72, prof. medicine, 1972-80, assoc. prof. rehab. medicine, 1964-74, prof., 1974-80; vis. lectr. U. Pa., 1964-80; prof. medicine, dir. div. rheumatology Hahnemann U., Phila., 1980-83; v.p. Anti-Inflammatory/Endocrine CIBA-Geigy Pharmaceuticals, Summit, N.J., 1983-86; head med. affairs CIBA-Geigy Ltd., Switzerland, 1987-88; pres. George E. Ehrlich Assocs., pharmaceutical cons.; adj. prof. clin. medicine NYU Med. Ctr., 1984—; lectr. in medicine U. Pa., 1989-91, adj. prof. medicine, 1992—; expert advisor, cons. Diabetes and Other Noncommunicable Diseases unit WHO, 1990-98, Chronic Disease Mgmt., 1998—; chmn. Internat. Low Back Pain Initiative; rep. of pres. Internat. League Assns. Rheumatology for Soft Tissue Rheumatisms, 1993-97, exec. com.; liaison to WHO, 1997-2001; mem. arthritis adv. com. FDA, 1993-96, chmn., 1993-96; expert, FDA, 1997-99; mem. coun. Chairs, FDA, 1996—; chmn. sci. adv. bd. Hochrheininstitut (Rheumatic Disease and Rehab. Rsch. Inst. of Upper Rhine in Germany, France and Switzerland for Treatment, Tchg., and Rsch.), 1993—; bd. dirs. Greenwich Inst. Am. Edn., 1994—; chmn., U.S. mem. Expert Adv. Panel on Chronic Degenerative Diseases, WHO, 1996—; bd. dirs. sci. adv. bds., several U.S. and internat. socs. Author: Differential Diagnosis of Rheumatoid Arthritis, 1972, Oculocutaneous Manifestations of Rheumatic Diseases, 1973, Total Management of the Arthritic Patient, 1973, Rehabilitation Management of Rheumatic Conditions, 1980, 2d edit., 1986, (with J. Fries) Prognosis, 1981, (with H.E. Paulus) Controversies in the Clinical Evaluation of Analgesic-Anti-Inflammatory-Antirheumatic Drugs, 1981; (with P. Utsinger, N. Zvaifler) Rheumatoid Arthritis, 1985, (with W. Simon) Medicolegal Consequences of Trauma, 1992; editor: Jour. Albert Einstein Med. Center, 1966-71; Arthritis and Rheumatic Diseases Abstracts, 1968-71; editorial bd.: Inflammation, 1974-88, Psychosomatics, 1977-83, Sexual Medicine Today, 1977-84, Jour. Rheumatology, 1982—, Immunopharmacology, 1985—, Med. Problems Performing Artists, 1985-92, Brazilian Jour. Rheumatology, 1992, 96—, Italian Jour. Rheumatic Diseases, 1999—; contbr. articles to profl. jours. Pres. Ea. Pa. chpt. Arthritis Found., 1970-72; mem. Phila. Mayor's Sci. and Tech. Adv. Coun., 1972-81; chmn. ad hoc adv. com. Bur. Drugs, FDA, 1971; mem. subcom. on redefinition of disability Social Security Adminstrn., 1982-86. Served to comdr. M.C. USNR, 1953-55; Res. to 1975, ret. Recipient citations City Phila., 1969, 74, Distinguished Alumnus award Chgo. Med. Sch., 1969; decorated Cavaliere Order of Star of Italian Solidarity. Fellow ACP, Royal Coll. Physicians Edinburgh, Phila. Coll. Physicians, Am. Coll. Rheumatology (elected master, 1994, com. for publ. Arthritis and Rheumatism, 1977-79, mem. editl. bd. 1980-83), Rheumatism Socs. Ecuador, India (hon.); mem. AMA (editl. bd. Jour. 1972-82), Am. Soc. Clin. Pharmacology and Therapeutics, Assn. Mil. Surgeons (Philip Hench award 1971), Brit. Assn. Rheumatology and Rehab. (overseas mem., editl. bd. 1979-82), Alpha Omega Alpha. Club: Harvard (Boston, N.Y.C.). Home: 38 Holly Dr Loveladies NJ 08008-6119 Office: 1 Independence Place #1101 Philadelphia PA 19106-3731 *Respect for the ideas of others, but ultimately responsible for my own ideas, thus, a liberal philosophy in a conservative setting. Like Brecht's Galileo, I should like to be remembered as a lover of old wines and new ideas.*

EHRLICH, GERALDINE ELIZABETH, management consultant; d. Joseph Vincent and Agnes Barbara (Campbell) McKenna; m. S. Paul Ehrlich, Jr., June 20, 1959; children: Susan Patricia, Paula Jeanne, Jill Marie. BS, Drexel Inst. Tech. Nutrition cons. hypertension rsch. team U. Calif. Micronesia, 1970; regional sales mgr. Marriott Corp., Bethesda, Md., 1976-78; dir. sales and profl. svcs. Coll. and Health Care divsn. Macke Co., Cheverly, Md., 1978, gen. mgr., 1978-79, v.p. ops. divsn., 1979-80, pres. Health Care divsn., 1980-81; regional v.p. Custom Mgmt. Corp., Alexandria, Va., 1981-83, v.p. mktg., 1983-87; v.p. mktg. and healthcare sales Morrison's Custom Mgmt., Mobile, Ala., 1987-88; v.p. sales ARA Svcs., Phila., 1988-93; v.p. bus. devel. ARAMARK, Phila., 1993-96; exec. dir. The Resource Group, Phila., 1995—; cons. mktg. The Green House, Tokyo, 1987-88; chmn. bd. Mktg. Matrix, Falls Church, Va., 1984—. Mem. Health Systems Agy. No. Va., 1976-77; chmn. Health Care Adv. Bd., Fairfax County, Va., 1973-77; vice chmn. Fairfax County Cmty. Action Com., 1973-77; treas. Fairfax County Dem. Com., 1969-73; trustee Fairfax Hosp., 1973-77; bd. dirs. Tennis Patrons, Washington, 1984-88, Phila. Singers, 1993-98, Physicians for Peace, 1993-98. Mem. NAFE, AAUW, Internat. Women's Assn., Am. Mgmt. Assn., Soc. Mktg. Profls. Home: 6512 Lakeview Dr Falls Church VA 22041-1102 Office: 6081 Hamilton Blvd Allentown PA 18106-9687

EHRLICH, GERT, science educator, researcher; b. Vienna, Austria, June 22, 1926; came to U.S., 1939; s. Leopold and Paula Maria (Kucera) E.; m. Anne Vogdes Alger, Apr. 27, 1957. AB with honors in Chemistry, Columbia U., 1948; AM, Harvard U., 1950, PhD, 1952. NIH postdoctoral fellow Harvard U., Cambridge, Mass., 1951-52; research assoc., Dept. Physics U. Mich., Ann Arbor, 1952-53; mem. research staff Gen. Electric Research Lab., Schenectady, N.Y., 1953-68; prof. materials sci. U. Ill., Urbana-Champaign, 1968—, research prof. Coordinated Sci. Lab., 1968—. Former mem. editorial adv. bd. Chem. Physics Letters, Jour. Chem. Physics, Jour. Vacuum Sci. & Tech., Surface & Colloid Sci., Progress in Surface & Membrane Sci.; contbr. numerous articles on molecular behavior at crystal surfaces and on properties of individual atoms and atom clusters. Served to cpl. U.S. Army, 1945-47, ETO. Guggenheim fellow, 1985. Fellow Am. Phys. Soc., N.Y. Acad. Scis.; mem. Nat. Acad. Scis., Am. Chem. Soc. (Kendall award 1982), Am. Vacuum Soc. (Medard W. Welch award 1979), Alexander von Humboldt Found. (Humboldt-Preis 1992), Sigma Xi, Phi Beta Kappa. Office: U Ill Materials Rsch Lab 104 S Goodwin Ave Urbana IL 61801-2902*

EHRLICH, GRANT C(ONKLIN), business consultant; b. Chgo., Aug. 16, 1916; s. Howard and Jenese (Conklin) E.; m. Gretchen Woerz, Sept. 14, 1940; children: Galen Wood, Gretel Ehrlich. B.S. in Adm. Engring. and Mech. Engring., Cornell U., 1938. Sales and engring. mgr. New Eng. Tape Co., Hudson, Mass., 1938-44; pres. Resin Industries, Inc., Santa Barbara, Calif., 1944-56, Industrial de Resinas. S.A., Mexico City, 1953-85; chmn. Templock Corp., Santa Barbara, Calif., 1977—; CEO Flow Gen. Inc., McLean, Va., 1983-85, chmn., 1983-88; chmn. Cerechem Corp., Santa Barbara, 1995—. Chmn. Young Republicans of Calif., 1950. Club: Valley Club of Montecito (treas., dir. 1980-82). *

EHRLICH, HENRY LUTZ, biology educator; b. Stettin, Pommerania, Germany, Aug. 31, 1925; came to U.S., 1940; s. Max and Gerda (Tannenwald) E. *His paternal grandparents were Sanitätsrat Dr. Franz Ehrlich, an internist, born in Silesia, and Lucie (Frankenstein) E, who died in the early 1900's. His maternal grandparents were Jakob Tannenwald, successful businessman, born in Rothenburg-an-der-Fulda, Hesse, and Leonore (Jessel) T. Franz E. was a victim of the Holocaust. He was deported from Stettin to Lublin, Poland in February 1940, where he died. Jacob T., upon retirement, moved with his wife from Stettin to Berlin. He died in 1935. Also a Holocaust victim, Leonore T. was deported from Berlin to Lodz, Poland in October 1941, her fate unknown.* BS cum laude, Harvard Coll., 1948; MS, U. Wis., 1949, PhD, 1951. From asst. prof. to prof. biology Rensselaer Poly. Inst., Troy, N.Y., 1951-94; prof. emeritus, 1994; cons. in field. Author: Geomicrobiology, 1981, 3d edit., 1995; author, co-editor: Workshop on Biotechnology for the Mining, Metal Refining and Fossil Fuel Processing Industries, 1986; co-author, co-editor: Microbial Mineral Recovery, 1990; co-editor-in-chiefGeomicrobiology Jour. Mem. interdisciplinary com. World Cultural Coun., Monterrey, Mex. Am. Acad. Microbiology fellow. Fellow AAAS; mem. Symposia for Environ. Biogeochemistry (v.p., treas.), Am. Soc. Microbiology, Soc. Indsl. Microbiology, Am. Inst. Biol. Scis., Sigma Xi. Jewish. Achievements include research on microbial manganese oxidation and reduction; microbial chromate reduction; microbial bauxite weathering;

bioleaching. Home: 2423 21st St Troy NY 12180-1826 Office: Rensselaer Polytech Inst Biology Dept 110 8th St Troy NY 12180-3522

EHRLICH, IRA ROBERT, mechanical engineering consultant; b. Washington, Sept. 1, 1926; s. Abraham Moses and Anna (Garonzik) E.; m. Sheila Lenor Kaminsky, June 11, 1950; children: Richard Mark, Heather Maureen Ehrlich Reiser. B.S., U.S. Mil. Acad., 1950; M.S., Purdue U., 1956; Ph.D., U. Mich., 1960; M.S. (hon.), Stevens Inst. Tech., 1982. Registered profl. engr., Mich., N.J. Supr. ITT, Paramus, N.J., 1960-62; mgr. transp. research group Stevens Inst. Tech., Hoboken, N.J., 1962-74, dean research 1974-83, head dept. mech. engring., 1979-83, v.p. research, 1983-85, v.p. acad. affairs, 1984-85, prof. emeritus, 1988—; pres. I. Robert Ehrlich P.A., Teaneck, N.J., 1988—; chmn. sci. adv. com. U.S. Army Tank-Automotive Rsch. and Devel. Command, 1970-77; cons. to industry; mem. N.J. Motor Vehicle Insp. Sta. Rev. Commn., chmn. safety com., 1977-80. Asso. editor Tire Sci. and Tech, 1972-80. Served to capt. U.S. Army, 1950-60. Themis grantee, 1967-72. Fellow Soc. Automotive Engrs., Internat. Soc. Terrain-Vehicle Systems (gen. sec. 1967-78, v.p. 1978-81, pres. 1981-84); mem. ASME, NSPE, ASTM, Nat. Safety Coun., Nat. Assn. Profl. Accident Reconstructionists (bd. dirs. 1997-99), B'nai Brith (chpt. pres. 1967-68,. Jewish. Home and Office: 859 Columbus Dr Teaneck NJ 07666-6612 *Make the most of your scraps of time.*

EHRLICH, JEFFREY, data processing company executive; married; 1 child. BSEE, U. R.I.; MS in Tech. Mgmt. and Computer Sci., Rensselaer Polytechnic Inst.; postgrad., GE Mgmt. Inst., Crotonville, N.Y. Formerly CIO GE Med. Syss. Bus., Milw.; chief technology officer Nat. Data Corp., Atlanta, 1995—. Designer on-line database transaction sys. for GE Capital. Office: Nat Data Corp 3rd Flr National Data Plz Atlanta GA 30329-2010*

EHRLICH, JOHN GUNTHER, writer; b. Berlin, Apr. 6, 1930; s. Walter Frederick and Henrietta (Fletch) E.; m. Frances Hendrika Vernon, Nov. 17, 1952 (div. Nov. 1978); children: Timothy Walter, Lisa Frances Gamble; m. Karen Ann Carr, Dec. 31, 1982. BJ, Syracuse U., 1952; JD, Bklyn. Law Sch., 1962. Bar: N.Y. 1962; Federal, 1962; U.S. Dist. Ct. (so. dist., ea. dist.), 1962. Reporter Newsday, Huntington, N.Y., 1955-60; exec. asst. Suffolk County Rep. Com., Blue Point, N.Y., 1960-63; bur. chief Suffolk County Dist. Atty., Hauppauge, N.Y., 1963-90; writer Little River, S.C., 1990—. Author: (as Jack Ehrlich) Revenge, 1959, Court Martial, 1960, Parole, 1961, Slow Burn, 1961, Cry, Baby, 1962, The Girl Cage, 1967, Close Combat, 1969, The Drowning, 1970, The Chatham Killing, 1976, The Fastest Gun in the Pulpit, (German, French, Swedish transl., movie script from novel), 1972, Bloody Vengeance, 1973, The Laramie River Crossing, 1973, Rebellion at Cripple Creek, 1979; contbr. short stories, non-fiction articles to mags. Capt. USAF, 1952-54. Recipient Investigative Reporting award Nat. Home Builders, 1958, Edgar Allan Poe award Mystery Writers, N.Y.C., 1970, Cert. Appreciation, Suffolk County Police Benevolent Assn., 1989. Republican. Episcopalian. Avocations: golf, gardening, music, horseback riding. Office: PO Box 62 Little River SC 29566-0062 also: Theron Raines 71 Park Ave # 4A New York NY 10016-2507

EHRLICH, LAWRENCE, retired cantor, educator; b. Bklyn., Sept. 28, 1917; s. Moses and Bella Riva Erlick; m. Pearl Barron, May 29, 1945 (dec. Dec. 1953); 1 child, Harriet Dale; m. Cecile Pincus, June 6, 1976. Grad., Hebrew Union Coll., 1952, B Sacred Music, 1955, D in Music (hon.), 1998. Cantor Temple Beth Sholom, Flushing, N.Y., 1950-52; cantor educator Congregation Rodef Sholom, Youngstown, Ohio, 1952-83, cantor emeritus, 1983—; cantor/rabbi substitute for Tri-State area; nat. rep. Fedn. Temple Youth, Starlight, Pa., 1951; regional rep. Fedn. Temple Youth, Rochester, Buffalo, Cleve., 1953-58; regional rep. Am. Conf. Cantors, 1955-65; aux. cantor (hon.) Heritage Manor, Youngstown, 1970—; holiday cantor Temple Israel, New Castle, Pa., 1983—, aux. cantor/leader, 1989; aux. cantor/leader Morse Geriatric Ctr., West Palm Beach, Fla., 1990; lectr. on Jewish music; advisor to Alumni Assn., 1983. Chmn. UNICEF, 1960; pres. UN Assn. Youngstown, 1960-67, Clergy Boy Scout Camp Retreats, 1954-57, Clergy Gold Star Mothers Meml. Day, 1954-74; area chmn. Am. Heart Assn., Youngstown, 1970; chmn. Youngstown area Commn. for Jewish Edn., 1980-82. Recipient Gates of Jerusalem State of Israel Bonds, Zionist Orgn. Am., 1972, Outstanding Svc. to Congregation Rodef Sholom Lt. Gov. Richard F. Celeste, Ohio, 1972, Shiliah Tzibur award Am. Conf. Cantors, 1977, Kol Hakavod award Cantorial alumni Assn., 1977, Appreciation award Congressman Lyle Williams, 1983, Retirement award Senator Harry Meshel, 1983, Proclamation of Appreciation award Mayor George Vukovich of Youngstown, 1983m Justice Brandeis award Zionist Orgn. Am., 1987, Kfar Silver scholarship plaque, 1987, Arthur award, 1971-72, 78-79; Cantor Lawrence Ehrlich Day proclaimed in his honor, May 25, Youngstown. Mem. Am. Conf. Cantors (charter), Nat. Assn. Temple Educators (charter, reform Jewish educator cert. 1989), Zionist Orgn. Am. (life), Jewish Chautauqua Soc. (life), Hadassah (life, assoc.), B'nai Brith, Congregation Rodef Sholom (life), Temple Israel (life), Rodef Sholom Brotherhood (life), Rodef Sholom Sisterhood (hon. life), Masons. Avocations: reading, collecting opera scores and records, entertaining geriatric groups, philately. Avocation: Jewish music. Summer Home: 1530 Fisher Dr Hubbard OH 44425-3303 Winter Home: 1530 Fisher Dr Hubbard OH 44425-3303 *For a meaningful and happy life, share with others their sorrows and share your joys with them; and listen!.*

EHRLICH, M. GORDON, lawyer; b. Springfield, Mass., Sept. 28, 1930; s. Robert and Ida (Gordon) E.; m. Eleanor Fradkin, Sept. 1, 1956; children: Kenneth, Virginia, Sarah, Alexandra. BS, Yale U., 1951; LLB, Harvard U., 1954. Bar: Mass. 1954. Atty. Bingham, Dana, Boston, 1957—; former chmn. Boston Tax Forum, Boston Estate and Bus. Planning Coun.; lectr. Harvard U. Law Sch. Contbr. articles to profl. jours. Former pres. Chestnut Hill Assn.; trustee Beth Israel Hosp., Boston. Mem. ABA (tax sect.), Am. Law Inst. Office: Bingham Dana 150 Federal St Fl 14 Boston MA 02110-1726

EHRLICH, MORTON, international finance executive; b. N.Y.C., Dec. 1, 1934; s. Milton and Anne (Tannenbaum) E.; children from previous marriage: Bruce, Ellen, Wendy; m. Paula Ehrlich, Feb. 25, 1991. BBA cum laude, CCNY, 1960; PhD in Economics (Ford Found. fellow), Brown U., 1965. Economist, Fed. Res. Bank of N.Y., 1965-67, Nat. Indsl. Conf. Bd., N.Y.C., 1967-68; v.p. Eastern Airlines, Miami, Fla., 1968-76, sr. v.p. planning, 1976-85; exec. v.p. Transworld Airlines, N.Y., 1985-88, also bd. dirs.; pres. LIFECO Svcs. Corp., 1988-91; chmn., chief exec. officer Integrated Mgmt. Corp., 1991—; trustee AETNA Mut. Funds. Bd. dirs. Nat. Bur. Econ. Rsch. With U.S. Army, 1953-56. Mem. Am. Econ. Assn., Nat. Assn. Bus. Economists, U.S. C. of C. Author: Discretionary Income, 1967, A Weekly Index of Business Activity, 1967, U.S. Foreign Trade, 1968, Computer Application in the Allocation of Airline Resources, 1975, An Integrated System for Airline Planning and Management Information, 1977, An Integrated Strategic Plan for Network Marketing, 1996, Paradigm Shift Syndrome, 1997. Home: Ste 1702 1000 Venetian Way Apt 1702 Miami FL 33139-1009 Office: Integrated Mgmt Corp 1000 Venetian Way Apt 1702 Miami FL 33139-1009

EHRLICH, PAUL, chemist, educator; b. Vienna, Austria, Feb. 26, 1923; came to U.S., 1940, naturalized, 1944; s. Jacob and Irma (Hutter) E.; m. Celia Lesley, Apr. 16, 1949; children—Daniel, James, Catherine, Margot, Paul R. B.S., Queens Coll., 1944; M.S., U. Wis., 1948, Ph.D., 1951. Phys. chemist Nat. Bur. Standards, Washington, 1951-53; postdoctoral fellow Harvard, 1953-54; research chemist, scientist Monsanto Co., Springfield, Mass. and St. Louis, 1955-67; assoc. prof., prof. SUNY, Buffalo, 1967-91, prof. emeritus, 1991—; adj. rsch. prof. U. Mass., Amherst. Mem. editl. bd. Jour. Macromolecular Sci, 1966-81; contbr. articles to profl. jours. Served with AUS, 1944-46. Rsch. grantee NSF, 1968, 72, 75, 77, 79, 86, 89, 92. Mem. AAAS, Am. Chem. Soc., Am. Phys. Soc. Home: 254 Poverty Ln Lebanon NH 03766-2702 Office: U Mass Dept Polymer Sci-Engring Amherst MA 01003-4530

EHRLICH, PAUL RALPH, biology educator; b. Phila., May 29, 1932; s. William and Ruth (Rosenberg) E.; m. Anne Fitzhugh Howland, Dec. 18, 1954; 1 dau., Lisa Marie. AB, U. Pa., 1953; AM, U. Kans., 1955, PhD, 1957. Research assoc. U. Kans., Lawrence, 1958-59; asst. prof. biol. scis. Stanford U., 1959-62, assoc. prof., 1962-66, prof., 1966—, Bing prof. population studies, 1976—, dir. grad. study dept. biol. scis., 1966-69, 1974-76, pres. Ctr. for Conservation Biology, 1988—; cons. Behavioral Rsch. Labs., 1963-67; corr. NBC News, 1989-92. Author: How to Know the Butterflies, 1961, Process of Evolution, 1963, Principles of Modern Biology, 1968, Population Bomb, 1968, 2d edit., 1971, Population, Resources, Environment: Issues in Human Ecology, 1970, 2d edit., 1972, How to Be a Survivor, 1971, Global Ecology: Readings Toward a Rational Strategy for Man, 1971, Man and the Ecosphere, 1971, Introductory Biology, 1973, Human Ecology: Problems and Solutions, 1973, Ark II: Social Response to Environmental Imperatives, 1974, The End of Affluence: A Blueprint for the Future, 1974, Biology and Society, 1976, Race Bomb, 1977, Ecoscience: Population, Resources, Environment, 1977, Insect Biology, 1978, The Golden Door: International Migration, Mexico, and the U.S., 1979, Extinction: The Causes and Consequences of the Disappearance of Species, 1981, The Machinery of Nature, 1986, Earth, 1987, The Science of Ecology, 1987, The Birder's Handbook, 1988, New World/New Mind, 1989, The Population Explosion, 1990, Healing the Planet, 1991, Birds in Jeopardy, 1992, The Birdwatchers Handbook, 1994, The Stork & the Plow, 1995, Betrayal of Science and Reason, 1996, World of Wounds, 1997; contbr. articles to profl. jours. Recipient World Wildlife Fedn. medal, 1987; co-recipient Crafoord prize in population biology and conservation biol. diversity, 1990, Volvo Environ. prize, 1993, World Ecology medal Internat. Ctr. Tropical Ecology, 1993, UN Sasakawa Environ. prize, 1994, Heinz prize for the environ., 1995, Tyler Environ. prize, 1998, Heineken prize for environ. sci., 1998, Blue Plant prize, 1999; MacArthur Prize fellow, 1990-95. Fellow Calif. Acad. Scis., Am. Acad. Arts and Scis., AAAS, Am. Philos. Soc., Entomology Soc. Am.; mem. Nat. Acad. Scis., Entomological Soc. Am., Soc. for Study Evolution, Soc. Systematic Zoology, Am. Soc. Naturalists, Lepidopterists Soc., Am. Mus. Natural History (hon. life mem.). Office: Stanford U Dept Biol Scis Stanford CA 94305

EHRLICH, RAYMOND, lawyer; b. Swainsboro, Ga., Feb. 2, 1918; s. Ben and Esther Ehrlich; m. Miriam Bettman, Nov. 27, 1975; stepchildren: Jack Bettman, Gerald Bettman, Zelda Bettman, Carol Ann B. Berkowitz. BS, U. Fla., 1939, JD, 1942. Bar: Fla. 1942, U.S. Dist. Ct., U.S. Ct. Appeals (11th cir.), U.S. Supreme Ct. Ptnr. Mathews Osborne Ehrlich et al., Jacksonville, Fla., 1946-81; justice Supreme Ct. Fla., Tallahassee, 1981-91, chief justice, 1988-90; ptnr. Holland & Knight, Jacksonville, Fla., 1992—; jurist-in-residence Fla. State U. Coll. Law, 1991. Spl. counsel to U.S. Senator Bob Graham, 1991. Served to comdr. USN, 1942-46. Mem. ABA, Fla. Bar Assn., Jacksonville Bar Assn., Am. Coll. Trial Lawyers, Internat. Acad. Trial Lawyers, Am. Law Inst. Office: Holland & Knight 50 N Laura St Ste 3900 Jacksonville FL 32202-3622

EHRLICH, ROBERT L., JR., congressman. Law clk. H. Russell Smouse, Esq., 1981; assoc. Ober, Kaler, Grimes, and Shriver, 1982-92, of counsel, 1992-94; mem. Md. Ho. of Dels., 1987-94, mem. Ho. Jud. Com., Joint Legis. Ethics Com., Gov.'s Coun. Child Abuse & Neglect, Gov.'s Adv. Panel for Justice Adminstrn., mem. Gov.'s Select Panel on Drug-Addicted Newborns, Gov.'s Select Panel on the Hickey Sch., also Ho. co-chmn. Joint Com. on Md.'s Procurement Laws; mem. U.S. Ho. of Reps., Washington, 1995—; mem. budget com. U.S. Ho. of Reps.; mem. Banking & Fin. Svcs. Com., subcoms. Fin. Insts. and Commercial Credit, Housing and Fin. Svcs., Spkrs. Spl. Adv. Com. on Corrections, U.S. Ho. of Reps., 104th Congress, asst. majority whip, Nat. Security Working Group. Named Guardian of Small Bus. Nat. Fedn. Ind. Bus., 1987-90, Legislator of Yr. Md. State's Attys. Assn., 1989, Fraternal Order of Police Md. State Lodge, 1994, Nat. Conf. for Prevention of Child Abuse, 1994, Outstanding Young Marylander Md. Jaycees, 1995, Outstanding Rep. Male Md. Rep. State Ctrl. Com., 1995, Disting. Svc. award German Soc. Md., 1997, Legislator of Yr. Nat. Assn. Mortgage Brokers, 1997; recipient Spirit of Enterprise award U.S. C. of C., 1996, 97, Thomas Jefferson award Food Distbrs. Internat., 1996, Congl. Tax Fighter award Nat. Tax Limitation Com., 1996, Taxpayer Hero award Citizens Against Govt. Waste, 1997. Office: US House Reps 315 Cannon Bldg Ofc Bldg Washington DC 20515-2002 also: 1407 York Rd Ste 304 Lutherville MD 21093-6054*

EHRLICH, THOMAS, educator; b. Cambridge, Mass., Mar. 4, 1934; s. William and Evelyn (Seltzer) E.; m. Ellen Rome, June 18, 1957; children—David, Elizabeth, Paul. AB, Harvard U., 1956, LLB, 1959; LLD (hon.), Villanova U., 1979, Notre Dame U., 1980, U. Pa., 1987. Bar: Wis. bar 1959. Law clk. Judge Learned Hand U.S. Ct. Appeals 2d Circuit, 1959-60; spl. asst. to legal adviser Dept. State, 1962-64; spl. asst. to under-sec. U.S. Dept. State, 1964-65; assoc. prof. law Stanford (Calif.) U., 1965-68, prof., 1968-75, also dean, 1971-75, Richard E. Lang dean and prof., 1973-75; pres. Legal Services Corp., Washington, 1976-79; dir. Internat. Devel. Coop. Agy., Washington, 1979-81; provost, prof. law U. Pa., Phila., 1981-87; pres., prof. law Ind. U., Bloomington and Indpls., 1987-94; vis. prof. Duke U., Durham, 1994; Disting. Univ. scholar Calif. State U., San Francisco, 1995—; vis. prof. Stanford Law Sch., 1994—; sr. scholar Carnegie Found. for Advancement of Tchg., 1997—. Author: (with Abram Chayes and Andreas F. Lowenfeld) The International Legal Process, 3 vols., 1968, (with Herbert L. Packer) New Directions in Legal Education, 1972, International Crises and the Role of Law, Cyprus, 1958-67, 1974; editor: (with Geoffrey C. Hazard Jr.) Going to Law School?, 1975, (with Mary Ellen O'Connell) International Law and the Use of Force, 1993, The Courage to Inquire, 1995. Office: Carnegie Found for the Advancement of Tchg 555 Middlefield Rd Menlo Park CA 94025

EHRLING, SIXTEN, orchestra conductor; b. Malmö, Sweden, Apr. 3, 1918; came to U.S., 1963; s. Gunnar and Emilia (Lundgren) E.; m. Gunnel Lindgren, Sept. 19, 1947; children: Elisabeth, Ann-Charlotte. Student, Royal High Sch. Music, Stockholm, 1936-40. Head conducting and orch. dept. Juilliard Sch., N.Y.C., 1973-88, Manhattan Sch. of Music, N.Y.C., 1993—. Condr. Royal Opera House, Stockholm, 1940-53, 90; prin. condr., music dir., 1953-60, condr., music dir. Detroit Symphony Orch., 1963-73; mus. advisor, prin. guest condr. Denver Symphony, 1978-89, music advisor, 1989—; guest condr. Met. Opera, N.Y.C., U.S., Europe, Japan, Australia, South Am., Vienna State Opera.

EHRMAN, JOACHIM BENEDICT, mathematics educator; b. Nuremberg, Germany, Nov. 12, 1929; emigrated to U.S., 1938, naturalized, 1943; s. Fritz Sally and Ilse (Benedict) E.; m. Gloria Jeanette Gould, Jan. 24, 1961; 1 son, Carl David. A.B., U. Pa., 1948; A.M., Princeton, 1949, Ph.D., 1954. Research physicist N.Am. Aviation, Inc., Downey, Calif., 1951-53; instr. physics Yale, 1954-55; research physicist U.S. Naval Research Lab., Washington, 1955-68; prof. dept. applied math. U. Western Ont., Can., London, 1968—; asso. prof. physics George Washington U., 1956-57; lectr. U. Md., 1963-64; vis. research staff Plasma Physics Lab., Princeton, 1975-76. Contbr. profl. jours. Mem. Phi Beta Kappa. Jewish. Office: U Western Ont, Dept Applied Math, London, ON Canada N6A 5B7

EHRMAN, JOHN, federal agency official, historian; b. Albuquerque, Nov. 23, 1959; s. Leonard and Peggy Zimmer Ehrman; m. Diane Marie Parsont, Mar. 12, 1989; children: Rachelle, Benjamin. BA, Tufts U., 1981; M in Internat. Affairs, Columbia U., 1983; PhD, George Washington U., 1993. With U.S. Govt., Washington, 1983—. Author: The Rise of Neoconservatism, 1995.

EHRMAN, LEE, geneticist; b. N.Y.C., May 25, 1935; m. Richard Ehrman, 1955; children: Esther, Judith. BS, Queens Coll., 1956; MS, Columbia U., 1957, PhD in Genetics, 1959; DSc (hon.), CUNY, 1989. Mem. faculty Barnard Coll., 1956-58; postdoctoral fellow in genetics Columbia U., N.Y.C., 1959-61; assoc. seminar on population biology Columbia U., 1981—; mem. faculty SUNY-Purchase, 1970—, prof. div. natural scis., 1972—; Disting. prof. biology SUNY, Purchase, 1995—; mem. spl. study sect. NIH, NIMH, 1979-80; vis. disting. prof. U. Miami, Coral Gables, Fla., 1981; vis. lectr. U. Puerto Rico, Rio Piedras, 1987; coordinator, panelist workshops, programs in field. Author: Behavior Genetics and Evolution, 2d edit., 1981, 2 other books; assoc. editor Evolution; assoc. editor for genetics and cytology Am. Midland Naturalist; co-editor: Behavior Genetics; assoc. editor, exec. com. Soc. Am. Naturalists, 1977-85, pres.-elect 1990; contbr. more than 500 articles to profl. jours. Recipient Lit. Soc. Found. medal in German, 1956; Shirley Farr postdoctoral fellow, 1961-62; USPHS postdoctoral fellow, 1959-61; faculty exch. scholar, 1974—; NSF grantee, 1979-84; Sr. Scientist awardee Whitehall Found., 1987, 93; NIH gen. med. scis. grantee, 1987—; SUNY travel grantee, 1988, 93, 96. Fellow AAAS, Inst. Soc. Ethics and Life Scis; mem. AAUW (life), Am. Soc. Naturalists (pres. 1990), Behavior Genetics Assn. (pres. 1978, Dobzhansky award for lifetime resch. 1988), Soc. for Study of Evolution (exec. council 1986—), Phi Beta Kappa, Sigma Xi. Home: 2 Jennifer Ln Rye Brook NY 10573-1916 Office: SUNY Div Natural Scis Purchase NY 10577

EHRMAN, MADELINE ELIZABETH, federal agency administrator; b. N.Y.C., July 4, 1942; d. Donald McKinley and Marie Madeleine (Brandeis) Ehrman. BA summa cum laude Brown U., 1964, MA, 1965; M of Philosophy, Yale U., 1967; PhD, The Union Inst., 1989. Sci. linguist U.S. Dept. State, Washington, 1969-73, regional lang. supr. U.S. Embassy, Bangkok, Thailand, 1973-75, lang. tng. supr. U.S. Dept. State, Washington, 1975-84, curriculum and tng. specialist, 1984-85, acting chmn. dept. Asian and African Langs., 1985, chmn. dept. Asian and African Langs., 1986-88, acting assoc. dean Sch. Lang. Studies, 1987-88, dir. rsch., evaluation and devel., 1989—. Author: The Meanings of the Modals in Present Day American English, 1966, Contemporary Cambodian, 1975, Indonesian Fast Course, 1982, Communicative Japanese Materials, 1984, Ants and Grasshoppers, Badgers and Butterflies: Qualitative and Quantitative Exploration of Adult Language Learning Styles and Strategies, 1989, Understanding Second Language Learning Difficulties, 1996, Interpersonal Dynamics in Second Language Education, 1998; mem. editl. bd. Jour. Psychol. Type, 1991—. Mem., ESOL/HILT Citizen's Adv. Coun., Arlington County, Va., 1985-89; psychotherapist Meyer Treatment Ctr. Washington Sch. Psychiatry, 1989-94. Woodrow Wilson Found. fellow, 1964; NSF fellow, 1964-69; recipient Meritorious Honor award U.S. Dept. State, 1972, 83, 98. Mem. Am. Psychol. Assn., Tchrs. of English to Speakers of Other Langs., Am. Assn. for Applied Linguistics, Assn. for Psychol. Type, Phi Beta Kappa, Psi Chi. Avocations: reading, computers, gardening. Office: Fgn Svc Inst 4000 Arlington Blvd Arlington VA 22204-1586

EHRNSCHWENDER, ARTHUR ROBERT, former utility company executive; b. Cin., Oct. 3, 1922; s. Arthur Michael and Lydia Carol (Widmer) E.; m. Grace Scholl Popplewell, Oct. 19, 1950; children: Barry N., Scott A. ME, U. Cin., 1948, BS in Commerce, 1959; MBA, Xavier U., 1959; D in Tech. Letters (hon.), Cin. Tech. Coll., 1980. Registered profl. engr., Ohio, Ky. Field engr. SKF Bearing Co., Cin., 1948-49; Chevrolet field rep. GM, Cin., 1949-50; with Cin. Gas and Electric Co., 1952-84, former sr. v.p.; bd. dirs. Porter Precision Products, Cin.; vice chmn., bd. dirs. OKI Supply Co., Cin.; chmn. Cin. Electric Inc. Past pres. Goodwill Industries, Cin., 1961-85; trustee Cin. Assn. for Blind, 1965—, Hamilton county YMCA, 1974—; chmn. bd. trustees Deaconess Hosp., Cin., 1970—. Capt. U.S. Army, 1943-46, 1950-52. Decorated Bronze Star, 1952; named Disting. Alumnus U. Cin., 1974, Xavier U. Mem. Soc. Automotive Engrs. (sect. chmn.), Engring. Soc. Cin., Edison Electric Inst. (divsn. chmn.), Am. Gas Assn. (sect. chmn.), Queen City Club, Cin. Country Club, The Club Pelican Bay, Naples Yacht Club, Stumps Boat Club, Masons (hon. 33d degree). Republican. Presbyterian. Home: 1201 Edgecliff Pl # 1083 Cincinnati OH 45206 also (winter): 5954 Pelican Bay Blvd Naples FL 34108-8153 Office: Cincinnati Electric Inc 9709 Reading Rd Cincinnati OH 45215-3594

EHSANI, MEHRDAD (MARK EHSANI), electrical engineering educator, consultant; naturalized, 1980; s. Heshmat and Didar (Ahmadi) E.; children: Evan Mancil, Nathaniel William. MS, U. Tex., 1974; PhD, U. Wis., 1981. Registered profl. engr., Tex. Rsch. engr. Fusion Rsch. Ctr. U. Tex., Austin, 1974-77; rsch. engr. Argonne (Ill.) Nat. Lab., 1977-81; prof. elec. engring. Tex. A&M U., College Station, 1981—, Halliburton prof. elec. engring., 1992, Dress Industries prof., 1994, dir. Tex. Applied Power Electronics Ctr.; lectr. in field. Author: Converter Circuits for Superconductive Magnetic Energy Storage, 1988; co-author: ANSI/IEEE Standards 936, 1987; contbr. over 180 articles to profl. jours.; 13 patents in field. Named Outstanding Young Engr. chpt. Tex. Soc. Profl. Engrs., 1984, Disting. Lectr. IEEE-Industry Applications Soc., Indsl. Electronics Soc. Fellow IEEE; mem. Power Electronics Soc. of IEEE (adminstrv. com. 1990-96), Industry Applications Soc. of IEEE (exec. coun. 1989-93, Disting. lectr.). Bahai. Office: Tex A&M U Dept Elec Engring College Station TX 77843

EHSANI, MICHAEL, quality assurance executive; b. Calif., Feb. 20, 1961. BSEE, U. Houston, 1983. Registered auditor. Quality assurance mgr. Golden Triangle Co., Irvine, Calif., 1983-90; sr. quality cons. ABS Indsl. Verification, Inc., Houston, 1990-91; pres., prin. cons. am. inst. Cons. Quality Svcs., inc., Houston, 1991—. Mem. Am. Soc. Quality. Office: AIC Quality Svcs Inc PO Box 940022 Houston TX 77094

EHST, ERIC RICHARD, aerospace engineer; b. Washington, Nov. 20, 1951; s. Richard Paul and Eileen Marjorie (Kohout) E.; m. Vickie Anita Bentley, Jan. 6, 1977; children: Nicholas Eric, Spencer Alexander. BS in Aerospace Engring., U. Md., 1973. Devel. engr. Flight Systems, Inc., Arlington, Va., 1977-78; sr. exptl. engr. Pratt & Whitney Aircraft, West Palm Beach, Fla., 1978-83; sr. devel. specialist Allied Signal Aerospace, Phoenix, 1983-98. Asst. scoutmaster Boy Scouts Am., Bethesda, Md., 1969-72, scoutmaster, 1973; pres. S.W. Outdoor Club, Tempe, Ariz., 1993; chmn. Ariz. Dist. 24 Dems., Phoenix, 1995-96; vice chmn. Ariz. Dem. Party, 1997—. Served with USAF, 1973-77. Avocations: hiking, backpacking, archaeology, history. Home: 14409 N 43rd St Phoenix AZ 85032-5468 Office: Allied Signal Engines MS 301-226 111 S 34th St Phoenix AZ 85034-2802

EIBEN, ROBERT MICHAEL, pediatric neurologist, educator; b. Cleve., July 12, 1922; s. Michael Albert and Frances Carlysle (Gedeon) E.; m. Anne F. Eiben; children: Daniel F., Christopher J., Thomas M., Mary, Charles G., Elizabeth A. BS, Western Res. U., 1944, MD, 1946. Diplomate Am. Bd. Pediatrics. Intern medicine Univ. Hosp., Cleve., 1946-47; asst. resident pediatrics and contagious diseases City Hosp., Cleve., 1947; asst. med. dir. div. contagious diseases City Hosp., 1949-50, visitant in pediatrics, 1949-50, acting dir. dept. pediatrics and contagious diseases, 1950-52; asst. resident pediatrics Babies and Children's Hosp., Cleve., 1948; clin. fellow pediatrics Babies and Children's Hosp., 1948-49; practice medicine specializing in pediatrics Cleve., 1949-90; asst. dir. dept. pediatrics and contagious diseases Cleve. Met. Gen. Hosp., 1952-60; med. dir. Respiratory Care and Rehab. Center, 1954-60, pres. med. staff, 1958-60, pediatric neurologist, 1963-90, acting med. dir. comprehensive care program, 1966-67, med. dir., 1968-73, mem. med. exec. com., 1974-76, acting dir. dept. pediatrics, 1979-80; USPHS fellow in neurology U. Wash., 1960-63; acting chief, sect. on clin. investigations and therapeutics Developmental and Metabolic Neurology br. Nat. Inst. Neurol. and Communicative Disorders and Strokes, NIH, Bethesda, Md., 1976-77; clin. instr. pediatrics Western Res. U., 1949-50, instr. pediatrics, 1950-51, asst. clin. prof., 1951-54, asst. prof., 1954-65, asst. prof. neurology, 1964-72, assoc. prof. pediatrics, 1965-75, assoc. prof. neurology, 1972-85, prof. pediatrics, 1975-90, prof. neurology, 1985-90, prof. emeritus pediatric neurology, 1991—; cons., project site visitor Nat. Found. Birth Defects Center Programs, 1961-66; mem. adv. com. on grants to train dentists to care for handicapped Robert Wood Johnson Found., 1975-80. Mem. coun. Bratenahl Village-County of Cuyahoga, 1982-98. Recipient Presdl. award Internat. Poliomyelitis Congress, Geneva, 1957, Clifford J. Vogt Alumni Svc. award Case Western Res. U., Cleve., 1985. Mem. Am. Acad. Pediatrics, Am. Acad. Neurology (chmn. residence exam. com. 1989-93), Am. Soc. Human Genetics, Am. Pediatric Soc., Am. Epilepsy Soc., No. Ohio Pediatric Soc., No. Ohio Neurol. Soc., Innominatum Soc., Pasteur Club, Child Neurology Soc. (chmn. tng. program com. 1976-77, sec.-treas. 1978-81, pres 1983-85), Case Western Res. U. Med. Alumni Assn. (pres. 1979). Home: 2 Oakshore Dr Bratenahl OH 44108-1118 Office: MetroHealth Med Ctr 2500 Metrohealth Dr Cleveland OH 44109-1900

EIBERGER, CARL FREDERICK, trial lawyer; b. Denver, Jan. 17, 1931; s. Carl Frederick and Madeleine Anastasia (Ries) E.; children: Eileen, Carl III, Mary, James. BS in Chemistry magna cum laude, U. Notre Dame, 1952, JD magna cum laude, 1954; MBA, Denver U., 1959. Sole practice, 1954-55; ptnr. Rovira, DeMuth & Eiberger, Denver, 1957-69, Eiberger, Stacy, Smith & Martin, Denver, 1979-96; prin. Carl F. Eiberger & Assocs., Denver, 1996—; chmn. CBA/DBA/Econs. of Law Practice Coms.; co-founder CBA/Steering Com. Labor Law Com., Denver; arbitrator Am. Arbitration Assn.; asst. bar examiner, 1963-68; lectr. on continuing legal edn. Contbr. articles to legal jours. Bd. dirs. Colo. Assn. Commerce and Industry; pres. Prospect Recreation and Park Dist.; founder Applewood Athletic Club, Jefferson County; gen. counsel Denver Symphony Orch. Recipient merit award Jefferson City Commrs., merit cert. Jefferson City Homeowners; named Man of the Yr. Notre Dame Club of Denver, Vol. of Yr. Channel 9TV, Denver., Citizen of Yr., Lions Club Internat. Mem. ABA, Colo. Bar Assn. (bd. govs.), Denver Bar Assn. (nominated pres.), Notre Dame Law Assn. (bd. dirs. 1965—), Gov. Adv. Coun. to Colo dept. of labor, Notre Dame Club (pres., bd. dirs.), Athletic Club (Denver), Rolling Hills Country Club. Roman Catholic. Home: 14330 Fairview Ln Golden CO 80401-2050 Office: 1775 Sherman St Ste 2900 Denver CO 80203-4324

EICH, SUSAN, public relations executive. Dir. corp. pub. rels. Dayton Hudson Corp., Mpls., 1995—. Office: Dayton Hudson Corp 33 S 6th PO Box 1392 Minneapolis MN 55440-1392*

EICH, WILBUR FOSTER, III, pediatrician; b. Tuskegee, Ala., June 26, 1938; s. Wilbur Foster and Lula Olivia (Dudley) E.; B.A., Huntingdon Coll., 1960; M.D., Tulane, 1964; m. Eugenia Glass Graves, May 31, 1963; children—Paul Foster, Mark Samuel, Donna Eugenia. Intern, Lloyd Noland Hosp., Fairfield, Ala., 1964-65; resident in pediatrics U.S. Naval Hosp., Portsmouth, Va., 1967-69; pediatrician Infants' and Children's Clinic, Florence, Ala., 1971—; pres. med. staff Eliza Coffee Meml. Hosp., 1980-81; ordained priest Episcopal Ch., 1981. Vol., Project Hope, Brazil, 1973; trustee Huntingdon Coll., Montgomery, Ala., 1977—. Served with USN, 1965-71. Diplomate Am. Bd. Pediatrics. Contbr. numerous articles and book revs. to med. and ch. jours. Fellow Am. Acad. Pediatrics, Am. Acad. Cerebral Palsy and Devel. Medicine; mem. AMA, So. Med. Assn., Med. Assn. Ala., Lauderdale County Med. Soc., Christian Med. Soc. Home: 120 Limerick Ct Muscle Shoals AL 35661-4105 Office: 421 W College St Florence AL 35630-5520

EICHBERG, RODOLFO DAVID, physician, educator; b. Pforzheim, Germany, July 26, 1937; came to the U.S., 1965; s. Julio and Ilse (Schonfarber) E.; m. Yvette Salama, May 21, 1965; children: William Amadeo, Matias David. Baccalaureate, St. Andrews Scots Sch., Argentina, 1955; MD, U. Buenos Aires, 1963. Intern, resident Grace Hosp. Wayne State U., Detroit, 1965-67; orthopedic surgeon Mar Del Plata, Argentina, 1968-73; resident physical medicine NYU, 1973-75; pvt. practice Rehab. and Electro Diagnosis Assocs., P.C., Tampa, 1975-96, 98—; prof. U. So. Fla., Tampa, 1975-93, clin. assoc. prof., 1994—; chief spinal cord injury rehab. Tampa Gen. Hosp., 1984-96; chief phys. medicine & rehab. VA Med. Ctr., New Orleans, 1997-98; med. dir. Meml. Hosp. Ctr. for Comprehensive Rehab., 1998—; mem. state adv. coun. Head Spinal Cord Injuries, Tallahassee, 1976-96; clin. assoc. prof. La. State U. Sch. Medicine, 1997-98; physician advisor State of Fla. Athletic Commn., 1998—. Contbr. articles to profl. jours. Bd. trustees Congregation Schaaraizedek, Tampa, 1980-82. Recipient Honors award City of La Paz, Bolivia, 1994. Mem. AMA, Am. Acad. Phys. Medicine Rehab. (health policy legis. com. 1990-95), Am. Spinal Injury Assn. (internat. rels. rep. S.C. 1990-95), Assn. Med. Latino Americana de Rehab., Colombian Phys. Medicine Rehab. Soc. (corr.), Argentine Soc. Rehab. Medicine (corr.), Fla. Med. Assn., Fla. Soc. Phys. Medicine Rehab. (pres. 1994-96), Hillsborough County Med. Soc. (bd. censors 1975—), So. Soc. of Phy. Medicine Rehab. Jewish. Avocations: boating, tennis, travel. Office: Rehab and Electro Diag Assocs PA Dept Medicine Rehabilitation 2914 N Boulevard Tampa FL 33602-1208

EICHBERGER, LEROY CARL, mechanical engineer, consultant, stress analyst; b. Chgo., Oct. 26, 1927; s. Roy George and Phyllis Zena (Goss) E.; m. Mary Ann Teresa Bronars, Sept. 10, 1955; children: Charles David, David Paul, Scott Thomas. BSME, U. Ill., 1951, MS, 1955, PhD, 1959. Registered profl. engr., Tex. Assoc. prof. U. Houston, 1959-77; mgr. engring. Weatherford Lamb USA, Houston, 1977-80; mgr. R&D Atlas Bradford, Houston, 1980-89; ind. cons. Houston, 1989—; tech. cons. Reed Roller Bit Co., Houston, 1959-61, Exxon Co. USA, Houston, 1968-77; staff cons. H.O. Mohr Rsch. and Engring., Houston, 1989—. Author monographs on methods for dynamic calibration of pressure transducers. With USCG, 1946-47. Recipient Arthur Lubinski award of excellence Offshore Tech. Conf., Houston, 1984. Mem. ASME, Soc. Exptl. Stress Analysis. Christian Scientist. Home and Office: 5310 Dumfries Dr Houston TX 77096-5107

EICHE, CANDACE ROSE, journalist; b. Milw.; d. F.M. and M.M. Eiche. Student, U. Wis., Green Bay, 1998. Stage mgr. Actor's Equity Assn., N.Y.C., 1979—; freelance journalist, 1994—, freelance computer programmer, 1996—; ceo Best Author Website Design Studio, 1998—. Editor: The Waushara Argus, 1997; contbr. news and feature stories to Ctrl. Wis. Resorter, 1995-97, The Berlin Jour., 1996, Green Bay Press Gazette, 1997. Chair Waushara County Habitat for Humanity, Inc., Wautoma, Wis., 1995-96; treas. Redgranite (Wis.) Civic Ctr., Inc., 1997; sec. Redgranite Friends of the Libr., 1997; sec. Marion (Wis.) Ac Hoc Bldg. Com., 1996-97. Faith Saunders scholar, 1996-97; grantee High Edn. Found., 1995-97, Chancellor's Leadership Medallion, 1998. Mem. Actor's Equity Assn., Nat. Fedn. Press Women. Home and Office: N914 Windwood Dr Neshkoro WI 54960-6418

EICHELBERGER, CHARLES BELL, retired career officer; b. LaGrange, Ga., Nov. 19, 1934; s. Charlie Wirt and Sybil Peavy (Johnson) E.; m. Jaqueline Ann Wood, July 17, 1955; children: Susan Christie Eichelberger Benator, Terrie Lynn Eichelberger Safranca. Cert. in Liberal Arts, Ga. Mil. Coll., 1955; BS in Law Enforcement, U. Nebr., 1971; MEd, Pepperdine U., 1977. Commd. 2d lt. U.S. Army, 1957, advanced through grades to lt. gen., 1989; comdr. U.S. Army Field Station, Berlin, 1978-80; div. chief Reconnaissance, Intelligence, Surveillance and Electronic Warfare Div., dep. chief of staff for ops. and plans, Dept. of Army, Washington, 1980-82; dep. comdt. U.S. Army Intelligence Ctr. and Sch., Ft. Huachuca, Ariz., 1982-84; dir. of intelligence (J-2) U.S. Cen. Command, MacDill AFB, Fla., 1984-86; dep. chief of staff for intelligence U.S. Army Europe, Heidelberg, Fed. Republic Germany, 1986-88, Dept. of Army, Washington, 1988-91; ret., 1991. Contbr. articles to profl. jours. Decorated D.S.M. with oak leaf cluster, Nat. Intelligence D.S.M. (CIA), Master Parachutist badge. Mem. Assn. Old Crows, Assn. U.S. Army, Ret. Officers' Assn. Home: 124 Sweetwater Oaks Peachtree City GA 30269-2110

EICHELBERGER, JOHN H., JR., county commissioner; b. Altoona, Pa., Sept. 1, 1958; s. John Henry Sr. and Faye Mardell Eichelberger; m. Martha Ann Snell, Nov. 27, 1982 (div. July 1992); 1 child, John Henry III; m. Charlotte Kim Ames, Dec. 7, 1996. BA, Pa. State U., 1985. Lic. ins. agt., Pa.; lic. ins. broker, Pa. 1st dep. register of wills and recorder of deeds County of Blair, Hollidaysburg, Pa., 1979-84; county commr. County of Blair, Hollidaysburg, 1996—; ins. agt., broker Cal G. Griffith Jr. Agy., Inc., Altoona, 1982-89; regional mgr. Sausman Ins. Agy., Inc., Altoona, 1989—; Exec. bd. mem. So. Alleghenies Planning and Devel. Commn., Altoona, 1996—; chmn. So. Alleghenies Regional Tourism Confederation, Altoona, 1996—, Blair County Salary Bd., Hollidaysburg, 1996—, Blair County Retirement Bd., Hollidaysburg, 1996—; bd. mem. So. Alleghenies Resource, Conservation and Devel. Area, Bedford, Pa., 1996—, Altoona Blair County Devel. Corp., 1998—; vice-chmn. Blair County Prison Bd., Hollidaysburg, 1996—; ex officio bd. mem. Allegheny Mountains Conv. and Visitors Bur., Altoona, 1996—; dir. Blair County Conservation Dist. Bd., Hollidaysburg, 1996—; voting mem. Met. Planning Orgn., Hollidaysburg, 1996—; mem. Blair County Heritage Com., Altoona, 1996—, Blair Sr. Svcs. Adv. Bd., Altoona, 1997—. Former pres. Blair County Young Rep. Club, Hollidaysburg, 1978-98; former dir. at large Pa. Fedn. Young Reps., Harrisburg, 1978-98; mem., former pres. Morrison's Cove Rep. Club, Roaring Spring, Pa., 1980—; active Ctrl. Pa. Rep. Conf., Harrisburg, 1982—, Pa. Rep. State Com., Harrisburg, 1982—, Friends of New Day, Inc., Altoona, 1997—, Blair County Law Enforcement Assn., Hollidaysburg, 1999—; chmn. Blair County Rep. Com., Duncansville, Pa., 1996—; bd. mem. Habitat for Humanity Blair County, Altoona, 1996—. Recipient Spark Plug award Am. Bus. Clubs, Kansas City, Mo., 1987. Mem. Am. Fedn. Musicians, Altoona A.M. Chpt. Am. Bus. Clubs (former v.p.), Altoona Area Claims Assn., Blair County C. of C. (ex officio bd. mem. 1996—). Republican. Brethren. Avocations: running, music. Home: 643 Hillside View Dr Duncansville PA 16635 Office: Commrs Office County Blair 423 Allegheny St Hollidaysburg PA 16648

EICHELBERGER, ROBERT JOHN, retired government research and development administrator, consultant; b. Washington, Pa., Apr. 10, 1921; s. John Eugene and Dorothy Louise (Failinger) E.; m. Estella Ann Westcott, May 14, 1943; children: William J., Charles R., Sara Jane Eichelberger Yosua, Mary Ann Eichelberger Nals. AB, Washington and Jefferson Coll., 1942; MS, Carnegie Inst. Tech., 1948, PhD, 1954. Rsch. supr. Carnegie Inst. Tech., Pitts., 1943-55; chief detonation physics br. U.S. Army Ballistic Rsch. Labs., Aberdeen Proving Ground, Md., 1955-62, assoc. tech. dir. labs., 1962-67, dir. labs., 1967-86, ret., 1986; cons. Bel Air, Md., 1986—; assoc. tech. dir. U.S. Army Armament R&D Command, 1976-80; lectr. in field. Contbr. articles to profl. jours. Recipient Disting. Civilian Svc. award Dept. Def., 1977, Exceptional Civilian Svc. award Dept. Army, 1971, R&D Achievement award, 1961, 71, Presdl. Meritorious Exec. award, 1982, Roger W. Jones award for exec. leadership Am. U., 1985, Clifford P. Gross award Am. Assn. Pub. Adminstrn., 1985, Comdr.'s award U.S. Army Materiel Command, 1986; Crozier prize Am. Def. Preparedness Agy., 1984; inductee U.S. Army Ordnance Hall of Fame, 1987. Mem. AAAS, Am. Phys. Soc., Nat. Coun. Advancement Rsch. (dir.), Soc. Natural Philosophy, Am. Def. Preparedness Assn. (cons.), Assn. U.S. Army, Combustion Inst., Internat. Ballistics Com. Democrat. Presbyterian. Home: 409 Catherine St Bel Air MD 21014-3613*

EICHENWALD, HEINZ FELIX, physician; b. Switzerland, Mar. 3, 1926; came to U.S., 1936, naturalized, 1945; s. Ernst M. and Stella E.; m. Linda E. Moragné, July 20, 1995; children: Kathryn S., Eric C., Kurt A., Michael M. BA in Biochem. Scis. magna cum laude, Harvard U., 1946; MD, Cornell U., 1950. Successively intern, sr. asst. resident, sr. resident pediatrician N.Y. Hosp., 1950-51; asst. in pediatrics Cornell U. Med. Sch., 1951-53, instr., then asst. prof., 1955-58, assoc. prof., then prof. pediatrics, 1958-64; USPHS instr. pediatrics Emory U. Med. Sch., 1953-55; also vis. physician Grady and Crawford Long hosps., Atlanta; mem. staff N.Y. Hosp., 1958-65, attending pediatrician, 1963-65; vis. asst. prof. Albert Einstein Med. Sch., 1956-58; cons. Hosp. Spl. Surgery, N.Y.C., 1956-64, Patterson (N.J.) Gen. Hosp., 1958-64; prof. pediatrics, chmn. dept. U. Tex. Southwestern Med. Sch., Dallas, 1964-83; chief-of-staff Children's Med. Ctr., Dallas, 1964—; chief pediatrics Parkland Meml. Hosp., Dallas, 1964—; cons. St. Paul, Irving Community, Presbyn. hosps., Dallas; chief hepatitis investigation unit, epidemiology br. USPHS, 1954-55; Richard Bruce Miller lectr. Harvard U. Med. Sch., 1960; lectr. Columbia U. Tchrs. Coll., 1960-64; chmn. Internat. Rsch. Confs. Mental Retardation, 1965-66; chmn. panel anti-infectives NAS-NRC, 1966-69; vis. prof. U. Saigon Med. Sch., 1968-72; Vanuxem lectr. Princeton U., 1970; bd. dirs. Dallas Free Clinic, 1970-74, Children's Devel. Ctr., Dallas, 1974—; mem. bd. maternal and child health NIH, 1974-78; cons. in field, mem. numerous profl. coms. Assoc. editor Pediatric Therapy, 1974; editor Practical Pediatric Therapy, 1985, Current Therapy in Pediatrics, 1989, Pediatric Therapy, 1993; mem. editorial bd. profl. jours.; contbr. numerous articles in profl. publs. Bd. dirs., chmn. exec. com. Lamplighter Sch., Dallas, 1971—; bd. dirs. Winston Sch., 1974. Recipient Career Rsch. award NIH, 1963-65, Alexander von Humboldt prize Govt. of Germany (then Fed. Republic Germany), 1979, Weinstein-Goldeson award United Cerebral Palsy Found., 1980; Markle scholar med. sci., 1953. Mem. Harvey Soc., Soc. Pediatric Rsch., Am. Pediatric Soc., Infectious Disease Soc. Am., N.Y. Acad. Scis., Tex. Pediatric Soc., Phi Beta Kappa, Sigma Xi, Alpha Omega Alpha. Office: 5323 Harry Hines Blvd Dallas TX 75235-7208

EICHER, GEORGE JOHN, aquatic biologist; b. Bremerton, Wash., Aug. 27, 1916; s. George John and Caroline Agnes (Wolfer) E.; m. Patricia Jane Davies, Feb. 17, 1951; children: George C., Kenneth. Student, Wash. State U., 1938; B.S., Oreg. State U., 1941. Research party leader in Alaska U.S. Bur. Fisheries, 1939-41; fish biologist Ariz. Game and Fish Commn., 1943-47; charge salmon research in Western Alaska U.S. Fish and Wildlife Service, 1947-56; chief aquatic biologist Gen. Electric Co., Portland, Oreg., 1956-72; mgr. dept. environ. services Gen. Electric Co., 1972-78; pres. Eicher Assos., Inc., Portland, 1978—; cons. in field, 1958—; Mem. Gov. Oreg. Outdoor Recreation Council, 1960—; sci. bd. cons. demonstration grants water quality and pollution control HEW, 1963—; adviser fisheries Nat. Izaak Walton League Am., 1960-65; mem. U.S. Com. on Large Dams. Free-lance writer, 1941-43; patentee turbine fish screen. Fellow Am. Inst. Fishery Research Biologists, Internat. Acad. Fishery Sci.; mem. Am. Fisheries Soc. (pres. 1965), Assn. Power Biologists (pres. 1958-60), Wildlife Soc., Explorers Club, Am. Soc. Limnology and Oceanography, Am. Inst. Biol. Scis., Pacific Fishery Biologists (sec. 1950), U.S. C. of C. (nat. resources com.), Portland C. of C. (chmn. recreational and natural resources com. 1962, chmn. water standards com. 1966-70), Sigma Chi.

EICHHORN, ARTHUR DAVID, music director; b. St. Louis, Oct. 13, 1953; s. Arthur Louis and Adele (Stankunas) E. BA, Concordia U., River Forest, Ill., 1975, MA, 1976; MA, Webster U., 1986; EdD, Calif. Coast U., 1997. Cert. elem. tchr., Ill., Mo. Dir. music St. John Luth. Ch., Mt. Prospect, Ill., 1974-76, Our Savior Luth. Ch., Springfield, Ill., 1976-81, Holy Cross Luth. Ch., St. Louis, 1981-91, Timothy Luth. Ch., St. Louis, 1991—; part-time instr., dir. St. Louis extension site Concordia U., Wis. Mem. Choristers Guild (pres. local chpt. 1990-92), Music Educators Nat. Conf., Mo. Music Educators Assn., Am. Guild Organists, Assn. Luth. Ch. Musicians. Republican. Home: 7116 Mardel Ave Saint Louis MO 63109-1123 Office: Timothy Luth Ch 6704 Fyler Ave Saint Louis MO 63139-2239

EICHHORN, BRADFORD REESE, management consultant; b. Cleve., Jan. 24, 1954; s. Charles Albert Jr. and Jeanne Yvonne (Reese) E.; m. Dawn Lynette Mattern, Feb. 25, 1980; children: Serena Ruth, Reese Aaron, Hannah Dawn, Charles Donald Nathan. BS in Computer Sci. magna cum laude, Cleve. State U., 1975, MS in Operations Research summa cum laude, 1977. Cert. data processor, systems profl. Mgr. applications devel. Control Data Corp., Lakewood, Ohio, 1976-83; sr. cons. Coopers & Lybrand, Cleve., 1983-84; mgr. bus. systems Ferro Corp., Independence, Ohio, 1984-89; mgr. systems and programming Forest City Enterprises, Cleve., 1989-95; mgr. Claremont Tech. Group, Cleve., 1995-96, sr. mgr., 1996-98; project mgmt. leader Key Svcs. Corp., Cleve., 1998; sr. mgr. Complete Bus. Solutions, Inc., Cleve., 1998—; treas. Blossom Property Devel., Cleve., 1985-87, Medina Alliance Fellowship, 1995—. Contbg. editor Hinckley Record, 1993. Chmn. fin. com. All Saints Luth. Ch., Olmsted Falls, Ohio, 1984-85; chmn. endowment fund Our Saviour Luth. Ch., Hinckley, Ohio, 1989-93, sec. stewardship and fin. com., 1986-87; Christian fin. counselor; chmn. deacons Medina Alliance Fellowship, 1993-94, elder, 1995—; dir. Compassion Inc., Ashland, Ohio, 1995-96, pres., 1996-97; dir. Precious Hands Child Care, 1997-98. Mem. Beta Gamma Sigma. Home: 149 Salem Ct Hinckley OH 44233-9639 Office: Complete Bus Solutions Inc 600 Superior Ave Ste 2550 Cleveland OH 44114-2611

EICHHORN, FREDERICK FOLTZ, JR., retired lawyer; b. Gary, Ind., Oct. 16, 1930; s. Frederick Foltz and Adele D. (DeLano) E.; m. Julia Abel, Aug. 27, 1955; children: Jill, Thomas, Timothy, Linda. B.S., Ind. U., 1952, J.D., 1957. Bar: Ind. 1957, U.S. Ct. Appeals (7th cir.) 1957, U.S. Dist. Ct. (no dist.) Ind. 1957, U.S. Supreme Ct. 1973. Assoc. Gavit, Eichhorn, Gary, 1957-62; ptnr. Eichhorn, Eichhorn & Link, and predecessor firm, 1963-76; sr. ptnr. Eichhorn, Eichhorn & Link and predecessor firm, 1977-96; ret., 1996. Bd. dirs. Gary Housing Authority, 1972-75, Planned Parenthood, Gary Police Civil Svc. Commn., 1975-82; bd. dirs., founder Miller Citizens Corp., 1971; mem. Ind. Sesquicentennial Commn.; chmn. Lake County Cmty. Devel. Com., 1984; bd. dirs. N.W. Ind. Symphony; chmn. N.W. Ind. Forum, World Affairs Coun., Gary Regional Airport Task Force, 1989-94; trustee Ind. U., 1990—. With USAF, 1952-54. Fellow Am. Bar Found., Ind. Bar Found.; mem. ABA (membership chmn. for Ind. ho. of dels.), Ind. Bar Assn. (inst. chmn. white collar crime 1979, treas. 1977-78, bd. mgrs. 1979-80, v.p. 1983-84, pres. 1985-86), Am. Gas Assn. (state rate litigation com. 1982, regulation of gas supplies com., state regulatory matters com.) Midwest Gas Assn. (legal affairs sect. 1982) Ind. Soc. Chgo., Lincoln Legal Found. (trustee 1989-92), Phi Delta Phi, Delta Tau Delta.

EICHHORN, GUNTHER LOUIS, chemist; b. Frankfurt am Main, Germany, Feb. 8, 1927; s. Fritz David and Else Regina (Weiss) E.; m. Lotti Neuhaus, June 25, 1964; children: David Mark, Sharon Julie. AB in Chemistry, U. Louisville, 1947; MS, U. Ill., 1948, PhD, 1950. From asst. prof. to assoc. prof. chemistry La. State U., 1950-57; commd. officer USPHS, 1954-57; assoc. prof. chemistry Georgetown U., 1957-58; guest scientist Naval Med. Rsch. Inst., 1957-58; chief sect. molecular biology Gerontology Rsch., NIH, Balt., 1958-78, chief lab. cellular and molecular biology and head sect. inorganic biochemistry, 1978-94; scientist emeritus NIH, 1994—; counsellor La. State U. Hillel Found., 1952-54; pres. Nat. Inst. Child Health and Human Devel. Assembly Scientists, 1972-73; mem. panel nickel NRC, 1974; disting. lectr. Mich. State U., 1972; lectr. Internat. Conf. on Biology and the Future of Mankind, Paris, 1974; Watkins vis. prof. Wichita State U., 1983; organizer symposium Internat. Conf. Bioinorganic Chemistry, The Netherlands, 1987; lectr. Internat. Conf. Molecular Mechanisms of Metal Toxicity and Carcinogenicity, Urbino, Italy, 1988, Bailar Symposium, Houston, 1992, G.L. Eichhorn Symposium on Metals, Nucleic Acids, Transcription and Aging, 1995; acting sci. dir. Nat. Inst. Aging, 1988; Henry Lardy lectr. S.D. U.; lectr. Metal Ion Nucleic Acid Interactions Conf., Amsterdam, The Netherlands, 1991; organizer, presenter and lectr. in field. Editor: Inorganic Biochemistry, 1973; co-editor: Advances in Inorganic Biochemistry, 1978—; mem. editl. bd. Mechanisms of Ageing and Development; contbr. articles to profl. jours. Gen. Aniline and Film Co. grantee, 1949; Ohio State U. fellow, summers 1951-52; recipient Woodcock medal U. Louisville, 1947, Md. Chemist award, 1978, NIH Dir.'s award, 1979, Sr. Exec. Svc. bonus award, 1982, 88. Fellow AAAS, Am. Inst. Chemists, Gerontol. Soc. (fin. com. 1980-82, research and edn. com. 1982-83); mem. Am. Chem. Soc., N.Y. Acad. Scis., Am. Inst. Biol. Chemists, Biophys. Soc. Achievements include reseach in metal-ion induced stabilization and destabilization of DNA double helix, mechanism of RNA degradation by metal ions, nucleic acid conformational changes induced by metal ions; structural basis by which RNA polymerase produces fidelity in transcription (of DNA to RNA), catalysis of double bond cleavage by metal ions, discovery of Schiff base tautomers in vitamin B6-metal coplexes; molecular age changes in metal ions, proteins and nucleic acids. Home: 10500 Rockville Pike Rockville MD 20852-3359 Office: NIH NIA Gerontology Rsch Ctr 5600 Nathan Shock Dr Baltimore MD 21224-6825

EICHINGER, MARILYNNE H., museum administrator; children: Ryan, Kara, Julia, Jessica, Talik. BA in Anthropology and Sociology magna cum laude, Boston U., 1965; MA, Mich. State U., 1971. With emergency and outpatient staff Ingham County Mental Health Ctr., 1972; founder, pres., exec. dir. Impression 5 Sci. and Art Mus., Lansing, Mich., 1973-85; pres. Oreg. Mus. Sci. and Industry, Portland, 1985-95; bd. dirs. Portland Visitors Assn., 1985-95; pres. Informal Edn. Products Ltd., 1995—, Portland, 1995—; bd. dirs. N.W. Regional Edn. Labs., 1991-97; instr. Lansing (Mich.) C.C., 1978; ptnr. Eyrie Studio, 1982-85; condr. numerous workshops in interactive exhibit design, adminstrn. and fund devel. for schs., orgns., profl. socs. Author: (with Jane Mack) Lexington Montessori School Survey, 1969, Manual on the Five Senses, 1974; pub. Mich. edit. Boing mag. Founder Cambridge Montessori Sch., 1964; bd. dirs. Lexington Montessori Sch., 1969, Mid-Mich. South Health Sys. Agy., 1978-81, Cmty. Referral Ctr., 1981-85, Sta. WKAR, 1981-85; active Lansing "Riverfest" Lighted Boat Parade, 1980; mem. state Health Coordinating Coun., 1980-82; mem. pres.'s adv. coun. Portland State U., 1986—, mem. pres.' adv. bd., 1987-91; bd. dirs. Portland Visitors Assn., 1994-97. Recipient Diana Cert. Leadership, YWCA, 1976-77, Woman of Achievement award, 1991, Community Svc. award Portland State U., 1992. Mem. Am. Assn. Mus., Oreg. Mus. Assn., Assn. Sci. and Tech. Ctrs. (bd. dirs. 1980-84, 88-93), Zonta Lodge (founder, bd. dirs. East Lansing club 1978), Internat. Women's Forum, Portland C. of C. Office: Informal Edn Products Ltd 2520 SW Sherwood Dr Portland OR 97201-1615

EICHLER, THOMAS P., state agency administrator; b. Utica, N.Y., Sept. 18, 1944; s. Paul S. and Irene (Rood) E.; m. Susan Aussiker, May 17, 1969; children: Matthew, Mark, Michael. BA, Syracuse U., 1966; MA, SUNY, Albany, 1968, M Pub. Adminstrn., 1974. Program assoc. Gov.'s Office, State of N.Y., Albany, 1969-73; dir. program devel. and planning N.Y. State Dept. Environ. Conservation, Albany, 1973-79; dir. environ. control Del. Dept. Natural Resources and Environ. Control, Dover, 1979-83; regional adminstr. U.S. EPA, Phila., 1983-85; sec. of health and social svcs. Del. Dept. Health and Social Svcs., New Castle, 1985-93; sec. svcs. for children, youth and their families Del. Dept. Svcs. for Children Youth and Their Families, Wilmington, 1993—; bd. dirs. U.S. Welfare Simplification and Coordination Adv. Com., 1992. Recipient Spl. Achievement award EPA, Washington, 1985, Disting. Svc. award Nat. Govs. Assn., 1992, Nat. Pub. Svc. award, 1998. Mem. Am. Soc. Pub. Adminstrn. (pub. svc. award 1998), Del. Soc. Pub. Adminstrn. Republican. Roman Catholic. Home: 32 Kimmie Ct Bear DE 19701-1746 Office: Dept Svcs for Children Youth and Their Families 1825 Faulkland Rd Wilmington DE 19805-1121

EICHMAN, CHARLES MELVIN, career assessment educator, school counselor; b. Ft. Hays, Kans., June 16, 1950; s. Melvin Joseph and Barbara Ann (Bennett) E. BA, U. No. Colo., 1972; MA, Fuller Theol. Sem., 1974; cert., U. Mo., 1989, 91. Cert. vocat. evaluator, vocat. guidance specialist, sch. counselor, job devel. specialist, rehab. counselor, job placement specialist, secondary sch. tchr. Youth activity coord. YMCA, Glendale, Calif., 1972-74; counselor U. Colo., Colorado Springs, 1975-76; resident hall advisor U. No. Colo., Greeley, 1976-77; secondary tchr., coach Jefferson County Dist. R-1, Lakewood, Colo., 1978-80; pres., owner Big Sky C.F.M. and Mgmt. Resources, Rock Springs, Wyo., 1980-85; secondary tchr. Boulder (Colo.) Valley Dist. RE-2, 1986-88; vocat. evaluator and dir. Platte County Dist. RE-111 Vocat. Evaluation Ctr., Platte City, Mo., 1988-92; pres., owner Career Assessment Svcs., Arvada, Colo., 1992-94; sch. counselor, head dist. elem. at-risk student program Albany Schs. Re-1, Laramie, Wyo., 1993-94; sch. counselor, dir. dist. model Kids at Risk program Sch. Dist. 25, Pocatello, Idaho., 1994—. Contbr. articles to profl. jours. Mem. NEA, Am. Vocat. Assn., Nat. Rehab. Assn., Nat. Assn. Vocat. Edn. Spl. Needs Pers. (region III com. chair 1989-90, cert. of recognition 1990), Nat. Assn. Vocat. Assessment in Edn., Am. Sch. Counselors Assn., Am. Assn. Marriage and Family Therapy, Vocat. Evaluation and Work Adjustment Assn. (Wyo. rep. 1993-94, conf. presenter 1991), Mo. Vocat. Spl. Needs Assn. (exec. v.p. 1990-92, conf. speaker 1989-92, Outstanding Achievement award 1990-91, certs. of appreciation 1988-91), Mo. State Tchrs. Assn., Mo. Sch. Counselors Assn. (conf. speaker 1989-91), Mo. Vocat. Assn. (conf. speaker 1992), Idaho Edn. Assn., Idaho Sch. Counseling Assn., Idaho Counseling Assn., Idaho Assn. Marriage and Family Therapy, Idaho Vocat. Guidance Assn. (com. chair 1997), Idaho Vocat. Assn., Kiwanis. Avocations: handball, skiing, outdoor adventure trips, creative arts activities, swimming. Home: PO Box 4931 Pocatello ID 83205-4931 Office: PO Box 4931 Pocatello ID 83205-4931

EICHNER, HANS, German language and literature educator; b. Vienna, Austria, Oct. 30, 1921; emigrated to Eng., 1938, to Can., 1950; s. Alexander and Valerie (Ungar) E.; m. Joan M. Partridge, May 29, 1957 (div. Aug. 1985); children: Jane Elizabeth, James Alexander; m. Kari Grimstad, Nov. 9, 1985. B.A., U. London, 1944, Ph.D., 1949; LL.D., Queen's U., 1974. Asst. lectr. Bedford Coll. London, 1948-50; mem. faculty Queens U., Kingston, Ont., Can., 1950-67; assoc. prof. Queens U., 1956-62, prof., 1962-67; chmn. grad. dept. German U. Toronto, Ont., Can., 1967-72; prof. U. Toronto, 1967-88, chmn. dept. German, 1975-84; univ. prof. U. Toronto, Ont., Can., 1981—; hon. prof. humanities U. Calgary, Alta., Can., 1978—; adj. prof. Queen's U., 1991—. Author: Thomas Mann, 1953, 61, Four German Authors, 1964, Friedrich Schlegel, 1970, Deutsche Literatur im Klassisch-romantischen Zeitalter I, 1795-1805, Vol. I, 1990; editor: Literary Notebooks (Friedrich Schlegel), 1957, Critical Edition of F. Schlegel Works, vols. 2-6, 16, 1959-81, Romantic: The European History of a Word, 1972. Recipient Goethe Inst. medal, 1973; William Riley Parker prize, 1982; Nuffield Found. fellow, 1952-53; Can. Council sr. fellow, 1959-60; McLaughlin Research prof., 1965-66. Fellow Royal Soc. Can.; mem. MLA, Can. Assn. U. Tchrs. of German (pres. 1976-78). Home: Box 41, Rockwood, ON Canada N0B 2K0

EICHNER, KAY MARIE, mental health nurse; b. Des Moines, Apr. 28, 1955; d. Earl C. and Rachel L. (Martens) E. BSN, Grand View Coll., 1979. Staff nurse U. Iowa Hosp., Iowa City, 1979-80; staff nurse, supr. nursery Oasis Day Care Ctr., Indianola, Iowa, 1985-86; staff nurse Iowa Meth. Med. Ctr., Des Moines, 1980-83, 87-96, Iowa Luth. Hosp., 1996-98; speaker on survivors of child sexual abuse. Mem. Nat. Nurses Soc. on Addictions. Republican. Mem. Christian Ch. Home: 3208 Fairlane Dr Des Moines IA 50315-7726

EICHOLD, SAMUEL, medical educator, medical museum curator; b. Mobile, Ala., May 27, 1916; s. Bernard H. and Myra (Solomon) E.; m. Charlotte Hartsig, Feb. 26, 1943; children: Beth, Alice, Bert. BS, Tulane U., 1937, MD, 1940; LLD (hon.), Spring Hill Coll., 1991. Intern Touro Infirmary, 1941; resident in internal medicine City Hosp. Mobile, 1941; pvt. practice medicine specializing in internal medicine Mobile, 1946-72; prof. medicine dept. internal medicine U. South Ala., Mobile, 1973-84, prof. emeritus, 1984—; hon. prof. Universidad Francisco Marroquin, 1985—; dir. continuing edn. U. South Ala., Mobile, 1975-82, perceptor history of medicine, 1976, perceptor rural and tropical medicine in developing nation, 1976—; med. dir. Central Plaza Towers Med. Ctr., 1981-98, Allen Meml. Home, 1973—, Cogburn Nursing Home, 1975-81, Hillhaven-Mobile, 1980-85, Mercy Med. Hosp., 1985-94; med. advisor Ala. Dept. Corrections, 1987—; bd. dirs. Mercy Med., 1989-98, vice chmn. Old Mobile Restoration; bd. trustees Spring Hill Coll., 1991—; pres. Mobile Revolving Fund for Hist. Properties, 1992-96. Author: Without Malice-100 Year History of Comic Cowboys of Mobile; mem. editorial bd. ADA Forecast mag., 1987-91, Ala. Treasure Forest Gulf Coast Hist. rev.; contbr. articles to profl. jours. Asst. county health officer Mobile County; bd dir. Preventable Disease, 1974-75; active Josiah C. Nott Found., 1980; founder, curator Heustis Med. Mus.; established Camp Seale Harris for Diabetic Children, 1947; sec./treas. Mobile Imfirmary, 1967-68; officer Mobile Tree Commn., 1968-73, chmn., 1973; bd. dirs. Mobile Symphony, Mobile Chamber Music Soc., Inc., 1952-75, Mobile Opera Assn., Hist. Mobile Preservation, 1977-84, Mobile chpt. ARC, 1951, Fine Arts Mus. of South, 1975-81, Mobile Mus., 1975-81, Mobile Hist. Mus., 1994—, Mobile Mus. Art, 1995—, Cmty. Found. S.W. Ala., 1998—, Friends Magnolia Cemetery, 1999—; active adv. bd. Ala. Hist. Commn., 1974—; pres. Mobile Hist. Devel. Found., 1973-75, bd. dirs., 1973-76; mem. council, chmn. regents Spring Hill Coll., 1984, trustee, 1991—. With USNR, 1941-69, comdr. ret. Recipient M.O. Beale Scroll of Merit award, 1951, 56, 59, Doc E award ADA, 1975, Ruth E. Hanson award 1978, Dept. Internal Medicine Faculty award, 1979, Comic Cowboy of Yr. award, 1982, Joe Treadwell award Ala. affiliate ADA, 1990; named Hon. Fellow Mobile Coll., 1977; named Mobilian of Yr. Mobile Civitan Club, 1989. Mem. AMA, ACP, Am. Assn. Diabetes Educators, Med. Soc. Mobile County (recognition award 1975), So. Med. Assn., Am. Diabetes Assn. (citation Mobile chpt. 1980, Becton Dickinson award 1981), Am. Soc. Internal Medicine, Ala. Diabetes Assn., Mobile County Physicians, Franklin Soc. (pres. 1975), Mobile Area C. of C. Republican. Jewish. Clubs: Country of Mobile, Mobile Yacht. Lodges: Masons, Shriners, Kiwanis. Home: 300 Chatham St Mobile AL 36604-3107

EICK, CHARLES F., federal judge; b. 1954. BA cum laude, Tulane U., 1975; JD with high honors, U. Tex., 1978. Bar: Calif. 1978. Ptnr. Mitchell, Silberberg and Knupp, L.A., 1978-88; magistrate judge for ctrl. Calif., U.S. Magistrate Ct., L.A., 1988—. Office: US Magistrate Ct 342 US Courthouse 312 N Spring St Los Angeles CA 90012-4701

EICKELBERG, W. WARREN BARBOUR, academic administrator; b. N.Y.C., Jan. 19, 1925; s. Graham Alexander and Lillian (Hayes) E.; student Harvard U., 1942-43; BA, Hope Coll., Holland, Mich., 1949; MA (Dennison fellow), Wesleyan U. Conn., 1951; children: William, Margaret, Robert, Janet.; m. Marilyn K. Banks. Prof. Adelphi U., Garden City, L.I., N.Y., 1952—, First Centennial prof. of life scis., 1996, now emeritus; dir. devel., v.p., 1958-66, dir. premed. curriculum, 1967-89; cons. devel. planning Nat. Ctr. for Disability Svcs., Albertson, N.Y., 1953-95; mem. biomechanics cons. group Pres.'s Com. on Disabled; mem. ad hoc com. N.Y. State Joint Legis. Com. on Transp. Chmn. Nassau County Museum Council, 1966-67; mem. founding com. Adelphi Suffolk Coll.; nat. cons. Nat. Council Cath. Men, 1969. Served to 1st lt. USAAF, 1943-46. Recipient Flambeau award Adelphi U., 1956, Disting. Service award, 1981, Disting. Teaching award, 1985; L.I. Gov.'s award, 1966, Alpha Epsilon Delta award, 1989, Joseph Serio award, 1990-91, 91-92, 92-93, 98; certificate of distinction Dictionary Internat. Biography, 1968; Wisdom award, 1970. Mem. N.Y. Acad. Scis., Internat. Soc. Biomechanics (charter), Nat. Soc. Fund Raisers, Public Relations Soc. Am. (accredited, pres. L.I. chpt. 1980), L.I. Pub. Relations Assn. (past pres., dir.), L.I. Sci. Tchrs. Assn. (past pres., dir.). Sigma Xi, Kappa Eta Nu. Clubs: Lions; Wesleyan (N.Y.C.); Unqua Yacht (Amityville). Home: 1720 City Park Blvd Alexandria LA 71301-4600 Office: Adelphi U Garden City NY 11530

EICKHOFF, THEODORE CARL, physician; b. Cleve., Sept. 13, 1931; s. Theodore Henry and Clara (Strassen) E.; m. Margaret Heinecke, Aug. 24, 1952; children: Stephen, Mark, Philip. BA, Valparaiso U., 1953; MD, Case Western Res. U., 1957. Diplomate: Am. Bd. Internal Medicine. Intern, then resident Harvard Med. Services, Boston City Hosp., 1957-59; fellow in medicine Harvard Med. Sch.-Boston City Hosp., 1961-64; epidemiologist Center for Disease Control, 1964-67; prof. medicine U. Colo. Med. Ctr., 1975—, head div. infectious disease, 1967-80; vice chmn. dept. medicine U. Colo. Med. Center, 1976-81; dir. internal medicine Presbyn./St. Luke's Med. Ctr., 1981-92; dir. medicine Denver Gen. Hosp., 1978-81; cons. FDA, Ctrs. for Disease Control, Am. Hosp. Assn.; mem. nat. commn. orphan diseases HHS, 1986-90, mem. vaccines adv. com., 1995—. Contbr. articles to med. jours. Served with USPHS, 1959-67. Recipient Commr.'s Spl. Citation, FDA, 1990, Trustee's award Am. Hosp. Assn., 1993. Mem. ACP (Disting. Internist award Colo. chpt. 1995), Am. Fedn. Clin. Rsch., Am. Soc. Clin. Investigation, Assn. Am. Physicians, Infectious Diseases Soc. Am. (sec. 1978-82, pres. 1983-84, Finland Lectureship award 1995), Am. Epidemiol. Soc. (pres. 1985-86). Home: 15 S Franklin Cir Greenwood Village CO 80121-1245 Office: Univ Colo Health Sci Ctr B 168 Div Infectious Disease Denver CO 80262

EIDE, IMOGENE GARNETT, nursing consultant; b. Missoula, Mont., Dec. 19, 1922; d. Lewis M. and Alice (Garnett) Felton; m. Bruce Eide, 1972 (div.); children: Pollie Sue Coons, Henry Hoy Harter (dec.). RN, St. Patricks Hosp., Missoula, 1943; BS in Nursing, Ariz. State U., Tempe, 1967. Cert. nurse adminstr., ANA. Dir. nursing Southside Dist. Hosp., Mesa, Ariz., 1956-66; cons. stationed in India WHO, Geneva, 1968-70; asst. dir. pub. health Maricopa County Health Dept., Phoenix, 1970-86; adminstr. home care and Hospice CIGNA Health Plan Ariz., Inc., Phoenix, 1986-90; pres., owner Home Care/Hospice Cons. Svc., Inc., Scottsdale, Ariz., 1991-92; insvc. nurse Thurshulp Oost Stichting Thruszorg, Rottedam, 1992; nurse adminstr., pres. Home Care/Hospice Consulting Svc., Inc., Scottsdale, 1991—; instr. CNA, Handmaker Jewish Home for the Aged, Tucson, 1994-95. Fellow Nat. Assn. Home Care U. (bd. dirs. 1982, Spl. Recognition NAHC award 1991); mem. ANA (exec. com. cmty. health), Ariz. Assn. Home Care (life, pres. 1986-90), Ariz. Nurses Assn. (life), Sigma Theta Tau (Beta Epsilon chpt.). Home: 7015 E Sweetwater Ave Scottsdale AZ 85254-5355 Office: 8102 E McDowell Scottsdale AZ 85257

EIDE, JOEL S., museum director. Dir. No. Ariz. U. Art Mus. and Galleries, 1975-98; prof. fine art No. Ariz. U., Flagstaff, 1998—. Home: 1926 N Crescent Dr Flagstaff AZ 86001-1114 Office: No Ariz U Art Mus and Galleries PO Box 6021 Flagstaff AZ 86011*

EIDECKER, MARTINA ELISABETH, foreign language educator; b. Drensteinfurt, Germany, Aug. 31, 1965; came to the U.S., 1992; d. Engelbert and Brigitta Agnes Eidecker. MA, Westfälische Wilhelms U., Muenster, Germany, 1989, Ariz. State U., 1992; PhD, UCLA, 1996. Author: Trauerarbeit und Sinnsuche, 1998; editor: Positionen, 1999. Mem. MLA, Pacific Ancient and MLA, S. Atlantic MLA, Am. Assn. Tchrs. German (German testing 1996—, bus. German exec. 1996—), Women in German. Avocations: interior design, music, reading, traveling, psychology. E-mail: meidecker@gsu.edu. Office: Ga State Univ University Plaza Atlanta GA 30303

EIDELHOCH, LESTER PHILIP, physician, educator, surgeon; b. N.Y.C., Jan. 7, 1932; s. Abraham David Eidelhoch and Ella (Sarah) Lovinger; m. Cecily Ruth Rosenberg, Apr. 28, 1963; children: Alison Marc, Arthur Mark, Meredith Marc. BA, Columbia U., 1952; MD, NYU, 1956. Diplomate Am. Bd. Med. Examiners. Intern Strong Meml. Hosp., Rochester, N.Y.; resident Harvard Surg. div. Boston City Hosp., 1958-62; pvt. practice New Hartford, N.Y., 1965—; med. dir. Walsh Med. Ctr., Rome, N.Y., 1991—; mem. faculty SUNY. Bd. dirs. Jewish Fedn., Utica (N.Y.) Symphony, Charles T. Sitrin Home. Lt. comdr. USN, 1962-64. Recipient Lindner Surg. award NYU. Fellow ACS, Royal Coll. Medicine; mem. N.Y. Cen. Soc. Surgeons, Cen. N.Y. Acad. Medicine, Oneida County Med. Soc. Republican. Avocations: skiing, sailing. Home and Office: 6 Old Willow Rd New Hartford NY 13413-2419

EIDSON, JAMES ANTHONY, lawyer; b. Atlanta, June 3, 1952; s. Howard Curtis and Emma Delores (Wilson) E.; m. Dianne Claudia Chesslock, Jan. 9, 1982. BS in Psychology cum laude, Ga. State U., 1977; JD cum laude, Mercer U., Macon, Ga., 1980. Bar: Ga. 1980; U.S. Ct. Appeals (11th cir.) 1984, U.S. Dist. Ct. (no. dist.) 1981, U.S. Dist. Ct. (mid. dist.) 1982, U.S. Dist. Ct. (so. dist.) 1982, U.S. Ct. Appeals (5th cir.) 1981. Assoc. atty. Powell, Goldstein, Frazier and Murphy, Atlanta, 1980-83; ptnr. Eidson & Assocs., P.C., Atlanta, 1983—; city atty. City of East Point, Ga., 1983-90, City of Fairburn, Ga., 1986-96; dir. First Bank of Ga., East Point, 1988—, First Bankshares, Inc., Hapeville, Ga., 1994—. Author: (Jour.) Mercer Law Review, 1978. Lt. USMC, 1969-80. Mem. Atlanta Lawyers Club, 191 Club. Republican. Methodist. Avocations: sailing, hunting. Home: 2515 Habersham Rd NW Atlanta GA 30305-3557 Office: Eidson & Assocs PC 600 S Central Ave Atlanta GA 30354-1928

EIDSVOLD, GARY MASON, physician, public health officer, medical educator; b. Morris, Minn., Sept. 28, 1938; s. Lyman Woodrow and Julia Magdalene (Mason) E. BA, St. Olaf Coll., 1960; MD, U. Minn., 1964; MPH, Johns Hopkins U., 1966. Diplomate Am. Bd. Preventive Medicine. Rotating intern Long Island Coll. Hosp., Bklyn., 1964-65; resident in preventive medicine Johns Hopkins U. Sch. Pub. Health, Balt., 1965-68; asst. prof. Haile Selassie U., Gondar, Ethiopia, 1967-68; dir. Indian Health Svc. Hosp., Tuba City, Ariz., 1968-70; South Bronx Health Officer N.Y.C. Health Dept., 1970-73, North Bklyn. Health Officer, 1973-74, Bronx and Staten Island dir., 1974-78; N.Y.C. med. dir. N.Y. State Health Dept., 1978-97, amb. care program dir., 1978-85, home health and HMO program dir., 1978-85, Medicaid program dir., 1978-95, alternative delivery sys. program dir., 1995, managed care program dir., 1995-97, family helath managed care program dir., 1997—; clin. asst. prof. dept. preventive medicine N.Y. Med. Coll., N.Y.C.; clinical asst. prof. dept. preventive medicine N.Y. Med. Coll., N.Y.C., 1971-73; asst. prof. SUNY Health Sci. Ctr., Bklyn., 1973—; lectr. Columbia U. Sch. Pub. Health, N.Y.C., 1973-83; faculty New Sch. Soc. Rsch., N.Y.C., 1974-75. Contbr. articles to profl. jours. Coun. and com. chmn. Trinity Ch. in the City of N.Y., 1972-76, St. John's Evang. Luth. Ch., N.Y.C., 1988—. Surgeon, USPHS, 1968-70. Recipient outstanding leadership award, East N.Y. Health Coalition, Bklyn., 1973. Fellow Am. Coll. Preventive Medicine, Am. Tchrs. Preventive Medicine; mem. Am. Pub. Health Assn. (chmn. Health Adminstrn. Sect. 1979-81), Pub. Health Physicians Assn. N.Y.C. (pres. 1973-76), Pub. Health Assn. N.Y.C. (bd. dirs. 1975-81), Nat. Assn. County Health Officers (bd. dirs. 1975-78), Lutheran Soc. Svcs. Metro N.Y. (bd. dirs. 1991-94), Norwegian Am. Hist. Soc. (life). Democrat. Lutheran. Avocations: Norwegian language, genealogy, cooking, gym, music. Home: 71 Grand St New York NY 10013-2219 Office: NY State Health Dept Penn Plz Fl 2 New York NY 10001-1803

EIERMANN-WEGENER, DARLENE MAE, paralegal; b. New Orleans, June 10, 1959; d. Wilbur Joseph and Dorothy M. (Walton-Palmer) Eiermann; m. Edmund T. Wegener, Jr., Apr. 26, 1991. Student, U. New Orleans, 1991—. Cert. paralegal. Adminstrv. asst. Jefferson Parish Coun., Gretna, La., 1980; sec. Robin Towing Corp., Harvey, La., 1980-83; legal sec. Oster & Wegener, APLC, New Orleans, 1983-86, paralegal, 1986—. Candidate for justice of the peace, Ward 8, St. Tammany parish, 1996. Mem. Assn. Trial Lawyers of Am., New Orleans Paralegal Assn., La. State Paralegal Assn., Nat. Paralegal Assn., Mensa, Beta Sigma Phi, others. Republican. Lutheran. Avocations: reading, researching, attaining political office, continuing education. Office: Oster & Wegener PO Box 5747 Slidell LA 70469-5747

EIFRIG, DAVID ERIC, ophthalmologist, educator; b. Oak Park, Ill., Jan. 4, 1935. BA, Carleton Coll., Northfield, Minn., 1956; MD, Johns Hopkins U., 1960. Diplomate Am. Bd. Ophthalmology. Mem. liaison svc. Johns Hopkins U. Hosp., Balt., 1957, mem. dept. pathology, 1958, mem. dog lab. dept. surgery, 1959-60; intern, then asst. resident Halsted Surg. Svc. Johns Hopkins U. Hosp., Balt., 1960-62, resident in ophthalmology Wilmer Eye Inst., 1964-67; retinal fellow Jules Stein Eye Inst., UCLA, 1967-68; asst. prof. dept. ophthalmology U. Ky. Sch. Medicine, Lexington, 1968-70; asst. prof. dept. ophthalmology U. Minn. Sch. Medicine, Mpls., 1970-73, assoc. prof., 1973-77; prof. dept. ophthalmology U. N.C. Sch. Medicine, Chapel Hill, 1977—, Sterling A. Barrett prof., 1980—, chmn. dept. ophthalmology, 1977—; Z80 com. Am. Nat. Stds. Inst., 1980-97, chmn. 1985-97; mem. Med. Devices Stds. d., 1986-98; mem. Internat. Stds. Orgn., 1986-97; adv. bd. Am. Coll. of Surgeons, 1994—. Contbr. articles to profl. jours.; lectr. to profl. confs. With M.C., USNR, 1962-64. Recipient Schwentker medal for rsch. Johns Hopkins U., 1967. Fellow ACS; mem. AMA, Am. Acad. Ophthalmology, Assn. Rsch. in Vision and Ophthalmology, Assn. Univ. Profs. in Ophthalmology (trustee, pres. 1994-95), Durham-Orange County Med. Soc., Johns Hopkins Med. and Surg. Assn., N.C. Med. Soc., N.C. Soc. Ophthalmology, Retina Soc., Mensa, Order Ky. Cols. Home: 128 New Castle Dr Chapel Hill NC 27514-6545 Office: U NC Sch Medicine Dept Ophthalmology 617 Clinical Scis 229H Chapel Hill NC 27514

EIG, BLAIR MITCHELL, pediatrician; b. Washington, Jan. 26, 1956; s. Blaine H. and Elizabeth Eig; m. Kaethe Enos, Aug. 5, 1979; children: Sarah, Joshua, Steven. BA in Biology and Biochemistry, Brandeis U., 1977, MA in Biochemistry, 1977; MD, Harvard U., 1983. Diplomate Am. Bd. Pediat., Nat. Bd. Med. Examiners. From intern to chief resident Children's Nat. Med. Ctr., Washington, 1983-87, pres. med. staff, 1998—; pvt. practice Hollander, Cohen, Eig & Madden, Silver Spring, Md., 1987—; co-chmn. lab. adv. com. State of Md., 1993—; chmn. med. adv. bd. Treatment and Learning Ctr., Rockville, Md., 1996. Contbr. chpt. to book Bridging the Parent-Professional Gap, 1999. Student activity theater sponsor Montgomery County Pub. Schs., Md., 1993—. Fellow Am. Acad. Pediat.; mem. Med. and Chirurgical Faculty Md., Montgomery-Prince Georges Pediat. Soc. (pres. 1992-93), Phi Beta Kappa. Avocations: opera, animation, roller coasters. Office: 10313 Georgia Ave Ste 303 Silver Spring MD 20902-5006

EIG, NORMAN, investment company executive; b. Passaic, N.J., Mar. 9, 1941; s. Edward H. and Mary (Friedman) E.; m. Barbara Minkin, Feb. 1, 1964; children: Andrew, Alissa, Karin. BS, Ohio State U., 1963; MBA, Columbia U., 1965. Asst. controller Silver Burdett Co., Morristown, N.J., 1965; controller Juliet Footwear, East Paterson, N.J., 1965-68; security analyst Brimberg and Co., N.Y.C., 1968; portfolio mgr. EFC Mgmt., N.Y.C., 1968-69, Scherl, Egener and Co., N.Y.C., 1970-71; exec. v.p. Internat. Research and Devel., Princeton, N.J., 1971-72; pres. Rotunda Advisors, Princeton, 1972-73; ptnr. Oppenheimer and Co., N.Y.C., 1973-82, Lazard Freres and Co., N.Y.C., 1982—; chmn. bd. dirs. Lazard Family of Funds, N.Y.C.; bd. dirs. Value Fund., N.Y.C., Edison Control Corp. Mem. corp. adv. bd. Sch. Social Work, Columbia U., N.Y.C., 1986-90, mem. bd. overseers Sch. Bus., 1994; bd. dirs. Friends of the Israel Def. Forces, Damon Runyon-Walter Winchell Found. Mem. The Columbia Club of N.Y., Mtn. Ridge Country Club, Metedeconk Nat. Golf Club (Jackson, N.J., bd. adv.), Medalist Golf Club, Hobe Sound (North Palm Beach, Fla.). Jewish. Avocations: golf, tennis, jazz, non-fiction reading. Office: Lazard Freres & Co 30 Rockefeller Plz Fl 59 New York NY 10112-5900

EIGEL, CHRISTOPHER JOHN, real estate executive; b. Evanston, Ill.; s. Jack William and Martha Eloise (English) E.; m. Carolyn Koenig, Mar. 23, 1968; children: Jeffrey Christopher, Edward Drummond, Amy Elizabeth. BA, U. Ill., 1967; MBA, U. Chgo., 1969. Mktg. rsch. officer The Northern Trust Co., Chgo., 1969-74; exec. v.p. and gen. sales mgr. Koenig and Strey Inc., Wilmette, Ill., 1974—. Mem. real estate adv. bd. Oakton C.C., Des Plaines, Ill. Mem. Ill. Assn. Realtors (bd. dirs. 1986-88), North Shore Bd. Realtors (bd. dirs. 1980-88, 96—, pres. 1987), U. Ill. Alumni Assn. (bd. dirs. 1993-96). Home: 630 Windsor Rd Glenview IL 60025-4453 Office: Koenig and Strey Inc 3201 Old Glenview Rd Wilmette IL 60091-2999

EIGEL, EDWIN GEORGE, JR., mathematics educator, retired university president; b. St. Louis, June 4, 1932; s. Edwin George and Catherine (Rohan) E.; m. Marcia Jeanne Duffy, May 30, 1959; children: Edwin George III, Mary Marcia. BS, MIT, 1954; postgrad., U. Marburg, Germany, 1954-55; PhD, St. Louis U., 1961. Lectr. math. George Washington U., 1961; asst. prof. math. St. Louis U., 1961-64, assoc. prof., 1964-69, asst. to dean Grad. Sch., 1965-67, prof., 1969-79, dean Grad. Sch., 1967-71, assoc. acad. v.p., 1971-72, acad. v.p., 1972-79, exec. v.p., 1973; assoc. prof. math. U. Bridgeport, Conn., 1979-82, prof., 1982—, Univ. prof., 1995—, v.p. acad. affairs, 1979-91, provost, 1981-91; pres., 1991-95; pres. emeritus U. Bridgeport, Conn., 1995—; mem. adv. com. on accreditation Conn. Dept. Higher Edn., 1989-92. Commr. McDonnell Planetarium, St. Louis, 1972-79; mem. Conn. Disting. Citizens Task Force on Quality Tchg., 1982-83; acting exec. dir. Bridgeport Area Consortium Colls. and Univs., 1989; bd. dirs. Bridgeport Pub. Edn. Fund, 1993-97, Bridgport Regional Bus. Coun., 1994-95, United Way Ea. Fairfield County, 1994-98, Univ. Bridgeport, 1995—. Mem. Am. Math. Soc., Math. Assn. Am., Rotary (bd. dirs. Bridgeport 1994-97), Phi Beta Kappa, Phi Beta Kappa Assocs., Sigma Xi, Pi Mu Epsilon, Phi Kappa Phi, Beta Gamma Sigma, Upsilon Pi Epsilon, Sigma Beta Delta. Achievements include: research in math. applications of computers. Home: 33 Pepperbush Ln Fairfield CT 06430-4036

EIGEL, MARCIA DUFFY, editor; b. Denver, July 15, 1936; d. Eugene and Margaret (Foley) Duffy; m. Edwin G. Eigel Jr., May 30, 1959; children: Edwin III, Mary. BA, Webster U., 1958. Dir. mktg. Greater Bridgeport (Conn.) Transp. Dist., 1979-81; security analyst Tucker, Anthony & R. L. Day, Stamford, Conn., 1981-84; fin. editor Evaluation Assoc., Westport, Conn., 1984-85; editor, writer corp. hdqrs. GE, Fairfield, Conn., 1985-92, copy editor, 1996—; dir. comms. Girl Scouts of Housatonic Coun., Bridgeport, Conn., 1994-97; instr. in bus. writing So. Conn. State U., New Haven, 1986, U. Bridgeport, 1990. Writer, editor newsletter Customer Fin. Svcs. News, 1987-92, Woman Traveler, 1990—; contbr. articles and poetry to profl. jours. Bd. trustees Greater Bridgeport (Conn.) Symphony, 1998—. Mem. NAFE. Home and office: 33 Pepperbush Ln Fairfield CT 06430-4036

EIGEN, HOWARD, pediatrician, educator; b. N.Y.C., Sept. 8, 1942; s. Jay and Libbie (Kantrowitz) E.; m. Linda Hazzard; children—Sarah Elizabeth, Lauren Michelle. B.S., Queens Coll., 1964; M.D., Upstate N.Y. Med. Ctr., Syracuse, 1968. Diplomate Am. Bd. Pediatrics, Am. Bd. Pediatric Pulmonology, Am. Bd. Critical Care Medicine, Nat. Bd. Med. Examiners (mem. pediatric test com. 1986-90). Resident in pediatrics Upstate Med. Ctr., Syracuse, 1968-71; fellow in pediatric pulmonology Tulane U., New Orleans, 1973-76; asst. prof. pediatrics Ind. U., Indpls., 1976-84, prof., 1984-96, Billie Lou Wood Prof. pediatrics, 1996—; assoc. chmn. of Pediatrics for Clin. Affairs, dir. pediatric intensive care, pulmonology sect. Riley Hosp. for Children, med. dir. ambulatory care, 1989—. Co-editor: Respiratory Disease in Children: Diagnosis and Management; assoc. editor Pediatric Pulmonology, 1984-91; contbr. articles to profl. jours. Served to maj. U.S. Army, 1971-73. Fellow Am. Acad. Pediatrics (pres. chest sect. 1983-85, pulmonology 1986—), Am. Thoracic Soc., Am. Bd. Pediatrics, Am. Lung Assn. (pres. Ind. 1984-85). Avocation: tennis. Office: Ind U Dept Pediatrics 702 Barnhill Dr Rm 2750 Indianapolis IN 46202-5128

EIGEN, MANFRED, physicist; b. Bochum, Germany, May 9, 1927; s. Ernst E. and Hedwig (Feld) E.; m. Elfriede Müller; 2 children. Studies in physics and chemistry, U. Gottingen, Germany; hon. degrees, U. Göttingen, U. Chgo., Washington U., St. Louis, Nottingham U., Bristol U., U.K., Hebrew U., Jerusalem, Cambridge U., U.K., Debrecen U., Techn. U., Munich, Bielefeld U., Utah State U. Sci. asst. Inst. Phys. Chemistry U. Göttingen, 1951-53; mem. staff, then chmn. Max Planck Inst. Phys. Chemistry, Göttingen, 1953—; vis. lectr. Cornell. Author tech. papers. Co-recipient Nobel prize in chemistry, 1967, Max-Planck-Forschungs-Preis, Alexander von Humboldt-Stiftung, 1994, Paul Ehrlich award, 1996. Mem. Bunsen Soc. Phys. Chemistry (Bodenstein Preis 1956), Faraday Soc., NAS, Royal Soc. London (fgn.). Achievements include studying evolution of biol. macromolecules; research on control of enzymes. Office: Max Planck Inst, 37077 Göttingen Germany

EIGER, RICHARD WILLIAM, retired publisher; b. N.Y.C., May 11, 1933; s. William and Helen M. (Fetten) E.; m. Ruth B. Engelke; 1 child, Keith R. BFA, Pratt Inst., 1955; MBA, NYU, 1960. With Western Pub. Co., N.Y.C., 1958-80, pub. dir., 1968-74, v.p. pub., 1975-80; pres. Macmillan Ednl. Co., N.Y.C., 1980-91; sr. v.p. Macmillan Pub. Co., N.Y.C., 1980-91; v.p. K-III Reference Corp. (now PRIMEDIA Reference Corp.), Mahwah, N.J., 1991-93; pub. The World Almanac, 1993-98; ret., 1998. Bd. dirs. alumni bd. The Pratt Inst., N.Y.C., 1986—, trustee, 1992—, mem. exec. com., 1995—, sec. 1996—, chmn. devel. com., 1997—; mem. pub. com. Brandeis U., Waltham, Mass., 1993—; trustee The Katharine Gibbs Sch., Montclair, N.J., 1995—, Piscataway, N.J., 1996—. Lt. U.S. Army, 1956-57. Home: 459 Franklin Ave Wyckoff NJ 07481-1306

EIGHMEY, GEORGE V., lawyer, state legislator; b. Chgo., May 3, 1941; ss. Orville Eugene and Sophie Mary (Voynovich) E.; m. Marie Going, Sept. 5, 1964 (div. Nov. 1976); children: Jasmine Ruthdotter, Gred; m. Peter Livingston, June 20, 1981. BS, U. Ill., 1969, JD, 1972. Bar: Ill., Oreg. Assoc. Thomas Mamer & Hangley, Champaign, Ill., 1972-82; pvt. practice Portland, Oreg., 1982—; mem. Oreg. Ho. of Reps., Salem, 1993-99; exec. dir. Compassion in Dying of Oreg., 1999—. With USAF, 1960-64. Democrat. Home: 1524 SE Poplar Ave Portland OR 97214-4863 Office: 1423 SE Hawthorne Blvd Portland OR 97214-3640

EIGLER, DONALD MARK, physicist; b. L.A., Mar. 23, 1953; s. Irving Baer and Evelin Muriel (Baker) E.; m. Roslyn Winifred Rubesin, Nov. 2, 1986. BA, U. Calif., San Diego, 1975, PhD in Physics, 1984. Rsch. assoc. U. Köln (Fed. Republic Germany), 1975-76; rsch. assoc. U. Calif., San Diego, 1977-84, postdoctoral rsch. assoc., 1984, assoc. rsch. physicist dept. physics, 1986; postdoctoral mem. tech. staff AT&T Bell Labs., Murray Hill, N.J., 1984-86; rsch. staff mem. IBM, San Jose, Calif., 1986-93, IBM fellow, 1993—; Alexander M. Cruickshank lectr. in phys. sci. (Gordon Rsch. Confs.), 1994. Co-winner 1993-94 Newcomb Cleveland prize AAAS; recipient Dannie Heineman prize Göttingen Acad. Scis., 1995, Outstanding Alumnus award U. Calif. San Diego alumni Assn., 1998, Nanoscience prize Conf. on Atomically Controlled Interfaces and Surfaces, 1999. Fellow Am. Phys. Soc. Office: IBM Almaden Rsch Ctr 650 Harry Rd San Jose CA 95120-6099

EIGSTI, ROGER HARRY, insurance company executive; b. Vancouver, Wash., Apr. 17, 1942; s. Harry A. and Alice E. (Huber) E.; m. Mary Lou Nelson, June 8, 1963; children: Gregory, Ann. BS, Linfield Coll., 1964. CPA, Oreg., Wash. Staff CPA Touche Ross and Co., Portland, Oreg., 1964-72; asst. to controller Safeco Corp., Seattle, 1972-78, controller, 1980; controller Safeco Life Ins. Co., Seattle, 1978-80; pres. Safeco Credit Co., Seattle, 1980-81, Safeco Life Ins. Co., Seattle, 1981-85; exec. v.p., CFO Safeco Corp., Seattle, 1985, CEO, chmn. bd. dirs. Ind. Colls. of Wash., Seattle, 1981-87, bus. dir. Seattle Repertory Theatre, 1981—, bd. dirs. 1981—. Mem. Am. Inst. CPA's, Life Office Mgmt. Assn. (bd. dirs. 1983—), Seattle C. of C. (chmn. metro budget rev. com. 1984—). Republican. Clubs: Mercer Island (Wash.) Country (treas., bd. dirs. 1981-84); Central Park Tennis. Home: 1503 Parkside Dr E Seattle WA 98112-3719

EIKENBERRY, ARTHUR RAYMOND, writer, service executive, researcher; b. Sebring, Fla., June 5, 1920; s. Leroy Albertus and Vernie Cordelia (Griffin) E.; m. Carol Jean Parrott, June 10, 1955; children: Robin Rene, Shari LaVon, Jan Rochelle, Karyn LaRae, Kelli Yvette. Student, Pasadena (Calif.) Jr. Coll., 1939, Kunming U., China, 1944-45. MSgt. Army Air Corps, 1941-45, re-enlisted in grade of TSgt., 1947; advanced through grades to SMSgt. USAF; ret., 1973, mgmt., pers., adminstrv. and security insp.; mgr. property control, real estate agent TR Devel. Co., Englewood, Colo., 1973-74; real estate agt. The Pinery, Parker, Colo., 1974-75; mgr., patient acctg. dept. Univ. Colo. Health Scis. Ctr., Denver, 1975-89. Author: Investment Strategies for the Clever Investor, 1989, LOTTO GURU (Omni-Personal Selection Systems & Strategies), 1989. Charter mem. U.S. Congl. Adv. Bd. Fellow Internat. Biog. Ctr. (hon. life patron, dep. dir. gen.); mem. Am. Biog. Inst. (life, dep. gov., nat. adviser), World Inst. of Achievement (disting.), Masons, Eastern Star, Royal Order of the Amaranth. Address: Apt 2085 9901 W Sahara Ave Las Vegas NV 89117-5912

EILEN, HOWARD SCOTT, lawyer, mediator; b. N.Y.C., Mar. 28, 1954; m. Sharon R. Kornbluth, Oct. 21, 1979; children: Michael, Jeffrey. BA summa cum laude, CUNY, 1975, MA, 1975; JD, St. John's U., 1979. Bar: N.Y. 1980, U.S. Tax Ct. 1980, U.S. Dist. Ct. (so., ea. dists.) N.Y. 1980, U.S. Dist. Ct. (ea. dist.) Mich. 1982. Assoc. Bloom & Tese, N.Y.C., 1980-83; ptnr. Bloom & Eilen, N.Y.C., 1983-86, 87-94; of counsel Spengler, Carlson, Gubar, Brodsky & Frischling, N.Y.C., 1986-87; ptnr. Lehman & Eilen, Uniondale, N.Y., 1994—; Arbitrator Nat. Assn. Securities Dealers, Inc., Nat. Futures Assn., Am. Arbitration Assn., U.S. Arbitration and Mediation, Inc., Mediator Nat. Assn. Sec. Dealers, Inc., Spl. Master N.Y. Supreme Ct., Faculty Practising Law Inst., Sec. Arbitration Program. Contbg. editor Futures Tribune Mag., Japan. Mem. N.Y. County Lawyers Assn. (com. on securities and exchanges 1983—, chmn. subcom. on commodities regulation, com. on arbitration and conciliation 1990—), Nassau County Bar Assn. (securities law com.). Office: Lehman & Eilen Ste 505 50 Charles Lindbergh Blvd Uniondale NY 11553-3612

EILTS, HERMANN FREDERICK, international relations educator, former diplomat; b. Weissenfels Saale, Germany, Mar. 23, 1922; came to U.S., 1926; naturalized, 1930; s. Friedrich Alex and Meta Dorothea (Pruser) E.; m. Helen Josephine Brew, June 12, 1948; children: Conrad Marshall, Frederick Lowell. BA, Ursinus Coll., 1942, LLD, 1960; MA, Johns Hopkins U., 1947; postgrad., U. Pa., 1950-51. Joined Fgn. Svc., Dept. State, 1947; 3d sec., vice consul Tehran, Iran, 1947-48, Jidda, Saudi Arabia, 1948-50; consul prin. officer Aden, 1951-53; 2d sec., consul Sana, Yemen, 1951-53; 2d sec., consul, chief polit. sect. Bahdad, Iraq, 1954-56; officer in charge Baghdad Pact affairs Dept. State, Washington, 1957-59, officer in charge Arabian Peninsula affairs, 1959-61; 1st sec. Am. Embassy, London, 1962-64; counsellor, dep. chief of mission Am. Embassy, Tripoli, Libya, 1964-65; amb. to Saudi Arabia, 1965-70; dep. commandant for internat. affairs, diplomatic adviser U.S. Army War Coll., Carlisle Barracks, Pa., 1970-73; amb. to Egypt Cairo, 1973-79; Disting. Univ. prof. internat. rels. Boston U., 1979—, chmn. dept. polit. sci., 1982-87, chmn. dept. internat. rels., 1989-93, acad. coord., mil. edn. div., 1990-93, prof. emeritus, 1993—. 1st lt. M.I., AUS, 1942-45. Decorated Purple Heart, Bronze Star; recipient Arthur Flemming award, 1958, Disting. Civilian Honor award Dept. Army, 1973, Disting. Honor award Dept. State, 1979, Joseph C. Wilson award, 1979, Disting. Alumnus award Johns Hopkins U., 1980, All-Pa. Coll. Alumni Assn. citation, 1987, Am. Foreign Svc. cup Dept. State, 1992; named Disting. Fellow U.S. Army War Coll., 1991. Fellow Royal Geog. Soc., Royal Asiatic Soc.; mem. Am. Fgn. Svc. Assn., Middle East Inst., Royal Cen. Asian Soc. Mem. Evang. Reformed Ch. Address: 67 Cleveland Rd Wellesley MA 02481-2434

EILTS, MICHAEL DEAN, research meteorologist, manager; b. La Chapelle, France, Aug. 22, 1959; (parents Am. citizens); s. Leonard Gene and Arlys Mamie (Ziegler) E. BS in Meteorology, U. Okla., 1981, MS in Meteorology, 1983, MBA in Fin. and Human Resource Mgmt., 1991. Rsch. asst., rsch. meteorologist Coop. Inst. for Mesoscale Meteorol. Studies, Norman, Okla., 1981-84; rsch. meteorologist Nat. Severe Storms Lab., Norman, 1984-87, mgr. weather hazards to aviation project, 1987-91, chief forecast applications rsch. group, 1991-93, asst. dir., chief stormscale rsch. and applications divsn., 1993—; mem. exptl. forecast facility mgmt. group, 1991-95; mem. Cleveland County YMCA Program Com., 1991-93; spl. mem. adj. faculty U. Okla. Sch. Meteorology, Norman, 1989—; mem. Okla. Mesonet Steering Com.; coun. mem., fellow Coop. Inst. Mesoscale Meteorol. Studies. Contbr. articles to profl. jours. Grantee FAA, 1987-99, NASA, 1990-91, 96-97, Nat. Weather Svc., 1991-99, Ga. Emergency Mgmt. Agy., 1999; recipient Dist. Authorship award Environ. Rsch. Labs., 1991, Adminstrs. award NOAA, 1998. Mem. Am. Meteorol. Soc. Lutheran. Avocations: golf, volleyball, softball. Home: 3405 S Bryant Ave Moore OK 73160-8401 Office: Nat Severe Storms Lab 1313 Halley Cir Norman OK 73069-8480

EILTS, SUSANNE ELIZABETH, physician; b. Council Bluffs, Iowa, Oct. 12, 1955; d. Ervin Edwin and Mary Margaret (Leonard) E. BS, Nebr. Wesleyan U., 1976; MD, U. Iowa, 1980. Diplomate Am. Bd. Internal Medicine. Intern, resident U. Nebr. Med. Ctr., Omaha, 1980-83; pvt. practice, Omaha, 1983—; clin. instr. internal medicine U. Nebr., Omaha, 1983—; med. dir. Amb. Nursing Home, Omaha, 1990-92; quality assurance reviewer Sunderbruch Corp. Nebr., Lincoln, 1990-92; v.p. quality assurance Internal Med. Assocs., 1993-95, bd. dirs.; chmn. dept. medicine Clarkson Hosp., 1994-95, sec.-treas. med. staff, 1996-98, mem. staff exec. com., 1994-98, med. outcomes coun., 1994-96; v.p. pvt. practice category Nebr. Health Sys., 1998—; bd. examiners in medicine and surgery Nebr. State Dept. Health, 1996—, sec., 1998, vice chair, 1999; mem. Nebr. Health Care Facility Licensure Reform Rationale Task Force, 1997, Health Professions Licensure Sys. Reengring., 1998; bd. dirs. Clarkson Regional Health Svcs., Pvt. Practice Assocs. LLC, chm. enrollment com. Mem. ACP, Am. Geriatric Soc., Nebr. Med. Assn. (alt. del. 1990-91, del. 1992, young physician com. 1989-93, com. health care reform 1993-94, legis. com. 1993—, legis. subcom. for HMO/PPO policy statement 1995-96, chmn. advocacy com. 1998—, vice spkr. ho. of dels. 1999—), Am. Women's Med. Assn. Nebr. (sec. 1987), Nebr. Soc. Internal Medicine (bd. dirs. 1994-98), Beta Beta Beta, Phi Kappa Phi, Phi Lambda Upsilon. Avocations: bicycling, playing the pennywhistle. Office: Internal Medicine Assocs PC 4242 Farnam St Ste 650N Omaha NE 68131-2802

EIMER, NATHAN PHILIP, lawyer; b. Chgo., June 26, 1949; s. Irving A. and Charlotte Eimer; m. Kathleen L. Roach; children: Micah Jacob, Noah Joseph, Daniel Jordan, Anna Beatrice. AB in Econs. magna cum laude, U. Ill., 1970; JD cum laude, Northwestern U., 1973. Bar: Ill. 1973, U.S. Supreme Ct. 1978, N.Y. 1985, Tex. 1998. Assoc. Sidley & Austin, Chgo., 1973-80, ptnr., 1980—; adj. prof. Law Sch., Northwestern U., Chgo., 1989-96. Note and comment editor Northwestern U. Law Rev., 1972-73. Bd. dirs. Chgo. Lawyers Com. for Civil Rights, 1991—, pres., 1993-94; bd. dirs. UNICEF, 1992-93, Infant Welfare Soc., Chgo., exec. v.p., 1992-96, pres., 1996-98; mem. adv. bd. Children & Family Justice Ctr., Northwestern U. Legal Clinic, 1996-98. Mem. ABA, Midday Club Chgo. Office: Sidley & Austin 1 First Natl Plz Ste 5300 Chicago IL 60603-2003

EIMERS, JERI ANNE, therapist; b. Berkeley, Calif., Jan. 20, 1951; d. Alfred D. Wallace and Marjorie E. (Nordheim) Stevens; m. Roy A. Neiman, June 12, 1969 (div. Aug. 1977); children: Lorien, Arwen; m. Richard A. Eimers, Mar. 2, 1996. AA, Palomar Jr. Coll., 1977; BA in Psychology with distinction, Calif. State U., Long Beach, 1979, MA in Psychology with distinction, 1981; postgrad. Human Sexuality Program, UCLA, 1991-92. Lic. marriage, family, child therapist, Calif.; cert. community coll. instr., counselor; cert. sex therapist. Rsch. asst. Calif. State U., 1978-82; tchr. Artesia (Calif.)-Bellflower-Cerritos Unified Sch. Dist., 1982-83; dir. Am. Learning Corp., Huntington Beach, Calif., 1983-85; social worker Los Angeles County Children's Protective Svcs., Long Beach, 1986-88; sr. social worker Orange County Social Svc. Agy., Orange, Calif., 1988-90; therapist Cypress Mental Health, Cypress, Calif., 1988—, cons., 1990—; cons., 1990—; group chair, leader Adults Abused as Children, Los Altos Hosp., Long Beach, 1991—, Coll. Hosp., Cerritos, 1993—; speaker, presenter in field. Mem. Child's Sexual Abuse Network, Orange, 1988—; mem. legis. com. Child Abuse Coun. of Orange County, 1988. Women's League scholar, 1980-81. Mem. AAUW, Am. Assn. Marriage, Family Therapists, Calif. Assn. Marriage, Family Therapists, Am. Profl. Soc. for Abused Children, Calif. Profl. Assn. for Abused Children, Phi Kappa Phi, Psi Chi. Republican. Methodist. Avocations: writing, theater, classical and jazz music, swimming. Office: Huntington Group 9191 Towne Centre Dr Ste 365 San Diego CA 92122-1229

EIMICKE, VICTOR W(ILLIAM), publishing company executive; b. N.Y.C., Feb. 4, 1925; s. Victor H. and Anna (Gille) E.; m. Maxine Howard Thome, Aug. 6, 1955; children: Laura Eimicke Klimley, Alicia Eimicke Barbieri. A.B., NYU, 1945, M.A., 1946, Ph.D., 1951; Litt.D. (hon.), Hope Coll., 1987. Lectr. NYU, 1945-47, Bklyn. Coll., 1946-49; dir. audio visual dept. CCNY, 1947-53; asst. prof. Pace Coll., 1953-56; v.p. Inst. Human Research in Industry, N.Y.C., 1947-48; pres. V.W. Eimicke Assocs. Inc., N.Y.C., 1951—, V.W. Eimicke Ltd., Peterborough, Ont., Can., 1978—; chmn. Eimicke Assocs. Ltd., London, 1956-69; pres. Action Aids, Inc., N.Y.C., 1969-73, Laurel Office Aids, Inc., N.Y.C., 1969-73, Action List Services, Inc., Yonkers, N.Y., 1976-80, Eimicke Pub. Co., Yonkers, 1976-78, Geschäftsführer, Envelo-Formulare GmbH, Krefeld, Ger., 1978-83, Geschäftsführer, V.W. Eimicke GmbH, 1983-93; dir. New England Grocer Supply Co., Worcester, Mass., 1964-68, Nathan's Famous, Inc., N.Y.C., 1974-79, 85-87, Wetson's, Inc., N.Y.C., 1975-79. Author: (with Laura Klimley) Managing Human Resources - Documenting the Personnel Function. Pres. bd. trustees Halsted Sch., Yonkers, 1969-74; bd. govs. Lawrence Hosp., Bronxville, N.Y., 1971-74, mem. corp., 1986—; bd. dirs. Japan International Christian U. Found., Inc., 1972-91, v.p., 1990; trustee Hope Coll., Holland, Mich., 1976-87, chmn. bd., 1978-87, hon. trustee, 1987—; bd. dirs. Community Fund of Bronxville, 1982-87, pres., 1983-86, hon. dir., 1987—; elder, mem. consistory Reformed Ch. of Bronxville, 1968—, mem.-at-large gen. synod coun. Reformed Ch. in Am., 1993-98; bd. dirs. Living Pulpit Inc., 1993-95; dir. Warwick (N.Y.) Conf. Ctr., 1993—. Mem. Assn. Churchill Fellows of Westminster Coll., 1986—. Mem. APA, Ea. Psychol. Assn., N.Y. State Psychol. Assn., Westchester Psychol. Assn., Nat. Inst. Social Scis., Nat. Bible Assn. (bd. dirs., treas. 1969-70, pres. 1982-94, chmn. 1994-98, trustee 1998—), Met. Opera Club, Union League, Univ. Club (N.Y.C.), Siwanoy Country Club (Bronxville, N.Y.), Lake Placid Club (N.Y.), Phi Beta Kappa, Kappa Delta Pi, Phi Delta Kappa. Home: 20 Hereford Rd Bronxville NY 10708-5408 Office: 35 E Grassy Sprain Rd Yonkers NY 10710-4611

EIN, DANIEL, allergist; b. Liege, Belgium, Nov. 26, 1938; came to U.S., 1941; s. Max Motel and Sabine (Toeman) E.; m. Marion Hess, June 25, 1961 (div. 1978); children: Mark David, Jon Spencer; m. Marina Wallach, Apr. 10, 1988; stepchildren: Jacqueline A. Newmyer, Tory Newmyer. AB, Columbia U., 1959; MD, Albert Einstein Coll. Medicine, 1964. Diplomate Am. Bd. Internal Medicine, Am. Bd. Allergy and Immunology. Intern Bronx Mcpl. Hosp., N.Y.C., 1964-65; staff assoc. Nat. Cancer Inst., Washington, 1965-67, clin. assoc., 1967-68; asst. resident Mass. Gen. Hosp., Boston, 1968-69; sr. investigator Nat. Cancer Inst., Washington, 1969-71; pvt. practice Washington, 1971—; clin. prof. medicine George Washington U., Washington, 1982—, Georgetown U., Washington, 1996—; founder, pres. Capital Physicians Network, 1994-99. Contbr. articles to profl. jours. and newspapers. Fellow ACP, Am. Acad. Allergy (AMA del. 1994), Am. Coll. Allergy; mem. Joint Coun. of Allergy (pres. 1998—), Med. Soc. of D.C. (pres. 1991), Greater Washington Allergy Soc. (pres. 1979), Cosmos Club. Jewish. Achievements include discovery of OZ factors on human immunoglobulin light chains. Home: 4636 Kenmore Dr NW Washington DC 20007-1924

EINACH, CHARLES DONALD, advertising and publishing executive; b. Buffalo, July 1, 1929; s. Joseph and Esther Riva (Liner) E.; m. Elen Simon, Mar. 15, 1971. BA, U. Buffalo, 1951; MA, Syracuse U., 1953. Broadcast dir. The Rumrill Co. Inc., Buffalo, 1954-60; dir. advt. J. Nelson Prewitt Inc., Rochester, N.Y., 1960-63; account supr., v.p. Grey Advt. Inc., N.Y.C., 1963-71; exec. v.p. Nadler & Larimer Inc., N.Y.C., 1971-84; sr. v.p. Mandelbaum, Wolf, Wiskowski Inc., Jersey City, 1986-87; pres. Headwork Svcs. Cons., N.Y.C., 1985-94; chief editor mut. fund. publs. Value Line Publ., Inc., N.Y.C., 1994—. Co-chmn. Citizens for Sane Residential Zoning, N.Y.C., 1984-85. Mem. Nat. Acad. TV Arts and Scis., Internat. Wine Soc. Club: Les Amis du Vin (N.Y.C.). Avocation: enology. Home: 301 E 66th St New York NY 10021-6216 Office: Value Line Publs Inc 220 E 42d St New York NY 10017-5891

EINEKE, ALVINA MARIE, public health nurse; b. Elmhurst, Ill., Mar. 31, 1951; d. Herbert Fred and Gertrude (Gittings) E. BSN, Valparaiso U., 1973. Credentialed early intervention specialist. Staff nurse pediatrics Wyler Children's Hosp.-U. Chgo. Hosps. and Cinics, Chgo., 1973-78; pub. health nurse Tuscola County Health Dept., Caro, Mich., 1978-82, Saginaw County Health Dept., Saginaw, Mich., 1982-86; pub. health nurse, prenatal care program coord. Tuscola County Health Dept., Caro, 1986-87; staff pediatrics St. Josephs Hosp., Elgin, Ill., 1988; pub. health nurse Dupage County Health Dept., Wheaton, Ill., 1988; pub. health nurse DeKalb County Health Dept., DeKalb, Ill., 1988-92, coord. Maternal Child Health program, 1992-93, early intervention health specialist, mem. communicable disease staff, 1993-98; childhood lead program case mgr. quality assurance Kane County Health Dept., Aurora, Ill., 1998—; co-founder, profl. cons. DeKalb County High Risk Parent to Parent Support Group, DeKalb, 1991-93; pvt. practice early intervention specialist. Bd. dirs. Assn. Care of Children's Health, Mich., 1979-81, family com. mem., Chgo., 1975-78; softball coach 7 to 10 yr. old girls Sch. Dist./Park Dist. Youth Softball, Caro, 1979; vol. Kane County Natural Area Vols., Geneva, Ill., 1989—; crisis vol. telephone and support Tuscola County, Caro, 1980-83. Mem. No. Ill. Perinatal Regional (agy. rep. 1988-93). Lutheran. Avocations: reading, camping, photography, environmental preservation, gardening. Office: 113 S Grove Ave Elgin IL 60120

EINHORN, DAVID ALLEN, lawyer; b. Bklyn., Dec. 11, 1961; s. Harold and Jane Ellen (Wiener) E. BA in Computer Sci. magna cum laude, Columbia U., 1983, JD, 1986. Bar: N.Y. 1987, D.C. 1988, U.S. Dist. Ct. (so. and ea. dists.) N.Y. 1989, U.S. Ct. Appeals (fed. cir.) 1992, U.S. Dist. Ct. (no. dist.) Calif. 1994. Assoc. Kaye, Scholer, Fierman, Hays & Handler, N.Y.C., 1986-89; ptnr. Anderson Kill & Olick, PC, N.Y.C., 1989—; columnist Grapevine; lectr. Am. Conf. Inst. Editor-in-chief Law and Technology for the New Millenium, 1997—; contbr. articles to profl. jours. Lt. col. N.Y. Guard, 1987—. Harlan Fiske Stone scholar Columbia U., 1985; recipient Nat. prize Nathan Burkan Copyright Essay Competition, 1985; named to Order of Merit, Les Amis du Vin, 1982. Mem. ABA (chmn. software patent subcom. 1988-91, software licensing subcom. 1991-97, software copyright subcom. 1995-96), Am. Israel Pub. Affairs Com., Am. Intellectual Property Law Assn. (chmn. software copyright subcom. 1999—), N.Y. Intellectual Property Law Assn., Internat. Trademark Assn. (chmn. com. on electronic info. 1994-95), D.C. Bar Assn. (computer law sect.), Columbia Soc. Law and Tech. (pres. 1985-86), Licensing Execs. Soc. (lectr.), N.Y. Soc. Mil. and Naval Officers (v.p. 1995—), Wine Lovers Internat. (v.p., bd. dirs. 1994—, Order of Merit 1997), Tasters Guild (v.p., bd. dirs. 1997—), Untitled Theater Co. #61, Ltd. (chmn. bd. dirs., producing dir., treas. 1994—). Jewish. Democrat. Avocations: tennis, racquetball, wine tasting, marksmanship. Home: 2373 Broadway Apt 802 New York NY 10024-2835 Office: Anderson Kill & Olick PC 1251 Ave of the Americas New York NY 10020-1182

EINHORN, JERZY, internist, endocrinologist, consultant; b. Sosnowiec, Poland, Mar. 17, 1919; s. Oskar Einhorn and Karola (Birman) Mazurkiewicz; m. Jadwiga Piaskowski, Mar. 17, 1946 (div. Apr. 1968); children: Janusz Richard, Robert Krzysztof, Ewa Krystyna; m. Ruth Mary Gregor, May 23, 1968; 1 child, Edward William. MD, Poznan (Poland) Med. Acad., 1951; PhD, Silesia Med. Acad., Katowice, Poland, 1963. Dir. State Endocrinology Consulting Ctr., Katowice, 1954-66; assoc. prof. 3rd Dept. Internal Medicine, Katowice, 1962-66; endocrine rschr. Royal Postgrad. Med. Sch., London, 1965, 67; assoc. prof. U. Pitts. Med. Sch., 1971-94; dir. Hazelwood & Greenfield Cmty. Health Ctrs., Pitts., 1971-84; dir. thyroid screening program U. Pitts. Med. Sch., 1976-93. Contbr. over 35 rsch. articles to profl. jours. Capt. Polish Light Horse Artillery, 1939, Polish Underground Army, 1940-44, Warsaw Uprising, 1944. Recipient Silver Cross of Merit, 1957, Endocrine rsch. awards Polish Endocrine Soc., 1962, 63, 1st Class prize Min. Health, 1967; recipient mil. awards Virtuti Military, 1939, Cross of Valour, 1944, Cross of the Warsaw Uprising, 1944. Avocations: woodworking, photography, horseback riding. Home: 415 Summit Dr Pittsburgh PA 15228-2617

EINHORN, STEPHEN EDWARD, mergers and acquisitions executive, consultant, investment banker; b. Bklyn., June 25, 1943; s. Benjamin and Rosalind (Nuss) R.; m. Nancy Lore, May 22, 1965; children: David, Daniel. BA, Cornell U., 1964; postgrad., U. Pa., 1964-65; MSChemE, Bklyn. Polytech. Inst., 1967. With Adelphi Paint Co., Carlstadt, N.J., 1965-75; pres. Einhorn Assocs., Inc., Milw., 1975—; mergers and acquisitions chem. industry specialist venture capital for LBO and MBO; assoc. Ed Prévost, Toronto, Thilo Kaffenberger-Termen, Switzerland; spkr. Can. Paint Assn., St. Johns, Newfoundland, 1997. Author: If You Try to Please Everybody..., 1983, Employee Stock Option Plans, 1985; contbr. articles to profl. jours.; patentee on handling latex paint, 1978. Chmn. technol. transfer subcom. Cornell U. Trustee Coun.; vol. Milwaukee Art Mus. Avocations: tennis, reading. Home: 8205 N River Rd Milwaukee WI 53217-2546 Office: 2675 N Mayfair Rd Ste 410 Milwaukee WI 53226-1305

EINIGER, CAROL BLUM, investment executive; b. Nov. 30, 1949; d. Bernard Michael and Bella (Karff) Blum; m. Roger William Einiger, Dec. 21, 1969; 1 child. BA, U. Pa., 1970; MBA, Columbia U., 1973. With Conde Nast Publs., N.Y.C., 1970-71, Goldman, Sachs & Co., N.Y.C., 1971-72; with 1st Boston Corp., N.Y.C., 1973-88, mng. dir., 1982-88, head short-term fin. dept., 1983-88, head capital markets dept., 1985-88; vis. prof., exec.-in-residence Columbia U. Bus. Sch., N.Y.C., 1988-89; mng. dir. Wasserstein Perella & Co. Inc., N.Y.C., 1989-92; CFO Edna McConnell Clark Found., N.Y.C., 1992-96; chief investment officer Rockefeller U., N.Y.C., 1996—. Trustee Horace Mann Sch., 1988-94, U. Pa., 1989—, mem. audit, budget and fin., investment, external affairs, and student life coms.; bd. overseers Columbia U. Bus. Sch., 1988—, nominating com.; vice chair investment com. Mus. Modern Art, 1994—. Office: Rockefeller Univ 1230 York Ave New York NY 10021-6399

EINODER, CAMILLE ELIZABETH, secondary education educator, small business owner; b. Chgo., June 15, 1937; d. Isadore and Elizabeth T. (Czerwinski) Popowski; student Fox Bus. Coll., 1954; BEd in Biology, Chgo. Tchrs. Coll., 1964; MA in Analytical Chemistry, Gov.'s State U., 1977; MA in Adminstrn. and Supervision, Roosevelt U., 1986; postgrad 1992—. m. Joseph X. Einoder, Aug. 5, 1978; children: Carl Frank, Mark Frank, Vivian Einoder, Joe Einoder, Tim Einoder, Sheila Einoder, Jude Einoder. Secretarial positions, Chgo., 1955-64; tchr. biology Chgo. Bd. Edn., 1964—, tchr. biology and agr., 1975-81, tchr. biology, agr. and chemistry, 1981—; human rels. coord. Morgan Park High Sch., Chgo., 1980—, tchr. biology Internat. Studies Sch., 1983—, mem. adv. bd., 1989—; owner Einoder Masonry, 1997—, Einoder Antiques, 1996—; career devel. cons. for agr. related curriculum; internat. baccalaureate tchr., Chgo. pub. schs. consulting tchr., 1997. Bd. dirs., founding mem., author constn. Community Coun., 1970—; bd. dirs., edn. cons. Neighborhood Coun., 1974; rep. Chgo. Tchrs. Union, 1969; exec. bd. dir. The Lira Ensemble, 1996—. Mem. AAAS, NSTA, Polish Inst. for Arts and Sci., Am. Chem. Soc., Am. Biology Tchrs. Assn., Nat. Assn. Women Bus. Owners, Copernicus Found., Kosciuszko Soc., Polish Arts Club, Phi Delta Kappa, Iota Sigma Pi. Home: 10637 S Claremont Ave Chicago IL 60643-3101 Office: 1744 W Pryor Ave Chicago IL 60643-3457

EINREINHOFER, NANCY ANNE, art gallery director; b. Paterson, N.J., Sept. 8, 1944; d. John Edward and Nora (Niland) Gleason; m. Robert Einreinhofer, Nov. 26, 1966; 1 child, Robert. BA in Art, William Paterson Coll., 1976, BA in English, 1977, MA in Visual Arts, 1978; cert. in supervisory mgmt., Rutgers U., 1986; PhD in Mus. Studies, Leicester U., England, 1993. Art critic N.J. News, 1973-76; gallery curator O.K. Harris Works of Art, N.Y.C., 1978; dir. gallery William Paterson U., Wayne, N.J., 1979—; bd. dirs. Mus. Council of N.J., 1984—; cons. Sussex County Arts Council, N.J., 1987. Author: The American Art Museum: Elitism and Democracy, 1997; contbr. articles to profl. jours. Recipient grant Nat. Endowment for Arts, 1979, NEH, 1984-85, 87-88, N.J State Ccouncil Arts, 1984-85, 85-86, 87-88. Mem. Am. Assn. Mus., Internat. Council Mus., Mid Atlantic Assn. Mus., Assn. Coll. and U. Mus. Galleries, Mus. Council of N.J. (exec. bd. 1984-88). Home: 1 Cheyenne Trl Sparta NJ 07871-2924 Office: William Paterson U Ben Shahn Galleries Wayne NJ 07470

EINREINHOFER, WILLIAM MICHAEL, JR., television producer and director, educator; b. Rutherford, N.J., Apr. 29, 1952; s. William Michael and Mary Alberta (Louise) E. BA, St. Peter's Coll., Jersey City, 1974; MA, U. Wis., 1976. Prodr. Sta. WNET-TV, PBS, N.Y.C., 1976-78, exec. prodr., 1982-85; sr. prodr. N.J. Pub. TV, PBS, Newark, 1978-82; exec. prodr. Innovation, PBS series, N.Y.C., 1985-96; sr. v.p. China TV Ventures, Chgo., 1996-97; mng. dir. Paradox Comm., N.Y.C., 1997—; host, prodr. Jazz Evolution, syndicated nat. radio series, 1972-78; adj. prof. media Parsons Sch. Design, N.Y.C., 1987-89; adj. honors prof. comm. St. Peter's Coll., 1996—; juror internat. Emmy awards, 1993-97; mem. bd. disting. judges and advisors N.Y. Festivals, juror Best of Festival, 1995—. Contbr. essays to N.Y. Times; exec. prodr. over 100 hours nat. TV programming, various programs, spls. and series, 1986—; prodr., dir. PBS documentary programs, 1985—. Mem. N.J. Peace Action, Montclair, 1982—; bd. dirs. N.J. Film and Video Festival, Newark, 1982-88. Recipient gold medal N.Y. TV and Film Festival, 1984, silver Hugo award Chgo. Internat. Film Festival, 1986, 1st place award Internat. Sci. TV Festival, Paris, 1995. Mem. NATAS (Emmy awards com. N.Y. chpt. 1984-90, Emmy awards 1984, 85, 87), Dirs. Guild Am. (juror documentary award 1994). Avocation: travel and study in Asia with particular emphasis on China and Japan. Fax: 201-659-1273. E-mail: einrein@concentric.net. Office: Paradox Comm 904 Hudson St Hoboken NJ 07030

EINS, STEFAN, painter, conceptual artist, arts curator, sculptor; b. Prague, Bohemia; came to U.S., 1967; s. Stefan and Daisy (Ganghofer) Schmid. MA in Theology, U. Vienna, 1965; BA in Sculpture, Acad. Bildenen Kuenste, Vienna, 1967. Founder, exec. dir. 3 Mercer St, N.Y.C., 1972-79, Fashion Moda, N.Y.C., 1978-84, 88-93; painter, 1980—. Sculptor: prin. works include Variables, 1966. Co-founder chpt. The Audubon Soc., N.Y.C., 1979. Recipient fellowship NEA, 1980, 87. Mem. Collaborative Projects, Inc. (pres. 1988-89). Achievements include research on liquids formation; discovery of formation process of vertebrae, 1985; uncovered stone age artifacts in Austria, 1987-94. Home: PO Box 33 New York NY 10013-0033

EINSEL, DAVID WILLIAM, JR., retired army officer and consultant; b. Tiffin, Ohio, Nov. 4, 1928; s. David William and Naomi Dorothy (Williams) E.; m. Elva yates Aylor, June 16, 1956; children: Susan Vagnier, Mary Kost. BA, MA in Chemistry, Ohio State U., 1950; MSc, U. Va., 1956. Commd. 2d lt. U.S. Army, 1950, advanced through grades to maj. gen., 1980; staff officer Orgn. of the Joint Chiefs of Staff, Washington, 1968-70; comdr. Harry Diamond Labs., Adelphi, Md., 1970-75; chief nuclear-chem. officer hdqrs. Dept. of the Army, Washington, 1975-76; dep. commanding gen. U.S. Army Armament R&D Command Picatinny (N.J.) Arsenal, 1976-80; asst. to sec. of def. Office of the Sec. of Def., Washington, 1980-85; officer Nat. Intelligence Coun., Washington, 1985-89; ret. U.S. Army, 1985; cons. Tiffin, Ohio, 1989—. Author: International Military Encyclopedia, 1991; contbr. article to Jour. Analytical Chemistry. Decorated Silver Star, Bronze Star, Purple Heart; named to U.S. Army Chem. Corps Hall of Fame, 1993; recipient Profl. Achievement award Ohio State U., 1998. Mem. AAAS, Assn. of the U.S. Army, Am. Def. Preparedness Assn., Kiwanis, Masons (33d degree), Phi Beta Kappa, Sigma Xi. Republican. Methodist. Achievements include patent in automatic electrolytic apparatus for determining acid prodn. rates. Home and Office: 594 S Washington St Tiffin OH 44883-3320

EINSPRUCH, BURTON CYRIL, psychiatrist; b. N.Y.C., June 27, 1935; s. Adolph and Mala (Goldblatt) E.; B.A., So. Meth. U., 1956, Sc.B., 1958; M.D., Southwestern Med. Sch., Dallas, 1960; m. Barbara Standen Traeger, Oct. 9, 1960; children: Julia E. Lewis, Alexander Louis, Robert Sands. Intern, Montefiore Hosp., N.Y.C., 1960-61; resident Nat. Hosp. Inst. Neurology, London, 1962, U. Tex., Dallas, 1961-64 (also fellow); sr. resident Parkland Meml. Hosp., Dallas, 1964; instr. psychiatry U. Pa., 1964-66; pvt. practice psychiatry, Dallas, 1966—; mem. staff Presbyn. and Parkland hosps., Timberlawn Psychiat. Hosp.; clin. asst. prof. U. Tex., Health Sci. Center, Dallas, 1966-70, dir. psychiat. div. Student Health Service, 1966-72, clin. assoc. prof., 1970—; dir. Southwestern Adult Psychiat. Clinic, Dallas, 1966-74; dir. psychiat. service Dallas Home for Jewish Aged, 1966-82, now cons. staff dir. Dallas Nat. Bank; research cons. Dallas Geriatric Research Inst., 1974-80; adj. prof. sociology N. Tex. State U., Denton, 1975-82; cons. staff Baylor U. Hosp., Golden Acres Hosp.; clin. prof. psychiatry U. Tex. Health Scis. Ctr., Dallas, 1971—; prof. psychiatry U. Tex. Southwestern Med. Ctr., Dallas, 1971—; bd. dirs., founder Dallas Nat. Bank; clin. assoc. prof. psychiatry NYU Med. Ctr., N.Y.C., 1990-96; chmn., bd. dirs. Planned Behavioral Health Care, Inc., Dallas; affiliate Tex. Inst. Rsch. and Edn. on Aging, Health Sci. Ctr. Fort Worth; Mem. editorial bd. Tex. Medicine. Bd. dirs. Mental Health Assn. Dallas, 1960-69, Jewish Family Service, 1969-71, 73-75. Trustee Evans Fedn., N.Y.C., 1986—, St. Mark's Sch. Tex., 1987—, Jaffe Collection McDermott Libr., U. Tex., Dallas, 1987—; mem. exec. bd. libr. So. Meth. U., 1992—; adv. dir. Leonhardt Fedn., N.Y.C., 1990, Children of Alcoholics Fedn., 1991; arbitrator, N.Y. and Am. Exchs., N.Y.C., 1884—; bd. dirs. Wyndham Internat. Served to lt. comdr. M.C., USNR, 1964-66. Diplomate Am. Bd. Psychiatry and Neurology (examiner, 1974—). Fellow Am. Psychiat. Assn., Am. Coll. Psychiatrists, Am. Soc. Adolescent Psychiatry, N. Tex. Soc. Adolescent Psychiatry (past pres.); mem. Royal Coll. Psychiatry London, AMA, Tex. Med. Assn. Contbr. profl. jours. Home: 3505 Lindenwood Ave Dallas TX 75205-3229 Office: 8330 Meadow Rd Ste 117 Dallas TX 75231-3750.

EINSPRUCH, NORMAN GERALD, physicist, educator; b. N.Y.C., June 27, 1932; s. Adolph and Mala (Goldblatt) E.; m. Edith Melnick, Dec. 20, 1953; children—Eric, Andrew, Franklin. B.A. in Physics, Rice U., 1953; M.S. in Physics, U. Colo., 1955; Ph.D. in Applied Math, Brown U., 1959. Mem. tech. staff, central research labs. Tex. Instruments, Inc., Dallas, 1959-62; mgr. electron transport physics br., central research labs. Tex. Instruments, Inc., 1962-68, dir. advanced tech. lab., central research labs., 1968-69, dir. tech., chem. materials div., 1969-72, dir. central research labs., 1972-75, asst. v.p., 1975-77, mgr. corp. devel., 1975-76, mgr. tech. and planning consumer products, 1976-77; prof. dept. elec. and computer engring. Coll. Engring. U. Miami, Coral Gables, Fla., 1977—; dean Coll. Engring. U. Miami, 1977-90, sr. fellow in sci. and tech., 1990—, chmn. dept. indsl. engring., 1994-99; chmn. panel on thin film microstructure sci. and tech. NRC, 1978-79, mem. panel on impact of Dod bery high speed integrated crcts. program, 1980-81, panel on edn. and utilization of the engr., 1981-82; bd. dirs. Ogden Corp. Author: Electronic Genie: The Tangled History of Silicon, 1998 editor: (series) VLSI Electronics: Microstructure Science, 24 vols., VLSI Handbook, 1985; contbr. articles to profl. jours. Recipient George Washington Honor medal Freedoms Found. Valley Forge. Fellow Am. Phys. Soc., Acoustical Soc. Am., IEEE, AAAS; mem. Inst. of Indsl. Engrs. (sr.), Am. Soc. Engring. Edn., Golden Key, Iron Arrow, Sigma Xi, Omicron Delta Kappa, Tau Beta Pi, Eta Kappa Nu, Phi Kappa Phi, Alpha Pi Mu, Tau Sigma Delta. Home: 1415 Trillo Ave Miami FL 33146-2312 Office: U Miami Coll Engring PO Box 248581 Coral Gables FL 33124-8581

EINSTEIN, ALBERT See BROOKS, ALBERT

EINSTEIN, CLIFFORD JAY, advertising executive; b. L.A., May 4, 1939; s. Harry and Thelma (Bernstein) E.; m. Madeline Mandel, Jan. 28, 1962; children: Harold Jay, Karen Holly. BA in English, UCLA, 1961. Writer Norman, Craig and Kummel, N.Y.C., 1961-62, Foote, Cone and Belding, L.A., 1962-64; ptnr. Silverman and Einstein, L.A., 1965-67; pres., creative dir. Dailey and Assos., L.A., 1968-93, chmn., CEO, 1994—, also bd dirs.; dir. Campaign '80, advt. agy. Reagan for Pres., 1980; lectr. various colls.; founder, bd. dirs. First Coastal Bank; bd. dirs. The Jewish Cmty. Found. Contbr. articles to Advertising Age; prodr.: (play) Whatever Happened to Georgie Tapps, L.A. and San Francisco, 1980; film appearances include Real Life, Modern Romance, Defending Your Life, Face/Off, 1997; T.V. appearance in Bizarre, Super Dave Show. Bd. dirs. Rape Treatment Ctr., Santa Monica Med. Ctr., Discovery Fund for Eye Rsch.; trustee Mus. Contemporary Art, L.A., 1994—. With U.S. Army, 1957. Recipient Am. Advt. award, 1968, 73, 79, Clio award, 1973, Internat. Broadcast Pub. Svc. award, 1970, 85, Nat. Addy award, 1979, Gov.'s award, 1987; named Creative Dir. of the West, Adweek Poll, 1982, Exec. of West, 1986, Western States Assn. Advt. Agys. Leader of Yr., 1992. Mem. AFTRA, ASCAP, SAG, Dirs. Guild Am., Am. Assn. Advt. Agys. (vice chmn. western region), Hillcrest Country Club, Calif. Club. Office: Dailey & Assocs 8687 Melrose Ave West Hollywood CA 90069-5701

EINSTEIN, STEPHEN JAN, rabbi; b. L.A., Nov. 15, 1945; s. Syd C. and Selma (Rothenberg) E.; m. Robin Susan Kessler, Sept. 9, 1967; children: Rebecca Yael, Jennifer Melissa, Heath Isaac, Zachary Shane. AB, UCLA, 1967; BHL, Hebrew Union Coll., L.A., 1968, DHL, 1995; MAHL, Hebrew Union Coll., Cin., 1971; DD (hon.), Hebrew Union Coll., Los Angeles, 1971. Ordained rabbi. Rabbi Temple Beth Am, Parsippany, N.J., 1971-74; rabbi Temple Beth David, Westminster, Calif., 1974-76, Congregation B'nai Tzedek, Fountain Valley, Calif., 1976—. Co-author: Every Person's Guide to Judaism, 1989; co-editor: Introduction to Judaism, 1983. Pres., trustee Fountain Valley (Calif.) Sch. Bd., 1984-90; chair Pers. Commn. Fountain Valley Sch. Dist., 1991—; chaplain Fountain Valley Police Dept. Honored for Maj. Contributions to Jewish Learning, Orange County (Calif.) Bur. Jewish Edn., 1986; recipient Micah Award for Interfaith Activities, Am. Jewish Com., 1988. Mem. Ctrl. Conf. Am. Rabbis (mem. exec. bd. 1989-91, mem. ethics com. 1993-98), Pacific Assn. Reform Rabbis (mem. exec. bd. 1987-91, 97—), Orange County Bd. Rabbis (pres. 1976-79, 97-98), Jewish Educators Assn. Orange County (pres. 1979-81), Orange County Bur. Jewish Edn. (v.p. 1982-84, 92-94, pres. 1994-97), Am. Cancer Soc. (v.p. West Orange County dist. 1994-98, co-chair Commn. on Reform Jewish Outreach 1999—), Phi Beta Kappa. Democrat. Office: Congregation Bnai Tzedek 9669 Talbert Ave Fountain Valley CA 92708

EIRICH, FREDERICK ROLAND, chemist, educator; b. Vienna, Austria, May 23, 1905; came to U.S., 1947, naturalized, 1953; s. Otto George and Hermine (Perlhefter) E.; m. Maria Dorothea Dehne, Feb. 1, 1936; children: Ursula D., Richard S. Moeller, Susan H. Ph.D., U. Vienna, 1929, Dr. Phil. habil., 1938; M.A., U. Cambridge, Eng., 1939. Research asso., lectr. U. Vienna, 1934- 38, U. Cambridge, 1939-47; mem. faculty Poly. Inst., Bklyn., 1948—; prof. Poly. Inst., 1952—; distinguished prof., 1969—, dean research, 1967-70; vis. prof. U. Uppsala, 1950; Unilever prof. U. Bristol, 1965; vis. scientist Lab. Chem. Evolution, U. Md., 1985—; cons. Govt. Com. Chems., Plastics and Rubber Industry. Author, editor numerous books and research papers. Recipient A. Humboldt Found. award, 1980; Bingham Medal, 1983, M. Huggins award, 1985. Fellow N.Y. Acad. Sci. (chmn. chem. sect. 1952-53), Faraday Soc., Internat. Inst. Fracture Mechanics (hon.); mem. Am. Chem. Soc. (chmn. colloid div. 1960, Distinguished Service award 1975, Merit award Rubber Div. 1978), AAAS (chmn., councillor Gordon Confs. 1959-65), Soc. Rheology (pres. 1972-73), Am. Phys. Soc. (gov. bd. 1970-74), Sigma Xi (research award 1970). Home: Meadow Lks Apt 45-01 Hightstown NJ 08520-3354 Office: Poly U Bklyn Campus 6 Metrotech Ctr Brooklyn NY 11201-3840

EISCH, JOHN JOSEPH, chemist, educator, consultant; b. Milw., Nov. 5, 1930; s. Frank Joseph and Gladys (Riordan) E.; m. Joan Terese Scheuerell, Sept. 5, 1953; children: Margaret (dec.), Karla, Paula, Joseph, Amelia. BS summa cum laude, Marquette U., 1952, PhD, 1956; P&G fellow, Iowa State U., 1956. Postdoctoral Union Carbide fellow Max Planck Inst. für Kohlenforschung, Mülheim, Germany, 1956-57; rsch. assoc. European Rsch. Assocs., Brussels, 1957; mem. faculty St. Louis U., 1957-59; faculty U. Mich., 1959-63, Cath. U. Am., Washington, 1963-72; chmn. dept. chemistry SUNY, Binghamton, 1972-78, prof., 1972—, disting. prof., 1983—; sr. rsch. fellow Japan Soc. for Promotion of Sci., 1979, Alexander von Humboldt Found., Germany, 1993-96; cons. in field, 1957—; legal expert witness. Author: The Chemistry of Organometallic Compounds, 1967, (with R. B. King) Organometallic Syntheses, Vol. I, 1965, Vol. II, 1981, Vol. III, 1986, Vol. IV, 1988; contbr. more than 300 articles to profl. publs.; patentee in field. Mem. Am. Chem. Soc., Am. Inst. Chemists, Sigma Xi, Phi Lambda Upsilon, Phi Kappa Phi. Republican. Roman Catholic. Achievements include research and publs. on the synthesis and properties of organometallic compounds (those with carbon-metal bonds) and heterocycles, with emphasis on the kinetics and stereochemistry of carbon-metal bond and hydrogen-metal bond additions to olefins, acetylenes; radical-anion, nonbenzenoid aromatic studies, photochemistry of organometallics; catalytic processes of polymerization, heteroatom removal, isomerizations and prebiotic organic synthesis. E-mail: jjeisch@binghamton.edu. Fax: 607-777-4865. Home: 212 Sheedy Rd Vestal NY 13850-5905 Office: SUNY Binghamton Dept Chemistry Binghamton NY 13902-6000

EISCHEN, MICHAEL HUGH, retired railroad executive; b. Chgo., Apr. 28, 1931; s. Michael A. and Marie (Tennent) E.; m. Rita A. Donohoe, Nov. 17, 1959; children: Mary Pat, Michael, James, Kathleen, Timothy, Denis. BS in Commerce, Loyola U., Chgo., 1957. Auditor Arthur Andersen & Co., Chgo., 1957-59; with Chgo. and N. Western Transp. Co., Chgo., 1959—, mgr. expenditures, 1975-84, asst. v.p. expenditures, 1985-88, v.p. and comptr., 1988-90; ret., 1990. Mem. bd. St. Hilary's Sch., Chgo., 1969; mem. fin. com. St. Hilary's Sch. and Ch., Chgo., 1970; mem. handball com. YMCA, Evanston, 1965-75. With USMC, 1951-53. Mem. Assn. Am. RR (chmn. 1982-83), Chgo. Disbursements Com., Tower Club. Republican. Roman Catholic. Avocations: handball, golf, fishing, gardening.

EISDORFER, CARL, psychiatrist, health care executive; b. Bronx, N.Y., June 20, 1930. B.A., NYU, 1951, M.A., 1953, Ph.D., 1959; M.D., Duke U., 1964; postgrad. in health systems mgmt., Harvard U., 1981. Lectr. in psychology Duke U. Med. Ctr., Durham, N.C., 1959-72, intern in medicine, 1964-65, psychiat. trainee, 1964-67, dir. tng., research coordinator Ctr. for Study Aging and Human Devel., 1965-70, prof. psychiatry and med. psychology, 1968-72, dir. med. studies behavioral scis. program, 1970-72, head div. med. psychology dept. psychiatry, 1970-72, dir. Ctr. for Study Aging and Human Devel., 1970-72; founding dir. Inst. on Aging, U. Wash., Seattle, 1977-79, prof., chmn. dept. psychiatry and behavioral scis. Sch. of Medicine, adj. prof. psychology, 1972-81; sr. scholar in residence Inst. Medicine, Nat. Acad. Scis., Washington, 1979-80; prof. psychiatry and neurosci. Albert Einstein Coll. Medicine, N.Y.C., 1981-85; chief exec. officer Montefiore Med. Ctr., N.Y.C., 1981-85; prof., chmn. dept. psychiatry U. Miami, Fla., 1986—; also dir. Ctr. on Adult Devel. and Aging U. Miami; chief div. mental health Jackson Meml. Med. Ctr., 1986—; coordinator Community Mental Health Services, Halifax County N.C., 1969-70; vis. prof. U. Calif., 1969-70, U. Calif.-Berkeley, 1969-70; H.T. Dozer vis. prof. geriatrics and psychiatry Ben Gurion U., Negev, Israel, 1980; cons. NIH, Bethesda, Md., Robert Wood Johnson Found., numerous others. Editor in chief Ann. Rev. Gerontology and Geriatrics, 1978—; cons. editor Ency. of Aging, 1984—; mem. editorial bd. Alzheimers Disease and Related Disorders-Internat. Jour., Aging and Human Devel., Western Jour. Medicine, Neurobiology of Aging: Exptl. and Clin. Research; contbr. numerous articles to profl. jours.; also books. Served with U.S. Army, 1954-56. Recipient Kesten award Ethel Percy Andrus Gerontology Ctr., U. So. Calif., 1976, Potamkin prize, 1982, Disting. Alumnus award Duke U. Sch. of Medicine, 1985. Fellow Soc. Behavioral Medicine, N.Y. Acad. Medicine, Am. Psychol. Assn. (chmn. div. adult devel. and aging 1970-71, task force on aging 1971-73, award for disting. contbns. 1981, award for contbns. on aging research 1985), Gerontol. Soc. Am. (pres. 1971-72, Robert W. Kleemeier award 1969, Joseph Freeman award div. clin. medicine 1979), Am. Geriatrics Soc. (Edward B. Allen award 1974, Edward Henderson Meml. award 1988), Am. Psychiat. Assn. (Jack Weinberg Meml. award 1984), Am. Coll. Psychiatrists, Am. Coll. Physicians (Menniger award 1990), AAAS; mem. Am. Soc. Aging (pres. 1980-82), Am. Fed. Aging Res. (pres. 1986-88), Sigma Xi, Alpha Omega Alpha. Office: U Miami Sch Medicine Dept Psychiatry D-28 PO Box 016960 # D28 Miami FL 33101-6960

EISELE, GARNETT THOMAS, federal judge; b. Hot Springs, Ark., Nov. 3, 1923; s. Garnett Martin and Mary (Martin) E.; m. Kathryn Freygang, June 24, 1950; children: Wendell A., Garnett Martin II, Kathryn M., Jean E. Student, U. Fla., 1940-42, Ind. U., 1942-43; AB, Washington U., 1947; LLB, Harvard U., 1950, LLM, 1951. Bar: Ark. 1951. Practiced in Hot Springs, 1951-52, Little Rock, 1953-69; assoc. Wootten, Land and Matthews, 1951-52, Owens, McHaney, Lofton & McHaney, 1956-60; asst. U.S. atty. Little Rock, 1953-55; pvt. practice law, 1961-69; judge U.S. Dist. Ct. (ea. dist.) Ark., 1970—, chief judge, 1975-91, sr. judge, 1991—; legal adviser to gov. Ark., 1966-69. Del. Ark. 7th Constl. Conv., 1969-70; trustee U. Ark., 1969-70. Served with AUS, 1943-46, ETO. Mem. ABA, Ark. Bar Assn., Pulaski County Bar Assn., Am. Judicature Soc., Am. Law Inst. Office: US Dist Ct PO Box 3684 Little Rock AR 72203-3684

EISELE, MILTON DOUGLAS, viticulturist; b. N.Y.C., Apr. 2, 1910; s. Charles Francis and Helen Agnes (Dolan) E.; B.A., U. Calif.-Berkeley, 1933; grad. San Francisco Stock Exch. Inst., 1938; m. Barbara Lois Morgan, July 26, 1941; children: Helen Frances Eisele Osthimer, Barbara Glennis, William Douglas. Investment cashier Wells Fargo Bank, San Francisco, 1934-39; coordinator cement sales Permanente Corp., 1940-41, constrn. supt., 1941-43; mgr. refractory div. Kaiser Aluminum, 1943-47, mgr. regional sales, Chgo., 1947-50, mgr. foil div., 1950-55, mgr. prodn., 1955-60, mgr. market and prodn. devel., 1960-65, mgr. investments, 1966-71; ret., 1971; former owner, operator Eisele Vineyards, Napa Valley, Calif., 1969-89. Dir., former pres. Napa Valley Found., 1981-85; bd. dirs., past chmn. Vintage Hall, Inc., 1973-85; bd. dirs., pres. Napa Valley Heritage Fund, 1973—; past pres., bd. dirs. Upper Napa Valley Assocs., 1976-80; mem. adv. coun. Napa County Land Trust, 1976-79; mem. Napa County Grand Jury, 1988-89, hon. co-chmn. 150th anny. planting first grapes. Mem. Am. Soc. Enologists, Napa Valley Grape Growers Assn. (dir.), Calif. Assn. Wine Grape Growers (dir., former sec., chmn. 1986-87), Calif. Vintage Wine Soc. (bd. dirs., pres. 1994—), Agrl. Coun. of Napa County, Wine and Winegrape Mktg. Order State of Calif. (dir. 1984), Napa Valley Growers and Vinters (chmn. bd. dirs., mktg. and promotion com. 1985—), Marin County Wine & Food Soc., Kappa Alpha Order. Republican. Episcopalian (vestryman, sr. warden 1966-69). Home and Office: PO Box 687 1865 St Helen Hwy Rutherford CA 94573

EISELT, MICHAEL HERBERT, optics scientist; b. Oldenburg, Germany, Jan. 25, 1963; s. Theodor and Ursula (Eiselt) Wuerdemann; m. Renate Viktoria Marianne Helm, Aug. 21, 1992. Diploma in elec. engring., U. Hannover, Germany, 1989; DEng, Tech. U. Berlin, 1994. Rsch. staff Heinrich-Hertz Inst., Berlin, 1989-97; prin. tech. staff mem. AT&T Labs Rsch., Red Bank, N.J., 1997—; vis. rschr. AT&T Bell Labs Rsch., 1995-96. Patentee in field. With German Army, 1982-83. Mem. IEEE (sr. mem.), Optical Soc. Am. Avocation: fencing. Fax: 732-345-3037. Office: AT&T Labs Rsch 100 Schulz Dr Red Bank NJ 07701

EISEN, ERIC ANSHEL, lawyer; b. N.Y.C., Apr. 9, 1950; s. Morton and Victoria (Goldstein) E.; m. Claire L. Shapiro, Jan. 6, 1979; children: Rebecca, Jennifer, Melissa. AB, U. Mich., 1971, JD magna cum laude, 1975. Bar: Alaska 1976, D.C. 1977, Md. 1988. Law clk. to presiding justice Alaska Supreme Ct., Fairbanks, 1975-76; assoc. Covington & Burling, Washington, 1976-81; assoc. Birch, Horton, Bittner, Washington, 1981-85, ptnr., 1985-93; ptnr. Eisen Law Offices, Bethesda, Md., 1993—; speaker various seminars and colloquia on energy and bus. matters. Contbr. articles legal publs. Pres. Wildwood Hills Citizens Assn., Bethesda, Md., 1987—; sec. N. Bethesda Cong. Citizens Assns., 1989-90. Mem. Fed. Bar Assn., Fed. Energy Bar Assn., D.C. Bar Assn., Montgomery County Bar Assn., Toastmasters, Order of Coif. Avocation: woodworking. Office: Eisen Law Office 10028 Woodhill Rd Bethesda MD 20817-1218

EISEN, GLENN PHILIP, management consultant, teacher; b. Chgo., Feb. 8, 1940; s. Sol Eisen and Lorraine (Winsberg) Lukinsky; m. Devera Arne Chiz, May 7, 1961 (div. 1974); children: Julia, Steven; m. Barbara Baxter McNear, June 7, 1987. BS in Indsl. Mgmt., Ill. Inst. Tech., 1972. Cert. mgmt. cons. Prodn. supr. Intercraft Industries, Chgo., 1961-64; sr. buyer Simoniz Co., Chgo., 1964-65; purchasing/packaging mgr. Paper Mate div. Gillette, La Grange Park, Ill., 1965-69; assoc. The Packaging House Inc., Chgo., 1969-73; cons. Israel Inst. of Packaging, Tel Aviv, 1973-74; prin. The Emerson Cons., N.Y.C., 1975-80, Arthur Andersen & Co., Chgo., 1980-87; chief exec. officer The Eisen Group, Wilton, Conn., 1987-96; prin. The Omega Cons., LLC, 1996—; internat. comml. arbitrator Am. Arbitration Assn., N.Y.C., 1985—. Author: Purchasing Negotiations, 1983, Group Buying in Health Care, 1985, Supply Market Management, 1989, Maximizing Your Value When Using Management Consultants, 1992, Ethical Practices and Conflicts of Interest Benchmark Study, 1994, Procurement Best Practices, 1997, Maintenance Planning and Management Best Practices, 1998; assoc. editor: In Bound Logistics Mag., 1990. With U.S. Army, 1958-61. Mem. The Australia Soc., Kiwanis Internat. Jewish. Office: The Omega Cons LLC 23 Telva Rd Wilton CT 06897-3733

EISEN, HERMAN NATHANIEL, immunology researcher, medical educator; b. Bklyn., Oct. 15, 1918; m. Natalie Aronson, 1948; 5 children. AB, NYU, 1939, MD, 1943. Asst. in pathology Coll. Physicians and Surgeons, Columbia U., N.Y.C., 1944-46; NIH fellow Coll. Medicine, NYU, 1947-48, fellow in chemistry, 1948-49, asst. prof. indsl. medicine, 1949-53, assoc. prof., 1953-55; prof. medicine Sch. Medicine, Washington U., St. Louis, 1955-61; dermatologist-in-chief Barnes Hosp., St. Louis, 1955-61; prof. microbiology, head dept. Sch. Medicine Washington U., St. Louis, 1961-73; prof. MIT, Cambridge, 1973-82, Whitehead Inst. prof. immunology, 1982-89; prof. emeritus, 1989—; mem. adv. bd. Mass. Gen. Hosp., Yale Med. Sch., Harvard Sch. Pub. Health, Children's Hosp., Boston, Merck, Sharpe and Dohme Rsch. Labs., Roche Inst. for Molecular Biology, Howard Hughes Med. Inst. Recipient Outstanding Investigator award Nat. Cancer Inst., NIH, 1986-93, Dupont award Clin. Ligand Soc., 1987, Med. Sci. Achievement award NYU, 1978, others. Mem. Nat. Acad. Sci. (editl. bd. Proceedings of the NAS), Am. Assn. Physicians, Inst. Medicine, Am. Acad. Arts and Scis., Am. Assn. Immunologists (pres. 1968, Behring-Heidelberger award 1993). Office: MIT Ctr Cancer Rsch E17-128 77 Massachusetts Ave Cambridge MA 02139-4307*

EISEN, HOWARD JOEL, physician, researcher; b. Forest Hills, N.Y., May 25, 1956; s. Ezra Michael and Gertrude Margaret (Schmidt) E.; m. Judith Ellen Wolf, June 26, 1983; children: Jonathan Ezra, Miriam Sarah. BA in Biology, Cornell U., 1977; MD, U. Pa., 1981. Diplomate Am. Bd. Med. Examiners, Am. Bd. Internal Medicine, Am. Bd. Cardiovascular Diseases. Med. intern Hosp. U. Pa., Phila., 1981-82, resident in medicine, 1982-84; fellow in cardiology Washington U. Sch. Medicine-Barnes Hosp., St. Louis, 1984-87; asst. prof. medicine U. Pa., Phila., 1990-93; assoc. prof. medicine and physiology Temple U., Phila., 1993-97, prof. medicine and physiology, 1997—, dir. heart failure care unit, 1993-99, med. dir. cardiac transplant program, 1993-99, assoc. dir. Gen. Clin. Rsch. Ctr., 1995—, med. dir. Cardiomyopathy and Transplant Ctr., 1999—, med. dir. advanced heart failure and transplant program, 1999—; mem. cryptosporidiosis adv. com. Dept. Pub. Health, Phila., 1995—. Fellow ACP, Am. Coll. Cardiology, Am. Heart Assn. (clin. coun., mem. rsch. com. 1995—, chmn. peer-review com. 1996—, Established Investigatorship award 1996—, grant-in-aid, Dallas 1990—); mem. Am. Fedn. Clin. Rsch. (mem. nat. coun. 1992-95, H. Christian award 1993, ea. chmn. 1993-94), Internat. Soc. Heart and Lung Transplantation, Phi Beta Kappa, Alpha Omega Alpha. Avocations: reading, rowing, classical music, running. Home: 507 Shortridge Dr Wynnewood PA 19096-1609 Office: Temple U Sch Medicine 3401 N Broad St # 9pp Philadelphia PA 19140-5103

EISEN, LEONARD, food and retail company executive; b. Toronto, Ont., Can., Oct. 14, 1934; s. Harry Mendle and Anne Miriam (Grossman) E.; m. Merle Faye Dover, June 18, 1958; children: Rhonda Lynn Eisen Shore, Beth Francis. Chartered Acct., Inst. Chartered Accts. Ont., Toronto, 1957; BA in Econs., York U., Toronto, 1977. Chartered acct. Mgr. corp. fin. Vise, Rumack, Seigel, Kurtz & Co., Toronto, 1960-63; ptnr. Bernard C. Kurtz & Co., Toronto, 1963-64; v.p. fin. and adminstrn. WIMCO Steel Sales Ltd., Toronto, 1964-68; v.p. fin., dir. Toronto Iron Works Ltd., 1965-68; dir. corp. acctg. The Oshawa Group Ltd., Toronto, 1968-70, asst. treas., 1970-74, treas., 1974-99. Bd. govs., treas., mem. audi com., chmn. budget and fin. coms. Beth Tzedec Synagogue, Toronto, 1983—, treas., 1999—. Fellow Inst. Chartered Accts. Ont.; mem. Can. Tax Found. (bd. govs., chmn. audit and fin. com. 1984-87, chmn. investment com. 1984—), Retail Coun. Can. (chmn. tax com., retail payments com.), Tax Execs. Inst. *

EISEN, RICH, reporter; b. N.Y.C., June 24, 1969. BA in Comms., U. Mich., 1990; MS in Broadcast Journalism, Northwestern U., 1994. Staff writer S.I. Advance, 1990-93; stringer pub. h.s. football and basketball Chgo. Tribune, 1993-94; prodn. asst. CBS Evening News with Dan Rather and Connie Chung, 1994; corr. Medill News Svc., Washington, 1994; sports anchor/reporter Sta. KRCR-RV, Redding, Calif., 1994-96; anchor/reporter SportsCenter ESPN, 1996—. Office: c/o ESPN ESPN Plz 935 Middle St Bristol CT 06010*

EISEN, STEVEN LESLIE, neurologist; b. N.Y.C., July 15, 1940; s. Sidney and Bernice Leffert E.; m. Emily Littman, July 23, 1967; 1 child, Andrew Wallace. BS, Union Coll., 1962; MD, Albany Med. Coll., 1966. Intern Montefiore Hosp., Bronx, N.Y., 1966-67; resident Albert Einstein Coll. Medicine, Bronx, 1967-70; attendint neurologist Waterbury (Conn.) Hosp., 1970—, St. Mary's Hosp., Waterbury, 1970—; chief staff Waterbury Hosp., 1999, chief medicine, 1988-94. Chmn. Planning Commn., Bethlehem, Conn., 1976-79. Avocations: fishing, sailing. Office: 1211 W Main St Waterbury CT 06708

EISENBERG, ADI, chemist; b. Wroclaw (Breslau), formerly Germany, Feb. 18, 1935; emigrated to U.S., 1951; s. Oscar and Helene E.; m. Sandra M. Kloner, June 9, 1957 (div. 1985); 1 son, Elliot. BSc, Worcester Poly. Inst., 1957; MA, Princeton U., 1959, PhD, 1960. Postdoctoral fellow U. Basel, Switzerland, 1961-62; asst. prof. chemistry UCLA, 1962-67; assoc. prof. chemistry McGill U., Montreal, Que., Can., 1967-74; prof. McGill U., 1975—; dir. Polymer McGill, 1991—, Otto Maass Prof. Chemistry, 1993—; cons. in field. Author 7 books in field; contbr. articles to profl. jours. NATO fellow, 1961-62; Killam Research fellow, 1987-88; recipient E.W.R. Steacie award, 1998. Fellow Am. Phys. Soc (chmn. div. high polymer physics 1975-76), Chem. Inst. Can. (Dunlop award 1988, E.W.R. Steacie award 1998); mem. Am. Chem. Soc., Sigma Xi. Achievements include patents in field. Office: McGill University, 801 Sherbrooke St W, Montreal, PQ Canada H3A 2K6

EISENBERG, ALAN, professional society administrator; b. N.Y.C., Apr. 15, 1935; s. Arthur and Mollie (Novak) E.; m. Rebecca Cooper, July 14, 1972 (div. May 19, 1980); m. Claire Copley, May 23, 1982; children: Mollie Copley, Emma Copley. AB, U. Mich., 1956; LLB, NYU, 1959. Bar: N.Y., Va., D.C. Assoc. Booth, Lipton & Lipton, N.Y.C., 1960, Hirson & Bertini, N.Y.C., 1960-64; atty. NLRB, Washington and Chgo., 1964-68; assoc. Seligman & Seligman, N.Y.C., 1968-72; ptnr. Eisenberg & Paul, Arlington, Va., 1972-81; exec. dir. Actors' Equity Assn., N.Y.C., 1981—; vis. prof. theatre adminstrn. Yale U. Sch. Drama, New Haven, 1982—; adj. faculty Sch. of Arts Columbia U., 1995-98. Gen. v.p. dept. for profl. employees AFL-CIO; dir. Actor's Equity Found., Non Traditional Casting Project, Inc., Career Transition for Dancers, Times Square Bus. Improvement Dist.; trustee Equity League Pension and Health Funds, Actors' Fund of Am.; trustee, v.p. Broadway Cares, Equity Fights AIDS. Office: Actors' Equity Assn 165 W 46th St New York NY 10036-2501

EISENBERG, ALBERT CHARLES, federal agency administrator; b. Jersey City, Oct. 15, 1946; s. Albert Simon and Henrietta (Kirschner) E.; m. Sharon Eileen Davis, Jan. 10, 1976; children: Matthew Davis, Alexander Davis. BA, U. Richmond, Va., 1968; MA, Hampton (Va.) U., 1971. Tchr. intern Nat. Tchr. Corps, Hampton, 1969-71; tchr. Chesapeake (Va.) City Schs., 1970-74; campaign dir. Robert Richards for Congress, Norfolk, Va., 1974; legis. asst. Office of U.S. Senator Harrison A. Williams, Jr., Washington, 1975-79; staff dir. U.S. Senate Subcom. on Housing and Urban Affairs, Washington, 1979-82; dir. fed. legis. affairs AIA, Washington, 1982-96; dep. dir., cons. Nat. Pks. and Conservation Assn., Washington, 1996-98; dep. asst. sec. for transp. policy U.S. Dept. of Transp., Washington, 1999—. Mem. Arlington (Va.) County Bd., 1984-99, chmn., 1987, 90, 95, 99, vice chmn., 1986, 89, 94, 98; mem. Lyon Pk. and Ashton Heights Civic Assns., 1983—; chmn. No. Va. Transp. Commn., Arlington, 1998; mem. Washington Met. Govts. Transp. Planning Bd., 1992-99, chmn. pub. safety policy com., 1984-86, chmn. land use and met. devel. policy coms., 1992-93; mem. No. Va. Transp. Coordinating Coun., Fairfax, 1992-99, No. Va. Planning Dist. Commn., 1984-99, chmn., 1995-97; commr. Va. Housing Devel. authority, Richmond, 1991-96, Arlington Tenant-Landlord Commn., 1977-79; mem. Arlington County Cmty. Devel. Citizens Adv. Commn., 1977-79; chmn. Arlington United Way Social Planning Com., 1981-83; co-founder, convenor No. Va. Housing Coalition, Fairfax, 1986-99; co-founder, vice chmn. Washington Area Housing Partnership, 1991-95; various offices Arlington County Dem. Com., 1975—, Va. Young Dems.; mem., sec. 10th Dist. Dem. Com., Arlington, 1981-84; mem. Va. State Dem. Ctrl. Com., Richmond, 1981-84; del. Va. State Dem. Conv., 1972, 76, 79, 84, 85, 89, 92, 93, Dem. Nat. Conv., N.Y.C., 1992; sec. Norfolk (Va.) Dem. Com., 1972-73. Recipient Bronze Good Citizenship medal Nat. Soc. SAR, 1986, Elizabeth and David Scull Pub. Svc. award Washington Met. Coun. Govts., 1992, Recognition of Leadership award Arlington Heritage Alliance, 1995; named Citizen of Yr., Arlington-Fairfax Elks, 1990, Citizen Ptnr. of Yr., Arlington Housing corp., 1990. Mem. Arlington C. of C., Arlington Hist. Soc., Arlington County NAACP, No. Va. Urban League. Jewish. Avocations: Civil War research and memorabilia, political activities.

EISENBERG, BERTRAM WILLIAM, lawyer; b. Phoenix, Feb. 22, 1930; s. Louis and Mary Ethel (Fiddle) E.; m. Carlene Brown, Feb. 28, 1953; children: Stephen W., Lawrence D. AB, Syracuse U., 1948; LLB, Harvard U., 1951. Bar: N.Y. 1951, U.S. Dist. Ct. (so. dist.) N.Y. 1973. Assoc. Harrison & Coughlin, Binghamton, N.Y., 1954-60; ptnr. Appelbaum & Eisenberg, Liberty, N.Y., 1960-95, Eisenberg & Kirsch, Liberty, N.Y., 1995—. Served as 1st lt. JAGC, 1951-54. Office: Eisenberg & Kirsch PO Box 715 Liberty NY 12754-0715

EISENBERG, CAROLA, psychiatry educator; b. Buenos Aires, Sept. 15, 1917; came to U.S., 1945; d. Bernardo and Teodora (Kahan) Blitzman; m. Manfred Guttmacher, Oct. 11, 1946 (dec. 1966); m. Leon Eisenberg, Aug. 31, 1967; children: Laurence, Alan. M of Social Work, Liceo de Senoritas; MD, U. Buenos Aires, 1945. Resident in psychiatry U. Md., 1946-48; fellow in child psychiatry Johns Hopkins Hosp., 1948-50; asst. prof. psychiatry and pediatrics Johns Hopkins Hosp., Balt., 1960-67; psychiatrist MIT, Boston, 1967-72, dean of students, 1972-78; dean student affairs Harvard Med. Sch., Boston, 1978-90, dir. internat. programs for students, 1990-92, lectr. psychiatry, 1970-92, lectr. social medicine, 1992—; co-chmn. women in biomed. careers workshop Office on Women's Health, NIH, 1992, mem. adv. com. on rsch. and women's health, 1995-98; mem. com. on human rights ACP; mem. com. on women in sci. and engring. NAS, 1992-95. V.p. Physicians for Human Rights, Boston, 1987—; pres. Examiners Club, Boston, 1993—.

Fellow Am. Psychiat. Assn. (life, mem. Coun. Internat. Affairs, com. on human rights), Am. Orthopsychiat. Assn. (life); mem. AAUP. Avocations: traveling, music, reading. Home and Office: 9 Clement Cir Cambridge MA 02138-2205

EISENBERG, DANIEL, filmmaker. Instr. in film Collective For Living Cinema, N.Y., 1978, Boston Film/Video Found., 1979; asst. prof. film Mass. Coll. Art, Boston, 1979-82, 93-94; spl. instr. in film and photography U. R.I., Kingston, 1984; instr. video Mass. Coll. Art, Boston, 1987; vis. artist in film San Francisco Art Inst., 1993; asst. prof. film, chair dept. filmmaking Sch. Art Inst. Chgo., 1994-97, assoc. prof. film, chair dept. filmmaking, 1998-99; editor various works WGBH, Boston, 1981-90; presenter in field. One-person shows include Collective for Living Cinema, N.Y.C., 1981, 89, MIT, Cambridge, 1984, Sch. Mus. Fine Arts, Boston, 1986, Boston Film/Video Found., 1987, Montserrat Sch. Art, Beverly, Mass., 1987, Brattle Theatre, Cambridge, 1988, Art Cinema, Binghamton, N.Y., 1988, Mass. Coll. Art, Boston, 1988, San Francisco Cinematheque, San Francisco, 1988, Pacific Film Archive, Berkeley, 1988, Kino Arsenal, Berlin, 1988, 91, Am. Mus. Moving Image, N.Y., 1988, Inst. Contemporary Arts, Boston, 1989, Mus. Modern Art, Cineprobe, N.Y., 1989, 98, Harvard U., Grad. Sch. Design, 1990, Boston Film/Video Found., 1991, London Filmmakers Coop, 1991, hochschule der Kunst, Berlin, 1991, Hochschule der Kunst, Braunschweig, 1991, Musée du Cinema, Brussels, 1991, Kommunales Kino, Hannover, 1991, Kommunales Kino, Kiel, 1991, De Unie, Rotterdam, 1992, 't Hoogt, Utrecht, 1992, Filmmuseum, Franfurt, 1992, Filmmuseum, Munich, 1992, Musee Nat. d'Art Moderne, 1992, Calif. Coll. Arts and Crafts, Oakland, 1993, Davis Mus., 1994, U. Iowa, Iowa City, 1996, L.A. Film Forum, 1997, Pacific Film Archive, Berkeley, Calif., 1997, Rocky Mountain Film Ctr., Boulder, Colo., 1998, Boston U., 1998, Harvard Film Archive, Cambridge, 1998, others; group shows at Viper, Lucerne, Switzerland, 1995, Sydney Internat. Film Festival, 1997, Vue Sur Les Docs Festival, Marseilles, 1998, Goethe Inst., Chgo., 1999, numerous others; represented in permanent collections; filmmaker Matrice, 1975, To A Brother in Asia, 1983, Film Studies, 1979, 90, Persistence, 1997, others; dir. The Conjuror, 1983; editor numerous films. Recipient Outstanding Film award New England Film Festival, 1981, CEBA awards for excellence, 1988, Hon. Mention, New England Film Festival, 1988, Grand prize Black Maria Film and Video Festival, 1988-89; New England Regional fellow Nat. Endowment Arts, 1982; fellow in film Mass. Artists Found., 1982; Mass. Prodns. grantee Mass. Coun. on Arts, 1986-88; Media Arts grantee Nat. Endowment Arts, 1989-92; artist fellow The MacDowell Colony, 1990; Berlin artist-in-residence Deutscher Akademischer Austauschdienst, 1991, 97; fellow in film Mass. Artists Found., 1991; Sch. Art Inst. Faculty Enrichment grantee, 1995, 97; John Simon Guggenheim Meml. Found. fellow, 1999—.

EISENBERG, DAVID SAMUEL, molecular biologist, educator; b. Chgo., Mar. 15, 1939; s. George and Ruth E.; m. Lucy Tuchman, Aug. 25, 1963; children: Jenny, Nell. A.B., Harvard U., 1961; Phil.D., Oxford U., Eng., 1964. NSF postdoctoral fellow Princeton U., 1964-66; research fellow chemistry Calif. Inst. Tech., Pasadena, 1966-69; asst. prof. UCLA, 1968-71, assoc. prof., 1971-76, prof. chemistry, biochemistry, 1976—, assoc. dir. Molecular Biology Inst., 1981-85; dir. UCLA-DOE Lab. of Structural Biology and Molecular Medicine, 1993—. Author: (with W. Kauzmann) Structure and Properties of Water, 1969, (with D.M. Crothers) Physical Chemistry with Applications in the Life Sciences, 1979. Chmn. Citizens for West Los Angeles Veloway, 1977—; bd. dirs. Westlake Sch., 1983-89, Harvard-Westlake Sch., 1990-91. Recipient USPHS Career Devel. awardee, 1972-77; Rhodes scholar, 1961-64; Guggenheim fellow, 1985, Stein & Moore award, 1996, Repligen award, 1998. Mem. NAS, Am. Acad. Arts and Scis., Am. Soc. Biol. Chemists, Am. Crystallographic Assn., Biophys. Soc. (councillor 1977-80), The Protein Soc. (pres. 1987-89, councillor 1989-94). Office: UCLALab Structural Biology and Molecular Medicine Box 951570 Los Angeles CA 90095-1570

EISENBERG, DOROTHY, federal judge; b. 1929. LLB, Bklyn. Law Sch., 1950. Bar: N.Y. 1951, U.S. Dist. Ct. (ea. and so. dists.) N.Y., U.S. Ct. Appeals (2nd cir.), U.S. Supreme Ct. Assoc. Otterbourg, Stiendler, Houston & Rosen, N.Y.C., 1950-51, Goldman, Horowitz & Cherno, Mineola, N.Y., 1970-80; pvt. practice Garden City, N.Y., 1981; ptnr. Shaw, Licitra, Eisenberg, Esernio & Schwartz, P.C., Garden City, 1981-89; bankruptcy judge ea. dist. U.S. Bankruptcy Ct., N.Y., 1989—; mem. Com. on Character and Fitness, Appellate divsn, 2nd Dept., 1983-89; panel trustee U.S. Bankruptcy Ct. (ea. dist.) N.Y., 1975-89, U.S. Bankruptcy Ct. (so. dist.) N.Y., 1979-89. Fellow Am. Bar Found.; mem. ABA, Nat. Assn. Women Judges, N.Y. State Assn. Women Judges, Bar Assn. Nassau County, Theodore Roosevelt Am. Inn Ct. Office: U S Bankruptcy Ct 1635 Privado Rd Westbury NY 11590-5298

EISENBERG, GERSON G., author, historian; b. Balt., Mar. 5, 1909; s. Abram and Helen (Gutman) E.; m. Sandy Frenkil, Sept. 15, 1967. BA, George Washington U., 1930; postgrad., Johns Hopkins U., 1936-38; MBA, NYU, 1944. With Am. Oil Co., Balt., 1931-33; v.p. Robinson's Dept. Store, Glen Burnie, Md., 1949-62. Author: Learning Vacations, 6th edit., 1989, Marylanders Who Served the Nation, 1992, tour tapes of Balt., 1st self-guided city tour in U.S., 1969. Bd. dirs. Hebrew Immigrant Aid Soc., Balt., Am. Jewish Com., Balt.; donor Eisenberg Med. Libr., Sinai Hosp., Balt., 1969; gift of seminar rm. to Milton Eisenhower Libr., Johns Hopkins U., art rm. of Balt. Hebrew Cong., 1955, gift of impressionist art collection, Balt. Mus. of Art; mem. Ecumenical Inst. of St. Mary's, Balt., instituted grant for Judaic Christian studies, Ecumenical Inst., 1974; edn. com. Md. Hist. Soc., Balt. Mem. Johns Hopkins U. Club, Suburban Club Baltimore County, The Authors Guild Inc. Home: 11 Slade Ave Apt 116 Baltimore MD 21208-5209

EISENBERG, HOWARD EDWARD, physician, psychotherapist, educator, consultant, author; b. Montreal, Que., Can., Aug. 5, 1946; s. Harold and Elsie (Goldbloom) E.; children: Taryn Noelle, Jory Michael, Meredith Kate, Tessa Chloe. BSc with honors in Psychology, McGill U., 1967, MSc, 1971, MDCM, 1972. Intern Sunnybrook Med. Ctr., U. Toronto, 1973; research asst. psychology dept. McGill U., 1966-69, research asst. gerontology unit Alan Meml. Inst. Psychiatry, McGill U., 1968, clin. fellow Clarke Inst. Psychiatry, U. Toronto, 1973; lectr. Centre for Continuing Edn., York U., 1973-78, Sheridan Coll., Oakville, 1974-76; supr. individual directed study Faculty Environ. Studies, York U., 1975; lectr. dept. interdisciplinary studies U. Toronto, 1975; instr. ind. studies program, Innis Coll., U. Toronto, 1975-78, lectr. 1976-81, spl. coord. coordinator, 1977-79, 88-89, lectr. Sch. Continuing Studies, 1977-89; lectr. continuing edn. U. Vt., 1990-92, 95; assoc. dir. edn. and growth opportunities program York U., 1975-76, dir. E.G.O. program, 1976-78; lectr. Sch. Adult Edn., McMaster U., 1980-89; instr. profl. and mgmt. devel. Humber Coll., 1982-85; pvt. practice psychotherapy and behavioral medicine, Toronto, Ont., 1973-91, Stowe, Vt., 1991-98; assoc. prof. dept. family practice, Coll. Med. Univ. Vt., 1993—; cons. staff dept. medicine Copley Hosp., Vt., 1990-96; pres. Synectia Cons., Inc., Toronto, 1980-84, Syntrek, Inc., Montpelier, Vt., 1989—, Synectia Prodns., Inc., Toronto, 1974—; co-founder Healthcare Knowledge Mgmt. Consortium, 1998. Author: Inner Spaces, 1977, The Tranquility Experience, 1987, Stress Mastery for the Real World, 1991, Creative Thinking Tools for Innovation, 1994, 2d edit., 1997, Fundamentals of High Performance Teamwork, 1995; contbr. articles to profl. jours. McGill scholar, 1966-67; Quebec scholar, 1967-68; Earle C. Anthony fellow, 1967-68; Ont. Arts Council grantee, 1977. Mem. Ont. Med. Assn. (former chmn. sect. ind. physicians), Vt. Med. Soc., Am. Soc. for Tng. and Devel. Office: Syntrek Inc, 7 B Pleasant Blvd Ste 1008, Toronto, ON Canada M4T 1K2

EISENBERG, HOWARD MICHAEL, neurosurgeon; b. N.Y.C., May 4, 1939; s. Monroe L. and Regina (Fish) E.; children: Nancy M. Hoy, John A.; m. Janet Lee Campbell, Feb. 17, 1982. BA, Syracuse U., 1960; MD, SUNY, N.Y.C., 1964. Diplomate Am. Bd. Neurol. Surgery. Intern N.Y. Hosp., N.Y.C., 1964-65; resident, fellow Cornell U. Med. Sch., N.Y.C., 1964-66; resident in neurosurgery Peter Bent Brigham Hosp., Boston, 1966-70; surgery instr. Harvard U., Boston, 1972-75; assoc. prof. U. Tex. Med. Br., Galveston, 1975-80, prof., chief of neurosurgery, 1980-92; head divsn. neurosurgery U. Md., Balt., 1992-96, dir. med. svcs. Shock Truama Ctr., 1992-96, prof. chair dept. neurosurgery, 1996—; chmn. neurology A study sect. NIH, Bethesda, Md., 1980-87; numerous vis. professorships and guest lectureships. Mem. editl. bd. Jour. Neurosurgery, 1989—, chair, 1997-99; editor: The Cerebral Microvasulature, 1980, Neurobehavioral Recovery from Head Injury, 1987, Mild Head Injury, 1989, Neurosurgery Clinics of North America-Management of Head Injury, 1991, The Frontal Lobes, 1991; contbr. over 250 articles to profl. jours. Mem. devel. bd. Houston Grand Opera, 1989-92. Lt. comdr. USN, 1970-72. Recipient William Cavernes award Nat. Head Injury Found., 1994, Wakeman award, 1990, numerous grants in field. Mem. ACS (chair neurosurg. adv. coun.), Am. Bd. Neurol. Surgery (mem. bd. dirs., sec.-treas., bd. dirs. 1990-95, chmn. 1995-96), ACGME (mem. residency rev. com. for neurosurgery), Soc. Neurol. Surgeons (v.p., pres.-elect), Acad. Neurol. Surgeons, Am. Surg. Assn., Cosmos Club, Annapolis Yacht Club, N.Y. Yacht Club. Office: U Md Med Systems Dept Neurosurgery 22 S Greene St Rm S10b11 Baltimore MD 21201-1544

EISENBERG, JAY LYNN, marketing professional; b. Mpls., Mar. 28, 1943; s. Benjamin Gene and Blanche (Goldfetter) E.; m. Gabriela Hubert,, Aug. 17, 1975. BA, U. Minn., 1966, MA, 1970. Jr. project dir. Gen. Mills Inc., Mpls., 1968-70; mktg. rsch. analyst Green Giant Co., Bloomington, Minn., 1970-72; project mgr. Am. Guidance Svc., Circle Pines, Minn., 1973-80; mgr. mkt. rsch. Nash Finch Co., Mpls., 1981—, sr. market rsch. mgr., 1999—. Co-author: Peabody Picture Vocabulary Test-Revised Technical Supplement, 1981; contbr. articles to profl. and popular publs. Co-coord. family coun. Sholom West Nursing Home, St. Louis Park, Minn., 1993-97. Grantee U. Minn. Computer Ctr., 1968; recipient Bronze award 40th Pacific Internat. Philatelic Exhb., 1980, others. Mem. Am. Mktg. Assn. (Minn. chpt.), Am. Philat. Soc., Am. Topical Assn., Classic Corvettes Minn., Chesstamp Rev. (charter). Achievements include development of Store Insight Assessment Model. Avocations: camping, stamp collecting, collecting chess sets, Corvette show cars, reading. Office: Nash Finch Co PO Box 355 7600 France Ave S Ste 200 Minneapolis MN 55435-5920

EISENBERG, JOHN MEYER, physician, educator; b. Atlanta, Sept. 24, 1946; s. Irvin and Roslyn Furchgott (Karesh) E. AB magna cum laude, Princeton U., 1968; MD, Washington U., 1972; MBA with distinction, U. Pa., 1976. Intern, resident in medicine Hosp. of U. Pa., 1972-75, fellow, 1975-77; asst. prof. medicine U. Pa., Phila., 1976-78, Sol Katz asst. prof. gen. medicine, 1978-81, Sol Katz assoc. prof., 1981-86, Sol Katz prof., 1986-92, chief sect. gen. internal medicine, 1978-92, interim chmn. dept. medicine, 1990-91; chmn. dept. medicine Georgetown U., Washington, 1992-97, Anton and Margaret Fuisz prof. medicine, physician-in-chief, 1992-97; adminstr. Agy. for Health Care Policy and Rsch. Dept. Health and Human Svcs., Rockville, Md., 1997—, spl. advisor to Sec. on quality, 1997—, acting Asst. Sec. for health, 1997-98; cons. Nat. Ctr. for Health Svcs. Rsch., 1981-85; commr. Physician Payment Rev. Commn., 1986-95, chmn., 1993-95; program dir. Robert Wood Johnson Found. Generalist Physician Faculty Scholars Program, 1992-97. Editor: The Physicians Practice, 1980; author: Doctors' Decisions and the Cost of Medical Care, 1986, Paying Physicians, 1992; co-editor Internal Medicine, 1998; contbr. articles to profl. jours. Recipient Alumni Achievement award Wharton Sch., U. Pa., 1992, Wash. U. Sch. Medicine, 1997; Robert Wood Johnson Found. clin. scholar, 1974-77; named Disting. Internist of Yr., Am. Soc. Internal Medicine, 1993. Fellow ACP (Master, bd. regents 1985-87, 1996-97, chmn. health care financing subcom. 1984-89, Laureate award 1998), Coun. of Med. Socs. (chmn. 1985-87); mem. Soc. Gen. Internal Medicine (sec.-treas. 1978-80, pres. 1982-83, Glaser award 1995), Soc. Med. Decision Making (v.p. 1980-81), Assn. Program Dirs. Internal Medicine (coun. 1987-90), Am. Coll. Preventive Medicine, Am. Pub. Health Assn., Am. Fedn. Med. Rsch., Assn. Health Svcs. Rsch. (sec. 1989-90, pres. 1991-92), Found. Health Svcs. Rsch. (pres. 1992-93, Alpha Ctr. bd. dirs., 1992-95), Am. Bd. Internal Medicine (bd. govs. 1987-93, exec. com. 1992-93), Inst. Medicine, Assn. Am. Physicians, Am. Soc. Clin. Investigation, Am. Soc. Internal Med., Am. Clin. and Climatological Assn, Washington Acad. Medicine, Interurban Club, Cosmos Club. Office: Agy for Health Care Policy and Rsch 2101 E Jefferson St Ste 600 Rockville MD 20852-4908

EISENBERG, JOSEPH MARTIN, psychologist; b. Bklyn., June 19, 1944; s. David and Dora (Levine) E.; m. Susan Joan Kahn, Aug. 16, 1980; children: Ian, Lara, Jason, Davida. BA in Psychology magna cum laude, C.W. Post Coll., 1966; M.A. in Psychology, U. Alta, 1969, PhD in Psychology, 1971. Cert., lic., Md.; cert. clin. hypnotherapist, Negotiation Inst. Psychol. diagnostician, counselor dept. psychology U. Alta, Can., 1969-70; field rschr. Dept. Youth Alta, 1969-70; assoc. dir. Toronto (Ont.) YMCA Ctr. for counseling and Human Rels., 1970-71; chief psychologist Salvation Army House of Concord, Toronto, 1971-72; dir. outpatient svc. St. Vincent Hosp. Cmty. Mental Health Ctr., Erie, Pa., 1972-73; dir. Erie County Ctr. for Learning Disabilities, 1973-74; pvt. practice psychology Erie and Balt., 1972—; v.p. in charge personnel and comm. Bridge Energy Corp., Balt., 1981—, Reason House, Balt., 1981-97; spl. cons. Md. Children and Family Svcs., Inc.; mem. profl. adv. bds. Balt. Assn. children with Learning Disabilities; cons. Mormac Ltd., 1979-97; forensic cons. Howard County/Balt. County/Carroll County, Office of Pub. Defenders and Balt. City Solicitor's Office, 1977—. Co-author computer software; contbr. articles to profl. jours. Chmn. Carroll County Child Abuse Consultation Com., 1978-80; dir. Psychol. Svcs. for the Metabolic Nutrition Program, 1986-89; mem. profl. adv. bd. Catonsville Group Home, 1980-81. Recipient Richard P. Runyon award, 1966. Mem. Am. Psychol. Assn., Md. Psychol. Assn., Am. Bd. Profl. Disability Cons., Am. Bd. Cert. Managed Care Providers, Psi Chi, Phi Theta. Office: 1402 York Rd Ste 207 Lutherville MD 21093-6031

EISENBERG, KAREN SUE BYER, nurse; b. Bklyn., Mar. 11, 1954; d. Marvin and Florence (Beck) Byer; m. Howard Eisenberg, May 11, 1974; children: Carly Beth, Mariel Bryn. Diploma, L.I. Coll. Hosp. Sch. Nursing, 1973; BS in Nursing, L.I. U., 1976, M in Profl. Studies, 1977. Nurse recovery room and surg. intensive care unit Downstate Med. Ctr., Bklyn., 1973-75; utilization rev. analyst Bezallel Health Related Facility, Far Rockaway, N.Y., 1975-76; utilization rev. analyst, R.N. supr. Seagirt Health Related Facility, Far Rockaway, 1976; staff nurse neurosurg. and rehab. nursing Downstate Med. Ctr., Bklyn., 1978, nurse intensive care unit, 1978-79; asst. nursing dir. pathology, clin. rsch. assoc. Rsch. Found., Bklyn., 1979-90; instrl. support specialist pathology Health Sci. Ctr. SUNY, Bklyn., 1990-92; nurse practitioner pathology SUNY Rsch. Found., Bklyn., 1992-95; nurse rsch. coord. surgery SUNY Health Sci. Ctr., Bklyn., 1995—. Contbr. articles to profl. jours. Mem. ANA, Oncology Nursing Soc., N.Y. State Nurses Assn., N.Y. Acad. Scis., L.I. Coll. Hosp. Alumnae Assn. Office: 450 Clarkson Ave Brooklyn NY 11203-2056

EISENBERG, LEE B., communications executive, author; b. Phila., July 22, 1946; s. George M. and Eve (Blonsky) E.; m. Linda Reville, June 7, 1986; children: Edmund George, Katherine Eve. AB, U. Pa., 1968; MA, Annenberg Sch. Communications, 1970. Assoc. editor Esquire Mag., N.Y.C., 1970-72, sr. editor, 1972-74, mng. editor, 1974-75, editor, 1976-77, v.p. devel., 1980-84, editor-in-chief, 1987-90; founding editor-in-chief Esquire U.K., London, 1990-91; founding ptnr. The Edison Project, Knoxville, Tenn., 1992-95; editor creative devel. Time Mag., N.Y.C., 1995-99; exec. v.p., creative dir. Lands' End, Dodgeville, Wis., 1999—; cons. N.Y. Times Co., 1977-78, Warner Bros., Los Angeles, 1978-79; founder Eisenberg, McCall & Okrent, N.Y.C., 1978-81. Author: Sneaky Feats, 1974, Atlantic City, 1978, Ultimate Fishing Book, 1981, Breakins Eighty, 1997. Founder Rotisserie League Baseball, N.Y.C., 1980—. Recipient One Show award Art Dirs. Club, 1976, Gold Cindy award Assn. Visual Comms., 1984, various nat. mag. awards, 1984-90. Office: Lands' End 1 Lands' End Ln Dodgeville WI 53595*

EISENBERG, LEON, psychiatrist, educator; b. Phila., Aug. 8, 1922; s. Morris and and Elizabeth (Sabreen) E.; m. Ruth Harriet Bleier, June 11, 1948 (div. 1967); children: Mark Philip, Kathy Bleier; m. Carola Blitzman Guttmacher, Aug. 31, 1967; children: Laurence, Alan. AB, U. Pa., 1944, MD, 1946; MA (hon.), Harvard U., 1967; DSc (hon.), U. Manchester, Eng., 1973, U. Mass., 1991. Diplomate: in child psychiatry and psychiatry Am. Bd. Psychiatry and Neurology. Intern Mt. Sinai Hosp., N.Y.C., 1946-47; instr. physiology U. Pa., 1947-48; resident psychiatry Sheppard-Pratt Hosp., Towson, Md., 1950-52; with Johns Hopkins, 1952-67, prof. child psychiatry Med. Sch., 1961-67; psychiatrist-in-charge children's psychiat. service Harriet Lane Home, 1958-67; prof. psychiatry Harvard U. Med. Sch., Boston, 1967—, Maude and Lillian Presley prof. psychiatry, 1975-80, chmn. exec. com. dept. psychiatry, 1973-80, Maude and Lillian Presley prof. social medicine, 1980-93, chmn. dept., 1980-91, prof. of social medicine emeritus, 1993—; psychiatrist-in-chief Mass. Gen. Hosp., 1967-74, mem. bd. consultation, 1974—; sr. assoc. in psychiatry Children's Hosp., Boston, 1974—; prof. emeritus, 1993—; Paley lectr. Cornell U., 1983; Schilder lectr. NYU, 1984; Eli Robins lectr. Washington U., St. Louis, 1985; Plenary session lectr. Internat. Pediat. Assn., Amsterdam, 1998; lectr. Italian Psychiat. Soc., Bologna, 1998, Alpha Omega Alpha lectr. U. Rochester, 1999; ; Plenary lectr. World Psychiat. Assn., Athens, 1999; vis. lectr. Yale U., 1987; R.W. Johnson vis. prof. U. Rochester, 1987; Carolyn Voorsanger lectr. Stanford U. Med. Sch., 1989; Willard Sears Simpkins lectr. Johns Hopkins U., 1989; William Potter lectr. Thomas Jefferson U., 1992; vis. prof. McMaster U., Can., 1991, Charles U. Prague; psychiat. cons. Crownsville (Md.) State Hosp., 1954-58, Rosewood State Tng. Sch., Owings Mills, Md., 1957-60, Balt. City Hosp., 1959-62, Children's Guild, Balt., 1954-61; cons. Sinai Hosp., Balt., 1963-67; Mapother-Lewis ann. lectr. Maudsley Hosp., London, 1977; Baan Meml. lectr. Netherlands Psychiat. Soc., Amsterdam, 1978; Royal Soc. Medicine vis. prof., London, 1983; mem. subcom. psychiat. nomenclature com. vital stats. USPHS; chmn. WHO Conf. Devel. Regulation, 1964-67; mem. Joint Commn. Mental Health of Children; cons. divsn. mental health WHO, 1974—, chmn. sci. group on evaluation of psychiat. treatment, 1989; mem. adv. com. to dir. NIH, 1977-80; lectr. Can. Royal Coll. Psychiatry, 1993, Italian Soc. for Biol. Psychiatry, Cagliari, Sardinia, 1994; Richard Goldbloom lectr. Dalhousie U., Halifax, N.S., Can., 1995; Wolfe Adler lectr. Sheppard-Pratt Hosp. Sys., Balt., 1995; spl. lectr. Health of the Child on the Eve of the Year 2000, Bologna, Italy, 1995. Editor Am. Jour. Orthopsychiatry, 1963-73; editorial bd.: Culture, Medicine and Psychiatry, Psychol. Medicine, Jour. Psychiat. Research. Capt. M.C., U.S. Army, 1948-50. Recipient Theobald Smith award Albany Med. Coll., 1979, Orton award Orton Soc., 1980, Disting. Alumnus award U. Pa., 1992, Presdl. Commendation Am. Psychiat. Assn., 1992, Agnes Purchell McGavin award, 1994, Camille Cosby World of Children award Judge Baker Children's Ctr., 1994, Salmon medal N.Y. Acad. Medicine, 1995, Mumford award and lecture, 1996. Fellow AAAS, Am. Psychiat. Assn. (life, trustee 1973-76), Am. Orthopsychiat. Assn. (life, Ittleson Meml. award 1996), Soc. Rsch. Child Devel., Royal Coll. Psychiatrists (hon., Eli Lilly lectr. 1986), Royal Soc. Medicine; mem. Inst. Medicine of NAS (coun. 1975-77, program and membership coms. 1979-82, bd. on health sci. policy 1989-91, Rhoda and Bernard Sarnat prize in mental health 1996), AAUP (past pres. Johns Hopkins chpt.), Am. Acad. Pediatrics (Aldrich award 1980, Dale Richmond lectr. 1989), Am. Pediatric Soc., Can. Pediatric Soc. (Queen Elizabeth II lectr. 1986), Assn. Rsch. Nervous and Mental Disease, Am. Psychopath. Assn., Md. Psychiat. Soc. (past pres.), Am. Acad. Arts and Scis. (communication sec. 1995—), Psychiat. Rsch. Soc. (past pres.), Soc. Neurosci., Mass. Med. Soc., Greek Soc. Neurology and Psychiatry (hon.), Ecuadorean Soc. Neurosci. (hon.), Johns Hopkins Soc. Scholars, Phi Beta Kappa (chpt. pres. 1958, vis. scholar 1994-95), I.O.M. (chair com. on planned childbearing 1993-95), Sigma Xi, Alpha Omega Alpha (lectr. Jefferson Med. Coll. 1994). Home: 9 Clement Cir Cambridge MA 02138-2205 Office: Harvard U Med Sch Dept Soc Med Boston MA 02115

EISENBERG, MARVIN JULIUS, art history educator; b. Phila., Aug. 19, 1922; s. Frank and Rosalie (Julius) E. B.A., U. Pa., 1943; M.F.A., Princeton, 1949, Ph.D., 1954. Mem. faculty U. Mich., Ann Arbor, 1949-89, prof. art history, chmn. dept., 1960-69, Collegiate prof., 1974-75, prof. emeritus, 1989—; mem. Inst. for Advanced Study, Princeton, N.J., 1970; vis. prof. Stanford U., 1973; mem. adv. com. Center for Advanced Study in Visual Arts, Nat. Gallery, Washington, 1981-84; mem. vis. com. dept. fine arts, Harvard U., 1975-81, Freer Gallery Art, Washington, 1970-96, Commn. on Preservation and Access, Washington, 1991-94, Ga. Mus. Art, 1997—; disting. Berg prof. Colo. Coll., 1990, 93, 95, 97; Hooker disting. vis. prof. McMaster U., 1993; Saunders lectr. St. Andrews U., 1998. Author: Lorenzo Monaco, 1989; co-author: The Confraternity Altarpiece by Mariotto Di Nardo, 1998; contbr. articles on early Italian painting to profl. jours. Served with AUS, 1943-46. Recipient Star of Solidarity II Italy, 1961; Coll. Art Assn. Disting. Teaching of Art History award, 1987; Guggenheim fellow, 1959. Fellow Japan Soc. for Promotion of Sci.; mem. Coll. Art Assn. Am. (dir. 1965-70, v.p. 1966-67, pres. 1968-69), Royal Soc. Arts (Benjamin Franklin fellow 1969), Phi Beta Kappa, Phi Kappa Phi. Home: 2200 Fuller Rd Apt 1201 Ann Arbor MI 48105-2304

EISENBERG, MELVIN A., law educator; b. New York, Dec. 3, 1934; s. Max and Laura (Wallance) E.; m. Helen Garlitz, Feb. 5, 1956; children: Bronwyn, David Abram (dec. 1997). AB, SCL, Columbia U., 1956; LLB, SCL, Harvard U., 1959, Faye Diploma in Law, 1959; LLD (hon.), U. Milan, 1998. Bar: N.Y. 1960. Assoc. Kaye Scholer Fierman Hays & Handler, 1959-63, 64-66; corp. counsel City of N.Y., 1966; acting prof. U. Calif.-Berkeley, 1966-69, prof. law, 1969-83, Koret prof. law, 1983—; vis. prof. Harvard U., 1969-70, U. Tokyo, 1992, Justin d'Atri vis. prof. law, bus. and society, Columbia U., 1998—; asst. counsel Pres. Commn. on Assassination President Kennedy, Warren Commn., 1964; counsel mayor's task force on reorganization N.Y.C. govt., 1966; mem. mayor's task force on N.Y.C. transp. reorganization, 1966; mem. mayors' task force on mcpl. collective bargaining, 1966; reporter Am. Law Inst., principles of corporate governance: analysis and recommendations, 1980-84, chief reporter, 1984-94, Ammi Cutter chair, 1991-93; adviser, restatement 3d of agy. 1996—; adviser, restatement 2d of restitution, 1998—; prof.-in-residence, Cologne U., 1984, U. Milan, 1992; mem. ABA com. on corp. laws, 1992—; U. Iowa Inaugural lectr., 1987, Roy R. Ray lectr. So. Meth. U., 1993, Robert L. Levine Distg. Lectures, Fordham Univ., 1993; chmn. AALS contracts sect., 1989, AALS contracts workshop, 1986; chmn. AALS bus. assns. sect., 1998; vis.-in-residence U. Murdoch, U. Western Australia, 1992, McGill U., 1981; Sobeloff lectr. U. Md., 1994; Freehill, Hollingsdale and Page vis. fellow U. New South Wales, Australia, 1994. Author: The Structure of the Corporation, 1977 (Coif Triennial Book award honorable mention 1980), The Nature of the Common Law, 1988, (with L. Fuller) Basic Contract Law, 1996, (with W. Cary) Corporations-Cases and Materials, 1995; also numerous articles. Pres. Queen's Child Guidance Ctr., 1963-66. Recipient Disting. Teaching award U. Calif., Berkeley, 1990; Guggenheim fellow, 1971-72, Canterbury vis. fellow U. Canterbury, New Zealand, 1988, Kimber fellow York U., Toronto, Ont., Can., 1989; Fulbright Sr. scholar, Australia, 1987, Mellon scholar U. Pitts., 1989; named Cooley lectr. U. Mich., 1985; Manuel F. Cohen vis. scholar George Washington U. Sch. Law; Baron de Hirsch Meyer lectr. U. Miami Sch. Law; TePoel lectr. Creighton U. Sch. Law; Rabin fellow Yale Sch. Law.; recipient Faye Diploma Harvard U. Law Sch. Fellow AAAS; mem. ABA (com. on corp. law, 1992-99), Am. Law Inst., Phi Beta Kappa. Home: 1197 Keeler Ave Berkeley CA 94708-1753 Office: U Calif Sch Law 331 Boalt Hall Berkeley CA 94720-7201 also: 201 E 79th St New York NY 10021-0830 Office: Columbia U Law Sch 435 W 116th St New York NY 10027

EISENBERG, MEYER, lawyer; b. Bklyn., Dec. 15, 1931; s. Samuel and Bella (Fishman) E.; m. Carolyn Schoen, Dec. 26, 1954; children—Julie S., Ellen M. BA, Bklyn. Coll., 1953; LLB, Columbia U., 1958. Bar: N.Y. 1960, D.C. 1970, U.S. Supreme Ct. 1963. Law clk. to Chief Justice William McAllister Supreme Ct. Oreg., Salem, 1958-59; atty. SEC, Washington, 1959-70; counsel spl. study securities markets SEC, 1962-64, asst. gen. counsel, 1966-68, exec. asst. to chmn., 1968-69, assoc. gen. counsel, 1969-70; with firm Lawler, Kent & Eisenberg, Washington, 1970-79, Rosenman, Colin, Freund, Lewis & Cohen, Washington, 1980-87, Ballard, Spahr, Andrews & Ingersoll, Washington, 1987-93, Kramer, Levin, Naftalis & Frankel, Washington, 1994-98; dep. gen. coun. sec. SEC, Washington, 1998—; adj. prof. law George Washington U., 1972-75, Georgetown U. Law Sch., 1988-90; vis. prof. law U. Calif., Berkeley; dir. Nat. Ctr. Fin. Svcs., 1985-86; mem. exec. com. Calif. Securities Regulation Inst.; cons. in field. Contbr. articles to profl. pubs. Mem. internat. bd. govs. B'nai B'rith, 1978-92; mem. nat. exec. com. Anti-Defamation League, 1980—, nat. vice chmn., 1994—; chmn. Nat. Civil Rights Com., 1992-94. Mem. ABA (chmn. com. on devels. in investment svcs. 1981-86, chmn. com. on long-range issues affecting bus. law practice 1986-90, coun. sec. bus. law 1990-94, chmn. com. on internat. tech. assistance 1994—, sec. bus. law), Fed. Bar Assn. (chmn. securities law com. 1984-85). Home: 8216 Lakenheath Way Potomac MD 20854-2740 Office: SEC 450 5th St NW Washington DC 20549

EISENBERG, MICKEY STEWART, municipal medical services director; b. Detroit, Oct. 16, 1945; three children. BA, U. Mich., 1967; MD, Case Western Res. U., 1971; MPH, U. Wash., 1978. Diplomate Am. Bd. Internal Medicine. Epidemic intelligence svc. officer Ctr. for Disease Control, USPHS, 1973-75; acting instr. U. Wash., Seattle, 1976-78, asst. prof. then assoc. prof., 1978-88, dir. emergency med. svcs. Med. Ctr., 1980—, prof., 1988—; co-dir. Ctr. for Evaluation of Emergency Med. Svcs., King County, Seattle, 1986—; med. dir. King County Emergency Med. Svcs., 1975-77; assoc. dir. Emergency Med. Svcs., U. Wash. Med. Ctr., 1978-80; adj. asst. prof., then adj. assoc. prof., dept. epidemiology, U. Wash., 1979-88, adj. prof., 1988—, sect. headdivsn. gen. internal medicine, 1990-94acting divsn. head, 1992-95. Contbr. articles to profl. jours. Recipient Baxter Found. Health Svcs. award, 1989. Fellow ACP; mem. AMA, Inst. Medicine Nat. Acad. Scis., Am. Heart Assn., Am. Pub. Health Assn., Soc. Acad. Emergency Medicine, Am. Coll. Emergency Physicians. *

EISENBERG, PABLO SAMUEL, non-profit organization executive; b. Paris, July 1, 1932; came to U.S. 1939; s. Maurice and Paula (Halpert) E.; m. Helen Leone Cierniak, June 5, 1960; 1 child, Marina. BA, Princeton U., 1954; BLitt, Oxford U., Eng., 1957. Fgn. svc. officer USIA, 1960-63; program dir. Operation Crossroads Africa, N.Y.C., 1963-65; coord. Pa. Office Econ. Opportunity, 1965-67; dep. dir. Rsch. and Demonstration Office, Office of Econ. Opportunity, Washington, 1967-68; asst. dir. Nat. Urban Coalition, Washington, 1968-73; ind. cons. Washington, 1973-75; pres. Ctr. for Cmty. Change, Washington, 1975-98; sr. fellow, cons. Georgetown Pub. Policy Inst., Washington, 1998Y. Contbr. articles to profl. jours., chpts. to book; columnist Chronicle of Philanthropy. Co-chmn. Nat. Com. for Responsive Philanthropy, Washington, 1976—; pres. Friends of VISTA, Washington, 1980—; vice chmn. Nat. Neighborhood Coalition, Washington, 1976—; bd. dirs. Environ. Support Ctr., Non-Profit Sector Rsch. Fund, Nat. Coun. for Non-Profit Assns., 1993—. Recipient John Gardner Leadership award, 1998; German Marshall Fund of U.S. travelling fellow, 1988. Democrat. Jewish. Avocations: tennis, antique books, movies, sports. Home: 3729 Massachusetts Ave NW Washington DC 20016-5004 Office: Ctr for Community Change 1000 Wisconsin Ave NW Ste B Washington DC 20007-3651

EISENBERG, PAUL RICHARD, cardiologist, consultant, educator; b. Rome, Mar. 9, 1955; came to U.S., 1956; s. David Marvin and Sonia Maria (Benesdetti) E.; m. Patricia Lynn Goodman, Apr. 25, 1982; 1 child, Jamie. BS, Tulane U., 1975, MPH, 1980; MD, N.Y. Med. Coll., Valhalla, 1980. Diplomate Am. Bd. Internal Medicine, Am. Bd. Cardiology. Intern in internal medicine Barnes Hosp., St. Louis, 1980-83, fellow in cardiology, pulmonary medicine, 1983-85, asst. dir. CCU, 1986-91, dir. CCU, 1991—; asst. prof. Washington U., St. Louis, 1985-91, assoc. prof., 1991-97, prof., 1997-98; med. dir. cardiovasc. therapeutics Eli Lilly & Co., Indpls., 1998—. Asst. editor: Medical Management of Heart Disease; contbr. over 100 articles to profl. jours. Fellow Am. Heart Assn. (clin. cardiology), Am. Coll. Chest Physicians, Am. Coll. Cardiology; mem. Am. Fedn. Clin. Rsch., Internat. Soc. Thrombosis and Haemostasis. Office: Lilly Rsch Labs Lily Corp Ctr Drop Code 2146 Indianapolis IN 46285

EISENBERG, RICHARD MARTIN, pharmacology educator; b. Weehawken, N.J., May 15, 1942; s. Herbert and Evelyn (Stecker) E.; m. Marsha Eisenberg, July 3, 1966; children: Marla, Aaron, Shana. BA, UCLA, 1963, MS, 1967, PhD, 1970; postdoc., U. Rochester, 1970-71. Asst. prof. pharmacology U. Minn., Duluth, 1971-76, assoc. prof., 1976-77, assoc. prof., acting dept. head, 1977-80, assoc. prof., dept. head, 1980-85, prof., dept. head, 1985—. Author-developer: (computer software) Mac Pharmacology, Mac MedVirology, Mac BrainLesion; presenter in field; contbr. articles to profl. jours. Recipient numerous rsch. grants Nat. Inst. Drug Abuse, 1978—, other instns., 1975—. Mem. Am. Soc. Pharmacology and Exptl. Therapeutics, Assn. Med. Sch. Pharmacology (treas. 1994-98, pres. 1998—), Endocrine Soc., Western Pharmacology Soc., Coll. on Problems of Drug Dependence. Avocations: cabinet making, microcomputers, photography. Office: U Minn Duluth Sch Medicine Dept Pharmacology 10 University Dr Duluth MN 55812-2403

EISENBERG, RICHARD S., chemistry educator; b. N.Y.C., Feb. 12, 1943; s. Paul and Norma (Frommer) E.; m. Marcia Landau, Aug. 6, 1966; children: Alan, Robert. A.B., Columbia U., 1963, M.A., 1964, Ph.D., 1967. Asst. prof. chemistry Brown U., Providence, 1967-71, assoc. prof., 1971-73; assoc. prof. chemistry U. Rochester (N.Y.), 1973-76, prof., 1976-96, chair, 1991-94, univ. mentor, 1986-87, assoc. dean Coll. Arts and Scis., 1989-91, Tracy H. Harris prof., 1996—; vis. scientist Calif. Inst. Tech., 1977-78; vis. scholar Cambridge (Eng.) U., 1978; vis. prof. Columbia U., 1985; vice chmn. Gordon Conf. on Organometallic Chemistry, 1987, chmn., 1988; cons. SOHIO, Cleve., 1982-83, Eastman Kodak, Rochester, 1982; mem. adv. bd. Petroleum Rsch. Fund, 1988-91; Closs lectr. U. Chgo., 1994; vis. prof. Chemistry Rsch. Promotion Ctr., Republic of China, 1994; Coates lectr. U. Wyo., 1966; Varon vis. prof. Weizmann Inst., 1997; Lady Davis fellow Hebrew U., 1997. Contbr. numerous articles on chemistry to profl. jours.; mem. editorial adv. bd.: Jour. Am. Chem. Soc., 1982-84, Inorganic Chemistry, 1997—, Organometallics, 1998—. NSF fellow, 1964-66, George B. Pegram Hon. fellow, 1964-65, Alfred P. Sloan fellow, 1972-74, Guggenheim fellow, 1977-78. Mem. Am. Chem. Soc. (chmn. organometallic subdiv. inorganic div. 1982, alt. councilor inorganic div. 1985-87, editorial adv. bd. jour. 1982-84, councilor inorganic div. 1988-90, chmn.-elect 1992, chmn. 1993), Am. Crystallographic Assn., Chem. Soc. Rsch. interests in homogeneous catalysts, organometallic compounds of platinum group elements, binuclear complexes, inorganic photochemistry; bond activiation and oxidative addition, parahydrogen induced polarization, metal hydrides, structure-function relationships in catalytically active systems. Home: 175 Parkwood Ave Rochester NY 14620-3403 Office: U Rochester River Campus Dept Chemistry Rochester NY 14627

EISENBERG, RUSSELL A., federal judge; b. 1937. BNS, Marquette U., 1945, LLB, 1948. Atty. Curran, Curran & Hollenback, 1948-83; bankruptcy judge U.S. Dist. Ct. (ea. dist.) Wis., 1983—. Served with USN, 1943-46. Office: 140 US Courthouse 517 E Wisconsin Ave Milwaukee WI 53202-4500

EISENBERG, SONJA MIRIAM, artist; b. Berlin, June 10, 1926; came to U.S., 1938, naturalized, 1947; d. Adolf and Meta Cecilie (Bettauer) Weinberger; student Queens Coll., 1943-46, Middlebury Coll., 1945; NYU, 1952-54; BA, NYU, 1954; postgrad. Nat. Acad. Sch. Fine Arts, 1961; m. Jack Eisenberg, Mar. 31, 1946; children: Ralph, Lynn, Lauren. One-woman shows: Bodley Gallery, N.Y.C., 1970, 73, 75, 80, Galerie Art du Monde, Paris, 1973, Buyways Gallery, Sarasota, Fla., 1973, 74, 75, 78, Galerie de Sfinx, Amsterdam, Netherlands, 1974, Huntsville (Ala.) Mus. Art, 1974, Anglo-Am. Art Mus., Baton Rouge, 1974, Comara Gallery, L.A., 1974, Palm Spring (Calif.) Desert Mus., 1975, Fordham U., N.Y.C., 1976, Omega Inst., New Lebanon, N.Y., 1979, Am. Mus., Hayden Planetarium, N.Y.C., 1980, Avila Graphics, Ltd., 1981, YWCA, N.Y.C., 1981, Cathedral of St. John the Divine, N.Y.C., 1983, 85, The Millbrook Gallery, N.Y., 1989, 94, Christopher Leonard Gallery, N.Y.C., 1993, Park Hotel, Vitznau, Switzerland, 1994, The Burgenstock (Switzerland) Hotels, 1995, Wainscott Gallery, N.Y., 1997, Galerie Dussmann, Kulturkaufhaus, Berlin, 1998; group shows include Mus. Fine Arts, St. Petersburg, Fla., 1973, Am. Watercolor Soc., 107th, 108th Exhbn., 1974, 75, Galerie Frederic Gollong, St. Paul de Vence, France, 1978, Betty Parson's Gallery, N.Y.C., 1981, Foster Harmon Galleries of Am. Art, Sarasota, Fla., 1988, Tokyo Met. Art Mus. 14th Internat. Art Friendship Exhbn., 1989, Galerie Herbert Leidel, Munich, Germany, 1991, Park Ave. Armory, N.Y.C., 1996, Akim-USA, N.Y.C., 1996; represented in permanent collections: Archives Am. Art, Smithsonian Inst., Jewish Mus., N.Y.C., Fordham U. Mus., N.Y.C., Palm Springs Desert Mus., Omega Inst., Cathedral of St. John the Divine; artist-in-residence Cathedral of St. John the Divine, N.Y.C.; designer WFUNA cachet for UN Water Power Conf., 1977, UN Internat. Yr. of Disabled Persons, 1981. Regent Cathedral of St. John the Divine, N.Y.C., 1990, commisioned painting to commemorate Crystal Night for Telecom Telefon Karte, Munich, 1993. Recipient gold medal for artistic merit Internat. Parliament for Safety and Peace, 1983, Palma D'Oro Europe, 1986. Mem. Accademia Italia delle Arti e del Lavoro (Gold medal 1981). Completed project Seeing the Gospel According to St. John (text and 41 paintings) for Cathedral of St. John, 1987; appointed art dir. Hermes Media B.V., Amsterdam, The Netherlands, 1992. Home and Office: 1020 Park Ave New York NY 10028-0913 *When you focus your mind, you may break through the Known with its borders of words and ideas, and get a glimpse of the "nothing" that is so creative.*

EISENDRATH, CHARLES RICE, journalism educator, manufacturer, farmer, consultant; b. Chicago, Ill., Oct. 9, 1940; s. William Nathan and Erna Sarah (Rice) E.; m. Julia Cardozo, Jan. 28, 1967; children: Benjamin Cardozo, Mark William. BA, Yale U., 1962; MA, U. Mich., 1965. Reporter Post-Dispatch, St. Louis, 1962, 64, Evening Sun, Balt., 1966-68; corr. Time Mag., Washington, London, Paris; bur. chief Time Mag., Buenos Aires, 1968-73; prof. U. Mich., Ann Arbor, 1975—; proprietor Overlook Farm, East Jordan, Mich., 1972—; chmn. Grillworks, Inc., Ann Arbor, 1978—; cons. Midland Bank of London, Pfizer, 1985-88. Contbr. articles to profl. jours.; inventor in field. Dir. Mich. Journalism Fellows, 1986—; founding dir. Livingston Awards, Ann Arbor, 1980—; judge nat. barbecue contest, 1994—. NEH Mich. Journalism fellow, 1974-75. Mem. Coun. Fgn. Rels., Century Assn. (N.Y.C.), Soc. Profl. Journalists, Com. of Concerned Journalists (founding), Project on the State of the Am. Newspaper (founding bd. dirs. 1998—), Lansdowne Club (London), Phi Kappa Phi. Jewish. Office: Wallace House 620 Oxford Rd Ann Arbor MI 48104-2623

EISENHOWER, CYNTHIA P., state official. MPA, Drake U., 1976. Dir. bus. and fin. Iowa State Bd. Regents; mgmt. dir. Iowa Dept. Mgmt., Des Moines, dir., 1999—; exec. dir. Iowa Campaign Fin. Disclosure Commn. IBM Harvard fellow, 1994; recipient Nat. Pub. Adminstr. of Yr., Nat. Employers Coun., Innovation in Govt. award Ford Found., Excellence in Pub. Svc. award Nat. Pub. Employees Roundtable. Office: Iowa Dept Mgmt Capitol Bldg Rm 12 Des Moines IA 50319

EISENHOWER, JOHN SHELDON DOUD, former ambassador, author; b. Denver, Aug. 3, 1922; s. Dwight David (34th Pres. of U.S.) and Mamie (Doud) E.; m. Barbara Jean Thompson, June 10, 1947 (div. 1986); children: Dwight David II, Barbara Anne, Susan Elaine, Mary Jean; m. Joanne Thompson, Apr. 9, 1990. BS, U.S. Mil. Acad., 1944; MA in English Lit., Columbia, 1950; LHD (hon.), Northwood Inst., 1970. Commd. 2d lt. U.S. Army, 1944, advanced through grades to lt. col., 1963; assigned 1st Army, Europe, 1945, Army of Occupation, Europe, 1945-47, Korean War, 1952-53, Army Gen. Staff, 1957-58, White House Staff, 1958-61; resigned, 1963; brig. gen. USAR, 1974; engaged in writing, 1965-69; U.S. ambassador to Belgium, 1969-71; cons. to the Pres.; also chmn. Interagency Classification Review Com., 1972-73; chmn. bd. Acad. Life Ins. Co., Atlanta; mem. adv. council Nat. Archives, 1974-77; chmn. President's Adv. Com. on Refugees, 1975; mil. editor Algonguin Books of Chapel Hill. Author: The Bitter Woods, 1969, Strictly Personal, 1974; editor: Letters to Mamie, 1978, Allies, 1982, So Far From God, 1989, Intervention!, 1993, Agent of Destiny, 1997. Mem. diplomatic coun., bd. govs. USO, 1983-85; trustee Alumni Fedn. Columbia U., 1976-80. Decorated Legion of Merit, Bronze Star, Combat Inf. badge, grand cross Order of Crown Belgium, Chungmu Disting. Service medal (Korea); recipient Grad. Faculties Alumni award for excellence Columbia U., 1970. Mem. Aircraft Owners and Pilots Assn., NAA, Authors Guild, Authors League Am., Capital Hill Club, Seabrook Island Ocean Club.

EISENMAN, PETER DAVID, architect, educator; b. Newark, Aug. 11, 1932; s. Herschel I. and Sylvia H. (Heller) E.; m. Elizabeth Henderson, 1963 (div. 1990); children: Julia, Nicholas; m. Cynthia Davidson, 1990; 1 child, Samuel Chapin. B.Arch. (Charles G. Sands Meml. medal 1955), Cornell U., 1955; M.S. in Architecture (Alumni tuition scholar 1959, William Kinne fellow 1960-61), Columbia U., 1960; M.A., Cambridge (Eng.) U., 1962, Ph.D., 1963. Prin. firm Eisenman/Robertson Architects, N.Y.C., 1980-88, Eisenman Architects, N.Y.C., 1988—; founder Inst. Architecture and Urban Studies, N.Y.C., 1967, dir., 1967-82; mem. faculty Cambridge U., 1960-63, Princeton U., 1965-67; faculty Cooper Union, 1970—, adj. prof., 1975-86, Irwin Chanin Disting. prof. 1986—; architect-in-residence Am. Acad. Rome, 1976; Kea prof. U. Md., 1978; Charlotte Davenport prof. Yale U., 1980; Arthur Rotch prof. Harvard U., 1982-85, Eliot Noyes vis. critic, 1993; Louis H. Sullivan rsch. prof. architecture U. Ill., Chgo., 1987-93; vis. prof. Ohio State U., 1991-93; John Williams prof. architecture U. Ark., 1997. Editor: Oppositions Books, House X Rizzoli, Houses of Cards; prin. works include pvt. residences Princeton, N.J., Hardwick, Vt., Lakeville and Cornwall, Conn., 1968-76; others Housing Koch-Friedrichstrasse, Berlin, 1980-86, Wexner Ctr. for Visual Arts, Columbus, Ohio, 1983-89, U. Cin. Coll. Design, Art, Architecture and Planning, 1988-96, Columbus (Ohio) Conv. Ctr., 1988-93, Koizumi Sangyo Bldg., Tokyo, 1989-90, Nunotani Office Bldg., 1990-92, Emory U. Art Ctr., 1991-95, Rebstock Pk., Frankfurt, Germany, 1991-95, U.S. Pavilion, Venice Biennale, 1991, Max Reinhardt Haus, Berlin, 1992—, Haus Immendorff, Dusseldorf, Germany, 1993-94, Jewish Mus., San Francisco, 1996—, BFL Software, Ltd. Hdqs., Bangalore, India, 1996—, Libr. UN Complex, Geneva, 1996—, Staten Island Inst. Arts and Scis., 1997—. . Served with U.S. Army, 1955-57. Fellow Graham Found., 1966; Guggenheim Found., 1976; grantee Princeton U., 1964, 66; recipient Arnold W. Brunner Meml. prize in architecture Am. Acad. and Inst. Arts and Letters, 1984. Fellow AIA; mem. Archtl. League N.Y. (v.p. 1970), Conf. Architects Study Environ. (co-founder 1964). Club: Century Assn. (N.Y.C.). Office: Eisenman Architects 41 W 25th St New York NY 10010-2021

EISENMANN, DALE RICHARD, dental educator, administrator, researcher; b. Watseka, Ill., Jan. 13, 1941; s. Chris Robert and Lydia Rose (Koehl) E.; m. Judith Ann Feller, June 25, 1961; children—Bradley, Todd, Luann. D.D.S., U. Ill.-Chgo., 1965, Ph.D., 1968. USPHS trainee U. Ill. Coll. Dentistry, Chgo., 1965-68, asst. prof. to prof., 1968—, head dept. histology, 1973-93, chmn. Coll. Dentistry Research Bd., 1978-95, assoc. dean for acad. affairs, 1994—. Contbr. chpts. Oral Histology-Development Structure and Function, 1994. Contbr. articles to profl. jours. Elder Apostolic Christian Ch. Am., Hillside, Ill., 1975—. Grantee NIH, 1984—. Mem. Internat. Assn. Dental Research, Phi Kappa Phi. Avocation: Gardening. Home: 6913 Wilmette Ave Darien IL 60561-4047 Office: Univ Ill College Dentistry 801 S Paulina St Chicago IL 60612-7210*

EISENPREIS, ALFRED, communications and marketing executive; b. Vienna, Austria, June 16, 1924; came to U.S., 1939, naturalized, 1942; s. Siegmund and Claire (Silberman-Günsberg) E.; 1 child, Steven. AB, St. Thomas Coll., 1943; MA, N.Y. Sch. Social Research, 1974; postgrad., Union Inst., 1997—. Exec. Pomeroy's Inc. (dept. store), Wilkes-Barre, Pa., 1943-57; with Allied Stores Corp., N.Y.C., 1957-74; v.p. planning and research Allied Stores Corp., 1963-69, v.p. mktg., 1970-74; adminstr. Econ. Devel. Adminstrn. City of N.Y., 1974-76; v.p. Newspaper Advt. Bur., 1977-86, sr. v.p., 1986-91; pres. Eisenpreis & Co., Ltd. Cons., N.Y.C., 1991—; editorial dir. Retail Ad-Week Eisenpreis & Co., Ltd., N.Y.C., 1991-95; dir. Henchy & Assocs., N.Y.C., 1982-86; v.p. City Innovation, 1992-95, vice chmn., 1995—; pres. Cmty. Action Network, 1996-98, vice chmn., 1998—; cons. N.Y. C. of C., Econ. Devel. Council N.Y.C., 1976; mem. faculty Grad. Sch. Mgmt. and Urban Professions, New Sch. Social Research, 1975-82, mem. adv. coms. on manpower and tourism programs, 1975-82, bd. overseers Grad. Sch. Mgmt. and Urban Professions, 1984-87; mem. policy com. City of N.Y., 1974-76; pres. N.Y.C. Indsl. Devel. Corp., 1974-76; mem. Port Devel. Council N.Y., 1974-76; vice chmn. Interagy. Rail Com., 1975; steering com. Westside Hwy., 1974-76; dir. N.Y.C. Indsl. Devel. Agy., 1974-76; chmn. Retail Research Inst., 1963-68; mem. com. dept. store statistics Fed. Res. System, 1960-65; chmn. adv. com. Center Econ. Projections, Nat. Planning Assn., 1963-68; mem. dept. urban research Nat. Acad. Scis., 1964-69; cons. U.S. Dept. Commerce, 1965-69; dir. Greater Jamaica Devel. Com., 1965-68; trustee Fed. Statis. Users Conf., 1965-67, N.Y. Met. Regional Statis. Center, 1965-67; mem. Census Adv. Com., 1966-68, 72-74; mem. nat. mktg. adv. com. U.S. Dept. Commerce, 1968-72; cons. Office of Emergency Preparedness-Fed. Emergency Mgmt. Agy., 1966-82; mem. Nat. Def. Exec. Res., 1966—, Fed. Emergency Mgmt. Agy. Res., 1990—, Nat. Mgmt. Council Mktg. Edn., chmn., 1972, 79-81; mem. Nat. Bus. Council on Consumer Interests, 1972-73; mem. local candidates com. Citizens Union, 1995—. Author: The Changing Consumer, 1961, Organization for Multi-Unit Stores, 1962, Evaluation of Retail Store Location Research, 1965, Retail Marketing, 1981, Print Advertising for Shopping Centers, 1993. Trustee Wilkes Coll., Wilkes Barre, Pa., 1968-74, Reece Sch., N.Y.C., 1968-72; dir. Jewish Publs. Soc., 1992-97; trustee, exec. com. Union Am. Hebrew Congregations, 1970-81, trustee, 1992-98; trustee French and Polyclinic Med. Sch. and Health Center, N.Y.C., 1972-73, chmn. libr. com., 1998—; trustee Pub. Devel. Corp., 1974-76; bd. dirs. N.Y.C. Conv. Center, 1974-76, N.Y.C. Conv. and Visitors Bur., 1974-76; bd. dirs. Nat. Found. Jewish Culture, 1974—, treas., 1977-86, v.p., 1986-88, mem. exec. com., 1992-93, life trustee, 1998—; adv. com. N.Y. Pub. Library, 1968-74; bd. dirs. Nat. Council for Urban Econ. Devel., 1975-76; trustee Emanu-El Congregation, N.Y.C., 1968—, treas., 1990—; mem. exec. com. N.Y.C. chpt. Am. Jewish Com., 1976-87, v.p., 1984-86, exec. bd. N.Y.C. Chpt., 1992—; mem. adv. com. Inst. Internat. Edn., N.Y.C., 1974-78; mem. N.Y.C. Jewish Community Relations Council, 1976-78; mem. president's council Sch. Social Work, NYU, 1977-80; v.p. Joyce Theater Found., N.Y.C., 1980-84; exec. council Am. Jewish Hist. Assn., 1983-85; sr. v.p. Mothers/Fathers Day Coun., 1986-96; exec. com., bd. dirs. Cancer Rsch. and Treatment Fund, 1987—; mem. exec. com. Pomesa Found., N.Y.C., 1995—. Recipient I.M. Lubin award New Sch., 1974, Trustees award Internat. Coun. Shopping Ctrs., 1991; named to Retail Advt. Hall of Fame, 1989; resident fellow Explorers Club, 1997—. Mem. Forecasters Club N.Y. (hon. life mem., pres. 1973-74), Am. Statis. Assn., Am. Econ. Assn., Am. Polit. Sci. Assn., Nat. Retail Mchts. Assn. (bd. dir. 1963-72, exec. com. 1968-72, v.p. 1970, Silver Plaque award 1966), U. Club Libr. Assocs. (chmn. program com. 1983-90), Am. Retail Fedn. (dir., exec. com. 1968-72), Retail Advt. Conf. (bd. dir. 1987-91), N.Y. Acad. Scis., Nat. Assn. Scholars, Retail Mktg. Soc. (hon.), Internat. Newspaper Advt. and Mktg. Execs. (hon. life), Newcomen Soc., Regional Plan Assn. N.Y.C. (com. 2d regional plan), Archaeol. Inst. Am. (bd. dirs. 1997—), Grolier Club, Univ. Club.

EISENREICH, STEVEN JOHN, chemistry educator, environmental scientist; b. Eau Claire, Wis., Sept. 9, 1947. BS, U. Wis., Eau Claire, 1969; MS, U. Wis., Milw., 1973; PhD, U. Wis., Madison, 1975. From asst. to assoc. prof. U. Minn., Mpls., 1975-83, prof. environ. engring. dept. civil engring., 1983-95; dir. Gray Freshwater Biol. Inst. U. Minn., 1990-95; prof. Cook Coll. Rutgers U., New Brunswick, N.J., 1995—, former chair dept. environ. scis. Recipient Am. Chem. Soc. award for Creative Advances in Environ. Sci. and Tech., 1994. Mem. Am. Chem. Soc., Am. Geophys. Union, Am. Soc. Limnology Oceanography, Internat. Assn. Great Lakes Rsch. Office: Rutgers U Dept Environ Scis 14 College Farm Rd New Brunswick NJ 08901-8551*

EISENSHTAT, SIDNEY HERBERT, architect; b. New Haven, June 6, 1914; s. Morris and Ella (Sobole) E.; m. Alice D. Brenner, Dec. 19, 1937; children: Carole Oken, Abby Robyn. BArch, U. So. Calif., 1935. Registered architect, Calif. Prin. Sidney Eisenshtat & Assocs. FAIA, Beverly Hills, Calif., 1941—; mem. architects panel Union Am. Hebrew Congregations; bd. dirs. Internat. Tech. Coop. Ctr., Tel Aviv; pres., chmn. bd. dirs. Beth Jacob Congregation; v.p. L.A. Assn. Jewish Edn.; chmn. bd., pres. West Coast Talmudical Sem.; co-chmn. Nat. Conf. Religious Architecture; cons. Great Synagogue, Jerusalem, Israel; chmn. bd. Torah U. (now Yeshiva of L.A.). Prin. works include House of the Book, Brandeis, Calif., 1970 (Landmark award 1979), Sinai Temple, Los Angeles, 1959 (25 yr. Landmark award 1984), Knox Presbyn. Ch., 1965 (Los Angeles Beauty award 1975), Wells Fargo Bldg., 1975 (Beverly Hills award 1978), Union Bank Bldg., 1960, Beverly Hills, Exec. Life Bldg., 1966, Beverly Hills, Hughes Aircraft Satellite Testing and Computer Ctr., El Segundo, Calif., Friars Club, Los Angeles, 1961, Marlton Sch. for Deaf, Los Angeles, 1968, Sven Lokrantz School for Handicapped, Univ. Judaism Master Plan & Bldgs., Los Angeles, 1977, B'nai Zion Temple, El Paso, Tex., 1983, Temple Mt. Sinai, El Paso, 1962, Ctrl. Jewish Community Ctr., L.A., Bnai David Synagogue, Southfield, Mich., Hillel House, U. So. Calif.; whole body of religious archtl. work in permanent collection at Skirball Mus., L.A. as core collection of Jewish Architecture in America. Chmn., charter agy. pres. Bur. Jewish Edn. Greater L.A.; v.p., lifetime bd. mem. Jewish Fedn. Coun.; bd. dirs. Hebrew Immigration Soc.; v.p. Coun. Pres. Affiliated Orgns.; vice chmn. R-1 Commn., City of Beverly Hills. Recipient Nat. Sch. Adminstrs. award, 1966, Pub. Svc. award City of Beverly Hills, Nat. Disting. Svc. award Union Orthodox Jewish Congregations; named Honoree Bur. Jewish Edn. 60th Anniversary Celebration. Fellow AIA (honor award 1960, 66). Home: 2736 Motor Ave Los Angeles CA 90064-3413 Office: 144 S Beverly Dr Beverly Hills CA 90212-3033 *When a sanctuary succeeds in helping the congregation to feel that it stands in the presence of God, its architect has received his lifetime award. For one who has been so rewarded a few times...*

EISENSTADT, G. MICHAEL, diplomat, author, lecturer, research scholar; b. Free City of Danzig (now Gdansk, Poland), Nov. 16, 1928; s. Isidor and Edith (Lange) E.; 1 child, Judith Luzann. BA, Queens Coll., 1951; MS, U. Wis., 1952; postgrad., Russian Inst. Columbia U., 1954-56, Fgn. Svc. Inst., 1982-83. Instr. history Queens Coll., Flushing, N.Y., 1955-60; jr. officer Am. Embassy, Belgrade, Yugoslavia, 1960-61; cultural officer Am. Consulate Gen., Guayaquil, Ecuador, 1962-63; asst. cultural affairs officer Am. Embassy, Belgrade, Yugoslavia, 1963-67; cultural attaché Am. Embassy, Warsaw, Poland, 1968-71; br. pub. affairs officer Am. Embassy, Bonn, Fed. Republic of Germany, 1973-76; counselor for pub. affairs Am. Embassy, Budapest, Hungary, 1977-80; dep. counselor for pub. affairs Am. Embassy, Bonn, 1983-84; counselor for pub. affairs Am. Embassy, Belgrade, 1984-88; dep. policy officer Voice of Am., Washington, 1971-73; dir. Office Internat. Visitors USIA, Washington, 1980-82; mem. sr. seminar State Dept., Washington, 1982-83; dir. Office European Affairs USIA, Washington, 1988-89; diplomat-in-residence NYU, 1989-90; dir. N.Y. Reception Ctr. USIA, 1990-92; sr. rsch. scholar Inst. East Cen. Europe Columbia U., 1992-94; cons. on the Balkans, Ea. and Ctrl. Europe, countries of the former Soviet Union; chmn. coordinating com., chmn. drafting com. Conf. on Peace and Tolerance, Istanbul, 1994; chmn. coordinating com. Conflict Resolution Conf., Vienna, 1995; election observer OSCE in Serbia, 1997; coord. Peace and Tolerance Conf. on Kosove, Vienna, Austria, 1999. Sec. Appeal of Conscience Del. to Switzerland, 1997. With U.S. Army, 1952-54. Mem. Internat. Conf. and Seminars Assn. (pres.). Home: 880 5th Ave Apt Phe New York NY 10021-4951

EISENSTADT, PAULINE DOREEN BAUMAN, investment company executive, state legislator; b. N.Y.C., Dec. 31, 1938; d. Morris and Anne (Lautenberg) Bauman; BA, U. Fla., 1960; MS (NSF grantee), U. Ariz., 1965; postgrad. U. N.Mex.; m. Melvin M. Eisenstadt, Nov. 20, 1960; children: Todd Alan, Keith Mark. Tchr., Ariz., 1961-65, P.R., 1972-73; adminstrv. asst. Inst. Social Research U. N.Mex., 1973-74; founder, 1st exec. dir. Energy Consumers N.Mex., 1977-81; dir., host TV program Consumer Viewpoint, 1980-82; host TV program N.Mex. Today and Tomorrow, 1992—; chmn. consumer affairs adv. com. Dept. Energy, 1979-80; v.p. tech. bd. Nat. Center Appropiate Tech., 1980—; pres. Eisenstadt Enterprises, investments, 1983—; mem. N.Mex. Ho. of Reps., 1985-92, chairwoman majority caucus, chair rules com. N.Mex. House of Reps., 1987—, chair sub. com. on children and youth, 1987; mem. exec. com., vice chair pvt. coun. Nat. Conf. State Legislators, 1987; mem. N.Mex. State Senate, 1996—, mem. senate fin. com., com. higher edn., com. econ. devel., sci. & tech., water & natural resources, electric deregulation com., chair conservation com.; vice chmn. Sandoval County (N.Mex.) Democratic Party, 1981—; mem. N.Mex. Dem. State Central Com., 1981—; N.Mex. del. Dem. Nat. Platform Com., 1984, Dem. Nat. Conv., 1984; pres. Sandoval County Dem. Women's Assn., 1979-81; vice chmn. N. Mex. Dem. Platform Com., 1984—; mem. Sandoval County Redistricting Task Force, 1983-84; mem. Rio Rancho Ednl. Study Com., 1984—.; pres. Anti Defamation League, N. Mex., 1994-95; mem. N.Mex. First. Recipient Gov.'s award Outstanding N. Mex. Women, Commn. on the Status of Women and Gov. Bruce King, 1992. Author: Corrales, Portrait of a Changing Village, 1980. Mem. Kiwanis (1st woman mem. local club), Rio Rancho Rotary Club (pres. 1995—, Rotarian of the Year, 1995). Home: PO Box 658 Corrales NM 87048-0658

EISENSTAT, BENJAMIN, artist; b. Phila., June 4, 1915; s. Philip and Rose (Muskett) E.; m. Jane Sperry, Aug. 23, 1940; children: Kathryn Krall, Alice Amanda Carter. Student, Fleisher Art Meml., Phila., 1932-36, Pa. Acad. Fine Art, 1936-37, Albert Barnes Found., 1937-38. Prof. emeritus U. of the Arts, Phila., 1946-84; tchr. Fleisher Art Meml., 1946-50, Phila. Mus. Art, 1962-66, Parson's Sch. of Design, 1976-81, Acad. of Art, San Francisco, 1986; vis. prof. Cambridge (Eng.) Coll. of Art, 1976, Syracuse U., 1981; lectr. Royal Coll. Art, London, N.Y. Hist. Soc., Montclair (N.J.) State Coll., others. Group shows include Met. Mus., Nat. Acad., Pa. Acad. Fine Arts, N.Y. Soc. Illustrators, Phila. Mus. Art, Norfolk Mus., Rutgers U.; represented in collections Phila. Mus. Art, Woodmere Mus., Phila., Jefferson Hosp. U., Ford Motor Co., Mich., New Britain Mus. Am. Art, Colo., Mus. U.S. Army, Washington; murals commissioned by Heritage Trust Co., N.J., Oreland Bapt. Ch., Pa., Burlington County Bank and Trust, N.J., Abraham Strause Co. Dept. Store, others; contbr. drawings, paintings and articles to popular and profl. mags. Cpl. U.S. Army, 1943-46, ETO. Recipient Harrison Morris prize (3) Pa. Acad. Fine Art Fellowship Anns., Thornton Oakely prize Phila. Watercolor Club, Medal of Achievement, Phila. Watercolor Club, 1st prize Phila. Art Dir.'s Ann., 1st prize Watercolor USA, Springfield Mus. Fellow Pa. Acad. Fine Art; mem. Am. Watercolor Soc.,

Phila. Watercolor Soc. Avocations: collecting art, lecturing and writing about art. Home: 3639 Bryant St Palo Alto CA 94306-4209

EISENSTAT, THEODORE ELLIS, colon and rectal surgeon, educator; b. N.Y.C., Sept. 24, 1942; m. Sharon Diane Leonard, July, 1966; children: Maren Elise, Loren Aline. BA, Vanderbilt U., 1964; MD, N.Y. Med. Coll., 1968. Diplomate Am. Bd. Surgery, Am. Bd. Colon and Rectal Surgery, Nat. Bd. Med. Examiners; lic. surgeon Md., N.J., Pa. Rotating intern St. Vincent's Hosp., Worcester, Mass., 1968-69; resident in surgery Thomas Jefferson U. Hosp., Phila., 1969-71; chief resident in surgery Pa. Hosp., Phila., 1971-73; fellow in colon and rectal surgery Muhlenberg Hosp.-Robert Wood Johnson Sch. Medicine, N.J., 1977-78; dir. surg. endoscopy U. Md., 1975-80, dir. colon & rectal svc., 1976-80; asst. prof. surgery U. Md. Sch. Medicine, 1975-80; sr. attending surgeon Muhlenberg Regional Med. Ctr., Plainfield, N.J., 1979—, John F. Kennedy Med. Ctr., Edison, N.J., 1979—; clin. assoc. prof. surgery U. Medicine and Dentistry of N.J., Newark, 1981—; clin. prof. surgery Robert Wood Johnson Med. Sch. U. Medicine and Dentistry of N.J., New Brunswick, N.J., 1979-91; clin. prof. surgery U. Medicine and Dentistry of N.J., New Brunswick, 1991—, dir. colon and rectal residency program, 1993—; cons. surgeon Lock Raven VA Hosp., Balt., 1975-80, U.S. Army, Kimbrough Army Hosp., Ft. Meade, Md., 1975-80; bd. dirs., ACS rep. Am. Bd. Colon and Rectal Surgery, 1990-96, pres., 1995-96; attending surgeon Robert Wood Johnson U. Hosp., New Brunswick, N.J., 1984—; exhibitor and presenter in field; vis. prof. U. Md. Sch. Medicine, 1983, Abington (Pa.) Meml. Hosp., 1985, York (Pa.) Hosp., 1990, Pa. Hosp., Phila., 1990, others. Contbr. articles to profl. jours. Maj. U.S. Army, 1973-75. Fellow ACS (adv. coun. colon and rectal surgery), Am. Soc. Colon and Rectal Surgeons (Walter A. Fansler award 1977, Purdue Frederick fellow 1977, 1st prize sci. exhibit 1979); mem. AMA, Soc. for Surgery of Alimentary Tract, Assn. for Acad. Surgery, Soc. Am. Gastrointestinal Endoscopic Surgeons (founder 1981, bd. govs. 1986-89), Am. Soc. Gastrointestinal Endoscopy, N.Y. Soc. Colon and Rectal Surgeons (mem. coun. 1983-85, sec.-treas. 1986-87, v.p. 1988-89, pres. 1990-92, 1st prize film 1978), Pa. Soc. Colon. and Rectal Surgeons, N.J. Soc. Colon and Rectal Surgeons (sec.-treas. 1983-85, pres. 1989-90), N.J. Soc. Gastroenterology, N.J. Soc. Gastrointestinal Endoscopy, Assn. Mil. Surgeons U.S., Soc. Surgeons N.J., Crohn's and Colitis Found. Am.

EISENSTEIN, BRUCE ALLAN, electrical engineering educator; b. Phila., Sept. 10, 1941; s. Ira S. and Rose Eisenstein; m. Toby Karet, Sept. 8, 1963; children: Eric, Andrew, Ilana. BEE, MIT, 1963; MEE, Drexel U., 1965; PhD, U. Pa., 1970. Registered profl. engr., Pa. Vis. asst. prof. Princeton (N.J.) U., 1970-71; asst. prof. Drexel U., Phila., 1971-77, assoc. dean grad. sch., 1976-78, prof., head dept. elec. and computer engring., 1980-95, Arthur J. Rowland prof., 1996—; cons. forensic engring. numerous lawyers; cons. electronics and signal processing projects various indsl. and legal firms, book pubs.; chmn. adv. com. for elect., communications and systems engring. divsn. NSF; mem. adv. com. for engring. directorate NSF, adv. coun. for engring. C.C. Phila., 1992-96. Bd. mgrs. Cen. High Sch. Alumni Assn., Phila, 1972-79, chmn. com. on sch. standards, 1974-76. Ford Found. fellow, 1965, NASA-Am. Soc. Engring. Edn. summer faculty fellow Stanford U., 1969. Fellow IEEE (bd. dirs. 1993-96, 1998—, v.p. tech. activities, chair tech. activities bd. 1995-96, treas. 1998, pres.-elect 1999, exec. com. bd. dirs., exec. com. Phila. sect., counselor); mem. Edn. Soc. IEEE (pres. 1984-85, bd. dirs. 1983-93, mem. AdCom, Achievement award 1987), Am. Soc. Engring. Edn., Sigma Xi, Eta Kappa Nu (C. Holmes McDonald award 1976), Tau Beta Pi. Republican. Jewish. Avocations: squash, tennis, skiing, classical music-piano. Home: Pine Rd Wyndmoor PA 19038-8527 Office: Drexel U Dept Elec & Computer Engring 32nd Chestnut Philadelphia PA 19104

EISENSTEIN, ELIZABETH LEWISOHN, historian, educator; b. N.Y.C., Oct. 11, 1923; d. Sam A. and Margaret V. (Seligman) Lewisohn; m. Julian Calvert Eisenstein, May 30, 1948; children: Margaret, John (dec.), Edward. A.B., Vassar Coll., 1944; M.A., Radcliffe Coll., 1947, Ph.D., 1953; Litt. D. (hon.), Mt. Holyoke Coll., 1979. From lectr. to adj. prof history Am. U., Washington, 1959-74; Alice Freeman Palmer prof. history U. Mich., Ann Arbor, 1975-88, prof. emerita, 1988—; scholar-in-residence Rockefeller Found. Center, Bellagio, Italy, June 1977; mem. vis. com. dept. history Harvard U., 1975-81, vice-chmn., 1979-81; dir. Ecole des Hautes Etudes en Sciences Sociales, Paris, 1982; guest speaker, participant confs. and seminars; I. Beam vis. prof. U. Iowa, 1980; Mead-Swing lectr. Oberlin Coll., 1980; Stone lectr. U. Glasgow, 1984; Van Leer lectr. Van Leer Fedn., Jerusalem, 1984; Hanes lectr. U. N.C., Chapel Hill, 1985 first resident cons. Center for the Book, Library of Congress, Washington, 1979; mem. Coun. Scholars, 1980-88; pres.'s disting. visitor Vassar Coll., 1988; Pforzheimer lectr. N.Y. Pub. Libr., 1989, Lyell lectr. Bodleian Libr., Oxford, 1990, Merle Curti lectr. U. Wis., Madison, 1992, Jantz lectr. Oberlin Coll., 1995, Clifford lectr. Austin, Tex., 1996; vis. fellow Wolfson Coll., Oxford, 1990. Author: The First Professional Revolutionist: F. M. Buonarroti, 1959, The Printing Press as an Agent of Change, 1979 , 2 vols. paperback edit., 1980 (Phi Beta Kappa Ralph Waldo Emerson prize 1980), The Printing Revolution in Early Modern Europe, 1983 (reissued as Canto Book, 1993), Grub Street Abroad, 1992; mem. editorial bd. Jour. Modern History, 1973-76, 83-86, Revs. in European History, 1973-86, Jour. Library History, 1979-82, Eighteenth Century Studies, 1981-84; contbr. articles to profl. jours., chpts. to books. Belle Skinner fellow Vassar Coll., NEH fellow, 1977, Guggenheim fellow, 1982, fellow Ctr. Advanced Studies in Behavioral Scis., 1982-83, 92-93, Humanities Rsch. Ctr. fellow Australian Nat. U., 1988. Fellow Am. Acad. Arts and Scis., Royal Hist. Soc.; mem. Soc. French Hist. Studies (v.p. 1970, mem. program com. 1974), Am. Soc. 18th Century Studies (nominating com. 1971), Soc. 16th Century Studies, Am. Hist. Assn. (com. on coms. 1970-72, chmn. Modern European sect. 1981, council 1982-85), Renaissance Soc. Am. (council 1973-76, pres. 1986), Am. Antiquarian Soc. (exec. com., adv. bd. 1984-87), Phi Beta Kappa. Office: U Mich Dept History Ann Arbor MI 48109

EISENSTEIN, ELLIOT MARTIN, pediatrician; b. Englewood, N.J., May 20, 1935; s. Max and Anne Lillian (Landau) E.; m. Carol Anita Isenberg, July 4, 1955 (div. Nov. 1996); children: Sheryl, Debbie, Alan, Michael, Jonathon, Robert; m. Marcie Anne Krommenohl, Dec. 6, 1996. BS cum laude, Franklin & Marshall, 1956; MD with distinction, George Washington U., 1960. Cert. Am. Bd. Pediatrics. Pvt. practice Wayne, N.J., 1965—. Bd. dirs. Jewish Family Svc. North Jersey, Wayne, 1985— (past v.p.); capt. U.S. Army, 1960-65. Mem. Shomrei Torah, Wayne, N.J., 1973— (past pres.). Rep. Jewish. Office: 1055 Hamburg Tpke Wayne NJ 07470-3211

EISENSTEIN, THEODORE DONALD, pediatrician; b. N.Y.C., July 4, 1930; s. Harry and Myra (Drexler) E.; married; children: Janet, Stephen. Student, NYU, 1948-49; A.B., Johns Hopkins U., 1952; M.D., Albany Med. Coll., 1956. Diplomate Am. Bd. Pediatrics. Pediatric intern Kings County Med. Ctr., Bklyn., 1956-57; resident in pediatrics N.Y. Hosp., N.Y.C., 1957-59; NIH vis. fellow in pediatric endocrinology Columbia-Presbyn. Med. Ctr., N.Y.C., 1961-62; practice medicine specializing in pediatrics West Caldwell, N.J., 1962—; full attending staff St. Barnabas Med. Ctr.; v.p. Pediatric Assos. West Essex, P.A.; asst. clin. prof. pediatrics Columbia U. Coll. Phys. and Surg., 1970—; clin. asst. prof. pediatrics N.J. Coll. Medicine and Dentistry, Rutgers U., 1970—. Research on pediatric endocrinology, human growth hormone. Mem. alumni coun. N.Y. Hosp.-Cornell Med. Ctr. Served with M.C., USAF, 1959-61. Fellow Am. Acad. Pediatrics; mem. AMA, Acad. Medicine N.J., Am. Diabetes Assn., AAAS, Soc. Practitioners Columbia-Presbyn. Med. Ctr., Albany Med. Coll. Alumni Assn., Am. Physicians Fellowship, N.J. Med. Sch. Faculty Orgn. Jewish. Home: 7 Byron Rd N Caldwell NJ 07006-4203 Office: St Barnabas Med Ctr Old Short Hills Rd Livingston NJ 07039

EISENSTEIN, TOBY K., microbiology educator; b. Phila., Sept. 15, 1942; d. Edward and Sylvia (Mandel) Karet; m. Bruce A. Eisenstein, Sept. 8, 1963; children: Eric, Andrew, Ilana. BA, Wellesley Coll., 1964; PhD, Bryn Mawr Coll., 1969. Instr. Med. Sch. Temple U., Phila., 1969-71, asst. prof., 1971-79, assoc. prof. microbiology and immunology Med. Sch., 1979-84, prof., 1984—, acting chair, 1990-92; mem. bacteriology and mycology study sect., NIH, 1976-80, 88-92, Drugs of Abuse and AIDS study sect., 1994—. Contbr. articles to profl. jours. NIH fellow, 1965-69; USPHS grantee, 1971—. Fellow Am. Acad. Microbiology; mem. AAAS, Am. Soc. Microbiology (pres. Ea. Pa. br. 1985-86, coun. policy com. 1993-96), Am. Assn. Immunologists, Soc. Leukocyte Biology (sec. 1998—), Internat. Endotoxin Soc., Coll. on Problems of Drug Dependence, Sigma Xi, (pres. Temple U. chpt. 1981-83). Office: Temple U Sch Medicine Dept Microbiology and Immunology 3400 N Broad St Philadelphia PA 19140-5104

EISENTHAL, KENNETH B., physical chemistry educator; b. N.Y.C., Mar. 23, 1933; s. Benjamin and Sarah (Shafer) E.; children: Julia, Jessica, Andrew. BS, Bklyn. Coll., 1954; MA, Harvard U., 1957, PhD, 1959. NIH postdoctoral fellow UCLA, 1959-61; rsch. scientist Aerospace Corp., El Segundo, Calif., 1961-63; rsch. assoc. UCLA, 1963-64; rsch. scientist, head of phys. scis IBM, San Jose, Calif., 1964-75; prof. Columbia U., N.Y.C., 1975—, chair dept. chemistry, 1996—; cons. IBM, Yorktown Heights, N.Y., 1985—. Author, editor: Picosecond Phenomena, 1982, Ultrafast Phenomena IV, 1984, Picosecond Spec. to Chemistry, 2984; contbr. articles on laser chemistry to jours. in field; mem. editorial adv. bd. Chem. Physics Letters, 1987—, Jour. Chem. Physics, 1985-87, Laser Chemistry, 1985—, Jour. Phys. Chemistry, 1980-83; editor adv. bd. Molecular Physics, 1992. Guggenheim fellow, 1984-85; recipient Bryce Crawford award in Spectroscopy, 1995' Oxford U. Hinshelwood lectr., 1996. Fellow Am. Phys.Soc. (chmn. div. chem. physics 1993); mem. Am. Chem. Soc. (Arthur W. Adamson award 1998), Phi Beta Kappa, Sigma Xi. Jewish. Avocations: reading, handball, biking. Office: Dept Chemistry Columbia Univ 3000 Broadway Mail Code 3107 New York NY 10027

EISERER, LEONARD ALBERT CARL, publishing executive; b. Polar, Wis., June 3, 1916; s. Herman Frederick and Anna Elizabeth (Schnieder) E.; m. Lorraine Elizabeth Hickey, June 28, 1941; children: Carol Jean, Elaine Roberta, Leonard Arnold, Beverly Arlene. B.A., Roosevelt U., Chgo., 1937; M.S. in Journalism, Northwestern U., 1939. Editor Am. Aviation Publs., Inc., Washington, 1939-51, v.p., gen. mgr., 1952-57, exec. v.p., sec., 1958-62; pres., pub. Sports Age, Inc., Washington, 1962-63; chmn., CEO Bus. Pubs., Inc., Silver Spring, Md., 1963—. Chmn. Carol Jean Cancer Found., Inc.; bd. dirs. U. N.C. at Greensboro Excellence Found.; pres., dir. Eiserer-Hickey Found., Inc.; dir. Univ. Club of Washington Found. Lt. USN, 1942-46. Named to Hall of Fame Newsletter Pubs. Found., 1994, Man of Yr. Univ. Club of Washington, 1995; inductee Hall of Achievement, Northwestern U. Medill Sch. Journalism, 1997. Mem. Air and Waste Mgmt. Assn., Water Environ. Fedn., Soc. Profl. Journalists, Nat. Press Club, Univ. Club, Newsletter Pubs. Assn. Home: 9101 Sligo Creek Pky Silver Spring MD 20901-3360 Office: Bus Pubs Inc 951 Pershing Dr Silver Spring MD 20910-4432

EISERT, EDWARD GAVER, lawyer; b. N.Y.C., May 26, 1948; s. Israel Jay and Bess (Gaver) E.; div.; children: Carolyn B., Stephen J. AB, Cornell U., 1969; JD, NYU, 1973. Bar: N.Y. 1974. Law clk. to Judge Charles L. Brieant U.S. Dist. Ct. (so. dist.) N.Y., N.Y.C., 1973-74; assoc. Simpson Thacher & Bartlett, N.Y.C., 1974-76; assoc. Schulte Roth & Zabel, N.Y.C., 1976-80, ptnr., 1981—; Bd. dirs. N.Y. Small Bus. Venture Fund LLC., 1998—. Note and comment editor NYU Law Rev., 1972-73. Mem. ABA (com. on fed. regulation of securities 1983—, subcom. on ann. rev. fed. regulation of securities 1983-89, subcom. on mcpl. and govtl. obligations 1984-92, subcom. on investment cos. and investment advisors 1992—), N.Y. Stat Bar Assn., Assn. Bar City N.Y., Nat. Assn. Bond Lawyers (joint ABA/Nat. Assn. Bond Lawyers task force on roles of counsel in state and local govt. securities transactions 1984-87), Univ. Club of N.Y.C. Club: University (N.Y.C.). Home: 302 Church St White Plains NY 10603-3525 Office: Schulte Roth & Zabel 900 3rd Ave Fl 19 New York NY 10022-4774

EISINGER, ROBERT PETER, nephrologist, educator; b. N.Y.C., Oct. 29, 1929; s. Jacob Samuel and Rose (Sapir) E.; m. Miriam Blumberg, Sept. 4, 1956; children: Ari, Dina. AB, Swarthmore Coll., 1951; MD, Columbia U., 1955. Diplomate Am. Bd. Internal Medicine, Am. Bd. Nephrology. From instr. to assoc. prof. NYU Sch. Medicine, N.Y.C., 1963-73; prof. medicine, chief nephrology U. Medicine & Dentistry N.J., Robert Wood Johnson Med. Sch., New Brunswick, 1973-98, prof. emeritus, 1998—. Capt. USAF, 1959-61.

EISLAND, JUNE M., councilwoman; b. Bklyn.; d. Harold R. and Ina (Hollander) Merahn; m. Paul Eisland; children: Marla, Bruce Margolin, Evan. Student, U. Miami, Fla. City councilwoman N.Y.C. Coun. Dist. 11, 1979—, dep. majority whip; chairwoman land use com., mem. transp., fin., pub. safety, rules, privileges and elections com. N.Y.C. Coun. Mem. NAACP, LWV, Bronx Women's Polit. Caucus (charter), Network Orgn. Bronx Women, Nat. League Cities (mem. adv. bd.), Nat. Coun. Jewish Women, B'nai B'rith Women. Office: 3636 Waldo Ave Bronx NY 10463-2247*

EISLER, COLIN TOBIAS, art historian, curator; b. Hamburg, Germany, Mar. 17, 1931; came to U.S., 1940, naturalized, 1946; s. George Bernard and Kate Minden (Basseches) E.; m. Benita J. Blitzer, 1960; 1 child, Rachel. Ed., Yale U., 1952; postgrad. (Henry fellow), Magdalen Coll., Oxford (Eng.) U., 1952-53; Ph.D., Harvard U., 1956. Instr. art Yale U., 1955-56, asst. prof., 1956-57, curator dept. print and drawings, 1955-57; fellow Saybrook Coll.; mem. faculty Harvard U., summer 1956; mem. faculty N.Y. U. Inst. Fine Arts, 1958-60, asst. prof., 1960-65; assoc. prof. to prof. NYU Inst. Fine Arts, 1965-70, Robert Lehman prof. art, 1977—; research curator paintings dept. Met. Museum Art, N.Y.C., 1958-60; sr. fellow ctr. for advanced study in the visual arts Nat. Gallery of Art, 1987-88; past mem. vis. com. Smith Coll. Art Mus., Wellesley Coll. Art Mus.; sec. Nat. Com. History of Art, 1958-92; exec. mem. Comité International pour l'histoire de l'art; fellow Inst. Advanced Study, 1957-58; Disting. vis. prof. George Washington U., 1987-88, Jewish Theol. Sem., 1992; mem. adv./selection com. Am. Acad. in Berlin. Author: Early Netherlandish Painting in New England Collections, 1960, The Seeing Hand, 1975, European Paintings Excluding Italian from the Samuel M. Kress Collection, 1976, The Master of the Unicorn, 1979, Sculptors' Drawings Over Five Centuries, 1981, Early Netherlandish Paintings in the Thyssen Collection, 1989, The Genius of Jacob Bellini, 1989, Cats Know Best, 1990, Paintings of the Hermitage, 1990, Durer's Animals, 1992, David's Songs, 1992, Masterworks in Berlin, 199 6(TV series) Art of the Western World-The Northern Renaissance, 1989; Editorial bd.: Coll. Art Bulletin, 1953-55, Studia Neerlandica, 1976—, Jour. Jewish Art, 1979—, Encyclopedia Americana, 1992—; assoc. editor Renaissance Quar., 1989-92; curator: The Grand Tour, Montgomery, Ala., Sculptor's Drawings, Drawing Ctr., 1986, Show and Tell: Artists' Illustrated Letters, Grey Art Gallery, NYU, 1990. Mem. exbn. com. Jewish Mus., 1990-93, Cooper-Hewitt Vis. Com., Internat. Ctr. for Photography, 1988-94; Jewish monuments com. World Monuments Commn. Commn. Relief Belge fellow, 1953, 55; Ford fellow, 1959; Guggenheim fellow, 1960-61; Nat. Endowment for Humanities sr. fellow, 1972-73; Am. Council Learned Socs. fellow, 1979; Delmas fellow, 1980; Kress travel grantee. Mem. Coll. Art Assn. (dir. 1958-61, editorial bd. 1978—). Club: Elizabethan. Office: NYU Inst Fine Arts 1 E 78th St New York NY 10021-0102

EISLER, DAVID LEE, provost; m. Patricia Johnson; children: Heather, Lindsay. BM high distinction, Univ. Mich., 1972; MM summa cum laude, Yale Univ., 1975; DMA high distinction, Univ. Mich., 1978. Coord. instrumental music Troy State, 1978-90, exec. dir. southeast band clinic, 1979-90, dir., grad. studies, 1980-90, asst. dean. of fine arts, 1982-90; dean. coll. fine arts Eastern New Mex., 1990-96; provost Weber State Univ., Ogden, Utah, 1996—; Host, Strike up the Band on NPR, 1979-90, clinician and cons., G. Leblanc Corp., 1984-94, concert soloist, recitalist. Contbr. articles to profl. jours. Judge Nat. Assn. Media Edn.; founding mem. High Plains Art Coun., exec.bd. Conquistador Coun., Boy Scouts Am. Named Vol. of Yr. Cmty. Svcs. Ctr., 1993-94, WSU Exemplary Collaboration Awd., 1999. Mem. Am. Assn. Higher Edn., Nat. Band Assn., Internat. Clarinet Soc., Coll. Band Dirs. Nat. Assn., Rotary Internatl., Phi Kappa Lambda, Kappa Kappa Psi, Phi Mu Alpha, Tau Beta Sigma. Office: Weber State Univ 1004 University Cir Ogden UT 84408-1004

EISLER, MILLARD MARCUS, financial executive; b. Toledo, Ohio, Mar. 31, 1950; s. Joseph R. and Marilynn (Gross) E. BS, Ind. U., 1972; MBA, Cornell U., 1977. CPA, Ill., Mass., N.H. Auditor Arthur Andersen & Co., Boston, 1977-79; mgr. internat. acctg. Wheelabrator-Frye, Inc., Hampton, N.H., 1979-81; mgr. ops. analysis and audit GCA Corp., Bedford, Mass., 1981-85; mgr. cost acctg. and fin. analysis Precision Sci., Inc., Chgo., 1985-86, contr., chief fin. officer, 1986-89; tax preparer H&R Block, Inc., Chgo., 1989-92; tax preparer H&R Block, Inc., Lincoln, Nebr., 1993, quality control mgr., 1994; franchise dir., dist. mgr. H&R Block, Inc., Madison, Wis., 1994-98; tax preparer H.R. Block, Madison, Wis., 1999—; fin. mgmt. cons. CUNA Mutual Group, Madison, 1998—; bd. dirs. Franklin Software Co., Arvada, Colo.; lectr. Northeastern Ill. U., Chgo., 1986-88. Mem. Ind. U. Alumni Assn., Cornell U. Alumni Assn. of Wis. Democrat. Jewish. Home: 834 S Gammon Rd Madison WI 53719-1381 Office: CUNA Mutual Group 5910 Mineral Point Rd Madison WI 53705

EISMA, JOSE A., physician; b. Jolo, Sulu, Philippines, Oct. 18, 1939; came to U.S., 1964, naturalized, 1973; s. Marcelo L. and Rosa A. (Albarracin) E.; A.A., Silliman U., Philippines, 1958; M.D., U. Santo Tomas (Manila), 1963; m. Lenora Womack, Sept. 14, 1977; children: Joseph Alan, John Mitchell, Gregory Mitchell, Teresa Lyn, Lorell Elizabeth, Julia Dawn. Diplomate Am. Bd. Family Practice. Rotating intern Wilson Meml. Hosp., Johnson City, N.Y., 1964-65, med. resident, 1965-67; med. resident Kingsbrook Jewish Med. Center, Bklyn., 1967-68; gen. internist Reynolds Army Hosp., Ft. Sill, Okla., 1971-73; resident in pulmonary disease Brooke Army Med. Center, Ft. Sam Houston, Tex., 1973-74; chief of medicine, med. dir. respiratory therapy dept. West (Tex.) Community Hosp., 1976—, bd. dirs., 1986. Served to col., M.C., 1975-80; surgeon Army N.G. State, 1991-93. Fellow Am. Acad. Family Physicians; mem. A.C.P., Res. Officers Assn., Tex. N.G. Assn., Assn. U.S. Army, Assn. Mil. Surgeons of U.S. Contbr. article to profl. publ. in field. Home: 1406 N Reagan St West TX 76691-1022 Office: 401 Meadow Dr West TX 76691

EISNER, DIANA, pediatrician; b. Houston, May 7, 1951; d. Elmer and Edith (Dubow) E. BA in Biology cum laude, Brandeis U., 1973; MD, Southwestern Med. Sch., 1977. Diplomate Am. Bd. Pediatrics. Intern, resident Baylor Coll. Medicine, Houston, 1977-80; pvt. practice Houston, 1981—; chmn. dept. pediatrics Meml. N.W. Hosp., Houston, 1990. Recipient Commendation award Children's Protection Com. Tex. Children's Hosp., 1978, Physician's Recognition award AMA, 1983. Mem. Am. Acad. Pediatrics, Tex. Med. Assn., Tex. Pediatric Soc., Houston Pediatric Soc., Harris County Med. Soc. Avocations: ballet, swimming, walking. Office: 2030 North Loop W Ste 125 Houston TX 77018-8107

EISNER, HENRY WOLFGANG, advertising agency executive; b. Germany, July 3, 1920; came to U.S., 1940, naturalized, 1943; s. Walter M. and Elsa J. E.; student U. Zurich, 1938-39, London Polytechnic U., 1939-40, Georgetown U., 1943, Johns Hopkins U., 1943-49; m. Harriet Sauber, July 11, 1943; children: Nancy Eisner, Steve C. Editor European story dept. 20th Century Fox, 1939; copywriter Balt. News Am., 1940-42; prodn. mgr. S.A. Levyne Co., Balt., 1946-48, copywriter, 1948-52, account mgmt. supr., 1952-60, exec. v.p., 1960-65; pres. Eisner & Assocs., Balt., 1965-85, chmn., 1986—. Bd. dirs. The Associated Jewish Cmty. Fedn. Balt.; trustee, mem. sr. adv. coun. Park Sch., Jewish Family Services, La Chaine des Rotisseurs; chmn. Levering Hall adv. com. Johns Hopkins U. Mem. Am. Assn. Advt. Agys. Club: Suburban of Baltimore County (pres.). Home: 3623 Anton Farms Rd Baltimore MD 21208-1705 Office: Eisner & Assocs Inc 509 South Exeter St Baltimore MD 21202

EISNER, HOWARD, engineering educator, engineering executive; b. N.Y.C., Aug. 8, 1935; s. Samuel Eisner and Mary (Isser) Wegodner; m. Joan Arlene Knopfer, Feb. 9, 1957(div. 1994); children: Seth Eric, Susan Rachel, Oren David; m. June B. Linowitz, Nov. 8, 1995. BEE, CCNY, 1957; MS, Columbia U., 1958; DSc, George Washington U., 1966. Teaching asst. Columbia U., 1957; lectr. dept. physics Bklyn. Coll., 1957-59; lectr., asst. professorial lectr. George Washington U., 1961-67; prof. U. Maryland, 1987-89; various engring. positions ORI, Inc., Rockville, Md., 1959-68, v.p., 1968-71, exec. v.p., 1971-84, corp. exec. v.p., 1984-85, also dir.; pres. Intercon Systems Corp. subs. ORI, Group, Inc., Rockville, 1985-89, Atlantic Research Services Corp., Alexandria, Va., 1987-89; Disting. rsch. prof. George Washington U., Washington, 1989—. Author: Advanced Algebra, 1960, Computer-Aided Systems Engineering, 1988, Essentials of Project and Systems Engineering Management, 1997; contbr. articles in field. Fellow IEEE, N.Y. Acad. Scis.; mem. AIAA, INFORMS, Sigma Xi, Tau Beta Pi, Eta Kappa Nu, Omega Rho. Avocations: personal computers, tennis, choral singing, writing. Office: George Washington U Rm 704 SEAS-EMGT Gelman Libr Washington DC 20052

EISNER, SISTER JANET MARGARET, college president; b. Boston, Oct. 10, 1940; d. Eldon and Ada (Martin) E. AB, Emmanuel Coll., 1963; MA, Boston Coll., 1969; PhD, U. Mich., 1975; LHD (hon.), Northeastern U. Joined Sisters of Notre Dame de Namur, Roman Cath. Ch. Dir. admissions Emmanuel Coll., 1967-71; lectr., teaching asst. U. Mich., Ann Arbor, 1971-73; dir. Emmanuel Coll. and City of Boston Pairings, 1976-78, asst. prof. English, 1976-78, chmn. dept., 1977-78, acting pres., 1978-79, pres., 1979—; mem. Mass. Bd. Regents, chmn. regents planning com., 1980-86; mem. adv. bd. Ctr. for Religious Devel., 1983—; mem. exec. com. Boston Higher Edn. Partnership, 1991—. Trustee Trinity Coll., 1979-85, mem. adv. coun. on enrollment planning, 1981-82; adv. coun. pres. Assn. Governing Bds., 1982-88; mem. commn. on women in higher edn. Am. Coun. on Edn., 1985-87; mem. adv. bd. Synod of Archdiocese of Boston, 1988, Anti-Defamation League Dinner Com., 1988-89; chair four-yr. coll. div. United Way Campaign, 1989; mem. NAICU/NIIC joint task force Minority Participation in Ind. Higher Edn., 1989; mem. govs. award com. Carballo Scholarships, 1989; bd. dirs. Med. Area Svc. Corp., 1989—; trustee Boston Cath. TV Ctr., 1990—. Rackham prize fellow, Ford Found. fellow, 1973-75. Mem. Nat. Assn. Ind. Colls. and Univs. (commn. on policy analysis 1991—), Assn. Ind. Colls. and Univs. in Mass. (chair 1991—), Women's Coll. Coalition (exec. com. 1991—). Office: Emmanuel Coll Office of the President 400 Fenway Boston MA 02115-5725*

EISNER, MICHAEL DAMMANN, entertainment company executive; b. Mt. Kisco, N.Y., Mar. 7, 1942; s. Lester and Margaret (Dammann) E.; m. Jane Breckenridge; children: Breck, Eric, Anders. BA, Denison U., 1964. Began career in programming dept. CBS; asst. to nat. programming dir. ABC, 1966-68, mgr. spls. and talent, dir. program devel.-East Coast, 1968-71, dir. program devel. East Coast, 1968-71; dir. feature films and program devel. ABC, $D, $D, 1969; v.p. daytime programming ABC, 1971-75, v.p. program planning and devel., 1975-76, sr. v.p. prime time prodn. and devel., 1976; pres., chief operating officer Paramount Pictures, 1976-84; chmn., chief exec. officer Walt Disney Co., Burbank, Calif., 1984—; governor Mighty Ducks of Anaheim, 1993. Trustee Denison U., Calif. Inst. Arts; bd. dirs. Am. Hosp. of Paris Found., Conservation Internat., UCLA Exec. Bd. for Med. Sci. Office: Walt Disney Co 500 S Buena Vista St Burbank CA 91521-0004

EISNER, NEIL ROBERT, lawyer; b. Syracuse, N.Y., Feb. 19, 1943; s. Martin Bert and Bertha Martha (Roniger) E.; m. Joan Merle Stock, Sept. 11, 1966; children: David Jeffrey, Jennifer Lauren; m. Janis Lynn Paushter, Feb. 8, 1981. AB, Syracuse U., 1964; JD, Columbia U., 1967. Bar: N.Y. 1967, D.C. 1972. Trial atty. FAA, Washington, 1967-72, chief accident counsel br., 1972-76, dep. asst. chief counsel, 1976, asst. chief counsel, 1976-78; asst. gen. counsel U.S. Dept. Transp., Washington, 1978—; mem. Adminstrv. Conf. U.S., Washington, 1982-95. Mem. ABA (coun. mem. sect. on adminstrv. law & regulatory practice 1989-92), D.C. Bar Assn., Pi Sigma Alpha (chpt. pres. 1963-64). Jewish. Home: 6356 Lakeview Dr Falls Church VA 22041-1333 Office: US Dept Transp 7th and D Sts SW Washington DC 20590

EISNER, PETER NORMAN, journalist, author, news agency executive; b. Jersey City, Aug. 27, 1950; s. Bernard and Lorraine (Gropper) E.; m. Musha Salinas, Aug. 27, 1982; children: Isabel, Marina. BA, Rutgers U., 1972. Reporter Hudson (N.Y.) Register-Star, 1974-75, Poughkeepsie (N.Y.) Jour., 1975-76; newsman AP, Columbus, N.Y.C., 1978-1979; Brazil corr. AP, Brasilia, 1979-81; Venezuela bur. chief. AP, Caracas, 1982; news editor, Mex., Cen. Am. AP, Mex. City, 1982-83; dep. fgn. editor Newsday, N.Y.C., 1984-85, sr. editor fgn. news, 1985-89, sr. corr., 1989-94; mng. dir. NewsCom, Coral Gables, Fla., 1994-98, Ctr. for Pub. Integrity, Washington, 1999—. Author, editor, translator: Death Beat, 1994, America's Prisoner, 1997. Mem. bd. advisors C.Am. Journalists Program, 1989-93. Mem. Interam. Press Assn. (freedom of press com. 1988-94, bd. dirs. 1988-94). Office: Ctr for Pub Integrity 910 17th St NW 7th Fl Washington DC 20006

EISNER, PHILIP NATHAN, management consultant; b. Springfield, Mass., Mar. 7, 1934; s. Samuel Cole and Esther (Hurwitz) E.; m. Elizabeth

Renwick Whittingham, Dec. 3, 1960; 1 child, Edward. BS, MIT, 1955; PhD, NYU, 1969. Rsch. scientist ITT Labs, Nutley, N.J., 1967-61; assoc. dir. Space Physics Lab Dewey Electronics Corp., Paramus, N.J., 1961-72; project mgr. Exxon Corp. Rsch. Lab., Linden, N.J., 1972-81; sr. staff advisor Exxon Rsch. & Engring. Co., Florham Park, N.J., 1981-86; pres. Eisner Consulting, Summit, N.J., 1986—. Patentee in field; contbr. articles to profl. jours. Active Bd. Edn., Summit, 1997—. Mem. AAAS. Home and Office: 30 Garden Rd Summit NJ 07901-3029

EISNER, RICHARD ALAN, accountant; b. N.Y.C., Feb. 25, 1934; s. Joseph and Helen (Cohen) E.; m. Carole Swid, May 7, 1961; children: Joseph, Susan, Douglas, Michael, Hallie. BA, Yale U., 1956; MBA, Harvard Bus. Sch., 1958. CPA, N.Y. Acct. Eisner & Lubin, N.Y.C., 1959-63; mng. ptnr. Richard A. Eisner & Co., N.Y.C., 1963—; mem. new sch. adv. bd. Columbia Sch. Pub. Health. Chmn. audit com. UJA of N.Y.; bd. trustees Jewish Fund for Justice, N.Y.C, Beth Israel Hosp.; hon. bd. trustees Horace Mann Sch., Bronx, N.Y.C. Mem. Harmonie Club, Yale Club. Democrat. Avocations: reading, classical music, tennis, chess. Office: Richard A Eisner & Co 575 Madison Ave Fl 7 New York NY 10022-2597

EISNER, THOMAS, biologist, educator; b. Berlin, June 25, 1929; s. Hans Edouard and Margarete (Heil) E.; m. Maria Lobell, June 10, 1952; children: Yvonne, Vivian, Christina. BA, Harvard U., 1951, PhD, 1955; DSc (hon.), U. Wüzburg, Germany, 1982, U. Zürich, Switzerland, 1983, U. Göteborg, Sweden, 1989, Drexel U., 1992. Postdoctoral fellow Harvard U., 1955-57; asst. prof. biology Cornell U., Ithaca, N.Y., 1957-62, assoc. prof., 1962-66, prof., 1966-76, Jacob Gould Schurman prof. chem. ecology, 1976—, dir. Cornell Inst. for Rsch. in Chem. Ecology, 1992—; sr. fellow Cornell Ctr. for the Environ., 1994—; vis. scientist dept. entomology Sch. Agr., Wageningen, The Netherlands, 1964-65; vis. scientist Smithsonian Tropical Rsch. Lab., Barro Colorado Island, C.Z., 1968; sr. vis. scientist Max Planck Inst. für Verhaltensphysiologie, Seewiesen, Fed. Republic Germany, 1971, Divsn. Entomology, CSIRO, Canberra, Australia, 1972-73; Rand fellow Marine Biol. Labs., Woods Hole, Mass., 1974; vis. rsch. prof. U. Fla., Gainesville, 1977-78; rsch. assoc. Archbold Biol. Sta., 1973—; vis. prof. Stanford U., 1979-80, U. Zürich, 1980-81. Co-author: Animal Adaptation, 1964, Life on Earth, 1973, and 6 other books; mem. editl. bd. Sci., 1970-71, Am. Naturalist, 1970-71, Jour. Comparative Physiology, 1974-80, Jour. Chem. Ecology, 1974—, Behavioral Ecology and Sociobiology, 1976-97, Sci. Yr. World Books, 1979-82, Human Ecology Forum, 1981-85, Living Bird Quar., 1982-88, Experientia, 1982-96, Quar. Rev. Biology, 1983-87, Chemoecology, 1997—; co-editor: Explorations in Chemical Ecology Series, 1987—; contbr. articles to profl. jours. Recipient Archie F. Carr medal, 1983, Procter prize Sigma Xi, 1986, Karl Ritter von Frisch medal, 1988, Centennial medal Harvard U., 1989, Tyler Environ. Achievement prize U. So. Calif., 1990, Esselen award, 1991, Silver medal Internat. Soc. Chem. Ecology, 1991, Nat. medal sci., 1994, NWF Nat. Conservation Achievement award, 1997, Green Globe award, 1997; Guggenheim fellow, 1964-65, 72-73. Fellow Am. Acad. Arts and Scis., Royal Soc. Arts, Animal Behavior Soc., Entomol. Soc. Am.; mem. NAS (rsch. opportunity in biology com. 1985, film com. 1986—, com. on human rights 1987-90), AAAS (chmn. biology sect. 1980-81, com. on sci. freedom and responsibility 1980-87, chmn. subcom. sci. and human rights 1981-87, judging com. sci. freedom and responsibility award 1985-87, Newcomb Cleveland prize 1967), Am. Philos. Soc., Explorers Club, Deutsche Acad. Naturforscher Leopoldina, Acad. Europaea, Zero Population Growth (bd. dirs. 1969-70), Nature Conservancy (nat. sci. adv. coun. 1969-74), Nat. Audubon Soc. (bd. dirs. 1970-75), Fedn. Am. Scientists (coun. mem. 1977-81), Ctr. on Consequences Nuclear War (steering com. 1983-90), World Wildlife Fund (sci. adv. coun. 1983-91), Am. Inst. Biol. Sci. (task force for 90s 1990—, disting. svc. award 1996), Mo. Botanical Garden Ctr. Plant Conservation (adv. bd. econ. potential rare and threatened plants 1992), Am. Soc. Naturalists (pres. 1989-90), Monell Chem. Senses Ctr. (adv. coun. 1988-95), World Resources Inst. (adv. coun. 1988-95), Com. Concerned Scientists (nat. sponsor 1988—), Union Concerned Scientists (bd. dirs. 1993—), Xerces Soc. (sci. adv. com. 1990—, pres. 1992—), Nat. Mus. Nat. Hist. (adv. coun. 1996—), Ctr. of Biodiv. Conserv. Amer. Mus. Natl. Hist. (adv. com. 1995—), Ctr. Adv. Studies in Amazonian Biodiv. (adv. bd., 1997—), Ency. of Biodiversity (internat. adv. bd. 1997—, ctr. adv. studies in Amazonian biodiversity adv. bd. 1997—), Am. Mus. Natural History (adv. coun. Ctr. Biodiversity and Conservation 1995—), Mo. Bot. Garden. Office: Cornell U W347 Seeley Mudd Hall Dept Neurobiology & Behavior Ithaca NY 14853 *I am a naturalist, interested primarily in field exploration and discovery. My research deals with the behavior and chemical ecology of insects, and with the photographic and cinematographic documentation of little-known aspects of the life of these animals. My chief goal in life is to relate my findings to the cause of wildlife and wilderness preservation.*

EISNER, WILL, publishing company executive; b. N.Y.C., Mar. 6, 1917; s. Samuel and Fannie (Ingber) E.; m. Ann Louise Weingarten, June 15, 1950; children: John David, Alice Carol (dec.). Student, Art Student's League, N.Y.C., 1935. Pres. Am. Visuals Corp., 1949—, N.Am. Newspaper Alliance, 1962-64, Ednl. Supplements Corp., 1965-72; exec. v.p. Koster-Dana Corp., 1962-64; chmn. bd. Croft Ednl. Services Corp., 1972—; Mem. faculty Sch. Visual Arts, N.Y.C., 1973—. Author, cartoonist (syndicated newspaper feature) The Spirit, 1940-52; pub.: Eisner-Arnold Comic Group; editor: U.S. Army Ordnance. 1942-45 (recipient award comic book artist of yr. Nat. Cartoonist Soc., N.Y. 1967, Best artist award 1968-69, Best Comic Book Story cartoonist 1979, ann. award for quality of art in comic books Soc. Comic Art Rsch., 1968, Internat. Cartoonist award Angouleme, France, 1974); author: America's Combat Weapons, 1960, America's Space Vehicles, 1961, Contract with God, 1978, Gleeful Guides Series, 1980, Life on Another Planet, 1982, Big City, 1983 (graphic novel), Life Force, 1984, Comics and Sequential Art, 1985, To the Heart of the Storm, 1991, Invisible People, 1993, Dropsie Avenue, 1995, Graphic Storytelling, 1996, A Family Matter, 1998. Trustee Internat. Mus. Cartoon Art, 1994. Recipient Life Work award Barcelona Internat. Comic and Illustration Conv., Spl. Lifetime Achievement award Lucca Internat. Salon, 1986, Best Comic Book Artist award Nat. Cartoonists Co., 1967-68, 79, 88, 89, Spl. Career Achievement award U.K. Comic Art Awards, 1994, Max and Mortiz Life-Work Achievement award, Erlangen, Germany, 1994, San Diego Comic Conv. Humanitarian award, 1994, Lifetime Achievement award Nat. Cartoonist Soc., 1995, Grand Prize Yellow Kid award, Rome, 1997; inducted into Hall of Fame, Cartoon Art Mus., 1989. Mem. Illustrators Soc. N.Y.C., Internat. Mus. Cartoon Art (bd. trustees), Scottish Cartoonist Soc. (hon. pres.), Svenska Serieaka demins Goteborg (diplomate), Princeton Club (N.Y.C.). Home and Office: 8333 W Mcnab Rd Ste 114 Fort Lauderdale FL 33321-3203

EISS, HARRY EDWIN, English educator; b. Mpls., May 17, 1950; s. Harry Earl and Helen Holmgren Eiss; m. Betty Jean Palm; children: Meghan, Israel, Angela, Jared, Ryan. BA, U. Minn., 1975; MS, Mankato State U., 1976; PhD, U. N.D., 1982. Asst. prof. No. Mont. Coll., Havre, 1983-87; asst. prof. Ea. Migh. U., Ypsilanti, 1987-91, assoc. prof., 1991-96, prof., 1996—; mem. Mont. Com. Humanities, 1985-87. Author: Language Games, Puzzlesl and Amusements, 1986, Mathematical Games, Puzzles and Amusements, 1988, Books on War and Peace for Youth, 1989; author/editor: Images of the Child, 1994. Mem. Am. Soc. Composers, Authors & Pubs., Popular Culture Assn., Modern Lang. Assn., People for the Am. Way, Sigma Tau Delta. Home: 5737 Schafer Rd W Howell MI 48843

EISSMANN, ROBERT FRED, manufacturing engineer; b. Bklyn., Jan. 17, 1924; s. Fred Arno and Katherine Elizabeth (Petersohn) E.; m. June I. Vreeland, Dec. 29, 1950; 1 child, Roy Norman. Student, Pratt Inst., 1942-43, 46. Wireman, Western Electric Co., Kearney, N.J., 1946-49; assembler Indsl. TV, Clifton, N.J., 1949-51; leadman Bogue Electric, Paterson, N.J., 1951-60, 65-68; wireman, engring. asst. Kearfott, Gen. Precion, West Paterson, N.J., 1960-65; assembler-wireman Henderson Industries, Fairfield, N.J., 1968-72; prodn. mgr. Mipco Inc., West Caldwell, N.J., 1972-80, plant mgr., 1980-84, product support mgr., 1984-85, value engr., 1985-86; advance product design engr., 1986-87, design engr. indsl., elec. products, Amerace Corp., 1987-90, ret., 1990; staff mem. Russellstoll div. Midland Ross Corp., Livingston, N.J., 1980-83. Mem. freight container standards com. Elec. Task Force. With Signal Corps, U.S. Army, 1943-46. Methodist.

EISSMANN, WALTER JAMES, consulting company executive; b. Newark, N.J., Apr. 20, 1939; s. Walter Curt Eissmann and Alice Delice (Irving) Clark; m. Dorothea Ann Donaldson, June 1, 1963; children: Patricia Helene Ridenhour, Walter William. BS in Indsl. Engring., Rutgers U., 1962. Account mgr. Gen. Electric, Engelwood Cliffs, N.J., 1962-67; regional sales mgr. Tymshare, Engelwood Cliffs, 1968-71, Buffalo, N.Y., 1971-73; v.p. mktg. svc. divsn. Tymshare, Cupertino, Calif., 1974-79, divsn. v.p., 1980-84; sr. v.p. McDonnell Douglas Corp., Cupertino, 1984-86; gen. ptnr. Archer Assocs., Cupertino, 1985-92; pres., chmn. bd. Walter J. Eissmann Inc., La Quinta, Calif., 1989—, Walter J. Eissmann, Inc., La Quinta, Calif., 1989—; bd. dirs. NSF Corp., Nutri/system Franchisee Corp.; chmn. bd. businesswise Inc., 1992-93; mng. gen. ptnr. Grand Tyme Partnership, 1992—. Bd. dirs. Saratoga Little League, Calif., 1976-81, Saratoga Boosters, 1981-84; active Vienna Theatre Players, Va., 1973; mem. Church Men's Choir, Saratoga, 1980-82. Named to President's club Tymshare, Golden Circle, Nutri/system Master of the Keys. Mem. Pi Tau Sigma. Republican.

EISWERTH, BARRY NEIL, architect, educator; b. Williamsport, Pa., Sept. 16, 1942; s. Eugene Lewis and Mary Jane (Winters) E.; m. Anne Caroline Essl, Apr. 8, 1967; children: Jason, Brendan. B.Arch., Pa. State U.-University Park, 1965. Registered architect, Pa. Assoc. H2L2 Architects/Planners, Phila., 1967-77, ptnr., 1977-88, sr. ptnr., 1988—; pres. H2L2 Design Co., Phila., 1980—; asst. prof. archtl. design Drexel U., 1975-81; mem. faculty, thesis advisor Phila. Coll. Art. Archtl. works include Children's Hosp., Phila., bldgs. Phila. '76 Bicentennial, Phila. Bourse Bldg., Cypress Sq. Townhouse Complex Phila. (recipient Design award Old Phila. Devel. Corp., Preservation Alliance award for Design Offices and Montgomery McCracken Warker & Rhodes), Constitutional Pavillion for We The People 200, Master Plan Cairo Am. Coll., Engring. and Computer Sci. Campus-Am. U. Cairo, Master Plan Am. Internat. Sch., Tel Aviv, Master Plan Am. Embassy Sch., New Delhi, Master Plan and Design new campus Am. Sch. of Warsaw. Trustee curator Phila. City Inst. Recipient awards for archtl. designs. Mem. AIA, Pa. Soc. Architects, Nat. Acad. Design, Phila. Club. Democrat. Roman Catholic. Office: H2L2 Architects/Planners 714 Market St Ste 4 Philadelphia PA 19106-2372

EITAN, TONY See FIORINO, ANTHONY SAVERIO

EITEL, ANTONIUS, diplomat. Perm. rep. of Germany to UN N.Y.C., 1995-98; diplomat rep of Germany UN, 1998—. Office: Perm Mission of Germany to UN 871 UN Plz New York NY 10017

EITEL, DOLORES J., healthcare consultant, educator; 1 child, Steven Maviglio. Grad., RN, Presbyn. Hosp. Sch. Nursing, Newark, 1956; BSN, Fairleigh Dickenson U., 1972; MA, Seton Hall U., 1980. Cert. adult nurse practitioner, family nurse practitioner, critical care forensic nurse. Asst. v.p. nursing Stamford (Conn.) Hosp.; adj. faculty Sacred Heart U., Bridgeport, Conn.; adminstr. Nephrology and Dialysis Cons., So. Conn. Dialysis Unit, Bridgeport, Conn.; v.p. nursing Lourdes Hosp., Binghamton, N.Y.; v.p. patient care Windham Hosp., Willimantic, Conn.; healthcare cons., healthcare mediator in ind. practice; tchr. Bloomfield Coll., 1994—; asst. prof. U. Conn.; prof. Bloomfield Coll. Mem. ANA, N.J. Nurses Assn. (bd. dirs., dist. pres.), Am. Orgn. Nurse Execs., Am. Orgn. Healthcare Execs., Am. Congress of Nurse Practitioners, Sigma Theta Tau.

EITINGON, DANIEL BENJAMIN, insurance consultant; b. N.Y.C., Nov. 20, 1950; s. Mark and Aimee Brigitte (Berline) E. BBA, Hofstra U., 1977; PhD, LaSalle U., Mandeville, La., 1997. CPCU; assoc. in risk mgmt.; assoc. in underwriting; accredited customer svc. rep.; accredited advisor in ins.; cert. ins. counselor. Dir. mktg. BHK&R Inc., Mpls., 1982-89; v.p., broking exec. Alexander & Alexander, Inc., Mpls., 1990-95; pres., CEO Outsource Ins. Svcs., Ltd., Mpls., 1995—. Mem. Soc. CPCUs (Minn. chpt. media contact com.), Soc. Ins. Trainers and Educators, Twin Cities Ins. Club. Democrat. Jewish. Avocations: piano playing, walking, classical music, travel, speaking French. Home: 3782 Kipling Ave South Saint Louis Park MN 55416-4848 Office: Outsource Ins Svcs Ltd 3208 W Lake St # 160 Minneapolis MN 55416-4512

EITNER, LORENZ EDWIN ALFRED, art historian, educator; b. Brunn, Czechoslovakia, Aug. 27, 1919; came to U.S., 1935, naturalized, 1943; s. Wilhelm and Katherina (Thonet) E.; m. Trudi von Kathrein, Oct. 26, 1946; children: Christy, Kathy, Claudia. AB, Duke U., 1940; MFA, Princeton U., 1948, PhD, 1952. Research unit head Nuremberg War Crimes Trial, 1946-47; from instr. to prof. art U. Minn., Mpls., 1949-63; chmn. dept. art, dir. mus. Stanford U., Calif., 1963-89; organizer exhbn. works of Gericault for museums of Los Angeles, Detroit and Phila., 1971-72. Author: The Flabellum of Tournus, 1944, Gericault Sketchbooks in the Chicago Art Institute, 1960, Introduction to Art, 1951, Neo-Classicism and Romanticism, 1969, Gericault's Raft of the Medusa, 1972, Gericault, His Life and Work, 1983 (Mitchell prize 1984, C.R. Morey award 1985), An Outline of 19th Century European Painting from David through Cezanne, 1987; (with others) The Arts in Higher Education, 1963, Stanford Mus. Art, The Drawing Collection, 1993; contbr. articles to profl. jours. Mem. Regional Area Arts Coun. San Francisco Bay Area. Officer OSS, AUS, 1943-46; sect. head ministries divsn. Nuremberg War Crimes Trial, 1946-47. Fulbright grantee, Belgium, 1952-53; Guggenheim fellow, Munich, Federal Republic Germany, 1956-57; recipient Gold Medal for Meritorious Service to Austrian Republic, 1990. Mem. AAAS, Am. Acad. Arts and Scis., Coll. Art Assn. Am. (bd. dirs., past v.p.), Phi Beta Kappa. Home: 684 Mirada Ave Stanford CA 94305-8475 Office: Stanford U Art Dept Palo Alto CA 94305*

EITRHEIM, NORMAN DUANE, bishop; b. Baltic, S.D., Jan. 14, 1929; s. Daniel Tormod and Selma (Thompson) E.; m. Clarice Yvonne Pederson, Aug. 23, 1952; children: Daniel, David, John, Marie. BA, Augustana Coll., 1951; BTh, Luther Sem., St. Paul, 1956; LHD (hon.), Augustana Coll., 1988. Pastor 1st English Luth. Ch., Tyler, Minn., 1956-63, St. Philips Luth. Ch., Fridley, Minn., 1963-76; asst. to pres. Luther Northwestern Sem., St. Paul, 1976-80; bishop S.D. dist. Am. Luth. Ch., Sioux Falls, 1981-87; bishop S.D. Synod Evang. Luth. Ch. in Am., Sioux Falls, 1988-95. Staff sgt. USAF, 1951-52.

EITTREIM, RICHARD MACNUTT, lawyer; b. Neptune, N.J., Feb. 10, 1945; s. Wilbur Lawrence and Leta Blanch (MacNutt) E.; m. Margaret Anne Nolan, June 11, 1967; children: Theodore Scott, Elisabeth Marie, Samantha Leta. AB, Yale U., 1967; JD, U. Va., 1973. Bar: N.J. 1973, U.S. Dist. Ct. N.J. 1973, U.S. Ct. Appeals (3d cir.) 1984, U.S. Supreme Ct. 1998. Assoc. McCarter & English, Newark, N.J., 1973-80, ptnr., 1980—. Trustee Children's Psychiat. Ctr., Eatontown, N.J., 1977-87, Riverview Hosp. Found., Red Bank, N.J., 1988-93. Mem. ABA, N.J. State Bar Assn., Essex County Bar Assn., Phi Alpha Delta, Sea Bright Lawn Tennis and Cricket Club (bd. govs. 1994—), Monmouth Boat Club (treas. 1983-86), Essex Club, Yale Club (pres. 1986-87). Democrat. Presbyterian. Home: Windmill Ln Rumson NJ 07760 Office: McCarter & English 4 Gateway Ctr 100 Mulberry St Newark NJ 07102-4004

EITZEN, DAVID STANLEY, sociologist, educator; b. Glendale, Calif., Aug. 4, 1934; s. David Donald and Amanda Emma (Heidebrecht) E.; m. Florine Kay Voran, May 29, 1956; children: Keith, Michael, Kelly. A.B. in History, Bethel Coll., 1956; M.S., Emporia State U., 1962; M.A. in Sociology, U. Kans., 1966, Ph.D. in Sociology, 1968. Recreational therapist Menninger Found., Topeka, Kans., 1956-58; tchr. Galva (Kans.) High Sch., 1958-60, Turner (Kans.) High Sch., 1960-65; asst. prof. sociology U. Kans., 1968-72, asso. prof., 1972-74; prof. sociology Colo. State U., Ft. Collins, 1974-95, prof. emeritus, 1995—. Author: Social Structure and Social Problems, 1974, Sociology of American Sport, 1978, In Conflict and Order: Understanding Society, 1978, Sport in Contemporary Society, 1979, Social Problems, 1980, Elite Deviance, 1981; Criminology: Crime and Criminal Justice, 1985, Diversity in American Families, 1987, Society's Problems: Sources and Consequences, 1989, Crime in the Streets and Crime in the Suites: Perspectives on Crime and Criminal Justice, 1989, The Reshaping of America: Social Consequences of the Changing Economy, 1989, Paths to Homelessness, 1994, Solutions to Social Problems: Lessons from Other Societies, 1997, Fair and Foul: Beyond the Myths and Paradoxes of Sport, 1999; editor Social Sci. Jour., 1978-84. Contbr. articles to profl. jours. NDEA fellow, 1965-67. Mem. Internat. Sociol. Assn., Am. Sociol. Assn., Midwest Sociol. Soc., Soc. Study Social Problems, Western Social Sci. Assn., Southwestern Social Sci. Assn., Internat. Com. for Sociology Sport., N.Am. Soc. for Sociology of Sport (pres. 1986-87). Democrat. Mennonite. Home: 924 Breakwater Dr Fort Collins CO 80525-3345 Office: Colo State U Dept Sociology Fort Collins CO 80523

EIZENBERG, JULIE, architect. BArch, U. Melbourne, Australia, 1978; MArch II, UCLA, 1981. Lic. architect, Calif., reg. architect, Australia. Principal, architect Koning Eizenberg Architecture, Santa Monica, Calif., 1981—; instr. various courses UCLA, MIT, Harvard U.; lectr. in field; jury member P/A awards. Exhbns. incl. Koning Eizenberg Architecture 3A Garage, San Francisco, 1996, "House Rules" Wexner Ctr., 1994, "The Architect's Dream: Houses for the Next Millenium" The Contemporary Arts Ctr., 1993, "Angels & Franciscans" Gagosian Gallery, 1992, Santa Monica Mus. Art, 1993, "Broadening the Discourse" Calif. Women in Environmental Design, 1992, "Conceptional Drawings by Architects" Bannatyne Gallery, 1991, Exhbn. Koning Eizenberg Projects Grad. Sch. Architecture & Urban Planning UCLA, 1990; prin. works include Digital Domain Renovation and Screening Room, Santa Monica, Lightstorm Entertainment Office Renovation and Screening Room, Santa Monica, Gilmore Bank Addition and Remodel, L.A., 1548-1550 Studios, Santa Monica, (with RTA) Materials Rsch. Lab. at U. Calif., Santa Barbara, Ken Edwards Ctr. Cmty. Svcs., Santa Monica, Peck Park Cmty. Ctr. Gymnasium, San Pedro, Calif., Sepulveda Recreation Ctr., L.A. (Design award AIA San Fernando Valley 1995, Nat. Concrete and Masonry award 1996, AIA Calif. Coun. Honor award 1996, L.A. Bus. Coun. Beautification award 1996, AIA Los Angeles Chpt. Merit Award, 1997), PS # 1 Elem. Sch., Santa Monica, Farmers Market, L.A. Additions and Master Plan (Westside Urban Forum prize 1991), Stage Deli, L.A., Simone Hotel, L.A. (Nat. Honor award AIA 1994), Boyd Hotel, L.A., Cmty. Corp. Santa Monica Housing Projects, 5th St. Family Housing, Santa Monica, St. John's Hosp. Replacement Housing Program, Santa Monica, Liffman Ho., Santa Monica, (with Glenn Erikson) Electric Artblock, Venice (Beautification award L.A. Bus. Coun. 1993), 6th St. Condominiums, Santa Monica, Hollywood Duplex, Hollywood Hills (Record Houses Archtl. Record 1988), California Ave. Duplex, Santa Monica, Tarzana Ho. (Award of Merit L.A. chpt. AIA 1992, AIA Calif. Coun. Merit Award, 1998, Sunset Western home Awards citation 1993-94), 909 Ho., Santa Monica (Award of Merit L.A. chpt. AIA 1991), 31st St. Ho., Santa Monica (Honor award AIACC 1994, Nat. AIA Honor award 1996), others. Recipient 1st award Progressive Architecture, 1987; named one of Domino's Top 30 Architects, 1989. Mem. L.A. County Mus. Art, Westside Urban Forum, Urban Land Inst., Architects and Designers for Social Responsibility, Mus. Contemporary Art, The Nature Conservancy, Sierra Club. Office: Koning Eizenberg Architecture 1548 18th St Santa Monica CA 90404-3404

EIZENSTAT, STUART E., ambassador, lawyer; b. Chgo., Jan. 15, 1943; m. Fran Eizenstat; children: Jay, Brian. AB cum laude, U. N.C., 1964; LLB, Harvard U., 1967; LLD (hon.), Yeshiva U., 1998, Weizmann Inst. Sci., 1999. Bar: Ga. 1967, D.C. 1981. Mem. White House staff, 1967-68; mem. nat. campaign staff Hubert H. Humphrey, 1968; law clk. U.S. Dist. Ct. No. Dist. Ga., 1968-70; ptnr. Powell, Goldstein, Frazer & Murphy, Washington, 1970-77, 81-93, vice chmn., 1991-93; asst. to Pres. U.S. for domestic affairs and policy, 77-81, dir. White House Domestic Policy Staff, 1977-81; amb. to European Union Brussels, 1993-96; spl. envoy Dept. State Property Claims in Ctrl. Europe, 1995—; undersec. for internat. trade Dept. Commerce, Washington, 1996-97; envoy Pres. of U.S. for Promotion of Democracy in Cuba, 1996-97; undersec. of state for econ., bus. and agrl. affairs Dept. Commerce, Washington, 1997—; alt gov. World Bank, 1998—, Regional Devel. Banks, 1998—; adj. lectr. J.F. Kennedy Sch. Govt., Harvard U., 1981-92; guest scholar Brookings Inst., Washington, 1981; mem. Energy Coord. Coun., Econ. Policy Group, 1977-81, Pres. Bush task force on U.S. Internat. Broadcasting, 1991; head U.S. del. CSCE Econ. Forum, 1994; lectr. coll., bus. and civic groups. Co-author: Andrew Young: The Path to History, 1973;Environmental Auditing Handbook, 1984; co-editor: The American Agenda: Report to the 41st President of the United States, 1988, reprint, 1989; contbr. articles to profl. jours. and newspapers. Vice-pres. Jewish Publ. Soc., 1981-85; chmn. Inst. U.S. Jewish-Israeli Relations, 1982-86; bd. dirs. Woodrow Wilson Center for Internat. Scholars, 1978-87, Jerusalem Found., 1992-93, Eurasia Found., 1993; pres. Greater Washington Jewish Community Ctr., 1989-91; mem. exec. com. Ctr. for Dem. Policy, 1982-93; bd. visitors U. N.C., Chapel Hill, 1987-90; co-dir. The American Agenda (with Pres. Ford and Pres. Carter), 1991; trustee Jerusalem Inst. Mgmt., 1987-93; mem. coun. Harvard Law Sch. Assn., 1988-92, Gov.'s Commn. on Fed. Funding, Commonwealth of Va., 1986, Com. on Federalism and Nat. Purpose, 1984-85; chmn. Econ. and Budget Strategy Com., Montgomery County Coun., 1986; v.p., bd. dirs. Am. Assocs., Ben-Gurion U. of the Negev. N.Y.C., 1981-89; trustee Washington Inst. for Jewish Leadership and Values, 1988—, Brandeis U., 1991—; commr. Commn. on Jewish Edn. in N.Am., 1988-90; v.p. Atlanta Bur. Jewish Edn., 1973-76; mem. exec. com. Atlanta Jewish Community Center, 1970-76; mem. B'nai Brith Youth Commn., Washington, 1981-82; bd. dirs. United Synagogues Am., 1981-84.; internat. bd. dir. Weizmann Inst., 1989-93; active in Dem. party and political campaigns. Recipient Man of Yr. award Nat. Capital Assn., Star award for Public Svs., 1996. B'nai B'rith Lodges, 1982, Outstanding Svc. to Summer Youth Program U.S. Dept. Labor, 1980, Outstanding Svc. award Hebrew Aid Immigration Soc., 1980, Outstanding Svc. award Opportunities Industrialization Ctrs., 1979, award Washington Internat. Bus. Coun., 1978, award Nat. Coalition Involved People, 1977, Young Man of Yr. award Am. Assn. Jewish Edn., 1973-74, Leadership award Acad. Jewish Religion, 1989, Tree of Life award Hadassah, Boston, 1989, Myrtle Wreath award Fla. Atlantic Region Hadassah, 1991, Benjamin Cardozo Professionalism award Atlanta Jewish Fedn., 1992, Export Finance award Coalition for Employment Through Exports, 1993, award for pub. svc. Sec. of State, 1996, Moral Statesman award Anti-Defamation League, 1997, Phillip Klutznick B'Nai B'Rith award for Outstanding Pub. Svc., 1996, award for transatlantic svc. European Inst., 1997, Myrtle Wreath award Hadassah, 1997, 98, Transatlantic Svc. award European Inst., 1997, award for courage and conscience Israeli Knesset, 1998; named one of Leaders of Atlanta, Atlanta Mag., 1976. Fellow Nat. Acad. Pub. Adminstn., Ctr. for Excellence in Govt.; mem. ABA (spl. com. on lawyers in govt., mem. com. govt. standards 1992-93), Atlanta Bar Assn., D.C. Bar Assn., Ga. Bar Assn., U.S. C. of C. (Internat. Policy Com. 1982-89), Nat. Fgn. Trade Coun. (Internat. Trade Com.), Washington Policy Coun. (Internat. Mgmt. and Devel. Inst.), Phi Beta Kappa, Phi Eta Sigma. Democrat. Jewish. Home: 9107 Brierly Rd Chevy Chase MD 20815-5654 Office: US Dept Commerce Ste 3805 14th Constitution Ave NW Washington DC 20011

EJABAT, MORY, communications executive. BS in Indsl. Engring., Calif. State U., Northridge, MS in Sys. Engring.; MBA, Pepperdine U. V.p. Micom Sys. Inc.; v.p. Ascend Comm., Alameda, Calif., 1990-92, exec. v.p., chief operating officer, 1992-95, pres., chief exec. officer, 1995—. Office: Ascend Comm 1701 Harbor Bay Pkwy Alameda CA 94502-3002*

EJIMOFOR, CORNELIUS OGU, political scientist, educator; b. Owerri, Nigeria, Oct. 10, 1940; came to U.S., 1963; s. Osuji and Helen Domaonu (Atashia) E.; m. Priscilla Loveth Amaugo, Mar. 10, 1966; children: Cornelia, Caroline, Cornelius Jr., Priscilla, Ebere. AA, Warren Wilson Coll., 1965; BA in Polit. Sci., Wilberforce U., 1966; MPA, U. Dayton, 1967; MA, PhD, U. Okla., 1971. Tchr. Cath. Mission Schs., Emekuku, Nigeria, 1959-63; rsch. asst. U. Dayton, Ohio, 1966-67; instr. polit. sci. Edward Waters Coll., Jacksonville, Fla., 1967-68, prof. polit. sci., 1992—; chmn. divsn. arts and scis. Edward Waters Coll., Jacksonville, 1992-93; grad. asst. U. Okla., Norman, 1968-70; asst. prof. William Paterson Coll., Wayne, N.J., 1970-72; from assoc. prof. to prof. Tuskegee (Ala.) U., 1972-80, dept. head polit. sci., 1972-77; sr. lectr., reader U. Nigeria, Nsukka, 1980-91, prof. polit. sci., 1991-92; coord., head, prof. sub-dept. pub. adminstrn. and local govt. U. Nigeria, 1990-92, coord. local govt. tng. programs, 1990-92. Author: British Colonia Objectives and Policies in Nigeria, 1987, Management of Human Resources: A Generic Approach, 1992. Mem. AAUP, Am. Soc. for Pub. Adminstrn. (state coun. mem. Ala. 1976-78), Am. Polit. Sci. Assn., Nigerian Polit. Sci. Assn., KC. Democrat. Roman Catholic. Avocations: swimming, reading and writing, discussing civics. Home: 157 Lamson St Jacksonville FL 32211-8066

E. JOSEPH, SAVIOE, state education agency administrator. BA in Edn., USL, M in Edn.; DEd in Edn. Adminstrn., Columbia U. Commr. of higher edn. State of La.; mem. Mike Fosters Higher Edn. Transition Team; staff former Gov. Edwin Edward's proaction Commn. for Higher Edn., Commn.

on Higher Edn. in the 21st Century. Office: Bd of Regents Higher Edn Commn 150 3rd St Ste 129 Baton Rouge LA 70801

EK, ALAN RYAN, forestry educator; b. Mpls., Sept. 5, 1942; cons. in field in U.S. and world; mem. forestry rsch. adv. coun. USDA. BS in Forestry, U. Minn., St. Paul, 1964, MS, 1965; PhD, Oreg. State U., Corvallis, 1969. Rsch. officer Can. Dept. Forestry and Rural Devel., Sault Ste Marie, Ont., Can., 1966-69; asst. prof., then assoc. prof. forestry U. Wis., Madison, 1969-77; assoc. prof., then prof. forestry U. Minn., St. Paul, 1977—, head dept. forest resources, 1984—; mem. USDA Forestry Rsch. Adv. Coun., 1994-96, 98, chair, 1998-99; cons. in field in U.S. and world. Contbr. chpts. to books, articles to profl. jours. Fulbright scholar to Finland, 1997. Fellow Soc. Am. Foresters (various coms., chmn. forest sci. and tech. bd. 1989-90); mem. AAAS, Nat. Assn. Profl. Forestry Schs. and Colls. (chmn. rsch. com. 1993-95), Am. Statis. Assn., Am. Soc. Photogrammetry and Remote Sensing, Sigma Xi, Xi Sigma Pi, Gamma Sigma Delta. Avocations: reading, sports. Home: 4744 Kevin Ln Saint Paul MN 55126-5849 Office: U Minn Dept Forest Resources Saint Paul MN 55108

EKANGER, LAURIE, state official; b. Salt Lake City, Mar. 4, 1949; d. Bernard and Mary (Dearth) E.; m. William J. Shupe, Nov. 6, 1973; children: Ben, Robert. BA in English, U. Oreg., 1973. Various pos. Mont. State Employment & Tng. Divsn., Helena, 1975-80, dep. adminstr., 1980-82; adminstr. Mont. State Purchasing Divsn., Helena, 1982-85, Mont. State Personnel Divsn., Helena, 1985-93; labor commr. Mont. Dept. Labor & Ind., Helena, 1993-97; dir. Mont. Dept. Pub. Health and Human Svcs., 1997—; council chair State Employee Group Benefits Coun., 1985-93; bd. dirs. Pub. Employee Retirement Bd., 1988. Home: 80 Pinecrest Rd Clancy MT 59634-9505 Office: Dept Pub Health and Human Svcs PO Box 4210 Helena MT 59604-4210

EKBATANI, GLAYOL, educator, program director, author; b. Tehran, Iran; d. Saed and Parvin (Sohai) E.; divorced; 1 child, Orkideh. MA, U. Ill., 1974, PhD, 1981. Dir., prof. English 2d lang. program U. Maine, Orano, 1987-90; dir. English 2d lang., bilingual programs C.C. Phila., 1990-92; dir., prof. English 2d lang. programs St. John's U., Jamaica, N.Y., 1992—; rschr. Georgetown U., Washington, 1986-87. Author: Dearnes Directed Assessment Time, 1999; contbr. articles to profl. jours.; author: (book) Learner Directed Assessment,. Mem. Nat. Assn. Fgn. Students Washington, Tchrs. English to Spkrs. of Other Langs. (pres. 1991-92). Home: 1 Bay Club Dr Apt 14T Bayside NY 11360-2910 Office: St John's U 8000 Utopia Pkwy Rm 377 Jamaica NY 11432-1343

EKBERG, SUSAN JANE, writer, publisher; b. Bismarck, N.D., Aug. 18, 1960; d. William Alan and Marietta Meyer E.; m. David Rolf Aanestad, Oct. 9, 1982 (div. Nov. 1991); children: Kari Ruth, Erik Alan Henning; m. Steve Olaf Risher, Oct. 7, 1995. BA, Concordia Coll., 1982; postgrad., Moorhead State U. Cert. 2d level Reiki practitioner Usui method. Mgr. Tupperware, Fargo, N.D., 1987-90; pres. Spiritseeker Pub., Inc., Fargo, 1990—; keynote spkr. Parents Murdered Children, Mpls., 1994. Author: Pink Stars and Angel Wings, 1992, The Trust Walk, 1994. Coord. Jr. Great Books, Fargo, 1991-96; bd. dirs. Town Hall, Fargo, 1996—. Mem. P.E.O. (chaplain 1994-96). Avocations: reading, athletic training, cooking, travelling, foreign films. E-mail: seeker@rrnet.com. Office: Spiritseeker Pub Inc 300 8th St S # 11 Fargo ND 58103

EKDAHL, JON NELS, lawyer, corporate secretary; b. Topeka, Nov. 15, 1942; s. Oscar S. and Dorothy O. (Ekdahl) M.; m. Marcia Opp, May 24, 1975; children: Kirsten, Erika, Kristofer. AB magna cum laude, Harvard U., 1964, LLB, 1968; MS in Econs., London Sch. Econs., 1965. Bar: Ill. 1969, U.S. Ct. Appeals (7th cir.) 1981, U.S. Supreme Ct. 1981. Assoc. Sidley & Austin, Chgo., 1968-75, ptnr., 1973-75; mng. ptnr., gen. counsel Andersen Worldwide SC, Chgo., 1975—. With USAR, 1968-74. Mem. ABA, Chgo. Bar Assn., Mid-Am. Club, Chgo. Club. Office: Andersen Worldwide SC 225 N Michigan Ave Fl 16 Chicago IL 60601-7668

EKE, KENOYE KELVIN, academic administrator; b. Otari, Atuba, Nigeria, Sept. 1, 1956; came to U.S., 1977; s. Joseph and Nancy (Owen) E.; m. Lycynthia Sampson (div.); m. Joy Makra Grimes, June 24, 1989; children: Kenoye Kelvin Joseph, Kebbin Henry Joseph. BA, Ala. A&M U., 1980; MA, Atlanta U., 1982, PhD, 1985. Asst. prof. polit. sci. Bethune-Cookman Coll., Daytona Beach, Fla., 1985-89; from assoc. prof. to prof. polit. sci., dean Savannah (Ga.) State U., 1989-98; asst. v.p. acad. affairs Calif. State U., Monterey Bay, 1998—. Author: Nigeria's Foreign Policy Under Two Military Governments, 1990; co-editor: Media Coverage of Terrorism, 1991. Founding pres. Pan-African Awareness Assn., Daytona Beach, 1987-88; bd. dirs. Savannah Coun. World Affairs, 1993-95; benefits coun. DFCS, Savannah, 1990-93. Fellow Am. Coun. Edn., 1994-95, PEW faculty fellow in internat. affairs John F. Kennedy Sch. Govt. Harvard U., 1992-93. Mem. Assn. Higher Edn., Am. Polit. Sci. Assn., Nat. Conf. Black Political Sci., Assn. Internat. Edn., Coun. Colls. Arts & Scis. Avocations: tennis, swimming, racquetball. Office: Calif State U-Monterey Bay 100 Campus Ctr Seaside CA 93955

EKELMAN, DANIEL LOUIS, lawyer; b. Cleve., May 1, 1926; s. William Harry and Edna Mae (James) E.; m. Ann Jane Farnacy, Aug. 5, 1950 (dec. June 1993); children: Sally, Karen, Barbara, Beth; m. Phyllis E. Patton, Oct. 18, 1997. BA, Ohio Wesleyan U., 1950; LLB, Case Western Res. U., 1952. Bar: Ohio 1952, U.S. Dist. Ct. (no. dist.) Ohio 1953, U.S. Tax Ct. 1955. Assoc. Calfee, Halter & Griswold, Cleve., 1952-59, ptnr., 1959-77, mng. ptnr., 1977-85, sr. ptnr., 1985-95; ret., 1996; gen. ptnr. Sawmill Creek Resort, Huron, Ohio, 1968-80. Trustee Brentwood Hosp., Cleve., 1960-94, Greater Cleve. Hosp. Assn., 1975-78 (Outstanding Trustee award 1992), Case Western Res. Law Sch., 1984-87, Merridia South Pointe Hosp., 1995, Brentwood Found., 1995-99. With USN, 1944-46, PTO. Fellow ABA; mem. Ohio Bar Assn., Cleve. Bar Assn., Soc. Benchers, Order of the Coif, The Country Club (Pepper Pike, Ohio, trustee 1988-91), Union Club, Jupiter Hills Club (Jupiter, Fla.). Republican. Home: 22029 Douglas Rd Shaker Heights OH 44122

EKERY, ADRIANA TERESA, healthcare administrator, oncology nurse; b. Terrell, Tex., Feb. 15, 1957; d. Fernando V. and Josefina (Quintero) Rodriguez; m. Alan D. Ekery, Sept. 23, 1989. Assoc. in Nursing, McLennan Community Coll., 1979; BSN, U. Tex., Arlington, 1983. Nurse administrator Caremark Home Care, El Paso, Tex., 1988; Medicare coord./supr. Mission Health Care Svcs., El Paso, 1989-93; DON (2 brs.) Columbia Health Care Svcs. (formerly Mission Health Care Svcs.), 1993-99; adminstr., dir. nursing Home Health Svc., Inc., 1992-99; title 1 compliance nurse El Paso Ind. Sch. Dist., 1999—; profl. in establishing home health aide competency test for all HHA's, City of El Paso. Mem. Am. Soc. Parenteral and Enteral Nutrition, Oncology Nursing Soc., Intravenous Nurses Soc., El Paso Home Health Assocs. (rec. sec.), Tex. Assn. Home Care (chair edn. com.).

EKEY, CARRIE RAE, elementary education educator; b. North Platte, Nebr., July 6, 1947; d. Chester O. and Alice A. (Johnson) Florom; m. Glenn W. Ekey, Mar. 22, 1970; children: Brian, Todd. BA in Elem. Edn. and Math., U. No. Colo., 1969; MA in Curriculum and Instrn., U. Colo., Denver, 1990. Cert. elem. tchr., Colo. 3d grade tchr. Jefferson County, Lakewood, Colo., 1969-73; 4th-6th grade tchr. Jefferson County, Wheatridge, Colo., 1981-85; 1st-2d grade tchr. Jefferson County, Arvada, Westminster, Colo., 1985-97; staff developer Jefferson County, Lakewood, Colo., 1992-93, 97-99; instr. Regis U., Denver, 1989—, curriculum coord. Masters in Whole Learning program, 1994—; cons. various sch. dists., Colo., 1989—. Mem. Nat. Coun. Tchrs. English, Nat. Coun. Tchrs. Math., Internat. Reading Assn., Assn. for Supervision and Curriculum Devel., Colo. Coun. Tchrs. English, Colo. Reading Assn. Avocations: reading, golfing, gardening, walking. Office: Jefferson County Schs 9650 W 97th Ave Broomfield CO 80021-4282

EKLOF, SVEA CHRISTINE, ballet dancer; b. L.A., May 31, 1951; d. Theodore Herman and Christiane (Simonpietri) E.; m. Michel Rahn, Aug. 27, 1976 (div. Jan. 1986); m. John Michael Grey, Jan. 29, 1986; 1 child, Georgina Germaine. Student, U. N.C., 1969-70. Mem. corps de ballet Pa. Ballet Co., Phila., 1970-71; soloist Ballet Classico de Mex., Mexico City, 1971-73, Ballet Du Grand Theatre, Geneva, Switzerland, 1973-74, Netherlands Dance Theatre, Den Haag, The Netherlands, 1974-75; prin. dancer Ballet Du Grand Theatre, Geneva, Switzerland, 1975-76, N.C. Dance Theatre, Winston-Salem, 1976-79, Alta. Ballet Co., Edmonton, 1979-83; soloist Royal Winnipeg Ballet, Man., 1983-85; prin. dancer Royal Winnipeg Ballet Co., Man., 1985-89; guest tchr. N.C. Sch. Arts, Winston-Salem, 1976-79, 89, Edmonton Sch. Ballet and Alta. Ballet Sch. Ballet, 1979-83, Nat. Ballet Sch., Toronto, 1989-93, W.Va. Dance Festival, 1992-96; guest coach Royal Winnipeg Ballet Sch.; prin. tchr. Dancespace, Toronto, 1991-94; artistic dir. Profl. Sch. of Toronto Ballet Ensemble, 1994—; judge new choreography on Dora Maria Moore awards panel, 1989-90; classical coach Ballet Jôrgen, 1989-91; coach for applicants of IV Internat. Ballet Competition, Jackson, Miss.; tchr. Ont. Ballet Theatre Co., 1989-90, 90-93. Guest appearances include Chgo. Ballet, 1976-77, Ballet Galaxie, Taiwan, 1981, New World Ballet, Miami, Fla., 1982, W.Va. Ballet, 1979-81, Edmonton Symphony Orch., 1987-90; prin. ballerina Internat. Opera Festival, 1989, Memphis Concert. Ballet, 1989. Guest tchr. ballet W.Va. Dance Festival, 1992-94, 96; accessor Ont. Arts Coun., 1993—, Met. Toronto Arts Coun., Canada Coun., 1996. Mem. Alta. Ballet Co. (adv. bd. 1986—), Manitoba Dance Assn. (ajudicator dance festival 1994), Can. Dance Tchrs. Assn. (guest tchr. 1995). Avocations: speaking fluent French and Spanish. Office: 296 Withrow Ave, Toronto, ON Canada M4J 1B7

EKLUND, CARL ANDREW, lawyer; b. Denver, Aug. 12, 1943; s. John M. and Zara (Zerbst) E.; m. Nancy Jane Griggs, Sept. 7, 1968; children: Kristin, Jessica, Peter. BA, U. Colo., 1967, JD, 1971. Bar: Colo. 1971, U.S. Dist. Ct. Colo. 1971, U.S. Ct. Appeals (9th cir.) 1975, U.S. Ct. Appeals (10th cir.) 1978, U.S. Supreme Ct. 1978. Dep. dist. atty. Denver Dist. Attys. Office, 1971-73; ptnr. DiManna, Eklund, Ciancio & Jackson, Denver, 1975-81, Smart, DeFurio, Brooks & Eklund, Denver, 1982-84, Roath & Brega, P.C., Denver, 1984-88, Faegre & Benson, Denver, 1988-94, LeBoeuf, Lamb, Greene & MacRae L.L.P., Denver, 1994—; local rules com. Bankruptcy Ct. D.C., 1979-80; reporter Nat. Bankruptcy Conf., 1981-82; lectr. ann. spring meeting Am. Bankruptcy Inst., Rocky Mountain Bankruptcy Conf., Continuing Legal Edn. Colo., Inc., Colo. Practice Inst., Colo. Bar Assn., Nat. Ctr. Continuing Legal Edn., Inc., Profl. Edn. Systems, Inc., Comml. Law Inst. Am., Law Edn. Inst., Inc., Bur. Nat. Affairs, Inc., Practising Law Inst., So. Meth. U. Sch. Law, Continuing Edn. Svcs., Lorman Bus. Ctr., Inc. Author: The Probelm With Creditors' Committees in Chapter 11: How to Manage the Inherent Conflicts Without Loss of Function, 1997; contbg. author: Collier's Bankruptcy Practice Guide, Representing Debtors in Bankruptcy, Letters Formbook and Legal Opinion, Advanced Chapter 11 Bankruptcy Practice, Wiley Law Pubs.; mem. adv. bd. ABI Law Rev., 1993—. Fellow Am. Coll. Bankruptcy; mem. ABA (bus. law and corp. banking sect. 1977—, bus. bankruptcy com. 1982—, subcom. on rules 1981—), Colo. Bar Assn. (bd. govs. 1980-82, corp. banking and bus. law sect. 1977—, ethics com. 1981-82, subcom. bankruptcy cts.), Am. Bankruptcy Inst. (dir. SW Bankruptcy Conf., Rocky Mountain Bankruptcy Conf.), Denver Bar Assn. (trustee 1983-86). Office: LeBoeuf Lamb Greene & MacRae LLP 633 17th St Ste 2000 Denver CO 80202-3620

EKMAN, RICHARD, foundation executive, educator; b. N.Y.C., Oct. 1, 1945; s. Sheldon Victor and Judith (Saturen) E.; m. Caroline Read, June 15, 1975; children: Nathaniel Paul, Peter Sheldon Read. AB magna cum laude, Harvard U., 1966, AM, 1967, PhD, 1972. Asst. to provost U. Mass., Boston, 1971-73; dep. dir. div. edn. programs NEH, Washington, 1973-78, dir. div. edn. programs, 1982-85, dir. div. rsch. programs, 1985-91; v.p., dean of coll. Hiram (Ohio) Coll., 1978-82; sec. of found. Andrew W. Mellon Found, N.Y.C., 1991—; mem. nat. adv. com. Yale-New Haven Tchrs. Inst., 1984—. Trustee Collegiate Sch., N.Y.C., 1992—. Mem. Am. Assn. Higher Edn. (bd. dirs. 1994—), Harvard Grad. Sch. Alumni Assn. (coun. 1997—). Mem. Harvard Club N.Y.C. Home: 180 Highland Ave Ridgewood NJ 07450-4002 Office: Andrew W Mellon Found 140 E 62nd St New York NY 10021-8142

ELACHI, CHARLES, aerospace engineer; b. Apr. 18, 1947. BS, U. Grenoble, France, 1968; MS, Calif. Inst. Tech., 1969, PhD in Elec. Sci., 1971; MBA, U. So. Calif., 1978; MS, UCLA, 1983. Rsch. fellow Calif. Inst. Tech., Pasadena, 1971-74, leader Radar Remote Sensing Team,, 1974-80, asst. lab. dir. space and sci. instruments, 1987-95, sr. scientist Jet Propulsion Lab.,, 1971-74, sr. rsch. scientist Jet Propulsion Lab.,, 1981—, dir. space and earth sci. programs, 1995—, Watson lectr., 1983—; prin. investigator various studies and devel. NASA, 1973-87, mem. Solar Sys. Exploration Com. Coun., 1988—, Astrophysics Coun., 1988—; mem. Electromagnetic Acad., 1990-95. Contbr. over 200 articles to profl. publs.; patentee in field. Recipient Prof. R.W.P. King award for outstanding contbrn. in field of electromagnetics, 1973. Mem. AIAA, NAE, IEEE (Geosensing and Remote Sensing Disting. Achievement award 1987, Engring. Excellence medal 1992), Am. Astronautical Soc., Electromagnetic Soc., Am. Geophys. Union, Planetary Soc., Sigma Xi. Office: Jet Propulsion Lab MS 180-704 4800 Oak Grove Dr Pasadena CA 91109-8001*

ELAM, FRED ELDON, retired career army officer; b. Seminole, Okla., July 10, 1937; s. Jack Eldon Elam and Maye (Gaskill) E.; m. Judy Teller, Feb. 21, 1959; children: Jacqueline Marie Elam Kabat, Justin Eldon. BS, U. Ark., 1960; MBA, Mich. State U., 1964; grad. strategy mgmt. and naval ops., Naval War Coll., 1977; grad., Harvard Grad. Sch. Bus. Admin., 1988. Commd. 2d lt. U.S. Army, 1960, advanced through grades to maj. gen., 1986; with Div. G-4, 101st Airborne (Air Assault) U.S. Army, Fort Campbell, Ky., 1976-77; comdr. Materiel Support Ctr. U.S. Army, Waegwan, Republic of Korea, 1977-79; dir. programs and evaluation Army Materiel Command U.S. Army, Alexandria, Va., 1979-82; comdg. gen. 19th Support Command, Taegu, Republic of Korea, 1982-84; dir. mgmt. Hdqrs. Dept. Army, Washington, 1984-85; chief U.S. Army Transp., Hdqrs. Transp. Ctr. Fort Eustis, Va., 1985-88; comdr. Joint U.S. Mil. Mission for Aid to Turkey Ankara, 1988-90; asst. dep. chief of staff for logistics, Dept. Army Washington, 1990-93; v.p. tech. and logistics svcs. Advancia Corp., Arlington, Va., 1993—; mem. lifetime staff and faculty Army Logistics Mgmt. Ctr., Fort Lee, Va., 1971—, Va. Mil. Commn., 1986-88; disting. mem. Transp. Corps Rgt., U.S. Army. Decorated D.S.M., Def. Superior Svc. medal, Legion of Merit, Bronze Star with two oak leaf clusters, Meritorious Svc. medal with two oak leaf clusters, Air medal, Army Commendation medal with three oak leaf clusters, Armed Forces expeditionary medal, Vietnam Svc. medal with four oak leaf clusters, Overseas Svc. ribbon with "4" device, Republic of Vietnam campaign medal, Republic of Korea Svc. medal, Medal of Merit of Turkish Armed Forces, Meritorious Svc. medal. Mem. Assn. U.S. Army, Air Traffic Control Assn., Soc. of 173d Airborne Brigade, Nat. Def. Transp. Assn., Res. Officers Assn., Am.-Turkish Friendship Assn., Beta Gamma Sigma. Avocations: running, reading, military history. Office: LB&M Assocs Arlington VA 22209

ELAM, JOHN CARLTON, lawyer; b. Ft. Wayne, Ind., Mar. 6, 1924; s. Bernard C. and Eunice (Gawthrop) E.; m. Virginia Mayberry, July 14, 1945; children: Nancy Lee, Patricia Scott, Mary Jane, John William. B.A., U. Mich., 1948, J.D. with distinction, 1949. Bar: Mich. 1949, Ohio 1950. Assoc. Vorys, Sater, Seymour & Pease, Columbus, Ohio, 1949-54, ptnr., 1954—, presiding ptnr., 1964-94, of counsel, 1995—. Trustee Columbus Coll. Art and Design, 1981-88. Fellow Am. Coll. Trial Lawyers (pres. 1980-81); mem. ABA (standing com. on fed. judiciary and ho. of dels.), Ohio Bar Assn., Columbus Bar Assn. (pres. 1964), 6th Cir. Jud. Conf. Home: 5000 Squirrel Bnd Columbus OH 43220-2278 Office: Vorys Sater Seymour & Pease 52 E Gay St Columbus OH 43215-3161

ELAM, KAREN MORGAN, food company executive, consultant; b. Watseka, Ill., Feb. 22, 1945; d. Howard Edgar and Margaret Lucille (Dilling) Johnson; m. Fred William Morgan, Jr., Aug. 26, 1967 (div. June 1974); 1 child, Todd Anthony; m. Rick Elam, Nov. 19, 1979; 1 stepchild, Paula Helene. B.S., Purdue U., 1967; M.S., Mich. State U., 1968; Ph.D., U. Mo., 1977. Instr. nutrition assessment and food policy research U. Mo., Columbia, 1973-74, grad. research asst., 1974-77, asst. prof., 1981-83, assoc. prof., 1983-86; asst. prof. Mich. State U., East Lansing, 1977-81; dir. consumer affairs Nabisco Brands, Inc., East Hanover, N.J., 1987-90; sr. dir. consumer and sci. affairs Nabisco, Inc., 1991—; cons. numerous food industries and pub. relation firms, 1979-87. Author: Nutrients in Foods, 1983; computerized nutrient data bank at Mich. State U., 1979 (yearly updates). Editor Nutrition Data Bank Conf. Proc., 1980. Contbr. articles to profl. jours. Grantee USDA, HHS. Fellow Am. Coll. Nutrition; mem. Am. Inst. Nutrition, Nat. Acad. Scis. (com. foods additives survey data), Am. Agrl. Econs. Assn., Inst. Food Technologists. Avocations: downhill skiing, reading. Office: Nabisco Consumer & Sci Affairs 100 Deforest Ave East Hanover NJ 07936-2897

ELAM, LESLIE ALBERT, museum administrator; b. Balt., May 12, 1938; s. Albert and Mary (Walker) E.; m. Judith Anne Clark, Apr. 4, 1964; children—Jennifer Helen, Jeffrey Walker. B.A., Lehman Coll., City U. N.Y., 1973. Editor J.J. Augustin, Inc. Pub., Locust Valley, N.Y., 1958-61; editorial asst. Am. Numis. Soc., N.Y.C., 1963-66; editor Am. Numis. Soc., 1966-89, adminstrv. officer, 1966-69, sec., 1969—, dir., 1972—, adminstr., 1963—, exec. dir., 1997-99. Editor: Am. Numis. Soc. Museum Notes, 1966-89. Served with AUS 1961-63. Mem. Phi Beta Kappa. Home: 1 Buck Run South Salem NY 10590 Office: The Am Numismatic Society Broadway At 155th St New York NY 10032

ELARABY, NABIL A., Egyptian diplomat; b. Cairo, Mar. 15, 1935; m. Nadia Teymour; children: May, Marwan, Hisham. Licencie en Droit, Cairo U., Egypt; LLM in Internat. Law, NYU, U.S.A., JSD. Legal advisor to Egyptian del. UN Mid. East Peace Conf., Ministry of Fgn. Affairs, Geneva, 1973-75; counsellor to mission from Egypt UN, Geneva, 1974-76; amb., dep. permanent rep. of Egypt UN, N.Y.C., 1978-81; amb. extraordinary and plenipotentiary, permanent rep. of Egypt UN, Geneva, 1987-91; permanent rep. UN, N.Y.C., 1991—; legal advisor, dir. legal and treaties dept. Ministry of Fgn. Affairs, Geneva, 1976-78, 83-87; Egyptian amb. India, 1981-83; arbitrator (Suez Canal dispute) ICC Internat. Ct. of Arbitration, Paris, 1989; judge Judicial Tribunal of the Arb Orgn. of Arab Petroleum Exporting Countries, 1990; represented Egypt in the following UN Orgns. The Gen. Assembly, Security Coun., Econ. and Social Coun., Human Rights Commn., 1966—; head Egyptian Del. UN Conf. on Disarmament, 1987-91; led Egyptian Delegation to Egyptian-Israeli Arbitration Tribunal Taba Talks, 1986-89; former chair numerous UN coms. and working groups; pres. Security Coun., 1996; lectr. The Hague Acad. of Internat. Law, Columbia U., NYU, Duke U., Yale U., The Egyptian Soc. Internat. Law, Am. Soc. Internat. Law, and many others. Contbr. to profl. jours. and internat. law publs. Adlai Stevenson fellow UN Inst. for Tgn. and Rsch., 1968, Spl. fellow, 1973. Mem. Egyptian Soc. Internat. Law (bd. dirs.), Am. Soc. Internat. Law, Internat. Law Assn. (am. br.), Inst. World Affairs (bd. dirs.). Address: Permanent Mission of Egypt to UN 36 E 67th St New York NY 10021*

ELARDO, RICHARD, psychology and education educator; b. Bklyn., Oct. 30, 1942; s. Ray and Diana (Davis) E.; m. Patricia Harrington, 1964 (div. 1965); 1 child, William Donald; m. Phyllis Thomson, 1970 (div. 1975). BA, Ariz. State U., 1965, MA, 1967, PhD, 1971. Asst. prof. U. Ark., Little Rock, 1971-75; assoc. prof. U. Mo., St. Louis, 1975-78; assoc. prof. edn. U. Iowa, Iowa City, 1978—; rsch. coord. Ctr. for Early Devel. and Edn., U. Ark., 1974-75; dir. Project Home, St. Louis Dept. of Mental Health, 1977-78; dir. Early Childhood Edn. Ctr., U. Iowa, 1978-81. Editor: Perspectives on Infant Day Care, 1976; contbr. articles to profl. jours. Co-founder after-sch. program Iowa City Schs., 1980, Good Shephard Day Care Ctr., Iowa City, 1981; co-chair Rep. Party Precinct, Iowa City, 1995. Grantee U.S. Bur. Edn. for the Handicapped, 1974, State of Mo., 1976; recipient Best Rsch. in Child Abuse award End Violence Against Next Generation, Inc., 1976. Mem. APA, Nat. Assn. for Edn. Young Children, Am. Ednl. Rsch. Assn., Nat. Assn. Early Childhood Tchr. Eductors, Iowa City Assn. for Edn. Young Children (pres. 1990-92). Avocations: boating, sports cars. Home: 2144 Plaen View Dr Iowa City IA 52246 Office: U Iowa Coll Edn Iowa City IA 52242

ELAYDI, SABER NASR, educator; b. Beersheba, Palestine, Jan. 7, 1943; s. Nasr and Nora E.; n. Salwa Arnous, Dec. 8, 1966; children: Tarek, Ghada, Raed. BS, Ain Shams U., Cairo, 1964; PhD, U. Mo., 1978. Asst. prof. Kuwait U., 1978-83; assoc. prof. U. Colo., Colorado Springs, 1984-89; assoc. prof. Trinity U., San Antonio, 1989-91, prof., chair, 1991-99; vis. prof. Case Western Res. U., Cleve., 1983-84. Author: An Introduction fo Difference Equations, 1996, Discrete Chaos, 1999; editor-in-chief Jour. Difference Equations and Apllications, 1994—; editor Jour. Computational Analysis and Applications, 1998—. Mem. Am. Math. Soc., Math. Assn. Am., Soc. Indls. & Applied Math., Soc. Math. Biology. Office: Trinity U Math Dept 715 Stadium Dr San Antonio TX 78212-7200

EL-BAGHDADI, MAHDI ABBAS, public administration educator; b. July 1, 1934. BA in Internat. Rels., Dartmouth Coll., 1958; M Pub. and Internat. Affairs, U. Pitts., 1982, PhD in Pub. and Internat. Affairs, 1986. Fgn. svc. officer Iraqi Ministry Fgn. Affairs, various countries, 1959-75; dir. internat. econ. orgns. and confs. Iraqi Ministry Trade, Baghdad, 1975-80; adj. prof. U. Pitts., 1986-88; assoc. prof. Grambling (La.) State U., 1988-99, prof., 1999—; mem. assoc. faculty Ctrl. Mich. U. Coll. Extended Learning, Mt. Pleasant, 1994—. Home: 401 Zephyr Ln Ruston LA 71270 Office: Dept. Pol. Sci./P.A. Grambling State U. Box 4266 Grambling LA 71245

EL-BAKRY, AMR SAAD, mathematician, researcher; b. Alexandria, Egypt, Oct. 7, 1963; arrived in the U.S., 1987; s. Saad El-Bakry and Gawaher Ali; m. Fadila Hasan Ali, July 13, 1987; children: Maryam, Abdul-Rahman, Sana. Bachelor, Alexandria U., 1984; MS, Rice U., 1990, PhD, 1991. Asst. prof. Alexandria U., 1993-96; rsch. assoc. Rice U., 1996-98; sr. rsch. math. Exxon Prodn. and Rsch., Houston, 1998—; editor Jour. Optimization and Engring./Kluwer Pubs., 1999—. Contbr. articles to profl. jours. E-mail: elbakry@caam.rice.edu.

ELBAUM, CHARLES, physicist, educator, researcher; b. May 15, 1926; married; 3 children. MASc, U. Toronto, Ont., Can., 1952; PhD in Applied Sci., U. Toronto, 1954; MA (hon.), Brown U., 1961. Research fellow in metal physics U. Toronto, Ont., Can., 1954-57; research fellow in metal physics Harvard U., 1957-59; asst. prof. applied physics Brown U., Providence, 1959-61; assoc. prof. physics Brown U., 1961-63, prof. physics, 1963—, chmn. dept. physics, 1980-86, also Hazard prof. physics, 1991—; cons. to industry. Fellow Am. Phys. Soc.; mem. AIME, Soc. Neurosci., AAAS. Office: Brown U Dept Physics PO Box 1843 Providence RI 02912-1843

ELBAUM, MAREK, electro-optical sciences executive, researcher; b. Kovel, U.S.S.R., May 8, 1941; came to U.S., 1969; s. Isaak Elbaum and Maria Rajbenbach; m. Lia Krusin, Jan. 2, 1969; 1 child, Martin Krusin-Elbaum. MSc, Warsaw (Poland) Tech. U., 1966; PhD, Columbia U., 1977. Rsch. assoc. Polish Acad. Sci., Warsaw, 1966-68; mem. rsch. staff Riverside Rsch. Inst., N.Y.C., 1969-79, mgr. electro-optics div., 1979-82, rsch. dir., 1982-90; pres. Electro-Optical Scis., Irvington, N.Y., 1990—. Contbr. more than 60 articles to profl. jours. Recipient Award Christopher Columbus Found., 1998. Achievements include patents for novel holographic technique, novel techniques for tracking space object in the visible and infrared; development of theory for direct detection laser radars; first demonstration of frequency diversity technique for laser speckle reduction and ultrasound applications; development of multi-spectral lesion imaging method for automatic detection of early melanoma; development digital fiber optics transillumination for detection of early caries. Office: Electro Optical Scis 1 Bridge St Irvington NY 10533-1543

EL-BAZ, FAROUK, research director, educator; b. Zagazig, Egypt, Jan. 1, 1938; came to U.S., 1967, naturalized, 1970; s. El-Sayed Mohammed and Zahia Abul-Ata (Hammouda) El-B.; m. Catherine Patricia O'Leary, 1963; children—Monira, Soraya, Karima, Fairouz. BSc, Ain Shams U., 1958; MS, U. Mo., 1961; PhD, U. Mo. and MIT, 1964; DSc (hon.), New England Coll., 1989. Demonstrator geology dept. Assiut U., Egypt, 1958-60; lectr. Mineralogy-Petrography Inst., U. Heidelberg, Germany, 1964-65; geologist exploration dept. Pan Am.-UAR Oil Co., Egypt, 1966; supr. lunar exploration Bellcomm and Bell Tel. Labs., Washington, 1967-72; rsch. dir. Center for Earth and Planetary Studies, Nat. Air and Space Mus., Smithsonian Instn., Washington, 1973-82; v.p. sci. and tech. Itek Optical Sys., Litton Industries, Lexington, Mass., 1982-86; cons. geology, prof. geology and geophysics U. Utah, 1975-77; prof. geology Ain Shams U., Egypt, 1976-81, 95—; sci. adviser Pres. Anwar Sadat of Egypt, 1978-81; sr. advisor Nat. Rsch. Inst. for Astronomy and Geophysics, Helwan, Egypt, 1996—; dir. Ctr. for Remote Sensing Boston U., 1986—. Author: Say It in Arabic, 1968, Astronaut Observations from the Apollo-Soyuz Mission, 1977, Egypt as Seen by Landsat, 1979, The Geology of Egypt: An Annotated Bibliography, 1984; co-author: Coprolites: An Annotated Bibliography, 1968, Glossory of

Mining Geology, 1970, The Moon as Viewed by Lunar Orbiter, 1970, Apollo Over the Moon: A View from Orbit, 1978; co-editor: Apollo-Soyuz Test Project Summary Science Report: Earth Observations and Photography, 1979, Desert Landforms of Southwest Egypt: A Basis for Comparison with Mars, 1982, Physics of Desertification, 1986, Remote Sensing and Resource Exploration, 1989, Sand Transport and Desertification in Arid Lands, 1990, The Gulf War and the Environment, 1994; editor: Deserts and Arid Lands, 1984; contbr. articles to profl. jours. Decorated Order of Merit 1st class Egypt; recipient certificate merit U.S. Bur. Mines, 1961, Exceptional Sci. Achievement medal NASA, 1971, Alumni Achievement award U. Mo., 1972, Honor citation Assn. Arab-Am. U. Grads., 1973, Outstanding Contbns. to Sci. and Space Tech. award Am.-Arab Anti-Discrimination Com., 1995, Achievement award Egyptian-Am. Profl. Soc., 1995, Human Needs award Am. Assn. Petroleum Geologists, 1996. Fellow AAAS (Pub. Understanding of Sci. and Tech. award 1992), Royal Astron. Soc., Geol. Soc. Am. (certificate commendation 1973); mem. World Aerospace Edn. Orgn. (cert. of merit, 1973), Internat. Inst. of Boston (Golden Door award 1992), Explorers Club, Sigma Xi. Office: Boston U Ctr Remote Sensing 725 Commonwealth Ave Boston MA 02215-1401

ELBAZ, SOHAIR WASTAWY, library director, consultant; b. Cairo, Nov. 7, 1954; came to U.S., 1981; s. Fahmy Elsayed Wastawy and Alia Ahmed Shaffie; m. Nabil Gamal, July 28, 1987; children: Kareim, Tahany. BA, Cairo U., 1975, MA, 1978; MLS, Cath. U., 1973; PhD, Simmons Coll., 1987. Micrographics specialist Cairo U., 1975-83; asst. prof. Inst. Pub. Administrn., Riyadh, Saudi Arabia, 1984-85; info. specialist, mktg. dir. Data Processing Services, Cairo, 1983-87; info. researcher Ill. Inst. Tech., Chgo., 1988-91, dir. libr., 1991—; cons. UN, 1989—. Mem. Egyptian Soc. Info. Sci., Ill. Libr. Assn. Republican. Office: Illinois Inst of Tech Paul V Galvin Libr 35 W 33rd St Chicago IL 60616-3739

ELBEIN, ALAN DAVID, medical science educator; b. Lynn, Mass., Mar. 20, 1933; s. Gersh and Golda (Stryer) E.; m. Elaine J. Brooks, June 21, 1953; children: Steven Conrad, Bradley Martin, Richard Craig. AB, Clark U., 1954; MS, U. Ariz., 1956; PhD, Purdue U., 1960. Rsch. assoc. in biochemistry Med. Sch. U. Mich., Ann Arbor, 1960-63; rsch. assoc. in biochemistry U. Calif., Berkeley, 1963-64; asst. prof., then assoc. prof. biology Rice U., Houston, 1964-69; prof. Health Sci. Ctr. U. Tex., San Antonio, 1969-90; prof., chmn. biochemistry dept. U. Ark. Med. Sci., Little Rock, 1991—; mem. study sect. NSF, 1972-75, NIH, 1983-87, 93-97; mem. editl. bd. Jour. Biol. Chemistry, Arch. Biochem. Biophysics, Plant Physiology, Glycobiology, Jour. Bacteriology, Eur. Jour. Biochem. Editor: Swainsonine; contbr. articles, revs. to profl. jours. Disting. Faculty scholar UAMS, 1996-97. Mem. Am. Chem. Soc., Am. Soc. Plant Physiology, Am. Soc. Biol. Chem. and Molecular Biology. Jewish. Achievements include numerous patents and pubs. Home: 23 Fontenay Cir Little Rock AR 72223-9569 Office: U Ark Med Scis Dept Biochem & Mol Biology 4301 W Markham St Little Rock AR 72205-7101

ELBERRY, ZAINAB ABDELHALIEM, insurance company executive; b. Alexandria, Egypt, Sept. 30, 1948; came to U.S., 1973; d. Abelhaliem Elberry and Nazieha Ahmed (Ezzat) E.; m. Mohammed Nour Naciri, Aug. 7, 1975; 1 child, Nadeam El Shami. BA, Ain Shams U., Cairo, 1971; MA, Am. U., Cairo, 1975. Cataloger Vanderbilt Joint U. Librs., Nashville, 1976-77; sales rep. Equitable Life Assurance Soc., 1977-80; with Met. Life Ins., Nashville, 1980—, account rep., 1981—, mgr., 1984; mem. adv. bd. Parkview Surgery Ctr., 1983-84. Chmn. com., bd. dirs. Nashville Internat. Cultural Heritage, 1983—, also bd. dirs.; chmn. Internat. Women Nashville Fair, 1977-78; bd. dirs. YWCA, Coun. for Nat. Interest; fundraiser Peace Links, 1989, YMCA Internat. House, 1987-89, Nashville Animal Shelter, 1979, Nashville League Hearing Impaired, 1976-81; mem. adv. bd. Nashville celebration Internat. Yr. of Disabled Persons; pres. Internat. Women Nashville. Recipient Spl. Contbn. award U.S. Coun. Internat. Disabled Persons, 1981. Mem. Nat. Assn. Life Underwriters, Nat. Assn. Profl. Saleswomen (Recognition award 1986), Gen. Agy. Mgrs. Assn., UN Assn. (bd. dirs. Nashville chpt.), Altrusa Club. Islam. Home: 5600 Kendall Dr # B Nashville TN 37209-4548

ELBERT, JAMES PEAK, independent insurance agent, minister; b. Pampa, Tex., Feb. 5, 1937; s. James Monteen and Nannie Pearle (Harwell) E.; m. Jean Coburn, June 25, 1960 (div. Jan., 1983); children: James Michael, Steven Lawrence; m. Ann English Smith, Apr. 23, 1983; 1 child, Jennifer English Aberle. BA, Southwestern U., Georgetown, Tex., 1959; MDiv, So. Meth. U., 1962. Minister First Meth. Ch., Glen Flora, Tex., 1962-65, Falvey Meml. Meth. Ch., Wells, Tex., 1965-67; assoc. minister First United Meth. Ch., Orange, Tex., 1967-69; minister of edn. Trinity United Meth. Ch., Beaumont, Tex., 1969-70; minister First United Meth. Ch., Murchiston, Tex., 1970-71; campus minister Henderson County Jr. Coll., Athens, Tex., 1970-71; v.p., owner Elbert Insur. Agy., Lake Jackson, Tex., 1971-76, Bennett-Elbert Co., Lake Jackson, 1976-83; v.p., gen. mgr. Jahn-Austin Insur., Galveston, Tex., 1983-96; prin., owner Brazoria (Tex.) Ins. Agy., 1998—; pres. Galveston Ins. Bd., 1986-88; Elbert Ins. Agy., Lake Jackson, Tex., 1995—, pres., owner; apptd. to Windstorm Study com. Tex. Dept. Ins., 1992, liaison to Tex. Dept. Ins. bldg. code study com., 1992—; supernumerary Tex. Conf. United Meth. Ch. Bd. dirs. Jr. Achievement of Brazoria County, 1980-81; active Lake Jackson Little League, 1974-77, Lake Jackson Teenage League, 1978-79, Lake Jackson Babe Ruth League, 1980; sec. Galveston Windstorm Action Com., 1988—; pres. Galveston Housing Fin. Corp., 1993-95, City of Galveston Property Fin. Authority, Inc., 1993-95; v.p. Bay Area coun. Boy Scouts Am., 1988—; pres. Ball H.S. Band Boosters, Galveston, 1991-92; mem. Mayor's Roundtable on Housing, City of Galveston, 1993-95; chmn. com. on ministries Moody Meml. First United Meth. Ch., 1994-95. Recipient Merit award Bay Area Coun. Boy Scouts Am. Quintana Dist., Lake Jackson, 1979, Silver Beaver award Bay Area Coun. Boy Scouts Am., Galveston, 1985. Mem. Cert. Ins. Counselors (cert., pres. Tex. chpt. 1992), Ind. Ins. Agts. Tex. (chmn. com. 1991-95), Tex. Windstorm Ins. Assn. (bd. dirs. 1998—), Tex. Assn. Ins. Agts. (liaison to Tex. Windstorm Pool Assn. 1993-95, bd. dirs. 1995-98, Chmn. of the Yr. 1993-94), Galveston C. of C. (bd. dirs. 1992-95), Rotary of Galveston Island (pres. 1993-94, Rotarian of Yr., Paul Harris fellow 1990, Bd. Mem. of Yr. 1991), Brazosport C. of C. (mem. bd. 1980-81), Phi Delta Theta. Avocations: family camping, gardening. Home: 7754 Beaudelaire Cir Galveston TX 77551-1625 Office: Elbert Ins Agy 127 Circle Way St Ste C Lake Jackson TX 77566-5233

ELBIN-SCHELL, CAROL GERTRUDE, television promotion manager; b. Morgantown, W.Va., Sept. 30, 1937; d. Harry C. and Gertrude I. (Simms) Elbin; 1 child, Karen Denise Schell. B.F.A., Cin. Coll.-Conservatory, 1959; student Foley Modeling Sch., 1961; postgrad. Tidewater Community Coll., 1976-77. Promotion mgr. Sta. WAVY-TV, Norfolk, Va., 1975-76; promotion pub. service mgr. Sta. WNYS-TV (now WIXT), Syracuse, N.Y., 1962-71; asst. promotion dept. Sta. KRCA (now KNBC-TV), Hollywood, Calif., 1959; asst. promotion-pub. service mgr. Sta. WCPO-TV, Cin., 1956-59, 60-61; promotion-pub. service mgr. Sta. KUSK-TV, Prescott, Ariz., 1982-83; promotion mgr. Sta. KMIR-TV, Palm Springs, 1984; sta. mgr., promotion mgr. Gt. S.W. Broadcasting, Bakersfield, Calif., 1987-88; freelance writer, Prescott, 1983—; writer Videoview Mag., Phoenix, 1985; gen. mgr. Prescott Cmty. Access Channel, 1988-91; campaign coord. Senator John W. Warner of Va., 1977-78; campaign worker Senator Barry Goldwater of Ariz., 1980. Author: Great Hospital Connection, 1976; Self Signs, 1976. Recipient Gabriel award Office of Catholic Dioceses, Washington, 1971; supr. personal appearances: Mike Douglas, Jack LaLanne, Vic Morrow, others, 1962-83; personal appearance coord., publicist to Elizabeth Taylor-Warner, 1977-78; exec. prodr., writer, editor tv series, specials, 1962-91. Mem. Women in Communications, Am. Women in Radio and TV, Broadcast Promotion Assn., Am. Film Inst., Delta Omicron. Republican. Methodist.

ELCANO, MARY S., lawyer, federal agency administrator. BA cum laude, Lynchburg Coll., 1971; JD, Cath. U., Washington, 1976; postgrad., Georgetown U. Litigation atty. Balt. Legal Aide Bur., 1976; staff atty. Office Solicitor Dept. Labor, 1979; gen. trial and appellate atty. Office Labor Law U.S. Postal Svc., 1982, exec. dir. Office EEO, 1984, regional dir. human resources N.E. region, 1987, sr. v.p., gen. counsel, 1992—. Office: US Postal Svc Gen Counsel 475 Lenfant Plz SW Rm 6004 Washington DC 20260-0004

ELCIK, ELIZABETH MABIE, fashion illustrator; b. Bklyn., Sept. 16, 1933; d. Cornelius Peter and Anna Julia (Cunningham) Mabie; m. John Joseph Elcik, Apr. 20, 1963. Grad., Jamesine Franklin Sch. Profl. Arts, N.Y.C., 1954; student in painting, NYU; student life class, Art Students League, N.Y.C. Fashion illustrator Vogue patterns Conde Nast Publs., 1954-59; freelance illustrator various clients, N.Y.C., 1960-74; fashion illustrator Butterick Fashion Mktg. Co., N.Y.C., 1974-82, McCall Pattern Co., N.Y.C., 1982—; monitor profl. sketch classes, N.Y.C., 1962-79. Scholar N.Y.C Art, 1951, Jamesine Franklin Sch., 1952. Mem. Nat. Mus. Women in Arts. Roman Catholic. Avocation: travel.

ELDEFRAWI, AMIRA TOPPOZADA, medical educator, toxicologist, pharmacologist; b. Giza, Cairo, Egypt, Feb. 10, 1937; came to U.S., 1968; d. Hussein Khairy and Fadila Ibrahim (Aref) Toppozada; children: Mosen M., Mona D. Hoff, Mohab M. BS, U. Alexandria, Egypt, 1957; PhD, U. Calif., Berkeley, 1960. Asst. prof. U. Alexandria, 1960-68; rsch. assoc. prof. Cornell U., Ithaca, N.Y., 1968-76; from rsch. assoc. prof. to rsch. prof. U. Md., Balt., 1976-88, prof., 1988—; cons. U.S. State Dept., Washington, 1982-83, Nat. Inst. Environ. Health Sci. Rev. Com., Research Triangle Park, N.C., 1987-91, 97, EPA Sci. Adv. Panel, 1997-98; scholar-in-residence Queen's U. Sch. Medicine, Kingston, Ont., Can., 1985. Author: Resistance of Insects to Insecticides, 1966; editor Myasthenia Gravis, 1983; assoc. editor Membrane Biochemistry, 1987-93; mem. editorial bd. Pesticide Biochemistry & Physiology, 1987—, Jour. Toxicology and Environ. Health, 1987—, Environ. Rsch., 1995—, Jour. Pesticide Management and Environ., 1996—; publ. scientific papers in field. Grantee NIH, 1975—, NATO, 1986-89, U.S. Army, 1995—. Mem. Am. Soc. Pharmacology and Exptl. Therapeutics, Soc. Neurosci., Entomol. Soc. Am., Soc. Toxicology (pres. neurotoxicology splty. sect. 1996-97). Office: U Md Sch Medicine 655 W Baltimore St Baltimore MD 21201-1509

ELDEN, GARY MICHAEL, lawyer; b. Chgo., Dec. 11, 1944; s. E. Harold and Sylvia Arlene (Diamond) E.; m. Phyllis Deborah Mandler, Apr. 20, 1975; children: Roxanna Mandler, Erica Mandler. BA, U. Ill., 1966; JD, Harvard U., 1969. Bar: Ill. 1969, U.S. Dist. Ct. (no. dist.) Ill. 1969, U.S. Ct. Appeals (7th cir.) 1973, U.S. Supreme Ct. 1973, U.S. Dist. Ct. (ea. dist.) Mich. 1985, U.S. Ct. Appeals (8th cir.) 1988, U.S. Ct. Appeals (6th and 10th cirs.) 1990, U.S. Dist. Ct. (ea. dist.) Wis. 1992. Ptnr. Kirkland & Ellis, Chgo., 1969-78, Reuben & Proctor, Chgo., 1978-86, Isham, Lincoln & Beale, Chgo., 1986-88, Grippo & Elden, Chgo., 1988—. Contbr. articles to profl. jours. Fellow Am. Coll. Trial Lawyers; mem. ABA, Chgo. Bar Assn. (sec. com. appellate procedures 1975-77), Chgo. Coun. Lawyers, Appellate Lawyers Assn. (bd. dirs. 1975-77), Met. Club. Home: 3750 N Lake Shore Dr Chicago IL 60613-4238 Office: Grippo & Elden 227 W Monroe St Ste 3600 Chicago IL 60606-5018

ELDER, BESSIE RUTH, pharmacist; b. Ovalo, Tex., June 28, 1935; d. William Kinsalow and Ima Ruth (Carter) Griffing; m. George Davis Elder, Sept. 15, 1950 (dec. Nov. 1991); children: Michael Davis, Linda Sue Elder Claborn. BS in Pharmacy, Southwestern Okla. U., 1989. Staff pharmacist Coleman Pharmacy, Dimmitt, Tex., 1989-90, United Pharmacy, Lubbock, Tex., 1990-92, St. Mary's Hosp. Pharmacy, Lubbock, 1992-95, Albertsons Pharmacy, 1996—. Home: 5713 87th St Lubbock TX 79424-4525

ELDER, ELDON, stage designer, theatre consultant; b. Atchison, Kans., Mar. 17, 1921; s. Clifford Phillips and Signe (Larsen) E. B.S., Emporia State Coll., 1944; postgrad., U. Denver, 1947; M.F.A., Yale U., 1958. Critic in stage design Yale U., New Haven, 1954, U. Denver, 1964-65; asst. prof. stage design Bklyn. Coll., CUNY, 1956-66, assoc. prof., 1966-69, prof., 1969-75; pres. Eldon Elder Assocs., N.Y.C., 1975—; theater designer and cons. Theatre Projects Cons., N.Y.C., 1982-86; participant cultural exch. tour Dept. State to USSR, Poland, 1965; vis. critic U. Ga., 1979; guest prof. design Ohio U., 1979; vis. prof. scene design Carnegie Mellon U., 1983-90, U. Ill., 1990-91; lecture tour China at invitation Chinese Theatre Assn., 1988, Internat. Design Exhbn., Shanghai, China, 1989; Fulbright disting. lectr. Ctrl. Acad. Drama and Sch. Architecture, Tsinghua U., Beijing, 1993. Scene, costume, lighting designer for over 250 plays, operas, TV prodns., including Broadway: The Affair, Fallen Angels, Legend of Lovers, Phoenix '55, Rugantino, The Girl in Pink Tights, Take a Giant Step, Time Out for Ginger, Venus Observed, Will Rogers' U.S.A., Every Good Boy Deserves Favour Shinbone Alley, Hizzoner!; Off Broadway prodns.: Delacorte Theater, N.Y.C., Am. Shakespeare Festival, Stratford, Conn., Santa Fe Opera Co., San Francisco Opera, Pitts. Pub. Theater, Seattle Repertory Theatre, Center Stage, Balt., Long Wharf Theatre, New Haven, Alliance Theatre, Atlanta, Asolo Theatre, Sarasota, Fla.; theatre designer, cons. Delacorte Theater, Tappan Zee Playhouse Redevel., Nyack, N.Y., Bininger Performing Arts Ctr., Eckard Coll. St. Petersburg, Fla., Harlem Performing Arts Ctr., N.Y.C., Theatre Devel. Project, Southeast Alaska, 42d Street Redevel. Project, N.Y.C., W. 63rd St YMCA Theatre, N.Y.C., Studio Theatre U. Okla., Norman, Nino Aquino Amphitheatre, Manila, Helen Hayes Performing Arts Ctr., Nyack, N.Y., Bldg. Code Study Dept. Cultural Affairs Chgo.; scene, costume, lighting designer one man exhbn., Performing Arts Mus., Lincoln Ctr., N.Y.C., 1978; group shows Contemporary Stage Design-U.S.A., N.Y.C., Washington, Prague, Czechoslovakia, 1975, Prague Quadrennial, 1987, 91; author: Will It Make a Theatre, 1979, 93; catalogue Eldon Elder: Designs for the Theatre, 1978. Served to lt. (j.g.) USNR, 1945-47, PTO. Guggenheim fellow, Greece and Italy, 1963; Ford Found. grantee, 1960; Fulbright Disting. lectr., Beijing, 1993-94. Mem. U.S. Inst. Theatre Tech. (bd. dirs. 1956), United Scenic Artists Am., Nat. Theater Conf. Office: Eldon Elder Assocs 27 W 67th St New York NY 10023-6258

ELDER, FRED KINGSLEY, JR., physicist, educator; b. Coronado, Calif., Oct. 19, 1921; s. Fred and Ethel S. (Tait) E.; m. Elinor Jean Goertz, July 5, 1947; children: Nancy Elisabeth Elder Backus, Jessie Custer Elder James, Jacqueline Lesesne Elder Shafer, Elinor Tait Elder Powell, Lydia Jean Elder Archer, Robert Abraham, Mary Grace Elder Graham, John Philip. B.S. in Physics, U. N.C., 1941; M.S. in Physics, Yale U., 1943, Ph.D., 1947. Instr., Yale U., 1943-44; instr. U. Pa., 1947-49; physicist Nat. Bur. Standards, summer 1949; asst. prof. U. Wyo., 1949-50; sr. physicist applied physics lab. Johns Hopkins U., 1950-53; assoc. prof. physics Wabash Coll., Crawfordsville, Ind., 1953-55; prof., chmn. physics dept. and div. natural scis. and math. Belhaven Coll., Jackson, Miss., 1955-59; research physicist U.S. Naval Ordnance Lab., White Oak, Md., summers 1957-59; head research br. antisubmarine warfare lab. U.S. Naval Air Devel. Center, Johnsville, Pa., 1959-65; prof. physics Rochester Inst. Tech., N.Y., 1965-91; prof. emeritus Rochester Inst. Tech., 1991—, head dept., 1965-72; scientist Physics Research Labs., Eastman Kodak Co., summer 1982; hon. vis. lectr. physics Aston U., Birmingham, Eng., 1985-86; vis. research fellow Lanchester Poly., Coventry, Eng., 1985-86. Scoutmaster, Nat. Capital Area council Boy Scouts Am., 1950-53; Scoutmaster Central Indiana council, 1953-55; trustee Westminster Theol. Sem., Phila., 1960—, sec. bd. trustees, 1981-83, mem. exec. com., 1965-78; trustee Presbyn. Guardian Pub. Corp., 1958-79; bd. dirs. Presbyn. Jour. Corp., 1979-87, mem. exec. com., 1979-84, mem. editorial com., 1984-87, mem. various denominational bds.; coms. gen. assembly Orthodox Presbyn. Ch., 1952—; trustee Great Commn. Publs., 1976—, v.p., 1975-76, 77-78, pres. 1978-79, 86-87, 90-91, 92-93. Served to lt. comdr. USNR, 1944-46; physicist U.S. Naval Research Lab. Washington. Mem. Am. Assn. Physics Tchrs. (vice chmn. N.Y. State sect. 1976-78, chmn. 1978-82), Netherlands, Am. phys. socs., Am. Geophys. Union, Am. Soc. for Engring. Edn., Inst. Physics (Gt. Britain), Franklin Inst., U.S. Naval Inst., Phi Beta Kappa, Phi Kappa Phi, Sigma Pi Sigma, Sigma Xi. Orthodox Presbyterian (ruling elder 1952—). Research, publs. on physics of fluids, physics edn. Home: 341 Barrington St Rochester NY 14607-3304 Office: Rochester Inst Tech Physics Dept Rochester NY 14623*

ELDER, IRMA, automotive company executive. Pres. Troy (Mich.) Motors. Office: Troy Motors 777 John R Rd Troy MI 48083-4302*

ELDER, JAMES CARL, lawyer; b. Detroit, Mar. 11, 1947; s. Carl W. and Alta M. (Bradley) E.; m. Margaret Ford, Apr. 6, 1974; children: James B., William J., Michael L., Samuel F. BA, U. Okla, 1969, JD, 1972. Bar: Okla. 1972, U.S. Dist. Ct. (we. dist.) Okla. 1972. Ptnr., dir. Crowe & Dunlevy, Oklahoma City, 1972-82; dir., mem. Mock, Schwabe, Waldo, et. al., Oklahoma City, 1982-96, 98—; ptnr. Gable Gotwals Mock Schwabe Kihle Gaberino, 1996-98. Nat. coun. rep. Last Frontier Coun. Boy Scouts Am., 1989—, pres., 1997-99; trustee Norman (Okla.) Pub. Sch. Found., 1989—, pres., 1995-97; elder Meml. Presbyn. Ch., Norman, clk. of session, 1992-95; dir. Cmty. Coun. Ctrl. Okla., 1998—. Recipient Silver Beaver award Boy Scouts Am., Oklahoma City, 1988, Silver Antelope award, 1999. Fellow Okla. Bar Found. (life), Baden Powell World Fellowship; mem. ABA (mem. title ins. com. real property, probate and trust law sect. 1993—, chmn. closing issues subcom. 1995—), Rotary, Beta Theta Pi Corp. of Okla. (trustee, v.p., chpt. counselor 1975-85, pres. 1995—). Avocations: scouting, skiing, reading. Office: Mock Schwabe Waldo et al 211 N Robinson 2 Leadership Sq 14th Fl Oklahoma City OK 73102

ELDER, JOHN BLANTON, psychologist, clergyman; b. Dallas, Dec. 27, 1926; s. Arthur Blanton and Inez (Staub) E.; m. Jeanine Copeland, June 9, 1950 (div. 1971); children: Nancy, Arthur, Jeanne; m. Thersia Dost, Sept. 21, 1974; 1 child, John Eric. BS, U. Tex., 1946; MDiv, Austin Sem., 1951; MA, U. Tex., 1966; PhD, U. Houston, 1974. Ordained to ministry Presbyterian Ch., 1951. Pastor Presbyn. chs., various locations, 1951-69; lectr. U. Md., College Park, 1976-88; clin. psychologist VA Med. Ctr., Grand Island, Nebr., 1989-90; clin. dir. Dept. of Army, Ft. Hood, Tex., 1990-91; pvt. practice Georgetown, Tex., 1991—; min. Leander (Tex.) Presbyn. Ch., 1994-98; organizing minister Presbyn. Ch., Sun City Georgetown, Tex. Moderator Brazos Presbytery, Houston, 1969; bd. dirs. Nebraskans for Ind. Living, 1989. Lt. (j.g.) USN, 1944-47. Mem. APA. Avocations: collecting coins, stamps, song sheets, travel. Home and Office: 1204 Power Rd Georgetown TX 78628-3145

ELDER, MARY LOUISE, librarian; b. Ann Arbor, Mich., Sept. 7, 1937; d. John Dyer and Elsie (Phelps) E. BA, St. Louis U., 1959; MA, U. Chgo., 1962; postgrad., U. Calif., Berkeley, 1965-69. Libr. U. Chgo., 1961-63; rare book cataloger U. Kans., Lawrence, 1963-65; rare books libr. St. Louis Pub. Libr., 1969-74; rare book cataloger Duke U., Durham, N.C., 1979-84, Smithsonian Inst., Washington, 1984-91, Libr. Congress, Washington, 1991—. Mem. ALA, Am. Printing History Assn., Bibliog. Soc., Bibliog. Soc. Am., Cath. Libr. Assn., Soc. History Authorship, Reading and Publishing, Alpha Sigma Nu. Office: Libr Congress Washington DC 20540

ELDER, REX ALFRED, civil engineer; b. Pa., Oct. 4, 1917; s. George Alfred and Harriet Jane (White) E.; m. Janet Stevens Alger, Aug. 10, 1940; children: John A., Carol S., Susan A., William P. BSCE, Carnegie Inst. Tech., 1940; MS, Oreg. State Coll., 1942. Hydraulic engr. TVA, Norris, Tenn., 1942-48; dir. hydraulic lab. TVA, 1948-61, dir. engring. lab., 1961-73; engring. mgr. Bechtel Civil & Minerals Inc., San Francisco, 1973-85; cons. hydraulic engr., 1986—. Contbr. numerous articles on hydraulic structures, hydraulic model studies, reservoir stratification and water quality, hydraulic research and hydraulic machinery to profl. jours. Served with USN, 1945-46. Fellow ASCE (hon. 1993, James Laurie prize 1949, Hunter Rouse lectr. 1984, Hydraulic Structures medal 1991), NAE, Internat. Assn. Hydraulic Rsch. (hon.). Home and Office: 501 Via Casitas Apt 424 Greenbrae CA 94904-1947

ELDER, ROBERT LAURIE, newspaper editor; b. Nashville, June 23, 1938; s. Charles Jerome and Dorothea Eloise (Calhoun) E.; m. Betty Ann Doak, Sept. 1, 1958 (div. May 1969); children—Mark Christopher, Jeffrey Cathcart. B.A., Washington and Lee U., 1960; M.A., Vanderbilt U., 1966; postgrad., Stanford U., 1976-77. Reporter Nashville Tennessean, 1964-68; asst. dir. So. Newspaper Pubs. Assn. Found., Atlanta, 1969; reporter The Miami Herald, Fla., 1970-76; editor San Jose (Calif.) Mercury News, 1978—, v.p. editor, 1987—; bd. dirs. RLM Ptnrs. Author: Crash, 1977. Bd. dirs. Santa Clara U. Ctr. for Applied Ethics, 1987—, Alliance for Cmty. Care, 1997, Nonprofit Devel. Ctr., 1997—. 1st lt. U.S. Army, 1960-62. Recipient Disting. Achievement award Fla. Soc. Newspaper Editors, 1973, White House Conf. on Librs. Pub. award, 1994, Pres. award Calif. Libr. Assn., 1995. Episcopalian. Home: 2007 University Ave San Jose CA 95128-1444 Office: San Jose Mercury News 750 Ridder Park Dr San Jose CA 95131-2432*

ELDER, ROBERT LEE, professional golfer; b. Dallas, July 14, 1934; s. Charles and Sadie E.; m. Rose Lorraine Harper, July 18, 1966. H.H.D. (hon.), Daniel Hale Williams U. Profl. golfer appearing in tournaments sponsored by United Golf Assn., 1961-67, Profl. Golfers Assn., 1967—; founder Lee Elder Celebrity Pro-Am Golf Classic, 1970—; pres. Elder Assocs. Inc. Founder Lee Elder Scholarship Fund, Inc.; Promoter Summer Youth Golf Devel. Programs, Washington; mem. nat. adv. bd. Goodwill Industries Am.; bd. dirs. Met. Washington Police Boys Club. Served with U.S. Army, 1959-61. Recipient Charles Bartlett award Golf Writers Am., 1977; Herman A. English Humanitarian award City of Los Angeles, 1977; A.G. Gaston Business of Year Nat. Bus. League, 1978; named Goodwill Ambassador to Africa, U.S. Dept. State, 1972; inducted into Washington Hall Stars, 1979. Mem. NAACP (life), Profl. Golfers Assn. Am. (dir.). Baptist. Club: Masons. Winning tournaments include Nigerian Open, 1971, Monsanto Open, 1974, Houston Open, 1976, Milw. Open, 1978, Westchester Classic, 1978, Denver Post Srs. tournament, 1985, Merrill Lynch/Golf Digest Srs. tournament, 1985, PGA Srs. tournament, 1985; 1st black golfer to qualify for Ryder Cup Golf Team, 1979. Office: Lee Elder 1440 S Ocean Blvd Apt 3C Pompano Beach FL 33062-7368*

ELDER, SHERI LYNNE, symphony orchestra official; b. Longview, Tex., Jan. 17, 1965; d. James Vayne and Bobbie Dean (Harris) E. BA, Baylor U., 1987; MA, Am. U., 1991. Adminstrv. coord. dept. performing arts Am. U., Washington, 1988-93; asst. dir. Givens Performing Arts Ctr., Pembroke, N.C., 1993-94; dir. mktg. Sacramento Theatre Co., 1994-96; mgr. prospect rsch. Dallas Symphony Orch., 1996-98, centennial coord., 1998—. Dir. plays, 1990-95; singer, actor musicals, operas, plays, 1990-95; prodr. spl. events, 1990-96. Mem. com. Sacramento Met. Arts Commn., 1995-96; panelist D.C. Commn. on the Arts and Humanities, Washington, 1991-92. Mem. AAUW, Am. U. Alumni Assn., Baylor U. Alumni Assn., Phi Kappa Phi. Democrat. Avocations: singing, acting. Home: 4303 Buena Vista St Apt 102 Dallas TX 75205-4463 Office: Dallas Symphony Assn 2301 Flora St Ste 300 Dallas TX 75201-2413

ELDER, STEWART TAYLOR, dentist, retired naval officer; b. Darlington, Pa., Aug. 6, 1917; s. William Carl and Olive Gertrude (Taylor) E.; m. Loretta Tersa Vitlo, Apr. 23, 1946; children: Donna Lou, Susan Loretta. BS, Mt. Union Coll., 1940; DDS, Ohio State U., 1945; postgrad., Naval Dental Sch., Nat. Naval Med. Center, Bethesda, Md., 1952-53. With Deming Pump Co., Salem, Ohio, 1935-36; prodn. mgr. Deming Pump Co., 1952-53; commd. lt. (j.g.) U.S. Navy, 1945; advanced through grades to capt. Dental Corps, 1960; prosthetics officer 50th Field Hosp., Paris, 1946-47; asst. dental officer Norfolk Naval Shipyard, Portsmouth, Va., 1948-50, U.S.S. Wisconsin, 1950-52; postgrad. resident in prosthodontics Naval Weapons Plant, Washington, 1953-54; prosthetics officer Norfolk Naval Shipyard, Portsmouth, 1954-55, 57-60; dental officer, prosthetics officer U.S.S. Vulcan, 1955-57; prosthetics officer, exec. officer Naval Dental Clinic, Guantanamo Bay, Cuba, 1960-62; prosthetics officer Naval Dental Clinic Marine Corps Base, Camp Pendleton, Calif., 1962-66; comdg. officer 11th Dental Co., Republic of Vietnam, 1966-67; chief dental service Naval Hosp., Camp Pendleton, 1967-71; exec. officer Naval Dental Clinic, Washington, 1971-73; comdg. officer Naval Dental Clinic, 1973-75, Naval Regional Dental Center, Washington, 1975-76, Nat. Naval Dental Center, Bethesda, Md., 1976-79; lectr., instr. Navy Dental Corps Continuing Edn. Program, 1963—, Dental Intern and Postdoctoral Fellowship Programs, 1967—; practice gen. dentistry, Salem, Ohio, 1947-48, lectr. and condr. clinics in field. Mem. ADA (life), Am. Prosthodontic Soc. (life), Fedn. Prosthodontic Orgns. (life). Home: 1436 Patriot Dr Melbourne FL 32940

ELDER, THOMAS WOODROW, real estate consultant; b. Boswell, Okla., Feb. 4, 1919; s. James Thomas and Tennie (Denton) E.; m. Croshia Ruth Davis, June 17, 1957. BS in Agrl. Econs., U. Tenn., 1948. Lic. real estate broker, Tenn. Asst. supt. Tenn. State Vocat. Tng. Sch., Pikeville, 1949-63; owner Elder Real Estate Co., Dayton, Tenn., 1964—; real estate appraiser TVA, Chattanooga, 1965-82, U.S. Dept. of Interior, Amarillo, 1982-83; reviewer of real estate appraisals, real estate appraiser State of Fla., Dept. Auditor Gen., Tallahassee, 1983-84; real estate cons. land br. of TVA, Chattanooga, 1985—. Lt. U.S. Army, 1941-46. Mem. Nat. Assn. Realtors, Nat. Assn. Review Appraisers, Internat. Right of Way Assn., Phi Beta Sigma, Phi Kappa Phi. Democrat. Methodist. Avocations: tennis, volleyball, quail hunting. Home: 680 Illinois Ave Dayton TN 37321-1534 Office: Tenn Valley Authority 1101 Market St Chattanooga TN 37401

ELDERKIN, CHARLES EDWIN, retired meteorologist; b. Seattle, Aug. 6, 1930; s. Andrew Charles and Hilda Olena E.; m. Mary DuPriest, May 28, 1959; 1 child, Christopher Charles. B.S., U. Wash., 1953, Ph.D., 1966. Meteorologist Gen. Electric Co., 1959-65; mgr. atmospheric physics sect. Battelle Pacific N.W. Lab., Battelle Meml. Inst., Richland, Wash., 1965-72; assoc. mgr. atmospheric scis. dept. Battelle Pacific N.W. Lab., Battelle Meml. Inst., 1972-79, program mgr. wind characteristics program element of fed. wind energy program, 1976-79, mgr. atmospheric scis. dept., 1979-82, assoc. mgr. geoscis. research and engring. dept., 1982-84, mgr. Hanford environ. oversight office, 1984-85, assoc. mgr. earth scis. dept., 1985-86, sr. program mgr. earth and environment scis. ctr., 1986-92; sci. dir. multi-lab. rsch. program Atmospheric Studies in Complex Terrain, Dept. Energy, 1989-92. Served with USAF, 1954-55. Recipient E.O. Lawrence award U.S. Energy Research and Devel. Adminstrn., 1975. Mem. Am. Meteorol. Soc. (chmn. com. atmospheric turbulence and diffusion 1972), Sigma Xi. Home: 531 Holly St Richland WA 99352-1822

ELDERKIN, E(DWIN) JUDGE, retired lawyer; b. Missoula, Mont., Oct. 25, 1932; s. Emerson Winston and Valma Agnes (Judge) E.; m. Marie Jane Fletcher, June 20, 1954; children: Susan Marie, Michael Judge. BS in History, U. Oregon, 1954; LLB, U. Calif., Berkeley, 1959. Bar: Calif. 1960, U.S. Ct. Appeals (9th crct.) Calif. 1960, U.S. Supreme Ct. 1967. Assoc. Brobeck, Phleger & Harrison, San Francisco, 1959-66, ptnr., 1966-92, mng. ptnr., 1984-88; pvt. judge Pvt. Adjudication Ctr., Inc.; advisor Ctr. Pub. Resources; lectr. in field; bd. dirs. MPC Ins. Ltd., The Renewal Project; mem. policy com. Aetna dental. Pscyhol. lay counsel for low income families. Named Counselor of the Yr. 1996. Fellow Am. Coll. Trial Lawyers, Am. Bar Found.; mem. Am. Cancer Soc. (driver, Driver of Yr. 1996). Mem. Evangel. Covenant Ch. Avocations: hiking, swimming, golf, tennis. Office: Brobeck Phleger & Harrison Spear St Tower 1 Market Plz Ste 341 San Francisco CA 94105-1193

ELDERKIN, HELAINE GRACE, lawyer; b. New Rochelle, N.Y., Sept. 18, 1954; d. EllsworthJay and Madelyn A. (Roberts) E.; m. Stefan Shrier, Feb. 23, 1985. BA, Fla. Atlantic U., 1975; JD, George Mason U., 1985. Bar: Va. 1985, U.S. Ct. Appeals (4th cir.) 1985, U.S. Ct. Fed. Claims 1994. Aide Carter/Mondale Presdl. Campaign Com., Atlanta, 1976, Presdl. Transition Staff, Washington, 1976-77; spl. asst. Agy. Internat. Devel. U.S. Dept. State, Washington, 1977; spl. asst. U.S. Dept. Def., Washington, 1977-79; mem. tech. staff System Planning Corp., Arlington, Va., 1980-83; dir. corp. rsch. Analytics, Inc., McLean, Va., 1983-85; v.p., gen. counsel Analytics, Inc., Fairfax, Va., 1985-91; of counsel Feith and Zell, P.C., Washington, 1986-91; asst. gen. counsel Computer Scis. Corp., 1991—; mem. Army Sci. Bd., 1994-98. Fellow Mil. Ops. Rsch. Soc. Democrat. Home: 624A S Pitt St Alexandria VA 22314-4138 Office: Computer Scis Corp 3170 Fairview Park Dr Falls Church VA 22042-4516

ELDRED, GERALD MARCUS, retired performing arts association executive; b. Cambridge, Ont., Can., Oct. 5, 1934; s. Albert Harold and Ethel Emily Hope (Bardwell) E.; m. Marjorie Christine Kidd, Aug. 4, 1956; 1 child, Peter Marcus (dec.). Diploma, Nat. Theatre Sch., Montreal, 1965. Adminstr. Nat. Ballet Can., Toronto, 1972-79; adminstrv. dir., acad. prin. Nat. Ballet Sch., Toronto, 1979-82; exec. dir. Stratford Festival, (Ont.), 1982-86; dir. fin. and ops. Harbourfront Corp., 1987-97; cons. in field; mem. arts adv. com. The Laidlaw Found., 1980-90. Stage producer, dir., adminstr. Canadian Players, Toronto, 1965-66, Man. Theatre Centre, Winnipeg, 1966-72, Shaw Festival, Niagara-on-the-Lake., Ont., 1967, Expo '67, Montreal, 1967, Rainbow Stage, Winnipeg, 1968, Kawartha Summer Festival, Lindsay, Ont., 1966, producer commd. opera for Nat. Arts Centre, Ottawa, 1969—. Mem. adv. com. program in art York U., 1982-90; mem., officer, bd. dirs. The Theatre Mus. Corp., 1988—, The Pleiades Theatre, Toronto, 1996. Mem. Can. Actors Equity Assn., Assn. Cultural Execs., Can. Coun. (adv. arts panel 1970-72, adv. bd. touring office 1983-85). Home: 346 Sugar Maple Ct, RR 5, Cambridge, ON Canada N1R 5S6

ELDRED, KENNETH MCKECHNIE, acoustical consultant; b. Springfield, Mass., Nov. 25, 1929; s. Robert Moseley and Jean McKechnie (Ashton) E.; m. Helene Barbara Koerting Fischer, May 31, 1957; 1 dau., Heidi Jean. B.S., MIT, 1950, postgrad., 1951-53; postgrad., UCLA, 1960-63. Engr. in charge vibration and sound lab. Boston Naval Shipyard, 1951-54; supervisory physicist, chief phys. acoustics sect. U.S. Air Force, Wright Field, Ohio, 1956-57; v.p., cons. acoustics Western Electro-Acoustics Labs., Los Angeles, 1957-63; v.p., tech. dir. sci. services and systems group Wyle Labs., El Segundo, Calif., 1963-73; v.p., dir. div. environ. and noise control tech. Bolt Beranek and Newman Inc., Cambridge, Mass., 1973-77; prin. cons. Bolt Beranek and Newman Inc., 1977-81; dir. Ken Eldred Engring.; mem. exec. stds. coun. Am. Nat. Stds. Inst., 1979-89, vice-chmn., 1981-83, chmn., 1985-87, bd. dirs., 1983-87; mem., past chmn. Acoustical Stds. Bd.; mem. com. hearing, bioacoustics and biomechanics NRC, 1963-88; chmn. Internat. Stds. Orgn. Tech. Com. TC108 Mechanical Shock and Vibration, 1994-99. Served with USAF, 1954-56. Fellow Acoustical Soc. Am. (stds. dir. 1987-93, past chmn. coordinating com. environ. acoustics, Silver Medal in Noise 1994); mem. NAE, Inst. Noise Control Engring. (pres. 1976, bd. dirs. 1987-91), Soc. Automotive Engrs., Soc. Naval Architects and Marine Engrs., Boothbay Harbor Yacht Club, Blue Water Sailing Club, Down East Yacht Club. Home: Meadow Cove East Boothbay ME 04544 Office: PO Box 501 East Boothbay ME 04544-0501

ELDRED, THOMAS GILBERT, secondary education educator, historian; b. Rochester, N.Y., Jan. 16, 1933; s. Millard Frederick and Helen Anna (Jenne) E. BA, SUNY, Albany, 1954; MA, Syracuse U., 1965. Cert. social studies tchr., N.Y. Social studies tchr. Union Springs (N.Y.) Ctrl. Sch., 1954-92; county historian Cayuga County, Auburn, N.Y., 1975—; coord. Nat. History Day, U. Md., College Park, 1990—. Author: (student textbooks) Citizen in Our Local Environment, 1960, East of Cayuga Bridge, 1987. Chmn. Planning Bd., Union Springs, 1970-75, Bicentennial Commn., Union Springs, 1975-77, Capuga County Bicentennial, 1997-99; founder Frontenac Hist. Soc., Union Springs, 1975—, Capuga County Model Senate, Auburn, N.Y., 1976—. Recipient Valley Forge Classroom Tchrs. medal Freedoms Found., 1962, Dewitt Clinton award for community svc. Warren Lodge F.A.M. #147, 1991; named Outstanding Secondary Educators of Am., 1974, Outstanding Tchr. of Am. History, N.Y. State DAR, 1982. Mem. Nat. Coun. for Pub. History, N.Y. State Coun. for Social Studies, Canal Soc. N.Y. State, Nat. Rwy. Hist. Soc., N.Y. State United Tchrs., N.Y. State Hist. Assn. (Yorker advisor 1955-92), County Historians Assn. of N.Y. State (v.p. 1990-93, pres. 1993-97). Republican. Episcopalian. Avocations: golf, travel, camping, baseball, basketball. Home: 10 Center St Union Springs NY 13160 Office: 157 Genesee St Auburn NY 13021-3423

ELDREDGE, BRUCE BEARD, museum director; b. Van Wert, Ohio, July 1, 1952; s. Thomas Harte and Barbara Louise (Beard) E.; m. Janet Duncan Roth, May 17, 1975; children: Lindsay Katherine, Barbara Roth. BA, Ohio Wesleyan U., 1974; MA, Tex. Tech U., 1976; postgrad., SUNY, 1980-81. Dir. Geneva (N.Y.) Hist. Soc. and Mus., 1976-78, Schenectady (N.Y.) Mus., 1978-80; coord. art and humanities Capital Dist. Humanities Program, SUNY, Albany, 1980-81; dir. Frederic Remington Art Mus., Ogdensburg, N.Y., 1981-84, Muskegon (Mich.) Mus. Art, 1984-87, Tucson Mus. Art, 1987-89, Portsmouth (Va.) Mus's., 1991-93, Stark Mus. Art, Orange, Tex., 1993-96, Hubbard Mus. Am. West (formerly Mus. of the Horse), Ruidoso Downs, N.Mex., 1996—; presenter Gov.'s Conf. on Tourism, Phoenix, 1989; mem. coun. Midwest Mus. Assn., 1986-87, chmn. program ann. meeting, Grand Rapids, Mich., 1987; chmn. Ruidoso Arts Commn., 1996—, Village Visioning Process, 1997—. Vice pres. Schenectady County coun. Boy Scouts Am., 1979-81, Seaway Valley coun., Canton, N.Y., 1982-84, West Mich. Shores coun., Grand Rapids, 1985-87, dist. com. Three Rivers coun., 1992—, v.p. Three Rivers coun., 1995-96; bd. dirs. Orange Cmty. Concert Assn., 1995-96. Mem. Am. Assn. Mus., Tex. Assn. Mus. (sourcebook editor 1993-96), N.Mex. Mus. Assn. (membership chair), Alto Lakes Country Club, Cree Meadows C.C., Rotary. Republican. Presbyterian. Home: 126 N Eagle Dr Ruidoso NM 88345-6831 Office: The Hubbard Museum PO Box 40 Ruidoso Downs NM 88346

ELDREDGE, CHARLES CHILD, III, art history educator; b. Boston, Apr. 12, 1944; s. Henry and Priscilla Marion (Bateson) E.; m. Jane Allen MacDougal, June 11, 1966; children: Henry Gifford, Janann Bateson. B.A., Amherst Coll., 1966; Ph.D., U. Minn., 1971. Curator asst. Minn. Hist. Soc., St. Paul, 1966-68; mem. edn. dept. Mpls. Inst. Arts, 1967-69; teaching assoc. art history U. Minn., 1968-70; asst. prof. art history, curator collections Spencer Mus. Art, U. Kans., Lawrence, 1970-71; dir. mus. Spencer Mus. Art, U. Kans., 1971-82, assoc. prof., 1974-80, prof., 1980-82; dir. Nat. Mus. Am. Art, Washington, 1982-88; Hall disting. prof. of Am. art U. Kans., Lawrence, 1988—; C.H. Hynson vis. prof. U. Tex., Austin, 1985; trustee Watkins Cmty. Mus., Lawrence, 1972-76, Assn. Art Mus. Dirs., 1982, 87, Reynolda House Mus. Am. Art, 1986-88, Amherst Coll., 1987-93; trustee Georgia O'Keeffe Found., 1989-95; rsch. assoc. Smithsonian Instn., 1988—; founder Smithsonian Studies in Am. Art, 1987. Author: Marsden Hartley: Lithographs and Related Works, 1972, Ward Lockwood, 1894-1963, 1974, American Imagination and Symbolist Painting, 1979, Charles Walter Stetson, Color and Fantasy, 1982, Pacific Parallels: Artists and the Landscape in New Zealand, 1991, Georgia O'Keeffe, 1991, Georgia O'Keeffe: American and Modern, 1992, Canyon Suite: Early Watercolors by Georgia O'Keeffe, 1994, The College on the Hill, 1996, Reflections on Nature: Small Paintings by Arthur Dove, 1997; co-author: The Arcadian Landscape: 19th Century American Painters in Italy, 1972, Art in New Mexico, 1900-1945, 1986, American Originals: Selections from Reynolda House, Mus. of American Art, 1990, Life Cycles: The Charles E. Burchfield Collection, 1996, John Stewart Curry: Inventing the Middle West, 1997, Ther Regionalist Vision of William Dickerson, 1997; gen. editor The Register of Mus. Art, 1971-82; editl. bd. Am. Studies, 1974-77, Am. Art, 1996—. Smithsonian Instn. fellow Nat. Collection Fine Arts, 1979; Fulbright scholar N.Z., 1983; Found. Visitor fellow U. Auckland, 1993, Smithsonian fellowship Nat. Mus. of Am. Art, 1995; recipient Outstanding Alumnus award u. Minn., 1986. Mem. Coll. Art Assn. Am., Am. Studies Assn., Am. Assn. Mus., Assn. Art Mus. Dirs., Authors Guild. Office: U Kans Dept Art History 209 Spencer Mus Art Lawrence KS 66045

ELDREDGE, GARTH MELVIN, rehabilitation counseling educator; b. Idaho Falls, Idaho, Oct. 1, 1935; s. Melvin A. and Eva L. (Bowles) E.; m. Ann Smith, Aug. 5, 1960; children: Merri L. Gillespie, Julianne Bond, Pamela Gosch. BS, U. Utah, 1959, MS, 1963, PhD, 1965. Cert. rehab. counselor; nat. cert. counselor. Tchr. Granite Dist. Schs., Salt Lake City, 1959-61; counselor Salt Lake C.C., 1963-66; prof. vocat. rehab. counseling U. No. Colo., Greeley, 1966-90, Utah State U., Logan, 1990—. Contbr. articles to profl. jours. Tng. grantee U.S. Office of Edn., Utah, 1991, 94, 95, Devel. Distance Edn. grantee U.S. Office of Edn., Utah, 1993. Mem. Nat. Coun. on Rehab. Edn. (adminstrv. sec. 1991-96). Mem. LDS Ch. Office: Dept Spl Edn and Rehab Utah State Univ Logan UT 84322-2865

ELDREDGE, ROBERT JOHN, social services administrator, psychologist; b. Salt Lake City, Apr. 20, 1947; s. John Eugene and Blythe Vivian (Wright) E.; m. Pamela Ellen Waterman, Sept. 9, 1969; children: Hilary Elizabeth, Christopher Robert, Eric Michael. BS, Brigham Young U., 1971, MA, 1973; PhD, U. Calif., L.A., 1984. Lic. psychologist; nat. cert. sch. psychologist; cert. sch. psychologist, S.D. Psychologist Dist. 251, Ribgy, Idaho, 1973-76, Bonneville Dist. 93, Idaho Falls, Idaho, 1976-78, S.D. Developmental Ctr., Redfield, 1983-87; lic. psychologist Northeastern Mental Health Ctr., Aberdeen, S.D., 1987—; clin. dir. Dakota House, Aberdeen, 1990—; adj. asst. prof. No. State U., Aberdeen, 1996. High councilor, Fargo (N.D.) Stake, LDS Ch., 1990-96; troop com. Boy Scouts Troop 81, Aberdeen, 1996—. Grad. sch. scholar Brigham Young U., Provo, Utah, 1972; univ. grantee U. Calif., L.A., 1978, Chanellor's grantee U. Calif., L.A., 1979; predoctoral fellow U.S. Dept. Edn., 1978-83. Mem. APA, Nat. Assn. Sch. Psychologists. Republican. Avocations: flyfishing, early Christian and Mormon history, playing keyboards, tennis, bicycling. Office: Northeastern Mental Health Ctr 703 3rd Ave SE Aberdeen SD 57401-4508

ELDRIDGE, DAVID CARLTON, art appraiser; b. Lansing, Mich., July 15, 1949; s. Carlton Brady and Blythe (Axford) E.; m. Suzanne Hamrick, Dec. 12, 1970; 1 child, Morgan Worth. B.F.A., Ill. Wesleyan U., 1971; postgrad., U. Denver, 1972-73; M.F.A., So. Ill. U., 1974. Curator exhibits Nature Sci. Park, Winston Salem, N.C., 1974; curator exhibits Tenn. State Mus., Nashville, 1974-80; exec. dir. Mus. Arts and Scis., Macon, Ga., 1980-82; dir. Eldridge Appraisals, Naples, Fla., 1982—. Mem. Am. Soc. Appraisers (sr.), Appraisers Assn. Am. Office: 1839 Imperial Golf Course Blvd Naples FL 34110-8140

ELDRIDGE, DOUGLAS ALAN, lawyer; b. Boulder, Colo., Mar. 15, 1944; s. Douglas Hilton and Clara Effie (Young) E.; m. Benna June Germann, June 24, 1967; children: Heather Dana, Ethan Douglas, Hilary Beca. BA, Yale U., 1966; LLB, U. Pa., 1969; cert. Nat. Inst. Trial Advocacy, Boulder, 1973. Bar: N.Y. 1972, U.S. Dist. Ct. (no. dist.) N.Y. 1973, U.S. Supreme Ct. 1975. Staff. atty. Onondaga Neighborhood Legal Svcs., Syracuse, N.Y., 1971-74, exec. dir., 1974-76; counsel N.Y. State Div. of Substance Abuse Services, Albany, 1976-79; dep. counsel N.Y. State Health Dept., Albany, 1979-80; dep. counsel N.Y. State Energy Office, Albany, 1980-82, asst. counsel, 1982-87; gen. counsel Commn. for Siting Low-level Radioactive Waste Disposal Facilities, Troy, N.Y., 1987-95. Contbr. articles to legal jours.; bd. dirs. Coun. Cmty. Svcs. United Way of Northeastern N.Y., Albany, 1980-90, pres., 1986-88; bd. dirs. United Way Ea. N.Y., 1986-88, Mohawk-Hudson Found., 1986-89; sole practice, Albany, 1995—; dir. govtl. affairs counsel N.Y. Rehab. Assn., Inc. Recipient Reginald Heber Smith Cmty. Lawyer fellowship OEO, 1969-71. Mem. N.Y. State Bar Assn., Albany County Bar Assn. (chair legis. com. 1998—), Onondaga County Bar Assn., Assn. of Bar of City of N.Y., Yale Alumni Schs. Com., Yale Alumni Assn. Northeastern N.Y., Assn. of Yale Alumni (rep. 1985-88, 94-97), University Club (bd. dirs. 1998—). Home: 9 Pinedale Ave Delmar NY 12054-3012

ELDRIDGE, JOHN COLE, judge; b. Balt., Nov. 13, 1933; s. Arthur Clement and Bertha Jean (Klitch) E.; m. Dayne S. Worsham, July 15, 1961; children: Kathryn Chandler, John Cole. B.A., Harvard U., 1955; LL.B., U. Md., 1959. Bar: Md. 1960, D.C. 1961. Law clk. to chief judge U.S. Ct. Appeals 4th Circuit, 1959-61; trial atty. appellate sect., civil div. Dept. Justice, 1961-67, asst. chief appellate sect., 1967-69; chief legis. officer, counsel Staff of Gov. of Md., 1969-74; judge Ct. Appeals Md., Annapolis, Md., 1974—; Chmn. Md. Adv. Bd. Correction, 1969-70; dir. Annapolis Fine Arts Found., 1974-77. Mem. Anne Arundel County Bar Assn., Annapolis Yacht Club. Democrat. Methodist. Office: Ct Appeals Md Court of Appeals Bldg 361 Rowe Blvd Annapolis MD 21401-1672*

ELDRIDGE, LARRY (WILLIAM LAWRENCE ELDRIDGE), journalist; b. Phila., Sept. 15, 1932; s. William Stauffer and Irene Elizabeth (Dougherty) E.; m. Joyce Meckling, Sept. 6, 1952 (div. 1966); children—William Lawrence, Janice Lynn, Scott Richard; m. Joyce Pearlswig Leffler, Aug. 23, 1970; children—Nicole Elizabeth, Ross Gregory, Robin Natalie. B.A., U. Pa., 1958. Sports clk. Phila. Inquirer, 1953-59; asst. dir. pub. relations Colby Coll., 1959-60; newsman AP, Portland, Maine and Boston, 1960-71; sports columnist Christian Sci. Monitor, Boston, 1971-75, sports editor, 1975-88, host, exec. producer Eldridge on Sports, 1989-92; sports writer Boston Herald, 1993-95; sr. sports editor AT&T New Media Svcs., 1995—. Contbr. articles to, Reader's Digest, Sports Illustrated, Sporting News; chess columnist, Me. Sunday Telegram; work included in Best Sports Stories, 1976-89. Mem. Baseball Writers Assn. Am., U.S. Ski Writers Assn., U.S. Chess Fedn. Winner several chess tournaments. Home: 36 Wedgewood Rd Newton MA 02465-1918 Office: One Cambridge Center Cambridge MA 02142

ELDRIDGE, RICHARD MARK, lawyer; b. Okmulgee, Okla., June 20, 1951; s. H.G. and Marcheta (Barnes) E.; m. Nellene Jane Mark, Aug. 20, 1971; children: Richard Mark Jr. (dec.), Christopher Bryan, Ryan Matthew, Michael Jonathan. BA, Okla. State U., 1973; JD, U. Tulsa, 1975. Bar: Okla. 1976; U.S. Dist. Ct. (no. dist.) Okla. 1976, U.S. Dist. Ct. (ea. dist.) Okla. 1989; U.S. Ct. Appeals (10th cir.) 1977, U.S. Dist. Ct. (we. dist.) Okla. 1991. Ptnr. Jacobus, Green & Eldridge, Tulsa, 1976-78; spl. judge Dist. Ct., Tulsa, 1979-82; ptnr. Rhodes, Hieronymus, Jones, Tucker & Gable, Tulsa, 1982—; adj. prof. Oral Roberts U., Tulsa, 1985. Tchr. Couples for Christ, Asbury United Meth. Ch., Tulsa, 1979—; pres., sec. Christian Businessmen's Com., Tulsa, 1981-93; chmn. Asbury Presch. Bd., Tulsa, 1985-95; trustee Metro Christian Acad., 1998—. Recipient Cert. of Achievement, Am. Acad. Jud. Edn., 1979. Mem. Okla. Bar Assn., Tulsa County Bar Assn. Democrat. Avocation: basketball. Home: 2916 E 88th St Tulsa OK 74137-2507 Office: Rhodes Hieronymus et al 100 W 5th St Ste 400 Tulsa OK 74103-4287

ELDRIDGE, RONNIE, councilwoman; b. N.Y.C., Jan. 30, 1931; m. Lawrence Eldridge (dec.); m. Jimmy Breslin; children: Daniel, Emily, Lucy. BA, Barnard Coll., 1952. Dist. leader Reform Ind. Dem., 1963-68; spl. asst. to mayor N.Y.C., 1969-72, dir. city adminstr., 1972; dir. cmty. and govt. affairs Port Authority WY & N.J., 1977-82; city councilwoman Dist. 6 N.Y.C. Coun., 1990—; chmn. subcom. on women, mem. econ. devel., gen. welfare, devel. and civil svc., women and youth svc. com. N.Y.C. Coun.; dir. spl. projects MS Mag.; bd. chmn. Women Care. E-mail: eldridge@c-su.council.nyc.ny.us. Office: Ste 1490 1841 Broadway Ste 1202 New York NY 10023*

ELDRIDGE, TRUMAN KERMIT, JR., lawyer; b. Kansas City, Mo., July 27, 1944; s. Truman Kermit and Nell Marie (Dennis) E.; m. Joan Ellen Jurgeson, Feb. 9, 1965; children: Christina Joanne, Gregory Truman. AB, Rockhurst Coll., 1966; JD, U. Mo., Kansas City, 1969. Bar: Mo. 1969, U.S. Dist. Ct. (we. dist.) Mo. 1969, U.S. Ct. Appeals (8th cir.) 1977, (10th cir.) 1995, U.S. S. Ct., 1992, U.S. Dist. Ct. Kans. 1998. Assoc. Morris, Foust, Moudy & Beckett, Kansas City, 1969-70; assoc. Dietrich, Davis, Dicus, Rowlands & Schmitt, Kansas City, 1971-74, ptnr., 1975; ptnr. Armstrong, Teasdale, LLP, Kansas City, 1989—. Author: (with others) Missouri Environmental Law Handbook, 1990, 2d edit., 1993, 3d edit., 1997; contbr. articles to profl. jours. Chmn. bd. dirs. Loretto Sch., Kansas City, 1981-83; mem. Friends of Art, Nelson Atkins Gallery, Kansas City, 1980—; mem. Energy and Environ. Commn. City of Kansas City, 1990-91, 1994, bd. dirs. Sheffield Pl., 1997—, vice chair, 1998—. Mem. ABA, Def. Rsch. Inst., Mo. Bar Assn., Kansas City Met. Bar Assn. (fed. ct. com., vice chair 1989-90, chair 1990-91), Mo. Orgn. Def. Lawyers, Greater Kansas City C. of C. (mem. environ. com. 1989—), Kansas City Club (athletic com. 1990—, chair 1995—, house com. 1993-96, 98—, long range planning com. 1993-97, bd. dirs. 1997—). Roman Catholic. Avocations: sailing, reading, photography, raquetball. Home: 448 W 68th Ter Kansas City MO 64113-1933 Office: Armstrong Teasdale LLP 2345 Grand Blvd Ste 2000 Kansas City MO 64108-2617

ELDRIDGE-HOWARD, JOYCE, principal; b. Apr. 14. BS in Elem. Edn., Ctrl. State U., 1965; MA in Edn., Seton Hall U., 1974; postgrad., Montclair (N.J.) State U., 1977. Cert. elem. tchr., N.J., cert. in supervision, adminstrn., student-personnel guidance and counseling. Tchr. kindergarten, grade 2, 6 Sch. # 2, Linden, N.J., 1965-72; tchr. grade 4, 6 Demarest Sch., Bloomfield, N.J., 1972-88, gifted/talented tchr./coord., 1988-90, elem. guidance counselor, 1990-92; asst. prin. K-6 Washington Sch., East Orange, N.J., 1992—; Mem. Essex County Steering Com. Gifted and Talented; judge N.J. Sch. Bds. Essay Contest, 1987. V.p. N.J. chpt. Jack and Jill of Am., Inc.; co-chairperson African Am. Month Bloomfield (N.J.) Pub. Libr., 1978; dir. Bloomfield, Glen Ridge (N.J.) unit Big. Bros. and Big Sisters, 1979. Selectee Gov.'s Tchr. Recognition Program, 1988. Mem. NEA, N.J. Educators of the Gifted and Talented, Bloomfield (N.J.) Edn. Assn. (Disting. Svc. award 1977, 88), Essex County Edn. Assn., Assn. Supervision and Curriculum Devel., N.J. Prins. Assn., East Orange Adminstrv. Assn. (sec.), Jack and Jill North Jersey (former 1st v.p.), Delta Sigma Theta Sorority (former journalist, chairperson arts and letters, ways and mean com. Montclair alumnae chpt.). E-mail: timbaone@aol.com. Home: 64 Park End Pl East Orange NJ 07018-1114

ELECCION, MARCELINO, security executive, computer consultant, music consultant, educator; b. N.Y.C., Aug. 22, 1936; s. Marcelino G. and Margaret J. (Krcha) E.; m. Marcia L. Smith, June 6, 1962; 1 child, Mark Eaton; m. Naomi E. Kor, Jan. 5, 1978; 1 child, Jordan Kai. BA, NYU, 1961; postgrad. Courant Inst. Math. Scis., 1962-64; AS, Coll. San Mateo, 1988; postgrad. San Jose State U., 1988-91. Electromech. draftsman Gen. Engring., NYU, Bronx, 1954-57, chief designer dept. elec. engring., 1957-60, tech. editor lab. for electrosci. research, 1960-62, editor publs. Sch. Engring. and Scis., 1962-67; asst. editor IEEE Spectrum, N.Y.C., 1967-69, assoc. editor, 1969-70, staff writer, 1970-76, contbg. editor, 1976—; dir. adminstrn. Internat. Bur. Protection and Investigation, Ltd., N.Y.C., 1976-78; account exec. Paul Purdom & Co., pub. relations, San Francisco, 1978-81, creative dir., 1981-83; dir. mktg. communications Am. Info. Systems, Palo Alto, 1983-85; dir. engring. Tech. Cons., Palo Alto, 1986—; cons. tech. artist, 1953—; music orchestration cons., 1956-70; cons. Ency. Britannica, 1969-70, Time-Life Books, 1973; spl. guest lectr. Napa Coll., 1979—. Aux. police officer, N.Y.C. Police Dept., 1964-70, aux. sgt., 1970-73, aux. lt., 1973-76, aux. capt., 1976-78. Recipient Mayor's commendation award N.Y.C., 1971. Mem. IEEE (sr.), N.Y. Acad. Scis., Am. Math. Soc., AAAS, Optical Soc. Am., Smithsonian Assocs., Am. Numis. Assn., Nat. Geog. Soc., U.S. Judo Fedn., Athletic Congress, AAU. Fedn. Home: PMB # 2004 3790 El Camino Real Palo Alto CA 94306-3314

ELEGANT, ROBERT SAMPSON, journalist, author; b. N.Y.C., Mar. 7, 1928; s. Louis and Lillie Rebecca (Sampson) E.; m. Moira Clarissa Brady, Apr. 16, 1956; children: Victoria Ann, Simon David Brady. A.B., U. Pa., 1946; diploma proficiency, Inst. Far Eastern Langs. and Lit., Yale U., 1948; M.A. in Chinese and Japanese, Columbia U., 1950; M.S. in Journalism, Columbia, 1951. Far East corr. Overseas News Agy., 1951-52; war corr. Internat. News Service, Korea, 1953; corr. in Singapore CBS, N.Am. Newspaper Alliance, McGraw-Hill News Service, 1954-55; South Asian corr., chief New Delhi (India) bur. Newsweek mag., 1956-57, Southeast Asian corr., chief Hong Kong bur., 1958-61, chief Central European bur., Bonn (Germany) bur., 1962-64; chief Hong Kong bur. Los Angeles Times, 1965-69; fgn. affairs columnist Los Angeles Times, Munich, 1970-72, Hong Kong, 1973-76; ind. author, 1977—; vis. prof. U. S.C., 1976, Boston U., 1994-95; lectr. in field, 1964—; sr. fellow Inst. of Advanced Studies, Berlin. Author: China's Red Masters, 1951, The Dragon's Seed, 1959, The Center of the World, 1964, rev. 1968, Mao's Great Revolution, 1971, Mao vs. Chiang, 1972, The Great Cities: Hong Kong, 1977, Pacific Destiny: Inside Asia Today, 1990; (novels) A Kind of Treason, 1966, The Seeking, 1969, Dynasty, 1977, Manchu, 1980, Mandarin, 1983, From a Far Land, 1987, Bianca, 1992, The Everlasting Sorrow, 1994, Last Year in Hong Kong, 1997; also numerous articles. Served with AUS, 1946-48. Pulitzer Travelling fellow, 1951-52; fellow Ford Found. 1954-55; rsch. fellow Am. Enterprise Inst. Pub. Policy Rsch., 1977-79; citation best mag. reporting from abroad Overseas Press Club, 1962, award for best interpretation of fgn. affairs, 1967, 69, 72; Edgar Allan Poe award Mystery Writers Am., 1967; Sigma Delta Chi award, 1967; sr. fellow Inst. Advanced Studies, Berlin, 1993-94. Mem. Authors League, Phi Beta Kappa. Clubs: Hong Kong Foreign Correspondents (pres. 1960), Royal Hong Kong Yacht. Address: Manor House, Middle Green, Buckinghamshire SL3 6BS, England

ELEQUIN, CLETO, JR., retired physician; b. Antique, Philippines, Oct. 18, 1933; s. Cleto and Enriqueta (Tengonciang) E.; m. Nancy Johnson, May 14, 1958; children: Tracy, Thomas Kyle, Stuart Scott. M.D., Far Eastern U., Philippines, 1957. Rotating intern Good Samaritan Hosp., Lexington, Ky., 1957-58; gen. practice resident Central Bapt. Hosp., Lexington, 1958-59; psychiat. resident State Hosp., Danville, Pa., 1959-60, 61-62; psychiat. resident with child psychiatry State Hosp., New Castle, Del., 1962-63; staff physician Eastern State Hosp., Lexington, 1960-61, dir. Fayette County Project, dir. intensive treatment service, 1964-67, supt., 1969-71; dep. commr. Dept. Mental Health, State Ky., 1967-69; practice medicine, specializing in family practice Pecos, Tex., 1971-72, Austin, Tex., 1974-89; ret.; cons. psychiatrist Texas Youth Commn., Peyote, Tex., Permian Basin Cmty. Mental Health-Mental Retardation, Odessa, Tex., Prude Ranch for Emotionally Disturbed Children and Adolescents, Ft. Davis, Tex., Dept. Mental Health-Mental Retardation State of Tex.; vis. lectr. in medicine and psychiatry Am. U. of the Caribbean, Plymouth, Montserrat; asst. dep. commr. Tex. Dept. Mental Health and Mental Retardation, Austin, 1973-74, dep. commr. mental health, 1974; pvt. practice family practice and psychiatry, Austin, 1974-85; mem. attending staff Brackenridge Hosp., St. David Med. Ctr., Seton Med. Ctr., Shoal Creek Hosp.; med. dir. Mary Lee Sch. and Found., 1974-80, bd. trustees, 1980-85; attending psychiatrist U. Ky. Med. Ctr., 1964-71, Good Samaritan Hosp., 1969-71, Ctrl. Bapt. Hosp., 1966-71; cons. psychiatrist U. Ky. Student Health Svc., 1965-71, Peace Corps, 1966-68, Bur. Rehab. State Ky., 1965-71, Blue Grass Cmty. Care Ctr., 1967-71, Covington (Ky.) Cmty. Care Ctr., 1969-71, Hazard Cmty. Care Ctr., 1969-71, Danville (Ky.) Cmty. Care Ctr., 1969-71, Maysville (Ky.) Cmty. Care Ctr., 1969-71; clin.

instr., asst. clin. prof. dept. psychiatry U. Ky. Med. Ctr., 1964-69, assoc. clin. prof., 1969-71; cons. psychiatrist Tex. Youth Commn. Tex. Dept. of MH-MR, State of Tex.; pvt. practice in psychiatry, Austin, 1974-85; mem. attending staff Brackenridge Hosp., St. David Med. Ctr., Seton Med. Ctr., Shoal Creek Hosp.; med. dir. Mary Lee Sch. and Found., 1974-80, mem. bd. trustees, 1980-85. Mem. Profl. Adv. Coun. Community Mental Health-Retardation Ctr., Lexington, 1967-71; mem. Lexington Hosp. Coun., 1969-71. Mem. AMA, Am. Psychiat. Assn., Am. Acad. Family Physicians (life), Assn. Med. Supts. Mental Hosps., Tex. Med. Assn., Travis County Med. Soc., Austin Psychiat. Soc. Home: 10101 Jupiter Hills Dr Austin TX 78747-1322

ELEUTERIO, MARIANNE KINGSBURY, retired genetics educator; b. Cassopolis, Mich., Aug. 7, 1929; d. Manning Marion and Marion Salina (Orr) Kingsbury; m. Herbert Souza Eleuterio, June 12, 1951; children: Susan, Kathi, Thomas, Mary Beth, John, Daniel. BS, Mich. State U., 1950; PhD, U. Del., 1971. Postdoctoral student Temple U. Sch. Medicine, Phila., 1971-72; post doctoral student U. Del., Newark, 1972-73; asst. prof. West Chester (Pa.) U., 1973-76, assoc. prof., 1976-88, prof., 1988-97; rsch. scientist Ctr. for Natural Products Rsch. Nat. U., Singapore, 1997-99; ret., 1999. Contbr. articles to profl. jours.; contbr. to book: Catalog of Chromosomal Variants and Anomalies, 1984. Mem. Am. Soc. for Microbiology, Am. Soc. Human Genetics, Sigma Xi, Phi Kappa Phi, Tau Sigma. Democrat. Roman Catholic. Home: 513 Ivydale Rd Wilmington DE 19803-4329

ELEWSKI, BONI ELIZABETH, dermatologist, educator; b. Cleve., Aug. 7, 1953; d. John Stanley and Alberta (Gulish) E.; married. BA summa cum laude, Miami U., Oxford, Ohio, 1975; MD cum laude, Ohio State U., 1978. Intern U. N.C., Chapel Hill, 1978-79, resident, 1979-82; staff dermatologist Akron (Ohio) Clinic, 1982-88; prof. dermatology Univ. Hosps. of Cleve., Case Western Res. U., 1988—. Author chpts. to books; editor: Cutaneous Fungal Infections, 1992, 2d edit., 1998; contbr. articles to profl. jours. Fellow Cleve. Dermatology Soc. (sec. bd. dirs., chair skin cancer screening program 1988—, pres. 1994), Am. Acad. Dermatology (bd. dirs. 1996—); mem. Am. Dermatol. Assn., Women's Dermatology Soc. (sec.-treas., pres.-elect 1998, pres. 1999), Dermatology Found. (trustee 1987-91). Roman Catholic. Home: PO Box 5475 Akron OH 44334-0475 Office: Univ Hosp 11100 Euclid Ave Cleveland OH 44106-1736

ELEY, LYNN W., political science educator, former mayor; b. Zearing, Iowa, Oct. 23, 1925; s. Wilbur Charles and Myrtle (Wolford) E.; m. Elizabeth Sherwood Hill, Aug. 25, 1950 (div. 1970); children—Thomas Wendell, David Matthew, Mary Sherwood; m. Janet Burdy, Aug. 26, 1971; children—Benjamin Charles, Margaret Burdy. B.A., Harvard U., 1949; M.A., U. Iowa, 1951; Ph.D., 1952. Orgn. and methods analyst Dept. Agr., Washington, 1952-55; research assoc., supr. Lansing Office, Inst. Pub. Adminstrn., 1955-58; assoc. dir. Extension Service; assoc. prof. polit. sci. U. Mich., 1959-64; dean Sch. Continuing Edn., and Summer Sch.; assoc. prof. polit. sci. Washington U., St. Louis, 1964-68; asst. chancellor U. Wis., Milw., 1968-72, prof. dept. govtl. affairs, 1972-91, prof. emeritus govtl. affairs, 1991—, chmn. dept., 1985-91; editorial asst. com. on appropriations U.S. Ho. of Reps., 1953; instr. U.S. Dept. Agr. Grad. Sch., 1954-55; mayor City of Mequon, Wis., 1980-86. Author: The Executive Reorganization Plan: A Survey of State Experience, 1967, The Regionalization of Business Services in the Agricultural Research Service, 1967, Local Ombudsmen in America, 1973, An Ombudsman for Milwaukee? 1974; with others Representation of the Poor in Milwaukee's War on Poverty, 1977, A Guide to Citizen Participation in Government: Administrative Rule Making, 1979, 80; Sr. editor: with others The Politics of Fair-Housing Legislation: State and Local Case Studies, 1968, Wisconsin Government and Politics, 4th edit., 1987; mem. editorial bd.: Pub. Adminstrn. Rev, 1969-72. Sec. Gov.'s Adv. Com. Reorgn. State Govt. Mich., 1958-62; city councilman Ann Arbor, Mich., 1961-63; mem. Milw. Model Cities Policy Commn., 1970-75; bd. dirs. Wis. Congress on Aging, 1979-82, N.W. Gen. Hosp., Milw., 1990-94; exec. dir. Mid-Moraine Mcpl. Assn., 1986-95; pres. Riveredge Nature Ctr., Newburg, Wis., 1993-95; mem. planning and zoning commn. City of Bisbee, Ariz., 1998—. With USNR, 1944-46. Ellis L. Phillips Found. Postdoctoral intern in acad. adminstrn., 1963-64. *The capacity to adapt affirmatively to conditions of change in one's life situation not only through childhood, but throughout adulthood, seems to me the essential ingredient in successful living.*

ELFERS, WILLIAM, retired investment company director; b. N.Y.C., June 6, 1918; s. Herman and Katherine (Evers) E.; m. Ann Rice, Dec. 8, 1944; children: William Rice, Joanne, Jane Fuller (Mrs. Herbert C. Muther III). Student, Hotchkiss Sch., 1933-37; B.A., Princeton U., 1941; M.B.A., Harvard U., 1943; LHD (hon.), Northeastern U., 1989. Advt. mgr. Modern Materials Handling, Boston, 1946-47; staff assoc. Am. Research and Devel. Corp., Boston, 1947-50; asst. v.p. Am. Research and Devel. Corp., 1950-52, v.p., 1952-65; gen. ptnr. Greylock and Co., Boston, 1965-79; gen. ptnr. Greylock Investors and Co., 1973-76, ltd. partner, 1977-85; pres. Greylock Mgmt. Corp., Boston, 1965-76; chmn. exec. com. Greylock Mgmt. Corp., 1977-87; ltd. ptnr. Greylock Capital Ltd. Partnership, 1987-97, Greylock Ventures Ltd. Partnership, 1984-95, Greylock Ltd. Partnership, 1990-96. Trustee emeritus Northeastern U. Boston, Hotchkiss Sch., Lakeville, Conn.; hon. trustee Mus. Fine Arts, Boston. Lt. USNR, 1943-46. Episcopalian. Clubs: Commercial, Algonquin (Boston); Longwood Cricket (Chestnut Hill, Mass.); Wellesley Country; Princeton, River (N.Y.C.). Home: 70 Greylock Rd Wellesley MA 02481-1323 Office: Greylock Mgmt Corp 1 Federal St Ste 2602 Boston MA 02110-2065

ELFERVIG, LUCIE THERESA SAVOIE, independent ophthalmic nursing consultant; b. Donaldsonville, La., Oct. 15, 1948; d. Charles Clarence Sr. and Ursula Marie (Prados) Savoie; m. John Lars Elfervig, May 19, 1972; children: John Lars II (dec.), Martye Elizabeth, Michelle Karene, Taylor Anders. BSN, U. Southwestern La., 1972, postgrad., 1979-80; MSN, Northwestern State U., 1975; D Nursing Sci., La. State U., 1996. RN, Utah, Ga., Ark., Ariz., Miss., Tenn., La., Mo.; cert. ophthalmic nurse, advanced practice RN, CNS, Tenn., La., Utah; cert. of fitness with prescription privile, Tenn. Nurse's aide St. Elizabeth's Hosp., Paincourtville, La., 1969, Charity Hosp., New Orleans, 1971; staff nurse Confederate Meml. Med. Ctr., Shreveport, La., 1972-73; staff nurse med./surg. dept. Dr.'s Hosp., Shreveport, 1973; pediatric clin. nurse specialist La. State U. Med. Ctr., Shreveport, 1975-76; instr. in nursing U. Southwestern La., Lafayette, 1980; pediatric clin. nurse specialist, emergency staff nurse LeBonheur Children's Med. Ctr., Memphis, 1984-85; pediatric clin. nurse specialist, agy. nurse emergency dept. So. Health Sys., Profl. Health Care, Memphis, 1985-90; ophthalmic clin. nurse specialist Hamilton Eye Clinic, Memphis, 1990-91; ind. ophthalmic cons. Memphis, 1992—; pediatric instr. Stanley Kaplan Ednl. Ctr., Memphis, 1986; ophthalmic clin. nurse specialist Mid-South Retina Assocs., Memphis, summer 1988, Albany (Ga.) Retinal Eye Ctr., summer 1989; cons. Rea & Assocs., Inc., Med. Mgmt. and Fin. Svcs., Memphis, 1992-94, Ridge Lake Ambulatory Surg. Ctr., Memphis, 1992-95, Vitreo-Retinal Found., Memphis, Van Dyck Eye Ctr., Paris, Tenn., So. Eye Assocs., Jonesboro, Ark., Physicians Surg. Ctr. Eye Clin., Jackson, Tenn.; lectr., cons., ophthalmic clin. nurse cons. People to People Citizen Ambassador Program. Contbr. articles to profl. publs.; mem. editl. bd. Insight Jour., 1997; jr. reviewer JAGS. Vol. blood pressure screening program La. Heart Assn., Shreveport, 1974; vol. Holy Rosary Sch., Memphis, 1981-92; tchr. math. Head Start of Memphis, 1986; track meet ofcl. Germantown (Tenn.) Track Club, 1988-92; vol. ophthalmic nurse specialist South Am. Mission/World Lens Project, Pupalla, Peru, 1991, Marantha Mission, Cadereyta, Mex., 1993; campaign vol. Gov.-Elect Don Sundquist, 1994; team leader silent auction bldg. fund benefit Christian Bros. H.S., Memphis, 1993, 94; mem. health ministry Our Lady of Perpetual Help Ch., 1996—. Recipient Endowment, Rep. Congl. Order of Liberty, 1993, Congl. Cert. of Appreciation U.S. Congress, 1993, Edna Ashy award for contbns. to ophthal. nursing. Mem. ANA (coun. nurses in advanced practice), Am. Soc. Ophthalmic RNs (mem. peer rev. com. jour. 1994—, nominating com. 1996—, approver com. 1998, Honor award 1998, pres. mid-south chpt. 1997, editl. bd. 1997), Tenn. Nurses Assn., NLN (coun. for nursing practice), West Tenn. League Nurses (chpt. chair 1994-95), Am. Geriatrics Soc. (jr. reviewer jour.), Nat. Assn. CNS, Am. Nurses Found., Nat. Assn. Pro-Life Nurses, Mid. Tenn. Advanced Practice Nurses, Nat. Assn. Cert. Nurse Specialists, Vision Group of U. Tenn. Memphis, Memphis Eye Soc., Greater Memphis Advanced Practice Nursing, Am. Acad. Ophthalmology, Am. Acad. Nurse Practitioners, Sigma Theta Tau. Avocations: cooking, reading, travel, hunting, family. Office: Vitreo-Retinal Found 825 Ridge Lake Blvd Ste 200 Memphis TN 38120-9440

ELFIN, MEL, magazine editor; b. Bklyn., July 18, 1929; s. Joseph and Bess (Margolis) E.; m. Margery Lesser, June 21, 1953; children: David, Dana. AB, Syracuse U., 1951; MA, Harvard U., 1952; postgrad., New Sch. Social Research, 1955-58; LHD, Ill. Wesleyan U., 1997. Copywriter Marvin and Leonard, Boston, advt. staff, 1953-54; successively reporter, travel editor, asst. city editor L.I. Daily Press, Jamaica, N.Y., 1954-58; mem. staff Newsweek mag., 1958—, gen. editor, 1964-65; chief Washington bur., 1965-85, sr. editor, 1985-86; editor spl. projects U.S. News and World Report, 1986-97; editor emeritus U.S. News Coll. Guides, 1997—; TV panelist; cons. Ednl. Facilities Lab., N.Y.C. Author: (with others) Bricks and Mortarboards, 1963; editor America's Best Colleges, 1987—, Guide to America's Best Graduate Schools, 1994—, Triumph Without Victory, 1992; contbr. articles to various publs. Served as officer SAC, USAF, 1952-53. Recipient George Polk Meml. award reporting, 1957, N.Y. Newspaper Guild Page One award, 1957; award Edn. Writers Assn., 1966. Mem. White House Corr. Assn., Phi Beta Kappa. Home: 4515 30th St NW Washington DC 20008-2126

ELFMAN, ERIC MICHAEL, lawyer; b. Phila., Oct. 24, 1954; s. Isaac Selig and Mae (Kline) E.; m. Barbara Cecile Feldstein, Oct. 9, 1982; children: Elizabeth, Bradley, Todd. BS in Econs., U. Pa., 1975, MS in Acctg., 1976; JD, George Washington U., 1980. Bar: Calif. 1980, U.S. Tax Ct. 1981, Mass. 1986; CPA, Pa. Acct. Peat, Marwick, Mitchell and Co., Phila., 1976-77; assoc. Pettit & Martin, San Francisco, 1980-83; assoc. office of tax legis. counsel U.S. Dept. of Treas., Washington, 1983-85; ptnr. Ropes & Gray, Boston, 1985—. Mem. ABA (chair corporate tax com. 1996-97, taxation sect.), AICPA, Mass. Soc. CPAs, Boston Bar Assn. Home: 19 Gypsy Trl Weston MA 02493-1607 Office: Ropes & Gray One Internat Pl Boston MA 02110-2624

ELFMAN, JENNA, actress; b. L.A., Sept. 30; m. Bodhi Rice Elfman. Studied with Milton Katselas, L.A. Actress in Dharma & Greg Moore Metavoy, L.A. TV appearances include Townies, The Single Guy; guest appearances include Roseanne, Murder One, NYPD Blue, Almost Perfect; TV films include Her Last Chance; films include Grosse Point Blank, Krippendorf's Tribe; starred in many music videos including Antrax video for Crossroads Films. Avocations: performing ballet. Office: Moore Metavoy 7920 W Sunset Blvd Los Angeles CA 90046-3300

ELFNER, ALBERT HENRY, III, mutual fund management company executive; b. Boston, Oct. 6, 1944; s. Albert Henry and Nellie May (Stewart) E.; m. Norma Elfner (div.); 1 child, Nicholas Stewart; m. Jane Colgrove, Oct. 10, 1980; 1 child, Kimberly Ann Druker. AB, Middlebury Coll., 1966; postgrad., Harvard U., 1993; D of Comml. Sci. (hon.), Merrimack Coll., 1999. CFA. Investment analyst Bank of Boston, 1966-69; portfolio mgr. Keystone Custodian Funds, Inc., Boston, 1969-81, pres., 1983-91; chmn. Keystone Investment Mgmt. Corp., Boston; pres. Keystone Group, Boston, 1990-95, pres., CEO, 1995—; CEO Keystone Investments, 1995; bd. dirs. Keystone Funds, Keystone Investments, Inc., Polanis Investment Trust Co., Taipei, Taiwan, ICI Mutual Ins. Co.; bd. govs. Investment Co. Inst., Washington, Unitil Corp., Hampton, N.H. Trustee Anatolia Coll., Middlesex Sch., Pres. New Eng. Colls. Fund, 1995; bd. dirs. Boston Children's Svc. Assn., 1976—; bd. govs. New Eng. Med. Ctr. Mem. Fin. Analysts Fedn., Boston Soc. Security Analysts, Union Boat Club (bd. dirs., pres. 1983-86), Somerset Club, Boston Econs. Club, Country Club (Brookline, Mass.). Republican. Episcopalian. Avocations: skiing, squash, golf, gardening. Home: 53 Chestnut St Boston MA 02108-3506 Office: Keystone Investments 200 Berkeley St Boston MA 02116-5022

ELFTMAN, SUSAN NANCY, physician assistant, childbirth-lactation educator; b. Oakland, Calif., Apr. 3, 1951; d. Arthur Gerhardt Samuel and Ella Johanna (Nelson) E. AA summa cum laude, Chabot Coll., 1971; BA in Zoology, U. Calif., Berkeley, 1973; BS in Med. Sci. magna cum laude, Alderson-Broaddus Coll., 1980; MPH, UCLA, 1990. Bd. cert. physician asst., Calif. Physician asst. So. Calif. Permanente Group, San Diego, 1981-82, Mem. Med. Ctr., Long Beach, Calif., 1982-88, Harriman-Jones Med. Group, Long Beach, 1988-90, Pamela Kushner, MD, Long Beach, 1990—. Spkr. Am. Cancer Soc., Long. Beach, Meml. Med. Ctr., Long Beach, March of Dimes. Fellow Am. Acad. Physician Assts., Calif. Acad. Physician Assts.; mem. Am. Soc. for Psychoprophylaxis in Obstetrics (cert. lactation and childbirth educator). Home: 275 Ximeno Ave Long Beach CA 90803-1657 Office: Pamela Kushner MD 2865 Atlantic Ave Ste 207 Long Beach CA 90806-1730

ELFVIN, JOHN THOMAS, federal judge; b. Montour Falls, N.Y., June 30, 1917; s. John Arthur and Lillian Ruth (Dorning) E.; m. Peggy Pierce, Oct. 1, 1949. B.E.E., Cornell U., 1942; J.D., Georgetown U., 1947. Bar: D.C. 1948, N.Y. 1949. Confidential clk. to U.S. Circuit Ct. Judge E. Barrett Prettyman, 1947-48; asst. U.S. atty., Buffalo, 1955-58; U.S. atty. Western Dist. N.Y., 1972-75; with firm Cravath, Swaine & Moore, N.Y.C., 1948-51, Dudley, Stowe & Sawyer, Buffalo, 1951-55, Lansdowne, Horning & Elfvin, Buffalo, 1958-69, 70-72; justice N.Y. Supreme Ct., 1969; judge U.S. Dist. Ct., Buffalo, 1975—, now sr. judge; Mem. bd. suprs. Erie County, N.Y., 1962-65, mem. bd. ethics, 1971-74, chmn., 1971-72; mem., minority leader Buffalo Common Council Delaware Dist., 1966-69. Mem. Am. Judicature Soc., Erie County Bar Assn., Engring. Soc. Buffalo (pres. 1958-59), Tech. Socs. Niagara Frontier (pres. 1960-61), Phi Kappa Tau, Delta Sigma Chi. Republican. Clubs: Cornell (pres. 1957-58); City (Buffalo), Buffalo Country, Saturn. Office: US Dist Ct 716 US Courthouse 68 Court St Buffalo NY 14202-3405

ELFVING, DON C., horticulturist; b. Albany, Calif., June 20, 1941. BS in Botany, U. Calif., Davis, 1964, MS in Horticulture, 1966; PhD in Plant Physiology, U. Calif., Riverside, 1971. From asst. prof. to assoc. prof. pomology Cornell U., Ithaca, N.Y., 1972-79; rsch. scientist Hort. Rsch. Inst. Ontario, Simcoe, Can., 1979-91; mgr. rsch. programs Hort. Rsch. Inst. Ontario, Vineland, Can., 1991-93; supt. tree fruit rsch. and extension ctr. Wash. State U., Wenatchee, 1993-97, horticulturist, 1997—; cons. U.S. AID, 1977; cons. Internat. Agrl. Devel. Svc., Ark., 1981-82. Author: Training and Pruning of Apple and Pear Trees, 1992. Recipient U.P. Hedrick 1st Pl. award Am. Pomological Soc., 1992. Mem. Am. Soc. for Hort. Sci. (bd. dirs. 1993-95, chair publs. com. 1993-95), Internat. Dwarf Fruit Tree Assn. (R.F. Carlson Disting. lectr. 1993). Office: Tree Fruit Rsch and Ext Ctr 1100 N Western Ave Wenatchee WA 98801-1230

ELGART, LARRY JOSEPH, orchestra leader; b. New London, Conn., Mar. 20, 1922; s. Arthur M. and Bessie (Aisman) E.; m. Lynn Walzer, June 28, 1963; children by previous marriage: Brock, Brad. Altosaxophonist, formed Les and Larry Elgart Orch., 1947, rec. artist for Decca, RCA, Victor, MGM, Columbia labels. Recipient Billboard award, 1959, Downbeat Most Played Band award Disc Jockey poll, 1959, Downbeat, Cashbox and Billboards awards in popularity polls, Gold record album for Hooked on Swing, 1982, Platinum, 1984.

ELGART, MERVYN L., dermatologist, educator; b. Bklyn., Aug. 12, 1933; s. Jacob and Sally R. E.; m. Sheila Ruth Cliff, June 13, 1954; children—Brian, George, Paul, Adam, James. A.B., Bklyn. Coll., 1953; M.D., Cornell U., 1957. Intern Buffalo Gen. Hosp., 1957-58; resident in dermatology Walter Reed Gen. Hosp., Washington, 1960-63; chief dermatology Andrews AFB Hosp., Washington, 1964-66; mem. faculty George Washington U. Med. Sch., 1967-97, prof. dermatology, 1974-97, chmn. dept., 1975-97, prof. pediatrics, 1974-97, prof. medicine, 1974-97; clin. prof. dermatology, medicine and pediatrics Univ. Dermatology Assocs., Washington, 1997—; clin. asst. prof. health care scis. George Washington U. Med.-Sch., 1997—. Served as officer M.C. USAF, 1958-66. Fellow Am. Acad. Dermatology; mem. AMA, So. Med. Assn., Internat. Soc. Dermatology, Washington Dermatol. Soc., Am. Dermatol. Assn., Phi Beta Kappa, Alpha Omega Alpha. Roman Catholic. Office: Univ Dermatology Assocs 1120 19th St NW Ste 250 Washington DC 20036-3605

ELGAVISH, ADA, molecular, cellular biologist; b. Cluj, Romania, Jan. 23, 1946; came to U.S. 1979; d. David and Malca (Neuman) Simchas; m. Gabriel A. Elgavish, Dec. 28, 1968; children: Rotem, Eynav. BSc, Tel-Aviv U., 1969, MSc, 1972; PhD, Weizmann Inst. Sci., Rehovot, Israel, 1978. Postdoctoral vis. fellow NIH, Balt., 1979-81; instr. U. Ala. Sch. Medicine, Birmingham, 1981-82, rsch. assoc., 1982-84, rsch. asst. prof., 1984-89, asst. prof. comparative medicine, 1989-92, assoc. prof., 1992—; scientist Cell Adhesion and Matrix Rsch. Ctr., Birmingham, 1995—, Ctr. Metabolic Bone Disease, Ctr. for Aging, 1996; mem. Cancer Ctr.; founder Diacell, Inc., 1998. Grantee Cystic Fibrosis Found., 1986-90, Am. Lung Assn., 1987-92, NIH, 1989—. Mem. AAAS, Am. Physiol. Soc., Am. Urol. Assn., Soc. for Basic Urol. Rsch., Sigma Xi. Home: 1737 Valpar Dr Birmingham AL 35226-2343 Office: U Ala Sch Medicine Dept Comparative Medicine Birmingham AL 35294

ELGAVISH, GABRIEL ANDREAS, physical biochemistry educator; b. Budapest, Hungary, July 29, 1942; arrived in Israel, 1957, came to U.S., 1979; s. László and Katalin Barbara (Szentmiklóssy) Schwarcz; m. Ada Stephanie Simcas, Dec. 28, 1967; children: Rotem László Abraham, Eynav Elgavish. BSc, Hebrew U., Jerusalem, 1967; MSc, Tel-Aviv U., 1972; PhD, Weizmann Inst. of Sci., 1978. Vis. fellow NIH, Balt., 1979-81; asst. prof. U. Ala., Birmingham, 1981-87, assoc. prof., 1987-95, prof., 1995—. Contbr. articles to profl. jours. 1st lt. Israeli Army, 1961-64. Mem. Am. Chem. Soc., Am. Soc. for Biochemistry and Molecular Biology, Am. Heart Assn./Basic Sci., Soc. Magnetic Resonance in Medicine. Jewish. Achievements include patents on Contrast Agents for Nuclear Magnetic Resonance Imaging; research in biomedical nuclear magnetic resonance spectroscopy. Office: U Ala THT 336 1900 University Blvd Birmingham AL 35233-2008

ELGEE, NEIL JOHNSON, retired internist and endocrinologist, educator; b. Oxford, N.S., Can., Apr. 3, 1926; came to U.S., 1946, naturalized, 1955; s. William Harris and Lucile (Nevers) E.; m. Leona Victoria Karlsson, Aug. 18, 1951; children—Joan, Susan, Laurie, Steven, Karen. B.Sc., U. N.B., Can., 1946; M.D., U. Rochester, 1950. Intern Peter Bent Brigham Hosp., Boston, 1950-51; resident Strong Meml. Hosp., Rochester, N.Y., 1951-52; fellow in endocrinology U. Wash., 1952-54; co-chief resident in medicine U. Wash., Seattle, 030, 1954-55; clin. prof. medicine U. Wash., Seattle, 1968-93, emeritus clin. prof. medicine, 1993—; practice medicine specializing in endocrinology Seattle, 1957-93; retired, 1993; pres. Ernest Becker Found., 1993—. Served as capt. USAF, 1955-57. Master ACP (gov. for Wash. and Alaska 1965-71, regent 1974-78); mem. Endocrine Soc., Inst. Medicine. Home: 3621 72nd Ave SE Mercer Island WA 98040-3330

ELGER, WILLIAM ROBERT, JR., accountant; b. Chgo., Mar. 20, 1950; s. William Robert and Grace G. (LaVaque) E.; m. Kathryn Michele Johnson, July 10, 1971; children: Kimberly, William, Kristin, Joseph. AS in Applied Sci., Coll. of DuPage, Glen Ellyn, Ill., 1970; BS magna cum laude, U. Ill.-Chgo., 1972. CPA, Ill. Staff acct. Ernst & Whinney, Chgo., 1973, in-charge acct., 1973-74, sr. acct., 1974-78, mgr., 1978-82, sr. mgr., 1982-88; chief fin. officer U. Ill. Eye and Ear Infirmary, 1988-89; CFO U. Mich. Med. Sch., Ann Arbor, 1989—; presenter various confs. in field Ernst & Whinney, Chgo., 1980-88. Author, developer: (tng. course) Auditing Third Party Reimbursement, 1986, 87. Active Union League Civic and Arts Found., Chgo., 1982-89, Union League Found. for Boys and Girls Clubs, Chgo., 1982-89; treas. Newport Assn., Carol Stream, Ill., 1982-83; coach Tri-City Soccer Assn., St. Charles, Ill., 1984, 87, Saline Soccer Assn., 1990, 91, 93, 94, 95, Saline H.S. Soccer Club, 1996, 97. Mem. AICPA, Healthcare Fin. Mgmt. Assn. (advanced mem., acctg. and reimbursement com. 1982-87, chpt. task force com. 1986, 87, auditing com. 1986, 87, Spl. Recognition award 1986), Ill. Soc. CPAs (mem. long term healthcare com. 1983, hosps. com. 1988-89), Nat. Coun. Univ. Rsch. Adminstrs., Assn. of Univ. Technology Mgrs., Med. Group Mgmt. Assn., Assn. Am. Med. Colls. Group on Bus. Affairs. Methodist. Avocations: golf, tennis. Office: U Mich Med Sch MSI Box 0624 1301 Catherine St Ann Arbor MI 48109-0600

ELGIN, GITA, psychologist; b. Santiago, Chile; came to U.S., 1968, naturalized 1987; d. Serafín and Regina (Urízar) Elguin; BS in biology summa cum laude, U. Chile, Santiago, DPs, 1964; PhD in Counseling Psychology, U. Calif., Berkeley, 1976; m. Bart Bödy, Oct. 23, 1971; children: Dio Christopher Károly, Alma Ilona Raia Julia. Clin. psychologist Barros Luco-Trudeau Gen. Hosp., Santiago, 1964-65; co-founder, co-dir. Lab. for Parapsychol. Rsch., Psychiat. Clinic, U. Chile, Santiago, 1965-68; rsch. fellow Found. Rsch. on Nature of Man, Durham, N.C., 1968; rschr. psychol. correlates of EEG-Alpha waves U. Calif., Berkeley, 1972-76; originator holistic method of psychotherapy Psychotherapy for a Crowd of One, 1978; co-founder, clin. dir. Holistic Health Assos., Oakland, Calif., 1979—, Montclair Mediation Group, Oakland, 1994; lectr. holistic health Piedmont (Calif.) Adult Sch., 1979-80; hostess Holistic Perspective, Sta. KALW-FM, Nat. Public Radio, 1980; co-creator Holistic Renewal, The Elgin Process of Creative Self Mastery. Author: (video documentary) Taking the Risk: Sharing the Trauma of Sexual & Ritualistic Abuse in Group Therapy, 1992. Lic. psychologist, Chile, Calif. Chancellor's Patent Fund grantee U. Calif., 1976, NIMH fellow, 1976. Mem. APA, Am. Holistic Psychol. Assn. (founder 1995—), Holistic Village (pres., co-founder 1997), Alameda County Psychol. Assn., Calif. State Psychol. Assn., Montclair Health Profls. Assn. (co-founder, pres. 1983-85), Sierra Club, U. Calif. Alumni Assn. Contbr. articles in clin. psychology and holistic health to profl. jours. and local periodicals. Presenter Whole Life Expo, 1986. Office: Montclair Profl Bldg 2080 Mountain Blvd Ste 107 Oakland CA 94611-2829

ELIAS, DONALD FRANCIS, environmental consultant; b. Cleve., Aug. 8, 1949; s. Richard Joseph and Marie Terese (Sievers) E. BS in Chemistry with honors, U. S.C., 1971; cert. in meteorology, St. Louis U., 1972; MS in Environ. Engring., Wash. State U., 1977. Chemist S.C. Dept. of Health and Environ. Control, Columbia, 1974-75; rsch. asst. Wash. State U., Pullman, 1975-77; sr. assoc. scientist I.I.T. Rsch. Inst., Chgo., 1977-78; mgr. USEPA Air Pollution Tng. Inst. Northrop Svcs., Research Triangle Park, N.C., 1978-80; prin. Dames & Moore, Houston and Bethesda, Md., 1980-82; mgr. Camp, Dresser & McKee, Denver and Edison, N.J., 1982-86; founding prin. Research Triangle Park Environ. Assocs., Inc., Green Brook, N.J., 1978-86, pres., prin., 1986—, pres., 1990-92, chmn. bd. dirs., 1992—; ptnr. Waverly Properties; founding ptnr. Waverly Properties, Columbia, S.C., 1994—; CEO, bd. dirs. Haztraacht, LLC, 1996—. Contbr. articles to profl. jours. Mem. Martinsville (N.J.) Rescue Squad, 1984—, lt., 1984-90, pres., 1991-95, del. 5th dist., 1998—; eucharistic min., lectr. Blessed Sacrament, Martinsville, 1986—; mem. Green Brook Rescue Squad, 1988-93; mem. ptnrs. coun. Habitat for Humanity. Lt. USAF, 1971-74. Mem. Am. Chem. Soc., Am. Meteorol. Soc., Natural Resources Def. Coun., Assn. Energy Engrs. (sr.), Air and Waste Mgmt. Assn. (vice chmn. waste source group 1989-94), Environ. Def. Fund, Amnesty Internat., Natural Resources Def. Coun., Consumer's Union (life), Sierra Club (life), Nat. Arbor Soc., Humane Soc. U.S. Avocations: playing golf, playing tennis, reading. Office: RTP Environmental Assoc Inc 239 Us Highway 22 Green Brook NJ 08812-1916

ELIAS, PAUL S., marketing executive; b. Chgo., July 5, 1926; s. Maurice I. and Ethel (Tieger) E.; m. Jennie Lee Feldschreiber, June 28, 1953; children—Eric David, Stephen Mark, Daniel Avrum. B.S., Northwestern U. Sch. Bus., 1950; hon. degree, N.Y. U. Sch. Continuing Edn., 1972. Buyer Mandel Bros., Chgo., 1950-53; salesman Internat. Latex Corp., Chgo., 1953-56; v.p. Hy Zeiger & Co., Milw., 1957-59; exec. v.p. K-Promotions, Inc., Milw., 1960-78, pres., 1979-80; chief exec. officer, pres. consumer promotions Carlson Mktg. Group, Milw., 1981-84, chief exec. officer promotions div., 1985-86; pres. K-Promotions Div. Carlson Promotion Group, 1987-88, Giftmaster Div. Carlson Promotion Group, 1989—, Elias Mktg., Inc., 1989—. Officer, dir. Milw. Jewish Community Center; pres. regional bd. Anti-Defamation League; pres. Regional Bd. Jewish Nat. Fund, 1993-96. Served with USAAF, 1945-46. Mem. Assn. Incentive Mktg., Direct Mail Advt. Assn., Am. Jewish. Developer inflight mail order mktg. programs for airlines. Office: Elias Mktg Inc 11512 N Port Washington Rd Mequon WI 53092-3453

ELIAS, PETER, electrical engineering educator; b. New Brunswick, N.J., Nov. 26, 1923; s. Nathaniel Mandel and Ann (Wahrhaftig) E.; m. Marjorie Forbes, July 8, 1950 (dec. Feb. 1993); children: Ellen, Paul, Daniel. Student, Swarthmore Coll., 1940-42; S.B., MIT, 1944; M.A., Harvard U., 1948, M.Engring. Sci., 1949, Ph.D., 1950. Jr. fellow Harvard U., 1950-53; asst. prof. MIT, Cambridge, 1953-56, assoc. prof., 1956-60, prof., head dept. elec. engring., 1960-66, Edwin S. Webster prof., 1974-92, Webster prof. emeritus, sr. lectr., 1992—; vis. prof. U. Calif.-Berkeley, 1958, Harvard U., Cambridge, Mass., 1967-68, 83-84, Imperial Coll., London, 1975-76. Editor, mem. editorial bd. Info. and Control jour., 1957—. Contbr. numerous articles on info. theory and communications to profl. jours. Served with USN, 1944-46. Fellow Am. Acad. Arts and Scis., IEEE (chmn. info. theory group 1965, Shannon award 1977, Centennial medal 1984), AAAS (mem. coun. 1983, mem. engring. sect. 1986), Assn. Computing Machinery; mem. Nat. Acad. Scis., Nat. Acad. Engring., Inst. Math. Stats. Democrat. Office: MIT Dept Elec Engring 77 Massachusetts Ave Cambridge MA 02139-4307

ELIAS, ROSALIND, mezzo-soprano; b. Lowell, Mass., Mar. 13, 1931; d. Salem and Shelahuy Rose (Namy) E.; m. Zuhayr Moghrabi. Student, New Eng. Conservatory Music, Accademia di Santa Cecilia, Rome; studies with, Daniel Ferro, N.Y.C. Singer New Eng. Opera, 1948-52, Met. Opera, 1954—; artistic dir. Am. Lyric Theatre. Debut with Boris Goldowsky, Boston, 1948; appeared in numerous roles including Cherubino, Dorabella, Rosina, Hansel, Cenerentola, Carmen, Amneris and Azucena (Verdi), Charlotte and Giulietta (Massenet), Herodias, 1987; originated role of Erika in Vanessa (Samuel Barber) and Cleopatra in Antony and Cleopatra (Barber); also appeared with Scottish Opera, Vienna Staatsoper, Glynbourne Festival, many others; prodr. Carmen, Cin., 1988, Il Barbiere di Siviglia, Opera Pacific, Costa Mesa, Calif., 1989; recs. for RCA and Columbia records include La Gioconda, La Forza del Destno, Il Trovatore, Falstaff, Madama Butterfly, Rigoletto, Der fliegende Holländer. Mem. Sigma Alpha Iota. Office: care Robert Lombardo Associates One Harkness Plaza 61 W 62nd St Apt 6F New York NY 10023-7017*

ELIAS, SAMY E. G., engineering executive; b. Cairo, June 28, 1930; came to U.S., 1956, naturalized, 1964; s. Elias Girgis and Tahia N. (Kassabgy) E.; m. Janice Lee Craig, Aug. 21, 1960; children: Mona Lee, Tresa Jean, Cecilia Ruth. BS in Aero. Engring., Cairo U., 1955; MS in Aero. Engring., Tex. A&M U., 1958; PhD in Indsl. Engring. and Mgmt., Okla. State U., 1960. Grad. asst. Tex. A&M U., College Station, 1957-58; grad. asst. Okla. State U., Stillwater, 1958-60; asst. prof., indsl. engring. Kans. State U., Manhattan, 1960-61; exec. asst. to chmn. bd. Orgn. of Mil. Factories, Egypt, 1961-62; asso. prof. indsl. engring. Kans. State U., 1962-65; assoc. prof. indsl. engring. W.Va. U., Morgantown, 1965-67; prof. W.Va. U., 1967-79, chmn. dept. indsl. engring., 1969-76, spl. asst. to univ. pres. for personal rapid transit, 1970-77, Claude Worthington Benedum prof. transp., 1976-82; dir. Harley O. Staggers Nat. Transp. Ctr., 1980-82; dir. transit engring. and safety Washington Met. Area Transit Authority, 1982-84; v.p. Transp. and Distbn. Assocs., Inc. subs. Day & Zimmermann,, Phila., 1984-87; prin. FAI Assocs., Inc., McLean, Va., 1987—; assoc. dean engring. rsch. U. Nebr., Lincoln, 1988—; cons. Kansas City Transit, N.Y. Transit Authority, N.Y. Transit Authority Police Dept., Omaha Transit Co., Cin. Transit Co., W.C. Gilman & Co., Inc., Brown Engring., Transp. and Distbn. Assocs., PRC Harris, Arab Petroleum Cons., Urban Transp. Devel. Corp., World Bank, also others. Contbr. over numerous publs. to profl. jours. Recipient Americanism medal DAR, 1977. Fellow Chartered Inst. Transp., Inst. Indsl. Engrs. (Transp. and Distbn. award 1979); mem. Soc. Am. Value Engrs., Am. Soc. Engring. Edn. (chmn. indsl. engring. divsn. 1972-73), Soc. for Computer Simulation, Nat. Soc. Propl. Engrs., Accreditation Bd. Engring. Tech. (engring. accreditation com. 1987-92, W.Va. Soc. Profl. Engrs. Coptic Orthodox. Home: 8111 Dorset Dr Lincoln NE 68510-5209 Office: U Nebr Engring Rsch Ctrs 150 W Nebraska Hall Lincoln NE 68588

ELIAS, THOMAS SAM, botanist, author; b. Cairo, Ill., Dec. 30, 1942; s. George Sam (dec.) and Anna (Clanton) E.; m. Barbara Ana Boyd (dec.); children: Stephen, Brian. BA in Botany, So. Ill. U., 1964, MA in Botany, 1966; PhD in Biology, St. Louis U., 1969. Asst. curator Arnold Arboretum of Harvard U., Cambridge, Mass., 1969-71; adminstr., dendrologist Cary Arboretum, N.Y. Botanical Garden, Millbrook, 1971-73, asst. dir., 1973-84; dir., CEO Rancho Santa Ana Bot. Garden, Claremont, Calif., 1984-93; chmn., prof. dept. botany Claremont Grad. Sch., 1984-93; dir. U.S. Nat. Arboretum, Washington, 1993—; lectr. in extension Harvard U., 1971; adj. prof. Coll. Environ. Science and Forestry, Syracuse, N.Y., 1977-80; coord. U.S.A/U.S.S.R. Botanical Exch., Program for U.S. Dept. of Interior, Washington, 1976—, U.S.A./China Botanical Exch., Program for U.S. Dept. of Interior, 1988—. Editor: Extinction is Forever, 1977 (one of 100 Best Books in Sci. and Tech. ALA 1977), Conservation and Management of Rare and Endangered Plants, 1987; author: Complete Trees of North America, 1980 (one of 100 Best Books in Sci. and Tech. ALA 1980), Field Guide to Edible Wild Plants of North America (one of 100 Best Books in Sci. and Tech. ALA 1983). Recipient Cooley award Am. Soc. Plant Taxonomist, 1970, Disting. Alumni award So. Ill. U., 1989. Home: 2447 San Mateo Ct Claremont CA 91711-1652 Office: US Nat Arboretum 3501 New York Ave NE Washington DC 20002-1958

ELIASON, JON TATE, electrical engineer; b. Menominee, Mich., Mar. 23, 1938; s. Edwin Adolph and Irene Albertyn (Longlais) E.; m. Barbara Ann Love, July 2, 1960 (div. Dec. 1980); children: Ellen Artimese, Eric Alan, Eileen Amber; m. Kathleen Ann Vitell, May 25, 1996. BS in Sci. Engring., U. Mich., 1960; MS in Physics, Oreg. State U., 1966. Registered profl. engr., Ala. Engr. Vallecitos Nuclear Lab. GE, Pleasanton, Calif., 1964-66; sr. staff engr., engring. cons. Sperry Rand Corp., Huntsville, Ala., 1966-76; sr. staff engr. Martin Marietta Corp., Denver, 1976-84; master program engr., group engr. Sundstrand Corp., Rockford, Ill., 1984-92; engr. Insight Industries, Inc., Platteville, Wis., 1993-96, Insight Info. Inc., Platteville, Wis., 1996; project engr. Barber-Colman Co., Loves Park, Ill., 1996—. Patentee in field. Recipient New Tech. award NASA, 1973, 75; Regents/Alumni scholar U. Mich., 1956-60. Mem. IEEE, AIAA, Am. Phys. Soc., Sigma Pi Sigma, (chpt. pres. 1963-64). Avocations: amateur radio, private pilot. Office: PO Box 7231 Rockford IL 61126-7231

ELIASON, RUSSELL ALLEN, judge; b. Mpls., Jan. 28, 1944; s. Walter Joseph and Hazel Agnes Pearl (Jensen) E.; m. Karen L. Stevens; children: Nathaniel, Heidi, Justine, Danielle. Student U. Minn., 1964-65, JD, 1970; BA, Yale U., 1967; student Wake Forest U. Sch. Law, 1967-68. Bar: Minn. 1970, Iowa 1971, N.C. 1973, Nebr. 1975, U.S. Dist. Ct. (no. dist.) Iowa 1971, U.S. Dist. Ct. (mid. dist.) N.C. 1974, U.S. Dist. Ct. Nebr. 1975, U.S. Ct. Appeals (8th cir.) 1971, U.S. Ct. Appeals (4th cir.) 1976. Law clk. to judge U.S. Ct. Appeals 8th Cir., 1970-71; asst. U.S. atty. Dept. Justice, Sioux City, Iowa, 1971-72; law clk. to judge U.S. Dist. Ct. Mid. Dist. N.C., 1972-74; assoc. Ryan, Scoville & Uhlir, South Sioux City, Nebr., 1974-75; asst. U.S. atty. Dept. Justice, Greensboro, N.C., 1975-76; U.S. magistrate judge U.S. Dist. Ct. Mid. Dist. N.C., Winston-Salem, 1976—; lectr. in field; active law-sch. skills programs. Trumpeter Salem Band, Old Salem Band. Mem. ABA, N.C. Bar Assn., Forsyth County Bar, Minn. Bar Assn., Nebr. Bar Assn., Sons of Norway, Phi Alpha Alpha Delta. Mem. Moravian Ch. Office: 224 Fed Bldg 251 N Main St Winston Salem NC 27101-3914

ELIASOPH, JEFFREY PAUL, television news anchor; b. N.Y.C., July 29, 1956; s. Ira Ingram E. and Ann Patricia (Levy) Klein; m. Elisa Robin Malinovitz, Aug. 8, 1988; children: Vivien Norma, Hannah Ida. BA in Polit. Sci., Johns Hopkins U., 1978. Reporter Sta. KCBQ-AM, San Diego, 1979-80; sports reporter Mutual Broadcasting, San Diego, 1980-81; features editor Copley News Svc., San Diego, 1982; reporter, anchor Sta. KGBT-TV, Harlingen, Tex., 1983-85; news anchor Tex. State Network, Dallas, 1986; reporter, anchor Sta. KTBS-TV, Shreveport, La., 1986-88; morning news anchor Sta. KXAS-TV, Dallas, 1989—; media cons. Dallas Jewish Coaliton for the Homeless, 1992—. Speaker and presenter in field. Master of ceremonies Fort Worth (Tex.) Clean City, 1993—, Tarrant County (Tex.) Employee's Day, 1993—; spokesman Tex. Red Ribbon Anti-drug Campaign, Dallas, 1991—; vol. Dallas Jewish Coalition for the Homeless, Vogel Family Alcove; bd. dirs. Richardson Children's Theatre, 1994-97. Recipient Spot News Excellence award Tex. AP, 1991, Planned Event Coverage 1st Place award La. AP, 1987, Spot News Story award, 1986, Exceptional Vol. Svc. award Tex. Gov. Mark White, 1984. Mem. NAACP, Soc. Profl. Journalists, So. Poverty Law Ctr. Avocations: baseball, classic films, musical theatre, working with children. Office: KXAS TV 5 3900 Barnett St Fort Worth TX 76103-1400

ELIASSEN, JON ERIC, utility company executive; b. Omak, Wash., Mar. 10, 1947; s. Marvin George and Helen Grace (Meyer) E.; m. Valerie A. Foyle, Aug. 14, 1971; 1 child, Michael T. BA in Bus., Wash. State U., 1970. Staff acct. Wash. Water Power Co., Spokane, 1970-73, tax acct., 1973-76, fin. analyst, 1976-80, treas., 1980-86, v.p. fin., CFO, 1986-96; sr. v.p., CFO Avista Corp., Spokane, 1996—; bd. dirs. Northwest Venture Ptnrs., Itron Corp., Pentzer Corp., Momentum. Trustee Wash. State U. Found., Pullman, 1987; treas. Wash. State U. Found., 1995-97; trustee Spokane Symphony, 1989-95, treas., 1990-95, mem. endowment bd.; pres. Spokane Intercollegiate Rsch. & Tech. Inst. Found., 1996—. Mem. Pacific Coast Gas Assn. (past chmn. adminstrv. svcs. com.), Fin. Exec. Inst. (bd. dirs., sec., past pres. Inland N.W. chpt. 1983—). Episcopalian. Avocations: skiing, traveling, bicycling, photography. Office: Avista Corp PO Box 3727 Spokane WA 99220-3727*

ELIBOL, TARIK, gastroenterologist; b. Turkey, Sept. 1, 1937; came to U.S., 1964, naturalized, 1970; s. Ismail Cemal and Nuriye (Tutkun) E.; m. Eileen Elibol, Aug. 30, 1997; children—Kimberly, Lisa, David, Adam, John. MD U. Istanbul, 1964. Resident in internal medicine E.J. Meyer Hosp. U. Buffalo, 1964-66, fellow in gastroenterology Cleve. Clinic, 1966-68; clin. asst. prof. medicine U. Buffalo, 1975—; practice medicine specializing in digestive diseases, Buffalo, 1969—; former chief of staff DeGraff Meml. Hosp.; mem. staff Erie County Med. Center, Kenmore Mercy Hosp. Fellow Am. Coll. Gastroenterology, Am. Coll. Physicians; mem. Western N.Y. Soc. Gastrointestinal Endoscopy (past pres.), Western N.Y. Gastrointestinal Liver Soc. (pres. 1980—), Western N.Y. Physician Found. (pres. 1980—); mem. ACP, Am. Soc. Internal Medicine, Erie County Med. Soc., N.Y. State Med. Soc., Am. Soc. Gastrointestinal Endoscopy. Contbr. articles to profl. jours. Home: 55 Leicester Rd Buffalo NY 14217-2111 Office: 2949 Elmwood Ave Kenmore NY 14217-1356

ELICKER, GORDON LEONARD, lawyer; b. Cleve., May 27, 1940. BA in Math., U. Mich., 1962, JD, 1965; postdoctoral, U. Aix-Marseille, Aix-En Provence, France, 1965-66. Bar: Mich. 1967, N.Y. 1968, U.S. Dist. Ct. (so. dist.) N.Y. 1973. Stagiaire EEC, Brussels, 1966-67; assoc. Shearman & Sterling, N.Y.C., 1967-77, ptnr., 1977-91; ptnr. Nixon, Hargrave, Devans & Doyle, N.Y.C., 1991—; speaker in field. Contbr. articles to profl. jours. Mem. legal com. U.S.-U.S.S.R. Trade and Econ. Coun., N.Y.C., 1978-91; chmn. legis. com. N.Y. Dist. Export Coun., N.Y.C., 1980-86; mem. Dem. Town Com., New Canaan, 1985-87; mem. bd. edn., New Canaan, Conn., 1986-90, chmn., 1989-90. Fulbright scholar, 1965. Mem. ABA, Internat. Bar Assn., Assn. of Bar of City of N.Y. Democrat. Office: Nixon Hargrave Devans Doyle 437 Madison Ave New York NY 10022-7001

ELIE, JEAN ANDRÉ, investment banker; b. Montreal, Que., Can., Oct. 8, 1943; s. Jean-Paul and Violet (Trempe) E.; m. Josée Langevin. BA, Coll. Jean de Brébeuf, 1962; BCL, McGill U., 1965; MBA, U. Western Ont., 1968. Bar: Que. 1966. With Rolland Inc., Montreal, 1968-81; sec. Rolland Inc., 1974-81, counsel, 1974-81, v.p. administrn., 1978-81; dir. corp. services Burns Fry Ltd., Montreal, 1981-88; v.p., dir. corp. and govt. svcs. Burns Fry Lte., Montreal, 1988-94; fin. cons. Birinco Holdings Internat., Inc., Montreal, 1994—; mem. adminstrv. coun. Coopers & Lybrand, 1996; mng. dir. Corp. and Investment Banking, Can., Soc. Genérale, 1998; chmn. adv. bd. Procrea Bioscis. Inc. Bd. dirs., vice chmn. Montreal Symphony Orch.; bd. dirs., v.p. Found. Hosp. Notre Dame; chmn. adv. bd. McGill U. Faculty of Music. Mem. Can. Bar Assn., Que. Bar Assn., Investment Dealers Assn. Can. (exec. com., bd. dirs.), Mt. Royal Club. Roman Catholic. Clubs: St. Denis. Home: 1929 Laird Blvd, Mount Royal, PQ Canada H3P 2V2 Office: 1501 McGill Coll Ave Ste 1800, Montreal, PQ Canada H3P 2V2

ELIEFF, LEWIS STEVEN, stockbroker; b. Sofia, Bulgaria, Aug. 2, 1929; s. Steven and Vera (Svetcoff) E.; B.B.A., U. Mich., 1953, M.B.A., 1954; m. Evanka Brown, May 25, 1958; children: Nancy Ann, Robert and Richard (twins). Statistician, tax acct. Gen. Motors Corp., Flint, Mich., 1954-60; stockbroker Roney & Co., Flint, 1960-73, ltd. ptnr., 1973-79, gen. ptnr., 1979—; tchr. stock market curriculum Flint Pub. Schs., 1960-68, Genesee County Community Coll., 1968-73, U. Mich. Extension and Grad. Study Ctr. Flint Campus, 1974—. Served with AUS, 1954-56. Mem. U. Mich. Alumni Club and Assn. Clubs: Genesee Valley Rotary. Home: 6612 Kings Point Rd Grand Blanc MI 48439-8711 Office: 3499 S Linden Rd Ste 4 Flint MI 48507-3022

ELIEFF, RICHARD GEORGE, energy industry consultant; b. Flint, Mich., July 11, 1960; s. Lewis Steven and Evanka Marie (Brown) E. BSCE summa cum laude, U. Mich., 1982; MBA, U. Pa., 1987. Cost/schedule engr. Bechtel Power Corp., Ann Arbor, 1982-85; constrn. scheduling cons. Hovnanian Enterprises, Inc., Red Bank, N.J., 1986; strategic planning cons. Mendenhall (Pa.) Assocs., Inc., 1987; devel. specialist Wesley Housing Devel. Corp., Alexandria, 1988-91; prin. Vertumnus Enterprises, Alexandria, 1991-97; pres. IntelliPro Software Inc., Alexandria, 1995-98; project mgr. Pace Global Energy Svcs., Fairfax, Va., 1997—; mem. adv. com. for multifamily loan program Va. Dept. of Housing and Cmty. Devel., Richmond, 1989-91. Author: (software) Secrets to a Happy Car, 1996. William J. Branstrom scholar U. Mich., 1979, scholarship 1980; fellowship Associated Gen. Contractors, 1981. Mem. Tau Beta Pi, Chi Epsilon. Republican. Orthodox. Avocations: stock market, automotive mechanics, piano. Home: 4203 Lauries Way Apt 102 Fairfax VA 22033-4361 Office: Pace Global Energy Svcs 4401 Fair Lakes Ct Ste 400 Fairfax VA 22033-3848

ELIEL, ERNEST LUDWIG, chemist, educator; b. Cologne, Germany, Dec. 28, 1921; came to U.S., 1946, naturalized, 1951; s. Oskar and Luise (Tietz) E.; m. Eva Schwarz, Dec. 23, 1949; children: Ruth Louise, Carol Susan. Student, U. Edinburgh, Scotland, 1939-40; degree in phys.-chem. sci., U. Havana, Cuba, 1946; PhD, U. Ill., 1948; DSc (hon.), Duke U., 1983, U. Notre Dame, 1990, Babes-Bolyai U., Cluj, Romania, 1993. Mem. faculty U. Notre Dame, South Bend, Ind., 1948-72, prof. chemistry, 1960-72, head dept., 1964-66; W.R. Kenan Jr. prof. chemistry U. N.C., Chapel Hill, 1972-93, prof. emeritus, 1993—; Le Bel Centennial lectr., Paris, 1974; Sir C.V. Raman vis. prof. U. Madras, India, 1981; Geoffrey Coates lectr. U. Wyo., 1989; Smith, Kline & French lectr. U. Ill., 1990; Richard and Doris Arnold lectr. U. South Ill., 1997. Author: Stereochemistry of Carbon Compounds, 1962, Elements of Stereochemistry, 1969, From Cologne to Chapel Hill, 1990; co-author: Conformational Analysis, 1965, Stereochemistry of Organic Compounds, 1994; co-editor: Topics in Stereochemistry, vols. I-XXI, 1967-94. Pres. Internat. Rels. Coun., St. Joseph Valley, Ind., 1961-63; chmn. bd. U.S.-Mex. Found. for Sci., 1994-96. Recipient Coll. Chem. Tchrs. award Mfg. Chemists Assn., 1965, Laurent Lavoisier medal French Chem. Soc., 1968, Amoco Teaching award U. N.C., 1975, Thomas Jefferson award U. N.C., 1991, N.C. award in Sci., 1986, Chirality medal Internat. Symposium on Chiral Discrimination, 1996; NSF sr. rsch. fellow Harvard U., 1958, Calif. Inst. Tech., 1958-59, E.T.H. Zurich, Switzerland, 1967-68, Guggenheim fellow Stanford U., Princeton U., 1975-76, Duke U., 1983-84; named One of Top 75 Disting. Contbrs. to Chem. Enterprise, Chem. and Engring. News, 1998. Fellow AAAS (chmn. chemistry sect. 1991-92), Royal Soc. Chems.; mem. NAS (award for chemistry in svc. to society 1997), AAUP (chpt. pres. 1971-72, 78-79), Am. Acad. Arts and Scis., Am. Chem. Soc. (chmn. St. Joseph Valley sect. 1960, councillor 1965-73, 75—, chmn. com. publs. 1972, 76-78, dir. 1985-93, chmn. bd. dirs. 1987-89, pres. 1992, Morley medal Cleve. sect. 1965, Harry and Carol Mosher award Santa Clara Valley sect. 1982, Herty medal Ga. sect. 1991, So. Chemist award Memphis sect. 1991, Madison Marshall award North Ala. sect., 1993, George C. Pimentel award in Chem. Edn. 1995, Priestley medal 1996), Coun. Sci. Soc. Pres.'s (pres. 1996), Royal Spanish Chem. Soc. (hon.), Argentine Chem. Assn. (hon.), Peruvian Chem. Soc. (corr.), Mex. Chem. Soc. (hon.), Mex. Acad. Scis. (corr.), Chilean Chem. Soc. (hon.), Sigma Xi (pres. U. Notre Dame chpt. 1968-69), Phi Lambda Upsilon, Phi Kappa Phi. Home: 725 Kenmore Rd Chapel Hill NC 27514-2019

ELIEN, MONA MARIE, air transportation professional; b. Atwood, Kans., June 13, 1932; d. Lawrence Wallace Berry and Adele Wright; m. R.J. Wright, Jan. 1952 (div. 1957); m. J.P. Kobus, Nov. 1968 (div. 1991); m. Robert Louis Tour, Oct. 3, 1992 (wid. Sept. 1998). BS, U. Ariz., 1961; grad., Swiss Mountain Climbing Inst., Rosenlaui, 1963; postgrad., No. Ariz. U., 1966-67, Ariz. State U., 1967-69, 86-87; MPA, Ariz. State U., 1981. Customer rels. rep. Ariz. Pub. Svc. Co., Casa Grande, Flagstaff, Ariz., 1961-67; owner/operator Mona's Clipping Svc., Phoenix, 1969—; various positions City of Phoenix, 1974—; contract mgr. Phoenix CETA/PSE/PNP, 1978-81; planning and devel. asst. Phoenix Sky Harbor Internat. Airport, 1986—; staff asst. 1988 Citizens Bond Com. for Aviation, Phoenix, 1987-88; chmn. aviation Dept. CSFD, 1996. Compiler, editor: Aviation Acronyms and Abbreviations, 1987, 2d rev. edit., 1992; editor, writer (newsletter) Rapsheet, 1972-75; author profl. columns, 1961-67. Pres. state home econs. related occupations adv. bd. Ariz. State U., 1983-84; mem. Phoenix City Mgr.'s Women's Issues Com., 1989-91; pres. elect Tri-City (Ariz.) Zonta Internat., 1964-65; vol. speaker's bur. Phoenix Cmty. Alliance and Prep. Acad. Partnership, 1992—; mem. exec. com. Cmty. Svc. Fund Drive, Phoenix, 1984-86, 97—; mem. precinct com. Yuma County Dem. Com., 1958; mem. employee-of-yr. com. Phoenix Aviation Dept., 1993, co-chmn., 1994; mem. Super Bowl XXX Host Com., 1996; vol. City of Phoenix Visions and Values Seminars. Recipient recognition pub. svc. award Ariz. Dept. Econ. Security, 1975, Heart and Soul award Barry M. Goldwater Terminal 4, 1990, Planning and Devel. divsn. Employee of Yr. 1996, 98, PHXcellence awards, 1993-99, Art Hero award Phoenix Sky Harbor Internat. Airport, 1993; named one of Outstanding Young Women of Am., 1966. Mem. ASPA (life; Phoenix chpt. awards banquet com. 1991, 92, 98, 99, nat. com. 1990-91, Task Force Nonviolence, 1998), Am. Assn. Family and Consumer Scis. (life), Ariz. Home Econs. Assn. (pres. no. region 1965-67), Sinagua Soc. Museum No. Ariz., Satisfied Frog Gold Mountain Club, Flagstaff C. of C. (chmn. Indian princesses, retail mchts. sect. 1965-67), So. Ariz. Hiking Club, Desert Bot. Gardens, Swinging Stars Square Dance Club, Delta Delta Delta. Republican. Lutheran. Home: 7300 N Dreamy Draw Dr # 101 Phoenix AZ 85020-5244 Office: Phoenix Sky Harbor Internat Airport 3400 E Sky Harbor Blvd Phoenix AZ 85034-4403

ELIKANN, LAWRENCE S. (LARRY ELIKANN), television and film director; b. N.Y.C., July 4, 1923; s. Harry and Sadye (Trause) E.; m. Corinne Schuman; Dec. 6, 1947; children—JoAnne Jarrin, Jill Barad. B.A., Bklyn. Coll., 1943; E.E., Walter Harvey Coll., 1948. Tech. dir. NBC-TV, N.Y.C., 1948-64; comml. dir. VPI-TV, N.Y.C., 1964-66, Filmex-TV, N.Y.C., 1966-68, Plus two TV, N.Y.C., 1968-70. Dir. mini-series Last Flight Out, The Great L.A. Earthquake, The Big One, The Inconvenient Woman, Fever, Story Lady, One Against the Wind, Bonds of Love, I Know My First Name is Steven, Hands of a Stranger, Kiss of a Killer, God Bless the Child, Out of Darkness, Menendez—A Killing in Beverly Hills, Tecumseh—The Last Warrior, A Mother's Prayer, Blue River, "Unexpected Family", Lies He Told. Mem. Mus. Contemporary Art of L.A., L.A. County Mus.; mem. rsch. coun. Scripps Clinic and Rsch. Found. With Signal Corps, U.S. Army, 1943-46. Recipient Emmy award, 1978-79, 89, Golden Globe award, 1989, 91, 94, Christopher award 1973-76, 77, 78-79, 91, Chgo. Internat. Film Festival award 1977, Internat. Film and TV Festival of N.Y. award, 1977, Dir. of Yr. award Am. Ctrs. for Children, 1978; Humanitas prize, 1988, 94, 96. Mem. NATAS (gov. 1961-63), Dirs. Guild Am., Am. film Inst., Nat. Hist. Preservation Soc., Smithsonian Inst., Scripps Inst. (bd. dirs.), Acad. TV Arts and Scis.

ELIN, RONALD JOHN, pathologist; b. Mpls., Apr. 14, 1939; s. John Matthew and Helen Sophia (Lind) E.; m. Susan May Krogh, June 14, 1969; children: Derek, Justin. BA, U. Minn., 1960, BS, 1962, MD, 1966, PhD, 1969. Diplomate Am. Bd. Pathology, Am. Bd. Clin. Chemistry. Intern U. Hosp. Calif., San Diego, 1969-70; commd. med. officer USPHS, 1970, advanced through grades to med. dir., 1975; staff assoc. Nat. Inst. Allergy and Infectious Diseases NIH, Bethesda, Md., 1970-73, resident clin. pathology dept., 1973-74, chief clin. pathology dept., 1975-97, chief chemistry svc., 1977-97; vice chmn. pathology U. Louisville, Ky., 1997—; clin. prof. Uniformed Svcs. U. of Health Scis., Bethesda, 1978-97; initiator, first chmn. Gordon Rsch. Conf. on Magnesium in Biomed. Processes and Medicine, 1978. Contbr. more than 180 articles to profl. jours. Decorated Commendation medal USPHS, 1980, Meritorious Svc. medal USPHS, 1984. Fellow Am. Coll. Nutrition, Coll. Am. Pathologists, Am. Soc. Clin. Pathologists; mem. Am. Assn. Pathologists, Am. Assn. Clin. Chemistry (Outstanding Contbns. to Clin. Chemistry in a Selected Area of Rsch. award 1994), Acad. Clin. Lab. Physicians and Scientists (sec.-treas. 1985-87, pres. 1990-91, Gerald T. Evans award 1995). Lutheran. Achievements include research on magnesium metabolism, properties of endotoxin. Office: U Louisville Hosp Dept Pathology and Lab Medicine 530 S Jackson St Rm C1D05 Louisville KY 40202-1675

ELINSON, JACK, sociology educator; b. N.Y.C., June 30, 1917; s. Sam and Rebecca (Block) E.; m. May Gomberg, July 5, 1941; children: Richard, Elaine, Mitchell, Robert. B.S., CCNY, 1937; M.A., George Washington U., 1946, Ph.D., 1954. Social sci. analyst Dept. Def., Washington, 1942-51; sr. study dir. Nat. Opinion Research Center, 1951-56; asst. prof. sociology U. Chgo., 1954-56; assoc. prof. adminstrv. medicine Columbia U., N.Y.C., 1956-64; prof. adminstrv. medicine Columbia U., 1964-68, prof. sociomed. scis. and sociology, 1968-86, prof. emeritus, 1986—; Service fellow Nat. Center Health Stats., 1977-81; vis. prof. behavioral scis. U. Toronto, 1969-77; Disting. vis. prof. Inst. Health Care Policy, Rutgers U., 1986-89, Disting. sr. scholar, 1990—; vis. prof. Robert Wood Johnson Med. Sch. (formerly Rutgers Med. Sch.), Univ. Medicine and Dentistry of N.J., 1986—; dir. program evaluation dept. patient care Harlem Hosp. Ctr., 1966-71; bd. dirs. Med. and Health Rsch. Assn., N.Y.C., 1977-89, Bergen County, N.J. Tb and Health Assn., 1960-65; mem. adminstrv. bd. Bur. Applied Social Rsch., Columbia U., 1970-75; co-dir. health care orgn. and adminstrn. track Program for Master's Degree in Pub. Health, Rutgers U.-U. Medicine and Dentistry of N.J., 1983-92. Author: (with R. E. Trussell) Chronic Illness in a Rural Area, 1959, (with J.J. Williams and R.E. Trussell) Family Medical Care under Three Types of Health Insurance, 1962, (with E. Padilla and M. Perkins) Public Image of Mental Health Services, 1967; editor: (with A.E. Siegmann) Sociomedical Health Indicators, 1979, (with A. Mooney and A. Siegmann) Health Goals and Health Indicators: Policy, Planning and Evaluation, 1977, (with N.K. Wenger, M.E. Mattson, and C.D. Furberg) Assessment of Quality of Life in Clinical Trials of Cardiovascular Therapies, 1984. Recipient nat. merit award Delta Omega Soc., 1982, Festschrift, spl. issue of Social Sci. and Medicine, 1989; Jack Elinson Sociomed. Scis. Libr. dedicated Columbia U. Sch. Pub. Health, 1998. Fellow Am. Sociol. Assn. (chmn. med. sociology, Leo G. Reeder award 1985), AAAS, APHA (1st award Assn. Social Scis. in Health 1984), Am. Assn. Pub. Opinion Rsch. (pres. 1979-80, Exceptionally Disting. Achievement award 1993); mem. Inst. of Medicine NAS, N.Y.C. Pub. Health Assn. (dir.), N.J. Pub. Health Assn. (exec. bd.Dennis J. Sullivan award 1990). Office: Columbia U Sch Pub Health Divsn Sociomed Scis 600 W 168th St New York NY 10032-3702

ELIOT, ALEXANDER, author, mythologist; b. Cambridge, Mass., Apr. 28, 1919; s. Samuel Atkins, Jr. and Ethel (Cook) E.; m. Jane Winslow Knapp, May 3, 1952; children: May Rose, Jefferson, Winslow. *Wife Jane Winslow Eliot is a travel writer, educator, and author of "Let's Talk, Let's Play," among other books. Daughter May Eliot Paddock is an educator involved in many good works. Son Jefferson Eliot is a noted theme park and museum designer. Daughter Winslow Eliot Stier is a novelist ("The Bright Face of Danger") published in seven languages.* Student, Black Mountain Coll., 1936-38, Boston Mus. Sch., 1938-39. Dir., Pinkney St. Artists Alliance, Boston, 1940-41; asst. to producer March of Time newsreel, 1941-42; asst. dir. films OWI, 1942-43; editor films (Coordinator Inter-Am. Affairs), 1943-45; art editor Time mag., 1945-60; prof. emeritus program Hampshire Coll., 1977. Editor Parabola mag., 1995-96; contbg. editor Harvard mag., 1988-95; author: Proud Youth, 1953, Three Hundred Years of American Painting, 1957, Sight and Insight, 1959, Earth, Air, Fire and Water, 1962, Greece, 1963, Love Play, 1966, Creatures of Arcadia, 1967, Socrates, 1967, A Concise History of Greece, 1972, Myths, 1976, Zen Edge, 1979, (with Jane Winslow Eliot) Fisher's Guide to Greece, 1984, Abraham Lincoln, 1985, The Universal Myths, 1990, The Global Myths, 1993, The Timeless Myths, 1996; (film with Jane Winslow Eliot) The Secret of Michaelangelo, Every Man's Dream, 1968. Guggenheim fellow, 1960; Japan Found. fellow, 1975. Mem. Century Assn., Soc. Am. Travel Writers, Dutch Treat Club (N.Y.C.). Home: 105 Paloma Ave Venice CA 90291-2572 *The moon, the planets, pass around my heart. The sun shines into me, and in me as well. Yet what am I? A goose-pimpled crazy on a skewed glass bicycle, continually crashing into scribbled walls. And this moment, this being is the thing.*

ELIOT, CHARLES WILLIAM JOHN, former university president; b. Rawalpindi, Pakistan, Dec. 8, 1928; s. William Edmund and Ann Catherine (McDougall) E.; m. Mary Williamson, Sept. 2, 1954; children: Charles, Sophia (dec.), Nicholas, Johanna, Luke. BA, U. Toronto, Ont., Can., 1949, MA, 1951, PhD, 1961; DCL, King's Coll., 1988. Lectr., asst. prof., assoc. prof., prof. U. B.C., Vancouver, Can., 1957-71; prof. archaeology Am. Sch. Classical Studies, Athens, Greece, 1971-76; prof. classics Mount Allison U., Sackville, N.B., Can., 1976-85, acad. v.p., 1981-83; pres. U. P.E.I., Charlottetown, Can., 1985-95; pres. emeritus U. P.E.I., 1996—; mem. Acad. Panel of the Social Scis. and Humanities Rsch., 1978-82, chmn., 1980-81. Author: Coastal Demes of Attika, 1962, Campaign of the Falieri and Piraeus in the Year 1827; or a Journal of a Volunteer, 1992. Contbr. revs. and articles to profl. jours. Mem. Sch. Bd. Dist. 14 N.B., 1983-85. Mem. Order of Can., 1994; scholar Am. Sch. Classical Studies, 1952-54, Can. Coun., 1965-66, Dumbarton Oaks, 1980, Social Scis. and Humanities Rsch. Coun. Can., 1984-85. Mem. Classical Assn. Can. (pres. 1992-94). Anglican. Avocations: works of John Galt.

ELIOT, LUCY, artist; b. N.Y.C., May 8, 1913; d. Ellsworth and Lucy Carter (Byrd) E. B.A., Vassar Coll., 1935; postgrad., Art Students League, 1935-40. tchr. painting and drawing Red Cross Bronx Vets. Hosp., N.Y.C., 1950, 51. Exhibited one-woman shows, Rochester Meml. Art Gallery, 1946, Cazenovia Coll., 1942, 47, 62, Syracuse Mus. Fine Arts, 1947, Wells Coll., 1953, Ft. Schuyler Club, Utica, N.Y., 1971, Nat. Shows, Pa. Acad. Fine Arts, Phila., 1946, 48, 49, 50, 52, 54, Corcoran Biennial, Washington, 1947, 51, Va. Biennial, Richmond, 1948, NAD, N.Y.C., 1971, 78, 90, Butler Inst. Am. Art, 1965, 67, 69, 70, 72, 74, 81, Cooperstown Art Assn. ann. exhbn., 1978, 80, 90; represented in permanent collections: Rochester Meml. Art Gallery, Munson-Williams-Proctor Inst., also pvt. collections. Bd. dirs. Artists Tech. Research Inst., 1975-79. Recipient First prize Rochester Meml. Art Gallery, 1946, Purchase prize Munson-Williams-Proctor Inst., 1949, Painting of Industry award Silvermine Guild, 1957, 1st prize in oils Cooperstown Art Assn., 1978. Mem. Nat. Assn. Women Artists (Moore-Greenblatt Meml. award 1993), N.Y. Soc. Women Artists, N.Y. Artists Equity, Audubon Artists (bd. dirs. oil 1983-85, chmn. award 1986-88, Elaine and James Hewitt award 1991, Michael M. Engel Meml. award 1994, Robert Philipp Meml. award 1995), Am. Soc. Contemporary Artists, Pen and Brush Club N.Y.C. (Liquitex Art award spring oil exhbn. 1989, 90, Cecilia Cardman Meml. award 1991, Grumbacher Art award Pen and Brush 1993), Cazenovia Club, Cosmopolitan Club. Episcopalian. Home: 131 E 66th St Apt 11G New York NY 10021-6129 also: 70 Sullivan St Cazenovia NY 13035-1038 *I feel that there has been slow but fairly steady improvement in my work as each painting has constituted a learning process (offering a better chance for the next.) I hope to be able to continue working for some time to come, as I have the same feeling now that I have had over the years: that I am just beginning to paint.**

ELITZUR, MOSHE, physicist, educator; b. Borzcow, Poland, Apr. 29, 1944; came to the U.S., 1977; s. Yechiel and Sofia (Brandwein) E.; m. Shlomit Yoskowitz, Apr. 7, 1970; children: Ofer, Haggai, Ben. BS, Hebrew U., Jerusalem, 1964; MSc, Weizman Inst., Rehovot, Israel, 1965; PhD, Weizmann Inst., Rehovot, Israel, 1971. Scientist Weizman Inst., 1973-75, sr. scientist, 1975-80; assoc. prof. U. Ky., Lexington, 1980-86, prof., 1986—. Author: Astronomical Masers, 1992. Lt. Israeli Army, 1965-70. NSF grantee, 1980—. Office: U Ky Dept Physics Astronomy Lexington KY 40506

ELIX, DOUGLAS THORNE, computer company executive; b. Adelaide, Australia, July 27, 1948; s. David Llewellyn and Margaret Thorne (Martin) E.; m. Robin Claire Wallace; children: Claire, Penelope, David, Sarah. Dir. banking region IBM Australia Ltd., 1987-89; dir. fin. industry IBM Asia Pacific, Tokyo, 1990-91; dir. of ops. IBM Australia Ltd., 1991-92, gen. mgr. fin. svcs., 1992-93, asst. mng. dir., CEO, 1993-96; dir. fin. industry IBM Asia Pacific, Tokyo, 1990-91; pres., CEO Integrated Sys. Solution Corp., Somers, N.Y., 1996; gen. mgr. IBM Global Svcs., N.A., 1997—; bd. dirs. IBM Global Svcs. Australia Ltd., Bus. Coun. Australia. Chmn. Roseville Coll. Found., Sydney, 1994—. Fellow Australian Inst. Mgmt. Office: IBM Global Svcs M/D 4305 Rt 100 Somers NY 10589

ELIXSON, E. MARSHA, pediatric cardiovascular consultant; b. Winthrop, Mass., Feb. 12, 1946; d. Toivo and Margaret Eva Elixson. Diploma, Children's Hosp. Med. Ctr., Boston, 1966; BSN, Salem State Coll., 1983; MS, Boston Coll., 1985. Lic. advance practice, clin. nurse specialist, cons. Advanced practice clin. nurse specialist Sibley Heart Ctr., Egleston Children's Hosp., Atlanta, 1998—; pediatric cardiac clin. nurse specialist Mass. Gen. Hosp., Boston, 1990-98; cons. Pediatric Critical Care Concepts, 1970-99; ICU specialist cardiovascular surgery Children's Hosp., Boston. Contbr. chpts. to books, articles, and profl. jours.; editl. bd. Critical Care Nursing Quar., Jour. Neonatal and Pediatric Critical Care, Mediplex. ICU cons. Project Hope, China. Mem. AACN (past pres. Greater Boston chpt.), N.E. Pediatric Cardiovascular Nurses Assn., Soc. Pediatric Cardiology Nurses, Soc. Critical Care, Am. Heart Assn. (PALS affiliate faculty, coun. cardiovascular nursing, chair pediat. subcom.), Soc. Critical Care (chair pediatric com.), S.E. Pediat. Cardiovascular Soc. Home: 1166 Mandalay Ct Lilburn GA 30047

ELIZABETH, HER MAJESTY II (ELIZABETH ALEXANDRA MARY), Queen of United Kingdom of Great Britain and Northern Ireland, and her other Realms and Territories, head of the Commonwealth, Defender of the Faith; b. Apr. 21, 1926; d. King George VI (formerly Duke of York) and Queen Elizabeth (formerly Duchess of York); m. Prince Philip, Duke of Edinburgh, Nov. 20, 1947; children: Charles Philip Arthur George, Anne Elizabeth Alice Louise, Andrew Albert Christian Edward, Edward Antony Richard Louis. Succeeded to throne following death of father, Feb. 6, 1952, crowned Queen, June 2, 1953. Address: Buckingham Palace, London SW1A 1AA, England

ELIZONDO, HECTOR, actor; b. N.Y.C., Dec. 22, 1936; s. Martin Echevarria and Carmen Medina (Reyes) E.; m. Carolee Campbell, Apr. 13, 1969; 1 son, Rodd. Student, CCNY, 1955-56, Ballet Arts Co. of Carnegie Hall. Appearances include (plays) The Price (Broadway), Drums in the Night, Steambath, 1970 (OBIE award), Prisoner of Second Avenue, 1974, The Great White Hope, 1977, Sly Fox (Dr. Desk-Nun award), Medal of Honor Rag, American Playhouse; (movies) Report to the Commissioner, 1975, The Taking of Pelham-1-2-3, 1975, Cuba, 1978, American Gigolo, 1979, The Fan, 1979, Young Doctors in Love, 1983, The Flamingo Kid, 1984, Nothing in Common, 1985, Leviathan, Pretty Woman, 1990 (Golden Globe nominee best supporting actor), Chains of Gold, Paydirt, Necessary Roughness, Frankie and Johnny, 1991, Being Human, 1992, Exit to Eden, 1993, Getting Even with Dad, 1993, Beverly Hills Cop III, 1993, Safe House, 1996, Turbulence, 1996, Dear God, 1996, Romy & Michelle, 1996, The Other Sister, 1998, Runaway Bride, 1998-99; (TV series) Popi, 1976, Freebie and the Bean, Foley Square, 1985, Great Performances, WCET, 1987, The Impatient Heart, All in the Family, Chicago Hope, 1994—; (TV films) Casablanca, Medal of Honor Rag, Mrs. Cage (Emmy nominee for best supporting actor), The Dain Curse, Courage, Honey Boy, Out of the Darkness, Death on a Day Pass, Natica Jackson, Addicted to His Love, Your Mother Wears Combat Boots, The Amnesty File, The Burden of Proof, Chicago Hope (winner Emmy best supporting 1997), Borrowed Hearts, CBS. Recipient Lifetime Achievement Image award, 1997, ALMA award for best actor, 1998. Mem. Amnesty Internat. Roman Catholic.

ELKES, TERRENCE ALLEN, communications executive; b. N.Y.C., Apr. 28, 1934; s. Sidney and Beatrice (Sachnin) E.; m. Ruth Jerkowsky, June 14, 1959; children: Steven Andrew, David Adam, Daniel Arthur. B.A. cum laude, CCNY, 1955; J.D., U. Mich., 1958. Bar: N.Y. 1959. Atty. Prentice Hall, Inc., 1958-59; counsel internat. div. Norwich Pharmacal Co., 1959-65; corp. counsel, also v.p., sec. Parsons & Whittemore, Inc., 1965-72; corp. counsel Black Clawson Co., 1965-72; treas. Prince Albert Pulp Co. Ltd., 1966-72; v.p., sec., gen. counsel Viacom Internat., Inc., N.Y.C., 1972-76, exec. v.p., 1976-78, pres., 1978-87, chief exec. officer, 1984-87; prin. Apollo Ptnrs., Ltd., N.Y.C., Conn., 1987—; bd. dirs. IDC Svcs. Corp., Doane Agrl. Svcs., Inc., Entertainment Ptnrs., Newstar Media Inc.; mng. dir. Apollo Radio, Ltd., 1989-96; chmn. Transmedia Ptnrs. Ltd., Compact Video Corp., 1991-93, Internat. Post Ltd., 1994-97; chmn. Video Svcs. Corp., 1997—. Trustee U. Mich. Law Sch., 1992, mem. pres. adv. group U. Mich., 1992, mem. investment adv. group & tech. transfer group, 1992. Mem. ABA, N.Y. State Bar Assn., Assn. of Bar of City of N.Y., Internat. Radio and TV Soc. (bd. govs.). Home: 12 Trails End Rye NY 10580-2227 Office: Apollo Ptnrs Ltd 500 5th Ave New York NY 10110

EL KHADEM, HASSAN SAAD, chemistry educator, researcher; b. Cairo, Mar. 24, 1923; naturalized, 1975; s. Saad S. and Nimet (Zulficar) El K.; m. Nadia M. Said, Sept. 6, 1951; children: Samiha, Saad. DSc Tech., ETH Zurich, Switzerland, 1950; PhD, Imperial Coll., London, 1952; DSc, U. London, 1967; BSc with honors, Cairo U., 1946; DSc, U. Alexandria (Arab Republic of Egypt), 1963. Lectr. Alexandria U., 1952-58, asst. prof., 1958-64, prof. organic chemistry, 1964-71; prof. chemistry Michigan Tech. U., Houghton, 1971-74; head dept. chemistry and chem. engring. Mich. Tech. U., Houghton, 1974-80, pres. prof. chemistry, 1980-84; Isbell prof. chemistry The Am. U., Washington, 1984-93, Isbell prof. chemistry emeritus, 1993—. Mem. editorial bd. Carbohydrate Rsch., 1966-92; contbr. over 160 articles on carbohydrates and medicinal chemistry to profl. jours.; author 15 books including Carbohydrate Chemistry: Monosaccharides and their Oligomers, Synthetic Methods for Carbohydrates, Anthracycline Antibiotics; patentee in field. Fulbright scholar U.S. Dept. State, Ohio State U., Columbus, 1963-64; recipient Phys. Sci. award Washington Acad. Sci., 1992. Mem. AAAS, Am. Chem. Soc. (chmn. carbonhydrate div. 1984-85, Melville L. Wolfrom award 1989), Sigma Xi. Achievements include discovery of a lost Greek manuscript by Zosimos (300 A.D.) translated to Arabic in a twelveth century Alchemy book (donated to the Libr. of Congress). Home: 4948 Sentinel Dr Apt 101 Bethesda MD 20816-3586 Office: Am U Dept Chemistry Beeghly Bldg 4400 Massachusetts Ave NW Washington DC 20016-8001 *One reason why most students stop asking questions in class is that they do not get good answers.*

ELKHADEM, SAAD ELDIN AMIN, foreign language and literature educator, author, editor, publisher; b. Cairo, May 12, 1932; emigrated to Can., 1968, naturalized, 1974; s. Amin Saad and Zahra Amin (Tharwat) E.; m. Madiha Mahmoud, July 16, 1962; 1 child, Sherifa. Ph.D., U. Graz, 1961. Press attache Egyptian Govt., Berne, 1962-65; dir. Office for Cultural Relations, Cairo, 1965-67; asst. prof. U. N.D., Grand Forks, 1967-68; assoc. prof. German U. N.B., Fredericton, Can., 1968-74, prof. dept. German and Russian, 1974-95, prof. emeritus, 1995—. Author: Sechs Essays ueber den deutschen Roman, 1969, Ajniha Min Rasas, 1972, Zur Geschichte des deutschen Romans, 1974, Tajarib Laylah Wahidah, 1975, Dictionary of Literary Terms, 1976, The York Press Style manual, From Travels of the Egyptian Odysseus, 1979, The York Companion to Themes and Motifs of World Literature, 1981, History of the Egyptian Novel, 1985, Ulysses' Hallucinations or the Like, 1985, The Ulysses Trilogy, 1988, The Plague, 1988, Canadian Adventures of the Flying Egyptian, 1990, Chronicle of the Flying Egyptian in Canada, 1991, The Concise Dictionary of Greek, Roman, Norse and Egyptian Mythology, 1991, Crash Landing of the Flying Egyptian, 1992, Wings of a Lead: A Modern Egyptian Novella, 1994, Five Innovative Egyptian Short Stories, 1994, An Egyptian Satire about a Condemned Building, 1996, The Blessed Movement: An Egyptian Micronovel, 1997, The Great Egyptian Novel, 1998; editor Internat. Fiction Rev., 1974-96; editor, gen. mgr. York Press, (also transl.) Life is Like a Cucumber: Colloquial Egyptian Proverbs, 1993, The Sayings of the Prophet Muhammad, 1994; gen. editor Authoritative Studies in World Literature; contbr. articles to profl. jours. Can. Council grantee, 1974-75; recipient Min. of State multiculturalism awards, 1989, 90. Mem. MLA, Writer's Union Can. Home: 152 Boardwalk Dr, Toronto, ON Canada M4L3X4

ELKIES, NOAM D., mathematics educator. Prof. dept. math. Harvard U., Cambridge, Mass. Recipient NAS award for Initiatives in Rsch. Nat. Acad. Sci., 1991. Office: Harvard U Sci Bldg/Dept Math 1 Oxford St Cambridge MA 02138*

ELKIN, JEFFREY H., lawyer; b. Bklyn., Jan. 24, 1946. BA, Am. U., 1967, JD cum laude, 1971. Bar: N.Y. 1971, D.C. 1972. Ptnr. Winston & Strawn, N.Y.C. Mem. ABA, N.Y. State Bar Assn., N.Y. County Lawyers Assn., Pi Gamma Mu, Pi Sigma Alpha, Phi Alpha Delta. Office: Winston & Strawn 200 Park Ave Rm 4100 New York NY 10166-0005*

ELKIN, LOIS SHANMAN, business systems company executive; b. Cin., Oct. 31, 1937; d. Jerome David and Mildred Louise (Bloch) Shanman; m. Alan I. Elkin, May 6, 1962; children: Karen A., Jeffrey R. BA in Math., Goucher Coll., 1959. Sys. engr. ea. region IBM, Balt. and Columbia, S.C., 1959-61, mgr. Computer Test Ctr. ea. region, 1961-64; exec. v.p. Advance Bus. Sys., Balt., 1964—, A&L Real Estate, Balt., 1970—; pres. Our World Gallery, Inc., Balt., 1995—; part owner, bd. dirs. ATMS, Balt., 1994—; mentor for math. and bus. Goucher Coll., Balt., 1982-86; guest lectr. MBA program Loyola Coll. Md., Balt., 1993-94, Towson U.; mem. steering com. Loyola Ctr. for Closely Held Cos., Balt., 1993—; bd. dirs. Hunt Valley Bus. Forum, Balt., The Hearing and Speech Agy. Balt. Vol. House of Ruth, Balt., 1990—, Image Recovery Ctr., Union Meml. Hosp., Balt., 1995—; exec. bd. dirs. Pride of Balt. II, 1994—; bd. dirs. Hearing and Speech Agy. Balt.; co-chair Multiple Sclerosis Class of '98 fundraiser, 1998. Recipient AAA Torch award for ethics inbus., 1997; named one of Top 500 Women-Owned Businesses in U.S., Working Woman Mag., 1998, 99, Mds. Top 100 Women for 1999. Mem. Nat. Assn. Women Bus. Owners (Woman of Yr. award Balt. chpt. 1985). Avocation: collecting art. Office: Advance Bus Sys 10755 York Rd Cockeysville Hunt Valley MD 21030-2114

ELKIN, MILTON, radiologist, physician, educator; b. Boston, Feb. 24, 1916; s. Philip and Rose (Dexter) E.; m. Gloria King, Nov. 12, 1943; children: Philip, Karen, Laura. A.B., Harvard Coll., 1937; M.D., Harvard U. Med. Sch., 1941. Diplomate Am. Bd. Radiology (trustee 1983-95). Assoc. radiologist Peter Bent Brigham Hosp., Boston, 1951-52; dir. radiology Cambridge (Mass.) City Hosp.; asst. radiologist New Eng. Med. Ctr., Boston, 1952-53; assoc. radiologist Cedars of Lebanon Hosp., L.A., 1953-54; prof., chmn. dept. radiology Albert Einstein Coll. Medicine, Yeshiva U., N.Y.C., 1954-86, prof., 1986—; dir. radiology Jacobi Med. Ctr., N.Y.C., 1954-86; attending radiologist Bronx Municipal Hosp. Center, N.Y.C., 1986—; spl. cons. radiology tng. com. Nat. Inst. Gen. Med. Scis., NIH, USPHS, 1966-70; cons. Gen. Med. Research Program-Project Com., 1970-72; radiology rep. to Council Med. Splty. Socs., 1976-81; mem. Residency Rev. Com. for Radiology, 1986-92. Author: Radiology of the Urinary System, 1980, Plain Film Approach to Abdominal Calcifications, 1983; Contbr. articles to profl. jours. Fellow Am. Coll. Radiology (bd. chancellors 1970-76, gold medal 1977); mem. AMA, Harvard Med. Soc., Am. Roentgen Ray Soc., Radiol. Soc. N.Am. (dir. 1975-82, chmn. bd. 1978-79, pres. 1980-81, Gold medal 1985), Assn. Univ. Radiologists, N.Y. Roentgen Soc. (pres.), Soc. Uroradiology (Gold medal 1998). Home: 13 Kingston Rd Scarsdale NY 10583-1148 Office: 1300 Morris Park Ave Bronx NY 10461-1926

ELKIND, DAVID, psychology educator; b. Detroit, Mar. 11, 1931; s. Peter and Bessie (Nelson) E.; children: Paul Steven, Robert Edward, Eric Allen. BA, UCLA, 1952, PhD, 1955; DSc (hon.), R.I. Coll., 1987. Diplomate: Am. Bd. Profl. Examiners in Psychology. Research asst. to David Rapaport, Austen Riggs Ctr., Stockbridge, Mass., 1956-57; staff psychologist Beth Israel Hosp., Boston, 1957-59; asst. prof. Wheaton Coll., Norton, Mass., 1959-61; asst. prof. med. psychology U. Calif. Med. Sch., Los Angeles, 1961-62; assoc. prof., dir. Child Study Ctr., U. Denver, 1962-66; prof., dir. grad. tng. in developmental psychology, dept. psychology U. Rochester, N.Y., 1966-78; chmn. Eliot Pearson dept. child devel. Tufts U., Medford, Mass., 1978-83; prof. child devel. sr. resident scholar Lincoln Filene Ctr. Eliot Pearson dept. child study Tufts U., Medford, Mass.; research dir. World of Inquiry Evaluation-NSF, 1970; project dir. Tng. of Early Childhood Specialists, U.S. Office Edn., 1970; psychol. cons. VA, 1962-74, Rochester Mental Health Center, 1966-74, Rochester Family Ct., 1967-73; headmaster Mt. Hope Sch., Rochester, 1974-77; co-host Lifetime TV series "Kids These Days". Author: (with H.J. Flavell) Studies in Cognitive Development, 1969, Children and Adolescents, 1974, A Sympathetic Understanding of the Child, 1974, (with I. Weiner) Child Development: A Core Approach, 1972, (with others) Psychology: An Introduction, 1973, Child Development and Education, 1976, (with D. Hetzel) Readings in Human Development: Contemporary Perspectives, (with I. Weiner) Development of the Child, 1978, The Child's Reality: Three Developmental Themes, 1978, The Child and Society, 1979, The Hurried Child, 1981, All Grown Up and No Place to Go, 1984, Miseducation: Preschoolers at Risk, 1987, Grandparenting: Understanding Today's Children, 1988; editor: Perspectives in Early Childhood Education, 1991, Parenting Your Teenager in the Nineties, 1993, Images of the Young Child, 1993, Understanding Your Child, 1994, A Sympathetic Understanding of the Child Birth to Sixteen, 1994, Ties that Stress: The New Family Imbalance, 1994, Reinventing Childhood, 1998. NSF Sr. Postdoctoral fellow Geneva, 1964-65. Fellow Am. Psychol. Assn. (recipient Nicholas Hobbs Award div. 26), AAAS, Nat. Assn. Edn. of Young Children (pres. 1986-88). Home: 7 Lloyd Ln East Sandwich MA 02537-1225 Office: Tufts U Dept Child Devel Medford MA 02155

ELKIND, ELIZABETH C., perinatal clinical specialist; b. Stamford, Conn., Feb. 8, 1961; m. Gary Neil Elkind, June 17, 1984; children: Andrew, Danyelle, Kaitlyn. BSN, Holy Family Coll., 1983; MSN in Perinatal Nursing, U. Pa., 1987; MBA, U. Phoenix, 1997. RN, Pa., N.J.; cert. inpatient obstetrics; cert. childbirth educator. Staff/charge nurse mother-infant unit Einstein Med. Ctr., Phila., 1983-85; staff/charge nurse labor and delivery Cooper Med. Ctr., Camden, N.J., 1985-87; perinatal clin. specialist Underwood-Meml. Hosp., Woodbury, N.J., 1987-90; perinatal clin. specialist Our Lady of Lourdes Med. Ctr., Camden, N.J., 1990-97, info. svc. clin. sys. analyst, 1997—. Mem. Assn. Women's Health, Obstetrics and Neonatal Nursing (co-chmn. edn. com. N.J. sect. 1990-94, vice chmn. 1995-97, N.J. sec./treas. 1998—). Office: Our Lady of Lourdes Med Ctr Info Svcs 1600 Haddon Ave Camden NJ 08103-3101

ELKIND, MORT WILLIAM, creative and business consultant; b. N.Y.C., Sept. 10, 1925; s. Samuel William and Leah Fannie (Meschen) E.; m. Mary Johanna Ruggiero, June 10, 1962; children: Lori Ann, Susan Marie, Edward William. BS in Chemistry summa cum laude, U. S.W. La., 1949; MS Analytical Chemistry, La. State U., 1951; postgrad., Georgetown U. Inst. Lang. & Linguistics, 1952, UCLA, 1954-55; Berkeley Coll., 1991-92. Intelligence officer CIA, Washington, 1952-53; head waiter Scaroon Manor Hotel, Schroon Lake, N.Y., 1956-57; copywriter J. B. Rundle; Sanders & Lowen; Cayton, Inc., N.Y.C., 1959-65; dir. profl. rels. Kings County Rsch. Labs., Bklyn., 1965-67; copywriter L.W. Frohlich, N.Y.C., 1967-74; sr. copywriter William Douglas McAdams, N.Y.C., 1974-76; copy supr. Kallir, Philips, Ross, Inc., N.Y.C., 1976-85; cons. Chestnut Ridge, N.Y., 1965—; co-founder Photocell Corp. of Am., 1965, Screen Features, Inc., 1966; founder, prin. MWE Assocs. Advt., 1970; co-founder Quadrisec, Inc., 1980, Modular Exports, Inc., 1988; v.p. mktg. Am. Investor Note Paper Corp., N.Y.C., 1985-86; dir. mktg. Air Baby, Inc., Blauvelt, N.Y., 1990-91. Author: Internecine, 1957; editor: McNeil Psychiatric Calendar, 1978-83; writer, producer: (TV series) Billy Bang-Bang, 1966-68; creator: (film) The Internecine Project, 1974, (TV series) Bringing Up Kids, 1989 (Disting. mem. Internat. Soc. Poets 1994). Polit. cons. N.Y. State Senator, Rockland County and Albany, N.Y., 1978-80. Sgt. C.E., U.S. Army, 1943-46, ETO. Named to U. S.W. La. Athletic Hall of Fame, 1978; recipient Andy award N.Y. Advt. Club, 1979. Mem. Internat. Soc. Poets (Disting. mem.), Blue Key, Phi Kappa Phi, Phi Lambda Upsilon. Avocations: reading, writing, math problem solving.

ELKIND, MORTIMER MURRAY, biophysicist, educator; b. Bklyn., Oct. 25, 1922; s. Samuel and Yetta (Lubarsky) E.; m. Karla Annikki Holst, Jan. 27, 1960; children—Sean Thomas, Samuel Scott, Jonathan Harald. BME, Cooper Union, 1943; MME, Poly. Inst., Bklyn., 1949; MS in Physics, MIT, 1951, PhD in Physics, 1953. Asst. project engr. Wyssmont Co., N.Y.C., 1943; project engr. Safe Flight Instrument Corp., White Plains, N.Y., 1946-47; head instrumentation sect. Sloan Kettering Inst. Cancer Rsch., 1947-49; physicist Nat. Cancer Inst. on assignment to MIT, 1949-53; on assignment to Donner Lab. U. Calif., Berkeley, 1953-54; physicist Lab. Physiology, Nat. Cancer Inst., Bethesda, Md., 1954-67; sr. research physicist Lab. Physiology, Nat. Cancer Inst., 1967-69; sr. biophysicist biology dept. Brookhaven Nat. Lab., Upton, L.I., N.Y., 1969-73; guest scientist MRC exptl. radiopathology unit Hammersmith Hosp., London, 1971-73; sr. biophysicist, divsn. biol. and med. rsch. Argonne (Ill.) Nat. Lab., 1973-76, from asst. dir. to head mammalian cell biology group, 1976-81; prof. radiology U. Chgo., 1973-82; prof., chmn. dept. radiology and radiation biology Colo. State U., 1981-89, Disting. prof. dept. radiological health scis., 1986—; radiation study sect. NIH, 1962-66, molecular biology study sect., 1970-71; mem. developmental therapeutics com. Nat. Cancer Inst., 1975-77. Author monograph. With USNR, 1944-46. Recipient E.O. Lawrence award AEC, 1967, Superior Service award HEW, 1969, L.H. Gray medal Internat. Com. Radiation Units and Measurements, 1977, E.W. Bertner award M.D. Anderson Hosp. and Tumor Inst., 1979, A.W. Erskine award Radiol. Soc. N. Am., 1980, Albert Soiland Meml. award Albert Soiland Cancer Found., 1984, 1st Henry S. Kaplan Disting. Scientist award Internat. Assn. Radiation Research, 1987, Charles F. Kettering prize Gen. Motors Cancer Rsch. Found., 1989, Honor Scientist award Colo. State U. chpt. Sigma Xi, 1991, Roentgen-Plakette award, 1997, Fermi award U.S. Dept. Energy, 1997, Third Kligerman award U. Pa., 1998; Outstanding Investigator grantee Nat. Cancer Inst., 1988; Nat. Cancer Inst. Spl. fellow, 1972-74. Fellow Am. Coll. Radiology (hon.); mem. AAAS, Biophys. Soc., Radiation Research Soc. (council 1965-66, assoc. editor jour. 1965-68, pres.-elect and pres. 1980-81, G. Failla Meml. award 1984), Am. Assn. Cancer Research (assoc. editor jour. 1980-81), Am. Soc. Therapeutic Radiology and Oncology (gold medalist 1983), Tau Beta Pi. Office: Colo State U Dept Radiol Health Sci Fort Collins CO 80523-1673

ELKINGTON, STEVE, professional golfer; b. Inverell, Australia, Dec. 8, 1962; m. Lisa Elkington. Grad., U. Houston, 1985. Winner Players Championship, 1991, Kmart Greater Greensboro Open, 1990, Infiniti Tournament Open, 1992, Buick Southern Open, 1994, Mercedes Championships, 1995, PGA Championships, 1995, Doral-Ryder Open, 1997, 99, Buick Challenge, 1998; mem. Pres. Cup Team, 1994. 3 time winner PGA Tour. Office: care PGA Tour 112 Tpc Blvd Ponte Vedra Beach FL 32082-3046 Office: PGA America PO Box 109601 100 Ave of The Champions Palm Beach Gardens FL 33410*

ELKINS, DAVID J., political science educator; b. Ft. Madison, Iowa, July 29, 1941. BA, Yale U., 1963; MA, U. Calif., Berkeley, 1964, PhD, 1971. Asst. prof. polit. sci. U. B.C., Vancouver, Can., 1969-75, assoc. prof., 1975-80, prof., 1980—, head dept. polit. sci., 1985-89; acting dean of arts U. B.C., Vancouver, 1989-90; vis. prof. Queen's U., Kingston, Ont., Can., 1984-85, U. Toronto, 1991. Author: Electoral Participation in a South Indian Context, 1975, Manipulation and Consent, 1993, Beyond Sovereignty, 1995; co-author: Survey Research, 1976, Small Worlds, 1980, Two Political Worlds, 1985; contbr. articles to profl. jours. Mem. Assn. Can. Studies Austrialia and New Zealand, Am. Polit. Sci. Assn., Am. Assn. Pub. Opinion Research, Can. Polit. Sci. Assn. (pres. 1988-89), Australasian Polit. Sci. Assn., Can. Civil Liberties Union, Can. Wildlife Fedn. Avocations: skiing, hiking. Home: 1904 Rivergrove Pl, North Vancouver, BC Canada V7H 2L4 Office: Univ BC, Dept Polit Sci, Vancouver, BC Canada V6T 1Z1

ELKINS, DONALD MARCUM, dean, agronomy educator; b. Woodville, Ala., Sept. 15, 1940; s. Lotus Marcum and Una (Troup) E.; m. Earline Mizell, Feb. 16, 1963; children: Mark Willis, Daniel Joseph. BS, Tenn. Polytech. Inst., 1962; MS, Auburn U., 1964, PhD, 1967. Rsch. asst., NASA fellow Auburn (Ala.) U., 1965-67; asst. prof. So. Ill. U., Carbondale, 1967-71, assoc. prof., 1971-74, prof., 1974—, assoc. dean for acad. programs, 1985-95; dean Coll. Agr. and Human Ecology Tenn. Technol. U., Cookeville, Tenn., 1995—; advisor Agr. Students Adv. Coun., 1985-95; chmn. North Ctrl. Region Deans and Dirs. Resident Instrn., 1990-91. Author: (with others) Growth Regulating Chemicals, 1982; co-author Crop Production Principles and Practices, 4th edit., 1980; author: Crop Science Laboratory Studies, 1990; contbr. articles to jours. in field. Fellow Am. Soc. Agronomy (resident edn. com. 1981, fellow award 1987); mem. Nat. Assn. Colls. and Tchrs. Agr. (Outstanding Tchr. award 1978), Ambassadors Club (advisor 1986-95), AG/HEC Ambs. Club (advisor 1995—), Sigma Xi, Phi Kappa Phi, Alpha Zeta, Alpha Gamma Rho (hon.), Omicron Delta Kappa (faculty sec. 1996—), Lambda Alpha Sigma (advisor 1996-97), others. Republican. Mem. Ch. of Christ. Home: 980 Woodwinds Dr Cookeville TN 38501-4000

ELKINS, FRANCIS CLARK, history educator, university official; b. Scranton, Ark., Feb. 24, 1923; s. Frank and Auby (Moore) E.; m. Norma Trice, Aug. 18, 1946; 1 dau., Annette. BA, U. Cen. Ark., 1943; MA, U. Ark., 1947; PhD, Syracuse U., 1953; postdoctoral, U. Minn., 1956. From instr. to prof., chmn. div. social sci. Henderson State U., Arkadelphia, Ark., 1946-61; pres. Chadron (Nebr.) State Coll., 1961-67, N.E. Mo. State Coll., Kirksville, 1967-69; coordinator Univ. Coll., Ark State U., 1969-70, v.p. instrn., 1970-78, v.p. univ. relations, 1979-80; v.p. univ. relations and devel. No. Ariz. U., Flagstaff, 1980-83, prof. history, 1980-88, president's coord. univ. rels., 1983-88; edn. cons., 1988—; mem. exec. com. Rocky Mountain Edn. Lab., 1965-67; examiner North Cen. Assn. Colls. and Schs.; examiner, cons. Nat. Council Accreditation Tchr. Edn., chmn. visitation and appraisal com., 1963-68; mem. Nebr. Ednl. TV Council Higher Edn., 1966-67, Ark. Council Econ. Edn., 1970-81. Mem. adv. coun. Mo. 4-H Found., 1968-69; mem. Ark Adv. Coun. on Career Edn.; bd. dirs. United Way, 1980-88. Served with USAAF, 1943-45. Decorated D.F.C., Air medal with four oak leaf clusters; recipient John Vaughn Excellence in Edn. award North Cen. Assn. Colls. and Schs. Commn. on Schs., 1988, Disting. Svc. award Chadron (Nebr.) State Coll., 1989. Mem. NEA (life), Am. Assn. Colls. for Tchr. Edn. (dir. 1968-71, state liaison rep. 1974-77), Assn. Orgns. Tchr. Edn. (adv. coun.), Ark. Edn. Assn. (life), Ark. Assn. Colls. for Tchr. Edn. (charter pres. 1973-75), Flagstaff C. of C. (dir. 1980-88), Craighead County Hist. Assn. (life), Elks, Rotary Internat. (Paul Harris fellow), Phi Delta Kappa, Kappa Delta Pi, Phi Alpha Theta, Alpha Chi, Phi Kappa Phi, Sigma Tau Gamma, Sigma Nu. Methodist. Home and Office: 3004 Hillridge Cv Jonesboro AR 72401-5937

ELKINS, GLEN RAY, service company executive; b. Winnsboro, La., May 23, 1933; s. Ceicel Herbert and Edna Mae (Luallen) E.; m. Irene Kay Hildebrand, Aug. 25, 1951; children: Steven Breen, Douglas Charles, Karen Anne, Michael Glen; m. Diane Hodgson, Mar. 2, 1992. AA in Indsl. Mgmt, Coll. San Mateo, 1958. Successively mgr. production control, mgr. logistics, plant mgr., asst. v.p. ops. Aircraft Engring. and Maintenance Co. (Aemco), 1957-64; successively mgr. field ops., v.p. ops., exec. v.p., pres. Internat. Atlas Svcs. Co., Princeton, N.J., 1964-85; sr. v.p. Atlas Corp., Princeton; chmn., chief exec. officer, dir. Global Assocs., 1973-85; pres. Global Assocs. Internat. Ltd., 1975-84; pres., chief exec. officer Triad Am. Svcs. Corp., 1985—; pres. Pacific Mgmt. Svcs. Corp., TASC Enterprises Inc., dba Gottschall Engraving Co., 1993—. Area chmn. Easter Seals drive, 1974; bd. dirs. Utah Children's Mus. With USN, 1950-54. Mem. Nat. Mgmt. Assn., Electronic Industries Assn., Lakeview Club, Willow Creek Country Club (bd. dirs.). Home: 1445 Harvard Ave Salt Lake City UT 84105-1917 Office: 388 Ironwood Dr Salt Lake City UT 84115-2913

ELKINS, JAMES ANDERSON, JR., banker; b. Galveston, Tex., Mar. 24, 1919; s. James Anderson and Isabel (Mitchell) E.; m. Margaret Wiess, Nov. 24, 1945; children—Elise, James Anderson III, Leslie K. B.A., Princeton U., 1941. With First City Nat. Bank, Houston, 1941—, v.p., 1946-50, pres. then chmn. bd., 1950-82; dir. First City Bancorp., Houston, 1982-88; bd. dirs. Central Houston Inc. Bd. dirs. Houston Grand Opera; trustee Tex. Children's Hosp., Tex. Med. Ctr., 1991; chmn. bd. trustees Baylor Coll. Medicine, 1970—; trustee Menil Found.; mem. vestry Christ Ch. Cathedral. Episcopalian. Address: 1001 Fannin St Ste 1166 Houston TX 77002-6708

ELKINS, JAMES ANDERSON, III, investment banker; b. Houston, May 21, 1952; s. James Anderson Jr. and Margaret K. (Wiess) E.; m. Mary Virginia Arnold, Dec. 8, 1984; children: Margaret Wiess, James Anderson IV, Buck Arnold, John Caldwell, Harry Carothers, Samuel Hill, Lucy Gray. BA, Princeton U., 1974; MBA, U. Tex., 1976. Asst. treas. Morgan Guaranty Trust Co., N.Y.C., 1976-79; exec. v.p. First City Tex., Houston, 1979-93; chmn. Houston Trust Co., 1994—. Bd. govs. Rice U., Houston, 1982—; pres. Tex. Children's Hosp., Houston, 1997—, trustee, 1989—; trustee Children's Mus., Houston, 1988—, Houston Mus. Natural Sci., 1993—, Houston Zool. Soc., 1993—; bd. advisors U. Tex. Health Sci. Ctr., Houston, 1990; vice chmn. Salvation Army, 1990—; treas. Houston Parks Bd. Mem. Am. Bankers Assn. (exec. bd. corp. council), Houston Club, Robert Morris Assocs., Tex. Bankers Assn., Forum Club. Methodist. Office: Houston Trust Co 1001 Fannin St Ste 700 Houston TX 77002-6777

ELKINS, JAMES PAUL, physician; b. Lincoln, Nebr., Mar. 20, 1924; s. James Hill and Antonia (Wohler) E.; MD, U. Va., 1947; m. May Hollingsworth Reynolds, June 15, 1946; children—Patricia May Elkins Riggs, Paulette Frances Elkins Rhinesmith, James Barrington. Cert. Emergency Med. Svcs. Commn. Intern, DePaul Hosp., Norfolk, Va., 1947-48; resident in ob-gyn Alexandria (Va.) Hosp., 1948-49, Franklin Sq. Hosp., Balt., 1949-50, St. Rita's Hosp., Lima, Ohio, 1950, Tripler Army Hosp., Honolulu, 1953-54; practice medicine specializing in ob-gyn, Indpls., 1954-73; chief ob-gyn St. Francis Hosp., Beech Grove, Ind., 1965-66; mem. teaching staff Gen. Hosp., Indpls., 1954-73; dep. coroner Marion County, 1965-74; ret. med. cons. disability determination div. Ind. Rehab. Svcs.; ringside physician Ind. State Athletic Commn., Ind. Golden Gloves, Indpls. Pal Club, 1976-86; retired med. cons. Served with AUS, 1949-54. Recipient Fred Deborde Award Ind. Golden Gloves, 1985. Mem. Am. Coll. Ob-Gyn, Ind. State Med. Assn., Marion County Med. Soc., Indpls. Press Club (hon. life), Police League Ind., Fraternal Order Police, Nat. Sojourners, Ind. Sports Corp. (charter gold mem.), U.S. Auto Club (life), Phi Chi. Clubs: Ind. Pacers Booster (charter), Thundering Herd Booster Indpls. Colts (charter mem.). Lodges: Masons, Shriners (life). Home: 11603 Boone Dr Indianapolis IN 46229-9610

ELKINS, KEN JOE, broadcasting executive; b. Prenter, W.Va., Oct. 12, 1937; s. Ernest Eugene Elkins and Gay (Avis) Dodrill; married; children: James, Diana. Student, Nebr. U., 1966-69. Engr. Sta. KETV-TV, Omaha, 1960-67, asst. chief engr., 1967-70, ops. mgr., nat. sales, gen. sales mgr., 1972-75, gen. mgr., 1975-80; chief engr. Sta. KOUB-TV, Dubuque, Iowa, 1970-71, gen. mgr., 1971-72; gen. mgr. Sta. KSDK-TV, St. Louis, 1980-81; v.p., CEO Pulitzer Broadcasting Co., St. Louis, 1981-84, pres., CEO, 1984—; bd. dirs. Commerce Bank St. Louis, Maximum Svc. Telecasters, Washington, BMI; pres. Nebr. Broadcasters, Omaha, 1979-80; chmn. NBC Affiliate Bd. Govs. Bd. dirs. BJC Health Sys. With USAF, 1957-61. Inducted into Nebr. Broadcasters Hall of Fame, 1990. Mem. Nat. Assn. Broadcasters (1st amendment com. Washington chpt. 1986-91, 1st amendment com. 1986, bd. dirs.), Found. Broadcasters Hall of Fame (bd. dirs., trustee 1990), TV Operators Caucus, Algonquin Club. Avocations: golf, water sports. Home: 720 Twin Fawns Dr Saint Louis MO 63131-4722 Office: Pulitzer Broadcasting Co 101 S Hanley Rd Ste 1250 Saint Louis MO 63105-3428

ELKINS, LINCOLN FELTCH, petroleum engineering consultant; b. Denver, Feb. 12, 1918; s. Edwin and Beulah M. (Feltch) Elkins; m. Ruth Gordon, June 23, 1942; children : Gordon, Robert, Marc. Degree in Petroleum Engring., Colo. Sch. Mines, 1940. Research engr. Amoco Prodn. Co., Tulsa, 1941-45; prodn. engr. Conoco, Ponca City, Okla., 1945-47; from tech. advisor to chief engr. to sr. cons. engr. Sohio Petroleum Co., Oklahoma City, 1947-83; cons. Oklahoma City, 1983-87, Lakewood, Colo., 1987—. Active bd. adjustment, Oklahoma City, 1973-82. Recipient Disting. Achievement medal Colo. Sch. Mines, 1965. Mem. soc. Petroleum Engrs. (pres. 1965, DeGolyer Disting. Service medal 1971), Nat. Acad. Engrs., AIME (hon., Lucas Gold medal 1992), SPE. Republican. Presbyterian. Home: 2615 Oak Dr Apt 28 Lakewood CO 80215-7182

ELKINS, LLOYD EDWIN, SR., petroleum engineer, energy consultant; b. Golden, Colo., Apr. 1, 1912; s. Edwin and Beulah M. (Feltch) E.; m. Virginia L. Crosby, May 27, 1934; children: Marylou, Barbara Lee, Lloyd Edwin Jr. Degree in Petroleum Engring., Colo. Sch. Mines, 1934; PhD in Sci., U. Ozarks. With Amoco Prodn. Co., 1934-77; successively field engr., petroleum engr. Tulsa gen. office, sr. petroleum engr., petroleum engring. supr., asst. chief prodn. engr., chief prodn. engr., mgr. prodn. rsch., 1949-77; energy cons., 1977-97. Contbr. articles to profl. jours. Named to Engring. Hall of Fame Okla. State U., 1961; recipient Distinguished Service medal Colo. Sch. Mines, 1961; named to Engring. Hall of Fame U. Tulsa. Mem. Am. Assn. Petroleum Geologists, Am. Petroleum Inst. (chmn. mid-continent dist. div. prodn. 1948-49, chmn. adv. com fundamental research on occurrence and recovery petroleum 1941), Am. Inst. Mining, Metall. and Petroleum Engrs. (hon., v.p. 1953-59, pres. 1962, Anthony F. Lucas gold medal 1966), Nat. Acad. Engring., Tulsa Geol. Soc., Australian Inst. Mining and Metallurgy (hon.). Methodist. Clubs: Engineers (Tulsa) (pres. 1950-51), Petroleum (Tulsa), Tulsa Country (Tulsa). Home and Office: 5 Primrose Pl Amarillo TX 79106-4000

ELKINS, S. GORDON, lawyer; b. Phila., Dec. 21, 1930; m. Ethel Bronstein, June 16, 1957; children: Tod, Adam, Peter, Douglas. BS, Temple U., 1952; LLB, Yale U., 1955. Bar: Pa. 1956, U.S. Dist. Ct. (ea. dist.) Pa. 1956, U.S. Ct. Appeals (3d cir.) 1956, U.S. Ct. Appeals (6th cir.) 1979, U.S. Supreme Ct. Assoc. Stradley, Ronon, Stevens & Young, Phila., 1955-62, ptnr., 1962—; speaker on surety and fidelity matters to ABA, Practicing Law Inst., Internat. Assn. Def. Counsel, also others, on antitrust matters to Wood Machinery Mfrs. Assn., Fluid Power Distbr. Assn., Am. Brush Mfrs. Assn., Nat. Welding Supply Assn.; former trial cons. Cmty. Legal Svcs. Phila.; bd. dirs. Entertainment Comm., Inc. Contbr. articles to legal publs. Past pres. Melrose Park Improvement Assn.; former panel mem. Philadelphians for Equal Justice; bd. dirs. Phila. and Pa. chpts. ACLU, pres. Greater Phila. chpt., 1976-81; frequent speaker at meetings, participant various TV and radio panels on civil liberties matters; mem. Cheltenham Twp. Govt. Study Commn., 1974-76. Mem. ABA (fidelity and surety law com. tort ins. practice sect., past vice chair), Phila. Bar Assn., Internat. Assn. Def. Counsel (fidelity and surety law com.), Fedn. Ins. and Corp. Counsel (fidelity com.), Forum Com. for Constrn. Industry, Def. Rsch. Inst., Defenders Assn. Phila. (past bd. dirs.). Office: Stradley Ronon et al 2600 One Commerce Sq Philadelphia PA 19103

ELKINS, STANLEY MAURICE, historian, educator; b. Boston, Apr. 27, 1925; s. Frank and Frances (Reiner) E.; m. Dorothy Adele Lamken, June 22, 1947; children: Susan Roselyn, Robert Joel, Barbara Marion, Sara Ann. A.B., Harvard, 1949; M.A., Columbia, 1951, Ph.D., 1959. Tchr. Fieldston Sch., N.Y.C., 1951-54; asst. prof. history U. Chgo., 1955-60; faculty Smith Coll., Northampton, Mass., 1960—; prof. history Smith Coll., 1964-69, Sydenham Clark Parsons prof. history, 1969-92; fellow Inst. for Advanced Study, 1970-71, 76-77. Author: Slavery: A Problem in American Institutional and Intellectual Life, 1959, The Age of Federalism, 1993 (Bancroft prize Soc. Cin. Book Prize 1995). Served with AUS, 1943-46. Social Sci. Research Council fellow, 1963-64; Rockefeller fellow, 1954-55; Guggenheim fellow, 1976-77. Mem. Orgn. Am. Historians, Am. Hist. Assn., Soc. of Am. Historians. Home: 17 Kensington Ave Northampton MA 01060-2905

ELKINS, TONI MARCUS, artist, art association administrator; b. Tifton, Ga., Feb. 22, 1946; m. Samuel M. Elkins, 1968; children: Stephanie Elkins Sims, Eric Marcus. Student, Boston U., 1965; ABJ, U. Ga., 1968; postgrad., Columbia (S.C.) Coll., Athens, 1980-82; postgrad. photography/silk screening, Columbia (S.C.) Coll. Owner, designer Designs by Elkins, Columbia, 1986—; water color artist, 1983—; supt. fine art S.C. State Fair Art Exhbn., 1987-96. Works include watercolors All American Things, And the Good Ones Look Alike, And the Good Ones with Lace. Auction chair The Elegant Egg McKissick Mus., Columbia, 1994; bd. dirs. Trustus Theatre, 1994-96; chmn. S.C. Playwright's Festival, 1994—. Recipient Best of Show award 18th Internat. Dogwood Festival, 1991, So. Water Color Assn. Pres.'s award, 1992, Purchase award Anderson County Arts Coun. 17th Ann. Exhibit, 1992, Meyer Hardware award Rocky Mountain National, 1992, Howard B. Smith award S.C. Watercolor Ann., 1992. Mem. Nat. Watercolor Soc., Watercolor U.S.A., S.C. Watercolor Soc., Nat. Watercolor Okla., Penn. Watercolor Soc., Ga. Watercolor Soc., Rocky Mountain Nat. Watercolor Soc., Cultural Coun. of Richland & Lexington Counties (exec. bd. sec. 1990-93), Southeastern Art and Craft Expn. (adv. bd. 1993-94, Elizabeth O'Neill Verner award for the arts 1999). Avocations: roller blading, reading, swimming, collecting porcelain and S.C. art. Home and Studio: 1511 Adger Rd Columbia SC 29205-1407

ELKINS-ELLIOTT, KAY, law educator; b. Dallas, Nov. 21, 1938; d. William Hardin and Maxidine (Sadler) E.; m. Michael Gail Hodgson, July 7, 1960 (div. Dec. 1974); children: Michael Brett, Ashley Kim, Samantha; m. Frank Wallace Elliott, Aug. 15, 1983. AA with honors, Stephens Coll., 1958; JD, U. Okla., 1964; LLM, So. Meth. U., 1984; MA, U. Tex., Dallas, 1990. Bar: Okla. 1964, Tex. 1982, U.S. Dist. Ct. (no. dist.) Tex. 1982, U.S. Supreme Ct. 1984, U.S. Dist. Ct. (we. dist.) Okla. 1989. Assoc. Ben Hatcher and Assocs., Oklahoma City, Okla., 1964-65; dir., gen. counsel Take-A-Tour Swaziland, Mbabane, Swaziland, 1966-74; atty. Dept. Health and Human Svcs., Dallas, 1975-80; hearing officer EEOC, Dallas, 1980-84; atty. pvt. practice, Dallas, 1984-92; vis. assoc. prof. Tex. Wesleyan U. Sch. Law, Dallas, 1992-95; arbitrator State Farm Ins., Dallas, 1991-96; adj. prof. Wesleyan U. Sch. Law, 1995—, coach nat. ABA champion negotiation team, 1998; mediator pvt. practice, Dallas, 1991—; coord. cert. in conflict resolution program Tex. Woman's U., 1996—; cons. in field. Author: (with others) West Texas Practice, 1995. Mem. ABA (peer mediation and cmty. com. 1997—, alternative dispute resolution sect.), Tex. Bar Assn. (ADR sect. coun. mem. 1998—, chair Cont. Legal Edn. com.), Tex. Bar Found., Tex. Initiatives for Mediation in Edn. (founder, planning com. 1993-95), Soc. for Profls. in Dispute Resolution (pres. Dallas region 1995-97, Tex. Assn. Mediators, Assn. Atty. Mediators, Dallas Bar Assn. (coun. mem. 1993-94), Acad. Family Mediators, Toastmasters (v.p. 1993-94, pres. 1996-97), AIM for Peacepath. Avocations: singing, public speaking, peer mediation training. Home: 2120 N Rough Creek Ct Granbury TX 76048-2903 Office: 2401 Turtle Creek Blvd Dallas TX 75219-4712

ELKINTON, JOSEPH RUSSELL, medical educator; b. Moylan, Pa., Oct. 12, 1910; s. Joseph Passmore and Mary Russell (Bucknell) E.; m. Mary Teresa Sturge, Dec. 14, 1940; children: Gwyneth Elkinton Loud, Joseph Sturge. AB, Haverford (Pa.) Coll., 1932; MD, Harvard U., 1937. Diplomate Am. Bd. Internal Medicine; lic. physician, Pa., Conn. Intern and resident Pa. Hosp., Phila., 1937-40; nat. rsch. coun. fellow Yale U., New Haven, Conn., 1940-42, from instr. to asst. prof. medicine, 1942-48; from asst. prof. to assoc. prof. medicine U. Pa., Phila., 1948-62, prof. medicine, 1962-72, prof. emeritus, 1972—; staff physician U. Pa. Hosp., Phila., 1948-72; ret., 1972. Author: Bird On A Rocking Chair, 1988, Footnotes on the Sands of Time, 1994; co-author: Body Fluids: Basic Physiology and Practical Therapeutics, 1955, The Quaker Heritage in Medicine, 1978; editor Annals of Internal Medicine, 1960-71, editor emeritus, 1972—. Mem. study sect. metabolism and nutrition NIH, Washington, 1954-58; bd. dirs. Elwyn (Pa.) Inst., 1956-68; mem. family planning com. Am. Friends Svc. Com., Phila., 1965-71. Recipient Jacob Ehrenzeller award Pa. Hosp., 1975, A. N. Richards Disting. Achievement award in Nephrology, U. Pa., 1998; faculty fellow U. Birmingham, Eng., 1973-85. Master ACP, fellow Royal Coll. Physicians London; mem. Am. Soc. Clin. Investigation, Am. Physiol. Soc (coun. biology editors 1966), Assoc. Am. Physicians. Democrat. Mem. Soc. of Friends. Avocations: camping, canoeing, bird watching, gardening, writing. Home: 4 Andover Ct Bedford MA 01730-2902

ELKINTON, STEVEN, government agency administrator; b. Phila., Oct. 14, 1947; s. David Cope and Marian (Dunham) E.; m. Deborah Rosen, July 6, 1980; children: Sarah, Veronica. BFA, Kalamazoo Coll., 1969; M of Landscape Arch., U. Pa., 1976. Landscape architect Environ. Planning and Design, Pitts., 1976-78; landscape architect Nat. Park Svc., Cuyahoga Valley, Ohio, 1981-85, Falls Church, Va., 1978-81, 85-89; program leader for nat. trail sys. programming Nat. Park Svc., Washington, 1989—. Guest editor CRM Bull., 1997. Recipient Partnership Leader award Nat. Park Found., 1997, Pub. Svc. award Nat. Trails Symposium, 1998. Office: National Park Svc MS 3622 US Dept Interior 1849 C St NW Washington DC 20240-0001

EL KODSI, BAROUKH, gastroenterologist, educator; b. Cairo, Aug. 24, 1923; s. Moussa and Zohra (Aslan Cohen) El K.; came to U.S., 1957, naturalized, 1963; M.D., Cairo U., 1945; m. Marie Menasha, Mar. 26, 1960; children—Sylvia, Robert, Karen. Intern, Univ. Hosp. Cairo Sch. Medicine, 1946; resident in gen. medicine Jewish Hosp., Cairo, 1947-50, attending physician, 1950-57; intern, Miriam Hosp., Providence, 1958; resident in internal medicine, Boston City Hosp., 1959-61, chief resident, 1961-62, fellow in gastroenterology, 1962-64; asst. dir. medicine Union Hosp., Framingham, Mass., 1964-65; asso. dir. medicine Maimonides Med. Center, Bklyn., 1965-67, dir. gastroenterology, 1968—; chief gastroenterology Coney Island Hosp., N.Y.C., 1967-68; instr. Boston City Hosp., 1962-65; instr. Downstate Med. Center, SUNY, Bklyn., 1965-69, asst. prof. medicine, 1969-76, assoc. prof., 1976—. Chmn. Bklyn. physicians com. United Jewish Appeal. Named One of Best Drs. N.Y. New Yorker, 1966-67, 68-89. Fellow Am. Coll. Gastroenterology, ACP; mem. Am. Fedn. Clin. Research, Am. Gastroent. Assn., Am. Soc. Gastrointestinal Endoscopy, Am. Soc. Study of Liver Disease, AMA, N.Y. Gastroenterologic Assn. (pres. 1985-86), Ostomy Club (mem. exec. council). Contbr. articles to profl. jours. Home: 118 Girard St Brooklyn NY 11235-3010 Office: 925 48th St Brooklyn NY 11219-2919

ELKOWITZ, SHERYL SUE, radiologist; b. N.Y.C., Apr. 20, 1962. BS in Biology summa cum laude, Adelphi U., Garden City, N.Y., 1982; MD, Wayne State U., Detroit, 1986. Diplomate Am. Bd. Radiology; lic. physician, N.Y. Intern internal medicine L.I. Jewish Hillside Med. Ctr., New Hyde Park, N.Y., 1986-87, resident diagnostic radiology, 1987-91; fellow pediatric radiology, chief fellow L.I. Jewish Hillside Med. Ctr., Schneider Children's Hosp., New Hyde Park, 1991-92; staff attending dept. diagnostic radiology L.I. Jewish Hillside Med. Ctr., New Hyde Park, 1992-96; asst. prof. radiology Albert Einstein Coll. Medicine, Yeshiva U., Bronx, N.Y., 1992—; presenter various orgns. Contbr. articles to profl. jours. Mem. AMA, Soc. Pediatric Radiology, Radiol. Soc. N.Am., Am. Coll. Radiology, Am. Roentgen Ray Soc., Am. Assn. Women in Radiology (bylaws com. 1995), N.Y. Met. Pediatric Radiology Group, Neuhauser Soc., N.Y. State Radiol. Soc. Home: 96 Deer Run Roslyn Hts NY 11577-1972 Office: LIJ-Manhasset Women's Imaging Ctr 1554 Northern Blvd Manhasset NY 11030*

ELKUS, HOWARD FELIX, architect; b. San Francisco, Apr. 12, 1938; s. Eugene S. and Felice (Kahn) E.; m. Lorna Wheatley, Apr. 25, 1971. BS in Mech. Engring., Stanford U., 1959; MArch with distinction, Harvard U., 1963. Registered architect, Ariz., Calif., Conn., Fla., Ill., Ky., Maine, Mass., N.J., N.Y., Ohio, R.I., Vt., Wis., U.K. With Wagner & Martinez, Palo Alto, Calif., 1957, A.B. Atomenergi, Stockholm, 1958, Wilsey, Ham & Blair, San Mateo, Calif., 1960, Fry Drew & Ptnrs., London, 1961; prin., v.p. The Architects Collaborative, Cambridge, Mass., 1962-88; ptnr. Elkus/Manfredi Architects Ltd., Boston, 1988—. Prin. works include City Place Master Plan-West Palm Beach, Fla., 730 N Michigan Ave., Chgo., Pacific Place retail/entertainment complex, Seattle, Arnold Advt. hdqrs. offices, Boston, EF Centre N. Am. hdqr. bldg., Cambridge, Mass., Putnam Investments Hqtrs. Offices renovation, Boston, The Maternity Svc. at New Eng. Med. Ctr., Boston, Am. Express Bldg., Providence, Sun Microsystems, Chelmsford, Mass., The Limited/Express at Dadeland Mall, Miami, Limited, Inc. Office and Distbn. Complex, Reynoldsburg, Ohio, Nat. Coun. of Archtl. Registration Bds. Hdqrs., Washington, Near West Campus Stanford U., The Taubman Bldg., Kennedy Sch. of Harvard U., Copley Pl. (Urban Land Inst. excellence award 1988), Boston, Heritage on the Garden, Boston (Boston Soc. Architects Hon. award 1989), Flagship Wharf, Charlestown Navy Yard, Boston, Johnson Wax Hdqrs. Complex Expansion, Racine, Wis., Liberty Ctr. Pitts., AIA Hdqrs., Washington, Limited Hdqrs., Columbus, Ohio, GSIS Hdqrs. and Fin. Ctr., Manila, The Philippines. Recipient Prestressed Concrete Inst. award, 1983, The Concrete Industry Bd. Spl. Recognition, 1983, citation Engring. News Record, 1982, Constrn. Man of Yr. award Engring. News Record, 1982, White House citation for contbn. to energy efficient environment, 1983, Passive Solar Design award, 1982, Owens-Corning Energy Conservation award, 1982, Nat. Landscape award, 1986, Progressive Architecture Urban Design award, 1987, others. Fellow AIA (honor award 1966, 74, citation 1973), mem. Royal Inst. Brit. Architects, Mass. Assn. Architects, Boston Soc. Architects, Urban Land Inst., Nat. Trust for Hist. Preservation. Office: Elkus/Manfredi Architects Ltd 530 Atlantic Ave Boston MA 02210-2218*

ELKUS, RICHARD J., JR., electronics company executive; b. San Francisco, Feb. 25, 1935; s. Richard J. and Ruth (Kahn) E.; m. Helen Morrison, Aug. 17, 1956; children: Miriam Lyster, Richard M., Kevin J. BA, Stanford U., 1957; MBA, Dartmouth Coll., 1959. Prodn. control mgr. Ampex Corp., Redwood City, Calif., 1959-64, asst. to pres., 1968-71, mem. ops. bd., 1969-71, gen. mgr. ednl. and indsl. products div., 1969-72; pres., CEO, dir. Eyrle Co., Santa Clara, Calif., 1964-67; gen. mgr. Gould Med. Systems, Santa Clara, 1973-74; exec. v.p., gen. mgr. Geometrics, Inc., Sunnyvale, Calif., 1974-80; bd. dirs., chmn. Pacific Measurements, Inc., Sunnyvale, 1974-83, chmn., 1980-83; chmn., CEO, bd. dirs. Prometrix Corp., Santa Clara, 1983-94; vice chmn. bd. dirs. Tencor Instruments, Milpitas, Calif., 1994-97; bd. dirs., chmn. bd. Integrated Systems, Inc., Santa Clara, 1985-92; bd. dirs. KLA-Tencor, San Jose, Calif., Lam Rsch., Fremont, Calif., SOPRA, Paris; co-chmn. Voyan Tech., Santa Clara. Mem. coun. on competitiveness, chmn. panel on High Definition products and systems, NSF; mem. adv. bd. Ctr. for Strategic and Internat. Studies, Econ. Strategy Inst., 1990—, Sch. Engring., Ga. Inst. Tech., 1996-98. Capt. USAR, 1957-65. Mem. Am. Mgmt. Assn. (pres.'s coun.), Am. Electronics Assn. (bd. dirs., co-chmn. task force high resolution systems), Electronics Assn. Calif. (vice chmn. nat. medal technology nomination evaluation com. 1992-94, chmn. 1994-97), Econ. Strategy Inst. (adv. bd.), Foothills Tennis and Swim Club (Palo Alto, Calif.), Menlo Circus Club (Atherton, Calif.), Commonwealth Club. Office: Voyan Tech 3255-2 Scott Blvd Ste 103 Santa Clara CA 95054

ELLEBRACHT, HAROLD MARK, marine engineer; b. St. Louis, Jan. 14, 1955; s. Floyd Harold and Lorraine (Lynch) E.; m. Carol Ann McCaffery; children: Gena, Mark, Sara. Student, Bailey Tech. Sch., St. Louis, 1977, Belleville (Ill.) C.C., 1988-89. Marine surveyor Marine Loss Control, Inc., St. Louis, 1979-84; dir. engring. & ops. Sauget (Ill.) Properties Ltd., 1984-92; sr. dir. marine ops. Empress River Casino Corp., Joliet, Ill., 1992-95; dir. marine ops. Trump Ind., Inc., Gary, 1995—. Mem. Internat. Shipmasters Assn., Passenger Vessel Assn., Soc. Naval Architects & Marine Engrs. Avocations: computers, flying, astronomy. Office: Global Marine Solutions Inc 3326 Pandola Ave Joliet IL 60431-8440

ELLEBY, GAIL, management consultant; b. Seattle, Sept. 15, 1949; d. William Lee and Marie (Davis) E.; 1 child, Courtney Champion. BA, U. Wash., 1973, MPA, 1975; MSA in Sports Adminstrn., Ohio U., 1980. Adminstrn. specialist Mayor's Office, City of Seattle, 1986-87; adminstrv. asst. Seattle 1990 Goodwill Games, 1987-88; adminstr. Met. Enrichment Ctr., San Francisco, 1988-90; assoc. v.p. United Way of the Bay Area, San Francisco, 1990-93; cons., pres. Gail Elleby & Assocs., Daly City, Calif., 1993—; orgnl. and program devel., cmty. devel., collaboration tng., non-profit founds., corp. programs; dir. Even Start San Francisco Unified Sch. Dist., 1997-98, mgmt. and tng. specialist Western Ky. U., 1998—. Mem. BBB, San Mateo County, Calif., 1995—; bd. dirs. Boys and Girls Club of San Mateo County, South San Francisco, Calif., 1993-97; mem. San Mateo County Child Care Coun., 1992-97; mem. San Mateo County Commn. on Status of Women, 1994-98; mem. Bay Area Blacks in Philanthropy, 1992—. Mem. SAMCEDA, Cons. Group (founder). Mem. Ch. of Christ. Avocations: music, sports, reading, cooking, collecting dolls. Fax: 404-297-6381. Home: 1444 Summit Chase Dr Snellville GA 30078

ELLEDGE, GLENNA ELLEN TUELL, journalist; b. Welch, W.Va., Aug. 2, 1931; d. William Jackson and Ellen Annabelle (Jackson) Tuell; div.; children: Carl Gene, Jerry E., Ernest Everett. Certificate in comptometer, Capital City Coll., 1949; student, Wytheville (Va.) C.C., S.W. Va. C.C., Richlands, Va. Intermont Coll. Accounts clk. Household Fin. Corp., Charleston, W.Va., 1951-52; with incest divsn. FBI, Washington, 1953; asst. bookkeeper and acctg. clk. Ft. McNair Officers Open Mess, Washington, 1953-54; stat. analyst Office Strategic Intelligence, Washington, 1954-55; stock control 836th Supply Squadron, Langley AFB, Va., 1957-59; acct., office asst. Comml. Contracting, Troy, Mich., 1970-71; office svcs. asst. Southwestern State Hosp., Marion, Va., 1971-95; staff writer, photographer Saltville (Va.) Progress, 1977-81, Saltville News-Messenger, 1981-93, Family Cmty. Newspapers, Marion, 1993—; fire brigade Southwestern State Hosp., Marion, 1986-93, instr. CPR, 1986-89, adv. bd., 1986-93. Vol. Air Force Family Svcs., 1956-69, den mother Cub. Scouts Am., 1962-67; bd. dirs. Smyth County Crisis Ctr., Marion, 1971-81; sec., pres. Smyth Coun. Santa's Elves, Marion, 1974-78, Family Oriented Group Home parent Group Home Juveniles 28th Juvenile Domestic Rels. Ct., Abingdon, Va., 1978-81; EMT, instr. Am. Heart Assn., Smyth, Wise, Grayson Counties, 1986-89; former sunday sch. tchr., supr. Laural Springs United Meth. Ch. Mem. Nat. Fedn. Press Women (del. 1978, awards), Va. Press Women (del. 1978, awards), Va. Press Assn. (awards), Nat. Press Assn. Republican. Avocations: writing, reading, gardening, camping, traveling. Office: PO Box 901 Marion VA 24354-0901

ELLEDGE, JIM, poet, literature educator; b. Granite City, Ill., Aug. 28, 1950; s. Richard Marvin and Mary Louise Elledge; life ptnr., David Dean. BA in English, Ea. Ill. U., 1971, MSLS, 1973; PhD in English and Creative Writing, U. Ill., Chgo., 1986. Prof. English Ill. State U., Normal, 1986—. Author: Nothing Nice, 1987, Various Envies, 1989, Earth as It Is, 1994 (Ashland Poetry Press award), Into the Arms of the Universe, 1995 (Stonewall award), Four Chapters of Coming Forth By Day, 1999. E-mail: jmelled@ilstu.edu. Office: Ill State U Dept English Campus Box 4240 Normal IL 61790-4240

ELLEGARD, ROY WHITNEY, appraiser; b. Hartford, Conn., Sept. 16, 1957; s. Roy Taylor and Jeanette (Whitney) E. BA in Econs., U. Richmond, 1980. Appraiser Stone & Webster, Inc., N.Y.C., 1980-82; cons. Arthur Andersen & Co., N.Y.C., 1983; sr. cons. Arthur D. Little, Inc., Metro Park, N.J., 1984-87; nat. dir. machinery and equipment valuation advisors Ernst & Young LLP, N.Y.C., 1987-98; mng. dir. corp. value consulting Pricewater House Coopers LLP, 1998—. Mem. Am. Soc. Appraisers (sr., pres. Princeton chpt. 1992-93, 98-99), Kappa Alpha Alumni Assn. (treas. Princeton chpt. 1990-92), Princeton Club N.Y. Republican. Episcopalian.

Home: 175 E 96th St Apt 8K New York NY 10128-6204 Office: Pricewaterhouse Coopers 1177 Avenue Of The Americas New York NY 10036-2714

ELLEGOOD, DONALD RUSSELL, publishing executive; b. Lawton, Okla., June 21, 1924; s. Claude Jennings and Iva Claire (Richards) E.; m. Bettie Jane Dixon, Dec. 11, 1947; children—Elizabeth Nemi, Francis Hunter, Kyle Richards, Sarah Helen. B.A., U. Okla., 1948, M.A., 1950. Asst. editor U. Okla. Press, 1950-51; editor Johns Hopkins Press, 1951-54; dir. La. State U. Press, 1954-63, U. Wash. Press, Seattle, 1963—. Contbr. articles to profl. jours. Served to 1st lt. USAAF, 1943-46. Decorated Air medal, D.F.C. Mem. Am. Univ. Pubs. Group London (dir.), Am. Assn. Univ. Presses (pres.), Phi Beta Kappa. Home: 17852 49th Pl NE Seattle WA 98155-4312 Office: U Wash Press PO Box 50096 Seattle WA 98145-5096

ELLEMAN, BARBARA, editor; b. Coloma, Wis., Oct. 20, 1934; d. Donald and Evelyn (Kissinger) Koplein; m. Don W. Elleman, Nov. 14, 1970. BS in Edn., Wis. State U., 1956; MA in Librarianship, U. Denver, 1964. Sch. libr. media specialist Port Washington (Wis.) High Sch., 1956-59, Homestead High Sch., Thiensville-Mequon, Wis., 1959-64; children's libr. Denver Pub. Libr., 1964-65; sch. libr. media specialist Cherry Creek Schs., Denver, 1965-70, Henry Clay Sch., Whitefish Bay, Wis., 1971-75; children's reviewer ALA, Chgo., 1975-82, children's editor, 1982-90, editor Book Links, 1990-96; vis. lectr. U. Wis., 1974-75, 81-82, U. Ill., Circle Campus, 1983-85; Disting. scholar children's lit., Marquette U., 1996—; cons. H.W. Wilson Co., 1969-75; mem. Libr. Congress Adv. Com. on selection for children's books for blind and physically handicapped, 1980-88, Caldecott Calendar Com., 1986; judge The Am. Book Awards, 1982, Golden Kite, 1987, Boston Globe/Horn Book, 1990; mem. faculty Highlights for Children Writers Conf., 1985-90; mem. orgn. com. MidWest Conf. Soc. Children's Books Writers, 1974-76; chair Hans Christian Andersen Com., 1987-88; advisor Reading Rainbow, 1986-96, Ind. R.E.A.P. project, 1987-93; jury mem. VI Catalonia Premi Children's Book Exbhn., Barcelona, Spain, 1994; adv. bd. Parent's Choice, Cobblestone Publ., Georgia Pub. TV's 2000, The New Advocate mag., 20th Century Children's Writers, Encyclopedia of Children's Literature, Cooperative Children's Book Ctr., U. Wis., Madison, Riverbank Rev., 1998—, Ency. of Children's Lit., 1998—; lang. arts com. NCTE Notable Books, 1997—; spkr. in field. Author: Reading in a Media Age, 1975, 20th Century Children's Writers, 1979, rev. edit., 1984, What Else Can You Do With A Library Degree?, 1980, Popular Reading for Children, 1981, Popular Reading II, 1986, Children's Books of International Interest, 1984; contbr. articles to profl. jours. Publicity chair Internat. Bd. Books for Young People Congress, Williamsburg, Va., 1990. Recipient Jeremiah Ludington award Ednl. Paperback Assn., 1996, Hope S. Dean award Found. Children's Lit., 1996. Mem. ALA (2000 Caldecott Com. 1999—), Soc. Children's Book Writers (mem. orgn. com. MidWest Conf. 1974-76), Internat. Bd. Books for Young People (U.S. assoc. editor Bookbird 1978-86, chair nominating com., 1985, bd. dirs. 1990-92), Children's Reading Round Table Chgo. (award 1987), Nat. Coun. Tchrs. English (bd. dirs. children's lit. assembly 1986-88, mem. editl. adv. bd. CLA bull. 1989-91, mem. using nonfiction in classroom com. 1990-96), AAUW. Office: 1884 Somerset Ln Northbrook IL 60062-6066

ELLEMAN, LAWRENCE ROBERT, lawyer; b. Hamilton, Ohio, Nov. 21, 1940; s. Robert A. and Genevieve Elizabeth (Dunlap) E.; m. Barbara Ellen Mann, Sept. 12, 1964; children: Laura Ellen, Robert Andrew. BS, Ohio State U., 1963, JD summa cum laude, 1966. Bar: Ohio 1967, U.S. Dist. Ct. (no. dist.) Ohio 1967, U.S. Dist. Ct. (so. dist.) Ohio 1969, U.S. Dist. Ct. (ea. dist.) Ky. 1972, U.S. Ct. Appeals (6th cir.) 1970, U.S. Ct. Appeals (8th cir.) 1983, U.S. Ct. Appeals (11th cir.) 1984. Law clk. U.S. Dist. Ct. Ohio, Toledo, 1966-68; assoc. Dinsmore & Shohl, Cin., 1968-75, ptnr., 1975—; commr. Cin. Tall Stacks, 1993—; mem. Ohio Supreme Ct. Bd. Bar Examiners, 1994-97. Pres. Ronald McDonald House, Cin., 1988; bd. dirs., pres. Cincinnatus Assn., 1993-94; bd. dirs. Hamilton County Law Libr.; mem. Ohio State Commn. on Certification of Lawyers' Specialties, 1998—. Fellow Ohio State Bar Found.; mem. ABA, Cin. Bar Assn. (chmn. fed. cts. com., chmn. improvement adminstrn. of justice), Univ. Club Cin. Democrat. Avocations: boating, fishing, reading. Home: 3812 Earls Court Vw Cincinnati OH 45226-1305 Office: Dinsmore & Shohl 1900 Chemed Ctr 255 E 5th St Cincinnati OH 45202-4700*

ELLENBERGER, DIANE MARIE, nurse, consultant; b. St. Louis, Oct. 5, 1946; d. Charles Ernst and Celeste Loraine (Neudecker) E.; RN, Barnes Hosp., St. Louis, 1970; BSN, St. Louis U., 1976; MSN, U. Colo., 1977. Cert. clin. nurse specialist. Staff nurse hosps., clin. nurse, St. Louis, 1973-76; nurse clinician, Sedalia, Mo., 1977-78; nurse clinician, educator Bothwell Hosp., Sedalia, 1977-78; clin. nurse specialist, coord. perinatal outreach edn. Cardinal Glennon Meml. Hosp. Children, St. Louis, 1978-80; instr. McKendree Coll., Lebanon, Ill., 1980; asst. prof. Maryville Coll., St. Louis, 1982-85; nurse cons. Carr, Korein, Tillery, Kunin, Montroy, Cates & Glass, Attys. at Law, 1986-97; owner, nurse cons. The Med-Legal Advantage, San Anselmo, Calif., 1997—; owner, operator Diane Designs Needlepoint, St. Louis, 1981-96. With Nurse Corps, USAF, 1970-72. Mem. ANA (Calif. affiliate bd. dirs. 1998—), AACN, Am. Assn. Legal Nurse Cons., Nat. Perinatal Assn., Assn. Women's Health, Obstetric and Neonatal Nurses, Mo. Nurses Assn. (bd. dirs. 1996-97, bylaws chair 1990—, del. to ANA 1996, 3d dist. pres. 1993-96), Mo. Perinatal Assn. (v.p. 1980), Sigma Theta Tau. Mem. Divine Sci. Ch. Contbr. articles profl. jours. Office: PO Box 1638 San Anselmo CA 94979-1638

ELLENBERGER, JACK STUART, law librarian; b. Lamar, Colo., Sept. 5, 1930; s. Emmert C. and Ruby F. (Overstreet) E. B.S., Georgetown U., 1957; M.L.S., Columbia U., 1959. Law libr. HEW, 1957; libr. Carter, Ledyard & Milburn, N.Y.C., 1957-60, Jones, Day, Reavis & Pogue (and predecessor firm), Cleve., 1960, Bar Assn. of D.C., Washington, 1961-63, Covington & Burling, Washington, 1963-78; libr. Shearman & Sterling, N.Y.C., 1978-93, law libr. emeritus, 1994-95; ret., 1995. Editor: (with Mahar) Legislative History of the Securities Act of 1933 and the Securities Exchange Act of 1934, 1973. Served with USAF, 1951-54. Mem. Am. Assn. Law Libraries (pres. 1976-77, M.G. Gallagher Disting. Svc. award 1994), Spl. Libraries Assn. *

ELLENBOGEN, GEORGE, poet, educator; b. Montreal, Que., Can., Nov. 19, 1934; came to U.S., 1966; s. Moses and Jenny (Borenstein) E.; m. Karia Doris Feinzig, Dec. 18, 1960 (div. 1984); children: Sara Rachel, Adam. B.A., McGill U., Montreal, 1955; M.A., U. Montreal, 1962; Ph.D., Tufts U., 1969. Mem. faculty Bentley Coll., Waltham, Mass., 1965—, prof. English, 1980—, chmn. dept., 1980-85, dir. Forum for Creative Writing, 1987—; poetry editor Boston Today, 1978-81; vis. prof., writer-in-residence U. Siegen, Germany, 1996. Author: Winds of Unreason, 1957, The Night Unstones, 1971, Along the Road from Eden, 1989, The Rhinogate Poems, 1996, La Porte aux rhinos et autres poemes (bilingual edit.), 1997; subject of German documentary film produced by Wolfgang Lippke George Ellenbogen: A Canadian Poet in America; contbr. numerous articles and poems to mags. and anthologies. Recipient award Karolyi Meml. Found., 1986, Va. Ctr. for Creative Arts, 1987, 92, 93, Montalvo Assn., 1987, Whiting Found., 1994. Mem. AAUP, MLA, Coll. English Assn., Nat. Council Tchrs. of English. Home: 21 Wren St West Roxbury MA 02132-2625 Office: Bentley Coll English Dept Waltham MA 02154

ELLENBOGEN, LEON, nutritionist, pharmaceutical company executive; b. N.Y.C., May 3, 1927; s. Martin and Bella (Zalesnick) E.; m. Roslyn Barban, June 30, 1951; children: Kenneth Alan, Richard Glen, Cheryl Sue. BS, CCNY, 1949; MS, NYU, 1951; PhD, Ind. U., 1954. Technician and med. corpsman USN, 1945-47; rsch. technician Columbia U., N.Y.C., 1949-51; teaching asst. gen. chemistry and biochemistry Ind. U., Bloomington, 1951-53; rsch. biochemist Lederle Labs., Am. Cyanamid Co., Pearl River, N.Y., 1953-59, sr. rsch. biochemist, group leader, 1959-77, chief nutritional sci., sr. assoc. dir. med.. pharm. devel., 1977-95; asst. v.p. nutritional scis. Lederle Consumer Health divsn. Whitehall Robins Health Care, Am. Home Products, Madison, N.J., 1995-97; ret., 1997; adj. prof. nutrition in medicine Cornell U. Med. Coll., 1978—; adj. prof. nutrition N.Y. Med. Coll., 1981—; adj. prof., adv. com. intrinsic factor Nat. Formulatory Com.; mem. sci. affairs com. Proprietary Assn., 1980-89. Contbr. numerous articles to profl. jours., tech. books; author, presenter abstracts and papers profl. meetings; editor Contemporary Issues in Clin. Nutrition, 1980—, guest editor vols. 2 and 12; editor Drug Nutrient Interactions, 1982-91; cons. editor Biochemistry, Jour. AMA, Am. Jour. Clin. Nutrition, Sci., The Med. Letter, Nutrition Reports Internat., Thrombosis Rsch., Jour. Medicinal Chemistry, Archives Biochem. and Biophys., Annals Internal Medicine, Jour. Biol. Chemistry, Biochem. Pharmacology. Pharmacists mate USN, 1945-47. Recipient Steuben apple for contbns. to sci. rsch. Coun. for Responsible Nutrition. Fellow Am. Soc. Nutritional Scis., N.Y. Acad. Scis. (steering com. biochem. pharmacology discussion group 1973-77); mem. Am. Heart Assn., Am. Soc. Hematology, Am. Inst. Nutrition (nomenclature com.), Am. Soc. Clin. Nutrition, Am. Soc. Biol. Chemists, Am. Soc. Pharmacology and Exptl. Therapeutics, Am. Chem. Soc. (chmn. biochem. discussion group N.Y. sect. 1959, counselor divsn. biol. labs. 1977-79), Soc. Exptl. Biology and Medicine (editor proc. 1961-62), U.S. Pharmacopeia (com. on revision 1990-95, U.S. Pharmacopia subcom. for nonprescription drugs and nutritional supplements 1995—), Sigma Xi, Phi Lambda Upsilon. Avocation: sports. Home: 16 Morris Dr New City NY 10956-4652 Office: Lederle Consumer Health Whithall Robins Healthcare Madison NJ 07940-0871

ELLENBOGEN, RUDOLPH SOLOMON, library curator; b. Bronx, N.Y., Oct. 17, 1943; s. Simon and Renia (Russak) E.; m. Alane Helen Dropkin, June 24, 1965; children: Amy Abigail, David Ezra. BA, CCNY, 1965; MA, NYU, 1968; MS, Columbia U., 1970. Tchr. math. and sci. Elizabeth Barrett Browning Jr. High Sch., Bronx, 1965-68; tchr. English Taft High Sch., Bronx, 1968-69; asst. libr. Coll. Libr. Columbia U., N.Y.C., 1970-73, reference libr. rare books, 1973-76, asst. libr. rare books, 1976-93, curator rare books, 1993—, asst. editor Columbia Libr. Columns., 1980-90, assoc. editor, 1991-92; editor, 1992-94; assoc. editor Grolier Club Gazette, N.Y.C., 1994—. Compiler, editor exhibition catalogues. Mem. Am. Printing History Assn., Bibliog. Soc. Am., Grolier Club. Home: 55 Coralyn Ave White Plains NY 10605-3823 Office: Columbia U Rare Book and Manuscript Libr 535 W 114th St New York NY 10027-7035

ELLENBOGEN, S. DAVID, electronics company executive; b. Bayonne, N.J., May 26, 1938; s. Louis and Freda (Tindell) E.; m. Elaine Barbara Kaplan, June 7, 1959; children: Sandra Lynn, Michael Phillip. BSME, Newark Coll., 1960. Engr. Gen. Precision, Inc., Little Falls, N.J., 1960-61; mktg. specialist EMR div. Schlumberger, Inc., Princeton, N.J., 1961-66; sr. v.p. Am. Sci. and Engring. Co., Cambridge, Mass., 1966-68; pres. Diagnostic Tech., Inc., Waltham, Mass., 1981-85; chmn., CEO Hologic Inc., Waltham, 1985—; also bd. dirs. Hologic, Inc., Waltham, 1985—; pres. Vivid Technologies Inc. Bd. trustees New Eng. Bapt. Hosp., Boston; chmn. bd. trustees NEB Enterprises; bd. overseers N.J. Inst. Tech. Mem. Am. Elec. Assn. Home: 9 Pauline Dr Natick MA 01760-3621 Office: Hologic Inc 35 Crosby Dr Bedford MA 01730-1401*

ELLENBROOK, EDWARD CHARLES, county official, small business owner; b. Lawton, Okla., Aug. 12, 1938; s. Edward Charles Ellenbrook and Lera Belle (Pair) Becker; m. Carolyn Kay Baker, Apr. 13, 1968; 1 child, Margaret Elizabeth. BA, Okla. Bapt. U., 1964. Social worker Dept. Human Svcs., Lawton, 1964-73; dir. Comanche County Juvenile Bur., Lawton, 1973—; author, owner, pub. In-The-Valley-Of-The-Wichitas, Lawton, 1983—. Author: Outdoor & Trail Guide to the Wichita Mountains, 1983, Endless Encounters, 1988; outdoors/nature columnist Lawton-Constitution-Wichita Mountains Field Notes newspaper, 1989. Bd. dirs. Lawton Heritage Assn., 1989, Southwestern Okla. Hist. Soc., Lawton, 1970, Okla. Ornithol. Soc., Ada, Okla., 1990, Friends of the Wichitas, Lawton, 1989, City of Lawton's Model Cities Com., 1968, Teen Ct., Inc.; mem. criminal adv. bd. Cameron U.; trustee Inst. of the Gt. Plains, Mus. of the Gt. Plains, 1995. With U.S. Army, 1962-64. Mem. Book Pubs. of Tex., N.Am. Butterfly Assn. Avocations: hiking, backpacking, nature, illustration/book design, arts. E-mail: ecebrook@sirinet.net. Home: 1603 NW Keystone Dr Lawton OK 73505-2445 Office: In Valley of Wichitas PO Box 6741 Lawton OK 73506-0741

ELLENS, J(AY) HAROLD, philosopher, educator, psychotherapist; b. McBain, Mich., July 16, 1932; s. John S. and Grace (Kortmann) E.; m. Mary Jo Lewis, Sept. 7, 1954; children: Debra, Jackie, Dan, Beckie, Rocky, Brenda. AB, Calvin Coll., 1953; BD, Calvin Sem., 1956; ThM, Princeton Sem., 1965; PhD, Wayne State U., 1970; M in Divinity, Calvin Seminary, 1986. Ordained to ministry Christian Reformed Ch., 1956. Pastor Newton (N.J.) Christian Reformed Ch., 1961-65, North Hills Ch., Troy, Mich., 1965-68, Univ. Hills Ch., Farmington Hills, Mich., 1968-78; pvt. practice psychotherapy, Farmington Hills, 1967—; religious broadcaster TV, weekly, 1970-74, periodically to date; lectr. humanities and classics Wayne State U., John Wesley Coll., 1970—, Oakland U., 1970-90; vis. lectr. Princeton U., 1977-79; lectr. U.S. and abroad. Author: Program Format in Religious Television, 1970, Models of Religious Broadcasting, 1974, Chaplain (Major General) Gerhart W. Hyatt: An Oral History, 1977, (with others) Internat. Standard Bible Encyclopedia, 1979-89, Eternal Vigilance, 1980, God's Grace and Human Health, 1982, Life and Laughter, 1983, Psychology in Worship, 1984, (with others) Baker's Encyclopedia of Psychology, 1984, Psychotherapy: Key Issues, 1986, (with others) Psychotherapy in Christian Perspective, 1987, (with others) Christian Counseling and Psychotherapy, 1987, Psychotheology: Key Issues, 1987, Love, Life and Laughter, 1988, (with others) Psychology and Religion, 1988, (with others) The Church and Pastoral Care, 1988, (with others) Moral Obligation and the Military, 1988, (with others) God se genade is genoeg, 1989, (with others) Counseling and the Human Predicament, 1989, (with others) Turning Points in Pastoral Care, (with others) Christian Perspectives on Human Development, 1992, The Ancient Library of Alexandria and Early Christian Theological Development, 1993, 95, Alexander The Great and Hellemistic Culture, 1997, Sin or Sickness: The Problem of Human Disfunction, 1998, Humanistic Psychology, 1998, Dictionary of Pastoral Care and Counseling, 1990, (with others) The Interpretation of the Bible, 1998, Sin or Sickness: The Problem of Human Dysfunction, 1998, three books in Portuguese and one in Spanish; editor: CAPS Internat. Directory vols. II-V, 1976-87, Ethical Reflections, 1977, The Beauty of Holiness, 2d edit., 1985, God's Grace in Free Verse, 1987; editor in chief Jour. Psychology and Christianity, 1975-88; contbr. articles to profl. jours. Served to col. AUS, 1956-61, ret., 1992. Created knight, Queen Juliana, The Netherlands, 1974. Mem. Christian Assn. Psychol. Studies (now exec. dir.), AAUP, Am. Psychol. Assn., Soc. Bibl. Lit., Speech Communication Assn., Mil. Chaplain Assn., Ret. Officers Assn., Archeol. Inst. Am., Am. Personnel and Guidance Assn., Mil. Order World Wars, Am. Sci. Assn., World Assn. Christian Communicators. Home and Office: 26705 Farmington Rd Farmington MI 48334-4329 Office: 1150 Delaney Orlando FL 32806 *Secular and religious communities alike tend continually to shift their focus toward some orthodoxy or other, usually in the form of according ultimate authority to an aspect of the community's traditional thought or behavior, thus imposing constraints upon the quest for growth and for truth which are not responsive to reality or authenticity or relevant and wholesome freedon. Orthodoxy is always, therefore, a form of idolatry; it is a psychological phenomenon; it is the posture of arrogance in those who see themselves as "the chosen" or the elect; it is lunge for security vs. growth; it is designed to guard against the destablizing effect of change; it is, therefore inherently imperialistic, arbitrary, propagandist, and abusive.*

ELLENTUCK, ELMER, journal editor; b. N.Y.C.; s. Max and Deena (Bregman) E.; m. Beatrice Reiner, Nov. 25, 1946 (dec. Feb. 1982); m. Tara Marcus, June 28, 1985; 1 child, Daniel. BBA, CCNY, 1939; LLB, St. John's U., N.Y.C., 1948. Bar: N.Y. Gen. asst. O.N. Heilbut, N.Y.C., 1948-49; pvt. practice law N.Y.C., 1949-60; editor Prentice Hall, Inc., N.J., 1960-64, Bus. Rsch. Pubs., 1964-96, Employee Rels., 1996—. Co-author: Business Management Handbook, 1968; author: Employee Discipline, 1968. Sgt. USAAF, 1945-46. Mem. N.Y. County Lawyers Assn., Nat. Press Club, Masons. Avocations: reading, fishing, walking. Home and Office: 750 Kappock St Apt 915 Riverdale NY 10463-4615

ELLER, M. EDWARD, JR., physician; b. Martinsville, Va., Oct. 20, 1954; s. Myron Edward and Clovis (Gregory) E. BA in Biology, U. Va., Charlottesville, 1977, MD, 1981. Diplomate Am. Bd. Family Practice; cert. in geriatrics Am. Bd. Family Practice and Am. Bd. Internal Medicine. Chief resident dept. family practice U. Va., Charlottesville, 1983-84; pres. Commonwealth Family Physicians, Inc., Martinsville, Va., 1984—; med. dir. Blue Ridge Rehab., Martinsville, 1988-96; chmn. dept. family practice Meml. Hosp. Martinsville and Henry County, 1990-92. Avocations: American empire and 19th Century antiques, gardening. E-mail: eeller@neocomm.net. Home: 309 Thomas Hts Martinsville VA 24112-3836 Office: Commonwealth Family Physicians Inc 445 Commonwealth Blvd Martinsville VA 24112

ELLERBEE, LINDA, broadcast journalist; b. Bryan, Tex., Aug. 15, 1944; children: Vanessa, Joshua. Ed., Vanderbilt U. Newscaster, disc jockey Sta. WVON, Chgo., 1964-67; program dir. Sta. KSJO, San Francisco, 1967-68; reporter Sta. KJNO and AP, Juneau, Alaska, 1969-72, Sta. KHOU-TV, Dallas, 1972-73, Sta. WCBS-TV, N.Y.C., 1973-76; Washington corr. NBC News, 1975-78; co-anchor Weekend, NBC News, NBC-TV, 1978-80; reporter NBC Nightly News, 1980-82; co-anchor NBC News Overnight, 1982-84; corr., reporter Today Show, NBC-TV; writer, anchor Our World, ABC-TV, 1986; founder, pres. Lucky Duck Prodns., N.Y.C., 1987—; commentator Cable News Network, 1989. Author: And So It Goes: Adventures in Television, 1986, Move On: Adventures in the Real World, 1991; exec. prod. (TV spls.) A Conversation with Magic (Cable ACE award 1992), It's Only Television (Peabody award 1992); exec. prod., writer, host (news/mag. program) Nick News (Columbia duPont award 1993, Parents' Choice Found. Gold TV award); writer, anchor, actress Our World (Emmy for best writing 1986); weekly syndicated columnist King Features, N.Y.; actress (t.v. series) Weekend (regular 1978-79), Summer Sunday U.S.A., 1984, (narrator) Baby Boom, 1987, Addicted, 1997, exec. prodr., writer, filmography prodr.; filmography prodr. (miniseries) Oh What a Time It Was, 1999; guest appearances Murphy Brown, 1989, 1993, Ellen, 1998. Office: Lucky Duck Prodns 96 Morton St Fl 4 New York NY 10014-3326*

ELLERBUSCH, FRED, environmental engineer; b. Germany, Mar. 5, 1951. BSCE in Environ. Engring., N.J. Inst. Tech., 1973, MS in Environ. Engring., 1980. Registered profl. engr., N.J. Staff engr. Elson T. Killam Assocs., Inc., Millburn, N.J., 1973-74; staff environ. engr. Indsl. Environ. Rsch. Lab. U.S. EPA, Edison, N.J., 1974-77; environ. systems engr. METREK div. MITRE Corp., McLean, Va., 1977-78; regulatory conformance coord. Bristol-Myers Products div. Bristol-Myers Squibb Co., Bridgewater, N.J., 1978-83, mgr. regulatory compliance and govt. affairs, 1983-85, dir. safety, security and environ. affairs, 1985-89; dir. corp. environ. affairs Rhone-Poulenc Inc. affiliate Rhone-Poulenc SA, Monmouth Junction, N.J., 1989-95, dir. environ. affairs and remediation, 1995-96; dir. health, safety, environ. affairs Rhone-Poulenc Inc. affiliate Rhone-Poulenc SA, Monmouth Junction, 1996-98; pres. Systemsthink, Warren, N.J., 1998—; scientist in residence N.J. Inst. Tech., 1998—, dir. Ctr. for Health Environ. and Societal Sustainability, 1999—; v.p. Nat. Environ. Policy Inst., 1999—; adj. prof. environ. engring. grad. div. N.J. Inst. Tech., Newark, 1980-83; seminar leader div. continuing edn. N.J. Inst. Tech., Newark, 1977-90; chair unified environ. statute sector Nat. Environ. Policy Inst., 1995—. Co-author: Electrotechnology Applications in Manufacturing, Vol. 2, 1978, Industrial/Hazardous Waste Impoundment, 1979, Biomass Applications and Technology, 1980; co-editor: Carbon Adsorption Handbook, 1978, Guide for Industrial Noise Control, 1982; contbr. articles to profl. publs. Mem. nat. panel consumer arbitrators Better Bus. Bur. Mem. Acad. Hazard Control Mgmt., Acad. Hazardous Materials Mgmt. (bd. examiners 1984-85), Am. Indsl. Health Coun. (govt. affairs com. 1987, sci. policy com. 1988—, vice chmn. 1989,), Am. Sci. Affiliation, Chem. Mfrs. Assn. (mem. various coms.), N.Y. Acad. Scis., Soc. for Risk Analysis, N.J. Water Control Assn., N.J. Inst. Tech. (indsl. adv. bd. 1986—), Nat. Environ. Tng. Assn., N.J. Acad. Scis., Pharm. Mfrs. Assn. (environ. control resource com. 1985-89), others. Home: 73 Ferguson Rd Warren NJ 07059-5501 Office: Systems Think LLC PO Box 4225 Warren NJ 07059-0225

ELLETT, ALAN SIDNEY, real estate development company executive; b. Seven Kings, Essex, Eng., Jan. 6, 1930; came to U.S., 1974, permanent resident, 1974; s. Sidney Walter and May (Fowler) E.; m. Linda Jacqueline Cortell, 1985; children by previous marriage: Denise, Michelle, Wayne. BSc in Bldg. Constrn., 1951, MBA. Mng. dir. Gilbert Ash Structures, 1960-68; dir., gen. mgr. Lyon Group (real estate), 1968-70; mng. dir. (pres.) Gilbert Ash Ltd., 1970-72; dir. Bovis Ltd.; chief exec. Bovis Property divsn. Audley Properties Ltd., 1972-74; chmn. bd. Forest City Dillon, Inc., 1974-88; exec. v.p., dir. Forest City Enterprises, Inc., Cleve., 1974-89; chmn. Forest City Rental Properties, 1982-89; chmn., pres. Forest City Comml. Constrn. Co., Inc., 1987-89; exec. v.p., COO Am. Malls Internat., Washington, 1988—; pres. Intercontinental Devel. & Investment Corp., Washington, 1997—. Contbr. articles to profl. jours. Fellow Inst. Builders, Inst. Dirs. Mem. Conservative Party. Mem. Church of England. (London).

ELLETT, JOHN SPEARS, II, retired taxation educator, accountant, lawyer; b. Richmond, Va., Sept. 17, 1923; s. Henry Guerrant and Elizabeth Firmstone (Maxwell) E.; m. Mary Ball Ruffin, Apr. 15, 1950; children: John, Mary Ball, Elizabeth, Martha, Henry. BA, U. Va., 1948, JD, 1957, MA, 1961; PhD, U. N.C., 1969; CPA, Va., La.; bar: Va. 1957. Lab. instr. U. Va., Charlottesville, 1953-58; instr. Washington and Lee U., 1958-60; asst. prof. U. Fla., 1967-71; assoc. prof. U. New Orleans, 1971-76, prof. taxation, 1976-94; prof. emeritus, 1994—; trainee Va. Carolina Hardware Co., Richmond, 1948-51; acct. Equitable Life Assurance Soc., Richmond, 1951-52; staff acct. Musselman & Drysdale, Charlottesville, 1952-54; staff acct. R.M. Musselman, Charlottesville, 1957-58; mem. U. New Orleans Oil and Gas Acctg. Conf., 1973-92; bd. dirs., publicity chmn. U. New Orleans Energy Acctg. and Tax Conf., 1993-94, bd. dirs. publicity com.; pres. Maxwelton Farm and Timber Corp., 1994—; treas. U. New Orleans Estate Planning Seminar, 1975-78, lectr. continuing edn.; CPCU instr. New Orleans Ins. Inst., 1975-78. Served with AUS, 1943-46. Mem. AICPA, Am. Acctg. Assn., Am. Assn. Atty.-CPAs (chmn. ptnrship. taxation continuing edn. com. 1989, ptnrship. taxation com. 1990, organized La. chpt., v.p. 1991-93), Va. Soc. CPAs, Soc. La. CPAs, Va. Bar Assn. Democrat. Episcopalian. Author books; contbr. articles to prof. jours. Home: 177 Maxwelton Rd Charlottesville VA 22903-7859

ELLEY, REED, member of parliament; b. Simcoe, Ont., July 22, 1945; m. Louise Plester, June 17, 1967; children: Jennifer, John, David, Stephen, Joel, Dana, Jamie, Jill. BA, McMaster U., 1967, BD, 1970. Youth pastor Temple Bapt. Ch., Windsor, 1970-73; pastor Fonthill Bapt. CH., 1973-76; sr. pastor Royal Oak Bapt. Ch., Victoria, 1976-84, Crescent Heights Bapt. Ch., Calgary, 1984-92, First Bapt. Ch., Nanaimo, 1994-97; M.P. for Nanaimo-Cowichan House of Commons, 1997—, dep. health critic, mem. reform family caucus com., 1997—, vice chmn. standing com. on health, 1997—, assoc. mem. standing com. on human resources devel., 1997—, assoc. mem. standing com. on aboriginal affairs, 1997—. Pres. Nanaimo-Cowichan Constituency Assn., 1993-94; bd. dirs. Reform Nanaimo-Cowichan Constituency Assn., 1993-97; active foster parent assns., 1968—. Office: House of Commons, Rm 519 Confederation Bldg, Ottawa, ON Canada K1A 0A6

ELLICKSON, BRYAN CARL, economics educator; b. Bklyn., Feb. 12, 1941; s. Raymond Thorwald and Loene (Gibson) E.; m. Phyllis Lynn Rutter, June 19, 1965; 1 child, Paul Bryan. BA, U. Oreg., 1963; PhD, MIT, 1970. From asst. prof. to assoc. prof. UCLA, 1968-83, prof., 1983—, chair econs. dept., 1996-99; cons. Rand, Santa Monica, Calif., 1970—. Author: Competitive Equilibrium, 1993; contbr. articles to profl. jours. Rsch. grantee HUD, 1979-81, NSF, 1982-87. Mem. Am. Econ. Assn., Econometric Soc. Avocation: scuba diving. Home: 18409 Wakecrest Dr Malibu CA 90265-5620 Office: UCLA Dept Econs 405 Hilgard Ave Dept Econs Los Angeles CA 90095-9000

ELLICKSON, ROBERT CHESTER, law educator; b. Washington, Aug. 4, 1941; s. John Chester and Katherine Heilprin (Pollak) E.; m. Ellen Zachariasen, Dec. 19, 1971; children—Jenny, Owen. A.B., Oberlin Coll., 1963; LL.B., Yale U., 1966. Bar: D.C. 1967, Calif. 1971. Atty. adviser Pres.'s Com. on Urban Housing, Washington, 1967-68; mgr. urban affairs Levitt & Sons Inc., Lake Success, N.Y., 1968-70; prof. law U. So. Calif., Los Angeles, 1970-81, Stanford U., Calif., 1981-85; Robert E. Paradise prof. of natural resources law, Stanford U., Calif., 1985-88; Walter E. Meyer prof. of property and urban law, Yale U., New Haven, Conn., 1988—, dep. dean, 1991-92. Author: (with Tarlock) Land-Use Controls, 1981, Order Without Law, 1991 (Triennial award Order of the Coif), (with Rose & Ackerman) Perspectives on Property Law, 2d edit., 1995. Mem. Am. Acad. Arts & Scis., Am. Law Inst. Office: Yale U Law Sch PO Box 208215 New Haven CT 06520-8215

ELLICOTT, JOHN LEMOYNE, lawyer; b. Balt., May 26, 1929; s. Valcoulon LeMoyne and Mary Purnell (Gould) E.; m. Mary Lou Ulery, June

19, 1954 (dec. Jan. 1995); children: Valcoulon, Ann; m. Beatrice Berle Meyerson, Sept. 14, 1996. AB summa cum laude, Princeton U., 1951; LLB cum laude, Harvard U., 1954. Bar: D.C. 1957, U.S. Supreme Ct. 1959. Assoc. Covington & Burling, Washington, 1958-65, ptnr., 1965-98, chmn. mgmt. com., 1986-90, sr. counsel, 1998—. Pres. Fairfax County Fedn. Citizens Assn., Va., 1964; mem. governing bd. Nat. Cathedral Sch., Washington, 1973-80, 85-88, 89-90, chmn., 1978-79; trustee Landon Sch., Bethesda, Md., 1972-76; bd. dirs. Protestant Episc. Cathedral Found., Washington, 1980-88. Mem. ABA (sect. internat. law and practice), Washington Inst. Fgn. Affairs, Phi Beta Kappa. Democrat. Home: 5117 Macomb St NW Washington DC 20016-2611 Office: Covington & Burling 1201 Pennsylvania Ave NW PO Box 7566 Washington DC 20044-7566

ELLIG, BRUCE ROBERT, personnel executive; b. Manitowoc, Wis., Oct. 15, 1936; s. Robert Louis and Lucille Marie (Westphal) E.; 1 child, Brett Robert; m. Janice Reals. BBA, U. Wis., 1959, MBA, 1960. With Pfizer, Inc., N.Y.C., 1960-96, mgr. compensation and pers. rsch., 1968-70, corp. dir. compensation and benefits, 1970-78, v.p. compensation and benefits, 1978-83, v.p. employee rels., 1983-85, v.p. pers., 1985-95, v.p. employee resources, 1995-96; ret., 1996; speaker in field; mem. Pfizer standing coms., 1985-96, corp. edn. Employee Compensation and Mgmt. Devel., Retirement Plan, Retirement Plan Assets, Savs. and Investment, Corp. Adv. Coun., 1996—; cons. Orgn. Resources Counselors Inc., 1996—; bd. dirs. Headway Corp. Resources Inc.; adv. panel Career Ctrl. Author: Compensation and Benefits: Analytical Strategies, 1978; Executive Compensation: A Total Pay Perspective, 1982; Compensation and Benefits: Design and Analysis, 1985, Future Focus: Human Resources in the 21st Century, 1998; contbg. author: Encyclopedia of Professional Management, 1978; Handbook of Business Administration, 1984, Tomorrow's Human Resources Management, 1997; cons. editor Compensation and Benefits Rev.; mem. adv. bd. Jour. Compensation and Benefits; contbr. articles to profl. jours. Mem. Mayor's Adv. Pay Commn., N.Y.C., 1977-78, chmn., 1980; mem. bus. sector staff Coun. on Wage and Price Stability, 1979-80; mem. Ctr. for Advanced Human Resource Studies Cornell U., 1985-95, Presdl. Quadrennial Pay Commn., 1976, U.S. Civil Svc. Commn. Merit Pay Task Force, 1979; adv. bd. Ky. Ednl. TV, 1987-90, Global Remuneration Orgn. Named Person of Yr., U. Wis. Alumni Club of N.Y., 1995, Human Resource Exec. of Yr., Human Resource Exec. Mag., 1995; recipient Am. Compensation's Keystone award, 1999; Aresty fellow Wharton Bus. Sch. Fellow Nat. Acad. Human Resources (life), Employer Benefits Rsch. Inst., Wharton's Aresty Inst.; mem. Am. Compensation Assn. (life, certification program developer 1996—), N.Y. Assn. Compensation Adminstrs. (charter pres.), Am. Mgmt. Assn., Wall of Fame, N.Y. C. of C. and Ind. (human resource com.), N.Y. Pers. Mgmt. Assn. (past pres.), N.E. Sr. Human Resources Exec. Mtg. Group, Bus. Roundtable, Conf. Bd. (adv. coun. human resource mgmt.), Human Resources Roundtable Group, Pers. Round Table (life), Soc. Human Resource Mgmt. (life mem., chmn. bd. dirs. 1996, faculty staff 1996—), Wharton/Spencer Stuart Dir. Inst., U. Ill. Ctr. Human Resource Mgmt. (past ptnr.), Sr. Execs. Forum, U. So. Calif. Ctr. for Effective Orgns. (adv. bd. emeritus), U. Wis. Bus. Sch. Alumni (bd. dirs. emeritus), Phi Beta Kappa, Beta Gamma Sigma, Phi Eta Sigma,, others. Republican. Roman Catholic. Office: 25 East End Ave New York NY 10028-7052

ELLIMAN, DONALD, magazine company executive. Exec. v.p. Time Inc. Office: Time Inc Time & Life Bldg 1271 Avenue Of The Americas New York NY 10020-1300

ELLIMAN, DONALD M., JR., magazine publisher and executive; b. Bronxville, N.Y., Sept. 4, 1944; s. Donald M. Elliman; m. Mary Elliman; children: Kristin, Lindsay,, Anderw, Mack. BA, Middlebury Coll., 1967. With mktg. svc. dept. Time, N.Y.C., 1967-70, mem. advt. staff, assigned to London, circulation dir. People mag., 1976-78, pub. People, 1985-88; circulation dir. Time Internat., N.Y.C., 1978-81; pres. Time Distbn. Svcs., Inc., N.Y.C., 1981-82; advt. sales dir. Time Internat., N.Y.C., 1982-85, pub. dir., 1985; exec. v.p. mktg. for mags. Time Inc., N.Y.C., 1988-91, responsible for People and Entertainment Weekly mags., 1988-91, group pub., 1990-92, pres. sales and mktg. div., 1991-92, pres., pub. Sports Illustrated, 1992, pres. Sports Illustrated; Exec. Vice Pres Time Inc., NYC, NY, 1988—. Bd. dirs. Operation Sail; trustee N.Y. Yacht Club, Jimmie Heuga Ctr; hon. chmn. United Hosp. Fund. N.Y. Avocations: skiing, sailing. Office: Time Inc 1271 Avenue Of The Americas New York NY 10020-1300

ELLIN, MARVIN, lawyer; b. Balt., Mar. 6, 1923; s. Morris and Goldie (Rosen) E.; m. Stella J. Granto, Aug. 2, 1948; children: Morris, Raymond, Elisa. JD, U. Balt., 1953. Bar: Md. 1953, U.S. Supreme Ct. 1978; diplomate Am. Bd. Forensic Examiners. Practice law Balt., 1953—; mem. firm Ellin & Baker, 1957—; specialist in med. malpractice law; cons. on med. and legal trial matters; lectr. ACS, U. Md. Law Sch., U. Balt. City, Yale U. Sch. Medicine, Johns Hopkins Hosp., U. Calif., San Francisco, U. N.J.; former mem. chmn.'s adv. coun. com. on judiciary U.S. Senate. mem. editl. adv. bd.: Ob/Gyn Malpractice Prevention; contbr. chpts. on med. malpractice to various profl. publs. including Radiation Therapy of Benign Diseases. Fellow Internat. Acad. Trial Lawyers; mem. ABA, Am. Soc. Law and Medicine. Home: 13414 Longnecker Rd Glyndon MD 21071-4805 Office: 1101 Saint Paul St Baltimore MD 21202-2662

ELLINGHAUS, WILLIAM MAURICE, communications executive; b. Balt., Apr. 19, 1922; m. Erlaine Dietrich, May 30, 1942; children: Marcia A. Barone, Eric J., Douglas A., Barbara E. Gurne, Raymond W., Mark D., Christopher C., Jonathan P. LLD, Iona Coll., 1974, Pace U., 1976, St. John's U., 1976, Poly. Inst. N.Y., 1976; LL.D., W.Va. Wesleyan Coll., 1981; L.H.D., Manhattan Coll., 1975, Union Coll., 1982; D.B.A., Curry Coll., 1978; D.Sc. (hon.), Washington Coll., 1979; D.Sc., NYU, 1981. With Bell System, 1940-84; comml. mgr. Chesapeake & Potomac Tel. Co. Md., Balt., 1950-51; pub. office mgr. Chesapeake & Potomac Tel. Co. Va., Norfolk, 1951-52; dist. comml. mgr. Chesapeake & Potomac Tel. Co. Va., Culpeper, 1952-55; from gen. comml. supr. to v.p. dir. Chesapeake & Potomac Tel. Co. W.Va., Charleston, 1955-62; from v.p. accts. to v.p. pers. Chesapeake & Potomac Tel. Cos., Washington, 1962-65; from asst. v.p. planning to exec. v.p. AT&T, N.Y.C., 1965-70; exec. v.p. AT&T, 1970, vice-chmn. bd., 1976-79, pres., also bd. dirs., 1980-84, pres., 1970-76; pres. N.Y. Telephone Co., 1970-76; exec. vice chmn. bd dirs. N.Y. Stock Exchange, 1984-86; 1st chmn. N.Y. Mcpl. Assistance Corp., 1975; mem. N.Y. Emergency Fin.Ctrl. Bd., 1975-76. Bd. trustees Lawrence Hosp. With USNR, 1943-45. Mem. Am. Soc. Corp. Execs., Monroe County Telecomm. Authority, Mount Sinai Med. Ctr. (bd. trustees), Sovereign Order Knights of Malta, Equestrian Order Holy Sepulchre of Jerusalem. Home: Apt 3-H Stoneleigh 2 Bronxville NY 10708

ELLINGS, RICHARD JAMES, political and economic research institution executive; b. Santa Barbara, Calif., Jan. 7, 1950; s. George MacMachan and Barbara Marie (Kollin) E.; m. Marta Anna Korduba; children: Katherine Nicole, John William, Julia Victoria, Ruric George. AB, U. Calif., Berkeley, 1973; MA, U. Wash., 1976, PhD, 1983. Lectr. Calif. Poly. State U., San Luis Obispo, 1980-81; lectr. U. Wash., Seattle, 1982-83, assoc. dir. Henry M. Jackson Sch. Internat. Studies, 1986-89; legis. asst. U.S. Senate, Washington, 1984-85; exec. dir. Nat. Bur. Asian Rsch., Seattle, 1989—; also bd. dirs.; dir. George E. Taylor Fgn. Affairs Inst., Seattle, 1986-89; lectr. USIA, 1992, 97; cons. in field. Author: Embargoes and World Power, 1985; co-author: Private Property and National Security, 1991, (monograph) Asia's Challenge to American Strategy, 1992; editor: Americans Speak to APEC: Building a New Order with Asia, 1993, MFN Status, Human Rights and U.S.-China Relations, 1994, Access Asia: A Guide to Specialists and Current Research, 1994—, NBR Analysis, 1990—, Southeast Asian Security in the New Millenium, 1996. Del. Rep. Party State Conv., Tacoma, 1988. Grantee Dept. Def., 1990-95, 97, 98, Dept. State, 1994, Henry M. Jackson Found., 1989—, Japan Found. Ctr. for Global Partnership, 1995-98, Lynde and Harry Bradley Found., 1998-99, USIA, 1992, 97. Mem. Internat. Studies Assn., Pacific Coun. on Internat. Policy. Avocations: hiking, skiing, tennis. Home: 1615 85th Ave NE Clyde Hill WA 98004 Office: Nat Bur Asian Rsch 4518 University Way NE Ste 300 Seattle WA 98105-4530

ELLINGSON, IRMGARD HEIN, secondary education educator; b. Osceola, Iowa, July 5, 1953; s. Albert Hein and Minna (Wedmann) H.; m. Wayne Thomas Ellingson, Dec. 30, 1972; children: Gregg Michael, Tina Rossalie, Angela Christine. BS, Winona State Coll., 1974; MA, Wartburg Theol. Sem., 1993. Lic. secondary educator, Iowa. Pvt. music tchr. Elkhorn, Nebr., 1978-80, Ellis, Kans., 1980-83, Sumner, Ia., 1983-88; med. records clk. Good Samaritan Home, Ellis, Kan., 1981-83; tchr. German and social studies S. Winneshiek H.S., Calmar, Iowa, 1993—; exec. com. South Winneshiek Edn. Assn., Calmar, 1997—; South Winneshiek 2000 New Iowa Schs. Devel. Corp., Calmar, 1995—. Author Clues and Jour., Wandering Volhynians, 1978—; author: (book) The Bukovina Germans in Kansas: A 200 Year History of the Lutheran Swabians; editor, translator: (book) Illischestie, A Rural Community in Bukovina, 1993; mem. editl. bd. Am. Hist. Soc. of Germans from Russia, 1994—. Pres. South Winneshiek Bd. Edn., Calmar, 1992-93. Recipient Ehrenurkunde & Ehrennadel, Landsmannschaft der Buchenland deutschen, 1989, Silberne Ehrennadel, City of Augsburg, 1989. Mem. South Winneshiek Edn. Assn. (exec. com. 1994—), Evang. Luth. Ch. in Am., Am. Hist. Soc. Germans from Russia (editl. com. 1990—), Bukovina Soc. of Americans (internat. dir. 1989—), Wandering Volhynians (U.S. rep. 1993-98). Lutheran. Avocations: pianist, organist, translator, author, speaker, traveler.

ELLINGSWORTH, ALAN D., police superintendent; b. Georgetown, Del., 1954. BA, Wilmington Col., 1981, MA, 1990; grad., FBI Nat. Acad., 1988. Trooper Del. State Police, Dover, 1975, supt., 1994—. Named Trooper of the Yr., Crimestoppers. Office: Delaware State Police PO Box 430 Dover DE 19903-0430*

ELLINGTON, CAROL J., artist, printmaker; b. LeMars, Iowa, Nov. 5, 1950; d. Richard Joseph and Mary Jane (Kreber) Meis; m. Richard Wayne Ellington, July 1, 1972; children: Michelle Kay Ellington McNeil, Gina Anne. BFA in Printmaking magna cum laude, Bellevue U., 1989. One person shows at Offutt AFB, Bellevue, Nebr., 1990 (1st Pl. award), Plattsmouth (Nebr.) State Bank, 1992; exhibited in group shows at N.Mex. Internat. Art Exhbn., Clovis, 1986, Charleston (S.C.) AFB, 1980 (1st Pl. award), Bellevue U., 1986, 89, 90, (Pres. award), 94, King Korn Karnival Art Show, Plattsmouth, Nebr., 1982-95, Offutt AFB, 1988 (hon. mention), Nebr. State Office Bldg., 1989, Bellevue Artists' Assn., 1990, (hon. mention), 91 (2 Bronze awards), 92 (2 Bronze awards), 93 (2 Silver metals), 94 (Bronze award), 95 (Bronze award, hon. mention), 96 (hon. mention), Peter Kiewit Conf. Ctr., Omaha, 1990, 91 (hon. mention), 92 (award of merit), St. Barnabus Episcopal Parish Ch., Omaha, 1990, Assn. Nebr. Art Clubs, Columbus, 1990, Sioux City (Iowa) City Art Ctr., 1990, 91, LAEX Gallery, Omaha, 1990, Mus. Nebr. Art, Kearney, 1992 (Merit award), Nebr. Wesleyan U., Lincoln 1993 (Purchase award), Assn. Nebr. Art Clubs, 1993, 94, 95 (hon. mention), 96 (hon. mention), U. S.D. Art Galleries, 1993, Great Plains Chautauqua Art Show, Plattsmouth, 1993, 1200 Landmark Ctr., Omaha, 1994, Mus. Nebr. Art U. Nebr., 1994, Omaha-Douglas County Bldg., 1994, 95, Wrightstone Fine Arts Gallery, McCook (Nebr.) C.C., 1995, 97 (Patron award), Artists Coop. Gallery, Omaha, 1995, 96, Assn. Nebr. Art Clubs, Fremont, 1996, Nicolet Coll. LRC Gallery, Rhinelander, Wis., 1996, Arts Coun. S.E. Mo., Cape Girardeau, Mo., 1996, Ea. N.Mex. U., Portales, 1996, Trenton (N.J.) State Coll. Art Gallery, 1997, Moss-Thorns Gallery, Ft. Hays, Kans., 1997, others. Mem. Bellevue Artists Assn. (sec.), Assn. Nebr. Artists, Joslyn Art Mus., Artists' Cooperative Gallery, Associated Artists Omaha, Alpha Chi. Roman Catholic. Avocations: reading, travel, sewing. Home: 120 Debra St Plattsmouth NE 68048-2427

ELLINGTON, CHARLES RONALD, lawyer, educator; b. Cuthbert, Ga., Sept. 3, 1941; s. Charles Bartlett and Annie Claire (Moore) E.; m. Jean Alice Spencer, Apr. 29, 1967; children—Gregory Spencer, Alicia Nicole. A.B. summa cum laude, Emory U., 1963; LL.B., U. Va., 1966; LL.M., Harvard U., 1978. Bar: Ga. 1967, D.C. 1967. Assoc. firm Sutherland, Asbill and Brennan, Atlanta, 1966-69; mem. law faculty U. Ga. Sch. Law, 1969—, prof. law, 1977—, Thomas R.R. Cobb prof. law, 1983-93, dean, 1987-93, J. Alton Hosch prof. law, 1993—; on leave as scholar in residence U.S. Dept. Justice, Washington, 1979-80; reporter, Standard of the Profession Com., State Bar of Ga., Commn. on Uniform State Laws. Harvard U. fellow in law and humanities, 1973-74. Mem. Am. Law Inst. Avocation: sailing. Office: Univ Ga Sch Law Herty Dr Athens GA 30602

ELLINGTON, EDWARD, federal judge; b. 1940. BS, Miss. State U., 1962; JD, U. Miss., 1967. Law clk. to Hon. J.P. Coleman U.S. Ct. Appeals (5th cir.); law clk. to Hon. Henry Lee Rodgers Miss. Supreme Ct., Jackson; pvt. practice Jackson, 1968-86; chief bankruptcy judge U.S. Dist. Ct. (so. dist.) Miss., Jackson, 1986—; mem. Miss. State Senate. With U.S. Army. Office: US Dist Ct (so dist) Miss 100 E Capitol St Rm 107 Jackson MS 39201

ELLINGTON, HOWARD WESLEY, architect; b. Anthony, Kans., Mar. 2, 1938; s. John Wesley and Cressie May (Wilson) E.; m. Nelda Lee Newlin, Sept. 5, 1959; children: Howard Wesley II, Eric John, Craig Alan, Amy Lee. BArch, U. Kans., 1961. Registered architect, Kans., N.Mex., Mo., Ohio. Prin. Howard W. Ellington, AIA, Architect, Wichita, Kans., 1979—; co-owner Gallery Ellington, Wichita; founding trustee Kans. Cultural Trust, Wichita, 1985—; mem. bldg. and grounds com. Wichita Ctr. for Arts, trustee, 1995-97, treas., 1997, acting exec. dir., 1997-98, exec. dir. 1998—; bd. dirs. arts com. Ulrich Mus., Wichita, 1992-97; founding trustee, exec. dir. Allen-Lambe House Found., Wichita, 1990—; mem. Wichita Wayfinding Design Adv. Group, 1997. Editor: The Prairie Print Makers, 1984. Trustee Wichita Ctr. for the Arts, 1995-97; bd. dirs. Wichita-Sedgwick County Arts & Humanities Coun., 1996—, Wichita Pub. Arts Adv. Bd., 1996. Recipient Kans. Preservation award, 1993, Pedestal award Wichita Hist. Preservation Bd., 1996. Mem. Friends of Wichita Art Mus., Western Penn. Conservation, Nat. Trust for Hist. Preservation, Chgo. Archtl. Found., Frank Lloyd Wright Home and Studio Found., Birger Sandzen Meml. Gallery. Republican. Episcopalian. Avocation: art collecting. Office: 255 N Roosevelt St Wichita KS 67208-3720

ELLINGTON, JOHN DAVID, retired state official; b. Cramerton, N.C., Dec. 24, 1935; s. Joseph Randolph and Lyda Eva (Skidmore) E.; m. Mary Frances Powell, June 14, 1959; children: Susan Gail, John David, Michael Jon. AA, Mars Hill Coll., 1956; AB, U. N.C., 1958, MEd, 1961. Tchr. social studies Chapel Hill High Sch., N.C., 1958-65; cons. social studies N.C. Dept. Pub. Instrn., Raleigh, 1965-72, asst. dir. social studies, 1972-76, dir. divsn. social studies, 1976-93; pub. sch. liaison N.C. State U. Humanities Extension Divsn., Raleigh, 1995—; mem. adv. bd. Mini-Page Inc., Washington, 1973-82. Mem., chmn. Enloe Area Adv. Coun., Raleigh, N.C., 1981-93; precinct officer Precinct 28, Raleigh, 1981-82; mem. U.S.-Japan Conf. Cultural and Ednl. Interchange, U.S. Office Edn., Tokyo, 1977, Educators to Africa, 1971. Reynolds fellow in econs. U. N.C., Chapel Hill, 1961. Mem. Nat. Council Social Studies (com. chmn. 1984-85), N.C. Council Econ. Edn. (trustee-exec. com. 1975-93, N.C. state geography bee coord. 1988—, nat. assessment in ednl. progress-civics planning com. 1995-96), Coun. State Social Studies Specialists, N.C. Citizenship Edn. Inc. (pres.) chmn., bd. dirs. Middle Creek/Swift Creek Cmty. Alliance. Democrat. Baptist. Avocations: gardening, recreational sports. Home: 3412 Garden Oaks Ln Apex NC 27502-6811

ELLINGTON, MILDRED L., librarian; b. Marion, Ohio, June 7, 1921; d. Edward J. and Julia Ellen (Oiler) E. BA, Olivet Nazarene Coll., Kankakee, Ill., 1943; MA in French, Ohio State U., 1952; MA in English, Bowling Green (Ohio) U., 1964; MLS, Rosary Coll., River Forest, Ill., 1976. English and French tchr. Morral (Ohio) High Sch., 1944-49, Reddick (Ill.) High Sch., 1949-55; English tchr. Bremen Community High Sch., Midlothian, Ill., 1955-58, Bloom Twp. High Sch., Chicago Heights, Ill., 1958-60, Willowbrook High Sch., Villa Park, Ill., 1960-66; English tchr., then library dir. Addison (Ill.) Trail High Sch., 1966-82; reference librarian Maywood (Ill.) Pub. Library, 1982—. Sunday sch. supt. Elgin (Ill.) Ch. of the Nazarene, 1985-92. Mem. Ill. Library Assn. Democrat. Mem. Ch. of the Nazarene. Avocations: opera, singing, genealogy, travel. Office: Maywood Pub Libr 121 S 5th Ave Maywood IL 60153-1307

ELLINGWOOD, BRUCE RUSSELL, structural engineering researcher, educator; b. Evanston, Ill., Oct. 11, 1944; s. Robert W. and Carolyn L. (Ehmen) E.; m. Lois J. Drager, June 7, 1969; 1 son, Geoffrey D. BSCE, U. Ill., 1968, MSCE, 1969, PhD, 1972. Profl. engr., D.C. Structural engr. Naval Ship Research and Devel. Ctr., Bethesda, Md., 1972-75; research structural engr., leader structural engring. group Ctr. Bldg. Tech., Nat. Bur. Standards, Washington, 1975-86; prof. civil engring. Johns Hopkins U., Balt., 1986—, chmn. dept., 1990-97; lectr., cons. Assoc. editor: Jour. of Structural Safety; contbr. articles to profl. jours. Recipient Dural Research prize U. Ill., 1968, Nat. Capital award for Engring. Achievement D.C. Joint Council Engring. and Archtl. Socs., 1980, Walter L. Huber prize ASCE, 1980, Silver medal U.S. Dept. Commerce, 1980, Markwardt Rsch. prize Forest Products Rsch. Soc., 1988; named Engr. of Yr. of U.S. Dept. Commerce, Nat. Soc. Profl. Engrs., 1986. Mem. ASCE (State of Art in Civil Engring. award 1983, 88, Norman medal 1983, 98, Moissieff award 1988), Am. Concrete Inst., Am. Nat. Stds. Inst., Am. Inst. Steel Constrn. (T.R. Higgins lectureship 1988), Sigma Xi, Chi Epsilon, Tau Beta Pi. Presbyterian. Achievements include administered the secretariat of American National Standard Committee A58 on minimum design loads from 1977-84 and was responsible for coordinating and directing revisions to the A58 Standard that culminated in the publication of ANSI A58.1-1982 (now ASCE Standard 7), the first load standard in the U.S. to contain probability-based load combinations for limit states. Such load combinations now are used in Canada, the U.S. and in the Eurocodes now being developed in the common market. Was instrumental in the move by the steel industry toward limit states design. Office: John Hopkins U Dept Civil Engring 3400 N Charles St Baltimore MD 21218-2608

ELLIOT, DAVID CLEPHAN, historian, educator; b. Larkhall, Scotland, Sept. 17, 1917; came to U.S., 1947, naturalized, 1954; s. John James and Edith Emily (Bell) E.; m. Nancy Franelle Haskins, Dec. 3, 1945 (dec.); children: Enid Frances, John Clephan, Nancy Elizabeth. M.A., St. Andrews U., 1939; A.M., Harvard U., 1948, Ph.D., 1951; M.A., Oxford U., 1956, postgrad. (Ford fellow), 1956-57. With Indian Civil Service, 1941-47; teaching fellow Harvard U., 1948-50; asst. prof. history Calif. Inst. Tech., Pasadena, 1950-53; asso. prof. Calif. Inst. Tech., 1953-60, prof., 1960-86, prof. emeritus, 1986—; chmn. Calif. Inst. Tech. (75th Anniversary), 1965-67, exec. officer for humanities and social scis., 1967-71. Trustee Westridge Sch., 1970-90, trustee emeritus, 1992—, pres., 1976-78. With Royal Arty., 1940. NATO fellow, 1980. Mem. Inst. Current World Affairs (gov. 1964-70, chmn. 1969-70, trustee 1979-82, hon. trustee 1992—). Home: 1251 Inverness Dr Pasadena CA 91103-1115 Office: Calif Inst Tech Div Humanities and Social Scis 1200 E California Blvd Pasadena CA 91125

ELLIOT, DAVID HAWKSLEY, geologist; b. Chilwell, Eng., May 22, 1936; came to U.S., 1966; m. Ann Elliot, 1963. B.A., Cambridge U., Eng., 1959; Ph.D., Birmingham U., 1965. Mem. faculty Ohio State U., Columbus, 1969—, prof. dept. geol. scis., 1979—, dir. Byrd Polar Reseach Ctr. (formerly Inst. Polar Studies), 1973-89. Mem. Geol. Soc. Am., Geol. Soc. London, Ohio Acad. Sci., Am. Geophys. Union, Sigma Xi. Office: Ohio State Univ Dept Geol Scis Columbus OH 43210

ELLIOT, DOUGLAS GENE, chemical engineer, engineering company executive, consultant; b. Medford, Oreg., June 3, 1941; s. Don Joseph and Eleanor Joan (Sheets) E.; m. Noma Warnken, July 16, 1966 (div. 1979); 1 child, Jennifer M.; m. Patricia Jean Nichols, Mar. 15, 1980; children: Steven V. Bates, Michael A. Castillo. BSChemE, Oreg. State U., 1964; MS, U. Houston, 1968, PhD, 1971. Reservoir/prodn. engr. Humble Oil & Refining Co., Beaumont, Tex., 1964-66; co-founder, v.p. and bd. dirs. S.W. Wire Rope, Inc., 1967-70; cons. Gas Processors Assn., Houston, 1971; process/project engr. Hudson Engring. Co., Houston, 1971-78; mgr. process engring. Davy-McKee Corp., Houston, 1978-83, v.p. oil and gas, 1983-85; pres. D. G. Elliot & Assocs. Inc., Houston, 1985-86; pres., COO, Internat. Process Svcs. Inc., Houston, 1986—, also bd. dirs.; adj. prof. Rice U., Houston, 1976-77; mem. indsl. adv. com. Okla. State U., Stillwater, 1979-83; mgmt. cons. Norsk Hydro Oil & Gas Div., Oslo, 1984—. Contbr. articles to profl. jours.; mem. editorial rev. bd. Energy Process mag., 1981—; patentee in field. Mem. Tex. Energy Adv. Com., Austin, 1978; founding mem., bd. dirs. Tex. Solar Energy Soc., Austin, 1978; mem. Ctr. of Excellence R&D rev. panel Okla Ctr. for Advancement of Sci. & Tech., Oklahoma City. Recipient Outstanding Achievement award Tex. Soc. Profl. Engrs., 1978, citation for merit Bechtel Corp., 1991, 92, 93; Bechtel fellow, 1997, GPA citation for svc., 1998. Fellow AIChE (sec.-treas. S. Tex. sect. 1979, chmn. elect 1980, chmn. 1981, bd. dirs. fuels and petrochem. divsn. 1982-85); mem. Soc. Petroleum Engrs., Gas Processors Assn. (sec.-treas. 1983, Citation for Svc. award 1998), N.Y. Acad. Scis., Sigma Zi. Avocations: hunting, fishing. Home: 506 Fairport Ln Houston TX 77079-2429

ELLIOT, ERNEST ALEXANDER, retired naval rear admiral; b. Hilo, Hawaii, Mar. 13, 1942; m. Betty Ann Baechler; children: Michael, Christie. B of Math. and Econs., Whitman Coll., 1964; MBA, U. Mass., 1965; MS in Computer Sys. Mgmt., Naval Park Grad. Sch., Monterey, Calif., 1973. Commd. ensign USN, 1966, advanced through grades to rear adm., 1992; asst. to supply officer Naval Sta., Pearl Harbor, 1967-69; officer in charge, precommissioning supply officer USS Gray (DE-1054), Bremerton, Wash., 1969-70; liaison officer for Navy Fin. Ctr., navy comptr. Bur. Naval Pers., Cleve., 1973-75; dir. of fin. sys. dept. Fleet Material Support Officer, 1978-81; supply officer USS CANOPUS (AS-34), 1981-83; project officer for naval integrated storage, tracking and retrieval sys. Naval Supply Sys. Command, 1983-87; chief Def. Logistics Agy. Readiness Supply, 1987-90; exec. asst. to dir. Def. Mgmt. Rev. Studies Office of Sec. of Def., 1987-90; comdr. Navy Fleet Material Support Office, 1990-92; vice-comdr. Joint Logistics Sys. Ctr., Wright-Patterson AFB, Ohio, 1992-94; comdr. Def. Constrn. Supply Ctr., Dayton, Ohio, 1994-98; v.p. logistics XPEDX, 1998—. Decorated Def. Superior Svc. medal, Legion of Merit with gold star, Meritorious Svc. medal. Mem. Armed Forces Comms. and Electronics Assn. (v.p. 1994-95), Rotary. Avocations: golf, running, bowling, racquet ball. Home: 2000 River Ridge Ct Villa Hills KY 41017-4450 Office: XPEDX 50 E Rivercenter Blvd Ste 700 Covington KY 41011-1649*

ELLIOT, JARED, financial management consultant; b. Albany, N.Y., Oct. 15, 1928; s. Henry Melvin and Gladys Dolores (Richter) E.; children: Michael B., Lynn Elliot Hancock, Blake R., Jared. B.C.E., Yale U., 1950; M.B.A., Stanford U., 1955. Mgr. electronic data processing and mfg. scheduling Lenkurt Electric Co. Inc., San Carlos, Calif., 1955-58; sec., treas. Spectracoat Inc., San Carlos, 1958-61; mng. asso. mgmt. services dept. Arthur Young & Co., San Francisco, 1961-69; v.p. Tex. Gas Resources Corp., Owensboro, Ky., 1969—; treas. Tex. Gas Resources Corp., 1979-84; v.p. fin. Lightnet, New Haven, 1984-86, ret., 1987; pvt. practice fin. mgmt. cons., 1988—. Bd. dirs. United Way, Owensboro, 1969-80, pres., 1972; bd. dirs. Community Concert Assn., Owensboro, 1974-77. Served with USN, 1950-53. Republican.

ELLIOT, JEFFREY M., political science educator, author; b. L.A., June 14, 1947; s. Gene and Harriet (Sobsey) E. BA, U. So. Calif., 1969, MA, 1970; ArtsD in Govt., Claremont Grad. Sch., 1978; LittD (hon.), Shaw U., 1985; LLD (hon.), City U. L.A., 1986; cert. in grantsmanship, Grantsmanship Tng. Ctr., 1980; cert. in internat. trade and devel., N.C. Ctrl. U., 1995; cert. in conflict resolution, Ctr. for Peace Edn., 1997. Rsch. asst. U. So. Calif., 1969-70; instr. polit. sci. Glendale Coll., 1970-72, Cerritos Coll., 1970-72; asst. prof. history and polit. sci. U. Alaska-Anchorage C.C., 1973-74; asst. prof. history and polit. sci., dean curriculum Miami-Dade C.C., 1974-76; asst. prof. polit. sci. Va. Wesleyan Coll., Norfolk, 1978-79; sr. curriculum specialist Edn. Devel. Ctr., Newton, Mass., 1979-81; prof. polit. sci., dir. grad. studies, dir. internat. progs. N.C. Ctrl. U., 1981—; disting. advisor fgn. affairs Congressman Mervyn M. Dymally (Dem. Calif.), 1985-94. Author: 118 books, including Keys to Economic Understanding, 1976, Science Fiction Voices, 1979, Literary Voices, 1980, Analytical Congressional Directory, 1981, Deathman Pass Me By: Two Years on Death Row, 1982, Tempest in a Teapot: The Falkland Islands War, 1983, Kindred Spirits, 1984, Black Voices in American Politics, 1985, Urban Society, 1985, The Presidential-Congressional Political Dictionary, 1985, Fidel Castro: Nothing Can Stop the Course of History, 1986, The State and Local Government Political Dictionary, 1986, The Third World, 1987, The Arms Control, Disarmament, and Military Security Dictionary, 1988, Dictionary of American Government, 1988, Fidel, 1988, Conversations with Maya Angelou, 1988, Voices of Zaire: Rhetoric or Reality?, 1990, Brown & Benchmark Reader in American Government, 1991, Brown and Benchmark Reader in International Relations, 1991, The Trilemma of World Oil Politics, 1991, Starclimber: The Autobiography of Raymond Z. Gallon, 1991, Adventures of a Free-Lancer: The Autobiography of Stanton A. Coblentz, 1991, The Work of Jack Dann: An Annotated Bibliography and Guide, 1991, The Work of George Zebrowski: An Annotated Bibliography and Guide, 1991, Brown & Benchmark Reader in American Government, 1992, Brown & Benchmark Reader in International Relations, 1992, The Third World, 1992, Into the Flames: The

Life Story of a Righteous Gentile, 1992, After All These Years: Sam Moskowitz On His Science Fiction Career, 1992, The Encyclopedia of African-American Politics, 1994, The Work of Raymond Z. Gallun: An Annotated Bibliography and Guide, 1994, Fidel By Fidel, 1994, The African-American Historical Atlas, 1994, The Historical Dictionary of OPEC, 1995, The Dictionary of State and Local Government, 1995, The Historical Dictionary of the Third World, 1995, The Work of Pamela Sargent: An Annotated Bibliography and Guide, 1996, The Work of George Zebrowski: An Annotated Bibliography and Guide, 1996, The Work of Jack Dann: An Annotated Bibliography and Guide, 1997; contbr. 550 articles and revs. to profl. and popular jours.; contbg. editor Negro History Bull., 1976-80, West Coast Writers' Conspiracy, 1978-80. Mem. community services adv. council Miami (Fla.) Community Services, 1974-76; mem. Los Angeles Mayor's Adv. Com., 1971-72; speechwriter, research asst., campaign strategist U.S. Sen. Howard W. Cannon of Nev., 1969—; cons. Calif. Clean Environment Act, 1970-72. Recipient 100 literary and scholarly awards including Fair Enterprise Medallion award, 1965, Outstanding Polit. Sci. Scholar citation, 1970, Outstanding Tchr. award, 1971, Outstanding Am. Educator citation, 1975, Disting. Svc. Through Community Effort award, 1976, Outstanding Rsch. prize, 1987, 91, Disting. Scholarship award, 1987, Outstanding Rsch. Prize, 1991, Nancy Susan Reynolds award, 1991, Disting Svc. award Acad. Help Ctr., 1992, Gen. News, Election Analysis Associated Press award, 1993, Documentary Profile Community Television award, 1994. Mem. AAUP, ASCD, Community Coll. Social Sci. Assn. (dir. 1970-77, pres. 1975-77), So. Assn. Colls. and Schs. (accreditation team 1974-76), Am. Polit. Sci. Assn., Nat. Coun. for Social Studies, Rocky Mountain Social Sci. Assn., Soc. Internat. Devel. (Excellence award 1995), Coun. Fgn. Affairs, Internat. Studies Assn., Assn. Third World Studies, Am. Hist. Assn., Pi Sigma Alpha, Phi Delta Kappa. Home: 511 N Water's Edge Dr Durham NC 27703-6722 Office: NC Cen Univ Dept Polit Sci Durham NC 27707 *I have attempted to live those ideals which inspire me to fight for a more humane world love, honor, courage, integrity, and truth. I have also taken to heart the wisdom of the prophets who implore us to live and love as though life and love were one. Although this is a difficult and frustrating task, it is the only way to live. And finally, I have come to recognize that what matters most, after everything is said, are people-close family and friends who reach out and say in a host of ways, "I care."*

ELLIOT, RALPH GREGORY, lawyer; b. Hartford, Conn., Oct. 20, 1936; s. K. Gregory and Zarou (Manoukian) E. BA, Yale U., 1958, LLB, 1961. Bar: Conn. 1961, U.S. Dist. Ct. Conn. 1963, U.S. Ct. Appeals (2d cir.) 1966, U.S. Ct. Appeals (Fed. cir.) 1993, U.S. Ct. Appeals (1st cir.) 1997, U.S. Supreme Ct. 1967. Law clk. to assoc. justice Conn. Supreme Ct., Hartford, 1961-62; assoc. Alcorn, Bakewell & Smith, Hartford, 1962-67, ptnr., 1967-83; ptnr. Tyler, Cooper & Alcorn, Hartford, 1983—; adj. prof. law U. Conn., Hartford, 1973—; sec. Superior Ct. Legal Internship Com., Conn., 1971—; chmn. Superior Ct. Legal Specialization Screening Com., Conn., 1981—, U.S. Dist. Ct. Panel Spl. Masters, Hartford, 1983-88. Chmn. bd. editors Conn. Law Tribune, 1986-87. Chmn. Constn. Bicentennial Commn., Conn., 1986-91; mem. Criminal Justice Commn. Conn., 1991-95. Recipient Fenton P. Futtner award Conn. Reps., 1993. Fellow Am. Bar Found.; mem. ABA (standing com. on ethics and profl. responsibility 1989-95, standing com. on profl. discipline 1998—, ho. of dels. 1983-87), Conn. Bar Assn. (officer, bd. govs. 1971-79, 83-87, pres. 1985-86, John Eldred Shields Disting. Profl. Svc. award 1993), Am. Law Inst., Yale Law Sch. Assn. (pres. 1988-90, chmn. exec. com. 1990-92), Yale Club (pres. 1977-79, Nathan Hale award 1984, Betty McCallip Meml. award 1991), Hartford, Grad. Club (New Haven), Phi Beta Kappa. Republican. Episcopalian. Office: Tyler Cooper & Alcorn City Pl Fl 35 Hartford CT 06103

ELLIOT, SEAN MICHAEL, professional basketball player; b. Tucson, Feb. 2, 1968. Student, U. Ariz. Basketball player San Antonio Spurs, 1989-93, 94—, Detroit Pistons, 1993-94, Houston Rockets, 1994. Named to Sporting News All-Am. First team, 1988, 89, NBA All-Rookie second team, 1990, NBA All-Star team, 1993; recipient Wooden award. Office: San Antonio Spurs Alamodome 100 Montana St San Antonio TX 78203-1031*

ELLIOT, WILLARD SOMERS, retired musician, composer; b. Ft. Worth, Tex., July 18, 1926; s. Chester Somers and Grace Roberta (Bruyere) E.; m. Patricia Joan Bills, Dec. 30, 1952; children: Joseph, Peter. MusB, North Tex. U., 1945; MusM, EAStman Sch. Music U. Rochester, 1946. Bassoonist Houston Symphony, 1946-49; instr. bassoon North Tex. U., Denton, 1949-52; bassoonist Dallas Symphony, 1951-56, prin. bassoonist, 1956-64; prin. bassoonist Chgo. Symphony, 1964-96; prof. bassoon Tex. Christian U., 1997—; instr. bassoon De Paul U., Chgo., 1973-76, Northwestern U., Evanston, 1979-84; mem. Chgo. Pro Musica. Composer: Elegy for Orchestra, 1960 (Kousevitzky award 1961), Bassoon Concerto, 1965, Snake Charmer, 1975, Five Impressions for Wind Octet, 1981; recorded Mozart Bassoon Concerto with Chgo. Symphony, Claudio Abbado conducting. Served to cpl. U.S. Army, 1953-55. Recipient Grammy award Nat. Acad. Rec. Arts and Scis., 1985. Methodist.

ELLIOTT, BARBARA JEAN, librarian; b. Bluffton, Ind., Oct. 2, 1927; d. Dale A. and Gwendolyn I. (Long); m. Robert J. Elliott, June 13, 1949; 1 son, Michael Roger. B.S. with honors, Ind. U., 1949, M.L.S., 1979. Dir. tech. info. svcs. uranium div. Mallinckrodt Chems., St. Louis, 1949-59; rsch. libr. Petrolite Corp., Webster Groves, Mo., 1961-63; head tech. services St. Francis Coll., Ft. Wayne, Ind., 1974-76; dir. Bluffton-Wells County Pub. Library, 1976-95, ret. Pres. Wells County Found., 1995; pres. Ch. Women United of Wells County. Mem. ALA, Ind. Libr. Assn. (fed. legis. coordinator), LWV of Ind. (state sec. 1981-83, chmn. health care 1983-89, 3d vice pres. 1985-86), Ind. Bus. and Profl. Women (pres. 1987-88, dist. dir. 1988-93), Wells County Hist. Soc. (pres. 1997—), Bluffton Garden Club (pres.), Wells Co. Coun. on Aging (sec. 1996—). Home: 6831 SE State Rd 116 Bluffton IN 46714-9420

ELLIOTT, BENJAMIN PAUL, architect; b. Washington, Dec. 27, 1920; s. Benjamin Sargent and Marguerite (Plenckner) E.; m. Mary Dickenson, July 22, 1943; children: Paul Charles, Sara. Cath. U. Am., Catholic U. Am., 1948. Pvt. practice Silver Spring, Md., 1950-81; pres. Duane, Elliott, Cahill, Mullineaux & Mullineaux, P.A., Architects, Planners, Cons., Rockville, Md., 1981-90; ind. archtl. cons. Rockville, 1990—; Chmn. Washington Regional Conf. Religious Architecture, 1966; bd. dirs., hon. chmn. Nat. Conf. Religious Architecture, Washington, 1968-70. Contbr. to Ency. Architecture, 1987; pub. Potomac Valley Architect, 1957-59; pub., bus. mgr. Faith and Form, 1966-71. Pres. West Montgomery Citizens Assn., 1962-63; chmn. trustees Potomac Elem. Sch., 1963-69; bd. dirs. Montgomery County Hist. Soc., 1986-90, 92-96, bd. trustees, 1999—; vestryman local Episc. Ch., 1956-59, 61-68, jr. warden, 1968-69. With AUS, 1942-45. Recipient Spl. citation Guild for Religious Architecture, 1971, E.B. Morris Disting. Svc. award, 1975, Masonry Inst. award, 1976, 79, 82, citation Combined Chambers of Commerce Montgomery County, 1980. Fellow AIA (sec. Md. divsn. 1952-57, mem. nat. com. on religious architecture 1963-66, pres. Potomac Valley chpt. 1957-58, chmn. com. on bylaws 1965-76, Disting. Svc. award 1970, E.B. Morris award Potomac Valley chpt.); mem. Md. Soc. Archs. (sec.-treas. 1975-78, bd. dirs., chmn. bylaws com. 1988-91, chmn. pub. com. 1992-93), Am. Arbitration Assn. (panelist 1992—), Bethesda Cosmopolitan Club (pres. 1993-95). Address: 9724 Watts Branch Dr Rockville MD 20850-3756

ELLIOTT, BENNY LEE, JR., mechanical engineer; b. Phila., Aug. 21, 1947; s. Benny Lee and Viola (Watkins) E.; m. Lola F. Foulks, Mar. 13, 1971; children: Angela L., Vanessa A., Benny L. III. BSME, Spring Garden Coll., 1971; MSE, N.C. A&T State U., 1974; MSIE, Purdue U., 1994; postgrad., Stevens Inst. Tech., 1994—. Tech. asst. N.C. A&T State U., Greensboro, 1974; devel. engr. IBM Corp., Research Triangle Park, N.C., 1974-80; advanced devel. engr. Intersoll-Rand Co., Davidson, N.C., 1980-82; physics instr. Johnson C. Smith U., Charlotte, 1982; product engr. AT&T Mfg., Greensboro, 1982-95; mem. tech. staff Bell Labs., Whippany, N.J., 1995—. Contbr. articles to profl. publs. Big Brother United Way, Greensboro, 1991-95. Mem. ASME (bd. tech. devel. 1996—, chair N.C. sect. 1994-95, vice chair N.C. sect. 1993-94). Democrat. Baptist. Achievements include 12 engineering cost reductions to AT&T Corp. Home: 1809 Melchior Cir Greensboro NC 27406-9071

ELLIOTT, BILL, professional rac car driver; b. Dawsonville, Ga., Oct. 8, 1955. Winner numerous auto races including Daytona 500, 1985, 87, Coca-Cola 500, 1985, Winston 500, 1985, Budweiser 500, 1985, 88, Van Scoy 500, 1985, Miller 400, 1985, 86, 89, Pocono 500, 1985, Champion Spark Plug 400, 1985, 86, 87, So. 500, 1985, 88, Atlanta Jour. 500, 1985, 87, The Winston, 1986, AC Delco 500, 1987, Oakwood Home 500, 1987, Talladega 500, 1987, Busch Clash, 1987, Del 500, 1988, Summer 500, 1988, Firecracker 400, 1988, 91, Valleydale 500, 1988, Autoworks 500, 1989, AC Spark Plug 500, 1989, Peak 500, 1990; named Winston Cup Champion, 1988. *

ELLIOTT, CARL HARTLEY, former university president; b. Columbus, Ind., Mar. 21, 1922; s. Herschel B. and Hazel (Hartley) E.; m. Elizabeth Schmitt, July 8, 1945 (dec. May 1984); children: Prudence, Lisa, Linda, Nancy; m. Meredith Geyer Kopper, July 20, 1985. AB, Ind. U., 1946, MBA, 1947; PhD, Purdue U., 1952, LittD, 1985. Jr. mgmt. cons. Dillard E. Bird Assos., Cin., 1947-48; asst. prof. psychology Miami U., Oxford, Ohio, 1948-51; assoc. prof. Purdue U., Hammond, Ind., 1952-55; chancellor, dean, dir. Purdue U. (Calumet Campus), Hammond, 1959-74; employee rels. mgr. East Chicago Refinery (Ind.), Socony Mobil Oil Co., Inc., 1955-57; supr. selection and placement Socony Mobil Oil Co., Inc., N.Y.C., 1957-59; pres. Tri-State U., Angola, Ind., 1974-83, pres. emeritus, 1983—; dir. No. Ind. Pub. Svc. Co., 1970-93. Adviser Lake County Community Devel. Com., 1965-74; Lake County Econ. Opportunity Council, 1965-71, pres., 1965; v.p. N.W. Ind. chpt. ARC, 1968-70, Gt. Lakes Health and Edn. Found., 1968-76; mem. citizens bd. St. Margaret Hosp., 1966-74, chmn., 1974; bd. dirs. Purdue Calumet Devel. Found., 1964-76, pres., 1973-76; bd. dirs. N.W. Ind. United Fund, 1970-73, v.p., 1970-72; pres. NWI Research, Inc., 1970-72; bd. dirs. Lake Area United Way, 1973-74, Indiana Forum, 1976-79, Steuben County Mental Health Assn., 1983-86; sec. exec. com. Associated Colls. Ind., 1978-80; exec. bd. Anthony Wayne Area coun. Boy Scouts Am., 1987-90, mem. adv. com.; exec. com. Ind. Conf. Higher Edn., 1978-80; bd. dirs. Northeastern Ctr., Inc., 1985-86; bd. dirs. Ind. Colls. and Univs. of Ind., 1979-81, vice chmn., 1981. Served with USAAF, 1942-46. Named Sagamore of the Wabash; recipient DeMolay Legion of Honor. Fellow APA; mem. Midwest Psychol. Assn., Soc. for Advancement Mgmt. (pres. Calumet chpt. 1964-65), Assn. Continuing Higher Edn. (dir. 1969-75, pres. 1973-74), Angola Area C. of C. (dir. 1978-81), Quest Club, Masons (33 deg., KYCH, master Angola lodge 1987), Rotary (pres. Hammond club 1972-73), Sigma Xi, Beta Gamma Sigma, Delta Mu Delta, Delta Sigma Pi, Kappa Kappa Psi, Psi Chi, Phi Eta Sigma, Alpha Sigma Lambda. Methodist. Home: 4980 N 300 W Apt 4 Fremont IN 46737-9615 *I believe that all one's actions must be based on a strong sense of morality and personal integrity. It is important to be honest and straightforward. Communication with others must be open and forthright, with the recognition of both our own dependence on others and the consequences of our behavior. Working with and through others magnifies our own actions and is the only real road to accomplishment.*

ELLIOTT, CAROL C., career officer. BS in Internat. Rels. and Polit. Sci., Iowa State U., 1972; disting. grad., Officer Tng. Sch., 1973, Squadron Officer Sch., 1977; MBA in Aviation, Embry-Riddle Aero. U., 1984; disting. grad., Air Command and Staff Coll., 1987; student, Nat. War Coll., 1992. Commd. 2d lt. USAF, 1973, advanced through grades to brig. gen., 1998; intelligence analyst 432d Tactical Fighter Wing, Udorn Royal Thai AFB, Thailand, 1974-75, USAF, Clark Air Base, The Philippines, 1975-76; chief target intelligence br. 388th Tactical Fighter Wing, Hill AFB, Utah, 1976-79, 52d Tactical Fighter Wing, Spangdahlem Air Base, W. Germany, 1979-82; target intelligence officer Armed Forces Air Intelligence Ctr., Lowry AFB, Colo., 1983; chief target devel. br. then target studies br. Hdqs. USAF Europe, Ramstein Air Base, W. Germany, 1983-86, directorate intelligence applications, dep. chief staff intellegence, 1983-86; various assignments Hdqs. USAF, Pentagon, Washington, 1987-91, 97, vice dir. intelligence J2 joint staff, 1997—; chief collection mgmt. div., asst. chief staff intelligence Hdqs. U.S. Forces Korea, Yongsan, S. Korea, 1992-94; dep. dir. intelligence Air Combat Command, Langley AFB, Va., 1994-95; comdr. 692d Intelligence Group, Hickam AFB, Hawaii, 1995-96; dir. intelligence Hdqs. Pacific Air Force Base, Hickam AFB, 1996-97. Decorated Legion of Merit. Office: Joint Staff/J2 IE880 Joint Staff Pentagon Washington DC 20318-2000

ELLIOTT, CHARLES HAROLD, clinical psychologist; b. Kansas City, Mo., Dec. 30, 1948; s. Joseph Bond and Suzanne (Wider) E.; 1 child, Brian Douglas. BA, U. Kans., 1971, MA, 1974, PhD, 1976. Cert. clin. psychologist, N. Mex. Asst. prof. East Ctrl. U., Ada, Okla., 1976-79, U. Okla. Health Scis., 1979-85; assoc. prof. dept. psychiatry U. Okla., 1983-85, U. N. Mex. Sch. Medicine, Albuquerque, 1985-87; adj. assoc. prof. dept. psychology U. N.Mex., Albuquerque, 1986—; faculty full appointment Fielding Inst., Santa Barbara, Calif., 1987—; consulting editor Jour. Clin. Child Psychology, 1987-89; ad hoc reviewer to profl. jours., 1983—; cognitive therapist NIMH Collaborative Study of Depression, Okla. City, 1980-85. Co-author: (with Maureen K. Lassen) Why Can't I Get What I Want, 1998; guest editor Psychiatric Annals, 1992; contbr. numerous articles to profl. jours. Mem. APA, Biofeedback and Behavioral Medicine Soc. N.Mex. (pres. 1988), Assn. for Advancement of Behavior Therapy, Assn. for Advancement Psychology, Soc. Behavioral Medicine, Soc. Pediat. Psychology, N.Mex. Psychol. Assn. (bd. dirs. 1992-96). Home: 4200 Killington Rd NW Albuquerque NM 87114-5563 Address: 215 Gold Ave SW Albuquerque NM 87102-3364 Office: 212 Gold Ave SW # 202 Albuquerque NM 87102-3320

ELLIOTT, CLIFTON LANGSDALE, lawyer; b. Kansas City, Mo., Oct. 26, 1938; s. John Miller and Kate (Langsdale) E.; m. Bronwyn Ann Reese, Mar. 31, 1963 (div. Mar. 1983); children—Evan R., Kate L.; m. Marjorie A. Critten, Apr. 4, 1987. B.A., Dartmouth Coll., 1960; J.D., Northwestern U., 1963. Bar: Mo. 1963, Wash. 1991, Calif. 1992, U.S. Dist. Ct. (we. and ea. dists.) U.S. Ct. Appeals (8th cir.) 1965, U.S. Ct. Appeals (4th cir.) 1968, U.S. Ct. Appeals (D.C. cir.) 1973, U.S. Ct. Appeals (10 cir.) 1975, U.S. Ct. Appeals (2d, 5th and 9th cirs.) 1980, U.S. Supreme Ct. 1979. Assoc., ptnr. Spencer, Fane, Britt & Browne, Kansas City, Mo., 1963-79; ptnr. Elliott & Kaiser, Kansas City, 1979-87, Smith, Gill, Fisher & Butts, Kansas City, 1987-88, Watson, Ess, Marshall & Enggas, Kansas City, 1988-91; of counsel, ptnr. Davis Wright Tremaine, Seattle, 1991—; instr. labor law U. Mo., 1966; spl. counsel Am. Hosp. Assn., 1973-75; mem. U.S. C. of C. Nat. Labor Relations Act Task Force, 1980—. Mem. ABA, Mo. Bar, Wash. State Bar, Calif. Bar, Am. Soc. Hosp. Attys. (ad hoc com. labor relations 1975—). Contbr. articles to profl. jours. Avocations: boating, fishing. Office: Davis Wright Tremaine 1501 4th Ave Ste 2600 Seattle WA 98101-1688

ELLIOTT, DANIEL WHITACRE, surgeon, retired educator; b. Greenville, Ohio, Aug. 5, 1922; s. James Scott and LaVirge (Whitacre) E.; m. Elizabeth Lucille Wolff, Aug. 11, 1961; children: James Calvin, Lisa Ann. Student, Ohio State U., 1942-43, M.Med. Sci., 1956; M.D., Yale, 1949. Diplomate: Am. Bd. Surgery. Intern surgery Columbia Presbyn. Hosp., N.Y.C., 1949-50; surgery resident Ohio State U. Hosp., 1951, 53-57; mem. faculty Ohio State U. Sch. Medicine, 1957-64; prof. surgery U. Pitts. Sch. Medicine, 1965-76; Chief surgery Pitts. VA Hosp., Pitts., 1971-76; staff Presbyn., Western Pa., Shadyside, Children's hosps., Pitts., to 1976; mem. staff Kettering Meml., Miami Valley, Good Samaritan, St. Elizabeth's, VA hosps., all Dayton, Ohio; chmn. dept. surgery Wright State U. Sch. Medicine, 1976-88. Editorial bd.: Am. Surgeon, Am. Jour. Surgery; Contbr. numerous articles to profl. jours. Pres. Ctrl. Surgical Assn. Found., 1993. Served with AUS, 1943-45; as capt. M.C. USAF, 1951-53. Fellow ACS; mem. Am. Surg. Assn., Cen. Surg. Assn. (pres. 1988), Western Surg. Assn., Internat. Surg. Assn., Am. Burn Assn., Soc. Univ. Surgeons, Assn. Acad. Surgery, Am. Gastroenterology Assn., Soc. Surgery Alimentary Tract, Sigma Xi., Alpha Kappa Kappa, Alpha Omega Alpha. Home: 5917 Yarmouth Dr Dayton OH 45459-1449

ELLIOTT, DAVID DUNCAN, III, science research company executive; b. L.A., Aug. 4, 1930; s. David Duncan Elliott II and Mildred B. (Young) Mack; m. Arline L. Leckrone, Aug. 18, 1962; children: Lauren, Elliott Croft. BS, Stanford U., 1951; MS, Calif. Inst. Tech., 1953, PhD, 1959. Mem. tech. staff Lockheed Rsch. Lab., Palo Alto, Calif., 1959-61; postdoctoral fellow U. Paris., 1962; dept. head Aerospace Corp., El Segundo, Calif., 1961-70; sci. advisor Nat. Aeronautics and Space Coun., Washington, 1970-72; sr. staff mem. exec. office of pres. NSC, Washington, 1972-77; v.p. SRI Internat., Menlo Park, Calif., 1977-86; sr. v.p. Sci. Applications Internat. Corp., San Diego, 1986-91, Syst Control Tech., Palo Alto, Calif., 1991-94; corp. v.p. Sci. Applications Internat. Corp., Palo Alto, Calif., 1994-95; cons., 1995-99; sr. rschr. ctr. internat. security & coop. Stanford (Calif.) U., 1999—; mem. Army Sci. Bd., The Pentagon, Washington, 1982-89; cons. NRC, NAS, 1988—; mem. bd. visitors U. Calif., Davis, 1997—. Mem. editorial bd. Jour. Def. Rsch., 1988—. Recipient Outstanding Civilian Svc. award U.S. Army, 1989. Mem. AIAA, AAAS, Am. Phys. Soc., Am. Geophys. Union. Home: 2434 Sharon Oaks Dr Menlo Park CA 94025-6829 Office: CISAC Encina Hall Stanford CA 94305-6165

ELLIOTT, DAVID H., insurance company executive; b. 1941. With Aetna Life & Casualty Co., 1969-86; chmn., CEO MBIA Inc., Armonk, N.Y., 1986-99, bd. dirs., 1999—. Office: MBIA Ins Corp 113 King St Armonk NY 10504-1610*

ELLIOTT, DAVID LEROY, mathematician, educator, engineering educator; b. Cleve., May 29, 1932; s. Reed LeRoy and Roma (Benjamin) E.; m. Kiyoko Akaeda, Mar. 24, 1956 (div. 1980); children: Marguerite, Philip David; m. Pauline Wei-Ying Tang, Oct. 31, 1984. B.A., Pomona Coll., 1953; M.A., U. So. Calif., 1959; Ph.D., UCLA, 1969. Mathematician U.S. Naval Ocean Systems Ctr., Pasadena, Calif., 1955-69; lectr. UCLA, 1969-71; mem. faculty Washington U., St. Louis, 1971—; prof. dept. systems sci. and math. Washington U., 1980-94, prof. emeritus, 1994—; with NSF, Washington, DC, 1987-89; vis. prof. Brown U., Providence, 1979, UCLA, 1987; vis. rsch. scientist U. Md., 1992—; sr. rsch. scientist NeuroDyne, Inc., 1993—. Editor: Neural Systems for Control, 1997. Fellow IEEE; mem. Am. Math. Soc., Soc. Indsl. Applied Math., Math. Assn. Am., Sigma Xi. Avocations: music; science fiction.

ELLIOTT, DENNIS DAWSON, communications executive; b. Evansville, Ind., Jan. 30, 1945; s. Thomas Ira and Mary Pauline (Dawson) Elliott; m. Rebecca Lynn Robinett, Jan 28, 1967 (div. Oct. 1987); children: Jodi Suzanne, Dawn Denise; m. Catherine A. Canfield, Feb. 24, 1996. AB in Journalism, Ind. U., 1969. From bus. intern to advt. mgr. pharm. divsn. Mead Johnson & Co., Evansville, 1967-80, dir., devel. affairs pharm. divsn., 1980-85; advt. dir. Bristol-Myers U.S.P. & G., Evansville, 1985-89; exec. v.p. Campus Group Cos., Tuckahoe, N.Y., 1989-92; pres. Interactive Edn., N.Y.C., 1992—; v.p. bus. devel. CME, Inc., Santa Ana, Calif., 1993-94; sr. dir. Scienta Healthcare Edn., Durham, N.C., 1994-97; v.p. mktg. Campus Group Cos., Tuckahoe, N.Y., 1997—. Bd. dirs. So. Ind. Region Sports Car Club of Am., Evansville, 1970s. Recipient news photography award AP, 1967, Ernie Pyle scholarship Ind. U. Sch. Journalism, Bloomington, 1967. Mem. Med. Mktg. Assn., Pharm. Advt. Coun., Ind. U. Alumni Assn. (life, pres. 1969-79, sec.-treas., bd. dirs. Vanderburgh County), Sigma Delta Chi. Methodist. Avocations: photography, sports car racing, bicycling, writing. Home: 2317 Primrose Valley Ct Raleigh NC 27613-8552 Office: 42 Oak Ave Tuckahoe NY 10707-4025

ELLIOTT, DIANE V., lawyer; b. June 28, 1952. AB in Psychology, Lafayette Coll., 1974; JD, U. Miami, 1977; MS in Environtl. Sci., N.J. Inst. and Tech., 1995. Atty., 1977-96; dir. cmty. devel. Northampton County Devel. Corp., Easton, Pa., 1996-98; dir. Lehigh Valley Recycling Intiative, Allentown, Pa., 1999—. E-mail: dvelliott@phoenixland.org.

ELLIOTT, DOLORES, disabilities advocate, film producer; b. N.Y.C., Nov. 13, 1950; d. Thomas Augustus Elliot and Vera A. Burll. BFA, NYU, 1972; MEd, Hunter Coll., 1996. Prodr. Ctr. for Study Music, N.Y.C., 1988—; assoc. prodr. Stanley Nelson Prodns., N.Y.C., 1990-93, SearchLight, San Francisco, 1993; tng. dir. Achilles Track Club, N.Y.C., 1994—; mentor Networking project, N.Y.C., 1993—. Mem. Manhattan Soc., 1994—, Teens, N.Y.C. Artworks, YWCA, 53rd St. Membership Com. Mem. Soc. Disability Studies. Roman Catholic. Completed 3 N.Y.C. marathons, 1993, 94, 95. Home: 535 W 110th St New York NY 10025-2086

ELLIOTT, DONALD HARRIS, utility executive; b. Wichita, Kans., Jan. 11, 1932; s. Frank Shields and Esther Edna Elliott; m. Barbara Ann Roberts, Dec. 27, 1954; children: David Wayne, Diana Mateel Elliott Fanning-Shogren. Student, Wichita State U., 1950-53. Sales supr., sales mgr., asst. mgr. Wichita Kans. Gas & Elec. Co., divsn. mgr. Wichita, regional mgr. Wichita, 1954-92. Mem. Wichita Wagonmasters, Scottish Rite/Consistory, Midian Shrine, Botanica-Wichita Gardens (dir. emeritus), Sedgwick Ext. Coun. (officer, treas. 1999), Kans. One Call Inc. (exec. dir. 1993-97, dir. emeritus). Republican. Presbyterian. Avocations: horticulture, fishing, traveling, music, Scottish history. Home and Office: 6226 Marjorie Wichita KS 67208

ELLIOTT, EDDIE MAYES, academic administrator; b. Grain Valley, Mo., Sept. 12, 1938; s. Franklin E. and Edna Mae (Rowe) E.; m. Sandra Temple, Nov. 23, 1960; children: Glenn, Gregg, Grant. AB, William Jewell Coll., 1960; MA, Columbia U., 1964; EdD, U. No. Colo., 1969. Tchr. Harrisonville (Mo.) High Sch., 1960-61, Excelsior Springs (Mo.) Pub. Schs., 1961-63, The Trinity Sch., N.Y.C., 1963-64; mem. faculty dept. phys. edn. CUNY, 1964-65; chmn. athletics, coach Mo. Valley Coll., Marshall, 1965-71; dir. grad. studies Wayne (Nebr.) State Coll., 1971-73, dean spl. studies, 1973-75, v.p., 1975-82, pres., 1982-85; pres. Cen. Mo. State U., Warrensburg, 1985—; assoc. Ctr. for Planned Change, 1975-82; mem. adv. bd., bd. dirs. Nebr. Coun. on Econ. Edn., 1977-83; bd. incorporators Higher Edn. Strategic Planning Inst., 1981—; mem. Coun. Pub. Higher Edn. Mo.; bd. advisors Apple Restaurants Europe. Mem. land-grant mission adv. com. U. Mo. Named outstanding faculty mem. Wayne State Coll., 1973, to U. No. Colo. Alumni Hall of Fame, 1989; recipient Disting. Svc. award Wayne State Coll., 1986, Cecil R. Martin award William Jewell Coll., 1960, citation for achievement, 1986, Disting. Alumni award, 1986, James C. Kirkpatrick Excellence in Governance Awd., 1999. Mem. AAUP, AAHPERD, Am. Assn. State Colls. and Univs. (task force on emerging issues, bd. dirs., past chair, chair pres.'s commn. tchr. edn. 1993-94), Assn. Governing Bds. (adv. com. on strengthening governance of pub. univs.), Am. Assn. Higher Edn., Am. Coll. Sports Medicine, North Cen. Assn. Evaluation Teams, Nat. Coun. Accreditation of Tchrs., Mo. Corp. for Sci. and Tech., Warrensburg C. of C., Phi Kappa Phi. Office: Cen Mo State U Office of Pres Warrensburg MO 64093

ELLIOTT, EDWARD, investment executive, financial planner; b. Madison, Wis., Jan. 11, 1915; s. Edward C. and Elizabeth (Nowland) E.; m. Letitia Ord, Feb. 20, 1943 (div. Aug. 1955); children: Emily, Ord; m. Melita Uihlein, Jan. 1, 1958; 1 dau., Deborah. B.S. in Mech. Engring, Purdue U., 1936. Engr. Gen. Electric Co., Schenectady, 1936-37; with. Pressed Steel Tank Co., Milw., 1937-41, 46-58; v.p. sales Cambridge Co. div. Carrier Corp., Lowell, Mass., 1958-59; mgr. indsl. and med. sales Liquid Carbonic div. Gen. Dynamics Corp., Chgo., 1959-61; v.p. Haywood Pub. Co., Chgo., 1961-63; pres. Omnibus, Inc., Chgo., 1963-67; gen. sales mgr. Resistoflex Corp., Roseland, N.J., 1967-68; investment exec. Shearson, Hammill & Co., Inc., Chgo., 1968-74; v.p. McCormick & Co., Inc., 1974-75; v.p. Paine Webber, Inc., Naples, Fla., 1975-91, ret., 1991. Mem. pres.' coun. Purdue U. Lt. col. USAAF, 1941-46. Decorated officer Order Brit. Empire; inducted Indiana Basketball Hall of Fame. Mem. ASME, Air Force Assn., Internat. Assn. Fin. Planning, Royal Poinciana Golf Club, Hole-in-Wall Golf Club, Naples Yacht Club, Naples Athletic Club, Family Club (San Francisco), Rotary, Phi Delta Theta. Episcopalian. Home: 1285 Gulf Shore Blvd N Apt 1B Naples FL 34102-4936

ELLIOTT, EDWIN DONALD, JR., law educator, federal administrator, environmental lawyer; b. Chgo., Apr. 4, 1948; s. Edwin Donald and Mary Jane (Bope) E.; m. Geraldine Gennet (div. 1980); m. Mary Ellen Savage, Nov. 22, 1980; children: Eve Christina, Ian Donald. BA, Yale U., 1970, JD, 1974. Bar: D.C. 1975, U.S. Dist. Ct. D.C. 1975, U.S. Ct. Appeals (2d cir.) 1982. Law clk. to judge U.S. Dist. Ct. D.C., Washington, 1974-75, U.S. Ct. Appeals, Washington, 1975-76; assoc. Leva, Hawes et al, Washington, 1976-80; assoc. prof. law Yale U., New Haven, 1981-84, prof. law, 1984-89, 91-92; asst. adminstr., gen. counsel U.S. EPA, Washington, 1989-91; Julien & Virginia Cornell chair environ. law and litigation Yale U., New Haven, 1992-94, adj. prof. law, 1994—; cons. Fried, Frank, Harris, Shriver & Jacobson, N.Y.C., Washington, 1991-93; ptnr., head of DC Environ. Practice Fried, Frank, Harris, Shriver & Jacobson, Washington, 1993-96; ptnr. Paul, Hastings, Janofsky & Walker, Washington, 1996—; adj. prof. law Georgetown U., Washington, 1997—; advisor Fed. Cts. Study Com., UN Environment Programme, 1993; cons. Asian Devel. Bank, 1994, Carnegie Com. Sci., Tech. and Govt., 1989-93, chair Role of Sci. and Risk Assessment; with Nat. Environ. Policy Inst., 1994—, Overseas Pvt. Investment Corp., Washington, 1983-85, Adminstrv. Conf. U.S., 1987-89, Aetna Ins. Co., 1987-89, G.D.

Searle Co., 1988-89; spl. litigation counsel GE Co., Fairfield, Conn., 1985-89; gen. series editor Prentice Hall Environ. Series. Co-author: Sustainable Environmental Law, 1993; contbr. articles on evolutionary theories of law, adminstrv. law, constl. law, environ. and toxic tort law to profl. jours. Resources for the Future fellow, 1989. Mem. ABA (vice chmn. com. on separation of powers 1985-89, jud. rev. 1992—, environ. values 1993—, chair govt. policy liaison), Environ. Law Inst., Gruter Inst. for Law and Behavioral Rsch. (adv. bd. 1986—), Nat. Environ. Policy Inst. (chair sci. and risk assessment), Yale Club N.Y.C., New Haven Lawn Club. Republican. Presbyterian. Home: 826 A St SE Washington DC 20003-1340 also: 56 Beach Ave Milford CT 06460 Office: Paul Hastings Janofsky & Walker 1299 Pennsylvania Ave NW Washington DC 20004-2400 also: Yale Law Sch PO Box 208215 New Haven CT 06520-8215*

ELLIOTT, EMERSON JOHN, education consultant, policy analyst; b. Ann Arbor, Mich., Nov. 13, 1933; s. Clarence Hyde and Ella Ruth (Kohl) E.; m. Joyce Ann Dodge, Aug. 19, 1956; children—Douglas, Stuart, Susan. B.A., Albion Coll., Mich., 1955; M.P.A., U. Mich., 1957. Chief edn. br. OMB, Washington, 1967-70, dep. chief human resources programs div., 1970-72; dep. dir. Nat. Inst. Edn., Washington, 1972-77; dir. ednl. staff seminar Inst. for Ednl. Leadership, Washington, 1977-79; dir. sch. fin. study U.S. Dept. Edn., Washington, 1979-81, dir. planning and evaluation, 1981-82, dir. issues analysis, 1982-84; head Nat. Ctr. for Edn. Stats., Washington, 1984-92; com. of edn. stats., 1992-95; dir. new tchr. stds. project Nat. Coun. Accreditation Tchr. Edn., Washington, 1995—, dir. NPT Standards Devel. Recipient Disting. Alumnus award Albion Coll., 1975; Dirs. Superior Service award Nat. Inst. Edn., 1979; Presdl. Rank awards for Meritorious Service U.S. Govt., 1983, 91. Disting. Service U.S. Govt., 1987. Office: Nat Coun Accred Tchr Edn Ste 500 2010 Massachusetts Ave NW Washington DC 20036-1018*

ELLIOTT, EMORY BERNARD, English language educator, educational adminstrator; b. Balt., Oct. 30, 1942; s. Emory Bernard and Virginia L. (Ulbrick) E.; m. Georgia Ann Carroll, May 14, 1966; children: Scott, Mark, Matthew, Laura, Constance. A.B., Loyola Coll., Balt., 1964; M.A., Bowling Green State U., 1966; Ph.D., U. Ill., 1972. Instr. Cameron Coll., Lawton, Okla., 1966-67, U.S. Mil Acad., West Point, N.Y., 1967-69; from asst. prof. to prof. English, Princeton U., N.J., 1972-89, chmn. Am. studies program, 1976-82, master Lee D. Butler Coll., 1982-86, chmn. English dept., 1987-89; Pres.'s chair English U. Calif., Riverside, 1989-91, disting. prof., 1992—; dir. Ctr. for Ideas and Soc., 1996—; writing cons. Bell Labs., Holmdel, N.J., 1975-79, RCA, Princeton, 1980-81; edn. cons. Western Electric Corp. Edn. Ctr., Hopewell, N.J., 1974-79. Author: Power and the Pulpit in Puritan New England, 1975, Puritan Influences in American Literature, 1979, Revolutionary Writers: Literature and Authority in the New Republic, 1982, The Literature of Puritan New England in The Cambridge History of American Literature, Vol. 1, 1994; editor: Dictionary of Literary Biography, 3 Vols., 1606-1810, 1983-84; editor: Columbia Literary History of the United States, 1988 (Am. Book award 1988), American Literature: A Prentice Hall Anthology 3 Vols., 1990, Columbia History of The American Novel, 1991, The Jungle, 1991, Wieland, 1994, Huckleberry Finn, 1998; series editor Am. Novel Series, 1985—, Critical Studies in Contemporary Am. Fiction, 1987—; mem. editorial bd. Am. Quar., 1976-80, PMLA, 1990-92, Am. Lit., 1995—, Modern Fiction Studies, 1993—, Ill. Studies Lang. Lit., 1993—, Studies in Am. Puritan Spirituality, 1991—; mem. adv. com. Gale Bibliography of Am. Lit., 1981—; editor-at-large Am. Studies Internat., 1993—. Served to capt. U.S. Army, 1966-69. Fellow Woodrow Wilson Found., 1971-72, Am. Coun. Learned Socs., 1973, Guggenheim Found., 1976, Nat. Humanities Ctr. 1979-80, NEH, 1986-87, Inst. for Rsch. in the Humanities, 1991-92; Richard Stockton preceptor Princeton U., 1975-78. Mem. MLA (chmn. Early Am. lit. div., Am. lit. div. 1991). Office: U Calif Dept English Riverside CA 92521-4009

ELLIOTT, FRANK NELSON, retired college president; b. Dunkirk, N.Y., Mar. 18, 1926; s. Warren D. and Ima M. (Wilson) E.; m. Mary Elizabeth Neish, July 26, 1952; children: Robert Frank (dec.), Susan Marie, Ann Neish. B.A. cum laude with dept. honors, Alfred U., 1949, LL.D., 1972; M.A., Ohio U., 1950; Ph.D., U. Wis., 1956; LLD (hon.), Rider U., 1994. Grad. asst. Ohio U., 1949-50; Draper fellow Wis. Hist. Soc., 1951-52, field rep., field supr., 1952-56; curator history, asst. prof. history Mich. State U., 1956-61; asso. dean Sch. Gen. Studies, Columbia U., 1961-64, acting dean, 1964; dir. div. arts and scis. State U. N.Y. Coll. at Cortland, 1964-65, acting dean, 1965-66; v.p. Hofstra U., Hempstead, N.Y., 1966-69; pres. Rider Coll., Lawrenceville, N.J., 1969-90. Contbr. articles to profl. jours. Mem. adv. coun. N.J. State Libr., 1972-87; bd. dirs. N.J. Coun. for Humanities, 1972-76, Deleware Valley United Way, 1986-92, Presbyn. Homes N.J., 1990-96, Granville Acad., Trenton, N.J., 1990-94; bd. dirs. Mercer Med. Ctr., 1980-97, chmn., 1992-95; trustee Alfred U., 1964-69; elder Presbyn. Ch. With AUS, 1944-46, PTO. Mem. Am. Assn. State and Local History (coun. 1960-62), Mich. Hist. Soc. (trustee 1959-61, award for TV lectures 1960), Mercer County C. of C. (dir. 1975-88, Citizen of Yr. 1990). Home: 425 Ramsey Rd Yardley PA 19067-4642

ELLIOTT, FRANK WALLACE, lawyer, educator; b. Cotulla, Tex., June 25, 1930; s. Frank Wallace and Eunice Marie (Akin) E.; m. Winona Trent, July 3, 1954 (dec. 1981); 1 child, Harriet Lindsey; m. Kay Elkins, Aug. 15, 1983. Student, N.Mex. Mil. Inst., 1947-49; BA, U. Tex., 1951, LLB, 1957. Bar: Tex. 1957, U.S. Supreme Ct. 1962, U.S. Ct. Mil. Appeals 1974, U.S. Dist. Ct. (no. dist.) Tex. 1987, U.S. Ct. Appeals (5th cir.) 1988. Asst. atty. gen. State of Tex., 1957; briefing atty. Supreme Ct. Tex., 1957-58; prof. U. Tex. Law Sch., 1958-77; dean, prof. law Tex. Tech U. Sch. Law, 1977-80; pres. Southwestern Legal Found., 1980-86; ptnr. Baker, Mills & Glast, Dallas, 1987-88; of counsel Ramirez & Assocs., 1988—; dean Dallas/Ft. Worth Sch. Law, 1989-92; dean Sch. Law Tex. Wesleyan U., 1992-94, prof., 1992—; parliamentarian Tex. Senate, 1969-73; dir. rsch. Tex. Constl. Revision Commn., 1973. Author: Texas Judicial Process, 2d edit., 1977, Texas Trial and Appellate Practice, 2d edit., 1974, Cases on Evidence, 1980, West's Texas Forms, 20 vols., 1977—, West's Texas Practice, vol. 11, 1990, vol. 14, 1996. Served with U.S. Army, 1951-53, 73-74. Decorated Purple Heart. Mem. ABA, Judge Advs. Assn., Am. Judicature Soc., Am. Bar Found., Tex. Bar Found., Dallas Bar Found., Am. Law Inst., N.Mex. Mil. Inst. Alumni Hall of Fame. Home: 2120 N Rough Creek Ct Granbury TX 76048 Office: 1515 Commerce Fort Worth TX 76102-6509

ELLIOTT, GEORGE ALGIMON, pathologist, toxicologist, veterinarian; b. Trappe, Md., June 6, 1925; s. George A. and Mattie Tileston (Sullivan) E.; m. Marguerite Van Zandt Hammond, Aug. 15, 1949; children: Kathleen, Elizabeth, Jennifer. DVM, U. Ga., 1953; MSc in Vet. Pathology, U. Pa., 1957. Diplomate Am. Coll. Vet. Pathologists. From instr. to asst. prof. U. Pa. Sch. of Vet. Medicine, Phila., 1955-60; asst. prof. comparative pathology Vanderbilt U. Sch. of Medicine, Nashville, 1960-62; rsch. scientist (sr. vet. pathologist, toxicologist) The Upjohn Co., Kalamazoo, Mich., 1962-90. Contbr. articles to profl. jours. With U.S. Navy, 1945-46 PTO. Mem. Am. Vet. Medicine Assn., Phi Kappa Phi, Sigma Xi. Democrat. Mem. Reformed Ch. of Am. Avocation: orchids. Home: 4430 Romence Rd Portage MI 49024-3834*

ELLIOTT, GEORGE ARMSTRONG, III, artist, journalist; b. Wilmington, Del., July 24, 1929; s. George Armstrong Elliott Jr. and Amy Lewis (Rupert) Thomas; m. Shirley Barbara Henin, Oct. 16, 1965. BA, Colgate U., 1951; cert. in journalism, Columbia U., N.Y.C., 1964. Reporter, copy editor, corr. local and nat. newspapers and news agys., 1950-66, Balt. Sun, 1955-62, N.Y. Herald Tribune, 1964, New York Daily News, 1965-66; adminstrv. asst./press sec. Spiro T. Agnew, Baltimore County Exec., Towson, Md., 1962-65; campaign press mgr. Spiro T. Agnew, Baltimore County Exec., 1962; campaign press sec., speechwriter Spiro T. Agnew, Gov. of Md., 1966; pub. affairs dir. Md. State Rds. Commn., Balt., 1967-69; legis. asst. U.S. Congresswoman from Mass. Margaret M. Heckler, Washington, 1969-71; spl. asst. U.S. Sec. of Commerce Peter G. Peterson, Washington, 1972; campaign writer John H. Chafee for U.S. Senator, Providence, 1972; speechwriter Chmn. of FTC Lewis Engman, Washington, 1973; dir. nat. campaign for 55 m.p.h. speed limit U.S. Dept. Transp., Washington, 1976-77; spl. asst., speechwriter U.S. Congressman from Minn. Albert H. Quie, Washington and Mpls.-St. Paul, 1978; press sec. Rep. Margaret M. Heckler, Washington, 1979-81; prin. writer Nat. Alcohol Fuels Commn., Washington, 1980; writer Nat. Commn. on Air Quality, Washington, 1980-81; internat. pub. rels. counsel A. F. Sabo Assocs., Washington, 1981; Washington and East Coast corr. Jet Cargo News, Washington, 1984-93; profl. Chinese brush painting artist, 1993—; writer former Md. Gov. Theodore R. McKeldin for Mayor, Balt., 1963; writer for numerous congrl. and local polit. campaigns, 1962-63. Exhibitions include M-Pac Fine Arts Shows, Sugarloaf Mt. Works Shows, Towson, Md., Invitational Art Exhibit, Waterford, Va., Art Mart and Garden tour, Wilmington, Brandywine Arts Festival, Sydney (NSW, Australia) Internat. Art Soc., 1996, Internat. Salon de Haute-Loire, Puy-en-Velay, France, 1997, 99, Lalit Kala Nat. Acad. Art, New Delhi, 1998, 99. With U.S. Army, 1951-54. Ford Found. fellow in advanced internat. reporting Grad. Sch. Journalism, Columbia U., 1963-64. Mem. Nat. Assn. Govt. Communicators, Overseas Press Club Am., Washington Ind. Writers, Montgomery County Art Assn., Internat. Artists Support Group (pres. 1999—), Sumi-e Soc. Am. Home and Office: 5800 Aberdeen Rd Bethesda MD 20814-2252

ELLIOTT, HERSCHEL, agricultural engineer, educator. BSChemE, U. Tenn., 1972; MS in Civil Environ. Engring., U. Del., 1976, PhD in Civil Environ. Engring., 1979. Registered profl. engr., Pa. Vis. prof. chemistry U. Cape Town, Rondebosch, South Africa, 1991, U. Newcastle (Australia), 1991-92; prof. agrl. engring., coord. environ. resource mgmt. program Pa. State U., University Park, 1990-94, prof. agrl. engring., coord. undergrad. environ. program, 1994-95, prof. agrl. engring., chmn. grad. environ. pollution control, 1995—. Contbr. numerous articles to profl. jours. Recipient Young Engr. of Yr. award North Atlantic Region Am. Soc. Agrl. Engrs. Mem. Am. Water Works Assn., Am. Soc. Agronomy, Soil Sci. Soc. Am., Pa. Assn. Environ. Profls. (bd. dirs. 1988-89), Tau Beta Pi, Alpha Epsilon. Office: 206 Agrl Scis & Industries Bldg Pa State U University Park PA 16802-3505

ELLIOTT, HOWARD, JR., gas distribution company executive; b. St. Louis, July 4, 1933; s. Howard and Ruth Ann (Thomas) E.; student Brown U., 1956; J.D., Washington U., 1962; m. Susan Jane Spoehrer, Sept. 2, 1961; children—Kathryn Elliott Love, Elizabeth Elliott Niedringhaus. Admit ted to Mo. bar, 1962; assoc. firm Boyle, Priest, Elliott & Weakley, St. Louis, 1962-65, partner, 1965-67; commr. Mo. Pub. Service Commn., 1967-70; commr. U.S. Postal Rate Commn., 1970-73; assoc. gen. counsel Laclede Gas Co., St. Louis, 1973-77, v.p. adminstrn., 1977-92, sr. v.p. adminstrn., 1992-93, cons., 1993-94, atty., counselor, 1994—. Mem. com. on electricity and nuclear energy Nat. Assn. Regulatory Utility Commrs., 1968-70, mem. exec. com., 1971-73. Charter mem. com. of 40 for Adoption of St. Louis and St. Louis County Jr. Coll. Dist., 1962. Served with U.S. Army, 1956-58. Mem. Am. Gas Assn., ABA, Mo. Bar, Fed. Energy Bar Assn., Fed. Energy Bar Assn., Bar Assn. Met. St. Louis. Republican. Presbyterian. Clubs: St. Louis, Noonday, St. Louis Country, Chevy Chase, Md. Athletic, Loblolly Pines Golf Club, Hobe Sound, Fla. Home: 46 Clermont Ln Saint Louis MO 63124-1351 also: 6820 SE Wood Lark Ln Hobe Sound FL 33455-8048

ELLIOTT, INGER MCCABE, designer, textile company executive, design consultant; b. Oslo, Feb. 23, 1933; came to U.S., 1941; naturalized, 1946; d. David and Lova (Katz) Abrahamsen; m. Osborn Elliott, Oct. 20, 1973; children by previous marriage: Kari McCabe, Alexander McCabe, Marit McCabe. AB in History with honors, Cornell U., 1954; postgrad., Harvard U., 1955; AM, Radcliffe Coll., 1957. Photographer, Photo Rschrs., 1960-98; pres. China Seas, Inc., N.Y.C., 1972-90, Gifted Textile Collection to L.A. County Mus. Art, 1991—; Textile Exhibit, L.A. County Mus. Art, 1996-97, cons. Sotheby's, Inc., 1992—; mem. Coun. Fgn. Rels. Mem. East Asia vis. com. Harvard U.; trustee The Asia Soc., Am. Scandinavian Found. Recipient Roscoe awards, 1978—. Mem. Am. Soc. Mag. Photographers, Am. Women's Econ. Devel. Corp., Com. of 200, Cosmopolitan Club, Ellis Island Yacht Club (lt. comdr.), Phi Beta Kappa. Author: A Week in Amy's World, A Week in Henry's World, Batik: Fabled Cloth of Java, 1985, Exteriors, 1992; contbr. photographic essays to Esquire, Vogue, Life, Newsweek, N.Y. Times, Infinity, House & Garden. Home: 36 E 72nd St New York NY 10021-4247

ELLIOTT, JACK, folk musician. Albums include Bull Durham Sacks and Railroad Tracks, Young Brigham, Me & Bobby McGee, South Coast, 1995 (Grammy award 1996). Recipient Grammy award Best Traditional Folk Album Of The Yr., 1996, Bill Graham Lifetime Achievement award Bay Area Music Awards, 1996, Nat. Medal of Arts award Pres. Clinton, 1998. Address: Hightone Records 220 4th St # 101 Oakland CA 94607

ELLIOTT, JAMES A., oceanographer, researcher; b. Pierceland, Sask., Can., Feb. 24, 1941; s. James John and Dorothy (Spear) E.; m. Gillian Hope, May 13, 1967; children: Rebecca Jean, Jonathan James Patrick. BSc, U. Sask., 1962; MSc, U. B.C., 1965, PhD, 1970. Rsch. sci. Bedford Inst. Oceanography, Dartmouth, N.S., Can., 1962-78, rsch. mgr., 1979-85, rsch. dir., 1985-97; project dir. Bedford Inst. Oceanography, Dartmouth, N.S., 1998, emeritus scientist, 1999—. Contbr. numerous articles to oceanographic jours. Dir. A.G. Huntsman Found., 1980-98. Office: Bedford Inst Oceanography, PO Box 1006, Dartmouth, NS Canada B2Y 4A2

ELLIOTT, JAMES HEYER, retired university art museum curator, fine arts consultant; b. Medford, Oreg., Feb. 19, 1924; s. Bert R. and Marguerite E. (Heyer) E.; m. Judith Ann Algar, Apr. 23, 1966 (div.); children: Arabel Joan, Jakob Maxwell. BA, Willamette U., Salem, Oreg., 1947, DFA (hon.), 1978; AM, Harvard U., 1949; DFA (hon.), San Francisco Art Inst., 1991. James Rogers Rich fellow Harvard U., 1949-50; Fulbright grantee Paris, 1951-52; art critic European edit. N.Y. Herald-Tribune, 1952-53; curator, acting dir. Walker Art Center, Mpls., 1953-56; asst. chief curator, curator modern art Los Angeles County Mus. Art, 1956-63, chief curator, 1964-66; dir. Wadsworth Atheneum, Hartford, Conn., 1966-76; dir. Univ. Art Mus., Berkeley, Calif., 1976-88, chancellor's curator, 1989-90, dir. emeritus, 1990—; adj. prof. Hunter Coll., N.Y.C., 1968, U. Calif., Berkeley, 1976-90; commr. Conn. Commn. Arts, 1970-76; fellow Trumbull Coll., Yale U., 1971-75; mem. mus. arts panel Nat. Endowment Arts, 1974-77; bd. dirs. San Francisco Art Inst., 1980-90; art adv. com. Exploratorium, 1982-91; adv. com. Artists TV Access, 1987-90. Author: Bonnard and His Environment, 1964, James Lee Byars: Notes Towards a Biography, 1990. Trustee Marcia Simon Weisman Found., 1991—, 23 FIVE Found., San Francisco, 1993—, di Rosa Preserve, Napa, Calif., 1996—; mem. adv. bd. Artspace San Francisco, 1989—. With USNR, 1943-46. Mem. Am. Assn. Mus., Artists Space N.Y. (bd. dirs. 1980-84), Arts Club (Berkeley). Home: 13 Yellow Ferry Harbor Sausalito CA 94965-1327

ELLIOTT, JAMES ROBERT, federal judge; b. Gainesville, Ga., Jan. 1, 1910; s. Thomas M. and Mamie Lucille (Glenn) E.; m. Brownie C. Buck, Aug. 3, 1949; children: Susan G., James Robert. Ph.B., Emory U., 1930, LL.B., 1934. Bar: Ga. 1934. Pvt. practice law Columbus, Ga., 1934-62; judge U.S. Dist. Ct. (mid. dist.) Ga., Columbus, 1962—; Mem. Ga. Ho. of Reps., 1937-43, 47-49; Democratic nat. committeeman, 1948-56. Served as lt. USNR, 1943-46, PTO. Mem. Ga. Bar Assn., Kiwanis, Lambda Chi Alpha, Phi Delta Phi, Omicron Delta Kappa. Home: 2612 Carson Dr Columbus GA 31906-1563 Office: US Dist Ct 120-12th St Rm 224 PO Box 2017 Columbus GA 31902-2017*

ELLIOTT, JEAN ANN, librarian emeritus; b. Martinsburg, W.Va., Jan. 18, 1933; d. Howard Hoffman and Dorothy Jean (Horn) E. AB in Edn., Shepherd Coll., Shepherdstown, W.Va., 1954; MS in Libr. Sci., Syracuse U., 1957; MS, Shippensburg (Pa.) U., 1974. Asst. libr. Fairmont (W.Va.) State Coll., 1957-60; reference asst. U. Pitts., 1960-61; acting libr. Shepherd Coll., 1961-62, coord. libr. sci., 1962-97; compiler Jefferson County Hist. mag., 1990. Nat. treas. Palatines of Am., Columbus, Ohio, 1986-88. Mem. ALA, AAUW, DAR (W.Va. treas. 1980-83, 86-89, 95-98, state regent 1998—), W.Va. Libr. Assn. (election chmn. 1988-90), Va. Edn. Media Assn., Jefferson County Hist. Soc., Nat. Geneal. Soc., Nat. Soc. Daus. Am. Colonies (nat. libr. 1991-94, hon. state regent 1991—), Nat. Soc. Daus. 1812 (nat. libr. 1994-96), W.Va. Soc. Daus. 1812 (state pres. 1991-94, hon. state pres. 1994—), Alpha Beta Alpha (nat. exec. sec. 1968-76). Presbyterian. Avocations: genealogy, travel, knitting, computers. Home: PO Box 239 Shepherdstown WV 25443-0239

ELLIOTT, JOHN, accountant, educator, dean; b. Sacramento, Calif., Sept. 27, 1945; s. John William and Martha (Arnold) E.; children: Elizabeth Dawn, Jesse John. BS Econs. with high honors, U. Md., 1967, MBA, 1972; PhD Acctg., Cornell U., 1982. CPA, N.Y. Instr. acctg. U. Md., 1970-72; asst. prof. St. Lawrence U., 1972-76, Ctrl. Washington State Coll., 1976-77; vis. prof. U. Chgo., 1983, 88; prof. Johnson Sch. Cornell U., 1982—, assoc. dean, 1997—; mem. Fin. Policies and Procedures Staff Westinghouse Electric, 1969-70; staff mem. Arthur Andersen & Co., 1967-69. Author (with C. Horngren, G. Sundem) Introduction to Financial Accounting; assoc. editor Contemporary Acctg. Rsch., 1996-97; edit. bd. The Acctg. Review, 1984-87, 89-92, Jour. Acctg. and Pub. Policy, 1983-85, Jour. Fin. Statement Analysis, 1995-98; contbr. articles to profl. jours. Trustee Hangar Theatre, Ithaca, N.Y., 1985-94, Cayuga Med., Ithaca, N.Y., 1992—. Mem. AICPA, Am. Acctg. Assn. Home: 220 Prospect Hill Rd Horseheads NY 14845-7979 Office: Johnson Grad Sch Mgmt Cornell U 346 Sage Hall Ithaca NY 14853-6201

ELLIOTT, JOHN, JR., advertising agency executive; b. N.Y.C., Jan. 25, 1921; s. John and Audrey Neilson (Osborn) E.; m. Eleanor Lansing Thomas, July 27, 1956. A.B., Harvard U., 1942. Copywriter Batten, Barton, Durstine & Osborn, 1945-49, account exec., 1949-60, v.p., 1956-60, dir., 1958-60; sr. v.p., dir. Ogilvy, Benson & Mather, 1960-65; chmn. Ogilvy & Mather (U.S.), N.Y.C., 1965-75, Ogilvy & Mather Internat., N.Y.C., 1975-82; chmn. emeritus Ogilvy & Mather Internat., 1982—; dir. Fireman's Fund Am. Life Ins. Co. N.Y., 1972-82. Trustee, pres. Alumni Assn. Browning Sch., 1950-60; trustee St. Paul's Sch., 1978-81, Internat. House, 1967—, Wildlife Conservation Soc., 1979—, Park Assn., N.Y.C., 1956-60, Sta. WNET/Channel 13, 1983—; v.p. Mus. City of N.Y., 1956-65; gen. chmn Red Cross Campaign for Mems. and Funds, N.Y.C., 1970-71; TV advisor Rep. Party, 1950-53; bd. overseers Meml. Sloan-Kettering Cancer Care Center, 1980-84; bd. dirs. Advt. Ednl. Found., 1984—, Ctr. for Communication, 1982-90; pres. Scottish Nat. Trust Golden Jubilee Found., 1980-93; mem. President's Adv. Council Pvt. Sector Initiatives, 1983-85, Pres.'s Adv. Bd., 1985-89. Served to maj. USMCR, 1942-45. Mem. Am. Assn. Advt. Agys. (chmn. 1974-75), Advt. Council (dir. 1972—, vice chmn. 1979-84, chmn. 1984-85), Advt. Hall Fame (elected 1983). Clubs: Bedford Golf and Tennis, Harvard (N.Y.C.), Century Assn., Hon. Company Edinburgh Golfers, Brook. Office: Oglivy & Mather 309 W 49th St Fl 12 New York NY 10019-7399*

ELLIOTT, JOHN ED, economics educator; b. Los Angeles, Oct. 22, 1931; s. James Edgar and Jessie Fisher (Metcalf) E.; m. Elda Rose Wilson, Dec. 22, 1975; children: John David, Richard Lee, Elizabeth Ann, James Hall. BA in Econs., Occidental Coll., 1952; MA in Polit. Sci., Harvard U., 1956, PhD in Econs., 1956. Instr. U. So. Calif., Los Angeles, 1956-59, asst. prof. econs., 1959-61, assoc. prof., 1961-66, prof., 1966—; dir. faculty seminar NEH, 1980, 82, 84, 86, 88, 93, 95. Author: Comparative Economic Systems, 1985, Marx and Engels Economics Politics Society, 1981, Competing Philosophies American Political Economics, 1975, The Life and Times of Soviet Socialism, 1997; contbr. articles to profl. jours. Mem. AAUP (nat. council 1985—, pres. Calif. conf. 1985—), Hist. Econs. Soc. (v.p. 1988), Assn. Social Econs. (exec. council. 1985—, v.p. 1988, pres. 1989), Am. Econ. Assn., Western Econ. Assn., Assn. for Evolutionary Econ., Atlantic Econ. Soc., Union Radical Polit. Econs. Democrat. Avocations: classical jazz, swimming, music. Office: U So Calif Dept Econs University Park Los Angeles CA 90089*

ELLIOTT, JOHN GREGORY, aerospace design engineer; b. Surabaya, Dutch East Indies, Nov. 9, 1948; came to U.S., 1956; s. Frans Jan and Charlotte Clara (Rosel) E.; m. Jennifer Lee Austin, May 7, 1988. AA, Cerritos Coll., 1974; BS, Calif. State U., Long Beach, 1978. Design engr. Boeing Airplane Co., Long Beach, 1978-82, lead engr., 1983-89, sect. mgr. elect. installations group, 1989—. With USN, 1969-73. Mem. So. Calif. Profl. Engring. Assn., The Boeing Co. Tennis Club, The Boeing Co. Surf Club, The Boeing Co. Mgmt. Club. Republican. Presbyterian. Avocations: sailing, guitar, reading, remote-control gliders, painting. E-mail: john.g.elliott@boeing.com. Office: Boeing Aircraft Co Long Beach Divsn Internal Internal Mail Code D0360017 Long Beach CA 90846-0003

ELLIOTT, JOHN MICHAEL, lawyer; b. Girardville, Pa., July 8, 1941; s. John T. and Clair C. E.; children: John P., Heather D., Kirwan B., Kyle M. A.B. in Econs. magna cum laude, St. Vincent Coll., 1963, LL.D. (hon.), 1985; LL.B. cum laude, Georgetown U., 1966. Bar: Pa. 1966, U.S. Dist. Ct. (ea. dist.) Pa. 1967, U.S. Ct. Appeals (3d cir.) 1967, U.S. Supreme Ct. 1968,. Chmn. Elliott, Reihner, Siedzkowski & Egan, Phila., 1990—; Pa. counsel Del. River Port Authority, 1987-95; mem. Phila. Coal Rail Task Force, Rockefeller Commn., White House Coal Adv. Commn., 1980; bd. dirs. James A. Finnegan Fellowship Found., Irish Edn. Devel. Found., Inc., chmn.; mem. Pa. Citizens Adv. Coun. Dept. Environ. Resources, 1970-78, chmn. urban com.; mem. environ. quality bd. Commonwealth of Pa., 1970-78; commr. Del. River Port Authority; rep. auditor Gen. Robert P. Casey; mem. Phila. City Planning Commn., 1970-75, Del. Valley Citizens Coun. for Clean Air; chmn. Disciplinary Bd. Supreme Ct. Pa., 1985-86, vice chmn., 1985, chmn. rules com., 1982, Pa. Bar Inst., 1988-94; mem. Commn. on Security and Coop. in Europe Conf. on the Human Dimension, Paris, 1989, Conf. on Democratic Institutions, Oslo, 1991. Contbr. articles to profl. jours. Bd. dirs. Mann Music Ctr., 1988-91, Walnut St. Theatre, 1988-93, Internat. League for Human Rights, 1988-95. Recipient St. Patrick's Coll. Maynooth Ireland Salamanca Archives Dedication, Cahal B. Cardinal Daly, 1995; Williston rsch. fellow, 1965. Fellow Pa. Bar Found.; mem. ABA (lectr. on trial practice), Pa. Bar Assn. (ho. of dels. 1983-91, task force on civil ct. rules), Pa. Bar Inst. (bd. dirs. 1987-93, course planner, faculty), Am. Law Inst. (ABA appelate practice program), Nat. Inst. Trial Advocacy (lectr.), Phila. Bar Assn. (environ. quality com.), Nat. Lawyers Com. for Civil Rights Under Law, Braehon Law Soc., Mil. History Soc. Ireland. Home: 1202 Penllyn Blue Bell Pike Blue Bell PA 19422-2108 Office: Elliott Reihner Siedzkowski & Egan 925 Harvest Dr Blue Bell PA 19422-1956

ELLIOTT, KATHY BRADSHAW, judge; b. Beecher, Ill., July 11, 1951; d. Harry A. and Alice Marie (Embry) Bradshaw; m. Roger Charles Elliott; children: Nicholas, Samantha. BS in Speech Edn., So. Ill. U., 1972; MSW, U. Hawaii, 1976; JD, Ill. Inst. Tech., 1984. Bar: Ill. 1995. Tchr. Waipahu (Hawaii) H.S., 1974-75; counselor Hawaii State Prison, Oahu, 1977-78; social worker Ill. Dept. Mental Health, Tinley Park, Ill., 1979-80; asst. state's atty. Kankakee County State's Atty. Office, Kankakee, Ill., 1988-92, 1st asst. state's atty., 1992-97; judge 21st Jud. Circuit Ct., State of Ill., Kankakee, 1997—. Mem. Kankakee Bar Assn. Office: Ill Jud Circuit Ct 450 E Court St Kankakee IL 60901-3917

ELLIOTT, LARRY PAUL, cardiac radiologist, educator; b. Manhattan, Kans., Oct. 16, 1931; s. Leonard Paul and Mary Elizabeth (Myers) E.; m. Betty Lou Hawkins, June 23, 1956; children: Laurie Lou, Mary Elizabeth, Larry Paul. BS, U. Fla., 1954; MD, U. Tenn., 1957. Intern John Gaston Hosp., Memphis, 1957-58; resident in pediat. and pediat. cardiology U. Fla. Hosp., 1958-61; resident in cardiac pathology and cardiovasc. radiology U. Minn. Hosp., 1961-65; asso. prof. cardiac radiology Washington U. Med. Sch., St. Louis, 1966-67; prof. cardiac radiology U. Fla. Med. Sch., 1967-76; prof. radiology, dir. divsn. cardiac radiology U. Ala. Med. Sch., Birmingham, 1976-81; prof., chmn. dept. radiology Georgetown U. Sch. Medicine, 1981—, clin. prof., chmn. emeritus, 1996—; clin. rpof. radiology Emory U. Med. Ctr., Atlanta, 1997—; chmn. Fac. Practice Group, 1989—. Author: The X-Ray Diagnosis Heart Disease, 1968, 79; editor: Radiology, 1967—, Cardiovascular and Interventional Radiology, 1979—, The Fundamentals of Cardiac Imaging in Infants, Children and Adults, 1990; assoc. editor cardiovasc. sect. Taveras Radiology, 1986; contbr. articles to med. jours. Recipient Disting. Alumnus award U. Fla., 1981, Outstanding Alumna award U. Tenn. Med. Sch., 1993; grantee cardiac radiology Nat. Heart Inst., 1968-76, Allied Health Profl. Act, 1970. Fellow N.Am. Soc. Cardiac Radiology (pres. 1977-78), Am. Coll. Cardiology; mem. Radiol. Soc. N.Am., Soc. Cardiac Angiography, Am. Heart Assn., Soc. Thoracic Radiology (founding mem., pres. faculty practice group 1989-93). Home: 3 Ocean Point Isle of Palms SC 29451 *In my own success, I have found 5 key ingredients. (1) A mentor who ignited the switch or literally turned me on. (2) Superb training, especially in sound fundamental principles. (3) An obsessive enthusiasm, a prime feature I look for in all postgraduate students. (4) An element of discipline, which has prevented succumbing to the siren song of private practice. (5) Reward, the only fountain of youth that exists - a close association with each generation of students.*

ELLIOTT, LEE ANN, government official. BA, U. Ill. V.p. Bishop, Bryant amd Assocs., Inc., 1979-81; mem. Fed. Election Commn., Washington, 1981—, chmn., 1884, 90, 96; lectr., author and inventor in field. Bd. dirs., pres. Chgo. Area Pub. Affairs Group; bd. dirs. Kids Voting, USA. Mem. Am. Med. Polit. Action Com. (asst. dir. 1961-70, assoc. exec. dir. 1970-79), Am. Assn. Polit. Cons. (bd. dirs.), Nat. Assn. Mfrs. (award of excellence), U.S. C. of C. (pub. affairs com.). Office: Fed Election Commn 999 E St NW Washington DC 20239-0004

ELLIOTT, LESTER FRANKLYN, plastic surgeon; b. Macon, Ga., Oct. 18, 1950; s. Sewell and Mary Grace E.; m. Elizabeth Wilkinson, May 30, 1981; children: Mary Grace, Elizabeth Ballard. BA, Princeton U., 1972; MD, Vanderbilt U., 1976. Resident Vanderbilt U., Nashville, 1976-77, 77-78, Tulane U., New Orleans, 1978-80, 80-81, Emory U., Atlanta, 1981-83; instr. surgery La. State U., New Orleans, 1983-85, asst. clin. prof. surgery, 1985-87; clin. instr. srugery Emory U., 1987—; researcher in field. Contbr. articles to profl. jours. Bd. dirs. Atlanta Ballet, 1996—. Clin. orthopaedic fellow Sahlgranska Hosp., Gothenberg, Sweden, 1975. Fellow Am. Coll. Surgeons; mem. Am. Soc. Aesthetic Plastic Surgery, Am. Cleft Palate Assn., Am. Soc. Plastic and Reconstructive Surgeons, Am. Soc. Maxillo-Facial Surgeons, Southeastern Soc. Plastic and Reconstructive Surgeons, La. State Med. Soc., Surg. Assn. La., Ga. Surg. Soc., Ga. Plastic Surgery Soc., New Orleans Surg. Soc., Orleans Parish Med. Soc., Maurice J. Jurkiewicz Soc., Alton Ochsner Surg. Soc., Southern Surgical Assn., Oneiro Travel Club, Cap and Gown Club, Kappa Alpha. Avocations: cycling, marathons, travel, hunting. Home: 3668 Tuxedo Rd NW Atlanta GA 30305-1068 Office: Atlanta Plastic Surgery 975 Johnson Ferry Rd NE Ste 500 Atlanta GA 30342-1616

ELLIOTT, MITCHELL LEE, financial analyst; b. Greenwood, Miss., Oct. 24, 1958; s. Charles Edward and Elizabeth Ann (Roberts) E.; m. Ann Bonham, June 7, 1986. BSBA, U. So. Miss., 1980. Mktg. analyst JFMA, Jackson, Miss., 1981-82; fin. analyst ERGON, Jackson, 1982-97; contr. Johns Manville, Jackson, 1997—; v.p. bd. ERGON Cos. Credit Union, Jackson, 1987-90, pres., 1990-97; v.p. ETE Devel., 1992—. Mem. Pine Ridge Homeowners Assn. (pres. 1994). Republican. Methodist. Avocations: golf, basketball, snow skiing, scuba diving, gardening. Home: 110 Meadowview Dr Brandon MS 39047-9224 Office: ERGON PO Box 23028 Jackson MS 39225-3028

ELLIOTT, MYRA TURNER, nursing educator; b. Martin, Ky., Aug. 19, 1958; d. Langley and Violet (Sparkman) Turner; m. Olin Andrew Elliott II, June 10, 1978; 1 child, Myranda Grance Elliott. ADN, Prestonsburg (Ky.) C.C., 1978; BSN, U. Ky., 1981; postgrad., U. Tenn., 1985; MSN, U. Ky., 1993. Clin. I/nursing care mgr. St. Joseph's Hosp., Lexington, 1978-83; clin. I/nursing care mgr., office nurse Dr. Andy Elliott, Martin, Ky., 1983-84; assoc. prof. Prestonburg C.C., 1984-97, chair divsn., 1997—, divsn. chair, 1997—; chairperson devel. and implementation of a clin. ladder program, Prestonburg, 1990—. Mem. Floyd County Cmty. Com. for Edn., 1992—; bd. dirs. Hospice of Big Sandy, 1987-95; Sunday sch. tchr., mem. choir First Bapt. Ch., Prestonburg. Recipient NISOD Excellence award, 1996. Mem. ANA, Ky. Dental Aux. (state historian), Ky. Nurses Assn., Coun. on Critical Care, Ky. Mountain Dental Aux. (pres.), Ky. Dental Alliance (pres.-elect). Avocation: camping. Home: 1391 Abbott Creek Rd Prestonsburg KY 41653-8930 Office: Prestonsburg Cmty Coll One Bert Combo Dr Prestonsburg KY 41653

ELLIOTT, OSBORN, journalist, educator, urban activist, former dean; b. N.Y.C., Oct. 25, 1924; s. John and Audrey N. (Osborn) E.; m. Deirdre M. Spencer, May 8, 1948 (div. Dec. 1972); children: Diana, Cynthia, Dorinda; m. Inger McCabe, Oct. 20, 1973; stepchildren: Kari, Alexander, Marit. Grad., St. Paul's Sch., 1942; A.B., Harvard U., 1946; LHD (hon.), Mich. State U., 1972; LittD (hon.), Marlboro Coll., 1996; LHD (hon.), Marymount Manhattan Coll., 1998. Reporter N.Y. Jour. Commerce, 1946-49; contbg. editor Time mag., 1949-52, assoc. editor, 1952-55; sr. bus. editor Newsweek mag., 1955-59; mng. editor Newsweek, 1959-61; editor Newsweek, N.Y.C., 1961-69, 72-75, editor-in-chief, vice chmn., pres., CEO, chmn. bd., 1969-76; former dir. Washington Post Co., A.S. Abell Co. (Balt. Sun); dep. mayor econ. devel. City of N.Y., 1976-77; dean Grad. Sch. Journalism, Columbia U., N.Y.C., 1979-86, George Delacorte prof., 1986-94, pub. Columbia Journalism Rev., 1979-86. Author: Men At the Top, 1959, The World of Oz, 1980; editor: The Negro Revolution in America, 1964. Bd. overseers Harvard Coll., 1965-71; trustee N.Y. Pub. Libr., 1968-72, 77-79, St. Paul's Sch., 1969-73, Am. Mus. Natural History, 1958-80, Asia Soc., 1966-93, Lincoln Ctr. Theater, 1987-92, Pulitzer Prize Bd., 1979-86; judge Livingston Journalism Awards; chmn. China Seas, Inc., 1973-90, Bernstein Book award N.Y. Pub. Libr.; chmn. bd. dirs. Citizens Com. for N.Y.C., 1975-79, 90—; organizer 250,000 person Save Our Cities! Save Our Children! March on Washington, 1992; sr. adviser City Vote, 1995-96. With USNR, 1944-46. Recipient Frederick Douglass award N.Y. Urban League, 1993, Editor's Hall of Fame award Am. Soc. of Mag. Editors, 1996, Carr Van Anda award Ohio U., 1969, Creative Spirit award Black alumni, Pratt Inst., 1997. Fellow Am. Acad. Arts and Scis.; mem. Coun. Fgn. Rels., Harvard Club, Century Assn., Ellis Island Yacht Club (commodore). Home: 36 E 72nd St New York NY 10021-4247

ELLIOTT, PEGGY GORDON, university president; b. Matewan, W.Va., May 27, 1937; d. Herbert Hunt and Mary Ann (Renfro) Gordon; children from previous marriage: Scott Vandling III, Anne Gordon. BA, Transylvania Coll., 1959; MA, Northwestern U., 1964; EdD, Ind. U., 1975. Tchr. Horace Mann H.S., Gary, Ind., 1959-64; instr. English Ind. U. N.W., Gary, 1965-69, lectr. Edn., 1973-74, asst. prof. edn., 1975-78, assoc. prof., 1978-80, supr. secondary student tchg., 1973-74, dir. student tchg., 1975-77, dir. Office Field Experiences, 1977-78, dir. profl. devel., 1978-80, spl. asst. to chancellor, 1981-83, asst. to chancellor, 1983-84, acting chancellor, 1983-84, chancellor, 1984-92; instr. English Am. Inst. Banking, Gary, 1969-70; pres. U. Akron, Ohio, 1992-96, S.D. State U., 1998—; sr. fellow Nat. Ctr. for Higher Edn., 1996-97; vis. prof. U. Ark., 1979-80, U. Alaska, 1982; bd. dirs. Lubrizol Corp., A. Schulman Corp., First Nat. Bank Brookings, Akron Tomorrow, Ohio Aerospace Consortium, Ohio Super Computer Com.; holder VA Harrington disting. chair in edn., 1994-96, Charles G. Herbrich chair in leadership mgmt., 1996—; pres. S.D. State U., 1998. Author: (with C. Smith) Reading Activities for Middle and Secondary Schools: A Handbook for Teachers, 1979, Reading Instruction for Secondary Schools, 1986, How to Improve Your Scores on Reading Competency Tests, 1981, (with C. Smith and G. Ingersoll) Trends in Educational Materials: Traditionals and the New Technologies, 1983, The Urban Campus: Educating a New Majority for a New Century, 1994, also numerous articles. Bd. dirs. Meth. Hosp., N.W. Ind. Forum, N.W. Ind. Symphony, S.D. Art Mus., Boys Club N.W. Ind., Akron Symphony, NBD Bank, John S. Knight Conv. Ctr., Inventure Pl., Akron Roundtable, Cleve. Com. Higher Edn. Recipient Disting. Alumni award Northwestern U., VA Disting. Alumni award, 1994, numerous grants; Am. Council on Edn. fellow in acad. adminstrn. Ind. U., Bloomington, 1980-81. Mem. Assn. Tchr. Educators (nat. pres. 1984-85, Disting. Mem. 1990), Nat. Acad. Tchrs. Edn. (bd. dirs. 1983—), Ind. Assn. Tchr. Educators (past pres.), North Ctrl. Assn. (mem. commn. at large), Am. Assn. State Colls. and Univs. (sr. fellow 1996-98, acting v.p. divsn. acad. and internat. programs 1997, bd. dirs.), Am. Coun. Edn. (bd. dirs.), Leadership Devel. Coun. ACE, Ohio Inter Univ. Coun. (chairperson), Internat. Reading Assn., Akron Urban League (bd. dirs.), P.E.O., Phi Delta Kappa (Outstanding Young Educator award), Delta Kappa Gamma (Leadership/Mgmt. fellow 1980), Pi Lambda Theta, Chi Omega. Episcopalian. Avocation: music. Home: 929 Harvey Dunn St Brookings SD 57006-1347

ELLIOTT, PETER R., athletic organization executive, retired; b. Bloomington, Ill., Sept. 29, 1926; s. Joseph Norman and Alice (Marquis) E.; m. s. Joan Connaught Slater, June 14, 1949; children: Bruce Norman, David Lawrence. B.A., U. Mich., 1949. Asst. football coach Oreg. State U., 1949-50, U. Okla., 1951-55; head football coach Nebr. U., 1956, U. Calif., Berkeley, 1957-59, U. Ill., 1960-66, U. Miami, Fla., 1973-74; dir. athletics U. Miami, 1974-78; asst. football coach St. Louis Cardinals, 1978; exec. dir. Pro Football Hall of Fame, Canton, Ohio, 1979-96, ret., 1996. Served with USNR, 1944-45. Named to Mich. Sports Hall of Fame, 1983, Coll. Football Hall of Fame, 1994. Mem. Am. Football Coaches Assn. (Region 8 Coach of Yr. 1958, Region 5 Coach of Yr. 1963). Presbyterian. Home: 3003 Dunbarton Ave NW Canton OH 44708-1818

ELLIOTT, R LANCE, lawyer; b. Chillicothe, Ohio, Aug. 1, 1943; s. Kenneth Leroy and Ethel Miriam (Knisley) Elliott; m. Susan Jeanne Ames, Aug. 24, 1968; children: Jocelyn, Amy, Peter. AB, MacMurray Coll., 1967; JD, Georgetown U., 1977. Bar: D.C. 1977, Va. 1992, Md. 1998. Tchr. Sch. Dist. 6, Waverly, Ill., 1968-69; dir. pub. relations Urban Land Inst., Washington, 1969-71; gen. counsel Bowling, Inc., Washington, 1971-98; of counsel Power & Power, Washington, 1990-95. Mem. ABA, Am. Soc. Assn. Execs. Episcopalian. Office: Preston and Elliott 5454 Wisconsin Ave Ste 650 Chevy Chase MD 20815-6910

ELLIOTT, RAY ANDREW, JR., retired surgeon, consultant; b. Milw., Nov. 6, 1926; s. Ray Andrew and Irene (Jacobs) E.; m. Elisabeth Bartlett, Sept. 2, 1950 (div. 1989); children: David Wayne, Daonald Warren, Ray Andrew III. BA, Drew U., 1948; MD, Union U., Albany, N.Y., 1951. v.p. Plastic Surgery Edn. Found., Chgo., 1976-77. Contbr. over 100 articles to med. jours., chpts. to books. Pres. Northeastern N.Y. Speech Ctr., Albany, 1967-68; bd. dirs. Vis. Nurse Assn., Albany, 1970-73; charter mem. Albany County Airport Authority, 1994-98, vice chmn., 1994-95; maj. CAP, 1993—; col. N.Y. N.G., 1995—. Recipient awards Drew U., 1948-98. Mem. AMA (ho. dels. 1972-94), Am. Assn. for Hand Surgery (pres. 1973-74), Am. Soc. Plastic and Reconstructive Surgery, Am. Soc. Aesthetic Plastic Surgeons, Internat. Soc. Aesthetic Plastic Surgeons (sec. gen. 1989-92, hon. citation 1992), PSEF (v.p. 1976-77). Avocations: private, commercial and instrument pilot. E-mail: raejrmd@aol.com. Home: PO Box 39 Slingerlands NY 12159

ELLIOTT, RICHARD HOWARD, lawyer; b. Astoria, N.Y., Apr. 30, 1933; m. Judith A. Kessler, Dec. 26, 1956; children—Marc Evan, Jonathan Hugh, Eve; m. 2d, Diane S. Schaefer, Nov. 18, 1978; children—Alexis, Sara Jane, Benjamin, David. B.S., Lehigh U., 1954; J.D. cum laude, U. Pa., 1962. Bar: U.S. Dist. Ct. (ea. dist.) Pa. 1962, Pa. Supreme Ct. 1962, U.S. Ct. Appeals (3d cir.) 1963, U.S. Dist. Ct. (mid. dist.) Pa. 1976. Assoc. Clark, Ladner, Fortenbaugh & Young, Phila., 1962-69; ptnr., 1970-75; ptnr. Elliott & Magee, Doylestown, Pa., 1976—; moderator Permanent Jud. Commn., Presbytery of Phila.; v.p., dir. Bucks County Soc. Prevention Cruelty to Animals; pres., dir. Pa. Soc. for Prevention of Cruelty to Animals. Gen. Counsel, dir. Pa. Fedn. Humane Socs., adj. faculty Bucks County Cmty. Coll.; mem. Pa. Navigation Commn., 1977-80. Lt. USN, 1954-59. Mem. ABA, Pa. Bar Assn., Phila. Bar Assn., Bucks County Bar Assn. Democrat. Home: 1205 Victoria Rd Warminster PA 18974-3923 Office: Elliott & Magee 1795 S Easton Rd Doylestown PA 18901-2837

ELLIOTT, ROBBINS LEONARD, consultant; b. Can., Aug. 12, 1920; s. Malcolm Robertson and Jean Steadman (Haley) E.; m. Myfanwy Esther Millward, Sept. 9, 1950; children: Michael, Wendy, Ruth, Robbins. BA, Acadia U., 1941; MA in Econs., U. Toronto, 1947. With Can. Fed. Govt., Ottawa, 1947-58, 63-76; exec. dir. Royal Archtl. Inst. Can., Ottawa, 1958-63; dir. planning and ops. Centennial Adminstrn., 1963-68; exec. v.p. Royal Archtl. Inst. Can., 1976-81; pres. Robbins Elliott Assos. Ltd., Ottawa, 1981-83; exec. dir. Can. Housing Design Council, 1982-86. Trustee Ottawa Bd. Edn., 1974-76; vice chmn. Ont. Heritage Found.; dir. Ont. Bicentennial Adv. Commn.; chmn. Wolfville Cent. Com., 1990-93; adv. com. on comms. Nat. Capital Commn.; Wolfville town councillor, 1994-97. Served to capt. Can. Army, World War II. Mem. Archaeol. Inst. Am. Progressive Conservative. Baptist. Home: 9 Westwood Dr Apt GL 3, Wolfville, NS Canada B0P 1X0

ELLIOTT, ROBERT BETZEL, retired physician; b. Ada, Ohio, Dec. 8, 1926; s. Floyd Milton and Rose Marguerite (Betzel) E.; m. Margaret Mary Robichaux, Aug. 26, 1954; children: Howard A., Michael D., Robert Bruce, Douglas J., John C., Joan O. BA, Ohio No. U., 1949; MD, U. Cin., 1953. Diplomate Am. Bd. Family Practice. Intern Charity Hosp., New Orleans, 1953-54; resident in pathology Bapt. Meml. Hosp., Memphis, 1958-59; practice medicine specializing in family practice, Ada, 1959—; mem. staff Ohio No. U. Health Service, Ada, 1960-70; coroner Hardin County, 1973-93. Mem. Ada Exempted Village Sch. Bd., 1960-76, pres., 1966-69, 72—, v.p. 1971—. Named Ohio Family Physician of Yr., 1985. Mem. AMA, Ohio Med. Assn., Hardin County Med. Soc. (pres. 1964), Am. Acad. Family Physicians, Ohio Acad. Family Physicians, Lima Acad. Family Physicians, Am. Coll. Health Assn., Masons, Elks. Democrat. Presbyterian. Home: 4429 State Route 235 Ada OH 45810-9516

ELLIOTT, ROBERT JOHN, lawyer; b. Jersey City, Jan. 1, 1934; s. John Elliott and Frances (Weilgus) Cardone; m. Linda M. Hall, Sept. 9, 1967; children: Robert Jr., Faye, Tiffany. AB, St. Mary's Coll., Techny, Ill., 1957; LLB, Georgetown U., 1961. Bar: D.C. 1961, Md. 1984. Assoc. Hogan & Hartson, Washington, 1961-69, ptnr., 1969—; gen. counsel Greater Washington Bd. Trade, 1991, 92. Mem. Md. Bar Assn., Bar of U.S. Supreme Ct., D.C. Bar Assn., Barristers' Club, Met. Club, Congl. Country Club (Bethesda, Md.), City Club Washington, Rotary. Avocations: golf, piano. Office: Hogan & Hartson 555 13th St NW Ste 800E Washington DC 20004-1161

ELLIOTT, RONALD DEAN, minister; b. Independence, Mo., Mar. 27, 1953; s. Morris Hayden and Lucille (Forman) E.; m. Deborah Ann Boehner, Dec. 30, 1977; children: Rachael Ann, Lydia Marie, Jeremiah Dean, Elizabeth Ann. BA, William Jewell Coll., Liberty, Mo., 1975; MDiv, Midwestern Sem., Kansas City, Mo., 1978; postgrad., Midwestern Bapt. Theol. Sem., 1998. Ordained to ministry So. Bapt. Conv., 1975. Youth pastor Spring Valley Bapt. Ch., Raytown, Mo., 1977-80; assoc. pastor Southview Bapt. Ch., Lincoln, Nebr., 1981-83; pastor Calvary Bapt. Ch., Lincoln, Nebr., 1983-90, Layton Hills Bapt. Ch., Layton, Utah, 1990-95, First Bapt. Ch., Bellevue, Nebr., 1995—; exec. bd. Kans. Nebr. Conv. So. Bapts., Topeka, 1987-89, Nebr. Coun. Alcohol and Drug Edn., Lincoln, 1987-90, Ea. Nebr. Bapt. Assn., Omaha, 1983-90. Chaplain Lincoln Police Dept., 1986-90, Boy Scouts Am., Lincoln, 1986-88; del. Lancaster County Rep. Party, 1988; trustee Midwestern Bapt. Theol. Sem., Kansas City, Mo. Home: 2501 Century Rd Bellevue NE 68123-1940 Office: First Bapt Ch 23d and Hancock Sts Bellevue NE 68005 *I have observed that it is only in understanding those things which are eternal that true meaning is found in the temporal.*

ELLIOTT, ROXANNE SNELLING, educational consultant to independent schools; b. Ft. Eustis, Va., Aug. 17, 1954; d. William Rodman and Anne Louise (Kurtz) Snelling; m. Vincent James Elliott, Oct. 1, 1983 (div.); children: Brian William, Lauren Elizabeth. BA, Denison U., 1976; MBA, Syracuse U., 1978. Internat. loan officer First Pa. Bank, Phila., 1978-82; ins. assoc. Ind. Sch. Mgmt., Wilmington, Del, 1982-83, dir. mgmt. insts., 1983-87, cons., exec. dir. consortium, 1984—, v.p., 1986-90, pres., 1990—. Republican. Episcopalian. Office: Ind Sch Mgmt 1316 N Union St Wilmington DE 19806-2594

ELLIOTT, R(OY) FRASER, lawyer, holding and management company executive; b. Ottawa, Ont., Can., Nov. 25, 1921. B.Comm., Queen's U., Kingston, Ont., Can., 1943; LLB, Osgoode Hall Law Sch., 1946; grad., Harvard U. Sch. Bus. Adminstrn., 1947. Bar: Ont. 1946, Que. 1948; created queen's counsel. Ptnr. Stikeman, Elliott, Toronto, Ont., 1952—; bd. dirs. CAE Inc., Toronto; lectr. co. law McGill U., Montreal, 1951. Contbg. author, editor: Que. Corp. Manual, 1948-53; co-editor: Doing Business in Canada. Mem. Montreal Bar Assn., Can. Bar Assn., Law Soc. Upper Can. Office: Commerce Ct W Ste 5300, Toronto, ON Canada M5L 1B9

ELLIOTT, THOMAS MICHAEL, executive, educator, consultant; b. Evansville, Ind., Aug. 4, 1942; s. Thomas Ira and Pauline (Dawson) E.; m. Susan M. Spiers, July 8, 1967 (div. Aug. 1975); 1 son, Christopher Michael; m. Loretta S. Glaze, Jan. 28, 1976. AB in Zoology, Ind. U., 1965, MS in Higher Edn., 1967, EdD, 1970. Asst. to pres. Purdue U., West Lafayette, Ind., 1972-73, asst. provost, 1973-74; exec. dir. Nat. Commn. United Methodist Higher Edn., Nashville, 1974-77; dep. commr. Mo. Dept. Higher Edn., Jefferson City, 1977-79; exec. dir. Ark. Dept. Higher Edn., Little Rock, 1979-82; exec. dir., CEO IEEE Computer Soc., Washington, 1982—; ptnr. Planning Mgmt. Services Group, Washington, 1976-82; cons. numerous colls. and univs. Author: Computer Simulation System, 1975; contbr. articles to profl. jours. Bd. dirs., mem. exec. com. So. Regional Edn. Bd., Atlanta, 1980-82; mem. Cabinet of Gov. Bill Clinton and Gov. Frank White, State of Ark., 1979-82. Mem. IEEE (sr.), IEEE Computer Soc., State Higher Edn. Exec. Officers Assn., Am. Soc. Assn. Execs., Am. Mgmt. Assn. Home: 1735 Q St NW Washington DC 20009-2407 Office: IEEE Computer Soc 1730 Massachusetts Ave NW Washington DC 20036-1903

ELLIOTT, VIRGINIA F. HARRISON, retired anatomist, kinesiologist and educator, investment advisor, publisher, philanthropist; b. St. Louis, Mar. 15, 1918; d. George Benjamin and Florence Gertrude (McManus) H.; m. William Hector Marsh, Dec. 1, 1963 (dec. Dec. 1986); m. George William Elliott, Oct. 27, 1991; stepchildren: Carolyn Frances Roberts, George William II, Robert Bonner (dec. Apr. 1995), Cathrine Susan Dimino. BS, U. Wis., 1940, PhD, 1959; MA, Columbia U., 1944. Lectr. Columbia U., N.Y.C., 1943-46; asst. prof. Mary Washington Coll. of U. Va., Fredericksburg, 1946-48; asst. prof. Oreg. State U., Corvallis, 1948-50, assoc. prof., 1950-59; instr. Army Med. Acad./Brooks Army Med. Ctr., San Antonio, 1959-60, assoc. prof., 1960-64; lectr. U. Tex. Med. Sch., Galveston, 1962-64, Hadassah Med. Sch., Hebrew U. of Jerusalem, 1965; lectr. grad. sch. U. Wis., Madison, 1964; pvt. practice stock market investment lectr. Washington, 1969-84, pub. stock market letter, 1969-84; ret., 1984; fashion model, 1936-47, with John Robert Powers Schs., Phila., Pitts., N.Y.C., 1943-47; cons. U. Tex. Med. Sch., 1962-64, U.S. Pentathlon Team, San Antonio, 1960-64, Dentists for Treatment of Pain from Muscular Tension, San Antonio, 1960-64; vis. prof. grad. sch. U. Wash., Seattle, 1961; lectr. in field. Contbr. articles to profl. jours. Mem. bd. visitors Sch. Edn., U. Wis., Madison, 1992-95, now emeritus; mem. Washington com. Nat. Coun. on Women's Giving. Recipient Civilian Meritorious Svc. award U.S. Civil Svc., 1965; Amy Morris Homans fellow, 1958; hon. fellow U. Wis., 1956, 58, 59. Fellow AAHPERD, Tex. Acad. Sci.; mem. Am. Alliance Health, Physical Edn., Recreation and Dance, Am. Assn. Anatomists divs. Fedn. Am. Socs. for Exptl. Biology, Cosmos Club, Achievement Rewards Coll. Scientists, Inc. (v.p. 1973-74, 78-80, bd. dirs. 1974-75, 76-78, 80-85, 87-89), Hospitality Info. Svc., Nat. Trust for Hist. Preservation, Rsch. Consortium, Bascom Hill Soc., Deans Club U. Wis., Friends Salvation Army, Arts for the Aging, Inc., Lake Bancroft Woman's Club. Avocations: designing clothing, furniture, landscaping and boats, sculpting, painting. Home: 6333 Cavalier Corridor Falls Church VA 22044-1301

ELLIOTT, WARREN G., lawyer; b. Pueblo, Colo., Jan. 3, 1927; s. Wallace Ford and Hazel (Ellsworth) E.; m. Martha McCabe, June 20, 1953 (div. Sept. 1980); children: Mark, Winthrop, Carolyn, Byron. Student, U. Nebr., 1944-45, U. Colo., 1947-49; AB, U. Colo., 1973; LLB, U. Mich., 1952. Bar: Colo. 1952, Conn. 1976, D.C. bar 1978. Asst. city mgr., city atty. Pueblo, 1952-55; adminstrv. asst., legislative counsel U.S. Senator Gordon Allott, 1956-61; asst. gen. counsel Life Ins. Assn. Am., Washington, 1961-68; gen. counsel Aetna Life & Casualty Co., Hartford, Conn., 1968-78; mem. firm Hedrick & Lane, Washington, 1978-79; of counsel Nossaman, Guthner, Knox & Elliott, Washington, 1979—; mem. Epstein, Becker & Green, P.C., Washington, 1986—. Corporator Hartford Hosp., St. Francis Hosp., Inst. for Living; dir. Friends of the Hopkins Ctr., Washington Area Tennis Patrons Found. Served with USAAC, 1944-46. Mem. ABA, Fed. Bar Assn., D.C. Bar Assn., Capitol Hill Club, St. Albans Tennis Club, Univ. Club (Washington), West Side Tennis Club (N.Y.C.), Phi Gamma Delta, Phi Alpha Delta. Home: 1 Chambers Rd Hanover NH 03755-2308 Office: Epstein Becker & Green 1227 25th St NW Ste 700 Washington DC 20037-1175

ELLIOTT-WATSON, DORIS JEAN, psychiatric, mental health and gerontological nurse educator; b. Caney, Kans., Dec. 6, 1932; d. Alva Orr and Mary Amelia (Boyns) Elliott; children Marsha Jean Watson, Sherwood Elliott Watson. BE, U. Miami, Fla., 1952, MEd, 1954; EdD, Pacific Western U., 1982; BSN, U. Kans., 1985; AS in Psychology, Kansas City (Kans.) C.C., 1989; AA in Music, Kansas City C.C., 1994; AA in Art, Johnson County C.C., 1997. RN, Kans., Mo.; cert. clin. specialist gerontology nurse, gerontology nurse generalist, psychiat.-mental health nurse, med.-surg. nurse, ANCC; cert. elem. to jr. coll. tchr., Kans., Mo.; lic. adult care home adminstr., Kans.; cert. master gardener. Tchr. learning disabled, gifted, emotionally disturbed Shawnee Mission, Kans., 1961-76; instr. hospitalized psychiat. and med.-surg. children U. Kans. Med. Ctr., Kansas City, 1979-82; pvt. practice, gerontol. nurse educator Bonner Springs, Kans., 1985—; libr. U. Miami, 1952, Kans. U., 1978; nurse ARC, Kansas City, 1985—; nurse educator Am. Heart Assn., Kansas City, 1985—; program designer mainstreaming spl. needs children into regular classrooms, 1969; specialist geriatric sexuality nursing homes, 1986. Author: The Thrifty Biker: Crossing America on a Three Speed, A Seventy Day, 3,730 Mile, $1,000 Adventure, 1999; editor Park Stylus, Parkville, Mo., 1952, Master Gardener's Back Fence, Columbia, Mo., 1997; author, speaker Kansas City area, 1950—. Tutor-organizer Tutoring Vol.Orgn. for Inner City Children, 1965-68; sustaining mem. Rep. Nat. Com., Washington, 1978—, rep. Congl. Com., 1978—, Rep. Senatorial Com., 1978—; pres. Young Reps., Kansas City, 1960; mem. Rep. Nat. Conv. Platform Planning Com., 1995; patron, charter mem. Kaw Valley Cmty. Choir, 1990-92; mem. Kansas City Cmty. Choir, 1992—, mem. tour of cathedrals Christ Ch., Oxford and King's Coll., Eng., 1993; mem. Mid. Am. Nazarene Coll. Cmty. Choir, 1993—, Leavenworth Cmty. Carnegie Choir, 1994—. Recipient Coast to Coast 2810 miles award Am. Running and Fitness Assn., 1994; inducted Rep. Nat. Hall of Honor, Rep. Nat. Conv., 1992. Mem. ANA (coun. on gerontol. nurses, coun. for cmty., primary care and long term care nursing practice, coun. for nursing rsch.), NEA (life, del. state conv. 1980, nat. conv. 1973), Kans. Nurses Assn., U. Kans. Alumni Assn., Bus. and Profl. Women, Order Ea. Star (Electra 1982, Martha 1994, Marshal 1995, Assoc. Conductress 1996, Assoc. Matron 1997, organist 1998), Order Rainbow for Girls (worthy advisor 1950), Am. Volkssport Assn. (Tri-Athlete 1993, 94, 95, 96, 4500 Km Walking award 1993, 5500Km 1994, 6500 Km 1996, Sunflower State Games Athlete 1993, 94, 95, 96, Sooner State Games Athlete award 1994, 95, 96, Mid-Am. Walking Marathon 1994, 6500 Km Walking award 1995, Kans. Female Athlete of Yr. 1997), Bike Across USA 1998, Bike Across Kans. 1997, Tiblow Trailblazers Walking Club (pres. 1993—), Nat. Wildlife Fedn. (cert. backyard wildlife habitat), Kappa Delta Pi, Pi Delta Epsilon, Phi Theta Kappa, Alpha Kappa Delta, Phi Alpha Theta. Avocations: holistic healing, gardening, camping, community involvement. Home and Office: 231 Sheidley Ave Bonner Springs KS 66012-1410

ELLIS, ALBERT, clinical psychologist, educator, author; b. Pitts., Sept. 27, 1913; s. Henry Oscar and Hettie (Hanigbaum) E.; life ptnr. Janet L. Wolfe. BBA, CCNY, 1934; MA, Columbia U., 1943, PhD, 1947. Diplomate: Am. Bd. Profl. Psychology; in clin. hypnosis Am. Bd. Psychol. Hypnosis; Am. Bd. Med. Psychotherapists, Am. Bd. Sexology. Free-lance writer, 1934-38; personnel mgr. Distinctive Creations, 1938-48; sr. clin. psychologist N.J. State Hosp., Greystone Park, 1948-49; instr. psychology Rutgers U., 1948-49, adj. prof., 1971-83; instr. psychology N.Y. U., 1949; adj. prof. Union Grad. Sch., 1971-77, U.S. Internat. U., 1974-80, Pittsburg State U., 1978—; chief psychologist N.J. State Diagnostic Center, Menlo Park, 1949-50, N.J. Dept. Instns. and Agys., Trenton, 1950-52; pvt. practice psychotherapy and marriage and family therapy N.Y.C., 1943-68; exec. dir. Albert Ellis Inst. for Rational Emotive Behavior Therapy, N.Y.C., 1959-89; pres., 1989—; Cons. clin. psychology VA, 1961-67. Author: An Introduction to the Principles of Scientific Psychoanalysis, 1950, The Folklore of Sex, 1951, (with A.P. Pillay) Sex, Society and the Individual, 1953, The American Sexual Tragedy, 1954, Sex Life of the American Woman and the Kinsey Report, 1954, New Approaches to Psychotherapy Techniques, 1955, (with Ralph Brancale) The Psychology of Sex Offenders, 1956, How to Live With a Neurotic, 1957, Sex Without Guilt, 1958, What Is Psychotherapy, 1959, The Place of Values in the Practice of Psychotherapy, 1959, The Art and Science of Love, 1960, (with Robert A. Harper) A Guide to Successful Marriage, 1961, (with R.A. Harper) A Guide to Rational Living, 1961, (with Albert Abarbanel) The Encyclopedia of Sexual Behavior, 1961, Reason and Emotion in Psychotherapy, 1962, The Intelligent Woman's Guide to Manhunting, 1963, If This Be Sexual Heresy, 1963, Sex and the Single Man, 1963, The Origins and the Development of the Incest Taboo, 1963, Nymphomania, A Study of the Over-Sexed Woman, 1964, Homosexuality, 1965, Suppressed: Seven Key Essays Publishers Dared Not Print, 1965, The Case for Sexual Liberty, 1965, The Search for Sexual Enjoyment, 1966, (with others) How to Raise an Emotionally Healthy, Happy Child, 1966, (with Roger O. Conway) The Art of Erotic Seduction, 1967, Is Objectivism a Religion, 1968, (with John M. Gullo) Murder and Assassination, 1971, (with others) Growth Through Reason, 1971, Executive Leadership: A Rational Approach, 1972, The Civilized Couple's Guide to Extramarital Adventure, 1972, How to Master Your Fear of Flying, 1972, The Sensuous Person: Critique and Corrections, 1972, (with others) Sex and Sex Education: A Bibliography, 1972, Humanistic Psychotherapy: The Rational-Emotive Approach, 1973, (with Robert A. Harper) A New Guide to Rational Living, 1975, Sex and the Liberated Man, 1976, Anger How to Live With and Without It, 1977, (with

Russell Grieger) Handbook of Rational-Emotive Therapy, 1977, (with W. Knaus) Overcoming Procrastination, 1977, (with E. Abrahms) Brief Psychotherapy in Medical and Health Practice, 1978, (with J.M. Whiteley) Theoretical and Empirical Foundations of Rational-Emotive Therapy, 1979, The Intelligent Woman's Guide to Dating and Mating, 1979, (with I. Becker) A Guide to Personal Happiness, 1982, (with M. Bernard) Rational-Emotive Approaches to the Problems of Childhood, 1983, (with M. Bernard) Clinical Applications of Rational-Emotive Therapy, 1985, Overcoming Resistance, 1985, (with Russell Grieger) Handbook of Rational-Emotive Therapy, Vol. 2, 1986, (with Windy Dryden) The Practice of Rational-Emotive Therapy, 1987, (with others) Rational-Emotive Treatment of Alcoholism and Substance Abuse, 1988, How To Stubbornly Refuse to Make Yourself Miserable About Anything-Yes Anything!, 1988, (with others) Rational-Emotive Couples Therapy, 1989, (with R. Yeager) Why Some Therapies Don't Work: The Dangers of Transpersonal Psychology, 1989, (with Windy Dryden) The Essential Albert Ellis, 1990, (with Patricia Hunter) Why Am I Always Broke: How to Be Sane about Money, 1991, (with Windy Dryden) A Dialogue with Albert Ellis: Against Dogma, 1991, (with Emmett Velten) What To do When AA Doesn't Work For You: Rational Steps to Quitting Alcohol, 1992, (with Lidia Dengelegi and Michael Abrams) The Art and Science of Rational Eating, 1992, (with Arthur Lange) How to Keep People from Pushing Your Buttons, 1994, (with Michael Abrams) How to Cope with a Fatal Illness, 1994, Reason and Emotion in Psychotherapy Revised, 1994, Better, Deeper and More Enduring Brief Therapy, 1996, (with Jack Gordon, Michael Neenan nd Stephen Palmer) Stress Counseling: A Rational Creative Behavior Therapy Approach, 1996, (with R.A. Harper) A Guide To Rational Living, 1997, (with R.C. Tafrate) How to Control Your Anger Before It Controls You, 1997, (with Catherine MacLaren) Rational Emotive Behavior Therapy: A Therapist's Guide, 1998, How to Control Your Anxiety Before It Controls You, 1998, (with Shawn Blau) The Albert Ellis Reader, 1998, Optimal Aging: How to Get Over Growing Older, 1998, How to Make Yourself Happy and Remarkably Less Disturbable, 1999. Fellow APA (pres. divsn. cons. psychology 1961-62, exec. com. divsn. psychotherapy 1969-73, coun. reps. 1963-64, 72-74), AAAS, Am. Assn. Marriage and Family Therapists (exec. com. 1957-59), Soc. Sci. Study Sex (exec. com. 1957-58, pres. 1958-60), Am. Orthopsychiat. Assn., Am. Sociol. Assn., Am. Assn. Applied Anthropology; mem. ACA, Am. Assn. Sex Educators, Counselors and Therapists (bd. dirs. 1981-82), Nat. Acad. Practice, Soc. Psychotherapy Rsch., N.Y. Assn. Clin. Psychologists in Pvt. Practice (chmn. 1952-54), N.Y. Joint Coun. Psychologists on Legislation (exec. com. 1951-53), Am. Group Psychotherapy Assn., Am. Acad. Psychotherapists (exec. com. 1954-64, v.p. 1962-64), Mensa, Am. Assn. Advancement Psychotherapy, N.Y. State Psychol. Assn., Soc. Exptl. and Clin. Hypnosis. Office: Albert Ellis Inst 45 E 65th St New York NY 10021-6508 *I now see that I have given up any addiction to MUSTurbation many years ago—to thinking that I must do well; that others must treat me considerately or fairly; and that the world must provide me with the things I want easily and quickly. I now almost always think that it would be better or nicer if I did well, others treated me fairly, and the world proved easy and pleasant. But it doesn't have to turn out those ways—and that makes quite a difference!.*

ELLIS, ALFRED WRIGHT (AL ELLIS), lawyer; b. Cleve., Aug. 26, 1943; s. Donald Porter and Louise (Wright) E.; m. Kay Genseke, June 1965 (div. 1976); 1 child, Joshua Kyle; m. Sandra Lee Fahey, Feb. 11, 1989. BA with honors, U. Tex., Arlington, 1965; JD, So. Meth. U., 1971. Bar: Tex., U.S. Dist. Ct. (no., so., ea. and we. dists.) Tex., U.S. Ct. Appeals (5th cir.), U.S. Supreme Ct.; cert. personal injury and civil trial lawyer. Atty. Woodruff, Kendall & Smith, Dallas, 1972; ptnr. Woodruff & Ellis, Dallas; pvt. practice Dallas, 1983-96; of counsel Howie & Sweeney, 1996—; instr. So. Meth. U. Law Sch. Trial Advocacy; past pres. Law Focused Edn., Inc. Past mem. City of Dallas Urban Rehab. Standards Bd., Dallas Assembly, Salesmanship Club, Dallas; bd. dirs. Habitat for Humanity, 1998—, treas., 1999; trustee Hist. Preservation League, 1992-94; tournament dir. Dallas Regional Golden Gloves Tournament, 1976-96; pres., bd. dirs. Dallas Coun. on Alcoholism, 1980. Capt. U.S. Army, 1965-69. Fellow Roscoe Pound Found.; named one of Outstanding Young Mem of Am., 1977, named Boss of Yr. Dallas Assn. Legal Secs., 1978; recipient Certs. of Recognition (8) D.I.S.D., 1971-83, Wall St. Jour. award So. Meth. U. Law Sch., 1972, Hayward McMurray award Dallas Jaycees, 1975-76, Spl. Recognition award All Sports Assn., 1977, Cert. of Appreciation for Exceptional and Disting. Vol. Svc. Gov. Mark White, 1983, Community Spirit award Dallas Bus. Jour., 1993, Disting. Svc. award Dallas All Sports Assn., 1993,award Nancy Garms Meml. for outstanding Contr. to Law Focus Edn., 1996-Leon Jaworski award. Fellow Tex. Bar Found. (sustaining life), Dallas Bar Found. (trustee); mem. ATLA, Am. Bd. Trial Advocates (diplomate, sec.-treas. Dallas chpt. 1998, pres. 1999), Am. Coll. Legal Medicine (assoc.), Legal Svcs. of North Tex. (bd. dirs., Outstanding Svc. award 1990), State Bar Tex. (lectr. seminars, bd. dirs. 1991-94, 95, Excellence in Diversity award 1994), Dallas Bar Assn. (bd. dirs. 1978, chmn. bd. dirs. 1986, v.p. 1987-88, pres. 1990), Dallas Trial Lawyers Assn. (pres. 1977, Disting. Cmty. Svc. award 1990), Tex. Trial Lawyers Assn., Tex. Equal Access to Justice Found. (bd. dirs. 1994-96), Coll. State Bar of Tex. (bd. dirs. 1997—), Dallas All Sports Assn. (pres.-1980). Avocations: tennis, skiing. Office: 2911 Turtle Creek Blvd Ste 1400 Dallas TX 75219-6258

ELLIS, ANDREW JACKSON, JR., lawyer; b. Ashland, Va., June 23, 1930; m. Dorothy L. Lichliter, Apr. 24. 1954; children: Elizabeth E. Attkisson, Andrew C., William D. AB, Washington and Lee U., 1951, LLB, 1953. Bar: Va. 1952. Ptnr. Campbell, Ellis & Campbell, Ashland, 1955-70, Mays, Valentine, Davenport & Moore, Richmond, Va., 1970-88; ptnr. Mays & Valentine, Richmond, 1988-96, sr. counsel, 1998—; substitute judge County of Hanover (Va.) Ct., 1958-63, commonwealth atty., 1963-70, county atty., 1970-78; substitute judge 15th jud. dist., 1990-96; judge 15th dist Juvenile and Domestic Rels. Ct., 1996-98; mem. capital adv. bd. NationsBank of Va., 1960-93. Mem. Ashland Town Coun., 1956-63, mayor, 1958-63; trustee J. Sargent Reynolds C.C., 1972-80. 1st lt. U.S. Army, 1953-55. Fellow Am. Coll. Trial Lawyers, Va. Law Found.; mem. Am. Judicature Soc., Va. Bar Assn., Va. State Bar (coun. 1968-74), Va. Trial Lawyers Assn., S.R., Kiwanis. Episcopalian. Home: 15293 Old Ridge Rd Beaverdam VA 23015-1610 Office: PO Box 1122 Richmond VA 23218-1122

ELLIS, ANNE ELIZABETH, fundraiser; b. Orngestad, Aruba, Aug. 21, 1945; d. Thomas Albert and Anne Elizabeth (Belis) Wolfe; m. Earl Edward Ellis, Feb. 14, 1970. BS, La. State U., 1967. Fashion coord. Baton Rouge, 1962-67; textile researcher La. State U., Baton Rouge, 1965-67; buyer I.H. Rubensteins., Baton Rouge, 1967-68; fashion distbr. J.C. Penney, Inc., Arlington, Tex., 1969-70; asst. buyer J.C. Penney, Inc., Dallas, 1970-73; exec. dir. Nassau County Mus. Fine Art Assn., Roslyn, N.Y., 1985-88; speaker C.W. Post U., Greenvale, N.Y., 1988—; cons. in field. Chmn., editor: (cookbook) Specialities of the House, 1981-83. Bd. dirs., com. chmn. Congregational Ch., Manhasset, N.Y., 1975-96; exec. v.p., bd. dirs., com. chmn. Jr. League Internat.; benefit gala chmn., com. chmn. Grenville Baker Boys & Girls Club, Locust Valley, N.Y., 1983-91; pres. bd., vice-chmn. cmty. outreach, benefit gala chmn. Tilles Performing Art Ctr. L.I. U., Greenvale, N.Y., 1985—; bd. dirs., benefit co-chmn. Nassau County Family Assn. Svcs., Hempstead, 1988-96; benefit vice-chmn. Glen Cove/North Shore Cmty. Hosp., 1989-93; mem. exec. bd., exec. v.p., trustee WLIW, L.I. Pub. TV, 1990—, chmn. bd. dirs., 1997-99; trustee Cmty. Found. of Oyster Bay, 1991-94; trustee Dowling Coll., Oakdale, N.Y., 1993-98, exec. bd., 1997-98; adv. bd. Westbury (N.Y.) Gardens, 1993-97; chmn. adv. bd. Long Island chpt. Save the Children, 1995—; trustee L.I. U., 1998—. Recipient Vol. of Yr. award Jr. League L.I., 1984, 85, Outstanding Vol. Svcs. and Commitment award County of Nassau, 1989, Juliette Low award Nassau County Girl Scouts, L.I., 1991, Disting. Leadership award, L.I., 1991, Outstanding Community Vol. award Jr. League of L.I., 1991-92, Disting. Svc. medal L.I. State Parks Found., 1999. Mem. P.E.O. (pres. 1985-87), The Creek Inc., Meadowbrook Club Inc., Lost Tree Club, Forest Creek Club, Kappa Kappa Gamma (alumna pres. 1971-72). Republican. Congregationalist. Avocations: golf, gardening, needlepoint.

ELLIS, ANTHONY JOHN, education educator; b. Scunthorpe, Eng., June 15, 1945; came to U.S., 1990; s. Jack and Nancy Doreen (Read) E.; m. Maureen Anne Twomey, July 16, 1966 (div.); children: Katherine, Seonaid; m. Alice Anne Findlay, Sept. 4, 1980; 1 child, Bridget Anne. BA, Kings Coll., London, 1967, MA, 1968. From lectr. to sr. lectr., dept. chmn. U. St. Andrews, Scotland, 1971-90; prof. Va. Commonwealth U., Richmond, 1990—. Contbr. articles to profl. jours.; editor: Philosophical Books, 1985—. U. Wollongong fellow, Australia, 1989; recipient Fulbright Travel award, 1989. Mem. Am. Philos. Assn., Royal Inst. Philosophy, Aristotelian Soc. Avocation: music. Office: Va Commonwealth Univ PO Box 842025 Richmond VA 23284-2025

ELLIS, ARTHUR BARON, chemist, educator; b. Lakewood, Ohio, Apr. 4, 1951; s. Nathan and Carolyn Joan (Agulnick) E.; m. Susan Harriet Trebach, Nov. 9, 1975; children: Joshua, Margot. BS, Calif. Inst. Tech., 1973; PhD, MIT, 1977. Asst. prof. chemistry U. Wis., Madison, 1977-82, assoc. prof., 1982-84, prof., 1984-86, Meloche-Bascom prof., 1986—. Editor: Chemistry and Structure at Interfaces, 1986; patentee in field; contbr. articles to profl. jours. Fellow A.P. Sloan Found., 1981, H.I. Romnes fellow U. Wis., 1985, Guggenheim fellow, 1989; recipient Nat. Catalyst Tchg. award Chem. Mfrs. Assn., 1994. Mem. Am. Chem. Soc. (Exxon fellow 1980, chmn. edn., Pimentel award 1997). Jewish. Achievements include creating 1-2-3 levitation kit based on high-temperature superconductors. Office: U Wis Dept Chemistry 1101 University Ave Madison WI 53706-1322

ELLIS, BERNICE, financial planning company executive, investment advisor; b. Bklyn.; d. Samuel and Clara H.; m. Seymour Scott Ellis; children: Michele, Wayne. BA, Bklyn. Coll.; MS, Queens Coll., 1970. Cert. fin. planner, N.Y. 1987, elem. educator, N.Y.C. Elem. tchr. L.I. Sch. Dists., Merrick, N.Y.; tchr. reading N.Y.C. Bd. of Edn., Bklyn., 1972-73; coordinator Reading is Fundamental, Lawrence, N.Y., 1973-75; pres., founder N.Y. State Assn. for the Gifted and Talented, Valley Stream, N.Y., 1974-87; pres. Ellis Planning, Valley Stream, N.Y., 1984—; cons. Nassau County Bd. Coop. Ednl. Svcs., Westbury, N.Y., 1973-74; adminstrv. intern region II U.S. Office Edn., 1977-78; adj. asst. prof. Nassau C.C., Garden City, N.Y., 1975-91, adj. assoc. prof., 1991-94, adj. full prof., 1995—; fin. commentator Money Talk radio program WHPC FM; arbitrator NASD, 1996. Contbr. articles to profl. jours and fin. newsletters. Mem. adv. com. Ams. for Ams. for Hope, Growth and Opportunity, 1998; mem. Nat. Rep. Party, Valley Stream Rep. Party. Recipient Ednl. Professions Devel. Act fellow CUNY Inst. for Remediations Skills for Coll. Personnel, Queensborough Community Coll., 1970-73. Mem. AAUW (North Shore bd., chmn. Money Talk 1991—), Nat. Assn. Securities Dealers (arbitrator 1996), Nat. Alliance of Sales Execs., Inst. for CFPs, Inst. for CFPs of L.I. (bd. dirs.), Internat. Assn. Fin. Planners (legis. com. L.I. chpt. 1986-87), N.Y. State Reading Assn., Adj. Faculty Assn. Nassau C.C., L.I. C. of C., Rotary. Avocations: reading, swimming. Office: Ellis Planning Inc 628 Golf Dr Valley Stream NY 11581-3594

ELLIS, CAROLYN MCCLAIN, educator; b. Charlotte, N.C., Aug. 11, 1952; d. James Odell and Wyonella (Alexander) McC.; m. Robert L. Ellis, Aug. 9, 1980; children: Lindsay Alexandria, Erin Daniel. BA, Johnson C. Smith U., 1975. Tchr. Charlotte-Mecklenburg Schs., 1976—, reading cons., 1980-85; field tester Nat. Bd. Tchg. Cert., Charlotte, 1993-94. Pres. Bahama/Havana Homeowners, Inc., Charlotte, 1997—. Democrat. Methodist. Home: 8217 Belle Vista Ct Charlotte NC 28216-2063

ELLIS, CAROLYN TERRY, lawyer; b. N.Y.C., Apr. 20, 1949; D. Francis Martin and Sarah Baker (Ames) E. m. H. Lake Wise, Feb. 27, 1982; children: Carolyn Campbell Wise, Burke Ames. BA, U. Chgo., 1971; JD, NYU, 1974. Bar: N.Y. 1975. Rsch. analyst Dept. Justice, N.Y.C., 1973-74; from assoc. to ptnr. Lord, Day & Lord, N.Y.C., 1974-86; ptnr. Coudert Bros., N.Y.C., 1986—; instr. Bklyn. Law Sch., 1980-82. Mem. ABA, N.Y. State Bar Assn., Assn. of Bar of City of N.Y. (antitrust and trade regulation com. 1989-92, internat. trade comm. 1993-95). Office: Coudert Bros The Grace Bldg 1114 Avenue of The Americas New York NY 10036-7703*

ELLIS, CHARLES RICHARD, publishing executive; b. N.Y.C., July 20, 1935; s. Charles and Ruth Frances (Allen) E.; m. Nathalie Likwas, Sept. 15, 1957 (div. 1963); 1 child, Kenneth; m. Jeanne Marie Laurent, May 28, 1963; stepchildren: Christopher, Patrick, Shannon, Nicholas Moore. AB, Princeton U., 1957; MA, Columbia U., 1961. Tchr. Barnard Sch., N.Y.C., 1958-63; mgr. Sci. Rsch. Assocs., Chgo., 1963-68; exec. editor D.C. Heath, Boston, 1968-70; chmn., mng. dir. D.C. Heath Ltd., U.K., 1970-75; co-mng. dir. Pergamon Press, U.K., 1975-78; internat. mktg. dir. Elsevier Pub., Amsterdam, 1978-81; pres. Elsevier Sci. Pub. Co., N.Y.C., 1981-88; exec. v.p. John Wiley & Sons, N.Y.C., 1988-90, pres., CEO, 1990-97, sr. advisor, 1998—; pres. bd. trustees Princeton Univ. Press, 1987—; vice chmn. Copyright Clearance Ctr., Salem, Mass., 1987-88. Contbr. articles to profl. jours. Mem. Assn. Am. Pubs. (vice chmn. 1986-87, 91, chmn. 1991-94), Internat. Pubs. Assn. (vice chmn. 1996—), Chevalier French Order Arts and Letters, Princeton Club N.Y. Democrat. Home: 213 Constitution Dr Princeton NJ 08540-5018 Office: John Wiley & Sons 605 3rd Ave Fl 6 New York NY 10158-0012*

ELLIS, CHRISTINE JO, middle school educator; b. South Bend, Ind., June 13, 1952; d. Dean E. DeLeury and Rita Lorraine Hall Kroll; children: William, Matthew. BS, Ball State U., 1974; MEd, Kent State U., 1994. Cert. tchr. English and reading, Ohio. Tchr. Marion (Ind.) Pub. Schs., 1974-77, Licking Hts. (Ohio) Schs., 1986-88; tchr. lang. arts Hudson (Ohio) Local Schs., 1991—; assoc./cons. nat. Writing Project, 1997—. Contbg. author: Ohio Teachers Write, 1997, Ohio Journal of English Language Art, 1998. Tchr. rep. Hudson PTO, 1997—. Named Outstanding Mid. Sch. English Arts Educator for Ohio, 1999. Mem. Nat. Mid. Sch. Assn., Ohio Coun. Tchrs. English Lang. Arts, Nat. Coun. Tchrs. English. Avocations: writing, roller blading. Office: Hudson Mid Sch 77 N Oviatt St Hudson OH 44236-3043

ELLIS, CLAUD M. BUDDY, diversified financial services company executive; b. Oklahoma City, July 2, 1947; s. Charles and Cloal Marie (Shirley) E.; 1 child, Carla Mohler. BA in Polit. Sci. and Mktg., Columbia U., 1970; MBA in Internat. Banking and Econs., London Sch. Econs., 1972. Dir. govt. rels. and pub. policy Aero Comdr. divsn. Rockwell Internat. Corp., Seal Beach, Calif., 1973-83; White Ho. fellow V.P. George Bush, Washington, 1984-85; pres., CEO Banco Resources Ltd., London, 1985—. Home: 9826 Hefner Village Pl Oklahoma City OK 73162 Office: Banco Resources Ltd. 18 Trafalgar St, London England

ELLIS, CLIFF, college basketball coach; m. Carolyn Ratzlaff; children: Chryssa Rutland, Clay, Anna Catherine. Grad., Fla. State U., 1968. Coach various high schs. and colls, 1968-75; head coach South Ala. Jaguars, 1975-84; played in Sun Belt Conf., 1977-78, played in NCAA Tournament, 1979; played in Sun Belt Conf. Clemson Tigers, 1984-94; reached Nat. Invitional Tournament Final 8, 1985-86, ranked 13th in NCAA, 1986-87, played in NCAA Tournament, played in Nat. Invitational Tournament; head coach Auburn (Ala.) Tigers, 1994—; SEC western divsn. champions, SEC champions, reached NCAA Final 4, 1998-99. Author: Zone Press Variations for Winning Basketball, The Complete Book of Fast Break Basketball. Named Sun Belt Coach of Yr., 1979, ACC Coach of Yr., 1987, 90, Nat. Coach of Yr., Sports Illustrated, 1999, SEC Coach of Yr., 1995, 99. Office: c/o Athletic Dept Auburn U PO Box 351 Auburn AL 36831-0351*

ELLIS, COURTENAY, lawyer; b. Cottingham, Eng., Jan. 4, 1946; came to the U.S., 1970; BA, Oxford U., Eng., 1967, MA, 1974; LLM, George Washington U., 1972. Bar: D.C. 1973; cert. solicitor, Eng. Solicitor's articled clk. Field, Fisher & Co., London, 1968-69; solicitor Farrer & Co., London, 1970; assoc. atty. Covington & Burling, Washington, 1972-76, Akin, Gump, Strauss, Hauer & Feld, 1976-78; ptnr. Akin, Gump, Strauss, Hauer & Feld, Washington, 1979-98; lawyer Oppenheimer Wolff Donnelly Bayh, Washington, 1998—. Bd. dirs. The Episcopal Ctr. for Children, Washington, 1986-92. Mem. ABA (internat., antitrust and litigation and energy sects.), Am. Soc. Internat. Law, Law Soc. London, Brit. Am. Bus. Assn. (bd. dirs., program chair 1997-98), Washington Fgn. Law Soc. (bd. govs., membership coord. 1993-95, program coord. 1995-96, pres. 1997-98), Assn. Internat. Petroleum Negotiators, Fed. Bar Assn. (internat. law sect., chair 1996-98), Met. Club, Annapolis Yacht Club. Office: Wolff Donnelly Bayh 1350 Eye St NW Ste 200 Washington DC 20005*

ELLIS, DAVID WERTZ, museum director; b. Huntingdon, Pa., Feb. 8, 1936; s. Calvert Nice and Elizabeth Oller (Wertz) E.; m. Marion Elizabeth Schmitt, June 24, 1961; children: Kathryn Dana, Lorna Beth, Audrey Heather. BA with honors in Chemistry, Haverford Coll., 1958; PhD in Chemistry, MIT, 1962; LLD (hon.), Lehigh U., 1979, Lafayette Coll., 1990; DSc (hon.), Susquehanna U., 1982, Ursinus Coll., 1985; LHD (hon.), Juniata Coll., 1989. Asst. prof. chemistry U. N.H., 1962-67, assoc. prof., 1967-78, acting asst. dean Grad. Sch., 1967, asst. dean Coll. of Tech., 1968, assoc. acad. v.p., 1968-71, vice provost, v.p. acad. affairs, 1971-78; pres. Lafayette Coll., Easton, Pa., 1978-90; pres., dir. Mus. of Sci., Boston, 1990—; mem. adv. com. for The Directorate on Edn. and Human Resources, NSF, 1998—. Author: (with others) Calculations of Analytical Chemistry, 7th edit., 1971; contbr. articles to profl. jours. Bd. dirs., chmn. mktg. com. Internat. Space Theater Consortium, 1993-94, chmn. liaison com., 1997-98; bd. dirs. Assn. Sci. Tech. Ctrs., 1992-93, 95—, v.p., 1997—; convener Nat. Health Scis. Consortium, 1994-96; bd. dirs. Sci. Mus. Exhibits Collaborative, 1990—, sec.-treas., 1992-93, chmn., 1993-95; bd. dirs. Elderhostel, 1983-87, 89—, chmn., 1990-95, 96—; bd. dirs. Mus. Film Network, 1990—, chmn., 1993-97; bd. dirs. Sta. WGBH, pub. broadcasting, 1990—, mem. exec. com., 1992—, chmn. audit com., 1993—; mem. bd. overseers Tufts U., Colls. of Arts and Sci., 1995—; mem. bd. U. N.H. Found., 1997—, vice chair 1999—. Dupont fellow, 1960-61. Mem. AAAS, Am. Chem. Soc., Am. Assn. Mus., Assn. Sci. Mus. Dirs., Nat. Assn. Ind. Colls. and Univs. (vice chmn. 1987-88, chmn. 1988-89), Harvard Club. Mem. United Ch. of Christ. Home: Thomas Graves' Landing 6 Canal Park # 710 Cambridge MA 02141-2211 Office: Museum of Sci Science Park Boston MA 02114-1099

ELLIS, DONALD LEE, lawyer; b. Dallas, Oct. 2, 1950; s. Truett T. and Rosemary (Tarrant) E.; children: Angela Nicole, Laura Elizabeth, Natalie Dawn, Donald Lee II. BS, U. Tulsa, 1973; JD, Oklahoma City U., 1976. Bar: Tex. 1979, Okla. 1977, U.S. Dist. Ct. (ea. dist.) Tex. 1978, U.S. Dist. Ct. (we. dist.) Okla. 1978, U.S. Ct. Appeals (5th cir.) 1984, U.S. Supreme Ct., 1984, U.S. Ct. Appeals (11th cir.). Spl. agt. FBI, Washington, 1976-78; asst. dist. atty. Smith County, Tyler, Tex., 1979-80; mem. firm Barron & Ellis, Tyler, 1980-84, Ellis & Woods law firm, 1984-85; sole practice, Tyler, 1985—. Bd. dirs. Mental Health Assn., Tyler, 1983-87. Mem. Assn. Trial Lawyers Am., Tex. Bar Assn., Okla. Bar Assn., Smith County Bar Assn., Soc. Former Spl. Agts. FBI, Tex. Trial Lawyers Assn., FBI Agents Assn., Lawyers-Pilot Bar Assn. Home: PO Box 131221 Tyler TX 75713-1221 Office: PO Box 131221 217 W Houston St Tyler TX 75702-8137

ELLIS, DORSEY DANIEL, JR., dean, lawyer; b. Cape Girardeau, Mo., May 18, 1938; s. Dorsey D. and Anne (Stanaland) E.; m. Sondra Wagner, Dec. 27, 1962; children: Laura Elizabeth, Geoffrey Earl. BA, Maryville Coll., 1960; JD, U. Chgo., 1963. Bar: N.Y. 1967, U.S. Ct. Appeals (2d cir.) 1967, Iowa 1976, U.S. Ct. Appeals (8th cir.) 1976. Assoc. Cravath, Swaine & Moore, N.Y.C., 1963-68; assoc. prof. U. Iowa, Iowa City, 1968-71, prof., 1971-87, v.p. fin. and univ. svcs., 1984-87, spl. asst. to pres., 1974-75; dean Washington U. Sch. Law, St. Louis, Mo., 1987—, prof. law, 1999—; vis. mem. sr. common room Mansfield Coll., Oxford U., Eng., 1972-73, 75; vis. prof. law Emory U., Atlanta, 1981-82. Contbr. articles to profl. jours. Trustee Mo. Hist. Soc., St. Louis, 1995—. Nat. Honor scholar U. Chgo., 1960-63; recipient Joseph Henry Beale prize, 1961, Alumni award Maryville Coll., 1988. Mem. ABA, Am. Law Inst., Bar Assn. Metro St. Louis, Mound City Bar Assn., Iowa Bar Assn., AALS Acad. Resource Corps., Order of Coif. Home: 1 Brookings Dr Saint Louis MO 63130-4862*

ELLIS, E. ADDISON, III, publishing executive. BA, Wooster U., 1975; MBA, Ohio State U., 1977. From product mgr. for sci. and math. to dir. mktg. Merrill Pub. Co., 1973-81, v.p., dir. sch. divsn., 1981-88, pres. ELHI divsn., 1988-94; sr. v.p., pres. Glencoe/McGraw-Hill Cos., Inc., Westerville, Ohio, 1994—. Office: Glencoe/McGraw-Hill Cos Inc 936 Eastwind Dr Westerville OH 43081-3329

ELLIS, EDWARD R. (BUSTER), career officer. BS in Bus. Mgmt., Va. Polytechnic Inst. and State U., 1968; MA in Bus. Stats., U. Ala., 1970; grad., Squadron Officer Sch., 1975, Air Command and Staff Coll., 1984, Air War Coll., 1986, Nat. War Coll., 1991. Commd. 2d lt. USAF, 1971, advanced through grades to brig. gen., 1998; instr. pilot then flight examiner 29th Flying Tng. Wing, Craig AFB, Ala., 1973-77; F-4E pilot, asst. flight comdr. 18th Tactical Fighter Squadron, Elmendorf AFB, Alaska, 1977-80; sect. comdr., ops. officer for dir. student ops. Squadron Officer Sch., Maxwell AFB, Ala., 1980-83; exec. officer to comdt., 1980-83; F-4E pilot, asst. ops. officer then ops. officer 36th Tactical Fighter Squadron, Osan Air Base, S. Korea, 1984-86; exec. officer to comdr. 51st Tactical Fighter Wing, Osan Air Base, 1984-86; faculty instr., comdr. 3823rd Air Command and Staff Coll. Student Squadron, Maxwell AFB, 1986-88; comdr. 35th Flying Tng. Squadron, Reese AFB, Tex., 1988-90; chief Caribbean Basin br. then chief We. Hemisphere div. Strategic Plans and Policy, Joint Staff, Pentagon, Washington, 1991-94; chief flying tng. div. Hdqs. Air Edn. and Tng. Command, Randolph AFB, Tex., 1994-95; comdr. 71st Flying Tng. Wing, Vance AFB, Okla., 1995-97; comdt. Squadron Officer Sch., Maxwell AFB, 1997; comdr. Air Force Accession and Tng. Schs., Maxwell AFB, 1997—. Decorated Legion of Merit. Office: AFOATS/CC 551 Maxwell Blvd Ste 1 Maxwell AFB AL 36112-6106

ELLIS, ELDON EUGENE, surgeon; b. Washington, Ind., July 2, 1922; s. Osman Polson and Ina Lucretia (Cochran) E.; m. Irene Clay, June 26, 1948 (dec. 1968); m. Priscilla Dean Strong, Sept. 20, 1969 (dec. Feb. 1990); children: Paul Addison, Kathe Lynn, Jonathan Clay, Sharon Anne, Eldon Eugene, Rebecca Deborah; m. Virginia Michael Ellis, Aug. 22, 1992. BA, U. Rochester, 1946, MD, 1949. Intern in surgery Stanford U. Hosp., San Francisco, 1949-50, resident and fellow in surgery, 1950-52, 55; Schilling fellow in pathology San Francisco Gen. Hosp., 1955; ptnr. Redwood Med. Clinic, Redwood City, Calif., 1955-87; med. dir. Redwood Med. Clinic, Redwood City, 1984-87; semi-ret. physician, 1987—; med. dir. Peninsula Occupl. Health Assocs., San Carlos, Calif., 1991-94; physician Peninsula Occupl. Health Assocs., San Carlos, 1995-99, Sequoia Med. Clinic, Redwood City, Calif., 1999—; asst. clin. prof. surgery Stanford U., 1970-80; dir. Sequoia Hosp., Redwood City, 1974-82. Pres. Sequoia Hosp. Found., 1983-92, bd. dirs.; pres., chmn. bd. dirs. Bay Chamber Symphony Orch., San Mateo, Calif., 1988-91; mem. Nat. Bd. Benevolence Evang. Covenant Ch., Chgo., 1988-93; mem. mgmt. com. The Samarkand Retirement Cmty., Santa Barbara, Calif.; past pres. Project Hope Nat. Alumni Assn., 1992-94, bd. dirs., 1994—; med. advisor Project Hope, Russia Commonwealth Ind. States, 1992. With USNR, 1942-46, 50-52. Named Outstanding Citizen of Yr., Redwood City, 1987. Mem. AMA, Calif. Med. Assn., Am. Coll. Chest Physicians, Am. Heart Assn. (v.p. 1974-75), Calif. Heart Assn. (pres. 1965-66), San Mateo County Heart Assn. (pres. 1961-63), San Mateo Med. Soc. (pres. 1969-70), San Mateo County Comprehensive Health Planning Coun. (v.p. 1969-70), San Mateo Surg. Soc., Stanford Surg. Soc., San Mateo Individual Practice Assn. (treas. 1984-97), Cardiovasc. Coun., Calif. Thoracic Soc., Commonwealth Club. Republican. Mem. Peninsula Covenant Ch. Home: 2305 Wooster Ave Belmont CA 94002-1549 Office: Sequoia Med Clinic 633 Veterans Blvd Redwood City CA 94063

ELLIS, ELLA THORP, writer, retired educator; b. L.A., July 14, 1928; d. William Dunham and Marian (Yates) Thorp; m. Lea Herbert Ellis, Dec. 17, 1949; children: Steven, David, Patrick. Student, U. Cordoba, Argentina, 1961-62; BA in English and History, UCLA, 1966; MA in English and Writing, San Francisco State U., 1975. Instr. creative writing U. Calif. Ext., Berkeley, 1972-77, lectr., instr. fiction, 1986-94; lectr. creative writing San Francisco State U., 1975-80; lectr. lit. Univ. Women Internat., Buenos Aires, 1981-85. Author: (novels) Roam the Wild Country, 1967, Riptide, 1969, Celebrate the Morning, 1972, Where the Road Ends, 1974, Hallelujah, 1976, Sleepwalker's Moon, 1980, Hugo and the Princess Nena, 1983, Swimming with the Whales, 1995, also fgn. and paperback edits. Recipient 6 Am. Libr. Honor Book awards, 2 Jr. Lit. Guild Book of Month awards, also state awards. Mem. Authors Guild, Soc. Childrens Book Writers, Soc. Woman Geographers, Opera Guild, Sierra Club, Amnesty Internat. Democrat. Episcopalian. Avocations: travel, gardening, opera, reading. E-mail: chellis@ieee.com. home: 1438 Grizzly Peak Berkeley CA 94708

ELLIS, ELMO ISRAEL, broadcast executive, consultant, columnist; b. Birmingham, Ala., Nov. 11, 1918; s. Samuel B. and Bertha F. (Seltz) Israel; m. Ruth M. Ballinger, Dec. 26, 1944; children: Janet Faye, William Bryan. A.B., U. Ala., 1940; M.A., Emory U., 1948; postgrad., Am. Mgmt. Assn., 1959, Emory U., 1965; LittD (hon.), Oglethorpe U., 1995. Dir. publicity, prodn. mgr. Sta. WSB-AM-FM, Atlanta, 1940-42; writer, prodr. "We, The People" CBS, 1946-47; prodn. mgr. Sta. WSB-TV, 1948-52; mgr.

programming Sta. WSB-AM-FM, 1952-63, v.p., gen. mgr., 1963—; v.p. Cox Broadcasting Corp., 1969-82; former chmn. Radio Advt. Bur.; syndicated radio commentator Jacor Communications, Inc., 1982-87; syndicated columnist Neighbor newspapers, 1982—; former chmn. NAFMB, NBC Radio Affiliates, Radio Code Bd. Nat. Assn. Broadcasters; mem. nat. adv. bd. Am. Women in Radio and TV, 1981-82; former instr. in radio-TV Emory U., Ga. State U.; lectr. Oglethorpe U., bd. trustees, 1975—; bd. visitors Coll. Comm., U. Ala., 1997; mem. journalism adv. bd. Emory U., 1997—. Writer, producer network radio programs NBC, ABC, CBS and Mut. Broadcasting System, 1942-47; co-author: Radio Station Management, 1960; author: Sleepy Hollow Poems, 1942, Removing the Rust from Radio, 1954, Happiness is Worth the Effort, 1970, Opportunities in Broadcasting Careers, 1986, 5th edit., 1999, The Youthful Option, 1997, The Phoenix-Civil War Centennial Pageant, 1961, Power of the South and other comml. films, articles, poems, TV and radio commercials; contbg. author: Diagnosis and Prognosis in Journalism, 1962, A Forward Look for Communications, 1967, Business and the Media, 1979. Radio-TV rep. Nat. Heart Assn., 1969; pres. Ga. Safety Coun., 1981-82; past chmn. S.E. regional adv. bd. Anti-Defamation League, B'nai B'rith, hon. life mem. nat. adv. commn., 1983; chmn. Atlanta Christmas Seals Drive, 1977, 78; asst. to dir. Dem. Nat. Convs., 1952, 56, 60, 64; bd. dirs. Atlanta Landmarks, Inc.; chmn. Friends of the Libraries, Emory U., 1985-90; past mem. exec. com., bd. dirs. Peach Bowl; founder Elmo Ellis Profl.-in-Residence Fund U. Ala., 1987; ret. bd. trustees Multiple Sclerosis Soc., Ga., Ga. State . Coll. Bus. Adminstrn.; bd. visitors Emory U., Oglethorpe U., Clark Coll. Comms. Dept., Ctr. for Holocaust Studies, Washington, Girl Scouts Greater Atlanta, Boy Scouts Metro Atlanta, Am. Jewish Com., Ga., Consumer Credit Svcs. Greater Atlanta, Ga. Coun. on Child Abuse, Gerontology Ctr. Ga. State U., Jr. Achievement Greater Atlanta. Capt. USAAF, 1942-46. Recipient Ga. Libr. Assn. award, 1965, Silver Medal award Atlanta Advt. Club, 1965, Peabody awards, 1954, 66, Alfred P. Sloan award, 1966, Sch. Bell award Ga. Edn. Assn., 1967, Citizen of Yr. award Ga. Assn. Broadcasters, 1965, Southeastern Father of Yr. award, 1978, Thomas Alva Edison award, 1966, Red Cross Disting. Svc. award, 1968, Abraham Lincoln awards So. Bapt. Radio-TV Commn., 1972, 77, Silver Beaver award Boy Scouts Am., 1972, Pioneer Broadcaster Ga. award Phi Gamma Kappa, 1972, Meritorious Svc. award Am. Heart Assn., 1970, Disting. Alumnus award U. Ala., 1971, Gavin Disting. Broadcaster award, 1971, 72, 84, Disting. Svc. award Nat. Safety Coun., 1973, George Washington Honor medals and Disting. Svc. awards Freedom's Found., 1973-86, Abe Goldstein award Anti-Defamation League, 1975, Gold Boot award March of Dimes, 1975, George Erwin award Ga. Assn. Realtors, 1975, 76, 77, 78, Humanitarian award Nat. Jewish Hosp., 1979, Operation Lifesaver award Ga. Safety Coun., 1979, 25 Year Svc. award ARC, 1967, Red Cross Big Drop award ARC, 1979, Mass Media award Protestant Radio-TV Ctr., 1981, Cmty. Svc. award of honor Emory U., 1985, Nat. Bronze award Jr. Achievement, 1985; 1st appointee to Atlanta chpt. U. Ala. Hall of Fame, 1987; named one of Atlanta's Leaders of Tomorrow Time mag.; Disting. Svc. award Arthritis Found., 1966, news and editl. awards AP, UPI, SDX; U.S. Presdl. Commendation, 1970, Heroes, Saints and Legends award Wesley Woods Found., 1995; named to Ga. Music Hall of Fame, 1995, U. Ala. Hall of Fame Coll. of Comm.; named lt. col. Aide-de-Camp Gov.'s Staff State of Ga., 1990. Mem. NARAS (Hall of Fame elections com. 1987-95), Broadcast Pioneers, Internat. Radio-TV Soc., Ga. Assn. Broadcasters (bd. dirs., past pres., Hall of Fame 1987), Am. Values Inc. (nat. adv. bd. 1987—), Emory U. Alumni Assn. (past pres.), Soc. Profl. Journalists (Ralph McGill award 1993), U. Ala. Alumni Assn. (Disting. Alumnus award 1993), Commerce Club, Phi Beta Kappa, Phi Eta Sigma, Tau Kappa Alpha, Omicron Delta Kappa. Home and Office: 6345 Aberdeen Dr NE Atlanta GA 30328-4208 *Just look around at the unfinished work of the world, and you can see our reason for being.*

ELLIS, EMORY LEON, retired biochemist; b. Grayville, Ill., Oct. 29, 1906; s. Walter Leon and Bertha May (Forman) W.; m. Marion Louise Faulkner, Sept. 17, 1930 (dec. Aug. 1994). BS, Calif. Inst. Tech., 1930, MS in Chemistry, 1932, PhD in Biochemistry, 1934. Registered profl. engr., Calif. Chemist U.S. FDA, L.A., 1934-35; rsch. assoc. CalTech, Pasadena, 1935-43; dept. head U.S. Navy Ordnance Test Sta., China Lake, Calif., 1943-54; dir. ordnance plan Rheem Ordnance Lab, Downey, Calif., 1954-57; project leader Inst. for Def. Analysis, Washington, 1957-63; cons. U.S. Navy Weapons Ctr., China Lake, 1966-68; ptnr. Devcom, La Habra, Calif., 1965-68. Contbr. chpt. in books and articles to profl. jours. Recipient Alumni Disting. Svc. award Calif. Inst. Tech., 1970; Paul Harris fellow Rotary Internat., 1993. Mem. AAAS, Am. Chem. Soc., Tau Beta Pi, Sigma Xi. Avocations: writing essays, travel. Home: 506 Pioneer Ct Santa Maria CA 93454-3442

ELLIS, FRANK HALE, English literature educator; b. Chgo., Jan. 18, 1916; s. Frank Hale and Gay (Shepherd) E.; m. Constance Dimock, Dec. 20, 1940; 1 dau., Gay. BS with honors, Northwestern U., 1939; PhD, Yale U., 1948. Mem. faculty U. Buffalo, 1941-42; mem. faculty Yale U., 1945-51; with Dept. State, Washington, 1951-54; mem. faculty Smith Coll., 1958-86, Mary Augusta Jordan prof. English lit., 1974-86. Author: Swift's Discourse, 1967, Twentieth Century Interpretations of Robinson Crusoe, 1969, Poems on Affairs of State, 1697-1714, 2 vols., 1970, 75, Swift vs. Mainwaring, 1985, Sentimental Comedy: Theory and Practice, 1991, John Wilmot Earl of Rochester: The Complete Works, 1994, New Dictionary of National Biography; contbr. articles to profl. jours. Served with AUS, 1942-45, ETO and PTO. Decorated Bronze Star; Morse fellow, 1950-51; Huntington Library fellow, 1975. Mem. Cum Laude Soc., Conn. Acad. Arts and Scis., Phi Beta Kappa. Clubs: Elizabethan, Lawn (New Haven). Home: 146 Elm St Northampton MA 01060-2904

ELLIS, FRANKLIN HENRY, JR., surgeon, educator; b. Washington, Sept. 20, 1920; s. Franklin Henry and Katherine (McClintock) E.; m. Mary Jane Walsh, Dec. 2, 1978; children: Katherine de Saulles (Mrs. Robert Manoff), Elizabeth Dunston (Mrs. Joseph Browning), Franklin Henry III, Margot McClintock (Mrs. Hugh Starkey), Laura Lawson (Mrs. David Milliken), Marie-Armide Longer (Mrs. Charles Storey), Hedrick Watson, Michael Garrison. A.B., Yale U., 1941; M.D., Columbia U., 1944; PhD, U. Minn., 1951. Diplomate: Am. Bd. Surgery, Am. Bd. Thoracic Surgery. Intern Bellevue Hosp., N.Y.C., 1944-45; fellow surgery Mayo Clinic, 1945-46, 48-52, fellow thoracic surgery, 1952-53, asst. to surg. staff, 1952-53, cons. surgery, 1953-70; mem. faculty Mayo Grad. Sch. Medicine, 1952-70, prof. surgery, 1964-70, chmn. thoracic surg. sect., 1966-70; chief cardiovascular surgery Lahey Clinic Found., Boston, 1970-75; chief thoracic and cardiovascular surgery Lahey Clinic Med. Ctr., 1975-86, sr. cons., 1986-90; chmn. dept. thoracic and cardiovascular surgery New Eng. Deaconess Hosp., Boston, 1971-90; lectr. surgery Harvard Med. Sch., 1970-74, asso. clin. prof. surgery, 1974-80, clin. prof. surgery, 1980-91, prof. emeritus, 1991—. Served with USNR, 1946-48. Mem. AMA (Billings Gold medal 1955), ACS, Am. Assn. Thoracic Surgery, Internat. Soc. Surgery, Boston Surg. Soc. (pres. 1985-86), New Eng. Surg. Soc., Soc. Clin. Surgery, Soc. Vascular Surgery (pres. 1971), Soc. Thoracic Surgeons (pres. 1977), Assn. Cardiothoracic Surgeons Gt. Britain and Ireland (hon.), Am. Surg. Assn., European Assn. Cardiothoracic Surgery, European Soc. Thoracic Surgeons (corr.), Internat. Soc. Diseases of Esophagus (hon.). Home: 21 Fairmount St Brookline MA 02445-5905 Office: BI-Deaconess Med Ctr 110 Francis St Ste 2C Boston MA 02215-5501

ELLIS, FREDERICK STEPHEN, retired judge; b. Amite, La., Oct. 20, 1924; s. Ezekiel Parke Ellis and Lelia Marguerite Rightor; m. Betty Blanche Dahzberg, June 11, 1948 (dec. Jan. 1978); children: Frederick Stephen II, Douglas Culver; m. Haydee Helen Lafaye, June 7, 1980. BS in Geology, Tulane U., 1948, LLB, 1951. Bar: La. 1951. Atty. Covington, La., 1951-60; judge 22nd Jud. Dist., Covington, La., U.S. Ct. Appeals (1st Cir.), Baton Rouge, 1966-82; judge-ad-hoc various cts., 1982-89; liquidator Champion Ins. Co., Baton Rouge, 1989-91; ind. counsel La. State Bd. Med. Examiners, New Orleans, 1991—; gen. ptnr. Litig. Arbiters, Covington, 1987—. Author: St. Tammany Parish, 1981. Sec. Covington Country Club, 1953; pres. Playmakers, Inc., La., 1954, Covington Cmty. Concert, 1972; comdr. Pontchartrain Yacht Club, Mandeville, La., 1970; Lt. (j.g.) USNR, 1945-46, PTO. Mem. The Boston Club, Pickwick Club. Avocations: history, music, writing. E-Mail: judge@gs.verio.net. Office: Litigation Arbiters 325 N New Hampshire St Covington LA 70434

ELLIS, FREDRIC LEE, lawyer; b. Springfield, Mass., Nov. 21, 1957; s. Irving Donald and Evelyn Gladys (Melnick) E.; m. Wendy J. Murphy, Oct. 21, 1988; children: Grant, Taylor, Reed, Cameron. BA, Hampshire Coll., Amherst, Mass., 1979; JD cum laude, Harvard U., 1983. Bar: Mass. 1983, U.S. Dist. Ct. Mass. 1983, U.S. Ct. Appeals (1st cir.) 1983, U.S. Ct. Appeals (11th cir.) 1994. Law clk. to Justice Raya Dreben Mass. Appellate Ct., Boston, 1983-84; asst. dist. atty. Dist. Atty.'s Office, Cambridge, Mass., 1984-86, dep. chief Appeals and Tng. Bur., 1986-87; ptnr. Gilman, McLaughlin & Hanrahan, Boston, 1987-96; owner Ellis & Rapacki, Boston, 1996—. Mem. bd. editors med./Legal Aspects of Breast Implants, 1996—. Named Lawyer of Yr., Mass. Lawyers Weekly, 1996, Outstanding Civil Trial Atty., Middlesex Bar Assn., 1998. Mem. ATLA, Mass. Bar Assn. Office: Ellis & Rapacki 85 Merrimac St Ste 300 Boston MA 02114-4715

ELLIS, GEORGE EDWIN, JR., chemical engineer; b. Beaumont, Tex., Apr. 14, 1921; s. George Edwin and Julia (Ryan) E. BSChemE, U. Tex., 1948; MS, U. So. Calif., 1958, MBA, 1965, MS in Mech. Engring., 1968, MS in Mgmt. Sci., 1971, Engr. in Indsl. and Systems Engring., 1979. Rsch. chem. engr. Tex. Co., Port Arthur, 1948-51, Houston and Long Beach, Calif., 1952-53; rsch. chem. engr. Space and Info. Divsn., N.Am. Aviation Co., Downey, Calif., 1959-61, Magna Corp., Anaheim, Calif., 1961-62; chem. process engr. AiResearch Mfg. Co., L.A., 1953-57, 57-59; chem. engr. Petroleum Combustion & Engring. Co., Santa Monica, Calif., 1957, Jacobs Engring. Co., Pasadena, Calif., 1957, Sesler & Assocs., L.A., 1959; rsch. specialist Marquardt Corp., Van Nuys, Calif., 1962-67; sr. project engr. Conductron Corp., Northridge, Calif., 1967-68; info. systems asst. L.A. Dept. Water and Power, 1969-92; instr. thermodynamics U. So. Calif., L.A., 1957. With USAAF, 1943-45. Mem. ASTM, ASME, AIChE, Nat. Assn. Purchasing Mgmt., Nat. Contract Mgmt. Assn., Am. Inst. Profl. Bookkeepers, Am. Soc. Safety Engrs., Am. Chem. Soc., Am. Soc. Materials, Am. Electroplaters and Surface Finishers Soc., Nat. Assn. Corrosion Engrs., Inst. Indsl. Engrs., Am. Prodn. and Inventory Control Soc., Am. Soc. Quality, Am. Indsl. Hygenists Assn., Steel Structure Painting Coun., Inst. Mgmt. Accts., Soc. Mfg. Engrs., L.A. Soc. Coating Tech., Assn. Finishing Processes, Chem. Coatings Assn. Internat., Pi Tau Sigma, Phi Lambda Upsilon, Alpha Pi Mu. Home: 1344 W 20th St San Pedro CA 90732-4408

ELLIS, GEORGE FITZALLEN, JR., retired energy services company executive; b. Salisbury, N.C., May 4, 1923; s. George F. and Lena (Ramsay) E.; m. Rachael Trexler, Oct. 27, 1945 (dec. Jan. 1995); children: Susan Ellis Snyder, George F. III; m. Carol Andrews, July 19, 1997. B.S., U.S. Naval Acad., 1944; M.S., Rensselaer Poly. Inst., 1957. Commd. ensign U.S. Navy, 1944, advanced through grades to rear adm., 1972; comdr. South Atlantic Force, U.S. Atlantic Fleet, 1975-76; staff supreme Allied Command Europe, 1974-75; ret. U.S. Navy, 1976; dir. internat. bus. Babcock & Wilcox Co., Lynchburg, Va., 1976-78; dir. govt. relations Babcock & Wilcox Co., Washington, 1978-79; v.p. govt. ops. McDermott Internat., Inc., Washington, 1979-88; bd. dirs. John Hanson Savs. Bank, Beltsville, MD., 1989-90. Trustee Am. U., 1982-91; trustee Ch. of the Covenant, Arlington, Va., 1981-82. Decorated Legion Merit with 4 clusters. Mem. Army-Navy Club (Washington), Vero Beach (Fla.) Yacht Club, Annapolis Yacht Club, Naval Acad. Faculty Club. Home: 1824 Milvale Rd Annapolis MD 21401-5923 also: 3554 Ocean Dr Vero Beach FL 32963-1673*

ELLIS, GEORGE HATHAWAY, retired banker and utility company executive; b. Orono, Maine, Jan. 29, 1920; s. Milton Ellis and Carrie (Voadecia) White; m. Sylvia Poor, Aug. 18, 1946; children—Rebecca Anne, George Milton, Randall Poor, Deborah Josephine. BA, U. Maine, 1941, LLD, 1962; MA, Harvard U., 1948, PhD, 1950; LLD, Nasson Coll., Springvale, Maine, 1961, Bates Coll., Univ. Mass., 1968; DCS, Western NE Coll., 1968. Pres. Fed. Res. Bank Boston, 1961-68; pres., chief exec. officer Keystone Funds, Boston, 1968-74, Home Savs. Bank, Boston, 1975-85; chmn. bd. Cen. Maine Power Co., Augusta, 1983-90, ret., 1990. Editor, contbg. author: The Economic State of New England, 1954; contbr. articles to profl. jours. Trustee Econ. Edn. Coun. Mass.; mem. devel. coun. U. Maine, Orono, 1960-84; corp. mem. Univ. Hosp., Boston, 1978-84; bd. dirs. Greater Boston Community Devel., 1979-86; chmn. bd. trustees United Ch. of Christ Pension Bds., N.Y.C., 1985-90. Maj. inf. U.S. Army, 1941-45; PTO. Nat. honoree Beta Gamma Sigma, U. Mass., 1968. Fellow Am. Acad. Arts and Scis.; mem. Phi Beta Kappa, Phi Kappa Phi. Congregationalist. Home: PO Box 250 Andover ME 04216-0250

ELLIS, GEORGE RICHARD, museum administrator; b. Birmingham, Ala., Dec. 9, 1937; s. Richard Paul and Dorsie (Gibbs) E.; m. Sherrill Edwards, June 20, 1961 (dec. 1973); m. Nancy Enderson, Aug. 27, 1975; 1 son, Joshua. BA, U. Chgo., 1959, MFA, 1961; postgrad., UCLA, 1971. Art supr. Jefferson County Schs., Birmingham, 1962-64; asst. dir. Birmingham Mus. Art, 1964-66; asst. dir. UCLA Mus. Cultural History, 1971-81, assoc. dir., 1981-82; dir. Honolulu Acad. Arts, 1981—. Author various works on non-western art, 1971—. Bd. dirs. Children's Lit. Hawaii, Japan Am. Soc.; humanities adv. com. mem. Hawaii Pacific U., 1995—; cmty. adv. bd. Japanese Cultural Ctr., 1997—; sec.-treas. Social Sci. Club, 1985—. Recipient Ralph Altman award UCLA, 1968; recipient Outstanding Achievement award UCLA, 1980; fellow Kress Found., 1971. Mem. Pacific Arts Assn. (v.p. 1985-89, exec. bd. 1989—), Hawaii Mus. Assn. (v.p. 1986-87, pres. 1987-88, bd. pres. 1996-97, 97-98), Assn. Art Mus. Dirs., Am. Assn. Mus., L.A. Ethnic Arts Coun. (hon.), Friends of Iolani Palace (bd. dirs.), Pacific Club. Office: Honolulu Academy of Arts 900 S Beretania St Honolulu HI 96814-1495

ELLIS, GLEN EDWARD, JR., insurance agent, financial planner; b. Austin, Tex., Sept. 7, 1960; s. Glen Edward and Virginia Lee (Walter) E.; m. Sherry Kay Testolin, Aug. 8, 1992. BS, Stanford U., 1983. ChFC. Registered rep., sr. field underwriter Aetna Investment Svcs., Inc., Hartford, Conn., 1987—; fin. planner Aetna Fin. Svcs., Inc., Hartford, Conn., 1996—. Mem. Internat. Assn. for Fin. Planning, Million Dollar Round Table, Nat. Assn. Life Underwriters (Nat. Sales Achievement award 1988-89, 93-98, Nat. Quality award 1990-98), Soc. Fin. Svc. Profls. Avocations: hiking, fishing. Office: Aetna Fin Svcs Inc Ste 2210 8911 N Capital Of Texas Hwy Austin TX 78759-7200

ELLIS, HAROLD DONALD, auto repair company executive; b. Lynwood, Calif., Aug. 10, 1946; s. Lloyd Jasper Ellis and Gladys (Beets) Worthington. BA in Sociology, Roosevelt U., 1970. Mgr. student svcs. M-W Edn. Corp., Chgo., 1973-79; mgr. customer svc. Midas Internat., Chgo., 1981-86, mgr. customer and consumer rels., 1986-87, dir. customer and consumer rels., 1987-89, dir. mktg. and adminstrn., 1989-95, v.p. consumer affairs, 1995-99, v.p. franchise support svcs., 1999—; chmn. Motorist Assurance Program, Washington, 1997—. Mem. Automotive Maintenance and Repair Assn. (chmn. 1994-97). Avocations: water gardening, collecting Koi. Office: Midas Internat 1300 Arlington Heights Rd Itasca IL 60143

ELLIS, HARRIETTE ROTHSTEIN, editor, writer; b. Memphis, Feb. 29, 1924; d. Samuel and Edith (Brodsky) Rothstein; m. Manuel J. Kaplan, June 1, 1944 (div. 1970); children: Deborah Elise Kaplan-Wyckoff, Claire Naomi Kaplan, Amelia Stephanie Kaplan; m. Theodore J. Ellis, Aug. 22, 1971 (div. Jan. 1992). Student, Memphis State U., 1941-42, Memphis Art Acad., 1940-43; BA, U. Ala., Tuscaloosa, 1944; postgrad., UCLA, 1949-50, Chouinard Art Inst., L.A., 1948. Advt. art/copy retail industry, New Orleans, Albuquerque, L.A., 1944-49; writer, graphic artist for newspapers and mags., L.A., 1944-49; editor Jewish Fedn. News, Long Beach, Calif., 1969-81; editor, writer Calif. Fashion Publs., L.A., 1982-86; editor Valley Mag., Granada Hills, Calif., 1987; pub. rels. Joan Luther & Assocs., Beverly Hills, Calif., 1988-90; editor Jewish Cmty. Chronicle, Long Beach, 1990—; dir. corp. comms. Startel Corp., Irvine, Calif., 1981-82. Active on com. to help implement infusion of fluoridated water in city water sys., mem. comty. interfaith com., Long Beach; bd. dirs. Hillel, 1994—, Camp Komaroff, 1994—, Temple Israel, Long Beach, Jewish Cmty. Ctr., Long Beach. Named Woman of Yr., Temple Israel, Long Beach, Pioneer Women; recipient newspaper awards Calif. Press Women, Nat. Fedn. Press Women, Coun. of Jewish Fedns. Mem. Calif. Press Women (bd. dirs., treas., v.p., pres. 1997—), Nat. Fedn. Press Women, Women of Reform Judaism (regional and nat. bd. dirs.). Avocations: theatre, music, travel, archeology. E-mail: jchron@net999.com. Office: 3801 E Willow St Long Beach CA 90815-1734

ELLIS, HELENE RITA, social worker; b. St. Paul, Sept. 20, 1935; d. Moe and Cele (Sidletsky) Weisman; m. Bernard M. Ellis, Sept. 30, 1956; children: Miriam, Arienne, Elia, Evie. BS, U. Minn., 1956; MSW, Loyola U., 1974; PhD, Inst. Clin. Social Work, Chgo., 1996. Lic. clin. social worker, Ill.; bd. cert. diplomate. Tchr. Roosevelt High Sch., Mpls., 1957-58, Barrington (Ill.) High Sch., 1958-59; social worker Dist. #39 Schs., Wilmette, Ill., 1974—; lectr. Loyola U. of Chgo., 1996—; chairperson Dist. 39 Health and Safety Curriculum Project, Wilmette, 1987-92. Named Ill. Sch. Social Worker of Yr., Ill. Assn. Sch. Social Workers, 1997-98. Mem. NASW, Am. Orthopsychiatric, N.Am. Soc. Adlerian Psychology, Sch. Social Work Assn. Am., Am. Group Psychotherapy Assn., Ill. Assn. Sch. Social Workers (Social Worker of Yr. 1997-98), Pi Lambda Theta, Phi Beta Kappa, Alpha Sigma Nu. Home: 2530 Wellington Ct Evanston IL 60201 Office: Dist 39 Schs 615 Locust Rd Wilmette IL 60091-2237

ELLIS, HOWARD WOODROW, evangelist, creative agent, clergyman, artist, author; b. Linton, Ind., Feb. 19, 1914; s. Lee and Effie (Walraven) E.; m. Susanna Goldsmith, Aug. 27, 1942; children: Patricia Sue Ellis Beebe, Mary Lou Ellis Bordwell. Student, Art Inst. Chgo., 1944-45, Am. Art Acad., 1945-46; AB, U. Evansville, 1943, HHD hon., 1962; BD, Garrett Bibl. Inst., 1946; postgrad., Peabody Coll., 1959-60, U. Tenn.-Nashville. Ordained to ministry United Methodist Ch., 1943. Mem. nat. staff Gen. Bd. Evangelism, Meth. Ch., Nashville, 1946-66; assoc. Central Avenue Meth. Ch., Indpls., 1966-68, Main Street United Meth. Ch., Boonville, Ind., 1968-74, Wall Street United Meth. Ch., Jeffersonville, Ind., 1974-78, Gobin United Meth. Ch., 1978-79; condr. evangelist missions to Sweden, Norway, Denmark, Finland, 1957, 59, 82, Mex., 1961, 65, 87, Korea, 1961, Gt. Britain, 1982, India, 1984, also throughout U.S. Exhibited in one-man travelling exhbn., 1973; group shows include, Nashville Fine Arts Festival, 1959, 60, 61, Tenn. State Fair, Nashville, 1959-66, painting in group shows, Smithsonian Instn., Washington, 1960, U. Evansville, Ind., 1960, Ewha U., Seoul, 1962, Inst. Mexican-Am. Cultural Relations, Mexico City, 1962, Nat. Convocation Meth. Youth, Purdue U., West Layayette, Ind., 1964, retrospective show North United Meth. Ch., Indpls., 1967, represented in numerous permanent collections including U. Evansville, Upper Room Mus., Nashville; author: Sallman Interpretations, 1944, The Witnessing Fellowship, 1961, Evangelism for Teen-Agers, 1958, rev. edit., 1966, The Last Supper, 1963; (with T. McEachern) Youth Evangelism, New Reflections, The Marks of the Christian, A Study of the Beatitudes,Christian Lit. Soc., India, 1987; (latest books) author, illustrator: How to Draw and Speak, 1961, He Took the Cup, 1961. Recipient Denman Evangelism award, 1984. *Died Oct. 2, 1998.**

ELLIS, JAMES ALVIS, JR., lawyer; b. Lubbock, Tex., Mar. 19, 1943; s. James Alvis and Myrle Alice (Peden) E.; m. Sandra Gay Gillespie, June 18, 1966; children: Claire Elizabeth, James Alvis III. B.A., Tex. Tech U., 1965; J.D., U. Tex., 1968. Bar: Tex. 1968, U.S. Dist. Ct. (no., so., ea. and we. dists.) Tex. 1969, U.S. Ct. Appeals 1970, U.S. Supreme Ct. 1980; cert. in civil trial law Tex. Bd. Legal Specialization. Law clk. to presiding judge U.S. Dist. Ct. (we. dist.) Tex., 1968-69; assoc. Carrington, Coleman Sloman & Blumenthal, Dallas, 1970-74, ptnr., 1975—. Pres. Dallas Jr. Bar Assn., 1972. Fellow Tex. Bar Found., Dallas Bar Found.; mem. ABA, State Bar Tex., Dallas Bar Assn. Presbyterian. Clubs: Cresent. Office: Carrington Coleman Sloman & Blumenthal 200 Crescent Ct Ste 1500 Dallas TX 75201-1848

ELLIS, JAMES D., communications executive, corporate lawyer; b. 1943. BBA, U. Iowa, 1965; JD, U. Mo., 1968. Bar: Mo. 1968, U.S. Ct. Appeals (D.C. cir.) 1977, Tex. 1980. Atty. AT&T, 1972-74, AT&T Long Lines, 1974-77; atty. gen. depts. AT&T, 1977-79; gen. atty. Southwestern Bell Telephone Co., San Antonio, 1979-83; v.p., gen. counsel Bellcore, 1983-84, Southwestern Bell Telephone Co., Tex., 1984-86; v.p., gen. counsel, sec. Southwestern Bell Corp., 1986-88; sr. v.p., gen. counsel Southwestern Bell Corp., 1988-89; sr. exec. v.p., gen. counsel SBC Comm., San Antonio, 1989—. With U.S. Army, 1968-72. Office: SBC Communications Inc 175 E Houston St San Antonio TX 78205-2233*

ELLIS, JAMES JOLLY, landscape resort official; b. Meadville, Pa., Mar. 3, 1937; s. Walter Harmon and Nerea Isabel (Farber) E. AA, Orlando Jr. Coll., 1959; BS in Bus. Adminstrn. and Econs., Rollins Coll., 1981. With Orlando (Fla.) Parks and Forestry Dept., 1961-70; supr. landscape dept. Walt Disney World, Fla., 1970-78, 81-82; supr. landscape dept. Walt Disney Village Comtys., Orlando, 1978-81, horticulture area mgr. over rd. maintenance/spl. projects, 1995—; owner, operator Chestnut Grove Co. Served with U.S. Army, 1959-60. Mem. Am. Mgmt. Assn., Fla. Turf Grass Assn. Republican. Lutheran. Home: 705 S Summerlin Ave Orlando FL 32801-4021 Office: PO Box 10000 Orlando FL 32830-1000

ELLIS, JAMES REED, lawyer; b. Oakland, Calif., Aug. 5, 1921; s. Floyd E. and Hazel (Reed) E.; m. Mary Lou Earling, Nov. 18, 1944 (dec.); children: Robert Lee, Judith Ann (dec.), Lynn Earling, Steven Reed. B.S., Yale, 1942; J.D., U. Wash., 1948; LL.D., Lewis and Clark U., 1968, Seattle U., 1981, Whitman Coll., 1992. Bar: Wash. 1949, D.C. 1971. Ptnr. Preston, Thorgrimson, Horowitz, Starin & Ellis, Seattle, 1952-69, Preston, Thorgrimson, Starin, Ellis & Holman, Seattle, 1969-72, Preston, Thorgrimson, Ellis, Holman & Fletcher, Seattle, 1972-79; sr. ptnr. Preston, Thorgrimson, Ellis & Holman, Seattle, 1979-90, Preston, Thorgrimson, Shidler, Gates & Ellis, Seattle, 1990-92; ret., of counsel Preston Gates & Ellis, Seattle, 1992—; chmn., CEO Wash. State Convention and Trade Ctr., Seattle, 1986—; dep. pros. atty. King County, 1952; gen. counsel Municipality of Met. Seattle, 1958-79; dir., mem. exec. com. Key Bank of Wash., 1969-94, KIRO, Inc., 1965-95; dir. Blue Cross of Wash. and Alaska, 1989-98. Mem. Nat. Water Commn., 1970-73; mem. urban transp. adv. council U.S. Dept. Transp., 1970-71; mem. Wash. Planning Adv. Council, 1965-72; mem. Washington State Growth Strategies Commn., 1989-90; pres. Forward Thrust Inc., 1966-73; chmn. Mayors Com. on Rapid Transit, 1964-65; trustee Ford Found., 1970-82, mem. exec. com., 1978-82; bd. regents U. Wash., 1965-77, pres., 1972-73; trustee Resources for the Future, 1983-92; mem. council Nat. Mcpl. League, 1968-76, v.p., 1972-76; chmn. Save our Local Farmlands Com., 1978-79, King County Farmlands Adv. Commn., 1980-82; pres. Friends of Freeway Park, 1976—; bd. dirs. Nat. Park and Recreation Assn., 1979-82; trustee Lewis and Clark U., 1988-94; pres. Mountains to Sound Greenway Trust, Inc., 1991—; trustee Henry M. Jackson Found., 1992—. 1st lt. USAAF, 1943-46. Recipient Bellevue First Citizen award, 1968, Seattle First Citizen award, 1968, Nat. Conservation award Am. Motors, 1968, Distinguished Service award Wash. State Dept. Parks and Recreation, 1968, Distinguished Citizen award Nat. Municipal League, 1969, King County Distinguished Citizen award, 1970, La Guardia award Center N.Y.C. Affairs, 1975, Environ. Quality award EPA, 1977, Am. Inst. for Public Service Nat. Jefferson award, 1974, U. Wash. Recognition award, 1981, State Merit medal State of Wash., 1990, Nat. Founders award Local Initiatives Support Corp., 1992, Henry M. Jackson Disting. Pub. Svc. medal, 1998. Fellow Am. Bar Found.; mem. ABA (ho. dels. 1978-82, past chmn. urban, state and local govt. law sect.), Nat. Assn. Bond Lawyers (com. standards of practice), Wash. Bar Assn., Seattle Bar Assn. (Pres.'s award 1993), D.C. Bar Assn., Am. Judicature Soc., Acad. Pub. Adminstrn., Coun. on Fgn. Rels., Mcpl. League Seattle and King County (past pres.), Order of Hosp. of St. John of Jerusalem, AIA (hon.), Order of Coif (hon.), Phi Delta Phi, Phi Gamma Delta, Rainier Club (Seattle). Home: 903 Shoreland Dr SE Bellevue WA 98004-6738 Office: 5000 Columbia Seafirst Ctr 701 5th Ave Seattle WA 98104-7016

ELLIS, JOHN, small business owner; b. Amherst, Ohio, Sept. 15, 1929; s. Edward Pierson and Jean (Scott) E.; m. Carolyn Elizabeth Collier, Dec. 29, 1951; children: Linda Ellis Wieand, Jeanine Ellis Klausing, Jeanette Ellis Hale, John Edward. BS, Bowling Green State U., 1953; MA, Case Western Res. U., Cleve., 1958; EdD, Harvard U., 1964. Tchr. pub. schs., Lorain, Ohio, 1953-54, prin., 1957-61, asst. supt. schs., Massillon, Ohio, 1963-64, supt. schs., 1964-66, Lakewood, Ohio, 1966-71, Columbus, Ohio, 1971-77; adj. prof. ednl. adminstrn. Ohio State U., Columbus, 1971-77; exec. dep. commr. edn. U.S. Office Edn., Washington, 1977-80; supt. schs., Austin, Tex., 1980-90; commr. N.J. Dept. Edn., 1990-92; owner Ellis Broadcasting Corp., Wimberley, Tex., 1992—. Elder local Presbyn. Ch. Served with USAF, 1947-49, 54-57. Recipient Massillon Young Man of Yr. award, 1965; named to Saturday Rev. Honor Roll, 1977. Mem. Phi Delta Kappa, Pi Kappa Alpha, Phi Alpha Theta, Kappa Delta Pi, Gamma Theta Upsilon. Lodge: Rotary. Home: 500 Leath Hollow Dr Wimberley TX 78676-5207

ELLIS, JOHN CARROLL, JR., life insurance sales executive; b. Portsmouth, Va., Aug. 11, 1948; s. John Carroll and Sarah Edith (Pittman) E.;

m. Janet Elizabeth Ackroyd, Nov. 17, 1973; 1 child, Mary Virginia. BA, Hampden-Sydney (Va.) Coll., 1970; postgrad., U. Richmond, 1971-72. CLU. Life ins. agt. Northwestern Mut. Life Ins. Co., Richmond, 1972-73, Conn. Mut. Life Ins. Co., Virginia Beach, Va., 1973-96, Mass. Mut. Life Ins. Co., Virginia Beach, Va., 1996—; bd. dirs. Jones Inst. devel. com. Med. Coll. Hampton Rds. Found. Bd. dirs. YMCA, Lynchburg, Va., 1981-89; elder First Presbyn. Ch., Virginia Beach, 1990—. Mem. CLU-ChFC (pres. Norfolk-Tidewater chpt. 1989-90), Norfolk C. of C. (bd. dirs. 1975-78), Million Dollar Round Table, Hampden-Sydney Coll. Alumni Assn. (pres.-elect 1989-91, pres. 1991-93, trustee 1995—), Cape Henry Racquet Club (pres. 1985-87), Virginia Beach Assembly (pres. 1996-97), Exch. Club Virginia Beach (pres. 1980-81), Leaders Club. Avocations: bird hunting, rugby, sailing, skiing. Home: 837 Greentree Arch Virginia Beach VA 23451-3787 Office: 3330 Pacific Ave Ste 401 Virginia Beach VA 23451-2983

ELLIS, JOHN MARTIN, German literature educator; b. London, May 31, 1936; came to U.S., 1966, naturalized, 1972; s. John Albert and Emily (Silvey) E.; m. Barbara Stephanie Rhoades, June 28, 1978; children: J. Richard, Andrew W., Katherine M., Jill E. B.A. with 1st class honours, U. London, 1959, Ph.D., 1965. Tutorial asst. German Univ. Coll., Wales, Aberystwyth, 1959-60; asst. lectr. U. Leicester, Eng., 1960-63; asst. prof. U. Alta., Edmonton, Can., 1963-66; mem. faculty U. Calif., Santa Cruz, 1966—; prof. German U. Calif., 1970-94, prof. emeritus, 1994, dean grad. div., 1977-86; vis. prof. U. Kent, Canterbury, Eng., 1970-71. Author: Schiller's Kalliasbriefe and the Study of His Aesthetic Theory, 1969, Kleist's Prinz Friedrich von Homburg: A Critical Study, 1970, Narration in the German Novelle, 1974, The Theory of Literary Criticism: A Logical Analysis, 1974, Heinrich von Kleist: Studies in the Character and Meaning of His Writings, 1979, One Fairy Story Too Many: The Brothers Grimm and Their Tales, 1983, Against Deconstruction, 1989, Language, Thought and Logic, 1993, Literature Lost: Social Agendas and the Corruption of the Humanities, 1997. Served with Brit. Army, 1954-56. Fellow Guggenheim Found., 1970-71; Fellow NEH, 1975-76, 92. Mem. NAS, ACLA, Am. Assn. Tchrs. German, Internat. Assn. Germanic Studies, Assn. Lit. Scholars and Critics (sec.-treas. 1994-99).

ELLIS, JOHN MUNN, III, insurance company financial executive; b. Morristown, N.J.; s. John M. and Mary Jane (Berg) E.; widowed; children: John Jaz M., Blair M. BA, Kans. Wesleyan U., 1973; BS, Kans. State U., 1978; postgrad., Harvard Bus Exec. Mgmt. Sch, 1975. CLU. Agt. N.Y. Life Ins. Co., Topeka, 1976-78, sales mgr., 1978-83, assoc. gen. mgr., 1983-85; exec. mgmt. cons. N.Y. Life Ins. Co., N.Y.C., 1985-88; gen. mgr. N.Y. Life Ins. Co., Fairfield, Conn., 1988-96; regional dir. tng. and devel. for ins. ops. in Middle East and Africa, agy. dir. for Oman, Qatar, Kuwait, Bahrain, United Arab Emirates, Pakistan Am. Life Ins. Co., Sharjah, United Arab Emirates, 1996-98; agy. dir., profit ctr. head v.p. AIG-AIA, China, 1998—. Mem. Fairfield bldg. com. YMCA. Mem. Nat. Assn. Life Underwriters (cert. life underwriters tng. coun.), Fairfield C. of C. (past pres., v.p. fin. 1989-93, bldg. com. 1993), Gen. Agts. and Mgrs. Assn. (bd. dirs. 1989-95, pres. 1994-95, nat. membership com. 1995-97), Am. Quarter Horse Assn. (life), Lions (pres. Auburn, Kans. 1989), Rotary, Optimists. E-mail: john-m.ellis@aig.com.

ELLIS, JOHN W., professional baseball team executive, utility company executive; b. Seattle, Sept. 14, 1928; s. Floyd E. and Hazel (Reed) R.; m. Doris Stearns, Sept. 1, 1953; children: Thomas R., John, Barbara, Jim. B.S., U. Wash., 1952, J.D., 1953. Bar: Wash. State bar 1953. Ptnr. Perkins, Coie, Stone, Olsen & Williams, Seattle, 1953-70; with Puget Sound Power & Light Co., Bellevue, Wash., 1970—, exec. v.p., 1973-76, pres., CEO, 1976-87, also dir., chmn., CEO, 1987-92, chmn. bd., 1992—; dir., chmn. Seattle br. Fed. Res. Bank of San Francisco, 1982-88; chief exec. officer Seattle Mariners, 1992—; mem. Wash. Gov.'s Spl. Com. Energy Curtailment, 1973-74; mem. Wash. Gov.'s Coun. on Edn., 1991—; chmn. Pacific N.W. Utilities Coordinating Com., 1976-82; bd. dirs. Wash. Mut. Savs. Bank, Seattle, SAFECO Corp., Nat. Energy Found., 1985-87, FlowMole Corp., Assoc. Electric & Gas Ins. Svcs. Ltd.; chmn. Electric Power Rsch. Inst., 1984—; chmn., CEO, The Baseball Club of Seattle, L.P.; regent Wash. State U., 1992—. Pres. Bellevue Boys and Girls Club, 1969-71, Seattle/King County Econ. Devel. Council, 1984—; mem. exec. dirs. Seattle/King County Boys and Girls Club, 1972-75; bd. dirs. Overlake Hosp., Bellevue, 1974—, United Way King County, 1977—, Seattle Sci. Found., 1977—, Seattle Sailing Found., Evergreen Safety Council, 1981, Assn. Wash. Bus., 1980-81, Govs. Adv. Council on Econ. Devel., 1984—; chmn. bd. Wash. State Bus. Round Table, 1983; pres. United for Washington; adv. bd. Grad. Sch. Bus. Adminstrn. U. Wash., 1982—, Wash. State Econ. Ptnrship., 1984—; chmn. Seattle Regional Panel White Ho. Fellows, 1985—; trustee Seattle U., 1986—. Mem. ABA, Wash. Bar Assn., King County Bar Assn., Nat. Assn. Elec. Cos. (dir. 1977-79), Edison Electric Inst. (dir. 1978-80, exec. com. 1982, 2d vice chmn. 1987, 1st vice chmn. 1988, now chmn.), Assn. Edison Illuminating Cos. (exec. com. 1979-81), Seattle C. of C. (dir. 1980—, 1st vice chmn. 1987-88, chmn. 1988—), Phi Gamma Delta, Phi Delta Phi. Clubs: Rainier (Seattle) (sec. 1972, v.p. 1984, pres. 1985), Seattle Yacht (Seattle), Corinthian Yacht (Seattle); Meydenbauer Bay Yacht (Bellevue), Bellevue Athletic. Lodge: Rotary (Seattle). Home: 901 Shoreland Dr SE Bellevue WA 98004-6738 Office: Seattle Mariners PO Box 4100 83 King St Seattle WA 98104-2860 also: Puget Sound Power & Light Co PO Box 97034 Bldg Bellevue WA 98009-9734*

ELLIS, JOSEPH NEWLIN, retired distribution company executive; b. Tenn., Oct. 19, 1928; s. Richard M. and Pearl A. (Fuqua) E.; m. Barbara Harpster, Sept. 17, 1955; 1 child, Patricia Anne. BS, Northwestern U., 1954. Co-founder LaSalle-Deitch Co., Inc., Elkhart, Ind., 1963; exec. v.p. LaSalle-Deitch Co., Inc., 1969-72, pres., chief exec. officer, 1972-89, chmn. of the bd., chief exec. officer, 1989-94. With U.S. Army, 1950-52. Home: 1160 Benders Ferry Rd Gallatin TN 37066-5703

ELLIS, JUDY, broadcast executive. V.p., gen. mgr. Sta. WQHT-FM, N.Y.C. Office: WQHT FM 395 Hudson St Fl 7 New York NY 10014-3600*

ELLIS, JUNE B., human resource consultant; b. Portland, Ind., June 17; children: Kenneth G., Reyn K. BS, Mary Washington Coll., 1942; MSW, Tulane U., 1953; PhD, Internat. U., 1977. Asst. dir. social services East La. State Hosp., Jackson, 1960-62; instr. Tulane U. Sch. Social Work, New Orleans, 1962-63, asst. prof. dept. psyhiatry, Sch. Medicine, 1963-68; exec. dir. Family Service-Travelers Aid, Ft. Smith, Ark., 1967-71; pres. Child and Family Cons., Ft. Smith, 1971—; dir. Human Resource Devel. Ctr., Ft. Smith; mem. adv. bd. Suspect Child Abuse and Neglect; cons. Volvo Health Care, Goteborg, Sweden, 1974-92, Kontura Personal, 1974-92, Christian Counseling Ctr., Vellore, India, 1974—; mem. Tulane Alumni Bd., 1978-88; mem. continuing profl. edn. com. Tulane Univ. Sch. Social Work, 1996—. Author: TA Tally, 1974, TA Talk, terms and references in transaction, 1976, BEING, 1982. Mem. Ark. Gov.'s Commn. on Status of Women, 1970-73, Ark. Gov.'s Com. Drug Abuse Prevention; cons. Cuban Resettlement Program, Ft. Chaffee, Ark., 1980; del. leader to China, 1984; mem. adv. bd. Jr. League Am.; mem. scholarship selection com. Whirlpool Corp.; bd. mem. Ctr. for Long Life Learning, Tulane U.; coord. Western Ark. Health Advocacy Svc., 1995—; mem. adv. bd. Ctr. for Long Life Living, Tulane U., 1996; cons. gerontology, Tulane U., 1998—; judge Odyssey of the Mind, Tex. Sch. Sys., 1998—. Named Outstanding Alumni, Tulane U., 1984. Mem. ASTD, AAUS, AAUW, Am. Acad. Psychotherapists, Am. Group Psychotherapy Assn., Am. Orthopsychiat. Assn., Acad. Cert. Social Workers, Western Ark. Mental Health Assn. (adv. bd.), Conf. for Advancement of Pvt. Practice in Social Work, Am. Assn. Ret. Persons, Am. Assn. of Individual Investors, Park Cities Club. Episcopalian. Office: 3437 Westminster Ave Dallas TX 75205-1336

ELLIS, KEM BYRON, public library administrator; b. Greensboro, N.C., Apr. 4, 1953; s. Laynelle Zenetues and Bernice (Godley) E.; m. Lelia Joanne Turner, June 4, 1977; children: Joseph Byron, Sarah Kathryn. AB in History and Polit. Sci., High Point (N.C.) U., 1975; MLS, U. N.C., Greensboro, 1977. Cert. librarian, N.C. Libr. asst. High Point Pub. Libr., 1972-77, head of gen. rsch., 1977-84, head of bus. rsch., 1984-88, head of rsch. svcs., 1988-92, dir., 1992—. Vol. C. of C., High Point; mem. Leadership High Point 1987—; bd. dirs. Cmtys. in Schs., 1998—; vol. United Way, High Point, 1986—. Named Vol. of Yr., Gov. of N.C., 1987. Mem. ALA, N.C. Libr. Assn., Pub. Libr. Assn., N.C. Pub. Libr. Dirs. Assn. (treas. 1997-98, pres. elect 1999), High Point Rotary Club (sec. 1988—, Paul Harris fellow 1992). Methodist.

ELLIS, LEE, publisher, editor; b. Medford, Mass., Mar. 12, 1924; s. Lewis Leeds and Charlotte Frances Ellis; m. Sharon Kay Barnhouse, Aug. 19, 1972. Child actor, dancer, stage, radio, movies Keith-Albee Cir., Ea. U.S., 1927-37; announcer, prodr., writer various radio stas. and CBS, Boston, N.Y.C., Miami, Fla., 1946-50; TV dir. ABC; mem. TV faculty U. Mo. Sch. Journalism, Columbia, 1950-55; mgr. Sta. KFSD/KFSD-TV, San Diego, 1955-60; gen. mgr. Imperial Broadcasting Sys., 1960-62; v.p., dir. advt. Media-Agys.-Clients, L.A., 1962-66; v.p., dir. newspaper rels. Family Weekly (name now USA Weekend), N.Y.C., 1966-89; pres., owner, editor Sharlee Publs., 1989—; voice of Nat. Date Festival, 1990-93; lectr. gen. semantics and comm., Idaho State U., Utah State U., San Diego State U., pres. emeritus, bd. dirs., Quadrille Acad., Indio. With USN, 1941-44, PTO. Mem. San Diego Press Club, Indio C. of C. Republican. Methodist. E-mail: indiolee@the-desert.net. Fax: 760-342-1600. Home and Office: 47-800 Madison St Unit 53 Indio CA 92201-6673

ELLIS, LESTER NEAL, JR., lawyer; b. Washington, Aug. 1, 1948; s. Lester Neal and Marie (Brooks) E. BS, U.s. Mil. Acad., 1970; JD, U. Va., 1975. Bar: Va. 1975, U.S. Ct. Appeals (5th cir.) 1977, D.C. 1978, U.S. Ct. Appeals (4th and D.C. cirs.) 1979, U.S. Ct. Appeals (11th cir.) 1982, N.C. 1985, U.S. Dist. Ct. (ea., mid., we. dists.) N.C., U.S. Dist. Ct. (ea., we. dists.) Va., U.S. Ct. Claims. Trial atty. litigation divsn. Office of JAG, U.S. Dept. Army, Washington, 1975-78; assoc. Hunton & Williams, Richmond, Va., 1978-84; ptnr. Hunton & Williams, Raleigh, 1984—. Maj. U.S. Army, 1970-78, col. USAR, 1993—. Recipient Judge Paul Brosman award U.S. Ct. Mil. Appeals, 1975. Mem. ABA (chair comml. torts commn., tort and ins. practice sect., editor-in-chief tort and Ins. Law Jour.), Va. Bar Assn. (spl. issues com. 1982—), D.C. Bar Assn. (ct. rules com. 1981—, Wake County bd. elections 1986—, chmn. 1987—), Phi Kappa Phi. Republican. Episcopalian. Home: 2608 Dover Rd Raleigh NC 27608-2032 Office: Hunton & Williams One Hanover Sq PO Box 109 Raleigh NC 27602-0109

ELLIS, LLOYD H., JR., emergency physician; b. Denver, Apr. 7, 1936; s. Lloyd Harris and Lura Lou (Wallace) E.; m. Nancy Kay Greenamyre, June 4, 1962 (div. June 1979); children: Peter, Amanda Hunt; m. Eva Marie Bevan, Sept. 1, 1984; children: Gwendolyn Ruth, David Bevan. BA, Yale U., New Haven, Conn., 1960, MA, 1961; MD, Case Western Reserve U., Cleve., 1970. Diplomate Am. Bd. Emergency Medicine. Farm mgr. Hastings, Nebr., 1961-62; vice consul Dept. of State, Lourenco Marques, Mozambique, 1963-64; intelligence analyst Dept. of State, Washington, 1965-66; dir. emergency dept. Univ. Hosps., Cleve., 1976-84, emergency physician, 1985-94; emergency physician Emergency Profl. Svcs., Chardon, Ohio, 1995—; instr. in surgery Case Western Reserve U., Cleve., 1976-78, asst. prof. surgery, 1979-94. Med. dir. Cleve. Emergency Svc., 1976-94; pres. Jeffrey Wallace Ellis Found., Hastings, 1993—. 1st Lt. Armor, 1956-59. Recipient Ford scholar Ford Found., New Haven, 1952-55. Mem. Am. Coll. Emergency Physicians, Am. Acad. Emergency Medicine. Republican. Episcopalian. Avocation: art history. Home and Office: 32250 Woodsdale Ln Cleveland OH 44139-1335

ELLIS, LONNIE CALVERT, educator; b. Oneida, Tenn., Sept. 18, 1945; s. Lewis Calvert and Alma Gean (Goad) E.; m. Karen Chambers, Dec. 16, 1967; children: Lonnie Christopher, James Gregory, Megan Lynn. BS, Cumberland Coll., 1968; MA, Tenn. Tech. U., 1974, EdS, 1985. Cert. Career Level II and III tchr. Coach Oneida Ind. Sch. Dist., Tenn., 1968-72, Scott County Sch. System, Huntsville, Tenn., 1972-78, 1979—, computer coord. Scott H.S., 1993—; mgr. pers. Tibbals Flooring Co., Oneida, 1978-79; instr. Roane State C.C., 1985-91, State Tech. Inst., Knoxville, 1985-86; bd. dirs. Scott Appalacian Industries, v.p., 1986. Chmn. Cissy Baker for Senate campaign, Huntsville, 1980; vice chmn. Scott County Recreation Com., 1984-90; active Huntsville Recreation Com., 1991—; pres. Scott County Youth Softball/Baseball League, 1992—. Recipient Dist. Coach of Yr. award Coca Cola Bottling Co., 1985, recognition award Tenn. Ho. of Reps., 1985, Citizens award E. Tenn. chpt. Nat. Football Found., 1978. Mem. Scott County Edn. Assn. (chmn. welfare com., state contact person, pres.-elect, chief negotiator 1987-88), East Tenn. Edn. Assn., Tenn. Edn. Assn., NEA. Baptist. Avocations: computers, athletics. Home: 357 Galloway Dr Helenwood TN 37755-5127 Office: Scott County High Sch Scott High Dr Huntsville TN 37756

ELLIS, LYNN WEBSTER, management educator, telecommunications consultant; b. San Mateo, Calif., Feb. 27, 1928; s. Lynn Webster Sr. and Mary Eleanor (Barstow) E.; m. Eileen Mary Gallagher; children: Lynn W. Jr., Margaret, Katherine. BEE, Cornell U., 1948; MS, Stevens Inst. Tech., 1954; D Profl. Studies in Mgmt., Pace U., 1979. Exec. ITT Corp., 1948-79; v.p. engring. Bristol Babcock Co., Waterbury, Conn., 1980-82; cons. Lynn W. Ellis Assocs., Westport, Conn., 1982-85; prof. U. New Haven, West Haven, Conn., 1985-94, scholar-in-residence, 1994-97, prof. emeritus, 1997—. Author: Evaluating R&D Processes, 1996, Financial Side of Industrial Research Management, 1984; contbr. and co-contbr. over 50 articles to profl. jours.; patentee in field. Chmn. adv. com.Dept. Commerce, Washington, 1973-75; mem. five panels and coms. NRC, Washington, 1970-95. Capt. U.S. Army, 1948-52. Fellow IEEE (internat. communication award 1983), AAAS. Home: 1301 Gulf Blvd Apt 115 Clearwater FL 33767-2803 Office: U New Haven 300 Orange Ave West Haven CT 06516-1916

ELLIS, MARY LOUISE HELGESON, insurance company executive; b. Albert Lea, Minn., May 29, 1943; d. Stanley Orville and Neoma Lois (Guthier) Helgeson; children: Christopher, Tracy; m. David Readinger, Nov. 5, 1994. BS in Pharmacy, U. Iowa, 1966; MA in Pub. Adminstrn., Iowa State U., 1982, postgrad., 1982-83. Faculty Duquesne U., Pitts., 1977; cons. in pharmacy, Colville, Wash., 1978-79; dir. pharmacy Mt. Carmel Hosp., Colville, 1978-79; clin. pharmacist Iowa Vets. Home, Marshalltown, Iowa, 1980-81; instr. Iowa Valley Community Coll., Marshalltown, 1981-83; dir. Iowa Dept. Substance Abuse, Des Moines, 1983-86; dir. State of Iowa Pub. Health, dir. Iowa Dept. Pub. Health, Des Moines, 1986-90; spl. cons. health affairs Blue Cross/Blue Shield of Iowa, 1990-91; v.p. Blue Cross/Blue Shield of Iowa and S.D., 1991—; chair Iowa Health Data Commn., Des Moines, 1986-90; bd. dirs. Health Policy Corp. Iowa, 1986-90; adj. asst. prof. U. Iowa, Iowa City, 1984—; comd. officer U.S. Food & Drug Adminstrn., 1989-90; mem. alumnae bd. dirs. U. Iowa Coll. of Pharmacy, 1989—; chair Nat. Commn. Accreditation of Ambulance Svcs., 1992—. Mem. Iowa State Bd. Health, 1981-83, v.p., 1982-83; mem. adv. council Iowa Valley Community Coll., 1983-85. Recipient Woman of Achievement award Des Moines YWCA, 1988. Mem. Iowa Pharmacists Assn., Am. Pub. Health Assn., Iowa Pub. Health Assn. (bd. dirs., Henry Albert award 1990), Alpha Xi Delta, Phi Kappa Phi, Pi Sigma Alpha. Republican. Home: 2912 Caulder Ave Des Moines IA 50321-2637 Office: Blue Cross and Blue Shield Iowa 636 Grand Ave Des Moines IA 50309-2551

ELLIS, MICHAEL DAVID, aerospace engineer; b. Sacramento, July 13, 1952; s. John David and Priscilla Agnes (Tupper) E.; m. Virginia Katherine Hanlon, Mar. 27, 1976; children: Gwendolyn Dawn, January Marie, Jennifer Noel. BS in Space Sci., Fla. Inst. Tech., 1975. With satellite ops., orbit analyst Western Union, Sussex, N.J., 1976-77; with satellite ops., 3 axis RCA Americom, Sussex, N.J., 1977-78; with satellite ops., Land Sat ATS-6 Goddard Space Flight Ctr., Greenbelt, Md., 1978-79; with Voyager System Lead Jet Propulsion Lab., Pasadena, Calif., 1979-82; STS ground ops. analyst Applied Rsch. Inc., El Segundo, Calif., 1982-83; mission ops. Aerospace Corp., El Segundo, Calif., 1983-88; space sta. mission ops. Johnson Spaceflight Ctr., Houston, 1988—. Mem. troop asst. San Jacinto Girl Scouts U.S., Houston, 1988-94; Confraternity Christian Doctrine tchr. St. Bernadette, Clear Lake, 1990; Clear Lake Drill Team support Starlettes, 1989-95, Clear Lake Flares, 1995-96. Mem. Soc. Automotive Engrs. (chmn. spacecraft com. 1986-87), Am. Inst. Aeronautics and Astronautics (chmn. 1972-75).

ELLIS, MICHAEL EUGENE, documentary film producer, writer, director, marketing executive; b. Murphysboro, Ill., Aug. 1, 1946; s. Robert Eugene and Lula May (Williams) E. BS, So. Ill. U., Carbondale, 1971. Asst. to pres. So. Ill. U., 1970; asst. dir. Ill. Info. Svc., Springfield, 1971-72; mgr. press rels. Ill. Ho. of Reps., Springfield, 1973-77; dep. dir. com. Rep. Nat. Com., Washington, 1977; pres. Lincana Corp., Springfield, 1978-80; mgr. mktg. presentations Ill. Dept. Commerce, Springfield, 1980-91; dir. devel. and comms. Sparc Inc., Springfield, 1993—. Co-author: Work and the College Student, 1975; author: Elements of Political Public Relations, 1977; editor: Springfield Eats, 1996; author film scripts, 1983—. Dir. comm. Pres. Ford Com. in Ill., Chgo., 1976; mem. Ill. Rep. Com., Springfield, Rep. Presdl. Task Force, Washington, Sangamon Rep. Found., Springfield. Recipient Gold Award Advt. Assn., Springfield, Ill., 1987-89. Mem. Internat. Communications Industry Assn., Am. Film Inst., Assn. for Multi Image Internat., World Affairs Coun., Nat. Soc. Fund Raising Execs. (bd. dirs. 1998-99), Ill. Soc. Assn. Execs. (bd. dirs. 1998-99, Excellence in Comms. award 1998). Avocations: writing, gardening, photography. Home: 627 Witherspoon Dr Springfield IL 62704-1424 Office: Sparc Inc 1 Sparc Ctr Plz 232 N Bruns Ln Springfield IL 62702-4613

ELLIS, NORMANDI, writer; b. Sept. 24, 1953. BA, U. Ky., 1976; MA, U. Colo., 1981. Exec. editor Bookmakers Guild, Longmont, Colo., 1986-88; tchr. fiction U. Ky., Lexington, 1992-98; artist in schs. Ky. Arts Coun., 1993—; lectr. in field. Author: Awakening Osiris, 1988, Sorrowful Mysteries, 1991, Dreams of Isis, 1994, Voice Forms, 1998, Feasts of Light, 1999. Recipient Bumbershoot Weyerhauser award, 1991. Address: PO Box 51 Frankfort KY 40602 also: 1042 Iroquois Trail Frankfort KY 40601-2545

ELLIS, PATRICIA WEATHERS, small business owner, electronic technician; b. Shelby, N.C., June 21, 1941; d. William Roy and Lucille Elzora (Allen) Weathers; m. Donald Eugene Ellis, Nov. 16, 1957; children: Dana Michelle, Lisa Maria. Student, Gaston Coll., Shelby, 1970-82. Tel. operator So. Bell, Greensboro, N.C., 1959-61; tel. operator So. Bell, Gastonia, N.C., 1961-63, dial clk., 1963-68, frame technician, 1968-79, test technician, 1980-84, maintenance adminstr., 1984-85, toll test technician, 1985-87; electronic technician BellSouth, Gastonia, 1987-91, Charlotte, N.C., 1991—; store mgr. Ellis-Bowen Carpet Svc., Gastonia, 1969-70. Commr. Gaston County, Gastonia, 1992-96; bd. dirs. Gaston County Health Dept., Airport Com., Gaston Mus. Art and History, 1992-96, Gaston County Dept. Social Svcs.; alt. Ctrl. Lina Coun. Govts., 1994-95; mem. Nat. Rep. Party, Gaston Good Neighbor, Courthouse Dedication Com.; com. mem. Right-Sizing County Govt. Mem. Tel. Pioners Am., Woman's Aux. Fedn. Postal Clks. (charter; pres. Gastonia 1966, State v.p. 1966-69), Nat. Republican Party. Republican. Avocations: art, writing poems and songs, collecting dolls and stamps.

ELLIS, BROTHER PATRICK (H. J. ELLIS), academic administrator; b. Balt., Nov. 17, 1928; s. Harry James and Elizabeth Alida (Evert) E. AB, Cath. U. Am., Washington, 1951; AM, U. Pa., 1954, PhD, 1960; postgrad., Barry Coll., 1963-64, Inst. Catholique, Paris, 1958; LHD (hon.), Assumption Coll., 1982, La Salle U., 1992; HHD (hon.), King's Coll., 1987; LLD (hon.), U. Scranton, 1988, C.C. Phila., 1992, Quincy U., 1993; PdD, Manhattan Coll., 1993; DEd, Anna Maria Coll., 1993, Loyola U., 1997. Joined Bros. of Christian Schs., Roman Cath. Ch., 1946. Tchr. English dept. West Cath. High Sch. for Boys, Phila., 1951-60; chmn. English dept. West Cath. High Sch. for Boys, 1956-58, guidance dir., 1959-60; dir. practice teaching, sch. prin. St. Gabriel's Hall, Phoenixville, Pa., summers 1960-61, 65-66; asst. prof. English La Salle U., Phila., 1960-62; assoc. prof. La Salle U., 1968-73, prof., 1973—, dir. housing, 1961-62, dir. honors program, 1964-69, dir. devel., v.p., 1969-76, pres., 1977-92; pres. Cath. U. Am., Washington, 1992-98; prin. La Salle High Sch., Miami, Fla., 1962-64. Condr.: series for How To Read Gt. Books, U. of the Air, WFIL-TV, Phila., 1961, 65; Contbr. articles to profl. publs. Trustee Manhattan Coll., N.Y.C., St. Mary's U., Minn., Calvert Hall H.S., Balt.; bd. dirs. Phila. Cath. Charities, 1986-92, Greater Phila. Urban Coalition, Police Athletic League, Phila., Free Libr. Phila., 1991-92, Del. Valley Citizens Crime Commn., Fed. City Coun., D.C. Econ. Club, D.C. Bd. Trade; former trustee Cmty. Leadership Seminars, BBB. Recipient Lindback award for disting. teaching LaSalle Coll., Phila., 1965. Mem. Union League, Sunday Breakfast Club (Phila.), Phila. Club, Univ. Club (Washington), Nat. Press Club, Phi Beta Kappa, Knights of Holy Sepulchre. Home and Office: Calvert Hall HS 8102 La Salle Rd Baltimore MD 21286-8022

ELLIS, PATRICK R., municipal official; b. Neenah, Wis., Sept. 11, 1942. BA in Comty. Planning and Devel., Columbus (Ga.) State U., 1986. Dir. comty. and econ. devel. dept. City of Columbus, Ga., 1987-99; exec. dir. Buick Challenge, Columbus, Ga., 1999—. Office: Buick Challenge PO Box 2056 Columbus GA 31902-1340*

ELLIS, PETER, editor. Mng. editor Argus Leader, 1993. Office: Argus Leader PO Box 5034 200 S Minnesota Ave Sioux Falls SD 57117-6314*

ELLIS, RICHARD W., lawyer; b. Raleigh, N.C., Apr. 20, 1942. AB, U. N.C., 1964, JD with high honors, 1969. Bar: N.C. 1969. Mem. Smith Helms Mulliss & Moore, Raleigh. Assoc. editor N.C. Law Rev., 1968-69. With USNR, 1964-66. Mem. Am. Coll. Trial Lawyers, Def. Rsch. Inst., N.C. Assn. Def. Attys., Order of Coif. Office: Smith Helms Mulliss & Moore PO Box 27525 2800 Two Hannover Sq Raleigh NC 27611-7525

ELLIS, ROBERT SMITH, allergist, immunologist; b. Shawnee, Okla., July 13, 1926. MD, Northwestern U., 1950. Diplomate Am. Bd. Allergy and Immunology, Am. Bd. Internal Medicine. Intern Henry Ford Hosp., Detroit, 1950-51, resident in medicine, 1951-52, 54-55; resident in allergy U. Mich. Hosp., Ann Arbor, 1955-56; with Presbyn. Hosp., Oklahoma City; allergist Okla. Allergy and Asthma Clinic, Oklahoma City, 1956—; clin. prof. medicine U. Okal. Coll. Medicine. Mem. AMA, Am. Acad. Allergy and Immunology, Southern Med. Assn. Office: Okla Allergy & Asthma Clin PO Box 26827 Oklahoma City OK 73126-0827

ELLIS, ROBERT WILLIAM, engineering educator; b. Richmond, Va., Oct. 16, 1939; s. Robert William and Odessa (Thompson) E.; m. Donna Lee Bell, Mar. 22, 1960; children: Robert William III, Richard Berkeley, John Stephen, Donna Elaine. B.S., Va. Poly. Inst., 1962, M.S., 1963, Ph.D., 1966. Registered profl. engr., Mich. Materials engr., engr. Polysci. div. Litton Industries, Blacksburg, Va., 1962-63; Nat. Def. Edn. Act fellow engring. Va. Poly. Inst., 1962-65; asst. prof. engring. U. South Fla., Tampa, 1965-66, assoc. prof., 1967-68, asst. dean engring., 1969-71, asst. v.p. acad. affairs, 1971-72; dean Sch. Bus., Fla. Internat. U., Miami, 1972-74; dean Sch. Tech., Fla. Internat. U., 1972-78, provost North Miami campus, 1977; exec. v.p. Detroit Inst. Tech., 1978-80, pres., 1980-81; sr. engr. U.S. Army Tank Automotive Research and Devel. Center, Warren, Mich., 1981-84; lectr. mech. engring. Lawrence Inst. Tech., 1981-84, dean Sch. Engring., 1984-89; provost Lawrence Tech. U., 1989-94, prof. mech. engring., 1994-99; cons. Gen. Dynamics Corp., 1984-89; tech. adv. bd. Fla. Solar Energy Ctr.; bd. govs. Nat. Inst. Cert. of Engring. Tech., 1994—, chmn., 1997. Mem. economy task force Met. Dade County Planning Adv. Bd.; bd. dirs. Fla. State U. System Inst. Oceanography; vice chmn. Metro Dade County Constrn. Licensing Bd. Recipient Nat. Faculty Service award Nat. Univ. Extension Assn., 1977; NASA fellow, 1969. Fellow Engring. Soc. Detroit, Mich. Soc. profl. Engrs. (Engr. of Yr. in Mich. 1987, pres. Detroit chpt. 1987, pres. state soc. 1990); mem. NSPE (vice chmn. Cen. region profl. engrs. in edn.), Am. Soc. Engring. Edn. (chmn. southeastern sect. tech. div. 1976, bd. dirs. coll. industry coun. 1975-78, chmn. div. on rels. with industry 1990-91), Soc. Automotive Engrs. (engring. edn. bd. 1987-90, chmn. scolarship com. 1989-91), Sigma Xi, Omicron Delta Kappa, Phi Kappa Phi, Sigma Pi Sigma, Tau Beta Pi, Sigma Lambda Chi, Alpha Sigma Mu. Home: 29383 Breezewood Farmington Hills MI 48331

ELLIS, RONALD L., federal judge; b. 1950. B Chem. Engring., Manhattan Coll., 1972; JD, NYU, 1975. Bar: N.Y. With NAACP Legal Def. and Ednl. Fund, N.Y.C., 1976-93, dir. fair employment program, 1984-90, dir. poverty and justice program, 1990-93; magistrate judge for so. dist. N.Y. U.S. Magistrate Ct., N.Y.C., 1993—; adj. prof. NYU Sch. Law, 1984-94. Office: 1970 US Courthouse 500 Pearl St New York NY 10007-1316

ELLIS, SARAH STEVENS, safety and risk analyst; b. Nashville, July 2, 1967; d. Michael Ventress Stevens and Kathy (Sohm) Farmer; m. Harold Maurice Ellis, Nov. 27, 1993. BA, Memphis State U., 1991; MA, U. Memphis, 1994. Safety asst. Fed. Express, Memphis, 1988-92; liability claims adjuster Nationwide Ins., Memphis, 1993-95; loss prevention specialist MS Carriers, Memphis, 1995-96, safety and risk analyst, 1996-98, safety mgr., 1998; investigative claims mgr. Travelers Property Casualty,

1998—. Contbr. articles to profl. jours. Chair ORgan Transplant Found., Batesville, Miss., 1996. Avocations: football, writing, reading.

ELLIS, SCOTT, theatrical director. Grad., Goodman Sch. of Drama, Chgo. Dir. plays 1776 (Drama Desk, Outer Critics Circle and Tony nominations), Steel Pier (Drama Desk, Outer Critics Circle and Tony nominations), Company, She Love Me (Tony nomination, Outer Critics Circle award Best Dir., Best Revival, Olivier award), Picnic (Outer Critics Circle nomination), A Month in the Country, Dark Rapture, The World Goes Round: The Music of Kander and Ebb (Drama Desk, Outer Critics Circle awards Best Director, Best Musical Revue), Flora, the Red Menace, 110 in the Shade, A Little Night Music (Drama Desk award Best Director, Best Revival), Sondheim: A Celebration at Carnegie Hall. Office: Nederlander Producing Co Am 810 7th Ave New York NY 10019-5818*

ELLIS, STEPHEN WALKER, corporate executive; b. 1966; s. Robert and Barbara Ellis; m. Crystal Leigh Turner, 1993; children: Robert Clay II, Edgar Turner. Student, U. Pa., Phila., 1984-86; BS in Acctg., La. State U., 1988; MBA, U. Memphis, 1998. CPA; cert. mgmt. acct.; cert. in fin. mgmt. Audit assoc. Coopers & Lybrand LLP, New Orleans, 1992-94; sr. acct. Ernst & Young LLP, Jackson, Miss., 1994-95; fin. contr. Horseshoe Casino, Robinsonville, Miss., 1995-98; dir. pricing svcs. Dobbs Internat. Svcs., Memphis, 1998-99, dir. strategic devel., 1999—. Mem. AICPA, Inst. Mgmt. Accts. (Memphis chpt.), Tenn. Soc. CPAs (bd. dirs. Memphis chpt.), Hernando Hills Country Club, Hernando United Meth. Ch. Republican. Methodist. Avocations: golf, tennis, sailing, travel. Home: 474 Fairway Oaks Dr Hernando MS 38632-7282 Office: Dobbs Internat Svcs 5100 Poplar Ave Memphis TN 38137

ELLIS, STEVEN GEORGE, public relations and international political consultant; b. Chattanooga, Mar. 14, 1949; s. George G. and Betty (Chew) E.; m. Sylvia Regina Ellis; children: Steven Andrew, Christopher John, Katharine Marie. BA, U. Ga., 1971. V.p. Burson-Marsteller, Washington, 1976-83; v.p., gen. mgr. Earle Palmer Brown Pub. Rels., Bethesda, Md., 1983-84, pres., 1987-88; v.p. corp. communications RKO Gen. Co. subs. GenCorp, Inc., N.Y.C., 1984-86; pres. Steve Ellis Communications Inc, 1988-95; sr. v.p. Jefferson-Waterman Internat., Washington, 1995-98; dir. corp. comms. SAGA Software, Inc., 1998—; adv. bd. Henry W. Grady Coll. Journalism and Mass Comm. Recipient Gold Key award Pub. Rels. News, 1985, 86. Office: 1341 G St NW Washington DC 20005-3105

ELLIS, SUSAN GOTTENBERG, psychologist; b. N.Y.C., Jan. 24, 1949; d. Sam and Sally (Hirschman) Gottenberg; m. David Roy Ellis, July 23, 1972; children: Sharon Rachel, Dana Michelle. BS, Cornell U., 1970; MA, Columbia U., 1971, Hofstra U., 1975; PhD, Hofstra U., 1976. Instr. health edn. Nassau C.C., Garden City, N.Y., 1971-73; sch. psychologist pub. schs., Somerville, N.J., 1976-77; clin. psychologist pub. schs., Pinellas County, Fla., 1977-78; instr. St. Petersburg (Fla.) Jr. Coll., 1978; clin. psychologist Largo, Fla., 1977—; cons. Fla. Dept. Health and Rehab. Services, Med. Center Hosp., Largo, Morton Plant Hosp., Clearwater, Fla., 1978-79, N.Y. State Regents scholar, 1966-71; adj. prof. Eckerd Coll. St. Petersburg, 1988. Author: Interpret Your Dreams, 1987, A Dream Primer, 1988, Makes Sense of Your Dreams, 1988. Mem. Am. Psychol. Assn., Fla. Psychol. Assn., Pinellas Psychol. Assn. 9treas. 1978, polit. action chmn. 1979), Cornell U. Suncoast Club (v.p. 1979-80), Kappa Delta Pi. Office: 3233 E Bay Dr Ste 100 Largo FL 33771-1900

ELLIS, SYDNEY, pharmacological scientist, former pharmacology educator; b. Boston, Apr. 20, 1917; s. George I. and Sarah (Gaull) E.; m. Marion Gardner, Oct. 8, 1942; children—Jeanne (Mrs. Richard P. Jaffe), Richard Jay. B.S., Boston U., 1938, M.A., 1939, Ph.D., 1941. Fellow, then asst. Harvard U. Med. Sch., 1941-44, NYU Nat. Def. Rsch. Com. project, 1942; asst. prof. Duke U. Sch. Medicine, 1946-49; assoc. prof. Temple U. Sch. Medicine, 1949-57; prof. pharmacology and toxicology, chmn. dept. Woman's Med. Coll. Pa., 1957-67; prof. pharmacology and toxicology U. Tex. Med. Br., Galveston, 1967-80; chmn. dept. U. Tex. Med. Br., 1967-77; dep. dir. div. drug biology FDA, 1980-89, dep. dir. div. rsch. and testing, 1989-95, sci. cons., 1995—; vis. prof. U. Paris Inst. Pharmacology, 1972; vis. scientist div. drug biology FDA, 1979-80; cons. in field; mem. pet study sect. NIH, 1960-64, med. chem. B study sect., 1964-68; mem. Nat. Bd. Med. Examiners, 1964-68. Served to capt. AUS, 1944-46. Recipient Lindback Found. award distinguished teaching, 1964; named to Collegium of Distinguished Alumni Boston U., 1974. Fellow AAAS, N.Y. Acad. Sci.; mem. Am. Soc. Pharmacology (councilor 1967-70, sec.-treas. 1976-79), Am. Chem. Soc., Soc. Exptl. Biology and Medicine, Catecholamine Club (pres. 1990-91), AAUP, Sigma Xi (pres. Temple U. chpt. 1957). Home: 4601 N Park Ave Chevy Chase MD 20815-4519

ELLIS, SYLVIA D. HALL, development and library education consultant; b. Kewanee, Ill., June 21, 1949; d. Martin Orrill and Elizabeth Jean (Boase) Dunn; m. J. Theodore Ellis, Dec. 24, 1990. BA, Rockford Coll., 1971; MLS, U. N. Tex., 1972; MA, U. Tex., San Antonio, 1975; PhD, U. Pitts., 1985. Libr. Holding Inst., Laredo, Tex., 1972-73; dist. coord. San Antonio Pub. Librs., 1973-76; divsn. libr. Corpus Christi Pub. Librs., Tex., 1976-78; asst. dir. So. Tier Libr. System, Corning, N.Y., 1978-81; devel. officer Pitts. Regional Libr. Ctr., 1981-85; dir. librs. Rocky Mountain Coll. of Art and Design, Denver, 1992-93; asst. prof. Sam Houston State U., Huntsville, Tex., 1993-96; devel. officer Region 1 Edn. Svc. Ctr., Edinburg, Tex., 1995-97; dir devel. Mid-Continent Regional Ednl. Lab., Aurora, Colo., 1997-98; mng. ptnr. 886, Inc., 1998—; dir. Tech. Prep of Rio Grande Valley, Inc., Harlingen, Tex., 1995—; cons. States of Colo., Mont., Iowa, S.D., Tex., Pa., 1981—. Author: Grant Writing for Small Libraries and School Library Media Centers, 1999; contbr. articles to profl. jours. Democrat. Episcopalian. Mailing Address: PO Box 61048 Denver CO 80206-1048 Office: PO Box 61048 Denver CO 80206-1048

ELLIS, THOMAS SELBY, III, judge; b. Bogota, Columbia, May 15, 1940; came to U.S., 1951; s. Thomas Selby and Anne Leete (Sachs) E.; m. Rebecca Lynn Garron, Sept. 23, 1995; children: Alexander Reed, Parrish Selby. B.S.E., Princeton U., 1961; J.D. magna cum laude (Knox fellow), Harvard U., 1969; diploma in law Magdalen Coll. Oxford (Eng.) U., 1970. Assoc., Hunton & Williams, Richmond, Va., 1970-76, ptnr., 1976-87; judge U.S. Dist. Ct. (ea. dist.) Va., Alexandria, 1987—; temporary mem. sr. common rm. U. Coll., Oxford, 1984. lectr. law Coll. William & Mary, Williamsburg, Va., 1981-83; mem. adv. coun. dept. astrophysics Princeton U., 1984—; speaker in field. Office: US Dist Court 401 Courthouse Sq Alexandria VA 22314-5704*

ELLIS, U. BERTRAM, JR., information technology company executive; b. Wilmington, N.C., Sept. 16, 1953. BA in Econs., U. Va., MBA. Chmn., CEO IXL, Atlanta, 1996—. Named Entrepreneur of Yr., Ernst & Young for Ga., 1997. Office: 1888 Emory St NW Atlanta GA 30318

ELLIS, WALTER LEON, minister; b. McKinney, Tex., Oct. 22, 1941; s. Erwin Ballard and Mary Edra (Bray) E.; m. Susan Elizabeth Elder, Nov. 23, 1960; children: Bruce Walter, David Anthony, Patrick Durward. BA, U. North Tex., 1964, MA, 1966; MDiv, Va. Sem., 1977; DMin, Austin Presbyn. Theol. Sem., 1993. Ordained to ministry Episc. Ch., 1977. Vicar St. Michael & All Angels', Longview, Tex., 1977-79, St. Mark's, Gladewater, Tex., 1977-79; rector St. Michael & All Angel's, Longview, 1979-82, St. Christopher, League City, Tex., 1982—; dean Galveston Convocation, League City, 1989-97; mem. Diocesan Standing Com., Houston, 1996-99, pres., 1998; mem. Order of St. Luke Chaplain, 1996—, Diocesan Exec. Bd., 1998—, Cursillo Secretariat, 1997-99; trustee St. James House, Baytown, Tex., 1983-84, 90-93, Camp Allen, Navasota, Tex., 1987-90, Bishop Quin Found., Houston, 1991-97, St. Vincent's House, Galveston, 1996-99; chmn. dept. environment Diocese of Tex., 1993-95; b.d dirs. Interfaith Caring Ministries, League City, 1993-94; stewardship cons. Episcopal Ch. Ctr., N.Y.C., 1990-95. Contbr. articles to profl. jours. Bd. dirs. pres. Parents Anonymous, Longview, 1980; mem. exec. bd. Bay Area coun. Boy Scouts Am., Tex., 1983-86; pres. Rotary Club, League City, 1989-90. Paul Harris fellow Space Ctr. Rotary Club, Houston, 1989. Mem. League City Ministers' Assn., Clear Lake Ministerial Alliance, Brotherhood of St. Andrew, Am. Acad. Ministry, Am. Assn. Christian Counselors, World Future Soc. Home: 18619 Prince William Ln Houston TX 77058-4224 Office: St Christopher Episc Ch 2100 Saint Christopher Ave League City TX 77573-4234 *You have been blessed by God through others. Find something you admire in each person you meet. Then bless those people by telling them what you admire in them.*

ELLIS, WILLIAM BEN, environmental educator, retired utility executive; b. Vicksburg, Miss., July 4, 1940; s. Conrad Ben and Viola Elizabeth (Stigall) E.; children by previous marriage: Bradford, Katherine, Emily, Ben; m. Elaine Klutsavage, July 10, 1988; children: John, David. BS, Carnegie Mellon U., 1962; PhD, U. Md., 1966; postgrad., Am. U., 1968. Rsch. asst. Olin Mathieson Chem. Corp., West Monroe, La., 1958, Comml. Solvents Corp., Sterlington, La., 1959; engr. Procter & Gamble Co., Cin., 1961; process engr. Standard Oil N.J., Baton Rouge, 1962-67; assoc. McKinsey & Co., Inc., Washington, 1969-75, prin., 1975-76; exec. v.p., cfo Northeast Utilities and Subs., Hartford, Conn., 1976-78, pres., cfo, 1978-80, pres., coo, 1980-83, chmn., ceo, 1983-93, chmn., 1993-95; sr. fellow Yale U. Sch. of Forestry and Environ. Studies, 1995—; trustee Northeast Utilities, Hartford, Conn., 1977-95; bd. dirs. Mass. Mutual Life Ins. Co., Hartford Steam Boiler Inspection and Ins. Co., Advest Group. Inc., Catalytica Combustion Sys., Inc. Mem. bd. Nat. Mus. Natural History, Smithsonian Instn.; mem. sci. adv. bd. The Nature Conservancy. With U.S. Army, 1967-69. Mem. Greater Hartford C. of C. (bd. dirs. 1978—, chmn. 1985).

ELLIS, WILLIAM GRENVILLE, academic administrator, management consultant; b. Teaneck, N.J., Nov. 29, 1940; s. Grenville Brigham and Vivian Lilian (Breeze) E.; m. Nancy Elizabeth Kempton, 1963; children: William Grenville, Bradford Graham. BS in Bus. Adminstrn., Babson Coll., 1962; MBA, Suffolk U., 1963; EdM, Westfield State Coll., 1965; EdD, Pa. State U., 1968; MS, Concordia U., 1991; MLE (Sears Roebuck Found. scholar), Harvard U., 1980, U. Chgo., 1983; IAL, MIT, 1984, Harvard U., 1988, 96. Asst. prof. bus. Rider U., 1968-69; div. dir., assoc. prof. Castleton State Coll., 1969-72; exec. v.p., prof. Coll. of St. Joseph the Provider, Rutland, Vt., 1972-73; acad. v.p., dean grad. sch. Thomas Coll., Waterville, Maine, 1973-82; pres. Wayland Acad., Beaver Dam, Wis., 1982-95; pres. New Eng. Coll., Henniker, N.H., 1995-97; dean Sch. Bus. and Legal Studies, Concordia U. Wisconsin, Mequon, 1997—; mem. adv. bd. CFX Bank, 1996-97; corporator 1st Consumers Savs., 1974-81, Maine Savs., 1981-82; bd. dirs. Bank One, 1983-95. Trustee C.C. Vt., 1972-73, Marian Coll., 1988-91, Wayland Acad., 1982-95, New. Eng. Coll., 1995-97; bd. dirs. Westra Constrn. Corp., 1989-94; auditor Town of Castleton (Vt.), 1969-71; pres. Kennebee Valley Youth Hockey, Augusta, Maine, 1975-77; pres. Beaver Dam C. of C., 1985, 86, Midwest Classic Athletic Conf., 1989, Wisc. Assoc. Ind. Schs., 1984-86; chair, bd. dirs. Beaver Dam Cmty. Hosp., 1985-95; dir. North Cen. Assn. of Colls. and Secondary Schs., 1991-94, Ind. Schs. Ctrl. States, 1991-95; dir. N.H. Coll. an U. Coun., 1995-97. Named Cons. of Yr., SBA, 1975, 77; recipient Cmty. Svc. award Rutland C. of C., 1973, Disting. Svc. citation Wayland Acad., 1995. Mem. APA, Nat. Assn. Intercollegiate Athletics (cert. of merit 1979), Cum Laude Soc., Alpha Chi, Pi Omega Pi, Alpha Delta Sigma, Delta Pi Epsilon, Phi Delta Kappa. Club: Pheasant City, Wis. Club: Rotary. Author: The Analysis and Attainment of Economic Stability, 1963; The Relationship of Related Work Experience to the Teaching Success of Beginning Business Teachers, 1968, Marketing for Educational Administrators, 1991, A Gunner's Moon, 1997; contbr. numerous articles, abstracts to profl. publs. Home: 8655 N Regent Rd Fox Point WI 53217-2362 Office: Concordia U Sch Bus & Legal Studies 12800 N Lake Shore Dr Mequon WI 53097-2418

ELLIS, WILLIS HILL, lawyer, educator; b. Detroit, Aug. 30, 1927; s. Seth Wiley and Mildred (Hill) 6E.; m. Gwyneth Fair Saylors, July 7, 1977; 1 stepson, Kevin Saylors; children by previous marriage—Richard Wiley, Jennifer Jean, Scott Mabry. A.B., Wabash Coll., 1951; J.D., Ind. U., 1954. Bar: Ind. bar 1954. Practice law Indpls., 1954-59; teaching fellow Harvard Law Sch., 1960-61; asst. prof. U. Denver, 1961-64, assoc. prof., 1964-65; assoc. prof. U. N.Mex. Coll. Law, Albuquerque, 1965-68, prof. law, 1968-95; prof. emeritus U. N.Mex. Coll. Law, 1995—; Presdl. prof. law U. N.Mex. Coll. Law, Albuquerque, 1988-89; vis. holder chair natural resources law Faculty Law U. Calgary (Alta., Can.), 1983; mem. program devel. and rev. bd. N.Mex. Water Resources Rsch. Inst., 1987-95. Contbr. chpts. to books, articles to profl. jours. Trustee Rocky Mountain Mineral Law Found., 1965-87. Mem. Am. Bar Assn. Home: 13408 Rebonito Rd NE Albuquerque NM 87112-4868 Office: U NMex Law Sch 1117 Stanford Dr NE Albuquerque NM 87106-3721

ELLIS, WINFORD G., career officer; b. Aug. 30, 1941. Graduate, Naval Acadamy, Annapolis, Md., 1964. Commd. ensign US Navy, advanced through grades to rear admiral, 1996—; oceanographer Naval Obs., Washington, 1998—. Office: Oceanographer of Navy, Naval Obs 3450 Massachusetts Ave NW Washington DC 20392-5420*

ELLISON, CYRIL LEE, literary agent, retired publisher; b. N.Y.C., Dec. 11, 1916; m. Anne N. Nottonson, June 4, 1942. Assoc. Watson-Guptill Publs., 1939-69, v.p., advt. dir., 1939-69, assoc. pub. Am. Artist mag.; exec. v.p. Communication Channels, Inc., N.Y.C., 1969-88; pub. emeritus Fence Industry, Access Control, Pension World, Trusts & Estates, Nat. Real Estate Investor, Shopping Center World; pres. Lee Comms., 1980—; assoc. Kids Countrywide, Inc., 1987-94; literary agent, 1994—; pub. cons., book rep., advt. and mktg. cons., 1987-94; assoc. Mark Clements Rsch. N.Y., Inc., 1994—; pub. cons. Mag. Rsch. Mktg. Co., 1994—. Served with USAAF, 1942-46, PTO. Named Gray-Russo Advt. Man of Year Ad Men's Post Am. Legion, 1954; recipient Hall of Fame award Internat. Fence Industry Assn., 1985. Mem. Am. Legion (life, comdr. advt. men's post 1954, 64). Home: 6839 N 29th Ave Phoenix AZ 85017-1213 Office: Lee Communications 5060 N 19th Ave Phoenix AZ 85015-3210

ELLISON, DAVID CHARLES, special education educator; b. Agana, Guam, Apr. 20, 1957; s. Leo Charles and Joan Ruby (Hendrickson) E.; m. Teresa Josephine Vos, Dec. 20, 1980; children: Johanna Marie, Matthew David. BAA in Social Sci., U. Minn., Duluth, 1980. Tchr. spl. edn. ISD #94, Cloquet, Minn., 1981—; spl. edn. adminstr. ISD # 94, Cloquet, Minn., 1991-93. Head coach Cloquet Lumberjacks Spl. Olympics, 1981—. Recipient Transition Excellence award Dept. Children, Families and Learning in Minn., 1997. Democrat. Roman Catholic. Avocations: fishing, camping, hiking, family outings. Home: 705 Jasper St Cloquet MN 55720-1212 Office: ISD # 94 Cloquet Sr H S 1000 18th St Cloquet MN 55720-2438

ELLISON, EARL OTTO, computer scientist; b. Elizabeth, N.J., Apr. 26, 1938; s. Thorleif and Reidun Ingeborg (Andersen) E.; m. Judith Roque Impoc, Feb. 2, 1997; 1 child, Reidun Impoc. BS, Am. U., Washington, 1964, postgrad., 1964-66. Head supplies and equipment at Pentagon C & P Telephone Co. (now Bell Atlantic), Arlington, Va., 1956-62; tax acct. Trust Dept. Nat. Bank of Washington, 1964-65; methods analyst Automation Industries, Consol. Am. Svcs. Mgmt. Cons. Subs., Washington, L.A., 1965; mgmt. instr. fed. supply svc. GSA, Washington, 1965-67, contract negotiator info. tech. svc., 1967-77, computer sys. contracting officer, 1977-97; pres. Teledesic Svcs., Inc., Washington, 1997—. Author: Revenue Code of 1962: Effects on the Multi-National Firm, 1965. Judge ballroom dancing U.S. Ballroom Dancing Assn., Eastern seaboard, 1986—; swimming and diving coach Pike Br. Swim and Tennis Club, Alexandria, Va., 1966—. With USNR, 1961-62. Mem. The Beethoven Soc. Am. (exec. bd. 1993—), Norwegian Soc., Sons of Norway (Washington chpt. pres. 1994—, counselor 1993—, investment adv. 1979—, internat. del. to conv. 1988). Presbyterian. Avocations: swimming, diving, ballroom dancing. Home: 6324 Telegraph Rd Alexandria VA 22310-2969 Office: 710 W Peachtree St NW Atlanta GA 30308-1139 also: Rosfjord, 4580 Lyngdal Norway

ELLISON, EDWIN CHRISTOPHER, physician, surgeon; b. Columbus, Ohio, Jan. 10, 1950; s. Edwin Homer and Molly (Scheeler) E.; m. Mary Pat Borgess, Dec. 23, 1978; children: Jonathan Scott, Eric Christopher. BS, U. Wis., 1972; MD, Med. Coll. Wis., 1976. Diplomate Am. Bd. Surgery. Resident surgery Ohio State U., Columbus, 1976-83, asst. prof. surgery, 1983-93, assoc. prof., 1993-99, prof., 1999—; chief divsn. gen. surgery, bd. dirs. Ohio Digestive Disease Inst., Columbus, 1987-93; chief-of-staff-elect Ohio State U. Med. Ctr., Columbus, 1996, vice chmn. dept. surgery, 1996—. Fellow ACS. Office: N-729 Doan Hall 410 W 10th Ave Columbus OH 43210-1240

ELLISON, HARLAN JAY, author, screenwriter; b. Cleve., May 27, 1934; s. Louis Laverne and Serita (Rosenthal) E.; m. Charlotte Stein, 1956 (div. 1959); m. Billie Joyce Sanders, 1961 (div. 1962); m. Lory Patrick, 1965 (div. 1965); m. Lori Horwitz, 1976 (div. 1977); m. Susan Toth, Sept., 1986. Student, Ohio State U., 1953-55. A founder Cleve. Sci.-Fiction Soc., 1950; pub. mag. Sci.-Fantasy Bull. (later retitled Dimensions); editor Rogue Mag., Chgo., 1959-60, Regency Books, Chgo., 1960-61; lectr. colls. and univs.; book critic Los Angeles Times, 1969-82; editl. commentator Canadian Broadcasting Co., 1972-78; pres. Kilimanjaro Corp., 1979—; instr. Clarion Writers Workshop, Mich. State U., 1969-77, 1984; TV spokesman Chevrolet GEO Imports, 1988-89; on-screen TV actor for numerous shows including Babylon 5 and Psi-Factor. Actor: Cleveland Playhouse, part-time 1944-49; scriptwriter: TV series Alfred Hitchcock Hour, Outer Limits, The Man From U.N.C.L.E., others, 1962-77; writer 7 scripts for Burke's Law; creator (under pseudonym Cordwainer Bird) The Starlost, NBC-TV series; scenarist 2-hour NBC spl. The Tigers Are Loose, 1974-75; writer motion pictures The Dream Merchants, The Oscar, Nick the Greek, Best by Far, Harlan Ellison's Movie; scenarist I, Robot, 1978, Bug Jack Barron, 1982-83; writer Nebula winning novella-into-film A Boy and His Dog, 1975 (Hugo award for film adaptation 1976); author: 74 books including Web of the City, 1958, The Sound of a Scythe, 1960, Gentleman Junkie, 1961, Memos from Purgatory, 1961, Spider Kiss, 1961, Ellison Wonderland, 1962, Paingod (translated into French, Japanese, German, Spanish), 1965, I Have No Mouth & I Must Scream (translated into Japanese, French, Italian, Spanish, German), 1967, From the Land of Fear, 1967, Love Ain't Nothing But Sex Misspelled, 1968, The Beast that Shouted Love at the Heart of the World, 1969, Over the Edge, 1970, Alone Against Tomorrow, 1971, Partners in Wonder, 1971, Approaching Oblivion, 1974, Deathbird Stories, 1975, No Doors, No Windows, 1976, Strange Wine, 1978, All The Lies That Are My Life, 1980, Shatterday, 1980, Stalking the Nightmare, 1982, Sleepless Nights in the Procrustean Bed, 1984, An Edge in My Voice, 1985, Medea: Harlan's World, 1985, The Essential Ellison, 1987 (Bram Stoker award Horror Writers Am. 1988), Night and the Enemy, 1987, Angry Candy, 1988 (World Fantasy award for best short story collection, 1989, Major Works in Am. Lit. award 1988), Harlan Ellison's Watching, 1989 (Bram Stoker award Horror Writers Am. 1990), The Harlan Ellison Hornbook, 1990, Harlan Ellison's Movie, 1990, Dreams with Sharp Teeth, 1991, Mefisto in Onyx (Bram Stoker award Horror Writers Am. 1994), (with artist Jacek Yerka) Mind Fields (Morpheus), 1994, The City on the Edge of Forever, 1995, Edgeworks: The Collected Ellison, Vol. 1 & Vol 2, 1996, Edgeworks, Vols. 3 and 4 , 1997, Slippage, 1997, Repent, Harlequin!, 1997; editor, compiler: anthology Dangerous Visions (transls. French, German, Japanese, Italian, Spanish, U.K. edits.), 1967, Again, Dangerous Visions, 1972; author 4 books on juvenile delinquency; writer weekly TV column The Glass Teat, L.A. Free Press, 1968-71, pub. in 2 vols., 1970, 75, weekly column Harlan Ellison Hornbook, L.A. Free Press, 1972-73, An Edge in My Voice, Future Life, 1980-81, L.A. Weekly, 1982-83, pub. in 1 volume, 1985; on-camera commentator, critic cable Sci-Fi channel, 1993—; creator (with Larry Brody) weekly series The Dark Forces, NBC-TV, 1986, (with Ben Bova) series Brillo, ABC-TV, 1974, computer game based on I Have No Mouth and I Must Scream for Cyberdreams, 1995; creative cons., writer, dir. The Twilight Zone, CBS-TV, 1984-85, Cutter's World, 1987, 88; conceptual cons. Babylon 5, Warner Bros., 1993—; creator, editor series Harlan Ellison Discovery Series of 1st novels for Pyramid Books, 1973-77; voiceovers for animated cartoons; various works credited as inspiration for The Terminator (1984, Orion Pictures). With AUS, 1957-59. Recipient Hugo awards World Sci.-Fiction Conv., 1966, (2) 67, 68, 73, 74, 76, 77, 86, Spl. Achievement awards, 1968, 72, Certificate of Merit Trieste Film Festival, 1970, Edgar Allan Poe award Mystery Writers Am., 1974, 88, Am. Mystery award, 1988, 5 Bram Stoker Awards Inc., Lifetime Achievement, 1988, VIRA award for best vintage TV, The Outer Limits: Demon with a Glass Hand, 2 Audie Awards Audio Publishers Assn., 1999, George Méliès awards for cinematic achievement, 1972, 73, Jupiter award Instrs. Sci. Fiction in Higher Edn., 1974, 77, award for journalism PEN Internat., 1982, Americana Ann. award, 1989; inducted to Swedish Nat. Encyclopedia, 1992; honored by PEN for continuing commitment to artistic freedom and battle against censorship, 1990; selection of short story The Man Who Rowed Christopher Columbus for inclusion in The Best American Short Stories, 1993. Mem. SAG, Writers Guild Am. (Most Outstandign Scripts awards 1965, 67, 73, 86, screen bd., mem. West coun. 1971-72, 85-87), Sci. Fiction Writers Am. (co-founder, Nebula awards 1965, 69, 77, v.p. 1965-66). Address: PO Box 55548 Sherman Oaks CA 91413-0548 *The two most common elements in the universe are hydrogen and stupidity.*

ELLISON, HERBERT JAY, history educator; b. Portland, Oreg., Oct. 3, 1929; s. Benjamin F. and Esther (Anderson) E.; m. Alberta M. Moore, June 13, 1952; children: Valery, Pamela. BA, U. Wash., 1951, MA, 1952; PhD (Fulbright fellow), U. London, 1955. Instr. history U. Wash., 1955-56; asst. prof. history U. Okla., 1956-62; assoc. prof. history, chmn. Slavic studies program U. Kans., 1962-67, dir. NDEA Lang. and Area Center Slavic Studies, 1965-67, prof., 1965-68, assoc. dean faculties internat. programs, 1967-68; prof. history, Russian and Eastern European studies U. Wash., 1968—, dir. internat. programs, 1968-72, vice provost for ednl. devel., 1969-72, dir. Inst. Comparative and Fgn. Area Studies, 1973-78, chmn. Russian and East European studies, 1979-83; sec. Kennan Inst. Advanced Russian Studies, Washington, 1983-85; trustee Nat. Coun. for Russian and East European Rsch., 1983-87; dir. Russian rsch. Nat. Bur. Asian Rsch., 1990—, bd. dirs., 1993—; chmn. bd. dirs. Internat. Rsch. and Exchs. Bd., 1992-98; dir. The New Russia in Asia rsch. and conf. project, 1993-96; chmn. acad. coun. Kennan Inst. for Advanced Russian Studies, 1997—; bd. govs. Blakemore Found., 1998—. Author: History of Russia, 1964, Sino-Soviet Conflict, 1982, Soviet Policy Toward Western Europe, 1983, Japan and the Pacific Quadrille, 1987; chief cons., exec. dir. (PBS/BBC TV series) Messengers from Moscow, 1995.; contbr. articles to profl. jours. Mem. AAUP, Am. Hist. Assn., Am. Assn. Advancement of Slavic Studies, Univ. Club. Home: 12127 SE 15th St Bellevue WA 98005-3821 Office: Univ Wash Jackson Sch Internat Study PO Box 353650 Seattle WA 98195-3650

ELLISON, JAMES OLIVER, federal judge; b. St. Louis, Mo., Jan. 11, 1929; s. Jack and Mary (Patton) E.; m. Joan Roberts Ellison, June 7, 1950; 1 son, Scott. Student, U. Mo., Columbia, 1946-48; B.A., U. Okla., 1951, LL.B., 1951. Bar: Okla. Pvt. practice law Red Fork, Okla., 1953-55; ptnr. Boone, Ellison & Smith, Davis & Minter, 1955-79; judge U.S. Dist. Ct. (no. dist.) Okla., Tulsa, 1979—, chief justice, now sr. judge. Trustee Hillcrest Med. Center, Institution Programs, Inc.; elder Southminster Presbyterian Ch. Served to capt., inf. AUS, 1951-53. Mem. ABA, Okla. Bar Assn., Tulsa County Bar Assn., Alpha Tau Omega. Office: US Dist Ct The Fed Bldg 224 S Boulder Ave Tulsa OK 74103-3006*

ELLISON, JEFFREY ALAN, educator; b. Bronx, Nov. 7, 1951; s. Eli Robert and Estelle (Appelbaum) E.; m. Rebecca Sporn (div. Sept. 1994); children: Erin, Felicia. BA in History and Art History, Lake Forest Coll., 1973; MA in Anthropology, Wash. State U., 1977; postgrad., Fla. Atlantic U. Rschr. Field Mus. Natural History, Chgo., 1977-78; tchr. Chgo. Latin Sch., 1979-85; mgr. Spornette Internat., Homewood, Ill., 1985-90; tchr. Benjamin Sch., Palm Beach Gardens, Fla., 1990-93; tchr., chair dept. social studies Bernard Zell Anshe Emet Day Sch., Chgo., 1994—, coach chess team. Ill. state scholar, 1969, Travelling scholar, 1977. Mem. Nat. Coun. Social Studies Tchrs. Avocations: reading, chess, tennis. Home: 628 Onwentsia Ave Highland Park IL 60035-2030 Office: 3760 N Pine Grove Ave Chicago IL 60613-4103

ELLISON, LAWRENCE J., computer software company executive; b. 1944. BS. With Amdahl, Inc., Santa Clara, Calif., 1967-71; systems architect Amdahl, Inc.; pres. systems div. Omex Corp., 1972-77; with Oracle Corp., Redwood, Calif., 1977—, chmn., chief exec. officer, 1978—, also bd. dirs. Recipient Disting. Info. Scis. award Assn. Info. Tech. Profls., 1996. Office: Oracle Corp 500 Oracle Pkwy Redwood City CA 94065-1675*

ELLISON, LORIN BRUCE, management consultant; b. Chgo., Jan. 5, 1932; s. Edward L. and Bertha A. (Hoverson) E.; m. Beverley A. Burtar, July 24, 1953; children—Richard, Glen, Kirk, Kevin. B.S. in Bus. Adminstrn, Drake U., 1954. C.P.A., Ill. Auditor Arthur Andersen & Co., Chgo., 1957-62; mem. corporate staff, div. controller Interlake Steel Co., Chgo., 1962-65; v.p. finance, chief fin. officer, sec., div. pres. Tappan Co., Mansfield, Ohio, 1965-77; asso. cons. A.T. Kearney, Inc., Cleve., 1978-80; corp. controller, v.p. fin., chief fin. officer, v.p. bus. systems Bausch & Lomb, Rochester, N.Y., 1980-83; chief fin. officer Design & Mfg. Corp., Willoughby, Ohio, 1984; chief exec. officer, chmn. bd. Wave Tek Inc., Mansfield, Ohio, 1984-87; pvt. practice mgmt. cons. Mansfield, 1988—; sr. v.p., chief fin. officer Premier Salons Internat., Minnetonka, Minn., 1994-95; CFO SRECO-Flexible, Inc., Marina Del Rey, Calif., 1996-98; exec. v.p., CFO CRS Industries, Tampa, Fla., 1998—. Mem. Fin. Execs. Inst. Home: 550 Beech Dr Mansfield OH 44906-3309

ELLISON, LUTHER FREDERICK, oil company executive; b. Monroe, La., Jan. 2, 1925; s. Luther and Gertrude (Hudson) E.; m. Frances Williams, July 18, 1948 (dec.); children: Constance Elizabeth, Carolyn Williams; m. Patsy Hunter, Nov. 23, 1996. Student, Emory U., 1943-44; B.S. in Petroleum Engring., Tex. A&M U., 1949, B.S. in Geol. Engring., 1950. Registered profl. engr., Tex., La. Jr. petroleum engr. Sun Prodn. Co., Kilgore and McAllen, Tex., 1950-52; area petroleum engr. Sun Prodn. Co., Garcia Field, Tex., 1952-54; Delhi (La.) unit engr. Sun Prodn. Co., 1954-60; asst. region supt. Sun Prodn. Co., Dallas, 1960-62; dist. drilling engr. Sun Prodn. Co., Corpus Christi, 1962-63; dist. engr. Sun Prodn. Co., McAllen, 1963-65; supr. engring. Sun Prodn. Co., Dallas, 1965-66, div. chief petroleum engr., 1966-70, regional mgr. engring., 1970-75, region mgr., 1975-78, dir. devel., 1978-80, v.p. devel., 1980-84; div. v.p., dir. Sun Exploration and Prodn. Co., 1984-86, pres., bd. dirs., 1986—; pres., chief exec. officer Oil & Gas Experts, Inc., Dallas, 1986—, Am. Energy Enterprises Inc., Dallas, 1988—; pres., dir., mem. exec. com. Nabors-Sun Drilling Co.; dir., mem. exec. com. East Tex. Salt & Water Disposal Co.; CEO, pres. Oil & Gas Experts Inc., 1986; speaker in field. V.p. Northwood Jr. High Sch. PTA, Dallas, 1967-68, pres., 1968-69; elder, trustee Preston Hollow Presbyn. Ch. Found.; bd. dirs. Glen Lakes Assn. With USNR, 1943-46. Mem. Tex.-Mid-Continent Oil and Gas Assn. (Outstanding Achievement award 1964, chmn. area 1964-65, mgr. north region, operating com., Outstanding Performance award 1985—), Am. Petroleum Inst., Soc. Petroleum Engrs., Dallas Engrs. Club, Petroleum Engrs. Club, Dallas Petroleum Club, Park City Club, Northwood Club (Dallas), Lions Cub, Premier Club (Dallas), Parents League, Sigma Alpha Epsilon (pres. 1944-45). Home: 3 Castlecreek Ct Dallas TX 75225-1808 Office: 6440 N Central Expy Ste 613 Dallas TX 75206-4135

ELLISON, R. CURTIS, medicine and public health educator; b. Anderson, S.C., Dec. 23, 1933; s. William Jones and Sara Novice (Pettigrew) E.; m. Alexandra Margaret Armour, July 20, 1961; children: Robert Matthew, Sarah Alexandra. BS, Davidson (N.C.) Coll., 1955; MD, Med. U. S.C., 1959; MS in Epidemiology, Harvard U., 1976. Assoc. prof. medicine and pediatrics Georgetown U. Sch. Medicine, Washington, 1972-75; assoc. prof. pediatrics Harvard med. Sch., Boston, 1976-84; prof. medicine U. Mass. Med. Sch., Worcester, 1984-89; prof. medicine and pub. health Boston U. Sch. Medicine, 1989—, chief sect. of preventive medicine and epidemiology, 1989—, dir. Inst. on Lifestyle and Health, 1994—. Capt. U.S. Army, 1961-63. Mem. Am. Heart Assn. (fellow coun. on epidemiology and prevention). Office: Sect Prev Med and Epidem 88 E Newton St Rm B-612 Boston MA 02118-2308

ELLIS-VANT, KAREN MCGEE, elementary and special education educator, consultant; b. La Grande, Oreg., May 10, 1950; d. Ellis Eddington and Gladys Vera (Smith) McGee; m. Lynn F. Ellis, June 14, 1975 (div. Sept. 1983); children: Megan Marie, Matthew David; m. Jack Scott Vant, Sept. 6, 1986; children: Kathleen Erin, Kelli Christine (dec.). BA in Elem. Edn., Boise State U., 1972, MA in Spl. Edn., 1979; postgrad. studies in curriculum and instruction, U. Minn., 1985-86. Tchr. learning disabilities resource room New Plymouth Joint Sch. Dist., 1972-73, Payette Joint Sch. Dist., 1973, diagnostician project SELECT, 1974-75; cons. tchr. in spl. edn. Boise Sch. Dist., 1975-90; tchr. 1-2 combination, 1990-91, team tchr. 1st grade, 1991-92, 95—, site-based leadership team 1997-99, chpt. 1 program cons., 1992-95, mem. Idaho Mgmt. Change Projet, 1997—; mem. profl. Standards Commn., 1983-86. Bd. dirs. Hotline, Inc., 1979-82; mem. Idaho Coop. Manpower Commn., 1984-85; mem. First United Meth. Ch. (childcare bd. 1998—). Recipient Disting. Young Woman of Yr. award Boise Jayceettes, 1982, Idaho Jayceettes, 1983; Coffman Alumni scholar U. Minn., 1985-86. Mem. NEA (mem. civil rights com. 1983-85, state contact for peace caucus 1981-85, del. assembly rep., 1981-85), NSTA, ASCD, Internat. Reading Assn. (v.p. Boise chpt. 1996-97), NCTE, Internat. Coop. Learning Assn., Idaho Edn. Assn. (bd. dirs. region VII 1981-85, pres. region VII 1981-82), Boise Edn. Assn. (v.p. 1981-82, 84-85, pres. 1982-83), Nat. Council Urban Edn. Assn., World Future Soc., Council for Exceptional Children (pres. chpt. 1978-79), Nat. Coun. Tchrs. English, Minn. Coun. for Social Studies, Calif. Assn. for Gifted, Assn. for Grad. Edn. Students, Phi Delta Kappa. Contbr. articles to profl. jours.; editor, author ednl. texts and communiques; conductor of workshops, leadership tng. coop. learning. and frameworks. Office: Highlands Elem 3434 Bogus Basin Rd Boise ID 83702-1507

ELLMAN, NORMAN KENNETH, psychologist, psychoanalyst; b. Yonkers, N.Y., June 29, 1932; s. Sidney Lionel and Sadelle (Volan) E.; children: Deborah, Sharon, Douglas; m. Donna E. Ellman, May 20, 1995; stepchildren: Cheryl Graybush, Christina Graybush. BSin Edn., SUNY, New Paltz, 1954; MEd, Queens Coll., N.Y.C., 1958; M.Psychology, Yeshiva U., 1967; PhD, NYU, 1972. Lic. psychologist, N.J., N.Y.; cert. tchr.; cert. in psychoanalysis. Tchr. 6th grade Malverne (N.Y.) Pub. Schs., 1956-57, East Williston (N.Y.) Pub. Schs., 1957-59; sch. psychologist Brentwood (N.Y.) Pub. Schs., 1959-62, Wantagh (N.Y.) Pub. Schs., 1962-67; pvt. practice psychotherapy Oakland, N.J., 1967—; co-dir. North Jersey Mental Health Assocs., 1972-83, Counseling and Psychotherapy Svcs., Oakland, 1983—, North Jersey Mental Health Assocs., 1972-83; chief psychologist, dir. child study team Glen Rock (N.J.) Pub. Schs., 1967-72, psychol. cons., 1972-82; head counselor and dir. day camp Long Beach, N.Y., 1959-67; tchr. N.J. Inst. Psycholotherapy, Teaneck, N.J., part-time, 1975; adj. faculty psychology Nassau C.C., Hempstead, N.Y., 1966, Paterson (N.J.) State Tchrs. Coll., 1969; staff therapist Lynbrook (N.Y.) Cons. Ctr., Bi-County Cons. Ctr., Amityville, N.Y., 1963-67. With U.S. Army, 1954-56. Mem. APA, N.J. Psychol. Assn., Bergen County Psychol. Assn., Assn. Advancement of Psychology, Nat. Assn. Advancement of Psycholoanalysis. Avocations: softball, chess, piano. Home and Office: 60 Tidy Island Blvd Bradenton FL 34210-3302

ELLMANN, DOUGLAS STANLEY, lawyer; b. Detroit, July 15, 1956; s. William Marshall and Sheila Estelle (Frenkel) E.; m. Claudia Joan Roberts, Feb. 16, 1985; children: Ben Bosworth, Liam Roberts. AB, Occidental Coll., 1978; JD, U. Mich., 1982. Bar: Mich. 1982, U.S. Dist. Ct. (ea. dist.) Mich. 1982, U.S. Ct. Appeals (6th cir.) 1982. Assoc. Butzel, Keidan, Simon, Myers & Graham, Detroit, 1982-84; ptnr. Ellmann & Ellmann, Detroit, 1984-86; atty. Wise & Marsac, Detroit, 1987-89; U.S. panel trustee, 1989—; prin. Ellmann & Ellmann, P.C., Ann Arbor, Mich., 1989—; spl. asst. atty. gen., 1986; sec. bankruptcy trustees U.S. Bankruptcy Ct. (ea. dist.) Mich., 1993—, mem. bench bar com., 1994—. Author: Selected Issues in Asset Protection, 1994, My Advice: Next Time Go Solo, 1994, LWUSA; co-author: Winning Labor Arbitrations, 1987. Founder Amnesty Internat., Detroit, Lawyer's Support Network; mem. nat. com. U. Mich. Law Sch. Fund, 1986—. Mem. ABA (vice chair bankruptcy com. 1995—), Mich. Bar Assn. (rep. assembly 1983-89, 90-92, exec. counsel young lawyers sect. 1985-87, mem. client security fund com. 1987-95), State Bar Mich. (mem. manditory CLE com. 1989-96, chmn. 1995-96), Washtenaw County Bar Assn. (chmn. banking, bus., bankruptcy com. 1995—). Home: 4575 W Loch Alpine Dr Ann Arbor MI 48103-9081 Office: 308 W Huron St Ann Arbor MI 48103-4204

ELLMANN, SHEILA FRENKEL, investment company executive; b. Detroit, June 8, 1931; d. Joseph and Rose (Neback) Frenkel; BA in English, U. Mich., 1953; m. William M. Ellmann, Nov. 1, 1953; children: Douglas Stanley, Carol Elizabeth, Robert Lawrence. Dir. Advance Glove Mfg. Co., Detroit, 1954-78; v.p. Frome Investment Co., Detroit, 1980-96, pres., 1996—. Mem. U. Mich. Alumni Assn., Nat. Trust Hist. Preservation. Home: 28000 Weymouth Ct Farmington Hills MI 48334

ELLMANN, WILLIAM MARSHALL, lawyer, mediator, arbitrator, researcher; b. Highland Park, Mich., Mar. 23, 1921; s. James I. and Jeannette (Barsook) E.; m. Sheila Estelle Frenkel, Nov. 1, 1953; children: Douglas S., Carol E., Robert L. Student, Occidental Coll., 1939-40; AB, U. Mich., 1946; LLB, Wayne State U., 1951. Bar: Mich. 1951. Pvt. practice law Detroit, 1951—; ptnr. Ellmann & Ellmann, 1970—; spl. com. atty. gen. Mich. to study use state troops in emergencies, 1964-65; mem. exec. Inst. Continuing Legal Edn., 1964-68; mem. Mich. Employment Rels. Commn., 1973—, chmn., 1983-86; commr. Mackinac Island State Park Commn., 1979-85, chmn., 1983-86; panel mem. numerous orgns. Author: Of Hemingway, Toscanni and Arbitration: Practical Considerations for Preparing Winning Cases, 1985, A Reply to the Ambassador on Russia, 1991, (with Douglas S. Ellmann) Winning Labor Arbitrations, 1987; contbr. articles to profl. jours. With USAAF, 1942-46. Fellow Am. Bar Found.; mem. ABA (ho. of dels. 1969-72), Am. Arbitration Assn. (mem. adv. council), Nat. Acad. Arbitrators, Detroit Bar Assn. (vice chmn. pub. relations com. 1959), State Bar Mich. (commr. 1959-69, pres. 1966-67, co-chmn. com. on qualification jud. candidates 1970-78, mem. Detroit News secret witness panel 1983), Practicing Law Inst. (adv. council 1969-70, spl. asst. atty. gen. 1970-78), Sigma Nu Phi. Home: 28000 Weymouth Ct Farmington Hills MI 48334-3267 Office: Ellmann & Ellmann 308 W Huron St Ann Arbor MI 48103-4204

ELLNER, CAROLYN LIPTON, university dean, consultant; b. N.Y.C., Jan. 17, 1932; d. Robert Mitchell and Rose (Pearlman) Lipton; m. Richard Ellner, June 21, 1953; children: D. Lipton, Alison Lipton. AB cum laude, Mt. Holyoke Coll., 1953; A.M., Columbia Tchrs. Coll., 1957; PhD with distinction, UCLA, 1968. Tchr., prof., adminstr., N.Y. and Md., 1957-62; prof. dir. tchr. edn., assoc. dean Claremont Grad. Sch. (Calif.) 1967-82; prof., dean sch. edn. Calif. State U., Northridge, 1982-98, dean emerita, 1998—; pres., CEO On-the-Job Parenting. Co-author: Schoolmaking, 1977; Studies of College Teaching (Orange County Authors award 1984), 1983. Trustee Ctr. for Early Edn., Los Angeles, 1968-71, Oakwood Sch., Los Angeles, 1972-78, Mt. Holyoke Coll., South Hadley, Mass., 1979-84; commr. Economy and Efficiency Com., Los Angeles, 1974-82, Calif. Commn. Tchr. Credentialing, 1987-90, 93—, vice chair 1995-96, chair, 1996-98; bd. dirs. Found. for Effective Govt., Los Angeles, 1982, Calif. Coalition for Pub. Edn., 1985-88, Valley Hosp. Found., 1992-94, Mt. Holyoke Alumnae Assn. Bd., 1993-96; founding dir. Decade of Edn., 1990; assoc. dir. New Devel. in Sci. Project NSF, 1985-94; bd. dirs., chair edn. com. Valley Industry and Commerce Assn., 1990-93, v.p., 1993-94; co-prin. dir. Mid South Calif. Arts Project, 1991-98; mem. coun., trustees L.A. Alliance for Restructing Now (LEARN), 1992—; bd. dirs. Inner City Arts Found., 1993-96; involved with L.A. Annenberg Met. Project (LAAMP), DELTA, 1995—. Ford Found. fellow, 1964-67, fellow Ednl. Policy Fellowship Program, 1989-90; recipient Office of Edn. award U.S. Office of Edn., 1969-72, Alumnae medal of honor Mt. Holyoke Coll., 1998; W. M. Keck Found. grantee, 1983, 94. Mem. ASCD, Am. Edn. Rsch. Assn., Am. Assn. Colls. for Tchr. Edn., Nat. Soc. for Study of Edn.

ELLNER, MICHAEL WILLIAM, art educator; b. N.Y.C., Apr. 1, 1938; s. Charles and Sylvia May (Golub) E.; m. Josephine Helene Bilello, Aug. 24, 1957; children: Eileen Lorraine, Deborah Lynn, Laurence Steven. AA in Engring., San Jose City Coll., 1963, AA in Art, 1966; BA, Coll. Notre Dame, 1970; MA, San Jose State U., 1971, postgrad., 1973-74; postgrad., U. Calif., Santa Cruz, 1980. Cert. secondary art tchr., c.c. art tchr., Calif. Chair art dept. John Muir Jr. High Sch., San Jose, Calif., 1973-80; assoc. prof. art San Jose State U., 1974; chair art dept. Willow Glen Edn. Park, San Jose, 1980-91; visual arts coord. A. Lincoln AVPA Magnet High Sch., San Jose, 1991-96; cons. Coll. Bd., San Jose, 1989-97, San Jose Unified Sch. Dist., Saturday Acad., San Jose, 1996—, San Jose City Coll. Painting Program, 1996—; advisor Nat. Art Honor Soc., San Jose, 1991—; intern advisor Casa Program, San Jose, 1991—; co-convenor Lincoln HS Magnet Curriculum Coun., San Jose, 1991-96; mentor tchr. San Jose Unified Sch. Dist., 1985-94. Paintings included in numerous pub. collections including San Jose Mus. Art, Calif., De Saisset Mus., Santa Clara, Calif., Foot Mus., Long Beach, Calif., Coll. Notre Dame, Belmont, Calif.; guest curator Egyptian Mus. Art Gallery, San Jose, Calif., New World Gallery, San Jose, Calif., San Jose Art League, Calif.; guest curator Macla Gallery, San Jose, Calif., Genesis Gallery, San Jose, Calif., 1970—; exhibited in more than 100 group and one-person shows; created 19 cmty. murals. Past pres. San Jose Art League; past treas. Cambrian Art League. Recipient Art grant City of San Jose, 1994, Mural grant Rose Garden Assn., San Jose, 1996, grant Nat. League Am. Pen Women, 1996, 98, Program awards Nat. Blue Ribbon Sch., 1998, Magnet Sch. of Am., 1991, 92, 93, Calif. Disting. Sch. award, 1992, 96, Golden Bell award, 1994, Kennedy Ctr. award for the arts, 1995; named Tchr. of Yr., Willow Glen Edn. Park PTA, 1985, San Jose Shrine, 1986; inductee Youth Mentor's Hall of Fame, Youth Focus, 1999. Mem. Calif. Tchrs. Assn., NEA, San Jose Tchrs. Assn., San Jose Inst. Contemporary Art, Nat. Art Edn. Assn. (Program Stds. award 1993, 94, 95, 96, State Farm Good Neighbor award 1996), Artists Alliance Calif., South Bay Artists Assn. (adv. com.), Cmty. Partnership Santa Clara County, San Jose Art League (past pres.), Cambrian Art League (past treas.), Phi Kappa Phi. Avocations: painting, poetry, murals. Home: 1429 Scossa Ave San Jose CA 95118-2456

ELLNER, PAUL DANIEL, clinical microbiologist; b. N.Y.C., May 2, 1925; s. George and Cele (Weis) E.; m. Estelle Ziswasser, 1948 (div. 1960); 1 child, Diane; m. Cornelia Johns, Jan. 15, 1965; children—David, Jonathan. B.S., L.I. U., 1948; M.S., U. So. Calif., 1952; Ph.D., U. Md. Coll. Medicine, 1956. Diplomate Am. Bd. Med. Microbiology; cert. clin. lab. dir. N.Y.C. Dept. Health. Clin. bacteriologist Los Angeles hosps., 1948-52; research asst. Mt. Sinai Hosp., N.Y.C., 1952-53; instr. microbiology U. Fla. Coll. Medicine, 1956-60; asst. prof. U. Vt. Coll. Medicine, 1960-63; asst. prof. Columbia U. Coll. Physicians and Surgeons, N.Y.C., 1963-66, assoc. prof., 1966-70, prof. microbiology, 1971-78, prof. microbiology and pathology, 1978-89, prof. emeritus, 1989, dir. clin. microbiology service, 1971-89; assoc. microbiologist Presbyn. Hosp., N.Y.C., 1966-70, attending staff, 1971-89; cons. in field; vis. prof. N.Y. Med. Coll., Valhalla, 1979; ASM Latin Am. vis. prof., Medellin, Colombia, 1982; Am. Bur. Med. Advancement in China vis. prof., Taiwan, 1982; regional coordinator Nat. Disaster Med. System; v.p. Am. BioSci. Cons. Author: Current Procedures in Clinical Bacteriology, 1978, Understanding Infectious Disease, 1992; editor: Infectious Diarrheal Diseases: Current Concepts and Laboratory Procedures, 1984; mem. editorial bd. Sexually Transmitted Diseases, 1982-84, European Jour. Clin. Microbiology, 1985-89; contbr. chpts. to books, numerous articles to sci. jours. Served with AC, USN, 1943-44; to capt. USPHS Res., 1956—; health project officer USCG, 1982-91. U.S. Navy research fellow, 1954-56. Fellow Am. Acad. Microbiology, Assn. Clin Scientists, N.Y. Acad. Medicine (assoc.), Infectious Diseases Soc. Am.; mem. AMA (spl. affiliate), Am. Soc. Microbiology (chmn. clin. divsn. 1980-81, Sonnenwirth Meml. award 1992), Acad. Clin. Lab. Physicians and Scientists, Am. Venereal Disease Assn., Sigma Xi. Republican. Jewish. Avocations: flying, fishing, gardening, photography. *The greatest satisfaction for the scientist is recognition by his peers for honesty and integrity in his studies, fairness and impartiality to his colleagues, and guidance and encouragement to his students.*

ELLROY, JAMES, writer; b. L.A., Mar. 4, 1948; s. Geneva (Hillaker) E.; m. Mary Doherty, 1988. Author: (novels) Brown's Requiem, 1981, Clandestine, 1982, Blood on the Moon, 1984, Because the Night, 1984, Killer on the Road, 1986, Suicide Hill, 1986, Silent Terror, 1986, The Black Dahlia, 1987, The Big Nowhere, 1988 (Prix Mystere award 1990), L.A. Confidential, 1990, White Jazz, 1992, Hollywood Nocturnes, 1994, Dick Contino's Blues, American Tabloid, 1995, My Dark Places, 1996, Crime Wave, 1999; contbr.: Fallen Angels: Six Noir Tales Told for Television, 1993. Office: care Warner Books 1271 Ave of Americas New York NY 10020*

ELLSAESSER, HUGH WALTER, retired atmospheric scientist; b. Chillicothe, Mo., June 1, 1920; s. Charles Theobald and Louise Minerva (Bancroft) E.; m. Lois Merle McCaw, June 21, 1946 (dec. May 1998); children: Corbin Donald, Adrienne Sue; 1 adopted child, Robin Keith. AA, Bakersfield (Calif.) Jr. Coll., 1941; SB, U. Chgo., 1943, PhD, 1964; MA, UCLA, 1947. Commd. 2d lt. USAF, 1943, advanced through grades to lt. col., 1960; weather officer USAF, Washington, Fla., Eng., 1942-63; ret., 1963; physicist Lawrence Livermore (Calif.) Nat. Lab., 1963-86, guest scientist, 1986-97; ind. atmospheric cons., 1997—. Editor: Global 2000 Revisited, 1992; contbr. numerous articles to profl. jours. Mem. Am. Meteorol. Soc., Am. Geophysics Union. Republican. Presbyterian. Avocation: languages. Home and Office: 4293 Stanford Way Livermore CA 94550-3463

ELLSBERG, ROBERT BOYD, religious press editor; b. Jacksonville, N.C., Dec. 13, 1955; s. Daniel Ellsberg and Carol Cummings; m. Margaret Rizza, June 2, 1984; 1 child, Nicholas Boyd. BA, Harvard U., 1982. Mng. editor Cath. Worker, N.Y.C., 1976-78; teaching fellow Harvard U. Div. Sch., Cambridge, Mass., 1984-87; editor in chief Orbis Books, Maryknoll, N.Y., 1987—. Author: All Saints: Daily Reflections on Saints, Prophets, and Witnesses for Our Time, 1997; co-author: Hearts on Fire: The Story of the Mary Knoll Sisters, 1993; editor: By Little and By Little: Selected Writings of Dorothy Day, 1983, Gandhi on Christianity, 1991, Works of Mercy, 1992, Carlo Caretto: Selected Writing, 1994, Charles de Foucauld: Selected Writings, 1999; co-editor: The Logic of Solidarity, 1989, A Penny a Copy: Readings from the Catholic Worker, 1995. Recipient Christopher award, 1984, 93, 98, Cath. Book award, 1993, 94, 98, Veritas medal Dominican Coll., 1998; Sheldon fellow Harvard Coll., 1982. Mem. Phi Beta Kappa. Roman Catholic. Office: Orbis Books Maryknoll NY 10545

ELLSWORTH, BOB See WISE, ROBERT ELLSWORTH, JR.

ELLSWORTH, FRANK L., non-profit executive; b. Wooster, Ohio, May 20, 1943; s. Clayton Sumner and Frances (Fuller) E.; 1 child, Kirstin Lynne. BA, Western Res. Coll., 1965; MEd, Pa. State U., 1967; MA, Columbia U., 1969; PhD, U. Chgo., 1976; LLD, Pepperdine U., 1997. Asst. dir. devel. Columbia Law Sch., 1968-70; dir. spl. projects, prof. lit. Sarah Lawrence Coll., N.Y., 1971; asst. dean Law Sch., U. Chgo., 1971-79, instr. social sci. collegiate div., 1975-79; pres., prof. polit. sci. Pitzer Coll., Claremont, Calif., 1979-91; pres. Ind. Colls. So. Calif., L.A., 1991-97; v.p. Capital Rsch. & Mgmt. Co., 1997—; pres. Endowments, Inc.; disting. vis. prof. Pepperdine U. Author: Law on the Midway, 1977, Student Activism in American Higher Education; contbr. articles to profl. jours. Trustee Japanese Am. Nat. Mus., Pitzer Coll., Southwestern U.; chmn. Am. Sch. Internat. Studies, Seattle, Global Ptnrs. Inst., Can. Global Ptnrs. Recipient Disting. Young Alumnus award Case Western Res. U., 1981, True of Life award United Jewish Fund, 1991. Mem. History of Edn. Soc., Coun. for Advancement of Secondary Edn., Young Pres.'s Orgn., Ukiyo-e Soc., Asia Soc., Univ. Club of L.A. Home: 254 La Mirada Rd Pasadena CA 91105-2708 Office: The Capital Group 333 S Hope St Fl 34 Los Angeles CA 90071-1406

ELLSWORTH, JOSEPH CORDON, real estate executive, lawyer; b. Washington, Aug. 13, 1955; s. Richard Grant and Betty (Midgley) E.; m. Rebecca Ann Moss, Nov. 2, 1979; children: Lindsey, Stephanie, Brian, Brittney. Grad., Brigham Young U., 1980; JD, Calif. Western U., 1983. Bar: Utah 1984, U.S. Dist. Ct. Utah 1984. Asst. legal counsel Meadow Fresh Farms, Inc., Salt Lake City, 1983; mgr. property and leasing Equitec Properties Co., Atlanta, 1984-85; sr. mgr. real estate and adminstrn. MCI Telecom. Corp., Atlanta, 1985—; with MCI Worldcom, Englewood, Colo.; v.p. Rebecca's Sunnybrook Yogurt, Inc., Atlanta, 1985-90. Mem. FBA, Internat. Rsch. Devel. Coun., Nat. Assn. Corp. Real Estate Execs. Internat., B.Y.U. Alumni Assn. (chmn. Atlanta region 1988-94), Phi Alpha Delta. Republican. Avocations: sports, outside business ventures. Office: MCI Telecom Corp Ste 600E 6312 S Fiddlers Green Cir Englewood CO 80111-4949

ELLSWORTH, ROBERT FRED, investment executive, former government official; b. Lawrence, Kans., June 11, 1926; s. W. Fred and Lucile (Rarig) E.; m. Vivian Esther Sies, Nov. 10, 1956; children: Robert William, Ann Elizabeth. BS, U. Kans., 1945; JD, U. Mich., 1949. Bar: D.C., Mass., Kans., U.S. Supreme Ct. Mem. 87th to 89th Congresses from 2d and 3d Dist., Kans., 1961-67; asst. to Pres. of U.S., Washington, 1969; U.S. ambassador to NATO, 1969-71; gen. ptnr. Lazard Freres & Co., N.Y.C., 1971-74; asst. sec. for internat. security affairs U.S. Dept. Def., Washington, 1974-75; dep. sec. Def. U.S. Dept. Def., 1975-77; pres. Robert Ellsworth & Co., Inc., Washington, 1977—; mng. dir. The Hamilton Group LLC; bd. dirs. Price Comm. Corp. Lay reader Episcopal Ch. Knight Honor Johanniterorden. With USNR, 1944-46, 50-53. Recipient Presdl. Nat. Security medal, 1977. Mem. Coun. Fgn. Rels., Internat. Inst. Strategic Studies (v.p.), Atlantic Coun. of the U.S. (dir.), Am. Coun. on Germany (dir.), Coun. of Am. Amb. Home: 24120 Old Hundred Rd Dickerson MD 20842-9663 Office: PO Box 21156 Baltimore MD 21228

ELLWANGER, J. DAVID, lawyer; b. St. Louis, Feb. 11, 1937; s. Walter Henry and Jessie Lorraine (Hanger) E.; m. Barbara Ann Koehneke, Apr. 11, 1970; children: Carrie Louise, Jay David. Student, Valparaiso U., 1956; BS, U. Ala., 1959, JD, 1962. Asst. atty. gen. State of Ala., Montgomery, 1962-66; staff atty. Office of Econ. Opportunity Legal Services Program, Washington, 1967, Nat. Legal Aid and Defender Assn., Chgo., 1967-68; from asst. dir. to dir. pub. svcs. activities divsn. ABA, Chgo., 1968-73; dir. Commn. on Nat. Inst. Justice, Washington, 1973-74, Office Relations with other Orgns., 1975; exec. dir. L.A. County Bar Assn., 1976-78, D.C. Bar, Washington, 1979-81; CEO State Bar of Calif., San Francisco, 1982-86; pres., trustee Southwestern Legal Found., 1988—; dir. Internat. and Comparative Law Ctr., Internat. Oil and Gas Edn. Ctr.; rsch. fellow, 1988—. Dem. primary candidate for state senate, Selma, Ala., 1966; bd. dirs. English dist. Luth. Ch. of the Mo. Synod, 1970-75; bd. dirs. English Synod of the Assn. of Evang. Luth. Chs., 1976-77, Luth. Deaconess Assn., 1969-72, Luth. Wheatridge Found., Chgo., 1974-83, Luth. Social Svc. Tex., 1991-92, divsn. global mission Evang. Luth. Ch. in Am., 1995—; pres. Preston Meadow Luth. Ch., Plano, Tex., 1990-91; ch. coun. Evang. Luth. Ch. in Am., 1992-95; U.S. rep. on bd. dirs. Internat. Ecumenical Devel. Coop. Soc., 1993—; mem. exec. bd. So. Meth. U. Law Sch., 1991—; mem. Dallas Com. Fgn. Rels.; bd. dirs. Dallas World Salute, 1989-97, Dallas Coun. World Affairs. Recipient award Merit, Ala. State Bar, 1975. Fellow Am. Bar Found. (life); mem. ABA (commn. Nat. Inst. Justice 1976-81, chair individual rights and responsibilities sect. 1984-85, chmn. editl. bd. Human Rights 1993-96, Ho. of Dels. 1984, Commn. on Pub. Understanding About the Law 1982-88, standing com. assn. comms. 1989-92, adv. bd. ctrl. and east European law initiative 1991—), Patrick E. Higginbotham Inn of Ct. (sec. 1988—), Dallas Bar Assn., Ala. State Bar, D.C. Bar, Nat. Legal Aid and Defender Assn., Am. Judicature Soc. Democrat. Avocation: photography. Home: 3408 Caleo Ct Plano TX 75025-2204 Office: Southwestern Legal Found PO Box 830707 Richardson TX 75083-0707*

ELLWANGER, THOMAS JOHN, lawyer; b. Summit, N.J., Feb. 26, 1949; s. James Warren and Lorean (Nicholson) E.; children: James Hunter, Margaret Lorean. BA, Northwestern U., 1970; JD, U. Fla., 1974. Bar: Fla. 1975, U.S. Dist. Ct. (mid. dist.) Fla. 1976, U.S. Ct. Appeals (11th cir.) 1976, U.S. Dist. Ct. (so. dist.) Fla. 1977, U.S. Tax Ct. Mem. Fowler, White, Gillen, Boggs, Villareal & Banker P.A., Tampa, Fla., 1975—; instr. law U. Fla., Gainesville, 1975; adj. prof. Stetson U. Coll. Law, 1997—. Editor: Gadsden County Times, 1970-72. Pres. Neighborhood Housing Services Hyde Park, Tampa, 1978. Fellow Am. Coll. Trust and Estate Counsel, Fla. Bar (cert. tax lawyer), Hillsborough County Bar Assn. (chmn. com. probate liaison 1985-86, real property probate and trust law sect. 1987-89), Tampa Bay Estate Planning Counsel (pres. 1994-95). Democrat. Avocations: music. lit., sports. Office: Fowler White Gillen Boggs Villareal & Banker PA 501 E Kennedy Blvd Ste 1700 Tampa FL 33602-5200

ELLWOOD, DAVID TABOR, public policy educator; b. Mpls., Sept. 16, 1953; s. Paul and Ann Ellwood; m. Marilyn Rymer. AB in Econs. summa cum laude, Harvard U., 1975, PhD in Econs., 1981. Rsch. asst. to prof. Martin S. Feldstein Harvard U., Cambridge, Mass., 1974-75, 77; rsch. assoc. health policy program U. Calif., San Francisco, 1975-76; tchg. fellow labor econs. Harvard U., Cambridge, 1977-79; rsch. asst. Nat. Bur. Econ. Rsch., Cambridge, 1978-80; asst. prof. pub. policy John F. Kennedy Sch. Govt., Harvard U., Cambridge, 1980-84, assoc. prof. pub. policy, 1984-88, prof. pub. policy, 1988-92, Malcolm Wiener prof. pub. policy, 1992-98, Lucius N. Littauer prof. polit. economy, 1998—; co-dir. Malcolm Wiener Ctr. Pub. Policy, Harvard U., Cambridge, 1992-93; acad. dean John F. Kennedy Sch. Govt. Harvard U., Cambridge, 1992-93, 95-97; asst. sec. planning and evaluation HHS, Washington, 1993-95; rsch. assoc. Nat. Bur. Econ. Rsch., 1984-93; faculty mem. retreat U.S. House Ways and Means com.; panel mem. Work and Welfare Demonstration Manpower Demonstration Rsch. Corp., 1985-93, 95—; bd. overseers panel study income dynamics, 1986-88; dir. domestic strategy group The Aspen Inst., 1998—; cons. in field. Author: Poor Support: Poverty and the American Family, 1988 (notable books N.Y. Times Book Review 1988, outstanding book 1988 Policy Studies Orgn.); co-editor Welfare Policies for the 90s; co-author Welfare Realities: From Rhetonic to Reform, 1994; contbr. numerous articles, book reviews to profl. jours. Panel Com. Status Black Ams., NAS, 1986-91; adv. bd. Children's Program Edna McConnell Clark Found., 1989-93; mem. Nat. Forum Future Children and Their Parents, Nat. Rsch. Coun., 1988-91; mem. Task Force Poverty and Welfare Mario Cuomo, gov. State N.Y., 1986-87, Project Welfare Families Bruce Babbitt, gov., State Ariz., 1986-87. Recipient George Kershaw award Assn. Pub. Policy Analysis and Mgmt.; Lehman fellow

Harvard U. Mem. NAS (panel poverty and family assistance), Phi Beta Kappa. Office: Harvard U John F Kennedy Sch Govt 79 John F Kennedy St Cambridge MA 02138-5801

ELLWOOD, EDITH MUESING, free-lance writer; b. Manhattan, N.Y., Sept. 18, 1947; d. Carl Earl and Elsbeth Helen (Bushbeck) Muesing; m. William Adonis Ellwood, Sept. 15, 1980; children: Jeanie, Colin, Caroline. BA, Fordham U., 1969; MA, NYU, 1971. Rschr. Acad. Rsch. Group, Rutherford, N.J., 1975-78, 80-82; pres. Colin Press, Bklyn., 1984-88; editor Ellwood Editing Svc., Bklyn., 1990-93; free-lance writer, editor Bushkill, Pa., 1993—; presenter numerous papers at symposiums. Author: The Alternative to Technological culture, 1986, U.S. Dem. Myth vs. Reality, 1985, Dragonfly, 1985 (Reader's Best of Issue award); contbr. poetry, articles, fiction and nonfiction prose to jours. and anthologies. Mem. Nat. Writers Union, Women in Scholarly Pub. (writer, editor newsletter 1990-93), Internat. Women's Writing Guild (newsletter contbr.), Interstitial Cystit is Assn., Nature Conservancy, St. John's Women's Guild (writer, editor of newsletter). Democrat. Roman Catholic. Avocations: water and oil painting, sketching, antiques. Home: RR 1 Box 178 Bushkill PA 18324-9801

ELLWOOD, PAUL MURDOCK, JR., health policy analyst, consultant; b. San Francisco, July 16, 1926; s. Paul Ellwood and Rebecca May (Logan) E.; divorced; children: David, Cynthia, Deborah. B.A., Stanford U., 1949, M.D., 1953. Dir. Kenny Rehab. Inst., Mpls., 1962-63; exec. dir. Am. Rehab. Found., Mpls., 1963-73; dir. Inst. Interdisciplinary Studies, Mpls., 1970-73; pres. InterStudy, health policy analysis Excelsior, Minn., 1973-85; pres. Paul Ellwood & Assocs., Excelsior, 1985-87; chmn. bd., pres. InterStudy, 1987-92; pres. Jackson Hole Group, Tenton Village, Wy., 1992—; founding dir. Found. for Accountability/Quality Measure for Healthcare, Portland, Oreg., 1997—; dir., mem. exec. com. Jackson Hole Ski Corp., Wyo., 1972-87; clin. prof. phys. medicine and rehab., neurology and pediatrics U. Minn. Med. Sch.; cons. in health and delivery systems. Co-author: Assuring The Quality of Health Care, 1973; Co-editor: Handbook of Physical Medicine and Rehabilitation, 2d edit, 1971. Served with USNR, 1944-46. Recipient award Ministry Pub. Health, Republic Argentina, 1957; 1st award sci. exhibit Am. Acad. Neurology, 1958; citation President's Com. Employment Handicapped, 1962; Gold Key award Am. Congress Rehab., 1971; named Distinguished fellow Am. Rehab. Found., 1973. Mem. Inst. Medicine, Group Health Assn. Am. (dir. 1975-76), Nat. Health Council (dir. 1971-76), Assn. Rehab. Centers (pres. 1960-61, U.S. Healthcare Quality award 1991). Home: PO Box 165 Bondurant WY 82922-0165 Office: Jackson Hole Group PO Box 270 Bonduant WY 82922*

ELLWOOD, SCOTT, lawyer; b. Boston, July 8, 1936; s. William Prescott and Doris (Cook) E.; m. Suzanne M. Timble; children: Victoria, William Prescott II, Marjorie. Student, Williams Coll., 1954-56; AB, Eastern Mich. U., 1958; LLB, Harvard U., 1961. Bar: Iowa 1961, Ill. 1961, U.S. Dist. Ct. (no. dist.) Ill., 1961. Assoc. McBride & Baker, Chgo., 1961-67, ptnr., 1968-84; ptnr. McDermott, Will & Emery, Chgo., 1984—; pres. Miller Investment Co., 1973-93, bd. dirs.; v.p. SMI Investment Corp., 1978—, bd. dirs., FRC Investment Corp., 1984-89. Pres., bd. dirs. 110 N Wacker Dr Found., 1974-84, Northfield Found., 1978-84, Leadership Found., 1979-84, Woodbine Found., 1980-84, The Cannon River Found., 1982-84, L.M. McBride Found., 1982-84, Bellarmine Found., 1982-84, Mark Morton Meml. Fund, 1982—. Mem. Iowa Bar Assn., Chgo. Bar Assn., Harvard Law Soc. Ill. (bd. dirs. 1983-98, treas. 1987-88, sec. 1988-89, v.p. 1989-93, pres. 1993-95), Harvard Club Chgo. (bd. dirs. 1993-95), Monroe Club (bd. dirs. 1988-98), Skokie Country Club (Glencoe, Ill.). Republican. Episcopalian. Home: 1296 Hackberry Ln Winnetka IL 60093-1606 Office: McDermott Will & Emery 227 W Monroe St Ste 3100 Chicago IL 60606-5096

ELMA, BAYANI BORJA, physician; b. Manila, Philippines, Nov. 3, 1942; s. Medardo Romero and Hiwaga Rada Borja E.; m. Maria Mercado Chavez-Elma, July 4, 1971; children: Michael Anthony, Mary Anne. Degree in Preparatory Medicine, U. Philippines, 1963; MD, U. of the East, Quezon City, Philippines, 1968. Diplomate Am. Bd. Quality Assurance, Utilization Review Physicians. Vice-chief of staff Md. Gen. Hosp., Balt., 1985-90, dir., trustee, 1988-95, chmn., prof. affairs com., 1992-95; mem. panel editl. advisers Internal Medicine for the Specialist, Livingston, N.J., 1990—; editl. bd. Md. Med. Jour., Balt., 1993-96; pres. Assn. of Philippine Physicians in Md., 1997-99. Pres. U. East Med. Alumni Assn., 1992-94; dir., trustee U. East Med. Alumni Found, 1994—; vice-chmn. Govs. Commn. on Asian-Pacific Am. Affairs, Balt., 1992—; alt. del. House Del. Balt. City Med. Soc., 1997-99. Named One of the Twenty Outstanding Filipino Am. U.S. and Can. Filipino Image mag., 1998-99. Mem. Am. Coll. Physician Execs. Republican. Roman Catholic. Avocations: reading, writing, traveling. Home: 10907 Tony Dr Lutherville MD 21093-3618 Office: 3023 Eastern Ave Baltimore MD 21224-3902

EL-MAHDI, ANAS MORSI, retired radiation oncologist; b. Tanta, Egypt, July 7, 1935; came to U.S., 1965; m. Nancy Dale Webb; children: Samia A., Sharif A. PNS, Cairo U., 1954, MB, B.CH., 1959, DMR, 1963; ScD, Johns Hopkins U., 1970. Intern Cairo Univ. Hosps., 1960-61, resident in therapeutic radiology, 1961-63; instr. Middle Eastern Regional Radioisotope Ctr. for Arab Countries, Cairo, 1963, Cancer Inst.-Cairo U., 1963-65; instr. radiology Johns Hopkins U., Balt., 1966-67, asst. prof. radiology, 1967-71; assoc. prof. U. Va., Charlottesville, 1971-75, prof., 1975-76; prof., chmn. dept. radiation oncology & biophysics Eastern Va. Med. Sch., Norfolk, 1975-98, ret., 1998; dir. dept. radiation oncology Sentara Hosps., Norfolk, 1975-97; ACS prof. clin. oncology Am. Cancer Soc., Norfolk, 1986-91; cons. Children's Hosp. of the King's Daughters, Norfolk, 1976—, Maryview Hosp., Portsmouth, Va., 1984—, Portsmouth Gen. Hosp., 1984—; co-editor Cancer Trends, 1979—; chmn. dept. radiation oncology Va. Beach Gen. Hosp., 1983-86, active staff mem. 1984—; adj. prof. dept. physics Old Dominion U., 1984—. Contbr. numerous articles to profl. jours. Fellow Am. Coll. Radiology; mem. AAUP, AMA (Physicians Recognition award 1969, 78, 81, 84, 87, 90, 97), AAAS, Am. Assn. Cancer Rsch., Am. Soc. Therapeutic Radiology and Oncology, Radiol. Soc. N.Am., Med. Soc. Va., Mid-Atlantic Soc. for Radiation Oncologists, N.Y. Acad. Scis., Norfolk Acad. Medicine, Radiation Rsch. Soc., Soc. for Chairmen of Acad. Radiation Oncology Programs. Avocations: research, pen and ink drawing, cooking, reading.

ELMAN, GERRY JAY, lawyer; b. Chgo., Oct. 7, 1942; s. Earl Samuel and Lucille Paulyne Elman; m. Lois Suzanne Bermet Levine; children: Jason Farrel, Floren Haley. BS, U. Chgo., 1963; MS in Chemistry, Stanford U., 1964; JD, Columbia U., 1967. Bar: N.Y. 1967, U.S. Patent Office 1967, Pa. 1969, U.S. Dist. Ct. (so. and ea. dists.) N.Y., 1971, U.S. Dist. Ct. (ea. dist.) Pa. 1973, U.S. Supreme Ct. 1973, U.S. Dist. Ct. (mid. dist.) Pa. 1974, U.S. Ct. Appeals (fed. cir.), 1987, U.S. Ct. Appeals (3rd. cir.) 1989. Assoc. Hubbell, Cohen and Stiefel, N.Y.C., 1967-68; patent atty., enzymes and health products Rohm and Haas Co., Phila., 1968-72; dep. atty. gen. Pa. Dept. Justice, Harrisburg, Pa., 1972-76; trial atty. Mid. Atlantic office antitrust div. U.S. Justice Dept., Phila., 1976-82; pvt. practice, Phila., 1982-83; mem. Elman Assocs., Phila., 1984-88, Lipton, Famiglio & Elman, Media, Pa., 1988-89, Elman Wilf & Fried, Media, Pa., 1990-95, Elman & Fried, 1995-96, Elman & Assocs., 1996—; instr. short course in computer law Temple U., Phila., 1984, faculty mem. Intellectual Property Mgmt. U. Phoenix Online Campus, 1995-98. Contbg. author: Lawyers' Microcomputer Users Group Jour., 1985-88; editor: Columbia Jour. Transnat. Law, 1966-67; mem. adv. bd. Jour. Computer Law Reporter, 1983-90; mem. editorial bd. Jour. Trademark Reporter, 1968; founder, editor in chief legal jour. Biotechnology Law Report, 1982—; mem. adv. bd. BNA Spl. Reports Biotechnology, 1989-90; mem. bd. advisors Santa Clara Computer and High Tech. Law Jour., 1994—; mem. Global CyberLaw Network, 1997—; mem. adv. bd. The Licensing Jour., 1998—. Chmn. Three Steps Nursery Sch., Phila., 1977; arbitrator Phila. Ct. Common Pleas, 1971-72, 1983-88, U.S. Dist. Ct. (ea. dist.) Pa., 1983—, Am. Arbitration Assn. for computer disputes, 1987-96, Delaware County Ct. Common Pleas, Pa., 1993—; with Sysop, Ideas Inventions and Innovations Forum, CompuServe online svc., 1994—. Mem. ABA, Am. Chem. Soc., Licensing Execs. Soc., Am. Intellectual Property Law Assn., Phila. Bar Assn. (chmn. jurimetrics com. 1975-77), Phila. Intellectual Property Law Assn. (chmn. biotech. subcom. 1982-86, continuing legal edn. com. 1995-97), Del. County Bar Assn., Computer Law Assn., Benjamin Franklin Am. Inn of Ct. Home: 406 Yale Ave Swarthmore PA 19081-2024 Office: Elman & Assocs 20 W Third St Media PA 19063-2824

ELMAN, ROBERT, writer, editor; b. N.Y.C., Nov. 14, 1930; s. Dave and Pauline (Reffe) E.; m. Loris Harrington, Mar. 4, 1957 (div. 1975); children—Natalie Harrington, Thomas Harrington; m. Ellen Catherine Schwartz, Sept. 18, 1976; children—Daniel Walter, Catherine Elaine. B.S., Columbia U., 1953. Mng. editor, editor-in-chief Maco Pub. Co., N.Y.C., 1960-69; outdoors editor Ridge Press, N.Y.C., 1969-72; assoc. editor, editor-in-chief Winchester Press, N.Y.C., 1973-75; writer-in-residence Ridge Press, N.Y.C., 1975-77; editor-in-chief Winchester Press, Tulsa and Piscataway, N.J., 1979-84; writer, cons. editor, 1984—; editorial and pub. cons. Abenaki Pubs., Bennington, Vt., also other mag. and book pubs. Author: The Great American Shooting Prints, 1972, The Hiker's Bible, 1974, 2d edit., 1981, The Living World of Audubon Mammals, 1976, America's Pioneering Naturalists, 1981, Bears, 1992, The Cyclists's Bible, 1995, others. With inf. U.S. Army, 1953-55. Mem. Authors League, Authors Guild. Home: 646 S Main St Stewartsville NJ 08886-2209

ELMARSAFY, ZIAD MAGDY, educator; b. Cairo, Egypt, Feb. 16, 1967; s. Magdy Ma'noun and Aya Ahmad Mahran E. BA in Physics, Cornell U., 1986; MA in French Lit., Johns Hopkins U., 1990; PhD in French Lit., Emory U., 1992. Asst. prof. U. Calif., Riverside, 1992-93, Wellesley (Mass.) Coll., 1993-98; vis. asst. prof. NYU, N.Y.C., 1998-99. Author: The historic Sensibility: Theatricality and IUdentity from Corneille to Rousseau, 1999. NEH grantee, 1996, 97; sr. rsch. fellow Wesleyan U. Ctr. Humanities, 1996-97, A.J.A. Perry found. fellow, 1991. Mem. Am. Soc. eighteenth-Century Studies, Egyptian Am. Profl. Soc., Soic. Interdisciplinart French Seventeenth-Century Studies (exec. coun. 1993—), Modenr Lang. Assn. Office: NYU French Dept 19 Univ Pl New York NY 10003

ELMER, BRIAN CHRISTIAN, lawyer; b. Washington, Apr. 18, 1936; s. Arthur Christian and Kathryn Aleen (O'Brien) E.; m. Sonja Kay Glass, Sept. 3, 1966; children—Mark Christian, Kimberly Kay, Robin Ann. B.A. in Arts and Sci., Cornell U., Ithaca, N.Y., 1960; J.D., U. Mich., 1962. Bar: D.C. 1963. Law clk. U.S. Ct. Appeals (D.C. cir.), 1962-64; ptnr. Jones, Day, Reavis, and Pogue, Washington, 1964-79, Crowell and Moring, LLP, Washington, 1979—. Author: Fraud in Government Contracting, 1985. Contbr. articles to profl. jours. Mem. ABA, D.C. Bar Assn. Club: Metropolitan (Washington). Avocations: sailing; skiing; reading. Office: Crowell & Moring LLP 1001 Pennsylvania Ave NW Washington DC 20004-2505

ELMES, DAVID GORDON, psychologist, educator; b. Newton, Mass., Feb. 15, 1942; s. Leslie and Ruth (Adams) E.; m. Anne Louise Lawrence, June 7, 1963; children: Matthew David, Jennifer Anne. B.A., U. Va., 1964; M.A., U.Va., 1966; Ph.D., U. Va., 1967. Mgmt. trainee C & P of Va., 1963; asst. prof. psychology Washington and Lee U., Lexington, Va., 1967-71, assoc. prof., 1971-74, prof., 1975—, head dept. psychology, 1990—, co-dir. cognitive sci., 1987—; rsch. assoc. Human Performance Ctr., U. Mich., 1973-74; vis. fellow Univ. Coll., Oxford (Eng.) U., 1987; dir. rsch. in psychology at numerous undergrad. instns., 1995. Author: Readings in Experimental Psychology, 1978, Methods in Experimental Psychology, 1981, Research Methods in Psychology, 1989, Experimental Psychology: Understanding Psychological Research, 1997, Research Methods in Psychology, 1998; contbr. articles to profl. jours. Bd. dirs. Rockbridge Mental Health Clinic, 1968-73. Mem. Psychonomic Soc., Am. Psychol. Soc., Va. Acad. Sci., Coun. on Undergrad. Rsch. (pres.), Phi Beta Kappa, Sigma Xi. Home: 3 Westside Ct Lexington VA 24450-1970 Office: Dept Psychology Washington and Lee University Lexington VA 24450-0303

ELMETS, CRAIG ALLAN, dermatologist; b. Des Moines, Aug. 16, 1949; s. Harry B. and Charlotte Irene (Musin) E.; m. Laurie Beth Melamed, June 30, 1985; children: Joshua Philip, Michael William, David Benjamin. BA, U. Iowa, 1967-71, MD, 1971-75. Intern U. Kans. Med. Ctr., Kansas City, 1975-76, resident internal medicine, 1976-78; resident dermatology U. Iowa Hosps., Iowa City, 1978-80; fellow immunodermatology U. Tex. Health Sci., Dallas, 1980-82; asst. prof. dermatology Case Western Res. U., Cleve., 1982-88, asst. prof. gen. med. scis., oncology, 1987-88, assoc. prof. gen. med. scis. oncology, dermatology, 1988-94, prof. gen. med. scis. oncology, dermatology, 1994-97, assoc. prof. environ. health scis., 1991-97; attending physician U. Hosps. Cleve., 1982-97, chief immunodermatology svc., 1987-97; attending physician Cleve. VA Med. Ctr., 1990-97, chief photodermatology svc., 1994-97; prof., chmn. dept. dermatology U. Ala., Birmingham, 1997—; attending physician Birmingham VA Med. Ctr., 1997—; adj. prof. dermatology Case We. Res. U., 1997—; dir. Skin Diseases Rsch. Ctr. N.E. Ohio, NIH, 1994-1997; mem. rsch. adv. panel Rainbow Babies and Childrens Hosp., Cleve., 1990-96; mem. NIH Chem. Pathology Study Sect.; co-dir. meeting on photocarcinogenesis Current Status and Prospects for the Future, Washington, 1995. Editor: Photoimmunology, 1995; mem. editl. bd. Photodermatology, Photoimmunology, Photomedicine, 1991—, Jour. Investigative Dermatology, 1996-97, sect. editor Exptl. Dermatology, 1991—; assoc. editor Photochemistry and Photobiology, 1994-1997, Jour. Immunology, 1995—; tech. adv. com. Edison Biotech. Ctr., 1991-97; rsch. adv. com. Diabetes Assn. Greater Cleve., 1991-96; ad hoc reviewer gen. medicine study sect., NIH; contbr. articles to profl. jours. Recipient Frederic E. Mohs award Skin Cancer Found., 1986, New Investigator Rsch. award NIH, 1983-86, Rsch. Career Devel. award NIH, 1987-92. Mem. ACP, AAAS, Am. Acad. Dermatology (com. on occupl. health, com. sci. and poster exhibits, chmn. com. on scientific and poster exhibits 1995-98, EPA/NIEHS liaison com. 1995—, rsch. adv. coun. 1997—), Am. Dermatology Assn., Am. Contact Dermatitis Soc., Photomedicine Soc., Med. Dermatology Soc., Soc. Investigative Dermatology (midwest chmn. 198-89, mem. com. 1991-94, com. chmn. 1993-94), Am. Assn. Immunologists, Am. Soc. Photobiology (coun. 1997—), Am. Assn. Cancer Rsch., Ala. Dermatol. Soc. Office: Univ Alabama Dept Dermatology Univ Station PO Box 50B-76 Birmingham AL 35294-0007 Hom: 3449 Oak Canyon Dr Birmingham AL 35243-4810

ELMETS, HARRY BARNARD, osteopath, dermatologist; b. Des Moines, Apr. 22, 1920; s. William and Sara Charlotte (Ginsberg) E.; m. Charlotte Irene Musin, Dec. 9, 1945; children: Craig Allan, Steven Kent, Douglas Gregory. BA, U. Iowa, 1942; DO with distinction, Coll. Osteo. Medicine and Surgery, Des Moines, 1946; DSc (hon.), U. Osteo. Medicine/Health Sci., 1994. Intern Des Moines Gen. Hosp., 1946-47; resident in dermatology Coll. Osteo. Medicine, Des Moines, 1947-52; practice osteo. medicine specializing in dermatology Des Moines, 1952—; chief of dermatology Iowa Methodist Med. Ctr., Iowa Lutheran Hosp., Broadlawns Polk County Med. Ctr., Mercy Hosp. Med. Ctr.; clin. prof. dermatology U. Osteo. Medicine and Health Scis., 1947—; vis. prof. dermatology Kirksville Coll. Osteo. Medicine; guest lectr. Coll. Medicine U. Iowa; cons. dermatology VA Med. Ctr., Knoxville, Iowa, Iowa Dept. Health re tanning bed regulations; mem. Iowa Task Force Venereal Disease. Editorial referee Jour. Am. Osteo. Assn.; editorial bd. CUTIS, 1982—. Trustee, bd. dirs. Coll. Osteo. Medicine and Surgery, Des Moines Ctr. Sci. and Industry; co-chmn. Des Moines-Polk County Immunization Program; mem. adv. com. Iowa Dept. Pub. Health, Sci. Ctr. (hon.). Named Alumnus of Yr., Coll. Osteo. Medicine and Surgery, 1980; recipient Life Svc. award Iowa Osteopathic Med. Assn., 1997. Fellow Am. Osteo. Coll. Dermatology (pres. 1963, 71, Lifetime Achievement award); mem. Am. Osteo. Bd. Dermatology (chmn. 1962-89), Am. Osteo. Assn. (life), Iowa Soc. Osteo. Physicians and Surgeons (life), Polk County Osteo. Assn. (past pres.), Iowa Acad. Sci., Am. Social Health Assn. (bd. dirs. 1968-77), Am. Venereal Disease Soc., Am. Acad. Dermatology (life), Iowa Dermatol. Soc., Missouri Valley Dermatol. Soc., Minn. Dermatol. Soc., Nat. Assn. VA Dermatologists (charter), Wakonda Country Club, Des Moines Club, Masons, Shriners. Republican. Jewish. Home: 4238 Park Hill Dr Des Moines IA 50312-2530 Office: 1010 Midland Fin Bldg 206 6th Ave Ste 1010 Des Moines IA 50309-4017

ELMORE, EDWARD WHITEHEAD, lawyer; b. Lawrenceville, Va., July 15, 1938; s. Thomas Milton and Mary Norfleet (Whitehead) E.; m. Gail Harmon, Aug. 10, 1968; children: Mary Jennifer, Edward Whitehead Jr. B.A., U. Va.-Charlottesville, 1959, J.D., 1962. Bar: Va. 1962. Assoc. firm Hunton & Williams, Richmond, Va., 1965-69; staff atty. Ethyl Corp., Richmond, 1969-78, asst. gen. counsel, 1978-79, gen. counsel, 1979-80, gen. counsel., sec., 1980-83, v.p., gen. counsel, sec., 1983-94, spl. counsel to exec. com., corp. sec., 1994—; sr. v.p., gen. counsel, sec. Albemarle Corp., Richmond, 1994-98. Served to capt. AUS, 1962-65. Decorated Army Commendation medal. Mem. ABA, Va. Bar Assn., Internat. Bar Assn., Va. State Bar, Am. Corp. Counsel Assn., Bar Assn. Richmond, Am. Soc. Corp. Secs., Raven Soc., Phi Beta Kappa. Home: 2901 W Brigstock Rd Midlothian VA 23113-6335 Office: Albemarle Corp 330 S 4th St Richmond VA 23219-4350

ELMORE, JAMES WALTER, architect, retired university dean; b. Lincoln, Nebr., Sept. 5, 1917; s. Harry Douglas and Marie Clare (Minor) E.; m. Mary Ann Davidson, Sept. 6, 1947; children: James Davidson, Margaret Kay. A.B., U. Nebr., 1938; M.S. in Architecture, Columbia U., 1948. Mem. faculty Ariz. State U., 1949-86, prof. architecture, 1959-86, founding dean Coll. of Architecture, 1964-74; cons. architect, 1956—. Trustee Heard Museum, Phoenix, 1968-79; bd. dirs. Valley Forward Assn., 1969-89 , pres., 1985; bd. dirs. Central Ariz. chpt. Ariz. Hist. Soc., 1973-89; bd. dirs. Ariz. Architects Found., 1978-86, Rio Salado Devel. Dist., 1980-87. Served to col., C.E. U.S. Army, 1940-46. Decorated Bronze Star. Fellow AIA; mem. Ariz. Acad. Home: 6229 N 29th Pl Phoenix AZ 85016-2251

ELMORE, WALTER A., electrical engineer, consultant; b. Bartlett, Tenn., Oct. 2, 1925; s. Walter Alcorn and Lucile (Tapp) E.; m. Jane Ann Huey, June 3, 1950; children: Robin, Jamie, Laura. BSEE, U. Tenn., 1949. Registered profl. engr., Fla. Mgr. cons. engring. sect. Protective Relay div. Westinghouse Elec. Corp., Newark, 1951-79, Protective Relay div. ABB Power T & D Co., Coral Springs, Fla., 1979-89; mgr. cons. engring. sect. protective relay divsn. ABB Power T&D Co., Coral Springs, Fla., 1989-94; cons. engr. high voltage protection ABB Power T&D Co., Coral Springs, 1994-96, ret., 1996. Author: (with others) Applied Protective Relaying, 1976, Protective Relaying Theory and Application, 1994. Fellow IEEE (chmn. IEEE/PES tech. coun. 1988-89, Gold medal for engring. excellence 1989); mem. NAE, Phi Beta Pi, Eta Kappa Nu, Phi Kappa Phi. Republican. Home: 104 Macgregor Dr Blue Ridge VA 24064-1525

ELMOUCHI, JOAN LESLIE, library director; b. Atlantic City, Feb. 18, 1952; d. William Nathaniel Solkin and Ann Herman; m. Gary William Stewart (div. 1984); m. Robert Alan Elmouchi, Sept. 21, 1986. BA, Rutgers U., 1974; MLS, U. Mich., 1975. Librs. permanent profl. cert. Children's libr. Troy (Mich.) Pub. Libr., 1976-78; reference libr. Waterford Twp. (Mich.) Libr., 1979-85; libr. dir. Auburn Hills (Mich.) Libr., 1985-93, Garden City (Mich.) Libr., 1993—; adv. coun. mem. Wayne (Mich.)-Oakland Libr. Fedn., 1989-90. Author: Beach Freaks' Guide to Michigan's Best Beaches, 1999. Grantee Dept. Edn. and State Mich., 1997. Mem. ALA, Mich. Libr. Assn. (pub. libr. rep. 1994-95), Metro-Detroit Book and Author Soc. (pres. 1995-99), No Kidding! (Detroit area rep. 1997-99). Avocations: reading, cross-country skiing, dancing. E-mail: elmouchi@tln.lib.mi.us. Office: Garden City Libr 2012 Middlebelt Rd Garden City MI 48135

ELMQUIST, JOHN GUNNAR, plastic surgeon, general surgeon; b. Redlands, Calif., July 24, 1936; s. Frans Gunnar and Dagmar Caroline E.; m. Carol Jean Grindahl, Aug. 11, 1962 (div. Apr. 1980); children: Karin, Jon, Thomas; m. Regina Barbara Gatto Allen, Dec. 27, 1992. AA, N. Park U., 1956; BA, Northwe. U., 1958, MD, 1961. Diplomate Am. Bd. Surgery, Am. Bd. Plastic Surgery. Pvt. practice W. Palm Beach, Fla., 1971-96; ret., 1996. Capt. U.S. Army, 1966-68. Fellow ACS; mem. Am. Soc. Plastic and Reconstructive Surgeons, Am. Soc. Aesthetic Plastic Surgery. Republican. Lutheran. Avocations: travel, golf. Home: 12501 Pineacre Ln Wellington FL 33414

ELMS, BEN, actor, director; b. Syracuse, N.Y., July 1, 1935; s. Benjamin Charles and Sarah Mildred (Nourse) E. BA, Syracuse U., 1957. Appeared in TV shows including Unsolved Mysteries, 1990; films include Man Who Knew Too Much, 1985, The Judgement, 1990; musicals include The Fantasticks, 1987, Jesus Christ Superstar, 1987; plays include Death of a Salesman, 1989, Foxfire, 1991, Noises Off, 1996; dir. plays including Butterflies Are Free, 1978, Extremities, 1987; also commls. Capt. U.S. Army, 1958-60. Mem. SAG, Actors Equity Assn. Republican. Roman Catholic. Home: 60 Presidential Plz Syracuse NY 13202-2292

ELMSTROM, GEORGE P., optometrist, writer; b. Salem, Mass., Dec. 11, 1925; s. George and Emily Irene (Wedgwood) E.; grad. So. Calif. Coll. Optometry, 1951; m. Nancy DePaul, Apr. 29, 1973; children—Pamela, Beverly, Robert. Pvt. practice optometry, El Segundo, Calif., 1951—; mem. staff So. Calif. Coll. Optometry, 1951—; book cons. Med. Econs. Books, 1970—; instrument and forensic editor Jour. Am. Optical Assn.; comml. airplane and balloon pilot, 1968—. Served with U.S. Army, World War II. Decorated Silver Star; named Writer of Year, Calif. Optometric Assn., 1957, Man of Year, El Segundo, 1956; recipient spl. citation Nat. Eye Found., 1955. Fellow Am. Acad. Optometry, AAAS, Southwest Contact Lens Soc., Disting. Service Found. of Optometry, Internat. Acad. Preventive Medicine; mem. Am. Optometric Assn., Assn. for Research in Vision, Am. Soc. Ultrasonography, Am. Pub. Health Assn., Optometric Editors Assn., Assn. Research in Vision, Internat. Soc. Ophthalmic Ultrasound, Profl. Airshow Pilots Assn., Flying Optometrists Assn. Am., Beta Sigma Kappa, So. Calif. Coll. Optometry Alumni (pres. 1955-56). Author: Optometric Practice Management, 1963; Legal Aspects of Contact Lens Practice, 1966; Advanced Management for Optometrists, 1974; Modernized Management, 1982; mgmt. editor Optometric Monthly, 1973. Home: 484 Washington St Ste B Monterey CA 93940-3052 Office: PO Box S-3061 Carmel CA 93921-3061

ELOFSON, NANCY MEYER, retired office equipment company executive; b. Glencoe, Ill., Jan. 27, 1923; d. Bernard Francis and Agnes (Ulbrich) Meyer; m. Carl L. Elofson, Nov. 27, 1946 (dec. Dec. 1991); 1 child, Peter Carl. BA, Western Coll., 1944; postgrad., SUNY, Jamestown, 1960-80. Sales corr. Scott, Foresman Pub., Chgo., 1944-46; sec., treas. Office Machines and Equipment Co., Jamestown, 1948-86; ret., 1986—. Mem. coun. camp com. Girl Scouts U.S.A., Jamestown, 1962-66, mem. alumnae archives com., 1992—; candidate Chautauqua County Legis., 1979; mem. choir 1st Congl. United Ch. of Christ, Jamestown, 1948—, moderator, 1978-79, ch. clk., 1995, mem. ch. coun., 1990-95, chmn. 175th anniversary com., 1990-91, mem. ch. growth com., mem. long range planning com., 1993-95, trustee, 1996—; mem. ch. and ministry com. Western area N.Y. conf. United Ch. of Christ, 1997—; founder, pres. bd. dirs. Chautauqua Adult Day Care Ctrs., Inc., Jamestown, 1981-91, bd. dirs., 1981—; pres. bd. dirs. YWCA, Jamestown, 1983-85, trustee, 1987—; mem. exec. bd./com. United Way, Jamestown, 1991-96, allocations chmn., 1991-95, chmn. planning com., 1996; active Chautauqua County Domestic Violence Guidance Team, 1994; pres. Inter-Club Coun., 1997—. Named Chautauqua County Caregiver of Yr., Chautauqua County Office of Aging, 1988, Vol. of Yr., United Way, 1992, Woman of 1996 Yr., Jamestown, 1997; recipient Caregiver's award N.Y. State Office of Aging, 1988, Women Making a Difference award Jamestown Post Jour., 1991. Mem. AAUW (sec. 1948), Women's Polit. Caucus, Jamestown Audubon Soc., Jamestown Koinonia, Roger Tory Peterson Inst., Lucille Ball Little Theatre Jamestown, The Fortnightly Allied Arts, Interclub Coun. (pres.). Avocations: human and elder svcs., sailing, gardening, singing, music. Home: 81 Gordon St Jamestown NY 14701-1641

ELROD, BEN MOODY, academic administrator; b. Rison, Ark., Oct. 13, 1930; s. Benjamin Searcy and Frances Othello (Sadler) E.; m. Betty Lou Warren, Aug. 7, 1951; children: Cynthia Lou, William Searcy. BA, Ouachita Baptist U., 1952; ThD, Southwestern Bapt. Theol. Sem., 1962; EdD, Ind. U., 1975. Ordained to ministry Baptist Ch., 1950; pastor First Bapt. Ch., Atkins, Ark., 1951-53, Tioga, Tex., 1955-57, Marlow, Okla., 1957-60; pastor South Side Bapt. Ch., Pine Bluff, Ark., 1960-63; pres. Oakland City (Ind.) Coll., 1968-70, Georgetown (Ky.) Coll., 1978-83, Ind. Colls. of Ark., 1983-88; v.p. devel. Ouachita Bapt. U., Arkadelphia, Ark., 1963-68, 70-78, pres., 1988-97, chancellor, 1998—; vis. lectr. in field; cons. higher edn. Contbr. articles to religion jours. Page U.S. Ho. of Reps., 1946-47; trustee Clark County (Ark.) Hosp., 1973-77, chmn., 1975-77; trustee Ark. Bapt. Med. System, 1978, 89—. Mem. Nat. Assn. Ind. Colls. and Univs. (chmn. tax policy commn. 1993), Ark. State C. of C. (bd. dirs. 1990—), Assn. So. Bapt. Colls. and Schs. (pres. 1996-97), Consortium for Global Edn. (chmn. bd. dirs. 1997—). Democrat. Home: 1008 Village Dr Arkadelphia AR 71923-3608 Office: Ouachita Bapt Univ Ouachita Sta Arkadelphia AR 71923-3221

ELROD, EUGENE RICHARD, lawyer; b. Roanoke, Ala., May 14, 1949; s. James Woodrow and Selma Fromer (Steinbach) E. AB, Dartmouth Coll., 1971; JD, Emory U., 1974. Bar: Ga. 1974, D.C. 1976, U.S. Ct. Appeals (D.C. cir.) 1985, U.S. Ct. Appeals (5th cir.) 1987, U.S. Dist. Ct. D.C. 1987, U.S. Ct. Appeals (11th cir.) 1987, U.S. Supreme Ct. 1987, U.S. Ct. Appeals

(10th cir.) 1997. Trial atty. Fed. Power Com., Washington, 1974-76; atty.-advisor Fed. Energy Adminstrn., Washington, 1977; assoc. Sidley & Austin, Washington, 1977-80, ptnr., 1981—; mem. adv. bd. The Keplinger Cos., Houston. Mem. selection com. for Woodruff scholars Emory U. Law Sch., Dartmouth '71 Exec. Com. Mem. ABA, D.C. Bar Assn., Ga. Bar Assn., Fed. Energy Bar Assn. (chmn. oil pipeline com. 1982-83, tax com. 1980-81, 92-95, liaison with adminstrv. law judges 1986-87, ethics com. 1997—), Dartmouth Club (exec. com. class of 1971), Book Club of Calif. Avocations: running, book collecting, gardening. Home: 4300 Hawthorne St NW Washington DC 20016-3571 Office: Sidley & Austin 1722 I St NW Fl 7 Washington DC 20006-3795

ELROD, JOHN WILLIAM, university president, philosophy and religion educator; b. Griffin, Ga., Jan. 21, 1940; s. John Charles and Carolyn (Barnette) E.; m. Mimi Cobb Milner, Aug. 3, 1963; children—Adam Milner, Joshua O'Beirne. BA, Presbyn. Coll., Clinton, S.C., 1962; MA, Columbia U., 1967, PhD, 1971. Asst. prof. philosophy Iowa State U., Ames, 1971-75, assoc. prof., 1975-81, prof., 1981-84, chmn. dept., 1979-84; prof. philosophy Washington and Lee U., Lexington, Va., 1984—, dean Coll., 1984-88, v.p. acad. affairs, dean, 1987-95, acting pres., 1988, pres., 1995—; acad. cons. So. Assn. Colls. and Schs. Author: Being and Existence in Kierkegaard's Pseudonymous Works, 1975, Kierkegaard and Christendom, 1981; assoc. editor Jour. Philosophy of Religion, 1974-83; mem. adv. bd. Kierkegaard's Writings, 1977-85, Internat. Kierkegaard Commentary, 1981-85; contbr. articles to profl. jours. NEH fellow, 1976; grantee Am. Philos. Soc., 1977, Iowa State U., 1977, 80, 82, Iowa Bd. for Pub. Programming in Humanities, 1980. Mem. Am. Philos. Assn., Am. Acad. Religion, Soc. Philosophy of Religion (v.p. 1985—), Metaphys. Soc. Am., Soc. for Christian Philosophy, Phi Beta Kappa, Omicron Delta Kappa. Democrat. Presbyterian. Avocations: tennis; jogging; music; birding. Home: 2 University Pl Lexington VA 24450-2114 Office: Washington & Lee U Office of President Lexington VA 24450

ELROD, LINDA DIANE HENRY, lawyer, educator; b. Topeka, Kans., Mar. 6, 1947; d. Lyndus Arthur Henry and Marjorie Jane (Hammel) Allen; divorced; children: Carson Douglas, Bree Elizabeth. BA in English with honors, Washburn U., 1969, JD cum laude, 1971. Bar: Kans. 1972. Instr. U. S.D., Topeka, 1970-71; research atty. Kans. Jud. Council, Topeka, 1972-74; asst. prof. Washburn U., Topeka, 1974-78, assoc. prof., 1978-82, prof. law, 1982-93; disting. prof., 1993—; vis. prof. law U. San Diego, Paris Summer Inst., 1988, 90, Washington U. Sch. Law, St. Louis, 1990, 98, summer 1991, 93. Author: Kansas Family Law Handbook, 1983, rev. edit., 1990, supplement, 1993, Child Custody Practice and Procedure, 1993, supplements, 1994-97, 99; co-author: Principle of Family Law, 1999, Kansas Family Law Guide, 1999; editor Family Law Quar., 1992—; contbr. articles to profl. jours. Pres. YWCA, Topeka, 1982-83; vice-chair Kans. Commn. on Child Support, 1984-87, Supreme Ct. Com. on Child Support, 1989—; chair Kans. Cmty. Svc. Orgn., 1986-87; adv. bd. CASA, 1997—. Recipient Disting. Service award Washburn Law Sch. Assn., 1986; named woman of distinction YWCA, 1997. Mem. ABA (coun. family law sect. 1988-92, sec. 1998, vice-chair, 1999, chair Schwab Meml. Grant Implementation 1984-87, co-chair Amicus Curiae com. 1987-92), Topeka Bar Assn. (sec. 1981-85, v.p. 1985-86, pres. 1986-87), Kans. Child Support Enforcement Assn. (bd. dirs. 1988—, Child Support Hall of Fame 1990), Kans. Bar Assn. (sec.-treas. 1988-89, com. ops. and fin. 1988, pres. family law sect. 1984-86, Disting. Svc. award 1985), NONOSO, Phi Kappa Phi, Phi Alpha Delta Alumni Assn. (justice 1976-77), Phi Beta Delta, Kappa Alpha Theta (pres. alumnae chpt. 1995-97). Presbyterian. Avocations: bridge, reading, quilting. Office: Washburn U Law Sch 17th and College Topeka KS 66621

ELROD, LU, music educator, actress, author; b. Chattanooga, Tenn., Apr. 23, 1935; d. John C. Elrod and Helen Pauline (Kohn). MusB, Ga. State U., 1960; M in Music Edn., U. Ga., 1970, EdD, 1971; PhD, U. London, 1975. Prof. music, music coach U. Md., Balt., 1972-78, Calif. State U., L.A., 1978—; singer with Dallas (Tex.) Opera, 1957. Appeared in movies Wag the Dog, 1997, The Big Lebowski, 1998, Brewster's Millions, 1986, Major Pettigrew and Me, 1976, Seduction of Joe Tynan, 1977, Atlanta Child Murders, 1985, Children Don't Tell, 1986, For Love or Money, 1986, High School High, 1996, Primary Colors, 1998, Lloyd the Ugly Kid, 1999; appeared on TV in Lazarus Syndrome, 1980, Hill Street Blues (Emmy award), 1988, Superior Court, 1988, TV Bloopers, 1989, Beakman's World (Emmy award), Dream On, 1993, Misery Loves Company, 1995, Caroline in the City, 1995, Louie, 1996, George and Alana, 1996, Maggie, 1998; appeared in TV comls. Recipient Leadership Devel. award Ford Found., 1967, Leadership Fellows award Ford Found., 1968; Tift Coll. voice scholar, 1953, Baylor U. voice scholar, 1956; Lu Elrod scholarship named at Calif. State U., L.A., 1989. Mem. AAUP, AFTRA, SAG, Am. Guild Variety Artists, Calif. Faculty Assn., Coll. Music Soc. Avocations: philanthropy, fundraising. Office: Calif State Univ 5151 State University Dr Los Angeles CA 90032-4226

ELS, THEODORE ERNEST, professional golfer; b. Kempton Park, South Africa, Oct. 17, 1969; s. Cornelius and Hester E. Diploma, Jan de Klerk Tech. Coll. Winner numerous matches, including U.S. Open 1994, World Match Play Championship, 1994-96, Buick Classic, 1996-97, U.S. Open, 1997; named PGA European Player of Yr., 1994; South African Sportsman of the Yr., 1994, winner Bay Hill Invitational, 1998. Mem. Kempton Park Golf. Avocations: squash, movies. Address: 46 Chapman Rd, Klippoortjie 1401, South Africa*

ELSAESSER, ROBERT JAMES, retired manufacturing executive; b. Canton, Ohio, June 25, 1926; s. Otto Louis and Rose Augusta (Hoera) E.; m. Norma Ruth Adams, June 25, 1934. BA, Denison U., 1949. With Janson Industries, Canton, Ohio, 1949, Ins. Co. North Am., Cleve., 1950-51; with The Hoover Co., San Francisco, 1952-88, br. office mgr., 1952-53; dist. mgr. The Hoover Co., Fresno, Calif., 1954, Santa Clara, Calif., 1954-55, Sacramento, 1956-60; br. mgr. The Hoover Co., San Francisco, 1961-63, Kansas City, Mo., 1964-66; div. mgr. of div. 5000 The Hoover Co., Kansas City, 1967-68; mgr. distributor sales and spl. accounts The Hoover Co., North Canton, Ohio, 1969-71; v.p. export western region The Hoover Co., North Canton, 1972-74, sr. v.p., 1975-82; dir. Hoover Worldwide Corp., North Canton, 1981; exec. v.p., dir. The Hoover Co., North Canton, 1982-88, pres., 1988, ret., 1988; Pres. Hoover Mexicana S.A. de C.V., Hoover Indsl. y Comml. S.A.; bd. dirs. The Hoover Co. and Hoover Worldwide Corp.; trustee Stark Devel., 1987-88; chmn. Juver Indsl. S.A. de C.V., 1985-88. Mem. adv. bd. Leadership Canton, 1987-88; exec. adv. council Jr. Achievement, 1985-88. With USAAF, 1944-45. Mem. U.S. and Mex. C. of C. (bd. dirs., exec. com. 1983-89), Blue Coats, Brookside Country Club (bd. dirs. 1977, 79), Phi Delta Theta. Republican. Avocation: golf. Home: 182 Turtle Creek Dr Tequesta FL 33469 also: 2730 Brentwood Dr NW Canton OH 44708-1310 Office: Hoover Co 101 E Maple St Canton OH 44720-2597

ELSAS, LOUIS JACOB, II, medical educator; b. Atlanta, Feb. 10, 1937; s. Herbert R. and Edith (Levy) E.; m. Nancy Terrell, July 15, 1961; children: Nancy Louise, Margaret Edith, Louis Jacob, III. B.A., Harvard U., 1958; M.D., U. Va., 1962. Diplomate: Am. Bd. Internal Medicine, Am. Bd. Med. Genetics. Intern Yale-New Haven Hosp., 1962-63, resident in internal medicine, 1963-65; NIH postdoctoral fellow in med. genetics Yale U., 1965-68, from instr. to assoc. prof. sect. genetics, dept. medicine and pediatrics, 1968-70; mem. faculty Emory U. Med. Sch., 1970—, prof. pediatrics and biochemistry, 1977—, dir. med. genetics, 1970—; dir. Ga. Comprehensive Genetic System, 1978; vis. prof. Japan Soc. Promotion Sci., 1976; Professore a contratto, Italy, 1985—; U.S. advisor Congress of Inborn Errors of Metabolism, 1980. Contbr. numerous articles to profl. jours. Recipient Rsch. Career Devel. award NIH, 1972-77, John Horsley Meml. prize U. Va. Med. Sch., 1972, A.E. Levy Faculty Rsch. award Emory U., 1989, Big Heart award Civitans, 1992; named hon. citizen Interlaken, Switzerland, 1980. Fellow Am. Acad. Pediat., Am. Coll. Med. Genetics (founder, bd. dirs. 1996—); mem. Soc. Inherited Metabolic Disorders (founding pres.), Am. Soc. Clin. Investigation, Soc. Pediat. Rsch., Am. Soc. Biol. Chemistry, Am. Soc. Human Genetics, Assn. Am. Physicians, Assn. Profs. Human and Med. Genetics (pres. 1998—), S.E. Genetics Group (chmn. 1983-94), Coun. Regional Networks (pres. 1994—), Sigma Xi (past chpt. pres.). Clubs: Emory U. Faculty, Druid Hills Golf, Civitan (Humanitarian award 1979, Big Heart award 1992), The Temple. Home: 858 Oakdale Rd NE Atlanta GA 30307-1210 Office: Emory U 2040 Ridgewood Dr NE Atlanta GA 30322-1028 *The successful biomedical scientist must develop a personal balance between science and humanism; innovation and application; learning and teaching. This goal can be met if one starts at an early age and continues as a student of fundamental science; is curious and tests central dogma; uses truth and the scientific method as standards of conduct and is sympathetic to the needs of individuals and society.*

ELSASSER, GLEN ROBERT, journalist; b. Marion, Ohio, Oct. 18, 1935; s. Glen Robert and Mary Louise (Hogan) E.; m. Katharine Macy Kersting, Sept. 8, 1973; 1 child, Daniel. BA, Ohio State U., 1957; MS, Columbia U. Sch. Journalism, 1961. Reporter UPI, Louisville, 1957-58; reporter, writer Indpls. Star, 1961-63; reporter, writer, editor Chgo. Tribune, Chgo., N.Y.C., Washington, 1963—. With U.S. Army, 1958-60, Kansas City, Mo. Recipient Gavel award ABA, 1979. Home: 319 C St NE Washington DC 20002-5709 Office: Chgo Tribune 1325 G St NW Ste 200 Washington DC 20005-3104

EL-SAYED, MOSTAFA AMR, chemistry educator; b. Zifta, Egypt, May 8, 1933; s. Amr and Zakia (Ahmed) El-Sayed; m. Janice Jones, Mar. 15, 1957; children—Lyla, Tarric, James, Dorea Jehan, Ivan Homer. BSc, Ein Shams U., Cairo, 1953; PhD, Fla. State U., 1959; Dr honoris causa, Hebrew U., 1993. Research fellow Yale U., 1957; research fellow Harvard U., 1959-60, Calif. Inst. Tech., 1960, 61; asst. prof. chemistry UCLA, 1961-64, assoc. prof. chemistry, 1964-67, prof. chemistry, 1967-94; Julius Brown prof. Ga. Inst. Tech., 1994—; vis. prof. Am. U. Beirut, 1967-68; fgn. prof. U. So. Paris, Orsay, 1976; Sherman Fairchild disting. scholar Calif. Inst. Tech., 1980; cons. Space Tech. Lab, 1962-63, Electro-Optical System, 1963-66, N.Am. Aviation, 1964-65, Navy Electronics Labs., 1969-73, Ford Research Labs., 1970, Northrop Corp., 1979-81; mem. adv. bd. Alexandria Research Ctr., 1979-83; trustee Associated Univs., 1988; mem. steering com. Internat. Ctr. Pure and Applied Chemistry, Trieste, Italy, 1988. Mem. adv. bd. Chem. Physics, Chem. Physics Letters and Accounts of Chem. Research; contbr. numerous articles to profl. jours., chpts. to books. Mem. chemistry grant selection com. NRC of Can.; mem. chemistry research evaluation panel for directorate of chem. scis. Air Force Office of Sci. Research; mem. rev. com. San Francisco Laser Ctr., radiation lab Notre Dame U., dept. energy and environment Lawrence Berkeley Lab.; mem. NRC com. to survey opportunities in chemistry; mem. vis. com. Brookhaven Nat. Lab., 1986—. Recipient Disting. Teaching award UCLA, 1964; Fresenius nat. award in pure and applied chemistry, 1967; McCoy Research award, chemistry dept. UCLA, 1969, Harris award U. Nebr., 1995; Alexander von Humboldt Sr. U.S. Scientist award Fed. Republic Germany, 1982; King Faisal Internat. Prize in Sci. (Chemistry), 1990. Mem. Am. Chem. Soc. (Gold Medal award Calif. sect. 1971, editor in chief Jour. Phys. Chemistry 1980—and editor Internat. Revs. Phys. Chemistry 1984-90, Tolman award 1990, Fla. sect. award 1999), NAS (elected), Am. Acad. Arts and Scis. (elected), AAUP, AAAS, Assn. for Harvard Chemists, Western Spectroscopy Assn., N.Y. Acad. Scis., Third World Acad. Scis. (elected), Phys. Chemistry Div. Internat. Union Pure and Applied Chemistry (elected, vice chmn. U.S. NRC com. 1987, chmn. 1992). Office: Ga Tech Sch of Chemistry & Biochemistry Atlanta GA 30332

ELSE, CAROLYN JOAN, library system administrator; b. Mpls., Jan. 31, 1934; d. Elmer Oscar and Irma Carolyn (Seibert) Wahlberg; m. Floyd Warren Else, 1962 (div. 1968); children: Stephen Alexander, Catherine Elizabeth. B.S. Stanford U., 1956; M.L.S., U. Wash., 1957. Cert. prof. librarian, Wash. Librarian Queens Borough Pub. Library, N.Y.C., 1957-59, U.S. Army Special Services, France, Germany, 1959-62; info. librarian Bennett Martin Library, Lincoln, Neb., 1962-63; br. librarian Pierce County Library, Tacoma, Wash., 1963-65, dir., 1965-94. Bd. dirs. Campfire, Tacoma, 1984-92, Cmty. Health Care, 1997—; mem. study commn. Wash. State Local Governance, 1985-88; mem. Higher Edn. Coun. South Puget Sound, 1988-92. Mem. ALA, Wash. Library Assn. (v.p. 1969-71), Pacific Northwest Library Assn. (sec. 1969-71), City Club (Tacoma), Tacoma Rotary # 8 Club (bd. dirs. 1995-97).

ELSEN, JON, editor, columnist; b. N.Y.C., Dec. 26, 1959; s. Sheldon H. and Gerri (Sharfman) E. BA, Columbia U., 1981. Reporter Jour. Inquiror, Manchester, Conn., 1981-86, The Hartford (Conn.) Courant, 1986-89, The Record, Hackensack, N.J., 1989-90; editor New York Times New Media Group, N.Y.C., 1991-95; reporter, editor Investment Dealer's Digest, N.Y.C., 1995-97; dep. bus. editor, columnist The New York Post, N.Y.C., 1997—. Mem. N.Y. Fin. Writers Assn. Jewish. Office: The New York Post 1211 Ave of the Americas 10th Fl New York NY 10036-8790

ELSEN, SHELDON HOWARD, lawyer; b. Pitts., May 12, 1928; m. Gerri Sharfman, 1952; children: Susan Rachel, Jonathan Charles. AB, Princeton U., 1950; AM, Harvard U., 1952, JD, 1958. Bar: N.Y. 1959, U.S. Supreme Ct. 1971. Ptnr. Orans, Elsen & Lupert, N.Y.C., 1965—; adj. prof. law Columbia U. Law Sch., 1969—; chief counsel N.Y. Moreland Act Commn. on UDC, 1975-76; asst. U.S. atty. So. Dist. N.Y., 1960-64; cons. Pres.'s Commn. Law Enforcement Adminstrn. Justice, 1967; mem. faculty Nat. Inst. Trial Advocacy, 1973; mem. 1st dept. disciplinary com. N.Y., 1990-96. Contbr. articles to legal jours. Fellow Am. Coll. Trial Lawyers; mem. Assn. of Bar of City of N.Y. (v.p. 1988-89, chmn. com. on fed. legislation 1969-72, chmn. com. on fed. cts. 1983-86, chmn. nominating com. 1986-87, chmn. com. amenities in land use process for N.Y.C. 1987-88), Am. Law Inst., Phi Beta Kappa. Home: 50 Fenimore Rd Scarsdale NY 10583-2251 Office: 1 Rockefeller Plz New York NY 10020-2102

ELSEY, GEORGE MCKEE, foundation administrator; b. Palo Alto, Calif., Feb. 5, 1918; s. Howard McKee and Ethel May (Daniels) E.; m. Sally Phelps Bradley, Dec. 15, 1951; children: Anne Bradley (Mrs. Roger Kranz), Howard McKee. A.B., Princeton U., 1939; A.M., Harvard U., 1940; L.H.D., Am. Internat. Coll., 1982. Mem. staff The White House, 1947-53; with ARC, 1953-61, v.p., 1958-61; with various divs. Pullman Inc., 1961-65, asst. to chmn. and pres., 1966-70; pres. Am. Nat. Red Cross, 1970-82, pres. emeritus, 1983—; bd. dirs. Security Storage Co.; bd. dirs. Suburban Health Found., chmn., 1996-98; mem. Washington adv. bd. MNC Fin., 1991-93; bd. dirs. The White House Hist. Assn., pres., 1990-95. cres. Meridian House Internat., Washington, 1961-66, vice chmn., 1967-68, counselor, 1971—; trustee Brookings Instn., 1971-83, George C. Marshall Rsch. Found., 1973-83, Harry S. Truman Libr. Inst., 1973-95, PCC Charitable Found., 1997—; mem. Nat. Archives Adv. Coun., 1974-79, mem. com. on presdl. librs., 1988-95; trustee emeritus Nat. Trust Hist. Preservation, 1976—; fin. chmn. League Red Cross and Red Crescent Socs., Geneva, 1977-87; bd. dirs. U.S. Capitol Hist. Soc., 1993-95. Comdr. USNR, 1941-47. Decorated Legion of Merit, Order Brit. Empire, medals from Red Cross Socs. Finland, Korea, Greece, Netherlands, Fed. Republic Germany, Can. and Magen David Adom (Israel), comdr. Order of St. John; recipient Disting. Pub. Svc. medal Dept. Def. Internat. Humanitarian award Am. Red Mogen David for Israel, Henry Dunant medal Internat. Red Cross and Red Crescent, 1989. Mem. AAAS, Hist. Soc. Washington, Nat. Geog. Soc. (trustee 1977-93), Nat. Alliance for Mentally Ill, Princeton Club (N.Y.), Met. Club (Washington), City Tavern Club (Washington), White House Mil. Aides Assn. (hon. chmn. 1998—), Phi Beta Kappa. Presbyterian. Home: 5351 Macarthur Blvd NW Washington DC 20016-2539

EL-SHERIF, MAHMOUD A., electrical engineering educator; b. Cairo, July 7, 1942; came to U.S., 1981; s. Abd-El-Rahman E. and Hakmat Kaleb (El-Saied) E.; m. Jeylan Talaat El-Mansoury, Mar. 15, 1950; children: Dina, Dalia, Mohamed. BSc in Comm. Engring., Cairo U., 1966; Diploma in Electronic Engring., Alexandria (Egypt) U., 1977, MSc in Electro-Physics, 1980; MSEE, U. Pa., 1983; PhD in Elec. Engring., Drexel U., 1987. Engr. The Egyptian Telecom. Orgn., Cairo, 1966-67; radar instr. Air Def. Inst., Alexandria, 1967-77, radar dept. chmn., 1977-81; dean engring. edn. Air Def. Coll., Alexandria, 1987-89; rsch. prof. Drexel U., Phila., 1989-94, dir., founder Fiber Optics and Photonics Lab., 1994—, dir., founder Fiber Optics and Photonics Mfg. Engring. Ctr., 1997—; prin. investigator NASA Lewis Rsch. Ctr., 1991-95, Dept. Def., 1990—; pres. Photonics, Inc., Wilmington, Del. and Phila., 1990—; cons. David Sarnoff Rsch. Ctr., Princeton, 1996—. Mem. laser tech. delegation U.S. Citizen Ambassador Program, Spokane, Wash., 1996—. Recipient 1st Class Medal of Disting. Performance, Pres. of Egypt, 1971, Medal and cert. of Appreciation, Egyptian Engring. assn., 1987. Fellow Optical Soc. Am.; mem. IEEE, Am. Ceramic Soc., Internat. Soc. Optical Engrs., Soc. for Advancement of Material and Processing Engrs. Achievements include research on optical fibers as active devices; inventor first fiber-optic modulator, coupler, switch and multiplexers; inventor novel structure of Bragg optical fibers; novel process for manufacturing of sapphire optical fibers (core, clad, jacket) for IR transmission and application up to 1700 degrees centegrade; leadership in design/development of intelligent and smart structures with fiber optic systems embedded in materials for in-situ real-time characterization and health monitoring of stuctures; development of smart soldier's uniform with embedded fiber optic biological sensors for automatic detection of battle field biological threats. Avocations: chess, travel, history, movies, classical music. Home: 1117 Hillcrest Rd Narberth PA 19072-1223 Office: Drexel Univ Dept Material Engring 32d and Chestnut Sts Philadelphia PA 19104

ELSHTAIN, JEAN BETHKE, social and political ethics educator; b. Windsor, Colo., Jan. 6, 1941; d. Paul G. and Helen L. Bethke; m. Errol L. Elsthain, Sept. 3, 1965; children: Sheri, Heidi, Jenny, Eric. BA in History, Colo. State U., 1963; MA in History, U. Colo., 1965; PhD in Politics, Brandeis U., 1973; LLD (hon.), Gonzaga U., 1996; DHL (hon.), Valparaiso U., 1996, Grinell Coll., 1997, Maryville U., 1997, Messiah Coll., 1999. Prof. polit. sci. U. Mass., Amherst, 1973-88, Vanderbilt U., Nashville, 1988-94; vis. prof. Harvard U., Cambridge, Mass., 1994; prof. ethics U. Chgo., 1995—. Author: Public Man, Private Woman: Women in Social and Political Thought, 1982, 2d edit., 1992 (Top Choice acad. book), Women and War, 1987, Japanese translation, 1994, Power Trips and Other Journeys, Essays on Feminism as Civic Discourse, 1990, Meditations on Modern Political Thought: Masculine/Feminine Themes Luther to Arendt, 1992, Democracy on Trial, 1995, Augustine and the Limits of Politics, 1996; co-author: But Was It Just? Reflections on the Morality of the Gulf War, 1992; editor: The Family in Political Thought, 1982, Just War Theory, 1991; co-editor: Women, Militarism and War, 1990, Politics and the Human Body, 1995, Promise to Keep, Decline and Renewal of Marriage in America, 1996, Real Politics, Political Theory and Everyday Life, 1997, New Wine in Old Bottles: International Politics and Ethical Discourse, 1998. Trustee Inst. for Advanced Study, 1994-99, Nat. Humanities Ctr., N.C., 1996—; chair Coun. on Civil Soc., N.Y.C. and Chgo., 1995—, Coun. on Families in Am., N.Y.C., 1995—. Fellow AAAS; mem. Am. Polit. Sci. Assn. (v.p. 1998—), Am. Soc. Polit. and Legal Philosophy (v.p. 1996-97). Avocations: movies, reading. Home: 4010 Wallace Ln Nashville TN 37215 Office: U Chgo Div Sch 1025 E 58th St Chicago IL 60637

ELSILA, DAVID AUGUST, editor; b. Detroit, Feb. 2, 1939; s. Edward J. and Sylvia (Mikkola) E.; m. Kathlyn Deutch, July 17, 1965; children: Mikael, Jamie and Kari (twins). B.A., Eastern Mich. U., 1960, postgrad., 1962. Tchr. pub. schs. Livonia, Mich., 1960-64; editor-in-chief Livonia Observer, 1964-65; dir. publs., editor Am. Tchr., also, Changing Edn., Am. Fedn. Tchrs., Washington, 1965-76; editor UAW Solidarity, 1976-97; asst. dir. pub. rels. and publs. dept. UAW, 1976-98; sr. editor Working USA, 1997—; editor ofcl. publs. ACLU, Ill., Mich., 1964-67; del. Greater Washington Ctrl. Labor Coun., AFL-CIO; mem. adv. bd. dirs. TV show We Do The Work, 1992—. Co-author: Union Town: A Labor History Guide to Detroit, 1980; contbg. author: Working Detroit, 1986, The New Labor Press, 1992. Nat. sec. Workers Edn. Local 189, 1978-86, Great Lakes bd. mem., 1986-88, Mich. chpt. bd. mem., 1992—, exec. bd., 1994—; co-chair Detroit Laborfest, 1997, 98, 99. Recipient Page 1 award Chgo. Newspaper Guild, 1967, 1st awards in journalism Internat. Labor Comm. Assn., 1968-69, 72-73, 75-76, 83-97, 1st awards in journalism Ednl. Press Assn. Am., 1968-76, Joady award Film Arts Found., 1991, Pollie award Am. Assn. Polit. Cons., 1992, Max Steinbock award, Saul Miller award Internat. Labor Comm. Assn., 1996, Eugene V. Debs award Dem. Socialists of Am., 1998. Mem. Washington-Balt. Newspaper Guild (mem. exec. bd. 1970-71), Detroit Newspaper Guild, Ednl. Press Assn. Am. (pres. Washington chpt. 1971), Internat. Labor Comms. Assn. (v.p. 1983-89, sec.-treas. 1990-91), ACLU (mem. exec. bd. Detroit chpt. 1993—), Phi Delta Kappa. Home: 1411 Three Mile Dr Grosse Pointe MI 48230-1125

ELSMAN, JAMES LEONARD, JR., lawyer; b. Kalamazoo, Sept. 10, 1936; s. James Leonard and Dorothy Isabell (Pierce) E.; m. Janice Marie Wilczewski, Aug. 6, 1960; children—Stephanie, James Leonard III. *Grandfather Leonard Elsman, immigrated into the US in early 1900s, from The Netherlands (Freesland), but mother's lineage was Native Indian, German, English and Irish. All Common people who believed the Bible re lineage: "And He made from one (common origin, one source, one blood) all nations of men to settle on the face of the earth." - The Amplified Bible - Zondervan Acts 17:26.* B.A., U. Mich., 1958, J.D., 1962; postgrad., Harvard Div. Sch., 1958-59. Bar: Mich. 1963. Clk. Mich. Atty. Gen.'s Office, Lansing, 1961; atty. legal dept. Chrysler Corp., Detroit, 1962-64; founding ptnr. Elsman, Young, O'Rourke, Bruno & Bunn, Birmingham, Mich., 1964-72; pvt. practice Elsman Law Firm, Birmingham, 1972—; owner Radio Sta. WOLY, Battle Creek, Mich. Author: The Seekers, 1962; screenplay, 1976, 200 Candles to Whom?, 1973; contbr. articles to profl. jours.; Composer, 1974, 76; talk show host Citizen's Court, TV-48, Detroit. Mem. Regional Export Expansion Coun., 1966-73, Mich. Ptnrs. for Alliance for Progress, 1969-80; cand. U.S. Senate, 1966, 76, 94, 96, U.S. Ho. of Reps. 1970, Rockefeller Bros. Found. fellow Harvard Div. Sch., 1959. Mem. ABA, Am. Soc. Internat. Law, Econ. Club Detroit, World Peace Through Law Center, Full Gospel Businessmen, Bloomfield Open Hunt Club, Pres. Club (U. Mich.), Circumnavigators Club, Naples Bath and Tennis, Rotary. Republican. Mem. Christian Ch. Home: 4811 Burnley Dr Bloomfield Hills MI 48304-3781 Office: 635 Elm St Birmingham MI 48009-6768 *Christianity is not a religion. It is knowing Jesus, i.e. God, personally. It does not hinge on man's works or effort. Christianity is the only way to God, as Christ is the only Mediator between God and man. Choose! You can be sincerely wrong and still go to Hell eternally. Just A country lawyer in a big city, representing the common man in mass tort and class actions and other litigation, whose priority client is Jesus.*

ELSON, ALEX, lawyer, educator, arbitrator; b. nr. Kiev, Russia, Apr. 17, 1905; came to U.S., 1906, naturalized, 1913; s. Jacob and Rebecca (Brodsky) E.; m. Miriam Almond, July 6, 1933; children: Jacova Silverthorne, Karen O'Neil. PhB, U. Chgo., 1925, JD, 1928. Bar: Ill. 1928. Bill drafter Legislative Reference Bur., Springfield, Ill., 1929; atty. Legal Aid Bur., Chgo., 1929-34; assoc. atty. Tolman, Chandler & Dickinson, 1934-38; regional atty. Wage-Hour Div., Chgo., 1938-41; regional atty., asst. gen. counsel OPA, 1941-45; of counsel Rosenthal & Schanfield; lectr. U. Chgo., intermittently 1933-48, Yale Law Sch., 1946, seminar-labor relations Northwestern U. Sch. Law, 1961-65; seminar constl. law Ariz U., 1971. Author: Civil Practice Forms, 1934; co-author: Civil Practice Forms, Illinois-Federal, 1952, rev., 1965; contbr.: articles to profl. jours., also to Ency. Brit. Former pub. mem. Regional War Labor Bd.; former chmn. Chgo. Rent Commn.; pres. Fund for Justice, 1972-76; former chmn. Ill. divsn. ACLU (hon. mem. bd. dirs. Ill. divsn.); former vice chmn. Ill. Commn. on Children; former chmn. Bd. Mental Health Commrs. State Ill., 1960-69; v.p. Law in Am. Soc. Found.; pres. Nat. Acad. Arbitrators Rsch. and Edn. Found., 1987-90; bd. govs. Orthogenic Sch., U. Chgo.; mem. instnl. rev. bd. divsn. social sci. U. Chgo., 1994-97; cons. Ford Found., 1963-68; bd. dirs. Hull House Assn., 1955-65. Fellow Am. Bar Found., Emeritus fellow Coll. of Labor and Employment Lawyers, 1998—; mem. ABA, Ill. Bar Assn., Chgo. Bar Assn. (bd. mgrs.), Am. Law Inst. (life), Nat. Acad. Arbitrators (v.p. 1983-85), Inst. Psychoanalysis (pres. 1976-79). Home: 5642 S Dorchester Ave Chicago IL 60637-1722 Office: 55 E Monroe St Chicago IL 60603-5713

ELSON, CHARLES, stage designer, educator; b. Chgo., Sept. 5, 1909; s. Jacob and Rebecca (Brodsky) E.; m. Diana Rivers, Aug. 12, 1938 (dec. Nov. 1996); 1 child, Alexandra. Student, Hull House Little Theatre, Chgo., 1914-32, U. Ill., 1929-30; PhB, U. Chgo., 1932; MFA in Theatre, Yale U., 1935. Instr., art dir. U. Iowa, 1935-36; assoc. prof. theatre, art dir. univ. theatre U. Okla., 1937-43; civilian design engr. tng. aids bur. USNR, 1943-45; prof., dir. theatre workshop Hunter Coll. CUNY, 1948-69, prof. emeritus, 1974—, established MA program in theatre, also Grad. Ctr. PhD program, 1965; vis. lectr. stage design dept. drama Yale U., 1950-51, vis. critic stage lighting Sch. Drama Yale U., 1964-67, vis. prof. design, 1967-69; Fulbright lectr., cons. design of 12 state and mcpl. theatres, India, 1959-60, organizer exhibit World Theatre Architecture, New Delhi, 1960; cons. Theatre Architecture, India, 1970; mem. design competition Internat. Theatre Inst. U.S.A., contbr. to Design jour., 1974; western theatre del. 3d Asian Symposium Arts, Seoul, Korea, 1974; U.S. Dept. State specialist S.E. Asia, 1974; art dir., stage lighting dir. fed. theatre project Works Projects Adminstrn., L.A., 1936-37; art dir. Ogunquit (Maine) Summer Theatre, 1939-41, 45; mem. Fulbright

Nat. Selection Theatre Com., 1957; mem. exhibit com. Yale Drama Sch. 50th Anniversary. Stage designer, 1946—; first N.Y. prodn. As You Like It; designed settings and or stage lighting for 101 Broadway and London plays including Kiss Me Kate, Music in the Air, Deep Blue Sea, His and Hers, Private Lives, The Lovers, Compulsion, Blue Denim, Troilus and Cressida, Henry IV, Richard II, Wildcat, Photo Finish, Met. Operas including Lohengrin, The Flying Dutchman, Don Giovanni, Madame Butterfly, Norma, Dialogues of the Carmelites, N.Y.C. Opera, also ballets; designer and/or producer 218 coll., univ., summer and community prodns.; exhbns., City Ctr. Gallery, U. Conn., 1955—; Am. editor: Stage Design Throughout the World (Belgium), Vols. 1, 1956, vol. 2, 1964. Pres. North Castle Friends of Libr., 1961-63, 65-67, bd. dirs., 1956-72; trustee, past pres. bd. trustees, North Castle Libr., 1972-89; pres. North Castle Citizens Coun., 1957-59; mem. theatre arts com. Young Artists Abroad Program, Inst. Internat. Edn., 1962; dir. Middle Patent Rural Cemetery Assn., 1965—; designer theatre Byram Hills High Sch., 1965; bd. dirs. North Castle Hist. Soc., 1972-76; vice chmn. North Castle Bicentennial Commn., 1973-76; chmn., producer North Castle July 4th celebration, 1975-76; former mem. landmark and beautifications coms. North Castle; chmn. theatre workshop for ex-convicts The Family, N.Y.C., 1974-81. Recipient Outstanding Contbn. to Theatre award U.S. Inst. Theatre, 1981, Am. Theatre Heritage award U.S. Inst. Theatre Tech., 1984, Disting. Svc. award North Castle Twp., 1988. Fellow Internat. Inst. Arts and Letters; mem. United Scenic Artists (chmn. exam. com. 1953-58), Century Assn. Home: 22 Faraway Rd Armonk NY 10504-1214*

ELSON, CHARLES MYER, law educator; b. Atlanta, Nov. 12, 1959; s. Edward Elliott and Suzanne (Goodman) E.; m. Aimee F. Kemker, Dec. 18, 1993. AB magna cum laude, Harvard U., 1981, postgrad., 1981-82; JD, U. Va., 1985. Bar: N.Y. 1987, D.C. 1988, U.S. Dist. Ct. (so. and ea. dists.) N.Y. 1987, U.S. Ct. Appeals (11th cir.) 1987. Law clk. to judge U.S. Ct. Appeals (11th cir.), Atlanta, 1985-86; assoc. Sullivan & Cromwell, N.Y.C., 1986-90; asst. prof. Stetson U. Coll. Law, St. Petersburg, Fla., 1990-93, assoc. prof., 1993-96, prof., 1996—; vis. prof. law U. Ill., Champaign-Urbana, 1995, Cornell U. Law Sch., Ithaca, N.Y., 1996, U. Md. Law Sch., Balt., 1998; cons. Holland & Knight, 1995—, Towers, Perrin, 1998; bd. dirs. Nuevo Energy Co., Sunbeam Corp., Gulfcoast Legal Svcs. Corp., Investor Responsibility Rsch. Coun. Bd. dirs. Big Apple Circus, Ltd., N.Y.C., 1987-93, Circon Corp., 1997-99; trustee Talladega Coll., 1994—, Tampa Mus. Art, 1993—. Salvatori fellow Heritage Found., 1993-94. Mem. ABA, Am. Law Inst., Assn. Bar City N.Y., Chevaliers du Tastevin, Down Town Assn., Nat. Assn. Corp. Dirs. (adv. coun. 1997—, commn. dir. compensation 1995, commn. dir. professionalism 1996, com. on securities litig. reform and fraud detection 1997, com. on succession planning 1998, com. on audit coms. 1999), Harvard Club N.Y.C., Univ. Club N.Y.C. Home: 3315 W Mullen Ave Tampa FL 33609-4657 Office: Law Coll 1401 61st St S Saint Petersburg FL 33707-3246

ELSON, HANNAH FRIEDMAN, research biologist; b. Lublin, Poland, July 10, 1943; came to U.S., 1949; m. Edward C. Elson; 2 children. BA, Vassar Coll., 1964; PhD, MIT, 1970. Arthritis Found. postdoctoral fellow Med. Rsch. Coun. Lab Molecular Biology, Cambridge, Eng., 1970-72; asst. prof., then asst. rsch. biologist U. Calif.-San Diego, La Jolla, 1972-79; rsch. sci. MEDSAT Rsch. Co., Bethesda, Md., 1986-90, 94—; sr. resident rsch. assoc. Nat. Rsch. Coun. Walter Reed Army Inst. Rsch., Washington, 1988-90; sr. staff fellow Nat. Heart, Lung, Blood Inst. NIH, Bethesda, 1990-92, expert Nat. Cancer Inst., 1992-94; pres. Kenwood Park Citizens Assn., Inc., Bethesda, 1995-99. Contbr. articles to sci. jours. Mem. AAAS, Am. Chem. Soc., Am. Soc. Cell Biology, Sigma Xi (treas. D.C. chpt.). Achievements include research on protein synthesis, membrane changes during development of skeletal muscle, membrane fusion by HIV, and gene therapy.

ELSON, JAMES MARTIN, historic foundation director, college music educator, fine arts administrator; b. N.Y.C., Nov. 25, 1932; s. John James and Elizabeth Jane (Slights) E.; m. Joan Mary Scott Elson, Aug. 21, 1965 (dec. Feb. 15, 1991); children: Elizabeth Joan Elson, Christina Marie Elson, James Scott Elson; m. Karen Sue Porter Elson, Aug. 22, 1992. BA, U. Tenn., 1955; MS, The Juilliard Sch., 1961; Mus. AD, W.Va. U., 1970. Chmn. vocal dept. Dana Sch. Music, Youngstown (Ohio) State U., 1962-68; grad. asst. Creative Arts Ctr., W.Va. U., Morgantown, 1968-70; chmn., vocal dept. Sch. Music, Winthrop Coll., Rock Hill, S.C., 1970-72; chmn., dept. visual and performing arts Huntingdon Coll., Montgomery, Ala., 1972-76; chmn., dept. fine arts High Point (N.C.) Coll., 1976-83; exec. dir. Acad. of Music Theatre, Lynchburg, Va., 1984-88; exec. v.p. Patrick Henry Meml. Fdn., Brookneal, Va., 1988—; performing arts critic High Point (N.C.) Enterprise, 1977-83. Author: Academy of Music, Lynchburg, VA: The Golden Age of Live Performance, 1993; author, editor: Patrick Henry Essays, 1994, Patrick Henry and Thomas Jefferson, 1997; contbr. articles to profl. jours. 1st lt. U.S. Army, 1955-57. Fulbright grant Fulbright Commn., 1961-62. Mem. Coll. Music Soc. (life), Res. Officers Assn. (life), Kappa Sigma Fraternity (life). Episcopalian. Home: 34 N Princeton Cir Lynchburg VA 24503-1547 Office: Red Hill Patrick Henry Nat Mem 1250 Red Hill Rd Brookneal VA 24528-9302

ELSON, SARAH LEE, art historian and consultant; b. Valley Forge, Pa., Oct. 1, 1962; d. John Everett and Ione (Coker) Lee; m. Louis Goodman Elson, Aug. 26, 1989; children: Isabel Coker Elson, Everett Esther Elson, Edward Lee Elson. BA, Princeton U., 1984; MA, Columbia U., 1990, MPhil in Art History, 1992. Prof. English Beijing Normal U., 1984-85; pub. affairs asst. Guggenheim Mus., N.Y.C., 1985-87; lectr. Met. Mus. Art, N.Y.C., 1990-92; freelance lectr. Nat. Gallery, London, 1994—; rschr. Met. Mus., 1990-92, Tate Gallery, London, 1992-93; fellow The Frick Collection, N.Y.C., 1990—. Author catalogs. Nat. Endowment for Arts fellow, 1988, Pres.'s fellow Columbia U., 1988-90, Luce Travel grant, 1992. Mem. Woolnoth Soc. in the City of London. Democrat. Home: 2 Kensington Gate, London W8 5NA, England

ELSON, SUZANNE GOODMAN, community activist; b. Memphis, Oct. 17, 1937; d. Charles F. and Isabel (Ehrlich) Goodman; m. Edward Elliott Elson, Aug. 24, 1957; children: Charles Myer, Louis Goodman, Harry II. Student Randolph-Macon Woman's Coll., Lynchburg, Va.; B.A., Agnes Scott Coll., 1959. Sec. Nat. Council Jewish Women, N.Y.C., 1977-79; pres., Nat. Mental Health Assn., 1980-82, pres., 1986-87; trustee, Randolph Macon Woman's Coll., 1986—, Am. Federation of Arts, 1992-96; chmn. Am. Craft Coun., 1989-92, honorary chmn., 1992-94, hon. trustee, 1994—; bd. dirs. Rosalynn Carter Inst., 1990—, Nat. Coun. Medicine Emory U., 1990-95; bd. trustees Project Interconnections, Inc., Atlanta, 1989—, Va. Mus. of Fine Art, 1992-96, High Mus. Fine Art, 1972-92; bd. regents U. System of Ga., 1993-97; adv. bd. Breast Cancer Rsch. Found., 1998—; bd. dirs. Friends of Art and Preservation in Embassies, 1999—. Home: 180 Cocoanut Row Palm Beach FL 33480-4121

ELSORADY, ALEXA MARIE, secondary education educator; b. San Francisco, Jan. 4, 1946; d. Willard John and Helen Mary (Bardmess) Saunders; m. R.M. Elsorady, Nov. 24, 1972; children: Tarik, Alexander. BA, San Jose State U., 1967, MA, 1976. Cert. secondary and cmty. coll. tchr. Tchr. biology, integrated sci., English, and social studies Fremont Union High Sch. Dist., San Jose, Calif., 1970—; mem. Workforce Silicon Valley Leadership Inst., summers 1996, 98; instr. School-Within-a-School sci. team Lynbrook H.S., 1994-99; mem. task force com. Calif. Health Occupations Resource Ctr. Mission Coll., 1998-99. Named Mentor Tchr., State of Calif., 1987-88, Mentor, 1993-94; grantee Superschs. Found. Sci.-Math.; fellow NSF, 1992, Evolution and Nature of Sci. Inst., San Jose State U., 1993, Mayor Susan Hammer's San Jose Edn. Network Tech. Inst., summer 1994. Mem. Nat. Sci. Tchrs. Assn., Calif. Sci. Tchrs. Assn., Calif. Acad. Scis. (mem. biology forum 1990-98), Santa Clara County Sci. Tchrs. Assn., San Jose State U. Alumni Assn. (life), Kappa Alpha Theta (life), Phi Kappa Phi (life), Phi Alpha Theta (life). Home: 1233 Redmond Ave San Jose CA 95120-2745 Office: Lynbrook High Sch 1280 Johnson Ave San Jose CA 95129-4199

ELSTE, GUENTHER HEINO ERICH, astrophysicist; b. Jauer, Germany, Apr. 21, 1923; came to the U.S., 1962; s. Arno Heino Erich and Charlotte Marie Anna (Kramer) E.; m. Annelie Luise Puhl, June 3, 1950; children: Volker, Brigitte Wallis. BS, Georgia Augusta U., Göttingen, Germany, 1952, PhD, 1954. From rsch. asst. dept. astronomy to rsch. assoc. U. Mich., Ann Arbor, 1954-56, asst. prof., 1962-68, assoc. prof., 1968-91, assoc. prof. emeritus, 1992—; Wissenschaftlicher asst. U. Sternwarte, Göttingen, 1957-62; cons. Environ. Rsch. Inst. Mich., Ann Arbor, 1994-95; guest investigator Orbiting Solar Obs., Boulder, Colo., 1976; mem. working group Radiative Inputs of Sun to Earth rsch. project, Boulder, 1990. Contbr. articles to profl. jours. Bd. dirs. Washtenaw Ski Touring Club, Ann Arbor, 1974-83; instr. Washtenaw County Ski Clinics, Ann Arbor, 1974-80. Mem. Astronomische Gesellschaft, Am. Astron. Soc., Internat. Astron. Union, Sci. Rsch. Club (pres. 1974-75). Avocations: track and field, cross country skiing, swimming, Deutsches Sportabz. Gold 10. Office: U Mich Dept Astronomy 1045 Dennison Bldg Ann Arbor MI 48109-1090

ELSTER, SAMUEL KASE, college dean, medical educator, physician; b. N.Y.C., Dec. 6, 1922; s. Morris and Rebecca (Post) E.; m. Maxine Lefkowitz, June 17, 1945; 1 child, Charles. B.S., CCNY, 1942; M.D., NYU, 1946. Diplomate Am. Bd. Internal Medicine, Cardiovascular Diseases. Intern Mt. Sinai Hosp., 1946-47, resident, 1950-52; asst. in pathology NYU Sch. Medicine, N.Y.C., 1947-48; instr. medicine Columbia U. Coll. Physicians and Surgeons, N.Y.C., 1959-66; clin. prof. medicine Mount Sinai Sch. Medicine, CUNY, N.Y.C., 1974-97; clin. prof. emeritus medicine Mount Sinai Sch. Medicine, CUNY, 1997—; dean Page and William Black Postgrad. Sch. of Medicine Mount Sinai Sch. Medicine, CUNY, N.Y.C., 1976-85, dean emeritus, 1985—; dean emeritus for continuous edn. Mount Sinai Sch. Medicine, CUNY, 1985—. Contbr. articles in field to profl. jours. Mem., pres. bd. edn., Tenafly, N.J., 1968-73. Served to capt., M.C. U.S. Army, 1948-50. Fellow Am. Coll. Cardiology, ACP, N.Y. Acad. Medicine; mem. Am. Heart Assn. (mem. council in clin. cardiology), Assn. Am. Med. Colls. Democrat. Jewish. Office: Mt Sinai Med Ctr Box 1030 1 Gustave Levy Pl New York NY 10029

ELSTON, MICHAEL JAMES, lawyer, educator; b. Rockford, Ill., Feb. 7, 1969; s. James L. and Barbara Emanuel. BA in Polit. Sci., Drake U., 1991; JD with high honors, Duke U., 1994. Bar: Ill. 1994, Mo. 1997, Kans. 1998, U.S. Ct. Appeals (10th and 11th cirs.) 1997, U.S. Dist. Ct. Mo. 1997, U.S. Ct. Appeals (7th and 8th cirs.) 1995, U.S. Dist. Ct. (no. dist.) Ill. 1995, U.S. Supreme Ct. 1997. Law clk. to Hon. Pasco. M. Bowman U.S. Ct. Appeals (8th cir.), Kansas City, Mo., 1994-96; assoc. Shughart Thomson & Kilroy, P.C., 1997-99; asst. U.S. Atty. No. Dist. Ill., 1999—; adj. prof. law U. Mo., Kansas City, 1995-99. Co-author: Grand Jury Law & Practice, 1997. Chmn. Nat. Adv. Bd. Student Life, Drake U., 1998—, vol. cook Kansas City Cmty. Kitchen, 1994-96. Mem. ABA (litigation sect. 1994—), Theta Chi (regional counselor 1993—, legal affairs com. 1994—). Avocation: baseball.

ELSTON, ROBERT C., medical educator. BA with honors, Cambridge (Eng.) U., 1955, diploma in agr., 1956, MA, 1957; PhD, Cornell U., 1959; postgrad., U. N.C., 1960. Asst. prof. U. N.C., Chapel Hill, 1960-62, assoc. prof., 1964-69, prof., dir. genetics lab. Sch. Pub. Health, 1969-79; sr. rsch. fellow biometric medicine U. Aberdeen, 1962-64; prof., head dept. biometry & genetics La. State U. Med. Ctr., New Orleans, 1979-95; prof. dept. epidemiology & biostats. Case Western Res. U., Cleve., 1995—; vis. prof. Yale U., 1965-66, London U., 1967, Cambridge U., 1970, Fourth Mil. Med. Coll. Xian, China, 1987, U. Calif., Irvine, 1988-89; dir. Ctr. Molecular & Human Genetics La. State U. Med. Ctr., 1991-95; mem. internat. adv. bd. Genetics Selection Evolution, 1992—; exec. com. mem. teaching of stats. in health scis. sect. Am. Stats. Assn., 1992-94, chair, 1993. Assoc. editor Biometrics, 1967-71, Am. Jour. Human Genetics, 1974-82; editl. bd. Thrombosis Rsch., 1972-76, Neuropsychobiology, 1975-78, Am. Jour. med. Genetics, 1977—, Genetic Epidemiology, 1984—; contbr. articles to profl. jours. Recipient Career Devel. award NIH, 1966-76, Rsch. Scientist award, NIMH, 1977-79, Hoch award Am. Psychopath. Assn., 1992, Wick R. Williams Meml. award Fox Chase Cancer Ctr., 1994, Leadership award Internat. Genetic Epidemiology Soc., 1995, William Allan Meml. award Am. Soc. Human Genetics, 1996; King George VI Meml. fellow, 1956-57, John Simon Guggenheim Meml. fellow, 1973-74; Coulthurst scholar, 1955-56, Cornell scholar, 1956-59. Fellow Am. Stats. Assn. Office: Case Western Res U Dept Epidemiology & Biostats 2500 Metrohealth Dr Rm R-258 Cleveland OH 44109-1900*

ELSTON, WILLIAM STEGER, food products company executive; b. Louisville, Sept. 1, 1940; s. Woodrow Lewis and Margaret Mary (Peake) E.; m. Charlynne White, Aug. 12, 1959 (div. Dec. 1976); m. Marilyn Kay Wood, Jan. 31, 1977. BS, U. Louisville, 1963. Mfg. engr. Pillsbury Co., Mpls., 1969-71; prodn. mgr. Pillsbury Co., Grand Forks, N.D., 1971-73; prodn. mgr. Pillsbury Co., Terre Haute, Ind., 1973-76, plant mgr., 1976-79; plant mgr. Frito-Lay Inc., Detroit, 1979-81; area v.p. mfg. Frito-Lay Inc., Dallas, 1981-84, v.p. process engring., 1984-85, v.p. mfg., 1985-89, sr. v.p. ops., 1989-90; pres. Assoc. Unit Cos., Jacksonville, Fla., 1990-91; pres., CEO The Unit Cos., Jacksonville, 1991-94, GATX Logistics, Jacksonville, 1993-94; exec. v.p. DHR Internat., Chgo., 1995—, bd. dirs.; pres., CEO Clean Shower, L.P., 1998—; bd. dirs. Landstar Sys., So. Petroleum Sys. Bd. dirs. Jr. Achievement, Terre Haute, 1976-78; chmn. United Way, Terre Haute, 1978; mem. Cooper Canyon (Tex.) City Coun., 1984-88. Mem. Univ. Club (bd. dirs. 1993—). Avocations: racquetball, jogging, water skiing, stamp collecting. Office: DHR Internat 2 Sawgrass Village Dr Ste 400 Ponte Vedra Beach FL 32082-3079

ELVERUM, GERARD WILLIAM, JR., retired electronic and diversified company executive; b. Mpls., Sept. 29, 1927; m. Mary Jean Proverbs, Dec. 28, 1948. Student, U. Nebr., 1945, S.D. State U., 1945; B in Physics, U. Minn., 1949. Engr. Jet Propulsion Lab., Pasadena, Calif., 1949-59; sect. head, mgr. dept. Space Tech. Lab., El Segundo, Calif., 1959-62; dir. lab. Systems Group TRW, Redondo Beach, Calif., 1963-66, mgr. ops. Def. and Space Systems Group, 1969-81, v.p., gen. mgr. Applied Tech. Div./Space and Tech. Group, 1981-91, ret., 1991; mem. adv. panel NASA/Aerospace Safety Bd., Washington, 1982-91; mem. NASA Access to Space Panel, 1995—; mem. Space Studies Bd., NRC, 1996—. Contbr. articles to profl. jours.; patentee in field. Commr. Commn. on Engring. and Tech. Systems, Nat. Rsch. Coun., 1991-94. Served with USAF, 1944-46. Recipient Spl. Achievement award ASME, 1971; named Outstanding Engr. Inst. Advancement Engring., 1972. Fellow AIAA (James H. Wyld Propulsion award 1973); mem. Am. Def. Preparedness Assn., Nat. Acad. Engring. *Preparation, perseverance, patience with others, and absolute integrity will create the career opportunities that many will simply attribute to being at the right place at the right time.*

ELVIG, MERRYWAYNE, real estate manager; b. Anoka, Minn., Jan. 16, 1931; d. Wayne Leroy and Erma Lou (Greenwald) Ridge; m. Donald Keith Elvig, June 15, 1955 (div. 1972); children: Amy, David. AA, Cottey Jr. Coll., 1951; BS, U. Minn., 1953. Tchr. Anoka Hennepin Sch. Dist., Anoka, 1953-56; with med. records div. East Main Clinic, Anoka, 1972-78; real estate mgr. Skurdal Properties, Anoka, 1978-79; mgr. ABC Travel, Anoka, 1979-93; chmn. Walker Meth. Residence Group, 1990—; chmn. Walker Plaza, 1994—, Walker on the River, 1994—; travel counselor Am. Automobile Assn., 1994—. Commr. Housing Redevel. Authority, Anoka, 1978, chmn., 1984—; bd. dirs. Walker Sr. Housing Corp., Anoka, 1986—; bd. dirs. Walker Meth. Sr. Housing, Inc., 1988—, sec., 1997—; chair Walker Meth. Sr. Property Mgmt. Group, 1990—; treas. Anoka Devel. Corp., 1986—; charter and life mem. aux. Mercy Med. Ctr., coon Rapids, Minn., 1965—, bd. dirs., 1965-71; mem. Greenhaven Study Com., Anoka, 1986-90, Anoka County Hist. Soc., 1987—, Anoka North Ctrl. Bus. Dist. Study Commn., 1993—, Anoka Floodplain Devel. Com., 1999—; vol. Anoka coun. Girl Scouts U.S., 1963-65; chmn. Am. Cancer Soc., 1962-65; moderator 1st Congl. Ch., Anoka, 1984-86; deacon 1st Congregational Ch., 1995-97, trustee, 1997—, trustee chair, 1999—. Mem. Am. Soc. Travel Agts. (bd. dirs. 1986—), Minn. Exec. Women in Travel (treas.), Minn. Exec. Women in Tourism, Internat. Fedn. Women's Orgns., Anoka Area C. of C. (pres. 1985), Kiwanis (bd. dirs.), Philanthropic Ednl. Orgn. Sisterhood (pres. 1966-68), Philolectian Club (pres. 1965-67), Greenhaven Women's Golf Club (pres. 1987-89, v.p. 1998, pres. 1999). Republican. Avocations: bridge, golf, reading, music. Home: 1933 Cressy Ave Anoka MN 55303-1920 Office: AAA Minnesota 3027 Coon Rapids Blvd NW Coon Rapids MN 55433-3400

ELVIN, PETER WAYNE, healthcare executive, consultant; b. Augusta, Maine, Mar. 10, 1955; s. Grahame Dennis and Clemence Marie (Poulin) E.; m. Suzanne Piché. Student, U. Maine, 1973-74, U. Cin., 1974-75; AA, Cin. Tech. Coll., 1977; MS in Mgmt., Lesley Coll., 1985. Physicians asst. Monson Devel. Ctr., Palmer, Mass., 1977-86; rep. Blue Cross and Blue Shield of Maine, Portland, 1986—; dir. physician practices TVM, Inc./Miles Health Care, Damariscotta, Maine, 1990—; pvt. practice cons., 1989—; health care analyst Mass. Dept. Health, Boston, 1984-86; cons. Med. Care Devel., Augusta, 1985-86, Rural Health Ctrs., Maine, 1985-86; adminstr. Harrington (Maine) Family Health Ctr. Mem. Maine Rep. Party, Rep. Nat. Com.; mem. Am. Humane Soc.; mem. Am. Soc. Prevention of Cruelty to Animals, Mass. Soc. Prevention of Cruelty to Animals. Mem. NRA, Am. Assn. Individual Investors, Investors Alliance, Physicians com. Responsible Medicine, Am. Acad. Physicians Assts., Am. Humane Soc., Am. Soc. Prevention Cruelty Animals (Mass. chpt.), Soc. Emergency Med. (physician assn., downeast assn.), Soc. emergency Medicine Physicians Assn., Downeast Assn. Physician Assts., Assn. MBA Execs., Inc., Lesley Coll. Alumni Assn., Rental Housing Assn. Greater Springfield, Bath/Brunswick Rental Housing Assn., Maine Apt. Owners and Mgrs. Assn., Maine Hosp. Assn., U.S. C. of C., Nat. Fedn. Ind. Bus., Boston Computer Soc., Profl. Cons. of Maine, NRA, Am. Assn. Individual Investors, Investors Alliance, Maine Apt. Owners Mgr. Assn., Republican. Episcopalian. Avocations: swimming, boating, gardening. Home: 60 Middle Rd Dresden ME 04342-3638 Office: Dresden Cons Group 60 Middle Rd Ste A Dresden ME 04342-3638

ELWAY, JOHN ALBERT, professional football player; b. Port Angeles, Wash., June 28, 1960; s. Jack Elway; m. Janet Elway; 2 daughters: Jessica Gwen, Jordan Marie. BA in Econs., Stanford U., 1983. Quarterback Denver Broncos, 1983—. Mem. Mayor's Council on Phys. Fitness, City of Denver; chmn. Rocky Mountain region Nat. Kidney Found. Played Super Bowl XXI, 1986, XXII, 1987, XXIV, 1989; named to Sporting News Coll. All-Am. team, 1980, 82, Sporting News NFL All-Pro team, 1987, Pro Bowl team, 1986, 87, 89, 91, 93, 94. Office: Denver Broncos 13655 Broncos Pky Englewood CO 80112-4150*

ELWELL, BARBARA LOIS DOW, community organizer; b. Purcell, Okla., Feb. 15, 1933; d. Henry Kenneth and Leah Maude (Caldwell) Dow; m. Robert G. Elwell, Apr. 7, 1956 (div. July 1977); children: David Robert, Kenneth Dow. Student, Endicott Coll., 1950-51, Jackson Von Ladau Sch. Design, 1952-54. Dir. Alternative House, Inc., Lowell, Mass., 1976-84; exec. sec. Encode Tech., Inc., Nashua, N.H., 1984-87; staff asst. Smithsonian Astrophys. Observatory, Cambridge, Mass., 1987—. Founder Alternative House, Lowell, 1978; founding mem. Mass Coalition of Battered Women/Svc. Groups, Boston, 1976, steering com., 1976-84, adv. bd. 1978-80. Recipient Outstanding Achievement award Mass. Coalition of Battered Women/Svc. Groups, 1976. Avocations: woodworking, antique collecting, minatures, gardening, painting. Home: 142 Graniteville Rd Chelmsford MA 01824-1122

ELWELL, ROBERT H., manufacturing executive; b. New Kensington, Pa., July 17, 1953; s. Howard McCabe and Edith Maizetta (Smith) E.; m. Nancy Ann Schwetz, May 27, 1978; children: Kathryn Elizabeth, Margaret Elaine. BS in Metall. Engring., Lafayette Coll., 1975; MBA, Widener U., 1979. Supt. casting and conditioning Lukens Steel Co., Coatesville, Pa., 1975-86; mfg. mgr. Haynes Internat., Kokomo, Ind., 1987-93; v.p. quality and tech. Freedom Forge Corp., Burnham, Pa., 1993-94; v.p. mfg. Cannon-Muskegon (Mich.) Corp., 1994-98; pres. Greenville Metals Inc., Transfer, Pa., 1998—. Clk. of session First Presbyn. Ch., Muskegon, 1997-98. Mem. Am. Iron and Steel Inst. (chmn. strand casting subcom. 1984-85). Presbyterian. Avocations: long-distance running, singing, piano.

ELWES, CARY, actor; b. London, Oct. 26, 1962; s. Dominic and Tessa (Kennedy) E. Stage debut in Equus, 1981; films include Another Country, 1984, Oxford Blues, 1984, The Bride, 1985, Lady Jane, 1986, Maschenka, 1987, The Princess Bride, 1987, Glory, 1989, Days of Thunder, 1990, Hot Shots!, 1990, Leather Jackets, 1991, Bram Stoker's Dracula, 1992, The Crush, 1993, Robin Hood: Men In Tights, 1993, Rudyard Kipling's Jungle Book, 1994, The Chase, 1994, Twister, 1996, Liar Liar, 1997, Kiss the Girls, 1997, The Informant, 1997, Liar LIar, 1997, Quest for Camelot (voice), 1998, Cradle Will Rock, 1999. Office: William Morris Agy c/o Michael Gruber 151 S El Camino Dr Beverly Hills CA 90212-2775*

ELWIN, JAMES WILLIAM, JR., dean, lawyer; b. Everett, Wash., June 28, 1950; s. James William Elwin and Jeannette Georgette (Zichy-Litscheff) Sherman; m. Regina K. McCabe, Oct. 25, 1986. BA, U. Denver, 1971, MA, 1972; JD, Northwestern U., 1975. Bar: Ill. 1975, U.S. Dist. Ct. (no. dist.) Ill. 1975, U.S. Ct. Appeals (7th cir.) 1977, U.S. Supreme Ct. 1980, U.S. Ct. Fed. Claims 1989. Trial atty. antitrust divsn. U.S. Dept. Justice, Chgo., 1975-77; asst. dean Sch. Law Northwestern U., Chgo., 1977-82, assoc. dean, 1982—; exec. dir. Corp. Counsel Ctr., 1984—; planning dir. Corp. Counsel Inst., Garrett Corp. and Securities Law Inst., Chgo., 1983—; dir. Short Course for Pros. Attys., 1981—, Short Course for Def. Lawyers in Criminal Cases, Chgo., 1979—. Bd. dirs. Legal Assistance Found. of Chgo., 1985-97; vice chmn. Gov.'s Adv. Coun. on Criminal Justice Legis., 1986-91. Fellow German Acad. Exch. Svc., 1986; Fulbright scholar, Germany, 1990. Mem. Chgo. Coun. Fgn. Rels. (mem. Chgo. com.), Chgo. Bar Assn. (bd. mgrs. 1983-85), Chgo. Bar Found. (bd. dirs. 1985-93, pres. 1989-91), Ill. Inst. Continuing Legal Edn. (bd. dirs. 1978-90, chmn. 1987-88), Am. Law Inst., Legal Club (pres. 1991-92), Univ. Club, Law Club City of Chgo., Phi Beta Kappa, Pi Gamma Mu. Office: Northwestern U Sch Law 357 E Chicago Ave Chicago IL 60611-3059

ELWIN, KEVIN THOMAS, broadcast engineering manager; b. N.Y.C., May 10, 1957; s. Cecil O.L. and Myrtle Ursurla (Vanterpool) E.; m. Alisa N.M.N. Thomas, July 2, 1988; children: André, Michele, Justin. BEEE, Pratt Inst., 1988. Broadcast maintenance engr. Capital Cities/ABC, N.Y.C., 1983-87, tech. opers. mgr., 1991-94, mgr. network tech. maintenance, 1994—; broadcast maintenance engring. supr. Fox Broadcastin Co., L.A., 1987-91. Aux. police officer Nassau County Police Dept., L.I., N.Y., 1994—; mentor N.Y.C. Bd. Edn., H.S. Performing Arts, 1996—; coach Westbury (L.I.) Little League, 1994-95. Served in USN, 1977-81, USNR, 1981-91, 95—. Mem. IEEE, Soc. Broadcast Engrs., Soc. Motion Picture and TV Engrs. Avocations: martial arts, sailing. Office: ABC Inc 47 W 66th St Rm 800 New York NY 10023-6290

ELWOOD, PATRICIA COWAN, education specialist, political consultant; b. Haverhill, Mass., Oct. 22, 1941; d. Raymond Bernard and Florence Eva Cowan; children: Robert Michael, Douglas Matthew. BS, Tufts U., 1963; MEd, Boston U., 1965; PhD, U. Md., 1978. Tchr./trainer Boston Pub. Schs., 1964-67; dir. Head Start Prog., various cities, Mass., 1968; adminstrv. asst. Dept. Child Study Tufts U., Medford, Mass., 1967-68; diagnostician, tchr./counselor Program for Hearing Impaired Richmond (Calif.) Pub. Schs., 1968-69, supr., 1970-73; asst. to dir. Berkeley (Calif.) Profl. Studies Abroad Program, New Delhi, 1969-70; curriculum writer Prince Georges County Pub. Schs., Upper Marlboro, Md., 1974; learning problems and hearing specialist Prince Georges County Pub. Schs., 1976-80, hearing therapist, 1980—; mktg. rschr., 1990-94, ednl. cons., 1985—; polit. cons., 1990—; lectr. Trinity Coll., Washington, 1980-84; cons. Pan Am. Health Orgn., Caribbean, 1978-80; coord. state conf. early childhood edn., grad. asst., 1978. Author: From a Professional Parent's Prospective, 1994; co-author: Social and Emotional Development of Young Children, 1968, Alameda County California Public Schools Health Curriculum, 1969, Piaget's Theory as It Relates to Early Childhood Curricula, 1979; co-editor: Parent-Centered Programs for Young Hearing Impaired Students, 1976; implemented approved self-authored grant for one of first Parent-Infant Programs in the U.S.; contbr. articles to profl. jours. Apptd. mem. Inst. for Dist. Affairs, U. D.C., 1981-82; mem. fin. com. Sidwell Friends Sch., 1985-90; elected mem. Dem. State Com., Washington, 1985—, fin. chmn., 1988-90; mem. St. Albans Sch. Parent Bd., 1993-94; 1st vice chmn. Ward III Dem. Com., Washington, 1988-91, 95—, fin. sec., 1994-95, treas., 1986-88; past mem. fin. and policy coms. presdl., senate, ho. reps., gubernatorial campaigns; campaign co-chmn., ward chmn. steering com. D.C. and Greater Washington area polit. candidate campaigns, 1980—; founder D.C. Soccer, 1978, D.C. Baseball Connection, 1994-95; head com. to bring Am. Legion Baseball to D.C., 1994-95; bd. dirs. Babe Ruth League, Little League and Boys and Girls Club, 1986-91, Nat. Child Rsch. Ctr., 1977-82, Washington Hearing and Speech Ctr., 1982-87, Washington Tufts Alliance, co-chairperson, 1986-88, vice chairperson, 1985-86, treas., 1988—, chair interviewing com., 1990—; apptd. Coun. Govts. Task Force Com. on Growth and Transp., 1990-92; commr. Mayoral Appointee, Nat. Capital Planning Commn., 1987—, exec. com., 1993—, vice chairperson, 1995—; mem. nominating com., trustee U.

D.C., 1988-92; presdl. appointee Selective Svc. Bd., 1988-91; bd. dirs. Ft. Myer Swim Team, 1983-85, 89-90; elected mem. alumni coun. Tufts U., 1988—, chmn. interviewing com.; mem. bd. trustees City Lights Sch., 1993-97, soccer adv. com., 1995-96; bd. dirs. D.C. Mental Health Assn., Anacostia Coord. Com., African-Am. Mus.; mem. adv. coun. Hist. Soc. of Washington, 1998; mem. adv. com. Y-Care 2000 Found.; adv. bd. Hist. Preservation Soc., 1998—; mem. D.C. Agenda. Named Outstanding Young Woman in Am., 1966. Mem. Nat. Assn. for Edn. Young Children, World Affairs Coun., Nat. Trust for Historic Preservation, Internat. Bus. Coun. (bd. dirs.), Citizens Against Gun Violence, Tufts U. Alumnae Assn. Democrat. Avocations: politics, swimming, walking, baseball. Home: 2740 34th St NW Washington DC 20008-2714 Office: Prince Georges County Bd Edn Upper Marlboro MD 20008

ELWOOD, WILLIAM NORELLI, medical researcher; b. East Orange, N.J., Aug. 21, 1962; s. William Rogers and Frances Emma (Norelli) E. BS in Comm., U. Fla., 1985; MA in Human Comm., U. South Fla., 1989; PhD in Human Communication, Purdue U., 1992. Grad. teaching asst. U. South Fla., 1988-89; grad. teaching instr. Purdue U., 1989-91; asst. prof. Auburn (Ala.) U., 1992-94; rsch. assoc. Affiliated Systems Corp., Houston, 1994-96; co-prin. investigator Nat. Inst. on Drug Abuse, 1994-96, 97—; sr. rsch. scientist NOVA Rsch. Co., Bethesda, Md., 1995—; adj. asst. prof. Ctr. for Health Promotion Rsch. and Devel. U. Tex.-Houston Sch. of Pub. Health, 1996—. Author: Rhetoric in the War on Drugs, 1994, Public Relations Inquiry as Rhetorical Criticism, 1995, Power in the Blood: A Handbook on AIDS, Politics and Communication, 1999; contbr. articles to profl. jours. Chmn. Grove St./Blossom Brook Neighborhood Improvement Project, Sarasota, Fla., 1990-92; poll sheriff Tippecanoe County, Ind. State Elections, 1990; precinct capt. Sarasota County, Fla., 1986-89. Recipient Alan H. Monroe Disting. Grad. scholar, and teaching award, 1990-91; Rsch. grantee, Auburn U., 1993, Nat. Inst. Drug Abuse, 1997. Mem. Houston Crackdown Com. on Treatment and Rsch., Tex. Drug Epidemiology Workgroup, U.S.-Mex. Border Drug Epidemiology Workgroup, City of Houston HIV Prevention Cmty. Planning Group. Home: 402 Tuam Ave Apt 1 Houston TX 77006-3433

ELY, DAVID (DAVID E. LILIENTHAL, JR.), writer; b. Chgo., Nov. 19, 1927; s. David Eli and Helen Marian (Lamb) Lilienthal; m. Margaret Anne Jenkins, Aug. 7, 1954; children: Michael, Pamela, David, Margaret. AB, Harvard U., 1949. Author: (novels) Trot, 1963, Seconds, 1963, The Tour, 1967, Poor Devils, 1970, Walking Davis, 1972, Mr. Nicholas, 1974, A Journal of the Flood Year, 1992, (short stories) Time Out, 1968, Always Home, 1991. Home: PO Box 1387 East Dennis MA 02641

ELY, DONALD J(EAN), clergyman, secondary school educator; b. Frederick, Md., July 15, 1935; s. George Kline and Jennie Mabel (Boyer) E. m. Lois Jean Kirkpatrick, Aug. 27, 1967; children: Kathleen Rose, Stephen David, Yvonne Elaine. AB, Gettysburg Coll., 1955; BD, Lancaster Sem., 1958; MEd, Bloomsburg State U., 1972. Ordained to ministry Evang. and Reformed Ch., 1958. Pastor St. John Evang. and Reformed Ch., Riegelsville, Pa., 1958-61, Zion's Reformed Ch., Ashland, Pa., 1961-64, Augusta Reformed Parish, Sunbury, Pa., 1964-74, Salem United Meth. Ch., Middleburg, Pa., 1974-79, Salem Ind. Brethren Ch., Middleburg, Pa., 1979-83; tchr. social studies Shikellamy High Sch., Sunbury, Pa., 1966-98. Bd. dirs. Sunbury Area YMCA, 1966—, sec., 1973-80, 88-99; bd. dirs. Northumberland County unit Am. Cancer Soc., 1971-74, Snyder County unit, 1974-84, Greater Susquehanna Valley YMCA, 1993—, sec., 1999—; rep. candidate state legis., 1982; vice chmn. Govt. Study Commn. of City of Sunbury, 1989-91; mem. Northumberland County Rep. com., 1989—, state committeeman, 1992—. Mem. SAR (chaplain 1971—, chpt. pres. 1981-86, 1992), Pa. Coun. Social Studies, Snyder County Hist. Soc. (pres. 1980-83, life mem.), Northumberland County Hist. Soc. (trustee 1972-83, life mem.), Union County Hist. Soc., Hist. Soc. Evang. and Reformed Ch., Hereditary Register of U.S., Ams. for Constl. Action, Am. Conservative Union, Masons. Home and Office: PO Box 765 Sunbury PA 17801-0765

ELY, DUNCAN CAIRNES, non profit/human services executive, civic leader; b. Phila., Apr. 3, 1951; s. Donald and Barbara Dercum (Mifflin) E.; m. Elizabeth Caroline Wickenberg, June 14, 1984; 1 child, Penn Wickenberg Ely. BA, U. Ariz., 1974; MDiv, Gen. Theol. Sem., N.Y.C., 1988; cert. mentor Edn. for Ministry, U. of South, 1985. Cert. in clin. pastoral edn. Bapt. Med. Ctr., 1985; cert. human svcs. adminstrn. Human Svcs. Inst., 1991. Nat. exec. dir. Assn. for Independence of Disabled, Inc., Tucson, 1974-77; exec. dir. Frat. of Alpha Kappa Lambda, Inc., Indpls., 1977-79; asst. St. Stephen's Episcopal Ch., Phila., 1979-80; exec. dir. The Youth Alternatives Camps, Inc., Tucson, 1980-83, Crisis Assistance Clothing Ministry, Charlotte, N.C., 1989-93, N.C. Harvest, Inc., Charlotte, 1993-96, Spartanburg (S.C.) Cmty. Events, Inc., 1996-98; dir. Camp Gravatt, Aiken, S.C., 1998—; chmn. bd. advisors Expanded Foods and Nutrition Edn. Program N.C. State U., 1989-96; mem. foster care rev. bd. child protective svcs. Dept. Social Svcs., Charlotte, 1991-96. Author, editor: The Truth and the Word, 1978; also numerous articles in books, jours., mag. and newspapers. Past pres. Ely Assn., Inc., N.Y.C.; trustee Wildlife Guard, Inc., 1973—, past nat. pres., also past chmn. bd. advisors The Relatives, Inc., Charlotte, 1989-96, Ret. Sr. Vol. Program, Charlotte, 1990-96, Vol. Ctr. Charlotte, 1990-96; bd. dirs. Charlotte Emergency Housing, Inc., 1989-96, Met. Music Ministries, Inc., 1993-96, Piedmont Area Girl Scouts, Inc., 1997—, S.C. Inst. Nonprofit Leadership, Share the Vision resource com. City of Spartanburg, 1997—; mem. Vol. Leadership Devel. Program, Charlotte, 1991; grad. class XIII, Leadership Charlotte, 1991; grad. class III Carolinas Leadership Program, 1994; grad. class I Leadership N.C., 1995; chmn. bd. dirs. Spartanburg Caregivers, Inc., 1996—; grad. class 17 Leadership Spartanburg, 1997; grad. class 19 Leadership S.C., 1998; commr. for nat. and cmty. svc. State of N.C.; mem. N.C. Gov.'s Commn. on Nat. and Cmty. Svc.; mem. christian formation steering com. Episcopal Diocese Upper S.C., 1998—, mem. mission and outreach steering com., 1998—, mem. peer ministry conf., 1998. Recipient gold pin Phila. State Hosp., 1973, One of Nine Who Care award Sta. WSOC-TV and United Way, Charlotte, 1991, 94. Mem. S.R., Internat. Festivals and Events Assn., Nat. Soc. Am. Royal Descent, Barorial Order Magna Charta, Colonial Order of the Crown, Soc. Mayflower Descendants, Am. Mgmt. Assn., Am. Soc. Assn. Execs., Nat. Christian Counselors Assn. (lic. pastoral counselor), Metrolina Assn. for Vol. Adminstrn. (past pres.), N.C. Assn. Vol. Adminstrs. (past v.p.), S.C. Festival Assn., Penn Laurel Poets, Soc. Nonprofit Execs., Soc. Cin., Pen and Pencil Club, Alpha Kappa Lambda (past pres.), Alpha Phi Omega (past pres.), Theta Kappa Psi (past pres.), Theta Omega (past pres.), Psi Chi (past pres.), Country Club of Spartanburg, Piedmont Club, Fripp Island Club (S.C.), numerous others. Republican. Episcopalian. Avocations: arts, genealogy, historic preservation horticulture, reading, sports and outdoor activities. E-mail: duncely@spartanburg.net. Home: Skidaway 605 Crystal Dr Spartanburg SC 29302-2716 Office: Camp Gravatt 1006 Camp Gravatt Rd Aiken SC 29805-8730

ELY, ELIZABETH WICKENBERG, priest; b. Columbia, S.C., June 14, 1953; d. Charles Herbert Jr. and Margaret Smith (Gall) Wickenberg; m. Duncan Cairnes Ely, June 14, 1984; 1 child, Penn Wickenberg Ely. BA, Agnes Scott Coll., 1975; MS, Columbia U., 1976; MDiv cum laude, Gen. Theol. Sem., N.Y.C., 1989. Ordained to priesthood Episcopal Ch. in U.S.A., 1990. Homes and real estate editor Providence Jour.-Bull., Providence, 1976-78; sports columnist Clarion-Ledger, Jackson, Miss., 1978-80; sports writer, copy editor Atlanta Jour., 1980; sports editor and columnist Natchez (Miss.) Dem., 1980-81; sports copy editor Dallas Times-Herald, 1982; sports copy editor/writer Ariz. Daily Star, Tucson, 1981-83; copy editor Phila. Inquirer, 1983-85; assoc. rector St. John's Episcopal Ch., Charlotte, N.C., 1989-93; vicar All Saints and St. Patrick Episcopal Chs., Charlotte, 1993-96; assoc. rector Episcopal Ch. of the Advent, Spartansburg, S.C., 1996—; mem. diocesan coun. Episcopal Diocese of N.C. Author: A Manual for Lay Eucharistic Ministers, 1991. Mem. instnl. rev. bd. Carolinas Med. Ctr., Charlotte, 1990-96. Home: Skidaway 605 Crystal Dr Spartanburg SC 29302-2716 Office: Episcopal Ch of the Advent 141 Advent St Spartanburg SC 29302-1904

ELY, GLEN SAMPLE, television and video producer; b. Princeton, N.J., May 14, 1956; s. Roland Taylor Ely and Sally Sample Aall; m. Melinda Ann Veatch, May 23, 1993. BS in Broadcasting, Ariz. State U., Tempe, 1981. Editor KBMT-TV, Beaumont, Tex., 1981-82, photographer, 1982-83, reporter, 1984-85, program anchor, 1985; owner, pres. Forest Glen Prodns., Ft. Worth, 1986—. Video prodns. include Bandits, Bootleggers and Businessmen: A History of the Big Bend, Texas 1848-1948, 1987, Pioneer Life in Texas: A Recreation, 1988, A History of the Guadalupe Mountains and Carlsbad Caverns, 1989, Graveyard of the West: The Pecos River of Texas, Where Myth Meets History, 1993, The Frontier Forts and American Indian Wars in Texas, 1994, The Settlement of Texas: Part One-The Native Americans, 1996, The Settlement of Texas: Part Two-The Hispanics and Americans, 1996, Working Texas: From Ranchers and Roughnecks to Sodbusters and Spacemen, 1996, The Home Front: Life in Texas During the Civil War, 1998, Fort Davis: West Texas Military Outpost 1854-1891, 1998, Stage Coaching in Texas, 1998; programs have run on The History Channel, PBS-TV, Discovery, Arts and Entertainment, Lifetime; producer Nat. Parks TV documentaries, 1989-94. Recipient Tex. award for Hist. Preservation, Tex. Hist. Commn., 1988, 90, The Wilder award Tex. Assn. Museums, 1994. Mem. Tex. State Hist. Assn., Friends of Ft. Concho, Friends of Ft. Stockton, Big Bend Nat. History Assn. Avocations: music, camping, hiking. Office: Forest Glen Prodns PO Box 101823 Fort Worth TX 76185-1823

ELY, JOE, singer and songwriter; b. Feb. 9, 1947. With Flatlanders Band, Joe Ely Band; albums include Joe Ely, 1977, Honky Tonk Masquerade, 1978, Down on the Drag, 1979, Live Shots, 1980, Musta Notta Gotta Lotta, 1981, Hi-Res, 1984, Lord of the Highway, 1987, Milkshakes & Malts, 1988, Dig All Night, 1988, Live at Liberty Lunch, 1990, Love and Danger, 1992, From Chippy, Letter to Laredo, 1995, Twistin' in the Wind, 1998, Los Super Seven, 1999 (Grammy 1999). Address: LC Media Attn: Lance Cowan PO Box 965 Antioch TN 37011

ELY, JOHN HART, lawyer, university dean; b. N.Y.C., Dec. 3, 1938; s. John H. and Martha Foster (Coyle) E.; children: John Duff, Robert Allan Duff. A.B. summa cum laude, Princeton U., 1960; LL.B. magna cum laude, Yale U., 1963, M.A. (hon.), 1971; M.A. (hon.), Harvard U., 1973; LLD, U. San Diego, 1988, Ill. Inst. Tech., 1991. Bar: D.C. 1965, Calif. 1967. Atty. Warren Commn., 1964; law clk. to Chief Justice Warren, 1964-65; Fulbright scholar London Sch. Econs., 1965-66; atty. Defenders, Inc., San Diego, 1966-68; asso. prof., then prof. law Yale U. Law Sch., 1968-73; prof. Harvard U. Law Sch., 1973-1982, Ralph S. Tyler, Jr. prof. constl. law, 1981-1982; Richard E. Lang prof. law Stanford U. Law Sch., Calif., 1982-87, dean, 1982-87; Robert E. Paradise prof. Stanford (Calif.) U. Law Sch., 1987-96; Richard A. Hausler prof. U. Miami (Fla.) Law Sch., 1996—; gen. counsel U.S. Dept. Transp., 1975-76. Author: Democracy and Distrust, 1980, War and Responsibility, 1993, On Constitutional Ground, 1996. Served with USAR, 1963-69. Fellow Woodrow WIlson Internat. Ctr. scholars (1978-79), Am. Acad. Arts and Scis., Coun. on Fgn. Rels. Office: U Miami Law Sch PO Box 248087 Coral Gables FL 33124-8087

ELY, LAURENCE DRIGGS, III, theoretical Christian astrologer; b. N.Y.C., Feb. 3, 1945; s. Laurence D. Ely Jr. and Winifred F. (Forgit) Ewing; m. Tamson Myers, Mar. 14, 1970; children: Nicholas Myers, Alexander Nash. AB with honors, Princeton U., 1967. Rsch. chemist Monsanto, Springfield, Mass., 1968-69; dir., tchr. Demeter Inst., Amherst, Mass., 1973—. Author: True Solar and Lunar Progressions, 1982, (anthology) Astrology's Special Measurements: Toward a General Theory of Rectification, 1994. Organizer Prison Vis. Chess Club, Boston, 1970-72; mem. choir South Congl. Ch., 1995—, chair arts com., 1998—; active Friends of Rudolf Steiner. With Peace Corps, 1967, USNG, 1969-72, conscientious objector discharge, 1972. Avocations: classical music, chess, choir, tennis.

ELY, LAWRENCE ORLO, retired surgeon; b. Guthrie Center, Iowa, Dec. 13, 1919; s. John Ermerson and Luella Mabel (Knapp) E.; m. Dorothy Maxine Jenkins, Aug. 23, 1942; children: Patricia Anne, Lawrence Orlo, Stephen Craig, Bennett Knapp, Carolyn Elizabeth. BA, State U. Iowa, 1942, MD, 1943; MS, 1948, PhD, 1950. Diplomate Am. Bd. Gen. Surgery. Intern Mt. Carmel Mercy Hosp., Detroit, 1943-44; instr. dept. physiology Med. Sch., State U. Iowa, Iowa City, 1946-48, resident, instr. dept. surgery, 1948-52; pvt. practice gen. surgery Des Moines, 1952-85; mem. staff Iowa Luth. Hosp., Des Moines, 1952-85, Mercy Med. Ctr., Des Moines, 1952-85, Iowa Meth. Med. Ctr., Des Moines, 1952-86; cons. Iowa Blue Cross-Blue Shield, 1985-86, Iowa Found. for Med. Care, 1985-86. Sect. head United Campaign, Des Moines, 1958-60; mem. Des Moines Opera Bd., 1973—, pres., 1973-78; mem. Health Planning Coun. of Iowa Med. Corp., 1970-78; bd. dirs., pres. Ramsey Home, 1988-94; bd. dirs. Civic Music Assn. Des Moines, 1984-98; mem. steering com. Friends of the Arts, Drake U., Des Moines. Capt. M.C., U.S. Army, 1944-46. Fellow ACS; mem. AMA, Iowa Med. Soc., Polk County Med. Soc. Republican. Mem. Disciples of Christ Ch. Avocation: singing. Home: 3500 Fleur Dr Des Moines IA 50321-2650

ELY, PAUL C., JR., electronics company executive; b. McKeesport, Pa., Feb. 18, 1932; s. Paul C. and Jean C. E.; m. Barbara Sheiry, Apr. 3, 1953; children: Paul C., Glenn E. BSEE, Lehigh U., 1953; MSEE, Stanford U., 1964. Research and devel. engr. Sperry Rand Corp., Great Neck, N.Y. and Clearwater, Fla., 1953-62; research and devel. sect. mgr., engring. mgr. microwave div. Hewlett-Packard Co., Palo Alto, Calif., 1962-73; gen. mgr. data systems div. Hewlett-Packard Co., 1973-74, gen. mgr. computer group, 1974-76, v.p., 1976-80, exec. v.p., also bd. dirs., 1980-85; chmn., chief exec. officer Convergent Technologies (name now Unisys), San Jose, Calif., from 1985; exec. v.p. Unisys Corp., San Jose, 1989; gen. ptnr. Alpha Ptnrs. Venture Capital, 1989-98; bd. dirs. Parker-Hannifin Corp., Tektronix, The Sabre Group. Chmn. Cupertino United Fund, 1976, Bay Area Sci. Fair, 1969; regent U. Santa Clara; mem. Calif. Econ. Devel. Commn., 1976. Mem. IEEE, Am. Electronics Assn. (bd. dirs., exec. com. 1985-89).

ELY, ROBERT POLLOCK, JR., physics educator, researcher; b. Freeport, Ill., Apr. 2, 1930; s. Robert Pollock and Katharyn (Wilson) E.; m. Margaret Little, Dec. 27, 1952; children: Kimberly Ann, Courtney Katharyn, Kirsten Margaret, William. BS, MIT, 1952, MS, 1953, PhD, 1959. Physicist Lawrence Berkeley Lab., Berkeley, Calif., 1960-62; asst. prof. physics U. Calif., Berkeley, 1962-65, assoc. prof., 1966-69, prof., 1970-93, prof. emeritus, 1993—; physicist Lawrence Berkeley Lab., 1993—; program dir. NSF, 1993-95. Served to 1st lt. USAF, 1952-56. Fellow Am. Phys. Soc. Office: Univ of Calif Dept Physics 50B5238 Lawrence Berkely Lb Berkeley CA 94720

ELYA, JOHN ADEL, bishop; b. Maghdoucheh, Lebanon, Sept. 16, 1928; came to U.S., 1958; s. Maroun Milhim and Abla (Moussa) E. Bacalaureat Etudes Secondaires, Seminaire St. Sauveur, Saida, Lebanon, 1946; Baccalaureate in Sacred Theology, Pontifical Gregorian U., Rome, 1950, Licentiate in Sacred Theology, 1952; MA in Sociology, Boston Coll., 1966. Ordained priest Melkite Greek Cath., 1952, ordained bishop, 1986. Prof. moral theology Séminaire St. Sauveur, 1952-56; asst. pastor, prin. parish sch. Sacred Heart Ch., Zarka, Jordan, 1956-58; dean studies, prof. moral theology St. Basil Sem., Methuen, Mass., 1958-67, rector, 1963-66, co-founder, dir. Ecumenical Inst. for Religious Studies, 1964-67; aux. bishop Diocese of Newton for Melkites in U.S., Roslindale, Mass., 1986; rector Melkite Cathedral of Annunciation, Roslindale, 1985-89; regional bishop of Eastern region Melkites in U.S., Rosindale, 1989-90; regional bishop Western region Melkites in U.S., North Hollywood, Calif., 1990-93; eparch Diocese of Newton, Melkite Greek Caths. in U.S., 1993—; pastor Our Lady of the Cedars Ch., Manchester, N.H., 1962-63, 69-72, 80-81, St. Joseph's Melkite Ch., Lawrence, Mass., 1972-79, 82-85; local superior Basilian Salvatorian Fathers, Metheun, 1979-81; tribunal officialis Melkite Diocese, Montreal, Que., Can., 1981-82. Editor-in-chief An-Nahlah Sem. Mag., 1953-56, Du'a Al'Ajras Mission Quar., 1956-58; contbr. numerous articles to religious publs. Recipient Immigrant City award Internat. Inst. Greater Lawrence, 1986, Ellis Is. Medal of Hon. Nat. Ethnic Coalition of Orgns. Found., Inc., N.Y.C., 1996. Mem. Greater Lawrence Clerical Fellowship (sec. 1973-78, pres. 1978-79, 84-85). E-mail: BishopElya@aol.com. Home and Office: Melkite Diocese of Newton 19 Dartmouth St West Newton MA 02465-2601

ELY-CHAITLIN, MARC ERIC, government official; b. Santa Monica, Calif., Apr. 18, 1959; s. Mel and Shirley Louvella (Ely) C. LLD (hon.), RUE, Dana Point, Calif. CEO FTEC, Dana Point, 1975—; exec. pres. MRMF, Inc., Dana Point, 1989; regent Nation of Am., Dana Point, 1993-94, CEO, 1994—. Author: TheConstitution Papers, 1987, Banned in America, 1996. Organizer homeless shelters Mildred Rose Meml. Found., Inc., Orange County, Calif., 1991-95. Mem. Universal Life Ch. Office: Nation of America 27036 Azul Dr Capo Beach CA 92624-1648

ELYN, MARK, retired opera singer, educator; b. Seattle, Feb. 4, 1932; s. Isadore and Goldie Elyn; m. Jaclyn Rendall, 1956. Student, U. Wash., 1948-51, Seattle U., 1951-52; student of Robert Weede. Debut, N.Y.C. Opera, 1956, leading roles, San Francisco Opera, NBC Opera, Phila. Lyric Opera, leading bass, Cologne, Munich, Hamburg, Stuttgart, Vienna, Monte Carlo, Geneva, Barcelona; roles include: Don Giovanni, Sarastro in The Magic Flute, Philip II in Don Carlo, Figaro in The Marriage of Figaro; prof. music, U. Ill., Urbana, 1977—, chmn. voice dept., 1990—. Mem. Am. Guild Mus. Artists, Deutsche Buehnengenossenschaft, Nat. Assn. Tchrs. of Singing. Home: 1238-10th Ave East Seattle WA 98102

ELY-RAPHEL, NANCY, diplomat; b. N.Y.C, Feb. 4, 1937; d. Thomas Clarkson and Margaret (Merritt) Halliday; widowed; children: John Duff Ely, Robert Duff Ely, Stephanie Joyce Raphel. AB, Syracuse U., 1957; JD, U. San Diego, 1968. Bar: Calif. 1968, U.S. Supreme Ct. 1976. Dep. city atty. City of San Diego, 1969-70; asst. U.S. atty. So. Dist. Calif., 1970-71; assoc. Tyler, Cooper, Grant, Bowerman and Keefe, New Haven, 1971-72; from asst. to assoc. dean Sch. Law Boston U., 1972-75; atty.-advisor U.S. Dept. State, Washington, 1975-77; spl. atty. Boston Strike Force U.S. Dept. Justice, 1977-78; asst. legal advisor African Affairs U.S. Dept. State, Washington, 1978-87, asst. legal advisor Nuclear Affairs, 1988-89; dep. asst. Sec. of State Bur. Democracy, Human Rights and Labor Affairs, Washington, 1989-93, prin. dep. asst., 1993-95; Balkan coord. Bur. European and Can. Affairs, Washington, 1995-98; U.S. amb. to Slovenia, Am. Embassy, Ljubljana, 1998—. Mem. Coun. on Fgn. Rels., 1988-96. Recipient Outstanding Alumni award U. San Diego Law Sch., 1979, Superior Honor award U.S. Dept. State, Washington, 1983, 84, Presdl. Meritorious Svc. award U.S. Govt., Washington, 1986, 94, Presdl. Disting. Svc. award, 1992. Home: 1304 30th St NW Washington DC 20007-3343 Office: US Dept State Am Embassy Ljubljana Washington DC 20521-7140

ELZERMAN, ALAN WILLIAM, environmental chemistry educator; b. Ann Arbor, Mich., Apr. 2, 1949; m. 1970; 2 children. BA, Williams Coll., 1971; PhD in Water Chemistry, U. Wis., 1976. Rsch. asst. water chemistry U. Wis., 1973-76; fellow scholar Woods Hole Oceanographic Inst., Mass., 1976-78; fellow Atomic Energy Rsch. Establishment, Eng., 1978; asst. prof., assoc. prof. Clemson U., Anderson, S.C., 1978-88, prof. environ. chemistry, environ. systems engring., 1988—; chair environ. engring. and sci., dir. Sch. of Environment Clemson U., Anderson, 1997—. Mem. Am. Chem. Soc., Water Pollution Control Fedn., Assn. Environ. Engring. Profs., Am. Geophys Union, Soc. Environ. Toxicology and Chemistry. Office: Clemson U Environ Engring & Sci 342 Computer Ct Anderson SC 29625-6510

EMANS, ROBERT LEROY, academic administrator, education educator; b. Madison, Wis., June 12, 1934; s. Lester Meeker and Anita Margaret (Jones) E.; m. Jeanne Elizabeth Faughnan, June 21, 1958; children: Charlotte, Jennifer, Rebecca. BS with honors, U. Wis., 1957; MA, U. Chgo., 1958, PhD, 1963; postdoctoral, Harvard U., 1980. Cert. elem. tchr. Tchr. 6th grade Montreal Pub. Schs., Que., Can., 1959-60; from instr. to asst. prof. edn. U. Wis., Milw., 1963-64; asst. prof. edn. Chgo. Tchrs. Coll., 1964-66; research assoc. U. Chgo., 1965-66; assoc. prof. edn. Temple U., Phila., 1966-68; prof. edn., chmn. Ohio State U., Columbus, 1968-74; dean, prof. edn. U. Md., College Park, 1974-76; assoc. dean, prof. edn. Coll. William and Mary, Williamsburg, Va., 1976-84; prof. edn., dean U. S.D., Vermillion, 1984-90, Tenn. State U., Nashville, 1990—; vis. asst. prof. U. Chgo., 1966, research assoc., 1965-66; vis. prof. U. Hawaii, Honolulu, 1971; mem. State Task Force on Tchr. Induction, S.D., 1986, State Task Force on Cert. of Tchrs., S.D., 1986, Gov.'s Scholarship com., S.D., 1987, Gov.'s Task Force on Tchr.'s Pay, S.D., 1987; cons. U.S. Office Edn., Washington, State Govts. of Ohio, Md., Va., S.D. Author: A Question of Competence, 1972; contbr. articles to profl. jours. Served to 1st lt. U.S. Army, 1958. Fellow Nat. Council Research in English (pres. 1974-75); mem. Am. Assn. Coll. for Tchr. Edn., Assn. Tchr. Educators, S.D. Assn. of Coll. for Tchr. Edn., Phi Delta Kappa. Avocations: time farming, traveling. Home: 4701 Michigan Ave Nashville TN 37209-2221 Office: Dean Edn Tenn State U Nashville TN 37209

EMANUEL, ABRAHAM GABRIEL, photo processing company executive, consultant; b. Bklyn., Feb. 25, 1930; s. Levy A. and Anna G. (Ullman) E.; m. Patricia Ann Clark, July, 1955 (dec. Jan. 1966); children: David C., Keith D. BChemE, Cornell U., 1952; MBA, Hofstra U., 1959. Chem. engr. E. I. DuPont, Wilmington, Del., 1952-53, mem. new bus. devel. staff, 1967-86; indsl. salesman Texaco, N.Y.C., 1955-59; product engr. Crown Cen. Petroleum Corp., Balt., 1959-63; product mgr. Carus Chem. Co., La Salle, Ill., 1963-66; v.p. Robinson Assoc., Newark, 1966-67; owner, pres., CEO Photo Bug, Inc., Wilmington, 1983—; mktg. cons., Wilmington, 1986—. Contbr. numerous articles to sci. and profl. jours. With U.S. Army, 1953-55. Mem. Am. Mktg. Assn., Am. Chem. Soc., Photographic Mktg. Assn. Avocations: skiing, tennis, photography. Office: Photo Bug Inc 2203 Concord Pike Wilmington DE 19803-2908

EMANUEL, EVELYN LOUISE, nurse; b. Curaçao, Netherlands Antilles, May 16, 1958; came to the U.S., 1980; d. Joshua George and Eileen Aurora (Phillip) E.; children: Jamal, Victor. AAS, Bronx (N.Y.) C.C., 1990; BSN, Coll. New Rochelle, 1994, postgrad., 1995—. RN, N.Y.; cert. med.-surg. nursing, ANCC.; chemotherapy cert.; respiratory cert., cardio pulmonary cert. Nursing asst. Our Lady of Mercy Med. Ctr., Bronx, 1987-89, LPN, 1989-90, RN oncology unit, 1990—. Tchr. Sunday Sch., Trinity Episcopal Ch., 1992—. Avocations: basketball, reading, netball. Home: 4140 Carpenter Ave Apt 3D Bronx NY 10466-2633 Office: Our Lady Mercy Med Ctr 600 E 233rd St Bronx NY 10466-2697

EMANUEL, KERRY ANDREW, earth sciences educator; b. Cin., Apr. 21, 1955; s. Albert II and Marny Catherine (Schonegevel) E.; m. Susan Boyd-Bowman, Dec. 29, 1990; 1 child, David Tristan Emanuel. SB in Earth and Planetary Scis., MIT, 1976, PhD in Meteorology, 1978. From adj. asst. prof. to asst. prof. dept. atmospheric scis. UCLA, 1978-81; postdoctoral fellow Coop. Inst. Mesoscale Meteorological Studies, U. Okla., 1979; asst. prof. dept. meteorology and physical oceanography MIT, 1981-83, from asst. prof. to assoc. prof. ctr. meteorology and physical oceanography, dept. earth, atmospheric & planetary scis., 1983-87, prof., 1987—, dir., 1989-97. Contbr. articles to profl. jours., textbooks, monographs. Fellow Am. Meteorol. Soc. (Meisinger award 1986, Banner I. Miller award with Richard Rotunno, 1992); mem. Sigma Xi, Phi Beta Kappa. Avocations: sailing, classical music. Office: MIT Dept Earth Atmosphere and Planet 77 Massachusetts Ave Cambridge MA 02139-4301

EMANUEL, MYRON, corporate communications specialist, consultant; b. N.Y.C., Oct. 25, 1920; s. Levy A. and Anna (Ullman) E.; B.A., N.Y. U., 1941; m. Maud Margaret Wenkenbach, Sept. 5, 1947; children—Christina Ann, Robin Duhamel, Anna Lee Chatty, Heather. Mem. editl. staffs Newsweek mag., 1941-42, Life mag., 1943-47, Sci. Illus., 1947-48, New Republic mag., 1949, Esquire, 1950-51; mgr. pub. affairs dept. E.I DuPont de Nemours & Co., Inc., Wilmington, Del., 1951-75; dir. bus. comm. programs Towers, Perrin, N.Y.C., 1975-81; pres. Myron Emanuel/Communications, Inc., 1982—; lectr. Hunter Coll., 1985—; lectr. various colls., univs., 1960—; condr. workshops, seminars, 1965—; vis. prof. Pub. Rels. John Curtin U., Perth, Australia, 1994—. Recipient Freedoms Found. medals, 1971, 72, 74; named Vis. Fellow of Pub. Rels. Inst. Australia. Fellow Internat. Assn. Bus. Communicators (named one of 25 most significant contbrs. to the success of Internat. Assn. Bus. Communicators 1995); mem. Council Communication Mgmt. (dir. 1972-80), Public Relations Soc. Am., AAAS, Nat. Assn. Sci. Writers. Club: Delaware Press (dir. 1952—). Author: Faces of Freedom, 1972; (with others) Corporate Economic Education Programs-An Evaluation and Appraisal, 1980, Communications Handbook for Human Resources Managers; contbr. chpt.: Inside Organizational Communications, 1981, 2d edit., 1985; contbr. numerous articles to profl. jours. Home: 8 Whitfield Pl Newport RI 02840-2963 Office: 350 E 30th St New York NY 10016-8323

EMANUEL, WILLIAM GILBERT, electrical engineer; b. Bklyn., July 9, 1956; s. William Victor and Lillian E.; m. Renee Marie Spears, Apr. 6, 1980. BS, Howard U., 1980, MS, 1986; DDiv (hon.), GMOR Theol. Inst., 1994. Elec. engr. Bechtel Power Corp., Gaithersburg, Md., 1980-81; constrn. engr. Bellefonte Nuclear Power Plant Tenn. Valley Authority, Scottsboro, Ala., 1982-84; sys. planning engr. Phila.-N.J.-Md. Interconnection Ofc. Phila. Electric Co., Norristown, Pa., 1986-92; project engr. prodn. dept. Phila. Electric Co., 1992-93; engring. cons. Howard U. Energy Sys. Network Lab.,

Washington, 1988-93; sys. engr. M&M Tech. Svcs., Lake Ridge, Va., 1998—; U.S. rep. to the 1st U.S./Sub-Sahara conf. on power sys.: Voltage Collapse and Voltage Regulation; founder The Faith of Jesus Ctr. and People of Color Tng. & Rsch. Inst.; lectr. to schs., coll., ch. and civic orgns., 1992—. Author: People of Color in the Bible series, Vol. 1 for Adults: Preliminaries (Establishing a Foundation), 1992, People of Color in the Bible for Children series, Vol. 1 In the Beginning; Vol. 2 Adam & Eve, Vol. 3 The Garden of Eden, 1995; (videos) People of Color In the Bible, 1993, Last Days Events and the New World Order Series Episode #1 God's Prophetic Timetable Revealed Through the Sanctuary Services, 1994, Episode #2 The Millenium Bug: The Year 2000 (Y2K), 1998. Office: The Faith of Jesus Center People of Color Tng/Rsch 136 The Farm Summertown TN 38483-9627

EMANUEL, WILLIAM JOSEPH, lawyer; b. Hawthorne, Calif., Oct. 31, 1938; s. Lawrence John and Henrietta (Moser) E.; m. Elizabeth Wolfe, Mar. 14, 1964; children—Christina, Michael, Steven. A.B., Marquette U., 1960; J.D., Georgetown U., 1963. Bar: Nebr. 1963, Calif. 1965, U.S. Supreme Ct. 1976. Assoc. Musick, Peeler & Garrett, L.A., 1963-70, ptnr., 1970-76; ptnr. Morgan, Lewis & Bockius, L.A., 1976-97; ptnr. Jones, Day, Reavis & Pogue, L.A., 1998—; mem. labor rels.. com. Am. Hosp. Assn., also mem. spl. subcom. to analyze report of Nat. Commn. on Nursing, Comparable Worth Task Force; mem. adv. com. NLRB, 1994—. Author: (with Michael L. Wolfram) California Employment Law, A Guide to California Laws Regulating Employment in the Private Sector, 1989. Mem. ABA (mem. com. on devel. of law under Nat. Labor Relations Act sect. on labor and employment law), State Bar Calif. (labor and employment law sect.), Los Angeles County Bar Assn. (chmn. labor law sect. 1983-84, mem. exec. com. 1974-86), So. Calif. Labor Law Symposium (founding chmn. 1980, 81), Am. Soc. Hosp. Attys., State Bar Nebr. Contbr. articles to profl. jours. Office: Jones Day Reavis & Pogue 555 W 5th St Ste 4600 Los Angeles CA 90013-1025

EMANUELE, R.M., business executive. V.p. rsch. and bus. devel. Cytrx Corp., Norcross, Ga. Office: Cytrx Corp Tech Park/Atlanta 154 Technology Pkwy Norcross GA 30092-2911*

EMANUEL-SMITH, ROBIN LESLEY, special education educator; m. Allen Weston Smith, Apr. 14, 1983; children: David, Ariel, Weston. BS in Engring., U.S. Mil. Acad., 1981; BS in Health-Phys. Edn. summa cum laude, Cameron U., Lawton, Okla., 1992; M Spl. Edn., Coll. of St. Rose, Albany, 1995. Cert. spl. edn., health and phys. edn. tchr., N.Y. Enlisted U.S. Army, 1974-76, commd. 2nd lt., 1981, advanced through grades to capt., 1984, resigned, 1990; tchr. spl. edn. Ulster County Bd. Coop. Ednl. Svcs., Port Ewen, N.Y., 1992—. Roman Catholic. Avocations: weightlifting, coaching and officiating youth soccer, softball and baseball. Office: Ulster County Bd Coop Ednl Svs Rt 32 New Paltz NY 12561

EMANUELSON, JAMES ROBERT, retired insurance company executive; b. Hammond, Ind., Sept. 12, 1931; s. Clarence Harry and Ethel Janet (Anderson) E.; m. Dolores Patricia Fordyce, Aug. 10, 1957; children: James Robert, John Thomas, Karen Lynn. B.S., Denison U., 1953. With Midland Mut. Life Ins. Co., Columbus, Ohio, 1953-67; mgr. gen. accounting Midland Mut. Life Ins. Co., 1957-62, dir. cost accounting, 1962-67; with Columbus Mut. Life Ins. Co., 1967—, comptroller, 1969—, apptd. v.p., 1970-76, v.p., elected officer, 1976-91, v.p., comptroller, treas., 1991-93, ret., 1993—. Mem. Ins. Acctg. and Statis. Assn. (mem. interco. fin. rev. com. 1972-82, chmn. com. 1978-82, mem. fin. planning and control coun. 1978-91, cost acctg. com. 1982-91), Sigma Chi. Republican. Home: 8232 Copperfield Dr Columbus OH 43235-1102

EMBER, CAROL R., anthropology educator, author; b. Bklyn., July 7, 1943; d. Hy and Elsie (Kardonsky) Ruchlis; m. Lawrence Baldwin, 1963 (div. 1969); m. Melvin Ember, Mar. 21, 1970; children: Katherine Ann, Julie Beth. BA, Antioch Coll., 1965; postgrad., Cornell U., 1965-66; PhD, Harvard, 1971. Lectr. Hunter Coll. CUNY, 1970-71; from asst. prof. to assoc. prof. CUNY, 1971-80; prof. Hunter Coll., 1981-97; exec. dir. Human Rels. Area Files Yale U., New Haven, Conn., 1997—. Author: Anthropology, 1973, Cultural Anthropology, 1973, (with M. Ember) Marriage, Family, and Kinship: Comparative Studies of Social Organization, 1983, Anthropology: A Brief Introduction, 1991, Anthropology, 9th edition, 1999, Cultural Anthropology, 9th edition, 1999, Anthropology: A Brief Introduction, 3rd edition, 1998; co-author: (with Burton Pasternak and M. Ember) Sex, Gender, and Kinship: A Cross-Cult Perspective; co-editor: Cross-Cultural Research for Social Science, 1998, Portraits of Culture, 1998, Research Frontiers in Anthropology, 1998. Woodrow Wilson Fellow, 1965-66, predoctoral fellow NIMH, 1969-70; rsch. grantee NSF, 1983-84, 86-98, U.S. Inst. Peace, 1990-92. Mem. Am. Anthrop. Assn., Soc. for Cross-Cultural Rsch. (pres. 1985), Soc. for Psychol. Anthropology. Office: Yale U Human Rels Area Files 755 Prospect St New Haven CT 06511-1225

EMBERLAND, GORM PETTER, software developer, computer programmer; b. Bergen, Norway, Aug. 28, 1958; came to the U.S., 1960; s. Rolf Bjarne and Sylvia Ekrheim Emberland; m. Joan Marie Judge, June 18, 1983; children: Ann Elizabeth, Colin Rolf. *Dr. Rolf Emberland, PhD Biochemistry, emigrated from Norway to the United Stateswith wife Sylvia and two sons Trond and Gorm in 1960. In 1964, daughter Anne wasadded to family. Dr. Emberland chose to move to the U.S. based on a position offered at the Worchester Foundation for Experimental Biology in Medicine. He was part of the team that developed the oral contraceptive pill. In the mid-1960s the family moved to Salisbury, Maryland where Dr. Emberland accepted the position of Laboratory Chief at Peninsula General Hospital. Dr. Emberland died in 1976. Slyvia Emberland remarried J. Ronald Fidler, Vice President of Wyoming Concrete in Dover, Delaware.* BS in Zoology, U. Md., 1981, BS in Computer Sci., 1986. Landsat computer ops. mgr. Earth Satellite Corp., Chevy Chase, Md., 1981-84; sys. programmer, mgr. prime ops. Program Resources, Inc., Annapolis, Md., 1984-87; prime applications mgr. AGB TV Rsch., Inc., Columbia, Md., 1987-88; sr. sys. analyst Unisys Corp., Washington, 1988-91; computer specialist, software engr. USDA, Agrl. Rsch. Svc., Nat. Germplasm Resources Lab., Beltsville, Md., 1991—. Contbr. numerous articles to EPA nat. newsletter. Laborer, vol. Christmas in April, Calvert County, Md., 1997, 98; soccer coach, vol. Spring Soccer, Calvert Soccer Assn., Calverty County, 1999; mem. Rep. Nat. Com. (Cert. Appreciation, 1988, Cert. of Recongition, 1990, 92). Recipient Cert. of Merit for Technol. Transfer Activities Aimed at Preservation and Use of Genetic Resources, USDA, 1996, Cert. of Merit Outstanding Support of Nat. Germplasm Resources Lab., 1996, Cert. Merit Using Data Processing Tecnnols.to Produce Databases of Nat. and Internat. Plant Germplasm Systems, 1997, Award of Merit for Excellence in Technol. Transfer Fed. Lab. Consortium, 1997, Cert. of Merit Devel. of Plant Germplasm Info. System Implemented On a Personal Computer, USDA, 1998. Mem. Nat. Trust for Hist. Preservation, Smithsonian Instn., The Civil War Trust (Friends of the Field award 1998), Disabled Am. Veterans (Commdrs. Club 1994). Republican. Lutheran. Achievements include development of Germplasm Resources Information Network for the Personal Computer. This software which has been translated into other languages is now a leading force in standardizing Germplasm management and documentation systems worldwide. Avocations: hiking, reading, biking, boating, horses. E-mail: emberland@olg.com. Home: 3151 Hunting Creek Rd Huntingtown MD 20639-9565

EMBLETON, TONY FREDERICK WALLACE, retired Canadian government official; b. Hornchurch, Essex, Eng., Oct. 1, 1929; emigrated to Can., 1952; s. Frederick William Howard and Lucy Violet Muriel (Wallace) E.; m. Eileen Loraine Blackall, Nov. 14, 1953; 1 dau., Sheila. B.Sc. with honours, U. London, 1950, Ph.D. in Physics, 1952, D.Sc., 1964. Postdoctoral fellow NRC, Ottawa, Ont., Can., 1952-53; asst. research officer NRC, 1954-57, asso. research officer, 1957-62, sr. research officer, 1962-74, prin. research officer, 1974-90, ret., 1990; vis. lectr. U. Ottawa, 1959-69, MIT, 1964, 67, 72; John Wiley Jones award lectr.Rochester Inst. Tech., 1976; adj. prof. Carleton U. 1977-90. Patentee in field; contbr. articles to profl. jours. Mem. Rockcliffe Park Pub. Sch. Bd., 1966-69; bd. dirs. Youth Sci. Found., 1967-72. Recipient Arch T. Coldwell award Soc. Automotive Engrs., 1974. Fellow Acoustical Soc. Am. (assoc. editor jour., mem. exec. coun., v.p. 1977-78, pres. 1980-81, stds. dir. 1993-97, Biennial award 1964, Silver medal in Noise 1986), Royal Soc. Can. (hon. treas. 1982-85); mem. NAE (fgn. assoc.), Can. Acoustical Assn. (founding sec. 1961-64, founding editor jour. 1971-74), Inst. Noise Control Engring. (dir. tech. group 1983-87, editl. bd. jour. 1983-93), Internat. Inst. of Noise Control Engring. (bd. dirs. 1992—). Home: PO Box 786, 80 Sheardown Dr, Nobleton, ON Canada L0G 1N0

EMBODY, DANIEL ROBERT, biometrician; b. Ithaca, N.Y., July 10, 1914; s. George Charles and Mary Madeline (Riceman) E.; m. Margaret Constance Gran, Mar. 21, 1946 (dec. Mar. 1961); children: James Michael, Daniel Robert, David Richard. BS, Cornell U., 1938, M.S., 1939, postgrad., 1939-42; postgrad., N.C. State Coll., summer 1940. Instr. limnology Cornell U., Ithaca, N.Y., 1940-42; sr. math. analyst Arnold Bernard & Co., N.Y.C., 1947-48; statistician Wash. Water Power Co., Spokane, 1949-53; head statistics sect. E.R. Squibb & Sons-Olin, New Brunswick, N.J., 1953-57, mgr. electronic data processing svc. ctr., 1958-63, coord. sci. computations, 1964-65; math. statistician Bur. Ships, Navy Dept., Washington, 1965-67; biometrician Dept. Agr., Beltsville, Md., 1967-72; staff biometrician animal and plant health inspection svc. Dept. Agr., Hyattsville, Md., 1972-87; sr. ptnr. EIC Assocs., Hyattsville, 1981—; cons. Idaho Fish and Game Dept., 1950-60, U.S. Geol. Survey, 1953-58, N.J. Dept. Fish and Game, 1953-60. Contbr. articles to profl. jours. Lt. comdr. USNR, 1942-46, ETO. Mem. IEEE, NRA, Am. Statis. Assn., Biometric Soc., Entomol. Soc. Am. (cert.; emeritus), N.Y. Acad. Scis., Assn. Computing Machinery, Am. Legion, Am. Fisheries Soc., Sigma Xi, Gamma Alpha. Home & Office: 7414 Jefferson St Hyattsville MD 20784-1758

EMBREE, AINSLIE THOMAS, history educator; b. N.S., Can., Jan. 1, 1921; came to U.S., 1958, naturalized, 1965; s. Ira Thomas and Margaret (Langley) E.; m. Suzanne Helene Harpole, May 24, 1947; children: Ralph Thomas, Margaret Louise. B.A., Dalhousie U., Halifax, N.S., 1941; B.D., Pine Hill Theol. Sem., Halifax, 1946; M.A., Union Theol. Sem., 1947, Columbia U., 1955; Ph.D., Columbia U., 1960; LL.D. hon., Juniata Coll., 1982. Prof. history Indore (India) Christian Coll., 1948-58; asst. prof., assoc. prof. history Columbia U., 1958-69, prof., 1972-91, prof. emeritus, 1991; assoc. dean Sch. Internat. Affairs, 1972-78, chmn., 1982-85, acting dean, 1989-90; prof. Duke U., 1969-72; counsellor for cultural affairs Am. Embassy, New Delhi, 1978-80, cons., 1994-95; vis. disting. prof. Brown U., 1996-97. Author: Charles Grant and British Rule in India, 1962, India, 1967, India's Search for National Identity, 1971; editor: The Hindu Tradition, 1966, Alberuni's India, 1971, Pakistan's Western Borderlands, 1978; editor in chief The Encyclopedia of Asian History, 4 vols., 1988, Imagining India, 1989, Utopias in Conflict, 1990. Served with RCAF, 1942-45. Recipient Van Doren award, 1985, Bancroft award, 1991, T. Das award, 1999, Tannenbaum award, 1999; Can. Council fellow, 1953-54; Am. Council Learned Socs. fellow, 1967; Am. Inst. Indian Studies fellow, 1968-69, 85-86; NEH fellow, 1977. Fellow AAAS; mem. Council Fgn. Relations, Assn. Asian Studies (pres. 1982-83), Am. Hist. Assn., Am. Inst. Indian Studies (pres. 1970-73). Home: 10450 Lottsford Rd #1008 Mitchellville MD 20721-7208

EMBREE, CATHERINE M., university official; b. St. Petersburg, Fla., July 18, 1966; d. Morton Thomas Embree and Wendy May (Sims) Dressel. BA, Drew U., 1988; MBA, Seton Hall U., 1996; postgrad., Columbia U., 1996—. Asst. mgr., auditor Anchor Savs. Bank, Wayne, N.J., 1988-90; compliance officer Life Instrs., Inc., New Providence, N.J., 1990-93; grad. asst. Seton Hall U., South Orange, N.J., 1993-96; assoc. Tchrs. Coll., Columbia U., N.Y.C., 1996—. Scholr N.J. Exec. Women's Assn., 1995, 96. Roman Catholic. Avocations: running, tennis, creative writing. Home: 72 W 105th St Apt 5B New York NY 10025-4016

EMBRY, MARCUS, English educator; b. Albuquerque, Apr. 18, 1960; s. Raymond Smiley and Elisama E.; m. Ulrike Seckler, Oct. 29, 1995; 1 child, Jonah Embry-Seckler. BA, Duke U., 1982, PhD, 1997. Asst. prof. English U. No. Colo., Greeley, 1995—. Editor: Latin Americanism as Cultural Practice, 1999. Fgn. Lang. Area Studies fellow U.S. Dept. Edn., 1994-95. Mem. MLA, Am. Studies Assn. Office: Dept English U No Colo Greeley CO 80639

EMBRY, ROBERT C., foundation administrator; b. Balt., 1937; m. Mary Ann Mears; children: Elizabeth, Katherine, Clair, Julia. Grad. with honors, Williams Coll., 1959; JD with honors, Harvard U., 1964; hon. degree, Md. Inst. Art, Morgan State U. Law clk. to Judge Simon E. Sobeloff U.S. Ct. Appeals (4th cir.), 1965; assoc. Venable, Baetjer and Howard, 1965-68; adj. prof. polit. sci. Loyola Coll., 1968-71; asst. sec. Dept. HUD for Cmty. Planning and Devel., 1977-81; ptnr. Cordish Embry & Assocs., 1981-87; pres. Abell Found., Balt., 1987—; exec. dir. Pres.' Task Force on Urban Policy, 1977-81. Exec. sec. Mayor's Task Force on Alcoholism, 1965-67; mem. Balt. City Planning Commn., 1967-68; commr. Dept. Housing and Cmty. Devel. Balt. City, 1968-77; chmn. Gov.'s Commn. on Quality Edn., Md., 1982; mem. bd. commrs. Balt. City Pub. Schs., 1983-85, pres., 1985-86; v.p. Md. State Bd. Edn., 1989-90, pres., 1990-95; bd. dirs. Greater Balt. Com., 1996—, Balt. City Empowerment Zone, 1995—; founding bd. dirs. 1000 Friends of Md. Named Balt. Young Man of Yr. Jr. Assn. Commerce, 1968, Md. Young Man of Yr. Jr. Assn. Commerce, 1969, One of 50 Outstanding Young Nat. Leaders Time mag., 1979; recipient Calvert medal State of Md., Andrew White medal Loyola Coll., J. Jefferson Miller award Greater Balt. Com., Frances M. Froelicher award Citizens Planning and Housing Assn. Mem. ABA, Balt. Bar Assn. Home: 903 Poplar Rd Baltimore MD Office: Abell Found 111 S Calvert St Ste 2300 Baltimore MD 21202

EMBRY, STEPHEN CRESTON, lawyer; b. Key West, Fla., Feb. 13, 1949; s. Jewell Creston and Julia Martine (Taylor) E.; m. Priscilla Mary Brown, Aug. 21, 1971; children: Nathaniel, Julia, Jessamyn. BA, Am. U., 1971; JD, U. Conn., 1976. Bar: Conn. 1976, U.S. Dist. Ct. Conn., 1976, U.S. Ct. Appeals (2d, 5th and 9th cirs.). Staff aide to Pres. The White House, Washington, 1969-72; assoc. Turner & Hensley, Great Bend, Kans., 1976, O'Brien, Shafner, Bartinik, & Stuart, Groton, Conn., 1976-85, Embry and Neusner, Groton, Conn., 1985—. Mem. editl. bd. Matthew Bender, BRB Reporter; contbr. articles to profl. publs. Mem. Groton Rep. com., 1976-83, North Stonington Rep. com., 1984-88; chmn. Groton Housing Authority, 1979-80. Mem. ATLA (chair workers compensation sect. 1984-85, bd. dirs. workplace injury litigation group), Maritime Claimants Attys. Assn. (bd. dirs. 1980—), Conn. Trial Lawyers, Conn. Bar Assn. (exec. bd.), Thames Club, Grange. Democrat.

EMBRY, WAYNE RICHARD, former basketball executive; b. Springfield, Ohio, Mar. 26, 1937; s. Floyd and Anna Elizabeth (Gardner) E.; m. Theresa Jackson, June 6, 1959; children: Deborah, Jill, Wayne Richard. BS, Miami U., Oxford, Ohio, 1958. Profl. basketball player Cin. Royals, 1958-66, Boston Celtics, 1966-68; Profl. basketball player Milw. Bucks, 1968-69, gen. mgr., 1972-77, v.p., cons., 1977-85; v.p., cons. Ind. Pacers, Indpls., 1985-86; v.p., gen. mgr. Cleve. Cavaliers, 1986-99, pres., COO, 1991-99; dir. recreation City Boston, 1969-70. Trustee Basketball Hall of Fame. Inductee Basketball Hall of Fame, 1999. *

EMCH, GERARD GUSTAV, mathematics and physics educator; b. Geneva, July 21, 1936; came to U.S., 1964; s. Martial Désiré and Violette Marie (Cornaglia) E.; m. Antoinette S. Dériaz, July 25, 1959; children: Florence Christiane, René-Didier Guillaume. PhD, U. Geneva, 1963. Asst. in theoreticlal physics. U.Geneva, 1959-63; chef des travaux in math. physics U. Geneva, 1963-64; research assoc. Princeton U., 1964-65; research assoc. dept. applied math. U. Md., 1965-66; asst. prof. math. and physics. U. Rochester, N.Y., 1966-71; assoc. prof. U. Rochester, 1971-78, prof., 1978-86; prof., chmn. dept. math. U. Fla., 1986-88, prof. math, 1988—; vis. prof. U. Nijmegen, U. Brussels, EPF-Lausanne, U. Bielefeld, U. Geneva, U. Sao Paulo, U. Vienna, U. Paris 7; Gauss prof. Akademie der Wissenschaften zu Göttingen, 1985. Author: Algebraic Methods in Statistical Mechanics and Quantum Field Theory, 1972, Mathematical and Conceptual Foundations of 20th-Century Physics, 1984; editor: On Klauder's Path, 1994, Selected Works of E.P. Wigner, vol. 6, 1994; contbr. chpts., numerous articles to profl. publs. Mem. Internat. Assn. Math. Physics (treas. 1988-94), Am. Phys. Soc., Am. Math. Soc., Am. Math. Assn. (hon.), Phi Beta Kappa. Presbyterian. Office: U Fla Dept Math Gainesville FL 32611

EMEAGWALI, GLORIA THOMAS, humanities educator; b. Trinidad, West Indies, Feb. 6, 1950; came to U.S., 1991; BA, U. W.I., 1973; edn. dipl., London U., 1975; MA, Toronto U., 1976; PhD, Ahmadu Bello U., Zaria, Nigeria, 1986. Asst. prof. Ahmadu Bello U., Zaria, Nigeria, 1979-86; assoc. prof. Nigerian Def. Acad., 1986, Ilorin U., Nigeria, 1986-89; vis. prof. U. W.I., Trinidad, 1989, Oxford U., U.K., 1990-91; assoc. prof. history and African studies Conn. State U., New Britain, 1991-96, tenured prof. history and African studies, 1996—; mem. editorial bd. Review of African Political Economy, U,K,, chief editor Africa Update, CCSU.; mem. adv. bd. Encyclopedia of the History of Science, Technology and Medicine, Hampshire Coll., Amherst. Editor: Historical Development of Science and Technology in Nigeria, 1992, Science and Technology in African History, 1992, African Systems of Science Technology and Art, 1993, Women Pay the Price: Structural Adjustment in Africa and the Caribbean, 1995, African Civilization, 1997. Fellow Oxford U., 1990; grantee Old Dominion U., 1986, 88, AAUP Conn. State award, 1992. Mem. AAUP (Conn. state award 1992, 97), Internat. Soc. for Study of Comp. Civilization (mem. governing body, exec. com. 1992—), World Anthrop. Soc., World Archeaol. Congress, Am. Hist. Assn., African Studies Assn. Avocations: keyboard playing, table tennis. Office: Cen Conn State U History/African Studies Dept New Britain CT 06050

EMEK, SHARON HELENE, business insurance and risk management specialist; b. Bklyn., Oct. 23, 1945; d. Hyman Sampson and Cynthia Gertrude (Roth) Rabinowitz; children: Aleeza Judith, Joshua Michael, Elana Yael. BA, CCNY, 1967; MA, Bklyn. Coll., 1970; EdD, Rutgers U., 1977; cert. ins. counselor. Dir. preliminary program for small coll. Bklyn. Coll., 1969-71, 73-74; dir. Am. Ctr. Reading Skills, Tel Aviv, 1972; asst. prof. Brookdale Community Coll., Lincroft, N.J., 1975-77, Rutgers U., New Brunswick, N.J., 1977-82; pres. The Emek Group, Inc., N.Y.C., 1980-98; pres., CEO Metro Ptnrs. Inc., N.Y.C., 1998—; apptd. to Mayor's Small Bus. Adv. Bd., N.Y.C., 1998—; mem. Small Bus. Rsch. and Tech. Adv. Coun. IBM, 1998—; speaker profl. meetings. Author: Answers For Managers, 1986; Dealing Successfully with Key Management Issues, 1986. Contbr. articles to profl. jours. Founding bd. dirs. Nat. Mus. Womens History, 1997—; bd. dirs. Nat. Assn. Women Bus. Owners, N.Y.C., pres. 1997-98, Family Bus. Coun. Greater N.Y., 1997-98; bd. dirs. econ. devel. com. sect. N.Y. Womens Agenda. Recipient Promising Research award Nat. Council Tchrs. of English, 1978, Mem. of Yr. award, NAWBO-NYC, 1997, Woman of Power and Influence award NOW, N.Y.C., 1999, Helen Garvin Outstanding Achiever in Ins. Industry award Nat. Assn. Ins. Women, 1999. Mem. Profl. Ins. Agents Assn., Nat. Assn. Women Bus. Owners (pres. 1997-98, Member of Yr. 1997), Ind. Ins. Agents Assn., Ins. Fedn. N.Y., Ins. Brokers Assn. N.Y., Assn. Profl. Ins. Women, Women's Pres. Orgn., Women, Inc., Women's Leadership Forum, Emily's List (majority coun.). Avocations: writing, reading, jogging, tennis, travel. Office: MetroPartners Inc. Wall St Plz Fl 20 New York NY 10005

EMEKLI, MAHI SUZANNE, counselor, researcher; b. Washington, Jan. 5, 1963; d. Hicabi and Dolores Patricia (Melvin) E. BA in English Edn., U. Del., 1984; MEd in Counseling and Personnel, Fordham U., 1991, MS PD in Adminstrn. and Supervision, 1993, PhD in lang. literacy and learning, 1995—. Counselor Fordham Prep. Sch., Bronx, N.Y., 1991—; j.v. tennis coach Fordham Prep. Sch., 1995—, mentor SADD, 1991—, diversity com., 1993—; tutor, tchr. English Sci. and Tech. Entry program Fordham U., Bronx, 1991—. Recipient Tchr. Supts. award for writing Montgomery County Bd. of Edn., 1987-88, SADD award N.Y. City Dept. Transp., 1996, 97. Mem. Am. Counseling Assn., Assn. Adminstrn. and Supervision. Avocations: tennis, soccer, doctoral research, reading, travel.

EMELY, CHARLES HARRY, trade association executive, consultant; b. Phila., Oct. 30, 1943; s. Charles Walter and Jane Beatty (Stott) E.; m. Susan Elizabeth Lawton, June 18, 1966 (dec. Mar. 1977); 1 child, Charles Walter II; m. Mary Ann Horvath, Sept. 1, 1979; 1 stepchild, Wendy A. Vellrath. Student, Drexel Inst. Tech., 1961-62; BA, Temple U., 1967; MA, Fairfield U., 1974; postgrad., NYU, 1974-76; PhD, Calif. Western U., 1978; postgrad., Ohio U., 1981-82. Adminstrv. asst. City of Phila., 1966-68; nat. rep. ARC, Washington, 1968-70; exec. dir., chief exec. officer Bridgeport, Conn., 1970-77; pres., chief exec. officer Comprehensive Bus. Cons., Ft. Washington, Pa., 1977-86; exec. v.p., chief exec. officer Adhesive & Sealant Council, Washington, 1987-88; pres., CEO Comprehensive Bus. Cons., Inc., Fairfax, Va., 1988—; exec. dir., CEO Internat. Assn. Law Firms, 1988—; exec. dir., COO Am. Soc. Hort. Sci., Alexandria, Va., 1994-97; chmn. Cmty. Cons. Corps, Ft. Washington, 1980—; sr. cons. Philippine Nutrition Ctr., Manila, 1980; adj. faculty Ohio U., Athens, 1982-83, bd. dirs. ICM Internat., Inc.; comunications officer, U.S.A. Nat. Disaster Med. Sys., 1992—. Mem. bd. mgrs. YMCA, Fairfield, Conn., 1971-75; bd. dirs. Hope Ctr., Inc., Bridgeport, 1972-76, Comprehensive Health Planning Agy., Bridgeport, 1973-74; mem. Mayor's Energy Adv. Com., Bridgeport, 1973-74, Fayetteville (N.Y.) United Meth. Ch., 1985; trustee, v.p. Mental Health Assn. Conn., 1973-77; mem. adminstrv. bd. Nichols United Meth. Ch., Trumbull, Conn., 1975-77; adv. com. campaign coun. Rep. Nat. Com.; mem. Patriots Soc. Germantown Acad., Ft. Washington, 1978-80; pres. Ambler (Pa.) Symphony Orchestra, 1979-80; mem. Pvt. Industry Council, Ambler, 1979-80, Zanesville, Ohio, 1981-83; mem. parents council Hartwick Coll., Oneonta, N.Y., 1987. Mem. Am. Mgmt. Assn., Adminstrv. Mgmt. Soc., Am. Soc. Assn. Execs. (cert. assn. exec. 1977), Nat. Assn. Corp. Dirs. (sec./treas. Washington chpt.), Am. Railway Engring. and Maint. of Way Assn.(ceo 1998—), Found. for Internat. Meetings, Mensa, Officers Club Nat. Naval Med. Ctr. (Bethesda), Am. Radio Relay League, Aircraft Owners and Pilots Assn., Armed Forces Comms. and Electronics Assn., Associated Pub. Safety Comm. Officers, Rep. Nat. Com. Campain Coun. Rep. Nat. Com. Pres.'s Club, U. of Conn. Alumni Assn. (life), Renewable Natural Resources Found. (bd. dirs.). Republican. Clubs: Phila. Aviation Country, Vesper, University, City of Washington, Nat. Assn. Execs. Lodges: Masons, Shriners, Rotary. Avocations: music, amateur radio, aviation, philately, travel. Home: 9715 Oak Bridge Pl Fairfax VA 22039-3400 Office: Computer Bus Cons Inc PO Box 2604 Fairfax VA 22031-0604

EMELY, MARY ANN, association executive; b. Bridgeport, Conn., Aug. 10, 1947; d. John and Stefanie Maria (Hutta) Horvath; m. Timothy Vellrath, Sept. 7, 1968 (div. Mar. 1975); 1 child, Wendy Amethyst Vellrath Delbrook; m. Charles H. Emely, Sept. 1, 1979. BA, U. Conn., 1969; postgrad., U. Bridgeport, 1975-76, Ohio U., 1982-83. Adminstrv. asst. ARC, Bridgeport, 1973-78; dir. mem. svcs. Comprehensive Assn. Cons., Ft. Washington, Pa., 1978-81; exec. dir. Muskingum County Respiratory Disease, Zanesville, Ohio, 1981-83; assoc. exec. dir. The Vol. Ctr., Syracuse, N.Y., 1984-86; dir. mem. programs NEA, Rockville, Md., 1986-91; dir. mem., mktg. Am. Geophys. Union, Washington, 1991-93; sr. dir. membership Coun. for Exceptional Children, Reston, Va., 1993-94; dep. exec. dir. Spl. Librs. Assn., Washington, 1994-95; exec. dir. Fedn. Govt. Info. Processing Couns., Fairfax, Va., 1995—; cons. Comprehensive Assn. Cons., Fairfax, Va., 1991—. Editor Husky P.A.W. Print, 1995-96, Fedn. Facts, 1995—; columnist Female Exec., 1994-95. Bd. dirs. Pub. Employees Roundtable, Washington, 1995—; mem. Nat. Rep. Coalition for Choice, Washington, 1993—, Jr. League of Washington, 1986—. Mem. NAFE, Am. Soc. assn. Execs. (cert., mentor diversity programs 1994-95), Am. Radio Relay League, Greater Washington Soc. Assn. Execs., Found. for Internat. Meetings, Mercedes Benz Club of Am., U. Conn. Alumni Assn. (Washington chpt., pres. 1996—), Kappa Alpha Theta. Methodist. Avocations: gardening, flower arranging, reading. Home: PO Box 420 Fairfax Station VA 22039-0420 Office: FGIPC 3601 Chain Bridge Rd Ste E Fairfax VA 22030-3243

EMENHISER, JEDON ALLEN, political science educator, academic administrator; b. Clovis, N.Mex., May 19, 1933; s. Glen Allen and Mary Opal (Sasser); m. Patricia Ellen Burke, Jan. 27, 1954; 1 child, Melissa Mary Emenhiser Westerfield. Student, Am. U., 1954; BA, U. Redlands, 1955; PhD, U. Minn., 1962. Cert. community coll. adminstr., Calif. Instr. to prof. polit. sci. Utah State U., Logan, 1960-77, acting dean, 1973-74; prof. Humboldt State U., Arcata, Calif., 1977—, dean, 1977-86; acting v.p. Humboldt State U., Arcata, 1984; chair Social Sci. Rsch. and Instrnl. Coun. Calif. State U., 1994-95; prof. Jr. Statesmen Summer Sch., Stanford U., 1989—; vis. instr. U. Redlands, Calif., 1959-60; vis. prof. U. Saigon, Vietnam, 1964-65; asst. dean Colgate U., Hamilton, N.Y., 1972-73; staff dir. Utah Legislature, Salt Lake City, 1967, cons., 1968-77; dir. Bur. Govt. and Opinion Rsch., Logan, 1965-70; cons. USCG, McKinleyville, Calif., 1982; v.p. Exch. Bank, New Franklin, Mo., 1970-76; reader advanced placement exam. U.S. Govt. Coll. Bd., 1990—; vis. fellow govt. divsn. Congl. Rsch. Svc. Libr. of Congress, 1996. Author: Utah's Governments, 1964, Freedom and Power in California, 1987; editor, contbr. Dragon on the Hill, 1970, Rocky Mountain Urban Politics, 1971; producer, dir. TV broadcasts The Hawks and the Doves, 1965-66; contbr. articles to profl. jours. Sec. Cache

County Dem. Party, Logan, 1962-63; chmn. Mayor's Commn. on Govt. Orgn., Logan, 1973-74; campaign mgr. various candidates and issues, Logan, 1965-75; bd. dirs. Humboldt Connections, Eureka, Calif., 1986-96, pres., 1989-92; elder Presbyn. ch. Sr. Fulbright-Hays lectr. Com. Internat. Exch. of Persons, Vietnam, 1964-65; Adminstrv. fellow Am. Coun. Edn., Colgate U., 1972-73; Paul Harris fellow Rotary Internat. Mem. Am. Polit. Sci. Assn., Western Polit. Sci. Assn., Am. Studies Assn., Phi Beta Kappa, Omicron Delta Kappa. Presbyterian. Avocations: gardening, photography, travel. Home: PO Box 250 Bayside CA 95524-0250 Office: Humboldt State U Dept Polit Sci Arcata CA 95521

EMERICK, NORMAN COOPER, consulting engineer; b. Springfield, Ill., Nov. 26, 1921; s. Athal Elder and Hazel Frances (Cooper) E.; m. Charlotte Lorraine Thompson, Feb. 19, 1950 (dec. Dec. 1996); children: Bruce Clay Cooper, Ingrid Anne. BS in Civil Engring., U. Ill., 1949, MS, 1950. Registered profl. engr., Md., Va. Consulting engr. Balt., 1960—; co-founder, founding pres. Mid-Atlantic Germanic Soc., 1982—. Fellow ASCE; mem. Chi Epsilon. Avocations: geneaology, hunting, fishing, biking. Office: 132 W 25th St Baltimore MD 21218-5006

EMERICK, ROBERT EARL, sociologist, educator; b. Cleve., Mar. 17, 1942; s. Merl Lowell and Virginia Melissa (Newmyer) E.; m. Carol Ann Carter, Nov.24, 1963; children: Laura Lee, Lynn Lee Emerick Hall. BA, U. Calif., Santa Barbara, 1964; PhD, Northwestern U., 1971. Prof. sociology San Diego State U., 1968—. Contbr. numerous articles to profl. jours. Home: 3829 Albatross St San Diego CA 92103-3017 Office: San Diego State U Dept Sociology San Diego CA 92182

EMERLING, CAROL G(REENBAUM), consultant; b. Cleve., Sept. 13, 1930; d. Bernard and Florence A. Greenbaum; m. Norton Harvey Noll, Oct. 1, 1950 (dec. July 1951); m. Stanley Justin Emerling, May 2, 1953 (div. Aug. 1971); children—Keith S., Susan C.; m. Jerrold A. Fadem, Aug. 24, 1974 (div. Oct. 1977). Student, Vassar Coll., 1948-49, Case Western Res. U., 1949-50; LL.B. summa cum laude, Cleve. State U., 1955. Bar: Ohio 1955, U.S. Supreme Ct. 1971, Calif. 1975, N.Y. 1982. Instr. Cleve. Coll., 1956-59; from staff atty. to atty.-in-charge Legal Aid Defenders Office, Cleve., 1962-70; regional dir. FTC, Cleve., 1970-74, L.A., 1974-78; sec. Am. Home Products Corp., N.Y.C., 1978-96; cons. Far Hills, N.J., 1997-98; adv. com. criminal rules Supreme Ct. Ohio, 1970-73; chmn. Cleve. Fed. Exec. Bd., 1973; internat. health policy cons.; bd. chair Global Health Coun.; bd. dirs. INMED. Co-author: The Allergy Cookbook, 1969; Contbr. articles to legal jours. Founder Pepper Pike (Ohio) Civic League, 1959; sec. Pepper Pike Charter Commn., 1966. Recipient Claude E. Clarke award Legal Aid Soc., 1967; Disting. Service award FTC, 1972. Mem. Assn. Bar City N.Y., State Bar Calif., N.Y. State Bar Assn, State Bar Ohio.

EMERSON, ALICE FREY, political scientist, educator emerita; b. Durham, N.C., Oct. 26, 1931; d. Alexander Hamilton and Alice (Hubbard) Frey; divorced; children: Rebecca, Peter. AB, Vassar Coll., 1953; PhD, Bryn Mawr Coll., 1964; LLD (hon.), Wheaton Coll., 1986, Middlebury Coll., 1998; DHL (hon.), Trinity Coll., 1992. Tchr., Newton (Mass.) High Sch., 1956-58; mem. faculty Bryn Mawr (Pa.) Coll., 1961-64; mem. faculty U. Pa., Phila., 1966-75, asst. prof. polit. sci., 1966-75, dean of women, 1966-69, dean of students, 1969-75; pres. Wheaton Coll., Norton, Mass., 1975-91, pres. emerita, 1991—; sr. fellow Andrew Mellon Found., N.Y.C., 1991-98, sr. advisor, 1998—; bd. dirs. AES Corp., BankBoston Corp., BankBoston, Champion Internat. Paper, Eastman Kodak Co.; adv. bd. HERS Mid-Am. Bd. dirs. Corp. for Pub. and Pvt. Ventures; bd. dirs. World Resources Inst., Salzburg Seminar, Nantucket Hist. Assn., MGH-Inst. Health Professions. Mem. Coun. on Fgn. Rels. Address: PO Box 206 Siasconset MA 02564

EMERSON, ALTON CALVIN, retired physical therapist; b. Webster, N.Y., Sept. 29, 1934; s. Homer Douglas and Pluma (Babcock) E.; m. Nancy Ann Poarch, Dec. 20, 1955 (div. 1972); children: Marcia Ann, Mark Alton; m. Barbara Irene Stewart, Oct. 6, 1972. BS in Vertibrate Zoology, U. Utah, 1957; cert. phys. therapy, U. So. Calif., 1959. Staff phys. therapist Los Angeles County Crippled Children's Services, 1958-65; pvt. practice phys. therapy Los Angeles, 1966-98; ret., 1998; cons. City of Hope, Duarte, Calif., 1962-72; trustee Wolcott Found. Inc., St. Louis, 1972-86, chmn. bd. trustees, 1980-85. Recipient Cert. of Achievement, George Washington U., Washington, 1986. Mem. Masons (pres. Temple City High Twelve Club 1971, master Camellia 1973, pres. Calif. Assn. High Twelve Clubs 1986, internat. pres. High Twelve 1990-91, mem. High Twelve Internat., Pasadena Scottish Rite Bodies, Venerable Master, Lodge of Perfection 1998, KCCH, Legion Merit), Royal Order Scotland, Al Malaikah Tmeple, Ancient Arabic order Nobles Mystic Shrine, DeMolay Legion of Honor, Order of DeMolay (hon. internat. supreme coun.), Conejo-Westlake Shrine Club (pres. 1996). Home and Office: 287 W Avenida De Las Flores Thousand Oaks CA 91360-1808

EMERSON, ANDI (MRS. ANDI EMERSON WEEKS), sales and advertising executive; b. N.Y.C., Nov. 1, 1932; d. Willard Ingham and Ethel (Mole) E.; m. George G. Fawcett, Jr. (div.); children—Ann Fawcett Ambia, George Gifford III, Christopher Babcock; m. Kenneth E. Weeks (div.); 1 child, Electra Ingham. Student, Barnard Coll. Successively v.p. Eugene Stevens, Inc., N.Y.C.; pres., dir. Emerson Mktg. Agy., Inc., N.Y.C., 1960—; pres., dir. Mail Order Operating Co. Ltd., N.Y.C. and London, 1976-88, Ingham Hall, Ltd., 1977-83; chmn. bd. dirs. Sonal World Mktg. Ltd., N.Y.C. and Delhi, India, 1983-87; instr. NYU, 1960-65, 87—; internat. lectr., seminar conductor Buenos Aires, Argentina, 1995—, Manila, Philippines, 1996. Vol. children's ward Meml. Hosp., 1964-66, Hosp. for Spl. Surgery, 1967; mem. adv. com. African Students League, 1965-67; bd. dirs. Violet Oakley Meml. Found., Phila., 1964-81; founder, pres., chmn. John Caples Internat. Awards, 1977—; elected N.Y. State Del. to White House Conf. on Small Bus., 1986. Inducted into Silver Apple Hall of Fame, 1985. Mem. N.Y. Acad. Scis., Direct Mktg. Assn. (Hall of Fame selection comn. 1989-91), Soc. Profl. Writers, Direct Mktg. Creative Guild (Andi Emerson award 1991, pres. 1975-81, bd. dirs. 1975-93), Direct Mktg. Club of N.Y. (treas. 1960-61), N.Y. Acad. Scis. Home: 16 E 96th St New York NY 10128-0753 Office: Emerson Mktg Agy Inc 636 Broadway Rm 1000 New York NY 10012-2623

EMERSON, ANNE, state director; m. Timothy H. Emerson; children: Tim, Andrew, Michael. BA, Pa. State U., 1960. Asst. creative dir. Fabergé, Inc., N.Y.C.; advt. copywriter J.C. Penney Co., Inc.; owner Emerson Advt., Ft. Scott, Kans., 1976-95; dist. dir. Office of U.S. Rep. Sam Brownback, Kans., 1995-96; state dir. Office of U.S. Senator Sam Brownback, Kans., 1996—. Office: 1001 N Broadway Pittsburg KS 66762

EMERSON, ARTHUR ROJAS, broadcast executive. Gen. mgr. San Antonio affiliate KVDA-TV 60 Telemundo, San Antonio, 1989—, v.p., gen. mgr., 1996—; prodr. spls. PBS network; dir. USAA Fed. Savs. Bank. Cochmn. Our Lady of the Lake U. Capital Campaign; bd. dirs. Avenida Guadalupe Assn.; trustee City Pub. Svc.; mem. U. Tex. San Antonio Devel. Bd. Recipient Emma McGaffey award Media Excellence Women in Communications, Inc., 1996. Mem. Greater San Antoinio C. of C. Office: KVDA-TV 60 6234 San Pedro Ave San Antonio TX 78216-7231*

EMERSON, DANIEL EVERETT, retired communications company executive; b. Passaic, N.J., Oct. 22, 1924; s. Daniel T. and Jennie (VanBeveren) E.; m. Patricia Thorston, June 14, 1947; children—Patricia Sue, Nancy Ellen, Pamela Thorston. B.E.E., Cornell U., 1949; postgrad., George Washington U., Boston U., N.Y. U., 1951-56, Dartmouth Coll., 1956, U. Pa., 1959-60. With A.T.&T., 1949—, v.p. fed. relations, 1968-74; v.p. network ops. N.Y. Telephone, N.Y.C., 1974-75; v.p. ops. analysis and methods N.Y. Telephone, 1975-76, exec. v.p. corp. devel., dir., 1976-83; exec. v.p. NYNEX Corp., 1983-86; chmn. bd. NYNEX Mobile Communications Co., 1983-86, NYNEX Info. Resources Co., 1983-86; bd. dirs. Adams Express Co., Petroleum and Resources Corp., Clifford of Vt. Bd. dirs., chmn. YMCA U.S.A.; former dir. trustee YMCA of Greater N.Y.; former trustee, pres. Kent Pl. Sch., Summit, N.J. 1st lt. USAAF, 1943-45. Decorated Air medal. Mem. U.S. C. of C. (communications com. 1972-74), Canoe Brook Country Club (Summit), Vero Beach (Fla.) Country Club, Riomar Bay Yacht Club, Cornell Club (N.Y.C.), Tau Beta Pi, Eta Kappa Nu, Theta Xi.

EMERSON, JAMES LARRY, beverage company executive; b. Garrett, Ind., Jan. 23, 1938; s. George Cary and Ellen A. (Bennett) E.; m. Madalyn Carol Brown, June 24, 1962; children: Todd Jeffrey, Kiersten Christine, Leisel Renee. Student in pre-vet medicine, Purdue U., 1958, MS, 1964, PhD, 1966; DVM, Ohio State U., 1962. Diplomate Am. Coll. Vet. Pathologists. Sr. rsch. specialist dept. pathology and toxicology Dow Chem. Co., Indpls., 1969-76; assoc. faculty mem. Ind. U., Purdue U., Indpls., 1972-76; mgr. dept. pathology Abbott Labs., North Chicago, Ill., 1976-79; mgr. life scis. Coca-Cola Co., Atlanta, 1979-81, assoc. dir. external tech. affairs, 1981-82, dir. sci. and regulatory affairs, 1982-99, sr. sci. fellow sci. and regulatory affairs, 1999—, asst. v.p.; chmn. saccharin tech. com. Internat. Life Scis. Inst., Washington, 1984—, mem. editl. bd., 1983—; trustee Health and Environ. Scis. Inst., 1990—; hon. prof. U. del Salvador, Buenos Aires, 1998; hon. prof. Kirov Med. Inst., Russia. Bd. dirs. Jacquelyn McClure Lupus Found., Atlanta, 1984—. Fellow Royal Soc. Medicine; mem. AVMA, Indsl. Vet. Assn., Soc. Toxicology, Internat. Acad. Pathologists, Flavor and Extract Mfrs. Assn. (bd. govs. 1987—, chmn. sec. com. 1984—, pres. 1994-95, bd. dirs. caloire control coun. 1998—). Methodist. Home: 290 Landfall Rd NW Atlanta GA 30328-1826 Office: Coca-Cola Co 1 Coca Cola Plz NW Atlanta GA 30313-2499

EMERSON, JO ANN, congresswoman; b. Sept. 16, 1950; d. Ab and Slyvia Hermann; m. Bill Emerson, 1975 (dec.); children: Victoria, Katherine; stepchildren: Elizabeth, Abigail. BA in Polit. Sci., Ohio Wesleyan U., 1972. Mem. 105th-106th Congress from 8th Mo. dist., 1997—; mem. agr. com. 105th Congress from 8th Mo. dist., mem. small bus. com., mem. transp. and infrastructure com.; sr. v.p. Am. Ins. Assn.; dir. state rels. and grassroots programs Nat. Restaurant Assn.; dep. dir. commn. Nat. Rep. Congl. Com. Mem. PEO Womens's Svc. Group (FY chpt.), Cape Girardeau; mem. adv. com. Children's Inn, NIH; mem. adv. bd. Arneson Inst. Practical Politics and Pub. Affairs, Ohio Wesleyan U.; bd. dirs. Presbyn. Children's Home, Farmington, Mo. Mem. Copper Dome Soc. Presbyterian. Office: 8th Congl Dist Mo 132 Cannon Bldg Washington DC 20515-2508*

EMERSON, JOHN WILLIAMS, II, lawyer; b. Greeneville, Tenn., Nov. 9, 1929; s. John Williams and Dorothy Mae (Moore) E.; m. Carolyn Rose Buchanan, Dec. 21, 1956; children: John Williams III, Amy Elizabeth, Emily Alicia. JD, Vanderbilt U., 1960. Bar: Fla. 1960, Tenn. 1960, U.S. Dist. Ct. (so. dist.) Fla. 1961, U.S. Ct. Appeals (5th cir.) 1961, U.S. Supreme Ct. 1968, U.S. Dist. Ct. (ea. dist.) Tenn. 1982, U.S. Ct. Appeals (6th cir.) 1983, U.S. Dist. Ct. (mid. dist.) Tenn. 1988, U.S. Dist. Ct. (mid. dist.) Fla. 1990. Ins. agt. Emerson Ins. Agy., Greeneville, 1949-56; instr. Peabody Coll., Nashville, 1958-59; assoc. Henderson, Franklin, Starnes & Holt, Ft. Myers, Fla., 1960-63; ptnr. Parks & Emerson, Naples, Fla., 1963-72, Treadwell, Emerson & Elkins, Naples, 1972-79, Emerson & Emerson P.C., Johnson City, Tenn., 1979-83, Emerson & Emerson P.A., Naples, 1983—; judge Small Claims Ct., Collier County, Naples, Fla., 1963-64. Col. aide de camp gov.'s staff State of Tenn., 1963-66; lt. gov. dist. 11 Fla. Dist. of Kiwanis, 1970-71. Capt. U.S. Army, 1950-54, Korea. Fellow Fla. Kiwanis Found. (life); mem. ABA, The Fla. Bar (bd. govs. young lawyers sect. 1963-66), Fla. Acad. Trial Lawyers, Assn. Trial Lawyers Am., Araba Temple (Ft. Myers, Fla.), Masons (32 Degree). Democrat. Presbyterian. Avocations: boating, travel. Home: 1935 Seville Blvd Unit 112 Naples FL 34109 Office: Emerson & Emerson PA PO Box 1675 Naples FL 34106-1675

EMERSON, PETER MICHAEL, counselor; b. Portland, Oreg., Feb. 16, 1956; s. George and Rayola (Jones) E. BS in Psychology, Brigham Young U., 1980; M in Counseling, Idaho State U., 1982, EdD in Counselor Edn., 1987. Cert. Nat. Bd. Cert. Counselors; lic. profl. counselor. Counselor Cedar Valley Boys Home, Fairfield, Utah, 1978-79; dir. drug abuse prevention Blackfoot (Idaho) Sch. Dist. # 55, 1980; dir. Trio Programs Upward Bound and Spl. Svcs., So. Utah State Coll., Cedar City, 1980-85; doctoral tchg. asst. of counselor edn. Idaho State U., Pocatello, 1985-87; asst. prof. Southeastern La. U., 1987-88; asst. prof. U. New Orleans, 1988-90; assoc. prof. Southeastern La. U., 1990-93, head dept., 1996—. Editor La. Jour. of Coun., 1989—. Mem. ACA, La. Lic. Profl. Counselors (chmn. bd. examiners), Am. Assn. for Marriage and Family Therapy (clin.), Assn. Adult Devel. and Aging (pres. 1994-95), Am. Assn. of State Counselin Bds. (pres. 1995-96). Mormon. Office: Southeastern La U PO Box 863 Hammond LA 70404-0863

EMERSON, PHILIP G., historic site director. Exec. dir. Jamestown Settlement, Yorktown Victory Ctr. Jamestown-Yorktown Found., Williamsburg, Va. Office: Jamestown-Yorktown Found Victory Ctr PO Box 1607 Williamsburg VA 23187-1607

EMERSON, RICHARD B., marketing company executive. Past positions in copywriting, pub. rels. and sales promotions; past v.p., past acct. supr. Cabot Advt.; founding ptnr., pres., CEO, acct. supr. Sperry Top Sider, Fidelity Investments, Marriott Corp., Stop & Shop, Thom McAn Emerson Lane Forkino, 1981-91; COO intergrated divsns., sr. accts. mgr. Century 21, The Hartford, Stop & Shop (merged with Arnold Advt.), 1991; mng. ptnr., COO Arnold Comm., Inc., Boston. Past pres. Leukemia Soc. Am., Mass. Mem. 4A's (past chmn. New England bd. govs.), Ad Club (chmn. bd. dirs.). Office: care Arnold Comm Inc 101 Arch St Boston MA 02110*

EMERSON, SHARON B., biology researcher and educator; b. Santa Monica, Calif., July 14, 1945. BA, U. Calif., Berkeley, 1966; MS, U. So. Calif., 1968, PhD, 1971. Rsch. assoc. Field Mus. Natural History, Chgo.; rsch. prof. Dept. Biology U. Utah; rsch. assoc. Field Mus. Nat. History, Chgo. Recipient John D. and Katherine T. MacArthur fellowship, 1995, award for excellence in environ. health rsch. Lovelance Inst., Albuquerque, 1995. Mem. Am. Soc. Zoology (elected chair divsn. vertebrate morphology). Office: U Utah Dept Biology 257 S 1400 E Salt Lake City UT 84112*

EMERSON, STERLING JONATHAN, lawyer; b. Pasadena, Calif., July 2, 1929; s. Sterling H. and Mary Foote (Randall) E.; m. Virginia Beabes, July 3, 1954; children: Margaret Ellen, Henry Rollins, Peter Randall. BA in Econs. with honors, U. Calif., Berkeley, 1955; JD, U. Mich., 1957. Bar: Pa. 1958, U.S. Dist. Ct. (ea. dist.) Pa. 1958, U.S. Ct. Appeals (3d cir.) 1958. Assoc. Montgomery, McCracken, Walker & Rhoads, Phila., 1958, ptnr., 1966-97; pvt. practice Media, Pa., 1998—. Asst. editor Law Rev. U. Mich., 1957. With U.S. Army, 1950-52. Fellow Am. Coll. Trust and Estate Counsel; mem. ABA, Fiduciary Law Soc., Pa. Bar Assn., Phila. Bar Assn. (former bd. govs., former chmn. sect. on probate and trust law), Delaware County Bar Assn. Republican. Avocations: tennis, gardening, travel. Home: 16 Oberlin Ave Swarthmore PA 19081-1512 Office: 117 N Monroe St Media PA 19063-3037

EMERSON, SUSAN, oil company executive; b. Bryan, Tex., Nov. 2, 1947; d. Joseph Nathanial and Lorraine Parks; m. John S. Emerson, June 5, 1970 (div. 1984); children: John H., Christopher P.; m. Gerald W. Parker, May 4, 1985. Owner Emerson Ins. Agy., San Antonio, 1970-84, Emerson Oil Co., San Antonio, 1970—; bd. dirs. Washington Hosp. Ctr. Mem. Washington Hosp. Ctr. Women's Aux., 1988—; mem. D.C. Rep. Com., 1991—, alt. del. Rep. Nat. Conv., Washington, 1992, 4th ward committeewoman, 1992; commr. Adv. Neighborhood Commn., Washington, 1990—; 2d v.p. 4D Commn., Washington, 1990—; founder Boarder Baby Project, 1991—; Rep. candidate for D.C. del. to Congress, 1992; vice chmn. Cheshire County Rep. Com.; chmn. Rindge Rep. Com.; Justice of the Peace, Notary Pub. Recipient Sr. Adv. Silver Fox award Wash. Hosp. Women's Aux., 1989, Vol. award, 1990. Mem. LWV, D.C. Hosp. Assn. (trustee 1989), Am. Hosp. Assn. (D.C. del. 1990-92), Vis. Nurses Assn. (bioethic com. 1991—), Rindge Hist. Soc. (life), Tex. Breakfast Club, Rindge Womens Club, Rindge Garden Club. Lutheran. Avocations: travel, gourmet cooking, gardening, needlepoint. Home: 571 Route 119 Rindge NH 03461-3704

EMERSON, WALTER CARUTH, artist, educator; b. Dallas, Jan. 24, 1912; s. Walter Caruth and Dale (Chisholm) E.; m. Mary Elizabeth Hicks, July 15, 1961; children: Mary Jane, William Ross. Student, Aunspaugh Sch. Art, Dallas, 1923-24; student, Olin Travis Sch. Art, Dallas, 1926-27, John Knott Art Classes, Dallas, 1932-33, Southwestern Sch. Theatre, Dallas, 1934-35; BA, So. Meth. U., 1941. Founder, dir. art dept. Pollock Paper Corp., Dallas, 1937-52; course designer, instr. art and art history So. Meth. U., Dallas, 1940-63; organizer, dir. art dept. USN, Washington, 1941-45; producer Pencil Personalities, Sta. WFAA-TV, Dallas, 1958; art dir. food and drug divsn. Hunt Oil Co., Dallas, 1963-69; course designer, instr. Christian Coll. S.W., Dallas, 1969-70; creator, instr. credit courses Dallas County C.C. Dist., 1972-74; founder, dir. Art Acad. Dallas, 1974—; editorial cartoonist Dallas Morning News, 1941, N.Y. Mirror, 1956-58; lectr. throughout U.S., Kim Dawson Agy., Dallas, 1977—; initiated instrn. leading to coll. degrees in art for inmates of Dallas County Jail, 1973. Author: The Truth About Santa Anna, 1973, 75, 85; author syndicated column Art Alive, 1979—; contbr. articles to profl. jours.; paintings in Tex. State Mus. and in various other museums and pvt. collections. Founder Americans Unified, Dallas, 1979. Served to lt. USN, 1941-45. Mem. Better Bus. Bur., Mus. N.Mex. Found., Kimbell Art Mus., Dallas Mus. Art, Dallas Zool. Soc., Dallas Arboretum and Bot. Soc., Dallas Symphony Assn., Rotary (pres. pres.'s club Dallas 1970-71), Dallas Knife and Fork Club (pres. 1973-74). Office: Art Acad Dallas 8222 Douglas Ave Dallas TX 75225-5923 *Let go and let God (Anon.).*

EMERSON, WILLIAM ALLEN, retired investment company executive; b. Columbia, Tenn., July 13, 1921; s. Henry Houston and Mabel N. (Allen) E.; m. Jane Stannard, Oct. 5, 1944; children: Marshal Henry, Shelley, Stacey, Kimberly. AA, St. Petersburg Jr. Coll., 1941; BSBA, U. Fla., 1946. With Merrill Lynch, Pierce, Fenner & Smith, Inc., 1947-87; dir. gen. services div. Merrill Lynch, Pierce, Fenner & Smith, Inc., N.Y.C., 1968-72; Southeast regional dir., corp. dir. Merrill Lynch, Pierce, Fenner & Smith, Inc., Atlanta, 1972-81; sr. v.p., nat. sales dir. Merrill Lynch, Pierce, Fenner & Smith, Inc., 1981-86; vice chmn. bd. trustees St. Joseph-St. Anthony Health Sys. Trustee Oglethorpe U., Atlanta, Salvador Dali Mus., St. Petersburg, Mus. Fine Arts, St. Petersburg; trustee, past pres. U. Fla. Found. Pilot with USMC, 1942-45. Republican. Baptist. Clubs: Capital City; Atlanta; St. Petersburg Yacht, Feather Sound Country (St. Petersburg); Biltmore Forest Country (Asheville, N.C.); Masons. Home: 3050 82nd Way N Saint Petersburg FL 33710-2220 *I believe that what you give away returns to bless you in many ways, and that what you have left is worth more than before the gift.*

EMERSON, WILLIAM HARRY, lawyer, retired, oil company executive; b. Rochester, N.Y., Jan. 13, 1928; s. William Canfield and Alice Sarah (Adams) E.; m. Jane Anne Epple, Dec. 27, 1956; children: Elizabeth Anne, Carolyn Jane. BA, Cornell U., 1951, LLB, 1956. Bar: Ill. 1974. Atty. Amoco Corp., 1956-91; sec., dir. Amoco Gas Co., 1979-91. Pres., dir. Undercroft Montessori Sch., Tulsa, 1965-67, Tulsa Figure Skating Club, 1969; bd. dirs. Lake Forest (Ill.) Found. for Hist. Preservation, 1983—; mem. vestry Ch. Holy Spirit, Lake Forest. Home: 593 Greenvale Rd Lake Forest IL 60045-1526

EMERSON, WILLIAM KARY, engineering company executive; b. Enid, Okla., July 15, 1941; s. Kary Cadmus and Mary Rebecca (Williams) E.; m. Marcie Louise Stogner, Mar. 13, 1965; children: Rebecca A., Phillip W. *William Emerson is a descended from James Emerson, a leader in the Regulator movement in North Carolina, 1770. Grandfather Earle E. Emerson became leading educator in Oklahoma, serving on the state Retirement Board for many years and superintendent of many schools including the Early E. Emerson School, Coalgate, Oklahoma. Father, Dr. K.C. Emerson, survived the Battan Death March and 3 years of Japanese prisoner of war camp, served as Acting Assistant Secretary of the Army (R & D) on several occasions and was elected as an Oklahoma State University Distinguished Alumnus. Daughter is Rebecca Emerson, MS MIT 1989, Ph.D. Oxford University, 1995.* BS, Okla. State U., 1965, MS, 1974; diploma, Command and Gen. Staff Coll., 1979, Defense Systems Mgmt. Coll., 1980. Commd. 2d lt. U.S. Army, 1965; advanced through grades to lt. col., 1985; prin. program mgr. Honeywell, Inc., Minnetonka, Minn., 1985-90; sr. program mgr. Alliant Techsystems, Inc., Minnetonka, 1990-92; dep. dir. engring. Teledyne Brown Engring. Co., Huntsville, Ala., 1992-96, dir. advanced engring., 1996-97; sr. program mgr. PEI Electronics, Huntsville, Ala., 1997—; disting. guest lectr. Def. Sys. Mgmt. Coll., 1997. Author: Chevrons, 1983, Encyclopedia of Insignia, 1995; contbr. articles to profl. jours. and ency. Mem. adv. com. Dist. 281 Sch. Bd., Minn., 1986-88, mem. summer sch. concept com., 1988-89; mem. Huntsville Land Trust, 1994—; chmn. recycling com. N. Ala. Sierra Club, 1994-98; citizen mem. City of Huntsville Ordinance Rewrite Com., 1995-97; lay leader Asbury Meth. Ch., 1997—; bd. mgmt. Anne S.K. Browne Collection, Brown U., Providence, 1998—. Decorated Legion of Merit, Bronze Star with V and one oak leaf cluster, Purple Heart with two oak leaf clusters; inducted into Madison County (Ala.) Hall of Heros, 1996; recipient Lit. award Orders & Medals Soc. Am., 1998. Fellow Co. Mil. Historians (bd. dirs. 1983-86, editor 1986-92, Miller award 1977); mem. Am. Soc. Mil. Insignia Collectors (editor jour. 1993—, Best Nat. Display award 1984), Am. Def. Preparedness Assn., Assn. U.S. Army, Mil. Order Purple Heart, Heritage Club, Sierra Club (local chmn. recycling com.). Methodist. Avocations: running, fishing, racquetball. Office: PEI Electronics Inc 110 Wynn Dr NW Huntsville AL 35805-1957

EMERT, GEORGE HENRY, biochemist, academic administrator; b. Tenn., Dec. 15, 1938; s. Victor K. Emert and Hazel G. (Shultz) Ridley; m. Billie M. Bush, June 10, 1967; children: Debra Lea Lipp, Ann Lanie Taylor, Laurie Elizabeth, Jamie Marie. BA, U. Colo., 1962; MA, Colo. State U., 1970; PhD, Va. Tech. U., 1973. Registered profl. chem. engr. Microbiologist Colo. Dept. Pub. Health, Denver, 1967-70; post doctoral fellow U. Colo., Boulder, 1973-74; dir. biochem. tech. Gulf Oil Corp., Merriam, Kans., 1974-79; prof. biochemistry, dir. biomass rsch. ctr. U. Ark., Fayetteville, 1979-84; exec. v.p. Auburn (Ala.) U., 1984-92; pres. Utah State U., Logan, 1992—; adj. prof. microbiology U. Kans., Lawrence, 1975-79. Editor, author: Fuels from Biomass and Wastes, 1981; author book chpt.; contbr. articles to profl. jours.; poet. Mem. So. Tech. Coun., Raleigh, N.C., 1985-92; dir. Ala. Supercomputer Authority, Montgomery, 1987-92, Blue Cross Blue Shield Utah, 1996—, Utah Partnership Econ. Devel.; trustee, adv. bd. First Security Bank. Capt. U.S. Army, 1963-66, Vietnam. Named to Educators Hall of Fame, Lincoln Meml. U., 1988. Fellow Am. Inst. Chemists; mem. Rotary (Paul Harris fellow, pres., v.p. 1989-90), Phi Kappa Phi, Sigma Xi. Republican. Achievements include patent for method for enzyme reutilization. Office: Utah State U 1400 Old Main Hill Logan UT 84322-1400

EMERT, TIMOTHY RAY, lawyer; b. Independence, Kans., Jan. 29, 1940; s. Walter Glen and Fern LaVon (Braschler) E.; m. BarbaraA. Meitner, Aug. 22, 1964; children: Kate, Jennifer, Babs. BS in Journalism, U. Kans., JD. Bar: Kans. 1965. Ptnr. Scovel, Emert, Heasty and Chubb, Independence. Senator 15th dist. State of Kans.; bd. dirs. Independence C. C. Found., Class LTD; commr. Uniform Laws Conf.; mem. Kans. Judicial Coun.; former bd. dirs. Independence Bd. Edn., Independence Pub. Libr., Kans. State Bd. Edn., Kans. State H.S. Activities Assn., Kans. Commn. on Pub. Broadcasting, William Inge Festival Found., Kans. Commn. on Edn. Restructuring and Accountability Corp. for Change, Kans.; vol. Kans. Advocacy and Protective Svcs.; mem. adv. bd. Manor Nursing Home, Independence. Mem. S.E. Kans. Bar Assn., Kans. Bar Assn., Independence C. of C., Rotary. Republican. Roman Catholic.

EMERY, ALAN ROY, museum executive; b. Trinidad, West Indies, Feb. 21, 1939; s. Roy W. and Ruth I. (Jackson); m. Frances D. Ruttan, June 23, 1962; children: Katherine, Timothy. BSc with honors, U. Toronto, Ont., Can., 1962; MSc, McGill U., Montreal, Que., Can., 1964; PhD, U. Miami, 1968. Rsch., teaching asst. Toronto and Montreal, 1959-65; rsch. asst. Inst. of Marine Scis., Miami, Fla., 1965-68; rsch. scientist Ont. Ministry of Natural Resources, Maple, 1968-72; from rsch. assoc. to assoc. curator Royal Ont. Mus., Toronto, 1969-80, curator, Ichthyology and Herpetology, 1980-83; assoc. prof. U. Toronto, 1976-83; pres. Can. Mus. Nature, Ottawa, 1983-96, KIVU Nature Inc., 1998—; bd. dirs. Ctr. Traditional Knowledge, sec.-treas., 1993—; pres. Kivu Nature Inc., 1997—; cons. in field. Author: The Coral Reef, 1981; contbr. articles to profl. jours. Recipient Citation Sports Fishing Inst., Washington, Marine Environ. award Found. for Ocean Rsch., Toronto, 1986, Reconocimiento de honor Fundacian Cultural Banesto, Spain, 1992. Mem. World Consservation Union (pres. nat. com. Can. 1995-98), Assn. Systematics Collections (pres. 1987-89), Royal Can. Inst. (pres. 1983), Am. Soc. Ichthyologists and Herpetologists (editor, bd. govs. 1976-86). Avocations: photography, writing, music. *

EMERY, FRANK EUGENE, publishing executive; b. Wichita, Kans., May 14, 1934; s. Frank A.C. and Nellie Mae (Bloss) E.; m. Sara Manette Marble, Nov. 3, 1956 (div. 1983); children: Frank Michael, Mark W., Timothy T., Todd A.; m. Sandra Kay Adamson, June 28, 1988. BA, U. Kans., 1955, MD, 1959. Diplomate Am. Bd. Orthopedic Surgery, Nat. Bd. Med. Examiners. Intern U. Kans. Med. Ctr., Kansas City, 1959-60, resident radiology, 1960-61, resident gen. surgery, 1961-62; resident orthopedic surgery U. Tex. Med. Br., Galveston, 1968; fellow Orthopedic Rsch. and Edn. Found. U. Edinburgh, Scotland, 1968; pvt. practice specializing in orthopedic surgery Springfield, Mo., 1969-73; asst. prof. surgery, orthopedics U. Tex. Med. Br., Galveston, 1973-77, assoc. prof. surgery, orthopedics, 1977-78, dir. Arthritis Minimal Care Unit, 1975-76; pub. Ft. Scott (Kans.) Tribune, 1980—; pres. Tribune Monitor Co., Ft. Scott, 1982—; bd. dirs. Tribune Monitor Co., Ft. Scott, Gateway Comm., Wichita; gen. ptnr. Hotel Ptnrs., I, II, III, IV, Wichita. Contbr. articles to med. publs. V.p. Mo. and Ark. River Basins Assn., 1984-86; co-chmn. Gov.'s Task Force Pub. Sector Funding, Kans., Main St. Program, Topeka, 1985-86; chmn. basin adv. com. Kans. Water Authority, Topeka, 1986-90; bd. dirs. Kans. C. of C. and Industry, Topeka, 1990-91; councilman S.E. Kans. Econ. Alliance, 1998—. Lt. comdr., surgeon USPHS, 1991-93. Pediatric psychiatry fellow NIH, 1957; fellow United Cerebral Palsy Found., 1967-68. Fellow Am. Acad. Orthopedic Surgeons; mem. Kans. Press Assn., Inland Press Assn., Am. Soc. for Surgery of the Hand, Sigma Xi, Nu Sigma Nu, Delta Upsilon. Avocations: boating, swimming, hiking, mountain climbing. Home: 4559 E Creeksbend Ln Springfield MO 65809-9801 Office: Fort Scott Tribune 6 E Wall St Fort Scott KS 66701-1423

EMERY, FRANK (MICHAEL), plastic surgeon; b. Aug. 8, 1957. BA, U. Tex., 1979; MD, U. Tex., Galveston, 1983. Resident in plastic surgery U. Mo., Columbia, 1989-90, chief resident, 1990-91; plastic, reconstructive surgeon Plastic Surg. Ctr., Cedar Rapids, Iowa, 1991-94; pvt. practice Cedar Rapids, 1994—. E-mail: fmemery@aol.com.

EMERY, HERSCHELL GENE, lawyer; b. Hobart, Okla., Oct. 19, 1923; s. W. Herschell and L. Norean (Lewis) E.; m. Charlotte Chrisney, Oct. 29, 1948; children—Kathy Emery Miller, Steve . A.B., U. Ill., 1945; LL.B., Harvard U., 1948. Bar: Ind. 1949, Tex. 1955, U.S. Tax Ct. 1956, U.S. Ct. Appeals (5th cir.) 1980, U.S. Ct. Claims, 1980. Assoc., Ross McCord Ice & Miller, Indpls., 1948-55; assoc., ptnr. Thompson Knight Wright & Simmons, Dallas, 1955-65; ptnr. Rain Harrell Emery Young & Doke, Dallas, 1965-87, ptnr. Locke Purnell Rain Harrell, 1987-98, Locke Liddell & Sapp, 1999—; lectr. various tax and legal insts. Former pres. Dallas Estate Council, North Tex. chpt. Arthritis Found. Served with U.S. Army, 1943. Fellow Am. Coll. Tax Counsel, Am. Coll. Trust and Estate Counsel; mem. ABA, Tex. Bar Assn., Dallas Bar Assn., Phi Beta Kappa. Presbyterian. Clubs: Dallas Country (pres. 1993), Dallas Petroleum, Old Baldy. Office: Locke Liddell & Sapp 2200 Ross Ave Ste 2200 Dallas TX 75201-2748

EMERY, HOWARD IVAN, JR., management consultant, telecommunications specialist; b. N.Y.C., June 21, 1932; s. Howard I. and Margaret E. (Kayser) E.; m. Jean L. Winters, Sept. 24, 1955; children: David P., Donald P. BCE, Cornell U., 1955; MS in Advanced Mgmt., Pace U., 1979; M of Engrng. (hon.), Cornell U., 1988. Registered profl. engr., N.Y. Various line and staff N.Y. Telephone, N.Y.C., 1957-77; div. mgr. regulatory strategy AT&T, N.Y.C., 1977-79; div. mgr. exec. edn. N.Y. Telephone, N.Y.C., 1979-82; corp. dir. strategic planning Nynex Corp., White Plains, N.Y., 1982-85; v.p. internat. Nynex Internat. Co., White Plains, 1985-90; mgmt. cons. Huntington, N.Y., 1990—; bd. dirs. KPN US Inc., N.Y.C., Internat Computers and Communications, Washington; chmn. civil engr. adv. coun. Cornell U., Ithaca, N.Y., 1991-93, guest lectr. in internat. strategy, 1986—. Bd. edn. Harborfields Pub. Schs., Greenlawn, N.Y., 1966-73; active admissions and alumni groups Cornell U., Ithaca, 1960—. 1st lt. U.S. Army, 1955-57. Avocations: golf, reading, travel. Home and Office: 119 Huntington Bay Rd Huntington NY 11743-2238

EMERY, NANCY BETH, lawyer; b. Shawnee, Okla., July 9, 1952; d. Paul Dodd Finefrock and Kathryn Jo (Saling) Hutchens; m. Lee Monroe Emery, May 18, 1974. BA with highest honors, U. Okla., 1974; JD, Harvard U., 1977. Bar: Okla. 1977, D.C. 1981. Atty. advisor Office Gen. Counsel, U.S. Dept. Agri., Washington, 1977-79; legal adv. to Fed. Energy Regulatory Commr. Matthew Holden, Jr., Washington, 1979-81; assoc. firm Pierson, Ball & Dowd, and predecessor Sullivan & Beauregard, Washington, 1981-83, Paul Hastings, Janofsky & Walker, Washington, 1983-87, ptnr., 1987-93; ptnr. Sutherland, Asbill & Brennan, Washington, 1993-97. nat. adv. bd. USAID Tng. Program, 1994—. Bd. dirs., sec. Park Place Condominium Assn., Inc., Washington, 1982-84; page Continental Congress, DAR, 1978-82, chpt. del. Continental Congress, 1981, 84. Mem. ABA (natural resources energy & environ. law sect., bd. editors Natural Resources & Environ., 1990-98, pub. util. law sect., vice-chmn., 1998—), Fed. Energy Bar Assn. (chair tax com. 1986-87, chair FERC ops. and adminstrn. com. 1991-93, chair elec. utility regulation com. 1995-97, chair program com. 1997-98), Soc. Profl. Journalists, Mortar Bd., Phi Beta Kappa. Democrat. Office: Vice President & General Counsel California Ind Sys Op Corp 151 Blue Ravine Rd Folsom CA 95630-4704

EMERY, SARAH MARTHA WATSON, retired philosophy educator, writer; b. Pleasant City, Ohio, Aug. 8, 1911; d. William James and Daisy Taylor (McComb) Watson; m. Stephen Albert Emery, Sept. 11, 1948 (dec. Mar. 1991); children: Stephen, John Loring. Student, Agnes Scott Coll., 1929-31; AB, Emory U., 1933; MA in Philosophy, Ohio State U., 1938, PhD in Philosophy, 1942. 2d grade tchr. Coosa (Ga.) Sch., 1933-36; math. tchr. Valley Point H.S., Dalton, Ga., 1936-37; grad. asst. philosophy Ohio State U., Columbus, 1938-42; grad. asst. psychology U. Ill., Urbana, 1942-43; philosophy and psychology tchr. Jr. Coll. of Packer Collegiate Inst., Bklyn., 1943-46; dir. girls camp N.Y. Protestant Episcopal City Mission Soc., Milford, Conn., summer 1945; instr. philosophy Syracuse (N.Y.) U., 1946-47; asst. prof. philosophy Hollins Coll., Roanoke, Va., 1947-48, Duke U., Durham, N.C., 1951-52; ret., 1952. Author: Blood on the Old Well, 1963, (as J. A. Cheadle) A Donkey's Life, A Story for Children, 1979, They Walked into the Rose Garden and Other Poems, 1992, Plato's Euthyphro, Apology and Crito, Arranged for Dramatic Presentation from the Jowett Translation with Choruses, 1996. Tchr. creative writing, Denton (Tex.) Sr. Ctr., 1977-83. Mem. Am. Philosophical Assn., Poetry Soc. Tex., Phi Beta Kappa. Home: PO Box 683 Denton TX 76202-0683

EMERY, SUE MCHAM, bulletin editor, owner bridge studio; b. Wichita County, Tex., Feb. 23, 1920; d. Billy J. and Trula V. (Mayfield) McHam; m. Horace B. Camp (div. 1958); children: Ann Camp McGrath, Connie Camp Phillis, Billy Brit; m. John Walter Emery (dec. 1972). B.A., Harding Coll., 1939. Tchr., 1939-40; with U.S. Civil Svc., 1941-45; reporter Wichita Daily Times, Tex., 1945-46; ind. bridge club owner-operator, freelance tournament dir., daily bull. editor; editor Am. Contract Bridge League Bridge Bull., Memphis, 1972-96; ret., 1996; staff mem. Tex. Bridge Mag., 1960's. Author, researcher: No Passing Fancy, 1977; contbr. articles to mags. Active Womanpower for Eisenhower, 1950's, Democrats for Eisenhower, Tex., 1950's. Mem. Internat. Bridge Press Assn. Home: 4114 Rivercrest Dr Wichita Falls TX 76309-2812 Office: Contract Bridge Bull 2990 Airways Blvd Memphis TN 38116-3838

EMERY, VICKI MORRIS, school library media specialist; b. Kansas City, Mo., Sept. 7, 1948; d. Arthur Paul and Merna Alva (Powell) Morris; m. Harvey William Emery Jr., July 19, 1974. BS in Edn., Emporia (Kans.) State U., 1970; M in Urban Affairs, Va. Poly. Inst. and State U., 1980; MS in Libr. Sci., Cath. U. Am., 1995; postgrad. student in ednl. leadership, U. Va., 1997—. Tchr. St. Pius X Sch., Mission, Kans., 1970-72, Shawnee Mission (Kans.) Pub. Schs., 1973-74; editing supr. CTB/McGraw-Hill, Monterey, Calif., 1975-76; sch. libr. media specialist Fairfax County (Va.) Pub. Schs., 1995—; mem. adv. bd. Fairfax County Sch. Bd., 1996—. Contbr. revs. and articles to profl. jours. Pres. PTA Sangster Sch., Springfield, Va., 1994-95, 96-98, scholarship chair Fairfax County Coun. PTAs, 1995—; pres., bd. dirs. Spring-Mar Coop. Presch., Springfield, 1989-90. Recipient Outstanding Svc. award Va. Coop. Presch. Coun., 1991. Mem. ALA, Am. Assn. Sch. Librs. (mem. pres.'s program com. 1998), Assn. Supervision and Curriculum Devel., Va. Ednl. Media Assn., Va. Soc. Tech. Edn., Va. Congress Parents and Tchrs. (hon. life mem.), Beta Phi Mu. Office: BelleView Elem Sch 6701 Fort Hunt Rd Alexandria VA 22307-1798

EMERY, VIRGINIA OLGA BEATTIE, psychologist, researcher; b. Cleve., Apr. 9, 1938; d. Joseph P. and Antoinette Pauline (Misja) Kennick; m. Paul Hamilton Beattie Sr., 1960 (div. 1975); children: Tamsan Beattie Tharin, Paul Hamilton Beattie Jr.; m. Paul E. Emery, 1979. BA, U. Chgo., 1962, PhD, 1982; MA, Ind. U., 1973. Diplomate Am. Bd. Disability Analysts, Am. Acad. Traumatic Stress; lic. psychologist, N.H., Ohio; cert. brief therapist Nat. Acad. Brief Therapists; cert. cognitive therapist Nat. Bd. Behavioral Therapists, cert. domestic violence counselor endorsement; cert. expert traumatic stress, cognitive therapist. Asst. prof. psychology Case Western Res. U., Cleve., 1986-89, asst. clin. prof. psychiatry, 1986-89; sr. faculty assoc. Ctr. on Aging and Health, Concord and Hanover, N.H., 1986-89, dir., 1989—; adj. clin. asst. prof. psychiatry Dartmouth Med. Sch., Lebanon, 1983-85; clin. assoc. prof. Dartmouth Med. Sch., Lebanon, N.H., 1989—; mem. com. human devel. NIMH, Adult Devel. & Aging Traineeship, U. Chgo., 1974-76; sub-project dir. Case Western Res. U. Sch. Medicine, 1986-90; sec. women's faculty assn. Case Western Res. U., 1987-89; cons. Vets. Affairs Med. Ctr., Manchester, N.H., 1989—; sub-project dir. NIMH Mental Health Clin. Rsch. Ctr. Grant, Case Western Res. U. Sch. Medicine, 1986-90; mem. Dartmouth Coll. and Dartmouth Med. Sch. Neurosci. Group, 1990—; lectr. on medicine Harvard U. Faculty of Medicine, 1996—; Paul Janssen lectr. U. Goteberg, Sweden, 1997. *Virginia Emery pioneered in systemic research on language deterioration, specifically syntax indementing illnesses and normal aging. Research findings on aging deterioration in language, included an inverse correlation between language deterioration and language development in Alzheimer syndrome. He also did research on the relation between major depression and dementing illness with the finding that depressive dementia is a transitional stage between depression and dementia. He did research on vascular dementia and redefined the nosologic entity of vascular dementia so that it includes noninfarct vascular disorders. He received several prizes (as listed in biographical information) for these research findings and publication.* Author: Language and Aging, 1985, Pseudodementia: A Theoretical and Empirical Discussion, 1988; editor: Dementia: Presentations, Differential Diagnosis, and Nosology, 1994; contbr. articles to profl. jours. Bd. dirs. Frontiers of Knowledge Civic Trust, Concord, N.H., 1990—, pres. 1990-95. Recipient Adult Devel. and Aging grant/traineeship NIH/NIMH, 1974-76, Rsch. prize Am. Aging Assn., 1983, Havighurst prize for aging rsch. U. Chgo., 1984; named Frontiers of Knowledge Atlee Zellers lectr., 1994, Paul Janssen Med. Inst. lectr., 1997; rsch. grantee Western Res. Coll., 1986-87, NIMH Mental Health Clin. rsch. grantee, 1986-89. Fellow Gerontol. Soc. Am. (Disting creative contbn. award 1989), Am. Psychol. Assn., N.H. Psychol. Assn. (bd. dirs. 1991-93, chair com. acad. rsch. interests 1992-94, sec. 1994—, Riggs Disting. Contbn. award 1991), APA (student rsch. award 1984); mem. AAAS, AAUW, Internat. Psychiat. Rsch. Soc., Internat. Psychogeriatric Assn. (Pfizer lectr. 1997, 2d place award for rsch. paper 1995, 2nd Pl. Rsch. award in psychogeriatrics for paper 1995, IPA/Bayer Rsch. award in psychogeriatrics 1995), Boston Soc. Gerontol. Psychiatry, Acad. Psychosomatic Medicine, N.Y. Acad. Scis., Am. Acad. Experts in Traumatic Stress, Assn. Alzheimer's Disease Scientists. Fax: (603) 625-8199. Home: 15 Buckingham Dr Bow NH 03304-5207 Office: Dartmouth Med Sch Dept Psychiatry Box HB 7750 Lebanon NH 03756

EMICK, WILLIAM JOHN, real estate investor, retired federal executive; b. Atlantic City, Apr. 17, 1931; s. William and Mable Jeanette (Myers) E.; divorced; children: Richard, Cherie, James. AA, San Antonio Coll., 1975; BApplied Arts and Scis. Bus. Mgmt., S.W. Tex. State U., 1977. Dep. div. chief U.S. Air Force, 1956-86; real estate investor Emick Investments, San Antonio, 1986—; pres. Kelly Mgmt. Assn., San Antonio, 1978-79, Kelly Apprentice Club, San Antonio, 1957-59. Chmn. Sr. Olympics Racquetball Regional Competitions, 1990-91, Regional Sr. Olympics Champion Singles and Doubles, 1991, Regional Sr. Olympics Champion Singles, 1992; pres. Bent Oak Condo. Assn., 1982, 88; program chmn. San Antonio Youth Opportunities, 1979; mem. United San Antonio, 1981-82. With USAF, 1951-55. Mem. North San Antonio C. of C., Animal Defense League. Avocations: travel, fishing, scuba, biking, poetry. Home and Office: 3426 Sunlit Grv San Antonio TX 78247-2953

EMIL, ARTHUR D., lawyer; b. N.Y.C., Dec. 29, 1924; s. Allan D'lugasch and Kate Silverman Emil; m. Jane Allen Emil, Sept. 15, 1948 (dec. 1973); children: David A., Jennie, Suzanne Emil Pleskunas; m. Lydia Moffat, July 6, 1976. BE, Yale U., 1947; LLB, Columbia U., 1950. Bar: N.Y. 1950, U.S. Dist. Ct. (so. dist.) N.Y. 1950, U.S. Ct. Appeals (2d cir.) 1950. Trial atty. Cahill, Gordon, Reindel & Ohl, N.Y.C., 1950-52, U.S. Dept. Justice, Washington, 1952-53; assoc. McLaughlin & Fougner, N.Y.C., 1953-55, Arthur D. Emil, N.Y.C., 1955-60, Emil & Kobrin, N.Y.C., 1960-70, 77-79, Emil, Kobrin, Klein & Garbus, N.Y.C., 1970-77, Surrey & Morse, N.Y.C., 1979-86, Jones, Day, Reavis & Pogue, N.Y.C., 1986-93; Kramer, Levin, Naftalis, Nessen, Kamin & Frankel, N.Y.C., 1994—. Co-chmn. fin. com. Gov. Hugh Carey re-election campaign, N.Y., 1977-78. Lt. (j.g.) USNR, 1943-46, ETO, NATOUSA. Office: Kramer Levin Naftalis et al 919 3rd Ave New York NY 10022-3902

EMILSON, HENRY BERTIL, artist; b. Sundals-Ryr, Dalsland, Sweden, June 1, 1933; came to U.S., 1951; s. Harry Cristoffer Emilsson and Hanna (Nilsson) Svensson. BFA, Okla. U., 1960; MFA, Inst. Allende San Miguel, Mexico, 1967. Dir. U.S. Army Arts and Crafts Recreation Svcs., U.S. and overseas, 1962-88; artist Bollungsnas, Bralanda, Sweden, 1988—. Exhibited in one-man shows in Erlangen, Germany, 1979, Bad Windsheim, Germany, 1981, Gothenburg, Sweden, 1990, Vanersborg, Sweden, 1994, also others; represented in nat. and internat. pub. and pvt. collections. With USAF, 1952-56. Office: Bollungsnas, 460 65 Bralanda Sweden

EMILSSON, ELIZABETH MAYKUTH, special education educator; b. Bozeman, Mont., Feb. 23, 1936; d. Frank Leopold and Dolores Muriel (Lawrence) Maykuth; m. Robert Gunnar Emilsson, May 8, 1961 (dec.); children: Gunnar R., Ingrid L., John. BS, Mont. State Coll., 1958; MEd, Mont. State U., 1974; Spl. Edn. Cert., U. Mont., 1976, postgrad., 1978. Tchr. grades 4-8 Virginia City (Mont.) Schs., 1958-59; tchr. grades 7-8 El Camino Jr. H.S., Santa Maria, Calif., 1959-60; tchr. grade 6 Miller St. Sch., Santa Maria, 1960-61; tchr. grades 1-3 Stevenson sch., Ransomville, N.Y., 1967-72; resource tchr. Three Forks (Mont.) Unified Schs., 1974-76; spl. edn. cons. Mont. Reg. Svcs., Glendive, Mont., 1976-79; spl. edn. tchr. cons. Big Country Edn. Coop., Miles City, Mont., 1979-89; spl. edn. dir. Big Country Edn. Coop., 1990—; exec. dir. Big Country Edn./Head Start, 1991-99; ret., 1999; ednl. cons., tech. adv. Mont. State Office of Pub. Instruction, 1999—; pres. bd. dirs. South Eastern Mont. Adv. Prog., Miles City, 1987-88. Bd. dirs. Miles City Youth Soccer Assn., 1986-88. Mem. Coun. for Exceptional Children (Mont. pres. 1985-86, Nat. Bd. Govs. 1991-94, distinguished svc. award state fedn. 1994), PEO Sisterhood, Delta Kappa Gamma. Democrat. Lutheran. Avocations: hiking, fishing, reading, gardening. Home: 2203 Main St Miles City MT 59301-3801 Office: Big Country Ednl Coop PO Box 668 Miles City MT 59301-0668

EMISON, EWING RABB, JR., lawyer; b. Vincennes, Ind., Feb. 3, 1925; s. Ewing and Tuley (Sheperd) E.; m. Kathleen M. Crowley, Nov. 28, 1952; children: Susan, Anne Emison Wishard. AB, DePauw U., 1947; LLB, Ind. U., 1950. Bar: Ind. 1950. Ptnr. Emison Doolittle Kolb & Roellgen, Vincennes; dep. atty. gen. State of Ind., 1968-69; lectr. CLE seminars. Contbg. columnist Res Gestae, Ind. State Bar mag. Mem. Wabash Valley Interstate Commn., 1959-62, Ind. Flood Control and Water Resources Commn., 1961-65; mem. bd. visitors Ind. Univ. Sch. Law, 1984-87. With USN, 1943-46, 52-53. Mem. ABA (sects. on litigation, econs. of law practice), Ind. State Bar Assn. (bd. of mgrs. 1975-77, chmn. ho. of dels. 1979, pres. 1986-87), Internat. Assn. Def. Counsel, Columbia Club, Phi Delta Phi, Phi Kappa Psi. Republican. Presbyterian. Avocations: golf, assistance to minority law students, military history. Office: Emison Doolittle Kolb & Roellgen PO Box 215 8th and Busseron Sts Vincennes IN 47591

EMISON, JAMES WADE, petroleum company executive; b. Indpls., Sept. 21, 1930; s. John Rabb and Catherine (Stanbro) E.; divorced; children: Catherine Emison Stoick, Elizabeth Ann, Thomas Weston, William Ash; m. Jane Bale Larson, Feb. 14, 1983. BA, DePauw U., 1952. Gen. mgr. C&C Oil Co. Inc., Huntington, Ind., 1954-59; pres. May Petroleum Co. Inc., Lima, Ohio, 1959-61; sales mgr. Oskey Bros. Petroleum Corp., St. Paul, 1961-66; v.p. mktg. Nfld. Refining Co. Ltd., N.Y.C., 1966-69; v.p. Oskey Gasoline & Oil Co., Mpls., 1969-76; pres. Western Petroleum Co. (successor to Oskey Gasoline & Oil Co.), Mpls., 1977—; pres. Western Internat. Trading Co., Eden Prairie, Minn., 1981—; bd. dirs. Hydrocarbon Trading & Transport Co., Houston, Community Bank Group, Inc., Eden Prairie, Minn. Trustee DePauw U., Greencastle, Ind., 1981—, USMC Marine Corps U. Found. Inc., Quantico, Va., 1984-95. Capt. USMC, 1952-54. Mem. Am. Petroleum Inst., Minn. Petroleum Assn., Marine Corps Assn. (gov. 1981-84), Assn. Governing Bds. of Univs. and Colls. (bd. dirs. 1993), DePauw U. Alumni Assn. (pres. 1979-81, bd. dirs. 1975-81), The Minikahda Club (Mpls.), Monterey, Peninsula Country Club, Ballybunion Golf Club, Tralee Golf Club, Spring Hill Country Club (Orono, Minn.), Woodhill Country Club (Orono). Avocations: golf, fly fishing. Home: 3340 Hill Ln Wayzata MN 55391-2602 Office: Western Petroleum Co 9531 W 78th St Ste 102 Eden Prairie MN 55344-3897

EMLEN, WARREN METZ, computer-related services company owner; b. Elizabeth, N.J., Oct. 12, 1932; s. Andrew Arnberg and Dorothy Emma (Metz) E.; m. Carol Ringold Taylor, Sept. 28, 1958; children: Deborah Emlen Baker, David Taylor, Anne Emlen Donohue. BS in Forestry, U. Calif., Berkeley, 1955; BSEE, Pa. State U., 1963; MS in Systems Mgmt., U. So. Calif., 1973; MA in Pub. Adminstrn., U. N.Mex., 1980. Jr. forester U.S. Forest Service, Klamath, Calif., 1955-56; electronic engr. USAF, Griffiss AFB, N.Y., 1967-87; cons. forester, ptnr. L&E Environ. Cons., Rome, N.Y., 1965-87; v.p., adminstrv. asst. BPLW Architects & Engrs., Inc., Albuquerque, 1988-94; adminstrv. asst. Lovelace Health Systems, 1994-95; adminstrv. coord. Molzen-Corbin & Assocs. P.A., 1995-96; cons. in field; sole propr. Bus. Solutions and Svcs., 1998—; trustee DEDANE Trust, ANDOREM Trust; co-chmn. Industry Looks at Rome Air Devel. Ctr., Griffiss AFB, 1981; sec. Def. Intelligence Tech. forum, Washington, 1981-86; automated data processing cons., 1987-88, 96-97; adminstrv. asst., v.p. BPLW Architects& Engrs., Inc., Albuquerque, 1988-94; adminstrv. coord. Molzen-Corbin & Assocs., P.A., 1995-96. Contbr. numerous articles to profl. jours. Served to capt. USAF, 1956-67. Mem. IEEE (sr., chmn. engrng. mgmt. group Mohawk Valley sect. 1975-76), Armed Forces Comm. and Electronics Assn. Republican. Methodist. Avocations: stamp and coin collecting, investments, hiking, reading. Home and Office: 1509 Monte Largo Dr NE Albuquerque NM 87112-6304

EMMA, LYNNE ANNE, healthcare administrator; b. Bethpage, N.Y., July 12, 1954; d. Charles P. and Evelyn M. (Calone) E. BSN, Tex. Christian U., 1976; MPH, UCLA, 1983. CCRN. Staff and charge nurse, critical care UCLA Med. Ctr., 1976-83; study nurse coord., vascular specialist VA Med. Ctr., West Los Angeles, Calif., 1983-86; nurse educator Hollywood Presybn. Med. Ctr., L.A., 1986-88, clin. nurse specialist, 1988-92; clin. dir. Good Samaritan Hosp., L.A., 1992-93, dir. case mgmt. and social svcs., 1993-96; v.p. population health HealthCare Ptnrs. Med. Group, L.A., 1996-97; dir. med. ops. Cedars-Sinai Med. Network Svcs., Beverly Hills, Calif., 1997—. Mem. AACN, sigma Theta Tau.

EMMANOUILIDES, GEORGE CHRISTOS, physician, educator; b. Drama, Greece, Dec. 17, 1926; came to U.S., 1955; s. Christos Nicholas and Vassiliki (Jordanopoulos) E.; married; children: Nicholas, Elizabeth, Christopher, Martha, Sophia. MD, Aristotelion U., 1951; MS in Physiology, UCLA, 1963. Diplomate Am. Bd. Pediatrics (pediatric cardiology and neonatal-perinatal medicine). Asst. prof. UCLA, 1963-69, assoc. prof., 1969-73, prof., 1973-95, prof. emeritus, 1995—; chief divsn. pediatric cardiology Harbor UCLA Med. Ctr., Torrance, Calif., 1963-95. Co-author: Practical Pediatric Electrocardiography, 1973; co-editor: Heart Disease in Infants, Children and Adolescents, 2d edit., 1977, Moss' Heart Disease in Infants, Children and Adolescents, 3d edit., 1983, 4th edit., 1989, 5th edit., 1995, Neonatal Cardiopulmonary Distress, 1988; contbr. more than 70 articles in field to profl. jours. Served as 2d lt. M.C., Greek Army, 1953-55. Recipient Sherman Mellincoff award UCLA Sch. Medicine, 1982, several rsch. awards Am. Heart Assn., 1965-83. Fellow Am. Acad. Pediatrics (cardiology sect., chmn. 1978-80, Founders award 1996), Am. Coll. Cardiology; mem. Am. Pediatric Soc., Soc. for Pediatric Rsch., Hellenic-Am. Med. Soc. (pres.), Acad. of Athens (corr. mem.). Democrat. Greek Orthodox. Clubs: Hellenic Univ. (Los Angeles) (bd. dirs.). Avocation: gardening. Home: 4619 Browndeer Ln Rllng Hls Est CA 90275-3911 Office: Harbor-UCLA Med Ctr 1000 W Carson St Torrance CA 90502-2004

EMMANUEL, JORGE AGUSTIN, chemical engineer, environmental consultant; b. Manila, Aug. 28, 1954; came to U.S., 1970; s. Benjamin Elmido and Lourdes (Orozco) E.; 1 child, Andres Layanglawin. BS in Chemistry, N.C. State U., 1976, MSChemE, 1978; PhD in Chem. Engrng., U. Mich., 1988. Registered profl. engr., Calif., environ. profl.; cert. hazardous materials mgr. Process engr. Perry Electronics, Raleigh, N.C., 1973-74; rsch. asst. N.C. State U., Raleigh, 1977-78; rsch. chem. engr. GE Corp. R & D Ctr., Schenectady, N.Y., 1978-81; Amoco rsch. fellow U. Mich., Ann Arbor, 1981-84; sr. environ. analyst TEM Assocs., Inc., Emeryville, Calif., 1988-91; pres. Environ. & Engrng. Rsch. Group, Hercules, Calif., 1991—; environ. cons. to the Philippines, UN Devel. Program, 1992, 94; rsch. assoc. U. Calif., Berkeley, 1988-90. Contbr. articles to profl. jours. Mem. Assn. for Asian Studies, Ann Arbor, 1982-88; sec. Alliance for Philippine Concerns, L.A., 1983-91; assoc. Philippine Resource Ctr., Berkeley, 1988-92; bd. dirs. ARC-Ecology, San Francisco, 1990—, Asia Pacific Ctr., Washington, 1995—; bd. advisors Urban Habitat, 1995—. N.C. State U. grantee, 1976, Phoenix grantee U. Mich., 1982. Mem. NSPE, AAAS, Air and Waste Mgmt. Assn., Calif. Acad. Scis., N.Y. Acad. Scis., Filipino-Am. Soc. Architects and Engrs. (exec. sec. 1989-90, Svc. award 1990). Avocations: classical guitar, ethnomusicology, Asian studies. Office: The Environ & Engrng Rsch Group 628 2nd St Rodeo CA 94572-1111

EMMANUEL, RAHM, federal official. Asst. to Pres., polit. affairs div., dep. dir. comms. Polit. Affairs Office, Washington, 1993-99; mng. dir. Wasserstein & Perella, Chgo., 1999—. Office: Wasserstein & Perella Ste 5700 3 1st National Plaza Chicago IL 60602*

EMMEL, BRUCE HENRY, secondary education mathematics educator; b. St. Cloud, Minn., Jan. 8, 1942; s. Henry Joseph and Mary Ann Emily (Kangas) E.; m. Phyllis Wanda Campbell, Aug. 29, 1982; children: Debra Lynn Huber, Kathi Marie, Brent Boyd, Daniel Henry Huber, Brandi Rose. BS, St. Cloud State U., 1967; MA in Edn., Ball State U., 1973. Cert. vocat. tchr., Minn. Tchr. Lincoln Jr. High Sch., Hibbing, Minn., 1967-70, West Concord (Minn.) High Sch., 1970-72; vocat. tchr. Moorhead (Minn.) Tech. Coll., 1972-90; tchr. Moorhead Pub. Schs., 1984—; mem. Dist. Math. Com., Moorhead, 1978—. Comdr. Fargo (N.D.) CAP, 1984-86, 89, 94—; dir. pub. affairs N.D. CAP, Mandan, 1986-89; precinct chmn. Dem. Com., Moorhead, 1968-90. Mem. Nat. Coun. Tchrs. Math., Kappa Delta Pi. Congregationalist. Avocations: flying, aircraft builder, hunting, walking, traveling. Home: 1121 3rd St S Moorhead MN 56560-4015 Office: Moorhead Sr High Sch 2300 4th Ave S Moorhead MN 56560-3298

EMMELUTH, BRUCE PALMER, investment company executive, venture capitalist; b. L.A., Nov. 30, 1940; s. William J. and Elizabeth L. (Palmer) E.; children: William J. II (dec.), Bruce Palmer Jr., Carrie E.; m. Canda E. Samuels, Mar. 29, 1987. Sr. investment analyst corp. fin. dept. Prudential Ins. Co. Am., L.A., 1965-70; with Seidler Amdec Securities, Inc., 1970-90, sr. v.p., mgr. corp. fin. dept., 1974-90, also bd. dirs.; mng. dir. corp. fin., mgr. corp. fin. dept., mem. exec. com. First Securities Van Kasper, L.A., 1990—, also exec. v.p., exec. v.p., mng. dir. corp. fin.; pres., bd. dirs. SAS Capital Corp., venture capital subs. Seidler Amdec Securities, 1977-90; bd. advisors Entrepreneurial Studies Program, Anderson Grad. Sch. Mgmt. UCLA, 1985—, past. bd. dirs. Active Calvary Ch., Pacific Palisades, Calif. With U.S. Army N.G., 1965-71. Home: 17146 Palisades Cir Pacific Palisades CA 90272-2141 Office: First Securities Van Kasper 10877 Wilshire Blvd Ste 1700 Los Angeles CA 90024-4372

EMMERICH, ANDRE, art gallery executive, author; b. Frankfurt, Germany, Oct. 11, 1924; came to U.S., 1940; s. Hugo and Lily (Marx) E.; m. Constance R. Marantz, Aug. 25, 1958; children: Adam Oliver, Tobias David Hugo, Noah Nicholas; m. Susanne Bross, Jul. 21, 1994. BA, Oberlin Coll., 1944. Writer, editor Time-Life Internat., N.Y.C., N.Y. Herald Tribune, N.Y.C., Realites Mag., Paris, 1944-53; with Andre Emmerich Gallery, Inc., N.Y.C., 1954-98; sr. v.p. Sotheby's, 1996—; art adv. panel of Commr. Internal Revenue, 1986-89; mem. vis. com. Allen Meml. Art Mus., Oberlin Coll., Ohio. Author: Art Before Columbus, 1963, Sweat of the Sun and Tears of the Moon, 1965. Mem. Nat. Assn. Dealers in Ancient, Oriental and Primitive Art (bd. dirs. 1972—), Century Assn. Fax: 212-452-1406. Home: Andre Emmerich Gallery 30 E 72d St New York NY 10021-4406

EMMERICH, KAROL DENISE, foundation executive, former retail executive; b. St. Louis, Nov. 21, 1948; d. George Robert and Dorothy (May) Van Houten; m. Richard James, Oct. 18, 1969; 1 son, James Andrew. BA, Northwestern U., 1969; MBA, Stanford U., 1971. Nat. divsn. account officer Bank of Am., San Francisco, 1971-72; fin. analyst Dayton Hudson Corp., Mpls., 1972-73, sr. fin. analyst, 1973-74, mgr. short term financing, 1974-76, asst. treas., 1976-79, treas., 1979—, v.p., 1980-93; exec. fellow U. St. Thomas Grad. Sch. Bus., 1993—; pres. Emmerich Found., Edina, Minn., 1993—; bd. dirs. Slumberland. Bd. dirs. Women's Opportunity Fund, Hemerocallis Soc. of Minn., Opportunity Internat., The Gathering, Royal Treasure; mem. adv. bd. Women Venture. Mem. Minn. Women's Econ. Roundtable. Home and Office: 7302 Claredon Dr Edina MN 55439-1722

EMMERICH, ROLAND, director, producer, writer; b. Stuttgart, Germany, Nov. 10, 1955. Prodr. The Thirteenth Floor, 1999, The High Crusade, 1994; dir. Raumpatrouille (TV series), 1998, Universal Soldier, 1992; dir., prodr., writer Godzilla, 1998 (Best Dir. Audience award European Film Awards), Independence Day, 1996, Moon 44, 1990; dir., writer Stargate, 1994 (Sci-Fi Universe Mag. Reader's Choice award), Hollywood-Monster, 1987, Joey, 1985, Das Arche Noah Prinzip, 1984; exec. prodr. Eye of the Storm, 1991; creator, exec. prodr. (TV series) The Visitor; editor, writer, dir. Franzmann, 1979; actor Die 120 Tage von Bottrop, 1997. Office: Creative Artists Agy 9830 Wilshire Blvd Beverly Hills CA 90212*

EMMERICH, WERNER SIGMUND, physicist; b. Dusseldorf, Germany, June 3, 1921; s. Adolph and Julia (Frank) E.; m. Eva G. Pauson, June 13, 1953; children—Fay Lillian, Ralph Austin, Bertram Frank. B.S., Ohio State U., 1949, M.S., 1950, Ph.D., 1953. Research physicist Westinghouse Research and Devel. Ctr., Pitts., 1954-57, adv. physicist, 1957-64, mgr. arc and plasma research, 1964-73, dir. applied physics, 1973-75, dir. corp. research, 1975-79, dir. power systems, 1979-83, dir. corp. and comml. research, 1983-86; retired, 1986. Author: Fast Neutron Physics, 1963; patentee in field. Served with AUS, 1942-46, ETO. Fellow Am. Phys. Soc.; mem. AAAS (life), Sigma XI, Phi Beta Kappa, Zeta Beta Tau. Home: 1883 Beulah Rd Pittsburgh PA 15235-5004

EMMERMAN, MICHAEL N, financial analyst; b. Bklyn., Oct. 7, 1945; s. Leon and Ida (Levine) E.; m. Janet Louise Goldman, Dec. 20, 1969 (div. Apr. 1978); children: Daniel Blake, Karen Stacey; m. Patricia Anne Stockhausen, Sept. 9, 1995; 1 child, Thomas Justin Stockhausen Emmerman. BBA, Pace U., 1966; MBA, L.I. U., 1967. Bd. cert. forensic examiner; diplomate Am. Bd. Forensic Examiners. Security analyst Standard & Poor's Inc., N.Y.C., 1965-68; sr. security analyst Arnhold & S. Bleichroeder Inc., N.Y.C., 1968-69; dir. managed accounts Lombard, Nelson, McKenna & Paganucci, N.Y.C., 1970-72; pres. Dominick Mgmt. Co., N.Y.C., 1972-74; gen. ptnr., money mgr. Neuberger Berman L.L.C., N.Y.C., 1974—; co-founder, bd. dirs. Kentek Info. Sys. Inc., Boulder, Colo.; spl. tech. advisor N.Y. Police Dept. Harbor Unit Scuba Team. Author: Flying and Diving: A New Look, 1987; contbr. articles to jours. in med. and underwater sci. fields. Sr. v.p. N.Y.'s Finest Found., Inc.; vice chmn. Fed. Drug Agts. Found., Inc. Fellow Fin. Analysts Fedn., Explorers Club; mem. N.Y. Soc. Security Analysts (accredited sr. security analyst), Undersea and Hyperbaric Med. Soc., Am. Acad. Underwater Scis., Nat. Assn. Underwater Instrs. (life), Profl. Assn. Diving Instrs. (instr. 1986—), Princeton Club. Avocations: underwater exploration, squash, music. Office: Neuberger Berman LLC 605 3d Ave Fl 21 New York NY 10158-3698

EMMERSON, RED, sawmill owner. CEO Sierra Pacific Industries, Redding, Calif. Office: Sierra Pacific Industries PO Box 496028 Redding CA 96049-6028*

EMMERT, GILBERT ARTHUR, engineer, educator; b. Merced, Calif., June 2, 1938; s. Allan Valentine and Mildred (Vanderbilt) E.; m. Nancy Sue Johnson, June 12, 1964; children: David Allan, Daniel Andrew. BS, U. Calif., Berkeley, 1961; MS, Rensselaer Poly. Inst., Troy, N.Y., 1964; PhD, Stevens Inst. Tech., Hoboken, N.J., 1968. Analytical engr. United Tech. Corp., East Hartford, Conn., 1961-64; asst. prof. U. Wis., Madison, 1968-72, assoc. prof., 1972-79, prof., 1979—, dept. chair, 1992—. Contbr. articles to profl. jours. Mem. Am. Physical Soc., Am. Nuclear Soc., Am. Assn. Univ. Profs., Am. Soc. Engrng. Edn. Office: U Wis Dept Engrng Physics 1500 Engineering Dr Madison WI 53706-1609

EMMERT, RICHARD EUGENE, retired professional association executive; b. Iowa City, Iowa, Feb. 23, 1929; s. Frank Thomas and Okie Leona (Seydel) E.; m. Marilyn Ruth Marner, June 19, 1949; children: Debra Sue Emmert Warrington, Andrea Gale Emmert Mazzuca, Lisa Alison Emmert Grant. BS, U. Iowa, 1951; MS, U. Del., 1952, PhD, 1954; DSc (hon.), Manhattan Coll., 1992. Supt. mfg. textile fibers dept. E.I. du Pont de Nemours & Co., Martinsville, 1966-67; mgr. engrng. tech. and materials rsch. E.I. du Pont de Nemours & Co., Wilmington, 1969-73, dir. rsch. and devel. pigments dept., 1973-75, dir. instrument products, photo products dept., 1975-77, dir. electronic products, photo products dept., 1977-79, gen. mgr. textile fibers dept., 1979-80, v.p. corp. plans, 1980-83, v.p. electronics dept., 1984-87; exec. dir. AIChE, N.Y.C., 1988-96, ret., 1996; trustee U. Del. Rsch. Found., Newark, 1987—, pres., 1994—; commencement spkr. Coll. Engrng., U. Iowa, 1995. Author: Gas Absorption and Solvent Extraction, 1963; contbr. articles to profl. jours. Vice chmn. Stanton Sch. Bd., Del., 1961-64; chmn. adv. bd. Coll. Engrng., U. Iowa, Iowa City, 1974-80; chmn. adv. bd. dept. chem. engrng. U. Calif., Berkeley, 1978-87, chmn., 1982-83; co-chmn. adv. bd. dept. chem. engrng. U. Del., Newark, 1984-88, mem. Coll. Engrng. adv. coun., 1995—; trustee Med. Ctr. Del., Wilmington, 1983—; pres. Del. Found. for Phys. Edn., Wilmington, 1984—. With U.S. Army, 1954-56. Recipient 1st Disting. Engrng. Alumni award U. Del., 1984, Medal of Distinction, U. Del., 1993, Disting. Alumni award U. Iowa, 1988, Kenneth Andrew Roe award Am. Assn. of Engrng. Socs., 1996. Fellow AIChE (Van Antwerpen award 1998); mem. Nat. Acad. Engrng., Del. Tennis Assn. (pres. 1982-83), Tau Beta Pi, Sigma Xi, Phi Eta Sigma. Republican. Presbyterian. Avocation: tennis. Home: 24 Brandywine Falls Rd Wilmington DE 19806-1002

EMMERT, ROBERTA RITA, health facility administrator; b. Buffalo, Aug. 28, 1953; d. Robert George and Rita Rose (Lambert) E. Diploma, St. Elizabeth Hosp. Sch. Nsg., 1974; BSN magna cum laude, SUNY, Utica, 1989; MS, Syracuse U., 1993, cert. PNP, 1997. RN, N.Y., Calif. Charge nurse, staff nurse pediatrics St. Joseph Hosp. Health Ctr., Syracuse, N.Y., 1974-83; charge nurse spl. care pediatrics St. Joseph Hosp. Health Ctr., 1983-89; adminstrv. supr., nurse educator St. Joseph Hosp. Health Ctr., Syracuse, N.Y., 1989—; instr. Am. Heart Assn. Mem. ANA (cert. pediat. nurse), Am. Orgn. Nurse Execs., N.Y. State Nurses Assn., Soc. Pediat. Nurses, Sigma Theta Tau. Home: 4750 Woodard Way Apt 9K Liverpool NY 13088-4630

EMMETT, MICHAEL, physician; b. Linz, Austria, Oct. 29, 1945; came to U.S., 1949; s. Issac and Pearl (Gladstone) E.; m. Rachel Kozuch, Aug. 2, 1969; children: Mira, Daniel, Joshua. BS, Pa. State U., 1967; MD, Temple U., 1971. Diplomate Am. Bd. Internal Medicine, Am. Bd. Internal Medicine, Nephrology. Intern, then resident Yale U. Med. Ctr., New Haven, 1971-74; nephrology fellow Hosp. U. of Pa., Phila., 1974-76; clin. asst. prof. medicine U. Tex. Southwestern Med. Sch., Dallas, 1976-80, clin. assoc. prof. medicine, 1980-85, clin. prof. medicine, 1985—; Ralph Tompsett prof. medicine Baylor U. Med. Ctr., Dallas, 1986—, dir., nephrology/metabolism, 1986-96, dir. nephrology endocrinology labs, 1986—, chief of medicine, 1996—; cons. physician Parkland Hosp., Dallas, 1976—, Presbyn. Hosp., Dallas, 1976—. Contbr. articles to profl. jours. Fellow ACP; mem. Am. Fedn. Clin. Rsch., Dallas County Med. Soc., Tex. Med. Assn., So. Med. Soc., Am. Soc. Nephrology, Internat. Soc. Nephrology. Avocations: tennis, skiing. Office: Baylor U Med Ctr 3500 Gaston Ave Dallas TX 75246-2017

EMMETT, RITA, professional speaker; b. Chgo., Apr. 12, 1943; d. Thomas Henry Dorney and Helen Fischer; m. Bruce Karder, May 21, 1994; children: Robb Sean, Kerry Shannon. BA in English, Northeastern Ill. U., 1979; MS in Adult and Cont. Edn, Nat. Louis U., Evanston, Ill., 1985. Coord. edn. programs Leyden Family Svc., Franklin Park, Ill., 1977-95; mem. adj. faculty Triton Coll., River Grove, Ill., 1977—, Wright Coll., Chgo., 1985—; pres. Emmett Enterprises, Inc., Des Plaines, 1994—; presenter seminars in field. Author: The Complete Procrastinator's Handbook, Family Communications Handbook, Great Speakers Anthology; contbr. articles to newspapers and mags. Pres. Parent's Club, River Grove, 1987-88; keynote spkr. Gov.'s Mansion, Springfield, Ill. Mem. Bus. and Profl. Women (Achievement award 1986), Assn. Consultation and Edn. (sec.), Ill. Prevention Network, Century Club, Nat. Spkr.'s Assn., Profl. Spkr.'s of Ill. (bd. dirs. 1995, 96). Roman Catholic. Avocations: reading, writing, travel, friends.

EMMETT, ROBERT ADDIS, III, lawyer; b. Washington, July 2, 1943; s. Robert Addis Jr. and Marjorie (Slater) E.; m. Anne Ellen Flanigan, Aug. 29, 1969; children: Jennifer, Laura, Robert, Andrew. BA, U. Mich., 1965; JD, Stanford U., 1968. Bar: Calif. 1969, D.C. 1976, U.S. Ct. Appeals (D.C. cir.) 1978, U.S. Supreme Ct. 1980, U.S. Ct. Appeals (8th cir.) 1981, U.S. Ct. Appeals (4th cir.) 1985, U.S. Ct. Appeals (3d and 6th cirs.) 1986. Vol. U.S. Peace Corps., Acarigua, Venezuela, 1969-70; atty. br. chief U.S. EPA, Washington, 1971-77; from assoc. to ptnr. Reed Smith Shaw & McClay, Washington, 1978—; bd. dirs. Detrex Corp., Southfield, Mich., 1984—. Mem. ABA, D.C. Bar Assn. Club: Edgemoor (Bethesda, Md.). Home: 5408 Moorland Ln Bethesda MD 20814-1336 Office: Reed Smith Shaw & McClay 1301 K St NW Ste 1100E Washington DC 20005-3373

EMMICH, LINDA L., secondary education educator, guidance counselor; b. Cin., Feb. 8, 1949; d. Jack C. and Edna E. (Wiese) E. BS, U. Cin., 1971, MA, 1986. Cert. secondary edn. tchr., permanent sch. counselor. Counselor Friars Club, Cin., 1986-89; tchr., counselor Nativity Sch. Archdiocese of Cin., 1986, mem. curriculum com., 1983, tch. Purcell Marian High Sch. summer program, 1991-95; tutor, facilitator Lang. and Learning Ctr. No. Ky., 1996-98; with Navitity Sch., Cin.; ednl. resource Creative Therapy Assocs., Cin., 1989, 90. Fed. Study grantee, 1978-79, 88. Mem. Nat. Coun. Tchrs. Math., Nat. Cath. Edn. Assn., Ohio Cath. Edn. Assn. (conv. speaker 1987). Office: Nativity Sch 5936 Ridge Ave Cincinnati OH 45213-1699

EMMONS, BEVERLY, lighting designer; b. Dec. 12, 1943; d. Howard W. and Dorothy (Allen) E.; m. Peter Gombosi, Sept. 1, 1973 (div. 1978); m. Peter Angelo Simon, Oct. 17, 1980; 1 child, Annie Corinne. BA, Sarah Lawrence Coll., 1965; student, Lester Polakov Sch. Theatrical Design. Lighting designer Broadway prodns. Elephant Man, A Day in Hollywood/A Night in the Ukraine, All's Well That Ends Well, The Heiress (Tony nomination - Lighting Design, 1995). Recipient Obie award, 1980, Bessie award, 1984. Mem. United Scenic Artists (exec. bd.).

EMMONS, JEANNE CARTER, English educator; b. Minden, La., Oct. 5, 1949; d. Winfred S. and Ethel May (Moore) E.; m. Adam Joseph Frisch, July 23, 1977; children: Austin, Eleanor. BA, U. Tex., 1971, MA, 1973, PhD, 1977. Asst. instr. U. Tex., Austin, 1977-78; instr. English Northwestern Coll., Orange City, Iowa, 1978; prof. English Briar Cliff Coll., Sioux City, Iowa, 1978—. Contbr. poems to profl. publs. Creative writing tchr. Girls, Inc., Sioux City, 1995—; bd. dirs. Friends of the Sioux City Public Libr., 1995—. Recipient 1st Prize Iowa Woman Poetry Competition, 1991, South Coast Poetry Rev. Competition, 1993, Winner Minn. Voices Poetry Competition, 1996. Mem. MLA, Sierra Club, Phi Beta Kappa, Phi Kappa Phi. Democrat. Lutheran. Avocations: gardening, singing. Office: Briar Cliff Coll 3303 Rebecca St Sioux City IA 51104-2324

EMMONS, JOANNE, state senator; b. Big Rapids, Mich., Feb. 8, 1934; d. Ray J. and Emma M. (Von Glahn) Gregory; m. John Francis Emmons, June 9, 1956; children: Sarah, Dorothy. BS, Mich. State U., 1956; degree in pub. svc. (hon.), Ferris State U., 1992. Tchr. Mecosta (Mich.) High Sch., 1956-58; treas. Big Rapids Twp., 1976-86; state rep. State of Mich., Lansing, 1987-91, state senator, 1991—. Chair Mecosta County Rep. Com., 1976-80; vice chair 10th dist. Rep. Com., 1984-86; bd. dirs. Luth. Child and Family Svcs., 1990—. Named Nat. Rep. Legislator of Yr., Nat. Assn. State Legislators, 1993, Legislator of Yr., Mich. Twp. Assn., 1993. Mem. Am. Legion Aux., Mich. Farm Bur. (legis. com. 1970—), Milk Haulers Assn. (Legislator of Yr. 1995), Omicron Delta Kappa. Avocations: reading, sewing. Home: PO Box 30036 Lansing MI 48909-7536 Office: Mich State Senate State Capitol Lansing MI 48909

EMMONS, ROBERT DUNCAN, diplomat; b. Los Angeles, Mar. 1, 1932; s. Richard Norman and Margaret Houston (Kelly) E.; m. Susan Mary Likeman, Aug. 23, 1958; 1 child, Robert Campbell; m. Carolyn Elizabeth Kingsley, Sept. 27, 1995. B.A., UCLA, 1954, LL.B., 1957. Contract adminstr. N.Am. Aviation, Inc., Los Angeles, 1958-60, 62-63; contract adminstr. Litton Industries, Los Angeles, 1961; fgn. service officer Dept. State, Washington, 1963-88; vice consul, 3d sec. Am. embassy, Beirut, 1963-65; consul Am. consulate, St. John, N.B., Can., 1966-68; program officer AID, Saigon, Vietnam, 1968-70; sr. watch officer Dept. State, Washington, 1970-71; chief consular sect. Am. embassy, Warsaw, Poland, 1972-74; counselor of embassy Am. embassy, Copenhagen, 1974-76; consul gen. Am. embassy, Kingston, Jamaica, 1976-78; office dir. Dept. State, Washington, 1978-80; chief immigration br. Am. embassy, London, 1980-84; consul gen. Am. consulate gen., Tijuana, Mex., 1984-87; retired, 1988. Recipient Vietnam award Dept. State, 1969. Mem. Am. Fgn. Service Assn., Calif. State Bar.

EMMONS, ROBERT JOHN, corporate executive; b. Trenton, N.J., Sept. 18, 1934; s. Charles Glunk and Ruth Marie (Heilhecker) E.; m. Christine Young Bebb, July 13, 1980; children: Bradley Thomas, Cathy Lynne, Christopher Robert, Ryan Hunter. A.B. in Econs, U. Mich., 1956, M.B.A., 1960, J.D., 1964. V.p. Baskin-Robbins Co., Burbank, Calif., 1964-68; pres. United Rent-All, Los Angeles, 1968-69, Master Host Internat., Los Angeles, 1969-71; prof. Grad. Sch. Bus., U. So. Calif., 1971-82; pres. LTI Corp., Monterey, Calif., 1982-84; chmn., CEO, dir. Casino USA/SFI Corp., Santa Barbara, Calif., 1984-98; CEO Emmons Capital Investments, Santa Barbara, Calif., 1999—. Author: The American Franchise Revolution, 1970, The American Marketing Revolution, 1980; poetry Other Places, Other Times, 1974, Love and Other Minor Tragedies, 1980. Mem. AAUP, Am. Mktg. Assn., European Mktg. Assn., Am. Econ. Assn., Calif. Yacht Club (L.A.), Hawaii Yacht Club (Honolulu), The Valley Club of Montecito (Calif.), Useppa Island Club (Fla.), St. Petersburg Yacht Club (Fla.), The Calif. Club, Beta Gamma Sigma, Pi Kappa Alpha. Office: Emmons Capital Investments PO Box 50243 Santa Barbara CA 93150

EMMONS, VICTORIA ANN, hospital administrator, marketing consultant; b. Carmel, Calif., Sept. 27, 1950; d. Herbert Glen and Miriam Box; m. Daniel Richard Stober, June 24, 1972 (div. July 1982); 1 child, Katharine Evans Stober; m. John Louis Emmons, May 16, 1987. BA in French, Fla. State U., 1972; student, U. Strasbourg, France, 1970-71; postgrad., U. South Fla., 1978-80, U. San Francisco, 1999—; student, U. San Francisco. Thcr. French and journalism Brookside Jr. H.S., Sarasota, Fla., 1974-79; thcr. French and journalism St. Stephen's Sch., Bradenton, Fla., 1980-81, dir. devel., 1982-84; comms. specialist Manatee Meml. Hosp., Bradenton, 1984-85; sr. dir. cmty. rels. Washington Hosp., Fremont, Calif., 1985-93; exec. dir. Washington Hosp. Found., Fremont, 1993-96; pres., owner E2 Cons., Los Altos, Calif., 1994—; v.p. mktg. and devel. El Camino Hosp., Mountain View, Calif., 1997—; bd. dirs. Mid-Peninsula Home Health and Hospice, Inc., Mountain View, 1997—, Fremont Healthy Start, 1992-94. Contbr. articles to Vim and Vigor Mag., Health Signs, others. Bd. dirs., chair pub. rels. Spl. Olympics of Alameda County, Fremont, 1995-96; mem. Jr. League of Manatee County, Fla., 1976-79; bd. dirs. Manatee County Cancer Soc., Bradenton, 1984-85, Ctr. for Cmty. Dispute Settlement, Livermore, Calif., 1996; chair March of dimes Walk-a-Thon, 1999. Recipient YWCA Tribute to Women and Industry award, San Jose, 1998; Bradenton Herald/Knight-Ridder journalism scholar, 1979. Mem. Healthcare Profls. of No. Calif., Women in Comms., Commonwealth Club, Assn. for Healthcare Philanthropy, No. Calif. Soc. for Healthcare Pub. Rels. and Mktg. (bd. dirs.), Fremont C. of C., Newark C. of C., Rotary Club (pres. Warm Springs chpt. 1993-94, L.A. chpt.), Kappa Alpha Theta (bd. dirs., chair pub. rels. of alumni club). Democrat. Episcopalian. Avocations: golf, reading, piano, speaking French, travel. Office: El Camino Hosp 2500 Grant Rd PO Box 7025 Mountain View CA 94039-7025

EMORY, HUGH MERCER, lawyer; b. Jackson, Miss., Nov. 10, 1945; s. George Bache and Elizabeth (Burlingame) E.; m. Jayne Kovanda, Aug. 4, 1969 (div. 1971); m. Pamela S. Fox, Aug. 6, 1973; children: Gail, Benjamin. BA, Cornell U., 1967; JD, Temple U., 1972. Bar: Pa. 1972, U.S. Dist. Ct. (ea. and mid. dists.) Pa., 1972, U.S. Ct. Appeals (3rd cir.) 1978, U.S. Supreme Ct., 1984. Assoc. Duane, Morris & Heckscher, Phila., 1972-80, ptnr., 1980-97; pvt. practice Wayne, Pa., 1997-98; ptnr. Ryan, Emory & Ryan LLP, Paoli, Pa., 1998—. Editor-in-chief Temple Law Rev., 1971-72; author, editor (newsletter) PASADWIP, 1991—. Committeeman Tredyffrin Twp. Rep. Com., Berwyn, 1980-94, area chmn., 1984-90; mem. Chester County Rep. Com., West Chester, Pa., 1984-90. With U.S. Army, 1967-69, Korea. Master Hon. John E. Stively Jr. Inn of Ct.; mem. Assn. Ski Def. Attys. (founding dir. 1986, bd. dirs. 1987-91). Republican. Episcopalian. Home: 745 Country Club Rd Phoenixville PA 19460-2725 Office: Ste 105 Station Square Three Paoli PA 19301

EMORY, MEADE, lawyer; b. Seattle, Feb. 26, 1931; s. DeWolfe and Marion (Burton) E.; m. Deborah Carley, Apr. 30, 1959; children: Ann, Campbell, Elizabeth. A.B., George Washington U., 1954, LL.B., 1957; LL.M. in Taxation, Boston U., 1963. Bar: D.C. 1958, Wash. 1958, Iowa 1966. Trial atty. IRS, Boston, 1961-64; teaching fellow N.Y.U. Sch. Law, 1964-65; mem. faculty U. Iowa Sch. Law, 1965-70; legislation atty. Joint Com. on Taxation, U.S. Congress, 1970-72; mem. faculty U. Calif. Sch. Law, Davis, 1972-75; asst. to commr. IRS, 1975-77; ptnr. firm LeSourd & Patten, Seattle, 1978-90; of counsel Lane Powell Spears Lubersky, Seattle, 1991—; prof. law and dir. grad. program in taxation U. Wash. Sch. Law, Seattle, 1995—; vis. prof. law UCLA, 1987, Tulane U. Law Sch., 1990, Duke U., 1991, 92, Northwestern U. Sch. of Law, 1993, Georgetown U. Law, 1993, U. Pa. 1995; Mason Ladd dist. vis. prof. U. Iowa Law, 1994; Earl Dunlap dist. vis. prof. U. Nebr. Law, 1994; Charles S. Lyon vis. prof. taxation from practice NYU, 1989. Co-author: Federal Income Taxation of Corporations and Shareholders-Forms, 1981, rev. edit., 1989; mem. bd. editors Jour. Taxation. Trustee Seattle Symphony Orch., 1978-89; bd. dirs. Cornish Inst. Art, Seattle, 1979—. Recipient Commr.'s award IRS 1976. Mem. Am. Bar Assn., Am. Law Inst. Clubs: Rainier (Seattle), Seattle Tennis (Seattle), Univ. (Seattle); Cosmos (Washington). Office: U Wash Sch Law 1100 NE Campus Pkwy Seattle WA 98105-6605 Office: U Wash Sch Law 1100 NE Campus Pkwy Seattle WA 98105-6605

EMORY, THOMAS MERCER, JR., data communications equipment manufacturing executive; b. Morristown, N.J., Sept. 5, 1940; s. Thomas Mercer and Marie Louise (Bates) E.; m. Nancy Florence Jowitt, July 24, 1965; children—Shawn Mercer, Drew Jowitt. B.S.E.E., Lafayette Coll., 1962; M.S.E.E., U. Pa., 1965. Registered profl. engr., Pa. Devel. engr. Gen. Electric, King of Prussia, Pa., 1962-68; pres. Digilog Inc., Willow Grove, Pa., 1968-96; dir. Upper Bucks Inst. Aeronautics, Quakertown, Pa., 1996—; bd. dirs. Sunburst Aviation, Inc. Avocations: skiing; flying; sailing. Home: 344 Sweetbriar Rd Perkasie PA 18944-3867 Office: Digilog Inc 2360 Maryland Rd Willow Grove PA 19090-1709

EMPERADO, MERCEDES LOPEZ, librarian; b. Manila, Aug. 9, 1941; came to U.S., 1969; d. Evaristo Villasor and Marina (Gallardo) Lopez; m. Conrado Emperado, June 30, 1968; children: Joshua Caleb, Marita Eve. BS in Elem. Edn., Philippine Normal Coll., 1963; MLS, Cath. U. Am., 1974. Libr. math. and computation lab. Fed. Preparedness Agy., Washington, 1976-79; libr. Fed. Emergency Mgmt. Agy., Washington, 1979—. Mem. ALA, Am. Soc. Info. Sci., Spl. Librs. Assn., Nat. Coordinating Coun. on Emergency Mgmt. Baptist. Home: 6303 Elm Way Clinton MD 20735-3928 Office: Fed Emergency Mgmt Agy Libr 500 C St SW Washington DC 20024-2523

EMPEY, DONALD WARNE, educational administrator; b. McMinnville, Oreg., Feb. 8, 1932; s. Earnest Warne and Anna May (Alsman) E.; m. Mary Catherine Reeh, July 14, 1956; children: Elizabeth, Margaret, Jennifer. BA, Willamette U., 1954; MA, Stanford U., 1955; EdD, U. Oreg., 1964. Tchr. history South Salem High Sch., Salem, Oreg., 1955-58; asst. prin. Bend Sr. High Sch., Oreg., 1958-61; prin. Bend Sr. High Sch., 1961-63; grad. asst. U. Oreg., Eugene, 1963-64; dir. instrn. Arcadia Sch. Dist., Calif., 1964-68; dep. supt. Lake Washington Sch. Dist., Kirkland, Wash., 1968-69; supt. Lake Washington Sch. Dist., 1969-76; dep. supt. Glendale Unified Sch. Dist., Calif., 1976—; vis. lectr. Claremont (Calif.) Grad. Sch., 1966-68, Calif. State U., Northridge, 1986—; mem. adv. com. on profl. growth Calif. Commn. on Tchr. Credentialing, 1985. Contbr. articles to profl. jours. Co-chmn. Glendale Youth Leadership Conf., 1986—; mem. exec. bd. Glendale Child Care Council, 1987-89; pres. Glendale Community Coordinating Council, 1987; vice chmn. Glendale Mayors Com. on Drug Free Glendale, 1991; mem. Glendale Task Force on Performing Arts Ctr., 1991. Recipient Golden Acorn award Lake Washington PTA Coun., 1975, hon. svc. award Glendale PTA Coun., 1980, spl. recognition award L.A. County Schs., 1991, Willamette U. Alumni Citation award, 1991, Outstanding Pub. Svc. award Calif. Farm Bur., 1993; Danforth Found. fellow, 1975; named Educator of Yr. Crescent Valley C. of C., 1994. Mem. Assn. Supervision and Curriculum Devel., Am. Assn. Sch. Adminstrs., Kiwanis (v.p. Glendale 1990—), Phi Delta Kappa. Republican. Presbyterian. Home: 5334 Ramsdell Ave La Crescenta CA 91214-1923 Office: Glendale Unified Sch Dist 223 N Jackson St Glendale CA 91206-4380

EMPEY, GENE F., real estate executive; b. Hood River, Oreg., July 13, 1923; BS in Animal Husbandry, Oreg. State U., 1949; M. of Tech. Journalism Iowa State U., 1950; m. Janet Halladay, Dec. 27, 1950; children: Stephen Bruce, Michael Guy. Publs. dir. U. Nev., Reno, 1950-55; mgr. Zephyr Cove Lodge Hotel, Lake Tahoe, Nev., 1955-65; owner Empey Co., real estate agy., Carson City and Tahoe, Nev., 1964—; land developer, owner investment and brokerage firm . Mem. Nev. Planning Bd., 1959-72, chmn., 1961-66; mem. Nev. Tax Commn., 1982—; participant People to People Program, China, 1996, Egypt, Jordan, 1997. Capt., inf. U.S. Army, 1943-47; PTO. Grad. Realtors Inst. Mem. Nat. Assn. Realtors, (cert. comml. investment mem.; pres. Nev. chpt.), Tahoe Douglas C. of C. (pres. 1962, dir.), Carson City C. of C., Carson-Tahoe-Douglas Bd. Realtors, Capital City Club, Rotary, Heavenly Valley Ski (pres. 1968) Club, The Prospector's Club (Reno). Republican. Home: PO Box 707 Zephyr Cove NV 89448-0707 Office: 512 S Curry St Carson City NV 89703-4614

EMPLIT, RAYMOND HENRY, electrical engineer; b. Darby, Pa., May 2, 1948; s. Henry Raymond and Caroline Winifred (Parker) E.; m. Patricia Jean Jezl, Aug. 7, 1976; children: Eric, Susan. BS summa cum laude in Engrng., U. Pa., 1978, MS in Engrng., 1979. Engr. Custom Controls Co., Broomall, Pa., 1972-75, tech. dir., 1975-78, v.p., 1979-82; chief engr. Robertshaw Controls, Havertown, Pa., 1982-87; pres. Electronic Devel. Corp., Edgemont, Pa., 1987-89; project engr. Gt. Lake Instruments, Edgemont, Pa., 1989-91; v.p. Interlink Techs., Broomall, Pa., 1991-97, pres., 1997—. Patentee indsl. level instrumentation in U.S. and Can. With U.S. Army, 1968-71. Recipient Hugo Otto Wolf Meml. prize U. Pa., 1978. Mem. IEEE, Eta Kappa Nu, Tau Beta Pi. Republican. Avocations: reading, wine, investing. Home: 71 Sweetwater Rd Glen Mills PA 19342-1710 Office: Interlink Techs 1000 Sussex Blvd Broomall PA 19008-4011

EMRICH, EDMUND MICHAEL, lawyer; b. N.Y.C., Apr. 12, 1956; s. Edmund and Mary Ann (Picarella) E. BA, SUNY, Albany, 1978; JD, Hofstra U., 1981. Bar: N.Y. 1982, U.S. Dist. Ct. (so. and ea. dists.) N.Y. 1982, U.S. Ct. Appeals (2d cir.) 1987. Law clk. to presiding justice U.S. Bankruptcy Ct. (ea. dist.) N.Y., Westbury, 1982-83; assoc. Levin & Weintraub & Crames, N.Y.C., 1983-90; assoc. Kaye, Scholer, Fierman, Hays & Handler, N.Y.C., 1990-92, ptnr., 1993—; local rules com. U.S. Bankruptcy Ct. (ea. dist.) N.Y., 1985-86; mem. local rules drafting subcom. U.S. Bankruptcy Ct. (so. dist.) N.Y., 1985-86, 95-98. Mem. Hofstra U. Law Rev., 1981-82. Mem. ABA, N.Y. State Bar Assn., Am. Bankruptcy Inst. Avocations: golf, tennis, wine collecting. Home: 300 E 85th St New York NY 10028-4500 Office: Kaye Scholer Fierman Hays & Handler 425 Park Ave New York NY 10022-3506

EMRICK, TERRY LAMAR, financial business consultant; b. Bowling Green, Ohio, Aug. 24, 1935; s. Everett Dale and Lois (Fry) E.; m. Alma Faye Adams, July 3, 1953; children—Jacquelyn, Kelly. B.S., Bowling Green State U., 1957. Jr. acct., supr. tax dept. Ernst & Young, C.P.A.s, Toledo, 1957-64; tax mgr., asst. controller, corporate controller and v.p. Champion Spark Plug Co., Toledo, 1964-83; v.p. fin. and adminstrn. CVI Inc., Columbus, Ohio, 1984-87; owner tax cons. service, 1967-72; v.p. Summit Christian Coll., Fort Wayne, Ind., 1988-92; bus. cons., 1993—. Mem. Perrysburg Sch. Bd., 1972-75; bd. dirs., treas. Toledo Zool. Soc., 1978-82; mem. Fresno Civil Svc. Bd., 1997—. Mem. Tax Forum (pres. 1970-71), Ohio Soc.

C.P.A.s, Fin. Execs. Inst. (dir., pres. Toledo chpt.). Home and Office: 645 E Champlain Dr Apt 138 Fresno CA 93720-1294

EMSLIE, WILLIAM ARTHUR, electrical engineer; b. Denver, Oct. 30, 1947; s. William Albert and Hazel Esther (Niles) E.; m. Tracey Jane Palmer, Feb 22, 1975; children: David Barrett, Andrew Niles, Charles William, Alexis Claire. BSEE, U.S. Naval Acad., 1971; MSEE, Mich. State U., 1972. Registered profl. engr., Colo. Commd. ensign USN, 1971, advanced through grades to capt., 1997; with USNR, 1978—; energy conversion engr. Pub. Svc. Co. of N.Mex., Albuquerque, 1978-79; mgr. engr. Horizon Tech., Ft. Collins, Colo., 1979-80; staff engr. Platte River Power Authority, Ft. Collins, 1980-85, planning supr., 1985-89, mgr. quality improvement, 1989-92, exec. engr., 1992-95, supr. engring. svcs., 1995-97, bus. planning mgr., 1997—; mem. renewable task force Electric Power Rsch. Inst., Palo Alto, Calif., 1982-85, mgt. com. Western Energy Supply and Transmission Assocs., Albuquerque, 1991—, vice chair, 1994-95, chair, 1996—; chmn. Am. Pub. Power Assn. Demonstration of Energy Efficient Devels. Bd., Washington, 1992-94. Chmn. campaign Ft. Collins Area United Way, 1986, pres. bd. dirs., 1988; chmn. Sch. Mill Levy Tax Com., Ft. Collins, 1988. Grantee State of Colo., Am. Public Power Assn./Demonstration of Energy Efficient Devels., Western Energy Supply and Transmission Assocs., U.S. Dept. Energy, City of Colorado Springs, 1986-90. Mem. IEEE, Foothills Rotary of Ft. Collins (pres. 1995-96). Achievements include research in photovoltaics which provided a solar insolation assessment that is more accurate than the typical meterological year and a comprehensive evaluation of the effectiveness of 4 types of photovoltaic systems. Home: 825 E Pitkin St Fort Collins CO 80524-3839 Office: Platte River Power Auth 2000 E Horsetooth Rd Fort Collins CO 80525-5721

ENAM, SYED ATHER, neurosurgeon, researcher; b. Sindri, Bihar, India, Nov. 21, 1961; s. Syed Enamul Haque and Razia Enam; m. Kishwar Fakhar, Jan. 1, 1989; children: Syed Faaiz, Syed Zayd, Syed Usman. MBBS, Dow Med. Coll., Karachi, Pakistan, 1987; PhD, Northwestern U., 1991. Resident in gen. surgery SUNY, Buffalo, 1991-92; resident in neurosurgery Henry Ford Hosp., Detroit, 1992-98; Senior Staff Henry Ford Hosp., 1998; chief Neurosurgery Assocs. of Macomb, 1998—. Contbr. chpts. to textbooks, articles to profl. jours. Recipient Outstanding Resident award Henry Ford Med. Assn., 1998, 1st prize Midwest Soc. Electron Microscopists, 1991; Am. Health Assn. Found. fellow, 1990, Northwestern U. Dean's fellow, 1987; Quaid-e-Azom scholar/medal Bd. of Edn., Punjab, 1977. Mem. Soc. for Neurosci., Am. Assn. Neurol. Surgeons, World Fedn. Neurology, Rsch. Soc., Congress of Neurol. Surgeons, Sigma Xi. (recipient Grad. Rsch. Symposium award). Islamic. Achievements include research on cell biology of Alzheimer's Disease, neuron interaction and neuronal development, cell biology of brain tumor invasion. Home: E-138 Block 7, Gulshan Iqbal, Karachi Pakistan Office: Henry Ford Hosp Dept Neurosurgery 2799 W Grand Blvd Dept Detroit MI 48202-2689

ENARSON, HAROLD L., university presidentemeritus; b. Villisca, Iowa, May 24, 1919; s. John and Hulda (Thorson) E.; m. Audrey Pitt., June 7, 1942; children: Merlyn Pitt Prentice, Elaine, Lisa. B.A., U. N.Mex., 1940, L.H.D., 1981; M.A., Stanford U., 1946; Ph.D., Am. U., 1951; L.H.D., Kent State U., 1972, U. Detroit, 1975, Ohio State U., 1981; D.P.S., Bethany Coll., 1975; LL.D., Miami U., Oxford, Ohio, 1978, U. Akron, 1981, Central State U., 1981; Dr. Pub. Service (hon.), U. W. Fla., 1986; LLD (hon.), SUNY, 1987; LHD (hon.), Cleve. State U., 1990, U. Nebr., CCNY, 1993; HHD, No. Mich. U., 1993. Teaching asst., research asst. Stanford U., 1940-41, asst. prof., 1949-50; examiner Bur. Budget, Washington, 1942-43, 46-49; asst. prof. Whittier Coll., 1949; exec. sec. Steel Industry Bd., summer 1949; cons. Nat. Security Resources Bd., summer 1950; spl. asst. White House, Washington, 1950-52; pub. mem. WSB, 1952-53; asst. dir. commerce City Phila., 1953; exec. sec. mayor Phila., 1954; exec. dir. Western Interstate Commn. Higher Edn., 1954-60, sr. advisor, 1981—; adminstrv. v.p. U. N.Mex., 1960-61, acad. v.p., 1961-66, past project dir.; Internships in Latin Am.; pres. Cleve. State U., 1966-72, Ohio State U., Columbus, 1972-81; pres. emeritus Ohio State U., 1981—; Carl Hatch chair pub. adminstrn. U. N.Mex., 1982-83; Regents' prof. U. Calif., San Francisco, spring 1984; Carnegie Corp. adminstrs. fellowship, 1958; mem. Nat. Dental Research Council, 1958-62, surgeon gen.'s cons. group on med. manpower, 1960; cons. Ford Found., Egypt, 1960, C.Am., summers 1961-63, AID, 1965; dir. edn. svcs. Office Human Resources and Social Devel., 1963-64; mem. nat. adv. health coun. USPHS, 1964-68, task force on reorgn., 1967, Nat. Com. on U.S.-China Rels., 1976—, Nat. Commn. for Coop. Edn., 1968-78, adv. com. U.S. Army Command and Gen. Staff Coll., 1975-78; bd. dirs., mem. planning com. Coun. for Fin. Aid to Edn., 1977-81; panelist nat. identification program for advancement women in higher edn. Am. Coun. on Edn., 1977-80, mem. commn. on internat. edn., 1965-67, past mem. commn. on acad. affairs, coun. overseas liaison com., 1977-80, bd. dirs., 1970-73, 79-82; chmn. Inter-Univ. Coun. Ohio, 1979-80; sr. cons. Kellogg Nat. Fellows program W.K. Kellogg Found., 1981-85; bd. dirs. Am. Mideast Ednl. and Tng. System, 1983-90; pub. mem. U.S. Med. Licensing Exams., 1991-94. Trustee Am. Coll. Testing Program, 1979-82; mem. Nat. Coun. on Ednl. Rsch., 1980-81; mem. nat. sponsors com. Coun. for Internat. Exch. of Scholars, 1981-84; co-chmn. Com. on Future of SUNY, 1984; bd. visitors Air U., 1968-70; chmn. bd. dirs. Acad. Ind. Scholars, 1984-88. With AUS, 1943-46. Recipient Disting. Svc. award Pub. Sector, Assn. of Governing Bds. of Univs. and Colls., 1992. Mem. Nat. Assn. State Univs. and Land-Grant Colls. (chmn. internat. affairs com., mem. com. on financing higher edn., commn. on arts and scis. 1978, chmn. assn. and exec. com. 1980-81), Coun. of Presidents (chmn. 1978-79, mem. exec. com. 1978-79), Nat. Acad. Pub. Adminstrn., Assn. Urban Univs. (pres. 1971-72), Assn. Am. Univs. (health policy joint com. 1978-88), Am. Optometric Assn. (coun. on optometric edn. 1984-88), Rotary. Home: 2994 Nogales Ct Boulder CO 80301-1518

ENBYSK, H. MONTE, writer; b. Oct. 22, 1953. BS in Journalism, U. Oreg., 1975, MS in Journalism, 1978. Reporter, editor Eastside Jour., Bellevue, Wash., 1984-95; mng. editor Wash. CEO Mag., Seattle, 1995-97; copy editor, writer MSN Money Ctrl., Redmond, Wash., 1997-98; staff writer Microsoft MicroNews, Redmond, 1998—. E-mail: amontee@microsoft.com. Office: One Microsoft Way Redmond WA 98052

END, HENRY, interior and industrial designer; b. Salford, Eng., Nov. 3, 1915; came to U.S. 1946; s. Maximillian and Adela (Blain) E.; m. Jessica Marion Claas, July 5, 1947; 1 child, Lindsay. Student architecture and art, St. Martin's Sch. Art, London, 1930; A.R.C.A., Royal Coll. Art, London, 1934. Founder, pres. Henry End Assoc, Miami, Fla., 1950—; founder Internat. Design Ctr. Los Angeles and Miami, 1960; designer sets 20th Century Fox, Warner Bros., Universal, Selznick. Interior designer hotels and restaurants, condominiums, office bldgs., including Cocoanut Grove, Los Angeles, Carlton Tower and Heathrow Hotel, London, Mayflower, Washington, Hotel Quito, Ecuador, El Conquistador, P.R., Carlton Beach, Bermuda, Lucayan Beach Hotel, Grand Bahama Island, Nassau Beach Hotel, Penta Hotels, London and Munich, Fed. Republic Germany, Ritz Carlton, Montreal, Que., Can., Seacoast Towers West, Seacoast Towers V, 733 Park Ave. Bldg., N.Y.C., The Whitehall, Chgo., Marriott chain motor hotels, tourist hotels for Govt. Tunisia, Hilton,Munich, Sheraton Brussels, Sheraton Buenos Aires, Rio de Janeiro, Hyatt Internat., Brussels, Montreal, Iran and Jamaica, Esso Hotel, Antwerp, Belgium, UN Hotel N.Y.C., S.S. Norway, Pavillion Hotel, Miami, Ledra Marriott, Athens, Lakeside Regent, Palm Beach, Fla.; designer feature exhibits Room of Tomorrow, Designs for Dining, Internat. Hotel Expn., N.Y.C., Chgo., Los Angeles, Internat. Restaurant Expn., Chgo., U.S. Rubber Pavilion, Coliseum, N.Y.C.; author: Interiors Book of Hotels and Motor Hotels, 1963, Interiors 2nd Book of Hotels, 1976, Hyatt Regency, Miami, Plaza Hotel, N.Y.C. Served with RAF, 1940-46. Recipient spl. citation AIA, awards Art Dirs. Club, Design Derby citation Société Culinaire Philanthropique, 13 design awards Instns. Mag.; named to Hall of Fame, Interior Design Mag., 1985. Fellow Royal Soc. Arts; mem. Am. Soc. Interior Designers (citation of merit, 2 design awards). *America has few boundaries for one who wishes to work hard. With the addition of little talent, success is unlimited.*

END, WILLIAM THOMAS, business executive; b. Milw., Oct. 31, 1947; s. Jack Arthur and Cecil (O'Brien) E.; m. Nancy Kolb, June 10, 1969 (div. 1974); 1 child, Laura; m. Elyse Soucy, Feb. 23, 1980; children—Alison, David. BA, Boston Coll., 1969; student, U. Vienna, Austria, 1967-68; MBA, Harvard U., 1971. Group product mgr. Gillette Toiletries, Boston, 1971-75; exec. v.p. L.L. Bean, Inc., Freeport, Maine, 1975-90; exec. v.p. Lands' End, Inc., Dodgeville, Wis., 1991-92, pres., CEO, 1992-95; chmn., CEO Internat. Cornerstone Group, Portland, Maine, 1995—, also bd. dirs.; bd. dirs. Hannaford Bros. Co., Scarborough, Maine, Ariel, Inc., Augusta, Maine, Cinmar, Cin., Travel Smith, San Rafael, Calif., Internat. Cornerstone Group, The Territory Ahead, Santa Barbara, Calif., Garnet Hill, Franconia, N.H., Ballard Designs, Atlanta. Republican. Roman Catholic. Avocations: hunting; fishing; skiing; camping; canoeing. Home: PO Box 339 34 Castle Rd South Freeport ME 04078 Office: Internat Cornerstone Group 415 Congress St Ste 600 Portland ME 04101-3538*

ENDAHL, LOWELL JEROME, retired electrical cooperative executive; b. Jerauld County, S.D., July 3, 1922; s. John Martin and Olga A. (Bunde) E.; m. Vronna Belle Lee, Oct. 16, 1948; children: John Raymond and Jay Jerome (twins), Mark Arnold. B.S. in Agrl. Engring., S.D. State U. Power use adviser Tri-County Electric Assn., Plankinton, S.D., 1948-51; mgr. power use dept. Sioux Valley Empire Electric, Colman, S.D., 1951-54; mgr., mem. services Nat. Rural Electric Coop. Assn., Washington, 1954-75, mgr. energy R & D., 1975-89; ret., 1989; cons., vol. Nat. Rural Electric Coop. Assn., Arlington, Va., 1990-98; U.S. rep. UN Working Party on Rural Electrification, Belgium and Netherlands, 1968; cons. Internat. Program divsn. NRECA, Ecuador and Columbia, 1969, cons. Internat. program divsn., Vietnam, 1970, Internat. program divsn., Ghana, Africa, 1994. Columnist: rural Electrification, 1975-89. Pres. Luther Pl. Meml. Ch., Washington, 1976-78; vol. NRECA Internat. Found., 1990-98. Capt. USMC, 1943-46, PTO. Fellow Am. Soc. Agrl. Engrs. (chmn. EPP div. 1873-74 George W. Kable Electrification award, vice-chmn. editorial bd. Agrl. Engr. 1981-82, past pres. Md.-D.C. chpt.).

ENDERS, ALLEN COFFIN, anatomy educator; b. Wooster, Ohio, Aug. 5, 1928; s. Robert Kendal and Abbie Gertrude (Crandell) E.; m. Alice Hay, June 15, 1950 (div. Dec. 1975); children: Robert H., George C., Richard S., Gregory H.; m. Sandra Jean Schlafke, Aug. 5, 1976. AB, Swarthmore Coll., 1950; AM, Harvard U., 1952, PhD, 1955. From asst. prof. to assoc. prof Rice Inst., Houston, 1954-63; from assoc. prof to prof. Washington U., St. Louis, 1963-75; prof., chmn. dept. human anatomy U. Calif., Davis, 1976-86, prof. cell biology and human anatomy, 1986—; cons. NIH, Bethesda, Md., 1964-68, 70-73, 76-80, 83-93. Author: (with others) Bailey's Microscopic Anatomy, 1984; editor: Delayed Implantation, 1964; contbr. numerous articles on anatomy and reproduction to profl. jours. Nat. pres. Perinatal Research Soc., 1981. Grantee NIH, 1959—. Fellow AAAS; mem. Am. Assn. Anatomists (v.p. 1980-82, pres. 1983-84), Soc. Study Reprodn., Am. Soc. Cell Biology. Home: 39707 Barry Rd Davis CA 95616-9415 Office: U Calif Sch of Medicine Cell Biology And Anato Davis CA 95616

ENDERS, ELIZABETH MCGUIRE, artist; b. New London, Conn., Feb. 18, 1939; d. Francis Foran and Helen Cuseck (Connolly) McGuire; m. Anthony Talcott Enders, June 9, 1962; children: Charles Talcott, Alexandra Eustis, Camilla, Ostrom II. BA, Conn. Coll., 1962; MA, NYU, 1987. Trustee Artists Space, N.Y.C., 1986-95, Conn. Coll., New London, 1988-93; assoc. dept. prints and illustrated books Mus. Modern Art, 1993—, Lyman Allyn Art Mus., 1994—. One-woman shows include Paul Schuster Gallery, Cambridge, Mass., 1966, Ulysses Gallery, N.Y.C., 1992, 94, Lyman Allyn Art Mus., New London, Conn., 1994, Charles Cowles Gallery, N.Y.C., 1995, Norbert Considine Gallery, Princeton, N.J., 1997; exhibited in group shows at Boston Symphony Orch., 1982, NYU, 1983, Conn. Conn., 1988, Bronx Coun. on Arts, 1990-91, Addison Gallery Am. Art, 1993, Angel Art, L.A., 1993, Lyman Allyn Art Mus., New London, Conn., 1994-95, So. Alleghenies Mus. Art, Loretto, Pa., 1994, Artists Space Multiple, 1995, New Mus. Contemporary Art, N.Y.C., 1995, Denise Bibro Fine Art, N.Y.C., 1995, N.Y. Studio Sch., N.Y.C., 1995, Divine Design '95, L.A., Spring Benefit Raffle, Sculpture Ctr., N.Y.C., 1996, 97, 98, Charles Cowles Gallery, N.Y.C., 1996, Fax Art Week, Copenhagen, Assn. Danish Graphic Artists, 1996, Open Studio, Downtown Arts Festival, N.Y.C., 1997, 98, Dieu Donne Papermill, 1997, Charles Cowles Gallery, N.Y.C., 1998, Denise Bibro Fine Art, 1998, Lyman Allyn Art Mus., 1998, David McKee Gallery, 1998, Lyman Allyn Art Mus., 1999, Robert Brown Gall., Wash. D.C., 1999, New York Acad. of Art Benefit Auction, 1999; traveling group show Artists Space, 1992, 94, Southeastern Ctr. Contemporary Art, Winston-Salem, N.C., 1993, Allentown (Pa.) Art Mus., 1994, Cleve. Ctr. Contemporary Art, 1994, Salt Lake Art Ctr., Salt Lake City, 1995, Kemper Ctr. Contemporary Art and Design, Kansas City, Mo., 1996, Bass Mus. of Art, Miami Beach, Fla., 1997, Flint (Mich.) Inst. Arts, 1998, Blaffer Gallery, U. Houston, TX, 1998, Contemporary Art Ctr., Va. Beach, 1998, Tampa Mus. of Art, 1998-99, Art Mus. of Southeast Tex., 1999; represented in permanent collections at Addison Gallery of Am. Art, Andover, Mass., Graham Gund, Cambridge, Daimler Benz North Am. Corp., Lyman Allyn Art Mus., Conn. Coll., New London. Mem. nat. fin. coun. Dem. Nat. Com., Washington, 1988—. Recipient Citation of Appreciation, Conn. Coll., 1990, medal, 1993. Fellow Frick Collection (N.Y.C.); mem. The Drawing Soc., The Bklyn. Mus., Williams Coll. Mus. of Art, Mus. Modern Art (assoc.), Williams Club. Democrat. Roman Catholic. Home: 530 E 86th St New York NY 10028-7535

ENDERS, JODY, French educator; b. Washington, May 22, 1955; d. Hward and Corinne Engelsberg Enders; m. Eric D.Hoker, Aug. 7, 1996. BA in French and Russian summa cum laude, U. Va., 1977, MA in French Lit., 1979; PhD in Romance Langs., U. Pa., 1986. Asst. prof. French U. Ill., Chgo., 1986-92; assoc. prof. French U. Calif., Santa Barbara, 1992-96, prof. French, 1996—; dramaturge Chgo. Medieval Players, 1989-92; vis. Inst. for Advanced Study, Princeton U., 1997. Author: Rhetoric and the Origins of Medieval Drama, 1992, The Medieval Theater of Cruelty, 1998; contbr. articles to profl. jours. John Simon Guggenheim fellow, 1999. Mem. Phi Beta Kappa (Mary Isabel Sibley award 1986-87).

ENDICO, MARY ANTOINETTE, artist; b. Bronx, N.Y., June 13, 1954; d. Felix and Katherine (Gluck) E.; m. Robert W. Fugett. BFA, Boston U., 1976. artist cons. D'Arches Fine Art Paper, France, 1983; demonstrator, lectr. art groups N.Y. State, 1980-97; sec. Sugarloaf (N.Y.) Guild, 1980-88. Self-employed artist, Sugar Loaf, 1977—; group shows include Art of Orange and Rockland N.Y. Invitational, 1986, Aqueous Annual, Ky., 1987, 88, 89, 94, Nat. Exhibit Am. Watercolors, N.Y., 1989, 90, 91, N.E. Watercolor Annual, N.Y., 1991, Nat. Watercolor Soc., Calif., 1992, San Diego Internat., 1997; permanent collections include Del Monte Corp., N.Y., IBM Corp., N.Y., The Ambra Found., N.H., Ashville (N.C.) Mus., Ky. Mus., Bowling Green. Mem. Northeast Watercolor Soc. (co-founder 1991), Knickerbocker Artists, Orange County Watercolor Soc., Salmagundi Club, Ky. Watercolor Soc. Avocation: dressage. Office: Fantasy Factory PO Box 31 1386 Kings Hwy Sugar Loaf NY 10981

ENDICOTT, JENNIFER JANE, education educator; b. Oklahoma City, Oct. 17, 1947; d. M. Ector and Jessie Ruth (Carter) Reynolds; m. William George Endicott, June 2, 1969 (dec. Sept. 1976); 1 child, Andrea A. BA History, U. Okla., 1969, MEd Adminstrn., 1975, PhD, 1987. Cert. secondary edn. tchr.: history, govt., geography, econs., adminstr., Okla. Mid. sch. tchr. Norman (Okla.) Pub. Schs., 1970-77, adminstr. elem. edn., 1977-80; grad. asst. U. Okla., Norman, 1984-88; adj. lectr. U. Ctrl. Okla., Edmond, 1988-90, asst. prof., 1990-94, assoc. prof., 1995-98, prof., 1999—; cons. Okla. Action Network, 1992—, Coop. Coun. Okla. Sch. Adminstrn., 1996—. Mem. adv. bd. The Annual Editions Series, Guilford, Conn., 1994—; co-editor Okla. Assn. Tchr. Educators Jour., 1997—; contbr. articles to profl. jours. Bd. dirs. Cleveland County Hist. Soc., Norman, 1980-88, Arts and Humanities Coun., Norman, 1982-88; bd. dirs. Jr. League, Inc., Norman, 1982-90; bd. dirs. Assistance League, Norman, 1982-90, pres. 1988-89. Recipient Harriet Harvey Meml. award U. Okla. Found., 1984; named Norman Cmty. Family of the Yr. Finalist, LDS Ch., Norman, 1985. Mem. ASCD, NAESP, Okla. ASCD, Okla. Assn. for Supr. and Curriculum Devel., Okla. Assn. Elem. Sch. Prins., Okla. Assn. Tchr. Educators (bd. dirs. 1994—, pres. 1996-97), Am. Assn. Tchr. Educators, Soc. for Philosophy and History of Edn., Am. Assn. Teaching and Curriculum (charter mem. 1994—), Am. Ednl. Rsch. Assn., Philosophy of Edn. Soc., Kappa Delta Pi (univ. sponsor 1991-96), Phi Delta Kappa (found. rep. Mid. State chpt. 1993-95, sec. 1995-96, v.p. 1997-99, Svc. Key 1998).

ENDICOTT, JOHN EDGAR, international relations educator; b. Cin., Aug. 9, 1936; s. Charles Lafayette and Alice Willa (Campbell) E.; m. Mitsuyo Tiffani Kobayashi, Aug. 24, 1959; children: Charlene Nobel, John Edward. BA, Ohio State U., 1958; MA in History, Omaha U., 1968; MA in Internat. Rels., Tufts U., 1972, MALD, 1973, PhD, 1973; student, Natl. War Coll., 1982, Air Command Staff Coll., 1978, Air War Coll., 1976, Squadron Officer Sch., 1963. Commd. USAF, advanced through grades to col.; dep. head polit. sci. and philosophy dept. USAF Acad., 1969-71, 73-78; dep. Air Force rep. mil. staff com. UN Security Coun., 1979-81; dir. internat. affairs divsn. Air Force Plans, The Pentagon, 1978-81; assoc. dean Nat. War Coll., 1981-83; dir. rsch. directorate Nat. Def. U., 1983-86; dir. Inst. Nat. Strategic Studies, Dept. Def., 1986-89; prof. Sam Nunn Sch. Internat. Affairs Ga. Inst. Tech., Atlanta, 1989—, founding dir. Ctr. Internat. Strategy Tech. and Policy, 1989—; apptd. Olympic attache Mongolian Olympic Com., Ulaan Bataar, 1995-96; co-chair Coun. U.S.-Japan Security Rels.; bd. dirs. Nat. Def. U. Found., UN Assn. Atlanta; cons. Dept. Def., Chmn. Joint Chiefs Staff, Process for Accreditation of Joint Edn. Program, NRC of NAS, Office Internat. Affairs, Def. Task Force, Inst. Def. Analysis, others; chmn. interim secretariat Agy. for Ltd. Nuclear Weapons-Free Zone for N.E. Asia, 1996—. Mem. editl. bd. The Japan Digest, Small Wars and Insurgencies, New South Mag.; author: Japan's Nuclear Option, 1975; co-editor, contbr.: American Defense Policy, 1977, Regional Security Issues, 1991; co-author: Politics of East Asia, 1978; contbr. articles to profl. jours. Decorated Def. Superior Svc. medal, Legion of Merit, Bronze Star, Meritorious Svc. medal, Air medal with oak leaf cluster, Air Force Commendation medal with oak leaf cluster; Vietnam Svc. Medal with 2 bronze stars; Natl. Defense Svc. Medal, Rep. of Vietnam gallantry cross with device; Rep. of Vietnam Campaign Medal; Dept. of the Army Exceptional Civilian Svc. Medal; W. Alton Jones rsch. grantee Ploughshares Found. Fellow Internat. Inst. Strategic Studies; mem. Internat. Studies Assn., Assn. Asian Studies, Army and Navy Club, Ga. Polit. Sci. Assn., Japan-Am. Soc. Ga. (recipient Mike Mansfield award 1996, exec. com., bd. dirs.), S.E. Korea-Am. Friendship Soc. (charter, bd. dirs.), Georgian Club, Phi Beta Kappa. Avocations: tennis, French horn, writing, language study. Office: Ga Inst Tech Ctr Internat Strategy Atlanta GA 30332

ENDICOTT, WILLIAM F., journalist; b. Harrodsburg, Ky., Aug. 26, 1935; s. William O. and Evelyn E.; m. Mary Frances Thomas, Dec. 27, 1956; children: Gene, Fran, Greg. Student, Am. U., 1955; BA in Polit. Sci., Transylvania U., 1957. With Lexington (Ky.) Leader, 1957; sports writer Louisville Courier-Jour., 1958-62; reporter Tulare (Calif.) Advance-Register, 1963; reporter, city editor Modesto (Calif.) Bee, 1963-66; city editor Sacramento Union, 1966-67; with Los Angeles Times, 1968-85; Capitol bur. chief Sacramento Bee, 1985-95, asst. mng. editor, 1995-98, dep. mng. editor, 1998—; Hearst vis. profl. U. Tex., 1993. Served with USMCR, 1957-58. Recipient various journalism awards Disting. Alumnus award Transylvania U., 1980. Episcopalian. Office: 21st and Q Sts Sacramento CA 95852

ENDIEVERI, ANTHONY FRANK, lawyer; b. Syracuse, N.Y., May 21, 1939; s. Santo and Anne Rose (Zeolla) E.; m. Arlene Rita McDonald, May 20, 1967; children: Anne C., Steven A. BA, Syracuse U., 1961, LLB, 1965, JD, 1968. Bar: N.Y. 1967, U.S. Dist. Ct. (no. dist.) N.Y. 1967, U.S. Ct. Appeals (2d cir.) 1969, U.S. Supreme Ct. 1970; cert. civil trial lawyer Nat. Bd. Trial Advocacy. Assoc. Ronald Crowley, Atty., North Syracuse, N.Y., 1965-67, Love, Balducci & Scacciz, Syracuse, 1967; pvt. practice law Camillus, N.Y., 1968—; appellate counsel Hiscock Legal Aid, Syracuse, 1968-70; asst. corp. counsel, housing code prosecutor City of Syracuse, 1970-74; participant Nat. Coll. Advocacy, 1981-83, 86; lectr. Melvin Belli seminar, San Francisco, 1987, 93, Kansas City, Mo., 1988, Boston, 1989, San Diego, 1990; spkr. in field. Mem. ministry program Syracuse Diocese Pre-Deacon Study, 1980-82. Maj. USMCR, 1972-88, ret. Mem. ATLA (spkr. nat. conv. 1990, seminar 1990, ultimate trial advocacy course 1 991), Assn. Trial Lawyers Am. Coll. Advocacy, N.Y. Bar Assn., N.Y. State Bar Assn., Onondaga County Bar Assn., N.Y. Trial Lawyers Assn., Nat. Brain Injury Assn., N.Y. Brain Injury Assn. Democrat. Roman Catholic. Home: 205 Emann Dr Camillus NY 13031-2009

ENDLER, NORMAN SOLOMON, psychology educator; b. Montreal, Que., Can., May 2, 1931; m. Beatrice Kerdman, June 26, 1955; children—Mark, Marla. B.Sc., McGill U., 1953, M.Sc., 1954; Ph.D., U. Ill., 1958. Registered psychologist, Ont., Can. Psychologist Pa. State U., 1958-60; lectr. psychology York U., Downsview, Ont., 1960-62; asst. prof. York U., 1962-65, assoc. prof., 1965-68, prof., 1968-95, Disting. rsch. prof., 1995—; cons. Toronto East Gen. Hosp., 1964-84, Clarke Inst., Toronto, 1972-81; vis. scholar Oxford (Eng.) U., 1993. Author: Holiday of Darkness, 1982, rev., 1990, (with E.J. Shipton, F.D. Kemper) Maturing in a Changing World, 1971, (with D. Magnusson) Interactional Psychology and Personality, 1976, (with L.R. Boulter, H. Osser) Contemporary Issues in Developmental Psychology, 1976, (with D. Magnusson) Personality at the Crossroads: Current Issues in Interactional Psychology, 1977, (with J. McV. Hunt) Personality and the Behavioral Disorders, 2d edit., 1984, (with E. Persad) Electroconvulsive Therapy: The Myths and the Realities, 1988, (with C.D. McCann) Depression: New Directions in Research, Theory, and Practice, 1990, (with J.D.A. Parker) Coping Inventory for Stressful Situations, 1990, (with J.M. Edwards, R. Vitelli) Multidimensional Anxiety Scales, 1991, (with M. Zeidner) Handbook of Coping, 1996. Recipient Can. Silver Jubilee medal, 1978; grantee Ont. Mental Health Assn., 1968-74, Can. Coun., 1969-78, Social Scis. and Humanities Rsch. Coun., 1979-80, 91—; Killam Rsch. fellow Can. Coun., 1987-89. Fellow Am. Psychol. Assn., Can. Psychol. Assn. (D.O. Hebb award for disting. contbn. to psychology as a sci. 1997), Ont. Psychol. Assn., Royal Soc. Can. (Innis-Gerin medal 1997). Home: 52 Sawley Dr, Willowdale, ON Canada M2K 2J5 Office: York U Dept Psychology, 4700 Keele St, Downsview, ON Canada M3J 1P3

ENDRENYI, JANOS, research engineer, educator; b. Budapest, Hungary, Nov. 9, 1927; came to Can., 1957; s. Sandor and Lilly (Szegvari) E.; m. Edith Bernat, Dec. 5, 1956. Diploma in Engring., Tech. U., Budapest, 1951; MASc, U. Waterloo, Ont., Can., 1965; PhD, U. Toronto, Ont., 1972. Registered profl. engr., Ont., Can. Instr. Tech. U., Budapest, 1949-52; rsch. engr. Rsch. Inst. for Electric Power, Budapest, 1952-56; engr. Toronto Hydro, 1957-59; rsch. engr. rsch. divsn. Ont. Power Hydro, Toronto, 1959-79, head reliability and stats. sect., 1979-90, prin. rsch. engr., 1990-92, prin. scientist emeritus, 1992—; lectr. U. Toronto, 1972-80, adj. assoc. prof., 1980-83, adj. prof., 1983—; spkr. at seminars worldwide. Author: Electric Shock Prevention (in Hungarian), 1956, Reliability Modeling in Electric Power Systems, 1978; contbr. papers to profl. jours. Fellow IEEE. Home: 80 Front St E Apt 201, Toronto, ON Canada M5E 1T4 Office: Ont Power Techs, 800 Kipling Ave, Toronto, ON Canada M8Z 5S4

ENDRESS, ANTON G., horticulturist, educator; b. Boise, Idaho, Aug. 19, 1945; s. Rudolph George and Ruth Marie (Wallace) E.; m. Nancy C. Statius-Muller; children: Gregory Anton, Bryan Anton. BS in Biology, Duquesne U., 1967; MS in Botany, U. Iowa, 1970, PhD in Botany, 1974. Instr. dept. biology U. Dubuque, Iowa, 1972; postgrad. rsch. biologist I-IV Dept. Biology U. Calif., Riverside, 1974-77, asst. rsch. biologist I-III Statewide Ari Pollution Rsch. Ctr., 1977-80, instr. dept. biology, 1978, 80; assoc. botanist Sect. Botany and Plant Pathology Ill. Natural History Survey, 1980-85, head Sect. Botany and Plant Pathology, 1985-89, asst. chief. for planning, 1989-90, affiliate profl. scientist Ctr. for Biodiversity, 1990—; affiliate prof. dept. agronomy U. Ill., 1986-90, prof., head dept. horticulture, 1990-96, prof. dept. natural resources and environ. scis., 1996—; mem. numerous coms. Ill. Natural History Survey, 1980-89, U. Ill., 1988—; participant numerous symposiums, confs. and workshops; lectr. in field. Contbr. articles to profl. jours., chpts. to books. Sci. Fair Judge, Champaign Schs., 1985-86, Ill. Jr. Acad. Sci., 1994; mem. Sci. Curriculum Revision Project, Unit 4 (Champaign) Sch. Dist., 1989-90; bd. mem., sec., v.p., coach Champaign Park Dist. Soccer League, 1980-85; founder, bd. mem., coach Little Illini Soccer Club, 1981-90; v.p., bd. dirs. Ctrl. Ill. Soccer League, 1986-90. Grantee USAF Office Sci. Rsch., 1977-80, U. Ill. Campus Rsch. Bd., 1980, Abandoned Mine Land Reclamation Coun., 1982, Ill. Dept. Energy and Natural Resources, 1982, 83, Nat. Arborist Assn., 1989-92, Environ. Protection Trust Fund Commn., 1990, UIUC Campus Rsch. Bd., 1994-95; recipient Amah-LO Nation Y-Indian Guides Achievement award Riverside (Calif.) YMCA, 1979, Disting. Svc. award, 1979, Vol. Svc. award Champaign Park Dist., 1983, Appreciation award Ill. Vegetable Growers Assn., 1995. Mem. AAAS, Am. Inst. Biol. Scis., Am. Soc. Agronomy, Am. Soc. Horticultural Sci., Crop Sci. Soc. Am. (Fred V. Grau Turfgrass Sci. Award Com. 1992—), Minorities in Agriculture and Natural Resources Assn., Soc. Ecological Restoration, Pi Alpha Xi, Gamma Sigma Delta. Office: U Ill 36 Envir & Agr Bld 36 EASB Madigan Lab MC-637 Urbana IL 61801*

ENDRST, JAMES BRYAN, television critic, columnist; b. N.Y.C., Sept. 17, 1956; s. Jaroslav Jan and Elsa Beatrice (Latzko) E.; m. Dru Ellen Nadler, May 21, 1983 (div. Dec. 1996); 1 child, Nina. BA, Fairfield U., 1979. Copy editor, asst. news editor The Greenwich (Conn.) Time, 1979-82; feature writer, editor The Times-Herald Record, Middletown, N.Y., 1982-85; TV critic The Hartford (Conn.) Courant, 1985—. Mem. TV Critics Assn., Soc. Profl. Journalists. Office: Hartford Courant Co 285 Broad St Hartford CT 06115-3785

ENDSLEY, JANE RUTH, nursing educator; b. Harrisburg, Ill., Oct. 14, 1942; d. Clifford B. Bond and Haroldene (Malone) Miller; m. William R. Endsley, June 6, 1964. Grad., Deaconess Hosp. Sch. Nursing, Evansville, Ind., 1963; student, So. Ill. U., 1968; BSN cum laude, U. Evansville, 1978. RN, Ind., Ill. Staff nurse Deaconess Hosp., 1963-64; psychiat. nurse med.-surg. emergency rm. and obstetrics Ferrell Hosp., Eldorado, Ill., 1964-68, DON, 1969-70; DON, Good Shepherd Nursing Home, Eldorado, 1971-72; instr. nursing Southea. Ill. U., Harrisburg, 1973—; pres., sec. Peartree Antiques, Inc., Eldorado, 1995—; cons. parents too soon Egyptian Pub. Health Dept., Eldorado, 1985. Vice chmn. Pvt. Industry Coun., Harrisburg, 1983-91; precinct committeeperson Harrisburg Dem. Com., 1986-90; donor chmn. ARC, Harrisburg, 1970—; instr. CPR to civic orgns. and students, 1980-87. Mem. Ill. Nurses Assn. (nominating com. 1975), Southeasterrn Ill. Coll. Edn. Assn. (pres. 1988-91), Faculty Wives and Women Southeastern Ill. Coll. (sec.-treas. 1974-75), Assn. Antique Dealers and Collectors, Ill. Preservation Coun., Nat. Hist. Soc., Sigma Theta Tau. Avocations: reading, gardening, travel, interior decorating, antiques. Home: PO Box 345 1075 Shawnee Hills Rd Harrisburg IL 62946-4943

ENEGESS, DAVID NORMAN, chemical engineer; b. Winchester, Mass., Aug. 25, 1946; s. Norman Leonard and Shirley Mildred (Lewis) E.; m. Jane Deborah Enegess, June 20, 1970; children: Deborah Marie, Christine Kerry. BSChemE, Tufts U., 1968, MSChemE, 1971. Registered profl. engr., Conn., Mich. Nuclear systems engr. Combustion Engring. Inc., Windsor, Conn., 1972-75, supr. radwaste systems devel. and design, 1975-77; project engr. Hazardous Waste Systems Group, WP Corp., Ramsey, N.J., 1977-79, mgr. projects, 1979-80, gen. mgr., 1980-82; co-founder, v.p. Waste Chem. Corp., Paramus, N.J., 1982-88, Envirogen, Inc., Princeton, N.J., 1988—; mem. EPA Bioremediation Action Adv. Com., Washington, 1990—, Waste Mgmt. Symposia Tech. Program Com., Tucson, 1980-88, Oak Ridge (Tenn.) Nat. Lab. Waste Form Adv. Com., 1988-90; adviser Tufts U. Career Adv., Medford, Mass., 1990—; mem. Tufts Alumni Admissions Program, 1996—; bd. dirs. Vapex Corp, CVT America. Contbr. articles to profl. jours. Mem. Wyckoff (N.J.) Environ. Commn., 1986-88, Com. on Extended Learning, Wyckoff, 1984-85; mem., co-chair High Sch. Music Program Fund Raising, Wyckoff, 1987-90; coach Jr. Soccer League, Wyckoff, 1981-82; mem. Tufts U. Alumni Admissions Program, 1996—. 1st lt. U.S. Army, 1969-72. NSF fellow, 1968-69. Mem. ASME (mem. radwaste systems com. 1978-85), Am. Inst. Chem. Engrs., Atomic Indsl. Forum (rep. 1976-77), Am. Nuclear Soc., Hazardous Materials Control Rsch. Inst., Applied Biotreatment Assn. (dir. 1989-90). Achievements include patents for a static device for separations of gas mixtures into individual components, system using membrane device for radwaste processing, and process involving thin-film evaporation for radioactive wastewaters. Office: Envirogen Inc 4100 Quakerbridge Rd Lawrenceville NJ 08648-4702

ENELOW, ALLEN JAY, psychiatrist, educator; b. Pitts., Jan. 15, 1922; s. Isadore M. and Rose (Kasdan) E.; m. Mary Cleveland, July 21, 1946 (div. Sept. 1965); children: David, James, Susan, Margaret, Patience, Abigail; m. Sheila Kearns, Oct. 1, 1966; stepchildren: Lauren, Lisa. A.B., W.Va. U., 1942; M.D., U. Louisville, 1944. Intern Michael Reese Hosp., Chgo., 1944-45; resident psychiatry Winter VA Hosp., Topeka, 1947-49; mem. staff Menninger Found. and Asso. Hosps., 1947-52; practice medicine specializing in psychiatry Beverly Hills, Calif., 1952-58, Pacific Palisades, Calif., 1956-64; faculty U. So. Calif., Los Angeles, 1960-67; prof., chmn. dept. psychiatry Mich. State U., East Lansing, 1967-72; prof. psychiatry U. of Pacific, 1972-78; chmn. dept. psychiatry Pacific Med. Center, San Francisco, 1972-82; clin. prof. psychiatry U. Calif., 1977-82; clin. prof. psychiatry U. So. Calif., 1982-89, clin. prof. emeritus, 1989—; cons. NIMH, VA, others. Author: Psychiatry in the Practice of Medicine, 1966, Interviewing and Patient Care, 1972, 3d edit., 1985, 4th edit., 1996, Elements of Psychotherapy, 1977; contbr. numerous articles to profl. jours. Served with M.C. AUS, 1945-47. Fellow Am. Psychiat. Assn. (life), ACP. Office: 1532 Anacapa St Santa Barbara CA 93101-1929

ENEMARK, RICHARD DEMERITT, educational administrator; b. New York, Feb. 17, 1949; s. Richard and Mary (Clayton) E.; m. Nancy J. Lawton, Feb. 28, 1950; children: Faith Lawton Demeritt Enemark, Forrest Lawton Demeritt Enemark. AB, Colgate Univ., 1972; MA, Univ. Vt., 1978; M. Phil, Columbia Univ., 1984, PhD with highest distinction, 1986. Dir. studies Burke Mtn. Acad., East Burke, Vt., 1974-79; instr. Columbia Univ., N.Y., 1980-85; dean Noble & Greenough Sch., Dedham, Mass., 1988-90; head of h.s. Elis Irwin H.S., N.Y., 1985-87; instr.,, dir. teaching fellow Phillips Acad., Andover, Mass., 1987-88; headmaster The York Sch., Monterey, Calif., 1990-93; assoc. head St. Christopher's Sch., Richmond, Va., 1993-95; cons. Advancement for Edn., Orleans, Mass., 1995—; headmaster The Doane Stuart Sch., Albany, N.Y., 1998—. Commn. Ind. Schs., Washington, 1992-93; trustee All Sts. Sch., Carmel, Calif., 1990-93, Burke Mtn. Acad., E. Burke, Vt., 1995—. Mem. NAIS, CASE, Phi Beta Kappa. Avocations: gardening, sailing. Home: 78 Willett St Albany NY 12210 Office: The Doane Stuart Sch 799 S Pearl St Albany NY 12202

ENENBACH, MARK HENRY, community action agency executive, educator; b. Chgo., July 28, 1949; s. Joseph Henry and Antonette Regina (Kasko) E.; children: Joy Elizabeth, Erin Regina; m. Kai Lindquist Bergin, Sept. 28, 1985; 1 child, Faith Marie. BA in Polit. Sci. with honors, Loyola U., Chgo., 1971, MA in Urban Studies with honors, 1973. Cmty. resource specialist Model Cities, Chgo., 1974-79; grad. prof. Govs. State U., Park Forest South, Ill., 1977-89; dir. energy program City of Chgo., 1980-83; prof. St. Augustine's Coll., Chgo., 1981-82; coord. cmty. svcs. Dept. Human Svcs., Chgo., 1984-91; prof. urban planning and pub. adminstrn. DePaul U., Chgo., 1987—; dir. cmty. svcs. block grant programs Cmty. and Econ. Devel. Assn. Cook County, Inc., Chgo., 1992-96, v.p./COO, 1997—; mem. adv. bd. City Colls. Chgo., 1984-88; spkr. Nat. Headstart Assn., Washington, 1995; mem. task force Ill. Dept. Commerce and Cmty. Affairs, Springfield, 1996-97. Pres. Lincoln Park Interagy. Coun., Chgo., 1986-91; mem. adv. bd. Salvation Army, Chgo., 1987-91. Grad. rsch. fellow Loyola U., 1972-73. Mem. Nat. Assn. Cmty. Action Agys. (spkr. 1996), Ill. Assn. Cmty. Action Agys. Avocations: urban research, writing and travel in over 30 countries. Office: Cmty and Econ Devel Assn 208 S Lasalle St Ste 1900 Chicago IL 60604-1104

ENFIELD, D(ONALD) MICHAEL, insurance executive; b. L.A., Jan. 24, 1945; s. Fred Donald Jr. and Suzanne Arden (Hinkle) E.; m. Roseanne Burke, Dec. 29, 1978; children: Susan Ann, Michael David, Peter Christian. BA in Polit. Sci., U. San Francisco, 1967. Mgmt. trainee Marsh & McLennan, Inc., San Francisco, 1967-70, acct. exec., 1970-77, asst. v.p., 1977-79, v.p., 1979-81, sr. v.p., 1981-82, mng. dir., 1982-89; chmn., CEO Frank B. Hall & Co. of No. Calif., San Francisco, 1989-92; founder, chmn., CEO Metro/Risk, Inc., San Francisco, 1992—; cons. in field. Contbr. articles to profl. pubs. Bd. dirs. Ronald McDonald House, San Francisco, 1989-92; chmn. bd. dirs. Midsummer Mozart Festival, San Francisco, 1985-90; trustee Lamplighters Music Theater, 1996—. Mem. San Francisco C. of C. (dir. bus./arts coun. 1987-93), Soc. Calif. Pioneers (county v.p. 1974—), Lotos Club of N.Y., City Club of San Francisco, Olympic Club of San Francisco. Avocation: classical music. Office: Metro/Risk Inc 750 Battery St Ste 550 San Francisco CA 94111-1526

ENFIELD, RONALD LEE, Internet software company executive; b. Wash., 1945; s. Leon Earl and Verneta May Enfield; m. Diane Lee Christopher, June 29, 1968; children: Jennifer Jay Palmer, Lauren Elizabeth. BA, UCLA, 1966; MS, Fairleigh Dickinson U., 1982; student, U. Calif., Berkeley, 1962-65. Computer programmer Sys. Devel. Corp., Santa Monica, Calif., 1967-69; programmer, analyst Control Data Corp., Mpls., 1969-72; computer programmer Peoples Nat. Bank, Seattle, 1972; systems supr. Port of Seattle, 1972-74; mgr. tech. support C.F. Braun & Co., Engrs., Alhambra, Calif., 1974-77; computer scientist Computer Scis. Corp., Moorestown, N.J., 1977-79; mem. tech. staff The Mitre Corp., McLean, Va., 1979-81; pres. Medford Software Works, Inc., Haddonfield, N.J., 1981—. Contbg. photographer: The Trouble in Berkeley, 1965. Commr. environ. commn., Medford Lakes, N.J., 1991-92. Recipient Math. and Sci. Achievement award Bank of Am., L.A., 1962; scholar U. Calif. Berkeley Alumni Assn., 1962. Mem. Assn. Computing Machinery, Soc. Tech. Comm. (award of achievement 1987, 93, award of distinction 1992), Computer Profls. for Social Responsibility, Sierra Club. Avocations: skiing, flyfishing, travel. Home and Office: 601 Maple Ave Haddonfield NJ 08033-1129

ENG, CALVIN, cardiologist, researcher; b. Canton, China, June 12, 1947; s. David and Alice (Yee) E.; m. Alice Dong, Aug. 14, 1977; children: Andrew, Elizabeth. SB, MIT, 1969; MA, Columbia U., 1971; MD, Albert Einstein Coll. Medicine, 1974. Cert. Am. Bd. Internal Medicine. Asst. prof. Albert Einstein Coll. Medicine, Bronx, N.Y., 1981-86, assoc. prof., 1986-93; assoc. prof. Mt. Sinai Sch. Medicine, N.Y.C., 1993—; chief cardiology VA Med. Ctr., Bronx, 1993—. Recipient young investigator rsch. award NIH, 1981-84, established scientist award N.Y. Heart Assn., 1984-89. Fellow Am. Coll. Cardiology, Am. Heart Assn., N.Y. Acad. Scis. Home: 55 Irene Ct Closter NJ 07624-3209 Office: VA Med Ctr Radiology Dept 130 W Kingsbridge Rd Bronx NY 10468-3992*

ENG, CATHERINE, health care facility administrator, physician, medical educator; b. Hong Kong, May 20, 1950; came to U.S., 1953; d. Doi Kwong and Alice (Yee) E.; m. Daniel Charles Chan; 1 child, Michael B. BA, Wellesley Coll., 1972; MD, Columbia U., 1976. Diplomate Am. Bd. Internal Medicine, Am. Bd. Gastroenterology; cert. added qualifications geriatrics. Intern in internal medicine Presbyterian Hosp./Columbia, Presbyterian Med. Ctr., 1976-77, resident in internal medicine, 1977-79; fellow in gastroenterology/hepatology N.Y. Hosp./Cornell U. Med. Coll., 1979-81; instr. medicine Cornell U. Coll. Medicine, N.Y.C., 1980-81; staff physician On Lok Sr. Health Svcs., San Francisco, 1981-86, supervising physician, 1986-91, med. dir., 1992—; asst. clin. prof. dept. family and cmty. medicine U. Calif., San Francisco, 1986—, asst. clin. prof. dept. medicine, 1992-95; assoc. clinical prof. dept. medicine, Univ. Calif., San Francisco, 1995—; primary care specialist Program of All-inclusive Care for the Elderly, San Francisco, 1987-94; asst. chief dept. medicine Chinese Hosp., San Francisco, 1993-98, chmn. com. credentials, 1994-98. Instr. BLS Am. Heart Assn., San Francisco, 1988-92; mem. nominating com. YWCA of Marin, San Francisco, San Mateo, 1991-95; mem. mgmt. com. YWCA-Chinatown/North Beach, San Francisco, 1989-95; bd. dirs. Chinatown Cmty. Children's Ctr., San Francisco, 1987-90. Durant scholar Wellesley Coll., 1972. Fellow ACP; mem. Am. Geriatrics Soc., Am. Soc. Aging, Am. Gastroent. Assn., Calif. Med. Assn. (assoc.), San Francisco Med. Soc. (assoc.), Sigma Xi, Alpha Omega Alpha. Avocations: reading, hiking. Office: On Lok Sr Health Services 1333 Bush St San Francisco CA 94109-5611

ENG, JOAN LOUISE, retired special education educator; b. Yakima, Wash., July 29, 1934; d. Vernon Ross and Vivian Thelma (Rust) Dent; children: Andrew, Jane, William, June, Vern, Eric, Fred. BEd in English and Social Studies, Seattle U., 1961; MEd in Exceptional Children, Cen. Wash. U., 1965; postgrad., U. Wash., 1962, LeVerne U., 1972-73, Ea. Wash. U., 1975-76, Seattle Pacific U., 1976, Yakima Valley Coll., 1977; U. South Sch. Theology, 1997. Cert. tchr., elem. prin., Wash. Tchr. English, Selah (Wash.) H.S., 1962-65; tchr. English Yakima Valley Coll., 1965-66; tchr. Adams Elem. Sch., Yakima, 1966-71, McKinley Elem. Sch., Yakima, 1971-72, Stanton Elem. Sch., Yakima, 1972-77, Franklin Jr. High Sch., Yakima, 1977-82, John F. Kennedy H.S., Seattle, 1984-85, Artz-Fox Elem. Sch., Mabton, Wash., 1988-98; ret., 1998; supt. St. Timothy's Episcopal Ch. Sch., Yakima, St. Michael's Episcopal Ch. Sch., Yakima; cons. Tonnemaker Corp., Seattle, life vowed Sister-Community of the Paraclete. Editor Yakima Deanry Newsletter, 1998—, Paracletian Focus, 1998—. Asst. min., guardian St. Stephen's Priory, 1992-96, Seattle; chpt. guardian Spirit-In-Life, 1996—, Yakima, 1994-97; coord. Sunday worship team Heritage Garden Nursing Home, 1998—; coord. ann. retreat Cmty. of Paraclete, 1999—, mem. pastoral care team, 1996—; tchr. St. Michael's Sunday Sch., 1998—; vestry mem. St. Michael's, 1998—; del. Diocesan Conv. 1998, 99; mem. com. on handicapped, confined and chonically ill Diocese of Spokane, WA, 1998—; hospice vol., 1999—; vol. Annie Tran Grief and Loss Ctr., 1999—. Mem. NEA, Mabton Edn. Assn., Wash. Edn. Assn., Retired Tchrs., Yakima, WA, Washington State Retired Tchrs., 1998—. Avocations: guitar, knitting, crocheting. Home: 802 N 40th Ave Unit 16 Yakima WA 98908-2455

ENG, LAWRENCE FOOK, biochemistry educator, neurochemist; b. Spokane, Wash., Feb. 19, 1931; s. On Kee and Shee (Hue) E.; m. Jeanne Leong, Aug. 30, 1957; children: Douglas, Alice, Steven, Shirley. BS in Chemistry, Wash. State U., 1952; MS in Chemistry, Stanford U., 1954, PhD in Chemistry, 1962. Chief chemistry sect. path. and lab. med. svc. PAVA Health Care Sys., Palo Alto, Calif., 1961—; rsch. assoc. dept. pathology Sch. Medicine Stanford (Calif.) U., 1966-70, sr. scientist dept. pathology Sch. of Medicine, 1970-75, adj. prof., 1975-82, prof. dept. pathology Sch. of Medicine, 1982—; mem. ad hoc neurol. sci. study sect. and neurology B study sect. NIH, 1976-79, mem. neurol. sci. study sect., 1978-83; mem. adv. bd. VA Office of Regeneration Rsch. Program, 1985-89; mem. VA Merit Rev. Bd. for Neurobiology, 1987-90; mem. Nat. Adv. Neurol. Disorders and Stroke Coun., 1991-94. Mem. editorial bd. Neurobiology, 1970-75, Jour. of Neurochemistry, 1978-85, Jour. of Neuroimmunology, 1980-83, Molecular and Chem. Neuropathology, 1982—, Glia, 1987—, Jour. for Neurosci. Rsch., 1991—, Neurochemical Rsch., 1993—. Capt. USAF, 1952-57. Mem. Am. Soc. for Neurochemistry (coun. 1979-83, 85-87, 93—, sec. 1987-93), Am. Soc. Biochemistry and Molecular Biology, Internat. Soc. for Neurochemistry, Soc. for Neurosci. Office: VAPA Health Care System Path & Lab Med Svc 3801 Miranda Ave Palo Alto CA 94304-1207

ENGAR, RICHARD CHARLES, insurance executive, dentist, educator; b. Salt Lake City, Apr. 2, 1953; s. Keith Maurice and Amy Kathryn (Lyman) E.; m. Elizabeth Ann Willardson, June 21, 1977; children: Robert Keith, Thomas William, Julia Elizabeth. BA in Psychology, U. Utah, 1976; DDS, U. Wash., 1980. Resident gen. practice Sinai Hosp., Detroit, 1980-81; pvt. practice Salt Lake City, 1981-91; cons. Profl. Ins. Exch., Salt Lake City, 1990-91, atty.-in-fact, 1991—; clin. instr. dept. pathology, dental gen. practice residency program U. Utah Med. Ctr., Salt Lake City, 1988—. Author: Dental Treatment of the Sensory Impaired Patient, 1977; (with others) General Dentistry, 1996; contbr. articles to profl. jours. Dist. trainer Spring Creek Dist., Great Salt Lake coun. Boy Scouts Am., 1989-92. Fellow Acad. Gen. Dentistry (regional dir. 1991-97, chair regional dirs. 1995-97, trustee 1997—, publs. com. 1997—), Pierre Fauchard Acad., Utah Acad. Gen. Dentistry (pres. 1987, Dentist of Yr. 1997); mem. ADA, Salt Lake Dist. Dental Soc. (treas. 1986-88), Utah Dental Assn. (editor 1985-88), Acad. of Dentistry Internat., Utah Scale Modelers Assn. (v.p. 1992, 94, 97), Phi Beta Kappa, Phi Kappa Phi. Mem. LDS Ch. Avocations: model airplane building, backpacking, photography, painting. Home: 1806 Glenbrook Cir Salt Lake City UT 84121-1213 Office: 445 E 4500 S Salt Lake City UT 84107-3129

ENGBER, CHERYL ANN, language educator, linguist; b. East Chicago, Ind., Oct. 12, 1945; d. James Ward and Beryl Ann (Crowe) Biddle; m. Michael David Engber, Nov. 25, 1967; children: Sara Ann, Kimberly Sue. BA in Spanish with honors, Ind. U., 1967, PhD in Linguistics, 1992, MA in Spanish, 1974; MA in Tchg. ESL, Ball State U., 1979. Instr. Spanish Anderson (Ind.) U., 1979-82; assoc. instr. intensive English program Ind. U., Bloomington, 1983-86, adminstrv. asst. com. for R & D, 1989-91, instr. semi-intensive English program, 1991-93; assoc. prof. linguistics Truman State U., Kirksville, Mo., 1993—; instr. ESL Ind. U., Kuala Lumpur, Malaysia, 1985-86; grader for Test of Written English Ednl. Testing Svc., Princeton, N.J., 1989—; asst. to editor Studies in Second Lang. Acquisition Ind. U., 1987-89; spkr. in field. Contbr. Understanding English: A Listening Approach to ESL, 1983; contbr. articles to profl. jours. Founder Muncie (Ind.) Internat. Ctr., 1974; vol. tchr., founder internat. summer workshops for children, Muncie, 1977; deacon, elder, mem. com. First Christian Ch., Bloomington, Ind., 1987-92. Ind. U. fellow, 1982; Truman State U. grantee, 1994. Mem. Linguistic Soc. Am., Tchrs. ESL, Am. Assn. for Applied Linguistics, Nat. Coun. Tchrs. English, Phi Beta Kappa, Phi Kappa Phi. Avocations: travel, gardening, gourmet cooking. Office: Truman State Univ Divsn Lang and Lit McClain Hall 310 Kirksville MO 63501

ENGBERS, JAMES AREND, lawyer; b. Grand Rapids, Mich., Dec. 11, 1938; s. Martin Hoffius and Harriet Jean (Riddering) E.; m. Harriet M. Wissink, Sept. 13, 1960; children: Charles M., James A., Nancy L. Falk, David W. LLB, Hope Coll., Holland, Mich., 1960; JD, Wayne U., 1963. Bar: Mich. 1963, U.S. Dist. Ct. (we. dist.) Mich. 1963. Mem. firm Miller, Johnson, Snell & Cummiskey, P.L.C., Grand Rapids, Mich., 1963—. Mem. State Bar Mich. (standing com. on character and fitness 1993-97), Grand Rapids Bar Assn. (trustee 1972-73), Rotary Club. Republican. Presbyterian. Avocations: golf, tennis, reading, photography. Office: Miller Johnson Snell & Cummiskey PLC 800 Calder Plaza Bldg Grand Rapids MI 49503-2250

ENGDAHL, TODD PHILIP, newspaper editor; b. Jamestown, N.Y., Feb. 8, 1950; s. George Philip and Janice Marie (Wallin) E.; m. Caroline C.N. Schomp, Dec. 29 , 1973; children: Anders Justus Schomp, Mats Philip Schomp. BA, Pomona Coll., 1971; MS, Northwestern U., 1972. Reporter Oregonian, Portland, 1972-75; reporter Denver Post, 1975-80, asst. city editor, 1980-83, night city editor, 1983-85, Sunday editor, 1985-86, city editor, 1986-90, exec. city editor, 1990-95, new media editor, 1995—; lectr. journalism Portland State U., 1974; bd. dirs. Augsburg Fortress Pubs. Democrat. Lutheran. Avocations: reading, gardening, woodworking. Office: Denver Post PO Box 1709 Denver CO 80201-1709

ENGE, VERNON REIER, editor health care publications; b. Bismarck, N.D., Dec. 12, 1942; s. Vernon Lewis and Aurella Luella (Potter) E.; m. Mary C. Mortensen, Nov. 29, 1968; children: Eric Vernon, Evan Morten. BS, BA, Dickinson State U., 1964; MA, N. D. State U., 1979. Instr. Mandan (N.D.) H.S., 1965-74; night editor Mandan Pioneer, 1974-75; pub. info. office Bismarck (N.D.) Region Social Svcs., 1976; instr. Valley City (N.D.) H.S., 1976-82; instr. tech. writing Miles City (Mont.) C.C., 1982-83; gen. reporter Richland Free Press, Sidney, Mont., 1983-84; city editor, health & sci. editor Evening Phoenix, Phoenixville, Pa., 1984-87; editor Advance for Respiratory Care Practitioners Merion Publs. Inc., King of Prussia, Pa., 1988—; editor Advance for Mgrs. of Respiratory Care Merion Publs. Inc., King of Prussia, 1992—; founding editor of several other health care mags. Merion Publs. Inc., King of Prussia, 1988—. Mem. Minimum Wage Bd., Bismarck, N.D., 1975; del. to Dem. state conv., 1979. Named Outstanding Young Educator, Mandan Jaycees, 1974. Mem. Elks. Methodist. Achievements include: development of a regional health care publication to a 14 publication network of nat. influence. Avocations: music, literature, art. Home: 34 Fords Edge Royersford PA 19468-2666 Office: Merion Publs Inc 2900 Horizon Dr King Of Prussia PA 19406-1434

ENGEBRETSON, DOUGLAS KENNETH, architect, interior designer; b. Dawson, Minn., Nov. 5, 1946; s. Melvin Kenneth and Mary Louise (Jackson) E.; m. Kathleen Stella Jefferies, June 14, 1969; children: Leif Erik, Kristin Ann. B.Arch., U. Ariz., 1969. Registered architect, Mass., Vt., N.H., Conn. Draftsman, William B. Tabler, FAIA, N.Y.C., summer 1969, Wheeler Petterson Coffeen, Tucson, 1968-69; assoc. Alderman & MacNeish, West Springfield, Mass., 1970-78; pres. Tessier Assocs., West Springfield, Mass., 1978—; mem. Mass. Bd. Registration Architects, 1996—; corporator Chicopee (Mass.) Savs. Bank. Works include Putnam Vocat. Tech. Sch., Springfield, Mass., Palmer H.S. and Elem. Schs., Cmty. Savs. Bank, South Hadley, Mass., Ring Nursing Home, Springfield, Mt. Everett Regional Sch., Sheffield, Mass., Heritage Bank Hdqs., Holyoke, Mass.; co-author: Norway, 1978; author article in field. Mem. Zoning Bd. Appeals, Southampton, Mass., 1976-84, Personnel Policy and Procedures Bd., 1983-85; trustee Bay Path Coll., Longmeadow, Mass., 1991—, Brightside for Families and Children, West Springfield, 1992-96, Sta. WGBY-TV, Springfield, Mass., 1992—. Served with USAF, 1969-73. Recipient Group Study Exchange award to Norway, Rotary Internat., Evanston, Ill., 1978, Philanthropist of Distinction award Nat. Soc. of Fundraising Execs., Hampden County, 1996. Fellow AIA (nat. dir. 1986-89, nat. sec. 1991-92, pres. New Eng. regional council 1985-86, Richard Upjohn fellow 1992); mem. Western Mass. Chpt. AIA (pres. 1980-82), Mass. State Assn. Architects (pres. 1982-83). Republican. Lutheran. Club: Rotary (pres. 1985-86). Home: 6 Madison Ave Southampton MA 01073-9520 Office: Tessier Assoc Inc 1578 Riverdale St West Springfield MA 01089-4905

ENGEBRETSON, KATHLEEN MARY MURRAY, women's health nurse, psychiatric nurse; b. Waterbury, Conn., Sept. 16, 1954; d. William J. and Josephine C. (Smith) Murray; m. Edward J. Engebretson, Feb. 20, 1999; children: Patrick, Stephanie. Diploma, N.H. Hosp. Sch. Nursing, Concord, 1976. Cert. psychiat. mental health nurse, ANA. Staff nurse surg. fl. St. Mary's Hosp., Waterbury, Conn., 1978; staff nurse obstetrics Elliot Hosp., Manchester, N.H., 1978-82, Cath. Med. Ctr., Manchester, 1982-87; staff nurse residential, liason psychiatry W.J. Moore Regional Svcs., Inc., Manchester, 1988-92; psychiat. nurse (part-time) Moore Ctr. Svcs., Manchester, N.H., 1991-93; psychiat. nurse Lake Shore Hosp., Manchester, N.H., 1992-93; office nurse, study coord., rsch. asst. Dr. Lawrence DuBuske, Londonderry, N.H., 1992—; counselor, sr. nurse Odyssey Family Ctr., Canterbury, N.H., 1994; per diem staff Greater Manchester (N.H.) Mental Health Ctr.; psychiat. nurse Alt. Care Med. Svcs., Mass., N.H., 1995-97; meeting liason Immunology Rsch. Inst. of New England, 1998—. Eucharistic min., lector St. Catherine, Manchester, N.H. Mem. Developmental Disabilities Nurses N.H., Nat. League for Nursing, N.H.H. Sch. Alumni Assn. Home and Office: 24 Mo-sett Ave Goffstown NH 03045-2716

ENGEL, ALBERT JOSEPH, federal judge; b. Lake City, Mich., Mar. 21, 1924; s. Albert Joseph and Bertha (Bielby) E.; m. Eloise Ruth Bull, Oct. 18, 1952; children: Albert Joseph III, Katherine Ann, James Robert, Mary Elizabeth. Student, U. Md., 1941-42; A.B., U. Mich., 1948, LL.B., 1950. Bar: Mich. 1951. Ptnr. firm Engle & Engel, Muskegon, Mich., 1952-67; judge Mich. Circuit Ct., 1967-71; judge U.S. Dist. Ct. Western Dist. Mich., 1971-74; circuit judge U.S. Ct. Appeals, 6th Circuit, Grand Rapids, Mich., 1974-88, chief judge, 1988-89, sr. judge, 1989—. Served with AUS, 1943-46, ETO. Fellow Am. Bar Found.; mem. ABA, Fed. Bar Assn., Mich. Bar Assn., Cin. Bar Assn., Grand Rapids Bar Assn., Am. Judicature Soc., Am. Legion, Phi Sigma Kappa, Phi Delta Phi. Episcopalian. Club: Grand Rapids Torch. Home: 5497 Forest Bend Dr SE Ada MI 49301-9079 Office: US Ct Appeals 100 E 5th St Ste 418 Cincinnati OH 45202-3988 also: 640 Federal Bldg 110 Michigan St NW Grand Rapids MI 49503-2313

ENGEL, ANDREW GEORGE, neurologist; b. Budapest, Hungary, July 12, 1930; s. Alexander and Alice Julia (Gluck) E.; m. Nancy Jean Brombacher, Aug. 15, 1958; children: Lloyd William, Andrew George. BSc, McGill U., 1953, MD, 1955. Diplomate: Am. Bd. Internal Medicine, Am. Bd. Psychiatry and Neurology. Intern Phila. Gen. Hosp., 1955-56; sr. asst. surgeon, clin. asso. USPHS, NIH, Bethesda, Md., 1958-59; fellow in neuropathology Columbia U., N.Y.C., 1962-64; with Mayo Clinic, Rochester, Minn., 1956-57, 60-62; cons. Rochester, Minn., 1965—; prof. neurology Mayo Med. Sch., Rochester, 1973—, William L. McKnight-3M prof. neurosci., 1984—; disting. investigator Mayo Clinic, 1995—; mem. sci. adv. com. Muscular Dystrophy Assn., 1973—; mem. rev. com. NIH, 1977-81. Mem. editl. bd. Neurology, 1973-77, Annals Neurology, 1978-84, 90-95, Muscle and Nerve, 1978—, Jour. Neuropathology, 1981-83, European Neurology, 1989—, Jour. Neuroimmunology, 1991-98; contbr. over 300 articles to med. jours. Served with USPHS, 1957-59. Mem. Am. Acad. Neurology, Am. Neurol. Assn., Am. Assn. Neuropathologists, Am. Soc. Cell Biology, Soc. Neurosci., AAAS. Home: 2027 Lenwood Dr SW Rochester MN 55902-1051 Office: Mayo Clinic 200 1st St SW Rochester MN 55905-0002

ENGEL, BERNARD THEODORE, psychologist, educator; b. Chgo., Apr. 18, 1928; s. Marvin I. and Hannah (Hollander) E.; m. Rae Goldberg, Mar. 10, 1951; children: Sandra E., Jeffrey P., Lauren C. BA, UCLA, 1954, PhD, 1956. Jr. rsch. psychologist UCLA, 1956; rsch. psychologist Inst. Psychosomatic and Psychiatric. Research and Tng., Michael Reese Hosp., Chgo., 1957-58; lectr. med. psychology, mem. sr. staff Cardiovasc. rsch. Inst., Sch. Medicine U. Calif., San Francisco, 1959-67; chief behavioral physiology sect., chief Lab. Behavioral Scis. Gerontology Research Center, Nat. Inst. Aging, NIH, Balt., 1967-95; assoc. prof. behavioral biology Johns Hopkins Sch. Medicine, Balt., 1970-82; prof. Johns Hopkins Sch. Medicine, 1982—; bd. dirs. Insts. for Behavioral Resources, Inc.; adj. prof. psychiatry and behavioral scis. Duke U. Sch. Medicine, Durham, N.C., 1999—. Contbr. 175 articles to sci. jours.; editorial bds. Applied Psychophysiology and Biofeedback, Jour. of Behavioral Medicine, Psychosomatic Medicine.

Served in U.S. Army, 1950-52. Recipient award Pavlovian Soc., 1979. Fellow AAAS, Gerontol. Sci.; mem. Soc. Psychophysiol. Rsch. (pres. 1970-71), Assn. Applied Psychophysiology and Biofeedback (pres. 1981-82), Am. Psychosomatic Soc. (sec.-treas. 1981-85, pres. 1985-86, Patricia R. Barchas award in sociophysiology 1999), Pavlovian Soc., Gerontol. Soc. Am., Acad. Behavioral Medicine Rsch., Sigma Xi.

ENGEL, BRENDA BOLTON, controller; b. Niles, Mich., Mar. 1, 1961; d. Charles Edward and Evelyn Laurie (Dolph) Bolton; m. John H. Engel, July 11, 1998. AA, Southwestern Mich. Coll., Dowagiac, 1981; BSBA, Ferris State U., 1985; MBA, Western Mich. U., 1997. Asst. contr. Gen. Signal Corp., Watertown, Wis./Riverside, Mich., 1990-96; contr. Interlogic Systems, Inc., Elkhart, Ind., 1996-97, Internat. Wire, Inc., South Bend, Ind., 1997—; ops. controller internat. wire group, harness divsn. Internat. Wire, Inc., South Bend, 1997—; mem. adv. bd. Sch. Bus., Southewestern Mich. Coll., 1984. Mem. Inst. Mgmt. Accts. (pres. 1994-96, regional dir. 1998—, Bldg. Bridges award 1995), United Meth. Women. Avocations: golf, collecting cobalt blue depression glass, travel. Home: 52475 Liberty Mills Ct Granger IN 46530-8727

ENGEL, CHARLES ROBERT, chemist, educator; b. Vienna, Austria, Jan. 28, 1922; s. Jean and Lucie (Fuchs) E.; m. Edith H. Braillard, Aug. 6, 1951; children: Lucie Tatiana Berthoud, Christiane Simonne, Francis Pierre, Marc Robert. BA, U. Grenoble, 1941; MSc, Swiss Fed. Inst. Tech., Zurich, 1947, DSc, 1951; State-DSc, U. Paris, 1970. Research fellow, asst. Swiss Fed. Inst. Tech., Zurich, 1948-51; asst. prof. med. research Collip Med. Research Lab. U. Western Ont., London, 1951-55, asso. prof. med. research, 1955-58; hon. spl. lectr. chemistry, dept. chemistry U. Western Ont., 1951-58; prof. chemistry Laval U., Quebec, Que., 1958-90, prof. emeritus, 1995—; vis. prof. Inst. de Chimie des Substances Naturelles CNRS, Gif-sur-Yvette, France, 1966-67. Mem. editorial bd. Steroids, 1964-91; hon. editorial bd. Current Abstracts of Chemistry, 1971-72, Index Chemicus, 1971-72; mem. editorial adv. bd. Can. Jour. Chemistry, 1974; editor Can. Jour. Chemistry, 1986-91.; mem. French govtl. commn. chem. terminology, 1992—. Lt. for Can.-Que., Equestrian Order of Holy Sepulchre of Jerusalem, 1970-89, mem. Grand Magisterium, Vatican, 1989-93; bd. dirs. Cath. Culture Ctr., London, Ont. Decorated comdr. Equestrian Order of Holy Sepulchre of Jerusalem, comdr. with star, knight grand cross; knight Legion of Honour (France); recipient medal Austrian Ministry Edn., Commemorative medal for 125th Anniversary of Confedn. of Can., 1992. Fellow Chem. Inst. Can. (chmn. organic divsn. 1965-66, exec. med. divsn. 1968-79), Royal Soc. Chemistry (London); mem. Am. Chem. Soc., French Chem. Soc., Swiss Chem. Soc., New Swiss Chem. Soc., Can. Soc. Biochem., Molecular and Cellular Biology, French-Can. Assn. for the Advancement of Scis., N.Y. Acad. Scis., Order Chemists Que., Sigma Xi. Home: 1098 Parc Thornhill, Quebec, PQ Canada G1S 3N7 Office: Laval U, Dept Chemistry, Quebec, PQ Canada G1K 7P4*

ENGEL, DAVID LEWIS, lawyer; b. N.Y.C., Mar. 31, 1947; s. Benjamin and Selma (Fruchtman) E.; m. Edith Greetham Smith, June 9, 1973; children: Richard William, Jonathan Martin. AB in Gen. Studies in Econ. cum laude, Harvard U., 1967, JD magna cum laude, 1973; Disting. Naval grad., U.S. Naval Officer Candidate Sch., 1969. Bar: Mass. 1975. Law clk. to Judge Henry J. Friendly U.S. Ct. Appeals (2nd cir.), N.Y.C., 1973-74; assoc. Goodwin, Procter & Hoar, Boston, 1974-76, 79-80; asst. prof. law Stanford U., Calif., 1976-79; ptnr. Berman, Dittmar & Engel, P.C., Boston, 1980-84, Bingham Dana LLP, Boston, 1984—. Contbr. article to Stanford Law Rev., 1979; pres. Harvard Law Rev., 1972-73. Mem. bd. visitors Stanford U. Law Sch., 1982-84; bd. dirs. Project Joy, 1995—. Lt. (j.g.) USNR, 1969-71. Named John Harvard scholar, Harvard Coll. scholar, Nat. Merit scholar, 1964-67; recipient Sears prize, 1968, John Bingham Hurlbut award, 1979. Mem. ABA, Boston Bar Assn. (working group of task force on revision of Mass. corp. statute 1987—), Phi Beta Kappa. Office: Bingham Dana LLP 150 Federal St Boston MA 02110-1713

ENGEL, ELIOT L., congressman; b. N.Y.C., Feb. 18, 1947; s. Philip and Sylvia (Bleend) E. BA, CUNY, 1969, MS, 1973. Counselor, advisor N.Y. Urban Corps, 1968; tchr., dept. chmn. N.Y. Bd. Edn., 1969-76; guidance counselor N.Y. Pub. Schs., 1973-75; mem. N.Y. State Assembly, 1977-89, 101st-106th Congresses from 19th (now 17th) N.Y. dist., 1989—; mem. econ. and ednl. opportunity com., commerce com., mem. internat. rels. com. Columnist Co-op City News, 1972. V.p. Park-East Ind. Dem. Club, N.Y., 1970-71; del. Bronx Com. for Dem. Voters, 1971-76, v.p., 1975-76; del., mem. steering com. Youth Caucus, Dem. Nat. Conv., 172; v.p. Ind. Dems. of Co-op City, 1972-73, pres., 1974-75; committeeman Bronx County Dem. Com., N.Y., 1972—; mem. exec. coun. N.Y. State New Dem. Coalition, 1973-75; founder New Dem. Club Co-op City, 1975, pres., 1975-76; jud. del. N.Y. Supreme Ct. Conv., 1st Jud. Dist., 1975-76, dist. leader, 1976—. Recipient Man of Yr. award FDR Ind. Dem. Club, 1976. Mem. United Fund Tchrs., Ams. for Dem. Action (bd. dirs. N.Y. 1974—), Zionist Orgn. Am., K.P. Jewish. Office: US Ho of Reps 2303 Rayburn Washington DC 20515-0004*

ENGEL, GEOFFREY BYRON, editor; b. La Jolla, Calif., Feb. 6, 1970; s. James Douglas and Kim Marie (Warner) E. BA in Broadcast Journalism, U. So. Calif., 1991. Copy editor Calif. Bus. Mag., L.A., 1991, 4-Wheel & Off-Road Mag., L.A., 1991-92, Hot Rod Mag., L.A., 1992-93; assoc. editor Petersen's Photographic, L.A., 1993-94; mng. editor Outdoor Photographer, L.A., 1994-95; editor Petersen's Photographic, 1995-97; sr. project mgr. Internal and External Comm., Inc., Marina Del Rey, Calif., 1997—; cons. Driver 8 Prodns., Sherman Oaks, Calif., 1993—. Mem. Am. Soc. Media Phorographers, Photo Mktg. Assn. Democrat. Avocations: flying, mountain biking, photography, hiking. Office: IEC 4215 Glencoe Ave Marina Del Rey CA 90292

ENGEL, JAMES HARRY, computer company executive; b. Rahway, N.J., June 11, 1946; s. August Joseph and Laura Ellen (Rigright) E.; m. Angela Marie Jenkins. AAS in Computer Sci., Union County Tech. Inst., 1966. Systems analyst State of N.Mex., Santa Fe, 1977; programmer analyst Los Alamos (N.Mex.) Nat. Lab., 1977-80; database analyst EG&G, Morgantown, W.Va., 1980-82; systems programmer U.S. Army AMCCOM, Dover, N.J., 1982-83, Cray Rsch. Inc., Mendota Heights, Minn., 1983-88; mgr. ECF support Grumman Data Systems, Houston, 1988-95; engring. mgr. E-Systems, Dallas, 1996-98, HIE, Inc., Dallas, 1998—. Active Clean Water Action, Houston, 1990-92, Assn. for Cmty. TV, Houston, 1990-94, Whale Adoption Project, Houston, 1990-94, Tex. State Trooper Assn., Houston, 1990-93. With U.S. Army, 1966-68, Vietnam. Mem. Nat. Mgmt. Assn. Avocation: boating. Home: 900 Henderson Ave Apt 913 Houston TX 77058-3806

ENGEL, JOHN, lawyer; b. N.Y.C., Mar. 8, 1943; s. Ralph and Ann (Unterman) E.; m. Gayle Iselin, May 25, 1980; children: Samuel Albert, Maxwell Robert. BA, Yale U., 1965; JD, Georgetown U., 1971. Bar: D.C., Va. Atty. The Rouse Co., Columbia, Md., 1971-75, Shaw Pittman Potts & Trowbridge, Washington, 1976-84; sr. real estate ptnr. Shaw Pittman Potts & Trowbridge, McLean, Va., 1984—; chair Real Estate Transaction Group; mem. regional adv. bd. Chgo. Title Ins. Co. Chmn. Va. Govt. affairs Internat. Coun. of Shopping, 1987-89; mem. task force City of Alexandria, Va.; bd. dirs. Family Respite Ctr. Mem. ABA, No. Va. Building Industry Assn. (mem. comml. com., head ad hoc task force on fire retard lumber issues). Office: Shaw Pittman Potts & Trowbridge 2300 N St NW Fl 5 Washington DC 20037-1172*

ENGEL, JOHN JACOB, communications executive; b. N.Y.C., June 9, 1936; s. Stewart I. and Beatrice (Schapiro) E.; m. Miriam Jarman, Aug. 17, 1986; children by previous marriage: Susan Lisa, Mark Alan; stepchildren: Alan Brett, Amy Ruth. BA, Adelphi U., Garden City, N.Y., 1957; MS, Boston U., 1959. Program dir. Sta. WLAD FM, DAnbury, Conn., 1954-57; account exec. Sta. WBRY AM, Waterbury, Conn., 1959-62, Sta. WNHC AM, New Haven, 1962-63; account exec. N.Am. Precis Syndicate, Inc., N.Y.C., 1963-68, exec. v.p., prin., 1968—; guest lectr. Publicity Club of N.Y., 1971. Mem. Manalapan-Englishtown Bd. Edn., N.J., 1971-77, pres., 1975-77; treas. Rosegate Condominium Assn., Old Bridge, N.J., 1986-87. Mem. Pub. Rels. Soc. Am., Publicity Club of N.Y. (bd. dirs.), B'nai B'rith (pres. 1967-69). Home: 13 Lindsey Cir Old Bridge NJ 08857-2678

ENGEL, L. PATRICK, state legislator; b. South Sioux City, Nebr., May 18, 1932; m. Dee Smith, 1952; children: Kathie, Kim, Jeff, Julie, Michael. Student, U. Nebr. Ins. agt. State Farm Ins., South Sioux City, Nebr.; commr. Dakota County, Nebr.; senator State of Nebr., Lincoln, 1994—; mem. appropriations com., exec. bd. Nebr. Senate. Mem. South Sioux City Sch. Bd., fin. com. St. Michael's Ch., South Sioux City Comty. Sch. Cardinal Found. Mem. KC (past grand knight, dist. dep.), Mended Hearts (chpt. 41), Sertoma, Toastmasters. Office: Nebr State Senate State Capitol Rm 2011 Lincoln NE 68509*

ENGEL, LINDA JEANNE, mining executive; b. Denver, Aug. 24, 1949; d. Thomas Mintor and Irene Evelyn (Esbenson) Kelley; m. William Stephen Engel, May 6, 1972; children: Kacey, Ryan. *Husband William Stephen (Steve) Engel is broker, manager, of ReMax West and has served as president of Denver Board of Realtors. Steve played professional football for two years with the Cleveland Browns. Daughter Kacey Lynn Engel (now Kacey Koonce) is married to Nathan Koonce, an electrical engineer. Kacey is an aerospace engineer and is currently employed in flight & systems operations at Lockheed Martin and is directly involved in Stardust & Genesis Satellite projects. Son Ryan Stephen Engel is a 1999 graduate in civil engineering of the U.S. Coast Guard Academy in New London, Connecticut. He is an ensign, aboard the USCGC ship "Diligence" in Wilmington, N.C., and would like to pursue a career in aviation.* BA in Polit. Sci., U. Colo., 1975. Statis. researcher Martin Marietta, Waterton, Colo., 1971; asst. dir. Fed. Drug Abuse Program, Denver, 1972-74; corp. sec./treas. Grayhill Exploration Co., Arvada, Colo., 1981-84; controller Western Internat. Gold-Silver, Westminster, Colo., 1985-86; investor rels. dir. and corp. sec. Canyon Resources Corp., Golden, Colo., 1986-94. Republican.

ENGEL, MICHAEL SCOTT, entomologist, paleontologist; b. St. Louis, Sept. 24, 1971; s. Alger Gayle and Donna Gail (Pratt) E. BA in Chemistry, U. Kans., 1993, BS in Cell Biology, 1993; PhD, Cornell U., 1998. Rsch. asst. 1, rsch. asst. 2 U. Kans., Lawrence, 1991-93, instr. NSF/Howard Hughes Young Scholars Program, 1993; tchg. asst. Cornell U., Ithaca, N.Y., 1993-94, 95; rsch. asst. Cornell U., Ithaca, 1994, NSF grad. fellow, 1995-98; rsch. scientist in entomology Am. Mus. Natural History, N.Y.C., 1998—. Editor: Proceedings of the Eickwort Symposium, 1996; contbr. articles to profl. jours. Recipient Ernst Mayr award Harvard U., 1996; undergrad. fellow Pew Found., 1992-93, fellow NSF, 1995-98, Smithsonian Tropical Rsch. Inst., Balboa, Panama, 1996. Mem. Am. Arachnological Soc., Am. Entomological Soc., Internat. Bee Rsch. Assn., Internat. Soc. Hymenopterists, Cambridge Entomological Club, Phi Beta Kappa. Avocations: playing violin, mathematics, traveling.

ENGEL, PAUL BERNARD, lawyer; b. Balt., Feb. 6, 1926; s. Robert and Ida (L) E.; m. Lorraine Goodman, Sept. 7, 1947; children—Seena Engel Kling, Cindy Engel Dubansky, Lon Craig. AA, U. Balt., 1947, JD, 1950. Bar: Md.1950, DC 1950. Ptnr. Engel and Engel P.A., Balt., 1950—. Bd. govs. Boca Highland Ctr. Assn., gov., 1992—, treas., pres.; chmn. legal com. Aberdeen Arms Condos, v.p. With AUS, 1944-45. Mem. ABA, Md. Plaintiffs Bar Assn., Balt. City Bar Assn., Bonnie View C. of C. (bd. dirs. 1964-67, 69-72). Club: Bonnie View Country (bd. dirs.). Lodge: Masons. Home: 3409 Deep Willow Ave Baltimore MD 21208-3116 Office: 11 E Lexington St Ste 200 Baltimore MD 21202-1718

ENGEL, PHILIP L., insurance company executive. BA, U. Chgo., 1961, MBA, 1980. With CNA, Chgo., 1961, asst. v.p. corp. planning and control divsn., 1972-76, v.p., 1976-78, v.p. mktg., 1978-90, v.p. sys. and svcs., 1990, exec. v.p. claims, mktg., svcs., sys., underwriting, 1990-92; pres. CNA Ins. Cos., Chgo., 1992—; bd. dirs. CNA Fin. Corp., Agy. Mgmt. Svcs., Inc. Vice chmn. bd. trustees Pacific Garden Mission, Chgo.; pres., bd. dirs. Shakespeare Repertory Theater, Chgo. Fellow Soc. Actuaries, Casualty Actuarial Soc.; mem. Am. Acad. Actuaries, Quality Ins. Congress (chmn. bd. dirs.). Office: CNA CNA Plz Chicago IL 60685-0001*

ENGEL, RALPH, manufacturers association executive; b. Balt., Mar. 19, 1934; s. William and Anna G. Engel; m. Patricia R. Kahn, June 21, 1959; children—William, Steven. P.D. in Pharmacy, U. Md., 1956, J.D., 1966. Bar: N.Y. bar 1966. Gen. practice pharmacy Balt., 1956-66; counsel, dir. regulatory affairs Purdue Frederick Co., Yonkers, N.Y., 1966-69; dir. Nat. Health Care Council, Washington, 1970-74; pres. Chem. Specialties Mfrs. Assn., Washington, 1974—, Consumer Spltys. Ins. Co. (RRG), Vt.; adj. prof. adminstrn. U. Md.; mem. pesticide policy advisory com. EPA; vice chmn. ISAC 7 com. Dept. Commerce; mem. com. environ. carcinogens Nat. Cancer Inst. Contbr. articles in field to mgmt. and tech. jours. Recipient Merck award Chemistry, 1956; L.S. Williams award Pharmacology, 1956. Fellow Am. Soc. Pharmacy Law; mem. Am. Soc. Assn. Execs. Clubs: Capitol Hill, Univ. Office: 1913 I St NW Washington DC 20006-2106

ENGEL, RALPH MANUEL, lawyer; b. N.Y.C., May 13, 1944; s. Werner Herman and Ruth Fredericke (Friedlander) E.; m. Diane Linda Weinberg, Aug. 10, 1968; children—Eric M., Daniel C., Julie R. BA in Econs. with highest honors, NYU, 1965, JD, 1968. Bar: N.Y. 1968, U.S. Supreme Ct. 1972. Assoc. Gilbert, Segall and Young, N.Y.C., 1968-71, Trubin Sillcocks Edelman & Knapp, N.Y.C., 1971-76; assoc., then ptnr. Summit Rovins & Feldesman and predecessor firms, N.Y.C., 1976-91; ptnr. Rosen & Reade, LLP, N.Y.C., 1991—; lectr. Sch. Law, Fordham U., 1990-91. Contbr. articles to legal and other publs.; editor-in-chief The Commentator, NYU, 1968. Mem. Planning Com., Larchmont, N.Y., 1992—. Fellow Am. Coll. Trust and Estate Counsel; mem. N.Y. State Bar Assn. (trust and estate law sect. com. on practice and ethics 1991—, elder law sect., com. on guardianships and fiduciaries 1991-97, com. on estates and tax planning 1997—), Assn. Bar City of N.Y. (com. on estate and gift taxation 1992-95, chmn. subcom. on splitting and combining trusts 1994-95, chmn., subcom. on spousal rights 1994-95, com. on trusts, estates and surrogate's cts. 1997—), Estate Planning Coun. Westchester County (bd. dirs. 1985-91). Home and Office: 6 Rockwood Dr Larchmont NY 10538-2537 Office: 757 3rd Ave New York NY 10017-2013

ENGEL, RICHARD L., career officer; b. L.A., July 2, 1946; s. Richard Leroy and Margret Ellen (Wilson) E.; m. Connie Jean Ricks, Sept. 8, 1973; children: Lindsey, Jennifer, Shelly. BS in Mech. Engring., Tex. A&M U., 1968; MS in Indsl. and Sys. Mgmt. Engring., Ariz. State U., Tucson, 1975; student, Air Force Test Pilot Sch., 1976-77, Armed Forces Staff Coll., 1981; M in Nat. Security Strategic Studies, Naval War Coll., 1988. Commd. 2d lt. USAF, 1968, advanced through grades to maj. gen., 1996; pilot spl. ops. USAF, South Vietnam, 1970-71; instr. pilot USAF, Williams AFB, Ariz., 1971-74; air staff officer Hdqs. Air Tng. Command, Randolph AFB, Tex., 1974-76; advanced simulator rsch. flight test officer Air Force Human Resources Lab., Williams AFB, 1978-81; chief of acads. Air Force Test Pilot Sch., Edwards AFB, Calif., 1981-83; dep. dir. F-16 LANTIRN Test Program, Edwards AFB, 1983-85; comdr. F-16 and LANTIRN Combined Test Forces, Edwards AFB, 1985-87; divsn. chief weapons sys. divsn. Office of Legis. Liaison for Sec. of Air Force, Washington, 1988-89; comdr. 3246th Test Wing, Air Force Devel. Test Ctr., Eglin AFB, Fla., 1989-92, 412th Test Wing, Edwards AFB, 1992-93, Air Force Flight Test Ctr., Edwards AFB, 1993-98; commandant Indsl. Coll. of the Armed Forces, Ft. McNair, 1998—. Decorated Legion of Merit, D.F.C. with two oak leaf clusters, Air medal with nine oak leaf clusters, Air Force Commendation medal. Mem. AIAA, Soc. Exptl. Test Pilots. Home: 4780 Command Ln Andrews Air Force Base MD 20762-5568 Office: Indsl Coll of the Armed Forces 408 4th Ave Fort McNair DC 20319-5062*

ENGEL, RICHARD LEE, lawyer, educator; b. Syracuse, N.Y., Sept. 19, 1936; s. S. Sanford and Eleanor M. (Gallop) E.; m. Karen K. Engel, Dec. 26, 1965; children: Todd Sanford, Gregg Matthew. BA, Yale U., 1958, JD, 1981. Bar: N.Y. 1961. Law asst. justices Appellate Divsn. N.Y. 4th Jud. Dist., 1961-63; law clk. judge N.Y. Supreme Ct., 1963-65; sr. ptnr. Nottingham, Engel, Gordon & Kerr LLP, Syracuse, 1970—; adj. prof. law Syracuse U. Coll. of Law; arbitrator, mediator law and medicine, equine law Coll. Law trial practice Am. Arbitration Assn., Resolute Sys., Inc.; lectr. in field. Contbr. articles to profl. jours. Pres. Temple Soc. Concord, 1985-87; bd. dirs. Am. Field Svcs. Intercultural Programs, Inc., 1974-81. Mem. ABA, Am. Coll. Legal Medicine, N.Y. State Bar Assn., Onondaga Bar Assn. (mem. trial lawyers com. 1978-80, chmn. med. legal liaison com. 1976-77, chmn. spl. isn. com. 1988, Bench and Bar com. 1991, found. bd. 1992-98, grievance com. 1998), N.Y. State Trials Attys. Assn., Upstate Trial Attys. Assn. (pres. 1973-74, chmn. bd. 1974-77), Thoroughbred Owners and Breeders Assn. (owners coun.), Def. Rsch. Inst., Inc., Cavalry Country, Saratoga Reading Rooms, Inc., Yale (pres. Ctrl. N.Y.). Home: Brockway Ln Fayetteville NY 13066 Office: One Lincoln Ctr 8th Flr Syracuse NY 13202

ENGEL, WALBURGA See VON RAFFLER-ENGEL, WALBURGA

ENGEL, WILLIAM KING, neurologist, educator; b. St. Louis, Nov. 19, 1930; s. William Ernst and Opal (King) E.; m. Valerie Askanas; children: W. Keith, Peter J., Bradford C., Eve M. Kerr. B.A., Johns Hopkins U., 1951; M.D., C.M., McGill U., 1955; M.D. (hon.), L'univ. d'Aix Marseille II, 1987. Diplomate: Am. Bd. Neurology and Psychiatry, Pan. Am. Med. Assn. (hon. life mem.). Intern U. Mich. Hosp., 1955-56; clin. assoc. Nat. Inst. Neurol. Diseases and Blindness, 1956-59; clin. clk. Nat. Hosp., London, 1959-60; with Nat. Inst. Neurol. Diseases and Stroke, 1960-81, chief med. neurology, 1963-78, chief neuromuscular diseases, 1978-81; clin. prof. neurology George Washington U., 1969-81; prof. neurology and pathology, chief div. neuromuscular diseases, dept. neurology U. So. Calif. Sch. Medicine, Los Angeles, 1981—; mem. med. bd. NIH, 1968-69;; founding dir. U. So. Calif. Neuromuscular Center, Hosp. of Good Samaritan, 1981—; mem. med. adv. bd. St. Jude's Children's Rsch. Hosp., Memphis, 1970-76, Myasthenia Gravis Found., 1970—, L.A. chpt. Muscular Dystropy Assn., 1981—, Amyotrophic Lateral Sclerosis Nat. Found., 1971-85, Amyotrophic Lateral Sclerosis Soc. Am., 1980-85, mem. sci. adv. bd., 1982-85; vis. prof., invited lectr., advisor internat. congresses in Europe, S.Am., Can., Australia, Far East; cons. Nat. Naval Med. Ctr. Former Mem. editorial bd.: Archives of Neurology; contbr. numerous papers to profl. lit., poems to mags. Past pres. Citizens Assn., Bethesda, Md., Longhouse chief YMCA Indian Guides, 1965-66; past chmn. troop com. Boy Scouts Am.; mem. edn. adv. bd. Phronesis, Spain; nat. corp. mem. Muscular Dystrophy Assn., 1985-88, nat. v.p. 1988—, med. adv. bd. Los Angeles chpt., 1981—, bd. dirs. 1985—. Recipient Meritorious Service medal USPHS, 1971, Gaetano Conte Gold medal for clin. rsch., 1999, various awards from Italian me . socs. Fellow Am. Acad. Neurology (S. Weir Mitchell award 1962; pres. VI Internat. Congress Neuromuscular Diseases 1986); mem. AMA, Histochem. Soc., Am. Soc. Cell Biology, Am. Assn. Neuropathologists, Soc. for Neurosci., World Commn. Neuromuscular Disease (exec. com.), Am. Neurol. Assn., L.A. County Med. Assn., Société Belge d'Electromyographie (assoc.), Asociación de Distrofia Muscular de la Republica Argentina (hon. pres.), Société Française de Neurologie (hon.). Office: U So Calif Neuromuscular Ctr Good Samaritan Hosp 637 Lucas Ave Los Angeles CA 90017-1912

ENGELAGE, JAMES ROLAND, business executive, consultant; b. Springfield, Mo., Dec. 5, 1945; s. Roland C. and Dorothy (Deeds) E.; m. Marcia Cooley, July 5, 1968. BS, SW Mo. State U., 1965; MS, Troy U., 1968; MA, Cen. Mich. U., 1978; PhD, St. Louis U., 1977. Dept. chmn. Montgomery (Ala.) Pub. Schs., 1968-69; asst. prin. Francis Howell Sch. Dist., St. Charles, 1969-74; asst. supt. Francis Howell Sch. Dist., 1974-75; adj. faculty Command & Gen. Staff Coll., Ft. Leavenworth, Kans., 1976-93; dean Randolph Macon Acad., Front Royal, Va., 1993-94; CEO JAMARC Mgmt. Corp., Winchester, Va., 1994—; evening dir. Temple Schs., Silver Spring, Md., 1982-84; adj. prof. Park Coll., Ft. Myer, Va., 1980-82. Editor: Operation Desert Shield, 1992; contbr. articles to publs. Served to col. U.S. Army, 1975-93. Recipient legion of merit award Dept. Army, Washington, 1993. Mem. Res. Officers Assn. (pres. Chgo. chpt. 1992, Louisville chpt. 1993), Civil Air Patrol (capt. 1973-74), Lions Club (charter 1970-71), Civitans. Republican. Methodist. Avocations: public speaking, computers, aviation. Home: 411 Windsor Ln Winchester VA 22602-2333 Office: JAMARC Mgmt Corp 2021 S Pleasant Valley Rd Winchester VA 22601-7001

ENGEL-ARIELI, SUSAN LEE, physician; b. Chgo., Oct. 7, 1954; d. Thaddeus S. Dziengiel and Marion L. (Carpenter) Kasper; m. Udi Arieli. BA, Northwestern U., 1975; MD, Chgo. Med. Sch., 1982. Diplomate Am. Bd. Gen. Practice. Med. technician G.D. Searle, Skokie, Ill., 1972, 73, assoc. dir., 1983-84; dir. U.S. Regional Clin. Support G.D. Searle, 1984-86; rsch. editorial asst. U. Chgo., 1974; rsch. assoc. Loyola U., Maywood, Ill., 1977-78; intern Rush Presbyn. St. Lukes Hosp., Chgo., 1982-83; resident U. Chgo., 1983; mgr. hosp. products div. Abbott Labs., Abbott Park, Ill., 1986-87; bd. govs., dep. gov. Am. Biog. Inst. Rsch. Assn., 1988; vis. prof. Rush Presbyn.-St. Luke's Hosp., Chgo., 1985, faculty assoc., 1985; assoc. investigator, asst. prof. medicine King Drew Med. Ctr., UCLA, 1985-90; practical cardiology panel experts, 1988; Med. World News Rev. panel, 1988; bd. dirs. Am. Soc. Handicapped Physicians, acting v.p.; bd. dirs. fundraising, chmn. Vestibular Disorders Assn. Author: How Your Body Works, 1994, C-D Rom version, 1995; contbr. articles to profl. and scholarly jours. Bd. govs. Art Inst. Chgo., 1985—, mem. aux. bd., 1988—, mem. multiple benefit coms., 1984—, vice chmn. Capital Campaign, 1984-85; mem. pres. com. Landmark Preservation Coun., Chgo., 1984-90, chmn. multiple coms. polit. candidates, 1986; bd. dirs. Marshall unit Chgo. Boys Clubs, 1984—; mem. benefit com. Hubbard St. Dance Co. 10th Gala, 1988, Victory Garden's Theatre Ann. Benefit, 1988. Recipient Gold award, 1995, Nat. Health Info. award, 1995; Internat. Coll. Surgeons fellow, 1982. Mem. AMA, ACP, Am. Fedn. for Clin. Rsch., Southern Med. Assn., Ill. State Med. Soc., Chgo. Med. Soc., Am. Acad. Med. Dirs., Nat. Acad. Arts and Scis., Am. Soc. Handicapped Physicians (bd. dirs., v.p.), Vestibular Disorders Assn. (bd. dirs., pub. rels. com., co-chmn. fundraising). Avocations: German language, organ playing, composing music, writing.

ENGELBART, DOUG, engineering executive; b. Portland, Oreg., Jan. 30, 1925. BSEE, Oreg. State U., 1948, D (hon.), 1994; degree in engring., U. Calif., Berkeley, 1952; PhD in Elec. Engring., U. Calif., 1955. Electronic/radar tech. USN, 1944-46; elec. engr. NACA Ames Lab., Mountain View, Calif., 1948-51; asst. prof. elec. engring. U. Calif., Berkeley, 1955-56; rschr. Stanford (Calif.) Rsch. Inst. (now SRI Internat.), 1957-59, dir. augmentation rsch. ctr., 1959-77; sr. scientist Tymshare, Inc., Cupertino, Calif., 1977-84, McDonnell Douglas ISC, San Jose, Calif., 1984-89; dir. Bootstrap Project Stanford U., 1989-90; dir. Bootstrap Project, Palo Alto, Calif., 1990-91, Bootstrap Inst., Fremont, Calif., 1991—. Contbr. numerous articles to profl. jours. Recipient Lifetime Achievement award for Tech. Excellence, PC Mag., 1987, Disting. Alumni of Yr. award Oreg. STate U., 1987, Disting. Svc. and Outstanding Contbns. in Field citation Sigma Phi Epsilon, St. Louis, 1989, Lifetime Achievement award for Vision, Inspiration and Contbn., Electronic Networking Assn., San Francisco, 1990, Software Sys. award Assn. Computing Machinery, 1990, Am. Ingenuity award Nat. Assn. Mfrs.' Congress of Am. Industry, Washington, 1991, Disting. Alumnus award U. Calif., Berkeley, 1991, Lifetime Achievement award Dominican Coll. of San Rafael, Calif., 1991, Lifetime Achievement award Price Waterhouse, Washington, 1994, cert. of appreciation Smart Valley, Inc., 1994, Editors' Choice award MacUser Awards Ceremony, 1995, SoftQuad Web award World Wide Web Conf., Boston, 1995, cert. of merit The Franklin Inst. Com. on Sci. and the Arts, 1996, Spl. award Am. Soc. for Info. Sci., 1996, Jerome H. Lemelson-MIT prize for excellence in invention and innovation, 1997; named Pioneer of the Electronic Frontier, Electronic Frontier Found., Washington, 1992; Engelbart award established in his honor Internat. Conf. on Hypertext and Hypermedia, 1994. Fellow Nat. Acad. Arts and Scis.; mem. IEEE (treas., vice chmn., chmn. San Francisco chpt. profl. group on electronic computers 1957-59, Computer Pioneer award 1993), NAS (com. on augmentation of human intellect 1989, panel on future role of computers in rsch. librs. 1968-70), Nat. Acad. Engring., Computer Profls. for Social Responsibility (adv. bd.), The Tech. Ctr. of Silicon Valley (adv. coun.), Phi Kappa Phi, Tau Beta Pi, Sigma Tau, Eta Kappa Nu, Blue Key, Sigma Xi. Achievements include visionary and pioneering work in organizational augmentation, including strategies for continuous improvement, human-tool co-evolution and interactive collaborative hypermedia computing to support the knowledge-intensive work of groups and individuals; 7 patents relating to bi-stable gaseous plasma digital devices, 12 patents relating to all-magnetic digital devices, 1 patent for invention of the Mouse. Home: 89 Catalpa Dr Atherton CA 94027-2167 Office: Bootstrap Inst 6505 Kaiser Dr Fremont CA 94555-3614

ENGELBRECHT, RUDOLF, electrical engineering educator; b. Atlanta, Apr. 18, 1928; s. Walter and Dorothea (Succo) E.; m. Christel M. Kluth, Sept. 10, 1950; children—Richard, Rolf, Erika. B.S., Ga. Inst. Tech., 1951, M.S. in Elec. Engring., 1953; Ph.D. in Elec. Engring., Oreg. State U., 1979.

Mem. tech. staff Bell Labs., Whippany, N.J., 1953-60, supr., Murray Hill, N.J., 1961-63, dept. head, 1964-69; dir. RCA Tech. Ctr., Somerville, N.J., 1970-72; group leader RCA Labs., Zurich, Switzerland, 1972-77; assoc. prof. Oreg. State U., Corvallis, 1977-93. Co-author: Microwave Devices, 1969; contbr. articles to profl. jours.; patentee in field. Named to Oreg. State U. Engring. Hall of Fame, 1998. Fellow IEEE (life, Centennial award 1984); mem. Sigma Xi. Home: 1920 NW Douglas Pl Corvallis OR 97330-1005 Office: Oreg State U Dept Elec Computer Eng Corvallis OR 97331

ENGELER, WILLIAM ERNEST, retired physicist; b. Bklyn., Nov. 13, 1928; s. William Ernest and Marguerite E.; m. Marilyn Ann McKee, Nov. 26, 1955; children: William R., Amy K., Elizabeth A., Mary P. BS, Poly. Inst. Bklyn., 1951; MS, Syracuse U., 1958, PhD, 1961. Physicist GE, Schenectady, N.Y., 1951-52, Syracuse, N.Y., 1952-55; physicist GE Corp. R&D Ctr., Schenectady, 1961-95; ret., 1995. Author, co-author 111 patents, 1953-92; contbr. articles to profl. jours., chpts. to books. With U.S. Army, 1955-56. Coolidge fellow GE, 1979. Fellow IEEE; mem. Am. Phys. Soc., Edison Club (Rexford, N.Y.). Avocations: woodworking, golf.

ENGELHARD, BARBARA JO, education educator; b. Mexico, Md., Feb. 24, 1956; d. Edgar Bricie and Mary Evelyn (Dougherty) Lewis; m. Randall Charles Engelhard, Jan. 20, 1979; children: Jared Michael, Amanda Dawn, Stacy Lynn. BS in Elem. Edn., N.E. Mo. State U., Kirksville, 1977, MA in Elem. Edn., 1980, cert. remedial reading, 1983. Cert. tech. elem. edn., remedial reading. Tchr. 6th grade Walt Disney Elem., Marceline, Mo., 1977-80, tchr. 2nd grade, 1980-83, tchr. Title I reading, 1983-97; presenter, cons. Select Tchrs. as Regional Resources Dept. Elem. and Secondary Edn., Truman State U., Kirksville, Mo., 1996—; coord. parent edn. program Walt Disney Elem., Marceline, 1995, 96; presenter various confs. and meetings. Bd. dirs., pres. Kinderland Presch., Marceline, 1988-92; troop asst. leader Girl Scouts Am., Marceline, 1977-78, troop vol., 1990-97; troop vol. Boy Scouts Am., Marceline, 1994-97; vol. Vacation Bible Sch., Bethany Bapt. Ch., Marceline, 1995, 96. Mem. ASCD, Internat. Reading Assn., Cmty. Tchrs. Assn. (treas., pres. 1977-97), Mo. State Tchrs. Assn., Alpha Sigma Alpha (corr. sec.). Home: RR 1 Box 239B Marceline MO 64658-9629 Office: Marceline R-V Sch Dist 420 E California Ave Marceline MO 64658-1594

ENGELHARDT, ALBERT GEORGE, physicist; b. Toronto, Ont., Can., Mar. 17, 1935; came to U.S., 1957, naturalized, 1965; s. Samuel and Rose (Menkes) E.; m. Elzbieta Szajkowska, June 14, 1960; children—Frederick, Leonard, Michael. B.A.Sc., U. Toronto, 1958; M.S., U. Ill., 1959, Ph.D. (grad. fellow), 1961. Research asst. elec. engring. U. Ill., Urbana, 1958-61; staff research and devel. center engr. Westinghouse Electric Co., Pitts., 1961-70; mgr. Westinghouse Electric Co., 1966-69, fellow scientist, 1969-70; sr. research scientist, group leader Hydro-Que. Research Inst., Varennes, Can., 1970-74; mem. staff Los Alamos Sci. Lab., 1974-86; adj. prof. elec. engring. Tex. Tech. U., Lubbock, 1976—; pres., chief exec. officer, founder Enfitek, Inc., Los Alamos, N.Mex., 1982—; vis. prof. U. Que., 1970-77. Contbr. articles to profl. jours. Group leader Boy Scouts Can., 1972-74. Mem. IEEE Nuclear and Plasma Scis. Soc., Am. Phys. Soc. Home and Office: 549 Bryce Ave Los Alamos NM 87544-3607 *Since 1959 my basic research interest has been plasma physics and concomitantly nuclear fusion. The importance of the latter is that it shows great promise for providing us with renewable energy resources with acceptably small environmental and ecological perturbation.*

ENGELHARDT, IRL F., coal company executive; b. Oct. 19, 1946; m. Suzanne C.; children: Joel, Erin, Evan. BS in Acctg., U. Ill., 1968; MBA, So. Ill. U., 1971. From mem. staff to pres., CEO Peabody Group, St. Louis, 1979-90, pres., CEO, 1990—; cons. in field; bd. dirs. Mercantile Bank of St. Louis, Citizens Power, St. Louis, U. Mo., St. Louis. Recipient Erskine Ramsay medal Am. Inst. Mining, Metaallurgical and Petroleum Engrs., 1998. Mem. Nat. Mining Assn. (bd. dirs., chmn. 1995-96), Nat. Coal Assn. (chmn. 1995-96), Internat. Energy Agy. (coal industry adv. bd., chmn., special com. mem.), Nat. Assn. Mfrs. (bd. dirs., chmn. environ. com.), St. Louis Arts and Edn. Council, St. Louis Area Council (exec. bd.), Boy Scouts of Am. E-mail: iengelha@peabodygroup.com. Fax: 314-342-7797. Office: Peabody Group 701 Market St Ste 700 Saint Louis MO 63101-1850

ENGELHARDT, JOHN HUGO, lawyer, banker; b. Houston, Feb. 3, 1946; s. Hugo Tristram and Beulah Lillie (Karbach) E.; m. Jasmin Inge Nestler, Nov. 12, 1976; children: Angelique D, Sabrina N. BA, U. Tex., 1968; JD, St. Mary's U., San Antonio, 1973. Bar: Tex. 1973. Tchr. history Pearsall H.S., Tex., 1968-69; pvt. practice, New Braunfels, Tex., 1973-75; examining atty. Comml. Title Co., San Antonio, 1975-78, San Antonio Title Co., 1978-82; pvt. practice, New Braunfels, 1982—; adv. dir. M Bank Brenham, Tex., 1983-89. Fellow Coll. State Bar Tex.; mem. ABA, Pi Gamma Mu. Republican. Roman Catholic.

ENGELHARDT, LEROY A., retired paper company executive; b. Saginaw, Mich., Mar. 15, 1924; s. Herman J. and Alma (Engelhard) E.; m. Arlene L. Papineau, July 12, 1947; children—Richard C., Kay C., Douglas R. B.B.A., U. Mich., 1949, M.B.A., 1950. Plant, div. or subsidiary controller Chrysler Corp., 1950-60; mgmt. controls cons. Diehl K.G., Nuremberg, Germany, 1960-63; sec. Genesee Brewing Co., Rochester, N.Y., 1963-67; v.p. fin. Consol. Papers, Inc., Wisconsin Rapids, Wis., 1967-89; also ret. dir. Consol. Papers, Inc. Served with AUS, 1943-46. Home: 444 Two Mile Ave Wisconsin Rapids WI 54494-6559

ENGELHARDT, REGINA, cosmetologist, artist, art restorer; b. Kiwerce, Poland, Oct. 1, 1928; came to U.S., 1949; d. Marian and Maria (Wardach) Engelhardt; m. Gerard Edward Twardon, May 30, 1953 (div. 1961); children: Miriam Teresa Twardon Bielski, Elizabeth Maria Twardon, Renee Marie Twardon Gilchrist. Grad., Laski Inst. Tech., 1951; lic. cosmetologist, Hamtramck Beauty Sch., 1960; art student, Mercy Ctr., 1980-84. Sec. Am. Savs., Detroit, 1950-55; cosmetologist Magic Touch Salon, Oak Park, Mich., 1960—; owner Regina's Fine Arts, Detroit, 1986—, Art Restorations, 1986—; art tchr. Farmington Activity Ctr., Farmington Hills, Mich., 1993—; spkr. in field. Artist lithographs; represented in permanent collection at Althorp Mus., Eng., 1998. Mem. Dem. Nat. Com., 1996—; mem. nat. com. to preserve social security and medicare, 1993—. Recipient Gold and Silver medals Internat. Art Challenge, 1987-88, 90, Kubinski award Friends of Polish Arts, 1989, First and Fourth awards Mich. State Exhibit, 1988. Mem. Sculptores Guild of Mich., Four Octave Club, Farmington Artists Club (6 Popular Vote awards 1985, 86, 97, merit award local art exhibit 1997, two merit awards 1998), Sierra Club, Internat. Platform Assn., Nature Conservancy. Roman Catholic. Avocations: music, needlework, dance, reading. Home: 17345 Wildemere St Detroit MI 48221-2722

ENGELHARDT, SARA LAWRENCE, organization executive; b. Phila., Aug. 23, 1943; d. Ruddick Carpenter and Barbara (Dole) Lawrence; m. Dean Lee Engelhardt, June 20, 1970; children: Barbara Elizabeth, Margaret Ann. BA, Wellesley Coll., 1965; MA, Tchrs. Coll., Columbia U., 1970. Staff asst. Carnegie Corp., N.Y.C., 1966-70; asst. sec. Carnegie Corp., 1972-74, assoc. sec., 1974-75, sec., 1975-87; exec. v.p. Found. Ctr., N.Y.C., 1987-91, pres., 1991—. Free-lance editor and writer, Storrs, Conn., 1970-72. Bd. dirs. Nat. Charities Info. Bur., 1984—, chairperson, 1987-91; trustee Found. Ctr., 1984-87; bd. dirs. Trust for Philanthropy AAFRC, 1989-98; trustee Consortium for Advancement of Pvt. Higher Edn., 1989-93, chairperson, 1992-93; mem. bd. overseers Ctr. Rsch. on Women, Wellesley Coll., 1979-88; nat. bd. dirs. Girls Inc., 1992-98, Ind. Sector, 1992-98, Coun. Ind. Colls., 1993-94; bd. dirs. NOW Legal Def. and Edn. Fund, 1994—, Amigos de las Americas, 1995—. Home: 173 Riverside Dr New York NY 10024-1615 Office: Foundation Ctr 79 5th Ave Fl 8 New York NY 10003-3076

ENGELHARDT, THOMAS ALEXANDER, editorial cartoonist; b. St. Louis, Dec. 29, 1930; s. Alexander Frederick and Gertrude Dolores (Derby) E.; m. Katherine Agnes McCue, June 25, 1960; children—Marybeth, Carol Marie, Christine Leigh, Mark Thomas. Student, Denver U., 1950-51, Ruskin Sch. Fine Arts, Oxford (Eng.) U., 1954-56, Sch. Visual Arts, N.Y.C., 1957. Free-lance cartoonist, comml. artist, N.Y.C., 1957-60, Cleve., 1961-62, asst. editorial cartoonist, Newspaper Enterprise Assn., Cleve., 1960-61; editorial cartoonist St. Louis Post-Dispatch, 1962-97; freelance cartoonist, 1998—; one-man exhbns. of cartoons at Fontbonne Coll. Art Gallery, St. Louis, 1972, Old Courthouse (Jefferson Nat. Meml.), St. Louis, 1981, Mark Twain Bank, Frontenac, Mo., 1989. Served with USAF, 1951-53. Recipient Ethical Humanist of Yr. award St. Louis Ethical Soc., 1986. Roman Catholic. Office: 7830 Lafon Pl Saint Louis MO 63130-3805

ENGELKES, DONALD JOHN, insurance company executive; b. Monroe Ctr., Ill., Jan. 23, 1938; s. William H. and Rita M. (Sauter) E.; m. Lucille A. Gibson, Aug. 19, 1939; children: James, Richard, Jeffrey. BS, No. Ill. U., 1961. Agt. Country Cos., Rochelle, Ill., 1962-66; agy. mgr. Country Cos., Lincoln, Ill., 1966-81; exec. asst. Country Cos., Bloomington, Ill., 1981-82, dir. agy. adminstrn., 1982-83; v.p. Country Life Ins. Co., Bloomington, 1983—, Country Capitol Mgmt. Co., 1988—; bd. dirs., chmn. Bromenn Healthcare. Bd. dirs., pres. Heartland C.C. Found.; dist. chmn. Boy Scouts Am., Lincoln, 1973-75; mem. Cmty. Resource Devel. Com., Lincoln; trustee 2d Presbyn. Ch.; pres. Ill. Life Ins. Coun. Mem. Nat. Assn. Life Underwriters, Ill. Life Underwriters Assn. (v.p. 1980-81, dir. Polit. Action Com. 1977, 78, 79), Am. Soc. CLU's, Gen. Agts. and Mgrs. Conf., Ill. Athletic Assn. Recreation Assn. (bd. dirs. 1983-90). Republican. Lodge: Elks. Home: 28 Ravenwood Cir Bloomington IL 61704-8424 Office: Country Life Ins Co 1701 N Towanda Ave Bloomington IL 61701-2090

ENGELL, JAMES THEODORE, English educator; b. Danville, Pa., Sept. 6, 1951; s. Frederick Jacob and Ruth Louise Engell; m. Ainslie Sheridan Brennan, June 2, 1984; children: Marleny Brennan, Alexander E. BA, Harvard Coll., 1973; PhD, Harvard U., 1978. Asst. prof. Harvard U., Cambridge, Mass., 1978-80, assoc. prof., 1980-83, prof. English and comparative lit., 1983—, chair degree program in history and lit., 1988-93, dir. undergrad. studies in English, 1995-97. Author: The Creative Imagination, 1981 (Thomas Wilson prize 1982), Forming the Critical Mind, 1989, The Committed Word: Literature and Public Values, 1999; editor: Coleridge: The Early Family Letters, 1994; co-editor: Coleridge, Biographia Literaria, 1983; editor, contbr.: Johnson and His Age, 1984, Teaching Literature: What Is Needed Now, 1988; editl. advisor Jour. History of Ideas, 1986—, Coll. Lit., 1990—, 1650-1850 Ideas, Aesthetics, and Inquiries in the Early Modern Era, Boston Book Review, Literature and Religion. Corporator Emerson Hosp. and Health System, Concord, Mass., 1989-94. Recipient Levenson Tchg. prize, 1995, Roslyn Abramson Tchg. award, 1997; Ford Found. grant, 1978. Mem. MLA, Am. Soc. 18th Century Studies, Johnsonians (chair 1990-91), Assn. Lit. Scholars and Critics, Friends of Coleridge. Avocations: travel, sports, music. Office: Harvard U Widener Libr 415 Cambridge MA 02138

ENGELMAN, JOHN HERRICK, chemist; b. White Cloud, Mich., Mar. 26, 1941; s. John Herrick Engleman and Margaret Harris; m. Alice Marie London, May 21, 1994. AAS, Ferris State U., 1964. Technician Dow Corning, Midland, Mich., 1964-76; inspector Midland Nuclear Power Plant, 1976-82; tech. specialist Quantum Composites, Inc., Midland, 1982-84, quality control mgr., 1984-89; sr. rsch. technologist Essex Specialty Products, Midland, 1989-94, Dow Brands, Midland, 1994-98; technician specialist S. C. Johnson, Racine, Wis., 1998—. Mem. allocations com. United Way, Midland, 1996-97. With U.S. Army, 1959-62. Mem. Am. Chem. Soc. (regional coord. 1997-98, com. on technician activities 1989-99), Mid Mich. Tech. Group (treas. 1995-96, dir. 1994-95), Dow Cen. Rsch. Tech. Group (chair 1995-96). Methodist. Office: S C Johnson 1525 Howe St Racine WI 53403

ENGELMAN, KARL, physician; b. N.Y.C., June 23, 1933; s. Samuel and Lillian (Wachs) E.; m. Elaine Kaufman, June 10, 1956; children—Harold Kent, Ross Mitchell, Jeffrey Steven. B.S., Men's Coll. Arts and Scis., Rutgers U., 1955; M.D., Harvard U., 1959; M.A. (hon.), U. Pa., 1971. Diplomate: Am. Bd. Internal Medicine. Intern, asst. resident, resident in medicine Mass. Gen. Hosp., Boston, 1959-64; clin. asso., sr. investigator, attending physician Nat. Heart Inst., NIH, Bethesda, Md., 1961-70; assoc. prof. medicine and pharmacology Sch. Medicine U. Pa., Phila., 1971-95; chief hypertension sect., dir. clin. research center Sch. Medicine U. Pa.; cons. physician Phila. VA Hosp., 1971-95, Children's Hosp., Phila., 1971-95; clin. prof. medicine Med. U. of S.C., 1996—; cons. Beaufort-Jasper Comprehensive Health Svcs., 1996—. Served with USPHS, 1961-63. Mem. ACP, Am. Coll. Clin. Pharmacology, Internat. Soc. of Hypertention (sci. coun. on hypertension), U.S. Pharmacopeia and Nat. Formullary (adv. coun.), Coun. for High Blood Pressure Rsch. (adv. bd.), Am. Heart Assn., Phila. Doctors Golf Assn., Sea Pines Club. Jewish. Patentee in field. Home: 20 Turnberry Ln Hilton Head Island SC 29928-4108

ENGELMAN, MELVIN ALKON, retired dentist, business executive, scientist; b. Waterbury, Conn., July 27, 1921; s. Herman B. and Marion (Halpern) E.; m. Muriel Phillips, Aug. 27, 1949; children: Curtis Land, Suzanne Ruth. AB, Ohio U., 1942; DDS, Western Res. U., 1944. Diplomate: Am. Bd. Oral Electrosurgery. Pvt. practice dentistry Wappingers Falls, N.Y., 1949-89; chmn. oral diagnosis and oral pathology sect., dir. oral diagnostic ctr. St. Francis Hosp., Poughkeepsie, N.Y., 1963-77, attending dentist, 1963-89, dir. dept. dentistry, 1967, 71-74, 78, hon. staff, 1989—; pres. Di-Equi Dental Products Inc., 1980-99, Dentifax Internat. Inc., 1982-99; observer Meml. Hosp. Cancer and Allied Diseases, N.Y.C., 1962-66; mem. adv. bd. Dutchess Community Coll., 1963-69, lectr. dental assts. program, 1960-63; dir. 1st regional sci. fair, Dutchess County, N.Y., 1960-61; project dir. USPHS community cancer demonstration project, St. Francis Hosp., 1963-66; asst. chief med. officer Dutchess County N.Y. CD, 1963-68; cons. Nat. Cancer Inst., mem. clin. cancer tng. com., 1968-71, Profl. edn. com. for cancer control, 1972-73; attending dentist Central Dutchess Nursing Home, 1970-85; cons. VA Hosp., Castle Point, N.Y., 1976-77, Lactona Corp., div. Warner Lambert, 1976-80; internat. lectr. on fixed prosthodontics, premedication, oral cancer, metallurgy. Co-author: Oral Cancer Examination Procedure, 16 edits., 1967-83; contbr. articles to profl. jours.; patentee for feeder bar, spruing assembly, sprue pin, and hollow movable reservoir. Chmn. Wappinger Red Cross Fund Drive, 1956; committeeman Troop 6, Boy Scouts Am., Chelsea, N.Y., 1963-67; pres. Dutchess County unit Am. Cancer Soc., 1969-71. From ensign to lt. Dental Corps, USNR, FMF PAC, 1942-46; lt. comdr. ret., 1986. Fellow AAAS (life), Royal Soc. Health (Eng.), Am. Pub. Health Assn., Acad. Gen. Dentistry; mem. ADA (life), Internat. Assn. Dental Research, Assn. Mil. Surgeons (life mem.), 9th Dist. Dental Soc. (life mem.), Dutchess County Dental Soc. (pres. 1965), Am. Acad. Dental Electrosurgery (pres. 1983), Wappinger Conservation Assn. (v.p. 1970-71), Wappingers Falls C. of C. (pres. 1952-54), Alpha Omega. Clubs: Masons (32 deg.), Shriners, B'nai B'rith (pres. So. Duchess lodge 1963-64). Address: Nutmeg Hill 76 Old State Rd Wappingers Falls NY 12590-3905 also: 5720 Cottonwood St Bradenton FL 34203-8806

ENGELMANN, PAUL VICTOR, plastics engineering educator; b. Ann Arbor, Mich., Jan. 15, 1958; s. Manfred David and Patricia (Park) E.; 1 child, David; m. Sarah C. Sanford, Oct. 24, 1998. AS in Geology, Lansing (Mich.) C.C., 1980; BS in Indsl. Edn., Western Mich. U., 1982, MA in Vocat. Edn., 1984, EdD in Ednl. Leadership, 1988. Owner H.L. & S. Auto Restoration & Fabrication, Lansing, Mich., 1977-82; tchg. asst. dept. engring. tech. Western Mich. U., Kalamazoo, 1982-83, part time instr., 1983-87, instr., 1987-89, asst. prof. plastics, 1989-93, assoc. prof. dept. indsl. and mfg. engring., 1993—; prin. investigator Rsch. and Tech. Inst., Grand Rapids, Mich., 1988-97; prin. investigator Performance Place, Grand Rapids, 1997—; rschr. Robert Morgan & Co., Battle Creek, Mich., 1990-94; prin. investigator Copper Devel. Assn. Inc., 1995—; cons. plastics Parker Hannafin Corp., Ostego, Mich., 1990-97; v.p. Western Mich. SPE Edn. Found., 1994-97. Author (book) Manufacturing Technology, 1989; contbr. articles to profl. jours.; patentee in field. Pres. Plainwell (Mich.) Hist. Preservation Soc., 1990-91, 97-99; pres. bd. dirs. Pipp Found., 1992—, sec. 1992—; chmn., bd. trustees 1st United Meth. Ch., Plainwell, 1996-97, vice chmn. bldg. com., 1997—. Presdl. scholar, 1982; recipient Protective Package of the Yr. award Children's Hosp. of Birmingham, 1990, Teaching Excellence award Western Mich. U., 1990. Mem. Soc. Plastics Engrs. (sr., past pres. 1992-93, pres. 1991-92, pres.-elect 1990-91, v.p. Western Mich. sec. 1988-89, edn. chmn. 1985-88, Sectional award 1986, 87, 88, Best Paper award 1992, Outstanding Member award 1994). Methodist. Avocations: antique auto restoration, old house preservation, environmental preservation. Home: 311 E Chart St Plainwell MI 49080-1703 Office: Western Mich U Dept Indsl and Mfg Engring 1201 Oliver St Kalamazoo MI 49008-3804

ENGELMANN, RUDOLF JACOB, meteorologist; b. Ward County, N.D, Mar. 11, 1930; s. Emil B. and Hazel Ella (Schwartz) E.; m. Virginia D. Fletcher, Dec. 27, 1952; children: Richard, Eric, Kurt, Peter, Aleta, Karsten. B.A., Augsburg Coll., 1950; postgrad., N.Y. U., 1952; Ph.D., U. Wash., 1964. Cert. cons. meteorologist. Meteorologist Gen. Elec. Co., Hanford, Wash., 1958-66; chief fallout studies AEC, 1967-73; dep. mgr. environ. programs Energy Research and Devel. Adminstrn., 1973-75; dir. outer continental shelf environ. assessment program Nat. Oceanic and Atmospheric Adminstrn., Boulder, Colo., 1975-80; sr. oceanographer Nat. Oceanic and Atmospheric Adminstrn., Washington, 1983-84, dir. program devel., 1984-87; sr. scientist Dept. Energy, Washington, 1987-88; pres. Global Atmospheric Response, Potomac, Md., 1989—; dep. dir. Div. Environ. Assessment, UN Environment Program, Nairobi, Kenya, 1980-82; cons. Environment and Emergency Preparedness, 1989—. Served to 1st lt. USAF, 1950-57. Named Distinguished Alumnus Augsburg Coll., 1976. Mem. Am. Meteorol. Soc., Am. Geophys. Union, Am. Nuclear Soc., Air Pollution Control Assn., Sigma Chi, Am. Conf. Govtl. Indsl. Hygienists. Achievements include research on precipitation scavenging and on vehicles and residences as shelters in airborne toxic releases. Home: 11701 Karen Dr Potomac MD 20854-3155 Office: Global Atmospheric Response 11701 Karen Dr Potomac MD 20854-3155

ENGELMANN, RUDOLPH HERMAN, electronics consultant; b. Hewitt, Minn., Mar. 5, 1929; s. Herman Emil Robert and Minna Louise (Kniep) E.; children: Guy Robert, Heidi Louise. BA, U. Minn., 1953. Electronic designer Lawrence Livermore (Calif.) Lab., 1959-61; cons. Atlantic Rsch. Corp., Manchester, N.H., 1961-64, Gen. Radio Co., West Concord, Mass., 1963-69, Possis Engring., Mpls., 1970—, 3M Co., St. Paul, 1977-78, Pako Photo, Mpls., 1977-78, Litton Microwave, Mpls., 1977-79; Presenter papers at confs., 1988-89, 89-90. Contbr. articles to profl. jours. 1st lt. USAF, 1946-53. Achievements include developments and patents in gigahertz digital frequency scalers and counters and time interval meters, touchtone telephone for U.S. Army, automatic photographic focus control, automatic temperature monitor and control for grain and petroleum storage safety and volume correction, optical character recognition, high efficiency battery charging systems, end-of-charge detector, rudderless flight control, ultra lightweight muscle prostheses, flight controls, power management, stealth penetrating radar, high efficiency shpae memory alloy modulation and linear circuitry, high-efficiency electronic orthetic muscle, digitally variable 90db A.C. power source, raster scanning microscope, linear wave blood pump. Office: World Effort Found 1171 Bush St Apt 2 San Francisco CA 94109-5926

ENGELS, LAWRENCE ARTHUR, metals company executive; b. Darlington, Wis., Sept. 26, 1933; s. Henry Morris and Nell Ellen (O'Connor) E.; m. Marilyn Rae Stellick, Sept. 6, 1958; children: Laurie, Michael, Thomas, Stephen. B.B.A., U. Wis., 1959; M.B.A., Northwestern U., 1970. Dist. credit mgr. U.S. Steel Corp., Chgo., 1959-69; asst. treas. Nat. Can Corp., Chgo., 1969-77; corp. treas. Comml. Metals Co., Dallas, 1977—; chief fin. officer and treas. Comml. Metals Co., 1979—; v.p., treas., chief fin. officer Comml. Metals Co., Dallas, 1981—. Served with USN, 1952-55. Fellow Nat. Inst. Credit; mem. Cash Mgmt. Practitioners Assn. (Chgo. sec. 1975), Chgo. Midwest Credit Mgmt. Assn. (dir. 1973-75), Chgo. Midwest Credit Service Corp. (dir. 1975), Fin. Execs. Inst., Nat. Assn. Corp. Treas. Office: Comml Metals Co PO Box 1046 7800 N Stemmons Fwy Dallas TX 75247-4227

ENGELS, THOMAS JOSEPH, sales executive; b. New Orleans, May 24, 1958; s. Ronald Henry and Sally (Jacobsen) E.; m. Tamara Lewis Engels, May 29, 1982; children: Kristen, Danielle. BS in Gen. Mgmt., Purdue U., 1980. Sales rep. Johnson & Johnson, New Brunswick, N.J., 1980-82, mgr., 1982-83; dist. sales mgr. Pepsi Cola U.S.A., Somers, N.Y., 1983-87; regional sales mgr. Rich Sea Pak Corp., St. Simons Island, Ga., 1988-89; cen. regional mgr. food svc. div. Sara Lee Bakery, Chgo., 1990-93; area mgr. Ctrl. Zone Sara Lee Bakery Food Svc., 1993-94, divsn. promotion mgr. East, 1995-96; no. zone mgr. food svc. Land O'Lakes, Inc., 1996—. Roman Catholic. Avocations: tri-athlons, golf, basketball, coaching soccer.

ENGEN, D(ONALD) TRAVIS, diversified telecommunications company executive; b. Pasadena, Calif., June 27, 1944; s. Donald Davenport and Mary (Baker) E.; m. Anne Elizabeth Erickson, June 4, 1967; 1 child, Leigh Elizabeth. BS in Aeronautics and Astronautics, MIT, 1967. Dir. electronics mktg. Bell Aerospace, Niagara Falls, N.Y., 1965-76; dir. mktg. Republic Electronic Industries Corp., Melville, N.Y., 1976-79; dir. govt. avionics Bendix Avionics divsn. Bendix Aircraft Systems Co., Ft. Lauderdale, Fla., 1979-83, v.p., gen. mgr., 1983-85; pres., gen. mgr. avionics divsn. ITT Corp., Nutley, N.J., 1985-87; sr. v.p. ITT Corp., Washington, 1987-91; pres., chief exec. officer ITT Def., Washington, 1987-91; exec. v.p. ITT Corp., N.Y.C., 1991-95; chmn., CEO ITT Industries Inc., 1994—. Avocation: triathlons, vintage car racing. Office: ITT Industries 4 W Red Oak Ln Ste 2 White Plains NY 10604-3617

ENGEN, LEE EMERSON, savings and loan executive; b. Clark, S.D., Sept. 8, 1921; s. Harold O. and Esther V. (Heig) E.; m. Elizabeth M. Eaton, Oct. 29, 1943; children: Barry Lee, Rodney Kent, Timothy Ray. BS, S.D. State U., 1947; postgrad. Ind. U., 1961. Furrier, Norris Furs, Sioux Falls, S.D., 1947-50; with Home Fed. Savs. and Loan Assn., Sioux Falls, 1953-86, pres., 1970-86; chmn. bd. Home Federal Fin. Corp. and Home Federal Savs. Bank, 1991-96; Treas., Sioux Empire United Way, 1968-73, campaign chmn., 1976, pres., 1982-83; bd. dirs. Sioux Valley Hosp., 1972-81; pres. Family Practice Ctr., 1977-78; treas. Children's Care Hosp. and Sch., 1975-83; pres., 1983-84; pres. Jr. Achievement, 1971-72, Crippled Children Hosp. and Sch. Found., 1989-90, Sioux Falls High Sch. Found., 1989-96; sec. Sioux Falls Community Hotel Corp., 1975-85; mem. Sioux Falls City Planning Commn., 1968-76; treas. Sioux Falls High Sch. Found., 1973-89, Mary Chilton Dar Found., 1991-94; chmn. Sioux Valley Hosp. Found., 1984-86, bd. dirs., 1984-87; pres. Nordland Fest, 1987-88, also bd. dirs. 1983-90; bd. dirs. MinnI-aKota coun. Girl Scouts U.S., 1985-89, Nordland Heritage Found., 1992-98, pres., 1996-98. Served with AUS, 1943-46, U.S. Army, 1950-53. Decorated Bronze Star with 2 oak leaf clusters, Purple Heart; named Boss of Yr., Sioux Falls Jaycees, 1967, Bus. Citizen of Yr., Sioux Falls Area C. of C. and Sioux Falls Sales & Mktg. Execs, 1985, Boss of Yr., Am. Bus. Womens Assn., 1986; recipient Bronze Leadership award Jr. Achievement, 1978, Silver Leadership award, 1985, Disting. Service award Sioux Falls Cosmopolitan Club, 1981. Mem. Sioux Falls Area C. of C. (pres. 1973-74). Mem. United Ch. of Christ. Club: Minnehaha Country. Lodges: Masons, Shriners, Elks, Am. Legion. Home: 3201 Woodcrest Way Sioux Falls SD 57105-4261 Office: 360 Boyce Greeley Bldg Sioux Falls SD 57102

ENGER, EDWARD HENRY, JR., editor, writer; b. Mpls., Mar. 16, 1930; s. Edward Henry Sr. and Anastasia (Barber) E.; m. Carolyn Sue Bush, June 1, 1964. BS in Edn., U. Minn., 1952. Cert. tchr., Calif. Tchr. Downers Grove (Ill.) Pub. Sch., 1956-58; editor Harper & Row, Evanston, Ill., 1958-62; author Harper & Row, N.Y.C., 1975-78; editor Silver Burdett Co., Morristown, N.J., 1962-68, Dell Pub. Co., N.Y.C., 1968-75; author Nat. Textbook Co., Chgo., 1979-81; editorial dir. Amsco Sch. Publs., N.Y.C., 1982-97. Author: Writing by Doing, 1981, (textbook series) Language Basics, 1975-78. Served to cpl. U.S. Army, 1954-56, Korea. Mem. Nat. Council Tchrs. English. Democrat. Avocations: gardening, cooking, hiking, jogging.

ENGERRAND, DORIS DIESKOW, business educator; b. Chgo., Aug. 7, 1925; d. William Jacob and Alma Willhelmina (Cords) Dieskow; BS in Bus. Adminstrn., N. Ga. Coll., 1958, BS in Elementary Edn., 1959; M Bus. Edn., Ga. State U., 1966, PhD, 1970; m. Gabriel H. Engerrand, Oct. 26, 1946 (dec. June 1987); children: Steven, Kenneth, Jeannine. Tchr., dept. chmn. Lumpkin County H.S., Dahlonega, Ga., 1960-63, 65-68; tchr., Gainesville, Ga., 1965; asst. prof. Troy (Ala.) State U., 1969-71; asst. prof. bus. Ga. Coll. and State U., Milledgeville, 1971-74, assoc. prof., 1974-78, prof., 1978-90, chmn. dept. info. systems and comms., 1978-89, ret., 1990; cons. Named Outstanding Tchr. Lumpkin County Pub. Schs., 1963, 66; Outstanding Educator bus. faculty Ga. Coll., 1975, Exec. of Yr. award, 1983. Fellow Assn. for Bus. Communication (v.p. S.E. 1978-80, 81-84, 89-92, bd. dirs.), Nat. Bus. Edn. Assn., Ga. Bus. Edn. Assn. (Postsecondary Tchr. of Yr. award 10th dist. 1983, Postsecondary Tchr. of Yr. award 1984), Am. Vocat. Assn., Ga. Vocat. Assn. (Educator of Yr. award 1984, Parker Liles award 1989), Profl. Secs. Internat. (pres. Milledgeville chpt. 1996-97), Ninety-nines Internat. (chmn. N. Ga. chpt. 1975-76, named Pilot of Year N. Ga. chpt. 1973). Methodist. Contbr. articles on bus. edn. to profl. publs. Home: 1674

Pine Valley Rd Milledgeville GA 31061-2465 Office: Ga Coll and State U Milledgeville GA 31061

ENGERSGARD, JORGEN, architect; b. Herning, Denmark, Dec. 31, 1954; came to U.S., 1989; s. Morten Engersgard and Ragna (Christensen) Jorgensen; m. Evelyn Lizette Calderon, Sept. 4, 1994; children: Christian, Gabriella. BSc in Math. and Physics, U. Herning, 1977; MSc, Arch. Sch., Aarhus, Denmark, 1984. Arch. M & N Furniture, Herning, 1984-86, Idea Furniture, Aarhus, 1986-88; arch., project exec. Walker Group/CMI, N.Y.C., 1989-97; arch. Innovative Marble, Hauppauge, N.Y., 1997—. With Danish Marines, 1977-78. Mem. Inst. Acad. Archs. Avocations: golf, skiing, sailing. Office: 455 Ocean Pkwy Brooklyn NY 11218-5151

ENGGAS, GRACE FALCETTA, university administrator; b. Hartford, Conn., May 25, 1946; d. Giacomo and Frances Catanzaro Falcetta; m. David Hirsh Enggas, Mar. 16, 1974. BA, U. Conn., 1971; MA, Ohio State U., 1973; grad., New Eng. mgmt. Inst., Wellesey, Mass., 1995. Cert. in Myers Briggs Type Inventory, 1987. Contract underwriter Travelers Ins. Cos., Hartford, 1965-71; asst. mgr., Jones Grad. Twr. Ohio State U., Columbus, 1972-73; resident counselor Worcester (Mass.) State Coll., 1974-77; area coord. Ea. Conn. State U., Willimantic, Conn., 1977-78, assoc. dir. housing, 1978-87, dir. housing, 1987—. Bd. dirs. and v.p. Literacy Vols. of Conn., 1990—; treas. Charter Cable Adv. Bd., 1989—. Mem. Nat. Assn. Student Pers. Adminstrs., Assn. Coll. and Univ. Housing Officers, Conn. Assn. Women in Edn. (treas. 1988—), Nat. Assn. Women in Edn., State U. Adminstrv. Faculty/Am. Fedn. State, County and Mcpl. Employees local #2836 Collective Bargaining Unit (treas. 1978, sec. 1986-92, v.p. 1992—, del. 1992). Democrat. Home: 58 Mountain Rd Mansfield Center CT 06250-1211 Office: Ea Conn State Univ 83 Windham St Willimantic CT 06226-2211

ENGH, FREDRIC CHARLES, educational association administrator; b. Johnstown, Pa., Aug. 13, 1935; s. Lynn Anderson and Rosealma (Harrigan) E.; m. Michaele Shortall, Jan. 3, 1960; children: Kathi, David, Eric, John, Darin, Joanna, Patrick. BS in Physical Edn., U. Md., 1963. Cert. tchr., phys. edn. Tchr. St. Francis Sch., Salisbury, Md., 1963-66; athletic dir. St. Elizabeth High Sch., Wilmington, Del., 1967-69; exec. dir. Cath. Youth Orgn., Del., 1970-73; nat. dir. youth sports Athletic Inst., Chgo., 1973-76; founder, pres., chief exec. officer Nat. Youth Sports Coaches Assn., West Palm Beach, Fla., 1980—; cert. agt. Major League Baseball Players Assn.; radio broadcaster, sports analyst WDEL, Wilmington, 1969-72; pres., CEO Nat. Alliance Youth Sports, 1993—. Contbr. articles to profl. jours., 1965—. Pres. PTA, Munster, Ind., 1974, local civic assn., Wilmington, 1968. With U.S. Army, 1954-56. Avocations: golf, tennis, skiing, bowling. Home: 200 Miramar Way West Palm Beach FL 33405-4712 Office: National Youth Sports Coaches Assn 2050 Vista Pkwy West Palm Beach FL 33411-2718*

ENGHETA, NADER, electrical engineering educator, researcher; b. Tehran, Iran, Oct. 8, 1955; came to U.S. 1978; s. Abdollah and Meymanat (Mesghali) E.; m. Susanne Hoshyar, Oct. 15, 1983; children: Alex Cameron, Sarah Katherine. BSEE, U. Tehran, 1978; MSEE, Calif. Inst. Tech., 1979, PhD in Elec. Enging., 1982. Grad. rsch. asst. Calif. Inst. Tech., Pasadena, 1979-82, postdoctoral rsch. fellow, 1982-83; sr. rsch. scientist Dikewood Divsn. Kaman Scis. Corp., Santa Monica, Calif., 1983-87; asst. prof. elec. enging. U. Pa., Phila., 1987-90, assoc. prof. elec. enging., 1990-95, prof. elec. enging., 1995—, UPS Found. Disting. Educator chair, 1999—; grad. group chmn. elec. enging. U. Pa., 1993-97; gen. chmn. Benjamin Franklin Symposium, Phila., 1990-91; vis. lectr., UCLA, spring 1986; condr. seminars in field; IEEE Antennas and Propagation Soc. Disting. lectr., 1997—. Guest editor spl. issue of Jour. of Electromagnetic Waves and Applications on Wave interaction with chiral and complex media, Vol. 6, No. 5/6, 1992, mem. editl. bd., 1993—; guest editor Jour. Franklin Inst. on Antennas and Microwaves, 13th Annual Benjamin Franklin Symposium, Vol. 332B, No. 5, 1995; assoc. editor Radio Sci., 1991-96, IEEE Trans. on Antennas & Propagation, 1996—; contbr. over 60 articles to profl. jours., chpts. to books. NSF Presdl. Young Investigator, 1989; AT&T Spl. Purpose grantee, 1988; U. Pa. Rsch. Found. grantee, 1988, 90, 93; recipient Enging. Tchg. Excellence award W.M. Keck Found., 1995, Fulbright Naples Chair award for Italy, 1998, Guggenheim Fellowship award 1999. Fellow IEEE (chmn. antennas and propagation/microwave theory and technique Phila. chpt. 1990-91), Optical Soc. Am.; mem. AAAS, Am. Phys. Soc., Internat. Union of Radio Sci. (commn. B and D of USNC), Sigma Xi. Achievements include five patents (with others) for method of measuring chiral parameters of chiral materials, novel electromagnetic shielding reflection and scattering control using chiral materials, waveguides using chiral materials; printed-circuit antenna using material and rodomes using chiral materials; patents pending (with others) for electromagnetically non-reflective material, novel antenna arrays using chiral materials, novel lenses using chiral materials and method of using polarization differencing to improve vision; research on applied and theoretical electromagnetics, optics, complex unconventional electromagnetic materials, electromagnetic chiral materials, microwave, polarization-difference imaging, waveguide theory, role of fractional calculus and fractional paradigm in electrodynamics. Office: Univ of Pa 200 S 33rd St Philadelphia PA 19104-6314

ENGIBOUS, THOMAS JAMES, electronics company executive; b. St. Louis, Jan. 31, 1953; s. James C. and Emma E. (Buck) E.; children: Ryan T., Christopher M. B of Elec. Enging., Purdue U., 1975, M of Elec. Enging., 1976, D of Enging. (hon.), 1997. Design engr. SCG, Tex. Instruments, Dallas, 1976-80, dept. mgr., 1980-86, v.p., 1986-91, sr. v.p., 1991-93; exec. v.p., pres. semi-condr. group Tex. Instruments, Dallas, 1993-96; pres., CEO Tex. Instruments Inc., Dallas, 1996-98, chmn., pres., CEO, 1998—; mem. vis. com. Purdue U. Enging., 1995—; bd. dirs. Catalyst. Mem. Dallas Citizens Coun., 1996—; trustee So. Meth. U. Mem. IEEE, Bus. Roundtable, Bus. Coun. Roman Catholic. Avocations: boating, water sports, snow skiing. *

ENGLAND, ANTHONY WAYNE, electrical engineering and computer science educator, astronaut, geophysicist; b. Indpls., May 15, 1942; s. Herman U. and Betty (Steel) E.; m. Kathleen Ann Kreutz, Aug. 31, 1962. SB SM, MIT, 1965, PhD, 1970. With Texaco Co., 1962; field geologist Ind. U., 1963; scientist-astronaut NASA, 1967-72, 79-88; with U.S. Geol. Survey, 1972-79; crewmember on Spacelab 2, July, 1985; adj. prof. Rice U., Houston, 1987-88; prof. elec. enging. and computer sci. U. Mich., Ann Arbor, 1988—, prof. atmospheric, oceanic and space sci., 1989—, assoc. dean Rackham Grad. Sch., 1995-98; mem. space studies bd. NRC, 1992-98. Assoc. editor Jour. Geophys. Rsch. Recipient Antarctic medal, Spaceflight medal NASA, Spaceflight award Am. Astron. Soc., Outstanding Scientific Achievement medal NASA. Fellow IEEE; mem. Am. Geophys. Union. Home: 7949 Ridgeway Ct Dexter MI 48130-9700 Office: U Mich Dept Elec Engring-Comp Sci Ann Arbor MI 48109-2122

ENGLAND, ARTHUR JAY, JR., lawyer, former state justice; b. Dayton, Ohio, Dec. 23, 1932; s. Arthur Jay and Elsbeth (Weiskopf) E.; m. Morley Tenenbom, June 24, 1959 (div.); children: Andrea, Pamela, Ellen, Karen; m. Deborah J. Miller, Mar. 31, 1984; children: Rachel, Aaron. BS, U. Pa., 1955, LLB, 1961; LLM, U. Miami, 1971; LLD (hon.), John B. Stetson Coll. Law, 1979, Nova U., 1982. Bar: Fla. 1961, N.Y. 1962. Assoc. Dewey, Ballantine, Bushby, Palmer & Wood, N.Y.C., 1961-64; ptnr. Culverhouse, Tomlinson, Taylor & DeCarion, Miami, Fla., 1964-69, Scott, McCarthy, Steel, Hector & Davis, Miami, 1969-70; spl. tax counsel Fla. Ho. Reps., 1971-72; consumer adviser, spl. counsel to gov. Fla., 1972-73; ptnr. Paul & Thomson, Miami, 1973-74; justice Supreme Ct. Fla., 1975-81, chief justice, 1978-80; ptnr. Steel, Hector & Davis, Miami, 1981-84; ptnr. Fine Jacobson Schwartz Nash Block England, Miami, 1984-92, pres., chief exec. officer, 1988-89; shareholder Greenberg Traurig Hoffman Lipoff Rosen & Quentel, Miami, 1992, Greenberg Traurig, P.A. (and predecessor firm), Miami, 1992—; dep. chmn. Conf. of Chief Justices, 1978-80; chmn. Coun. of State Ct. Reps., Nat. Ctr. for State Cts., 1979-80; mem. Commn. on Interest on Lawyers' Trust Accounts, 1986-90, chmn., 1989-90; chmn. adv. bd. Nat. Interest on Lawyers' Trust Accounts Clearinghouse, 1983-86; adj. prof. Coll. Law, Fla. State U. Contbr. articles to legal jours. With AUS, 1955-57. Recipient Medal of Honor, Fla. Bar Found., 1983, Herbert Harley award Am. Judicature Soc., 1986, Jurisprudence award Anti-Defamation League, 1991. Mem. ABA (Pro Bono Pub. award 1988), Am. Acad. Appellate Lawyers (pres. 1990-92), Am. Law Inst., Fla. Bar Assn. (chmn. appellate practice cert. com. 1993-94, cert. appellate lawyers), N.Y. State Bar Assn., Order of Coif, Beta Gamma Sigma. Jewish. Home: 4897 SW 82nd St Miami FL 33143-8603 Office: Greenberg Traurig PA 1221 Brickell Ave Miami FL 33131-3224

ENGLAND, CHERYL, publisher, editorial director; b. Hopewell, Va., Nov. 29, 1960; d. R. Stanford and Joyce (Hall) E. BA in English, U. Va., 1983. Staff writer, sr. staff writer Bus. Software Mag., Redwood City, Calif., 1984-85, database sect. editor, 1985-86; assoc. editor Personal Computing Mag., San Jose, Calif., 1986-87; assoc. editor reviews Macworld Mag., San Francisco, 1987-88, sr. assoc. editor, 1988-91, sr. editor features, 1992-93; sr. editor integration Corp. Computing Mag., Foster City, Calif., 1993; sr. editor features MacUser Mag., Foster City, 1993, exec. editor features, 1994-95, editor, 1995-96; editor-in-chief MacAddict mag., Brisbane, Calif., 1996-97, pub., editl. dir., 1998—; mem. adv. panel CD-ROM Expo, 1993; lectr. in field; bd. dirs. Berkley Mac Users Group. Recipient Best Hardware Product Review award Computer Press Assn., 1990, 93, 94, Best Feature award, 1992, Reporting award Am. Soc. Bus. Press Editors, 1991, Best Feature Series award, 1992, Best Overall Mag., Computer Press Assn., 1996. Avocations: scuba diving, running, travel. Office: Imagine Media 150 N Hill Dr Brisbane CA 94005-1018*

ENGLAND, DAN BENJAMIN, accountant; b. Duncan, Okla., Aug. 23, 1955; s. Haskell Thomas and Lillian Lucille (Rouw) E.; m. Mary Elizabeth Metcalf, May 24, 1980; 1 child, Stuart Benjamin. BA, Southeastern Okla. State U., 1977, BS, 1982. CPA, Okla. Br. mgr. Curtis Distbg. Co., Durant, Okla., 1978-79; dist. agt. Prudential Ins. Co., Durant, 1980-82; acct. Reedrill Inc., Sherman, Tex., 1982; mgr. Williams and Co. CPAs Inc., Durant, 1983-85; v.p. England Enterprises Inc., Durant, 1985—; pvt. practice acctg., Durant, 1985—; adj. instr. Southeastern Okla. State U., Durant, 1985-86; investment advisor rep., 1993—. Bd. dirs. Red River Arts Coun., Durant, 1986-94. Mem. Nat. Assn. Tax Practitioners, Okla. Soc. CPAs, Durant Jaycees (bd. dirs. 1985), Durant C. of C. Republican. Mem. Ch. of Christ. Lodge: Kiwanis (treas. Durant, 1985, sec. 1986, v.p. 1988, pres. 1989). Avocations: golf, tennis, music, art. Office: 206 N 10th Ave Durant OK 74701-4328

ENGLAND, JAMES C., federal judge; b. 1947. JD, U. Mo., 1972. Magistrate judge U.S. Dist. Ct. (we. dist.) Mo., Springfield, 1976—. Office: 2200 US Courthouse 222 N John Q Hammons Pkwy Springfield MO 65806-2541

ENGLAND, JOHN DAVID, neurologist; b. Clarksburg, W.Va., Jan. 20, 1954; s. John Draper and Imogene Lucille (Alexander) E.; m. Cathy Ann Drummond, Nov. 22, 1975. BA in Chemistry, W.Va. U., 1976, MD, 1980. Diplomate Nat. Bd. Med. Examiners, Am. Bd. Psychiatry and Neurology, Am. Bd. Electrodiagnostic Medicine; lic. physician, S.C., Pa., Colo., La. Intern Med. U. S.C., Charleston, 1980-81, resident in neurology, 1981-84; clin. neuromuscular fellow dept. neurology Hosp. of U. Pa., Phila., 1984-85, postdoctoral rsch. fellow dept. neurology, 1985-87; asst. prof. neurology U. Colo., Denver, 1987-92; assoc. prof. neurology La. State U., New Orleans, 1992-98, prof. neurology and neuroscience, 1998—; attending physician U. Colo. Health Scis. Ctr., Denver, 1987-92, dir. electromyography lab., 1987-92; attending physician Med. Ctr. La., New Orleans, 1992—; prof. neurology and neurosci. La. State U., New Orleans, 1998—; lectr. in field. Contbr. numerous articles to profl. jours.; editl. cons. Muscle and Nerve, 1987—, Ann. Neurol., 1990—, Brain, 1993—. Recipient Koehler award in chemistry, Handbook award Chem. Rubber Co., Whitehall award of dept. chemistry; W.Va. U. Bd. Regents scholar, Masonic scholar, others; grantee Muscular Dystrophy Assn., 1985-87, NIH, 1987-88, Nat. Inst. Neurol. Disorders and Stroke, 1988-93, Nat. Inst. Aging, 1991-94, La. State U. Neurosci. Ctr. for Excellence, 1993-94, Dept. Def., 1993—. Mem. AMA, Am. Neurol. Assn., Am. Assn. Electrodiagnostic Medicine (profl. practice com. 1988-91, liaison rep. 1991-92, spl. interest group com. 1992-93, tng. program com. 1993-96, program com. 1996—), Am. Acad. Neurology, Am. Neurol. Assn., N.Y. Acad. Scis., Am. Soc. Neurol. Investigation, Soc. for Neurosci., W.Va. U. Alumni Assn., Alpha Omega Alpha, Phi Kappa Phi, Phi Lambda Upsilon, Phi Beta Kappa. Democrat. Methodist. Avocations: skiing, running, hunting, reading. Office: Louisiana State U Med Ctr Dept Neurology 1542 Tulane Ave New Orleans LA 70112-2825

ENGLAND, JOHN MELVIN, lawyer, clergyman; b. June 29, 1932; s. John Marcus and Frances Dorothy (Brown) E.; m. Jane Cantrell, Aug. 2, 1953; children: Kathryn Elizabeth, Janette Evelyn, John William, Kenneth Paul, James Andrew, Samuel Robert. Student, Ga. State U., 1951-53; JD, U. Ga., 1956; BD magna cum laude with honors Theology, Columbia Theol. Sem., Decatur, Ga., 1964. Bar: Ga. 1959, U.S. Dist. Ct. (no. dist.) Ga. 1967, U.S. Ct. Mil. Appeals 1976, U.S. Ct. Appeals (5th cir.) 1967, U.S. Ct. Appeals (11th cir.) 1981, U.S. Supreme Ct. 1977, U.S. Dist. Ct. (mid. dist.) Ga. 1986, U.S. Dist. Ct. (so. dist.) Ga. 1991, U.S. Dist. Ct. (no. dist.) Tex. 1991; ordained to ministry Presbyn. Ch., 1964. Spl. agt. FBI, Washington, 1956-57, Indpls., 1957-59, Charlotte, N.C., 1959, Greenville, S.C., 1959-60; student supply pastor Bethel and Buford Presbyn. Chs., Atlanta, 1960-63; pastor Mullins (S.C.) Presbyn. Ch., 1964-67; asst. dist. atty. Fulton County, Ga., 1967-75; sr. ptnr. England and Weller, Atlanta, 1975-88, England, Wearer & Kytle, 1988-94, England & McKnight, 1994—; legal seminar lectr. and spkr. throughout the country under auspices of Christian orgns.; spl. pros. for gov. Ga., 1976-79; spl. cons. on appellate reform Supreme Ct. Ga., 1979-80; state bar rep. to Superior Ct. Uniform Rules Com. Coun. Superior Ct. Judges, 1984, 93. Elder, tchr., evangelism coord. Presbyn. Ch. USA; chmn. Christian Bus. Men's Coms. of U.S.A., Atlanta, 1971-73, chmn. internat. conv., Atlanta, 1979, bd. dirs., 1971-81. Mem. ABA, ATLA, State Bar Ga., Atlanta Bar Assn., Lawyers Club Atlanta, Ga. Trial Lawyers Assn., Nat. Assn. Criminal Def. Lawyers, Ga. Assn. Criminal Def. Lawyers, North Fulton Bar Assn. Office: 9040 Roswell Rd Ste 410 Atlanta GA 30350-1863

ENGLAND, LYNNE LIPTON, lawyer, speech pathologist, audiologist; b. Youngstown, Ohio, Apr. 11, 1949; d. Sanford Y. and Sally (Kentor) Lipton; m. Richard E. England, Mar. 5, 1977. BA, U. Mich., 1970; MA, Temple U., 1972; JD, Tulane U., 1981. Bar: Fla. 1982, U.S. Dist. Ct. (mid. dist.) Fla. 1982, U.S. Ct. Appeals (11th cir.) 1982; cert. clin. competence in speech pathology and audiology. Speech pathologist Rockland Children's Hosp., N.Y., 1972-74, Jefferson Parish Sch., Gretna, La., 1977-81; audiologist Rehab. Inst. Chgo., 1974-76; assoc. Trenam, Simmons, Kemker, Scharf, Barkin, Frye & O'Neill, Tampa, Fla., 1981-84; asst. U.S. atty. for Middle Dist. Fla. Tampa, 1984-87; asst. U.S. trustee, 1987-91; ptnr. Stearns, Weaver, Miller, Weissler, Alhadeff & Sitterson, P.A., 1991-94, Prevatt, England & Taylor, Tampa, Fla., 1994—. Editor Fla. Bankruptcy Casenotes, 1983. Recipient clin. assistantship Temple U., 1972-74. Mem. ATLA, Comml. Law League, Am. Speech and Hearing Assn., Tampa Bay Bankruptcy Bar Assn. (dir. 1990-95), Am. Bankruptcy Inst., Fla. Bar Assn., Hillsborough County Bar Assn., Order of Coif. Jewish. Avocations: tennis, golf, playing French horn and piano. Office: PO Box 2920 1 Tampa City Ctr Ste 1700 Tampa FL 33602-5815

ENGLAND, RICHARD C., JR., special education educator; b. Birmingham, Ala., Mar. 16, 1955; s. Richard C. Sr. and Martha C. (Darnall) E.; m. Barbara L. England, Aug. 25, 1974; children: Richard III, Amy, Micah, Kathryn. Student, Freed-Hardeman U., 1972-74; MusB, Union U., 1976; MusM, Memphis State U., 1982, EdD, 1985. Pub. sch. tchr., 1978-84; mem. staff Ala. Commn. on Higher Edn., Montgomery, 1984-91; prin. Jackson (Tenn.) Christian Sch., 1991-93; headmaster Clifton Ganus Sch., New Orleans, 1993-94; prof. spl. edn. Freed-Hardeman U., Henderson, Tenn., 1994—. Contbr. articles to profl. jours., chpt. to textbooks. Commr. So. Assn. Colls. and Schs., 1994-95, Coun. on Occupl. Edn., 1995—; vol. Madison County Juveline Ct., Jackson. Mem. ASCD, Nat. Assn. Sch. Psychologists, Tenn. Assn. Sch. Psychologists. Mem. Ch. of Christ. Avocations: ham radio, fly fishing, reading, camping. Office: Freed-Hardeman U Dept Spl Edn Henderson TN 38340

ENGLAND, RUDY ALAN, lawyer; b. Snyder, Tex., Sept. 29, 1959; s. Bud and Imo D. (Witcher) E.; m. Zenda Cherie Ball, Mar. 24, 1978 (div. June 1988); children: Aaron, Kyle; m. Susan Ann Steadman, Mar. 10, 1990 (div. Dec. 1998). AA summa cum laude, Western Tex. Coll., 1979; BS summa cum laude, U. Houston, 1986, JD, 1989. Bar: Tex. 1990, U.S. Dist. Ct. (so. dist.) Tex. 1990, U.S. Dist. Ct. (no., ea. and we. dists.) Tex. 1994, U.S. Ct. Appeals (5th cir.) 1990. Adminstrv. asst. Tartan Oil & Gas, Houston, 1981-82; div. order analyst Moran Exploration, Inc., Houston, 1982-83; sr. lease analyst Integrated Energy Inc., Houston, 1983-84; landman Cambridge Royalty Co., Houston, 1984-85; supr. div. orders MCO Resources Inc., Houston, 1985-87; assoc. Hutcheson & Grundy, L.L.P., Houston, 1989-96, ptnr., 1997-98; of counsel Haynes and Boone LLP, Houston, 1998—. Mem. Houston Law Rev., 1988-89, bd. dirs. Houston Law Rev. Alumni Assn., 1996-97, v.p. 1997-98, pres., 1998-99. Mem. taxi squad U. Houston, 1991; mgr. Little League Baseball, 1993-96; bd. dirs. Braeburn Little League, 1995-96. Mem. Am. Assn. Profl. Landmen, Coll. of State Bar, State Bar Tex. (professionalism com. 1996—), Houston Bar Assn. (lawyers for literacy com. 1991-92, lawyers in pub. schs. com. 1995-98), Tex. Young Lawyers Assn. (bd. dirs. 1993-95, liaison to Tex. lawyer's creed com. of State Bar 1994-95, co-chmn. profl. and grievance awareness com. 1994-95, chmn. profl. com. 1993-94, mem. legis. com. 1990-93, vice chmn. legis. com. 1993-94, mem. local affiliates com. 1991-92, dropout prevention com. 1991-92, Tex. Young Lawyer Assn. sect. Tex. Bar Jour. com., 1991-93, profl. and ethics com. 1995-96, outstanding young lawyer com. 1995-96), Houston Young Lawyers Assn. (bd. dirs. 1991-93, sec. 1993-94, chmn. professionalism com. 1991-92, chmn. Law Day com. 1992-93, award achievement com. 1993-94, chmn. ops. com. 1993-94, outstanding young lawyers com. 1991-92, Liberty Bell award com. 1992-93), Houston Prodrs.' Forum, U. Houston Law Ctr. Alumni Assn. (bd. dirs. 1997-98), Cougar Cager Club. Mem. Unity Ch. of Christianity. Avocations: golf, snow skiing. Office: Haynes & Boone LLP 1000 Louisiana Ste 4300 Houston TX 77002-4313

ENGLANDER, ROGER LESLIE, television producer, director; b. Cleve., Nov. 23, 1926; s. Will C. and Frieda (Osteryoung) E. Student, Chgo. Mus. Coll., 1945-48; PhB, U. Chgo., 1946; postgrad., Goodman Theater of Art Inst. Chgo., 1947-48, U. Chgo., 1947-49. Freelance TV producer, dir. for Leonard Bernstein N.Y. Philharm. Young People Concerts, 1958-75; asst. to gen. mgr. Chgo. Opera Co., 1946-47; asst. to Gian Carlo Menotti N.Y.C., 1947-49; assoc. dir. ABC-TV, N.Y.C., 1949-50; producer, dir. CBS-TV, N.Y.C., 1950-75; freelance TV producer, dir., writer major networks, theatrical orgns., U.S., Eng., Israel, Italy, Japan, 1975—; chmn. panel Nat. Endowment for the Arts, Washington, 1962-72; tchr. broadcasting NYU, Fairfield U.; founder Am. Dance Theater, N.Y.C., 1964-66; producer N.Y. Philharm. Promenade Concerts, N.Y.C., 1963-67; dir. Music Theater, N.Y.C., 1964-65. Author: Opera: What's All the Screaming About?, 1983. Pres. St. Lukes Pl. Assn., N.Y.C., 1970—; mem. vis. com. U. Chgo., 1982—. Recipient Emmy award NATAS, 1961, 63, 65, 69, 73, Peabody award, 1979, Dirs. Guild Am. award, 1980, Profl. Achievement award U. Chgo., 1980. Avocation: writing. Home and Office: 15 Saint Lukes Pl New York NY 10014-3974*

ENGLAR, JOHN DAVID, textile company executive, lawyer; b. Baldwin, N.Y., Feb. 19, 1947; s. Jack Donald and Edith (Blackwell) E.; m. Linda Meter, May 10, 1986. BA magna cum laude, Duke U., 1969, JD, 1972. Bar: N.Y. 1973. Assoc. Davis Polk and Wardwell, N.Y.C. and Paris, 1972-78; corp. atty. Burlington Industries, Inc., Greensboro, N.C., 1978—, v.p., gen. counsel, sec., 1984-93, CFO, 1994-96; sr. v.p. corp. devel. and law, 1995—; also bd. dirs. Burlington Industries, Inc., 1990—. Chmn. bd. trustees Cen. N.C. chpt. Nat. Multiple Sclerosis Soc., 1984-86, mem. nat. adv. coun., 1988-89; mem. bd. visitors Wake Forest U. Sch. Law, 1984-95, Duke U. Fuqua Sch. Bus., 1995—. Mem. N.C. Bar Assn., Order of Coif, Phi Beta Kappa. Home: 215 Ridgeway Dr Greensboro NC 27403-1526 Office: Burlington Industries Inc PO Box 21207 3330 W Friendly Ave Greensboro NC 27410-4800*

ENGLE, CINDY, medical transcriptionist; b. Denver, Aug. 12, 1958; d. Wallace Clyde and Mary Margaret (Ingram) E. AA, Arapahoe C.C., 1979; BA in Kinesiology, U. No. Colo., 1992. Cert. paralegal; former cert. paramedic, Colo. EMT/paramedic Ambulance Svc. Co., Denver, 1978-80; pers. asst. payroll Burns Security Svc., Denver, 1980-82; part-time asst. mgr. Tokoyo Bowl Restaurant, Denver, 1982-85; paramedic Platte Valley Ambulance, 1982-85; part-time flight paramedic for Air Life North Colo. Med. Ctr., Greeley, Colo., 1986-91; paramedic Weld County Ambulance, Greeley, 1985-92; intern exercise svcs. Greeley (Colo.) Med. Clinic, 1992, med. transcriptionist, 1993-94; med. transcriptionist North Colo. Med. Ctr., Greeley, 1994—; cert. bioenergetic and wellness cons. and practitioner Bio-Lines, L.L.C., 1998—; part-time EMS/criminal justice instr. Aims C.C., Greeley, 1987-96; founder The Human Factor, 1992-98. Author ednl. game: The Reality Game, 1993. Avocations: reading, walking dogs. Office: The Human Factor 2626 23rd Ave Greeley CO 80631-7918

ENGLE, DONALD EDWARD, retired railway executive, lawyer; b. St. Paul, Mar. 5, 1927; s. Merlin Edward and Edna May (Berger) E.; m. Nancy Ruth Frank, Mar. 18, 1950; children: David Edward, Daniel Thomas, Nancy Ann. B.A., Macalester Coll., St. Paul, 1948; J.D., U. Minn., 1952, B.S.L., 1950. Bar: Minn. 1952, Mo. 1972. Law clk., spl. atty. Atty. Gen.'s Office Minn., 1951-52; atty., asst. gen. solicitor, asst. gen. counsel G.N. Ry., St. Paul, 1953-70; asso. gen. counsel Burlington No., Inc., 1970-72; v.p., gen. counsel S.L.-S.F. Ry., St. Louis, 1972-80, v.p. law, sec., 1979-80; v.p. law Burlington No., Inc., St. Paul, 1980-81; v.p. law Burlington No. Ry., St. Paul, 1981-83, sr. v.p. law and govt. affairs, sec., 1983-86, also dir.; ptnr., chmn., chief exec. officer Oppenheimer, Wolff & Donnelly, 1986-93, chmn., chief exec. officer, 1991-93, of counsel, 1993—; continuing edn. lectr. U. Minn. Bd. dirs. YMCA, St. Paul, 1981-84, ARC, 1981-84; bd. dirs. Boy Scouts Am., 1991—. Mem. ABA, Mo. Bar Assn., Minn. Bar Assn., Ramsey County Bar Assn., St. Louis Bar Assn., St. Paul C. of C. (bd. dirs. 1994-97), North Oaks Golf Club, Minn. Club, Bellerive Country Club, Phi Delta Phi. Republican. Lutheran. Home: 9 W Bay Ln Saint Paul MN 55127-2601

ENGLE, HOWARD A., retired pediatrician; b. Wis., Sept. 11, 1919; married; three children. BS, U. Wis., 1939, MS, 1941, MD, 1943. Diplomate Am. Bd. Pediatrics. Intern Michael Reese Hosp., Chgo., 1943, resident in pediatrics, 1943-44; pvt. practice Miami Beach, Fla., 1947—; assoc. clin. prof. U. Miami Sch. of Medicine, assoc. prof. pediatrics emeritus; sr. cons., past chmn. dept. pediatrics, Mount Sinai Med. Ctr., Miami Beach; com. mem., operation newborn U. Miami Sch. of Medicine; instr. dept. pediatrics U. Fla. Sch. of Nursing; pediatric preceptor Fla. Internat. U. Sch. Nursing; sr. cons. pediatrics Mount Sinai Med. Ctr.; courtesy staff Miami Childrens Hosp.; sr. attending pediatrics Jackson Mem. Hosp.; cons. Fla. Atlantic U. Dept. Spl. Edn., neuropediatrics, Childrens Home Soc. of Fla.; cons., lectr. Dupont de Nemours Found., State Miss.; cons. pediatric neurology Hope Sch.; dir. Symposium Cerebral Palsy, Miami; med. rep. Symposia Cerebral Palsy, State of Tex.; lectr. in field. Contbr. articles to profl. jours. Com. mem. Edn. and Therapy for the Handicapped, Dade County Sch. Bd.; past med. dir. United Cerebral Palsy of Miami; cons. neuropediatrics United Cerebral Palsy of Fla.; past. mem. clin. adv. bd. United Cerebral Palsy; nat. del. World Commn. on Cerebral Palsy, Copenhagen, 1963; med. cons. divsn. exceptional student edn. Dade County Sch. Bd. Recipient Ralph Hawley Dist. Svc. award for 50 yrs. svc. to medicine and the cmty. U. Wis., 1993. Mem. Am. Acad. Pediat., Child Neurology Soc., Am. Acad. Cerebral Palsy (exec. com.), Am. Acad. Neurology, Am. Assn. on Mental Retardation, Am. Population and Reproduction Assn. (pres., founder), Fla. Rehab. Assn., Internat. Soc. for Rehab. of Crippled and Disabled, Am. Acad. Phys. Medicine and Rehab., Internat. Soc. for Cerebral Palsy, Internat. Child Neurology Assn. (assoc.), Japanese Soc. Child Neurology, Dade County Med. Assn., Fla. Med. Assn., Fla. Pediatric Soc., Miami Pediatric Soc. (past pres.), Southeastern Med. Assn., European Paediatric Neurology Soc., World Med. Assn., Internat. Population and Reproduction Com. (chmn. edn. programs, bd. dirs., past pres. 1981-82), Alpha Omega Alpha, Sigma Sigma.

ENGLE, JAMES BRUCE, ambassador; b. Billings, Mont., Apr. 16, 1919; s. Bruce Wilmot and Verbeaudah Margaret (Morgan) E.; m. Priscilla Joyce Wright, June 10, 1950; children—Stephen, Judith, Philip, Susan, John, Peter. Diploma, Burlington (Iowa) Jr. Coll., 1938; B.A., U. Chgo., 1940, postgrad., 1940-41, 46; diploma, Grad. Sch. Bus. Adminstrn., Harvard, 1945; Honours B.A. (Rhodes scholar), Exeter Coll., Oxford (Eng.) U., 1950; Honours M.A., Oxford (Eng.) U., 1954; diploma, U. per Stranieri, Perugia, Italy, 1949; Fulbright scholar, Istituto Italiano Studi Storici, Naples, 1950-53; postgrad., Am. U., Washington, 1956-58; diploma, Goethe Institut, Germany, 1958; postgrad., King's Coll., Cambridge (Eng.) U., 1958-59. Dept. State liaison officer with Bd. Econ. Warfare, Washington, 1941-42; vice consul Quito, Ecuador, 1942-44, Rio de Janeiro, Brazil, 1946-47, Naples, 1951-53; 2d sec. Am. embassy, Rome, 1953-54; Italian desk officer Dept.

State, Washington, 1955-58; 1st sec. Am. embassy, London, 1958-59; consul Frankfurt, Germany, 1959, Duesseldorf, Germany, 1959-60; labor attache Am. embassy, Bonn, Germany, 1960-61; 1st sec. Am. embassy, Accra, Ghana, 1961-62; acting dep. chief mission Am. embassy, 1962-63, charge d'affaires, 1963; dep. chief mission, counselor embassy Managua, Nicaragua, 1963-67; charge d'affaires, 1967; mem. sr. seminar in fgn. policy Dept. State, Washington, 1967-68; dep. chief reports and analysis div. CORDS, Mil. Assistance Command, Saigon, Vietnam, 1968; province sr. advisor Phu Yen mil. region II, Tuy Hoa, Vietnam, 1969-70; dir. Vietnam working group Dept. State, sec. Nat. Security Council com. on Indochina, Washington, 1970-71; spl. advisor to ambassador-at-large on trade and currency negotiations, 1971-72, diplomatic advisor to sec. of treasury, 1972; spl. asst. to U.S. ambassador to North Atlantic Council, Brussels, Belgium, 1972; exec. sec. spl. interdepartmental task force on Indochina Dept. State, Washington, 1972-73; consul gen. Nha Trang, Vietnam, 1973; dep. chief mission, counselor of embassy Phnom Penh, Cambodia, 1973-74; charge d'affaires, 1974; ambassador to People's Republic of Bénin (Dahomey), Cotonou, 1974-76; polit. advisor with rank of ambassador to U.S. Comdr.-in-Chief Atlantic and Supreme Allied Comdr. Atlantic, 1976-78; sr. fgn. service insp. Dept. State, Washington, 1978-82; cons. on war gaming, 1983-84; dir. U.S. representation U.S.—Saudi Arabian Joint Commn. on Econ. Cooperation Riyadh, Saudi Arabia, 1984-85; Joint Commn. Advisor to Sr. Level Coms. U.S. and Saudi Arabian govts., 1985-87, cons. on fgn. affairs, 1987—; pres. Vermont Coverts: Woodlands for Wildlife, 1991—; mem. Vt. Forestry Communications Coun., 1991-95. Mem. Vt. Citizens Adv. Com., No. Forest Lands Coun., 1992-94, U. Vt. Extension Adv. Coun., 1993—. Served to lt. (j.g.) USN, 1944-46; mil. govt. officer Japan, 1945-46. Recipient Rockefeller Pub. Service award, 1958; named Tree Farmer of Yr. Caledonia County, Vt., 1997. Mem. The Oxford Union, Phi Beta Kappa. Episcopalian. Leader U.S. Andean expdns. in Ecuador, 1942-43. Home: PO Box 64 Peacham VT 05862-0064

ENGLE, JANE, research nurse; b. L.A., June 15, 1942; d. John Dean and Florence (Updike) E. BA with honors, U. N.C., 1965; BSN, Cornell U., 1970; MS in Nursing, U. Ill., Chgo., 1974; MDiv cum luade, Wesley Theol. Sem., 1988. RN. Tchr., vol., trainer Peace Corps, Afganistan, 1965-68; pub. health nurse Tufts Delta Health Ctr., Mound Bayou, Miss., 1969; coord. pub. health nursing Ill. Community Clinic, Chgo., 1970-72; nursing cons. rsch. edn. Dept. Pub. Health, Chgo., 1974-78; rsch. nurse AIDS NIH, Bethesda, Md., 1989-97; AIDS task force Interfaith Conf. Met. Washington, 1988-90. Author: Outcome Measures in Home Care, 1987, Immune-Based Therapy for HIV, 1996; contbr. article to profl. jour. V.p. women's bd. Episcopal Ch., Washington, 1981-82; mem. bd. deacons Nat. Presbyn. Ch., Washington, 1982-86; mem. Mayor's Task Force on Standards, Washington, 1985-87; vol. homeless agys. Wesley Theol. Sem. Biblical scholar, 1988; named Person of Week Washington Times, 1992. Mem. ANA (pres. local chpt. 1976-78), Assn. Nurses in AIDS Care, Phi Beta Kappa, Sigma Theta Tau. Democrat. Avocation: watercolorist. Home: 4831 Sedgwick St NW Washington DC 20016-2323

ENGLE, JEANNETTE CRANFILL, medical technologist; b. Davie County, N.C., July 7, 1941; d. Gurney Nathaniel and Versie Emmaline (Reavis) Cranfill; m. William Sherman Engle (div. 1970); children: Phillip William, Lisa Kaye. Diploma, Dell Sch. Med. Tech., 1960; BA, U. N.C., Asheville, 1976; MS in Biomed. Sci.-Genetics, Marshall U., 1999. Instr. Dell Sch. Med. Tech., Asheville, 1960-67; rotating technologist Meml. Mission Hosp., Asheville, 1967-68, asst. supr. hematology, 1968-71; supr. Damon Subs. Pvt. Clinic Lab., Asheville, 1971-73; chemistry technologist VA Med. Ctr., Durham, N.C., 1973-74, 75-76, supr., 1974-75; asst. supr. microbiology VA Med. Ctr., Salem, Va., 1976-79; supr. rsch. Med. Svc. Lab., Salem, 1979-90; flow cytometrist VA Med. Ctr., Huntington, W.Va., 1990-92, cons. to clin. lab. flow cytometry dept., 1992—; reviewer Jour. Club, Roanoke-Salem, Va., 1980-90. Author: (poem) Reflections on a Comet, 1984; contbr. numerous articles and abstracts on med. tech. to profl. jours., 1982—. Mem. The Acting Co. Ensemble. Democrat. Episcopalian. Avocations: reading, flower arranging, interior design, art, music. Home: 4775 Green Valley Rd Huntington WV 25701-9793

ENGLE, MARY ALLEN ENGLISH, physician; b. Madill, Okla., Jan. 26, 1922; d. Russell C. and Vera (Apperson) English; m. Ralph Landis Engle, Jr., June 7, 1945; children: Ralph Landis III (dec.), Marilyn Elizabeth. A.B. cum laude, Baylor U., 1942; M.D., Johns Hopkins U., 1945; D.Sc. (hon.), Iona Coll., 1982. Diplomate: in pediatric cardiology Am. Bd. Pediatrics. Intern pediatrics Johns Hopkins Hosp., 1945-46, asst. dir. pediatrics outpatient dept., 1946-47, fellow pediatric cardiology, 1947-48; instr. pediatrics Johns Hopkins U., 1946-48; asst. resident Sydenham Hosp. Contagious Diseases, Balt., 1946; asst. resident N.Y. Hosp., 1948-49, asst. attending pediatrician, 1952-60, assoc. attending pediatrician, 1960-62, attending pediatrician, 1962-92, hon. staff, 1992—; fellow in pediatrics Cornell U., N.Y.C., 1949-50, mem. faculty, 1950-92, prof., 1969-92, prof. emeritus, 1992—, Stavros S. Niarchos prof. pediatric cardiology, 1979-92, emeritus, 1992—; med. dir. Insts. in Care Premature Infant, 1952-55, dir. pediatric cardiology, 1963-92. Recipient Spence-Chapin award for contbns. to pediatrics, 1958, award of merit Philoptochos Soc. N. and S. Am., 1978, Woman of Conscience award Nat. Council Women, 1979, citation Nat. Bd. Med. Coll. Pa., 1979, Disting. Achievement award Baylor U., 1981, Disting. Alumna award Baylor U., 1988, Maurice Greenberg award N.Y. Hosp.-Cornell Med. Ctr., 1991; hon. fellow Cornell U. Med. Coll. Alumni; Mary Allen Engle Div. Pediatric Cardiology, N.Y. Hosp.-Cornell U. Med. Coll. dedicated in her honor, 1992, Johns Hopkins U. Soc. Scholars award, 1992, Alumni Assoc. Detlev Bronk award, 1993. Mem. Am. Acad. Pediat. (charter sect. cardiology, Founder's award cardiology sect. 1983), Am. Clin. and Climatological Assn. (recorder 1992—), Am. Heart Assn. (bd. dirs. 1975-78, award of merit 1975, Helen B. Taussig award 1976), N.Y. Heart Assn. (bd. dirs. 1980-86), N.Y. Acad. Medicine, N.E. Pediatric Cardiology Soc., Harvey Soc., Soc. Pediatric Rsch., Assn. European Pediatric Cardiologists (corr.), Royal Soc. Medicine (bd. dirs. Found. 1983-92, hon. bd. dirs. 1992—), Am. Coll. Cardiology (master tchr. 1969, 73, 76, trustee 1974-79, bd. govs. 1990-94, pres. N.Y. State chpt. 1991-92, Theodore and Susan Cummings Humanitarian award 1973, 76), Am. Pediatric Soc., Pediatric Cardiology Soc. Greater N.Y., N.Y. Cardiology Soc. (bd. dirs., pres. 1986-87), Soc. Scholars, Phi Beta Kappa, Alpha Omega Alpha. Presbyterian. Home: 2451 Brickell Ave PH-A Miami FL 33129 Home (summer): 27213 Baileys Neck Rd Easton MD 21601-8503

ENGLE, MOLLY, program evaluator, preventive medicine researcher, medical educator; b. Ft. Leavenworth, Kans., Apr. 12, 1947; d. Robert Thomas and Phyllis Adele (Germann) E. BSN, U. Ariz., 1971, MS, 1973, PhD, 1983. RN, Ariz. Rsch. assoc. U. Ariz., Tucson, 1979-82; program assoc. Am. Coll. Testing, Iowa City, 1982-84; instr. Sch. Medicine U. Ala., Birmingham, 1984-87, asst. prof. Sch. Medicine, 1987-94; dir. rsch. and evaluation Health East, Mpls., 1992-93; assoc. prof. dept. medicine Sch. Medicine U. Ala., Birmingham, 1994-98; assoc. prof. extension svc., dept. pub. health Oreg. State U., Corvallis, 1998—; co-dir. Geriat. Edn. Ctr., U. Ala., Birmingham, 1990-91; evaluation cons. Am. Soc. Aging, San Francisco, 1990-94, USPHS Health Resources and Svcs. Adminstrn., Bur. of Health Professions, Rockville, Md., 1996-98; cons. health svcs. rsch. and evaluation HealthEast, 1993-94. Prodr. (video series) Substance Abuse and the Pregnant Woman: A Series, 1994. Co-chair Adam Elem. Sch. Parent Tchr., Corrallis, 1999. Recipient fellowship NIMH, 1972-73, fellowship Health Scis. Consortium, 1989, Postdoctoral fellowship Gerontol. Soc. Am., 1990. Mem. Am. Evaluation Assn. (topical interest group program chair 1986—, bd. dirs. 1992-94, Svc. Recognition award 1994). Avocations: gardening, reading, travel, violin. Office: Oreg State U Extension Svc 125 Ballard Extension Hall Corvallis OR 97331-8538

ENGLE, RALPH LANDIS, JR., internist, educator; b. Phila., June 11, 1920; s. Ralph Landis and Ruth (Enck) E.; m. Mary Allen English, June 7, 1945; children: Ralph Landis III (dec.), Marilyn Elizabeth. BS, U. Fla., 1942; MD, Johns Hopkins U., 1945. Intern pathology N.Y. Hosp., 1945-46, intern medicine, 1948-49, asst. resident medicine, 1949-51, asst. attending physician, 1952-57, assoc. attending physician, 1957-69, attending physician, 1969-90, hon. staff, 1990—; Am. Cancer Soc. rsch. fellow anatomy Washington U. Med. Sch., St. Louis, 1951-52; chief div. hematology, 1960-67, chief div. med. systems and computer sci. dept. medicine N.Y. Hosp.-Cornell U. Med. Ctr., 1967-74; asst. prof. medicine Cornell U. Med. Coll., 1952-57, assoc. prof. medicine, 1957-69, prof. medicine, 1969-90, prof. emeritus, 1990—, prof. pub. health, 1973-90, prof. emeritus, 1990—, assoc. dir. Office Rsch. and Sponsored Programs, 1975-90; mem. com. sci. and tech. communications Nat. Acad. Scis.-Nat. Acad. Engring., 1967-70; chmn. Ad Hoc Task Group on Toxicol. Info., 1969-70; mem. toxicol. info. program com., div. med. scis., 1969-72, 76-78; mem. cancer clin. investigation rev. com. Nat. Cancer Inst., 1968-72, chmn. cancer control supportive svcs. rev. com., 1974-76, chmn. cancer control community activities rev. com., 1975, chmn. cancer control prevention, detection and pretreatment evaluation rev. com., 1976-78; mem. data rev. bd. statewide planning and rsch. coop. system State of N.Y. Dept. Health, 1990-92. Author: (with L.A. Wallis) Immunoglobulins, Immune Deficiency Syndromes, Multiple Myeloma and Related Disorders, 1969; also numerous articles. Served from 1st lt. to capt., M.C. AUS, 1946-48. Markle scholar in med. sci., 1952-57. Fellow ACP, N.Y. Acad. Medicine; mem. Internat. Soc. Hematology, Am. Soc. Hematology, N.Y. Soc. for Study Blood (past pres.), Soc. Exptl. Biology and Medicine, AAAS, AMA, Harvey Soc. (past sec.), Am. Clin. and Climatol. Assn., New York County Med. Soc. (past chmn. pub. health com.), Sigma Xi, Chi Phi, Nu Sigma Nu. Presbyterian. Achievements include patents for electronic perpetual calendar. Home: 2451 Brickell Ave PH-A Miami FL 33129 Home (summer): 27213 Baileys Neck Rd Easton MD 21601-8503 *Faith in God, trust in man, commitment to the responsibilities of life in the face of risk, and love of one's fellowmen are the keys to a successful and happy life.*

ENGLE, REED LAURENCE, landscape architect; b. Upper Darby, Pa., Jan. 4, 1944; s. Alexander Reed and Alice Lucille (Pickell) E.; m. Dolores Gill Dyson, Dec. 21, 1946; children: Elizabeth Gresham, Louisa Jefferis. BA, Lafayette Coll., Easton, Pa., 1967; MA in Am. History, Lehigh U., Bethlehem, Pa., 1977; M of Landscape Arch., U. Pa., 1986. Archtl. historian John M. Dickey, Media, Pa., 1976-83; hist. architect Nat. Park Svc., Phila., 1983-88, regional hist. landscape architect, 1988-89; chief cultural resources Gettysburg (Pa.) Nat. Mil. Park, 1989-94; cultural resource specialist Shenandoah Nat. Park, Luray, Va., 1994—. Author: Everything Was Wonderful: The C.C.C. in Shenandoah National Park, 1933-1942, 1999; coauthor: Story Behind the Scenery, 1998; author 22 books/hist. structure reports; contbr. numerous articles to profl. jours. Mem. Am. Soc. Landscape Architects (perservation com. 1986—). Avocations: gardening, reading, travel. Home: PO Box 44 Boston VA 22713-0044

ENGLE, STEPHEN DOUGLAS, history educator; b. Charlestown, W.Va., Feb. 26, 1962; s. Donald A. Engle; m. Stephanie D. Mickey, July 27, 1985; children: Tayla Benjamin, Caroline Claire. BA, Stepherd Coll., 1984; MA, Fla. State U., 1985, PhD, 1989. Assoc. prof. Am. history Fla. Atlantic U., Boca Raton, 1990—. Author: Yankee Dutchman, 1993, Most Promising Dutchman of All, 1999. Fulbright scholar, 1995-96. Mem. Am. Hist. Assn., Orgn. Am. Historians, Soc. Civil War Historians, Soc. German-Am. Studies. Office: Fla Atlantic U Dept History 777 Glades Rd Boca Raton FL 33431-6498

ENGLEHART, JOAN ANNE, trade association executive; b. Susquehanna, Pa., Sept. 15, 1940; d. George Louis and Muriel Elois (Washburn) Wanatt; m. Dale John Englehart, Nov. 24, 1958. AAS, Broome C.C., 1981; BS in Cultural Studies, Empire State Coll., 1984; postgrad., SUNY, Binghamton, 1984; PhD in Bus. Adminstrn., Century U., 1994. Office mgr., coord. sales Bush Transformer Corp., Endicott (N.Y.), Boston, 1959-65; mgr., cons. Snelling & Snelling, Binghamton, Endicott, 1965-71; mgr., tchr. Can. Acad., Kobe, Japan, 1971-72; owner Typewriting, Endicott, 1980-85; exec. v.p. Tioga County C. of C., Owego, N.Y., 1985-87, pres., 1988-99; exec. v.p. Chamber Found., 1987-99; cons. specializing in non-profit orgns., 1999—. Mem. scholarship com. Civic Club Binghamton, 1984-87; adv. bd. Broome and Tioga County Health Fairs, 1985-87; sec.-treas. Tioga County C. of C. Found., 1987-99; chmn. sustaining membership com. Broome United Way, Binghamton, 1986-87; planning process com. Broome-Delaware Tioga BOCES vocat. edn. coms., 1989, 92; bd. dirs. NYPENN Health Sys. Agy., 1989-91, Pvt. Industry Coun., 1994-99, Sch. to Careers, 1997-98, Tioga County Rural Ministry, 1992-97, chmn., 1993-97; pres. Tioga County divsn. Am. Heart Assn., 1994—; active Tioga County Tourism Coun., 1994-99, County Comprehensive Plan, 1994-97; v.p. Tioga County Revitalization Task Force, 1997-98; adv. com. So. Tier Rail, 1997; active Binghamton Met. Transp. Study, 1997. Recipient award Boy Scouts Am., 1979, Evening Student Assn., 1991, Friends Binghamton Libr., 1982, ATHENA award C. of C., 1986; named Woman of Achievement Broome County Status of Women Coun., 1978. Mem. AAUW (life, pres. 1986-87), So. Tier World Commerce Assn. (bd. dirs. 1992-99), Nat. Assn. Women in C. of C.'s (charter mem., Nat. Achievement award 1993, com. chmn. 1994-96), Am. C. of C. Execs., N.Y. State C. of C. Execs. (bd. dirs. 1991), Zonta (pres. Tioga County area club 1985-89, mem. internat. bd. dirs., gov. dist. II 1982-84, Woman of Achievement 1985-88). Republican. Baptist. Avocations: reading, interior design, music, photography, sports car activities. Home and Office: 4 Lancaster Dr Endicott NY 13760-4320

ENGLEHART, ROBERT WAYNE, JR., cartoonist; b. Ft. Wayne, Ind., Nov. 7, 1945; s. Robert Wayne Englehart, Sr. and Shirley Rose (Rogers) Bowers; m. Judith Ann King (div. 1986); children: Mark, Sherri; m. Patricia Ann McGrath, Mar. 16, 1947; 1 stepchild, Brian Loftus. Student, Am. Acad. Art, Chgo. Cartoonist, illustrator Chgo. Today, 1966-72; freelance artist, editorial cartoonist Jour. Gazette, Ft. Wayne, 1972-75; editorial cartoonist Jour. Herald, Dayton, Ohio, 1975-80, Hartford (Conn.) Courant, 1980—; syndicated L.A. Times-Washington Post News Svc. Author: Never Let Facts Get In The Way of A Good Cartoon, 1979, A Distinguished Panel of Experts, 1985; illustrator (children's book) 1,2,3 I Can Count, 1972; cartoons have appeared in Time, Newsweek, N.Y. Times, Washington Post, Playboy; cartoons exhibited at Widener Gallery Trinity Coll., Hartford, 1988; prodr. (video comic strip) Out There with Englehart, Conn. Pub. TV, 1986-91, (New Eng. Emmy award 1989, 90, 1st Pl. award Conn. AP Broadcasters Assn. 1988, 89); prodr. (sports video comic strip) Last Row With Englehart & McGrath, 1991-95; appeared in Broadway polit. comedi rev. Raucous Caucus, 1992. Finalist Pulitzer Prize, 1979; recipient H.L. Mencken award Free Press Assn., 1979, various awards Overseas Press Club, UN Population Inst., John Fischetti Contest, Planned Parenthood Conn. Mem. Assn. Am. Editorial Cartoonists, Nat. Cartoonists Soc. Office: Hartford Courant Co 285 Broad St Hartford CT 06115-3785*

ENGLEMAN, DENNIS EUGENE, electrical engineer; b. Falls City, Nebr., July 24, 1948; s. Eugene Adolf and Mary Alice (Franklin) E.; m. Deborah Faye Paulson, May 4, 1985; children: John Nicholas, Lily Eugenia, Mary Victoria. Student, U. Nebr., 1966-70; B in Engring. Tech., Wichita State U., 1982. Ordained to ministry Holy Order of Mans, 1977, ordained acolyte/reader Ea. Orthodox Ch., 1988. Minister various parishes, 1977-81; elec. technician Kans. Gas & Elec. Co., Wichita, 1981-82; elec. engr. Boeing Mil. Airplane Co., Wichita, 1982; design engr. Nat. Data Corp., Atlanta, 1983, Raymond Carousel Corp., Atlanta, 1984; elec. designer Cons. & Designers, Inc., Atlanta, 1984; from project engr. to engring. supr. Nordson Corp., Norcross, Ga., 1984-92, sr. engring. supr., 1992-94; project engr. ACE group, 1994-98; pres. Holy Mountain Imports, Atlanta, 1987-93, Engleman Photography Internat., Atlanta, 1989—, Liberty Imports, Atlanta; mem. dept. of ministry and evangelism Greek Orthodox Archdiocese of Vasiloupolis, 1992. Author: Ultimate Things, 1995, Beautiful America's Atlanta, 1996; co-editor: Tree of Life, 1992-97; prodr. programming People TV, Pub. Access TV, 1990-93; singer, songwriter, arranger, 1992, Pristine Records, 1993; prodr. various slide shows; writer, prodr. folk opera; contbr. over 95 articles to profl. publs. Dir. St. Cyril's Village Orch., 1987-91; mem. Atlanta Balalaika Soc. Orch., 1984-87; mem. Atlanta Mandolin Soc. Orch., 1994—; pres. Christian Cmty. Atlanta, 1985-87. Republican. Orthodox Christian. Avocations: folk music, photography.

ENGLEMAN, DONALD JAMES, lawyer, corporate executive; b. Boston, Jan. 25, 1947; s. Robert Tucker and Lillian E. (Peters) E.; m. Linda K. Knight, 1977; children: Eric, Kurt, Tracy, Jon. BA, Columbia U., 1968; JD, UCLA, 1971. Bar: Calif. 1972, D.C. 1972, N.C. 1978, Hawaii 1983. From atty. to sr. atty. to asst. gen. counsel U.S. Postal Service, Washington, 1971-77; assoc. gen. counsel Gen. Telephone Co. SE, Durham, S.C., 1977-79; sr. regulatory counsel GTE Service Corp., Stamford, Conn., 1979-82; v.p., gen. counsel Hawaiian Telephone Co., Honolulu, 1982-85, GTE Directories Corp., Dallas, 1985-89, GTE Info. Svcs., Tampa, Fla., 1985-91; v.p. law and govt. rels. GTE Info. Svcs., Dallas, 1991—. Mem. Order of Barristers, John Jay Assocs. Office: GTE Info Svcs Inc D/FW Airport PO Box 619810 Dallas TX 75261-9810

ENGLEMAN, EPHRAIM PHILIP, rheumatologist; b. San Jose, Calif., Mar. 24, 1911; s. Maurice and Tillie (Rosenberg) E.; m. Jean Sinton, Mar. 2, 1941; children—Ephraim Philip, Edgar George, Jill. B.A., Stanford U., 1933; M.D., Columbia U., 1937. Intern Mt. Zion Hosp., San Francisco; resident U. Calif., San Francisco, Jos. Pratt Diagnostic Hosp., Boston; research fellow Mass. Gen. Hosp., Boston, 1937-42; practice medicine specializing in rheumatology San Francisco, 1948—; mem. faculty U. Calif. Med. Center, San Francisco, 1949—; clin. prof. medicine U. Calif. Med. Center, 1965—; dir. Rosalind Russell Arthritis Center, 1979—; mem. staff U. Calif., Mills Meml., Peninsula hosps.; Chmn. Nat. Commn. Arthritis and Related Diseases, 1975-76. Author: The Book on Arthritis: A Guide for Patients and Their Families, 1979; also articles, chpts. in books. Served to maj. M.C. USMCR, 1942-47. Nat. Inst. Arthritis grantee; recipient citation Arthritis Found., 1973; Ephraim P. Engleman Disting. Professorship in Rheumatology established in his honor U. Calif., San Francisco, 1991. Fellow ACP; Mem. Internat. League Against Rheumatism (pres. 1981-85), Am. Coll. Rheumatology (founding fellow, master, pres. 1962-63), Nat. Soc. Clin. Rheumatologists, AMA, Am. Fedn. Clin. Research; hon. mem. Japanese Rheumatism Soc., Spanish Rheumatism Soc., Uruguay Rheumatism Soc., Australian Rheumatism Assn., Chinese Med. Assn., French Soc. Rheumatology, Internat. League against Rheumatism, Gold-Headed Cane Soc. (U. Calif., San Francisco). Republican. Jewish. Club: Family (San Francisco). Office: U Calif Rosalind Russell Med Rsch Ctr Arthritis 350 Parnassus Ave Ste 600 San Francisco CA 94117-3608

ENGLER, BRIAN DAVID, systems operations executive; b. Palmerton, Pa., Oct. 9, 1947; s. David James and Doreen Estelle (Sheldon) E.; m. Margaret Mary Hurlock, Dec. 31, 1969 (div. Apr. 1981); children: Donna, David; m. Maxine Sue Richard, May 24, 1981; children: Rachel, Stacey. BS with merit, U.S. Naval Acad., 1969; MS in Ops. Rsch., Naval Postgrad. Sch., Monterey, Calif., 1978; MBA in Fin., Acctg., Marymount U., 1986. Commd. ensign USN, 1969, advanced through grades to comdr., 1983, naval flight officer, mission comdr., ops. analyst, 1969-89, ret., 1989; ops. analyst, project leader Systems Planning and Analysis., Alexandria, Va., 1989-90; asst. program mgr. Systems Planning and Analysis., Falls Church, Va., 1990-91, program mgr., 1991—. Assoc. editor (alumni newsletter) O.R. News, 1976-78. Mem. Big Bros./ Big Sisters of Balt., Annapolis, Md., 1968-69; sec.-treas. bd. dirs. Gov.'s Sq. Homeowners Assn., Williamsburg, Va., 1989-97. Decorated Navy Commendation medals (2), Meritorious Svc. medal; recipient Juvenile Decency award Kiwanis Club, 1965, Cert. of Proficiency, Civil Air Patrol, 1963, Best Cadet award Temple U., 1965. Mem. Mil. Ops. Rsch. Soc. (bd. dirs. 1991—, sec.-treas. 1993-94, v.p. for adminstrn. 1994-95), VFW, post Junior Vice Commdr., Am. Legion, Delta Epsilon Sigma. Avocations: running, sailing, reading, music, fencing, bowling. Home: 5918 Clermont Landing Ct Burke VA 22015-2565 Office: Systems Planning and Analysis Inc 2000 N Beauregard St Ste 400 Alexandria VA 22311-1712

ENGLER, BRIAN KEITH, radio broadcast personality; b. Allentown, Pa., Dec. 3, 1966; s. Keith Roger and Darlene Ann (Williamson) E.; m. Jennifer Cavacini, June 30, 1993 (div. May 1996). Diploma, Northwestern Lehigh H.S., 1984. Prodn. editor Dun & Bradstreet, Bethlehem, Pa., 1985-96; on-air personality WODE-FM/WEEX-AM Radio, Easton, Pa., 1996—. Republican. Avocations: music, science fiction, computers, sports. Office: WODE-FM/WEEX-AM 107 Paxinosa Rd W Easton PA 18040-1344

ENGLER, JOHN, governor; b. Mt. Pleasant, Mich., Oct. 12, 1948; s. Mathias John and Agnes Marie (Neyer) E.; m. Michelle; children: Margaret Rose, Hannah Michelle, Madeleine Jenny; B.S. in Agrl. Econs., Mich. State U., 1971; J.D., Thomas M. Cooley Law Sch., 1981. Mem. Mich. Ho. of Reps., 1971-78; mem. Mich. Senate, 1979-90, Republican leader, 1983, majority leader, 1984-90; ; state senator, 1979-90; gov., 1990—. Del. White House Conf. on Youth, 1972; U.S. Trade Reps.' Intergovernmental Policy Adv. com., 1988, Intergovernmental Adv. Coun. on Edn., 1988. Bd. dirs. Mich. Spl. Olympics; chmn. Presdl. Scholars, 1991-92. Recipient Disting. Service to Agr. award Mich. Agr. Conf., 1974; named Legislator of Yr., Police Officers Assn. Mich., 1981; One of 5 Outstanding Young Men of Mich., Mich. Jaycees, 1983. Fellow State Bar Mich.; mem. Nat. Gov.'s Assn. (welfare reform task force 1993—, edn. goals panel 1993—). Republican. Roman Catholic. Club: Detroit Economic.*

ENGLER, ROBERT, political science educator, author; b. N.Y.C., July 12, 1922; s. Isidore and Esther (Haber) E.; m. Rosalind Elowitz, May 16, 1946 (div. June 1960); children: Richard J., Elise P.; m. Inea Bushnaq, Sept. 5, 1968; 1 dau., Nadya Kate. B.S.S., CCNY, 1942; M.A., U. Wis., 1946, Ph.D., 1947. Mem. faculty U. Wis., 1946-47, Syracuse U., 1947-50, Columbia U., 1959-63; prof. polit. sci. Queens Coll., CUNY, 1964-69; prof. polit. sci. Grad. Sch. and Bklyn. Coll., CUNY, 1969-91, prof. emeritus, 1991—; prof. polit. sci. Sarah Lawrence Coll., 1951-71; mem. faculty New Sch. Social Research, 1961-64; chair, vis. prof. world politics of peace and war Princeton U., 1988-89; vis. prof. U. P.R., 1961, U. Sask., 1973, Ctr. for Rsch. in Rural and Indsl. Devel., India, 1992, U. Havana, 1992, 93,; disting. vis. prof. Am. U., Cairo, 1978. Author: The Politics of Oil: Private Power and Democratic Directions, 1961, The Brotherhood of Oil: Energy Policy and the Public Interest, 1977; also articles, reviews; contbg. author: The Dissenting Academy, 1968, Winning America, 1988; editor: America's Energy: 100 Years of Struggle for the Democratic Control of Our Resources, 1980. Asst. to pres. Nat. Farmers Union, Washington, 1950-51; dir. Encampment for Citizenship, N.Y.C., 1961, 64. Served with AUS, 1943-46, ETO. Recipient Sidney Hillman Found. prize award polit. writing, 1955. Home: 444 Central Park W Apt 12F New York NY 10025-4358 Office: CUNY Grad Ctr 33 W 42nd St New York NY 10036-8099

ENGLERT, HELEN WIGGS, writer; b. Nashville, June 1, 1927; d. Lawrence Raymond and Frances Eloise (Smith) Wiggs; m. Roy Theodore Englert Sr., Sept. 25, 1948; children: Lee Ann Englert Regan, Roy Theodore Jr. AA, Ward Belmont Coll., Nashville, 1948; AB, George Washington U., Washington, 1954, postgrad., 1969-71. Lectr. Weight Watchers, Washington & Va., 1972-84. Author: Hey, Wait a Minute! Dealing with Feelings and Weight Control, 1992; contbr. articles to profl. jours. Elder Old Presbyn. Meeting House, Alexandria, Va., 1982—; bd. mem. Sr. Citizens Employment & Svcs. Inc., Alexandria, 1994-97. Mem. George Washington U. Club, Campagna Ctr. (Alexandria), Nat. Mus. Women in Arts, Phi Theta Kappa. Avocations: walking, travel, tennis, grandchild, geneology. Home: 12183 Cathedral Dr Lake Ridge VA 22192-2227

ENGLERT, ROY THEODORE, lawyer; b. Nashville, Sept. 11, 1922; s. Roy T. and Ruth Rowe (Tindall) E.; m. Helen Frances Wiggs, Sept. 25, 1948; children: Lee Ann, Roy Jr. BA, Vanderbilt U., 1943; JD, Columbia, 1951; LLM, George Washington U., 1953. Bar: Tenn. 1951, U.S. Dist. Ct. D.C. 1951, U.S. Supreme Ct. 1955, Internat. Trade 1975. Asst. counsel Office Comptroller of Currency, U.S. Treasury Dept., 1951-58, chief counsel, 1958-62, asst. gen. counsel of dept., 1962-66, dep. gen. counsel, 1966-73; sole practice Washington, 1973-96; bd. dirs., sec. Walker/Potter Assocs., Inc., Washington, 1973-96; mem. Sr. Seminarin Fgn. Policy, Dept. State, 1963-64, U.S. Assay Commn., 1975; lectr., writer on banking law. Contbr. articles to profl. jours. Judo tech. ofcl. Atlanta Olympics. Lt. USNR, 1943-46. Recipient Exceptional Service award U.S. Treasury, 1972, Gen. Counsel's award, 1973. Mem. ABA, Tenn. Bar Assn. Presbyterian. Home: 12183 Cathedral Dr Lake Ridge VA 22192-2227 Office: 6720 Bellamy Ave Springfield VA 22152-3023

ENGLERT, WALTER GEORGE, classics and humanities educator; b. Oakland, Calif., June 30, 1952; s. Walter George and Isobel Ann (O'Hearne) E.; m. Mary Ellen Mecchi; children: Francesca, Molly. BA summa cum laude, St. Mary's Coll. Calif., 1974; MA, U. Calif. Santa Barbara, 1976; postgrad., Am. Sch. Classical Studies, Athens, 1979; PhD, Stanford U., 1981. Teaching asst. U. Calif., Santa Barbara, 1974-76, Stanford U., 1977-78; vis. lectr. U. Mich., Ann Arbor, 1980-81; vis. assoc. prof. U. Calif., Berkeley, 1986, Intercollegiate Ctr. Classical Studies, Rome, 1992-93; Omar and Althea Hoskins prof. Reed Coll., Portland, Oreg., 1981—; organizer and lectr. Reed Latin Symposium for H.S. Students, 1988-97; participant TAG Spring Interdisciplinary confs., 1988; tchr. Paideia Class, 1989, 91, 96, 97, Reed MALS Seminar, 1988, 93, Reed Elderhostel Program, 1989; mem.

faculty Reed Alumni Coll., 1989, 95; lectr. Seattle Reed Alumni Group, 1991; guest Town Hall TV show, 1991. Contbr. articles to profl. jours. Grantee NEH, 1983, 95, Mellon Faculty Seminar, 1986-87, Sloan Found., 1987-88. Office: Reed Coll 3203 SE Woodstock Blvd Portland OR 97202-8138

ENGLESMITH, TEJAS, actor, producer, curator; b. London, Nov. 28, 1941; came to U.S. 1957; s. George and Lydia Julia (Johnson-Briet) E. Student in art history, U. St. Thomas, Houston, 1959-63. Asst. dir. Whitechapel Gallery, London, 1963-69; curator Contemporary Art Jewish Mus., N.Y.C., 1969-70; dir. Leo Castelli Gallery, N.Y.C., 1970-76, Max Hutchinson Gallery, Houston, 1976-78; pvt. art cons. Houston, 1978-80; auction mgr. Sta. KUHT-TV, Houston, 1980-84, exec. prodr., 1980-86, assoc. dir., devel. managing editor Public Times, 1984-86; prodr., announcer Sta. KUHF-FM, Houston, 1987-90; ind. broadcast cons. and prodr. Houston, 1990—; subscriber svcs./pub. rels. rep. Theatre Under the Stars, Houston, 1992-99; judge Roanoke (Va.) Art Festival, 1972; judge, lectr. S.W. Tex. State U., San Marcos, 1978. Narrator: (film) Pas de Deux: A Dance of Two Countries: China and America, 1980, Just a Closer Walk With Thee, 1989, The English Countryside, 1992 (Silver Telly award narration 1994), Hall of the Americas Houston Mus. of Natural Sciences, 1998, numerous travel and indsl. videos; interviewee: Inflatable Sculpture, CBS-TV, 1969, Views on Art, Sta. WNYC-FM, 1975, Curtain!, Sta. KUHT-TV, 1980-81; prodr./host: Conversations with People in Arts, Sta. KPFT-FM, 1977; exec. prodr. 30th Anniversary Sta. KUHT Sock Hop, 1983; writer mus. catalogues; organizer various exhbns. Mem. selection com. N.Y. Drawing Soc., 1970; reader Taping For the Blind, 1987—; adv. bd. Cultural Arts Council Houston, 1978. Recipient Silver award Assn. for Community TV, 1981, Gold award Assn. for Community TV, 1982. Fellow Royal Soc. Arts. Club: TLC Four Seasons. E-mail: tejase@msn.com. Home: 7839 Fondren Rd Houston TX 77074-4601 Office: Pastorini/Bosby Talent Agy 3013 Fountain View Dr Houston TX 77057-6124 *The learning and practice of good manners would alleviate most of the problems we face today . . . and tomorrow.*

ENGLISH, BETTY JO BOONE, programming educator; b. Suffolk, Va., Sept. 22, 1952; d. Robert Simon and Katherine Irene (Stringfield) B.; m. William Edwin English, Sept. 10, 1977; children: Robin, Melissia, William, Stephen, Katherine. BS, James Madison U., Harrisonburg, Va., 1974. Teaching cert. in Bus. edn., Va. Jr. programmer Smith Transfer Corp., Staunton, Va., 1974-75; programmer, analyst S & K Sales Inc., Norfolk, Va., 1976; programming instr. ECPI or Norfolk, 1976-77; bus. edn. tchr. The Pruden Ctr. for Industry and Tech., Suffolk, Va., 1977—; ednl. presenter Classroom Connect, El Sequndo, Calif., 1997-98. Contbr. articles to profl. jours. Bd. dirs., pres. The Suffolk Va. Employees Fed. Credit Union, 1991—; co-chmn. Goober Gang, The Peanut Fest, Inc., Suffolk, Va., 1996-98. Named Walter Shell Va. Bus. Educator of Yr., Va. Bus. Edn. Assn., Fiarfax, 1997, Suffolk Pub. Sch. H.S. Tchr. of Yr., 1999. Mem. Va. Bus. edn. Assn., Va. Soc. of Tech. in Edn. E-mail address: benglish@whro.net. Fax: 757-539-0733. Home: 5403 Pruden Blvd Suffolk VA 23434 Office: The Pruden Ctr for Industry and Tech 4169 Pruden Blvd Suffolk VA 23434

ENGLISH, BRUCE VAUGHAN, environmental consultant; b. Richmond, Va., Aug. 6, 1921; s. Pollard and Lucy Kelly (Rice) E.; m. Virginia Tejas McCall Shaw, Feb. 6, 1949. BS in Physics and Math., Randolph-Macon Coll., 1942; MS in Physics and Math., Ind. U., 1943; PhD in Physics, U. Va., 1958. Grad. asst. instr. army specialized tng. program/rsch. asst. Manhattan Dist. Engrs. Project; physics instr. Ind. U., Bloomington; asst. prof. physics army specialized tng. program Randolph-Macon Coll., Ashland, Va., 1943-44, assoc. prof., acting chmn. dept. physics, 1948-58, prof., chmn. dept., 1958-64; physicist, head high pressure lab. U.S. Navy Underwater Sound Reference Lab., Orlando, Fla., 1946-48; physicist, cons. historic preservation, pollution control and environment Ashland, 1964—; dir. Poe Found., Inc., Richmond, 1968-97, pres., 1973-92, life hon. pres., 1998—; pres., dir. Edgar Allan Poe Mus., Richmond, 1973-92; pres. Pollution Control Assocs., Richmond, 1967-70. Co-pub.: Poe's Richmond, 1978; columnist Herald-Progress, 1971—; contbr. numerous articles to Poe Messenger mag. Founding mem. Richmond Symphony, 1956; mem. Patrick Henry Scotchtown Com., Hanover County, Va., 1958—; pres. Hist. Richmond Found., 1967-70; bd. dirs. Church Hill Model Neighborhood Bd., Richmond, 1968-73; chmn. Bicentennial Com. for Hanover County, 1974-92, Drainage Com., Ashland, 1980s, Courthouse Com. for Hanover County, 1985—; lay reader, mem. vestry St. John's Ch., Church Hill, Richmond, Va., 1969-70; hon. pres. Poe Found., Inc., 1998. With USN, 1944-45. Named Hon. Citizen State of Md., 1990; Ford Faculty fellow, 1951-52, Danforth fellow, 1956-57, du Pont fellow, 1957-58. Mem. AAAS, Am. Phys. Soc., Va. Acad. Sci., Va. Hist. Soc., Nat. Trust for Hist. Preservation, Irish Georgian Soc., Cousteau Soc. (founding), Air and Waste Mgmt. Assn., Nat. Soc. for Clean Air Gt. Britain, Soc. Descendants of Peter Francisco (founder, advisor), City Tavern Club, Commonwealth Club, Farmington Country Club, Downtown Club, Phi Beta Kappa, Sigma Xi, Omicron Delta Kappa, Chi Beta Phi, Pi Delta Epsilon. Episcopalian. Achievements include research for project developing atomic bomb; increasing awareness of hazards of pollution since 1955, of Edgar Allan Poe's cosmology, cryptography, and other scientific writings.

ENGLISH, CHARLES BRAND, retired lawyer; b. Urbana, Ohio, June 10, 1924; s. Edwin L. and Margaret (Br) E.; m. Constance Coulter, 1946 (dec. 1953); 1 child, Thomas C.; m. Eva Uber, Oct. 3, 1954; children: Gwendolyn, Carolyn (dec.). Student, Dartmouth, 1941-42, Denison U., 1942-43; AB, U. Mich., 1944, LLB., 1947; LHD (hon.), Urbana U., 1978. Bar: Ohio 1947. Pvt. practice law Urbana, 1947-87; ret., 1987, farm mgr., 1950-60; bd. dirs. Milk Producers Union, Cin., 1957-62, Nat. Milk Producers Fedn., 1966-69; v.p. Cin. Milk Sales Assn., 1966-72, dir., 1962-72. Contbr. articles to jours. Mem. bd. edn. Triad Sch. Dist., 1951-59, Glen Helen Adv. Bd. Antioch Coll., 1959-76; open space legal adviser Com. for Country Common, 1963-76; mem. Ohio Land Use Rev. Adv. Council, 1976-77; trustee Urbana Coll., 1966-77, vice chmn., 1969-73, sec., 1973-76; bd. dirs. Assn. Ind. Colls. and Univs. Ohio, 1969-77, Ohio Citizens' Council for Health and Welfare, 1973-77; mem. Champaign County Bd. Mental Retardation, 1967-75. Named One of Hon. 100 alumni Ohio State U. Sch. Natural Resources, 1970; co-honoree The Eva and Charles B. English Fine Arts Scholarship Champaign County Arts Coun., 1988. Mem. ABA, Ohio Bar Assn., Champaign County Bar Assn. (pres. 1958), Ohio Conservation Found. (trustee 1969-85, sec.-treas. 1969-73), Am. Humanist Assn. (bd. dirs. 1957-66, sec. 1959-66), Fellowship of Religious Humanists (bd. dirs., sec. 1967-72), Community Water Resources Com. Champaign County (co-chmn. 1970-71), S.W. Ohio Water Devel. Study (adv. bd. 1969-72), The Legacy Club, Nature Conservancy. Unitarian. Home: Raiffeisenweg 7, 86923 Finning Germany

ENGLISH, CHERYL ANN, medical technologist; b. West Palm Beach, Fla., Sept. 18, 1960; d. William Ernest III and Sandra (McLaren) Tydings; m. Gary Marvin English, Dec. 22, 1984; 1 child, Nathan Kyle. AAS, Southwestern Tech. Coll., Sylva, N.C., 1984. Cert. med. technologist, Am. Med. Technolgists. Med. technologist Ridgecrest Hosp., Clayton, Ga., 1985-93, Stephens County Hosp., Toccoa, Ga., 1993-97, 1998—; med. technologist Rabun County Meml. Hosp., Clayton, 1997—. Baptist. Avocations: photography, hiking, camping, swimming, roller skating. Home: RR 2 Box 2292 Clayton GA 30525-9627

ENGLISH, DONALD MARVIN, loss control representative; b. Raleigh, N.C., July 31, 1951; s. Marvin Lee and Lois (Woodard) E.; m. Rebecca Pritchard, Sept. 3, 1970 (div. 1977); m. Kathryn A. Sumner, July 3, 1993 (div. 1998). Student, Miami U., Oxford, Ohio, 1969-70, 73-74, U. Cin., 1977-78, Calif. State U., Fresno, 1980—; AA, Fresno City Coll., 1991. Cert. safety profl. Bd. Cert. Safety Profls. Ins. inspector Comml. Services, Cin., 1974-78, Ohio Casualty Ins. Co., Fresno, 1978-93; owner Loss Control Systems, Renton, Wash., 1993; sr. loss control specialist Scott Wetzel Svcs., Inc., Federal Way, Wash., 1993-96; loss control territory mgr. Am. States Ins. Co., Seattle, 1996—. Served with U.S. Army, 1970-73. Mem. Am. Soc. Safety Engrs., Soc. CPCU (cert.), Ins. Inst. Am. (assoc. in loss control mgmt. 1990), East Fresno Exch. Club (pres. 1984-85). Avocation: internat. traveling. Home: 6520 146th St SW Edmonds WA 98026-3523 Office: 6021 244th St SW Mountlake Terrace WA 98043-5400

ENGLISH, FLOYD LEROY, telecommunications company executive; b. Nicholas, Calif., June 10, 1934; s. Elvan L. and Louise (Corliss) E.; children from previous marriage: children: Roxane, Darryl; m. Elaine Ewell, July 3, 1981; 1 child, Christine. AB in Physics, Calif. State U., Chico, 1959; MS in Physics, Ariz. State U., 1962, PhD in Physics, 1965. Divsn. supr. Sandia Labs., Albuquerque, 1965-73; gen. mgr. Rockwell Internat.-Collins, Newport Beach, Calif., 1973-75; pres. Darcom, Albuquerque, 1975-79; cons in energy mgmt. and acquisitions Albuquerque, 1979-80; v.p. U.S. ops. Andrew Corp., Orland Park, Ill., 1980-82, pres., 1982—, COO, 1982-83, CEO, 1983—, also bd. dirs., 1982—, chmn. bd. dirs., 1994—; bd. dirs. Internat. Engrng. Consortium. Contbr. articles to profl. jours. Bd. dirs. Ill. Math. and Sci. Acad. Fund for Advancement of Edn. 1st lt. U.S. Army, 1954-57; capt. Res., 1957-69. Mem. IEEE, Execs. Club of Chgo. (bd. dirs.). Republican. Presbyterian. Office: Andrew Corp 10500 W 153rd St Orland Park IL 60462-3071

ENGLISH, HENRY L., not-for-profit association executive; b. West Point, Miss., May 27, 1942; s. Flozell and Julie Pearl (Smith) E.; m. Denise Tulloch, Sept. 11, 1989; children: Nkrumah, Kenya, Jumaane, Kalmilah. Student, Malcolm X Coll., 1966-69; BA, U. N.H., 1972; MPA, Cornell U., 1974. Asst. dir. devel. Kittrell (N.C.) Coll., 1974-75; asst. adminstr. Jackson Park Hosp., Chgo., 1975-77; dir. planning, mktg. South Chgo. Hosp., 1977-85; pres., CEO Black United Fund of Ill., Chgo., 1985—. Co-chmn. United Black Voters of Ill., 1077-79; mem. Coalition to Save S. Shore Country Club, 1980-84; bd. dirs. COMPRAND, Ill., 1981-86; commr. Calumet Dist. Boy Scouts Am., Chgo., 1982-84. Named fellow Woodrow Wilson Nat. Fellowship Found., 1972-74; recipient Leadership award Boy Scouts Am., Chgo., 1983, Appreciation award, Svc. award Clara's House Shelter, Chgo., 1995. Mem Nat. Health Care Execs., Blacks in Devel. (Appreciation award 1993). Office: Black United Fund Ill 1809 E 71st St Chicago IL 60649-2000

ENGLISH, JAMES FAIRFIELD, JR., former college president; b. Putnam, Conn., Feb. 15, 1927; s. James Fairfield and Alice Bradford (Welles) E.; m. Isabelle Spotswood Cox, July 9, 1955; children: Alice, James Fairfield, Margaret, William. Grad., Loomis Sch., 1944; BA, Yale U., 1949; MA, Cambridge (Eng.) U., 1951; JD, U. Conn., 1956; HLD, Northeastern U., 1982, Trinity Coll., 1989; LLD, U. Hartford, 1971, St. Joseph Coll., West Hartford, Conn., 1982. With Conn. Bank & Trust Co., Hartford, 1951—, sr. v.p., 1961-63, exec. v.p., 1963-66, pres., 1966-70, chmn. bd., 1970-80; v.p. fin. and planning Trinity Coll., Hartford, 1977-81, pres., 1981-89. Bd. dirs. Mystic Seaport Mus. With AUS, 1944-46. Episcopalian. Home: 31 Potter St Groton CT 06340-5734 also: 777 Prospect Ave West Hartford CT 06105-4204

ENGLISH, JOHN DWIGHT, lawyer; b. Evanston, Ill., Mar. 28, 1949; s. John Francis English and Mary Faye (Taylor) Butler; m. Claranne Kay Lundeen, Apr. 22, 1972; children: Jennifer A., Katharine V., Margaret E. BA, Drake U., 1971; JD, Loyola U., 1976. Bar: Ill. 1976, U.S. Dist. Ct. (no. dist.) Ill. 1976, U.S. Tax Ct. 1977. Assoc. Bentley DuCanto Silvestri & Forkins, Chgo., 1976-79; ptnr. Silvestri Mahoney English & Zdeb, Chgo., 1979-81; assoc. Coffield Ungaretti & Harris, Chgo., 1981-83, ptnr., 1983—; instr. estate planning Loyola U., Chgo., 1982-87. Bd. dirs. Prince of Peace Luth. Sch., Chgo., 1977-83, Bethesda Home for the Aged, Chgo., 1981-89, Luth. Family Home Mission, Chgo., 1985-91; alderman Park Ridge (Ill.) City Coun., 1991-95. Mem. Ill. State Bar Assn., Chgo. Bar Assn. (chmn. div. II probate practice com.), Phi Beta Kappa. Lutheran. Home: 631 Wisner St Park Ridge IL 60068-3428 Office: Ungaretti & Harris 3500 Three 1st Nat Bank Plz Chicago IL 60602

ENGLISH, JOSEPH THOMAS, physician, medical administrator; b. Phila., May 21, 1933; m. Ann Carr Sanger, Dec. 20, 1969; 3 children. AB, St. Joseph's Coll., 1954; MD, Jefferson Med. Coll., 1958. Intern Jefferson Med. Coll. Hosp., Phila., 1958-59; resident in psychiatry Inst. of Pa. Hosp., Phila., 1959-61, NIMH, Bethesda, Md., 1961-62; practice psychiatry, 1962—; psychiatrist Office of Dir., NIMH, 1964-65, asst. chief policy and program coordination, 1965-66, dept. chief office interagy. liaison, 1966; chief psychiatrist med. program div. Peace Corps, Washington, 1962-66; dep. asst. dir. health affairs OEO, Washington, 1966, asst. dir., 1966-68; adminstr. Health Services and Mental Health Adminstrn., HEW, 1968-70; pres. N.Y.C. Health and Hosps. Corp., 1970-73; chmn. dept. psychiatry St. Vincent's Hosp. and Med. Ctr., N.Y.C., 1973—; prof. psychiatry, chmn. dept. psychiatry N.Y. Med. Coll., N.Y.C., 1979—, assoc. dean, 1979—; adj. prof. psychiatry Cornell U.; lectr. psychiatry Harvard U., 1978-89; vis. fellow Woodrow Wilson Nat. Fellowship Found., 1979—; chmn. interagy. task force emergency food and med. program for U.S. OEO-HEW, U.S. Dept. Agrl., 1968-69; chmn. Alaska Subcom. Fed. Health Programs Pres.'s Rev. Commn. Alaska, 1969-71; chmn. adv. com. on accessible environments for disabled Bldg. Rsch. Adv. Bd., Washington, 1974-76; chmn. exec. coord. panels on mental health svcs. delivery Pres.'s Commn. on Mental Health, 1977; mem. Health Adv. Coun. Gov. State N.Y., 1981; mem. profl. and tech. adv. com. for hosps. and accreditation program Joint Commn. Accreditation Hosps., 1984-86, vice chmn., 1986-88, chmn., 1988-89; mem. adv. panel on financing of psychiat. care NIMH, 1985-87; mem. commr.'s adv. com. N.Y.C. Dept. Mental Health, Mental Retardation and Alcoholism Svc., 1980-92; bd. dirs., chmn. nat. clin. adv. bd. Healthcare Svcs. Am., Inc., 1985-87. Author spl. reports on Peace Corps, other govtl. programs; editorial bd. The Psychiatric Times, 1985—; contbr. articles to profl. jours. Bd. dirs. Kennedy Child Study Ctr., 1975-93; trustee Menninger Found., 1993—, Sarah Lawrence Coll., 1986-90. Served to capt. USAF Res., 1958-63; sr. surgeon USPHS, 1963-66. Named One of Outstanding Young Men of Year U.S. Jr. C. of C., 1964; recipient John XXIII medal Coll. New Rochelle, N.Y., 1966; Meritorious award for exemplary achievement pub. adminstrn. William A. Jump Meml. Found., 1966; Flemming award, also personal commendation Pres. of U.S., 1968. Fellow Am. Psychiat. Assn. (pres. 1992-93, chmn. coun. on econ. affairs 1983-85, chmn. task force on prospective payment 1983—, chmn. task force and strategic planning 1993—), N.Y. Acad. Medicine, Am. Coll. Psychiatrists, Inst. Medicine of Nat. Acad. Scis.; mem. AMA, N.Y. Psychiat. Soc., Hosp. Soc. N.Y., Assn. for Acad. Psychiatry, N.Y. State Med. Soc., Am. Assn. Gen. Hosp. Psychiatrists, Group Advancement Psychiatry, Am. Coll. Mental Health Adminstrs., Am. Hosp. Assn., Greater N.Y. Hosp. Assn. (chmn. mental health and substance abuse svcs. com. 1975—), Cath. Health Assn. (com. on govt. rels. 1984-87), World Psychiatric Soc. (chmn. sect. on religion and psychiatry 1994—), Alpha Omega Alpha, Kappa Beta Phi, Alpha Sigma Nu. Office: St Vincent's Hosp & Med Ctr 203 W 12th St New York NY 10011-7762*

ENGLISH, JUJUAN BONDMAN, women's health nurse, educator; b. El Dorado, Ark., Dec. 16, 1947; d. Irvin Raymond and Ida Ruth (Payton) Bondman; m. Frederick J. English, Aug. 28, 1976; children: Michael, Christopher, Meagan. ADN, So. State Coll., Magnolia, Ark., 1970; BSN, U. Ark., 1988; MSN, U. Miss., 1992. Cert. childbirth educator. Charge nurse Union Med. Ctr., El Dorado; charge nurse Warner Brown Hosp., El Dorado, labor and delivery supr.; instr. nursing U. Ark., Monticello, asst. prof. nursing, 1993-95; dir. nursing edn. Area Health Edn. Ctr.-South Ark., 1995—; coord. Parenting Coalition of South Ark. Chair teen pregnancy prevention com. TEA Coalition for Union County. Mem. ANA (Ho. Dels. 1997, 98), Nat. Perinatal Assn., Ark. State Nurses Assn. (mem. strategic planning com., sec. 1994-96, pres.-elect 1996-97, pres. 1997-99, mem. exec. com., Outstanding Dist. Pres. 1994), Ark. Nursing Coalition (steering com., Salute to Nursing com. chair), So. Nursing Rsch. Soc. (rsch. reviewer for D. Jean Wood award 1993), Nat. League Nursing, Ark. League Nursing, So. Regional Heideggerian Hermeneutrical Inst., So. Ark. Breast Feeding Coalition (chair edn. com.), Assn. Women's Health, Obs. & Neonatal Nurses, Sigma Theta Tau.

ENGLISH, MARK EDWARD, Latin educator; b. New Haven, Conn., Jan. 21, 1953; s. Hubert M. and Betty Jo (Richards) E. BA, Yale U., 1975, Cambridge (Eng.) U., 1977; MA, Cambridge (Eng.) U., 1982. Rsch. fellow Wing Short-Title Catalog Revision Project, New Haven, 1981-94; instr. English U. New Haven, 1986-90; instr. Latin Laurelton Hall, Milford, Conn., 1989, So. Ct. State U., New Haven, 1990-96. Mem. Am. Classical League, Classical Assn. of New Eng. Anglican. Avocations: piano, opera, literary translation. Home: 6337 Yale Sta New Haven CT 06520

ENGLISH, MARLENE CABRAL, management consultant; b. Lawrence, Mass., Apr. 28, 1954; d. Amick John and Mary Rose (Vasconcelos) Cabral; m. Richard Gayle English, June 24, 1978. BBA, U. Mass., 1976. Acct. mgr. Revlon, Inc., N.Y.C., 1977-79; tech. rep. Rapidata, Inc., N.Y.C., 1979-80; mgr.acctg. systems group Pannell, Kerr, Forster, Dallas, 1980-83; mgmt. cons. Blythe/Nelson, Dallas, 1983-84, Prism Cons., Arlington, Tex., 1984—; sec., treas. Highland-Avery Industries, Inc., Dallas, 1988-95. Author: And God Created Woman, 1995. Tech. systems procurement & installation Rep. Nat. Conv., Dallas, 1984; dir. Faith Harvest Ministries, Inc., Dallas, 1990-95; sys. cons. Van Cliburn Internat. Piano Competition, Ft. Worth, 1985. Catholic. Avocations: antique linen restoration, gardening, writing, Christian works for children, classical piano. Home: 4320 Rambling Creek Dr Arlington TX 76016-3418 Office: Prism Cons 4320 Rambling Creek Dr Arlington TX 76016-3418

ENGLISH, NICHOLAS CONOVER, lawyer; b. Elizabeth, N.J., Apr. 12, 1912; s. Conover and Sara Elizabeth (Jones) E.; m. Agnes N. Perry, Mar. 18, 1939 (div. 1947); children—Henry H. P., Anne Whitall (Mrs. Edward J. Wardwell); m. Eleanor Morss, May 1, 1948; children—Priscilla English Vincent, Sara (dec.), Sherman, Eleanor English Folta. Grad., Pingry Sch., 1929; AB magna cum laude, Princeton, 1934; LL.B., Harvard, 1937. Bar: N.J. bar 1937. Since practiced in Newark; partner firm McCarter & English, 1947-77, of counsel, 1978—. Bd. dirs. Summit (N.J.) YMWCA, 1950-57, Newark YMCA; chmn. exec. com. Ctrl. Atlantic Area YMWCA, 1957-63; mem. nat. coun. YMCA, 1954, 58-81, v.p., 1959-60, mem. nat. bd., 1960-71, 73-81, vice chmn., 1969-71, treas., 1977-81; trustee N.J. Nat. Land Trust, 1983-93, Kent Place Sch., 1959—, pres., 1961-72, Pingry Sch., 1954-73; bd. dirs. Nat. Legal Aid Assn., 1953-56. Lt. USNR, 1943-46. Mem. ABA (ho. of dels. 1957-58), N.J. Bar Assn., Essex County Bar Assn., Am. Bible Soc. (bd. trustees 1964-93, sr. trustee 1993—), Am. Law Inst., Princeton Club (N.Y.C.). Republican. Congregationalist. Home: 46 Meadow Lks Apt 04L Hightstown NJ 08520-3332 Office: McCarter & English 4 Gateway Ctr 100 Mulberry St Newark NJ 07101-0652

ENGLISH, PHILIP SHERIDAN, congressman; b. Erie, Pa., June 20, 1956; s. John Sr. and Otilie English; m. Christiane Weschler. BA in Polit. Sci., U. Pa., 1978. Contr. City of Erie, Pa., 1986-90; chief of staff Senator Melissa Hart, Harrisburg, Pa., 1990-92; ex-dir. Pa. Senate Fin. Com., Harrisburg, 1992-94; rep. Pa. 21st dist. 104th-106th Congress, 1995—; mem. ways and means com. Republican. Roman Catholic. Avocations: hiking, history, archaeology. Office: US Ho of Reps 1410 Longworth HOB Washington DC 20515-3821*

ENGLISH, RAY, library administrator; b. Brevard, N.C., Dec. 11, 1946; s. Daniel Leon and Lois (Dorsett) E.; m. Allison Scott Ricker, Oct. 19, 1985; children: John, Michael. AB with honors in German, Davidson Coll., 1969; MA in German Lit., U. N.C., 1971, MSLS, 1977, PhD, 1978. Teaching asst. German dept. U. N.C., Chapel Hill, 1970-73, 74-75, rsch. asst., 1976; reference libr. Alderman Libr. U.Va., Charlottesville, Va., 1977-79; head reference libr. Oberlin (Ohio) Coll. Libr., 1979-89, assoc. dir., 1986-90; dir. librs. Oberlin (Ohio) Coll., 1990—; acad. advisor Oberlin Coll., 1980—, lectr. in German, 1986—; vis. lectr. Sch. Libr. Sci., U. N.C., Chapel Hill, 1981. Contbr. articles to profl. jours. German Acad. Exchange Svc. fellow, 1973-74. Mem. ALA, Assn. Coll. and Rsch. Librs., Libr. Adminstrn. and Mgmt. Assn., Acad. Libr. Assn. Ohio. Home: 83 S Cedar St Oberlin OH 44074-1559 Office: Oberlin Coll Library 148 W College St Oberlin OH 44074-1575

ENGLISH, R(OBERT) BRADFORD, marshal; b. Jefferson City, Mo., Apr. 12, 1952; s. Robert Deaton and Peggy Louise (Dickson) E.; m. Marsha Lynn Mills, Mar. 17, 1979; children: Lindsay Renee, Amy Leigh. BS in Criminal Justice, Lincoln U., 1982; MPA, U. Mo., 1984. Residential juvenile counselor Cole County Juvenile Ctr., Jefferson City, Mo., 1972-74; patrolman Jefferson City Police Dept., 1975-76, detective, 1976-78; comdr. Mo. Capitol Police, Jefferson City, 1978-79, police chief, 1979-94; marshal U.S. Marshal Svc., Kansas City, Mo., 1994—; chmn. ct. security com. U.S. Dist. Ct. (we. dist.) Mo., Kansas City, 1995—. Chmn. bd. dirs. Capitol Area Cmty. Svc. Agy., Jefferson City, 1994. Named Statesman of Month, News Tribune Co., 1994. Mem. Am. Soc. Indsl. Security (cert. protection profl.), Internat. Assn. Chiefs of Police, Internat. Assn. Bomb Technicians and Investigators, Masons. Democrat. Avocations: golf, scuba diving, walking, weight lifting. Office: US Marshal Svc 811 Grand Blvd Ste 509 Kansas City MO 64106-1904*

ENGLISH, ROBERT JOSEPH, electronic corporation executive; b. Jersey City, Dec. 5, 1932; s. John Joseph and Mary (Budrawiz) E.; m. Robyn Adele Allan, Dec. 27, 1958; children: Robert Joseph, Mark Allan, John Frederick. B.S., St. Peters Coll., 1954; LL.B., Georgetown U., 1958; M.B.A., NYU, 1963. Bar: D.C. 1958, N.J. 1959, N.Y. 1984. Subcontract adminstr. ITT Fed. Labs. div. Nutley, N.J., 1959-60; with Fed. Electric Corp., Paramus, N.J., 1960—; sec., gen. counsel Fed. Electric Corp., 1964-66, dir. legal contracts, 1967-70; gen. counsel ITT Govt. and Comml. Services Group, 1970-72; v.p., sec., gen. counsel ITT Def. Communications and ITT Avionics divs., Nutley, 1972—; sec., gen. counsel Internat. Electric Corp., 1972—; dir. ITT Fed. Support Services Inc., ITT Tech. Services Inc., Intelex Systems Inc., Providence, Base Services Inc., Paramus, Internat. Standard Engrng. Inc., Paramus. Author: Business Contract Forms, Federal Government Subcontract Forms; contbr. articles to profl. jours. Trustee Mahwah Hist. Soc., N.J., 1978—. Served to 1st lt., Chem. Corps, U.S. Army, 1954-56. Mem. Am., Bergen, N.J., D.C., N.Y. bar assns., Phi Delta Phi. Home: 36 Sunnyside Rd Mahwah NJ 07430-1418 Office: 492 River Rd Nutley NJ 07110-3609

ENGLISH, STEPHEN F., lawyer; b. Portland, Oreg., Jan. 17, 1948. BA with honors, U. Oreg., 1970; JD, U. Calif., San Francisco, 1973. Bar: Oreg. 1973; U.S. Dist. Ct. Oreg. 1973; U.S. Ct. Appeals (9th cir.) Oreg. 1980; U.S. Supreme Ct. 1982. Ptnr. Bullivant Houser Bailey, Portland, Oreg., 1983—; mem. faculty Hastings Coll. Trial Advocacy, 1998—. Mem. ABA (vice-chair products liability com., 1996—, chair self insurers and risk mgrs. com. 1994-95, editor Self Insurers Newsletter 1987-89, chair non-profit, charitable and religious orgns. com. 1990-92), Multnomah County Bar Assn., Oreg. State Bar Assn. (chair 1990-91, exec. com. 1987-91), Am. Bd. of Trial Adv. (treas. Oreg. chpt. 1996-98, sec. Oreg. chpt. 1998—), Oreg. Assn. of Def. Counsel (chair products liability practice group 1997-98), Def. Rsch. Inst. Office: Bullivant Houser Bailey 300 Pioneer Tower 888 SW 5th Ave Ste 300 Portland OR 97204-2089

ENGLISH, STEPHEN RAYMOND, lawyer; b. Key West, Nov. 25, 1946; s. Jack Raymond and Jean Clyde (Peightal) E.; m. Molly Munger, Oct. 7, 1978; children: Nicholas, Alfred. BA, UCLA, 1975; JD, Harvard U., 1975. Bar: Calif. 1975, U.S. Dist. Ct. (cen. dist.) Calif. 1976, U.S. Dist. Ct. (so. dist.) Calif. 1978, U.S. Dist. Ct. (ea. dist.) Calif. 1988, U.S. Ct. Appeals (9th cir.) 1992. Assoc. Agnew, Miller & Carlson, L.A., 1975-78; assoc. Morgan, Lewis & Bockius, L.A., 1978-85, ptnr., 1985-98; ptnr. English, Munger & Rice, L.A., 1998—; lawyer rep. Ninth Cir. Jud. Conf., 1996-97. Pres. bd. dirs. Pub. Counsel, L.A., 1988-89, Inner City Law Ctr., L.A., 1992-93. Mem. L.A. County Bar Assn. (mem. barristers exec. com. 1980-82, trustee 1990-92, chair pro bono coun. 1990-92, chair legal svcs. for poor 1993-95, mem. exec. com. litigation sect. 1994—), L.A. County Bar Found. (pres. 1998—). Office: English Munger & Rice 801 S Grand Ave Los Angeles CA 90017-4613

ENGLISH, WILLIAM DESHAY, lawyer; b. Piedmont, Calif., Dec. 25, 1924; s. Munro and Mabel (Michener) English; m. Nancy Ames, Apr. 7, 1956; children: Catherine, Barbara, Susan, Stephen. AB in Econs., U. Calif., Berkeley, 1948; JD, U. Calif., 1951. Bar: Calif. 1952, D.C. 1972. Trial atty, spl. asst. to atty. gen. U.S. Dept. Justice, Washington, 1953-55; sr. atty. AEC, Washington, 1955-62; legal advisor U.S. Mission to European Communities, Brussels, 1962-64; asst. gen. counsel internat. matters COMSAT, Washington, 1965-73; counsel Internat. Telecommunication Satellite Orgn., 1965-73; v.p., gen. counsel, dir. COMSAT Gen. Corp., 1973-76; sr. v.p. legal and govtl. affairs Satellite Bus. Systems, McLean, Va., 1976-86; v.p., gen. counsel Satellite Transponder Leasing Corp. (IBM), McLean, 1986-87; pvt. practice, McLean, 1987—; counsel Am. Space Transp. Assn., 1987-93, Washington Space Bus. Roundtable; gen. counsel Iridium, LLC, 1992-96, spl. counsel, 1996—. With USAAF, 1943-45. Decorated air medal. Fellow Coun. on Econ. Regulation, 1985-91; mem. ABA, AIAA (chmn. com. legal aspects aeronautics and astronautics, chmn. allocation space launch risks subcom. 1987, chmn. orbital debris legal subcom.), Am. Competitive Telecommunications Assn. (bd. dirs. 1976-84, pres. 1983), D.C. Bar Assn.,

Fed. Communications Bar Assn., State Bar Calif., Fgn. Policy Discussion Group, Metropolitan. Home: 7420 Exeter Rd Bethesda MD 20814-2352*

ENGLISH, WOODROW DOUGLAS, lawyer; b. San Antonio, Dec. 1, 1941; s. Woodie Douglas Jr. and June Louise (Wasik) E.; m. Marcia Anne Mathwig, Dec. 19, 1969 (div. Aug. 1981); children: Kristina Renee, David Douglas; m. Carol Jordan, July 11, 1987; children: Leanne Alexander Cassidy, Lisa Alexander Cook. BS in Physics, Trinity U., 1967; JD, Western State U., 1981. Bar: Calif. 1989, U.S. Patent Office 1982, U.S. Supreme Ct. 1992. Sales engr. Mfrs. Rep., Seattle, 1972-75; real estate salesperson, broker Sherwood & Roberts Realtors & Coldwell Banker, Seattle, 1975-78; safety engr. Boeing Aerospace, Seattle, 1978-79; ins. agt., broker Farmers Ins. Group, San Diego, 1979-81; U.S. patent agt. Dept. Def., China Lake, Calif., 1981-87; corp. counsel Del Mar Avionics, Irvine, Calif., 1987-97; pvt. practice Ventura, Calif., 1991—; real estate broker, Ventura, ins. broker, Ventura. Capt. USAF, 1961-65. Mem. Masons, Shriners, Elks, Kiwanis, Am. Legion, Sigma Pi Sigma, Phi Alpha Delta, Nu Beta Epsilon. Republican. Avocation: flying. Home: 1215 Lost Point Ln Oxnard CA 93030-6770 Office: County Sq Profl Offices 674 County Square Dr Ventura CA 93003-5454

ENGLUND, GAGE BUSH, dancer, educator; b. Birmingham, Ala., Sept. 7, 1931; d. Morris Williams and Margaret Wallace (Gagé) Bush; student Sweet Briar Coll.; student (Ford Found. scholar) Sch. Am. Ballet, 1960; m. Richard Bernard Englund, Dec. 1, 1959; children: Alixandra Gage, Rachel Rutherford. Founder, Birmingham Civic Ballet, 1952; mem. Robert Joffrey Ballet, N.Y.C., 1957-60, soloist, 1959-60; mem. Am. Ballet Theatre, N.Y.C., 1960-63, Huntington Dance Ensemble, L.I., N.Y., 1968-69; soloist Dance Repertory Co., 1969-72; tchr. ballet, assoc. chmn. Friends of Am. Ballet Theatre, N.Y.C., 1972—; rehearsal coach Am. Ballet Theatre II, 1973-85; mem. scholarship com. Am. Ballet Theatre Sch., N.Y.C., 1974—; dir. Ala. By-products Corp., 1971-77; rehearsal coach Joffrey Ballet II, 1985-95, Am. Ballet Theatre Studio Co., 1995—. Bd. dirs. Children's Hosp. Clinic, Birmingham, 1955-57, Spoleto Festival, U.S.A., 1980-83, Ala. State Ballet, 1967—, Birmingham Civic Ballet, 1952-67; trustee Ballet Theatre Found., 1974-87, v.p., 1980-81; trustee Episcopal Sch. of N.Y., 1979-83, Chapin Sch., 1982—, Animal Med. Ctr., N.Y.C., 1982—, Cancer Rsch. Inst., 1984—. Recipient Silver Bowl award Birmingham Festival of Arts, 1955; named Queen of Birmingham Festival of Arts, 1957. Mem. Am. Guild Mus. Artists, Colonial Dames Ala., Jr. League N.Y.C. Episcopalian. Clubs: Lakewood Country, The Colony. Home: PO Box 469 17367 Scenic Hwy 98 Point Clear AL 36564

ENGLUND, KENNETH JOHN, retired geologist; b. Ironwood, Mich., Oct. 10, 1925; s. Carl Gustaf and Anna Maria (Johnson) E.; m. Virginia Mae Brehm, June 15, 1951; children: Lynn Ann, Karen Elaine. BA in Geology, U. Wis., 1949, MA in Geology, 1950. Cert. profl. geologist, Va. Geologist U.S. Geol. Survey, Lexington, Ky., 1950-58, Washington, 1958-84; supervisory geologist U.S. Geol. Survey, Reston, Va., 1985-89, scientist emeritus, 1989—. Author 140 articles in profl. jours. and publs. Sgt. med. corps, 1944-46. Recipient Meritorious Svc. award U.S. Dept. Interior, Washington, 1982. Fellow Geol. Soc. Am.; mem. Am. Assn. Petroleum Geologists, Geol. Soc. Washington, Cosmos Club.

ENGLUND, PAUL THEODORE, biochemist, educator; b. Worcester, Mass., Mar. 25, 1938; s. Theodore John and Mildred Elizabeth (Anderson) E.; m. Jean Elizabeth Nelson, Aug. 12, 1961 (div. 1987); children: Suzanne Elizabeth, Maria Jean; m. Christine R. Schneyer, Nov. 24, 1990; stepchildren: Jennifer, Peter. B.A., Hamilton Coll., 1960; Ph.D., Rockefeller U., 1966. Postdoctoral fellow Stanford U., 1966-68; asst. prof. Johns Hopkins Sch. Medicine, Balt., 1968-74; asso. prof. Johns Hopkins Sch. Medicine, 1974-80, prof., 1980—; co-dir. biology of parasitism course Marine Biol. Lab., Woods Hole, Mass., 1985-88; bd. dirs. Internat. Lab. for Rsch. on Animal Diseases, Nairobi, Kenya, 1987-93. Editorial bd.: Jour. Biol. Chemistry, 1981-87, Molecular and Biochem. Parasitology, 1982—, Nucleic Acids Research, 1986-94, Sci., 1988—; contbr. articles to profl. jours. Faculty research grantee Am. Cancer Soc., 1969-74, grantee NIH, MacArthur Found.; Fogarty Sr. Internat. fellow, 1980; Burroughs-Wellcome scholar in molecular parasitology, 1982-87. Mem. Am. Chem. Soc., Am. Soc. for Biochemistry and Molecular Biology. Home: 105 Longwood Rd Baltimore MD 21210-2119 Office: 725 N Wolfe St Baltimore MD 21205-2105*

ENGORON, EDWARD DAVID, food service consultant, television and radio broadcaster; b. Los Angeles, Feb. 19, 1946; s. Leo and Claire (Gray) E.; m. Charlene Scott, Oct. 7, 1970 (div. July 1982). BArch., U. So. Calif., 1969, MBA, 1973, PhD, 1974; MA, Cordon Bleu, Paris, 1975. Art dir. ABC, L.A., 1964-67, Paramount Pictures, L.A., 1967-68, Warner Bros. Pictures, Burbank, Calif., 1968-69; mktg. dir. Lawry's Foods Inc., Burbank, 1969-74; v.p. Warehouse Restaurants, Marina del Rey, Calif., 1968-72; pres. Perspectives, San Francisco, 1974-82, Perspectives Comm. Syndicated Talk Shows, L.A., 1986—, China Rose Inc., Dallas, 1982-86; exec. v.p. T.G.I. Fridays Inc., Dallas, 1986-87; pres., chief exec. officer, bd. dirs. Guilt Free Goodies, Ltd., Vancouver, B.C., Can., 1986-90, Sugarless Co., L.A., 1986-90; cons. Southland Corp., Dallas, 1982-86, Pizza Hut Inc., Wichita, Kans., 1975-87, Frank L. Carney Enterprises, Wichita, 1982-87, Safeway Stores, Inc., Freemont, Calif., Romacorp, Dallas, Bel-Air Hotel Co., L.A., Capital Cities-ABC, Hollywood, Nestle Foods, White Plains, Screiber Foods, Green Bay, Rich's Food Products, Buffalo, Arby's Inc., Ft. Lauderdale, Fla., Sizzler Internat., L.A., ednl. found. Nat. Restaurant Assn., Taco Bell, Inc., Irvine, Calif., Basic Am., Inc. San Francisco, Nat. Super Markets, St. Louis, Wok Fast, Inc., L.A., The Vons Cons., L.A., 1989—; pres. Sweet Deceit, Inc., Guilt-Free Goodies, Ltd.; co-host nationally syndicated radio talk show The Super Foodies, ABC. Author: (cookbook) Stolen Secrets, 1980; patentee pasta cooking sta., 1981, micro-wave controller, 1982. Bd. govs. Los Angeles Parks, 1971-74; mem. Fine Arts Commn., Tiburon, Calif., 1974-76. Mem. Foodsvc. Cons. Soc. Internat., Soc. Motion Picture Art Dirs., Food, Wine and Travel Writers Assn., Internat. Assn. Culinary Profls., Masons. Republican. Office: 11030 Santa Monica Blvd Ste 301 Los Angeles CA 90025-7514

ENGS, RUTH CLIFFORD, health educator; b. Ridgeway, Pa., Sept. 15, 1939; d. Theodore Alexander and Elinor Kay Clifford; m. William Denis Engs, July 24, 1965 (div. 1973); m. Jeffrey Lee Franz, Oct. 2, 1987. BA, U. Vt., 1961; diploma in nursing, Merritt Coll., 1968; MA, MS, U. Oreg., 1970; EdD, U. Tenn., 1973. RN, Ind. Rsch. asst. Harvard Med. Sch., Boston, 1961-63; asst. prof. Dalhousie U., Halifax, N.S., Can., 1970-71; asst. prof. Ind. U., Bloomington, 1973-80, assoc. prof., 1980-90, prof. applied health sci., 1990—; vis. prof. U. Queensland (Australia), 1980. Author: Teaching Health Education in the Elementary Schools, 1978, Responsible Drug and Alcohol Use, 1979, Alcohol and Other Drugs: Self Responsibility, 1987; editor: Controverseys in the Addiction Field, 1990, Women: Alcohol and Other Drugs, 1992; contbr. over 150 articles to profl. jours. Mem. Am. Sch. Health Assn., Am. Alliance Health Phys. Edn. and Recreation. Unitarian. Avocations: flying, golfing, ranching, acting, hiking. Office: Dept Applied Health Sci Ind U Poplars 615 Bloomington IN 47405

ENGSTRAND, BEATRICE C., neurologist, educator; b. Oceanside, N.Y., July 16, 1960; d. Donald Daniel and Claudia Helen Engstrand. BA, Lehigh U., 1982; MD, Med. Coll. Pa., 1984; hon. doctorate, Lehigh U. Diplomate Am. Bd. Psychiatry and Neurology, bd. cert. in neurology; lic. physician, N.Y. Resident in medicine North Shore U. Hosp., Manhasset, N.Y., 1984-85; resident in neurology N.Y. Hosp., N.Y.C., 1985-86, SUNY Health Sci. Ctr., Bklyn., 1986-88; attending physician Met. Hosp., N.Y.C., 1988-92; asst. prof. neurology N.Y. Med. Coll., Valhalla, 1988—; pvt. practice Huntington, N.Y., 1992—; founder, pres. Neuro-Degenerative Disease Found., 1993—; presenter and lectr. in field. Author: (book) A Gift of Healing—A Legacy of Hope, 1990. Mem. adv. bd. arts and sci. Lehigh U., Bethlehem, Pa., 1992—, women's adv. study bd., 1993—; mem. legis. com. Suffolk County Med. Soc., 1994-97; com. fundraiser Gov. George Pataki Election, 1995; mem. People for Ethical Treatment of Animals, Physicians for Responsible Medicine, other animal rights groups. Recipient Woman of Distinction award Soroptimist Internat.; named one of Outstanding Young Woman of Am., 1997. Fellow Am. Acad. Neurology (diplomate); mem. AMA, ACP, Am. Med. Student Assn., Am. Acad. Neurology, Nat. Bd. Med. Examiners (diplomate), Med. Soc. N.Y. State, N.Y. County Med. Soc. (pub. rels. com.), Westchester County Med. Ctr. (bioethics com.), Bklyn. Neurol. Soc., Med. Coll. Pa. Alumni Assn., Cornell U. Alumni Assn., Rotary Club Upper Manhattan (v.p. 1990-91, pres. 1991-92, Paul Harris award 1991). Republican. Avocations: traveling, animals, languages, opera, writing. Office: Ste 1 76 E Main St Huntington NY 11743

ENGSTROM, ERIK, publishing company executive; b. Taby, Stockholm, Sweden; s. Kjell and Alice (Klarstrom) E. BS in Econs. & Bus. Adminstrn., Stockholm Sch. Econs., 1986; MS in Engring., Royal Inst. Technology, 1986; diploma Internat. Mgmt. Program, Ecole des Hautes Etudes Comml., Paris, 1986; MBA, Harvard U., 1988. Cons. and engagement mgr. McKinsey & Co., N.Y., 1988-91; v.p. corp. devel. Bantam Doubleday Dell Pub. Group, Inc., N.Y., 1991-92, sr. v.p., CFO, 1992-93, exec. v.p., chief adminstrv. officer, 1993-94, exec. v.p., COO, 1994-96; pres., COO, 1996-98; pres., CEO BDD N.Am., 1998; pres., COO Random House Inc., N.Y.C., 1998—; bd. dirs. Telemedia Comm. Inc. Bd. dirs. Graham-Windham Svcs. to Families and Children, 1999—; mem. bus. com. Met. Mus. of Art, 1998—. Sgt. Swedish Army, 1983-84. scholar Fulbright Commn., 1986. Mem. Swedish-Am. C. of C. (bd. dirs. 1998—). Office: Random House Inc 1540 Broadway New York NY 10036-4040

ENHORNING, GORAN, obstetrician, gynecologist, educator; b. Birkdale, Eng., Mar. 18, 1924; came to U.S. 1986; s. Emil Augustin and Maria Rosina (von Haartman) E.; m. Louise Christina Carlberg, Apr. 16, 1955; children: Ulf, Dag and Peder (twins), Marianne. MD, Karolinska Inst., Stockholm, 1952, PhD in Physiology, 1961. Asst. prof. ob/gyn. Karolinska Inst., Stockholm, 1952-61; Fulbright scholar U. Utah, Salt Lake City, 1961-63, UCLA, 1963-64; assoc. prof. ob/gyn. Karolinska Inst., 1964-71; assoc. prof. ob/gyn. U. Toronto, Ont., Can., 1971-75, prof. ob/gyn., 1975-86; prof. ob/gyn. SUNY, Buffalo, 1986—. Contbr. articles to profl. jours. Achievements include contribution to understanding of urinary bladder's closure mechanism; methods for evaluating surface properties of pulmonary surfactant; initiation of concept that neonatal respiratory distress syndrome can be prevented/treated by instillation of pulmonary surfactant into upper airways, and concept that symptoms of asthma and infectious bronchiolitis may be caused by a surfactant dysfunction. Home: 21 Oakland Pl Buffalo NY 14222-2008

ENIS, THOMAS JOSEPH, lawyer; b. Maryville, Mo., July 2, 1937; s. Herbert William and Loretta M. (Fitzmaurice) E.; m. Harolyn Gray Westhoff, July 24, 1971; children: Margaret Elizabeth, David Richard, John Anthony, Brian Edward. B.S., Rockhurst Coll., 1958; J.D., U. Mo.-Columbia, 1966. Bar: Mo. 1966, Okla. 1973. Law clk. U.S. Dist. Ct. (we. dist.) Mo., 1966-67; prof. coll. law U. Okla., Norman, 1967-74, assoc. dean, 1970-74; atty. Southwestern Bell Tel. Co., Oklahoma City, 1974-79; ptnr. Bulla and Enis, Oklahoma City, 1979-81; pvt. practice Law Offices of Thomas J. Enis, Oklahoma City, 1981-87; of counsel Fellers, Snider, Blankenship, Bailey & Tippens, Oklahoma City, 1988-89, ptnr., 1990—; lectr. Okla. Bar Rev., 1968-96, 98—. Bd. dirs. Okla. Symphony Orch., 1978-88, legal counsel, 1981-88; spl. counsel Okla. Ethics Commn., 1986-88; trustee Okla. County Law Libr., 1989-91; Judge Temp. Ct. of Appeals Okla., 1991-92. Mem. ABA, Okla. Bar Assn., Mo. Bar Assn., Oklahoma County Bar Assn., Order of Coif, Phi Delta Phi. Republican. Roman Catholic. Editor-in-chief Mo. Law Rev., 1965-66. Home: 3016 Stoneybrook Rd Oklahoma City OK 73120-5716 Office: 100 N Broadway Ave Ste 1700 Oklahoma City OK 73102-8606

ENLOW, DONALD HUGH, anatomist, educator, university dean; b. Mosquero, N.Mex., Jan. 22, 1927; s. Donald Carter and Martie Blairene (Albertson) E.; m. Martha Ruth McKnight, Sept. 3, 1945; 1 child, Sharon Lynn. B.S., U. Houston, 1949, M.S., 1951; Ph.D., Tex. A&M U., 1955. Instr. biology U. Houston, 1949-51; asst. prof. biology West Tex. State U., 1955-56; instr. anatomy Med. Coll. S.C., 1956-57; asst. prof. U. Mich. Med. Sch., Ann Arbor, 1957-62; assoc. prof. U. Mich. Med. Sch., 1962-67, prof. anatomy, 1969-72; dir. phys. growth program Center for Human Growth and Devel., 1966-72; prof., chmn. dept. anatomy W.Va. U. Sch. Medicine, Morgantown, 1972-77; Thomas Hill disting. prof., chmn. dept. orthodontics Case Western Res. Sch. Dentistry, Cleve., 1977-89, prof. emeritus, 1989—; asst. dean for rsch. and grad. studies Case Western Res. Sch. Dentistry, 1977-85, acting dean, 1983-86; adj. prof. U. N.C., 1992—; guest lectr. 29 fgn. countries, 1963—. Author: Principles of Bone Remodeling, 1963, The Human Face, 1968, Handbook of Facial Growth, 1975, 3d edit., 1990, Essentials of Facial Growth, 1996; contbr. chpts. to 28 books, numerous articles to profl. jours. Served with USCGR, 1945-46. Recipient Outstanding Research award Tex. Acad. Sci., 1952. Fellow Royal Soc. Medicine, Am. Assn. Anatomists, Internat. Assn. Dental Research; hon. mem. Am. Assn. Orthodontists (Mershon Meml. lectr. 1968, Spl. Merit award 1969, award for outstanding contbns. to orthodontia, 1984), Gt. Lakes Orthodontic Soc., Cleve. Dental Soc., Cleve. Orthodontic Soc., Omicron Kappa Upsilon. Republican. Methodist. Home: 36 Martin Dr Whisper Pines NC 28327-9335

ENNA, SALVATORE JOSEPH, research pharmacologist, pharmaceutical company executive; b. Kansas City, Mo., Dec. 19, 1944; s. Veto Anthony and Fannie Sylvia (Bonello) E.; m. Colleen Anne Nestor, July 26, 1969; children: Anne, Matthew, Katharine. BA in Biology, Rockhurst Coll., 1965; MS in Pharmacology, U. Mo., 1967, PhD in Pharmacology, 1970. Postdoctoral fellow U. Tex. Southwestern Med. Sch., Dallas, 1970-72, R. Hoffmann-LaRoche & Co., Basel, Switzerland, 1973-74; postdoctoral fellow Johns Hopkins U. Sch. Med., Balt., 1974-76, adj. prof. neurosci., 1986-92; prof. pharmacology and neurobiology U. Tex. Med. Sch., Houston, 1976-86; sr. v.p., sci. dir. Nova Pharm. Corp., Balt., 1986-90, exec. v.p., 1990-92; prof., chmn. dept. pharmacology and toxicology U. Kans.; cons. Merck-Bristol Mfrs., 1976-86; adj. prof. pharmacology Tulane U. Med. Sch., New Orleans, 1986—. Editor: 10 books on pharmacology and neurosci.; contbr. over 200 articles to med. jours. Bd. overseers Md. Sch. Math. and Sci., Balt., 1988; mem. biotech. adv. com. Balt. Community Coll., 1988—. Recipient rsch. career devel. awards NIH, 1978-84; rsch. grantee NIH, NSF, Dept. Def., pvt. industry, others, 1976—. Mem. Am. Soc. Pharmacology and Exptl. Therapeutics (John J. Abel award 1980), Soc. for Neurosci., Am. Coll. Neuropsychopharmacology (Daniel H. Efron award 1989), Am. Soc. for Neurochemistry. Roman Catholic. Avocation: travel. *

ENNEY, JAMES CROWE, former air force officer, business executive; b. Youngstown, Ohio, Oct. 1, 1930; s. Edgar Earl and Mildred (Crowe) E.; m. Margaret Ann Reeve, Oct. 31, 1975. B.G.E., U. Nebr., Omaha, 1963; grad., Air Command and Staff Coll., 1964, Indsl. Coll. Armed Forces, 1971. Commd. 2d. lt. USAF, 1953, advanced through grades to maj. gen., 1980; chief Target Intelligence Ctr., 7th Air Force, Republic of Vietnam, 1965-66, Targets; spl. asst. to asst. chief staff Intelligence, Hdqrs. USAF, Washington, 1966-70; chief plans div. U.S. European Command, Stuttgart, Fed. Republic of Germany, 1971-74; chief Soviet/Warsaw Pact div. Def. Intelligence Agy., Washington, 1974-75, dep. dir. for info. systems, 1975-76; dep. dir. Nat. Strategic Target List, Joint Strategic Target Planning Staff, Offutt AFB, Nebr., 1976-79; dep. chief staff Intelligence SAC, 1979-82; v.p. Sci. Applications, Inc., McLean, Va., 1982-84, Planning Rsch. Corp., McLean, 1984-90; nat. security cons., 1990—. Decorated Def. Superior Service medal, D.S.M., Legion of Merit with two oak leaf clusters, Joint Service Commendation medal, Air Force Commendation medal with one oak leaf cluster. Mem. Air Force Assn., Security Affairs Support Assn., Assn. Former Intelligence Officers, Retired Officers' Assn., Nat. Mil. Intelligence Assn., Armed Forces Communications-Electronics Assn. Episcopalian. Home and Office: 1914 Rose Mallow Ln Orange Park FL 32073-7066

ENNIS, BRUCE CLIFFORD, lawyer; b. Dover, Del., Mar. 22, 1941; s. Clifford Morgan and Mary Elizabeth (Jones) E.; m. Diane Wallace, July 19, 1969; 1 dau., Heather Diane. B.A., W.Va. Wesleyan Coll., 1963; J.D., Dickinson Sch. Law, 1966. Bar: Del. 1969, U.S. Dist. Ct. Del. 1971. Ptnr. Schmittinger & Rodriguez, P.A., Dover, 1969—; instr. Wesley Coll., Dover, 1970-78, Del. Tech. and C.C., Dover, 1978—. Active United Meth. Ch., Dover. Served with U.S. Army, 1966-68. Mem. Del. State Bar Assn., Kent County Bar Assn. Democrat. Office: Schmittinger & Rodriguez PA PO Box 497 Dover DE 19903-0497

ENNIS, EDGAR WILLIAM, JR., lawyer; b. Macon, Ga., May 20, 1945; s. Edgar W. and Nelle (Branan) E.; m. Judith Anne Godfrey, June 29, 1974; children: William, Branan. BS in Engring. Sci., USAF Acad., Colorado Springs, Colo., 1967; JD, U. Ga., 1971. Bar: Ga. 1971. Commd. 2d lt. USAF, 1967, advanced through ranks to capt., 1970, resigned, 1975; asst. U.S. atty. U.S. Atty.'s Office-Mid. Dist. of Ga., Macon, 1975-88; U.S. atty. U.S. Dept. Justice, Macon, 1988-93; of counsel Haynsworth, Baldwin, Johnson & Harper, Macon, 1993-97; ptnr. Haynsworth, Baldwin, Johnson & Greaves LLC, Macon, 1998—. Office: Haynsworth Baldwin Johnson & Greaves LLC 577 Mulberry St Ste 710 Macon GA 31201-8588

ENNIS, SHARON LYNN, elementary education educator; b. Washington, Oct. 27, 1951; d. Bobbie Herbert and Irene Roslyn Belcher; children: John R. Jenkins, Michele L. Jenkins; m. W. Frank Ennis, Sept. 1, 1995. BS Elem. Edn. cum laude, Carson-Newman Coll., 1973; Masters equivalent/music endorsement, Cen. Wash. U., 1982. Cert. elem. tchr. 1-6, mid. sch., tchr. music K-6. Tchr. kindergarten and music Green Acres Kindergarten, Louisville, 1974-75; elem. grade Grant County Sch. Dist., Corinth, Ky., 1976-78; long-term elem. substitute tchr. Bracken County Sch. Dist., Brooksville, Ky., 1978-79; long-term substitute bilingual-Spanish tchr. Moses Lake (Wash.) Sch. Dist., 1980-81, long-term substitute elem. tchr., 1981-84; elem. tchr. Wicomico County Sch. Dist., Salisbury, Md., 1984-88, tchr. elem. sch. music, 1988—; music dir. of choirs and congregations/pianist, Ky., Tenn., Wash. and Md., 1971-88; tchr. pvt. piano lessons various communities; tchr. Vacation Bible Sch., Tenn., Wash., Ky. and Md., 1971-88; presenter 1st U.S./Russia Joint Conf. on Edn., Moscow. Organizer/author: Vocabulary and Science Activities (curriculum to accompany textbook), 1982; author: (elem. holiday musical program) Symbols of Holidays, 1995, To Russia with Music, 1997; author/organizer music curriculum, 1994, lessons on multicultural music activities and traditions, 1988—, others. Mem. Delmar (Md.) elem. Sch. PTA, 1990-95; singer Salisbury Choral Soc., 1985-95; adult choir dir. Oak Ridge Bapt. Ch., Salisbury, 1994-95. Del. to 1st U.S./Russia Joint Conf. on Edn., Citizen Ambassador Program, Moscow, 1994. Mem. NEA, Md. State Tchrs. Assn., Wicomico County Edn. Assn., People-to-People Internat., Md. State Music Tchrs. Assn., Music Educators Nat. Conf., Md. Music Educators Assn., Delta Omicron. Avocations: collecting music in various mediums, sewing, cooking, movies, travel. Office: Delmar Elem Sch 811 S 2nd St Delmar MD 21875-1782

ENNIS, THOMAS MICHAEL, management consultant; b. Morgantown, W.Va., Mar. 7, 1931; s. Thomas Edson and Violet Ruth (Nugent) E.; m. Julia Marie Dorety, June 30, 1956; children: Thomas John, Robert Griswold (dec.). Student, W.Va. U., 1949-52; AB, George Washington U., 1954; JD, Georgetown U., 1960. With Gov. Employees Ins. Co., Washington, 1956, 59, Air Transport Assn. Am., Washington, 1959-60; dir. ann. support program George Washington U., 1960-63; nat. dir. devel. Project HOPE, People to People Health Found., Inc., Washington, 1963-66; nat. exec. dir. Epilepsy Found. Am., Washington, 1966-74; exec. dir. Clinton, Eaton, Ingham Community Mental Health Bd., Lansing, Mich., 1974-83; nat. exec. dir. Alzheimer's Disease and Related Disorders Assn., Inc., Chgo., 1983-86; exec. dir., pres. The John Douglas French Alzheimers Found., L.A., 1986-96, pres. emeritus, 1996—; clin. instr. dept. cmty. medicine and internat. health Georgetown U., 1967-74; adj. assoc. prof. dept. psychiatry Mich. State U., 1975-84; lectr. Univ. Ctr. for Internat. Rehab., 1977; cons. health and med. founds., related orgns.; cons. Am. Health Found., 1967-69, Reston, Va.-Georgetown U. Health Planning Project, 1967-70. Editl. bd. Am. Jour. Alzheimer's Disease, 1997—. Mem. adv. bd. Nat. Center for the Law and the Handicapped, 1971-74; advisor Nat. Reye's Syndrome Found.; mem. Nat. Com. for Research in Neurol. Disorders, 1967-72; mem. nat. adv. bd. Developmental Disabilities/Tech. Assistance System, U. N.C., 1971-78; nat. trustee Nat. Kidney Found., 1970-74, mem. exec. com. and bd. Nat. Capitol Area chpt., pres., 1972-74; bd. dirs. Nat. Assn. Pvt. Residential Facilities for Mentally Retarded, 1970-74; bd. dirs., mem. exec. com. Epilepsy Found. Am., 1977-84, Epilepsy Center Mich., 1974-83; nat. bd. dirs. Western Inst. on Epilepsy, 1969-72; bd. dirs., pres. Mich. Mid-South Health Systems Agy., 1975-78; sec. gen. Internat. Fedn. Alzheimer's Disease and Related Disorders, 1984-86; mem. panel Alzheimer's Disease Edn. and Referral Ctr., 1990-93; mem. Calif. State Coun. on Developmental Disabilities, 1997—; med. adv. bd. EdenCare Sr. Living Svcs., advisor Ctr. Aging, Washington, 1998—. World Rehab. Fund fellow Norway, 1980. Mem. Nat. Epilepsy League (bd. dirs. 1977-78), Mich. Assn. Cmty. Mental Health (pres. 1977-79), Nat. Coalition Rsch. Neurol. Disorders (dir. at-large 1991—), Scan Health Plan (bd. govs.), Phi Alpha Theta, Phi Kappa Psi. Home and Office: 23740 Killion St Woodland Hills CA 91367-5822

ENO, AMOS STEWART, natural resource foundation administrator; b. Princeton, N.J., Jan. 26, 1950; s. Amos and Alice Pardee (Stewart) E.; m. Marjorie Theresa Belli, Sept. 18, 1982; children: Amos Pinchot L., Angus Connelly. BA, Princeton U., 1972; MA, Cornell U., 1977. Staff asst. to asst. sec. U.S. Dept. Interior, Washington, 1974-76, spl. asst. to chief, office of endangered species, 1978-81; asst. dir. wildlife affairs Nat. Audubon Soc., Washington, 1981-82, dir. wildlife programs, 1982-86; dir. conservation programs Nat. Fish and Wildlife Found., Washington, 1986-91, exec. dir., 1991—; bd. dirs. Strategic Environ. Rsch. and Devel. Program, U.S. Dept. Def.; mem. coun. N.Am. Wetlands Conservation Coun., U.S. Dept. Interior. Editor FY 1987-93 Federal Agency Needs Assessment; editor reports. Recipient Frederick Douglas award, Princeton, 1972, Profl. Conservationist award Chevron, 1992, Pres. Conservation Achievement Awd., 1993, Nature Conservancy. Mem. Ivy Club. Avocations: tennis, running, photography. Office: Nat Fish & Wildlife Found 4 Fundy Rd Falmouth ME 04105-1764

ENO, WOODROW E., lawyer; m. Ann Eno; 3 children. BA in History/Econs., Pittsburg (Kans.) State U., 1968; JD, U. Nebr., 1971; LLM, Judge Advocate Gen. Sch., Charlottesville, Va. Trial atty., regional counsel criminal investigation command U.S. Army; dir. law dept. market support div. CNA Ins. Co.; with legal/state affairs dept. Health Ins. Assn. Am., Appleton, Wis., 1975, v.p., gen. counsel, dir. state affairs; developer model laws and regulators on timely issues Nat. Assn. Ins. Commrs. Contbr. articles to profl. jours. Fundraiser several Washington area charities. Lt. col. JAGC U.S. Army. Mem. Nat. Health Lawyers Assn. (bd. dirs. 1992). Methodist. Office: Aid Association for Lutherans 4321 N Ballard Rd Appleton WI 54919-0001*

ENOCH, CRAIG TRIVELY, state supreme court justice; b. Wichita, Kans., Apr. 3, 1950; s. Donald Kirk and Margery (Trively) E.; m. Kathryn Stafford Barker, Aug. 2, 1975. BA, So. Meth. U., 1972, JD, 1975; LLM, U. Va., 1992. Bar: Tex. 1975, U.S. Dist. Ct. (no. dist.) Tex. 1976, U.S. Ct. Appeals (5th cir.) 1979. Assoc. Burford, Ryburn & Ford, Dallas, 1975-77; ptnr. Moseley, Jones, Enoch & Martin, Dallas, 1977-81; judge 101st Dist. Ct., Dallas, 1981-87; chief justice Tex. Ct. Appeals (5th dist.), 1987-92; justice Tex. Supreme Ct., Austin, 1993—. Mem. exec. bd. Sch. Law So. Meth. U., 1990—; chmn. Canterbury House Collegiate Chapel, Dallas, 1982-84; chmn. subcom. Scouting for the Handicapped, Circle 10 Coun., Dallas, 1982-84; exec. vice chmn. track and field events area 10 Spl. Olympics, Dallas, 1984-85. Capt. USAFR, 1973-81. Recipient Disting. Alumni award for judicial svc. So. Meth. U. Sch. of Law, 1999. Fellow Am. Bar Found., Tex. State Bar Found., Dallas Bar Found.; mem. ABA (mem. exec. bd. appellate judges conf. jud. divsn.), Am. Law Inst., Dallas Bar Assn. Republican. Episcopalian. Home: 2614 Maria Anna Rd Austin TX 78703-1656

ENOCH, JAY MARTIN, vision scientist, educator; b. N.Y.C., Apr. 20, 1929; s. Jerome Dee and Stella Sarah (Nathan) E.; m. Rebekah Ann Feiss, June 24, 1951; children: Harold Owen, Barbara Diane, Ann Allison. BS in Optics and Optometry, Columbia U., 1950; postgrad., Inst. Optics U. Rochester, 1953; Ph.D. in Physiol. Optics, Ohio State U., 1956; DSc honoris causa, SUNY, 1993. Asst. prof. physiol. optics Ohio State U., Columbus, 1956-58; assoc. supr. Ohio State U. (Mapping and Charting Rsch. Lab.), 1957-58; fellow Nat. Phys. Lab., Teddington, Eng., 1959-60; rsch. instr. dept. ophthalmology Washington U. Sch. Medicine, St. Louis, 1958-59, rsch. asst. prof., 1959-64, rsch. assoc. prof., 1965-70, rsch. prof., 1970-74; fellow Barnes Hosp., St. Louis, 1960-64, cons. ophthalmology, 1964-74; rsch. prof. dept. psychology Washington U., St. Louis, 1970-74; grad. rsch. prof. ophthalmology and psychology Coll. Medicine U. Fla., Gainesville, 1974-80, grad. rsch. prof. physics, 1979-80; dir. Ctr. for Sensory Studies, 1976-80; dean Sch. Optometry, chmn. Grad. Group in Vision Sci. U. Calif., Berkeley, 1980-92, prof. optometry and vision sci., 1980-94, prof. of Grad. Sch., 1994—; prof. physiol. optics in ophthalmology U. Calif., San Francisco, 1980—; exec. sec. subcom. on vision and its disorders of nat. adv.Nat. Inst. Neurol. Diseases and Blindness Coun., NIH, 1963-66; chmn. subcom. contact lens stds. Am. Nat. Stds. Inst., 1970-77; mem. nat. adv. eye coun. Nat. Eye Inst., NIH, 1975-77, 80-84; exec. com., com. on vision NAS-NRC, 1973-76; mem. U.S. Nat. Com. Internat. Commn. Optics, 1976-79; health scis. com. systemwide adminstrn. U. Calif., 1989-93, co-chmn. subcom. on immigrant health in Calif., 1993-94; mem. sci. adv. bd. Fight-for-Sight, 1988-92, Allergan Corp., 1991-93; mem. Lighthouse for Blind, N.Y., 1989-96, chair, 1995, Pisart award com. Contbr. numerous chpts. and articles on visual sci., receptor optics, perimetry, contact lenses and infant vision to sci. jours.; contbr. chpts. in field to med. books; assoc. editor: Investigative Ophthamology, 1965-75, 83-88, Sight-Saving Rev., 1974-84, Sensory Processes, 1974-80; mem. editl. bd. Vision Rsch., 1974-80, Internat. Ophthamology, 1977-93, Binocular Vision, 1984—, Clin. Vision Sci., 1986-93, Biomed. Optics, 1988-90; mem. editl. bd. optical scis. Springer-Verlag, Heidelberg, 1978-87, biomed. scis., 1988-95, Annals of Ophthalmology, 1997—; assoc. editor for vision Handbook of Optics, Optical Soc. Am., 1997—. Mem. nat. sci. adv. bd. Retinitis Pigmentosa Found., 1977-95; U.S. rep. Internat. Perimetric Soc., 1974-90, also exec. com., chmn. Rsch. Group Standards; bd. dirs. Friends of Eye Rsch., 1977-88; trustee Illuminating Engrng. Rsch. Inst., 1977-81; bd. dirs. Lighting Rsch. Bd., 1988-95; mem. bd. counselors U.C. San Francisco Sch. Dentistry, 1995—. 2d lt. U.S. Army, 1951-52. Recipient Career Devel. award NIH, 1963-73, Everett Kinsey award Contact Lens Assn. Ophthalmologists, 1991, Berkeley citation, Festschrift U. Calif. Berkeley, 1996. Fellow AAAS, Am. Acad. Optometry (Glenn A. Fry award 1972, Charles F. Prentice medal award 1974), Optical Soc. Am. (chmn. vision tech. sect. 1974-76, mem. book pub. com. 1996—), Am. Acad. Ophthalmology (honor award 1985); mem. Assn. for Rsch. in Vision and Ophthalmology (trustee 1967-73, pres. 1972-73, Francis I. Proctor medal 1977), Concilium Ophthalmologicum Universale (chmn. visual functions com. 1982-86), Am. Optometric Assn. (low vision sect., Vision Care award 1987), Ocular Heritage Soc. (medal 1997), Cogan Ophthalmic History Soc., Sigma Xi. Home: 54 Shuey Dr Moraga CA 94556-2621 Office: U Calif Sch of Optometry Berkeley CA 94720-2020

ENOMOTO, JERRY JIRO, protective services official; b. San Francisco, Jan. 24, 1926. BA, U. Calif., Berkeley, 1949, MA, 1951. Counselor San Quentin Prison Calif. Dept. Corrections, 1952-54, parole officer, 1955-56, supr. San Quentin Prison, 1956-58, supr. Deuel Vocat. Inst., 1958-59, supr. counselor San Quinten Prison, 1959-60, assoc. warden Deuel Vocat Inst., 1960-65, chief classification svcs., 1965-70, deputy supt. Soledad Prison, 1970-71, warden Calif. Correctional Inst., 1971-74, acting supt. Calif. Inst. Women, 1974-75, dir., 1975-80; ind. cons., 1980-94, fed. ct. monitor, 1994; U.S. marshal Ea. Dist. Calif., 1994—. Pres., chmn. Japanese Am. Citizens League, 1987—. Mem. Am. Correctional Assn. Office: US Marshalls Office US Courthouse 650 Capitol Mall Sacramento CA 95814-4708

ENOS, PAUL, geologist, educator; b. Topeka, July 25, 1934; s. Allen Mason and Marjorie V. (Newell) E.; m. Carol Rae Curt, July 5, 1958; children—Curt Alan, Mischa Enos Martin, Kevin Christopher, Heather Lynne. BS, U. Kans., 1956; postgrad., U. Tubingen, W.Ger., 1956-57; MS, Stanford U., 1961; PhD, Yale U., 1965. Geologist Shell Devel. Co., Coral Gables, Fla., 1964-68; research geologist Shell Devel. Co., Houston, 1968-70; from assoc. prof. to prof. geology SUNY, Binghamton, 1970-82; Haas Disting. prof. geology U. Kans., Lawrence, 1982—; cons. to industry; sedimentologist Ocean Drilling, 1975, 92; rsch. vis. Oxford U., 1989, U. Erlangen, Germany, 1995-96; fgn. scientist Ministry Geology, People's Republic China, 1988; with Global Sedimentary Geology Project, 1988—, co-convener Working Group 4, 1992—. Co-author: Quaternary Sedimentation of South Florida, 1977, Mid-Cretaceous, Mexico, 1983; editor: Field Trips: South-Central New York, 1981, Deep-Water Carbonates, 1977; contbr. articles to sci. jours. Served to 1st lt. C.E., U.S. Army, 1957-59. U. Liverpool fellow, 1976-77; NSF fellow, 1959-62; Fulbright fellow, 1956-57; Summerfield scholar, 1954-56. Mem. Soc. Econ. Paleontologists and Mineralogists (assoc. editor 1976-80, 83-87, Best Paper award 1969), Internat. Assn. Sedimentologists (assoc. editor 1983-87), Am. Assn. Petroleum Geologists, AAAS, Sigma Xi, Omicron Delta Kappa. Avocations: photography, diving, cycling, history. Home: 2032 Quail Creek Dr Lawrence KS 66047-2139 Office: U Kans Dept Geology Lawrence KS 66045-2124

ENOS, RANDALL, cartoonist, illustrator; b. New Bedford, Mass., Jan. 30, 1936; s. Eugene and Isabel (Da Costa) E.; m. Leann Walker, June 23, 1956. Student, Boston Mus. Sch. Fine Arts, 1954-55. Art tchr. Famous Artists Schs., Inc., Westport, Conn., 1956-64; film designer Pablo Ferro Films, Inc., N.Y.C., 1964-66; free-lance illustrator and film designer Westport, 1966—; part-time tchr. Parsons Sch. Design, N.Y.C., 1975-84; lectr., tchr. Syracuse U. Designed films for maj. Am. corps.; illustrator for maj. publs. including N.Y. Times, Time Mag., also children's books, posters; represented in numerous illustrators and art dirs. anns., other anthologies and mus. collections; created comic strips. Recipient Cannes TV award, 1964. Democrat. Avocations: acting; juggling. Home: 402 N Park Ave Easton CT 06612-1248

ENOUEN, WILLIAM ALBERT, paper corporation executive; b. Columbus, Ohio, Nov. 7, 1928; s. John J. and Bertha (Thiry) E.; m. Joan Claire Batsche, June 20, 1953; children: William A., Robert, Kathryn, James, Patricia. B.S., U. Dayton, 1952; student advanced mgmt. program, Harvard, 1975. Various accounting positions Touche, Ross & Co., Dayton, Ohio, 1952-59; asst. to controller, asst. to group v.p. and fin. cons. affiliated cos. Mead Corp., Dayton, 1959-68; controller Mead Corp., 1969-72, v.p., controller, 1972-81, 1981-82, v.p. fin. resources and control, 1981-82, v.p. Pulp affiliates, 1982-86, sr. v.p., chief fin. officer, 1986-93; v.p. Brunswick Pulp & Paper Co., 1968-69; chmn. bd. Northwood Forest Industries Ltd., 1969-86; chmn. bd. dirs. Morris Bean; bd. dirs. Monarch Machine Tool Co. With AUS, 1946-47. Mem. Ohio Soc. CPAs (v.p. Dayton chpt. 1959-60). Home: 700 Murrell Dr Dayton OH 45429-1322

ENRICO, ROGER A., soft drink company executive. Former v.p. sales and mktg. Pepsi-Cola Metropol Bottling Co. Inc., Purchase, N.Y.; now pres., chief exec. officer Pepsico Worldwide Beverages, Purchase, N.Y.; CEO Pepsico, Inc., 1994—; also chmn. bd. dirs. Office: Pepsico Inc 700 Anderson Hill Rd Purchase NY 10577-1444*

ENRIGHT, GEORGANN MCGEE, mental health nurse; b. Chgo., Nov. 8, 1943; d. George Daniel and Marjorie (Altenburg) McGee; m. John Joseph Enright, Apr. 8, 1967; children: Sean, Erin, Emily, Katherine. BSN cum laude, U. Mich, 1965; cert., Patricia Stevens Career Coll., 1966; postgrad., Edison State Community Coll.; MS, Wright State U., 1994. Cert. psychiat. nurse ANCC. Staff nurse, med. surg. U. Hosp., Ann Arbor, Mich., 1965-66; float nurse, med. surg. ICU Christ Community Hosp., Oak Lawn, Ill., 1966; staff nurse, med. surg. Saratoga Gen. Hosp., Detroit, 1967; med.-surg. float nurse, staff nurse neurosurgery and neurology Ohio State U. Hosp., Columbus, 1967-68; clin. nurse, team leader Planned Parenthood Miami Valley, Dayton, Ohio, 1970-71; float nurse, med. surg. pediatrics Stouder Hosp., Troy, Ohio, 1974-75; staff nurse adolescent and adult mental health unit Upper Valley Med. Ctr., Troy, 1983—; instr. Edison State C.C., Piqua, Ohio, 1990-95; instr. Sinclair C.C., Dayton, 1993-96, regular adj. faculty, 1996—. Mem. Am. Psychiat. Nurses Assn., Nat. Alliance for Mentally Ill, Ohio Psychiat. Nurses Network, Dayton Area Psychiatric Nurses Assn., Sigma Theta Tau, Phi Kappa Phi, Alpha Lambda Delta. Home: 103 S Monroe St Troy OH 45373-2932

ENRIGHT, MICHAEL JOSEPH, radiologist; b. Richmond, Va., Mar. 27, 1955; s. Wlliam Joseph and Margaret (O'Connell) E.I (div.); children: Kelly Ann, Margeaux Elizabeth; m. Susan Ross Lemon, June 29, 1991; 1 child, Darby Michelle. BS in Pharmacy, Ohio State U., 1978; MD, Ea. Va. Med. Sch., 1981. Diplomate Nat. Bd. Med. Examiners, Am. Bd. Radiology, Va. Bd. Pharmacy. Resident in radiology Ea. Va. Grad. Sch. Medicine, Norfolk, 1981-85; radiologist U.S. Navy, Charleston, S.C., 1985-88; body imaging fellow U. Va. Med. Ctr., Charlottesville, 1988-89; radiologist Radiology Assocs. of Roanoke, Va., 1989—; treas. Low Country Imaging Soc., Charleston, 1986-87; sect. head Body and Musculoskeletal Magnetic Resonance Imaging, Radiology Assn. Roanoke, 1993—. Author (exhibit) Scrotal Ultrasonography at Am. Roentgen Ray Soc. Meeting, 1989. Lt. commdr. USN, 1985-88. Mem. AMA, Am. Coll. Radiology, Radiol. Soc. N. Am., Roanoke Soc. Medicine, Radiol. Soc. Roanoke (bd. dirs. 1995—, treas. 1998), Clin. Magnetic Resonance Soc., Radiology Assocs. Roanoke (treas. 1998). Republican. Avocations: running, tennis, archery, golf, boating. Home: 4400 Kings Chase Dr Roanoke VA 24014-6530 Office: Radiology Assocs of Roanoke Ste 435 2037 Crystal Spring Ave SW Roanoke VA 24014-2411

ENRIGHT, STEPHANIE VESELICH, investment company executive; b. L.A., Mar. 24, 1929; d. Stephen P. and Violet (Guthrie) Veselich; m. Robert James Enright (dec. Sept. 1982); children: Craig James, Brent Stephen, Erin Suzanne, Kyle Stephen. BA, U. So. Calif., 1952, MS, 1975. Fin. and engrng. cons. Orange County, Santa Ana, Calif., 1976-79; fin. cons. The SimEhrflo Group, Newport Beach, Calif., 1979-81; pres. Enright Fin. Cons., Torrance, Calif., 1981—; fin. columnist Copley Newspapers, 1982—; pres. Enright Fin. Cons., Torrance; adj. faculty mem. UCLA, U. So. Calif.; pres. Pacific Home Builders. Contbr. articles to profl. jours. Mem. Com. Assn. of the Peninsula, Palos Verdes, Calif., 1986; found. dir. Little Co. of Mary Hosp., Torrance; bd. dirs. local chpt. YWCA; dir. endowment com. Pa. Art Assn.; housing bd. Assistance League; bd. dirs. Pa. Symphony Soc., 1991, El Camino Coll. Found. Mem. Internat. Assn. Fin. Planning (bd. dirs., officer 1982-84, Planner of Month award 1984), Inst. Cert. Fin. Planners, Nat. Assn. Women Owners, Nat. Assn. Fin. Edn., Registry Profl. Planners, Torrance C. of C., Assistance League (bd. dirs. South Bay), Women in Constrn., Trojan Club and League (bd. dirs. 1978-79, 91—). Republican. Avocations: traveling, writing. Office: 21515 Hawthorne Blvd Ste 1050 Torrance CA 90503-6517

ENRIGHT, WILLIAM BENNER, judge; b. N.Y.C., July 12, 1925; s. Arthur Joseph and Anna Beatrice (Plante) E.; m. Bette Lou Card, Apr. 13, 1951; children—Kevin A., Kimberly A., Kerry K. BA, Dartmouth, 1947; LLB, Loyola U. at L.A., 1950. Bar: Calif. 1951; diplomate: Am. Bd. Trial Advs. Dep. dist. atty. San Diego County, 1951-54; ptnr. Enright, Levitt, Knutson & Tobin, San Diego, 1954-72; judge U.S. Dist. Ct. (so. dist.) Calif., San Diego, 1972-90, sr. judge, 1990—; Mem. adv. bd. Joint Legis. Com. for Revision Penal Code, 1970-72, Calif. Bd. Legal Specialization, 1970-72; mem. Jud. Council, 1972; Bd. dirs. Defenders, 1965-72, pres., 1972. Served as ensign USNR, 1943-46. Recipient Honor award San Diego County Bar, 1970; Extraordinary Service to Legal Professions award Mcpl. Ct. San Diego Jud. Dist., 1971. Fellow Am. Coll. Trial Lawyers, Am. Bar Found.; mem. ABA, San Diego County Bar Assn. (dir. 1963-65, pres. 1965), State Bar Calif. (gov. 1967-70, v.p. 1970, exec. com. law in a free soc. 1970—), Dartmouth Club San Diego, Am. Judicature Soc., Alpha Sigma Nu, Phi Delta Phi. Club: Rotarian. Office: US Dist Ct 4145 US Courthouse 940 Front St San Diego CA 92101-8994*

ENRIQUEZ, CAROLA RUPERT, museum director; b. Washington, Jan. 2, 1954; d. Jack Burns and Shirley Ann (Orcutt) Rupert; m. John Enriquez, Jr., Dec. 30, 1989. BA in History cum laude, Bryn Mawr Coll., 1976; MA, U. Del., 1978, cert. in mus. studies, 1978. Pers. mgmt. trainee Naval Material Command, Arlington, Va., 1972-76; tchg. asst. dept. history U. Del., Newark, 1976-77; asst. curator/exhibit specialist Hist. Soc. Del., Wilmington, 1977-78; dir. Macon County Mus. Complex, Decatur, Ill., 1978-81, Kern County Mus., Bakersfield, Calif., 1981—. Pres. Kern County Mus Found., 1991—; advisor Kern County Heritage Commn., 1981-88; chmn. Hist. Records Commn., 1981-88; sec.-treas. Arts Coun. of Kern, 1984-86, pres., 1986-88; county co-chmn. United Way, 1981, 82; chmn. steering com. Calif. State Bakersfield Co-op Program, 1982-83; mem. cmty. adv. bd. Calif. State U.-Bakersfield Anthrop. Soc., 1986-88; bd. dirs. Mgmt. Coun., 1983-86, v.p., 1987, pres., 1988; bd. dirs. Calif. Coun. for Promotion of History, 1984-86, v.p., 1987-88, pres., 1988-90; mem. cmty. adv. bd. Calif. State U.-Bakersfled Sociology Dept., 1986-88; mem. women's adv. com. Girls Scouts U.S., 1989-91; bd. dirs. Greater Bakersfield Conv. and Visitors Bur., 1993-95; co-chair 34th St. Neighborhood Partnership, 1994—. Hagley fellow Eleutherian Mills-Hagley found., 1977-78; Bryn Mawr alumnae reg. scholar, 1972-76. Mem. Calif. Assn. Mus. (reg. rep. 1991—, v.p. legis. affairs 1992—), Am. Assn. State and Local History (chair awards com. Calif. chpt. 1990, reg. vchair 1999—). Presbyterian. Office: Kern County Museum 3801 Chester Ave Bakersfield CA 93301-1345

ENRIQUEZ, CRISTINO CATUD, radiologist, internist, cardiologist; b. Batangas, Philippines, 1941. MD, U. of the East, Philippines, 1964. Diplomate Am. Bd. Radiology. Internist St. Mary's Hosp., Waterbury, Conn., 1965-66; res. internal med. Hosp. St. Raphael, New Haven, Conn., 1966-68; res. diagnostic radiol. Jackson Meml. Med. Ctr. U Miami, 1974-77; fellow in cardiology Baylor U., 1969-70; fellow in pulmonary disease Yale U. Hosp., 1971-72; founder Rapha Health & Longevity Inst. Fellow Am. Coll. Internat. Physicians; mem. AMA, Am. Coll. Cardiology, Am. Coll. Radiology, Interam. Coll. Radiology, Assn. Philippine Physicians in Am., Full Gospel Businessmen's Fellowship, Christian Med. and Dental Assn. Office: 8 Harborage Fort Lauderdale FL 33316-2306

ENRIQUEZ, MANUEL HIPOLITO, physician; b. Angeles City, Philippines, Aug. 19, 1953; came to U.S., 1982; s. Antonio S. and Milagros D. (Hipolito) E.; m. Mary Diane Maloney, June 22, 1985; children: Steven, Katie. BS, U. of the East, 1974, MD, 1979. Diplomate internal medicine, pulmonary disease and critical care medicine. Intern Philippine Gen. Hosp., Manila, 1980; resident Mercy Hosp., Buffalo, 1982-85; fellow Wayne State U. Sch. Medicine, Detroit, 1985-87; dir. respiratory therapy Humana Hosp. Clinch Valley, Richlands, Va., 1987-88; staff pulmonologist VA Med. Ctr., Asheville, N.C., 1989—, also dir. med. ICU, 1990—, med. dir. respiratory therapy, 1997—; flight surgeon USAF Clinic, Charleston AFB, S.C., 1991—; cons. assoc. Duke U. Med. ctr., Durham, N.C., 1989—; cons. in field. *A Lieutenant Colonel and Senior Flight Surgeon in the U.S. Air Force Reserve, he serves as Chief of Professional Services at the 315 Medical Squadron, Charleston AFB, South Carolina. He completed Squadron Officer School in 1993 and Air Command and Staff College in 1997. He also completed "Top Knife," the Air National Guard Fighter Surgeon School, in August, 1997. He has been awarded the Air Force Achievement and Meritorious Service Medals for distinguished service. He holds a commercial pilot certificate with instrument rating.* Med. officer CAP, Asheville, 1990—, sr. programs officer, 1993—. Fellow ACP, Am. Coll. Chest Physicians; mem. Aerospace Med. Assn., Am. Thoracic Soc., Res. Officers Assn., Soc. USAF Flight Surgeons. Roman Catholic. Avocations: flying, jogging, reading, computers. Office: VA Med Ctr 1100 Tunnel Rd Asheville NC 28805-2043

ENROTH-CUGELL, CHRISTINA ALMA ELISABETH, neurophysiologist, educator; b. Helsingfors, Finland, Aug. 27, 1919; came to U.S., 1956, naturalized, 1962; d. Emil and Maja (Syren) E.; m. David W. Cugell, Sept. 5, 1955. MD, Karolinska Inst., 1948, PhD, 1952; Hon. Doctors Degree, U. Helsinki, Finland, 1994. Resident Karolinska Sjukhuset, 1949-52; intern Passavant Meml. Hosp., 1956-57; with Northwestern U., Evanston, Ill., 1959-91; prof. emeritus Northwestern U., 1991—, prof. neurobiology and physiology dept. biomed-engring., 1974—; mem. vision research program com. Nat. Eye Inst., 1974-78, mem. nat. adv. eye council, 1980-84. Contbr. articles to profl. jours. Recipient Ludwig von Sallman award Internat. Assn. Rsch. in Vision and Ophthalmology, 1982. Fellow Am. Inst. Med. and Biol. Engrng., Am. Acad. Arts and Scis.; mem. Am. Assn. Rsch. in Vision and Ophthalmology (co-recipient Friedenwald award 1983, recipient W.H. Helmerich III award 1992), Soc. Neuroscis., Am. Physiol. Soc., Physiol. Soc. (U.K.). Office: Northwestern U McCormick Sch Engring Technl Inst 2145 Sheridan Rd Evanston IL 60208-0834

ENSENAT, LOUIS ALBERT, surgeon; b. Merida, Mexico, Oct. 24, 1916; s. Frank and Guadalupe F. (Ensenat) E.; B.S., Tulane U., 1938, M.D., 1941; M.Sc. in Medicine, U. Pa., 1953; m. Ruth Ogden, July 9, 1943; children—Gloria Louise, Tinita Ruth, Louis Albert, Rita Joan, Barbara Jean, Michael Monroe. Intern, Charity Hosp., New Orleans, 1941-42; resident surgery Charity Hosp., Monroe, La., 1942, Lakeshore Hosp., New Orleans, VA hosp., New Orleans, Batavia, N.Y.; fellow in surg. pathology Tulane U. Sch. Med.; preceptorship in surgery Biloxi (Miss.) VA Hosp.; staff surg. VA Hosp., Montgomery, 1946-52; pvt. practice surgery, Pasadena, Tex., 1952-63, New Orleans, 1963—; adminstr. Mercy Hosp. Pasadena, 1954-63, chief surgery, 1954-63; founder, dir. Gulf Coast Home Builders, Inc.; trustee Angiology Research Found., 1986—. Trustee, Big State Factors Corp. Served from lt (j.g.) to lt. comdr. USN, 1942-46. Decorated Purple Heart, Bronze Star. Diplomate Am. Bd. Surgery, Am. Bd. Abdominal Surgery. Fellow French Soc. Phlebology, Am. Coll. Angiology (pres.); mem. AMA, Hawthorne Surg. Soc., Am. Soc. Abdominal Surgeons, N.Y. Acad. Scis., Am. Med. Writers Assn. Author articles in field. Home and Office: 7630 Jeannette St New Orleans LA 70118-4064

ENSIGN, JERALD C., bacteriology educator. Prof. dept. bacteriology U. Wis., Madison, 1990—. Recipient Disting. Tchr. award Carski Found., 1992. Office: Univ Wis Dept Bacteriology 114 E Fred Hall 1550 Linden Dr Madison WI 53706-1521*

ENSIGN, JOHN E., former congressman; b. Roseville, Calif., Mar. 25, 1958; s. Mike and Sharon E.; m. Darlene Sciarretta Ensign; 1 child, Trevor. Student, UNLV; B in Gen. Sci., Oreg. State U., 1981; D of Veterinary Medicine, Colo. State U., 1985. Owner animal hosp., Las Vegas; gen. mgr. Gold Strike Hotel & Casino, 1991, Nev. Landing Hotel & Casino, 1992; mem. U.S. Congress from 1st Nev. dist., Washington, 1994-98; mem. ways and means com., subcom. health, subcom. human resources, mem. com. on resources, 1995-98. Candidate for U.S. Sen., 1998-99. Office: 7515 Coley Ave Las Vegas NV 89117*

ENSIGN, RICHARD PAPWORTH, transportation executive; b. Salt Lake City, Jan. 20, 1919; s. Louis Osborne and Florence May (Papworth) E.; m. Margaret Anne Hinckley, Sept. 5, 1942; children: Judith Ensign Lantz, Mary Jane Ensign Hofmeister, Richard L., James R., Margaret. B.S., U. Utah, 1941. With Western Air Lines, 1941-70, v.p. in-flight service, 1963-70, v.p. passenger service, 1970; v.p. passenger service Pan Am. World Airways, 1971, sr. v.p. field mgmt., 1972-74, sr. v.p. mktg., 1974-75; exec. v.p. Western Airlines, 1975-82; pres. R.P. Ensign & Assocs., 1982—; spl. asst. to pres. Marriott-Host, Marriott Corp., 1990-91; spl. asst. to chmn. Caterair Internat. Corp., 1991-96; chmn. Utah Nat. Adv. Coun., 1984-86; bd. dirs. Western Airlines, 1980-81, Pacific Area Travel Assocs., 1976-81, Marriott Airport Svc. Co., Osaka, Japan, 1986-92; resident dir. Marriott Internat. Corp., Seoul, People's Republic of Korea. Nat. fund raising chmn. U. Utah, 1982-83, 83-84. Recipient Disting. Service award Fla. Internat. U., 1973; named Disting. Alumnus U. Utah, 1976, 86, recipient merit award of honor, 1985. Mem. Nat. Aeros. Assn. Republican. Mormon. Club: Lochinvar. Patentee in field. Home: 3848 Malibu Country Dr Malibu CA 90265-4717 Office: PO Box 566 Malibu CA 90265-0566

ENSIGN, WILLIAM LLOYD, architect; b. Trinidad, W.I., Dec. 14, 1928; s. Lloyd Gordon and Evelyn Barbara (Hobson) E.; m. June G. Pollinger, July 10, 1954; children: David Gordon, Evan Alexander. B.S.A.E., B.S.C.E., U. Colo., 1950; M. Arch., Columbia U., 1952. Mem. firm McLeod & Ferrara (Architects), Washington, 1955-65; ptnr. McLeod Ferrara & Ensign, 1965-72; pres. McLeod Ferrara Ensign, 1972-80; asst. architect of the Capitol Washington, 1980-95; acting architect of the Capitol Washington, 1995-97; ind. cons. Md., 1997—; trustee Tax-Free Trust Ariz., Tax-Free Fund Utah; mem. D.C. Zoning commn., U.S. Capitol Police Bd., Nat. Capital Meml. Commn.; bd. dirs. Pa. Ave. Devel. Corp. Mem. Adv. Coun. Hist. Preservation, U.S. Capitol Guide Bd.; acting dir. U.S. Bot. Garden; trustee Nat. Bldg. Mus. With C.E.C., USNR, 1952-55. Fellow AIA (dir., past pres. Washington chpt., chmn. various coms.); mem. Nat. Trust Hist. Preservation, Nat. Capitol. Hist. Soc., Lambda Alpha Internat. (v.p.). Episcopalian.

ENSLEN, RICHARD ALAN, federal judge; b. Kalamazoo, May 28, 1931; s. Ehrman Thrasher and Pauline Mabel (Dragoo) E.; m. Pamela Gayle Chapman, Nov. 2, 1985; children—David, Susan, Sandra, Thomas, Janet, Joseph, Gennady. Student, Kalamazoo Coll., 1949-51, Western Mich. U., 1955; LL.B., Wayne State U., 1958; LL.M., U. Va., 1986. Bar: Mich. 1958, U.S. Dist. Ct. (we. dist.) Mich. 1960, U.S. Ct. Appeals (6th cir.) 1971, U.S. Ct. Appeals (4th cir.) 1975, U.S. Supreme Ct 1975. Mem. firm Stratton, Wise, Early & Starbuck, Kalamazoo, 1958-60, Bauckham & Enslen, Kalamazoo, 1960-64, Howard & Howard, Kalamazoo, 1970-76, Enslen & Schma, Kalamazoo, 1977-79; dir. Peace Corps. Costa Rica, 1965-67; judge Mich. Dist. Ct., 1968-70; U.S. dist. judge Kalamazoo, 1979—, chief judge, 1995—; mem. faculty Western Mich. U., 1961-62, Nazareth Coll., 1974-75; adj. prof. polit. sci. Western Mich. U., 1982—. Co-author: The Constitution Law Dictionary: Volume One, Individual Rights, 1985; Volume Two, Governmental Powers, 1987, Constitutional Deskbook: Individual Rights, 1987, (with Mary Bedikian and Pamela Enslen) Michigan Practice, Alternative Dispute Resolution, 1998. Served with USAF, 1951-54. Recipient Disting. Alumni award Wayne State Law Sch., 1980, Disting. Alumni award Western Mich. U., 1982; Outstanding Practical Achievement award Ctr. Pub. Resources, 1984; award for Excellence and Innovation in Alternative Dispute Resolution and Dispute Mgmt., Legal Program: Jewel Corp. scholar, 1956-57; Lampson McElhorne scholar, 1957. Mem. ABA (standing com. on dispute resolution 1983-90), Mich. Bar Assn., Am. Judicature Soc. (bd. dirs. 1983-85), Sixth Cir. Jud. Coun. Office: US Dist Ct 410 W Michigan Ave Kalamazoo MI 49007-3757

ENSLIN, JON S., bishop; b. Apr. 4, 1938; m. Crystal Enslin; children: Jonathan, Joshua. Piano teaching cert., Wis. Conservatory Music; BA magna cum laude, Carroll Coll., Waukesha, Wis.; MDiv, Northwestern Luth. Theol. Sem., Mpls. Mission devel., then pastor Christ the Servant Luth. Ch., Waukesha, Wis., 1964-75; sr. pastor St. Stephen's Luth. Ch., Monona, Wis., 1975-87; asst. to bishop, adminstrv. dean South-Ctrl. Synod, Wis., 1988-91, bishop, 1991—; trainer Clergy in Transition Growth in Excellence in Ministry Program, ELCA; mem. transition team South-Ctrl. Synod Wis. ELCA; mem. exec. bd. Wis.-Upper Mich. Synod of LCA, chmn. adminstrn. and fin. sect. exec. bd. Office: Evangelical Lutheran Church 2909 Landmark Pl Ste 202 Madison WI 53713-4200*

ENSLIN, THEODORE VERNON, poet; b. Chester, Pa., Mar. 25, 1925; s. Morton Scott and Ruth May (Tuttle); m. Mildred Marie Stout, Aug. 1, 1945 (div.); children—Deirdre, Jonathan Morton; m. Alison Jane Jose, Sept. 14, 1969; 1 son, Jacob Hezekiah. Studied mus. composition with Nadia Boulanger, Cambridge, Mass., 1943-44. Author: New Sharon's Prospect, 1965, To Come To Have Become, 1966, Forms (5 vols.), 1970-74, The Country of Our Consciousness, 1971, The Median Flow, 1975, Synthesis, 1975, Carmina, 1976, Ranger, 2 vols., 1978-80, Music for Several Occasions, 1985, Small Suite for Solo Flute, 1985, The Weather Within, 1986, Case Book, 1987, From Near the Great Pine, 1988, Love and Science, 1990, Little Wandering Flake of Snow, 1991, Gamma-UT, 1992, The House of the Golden Windows, 1993, Music in the Key of C, 1995, Communitas, 1996, Propositions for John Taggart, 1996, Thumbprint on Landscape, 1997, Skeins, 1998, Then and Now Selected Poems, 1999, Sequentiae, 1999; readings and seminars various colls. and univs. Recipient Niemann award for weekly newspaper column The Cape Codder, 1955, Hart Crane Meml. award, 1969; Disting. Vis. Prof. Bowling Green State U., 1989. Mem. Am. Found. for Homoeopathy. Address: RFD Box 289 Kansas Rd Milbridge ME 04658

ENSMINGER, DALE, mechanical engineer, electrical engineer; b. Mt. Perry, Ohio, Sept. 26, 1923; s. Charles Henry and Mary Elpha (Koehler) E.; m. Lois Elizabeth Hamilton, Mar. 25, 1948; children: Martha Jean, Laura Lee, Charles Robert, Jonathan Dale, Mary Ann, Daniel Joseph. BSME, BSEE, Ohio State U., 1950, postgrad., 1950-53. Registered profl. engr., Ohio. Rschr. Battelle Meml. Inst., Columbus, Ohio, 1950, prin. rschr.; sr. rschr. Battelle Columbus Labs., mgr. ultrasonics, sr. rsch. scientist, 1984-88; cons. in field. Author: Ultrasonics, 1973, 2d edit. 1988; contbr. articles to profl. jours., chpts. to books; patentee in field; contbr., reviewer Am. Soc. Non-Destructive Testing Handbook, 1989—. Sec. Columbus Prison Assn., 1950—; dean, dir. Columbus Bible Inst., 1952-97; mem. bd. Fundamental Bapt. Mission of Trinidad and Tobago. With U.S. Army, 1943-46. Recipient Cert. of Recognition, NASA, 1975. Mem. Acoustical Soc. Am., Soc. for Non-Destructive Testing, Ultrasonic Industry Assn. Home: 198 E Longview Ave Columbus OH 43202-1236

ENSMINGER, LUTHER GLENN, chemist; b. Mt. Perry, Ohio, Oct. 17, 1919; s. Charles Henry and Mary Elfa (Koehler) E.; m. Emma Jean Couch, May 12, 1951 (div. Apr. 1973); children: Luther, Douglas, Phillip, Deborah; m. How Leng Cheng, Nov. 11, 1983 (div. Dec. 1988); m. Lee Rose Olson, Oct. 19, 1992. B.Sc., Ohio State U., 1942, Ohio State U., 1948. Chemist FDA, Cin., 1948-56; chemist, lab. supr. FDA, Los Angeles, 1956-59; sci. adminstr. FDA, Washington, 1959-79; sci. cons. Arlington, Va., 1979—; vol., tutor for immigrant high sch. and coll. students (YMCA awards for outstanding tutoring work 1992, 93). Contbr. articles to profl. jours. Sec. Lee-Ballston Citizens Assn., 1965-75. Served with U.S. Army, 1942-45. Recipient Seven Who Care award, 1990, Outstanding Svc. to Cmty. award

YMCA Met. Washington, 1996. Fellow Assn. Ofcl. Analytical Chemists (exec. sec. 1967-79, mem. exec. com. 1960-79), Beta Gamma Sigma; mem. Am. Shoppers Panel. Republican. Presbyterian. Address: 631 N Edison St Arlington VA 22203-1430

ENSOR, ALLISON RASH, English language educator; b. Cookeville, Tenn., Oct. 3, 1935; s. Allison Rash Sr. and Rosenell (Johnson) E.; m. Anne Lovell, Aug. 20, 1958; children: Elizabeth Anne, Edward Mark. BA, Tenn. Tech. U., 1957; MA, U. Tenn., 1959; postgrad., Union Theol. Sem., N.Y.C., 1959-60; PhD, Ind. U., 1965. Asst. prof. English U. Tenn., Knoxville, 1965-71, assoc. prof., 1971-80, prof., 1980—. Author: Mark Twain and the Bible, 1969; editor: A Connecticut Yankee in King Arthur's Court by Mark Twain, 1982. Mem. MLA, South Atlantic MLA, Tenn. Philol. Assn. (pres. 1977-78), Ky.-Tenn. Am. Studies Assn. (pres. 1984-85), Tenn. Coll. English Assn. (sec.-treas. 1975—), Soc. for Study of So. Lit., Mark Twain Circle Am. Democrat. Methodist. Avocation: music. Home: 7109 Sheffield Dr Knoxville TN 37909-2531 Office: U Tenn Dept English Knoxville TN 37996

ENSSLIN, ROBERT FRANK, JR., retired association executive and military officer; b. Jacksonville, Fla., Feb. 22, 1928; s. Robert Frank Sr. and Pauline (Harper) E.; m. Fae Finter, Sept. 29, 1951; children: Robert III, Clyde, Paul, John. BA in Art, U. N.C., 1950; grad., F.A. Officer Candidate Sch., Ft. Sill, Okla., 1952, U.S. Army Command Staff Coll., 1969, U.S. Army War Coll., 1978. Commd. U.S. Army, 1952, advanced through grades to maj. gen., 1992; sales and adv. mgr. Sears, Roebuck & Co., Durham N.C. and Tampa, Fla., 1953-60; v.p. Louis Benito Advt., Tampa, 1960-67; pres. Ensslin & Hall Advt., Tampa, 1967-81; adj. gen. Fla. Nat. Guard, St. Augustine, Fla., 1982-92; exec. dir. Nat. Guard Assn. U.S., Washington, 1992-95; chair mil. adv. com. Office of Gov., Tallahassee, Fla., 1982-92. Pub. Nat. Guard mag., 1990-95; contbr. articles to profl. jours. Pres. Guidance Ctr. of Hillsborough, Tampa, 1964, Am. Cancer Soc., Tampa, 1968; gov. Fla. Advt. Fedn., 1964-65; mem. res. forces policy bd. Dept. Def., Washington, 1987-90; pres. Mcht.'s Assn. Fla., 1963-64. Decorated D.S.M., Legion of Merit. Mem. Am. Assn. Advt. Agys. (bd. dirs. 1978-81), Assn. of U.S. Army (trustee 1985-91, dir. Sunshine chpt.), N.G. Assn. U.S. (sec. 1986-88, v.p. 1988-90, pres. 1990-92, exec. dir.), Army and Navy Club. Home: 5903 Mount Eagle Dr Apt 414 Alexandria VA 22303-2527

ENSTROM, JAMES EUGENE, cancer epidemiologist; b. Alhambra, Calif., June 20, 1943; s. Elmer Melvin, Jr. and Klea Elizabeth (Bissell) E.; B.S., Harvey Mudd Coll., Claremont, Calif., 1965; M.S., Stanford U., 1967, Ph.D. in Physics, 1970; M.P.H., UCLA, 1976; m. Marta Eugenia Villanea, Sept. 3, 1978. Research asso. Stanford Linear Accelerator Center, 1970-71; research physicist, cons. Lawrence Berkeley Lab., U. Calif., 1971-75; Celeste Durand Rogers cancer research fellow Sch. Pub. Health, UCLA, 1973-75, Nat. Cancer Inst. postdoctoral trainee, 1975-76, cancer epidemiology researcher, 1976-81, assoc. research prof., 1981—; program dir. for cancer control epidemiology Jonsson Comprehensive Cancer Center, 1978-88, research epidemiologist, 1988—, sci. dir. tumor registry, 1984-87, mem. dean's council, 1976—; cons. epidemiologist Linus Pauling Inst. Sci. and Medicine, 1976-94; cons. physicist Rand Corp., 1969-73, R&D Assos., 1971-75; mem. sci. bd. Am. Council on Sci. and Health, 1984—. NSF predoctoral trainee, 1965-66; grantee Am. Cancer Soc., 1973—, Nat. Cancer Inst., 1979—; Preventive Oncology Acad. award, 1981-87. Fellow Am. Coll. Epidemiology; mem. Soc. Epidemiologic Research, Am. Heart Assn., Am. Pub. Health Assn., Am. Phys. Soc., AAAS, N.Y. Acad. Scis., Galileo Soc. Author papers in field. Office: U Calif Sch Pub Health Los Angeles CA 90024

ENTE, GERALD, pediatrician; b. N.Y.C., July 18, 1930; s. Louis M. and Minnie (Lackfish) E.; m. Phyllis Warch, Aug. 27, 1995; children: Peter, William. BS, Union Coll., 1951; MD, NYU, 1955. Diplomate Am. Acad. Pediatrics. Intern Kings County Hosp., Bklyn., 1955-56, resident in pediatrics, 1958-59; resident in pediatrics Bronx Mcpl. Hosp., 1959-60; pvt. practice, Westbury, N.Y., 1960—; clin. instr. pediatrics Einstein Med. Sch., 1960-64; clin. instr. pediatrics Meadowbrook, 1960-65, asst. attending pediatrics, 1965-68, clin. assoc. dir. of newborn svcs., 1968-70; clin. dir neonatology Nassau County Med. Ctr., 1970-88, attending physician pediatrics, 1974—; assoc. clin. prof. pediatrics SUNY Med. Coll., Stony Brook, N.Y., 1985-99; attending pediatrician Winthrop U. Hosp., 1997—, Schneider Children's Hosp., 1997—; med. dir. Trya Hostel, 1974-77, Fellowship Med. Labs, 1974-80; pediatric cons. Project Headstart, 1972, Westbury med. dir., 1966-76; cons. staff physician SUNY Coll. at Old Westbury, 1971-82, physician in-charge, 1972-79; cons. Westinghouse Electric Co., 1971-72, GenTel Electric Co., 1972; mem. Westbury Health Coun., 1974-78; dir. neonatology Ctrl. Gen. Hosp., 1980-90, chmn. pediats., 1990-94; profl. adv. bd. L.I. Inst. for Tng. in the Psychotherapies, 1979-81; mem. rsch. panel Med. World News, 1979-81. Author: (with others) Handbook of Neonatology, 1974, Pediatricians Manual Vol. I & II, 1977, Management of Prader Willi Syndrome, 1988; contbr. numerous articles to profl. jours. Bd. dirs. Offspring Dance Group, 1976-92; chmn. L.I. physicians United Way, 1983-84. Capt. U.S. Army Res., 1956-58. Recipient Samaritan award N.Y. Assn. Brain Insured Children, 1968, Man of Yr.; Resident's Teaching award Nassau County Medical Soc., 1972, Outstanding Attending of the Yr. Winthrop Univ. Hosp., 1998. Fellow Am. Acad. Pediatrics (PREP fellowship award 1979-85, PREP awards 1980-86, 93, 96, 98, exec. bd. chpt. 2), Royal Soc. of Pediatrics, Royal Soc. of Health, Internat. Coll. Pediatrics, Nassau Acad. of Medicine; mem. AMA (Physicians Recognition award 1980-84, 86, 87, 89, 91, 93, 96, 98), N.Y. State Med. Soc., Nassau County Med. Soc., World Med. Assn., Nassau Acad. Medicine (sect. on pediatrics), Pan Am. Med. Assn. (diplomate), Assn. Am. Soc. Photobiology, Internat. Transactional Analysis Assn., Am. Holistic Med. Assn., Nassau Acad. Medicine (bd trustees). Office: 530 Old Country Rd Westbury NY 11590-4500

ENTEMAN, WILLARD FINLEY, philosophy educator; b. Glen Ridge, N.J., Oct. 21, 1936; s. Verling Clair and Elizabeth Vance Rutherford (Dailey) E.; m. Kathleen Ffolliott, June 18, 1960; children: Sally Holyoke, David Finley. B.A., Williams Coll., 1959, LL.D. (hon.), 1978; M.B.A., Harvard U., 1961; M.A., Boston U., 1962, Ph.D., 1965; LL.D. (hon.), Colby Coll., 1980. Instr. in philosophy Wheaton Coll., 1963-65, asst. prof., 1965-69, assoc. prof., 1969-70; assoc. prof., chmn. dept. philosophy Union Coll., Schenectady, 1970-72; provost and assoc. prof. Union Coll., 1972-78; pres., prof. Bowdoin Coll., 1978-81; provost, v.p. acad. affairs R.I. Coll., 1982-90, prof. philosophy, 1982—; exec. v.p., dir. Bibliotech, Inc.; mem. New Eng. Bd. Higher Edn., 1978-81 ; 2d v.p., trustee Colby-Bates-Bowdoin Ednl. Telecasting Corp., 1978-81. Author: Managerialsim: The Emergence of a New Ideology, Retirement 101: How TIAA-CREF Members Should Deal with the Dramatic Changes in Their Pensions; editor: The Problem of Free Will, 1967; contbr. articles to profl. publs. Trustee Regional Meml. Hosp., Brunswick, Maine, 1978-81, Hotchkiss Sch., 1980-90, Eckerd Coll., 1987—; mem. long-range planning com. Portland (Maine) Sch. Art, 1979-81; vice chmn. bd. trustees R.I. Coun. on Econ. Edn. Named One of 100 Top Young Leaders in Higher Edn., Change mag., 1978. Mem. Nat. Assn. Ind. Colls. and Univs. (dir.), Brunswick C. of C. (trustee 1978-81). Office: RI Coll 600 Mt Pleasant Ave Providence RI 02908-1924

ENTERLINE, SUSAN CAROLE, elementary educator, writer; b. Sunbury, Pa., Aug. 10; d. Theodore Benjamin and Evelyn Jean (Janson) Picton; m. William Ralph Enterline, June 22; children: Christy Sue, Lori Ann. BS, Lock Haven U.; cert., Inst. Children's Lit., 1980, Long Ridge Writer's Group, West Redding, Conn., 1997; master's equivalency, Pa., 1989. Cert. tchr., Pa. Tchr. Muncy (Pa.) Sch. Dist., 1984-99, mem. homework com., 1996-99, mem. reading com., 1993—, mem. hiring interview com., 1992-94, writing specialist, 1998-99. Pres. PTO, Muncy, 1983-84, v.p., 1982-83; Bible sch. dir. Luth. Ch., Muncy, 1983; mem. St. Andrew Luth. Ch., Muncy, 1976-99, Sunday sch. tchr., 1978-80. Mem. ASCD, Pa. State Edn. Assn., Nat. Wildlife Fedn., Smithsonian Inst., Humane Soc. Republican. Avocations: writing, reading, gardening, swimming. Address: 7225 Sheffield Pl Cumming GA 30040

ENTHOVEN, ALAIN CHARLES, economist, educator; b. Seattle, Sept. 10, 1930; s. Richard Frederick and Jacqueline (Camerlynck) E.; m. Rosemary Fenech, July 28, 1956; children: Eleanor, Richard, Andrew, Martha, Nicholas, Daniel. B.A. in Econs, Stanford U., 1952; M.Phil. (Rhodes scholar), Oxford (Eng.) U., 1954; Ph.D. in Econs, MIT, 1956. Instr. econs. MIT, Cambridge, 1955-56; economist The RAND Corp., Santa Monica, Calif., 1956-60; ops. research analyst Office of Dir. Def. Research and Engring., Dept. Def., Washington, 1960; dep. comptroller, dep. asst. sec. U.S. Dept. Def., Washington, 1961-65, asst. sec. for systems analysis, 1965-69; v.p. for econ. planning Litton Industries, Beverly Hills, Calif., 1969-71; pres. Litton Med. Products, Beverly Hills, 1971-73; Marriner S. Eccles prof. pub. and pvt. mgmt. Grad. Sch. Bus. Stanford (Calif.) U., 1973—, prof. health care econs. Sch. Medicine, 1973—; cons. The Brookings Instn., 1956-60; vis. assoc. prof. econs. U. Wash., 1958; mem. Stanford Computer Sci. Adv. Com., 1968-73; cons. The RAND Corp., 1969—; mem. vis. com. in econs. Mass. Inst. Tech., 1971-78; mem. vis. com. on environ. quality lab. Calif. Inst. Tech., 1972-77; mem. Inst. Medicine, Nat. Acad. Scis., 1972—; mem. vis. com. Harvard U. Sch. Pub. Health, 1974-80; cons. Kaiser Found. Health Plan, Inc., 1973—; vis. prof. U. Paris, 1985, London Sch. Hygiene and Tropical Medicine, 1998-99; vis. fellow St. Catherine's Coll., Oxford U., Eng., 1985, New Coll., 1998-99; dir. Hotel Investors Trust, 1986-87, PCS Inc., 1987-90, Caresoft, 1996—. Contbr. numerous articles on def. spending and on econs. and pub. policy in health care to profl. jours.; author: (with K. Wayne Smith) How Much is Enough? Shaping the Defense Program 1961-69, 1971, Health Plan: The Only Practical Solution to the Soaring Cost of Medical Care, 1980; editor: (with A. Myrick Freeman III) Pollution, Resources and the Environment, 1973, Theory and Practice of Managed Competition in Health Care Finance, 1988. Bd. dirs. Georgetown U., Washington, 1968-73, Jackson Hole Group, 1993—; bd. regents St. John's Hosp., Santa Monica, 1971-73; vis. com. Harvard U. Kennedy Sch. Govt. Rock Carling fellow Nutfield Trust, 1999; recipient President's award for disting. fed. civilian svc., 1963, Disting. Pub. Svc. medal Dept. Def., 1990, Baxter prize for health svcs. rsch., 1994, Bd. Dirs.' award Healthcare Fin. Mgmt. Assn., 1995, Ellwood award Found. for Accountability, 1998; chmn. Gov.'s Taskforce Managed Care Improvement, 1997-98. Mem. Council on Fgn. Relations, Am. Assn. Rhodes Scholars, Am. Acad. Arts and Scis., Phi Beta Kappa. Home: 1 Mccormick Ln Atherton CA 94027-3033 Office: Stanford Univ Grad Sch Business Stanford CA 94305

ENTMAN, ROBERT MATHEW, communications educator, consultant; b. Bklyn., Nov. 7, 1949; s. Bernard and Rose (Jacobson) E.; m. Francie Seymour, June 1, 1979; children: Max, Emily. AB, Duke U., 1971; PhD, Yale U., 1977; M in Pub. Policy, U. Calif., Berkeley, 1980. Asst. prof. Dickinson Coll., Carlisle, Pa., 1975-77, Duke U., Durham, N.C., 1980-89; postdoctoral fellow U. Calif., 1978-80; assoc. prof. comm. Northwestern U., Evanston, Ill., 1989-94; prof. comm. N.C. State U., Raleigh, 1994—, dir. Ctr. for Info. Tech. and Policy, 1999—; adj. prof. U. N.C., Chapel Hill, 1995-98; Lombard vis. prof. Harvard U., 1997; cons. subcom. on telecom. U.S. Ho. of Reps., Washington, 1982, Nat. Telecom. and Info. Adminstrn., Washington, 1984-85, Aspen Inst., Washington and Aspen, Colo., 1986—; mem. working group Commn. on TV Policy, 1990-96; guest scholar Woodrow Wilson Ctr., Washington, 1989; Lombard vis. prof. Harvard U., 1997. Author: Democracy without Citizens, 1989, (monograph) Blacks in the News, 1991, Diversifying Broadcast Media, 1998; co-author: Media Power Politics, 1981; co-editor Mediated Politics: Communication in the Future of Democracy, 1999, (book series): Communication, Society and Politics, 1998—; also articles. Recipient McGannon award for comm. policy rsch., 1993; rsch. grantee Markle Found., 1984, 86, 88, 95, Chgo. Cmty. Trust, 1989-92, 95-97; rsch. fellow Ameritech., 1989-90. Mem. Am. Polit. Sci. Assn. (coun. polit. comm. sec. 1990-91, mem. editl. bd. Polit. Comm. 1992—, mem. editl. bd. Jour. Comm. 1994—, mem. editl. bd. Comm. Law and Policy 1994—, sec.-treas. polit. comm. sec. 1996-99, vice chair 1999-2000, chair 2000—), Social Sci. Rsch. Coun. (mem. working group on media and fgn. policy 1990-93). Avocations: wine collecting and tasting, tennis. Office: NC State U Dept Comm Box 8104 Raleigh NC 27695

ENTORF, RICHARD CARL, retired management consultant; b. Gettysburg, S.D., Feb. 11, 1929; s. Carl Luke and Violet (Carr) E.; m. Dorothy Ann Alexander, Nov. 23, 1951; children: Mark, Kimberly. B.S., U. Calif. at Berkeley, 1952. Methods engr. Boeing Aircraft Corp., 1957; successively prodn. mgr., dir. mfg., v.p. ops., v.p., gen. mgr., pres. Riverside Cement Co. div. Amcord, Inc., Los Angeles, 1957-75; successively v.p., gen. mgr. Fla. div., sr. v.p. Gen. Portland Inc., Dallas, 1975-81; sr. v.p. Fla. Crushed Stone Co., Leesburg, Fla., 1982-84, pres., 1984-89; pvt. practice mgmt. cons. Leesburg, 1989-99, retired, 1999. Served with USAF, 1953-57. Home: 33627 Overton Dr Leesburg FL 34788-3507

ENTREMONT, PHILIPPE, conductor, pianist; b. Rheims, France, June 7, 1934; came to U.S., 1953; s. Jean and Renée (Monchamps) E.; m. Andree Ragot, Dec. 21, 1955; children: Félicia, Alexandre. Student, Conservatoire National Superieur de Musique, Paris, Jean Doyen. Profl. debut at 17, Barcelona, Am. debut at 19, Nat. Gallery, Washington, 1953, pianist-condr. debut Mostly Mozart Festival, N.Y.c, 1971; rec. artist CBS, Teldec, EMI, Schwann and ProArte records; guest condr. Pitts. Symphony, Royal Philharm. Orch. Nat. de France, Montreal Symphony, San Francisco Symphony, Phila. Orch., Detroit Symphony, numerous others; prin. condr. Netherlands Chamber Orch., 1993—; prin.-guest condr. Israel Chamber Orch., 1994—; lifetime mus. dir. Vienna Chamber Orch., 1975—; mus. dir. New Orleans Symphony Orch., 1981-85, Denver Symphony, 1986-89, others. Decorated Officer of the Legion of Honor, Legion of Honor, Officer de l'Orde National du Merite: Austrian First Class Cross of Honor for the Arts and Scis., Comdr. in Order of Arts and Letters, 1998; A finalist Queen Elizabeth of Belgium Internat. Concours, 1952; Grand Prix Marguerite Long-Jacques Thibaud Competition, 1953; Harriet Cohen Piano medal, 1953; 1st prize Jeunesses Musicales; Grand Prix du Disque, 1967, 68, 69, 70; Edison award, 1968; Nominee Grammy award, 1972. Former mem. Academie Internationale de Musique Maurice Ravel (pres. 1975-80). Office: care Audrey Michaels 122 E 76th St New York NY 10021-2833 also: Amaro-Chantaco, 64500 Saint-Jean-de-Lux France*

ENTRIKEN, ROBERT KERSEY, retired management educator; b. McPherson, Kans., Jan. 15, 1913; s. Frederick Kersey and Opal (Birch) E.; m. Elizabeth Freeman, May 26, 1940 (div. Nov. 1951); children—Robert Kersey, Jr., Edward Livingston Freeman, Richard Davis; m. Jean Finch, June 5, 1954; 1 child, Birch Nelson. B.A., U. Kans. 1934; M.B.A., Golden Gate U., 1961; postgrad. City Univ. Grad. Bus. Sch., London, 1971-73. C.P.C.U. Ins. broker, Houston, Tex. and McPherson, Kans., 1935-39; asst. mgr. Cravens, Dargan & Co., Houston, 1939-42; br. mgr. Nat. Surety Corp., Memphis and San Francisco, 1942-54; v.p. Fireman's Fund Ins. Co., San Francisco. 1954-73; adj. prof. Golden Gate U., San Francisco, 1953-73, prof. mgmt., 1974-89; resident dean Asia Programs, Singapore, 1987-88; prof. emeritus 1989—, underwriting mem. Lloyd's of London, 1985-98; cons./ expert witness gen. mgmt. and surety bonding, 1987-97; ret., 1997. Contbr. articles to trade and profl. jours. Bd. dirs., sec., treas. Northstar Property Owners Assn., Calif., 1982-86. Served to capt. USNR, 1944-73, ret., 1973. Mem. Ins. Forum San Francisco (pres. 1965, trustee 1975-78, 84-88), Surety Underwriters Assn. No. Calif. (pres. 1956), CPCU Soc. (pres. No. Calif. chpt. 1957, Ins. Profl. of Yr., San Francisco chpt. 1981, bd. dirs., 1989-93), Chartered Ins. Inst., Ins. Inst. London, Musicians' Union Local No. 6 (life), U.S. Naval Inst., Assn. Naval Aviation, Phi Delta Theta. Episcopalian. Clubs: University, Marines' Meml. (San Francisco); Commonwealth. Lodge: Naval Order U.S. Office: 109 Minna St Ste 525 San Francisco CA 94105-3728

ENTRIKEN, ROBERT KERSEY, JR., motorsport writer, retired newspaper editor; b. Houston, Feb. 13, 1941; s. Robert and Jean (Finch) (stepmother) E.; married 1972 (div., 1982); 1 child, Jean Louise; m. Sandra Jo Miller, Mar. 4, 1989; children: Caitlyn Miller, Matthew Kersey; 1 adopted child, Stephanie Lynn; stepchild: Jared Ray Adamson. Student Sch. Journalism, U. Kans., 1961-69. Gen. assignment reporter Salina Jour., Kans., 1969-71, motorsport columnist, 1970-83, courts reporter, 1971-82, Sunday editor, 1972-75, spl. sects. editor, 1975-94, neighbors editor, 1982-95, TV editor, 1994-95; contbg. editor Sports Car Mag., Tustin, Calif., 1972—; motorsport columnist Motorsports Monthly, Tulsa, Okla., 1983-85, Nat. Speed Sport News, 1996—; operator Ikke så Hurtig Racing; Contbr. Performance Racing Industry mag., Sports Car World mag, Car Collector mag., Parts & People mag., Kansas! mag., Jox mag.; editor Kansas Motor Sports Ann, 1996. With USN, 1969-71, Guam. Mem. Am. Auto Racing Writers and Broadcasters Assn. (gen. v.p. 1982-86, Midwest v.p. 1980-82, chmn. All-Am. Team selections 1983—, chmn. Legends in Racing selections hall of fame 1989—), Soc. of Profl. Journalist Sigma Delta Chi, Sports Car Club Am. (Best Story award 1972, 73, 76-78, 83-87, 89, 92, inaugural recipient Vern Jacques SportsCar Contbr. of Yr. nat. award, 1999, Solo Cup nat. award 1981, England-Stipe award 1989, Nat. Solo I champion 1986, Road Racing Driver of the Year (Salina Region) 1995, Solo Driver of Yr. Wichita Region 1976, 82, Solo II Champion, Kans. 1978, 84, Midwest div. 1984, regional exec. of Kans. Region, 1974, founding mem. Salina Region 1990, regional exec. Salina Region 1994, Midwest divsn. Mid-Am. pointskeeper 1974—, nat. pointskeeper 1995—). Avocations: sports car racing, autocrossing, skiing. Home and Office: 2731 Scott Ave Salina KS 67401-7858

ENTWISLE, DORIS ROBERTS, sociology educator; b. Wilbraham, Mass., Sept. 28, 1924; d. Charles Edwin and Helen (McMenigall) Roberts; m. George Entwisle, Aug. 31, 1946; children: Barbara, Beverly, George H.; m. 2d Donald Roberts, Nov. 12, 1993. B.S., U. Mass., 1945; M.S., Brown U., 1946; Ph.D., Johns Hopkins U., 1960. Postdoctoral fellow Social Sci. Research Council Johns Hopkins U., Balt., 1960-61, research assoc. edn. and elec. engring., 1961-64, part-time asst. prof., 1964-67, assoc. prof., 1967-71, prof. sociology and engring. sci., 1971-98, prof. emerita, 1998—; mem. com. on child devel. and pub. policy NRC, 1982-87. Harvard vis. com. for sociology dept., 1986-91. Author: (with S.G. Doering) The First Birth, 1981, (with L.A. Hayduk) Early Schooling, 1982, (with K.L. Alexander and Susan Dauber) The Success of Failure, 1984, (with K.L. Alexander, L.S. Olson) Children, Schools and Inequality, 1997; editor: Sociology of Education, 1975-78; assoc. editor Am. Sociol. Rev., 1972-75, 95-98; co-editor Jour. Rsch. in Adolescence, 1990-94. Guggenheim fellow, 1976-77. Fellow APA, Am. Sociol. Assn. (chair sect. children); mem. Am. Ednl. Rsch. Assn., Soc. Rsch. in Child Devel. (pub. com. 1987-93, chair 1989-91, governing coun. 1993-99). Office: Johns Hopkins U 541 Mergenthaler Baltimore MD 21218

ENTZMINGER, JOHN NELSON, JR., federal agency administrator, electronic engineer, researcher; b. Memphis, Dec. 17, 1936; s. John Nelson and Josephine Chambers (Marshall) E.; m. Nancy May Burg, Sept. 9, 1961; children: David Marshall, Rebecca Louise. BSEE magna cum laude, U. S.C., 1959; MSEE, Syracuse U., 1968. Elec. engr. Bell Telephone Labs., Winston-Salem, N.C., 1959; project engr. Rome Air Devel. Ctr., Griffiss AFB, N.Y., 1960-66, sect. chief, communications, 1966-73, br. chief, communications and control, 1973-81, tech. dir. intelligence and reconnaissance, 1981-83; dir. tactical tech. Def. Advance Rsch. Project Agy., Washington, 1983-91, chief advanced tech., 1991-95; sr. staff mem. Inst. for Def. Analyses, Alexandria, Va., 1996-98; dep. for technology Def. Airborne Reconnaissance Office, Washington, 1996-98; pres. Entzminger Assocs. Consulting Firm, 1998—. Contbr. articles to profl. jours.; patentee in field. Elder Christian Assembly, Vienna, Va., 1985—. Fellow IEEE; mem. AAAS (sr.), Phi Beta Kappa, Tau Beta Pi. Republican. Avocations: flying, carpentry, mechanics, skiing. Home: 3203 Dominy Ct Oakton VA 22124-2008

ENYEART, JAMES L., museum director; b. Auburn, Wash., Jan. 13, 1943; s. Lyle F. and Emma A. (Ham) E.; m. Roxanne Enyeart Malone, Sept. 7, 1964; children: Mara, Sascha, Megan. BFA, Kansas City Art Inst., 1965; MFA, U. Kans., 1972. Dir. Albrecht Gallery Art, St. Joseph, Mo., 1967-68; curator photography, assoc. prof. Spencer Mus. Art, U. Kans., 1968-76; exec. dir. Friends of Photography, Carmel, Calif., 1976-77; dir., adj. prof. art Ctr. for Creative Photography, U. Ariz., 1977-89; dir. Internat. Mus. Photography at George Eastman House, Rochester, N.Y., 1989-95; Anne and John Marion prof., dir. Marion Ctr. Photo. Art Coll. Santa Fe, 1995—; prof. Photographic Arts, dir. Ann and John Marion Ctr., Coll. Santa Fe, 1995—; mem. numerous panels, adv. bds. and commns. in field, including peer panel, Nat. Endowment for Arts, Mus. Challenge Grants, 1993, adv. bd. Am. Photography Inst., NYU, 1991—, others; cons. in field. Author: Creative Camera, 1976, Francis Bruguiere, 1977, Jerry Uelsmann: Twenty-Five Years, A Retrospective, 1982, Edward Weston's California Landscapes, 1984 (Am. Inst. Graphic Arts award), Land, Sky, and All That Is Within: Visionary Photographers of the Southwest, 1998, The Nature of Photographs, 1998, others; (with R.D. Monroe, Philip Stokes) Three Classic American Photographs: Texts and Contexts, 1982; contbr. Edward Weston Omnibus, 1984, Contemporary Photographers, 1983, 2d rev. edit., 1986-87; editor: Decade by Decade: A Survey of Twentieth Century American Photography, 1989; co-editor: Henry Holmes Smith: Collected Writings 1935-1985, 1986; contbr. introductions to Andreas Feininger: A Retrospective, 1986, Aaron Siskind: Terrors and Pleasures, 1931-1980, 1982, W. Eugene Smith: Master of the Photographic Essay, 1981, Landscapes 1975-1979, 1981, Photography of the Fifties: An American Perspective, 1980, George Fiske, Yosemite Photographer, 1980, Peekamoose, 1973; editor Kans. Album, 1977, Heinecken, 1980, The Archive, 1988, Image, 1989—; designer print study rm. Spencer Mus. Art, U. Kans., 1976, Ctr. Creative Photography, U. Ariz., 1989; author, curator exhbn. Judy Dater: Twenty Years; represented in collections Albrecht Gallery, St. Joseph, Mo., Mus. Art, U. Kans., Bibliotheque Nationale, Paris, Internat. Mus. Photography at George Eastman House, Rochester, Sheldon Meml. Gallery, Lincoln, Nebr., Nat. Mus. Am. Art; numerous other publs. Commr. Kans. Arts Commn., 1973-74; selection com. Ariz. Gov.'s Arts Awards, 1984; creative arts award com. Brandeis U., Waltham, Mass., 1990—; adv. bd. Aaron Siskind Found., 1981—, W. Eugene Smith Meml. Fund, Inc., 1983—; nom. com. MacArthur Found., 1982; rev. panel Bush Found. Fellowships, St. Paul, 1980. Recipient Josef Sudek medal Ministry Culture, Union Visual Arts, Czechoslovakia, 1989, Photokina Obelisk award, Fed. Republic Germany, 1982, Internat. Achievement award Photographic Soc. Japan, 1994, others; grantee NEA, 1973, 74, 75; Hon. Rsch. fellow U. Exeter, 1974, OAS fellow, 1966-67, John Simon Guggenheim Meml. fellow, 1987; fellow John S. and James L. Knight Found. Nat. Millennium Survey, 1998; named 100 Most Important People in Photography Am. Photo, 1998; grantee Nat. Endowment for the Arts, 1973—; other awards in field. Mem. Am. Assn. Art Mus. Dirs., Am. Assn. Art Mus., Am. Photography Inst. (adv. bd. 1991—), Am. Photog. Hist. Soc. (hon. life), Oracle (co-founder), Deutschen Gesellschaft fur Photographie (hon. mem.), others. Office: Coll Santa Fe Marion Ctr Photographic Art 1600 Saint Michaels Dr Santa Fe NM 87505-7615 Office: Internat Mus Photography 900 East Ave Rochester NY 14607-2219

ENYEDI, ALEXANDER JOSEPH, plant physiologist, researcher; b. Brantford, Ont., Can., Feb. 18, 1958; came to U.S., 1986; s. Alexander Joseph and Helen Ann Enyedi; m. Andrea Louise Bower, Nov. 5, 1983; 1 child: Nathaniel Alexander Enyedi. BSc in Agr., U. Guelph, Ont., Can., 1981, MSc in Plant Physiology, 1985; PhD in Plant Pathology, Pa. State U., 1991. Lic. pvt. fixed-wing pilot. Grad. asst. U. Guelph, Ont., Can., 1980-83; rsch. scientist Govt. of Ont., 1983-86; grad. asst. Pa. State U., State College, 1986-90; postdoctoral scientist Rutgers U., New Brunswick, N.J., 1991-93; asst. prof. Western Mich. U., Kalamazoo, 1993-99, assoc. prof., 1999—. Author abstracts; contbr. articles to profl. jours. Recipient Am. Phytopathology Found. award, St. Paul, 1994; grantee Asgrow Seed Co., Kalamazoo, 1996, U.S. Dept. Def., Washington, 1997, Dow AgroScis., Indpls., 1998. Mem. Am. Soc. Plant Physiologists, Sigma Xi (pres.-elect 1997-98, pres. 1998-99). Office: Western Mich Univ Dept Biol Scis 3927 Wood Hall Kalamazoo MI 49008

ENYEDY, GUSTAV, JR., chemical engineer; b. Cleve., Aug. 23, 1924; s. Gustav and Mary (Silay) E.; m. Zoe Agnes Zachlin, Aug. 25, 1956 (div.); children: Louise Elaine, Roseann Marie, Arthur Gustav, Lillian Alice, Edward Anthony; m. Barbara Martha Ludwig Holley, May 9, 1987. B.S. in Chem. Engring., Case Inst. Tech., 1950, M.S., 1955. Registered profl. engr., Ohio. Engr., Rayon Tech. div. E.I. duPont, Richmond, Va., 1950-51; project engr. Grasselli Chem. Div., Cleve., 1951-54; devel. engr. Diamond Alkali (Soda Products), Painesville, Ohio, 1954-60; process engr. Central Engring., Cleve., 1960-61; staff engr. research dept. Central Engring., Painesville, 1961-65; supr. computer services Central Engring., 1965-68; mgr. Diamond Shamrock Corp., Painesville, 1968-73; engring. cons., 1973-85; pres. PDQS, Inc., 1975—; lectr. chem. engring. Fenn Coll., Cleve., 1957-61, Cleve. State U., 1975-76. Contbr. articles to tech. jours., textbooks. Treas., cubmaster, chmn. Gates Mills Cub Scout Pack, 1970-71, 75-78. Served with AUS, 1943-46. Decorated Bronze Star medal, Combat Inf. badge. Fellow Am. Inst. Chem. Engrs., Am. Assn. Cost Engrs. (tech. v.p. 1966-68, pres. 1969-70, speakers' bur. program 1971-89, O.T. Zimmerman Founder's award and hon. life mem., 1992); mem. Hungarian Geneal. Soc. of Greater Cleve. (founder 1996), Tau Beta Pi, Pi Delta Epsilon. Home and office: 7830 Sugarbush Ln Gates Mills OH 44040-9317 *Do each job with complete integrity. Do not gain favor by giving in to outside pressure to slant results.*

ENZI, MICHAEL BRADLEY, senator, accountant; b. Bremerton, Wash., Feb. 1, 1944; s. Elmer Jacob and Dorothy (Bradley) E.; m. Diana Buckley,

June 7, 1969; children: Amy, Bradley, Emily. BBA, George Wash. U., 1966; MBA, Denver U., 1968. Cert. profl. human resources, 1994. Pres. NZ Shoes, Inc., Gillette, Wyo., 1969-95, NZ Shoes of Sheridan, Inc., Wyo., 1983-96; acctg. mgr. Dunbar Well Svc., Inc., Gillette, 1985-97; mem. Wyo. Ho. of Reps., Cheynne, 1987-91, Wyo. State Senate, Cheynne, 1991-96, U.S. Senate, 1997—; chmn. bd. dirs. 1st Wyo. Bank, Gillette, 1978-88; chmn. Senate Revenue Com., 1992-96. Mayor City of Gillette, 1975-82; pres. Wyo. Assn. Mcpls., Cheyenne, 1980-82. Sgt. Wyo. Air NG, 1967-73. Mem. Wyo. Order of DeMolay (state master councilor 1963-64), Wyo. Jaycees (state pres. 1973-74), Masons (Sheridan and Gillette lodges), Scottish Rite, Shriners, Lions, Sigma Chi. Republican. Presbyterian. Avocations: fishing, bicycling, soccer. Home: 431 Circle Dr Gillette WY 82716-4903 Office: US Senate US Capitol Washington DC 20510

EPEL, DAVID, biologist, educator; b. Detroit, Mar. 26, 1937; s. Jacob A. and Anna K. (Karse) E.; m. Lois S. Ambush, Dec. 18, 1960; children: Andrea, Sharon, Elissa. A.B., Wayne State U., 1958; Ph.D., U. Calif.-Berkeley, 1963. Postdoctoral fellow Johnson Research Found., U. Pa., 1963-65; asst. prof. Hopkins Marine Sta., 1965-70; assoc. prof., then prof. Scripps Instn. Oceanography, 1970-77; Jane and Marshall Steel Jr. prof. marine scis. Hopkins Maine Sta., Stanford U., Pacific Grove, Calif., 1977—; acting dir. Hopkins Marine Sta., Pacific Grove, 1984-88; co-dir. embryology course Marine Biol. Lab., Woods Hole, 1974-77. Mem. editorial bd. Animal Biology, Biol. Bull, Zygote. Bd. dirs. Rsch. Inst., Monterey Bay Aquarium, 1987-89, trustee, 1985-88. Guggenheim fellow, 1976-77, Overseas fellow Churchill Coll., Cambridge, Eng., 1976-77; recipient Allen Cox medal for fostering excellence in undergrad. rsch. Stanford U., 1995. Fellow AAAS (mem.-at-large, sect. G 1979-84, chmn. sect. on biol. scis. 1998—); mem. Am. Soc. Cell Biology (mem. council 1978-80), Soc. Devel. Biology, Internat. Soc. Devel. Biology, Soc. Integrative and Comparative Biology (chairperson devel. and cell biology sect. 1990-92). Home: 25847 Carmel Knolls Dr Carmel CA 93923-8845 Office: Hopkins Marine Sta Pacific Grove CA 93950

EPEL, LIDIA MARMUREK, dentist; b. Buenos Aires, Argentina, Sept. 30, 1941; came to U.S., 1966; d. Israel and Ita Rosa (Sonabend) Marmurek; children: Diana, Bryan. BS, Buenos Aires U., 1959, DDS, 1964. Lic. dentist, N.Y. Gen. practice dentistry Argentina, 1965-66, Long Beach, N.Y., 1967-70, Lynbrook, N.Y., 1970-73, Rockville Centre, N.Y., 1973—. Bd. dirs. Rosa Lee Young Childhood Ctr., Rockville Centre, 1982-94, Rockville Centre Edn. Found., 1990—; mem. adv. com. on HIV/AIDS Bd. Edn. Rockville Centre Pub. Schs., 1994—; past pres. Queens-L.I. Women's Dental Study Group. Fellow Internat. Coll. Dentists, Pierre Fauchard Acad., Am. Coll. Dentistry, L.I. Acad. Odontology; mem. ADA (ho. of dels. 1996—), Fedn. Dentaire Internat., Nassau County Dental Soc. (bd. dirs., chair com. on pub. and profl. rels. 1990-96, chairperson com. on health, 1989-92, chair membership com. 1993, treas. exec. com. 1993, sec. exec. com. 1994, v.p. 1995, mem. membership task force 1994-95, pres-elect 1996, pres. 1997, dir. Greater L.I. dental meeting), Overseas Dentist Assn. (pres. N.Y. chpt. 1968-72), Dental Soc. of State of N.Y. (coun. for pub. and profl. rels. 1990—, chair children's dental health month campaign 1991, chair mem. recruitment and retention 1995—, bd. govs. 1998—, chair reference com. 198, mem. coun. on nominations 1998, coun. on constitutional by-laws 1999), Child Care Coun. of Nassau (bd. dirs. 1996—, reference coms. 1999), Hadassah (bd. dirs. Rockville Ctr. 1983-84, 92-93). Democrat. Jewish. Avocations: painting, traveling. Office: 165 N Village Ave Rockville Centre NY 11570-3761

EPHRAIM, CHARLES, lawyer; b. Chgo., Sept. 18, 1924; s. Max H. and Margaret Mary (O'Neill) E.; m. Marguerite Marie Lamont, Dec. 23, 1944; children: Linda Patrice O'Dea, Charles Lamont. Ph.B., U. Chgo., 1948, J.D., 1951. Bar: D.C. 1951, Ill. 1984, Tex. 1985. Sole practice D.C., Ill. and Tex. Mng. editor: U. Chgo. Law Rev, 1950-51; Contbr. to profl. publs. Bd. dirs. Christ Ch. Child Center (now The Ivymount Sch.), Bethesda, Md., 1961-68, chmn., 1961-62; v.p., bd. dirs. Bethesda Fellowship House, 1976-78. Served to 1st lt. USAF, 1943-47. Mem. Ill. Bar Assn., D.C. Bar Assn., Tex. Bar Assn., Transp. Lawyers Assn. (pres. 1978-79), Phi Beta Kappa, Order of Coif. Home: 1332 Bayview Dr Apt 303 Fort Lauderdale FL 33304-1634

EPHREMIDES, ANTHONY, electrical engineering educator; b. Athens, Greece, Sept. 19, 1943; came to U.S., 1967; s. John and Eva (Tsagris) E.; m. Jane Tsuchiyama, June 14, 1974. BS, Nat. Tech. Inst., Athens, 1967; MA, Princeton U., 1969, PhD, 1971. Registered profl. engr., Md. Asst. prof. U. Md., College Park, 1971-74, assoc. prof., 1975-80, prof. elec. engring., 1980—; pres. PONTOS, Inc., North Bethesda, Md., 1981—; vis. prof. Nat. Tech. U., 1978, U. Calif., Berkeley, 1979, MIT, Boston, 1985, Swiss Fed. Inst. Tech., Zurich, 1986; cons. Naval Rsch. Lab., Washington, 1977—; dir. Ctr. for Comml. Devel. of Space, NASA, 1991—; advisor U. Crete, Iraklion, Greece, 1983—; dir. Fairchild Scholars Program, College Park, 1980-85. Editor: Random Processes, 1974; editor IEEE Trans., 1979-80, 86-87, 88—; contbr. articles to profl. jours. Mem. Met. Opera Guild, N.Y.C., 1975—, Washington Opera Guild, 1975-83. Recipient Excellence awards Nat. Rsch. Labs., 1981, 83, 87; NSF grantee 1971—, Office Naval Rsch. grantee, 1988—. Fellow IEEE (pres. and bd. dirs. 1989—, chmn. symposia 1986, 91, Donald Fink award for best tutorial paper 1991); mem. Nat. Tech. Chamber Greece. Avocations: travel, outdoor sports, opera, arts. Home: 5809 Nicholson Ln Apt 1004 N Bethesda MD 20852-5712 Office: U Md Elec Engring Dept College Park MD 20742

EPHRON, NORA, writer, director; b. N.Y.C., May 19, 1941; d. Henry and Phoebe (Wolkind) E.; m. Dan Greenburg (div.); m. Carl Bernstein (div.); children: Jacob, Max; m. Nicholas Pileggi. BA, Wellesley Coll., 1962. Reporter N.Y. Post, 1963-68; free-lance writer, 1968—; contbg. editor, columnist Esquire mag., 1972-73, sr. editor, columnist, 1974-78; contbg. editor N.Y. mag., 1973-74. Author: Wallflower at the Orgy, 1970, Crazy Salad, 1975, Scribble Scribble, 1978, Heartburn, 1983, Nora Ephron Collected, 1991; screenwriter: (with Alice Arlen) Silkwood (nominated Acad. award for best original screenplay), 1983, Heartburn, 1986, Cookie, 1989, When Harry Met Sally (nominated Acad. award, BAFTA award for best screenplay), 1989, My Blue Heaven, 1990; dir., screenwriter (with Delia Ephron) This Is My Life, 1992, Mixed Nuts, 1994, Michael, 1996, You've Got Mail, 1998; co-screenwriter, dir. Sleepless in Seattle (nominated Acad. award for best original screenplay), 1993. Mem. Writers Guild Am., Authors Guild, Dirs. Guild of Am., Acad. Motion Picture Arts and Scis.

EPHROSS, PAUL HULLMAN, social work educator; b. Boston, Oct. 22, 1935; s. Israel Wolfson and Bessie (Hullman) E.; m. Joan Weiss, Dec. 30, 1990; children: Sara Anne, Peter Joseph, David Benjamin. AB, Harvard Coll., 1955; M.S.S.S., Boston U., 1957; PhD, U. Chgo., 1969. Lic. cert./clin. social worker, Md. Social worker Jewish Community Ctr., Boston, 1957-59; social worker, social work adminstr. Jewish Community Ctrs., Chgo., 1959-66; lectr. Chgo. City Coll., 1966-68; instr. Loyola U., Chgo., 1967-68; from asst. prof. to assoc. prof. U. Md., Balt., 1968-74, prof. social work, 1974—, clin. prof. psychiatry, 1989-94, dir. PhD program, 1976-81; psychotherapist, cons. Md. Sexuality Resource Ctr., Balt., 1987-93; adj. prof. Balt. Hebrew U., 1998—; cons. Md. State Dept. Edn., Balt. city and various other Md. counties, 1970-94, Juvenile Svcs. Agy. State of Md., Balt., 1972-82, Associated Cath. Charities, Inc., Balt., 1975-76, Nat. Assn. Social Workers, Silver Spring, Md., 1985-87, Md. State Dept. Health and Mental Hygiene, 1989—. Co-author: Working Effectively with Administrative Groups, 1987, Groups that Work, 1988, Human Behavior Theory and Social Work Practice, 1991, Group Work With Populations at Risk, 1997, Ethnicity and Social Work Practice, 1998; co-editor: Group Work: Expanding Horizons, 1993; contbr. articles to profl. jours. Bd. dirs. Balt. Hebrew Congregation, 1969-71, Associated Jewish Charities, Inc., Balt., 1980-84, Balt. Jewish Community Relations Coun., 1984—; mem. Amateur Chamber Music Players, 1965-94. Named Alumnus of Yr., Sch. of Social Work, Boston U., 1984; research and training grantee fed. & State of Md. agencies, 1977—. Mem. Nat. Assn. Social Workers, Coun. on Social Work Edn., Assn. for the Advancement of Social Work with Groups (bd. dirs. 1987-93, sec. 1989-93), Soc. for the Scientific Study of Sex, Am. and Eastern Sociol. Assns., U. Club (bd. dirs. Balt. 1987-93). Democrat. Jewish. Avocations: chamber music (flute, piano), Jewish & European history, Boston Red Sox. PEPHROSS@SS-W.UMARYLAND.EDU. Office: 525 W Redwood St Baltimore MD 21201-1777

EPLER, GARY ROBERT, physician, writer, educator; b. Chico, Calif., Apr. 5, 1944; s. Deane Chandler and Kathryn Louise (McNeil) E.; m. Joan Susan Weidman, Sept. 10, 1983; children: Gregory C., Brett H. MD, Tulane U., 1971; MPH, Harvard U., 1978. Diplomate in internal medicine and pulmonary medicine Am. Bd. Internal Medicine. Intern Harlem Hosp., Columbia U., 1971-72; resident U. Hosp., Boston, 1974-76, pulmonary medicine fellowship, 1975-78; asst. prof. medicine Sch. Medicine Boston U., 1978-85, assoc. clin. prof. medicine, 1985-96; assoc. clin. prof. medicine Harvard U., Boston, 1995—; med. dir. respiratory therapy, chmn. dept. medicine New England Bapt. Hosp., Boston, 1983-98, med. dir. rehab. unit, 1983-98; parasitology rsch. fellow Tulane U., Cali, Colombia, 1969-70, USPHS, Ctrs. Disease Control, 1972-74; tuberculosis cons. CDC Vietnamese Refugee Camps, Eglin AFB, Fla. and Indiantown Gap, Pa., 1975, Cuban Refugee Camp, Indiantown Gap, 1980; med. cons. CDC, Vietnamese Refugee Programs in Hong Kong, Thailand, Philippines, Malaysia, Indonesia; vis. attending physician U. Hosp., Boston City Hops. and Boston VA Hosp., 1978-98, Brigham and Women's Hosp., Boston, 1999—; med. dir. Occupational Health Ctr., Wilmington, Mass; vis. prof. Kyoto (Japan) U., 1990; many others. Author book on diseases of bronchioles, 1994; editor book on occupational lung diseases; editl. reviewer New England Jour. Medicine, Annals of Internal Medicine, Jour. AMA, Am. Rev. Respiratory Diseases, Chest, Jour. Respiratory Medicine, Jour. Western Medicine, Jour. Rheumatology, European Respiratory Jour.; contbr. chpts. to books, more than 85 articles to sci. jours. Lt. comdr. USPHS, 1972-74. Recipient cert. of appreciation Am. Lung Assn. Mass.; named one of Outstanding Med. Specialists in U.S., Town and Country Mag., 1989. Fellow ACP, Am. Coll. Chest Physicians (chmn. com. on occupational and environ. health 1987-88, v.p. New England States chpt. 1989-91, pres. chpt. 1991-93); mem. AMA (alt. del. 1987-93), Am. Soc. Law and Medicine (treas. 1983-85, Disting. Svc. award 1985), Am. Coll. Physician Execs., Mass. Thoracic Soc. (mem. coun. 1980-84, sec.-treas. 1984-85, pres. 1986-88), Mass. Med. Soc. Office: Brigham and Women's Hosp Pulmonary/Critical Care Med 75 Francis St Boston MA 02115

EPLEY, LEWIS EVERETT, JR., lawyer; b. Ft. Smith, Ark., Apr. 28, 1936; s. Lewis Everett and Evelyn (Wood) E.; m. Donna Louise Swopes, Feb. 24, 1962. B.S., J.D., U. Ark., 1961. Bar: Ark. 1961. Practiced in Eureka Springs, city atty., 1969-71; chmn. bd. Bank of Eureka Springs, Ark., 1990-93, vice-chmn., 1993—, also bd. dirs.; del. Ark. Constl. Conv., 1969-70; apptd. spl. assoc. justice Ark. Supreme Ct., 1984. Mem. Ark. Bldg. Svcs. Coun., 1975-80, chmn., 1976-78; mem. Carroll County Cen. Dem. Com., 1964-68; bd. dirs. Eureka Springs Ozark Folk Festival, 1964-69, Ark. Cancer Rsch. Ctr., N.W. Ark. Radiation Therapy Inst., 1984-91, pres. bd. dirs., 1989; chmn. adv. bd. Eureka Springs Mcpl. Hosp., 1963-71; mem. Beaver Lake Adv. Com., 1982-89; trustee U. Ark., 1989-99, chmn. bd. trustees, 1996-98; bd. dirs. U. Ark. Found., 1994—, Mashburn Scholarship Found., 1993—; dir. Washington Regional Med. Found.; chmn. Carroll County adv. com. Ark. Good Rds. Transp. Coun.; mem. Carroll County Com. for Study of Long-Term Health Care Needs, 1990-93; com. mem. Carroll County Centralized Health Feasibility, 1990-93; mem. devel. coun. Eureka Springs Hosp., 1997—. Fellow Ark. Bar Assn. (del. 1975-78), Am. Inns of Ct. (mem. emeritus W. B. Putnam chpt. 1990-97), Carroll County Bar Assn. (past pres.), Eureka Springs C. of C. (dir., past pres.), Eureka Springs Rotary Club (past pres.), Phi Alpha Delta, Kappa Kappa Psi. Baptist. Home: 1110 Pivot Rock Rd Eureka Springs AR 72632-9506 Office: PO Box 3159 20 Blue Water Circle Holiday Island AR 72631-3107

EPLEY, THELMA MAE CHILDERS, retired gifted and talented education educator; b. Ft. Wayne, Ind., Dec. 28, 1918; d. Harley Ellsworth and Bessie Mae (Corathers) Childers; m. Joseph Mendel Epley, Sept. 14, 1946. BS, Ind. U., 1941; MA, Calif. State U., Northridge, 1958; postgrad., U. So. Calif., 1964-65. Cert. elem., secondary tchr., adminstr., Calif. Tchr. Ft. Wayne Pub. Schs., 1941-42, 43-46; tchr., counselor Muncie (Ind.) Pub. Schs., 1942-43; tchr. L.A. Unified Sch. Dist., 1948-56, reserve tchr., 1955-57, specialist gifted program, 1958-70, tchr. adult edn., 1964-69, instrnl. adviser, 1970-75; instr. Occidental Coll., Eagle Rock, Calif., 1952-61, Calif. State U., 1958; newspaper edn. coord. Copley LA Newspapers, Santa Monica, Calif., 1978-93; ret.; mem. adv. bd. gifted parents groups, L.A., 1958-75; ednl. cons. state bds. edn., 1975-86; project affiliate Nat. and State Leadership Tng. Inst. for Gifted and Talented, 1976-87; instr. U. Calif., L.A., 1964-75, Mt. St. Marys Coll., Doheny, 1970-71, U. Tucson, 1983-85, U. Calgary, Can., 1985. Author: Annotated Bibliography on Gifted, 1958, Models For Thinking, 1982, Futuristics, 1985, Promoting Productive Thinking, 1988; contbr. articles to profl. jours. Active Nat. Rep. Com., Washington, 1982-93, Citizen Amb. Program, Washington, 1990-93. Mem. Nat. Assn. for Gifted (Achievement award 1958-75), World Coun. on Gifted, World Future Soc., Calif. Ret. Tchrs. Assn., Calif. Coords. of Newspaper in Edn., Assoc. Adminstrs. of L.A. Unified Sch. Dist., Delta Kappa Gamma (pres. Gamma Lambda chpt. 1963-65, Woman of Yr. award 1990). Republican. Avocations: reading, traveling, painting, decorating, gardening. Home: 5067 Avenida del Sol Laguna Woods CA 92653

EPLING, RICHARD LOUIS, lawyer; b. Waukegan, Ill., Aug. 16, 1951; s. Carrol Franklin and Mary Teresa Epling; m. Suzanne Braley, Aug. 4, 1973. BA in English and History magna cum laude, Duke U., 1973; JD, U. Mich., 1976. Bar: Ill. 1977, U.S. Dist. Ct. (no. dist.) Ill. 1977, U.S. Ct. Appeals (7th cir.) 1979, Ariz. 1981, U.S. Dist. Ct. Ariz. 1981, U.S. Ct. Appeals (9th cir.) 1982, N.Y. 1988, U.S. Ct. Appeals (2d cir.) 1988, U.S. Dist. Ct. (ea. and so. dists.) N.Y. 1989. Law clk. to presiding justice Mich. Supreme Ct., Southfield, 1976-77; assoc. Katten, Muchin & Zavis, Chgo., 1977-81; ptnr. Brown & Bain, P.A., Phoenix, 1981-88, Sidley & Austin, N.Y.C., 1988-92, Winthrop, Stimson, Putnam & Roberts, N.Y.C., 1992—; assoc. conferee Nat. Bankruptcy Conf., Washington, 1985-93. Contbr. articles to profl. jours. Mem. Am. Bankruptcy Inst., Phi Beta Kappa. Office: Winthrop Stimson Putnam & Roberts One Battery Park Plz New York NY 10004

EPNER, STEVEN ARTHUR, computer consultant; b. Buffalo, July ; s. Robert and Rosann (Krohn) E.; m. Louise Berke, June 20, 1970; children: Aaron J., Brian D. BS, Purdue U., 1970. Computer operator/programmer Union Carbide, Chgo. and London, 1966-68; system analyst process design III, Chgo., 1969; analyst, sr. systems analyst Monsanto Co., St. Louis, 1970-74; lead analyst Citicorp., St. Louis, 1974-76; cons., pres. The User Group, Inc. (name changed to BSW Consulting, Inc. 1995), St. Louis, 1976—; lectr. U. Mo., St. Louis Bus. Program, AICPA, Mo., 1983-93; SBA Task Force on Small Bus.; dir. Programming and Systems Cons., Inc. Editor: The Independent, 1977-84; contbg. editor St. Louis Bus. Jour., St. Louis Computing; contbr. articles to profl. jours. Trustee Steven A. Epner/ICAA Scholarship fund; mem. tech. com., founding rep. EDI Coalition of Assns. Mem. Ind. Computer Cons. Assn. (dir., pres. chpt., nat. pres.), Nat. Cons. Council, Nat. Spkrs. Assn., Internat. Brotherhood Magicians. Office: BSW Cons Inc 1050 N Lindbergh Blvd Saint Louis MO 63132-2912 *I am often asked about starting businesses. My normal reply is, "If it were easy and guaranteed, then it would already be done." Therefore, building a successful organization takes time, effort, and risk.*

EPP, DONALD JAMES, economist, educator; b. Hastings, Nebr., June 23, 1939; s. Abram W. and Edith Elizabeth (Harrison) E.; B.S., U. Nebr., 1961; M.S. (NDEA fellow), Mich. State U., 1964, Ph.D., 1967; m. Cathryn Jean Cronn, Dec. 10, 1961; children—Eric Alan, Amy Elizabeth. Instr., Mich. State U., East Lansing, 1965-67; asst. prof. agrl. econs. Pa. State U., University Park, 1967-71, assoc. prof., 1971-81, prof., 1981—, asst. dir. Environ. Resources Rsch. Inst. (formerly Inst. for Research on Land and Water Resources), 1981—; cons. to environ. firms, state and fed. agys. Served with F.A., U.S. Army, 1961-62. Mem. Am. Econ. Assn., Am. Agrl. Econ. Assn., NE Agrl. and Resource Econs. Assn. (pres. 1995-96), Assn. Environ. and Resource Economists, Sigma Xi, Gamma Sigma Delta. Author: (with John W. Malone, Jr.) Introduction to Agricultural Economics, 1981; contbr. articles to profl. jours. and tech. publs. Home: 550 Brittany Dr State College PA 16803-1423 Office: Pa State U 105 Armsby Bldg University Park PA 16802-5600

EPP, ELDON JAY, religion educator; b. Mountain Lake, Minn., Nov. 1, 1930; s. Jacob Jay and Louise (Kintzi) E.; m. ElDoris Balzer, June 13, 1951; children: Gregory Thomas, Jennifer Elizabeth. AB magna cum laude, Wheaton Coll., 1952; BD magna cum laude, Fuller Theol Sem., 1955; STM, Harvard U., 1956, PhD, 1961. Spl. rsch. asst. Princeton Theol. Sem., 1961-62; vis. instr. Drew U. Theol. Sch., 1962; asst. prof. religion U. So. Calif. Grad. Sch. Religion, 1962-65, assoc. prof., 1965-67, assoc. prof. classics, 1966-68; assoc. prof. religion Case Western Res. U., Cleve., 1968-71, prof. religion, Harkness prof. bibl. lit., 1971-98, prof. emeritus, 1998—, dean humanities and social scis., 1977-85, dean emeritus, 1998—, acting dean, 1984, chmn. dept. religion, 1982-98; Am. exec. com. Internat. Greek New Testament Project, 1968-88; mem. N.Am. Com., 1989—; mem. accreditation rev. coun. North Ctrl. Assn. Commn. on Insts. Higher Edn., 1986-90, mem. appeals panel, 1992-95, cons. evaluator corps, 1983-98; Kenneth W. Clark lectr. Duke U., 1986; Ratner lectr. Case Western Res. U., 1998; bd. dirs. New Testament Lang. Project. Author: The Theological Tendency of Codex Bezae Cantabrigiensis in Acts, 1966; co-author: Studies in the Theory and Method of New Testament Textual Criticism, 1993; co-editor: New Testament Textual Criticism: Its Significance for Exegesis, 1981, The New Testament and Its Modern Interpreters, 1989; assoc. editor Jour. Bibl. Lit., 1971-90; editor Critical Rev. of Books in Religion, 1991-94, Studies and Documents, 1991—; mem. editl. bd. Soc. Bibl. Lit. Monograph Series, 1969-72, Soc. Bibl. Lit. Centennial Publs., 1975-86, Studies and Documents, 1971—, Critical Rev. of Books in Religion, 1987-94; exec. sec. Hermeneia: A Critical and Historical Commentary on the Bible, 1962—, mem. editl. bd., 1966—; contbr. articles to profl. jours. Active Boy Scouts Am., 1975-78; Bd. mgrs. St. Paul's Episcopal Cathedral, L.A., 1964-68, clk., 1967-68. Harvard Faculty Arts and Scis. fellow, 1958-59, Rockefeller doctoral fellow in religion, 1959-60; postdoctoral fellow Claremont Grad. Sch., 1966-68; Guggenheim fellow, 1974-75; NEH grant, 1988. Mem. AAUP (mem. chpt. exec. com. 1970-72), Am. Acad. Religion (sect. pres. 1965-66), Soc. Bibl. Lit. (chmn. textual criticism seminar 1966, 71-84, mem. permanent Centennial com. 1975-80, mem. coun. 1980-82, 85-87, del. Coun. on Study of Religion 1980-82), Studiorum Novi Testamenti Societas, Cath. Bibl. Assn., Am. Soc. Papyrologists, New Testament Colloquium (chmn. 1974), Soc. Mithraic Studies, Inst. Antiquity and Christianity, Egypt Exploration Soc., Phi Beta Kappa. *Personal philosophy: Two essentials for life and livelihood are integrity and maturity. Integrity, in the abstract, is soundness, but in practical terms means incorruptibility, while maturity is basically the capacity to tolerate ambiguity. As individuals and as a society, we cannot afford to abandon integrity or to stifle maturity.*

EPP, MENNO HENRY, clergyman; b. Lena, Man., Can., Apr. 11, 1932; s. Henry Martin and Anna (Enns) E.; m. Irma Mary Wiens, July 26, 1957 (dec. Sep. 1990); children: Charlene and Beverly (twins), Darrell; m. Elsie Neufeld, Apr. 10, 1993. BTh, Can. Mennonite Bible Coll., 1957; BA, Bethel Coll., 1964; MDiv, Assoc. Mennonite Bible Sem., 1971; D of Ministry, St. Stephens Coll., 1983. Tchr., prin. Bethel Bible Inst., Abbotsford, B.C., 1957-69; dir. Camp Squeah, Yale, B.C., 1963-69; youth pastor Bethel United Meth., Elkhart, Ind., 1969-71; pastor Foothills Mennonite Ch., Calgary, Alta., 1971-84, Leamington (Ont.) United Mennonite Ch., 1984-98; retired, 1998; bd. dirs., chmn. Assoc. Mennonite Biblical Sem., Elkhart, 1977-89; moderator Conf. of Mennonites in Can., Winnipeg, 1990-96. Office: 242 Haight Pl Saskatoon, SK Canada S7H 4W2

EPPELE, DAVID LOUIS, columnist, author; b. Jersey City, Apr. 4, 1939; s. Joseph Anton and Lena Marie (Tadlock) E.; m. Gladys Emily Padilla (div. 1975); children: David D., Joseph E.; m. Geneva Mae Kirsch, July 7, 1977. Student, N.Mex. State U., 1958, U. N.Mex., 1966, U. Portland, 1972. Field botanist SW Deserts and Mex., 1947-99, N.Mex. Cactus Rsch., Belen, 1953-62; dir. Ariz. Cactus and Succulent Rsch., Bisbee, 1984—; editor Ariz. Cactus News, 1984—; columnist Western Newspapers, 1987—. Author (newspaper column) On the Desert, 1986—; author: On the Desert, 1991; editor: Index of Cactus Illustrations, 1990, Desert in Bloom, 1989. Mem. Mule Mountain Dem. Party, Bisbee, 1978—. With USN, 1958-59. Mem. AAAS, Cactus and Succulent Soc. Am., N.Mex. Acad. Sci., Bisbee C. of C. Avocations: photography, music. Home and Office: Ariz Cactus 8 S Cactus Ln Bisbee AZ 85603-6356

EPPEN, GARY DEAN, business educator; b. Austin, Minn., Apr. 28, 1936; s. Marldene Fredrick and Elsie Alma (Wendorf) E.; m. Ann Marie Sathre, June 14, 1958; children: Gregory, Peter, Paul, Amy. A.A., Austin Jr. Coll., 1956; B.S., U. Minn., 1958, M.S.I.E., 1960; Ph.D., Cornell U., 1964. Prof. mgmt. European Inst. Advanced Studies, Brussels, 1972-73; assoc. dean Grad. Sch. Bus., U. Chgo., 1969-75, prof. indsl. adminstrn., 1970—, assoc. dean Ph.D. studies, 1978-85, dir. internat. bus. exchange program, 1977-92, dir. Life Officers Investment Seminar, 1975-88, dir. Fin. Analysts Seminar, 1982-88, Robert Law prof., 1989-97, dir. exec. program, 1989-94, Keller Disting. Svc. prof., 1997—, dep. dean part-time programs, 1998—; Francqui prof. Cath. U. Leuven, Belgium, 1979; Urwitz vis. prof. Stockholm Sch. Econs., 1994; external examiner U. W.I., 1979-82; dir. Landauer, Inc., Hub Group, Inc., ROZ Trading Ltd. Author: (with F.J. Gould) Quantitative Concepts for Management, 1979, (with Metcalfe and Walters) The MBA Degree, 1979, (with F.J. Gould and C.P. Schmidt) Introductory Management Science, 1984; editor: Energy the Policy Issues, 1975; contbr. articles to profl. jours. FMC Faculty Rsch. scholar, 1986-89. Mem. Ops. Rsch. Soc. Am., Inst. Mgmt. Sci. Home: 5121 S Cornell Ave Chicago IL 60615-4215 Office: U Chgo Grad Sch Bus 1101 E 58th St Chicago IL 60637-1511

EPPERSON, DAVID ERNEST, dean, educator; b. Pitts., Mar. 14, 1935; s. Robert N. and Bessie Lee (Tibbs) E.; m. Cecelia Trower, July 11, 1964; children: Sharon, Lia. BA, U. Pitts., 1960, MSW, 1964, MA in Polit. Sci, 1971, PhD in Polit. Sci, 1975. World service worker YMCA, Hong Kong, 1961-62; coord. equal opportunities program U. Pitts., 1964-65; dep. dir. Pitts. program OEO, 1965-67, exec. dir., 1967-69; univ. fellow in urban affairs U. Pitts., 1969-72, prof., dean Sch. Social Work, 1972—; cons. specialist in social welfare, pub. policy, planning and adminstrn., urban affairs. Trustee, bd. dirs. Pitts. Theol. Sem.; vice chmn. Urban Redevel. Authority of Pitts., YMCA; chmn., bd. dirs., YMCA Pitts.; chmn. internat. com. YMCA U.S.A. With USAF, 1954-58. Mem. Coun. Social Work Edn., Nat. Assn. Social Workers. Democrat. Office: U Pitts Sch Social Work Cathedral of Learning Pittsburgh PA 15260*

EPPERSON, ERIC ROBERT, financial executive, film producer; b. Oregon City, Oreg., Dec. 10, 1949; s. Robert Max and Margaret Joan (Crawford) E.; m. Lyla Gene Harris, Aug. 21, 1969; 1 child, Marcie. BS, Brigham Young U., 1973, M of Acctg., 1974; MBA, Golden Gate U., 1977, JD, 1981. Instr. acctg. Brigham Young U., Provo, Utah, 1973-74; supr. domestic taxation Bechtel Corp., San Francisco, 1974-78; supr. internat. taxation Bechtel Power Corp., San Francisco, 1978-80; mgr. internat. tax planning Del Monte Corp., San Francisco, 1980-82, mgr. internat. taxes, 1982-85; internat. tax specialist Touche Ross & Co., San Francisco, 1985-87; dir. internat. tax Coopers & Lybrand, Portland, 1987-89; exec. v.p., chief fin. officer Epperson Dayton Sorenson Prodns., Inc., Salt Lake City, 1989-90, Epperson Prodns., 1990-92; exec. dir. The Oreg. Trail Found., Inc., Oregon City, 1992-93; pres. MFD Ltd., Portland, Oreg., 1993—, Oreg. Trail Films, Ltd., 1998—, Morgan's Ferry Prodns., LLC, L.A., 1998—. Author: (with T. Gilbert) Interfacing of the Securities and Exchange Commission with the Accounting Profession: 1968 to 1973, 1974; producer (motion pictures) Without Evidence, 1995, Morgan's Ferry, 1999; exec. producer (motion picture) Dream Machine, 1989. Scoutmaster, Boy Scouts Am., Provo, 1971-73, troop committeeman, 1973-74, 83—; mem. IRS Vol. Income Tax Assistance Program, 1972-75; pres. Mut. Improvement Assn., Ch. Jesus Christ of Latter-day Saints, 1972-74, pres. Sunday sch., 1977-79, tchr., 1974-80, ward clk., 1980-83, bishopric, 1983-87; bd. dirs. Oreg. Art Inst. Film Ctr., Oreg. Trail Coordinating Coun., Hist. Preservation League of Oreg.; vice chmn. ranch devel. com. Boy Scouts Am., Butte Creek. Mem. World Affairs Coun., Japan/Am. Soc., Internat. Tax Planning Assn., Internat. Fiscal Assn., Oreg. Trail Coordinating Coun. (exec. bd.), Oreg. Hist. Soc., U.S. Rowing Assn., Oreg. Calif. Trail Assn., Commonwealth Club, Multnomah Athletic Club. Republican. Office: PMB 180 25 NW 23d Pl Ste 6 Portland OR 97210-5599

EPPERSON, MARGARET FARRAR, civic worker; b. Hickman, Ky., Feb. 9, 1922; d. John Henry and Helen Margaret (Thompson) White; m. Liberty Weir Birmingham III, June 14, 1947 (dec. Feb. 1965); children: Margaret W., Elizabeth J., Richard L. (dec. Feb. 1997); m. Ralph Cameron Epperson, Sept. 18, 1971. Student, Washington Sch. Art, 1940; BA magna cum laude, Judson Coll., Marion, Ala., 1945; postgrad., Lambuth Coll., Jackson, Tenn., 1964. Cert. secondary tchr., Ky. Tchr. biology and typing Robert L. Osborne High Sch., Marietta, Ga., 1945-46; tchr. typing Hickman High Sch.,

1946-47; tchr. day care ctr. Southside Bapt. Ch., Jacksonville, Fla., 1972-73; sec. to min. of Edn. Jacksonville, Fla., 1973; file clk. Epperson Appraisers, Pensacola, Fla., 1986-87; formerly substitute tchr. various high schs. and jr. high schs., staff mem. Ridgecrest Bapt. Assembly, summer 1946, 1971. Exhibited in art shows, Jackson, Tenn., 1957, 58, West Tenn. Exec. Club, 1958-59. Pres. Alexander Sch. PTA, Jackson, 1959-60, devotional chmn., 1956-57, chmn. rm. mothers, 1957-58, 1st v.p., 1958-59; sec. Reelfoot Lake coun. Girl Scouts U.S.A., 1969-71, troop mother cookie chmn. 1958-65; PTA sec. Jackson, Tenn. H.S., 1967-68, 70-71; PTA 1st v.p. Jackson, Tenn. Ctrl. Coun., 1960-61; mem. aux. assn. Jackson-Madison County Bar, 1960-65; vol. ARC, Jackson, 1955, Meml. Med. Hosp. Aux., Jacksonville, 1978-86, Am. Heart Assn., 1987-90, Sacred Heart Hosp. Aux., Pensacola, 1986—; life mem. Jacksonville Children's Hosp. Aux., 1974—; hostess designer show house Jacksonville Symphony Guild, 1979-80; show house com. Pensacola Symphony Guild, 1996, 97, 99, dir. Women's Missionary Union, Bapt. Ch., 1976-78, mission support chmn., 1992, 93, 94, sec., 1995; Newcomers Club Greater Pensacola Area, 1988-89, Bon Appetit Luncheon Group, 1986-87, sunshine chmn., 1987-88, sec., 1988-89, nom. com., 1993-94, scholarship com., 1993-94, newcomer's book club group program chmn., 1995-96; publicity chmn. MacDowell Music Club, Jackson, 1954-55, program chmn. 1957-58, social chmn. 1959-60, parliamentarian 1961; com. mem. Jackson Cmty. Concert Assn., 1958-64; mem. women's bd. Bapt. Health Care Found., 1993—, mem. invitations and tickets com. for Style Show Friends of Libr., 1993-94, life mem., 1996—; active Friday Musicale of Jacksonville, Fla., 1979-86, Friends of Libr., 1995—, Escambia Coun. on Aging, 1996, 98-99. Mem. AAUW (sec. 1988-90, 2d v.p. 1990-92, tel. com. 1993—, br. area rep. cmty. problems Tenn. 1970-71, chmn. Tenn. divsn. cultural interests 1969-70, Fla. chmn. interest groups 1977-78), DAR (treas. 1981-82, chmn. Am. Heritage 1989-91, chmn. mag. 1991-93, chmn. vol. cmty. svcs. 1998-99), UDC (sec. Jacksonville chpt. 1979-81, historian Jacksonville chpt. 1981-83, sec. Pensacola chpt. 1989-90, corr. sec. Pensacola chpt. 1992-94, mem. com. chmn. 1993-94, chmn. patriotic activities 1998-99), Christian Women's Club (prayer chmn. 1991—, book chmn. 1987, 88, 92-94, hostesses asst. chmn. 1994—), Pensacola Fedn. Garden Clubs (pres. Poinciana Circle 1989-91, pres. Bells of Ireland Circle 1978-80, civic chmn., 1991, sec. Alderman Park Cir., Jacksonville 1980-82), Judson Coll. Alumnae Assn. of Pensacola (pres. 1993—, exec. bd. 1993—), Tenn. Fedn. Garden Clubs (pres. Jackson Jr. 1958-60, 60-70, chmn. exec. bd. 1970-71, chmn. flower show 1968). Avocations: giving book reviews, coal mining industry, volunteering.

EPPERSON, STELLA MARIE, artist; b. Oakland, Calif., Nov. 6, 1920; d. Walter Peter and Martha Josephine (Schmitt) Ross; m. John Cray Epperson, May 10, 1941; children: Therese, John, Peter. Student, Calif. Coll. Arts & Crafts, 1939, 40-41, 56; postgrad., Art Inst., San Miguel d'Allende, Mex., 1972. Portrait artist Oakland Art Assn., 1956—, San Francisco Women Artists, 1962—, Marin Soc. Artists, Ross, Calif., 1971—; art docent Oakland Mus., 1969-71, mem. women's bd., 1971—, art chmn. fund raiser, 1971-89, art guild chmn., 1965-69, chmn. exhbt. Japanese artists in Brazil, Kaiser Ctr., Oakland, for honoring artist Xavier Martinez, event honoring Neil Armstrong, Calif. Coll. Arts and Crafts. One-woman shows include Oakland Mus. Auction, 1993, Univ. Club, San Francisco, 1994; exhbns. include Women's Art Gallery, San Francisco, Kaiser Ctr., St. Mary's Coll. Hearst Gallery, numerous others; commd. portrait Mrs. Evangelina Macapagal, Malacalang Palace. Recipient San Francisco Women Artists award, 1989, Oakland Art Assn. award, 1991, 97, Marin Soc. Artists award, 1992. Mem. Oakland Art Assn. (1st award in small format show 1998, 1999 Artistic award in Kaiser Ctr. Gallery Exhibit), San Francisco Women Artists, Marin Art Assn., U. Calif. Berkeley Faculty Club, Orinda Country Club. Republican. Roman Catholic. Avocations: dress design, gourmet cooking, tennis. Home: 31 Valley View Rd Orinda CA 94563-1432

EPPERSON, VAUGHN ELMO, civil engineer; b. Provo, Utah, July 20, 1917; s. Lawrence Theophilus and Mary Loretta (Pritchett) E.; m. Margaret Ann Stewart Hewlett, Mar. 4, 1946; children: Margaret Ann Epperson Hill, Vaughn Hewlett, David Hewlett, Katherine (Mrs. Franz S. Amussen), Lawrence Stewart. BS, U. Utah, 1953. With Pritchett Bros. Constrn. Co., Provo, 1949-50; road design engr. Utah State Road Commn., Salt Lake City, 1951-53, bridge design engr., 1953-54; design engr. Kennecott Copper Corp., Salt Lake City, 1954-60, office engr., 1960-62, sr. engr., 1962, assigned concentrator plant engr., 1969-73, assigned concentrator project engr., 1973-78; cons. engr. Vaughn Epperson Engring. Service, Salt Lake City, 1978-87; project engr. Newbery-State Inc., Salt Lake City, 1980, geneal. computerized research programs, 1983-88, ancestral file programs family history dept. Ch. Jesus Christ of Latter-Day Saints, 1989-95. Scoutmaster Troop 190, Salt Lake City, 1949-51. Served to capt. AUS, 1941-45; maj. N.G., 1951; col. Utah State Guard, 1952-70. Decorated Army Commendation medal; recipient Service award Boy Scouts Am., 1949, Community Service award United Fund, 1961, Service award VA Hosp., Salt Lake City, 1977. Mem. ASCE, Am. Soc. Mil. Engrs., N.Y. Acad. Scis., Sons of Utah Pioneers. Republican. Mormon. Home: 1537 Laird Ave Salt Lake City UT 84105-1729

EPPES, THOMAS EVANS, advertising executive, public relations executive; b. N.Y.C., Aug. 10, 1952; s. Benjamin F. and Eileen (Evans) E.; m. Jennie Spradling, Aug. 2, 1980; children: Benjamin, Jared, Michael. BS, U. So. Miss., 1974. Reporter Jackson (Miss.) Daily News, 1974-75, 76-77, Clearwater (Fla.) Sun, 1975-76; pub. info. coord. Miss. Rsch. and Devel. Ctr., Jackson, 1976-78; press sec. Gov. Bill Waller for U.S. Senate, Jackson, 1978, Maurice Dantin for U.S. Senate, Jackson, 1978; dir. pub. rels. Days Inns Am., Atlanta, 1978-82, Mgmt. Sci. Am., Atlanta, 1982-85; pres., pub. rels. Price-McNabb, Asheville, N.C., 1985-91, pres., 1992—; spkr. nat. confs. on comms. and mktg. Bd. dirs., communications chmn. United Way of Asheville and Buncombe, 1986-87; campaign dir. Jacksonians for Mayor, Jackson, 1976; bd. advisors U. of Colo., Boulder Inc. Sch. Mem. Pub. Rels. Soc. Am. (counselor's acad., exec. bd. counselor's acad. 1998-2000, Silver Anvil award 1993), Internat. Assn. Bus. Communicators (Gold Quill award 1980, 81), Charlotte C. of C. (bd. dirs. 1997). Avocation: golf. Office: Price-McNabb 2800 NationsBank Comp Ctr Charlotte NC 28202

EPPES, WALTER W., JR., lawyer; b. Meridian, Miss., Oct. 9, 1929; s. Walter W. Sr. and Mary (Seymour) E.; m. Katherine Bailey, Oct. 17, 1952; children: Kathy Eppes Yarborough, Susan Eppes Whitehead. Student, U. Ala., Tuscaloosa, 1947-50; LLB, U. Miss., 1952. Bar: Miss. 1952, U.S. Dist. Ct. (so. dist.) Miss. 1952, U.S. Ct. Appeals (5th cir.) 1952. Adjuster U.S. Fidelity & Guaranty, Co., Meridian, 1952-54; ptnr. Shumate & Eppes, Meridian, 1954-63, Huff, Williams, Gunn, Eppes & Crenshaw, Meridian, 1963-73, Eppes, Watts & Shannon, Meridian, 1973-95, Eppes & Carter, Meridian, 1995—. Author: (with others) Mississippi Law Institute, 1975. Pres. Roundtable Investors, Meridian, 1992. Mem. Am. Bd. Trial Advs. (diplomate), Miss. Bar (pres. 1985-86), Internat. Soc. Barristers (gov. 1968—), Internat. Assn. Def. Counsel (comm. chmn. 1960—), Downtown Club Meridian (pres. 1972), Northwood Country Club (bd. dirs. 1972). Republican. Presbyterian. Avocation: hunting. Home: 4833 15th Pl Meridian MS 39305-1736 Office: Eppes & Carter Attys PO Box 3037 Broadmoor Mart Meridian MS 39303*

EPPES, WILLIAM DAVID, civic worker, writer; b. 1918; s. Talmadge DeWitt and Annie Lou (McCord) E. AB, Coll. of William and Mary, 1939; BS in LS, Vanderbilt U., 1940; student, U. Miami, U. Manchester (Eng.), 1950, Columbia U., 1950; MA, NYU, 1959; student, U. Durham, Eng., 1987. Reference asst. George Washington U., 1943-45, Calif. State U., San Francisco, 1945-46; cons. Z.D. McCord Co., San Francisco, 1945-47; head stack personnel Butler Libr. Columbia U., N.Y.C., 1954-58; assoc. prof. Kean (N.J.) State Coll., 1958-61; asst. libr. Cooper Union, N.Y.C., 1961-70; founder Film Classics League, St. Petersburg, Fla., 1950; co-founder Backstage Gallery, St. Petersburg Jr. Coll., 1950, Littlebury Eppes Meml. Libr., Westover Ch., Va.; adv. bd. Coral Gables (Fla.) Hist. Preservation Bd. Rev., 1979-81; trustee Greenwich Village Trust for Hist. Preservation, Inc., 1980, pres., 1980-84, adv., 1984-90, Landmark Coll., Putney, Vt., 1994-98; cons. Hist. Buckingham (Va.) Inc., 1987—; hon. commr. Eleanor Roosevelt Monument Fund, Inc., N.Y.C. Author: The Empire Theatre (1893-1953), 1978, Gertrude Michael-A Star of the Golden Age of Hollywood, 1985, Montgomery (Ala.) Theatre 1822-1985, 1986; contbr. articles to mags. and hist. jours. Bd. dirs. St. Petersburg Symphony Orch., 1950-54; exec. bd. Assn. Village Homeowners, N.Y.C., 1969-82, Assocs. of Earl Gregg Swem Libr., Coll. of William and Mary, 1973-86; benefactor Jonathon Daniels Sch., Keene, N.H., 1998, Apple Hill Chamber Orch., Sullivan, N.H., 1998. Mem. Theater Hist. Soc. (rsch. and reference com. 1977-81), Author's Guild, Inc., The Drama League, Soc. Descs. Francis Epes I of Va., W&M Choir, Hist. Hopewell Inc., Va. Hist. Soc. (exec. coun. 1995), Peterborough Hist. Soc. (benefactor 1997—), Ala. Preservation Soc. (Opelika chpt.),. Episcopalian. Home: 14 Rivermead Rd Peterborough NH 03458-1701

EPPLER, JEROME CANNON, private financial advisor; b. Englewood, N.J., Mar. 16, 1924; s. William E. and Aileen (Vaughan) E.; children: Stephen Vaughan, William Durand, Margaret Nye, Elizabeth Scott, Edward Curtis. BSME, Tex. A&M U., 1946; MBA, U. Pa., 1949. With Gen. Electric Supply Corp., Newark, 1949-50; investment banker Equitable Securities Corp., Nashville; mgr. Equitable Securities Corp., Houston, 1950-53; gen. partner Cyrus J. Lawrence & Sons, N.Y.C., 1953-61; mem. N.Y. Stock Exchange; owner Eppler & Co., Denver, 1961; ltd. ptnr. Alex Brown & Sons, Balt., 1982-84; bd. dirs. Chgo. Milw. St. Paul & Pacific Ry., 1958-63, Chemex Pharms., 1984-88; prin. Olympic Capital Ptnrs., Seattle; dir. Advanced Rsch. Sys., Inc., Seattle, Pvt. Asset Mgmt., Inc., Bellevue, Wash.; chmn. bd. United Screen Arts, Inc., L.A., 1966-73; bd. dirs. D.E. Frey Group Inc., Denver, VisionTek, Inc., Boulder, Colo.; chmn., bd. dirs. Life Ins. Co. Calif., 1967-77, I.S.I. Corp., 1967-77, Tessco Techs. Inc., Hunt Valley, Md., World Wide Life Assurance Co., London, 1972-77, Windsor Life Ins. Co., London, 1972-77; mem. indsl. adv. com. U. Calif., San Diego, 1978-93; dir. Telecredit, Inc., L.A., 1976-90, Brooktree Corp., San Diego, 1983-86, QTron, Inc., San Diego, 1995-97. Trustee emeritus Scripps Clinic and Research Found., La Jolla; former trustee Drew U. (N.J.), 1966-67, Morris Mus. Arts & Scis. (N.J.), 1954-76, Met. Opera Assn., 1980-82, Wharton Grad. Sch. Bus. N.Y., 1972-86. Lt. (j.g.) USNR, 1942-46. Mem. Wharton Grad. Bus. Sch. Club, Castle Pines Golf Club, Green Spring Valley Hunt Club, Wash. Athletic Club. Presbyterian. Office: Eppler & Co Castle Pines 1004 Hummingbird Dr Ste A Castle Rock CO 80104-9003 also: Olympic Capital Ptnrs PLLC 1325 4th Ave Ste 1900 Seattle WA 98101-2509

EPPLER, RICHARD ANDREW, chemical engineer, educator, consultant; b. Lynn, Mass., Apr. 30, 1934; s. Walter T. and Faith E. (Marden) E.; m. Ruth Marilyn Coon, June 20, 1959; children: Katherine R., Rebecca E., Walter R., Douglas R., Bruce A. BS, Carnegie-Mellon U., 1956; MS, U. Ill., 1958, PhD, 1960. Registered profl. engr., N.Y. Research chemist Corning (N.Y.) Glass Works, 1959-65; research scientist Mobay Chem. Corp., Balt., 1965-84; supr. ceramics Olin Corp., New Haven, 1984-86; cons. Eppler Assocs., Cheshire, Conn., 1986—; assoc. prof. chem. engring. U. Lowell, Mass., 1986-89. Over 20 patents in field; contbr. articles to profl. jours. Served with USAR, 1960. Fellow Am. Ceramic Soc. (v.p. 1984-85, John Marquis award 1974), ASTM (chmn. com. 1980-85, 92-97, merit award 1984); mem. Am. Chem. Soc., Electrochem. Soc., Sigma Xi. Republican. Congregationalist. Home and Office: Eppler Assocs 400 Cedar Ln Cheshire CT 06410-2222

EPPLEY, FRANCES FIELDEN, retired secondary education educator, author; b. Knoxville, Tenn., July 18, 1921; d. Chester Earl and Beulah Magnolia (Wells) Fielden; m. Gordon Talmage Couble, July 25, 1942; children: Russell Gordon Eppley, Carolyn Eppley Horseman; m. Fred Coan Eppley, Mar. 8, 1953; 1 child, Charlene Eppley Sellers. BA in English, Carson Newman Coll., 1942; MA, Winthrop U., 1963. Tchr. East Corinth (Maine) Acad.), 1942-43; tchr. pub. schs., Charlotte, N.C., 1950-53, 59-83, Greenville, S.C., 1954-56, Spartanburg, S.C., 1957-58; Head Start tchr., summers 1964-68. Mem. hist. com. N.C. Bapt. Conv., 1985-88. Alpha Delta Kappa Grantee, 1970. Mem. NEA, N.C. Social Studies Conf., Writers Assn., Alpha Delta Kappa, Pi Kappa Delta, Alpha Psi Omega. Baptist. Home: 6611 Rollingridge Dr Charlotte NC 28211-5428

EPPLEY, ROLAND RAYMOND, JR., retired financial services executive; b. Balt., Apr. 1, 1932; s. Roland and Verna (Garrettson) E.; m. LeVerne Pittman, June 20, 1953; children: Kimberly, Kent, Todd. B.A., Johns Hopkins U., 1952, M.A., 1953; D.C.S. (hon.), St. John's U., 1984. Pres., chief exec. officer Comm. Credit Computer, Balt., 1962-68; pres., chief exec. officer CIPC, Balt., 1968-71; vice chmn. Eastern States Monetary, Lake Success, N.Y., 1981-88; pres., chief exec. officer, dir. Affiliated Financial, Wilmington, Del., 1983-85, Eastern States Bankcard, Lake Success, N.Y., 1971-88; ret., 1988; chmn. bd. Eppley-Tongue Assocs., Inc.; adj. prof. St. John's U., 1973-88; bd. dirs. Ea. States Monetary, Veritas Inc., Hanover Investment Funds, Janel Hydraulics, Vista Funds; chmn. bd. Hanover Funds, 1989-96, Eppley-Tongue Assocs., Inc., 1992-95. Chmn. bd. trustees Calgary Bapt. Ch., Balt., 1969-71; chmn. investment com. Community Ch., Manhasset, N.Y., 1983-88; bd. advisors St. John's U., 1973-88; active Trinity Meth. Ch., Palm Beach Gardens, Fla.; mem. Johns Hopkins U. Alumni Coun., 1996-99. Recipient Disting. Service award St. John's U., 1981, 84 Laucheimer grantee, 1952-53. Mem. Am. Bankers Assn., Data Processing Mgmt. Assn., Am. Mgmt. Assn. Pres.'s Assn., Electronic Funds Transfer Assn., Mensa, Madison Sq. Garden Club, Meadowbrook Club, Plandome Country Club (dir. 1977-86), Hillendale Country Club, PGA Country Club, Cypress Links Country Club, City Club of Palm Beaches, Ibis Country Club, Cyress Yacht Club, Palm Beach Yacht Club, Masons, Shriners, Phi Beta Kappa, Omicron Delta Epsilon, Beta Gamma Sigma, Sigma Phi Epsilon (citation). Republican. Home: 105 Coventry Pl West Palm Beach FL 33418-8001 also: 510 Greenwood Rd Towson MD 21204 *Throughout my life, most of what I had planned did not work out. However, by being prepared for opportunities, I was able to take advantage of the unexpected.*

EPPS, AUGUSTUS CHARLES, lawyer; b. Richmond, Va., Feb. 2, 1916; s. John Lindsey and Lily Madeline (Becker) E.; m. Rosalie Suzanne Garrett, Aug. 17, 1946; children: Augustus Charles, George Garrett, John Daniel. B.S., U. Va., 1936, LL.B., 1938. Bar: Va. 1937, U.S. Supreme Ct. 1950. Practice in Richmond, 1938-42, 46—; assoc. atty. Christian, Barton & Parker, 1938-42; ptnr. Christian, Barton, Epps, Brent & Chappell, 1946-91; of counsel Christian and Barton, LLP, 1991—; bd. dirs., gen. counsel Richmond Life Ins. Co., 1952-69; bd. dirs. Wainwright Investment Co., Va. Legal Services Corp., Garrett Groves, Inc.; trustee emeritus U. Va. Law Sch. Found. Editorial bd., bd. mng. editors: Va. Law Rev, 1936-38; contbr. articles to profl. jours. Mem. Richmond Sch. Bd., 1963-70; past pres. Met. Richmond Legal Aid Project; past pres., bd. dirs. Crippled Children's Hosp., Friends Richmond Pub. Library; past vice chmn., bd. dirs. Richmond YMCA; bd. dirs., exec. com. Legal Aid Soc. Met. Richmond, 1967-76, Richmond Symphony; Richmond Urban Forum; former bd. dirs. Carpenter Ctr. for Performing Arts, 1981-87; mem. Richmond Public Library Bd., 1978-84; past bd. dirs. Richmond Offender Aid and Restoration, 1969-75; trustee Va. Diocesan Ctr., Episcopal Diocese Va.; bd. dirs., sec. Va. Math. & Sci. Coalition; v.p., bd. dirs. V.O.I.C.E.; active U. Va. Coun. Arts and Scis. Served to maj. AUS, 1942-46. Fellow Am. Bar Found., Am. Coll. Trial Lawyers, Va. State Bar; mem. ABA (past mem. com. on specialization, past mem. grievance com., past chmn. state com. legal edn., admission to bar, commn. on law and the economy), Va. Bar Assn. (pres. 1966-67, chmn. com. on specialization, past chmn. joint com. legis., law reform, past mem. exec. com.), Richmond Bar Assn. (past chmn. legal aid com., past pres.), Am. Judicature Soc., Assn. Life Ins. Counsel, Fed. Jud. Conf. 4th cir., U. Va. Law Sch. Assn. (council, chmn. Law Day 1972, 73, past chmn. com. scholarships, pres. 1977-79, nat. chmn. ann. giving appeal, 1984-85, 85-86), Phi Beta Kappa (pres. Richmond assocs. 1987-88), Order of Coif, Phi Delta Phi, Alpha Tau Omega. Episcopalian. Home: 6323 Ridgeway Rd Richmond VA 23226-3201 Office: 1200 Mutual Bldg 9th and Main Sts Richmond VA 23219-3012

EPPS, CHARLES HARRY, JR., orthopaedic surgery educator; b. Balt., July 24, 1930. BS magna cum laude, Howard U., 1951, MD, 1955. Intern Freedmen's Hosp., 1955-56, resident, 1956-57, mem. staff, 1961—; resident D.C. Gen. Hosp., Washington, 1958-60, vis. staff, 1961—, orthopaedic med. officer for handicapped and crippled children's svc., 1961—; chief orthopaedic surgeon Howard U., Washington, instr. orthopaedic surgery, 1961-64, asst. prof., 1964-68, assoc. prof., 1968-73, prof., 1973—, chief divsn. orthopaedic surgery, 1968-88, dean Coll. Medicine, 1988-94, exec. dean Coll. Medicine, 1994-95, v.p. health affairs, acting exec. dir., CEO, 1994-96; spl. asst. to pres. for health affairs Howard U., 1996—; assoc. prof. Johns Hopkins U., 1971; mem. staff VA Hosp., Washington, Cafritz Meml. Hosp., Providence Hosp.; cons. USN Med. Ctr., Bethesda, Md., Walter Reed Army Med. Ctr. Capt. M.C., U.S. Army, 1961-62. Fellow ACS; mem. AMA, Nat. Med. Assn., Ea. Orthop. Assn., Am. Orthop. Assn., Am. Acad. Orthop. Surgery. Office: Howard U Hosp Tower 6000 2041 Georgia Ave NW Washington DC 20060-0001

EPPS, JAMES HAWS, III, lawyer; b. Johnson City, Tenn., Sept. 15, 1936; s. James Haws and Anne Lafayette (Sessoms) E.; m. Jane Mahoney, Oct. 9, 1976; children from previous marriage--James Haws IV, Sara Stuart. B.A., U.N.C., 1955-59; J.D., Vanderbilt U., 1962. Bar: Tenn. 1962, U.S. Dist. Ct. Tenn. 1962, U.S. Ct. Appeals (6th cir.) 1971, Interstate Commerce Commn. Bar 1962, U.S. Supreme Ct. 1967. Prin. Epps & Epps, Johnson City, Tenn.; city atty. Johnson City, 1967—, Johnson City Bd. Edn., 1967-86; spl. counsel State of Tenn., 1966-70; former gen. counsel Appalachian Flying Svc. Inc., ET&WNC Transp. Co., Inc. First bd. govs. Transp. Law Jour. Past bd. dirs. Washington County Mental Health Assn., East Tenn. and Western N.C. Transp. Co., East Tenn. and Western N.C. R.R., Tennolina Corp., Appalachian Air Lines, Inc., Appalachian Flying Svc., Inc., Farmers and Mchts. Bank, Limestone, Tenn., Tenn. Mental Health Assn., budget com. United Fund of Johnson City, 1964-68, Assault Crime Counsel Early Support Svcs. Inc., Safe Passage Inc., Johnson City Homeless Coalition, Home Base Adv. Coun.; former legal adviser Appalachian Council Girl Scouts U.S.A.; mem. Tenn. Law Revision Commn., 1970-71; legal counsel Salvation Army, mem. adv. bd. 1974—, exec. com. 1977—, 1st v.p. adv. bd. 1991, pres. adv. bd. 1993, 94, mem. property com.; chmn. Family Violence Coun.; mem. Civil Def., 1967—; chmn. Washington County for Tenn. Leukemia Soc., 1991; mem. exec. com. Washington County Dem. Party, Tenn. Bicentennial Commn., exec. and fin. coms. Fellow Tenn. Bar Found.; mem. ABA, Fed. Bar Assn., Nat. Orgn. Legal Problems Edn., Nat. Assn. R.R. Trial Counsel, Internat. Mcpl. Lawyers Assn., (stata chmn. Tenn. 1988-89, ethics and environ. coms. 1989—, regional v.p. 1989-92, chmn. resolutions com. 1989-90, chmn. dues and alternatives revenue 1996—, chmn. budget and fin. 1996—, mem. federalism com. 1996—, state league counsel rev. com. 1997, lectr., trustee, 1992—), Nat. Legal Aid Defender Assn., Tenn. Bar Assn., Am. Judicature Soc., Washington County Bar Assn. (past pres.), Tenn. Mcpl. Attys. Assn., Assn. ICC Practitioners (past com. profl. ethics and grievences), Transp. Lawyers Assn., Motor Carrier Lawyers Assn., Am. Counsel Assn., Johnson City C. of C. (Disting. Service award 1968), Internat. Platform Assn., Lawyers Com. for Civil Rights Under Law, World Peace Through Law Ctr., Tenn. Lung Assn., Tenn. Correctional Assn., Tenn. Taxpayers Assn. (past bd. dirs.), Tennesseans for Better Transp., U.S. Supreme Ct. Hist. Soc., Def. Research Inst., Tipton Haynes Hist. Assn. (past dir.), Phi Delta Phi, Phi Delta Theta. Episcopalian. Clubs: Hurstleigh, J.C. Country, Unaka Rd. and Gun, Highland Stable, North Johnson City Bus. (dir., past pres. 1966-67), Nat. Lawyers, East Tenn. State U. Centry, Boys' Club (charter) (Johnson City/Washington County). Lodges: Masons, Elks (legal counsel 1963-67). Office: 115 E Unaka Ave Johnson City TN 37601-4623 also: PO Box 2288 Johnson City TN 37605-2288

EPPS, ROSELYN ELIZABETH PAYNE, pediatrician, educator; b. Little Rock, Dec. 11, 1930; d. William Kenneth and Mattie Elizabeth (Beverly) Payne; m. Charles Harry Epps, Jr., June 25, 1955; children: Charles Harry III (dec.), Kenneth Carter, Roselyn Elizabeth, Howard Robert. BS, Howard U., 1951, MD, 1955; MPH, Johns Hopkins U., 1973; MA, Am. U., 1981. Intern Freedmen's Hosp., Howard U., Washington, 1955-56, pediatric resident, 1956-59, chief resident, 1958-59; practice medicine specializing in pediatrics Washington, 1960; med. officer, pediatrics D.C. Dept. Pub. Health, Washington, 1961-64, dir. Clinic for Retarded Children, 1964-67, chief Infant and Pre-Sch. div., 1967-71, dir. children and youth project, 1970-71, dir. maternal and crippled children services, 1971-75; chief Bur. Clin. Services D.C. Dept. Human Services, Washington, 1975-80, acting commr. pub. health, 1980; instr., asst. research investigator Howard U. Coll. Medicine, Washington, 1960-61, prof. Dept. Pediatrics and Child Health, 1980-98, chief divsn. child devel., dir., 1985-89, dir. Child Devel. Ctr., 1985-89; rsch. assoc., vis. scientist smoking tobacco and cancer program, div. cancer prevention and control Nat. Cancer Inst. NIH, Washington, 1989-91; expert Nat. Cancer Inst. NIH, Pub. Health Applications Br., Bethesda, Md., 1991-97; scientific program adminstr. Nat. Cancer Inst. Pub. Health Applications Branch, Bethesda, Md., 1997-98; chmn. task force to prepare comprehensive child care plan for D.C. Dept. Human Services, 1973-74; mem. nat. task force on pediatric hypertension Heart, Lung and Blood Inst., NIH, 1975; chmn. rsch. grants rev. com. maternal and child health and crippled children's svcs. HEW, Rockville, Md., 1978-80; sec. Commn. Licensure to Practice Healing Arts, Washington, 1980; trustee med. svc. D.C. Blue Shield Plan Nat. Capital Area, 1980; chmn. sec.'s adv. com. on rights and responsibilities of women HEW, Washington, 1981; dir. high-risk young people's project Howard U. Hosp., 1981-85; Washington coord. Know Your Body Program Am. Health Found., N.Y.C., 1982-91; mem. bd. advs. Coll. Home Econs. Ohio State U., Columbus, Ohio, 1983-87; adv. com. Nat. Ctr. for Edn. in Maternal and Child Health Georgetown U., Washington, 1983-89; nat. steering com., subcom. chmn. Healthy Mothers, Healthy Babies Coalition, Washington, 1983-90, mem. nominating com., 1991; cons. sickle cell disease NIH, 1984-88, Govt. Liberia and World Bank, 1984, UN Fund for Population Activities, N.Y. and Caribbean, 1984, filmstrip Miriam Berg Varian/Parents Mag. Films, 1978; bd. dirs. Vis. Nurse Assn., Inc., Washington, 1983-89; pres. bd. dirs. Hosp. for Sick Children, Washington, 1986-90, bd. dirs., 1984-94; frequent guest lectr. Weekly columnist Your Child's Health, Afro-Am. Newspaper, Washington, 1960-63; contbr. articles syndicated column Nat. Newspaper Pubs. Assn., 1982, Nat. Newspaper Assn., 1986-87; co-author audiocassettes; exhibitor sci. program; contbr. more than 90 articles to profl. jours. Trustee nat. bd. Palmer Meml. Inst., Sedalia, N.C., 1969-71, Ford's Theatre, Washington, 1973-79; U.S. trustee Children's Internat. Summer Villages, Casstown, Ohio, 1969-76, pres., 1974-75; bd. mgrs. YWCA of D.C., 1970-76, 77-83, vice chmn., 1975-76; v.p. Jack and Jill of Am., Inc., Washington, 1970-71; nat. bd. dirs. Ctr. Population Options, Washington, 1980-86, Alexander Graham Bell Assn. for Deaf, Washington, 1974-78; bd. dirs. Washington Performing Arts Soc., 1971-81, v.p., 1979-81, hon. dir., 1981—; nat. bd. dirs. Meridian House Internat., Washington, 1974-81, counselor, 1981—; bd. dirs. YWCA Capital Area, 1975-76, United Negro Coll. Fund D.C., 1981-85; nat. bd. dirs. Girls Inc. (Formerly Girls Clubs Am., Inc.), N.Y.C., 1984-95, asst. sec., 1986-88, sec., 1988-90, pres., 1990-92; bd. dirs. Nat. Assembly Vol. Health and Welfare Agys., 1985-90, exec. bd., 1986-90, sec., 1988-90; bd. dirs. Mut. of Am., 1992—. Recipient Leadership and Meritorious Service in Medicine award Palmer Meml. Inst., 1968, 14th Ann. Fed. Women's award CSC, Washington, 1974, Superior Performance award D.C. Govt., 1975, Meritorious Community Service award Howard U. Sch. Social Work Alumni Assns. and vis. com., 1980, Cert. Commendation Mayor of D.C., 1981, Roselyn Payne Epps M.D. Recognition Resolution of 1983 Council D.C., 1983, Disting. Vol. Leadership award March of Dimes Birth Defects Found., 1984, Community Svc. award D.C. Hosp. Assn., 1990, Physician of Yr. award Women's Med. Assn. N.Y.C., 1990, 91; named Outstanding Vol. in Leadership category YWCA Nat. Capital Area, 1983; inducted into D.C. Women's Hall of Fame D.C. Commn. for Women, 1990; grantee Robert Wood Johnson Found., Princeton, N.J., 1982, div. maternal and child health HHS, Rockville, Md., 1986; honored Tribute Resolution of 1981 declaring Feb. 14 Dr. Roselyn Payne Epps Day, Council of D.C., 1981; recipient Ophelia Settle Egypt award Planned Parenthood of Met. Washington, 1991, Advocacy award Soc. Advancement Women's Health, 1996, Horizon award Nat. Assn. Negro Bus. and Profl. Women's Clubs, 1999. Fellow Am. Acad. Pediatrics (alt. state chmn. D.C. 1973-75, exec. com. D.C. chpt. 1983-94, pres. D.C. chpt. 1988-91, sec. cmty. pediatrics sect. 1973-75, cert. appreciation 1979, mem. coun. of child and adolescent health, cmty. and internat. health sect., charter mem., exec. com. 1992-94); mem. Acad. Medicine, AMA (alt. del. Nat. Med. Assn. 1983-85), Am. Med. Women's Assn. (chmn. pub. health com. 1973-75, pres. br. 1 1974-76, sec. 1988, v.p. 1989, pres-elect nat. 1990, pres. 1991, found. founding pres. 1992, bd. dirs. 1992-97, chmn. nominating com. 1993, Physician of Yr. award 1991, Cmty. Svc. award 1990, Elizabeth Blackwell award 1992), Women's Forum Washington, Med. Soc. D.C. (exec. bd. 1990, sec. 1990, pres.-elect 1991, pres. 1992, chair exec. bd. 1993, ann. Cmty. Svc. award 1982), Am. Pediatric Soc., D.C. Hosp. Assn. (Cmty. Svc. award 1990), Am. Pub. Health Assn. (action bd. 1977-79, joint policy com. 1978-79, gov. council 1978-81), Met. Washington Pub. Health Assn. (gov. council 1975-78, 81-83, ann. award 1981), Nat. Med. Assn. (chmn. pediatric sect. 1977-79, Ross Labs. award 1979, Outstanding Svcs. to Children during Internat. Yr. of Child award 1979, Meritorious Service Appreciation award 1979, W.M. Cobb co-lectr. 1985, mem. Coun. on Maternal and Child Health, 1974-92, chmn. 1979-89, ann. Roselyn Payne Epps Symposium 1994—, Grace Marilyn James award for Disting svc. Pediatric sect. 1991, Achievement award 1993, ann. Roselyn Payne Epps symposium 1994—), Am. Hosp. Assn. (maternal and child health sect. governing coun. 1989, 1992-94, maternal and child health nominating com. 1991), Soc. for the Advancement of Women's Health Rsch. (award for advocacy 1996), The Women's Forum of Washington, Alpha Omega Alpha, Delta Omega, Alpha

Kappa Alpha. Mem. United Ch. of Christ. Clubs: Pearls (pres. 1984-86), Carrousels (corr. sec. 1978-80), Links (pres. Met. chpt. 1986-89) (Washington), Cosmos. Lodge: Zonta, Internat. Women's Forum. Home and Office: 1775 N Portal Dr NW Washington DC 20012-1014

EPPS, WILLIAM DAVID, priest; b. Jan. 15, 1951; s. William E. Epps Jr.; m. Cynthia Scott Douglas; children: Jason, John, James. B in Social Work, East Tenn. State U., 1975; ThM, Internat. Sem., 1981; D Ministry, Berean Christian Coll., 1981; postgrad., Assemblies of God Theol. Sem. Lic. to ministry Assemblies of God, 1978, ordained, 1980; ordained priest Evangelical Episcopal Ch., 1995, received into Charismatic Episcopal Ch., 1996. Youth worker State St. United Meth. Ch., Bristol, Va., 1971-72; minister youth Wesley Meml. United Meth. Ch., Johnson City, Tenn., 1973-74; pastor Taylor Meml. United Meth. Ch., Johnston City, 1974-75, Chuckey United Meth. Cir., Greene County, Tenn., 1975-77, Orebank Assembly of God, Kingsport, Tenn., 1978-79; minister edn. Trinity Assembly of God, Johnson City, 1979-80; minister outreach 1st Assembly of God, Grand Junction, Colo., 1980-83; sr. pastor Trinity Fellowship, Peachtree City, Ga., 1983-96; rector Christ the King CEC, Peachtree City, Ga., 1996—; mem. bishop's coun. Ga. Diocese, 1997—; canon missioner Diocese of Armed Forces CEC; presbyter South Atlanta sect. Ga. Dist. Assemblies of God; chaplain Peachtree City Police Dept., Fayette County Sheriff's Dept., Atlanta divsn. FBI, Fulton County Police Acad.; chmn. 1990 N. Ga. Intercessory Prayer Gathering, Atlanta; mem. Ga. Dist. Evangelism Com., area evangelism rep.; mem. Coll. of Fellows of The Acad. Parish Clergy. Contbg. editor, Strategies for the 90's: A Pastoral Evangelism Handbook; contbr. articles to profl. jours. With USMC; U.S. Army N.G. Recipient Ga. Press Assn. Editorial award 1986, Cert. of Appreciation, Ga. Dist. Women's Ministries, 1989, many others. Mem. Fellowship Christian Athletes, Evang. Tchr. Tng. Assn. (honor mem.), Internat. Conf. Police Chaplains (Ga. post cert. police officer, Ga. post cert. chaplain, cert. sr. chaplain), Fayette County Ministerial Assn. (past pres.).

EPRIGHT, CHARLES JOHN, aerospace engineer; b. Bklyn., Jan. 11, 1932; s. Charles and Margaret Mary (Tripoli) E.; m. Mary Lucy Bono, May 29, 1954; children: Daniel John, Michael James, Marisa Epright Becker, Victoria Epright Carmona, Maria Carmela. BS in Math., U. Nev., 1965; MS in Engring. Mgmt., Northeastern U., 1971. Sr. engr. Raytheon, Andover, Mass., 1970-78, Delmo-Victor, Belmont, Calif., 1978-79; advanced systems engrng. specialist Lockheed Missile and Space Co., Austin and Sunnyvale, Tex. and Calif., 1979-87; engring. scientist Tracor Aerospace, Austin, 1987-89; staff engr. Lockheed Engring. and Sci. Co., Houston, 1989—. Civic adv. Salem-in-Action, N.H., 1977-79; dir. Reachout, Salem, 1976-79; cmty. action com. mem. N.H. Com. for Adopted and Foster Children, Manchester, 1978-79, Runaway Hotline, Austin, 1984-88, Middle Earth Spectrum Shelter, 1987-89; mem. pub. responsibility com. Mental Health/Mental Retardation, Austin, 1988-89; bd. dirs., v.p. Assn. Retarded Citizens, 1989-93; mem. outreach Covenant House Tex., Houston, 1990—. With USAF, 1950-70. Decorated Legion of Merit; recipient Family of Yr. award Sons of Italy, 1968, 69. Mem. Air Force Assn. (life), DAV, Am. Legion. Roman Catholic. Lodge: KC (grand knight 1968-69). Avocations: stamp collecting, photography, collecting old books. Home: 2012 Fairfield Ct N League City TX 77573-3504 Office: Lockheed Engring and Sci Co 2400 Nasa Rd One Houston TX 77258-8561

EPSTEIN, ALAN BRUCE, lawyer; b. Passaic, N.J., Sept. 20, 1944; s. Jerome P. and Stella M. (Goldfinger) E.; m. Eve Teichholz, June 21, 1966; children: Jason, Dylan. BA, Temple U., 1967, JD, 1969. Bar: Pa. 1970, U.S. Dist. Ct. (ea. dist.) Pa. 1970, U.S. Ct. Appeals (3d cir.) 1972, U.S. Ct. Appeals (5th cir.) 1977, U.S. Dist. Ct. (cen. and we. dists.) Pa. 1987, U.S. Supreme Ct. 1988. Assoc. firm Freedman, Borowsky & Lorry, Phila., 1969-77; ptnr. firm Jablon, Epstein, Wolf, & Drucker, Phila., 1977—; pres. Judicate Nat. Pvt. Ct. System, Phila., 1983-88. Fellow Pa. Bar Found.; mem. Phila. Trial Lawyers Assn. (bd. dirs. 1980-84), Pa. Trial Lawyers Assn. (bd. govs. 1984-86), Assn. Trial Lawyers Am., ABA, Phila. Bar Assn., Pa. Bar Assn., Temple Am. Inn of Ct. (bd. dirs. 1994—). Jewish. Home: 404 S Camac St Philadelphia PA 19147-1112 Office: Jablon Epstein Wolf & Drucker The Bellevue 9th Fl Broad St At Walnut Philadelphia PA 19102

EPSTEIN, ALVIN, actor, director, singer, mime; b. Bronx, N.Y., May 14, 1925; s. Harry and Goldie (Rudnick) E. Student, Queens Coll., 1941-43, Ecole de Mime Etienne Decroux, Paris, 1947-51, Sanford Meisner Profl. Class, N.Y.C., 1951-52. Tchr. Chamber Theatre, Israel, Neighborhood Playhouse, N.Y.C., Circle in Sq. Theatre Sch., N.Y.C., Yale Drama Sch., 1968-77, Am. Repertory Theatre Inst.; acting artistic dir. Yale Repertory Theatre, 1972-73, assoc. artistic dir., 1973-77; artistic dir. Guthrie Theatre, Mpls., 1978-79; mem. faculty Salzburg Am. Seminar, 1972, Aspen Music Festival, 1980-82. Actor Theatre de Mime Etienne Decroux, Paris, 1947-51, Habima Theatre, Israel, 1952-55; made Am. profl. debut with Marcel Marceau, Phoenix Theatre, N.Y.C., 1955; has appeared in many Broadway, off-Broadway touring and regional prodns., including The Fool in Orson Welles' King Lear, N.Y.C., 1956, Lucky in original Broadway prodn. Waiting for Godot, 1956, Puck in A Midsummer Night's Dream, Empire State Music Festival, N.Y., 1956, O'Killigain in Purple Dust, N.Y.C., Clov in Endgame, N.Y.C., Luc Delbert in No Strings, N.Y.C., title role in Enrico IV, Milw., Chgo., Beranger in The Pedestrian in the Air, Chgo., Theseus and Oberon in A Midsummer's Night Dream, N.Y.C., Octave in Clerambard, N.Y.C., various roles in Postmark Zero, N.Y.C., Landau in The Latent Heterosexual, Los Angeles, Sgt. in Dynamite Tonite, N.Y.C.; appeared in Whores, Wars and Tin Pan Alley, Chgo., New Haven, N.Y.C., Easthampton, A Place Without Doors, Long Wharf Theatre, New Haven, Staircase Theatre, N.Y.C., Goodman Theatre, Chgo., on U.S. tour, Los Angeles, Washington, 3 Plays by Samuel Beckett, Harold Clurman Theater N.Y.C., 1983-84, Mark Taper Forum Los Angeles, Library of Congress, Washington, 1984, Jerusalem Festival, 1985; directed and acted Hamm in Endgame, Samuel Beckett Theatre, Cherry Ln. Theater, N.Y.C., New Mayfair Theater, Los Angeles, Jerusalem Festival, 1985; mem. Yale Repertory Theatre, New Haven, 1968-77; playing leading parts Dynamite Tonite, God Bless, Story Theatre, The Bacchae, Greatshot, Crimes and Crimes, Olympian Games, Gimpel the Fool, Woyzeck, Don Juan, Macbett (Ionesco), The Tempest, Happy End, The Possessed, Bingo, Ivanov. Crossing Niagara, N.Y.C. Manhattan Theatre Club, Ghosts, Three Sisters, School for Scandal, Good Woman of Setzuan, 6 Characters in Search of an Author, Right You Are (If You Think You Are), Uncle Vanya, King Stag (Gozzi), Platanov, Mastergate, In Twilight (Chekhov Short Stories), The Miser (Moliere), Once In A Lifetime (Kaufman and Hart), When We Dead Awaken (Ibsen), Gloucester in King Lear, Polonius in Hamlet, Lord Summerhays in Misalliance (Shaw), Media Amok (C. Durang), Judge Brack in Hedda Gabler, Dr. Lombardi in The Servant of Two Masters (Goldoni), Dream of the Red Spider (Ribman), Iva Vasilyevich in Black Snow (Bulgakov-Dewhurst), Silence, Cunning, Exile (S. Greenman), directed and played Duncan and Scottish Doctor in Macbeth, King Henry in Henry IV Parts 1 & 2 (Shakespeare), Dr. Rance in What the Butler Saw (Orton), Firs in the Cherry Orchard (Chekhov), Patty O'Dowd in "A Touch of the Poet (O'Neill), Krapp's Last Tape, Ohio Impromptu, Agamemnon, Waiting for Godot, Henry V, Threepenny Opera, Beckett Trio: Eh Joe, Ghost Sonata, Nacht Und Träume, The Tempest, Tartuffe, Slaughter City, Am. Repertory Theatre, Cambridge, Mass., Value of Names, Androcles and the Lion, Hartford Stage Co., Waltz of the Toreadors, Roundabout Theatre, N.Y.C., Peachum in Three Penny Opera, Lunt-Fontanne Theatre, 1989; dir. The Rivals, Caligula, Seven Deadly Sins, Bourgeois Gentleman, Rise and Fall of the City of Mahagonny, The Tempest, A Midsummer Night's Dream, Troilus and Cressida, Julius Caesar, Old Times, Marriage of Figaro, Boys From Syracuse, Endgame, Importance of Being Earnest, Heartbreak House, others at Yale Repertory Theatre, Am. Repertory Theatre, Williamstown Theatre Festival, Richard III, Becket Trio; narrator Oedipus Rex, Cantata Singers; appeared in many TV shows on all networks, including The Doctors on NBC-TV, 1981-82, Doing Life NBC-TV film, 1986; dir. The Pretenders, Beggars Opera; appeared in Marriage, A Kurt Weill Cabaret for Guthrie Theatre, with Martha Schlamme in A Kurt Weill Cabaret for Bijou Theater, N.Y.C., on tour throughout U.S., Argentina, Brazil, Israel, 1979-85; co-founder, actor Berkshire Theatre Festival, Stockbridge, Mass., 1966, playing Antrobus in Skin of Our Teeth, Shylock in Merchant of Venice; dir. Colette, Berkshire Theatre Festival, Stockbridge, Mass., 1974; appeared in Schlamme and Epstein Sing Bernstein and Blitzstein, Aspen Music Festival, HB Studio N.Y.C., Am. Repertory Theatre, Cambridge, Mass., 1981, When the World Was Green, Olympic Arts Festival, The Cabinet of Dr. Caligari, Man and Superman; (film) Never Met Picasso, Thomas Edison in The Wizard of Menlo Park with Boston Pops, The Devil in Stravinsky's Soldier's Tale, Jordan Hall, Boston, Alice Tully Hall, N.Y.C., GBS in Dear Liar, on U.S. tour, Cadmus in The Bacchae, Shlink in In The Jungle of Cities, Lee Strasberg in Nobody Dies on Friday, Old Man in When The World was Green, Internat. Festival, Moscow Art Theatre, Russia, 1997-98, voice overs for documentary Africans in America, Old Gobbo and Tubal in Merchant of Venice, Am. Repertory Theatre, Cambridge Mass., narrator Philosopher's Stone by Mozart et al, Boston Baroque, Jordan Hall, Boston, Old Man in Charlie in The House of Rue, American Repertory Theatre, Cambridge, Leonard in film The Living Room Waltz, 1998-99; various roles in series of Samuel Beckett Radio Plays for Nat. Pub. Radio, 1987-88, Voice of the Bookseller in Walt Disney's Beauty and the Beast, 1991. Bd. dirs. Theatre Communications Group, N.Y.C., 1975-77. Served with AUS, 1943-46, ETO. Recipient Brandeis Creative Arts award, 1966, Obie award for Dynamite Tonite, 1968, Torch of Hope award, 1994, Elliot Norton prize Boston Theatre Critics, 1996; Ford Found. grantee, 1959-60; Trumbull Coll. fellow, Yale U.; named Most promising Actor, Variety poll, 1956. Address: 82 Highland Rd Brookline MA 02445-7041

EPSTEIN, ARTHUR BARRY, optometrist; b. N.Y.C., May 28, 1951; s. Morris Leo and Sadelle Jeanette (Posner) E.; m. Marilyn Sue Golomb, May 25, 1974; children: Rebecca Meryl, Emily Louise. BS in Psychology, CUNY, 1973; OD, SUNY, N.Y.C., 1977. Clin. instr. optometry SUNY, N.Y.C., 1977-78; pvt. practice in gen. optometry L.I., 1978-82; pvt. practice limited to contact lenses North Shore Contact Lens & Vision Cons., P.C., Roslyn, N.Y., 1982—, Ophthalmic Cons. L.I., Rockville Centre, N.Y., 1990—; attending staff North Shore U. Hosp., Manhasset, N.Y., 1990—, dir. contact lens svc., 1992—; clin. adj. asst. prof. Northeastern State U., Talequah, Okla.; mem. adv. com. Rigid Gas Permeable Lens Inst.; med. adv. bd. Nat. Keratoconus Found. Contbg. editor Contact Lens Forum, 1989-91; clin. editor Optometric Mgmt., 1995—, chief optometric editor, 1998; directing editor Optometric Mgmt., 1995—; contbg. author Specialty Contact Lenses: The Fitter's Guide, 1995, Clinical Contact Lens Practice, 1997; chief optometric editor: Optometric Management, 1998—; contbr. over 70 articles to profl. jours. Fellow Am. Acad. Optometry, N.Y. Acad. Optometry; mem. Internat. Acad. Sports Vision, Am. Optometric Assn. (contact lens section, editor Cross Section newsletter), N.Y. State Optometric Assn., Nassau County Optometric Soc., Assn. Rsch. in Vision and Ophthalmology, L.I. Contact Lens Soc. (pres., founder), Contact Lens Assn. Ophthalmologists (assoc.), Contact Lens Soc. Am., Internat. Acad. Sports Vision. Avocations: cycling, amateur radio. Office: North Shore Contact Lens 1025 Northern Blvd Ste 94 Roslyn NY 11576-1506

EPSTEIN, ARTHUR WILLIAM, physician, educator; b. N.Y.C., May 15, 1923; s. Jacob E. and Anne (Bass) E.; m. Leona Cruce, Mar. 2, 1955; children: David Byron, Nona Kathryn, Emily Vera, James Jacob. A.B., Columbia U., 1944, M.D., 1947. Intern Mt. Sinai Hosp., N.Y.C., 1947-48; resident Mt. Sinai Hosp., 1949-50; clin. asst. Norristown (Pa.) State Hosp., 1948-49; faculty Tulane U., New Orleans, 1954—; asso. prof. psychiatry and neurology, 1959-64, prof. Tulane U., 1964—; pvt. practice medicine, specializing in neuropsychiatry New Orleans, 1964—; prof. emeritus Tulane U., 1993—; vis. physician Charity Hosp., New Orleans, 1951—; cons. U.S. Army Hosp., New Orleans, 1958-64; mem. med. staff Tulane Med. Center Hosp., 1976—. Author: An Anatomist's Dream of Love, 1966, The Dissecting Room, 1978, The Lady and the Serpent, 1981, A Contemporary Religious Svc., 1987, Bridge Cross, 1989, Dreaming and Other Involuntary Mentation: An Essay in Neuropsychiatry, 1996; contbr. articles to profl. jours. Med. adviser Social Security Adminstrn., 1968-93; bd. dirs. Ednl. Rsch. and Treatment Ctr., New Orleans. Served with M.C. USNR, 1956-58. Named Psychiatrist of Yr. La. Psychiatric Assn., 1992. Fellow AAAS, Am. Psychiat. Assn. (life, leisure time and its uses com.), Am. Acad. Psychoanalysis (pres. 1987-88, Silverberg award 1985), Am. Acad. Neurology; mem. Soc. Biol. Psychiatry (v.p. 1979-80, pres.-elect 1980-81, pres. 1981-82), Am. Epilepsy Soc., Alpha Omega Alpha. Home: 1664 Robert St New Orleans LA 70115-4975 Office: DePaul-Tulane 1040 Calhoun St New Orleans LA 70118-5914 *Amid the hurly-burly, keep awe and wonder. Pursue the ideal.*

EPSTEIN, BARBARA, editor; b. Boston, Aug. 30, 1929; d. Harry W. and Helen (Diamond) Zimmerman; children: Jacob, Helen. B.A., Radcliffe Coll., 1949. Editor N.Y. Rev. Books, N.Y.C., 1963—. Office: NY Rev of Books 1755 Broadway Fl 5 New York NY 10019-3743

EPSTEIN, BRUCE HOWARD, lawyer, real estate broker; b. Dallas, Jan. 30, 1952; s. Raymond Howard and Thelma (Romotsky) E.; m. Toni Rosas, Aug. 28, 1988; children: Marianne Corinne, Peter Louis. Student, U. Calif., San Diego, 1970-71; AB in Polit. Sci. with honors, U. Calif., Riverside, 1974; JD, U. Calif., San Francisco, 1977. Bar: Calif. 1977, U.S. Dist. Ct. (no. dist.) Calif. 1977, U.S. Dist. Ct. (cen., ea. and so. dists.) Calif. 1990, U.S. Ct. Appeals (9th cir.) 1990, U.S. Supreme Ct. 1990; lic. real estate broker, Calif. Dep. dist. atty. San Bernardino County Dist. Atty.'s Office, San Bernardino, Calif., 1977-83; sr. assoc. Atwood, Hurst, Knox & Anderson, San Jose, Calif., 1983-85; dep. city atty. San Jose City Atty.'s Office, 1985-86; sole practitioner Campbell, Calif., 1985-87; asst. v.p. Lawyers Title Ins. Corp., Pasadena, Calif., 1987—; counsel, sec. Lawyers Title Co., Pasadena, 1987—, Land Title Ins. Co., Pasadena, 1987—, Land Am. Fin. Group, Pasadena, 1998—, Transnation Title Ins. Co., Pasadena, 1998—, Commonwealth Land Title Ins. Co., Pasadena, 1998—; asst. v.p. Land Am. Fin. Group, Pasadena, 1998—; real estate broker, Burbank, Calif., 1983—; lectr. Evergreen Coll., San Jose, 1986-87; instr. Minimum Continuing Legal Edn., 1997—, Escrow Agent Profl. Devel., 1997—; mem. claims awareness com. Calif. Land Title Assn., 1997—; pres. Robert Louis Stevenson Sch. Site Coun., 1997—. Mem. Am. Diabetes Assn., 1977—, Nat. Space Soc., 1992—, Smithsonian Instn., 1990—, Jewish Found. for the Righteous, 1990—, Am. Air Mus. in Britain; v.p. Temple Beth Emet, Burbank, Calif. Mem. Calif. State Bar Assn., Los Angeles County Bar Assn., Nat. Air and Space Soc., Am. Mus. Natural History, Anti Defamation League, Greater Los Angeles Zool. Assn., Descanso Gardens Guild, Natural History Mus. Los Angeles County, Calif. Sci. Ctr., Zool. Soc. of San Diego. Democrat. Jewish. Avocations: writing, sports, painting. Office: Land Am 55 S Lake Ave Ste 600 Pasadena CA 91101-2688

EPSTEIN, CARL PLAKCY, public information officer; b. Waterbury, Conn., Apr. 30, 1920; s. Benjamin and Eva (Plakcy) E. BA, Tulane U., 1947; MA, Johns Hopkins U., 1950; PhD, Am. U., 1964. Assoc. prof. U. Md.; prof. pub. speaking and internat. rels. Soochow U., Taipei, Taiwan, Republic of China, 1980-90, Tamkang U., Tamsui, Taipei, 1980-90, Fuhtsingkang U., Taipei, 1982-90; prof. internat. law and internat. adminstrn. Mil. Lang. Sch., Taipei, 1980-90; adj. prof. Southeastern U. Internat. Fin. and Mgmt. Author: Epstein Dialogues, 1988. 2d lt. U.S. Army, 1944, col. 1971, ret. 1977. Mem. VFW (life), Am. Legion, Res. Officer's Assn. (life mem.), Pi Sigma Alpha. Avocations: swimming, traveling, writing. Fax: 203-753-2072. Home: 76 Farmington Ave Waterbury CT 06710

EPSTEIN, CHARLES JOSEPH, physician, medical geneticist, pediatrics and biochemistry educator; b. Phila., Sept. 3, 1933; s. Jacob C. and Frieda (Savransky) E.; m. Lois Barth, June 10, 1956; children: David Alexander, Jonathan Akiba, Paul Michael, Joanna Marguerite. A.B., Harvard U., 1955, M.D., 1959; DS, Northeastern Ohio U., 1997. Diplomate: Am. Bd. Medical Genetics. Intern in medicine Peter Bent Brigham Hosp., Boston, 1959-60; asst. resident in medicine Peter Bent Brigham Hosp., 1960-61; research assoc., med. officer and sect. chief Nat. Heart Inst. and Nat. Inst. Arthritis and Metabolic Diseases, NIH, Bethesda, Md., 1961-67; research fellow in med. genetics U. Wash., 1963-64; assoc. prof. pediatrics and biochemistry U. Calif., San Francisco, 1967-72; prof. U. Calif., 1972—, chief divsn. med. genetics. dept. pediatrics, 1967—, co-dir. program in human genetics, 1997—; investigator Howard Hughes Med. Inst., 1976-81; mem. human embryology and devel. study sect. NIH, 1971-75; mem. mental retardation research com. Nat. Inst. Child Health and Devel., 1979-83, chmn., 1981-83; mem. com. for study inborn errors of metabolism NRC, 1972-75; mem. sci. adv. bd. Nat. Down Syndrome Soc., 1981—, chmn., 1984—, also bd. dirs.; mem. recombinant DNA adv. com. NIH, 1985-90, mem. human gene therapy subcom., 1987-91, chmn. residency review com. med. genetics, 1993-99; Stanley Wright Meml. lectr. Western Soc. Pediatric Research, 1986; William Potter lectr. Thomas Jefferson U., 1987; George H. Fetterman lectr. U Pitts., 1989; faculty rsch. lectr. U. Calif., San Francisco, 1994; Mary Hulings Edens lectr., U. of Tex. Med. Br., Galveston, 1996; Ida Cordelia Beam lectr., U. Iowa, 1998; Donald L. Thurston meml. lectr. Washington U., St. Louis, 1999. Author: The Consequences of Chromosome Imbalance: Principles, Mechanisms and Models, 1986; editor: Human Genetics, 1984-95, The Neurobiology of Down Syndrome, 1986, Oncology and Immunology of Down Syndrome, 1987, Am. Jour. Human Genetics, 1987-93, Molecular and Cytogenetic Studies of Non-disjunction, 1989, Molecular Genetics of Chromosome 21 and Down Syndrome, 1990, Morphogenesis of Down Syndrome, 1991, Down Syndrome and Alzheimer Disease, 1992, Phenotypic Mapping of Down Syndrome and other Aneuploid Conditions, 1993, Etiology and Pathogenesis of Down Syndrome, 1995; assoc. editor Rudolph's Textbook of Pediatrics, 18th edit., 1986, 20th edit., 1996; mem. editorial bd. Biology of Reproduction, 1974-78, Cytogenetics and Cell Genetics, 1975-80, Am. Jour. Med. Genetics, 1977—, sr. editor, 1995—, Devel. Genetics, 1983-85, Jour. Embryology and Exptl. Morphology, 1983-85, Human Gene Therapy, 1990-98, Human Mutation, 1992—, Human Genetics, 1995—, Down Syndrome Quar., 1996—, Trends in Genetics, 1997—, Cmty. Genetics, 1998—, Annual Review of Human Genetics and Genomics, 1999—. Served with USPHS, 1961-63. Recipient Henry A. Christian award Harvard Med. Sch., 1959, Rsch. Career Devel. award NIH, 1967-72, Nancy and Daniel Weisman Charitable Found. award, 1990, Lifetime Achievement award in genetic scis., March of Dimes Birth Defects Found, Col. Harland Sanders, 1995, 6th World Congress on Down Syndrome award, 1997, Disting. Rsch. award The Arc of the U.S., 1998. Fellow AAAS; mem. AMA, Am. Bd. Med. Genetics (bd. dirs. 1988-93, v.p. 1989, pres. 1990-91), Genetics Soc. Am., Am. Fedn. Clin. Rsch., Am. Soc. Human Genetics (bd. dirs. 1972-75, 87-93, 97-98, pres.-elect 1995, pres. 1996), Am. Soc. Biochemistry and Molecular Biology, Soc. Pediatric Rsch. (coun. 1972-75), Am. Coll. Med. Genetics, Western Soc. Clin. Investigation, Western Soc. Pediatric Rsch., Am. Soc. Clin. Investigation, Am. Soc. Cell Biology, Soc. Devel. Biology, Am. Pediatric Soc., Western Assn. Physicians (coun. 1993-95), Assn. Am. Physicians, Soc. Inherited Metabolic Disorders, Inst. Medicine (Nat. Acad. Scis.), Calif. Acad. Medicine, Phi Beta Kappa, Alpha Omega Alpha. Jewish. Research, numerous publs. on human and med. genetics, devel. genetics and biochemistry. Office: U Calif Dept Pediatrics U585L San Francisco CA 94143-0748

EPSTEIN, CYNTHIA FUCHS, sociology educator, writer. B.A. in Polit. Sci., Antioch Coll., 1955; postgrad., U. Chgo. Law Sch., 1955-56; M.A. in Sociology, New Sch. Social Research, 1960; Ph.D., Columbia U., 1968. Instr. anthropology Finch Coll., 1961-62; assoc. in sociology Columbia U., 1964-65, instr. Barnard Coll., 1965; instr. sociology Queens Coll., N.Y.C., 1966-67, asst. prof., 1968-70, assoc. prof., 1971-74, prof., 1974-84; prof. grad. ctr. CUNY, 1974, Disting. prof. Grad. Ctr., 1990; resident scholar Russell Sage Found., 1982-88; co-dir. Program in Sex Roles and Social Change Ctr. Social Scis., Columbia U., 1977-82, co-dir. NIMH tng. grant on sociology and econs. of women and work Grad. Ctr., disting. prof. Grad. Ctr., 1990—; vis. prof. Health Sci. Ctr., SUNY-Stony Brook, 1975, Stanford Law Sch., 1997; vis. scholar Stanford U., 1991; Phi Beta Kappa vis. scholar, 1991-92; cons., lectr. and speaker in field; mem. com. on women's employment and related social issues NRC-Nat. Acad. Scis., 1981-88; adv. com. on econ. role of women Pres.' Council Econ. Advisers, 1973-74. Author: Woman's Place: Options and Limits in Professional Careers, 1970, Women in Law, 1981, 2d edit., 1993, Deceptive Distinctions: Sex, Gender and the Social Order, 1988, The Part-time Paradox: Time Norms, Professional Life, Family and Gender, 1999; editor: (with William J. Goode) The Other Half: Roads to Women's Equality, 1971; (with Rose Laub Coser) Access to Power: Cross-National Studies of Women and Elites, 1981; mem. editorial bds.: Signs, Women's Studies, Internat. Jour. Work and Occupations, Sociol. Focus, Women 1974, Dissent, Am. Jour. Sociology, CUNY Mag., Gender and Soc.; contbr. chpts. to books, articles to profl. jours. Trustee Antioch U., 1984—. Recipient Award for Disting. Contb. to Study of Sex and Gender, ASAN, 1994, REbecca Rice award Antioch Coll., 1997; grantee Inst. Life Ins., 1974, Ford Found., 1975-77, Rsch. Found. City of N.Y., 1974-76, 90-93, Guggenheim Meml. Found., 1976-77, Ctr. Advanced Study in Behavioral Scis., 1977-78, Russell Sage Found., 1982-90, Sloan Found., 1995—; fellow NIH, 1963-66, MacDowell Colony, 1973, 74, 77, 80, Guggenheim Found., 1976-77, Ctr. Advanced Study in Behavioral Sci., 1977-78, Va. Ctr. Creative Arts, 1984. Mem. AAAS, Eastern Sociol. Soc. (v.p. 1977-79, exec. coun. 1973-74, pres. 1983-84, I Peter Gellman award), Am. Sociol. Assn. (coun. 1974-77, com. exec. office and budget 1978-81, chmn. sect. on orgns. and occupations, chmn. sect. on sociology of sex roles 1973-74), Social Rsch. Assn., Internat. Sci. Commn. on Family. Office: CUNY Grad Ctr 33 W 42nd St New York NY 10036-8099

EPSTEIN, DANIEL MARK, poet, dramatist; b. Washington, Oct. 25, 1948; s. Donald David and Louise Marietta (Tillman) E.; m. Wendy Roberts, May 29, 1976 (div. 1994); children: Johanna Ruth, Benjamin Robert; m. Jennifer Bishop, 1994; 1 child, Theodore John. A.B. magna cum laude with highest honors in English, Kenyon Coll., 1970; postgrad., U. Va., 1970-71; M.F.A. h.c., Norwich U. Asst. mgr. Automatic Enterprises, Washington, 1967-70; disting. scholar-in-residence Randolph-Macon Woman's Coll., 1982; writer-in-residence Towson State U., 1983-90; cons. lit. div. Nat. Endowment for Arts, Washington, 1973; lectr. USIS tour German univs., 1977, tour, Africa, 1978; asst. prof. Johns Hopkins U.; bd. dirs. Balt. Theatre Project; co-founder Balt. Poet's Theatre. Poet-in-residence, NDEA grantee, Garrett County, Md., 1972; master poet Md. Arts Coun. Artists-in-the Schs. program, 1974-77; appeared in numerous poetry readings; books of poetry include Appearances, 1969, No Vacancies in Hell, 1973, The Follies, 1977, Young Men's Gold, 1978, The Book of Fortune, 1982, Spirits, 1987, The Boy In The Well, 1995, stories and essays include Star of Wonder, 1986, Love's Compass, 1990; biographies include Sister Aimee, 1993, Nat King Cole, 1999; plays include Jenny and the Phoenix, 1977, The Midnight Visitor, 1981, The Leading Lady 1999, others; translator Euripides' The Bacchae, 1998. Recipient Robert Frost prize, 1969; Prix de Rome AAAL, 1977; Danforth Found. grantee, 1971; Nat. Endowment for Arts fellow, 1974; Guggenheim fellow, 1983. Fellow Am. Acad. in Rome; mem. Phi Beta Kappa. Address: 843 W University Pkwy Baltimore MD 21210-2911

EPSTEIN, DAVID GUSTAV, lawyer; b. Alexandria, La., Dec. 7, 1943; s. Isaac and Alice (Fried) E.; m. Diane Floca, Feb. 16, 1969; children: Daniel Stewart, Charles Abraham. LL.B., U. Tex., 1966; LL.M., Harvard U., 1969. Bar: Tex. 1966, Ariz. 1967, Ark. 1979, Ga. 1989. Asst. prof. N.C. Sch. Law, 1970-74; prof. law U. Tex., 1974-79, Fulbright and Jaworski prof. law, 1982-85; dean Sch. Law, U. Ark., 1979-82; dean and prof. bankruptcy law Southeastern Bankruptcy Law Inst., Emory U., Atlanta, 1985-89; ptnr. King & Spalding, 1989-97, of counsel, 1998—; Charles E. Tweedy Jr. chair in law, Law Sch. U. Ala., 1998—. Author: Basic Uniform Commerical Code Teachng Materials, 1977, 3d rev. edit., 1988, Cases and Materials on Debtors and Creditors, 1973, 4th edit., 1994, Debtor Creditor Law in a Nutshell, 1973, 5th rev. edit., 1995, Bankruptcy (3 vols.), 1992; mem. editl. bd. Collier on Bankruptcy. Mem. ABA, Ga. Bar Assn., Tex. Bar Assn., Nat. Bankruptcy Conf., Am. Law Inst., Am. Coll. Bankruptcy, Order of Coif. Democrat. Jewish. Office: King & Spalding 191 Peachtree St NE Atlanta GA 30303-1740

EPSTEIN, DAVID M., publishing executive; b. Chgo., Feb. 20, 1946; s. Bernard G. and Marjorie P. (McCormack) E.; m. Ryba L. Tregilgas, Apr. 11, 1968; children: Daniel, Miriam. AB, UCLA, 1968; MA, U. Ill., 1971. Assoc. editor Scott, Foresman and Co., Glenview, Ill., 1971-80, courseware splst., 1980-81; editor Richard D. Irwin Inc., Homewood, Ill., 1981-83, mgr. composition, 1983-89; assoc. pub. Am. Libr. Assn., Chgo., 1989-98; mgr. Global HR Solutions Publs. Ctr., PricewaterhouseCoopers LLP, Chgo., 1998—. Author: Electronic Text Management, 1984; editor: U.S. in Literature, 1978, Books of the Fairs, 1991; mng. editor: World Encyclopedia Libr. and Info. Sci., 1996. Mem. Chgo. Book Clinic (v.p. 1986-88, bd. dirs. 1985-90). Jewish. Avocations: aviation history, writing. Office: Price Waterhouse Coopers LLP 203 N LaSalle St Chicago IL 60601-1210

EPSTEIN, DAVID MAYER, composer, conductor, music theorist, educator; b. N.Y.C., Oct. 3, 1930; s. Joshua S. and Elizabeth (Mayer) E.; m. Anne Louise Merrick, June 21, 1953; children: Eve Miriam, Beth Sara. AB, Antioch Coll., 1952; MMus, New England Conservatory Music, 1953; MFA, Brandeis U., 1954, Princeton U., 1956; PhD, Princeton U., 1968. Asst. editor, music critic Musical America, N.Y.C., 1956-57; asst. prof. music Antioch Coll., 1957-61, assoc. prof., 1962; music dir. Ednl. Broadcasting Corp., N.Y.C., 1962-64; assoc. prof. music MIT, Cambridge, 1965-69; prof.

MIT, 1970—; vis. fellow Max-Planck Inst., Seewiesen, West Germany, 1980-81, Neurosci. Inst., La Jolla, Calif., 1996; vis. prof. U. Munich. 1980-82, 87-89, 92, U. Lisbon, 1980, U. Iowa Sch. Music, 1989, U. Dusseldorf, 1994; guest condr. Nouvel Orch. Philharm. de Paris, 1982, 84, Haifa Symphony Orch., 1979, 81; participant Salzburg Easter Festival, 1983-87, Herbert von Karajan Music Symposium, Vienna, Austria, 1988, Hannover Congress (Geist und Natur), 1988, Rochester U. Conf. on Time, 1988, Inst. for Advanced Study, Budapest, Hungary, 1996; master classes in conducting Salzburg Mozarteum, 1984-85, 87, 92, Dresden Hochschule for Music, 1988, 90, 92-93, Berlin Hochschule for Music, 1992, Weimar Hochschule for Music, 1996, Am. Symphony Orch. League, 1989, 93, Vogtland Philharm., 1994. Guest condr. Berlin Radio Orch., 1967, Czech Radio Orch., Pilsen, 1966, Cleve. Orch., 1961, N.Y.C. Ctr., 1966, N.J. Symphony, 1961, Bavarian Radio Symphony, 1973, Vienna Tonkuenstlerorchester, 1973, Israel Broadcasting Orch., 1971, Jerusalem Orch., 1982, Royal Philharm. Orch., 1974, Am. Symphony Orch., 1978, Bamberg Symphony Orch., 1978, Orch. de la Suisse Romande, 1981, 88, Symphony Orch. Radio Brussels, 1984, Robert Schumann Philharmonie, Karl-Marx-Stadt, Germany, 1986, 87, 90, Orch. Nat. Lyon, 1986, Danish Radio Orch., 1987, Helsinki Festival, 1987, Nat. Orch. State Mex., 1989, Neubrandenburg Philharmonie, Germany, 1993, Xalapa Symphony Orch., Mex., 1994, Mittelsachsische Philharmonie, 1995, Vogtland Philharmonie 1994, 95, 96; also Antioch Shakespeare Festival, 1957, Jena Philharmonic, 1995, Szeged (Hungary) Philharmonic, 1996, Orquestra Metro. de Lisboa, 1996. Orquestra Sinfonica de Portuagal, 1999; music dir. Harrisburg Symphony Orch., 1974-78, Worcester Orch. and Worcester Festival, 1976-80, New Orch. Boston, 1984—; composer documentary films, Nat. Ednl. TV, 1964-65; founder, dir. N.Y. Youth Symphony Orch., 1963-66; recs. on EMI, Desto, AR/DGG, Vox, Turnabout, Pantheon Internat., Newport Classic labels; author: Beyond Orpheus: Studies in Musical Structure, 1979; Shaping Time: Music, The Brain and Performance, 1995; mem. editl. bd. Music Theory Spectrum; contbr. articles to profl. jours.; editor Beauty and the Brain: Biological Aspects of Aesthetics, 1988. Bd. dirs. New England Lyric Theatre, Adirondack Found. of Arts, Young Audiences Boston, Conductors Guild, 1998—; alumni bd. Antioch Coll., 1996-99, bd. trustees, 1999—. Recipient Louisville Orch. award, Fromm Found. award, BMI award, N.Y. State Coun. for Arts Commn., 1973, Sr. Scientist award Alexander Von Humboldt Found., 1985, Deutsche Forschungsgemeinschaft award, 1980-82, 91, 94, Mass. Arts and Humanities Found. award, 1977, Boston Symphony Orch. Young People's Concerts Commn., 1972, ASCAP Deems Taylor award, 1996; Rockefeller Found. grantee, 1971, Ford Found. rec. grantee, 1971, 76; Kulas Found. fellow, sr. fellow in arts and humanities MIT, 1998. Mem. ASCAP, Am. Soc. Univ. Composers (exec. com. 1967-69), Am. Symphony Orch. League (chmn. univ. orch. sect. 1960-62), Am. Fedn. Musicians, Am. Music Ctr., Am. Brahms Soc. (bd. dirs. 1983—), Robert Schumann-Gesellschaft, Internat. Soc. for Study of Time (exec. bd. 1979-83), Soc. for Music Theory, Soc. for Music Perception and Cognition. Office: MIT Music Dept Cambridge MA 02139 *Communication with colleagues, with audiences, and with the brilliant creative minds that have given us our repertoire makes music an immensely satisfying profession. It is a profession that also demands self-discipline and continual striving for the highest standards.*

EPSTEIN, EDWARD JOSEPH, textile company executive; b. Newark, N.J., Apr. 18, 1920; s. Herman and Rose (Jennis) E.; children: Jonathan, Judith, Robert. Student, NYU, 1938; BS, Lowell U., 1941; MBA, Seton Hall U., 1970. Cert. Pub. Mgr. V.p. Nat. Rayon Dyeing Co., Inc., Newark, 1950-57, No. Yarn Mills, Newark, 1957-70; pres. Spacetronics Industries, Newark, 1970-81; dir. revenue and patent accounts State of N.J., 1981—. Patentee in field. Served with USN, 1942, lt. USNR, 1946. Mem. Leaders Textile Industry, Tau Epsilon Sigma. Jewish. Home: 8 Mitchell Ave Piscataway NJ 08854-5523 Office: 200 Sanatorium Rd Glen Gardner NJ 08826-3288

EPSTEIN, EDWARD LOUIS, lawyer; b. Walla Walla, Wash., Jan. 10, 1936; s. Louis and Marie (Barger) E.; m. Marilyn K. Young, Dec. 29, 1962; children: Lisa Marie, Rachel Ann. BA with great distinction, Stanford U., 1958; LLB magna cum laude, Harvard U., 1961. Bar: Oreg. 1962, U.S. Dist. Ct. Oreg. 1962, U.S. Ct. Appeals (9th cir.) 1963. Assoc. Stoel Rives LLP, Portland, Oreg., 1962-67, ptnr., 1967—. Past sec., bd. dirs. Portland Hosp. Facilities Authority; trustee Good Samaritan Hosp. and Med. Ctr., Portland, 1972-78, pres., 1978; past trustee Morrison Ctr. for Youth and Family Svcs., Oreg. Assn. Hosps. Found. Mem. ABA, Am. Bar Found., Nat. Health Lawyers Assn., Oreg. Bar Assn., Multnomah County Bar Assn., Multnomah Athletic Club, Univ. Club, Harvard Law Rev., Phi Beta Kappa. Democrat. Jewish. Office: Stoel Rives LLP 900 SW 5th Ave Ste 2600 Portland OR 97204-1235

EPSTEIN, EDWARD S., meteorologist; b. N.Y.C., Apr. 29, 1931; s. Herman and Julia Epstein; m. Alice Katzenstein, June 6, 1954; children: Debra, Harry, Nancy, William. AB, Harvard U., 1951; MBA, Columbia U., 1953; MS, Pa. State U., 1954, PhD, 1960. Lectr. U. Mich., 1959-61, asst. prof., 1961-63, assoc. prof., 1964-68, prof., 1969-73, chmn. dept. atmospheric and oceanic sci., 1971-73; assoc. adminstr. for environ. monitoring and predictions NOAA, 1973-77, acting asst. adminstr. for rsch. and devel., 1977-78; dir. Nat. Climate Program Office NOAA, Rockville, Md., 1978-81; chief Climate and Earth Scis. Lab. NOAA, 1981-83; acting dir. rsch. and applications Nat. Environ. Satellite, Data and Info. Svcs., 1982-83; sr. scientist Climate Analysis Ctr., Nat. Weather Service, 1983-93; prin. Prediction and Evaluation Systems, 1994-98; bd. dirs. Univ. Corp. for Atmospheric Rsch., 1969-73. Author: Statistical Inference and Prediction in Climatology: A Bayesian Approach, 1985; editor Jour. Applied Meteorology, 1971-73, Jour. Climate, 1995-98; contbr. articles to profl. jours. With USAF, 1953-57. Fellow AAAS (chmn. sect. hydrospheric scis. 1980), Am. Meteorol. Soc. (councillor 1974-77). Jewish. Home and Office: 8216 Inverness Hollow Ter Potomac MD 20854-2726

EPSTEIN, EMANUEL, plant physiologist; b. Duisburg, Germany, Nov. 5, 1916; came to U.S., 1938, naturalized, 1946; s. Harry and Bertha (Lowe) E.; m. Hazel M. Leask, Nov. 26, 1943; children: Jared H. (dec.), Jonathan H. BS, U. Calif., Davis, 1940, MS, 1941; PhD, U. Calif., Berkeley, 1950. Plant physiologist Dept. Agr., Beltsville, Md., 1950-58; lectr., assoc. plant physiologist U. Calif.-Davis, 1958-65, prof. plant nutrition, plant physiologist, 1965-87, faculty rsch. lectr., 1980, prof. botany, 1974-87, prof. and plant physiologist emeritus (active), 1987—; cons. to govt. and pvt. agys. Author: Mineral Nutrition of Plants: Principles and Perspectives, 1972; mem. editorial bd. Plant Physiology, 1962-71, 76-92, CRC Handbook Series in Nutrition and Food, 1975-84, The Biosaline Concept: An Approach to the Utilization of Underexploited Resources, 1978, Saline Agriculture: Salt-Tolerant Plants for Developing Countries, 1990; contbr. articles to profl. jours. including Plant Sci., 1981-89, Advances in Plant Nutrition, 1981-94, Soil Science and Plant Nutrition, 1998—. With U.S. Army, 1943-46. Recipient Gold medal Pisa (Italy) U., 1962; Guggenheim fellow, 1958; Fulbright sr. research scholar, 1965-66, 74-75. Fellow AAAS (pres. Pacific divsn. 1990, Fifty-Yr. Life mem. award 1999); mem. Nat. Acad. Scis., Am. Soc. Plant Physiologists (Charles Reid Barnes Hon. Life Membership award 1986), Scandinavian Soc. Plant Physiology, Am. Inst. Biol. Scis., Common Cause, Save-the-Redwoods League, U. Calif. Davis Club, Nature Conservancy, Nat. Parks and Conservation Assn., Sigma Xi. Rsch., publs. on ion transport in plants, mineral nutrition and salt rels. of plants, salt tolerant crops, and silicon in plant biology. Office: U Calif Soils and Biogeochemistry Land Air & Water Resources One Shields Ave Davis CA 95616-8627

EPSTEIN, FRANKLIN HAROLD, physician, educator; b. Bklyn., May 5, 1924; s. Max and Fannie (Geduld) E.; m. Sherrie Spivack, Aug. 12, 1951; children: Mark, Ann, Sara, Jonathan. B.A., Bklyn. Coll., 1944; M.D., Yale U., 1947; Doctor Honoris Causa, Med. Acad., Gdansk, 1992. Diplomate: Am. Bd. Internal Medicine (chmn. subsplty. bd. in nephrology 1969-72). Asst. prof. medicine Yale U., 1954-59, assoc. prof., 1959-66, prof. medicine, 1966-72, chief, divsn. metabolism, 1965-72; prof. medicine Harvard U., 1972—, H.L. Blumgart prof. medicine, W. Applebaum prof. medicine; dir. Thorndike Meml. Lab., Boston City Hosp., 1972; physician-in-chief Beth Israel Hosp., 1973-80, dir. renal divsn., 1980-93; Macy Found. fellow and vis. scientist Oxford (Eng.) U., 1980-81; cons. to surgeon gen. U.S. Army, 1964-80; mem. metabolism study sect. USPHS, 1962-66; pres. Mt. Desert Island Biol.Lab., 1986-95. Editor: Yearbook of Medicine, 1967-96; assoc. editor: Jour. Clin. Investigation, 1957-62, New Eng. Jour. Medicine, 1982—, Quar. Jour. Medicine, 1984-93; contbr. papers, book chpts. on renal physiology, disease of kidneys. Capt. M.C., U.S. Army, 1950-53. Recipient rsch. career award USPHS, 1964, John P. Peters award Am. Soc. Nephrology, 1985, Bywaters award Internat. Soc. Nephrology, 1999. Fellow AAAS, Assn. Physicians Gt. Britain and Ireland, Royal Coll. Physicians; mem. Am. Soc. Clin. Investigation (v.p. 1970), Assn. Am. Physicians, Interurban Clin. Club, Sigma Xi, Alpha Omega Alpha. Jewish. Home: 294 Buckminster Rd Brookline MA 02445-5801 Office: 330 Brookline Ave Boston MA 02215-5400

EPSTEIN, GARY MARVIN, lawyer; b. Bklyn., Nov. 28, 1946; s. Arthur and Juliett (Winick) E.; m. Jeralyn Needel, June 29, 1969; children: Daniel, Deborah. BSEE, Lehigh U., 1968; JD, Harvard U., 1971. Bar: D.C. 1971, U.S. Ct. Appeals (3d cir.) 1973, U.S. Supreme Ct. 1975, U.S. Ct. Appeals (9th cir.) 1988. Engr. Gordon Engring. Co., Wakefield, Mass., 1967-70; assoc. Arent, Fox, Kinter, Plotkin & Kahn, Washington, 1971-79, ptnr., 1979-81; chief Common Carrier Bur. FCC, Washington, 1981-83; ptnr. Latham & Watkins, Washington, 1983—; pub. mem. Adminstrv. Conf. U.S., 1983-86; chmn. adv. com. reduced orbital spacing FCC, 1983-86; chmn. adv. Com. World Radiocomms. Conf., FCC, 1994-96. Mem. ABA, D.C. Bar Assn., Eta Kappa Nu, Tau Beta Pi. Home: 7122 Arrowood Rd Bethesda MD 20817-2809 Office: Latham & Watkins Ste 1300 1001 Pennsylvania Ave NW Washington DC 20004-2585

EPSTEIN, HENRY DAVID, electronics company executive; b. Frankfurt, Germany, Apr. 5, 1927; came to U.S., 1940, naturalized, 1945; s. Julius S. and Lola C. (Heilbronner) E.; m. Henny Wenkart, Sept. 6, 1952; children: Jonathan, Heitzi, Ari. BS in Engring., Brown U., 1948; MS in Bus. Adminstrn., Harvard U., 1950. Mgr. devel. engring. Metal & Controls Corp., Attleboro, Mass., 1952-59, Tex. Instruments, Attleboro, 1959-67; mgr. div. control products, 1967-77, asst. v.p., 1969-77; sr. group v.p. Loral Corp., N.Y.C., 1977-85; pres. Ideonics, 1985-87; chmn., chief exec. officer Computer Communications Inc., Torrance, Calif., 1988-90; chmn., pres., chief exec. officer Penril Corp., Potomac, Md., 1987-96; pres. Memotec Communications INc., Montreal, 1996—. Patentee in elec. controls, automotive safety, pollution control. Pres. Ideonies Lake City, Fla.,1985—. Served with Signal Corps U.S. Army, 1945-46. Fellow IEEE; mem. Friends of Harvard Hillel, Am. Electronic Assn., Sigma Xi, Tau Beta Pi. Home: 4 Shady Hill Sq Cambridge MA 02138-2036

EPSTEIN, IRVING ROBERT, chemistry educator; b. Bklyn., Aug. 9, 1945; s. Milton and Marion (Hillsberg) E.; m. Ellen Bea Fisher, Oct. 31, 1971; children: David, Peter. AB, Harvard U., 1966, MA, 1968, PhD, 1971; diploma Oxford U., 1967. NATO postdoctoral fellow Cambridge U., 1971; asst. prof. dept. chemistry Brandeis U., Waltham, Mass., 1971-75, assoc. prof., 1975-81, prof., 1981—, Helena Rubinstein prof., 1989—, chmn., 1983-87, dean arts and scis., 1992-94, provost, sr. v.p. for acad. affairs, 1994—; NSF faculty profl. devel. fellow Max Planck Inst., Göttingen, Germany, 1977-78. Recipient Tchr.-Scholar award Dreyfus Found., 1973; Nat. Merit scholar, 1962-66, Marshall scholar, 1966-67, Woodrow Wilson fellow, 1968, Guggenheim fellow, 1977, 87, Humboldt fellow, 1977, NSF fellow, 1977-78. Mem. Am. Chem. Soc. (Liebmann award), Phi Beta Kappa. Mem. editorial adv. bd. Jour. Phys. Chemistry, 1982-89; assoc. editor Chaos, 1990—; mem. editl. bd. Interjour. Complex Sys., 1995—; contbr. articles to profl. jours. Home: 28 Otis St Newton MA 02460-1803 Office: Brandeis U MS134 Waltham MA 02254

EPSTEIN, JASON, publishing company executive; b. Cambridge, Mass., Aug. 25, 1928; s. Robert and Gladys (Shapiro) E.; children: Jacob, Helen. BA, Columbia U., 1949, MA, 1950. Editor Doubleday & Co., 1951-58; v.p., editorial dir. Random House, Inc., N.Y.C., 1958-97; co-founder N.Y. Rev. Books; founder Libr. of Am.; founder Reader's Catalog. Author: The Great Conspiracy Trial, 1970; co-author: Easthampton, a history and guide, 1975; contbr. articles to various publs. Recipient John Jay award Columbia Coll., 1988, Lifetime Achievement award Nat. Book, 1988, Curtis Benjamin award, 1993. Mem. Council Fgn. Relations, Phi Beta Kappa. Home: PO Box 1143 Sag Harbor NY 11963-0039 Office: 201 E 50th St New York NY 10022-7703

EPSTEIN, JAY STUART, medical researcher; married; 2 children. BA cum laude, Harvard U., 1969; MD, Downstate Med. Coll., 1976. Resident internal medicine George Washington U. Hosp., Washington, 1976-79, clin. fellow infectious diseases, 1979-81; sr. staff fellow rsch. divsn. virology office biologics rsch. & review FDA, Rockville, Md., 1981-85, chief immunochemistry lab., 1984-86, chief retrovirology lab. divsn. transfusion sci., 1986-92, acting dept. dir., 1990-92, dir. divsn. transfusion transmitted diseases Office Blood Rsch. & Review, 1993-95, acting. dir., 1993-95, dir., 1995—; rsch. asst. Moffit Hosp., San Francisco, 1971-73; part time physician Potomac (Md.) Village Med. Ctr., 1981-83; part time house physician Capitol Hill Hosp., Washington, 1981-83. With USPHS, 1985-88. Nat. Merit scholar, 1965, Harvard Coll. scholar, 1965, N.Y. State Regents Medicine scholar, 1969. Mem. AAAS, Infectious Diseases Soc. Am., Greater Washington Area Infectious Diseas Soc., Alpha Omega Alpha. Home: 1922 Foxhall Rd Mc Lean VA 22101-5535 Office: Office Blood Rsch & Review FDA CBER HFM-300 1401 Rockville Pike Rockville MD 20852-1428*

EPSTEIN, JAYE MARK, city planner; b. Washington, Dec. 30, 1950; s. Samuel and Doris Lee (Peck) E.; m. Mona Remer, June 30, 1974; children: Brian, Elizabeth, Sara. BA in Sociology, U. Md., 1974; M City and Regional Planning, Cath. U. Am., 1976. Cert. urban planner. Transp. planner Md. Dept. Transp., Office of Sec., Balt., 1978-82; assoc. planner Broward County Office of Planning, Ft. Lauderdale, Fla., 1982-83, Broward County Planning Coun., Ft. Lauderdale, 1983-85; chief planner City of Coral Springs, Fla., 1985-89; dir. planning City of Coral Springs, 1989-92, dir. community and econ. devel., 1992-93, dir. devel. svcs., 1993—; vice chmn. Broward County Tech. Coordinating Com., 1989—; chmn. Coral Springs Devel. Rev. Com., 1989—. Mem. Am. Inst. Cert. Planners (cert.), Am. Planning Assn., Fla. Planning Assn., Broward County Planning Assn., Cath. U. Am. Alumni Assn., U. Md. Alumni Assn. (life).

EPSTEIN, JEFFREY MARK, neurosurgeon; b. Newark, Apr. 7, 1951; s. Herbert Joseph and Roberta Laura (Sank) E.; m. Ronit Adler. BA, Johns Hopkins U., 1973; MD, Autonomous U. Guadalajara, Mex., 1979. Diplomate Am. Bd. Neurol. and Orthopedic Surgery, Am. Bd. Pain Mgmt. 5th channel clerkship Newark Beth-Israel Med. Ctr., 1979-80; intern in surgery Muhlenberg Hosp., Plainfield, N.J., 1980-81; resident in neurosurgery SUNY-Downstate and Kings County Hosp. Ctr., Bklyn., 1981-85, chief resident neurosurgery, 1985-86; instr. neurosurgery SUNY-Downstate Med. Ctr., 1986-87, asst. prof. neurosurgery, 1987-88; pvt. practice, Babylon, N.Y., 1988—. Contbr. articles to Anesthesia Jour., 1985. Mem. N.Y. State Neurosurgery Soc., Med. Soc. State N.Y., Suffolk County Med. Soc., Magoun Landing Yacht Club, Alpha Epsilon Delta (v.p. 1973). Jewish. Avocations: sailing, skiing. Office: 51 John St Ste 4 Babylon NY 11702-2928

EPSTEIN, JEREMIAH FAIN, anthropologist, educator; b. N.Y.C., Feb. 14, 1924; s. Joseph and Carol (Fain) E.; divorced; children—Anne, Louise, Suzanne; m. Kathleen Wheeler. B.S. in Agr, U. Ill., 1949, M.A. in Anthropology, 1951; Ph.D., U. Pa., 1957. Lectr. Hunter Coll., N.Y.C., 1954-58; research scientist anthropology U. Tex., Austin, 1958-60; mem. faculty U. Tex., 1958—, prof. anthropology, 1970-93; prof. emeritus, 1993—; fieldwork in, Mex., Belize, Honduras, France, U.S. Contbr. articles to profl. jours. Served with AUS, 1942-45. Decorated Purple Heart; grantee NSF, 1963, 64; grantee Wenner Gren Found., 1961; grantee U. Tex. Inst. Latin Am. Studies, 1963, 75; grantee U. Tex., 1988; Fulbright-Hays fellow, 1964; Mellon Found. fellow in Latin Am. studies, 1988; U. Tex. faculty rsch. assignment, 1988. Mem. Am. Anthrop. Assn., Soc. Am. Archaeology, AAAS, Soc. Mexicana Anthropologia. Office: U Tex Dept Anthropology Austin TX 78712

EPSTEIN, JEREMY G., lawyer; b. Chgo., Sept. 28, 1946; s. Joseph and Gayola (Goldman) E.; m. Amy Kallman, Sept. 15, 1968; children: Joshua, Abigail. BA summa cum laude, Columbia U., 1967; BA, Cambridge U., Eng., 1969, MA, 1973; JD, Yale U., 1972. Bar: N.Y. 1973. Law clk. to judge Arnold Bauman U.S. Dist. Ct. (so. dist.) N.Y., 1972-74; asst. U.S. atty. so. dist. N.Y. U.S. Dist. Ct., 1974-78; ptnr. Shearman & Sterling, N.Y.C., 1982—. Bd. dirs. Fund for Modern Cts., Legal Aid Soc.; vol. Lawyers for the Arts. Fellow Am. Coll. Trial Lawyers, Columbia Coll. Alumni Assn. (bd. dirs.), Phi Beta Kappa. Office: 599 Lexington Ave Fl C2 New York NY 10022-6030

EPSTEIN, JOHN HOWARD, dermatologist; b. San Francisco, Dec. 29, 1926; s. Norman Neman and Gertrude (Hirsch) E.; m. Alice Thompson, Nov. 1953; children: Norman H., Janice A., Beverly A. BA, U. Calif., Berkeley, 1949, MD, 1952; MS, U. Minn., 1956. Diplomate Am. Bd. Dermatology (dir. 1974-84, pres. 1981-82). Intern Stanford U. Med. Ctr., 1952-53; resident in dermatology Mayo Clinic, Rochester, Minn., 1953-56; practice medicine specializing in dermatology San Francisco, 1956—; chief dermatology Mt. Zion Hosp., 1970-80; clin. prof. U. Calif. Med. Sch., San Francisco, 1972—; cons. Letterman Army Med. Center, U.S. Naval Hosp., San Diego. Chief editor Archives of Dermatology, 1973-78; asst. editor Jour. Am. Acad. Dermatology, 1978-88; contbr. over 260 articles to profl. jours. With USNR, 1944-46. Fellow ACP; mem. Am. Acad. Dermatology (pres. 1981-82, Silver award for exhibit 1962, Gold award 1969), Soc. Investigative Dermatology (v.p. 1979-80), Am. Dermatol. Assn. (bd. dirs. 1983-88, pres. 1990-91), N.Am. Dermatology Soc., Pacific Dermatol. Assn. (pres. 1985-86), Brit. Dermatol. Soc., Danish Dermatol. Soc., Polish Dermatol. Soc., San Francisco Dermatol. Soc. (pres. 1963-64), Am. Soc. Photobiology (councilor 1983-86), Academia Mexicana and Dermatologia (hon.), European Acad. Dermatology and Venerology (hon.), La Societe Francaise de Dermatologie & de Syphiligraphie, Spanish Dermatol. Soc. Office: 450 Sutter St Rm 1306 San Francisco CA 94108-4002

EPSTEIN, JONATHAN DANIEL, journalist; b. Schenectady, N.Y., July 20, 1971; s. Gilbert Howard and Celia (Feiner) E. BA in Polit. Sci., History, U. Rochester, N.Y., 1993; MS in Print Journalism, Columbia U., N.Y.C., 1994. Reporter Am. Banker, Washington, 1994-96, deputy sect. editor, 1996-97; reporter News Journal, Wilmington, Del., 1997—. Cmty. bd. mem. U. Del. Hillel, Newark, 1998—. Fellow Stonies Grad. Sch. Banking, Newark, 1997. Mem. Soc. Profl. Journalists. Jewish. E-mail address: jdepstein@aol.com. Office: News Journal 950 W Basin Rd New Castle DE 19720

EPSTEIN, JUDITH ANN, lawyer; b. L.A., Dec. 23, 1942; d. Gerald Elliot and Harriet (Hirsh) Rubens; m. Joseph I. Epstein, Oct. 4, 1964; children: Mark Douglas, Laura Ann. AB, U. Calif., Berkeley, 1964; MA, U. San Francisco, 1974, JD, 1977. Bar: Calif. 1978, U.S. Dist. Ct. (no. dist.) Calif 1978, U.S. Supreme Ct. 1983, U.S. Ct. Appeals (9th cir.) 1984. With social svcs. dept. Sutter County, Yuba City, Calif., 1964-66; bus. devel. assoc. Yuba County C. of C., Marysville, Calif., 1968-70; rsch. clk. Calif. Supreme Ct., San Fransisco, 1977; ptnr. Crosby, Heafey, Roach & May, Oakland, Calif., 1978-91; gen. counsel and sec. Valent USA Corp., 1991-98; exec. dir. East Bay/The Commonwealth Club of Calif., 1998—; lectr. U. Calif. Grad. Sch. Journalism in Media Law, Berkeley, 1987-91; bd. dirs. Sierra Pacific Steel, Hayward, Calif.; adj. prof. U. San Francisco, 1999—. Bd. dirs., v.p. Oakland Ballet, 1980-92; mem. bd. counselors U. San Francisco Sch. Law, 1994; trustee U. San Francisco, 1996—; bd. dirs. San Francisco Bay area Girl Scouts U.S., 1998—. Recipient Pres.'s award Oakland Ballet, James Madison Freedom of Info. award Soc. Profl. Journalists, 1992; award for Disting. Achievement, Girl Scouts U.S., 1995. Fellow Am. Bar Found.; mem. Calif. Women Lawyers Assn., Alameda Bar Assn., Berkeley Tennis Club. Office: Valent USA Corp 1333 N California Blvd Ste 600 Walnut Creek CA 94596-4558

EPSTEIN, KALMAN NOEL, newspaper publishing company executive; b. N.Y.C., Nov. 5, 1938; s. Joseph and Ceil (Platkin) E.; m. Anita Kaminski; children: Stephanie Irene, Pamela Dyan. BS in Journalism, NYU, 1961. Copy boy Herald Tribune, N.Y.C.; with Wall St. Jour., N.Y.C., from 1961, asst. nat. editor, to 1965; head news desk Wall St. Jour., Washington, from 1965, gen. reporter, to 1969; writer, editor White House Conf. Children and Youth, Washington, 1969; asst. nat. editor Washington Post, 1970—, edn. editor, 1973-76, editor Sunday opinion sect., 1971-73, 77-83, editor nat. weekly edit., 1984-86, pub. Nat. Weekly edit., 1986-96; dir. Washington Post Books, 1997—; journalist-in-residence George Washington U., Washington, 1986. Author: Language, Ethnicity, and the Schools, 1977. Mem. exec. bd. Washington chpt. Am. Jewish Com., 1986—. Home: 301 Ellsworth Dr Silver Spring MD 20910-4200 Office: The Washington Post 1150 15th St NW Washington DC 20071-0002

EPSTEIN, LEON JOSEPH, psychiatrist; b. Jersey City, June 7, 1917; s. Irving and Sara (Pomerantz) E.; children: Lisa, David. A.B., Vanderbilt U., 1937, M.A., 1938; Ph.D., Peabody Coll., 1941; M.D., U. Tenn., 1949. Intern Wesley Meml. Hosp., Chgo., 1950; resident in psychiatry St. Elizabeths Hosp., Washington, 1951-54; staff psychiatrist St. Elizabeths Hosp., 1954-56; dep. dir. Calif. Dept. Mental Hygiene, Sacramento, 1956-61; prof. psychiatry, asso. dir. Langley Porter Inst. U. Calif. Sch. Medicine, San Francisco, 1961-83, interim chmn., dir., 1985-86, prof. psychiatry, emeritus, 1987—. Author books and articles in psychogerontology and psychopharmacology. Mem. San Francisco Crime Commn., 1969-71. Served to lt. comdr. USN, 1941-46. Recipient Sullivan award Peabody Coll., 1941; William A. White award St. Elizabeths Hosp., 1952, 53; J. Elliott Royer award U. Calif., 1976; Outstanding Achievement award Northern Calif. Psychiatric Soc., 1985. Mem. Am. Coll. Psychiatry, Am. Coll. Neuropsychopharmacology, Am. Psychiat. Assn., Am. Psychopath. Assn., Gerontol. Soc. Jewish. Home: 2251 Steiner St San Francisco CA 94115-2219 Office: 350 Parnassus Ave Ste 309 San Francisco CA 94117-3608

EPSTEIN, LIONEL CHARLES, lawyer; b. N.Y.C., Apr. 7, 1924; s. David and Carrie (Roth) E.; m. Sarah Louise Gamble, June 10, 1951 (div. Apr. 12, 1983); children: David Bradley, James Roth, Richard Aldis, Miles Owen, Sarah Carianne; m. Elizabeth Pendelton Streicher, Nov. 10, 1990. B.A., NYU, 1947; LL.B., Harvard U., 1950. Bar: N.Y. 1950, D.C. 1953, U.S. Supreme Ct. 1955. With office gen. counsel U.S. Navy Dept., 1950-52; tax div. U.S. Justice Dept., 1952-57; mem. firms Ginsburg & Leventhal, 1957-67, Epstein, Friedman, Duncan & Medalie, Washington, 1967-74; mem. firm Jones, Day, Reavis & Pogue, Washington, 1975-84, of counsel, 1984-86; chmn. EFO Capital Mgmt. Inc., Washington, 1984—; spl. asst. to R. Sargent Shriver Peace Corps, 1962; Bd. dirs. Expt. in Internat. Living, Mus. Modern Art, N.Y.C., Com. on Illustrated Books and Prints, Washington Print Club. Author art exhbn. catalogs. Served with inf. AUS, 1942-45. Decorated Purple Heart, Knight's Cross 1st class Order St. Olav (Norway). Mem. ABA, Harvard Club (N.Y.). Clubs: Lawyers (founding mem.), Internat, 1925 F St, Harvard. Home: 700 New Hampshire Ave NW Washington DC 20037-2406 Office: 21 Dupont Cir NW # 330 Washington DC 20036-1109

EPSTEIN, LOUIS RALPH, retired wholesale grocery executive; b. Sharon, Pa., Jan. 28, 1926; s. Samuel W. and Bess (Rosenblum) E.; m. Marlene Lurie, Aug. 13, 1950; children: Richard, Susan, Georgia. BS, U. Rochester, 1949. v.p. Peter J. Schmitt Co., 1982-92; dir., past pres. Harry M. Pollock Co., Kittaning, Pa. pres. Golden Dawn Foods, Inc., 1978-82; officer Mercer County United Way, 1955—; v.p., treas. F.H. Bull Trustees, Sharon. Recipient Merit award Pitts. Food Brokers Assn., 1975. Mem. Pa. Econ. League (chmn. Mercer County branch), Youngstown Area Jewish Fedn. (pres.), Sharon County Club (past pres.), Kiwanis. Avocations: photography; piano; travel. Home: 1754 Mcdowell St Sharon PA 16146-3858

EPSTEIN, MARC A., school system administrator; b. N.Y.C., Apr. 4, 1962; s. Robert and Ellen G. (Mark) E.; m. Yvonne M. Beaver, June 24, 1990; children: Amanda M., Matthew B. BS in Elem. Edn., Boston U., 1983; MA in Computers in Edn., Columbia U., 1984; specialist diploma, Queens Coll., 1993. Cert. tchr., sch. dist. adminstr., supr., N.Y., tchr., Mass. Computer cons. Pub. Sch. # 8, Bklyn., 1984; computer tchr. Clara H. Carlson Sch. and Gotham Ave. Sch., Elmont, N.Y., 1984-89; computer coord. Elmont Sch. Dist., 1988-89, South Mid. Sch., Great Neck, N.Y., 1989-96; dist. tech. cons. Great Neck Sch. Dist., 1994-98, dist. tech. dir., 1998—; curriculum writer Elmont Pub. Schs., 1985, 88; technology tash force chmn. Great Neck Pub. Schs., 1990-91, founder, sys. operator GNPS Online, 1994—, webmaster, 1998—; webmaster Great Neck Pub. Sch. Website, 1998—. Grantee NYNEX, 1994. Avocations: computers, sports, travel, music, reading. Office: Great Neck Pub Schs 345 Lakeville Rd Great Neck NY 11020-1639

EPSTEIN, MARK DANIEL, plastic surgeon; b. New Hyde Park, N.Y., Sept. 17, 1959; s. Irwin Louis and Barbara Ann Epstein; m. Elyse Rafal. MD, SUNY, Bklyn., 1984, SUNY, Bklyn., 1984. Diplomate Am.

Bd. Surgery, Am. Bd. Hand Surgery, Am. Bd. Plastic Surgery. Intern then resident in gen. surgery U. Cin. Med. Ctr., 1984-90; resident in plastic and reconstructive surgery Milton S. Hershey Med. Ctr. of Pa. State U., 1990-92; fellow in reconstructive microsurgery Chang Gung Meml. Hosp., Taipei, Taiwan, Republic of China, 1991; fellow in hand surgery Union Meml. Hosp. Raymond Curtis Hand Ctr., Balt., Taiwan, 1992-93; fellow in microsurgery div. plastic/reconstructive surgery Brigham and Women's Hosp., Boston, 1993-94; asst. prof. div. plastic and reconstructive surgery SUNY Health Scis. Ctr., Stony Brook, N.Y., 1994-97; with Musculoskeletal Inst., North Shore, N.Y., 1997-98; pvt. practice Stony Brook, N.Y.; lectr. in field. Inventor Epstein Carpal Tunnel Knife Guide, 1991; contbr. to books and manuscripts. Fellow SUNY Downstate Med. Ctr., Brooklyn, N.Y., 1978-82, NYU Med. Ctr., N.Y.C., 1984, Shriners Burn Inst., Cinn., 1987-88. Mem. ACS (assoc. fellow, hon. mention resident essay contest 1989), Am. Soc. Plastics and Reconstructive Surgeons. Fax: 516-689-1153. E-mail: mepstein@erols.com. Office: 2500-22 Rt 347 Ste 82 Stony Brook NY 11790

EPSTEIN, MARSHA ANN, public health administrator, physician; b. Chgo., Feb. 4, 1945; 1 child, Lee Rashad Mahmood. BA, Reed Coll., 1965; MD, U. Calif., San Francisco, 1969; MPH, U. Calif., Berkeley, 1971. Diplomate Am. Bd. Preventive Medicine. Intern French Hosp., San Francisco, 1969-70; resident in preventive medicine Sch. Pub. Health, U. Calif., Berkeley, 1971-73; fellow in family planning dept. ob-gyn. UCLA, 1973-74; med. dir. Herself Health Clinic, L.A., 1974-79; pvt. adult gen. practitioner L.A., 1978-82; dist. health officer L.A. County Pub. Health, Inglewood, Calif., 1982—; part-time physician U. Calif. Student Health, Berkeley, 1970-73; co-med. dir. Monsenior Oscar Romero Free Clinic, L.A., 1992-93. Mem. APHA, Am. Coll. Physician Execs., Am. Med. Women's Assn., So. Calif. Pub. Health Assn., Calif. Acad. Preventive Medicine, L.A. County Med. Women's Assn., L.A. County Sr. Women Mgrs. Democrat. Jewish. Avocations: camping, native plants, meditating. Office: Tucker Health Ctr 123 W Manchester Blvd Inglewood CA 90301-1753

EPSTEIN, MARVIN MORRIS, retired construction company executive; b. Cleve., June 2, 1928; s. Isadore Elchanan and Rose (Gevelber) E.; m. Lois M. DeSure, June 10, 1957; children: Deborah L. Epstein Merkin, David A. BA with highest honors, U. Mich., 1951; attended Western Res. U., 1947-49, Ohio State U. 1953, Cleve. State U., 1995-98. Reporter Cleve. Plain Dealer, 1951-52; editor AP, Columbus, Ohio, 1953-55; asst. mng. editor Times-Star, Cin., 1956-57; cons. Eden & Assocs., Cleve., 1959-60; sr. exec. The Austin Co., Cleve., 1961-93; v.p. pub. rels./advt., 1992-93; ret., 1993. Editor Internat. News Milw. Jour., 1958-59; contbr. articles to profl. jours. Active Greater Cleve. Growth Assn., 1975-90; mem. bd. overseers, visiting com. Case Western Res. U., Case Inst. Tech., Cleve., 1981-85. Bd. dirs. The Stearns Collection, Ann Arbor, Mich., 1990-93; trustee Cleve. Music Sch. Settlement, 1989-90; mem. Presdl. Societies, Univ. Mich., 1980—, Vis. Com. Coll. Lit., Sci. and the Arts, U Mich., 1989-92; trustee Cleveland Heights-University Heights Pub. Libr., 1997—. With U.S. Army, 1946-47. Recipient McNaught Gold medal U. Mich., 1951, Disting. Svc. award, 1998. Mem. Soc. Profl. Journalists, U. Mich. Alumni Assn. (pres. Cleve. chpt. 1975-76), Heights Regional C. of C. (pres. 1992). Democrat. Jewish. Home: 4161 Hadleigh Rd University Heights OH 44118

EPSTEIN, MELVIN, lawyer; b. Passaic, N.J., Jan. 4, 1938; s. Hyman and Lillian (Rozenblum) E.; m. Rachel Judith Stein, Dec. 20, 1964; children: Jonathan Andrew, Emily Sarah. AB, Harvard U., 1959, LLB, 1962. Bar: N.Y. 1963. Assoc. Stroock & Stroock & Lavan, L.L.P., N.Y.C., 1962-71, ptnr., 1972—. Bd. dirs. Hillel of N.Y.C.; mem. schs. com. Harvard U., 1984—. Mem. N.Y. State Bar Assn., Assn. of Bar of City of N.Y. Democrat. Jewish. Office: Stroock & Stroock & Lavan LLP 180 Maiden Ln New York NY 10038-4925

EPSTEIN, RAYMOND, engineering and architectural executive; b. Chgo., Jan. 12, 1918; s. Abraham and Janet (Rabinowitz) E.; m. Betty Jadwin, Apr. 7, 1940; children: Gail, David, Norman, Harriet. Student, MIT, 1934-36; B.S., U. Ill., 1938. Registered architect registered profl. engr. With A. Epstein & Sons Internat., Inc., Chgo., 1938—; chmn. bd. A. Epstein & Sons Internat., Inc., 1961-83, chmn. exec. com., 1983—. Bd. dirs., life trustee United Israel Appeal; past sec., hon. dir. Am. Jewish Joint Distbn. Com.; mem. exec. com. Nat. Jewish Cmty. Rels. Adv. Coun.; v.p. nat. bd. Jewish Telegraphic Agy.; mem. citizens bd. Loyola U.; past pres. Coun. Jewish Fedns., Welfare Funds, Inc., Jewish Welfare Fund Met. Chgo., Jewish United Fund, Young Men's Jewish Coun.; past sec. Jewish Fed. Met. Chgo.; past chmn. budget com., bd. govs. Jewish Agy.; past trustee Chgo. Med. Sch; past bd. dirs. United Jewish Appeal; past exec. com. Meml. Found. Jewish Culture; past chmn. pub. affairs com., past chmn. campaign Jewish United Fund Met. Chgo.; past. sec. Welfare Coun. Met. Chgo.; past bd. dirs. Chgo. Bldg. Congress; life dir. Mt. Sinai Med. Rsch. Found.; trustee, past dir. Ampal-Am. Israel Corp. Decorated comdr. Legion of Honor Ivory Coast, 1982; recipient Disting. Alumnus award U. Ill., 1974, Julius Rosenwald Meml. award Jewish Fedn. Chgo., 1974, Citation Brandeis U., 1992; named to City of Chgo. Sr. Citizens Hall of Fame, 1991. Fellow Soc. Civil Engr. France, Soc. Am. Registered Architects; mem. NSPE , ASCE, Am. Concrete Inst., Western Soc. Engrs., Assn. Engrs. and Architects in Israel, French Engrs. in the U.S., Inc., Pi Lambda Phi. Clubs: Standard (past trustee), Illini, MIT, Caxton (Chgo.). Home: 4950 S Chicago Beach Dr Chicago IL 60615-3207 Office: 600 W Fulton St Chicago IL 60661-1100

EPSTEIN, RICHARD A., law educator; b. 1943. AB, Columbia U., 1964; BA, Oxford U., 1966; LLB, Yale U., 1968. Bar: Calif. 1969. Asst. prof. Sch. Law U. So. Calif., L.A., 1968-70; assoc. prof., 1970-73; prof. Law Sch. U. Chgo., 1973-82; James Parker hall prof. law, 1982-88, James Parker Hall Disting. Svc. prof., 1988—; vis. assoc. prof. Law Sch. Chgo. U., 1972-73. Author: Cases and Materials in Torts, 6th dit., 1995, Takings: Private property and the Power of Eminent Domain, 1985, Simple Rules for a Complex World, 1995, Mortal Peril: Our Inalienable Right to Health Care, 1997, Principles for a Free Society: Reconciling Individual Liberty with the Common Good, 1998; editor: Jour. Legal Studies, 1981-91, Jour. Law and Econs., 1991—; mem. editl. bd. Yale Law Jour. Mem. Am. Acad. Arts and Scis., Order of Coif. Office: U Chgo Law Sch 1111 E 60th St Chicago IL 60637-2776*

EPSTEIN, ROBERT MARVIN, anesthesiologist, educator; b. N.Y.C., Mar. 10, 1928; s. Nathan Batlan and Rebecca (Dickes) E.; m. Lillian Ray Cohen, Dec. 31, 1950; children: Judith Susan, Neal Myron, Charles Benjamin. BS with distinction, U. Mich., 1947, MD cum laude, 1951. Diplomate: Am. Bd. Anesthesiology (dir. 1972-84, pres. 1979-80). Intern U. Mich. Hosp., 1951-52; resident in anesthesiology Presbyterian Hosp., N.Y.C., 1952-53, 55-56; instr. in anesthesiology and fellow in medicine Columbia U., 1956-57, assoc., 1957-59, asst. prof., anesthesiology, 1959-65, assoc. prof., 1965-70, prof., 1970-72; prof. U. Va., Charlottesville, 1972-74, Alumni prof., 1974-87, Disting. prof., 1987-92, Harold Carron prof., 1992—, dept. chmn., 1972-96; mem. anesthesiology tng. com. Nat. Inst. Gen. Med. Scis., NIH, 1966-69; mem. com. on anesthesia NRC, 1970-71; mem. Nat. Bd. Med. Examiners, 1982-90; chmn. dept. anesthesiology U. Va., Charlottesville, 1972-96. Editor Anesthesiology, 1974-79; contbr. numerous articles to profl. jours. Bd. dirs., sec. U.Va. Health Svcs. Found., 1980-90, pres., 1990-93; trustee Ednl. Commn. for Fgn. Med. Grads., 1991-95, vice chmn., 1993-95. With U.S. Army, 1953-55. Guggenheim fellow Oxford (Eng.) U., 1966-67; N.Y. Heart Assn. fellow, 1956-57; Scholar-in-Residence, Inst. Medicine NAS, 1997. Fellow Royal Coll. Anaesthetists (Eng.); mem. AAAS, Inst. Medicine NAS, Am. Physiol. Soc., Am. Soc. Anesthesiologists, Soc. Acad. Anesthesia Chmn. (mem. coun., rep. to Coun. Acad. Soc. Assn. Am. Med. Colls. 1984-91), Am. Soc. Pharmacy and Exptl. Therapeutics, Anaesthetic Rsch. Soc. (U.K.), Assn. Univ. Anesthesiologists (pres. 1973-74), W.T.G. Morton Soc., Phi Beta Kappa, Sigma Xi, Alpha Omega Alpha. Office: U Va Hosp Jefferson Park Ave Charlottesville VA 22908*

EPSTEIN, SAMUEL, geologist, educator; b. Poland, Dec. 9, 1919. BSc, U. Man., Can., 1941, MSc, 1942; PhD in Phys. Chemistry, McGill U., Can., 1944; LLD (hon.), U. Man., 1980. Rsch. chemist Natural Rsch. Coun. Can., 1944-47; rsch. assoc. Inst. Nuclear Studies, U. Chgo., 1948-52, rsch. fellow, 1952-53, sr. rsch. fellow, 1953-54, assoc. prof., 1954-59; prof. geochemistry Calif. Inst. Tech., Pasadena, 1959-84, William E. Leonhard prof. geology, 1984—. Recipient Wollaston medal Geol. Soc., London, 1993. Fellow Am. Acad. Arts Scis., Am. Geophys. Union, European Union Geoscis. (hon. gdn., Urey medal 1995), Royal Soc. of Can. (fgn. fellow); mem. NAS, Geol. Soc. Am. (Arthur L. Day medal 1978), Geochem. Soc. (Goldschmidt medal 1977). Office: Divsn Geol & Planetary Sci Calif Inst Tech Pasadena CA 91125

EPSTEIN, SAMUEL ABRAHAM, stock and bond broker, petroleum consultant; b. N.Y.C., Sept. 14, 1956; s. Isidore and Mamie (Kosofsky) E.; m. Peggy Ann Eisenberg, July 4, 1979; children: David, Daniel, Rebecca. BS in Geology, Bklyn. Coll., 1977; MS in Geology, Rensselear Poly. Inst., 1979. Rsch. asst. Steinetz Marine Lab., Elat, Israel, 1978-79; petroleum geologist Cities Svc. Co., Houston, 1979-82; sr. petroleum geologist Getty Oil Co./Texaco, Houston, 1982-85; first v.p. investments, retirement planning specialist Morgan Stanley Dean Witter, N.Y.C., 1998—, Word Trade Ctr. br. taxable fixed income coord., 1996-98, CPA continuing edn. instr. N.Y. State Investment Adv. Svcs., 1996-97, equity coord., 1998—. Contbg. author articles on interest rates; contbr. articles to petroleum industries profl. publs. Mem. Prime Mins. Club State of Israel Bonds, 1987-92. Recipient Bklyn. Coll. Disting. Geol. Alumni award, CUNY, 1990. Mem. Am. Assn. Petroleum Geologists (cert.), Metro Mus. of Art, N.Y. Acad. Scis. (co-chmn. geol. scis. sect.). Jewish. Avocations: weight training, walking, geology, oceanography. Home: 426 Beach 121st St Far Rockaway NY 11694-1965

EPSTEIN, SETH PAUL, immunologist, infectious disease researcher; b. N.Y.C., Sept. 11, 1958; s. Donald and Eileen (Schulman) E. BA in Chemistry with high honors, Brandeis U., 1980; MD, Autonomous U. Guadalajara, Mex., 1984. Med. extern Pontiac (Mich.) Gen. Hosp., 1984; postdoctoral rsch. fellow Mich. Cancer Found., Detroit, 1985-86; postdoctoral rsch. fellow NYU Med. Ctr., N.Y.C., 1987-91, asst. rsch. scientist, 1991; rsch. asst. Mt. Sinai Med. Ctr., N.Y.C., 1991-96, instr., asst. prof., 1997—. Contbr. articles to profl. jours. Tng. fellow NIH, 1987; grantee Dermatology Found., Inc., 1990. Mem. Assn. Rsch. in Vision and Ophthalmology, Phi Beta Kappa. Achievements include rsch. on cyclosporine A rapamycin transforming growth factor interferon-gamma relating to cytokine-induced upregulation of Langerhans cells, cell chemotaxis into the cornea and skin and treatment of herpetic keratitis; sunscreen prevention of Ultraviolet-activated herpes simplex; novel treatments for herpes simplex ocular infections. Office: Mount Sinai Med Ctr Dept Ophthalmology 1 Gustave L Levy Pl New York NY 10029-6500

EPSTEIN, SIDNEY, architect and engineer; b. Chgo., 1923; m. Sondra Berman, Sept. 4, 1987; children from previous marriage: Donna Epstein Barrows, Laurie Epstein Lawton. BS in Civil Engring. with high honors, U. Ill., 1943. Various positions A. Epstein & Sons Internat.; chmn. bd. dirs. A. Epstein & Sons Internat., Inc., Chgo.; dir. Amal. Trust & Savs. Bank, Polk Bros. Found., Michael Reese Found.; trustee emeritus Northwestern Mut. LIfe Ins. Co. Founder, bd. dirs., past chmn. Chgo. Youth Ctrs.; past chmn. bd. trustees Michael Reese Hosp. and Med. Ctr.; bd. govs., life mem. U. Chgo. Hosps. and Clinics; bd. dirs. Lyric Opera Chgo.; life trustee Orchestral Assn. Chgo. Mem. Polish-U.S. Econ. Coun., Standard Club (life; past pres.), Sigma Xi, Tau Beta Pi, Sigma Tau, Phi Kappa Phi, Phi Eta Sigma, Chi Epsilon. Home: 1430 N Lake Shore Dr Chicago IL 60610-6658 Office: A Epstein & Sons Internat Inc 600 W Fulton St Chicago IL 60661-1100

EPSTEIN, SIDNEY, editor; b. Wilmington, Del., Oct. 11, 1920; s. Abraham and Ida (Kelrick) E.; m. Eleni Sakes, Mar. 30, 1957; 1 dau., Diane. Student, George Washington U., 1937-41. With Washington Herald, 1937-54; city editor Washington Times-Herald, 1952-54; city editor Washington Star, 1958-68, asst. mng. editor, 1968-74, mng. editor, 1974-78, exec. editor, 1978-81, assoc. pub. and editor, 1981, also dir. Served to capt. USMCR, 1942-46. Mem. Sigma Delta Chi (hall of fame 1981). Home: 2807 Cathedral Ave NW Washington DC 20008-4121

EPSTEIN, STEPHEN ROGER, financial executive; b. Chgo., Nov. 25, 1947; s. Maurice and Gertrude (Ades) E.; m. Christine Marie Kudrys, June 10, 1979; 1 child, Jorie Anne. Student, U. Ill., 1965-69; BSBA, Roosevelt U., 1977. Mgr. collection and billing Field Enterprises Ednl. Corp., Chgo., 1971-73; asst. mgr. cost acctg. dept. Sun Electric Corp., Crystal Lake, Ill., 1973-77; fin. analyst Wilson Sporting Goods Co., River Grove, Ill., 1978-79; mgr. cost acctg. dept. Salerno-Megowen Biscuit Co., Niles, Ill., 1980-81; mgr. fin. planning dept. Nachman Corp., Des Plaines, Ill., 1981-82, controller, 1982-83; controller ops. div. Helene Curtis, Inc., Chgo., 1983-88, dir. cost mgmt., 1988-90; dir. cost and performance mgmt. svcs. Checkers, Simon & Rosner, Chgo., 1990-93; sr. mgr., practice leader advanced cost mgmt. Grant Thornton, Chgo., 1993-95; CFO Aquion Ptnrs., L.P., Elk Grove Village, Ill., 1995-97, CIO, 1998; dir. mfg. cons. FERS Bus. Svcs., Inc., Chgo., 1998—; speaker in field. Assoc. mem. Leukemia Rsch. Found., Chgo., 1974—. Staff sgt. Ill. N.G., 1970-77. Mem. Inst. Mgmt. Accts., Am. Prodn. and Inventory Control Soc., Inst. Mgmt. Cons., Am. Mgmt. Assn., Am. Radio Relay League. Avocations: electronics, photography, physical fitness. Office: Fers Bus Svcs Inc 401 N Michigan Ave Chicago IL 60611

EPSTEIN, WILLIAM, experimental psychologist; b. N.Y.C., Nov. 23, 1931; s. Jacob and Sarah (Kaplan) E.; m. Sheena J. Rogers, Apr. 22, 1989; 1 child: Maggie Eliana Rogers; children from previous marriage: Sara Ann, Edith Lynn. BA, NYU, 1955; MA, New Sch. Social Research, 1957, PhD, 1959; PhD (hon.), U. Uppsala, Sweden, 1992. Asst. prof. psychology U. Kans., 1959-68, asso. prof., 1962-65, prof., 1965-68; prof. psychology U. Wis.-Madison, 1968-96, prof. emeritus, 1996—, chmn. dept., 1975-79; vis. prof. Cambridge (Eng.) U., 1972-73, U. Va., 1997—; Fulbright rsch. fellow, vis. prof. Delhi (India) U., 1981-82; vis. fellow Wolfson Coll., Oxford U., Eng. Author: Varieties of Perceptual Learning, 1967, (with F.C. Shontz) Psychology in Progress, 1971, Stability and Constancy in Visual Perception, 1977, (with G. Jansson and S.S. Bergstrom) Perceiving Events and Objects, 1994; (with S. Rogers) Handbook of Perception and Cognition, Vol. 5 Perception of Space and Motion, 1995; cons. editor Perception and Psychophysics, 1971-82; editor Jour. Exptl. Psychology: Human Perception and Performance, 1982-88. NSF sr. postdoctoral fellow U. Uppsala, Sweden, 1966-67; grantee NIMH, 1959—, NSF, 1987—. Fellow Am. Psychol. Assn., Soc. Exptl. Psychologists; mem. AAAS, Psychonomic Soc., Sigma Xi. Office: Univ Va Gilmer Hall Charlottesville VA 22840

EPSTEIN, WILLIAM ERIC, health care executive; b. N.Y.C., Nov. 10, 1949; s. Felix Epstein and Betty Elizabeth Moses. BS in Indsl. Engring., Northeastern U., 1972; MBA, NYU, 1975. Sys. engr. Peter B. Brigham Hosp., Boston, 1969-72; sr. mgmt. cons. N.Y.C. Heath Hosp., 1972-76; asst. to v.p. planning Mt. Sinai Hosp., N.Y.C., 1976-80, asst. dir., 1980-82, adminstr., 1982-87, assoc. dir., 1987-91; asst. v.p. Hahnemann U., Phila., 1991-93, v.p. mgmt., regional v.p. corp. svcs. Allegheny HERF (Health Edn. Res. Found.), 1994-95; prin. Fineman & Assoc., Bronxville, N.Y., 1996-98; sr. mgr. Computer Assocs., Islandia, N.Y., 1998—; preceptor Baruch Coll. CUNY, N.Y.C., 1984-91; adj. lectr. Mt. Sinai Sch. Medicine, N.Y.C., 1987-91; advisor, panel mem. healthcare adminstrn. program New Sch. for Social Research Grad. Sch. Mgmt., N.Y.C., 1988; lectr. Seton Hall U.; spkr. in field. Pres. Harmon Cove Condominium Assn., Secaucus, N.J., 1986-91; mem. campaign com. Young Leadership Nat. Bd.-State of Israel, 1991—. Fellow Am. Coll. Health Care Exec. (examiner, regents adv. coun. Rsch. Bd.); mem. Health Care Infosystems Soc. (cert., sr. mem.), Hosp. Materials Mgmt. Soc. (sr. mem.), Health Care Mgmt. and Info. Systems Soc., Am. Hosp. Assn., NYU Alumni Assn. Stern Grad. Sch. Bus. Avocations: photography, flute, tennis, golf. Office: PO Box 1617 Clifton NJ 07015-1617

EPSTEIN, WOLFGANG, biochemist, educator; b. Breslau, Germany, May 7, 1931; came to U.S., 1936, naturalized, 1943; s. Stephan and Elsbeth (Lauinger) E.; m. Edna Selan, June 12, 1961; children: Matthew, Ezra, Tanya. B.A. with high honors, Swarthmore Coll., 1951; M.D., U. Minn., 1955. Postdoctoral fellow in physiology U. Minn., Mpls., 1959-60; postdoctoral fellow Pasteur Inst., Paris., 1963-65; postdoctoral fellow in biophysics Harvard Med. Sch., 1961-63, research asso., then asso. in biophysics, 1965-67; asst. prof. biochemistry U. Chgo., 1967-73, asso. prof., 1973-79, prof., 1979-84, prof. dept. molecular genetics and cell biology, 1984—. Served with M.C. U.S. Army, 1957-59. Mem. AAAS, Am. Soc. for Biochemistry and Molecular Biology, Am. Soc. for Microbiology. Home: 1120 E 50th St Chicago IL 60615-2804 Office: 920 E 58th St Chicago IL 60637-5415*

EPSTIEN, JAY ALAN, lawyer; b. Newark, May 23, 1951; s. Leonard and Lorraine (Pedd) E.; children: Jessica, Shira; m. Nancy Elizabeth Kirsch, June 1, 1996. BS, Case Western Res. U., 1973; JD, Cornell U., 1976. Bar: D.C. 1976, N.J. 1976, U.S. Supreme Ct. 1977. Indsl. engr. Ortho Pharm., Somerset, N.J., 1973; assoc. Shaw, Pittman, Potts & Trowbridge, Washington, 1976-83, ptnr., 1984-95, chmn. real estate dept., 1990-94, chmn. bus. dept., 1994-95; mng. ptnr. Rudnick, Wolfe, Epstien & Zeidman, Washington, 1996—. Mem. Internat. Coun. Shopping Ctrs. (chmn. D.C. govt. affairs 1989-96), Am. Coll. Real Estate Lawyers. Avocations: tennis, golf. Home: 3617 Shepherd St Chevy Chase MD 20815-4131 Office: Rudnick Wolfe Epstien & Zeidman 1201 New York Ave NW Ph Washington DC 20005-6162

EPTING, C. CHRISTOPHER, bishop; b. Greenville, S.C.; m. Pam Flagg; children: Michael, Amanda. Grad., U. Fla., Seabury-Western Theol. Sem., Evanston, Ill., 1952; STM, Gen. Theol. Sem., N.Y.C., 1984. Formerly curate Holy Trinity Ch., Melbourne; vicar Ch. of St. Luke the Evangelist, Mulberry, Fla., 1974-78; founding vicar St. Stephen's Ch., Lakeland, Fla.; canon residentiary St. John's Cathedral, from 1978; rector St. Mark's Episc. Ch. and Sch., Cocoa, Fla.; bishop coadjutor, then bishop Episc. Diocese of Iowa, Des Moines, 1988—; formerly dean Inst. Christian Studies, St. Luke's Cathedral, Orlando, Fla. Address: Episc Diocese of Iowa 225 37th St Des Moines IA 50312-4305*

EPTON, GREGG, performing company executive. Prodn. and tour. mgr. Alberta Ballet, Calgary, Can., 1987, gen. mgr., 1989, exec. dir., 1991—; co-founder Alberta Ballet Sch., 1991. Mem. Can. Assn. Profl. Dance Orgns. (corp. sec. 1992-94). Office: Alberta Ballet, 141 18th Ave SW, Calgary, AB Canada T2S 0B8*

ERASMUS, CHARLES JOHN, anthropologist, educator; b. Pitts., Sept. 23, 1921; s. Percy Thomas and Alice E.; m. Helen Marjorie O'Brien, Feb. 18, 1943; children: Thomas Glen, Gwendolyn. B.A., UCLA, 1942; M.A., U. Calif., Berkeley, 1950, Ph.D., 1955. Field ethnologist Smithsonian Instn., Colombia, 1950-52; applied anthropologist AID, Western S.Am., 1952-54; research assoc. culture exchange project U. Ill., Champaign-Urbana, 1955-59; vis. prof. anthropology Yale U., New Haven, 1959-60; assoc. prof. U. N.C., Chapel Hill, 1960-62; assoc. prof. U. Calif., Santa Barbara, 1962-64, prof., 1964-87, prof. emeritus, 1987—, chmn. dept. anthropology, 1964-68. Author: Man Takes Control: Cultural Development and American Aid, 1961, In Search of the Common Good: Utopian Experiments Past and Future, 1977, Contemporary Change in Traditional Communities of Mexico and Peru, 1978. Served with USN, 1942-45. Home: 6190 Barrington Dr Santa Barbara CA 93117-1758 Office: U Calif Dept Anthropology Santa Barbara CA 93106

ERB, DONALD, composer; b. Youngstown, Ohio, Jan. 17, 1927; s. Tod and Janet (Griffith) E.; m. Lucille Hyman, June 10, 1950; children: Christine, Matthew, Stephanie, Janet. BS, Kent State U., 1950; MusM, Cleve. Inst. Music, 1953, MusD (hon.), 1984; MusD, Ind. U., 1964. Tchr. Cleve. Inst. Music, 1953-61, composer-in-residence, 1966-81, disting. prof. of composition, 1987-96; Meadows prof. composition So. Meth. U., 1981-84; composer-in-residence St. Louis Symphony, 1988-91; resident composer Am. Acad., Rome, 1991; vis. asst. prof. rsch. electronic music Case Inst. Tech., 1965-67; composer-in-residence Dallas Symphony, 1968-69, Aspen Music Festival, 1993, Schweitzer Inst., 1994, 95; vis. prof. Ind. U., 1975-76, Calif. State U., L.A., 1977; prof. composition Ind. U., 1984-87; staff composer Bennington Composers Conf., 1969-73; resident composer June in Buffalo, 1984-96, composer-librettist panelist Nat. Endowment for Arts, 1973-79, chmn., 1977-79; performed at Warsaw Autumn Festival, 1971, 73, 94—; artist-in-residence Atlantic Ctr. for Arts, 1995. Composer: Dialogue for Violin and Piano, 1958, Correlations for Piano, 1959, Music for Violin and Piano, 1959, String Quartet No. 1, 1960, Sonata for Harpsichord and String Quartet, 1962, Chamber Concerto, 1961, Sonneries for Brass Choir, 1961, Four for Percussion, 1962, Bakersfield Pieces, 1962, Cumming's Cycle, 1963, Concertant for Harpsichord and Strings, 1963, Symphony of Overtures, 1964, VII Misc, 1964, Fallout?, 1964, Reticulation, 1965, Phantasma, 1965, Concert Piece 1, 1966, Diversion for Two, 1966, Stargazing, 1966, Concerto for Solo Percussion and Orchestra, 1966, Andante for Piccolo, Flute and Alto Flute, 1966, String Trio, 1966, Summermusic, 1966, Kyrie, 1967, Reconnaissance, 1967, In No Strange Land, 1968, the Seventh Trumpet, 1969, Basspiece, 1969, Klangfarbenfunk I, 1970, God Love You Now, 1971, Fanfare, 1971, The Purple-Roofed Ethical Suicide Parlor, 1972, Harold's Trip to the Sky, 1972, Concerto for Trombone and Orchestra, 1976, Quintet, 1976, Music for a Festive Occasion, 1976, Concerto for Violoncello and Orchestra, 1976, The Hawk, 1979, Cenotaph, 1979, Sonata for clarinet and percussino, 1980, Concerto for trumpet and orch., 1980, The Devil's Quickstep, 1982, Prismatic Variations, 1983, Concerto for clarinet and orch., 1984, The Rainbow Snake, 1985, The Dreamtime, 1985, Concerto for orch., 1985, Concerto for brass and orch., 1986, Three Poems for violin and piano, 1987, Solstice, 1988, Woody, 1988, Symphony for winds, 1989, String Quartet # 2, 1989, Five Red Hot Duets, 1989, Ritual Observances, 1991, Drawing down the Moon, 1991, Concerto for violin and orch., 1992, Evensong, 1993, Sonata for solo violin, 1994, Remembrances, 1994, Changes, 1994, Sonata for harp, 1995, Sunlit Peaks and Dark Valleys, 1995, String Quartet # 3, 1995, Suddenly It's Evening, 1997, others. Served with USNR, 1945-46. Recipient Disting. Alumni award Ind. U. Sch. Music, Naumberg Rec. award, 1974, Disting. Alumnus award Kent Sate U., 1982, Ohioana citation, 1978, award Am. Acad. Inst. Arts and Letters, 1985, Libr. of Congress Commn., 1987, Grammy nominee, 1994, Koussevitzky Commn., 1994, Fromm Found. Commn., 1994, Meet the Composer Commn., 1994, Ohioana Libr. Career award 1998; Ford Found. composer-in-residence Bakersfield, Calif., 1962-63; Rockefeller Found. grantee for performance Symphony of Overtures, 1965, grantee Nat. Coun. on Art, 1967-68, Nat. Endowment for Arts, 1980, 84, 91; Guggenheim fellow, 1965-66, fellow Bellagio Study and Conf. Ctr., 1979, 89, USA-Can. fellow NEA, 1995. Mem. Am. Music Center (pres. 1982-85), Broadcast Music, Cleve. Composers Guild, League ICSM (nat. adv. bd.). Home: 4073 Bluestone Rd Cleveland OH 44121-2465

ERB, DORETTA LOUISE BARKER, polymer applications scientist; b. Upper Darby, Pa., June 21, 1932; d. Ralph Merton and Pauline Kaufman (Isenberg) B.; m. Robert Allan Erb, June 27, 1953; children: Sylvia Ann, Susan Doretta, Carolyn Joy. BS in Pharmacy, Phila. Coll. Pharmacy and Sci., 1954. Registered pharmacist, Pa. Pharmacist Borland's Pharmacy, Upland, Pa., 1954-65; assoc. scientist Franklin Rsch. Ctr., ATC div. Calspan Corp., Norristown, Pa., 1974-93; owner, pres. SiliClone Studio, Valley Forge, Pa., 1982—. Mem. Am. Anaplastology Assn., Sigma Xi (chpt. sec. 1990-93). Presbyterian. Achievements include co-invention of intrinsic coloration techniques for highly realistic external prostheses including production of Human Coloration System for silicone prosthetics and special effects; inventor Feclone/simulated fecal material for product testing. Home and Office: PO Box 86 Jug Hollow Rd Valley Forge PA 19481-0086

ERB, RICHARD LOUIS LUNDIN, resort and hotel executive; b. Chgo., Dec. 23, 1929; s. Louis Henry and Miriam (Lundin) E.; m. Jean Elizabeth Easton, Mar. 14, 1959; children: John Richard, Elizabeth Anne, James Easton, Richard Louis II. BA, U. Calif., Berkeley, 1951, postgrad., 1952; student, San Francisco Art Inst., 1956. Cert. hotel adminstr. Asst. gen. mgr. Grand Teton Lodge Co., Jackson Hole, Wyo., 1954-62; mgr. Mauna Kea Beach Hotel, Hawaii, 1964-66; v.p., gen. mgr. Caneel Bay Plantation, Inc., St. John, V.I., 1966-75; gen. mgr. Williamsburg (Va.) Inn, 1975-78; exec. v.p., gen. mgr. Seabrook Island Co., Johns Island, S.C., 1978-80; v.p., dir. hotels Sands Hotel and Casino, Inc., Atlantic City, 1980-81; v.p., gen. mgr. Disneyland Hotel, Anaheim, Calif., 1981-82; COO Grand Traverse Resort, Grand Traverse Village, Mich., 1982-93; gen. mgr. Stein Eriksen Lodge, Deer Valley, Utah, 1993-96; pres. The Erb Group, 1996—; pres. Spruce-Park Mgmt. Co., 1989; mem. adv. bd. travel and tourism Mich. State U., 1992-96; vice-chmn. Charleston (S.C.) Tourism Coun., 1979-81; bd. dirs. Anaheim Visitors and Conv. Bur., 1981-82, Grand Traverse Conv. and Visitors Bur., 1985-90, U.S. 131 Area Devel. Assn., 1983-93; sr. cons. Cayuga Hosp. Advisors, 1996—. Contbr. articles to trade jours. Vice-pres. V.I. Montessori Sch., 1969-71, bd. dirs., 1968-76; bd. dirs. Coll. of V.I., 1976-79; adv. bd. U. S.C., 1978-82, Calif. State Poly. Inst., 1981-82, Orange Coast C.C., 1981-82, Northwestern Mich. Coll., 1983-93; adv. bd. hospitality mgmt. program Ea. Mich. U., 1989-93; trustee Munson Med. Ctr., Traverse City, 1985-93; bd. dirs. Traverse Symphony Orch., 1984-88, N.A. Vasa,

1987-89; adv. panel Mich. Communities of Econ. Excellence Program, 1984-88; mem. hospitality adv. bd. Utah Valley State Coll., 1994-98. Lt. arty. U.S. Army, 1952-54. Named hon. prof. Mich. State U. Hotel Sch., 1992—. Fellow Edn. Inst.; mem. Am. Hotel and Motel Assn. (dir. 1975-77, , 90-94, exec. bd. 1991-94, Service Merit award 1976, Lawson Odde award 1993, Gold Medalist Membership award 1993, trustee Ednl. Inst. 1977-83, mktg. com., exec. com. 1978-83, chmn. projects and programs com. 1982-83, AH&MA resort com. 1986-96, AH&MA condominium com. 1985-96, chmn. ratings com. 1988-96, Ambassador award 1986, Blue Ribbon task force 1988-89, Resort Exec. of Yr. 1988), Caribbean Hotel Assn. (1st v.p. 1972-74, dir. 1970-76, hon. life mem., Extraordinary Service Merit award 1974), V.I. Hotel Assn. (pres. chmn. bd. 1971-76, Merit award 1973), Calif. Hotel Assn. (dir. 1981-82), Caribbean Travel Assn. (dir. 1972-74), Internat. Hotel Assn. (dir. 1971-73), S.C. Hotel Assn. (dir. 1978-82), Am. Hotel Assn. Edn. Inst., (Lamp of Knowledge award 1988), Va. Hotel Assn., Williamsburg Hotel Assn. (bd. dirs. 1975-78), Atlantic City Hotel Assn. (v.p. 1981-82), Atlantic City Casino Assn. (dir. 1981-82), Cornell Soc. Hotelmen, Mich. Travel and Tourist Assn. (bd. dirs. 1983-94, treas. 1986, sec. 1987, v.p. 1988, mktg. com. 1986-93, govtl. affairs com. 1986-93, chmn. edn. com. 1983-84, chmn. bd. 1989-90, Mich. Hotelier of Yr. 1991), Mich. Restaurant Assn. (bd. dirs. 1989-91, chmn. adminstrv. com. 1989-90), Mich. Gov.'s Task Force on Tourism, 1986-87, Grand Island Adv. Commn., Grand Traverse C. of C. (bd. dirs. 1984-89), Nat. Restaurant Assn., Utah Hotel and Motel Assn. (bd. dirs. 1994-96, treas. 1996), Leadership Grand Traverse (exec. com. 1984-92, fellow 1992), Park City Lodging Assn. (bd. dirs. 1993-96), Park City C. of C. (bd. dirs. 1994-97), Tavern Club, Rotary (Paul Harris fellow 1990), Beta Theta Pi. Congregationalist.

ERB, ROBERT ALLAN, physical scientist; b. Ridley Park, Pa., Jan. 30, 1932; s. John Walter and Roma (Chapman) E.; m. Doretta Louise Barker, June 27, 1953; children—Sylvia Ann, Susan Doretta, Carolyn Joy. B.S. in Chemistry, U. Pa., 1953; M.S., Drexel Inst. Tech., 1959; Ph.D., Temple U., 1965. Chemist Gates Engring. Co., Wilmington, Del., 1953-54; with Franklin Research Center, div. Franklin Inst. (later div. Arvin/Calspan), Phila., 1954-93; sr. staff chemist Franklin Research Center, div. Franklin Inst. (later div. Arvin/Calspan), 1965-68, prin. scientist, 1968-81, Inst. fellow, 1981-84, staff scientist, 1985-93; tech. dir. SiliClone Studio, Valley Forge, Pa., 1993—. Mem. AAAS, Am. Anaplastology Assn. (pres. 1996-97), Am. Chem. Soc., Soc. Rheology, Soc. Plastics Engrs., The Franklin Inst., Sigma Xi. Presbyterian. Inventor human simulators, medical and prosthetic devices, solar collectors, permanent systems for dropwise condensation, contraceptive systems composites using waste plastics. Home and Office: PO Box 86 Valley Forge PA 19481-0086 *Success is to know God's will for your life and to do it.*

ERBE, EDWARD ROBERT, social studies educator, music percussion educator; b. Passaic, N.J., Jan. 22, 1944; s. Charles Edward and Dorothy Ethel (Dolan) E.; m. Helen Irene Moore, July 23, 1992; children from previous marriage: Christopher, Alana, Sheperd. BS in Econs. magna cum laude, Fairleigh Dickinson U., 1965; MA in Econs., Columbia U., 1967; MS in Edn., Monmouth Coll., 1984; PhD in Music Theory, Pacific Western U., 1989; postgrad., Cambridge (Eng.) U., 1984, 97, Caldwell Coll., 1996, U. Calif., 1997, Nova Southeastern U., 1998-99. Cert. tchr. social studies, N.J., cert. supr. and adminstr., N.J. Tchr. math. Red Bank (N.J.) H.S., 1967-68, Toms River (N.J.) H.S., 1968-69; profl. drummer recordings and TV Toronto, Ont., 1969-70; tchr. social studies Jackson (N.J.) Meml. H.S. and Mid. Sch., 1970—; dir. Bob Erbe Drum Sch., Toms River, 1971-92; instr. econs. Ocean County Coll., Toms River, 1990—; instr. percussion Stockton State Coll., Pomona, N.J., 1992-93; ednl. cons. Capella Drum Sticks, Marlboro, N.J., 1990-92; ednl. spkr. Barnegat (N.J.) Sch. Dist., 1983, Allentown (N.J.) H.S., 1996; presenter in field. Author: Beat Sheets, Beat Sheets II, Beat Sheets III, Roll Control I, Roll Control II, Rudiment Companion for the Drum Set, 1973-87. Scholar Nat. Coun for the Humanities, 1997; recipient Tchg. Project award Mayor of Jackson Twp., N.J., 1997, Found. Tchg. Econs. award, 1997, 98. Mem. NEA, ASCD, Nat. Coun. History Edn., Nat. Coun. Social Studies, N.J. Edn. Assn., Assn. Supervision and Curriculum Devel., Jackson Edn. Assn. Home: 7 Joseph Ct New Egypt NJ 08533-1817

ERBE, JANET SUE, medical surgical, orthopedics and pediatrics nurse; b. Hamilton, Ohio, Aug. 25, 1952; d. Robert A. and Evon R. (Walls) Schlotterbeck; m. Gene Erbe. ADN, Miami U., Hamilton, 1972; BS summa cum laude, Coll. Mt. St. Joseph, 1989. Cert. in neonatal resuscitation, Am. Heart Assn., basic life support. Asst. nurse mgr. Ft. Hamilton-Hughes Hosp., Hamilton, 1972-97; med. analyst Anthem Blue Cross-Blue Shield, Mason, Ohio, 1997—. Mem. ANA, ONA (legiis. liason). Home: 549 Beeler Blvd Hamilton OH 45013-6075 Office: 4361 Irwin Simpson Rd Mason OH 45040-9479

ERBE, YVONNE MARY, music educator, marketing specialist; b. Wausau, Wis., Nov. 18, 1947; d. Rudolph Anton and Lucille Virginia Karlen; children: Daniel, Heather. BMus Edn., U. Wis., Madison, 1969, postgrad.; MA in Guidance/Counseling Edn Psychology, Eastern Ky. U., Richmond. Lic. music educator, Wis. Music-vocal tchr. Bayport H.S., Greenbay, Wis., 1969-70; tchr. bassoon, oboe U. Wis., Greenbay, 1969-70; jr. high choral dir. Kenosha Unified Schs., Wis., 1970-76; adjudicator, clinician, 1969—; univ. supr.-edn. U. Wis.-Parkside, Kenosha, 1976-78; parent adv. com. mem. Northern Hills Sch. and Onalaska Mid. Sch., 1987-88; mktg. specialist Metro Prodns., La Crosse, Wis., 1984-85; tchr. music elem., jr. high sch., sr. high, LaCrosse, Wis., 1988-89, secondary high sch. choral dir., Lexington, Ky., 1989—. Parent vol. coord. Fauver Hill Sch., 1983-84; sec. exec. bd. Great River Festival of Arts, La Crosse, 1982-83, 1st v.p. exec. bd., chmn. adult choral workshop and performance, chmn. swing choir workshop, 1983-84, pres. bd. dirs., 1984-85; pres. La Crosse Area Newcomers Club, 1982-83; tchr. Confraternity of Christian Doctrine, 1985-88, bd. dirs. La Crosse Boy Choir, 1985-88; condr. Lexington Children's Choir, 1995-96; upward bound instr. Eastern Ky. U., 1994-95; conductor Ctrl. Ky. Youth Choruses, 1995-98. Mem. NEA, Am. Choral Dirs. Assn., Ky. Music Educators Assn., Ky. Edn. Assn., Ky. Mental Health Counselors Assn., Phi Delta Kappa, Sigma Alpha Iota. Roman Catholic. Avocations: tennis, cross-country skiing, aerobic exercises, needlecrafts, gourmet cooking.

ERBER, THOMAS, physics educator; b. Vienna, Austria, Dec. 6, 1930; m. Audrey Burns. B.Sc., MIT, 1951; M.S., U. Chgo., 1953, Ph.D. in Physics, 1957. Asst. prof. physics Ill. Inst. Tech., Chgo., 1957-62; assoc. prof. Ill. Inst. Tech., 1962-69, prof., 1969—, prof. math., 1986—; vis. scientist Stanford Linear Accelerator Ctr., 1970; prof. physics U. Graz, 1971, 82, prof. honoris causa, 1971—; prof. physics UCLA, 1978-79, 84-85, 87—, U. Grenoble, 1982; prof. physics U. Chgo., 1998—; mem. adv. bd. rsch. corp. Mem. editorial bd.: Acta Physica Austriaca. Rsch. fellow, Brussels, Belgium, 1963-64. Fellow Am. Phys. soc., Am. Math Soc.; mem. IEEE (sr.), European Phys. Soc., Oesterreichische Physikalische Gesellschaft, Magnetics Soc., N.Y. Acad. Sci., Am. Radio Relay League, Am. Acad. of Mechanics, Nuclear, Plasma & Magnetics Soc. Office: Ill Inst Tech Dept Physics Chicago IL 60616

ERBER, WILLIAM FRANKLIN, gastroenterologist; b. N.Y.C., June 1, 1941; s. Sigmund and Marcia (Picard) E.; m. Ingrid Amelia Friedler, Dec. 25, 1967; children: Gregory, Karina, Jonathan, Joanna, Jeremy. BS, Muhlenberg Coll., 1963; MD, U. Health Sci., Chgo., 1967. Diplomate Am. Bd. Internal Medicine and Gastroenterology. Intern Maimonides Hosp., 1967-68, resident, 1968-69, 71-72; fellowship in gastroenterology Albert Einstein Coll. of Medicine, 1973-75; rsch. fellow Hadassah Hosp., Jerusalem, 1971-72; clin. asst. prof. Health Sci. Ctr., Bklyn., 1975—; cons. Crohn's Colitis Found., N.Y.C., 1975—, H.I.P., N.Y.C., 1975—; attending gastroenterologist Maimonides Med. Ctr., Bklyn., 1975—. Author: Internal Medicine Review, 1979; contbr. articles to profl. jours. Maj. USAF, 1969-71. Fellow ACP, Am. Coll. Gastroenterology. Avocations: music, piano, skiing. Office: 591 Ocean Pkwy Brooklyn NY 11218-5913

ERBES, JOHN ROBERT, engineering executive; b. LaSalle County, Ill., Sept. 13, 1946; s. Robert William and Jeanette Marie (Brey) E. Cert. of Indsl. Engring. Tech., Allied Inst. Tech., 1966; BS in Gen. Engring., Kennedy Western U., Utah, 1993. Engring. project mgr. Methode Electronics, Inc., Carthage, Ill., 1977—. Vol. Reading is Fundamental, Bus. Ptnrs. Com., Boy Scouts Am. Recipient Award of Merit, Silver Beaver award, 1989. Mem. Soc. automotive Engrs., Soc. Plastics Engrs. Roman Catholic. Avocations: gardening, storytelling, woodworking. Home: 1260 E County Road 1200 Warsaw IL 62379-3409 Office: Methode Electronics Inc PO Box 130 Carthage IL 62321-0130

ERBSEN, CLAUDE ERNEST, journalist; b. Trieste, Italy, Mar. 10, 1938; came to U.S., 1951, naturalized, 1956; s. Henry M. and Laura Elena (Treves) E.; m. Jill J. Prosky, July 16, 1959; 1 dau., Diana Lisa; m. Hedy Miriam Cohn, Apr. 7, 1970; children—Allan Henry, Michael David. BA cum laude, Amherst Coll., 1959; Inter-Am. Press Assn. scholar, U. Andes, Bogota, Colombia, 1960. Reporter-printer Amherst Jour.-Record, 1955-57; staff reporter El Tiempo, Bogota, 1960; with AP, 1960-1965; newsman in AP, N.Y.C., Miami, Fla., Washington; to chief of bur. Brazil, 1965-69; exec. rep. for Latin Am., 1969-70; bus. mgr., adminstrv. dir. AP-Dow Jones Econ. Report, London, 1970-75; dep. dir. world services AP, N.Y.C., 1975-80; v.p., dir. AP-Dow Jones News Services, 1980-87; v.p., dir. world services AP, N.Y.C., 1987—; bd. dirs. World Press Inst., St. Paul. Served to lt. USNR, 1961-65. Recipient San Giusto D'Oro award City of Trieste, 1995. Mem. Internat. Press Inst., Coun. Fgn. Rels., World Assn. of Newspapers, U. Club. Home: 27 Stratton Rd Scarsdale NY 10583-7556 Office: AP 50 Rockefeller Plz New York NY 10020-1605

ERCK, WALTER W., air force officer; b. Joliet, Ill., Aug. 3, 1957; s. Walter Sr. and Joan (Haas) E. BA, William Patterson Coll., Wayne, N.J., 1979; MA, Chapman U., Orange, Calif., 1982; MBA, Golden Gate U., San Francisco, 1988. Commd. 2d lt. USAF, 1979, advanced through grades to maj., 1991; chief MWR Inspection Br., Langley AFB, Va., 1989-91, 49th MWR and Svcs. Squadron, Holloman AFB, N.Mex., 1991-93, Svcs. Inspection Br., Kirtland AFB, N.Mex., 1993—. Mem. cmty. bd. dirs. Boy Scouts Am. Decorated Air Force Commendation medal with 3 oak leaf clusters. Lutheran. Avocations: backpacking, whitewater rafting and canoeing. Address: 501 Brafferton Cir Hampton VA 23663-1921

ERCKLENTZ, ALEXANDER TONIO, investment executive; b. N.Y.C., July 13, 1936; s. Enno Wilhelm and Hildegard (Schlubach) E.; children—Alexander Tonio Jr., Christina Titaua, Nicholas Ley. BA, Yale U.; postgrad, NYU. Various positions Brown Brothers Harriman & Co., N.Y.C., 1959-77, ptnr., 1978—; bd. dirs. AXA Nordstern Art Ins. Corp., AXA Global Risks US Co., Deutsche Fonds Holding. Pres. Am. Berlin Opera Found.; trustee Am. U. Beirut. Mem. The Links Club, Down Town Assn., Stanwich Club (Greenwich), Field Club Greenwich. Republican. Roman Catholic. Office: Brown Brothers Harriman & Co 59 Wall St New York NY 10005-2808

ERCKLENTZ, ENNO WILHELM, JR., lawyer; b. N.Y.C., Jan. 27, 1931; s. Enno Wilhelm and Hildegard (Schlubach) E.; m. Mai A. Vilms, Sept. 20, 1969; children: Cornelia, Stephanie. AB, Columbia U., 1954; JD, Harvard U., 1957. Bar: N.Y. 1958. Assoc. Curtis, Mallet-Prevost, Colt & Mosle, N.Y.C., 1957-60; sec., gen. counsel Channing Fin. Corp., N.Y.C., 1960-69; v.p., sec., gen. counsel Inverness Mgmt. Corp., N.Y.C., 1969-75; sole practice, N.Y.C., 1975-78; ptnr. Whitman & Ransom, N.Y.C., 1978-87, Greeven & Ercklentz, N.Y.C., 1987-98; atty. pvt. practice, N.Y.C., 1998—. Author: Modern German Corporation Law, 1979. Mem. ABA, N.Y. State Bar Assn., Assn. of Bar City of N.Y., Am. Fgn. Law Assn. Republican. Roman Catholic. Office: Enno & Ercklentz Jr 630 5th Ave Ste 1905 New York NY 10111-0100

ERDELJAC, DANIEL JOSEPH, retired manufacturing company executive; b. Farmington, W.Va., Aug. 27, 1932; s. Phillip John, Mary M. (Hudak) E.; m. Constance June Sabatino, June 25, 1955; children—Daniel J. II, James M., Mary L., Laurie A. Grad. high sch., Farmington, W.Va. Materials mgr. South Union Coal Co., Edna, W.Va., 1952-60; plant mgr. Interpace Corp., various locations, 1960-70; pres., exec. v.p. Hydro Conduit Corp., Houston, 1970-92, pres., 1980-82, ret., 1992; divsn. mgr. Brooks Products, Houston, 1995-96, ret., 1996. Past chmn. Am. Concrete Pipe Assn. Roman Catholic. Avocations: grandchildren, investments.

ERDELY, STEPHEN LAJOS, music educator; b. Szeged, Hungary, May 6, 1921; came to U.S., 1949, naturalized, 1954; s. Jeno and Vilma (Lengyel) Erdelyi; m. Beatrice Eppinelle, Sept. 28, 1952. Absolutorium, Nat. Franz Liszt Music Acad., 1939-44, Franz Josef U., 1944; Ph.D., Case Western Res. U., 1962. Faculty Ohio State U., Toledo, 1966-73; prof. music M.I.T., Cambridge, Mass., 1973—; dir. music M.I.T., 1976—; mem. faculty Divsn. Continuing Edn. Harvard U.; rsch. assoc. Milman Perry Collection, Harvard U., faculty mem. divsn. continuing edn. Soloist, Munich (Ger.) Chamber Music Dept., 1946-49, Cleve. Orch., 1951-66, concert artist with, The Erdely Duo, 1951—; Author: Methods and Principles of Hungarian Ethnomusicology, 1965, Music of South Slavic Epics From The Bihac Region of Bosnia, 1995; contbr. articles to profl. jours. Am. Philos. Soc. grantee, 1962; Am. Council Learned Socs. grantee, 1964; Nat. Endowment for Arts grantee, 1974-77, 83-85. Mem. Am. Musicol. Soc. Soc. for Ethnomusicology (councilor 1970-73), Internat. Folk Music Council, Ohio Folklore Soc. (pres. 1967-69), Internat. Musicology Soc., Coll. Music Soc. Fax: 978-371-7046. Office: MIT Dept Humanities Cambridge MA 02139

ERDLEY, CYNTHIA ANNE, psychology educator; b. Harrisburg, Pa., Nov. 24, 1964; d. Larry Lee and Karen Marie (McMorris) E.; m. Sandy Edward Gardella, Oct. 12, 1996; 1 child, Kathryn Elizabeth Gardella. BA in Psychology summa cum laude, Gettysburg Coll., 1986; MA in Psychology, U. Ill., 1988, PhD in Psychology, 1992. NICHHD trainee dept. psychology U. Ill., Champaign, 1987-92, rsch. asst. dept. psychology, 1988-91; asst. prof. dept. psychology U. Maine, Orono, 1992-98, assoc. prof. dept. psychology, 1998—. Contbr. chpt. to book and articles to profl. jours. Mem. APA, Am. Ednl. Rsch. Assn., Soc. for Rsch. in Child Devel., Phi Beta Kappa, Psi Chi. Avocations: reading, travel, hiking, boating. Office: Univ Maine Dept Psychology 5742 Little Hall Dept Orono ME 04469-5742

ERDMAN, CARL L. N., retired banker; b. Reading, Pa., Aug. 3, 1915; s. Lee Marcus and Ella (Nolde) E.; m. Carolyn M. Wilson, Sept. 10, 1938; children—Lee W., Christine N. (Mrs. Robert D. Keeler). B.A., Dartmouth, 1937. With Am. Bank and Trust Co. Pa., Reading, 1953-81; exec. v.p. Am. Bank and Trust Co. Pa., 1966-81, ret., 1981. Mem. borough council, Wyomissing, Pa., 1964-81; bd. regents Mercersburg Acad., 1966-88. Served with USNR, 1943-46, 50-52. Recipient Silver Beaver award Boy Scouts Am., 1961. Mem. Beta Theta Pi. Club: Rotarian. Home: 1415 Parkside Dr N Reading PA 19610-2457

ERDMAN, JOSEPH, lawyer; b. Havana, Cuba, Dec. 14, 1935; s. Jonas and Miriam (Rimsky) E.; children: Harley, Andrew; m. Rosemary Hill, Apr. 20, 1992. BA, U. Va., 1956; postgrad., U. Mich., 1956-57; LLB, Fordham U., 1960. Bar: N.Y. 1960, Fla. 1975. Assoc. Wormser Koch Kiely-Alessandroni, N.Y.C., 1960-62; ptnr. Greenbaum, Wolff & Ernst, N.Y.C., 1962-82; ptnr. Proskauer Rose LLP, Fla. and N.Y.C., 1982—, chmn. personal planning dept., 1991—; lectr. radio, panels, NYU Inst. Taxation, 1978. Author: Complete Guide to Marital Deduction in Estate Planning, 1978, Effective Drafting Under the Revised Uniform Principal and Income Act, 1991; contbr. articles to profl. jours. Co-chmn. Westchester for Carter Campaign, 1976; pres. Scarsdale Synogogue, 1978-79; planned giving coun. U. Va., 1992—, arts and scis. alumni coun.; adv. coun. Bayly Mus. With U.S. Army, 1957-58. Fellow Am. Coll. Trust and Estate Coun.; mem. N.Y. State Bar Assn., Fla. Bar Assn., Jefferson Soc. Va., Phi Beta Kappa, Boca West Club, Farmington Country Club (Va.). Home: 19539 Island Court Dr Boca Raton FL 33434-5153 also: 4 Farmington Dr Charlottesville VA 22901-3241 Office: Proskauer Rose LLP One Boca Pl 2255 Glades Rd Ste 340 Boca Raton FL 33431-7382 also: 1585 Broadway New York NY 10036-8200*

ERDMAN, LOWELL PAUL, civil engineer, land surveyor; b. Wesley, Iowa, Aug. 11, 1926; s. Paul William and Olive Jane (Stillwell) E.; m. Audrey Lucille Stephenson, Aug. 18, 1956; children: Lindsay, Paul, Jeffrey. BS in Civil Engring., Iowa State U., 1950. Profl. engr., Iowa, Minn., Wis.; registered land surveyor, Iowa, Wis. Inspector Iowa Hwy. Commn., Jefferson, 1950-52; field engr. Phillip Petroleum Co., Bartlesville, Okla., 1952-55; cons. engr., pres. Erdman Engring., P.C., Decorah, Iowa, 1955-92; city engr., Decorah, 1955-90; mem. delegation environ. engrs. to People's Republic of China, 1986, People to People Land Surveys del. Egypt and Greece, 1989. Co-chmn. Brandstad for Gov. Com., Winneshiek County, 1982. Served with USAAF, 1945. Fellow ASCE; mem. Nat. Soc. Profl. Engrs., Iowa Engring Soc., Soc. Land Surveyors of Iowa. Republican. Lutheran. Club: Oneota Golf and Country. Avocations: Golf; bowling; fishing; fly tying. Home: PO Box 222 Decorah IA 52101-0222 Office: Erdman Engring PC 708 Commerce Dr PO Box 246 Decorah IA 52101-0246

ERDMAN, PAUL EMIL, author; b. Stratford, Ont., Can., May 19, 1932; (parents Am. citizens); s. Horace Herman and Helen E.; m. Helly Elizabeth Boeglin, Sept. 11, 1954; children: Constance Anne Catherine, Jennifer Michele. Student, Concordia Coll., Ft. Wayne, Ind., 1950-51, Concordia Sem., St. Louis, 1952-53; BA, Concordia Coll., St. Louis, 1954; BS, Georgetown U., 1956; MA, PhD, U. Basel, Switzerland, 1958. Econ. cons. European Coal and Steel Community, Luxembourg, Luxembourg, 1958; internat. economist Stanford Research Inst., Menlo Park, Calif., 1958-61; exec. v.p. Electronics Internat. Capital Ltd., Hamilton, Bermuda, 1962-64; vice chmn. United California Bank in Basel A.G., 1965-70; Cons. RAI Corp., TV corp., Italy.; host Moneytalk Sta. KGO, ABC, San Francisco, 1983-86, commentator, 1987—. Author: Swiss-American Economic Relations, 1959, Die Europaeische Wirtschaftsgemeinschaft und die Drittlaender, 1960, The Billion Dollar Sure Thing, 1973, The Silver Bears, 1974, The Crash of '79, 1976, The Last Days of America, 1981, Paul Erdman's Money Book: An Investor's Guide to Economics and Finance, 1984, The Panic of '89, 1987, The Palace, 1988, What Next? 1988, The Swiss Account, 1991, Warning to the Yen, 1992, Zero Coupon, 1993, Tug of War, 1996, The Set-Up, 1997; contbg. editor, columnist M Inc. mag., 1987-92; columnist The Nikon Keizai Shimbun, 1987-88, The Japan Post, 1989—, CBS Market Watch, 1998—, Bloomberg Personal, 1998—; contbr. articles, revs. to popular mags. Mem. bd. advisors program in internat. bus. diplomacy Sch. fgn. Service, Georgetown U., Washington, 1980—, faculty mem. Georgetown leadership seminar, 1982—; trustee Seneca Funds. Recipient Champion Media award for econ. understanding Amos Tuck Sch. Bus. Administrn., Dartmouth Coll., 1984. Mem. Authors Guild, Mysters Writers Am. (Edgar award 1974), PEN Am. Ctr., Commonwealth Club Calif. (bd. govs.). Lutheran. Address: 1817 Lytton Springs Rd Healdsburg CA 95448-9145

ERDMAN, TERRI SUE, pediatric and neonatal nurse, consultant; b. Casper, Wyo., June 27, 1954; d. Frederick Robert and Gretchen May (McCabe) Braunschweig; m. Steven H. Erdman, Oct. 2, 1982; 1 child, Samuel Cody. BS, U. Wyo., 1976; MS, U. Utah, 1981. RN, Calif.; cert. neonatal nurse practitioner. Staff nurse, charge nurse, transport nurse U. Utah Med. Ctr., Salt Lake City, 1976-80; neonatal nurse practitioner Primary Children's Med. Ctr., Salt Lake City, 1981-85; program coord. U. Utah Coll. Nursing, Salt Lake City, 1981-85; unit dir. med. transport svcs. dept. U. Nebr., Omaha, 1985-88, program dir. SKYMED, 1985-88; asst. prof. nursing, clin. instr. pediatrics Loma Linda (Calif.) U., 1988-90, acad. coord., 1988-90; cons. Tucson, Ariz., 1990—. Editl. cons., mem. rev. bd. Neonatal Network, 1985—, home study course reviewer, 1991—. Bd. dirs. Tucson Cmty. Sch., 1994-95, bd. trustees, 1995—, pres. bd. trustees, 1996-97, sec., 1997—. Mem. Nat. Assn. Neonatal Nurses (v.p. spl. interest group for advanced practice 1984-88, pres. 1989-91, bd. dirs. 1989-91, chair econ. task force 1992-95), Nat. Alliance Nurse Practitioners (bd. dirs., sec. 1992-95), Sigma Theta Tau Internat., Phi Kappa Phi. Democrat.

ERDMANN, ANDREW PATRICK NICHOLAS, historian; b. Royal Oak, Mich., Nov. 22, 1966; s. Charles R. and Naomi (Bennett) E.; m. Petra Anne Levin, Sept. 2, 1995. BA, Williams Coll., 1988, Oxford (Eng.) U., 1990; AM, Harvard U., 1991, PhD, 1999. Tutor Harvard U., Cambridge, 1993-94, chmn. Olin Nat. Security Group, 1997-98; cons. U.S. Army, Tng. and Doctrine Command, 1998; assoc. Weatherhead Ctr. Internat. Affairs, Harvard U., affiliate Olin Inst. Mellon fellow Mellon Found., 1990-94; Javits fellow U.S. Dept. Edn., 1994-98; Nat. Security fellow Harvard U., 1996-97; Peace scholar U.S. Inst. Peace, 1998-99. Mem. Am. Hist. Assn., Orgn. Am. Historians, Soc. Historians Am. Fgn. Rels., Soc. Mil. History. Avocations: running, rowing. E-mail: apnerdmann@aol.com. Home: 393 Broadway # 4 Cambridge MA 02139 Office: Harvard U Dept History Robinson Hall Cambridge MA 02138

ERDMANN, JAMES BERNARD, educational psychologist; b. Oct. 27, 1937; s. George C. and Emma (Hiltebrand) E.; m. Rebecca Susan Lindsay; children: Theodore Michael, Carolyn Louise, Christopher Joseph, Timothy James. Grad. cum laude, Pontifical Coll., Josephinium, 1959; MA, Loyola U., Chgo., 1964, PhD, 1966. Rsch. asst. Psychometric Lab. Loyola U., 1960-63, rsch. assoc., project dir., 1963-65, acting dir., 1965-66, assoc. dir., 1967-69, instr. dept. psychology, 1964-66, asst. prof. measurement program, 1967-69; assoc. prof. Sch. Edn. and Sch. Human Medicine, eval. coord. Office Med. Edn., R & D, Mich. State U., 1969-70; dir. divsn. ednl. measurement and rsch. Assn. Am. Med. Colls., Washington, 1970-87; clin. assoc. prof. psychiatry and behavioral scis. George Washington U. Sch. Medicine and Health Scis., 1973-87; assoc. dean adminstrn. and spl. projects Jefferson Med. Coll., Thomas Jefferson U., Phila., 1987-89, assoc. dean adminstrn. and univ. registrar, 1990—, prof. medicine (edn.) dept. medicine, 1993—. Contbr. articles to profl. jours. Mem. Am. Ednl. Rsch. Assn., Nat. Coun. Measurement in Edn. Assn., Am. Med. Coll. Roman Catholic. Home: 408 Bickmore Dr Media PA 19086-6909 Office: 1025 Walnut St Philadelphia PA 19107-5083

ERDMANN, JOACHIM CHRISTIAN, physicist; b. Danzig, June 5, 1928; s. Franz Werner and Maria Magdalena (Schreiber) E.; doctorate Tech. U. Braunschweig (Germany), 1958; m. Ursula Maria Wedemeyer, Aug. 24, 1957; children—Michael Andreas, Thomas Christian, Maria Martha Dorothea. Physicist, Osram Labs., Augsburg, Germany, 1954-60; sr. research scientist Boeing Sci. Research Labs., Seattle, 1960-72; sr. research scientist Boeing Aerospace Co., Seattle, 1972-73; prin. engr. Boeing Comml. Airplane Co., Seattle, 1973-81, sr. prin. engr., 1981-84; sr. prin. engr. Boeing Aerospace, Seattle, 1984-90; tech. cons., 1990—; vis. prof. Max Planck Inst. for Metals Research, Stuttgart, Germany, 1968-69; lectr. Tech. U. Stuttgart, 1968-69; pres. Optologics Inc., Seattle, 1973-94 . Mem. Am. Phys. Soc., Optical Soc. Am., Soc. Photo Optical Instrumentation Engrs. Author: Heat Conduction in Crystals, 1969. Contbr. articles to profl. jours. Research in cryogenics, statis. physics and opto electronics. Home: 14300 Trillium Blvd SE Apt 8 Bothell WA 98012-1300 Office: Boeing Def and Space Group PO Box 3999 Seattle WA 98124-2499

ERDOGAN, FAZIL, mechanical engineer; b. Kars, Turkey, Feb. 5, 1925; m. 1994; 2 children. MS, Tech U., Istanbul, Turkey, 1948; PhD in Mech. Engring., Lehigh U., 1955. Instr. engring. Tech U., Istanbul, Turkey, 1948-52; asst. Lehigh U., Bethlehem, Pa., 1952-55, assoc. prof. mech. engring., 1957-63, chmn. dept., 1983-89, dean. Coll. Engring., 1989-91, prof. mech. engring., 1963—, interim dean engring., 1990—. Recipient Alexander von Humboldt sr. U.S. scientist award, 1983, Lehigh U. Rsch. award, 1982. Mem. ASME, ASTM, Am. Acad. Mechanics, Soc. Engring. Sci. (Eringen medal 1993), Nat. Acad. Engrs., Am. Math. Soc. Home: RR 9 Bethlehem PA 18015-9805 Office: Packard Lab Dept Chem and Mech Engring 19 Memorial Dr W Bethlehem PA 18015*

ERDÖS, ERVIN GEORGE, pharmacology and biochemistry educator; b. Budapest, Hungary; came to U.S., 1954; naturalized, 1959; s. Andor and Aranka (Breuer) E; m. Sara F. Rabito, May 30, 1986; children from previous marriage: Martin, Peter, Philip. Grad., U. Budapest Sch. Medicine, 1950; MD, U. Munich, 1950. With hosp. Munich, 1951; rsch. assoc. in biochem. rsch. lab. U. Munich, 1952-54; rsch. assoc. Mercy Hosp., Pitts., 1955-58; fellow in biochemistry, ind. rsch. Mellon Inst., Pitts., 1958-63; asst. prof. pharmacology U. Pitts., 1958-61, assoc. prof., 1961-63; prof. pharmacology U. Okla. Sch. Medicine, Oklahoma City, 1963-73, George Lynn Cross rsch. prof., 1970-73; prof. pharmacology, internal medicine U. Tex., Southwestern Med. Sch., Dallas, 1973-85; prof. pharmacology and anesthesiology, dir. Peptide Rsch. Lab. U. Ill. Coll. Medicine, Chgo., 1985—; vis. prof. Tulane U., 1963; Disting. Fulbright prof., 1975; vis. scientist U.S.-Japan Coop. Sci. Program, NSF, 1966; vis. prof. dept. pharmacology Rush Med. Coll., Chgo., 1993—; cons. in field; mem. coms. Nat. Heart and Lung Inst. Editor books; mem. editorial bd. jours. Recipient gold medal Frey-Werle Found., Munich, 1988, Disting. Faculty award U. Ill. Coll. Medicine, 1992; Deutsche Forschungsgemeinschaft fellow, 1954; Wellcome Rsch. travel grantee, 1964; Univ. scholar U. Ill., 1990. Mem. Am. Soc. Pharmacology and Exptl. Therapeutics and Medicine, Am. Heart Assn. (med. adv. bd. Coun. for High

Blood Pressure Rsch. 1972—, Ciba award for hypertension rsch. 1994, Rsch. Achievement award 1995), Am. Soc. Biochemistry and Molecular Biology, Hungarian Acad. Sci. (fgn. mem.). Office: U Ill Coll Medicine Dept Pharmacology MC 868 835 S Wolcott Ave Chicago IL 60612-7340

ERDREICH, BEN LEADER, federal agency executive; b. Birmingham, Ala., Dec. 9, 1938; s. Stanley Marx and Corinne (Leader) E.; m. Ellen Cooper, May 30, 1965; children: Jeremy Cooper, Anna Bethia. BA, Yale U., 1960; JD with honors, U. Ala., 1963. Bar: Ala. 1963, D.C. 1984. Assoc. Kaye, Scholer, Fierman, Attys., N.Y.C., 1965-66; ptnr. Cooper, Mitch & Crawford, Birmingham, 1966-74; mem. 98th-102nd Congresses from 6th Dist. Ala., 1983-93; chmn. U.S. Merit Sys. Protection Bd., 1993—. Mem. Ala. Ho. of Reps., Birmingham, 1970-74, Jefferson County Commn., Birmingham, 1974-82. 1st lt. U.S. Army, 1963-65. Mem. D.C. Bar Assn., Ala. Bar Assn., Birmingham Bar Assn. Democrat. Jewish. Home: 2900 Redmont Park Cir Apt 202 Birmingham AL 35205-2155 Office: US Merit Systems Protection Bd 1120 Vermont Ave NW Washington DC 20005-3523

ERDRICH, (KAREN) LOUISE, fiction writer, poet; b. Little Falls, Minn., June 7, 1954; d. Ralph Louis and Rita Joanne (Gourneau) E.; m. Michael Anthony Dorris, Oct. 10, 1981 (dec. Apr. 1997); children: Abel (dec.), Sava, Madeline, Persia, Pallas, Aza. BA, Dartmouth Coll., 1976; MA, Johns Hopkins U., 1979. Vis. poet, tchr. N.D. State Arts Council, 1977-78; tchr. writing Johns Hopkins U., Balt., 1978-79; communications dir., editor Circle-Boston Indian Council, 1979-80; textbook writer Charles Merrill Co., 1980. Author: (textbook) Imagination, 1981; (poetry) Jacklight, 1984, Baptism of Desire, 1989; (novels) Love Medicine, 1984 (Nat. Book Critics Circle award for fiction 1984, Virgina McCormick Scully prize 1984, L.A. Times award for best novel 1985, Sue Kaufman prize for first fiction Am Acad. and Inst. of Arts and Letters 1985), The Beet Queen, 1986, Tracks, 1988, (with Michael Dorris) The Crown of Columbus, 1991, (with Dorris) Route 2, 1991, The Bingo Palace, 1994, The Blue Jay's Dance: A Writer's Year with Baby, 1995, Tales of Burning Love, 1996, The Antelope Wife, 1998; (children's) Grandmother's Pigeon, 1997, The Birchbark House, 1999; contbr. short stories, essays and poems to popular mags., other publs. Johns Hopkins U. teaching fellow, 1979; Macdowell Colony fellow, 1980; Yaddo Colony fellow, 1981; vis. fellow Dartmouth Coll., 1981; Guggenheim fellow, 1985-86; recipient numerous awards for profl. excellence including Nelson Algren award, 1982, Pushcart prize, 1983, Nat. Mag. Fiction award, 1983, 87, First prize O. Henry awards, 1987. Mem. PEN (exec. bd. 1985-90),, Am. Acad. Arts and Letters, Authors Guild, Western Lit. Assn. Address: c/o Rambar and Curtis 19 W 44th St New York NY 10036-4904

ERENBURG, STEVEN ALAN, retired communications executive; b. Bklyn., Sept. 8, 1937; s. Harry and Sophie (Karp) E.; m. Mary Kabasakalian, Nov. 10, 1970; children: Aram Lee, Mariam Jennifer. BEE, Pratt Inst., 1957; MS in Systems Sci., Bklyn. Poly. Inst., 1970. Project engr. Kearfott Co., Wayne, N.J., 1957-66; program mgr. Kollsman Instrument Corp., Syosset, N.Y., 1966-70; editor Electronic Design mag., N.Y.C., 1970-71; mng. editor EDN mag., Boston, 1971-73; mgr. pub. relations AT&T Bell Labs., Murray Hill, N.J., 1973-77; v.p., dir. corp. rels. ITT Corp., N.Y.C., 1977-98; ret., 1998; bd. dirs. Hybrid Data Systems, Inc., Rahway, N.J. Patentee Gyrocompass, 1965. Mem. IEEE (sr. mem., dir. external affairs com. 1974-79), Belgian Am. C. of C. (bd. dirs.). Democrat. Avocation: photography. Home: 35 S Mountain Rd Millburn NJ 07041-1505

ERENS, JAY ALLAN, lawyer; b. Chgo., Oct. 18, 1935; s. Miller S. and Annette (Goodman) R.; m. Patricia F. Brett, Aug. 21, 1960 (div. May 1985); children: Pamela B., Bradley B.; m. Patrice A. Krumm, June 15, 1985; 1 child, Cameron Jay. BA, Yale U., 1956; LLB, Harvard U., 1959. Bar: Ill. 1960. Law clk. to Justice John M. Harlan U.S. Supreme Ct., Washington, 1959-60; pvt. practice Chgo., 1960-64; founding and sr. ptnr. Levy and Erens (name changed to Erens and Miller 1985), Chgo., 1964-86; sr. ptnr. Hopkins & Sutter, Chgo., 1986—; lectr. law Northwestern U., Chgo., 1961-63; spl. asst. atty. gen. State Ill., Chgo., 1964-70. Trustee Latin Sch. Chgo., 1975-80. Mem. ABA, Chgo. Bar Assn. Office: Hopkins & Sutter 3 First National Plz Chicago IL 60602

ERENSTEIN, ALAN, emergency room nurse, medical education consultant. Grad., Aliquippa Hosp Sch. Radiology, Pa., 1974; student, Aliquippa Hosp. Sch. Radiology, New Wilmington, Pa., 1974; AA in Gen. Studies, LPN, Beaver County C.C., Monaca, Pa., 1977, AS in Nursing, RN, 1979. RN, Fla.; registered radiologic technologist. LPN Hamot Med. Ctr., Erie, Pa., 1977-78; team leader Trauma-Neuro ICU and Stepdown Unit Allegheny Gen. Hosp., Pitts., 1979-81, staff nurse Emergency Room, 1981; flight nurse LifeWATCH HCA Wesley Med. Ctr., Wichita, Kans., 1981-91, contigency and float pool, 1991-92, hyperbaric nurse, 1991-92; ER nurse, relief charge nurse, clin. coord., team leader JFK Med. Ctr., Atlantis, Fla., 1992-95; aeromed. specialist Bizjet Air Ambulance, West Palm Beach, Fla., 1994-95; med. edn. cons. Med. Edn. Cons. Am., Tampa, 1994-97; with disaster team Cutler Ridge (Fla.) Field Hosp., 1992; response team Kans. Tornado Wesley Med. Ctr., Wichita, 1991; emergency rm./trauma nurse DelRay Med. Ctr., 1996—; paramedic clin. coord. Hutchinson (Kans.) C.C., 1989; skills lab coord. Advanced Trauma Life Support Course, HCA Wesley Med. Ctr., Wichita, 1989-92; lectr. various med. ctrs., univs. and confs. Author: Trauma in Pregnancy, 1990; co-author: LifeWATCH Transport Manual, 1988; contbr. Society Trauma Nurses: Instructor's Resource Manual for Trauma Nursing, The Pregnant Trauma Patient Module, 1998. Mem. Soc. Trauma Nurses, Nat. Flight Nurses Assn. Home: 308 Island Shores Dr West Palm Beach FL 33413-2105 Office: Delray Med Ctr 5352 Linton Blvd Delray Beach FL 33484-6514

ERFANI, SHERVIN, electrical engineer, educator, scientist, writer; b. Tehran, Iran, Mar. 28, 1948; came to U.S. 1982; s. Ibrahim and Rashedeh (Naraghi) Erfani; m. Janet E. Kovar, Dec. 30, 1982. MSEE, U. Tehran, Iran, 1971; MS, So. Meth. U., 1974, PhD in EE, 1976. Asst. prof. Nat. U. Iran, Eveen, 1978-82; research assoc. So. Meth. U., Dallas, 1982-83; asst. prof. U. Mich., Dearborn, 1983-85; mem. tech. staff Lucent Techs. Bell Labs., Holmdel, N.J., 1985—; vis. prof. U. P.R., 1992-93; adj. prof. dept. elec. engring. and computer sci. Stevens Inst. Tech., Hoboken, N.J., 1996—; mem. rsch. staff Racal-Datacom, Ft. Lauderdale, Fla., 1997-98. Translator: Elec. Engring. textbook, Circuit Design & Synthesis, 1985; assoc. editor Computers and Elec. Engring.: An Internat. Jour.; sr. editor Jour. of Network and Systems Mgmt.; contbr. articles to profl. jours. 2nd lt. Signal Corps Iran Army, 1972-73. Mem. IEEE (sr. mem., v.p. S.E. Mich. chpt. 1985), Inst. Elec. Engrs. U.K. (chartered engr.), N.Y. Acad. Scis., Tau Beta Pi, Eta Kappa Nu. Islam. Avocations: flying, numismatics, antiques, philately. Office: Lucent Techs Bell Labs 101 Crawfords Corner Rd Holmdel NJ 07733-1900

ERGAS, ENRIQUE, orthopedic surgeon; b. Santiago, Chile, Oct. 8, 1938; came to U.S., 1964; s. Jaime and Rebecca E.; m. Joscelyn Krauss, June 20, 1955; children: Eileen, Jamie, Arielle. MD, U. Chile, 1964. Diplomate Am. Bd. Orthopaedic Surgery. Intern Methodist Hosp., Bklyn., 1964-65; resident in gen. surgery Mt. Sinai Hosp., N.Y.C., 1965-67; resident in orthopaedic surgery Albert Einstein Coll. Medicine, N.Y.C., 1967-71; practice medicine specializing in orthopaedic surgery N.Y.C., 1971—; asst. clin. prof. orthopaedic surgery Albert Einstein Coll. Medicine, N.Y.C., 1973-87, NYU, 1987—; dir. Latin Am. programs, Latin Am. fellowships Hosps. for Joint Diseases Orthopaedic Inst.; lectr., moderator various hosps. and colls. Sci. exhibit Am. Acad. Orthopaedic Surgery, New Orleans, 1982; contbr. articles to profl. jours. Bd. dirs., sec. med. bd. Trafalgar Hosp., 1976-77; mem. panel determination mal practice Supreme Ct., N.Y., 1987. Recipient Masada award Hadassah Hosp., 1974, Order of Merit cum laude, Orthopaedic Research Soc., 1985. Fellow Am. Acad. Orthopaedic Surgeons, ACS; mem. Arthroscopy Assn. N.Am., Internat. Arthroscopy Assn., Gericare (pres. 1987-89), AMA, N.Y. State Soc. Orthopaedic Surgeons, Med. Soc. County New York, N.Y. Acad. Medicine, Soc. Latim Am. Orthopedia Traumatologia, Spanish Am. Med. Soc., Chilean Soc. Orthopaedic and Traumatology (corr.), Am. Assn. French Speaking Health Profls., Montefiore Orthopaedic Alumni Assn. (regional bd. dirs.). Office: 1056 5th Ave New York NY 10028-0112

ERHARD, THOMAS AGNEW, English educator; b. West Hoboken, N.J., June 11, 1923; s. Herbert Charles and Grace Clarabelle (Agnew) E.; m. Jean Marie Beebe, July 25, 1945 (div. Sept. 1971); children: Bruce, Lawrence, Daniel; m. Evelyn Madrid, July 14, 1979. BA, Hofstra Coll., 1947; MA, U. N.Mex., 1950, PhD, 1960. Dir. pub., tchr. English Highland H.S., Albuquerque, 1949-53; dir. pub. info. Albuquerque Pub. Schs., 1953-57; asst. dir. press & radio NEA, Washington, 1957-58; prof. English, theatre N.Mex. State U., Las Cruces, 1960—. Author over 40 plays; contbr. articles to profl. jours.; sports announcer, Albuquerque, Las Cruces, 1955-95. Sgt. AUS, 1943-46. Mem. NEA, Soc. Profl. Journalists. Avocation: photography. Office: N Mex State U Box 3001 Las Cruces NM 88003

ERIBES, RICHARD, dean. Dean architecture and planning U. N.Mex., Albuquerque, 1996; dean Coll. Architecture U. Ariz., Tucson, 1997—. Office: U Ariz Sch Architecture PO Box 210075 Tucson AZ 85721-0075*

ERIBO, FESTUS, mass communication educator, journalist; b. Benin City, Edo, Nigeria, June 16, 1950; came to the U.S., 1985; s. Wilfred Omovbe and Grace Iroguehi Eribo; m. Luba N. Eribo, Aug. 24, 1978; children: Brenda, Hilda. MA, Leningrad (Russia) State U., 1979; PhD, U. Wis., 1989. Tchr. Edo Coll., Benin City, 1971; pub. rels. mgr. Ribway Group Cos., Benin City, 1971-73; prin. info. officer Dept. Info., Benin City, 1980-89; asst. prof. East Carolina U., Greenville, 1990-95, assoc. prof., 1995—. Author: Window on Africa: Democratization and Media Exposure, 1993, Press Freedom and Communication in Africa, 1997. Mem. Assn. for Edn. in Journalism and Mass Comm. Home: 402 Lancelot Dr Greenville NC 27858 Office: Dept Comm East Carolina Univ Greenville NC 27858

ERICH, LOUIS RICHARD, physician; b. Shanghai, China, Nov. 7, 1928; (parents Am. citizens); s. Otis G. and Julia A. (Cunningham) E.; m. Lillian Annie McFeters, June 7, 1951; children: Jonathan, Kevin, Timothy, Janine. BA, Pacific Union Coll., 1950; MD, Loma Linda U., 1955. Diplomate Am. Bd. Ob-Gyn. Intern Spartanburg (S.C.) Gen. Hosp., 1955-56; resident in internal medicine Loma Linda Clin. Med. Ctr., 1965-66, resident in ob-gyn., 1970-73; physician Sonora (Calif.) Med. Group, Inc., 1977—. Capt. U.S. Army, 1956-58. Fellow Am. Coll. Ob-Gyn. Office: Sonora Med Group Inc 4 S Forest Rd Sonora CA 95370-4827

ERICHSEN, PETER CHRISTIAN, university official, lawyer; b. Kentfield, Calif., Aug. 4, 1956; s. Hans Skabo and Ruth Elsie (Henderson) E. AB magna cum laude, Harvard U., 1978, JD cum laude, 1981. Bar: Mass. Assoc. Ropes & Gray, Boston, 1981-90, ptnr., 1990-93; dep. asst. atty. gen. U.S. Dept. Justice, Washington, 1993-96; assoc. counsel to Pres. The White House, 1996-97; v.p., gen. counsel U. Pa., U. Pa. Health Sys., 1997—; bd. govs. Phila. Stock Exch., 1999—. Vestryman Trinity Ch., Boston, 1987-91, 92-93, mem. bd. gov., also mem. search com., 1992-93; founding dir. Trinity Hospice, Boston, 1988-93. Mem. Groton Sch. Alumni Assn. (v.p. 1985-89). Office: 100 College Hall Philadelphia PA 19104

ERICK, MIRIAM ANNA, dietitian, medical writer; b. Norwich, Conn., Apr. 1, 1958; d. Eugene A. and Toini (Lampi) E. BS, U. Conn., Storrs, 1970; MS, U. Bridgeport, 1992. Morning sickness cons. Brigham and Women's Hosp., Boston, perinatal dietitian. Author: No More Morning Sickness: A Survival Guide for Pregnant Women, 1993, Take Two Crackers and Call Me in the Morning!, 1998, A Real Life Guide for Surviving Morning Sickness, 1995; contbr. articles to profl. jours. Mem. Am. Dietetic Assn., Am. Botanical Coun., Am. Coll. Ob/gyn. Avocations: horseback riding, culinary experimentation, hiking, horse statue photography. Home: 36 Winchester St Apt 8 Brookline MA 02446-2864 Office: Brigham and Women's Hosp 75 Francis St Brookline MA 02446-6638

ERICKSEN, JERALD LAVERNE, educator, engineering scientist; b. Portland, Oreg., Dec. 20, 1924; s. Adolph and Ethel Rebecca (Correy) E.; m. Marion Ella Pook, Feb. 24, 1946; children: Lynn Christine, Randolph Peder. BS, U. Wash., 1947; MA, Oreg. State Coll., 1949; PhD, Ind. U., 1951; DSc (hon.), Nat. U. Ireland, 1984, Heriot-Watt U., 1988. Mathematician, solid state physicist U.S. Naval Research Lab., 1951-57; faculty Johns Hopkins U., 1957-83, prof. theoretical mechanics, 1960-83; prof. mechanics and math. U. Minn., Mpls., 1983-90; cons. Florence, Oreg., 1990—. Served with USNR, 1943-46. Recipient Bingham medal, 1968, Timoshenko medal, 1979, Engring. Sci. medal, 1987. Mem. Nat. Acad. Engring., Soc. Rheology, Soc. Natural Philosophy, Soc. Interaction Mechanics and Math., Soc. Engring. Sci., Royal Irish Acad. (hon.). Home and Office: 5378 Buckskin Bob Dr Florence OR 97439-8320

ERICKSON, ALAN ERIC, librarian; b. Boston, Feb. 6, 1928; s. Elmer Eric and Ethel M. (Winch) E.; m. June Andersen, July 14, 1951; children—Kim, John, Martha, William. A.B., Middlebury Coll., 1949; M.A., Boston U., 1955, Ph.D., 1960; M.S.L.S., Simmons Sch. Library Sci., 1968. Cert. tchr., Mass. Instr. Boston U., 1954-60; staff scientist Worcester Found. for Exptl. Biology, Shrewsbury, Mass., 1960-66; sci. specialist library Harvard U., Cambridge, Mass., 1966-91; librarian Cabot Sci. Library, 1973-91; assoc. librarian for adminstrn. Harvard Coll., Cambridge, Mass., 1970-72; assoc. librarian Harvard Coll. Sci., 1984-91; ret., 1991; cons. Marine Biol. Labs., Woods Hole, Mass., 1981-82, 89; trustee BIOSIS Info. Svc., 1988-93, chmn. bd., 1993. Contbr. articles to profl. jours. Trustee Carter Meml. Meth. Ch., Needham, Mass., 1964-66, David Turner Scholarship Fund, Needham, 1970—. Lt. col. USAFR, 1951-73, ret. Recipient Woolsey Bible prize Middlebury Coll., Vt., 1949. Mem. Harvard U. Retirees Assn. (pres. 1995-97), Needham Ret. Men's Club (pres. 1999—), Sigma Xi. Avocations: gardening; woodworking; bicycling.

ERICKSON, ARTHUR CHARLES, architect; b. Vancouver, B.C., Can., June 14, 1924; s. Oscar and Myrtle (Chatterson) E. Student, U. B.C., Vancouver, 1942-44; B.Arch., McGill U., Montreal, Que., Can., 1950; LL.D. (hon.), Simon Fraser U., Vancouver, 1973, U. Man., Winnipeg, Can., 1978, Lethbridge U., 1981; D.Eng. (hon.), Novia Scotia Tech. Coll., McGill U., 1971; Litt.D. (hon.), U. B.C., 1985. Asst. prof. U. Oreg., Eugene, 1955-56; assoc. prof. U. B.C., 1956-63; ptnr. Erickson-Massey Architects, Vancouver, 1963-72; prin. Arthur Erickson Architects, Vancouver, 1972-91, Toronto, Ont., Can., 1981-91, Los Angeles, 1981-91; prin. Arthur Erickson Archtl. Corp., Vancouver, 1991—. Prin. works include Can. Pavilion at Expo '70, Osaka (recipient first prize in nat. competition, Archtl. Inst. of Japan award for best pavilion), Robson Square/The Law Courts (honor award), Mus. of Anthropology (honor award), Eppich Residence (honor award), Habitat Pavilion (honor award), Sikh Temple (award of merit), Champlain Heights Community Sch. (award of merit), San Diego Convention Ctr., Calif. Plz., L.A., Fresno City Hall; subject of Time mag. cover article and New Yorker profile; contbr. articles to profl. publs. Mem. com. on urban devel. Coun. of Can., 1971; bd. dirs. Can. Conf. of Arts, 1972; mem. design adv. coun. Portland Devel. Commn., Can. Coun. Urban Rsch.; trustee Inst. Rsch. on Pub. Policy. Capt. Can. Intelligence Corps., 1945-46. Recipient Molson prize Can. Coun. Arts, 1967, Triangle award Nat. Soc. Interior Design, Royal Bank Can. award, 1971, Gold medal Tau Sigma Delta, 1973, residential design award Can. Housing Coun., 1975, August Perret award Internat. Union Archiects Congress, 1975, Chgo. Architecture award, 1984, Gold medals Royal Archtl. Inst. Can., 1984, French Acad. Architecture, 1984, Pres. award excellence Am. Soc. Landscape Architects, 1979; named Officer, Order of Can., 1973, Companion Order of Can., 1981. Fellow AIA (hon., Pan Pacific citation Hawaiian chpt. 1963, gold medal 1986), Royal Archtl. Inst. Can. (recipient award 1980); mem. Royal Inst. Brit. Archs., Archtl. Inst. B.C., Royal Inst. Scottish Archs. (hon.), Coll. d'arquitectos de España (hon.), Coll. d'architectos de Mex. (hon.), Royal Can. Acad. Arts (academician), Heritage Can., S.F.U. Faculty Club. Office: Arthur Erickson Archtl Corp, 1672 W 1st Ave, Vancouver, BC Canada V6J 1G1

ERICKSON, BARBARA MARTHA, historian, writer, florist; b. Knoxville, Tenn., July 17, 1932; d. William Vivian and Elza Cleo (Nichols) Slatery; m. Eugene William Erickson, Aug. 21, 1954; children: Randall William, Jacqueline Barbara. BA, U. Tenn., 1954. Asst. bridal cons. LeGrands Jewelers, Chattanooga, Tenn., 1952-54; organizer patient file room Erlanger Hosp., Chattanooga, 1954; floral arranger Stevens Florists, Spring Valley, N.Y., 1956-58; sec. treas. Erickson Olds, Inc., Monsey, N.Y., 1968-92, Toyota of Rockland, Monsey, 1992; floral arranger Schweizers Florist, Pearl River, N.Y., Dykstras Florists, Spring Valley, N.Y. Author: 200 Years of Brick Church History, 1974, What in the World is a Rotary Ann?, 1983; editor Rockland Rep. Reporter Rockland County Young Rep. Club, 1950's, 60's, The Tempo of Brick Church West New Hempstead Reformed Ch., Spring Valley, N.Y., 1958—; contbr. articles to mags., jours., chpt. to book. Historian West New Hempstead Reformed Ch., 1961—; co-chmn. bi-centennial Town of Ramapo, N.Y., 1976. Recipient Gov.'s Newsleter award Dist. Gov. Rotary Internat., 1984, Town Svc., Humanitarian awards Town of Ramapo, 1991; named First Families of Tenn. East Tenn. Hist. Soc., 1995; Paul Harris fellow, 1982. Mem. Valley Garden Club (hon., pres. 1962-65), Valley Star Order of the Ea. Star (matron, pres. 1960), Suffern Woman's Club (mem. exec. bd. 1996—), other hist., geneal. assns. Mem. Reformed Ch. in Am. Avocations: writing, golf, scuba diving, camping, travel. Home: 179 W Maple Ave Monsey NY 10952-1733

ERICKSON, DAVID BELNAP, lawyer; b. Ogden, Utah, Oct. 13, 1951; s. Eldred H. and Lois (Belnap) E.; m. Julie Ann Hill, Apr. 19, 1974; children: Rachel, John, Michael, Jared, Emily, Steven, Katherine, Daniel, Elizabeth. BA, Brigham Young U., 1975; MEd, Utah State U., 1979; JD, Gonzaga Sch. Law, 1982. Bar: Utah 1982, U.S. Claims Ct. 1990, U.S. Dist. Ct. Utah 1982, U.S. Ct. Appeals (10th cir.) 1984, U.S. Ct. Appeals (9th cir.) 1987, U.S. Supreme Ct. 1987. English tchr., debate coach Bonneville High Sch., Ogden, 1976-79; law clk. U.S. Atty.'s Office, Spokane, Washington, 1980-81; law clk. to judge U.S. Dist. Ct., Salt Lake City, 1982-83; with Kirton, McConkie & Poelman, Salt Lake City, 1983-92; sr. counsel Intermountain Health Care, Salt Lake City, 1992—. Co-author: Utah Appellate Practice Manual, 1986, Utah Sr. Citizen's Handbook, 1987; editor-in-chief Gonzaga Law Rev., 1981-82; assoc. editor: Utah Barrister, 1986-87, Utah Bar Jour., 1988—. Mem. LDS Hosp. Bioethics Com.; mem. planning and zoning commn. Pleasant View City, 1991-95, chmn., 1994-95, mem. city coun., mayor protempor, 1998—; chmn. Weber View Dist. Boy Scouts Am., 1993-95; trustee Utah Alliance for Health Care, 1994-99. Mem. ABA (litigation sect.), Utah Bar Assn. (law jour. com., bridging the gap com., needs of the elderly com., legal and med. com., examiner constl. law bar, assoc. editor Utah Bar jour.), Salt Lake County Bar Assn., Weber County Bar Assn.,Am. Health Lawyers Assn., Phi Delta Phi. Mem. LDS Ch. Office: Intermountain Health Care 36 S State St Fl 22 Salt Lake City UT 84111-1401

ERICKSON, DONNA JOY, writer, educator; b. Boston, June 8, 1955; d. Samuel Jacob and Lillian Doris (Koven) Gilman; m. Jeffrey W. Erickson, Oct. 26, 1975; 1 child, Ryan S. Assoc. in Bus. with high honors, Massasoit C.C., Brockton, Mass., 1979. Asst. to meteorologist, pub. rels. coord. New Eng. Weather Sci., Hull, Mass., 1986-88; freelance feature writer South Shore News, Rockland, Mass., 1988-91; staff feature writer Abington/Rockland Mariner, Marshfield, Mass., 1992-94; staff writer South Shore Baby Jour., Kingston, Mass., 1992-98; owner A Flair For Writing, 1989—. Author hist. essay, 1989; radio Job Hour Program gues WMSX Radio AM, Brockton, Mass., 1992. Mem. Abington Cmty. Playground Com., 1989; facilitator Alliance for Mentally Ill-Sibling/Adult Children Group, Brockton, Mass., 1986. Mem. Nat. Writers Union, Cassel Comm. Network of Writers and Panel of Experts, South Shore Ad Club (mem. bd. dirs. 1992-94, newsletter editor 1992-94). Avocations: walking, meditation, alternative therapies.

ERICKSON, EDWARD LEONARD, biotechnology company executive, consultant; b. Chgo., Dec. 7, 1946; s. Leonard Gerald and Eleanore Antoinette (Picek) E.; m. Helen Leonora Masten, Dec. 29, 1979. BS in Math. and Physics, Ill. Inst. Tech., 1968, MS in Math., 1970; MBA in Gen. Mgmt., Harvard U., 1980. Mktg. rep. IBM, Miami, Fla., 1975-76; sr. systems engr. Advanced Tech., Inc., McLean, Va., 1976-78; cons. Bain & Co., Boston, 1979-80; sr. assoc. Resource Planning Assocs., Washington, 1980-82; dir. RPA Mgmt. Cons., London, 1982-83; dir. corp. devel. Amersham Internat. plc., Little Chalfont, Eng., 1983-86, gen. mgr. internat. ops., 1986-88; v.p. fin. ops. The Ares-Serono Group, Boston, 1988-90; pres. Serono-Baker Diagnostics (The Ares-Serono Group), Allentown, Pa., 1990-91; pres., chief exec. officer, dir. Cholestech Corp., Hayward, Calif., 1991-93; pres., CEO, DepoTech Corp., La Jolla, Calif., 1993-98, also bd. dirs.; bd. dirs. Megabios Corp., Burlingame, Calif.; chmn. Immunicon Corp., 1998—. Contbr. articles to profl. jours. Lt. USN, 1970-75. John L. Loeb fellow Harvard U., 1980, George F. Baker scholar, 1980, NASA fellow, 1968-70. Mem. Am. Soc. Clin. Oncology (affiliate), Am. Assn. Pharm. Scientists. Republican. Avocations: tennis, skiing. Home: 6887 Tohickon Hill Rd Pipersville PA 18947-1415

ERICKSON, GARWOOD ELLIOTT, manufacturing company executive; b. Little Silver, N.J., Jan. 8, 1946; s. Gustaf Walter and Martha Lake (Adams) E.; m. Carol Wyborski, July 21, 1973; children: Christopher Lake, Jason Edward. AB, Dartmouth Coll., 1967; BE, Thayer Sch. Engring., 1968, ME, 1969; MBA, U. Mich., 1974. Systems analyst Ford Motor Co., Dearborn, Mich., 1969-72, sect. supr., 1972-82, mgr., 1982-83; corp. dir. mgmt. info. services Hoover Universal, Ann Arbor, Mich., 1983-86, Vickers, Inc., Troy, Mich., 1986-89, dir. sales, 1989-90, dir. quality mgmt., 1990-93; chief info. officer R.L. Polk & Co., Taylor, Mich., 1993-96, owner Great Lakes Technols. Group, 1996—. Sec. Trayer Lakes Community Assn., Ann Arbor, Mich., 1977. Advanced Research Projects Agy. fellow, 1967-69. Mem. Dartmouth Club (pres. Ann Arbor 1982-86). Office: 26999 Central Pk Blvd Southfield MI 48076

ERICKSON, GEORGANNE MORRIS, nursing administrator, nursing educator, psychiatric-mental health consultant; b. Dayton, Ohio, Dec. 23, 1939; d. Arthur McKinley and Fannie Thelma (Shroyer) Morris; children: Heather Lee Smith, Kimberly Reneé Smith; m. Miles Alden Erickson. BSN, Ohio State U., 1963; postgrad., Wright State U., 1983-85; MS in Nursing Svc. Adminstrn., U. So. Miss., 1989. Cert. psychiat.-mental health nurse ANA. Several med. positions, 1960-75; asst. dir. insvc. edn. Grandview Hosp., Dayton, Ohio, 1975-79; asst. dir. nursing svc. Kettering (Ohio) Convalescent Ctr., 1979; PSRO nurse reviewer long-term care Region II Med. Rev. Corp., Dayton, 1979-81; psychiat. nurse VA Med. Ctr., Dayton, 1981-85; chem. dependency nurse Gulf Oak Hosp., Biloxi, Miss., 1987-88; psychiat.-mental health nurse cons., contract home health nurse Quality Home Health Care, Biloxi, 1988-90; clin. instr. Miss. Gulf Coast Community Coll., Gulfport, 1989-90; contract home health nurse Coastal Plains Pub. Health Dist. IX, Miss. State Dept Health, Gulfport, 1989-90; dir. quality assurance/edn. Profl. Home Health Agy., Biloxi, 1990; dir. nursing Sand Hill Hosp., Gulfport, 1990; adj. clin. faculty William Carey Coll., Gulfport, 1990, night shift charge nurse med.-surg. and psychiatry Biloxi Regional Med. Ctr., 1992-95; vol. regional liaison officer peer assistance program Ohio Nurses Assn., 1983-85, La. Nurses' Network Impaired Profls. La. State Nurses Assn., 1990. Vol. divsn. probation Harrison County Family Ct., 1990-92, ARC Disaster Health Svcs., 1994—, Keesler AFB Health Promotion Program, 1995-96, ARC Blood Svc., 1996—; mem. Miss. Gulf Coast C. of C. Maturity Health Resource Coun., 1998—, Miss. Gulf Coast Helpline, 1999—. Mem. ANA, Miss. Nurses Assn., Ohio Nurses Assn., Ohio State U. Sch. Nursing Alumni Assn., Sigma Theta Tau, Gamma Beta Phi. Home: 2434 W Shore Dr Biloxi MS 39532-3022

ERICKSON, GERALD MEYER, classical studies educator; b. Amery, Wis., Sept. 23, 1927; s. Oscar Meyer and Ellen Claire (Hanson) E.; m. Loretta Irene Eder, Feb. 11, 1951; children: Rachel, Viki, Kari. BS, U. Minn., 1954, MA, 1956, PhD, 1968. Cert. secondary sch. tchr., Minn. Tchr. Edina-Morningside Pub. Sch., Minn., 1956-65, 66-67; vis. lectr. U. Minn., Mpls., 1965-66, asst. prof., 1968-71, assoc. prof., 1971-83, prof. classical studies, 1983-95, prof. emeritus, 1995—; exchange prof. Moscow State U., 1980, 86; vis. prof. U. Ill., 1967, 68, Coll. of William and Mary, 1984; bd. regents La. Univ. System, 1981, chmn. evaluation team for classics programs; reader Coll. Bds. Advanced Placement Program, 1975-77, chief reader, 1978-81; cons., lectr. in field. Assoc. editor, mem. editorial staff Nature, Society and Thought, 1987—; author, lectr. various TV and radio courses. Served with U.S. Mcht. Marine, 1945-46, U.S. Army, 1946-47, PTO; served to capt. USAF, 1951-53. NEH grantee, 1977-79; recipient award Horace T. Morse Amoco Found., 1984. Mem. Minn. Classical Conf. (pres. 1971-74), Minn. Humanities Conf. (pres. 1974-75), Classical Assn. Midwest/South (Ovatio award 1971). Avocations: short-wave radio listening; bicycling. Home: 121 E 51st St Minneapolis MN 55419-2605 Office: 330 Folwell Hall 9 Pleasant St SE Minneapolis MN 55455-0194

ERICKSON, HOWARD HUGH, veterinarian, physiology educator; b. Wahoo, Nebr., Mar. 16, 1936; s. Conrad and Laurene (Swanson) E.; m. Ann E. Nicolay, June 6, 1959; children: James, David. BS, DVM, Kans. State U., 1959; PhD, Iowa State U., 1966. Commd. 1st lt. U.S. Air Force, 1959, advanced through grades to col., 1979; area veterinarian U.K., 1960-63; vet.

scientist Sch. Aerospace Medicine, Brooks AFB, Tex., 1966-75; dir. rsch. and devel. aerospace med. divsn. Sch. Aerospace Medicine, Brooks AFB, 1975-81; prof. physiology Kans. State U., Manhattan, 1981—, acting head dept. anatomy and physiology, 1989-90; mem. sci. adv. bd. Morris Animal Found., Englewood, Colo., 1990-93; cons. Tex. Higher Edn. Coordination Bd., Austin, 1990-91; clin. asst. prof. U. Tex. Health Sci. Ctr., San Antonio, 1972-81; vis. mem. grad. faculty Tex. A&M U., College Station, 1967-81; affiliate prof. Colo. State U., Fort Collins, 1970-75. Editor: Animal Pain, 1983; contbr. articles to profl. jours. Recipient Alumni Achievement award Midland Luth. Coll., Fremont, Nebr., 1977, Merck award for Creativity, 1993. Fellow AAAS, Royal Soc. Health, Aerospace Med. Assn. (assoc.); mem. Am. Vet. Med. Assn. (chmn. coun. on rsch. 1984), Am. Physiol. Soc., Optimists Club (Manhattan). Republican. Lutheran. Home: 2017 Arthur Dr Manhattan KS 66502-3918 Office: Kans State U Coll Vet Medicine Dept Anatomy and Physiology Manhattan KS 66506

ERICKSON, JAMES GARDNER, retired artist, cartoonist; b. International Falls, Minn., Apr. 11, 1925; s. Albin Edwin and Edna Lucille (Thomas) E. Student, Hundredmark Art Sch., Mpls., 1946-47. Comml. artist Pillsbury Co., Mpls., 1947-50; sign painter Tri-State Display Ctr., Mpls., 1950-64, Displaymasters, Inc., Mpls., 1964-80, Signdesign, Inc., St. Paul, 1980-90; ret., 1990. Contbr. cartoons to numerous publs. including Daily Worker, 1949-67, E.H.J. Am. Freeman. With U.S. Army, 1943-46, MTO. Decorated Inf. Combat Badge. Mem. ACLU, 36th Divsn. Assn. (life). Avocations: oil painting, cartoons, reading. Home: Hot Springs Lodge PO Box 336 406 Broadway Hot Springs MT 59845-0336

ERICKSON, JAMES HUSTON, clergyman, physician; b. Omaha, Sept. 7, 1931; s. Paul Ferdinand and Naomi Marie (Berglund) E.; m. Shirley Arlene Nordling, Dec. 26, 1959; children: Jonathan, Sonja, Ingrid. AA, North Park Coll., 1950; AB, Stanford U., 1952; MD, U. Colo., 1959; MPH, U. Minn., 1975; MS, Loyola Coll., Balt., 1982. Ordained to ministry Evang. Covenant Ch., 1985; Diplomate Am. Bd. Preventive Medicine, Am. Bd. Med. Psychotherapists. Intern Swedish Covenant Hosp., Chgo., 1959-60; resident in surgery VA Hosp., Hines, Ill., 1963; resident in gen. practice Swedish Covenant Hosp., Chgo., 1964-65; asst. minister Bethel Covenant Ch., Orange, Calif., 1960-61; commd. USN, 1960-63, 69-70, advanced through grades to commdr.; med. missionary Christian Med. Coll., Ludhiana, India, 1965; dir. med. edn. Swedish Covenant Hosp., Chgo., 1965-69; supply pastor Covenant and Presbyn. Chs., various locations, 1965-81; commd. USPHS, 1970-93; dir. USPHS Indian Med. Ctr., Phoenix, 1971-74, USPHS Hosp., Seattle, 1975-76; advanced through grades to asst. surgeon gen. USPHS, 1976, dir. Bur. Med. Svcs., 1976-81, ret., 1993; chaplain Boy Scouts Am., Laurel, Md., 1977-81; dir. health svcs., prof. community health No. Ill. U., DeKalb, Ill., 1981-85; assoc. minister Hillcrest Covenant Ch., DeKalb, 1982-85; interim minister Community Covenant Ch., Springfield, Va., 1988-89, Bethany Covenant Ch., Bedford, N.H., 1993, Bethesda Covenant Ch., Rockford, Ill., 1998-99; dir. health svcs. and pastoral care Atlantic Fleet NOAA, Norfolk, Va., 1986-88; dir. health svcs. and pastoral care hdqrs. NOAA, Rockville, Md., 1988-93; dir. Memphis Space Ctr., 1995-96; dir. med. edn. Swedish Covenant Hosp., Chgo., 1965-69; bd. dirs. The Holmstad, Batavia, Ill.; mem. commn. Christian action Evang. Covenant Ch., Chgo., 1984-90, 96—, ministerial ethics com., 1990-93; prof. family practice Uniformed Svcs. U., 1988-93; prof. pastoral care Memphis Theol. Sem., 1995-98; assoc. prof. cmty. health Eastern Va. Med. Sch., 1986-88. Vol. advisor Memphis chpt. ARC, 1994-98, Ch. Health Ctr., 1994-98. Fellow Am. Coll. Preventive Medicine, Royal Soc. Health, Am. Acad. Family Physicians, Am. Bd. Med. Psychotherapists; mem. Aerospace Med. Soc., Greater Rockford Ministries Assn., Commd. Officers Assn. USPHS, Civil Air Patrol, Civil Aviation Med. Assn., Aerospace Human Factors Assn., Assn. Mil. Surgeons U.S., Mil. Chaplains Assn., Acad. Parish Clergy. Avocations: reading, running, bicycling.

ERICKSON, JAMES PAUL, retired financial service company executive; b. Williston, N.D., Dec. 19, 1929; s. Carl Henry and Alice Ione (Borden) E.; m. Shirley Patricia Julian, Oct. 16, 1954; children—Christopher, Lisa Kasl. BS in Humanities and Social Sci., N.D. State U., 1991. Underwriter Mut. of Omaha, 1957-62, staff asst., 1962-68; asst. treas. Mut. of Omaha Fund Mgmt. Co., 1968-72, v.p., 1972-76, exec. v.p., 1976-81, exec. v.p., chief operating officer, 1981-87, pres., 1987-93; pres., CEO Mut. of Omaha Investors Svcs., 1993-96; bd. dirs. Am. Bapt. Homes of Midwest. Mem. Midwest region blood svcs. ARC, Omaha, 1985; trustee N.D. State U. Devel. Found. Served with USAF, 1952-56. Mem. Happy Hollow Country Club. Republican. Home: 6220 S 118th Plz Omaha NE 68137-4403

ERICKSON, JOHN DUFF, retired educational association administrator; b. Crawford, Nebr., Apr. 1, 1933; s. Harold Edward and Ruth Isabel (Duff) E.; m. Janet Eileen Lind, Dec. 28, 1955 (dec. Mar. 1992); children: Gregory Duff, Sheryl Ann; m. Bettie M. Hankins, July 7, 1994. BS in Mining Engring., S.D. Sch. Mines and Tech., 1955; MS in Indsl. Mgmt., MIT, 1965. Mine planning engr. Kennecott Copper Corp., Salt Lake City, 1965-67, truck ops. supt., 1968-69; mine mgr. Bougainville (New Guinea) Copper Ltd., Bougainville, Papua, New Guinea, 1970-72, exec. mgr. tech. services, 1973-75, asst. gen. mgr., 1976-77; head dept. mining engring. S.D. Sch. Mines and Tech., Rapid City, S.D., 1978-94; exec. dir. S.D. Sch. of Mines and Tech. Alumni Assn., Rapid City, S.D., 1984-98, prof. emeritus, 1998—; mining cons. Bechtel Civil and Minerals, San Francisco, 1979—, Fluor Daniel Engrs., Redwood City, Calif., 1983—, Davy McKee, San Ramon, Calif., Mineral Resources Devel., San Mateo, Calif.; bd. dirs. South Hills Mining Co., Rapid City. Bd. dirs. Nat. Mining Hall of Fame and Mus., S.D. Sch. Mines and Tech. Alumni Assn., Rapid City. Capt. U.S. Army, 1961-62. Sloan fellow MIT, 1964-65. Mem. SME/AIME (chmn. Black Hills sect. 1983), S.D. Mining Assn. (bd. dirs.), Arrowhead Country Club, Elks. Republican. Home: 2958 Tomahawk Dr Rapid City SD 57702-4276 Office: SD Sch Mines and Tech 501 E Saint Joseph St Rapid City SD 57701-3901

ERICKSON, KIM, consumer products company executive. Sr. v.p. fin. SuperValu Inc., Eden Prairie, Minn.; sr. v.p. strategic planning, treas. SuperValu Inc., Eden Prairie, 1998—. Office: SuperValu Inc 11840 Valley View Rd Eden Prairie MN 55344-3691*

ERICKSON, LARRY ALVIN, electronics sales and marketing executive; b. La Crosse, Wis., May 13, 1950; s. Leslie Louis and Alida Lillian Erickson; m. Sharon Kay Bakke, June 5, 1973 (div. Dec. 1980); children: Melissa J., Amy J., Brian D.; m. Sherri Sue Hillberg, Sept. 10, 1983; children: Mark E., Stephanie L. Student, Winona (Minn.) State Coll., 1968-72, Austin (Minn.) Vo-Tech. Sch., 1988-89, Austin C.C., 1990-91. Driver, mechanic Preston (Minn.) Equipment, 1977-80; truck driver Internat. Transport, Rochester, Minn., 1980-81, Comml. Svcs., Storm Lake, Iowa, 1981-82; meat cutter Hormel, Austin, 1982-85; gen. mgr. McPherson Archery Co., Austin, 1985-89; substitute tchr. Austin Vo-Tech. Sch., 1989-90; bookkeeper Hanson Constrn., Lyle, Minn., 1990-95; pres., CEO LeRoy (Minn.) Products Corp., 1990—; v.p., pres. sales Compact Cirs. Corp., Decorah, Iowa, 1996-97; owner Auscon, Inc., 1995—; ind. sales rep. Tech. Tool, Austin, 1992-95; small bus. cons., 1992—. Dir. communion distbn. St. Olaf Luth. Ch., Austin, 1992; 5th grade Sunday sch. tchr., 1996-98; vol. coach Austin Youth Hockey, 1992-96; coach Austin Youth Basketball, 1997-98. Recipient certificate of commendation Gov. State of Minn., 1987; named Outstanding Mem. of Month and Yr., Austin Jaycees, 1990. Mem. Am. Prodn. and Inventory Control Soc. (bd. dirs. 92), Minn. Archers Assn. (bd. dirs. 1989-91). Republican. Avocations: computer software applications, archery, basketball, handguns. Home: RR 4 Box 270A Austin MN 55912-9805 Office: Le Roy Products Corp Highway 56 And Country Rd Le Roy MN 55951

ERICKSON, LEIF B., federal judge; b. 1942. Law clk. Mont. Supreme Ct., 1967-68; pub. defender, 1969-70, dep. city atty., 1970-75, 79-85; judge 11th jud. dist. U.S. Dist. Ct. Mont., apptd. magistrate judge, 1992. Fax: (406) 542-7272. Office: Russell Smith Federal Bldg 201 E Broadway St Missoula MT 59802-4506

ERICKSON, PAMELA SUE, state agency administrator; b. Corpus Christi, Tex., Mar. 19, 1945; d. Walter Frederick Erickson and Barbara Jean (Roth) Carrigan; m. Kenneth Robert Gervais, Mar. 26, 1968 (div. Dec. 1990); 1 child, Lise Catherine Gervais; m. Gary William Domstrand Jr., Feb. 14, 1994. BA in Polit. Sci., Portland State U., 1967; MA in Govt., Georgetown U., 1974. Dep. adminstr. wage and hour divsn. Bur. Labor & Industries, Portland, Oreg., 1981-84; asst. adminstr. Oreg. Employment Divsn., Salem, 1984-91; project mgr. Metro, Portland, 1991-96; adminstr. Oreg. Liquor Control Commn., Milwaukie, 1996—. Mem. faculty Nat. Jud Coll., Reno, 1986, 87. Mem. Am. Soc. Pub. Adminstrs. (pres. Oreg. chpt. 1983, 91, mem. nat. coun. 1984-86), Oreg. Women in Pub. Svc. (founder, pres. 1990-93). Democrat. Mem. Unity Ch. Avocations: skiing, hiking, photography, knitting, reading. Office: Oreg Liquor Control Commn 9079 SE Mcloughlin Blvd Portland OR 97222-7355

ERICKSON, PETER BROWN, librarian, scholar, writer; b. Worcester, Mass., Aug. 11, 1945; s. Irving Peter and Elinor (Brown) E.; m. Tay Gavin, June 30, 1968 (dec. Oct. 1998); children: Andrew Sven, Ingrid Adriana, Benjamin Peter. BA, Amherst Coll., 1967; postgrad., U. Birmingham, Birmingham, Eng., 1967-68; PhD, U. Calif., 1975; MSLS, Simmons Coll., 1984. Asst. prof. Williams Coll., Williamstown, Mass., 1976-81; fellow Wesleyan U., Middletown, Conn., 1981-82; vis. asst. prof. Wesleyan U., Middletown, 1982-83; rsch. lib. Clark Art Inst., Williamstown, Mass., 1985—. Author: Patriarchal Structures in Shakespeare's Drama, 1985, Rewriting Shakespeare Rewriting Ourselves, 1991 (paperback edition, 1994); contbr. essays and book and theater reviews to profl. jours; editor: Festschrift: Shakespeare's Rough Magic, Renaissance Essays in Honor of C.L. Barber, 1985, Making Trifles of Terrors: Redistributing Complicities in Shakespeare, 1997. Recipient Amherst Meml. Fellowship, Amherst Coll., 1967-68, Kent Fellowship, Soc. for Values in Higher Edn., 1981-82. Mem. Shakespeare Assn. of Am., Renaissance Soc. of Am., Modern Language Assn., Appalachian Mt. Club, Phi Beta Kappa. Avocations: running, hiking, canoeing. Home: 81 Buxton Hill Rd Williamstown MA 01267-2773 Office: Clark Art Inst 225 South St # 8 Williamstown MA 01267-2891

ERICKSON, RALPH D., retired physical education educator, small business owner, consultant; b. Beresford, S.D., June 25, 1922; s. John Henning and Ester Christina (Lofgren) E.; m. Nancy Erickson, Sept. 1949 (div. 1961); m. Patricia Erickson, Apr. 1973 (div. 1975); m. Karen Ann Erickson, June 1, 1989; 1 child, Karina Ann. BS in Phys. Edn., Northwestern U., 1949, MA in Edn., 1953. Swim instr., coach Chgo. Park Dist., 1946-54; social studies tchr., swim coach Elmwood Park (Ill.) High Sch., 1954-65; swimming, water polo coach Loyola Univ., Chgo., 1965-87, assoc. prof. phys. edn., 1971-87; salesman Alexander Hamilton Inst., Chgo., 1966-69; tchr. Chgo. Bd. Edn., 1969-70; bd. dirs. Capital Investments & Ventures Corp., Santa Ana, Calif., 1983-93, Cosmopolitan Comm., Santa Ana, 1991-93; vice chmn. Internat. Profl. Assn. Diving Inst., Santa Ana, 1966-93. Author: Under Pressure, 1961, Discover the Under Water World, 1971, V/W Navigation, 1972, Search and Recovery, 1973. Sgt US Army, 1942-45. Recipient Reach Out award Diving Equipment Mfg. Assn.; named to Ill. H.S. Swimming Coaches Hall of Fame, 1982, Athletic Hall of Fame Loyola U. Chgo., 1986. Mem. Profl. Assn. Diving Instrs. (co-founder). Home and Office: 17307 Whippoorwill Trl Leander TX 78645-9734

ERICKSON, RALPH O., botany educator; b. Duluth, Minn., Oct. 27, 1914; s. Charles W. and Stella (Sjostrom) E.; m. Elinor M. Borgstedt, June 17, 1945; children: Diane Erickson Field, Elizabeth Erickson. B.A., Gustavus Adolphus Coll., 1935; M.S., Washington U., St. Louis, 1941; Ph.D., Washington U., 1944. Instr. Gustavus Adolphus Coll., 1935-39; asst. chemist Western Cartridge Co., East Alton, Ill., 1942-44; instr., then asst. prof. botany U. Rochester, N.Y., 1944-47; mem. faculty U. Pa., Phila., 1947—, prof. botany, 1954-85; prof. emeritus U. Pa., 1985—, chmn. grad. group botany, 1957-68, acting dir. div. biology, 1961-63, chmn. grad. group biology, 1968-76, acting chmn. dept. biology, 1977-78. Contbr. articles to profl. jours. Guggenheim fellow Calif. Inst. Tech., 1954-55. Mem. AAAS, Bot. Soc. Am., Soc. Devel. Biology (pres. 1959), Am. Inst. Biol. Scis., Sigma Xi. Home: 3300 Darby Rd Apt 3319 Haverford PA 19041-1071 Office: U Pa 307 Leidy Philadelphia PA 19104

ERICKSON, RAYMOND, academic dean, music historian, musician; b. Mpls., Aug. 2, 1941; s. Ray F. and Irene E. (Banko) E.; m. Carole A. DeSaram, May 15, 1982. BA with high honors, Whittier (Calif) Coll., 1963; PhD, Yale U., 1970. Acting instr. history music Yale U., New Haven, 1968-70; rsch. fellow IBM Sys. Rsch. Inst., N.Y.C., 1970-71; asst. prof. music Queens Coll., CUNY, Flushing, 1971-75, elected mem. Doctoral Programs in Music, 1976—, prof., 1981, chair dept. music, dir. Aaron Copland Sch. Music, 1978-81, dean faculty Coll. Arts and Humanities, 1993—; mem. Queens Coll. Corp. Adv. Bd., 1986—, Queens Coll. Arts Adv. Bd., 1992—. Author: "Musica enchiriadis" and "Scolica enchiriadis", 1995, DARMS: A Reference Manual, 1976; editor: Schubert's Vienna, 1997; artist (CD) Form rosey Bow'rs: Music of Henry Purcell, 1994; contbr. articles to profl. jours. Acad. dir. Aston Magna Found. for Music and Humanities, Inc., Great Barrington, Mass., 1978—; bd. dirs. ex officio Godwin-Ternbach Mus., Flushing, 1993—. Rsch. fellow Alexander von Humboldt Stiftung, Freiburg and Munich, Germany. 1977-78, 84-85. Mem. Alexander von Humboldt Assn. Am. (v.p.), Am. Musicology Soc., Early Music Am., Phi Beta Kappa (hon.), Pi Delta Phi (hon.), Omicron Delta Kappa. Avocations: wine, travel, languages. Office: Queens Coll CUNY Flushing NY 11367-1597

ERICKSON, RICHARD AMES, physicist, emeritus educator; b. Bryant, S.D., Sept. 12, 1923; s. Ray and Mabel Gabriella (Arneson) E.; m. Frances Irene Boyd, June 13, 1943; children: Donna Mae, Jeanne Marie (Mrs. Paul Mahoney), David Ray, Kristine Ann (Mrs. Scott Stewart). B.Sc., S.D. Sch. Mines and Tech., 1944; Ph.D., Tex. A. and M. U., 1952. Predoctoral fellow Oak Ridge Inst. Nuclear Studies, 1949-51; asst. prof. physics U. Tenn., 1951-54; asst. prof. Ohio State U., 1954-61, assoc. prof., 1961-74, prof., 1974-79, prof. emeritus, 1979—; prof. of physics Ind. U. (ITM/MUCIA), Shah Alam, Malaysia, 1987-89; sec. faculty Ohio State U., 1975-77; cons. Lockheed Research Lab., Palo Alto, Calif., 1964, AID, India, 1965; Mem. Univ. Area Commn., Columbus, Ohio, 1973-74. Contbg. author: Methods of Experimental Physics, vol. 3, 1961; Contbr. articles to profl. jours. Served with USNR, 1944-46. Home: 440 N Meier St Spearfish SD 57783-1979

ERICKSON, RICHARD BEAU, insurance and financial company executive; b. Chgo., May 14, 1952; s. Charles Arthur and Carole Annette (Beaumont) E. BS, U. Ky., 1974, MBA, 1975. CLU. Sales rep. Met. Life and affiliated cos., Chgo. Hgts., Ill., 1975-78; sales mgr. Met. Life and affiliated cos., Flossmoor, Ill., 1978-80; mktg. specialist Met. Life and affiliated cos., Aurora, Ill., 1980-81; branch mgr. Met. Life and affiliated cos., Orland Park, Ill., 1981-84; corp. dir. Met. Life Gen. Ins. Agy. Inc., N.Y.C., 1984-86; regional sales mgr. Met. Life Gen. Ins. Agy. Inc., L.A., 1986-89, agy. v.p., sr. mktg. and sales exec., 1989-98, agy. v.p., 1989-95, regional v.p., 1996-98; CEO, pres. Greater L.A. Fin. Group, Inc., L.A., 1999—; rep. (Midwest) Sales Mgr. Adv., N.Y.C., 1979; dir. South Cook County Assn. Life Underwriters, Chgo., 1983. Author: Met. Manpower Development, 1981, Met. Manpower Development: A Guideline for Success, 1986. Mem. Nat. Assn. Securities Dealers, Life Underwriters Tng. Counsel, Chartered Life Underwriters, Nat. Assn. Life Underwriters, Gen. Agts. & Mgrs. Assn., Sigma Nu. Avocations: coaching soccer, hiking, Norwegian Elkhound dog shows, mountain climbing. Fax: 310-789-7999. Office: Greater LA Fin Group 1801 Ave of the Stars Ste 1444 Los Angeles CA 90067

ERICKSON, ROBERT ALLEN, English literature educator; b. Fargo, N.D., Apr. 1, 1940; s. Allen Gerald and Ruth Dorothy (Dahl) E.; m. Liisa Raatikainen, Nov. 21, 1966; children: Martin, Stephen, Annaliisa. AB, Boston U., 1962; MA, Yale U., 1964, PhD, 1966. Asst. instr. in English Yale U., New Haven, 1965; asst. prof. of English U. Calif., Santa Barbara, 1966-73, lectr. in English with security, 1973-77, assoc. prof. of English, 1977-85, prof. English, 1985—. Author: Mother Midnight, 1986, (with others) The History of John Bull, 1976, The Language of the Heart, 1600-1750, 1997; contbr. articles to profl. jours. Woodrow Wilson fellowship, 1962-63, Fulbright fellowship, U.S. Govt., 1965-66; Augustus Howe Buck scholarship Boston U., 1958-60, Fulbright Fellow (Finland), 1999—. Mem. Am. Soc. for Eighteenth Century Studies. Home: 2517 Medcliff Rd Santa Barbara CA 93109-1819 Office: Dept English U Calif Dept English Santa Barbara CA 93105

ERICKSON, ROBERT ANDERS, optical engineer, physicist; b. Benson, Minn., Aug. 6, 1962; s. Wilton Robert and Irene Dorothy (Fenstra) E.; m. Deborah Popovchak, June 18, 1994; 1 child, Jeremy. BS in Physics, S.D. Sch. Mines and Tech., 1985; MS in Physics, U. Mo., St. Louis, 1989. Instr. physics S.D. Sch. Mines and Tech., Rapid City, 1984-85; optical software devel. engr., physicist McDonnell Douglas Corp., St. Louis, 1985—. Twin Cities scholar, 1981, Frank & Portia Vanlueve scholar, 1983. Mem. IEEE, Optical Soc. Am., Am. Inst. Physics, Sigma Pi Sigma (chpt. pres. 1984-85). Republican. Lutheran. Home: 3120 Wabash Ave Granite City IL 62040-5100 Office: Boeing Co Dept 312 M/C 51069253 PO Box 516 # 257 Saint Louis MO 63166-0516

ERICKSON, ROBERT STANLEY, lawyer; b. Kemmerer, Wyo., Apr. 17, 1944; s. Stanley W. and Dorothy Marie (Johnson) E.; m. Alice Norman, Dec. 27, 1972; children: Robert Badger, Erin Elizabeth, Andrew Carl, Scott Stanley, Courtney Ellen, Brennan Marie. BS in Bus., U. Idaho, 1966; JD, U. Utah, 1969; LLM in Taxation, George Washington U., 1973. Bar: U.S. Supreme Ct. 1973, U.S. Ct. Appeals (9th cir.) 1980, U.S. Dist. Ct. Idaho 1973, U.S. Tax Ct. 1969, Idaho 1973, Utah 1969. Assoc. atty. Office of Chief Counsel, Dept. Treasury, Washington, 1969-73; assoc. Elam, Burke, Jeppesen, Evans & Boyd, Boise, Idaho, 1973-77; ptnr. Elam, Burke, Evans, Boyd & Koontz, Boise, 1977-81; spl. counsel Holme Roberts & Owen, Salt Lake City, 1981-83; ptnr. Hansen & Erickson, Boise, 1983-85, Hawley Troxell Ennis & Hawley, Boise, 1985—. Contbr. articles to profl. jours. Named Citizen of Yr., Boise Exch. Club, 1980. Fellow Am. Coll. of Trust and Estate Counsel (past Idaho chmn. 1993—); mem. ABA (sect. on taxation, com. state and local taxes), IRS/Western Region Bar Assn. (mem., past chmn. liaison com. Idaho co-chair local task force IRS non-filer program 1993), Idaho State Bar (founding chmn. taxation, probate and trust law sect.), Utah State Bar (tax and estate planning sect.), Boise Estate Planning Council, Idaho State Tax Inst. (exec. com., numerous other local and nat. coms.). Mem. LDS Ch. Office: Hawley Troxell Ennis & Hawley First Interstate Ctr 877 Main St Ste 1000 Boise ID 83702-5884

ERICKSON, RODNEY ALLEN, dean, educator; b. Frederic, Wis., Oct. 3, 1946; s. Reuben Alexander and Elva Imogene (Bergman) E.; m. Sharon Lea Young, May 3, 1969; children: Craig, Jeffrey. BA, U. Minn., 1968, MA, 1970; PhD, U. Wash., 1973. Asst. prof. U. Wis., Madison, 1973-77; asst. prof. Pa. State U., University Park, 1977-79, assoc. prof., 1979-84, prof., 1984—, dean grad. sch., 1995-99, v.p. for rsch., 1997-99, exec. v.p., provost, 1999—. Staff sgt. USAR, 1966-72. Simon Sr. rsch. fellow U. Manchester (England), 1982, Census rsch. fellow NSF, Washington, 1989; sr. rsch. scholar Fulbright Commn., Washington, 1982. Mem. Am. Geographical Soc. (councilor 1984-96). Avocations: grain farming, windsurfing, skiing. E-mail: rae@psu.edu. Fax: (814) 863-9659. Office: Pa State U 304 Old Main University Park PA 16802-3300

ERICKSON, RONALD A., retail executive. CEO Holiday Cos., Mpls. Office: Holiday Companies PO Box 1224 Minneapolis MN 55440-1224*

ERICKSON, VIRGINIA BEMMELS, chemical engineer; b. Sleepy Eye, Minn., June 19, 1948; d. Gordon Boothe and Marion Mae (Rieke) Bemmels; m. Larry Douglas Erickson, Sept. 6, 1969; children: Kirsten Danielle, Dean Michael. Diploma in Nursing, Swedish Hosp. Sch. Nursing, 1969; BSChemE, U. Wash., 1983, MChemE, 1985. RN. Asst. head nurse N. Meml. Hosp., Mpls., 1970-73; intensive care RN Swedish Med. Ctr., Seattle, 1973-83; research asst. U. Wash., Seattle, 1983-85; instrumentation and control engr. CH2M Hill, Bellevue, Wash., 1985—, mgr. dept., 1988-93, mgr. info. mgmr., 1994—, v.p., 1995—; cons. instrumentation and control engr. Mem. editorial adv. bd. Control. Leader Girl Scouts U.S., Seattle, 1985; supt. Seattle Ch. Sch., 1983; rep. United Way, 1986—. Recipient Cert. Achievement, Soc. Women Engrs., 1983, Teenfeed, 1990. Mem. AAUW, Instrument Soc. Am., Tau Beta Pi. Democrat. Mem. United Methodist Ch. Avocations: running, soccer, music, cooking. Home: 6026 24th Ave NE Seattle WA 98115-7009 Office: CH2M Hill PO Box 91500 777 108th Ave NE Bellevue WA 98009-2050

ERICKSON, W(ALTER) BRUCE, business and economics educator, entrepreneur; b. Chgo., Mar. 4, 1938; s. Clifford Eric and Mildred B. (Brinkmeier) E. BA, Mich. State U., 1959, MA, 1960, PhD in Econs., 1965. Rsch. assoc. subcom. on antitrust and monopoly U.S. Senate, 1960-61; asst. prof. econs. Bowling Green (Ohio) U., 1964-66; asst. prof. bus. and govt. Coll. Bus. Adminstrn., U. Minn., Mpls., 1966-70; assoc. prof. Coll. Bus. Adminstrn., U. Minn., 1971-75, prof. dept. mgmt., 1975—, prof., chmn. dept. mgmt., 1977-80, co-chmn., then chmn., 1988-92; bd. dirs. various bus., non-profit and venture capital orgns.; cons. rock salt antitrust cases for atty. gens. Mich., cons. rock salt antitrust cases for atty. gens. Calif., Ill., Wis., Minn.; cons. U.S. Justice Dept. Author: An Introduction to Contemporary Business, 4th edit., 1985, Government and Business, 1980, 2d edit., 1984, International Business, 1998; co-author: International Business, 1998; bd. editors Antitrust Law and Econs. Rev., Jour. Indsl. Orgn.; contbr. articles to profl. jours. Bd. dirs. Found. for Constl. Edn. and the Citizens League, 1991-92; mem. ethics com. Ebenezer System, Minn. Mem. Am. Econ. Assn., Royal Econ. Soc. Office: Carlson Sch Mgmt 321 19th Ave S Minneapolis MN 55455-0438

ERICKSON, WILLIAM HURT, retired state supreme court justice; b. Denver, May 11, 1924; s. Arthur Xavier and Virginia (Hurt) E.; m. Doris Rogers, Dec. 24, 1953; children: Barbara Ann, Virginia Lee, Stephen Arthur, William Taylor. Degree in petroleum engring., Colo. Sch. Mines, 1947; student, U. Mich., 1949; LLB, U. Va., 1950. Bar: Colo. 1951. Pvt. practice Denver; justice Colo. Supreme Ct., 1971-96, chief justice, 1983-86; faculty NYU Appellate Judges Sch., 1972-85; mem. exec. Commn. on Accreditation of Law Enforcement Agys., 1980-83; chmn. Pres.'s Nat. Commn. for Rev. of Fed. and State Laws Relating to Wiretapping and Electronic Surveillance, 1976. Chmn. Erickson Commn., 1997. With USAAF, 1943. Recipient Disting. Achievement medal Colo. Sch. Mines, 1990. Fellow Internat. Acad. Trial Lawyers (former sec.), Am. Coll. Trial Lawyers, Am. Bar Found. (chmn. 1985), Internat. Soc. Barristers (pres. 1971); mem. ABA, (bd. govs. 1975-79, former chmn. com. on standards criminal justice, former chmn. coun. criminal law sect., former chmn. com. to implement standards criminal justice, mem. long-range planning com., action com. to reduce ct. cost and delay), Colo. Bar Assn. (award of merit 1989), Denver Bar Assn. (past pres., trustee), Am. Law Inst. (coun.), Practising Law Inst. (nat. adv. coun., bd. govs. Colo.), Freedoms Found. at Valley Forge (nat. coun. trustees, 1986—), Order of Coif, Scribes (pres. 1978). Home: 10 Martin Ln Englewood CO 80110-4821

ERICKSTAD, RALPH JOHN, judge, retired state supreme court chief justice; b. Starkweather, N.D., Aug. 15, 1922; s. John T. and Anna Louisa (Myklebust) E.; m. Lois Katherine Jacobson, July 30, 1949; children: Student, U. N.D., 1940-43; B.Sc. in Law, U. Minn., 1947, JD, 1949. Bar: N.D. 1949. Practiced in Devils Lake, 1949-62; State's atty. Ramsey County, 1953-57; mem. N.D. Senate from, Ramsey County, 1957-62; asst. majority floor leader N.D. Senate from, 1959, 61; assoc. justice Supreme Ct. N.D., Bismarck, 1963-73, chief justice, 1973-93, surrogate judge; treas. N.D. States Attys. Assn., 1955, v.p., 1956; mem. N.D. Legislative Research Com., 1957-59, N.D. Budget Bd., 1961-63, Gov. N.D. Spl. Com. Labor, 1960. Past mem. exec. com. Mo. Valley council Boy Scouts Am.; chmn. bd. trustees Mo. Valley Family YMCA, 1966-77. Served with USAAF, 1943-45, ETO. Recipient Silver Beaver award Boy Scouts Am., 1967, Sioux award U. N.D., 1973, 1st Disting. Service award Missouri Valley Family YMCA, 1978, Disting. Service award Nat. Ctr. for State Cts., 1989, N.D. Nat. Leadership award of excellence, 1987, "Chief Justice Ralph J. Erickstad Eagle Class" named in his honor, Frontier trails dist., No. Lights council, Boy Scouts Am., 1983. Mem. ABA, N.D. Bar Assn. (disting. svc. award 1988), Burleigh County Bar Assn., State Justice Inst. (bd. dirs. 1987-90), Nat. Conf. Chief Justices (exec. council 1977-78, 1980-82, pres. 1983-84), Am. Judicature Soc. (Herbert Harley award 1992), Am. Law Inst., Nat. Ctr. for State Cts. (pres. 1983-84), Task Force on Pub. Image of Cts., Williamsburg Conf.-State Courts: A Blueprint for the Future, 1978, Am. Legion (life). Lutheran (del. 1st biennial conv., mem. nominating com.). Clubs: Am. Legion, VFW, Kiwanian. Office: ND Supreme Ct Judicial Wing 1st Fl 600 E Boulevard Ave Bismarck ND 58505-0660*

ERICSON, BRUCE ALAN, lawyer; b. Buffalo, Feb. 28, 1952; s. Carl H. and Jean (Herman) E.; m. Elizabeth Whitney Burton, Feb. 6, 1988; children: John Cotton, Whitney Burton. AB, U. Pa., 1974; JD, Harvard U., 1977. Bar: Calif. 1977, U.S. Dist. Ct. (no. dist.) Calif, 1977, U.S. Dist. Ct. (ea. dist. and so. dist.) Calif. 1988, U.S. Dist. Ct. Ariz. 1992, U.S. Ct. Appeals (9th cir.) 1981, U.S. Ct. Appeals (11th cir.), 1991, U.S. Ct. Appeals (D.C. cir.) 1994, U.S. Supreme Ct. 1982. Assoc. Pillsbury, Madison & Sutro, San Francisco, 1977-84, ptnr., 1985—; judge pro tem. San Francisco Mcpl. Ct., 1984—. Mem. ABA, San Francisco Bar Assn., Phi Beta Kappa. Republican. Club: Olympic (San Francisco). Avocations: skiing, squash. Office: Pillsbury Madison & Sutro LLP 235 Montgomery St Fl 16 San Francisco CA 94104-3074

ERICSON, HAROLD LOUIS, telephone engineer; b. Hector, Minn., Dec. 11, 1909; s. Alfred Louis and Mabel (Grover) E.; m. Ella Louise Benson, Aug. 6, 1931 (div. 1968); children: Charles, James, Rolfe; m. Lillian Leiferman, June 5, 1968. BA, Cornell Coll., Mt. Vernon, Iowa, 1936. Pres. Minn. Ctrl. Telephone Co., Hector, 1952-68, N.Am. Commun. Corp., Mpls., 1968-70, Frontier Telephone Co., Mpls., 1970-73; pres. Cencom Corp., Rushford, Minn., 1973-75, chmn. bd., 1975-77; pres. Hecto Co., Castle Rock, Minn., 1970—, Futures Found., Castle Rock, 1980—. Author: Handbook for Survival, 1989. Mem. Acoustical Soc. Am., Rotary (pres. 1992-93). Achievements include patent for instrument for gliders. Home: 4436 280th St W Castle Rock MN 55010 Office: Hecto Co Futures Found 4430 280th St W Castle Rock MN 55011

ERICSON, JAMES DONALD, lawyer, insurance executive; b. Hawarden, Iowa, Oct. 12, 1935; s. Elmer H. and Martha (Sydness) E.; children: Linda Jean, James Robert. B.A. in History, State U. Iowa, 1958, J.D., 1962. Bar: Wis. 1965. Assoc. Fitzgerald, Brown, Leahy, McGill & Strom, Omaha, 1962-65; with Northwestern Mut. Life Ins. Co., Milw., 1965—, asst. to pres., 1972-75, dir. policy benefits, 1975-76, v.p., gen. counsel, sec., 1976-80, sr. v.p., 1980, exec. v.p., 1987, pres., 1990; chief operating officer Northwestern Mut. Life Ins. Co., 1991-93, pres., CEO, 1993—; dir. MGIC Investment Corp., Green Bay Packaging Inc., Am. Coun. Life Ins., Kohl's Corp., Consol. Papers, Inc., Northwestern Mut. Investment Svcs.; chair Am. Coun. Life Ins. Bd. dirs. Wis. Taxpayers Alliance, Competitive Wis., Inc., Greater Milw. Com., Milw. Redevel. Com., Marcus Ctr. for the Performing Arts, United Way, Met. Milw. Assn. Commerce, Med. Coll. Wis., Milw. Sch. Engring.; trustee Lawrence U., Com. for Econ. Devel., Boys and Girls Club Greater Milw. Mem. ABA, Assn. Life Ins. Counsel (hon.), Wis. Bar Assn., Milw. Club (bd. dirs.), Phi Beta Kappa. Republican. Presbyterian. Office: Northwestern Mut Life Ins Co 720 E Wisconsin Ave Milwaukee WI 53202-4797

ERICSON, JON MEYER, academic administrator, rhetoric theory educator; b. Three Forks, Mont., Aug. 1, 1928; s. George Edward and Olga Young (Meyer) E.; m. Amy Knutson, Aug. 19, 1951; children: Jon, Beth, Joel, Ingrid. BA, Pacific Luth. Coll., 1952; MA, Stanford U., 1953, PhD, 1961. Instr. argumentation, pub. speaking, rhetorical theory and criticism Tex. Luth. Coll., Seguin, 1953-54; asst. prof., dir. forensics Pacific Luth. Coll., Tacoma, Wash., 1954-57; instr. Stanford (Calif.) U., 1959-61, asst. prof., 1961-64; from assoc. prof. to prof., dept. head Cen. Wash. State U., Ellensburg, 1964-70, prof. dept. speech communication, 1988-95; dean sch. liberal arts Calif. Poly. State U., San Luis Obispo, 1970-88, dept. dir. London Study Program, 1984-96. Co-author: The Debater's Guide, 1961; contbg. author: Demosthenes on the Crown, 1967, Public Speaking as Dialogue, 1970; contbr. articles to profl. jours. and books. Pres. Pacific Forensic League, 1961-62, No. Calif. Forensic Assn., 1962-63; mem., trustee Pacific Luth. Theol. Sem., Berkeley, 1961-64. Served with USN, 1946-48. Danforth tchr., 1957; Univ. Honors scholarship Stanford U., 1957-61. Lutheran. Avocations: tennis, gardening. Home: 741 Pasatiempo Dr San Luis Obispo CA 93405-1033

ERICSON, PHYLLIS JANE, psychologist, psychotherapist, consultant; b. Ft. Worth, Aug. 16, 1947; d. John H. and Charlotte Marie (Turner) E.; divorced; children: Colleen Nichole Murphy Pass, Sean Matthew Murphy Pass. B. Gen. Studies in Bus. Mgmt. and Advt., U. Tex., Arlington, 1981; MA in Psychology and Psychotherapy, Antioch U., 1990; Grad. in Psychology, Union Inst., Cin., 1995. Registered and cert. hypnotist, Calif.; cert. chem. dependency counselor, Tex.; lic. profl. counselor, marriage and family therapist, chem. dependency counselor, Tex.; cert. nat. and neurolinguist programming master strategist. Clk.-typist Gen. Dynamics Corp., Ft. Worth, 1965-69; counselor Snelling & Snelling Pers., Ft. Worth, 1970-72; account exec. Ft. Worth Star Telegram, 1972-79; v.p., prin. Ericson Assocs., Inc., Hurst, Tex., 1979-83; account exec. L.A.Times, Times Mirror Corp., 1983; nat. advt. dir. Baker Comm., Beverly Hills, Calif., 1984; owner, prin., builder GE Rehabs, Ft. Worth, 1984-86; counselor Comprehensive Counseling (later Ctrl. Psychol. Svcs.), Hurst, 1988-91; dir., counselor, cons., awareness counseling of DFW Ctrl. Psychol. Svcs., St. Marteen, Netherlands, Antilles & Ft. Lauderdale, Fla., 1988—; counselor J. Marszalek & Assoc., Dallas, 1984-87, Wynrose Outpatient Program, Arlington, Tex., 1988-89, HCA Richland Hosp., North Richland Hills, Tex., 1988-89; crisis intervention counselor Suicide and Crisis Ctr., Dallas, 1987-88; pvt. practice Ctr. for Counseling Devel. Svcs., Ft. Worth, 1987-88; group facilitator, clin. cons. Bedford Meadows Hosp., 1989-91; instr. psychology dept. Tex. Wesleyan U., 1989; mem. allied staff, group facilitator Charter Hosp.-Grapevine, Tex., 1991-92. Mem. The Am. Psychotherapy Assn. (diplomat). Avocations: travel, education, writing, lecturing, water and snow sports. Address: 1100 E Lamar Blvd Apt 4 Arlington TX 76011-4322

ERICSON, RICHARD VICTOR, social science-law educator, university official; b. Montreal, Que., Sept. 20, 1948; s. John William and Elizabeth Mary (Hinkley) E.; m. Diana Lea McMillan, May 31, 1969; 1 child, Matthew Simon. BA, U. Guelph, Ont., 1969; MA, U. Toronto, 1971; PhD, Cambridge U., Eng., 1974, LittD, 1991. Asst. prof. U. Toronto, 1974-79, assoc. prof., 1979-82, prof. sociology, prof. criminology, 1982-93, dir. Ctr. of Criminology, 1992-93; prof. sociology, prof. law U. B.C., Vancouver, 1993—, prin. Green Coll., 1993—; vis. rsch. prof. Coll. Pub. Programs Ariz. State U., Tempe, 1991; vis. fellow Inst. Criminology Cambridge U., 1979, 84-85, Churchill Coll. Cambridge U., 1979, 84-85, All Souls Coll., Oxford, 1998—. Author: Making Crime (2d edit.), 1993; co-author: Negotiating Control, 1989, Representing Order, 1991, Policing the Risk Society, 1997. Hon. vis. fellow Green Coll., Oxford, 1993—, assoc. sr. fellow Massey Coll., Toronto, Ont., Can. Fellow Royal Soc. Can. Home: Principal's Residence, Green College at U BC, Vancouver, BC Canada V6T 1Z1 Office: Green College at U BC, 6201 Cecil Green Park Rd, Vancouver, BC Canada V6T 1Z1

ERICSON, ROBERT WALTER, lawyer; b. Highland Park, Ill., June 24, 1948. BA, Johns Hopkins U., 1970, MA, 1971; JD, U. Va., 1976. Bar: Ill. 1976, N.Y. 1992. Ptnr. Winston & Strawn, N.Y.C. Mem. ABA, N.Y. State Bar Assn. Office: Winston & Strawn 200 Park Ave Rm 4100 New York NY 10166-0005*

ERICSON, ROGER DELWIN, lawyer, forest resource company executive; b. Moline, Ill, Dec. 21, 1934; s. Carl D. and Linnea E. (Challman) E.; m. Norma F. Brown, Aug. 1, 1957; children: Catherine Lynn, David. AB, Stetson U., DeLand, Fla., 1958, JD, 1958; MBA, U. Chgo., 1971. Bar: Fla. 1958, Ill. 1959, Ind. 1974. Atty. Brunswick Corp., Skokie, Ill., 1959-62; asst. sec., asst. gen. counsel Chemetron Corp., Chgo., 1962-73; asst. v.p. Inland Container Corp., Indpls., 1973-75, v.p., gen. counsel, sec., 1975-83; v.p., gen. counsel, sec. Temple-Inland, Inc., 1983-94, of counsel, 1994—; v.p., sec. bd. dirs. Inland Container Corp.; dir., pres., co-CEO Kraft Land Svcs., Inc., Atlanta, 1978-88; bd. dirs., v.p. Guaranty Holdings Inc., Dallas; v.p. Temple-Inland Fin. Svcs., Inc., Austin, 1990-94; bd. dirs. Temple-Inland Forest Products, Temple-Inland Real Estate Investment, Inc., Temple-Inland Realty Inc. Trustee Chgo. Homes for Children, 1971-74; mem. alumni coun. U. Chgo., 1972-76; mem. Palatine Twp. Youth Comm., 1969-72; sect. chmn. Chgo. Heart Assn., 1972, 73; alumni bd. dirs. Stetson U.; bd. dirs. Temple-Inland Found; mem. Safe and Drug-Free Comm. Collier County Sch. Bd., 1996—. Mem. ABA, Am. Arbitration Assn. (nat. panel of comml. arbitrators), Am. Soc. corp. Secs., Am. Forest Products Assn. (past mem. govt. affairs com. and legal com.), Am. Corp. Counsel Assn., Ill Bar Assn., Ind. Bar Assn., Fla. Bar Assn., Chgo. Bar Assn., Indpls. Bar Assn. (chmn. corp. counsel sect., mem. profl. responsibility com. 1982), Collier County Bar Assn., Indpls. C. of C. (mem. govt. affairs com.), Plum Grove Club (pres. 1967), Collier's Reserve Country Club, Omicron Delta Kappa, Phi Delta Phi. Home: 12502 Colliers Reserve Dr Naples FL 34110-0915 Office: Temple-Inland Inc Drawer N Diboll TX 75941 *Concentrate on the desired final result of any activity. Never forget your family, co-workers, friends.*

ERIE, GRETCHEN ANN, cardiovascular clinician; b. Mason City, Iowa, June 18, 1945; d. Donald W. and Eloise M. Schultz; m. Thomas H. Erie, Aug. 19, 1990; stepchildren: Aaron, April. BSN, U. Iowa, 1967. RN; cert. basic life support, St. Paul. Staff nurse U. Iowa Hosp., Iowa City, 1967-68, Meth. Hosp., Houston, 1968-69; staff nurse cardiovascular surgery U. Minn. Hosp., Mpls., 1969-72, insvc. nurse cardiovascular surgery, 1972-75, head nurse cardiovascular surgery, 1975-81; nurse clinician Cardiac Surg. Assn., Mpls., 1981—; speaker U. Minn. Hosp. Community Edn. Dept., various cities in Minn., 1975-81, United Hosp., St. Paul, 1982, 87. Pianist Pleasant Hills Nursing Home, St. Paul, 1987-89; flutist North Heights Luth. Ch., St. Paul, 1987—; mem. Gloryland Band, 1994—; patterning exerciser Handicapped Toddler, St. Paul, 1987-88; leader singles group North Heights Luth. Ch., 1984-88, paticipant Splendor of Christmas and Passion play, co-leader Bible study group, 1993—. Mem. AACN, Am. Heart Assn. Republican. Lutheran. Avocations: biking, gardening, downhill skiing, flute playing, travel. Home: 3220 Orchard Ct White Bear Lk MN 55110-5385 Office: Cardiac Surg Assn 920 E 28th St Ste 420 Minneapolis MN 55407-1187

ERIE, STEVEN PHILIP, political science educator; b. Bakersfield, Calif., Jan. 28, 1946; s. Harlan Eugene Erie (dec.) and Carmen Joyce (O'Brien) Barr. BA, UCLA, 1967, MA, 1969, PhD, 1975. Asst. prof. pub. adminstrn. U. So. Calif., L.A., 1975-78; asst. prof. polit. sci. SUNY, Albany, 1978-80; policy analyst U.S. Dept. Health and Human Svcs., Washington, 1980-81; asst. prof. U. Calif. San Diego, La Jolla, 1981-89, assoc. prof. polit. sci., adj. prof. history, 1989—; cons. L.A. Pub. Commn. on County Govt., 1975-76, Ednl. Testing Svc., Princeton, N.J., 1989-91; faculty, cons. Inst. for Ct. Mgmt., Denver, 1978-80; cons. RAND, Santa Monica, 1997—, Metropolitan Forum Project, L.A., 1997—; sr. fellow So. Calif. Studies Ctr., L.A., 1997—. Author: Rainbow's End, 1988 (Best Book on Urban Politics, Am. Polit. Sci. Assn. 1989); contbg. editor Metro Investment Report, 1994—; mem. editl. adv. bd. U. Press of Va., Charlottesville, 1993—. Active Citizens Charter Reform Com., San Diego, 1993, San Diego Dialogue, 1995—, Citizens Coordinate for Century Three, San Diego, 1996; bd. dirs. Water and Power Assocs., L.A., 1994—. Charles F. Scott Meml. fellow UCLA Pacific Coun. on Internat. Pol., 1972-73; Faculty fellow Nat. Assn. Schs. of Pub. Affairs and Adminstrn., Washington, 1980-81; Faculty Rsch. grantee Calif. Policy Seminar, Berkeley, 1990, 94. Mem. Am. Polit. Sci. Assn. (exec. coun. urban politics sect. 1989-91, chair book prize com. 1991), Western Polit. Sci. Assn., Orgn. Am. Historians, Calif. Hist. Soc. Avocations: reading, tennis, swimming. Office: Univ Calif San Diego Dept Polit Sci La Jolla CA 92093

ERIKSEN, CHARLES WALTER, psychologist, educator; b. Omaha, Feb. 4, 1923; s. Charles Hans and Louella (Carlson) E.; m. Garnita Tharp, July 22, 1945 (div. Jan. 1971); children: Michael John, Kathy Ann; m. Barbara Becker, Apr. 1971. BA summa cum laude, U. Omaha, 1943; PhD, Stanford, 1950. Asst. prof. Johns Hopkins U., Balt., 1949-53, research scientist, 1954-55; lectr. Harvard U., Cambridge, Mass., 1953-54; mem. faculty U. Ill., Urbana, 1956—, prof., 1959-93, prof. emeritus, 1993—; rsch. cons. VA, 1960-80; mem. psycho-biology panel NSF, 1963; mem. exptl. psychology study sect. NIH, 1958-62, 66-70; Pillsbury Meml. lectr. Cornell U., 1966; keynote address 1st Internat. Congress on Visual Search, U. Durham, U.K., 1988, European Congress for Cognitive Psychology, Elsinore, Denmark, 1993; invited lectr. Max Plank Inst., Munich, 1993, Universidad Autonoma de Madrid, 1993, U. of Salamanca, Spain, 1993. Author: Behavior and Awareness, 1962; editor Am. Jour. Psychology, 1968; prin. editor Perception and Psychophysics, 1971-93; cons. editor Jour. Exptl. Psychology, 1965-71, Jour. Gerontology, 1980—; contbr. articles to profl. jours. Recipient Stratton award Am. Psychopath. Assn., 1964, NIMH Research Career award, 1964. Fellow AAAS; mem. Am. Psychol. Soc., Psychonomic Soc., Soc. Exptl. Psychologists, Midwestern Psychol. Assn., Sigma Xi. Home: 22485 State Highway 133 Oakland IL 61943-6822 Office: U Ill Psychol Bldg 603 E Daniel St Champaign IL 61820-6232

ERIKSEN, DAN OLUF, film director; b. Seattle, Sept. 24, 1925; s. Oluf and Esther K. (Andersen) E.; m. Delphina I. Brownlee, Apr. 20, 1954 (div. 1960); 1 child, Lynn Michele. Student, U. Wash., 1946-47. Film dir. numerous feature films and commls.; asst. dir. including The Pawnbroker, 1965, A Thousand Clowns, 1965, Truman Capote's Christmas Memory, 1966; dir. A Midsummer Night's Dream, 1966. USMC, 1943-45. Mem. Dirs. Guild Am. Lutheran. Avocations: reading, listening to classical music, walking, bike riding. Home: 39 Union St Boothbay Harbor ME 04538-2117

ERIKSEN, LISA MARY, museum director; b. Lynwood, Calif., Jan. 15, 1962; d. Villy and Nora (Welsh) E. BA in History with distinction, U. Calif., Santa Barbara, 1989; M in Mus. Edn., John F. Kennedy U., 1992. Collections processor Oakland (Calif.) Mus., 1989-91; interpretive intern Fowler Mus. Cultural History, UCLA, 1991; asst. dir. Vallejo (Calif.) Naval and Hist. Mus., 1991-92; dir. Benicia (Calif.) Camel Barn Mus., 1992—; interpretive intern, classroom thcr. Oakland Mus., 1990; spkr. in field. Vol. evaluator Western Mus. Conf., L.A., 1990; vol. Benicia Welcome Wagon; mem. hist. home tour com. Benicia Hist. Soc., 1993; mem. libr. opening celebration com. Friends of the Benicia Pub. Libr., 1993; charter mem. sibling devel. com. Assn. for Retarded Citizens Calif., 1993; mentor dept. mus. studies John F. Kennedy U. Recipient Cert. of Appreciation Vallejo Unified Sch. Dist., 1992. Mem. Am. Assn. Mus., Calif. Assn. Mus. (co-host ann. conf. 1993), Amnesty Internat., Benicia C. of C. (mem. tourism com. 1992—).

ERIKSEN, NORMAN JOHN, librarian, research historian; b. Freeport, N.Y., Mar. 21, 1959. BA in Edn., State U. Coll., Fredonia, N.Y., 1981; MLS, C.W. Post Coll., L.I. U., Brookville, N.Y., 1990. Cert. libr. Sales assoc. Svc. Mdse., Huntington, N.Y., 1982-84; retail dept. mgr. Svc. Mdse., East Meadow, Lake Grove, N.Y., 1984-86; office mgr. Conran's Habitat, Manhasset, N.Y., 1986-89; reference libr. Bklyn. Pub. Libr., 1989-92, divsn. chief, 1992—; mem. steering com. TRAIN, N.Y.C., 1993—. Vol. hist. interpreter Old Bethpage (N.Y.) Village Restoration, 1988—. Mem. ALA (social responsibilities round table 1997—), Pub. Libr. Assn., N.Y. Libr. Assn., Greenlawn Centreport Hist. Assn., 119th N.Y. State Vols. Hist. Assn. (treas. 1994—). Office: Bklyn Pub Libr Edn Job Info Ctr Grand Army Plz Brooklyn NY 11238

ERIKSEN, OTTO LOUIS, retired manufacturing company executive; b. Pitts., Jan. 28, 1930; s. Gabriel Soma and Catherine Lilian (Veatch) E.; m. Carmen Licano, July 4, 1981; children by previous marriage: Victor Soma, Catherine Ethel, Gregory Louis. Cert. in indsl. engring., Internat. Corr. Schs., 1965; student law, LaSalle U., 1966-68. Product line mgr. ITT Marlow Co., Midland Park, N.J., 1964-69; gen. mgr. ITT Jabsco, Costa Mesa, Calif., 1969-71; pres. ITT Marine & Recreation Components, Costa Mesa, 1971-83, ITT Jabsco Worldwide, 1983-90. Mem. Granite Falles and Desert Springs Golf Clubs (Surprise, Ariz.). Republican. Episcopalian. Home and Office: 18315 N Key Estrella Dr Surprise AZ 85374-6314

ERIKSON, G(EORGE) E(MIL) (ERIK ERIKSON), anatomist, archivist, historian, educator, information specialist; b. Palmer, Mass., May 3, 1920; s. Emil and Sofia (Gustafson) E.; m. Suzanne J. Henderson, Apr. 23, 1950; children: Ann, David, John, Thomas. BS, Mass. State Coll. (now U. Mass.), 1941; MA in Biology, Harvard U., 1946, PhD in Biology, 1948. Reader in history of sci. and learning Harvard U., 1943-45, asst. prof. gen. edn. in biology, 1949-52, lectr. anthropology, 1965; instr. anatomy Harvard Med. Sch., 1947-49, rsch. fellow anatomy, 1949-52, assoc. in anatomy, 1952-55, asst. prof. anatomy, 1955-65, assoc. curator Warren Anat. Mus., 1961-65; prof. med. sci. Brown U., Providence, 1965-90, prof. emeritus, 1990—, chmn. sect. morphology, 1968-85, co-chmn. sect. population biology, morphology & genetics and chmn. for anatomy, 1985-90; visiting prof., Dept. Anatomy and Cellular Biology Harvard U. Med. Sch., 1990-91; visiting lectr. in surgery Med. Sch. Harvard U., 1991—; anatomist dept. surgery Mass. Gen. Hosp., Boston, 1990—; pres. Erikson Biographical Institute, Inc., Providence, 1990—; adv. bd. Reed Elsevier, 1990; anatomist various Boston hosps., 1952-82, Mass. Gen. Hosp. Sch. Med. Illus., 1947-60, Mass. Gen. Hosp., 1990—, Lahey Clinic, Boston, 1947-60; anatomist depts. surgery, orthopedics & rehab., and neurosurgery R.I. Hosp.; cons. anatomist Surg. Techniques Illus., 1976-80; cons. Dorlands Illus. Med. Dictionary; Rockefeller Found. cons. med. and pub. health, S. Am., 1959; specialist State Dept., Brazil, 1962, (Fulbright Fellow); adj. mem. faculty R.I. Sch. Design, 1970—; Kate Hurd Mead lecturer Coll. Physicians Phila., 1977; Raymond C. Truex lecturer Hahnemann U. Sch. Med., 1985; adj. mem. faculty R.I. Sch. of Design, Providence, 1970—. Sheldon traveling fellow, Cent. Am., 1946; Guggenheim fellow, S. Am., 1949. Mem. AAAS, Am. Assn. Phys. Anthropologists (archivist and co-historian 1981—), History Sci. Soc. (life mem.), Am. Soc. Zoologists, Am. Assn. Anatomists (historian and archivist 1972-86, archivist 1986-90, historian and archivist 1990—), Am. Assn. History Medicine (council 1972-74), Oral Hist. Assn., Assn. of Anatomy Chairmen (emeritus), Sigma Xi, Alpha Omega Alpha Honor Med. Soc. (faculty election 1957). Achievements include special research in new world primates and gen. intellectual history, especially biology and medicine, developing database on over 400,000 careers without limits of time, place, or field with extensive institutional, subject, geographical analyses. Home: 153 Bay Rd Norton MA 02766-3029 Office: Brown U Sch Medicine Providence RI 02912 also: Erikson Biog Inst 242B Meeting St Providence RI 02906-2221*

ERIKSON, KAI, sociologist, educator; b. Vienna, Austria, Feb. 12, 1931; came to U.S., 1933, naturalized, 1937; s. Erik H. and Joan (Serson) E.; m. Joanna M. Slivka, Jan. 27, 1961; children: Keith S., Christopher J. BA, Reed Coll., 1953; MA, U. Chgo., 1955, PhD, 1963. Instr. psychiatry U. Pitts., 1959-63; assoc. prof. Emory U., Atlanta, 1963-66; prof. sociology Yale U., New Haven, 1966—; master Trumbull Coll. Yale U., 1969-73; editor Yale Rev., 1979-89. Author: Wayward Puritans, 1966, Everything in Its Path, 1976, A New Species of Trouble, 1994. With AUS, 1955-57. Fellow Am. Sociol. Assn. (MacIver award 1967, Sorokin award 1977, pres. 1984-85); mem. Soc. Study Social Problems (pres. 1970-71), Eastern Sociol. Soc. (pres. 1980-81). Home: 53 Quarry Dock Rd Branford CT 06405-4655 Office: Yale U Dept Sociology PO Box 208265 New Haven CT 06520-8265

ERIKSON, RAYMOND LEO, biology educator; b. Eagle, Wis., Jan. 24, 1936; m. 1958. BS, U. Wis., 1958, MS, 1961, PhD in Molecular Biology, 1963. Asst. prof. to assoc. prof. U. Colo., Denver, 1965-72, prof. pathology, 1972-82; Am. Cancer Soc. prof. cellular and devel. biology Harvard U., Cambridge, Mass., 1982—. USPHS fellow, 1963-65; recipient Papaicolau award, 1980, Albert Lasker award, 1982, Robert Koch prize, 1982, Alfred P. Sloan Jr. prize GM Cancer Rsch. Found., 1983, Hammer Cancer Rsch. prize, 1984. Mem. NAS, Am. Academia of Arts and Scis., Am. Soc. Biol. Chemists, Am. Soc. Microbiology. Office: Harvard U Biol Labs Rm 244 16 Divinity Ave Cambridge MA 02138-2020

ERIKSSON, ANNE-MARIE, social services executive, educator; b. Dunkirk, N.Y., Mar. 30, 1932; d. J. Kenneth and Kate Findley; m. Erik A. Eriksson, Jan. 1, 1984; 3 children from prior marriage. BS, SUNY, Fredonia, 1955; postgrad., Hunter Coll. CUNY, 1960. Social worker N.Y. State Dept. Social Welfare, N.Y.C., 1960-64; probation officer N.Y., 1972-84; founder, pres. Incest Survivors Resource Network Internat. a Quaker witness ednl. resource, N.Y.C., 1983—; cons. mental health needs UN Hdqs., 1987; presenter 1st and 3d Internat. Conf. Incest and Related Problems, Zurich, 1987, London, 1989; founder first internat. incest tel. helpline, 1983; coconvenor Quaker Sexual Child Abuse Prevention Network. Mem. Quaker Studies Human Betterment, Internat. Soc. Traumatic Stress Studies (founding co-chair bldg. bridges between profls. and self-help interest area), World Fedn. Mental Health, others. E-mail: http://www.zianet.com/ISRNI. Office: Incest Survivors Resource Network Internat PO Box 7375 Las Cruces NM 88006-7375

ERIKSSON, KARL-ERIK LENNART, biochemist, educator; b. Bohus-Malmön, Sweden, May 27, 1932; came to U.S., 1988; s. Erik Mårten and Lilly Kristina (Lund) E.; m. (Aina) Gunilla Strand, Dec. 31, 1958; children: Mats Erik Rudolf, Pia Gunilla, Aina Lisa Kristina. BS, U. Uppsala, Sweden, 1958, PhD (fil. lic.), 1963; Dr. Sci., U. Stockholm, 1967. Rsch. asst. Swedish Forest Products Rsch. Lab., Stockholm, 1958-64, head biol. rsch., 1964-88; postdoctoral fellow Calif. Inst. Tech., Pasadena, 1968-69; prof. biochemistry, eminent scholar biotechnology U. Ga., Athens, 1988-99, prof. emeritus, 1999—; originated series of internat. meetings on biotech. in pulp and paper industry, 1980; adj. prof. biochemistry Inst. Paper Sci. and Tech., Atlanta, 1990—; adj. prof. biol. agrl. engring. U. Ga., 1992-98, adj. prof. Warnell Sch. Forest Resources; cons. UN FAO, UNIDO for India, 1977-84; cons. to pulp and paper industry worldwide, 1960—; organizer sci. coop. between Sweden and developing Countries, 1984-87; co-founder (with Jan L. Yang) Enzymatic Deinking Tech. Co., Norcross, Ga. Co-author: Microbial and Enzymatic Degradation of Wood and Wood Components, 1990; contbr. over 275 articles to profl. publs. Fulbright fellow Calif. Inst. Tech., 1968-69; Am.-Scandinavian Found. fellow Calif. Inst. Tech., 1968-69; named hon. Gadolin lectr. Chem. Soc., Turku, Finland, 1982; recipient Internat. M. Wallenberg prize STORA, Falun, Sweden, 1985; named Cameron-Gifford lectr. U. Newcastle, Eng., 1986. Fellow Royal Swedish Acad. Engring. Sci. (bd. dirs. 1982-85, chmn. forestry and forest industry scis. sect. 1982-85), Internat. Acad. Wood Sci., World Acad. Arts and Scis. Lutheran. Achievements include patent on method for producing cellulose pulp, 5 Swedish patents in field; developer and applied for patents on techniques for enzymatic deinking of recycled papers; discovery of new enzymes involved in cellulose and lignin degradation, discovery of cellobiose quinone oxidoreductase, cellobiose dehydrogenase. Home: Rödbosundsvägen 17, Margretelund, 18460 Åkersberga Sweden Office: Univ Ga PO Box 304 Athens GA 30603-0304

ERION, CAROL ELIZABETH, music educator; b. Quincy, Ill., Jan. 16, 1943; d. Alva Eugene and Margaret Althea (Kaempfer) McKenney; m. David F. Erion, June 19, 1965; children: Elizabeth Celia Erion Matthews, Paul Frederick. MusB, Oberlin Coll., 1965; MusM, New England Conservatory Music, 1982; cert., U. Toronto, Ont., Can., 1978, Mozarteum Acad. Music, Salzburg, Austria, 1979. Music tchr. Montessori Sch. No. Va., Annandale, 1972-84, St. Agnes Episcopal Sch., Alexandria, Va., 1984-85, The Sidwell Friends Sch., Washington, 1985-87; music and fine arts tchr. Arlington (Va.) Pub. Schs., 1988—; music dir. All Saints Episcopal Ch., Alexandria, 1983-90; workshop clinician various music edn. orgns. in U.S., 1980—; adj. prof. George Mason U., Fairfax, Va., 1983—; cons. WETA-TV, Washington, 1987. Author: Tales to Tell, Tales to Play, 1982; contbr. articles to profl. jours. Humanities fellow Coun. Basic Edn., 1989. Mem. NEA, AAUW, ASCD, Am. Recorder Soc., Am. Orff Schulwerk Assn. (pres. 1993-95), Arlington Edn. Assn. (pres. 1998—). Democrat. Episcopalian. Home: 19 W Linden St Alexandria VA 22301-2621

ERISTOFF, ANDREW S., councilman; b. N.Y.C., Feb. 20, 1963. BA cum laude, Princeton U., 1985; JD cum laude, Georgetown U., 1989. Legis. analyst N.Y. State Senate, 1987; assoc. Webster & Sheffield Law Firm, 1989-91; counsel to Senator Roy M. Goodman, 1991-93; councilman dist. 4 City of N.Y., 1993—. Mem. ABA, N.Y. State Bar Assn., N.Y. County Lawyers Assn., Assn. Bar City N.Y. Office: 370 Lexington Ave Rm 2001A New York NY 10017-6503*

ERK, FRANK CHRIS, biologist, educator; b. Evansville, Ind., Dec. 17, 1924; s. Carl Benjamin and Matilda (Schumacher) E.; m. Ruth Parker Hobgood, June 12, 1948; children: Susan Patrick Erk Tierney, Elisabeth Carlene Erk Smith, Stephanie Diane Erk Lutostanski. AB magna cum laude, U. Evansville, 1948; PhD in Genetics, Johns Hopkins U., 1952. Jr. instr. Johns Hopkins U., Balt., 1948-51, Adam T. Bruce fellow, 1951-52, Lalor faculty fellow, 1956; assoc. prof. biology, chmn. dept. Washington Coll., Chestertown, Md., 1952-57; dir. coll. choir Washington Coll., Chestertown, 1952-57; prof. biology SUNY, L.I. Ctr., Oyster Bay, 1957-61, chmn. divsn. sci. and math., 1958-59, chmn. dept. biology, 1958-61, dir. univ. choir, 1957-61; prof. biol. scis. SUNY, Stony Brook, 1962-81, prof. biochemistry and cell biology, 1981-90, prof. emeritus, 1990—, chmn. dept. biology, 1962-67, 76-78; vis. assoc. prof. biology, Carnegie intern in gen. edn. U. Chgo., 1954-55; rsch. collaborator Masonic Med. Rsch. Lab., Utica, N.Y., 1968-71; vis. investigator Poultry Rsch. Ctr., Agrl. Rsch. Coun., U. Edinburgh, Scotland, 1964-65, Genetics Inst., U. Milan, Italy, 1965, U. Sussex, Eng., 1971-72, 85-86, Galton Lab., U. Coll. London, Eng., 1978-79, U. Edinburgh, 1979-80; vis. prof. U. Essex, Eng., 1978-79; asst. examiner Internat. Baccalaureate Program, Geneva, 1977-82, cons., 1976-84; cons., writer Biol. Scis. Curriculum Study, Boulder, Colo., 1960-70, 85-90; senator statewide SUNY Faculty Senate, 1967-69, pres., 1969-71; chair Emeritus Faculty Assn. SUNY, Stony Brook, 1990—, acting master honors coll., 1991-92; dir. Madrigal Singers, Stony Brook, 1963-71; mem. examining com. Advanced Placement Biology Coll. Entrance Exam. Bd., 1967-71, chmn., 1973-77; genealogy chair Three Village Hist. Soc., E. Setauket, N.Y., 1996—. Author: (with others) Biological Science: Molecules to Man, 1963, 68, (with others)

Biological Sciences: Interaction of Experiments and Ideas, 1965, 70, Biological Science: An Ecological Approach, 1987; editor: (with others) Evolution, Mammals and Southern Continents, 1972; exec. editor Quar. Rev. Biology, 1966-69, editor, 1969-99; mem. editl. bd. Jour. Biol. Edn., London, 1976-90. 1st lt. USAAF, 1943-46, PTO. Mem. AAAS, AAUP, Am. Genetics Assn. (coun. 1978-81), Genetics Soc. Am., Soc. Genetics Can., Nat. Assn. Biology Tchrs., Am. Soc. Zoologists, Soc. for Study Evolution, Human Biology Coun., SUNY Emeritus Faculty Assn. (chmn. 1990—), Sigma Xi, Phi Beta Chi, Omicron Delta Kappa. Home: 33 Yorktown Rd Setauket NY 11733-1215 Office: SUNY Dept Biochemistry & Cell Biology Stony Brook NY 11794-5215

ERKFRITZ, DONALD SPENCER, mechanical engineer; b. Highland Park, Mich., Mar. 16, 1925; s. Clarence Frederick and Dorothy N. (Spencer) E.; m. Marjorie Alethea Isard, Dec. 24, 1948; children: Jeannette, D. Michael, Lisa. Student, Henry Ford Trade Sch., 1938-42; lic. mechanic & ground sch. instr., A&E Mechanics Sch., Chillicothe, Ohio, 1945. Cert. mfg. engr. Design engr. Beaver Tool & Engring., Big Beaver, Mich., 1950-52; chief engr. Delman Co. Labs., Detroit, 1952-60, Futurmill, Inc., Farmington, Mich., 1960-68; R&D engr. Ingersoll Milling Machine Co., Rockford, Ill., 1968-72, Southfield, Mich., 1974-78; chief engr. Valenite div. Valeron Corp., Troy, Mich., 1972-74; milling programs mgr. Carboloy div. Gen. Electric, Warren, Mich., 1978-85; metalworking cons. Dba Rsch., Etc., Clarkston, Mich., 1985—; cons. Gen. Motors Tech. Ctr., Warren, 1985-88, Focus Hope, Detroit, 1990-92; devel. engr. Ingersoll Milling Machine Corp., Rockford, 1988-90; exptl. machinist AP Products, Auburn Hills, Mich., 1994-95; tooling engr. spl. projects Dijet, Inc., Plymouth, Mich., 1997-98; engring. cons. Wolverine Cutting Tool Inc., Oxford, Mich., 1998—; v.p. Laser Ink Corp.; adj. tchr. Oakland C.C., Auburn Hills, Mich., 1997-98. Patentee in field. instr. first aid ARC, Pontiac, 1958-68; co-chair High Fever Follies PGH Aux., Pontiac, Mich., 1962; host family Youth for Understanding Fgn. Exch. Student Program, 1967-68; mem. Pontiac Police Res., 1959-63. Mem. Henry Ford Trade Sch. Alumni Assn, Descs. and Founders Ancient Windsor, Mayflower Soc., Found. Geneal. and Hist. Rsch., Huntley Nat. Assn., Spencer Family Assn., Geneal. Soc. Vt., Ont. Geneal. Soc., Elder William Brewster Soc. Avocations: genealogy, music, woodcrafts, piano technician, machinist. Home and Office: 7905 S Eston Rd Clarkston MI 48348-4012

ERKONEN, WILLIAM E., radiologist, medical educator. BS, U. Iowa, 1955, MD, 1958. Diplomate Am. Bd. Radiology. Intern U. Oreg., Portland, 1959; pvt. practice; resident in radiology U. Iowa Coll. Medicine, Iowa City, 1968-71; pvt. practice, 1971-87; faculty U. Iowa Coll. Medicine, 1988-90, asst. prof. radiology, 1990-95, assoc. prof., 1995-98, co-dir. Electric Differential Multimedia Lab., 1993—, assoc. prof. emeritus, 1998—; rschr. in med. informatics and med. student instrn. and edn. Editor: (textbook) Radiology 101; contbr. articles to profl. jours.; developer electronic med. textbooks. Recipient numerous certs. of merit Radiology Soc. N.Am.; named Tchr. of Yr., U. Iowa Coll. Med., 1990, 93, 96; recipient Disting. Tchr. award for jr. faculty in clin. scis. Alpha Omega Alpha. Fellow Am. Coll. Radiology. Office: Univ Iowa Coll Medicine Dept Radiology Iowa City IA 52240

ERLA, KAREN, artist, painter, collagist, printmaker; b. Pitts., Nov. 17, 1942; d. Jack and Lenore (Kamons) Franklin; children: Stephanie, Joan. BFA, George Washington U., 1965; postgrad., Parsons Sch. Design, 1979-81, Carnegie Inst., 1958-59, Boston U., 1960-62, Pratt Inst., 1980-82, NYU, 1982. Solo exhbns. include Phoenix Gallery, N.Y.C., 1985, E.L. Stark Gallery, N.Y.C., 1988, Bertha Urdang Gallery, N.Y.C., 1986, Bennett and Siegel Gallery, 1989, 90, U. of South, Sewanee, Tenn., Manhattanville Coll., Purchase, N.Y., 1982, Printmaking Council of N.J., 1982, Bennet Siegel Gallery, N.Y.C., 1990, Bryant Gallery, N.Y.C., 1990, Queens Coll., N.Y.C., 1991; group shows include Herbert Johnson Mus. Art, Atlanta Coll. Art, Van Straaten Gallery, Chgo., Greene Gallery, Guilford, Conn., Nat. Mus. of Am. Art, Washington, D.C., Fine Arts Museum of L.I., N.Y., Zimmerli Mus., New Brunswick, N.J., Printmaking Council of N.J., Somerstown Studios and Gallery, Somers, N.Y., Cork Exhbn. in Lincoln Ctr., Fay Gold Gallery, Atlanta, 1984, Boston Printmakers 37th Nat. Exhbn., 1985, The Print Club's 61st Internat. Juried Exhbn., Phila., Schering-Plough Corp. Gallery, Madison, N.J., New Brunswick, N.J., Australian Nat. Gallery, 1989, E.L. Stark Exhbn., 1990, Am. Embassy, 1990, others; represented in permanent collections at Balt. Mus. of Art, Herbert F. Johnson Mus., Cornell U., Bklyn. Mus. Art, Huntsville Mus. Art, Ala., L.A. County Mus. Art, Met. Mus. Art, N.Y., Nat. Museum Am. Art, Australian Nat. Gallery, Smithsonian Inst., New Orleans Mus. Art, Phila. Mus. Art, Tampa Mus., Fla.; featured in Monograph of Karen Erla (text by Ronnie Cohen) 1988, Monoprints Karen Erla (text by Dr. Mary Lee Thompson), Paintings: Karen Erla (text by Bertha Urdang and E.L. Stark); featured in Newsday as New Yorker mag.; solo exhibitions E.L. Stark Gallery, Bertha Urdang Gallery, N.Y.C. Harrison Library, Harrison, N.Y. Manhattanville Coll., Purchase, N.Y., Sound Shore Gallery, N.Y.C., The Print Club 62d Internat., Phila. Recipient Nat. Art award, Pa., 1959, Herbert F. Johnson Mus., Cornell U.; Mamroneck Artists Guild award, 1983. Mem. World Print Council, Printmaking Council N.J., Artists Equity, Pratt Graphic Ctr., L.A. Printmaking Soc. Avocations: music, reading, traveling. Address: PO Box 202 White Plains NY 10603-0202

ERLAND, SHIRLEY MAY, nurse; b. N.Y.C., Sept. 24, 1947; d. Endre and Sigrid (Hoiland) E. Diploma, Meth. Hosp. Sch. Nursing, Bklyn., 1968; BS, Molloy Coll., 1981; MS, Adelphi U., 1987; postgrad., N.Y. Coll. Wholistic Health, Edn. & Rsch., 1998—. RN, N.Y. Surg. nurse Meth. Hosp., Bklyn., 1968-70; staff nurse J.B. Thomas Hosp., Peabody, Mass., 1971-73; staff nurse Mercy Med. Ctr., Rockville Centre, N.Y., 1973-75, critical care nurse, 1975-78, staff nurse CCU, 1978-86, asst. head nurse, 1986-87, instr. staff edn., 1987-97, ednl. mgr., 1998—. Contbr. articles to profl. jours. Mem. Nurses Assn. of the Counties of L.I., Transcultural Nursing Soc., Wholistic Nursing Soc., Sierra Club, Sons of Norway, Sigma Theta Tau, Phi Sigma Tau. Home: 2120 Wantagh Ave Wantagh NY 11793-3916 Office: Mercy Med Ctr 1000 N Village Ave Rockville Centre NY 11570-1000

ERLANDSON, DAVID ALAN, education administration educator; b. Chgo., Jan. 10, 1936; s. Gerald Kenneth and Anna Marie Schlichting E.; m. Gwyneth Ellen Jones, Sept. 21, 1957; children: Paul William, Linda Ann, Daniel Lindsay, Charles David. AB, Wheaton (Ill.) Coll., 1956; MS, No. Ill. U., 1962; EdD, U. Ill., 1969. Cert. supr. all grades, Ill. Tchr. jr. high sch. Geneva (Ill.) Pub. Schs., 1959-62; tchr. jr. high sch. Unit 4 Schs., Champaign, Ill., 1962-63, dir. gifted program, 1965-68, asst. prin., 1969-71; tchr. Univ. High Sch., Urbana, Ill., 1963-64; asst. prof. SUNY, Buffalo, 1964-65; dir. Ctr. for Upgrading Ednl. Services, Champaign, 1968-69; asst. prof. Queens Coll. CUNY, Flushing, 1971-76; prof. ednl. adminstrn. Tex. A&M U., College Station, 1977—, head dept. ednl. adminstrn., 1984-92; dir. Prins.' Ctr., Tex. A&M U., 1983-85, 93—. Author: Strengthening School Leadership, 1976, Doing Naturalistic Inquiry, 1993, Organizational Oversight, 1996; co-author: School Special Services, 1979; co-editor School Leadership Library; contbr. 124 articles to books and profl. jours. Served to 1st lt. USMC, 1956-59. Mem. Nat. Assn. Secondary Sch. Prins. (commn. on standards for principalship 1985-88), Am. Ednl. Rsch. Assn., Phi Delta Kappa, Phi Kappa Phi. Democrat. Home: 1107 Glade St College Station TX 77840-4434 Office: Tex A&M U Dept Ednl Adminstrn College Station TX 77843-4226

ERLANGER, BERNARD FERDINAND, biochemist, educator; b. N.Y.C., July 13, 1923; s. Leo and Frieda (David) E.; m. Rachel Fenichel, June 23, 1946; children—Laura, Louis, Leon. BS with highest honors, CCNY, 1943; MA, NYU, 1949; PhD, Columbia U., 1951. Chemist U.S. Indsl. Chems. Co., Inc., Newark, 1943-44; tech. adviser Manhattan Project, U.S. Army, Los Alamos, 1944-46; prodn. mgr. Hexagon Labs., Inc., N.Y.C., 1946-48; faculty Columbia, 1951—, prof. microbiology, 1966—; vis. scientist Instituto Superiore di Sanita, Rome, 1961-62, Inst. Cell Biology, Shanghai, People's Republic of China, 1978; mem. Fulbright-Hays Award Com., 1966-72; invited expert analyst biochem. and molecular biology edit. Chemtracts; mem. study sect. neurol. C, NIH, 1985-88. Recipient 600th Anniversary medal Copernican Med. Acad., Cracow, Poland, 1979,Sigma Alpha/Mu Gamma award N.Y. Heart Assn., Townsend Harris medal CUNY, 1995; Fulbright scholar U. Republic of Uruguay, 1967, Guggenheim fellow Inst. Phys.-Chem. Biology, Paris, 1969, Am. Cancer Soc. scholar Pasteur Inst., Paris, 1979. Recipient Physicians and Surgeons Disting. Svc. award Columbia U., 1996. Mem. Am. Chem. Soc., Am. Soc. Biol. Chemists, Biochem. Soc., N.Y. Acad. Scis. (mem. conf. com. 1978), Soc. Exptl. Biol. Medicine (assoc. editor proceedings 1981-88), Harvey Soc., Am. Soc. Immunologists, N.Y. Heart Assn., Am. Soc. Photobiology, Phi Beta Kappa, Sigma Alpha Mu (Gamma award). Achievements include research on mode of action of antibiotics and on cancer; investigation of mechanisms of enzyme catalysis, immunochemistry of macromolecules concerned with genetics, photoregulation, biological receptors. Home: 16316 15th Dr Flushing NY 11357-2935 Office: Columbia U 701 W 168th St New York NY 10032-2704 *The scientist, like the artist, contributes most when he allows his work to be an extension of his individuality. The risks to his ego and security are great, but success brings with it the satisfaction of making a personal imprint on the future of society.*

ERLANGER, STEVEN JAY, journalist; b. Waterbury, Conn., Oct. 14, 1952; s. Jay Herman and Florence (Cohen) E.; m. Elisabeth Carroll, Nov. 18, 1973. A.B. magna cum laude, Harvard U., 1974. Analyst Bur. Labor Stats., Dept. Labor, Boston, 1973-74; teaching fellow Harvard U., Cambridge, Mass., 1975-83; asst. editor Nieman Reports, Nieman Found., Cambridge, 1975; dep. nat.-fgn. editor Boston Globe, 1976-83; European corr. Boston Globe, London, 1983-87, N.Y. Times, 1987-88; S.E. Asia corr. N.Y. Times, Bangkok, Thailand, 1988-91; sr. assoc. mem. St. Antony's Coll., Oxford, 1991-92; Moscow corr. N.Y. Times, 1992-94, chief of bur., 1994-95, chief diplomatic corr., 1995—. Author: (monograph) The Colonial Worker in Boston, 1775, 1975; also articles. Recipient Livingston award Mollie Parnis Livingston Found., 1981. Mem. Internat. Press Inst., Assn. Am. Corrs. in London (exec. com. 1985-87, v.p. 1987), RAC London, Harvard Club N.Y., Phi Beta Kappa. Jewish. Office: NY Times 1627 I St NW Washington DC 20006-4007

ERLANSON, DEBORAH MCFARLIN, state program administrator; b. Watertown, N.Y., Oct. 17, 1943; d. Raymond Thomas and Alberta Antoinette (Schultz) McF.; m. David Norman Erlanson, Sept. 10, 1966 (dec. Aug. 1998); 1 child, Joshua David. AA in Liberal Arts, Dutchess C.C., 1964; BA in Psychology, Am. Internat. Coll., 1966; MS in Edn., So. Ill. U., 1972. Coord. occupancy tng. Decatur (Ill.) Housing Authority, 1975-76, coord. target projects program, 1976-77, coord. spl. svcs., 1977-78, asst. dir. planning, 1978-82, dir. program devel., 1982—; spkr. in field; cons. Piatt County Housing Authority, Monticello, Ill., 1985-89, Woodford Homes, Inc., Decatur, 1985-86. Steering com. Near West Restoration and Preservation Soc., Decatur, 1985-86, bd. dirs., 1986—, v.p., 1992—; mem. steering com. Cmtys. in Partnership, 1991—, bd. dirs., 1993—; mem. Decatur Advantage 20/20, 1993, Macon County Literacy Coun., 1992-95; parent group counselor Macon County Parents Anonymous, Decatur, 1976-80; mem. health divsn. Decatur Coun. Cmty. Svcs., 1978-84; bd. dirs. YWCA, Decatur, 1992-95; adv. bd. Ill. Housing Devel. Authority, 1993—. Mem. Nat. Assn. Housing/Redevel. Ofcls. (mem. state exec. bd. 1983-93, mem. profl. devel. com. 1983-93, state exec. bd. 1983-93, state pres. 1984-87, regional pres. 1993-95, profl. devel. faculty 1986—, nat. bd. govs. 1987—, vice chair 1987-89, v.p. profl. devel. 1987-89, task force on product devel. 1987, mem. task force on elderly housing issues 1990-91, mem. Award of Excellence jury 1991-98, regional pres. 1993-95, sr. v.p. 1995-97, chair future working group 1996-97, pres. 1997—, Charles A. Thompson award 1991, William R. Hammond award 1993), Decatur Women's Network, Internat. City Mgmt. Assn. Avocations: historic preservation, swimming. Home: 465 W Macon St Decatur IL 62522-3122 Office: Decatur Housing Authority 1808 E Locust St Decatur IL 62521-1565

ERLEBACHER, ALBERT, history educator; b. Ulm, Württemberg, Fed. Republic of Germany, Sept. 28, 1932; came to U.S., 1937; s. Alfred Samuel and Rosa (Wertheimer) E.; m. Dolores Adler, Aug. 20, 1961; children: Seth Allen, Steven John, Ross Maier. BA, Marquette U., 1954, MA, 1956; PhD, U. Wis., 1965. Cert. prin., Wis. Tchr. Independence (Wis.) H.S., 1954-55, Cen. H.S., Sheboygan, Wis., 1956-59; prin. Lone Rock (Wis.) H.S., 1960-62; asst. prof. U. Wis., Oshkosh, 1962-65; prof. DePaul U., Chgo., 1965—, chmn. history dept., 1982-88; dist. 69 Sch. Bd., Skokie, Ill., 1978-81; faculty adv. com. State Bd. Higher Edn., Champaign, Ill., 1974-80, 92-97. Mem. Temple Judea-Mizpah. Mem. AAUP, Am. Hist. Assn., State His. Soc. Wis. Home: 8232 Kilbourn Ave Skokie IL 60076-2614 Office: DePaul U 2320 N Kenmore Ave Chicago IL 60614-3210

ERLEBACHER, ARLENE CERNIK, retired lawyer; b. Chgo., Oct. 3, 1946; d. Laddie J. and Gertrude V. (Kurdys) Cernik; m. Albert Erlebacher, June 14, 1968; children: Annette Doherty, Jacqueline Erlebacher. BA, Northwestern U., 1967, JD, 1973. Bar: Ill. 1974, U.S. Dist. Ct. (no. dist.) Ill. 1974, U.S. Ct. Appeals (7th cir.) 1974, Fed. Trial Bar, 1983, U.S. Supreme Ct. 1985. Assoc. Sidley & Austin, Chgo., 1974-80, ptnr., 1980-95, ret., 1996. Fellow Am. Bar Found.; mem. Order Coif.

ERLEBACHER, MARTHA MAYER, artist, educator; b. Jersey City, Nov. 21, 1937; d. Desiderius and Mary (Persa) Mayer; m. Walter Erlebacher, June 26, 1961 (dec. Aug. 1991); children: Adrian Immanuel, Jonah Daedalus. Student, Gettysburg (Pa.) Coll., 1955-56; B of Indsl. Design, Pratt Inst., 1960, MFA, 1963. Indsl. designer, illustrator Arthur Wagner Assocs., N.Y.C., 1956-61; tchr. anatomy and figure drawing U. of Arts, Phila., 1978-94; tchr. Phila. Coll. Art, 1966-68, 75-78; tchr. anatomical drawing and painting Grad. Sch. Figurative Art, N.Y. Acad. Art, N.Y.C., 1992—, others; guest lectr. Grad. Sch. Art Yale U., 1974, Vassar Coll., Poughkeepsie, N.Y., 1975, Phila. Coll. Art, 1976, U. Conn., Storrs, 1977, Tyler Sch. Art Temple U., 1978, Med. Coll. Pa., Phila., 1987, N.Y. Acad. Art, 1990, others; vis. artist colls. and univs. including U. Wis., Oshkosh, 1979, Syracuse U., 1986-87, U. Mich., 1988, Calif. State U., 1989, 91, Tulane U., New Orleans, 1992, Kalamazoo Inst. Arts, 1989; panelist arts shows, 1978—; juror U. Del., 1979, N.Y. Statewide Bi-Annual, Trenton, 1984, Moss Rehab. Hosp., Phila., 1985, Tex. Nat. '98, Nacogdoches. Exhibited in one-person shows at Robert Schoelkopf Gallery, N.Y.C., 1973, 75, 78, 80, 82, 85, Dart Gallery, Chgo., 1976, 78, 83, Koplin Gallery, L.A., 1989, 91, Kalamazoo Inst. Arts, 1989, Fischbach Gallery, N.Y.C., 1993, 95, The More Gallery, Phila., 1993, 97, Hackett-Freeman Gallery, San Francisco, 1999, others; exhibited in group shows Bklyn. Mus., 1960, Phila. Art Alliance, 1967, Suffolk Mus., Stony Brook, N.Y., 1971, Pratt Manhattan Ctr., 1971, Am. Acad. Arts & Letters, N.Y.C., 1973, 76, 87, Yale U. Art Gallery, 1973, Phila. Civic Ctr., 1974, Mus. Art, Penn. State U., 1974, 76, N.Y. Cultural Ctr., 1975, Libr. Congress, 1975, U. Notre Dame, 1976, Ringling Mus. Art, Sarasota, Fla., 1976, Fogg Art Mus. Harvard U., Cambridge, Mass., 1976, Art Gallery Boston U., 1977, Penn. Acad. Fine Arts, 1978, 81, 82, Phila. Mus. Art, 1979, Centro Colombo Americano, Bogota, Colombia, 1979, Fendrick Gallery, Washington, 1980, Print Club, Phila., 1980, 88, Albright-Knox Gallery, Buffalo, 1981, Woodmere Art Gallery, Phila., 1982, Univ. Art Mus., Santa Barbara, Calif., 1983, N.J. State Mus., Trenton, 1984, Hudson River Mus., Yonkers, N.Y., 1986, Sch. Fine Arts Gallery Ind. U., 1987, Sherry French Gallery, N.Y.C., 1988, 91, 92, Jack Wright Gallery, Palm Beach, Fla., 1992, Contemporary Realist Gallery, San Francisco, 1993, 94, Gerald Peters Gallery, Sante Fe, 1993, Fletcher Gallery, Sante Fe, 1994, Arnot Mus., Elmira, N.Y., many others; represented in pvt. and pub. collections including Cleve. Mus. Art, Ball State U., Muncie, Ind., AT&T Co., Inc., Chgo., U. Notre Dame, Art Inst. Chgo., Fogg Mus. of Art, Fed. Reserve Bank, N.Y.C., Penn. Acad. Fine Arts, Phila., Valparaiso U., Phila. Mus. Art, Libr. Congress, Flint Inst. Arts, N.J. State Mus., others. Recipient Bertha Shay award Cheltenham Art Ctr., 1967, Netsky-Sernaker Meml. prize, 1973, Vivian and Meyer P. Potamkin prize, 1974; Yaddo fellow, 1966, 73, sr. fellow Nat. Endowment for Arts, 1982, fellow Pa. Coun. on Arts, 1988; grantee Ingram Merrill Found., 1978, Mellon Venture Fund, 1987; also other grants and awards. Home: 7733 Mill Rd Elkins Park PA 19027-2708

ERLENBORN, JOHN NEAL, lawyer, educator, former congressman; b. Chgo., Feb. 8, 1927; s. John H. and Veronica M. (Moran) E.; m. Dorothy C. Fisher, May 10, 1952; children: Debra Lynn, Paul Nelson, David John. Student, U. Notre Dame, 1944, U. Ill., 1945-46; JD, Loyola U., Chgo., 1949. Bar: Ill. 1949. With law office Joseph S. Perry, Wheaton, 1949-50; partner firm Erlenborn & Bauer, Elmhurst, 1952-63, Erlenborn, Bauer and Hotte, 1963-71; mem. 89-97th congresses from 14th Dist., Ill., 1965-83, 98th congress from 13th dist., Ill., 1983-85; asst. states atty. DuPage County, Ill., 1950-52; mem. Ill. Ho. of Reps. from DuPage County, 1956-64; ptnr. Seyfarth, Shaw, Fairweather & Geraldson, Washington, 1985-92, of counsel, 1993-94; bd. dirs. Custodial Trust Co., Princeton, N.J., Internat. Found. Employee Benefit Plans; mem. U.S. Dept. Labor Employee Retirement Income Security Act Adv. Coun., 1985-89, chmn., 1985-86; adj. prof. Georgetown U. Law Ctr., 1994—; mem., vice chair Legal Svcs. Corp., 1989-90, 1996—. Trustee The Aerospace Corp., 1990—, chair audit and fin. com., 1998—; advisor U.S. Delegation to ILO 78th and 79th Session, Geneva. With USNR, 1944-46. Mem. Former Mems. of Congress (trustee 1993—, sec. 1995-96, treas. 1996-97, v.p. 1998—).

ERLENMEYER-KIMLING, L., psychiatric and behavior genetics researcher, educator; b. Princeton, N.J.; d. Floyd M. and Dorothy F. (Dirst) Erlenmeyer; m. Carl F. E. Kimling. B.S. magna cum laude, Columbia U., 1957, Ph.D., 1961; DSc (hon.), SUNY, Purchase, 1997. Sr. research scientist N.Y. State Psychiat. Inst., N.Y.C., 1960-69; assoc. research scientist N.Y. State Psychiat. Inst., 1969-75, prin. research scientist, 1975-78, dir. div. devel. behavioral studies, 1978—, acting chief med. genetics, 1991—; asst. in psychiatry Columbia U., 1962-66, rsch. assoc., 1966-70, asst. prof., 1970-74, assoc. prof. psychiatry and genetics, 1974-78, prof., 1978—; vis. prof. psychology New Sch. Social Research, 1971-97; mem. peer rev. group NIH, 1976-80; mem. work group on guidance and counseling Congl. Commn. on Huntington's Disease, 1976-77; mem. task force on intervention Pres.'s Commn. on Mental Health, 1977-78; mem. initial rev. group NIMH, 1981-85; mem. adv. bd. Croatian Inst. Brain Rsch., 1991-93. Editor: Life-Span Research in Psychopathology, 1986; issue editor: Differential Reproduction, Social Biology, 1971, Genetics and Mental Disorders, Internat. Jour. Mental Health, 1972, Genetics and Gene Expression in Mental Illness, Jour. Psychiat. Rsch., 1992, Measuring Liability to Schizophrenia: Progress Report 1994, Schizophrenia Bull., 1994; mem. editorial bd. Social Biology, 1970-79, Schizophrenia Bull., 1978—, Jour. Preventive Psychiatry, 1980-84, Croatian Med. Jour., 1991—, Neurology/Psychiatry/Brain Research, 1991—, Neuropsychiat. Genetics, Am. Jour. Med. Genetics, 1992—. Recipient Merit award NIMH, 1989-96, William K. Warren Schizophrenia Rsch. award Internat. Congress on Schizophrenia Rsch., 1995; grantee NIMH, 1966-69, 71—, Scottish Rite Com. on Schizophrenia, 1970-74, 84-87, 89-94, W.T. Grant Found., 1978-86, MacArthur Found., 1981, Stanley Found., 1995—, NARSAD, 1996—. Fellow APA, Am. Psychopath. Assn., Am. Psychol. Soc.; mem. AAAS, Am. Soc. Human Genetics, Behavior Genetics Assn. (mem.-at-large 1972-74, Theodosius Dobzhansky award 1985), Internat. Soc. Psychiat. Genetics, N.Y. Acad. Scis., Soc. Study Social Biology (bd. dirs. 1969-84, 92-96, sec. 1972-75, pres. 1975-78), Phi Beta Kappa, Sigma Xi.

ERLICH, FREDRICK WILLIAM, human services administrator; b. Bklyn., Mar. 14, 1948; s. William and Raechel (Goldstein) E.; m. Elizabeth Anne Vandercar, Dec. 9, 1977; children: Maggie, Jacob, Seth. Student, CUNY, 1965-67; BA in Polit. Sci., SUNY, Albany, 1969, M Social Welfare, 1972, MBA, 1994. Asst. dir. for program devel. N.Y. State Office Mental Retardation and Devel. Disabilities, Albany, 1978-80; exec. dir. N.Y. State chpt. Nat. Soc. for Autistic Children, Albany, 1980-81; exec. dir. Living Resources Corp., Albany, 1981—, assoc. dir., 1973-77; faculty Sch. Bus., SUNY-Albany, 1994-98; guest lectr. devel. disabilities, 1975, SUNY, Binghamton, 1976, U. Maine, Orono, 1977; conf. presenter N.Y., 1980—; cons. Mercy House Shelter for Women, Albany, 1976-77; mem. commr.'s day svcs. adv. panel Office Mental Retardation and Devel. Disabilities, 1986-88. Contbr. articles to profl. jours. V.p. Nat. Barrier Awareness Found., 1988-90, chmn. Barrier Awareness Day, 1990; pres. Capital Area Residence, 1985-86; bd. mem. Ctr. for Independence, 1996-97. Recipient Disting. Alumni award Rockefeller Coll. Pub. Afffairs, SUNY, Albany, 1989; Exec. Peer recognition Albany Exec. Assn. and Northeastern N.Y. Coun. Community Svcs., 1990. mem. faculty Sch. Bus. SUNY, Albany, 1994; guest lectr. devel. disabilities, 1975, SUNY, Binghamton, 1976, U. Maine, Orono, 1977; conf. presenter N.Y., 1980—; cons. Mercy House Shelter for Women, Albany, 1976-77; mem. commr.'s day svcs. adv. panel Office Mental Retardation and Devel. Disabilities, 1986-88; guest lectr. Eldridge Found., Calif., 1995. Avocations: parenting, real estate investing and managing, renovating historic buildings, golf, hiking. E-mail: Erlicf@livingresources.com. Home: 37 The Crossway Delmar NY 12054-3613

ERLICH, REESE WILLIAM, journalist; b. L.A., July 5, 1947; s. Israel Erlich; m. Elizabeth Erlich, Jan. 20, 1972; 1 child, Jason. BA, U. Calif., Berkeley, 1970. Staff writer Ramparts mag., San Francisco, 1968-69; freelance journalist Calif., 1969—, Christian Sci. Monitor, Boston, 1983—, Monitor Radio, 1986-97, Nat. Pub. Radio, 1987—; lectr. in mass comm. Calif. State U., Hayward, 1988—. Prodr.: (TV documentary) Prison Labor/Prison Blues, 1995; contbr. articles to profl. jours. Recipient Silver Hugo, Chgo. Internat. Film Festival, 1996. Mem. Soc. Profl. Journalists, Nat. Writers Union, Assn. Ind. in Radio, Calif. Faculty Assn. (Hayward chpt. v.p. 1993-95). Office: PO Box 19261 Oakland CA 94619-0261

ERLICH, VICTOR, Slavic languages educator; b. Petrograd, Russia, Nov. 22, 1914; came to U.S., 1942, naturalized, 1943; s. Henryk and Sophie (Dubnov) E.; m. Iza Sznejerson, Feb. 27, 1940; children: Henry Anthony, Mark Leo. M.A., Free Polish U., Warsaw, 1937; Ph.D., Columbia U., 1951; M.A. (hon.), Yale U., 1963. Asst. lit. editor New Life mag., Warsaw, 1937-39; research writer Yiddish Ency., 1942-43; from asst. prof. to prof. Slavic lit. and langs. U. Wash., 1949-63; Bensinger prof. Russian lit. Yale U., 1963-85, chmn. dept. Slavic langs., 1963-68, 78-81, prof. emeritus, 1985—; Del. congress Fedn. Modern Lang. and Lit., 1957; Del. congress Internat. Congress Slavists, Sofia, 1963, Warsaw, 1973; Del. congress Internat. Comparative Lit. Assn., Belgrade, 1967. Author: Russian Formalism: History, Doctrine, 1955, The Double Image: Concepts of The Poet in Slavic Literatures, 1964, Gogol, 1969, Modernism and Revolution: Russian Literature in Transition, 1994; editor: Twentieth Century Russian Criticism, 1975, Pasternak: Twentieth-Century Views, 1977. Served with AUS, 1943-45, ETO. Decorated Purple Heart.; Ford Fellow, 1953-54; Fulbright lectr. U. Leyden, 1957-58; Guggenheim fellow, 1958, 64, 76-77; Nat. Endowment for Humanities fellow, 1968-69. Mem. Am. Assn. Advancement Slavic Studies (v.p.), MLA (exec. council), Internat. Assn. Slavic Langs. and Lits. (exec. council 1957-62), AAUP, Am. Comparative Lit. Assn., Am. Soc. Aesthetics. Home: 25 Glen Pky Hamden CT 06517-1402 Office: Yale Univ Dept of Slavic Languages New Haven CT 06520

ERLICHT, LEWIS HOWARD, broadcasting company executive; b. N.Y.C., Aug. 6, 1939; s. Harry and Estelle (Silk) E.; m. Wilma Binder, June 10, 1961; children: Paul Jon, Jamie Blake. B.A. in Psychology, L.I. U., 1962. With ABC-TV, 1962—, account exec., 1965-70; sales mgr. Sta. WABC-TV, 1970-73, gen. sales mgr., 1973-74; gen. mgr. Sta. WLS-TV, Chgo., 1974-77; v.p. programming Sta. WLS-TV, N.Y.C., 1977-79; v.p., asst. to pres. ABC Entertainment, Los Angeles, 1979-80, sr. v.p., asst. to pres., 1980-81, sr. v.p. prime time programming, 1981-83, pres., 1983-85; pres. ABC Circle Films, Los Angeles, 1985-86; pres., chief operating officer New World Broadcasting, Los Angeles, 1986-87; pres. LHE, Inc., 1986—; cons. Scandinavian Broadcasting Systems, 1989-91. Served with USAF, 1956-60.

ERLICK, EVERETT HOWARD, broadcasting company executive; b. Birmingham, Ala., Sept. 12, 1921; s. Julian H. and Bertha Lorraine (Engel) E.; m. Nancy Ruth Jacobs, July 11, 1953; children—James M., Lorre Bert. BA, Vanderbilt U., 1942; LLB, Yale, 1948. Bar: N.Y. 1948. Assoc. Engel, Judge & Miller, N.Y. C., 1948-51; asst. gen. counsel Young & Rubicam, N.Y.C., 1951-55, v.p., assoc. dir. media relations dept., 1955-58, v.p. radio-TV dept., 1959-61; v.p., gen. counsel Am. Broadcasting-Paramount Theatres, Inc. (now CCC/ABC Inc.), 1961-86, dir., 1962—, group v.p., gen. counsel, 1968-72, sr. v.p., gen. counsel, 1972—, exec. v.p., 1983-86, cons., 1986-88; dir. AB-PT, Inc., WLS, Inc.; mem. Pres.'s Bus. Adv. Com. on Desegregation, 1963, Pres.'s Nat. Citizens Com. for Community Relations, 1964, Nat. Com. for Immigration Reform, 1965. Mem. campaign Am. Cancer Soc., 1965—; nat. chmn. parents com. Duke U., 1974-76, pres.'s assoc., 1976-82; trustee Everglades Protection Assn., 1980-86, vice chmn., 1983-86. Mem. Phi Beta Kappa. Home: 2812 SE Dune Dr Apt 1102 Stuart FL 34996-1930

ERLINGER, MELVIN HERBERT, pastor, educator; b. St. Louis, Oct. 14, 1921; s. Herbert Charles and Martha Louise (Lange) E.; m. Ruth Audrey Jones, June 24, 1944; children: John M., Paul T. BA, Harris Tchrs. Coll., 1945; MA, Washington U., 1948, guidance and counseling cert., 1960. Acctg. clk. Fed. Res. Bank, St. Louis, 1940-42; tchr. St. Louis Schs., 1946-56, guidance counselor, 1956-63; guidance coord. Pinellas County Schs., St. Petersburg, 1963-87; coord. pastoral care Cornerstone Ch., St. Petersburg, 1987—. Contbr. articles to profl. jours. Vol. Edn. Found., St. Petersburg,

1987-94. With USNR, 1944-46. Mem. Phi Delta Kappa. Republican. Avocation: writing. Home: 12284 69th Ter Seminole FL 33772-5626 Office: Cornerstone Cmty Ch 6745 38th Ave N Saint Petersburg FL 33710-1536

ERMATINGER, JOHN, apparel executive. BS in Econs. magna cum laude, Linfield Coll., 1975. Stocktaker for men's jeans Levi Strauss & Co., 1973-74, sales rep. youthwear divsn., 1975-85, mdse. mgr. Silver Tab, 1986-91; gen. mgr. Levi Strauss Istanbul, 1991; spl. projects mgr. Levi Strauss, 1992, v.p. ops. and sourcing U.S.A., 1992-98, pres. Levi Stauss the Americas, 1998—. Mem. Am. Apparel Mfrs. Assn. (bd. dirs.). Office: Levi Strauss & Co 1155 Battery St San Francisco CA 94111

ERMOLAEV, HERMAN SERGEI, Slavic languages educator; b. Tomsk, Russia, Nov. 14, 1924; came to U.S., 1949, naturalized, 1956; s. Sergei and Vera (Kozminykh) E.; m. Tatiana Kuzubova, June 8, 1975; children: Michael, Natalia, Katherine. Student, U. Graz, Austria, 1949; BA, Stanford U., 1951; MA, U. Calif.-Berkeley, 1954, PhD, 1959. Mem. faculty Princeton U., 1959—, prof. Slavic langs. and lits., 1970—. Author: Soviet Literary Theories, 1917-1934, The Genesis of Socialist Realism, 1963, 77, Mikhail Sholokhov and His Art, 1982, Censorship in Soviet Literature, 1917-1991, 1997; co-author: Sholokhov's Tikhii Don, A Commentary, 1997; also articles; translator: Untimely Thoughts (Gorky), 1968, 95. McCosh fellow, 1967-68. Mem. Am. Assn. Advancement Slavic Studies, Am. Assn. Tchrs. Slavic and East European Langs. (pres. 1971-72). Home: 206 Moore St Princeton NJ 08540-3404

ERNEST, DOUGLAS JEROME, librarian; b. Billings, Mont., Mar. 31, 1947; s. Clarence Henry and Ruth (Imhof) E. BA in History, U. Colo., 1969, MA in History, 1975; MA in Libr. Sci., U. Denver, 1970. Reference libr. Florence (S.C.) County Libr., 1970-73, Mo. Western State Coll., St. Joseph, 1975-81; social scis. , humanities libr. Colo. State U., Ft. Collins., 1981—. Author: (book) Agricultural Frontier to Electronic Frontier, 1996; also articles. Recipient Lit. award Colo. Libr. Assn., 1996. Mem. Wilderness Soc., Nature Conservancy, Phi Beta Kappa, Beta Phi Mu. Democrat. Unitarian. Avocations: hiking, nature study. Home: 1625 W Elizabeth St Apt J-1 Fort Collins CO 80521-4465 Office: Colo State U Morgan Libr Fort Collins CO 80523

ERNEST, J. TERRY, ocular physiologist, educator; b. Sycamore, Ill., June 26, 1935; married, 1965; 2 children. BA, Northwestern U., 1957; MD, U. Chgo., 1961, PhD in Visual Sci., 1967. Prof. ophthalmology U. Wis., 1977-79; prof., chmn. ophthalmology Ind. U., 1980-81; prof. ophthalmology U. Ill., 1981-85; prof., chmn. ophthalmology U. Chgo., 1985—; mem visual sci. A study sect., NIH, 1975-78, chmn. 1978-79, chmn. visual disorders study sect., 1979-80; rsch. prof. Rsch. to Prevent Blindness, Ind., 1981-84; mem. Vision Rsch. Program Com., 1982-84. Founding editor, Key, 1986-88; editor, Year Book of Ophthamology, 1982-88, Investigative Ophthalmology and Visual Sci., 1988-92. Recipient Rsch. Career Devel. award NIH, 1972. Mem. AAAS, Am. Ophthalmol. Soc., Am. Acad. Ophthalmology (Honor award 1982), Assn. Rsch. Vision and Ophthalmology. Achievements include research in ocular circulation with special emphasis on glaucoma and diabetic retinopathy using various methods of in vivo blood flow measurements. Office: University of Chicago Visual Sciences Ctr 939 E 57th St Chicago IL 60637-1454

ERNEST, WELDEN ARENAS, retired history educator; b. Medina, N.Y., July 1, 1922; s. Arenas Hayes and Grace (Brown) E.; m. Andrea Joan Molnar, Nov. 22, 1951; children: Martha E. Monsson, Paul Arenas, Jonathan Alexander. BA magna cum laude, U. Buffalo, 1953; AM, Harvard U., 1954, PhD, 1967. Asst. prof. history U. Hawaii Manoa, Honolulu, 1958-68, assoc. prof. history, 1968-88; ret., 1988. Contbr. articles to profl. jours. Cpl. U.S. Army Air Force, 1943-45, ETO. Mem. Am. Hist. Assn., Medieval Acad. Am., 8th Air Force Hist. Soc., Phi Beta Kappa. Avocations: photography, travel. Home: 8085 Old Post Rd W East Amherst NY 14051-1532

ERNST, CALVIN BRADLEY, vascular surgeon, surgery educator; b. Detroit, May 12, 1934; s. Edward William and Irene Marie (Doelker) E.; m. Elizabeth Abbott, Dec. 21, 1957; children: Lisa Anne, Matthew Abbott, David William, Susan Elizabeth. M.D., U. Mich., 1959. Diplomate Am. Bd. Surgery (bd. dirs. 1991-97). Intern Ohio State U. Med. Ctr., Columbus, 1959-60; resident U. Mich. Med. Ctr., Ann Arbor, 1960-65; instr. surgery U. Mich., 1968-69, asst. prof., 1969-72, assoc. prof., 1972; assoc. prof. U. Ky., Lexington, 1972-74; prof. U. Ky., 1974-79; prof. surgery Johns Hopkins U., 1979-85, surgeon hosp., 1979-85; chmn. surg. scis. Balt. City Hosps., 1979-85; clin. prof. surgery U. Mich., Ann Arbor, 1985-97; prof. surgery Case Western Res. U., Cleve., 1994-97; head vascular surgery Henry Ford Hosp., Detroit, 1985-97; prof. surgery, chief vascular surgery Med. Coll. Pa., Hahnemann Univ., Phila., 1997—; cons. surgeon Loch Raven VA Hosp., Balt., 1979-85. Assoc. editor Jour. Vascular Surgery, 1986-91, editor, 1991-97, emeritus editor, 1997—; mem. editl. bd. Archives of Surgery, 1983-93, Surgery, 1983-93; editor 6 vascular surgery textbooks; contbr. chpts. to books. Dir. Am. Bd. Surgery, 1991-97. Served to capt. U.S. Army, 1966-68. Fellow ACS; mem. Soc. Vascular Surgery (sec. 1984-88, pres.-elect 1989-90, pres. 1990-910, Am. Surg. Assn., Internat. Cardiovascular Soc. (recorder 1977-82), So. Assn. Vascular Surgery (sec. treas. 1976-81, pres. 1982-83), Alpha Omega Alpha. Home: 1 Greythorne Woods Cir Wayne PA 19087-4758 Office: MCP/Hahemann U The Health Scis Broad and Vine Mail Stp 468 Philadelphia PA 19102

ERNST, CARL F., career officer; b. New Orleans, Sept. 23, 1943. Commd. officer U.S. Army, advanced through grades to maj. gen.; commdg. gen. U.S. Army Infantry Ctr., 1996—. Office: US Army Infantry Ctr Fort Benning GA 31905

ERNST, DANIEL PEARSON, lawyer; b. Des Moines, Sept. 30, 1931; s. Daniel Ward and Thea Elaine (Pearson) E.; m. Ann Robinson, April 14, 1956; children: Ellen, Daniel R., Ruth Ann. BA, Dartmouth Coll., 1953; JD, U. Mich., 1956. Bar: Iowa 1956, Ill. 1964, Mich. 1980. Assoc. Clewell Cooney & Fuerste, 1960-64; ptnr. Nelson Stapleton & Ernst, Stapleton & Ernst, Stapleton Ernst & Sprengelmeyer, East Dubuque, Ill., Nelson Stapleton & Ernst & Sprengelmeyer, Dubuque, Iowa, 1964-79; pvt. practice Dubuque, 1979-80; ptnr. Ernst & Cody, Dubuque, 1981-84, Daniel P. Ernst, P.C., Dubuque, 1984-90, Vincent Roth & Ernst, P.C., Galena, Ill., 1991; pub. defender State of Iowa, Dubuque, 1991-96; pvt. practice Dubuque, 1997—; U.S. trustee 1979-91. Capt. USAF, 1957-60. Mem. ABA, Iowa State Bar Assn. (bd. govs. 1985-89), Dubuque County Bar Assn. (2d v.p. 1979-80, 1st v.p. 1980-81, pres. 1981-82), Ill. State Bar Assn., Jo Daviess County Bar Assn., State Bar Assn. Mich., Grand Traverse-Leelanau-Antrim Bar Assn., Nat. Assn. Criminal Def. Lawyers, Nat. Legal Aid and Defenders Assn. Democrat. Avocations: swimming, sailing. Office: Attorney-at-Law 899 Mount Carmel Rd Dubuque IA 52003-7946

ERNST, EDWARD WILLIS, electrical engineering educator; b. Great Falls, Mont., Aug. 28, 1924; s. Paul Wilson and Grace Vio (Woodmore) E.; m. Helen Kitty Todd, Jan. 29, 1950 (dec. Mar. 1975); children: Deborah Kitty, Thomas Edward (dec.); m. Margaret Frances Patton, Sept. 13, 1975; children: Alan Harmon, Ruth Margaret, Betty Carol. BS, U. Ill., 1949, MS, 1950, PhD, 1955. Rsch. engr. GE, Syracuse, N.Y., 1955, Stewart-Warner, Chgo., 1955-58; assoc. prof. U. Ill., Urbana, 1958-68, prof., 1968-89, assoc. head elec. engring., 1970-85, assoc. dean engring., 1985-89; Allied-Signal prof. engring. U. S.C., Columbia, 1990—; program dir. NSF, Washington, 1987-90; chmn. Engring. Accreditation Commn., Accreditation Bd. for Engring. Tech., N.Y.C., 1985-86, pres., 1989-90. Pres. Mckinley Found., Champaign, Ill. 1968-72. Recipient Linton Grinter award Accreditation Bd. Engring. and Tech., 1992. Fellow IEEE (v.p. 1981-82, Centennial medal 1984, EAB Meritorious Achievement award in accreditation activities 1985), AAAS, ABET, Internat. Engring. Consortium (bd. dirs.), Am. Soc. for Engring. Edn. (editor Jour. Engring. Edn. 1992-96). Presbyterian. Avocations: photography, hiking, reading. Office: U SC Swearingen Engring Ctr Columbia SC 29208

ERNST, JOHN ALLAN, clinical neuropsychologist; b. Seattle, June 27, 1955; s. Gene Allan and Maxine Joan (Weedon) E. BA magna cum laude, U. Calif., San Diego, 1977; MS, San Diego State U., 1979; PhD, U. Mont., 1983. Diplomate Am. Bd. Clin. Neuropsychology, Am. Bd. Profl. Psychology; lic. psychologist, Calif., Wash., Queensland, Australia. Postdoctoral fellow U. Wash., Seattle, 1983-84; psychologist Western State Hosp., Lakewood, Wash., 1984-85; postdoctoral rsch. fellow Univ. Queensland, Brisbane, Australia, 1985-87; neuropsychologist St. Joseph Med. Ctr., Tacoma, Wash., 1987—; mem. Wash. State Examining Bd. of Psychology, 1995—. Contbr. articles to Behavioral Assessment, Psychology and Aging, others; mem. editl. bd. Rehab. Psychology, 1991-98, SCI Psychosocial Process, 1994-98. Mem. Am. Psychol. Assn. (cert. of appreciation rehab. divsn. 1991, 93), Am. Acad. of Clin. Neuropsychol., Nat. Register Health Svc. Providers in Psychology, Internat. Neuropsychol. Soc., Nat. Acad. Neuropsychology, Pacific N.W. Neuropsychol. Soc., many others. Avocations: music and art appreciation. Office: St Joseph Med Ctr Dept Psychology PO Box 2197 Tacoma WA 98401-2197

ERNST, JOHN LOUIS, management consultant; b. Pine Bluff, Ark., Dec. 24, 1932; s. Albert C. and Christine (Vinent) E.; m. Lois R. Geraci, June 12, 1971; children: Ann Marie, Catherine Teresa, Laura Elizabeth, Christine Margaret. BS, Spring Hill Coll., Mobile, Ala., 1954; postgrad., Georgetown U. Law Sch., 1956-57. Stockbroker Washington Planning Co., 1957-58; pub. rels.-sales exec. Am. Airlines, Washington, Phila. and N.Y.C., 1958-62; account exec. Ted Bates Advt. Agy., N.Y.C., 1962-65; sr. v.p., mgmt. dir. Marschalk Advt. Agy., N.Y.C., 1965-68; dir. Interpub. Svc. Corp., 1967-69; sr. v.p., mng. dir. McCann-Erickson Advt. Agy., N.Y.C., 1969-70; pres. Ernst-Van Praag, N.Y.C., 1970-75; chmn. bd. A.V.E. Corp., N.Y.C., 1974-75, Advt. to Women, Inc., N.Y.C., 1975-86; pres. Bellvinent Communications, Inc., N.Y.C., 1986—, Art Vault Internat., N.Y.C., 1996—. Capt. USMC, 1954-57. Mem. Amyotrophic Lateral Sclerosis (Lou Gehrig's Disease) Assn. (chmn. bd. dirs., CEO Greater N.Y.C. chpt. 1997—), Players Club. Home: 20 Monroe Ave Spring Lake NJ 07762-1717

ERNST, RALPH AMBROSE, poultry specialist; b. Saline, Mich., July 5, 1938; s. Ambrose William and Catherine (Prosser) E.; m. Patricia F. Ernst, Feb. 20, 1988. BS in Agrl. Edn., Mich. State U., 1959, MS in Poultry Sci., 1963, PhD in Poultry Sci., 1966. Rschr., tchg. asst. Mich. State U., East Lansing, 1961-66; poultry specialist U. Calif., Davis, 1966—. Mem. Calif. Assn. Farm Advisors and Specialists (Extension award 1978), Poultry Sci. Assn. (bd. dirs. 1985-86, newsletter editor 1986-91)), World Poultry Sci. Assn., Coun. Agrl. Sci. & Tech., Alpha Zeta. Office: Univ Calif Dept Animal Sci Davis CA 95616

ERNST, RICHARD JAMES, academic administrator; b. Niagara, Wis., Feb. 3, 1933; s. Seymour and Rose Marie (Berger) E.; B.S. with high honors, U. Fla., 1956, M.Ed. (univ. fellow), 1959; Ed.D., Fla. State U., 1965; m. Elizabeth Lyle McGeachy, Dec. 23, 1959; children—Marie Elizabeth, Theresa Ann, Richard James. Tchr., Pinellas and Hillsborough County pub. schs., Fla., 1958-62; adminstrv. intern Pinellas County Pub. Schs., 1962-63; instr., asst. dean instrn. St. Petersburg (Fla.) Jr. Coll., 1963-65, dean acad. affairs, 1965-68; pres. No. Va. C.C., Annandale, 1968—. Bd. dirs. Consortium for Continuing Higher Edn. in No. Va., 1972—, chmn. bd., 1978; mem. extension and pub. service adv. com. Va. Council Higher Edn., 1972-73, mem. gen. profl. adv. council, 1978—; mem. nat. commn. on acad. affairs Am. Council on Edn., 1972-74, mem. commn. on mil.-higher edn. relations, 1978—; mem. adv. com. nat. orgns. Corp. for Pub. Broadcasting, 1972-74; mem. Va. Adv. Council Vocat. Edn., 1976—; mem. Va. adv. com. Nat. Identification Program for Advancement of Women in Higher Edn. Adminstrn., 1977—; mem. Va. Forum on Edn., 1978—; chmn. fin. com., chmn. personnel com., mem. exec. com., adv. council pres.'s, mem. research and edn. com., acad. and student affairs com., chmn. intellectual property task force on continuing edn. and non-credit instrn. Va. C.C. Sys.; adv. bd. Jr. Service League No. Va., 1969-71; v.p. bd. trustees Fairfax Hosp., 1972—, also mem. exec. com., chmn. planning and program devel. com., chmn. joint conf. com.; mem. fin. com., mem. adv. panel on hosp.-physician contracts Fairfax Hosp. Assn., 1978—; bd. dirs. Interfaith Ctr. on Corp. Responsibility, 1975—. Coop. for Advancement Cmty.-Based C.C. Edn., 1975—; chmn. acad. affairs com., trustee Mary Baldwin Coll., 1976—; mem. exec. com. bd. trustees; mem. gen. assembly misson bd. Presbyn. Ch. in U.S., 1974—, chmn. investment com., 1974—, chmn. long-range planning task force, vice chmn. div. central support services, chmn. fiscal and data sub-div.; mem. trustees' assembly United Way Nat. Capitol Area; mem. Washington Dulles Task Force Adv. Com., 1983-84, Gov.'s Task Force Sci. and Tech., 1982-83; founding mem. Congl. award Council; bd. dirs. Am. Cancer Soc. Served with AUS, 1956-58. Fla. Ho. of Reps. scholar, 1952-56. Mem. No. Va. Ednl. TV Assn., So. Assn. Colls. and Schs. (com. on standards and reports, chmn. commn. on colls., chmn. accrediting coms.), Am. Assn. Community Colls. (nat. commn. on instrn., community coll. satellite network commn.), Nat. Coun. on Community Services and Continuing Education (Regional Person of the Yr. awd., 1992), Am. Coun. on Edn. (commn. on ednl. credit and credentials), Va. Coun. Pres., Assn. Va. Colls. (past pres.), Servicemembers Opportunity Colls. (past chmn. adv. bd. dirs.), George Mason Inst. (indsl. policy bd.), Va. Community Colls. Assn. (legis. action commn.), Va. Community Coll. System (exec. com., adv. coun. pres., acad. and student affairs com., adv. coun. pres., chmn., intellectual property task force, chairman task force on continuing edn. and non-credit instrnl.), Phi Eta Sigma, Phi Kappa Phi, Kappa Delta Pi, Phi Delta Kappa. Presbyterian (deacon, elder). Home: 8524 Pappas Way Annandale VA 22003-4433 Office: No Va C C 4001 Wakefield Chapel Rd Annandale VA 22003-3744

ERNST, RICHARD ROBERT, chemist, educator; b. Winterthur, Zurich, Switzerland, Aug. 14, 1933; s. Robert and Irma (Brunner) E.; m. Magdalena Kielholz, Oct. 9, 1963; children: Anna Magdalena, Katharina Elisabeth, Hans-Martin Walter. Diploma Chemistry, ETH-Zurich, 1956, DSc in Tech., 1962; PhD (hon.), ETH-Lausanne, Switzerland, 1986, Technische Hochschule, Munich, 1989, U. Zurich, 1994, U. Antwerp, 1997, U. Cluj-Napoca, 1998, U. Montpellier, 1999. Scientist ETH-Zurich, 1962-63, privatdozent, 1968-70, asst. prof., 1970-72, assoc. prof., 1973-76, prof., 1976—; scientist Varian Assocs., Palo Alto, Calif., 1963-68; cons. Spectrospin AG, Fällanden, Switzerland, 1978—, v.p. bd. dirs. Numerous inventions, patents in field. 1st lt. ACS-Dienst, 1953-88, Swiss mil. Recipient Silver medal ETH-Zurich, 1962, Ruzicka prize, 1968, Gold medal Soc. Magnetic Resonance in Medicine, San Francisco, 1983, Benoist prize Swiss Fedn. Confedn., Berne, 1986, Kirkwood award Yale U., 1989, Ampere prize, 1990, Wolf prize in chemistry, 1991, Louisa Gross Horwitz prize Columbia U., 1991, Nobel prize in chemistry, 1991, award for Achievements in Magnetic Resonance EAS, 1992. Mem. NAS (India), Deutsche Akademie Leopoldina, Acad. Europaea, Schweizerische Chemische Gesellschaft, Royal Soc. London, Österreichische Gesellschaft für Analytische Chemie, Am. Phys. Soc., U.S. Nat. Acad. Sci., Am. Acad. Arts and Scis., Schweizerische Akademie d. Tech. Wiss. Avocations: Tibetan art, music. Office: Lab F Phys Chem ETH-Zentrum, 8092 Zurich Switzerland

ERNST, ROGER CHARLES, former government official, natural resources consultant, association executive; b. 1914; s. Alexander Frederick and Elizabeth Jackson (Rogers) E.; m. Mary Louise Young, Apr. 4, 1942; children—Michael, Judith, Jeanne. B.S. in Commerce, U. Denver, 1937. Investment counselor, 1937-39; tech. report writer R.J. Tipton, Denver, 1940-42; exec. sec. Frying-Pan-Ark. Project, Pueblo, Colo., 1947-50; asst. to gen. mgr. Salt River Project, Phoenix, 1950-52; mgr. Wellton-Mohawk Irrigation Dist, Wellton, Ariz., 1952-53; land commr. Ariz. Phoenix, 1953-57; asst. sec. interior Washington, 1957-60; cons. Ariz. Pub. Svc. Co., Phoenix, 1961-89; mem. Alaska Rail and Hwy. Commn., 1957-60, Nat. Water Commn., 1969-73; mem. bd. Central Ariz. Water Conservation Dist., 1971-84, pres., 1971-77. Served with AUS, 1943-46. Mem. Assn. Am. Indian Affairs (bd. dirs. 1961-75, pres. 1968-73), Sigma Alpha Epsilon. Republican. Episcopalian. Home: 141 S Granados Ave Solana Beach CA 92075-2008

ERNST, WALLACE GARY, geology educator; b. St. Louis, Mo., Dec. 14, 1931; s. Fredrick A. and Helen Grace (Mahaffey) E.; m. Charlotte Elsa Pfau, Sept. 7, 1956; children: Susan, Warren, Alan, Kevin. B.A., Carleton Coll., 1953; M.S., U. Minn., 1955; Ph.D., Johns Hopkins U., 1959. Geologist U.S. Geol. Survey, Washington, 1955-56; fellow (Geophys. Lab.), Washington, 1956-59; mem. faculty UCLA, 1960-89, prof. geology and geophysics, 1968-89, chmn. geology dept. (now earth and space scis. dept.), 1970-74, 78-82, dir. Inst. Geophysics and Planetary Physics, 1987-89; dean Stanford Sch. of Earth Scis., 1989-94; prof. geol. and environ. scis. Stanford (Calif.) U., 1989—, dean Sch. of Earth Scis., 1989-94. Author: Amphiboles, 1968, Earth Materials, 1969, Metamorphism and Plate Tectonic Regimes, 1975, Subduction Zone Metamorphism, 1975, Petrologic Phase Equilibria, 1976, The Geotectonic Development of California, 1981, The Environment of the Deep Sea, 1982, Energy for Ourselves and Our Posterity, 1985, Cenozoic Basin Development of Coastal California, 1987, Metamorphic and Crustal Evolution of the Western Cordillera, 1988, The Dynamic Planet, 1990, Integrated Earth and Environmental Evolution of the Southwestern United States, 1998, Planetary Petrology and Geochemistry, 1999. Trustee Carnegie Instn. of Washington, 1990—. Recipient Geol. Soc. Japan medal, 1998. Mem. NAS (chmn. geology sect. 1979-82, sec. class I 1997—), AAAS (chair-elect), Am. Philos. Soc., Am. Geophys. Union, Am. Geol. Inst., Geol. Soc. Am. (pres. 1985-86), Am. Acad. Arts and Sci., Geochem. Soc., Mineral Soc. Am. (recipient award 1969, pres. 1979-80). Office: Stanford U Dept Earth and Environ Scis 209 Green St Palo Alto CA 94305-2115

ERNSTBERGER, ERIC, architectural company executive. Prin. Rundell Ernstberger & Assocs., Muncie, Ind. Office: Rundell Ernstberger 315 S Jefferson St Muncie IN 47305-2470*

ERNSTHAUSEN, CAROL KNASEL, educator; b. Sidney, Ohio, Aug. 22, 1938; d. Willis G. and Izetta Rosanna (Tabler) Knasel; m. Gerald William Ernsthausen, Aug. 20, 1960; children: Catherine, David, Mary, Mark. BS in Edn., Ohio State U., 1959; MS in Edn., SUNY, Brockport, 1982. Cert. devel. edn. specialist. Tchr. 2d grade North College Hill (Ohio) Schs., 1959-60; tchr. Worthington (Ohio) Pub. Schs., 1960-61; substitute tchr. Spencerport (N.Y.) Ctrl. Schs., 1970-80; grad. asst. SUNY Coll. at Brockport, 1980-82, learning specialist, summer 1984; comms. coord. Roberts Wesleyan Coll., Rochester, N.Y., 1983-87, dir. Learning Ctr., 1987—. Presenter at confs. Mem., tchr., choir mem. Trinity Luth. Ch., Spencerport, 1961—; mem. Friends of the OgdenFarmers' Libr., Spencerport, 1980s. Leader's scholar Kellog Inst./Appalachian State U., 1988. Mem. Nat. Assn. for Devel. Edn., N.Y. Coll. Learning Skills Assn. (v.p. 1987-88, reigonal rep. 1985-86), Advocacy Consortium for Students with Disabilities. Avocations: travel, cooking, gardening. Home: 38 Morningside Dr Spencerport NY 14559-2126 Office: Roberts Wesleyan Coll 2301 Westside Dr Rochester NY 14624-1933

ERNSTOFF, RAINA MARCIA, neurologist; b. N.Y.C.; m. Sandy Hansell; children: Saul, Jenny, Amy. MD, Wayne State U. Dir. Myasthenia Gravis Treatment Ctr., Royal Oak, Mich., 1978—; assoc. clin. prof. Wayne State U. Office: 735 Beaumont Med Bldg 3535 W 13 Mile Rd Royal Oak MI 48073-6710

ERNSTTHAL, HENRY L., management educator; b. N.Y.C., Nov. 7, 1940; s. Arthur Stanley and Lenore Amelia (Isaacsen) E.; m. Mary Lynn Miller, Sept. 3, 1963; children—Lisa Catherine, Logan Scott. B.A. in English, Wesleyan U., Middletown, Conn., 1962; J.D., Stanford U., 1965. cert. assn. exec. Asst. mgr. The Emporium, Palo Alto, Calif., 1966-67; mgr. Pacific Telephone Co., Berkeley, Calif., 1967-71; assoc. dir. Calif. Dental Assn., L.A., 1971-74, exec. dir., 1974-78; pres. Ernstthal & Assocs., Washington, 1978—; exec. dir. Soc. Nuclear Medicine, N.Y.C., 1979-89; assoc. prof. dir. Master of Assn. Mgmt. program George Washington U., 1989-95; cons. to assns.; mem. adv. com. Allied Dental Health, Sacramento, 1975-76. Author: Principles of Association Management, 3d edit., 1996; contbr. chpts. to books, articles to Jour. Nuclear Medicine, Assn. Mgmt., others.$Dfl. publs. Bd. dirs. Women's Crisis Ctr., Norwalk, Conn., 1985-87, A Better Chance of Darien, 1984-87. Fellow Am. Soc. Assn. Execs. (chmn. com. 1983-85, bd. dirs. 1985-89); mem. N.Y. Soc. Assn. Execs. (bd. dirs. 1982-85, v.p. 1985-86, Exec. of Yr. award 1984, pres.-elect 1986-87, pres. 1987-89, vice chmn. 1988-89), Issue Mgmt. Assn. (bd. dirs. 1982-87, treas. 1985-86). Republican.

ERNZEN, MARY ANNE, women's health nurse, clinical nurse specialist; m. Phillip Ernzen; children: Becky, Ted. BSN magna cum laude, Wichita State U., 1986, MSN, 1991. Cert. childbirth educator; cert. in ambulatory women's health. Clin. nurse specialist, patient educator for assocs. in women's health Wichita; mgr. post-partum home visit program birth ctr. planning com. Wesley Med. Ctr., Wichita; lectr. in transcultural nursing; rschr. post partum adaptation; adj. faculty Wichita State U. Dept. Nursing. Contbr. articles to profl. jours. Mem. AWHONN, ASPO, ICEA, Transcultural Nursing Soc., Sigma Theta Tau, Phi Kappa Phi.

ERON, LEONARD DAVID, psychology educator; b. Newark, May 22, 1920; s. Joseph I. and Sarah (Hilfman) E.; m. Madeline Marcus, Mar. 21, 1950; children: Joan Hobson, Don, Barbara. B.S., CCNY, 1941; M.A., Columbia U., 1946; Ph.D., U. Wis., 1949. Diplomate Am. Bd. Profl. Psychology. Asst. prof. psychology and psychiatry Yale U., New Haven, 1948-55; dir. research Rip Van Winkle Found., 1955-62; prof. psychology U. Iowa, Iowa City, 1962-69; research prof. U. Ill.-Chgo., 1969-89; emeritus rsch. prof. of the social sci. in psychology, 1989—; rsch. scientist, prof. psychology Inst. for Social Rsch., U. Mich., Ann Arbor, 1992—. Author 8 books; editor Jour. Abnormal Psychology, 1973-80; assoc. editor Am. Psychologist, 1986-90; contbr. numerous articles to profl. jours. Served to 1st lt. AUS, 1942-45. Fulbright lectr., Free U. Amsterdam, 1967-68; recipient Fulbright Sr. Scholar award, Queensland U., Australia, 1976-77, James McKeen Cattell Sabbatical award, U. Rome, 1984-85. Fellow AAAS, Am. Psychol. Assn. (chair commn. violence and youth 1991-93, Disting. Contbns. to Knowledge award 1980, Gold medal award for Life Contbn. to Psychology in the Pub. Interest 1995), Am. Orthopsychiat. Assn.; mem. Midwestern Psychol. Assn. (pres. 1985-86), Internat. Soc. for Rsch. in Aggression (pres. 1989-90). Office: U Mich Inst for Social Rsch 426 Thompson St Ann Arbor MI 48104-2321

ERPENBACH, STEVE W., state director; b. Mitchell, S.D., Sept. 21, 1962; m. Michelle Harvey, Aug. 9, 1986; children: Max, Jack, Grace. BJ, S.D. State U. Reporter The N'West Iowa Rev., Sheldon, 1985-86; reporter Sioux Falls (Iowa) Argus Leader, 1986-89, asst. city editor, 1989-90; press sec. Ted Muenster for U.S. Senate Campaign, 1990; exec. dir. S.D. Dem. Party, 1991-93; polit. dir. U.S. Senator Tom Daschle, Washington, 1993-96; state dir. U.S. Senator Tom Daschle, Sioux Falls, 1996—. Sports editor S.D. State U. The Collegian, 1983-84, editor, 1984-85. Recipient awards S.D. Newspaper Assn. Office: 810 S Minnesota Ave Sioux Falls SD 57101-1274

ERSEK, GREGORY JOSEPH MARK, lawyer, business administrator; b. Cleve., Aug. 30, 1956; s. Joseph Francis and Mary H. (Hurchanik) E. AB, Columbia U., 1977; MBA, U. Pa., 1979; JD, U. Fla., 1984; cert. cir. civil mediator, Fla. Internat. U., 1998. Bar: Fla. 1986, U.S. Dist. Ct. (so. dist.) Fla. 1987. Cons. fin. valuation Am. Appraisal Co., Princeton, N.J., 1979-80; mgr. import-export Marie L. Veslie Co., Coral Gables, Fla., 1980-85; assoc. Lunny, Tucker, Karns & Brescher, Ft. Lauderdale, Fla., 1986; dir. legal dept. Horizons Rsch. Labs. Inc., Ft. Lauderdale, 1986-89, sr. corp. planner, 1988-89; gen. counsel Unisco Corp., Ft. Lauderdale, 1989-93, TRICORD Corp., Ft. Lauderdale, 1990-93, Irish Times, Inc., Ft. Lauderdale, 1993-97; dir. corp. fin. dept. & sr. corp. counsel Canton Fin. Svcs. Corp., subs. Cyber Am. Corp., Salt Lake City, 1995-96; gen. counsel Greenstreet Capital Corp., Investment Bankers, Las Vegas, 1996—, Gaelic Pub. Devel., Inc., Ft. Lauderdale, 1998—; sec.-treas., dir. Sorkar Group, Inc., Ft. Lauderdale, 1987-89; CEO Am. CompuShopper, Inc., 1989-98; with legal dept. Pfizer Inc., N.Y.C., 1983; co-founder, mgr. Poland/U.S. Trade and Mktg. Consortium, 1989—; mem. Philip C. Jessup Internat. Moot Ct. team, 1983; gen. counsel Biltmore Vacation Resorts, Inc., f/k/a Cyber Information, Inc., Las Vegas, 1997—, Avalon Group, Inc., Cedar Rapids, Iowa, 1997—. Editor Medscanner, med. industry newsletter, 1987-89. Mem. venture coun. forum. Mem. Fla. Bar Assn., Utah Bar (securities sect.), Nat. Assn. Securities Dealers (nat. arbitration com.), Coun. on Fgn. Rels. (local com.), Wharton Club South Fla. Republican. Episcopalian. Avocations: travel, books, entrepreneurship, internat. bus. ventures, mergers and acquisitions. Home and Office: 17820 NW 18th Ave Miami FL 33056-4949

ERSEK, ROBERT ALLEN, plastic surgeon, inventor; b. Ridley Twp., Pa., June 19, 1938; s. Joseph Martin and Theda Louise (Kromes) E.; m. Gerry Avenelle Mullins, Mar. 28, 1958; children: Stephanie Louise, Cynthia Leigh. B.S., Morris Harvey Coll., 1961; M.D., Hahnemann Med. Coll., 1966. Diplomate Nat. Bd. Med. Examiners; cert. Am. Bd. Plastic Surgery. Intern surgery U. Minn. Hosps., Mpls., 1966-67; research fellow U. Pa., 1962, Hahnemann Med. Coll., Phila., 1963-65; med. fellow dept. surgery U. Minn., 1967-73; resident dept. plastic and reconstructive surgery Tulane U.,

New Orleans, 1975-77; fellow in plastic surgery U. Miss., Jackson, 1978; clin. instr. plastic surgery U. Tex. Health Sci. Center, San Antonio, 1979; chmn. bd., dir. Med. Gen. Inc., 1969—; dir., med. dir. Genetic Labs., 1970—, Emerald Airlines, Inc.; chmn. bd. Remedco, 1980—; bd. dirs., med. dir. Genetic Labs Wound Care; chmn. Personique Inc., 1996. Author: Pain Control, 1981; Co-editor: Organ Perfusion and Preservation, 1969; contbr. articles to med. jours. Bd. dirs. Austin Civic Ballet. Served to maj. USAF, 1973-75. Recipient Alan Edelsohn prize Hahnemann Med. Coll., 1966; Grand award for exhibit Student Am. Med. Assn. Squibb Nat. Contest, 1967; award of excellence in med. writing Minn. Medicine, 1970. Fellow ACS; mem. AMA, AAUP, NAS, Am. Coll. Emergency Physicians, La. Med. Soc., Soc. for Cryosurgery, Am. Soc. Plastic and Reconstructive Surgeons, Am. Soc. Artificial Internal Organs, Am. Med. Writers Assn., Smithsonian Inst., Nat. Assn., Flying Physicians, Am. Trauma Soc., Tex. Med. Assn., Travis County Med. Soc., Am. Burn Assn., Lipoplasty Soc. N.Am. (bd. dirs.), Serpent Soc., Aesculpulation Soc., Austin Knights of Symphony, Phi Kappa Delta. Patentee numerous surg. devices. Office: 630 W 34th St Austin TX 78705-1229

ERSHLER, WILLIAM BALDWIN, biogerontologist, educator; b. Syracuse, N.Y., Jan. 13, 1949; s. Irving Leonard and Eunice (Baldwin) E.; m. Joan Lipstein, Nov. 6, 1971; children: Rachel Eve, Leah Rose. BA, Case Western Res. U., 1970; MD, SUNY Upstate Ctr., Syracuse, 1974. Diplomate Am. Bd. Internal Medicine, Am. Bd. Med. Oncology, Am. Bd. Hematology. Asst. prof. U. Vt., Burlington, 1980-85; assoc. prof. U. Wis., Madison, 1985-89, prof. medicine, 1989-96, dir. Inst. on Aging, 1989-96, head geriatrics, 1989-96; dir. geriatric rsch. Edn. and Clin. Ctr. William Middleton VA Hosp., Madison, 1991-96; prof. medicine, dir. Glennan Ctr. Geriatrics & gerontolog Eastern Va. Medical Sch., Norfolk, 1996-97; dir. Inst. Advanced Studies in Geriatric Medicine & Aging, Washington, 1998—; dir. Inst. Advanced Studies in Aging and Geriatric Medicine. Editor Jour. Gerontology, 1996—; contbr. articles to profl. jours. Recipient Geriatric Leadership award NIH, 1990—; NIH grantee, 1989—. Fellow Gerontologic Soc. Am.; mem. Am. Geriatrics Soc., Am. Assn. Cancer Rsch., Am. Soc. Clin. Oncology, Am. Soc. Hematology, Assn. Dirs. Acad. Geriatrics (councilor). Jewish. Avocations: running, photography, travel. Office: Ste 400 1819 Pennsylvania Ave NW Washington DC 20006-3611

ERSKINE, JAMES LORENZO, physics educator; b. Seattle, Oct. 25, 1942; s. Lawrence A. and Elizabeth (Woodbury) E.; m. Julie Ann Grant; children: Michael Grant, John Lawrence. BSEE, U. Wash., 1964, MSEE, 1966, PhD in Physics, 1973. Sr. engr. and cons. Boeing Co., Seattle, 1967-74; rsch. asst. prof. dept. physics U. Ill., Urbana, 1974-77; asst. prof. dept. physics U. Tex., Austin, 1977-82, assoc. prof., 1982-86, prof., 1986—; Trull Centennial prof. Trull Found. U. Tex., 1986. Contbr. numerous articles in fields of solid state physics, magnetism and magnetic materials, surface physics, surface chemistry, and instrumentation. Grantee NSF, R.A. Welch Found., other fed. and pvt. agys. Fellow Am. Phys. Soc.; mem. Am. Vacuum Soc. Office: U Tex Grad Sch Dept Of Physics Austin TX 78712

ERSKINE, WILLIAM CRAWFORD, academic administrator, accountant, health facility administrator; b. Seattle, Feb. 29, 1924; s. Alwin Crawford and Emilie Hildred (Davies) E.; m. Mary Jean Hopkins, Feb. 28, 1946; children: Scott Crawford, Nancy Page. BA in Bus. Adminstrn., U. Wash., 1950. CPA, Tex. Auditor Arthur Andersen & Co., 1950-54; sr. auditor Ansell Johnson & Co., C.P.A.s, Seattle, 1956-59; contr. Food Giant Stores, Seattle, 1959-64; comptr. U. Wash., Seattle, 1964-70; v.p. bus. U. Colo., Boulder, 1970-74; exec. v.p. U. Nebr. system, Lincoln, 1974-80; v.p. bus. affairs U. Tex., El Paso, 1980-88; ret., 1988; dir. West Tex. Higher Edn. Authority, El Paso, 1982-88, Sunwest Bank El Paso, 1986-96, Providence Hosp. P.H.A., Inc., 1994-96; cons. Educator Cons. Panel GAO, 1978-86. Treas. St. Francis on the Hills Episcopal Ch., 1996-99. With U.S. Air Corps, WWII. Mem. Wash. State Soc. CPAs, Western Assn. Colls. and Univ. Bus. Assn., Nat. Assn. Colls. and Univ. Bus. Officers, Tex. Assn. Colls. and Univ. Bus. Officers, Nat. Assn. State Univ. and Land Grant Colls. (exec. com. 1977-80), Coronado Country Club (treas. 1990-93), Rotary Club of El Paso. Home: 6136 Los Robles Dr El Paso TX 79912-1933

ERSPAMER, PETER ROY, humanities educator, writer; b. Duluth, Minn., Sept. 28, 1959; s. Ernest Gordon and Jean Alice (McDonell) E. BA, Grinnell Coll., 1982; MA, U. Wis., 1986, PhD cum laude, 1992. Vis. asst. prof. humanities Winona (Minn.) State U., 1992-93, U. Mo., Columbia, 1993-94; vis. asst. prof. German Ft. Hays State U., Hays, Kans., 1994-96, organizer holocaust symposium, 1996; vis. scholar Boston U., summer 1997; lectr. German Ind. U./Purdue U., Indpls., 1997-98. Author: The Elusiveness of Tolerance: The Jewish Question from Lessing to the Napoleonic Wars, 1997 (Choice mag. Outstanding Acad. Book of 1997); contbg. author: The Yale Companion to Jewish Writing and Thought in German Culture, 1997, Literature and Ethnic Discrimination, 1997, Reader's Guide to Judaism, 1999. vol. tutor NAACP, Madison, 1986. Rsch. grantee Fulbright Commn., Bonn, Germany, 1989-91, pub. grantee Lucius N. Littauer Found., 1996, summer seminar grantee NEH, 1997. Mem. MLA, Lessing Soc., Goethe Soc., Western Jewish Studies Assn. Democrat. Unitarian. Avocations: writing, swimming, bookworming. Home: PO Box 48 Chetek WI 54728-0048

ERSTAD, LEON ROBERT, lawyer; b. Tyler, Minn., Aug. 3, 1947; s. Clifford and Josie (Dellberg) E.; m. Nancy Youel, July 19, 1969; children: Eric, Andrew, Jonathan. BSBA, U. Minn., 1969; JD cum laude, Temple U., 1976. Bar: Minn. 1976, U.S. Dist. Ct. Minn. 1976, U.S. Ct. Appeals (8th cir.) 1992, U.S. Supreme Ct. 1994; cert. ct. mediator. Ptnr. Chadwick, Johnson & Condon, P.A., Mpls., 1976-90, Erstad & Riemer P.A., 1990—; adj. instr. law William Mitchell Coll., St. Paul, 1985-94; spkr. at profl. seminars. Contbr. articles to profl. jours. Bd. dirs. Loring Nicollet Cmty. Ctr., Mpls., 1981-91, Minn. Returned Peace Corps Vols., Mpls., 1980-86, pres., 1980-81; trustee Lynnhurst Congrl. Ch., 1997—, deacon, 1994-97. Named alumni of notable achievement U. Minn. Mem. ABA, Minn. State Bar Assn., Minn. Def. Lawyers Assn., Def. Rsch. Inst. Home: 4700 Dupont Ave S Minneapolis MN 55409-2324 Office: Erstad & Riemer PA 1000 Northland Plz Minneapolis MN 55431

ERTEL, ALLEN EDWARD, lawyer, former congressman; b. Williamsport, Pa., Nov. 7, 1936; s. Clarence and Helen (Froehner) E.; m. Catharine Bieber Klepper, June 20, 1959; children: Taylor John (dec.), Edward Barnhardt, Amy Sara. BA, Dartmouth Coll., 1958, MSBA, MS, 1959; LL.B., Yale U., 1965. Bar: Pa., Del., U.S. Supreme Ct. Law clk. U.S. Dist. Ct. of Del., 1965-66; ptnr. Candor, Youngman, Gibson & Gault, Williamsport, 1967-72, Ertel & Kieser, Williamsport, 1972-76; dist. atty. Lycoming County, Pa., 1967-76; mem. 95th-97th Congresses from 17th Pa. Dist.; ptnr. Reed Smith Shaw & McClay, Williamsport, 1985-88; pvt. practice Williamsport, 1988—. del. Democratic. Nat. Conv., 1972; Dem. nominee for gov. of Pa., 1982, for atty. gen. of Pa., 1984. Served with USN, 1959-62. Mem. Pa. Bar Assn., Del. Bar Assn., Dartmouth Soc. Engrs., Lions. Lutheran. Home: 2245 Heim Hill Rd Montoursville PA 17754-9699 Office: 605 W 4th St Williamsport PA 17701-5901

ERTEL, GARY ARTHUR, accountant; b. Racine, Wis., Feb. 16, 1954; s. Arthur and Jean Ann (Potterville) E.; m. Judith Marie Vasy, Aug. 9, 1975; children: James Arthur, Emily Marie. BSBA in Acctg. cum laude, Drake U., 1975; MBA, Marquette U., 1984. CPA, Wis.; cert. cash mgr. Mem. staff Arthur Andersen & Co., Milw., 1975-77; mgr. Jezzo, Deppisch & Co., Cedarburg, Wis., 1978; gen. actg. mgr. to asst. sec.-treas. and contr. Grede Foundries, Inc., Milw., 1978—. Mem. Amateur Radio Emergency Svc., Milw., 1984—; bd. dirs. Grace Evang. Luth. Ch., Milw., 1984-87, stewardship com., 1980-89. Mem. AICPAs, Wis. Inst. CPAs (chmn. acctg. careers com. 1979-87, bd. dirs. southeastern chpt. 1988, chmn. long-range planning com. 1987-90, sec.-treas. 1989-90, pres. 1991-93, fin. com. 1993-95, Svc. award 1989-94), Nat. Cash Mgmt. Assn. (edn. com. 1989-93), Am. Foundrymens Soc. (treas. Wis. chpt. 1994-96), Wis. Cash Mgmt. Assn. (program com. 1985-87, v.p. 1987, pres. 1988, bd. dirs. 1989-98), Risk and Ins. Mgmt. Assn., Western Raquet Club (fin. com. 1993—, bd. dirs. 1993-98, v.p. 1995, pres. 1996). Avocations: skiing, tennis, amateur radio, golf. Home: 765 Talon Trl Brookfield WI 53045-6648 Office: Grede Foundries Inc 9898 W Bluemound Rd Milwaukee WI 53226-4365

ERTEL, ROSS STEVEN, printing sales executive; b. Williamsport, Pa., Apr. 19, 1957; s. Donald William and Betty Jane (Meck) E.; m. Carole Lynn Mostella, July 12, 1987; children: Benjamin, Bonnie. AS, Robert Morris Coll. Furniture mover N.Am. Van Lines, State College, Pa., 1975-78; comml. fisherman Cape May, N.J., 1978-82; supr. Rexham Packaging, Flemington, N.J., 1982-84, Greensboro, N.C., 1984-86; copier salesman Gray & Creeck, Greensboro, N.C., 1986-87; print salesman Fisher Harrison Printing, Greensboro, 1987-95, Gate City Printing, Greensboro, 1995-97; games designer, prodr. Ertel Games Co., Greensboro, 1997—. Author (game board) Checkered Flag. Office: Gate City Printing 2407 Greengate Dr Greensboro NC 27406-5250

ERTL, RITA MAE, elementary education educator; b. Appleton, Wis., Dec. 22, 1939; d. Irving John and Bertha Helen (Van Ryte) Petrie; m. Andrew Philip Ertl, June 12, 1971; children: Kristyn Marie, Jessica Lynn. Student, Silver Lake Coll., 1961-71. Religious instr. for mentally handicapped Holy Name Parish, Sheboygan, Wis., 1965-69; tchr. grade 3 Holy Name Sch. (name now Holy Family Sch.), Sheboygan, 1969-72, learning ctr. coord., 1984—; tchr. grade 2 St. Mary's Sch., Sheboygan Falls, 1961-69; mem. CCD bd. Holy Name Sch. Co-founder Human Rights Assn., Sheboygan, 1960-69. Avocations: sewing, reading, good music, volunteer work, gardening.

ERTL, WOLFGANG, German language and literature educator; b. Sangerhausen, Germany, May 27, 1946; came to U.S., 1969; m. Mary R. Clough, Aug. 30, 1969. BA in German and English, Philipps U., Marburg, Germany, 1969; MA in German, U. N.H., 1970; PhD in Germanic Langs. and Lits., U. Pa., 1975. Lectr. German U. Pa., Phila., 1974-76; asst. prof. German Swarthmore (Pa.) Coll., 1976-77; asst. prof. German U. Iowa, 1977-82, assoc. prof., 1982-88, prof., 1988—, chmn. dept. German, 1988-96. Author: Stephan Hermlin und die Tradition, 1977, Natur und Landschaft in der Lyrik der DDR: Walter Werner, Wulf Kirsten und Uwe Gressmann, 1982, (with Christine Cosentino) Zur Lyrik Volker Brauns, 1984, DDR-Lyrik im Kontext, 1988; also chpts. to books; contbr. articles to profl. jours. May Brodbeck Humanities fellow, 1987. Mem. MLA, N.E. MLA, Am. Assn. Tchrs. German, German Studies Assn. Office: U Iowa Dept German 526 Phillips Hall Iowa City IA 52242-1323

ERUMSELE, ANDREW AKHIGBE, development policy analyst; b. Auchi, Nigeria, Nov. 18, 1944; came to U.S., 1966; naturalized, 1971; s. Erumsele Bello and Itete (Isadoh) Iyoke; m. Mary Catherine Wimbley, Dec. 6, 1969 (div. 1975); 1 child, Uwadia Alexis; m. Laura Ann Stepanski, Jan. 21, 1987 (div. 1996); children: Ashley Idiagbon, Tristan Iyoke. BA magna cum laude, Loyola U., L.A., 1969; MPA, UCLA, 1971; MA, Am. U., 1974, PhD, 1977. Leadership fellow L.A. County Planning Commn., 1969-70; rsch. fellow UN Inst. for Tng. and Rsch., 1970; mem. staff U.S. Congrl. Commn. on Reorgn. of D.C. Govt., 1972-73; mgmt. and policy analyst U. D.C., Washington, 1973-97, also asst. to dean Coll. Life Scis., asst. to dean Coll. of Arts and Scis., 1994-97; founder, pres. Devel. Analytics, Inc., 1983—; exec. dir. Inst. Nigerian Affairs, 1992—; cons. Internat. City Mgmt. Assn., Orgn. of African Unity, Inst. for Public Adminstrn.; mem. World Affairs Coun., Washington. Spl. corr. for various African newspapers. Univ. scholar Nigerian Govt. scholar UCLA; recipient Hall of Nations award Am. U., Washington, 1972. Mem. Am. Soc. for Pub. Adminstrn., Acad. Polit. Sci., Soc. for Internat. Devel., Am. Soc. for Internat. Law, Pi Gamma Mu. Democrat. Moslem. Office: PO Box 39067 Washington DC 20016-9067

ERVANS, MARY SUE (TRIPOLINO), health facility administrator; b. Cedar Rapids, Iowa, May 28, 1959; d. Jack Joseph and Marylou (Colson) Tripolino; m. Bruce Edward Ervans, Mar. 3, 1995. Student, St. Ambrose Coll., 1977-78, U. Iowa, 1979-80; diploma, Allen Sch. Nursing, Waterloo, Iowa, 1983; BSN, Mt. Mercy Coll., 1991. RN, Mo. Staff nurse med. ICU/critical care unit Jerry L. Pettis VA Hosp., Loma Linda, Calif., 1985-86; staff nurse ICU John F. Kennedy Meml. Hosp., Indio, Calif., 1987-88, Allen Hosp., Waterloo, 1988; staff nurse cardiac surg. ICU St. Mary's Hosp., Rochester, Minn., 1988; staff nurse ICU St. Luke's Hosp., Cedar Rapids, 1989; DON Iowa City (Iowa) Care Ctr., 1989-90; staff nurse ICU Covenant Med. Ctr., Waterloo, 1989-91; staff nurse trauma Mercy Med. Ctr., Cedar Rapids, 1991-93; DON Cameron (Mo.) Cmty. Hosp., 1993—; adv. bd. North Ctrl. Mo. Coll., Trenton, 1993—; HIV/STD task force State of Mo., Jefferson City, 1994—; child fatality rev. bd. Clinton County, Plattsburg, Mo., 1994—. Contbr. articles to profl. jours. Asst. scout leader Girl Scouts Am., Cameron, 1993. Mem. ANA, Mo. Nurses Assn., Mo. Assn. Healthcare Educators, Sertoma (recruitment dir. 1993, sec.-treas. 1994), Mo. Assn. Risk Mgrs. Roman Catholic. Avocations: vocal music, reading, camping, running, traveling. Office: Cameron Cmty Hosp 1015 W 4th St Cameron MO 64429-1498

ERVIN, BILLY MAXWELL, aerospace executive; b. Dante, Va., July 29, 1933; s. Willie Beldon and Ollie Lowel (Biggs) E.; m. Barbara Frances Walsh, June 27, 1971; 1 child, Honore McDonough; 1 stepchild, Kerry Thompson. BS, U.S. Naval Acad., 1955; grad., Navy Nuclear Power Training, 1961; M in Marine Affairs, U. R.I., 1971; MBA, U. Mass., 1989. Commd. ensign USN, 1955, advanced through grades to capt., 1975; chief engr. aircraft carrier USN, Pacific, 1969-70; destroyer capt. USN, Atlantic/Pacific, 1971-73; project mgr. USN, Washington, 1973-78, head logistics br., 1978-80, head rsch. and devel. br., 1980-82; insp. gen. Europe USN, London, 1982-85; ret. USN, 1985; adminstr. Baystate Eye Care, P.C., Springfield, Mass., 1986-88; mgr. engring. adminstrn. and planning Kaman Aerospace Corp., Bloomfield, Conn., 1990-92; chief oper. officer Conn. Orthopaedic and Sports Medicine Ctr., Vernon, CT, 1992-97; bus. mgr. engring. Kaman Aerospace Corp., Bloomfield, 1997—. Decorated Bronze Star; recipient Meritorious Svc. Medal award Pres. of the U.S., 1985. Mem. Naval War Coll. Found., Navy League, St. Andrew's Soc., Clan Irwin Assn. Avocations: antique cars, genealogy. Home: 20 Magnolia Ter Springfield MA 01108-2512 Office: Kaman Aerospace Corp PO Box 2 Bloomfield CT 06002-0002

ERVIN, DAVID EUGENE, economist, educator, researcher; b. Mansfield, Ohio, July 28, 1945; s. Charles Raymodn and Dorothy Isabel (Ramsey) E.; m. Christine Alice Halsten, Sept. 12, 1971. BS, Ohio State U., 1967, MS, 1969; PhD, Oreg. State U., 1974. Postdoctoral fellow Oreg. State U., Corvallis, 1974-76; from asst. prof. to prof. U. Mo., Columbia, 1977-88; chief resource policy br. Econs. Rsch. Svc. Dept. Agr., Washington, 1988-91; prof., head Dept. Agr. Resource Econs. Oreg. State U., Corvallis, 1991-94, 96; dir. policy studies Henry Wallce Inst., Greenbelt, Md., 1996—; vis. sr. analyst Office Tech. Assessment, U.S. Congress, Washington, 1994-95; cons. Orgn. Econ. Coop. and Devel., Paris, 1988-97, European Union, Brussels, 1991, 98; vis. scholar Cambridge U., 1986-87; mem. adv. bd. USAID, Washington, 1991-92. Author: Land Use Control, 1997; contbr. articles to profl. jours. Tech. adviser Greenbelt Land Trust, Corvallis, Oreg., 1991-93. Staff Sgt. U.S. Army, 1968-74. Recipient Outstanding Ext. Program award Western Agr. Econs. Assn., 1981, Presdl. citation Soil and Water Conservation Soc., 1996. Mem. Am. Agr. Econs. Assn. (hon. mention awards 1969, 85), Internat. Soc. for Ecol. Econs., Assn. Environ. and Resource Economists, Resource and Policy Consortium (chair 1995). Avocations: biking, hiking, travel. Office: Henry Wallce Inst 9200 Edmonston Rd Ste 117 Greenbelt MD 20770-4575

ERVIN, MARGARET HOWIE, elementary education educator, special education educator; b. L.A., May 13, 1924; d. James Stanley and Margaret (Goff) H.; m. E. Frank Ervin, Mar. 22, 1947 (div. 1957); children: Frank, Daniel, Charles. BA, Fresno (Calif.) State U., 1958; grad. student, Purdue U., 1965-66, San Francisco State U., 1974-75. Cert. elem. and spl. edn. tchr. Elem. tchr. (Calif.) Schs., 1958-60, Fremont (Calif.) Unified Schs., 1960-83; spl. tchr. in summers Dominican Coll., San Rafael, Calif., 1972-78; asst. dir., cons. Arena Sch. and Learning Ctr., 1974-75, dir. Ervin Sch. and Learning Ctr., San Rafael, 1983-88; researcher, tchr. Primaria Sch. #110 PRI9745, Celaya, Mex., 1988; elem., spl. tchr. Napa (Calif.) City/County Schs., 1989—; diagnosis cons. Ervin Learning Ctr., Napa, 1989—; spl. edn. guest speaker various cities, U.S., Can., 1974-98; learning seminar Parents and Tchrs., Mexico, summer 1992, Psycho-motor Tgn. Don Bosco Home for Girls, Mexico, summer 1993. Vol. Option Inst. and Fellowship, "Sonrise" autism/devel. disabilities, Sheffield, Mass., summer 1994; pres. Children Handicapped Learning Devel., Calif., 1971-72, tchr. parents, 1970-80, 94—; bay area rep. Calif. Tchrs. Assn., Burlingame, 1970-74. Recipient cert. of merit Calif. Tchrs. Assn., Burlingame, 1974, $5,000 gift to Ervin Sch. Calif. Assn. Neurol. Handicapped Children, Fremont, 1984. Mem. AAUW, NOW, Assn. Children with Learning Abilities. Democrat. Unitarian. Avocations: tennis, biking, swimming. Home and Office: Ervin Learning Ctr 3361 Rohlffs Way Bldg 31 Napa CA 94558-4494

ERVIN, PATRICK FRANKLIN, nuclear engineer; b. Kansas City, Kans., Aug. 4, 1946; s. James Franklin and Irma Lee (Arnett) E.; m. Rita Jeanne Kimsey, Aug. 12, 1967; children: James, Kevin, Amber. BS in Nuclear Engring., Kans. State U., 1969, MS in Nuclear Engring., 1971; postgrad., Northeastern U., 1988. Registered profl. engr., Ill., Colo., Calif., Idaho, Wash.; cert. paleontology paraprofl., Colo. Reactor health physicist Dept. Nuclear Engring. Kans. State U., Manhattan, 1968-69, rsch. asst. Dept. Nuclear Engring., 1969-72, sr. reactor operator, temp. facility dir. Dept. Nuclear Engring., 1970-72; system test engr. Commonwealth Edison Co., Zion, Ill., 1972-73, 73-74; shift foreman Commonwealth Edison Co., Zion, 1973, shift foreman with sr. reactor operator lic., 1974-76, prin. engr., 1976-77, acting operating engr., 1977; tech. staff supr. Commonwealth Edison Co., Byron, Ill., 1977-81; lead test engr. Stone & Webster Engring. Corp., Denver, 1982-83, project mgr., 1982-95, ops. svcs. supr., 1982-86, asst. engring. mgr., 1986-89, cons. engr., 1989-94; sr. cons., 1994-96; decommissioning program mgr. Rocky Flats Closure project Kaiser-Hill Co., Denver, 1996—. Contbr. articles to profl. jours. Served with U.S. Army N.G., 1971-77. Mem. Am. Nuclear Soc. (Nat. and Colo. chpts.), Am. Nat. Standards Inst. (working group on containment leakage testing). Independent. Roman Catholic. Avocations: paleontology, hunting, fishing, camping, stamp collecting. Home: 2978 S Bahama St Aurora CO 80013-2340 Office: Kaiser Hill Co PO Box 464 Golden CO 80402-0464

ERVIN, RITA ANN, occupational health nurse; b. Chester, Ill., Nov. 22, 1949; d. Ray Landis and Myrtle R. (Hindman) E.; divorced; children: Amanda Lynn, Raymond William. ADN, Ill. Cen. Coll., 1987. RN, Ill. Staff nurse St. Francis Med. Ctr., Peoria, 1986-88, Midwest Health Svc., Peoria, Ill., 1988-90; nurse Bendix Field Engring. Corp., 1988-91; occupational/indsl. nurse BFEC, Caterpillar, Inc., Peoria, 1990—. Instr. in CPR, Am. Heart Assn.; 1st aid instr. ARC, ACLS.

ERVIN, ROBERT MARVIN, lawyer; b. near Ocala, Fla., Jan. 19, 1917; s. Richard William and Carrie (Phillips) E.; m. Frances Anne Cushing, Dec. 25, 1941; children: Anne Cushing (Mrs. Henry Lamar Rowe), Robert Marvin. B.S. in Bus. Adminstrn, U. Fla., 1941, LL.B., 1947. Bar: Fla. 1947. Of counsel Ervin, Varn, Jacobs & Ervin and predecessor firms, Tallahassee, 1947—; U.S. referee in bankruptcy No. Dist. Fla., part time, 1952-72. Mem. Fla. Constn. Revision Commn., 1966-68; Trustee U. Fla. Law Center Assn.; mem. founders com., mem. bd. visitors Fla. State U. Coll. Law. Served with USMCR, 1941-45, PTO; col. Res.ret. Recipient Distinguished Service award for legal edn. John B. Stetson U., 1966; Distinguished Service award Armed Forces League, 1966. Fellow Am. Bar Found. (chmn. 1989-90); mem. ABA (ho. of dels., bd. govs., chmn. sect. criminal justice 1975-76, mem. resource devel. coun., audit com., vice chmn. sr. lawyers div., chmn. spl. com. on fiscal policy 1984-85), Am. Coll. Trial Lawyers (bd. regents 1983-84), Am. Law Inst., Am. Judicature Soc., Fla. Bar (pres. 1965-66, Disting. Svc. award 1966), Fla. Supreme Ct. Hist. Soc. (chmn. trustees 1987-98), Am. Bar Retirement Assn. (pres. 1980-82), Nat. Conf. Referees in Bankruptcy (pres. 1963-64), Res. Officers Assn., Marine Corps Res. Officers Assn., Elks, Fla. Blue Key, Phi Alpha Delta, Alpha Kappa Psi. Baptist. Home: 530 N Ride Tallahassee FL 32303-5127 Office: PO Box 1170 305 S Gadsden St Tallahassee FL 32301-1811

ERVIN, SAMUEL JAMES, III, federal judge; b. Morganton, N.C., Mar. 2, 1926; s. Sam Ervin. B.S., Davidson Coll., 1948; LL.B., Harvard U., 1951. Bar: N.C. Pvt. practice law Morganton, 1952-57; solicitor Burke County (N.C.) Criminal Ct., 1954-56; mem. firm Patton, Ervin & Starnes and predecessors, Morganton, 1957-67; judge Superior Ct. 25th Jud. Dist. N.C., 1967-80; judge U.S. Ct. Appeals (4th cir.), Morganton, N.C., 1980-89, 96—, chief judge, 1989-96. Pres. Davidson Coll. Nat. Alumni Assn., 1973-74; trustee Davidson Coll., 1982-94, Grace Hosp., Inc., 1992—. Named Young Man of Yr. Morganton Jaycees, 1954. Office: US Ct Appeals One North Square PO Box 1488 Morganton NC 28680-1488*

ERVIN, WILMA JEAN, painter, photographer; b. McKeesport, Pa., Aug. 28, 1929; d. Walter Fulerton Dickson and Minnie Schwenk; m. Donald H. Ervin, Aug. 28, 1954; children: Jed, Gretchen, Aaron, Kirsten. BFA, Carnegie Mellon U., 1951; student, New Sch. Social Rsch., N.Y.C., 1957-58, Yale U., 1988-89. Textile designer Seneca Fabrics, N.Y.C., 1951-57; tchr. piano New Canaan, Conn., 1970-74; art and substitute tchr. New Canaan H.S., 1975-80; freelance book jacket design illustrator N.Y.C., 1990-94; tchr. photography Silvermine Sch., New Canaan, 1992; children's art tchr. Carver Cmty. Ctr., Norwalk, Conn., 1985-86. Author, illustrator: Zoo's Who, 1955; photographer: On the Edge, 1985; photographs featured on Sunday Morning, CBS-TV, 1988; exhbns. include L.A. Contemporary Gallery, 1983, Christ-Janner Gallery, New Canaan, 1983, Chenil Gallery, London, 1984, Hewlitt Gallery, Carnegie Mellon U., Pitts., 1987, Renquist Gallery, N.Y.C., 1987, Picasso Mus., Mougins, France, 1989; portrait painter, clients include: Carter Burden, Margaret Childs, Flora Biddle, Don Chung, Steven Rubin, Bruce Davidson; portraits of famous women artists include: Agnes Martin, Georgia O'Keefe, Louise Nevelson, Dianne Arbus, Gertrude Vanderbilt Whitney, Louise Bourgeois, Lisette Model. Recipient Grumbacher award Silvermine Gallery, 1980. Mem. Silvermine Guild (Art of N.E. award 1982). Democrat. Presbyterian. Avocations: piano, collecting 19th century photos. Home: 331 Park St New Canaan CT 06840

ERVING, JULIUS WINFIELD, II (DR. J. ERVING), business executive, retired professional basketball player; b. East Meadow, N.Y., Feb. 22, 1950; s. Callie Erving Lindsey; m. Turquoise Erving; 4 children. Grad., U. Mass., 1986; hon. doctorate, U.Mass., 1983, Temple U., 1983. With Va. Squires, Am. Basketball Assn., 1971-73, N.Y. Nets, Am. Basketball Assn., 1973-76, Phila. 76ers, NBA, 1976-87; mem. NBA Championship team, 1983; broadcaster NBC, 1993; exec. v.p. Orlando Magic, 1997—; v.p. RDV Sports, Orlando, 1997—; bd. dirs. Meridian Bancorp, Phila. Coca-Cola Bottling Co., DJ Group, Inc.; pres. mgmt. and mktg. firm JDREGI; spokesman Coca-Cola Co., Converse Shoe Co., Advanced Golf Techs., Hardee's. Appeared in film The Fish That Saved Pittsburgh, 1979. Trustee NBA Internat., Basketball Hall of Fame; bd. dirs. N.Y. State Sports Commn. Named Rookie of Yr. Am. Basketball Assn., 1972, Most Valuable Player Am. Basketball Assn., 1974, 76 and mem. championship team, 1974, 76; named to NBA 35th Anniversary All-Star Team, 1980; named Most Valuable Player NBA, 1981, Most Valuable Player All-Star Game NBA, 1971, 83; recipient Cert. Appreciation Easter Seals, 1982, Best Friend award Police Athletic League Phila, 1982, Walter Kennedy Citizenship award, 1983, Jackie Robinson award for Am. Black Achievement Ebony mag., 1983, Whitney M. Young award Urban League, 1984, Father Flanagan award Boys Town Nebr., 1984, Biddy Basketball award, 1984, Sports award Big Bros. Inc., N.Y.C., 1985, Man of Yr. award Am. Express, 1985, Appreciation award Lupus Found. Am., 1985, Sportsman of Yr. award David Zinkoff Meml. Found., 1986; presented Liberty Bell award Mayor Frank Rizzo, Phila., 1978; named to Hall of Fame, U. Mass., 1980, Basketball Hall of Fame. One of 3 players to score 30,000 points in his profl. basketball career; holds NBA All-Star game record for most free-throws attempted in one half, 11, in 1978; shares NBA All-Star game record for most free-throws made in one half, 9, in 1978; one of 7 players to average over 20 points and 20 rebounds per game during NCAA career. Office: care Erving Group Inc PO Box 8269 Cherry Hill NJ 08002-0269 also: Orlando Magic Orlando Arena One Magic Pl Orlando FL 32801*

ERWIN, DONALD CARROLL, plant pathology educator; b. Concord, Nebr., Nov. 24, 1920; s. Robert James and Carol (Sexson) E.; m. Veora Marie Endres, Aug. 15, 1948; children: Daniel Erwin, Myriam Erwin Casey. Student, Wayne State (Nebr.) Tchrs.Coll, 1938-39; BSc, U. Nebr., 1949, MA, 1950; PhD, U. Calif.-Davis, 1953. Jr. plant pathologist U. Calif., Riverside, 1953-54; asst. plant pathologist U. Calif., 1954-60, assoc. plant pathologist, 1960-66, prof. plant pathology, 1966—, emeritus prof., 1991. Sr. author: Phytophthora Diseases Worldwide, 1996; editor: Phytophthora: Its Biology, Taxonomy, Ecology and Pathology, 1983; contbr. articles to profl. jours. With U.S. Army, 1942-46: ETO. Nathan Gold fellow, 1949, Guggenheim fellow, 1959. Fellow Am. Phytopathol. Soc., Sigma Xi. Democrat. Roman Catholic. Office: U Calif Dept Plant Pathology Riverside CA 92521

ERWIN, ELIZABETH JOY, early childhood and special education specialist; b. Stamford, Conn., May 15, 1962; d. Jules and Harriet (Bakerson) E. BS, Syracuse U., 1983; MA, Columbia U., 1987, postgrad., 1987—. Cert. spl. edn. tchr., N.Y. Tchr. early childhood spl. edn. Stamford Pub. Schs., 1984-85; tchr. presch. spl. edn. Stepping Stone Day Sch., Queens, N.Y., 1985-88; tchr. early intervention Step By Step Infant Devel. Ctr., Bklyn., 1986-88; grad. asst./practicum Tchrs. Coll. Columbia U., N.Y.C., 1988-89, coord. masters program spl. edn., grad. asst./practicum Tchrs. Coll., 1989-91; coord. masters program early childhood spl. edn., rsch. assoc. N.Y. Med. Coll., Mental Retardation Inst., Valhalla, 1990; asst. prof. early childhood spl. edn. Queens Coll./CUNY, Flushing, 1993—; vis. asst. prof. Adelphi U., Garden City, N.Y.; cons. La Peninsula Head Start, South Bronx, N.Y., 1989-90. Peer reviewer Jour. Visual Impairment and Blindness, 1989—; contbr. articles to profl. jours. Mem. Assn. for Persons with Severe Handicap (bd. dirs. N.Y.C. chpt. 1987—, nat. media com. 1990—, Alice H. Hayden Fellowship award 1990), Assn. for Edn. and Rehab. of the Blind and Visually Impaired, Coun. For Exceptional Children (div. visually handicapped, early childhood, tchr. edn.). Jewish. Avocations: theatre, film, museums, traveling, yoga. Home: 29 Columbus Ave Montclair NJ 07042-5005 Office: Sch Edn/Ednl and Comty Prog Queens College Flushing NY 11367

ERWIN, ELMER LOUIS, vintager, cement consultant; b. Visalia, Calif., Oct. 6, 1926; s. Louis Nelson and Myra Erla (Hector) E.; m. Jeanne Prothero, Feb. 27, 1954; children: Catherine Lynn, Christopher Lawrence. B.S., U. Calif.-Berkeley, 1950. Registered profl. engr., Calif. With Kaiser Cement Corp., Oakland, Calif., 1957-80, v.p. mfg. and distbn., 1980-87; freelance vintager; cons. internat. cement plant projects.

ERWIN, FRANCES SUZANNE, artist; b. Stockton, Calif.; d. Frederick Bedford and Clara Jackquiline (Seale) Davis; widow; 9 children. Student, Thomas Leighton Sch. Fine Arts, San Francisco, 1964-70, Sergie Bongart Sch., Rexburg, Idaho, 1972-73, various master artists, various cities, 1972—. Portrait painting instr. Roy Johnson Sch., Castro Valley, Calif., 1993—, San Lorenzo (Calif.) Sch., 1995—; lectr. on visual arts, various San Francisco Bay area locations, 1987—. Portrait painter numerous pvt. commns.; commns. include Alameda County Ct. House, 1990, recreation facilities in Castro Valley and Hayward, 1991-92, Moreau H.S., Hayward, 1993, San Francisco World Trade Club, 1994, Eden Hosp., Castro Valley, 1994, Sakura Corp. Mus., Osaka, Japan, 1996; designed image for Sakura Corp. Judge various county fairs and open art shows, Alameda County, Contra Costa County, and Santa Clara County (all in Calif.), 1988—. Recipient Best of Show award Alameda County Fair, Pleasanton, Calif., 1989, Best of Class, 1990; recipient Purchase and Founders awards Pastel Soc. Fla., 1996. Mem. Pastel Soc. of Am., Pastel Soc. of the West Coast (co-founder, bd. dirs., events chair 1985-87, v.p. 1987-88, pres. 1988-89, adv. bd. mem. 1989—, Plaques 1988, 89, Art of the West award 1994), Knickerbocker Artists USA. Republican. Roman Catholic. Avocations: photography, sculpting, gardening. Home and Studio: The Studio 22125 Orange Ave Castro Valley CA 94546-6937

ERWIN, FRANK WILLIAM, personnel research and publishing executive; b. Elizabeth, N.J., Nov. 22, 1931; s. Frank J. and Jessie (Rugero) E.; m. Bridget E. Taddeo, June 26, 1965. B.A. cum laude, N.Y. U., 1957. With MBS, 1957-62, asst. to pres., asst. sec. to bd. dirs., 1960-62; dep. dir. div. selection, dir. recruiting ops. Peace Corps, 1962-65; exec. asst. to sec. labor, 1965-68; pres., chmn. Richardson, Bellows, Henry & Co., Inc., 1968—. Served with AUS, 1949-52. Mem. Am. Psychol. Assn., Internat. Assn. for Advancement Pschology, Soc. for Indsl. and Organizational Psychology, Internat. Personnel Mgmt. Assn. Home: 1400 S Joyce St Apt 118 Arlington VA 22202-1803 Office: Richardson Bellows Henry & Co Inc 2700 S Quincy St Arlington VA 22206-2226

ERWIN, JOAN LENORE, artist, educator; b. Berkeley, Calif., Feb. 12, 1932; d. Ralph Albert and Dorothy Christine (Wuhrman) Potter; m. Byron W. Crider, Jan. 28, 1956 (div. May 1975); children: Susan Lynne Crider Adams, Gayle Leann Crider; m. Joseph G. Erwin Jr., May 28, 1976; children: Terry, Ray, Steve, Tim. BS, U. So. Calif., 1954; MS in Sch. Adminstrn., Pepperdine U., 1975. Cert. tchr., Calif.; registered occupational therapist, Calif. Occupational therapist Calif. State Hosp., Camarillo, 1955-56, Harlan Shoemaker Sch., San Pedro, Calif., 1956-57; tchr. Norwalk (Calif.) Sch. Dist., 1957-59, Tustin (Calif.) Sch. Dist., 1966-68, Garden Grove (Calif.) Sch. Dist., 1968-92; freelance artist Phelan, Calif., 1976—; comml. artist Morningstar Creations, Fullerton, Calif., 1982-92; substitute tchr. Snowline Sch. Dist., Phelan, Calif., 1994—; artist Y.U.G.O., Los Alamitos, 1977-87. Pet portrait artist, U.S. and Eng., 1978-85; author, artist Biblical coloring books, 1985-90; exhibited in group shows San Bernardino County Mus., Riverside, Calif., Riverside Fine Arts Mus. Bd. dirs. San Bernardino County Mus., Fine Arts Inst. Calif. Elks scholar, 1952-53; grantee Ford Found., 1957-58, Mentor Tchr. Program, 1986. Republican. Baptist. Avocations: gardening, travel. Home: 10080 Monte Vista Rd Phelan CA 92371-8371

ERWIN, JOSEPH MARVIN, neurobiologist, primatologist; b. Scotia, Calif., Apr. 20, 1941; s. James Alexander and Shirley Virginia (McCann) E.; m. Norma Leah Schroeder, Aug. 31, 1964 (div. Dec. 1969); m. Nancy Jean Amaden, Mar. 10, 1973; children: Kristin Elizabeth Wroe Martens, Kendrick Lee Wroe. BA in Psychology, U. Pacific, Stockton, Calif., 1967; MA in Psychobiology, U. Calif., Davis, 1971, PhD in Psychobiology, 1974. Behavioral biologist Sch. of Medicine U. Calif., Davis, 1973-74; rsch. assoc. U. Wash., Seattle, 1974-77; asst. prof., scientist Peabody Coll., Nashville, 1977-78; adj. assoc. prof. Humboldt State U., Arcata, Calif., 1978-82; curator of primates Chgo. Zool. Soc., Brookfield, Ill., 1982-85; assoc. editor Nat. Geog. Rsch. Nat. Geog. Soc., Washington, 1985-88; primatologist, v.p., head divsn. neurobiology/behavior Diagnon Corp. and Bioqual, Inc., Rockville, Md., 1988—; rsch. prof. psychology Am. U., Washington, 1985-89; courtesy assoc. prof. anthropology U. Oreg., Eugene, 1992—; chmn. adv. bd. Nat. Ctr. for Study of Aging in Chimpanzees, Alamogordo, N.Mex., 1996—; U.S. coord. Sulawesi (Indonesia) Primate Project, 1985—; lectr., study leader Smithsonian Study Tours, Australia, Indonesia, Singapore, Malaysia, 1992, 98; prin. investigator Great Ape Aging Project, 1997—. Founding editor Am. Jour. Primatology, 1980-88; series editor, vol. co-editor: Comparative Primate Biology, 5 vols., 1982-87; mem. editl. bd. Tropical Biodiversity, 1989—; assoc. editor Nat. Geog. Rsch., 1985-88. Trustee Mattole Union Sch. Dist., Petrolia, Calif., 1980-82; canvaser Eugene McCarthy for Pres., Stockton, Calif., 1968. With U.S. Army, 1962-64. Nat. Geog. Soc. grantee, 1987-89; grantee Nat. Inst. on Aging, 1997, 98—. Mem. AAAS, Am. Assn. for Lab. Animal Sci., Soc. for Conservation Biology, Am. Soc. Primatologists (founder 1976, pres. 1994-96), Am. Zool. and Aquarium Assn., Species Survival Commn., Soc. for Neurosci. Democrat. Achievements include devel. of a comparative neurobiology of aging resource; patents for improved environments for laboratory animals; unexpected patterns of aggressive behavior in primates; limited intergradation among Sulawesi macaque populations. Avocations: photography, travel, nature study, design. Office: Diagnon Corp and Bioqual Inc 9600 Medical Center Dr Rockville MD 20850-3336

ERWIN, JUDITH ANN (JUDITH ANN PEACOCK), writer, photographer, lawyer; b. Decatur, Ga., Jan. 4, 1939; d. Milo Eugene and Lucy Isabelle (Simpson) Peacock; m. William Wofford Erwin, Sept. 5, 1959 (div. Mar. 1982); children: William Wofford Jr., Allison Sheridan (Norton). AA, Fla. C.C., 1987; BA summa cum laude, Jacksonville U., 1989; JD, U. Fla., 1993. Photography instr., freelance writer Jacksonville, Fla., 1986-91, freelance dance photographer, 1984-91; theater and dance critic Folio Weekly, Jacksonville, Fla., 1987-89; writer dance VUE mag.; founder On Our Own, 1991; pvt. practice lawyer; pres. Ballet Guild, Jacksonville, 1973-75, Ballet Repertory Jacksonville, 1979-80; freelance costume designer, Jacksonville, 1981-86; mem. grand rev. dance panel Fla. Dept. Cultural Affairs, 1996, 97; seminar spkr. in field. Mem. editorial staff Kalliope, Jour. Women's Art, 1989-91; editor-in-chief U. Fla. Jour. of Law and Pub. Policy, fall 1993; editor Jacksonville Trial Lawyers Newsletter. Mem. del.'s council Art's Assembly Jacksonville, 1979-80. Mem. AAUW, ATLA, Nat. Soc. Arts and Letters, Nat. League Am. Pen Women, Fla. Bar Assn., Jacksonville Bar Assn., Jacksonville Women Lawyers Assn., Phi Kappa Phi, Phi Theta Kappa. Democrat. Episcopalian.

ERWIN, RICHARD CANNON, SR., federal judge; b. McDowell County, N.C., Aug. 23, 1923; s. John Adam and Flora (Cannon) E.; m. Demerice Whitley, Aug. 25, 1946; children: Richard Cannon, Jr., Aurelia Whitley. BA, Johnson C. Smith U., 1947; LLB, Howard U., 1951; LLD, Pfeiffer Coll., 1980, Johnson C. Smith U., 1981. Bar: N.C. 1951, U.S. Supreme Ct. 1974. Practice law Winston-Salem, N.C., 1951-77; judge N.C. Ct. Appeals, 1978; judge U.S. Dist. Ct. (mid. dist.) N.C., 1980-88, chief judge, 1988-92, sr. judge, 1992—; rep. N.C. Gen. Assembly, chmn. hwy. safety com.; mem. law bd. vis. Wake Forest U., 1984—. Trustee Forsyth County Legal Aid Soc., Amos Cottage, Inc.; chmn. bd. trustees Bennett Coll.; bd. dirs. N.C. 4-H Devel. Fund, Inc.; bd. visitors Div. Sch., Duke U.; trustee Children's Home, Winston-Salem; mem. steering com. Winston-Salem Found.; bd. dirs. United Fund; bd. dirs., pres. Citizens Coalition Forsyth County and Anderson High Sch., PTA; mem. N.C. Bd. Edn., 1971-77, N.C. State Library Bd. Trustees, 1968-69; mem., chmn. personnel com. Winston-Salem/Forsyth County Sch. Bd.; chmn. bd. trustees St. Paul United Methodist Ch. Mem. N.C. Bar Assn. (v.p. 1983-84), N.C. Assn. Black Lawyers, Forsyth County Bar Assn. (pres.), N.C. State Bar. Office: US Dist Ct Federal Bldg #246 251 N Main St Winston Salem NC 27101-3914*

ERWIN, SHON T., federal judge. Part-time magistrate judge U.s. Dist. Ct. (we. dist.) Okla. Office: 207 US Courthouse 410 SW 5th St Lawton OK 73501-4628

ERXLEBEN, WILLIAM CHARLES, lawyer; b. Chgo., Dec. 18, 1942; s. Walter Oscar and Sarah Louise (Githens) E.; m. Gayle Amelia Reichmuth, Aug. 28, 1965; children: David William, Jennifer Renée. BS in Bus., Miami U., Oxford, Ohio, 1963; JD, Stanford U., 1966. Bar: Wash. 1966. Asst. state atty. gen. Wash. State Atty. Gen.'s Office, Olympia, 1968-70; exec. asst. U.S. atty. Dept. Justice, Seattle, 1970-72; regional dir. FTC, Seattle, 1972-79; lectr. Grad. Sch. Bus., U. Wash., Seattle, 1979-85; ptnr. Foster, Pepper & Shefelman, Bellevue, Wash., 1985-91; ptnr. Lane Powell Spears Lubersky, Olympia, 1991-93; pres., CEO Data I/O Corp., 1993-98; chmn., dir. Advanced Digital Tech., Bellevue, Wash., 1983-85; dir. Data I/O Corp., Redmond, Wash., 1979-98, cons., 1998—. Contbr. articles to law revs. Counsel Wash. Assn. for Children and Adults with Learning Disabilities, Seattle, 1985-93; chmn. Portwatch, Seattle, 1985; mem. advt. rev. com. Better Bus. Bur., Seattle, 1982; bd. dirs. Wash. Citizens for Recycling, Seattle, 1980-84; dem. nominee for Wash. State Atty. Gen., 1988. Served with USAF, 1966-68. Recipient Excellence in Supervision award FTC, 1975, Disting. Service award, 1979; Sloan exec. fellow Stanford U. Grad. Sch. Bus., 1975-76. Mem. ABA, Wash. State Bar Assn. (sec.-treas. antitrust subcom. 1981-83). Home: 16502 NE 46th St Redmond WA 98052-5440

ERZBERGER, HEINZ, aeronautical engineer. Chief designer of Ctr.-Tracone Automation System Ames Rsch. Ctr., Moffet Field, Calif.; sr. scientist for air traffic mgmt. Ames Rsch. Ctr., Calif., 1996—. Recipient Hugh L. Dryden Lectureship in Rsch. award Am. Inst. of Aeronautics and Astronautics, 1997. Office: NASA Ames Rsch Ctr M/S 210/9 Moffett Field CA 94035

ESAHAK, GEORGE MICHAEL, lawyer; b. Tucson, July 27, 1958; s. James and Bernice (Lindquist) E. BA, Yale U., 1980; JD, Northwestern U., 1983. Bar: Ariz. 1983, U.S. Ct. Appeals (9th cir.) 1983, U.S. Dist. Ct. Ariz. 1983. Assoc. Jennings Strouss & Salmon, Phoenix, 1983-88, ptnr., 1988—. Campaign vol. John McCain for Senator, Phoenix, 1984, Jon Kyl for Congressman, 1986. Mem. ABA, Ariz. Bar Assn., Maricopa County Bar Assn., Maricopa County Bar Found., Am. Judicature Soc., Phoenix C. of C., Captain's Club, IBM Ring 55 Club, Phi Beta Kappa. Republican. Avocations: triathlete, magic. Office: Jennings Strouss & Salmon 2 N Central Ave Ste 1600 Phoenix AZ 85004-2393

ESAKI, LEO, physicist, foundation executive; b. Osaka, Japan, Mar. 12, 1925; came to U.S., 1960; s. Soichiro and Niyoko (Ito) E.; m. Masako Kondo, May, 31, 1986; children from previous marriage: Nina Yvonne, Anna Eileen, Eugene Leo. B.S., U. Tokyo, 1947, Ph.D., 1959. With Sony Corp., Japan, 1956-60; with Thomas J. Watson Research Center, IBM, Yorktown Heights, N.Y., 1960-92; IBM fellow Thomas J. Watson Research Center, IBM, 1967-92, mgr. device research, 1965-92; dir. IBM-Japan, 1975-92; pres. U. Tsukuba, Ibaraki, Japan, 1992-98; chmn. Sci. and Tech. Found. of Ibaraki, 1998—. Recipient Stuart Ballantine medal Franklin Inst., 1961, Japan Acad. award, 1965, Nobel prize in physics, 1973; decorated Order of Culture Govt. of Japan, 1974. Fellow IEEE (Morris N. Liebman Meml. prize 1961, Medal of Honor 1991), Am. Phys. Soc. (councillor-at-large 1971-74), internat. prize for new materials 1985, Japan prize, 1998), conferred Grand Cordon Order of Rising Sun, Japan Phys. Soc., Am. Vacuum Soc. (bd. dirs. 1973-74); mem. NAS (fgn. assoc.), NAE (fgn. assoc.), Am. Acad. Arts and Scis., Am. Philos. Soc., Max-Planck Gesellschaft, Russian Acad. Scis. (fgn.), Academia Nacional de Ingenieria Mex. (corr.), Japan Acad. Achievements include invention of Esaki tunnel diode, 1957. Home: 2484 Uenomuro, Tsukuba Ibaraki 305-0023, Japan Office: Sci and Tech Promotion Fnd, Ibaraki, 2-1-6- Sengen, Tsukuba 305-0047, Japan also: PO Box 851 Katonah NY 10536-0851

ESBER, EDWARD MICHAEL, JR., software company executive; b. Cleve., June 22, 1952; s. Edward Michael and Joanne Helen (Saah) E.; m. Margaret Renfrow, July 19, 1980; children: Dianne Michelle, Paul Andrew, Alexander Joseph. BS in Computer Engring., Case Western Res. U., Cleve., 1974; MSEE, Syracuse U., N.Y., 1976; MBA, Harvard U., Cambridge, 1978. Assoc. engr. IBM, Poughkeepsie, N.Y., 1974-76; mktg. mgr. Tex. Instruments, Lubbock, Tex., 1978-79; v.p. mktg. Visi Corp., San Jose, Calif., 1979-83; ptnr. Esber-Folk Assocs., Dallas, 1983-84; exec. v.p. mktg. and sales Ashton-Tate, Torrance, Calif., 1984, pres., COO, 1984—, pres., chief exec. officer, 1984—, chmn., chief exec. officer, 1986-90; pres., COO Creative Labs, Milpitas, Calif., 1993-94; chmn., CEO Creative Insights, Sunnyvale, Calif., 1994-95; CEO, pres. Solo Point, Los Gatos, Calif., 1995—; chmn. Solo Point, Los Gatos, Calif., 1995-98; bd. dirs. Quantum Inc., Portivity, Integrated Circuit Sys., Inc., Socket Comm. Trustee Case Western Res. U. Mem. Am. Electronic Assn. Republican. Office: The Esber Group 13430 Country Way Los Altos Hills CA 94022

ESCALANTE, JUDSON ROBERT, business consultant; b. Schenectady, N.Y., Jan. 31, 1930; s. James S. and Katherine H. (Judson) E.; m. Charlotte D. Carpenter, June 7, 1958; children: David J., Katherine Anne. BA, Union Coll., 1953. Asst. estate planning officer Nat. Comml. Bank, Albany, N.Y., 1955-65; founder, v.p., sec., dir. Fidelity Bank of Colonie, Latham, N.Y, 1966-69; area dir. Gen. Bus. Svcs., Latham, 1969-81, Micro Bus. Svcs., 1981—; v.p. fin. Gad Cruise Lines, Inc., 1987-88; instr. in field. Bd. dirs., treas. Capital Artists Opera Co., 1970-74, 79; mem. fund dr. com. Union Coll., 1979-80; vestryman, treas. Episcopal Ch.; treas., chief fin. officer Chatham Vis. Nurse Assn., 1983-89; trustee Chatham Vis. Nurse Assn. Profit Trust, 1985-96; auditor Chatham Conservation Found., 1985-95. With U.S. Army, 1953-55. Mem. Colonie C. of C. (treas., bd. dirs. 1972-76), Union Coll. Alumni Soc. (pres. 1971-73, Alumni Gold medal 1978), Dutch Settlers Soc. Albany. Home: 400 Old Comers Rd Chatham MA 02633-1315

ESCALET, FRANK DIAZ, art gallery owner, artist, educator; b. Ponce, P.R., Mar. 16, 1930; s. Frank Thillet and Concepcion Rodriquez (Diaz) E.; m.Shirley Leslie Fanner, Sept. 29, 1953 (div. Aug., 1955); children: Judith Alicia, Sudan Edith Escalet Barry; m. Marjorie Janet Gaydash-Huebner, July 19, 1964; 1 child, Frank Daniel (dec.). Owner, operator Talent Shop, N.Y.C., 1955-58, House of Escalet, N.Y.C., 1958-71, Pandora's Box, Eastport, Maine, 1971-73, Cobbler's Bench Art Gallery, Pembroke, Maine, 1973-82, House of Escalet Gallery, Kennebunkport, Maine, 1982-84, House of Escalet Studios, Kennebunkport, 1984—; tchr. leathercraft Pasamaquoddy Reservation, Perry, Maine, 1971-72, Vocat. Sch. for Retarded Children, Calais, Maine, 1972-73. Works include solo traveling exhibit, Czechoslovakia, Russia, Poland, Yugoslavia, Hungary, Ukraine, 1991—; represented in permanent collections at Naprstkovo Mus., Prague, Union of Artists, Moscow, Bratslavia Primitive Mus., Slovakia, Frydek-Mistek Mus. No. Moravia, Museo Chicano, Phoenix, S.E. Tex. Art Mus., Beaumont, Arch. M. Huntington Gallery, Austin, Tex., Housatonic Mus., Bridgeport, Conn., Orgn. of Am. States Art Mus., Washington, Maryknoll (N.Y.) Sisters Ctr., The Mus. of City of N.Y., 1998; featured on pub. TV, 1978, 82, 89; works in permanent collection of Mus. of City of N.Y.: artist: Song and Dance Man acrylic, 1996. With US Air Force, 1947-54. Recipient numerous internat. and U.S. awards. Avocations: photography, antiques, gardening, traveling, reading. Home and Office: House of Escalet Studios PO Box 26 13 Fletcher St Kennebunk ME 04043-6705

ESCALÓN DELGADO, CLARA S., English language education specialist; b. Dayton, Ohio, Sept. 26, 1952; d. Paul and Jo Ellen (Wilson) Liesenhoff; m. Raúl Escalón, Sept. 18, 1977 (div. Sept. 1988); 1 child, Tania; m. Máximo Delgado, Feb. 23, 1990; stepchildren: Max Brian, Bridget Patricia. Degree in Spanish lit., U. Valencia, Spain, 1972-74; BA, Murray State U., 1974; MA, Wright State U., 1984. Instr. Global Sch. of Idioms, Valencia, 1972-74; instr., interim dir. ESL program Miami U., Greenville, Ohio, 1974-77; instr. English Inst., Reynosa, Mexico, 1978; outreach worker La Raza Unida, Dayton, 1979; instr., acting dir. The English Lang. and Multicultural Inst., Dayton, 1982-86, dir., 1986—; cons. to member schs. Southwestern Ohio Coun. Higher Edn., Dayton, 1985—; cons., presenter Ohio Pub. Sch. Systems, 1985—; cons. Dayton ESL Providers, 1985—; presenter numerous cross-cultural, communication and management workshops and seminars, 1984—. Author: (book and cassette program) Speaking American English, 1985 (Program of Yr. award 1986), Hispanics in the U.S.A., 1991, CDROM: The Sounds of American English Interactive Program, 1999. Founder, vol. instr. Spanish/English GED (Gen. Edn. Devel.) Program, Dayton, 1979-84; founding mem., vol. Project READ (Reading Edn. for Adults in Dayton), 1988—; founding dir. La Casa del Pueblo, Dayton, 1975-78; vol. emergency translator Vol. Bank/Dayton Cts., 1982—. Named one of Top 10 Women in Greater Dayton Area, Dayton Daily News, 1992. Mem. NAFE, Nat. Assn. Fgn. Student Affairs, Bus. and Profl. Women, Tchrs. of English to Speakers of Other Langs., Assn. Ind. Colls. and Schs. (cons./evaluator 1989—), Dayton Coun. World Affairs, Nat. Image. Avocations: aerobics, creative writing, reading. Office: English Lang and Multi- Cultural Inst 300 College Park Ave Rm 117 Dayton OH 45469-0001

ESCARRAZ, ENRIQUE, III, lawyer; b. Evergreen Park, Ill., Aug. 30, 1944; s. Enrique Jr. and Mary Ellen (Bandy) E.; children from previous marriage; Erin Christine, Martina Mary; m. Patricia Jane Escarraz; children: Sarah Ellen, James Lee, Jason F. BA, U. Fla., 1966, JD, 1968. Bar: Fla. 1969, U.S. Dist. Ct. (so. and mid. dists.) Fla. 1969, U.S. Ct. Appeals (5th cir.) 1971, U.S. Ct. Appeals (11th cir.) 1981. VISTA atty. Community Legal Counsel, Chgo., 1968-69; mng. atty. Fla. Rural Legal Services, Ft. Myers, 1969-71; pvt. practice law St. Petersburg, Fla., 1971-82, 85-87, 88—; ptnr. Anderson & Escarraz, St. Petersburg, 1982-85; asst. gen. counsel U. South Fla., 1987-88; assoc. James L. Eskald Law Office, Largo, Fla., 1988; part-time atty. Pub. Defender's Office Fla. 6th Cir., St. Petersburg, 1973-74; bd. dirs. Gulf Coast Legal Svcs., Inc., 1989—, pres., 1994-96. Vol. Cmty. Law Prog., Inc.; coord. James B. Sanderlin for Judge, Pinellas County, Fla., 1972-76; mem. ACLU Legal Panel, St. Petersburg, 1972—; cooperating atty. NAACP Legal Panel, St. Petersburg, 1972—; cooperating atty. NAACP Legal Def. Edn. Funds, Inc., N.Y.C., 1973—; pres. Creative Care, Inc., Clearwater, Fla., 1974-80; mem. allocations com. United Way, Pinellas County, 1976, 1978-81; pres., treas. Cmty. Youth Svcs., Inc., St. Petersburg, 1977-82; co-chmn. Blue Ribbon Com. Pinellas County Dem. Exec. Com., 1977-82; mem. Fla. HRS Dist. V Adv. Coun., Pinellas County, 1982, St. Petersburg Human Rels. Rev. Bd., 1984, 90—, St. Petersburg Adult Cmty. Band, 1989—, Greater St. Petersburg Second Time Around Marching Band, 1990-92; mem. adv. bd. Jacquelyn Elvera Hodges Johnson Fund, 1990—. Mem. ABA, ATLA, FBA, Nat. Assn. Social Security Claimant Reps., Pinellas County Trial Lawyers Assn., St. Petersburg Bar Assn. (pro bono com. 1988, 95—), Bayshore Runners Club, Greater Pinellas County Dem. Club (sec.-treas. 1989-97, bd. dirs. 1997—), Road Runners Club Am. Office: 2121 5th Ave N Saint Petersburg FL 33713-8013 also: PO Box 847 Saint Petersburg FL 33731-0847

ESCHBACH, JESSE ERNEST, federal judge; b. Warsaw, Ind., Oct. 26, 1920; S. Jesse Ernest and Mary W. (Stout) E.; m. Sara Ann Walker, Mar. 15, 1947; children: Jesse Ernest III, Virginia. BS, Ind. U., 1943, JD with distinction, 1949, LLD (hon.), 1986. Bar: Ind. 1949. Ptnr. Graham, Rasor, Eschbach & Harris, Warsaw, 1949-62; city atty. Warsaw, 1952-53; dep. pros. atty. 54th Jud. Circuit Ct. Ind., 1952-1954; judge U.S. Dist. Ct. Ind., 1962-81; chief judge judge U.S. Dist. Ct. Ind., 1974-81; judge U.S. Ct. Appeals (7th cir.), W. Palm Beach, Fla., 1981-85, sr. judge, 1985—; Pres. Endicott Church Furniture, Inc., 1960-62; sec., gen. counsel Dalton Foundries, Inc., 1957-62. Editorial staff: Ind. Law Jour, 1947-49. Trustee Ind. U., 1965-70. Served with USNR, 1943-46. Hastings scholar, 1949; Recipient U.S. Law Week award, 1949. Mem. U.S. C. of C. (labor relations com. 1960-62), Warsaw C. of C. (pres. 1955-56), Nat. Assn. Furniture Mfrs. (dir. 1962), Ind. Mfrs. Assn. (dir. 1962), ABA, Ind. Bar Assn. (bd. mgrs. 1953-54, ho. dels. 1950-60), Fed. Bar Assn., Am. Judicature Soc., Order of Coif. Presbyn. Club: Rotarian (pres. Warsaw 1956-57). Home: 11709 N Lake Dr Boynton Beach FL 33436-5518 Office: US Ct Appeals 7th Cir 253 US Courthouse 701 Clematis St West Palm Beach FL 33401-5101

ESCHBACH, JOSEPH WETHERILL, nephrology educator; b. Detroit, Jan. 21, 1933; s. Joseph William and Marguerite (Wetherill) E.; m. Mary Ann Charles, June 16, 1956; children: Cheryl Louise, Ann Elizabeth, Joseph Charles. BA, BS, Otterbein Coll., 1955; MD, Jefferson Med. Coll., 1959. Practitioner nephrology and internal medicine Minor and James Med., Seattle, 1965—; dir. home dialysis U. Wash., Seattle, 1965-72, clin. asst. prof. div. nephrology, 1967-70, clin. assoc. prof. div. nephrology, 1970-75, clin. prof. div. nephrology, 1975-85, clin. prof. divs. nephrology and hematology, 1985—; cons. Ortho Pharm., Raritan, N.J., 1987-88, Amgen, Thousand Oaks, Calif., 1985-91. Co-editor: Erythropoietin: Molecular, Cellular and Clinical Biology, 1991; contbr. articles to jours. in field, chpts. to textbooks. Trustee First Ave. Svc. Ctr., 1976-86; pres. bd. trustees Northwest Kidney Ctr., Seattle, 1985-87 (Haviland award 1991). Recipient Disting. Svc. award Seattle Jaycees, 1979, Alumni Achievement award Otterbein Coll., 1991. Fellow ACP; mem. Inst. Medicine of NAS, AMA, Am. Soc. Nephrology, Internat. Soc. Nephrology, King County Med. Soc. (pres. 1987). Presbyterian. Avocations: squash, woodworking, singing. Home: 770 96th Ave SE Bellevue WA 98004-6502 Office: Minor & James Med 515 Minor Ave Seattle WA 98104-2138

ESCHEN, ALBERT HERMAN, optometrist; b. N.Y.C., Dec. 3, 1921; s. Sam and Frances (Lazelle) E.; m. Florence Askwyth, Nov. 22, 1950; children: Burt, Andrew. DOptometry, Ill. Coll. Optometry, Chgo., 1948. Optometrist Optometric Ctr. of N.Y., N.Y.C., 1960-65; dir. Brownsville Eye Clinic, Bklyn., 1960-72; optometrist Crown Nursing Home Staff, Bklyn., 1968-78, Coronet Nursing Home Staff, Bklyn., 1958-68, N.Y.C. Health Ins. Program, Bklyn., 1964-74, N.Y.C. Dept. Health, Bklyn. and N.Y.C., 1962-82; pvt. practice optometry Bklyn., 1950—; cons N.Y.C. Dept. Rehab. and Guidance, Bklyn., 1963-73; bd. dirs. Brownsville Mental Health Clinic, Bklyn., 1965-75. Author short stories; engraver. Served to capt. USAF, 1942-46. Named Alumnus of Yr., Ill. Coll. Optometry, 1993. Fellow Internat. Coll. Ocular Sci.; mem. Am. Optometrists Assn., N.Y. State Optometric Assn. (dir. 1957-58), Bklyn. Optometric Soc. (life; pres. 1957-58, Svc. award 1957), Masons. Avocations: engraving, writing, drawing, antique collecting. Home: 2821 Avenue U Brooklyn NY 11229-5053

ESCHENBACH, CHRISTOPH, conductor, pianist; b. Breslau, Silesia, Germany, Feb. 20, 1940. Attended, Hamburg (Fed. Republic Germany) Conservatory, State Conservatory Music, Cologne, Fed. Republic Germany; Doctorate, U. Houston. Performed with leading orchs., including Concertgebouw, Amsterdam, The Netherlands, Paris Orch., London Symphony, Berlin Philharm., Cleve. Orch., London Philharm., Orchestre National de France; soloist with Cleve. Orch. during European Festival Tour, 1967; N.Am. debut Expo '67, Montreal, Que., Can., 1967; soloist with Cleve. Orch., 1969; Carnegie Hall debut with Cleve. Orch., 1969; toured Europe, North and South Am., Israel, Japan; appeared at festivals including Salzburg, Austria, Lucerne, Switzerland, Bonn, W. Ger., Aix-en-Provence, France; chief condr. Staatsphilharmonie Rheinland-Pfalz, Fed. Republic Germany, 1979; first prin. guest condr. Tonhalle Orch., Switzerland, 1981, chief condr., 1982; rec. artist, Deutsche Grammophon, Polydor, EMI, Virgin Classics, London, 1989; music dir. Houston Symphony Orch., 1988-99, conductor laureate, 1998—, tours in Japan; music dir. NDR Symphony, Hamburg, Germany, Orchestre de Paris, France; artistic dir. Schleswig-Holstein Music Festival, Germany. Participant Pacific Music Festival, 1990, 91, 92, 93, 94. Winner Munich Internat.; named artistic dir. Ravinia Music Festival, 1995. Office: care Columbia Artists Mgmt Inc 165 W 57th St New

York NY 10019-2201 also: Houston Symphony Orch Jesse H Jones Hall 615 Louisiana St Ste 102 Houston TX 77002-2715*

ESCHENMOSER, ALBERT, chemist; b. Erstfield, Aug. 5, 1925; s. Alfons and Johanna (Oesch) E.; m. Elizabeth Baschnonga, 1954; 3 children. Dr. Nat. Sci., Swiss Fed. Inst. Tech., 1951; student Collegium Altdorf, Kantonsschule St. Gallen, ETH Zurich; Dr.rer.nat. (hon.), U. Fribourg, 1966; DSc (hon.), U. Chgo., 1970, U. Edinburgh, 1979, U. Bologna, 1989, U. Frankfurt, 1990, U. Strasbourg, 1991, Harvard U., 1993. Privatdozent organic chemistry Swiss Fed. Inst. Tech., 1956, assoc. prof., 1960, prof. organic chemistry, 1965; prof. Skaggs Inst. Chem. Biology Scripps Rsch. Inst., La Jolla, Calif., 1996. Contbr. articles to profl. jours. Recipient Kern award Swiss Fed. Inst. Tech., 1949, Werner award, 1956, Ruzicka award Swiss Fed. Inst. Tech., 1958, Fritzsche award Am. Chem. Soc., 1966, Marcel Benoist prize Swiss Govt., 1973, R.A. Welch award in Chemistry, Houston, 1974, Kirkwood medal Yale, 1976, A.W.V. Hofmann-Denkmunze, GDCh., 1976, Dannie Heinemann prize Akademie der Wissenschaften Göttingen, 1977, Davy medal Royal Soc. London, 1978, Tetrahedron prize Pergamon Press, 1981, G. Kenner award U. Liverpool, 1982, Arthur C. Cope award Am. Chem. Soc., 1984, Wolf prize for chemistry, Wolf Found., Israel, 1986, Cothenius medal Leopoldina Halle, 1991, Orden Pour le mérite fur Wissenschaften und Künste, 1992, Oesterreichisches Ehrenzeichen für Wissenschaft und Kunst, 1993, Nakanishi prize Chem. Soc. Japan, 1998, Paracelsus prize Swiss Chem. Soc., 1999. Mem. Am. Acad. Arts and Scis. (fgn.), Nat. Acad. Scis. U.S. (fgn. assoc.), Akademie der Wissenschaften (corr. mem. Göttingen), Deutsche Akademie der Naturforscher Leopoldina (Halle), Royal Soc. (fgn. London), Pontificial Acad. (Vatican), Acad. Europe (London), Croatian Acad. Sci. Arts (corr. mem. Zagreb). Home: Bergstrasse 9, 8700 Küsnacht Switzerland

ESCHMEYER, WILLIAM NEIL, marine scientist; b. Knoxville, Tenn., Feb. 11, 1939; s. Reuben William and Ruth Elizabeth (Willey) E.; m. Lydia R. Berardelli, Sept. 9, 1967 (div. 1981); children: Lisa Ruth, David Paul, Lanea Cathleen. B.S., U. Mich., 1961; M.S., U. Miami, Fla., 1964, Ph.D., 1967. Asst. curator, then asso. curator Calif. Acad. Scis., San Francisco, 1967-73; curator Calif. Acad. Scis., 1973—, dir. research, 1977-83, sr. curator, 1983—. Author books, research papers, articles in field. Grantee NSF. Mem. Am. Soc. Ichthyologists and Herpetologists, other biol. socs., Zeta Psi. E-mail: weschmeyer@calacademy.org. Address: Calif Acad Scis Golden Gate Park San Francisco CA 94118

ESCOBAR, MARISOL See MARISOL

ESCOBAR, MARISOL, sculptor; b. Paris, 1930. Student, Ecole Beaux Arts, 1949, Art Students League, 1950, New Sch. Hans Hofmann Sch., 1951-54; hon. DFA, Moore Coll. Art, 1969; hon. dr. arts, R.I. Sch. Design, Providence, 1986; hon. DFA, SUNY, Buffalo, 1992. One man exhibits include Sidney Janis Gallery, N.Y., 1966, 67, 73, 75, 81, 84, 89, Columbus Gallery Fin Arts, Ohio, 1974, Makier Gallery, Phila., 1982, Boca Raton Mus. ARt, 1988, Galerie Tokoro, Tokyo, 1989, Hasagawa Gallery, Tokyo, 1989, Natl. Portrait Gallery, Washington, 1991, Forms in Wood, Am. Scultpure of the 1950's, Phila. Art Mus., 1985, The Artist's Mother: Portraits and Homages, Heckscher Mus. Huntington, N.Y. and Nat. Portrait Gallery, Washington, 1987, Urban Figures, Whitney Mus. Am. Art at Philip Morris, 1988, Body Language: The Figure in the ARt of Our Time, Rose ARt Mus., Waltham, Mass., 1990, Figures of Contemporary Sculpture, 1978-90, Images of Man, Isetan Mus. Art, Tokyo, Dakimoru Mus. Art, Osaka-Umeda & Hiroshima City Mus. Contemporary Art, 1992, many other exhibits; contbr. articles to profl. publs. Mem. Am. Acad. Arts and Letters. Office: Marlborough Gallery 40 W 57th St Fl 2 New York NY 10019-4069*

ESCOTET, MIGUEL-ANGEL, psychologist, educator; b. Leon, Spain, Mar. 27; came to U.S., 1967; s. Miguel and Mercedes (Alvarez) E.; m. Martha Ardila, Dec. 21, 1963; 1 child, Marta I. Student, Poly. Zulia, Madrid, 1958-60; lic. in clin. psychology, Javeriana U., Bogota, Colombia, 1964; MA in Psychology, Edn., U. Tex., 1969; PhD in Psychology, Rsch., U. Nebr., 1972; D (hon.), Maran U., Brazil; hon. degree, Palermo U., Buenos Aires. Acad. dean U. Oriente, Cumana, Venezuela, 1970-72; pvt. practice Miami, Madrid, Caracas, 1972-93; assoc. prof. Fort Lewis Coll., Durango, Colo., 1972-74; sub-sec. edn. Min. Edn., Caracas, Venezuela, 1974-76; v.p. Open U. Venezuela, Caracas, 1976-81; vis. prof. Fla. Internat. U., Miami, 1981-83, prof., dir. IIDE grad., 1993—; sec. gen. Orgn. Iberoam. States, Madrid, 1983-88; pres. Iberam. U., Salamanca, Spain, 1988-91; spl. adv. UNESCO, Paris, 1991-93; cons. UNESCO, Paris, 1976—, World Bank/Internat. Bank, Washington, 1976-82; adv. bd. UNESCO Higher Edn., Paris, 1992—. Author: Learning for the Future, 1993, University and Future, 1996, The End of the University, 1997, Auto-Evaluacion Universitaria, 1998; editor: Cultural and Social Foundations of Education, 1997. Pres. The Escotet Found., 1997—. Recipient Andres Bello Gold award Pres. Venezuela, 1986, Gold medal Orgn. Iberoam. States, 1988. Mem. Am. Psychol. Assn., Latin Am. Assn. Edn. (v.p. 1991—), Latin Am. Assn. Psychology (pres. 1986-90), Comparative Internat. Edn. Soc., Club Rome. Avocations: chess, cycling, jai-lai, ecology. Office: Fla Internat U ZEB 345A Univ Park Miami FL 33199

ESHBAUGH, W(ILLIAM) HARDY, botanist, educator; b. Glen Ridge, N.J., May 1, 1936; -; s. William Hardy Eshbaugh Jr. and Elizabeth (Wakeman) Henderson; m. Barbara Keller, Sept. 6, 1958; children: David Charles, Stephen Hardy, Elizabeth Wendy, Jeffrey Raymond. BA, Cornell U., 1959; MA, Ind. U., 1961, PhD, 1964. Lectr. in botany Ind. U., Bloomington, 1962; spl. asst. to chief ecology and epidemiology br. Dugway (Utah) Proving Ground, 1964-65; asst. prof., curator botany So. Ill. U., Carbondale, 1965-67; asst. prof., curator botany Miami U., Oxford, Ohio, 1967-71, assoc. prof., 1971-77; prof. botany, curator Willard Sherman Turell Herbarium, Oxford, Ohio, 1977-98; chmn. dept. botany Miami U., Oxford, Ohio, 1983-88; prof. emeritus Willard Sherman Turell Herbarium, Oxford, Ohio, 1998; assoc. program dir. NSF, Washington, 1982-83; mem. sci. rsch. bd. Amazon Ctr. Environ. Edn. and Rsch.; co-chmn. steering com. Systematics Agenda 2000-Charting the Biosphere; adv. bd. Am. Bot. Coun., 1996—; instr. Internat. Rainforest Workshops, 1991-99. Co-author: The Vascular Flora of Andros Island, Bahamas, 1988; contbr. articles to profl. jours. Bd. dirs. Childrens Environ. Trust Found., 1992-94; troop com. Oxford area Boy Scouts Am., 1986-90. Capt. U.S. Army, 1964-65. Fellow AAAS, Ohio Acad. Sci., Inst. Environ. Scis.; mem. Am. Inst. Biol. Scis. (pres. 1995), Am. Soc. Plant Taxonomists (pres. 1991-92), Soc. Econ. Botany (v.p. 1982-83, pres. 1983-84), Bot. Soc. Am. (pres. 1988-89, Merit award 1992), Nat. Audubon Soc. (bd. dirs. 1993—), Nature Conservancy (vice chmn. Ohio chpt. 1970-75, trustee 1970-77), Assn. Systemics Collections (bd. dirs. 1981-84, rep.-at-large), Internat. Orgn. Plant Biosystematists (coun. 1987-89, ad hoc com. 1989-92), N.Am. treas. 1992-95), Internat. Field Studies (trustee 1989-95). Methodist. Avocations: camping, sailing, skiing, fly-fishing, photography. Home: 209 Mckee Ave Oxford OH 45056-9059 Office: Miami U Dept Botany Oxford OH 45056

ESHELMAN, ENOS GRANT, JR., prosthodontist; b. Birmingham, Ala., Oct. 18, 1943; s. Enos Grant and Kathleen Marie (Lokey) E.; m. Mary Darlene Duncan, Nov. 22, 1975; children: Duncan Grant, Hunter Nicholas, Parker Jacob. AB, Franklin and Marshall Coll., Lancaster, Pa., 1965; DDS, Columbia U., 1969; MS, U. Mo., 1980. Commd. 2d lt. USAF, advanced through grades to col., 1969-97; gen. dental officer USAF, Lackland AFB, Tex., 1969-72; asst. base dental surgeon, oral surgeon, dental officer USAF, Korat Air Base, Thailand, 1972-73; asst. base dental surgeon, prosthodontics and lab. officer USAF, Sembach Air Base, Germany, 1973-78; chief prosthodontics USAF, Norton AFB, Calif., 1980-83; prosthodontics tng. officer USAF Hosp., Davis Monthan AFB, Ariz., 1983-89; chief prosthodontics, dental lab. officer 36 TFW Hosp., Bitburg Air Base, Germany, 1989-93; tng. officer prosthodontics USAF Hosp., Langley AFB, Va., 1993-97; asst. prof. Loma Linda (Calif.) U. Sch. Dentistry, 1981-83, Med. Coll. Va. Sch. of Dentistry, 1995-96, U. Mo. Sch. Dentistry, Kansas City, 1997—; prosthodontics cons. Jerry Pettis Vets. Hosp., Loma Linda, 1982-83, Vets. Affairs Med. Ctr., Tucson, 1983-89; pres. Fed. Svcs. Regional Dental Conf., Davis Monthan AFB, Ariz., 1983-85. Editor and contbr. to profl. sci. publs. Pres. Jr. Officers Coun. Korat Air Base, Thailand, 1973; asst. coach Sabino Little League Baseball, Tucson, 1988-89; pres. Cmty. Summer Swim Team, 1995, 96. Rinehart Found. rsch. grantee U. Mo. Sch. Dentistry, 1978; decorated Meritorious Svc. medal. Mem. ADA, Am. Coll. Prosthodontics, Internat. Coll. Dentists, Air Force Assn., Psi Omega. Avocations: WWII history, bicycle tng., photography, Little League baseball coaching. Home: 14416 W 72nd St Shawnee KS 66216-5505

ESHELMAN, RALPH ELLSWORTH, maritime historian, educator, consultant; b. Mt. Holly, N.J., Mar. 20, 1947; s. Ralph Mengel and Grace Elizha (Bozarth) E.; m. Evelyne Margaret Herman, June 3, 1974; 1 child, Erich Ellsworth. AA, Prince George's C.C., 1967; BS, SUNY, Stony Brook, 1969; MS, U. Iowa, 1971; PhD, U. Mich., 1974. Phys. sci. aide U.S. Geol. Survey, Washington, 1965-69; dir. Calvert Marine Mus., Solomons, Md., 1974-90; rsch. assoc. Smithsonian Inst., Washington, 1976—; rsch. assoc. Benedict (Md.) Estuarine Rsch. Lab. Acad. Natural Scis. Phila., 1993-95; owner Eshelman & Assocs., 1994—; lectr. on expedition cruise ship Explorer, 1991—; cons. Nat. Maritime Initiative, Nat. Park Svc., 1993—, USCG, 1995-98. Contbr. articles to profl. jours. Grantee Sigma Xi, 1972, Nat. Geog. Soc., 1981, 86. Mem. Nat. Maritime Preservation Task Force (vice chmn. 1983-84), Md. Soc. Underwater Archeology (trustee 1984-86), Md. Humanities Coun. (trustee 1984-89, 2d v.p. 1987-89), Coun. Am. Maritime Mus. (exec. com. 1983-89, v.p. 1988-89, pres. 1990), Nat. Maritime Alliance (co-chair 1994-95), Nat. Lighthouse Mus. (pres. steering com.), Nat. Lighthouse Ctr. and Mus. (trustee 1998—, 2nd v.p.). Avocations: spelunking, snorkeling, canoeing, hiking, swimming. Home and Office: 12178 Preston Dr Lusby MD 20657-2905

ESHELMAN, WILLIAM ROBERT, librarian, editor; b. Oklahoma City, Aug. 23, 1921; s. Cyrus Lenhert and Fern (Reed) E.; m. Mimi Blau, July 3, 1952 (div. Aug. 1956); m. Eve Kendall, June 21, 1957 (div. Apr. 1975); children: Ann, Benjamin, Zachary; m. Pat Rom, Dec. 29, 1977. BA, Chapman Coll., L.A., 1943; MA, UCLA, 1950; BLS, U. Calif. at Berkeley, 1951. Conscripted in civilian pub. service Waldport, Oreg., 1943-46; asst. dir., 1944-45; ptnr. Untide Press, Pasadena, Calif., 1946-65; teaching asst. UCLA, 1949-50, library asst., 1950; faculty Los Angeles State Coll., 1951-65, asst. librarian, 1954-59, coll. librarian, 1959-65; librarian, prof. bibliography Bucknell U., 1965-68; editor Wilson Library Bull., 1968-78; pres. Scarecrow Press, Metuchen, N.J., 1979-86; proprietor The Press at the Camperdown Elm, Wooster, Ohio, 1987-93. Editor: Take Hold Upon the Future: Letters on Writers and Writing by William Everson and Lawrence Clark Powell, 1938-1946, 1994; author: No Silence! A Library Life, 1997; contbg. author: Perspectives on William Everson, 1992; mem. editl. bd. Choice, 1966-71. Bd. dirs. Grolier Edn. Corp., 1979-86; mem. adv. council edn. for librarianship U. Calif., 1961-64; mem. acad. senate Calif. State Colls., 1964-65. Mem. AAUP (v.p. L.A. State Coll. 1958-59, pres. 1964-65), ALA (winner Libr. Periodicals award 1960, editorial com. 1964-66, mem. coun. 1972-76, com. accreditation 1977-79), Calif. Libr. Assn. (chmn. intellectual freedom com., pres. so. dist. 1965, editor Calif. Libr. jour. 1960-63), Assn. Coll. and Rsch. Librs. (publs. com.), Assn. Calif. State Coll. Profs., ACLU, Friends Com. Legis., N.J. Libr. Assn. (hon.), Rounce and Coffin Club (L.A.; sec.-treas. 1953-56), Typophiles CLub (N.Y.C.). Home and Office: 3645 SW 52nd Pl Portland OR 97221-2113

ESHER, BRIAN RICHARD, environmental company executive; b. N.Y.C., Sept. 1, 1948; s. John Conrad and Elizabeth (Carley) E.; m. Sharon Ann Scally, Sept. 4, 1977; children: Justin John, Christopher Ryan. B.S. in Bus. Mgmt. magna cum laude, Fairleigh Dickinson U., Madison, N.J., 1971, M.B.A. summa cum laude, 1975. Mgr. master planning Litton Industries, Morristown, N.J., 1972-75; industry mgr. AT&T Long Lines, Somerset, N.J., 1975-77, v.p. Transaction Mgmt., Inc., Montgomeryville, Pa., 1977-79; dir. mktg. Burroughs Corp., Detroit, 1980-82, exec. asst., 1982-84, v.p. Rochester, N.Y., 1984-85; sr. v.p., gen. mgr. ITEK Graphic Systems Div., 1985-88; exec. v.p. A.B. Dick Co., Chgo., 1988-89; chmn., pres., CEO Environ. Control Group, Inc., Maple Shade, N.J., 1989, pres., CEO, chmn., 1990-96; dir., chmn., pres., CEO MLX Corp., 1990-96, bd. dirs.; chmn., pres., CEO Pameco Corp., Norcross, Ga, 1992-96; pvt. investor; mem. adv. bd. Evergreen Equities, LLC, 1997—; adv. ptnr. Indsl. Growth Ptnrs., 1998—. With U.S. Army, 1967-69, Vietnam. Decorated D.S.C., Silver Star, Bronze Star, Purple Heart (3). Mem. Assn. of M.B.A. Execs., Phi Omega Epsilon (Membership award 1971). Republican. Avocation: tennis. Home: 9185 Old Southwick Pass Alpharetta GA 30022-6253

ESHLEMAN, VON RUSSEL, electrical engineering educator; b. Darke County, Ohio, Sept. 17, 1924; married; 4 children. BEE, George Washington U., 1949; MS, Stanford U., 1950, PhD in Elec. Engring., 1952. Rsch. assoc. Radio Propagation Lab. Stanford (Calif.) U., 1952-56, from instr. to prof. elec. engring., 1956-61, prof. elec. engring., co-dir. Ctr. Radar Astronomy, 1961-82, dir. Radioscience Lab., 1974-83; cons. NAS, Nat. Bur. Stds., SRI Internat., Jet Propulsion Lab.; mem. Internat. Astronaut Congress, Internat. Astron. Union, Internat. Sci. Radion Union; dir. emeritus Watkins-Johnson Co.; mem. radio sci. team Galileo Mission to Jupiter, 1979—. Fellow AAAS, IEEE, Am. Geophys. Union, Royal Astronomy Soc.; mem. NAE. Achievements include rsch. in radar astronomy, planetary exploration, ionospheric and plasma physics, radio wave propagation, astronautics. Office: Stanford U Ctr for Radar Astronomy Packard EE Bldg 309 Stanford CA 94305-9515

ESHOO, ANNA GEORGES, congresswoman; b. New Britain, Conn., Dec. 13, 1942; d. Fred and Alice Alexandre Georges; children: Karen Elizabeth, Paul Frederick. AA with honors, Canada Coll., 1975. Chmn. San Mateo County Dem. Ctrl. Com., Calif., 1978-82; chair Human Rels. Com., 79-82; mem. Congress from 14th Dist. Calif., 1993—, at-large minority whip; mem. commerce com. 106th Congress from 14th Dist. Calif.; chief of staff Calif. Assembly Spkr. Leo McCarthy, 1981; regional majority whip No. Calif., 1993-94. Co-founder Women's Hall of Fame; chair San Mateo County (Calif.) Dem. Party, 1980; active San Mateo County Bd. Suprs., 1982-92, pres., 1986; pres. Bay Area Air Quality Mgmt. Dist., 1982-92; mem. San Francisco Bay Conservation Devel. Commn., 1982-92; chair San Mateo County Gen. Hosp. Bd. Dirs. Roman Catholic. Office: US Ho of Reps Office of House Mems 308 Cannon 10B Washington DC 20515-0514

ESIASON, BOOMER (NORMAN JULIUS ESIASON), professional football player; b. West Islip, N.Y., Apr. 17, 1961; m. Cheryl Esiason. Student, U. Md. Football player Cin. Bengals, 1984-92, N.Y. Jets, 1993-97; broadcaster Monday Night Football ABC Sports, N.Y.C., 1997—; host In the Huddle with Boomer Esiason and Chris "Mad Dog" Russo, CBS Sports Radio/Westwood One, 1999—; played in Super Bowl XXIII, 1988. Co-chmn. Boomer Esaison Found., 1993—. Named to Pro Bowl, 1986, 88, 89, 93; Sporting News All-Pro team, 1988; named Sporting News Player of Yr., 1988. Office: Boomer Esiason Found 1 World Trade Ctr 101st Fl New York NY 10048*

ESKANDARIAN, EDWARD, advertising agency executive; b. Telford, Pa., Nov. 20, 1936; s. Michael and Katherine (Arslanian) E.; m. Nancy Rose Boujicanian, June 20, 1965; children: Wendy, Christopher, Jill. BS, Villanova U., 1958; MBA, Harvard, 1965. Engr. Pitman Dunn Labs., Phila., 1958-60; project engr. GE, Phila., 1961-63; v.p., account supr. Compton Advt., Inc., N.Y.C., 1965-71; chmn., chief exec. officer HBM/Creamer Inc., Boston, 1971-88; chmn. Della Femina McNamee, Boston, 1988-89; chmn., CEO Arnold Comm., Boston, 1989—. Overseer Boston Symphony, 1987—, Boston Mus. Sci., 1987—; trustee U. Richmond. With USAF, 1959-60. Mem. Am. Assn. Advt. Agys. (sec.-treas. 1988-89, ea. region gov.-at-large 1989-91), New Eng. Broadcasters Assn. (pres. 1982-83), Advt. Club Boston (pres. 1977-78, trustee 1980—), Harvard Bus. Sch. Assn. Boston (pres. 1984-85), Harvard Club, Algonquin Club, Weston Golf Club, Jupiter Hills Club, Oyster Harbors Club, Willowbend Club, Caves Valley Club. Home: 300 Boylston St Boston MA 02116 Office: Arnold Comm 101 Huntington Ave Boston MA 02199-7606

ESKEW, BENTON, judge; b. Bastrop, Tex., Sept. 2, 1961; s. Charles Allen and Vina M. (Sims) E. BBA, Baylor U., 1984, JD, 1986. Bar: Tex., U.S. Dist. Ct. (no. and we. dists.) Tex.; ordained Bapt. minister. Assoc. McCamish, Ingram, Martin & Brown, Austin, Tex., 1986-88, Naman, Howell, Smith & Lee, Austin, 1989-91; ptnr. Eskew & Goertz, Bastrop, Tex., 1992-94; judge Bastrop County, Tex., 1994—. Bd. dirs. Child Protective Svcs. Bd., Bastrop, 1994—, Bastrop Boys and Girls Club, 1998—. Mem. Bastrop C. of C., Masons, York Rite, Scottish Rite, Shriners, Lions Club, Kiwanis Club. Home: PO Box 1120 Bastrop TX 78602 Office: Bastrop County Ct Law 804 Pecan St Bastrop TX 78602-3846

ESKEW, RHEA TALIAFERRO, newspaper publisher; b. Lebanon, Tenn., Nov. 16, 1923; s. Robert Edward and Sammie (Taylor) E.; m. Nancy Portlock Hall, June 13, 1953; children: Rhea Taliaferro, Elizabeth Vaughan Overman, Tucker Alexander, Hall Edward. Student, U. Tenn., 1941-42; B.A., Emory U., 1948. With UPI, 1948-55; bus. rep. UPI, N.C., S.C., Va., 1951-55; dept. pub. relations So. Bell Telephone Co., 1955-56; with UPI, 1956-73; gen. mgr. communications UPI, N.Y.C., 1963-64; So. div. mgr. UPI, Atlanta, 1964-73; v.p., gen. mgr. Greenville (S.C.) News-Piedmont, 1973-77, pub., 1978-84; pres. Multimedia Newspaper Co., 1978-85, sr. exec., 1984-88; bd. dirs. Order of the Palmetto. Pres. Greenville Community Planning Coun., 1989. With AUS, 1942-45, ETO. Mem. S.C. Press Assn. (pres. 1981), So. Newspaper Pubs. Assn. (pres. 1982-83), Greenville Country Club, Poinsett Club, Atlanta Commerce Club, Greenville City Club. Methodist. Home: 400 Huntington Rd Greenville SC 29615-4210

ESKIN, BERNARD ABRAHAM, obstetrics and gynecology educator, medical researcher; b. Atlantic City, Feb. 12, 1928; s. Joseph H. and Goldie Celia (Schwartz) E.; m. Debra Lynn Kimelblot, June 11, 1955; children: Gregg Carl, JoAnne Hillary, Catherine Ruth. BS in Chemistry and Biology, Princeton U., Rutgers U., 1947; MS in Endocrinology, Rutgers U., 1949; MD, Albany Med. Coll., 1955. Diplomate Nat. Bd. Medicine, Am. Bd. Ob./Gyn; MD Pa., N.J., N.Y. Teaching and rsch. fellow Rutgers U., New Brunswick, N.J., 1948-49, Woods Hole (Mass.) Marine Biology, 1950, Brown U., Providence, 1950-51; teaching and rsch. fellow Woman's Med. Coll., Phila., 1960-67, asst. prof. ob./gyn. and reproductive endocrinology, 1965-70, assoc. prof., 1971-79; chief sect. reproductive endocrinology, ob./gyn. Med. Coll. of Pa. and Albert Einstein Med. Ctr., Phila., 1967-82; prof. ob./gyn., reproductive endocrinology Med. Coll. Pa./Hahnemann U. Sch. Medicine, Phila., 1979—, assoc. prof. psychiatry, 1976—; prof. pharmacology Med. Coll. Pa./Hahneman U. Sch. Medicine, Phila., 1993—; clin. prof. ob./gyn. Robert Wood Johnson Med. Sch., New Brunswick, 1967—. Author: Midlife Can Wait, 1995, Breast Disease for Primary Care Physicians, 1999; author, editor: Menopause (3d rev. edit.), 1995, others; numerous patents in field. Bd. dirs. Main Line Symphony Orch., Wayne, Pa., 1982—. Lt. USNR, 1943-46. Recipient Fogarty Internat. Rsch. award, 1998; grantee NIH, ACS, others, 1965—; Hartford Found. fellow, 1960-65; Nat. Found. for Infantile Paralysis fellow, 1951. Fellow Am. Coll. Ob./gyn. (life), Soc. Senologie (bd. dirs. 1984-88), Phila. Coll. Physicians; mem. Am. Thyroid Assn., Am. Assn. Cancer Rsch., Endocrine Soc., Am. Soc. Reproductive Medicine (life), Pa. Med. Soc. (state rep. 1987—), Phila. County Med. Soc. (bd. dirs. 1991—), Rutgers Univ. Fedn. (bd. dirs. 1993—), Rutgers U. Regional Alumni Clubs (chmn. 1994—). Jewish. Avocations: classical viola, jazz alto saxophones, clarinet. Office: MCP Hahnemann Sch Medicine Dept Ob/gyn 3300 Henry Ave Philadelphia PA 19129 also: 3900 City Ave D-124 Philadelphia PA 19131

ESLER, ANTHONY JAMES, historian, novelist, educator; b. New London, Conn., Feb. 20, 1934; s. Jamie Arthur and Helen Wilhelmina (Kreamer) E.; m. Carol Eaton Clemeau, June 17, 1961 (div. 1988); children: Kenneth Campbell, David Douglas; m. Helen Campbell Walker, July 24, 1992. B.A., U. Ariz., 1956; M.A., Duke U., 1958, Ph.D., 1961. Mem. faculty Coll. William and Mary, 1962—, prof. history, 1972—; vis. prof. Northwestern U., 1968-69. Author: The Aspiring Mind of the Elizabethan Younger Generation, 1966, Bombs, Beards and Barricades: 150 Years of Youth in Revolt, 1971, The Youth Revolution: The Conflict of Generations in Modern History, 1974, Castlemayne, 1974, Hellbane, 1975, Lord Libertine, 1976, Forbidden City, 1977, The Freebooters, 1979, Babylon, 1980, Bastion, 1980, Generations in History: An Introduction to the Concept, 1982, The Generation Gap in Society and History: A Select Bibliography, 1984, The Human Venture, 3d edit., 1996, The Western World: A Narrative History, 2d edit., 1997; co-author: A Survey of Western Civilization, 1987, World History: Connections to Today, 1997. Fulbright fellow U. London, 1961-62; research fellow Am. Council Learned Socs., 1969-70; Fulbright travel grantee Ivory Coast and Tanzania, 1983. Mem. World Hist. Assn., Am. Hist. Assn., Authors Guild, Amnesty Internat. Home: 416 Harriet Tubman Dr Williamsburg VA 23185 Office: Coll William and Mary Dept History Williamsburg VA 23187-8795

ESMAN, MARJORIE RUTH, lawyer; b. N.Y.C., Nov. 22, 1954; d. Aaron Hirsh and Rosa Hannah (Mencher) E. BA, Cornell U., 1975; MA, Tulane U., 1977, PhD, 1981, JD, 1987. Adj. asst. prof. La. State U., Baton Rouge, 1981-84; assoc. McGlinchey, Stafford et al, New Orleans, 1987-88, Walker, Bordelon, Hamlin, Theriot, Hardy, New Orleans, 1988-94; pvt. practice New Orleans, 1994—; of counsel Patrick, Miller, Burnside & Belleau, 1997—; lectr. on intellectual property issues; mem. faculty Tulane U. Sch. Law, 1999—. Author: Henderson, Louisiana, 1986; contbr. articles to profl. jours. Bd. dirs. ACLU of La., 1994—; pro bono atty. La. Vol. Lawyers for the Arts, 1988—. Mem. ABA, La. State Bar Assn. (intellectual property law sect.), New Orleans Bar Assn. (intellectual property law com. 1990). Office: 701 S Peters St New Orleans LA 70130-1588

ESMAN, ROSA MENCHER, art gallery executive; b. N.Y.C., Nov. 29, 1927; d. Maurice and Edith (Goldstein) Mencher; m. Aaron H. Esman, June 14, 1951; children: Susanna Singer, Marjorie, Abigail. BA, Smith Coll., 1948. Adminstrv. asst. to dir. Mus. Modern Art, N.Y.C., 1951-52; pres. Tanglewood Press, Inc., N.Y.C., 1964—; dir. original edits. Harry N. Abrams, Inc., N.Y.C., 1970-72; pres. Rosa Esman Gallery, N.Y.C., 1972-93; founding ptnr. UBU Gallery, N.Y.C., 1994—; bd. dirs. Artable, N.Y.C., 1987-88. Pub. original prints and multiples by maj. internat. artists. Mem. Art Dealers Assn. Am. Office: UBU Gallery 16 E 78th St New York NY 10021-1706*

ESMERIAN, RALPH O., museum administrator; b. Paris, Apr. 7, 1940. Grad., Princeton U., 1962. Owner R. Esmerian, Inc., N.Y.C., 1976—; pres., mem. bd. trustees Mus. Am. Folk Art, N.Y.C., 1978—; lectr. on jewelry and precious stones Met. Mus. Art, The Cooper Hewitt Mus., Gemological Inst. Am., Sotheby's, Christie's; mem. panel of judges De Beers Diamonds Internat. Awards, 1994. Author: (introduction) American Jewelry: Glamour and Tradition, 1987. Co-founder, dir. Gemcore; trustee Groton (Mass.) Sch. Office: Museum of American Folk Art 61 W 62d St New York NY 10023*

ESMOND, CHERI SUE, secondary school educator; b. Oak Park, Ill., Oct. 16, 1943; d. Fred W. and Shirley C. (Reiser) Wassmundt; m. Jack B. Esmond, Aug. 22, 1964; children: Jill Esmond Letbetter, Heather Esmond Camden. BS in Maths., U. Ill., 1965, MEd in Secondary Edn., 1966. Cert. secondary edn. tchr., Tex., Ill., N.Y., Mich.; lic. real estate broker, Ill. Tchr. Mahomet (Ill.) Seymour H.S., 1965-67, Ottawa (Ill.) H.S., 1972-73, Klein (Tex.) H.S., 1977—; yearbook judge Nat. Scholastic Press Assn., Mpls., 1967-73. Treas. Jr. Guild Adv. Bd., Houston, 1989-90, provisional coord., 1990-92. Mem. Nat. Coun. Tchrs. of Math., Tex. Assn. Gifted and Talented, Tex. Math. and Sci. Coachess Assn. (Number Sense Coach of Yr. 1997, 99, Sweepstakes Coach of Yr. 1997-99), Raveneaux Country Club, U. Ill. Alumni Assn., Chi Omega Alums (pres. 1995-97), Kappa Delta Pi. Avocations: travel, scuba diving, golf. E-mail: esmond@hal-pc.org. Home: 17814 Theiss Mail Route Rd Spring TX 77379-6111 Office: Klein H S 16715 Stuebner Airline Rd Klein TX 77379-7376

ESOLEN, ANTHONY MICHAEL, English educator; b. Archbald, Pa., Mar. 18, 1959; s. Anthony Thomas and Jane (Conserette) E.; m. Debra Kay Hower, Dec. 20, 1986; children: Jessica, David. AB summa cum laude, Princeton U., 1981; PhD, U. N.C., 1987. Asst. prof. Furman U., Greenville, S.C., 1988-90; asst. prof. Providence Coll., 1990-92, assoc. prof., 1992-95, prof. English, 1995—. Author: (poetry) Peppers, 1992; translator, editor: De Rerum Natura, 1995; contbr. articles and over 100 poems to profl. publs. Morehead fellow, 1981-85. Republican. Roman Catholic. Avocations: coin collecting, baseball, carpentry. Office: Providence Coll Dept English Providence RI 02908

ESP, BARBARA ANN LORRAINE, research scientist, educator; b. Bklyn., Nov. 10, 1947; d. Lawrence Joseph and Evelyn (Webber) Barbeire; m. Edward J. Esp, Aug. 31, 1968; children: Jacqueline, Michelle. BA, Adelphi U., 1969; PhD, Hofstra U., 1978. Counselor, tchr. U.S. Army Dept. Def., Wildflecken, Fed. Republic of Germany, 1970-73; adj. asst. prof. Hofstra U., Hempstead, N.Y., 1974-81; cons., rsch. program evaluator various sch. dists. N.Y., 1982-86; program rsch. analyst N.Y. State Div. Parole, N.Y.C., 1986-

88; dir. pupil pers. svcs., ednl. evaluator Cleary Sch. for Deaf, Nesconset, N.Y., 1989—. Contbr. articles to profl. jours. Leader Girl Scouts U.S., Farmingville, N.Y., 1976-78; bd. dirs. Nassau-Suffolk Counties Alzheimers Assn., Patchogue, N.Y., 1984-86. Hofstra U. fellow, 1975-76. Mem. Am. Ednl. Rsch. Assn. Republican. Roman Catholic. Home: 2 Jacqueline Dr Manorville NY 11949-2615

ESPAILLAT, RHINA POLONIA, poet; b. Dominican Republic, Jan. 20, 1932; came to the U.S., 1939; m. Alfred Moskowitz; three children. BA, CUNY, N.Y.C., 1953, MS in Edn., 1964. English tchr. Jamaica H.S., N.Y.C., 1965-80; poetry instr. United Fedn. Tchrs., Queens (N.Y.) Outreach Ctr., 1986-89; cons., asst. coord. annual poetry contest for intermediate grades N.Y.C. Bd. Edn., 1987-89. Author: (poetry collection) Lapsing to Grace, 1992, Where Horizons Go, 1998 (T.S. Eliot prize in poetry 1998); contbr. poetry to mags. and anthologies. Co-founder The Fresh Meadows Poets, Queens, The Powow River Poets, Newburyport. E-mail: espmosk@juno.com.

ESPALDON, ERNESTO MERCADER, former senator, plastic surgeon; b. Sulu, Philippines, Nov. 11, 1926; arrived in Guam, 1963; s. Cipriano Acuna Espaldon and Claudia (Cadag) Mercader); m. Leticia Legaspi Virata, May 31, 1952; children: Arlene Espaldon Ramos, Vivian Espaldon Wolff, James, Diane, Karl, Ernesto Jr. AA, U. Philippines, Manila, 1949; MD, U. Santo tomas, Manila, 1954; postgrad. in gen. surgery, U. Okla., 1959; postgrad. in plastic and recon. surgery, Washington U., St. Louis, 1961. Diplomate Am. Bd. Plastic Surgery. Plastic surgeon Guam Meml. Hosp., Agana, 1963—, chief surgery, 1965-69; pres., plastic surgeon Espaldon Clinic, Agana, 1969—; senator Guam Legislature, Agana, 1974-80, 86-92, chmn. Com. on Health, Welfare and Ecology and Com. on Ethics and Standards, 1974-80; vis. prof. Bicol Med. and Edn. Ctr., Legaspi City, The Philippines, 1980—; cons. plastic surgery U.S. Naval Hosp., Guam, 1972-76; chmn. com. on advance health care Assn. Pacific Islands Legislators, 1988-92. Author: With The Bravest, 1996. Pres., founder Guam Balikbayan Med. Mission, Agana, 1974—; organizer, co-founder Aloha Med., Mission, Honolulu, 1982—. Guerrilla comdr. Sulu (Philippines) Area Command, 1943-46, 2d lt. Philippine Army, 1946-47. Recipient Thomas Jefferson award for pub. svc., Am. Inst. Pub. Svc., Washington, and Honolulu Advertiser, 1983, Raja Baguinda award for humanitarian svc. 6th Centennial Celebration of Islam in The Philippines, 1980; named Outstanding Filipino Overseas Philippine Govt. and Philippine Jaycees, 1982, Most Outstanding Cmty. Filipino Leader of Guam Philippine-Am. Cmty., 1979, Man of Yr. and Disting. Svc. award Inst. Philippine Am. Affairs, Hawaii, 1983; named Most Outstanding Alumni Achiever for Humanitarian Svc., U. Santo Tomas, 1981, Ernesto M. Espaldon profl. chairship in plastic and reconstructive surgery U. Santo Tomas, 1995. Fellow ACS, Philippine Coll. Surgeons; mem. AMA, Pan Pacific Surg. Assn., Guam Med. Soc. (pres. 1970-72, chief del. to AMA 1973-76), KC. Republican. Roman Catholic. Home: PO Box Ce Agana GU 96932-8982 Office: GCIC Bldg Ste 709 Agana GU 96910

ESPAT, N. JOSEPH, surgeon; b. Guatemala, Guatemala, Jan. 8, 1964; came to U.S., 1971; s. Nocif and Elba Marina (Godoy) E.; m. Jacqueline A. Ellis, Apr. 5, 1997. BS in Biology, U. South Fla., 1985, BA in Philosophy, 1986; MD, U. Fla., 1990. Diplomate Am. Bd. Surgery. Intern U. Fla. Shands Hosp., Gainesville, Fla., 1990-91, resident, 1991-92; rsch. fellow U. Fla. Labs., Gainesville, Fla., 1992-94; sr. resident U. Fla. Shands Hosp., Gainesville, Fla., 1994-96, chief resident, 1996-97; fellow surg. oncology Meml. Sloan Kettering Hosp., N.Y.C., 1997-99; asst. prof. hepatobiliary surgery U. Ill., Chgo., 1999—; mem. Shands Institutional com. grad. medical edn., 1996-97, code com. Shands Hosp., 1995-96; med. team NASA Space Shuttle Univ. Fla., 1992-95, lectr. Project Smoke Free 2000, 1992-94. Contbr. numerous articles to profl. jours. Recipient Harry M. Vars Rsch. award, 1993, James Euwing travel award, 1993. Mem. Assn. Acad. Surgery, Am. Coll. Surgeons, AMA, Soc. Leukocyte Biology, Soc. Surgical Oncology, Southern Medical Assn., Southeastern Surgical Congress. Office: U Ill Dept Surgery 840 Wood St Rm 435 E Chicago IL 60612

ESPENLAUB, MARGO LINN, women's studies educator, artist; b. Decorah, Iowa, May 1, 1944; d. Lloyd Wilson and Margaret Mary (Seegmiller) Ruid; m. Alan Ludwig Espenlaub, Aug. 8, 1988; children: Arn R. Johnson, Cara C. Johnson. BA in Philosophy, U. Colo., 1983, M in Humanities, 1985; PhD in Women's Studies, The Union Inst. Grad. Sch., 1995. Adj. prof. women's studies Met. State Coll., Denver, 1987-99; adj. prof. U. Denver, The Women's Coll., 1996—; colloquium coord. Front Range Feminist Scholars, Denver, 1991-98; faculty coord. TWC Student Writer's Club. Co-author: Women's Studies: Thinking Women, 1993; gen. editor Voices of the Women's Coll., 1999. Mem. biomed. ethics com. Kaiser Permanente, Denver, 1986-96. Mem. Nat. Women's Studies Assn., Colo. Women's Studies An., Colo. Women's Agenda, Women's Caucus for Art (Colo. chpt., nat. bd. dirs.), Front Range Women in the Visual Arts. Avocations: drawing, writing, nature walking, snow shoeing. Office: The Womens Coll U Denver 7150 Montview Blvd Denver CO 80220-1866

ESPENSHADE, EDWARD BOWMAN, JR., geographer, educator; b. Chgo., Oct. 23, 1910; s. Edward B. and Mary E. (Jones) E.; m. Dorothy Elizabeth Barrows, June 17, 1939 (dec.); children—Jean Ellen, Nancy Elizabeth. B.S., U. Chgo., 1931, Ph.D., 1944. Asso. prof. geography Northwestern U., 1948-55, prof., 1958-78, prof. emeritus, 1979—, chmn. dept., 1958-76; geog. cons., geog. editor Rand McNally & Co.; chmn. div. earth scis. Nat. Acad. Sci.-NRC, 1960-62; mem. exec. bd. N. Cen. Assn. Commn. Higher Edn., 1972-77. Editor: Goode's World Atlas, 1947—. Fellow Geog. Soc. Chgo. (past sec., pres. 1969-71); mem. Assn. Am. Geographers (pres. 1964-65, chmn. commn. on coll. geography 1967-69). Home: 1440 Sheridan Rd Apt 605 Wilmette IL 60091-1858

ESPESETH, ROBERT D., park and recreation planning educator; b. Cameron, Wis., July 11, 1930; s. Robert I. and Mary (Willemssen) E.; m. Mary Ann Krepps, Dec. 30, 1952; children: Robert D. Jr., Steven R., Michael W., Karen S. BS in Landscape Architecture, U. Wis., 1952, MS in Landscape Arch./Regional Planning, 1956. Registered landscape architect, Ill., Neb. Park planner div. state forest and parks Wis. Conservation Dept., Madison, 1955-56; chief park planning bureau state parks and recreation Wis. Dept. Natural Resources, Madison, 1956-67; with Genessee County Park and Recreation Commn., Flint, Mich., 1967-73; asst. prof. dept. leisure studies U. Ill., Champaign, 1973-79, assoc. prof., 1979-95; ret., 1995; expert witness, Champaign, Ill., 1974—. Author monographs, Site Planning of Park Areas, 1987, Developing a Bed and Breakfast Business Plan, 1988, Use of Conservation Easements, 1990, Community Park and Recreation Planning, 1994. Commr. Champaign County Forest Preserve Dist., Mahomet, Ill., 1974-86; bd. dirs. Green Meadows coun. Girl Scouts USA, 1975-83. With USN, 1952-54, capt. USNR, ret. Recipient Disting. Svc. award Am. Inst. Park Execs., 1965, Scroll Honor award Navy League U.S., 1973. Fellow Ill. Park and Recreation Assn. (bd. dirs. 1977); mem. Nat. Soc. Park Resources (Meritorious Svc. award 1985), Nat. Recreation and Park Assn. (trustee 1989-95, Park Profl. of Yr. award 1992), Univ. Club (past pres. U. Ill.). Avocations: golf, gardening, fishing, biking. Office: U Ill 1206 S 4th St Ste 104 Champaign IL 61820-6920*

ESPEY, JOHN JENKINS, writer, English educator; b. Shanghai, Jan. 15, 1913; s. John Morton Espey and Mary Lucretia Jenkins; m. Alice Martha Rideout, Aug. 6, 1938 (dec. June 1973); children: Alice Maude, Susan Mary. AB, Occidental Coll., 1935, HLD (hon.); BLitt, Oxford (Eng.) U., 1939, MA, 1941; HLD (hon.), Occidental Coll., 1996. Instr. English Occidental Coll., L.A., 1938-41, asst. prof., 1941-44, assoc. prof., 1944-48; asst. prof. UCLA, 1948-50, assoc. prof., 1950-56, prof., 1956-73, prof. emeritus, 1973—. Author: Minor Heresies, 1945 (Commonwealth Silver medal 1946), Tales Out of School, 1947, The Other City, 1950, Ezra Pound's Mauberley, 1955, the Anniversaries, 1963, An Observer, 1965, Winter Return, 1992, others. Rhodes scholar, 1935-38; Guggenheim Found. fellow, 1958-59. Mem. MLA, Long Christmas Dinner Soc. (co-founder), Phi Beta Kappa. Democrat. Avocations: American book cover artists, bird watching. E-mail: espey@ucla.edu. Office: UCLA Dept English 405 Hilgard Ave Los Angeles CA 90095

ESPEY, LINDA ANN GLIDEWELL, accountant; b. Birmingham, Ala., Aug. 11, 1944; d. Emmett O'Neal and Iola Florence (Harris) Glidewell; m. Lindsey Stribling Smith, Nov. 5, 1966 (div. Dec. 1990); 1 child, Lindsey Nelson; m. Charles G. Espey, Sept. 11, 1997; 1 stepchild, Heidi Espey Holladay. BA cum laude, Birmingham-So. Coll., 1984. Stenographer Cook's Pest Control, Decatur, Ala., 1962, Nelson-Weaver Cos., Birmingham, Ala., 1963-69; resident mgr. Twin Homes of Mt. Brook, Ala., 1966-69; bookkeeper, sect. to v.p. Molton, Allen & Williams, 1969-72; sec. quality assurance dept. So. Co. Svc., Birmingham, 1972-74, sec. sys. constrn. budget, 1974-82, sr. sec. treasury dept., 1982-83; jr. acct. major projects-acctg. Ala. Power Co., Birmingham, 1983-87, sr. acct. fuel dept., 1987-90, sr. acct. stats. dept., 1990-92; fin. adminstr., comptr. Ala. Bapt., Inc., Birmingham, 1992-99. Asst. treas. So. Co. Svcs. State and Fed. PAC., Ala. PowerCo. State and Fed. PAC. Mem. Am. Soc. Women Accts., The Club, Inc., Alpha Lambda Delta, Birmingham So. Alumni Assn. (coun. mem.). Baptist. Avocations: travel, culinary art, walking, fishing. Office: Ala Bapt Inc 3310 Independence Dr Birmingham AL 35209-5602

ESPINOSA, GUSTAVO ADOLFO, radiologist, educator; b. Colombia, June 8, 1944; came to U.S., 1969, naturalized, 1976; s. Hector Octavius and Olga I. (Milanes) E.; m. Cecilia Troncoso, June 4, 1968; children: Gustavo Aldolfo, David A., Susan M. B.S., St. Joseph Coll., Colombia, 1960; MD magna cum laude, U. Xaveriana, Colombia, 1968. Diplomate Am. Bd. Radiology, Am. Bd. Radiology and Cardiovasc. and Interventional Radiology, Am. Bd. Forensic Experts. Intern Providence Hosp., Washington, 1969-70; resident in radiology Cook County Hosp., Chgo., 1971-75; attending radiologist Cook County Hosp., 1976—, West Side VA Hosp., Chgo., 1977—; chmn. dept. West Side VA Hosp., 1977—; attending U. Ill. Hosp., 1977—; assoc. prof. U. Ill. Med. Sch.; prof. radiology, 1988—; med. dir. Sch. X-ray Tech. Malcolm X Coll., Chgo. Fellow Am. Coll. Radiology, Am. Coll. Forensic Experts; mem. AMA, Radiol. Soc. N.Am., Am. Inst. Ultrasound in Medicine, Cardiovasc. and Intervention Radiol. Soc., Ill. Med. Soc., Ill. Radiol. Soc., Chgo. Med. Soc., Chgo. Roentgen Soc., Chgo. Ultrasound Soc., Alpha Omega Alpha. Office: 820 S Damen Ave Chicago IL 60612-3728

ESPINOZA, GALINA, magazine writer; b. N.Y.C., Apr. 13, 1970; d. Milton and Helene (Boxer) E. BA, U. Pa., 1991; MS, Columbia U., 1992. Corr. The Phila. (Pa.) Inquirer, 1992-94; staff writer Tribune Newspapers, Mesa, Ariz., 1994-95, Money mag., N.Y.C., 1995-99, People mag., N.Y.C., 1999—. Davidoff fellow Wesleyan U., 1993. Office: People Mag 1271 Ave Americas 29th Fl New York NY 10020

ESPINOZA, LUIS ROLAN, rheumatologist; b. Pisco, Peru, July 3, 1943; came to U.S.A., 1969; s. Luis R. and Luz Lelia (Bernales) E.; m. Carmen G. Gonzalez, Dec. 20, 1969; children: Luis M., Gabriela M. MD, Cayetano Heredia, Lima, Peru, 1969. Intern Jersey City (N.J.) Med. Ctr., 1969-70; resident Washington U., St. Louis, 1970-72, rheumatlogy fellow, 1972-73; rheumatlogy fellow McGill U., Montreal, Can., 1973-74, asst. prof., 1976-78; immunology fellow The Rockefeller U., N.Y.C., 1974-76; assoc. prof. U. South Fla., Tampa, 1978-83, prof. medicine, 1983-90; prof. medicine La. State U. Sch. Medicine, New Orleans, 1991—, also chief rheumatology sect. Editor: Infection in the Rheumatic Diseases, 1988, Psoriatic Arthritis, 1985, Immun Complexes, 1983; guest editor Infectious Arthritis Rheumatic Disease Clin. N. Am., 1993, 98. Chmn. Lupus Found. Am., Tampa, 1979-90. Recipient Rsch. award NIH, Tampa, 1981, Arthritis Found., Tampa, 1990. Fellow ACP, Am. Coll. Rheumatology; mem. Am. Assn. Immunologists, So. Soc. for Clin. Investigation, Soc. for Clin. Rsch., Can. Soc. Rheumatologists, Can. Soc. for Clin. Investigation. Avocations: music, swimming, chess. Home: 1212 Conery St New Orleans LA 70115-3340 Office: La State U Med Ctr 1542 Tulane Ave New Orleans LA 70112-2825

ESPINOZA, NOEMI RUTH, diplomat, researcher; b. Tegucigalpa, Honduras, Dec. 4, 1972; came to U.S., 1990; d. Felipe Vinicio and Noemi Ruth Espinoza. BA, Calvin Coll., 1994; MA, Vanderbilt U., 1997. Rschr. Christian Commn. for Devel., Tegucigalpa, 1993—; chancellor Honduran Consulate, N.Y.C., 1996-97; econ. counselor Permanent Mission of Honduras to UN, N.Y.C., 1997-98, amb., alt. permanent rep., 1998—; hon. mem. N.Y. and N.J. World Trade Coun., 1997. Mem. Calvin Investment Club. Avocations: Tae Kwon Do (black belt), scuba diving, Karate, bicycling. E-mail: nespinoza@att.net. Home: 188 Sixth Ave # 2RS New York NY 10013 Office: Mission Honduras to UN 866 UN Plz Ste 417 New York NY 10017

ESPOSITO, AMY SKLAR, lawyer; b. Bklyn., Nov. 9, 1955; d. Sidney and Rhoda (Weiner) Sklar; m. Francis Benedetto Esposito, May 4, 1985; children: Melissa, Anthony. BA, U. Vt., 1977; JD, Hofstra U., 1980. Bar: N.Y. 1981, Fla. 1983. Assoc. Herman & Natale, Esqs., Garden City, N.Y., 1980-81, Law Offices of Gabriel Kohn, Mineola, N.Y., 1981-84; ptnr. Ostor & Sklar, Esqs., Deer Park, N.Y., 1984-93; pvt. practice Deer Park, 1993-94; assoc. Naiburg & Rosenblum, Hauppauge, N.Y., 1994-95, Law Office of Lynne Adair Kramer, Commack, N.Y., 1994-95; pvt. practice Deer Park, N.Y., 1995-96, Commack, N.Y., 1996—. Coach mock trials Nassau County (N.Y.) High Schs., 1984-86. Mem. N.Y. State Bar Assn., Nassau-Suffolk Women's Bar Assn. (assoc., speaker on matrimonial law). Jewish. Avocations: painting, sewing.

ESPOSITO, BONNIE LOU, marketing professional; b. Chgo., July 20, 1947; d. Ralph Edgar and Dorothy Mae (Groh) Myers; m. Frank Merle Esposito, Aug. 15, 1969 (div. Sept. 1985); children: Mario Henry, Elizabeth Ann. BA, George Williams Coll., 1969. Caseworker Little Bros. of the Poor, Chgo., 1969-72; dir. Little Bros.-Friends of the Elderly, Mpls., 1972-78; organizer Community Crime Prevention, Mpls., 1978-81; owner Espo Inc./Mario's Ristorante, Mpls., 1978-85; mktg. mgr. City of Mpls. Energy Office, 1981—; dir. mktg. and tng. The Energy Collaborative, 1987-93; dir. mktg. Ctr. for Energy and Environment, Mpls., 1989-95; dir. WINGS program Employment Action Ctr., Mpls., 1995-97; dir. Minn. Office Citizenship and Vol. Svcs., Mpls., 1997—; v.p., bd. dirs. Resource Alternatives, Inc. Mem. NAFE (bd. dirs. Monday Night Network 1988), Midwest Direct Mktg. Assn., Minn. Multi-Housing Assn., Nat. Apt. Assn., Profl. Assn. for Consumer Energy Edn. (bd. dirs. 1993—, chmn. fin. com.). Office: Minn Office Citizenship and Vol Svcs Dept Adminstrn 117 University Ave W Saint Paul MN 55155-2202

ESPOSITO, DENNIS HARRY, lawyer; b. Providence, June 30, 1947; s. Harry Victor and Irene Rose (Radoccia) E.; m. Susan Audrey Cohen, Sept. 28, 1985; children: Matthew Perry, Lauren Elizabeth, Adam Aarons. BS, Boston Coll., 1969; JD, Boston U., 1974. Bar: R.I. 1974, U.S. Dist. Ct. R.I. 1974, Mass. 1984. Assoc. Goldman & Biafore, Providence, 1974-81; ptnr. Vrana, Cunha & Esposito, Providence, 1981-84; pvt. practice, Providence, 1984-91; of counsel McGregor, Shea & Doliner, Boston, 1987-91; ptnr., chmn. environ. practice group Adler Pollock and Sheehan, 1991—; legal counsel Coastal Resources Mgmt., Providence, 1974-81, Narragansett Bay Water Quality Mgmt. Dist. Commn., Providence, 1980-85; adj. prof. environ. law Sch. Law Roger Williams U. Alt. designee R.I. State Planning Council, 1980; legal advisor R.I. Constl. Conv. Commr., 1986-87, R.I. Environ. Quality Study Commn., 1988-90; administrv. hearing officer R.I. Dept. of Environ. Mgmt., 1987-89; gov.'s task force for Statutory Reorgn. R.I. Dept. Environ. Mgmt. and Coastal Resources Mgmt. Coun., 1989-90; mem. Gov.'s Commn. on Individual Sewage Disposal Systems and Freshwater Wetlands, 1995. Maj. USAFR, ret. Mem. ABA, R.I. Bar Assn. (chmn. environ. law com. 1985-95), R.I. Trial Assn. Office: Adler Pollock & Sheehan 2300 Hospital Trust Tower Providence RI 02903-2443

ESPOSITO, JOSEPH JOHN, publishing company executive; b. Englewood, N.J., June 19, 1951; s. Ross and Ann (Tamborinno) E.; m. Kim Ann Loretucci. AB, Rutgers U., 1973, MA, 1977, M in Philosophy, 1978. Editor Rutgers U. Press, New Brunswick, N.J., 1978-81, Dover Publs., N.Y.C., 1981-82; v.p. spl. projects New Am. Libr., N.Y.C., 1982-85; pres. reference div. Simon & Schuster, N.Y.C., 1985-88; v.p. reference, pres. Fodor's Travel Pubs. Random House Pub. Co., N.Y.C., 1988-90; with Ency. Britannica, 1990-96; pres. Merriam-Webster sub., 1990; CEO Ency. Britannica, 1995-96; pres., CEO Tribal Voice, Scotts Valley, Calif., 1997—; mem. mgmt. bd. MIT Press. Mem. ACLU, Dictionary Soc. N.Am. Office: Tribal Voice 1 Victor Sq Scotts Valley CA 95066-3532*

ESPOSITO, MARK ALAN, stock market executive; b. Youngstown, Ohio, July 8, 1962; s. Frank C. and Betty J. E.; m. Victoria Esposito, Nov. 30, 1996. BS in Acctg. and Fin., Slippery Rock U., 1984; MBA in Fin., Am. U., Washington, 1989. Auditor, acct. Riggs Nat. Bank, Washington, 1984-86; fin. analyst, mng. analyst, mng. dir. mkt. svcs. NASDAQ Stock Mkt., Washington, 1986—, v.p., 1999—. Roman Catholic. Avocations: skiing, golf, softball, cycling, investment clubs. Home: 7516 Blaise Trl McLean VA 22102-2101 Office: NASDAQ Stock Mkt 1735 K St NW Washington DC 20006-1516

ESPOSITO, RICHARD JOSEPH, journalist, executive; b. N.Y.C., Dec. 28, 1954; s. Richard and Marie (Croci) E.; m. Diana Claire von Mueffling, Aug. 29, 1992; 1 child, Tatiana Maria von Mueffling. BA with honors, NYU, 1975; postgrad., U. Calif., Berkeley, 1976-77. Clk. N.Y. Daily News, 1977-80, reporter, 1980-81; police bur. chief Phila. Bull., 1981; asst. editor Crains Bus. Mktg., N.Y.C., 1981-82; assoc. editor CBS Venture One, Fairlawn, N.Y., 1982-83; investigative reporter N.Y. Post, 1983-86; police bur. chief N.Y. Newsday, 1986-90, city editor, 1990-93; metro editor N.Y. Daily News, 1993, Sunday editor, 1993-95; sr. v.p. Warner Music Group, N.Y.C., 1995; exec. v.p., CEO Constant Mgmt. (formerly Maroley Media Group), 1995—; lectr. in field. Author: Dead on Delivery, 1992—. Recipient Silurian award, 1992, AP award, 1990-94; co-recipient Pulitzer Prize city editor Newsday, 1992. Mem. N.Y. Press Club, Internat. Crime Writers, Soc. Profl. Journalists. Avocations: skiing, tennis, sport fishing, shooting. Home: 110 E End Ave New York NY 10028-7412 also: Constant Mgmt Ste 6D 110 East End Ave New York NY 10028*

ESPY, CHARLES CLIFFORD, English language educator, author, consultant, lecturer, administrator; b. Centerville, Iowa, June 18, 1910; s. John Wesley and Hulda (Boyer) E.; m. Ruby Johnson, Aug. 5, 1939; children: Charles Clifford, Bruce William. BA in English, Iowa Wesleyan Coll., 1932, LLD, 1966; postgrad., State U. Iowa, 1934; MS in Edn., U. So. Calif., 1939, U. Va., 1980; postgrad., U. Calif., Berkeley, 1941, U. Ariz., 1944, N.H. State Coll., 1949, U. Wis., 1951-52, Chgo. State U., 1968, Cambridge (Eng.) U., 1981, Strathclyde U., Scotland, 1981, Univ. Kent, Eng., 1981, Univ. London, 1981, Trinity Coll., Rome, 1985. Tchr. high sch. Iowa, Calif., Utah, 1934-40; instr. Weber State Coll., Ogden, Utah, 1940-43, dormitory supr., 1943-44; telegrapher S.P.R.R., Ogden, 1944; with sales purchasing dept. W.P. Beto, Rockford, Ill., 1946-47; with sales and promotion dept. Rockford Sch. Bus., 1947-48; instr. Dale Carnegie Courses, 1947-60; tchr. speech pub. schs. Rockford, 1948-63; supt. Winnebago County (Ill.) Schs., 1963-67; prof. English Prairie State Coll., 1967-73; prof. English U. Hawaii, 1973-74, vis. lectr., 1977-78; vis. lectr. Rockford Coll., 1948, Ill. Inst. Tech., 1948, Tolentine Coll., 1968-73; founding supt. Rock Valley Coll.; bd. dirs. Intermountain Jr. Coll. Conf., 1941-44, pres., 1944; mem. Dunedin Coun. Orgns., 1978—. Author: Intermountain Jr. Collegiate Conference Constitution and By-Laws; History of Public Education in Winnebago County, 1967; producer TV series, 1965-67; contbr. articles to profl. jours. Active Boy Scouts Am., 1926-79, YMCA, Lone Scouts Am., 1918-26, 85-95; mem. Am. Bicentennial Commn., dir., 1975-76; mem. Seacoast Bird Sanctuary, Friends of Libr.; mem. DeMolay Found, U.S.C. Stray Greeks, 1937-38, pres., 1937; founder Protestant Athletic League, Ogden, 1936; bd. dirs. Big Bros. and Sisters of Ill., 1963-67, Mental Health Soc., 1964-67, Rock River chpt. ARC, 1964-67, Winnebago County TV Assn., 1964-67, Econ. Opportunity Corp., 1964-67; trustee Iowa Wesleyan Coll., 1968-70; sec. bd. dirs. Spl. Edn. Coun., 1964-67; bd. dirs. Toronto Blue Jays Boosters, Inc. Lt. comdr. USNR, 1944-46, res. 1946-57. Recipient George Washington medals Freedoms Found., 1953, 60, Alumni Service award Iowa Wesleyan Coll., 1959, Youth award Rockford C. of C., 1965, U.S. Olympics awards, 1932, 36, City of Dunedin Amazing Sr. award, 1995; named to Iowa Wesleyan Coll. Hall of Fame, Centerville H.S. Hall of Fame, 1996. Mem. NEA, Internat. Exec. Svc. Corps, Am. Boyers Assn., Ill. (exec. bd. N.W. div. 1964-67), Weber State Coll. Fac. Assn. (pres. 1942-43), Rockford Edn. Assns. (pres. 1949-50), Pinellas Suncoast C. of C., Dunedin (Fla.) C. of C. (life), Am. Legion, VFW, Am. Fedn. Tchrs. (life), Iowa Wesleyan Coll. Alumni Assn. (dir. 1959-70, pres. 1968-70), Ill. Univs. Annuitants (life), AAUP, SAR, Mauh-Nah-Tee-See Country Club (dir. 1957-58), Navy Club (Rockford), Dunedin Hist. Soc. (life), Am. Boyers Assn. (life), Profl. Dirs. Assn., Crystal Lake Country Club (dir. 1973-76) (Beulah, Mich.), West Fla. YMCA Runners (life), Dunedin Country Club, Chgo. Heights Country Club, Road Runners Am., Nat. Sr. Sports Assn. (charter mem.), Masons (32 deg.), Shriners, Scottish Rite, Elks, Kiwanis, Order Eastern Star (assn. patron 1935-36), Phi Delta Kappa (Ten Yrs. award), Chi Gamma Iota, Sigma Phi Epsilon (alumni bd. dirs.), Phi Theta Kappa, Beta Phi Gamma, Phi Rho Pi, Blue Key. Democrat. Lutheran. Avocations: reading, running, golf, dancing. Home: 1121 Ford Ln Dunedin FL 34698-2217

ESPY, SIRI NORINE, marketing professional; b. Rochester, Pa., July 3, 1953; d. Fred Warren and Charlotte Vanetta (Harris) Sainer; m. William Neal Espy, May 7, 1977; 1 child, Caitlin Colleen. BS in Psychology, U. Pitts., 1974; MA in Clin. Psychology, Miami U., Oxford, Ohio, 1976; MBA in Mgmt., Robert Morris Coll., Pitts., 1989. Adult outpatient therapist Jefferson County Mental Health Ctr., Steubenville, Ohio, 1976-78; sr. therapist Gateway Rehab. Ctr., Aliquippa, Pa., 1978-81; dir. planning and quality Gateway Rehab. Ctr., Aliquippa, 1981-86; adminstr., trainer C.C. of Allegheny County, Pitts., 1987-89; sr. planner Shadyside Hosp., Pitts., 1989-93, dir. planning and mktg., 1993-97; asst. dir. corp. planning and mktg. U. Pitts. Med. Ctr. Health Sys., Pitts., 1997; corp. dir. mktg. St. Margaret Retirement Corp., Pitts., 1998-99; sr. proj. dir. Campos Market Rsch., Pitts., 1999—; mem. adj. faculty Robert Morris Coll., 1988-89, 93-94, C.C. of Allegheny County, 1988-89; cons. Sewickley (Pa.) Valley Hosp., 1987-88, Hosp. Coun. Western Pa., Wexford, 1988; planning facilitator, Pitts., 1988-92. Author: Handbook of Strategic Planning for Nonprofit Organizations, 1986, Marketing Strategies for Nonprofit Organizations, 1992; contbr. articles to profl. jours. Mem. Health Exec. Forum. Democrat. Presbyterian. Avocations: reading, writing. Office: 216 Blvd of the Allies Pittsburgh PA 15222

ESPY, WILLARD RICHARDSON, author; b. Olympia, Wash., Dec. 11, 1910; s. Harry Albert and Helen Medora (Richardson) E.; m. Ann A. Hathaway, 1933; 1 child, Ian Alden; m. Hilda S. Cole, 1940; children: Mona Margaret, Freddy Medora, Joanna Page, Cassin Richardson, Jefferson Taylor (dec.); m. Louise J. Manheim, 1962. BA, U. Redlands, 1930; student, U. Paris, Sorbonne, 1930-31. Reporter Tulare (Calif.) Times, 1932, Brawley (Calif.) News, 1932; asst. editor World Tomorrow, N.Y.C., 1933-35; copy editor L'Agence Havas, 1937-40; mgr. promotion and pub. rels. Reader's Digest, 1941-57; producer, interviewer radio program Personalities in Print, 1957-58; creative advt. dir. Famous Artists Schs., 1958-63; publisher Charter Books, 1963-66; pub. relations cons. N.Y.C., 1963-75; panelist Harper Dict. Contemporary Usage, 1976, 83. Contbg. editor: Harvard Mag, 1978-85, Writer's Digest, 1985-92; author: Bold New Program, 1951, The Game of Words, 1972, An Almanac of Words at Play, 1975, Oysterville: Roads to Grandpa's Village, 1977, The Life and Works of Mr. Anonymous, 1977, O Thou Improper, Thou Uncommon Noun, 1978, Say It My Way, 1980, Another Almanac of Words at Play, 1980, Have a Word on Me, 1981, Espygrams, 1982, A Children's Almanac of Words at Play, 1982, Word Puzzles, 1983, The Garden of Eloquence, 1983, Words to Rhyme With, 1986, The Word's Gotten Out, 1989, Omak Me Yours Tonight, 1993, Skulduggery on Shoalwater Bay, 1998, A New Almanac of Words at Play, 1999; contbr. articles to periodicals. Recipient Gov.'s award for contbn. to cultural life of Wash., 1973, 76; Capt. Robert Gray medal Wash. State Hist. Soc., 1979. Mem. PEN, Nat. Book Critics' Circle, Authors Guild. Clubs: Century Assn., Dutch Treat, Book Table, Coffee House (N.Y.C.). Home: 420 E 79th St New York NY 10021-1472

ESQUER, DEBORAH ANNE, elementary education educator; b. Omaha, Oct. 28, 1950; d. Thomas Ross and Carolyn Mae (Wright) Woods; m. Mario H. Esquer, Aug. 21, 1971 (div. Apr. 1991); children: Mario, Michael. BA, Ariz. State U., 1972, MA in Edn., 1972, 78; postgrad., Ottawa U., Phoenix, 1990-92. Cert. elem. tchr., spl. edn. Tchr. Paradise Valley Sch. Dist., Phoenix, 1972—. Dem. precinct com. person; state Dem. com. person, Valley Leadership Class, 1999—. Tchr. venture grantee, Phoenix, 1988. Mem. NEA, Ariz. Edn. Assn., Ariz. Reading Coun., Paradise Valley Edn. Assn., Paradise Valley Reading Coun., Phoenix Art Mus., Ariz. Hist. Soc., Ariz. Forum, Paradise Valley Jr. Women's Club (corr. sec. 1991-92), Alpha Delta Kappa (pres. 1986-88, crtl. dist. treas. 1986-88, corr. sec. 1992-94, treas. 1994—, state com.), Alpha Phi. Democrat. Methodist. Office: Desert Springs 6010 E Acoma Dr Scottsdale AZ 85254-2599

ESQUIBEL, EDWARD V., psychiatrist, clinical medical program developer; b. Denver, May 28, 1928; s. Delfino C. and Beatrice (Solis) E.; m. Elaine F. Telk (div. 1961); children: Roxanne, Cyndi, Allen, James; m. Lillian D. Robb, 1961; children: Amanda, Ramona. MD, U. Colo., 1958. Diplomate Am. Bd. Psychiatry and Neurology. Assoc. chief svc. Ill. State Psychiat. Inst., Chgo., 1964-66; dir. undergrad. program psychiatry, asst. prof. psychiatry Chgo Med. Sch., 1966-68; cons. and supr. group therapy Lake County Mental Health Clinic, Gary, Ind., 1968-72; pvt. practice Daytona Beach, Jacksonville, Fla., 1972-82; chief forensic svcs., dir. div. maximum security and inst. rsch. Colo. State Hosp., Pueblo, 1981; assoc. clin. prof. psychiatry Quillen-Dishner Coll. Medicine, Johnson City, Tenn., 1982-84; clin. psychiatrist VA Outpatient Clinic, Riviera Beach, Fla., 1984-86; mental health coord., supr. VA, Pensacola, Fla., 1986-88; assoc. chief staff, ambulatory care VA Med. Ctr., Ft. Lyon, Colo., 1988-90, Carl Vinson VA Med. Ctr., Dublin, Ga., 1990-91; staff physician VA Med. Ctr., Sheridan, Wyo., 1993—; chief psychiat. svcs. VA Med. Ctr., Lake City, Fla., 1993-94; contract physician, 1995—. *Dr. Esquibel for a number of years has been developing a body of thought that would lead to a restructuring of the psychiatric programs of Veterans which in his opinion would lessen the dibilitating facets of the current abuse-prone system of the government which has been in place since WWII. His current effort includes a still to be published atypical novel entitled The Ticket to Nowhere. As such goals require consortial coupling, he welcomes contact from related professionals dissatisfied with the current VA format of psychiatric care.* Contbr. articles to profl. jours. Sgt. U.S. Army, 1948-52. Recipient Plaque Recognition award Southeastern Psychiat. Inst., 1964, Internat. Pers. Creative award, 1972, Key to City Daytona Beach, 1975, Hosp. Dirs. commendation VA, 1991. Mem. Am. Soc. Psychoanalytic Physicians. Avocations: gardening, arts and crafts, reading. Home and Office: 801 Gospel Island Rd Inverness FL 34450-3592

ESQUIVEL, AGERICO LIWAG, retired research physicist; b. Manila, June 5, 1932; came to U.S., 1957, naturalized, 1971; s. Enrique Frias and Pacita Ramos (Liwag) E. AB, Berchmans Coll., Manila, 1955; MA, Berchmans Coll., 1956; PhD, St. Louis U., 1963. Research assoc. St. Louis U., 1961-63; research scientist Research Inst. Advanced Studies, Balt., 1963, Materials Research Lab., Martin Co., Orlando, Fla., 1964-65; sr. research engr. Materials Tech. Labs., Boeng Co., Seattle, 1965-71; postdoctoral fellow Advanced Research Projects Agy., U. So. Calif., Los Angeles, 1971-73; mem. tech. staff Hughes Aircraft Co., Culver City, Calif., 1973-76, Semiconductor Process and Device Ctr., Tex. Instuments Inc., Dallas, 1976-98. NSF postdoctoral fellow, 1963. Mem. IEEE Elec. Devices Soc. (sr. mem.), Am. Phys. Soc., Electrochem. Soc., Sigma Xi, Pi Mu Epsilon. Achievements include U.S. and Japan patents, issued and pending, submicron CMOS process integration, development, device characterization, process/device computer simulation, trench isolation, buried multilevel interconnect systems, nonvolatile memory devices; contbr. papers to jours. and procs. on X-ray, electron diffaction, radiation hardening, cathodoluminescence in GaAs, deep level transient spectroscopy, x-ray lithography, high density nonvolatile memories, trench isolated electronically programmable read-only memories, sub-0.25 micron Complementary Metal Oxide Semiconductor (CMOS) transistors and fabrication process, 0.18 micron CMOS logic transistor technology, Ultra Large Scale Integrated (ULSI) CMOS device process integration and characterization; author, co-author 45 tech. pubs., 23 sci. papers presented at internat. symposia in U.S., Japan and Europe; patentee in field.

ESREY, ELIZABETH GOVE GOODIER, chemist, biologist; b. West Chester, Pa., Mar. 25, 1964; d. Robert Egan and Mary Ellen (Winslow) Goodier; m. James David Esrey, Nov. 28, 1987; children: Briana, Steven. BA in Biology, Maryville Coll., 1986. Lab. tech. Franklin Co., Wilmington, Del., 1987; lab. tech. Stine/Haskell Rsch., DuPont, Newark, Del., 1987-91, chemist, 1991-93, biochemist, 1993—; owner Beth's Homemade Breads & Pies, Middletown, Del., 1987—; biochemist herbicide biomechanisms Agrl. Product Discovery, 1993-94, biologist plant and fungal biochemistry, 1994-97; biologist high throughput screening/assay devel. Biol. Leads Discovery, 1998—; mem. safety resource team Stine-Haskell Rsch. Ctr., 1996-98. Recipient DuPont Agr. Products Global Tech Divsn. Achievement award, 1997. Mem. Circle K. (pres. 1985-86). Republican. Episcopalian. Office: Stine Haskell Rsch Labs PO Box 30 S300/476 Newark DE 19714-0030

ESREY, WILLIAM TODD, telecommunications company executive; b. Phila., Jan. 17, 1940; s. Alexander J. and Dorothy (B.) E.; m. Julie L. Campbell, June 13, 1964; children: William Todd, John Campbell. BA, Denison U., Granville, Ohio, 1961; MBA, Harvard U., 1964. With Am. Tel & Tel. Co., also N.Y. Tel. Co., 1964-69; pres. Empire City Subway Ltd., N.Y.C., 1969-70; mng. dir. Dillon, Read & Co. Inc., N.Y.C., 1970-80; exec. v.p. corp. planning United Telecommunications, Inc., Westwood, Kans., 1980-81, exec. v.p., chief fin. officer, 1981-82, 84-85; pres., chief exec. officer United Telecommunications, Inc., 1985—; pres. United Telecom Communications, Inc., Kansas City, Mo., 1982-85; chmn., chief exec. officer Sprint Corp., Westwood, Kans., 1990—; bd. dirs. Earthlink Network, Inc., Exxon Corp., Duke Energy Corp., Gen. Mills, Inc., Everen Capital Corp. Bd. dirs. Midwest Rsch. Com. for Econ. Devel. Mem. Mission Hills Country Club, River Club, Links Club, Kans. City Country Club, Phi Beta Kappa. Office: Sprint 2330 Shawnee Mission Pkwy Westwood KS 66205-2090*

ESRICK, JERALD PAUL, lawyer; b. Moline, Ill., Oct. 1, 1941; s. Reuben and Nancy (Parson) E.; m. Ellen Feinstein, June 18, 1966; children: Sara Elizabeth, Daniel Michael. BA, Northwestern U., 1963; JD, Harvard U., 1966. Bar: Ill. 1966, U.S. Dist. Ct. (no. dist.) Ill. 1967, U.S. Supreme Ct. 1974, U.S. Ct. Appeals (9th cir.) 1985, U.S. Ct. Appeals (7th cir.) 1967. Law clk. U.S. Dist. Ct. (no. dist.) Ill., 1966-68; assoc. Wildman, Harrold, Allen & Dixon, Chgo., 1968-73, ptnr., 1973—, also chmn. firm mgmt. com., 1987-90; lectr. Northwestern U., 1984-93, Coll. Arts and Scis. bd. advs., 1993—, Nat. Panel Comml. Arbitrators, Am. Arbitration Assn. Pres. bd. trustees Nat. Lekotek Ctr., Evanston, Ill., 1989-93, U.S. Toy Libr. Assn., 1987-88; bd. dirs. Evanston Mental Health Assn., 1984-86, Fund for Justice, 1969-95, Lawyers' Com. for Civil Rights, 1974-84. Fellow Am. Coll. Trial Lawyers; mem. ABA, Ill. State Bar Assn., Chgo. Coun. Lawyers (bd. dirs., sec., founding mem.), Chgo. Bar Assn., Legal Club Chgo. Avocations: running, skiing, sailing, windsurfing, classical music. E-mail esrick@whad.com. Home: 1326 Judson Ave Evanston IL 60201-4720 Office: Wildman Harrold Allen & Dixon 225 W Wacker Dr Ste 3000 Chicago IL 60606-1224

ESSANDOH, HILDA BRATHWAITE, kindergarten educator; b. N.Y.C., Feb. 19, 1925; d. Charles Christopher and Millicent Marian (Boxill) Brathwaite; m. Samuel O. Essandoh, June 11, 1959; children: Millicent Efua, Yvonne Araba, Dorothy Esi. BA, Hunter Coll., 1959; MS, Bank Street Coll. Edn., 1976, profl. diploma in supervision-adminstrn., 1980. Cert. nursery, kindergarten, 1st-6th grades, sch. adminstrn. and supervision. Tchr. kindergarten N.Y.C. Bd. Edn., 1962-91. Recipient Ely Trachtenberg award. Home: 548 W 165th St New York NY 10032

ESSENFELD, ANN PAULA, government official; b. N.Y.C., Aug. 20, 1945; d. Sam and Sonia (Schiller) E. BA, Tel-Aviv U., Israel, 1971; JD, John Marshall Law Sch., Atlanta, 1978. Bar: Ga. 1980, U.S. Ct. Appeals Ga. 1980. Sec. to chief of medicine Crawford W. Long Meml. Hosp., Atlanta, 1978-79; tech. writer Ga. Power Co., 1979-80; pvt. practice law, 1980-81; tech. writer Burroughs Corp., 1981-82, First Fin. Mgmt. Corp., Atlanta, 1982-85; contracting officer Dept. Def., Ft. Meade, Md., 1985-98, adminstrv. judge, 1991—; bus. mgr. Dept. Def., Ft. Meade, 1998—; vol. mediator Jewish Arbitration and Mediation Bd., Balt., 1998—; pro bono atty. Pro Bono Action Ctr., Balt., 1998—. Mem. State Bar of Ga. Avocations: physical fitness, classical music, ballet, home decorating, the Arts.

ESSER, ARISTIDE HENRI, psychiatrist; b. Padalarang, Java, Indonesia, May 11, 1930; came to U.S., 1961; s. Samuel Jonathan and Anganita (Tawalujan) E.; m. Ada Reif; children: Jonathan Hendrik, Jessica. MD, U. Amsterdam, The Netherlands, 1955. Diplomate Am. Bd. Psychiatry and Neurology. Med. dir. N.S. Kline Rsch. Inst., Orangeburg, N.Y., 1962-69; dir. rsch. Letchworth Village, Thiells, N.Y., 1969-71; dir. Ctrl. Bergen Cmty. Mental Health Ctr., Paramus, N.J., 1971-77; med. dir. Mission for Immaculate Virgin, S.I., N.Y., 1977-80; dir. quality assurance Bronx (N.Y.) Psychiat. Ctr., 1980-85; unit chief for supportive rehab. Rockland Psychiat. Ctr., Orangeburg, 1985-88, chief geriat. divsn., 1988-90; pvt. practice, 1989; cons. psychiatrist St. Dominic's Home, Blauvelt, 1990—; attending psychiatrist Rye (N.Y.) Hosp. Ctr., 1990—, Good Samaritan Hosp., Suffern, N.Y., 1990—; rsch. prof. NYU Med. Ctr., N.Y.C., 1985-94; pres. Psychiatry P.C., 1989—, Pediats. Practice Mgmt., Inc., 1998—, Psychiatry Evaluation Treatment of Rehab. Assocs., PLLC, 1999—. Co-author: Mental Illness: A Homecare Guide, 1989, Chi Gong: The Ancient Chinese Way to Health, 1990; co-editor: Behavior and Environment, 1971, Design for Communality and Privacy, 1978; editor Jour. Man-Environment Sys., 1969— (Internat. Design award 1973). Recipient travel grant City of Leyden, The Netherlands, 1960; Lederle Labs. fellow Yale U., 1961. Fellow AAAS (life), Am. Psychiat. Assn. (life); mem. Soc. for Biol. Psychiatry, Soc. for Gen. Systems Rsch., Am. Acad. Acupuncture (founding), Assn. for Study Man-Environment Rels. (founding). Home: 435 S Mountain Rd New City NY 10956 Office: 337 N Main St Ste 2 New City NY 10956-4310

ESSER, CARL ERIC, lawyer; b. Montclair, N.J., Feb. 12, 1942; s. Josef and Elly (Graber) E.; m. Barbara A. B. Stelzer, Oct. 12, 1968; children: Jennifer, Eric, Brian. AB, Princeton U., 1964; JD, U. Mich., 1967. Bar: Pa. 1967. Assoc. firm Reed Smith Shaw & McClay LLP, Phila., 1967-72, ptnr., 1973—. With USMCR, 1960-66. Mem. ABA, Pa. Bar Assn., Phila. Bar Assn., Pa. Soc. Healthcare Attys. (bd. dirs.), Pa. Lawyers Fund for Client Security (bd. dirs., chmn.), Octavia Hill Assn. (bd. dirs., asst. sec.), Racquet Club, Penllyn Club (bd. govs.), Mfrs. Golf and Country Club. Republican. Office: Reed Smith Shaw & McClay LLP 2500 One Liberty Pl Philadelphia PA 19103

ESSER, JAMES MARK, cardiovascular and interventional radiologist; b. Madison, Wis., Aug. 1, 1960; s. John Michael Esser and Helen Josephine (Brown) Butterworth. MD, SUNY, Buffalo, 1985. Diplomate Am. Bd. Radiology, Nat. Bd. Med. Examiners. Transitional resident John Burns Sch. Medicine-U. Hawaii, Honolulu, 1985-86, asst. clin. instr. surgery, 1985-86; resident in diagnostic radiology Beth Israel Med. Ctr.-Mt. Sinai Sch. Medicine, N.Y.C., 1986-90; fellow in vascular and interventional radiology St. Luke's-Roosevelt Hosp., N.Y.C., 1990-91; attending staff emergency dept. Bellvue Hosp., N.Y.C., 1988-91; attending radiologist Elmhurst Hosp., N.Y.C., 1990-91, St. Mary's Hosp., West Palm Beach, Fla., 1991-92, Med. Ctr. Hosp., Punta Gorda, Fla., 1992-93, Welborn Hosps. & Clins., Evansville, Ind., 1993-94, St. Mary's Med. Ctr., Evansville, 1993—, Cmty. Meth. Hosp., Henderson, Ky., 1994—, Perry County Meml. Hosp., Tell City, Ind., 1995—, St. Mary's Ctr. for Her, Evansville, 1995—, Vencor Hosp., Louisville, 1998—, Jasper (Ind.) Meml. Hosp., Louisville, 1998—. Pres., v.p. N.Y.C. Soc. Physicians for Social Responsibility, 1987-90. Clin. fellow Columbia Coll. Physicians and Surgeons, 1990-91. Mem. AAAS, Am. Coll. Radiology, Radiol. Soc. N.Am., Soc. Cardiovasc. and Interventional Radiology, Am. Roentgen Ray Soc., Ky. Med. Assn., Henderson County Med. Soc., N.Y. Roentgen Soc., Nat. Trust Historic Preservation. Roman Catholic. Avocations: jogging, surfing, rock climbing. Home and Office: PO Box 495 Henderson KY 42419-0495

ESSER, JOSEPH ALLEN, editor; b. Arnold, Pa., Jan. 9, 1939; s. Joseph Frank and Helen Elizabeth Esser. BS in Social Sci., John Carroll U., 1961. From staff writer to assoc. editor Broadcasting Publs. Inc., Washington, 1965-91; assoc. editor Reed Elsevier, New Providence, N.J., 1991—. Mem. Soc. Profl. Journalists, Washington Ind. Writers, Deadline Club. Avocations: shortwave radio, tennis, jazz. Office: Broadcasting & Cable Yearbook 121 Chanlon Rd New Providence NJ 07974

ESSEX, JOSEPH MICHAEL, visual communication planner; b. Santa Barbara, Calif., May 27, 1947. Student, Montgomery Coll., Rockville, Md., Va. Commonwealth U., Richmond. Art dir. Met. Pitts. Pub. Broadcasting, 1970-73; sr. designer Ctr. for Comm. Planning, 1973-76; assoc. creative dir. Jim Johnston Advt., 1976; design dir. Burson-Marsteller Design Group, Chgo., 1976-86, v.p., dir. visual comm. planning Americas, 1980-88; prin. Design By Objectives, Chgo., 1986-88; ptnr. Essex Partnership, Chgo., 1988-89, Essex Two Incorporate, Chgo., 1989—. One man poster exhbn. Chgo., 1979; exhibited in group shows: Japan, 1976, Ireland, 1977, Cooper-Hewitt Mus., N.Y.C., 1981. Recipient Silver medals, Merit award Art Directors Club, N.Y.C., 1979, 80, over 300 other awards from design and advt. orgns. Office: Essex Two Inc 2210 W North Ave Chicago IL 60647-5430

ESSEX, MYRON ELMER, microbiology educator; b. Coventry, R.I., Aug. 17, 1939; s. Myron Elmer and Ruth Hazel (Knight) E.; m. Elizabeth Katherine Jordan, June 19, 1966; children—Holly Anne, Carrie Lisa. BS, U. R.I., Kingston, 1962; DVM, Mich. State U., East Lansing, 1967; MS, Mich. State U., 1967, DSc (hon.), 1988; PhD, U. Calif., Davis, 1970; MA (hon.), Harvard U., 1979; DSc (hon.), U. R.I., 1987, U. Madrid, 1989, U. Md., 1992, U. Kinshasa, Zaire, 1995. Research fellow Karolinska Inst., Stockholm, 1970-72; asst. prof. Harvard U., Cambridge, Mass., 1972-76, assoc. prof., 1976-78, prof., chmn. dept. microbiology, 1978-81, chmn. dept. cancer biology, 1981-97, chmn. dept. immunology and infectious diseases, 1997—, Mary Woodard Lasker prof. health scis., 1989—, chmn. AIDS Inst., 1988—; mem. sci. adv. bd. Cambridg Biosci. Corp., 1982-93, Virus Rsch. Inst., 1993—; cons. Diacrin, Inc. Co-editor: Viruses in Cancer, 1980, AIDS: Etiology, Diagnosis, Treatment and Prevention, 1992, 97, Human T-cell Leukemia Viruses, 1984, AIDS in Africa, 1994; contbr. articles to profl. jours.; patentee test for human T leukemia virus infection and AIDS blood tests and vaccines. Bd. sci. counselors Nat. Cancer Inst., 1982-93; mem. Lasker award jury Albert & Mary Lasker Found., 1982-84, 87-92; sci. adv. bd. ARC, 1985-89; bd. dirs. Pierre Dick/Virbac Found; mem. adv. bd. AIDS Assn., 1990—; mem. sci. adv. bd. Until There's a Cure, 1995—, Internat. AIDS Vaccine Initiative, Rockefeller Found., 1996—, Sabin Found., 1996—, Inst. for Internat. Vaccine Devel., 1997—; Virus Rsch. Inst., 1992—; bd. dirs. Hong Kong Cancer Ctr., 1994—; v.p. sci. affairs Internat. Retroviral. Assn. HTLV and Related Viruses, 1995—; sec. gen. Internat. Assn. Rsch. on Leukemia, 1995-97, pres., 1997. Leukemia Soc. Am. scholar, 1972; Am. Cancer Soc. Nat. Cancer Inst. grantee, 1973—; recipient Bronze medal Am. Cancer Soc., 1978, Ralston-Purina rsch. award, 1985, Outstanding Investigator award Nat. Cancer Inst., 1985, Lifetime Rsch. award, 1995, Disting. Alumnus award Mich. State U., Lasker award, 1986, Carnation Rsch. award, 1987, Disting. Alumnus award U. Calif., Davis, 1987, Presdl. medal of honor Govt. of Senegal, 1991, ann. award Am. Assn. Vet. Epidemiologists, 1992, Gold-Headed Cane award, 1995, U. R.I. Alumni Excellence award, 1994. Fellow AAAS, Am. Assn. Microbiology, Infectious Disease Soc. Am.; mem. Inst. Medicine of NAS, AVMA, Am. Assn. Cancer Rsch., Am. Assn. Immunologists, Internat. Assn. Rsch. in Leukemia (pres.), Am. Soc. Virology, Nat. Acad. Practitioners, Reticuloendothelial Soc., Soc. Gen. Microbiology, Am. Cancer Soc. (mem. rsch. com. Mass. br. 1975-86), Leukemia Soc. Am. (adv. bd. 1978-83, 85—), Internat. Retrovirology Assn. (v.p.). Office: Harvard Sch Pub Health Immunology & Infectious Dis 651 Huntington Ave Boston MA 02115-6009*

ESSEY, BASIL, bishop; b. North Charleroi, Pa., Nov. 26, 1948; s. William Frederick and Genevieve Alberta (Lhota) E. BA, California U. of Pa., 1970; MDiv, St. Vladimir's Sem., Crestwood, N.Y., 1973. Tonsured reader Antiochian Orthodox Ch., Monessen, Pa., 1964; ordained subdeacon, then deacon Antiochian Orthodox Ch., Ligonier, Pa., 1979; ordained priest Antiochian Orthodox Ch., Bergenfield, N.J., 1980; elevated to archimandrite Antiochian Orthodox Ch., Wichita, Kans., 1987; consecrated bishop Antiochian Orthodox Christian Archdiocese of N.Am., Wichita, 1992—. Translator, editor: The Liturgikon, 1989. Recipient Jackman award for disting. alumnus California Univ. of Pa., 1993. Office: Antiochian Orthod Chancery 1559 N Woodlawn Blvd Wichita KS 67208-2429

ESSIEN, FRANCINE B., geneticist, educator. BA in Biology, Temple U.; PhD in Genetics, Yeshiva U.; postgrad., U. Conn. Prof. dept. biol. scis. Rutgers U., New Brunswick, N.J., 1997—; dir. Minority Undergrad. Sci. Programs, Rutgers U., 1988—, founder, co-founder Success in the Scis., Biomed. Careers Program, Rsch. Apprentice Program, ACCESS-MED, mem. adv. bd. Douglass Project for Rutgers Women in Math, Sci. and Engring.; mem. rev. panel NSF/NIH; cons. CUNY, Atlanta U.; lectr. in field. Contbr. articles to profl. jours. Fulbright scholar; recipient Spina Bifida Assn. Am. award, N.J. Women of Achievement award Woodrow Wilson Found. Instns.; named Black Achiever in Sci., Chgo. Mus. Sci. and Industry, U.S. Prof. of Yr. for Rsch. and Doctoral Univs., Carnegie Found. Advancement of Teaching.; Disting. Black Scholar-in-Residence, U. Cin., 1988; CASE Professor of the Yr. 1994-95; recipient W.E.B. DuBois award for edn. NAACP of Cen. N.J., 1997. Office: Rutgers U Nelson Lab/Busch Campus 604 Allison Rd Piscataway NJ 08854-8000*

ESSIG, ERHARDT HERBERT, English educator; b. Sawyer, Mich., May 24, 1913; s. William Gustav and Wilhelmina Augusta (Kirchner) E.; m. Viola Katherine Waldschmidt, Aug. 24, 1946. MA, U. Tex., 1939; DPhil, Northwestern U., 1951. Instr., dean students Concordia Coll., Austin, Tex., 1936-40; instr. Concordia High Sch., Ft. Wayne, Ind., 1940-46; asst. prof. Valparaiso (Ind.) U., 1946-51, assoc. prof., 1951-56; prof., chmn. humanities Concordia Sr. Coll., Ft. Wayne, 1956-77; assoc.faculty Ind. U.-Purdue U., Ft. Wayne, 1976-83; vis. prof. St. Francis Coll., Ft. Wayne, 1964-77; cons., spkr. in field. Author: History of Holy Cross Lutheran Church, 1995; contbr. articles to profl. jours. Grad. scholar Northwestern U., 1949-50. Mem. Modern Lang. Assn., Colonial Park Assn. (bd. dirs. 1972-74, pres. bd. dirs. 1972-73). Independent. Lutheran. Avocations: sports, travel, reading. Home: 1905 Colony Dr Fort Wayne IN 46825-5009

ESSIG, KATHLEEN SUSAN, university official, education consultant; b. Denver, July 5, 1956; d. Robert and Ethel Essig. BS in BA, Colo. State U., 1979, MS, 1987. CPA, Colo. Personal fin. planner, v.p. fin. Successful Money Mgmt., Ft. Collins, Colo., 1987-88; accts. payable technician Colo. State U., Ft. Collins, 1980-81, supr. comml. accts. receivable, 1981-83, gen. acct. II, 1983-85, supr. student loans, 1985-87, supr. accts. receivable, acct. II, 1988-89, cost acct. III, 1989-94, univ. ofcl., contr., 1994; univ. mgmt. cons. KPMG Peat Marwick, Denver, 1994-97, U.K., 1995-97; mgr. prin. cons. Oracle Corp., Redwood Shores, Calif., 1998—. Mem. Am. Bus. Women's Assn. (v.p. 1985, Woman of Yr. 1985), Nat. Assn. Accts. Avocations: photography, golf, skiing, scuba diving.

ESSLINGER, JOHN THOMAS, lawyer; b. Ephrata, Pa., Aug. 11, 1943; s. Doster Alvin and Lucy Mildred (Ream) E.; m. Patricia Lynn Smith, Aug. 15, 1970; 1 child, John David. BA, Yale U., 1965; JD, Georgetown U., 1973. Bar: D.C. 1973, U.S. Dist. Ct. D.C. 1974, U.S. Supreme Ct. 1974, U.S. Ct. Appeals (D.C. cir.) 1974. Assoc. Morgan, Lewis & Bockius, Washington, 1973-76; ptnr. Schmeltzer, Aptaker & Shepard, P.C., Washington, 1976—. Capt. USMC, 1966-70, Vietnam. Decorated Purple Heart, Bronze Star, Gold Star. Mem. ABA, Bar Assn. D.C., D.C. Bar Assn., Maritime Adminstrv. Bar Assn. Episcopalian. Avocations: golf, wine, baseball. Home: 9102 Brierly Rd Chevy Chase MD 20815-5655 Office: Schmeltzer Aptaker & Shepard PC 2600 Virginia Ave NW Ste 1000 Washington DC 20037-1905

ESSMYER, MICHAEL MARTIN, lawyer; b. Abilene, Tex., Dec. 6, 1949; s. Lytle Martin Essmyer and Roberta N. Essmyer Nicholson; m. Cynthia Rose Piccolo, Dec. 27, 1970; children: Deanna, Mike, Brent Austin. BS in Geology, Tex. A&M U., 1972; postgrad., Tex. Christian U., 1976; JD summa cum laude, South Tex. Coll. Law, 1980. Bar: Tex. 1980, U.S. Dist. Ct. (no., so., ea. we. dists) Tex. 1982, U.S. Ct. Appeals (5th cir.) 1981, U.S. Ct. Appeals (9th cir.) 1990, U.S. Ct. Appeals (1st cir.) 1993, U.S. Ct. Appeals (7th cir.) 1995, U.S. Ct. Appeals (fed. cir.) 1985, U.S. Ct. Claims, 1981, U.S. Supreme Ct. 1991. Briefing atty. Supreme Ct. Tex., Austin, 1980-81, Haynes & Fullenweider, Houston, 1981-89, Essmyer & Hanby, Houston, 1989-92; atty. Essmyer & Assocs., Houston, 1992-94; pres. Essmyer & Tritco, LLP, Houston, 1994-95, Essmyer, Tritco & Clary, LLP, Houston, 1995-99, Essmyer & Tritco, LLP, Houston, 1999—. Lead article editor South Tex. Law Jour., 1979. Dem. candidate for state rep., Bryan, Tex., 1972; del. Dem. Party, Houston, 1982, 84; precinct chmn. Harris County Dem. Exec. Com., Houston, 1983-86. Capt. USAF, 1972-78. Nat. Merit Scholar, 1968-72. Mem. ABA, Houston Bar Assn., Tex. Trial Lawyers Assn. (assoc. dir. 1996—), Harris County Trial Lawyers Assn. (dir. 1997—), Assn. Trial Lawyers Am., Tex. Criminal Def. Lawyers Assn., Tex. Bar Found., Harris County Criminal Lawyers Assn. (dir. 1986-87), Fed. Bar Assn., Houstonian Club, The Doctor's Club of Houston. Roman Catholic. E-mail: essmyer@flash.net. Home: 1122 Glourie Dr Houston TX 77055-7506 Office: Essmyer & Tritico LLP 4300 Scotland St Houston TX 77007-7328

ESTABROOK, REED, artist, educator; b. Boston, May 31, 1944; s. F. Reed and Nancy (Vogel) E.; 1 son, August. B.F.A., R.I. Sch. Design, Providence, 1969; M.F.A., Art Inst. Chgo., 1971. Instr. U. Ill., 1971-74; asst. prof. U. No. Iowa, Cedar Falls, 1974-78, assoc. prof., 1978-83, head dept. photog. program, 1974-83; advisor visual arts Iowa Arts Council, Des Moines, 1977-78, mem. art purchase com., 1977-78; chmn. photog. dept. Kansas City Art Inst., Mo., 1983-84; prof., coordinator Photo Dept. San Jose State U., 1984-89, 92-95; bd. dirs. San Francisco Camera Work, 1987-90; Fulbright exch. tchr. Sheffield Poly., Eng., 1990-91. Exhibited one-man shows, Sioux City Art Ctr., Iowa, 1981, Klein Gallery, Chgo., 1982, James Madison U., Harrisonburg, Va., 1983, Orange Coast Coll., Costa Mesa, Calif., 1983, Portland State U., Oreg., 1983, others, group shows, Isetan Mus. of Art, 1993, U. Colo., Boulder, 1977, 82, Mus. Modern Art, N.Y.C., 1978, 82, 84, Santa Barbara Mus. Art, Calif., 1979, San Francisco Mus. Modern Art, 1982, 90, Hokkaido Obihito Mus. of Art, 1993, Royal Coll. Art, London, 1994, Mus. Fine Art, Santa Fe, N.Mex., 1994, 96, San Jose Inst. Contemporary Art, 1996, San Francisco Mus. Modern Art, 1996, others; represented permanent collections, Mus. Modern Art, N.Y.C., Mpls. Inst. Arts, Hallmark Collection, Kansas City, Mo., Boise Gallery Art, Idaho, Walker Art Ctr., Mpls., R.I. Sch. Design, U. Colo., Fogg Mus. Art, Harvard U., Spencer Mus. Art, U. Kans., Lawrence, Internat. Mus. Photography, Rochester, N.Y., Art Inst. Chgo., Humbolt State U., Arcata, Calif., Smithsonian Instn., Washington, San Francisco Mus. Modern Art. W.R. French fellow Art Inst. Chgo., 1971; Nat. Endowment for Arts fellow, 1976. Fellow Soc. Contemporary Photo; mem. Soc. for Photog. Edn. Home: 482 Chetwood St Oakland CA 94610-2649 Office: San Jose State U Sch Art and Design San Jose CA 95192-0089

ESTABROOK, ROBERT HARLEY, journalist; b. Dayton, Ohio, Oct. 16, 1918; s. Charles and Christianne M. (Harley) E.; m. Mary Lou Stewart, Dec. 22, 1942; children: John Stewart, James Ross, David Morse, Margaret Harley. AB, Northwestern U., 1939; postgrad., Am. Press Inst., Columbia, 1947; LHD (hon.), Colby Coll., 1972. City editor Emmet County Graphic, Harbor Springs, Mich., 1936; editor Daily Northwestern, Northwestern U., 1938-39; reporter Cedar Rapids (Iowa) Gazette, 1939-40, editorial writer, 1940-42; editorial writer Washington Post, 1946-53, editor editorial page, 1953-61; corr. Washington Post, London, 1961-62, chief fgn. corr., 1962-65, UN and Can. corr., 1966-71; editor, pub. Lakeville (Conn.) Jour., 1971-86, pub. emeritus, cons., 1987—; lectr. journalism U. Md., 1948-49; India Editor Exchange Program, 1987. Served from pvt. to capt. AUS, 1942-46; in charge Army newspaper and radio sta. 1945, Brazil. Recipient John Peter Zenger award U. Ariz., 1979, Eugene Cervi award, 1980, Horace Greeley award, 1980, Yankee Quill award Acad. New Eng. Journalists, 1983. Mem. Nat. Conf. Editorial Writers (founder, life mem. pres. 1951), Council Fgn. Relations, Conn. Council on Freedom of Info. (chmn. 1981-82, Stephen Collins award, 1989), New Eng. Press Assn. (pres. 1983), Rotary Club, Phi Beta Kappa, Sigma Delta Chi (award for best editorial 1954), Deadline Club (Pulitzer Prize juror 1988, 89, award for UN corr. 1969, Golden Quill award for best editorial 1973, 78, Herbert Brucker award 1977), Delta Tau Delta. Unitarian. Office: Lakeville Jour 33 Bissell St Lakeville CT 06039-1212

ESTABROOK, RONALD WINFIELD, chemistry educator; b. Albany, N.Y., Jan. 3, 1926; s. George Arthur and Lillian Florence (Childs) E.; m. June Elizabeth Templeton, Aug. 23, 1947; children: Linda Estabrook Gilbert, Laura Estabrook Verinder, Jill Estabrook Wisehart, David. B.S., Rensselaer Poly. Inst., 1950; Ph.D., U. Rochester, 1954, D.Sc. (hon.), 1980; M.D. (hon.), Karolinska Inst., Stockholm, 1981. Johnson Research Found. fellow U. Pa. Sch. Medicine, 1955-58; research assoc., 1958-59, asst. prof. phys. biochemistry, 1959-62, assoc. prof., 1961-65, prof., 1965-68, Virginia Lazenby O'Hara prof. biochemistry, 1968—; chmn. biochemistry U. Tex. Southwestern Med. Ctr., Dallas, 1968-82; dean U. Tex. Health Sci. Center (Grad. Sch. Biomed. Scis.), 1973-76; Cecil and Ida Green Chair of Biomedical Scis., 1990—; acting dir. Green Ctr. for Reproductive Biology Scis. U. Tex. Southwestern Med. Ctr., Dallas, 1997—; chmn. basic sci. rev. com. VA, 1972-74; cons. in field; bd. sci. advisors St. Judes Hosp., Memphis, 1978-81; chmn. bd. toxicology and environ. health NAS, 1980-85; mem. governing bd. NRC, NAS, 1986-89; mem. Atlantic Richfield Sci. Adv. Coun., 1981-87; mem. coun. Inst. Medicine, NAS, 1984-89, mem. report rev. com.; chmn. bd. sci. overseers Med. Rsch. Inst. San Francisco; mem. Robert Wood Johnson Found. Commn. on Med. Edn., bd. sci. advisors ILSI Found.; treas. Fedn. Am. Socs. Exptl. Biology, 1992-94; treas. 17th Internat.

Congress of Biochemistry and Molecular Biology. Exec. editor Archives of Biochemistry and Biophysics, 1966-73, 77-92, chmn. editorial bd., 1984-90; exec. editor Cancer Research, 1980-84; editor Jour. Pharmacology and Exptl. Therapeutics, 1969-74, Xenobiotica, 1970—, Life Scis., 1973-84; contbr. articles to profl. jours. Served with USNR, 1943-46. Recipient Disting. Scientist award Fedn. Am. Socs. Exptl. Biology, 1977, Claude Bernard medal U. Montreal, 1969. Mem. NAS, Inst. Medicine, Pan Am. Assn., Biochem. Socs. (sec.-gen. 1972-75), Am. Assn. Med. Schs. (adminstrv. bd. council acad. socs.; task force cost med. edn. 1971-72, liaison com. med. edn. 1975-80), Am. Soc. Biol. Chemists (treas. 1985-91), Internat. Soc. for Study Xenobiotics (pres. 1988-90), Am. Soc. Pharmacology and Exptl. Therapeutics, OXYgene (founder 1989), Sigma Xi. Home: 5208 Preston Haven Dr Dallas TX 75229-3040 Office: U Tex Southwestern Med Ctr 5323 Harry Hines Blvd Dallas TX 75235-7208*

ESTAVER, PAUL EDWARD, writer, poet; b. Springfield, Mass., Mar. 7, 1924; s. Edward Andrew and Lillian Marguerite (Moore) E.; m. Marina Brodie, Feb. 15, 1964 (div. Feb. 1973); 1 child, Donna Estaver Hall; m. Lynn Inez Lala Tabb, May 24, 1975; children: Emile R. Tabb, Tari Tabb Brewer, Todd Tabb. AB, Boston U., 1948, MA, 1949. Dept. dir. Office of Law Enforcement Programs Law Enforcement Assistance Adminstrn., Washington, 1968-69, dir. civil disorders divsn., 1969-71; dep. dir. Nat. Ctr. for Dispute Settlement, Washington, 1973-75; dir. reference and dissemination divsn. Nat. Inst. Justice, Washington, 1976-95; Author: (poetry) Salisbury Beach-1954, 1984, (novel) His Third, Her Second, 1989. Cpl. U.S. Army, 1943-46, ETO. Recipient Va. prize for fiction Va. Commn. for Arts, 1984, fellowship in poetry Nat. Endowment for Arts, 1987, Asst. Atty. Gen.'s award U.S. Dept. Justice, 1987, Heroes of Reinvention award V.P. of U.S., 1995. Mem. Internat. Soc. for Panetics. Avocations: jazz musician, antique clock restoration, horse farming, breeding standard poodles. Home: 6309 Pilgrims Rest Rd E Warrenton VA 20187-2854

ESTEBAN, MANUEL ANTONIO, university administrator, educator; b. Barcelona, Spain, June 20, 1940; came to U.S., 1970; s. Manuel and Julia Esteban; m. Gloria Ribas, July 7, 1962; 1 child, Jacqueline. BA with 1st class honors in French, U. Calgary, Can., 1969, MA in Romance Studies, 1970; PhD in French, U. Calif., Santa Barbara, 1976. From asst. prof. to prof. French and Spanish langs. and lit. U. Mich., Dearborn, 1973-87, assoc. dean, 1984-86, acting dean coll. arts, scis., and letters, 1986-87; dean arts and scis. Calif. State U., Bakersfield, 1987-90; provost, v.p. acad. affairs Humboldt State U., Arcata, Calif., 1990-93; pres., prof. French and Spanish Calif. State U., Chico, 1993—; bd. dirs. Calif. Joint Policy Coun. on Agr. and Edn., 1995—, Sierra Health Found., 1998—. Author: Georges Feydeau, 1983; contbr. books revs. and articles to profl. publs. Woodrow Wilson fellow, 1969, doctoral fellow U. Calif., Santa Barbara, 1970-73, Can. Coun doctoral fellow, Govt. Can., 1970-73; Rackham grantee U. Mich., 1979, fellow, 1982-83. Mem. Am. Coun. Edn., Am. Assn. State Colls. and Univs., Greater Chico C. of C., U.S. Distance Learning Assn., Sierra Health Found. (bd. dirs. 1998—). Avocations: golf, woodworking, glassblowing. Office: Calif State Univ Office of Pres Chico CA 95929-0150

ESTELL, DORA LUCILE, retired educational administrator; b. Ft. Worth, Mar. 3, 1930; d. Hugh and Hattie Lucile (Poole) E. BA, East Tex. Bapt. U., 1951; MA, U. North Tex., 1959; EdD, East Tex. State U., 1988. Tchr. Mission (Tex.) Ind. Sch. Dist., 1951-53; tchr., adminstr. Marshall (Tex.) Ind. Sch. Dist., 1953-68; dep. dir. Region VII Edn. Svc. Ctr., Kilgore, Tex., 1968-94, ret., 1994. Contbr. articles to profl. jours. Mem. Phi Delta Kappa. Baptist. Avocations: photography, gardening. Home: 611 W Bell Ave Rockdale TX 76567-2809

ESTENSON, NOEL K., refining and fertilizer company executive; b. 1938. BS, N.D. U. Pres., CEO Cenex, Inc., St. Paul, 1987-98, CEO, 1998—. Office: Cenex Harvest States Cooperative PO Box 64089 Saint Paul MN 55164-0089*

ESTEP, JOHN HAYES, religious denomination executive, clergyman; b. Bellwood, Pa., June 30, 1930; s. Kenneth and Anna Emily Estep; m. Dorothy L. Nash, Aug. 21, 1951; children: Heidi Ann, John H. Jr. BA, Wheaton (Ill.) Coll., 1953; MDiv, Denver Sem., 1956, DD (hon.), 1980. Ordained to ministry Bapt. Ch., 1956. Asst. pastor Forest City Bapt. Ch., Rockford, Ill., 1956-62; pastor, sr. min. Calvary Bapt. Ch., Longmont, Colo., 1962-69; dir. ch. rels. Mission to the Americas, Wheaton, 1969-80, CEO, 1980-95. Bd. dirs. Colo. Christian U., Denver, 1964-71, Denver Sem., 1968-70. Mem. Nat. Assn. Evangelicals (officer 1988-96), Nat. Black Evang. Assn. (bd. dirs. 1992—). Avocations: golf, travel, reading, music. Office: CB Ministries Box 66 25W560 Geneva Rd Wheaton IL 60189

ESTEP, LAWRENCE ROBERT, videographer, video producer; b. New Albany, Ind., Mar. 15, 1973; s. Karen Sue (Estep) Spry. Grad. H.S., New Albany. Pub. svc. dir. WNAS Radio/TV, New Albany, 1989-90, weather dir., 1989-91, ops. dir., 1990-91; weather dir., master control operator WBNA-TV, Louisville, 1992-95, pub. svcs. dir., 1993-95; master control operator WFTE-TV, Louisville, 1996-99, Sta. WDRB-TV, Louisville, 1997-98; owner Estep Enterprises, New Albany, Ind. Mem. Am. Legion Post 42, Sons of the Am. Legion (squadron comdr. 1983-84, dir. Alert Ind. Tornado Rsch. 1992-96). Avocations: severe weather rsch., hot air ballooning, amusement parks, photography, NASCAR. Home: 2004 D Mapleton Ct Crawfordsville IN 47933 Office: Estep Enterprises 524 Roseview Ter New Albany IN 47150-4457

ESTEP, MARK RANDALL, secondary education educator; b. Springfield, Mo., June 18, 1962; s. Wendall Eugene Estep and Martha Anne (Wheeler) Johns; m. Shawna Lea Dittmar, June 18, 1988; children: Cheyanne Elizabeth, Shelby Lea, Jamie Lee. BS in Edn., S.W. Mo. State U., 1990; MEd, U. Mo., 1996. Cert. secondary tchr., Mo. Supr. Harry Cooper Supply Co., Springfield, 1985-90; co-owner Shawn-Mar Dairy Farm, Marionville, Mo., 1986-97; tchr. agriculture McDonald County Schs., Anderson, Mo., 1990-93, Marionville (Mo.) Schs., 1993—; advisor McDonald County Future Farmers Am., Anderson, 1990-93; advisor Marionville Future Farmers of Am., 1993—. Treas. McDonald County Fair Bd., Anderson, 1991-92; advisor Area 9 Future Farmers Am., 1995-96. Recipient Hon. State FFA Degree, 1998. Mem. Nat. Vocat. Assn., Nat. Assoc. of Agriculture Educators., Mo. Vocat. Agr. Tchrs. Assn. (Outstanding Agr. Program award 1992-93), Teaching Ideas Award Winner, 1997; Area 9 Agr. Tchrs. Assn. (sec.-treas. 1995-96, v.p. 1996-97, pres. 1997), Mo. Ayrshire Assn. (pres. 1989-90). Home: 20920 Lawrence 1235 Aurora MO 65605 Office: Marionville Future Farmers PO Box J Marionville MO 65705-0409

ESTEP, MICHAEL R., church administrator. Dir. comm. divsn. Ch. of the Nazarene, Kansas City, Mo., 1994—; exec. dir. Beacon Hill Press, Kansas City, Mo., 1994; adminstrv. dir. World Mission Radio, Kansas City, 1994; dir. Nazarene Comm. Network, Kansas City, 1995. Office: Church of Nazarene 6401 Paseo Blvd Kansas City MO 64131-1213

ESTEP, MYRNA LYNNE, systems analyst, philosophy educator; b. Whitesville, W.Va., Jan. 7, 1944; d. Modest Schaeffer and Mary Magdalene E.; m. Richard Keith Schoenig, June 5, 1971; 1 child, Debora Lynne. BA, Ind. U., 1970, MS, 1971, PhD, 1975; postgrad., U. Tex., 1993—. Assoc. instr. Ind. U., Bloomington, 1972-75; asst. prof. U. Tex., San Antonio, 1975-78; rsch. edn. specialist Acad. Health Scis., San Antonio, Tex., 1979-84; program systems analyst, field researcher USMC, U.S. Navy, Quantico, Va., 1984-87; grad. faculty, advisor U. Zimbabwe, 1987-89; rsch. systems analyst San Antonio, 1990—; adj. faculty in philosophy U. of Incarnate Word, San Antonio, 1996—, Our Lady of the Lake U., San Antonio, 1996-98; grad. faculty U. Zimbabwe, Harare; advisor to ministries of higher edn. and labour, manpower planning and social welfare, Zimbabwe, 1987-89. Author: The Relation Between Theoretical and Procedural Knowing, 1975; co-editor: (with E.S. Maccia and others) Women and Education, 1975; reviewer for jours.; contbr. sci. papers and monographs to profl. publs., including Feminista: The On-Line Jour. of Feminist Reconstrn., 1998—. Recipient Best Paper award U. Vienna, Austria, 1992. Mem. AAAS, Internat. Soc. Gen. Systems Rsch., Austrian Soc. Cybernetics, Math. Assn. Am., N.Y. Acad. Sci., Phi Kappa Phi. Home: 16022 Oak Grove Dr San Antonio TX 78255-1128

ESTEP, SARAH VIRGINIA, association executive; b. Altoona, Pa., Mar. 1, 1926; d. Benner Marshal and Helen Rebecca (Sellers) Wilson; m. Charles Sheldon Estep, Apr. 12, 1952; children: Cynthia Jane, Rebecca Anne, Robert Wilson. BA, Mary Washington U., Fredericksburg, Va., 1947. Social worker Blair County Childrens's Aid Soc., Altoona, Pa., 1947-52; tchr. Anne Arundel Bd. Edn., Annapolis, Md., 1952-75; pvt. camp dir. Hartford County, Md., summer 1963; camp dir. Girl Scouts of Cen. Md., Balt., summer 1964; dir. camping Camp Fire Girls Md., Balt., 1966-67; founder, dir. Am. Assn. Electronic Voice Phenomena, Severna Park, Md., 1982—; cons. in field; lectr. in field; conductor workshops in field. Author: Voices of Eternity, 1988; editor/pub. quar. newsletter, AA-EVP News, 1982; contbr. articles to profl. jours. Recipient Dr. A. Hedri prize for Epipsychology, 1996, Epipsychology award Swiss Found. for Parapsychology, 1996, Berne. Avocations: reading, music, electronics, travel.

ESTERHAI, JOHN LOUIS, JR., surgeon, medical educator; b. Phila., Oct. 23, 1946; s. John Louis and Louise K. (Moyer) E.; m. Carol Jean Keely, Apr. 12, 1969; children: Staci June, Gregory Wayne. BA, Gettysburg Coll., 1968; MD, Temple U., 1972. Intern in surgery Temple U. Health Sci. Ctr., Phila., 1973; flight surgeon USAF, Kadena AFB, Okinawa, Japan, 1973-76; resident in orthop. surgery U. Pa. Sch. Medicine, 1977-80; asst. prof. orthopedic surgery Hosp. U. Pa., Phila., 1980-87; assoc. prof. orthopedic surgery Hosp. U. Pa., 1987—. Editor: Musculoskeletal Infection, 1992. Maj. USAF, 1973-76. Recipient award Am. Orthopedic Assn., 1989, Assn. Bone and Joint Surgeons, 1994. Fellow Am. Acad. Orthopedic Surgeons, ACS; mem. Internat. Soc. Fracture Repair, Orthopaedic Rsch. Soc., Musculoskeletal Infection Soc. (pres. 1997-98). Office: Hosp U Pa Dept Orthopaedic Surgery 3400 Spruce St Philadelphia PA 19104-4204

ESTERLINE, SHIRLEY JEANNE, lithograph company executive; b. Paulding, Ohio, June 6, 1936; d. George Gary and Catherine Genevieve (Durbin) Sontchi; m. Meredith Esterline, Apr. 1, 1956; children: Gordon Alan, Amy Jeanne. Cert. med. technologist, Elkhart U., Ind., 1956. Lab technician Ft. Wayne, Ind., 1956-57; sec. Zollner Corp., Ft. Wayne, 1957-58, Magnavox Corp., Ft. Wayne, 1958-61; sales coord. Doty Lithograph Inc., Ft. Wayne, 1975-77; sales mgr. Dot Line div. Dot Corp., Auburn, Ind., 1977-87; Midwest sales mgr. Falco/Sunbelt div. Fl. Cos., Nashville, 1987-89; pvt. cons., 1989-98, ret., 1995. Mem. Specialty Advt. Assn. Internat. (suppliers com. 1983—, cert. advt. specialist 1985, master advt. specialist 1986, chmn. 100 club 1983—, seminar facilitator calendar advt. coun. 1985-89, CAS Alumni 1985—, mgmt. awards 1984, 85, 86). Methodist. Avocations: reading, sewing.

ESTERLY, NANCY BURTON, physician; b. N.Y.C., Apr. 14, 1935; d. Paul R. and Tanya (Pasahow) Burton; m. John R. Esterly, June 16, 1957; children: Sarah Burton, Anne Beidler, John Snyder, II, Henry Clark, II. AB, Smith Coll., 1956; MD, Johns Hopkins U., 1960. Intern, then resident in pediatrics Johns Hopkins Hosp., 1960-63, resident in dermatology, 1964-67; instr. pediatrics Johns Hopkins U. Med. Sch., 1967-68; instr., trainee La Rabida U. Chgo. Inst.; also dept. pediatrics U. Chgo. Med. Sch., 1968-69; asst. prof. Pritzker Sch. Medicine, U. Chgo., 1969-70, asso. prof., 1973-78; asst. prof. dermatology Abraham Lincoln Sch. Medicine, U. Ill., 1970-72, asso. prof. dermatology and pediatrics, 1972-73; dir. div. dermatology, dept. pediatrics Michael Reese Hosp. and Med. Ctr., Chgo., 1973-78; prof. pediatrics and dermatology Northwestern U. Med. Sch., 1978; head div. dermatology, dept. pediatrics Children's Meml. Hosp., Chgo., 1978-87; prof. pediatrics and dermatology Med. Coll. Wis., Milw., 1987—; head div. dermatology, dept. pediatrics Children's Hosp. Wis., Milw., 1987—. Contbr. numberous articles to profl. jours. Mem. Internat. Soc. Pediatric Dermatology, Am. Acad. Dermatology, Am. Dermatol. Assn., Wis. Dermatol. Soc., Soc. Investigative Dermatology, Am. Acad. Pediatrics, Soc. Pediatric Rsch., Soc. Pediatric Dermatology, Women's Dermatol. Soc., Wis. Pediatric Soc., Sigma Xi. Office: 9200 W Wisconsin Ave Milwaukee WI 53226-3522

ESTEROW, MILTON, magazine editor, publisher; b. Bklyn., July 28, 1928; s. Bernard and Yetta (Barash) E.; m. Jacqueline Levine, Jan. 6, 1951; children: Judith, Deborah. Student, Bklyn. Coll., 1946-49. Reporter N.Y. Times, N.Y.C., 1948-63, asst. to cultural news dir., 1963-68; assoc. dir. Kennedy Galleries, N.Y.C., 1968-72; editor, pub. ARTnews, N.Y.C., 1972—; chmn. ARTnewsletter, 1975—, Esterow Communications Corp., 1981, Annellen Publs., 1982, ARTnews for Students, 1995—; lectr. numerous colls., univs., museums. Author: The Art Stealers, 1966. Office: ARTnews LLC 48 W 38th St New York NY 10018-6211

ESTES, CAROLYN ANN HULL, retired elementary school educator; b. Memphis, June 11, 1933; d. Elmer Franklin and Annie Vernon (Jeter) Hull; m. Robert Marion Estes, June 4, 1955; children: Robert Franklin, David Carlton. BS, Memphis State U., 1955; postgrad., U. Tenn., 1958, Nat. Coll. Edn., 1968, N. Tex. State U., 1970, Tex. Christian U., 1984, U. Tex., Arlington, 1985. Cert. elem. and secondary tchr., Tex. 4th grade tchr. Memphis City Schs., 1955-56, 63-66; 6th grade tchr. Knoxville (Tenn.) City Schs., 1957-58; 3d grade tchr. Elk Grove Village (Ill.) Schs., 1968-69; sci. tchr. Stripling Middle Sch., Ft. Worth Ind. Sch. Dist., 1970-76; 5th grade magnet tchr. Eastern Hills Sch., Ft. Worth Ind. Sch. Dist., 1976-78; 5th grade honors tchr. Westcreek Elem. Sch., Ft. Worth Ind. Sch. Dist., 1978-91, computer instr., technol. coord., 1991-96; ret., 1996. Author: Hull's Heritage, 1986; contbg. author: Hardeman County History, 1979, also curriculum materials. Life mem. Tex. Coun. PTA, program chairperson, 1984-86; mem., bd. dirs. Ft. Worth Geneal. Assn. Named Walt Disney Salutes the Am. Tchr. Alternate, 1994. Mem. Nat. Edn. Assn., DAR (Outstanding Am. History Tchr. award 1988), Tex. State Tchrs. Assn., Ft. Worth Classroom Tchrs. (faculty liaison 1983-86, chmn. Tchr. Ethics and Profl. Standards 1989, Tchr. of Yr. 1985), Sigma Kappa (alumnae chpt., Significant Sigma award 1990). Home: 141 Club House Dr Weatherford TX 76087-4001

ESTES, CARROLL LYNN, sociologist, educator; b. Fort Worth, May 30, 1938; d. Joe Ewing and Carroll (Cox) E.; 1 child, Duskie Lynn Gelfand Estes. AB, STanford U., 1959; MA, So. Meth. U., 1961; PhD, U. Calif., San Diego, 1972; DHL (hon.), Russell Sage Coll., 1986. Rsch. asst., asst. study dir. Brandeis U. Social Welfare Rsch. Ctr., 1962-63, rsch. assoc., 1964-65, project dir., 1965-67; vis. lectr. Florence Heller Grad. Sch., 1964-65; rsch. dir. Simmons Coll., 1963-64; asst. prof. social work San Diego State Coll., 1967-72; asst. prof. in residence dept. psychiatry U. Calif., San Francisco, 1972-75, assoc. prof. dept. social and behavioral scis., 1975-79, prof., 1979-92, chair dept. social and behavioral scis., 1981-93, coord. human devel. tng. program, 1974-75; dir. Aging Health Policy Rsch. Ctr., 1979-85, Inst. for Health and Aging, 1985-99; faculty rsch. lectr. U. Calif., 1993. Author: The Decision-Makers: The Power Structure of Dallas, 1963; co-author: Protective Services for Older People, 1972, U.S. Senate Special Committee on Aging Report, Paperwork and the Older Americans Act, 1978, The Aging Enterprise, 1979 Fiscal Austerity and Aging, 1983, Long Term Care of the Elderly, 1985, Political Economy, Health and Aging, 1984, The Long Term Care Crisis, The Nation's Health, 1993, 5th edit., 1997, Critical Gerontology, 1998, Nursing & Health Policy, 1997; contbr. articles to profl. jours. Mem. Calif. Commn. on Aging, 1974-77; cons. U.S. Senate Spl. Com. on Aging from 1976, Notch Commn. U.S. Commn. Social Security, 1993-94. Recipient Matrix award Theta Sigma Phi, 1964, award for contbns. to lives of older Californians, Calif. Commn. on Aging, 1977, Helen Nahm Rsch. award U. Calif., San Francisco, 1986, Woman Who Would Be Pres. League of Women Voters, 1998. Mem. Inst. Medicine of NA, ACLU, Am. Sociol. Assn., Assn. Gerontology in Higher Edn. (pres. 1980-81, recipient Beverly award 1993), Am. Soc. on Aging (pres. 1982-84, Leadership awrad 1986), Geronotol. Soc. Am. (Kent award 1992, pres. 1995-96), Older Women's League (v.p. 1994-97), Soc. Study Social Problems, Alpha Kappa Delta, Pi Beta Phi. Democrat. Office: U Calif San Francisco Inst Health & Aging 3333 California St Ste 340 San Francisco CA 94118-1944

ESTES, CHRISTOPHER J., landscape architect; b. Bishops Stortford, Essex, Eng., June 14, 1963; came to U.S., 1970; s. James Hugh and Christine June (Barker) E.; m. Diane Renee Thortsen, May 7, 1994. BA, U. Ga., 1988; postgrad., U.N.C., Charlotte. Registered landscape architect, N.C., S.C. Intern. Brian Clouston & Assn., Chester, England, 1986; with Land Design Inc., Charlotte, 1988-89, DPR Assocs., Charlotte, 1989-90; contracts adminstr. City of Charlotte Engring. Dept., 1990-93; drainage specialist for spl. duties City of Charlotte Storm Water Svcs., 1993—; cons. Wetland ID. & Delineation. Founder Charlotte's rsch. program for urban stream morphology and bio-engring. channels program; designer Spirit Square exterior restoration, 1992, Dairy Branch Wetland Stream rehab. and constrn., 1995, Bid-Engineering Standards for City of Charlotte, Natural Channel Design for City of Charlotte; co-author: Charlotte-Meck Devel. Stds, 1999, Landscape Standards Manual for City of Charlotte, 1993. Recipient Merit award City of Charlotte, 1992, Blue Thumb award Mecklenburg County Water Quality Coalition, 1997. Mem. Am. Soc. Landscape Architects (Merit award 1996). Avocations: flying, scuba, backpacking, fishing, shooting. Office: City of Charlotte Engring 600 E 4th St Charlotte NC 28202-2800 Home: 515 Pembroke Ln Waxhaw NC 28173-6532

ESTES, EDWARD HARVEY, JR., medical educator; b. Gay, Ga., May 1, 1925; s. Edward Harvey and Veola (Jarrell) E.; m. Jean Anderson, Oct. 15, 1948; children: Sara Estes Malone, Susan Estes Jones III, Rebecca Estes Dunn, John, Elizabeth Estes Smith. B.S., Emory U., 1944, M.D., 1947. House officer, research fellow Grady Meml. Hosp., Atlanta, 1947-50; mem. faculty dept. medicine Duke U., 1952-90, Univ. Disting. Service prof., chmn. dept. community and family medicine, 1966-85, Univ. Disting Svc. prof. community and family medicine emeritus, 1990—, dir. family medicine div., 1985-88. Author: (with R.P. Grant) Spatial Vector Electrocardiography, 1950. Mem. AMA (ho. of dels. 1979-94, chmn. coun. sci. affairs 1992-94, Sci. Achievement award 1997), ACP, Inst. Medicine, Am. Soc. Internal Medicine (Disting. Internist of Yr. award 1975), Am. Acad. Family Physicians, Soc. Tchrs. Family Medicine (bd. dirs. 1987-89), N.C. Med. Soc. (pres. 1977-78). Home: 3542 Hamstead Ct Durham NC 27707-5137

ESTES, ELAINE ROSE GRAHAM, retired librarian; b. Springfield, Mo., Nov. 24, 1931; d. James McKinley and Zelma Mae (Smith) Graham; m. John Melvin Estes, Dec. 29, 1953. BSBA, Drake U., 1953, tchg. cert., 1956; MSLS, U. Ill., 1960. With Pub. Libr. Des Moines, 1956-95, coord. extension svcs., 1977-78, dir., 1978-95, ret., 1995; lectr. antiques, hist. architecture, libraries; mem. conservation planning com. for disaster preparedness for libraries. Author bibliographies of books on antiques; contbr. articles to profl. jours. Mem. State of Iowa Cultural Affairs Adv. Coun., 1986-94, Nat. Commn. on Future Drake U., 1987-88; chmn. Des moines Mayor's Hist. Dist. Commn.; bd. dirs. Des Moines Art Ctr., 1972-83, hon. mem., 1983—; bd. dirs. Friends of Libr. USA, 1986-92, Henry Wallace Housing Found.; mem. Iowa Libr. Centennial Com., 1990-91; nominations rev. com. Iowa State Nat. Hist. Register, 1983-89; chmn. hist. subcom. Des Moines Sesequecentennial com., 1993, Iowa Sister State Commn., 1993-95; mem. 45th anniversary com. Des Moines Art Ctr., 1993; mem. com. 40th anniversary Drake U. alumni weekend; mem. Iowa Sesequecentennial July 4 com., 1996; nat. exch. dir. Friendship Force, 1997; mem. nat. adv. bd. Cowles Libr.; mem. Gov.'s Iowa Centennial Meml. Found., 1998—; mem. cultural ctr. task force African Am. Hist. Mus., 1999. Recipient recognition for outstanding working women - leadership in econs. and civic life of Greater Des Moines, YWCA, 1975, Disting. Alumni award Drake U., 1979, Woman of Achievement award YWCA, 1989, City of Des Moines Excellence in Hist. Preservation award, 1994, Connect Found. Contribution to Cmty. award, 1995. Mem. ALA, Iowa Libr. Assn. (pres. 1978-79), ILA (life), Iowa Urban Pub. Libr. Assn., Libr. Assn. Greater Des Moines Metro Area (pres., chmn. 1992), Iowa Soc. Preservation Hist. Landmarks (bd. dirs. 1969-97), Terrace (Gov.'s Mansion) Soc. (v.p. 1991-93, pres. 1993-96), Links Inc. (40th ann. com. 1997), Questers, Inc. Club (pres. 1982, 1997, state 2nd v.p. 1984-86, 1st v.p. 1999), Iowa Antique Assn., Proteus, Rotary.

ESTES, GERALD WALTER, newspaper executive; b. Memphis, Apr. 21, 1928; s. Edward Leon and Grace Virginia (Knight) E.; m. Mary Charlene Owen, Nov. 7, 1953 (div. July 1975); children: Patricia Estes Tischler, Charles, Susan, Jacqueline; m. Bernice Pendleton O'Mery, Mar. 20, 1976 (div. Nov. 1984); m. Mary Owen Estes, Nov. 17, 1984. Student, Memphis State U., 1949-50. Research asst. Washington Star, 1954-56, asst. prodn. mgr., 1956-68; prodn. mgr. Richmond (Va.) Newspapers, 1968-69; v.p., gen. mgr. SE Media, Inc., Richmond, 1969-73; v.p. newspaper div. Media Gen., Inc., Richmond, 1974-77; sr. v.p. Media Gen., Inc., 1977-89; pres. ESC Restaurants, Inc., 1993—; chmn. LBE, Inc., 1993—. Served with USAF, 1946-49. Mem. Brandermill Country Club, Foundry Golf Club, Bull and Bear Club. Republican. Methodist. Clubs: Bull and Bear, Willow Oaks Country. Home: 13636 Northwich Dr Midlothian VA 23112-4932 Office: Media Gen Inc PO Box 85333C Richmond VA 23293-5333

ESTES, JOSEPH O'BRYANT, II, mortgage corporation executive; b. Greenville, S.C., July 14, 1974; s. Thomas Mack Casey and Amy Jo Estes. Student, Clemson U., 1992-94. Notary pub., Gwinnett County, Ga. Ops. mgr. Reliance Acceptance, Charlotte, N.C., 1995-96; sr. loan officer The Mortgage Team, Atlanta, 1996-97; sr. v.p. Pine Valley Mortgage, Atlanta, 1997—. Republican. Roman Catholic. Home: 2759 Porter Dr Lawrenceville GA 30044 Office: Pine Valley Mortgate Corp Ste A-14 4126 Pleasantville Rd Atlanta GA 30340

ESTES, MOREAU PINCKNEY, IV, real estate executive, lawyer; b. Nashville, Oct. 10, 1917; s. Moreau Pinckney III and Lillian (Cole) E.; m. Bertha Lewis, Jan. 14, 1941; children: Moreau Pinckney V, Robert Lewis, Victoria Susanne. Student, Vanderbilt U., 1935-36; LLB, Cumberland U., 1938. Bar: Tenn. 1938. Sole practice law Nashville, 1938-41, bldg. contractor, 1940-43, 46-53; dir. Davidson County Farm Bur., Nashville, 1950-56; v.p. Davidson Farmers Coop., 1955-56; gen. mgr. Harpeth Valley (Tenn.) Utilities Dist., 1963-67; founder, pres. Hillsboro-Harpeth Corp., 1964—; founder, sec.-treas. Alpha Publishing Co., Brentwood, Tenn., 1986—, also bd. dirs.; founder, owner Realty Investment Co., Nashville, 1964—. Mem. residents adv. bd. Tenn. Selective Svcs. System, 1941; atty. property div. State of Tenn., 1963-67, property adminstr., 1964-67; asst. commr. Tenn. Dept. Conservation, 1975; Dem. primary cand. U.S. Ho. of Reps., 1950; del. State Dem. Conv., 1951; sec. Williamson County Dem. Primary Commn., 1967-69; asst. dir. communications Tenn. Dem. Gubernatorial Campaign, 1974; Williamson County coord. Tenn. Dem. Primary Gubernatorial candidate, 1978; middle Tenn. coord. Dem. Primary and Gen. Election Gubernatorial candidate, 1982; bd. stewards, Sunday sch. tchr. Hobson Meth. Ch., 1940-42, 46-50; founder, chmn. bd., 1st pres. Rivermont Watershed Dist., Davidson County, Tenn., 1990-94; apptd. col., aide de camp Staff of Tenn. Gov. Frank Clement, 1963-67, Gov. Ray Blanton, 1975-79, Gov. Lamar Alexandar, 1979-87. Served to 1st lt. Signal Corps U.S. Army, 1942-46, with Res., 1946-51. Named Nashville Mcpl. Tennis Singles and Doubles champion, 1939, 40, Middle Tenn. Singles and Doubles Mcpl. Tennis champion, 1940. Mem. Nashville Home Builders Assn. (pres. 1950), Tenn. Horsemen's Assn. (dir. 1964), Tenn. Hist. Soc., Tenn. Bar Assn., Nashville Bar Assn., Bibl. Archaeology Soc., Nat. Audubon Soc., Smithsonian Assocs., Vanderbilt U. Alumni Assn., Nat. Geographic Soc., SAR, Internat. Bible Assn., Nature Conservancy, Sierra Club, Am. Legion, Wildwood Swimming and Tennis Club (founder, 1st chmn.), Delta Kappa Epsilon. Democrat. Methodist. Home: 6434 Panorama Dr Brentwood TN 37027-4823 Office: 4219 Hillsboro Pike Ste 228 Nashville TN 37215-3328

ESTES, NATHAN ANTHONY MARK, III, cardiologist, medical educator; b. Newport, R.I., Aug. 20, 1949; s. Nathan Anthony Jr. and Ione (Lewis) E.; m. Noël Evangeline Thorbecke, June 22, 1974; children: Elise Thorbecke, N.A. Chace, Kathryn Elizabeth. BA cum laude, U. Pa., 1971; MD magna cum laude, U. Cin., 1977. Diplomate Am. Bd. Internal Medicine, Am. Bd. Cardiovascular Disease, Am. Bd. Cardiac Electrophysiology. Med. intern New Eng. Deaconess Hosp.-Harvard Med. Sch., Boston, 1977-78, med. resident, 1978-80; fellow in cardiology New Eng. Med. Ctr.-Tufts U., Boston, 1980-82; fellow in electrophysiology Mass. Gen. Hosp.-Harvard Med. Sch., Boston, 1982-83; dir. cardiac arrhythmia New. Eng. Med. Ctr. Svc., Boston, 1983-96, dir. heart station, 1983-91; assoc. prof. medicine Tufts U. Sch. Med., Boston, 1983-90, prof., 1990-96, chief New Eng. Cardiac Arrythmia Ctr., 1996-97; chief divsn. cardiovascular medicine New. Eng. Med. Ctr., Boston, 1997—; chief Lifespan Cardiac Arrhythmia Consortium, Boston, 1998; ednl. cons., 1985-96; mem. internat. safety monitoring bd. 3M Pharms., Mpls., 1990-96; co-chmn. pubs. com. NIH, Bethesda, 1993-96; chmn. human investigations rev. com. Tufts U. Sch. Medicine, 1996—. Contbr. over 140 articles to sci. jours.; contbr. over 30 chpts. to books; editor books, 1994-96; editl. bd. Jour. Interventional Electrophysiology, 1995—, Pacing and Cardiac Electrophysiology, 1995—, Jour. Cardiovasc.

Electrophysiology, Am. Jour. Sports and Medicine, 1998, Am. Jour. Cardiology. Vestry mem. Trinity Ch., Newton, Mass., 1985-87; coach Baystate Tournament of Champions, Waltham, Mass., 1990-94; judge N.H. Racing Assn., Lincoln, 1993-95; bd. trustees Moses Brown Sch., Providence, R.I., 1997—. Fellow Am. Coll. Cardiology; mem. Am. Heart Assn. (chmn. bd. trustees Boston chpt. 1998), N. Am. Soc. Pacing and Electrophysiology (chmn. publs. com.), New Eng. Electrophysiology Soc. (pres. 1994-97), Alpha Omega Alpha. Episcopalian. Avocations: sailing, skiing, tennis, running. Office: New Eng Med Ctr 750 Washington St Boston MA 02111-1526

ESTES, RICHARD, artist; b. Kewanee, Ill., 1932. Student, Chgo. Art Inst., 1951-55. Exhbns. include Whitney Mus. Am. Art, Mus. Modern Art, Guggenheim Mus., all N.Y.C., Rockhill Nelson Mus., Kansas City, Mo., Toledo Mus., Chgo. Art Inst., Des Moines Art Ctr., Mus. Contemporary Art, Chgo., High Mus. Art, Atlanta, Hirshorne Mus., Washinton, Richmond, Va. Mus. Art, Mus. Contemporary Art, Vienna, Austria, Ludwig Collection, Cologne, Fed. Republic Germany; numerous exhbns. including Documenta V, Kassel, Fed. Republic Germany, 1972, Venice Biennale, 1972, Whitney Mus. Ann., 1972, Va. Mus. Fine Arts, 1974, Boston Mus. Fine Arts, 1975, 78, Allan Stone Gallery, 1983, Adams-Middleton Gallery, Dallas, 1984, Greenville (S.C.) County Mus. Art, 1984, Whitney Mus. Am. Art, N.Y., 1982, Martha White Gallery, Louisville, 1984, Heckscher Mus., Huntington, N.Y., 1984, Walter Moos Gallery, Toronto, Ont., Can., 1984, Byer Mus. Arts, Evanston, 1984, Daimaru Mus., Osaka, Japan, 1985, Mus. Art, Ft. Lauderdale, 1986. Contemporary Art Ctr., New Orleans, 1986, San Francisco Mus. Modern Art, 1986-87, 90, Carpenter Ctr., Harvard U., 1990, Portland (Maine) Mus. Art, 1991, Whitney Mus., Stamford, Conn., 1991-92; traveling retrospective exhibit in Japan, Tokyo, Osaka and Hiroshima, Am. Fedn. of Arts; traveling print show various mus., 1993-95; one-man show at Marlborough Gallery, 1995, 97, 98. Address: 300 Central Park W New York NY 10024-1513

ESTES, RICHARD MARTIN, lawyer; b. N.Y.C., June 27, 1933; s. Jack Estes and Irene Eva (Dessauer) Schwarz; m. Pamela Jane Graine, Mar. 18, 1965; children: Kenneth Murray, William Jonathan, Jessica Jane. BA, Yale Coll., 1955; LLB, Columbia U., 1959; LLM in Taxation, NYU, 1962. Bar: N.Y. 1959, Fla. 1976; U.S. Supreme Ct. 1962. Assoc. White & Case, N.Y.C., 1959-62, Root, Barrett, Cohen Knapp & Smith, N.Y.C., 1962-65; asst. tax counsel Rockefeller Family & Assocs., N.Y.C., 1965-68; tax counsel Bear, Stearns & Co., N.Y.C., 1968-70; assoc. to ptnr. Spear & Hill, N.Y.C., 1970-75; founding ptnr. Christy & Viener, N.Y.C., 1976-98, Salans, Hertzfeld, Heilbronn, Christy & Viener, N.Y.C., 1999—; lectr. in field. Contbr. articles to profl. jours. Trustee, sec., nomination com. N.Y.C. Police Found., 1971—; bd. mem., v.p., sec. Yale Project 55, Inc., N.Y.C., 1993—; trustee, treas. 1010 Tenants Corp., N.Y.C., 1988—. Maj. USAR, 1955-65. Honored as co-founder N.Y.C. Police Found., 1991. Mem. ABA, Assn. of the Bar of the City of N.Y. (libr. com.), N.Y. State Bar Assn. (tax sect.), Fla. Bar Assn., Univ. Club (coun., libr. and art com. 1976—), Grolier Club, Harmonie Club, Beach Point Club. Avocations: antiquarian book collector, fitness, reading, travel. Office: Salans Hertzfeld Heilbronn Christy & Viener 620 5th Ave New York NY 10020-2402

ESTES, SHIRLEY REID, medical/surgical nurse; b. Caldwell County, N.C., Apr. 22, 1959; d. William Sherrill and Betty (Brooks) Reid; m. Chris V. Estes, Sept. 13, 1980; children: Erica, Christopher. A.Nursing, Caldwell Community Coll., 1979. Staff nurse North Arunde Hosp., Glen Burnie, Md.; asst. charge nurse Frye Regional Med. Ctr., Hickory, N.C.; office nurse med.-surg. Hickory (N.C.) Orthopaedic Ctr. Home: 5701 Reid Rd Granite Falls NC 28630-9801

ESTES, SIMON LAMONT, opera singer, bass-baritone; b. Centerville, Iowa, Feb. 2, 1938. Studied with Charles Kellis, U. Iowa, 1956-63; student, Juilliard Sch., 1964-65. Appeared with major European and Am. operas including Deutche Opera, Boston Opera, Chgo. Lyric Opera, Met. Opera, Zurich Opera, Vienna Staatsoper, Paris Opera, numerous others; roles include Ramphis in Aida, Figaro in The Barber of Seville, Banquo in Macbeth, Oroveso in Norma, Dutchman in The Flying Dutchman, Amonasro in Aida, Wotan in Ring of the Nibelungen, Amonsaro in Aida, Gremin in Eugene Onegin, Porgy in Porgy and Bess, Amfortas in Parisfal, Orest in Elektra, King Philip in Don Carlos, Fiesco in Simon Boccanegra, Macbeth in Macbeth, London Promenade Concerts, 1989—; recs. include Spirituals, 1986. Recipient Munich competition prize, 1965; Silver medal Tchaikowsky Competition, Moscow, 1966. Address: IMG Artists Europe, 3 Burlington Ln, Chiswick W4 2TH, England Address: 1 Deer Ridge Rd Basking Ridge NJ 07920-3404*

ESTES, WILLIAM KAYE, psychologist, educator; b. Mpls., June 17, 1919; s. George D. and Mona; m. Katherine Walker, Sept. 26, 1942; children: George E., Gregory W. Mem. faculty Ind. U., 1946-62, prof. psychology, 1955-60, research prof. psychology, 1960-62; faculty research fellow Social Sci. Research Council, 1952-55; lectr. psychology U. Wis., summer 1949; vis. prof. Northwestern U., spring 1959; fellow Center Advanced Study Behavioral Scis., 1955-56; spl. univ. lectr. U. London, Eng., 1961; prof. psychology, mem. Inst. Math. Studies Social Scis., Stanford, 1962-68; prof. Rockefeller U., 1968-79; prof. Harvard U., 1979-89, prof. emeritus, 1989—; prof. Ind. U., 1999—; chmn. Office Sci. and Engring. Personnel NRC, 1982-85, chmn. com. on prevention of nuclear war, 1984-89. Author: An Experimental Study of Punishment, 1944, Learning Theory and Mental Development, 1970, Models of Learning, Memory and Choice, 1982, Statistical Models in Behavioral Research, 1991, Classification and Cognition, 1994; co-author: Modern Learning Theory, 1954; also numerous articles in profl. jours.; editor: Handbook of Learning and Cognitive Processes, 1962-68, Psychol. Rev., 1977-82, Psychol. Sci., 1990-94; assoc. editor Jour. Exptl. Psychology, 1958-62. Served with AUS, 1944-46. Recipient U.S. Nat. medal of Sci., 1997. Fellow APA (pres. div. exptl. psychology 1958-59, Disting. Sci. Contbn. award 1962, gold medal for lifetime achievement in psychol. sci. 1992), AAAS, Am. Acad. Arts and Scis.; mem. NAS, N.Y. Acad. Scis. (hon. life), Soc. Exptl. Psychologists (Warren medal 1963), Midwestern Psychol. Assn., Fedn. Behavioral Psychol. and Cognitive Scis. (v.p. 1988-91). Home: 2714 Pine Ln Bloomington IN 47401 Office: Ind U W James Hall Psychology Bldg Bloomington IN 47405

ESTESS, ROY S., federal agency administrator; m. Zann Estess; 2 children. Degree in aerospace engring., Miss. State U.; advanced mgmt. program, Harvard Grad. Bus. Sch. Registered profl. engr., Miss. Various positions U.S. Govt., 1960-66; various positions NASA, 1966-80; dep. dir. Stennis Space Ctr. NASA, Miss., 1980-88; dir. Stennis Space Ctr. NASA, 1988—; spl. asst. to NASA adminstrs. NASA, Washington, 1992-93; mem., past chmn. adv. com. Coll. Engring., Miss. State U. Ch. deacon. Recipient Nat. Disting. Exec. Svc. award for pub. svc., Alumni Fellow award Miss. State U., Picayune (Miss.) Citizen of Yr. award. Mem. Am. Inst. Aeronautics and Astronautics, Miss. Acad. Scis., Nat. Space Club (bd. dirs.), Tau Beta Pi. Office: John C Stennis Space Ctr Stennis Space Center MS 39529-6000*

ESTEVENS, ELLEN MUNSIL, healthcare professional; b. N.Y.C., Aug. 7, 1946; d. Bruce and Virginia Elizabeth (Claisse) Munsil; m. William P. Estevens, Jr., Nov. 24, 1971. BA, U. Houston, 1969; MSW, Tulane U., 1974. Caseworker child welfare svcs. La. Dept. Pub. Welfare, New Orleans, 1971-76; supervisor child welfare svcs. La. Dept. Health & Human Resources, Gretna, 1976-78; dir. social svcs. So. La. Med. Ctr., Houma, 1978-81; from regional coord. to program mgr. ops. La. Dept. Health & Hosps., Baton Rouge, 1981-90, mgr. Medicaid Policy program, 1990-97; program opers., program mgr., 1997-98, program mgr. Medicaid Waiver Divsn., 1998—; appts. La. Statewide Ind. Living Coun., Baton Rouge, 1996—; mem. La. Planning Coun. for Devel. Disabilities, 1998—. Mem. NASW, La. Assn. Social Workers, Nat. Rehab. Assn., La. Rehab. Assn., Mensa. Roman Catholic. Avocations: needlework, cultural events. Office: La Bur Health Svcs Financing PO Box 91030 Baton Rouge LA 70821-9030

ESTEVES, VERNON XAVIER, financial consultant, investment advisor; b. San Juan, P.R., May 26, 1950; came to U.S., 1979; s. Vernon Rafael and Isabel Dolores (Loyd) E.; m. Sylvia Mercedes Moscoso, June 11, 1977 (div. Apr. 1984); children: Sean, Alexandra; m. Victoria Anne Chemerys, Aug. 30, 1986 (div. Feb. 1996); 1 child, Max. BA, U. Pa., 1972. Account exec. Citibank N.A., San Juan and Mexico City, 1974-79; v.p. CitiBank N.A., N.Y.C., 1979-83; v.p., fin. cons. Salomon Smith Barney Inc., Miami, Fla., 1983—. Co. dir. United Way, N.Y.C., 1980. Mem. U. Pa. Alumni Club (secondary sch. com. 1990—), Andover Alumni Coun. Republican. Roman Catholic. Avocations: tennis, auto cross, sprint triathlons. Home: 701 Brickell Key Blvd Apt 2609 Miami FL 33131-2683

ESTEVEZ, CARLOS IRWIN See SHEEN, CHARLIE

ESTEVEZ, RAMON See SHEEN, MARTIN

ESTEY, AUDREE PHIPPS, artistic director; b. Winnipeg, Man., Can., Jan. 7, 1910; d. Robert and Anna (Harrington) Phipps; student Immaculate Heart Coll., 1927-29, Ernest Belcher Ballet Sch., 1928-31, Robert Major Drama Sch., 1929-31, Koslov Ballet Sch., 1930-31; m. L. Wendell Estey, Sept. 18, 1933; children: Lawrence Mitchell, Carol.Dancer Ernest Belcher Ballet Co., L.A., 1930, Fanchon and Marco Co., L.A., 1930-31; actress-dancer Fox Studio, Hollywood, Calif., 1931-32; ballet tchr. Lawrenceville and Princeton, N.J., 1938-80, Perry Mansfield Camp, Steamboat Springs Colo., summers 1949-50; head dance dept. Les Chalets Francais, Deer Isle, Maine, 1951-73; founder non-profit Princeton (N.J.) Ballet Soc., 1954, dir., cons.; founder Princeton Regional Ballet Co., 1963; founder profl. co., Princeton Ballet, 1979, Am. Repertory Ballet Co. Host Northeast Regional Ballet Festival-Princeton, 1968; coordinator Northeast Regional Ballet Festival-Jacob's Pillow, 1970. Apptd. by gov. N.J. State Commn. to Study Arts, 1968, trustee N.J. Sch. of the Arts, 1980; bd. dirs. Sarasota Ballet of Fla., 1989-91, co-chair resource com., 1992-93, mem. artistic com., 1993—. Recipient Rutgers U. award for contbn. to arts in N.J., 1982. Mem. N.E. Regional Ballet Assn. (pres., 1967-68, exec. v.p., 1968-71), Sarasota-Manatee Dance Tchrs. Assn. (pres. 1990-93). Episcopalian. Choreographer over 20 ballets for children and young dancers including: Festival of the Gnomes, Pastels, Peter and the Wolf, Sleeping Beauty, Cinderella, Pied Piper, The Nutcracker (choreography for Act I currently used by Princeton Ballet), Chanson Innocente, Graduation Ball, Coppelia. Office: 301 N Harrison St Princeton NJ 08540-3512

ESTIN, HANS HOWARD, investment executive; b. Prague, Czechoslovakia, Sept. 8, 1928; came to U.S., 1941, naturalized, 1946; m. Martha McCormick, Oct. 1990; children from previous marriage: Hilary Parker, Alexandra Howard; stepchildren: Sargent L. Goodchild, Jr., Abigail Goodchild, McKay Goodchild. A.B., Harvard U., 1949; LL.D., Merrimac Coll., 1972, Boston U., 1977. Vice chmn., pres., chmn. bd. Harbor Nat. Bank, Boston, 1964-67; vice chmn. N.Am. Mgmt. Corp., Boston, 1974—; trustee Putnam Group Mut. Funds. Trustee New Eng. Aquarium; chmn. bd. trustees Boston U., 1969-76; mem. corp. Mass. Gen. Hosp., Schepens Eye Rsch. Inst.; bd. overseers Boys and Girls Clubs Boston, Inc. 1st lt. USAF, 1951-55. Decorated Knight, Order of Crown, Belgium, 1983, Order of Leopold, Belgium, 1990; named Hon. Consul of Belgium at Boston, 1970-90. Mem. Somerset Club (Boston), Essex County Club (Manchester, Mass.). Home: 600 Summer St Manchester MA 01944-1626 Office: NAm Mgmt Corp Ten Post Office Sq Boston MA 02109

ESTIN-KLEIN, LIBBYADA, advertising executive, medical writer; b. Newark, July 13, 1937; d. Barney and Florence B. (Tenkin) Straver; m. Harvey M. Klein, Sept. 9, 1984. Student Syracuse U., 1955-57; BS, Columbia, 1960; RN, Columbia-Presbyn. Med. Ctr., 1960; cert., N.Y. Sch. Interior Design, 1962. Med. rsch. tech. writer, N.Y.C., 1960-62; pres. Libbyada Estin Interiors, N.Y.C., 1962-65; v.p. advt. and pub. relations Behrman/Estin Inc., N.Y.C., 1965-67; account exec., dir. pub. rels. J.S. Fullerton, Inc., N.Y.C., 1967-68; med. writer L.W. Frohlich & Co., Intercon Internat. Inc., N.Y.C., 1968-69, Kallir Philips Ross Inc., N.Y.C., 1969-71; copy supr. William Douglas McAdams Inc., N.Y.C., 1971-75, Sudler & Hennessey Inc., N.Y.C., 1975-80; v.p., exec. adminstr., creative dir. Grey Med. Advt. Inc., N.Y.C., 1980-84; founder, ptnr. Estin Sandler Comm. Inc., N.Y.C., 1984; v.p. Barnum Comm. Inc., N.Y.C., 1984-86; sr. v.p. ICE Comm., Inc., Rochester, N.Y., 1986-87; pres. Estin-Klein Comm. Inc., Rochester and Pittsford, N.Y., 1987—; dir. health group Roberts Comm., Inc., East Rochester, N.Y., 1993-95; bd. dirs. Pathways to Health Inc., Perinatal Network of Monroe County, Pathways to Health. Mem. Pub. Rels. Soc. Am., Advt. Women N.Y., Am. Advt. Fedn., Advt. Coun. of Rochester, Rochester Sales and Mktg. Execs. Club, Mktg. Communicators of Rochester, Am. Med. Writers Assn., Women in Comm., Healthcare Mktg. and Comms. Coun., Healthcare Bus. Women's Assn., Am. Nurses Assn., Allied Bd. Trade, Columbia-Presbyn. Hosp. Alumnae Assn., Columbia U. Alumnae Assn., Syracuse U. Alumnae Assn., Sigma Theta Tau, Delta Phi Epsilon. Home and Office: 289 Garnsey Rd Pittsford NY 14534-4540

ESTLE, THOMAS LEO, physicist, educator; b. Columbus Junction, Iowa, Jan. 8, 1931; s. Vincent Lambert and Ruby Jean (O'Neill) E.; m. Arlene Ruth Poggemiller, Oct. 10, 1953; children: Mark David, Ann Elizabeth, Laura Kay, Karen Ruth. BA, Rice Inst. (now U.), 1953; MS, U. Ill., 1954, PhD, 1957. Mem. tech. staff Tex. Instruments, Inc., Dallas, 1958-62, br. mgr., 1962-66, sr. rsch. physicist, 1966-67; physics dept. chair Rice U., Houston, 1982-86, prof. physics, 1967-96, prof. emeritus, 1996—; chair solid state physics and material sci. com. Los Alamos Meson Physics Facility, 1978-80; mem. subcom. on Muon Sources, Nat. Rsch. Coun., 1982-84. Author: The Physical Principles of Electron Paramagnetic Resonance, 1973, Quantum States of Atoms, Molecules and Solids, 1976, Understanding More Quantum Physics, 1991, (with others) Hydrogen in Semiconductors, 1991, Optical Properties of Ions in Solids, 1975; contbr. articles to profl. jours. Rsch. grantee NSF, 1969-99, Robert A. Welch Found., 1981-95, Rsch. Corp., 1980. Fellow Am. Phys. Soc. Achievements include rsch. on solid state physics. Home: 5334 Queensloch Dr Houston TX 77096-4134 Office: Rice U PO Box 1892 Physics Dept MS-61 Houston TX 77251-1892

ESTREN, MARK JAMES, business and media consultant, TV producer, author; b. N.Y.C., July 12, 1948; s. Solomon and Elaine Estren; m. S. Amber Gordon, July 4, 1986; children: Meredith, Nicholas. BA in Classics and English cum laude, Wesleyan U., 1968; MS in Journalism, Columbia U., 1970; MA in English and Psychology, U. Buffalo, 1973, PhD in English and Psychology, 1978. Producer, reporter, anchor Stas. WBEN & WBEN-TV, Buffalo, 1971-75; exec. producer Stas. WCBS-Radio and TV, N.Y.C., 1975-76, Sta. WCAU-TV, Phila., 1976-79; sr. producer ABC News, N.Y.C. and Washington, 1979-80; editor Phila. Inquirer, 1980-81, Miami (Fla.) Herald, 1980-81; exec. producer The Nightly Bus. Report, Miami, Fla., 1981-84; sr. v.p., gen. mgr. Fin. News Network, N.Y.C. and L.A., 1984-87; editor-in-chief High Tech. Bus. mag., Boston and N.Y.C., 1987-89; exec. v.p. Infotechnology, Inc., N.Y.C. and Washington, 1987-90, UPI, Washington, 1988-90; founder, pres. UPI TV, Fairfax, Va., 1989-90; pres., chief exec. officer TransCentury Comm., Inc., Easton, Conn. and McLean, Va., 1984—; adj. prof. Columbia U., 1987-89. Author: A History of Underground Comics, 1974, rev. edit., 1987, 89, 93; co-author: In a Word, 1992; contbg. editor Miami Herald, Bottom Line/Personal, Bottom Line/Tomorrow, Boardroom Reports, Bottom Line/Business, Washington Office Mag., Moneysworth, Parent Weekly, Va. Parent News. Trustee Boston Cath. TV Ctr., 1987-89; vice chmn. Arthritis Found., Washington, 1992-94, chmn. commn. com., 1990-92. Pulitzer Found. fellow, 1970. Avocations: classical music, herpetology. Office: 1163 Old Gate Ct Mc Lean VA 22102-2532

ESTRIN, DEBORAH PERRY, human resources executive; b. Waynesboro, Va., Dec. 28, 1948; d. James William and Annie Lee (Miller) Perry; m. Abbott Simon Estrin, Feb. 6, 1982. BS in Humanities, U. Tenn., 1982; MBA, Fairleigh Dickerson U., 1988. Dir. human resources Ciba Geigy Pharms., Summit, N.J., 1983-89; v.p. human resources Geneva Pharms. divsn. Ciba Geigy Pharms., Broomfield, Colo., 1989-91, USPCI subs. Union Pacific, Houston, 1994-96, N.Y. Power Authority, White Plains, 1994-96; sr. v.p. human resources Phila. Gas Works, 1996—; adj. prof. Audrey Cohen Coll., 1994-96; dir. ENS Charon Found. for Global Mgmt. Studies; dir. Found. Global Mgmt. Studies, Paris. Adv. bd. mem. Salvation Army. Office: Phila Gas Works 800 W Montgomery Ave Philadelphia PA 19122-2898

ESTRIN, GERALD, computer scientist, engineering educator, academic administrator; b. N.Y.C., Sept. 9, 1921; married; 3 children. B.S., U. Wis., 1948, M.S., 1949, Ph.D. in Elec. Engring., 1951. Rsch. engr. Inst. Advanced Study, Princeton, N.J., 1950-53, 55-56; dir. electronic computing project Weizmann Inst. Sci., Israel, 1953-55; assoc. prof. engring. UCLA, 1956-58, prof., 1958-91, prof. emeritus, 1991—, chmn. dept. computer sci., 1979-82, 85-88; mem. adv. bd. applied math. div. Argonne Nat. Lab., 1966-68, mem. assoc. univs. rev. com. for chmn., 1976-77, mem. adv. bd. applied math. div., 1974-80, adv. com. NASA space Applications, 1983-86; dir. Computer Communications, Inc., 1966-67, Systems Engring. Labs., 1977-80; mem. internat. program com. Internat. Fedn. Info. Processing Congress, 1968; internat. program chmn. Jerusalem Conf. Info. Tech., 1971; mem. math. and computer sci. research adv. com. AEC; mem. sci. com., operating bd. Gould, Inc., Rolling Meadows, Ill., 1981-86; bd. govs. Weizmann Inst. Sci., 1971-96, gov. emeritus, 1996—. Lipsky fellow, 1954, Guggenheim fellow, 1963, 67; recipient Disting. Svc. award U. Wis., 1975, Jerusalem Conf. on Info. Tech. Spl. Recognition award, 1978, NASA Commendation, 1986, Computer Pioneer award IEEE Computer Soc., 1995. Fellow AAAS, IEEE (disting. spkr. 1980), Assn. Computing Machinery (nat. lectr. 1966-67). Office: UCLA BH4731 Dept Computer Sci Los Angeles CA 90095

ESTRIN, HERBERT ALVIN, financial consultant, entertainment company executive; b. Jamaica, N.Y., May 4, 1925; s. Joseph and Minnie (Haskell) E.; m. Phyllis Glassman, Jan. 28, 1951; children—Myrna Hope, Richard Lawrence. B.S. in Acctg, N.Y. U., 1949. With Columbia Pictures Industries, Inc., N.Y.C., 1953-73, v.p., 1971-73; v.p., treas., chief fin. officer Prudential Bldg. Maintenance Corp., N.Y.C., 1973-79; v.p., treas. Bolt Corp., South Laguna, Calif., 1979; sr. v.p. fin. and adminstrn. Warner Home Video Inc. subs. Warner Communications, 1981-83; dir. ops. adminstrn. United Satellite Communications Inc., 1983-85; v.p. fin. and adminstrn. Rainbow Home Video div. Rainbow Program Enterprises Co., 1986-88; fin. cons., 1986—. Served with U.S. Army, 1943-46.

ESTRIN, MELVYN J., computer products company executive. Co-chmn., co-CEO Nat. Intergroup, Inc., Carrollton, Tex.; co-chmn, co-CEO McKesson Health Corp., Carrollton, Tex., 1996; also bd. dirs.; chmn. U. Rsch. Corp., Bethesda, Md.; mng. ptnr. Centaur Ptnrs., L.P.; chmn., pres., CEO Am. Health Svcs.; v.p., dir. Spectro Industries; founder First Women's Bank of Md.; pres. FWB Bancorporation, Rockville, Md.; chmn. FWB Bancorporation.; chmn. Estrin Internat., Inc.; with Estrin Realty and Devel. Corp.; bd. dirs. Washington Gas Light Co. Trustee U. Pa.; active Endowment Bd. of the Kennedy Ctr., The Econ. Club of Washington, The Washington Opera; nat. vice chmn. State of Israel Bonds; apptd. by Pres. Bush commr.Nat. Capital Planning Commn.; apptd. Nat. Coun. for the Performing Arts, John F. Kennedy Ctr. Recipient Eleanor Roosevelt Humanities award for Community Svc., 1986. Office: Univ Rsch Corp 7200 Wisconsin Ave Ste 600 Bethesda MD 20814-4811 also: Foxmeyer Health Corp 1220 Senlac Dr Carrollton TX 75006-7019

ESTRIN, MORTON, pianist, music educator; b. Burlington, Vt., Dec. 29, 1923; s. Nathan and Gertrude Ada (Lapidow) E.; m. Eleanor Sylvia Glassman, June 17, 1944 (div. Nov. 1986); 3 children; Steven Paul (dec.), Coren Gail, Robert Allan; m. Roberta Barbara Green Zaltzman, Dec. 28, 1986. Student, NYU, 1942-44; pvt. study, Vera Maurina Press, 1941-49. Prof. music Hofstra U., Hempstead, N.Y., 1958—; pvt. tchr., Hicksville, N.Y., 1941—. Debut Town Hall, N.Y.C., 1949; tours of U.S. and Europe; appeared in Carnegie Hall, Lincoln Ctr., Merkin Hall, N.Y.C.; performed all 24 Preludes by Rachmaninoff Nat. Gallery Art, Washington, Alice Tully Hall, N.Y.C., 1985; CDs include Etudes, Opus 8, Scriabin, 1989, Suite in D minor Opus 91, Raff, 1989, Sonata in G, Tchaikowsky, 1991, Six Etudes, Rubinstein, 1991. Mem. Am. Fedn. Musicians, AAUP, Bohemian Club N.Y., Pi Kappa Lambda. Home: 9 Clotilde Ct Hicksville NY 11801-5515

ESTRIN, RICHARD WILLIAM, retired newspaper editor, real estate broker; b. N.Y.C., Apr. 16, 1932; s. Max and Ruth (Lillienthal) E.; m. Alison Kiendl Stewart, Mar. 13, 1971. B.A., CCNY, 1953. Reporter Park Row News Service, N.Y.C., 1953-55; with Newsday, Inc., Long Island, N.Y., 1955-85, sucessively Sunday news editor, Part II editor, sr. editor news, until 1983, exec. news editor N.Y.C. Newsday, 1983-85; weekend editor Herald-Tribune, Sarasota, Fla., 1985-86, news editor, 1986-90, asst. mng. editor, 1990-97; v.p. Longview Realty, Longboat Key, Fla., 1999—. Recipient First Place Lifestyle Journalism awards J.C. Penney-U. M., 1974, 75. Mem. Phi Beta Kappa. Home: 6555 Bayou Hammock Rd Longboat Key FL 34228-1201

ESTY, DAVID CAMERON, marketing and communications executive; b. Mt. Kisco, N.Y., May 26, 1932; s. John Cushing and Virginia (Place) E.; m. Elizabeth Gunn; children: John Philip, Mary Virginia, David Cameron, Cynthia Elizabeth. B.A., Amherst Coll., 1954. Sr. v.p. J. Walter Thompson, N.Y.C., 1960-68; pres. CEO T.D.I., N.Y.C., 1968-75; CEO Douglas Leigh, Inc., N.Y.C., 1975-76; founder Catalyst Corp., 1976-78; CEO BIS Communications Corp., N.Y.C., 1979-82; owner, CEO Esty Assocs., Inc., Darien, Conn.; chief operating officer The Alden Group, N.Y.C., 1990-92; owner, CEO MarkeTeam, Inc., 1992—; prin. Adventure Assets, Inc., Cambridge, Mass., 1997—; bd. dirs. World Sports Humanitarian Hall of Fame, Boise. Author: Somebody Close to You is on Drugs, 1971. Mem. Nat. Ski Patrol (dist. svc. award 1995); EMT; chmn. class officers com. Amherst Coll., pres. Class of '54 (dist. soc. awd., 1999); mem. alpine ski com. Spl. Olympics Internat.; mem. disaster action team ARC, 1997. Capt. USAF Res., 1950-67. Mem. Ad Coun. (dir., mem. exec. com.), Young Pres. Orgn. (49er). Home: 18 Monkey Wrench Ln Bristol RI 02809-2911

ESTY, JOHN CUSHING, JR., writer, teacher, advisor to non-profit boards; b. White Plains, N.Y., Aug. 9, 1928; s. John Cushing and Virginia (Place) E.; m. Katharine Woolsey Cole, Dec. 21, 1955; children: Daniel Cushing, Paul Cameron, Benjamin Cole, Joshua Dwight. BA, Amherst Coll., 1950, LHD (hon.), 1970; MA, Yale U., 1951; postgrad., U. Calif., Berkeley, 1959-60. Asst. dean, asst. dir. admissions Amherst Coll., 1953-58, asso. dean, 1958-63, lectr. math., 1958-63; headmaster Taft Sch., Watertown, Conn., 1963-72; research asso. in edn. Harvard U., 1972-73; scholar-in-residence U. Mass. Sch. Edn., 1972-73; sr. staff asso. Edn. Devel. Center, Newton, Mass., 1973-74; staff asso. Rockefeller Bros. Fund, N.Y.C., 1973-78; pres. Nat. Assn. Ind. Schs., 1978-91; adj. lectr. U. Mass., 1978—; pres. bd. Coun. for Am. Pvt. Edn., 1987-89. Author: Choosing Private School, 1974. Trustee, treas. Charles Hayden Found., N.Y.C., 1991—; trustee, bd. chmn. Greeley Found., Mass., 1991—; dir., founder Recruiting New Tchrs., Inc., 1988—; assoc. for bd. devel. Nat. Ctr. Nonprofit Bds., 1993—. 1st lt. USAF, 1951-53. Mem. Phi Beta Kappa, Sigma Xi. Clubs: Univ. (N.Y.C.), Century Assn. (N.Y.C.).

ESWEIN, BRUCE JAMES, II, human resources executive; b. San Mateo, Calif., Oct. 26, 1951; s. Bruce James and Janet Gordon (Copeland) E.; m. Sarah Anne Shames, Feb. 7, 1981 (div.); children: Thomas Jonathan, Elizabeth Anne. Student, U. Wash., 1969-71; A.B., U. Calif.-Berkeley, 1973, M.B.A., 1977. Brand asst. Clorox Co., Oakland, Calif., 1977-79, coll. rels. mgr., 1979-83; mgr. exec. recruitment and devel. BBDO Worldwide, N.Y.C., 1983-84, v.p., 1984-87, v.p. personnel adminstrn., 1987-88, v.p. human resources, mgr. worldwide tng. and devel., 1988-89, v.p. human resources internat., 1989-90, v.p., dir. human resources internat., 1990-95, sr. v.p., dir. human resources internat., 1995—. Mem. Soc. for Human Resources Mgmt., U. Calif. at Berkeley Bus. Sch. Alumni Assn. (bd. dirs. 1980-83), Phi Beta Kappa, Chi Psi (v.p. 1972-73, bd. dirs. 1979-82, trustee ednl. trust 1983-84, trustee emeritus 1984—). Episcopalian. Home: 27 Scenic Dr Apt H Croton On Hudson NY 10520-1822 Office: BBDO Worldwide 1285 Ave of Americas New York NY 10019-6028

ETCHELLS, JOYCE LYNN, peri-operative nurse; b. Berkeley, Calif., Aug. 29, 1959; d. William John and Patricia Louis (Waller) Stirton; 1 child, Justin. BS in Nursing, San Diego State U., 1982; MSN, Calif. State U., Dominguez Hills, 1999. Cert. operating rm. nurse. Staff nurse Vets. Affairs Med. Ctr., San Diego, 1981-84; staff nurse operating rm. French Hosp., San Francisco, 1985-86, Vets. Affairs Med. Ctr., Martinez, Calif., 1986-91; head nurse operating rm. VA Med. Ctr., Fresno, Calif., 1991—; laser safety officer Vets. Affairs Med. Ctr., Martinez. Mem. Assn. Operating Rm. Nurses, San Joaquin Health Ministries Assn., Calif. Coalition of Nurse Practitioners, Sigma Theta Tau.

ETCHESON, WARREN WADE, business administration educator; b. Bainbridge, Ind., May 15, 1920; s. Raymond W. and Rosetta (Evans) E.; m. Marianne Newgent, May 30, 1947; children: Denise Elene, Crayton

Wade. BS, Ind. U., 1943; MA, U. Iowa, 1951, PhD, 1956. Adminstrv. sec., exec. sec., nat. sec. Delta Chi Nat. Fraternity, 1946-56; lectr. Santo Tomas U., Manila, 1946, U. Iowa, 1951-54; asst. prof. U. Wash., 1954-56, assoc. prof., 1956-60, prof. Sch. Bus. Adminstrn., 1960-90; assoc. dean Bus. Adminstrn., 1974-87; Fulbright prof. Istanbul, Turkey, 1963-64. Author: Pazarlama, 1964, Consumerism, 1972. Served to lt. U.S. Army, 1942-46. Mem. Alpha Kappa Psi, Phi Eta Sigma, Beta Gamma Sigma, Delta Chi. Home: 6625 NE 132nd St Kirkland WA 98034-1614 Office: Univ Wash Seattle WA 98195

ETCHEVERRY, LOUIS P., federal judge; b. 1940. BS, St. Mary's Coll., 1970; JD, U. Idaho, 1973. Apptd. part-time magistrate judge ea. dist. U.S. Dist. Ct. Calif., 1984. With USMC, 1960-70. Fax: (805) 322-3930. Office: # 350 1706 Chester Ave Ste 500 Bakersfield CA 93301-5239

ETCHEVERRY, MARCO, professional soccer player; b. Santa Cruz, Bolivia, Sept. 26, 1970. Grad., Tahuichi Acad., Santa Cruz. Team capt., midfielder D.C. United, 1996—; played in Maj. League Soccer Cup, 1996. Founder Acad. de Futbol Maco Etcheverry, Washington met. area. Named Maj. League Soccer's Most Valuable Player, 1998,. Holder single-season record for assists. Office: c/o DC United 13832 Redskin Dr Herndon VA 20171*

ETEFIA, FLORENCE VICTORIA, academic and behavior specialist; b. Alton, Ill., Feb. 13, 1946; d. Esau and Pearl (Taylor) Anthony. BA, Mich. State U., 1968; MAT, Oakland U., Rochester, Mich., 1972; EdS, Wayne State U., 1977, MA, 1987, postgrad. Cert. tchr. mentally impaired, Mich.; spl. edn. supr., Mich.; cert. tchr. mentally impaired, learning disabled, K-8 gen. edn., psychology, Mich. Special edn. tchr. Sch. Dist. of Pontiac, Mich. Mem. NEA, Mich. Edn. Assn., Pontiac Edn. Assn., Delta Sigma Theta. Home: 3035 Debra Ct Auburn Hills MI 48326-2044

ETESSAMI, RAMBOD, endodontist; b. Tehran, Iran, Mar. 20, 1960; came to U.S., 1977; s. Abdollah and Mahin E.; m. Pegah Etessami, Dec., 1991. BA in Math., Ind. U., 1980; DDS, Georgetown U., 1984; cert. in advanced endodontics, U. So. Calif., 1986. Head research & devel., chief sci. researcher, bd. dirs. Laseronics, Inc., Torrance, Calif., 1983—; assoc. clin. prof. endodontics U. So. Calif., L.A., 1986—; assoc. clin. prof. Sch. Dentistry UCLA, 1989—; pvt. practice L.A. and Beverly Hills, Calif., 1986—; lectr. Sch. Dentistry UCLA, 1995—. Chmn. Ind. U. chpt. United Jewish Appeal, 1978-79, chmn. Georgetown U. chpt., 1982-83; chmn. Young Dental divsn. Jewish Fedn. Coun.; bd. dirs. dental cabinet L.A. chpt.' 1987—; mem. Magbit Found.; bd. dirs. Iranian Jews Am., Washington, 1980-83, Am.-Israel Pub. Affairs Com., Washington, 1982-84; bd. dirs., chmn. Iranian immigration sect. Jewish Vocat. Svc., L.A., 1987-92. NIH grantee, 1978-79; B. Baj Bhussry fellow George U., 1981; Alpha Omega scholar, 1984. Mem. ADA (cert. Recognition and Appreciation 1984, 86), Am. Assn. Endodontists, Am. Dental Profls. Israel, Calif. Dental Assn., L.A. Dental Soc., B'nai Brith (bd. dirs. Fred Matloob chpt. 1990-94), Study Club for Oral Facial Rsch. Jewish. Avocations: tennis, swimming, traveling, painting, horseback riding. Office: Beverly Sunset Med Bldg 9201 W Sunset Blvd Ste 908 West Hollywood CA 90069-3710*

ETGEN, ANN, ballet educator, artistic director, choreographer; b. Dallas; d. Eddy R. and Myrtle (Applegate) Etgen; m. Bill Atkinson, Aug. 16, 1961. Dancer, Met. Opera Ballet N.Y.C., 1958-60, Broadway musicals Brigadoon, Carousel; guest dancer Omnibus History of Dance for Agnes De Mille, 1957; artistic dir. Etgen-Atkinson Sch. of Ballet, Dallas, 1962—, Dallas Met. Ballet, 1964—; host S.W. Regional Ballet Festival, 1973. Dance panel Tex. Fine Arts Com., 1978-79; active Arts Magnet Sch., 1980, 81, 82, 83. NEA choreography grantee, 1976, grantee Tex. Fine Arts Commn., 1973, 76-77, Mobile Oil, 1979, 500 Inc., 1978-79; recipient choreography plan award Nat. Assn. Regional Ballet, 1983. Mem. Nat. Assn. Regional Ballet, S.W. Regional Ballet Assn. (membership chmn. 1986-87). Presbyterian. Creator ballets for Dallas Met. Ballet. Office: Dallas Met Ballet 6815 Hillcrest Ave Dallas TX 75205-1308*

ETGES, FRANK JOSEPH, parasitology educator; b. Chgo., June 18, 1924; s. Joseph Peter and Anna Marie (Foss) E.; m. Ruth Camille Storkan, Sept. 20, 1948 (div. June 1984); children: Robert J., William J., Anne C., David J., Thomas J.; m. Lesta Judith Cooper-Freytag, July 6, 1985. AB, U. Ill., 1948, MS, 1949; PhD, NYU, 1953. Asst. prof. U. Ark., Fayetteville, 1953-54; asst. prof. U. Cin., 1954-59, assoc. prof., 1959-66, prof. parasitology, 1966-95; prof. emeritus, 1995—; rsch. assoc. U.S. Army Tropical Rsch. Med. Lab., San Juan, P.R., 1961-62; guest investigator London Sch. Tropical Medicine and Hygiene, 1971-72. Sgt. U.S. Army, 1943-46, ETO, PTO. NSF rsch. grantee, 1959-65; La. State U. Med. Sch. rsch. fellow, Santo Domingo, P.R., 1961-62, 64, 65, 67, 69; postdoctoral fellow NIH, London, 1971-72, WHO, Egypt, Sudan, Rhodesia, 1975. Mem. Am. Soc. Parasitologists (editorial com.), Am. Soc. Tropical Medicine and Hygiene, Am. Microscopical Soc. (v.p. 1970), Royal Soc. Tropical Medicine and Hygiene, Australian Soc. Parasitology, Soc. Protozoologists, Midwestern Parastiologists (pres. 1969), Helminthol. Soc. Washington, Sigma Xi. Avocations: travel, golf. E-mail: cooperlj@ucfwcu.rwc.uc.edu. Home: 8284 Sunfish Ln Maineville OH 45039-8978 Office: U Cin Dept Biol Scis Cincinnati OH 45221

ETHAN, CAROL BAEHR, psychotherapist; b. N.Y.C., May 30, 1920; d. Irving an dSadie (Goldman) Baehr; m. Sy Ethan, Mar. 18, 1955; children: Willa Capraro, Barbara Ethan. Student, Greenwich Inst. Psychanalytic, 1965-70; BA in Psychology with honors, NYU, 1978; MA in Psychology, New Sch. Social Rsch., 1981. Tchr. Queens Coll., 1956-57; consumer psychology rschr., cons., 1950-70; staff psychologist Fifth Ave. Ctr. Counseling & Psychotherapy, 1965-70; psychotherapyst pvt. practice, N.Y.C., 1967—. Writer Irvington (N.J.) Harold, 1946, Walt Farmer Prodns., 1949-50; columnist Rhinebeck Gazette-Advertiser, 1981-86. Dem. committeewoman for Queens County, 1960; vol. social rehab. program Queens County Mental Health Soc., 1965-66. Recipient Founders Day award NYU, 1978; fellow Internat. Coun. Sex Edn. & Parenthood Am. U. Fellow Am. Orthopsychiat. Assn.; mem. APA, N.Y. State Assn. Practising Psychotherapists (cert.), Am. Mental Health Counselors Assn., Family & Divorce Mediation Coun. N.Y., Internat. Acad. Behavioral Med., Counseling and Psychotherapy (clin. mem.), N.Am. Asns. Masters in Psychotherapy (cert.), Am. Psychotherapy Assn. (cert. diplomate). Address: 235 W 76th St New York NY 10023-8210

ETHEREDGE, FOREST DEROYCE, former state senator, university administrator; b. Dallas, Oct. 21, 1929; s. Gilbert Wybert and Theta Erlene (Tate) E.; m. Joan Mary Horan, Apr. 30, 1955; children: Forest William, John Bede, Mary Faith, Brian Thomas, Regina Ann. BS, Va. Poly. Inst. and State U., 1951; MS, U. Ill., 1953; postgrad., Northwestern U., 1953-55; PhD, Loyola U., Chgo., 1968. Mem. faculty City Colls. Chgo., 1955-65, chmn. phys. sci. dept., 1963-65; dean instrn. Rock Valley Coll., 1965-67, v.p., 1966-67; pres. McHenry County Coll., 1967-70, Waubonsee Community Coll., 1970-81; Ill. state senator, 1981-93, higher edn. com., 1981-91, mem. intergovtl. coop. commn., 1982-91, co-chmn. legis. info. system, 1983-93, minority spokesman appropriations I com., 1986-93; prof. pub. adminstrn. Aurora (Ill.) U., 1991—; dean Sch. of Bus. and Profl. Studies, 1994—. Author: School Boards and the Ballot Box, 1989. Bd. dirs. Ill. Math. and Sci. Acad., Dreyer Med. Found., Aurora. Republican. Roman Catholic. Lodge: Rotary (pres. Aurora chpt. 1978-79). Home: 843 Hardin Ave Aurora IL 60506-4936 Office: Aurora U Dunham Hall Rm 231 Aurora IL 60506-4892

ETHERIDGE, BOB, congressman; b. Lilington, N.C., Aug. 7, 1941. Supt. Pub. Inst. Dept., Raleigh, N.C., 1996; mem. from N.C. 2nd dist. House of Reps., Washington, 1996—; chmn. gen. farm commodities com. Office: US House of Reps 1641 Longworth House of C Bldg Washington DC 20515-3302*

ETHERIDGE, JACK PAUL, arbitrator, mediator, former judge; b. Atlanta, Mar. 16, 1927; s. Anton Lee and Jessie Shephard (Brown) E.; m. Ursula Schlatter, Feb. 2, 1952; children: Jack Paul, Margaret Ann, Mary Elizabeth. Grad., Darlington Sch., Rome, Ga., 1945; B.S., Davidson Coll., 1949; J.D., Emory U., 1955. Bar: Ga. 1955. Since practiced in Atlanta; mem. firm Hale, Etheridge & Harland, 1959-66; mem. Ga. Gen. Assembly from Fulton County, 1963-66; judge Fulton Superior Ct., 1966-76, sr. judge, 1977-91, litigation mgr., 1991; faculty Nat. Jud. Coll., Coll. Criminal Justice, Law Sch., U. S.C., 1977-80; assoc. dean Emory U. Law Sch., Atlanta, 1981-88; chief jud. officer Jud. Arbitration and Mediation Svcs., Inc., Atlanta, 1992-98; mem. Ga. Crime Commn., 1971-73; bd. dirs. Atlanta Legal Aid Soc., 1960-70. Trustee Davidson Coll., 1966-75; trustee Arts Festival of Atlanta, 1971-74, Atlanta U., 1977-87; chmn. bd. dirs. Atlanta Neighborhood Justice, Inc., Wolfcreek Wilderness Schs., Inc.; Fellow Harvard Law Sch., 1980. Served with USNR, 1945-46; Served with with AUS, 1949-52. Named Young Man of Year in Professions Atlanta Jr. C. of C., 1962. Fellow ABA, Am. Bar Found., Ga. Bar Assn., Internat. Acad. Trial Judges, Ctr. for Pub. Resources; mem. Atlanta Bar Assn. (pres. 1962-63), Nat. Conf. State Trial Judges (chmn. 1978-79), Atlanta Hist. Soc. (trustee 1969-75), Nat. Acad. Pub. Adminstrn., Beta Theta Pi, Omicron Delta Kappa, Phi Alpha Theta. Presbyterian. Home: 4715 Harris Trl NW Atlanta GA 30327-4409

ETHERIDGE, MARGARET DWYER, medical center director; b. Atlanta, Jan. 5, 1938; d. Philip Fitzgerald and Mary Catharine (Dwyer) E.; m. Roy Charles McCracken, May 5, 1975; m. William Bertram Smitheram, Aug. 17, 1985. BA, Emory U., 1960; M in Health Adminstrn., Washington U., St. Louis, 1973. Registered record adminstr., 1960-71. Spl. asst. to dir. VA Med. Ctr., Roseburg, Oreg., 1973-74; hosp. adminstrn. specialist VA Central Office, Washington, 1974-75; asst. dir. trainee VA Med. Ctr., Phila., 1976; assoc. dir. VA Med. Ctr., Hampton, Va., 1976-80, Buffalo, N.Y., 1980-81; Presdl. exchange exec. Kimberly Clark Corp., Neenah, Wis. and Roswell, Ga., 1981-82; dir. VA Med. Ctr., Grand Island, Nebr., 1982-94; interim dir. Grand Island-Hall County Health Dept., 1996-97; instr. Cerritos Coll., Calif., 1969-70. Bd. dirs. Project 2M Coordinating Coun., Inc., Grand Island, 1985-87; bd. dirs. Hall County Leadership Unlimited, Inc., 1990; bd. dirs., Grand Island Area United Way, 1987-90, pres. 1989; bd. dirs. Grand Island Concert Assn., 1987-92; bd. dirs. Ctrl. Nebr. Goodwill Industries, Inc, 1987-93, pres. 1991-92; mem. rev. bd. State of Nebr. Foster Care. Fellow Am. Coll. Healthcare Execs.; mem. Am. Hosp. Assn., Fed. Exec. Assn. (pres. Grand Island chpt. 1987), Nebr. Hosp. Assn., Grand Island C. of C. (bd. dirs. 1988-92, legis. affairs com. 1984-85, priorities com. 1984-85, govtl. affairs com. 1984-88, nominating com. 1991-92, 94-95, audit com. 1992-93, pres.' club 1993, 94), Rotary (v.p. internat. club 1485 1998-99, team leader group study exch. Korea internat. dist. 5630 1999), Riverside Golf Club. Roman Catholic. Home: 1429 Stagecoach Rd Grand Island NE 68801-7374

ETHERIDGE, MELISSA LOU, singer, songwriter; b. Leavenworth, Kans., 1962; d. John and Elizabeth Etheridge; life partner Julie Cypher; 1 child, Bailey Jean. Student, Berklee Coll. of Music, Boston, 1970. Wrote songs for the film, Weeds; albums include Melissa Etheridge, 1988, Brave and Crazy, 1989, Never Enough, 1992, Yes I Am, 1993, Your Little Secret, 1995. Named Entertainer of Year Can. Acad. Recording Arts and Scis., 1990; Grammy award, Best Female Rock Vocal for "Aint It Heavy," 1993, Female Rock Vocal Performance for "Come to My Window," 1994. Address: MEIN PO Box 884563 Dept H San Francisco CA 94188-4563*

ETHERINGTON, EDWIN DEACON, lawyer, business executive, educator; b. Bayonne, N.J., Dec. 25, 1924; s. Charles K. and Ethel (Bennett) E.; m. Katherine Colean, Sept. 11, 1953; children: Edwin Deacon Jr., Kenneth C. (dec.), Marion L. (dec.), Robert M. B.A. with honors and distinction, Wesleyan U., 1948; J.D., Yale U., 1952. Bar: D.C 1953, N.Y. 1955. Asst. dean, instr. English, Wesleyan U., 1948-49; asst. instr. Yale Law Sch., 1951-52; law clk. to judge Ct. Appeals, Washington, 1952-53; asso. Wilmer & Broun, Washington, 1953-54, Milbank, Tweed, Hope & Hadley, N.Y.C., 1954-56; sec. N.Y. Stock Exchange, 1956-58, v.p., 1958-61; ptnr. Pershing & Co., 1961-62; pres. Am. Stock Exchange, 1962-66; pres. Wesleyan U., Middletown, Conn., 1966-70, now pres. emeritus; pres. Nat. Center for Voluntary Action, Washington, 1971, chmn., 1972; chmn. bd. advisors U.S. Trust Co. of Fla.; chmn. Conn. Gov.'s Commn. on Svcs. and Expenditures, 1971-72, Nat. Advt. Rev. Bd., 1973-74. Named Conn. Citizen of Yr., 1973. Mem. Order of Coif, Yale Club, Black Hall Golf Club, Old Lyme (Conn.) Country Club, Old Lyme Beach Club, Island Club (v.p.), Jupiter Island (Fla.) Club, Hobe Sound (Fla.) Yacht Club (bd. dirs.), Hobe Sound (Fla.) Golf Club, Seminole Golf Club, North Palm Beach (Fla.) Club, Phi Beta Kappa Assocs., Phi Beta Kappa, Kappa Beta Pi, Phi Delta Phi. Congregationalist. Home: 102 Bassett Creek Trl Hobe Sound FL 33455-2201 also: 46 Bill Ln Old Lyne CT 06371

ETHINGTON, RAYMOND LINDSAY, geology educator, researcher; b. State Center, Iowa, Aug. 28, 1929; s. Lindsay E. and Hilda Ruby (Weuve) E.; m. Leslie Ann Nielsen, June 15, 1955; children: Elaine Marie, Mary Frances. BS, Iowa State U., 1951, MS, 1955; PhD, U. Iowa, 1958. Asst. prof. geology Ariz. State U., Tempe, 1958-62; asst. prof. U. Mo., Columbia, 1962-65, assoc. prof., 1965-68, prof., 1968—. With U.S. Army, 1951-53. NSF grantee, 1966, 87. Fellow Geol. Soc. Am.; mem. Soc. Econ. Paleontologists and Mineralogists (editor Jour. Paleontology 1969-74, spl. publs. editor 1980-83, chmn. publs. com. 1974-76, pres. 1989-90), Pander Soc. (chief panderer 1990-98), Am. Assn. Petroleum Geologists, Palaeontol. Assn. G.B., Paleontol. Soc. Mem. LDS Ch. Home: 1012 Pheasant Run Columbia MO 65201-6252 Office: U Mo Dept Geol Sci Columbia MO 65211

ETHRIDGE, BRENDA KAY, advertising employee; b. Hugo, Okla., July 27, 1967; d. Lee Washington Boyd and Jeanne (Bass) Rowe; m. Larry Charles Ethridge, Jan. 11, 1992. BS, E. Cen. U., 1990. Account exec. Cen. Telephone, Bartlesville, Okla., 1990; supr. Cen. Telephone, Cape Girardeau, Mo., 1990-91; account exec. Sch. Supplies Advantage, Oklahoma City, 1991-92; asst. mgr. Pepsico, Oklahoma City, 1992; telemktg. adminstr. Southwestern Bell, Oklahoma City, 1993-94, sales rep., 1994. Mem. Nat. Assn. Investment Clubs, Tycoons In Training Club (treas. 1997—). Avocations: reading, kick-boxing, Ju-Jitsu, theatre.

ETHRIDGE, MARK FOSTER, III, writer, publisher, media consultant; b. Winston-Salem, N.C., May 28, 1949; s. Mark F. Jr. and Margaret Burns (Furbee) E.; m. Kay Stover, Aug. 12, 1972; children: Emily Vigland, Mark Furbee. Grad., Phillips Exeter Acad., 1967; AB cum laude, Princeton U., 1971. Reporter AP, Boston, 1971-72; reporter The Charlotte (N.C.) Observer, 1972-88, dep. metro editor, 1978-79, mng. editor, 1979-88; pub. The Bus. Jour. of Charlotte, 1989-98; pres. Carolina Parenting, Inc., 1991—, Cotter Grp., 1998—; bd. mem. Bioethics Resource Group, Ltd. Mem. editorial adv. bd. PBS documentary series Frontline. Nieman fellow Harvard U., 1986. Mem. Princeton Alumni Assn. of Charlotte (pres. 1983-84). Presbyn. Home: 5516 Gorham Dr Charlotte NC 28226-6414 Office: Cotter Grp 6525 Hudspeth Rd Harrisburg NC 28075

ETLING, RUSSELL HULL, museum executive, production company executive; b. Coral Gables, Fla., May 25, 1955; s. Walter and Antionette (Hull) E. BFA magna cum laude, U. Miami, 1977; postgrad., Disney U., 1980. Asst. stage mgr. Deauville Star Theatre, Miami Beach, Fla., 1976; lighting dir. The Charo Show, various locations, U.S., 1977; stage mgr. Walt Disney Prodns., Orlando, Fla., 1978-80, The Shaklee Shows, various locations, 1980-83; pres. Etling Prodns., Miami, Fla., 1983—; exec. dir. Miami Mus. Sci., 1988-98, pres., CEO, 1998—; prodn. mgr. Perry Como in Concert, 1985-89; gen. mgr. Hyde Park (N.Y.) Festival Theatre, 1986, Ctr. for Health Tech. Affiliate Rev. Panel, 1991-97. Contbg. writer SciLights, 1988—; producer, dir. nat. TV halftime show for CBS Sports, 1983. Founding mem. Dade County Cultural Alliance, Miami, 1991; fundraiser Big Bros./Big Sisters Am., Miami, 1982—; mem. Orange Bowl Comm.; mem. Cape Fla. Ecol. Restoration Adv. Bd.; exec. bd. dirs. Fla. Assn. Mus. Recipient spl. recognition Big Bros./Big Sisters, 1987, Metro Dade Cmty. Action Agy., 1991, Outstanding Innovator award Fla. Assn. Mus., 1995. Mem. Assn. Sci. Tech. Ctr.'s, Fla. Assn. Mus.'s Bds., Actor's Equity Assn., Greater Miami C. of C. (cultural action com. 1990—), Explorers Club. Democrat. Methodist. Avocations: collecting fine art, graphics and natural history artifacts, film, theatre, music. Home: 3621 Viscaya Ct Coral Gables FL 33134-7188 Office: Museum of Science 3280 S Miami Ave Miami FL 33129-2899

ETLING, TERRY DOUGLAS, state agency administrator; b. Akron, Ohio, Jan. 24, 1943; s. Harold A. and Betty Jean (Newton) E.; m. Rosalind Joyce Gallogly, Dec. 26, 1966 (div. Mar. 1983); children: Allison Irene, Bret Newton. BS, Ohio State U., 1966; MEd, Kent (Ohio) State U., 1968. Vocat. rehab. counselor Apple Creek (Ohio) State Hosp., 1966-67, rehab. unit supr., 1967-69; coord. facility and program devel. Ohio Bur. Vocat. Rehab., Columbus, 1969-71; supr. rsch., planning and devel. div. Ohio Rehab. Svcs. Commn., Columbus, 1971-73, chief rsch., planning and devel. div., 1973-77, dep. adminstr., 1977-80, dir. bur. program support, 1980-91; retired Ohio Rehab. Svcs. Commn., 1991; cons. pvt. practice, 1991—; mgr. program devel. MEDVOC Mgmt., Inc., Columbus, 1992-93, dir. program devel., 1993—; mem. nat. adv. com. The Therapeutic Community of Upper Valley Med. Ctrs., J.M. Found. Search for Excellence in Vocat. Programs; mem. exec. com. chmn. standards com., trustee Commn. on Accreditation Rehab. Facilities, Tucson, 1985-89; chmn. Nat. State Facility Specialists Conf., Chgo., 1989; regional adv. coun. Rehab. Inst. Chgo. Rsch. and Tng. Ctr. in Prevention and Treatment of Spinal Cord Injury; dir. program devel. project boss Community Bankers Assn. Ohio, 1993-94; cons. Fla. Divsn. Vocat. Rehab., 1994—, Fla. Rehab. Adv. Coun., 1997—; adv. bd. dirs. Nat. Results Coun., St. Paul. Contbr. articles to profl. jours.; commentator for profl. papers Jour. of Rehab. Adminstrn., 1991—. Past pres. Assn. for Developmentally Disabled, Columbus, bd. dirs., 1977-88; ins. adv. coun. Good Samaritan Med. Ctr., Zanesville, Ohio, State Com. Purchase Products and Svcs. Severly Handicapped, 1977-88; chmn. Nat. Results Coun., Mpls., 1995—, apptd. CEO, 1996. Recipient Spl. Recognition award Commn. on Accreditation Rehab. Facilities, 1976, Meritorious Svc. award Ohio Industries for Handicapped, 1984, Disting. Svc. award Ohio Rehab. Counselors Assn., 1988, Mary Thiel award Fla. Assn. Rehab. Facilities, 1997. Mem. Coun. State Adminstrs. Vocat. Rehab. (mem. facility com.), Ohio Assn. Rehab. Facilities (agy. liaison to bd. dirs.), Nat. Rehab. Assn., Assn. for Developmentally Disabled (bd. dirs. 1987-88), SAR, Ohio State U. Alumni Assn., Union League Club, Delta Sigma Phi. Home: 733 NE 16th Terr Fort Lauderdale FL 33304-2940

ETO, HAJIME, information scientist, educator; b. Tokyo, June 16, 1935; s. Yoshio and Kikuko (Tamari) E. BA, U. Tokyo, 1959, MA, 1962; MS, U. Calif., Berkely, 1967; PhD, Tokyo Inst. Tech., 1979. Rschr. Hitachi Ltd., Tokyo, 1962-76; prof. U. Tsukuba, Japan, 1976-99, Chiba Keizai U., Japan, 1999—. *Based on the knowledge of classics of Eastern and Western, mathematical or statistical analyses on decision and policy of government or corporations concerning innovation research and development are uniquely prudent. A political and science philosophy for technological and organizational innovations is presented in the book "Research and Development Strategies of Japan" (Elsevier, Amsterdam, 1993). Conceptual analyses of legal systems promoting or inhibiting innovations such as the national tax system and unlawfully corrupt Tax Administration Agency are under preparation. He is extending his interest in technology innovation to organizational innovation and applying managerial technology to civil services via a case study.* Author, editor: R & D Management Systems in Japanese Industry, 1984, R & D Strategies in Japan, 1993; mem. editl. bd. Scientometrics Jour., 1979—, Human Sys. Mgmt., 1980-84, Internat. Jour. of the Sci. of Scis., 1994—, Internat. Jour. Svc. Tech. & Mgmt., 1998—; contbr. sci. articles to profl. jours. Recipient Fulbright scholarship U.S.-Japan Edn. Com., 1966. Mem. AAAS, Internat. Soc. Scientometrics and Informetrics (mem. coun. 1993—, mem. editl. bd. 1995—), Japan Assn. for Philosophy Sci. (mem. coun. 1970-92), Japan Soc. for Sci. Policy (bd. dirs. 1994-96, coun. 1997—), Assn. of France on Cybernetics, Econs. and Tech. (mem. editl. bd. 1985—), N.Y. Acad. Sci. Home: Nakano 3-43-17-305, Nakano-ku, Tokyo 164-0001, Japan

ETRA, DONALD, lawyer; b. N.Y.C., July 23, 1947; s. Harry and Blanche (Goldman) E.; m. Paula Kenee Wiener, Dec. 28, 1985; children: Harry, Dorothy, Anna, Jonathan. BA, Yale U., 1968; MBA, JD, Columbia U., 1971. Atty. to Ralph Nader Washington, 1971-73; trial atty. U.S. Dept. Justice, Washington, 1973-77; asst. U.S. atty. U.S. Dept. Justice, L.A., 1978-81; ptnr. Sidley & Austin, L.A., 1983-95, Law Offices of Donald Etra, L.A., 1995—. Co-author: Citibank, 1973. Office: 2029 Century Park E Ste 2710 Los Angeles CA 90067-3013

ETRIS, SAMUEL FRANKLIN, trade association administrator; b. Port Huron, Mich., Dec. 3, 1922; s. Samuel and Mildred Susan (Davis) E.; m. Mary Jane Lytle, June 29, 1957; children—Andrew Brooke, Edward Lytle. A.B., Temple U., 1947; M.S., Rutgers U., 1951. With Foote Mineral Rsch. Labs., Phila., 1947-49, spl. asst. to mng. dir. for nat. affairs, editor, 1967-80; editor ASTM, Phila., 1967-76; sr. cons. Klein of Saks, Inc., Washington; mgrs. Silver Inst., Gold Inst.; mem. numerical data adv. bd. NRC. Contbr. articles and editorials to profl. publs. Tchr. measurement course Phila. Pkwy. Sch.; Scoutmaster Boy Scouts Am., 1954-57, troop com. chmn., 1957-61; convenor 1st Internat. Conf. on Gold and Silver in Medicine, Bethesda, Md., 1987. Served to 1st lt. USAAF, 1944-46, CBI; Served to 1st lt. USAF, 1951-52. Recipient Scoutmaster's Key award, 1957. Mem. Am. Ceramic Soc. (emeritus). Home and Office: 115 Runnymede Ave Wayne PA 19087-4014

ETTENGER, ROBERT BRUCE, physician, nephrologist; b. Phila., Sept. 17, 1942; s.Ervin Earl and Sylvia (Goodstein) W.; m. Angela Joan Castellano Ettenger; children: Allison, Jessica. BA, U. Pa., 1964; MD, 1968. Maj. U.S. Army, El Paso, 1971-73; asst. prof. pediat. Children's Hosp. of L.A., 1976-80; asst. prof. pediat. Sch. Medicine UCLA, 1980-84, asst. prof., 1984-89, prof., 1989—, head divsn. pediat. nephrology dept. pediat., 1990—, vice chmn. clin. affairs, 1990—; dir. historcompatibility lab. UCLA Med. Ctr., 1987—; mem., chairperson sub bd. nephrology Am. Bd. Pediat., Chapel Hill, N.C., 1986-91; cons. Immunosuppressive Adv. Com. Food and Drug Adminstrn., Bethesda, Md., 1994—, Biologics and Immune Response Modifiers, Food and Drug Adminstrn., Bethesda, 1994—; mem. biol. sci. adv. com. U.S. Renal Data Sys., Ann Arbor, Mich., 1993—. Mem. editl. bd. Transplantation, Pediat. Nephrology, Pediat. Transplantation; contbr. articles to profl. jours. Coach, mem. exec. bd. AYSO Soccer, Santa Monica, Calif., 1994—, Bobby Sox Softball, 1995-97, YWCA Basketball, 1995—; mem. adv. bd. Nat. Kidney Found., L.A., 1993— . Recipient Ortho Biotech Lectureship Urologic Soc. for Transplantation, 1990, Continuing Svc. award Nat. Kidney Found., L.A., 1991, 92, 94. Fellow Internat. Soc. of Nephrology, Internat. Pediat. Nephrology Assn., Am. Acad. Pediat., Am. Soc. Transplant Physicians (pres. 1984-85), Am. Pediat. Soc., Am. Soc. of Nephrology, Am. Soc. of Pediat. Nephrology, Soc. for Pediat. Rsch., Transplantation Soc (Best Drs. in Am. 1992, 96). Jewish. Avocations: distance running, youth sports. Office: UCLA Med Ctr A2-383 Dept Pediatrics 10833 Le Conte Ave Los Angeles CA 90095-3075*

ETTENSON, GORDON MICHAEL, air force officer; b. Feb. 6, 1952. BS, USAF Acad., 1974; MA, U. Pitts., 1976. Commd. 2d lt. USAF, 1974, advanced through grades to col., 1996; chief joint doctrine U.S. Spl. Ops. Command, MacDill AFB, Fla., 1989-92; dep. comdr. 353d Spl. Ops. Group, Kadena Air Base, Japan, 1994-95; fellow Australian Coll. Def. and Strategic Studies, Canberra, 1996; cmdr. 43d Ops. Group, Pope AFB, N.C., 1997-99; chief spl. opers. divsn. HQ USAF, 1999—. E-mail: gordon.ettenson@pope.af.mil. Home: 2805 Glade Vale Way Vienna VA 22181 Office: HQ USAF/XOOS 1480 AF Pentagon Washington DC 20330-1480

ETTER, ALAN YANCY, legal administration executive; b. Fayette, Mo., May 25, 1949; s. Kern W. and Nina B. Etter; m. Linda L. Glisan, Dec. 28, 1971; children: Christy L., Katie A. BS in Edn., S.E. Mo. State U., 1971; M Equivalent, Indsl. Coll. Armed Forces, 1991; MPA, Troy State U., 1996. Comms. ens. USN, 1971, advanced through grades to capt., 1993; commanding officer USS Lawrence, Norfolk, Va., 1989-90, USS Pharris, Norfolk, 1991-92; dep. sr. mem. Propulsion Examining Bd., Norfolk, 1992-95; commanding officer Atlantic Bd. Inspection and Survey, Norfolk, 1995-98; ret. USN, 1998; dir. adminstrn. Jackson & Kelly PLLC, Charleston, W.Va., 1998—; surface warfare officer Navy Mil. Pers. Command, Washington, 1988. Referee U.S. Soccer Fedn., Va., 1987-98; girls coord. Beach FC youth soccer orgn., Virginia Beach, Va., 1992-93. Decorated Legion of Merit. Mem. Assn. Legal Adminstrs., Ret. Officers Assn., Indsl. Coll. Armed Forces Alumni, Ducks Unltd. Avocation: decoy carving. E-mail: aetter@jacksonkelly.com. Home: 9 Beacon Hill Charleston WV 25311 Office: Jackson & Kelly PLLC 1600 Laidley Tower Charleston WV 25322

ETTER, PETER ERICH, school district administrator; b. Lauenstein, Germany, Sept. 11, 1941; came to U.S., 1950; s. Friedrich Wilhelm and Luise Emma Bertha (Etter) Schnook; m. Sharon Emily Sperle, Aug. 1, 1964; children: Michael Erich, Kristina Elaina, Marcus Edward. Student, U. Wis. Milw., 1960-62; BS, U. Wis. Whitewater, 1965, MS, 1969. Cert. elem. tchr., jr. high tchr., German tchr., elem. prin., sch. dist. adminstr. Tchr. Germantown (Wis.) Schs., 1964-66; tchr., prin., adminstr. Darien (Wis.) Consol. Sch., 1966-79; sch. dist. adminstr. New Glarus (Wis.) Pub. Sch., 1979—; bd. dirs. Amcore Bank, New Glarus; bilingual tour guide Swiss Air, New Glarus, 1988, 90—; tchr. German Madison (Wis.) Area Tech. Coll., 1983—. Pres. Wilhelm Tell Guild, New Glarus, 1986—; mem. Green County Libr. Bd., Monroe, Wis., 1989—. Mem. Wis. Dept. Pub. Instrn. (Leadership Acad.), Wis. Assn. Sch. Dist. Adminstrs. Lutheran. Home: N9111 Old Madison Rd New Glarus WI 53574-9739 Office: Sch Dist New Glarus 1420 2nd St New Glarus WI 53574-9764

ETTER, ROBERT MILLER, retired consumer products executive, chemist; b. Chambersburg, Pa., July 13, 1932; s. John Edgar and Grace Elizabeth (Miller) E.; m. Jeane E. Beard, June 15, 1957; children: Robert Douglas, Jeffrey Beard, Roberta Marie. AB, Gettysburg Coll., 1954; postgrad., Harvard U., 1975; PhD, Pa. State U., 1959. Rsch. scientist Am. Cyanamid, Bound Brook, N.J., 1958-63; with S.C. Johnson & Son, Inc., Racine, Wis., 1963-89, dir. R & D Europe and Africa, Eng. and The Netherlands, 1972-78, dir. R & D worldwide indsl. products, 1978-80, v.p. R & D worldwide indsl. products, 1980-82, v.p. corp. rsch., 1982, v.p. R & D U.S. Consumer Products, 1982-88, v.p. external affairs, R & D, 1988-89. Mem. Am. Chem. Soc., AAAS, N.Y. Acad. Sci., Indsl. Research Inst., Chem. Specialties Mfrs. Assn. (dir. 1986-89), Sigma Xi. Home: 544 Bluebird Rdg Asheville NC 28804-1040

ETTERS, RONALD MILTON, lawyer, government official; b. San Antonio, Nov. 6, 1948; s. Milton William and Ilse Charlotte (Ostler) E.; m. Anna Colleen Wesson, Feb. 12, 1977; children: William Lawrence, Elizabeth Charlotte, Margaret Lawreen. BA magna cum laude, Am. U., 1971, JD, 1976. Bar: Va. 1976, U.S. Ct. Appeals (D.C. cir.) 1977, U.S. Dist. Ct. (ea. dist.) Va. 1978, U.S. Ct. Appeals (4th and 9th cirs.) 1978, U.S. Supreme Ct. 1979, D.C. 1980, U.S. Dist. Ct. D.C. 1980, U.S. Ct. Appeals (1st and 2d cirs.) 1980, U.S. Ct. Appeals (7th cir.) 1981, U.S. Ct. Appeals (3rd, 11th and Fed. cirs.) 1982, U.S. Ct. Appeals (5th cir.) 1983. Intern to gen. counsel Adminstrv. Office of U.S. Cts., Washington, 1970-71; fed. mgmt. intern IRS, Washington, 1971-72, labor rels. officer, 1972-75; ptnr. Nusbaum & Etters, Burke, Va., 1976-80; hearing officer, chief hearing officer Nat. Mediation Bd., Washington, 1975-80, gen. counsel, 1980—; with Sigma Alpha, 1971; justice Phi Alpha Delta, 1975; professorial lectr. Am. U., Washington, 1978-83; adj. prof. law Georgetown U., Washington, 1985-88. Sr. bd. editors The Railway Labor Act, 1991—. Mem. ABA (co-chmn. com. on railway and airline labor law 1987-93), Christian Legal Soc., Nat. Lawyers Assn. Home: PO Box 2374 Centreville VA 20122-2374 Office: Nat Mediation Bd 1301 K St NW East Tower Washington DC 20005

ETTINGER, DAVID A., lawyer; b. Detroit, 1951. AB with high distinction, U. Mich., 1973, JD cum laude, 1976. Bar: Mich. 1976. Mem. Honigman Miller Schwartz and Cohn, Detroit. Editor Mich. Law Rev., 1974-76; contbr. articles to profl. jours. Mem. ABA (head merger task force health care com. antitrust sect. 1992—), State Bar Mich. (chmn. antitrust law sect. 1989—). Address: Honigman Miller Schwartz & Cohn 600 Woodward Ave 2290 1st National Bldg Detroit MI 48226*

ETTINGER, HARRY JOSEPH, industrial hygiene engineer, project manager; b. N.Y.C., July 20, 1934; s. Morris and Pauline (Waxman) E.; m. June Kopf, June 14, 1958; children: Linda E., Steven E., Robert A. BCE, CCNY, 1956; MCE, NYU, 1958. Registered profl. engr., N.Mex.; cert. indsl. hygienist. Sanitary engr. USPHS, Bethesda, Md., 1958-61; staff mem. Los Alamos (N.Mex.) Nat. Lab., 1961-71, alt. group leader, 1971-74, group leader, 1974-80, program mgr., 1981-87; project dir. Occupational Safety and Health Adminstrn., Washington, 1987-89; tech. rsch. coord. Los Alamos (N.Mex.) Nat. Lab., 1989-91, program mgr., 1991-93, chief scientist environ., safety and health divsn., 1993-97, acting dep. divsn. dir., 1995-96, lab. assoc., 1997—; cons. divsn. reactor licensing USAEC, 1970-71, cons. EPA, 1972-74, various industries, 1970—; cons. to adv. com. on nuclear facility safety DOE, 1990-91; mem. adj. faculty U. Ark., Little Rock, 1969-90, San Diego State U., 1981-86; vis. faculty Tex. A&M U., College Station, 1981—; faculty affiliate Colo. State U., Ft. Collins, 1983—; mem. exec. com. toxic substances rsch. and tchg. program U. Calif., 1984-90; mem. stds. steering group DOE Lab. Dirs. Environ. and Occupational Health, 1990-96. Contbr. jour. articles and tech. reports on indsl. hygiene, aerosol physics, respiratory protection. Chmn. Los Alamos County Utility Bd., 1970; vice chmn. Los Alamos County planning and Zoning Commn., 1974-76, mem., 1997—. Fellow Am. Indsl. Hygiene Assn. (editl. rev. bd. 1979-87, 90-91, 95—, bd. dirs. 1987-90, v.p. 1991-92, pres.-elect 1992-93, pres. 1993-94, aerosol tech. com. 1968-78, 80-84, chmn. 1968-70, respirator com. 1995-98, Edward Baier award 1990); mem. Am. Acad. Indsl. Hygiene (editor newsletter 1997—), Am. Assn. Aerosol Rsch., Am. Bd. Indsl. Hygiene (bd. dirs. 1979-85, chmn. 1983-85), Am. Conf. Govtl. Indsl. Hygiene (Meritorious Achievement award 1985), Internat. Soc. Respiratory Protection (bd. dirs. 1985-88, 95-97), Internat. Occupational Hygiene Assn. (bd. dirs. 1994-97). Democrat. Jewish.

ETTINGER, JAYNE GOLD, physical education educator; b. N.Y.C., Oct. 18, 1954; d. Benjamin and Joan Louise (Hyman) Gold; m. Brian K. Ettinger, July 10, 1988; 1 child, Bradley Joseph. AA, Green Mountain Coll., Poultney, Vt., 1973; BS, Cortland State Coll., 1975; MS, Western Conn. State Coll., 1981. Lic. phys. edn. tchr., N.Y. Phys. edn. tchr. Lakeland Cen. Schs., Shrub Oak, N.Y., 1975—; volleyball ofcl. Hudson Valley Bd. of Ofcls., 1984-88, pres., 1987-89. Coord. Jump Rope for Heart, Mohegan Lake, N.Y., 1988—, Basketball Shoot Contest, Easter Seal Soc., 1989—, Hopping-Disability Awareness, 1992—. Mem. AAHPERD, N.Y. State Assn. Health, Phys. Edn., Recreation and Dance, Lakeland Fedn. Tchrs. (sec. 1985-97), Kappa Delta Pi. Office: George Washington Elem Sch 3634 Lexington Ave Mohegan Lake NY 10547-1244

ETTINGER, JOSEPH ALAN, lawyer; b. N.Y.C., July 21, 1931; s. Max and Frances E.; children: Amy Beth, Ellen Jane. BA, Tulane U., 1954, JD with honors, 1956. Bar: La. 1956, Ill. 1959. Asst. corp. counsel City of Chgo., 1959-62; pvt. practice, Chgo., 1962-73, 76-80; sr. ptnr. Ettinger & Schoenfield, Chgo., 1980-92; pvt. practice, Chgo., 1993—; assoc. prof. law Chgo.-Kent Coll., 1973-76; chmn. Village of Olympia Fields (Ill.) Zoning Bd. Appeals, 1969-76; chmn. panel on corrections Welfare Coun. Met. Chgo., 1969-76; spl. state appellate defender State of Ill., 1997-98. Contbr. articles to profl. publs. Capt. JAGC, U.S.Army, 1956-59. Recipient svc. award Village of Olympia Fields, 1976. Mem. Chgo. Bar Assn., Assn. Criminal Def. Lawyers (gov. 1970-72).

ETTINGER, LAWRENCE JAY, pediatric hematologist and oncologist, educator; b. Bklyn., Dec. 17, 1947; s. Joseph and Blanche (Mittman) E.; m. Alice G. Renick. BA, Case Western Res. U., 1969, MD, 1973. Intern in pediatrics U. Md. Hosp., Balt., 1973-74, resident in pediatrics, 1974-75; resident in pediatrics Children's Hosp. Buffalo, 1975-76; fellow in pediatric hematology-oncology Roswell Park Meml. Inst. and Children's Hosp. Buffalo, 1976-78; asst. prof. pediatrics U. Rochester (N.Y.) Sch. Med. and Dentistry, 1978-81, U. So. Calif., L.A., 1981-84; assoc. prof. U. Medicine and Dentistry N.J., Robert Wood Johnson Med. Sch., New Brunswick; chief div. pediatric hematology-oncology U. Medicine and Dentistry N.J., Robert Wood Johnson Med. Sch., 1984-98; lectr. in pediats. Coll. Physicians and Surgeons Columbia U., 1998—; chief divsn. pediat. hematology/oncology St. Peter's Univ. Hosp., 1998—; sickle cell adv. com. N.J. State Dept. Health, 1998—. Contbr. articles to profl. jours.; manuscript reviewer Cancer, Mayo Clinic Proceedings, Jour. Pediat. Hematology-Oncology, Brit. Jour. Cancer, Med. Pediat. Oncology. Mem. adv. com. Pediatric Oncology Adv. Group, N.J. Commn. Cancer Rsch., 1986—; mem. med. adv. bd. Inst. for Children with Cancer and Blood Disorders, 1991-98; field reader Office of Orphan Products Devel. FDA, 1988—; mem. spl. rev. com. NIH, 1992, 95; mem. cancer ad hoc com. Ocean County (N.J.) Health Dept., 1996-98. Recipient Univ. Excellence award for patient care U. Medicine and Dentistry, N.J., 1991, Pride of N.J. award and Clara Barton Med. Svc. award Gov. of N.J., 1992, N.J. Pride award in health, 1993; grantee N.J. Commn. on Cancer Rsch., Trenton, 1987-89, Valerie Fund, Maplewood, N.J., 1985-90, The Upjohn Co., Kalamazoo, 1984-86, Wyeth-Ayerst Rsch., Phila., 1992-94, Enzon Inc., Piscataway, N.J., 1992-94, Amgen, Inc., Thousand Oaks, Calif., 1992-94, Inst. for Children with Cancer and Blood Disorders, 1991-98, Sanofi Winthrop, 1996; Jr. Faculty Clin. . Fellow Am. Cancer Soc., 1980-83. Fellow Am. Acad. Pediatrics (exec. com. sect. on hematology-oncology 1997—); mem. AMA, Acad. Medicine N.J., Ea. Soc. Pediatric Rsch., Am. Assn. Cancer Rsch., Am. Soc. Clin. Oncology, Am. Soc. Hematology, Am. Soc. Pediatric Hematology-Oncology, Am. Cancer Soc. (svc. and rehab. com. N.J. divsn. 1985-96, vice chmn. 1988-89, 92-94, chmn. 1994-96, bd. trustees, exec. com. 1994-96), Oncology Soc. N.J., Children's Cancer Group (prin. investigator 1997-98), Phi Beta Kappa. Avocations: photography, travel. Office: St Peter's U Hosp 254 Easton Ave PO Box 591 New Brunswick NJ 08903-0591

ETTINGER, MORT, marketing educator; b. Chelsea, Mass., May 6, 1924; s. Louis Edward and Rose (Rosnitsky) E.; m. Charlotte Kahn, Nov. 12, 1950; children: Linda Joyce (dec.), Steven Alan, Jonathan Mark. BA, U. Maine, 1949; MS in Retailing, NYU, 1950. V.p. sales Ship 'n Shore, Aston, Pa., 1972-77, sr. v.p. internat., 1977-78; sr. v.p. Ship'n Shore, Aston, Pa., 1978-80; v.p. J.G. Hook, Phila., 1980-82; pres. Ettinger Enterprises, Lynn, Mass., 1982-86; prof. Suffolk U., Boston, 1986-87; pvt. Salem (Mass.) State Coll., 1986—, chairperson mktg. dept., 1987-97; pres. The Exec. Woman, The Boston Collection. Mem. Dem. Town Com., Marblehead, Mass., 1987—; hon. ambassador-at-large Govt. of Guam. With USN, 1943-46, PTO. Fellow Acad. Mktg. Sci.; mem. Am. Collegiate Retailing Assn., Am. Mktg. Assn. (exec. v.p. Boston chpt. 1994-95), World Comm. Assn., Sr. Exec. Inner Cir. (all coll. com. 1994-96, 97—), VFW, Masons, Shriners, Alpha Mu Alpha, Mu Kappa Tau, Delta Mu Delta (hon.). Democrat. Jewish. Home: 52 Auburndale Rd Marblehead MA 01945-1802 Office: Salem State Coll Sch Bus Dept Mktg Salem MA 01970

ETTLICH, WILLIAM F., electrical engineer; b. Spokane, Wash., Jan. 7, 1936; s. Fred Ernest Ettlich and Dorothy Sue (Olney) Nicholls; m. Alice Dianne Lawton, Aug. 24, 1958; children: Pamela, Daniel. BS, Oreg. State U.; PMD-25, Harvard U. Registered profl. engr., Oreg., Calif., Nev., Colo., Ohio. Project engr. CH2M-Hill Corp., Corvallis, Oreg., 1959-65; pres. Neptune Microfloc, Corvallis, 1965-74; v.p. Culp Wesner Culp, Cameron Park, Calif., 1974-86; exec. v.p. CWC-HDR, Inc., Cameron Park, 1986-88, HDR Engring., Inc., El Dorado Hills, 1988—; pres. Cameron Estates CSD, Cameron Park, 1977-80. Contbr. tech. articles to jours.; patentee in field. Bd. dirs. Marshall Hosp.; trustee Marshall Hosp. Found. Mem. IEEE (sr.), Instrument Soc. Am., Rotary (pres. Cameron Park club 1987-88). Republican. Presbyterian. Avocations: skiing, woodworking. Home: 3417 Strolling Hills Rd Cameron Park CA 95682-9632 Office: HDR Engring 271 Turn Pike Dr Folsom CA 95630-8098

ETTRE, LESLIE STEPHEN, chemist; b. Szombathely, Hungary, Sept. 16, 1922; came to U.S., 1958, naturalized, 1965; s. Stephen and Mary Therese (Dunay) E.; m. Kitty Polonyi, May 16, 1953; 1 child, Julie Suzanne. Diploma Chem. Engring, U. Tech. Scis., Hungary, 1945, D.Tech. Scis. Chemist G. Richter Pharm. Works, Budapest, Hungary, 1946-49; rsch. chemist Rsch. Inst. for Heavy Chem. Industries, Veszprem, Hungary, 1949-51, head tech. office, 1951-53; sr. lectr. chemistry U. Veszprem, 1951-53; head indsl. dept. Research Inst. for Plastics Industry, Budapest, 1953-56; chemist Lurgi Cos., Frankfurt, Fed. Republic Germany, 1957-58; applications chemist Perkin-Elmer Corp., Norwalk, Conn., 1958-60, product specialist, 1960-62, chief applications chemist, 1962-68, sr. staff scientist, 1972-87, sr. scientist, 1987-90; exec. editor Ency. Indsl. Chem. Analysis John Wiley & Sons, N.Y.C., 1968-72; rsch. assoc. dept. engring. and applied scis. Yale U., New Haven, 1977-78, adj. prof., 1989-95, rsch. affiliate, 1995—; adj. prof. U. Houston, 1978-88; chmn. various symposia on chromatography, intermittantly, 1972-93; co-chmn. Summer Symposium on Analytical Chemistry Miami U., Oxford, Ohio, 1973; lectr. in U.S., Can., Europe, Asia, Africa, Australia; participant lecture tours of Chromatography Coun. of Acad. Scis., USSR, 1976, 78, 79, 80, 81, 86, 88, Estonian Acad. Scis., 1979-81, Chinese Acad. Scis., 1980, 85, 87, Georgian Acad. Sci., 1981. Author: Open Tubular Columns in Gas Chromatography, 1965; (with A. Zlatkis) The Practice of Gas Chromatography, 1967; (with W.H. McFadden) Ancillary Techniques of Gas Chromatography, 1968 (trans. into Russian, 1972); Practical Gas Chromatography, 1972; Introduction to Open Tubular Columns, 1974, 2d edit., 1978, (transl. into German, 1976, Spanish, 1978, Chinese, 1981); (with A. Zlatkis) 75 Years of Chromatography-A Historical Dialogue, 1979; Basic Relationships of Gas Chromatography, 1977, (transl. into Chinese, 1988, rev. new edit. with J.V. Hinshaw 1993, transl. into German, 1996); (with R.W. Yost and R.D. Conlon) Practical Liquid Chromatography, 1980 (transl. into Spanish and French, 1981); (with J.J. DiCesare, M.N. Dong) Introduction to High-Speed Liquid Chromatography, 1981 (transl. into Spanish, 1982, Italian, 1983); (with Cs. Horvath) Chromatography in Biotechnology, 1993; (with J.V. Hinshaw) Introduction to Open Tubular Column Gas Chromatography, 1994, (with B. Kolb) Headspace-Gas Chromatography, 1997; mem. editl. bd. Jour. Chromatography Sci., 1963-95, LC/GC Mag., 1981—, Jour. Liquid Chromatography, 1986-93; editor: Chromatographia, 1970—, Hungarian Jour. of Chemists, 1993—; contbr. numerous articles to profl. jours. Recipient commemorative chromatography medal Acad. Scis., USSR, 1978, M.S. Tswett award in chromatography, 1978, L.S. Palmer award Minn. Chromatography Forum, 1980, A.J.P. Martin award Brit. Chromatography Discussion Group, 1982, Outstanding Svc. award Western Carolinas Chromatography Discussion Group, 1987, M.J.E. Golay award, 14th Internat. Symposium on Capillary Chromatography, 1992, Golden Diploma U. Tech. Scis., Budapest, 1995, Dimick award Pitts. Conf. on Analytical Chemistry and Applied Spectroscopy, 1998, Jubilee award 20th Internat. Symposium on Capillary Chromatography, 1998. Fellow Am. Inst. Chemists; mem. ASTM (chmn. subcom. rsch. com. E-19, 1966-70, subcom. on nomenclature of com. E-19, 1970-73), Am. Chem. Soc. (award in chromatography 1985), Chromatography Soc. (exec. com. 1982-89), N.Y. Acad. Scis., Internat. Union Pure and Applied Chemistry (nomenclature com. 1981-91), Hungarian Chem. Soc. (hon.). E-mail: lsettre@snet.net. FAX: 203-371-5765. Office: Beardsley Station PO Box 6274 Bridgeport CT 06606-0274

ETULAIN, RICHARD WAYNE, historian, educator; b. Wapato, Wash., Aug. 26, 1938; s. Sebastian and Mary Lou (Gillard) E.; m. Joyce Oldenkamp, Aug. 18, 1961; 1 child, Jacqueline Joyce Etulain Partch. BA in History, BA in English, N.W. Nazarene Coll., Nampa, Idaho, 1960; MA in Am. Lit., U. Oreg., 1962, PhD in Am. History and Lit., 1966. Grad. asst. U. Oreg., Eugene, 1963-66; asst. prof. N.W. Nazarene Coll., 1966-68; assoc. prof. Eastern Nazarene Coll., Quincy, Mass., 1968-69; postdoctoral grantee Dartmouth Coll., Hanover, N.H., 1969-70; from assoc. prof. to prof. history Idaho State U., Pocatello, 1970-79; prof. history U. N.Mex., Albuquerque, 1979—; postdoctoral fellow U. Nev., Reno, 1973-74. Author: Owen Wister, 1973, Ernest Haycox, 1988, The American West: A Twentieth-Century History, 1989, Re-imagining the Modern American West: A Century of Fiction, History, Art, 1996, Telling Western Stories: From Buffalo Bill to Larry McMurtry, 1999; editor/co-editor: Basque Americans, 1981, Conversations: Wallace Stegner on Western History and Literature, 2d edit., 1990, The Twentieth-Century West: Historical Interpretations, 1989, Basques of the Pacific Northwest, 1991, Religion in Modern New Mexico, 1997, By Grit and Grace: Eleven Women Who Shaped the American West, 1997, Myths and the American West, 1998, Portraits of Basques in the New World, 1999, Does the Frontier Experience Make America Exceptional?, 1999, With Badges and Bullets: Lawmen and Outlaws in the Old West, 1999; contbr. more than 100 essays and 300 revs. to scholarly jours. Sunday sch. tchr., mem. ch. bd., Pocatello and Albuquerque, 1970—. Recipient Wrangler/Western Heritage award Nat. Cowboy Hall of Fame, 1997, Excellence in Humanities award N.Mex. Endowment for Humanities, 1998; NEH Minority fellow, 1973-74; NHPC Hist. Editing fellow, 1969-70. Mem. Western Lit. Assn. (pres. 1979-80), Western History Assn. (pres. 1998-99, Best Book in Western History award 1997), Orgn. Am. Historians. Democrat. Mem. Ch. of the Nazarene. Avocations: book collecting, travel, writing. Email: baldbasq@unm.edu. Home: 1705 Stagecoach Rd SE Albuquerque NM 87123 Office: U NMex Dept History Albuquerque NM 87131

ETZ, (HELEN) JANE, hospital utilization; b. Riverside, Calif., Feb. 21, 1938; d. James Wycoth Van Derpool and Mildred Thelma Carr; m. William Arthur Ward, Aug. 9, 1958 (div. 1978); children: Arthur Scott Ward, Wendolyn Zee (Ward) Warwick; m. Charles Frederick Etz, Jan. 26, 1980. BSN, Calif. State U., Dominguez Hills, 1996. RN Calif; cert. Profl. Healthcare Quality, Calif., Pub. Health Nurse, Calif.; cert. case mgr. Clinic nurse Gridley (Calif.) Farm Labor Camp, 1965-67; staff nurse Chico (Calif.) Cmty. Hosp., 1972-75, patient care coord., 1975-80; head nurse King Abdulaziz Air Base Hosp., Dhahran, Saudi Arabia, 1980-81; utilization mgr. Chico Cmty. Hosp., 1981-91, dir. quality mgmt., 1991-94; dir. utilization mgmt. discharge planning and social svcs. Chico Cmty. Hosp., Inc., 1994-98; utilization mgr. Enloe Med. Ctr., Chico, 1998—; v.p., bd. dirs. Peg Taylor Adult Day Health, Chico, 1996—, sec. and bd. mem., 1993-96; pres. elect Butte/Glenn/Tehema County (Calif.) chpt. Am. Diabetic Assn., 1996—, pres. 1999—. Mem. Nat. and State Assn. HealthCare Quality, Continuing Care Assn., Calif. Assn. HealthCare Quality, North Sierra Quality/Utilization Assn. (pres. 1981-82), Case Mgrs. Soc. Am., Chico Book Club, Caribou Investment Club. Episcopalian. Avocations: books, investing, bicycle touring, birding, gardening. Home: 508 W Shasta Ave Chico CA 95973-8608 Office: Enloe Med Ctr 560 Cohasset Rd Chico CA 95926-2212

ETZ, LOIS KAPELSOHN, architectural company principal; b. Newark, Feb. 7, 1944; d. Sol D. and Matilda (Zlotnick) Kapelsohn; m. Leonard Etz, Dec. 4, 1967 (dec. May 1976); children: Rachel Jennie, Rebecca Sarah. BA, Mount Holyoke Coll., 1966; MA, Seton Hall U., 1968. Counselor N.J. Rehab. Commn., Trenton, 1966-68; pvt. antique dealer Princeton, N.J., 1968-78; pres. Nat. Code Cons., Princeton, 1971-78; dir. purchasing, aux. svcs. Mercer County Community Coll., Trenton, 1978-81; v.p. Hillier Group Architects, Princeton, 1981—. Bd. dirs. Vols. in Probation, Princeton, 1981, N.J. Printmaking Coun., Princeton Arts Coun., Mercer County Spl. Svc. Com., Hadassah; v.p. McCarter Theatre Assocs., Princeton, 1986-89; bd. dirs. McCarter Theatre Trustees, Princeton, 1989-91; past v.p., bd. dirs. Jewish Ctr. Commendation Chief Justice N.J. Supreme Ct., 1982. Commendation Chief Justice N.J. Supreme Ct., 1982. Mem. Mt. Holyoke Alumnae Assn. (past pres. Princeton chpt.), Record Mgmt. Assn. (founding officer), Princeton Pers. Assn. Democrat. Jewish. Home: 1038 Princeton Kingston Rd Princeton NJ 08540-4130 Office: The Hillier Group CN23 500 Alexander Pk Princeton NJ 08540

ETZEL, JAMES EDWARD, environmental engineering educator; b. Reading, Pa., Nov. 9, 1929; s. Edward John and Ruth Anna (Getrost) E.; m. Barbara Dawn Shoup, Sept. 3, 1950; children: Pamela Dawn, Gregory John, Mark Raymond, Scott Edward, Christopher James. BS in Sanitation Engring., Pa. State U., 1951; MSCE, Purdue U., 1955, PhD, 1957. Registered profl. engr., Ind. Engr. Capitol Engring. Co., Dillsburg, Pa., 1951, du Pont Co., Wilmington, Del., 1957-58; engr., dir. research Roy F. Weston, engrs., Newtown Sq., Pa., 1958-59; mem. faculty Purdue U., 1959-90, prof. environ. engring., 1964-90, Water Refining Co. prof., 1978-83, head environ. engring. area Sch. Civil Engring., 1971-90, prof. emeritus environ. engring., 1990—; v.p. Heritage Environ. Svcs., Inc., 1990—; chmn. Tippecanoe County (Ind.) Solid Wastes Com., 1971-86; mem. W. Lafayette Environ. Commn., 1968-76; cons. to industry, 1960—. Served with C.E., 1951-53, AUS. Named Outstanding Prof. in Civil Engring. Purdue U., 1979. Mem. Water Pollution Control Fedn. Ind. Water Pollution Control Assn. (past pres.). Lutheran. Patentee in field. Home: 710 Cardinal Dr Lafayette IN 47905-9036

ETZEL, RUTH ANN, pediatrician, epidemiologist; b. Milw., Apr. 6, 1954; d. Raymond Arthur and Marian Dorothy (Neu) E. Student, St. Olaf Coll., 1972-73; BA in Biology summa cum laude, U. Minn., 1976; MD, U. Wis., 1980; PhD, U. N.C., 1985. Pediatrics resident N.C. Meml. Hosp., Chapel Hill, 1980-83; adj. asst. prof. pediatrics Emory U. Sch. Medicine, Atlanta, 1985-87; epidemic intelligence svc. officer Ctr. Environ. Health Ctrs. for Disease Control, Atlanta, 1985-87, med. epidemiologist Ctr. Environ. Health and Injury Control, 1987-90; chief air pollution and respiratory health br. Ctrs. for Disease Control and Prevention, Atlanta, 1991-96, asst. dir. preventive medicine residency program, 1992-97; dir. divsn. epidemiology and risk assessment Office Pub. Health and Sci., Food Safety and Inspection Svc., USDA, Washington, 1998—; mem. preventive medicine and pub. health test com. Nat. Bd. Med. Examiners, 1992-94; mem. U.S. Med. Licensing Exam. Step 2 Preventive Medicine and Pub. Health Test Material Devel. Com., 1992-94. Contbr. articles to profl. publs. Robert Wood Johnson clin. scholar U. N.C., 1983-85, MacPherson scholar, 1972; recipient Arthur S. Flemming award D.C. Jaycees, 1991. Fellow Am. Acad. Pediat. com. on environ. hazards, Ctrs. for Disease Control and Prevention liaison 1986-92, chmn. sect. on epidemiology 1988-92, ex-officio 1993-94, chmn. com. on environ. health 1995—); mem. APHA, Ambulatory Pediatric Assn. (rsch. com. 1987—), Soc. for Pediatric Epidemiol. Rsch., Phi Beta Kappa, Delta Omega. Office: Rm 5043 1400 Independence Ave SW Stop 3718 Washington DC 20250-3718

ETZIONI, AMITAI, sociologist, educator; b. Cologne, Germany, Jan. 4, 1929; s. Willi Falk and Gertrude Hannauer (Falk) E.; m. Minerva Morales, Sept. 14, 1965 (dec. Dec. 20, 1985); children: Ethan, Oren, Michael, David, Benjamin; m. Patricia Kellogg, Nov. 6, 1992. BA, Hebrew U., Jerusalem, 1954, MA, 1956; PhD in Sociology, U. Calif., Berkeley, 1958; LittD (hon.), Rider Coll., 1980, Gov.'s State U., 1987; LLD (hon.), U. Utah, 1991; LHD (hon.), Colo. Coll., 1994, Conn. Coll., 1994. Mem. faculty Columbia U., 1958-80; rsch. assoc. Inst. War and Peace Studies, 1961, prof. sociology, 1967, chmn. dept., 1969-78; dir. Ctr. for Policy Rsch., 1968—; guest scholar Brookings Instn., 1978-79; sr. advisor White House, 1979-80; univ. prof. George Washington U., Washington, 1980—, dir. Inst. for Communitarian Policy Studies, 1995—; Thomas Henry Carroll Ford Found. vis. prof., grad. sch. bus. Harvard U., Cambridge, Mass., 1987-89; bd. dirs. Ctr. for Policy Rsch., Washington; mem. Econ. Forum The Conf. Bd., 1983-85; founder Ctr. for Comm. Policy Studies, George Washington U., 1995—; dir., founder Inst. Communitarian Policy Studies, 1995; developed organizational analysis, a typology based on means used to control participants in orgns., how orgns. change, survive and are integrated into larger social units. Author: A Comparative Analysis of Complex Organizations, 1961, Modern Organizations, 1964, Political Unification, A Comparative Study of Leaders and Forces, 1965, Studies in Social Change, 1966, the Active Society, 1968, Genetic Fix, 1973, Social Problems, 1975, An Immodest Agenda, 1982, Capital Corruption, 1984, The Moral Dimension, 1988, The Spirit of Community, 1993, The New Golden Rule, 1996, The Limits of Privacy, 1999; editor: The Responsive Community, 1990—; editorial bd. Sci. Mag., 1969-71; contbr. numerous articles to profl. jours. With Israeli Army. Social Sci. Rsch. Coun. faculty fellow, 1960-61, 67-68; fellow Ctr. for Advanced Study in Behavioral Scis., 1965-66; Guggenheim fellow, 1968. Fellow AAAS; mem. Am. Sociol. Assn. (pres. 1995), Soc. for the Advancement Socio-Econs. (founder 1989), The Communitarian Network (founder 1993), Inst. Medicine. Office: George Washington U 2130 H St NW Gelman Libr Rm 714 Washington DC 20052

ETZKORN, K. PETER, sociology educator, author; b. Karlsruhe, Germany; naturalized, 1958; s. Johannes and Luise (Schlick) E.; m. Hildegard Elizabeth Garve; children: Kyle Peter, Lars Peter. A.B., Ohio State U.; student, Ind. U.; A.M., Princeton, Ph.D. Asst. prof. U. Calif., Santa Barbara; assoc. prof. Am. U. Beirut, Lebanon; dir. Office Instl. Research; chmn. dept. sociology and anthropology U. Nev.; prof., chmn. faculty sociology and anthropology U. West Fla., 1967-68; prof. sociology San Fernando Valley State Coll., 1968-69; prof. sociology U. Mo., St. Louis, 1969—, asso. dean Grad. Sch., 1978-87, dir. Office Rsch., 1979-87; vis. prof. U. Münster, Germany, 1975-76, U. Vienna, Austria, 1987-88; cons. in field; prof. tng. adv. panel music divsn. NEA, 1994-97. Author: The Conflict in Modern Culture, 1968, Music and Society, 1973, Sociologists and Music, 1989; editor Jour. Ethnomusicology, 1984-87, Current Studies in the Sociology of Arts and Music, 1988—; contbr. articles to profl. jours. Mem. Gov. Nev. Com. on Dept. Correction, 1966; Mo. Gov. liaison German-Am. Tricentennial Task Force, 1983; mem. Mo. Adv. Com. on Humanities; chmn. Univ. Symposia Com. Bicentennial Horizons Am. Music; mem. St. Louis-Stuttgart Sister City Com.; Mo. state rep. Sister Cities Internat., 1976-81; cons. Nat. Endowment Arts, NSF; pres. St. Louis New Music Circle; bd. dirs. Am. Kantorei, MEDIACULT, Vienna; v.p. Internat. Inst. Met. St. Louis, 1982-86; pres. MEDIACULT, 1995—; exec. com. The Coun. on Fgn. Rels. St. Louis Com., 1996—; bd. dirs. St. Louis Soc. for Blind and Visually Impaired, 1996—. Fulbright scholar, Vienna, Austria, 1987. Fellow Am. Sociol. Assn., Am. Anthrop. Assn.; mem. Soc. Ethnomusicology (coun. 1963-71, 76-79, 81-86, editor spl. publs.), Inst. Internat. Sociologie (mem. bur.), Internam. Orgn. Higher Edn. (dep. coun. 1980-87), Town Affiliation Assn. U.S. (bd. dirs. 1981-93, v.p. 1987-90, sec. 1990-93), St. Louis Coun. Sister Cities (chmn. 1981-86), Internat. Soc. for Music Edn. (chmn. commn. on media, culture and pub. policy 1990-96), St. Louis Princeton Club (bd. dirs. 1987—). Home: 21 Ladue Ridge Rd Saint Louis MO 63124-1449

ETZWILER, DONNELL DENCIL, pediatrician; b. Mansfield, Ohio, Mar. 29, 1927; s. Donnell Seymour and Berniece Jean (Meek) E.; m. Helen Brown Beard, Mar. 3, 1989; children from previous marriage: Nancy, Lisa, Diane,

David. BA cum laude, Ind. U., 1950; MD, Yale U., 1953. Intern dept. pediatrics Sch. Medicine Yale U., New Haven, 1953-54; resident dept. pediatrics N.Y. Hosp. Cornell Med. Sch., N.Y.C., 1954-55, instr. pediatrics N.Y. Hosp., 1956-57; mem. faculty Clin. Inst. Med. Sch. U. Minn., Mpls., 1957-74, clin. instr., asst. clin. prof. pediatrics, 1974-84, clin. prof. dept. pediatrics, 1985-99, clin. prof. dept. family practice and cmty. medicine, 1990-99, clin. prof. emeritus pediatrics and family practice, 1999—; pediatrician Nicollet Med. Ctr., 1957-96; founder, pres., chief med. officer Internat. Diabetes Ctr., 1967-96, pres. emeritus, 1996—; instr. Project Hope, Trujillo, Peru, 1962; mem. Nat. Commn. on Diabetes, 1975-77; dir. WHO Diabetes Collaborating Ctr. in Diabetes Edn., Translation & Computer Tech., chmn., 1988—; chmn. WHO Collaborating Ctr. for Diabetes, 1988-94; co-dir. Internat. Diabetes Programme, Russia; mem. expert com. Compass Project, pres., 1998—. Author: Education and Management of the Patient with Diabetes Mellitus, 1967, 3d edit., 1992; editor: Learning to Live With Diabetes (in Russian), 1985, 2d edit., 91; co-editor: Staged Diabetes Management, 1992; contbr. articles to profl. jours. Bd. dirs. Minn. Soc. for the Blind, 1977-85, Diabetes Edn. and Rsch. Found., 1985-88, Chronimed, 1988-98; chmn. Med. and Sci. adv. bd., 1998—; bd. dirs., pres. Compass Project, 1998—; trustee FIT USA, 1999—. With USNR, WWII. Recipient Good Neighbor award Sta. WCCO, 1977, 85, Park Nicollet Med. Ctr. Community award, 1987, Park Nicollet Med. Found. Rsch. award, 1991, Educator award, 1993, Circle of Leadership award Am. Diabetes Assn., 1997; NIH fellow, 1955-56. Fellow All India Inst. Diabetes; mem. AMA, Am. Diabetes Assn. (pres. 1976-77, Disting. Svc. Youth award 1976, Banting medal 1977, Becton-Dickinson award 1978, Upjohn Educator award 1983, Med. Alley Honor award 1988, hon., Russian award for peace efforts 1994), Am. Assn. Diabetes Educators (hon.), Am. Dietetic Assn. (hon.), Internat. Diabetes Fedn. (exec. com., dir., bd. mgmt., chmn. internat. com. juvenile diabetes 1978-85, v.p. 1976-85), Soc. Pub. Health Educators, Am. Group Practice Assn., Am. Pub. Health Assn., Inst. of Medicine of NAS (camp dir. Minn. affiliate 1959-84, bd. dirs.), Am. Acad. Pediats., Minn. Med. Assn., Internat. Soc. Pediat. and Adolescent Diabetes, European Assn. for Study of Diabetes. Congregationalist.

EU, MARCH FONG, ambassador, former state official; b. Oakdale, Calif., Mar. 29, 1929; d. Yuen and Shiu (Shee) Kong; children by previous marriage: Matthew Kipling Fong, Marchesa Suyin Fong; m. Henry Eu, Aug. 31, 1973; stepchildren: Henry, Adeline, Yvonne, Conroy, Alaric. Student, Salinas Jr. Coll.; BS, U. Calif.-Berkeley, 1943; MEd, Mills Coll., 1947; EdD, Stanford U., 1956; postgrad., Columbia U., Calif. State Coll.-Hayward; LLD, Lincoln U., 1984; LLB (hon.), Western U., 1985; DHL (hon.), Northrup Coll., 1991; LLB (hon.), Pepperdine U., 1993. Chmn. divsn. dental hygiene U. Calif. Med. Center, San Francisco, 1948-56; dental hygienist Oakland (Calif.) Pub. Schs., 1948-56; supr. dental health edn. Alameda County (Calif.) Schs.; lectr. health edn. Mills Coll., Oakland; mem. Calif. Legislature, 1966-74, chmn. select com. on agr., foods and nutrition, 1973-74; mem. com. natural resources and conservation, com. commerce and pub. utilities, select com. med. malpractice; chief of protocol State of Calif., 1975-83, sec. of state, 1975-94; amb. to Federated States of Micronesia, Am. Embassy, Pohnpei, 1994—; chmn. Calif. State World Trade Commn., 1983-87; ex officio mem. Calif. State World Trade Commn., 1987—; spl. cons. Bur. Intergroup Relations, Calif. Dept. Edn.; ednl., legis. cons. Sausalito (Calif.) Pub. Schs., Santa Clara County Office Edn., Jefferson Elementary Union Sch. Dist., Santa Clara High Sch. Dist., Santa Clara Elementary Sch. Dist., Live Oak Union High Sch. Dist.; mem. Alameda County Bd. Edn., 1956-66, pres., 1961-62, legis. adv., 1963, Assembly Retirment Com., Assembly Com. on Govtl. Quality Com., Assembly Com. on Pub. Health; pres. Alameda County Sch. Bds. Assn., others; U.S. advisor Shenzhen Internat. Ent. Co., Ltd., Shenzhen, Guangzhou, China, 1997; internat. hon. advisor 4th World Chinese Entrepreneurs Conv., Vancouver, B.C., 1997; hon. chmn. Sino-Am. Inst. Human Resources, L.A., 1997; U.S. advisor Internat. Hort Exposition for 1999, Kunming, Yunnan, 1997; mem. exec. adv. bd. Asian Am. Policy Rev. Bd., Washington, 1998, others. Mem. budget panel Bay Area United Fund Crusade; mem. Oakland Econ. Devel. Coun.; mem. tourism devel. com. Calif. Econ. Devel. Commn.; mem. citizens com. on housing Coun. Social Planning; mem. Calif. Interagy. Coun. Family Planning; edn. chmn., mem. coun. social planning, dir. Oakland Area Baymont Dist. Cmty. Coun.; charter pres., hon. life mem. Howard Elem. Sch. PTA; charter pres. Chinese Young Ladies Soc., Oakland; mem., vice chmn. adv. com. Youth Study Ctrs. and Ford Found. Interagy. Project, 1962-63; chmn. Alameda County Mothers' March, 1971-72; bd. councillors U. So. Calif. Sch. Dentistry, 1976; mem. exec. com. Calif. Dem. Ctrl. Com., mem. ctrl. com., 1963-70, asst. sec.; del. Dem. Nat. Conv., 1968; dir. 8th Congl. Dist. Dem. Coun., 1963; v.p. Dems. of 8th Congl. Dist., 1963; dir. Key Women for Kennedy, 1963; women's vice chmn. No. Calif. Johnson for Pres., 1964; bd. dirs. Oakland YWCA, 1965; mem. nat. vice-chmn. Clinton/Gore Reelection Campaign Com., 1996; U.S. Ambassador to Federated States Micronesia, 1994; mem. exec. adv. bd. Asian Policy Review, Washington, 1994; chmn. Investment Devel. Fund Fed. States Micronesia, 1995; chmn. March Fong Eu com. to promote Asian Am. Agenda, 1996; U.S. advisor Internat. Hort. Expn., Kumming, China, 1977; hon. chmn. Sino-Am. Inst. Human Resources, L.A., 1997; internat. hon. advisor 4th World Chinese Entrepreneurs Convention, Vancouver, Can., 1997; U.S. advisor Shenzhen Internat. Enterprises Co. Ltd., China, 1997; U.S. advisor in S.E. Asia Heart to Heart Internat. Found., Olathe, Kans. and San Diego, 1997; mem. bd. govs. Natural Hist. Mus. of L.A. County, 1998—. Recipient Citizen of Yr. award Chinese-Am. United for Self Employment, 1996, Govt. Svc. award friends of Mus. of Chinese Am. History, L.A., 1997, Cmty. Svc. award Coll. of San Mateo, Ann. Humanitarian award Women's Ctr., Coll. of Law, San Diego, Asian Am. on the Move award for politics L.A. City Employees Asian Am. Assn., Outstanding Svc. to Cmty. award Irish-Israeli Italian Soc.. San Francisco, Disting. C.C. Alumni award Calif. C.C. and Jr. Coll. Assn., Outstanding Woman award Nat. Women's Polit. Caucus, Daisy award Calif. Landscape Contrs. Assn., 1980, Milton Shoong Hall of Fame Humanitarian award, 1981, Citizen of the Yr. award Coun. for Civic Unity of San Francisco Bay Area, 1982, Woman of the Yr., Dems. United, San Bernardino, 1986, Woman of Achievement Award of Distinction, San Gabriel Valley YWCA, 1987, Disting. svc. award Rep. of Honduras, 1987, Woman of the Yr. award Santa Barbara County Girls Club Coalition, 1987, Polit. Achievement award Calif. Dem. Party, Black Caucus, 1988, 1989 JFK Am. Leadership award Santa Ana Dem. Club, 1989, Cmty. Leadership award Torat-Haijun Hebrew Acad., 1990, Mother of the Yr. award No. Am. TV Corp., 1999numerous others; March Fong Eu ann. achievement award named in her honor Nat. Notary Pub. Assn., 1998. Fellow Internat. Coll. Dentists; mem. Navy League (life), Am. Dental Hygienists Assn. (pres. 1956-57), No. Calif. Dental Hygienists Assn., Oakland LWV, AAUW (area rep. in edn. Oakland br.), Calif. Tchrs. Assn., Calif. Agrl. Aircraft Assn. (hon.), Calif. Sch. Bd. Assn., Alameda County Sch. Bd. Assn. (pres. 1965), Alameda County Mental Health Assn., Calif. Pub. Health Assn. Northern Divsn. (hon.), So. Calif. Dental Assn. (hon.), Bus. and Profl. Women's Club, Soroptimist (hon.), Hadassah (life), Ebell Club (L.A.), Chinese Retail Food Markets Assn. (hon.), Chinese Women's Assn. Singapore, Am. Assn. Singapore, Pilot Club Internat., Clara Barton Soc. Am. Red Cross (L.A. chpt.), Delta Kappa Gamma, Phi Alpha Delta (hon.), Phi Delta Gamma (hon.), others. Avocation: painting.

EUANS, ROBERT EARL, architect; b. Columbus, Ohio, July 6, 1941; s. William Weldon Euans and Hilda Aurelia (Daugherty) Roberts; m. Carol May Chamberlain, Dec. 18, 1964; children: Bradley James, Lori Ellen, Bryant Scott, Bruce Allen. BArch, Ohio State U., 1967. Registered architect, Ohio, Mich., Pa., Ind., Ill., Minn, Mo., Ky., Fla. Draftsman Blaw-Knox Corp., Pitts., 1967-68; chief draftsman Schofield & Assocs., Columbus, Ohio, 1968-70; project architect Karlsberger & Assocs., Columbus, 1970-74, dir. tech., 1974-77; pvt. practice architecture Columbus, 1977—. Mem. AIA (bd. dirs. Columbus chpt. 1984-86), Architects Soc. Ohio, Constrn. specification Inst. Lutheran. Avocations: camping, sports, swimming.

EUBANK, J. THOMAS, lawyer; b. Port Arthur, Tex., Mar. 17, 1930; s. J.T. and Ada (White) E.; m. Nancy Moore, Feb.10, 1956; children: John, Marshall, Stephen, Laura. B.A., Rice U., 1951; J.D., U. Tex., 1954. Bar: Tex. 1954, U.S. Supreme Ct. 1960. Assoc. Baker & Botts, Houston, 1954-66, ptnr., 1966-79, sr. ptnr., 1979-90; ret. sr. ptnr., 1991—; mem. adv. coun. Rice U. Sch. Engring, Houston, 1990—. Mem. joint editorial bd. Uniform Probate code, 1972-86. Bd. govs. Rice U., 1985-91. Mem. ABA (chmn. sect. real property, probate and trust law 1978-79), Am. Coll. Trust and Estate Counsel (pres. 1984-85, pres. Found. 1986-89), State Bar Tex. (chmn. sect. real estate, probate and trust law 1972-73), Am. Bar Found., Tex. Bar Found., Houston Philos. Soc., Rice U. Alumni Assn. (pres. 1979-80, Rice Gold medal 1992), Am. Law Inst., Internat. Acad. Estate and Trust Law, Houston Country, CoronadoAllegro, Thalia. Home: 26 Liberty Bell Cir Houston TX 77024-6303 Office: 711 Louisiana St Ste 1745 Houston TX 77002-2759

EUBANKS, EUGENE EMERSON, education educator, consultant; b. Meadville, Pa., June 6, 1939; s. Nelson Eubanks and Emily (Princes) Jackson; m. Audrey Hunter, Aug. 4, 1962; children: Brian, Regina. BS, Edinboro (Pa.) State U., 1963; PhD, Mich. State U., 1972. Tchr. Cleve. Pub. Schs., 1963-68, unit prin., 1968-70; asst. prof. U. Del., Newark, 1972-74; asst. dean U. Mo., Kansas City, 1974-79, dean, 1979-88, prof. edn. and urban affairs, 1988—; dept. supt. Kansas City Pub. Schs., 1984-85. Contbr. articles to profl. jours. Cons. Urban League, 1978—, legal def. fund NAACP, 1978, Cleve. Found., 1978, U. Wis., 1988; bd. dirs. Operation PUSH, 1982-87, Mid-Continent Girl Scouts, Kansas City, 1983—, Genesis Sch., 1984—; chair Desegration Monitoring Com., 1985—. Mem. Am. Assn. Coll. Tchr. Edn. (pres. 1988-89), Nat. Alliance Found. (chmn. 1984-85), Black Sch. Educators (edn. commn.). Home: 12737 Oakmont Dr Kansas City MO 64145-1140 Office: U Mo Sch Edn 5100 Rockhill Rd Kansas City MO 64110-2446

EUBANKS, OMER LAFAYETTE, data communications consultant, systems engineer; b. Atlanta, Nov. 28, 1956; s. Omer LaFayette and Frances (Dix) EuB.; m. Joy Kay Gantt, Nov. 15, 1979; children: Matthew Christopher, Timothy Mark. BS, Vanderbuilt U., 1979. Cert. computer profl., Ga. Sys. programmer U. Tenn., Nashville, 1978-79, Equifax, Inc., Atlanta, 1979-85; sr. sys. programmer Advanced Techs., Inc., Norcross, Ga., 1985-86; sr. comm. sys. programmer Atlanta Jour. Constitution, 1987-89; sys. programmer Suntrust Banks, Atlanta, 1989-90; sr. comm. analyst Life Ins. Co. of Ga., Atlanta, 1990-91; cons. Sys. Ctr., Inc., Reston, Va., 1991-93; cons. Corinthian Software, Marietta, Ga., 1987, North Fulton Healthcare Assn., Roswell, Ga., 1990-99, ISSC-Windward Tech. Ctr., 1994, AT&T Universal Card Svcs., 1994, WORLDSPAN, 1994-96, Advantis, 1996, IBM, 1997, GE Capital, 1997, Candle Corp., 1997—. Bd. dirs. Wills Park Youth Baseball Assn., 1995-96—; deacon Roswell First Bapt., 1989—, vice chair deacon bd., 1994, chmn. student minister search com., 1996, mem. future devel. com., 1991-94, chair, 1994, mem pers. com., 1995-98, vice chair, 1998. NSF grantee, 1974. Mem. NRA (patron), N.Am. Hunting Club (life), Pi Kappa Alpha. Baptist. Avocations: hunting, fishing, camping, baseball. Home: 355 Hickory Flat Rd Alpharetta GA 30004-2612

EUBANKS, RONALD W., lawyer, broadcaster; b. Montgomery, Ala., Sept. 17, 1946; s. William Shell and Violet Lavern (Walker) E.; 1 child, Edward Todd; m. Anna Shaw; stepdaughter, Jennifer Shaw. Student, Auburn U., 1964-65; BA, U. Ala., 1968; JD, U. Utah, 1974. Bar: Utah 1974, Nebr. 1979, Minn. 1983, Wash. 1985, U.S. Ct. Appeals (10th cir.) 1977, U.S. Ct. Appeals (8th cir.) 1979, U.S. Supreme Ct. 1977, U.S. Ct. Appeals (9th cir.) 1985. Gen. mgr. Sta. WVMI and Sta. WQID, Biloxi Gulfport, Miss., 1968-71; with FCC, Washington, 1974-75; assoc. Hansen & Hansen, Salt Lake City, 1975-77; with law dept. Union Pacific R.R., Omaha, 1977-83; asst. gen. counsel Burlington No. R.R. Co., St. Paul, 1983-84, gen. counsel western region, 1984-87; v.p. law and corp. affairs Glacier Park Co., 1987-88; exec. v.p. Ecos Corp., 1988; CEO Capital Comms., Montgomery, 1991-97; pres. ET Comms., Montgomery, 1988-97; sr. regional v.p. So. Star Comm., 1997—; dir. Camas Prairie R. R., Longview Switching Co. Co-author: Practical Law in Utah, 1978, Defense of Mary Carter, 1984; contbr. articles to profl. publs. Bd. dirs., mem. exec. com., legal counsel Utah Boys Ranch, Salt Lake City, 1977-79; bd. dirs. Children and Youth Svcs., Salt Lake City, 1977-84, Nebr. affiliate Am. Diabetes Assn., 1982-83, Greater Montgomery Sickle Cell Found., 1990—, Ala. Broadcasters Assn., 1998—; co-chmn. Montgomery Father and Son Banquet Com., 1993—; bd. dirs., mem. exec. com. Montgomery Mental Health Assn., 1995—, treas., 1996—; bd. dirs., mem. exec. com. Montgomery Area Coun. on Aging; bd. advisors, dept. comm. Ala. State U., 1995—. Recipient Friend of Youth award YMCA, 1993; named Role Model of Yr. Southlawn Sch., 1996-97. Mem. ABA (sect. on litigation, coms. on publs. and trial techniques, sect. on tort and ins. practice, com. on r.r. law), Washington State Bar Assn., Seattle-King County Bar Assn., Wash. R.R. Assn. (chmn. 1984-87), Def. Rsch. Inst. (chmn. com on r.r. law 1984-86, mem. com. on practice and procedure), Jason's Soc., Phi Alpha Delta, Alpha Tau Omega. Presbyterian. Home: 9750 Vaughn Rd Pike Road AL 36064-2751 Office: Capital Comm 648 Perry St Montgomery AL 36104

EULAU, HEINZ, political scientist, educator; b. Offenbach, Germany, Oct. 14, 1915; s. Arthur and Martha (Spier) E.; m. Cleo Mishkin, June 8, 1946; children—Lauren, Peter. A.B., U. Calif. at Berkeley, 1937, M.A., 1938, Ph.D., 1941. Research asso. Library of Congress, 1941-42; sr. analyst Spl. War Policies Unit, Dept. Justice, 1942-44; asst. editor New Republic, 1944-47; from asst. prof. to prof. Antioch Coll., 1947-57; prof. polit. sci. Stanford U., 1958-86, William Bennett Munro prof., 1973-86, prof. emeritus, 1986—; vis. legis. research prof. U. Calif. at Berkeley, 1961-62; vis. prof. Inst. Advanced Studies, Vienna, Austria, 1964-65; vis. prof. Erasmus U., Rotterdam, Netherlands, 1985; mem. behavioral sci. div. NRC, 1969-73; bd. overseers, chmn. Nat. Election Studies, 1977-84; assoc. dir. Inter-Univ. Consortium for Polit. and Social Research, 1978—. Author: Class and Party in the Eisenhower Years, 1962, The Legislative System, 1962, Journeys in Politics, 1963, The Behavioral Persuasion in Politics, 1963, Micro-Macro Political Analysis, 1969, Labyrinths of Democracy, 1973, Technology and Civility, 1977, The Politics of Representation, 1978, Politics, Self, and Society, 1986, Crossroads of Social Science, 1989, Micro-Macro Dilemmas in Political Science, 1996, The Politics of Academic Culture, 1998. Fund Advancement Edn. fellow, 1951-52; Center Advanced Study Behavioral Scis. fellow, 1957-58; Guggenheim Found. fellow, 1979-80. Fellow AAAS, Am. Acad. Arts and Scis.; mem. Am. Polit. Sci. Assn. (pres. 1971-72). Home: 753 Frenchmans Rd Palo Alto CA 94305-1004

EULE, NORMAN L., lawyer; b. Bklyn., Jan. 5, 1947; m. Ellen D. Luks, June 21, 1971; 1 child, Alex. BA in Polit. Sci. cum laude, Bklyn. Coll., 1968; JD with highest honors, George Washington U., 1974. Bar: D.C. 1974. Assoc. Pierson, Ball & Dowd, Washington, 1974-81, ptnr., 1981-89; ptnr. Reed, Smith, Shaw & McClay, 1989-94, Ridberg, Press & Sherbill, Bethesda, Md., 1995—; profl. lectr., Am. U./Wash. Coll. of Law; speaker and author tax, bus. and employee benefits matters. Mem. editl. bd. Taxation for Lawyers; contbr. articles to profl. jours. Pres. Congregation Beth El, Montgomery County, Md. Mem. ABA, Fed. Comm. Bar Assn., Bar Assn. of D.C., Bar Assn. of Md., Order of Coif. Office: Ste 650 Three Bethesda Metro Ctr Bethesda MD 20814

EULER, DIANA LEONE, nursing educator; b. Freeport, Ill., Jan. 5, 1945; d. Leroy Melvin and Virginia Mae (Thruman) Veer; m. Paul E. Euler, Jr., Feb. 18, 1963; children: Patrick James, Tawna Suzanne, Darin Allen. ADN, Western Wis. Tech. Coll., 1986; student, Viterbo Coll., La Crosse, Wis., 1984-85, 87, Winona State U., 1990-92. RN, Wis., Minn.; lic. vocat. tchr., Minn. Staff nurse acute care unit, charge nurse geriatric unit St. Mary's Hosp., Sparta, Wis., 1986-88; dir. nursing svcs. acute care and long term care Caledonia (Minn.) Health Care Ctr., 1988-89; quality improvement coord. Good Shepherd Luth. Home, Rushford, Minn., 1989-93; support nurse/edn. Bethany-St. Joseph, LaCrosse, Wis., 1993—. Home: Valley High Estates RR 2 Box 214 Houston MN 55943-9644

EURICH, NELL P., educator, author; b. Norwood, Ohio, July 28, 1919; d. Clayton W. and Adah (Palmer) Plopper; m. Alvin C. Eurich, Mar. 15, 1953 (dec. 1987); children: Juliet Ann, Donald Alan; m. Maurice Lazarus, 1988. AA, Stephens Coll., 1939; BA, Stanford U., 1941, MA, 1943; PhD, Columbia U., 1959. Dir. student union U. Tex., 1942-43; resident counselor Barnard Coll., 1944-46; asst. to pres. Woman's Found., 1947-49; officer charge pub. relations State U. N.Y., 1949- 52; acting pres. Stephens Coll., 1953-54; asst. prof. English NYU, 1959-64; academic dean New Coll., Sarasota, Fla., 1965; dir. project to reorganize curriculum Aspen (Colo.) Pub. High Sch., 1966; dean faculty, prof. English Vassar Coll., 1967-70; provost, dean faculty, prof. English, v.p. acad. affairs Manhattanville Coll., N.Y., 1971-75; sr. cons. Internat. Council for Ednl. Devel., 1975-82, Acad. for Ednl. Devel., 1982-88; mem. nat. selection com., chmn. Rocky Mountain regional com. Nat. Endowment Humanities, 1966-67, cons., 1970-71; mem. Middle States commn. Marshall Scholarships, 1967-68; chmn. Northeastern region, 1969-71; mem. U.S. Commn. on Ednl. Tech., HEW, 1968-69; mem. overseer's vis. com. on summer sch. and univ. extension Harvard, 1969-75; mem. panel of judge's Fed. Woman's award, 1969; cons. Acad. for Ednl. Devel., 1970-71; mem. career minister rev. bd. U.S. Dept. State, 1972; participant Ditchley Conf. V, 1973; mem. Rhodes Scholarship Selection Com., 1976; moderator exec. seminar Aspen Inst. for Humanistic Studies, 1977, 79, 80; dir. Adult Learning Project Carnegie Found. for Advancement Teaching, 1985-90; advisor Nat. Acad. of Engring., 1987-88; vis. com. Neuro Scis., Mass. Gen. Hosp. Author: Science in Utopia, 1967, Higher Education in Twelve Countries: A Comparative View, 1981, (with B. Schwenkmeyer) Great Britain's Open University, 1971, Corporate Classrooms, 1985, The Learning Industry, 1991; contbg. author: (Alvin Toffler) Learning for Tomorrow, 1974, From Parnassus: Essays for Jacques Barzun, 1976; contbr. articles to profl. jours. Past trustee Bank Street Coll., Salisbury Sch., Hudson Guild Neighborhood House, Colo. Rocky Mountain Sch., Bennington Coll., Carnegie Coun. on Policy Studies in Higher Edn., 1977-80, Carnegie Found. for Advancement Teaching, 1978-84; trustee New Coll. Found. Mem. MLA, Am. Assn. Colls. (spl. com. on liberal studies 1966-70), World Soc. Ekistics, Nat. Coun. Women (hon.), Century Assn. N.Y.C. Home: 144 Brattle St Cambridge MA 02138-2202

EURICH, RICHARD REX, lawyer; b. Lancaster, Pa., Apr. 12, 1947; s. Richard Roy and Mary Elizabeth (Kiehl) E.; m. JoAnn Samsa, June 27, 1970; 1 child, Richard. BA cum laude, Am. U., 1969; JD cum laude, Harvard U., 1972. Bar: Mass. 1972, U.S. Dist. Ct. Mass. 1973, U.S. Ct. Appeals (1st cir.) 1975. Assoc. Morrison, Mahoney and Miller, Boston, 1972-76, ptnr., 1976—. Elected Town Meeting Mem., Town of Lexington, 1996-99; mem. exec. bd. Lexington Town Meeting Mems. Assn., 1998-99. Fellow Mass. Bar Found.; mem. ABA, Mass. Bar Assn. (chmn. ins. com.), Def. Rsch. Inst., Mass. Def. Lawyers Assn., Internat. Assn. Def. Counsel. Roman Catholic. Home: 7 Pitcairn Pl Lexington MA 02421-7108 Office: Morrison Mahoney and Miller 250 Summer St Fl 1 Boston MA 02210-1181

EUSIBIO, RAUL ANTONIO, baseball player; b. San Jose, Dominican Rep., Apr. 27, 1967. Grad. H.S., Dominican Rep. Catcher Houston Astros, 1994—. Office: Houston Astros Astrodome PO Box 288 Houston TX 77001-0288*

EUSTER, JOANNE REED, retired librarian; b. Grants Pass, Oreg., Apr. 7, 1936; d. Robert Lewis and Mabel Louise (Jones) Reed; m. Stephen L. Gerhardt, May 14, 1977; children: Sharon L., Carol L., Lisa J. Student, Lewis and Clark Coll., 1953-56; BA, Portland State Coll., 1965; MLibrarianship, U. Wash., 1968, MBA, 1977; PhD, U. Calif.-Berkeley, 1986. Asst. libr. Edmonds Community Coll., Lynnwood, Wash., 1968-73, dir. libr.-media ctr., 1973-77; univ. libr. Loyola U. of New Orleans, 1977-80; libr. dir. J. Paul Leonard Libr., San Francisco State U., 1980-86; univ. libr. Rutgers State U. N.J., New Brunswick, 1986-89, v.p. info. svcs., 1989-91, v.p. univ. librs., 1991-92; univ. libr. U. Calif., Irvine, 1992-97; ret., 1997; cons. Coll. S.I., Union Ejidal, La Penita, Nayarit, Mexico, 1973, Univ. D.C., 1988; co-cons. Office of Mgmt. Svcs. Assn. of Rsch. Librs., 1979—; bd. regents, Kansas; mem. adv. coun. Hong Kong U. Sci. and Tech. Librs., 1988—, Princeton U. Libr., 1988-92, U. B.C., Can., 1991—. Author: Changing Patterns of Internal Communication in Large Academic Libraries, 1981, The Academic Library Director, Management Activities and Effectiveness, 1987; columnist Wilson Libr. Bull., 1993-95; contbr. articles to profl. jours. Mem. ALA, Calif. Libr. Assn., Assn. Coll. and Rsch. Librs. (pres. 1987-88), Rsch. Librs. Group (chmn. bd. dirs. 1991-92). Home: 7515 25th Ave NE Seattle WA 98115-4607

EUSTICE, DAVID C., pharmaceutical researcher; b. Wharton, N.J., Sept. 26, 1952; s. Clarence William and Helen (Hobbs) E.; m. Phylliss Paeth, Mar. 21, 1984 (div. Dec. 1994); children: Alexander, Shannon. BS, SUNY, Geneseo, 1974, MA, 1976; PhD, SUNY, Binghamton, 1980. Post doctoral fellow Dartmouth Med. Sch., Hanover, N.H., 1980-82, U. Rochester, N.Y., 1982-85; prin. investigator Dupont Co., Wilmington, Del., 1985-91; sr. rsch. investigator Bristol-Myers Squibb, Wallingford, Conn., 1991-94; sr. staff scientist Bayer Corp., West Haven, Conn., 1994—. Contbr. articles to sci. jours. Home: 58 Middle Rd Guilford CT 06437-1708

EUSTICE, JAMES SAMUEL, legal educator, lawyer; b. Chgo., June 9, 1932; s. Burt C. and Julia (Bohon) E.; m. LaVaun Schild, Jan. 29, 1956 (dec. 1994); m. Carol Fonda, Nov. 1995; children: Cynthia, James M. BS, U. Ill., 1954, LLB, 1956; LLM in Taxation, NYU, 1958. Bar: Ill., 1956, N.Y., 1958. Assoc. White & Case, N.Y.C., 1958-60; prof. law NYU, N.Y.C., 1960—; counsel Kronish Lieb, N.Y.C., 1970—. Mem. ABA, N.Y. State Bar Assn., Am. Coll. Tax Counsel, Order of Coif. Republican, Presbyterian. Club: University (N.Y.C.). Author: (with Bittker) Federal Income Taxation of Corporations and Shareholders, 1994, (with Kuntz) Federal Income Taxation of Subchapter S Corporations, 1993. Office: NYU Sch Law 40 Washington Sq S New York NY 10012-1005

EUSTICE, RUSSELL CLIFFORD, consulting company executive, academic director; b. Hackensack, N.J., July 11, 1919; s. Russell C. and Ethel (Hutchison) E.; m. Veronica B. Dabrowski, Mar. 14, 1946; children: Russell Clifford, David A., Paul M. BA, Colgate U., 1941; MBA, Am. U., 1973. With Vick Chem. Corp., N.Y.C., 1941-42, 46-47; with Johnson & Johnson, 1947-61, div. sales mgr., 1954-61; nat. sales mgr. Park & Tilford div. Schenley Affiliates, N.Y.C., 1961-62; pres. Mid-Atlantic Assos., Inc., Prospect Harbor, Maine, 1962—; dir. Small Bus. Inst., Husson Coll., Bangor, Maine, 1979-88, alt. regional rep. New England Region - Svc. Corps. Ret. Execs., SBA, 1991—; asst. prof. bus. adminstrn., 1979-88; part-time instr. mktg. The Am. U., Washington, 1970-74; active VISTA; bus. develop. specialist Washington-Hancock Community Agy., 1989. Capt. AUS, 1942-46. Mem. Assn. Mil. Surgeons, Res. Officers Assn., Assn. Mktg. Educators, SBA, Alpha Tau Omega. Republican. Presbyterian. Home: HC 35 Box 83E Gouldsboro ME 04607-9603 also: 427 N Cameron St Hillsborough NC 27278

EUSTIS, ALBERT ANTHONY, lawyer, diversified industry corporate executive; b. Mahanoy City, Pa., Nov. 8, 1921; m. Mary Hampton Stewart, Apr. 25, 1959; children: Thomas Stewart, David Anthony. B.S., Columbia U., 1948; LL.B., Harvard U., 1951. Bar: N.Y. 1952, U.S. Dist. Ct. (So. dist.) N.Y 1955. Atty. firm Kelley, Drye & Warren, N.Y.C., 1951-61; atty. W.R. Grace & Co., N.Y.C., 1961-66; asst. gen. counsel W.R. Grace & Co., 1966-76, v.p., gen. counsel, sec., 1976-78, sr. v.p., gen. counsel, sec., 1978-82, exec. v.p., gen. counsel, sec., 1982-87; of counsel Holland & Knight, Washington, 1987—; chmn. bd. trustees, spl. counsel Found. for President's Pvt. Sector Survey on Cost Control; adj. prof. law Fordham Law Sch. Served with AUS, 1942-46. Mem. ABA, Am. Arbitration Assn. (bd. dirs., comml. arbitration panel).

EUSTIS, RICHMOND MINOR, lawyer; b. New Orleans, Nov. 24, 1945; s. David and Molly Cox (Minor) E.; m. Catherine Luise Baños, Apr. 15, 1971; children: Richmond Minor Jr., Julie Bransford, Joshua Leeds, Molly Minor. BA in Econs., U. Va., 1967; JD, Tulane U., 1970. Bar: La. 1970. Assoc. Phelps Dunbar, New Orleans, 1970-75; ptnr. Monroe and Lemann, New Orleans, 1975-96; founder, ptnr. Eustis & O'Keefe, LLC, New Orleans, 1996—. Bd. dirs. Children's Bur., 1976-88, treas., 1984. Mem. ABA, La. Bar Assn., New Orleans Bar Assn. (chmn. torts and ins. com. 1992-95), Maritime Law Assn., S.E. Admiralty Law Inst., Boston Club, La. Club. Republican. Episcopalian. Avocation: fishing. Home: 289 Audubon St New Orleans LA 70118-4841 Office: Eustis & O'Keefe 228 Saint Charles Ave Ste 1010 New Orleans LA 70130-2686

EUSTIS, ROBERT HENRY, mechanical engineer; b. Mpls., Apr. 18, 1920; s. Ralph Warren and Florence Louise E.; m. Katherine Vik Johnson, Mar. 20, 1943; children—Jeffrey Nelson, Karen V. B.M.E., U. Minn., 1942, M.S., 1944; Sc.D., M.I.T., 1953. Instr. U. Minn., 1942-44; research scientist NASA, 1944-47; asst. prof. M.I.T., 1947-51; chief engr. Thermal Research and Engring. Corp., 1951-53; mgr. heat and mech. sect. S.R.I. Internat., 1953-55; mem. faculty dept. mech. engring. Stanford U., 1955-90, prof., 1962, dir. high temperature gasdynamics lab, 1961-80, assoc. dean engring., 1984-88; chmn. tech. adv. coun. Emerson Electric Corp.; prin Eustis Designs, 1990—. Contbr. articles to profl. jours. Recipient medal Soviet Sci. Acad., 1973. Fellow AIAA, ASME, AAAS; mem. Am. Soc. Engring. Edn. Home:

862 Lathrop Dr Palo Alto CA 94305-1053 Office: Stanford Univ Mech Engring Dept Stanford CA 94305

EUTSLER, MARK LESLIE, business services executive, real estate broker; b. Crawfordsville, Ind., May 17, 1958; s. David Lee and Lilian Agnus May (Grant) E., m. Therese Anne Wagner, Oct. 3, 1987. BS, Ind. State U., 1980; MS in Edn., Purdue U., 1984; postgrad., Butler U., 1985. Cert. life tchr., Ind. Broker, assoc. Eutsler Real Estate, Linden, Ind., 1977-86; sec., treas. DEW Advt. Corp., Linden, 1978—; music dir. Frontier Sch. Corp., Chalmers, Ind., 1980-83; band and music dir. McCutcheon High Sch., Lafayette, Ind., 1983-84; acting pub. health sanitarian Montgomery County Dept. Health, Safety and Environ. Mgmt., Crawfordsville, Ind., 1985; asst. editor Lafayette Bus. Digest, 1985-86; field rep. Cen. Ind. Regional Blood Ctr., Lafayette, 1986-87; cons. DEW Advt. Corp., Linden, Ind., 1987—; v.p. mktg. and devel. Wesley Manor Retirement Cmty., 1999—; bd. dirs. Hist. Linden, Inc. dba Railway Heritage Network, pres., 1986—; rep. Pub. Assistance Ind., Inc., Crawfordsville, 1984—; program mgr. Arts Ind. Mag. in the Classroom, 1995—. Contbr. articles to profl. jours. Sec., bd. dirs. John T. Conner Ctr. for U.S.-USSR Reconciliation, Inc., 1985—; mem. Ind. State Police Coun. Emergency Response Team; bd. dirs. U.S. Selective Svc., 1993—; mem. proficiency overview com. Ind. Dept. Edn., 1998—; co-chair bands com. 500 Festival Parade, 1996—; Fanfest/Mus. chair 500 Festival Cmty. Day, 1998—; chair family concerts bands com. 500 Festival, 1998—. Named to Hon. Order of Ky. Cols., Gov. of Ky., Frankfort, 1985; named Disting. Hoosier by Gov. Evan Bayh, 1989; recipient Meritorious Hoosier award Ind. Sec. of State, Indpls., 1985, Cmty. Svc. award Gov.'s Voluntary Action Program, 1996; named Hoosier Hero, U.S. Senator Dan Coats, 1997. Mem. New Richmond Coal Creek Twp. Hist. Soc. Inc. (pub. rels. dir. 1984-87), Crawfordsville-Montgomery County C. of C. (tourism brochure com.), Greater Lafayette C. of C. (ambassador 1985-87), Young Audiences Ind. Arts Ptnrs. (steering com. 1995—), Railway Heritage Network (founding prse. 1986—), Arts Coun. Indpls. Task Force, Ind. Arts Commn. (adv. panelist 1997), Masons. Methodist. Home: PO Box 61 Linden IN 47955-0061 Office: DEW Advt Corp 207 N Main St Linden IN 47955

EUTSLER, R(ALPH) KERN, retired bishop, church finance consultant; b. Bridgewater, Va.; s. Robert L. and Norah Lillian (Zepp) E.; m. Eva Rebecca Vines, Oct. 10, 1945; children: Rebecca Ann Eutsler Coulter, Mary Margaret Eutsler Abramson. BA, Berea Coll., 1940; MDiv, Union Theol. Sem., N.Y.C., 1943; DD (hon.), Randolph Macon Coll., 1963. Ordained to ministry Meth. Ch., 1943. Min. Meth. chs., Greenville, 1943-45, Elkton, 1945-49; min. Luray, Va., 1949-53, South Roanoke, Va., 1953-60; min. Ginter Park United Meth. Ch., Richmond, Va., 1960-65, Washington Street United Meth. Ch., Alexandria, Va., 1965-66; exec. dir. Va. Meth. Homes, 1966-73; supt. Alexandria dist. United Meth. Ch., 1973-78; min. Reveille United Meth. Ch., Richmond, 1978-82, interim sr. min., 1988-89; dir. Va. Conf. Coun. on Ministries, 1982-84; bishop Southeastern Jurisdiction, United Meth. Ch., Holston, Va., 1984-88; ret., 1988; dir. interpretation and promotion United Meth. Vols. in Mission, 1989; cons. in ch. fin. United Meth. Ch., Richmond, 1991—; held numerous positions on conf. and gen. ch. agys. United Meth. Ch., elected to every jurisdictional and gen. conf., 1964-88. Address: United Meth Ch 10709 Sydelle Dr Richmond VA 23235-3323

EVAN, WILLIAM MARTIN, sociologist, educator; b. Ostrow, Poland, Dec. 17, 1922. BA, U. Pa., 1946; PhD, Cornell U., 1954. Instr. sociology Princeton U., 1954-56; asst. prof. Columbia U., 1956-59; research sociologist Bell Telephone Labs., Murray Hill, N.J., 1959-62; assoc. prof. sociology and mgmt. MIT, 1962-66; prof. U. Pa., Phila., 1966—; cons. to govt. agys. and pvt. industry, 1960—; Ford vis. prof. sociology Grad. Sch. Bus., U. Chgo., 1971-72; vis. fellow Wolfson Coll., U. Oxford, 1978-79. Author: (with others) Preventing World War III, 1962, Law and Sociology, 1962, Organizational Experiments, 1971, Interorganizational Relations, 1976, Organization Theory, 1976, Frontiers in Organization and Management, 1980, The Sociology of Law, 1980, Knowledge and Power in a Global Society, 1981, The Arms Race and Nuclear War, 1987, Social Structure and Law, 1990, Organization Theory: Research and Design, 1993, (with Ved P. Nanda) Nuclear Proliferation and the Legality of Nuclear Weapons, 1995. Social Sci. Rsch. Coun. tng. fellow, 1951-52, Fulbright fellow, 1952-53; Russell Sage Found. resident, 1956-58. Fellow AAAS; mem. Am. Sociol. Assn., Internat. Sociol. Assn., Internat. Inst. Mgmt. Scis., Law and Soc. Assn., Internat. Studies Assn. Clubs: U. Pa. Faculty, Phila. Art Alliance. Home: 311 South Smedley St Philadelphia PA 19103-6717 Office: Dept Sociology and Dept Mgmt Univ Pa Philadelphia PA 19104

EVANGELISTA, ALLAN, clergy member, medical researcher; b. Quezon City, Manila, The Philippines, June 23, 1970; arrived in U.S., 1990.; s. Go Guan and Ana Evangelista. BA in Biology, U. La Verne, Calif., 1991; MDiv in Family, Pastoral Care and Counseling, Fuller Theological Seminary, Calif., 1996; MPH (Master Pub. Health) in rsch., Loma Linda U., Calif., 1998—; DPM (Doctor of Podiatric Med.), Temple U. Sch. of Podiatric Med., Phila., PA. Ordained and lic. Evangelical minister. Supr., administrv. asst. D. G. Engering. Works, Butuan City, The Philippines, 1988-90; host, server, cashier Coco's Bakery & Family Restaurant, Pomona, Calif., 1991-92; tchg. asst. U. La Verne, Calif., 1991; project supr., computer graphic designer Interior Corner, Monterey Park, Calif., 1992-93; inter library loan processor Fuller Seminary Libr., Pasadena, Calif., 1995-96; assoc. pastor New Life Christian Ctr., El Monte, Calif., 1992—; rsch. assoc. USC Cardiovascular Lab, L.A., Calif., 1993—; fin. investment analyst, San Gabriel, Calif., 1993—; fin. trustee New Life Christian Ctr., El Monte, Calif., 1994—, pastoral care/marriage counselor First Assembly of God Ch., El Monte, Calif., 1994—. Contbr. to professional medical jours. Vol. San Gabriel Valley Med. Ctr., Calif., 1992; med. outreach coord. First Assembly of God Ch., El Monte, Calif., 1994—; youth pastoring/bible tchr. Christian Reform Ch., West Covina, Calif., 1995—; chaplain UCLA Med. Ctr., Westwood, Calif., 1996. Recipient Ednl. Excellence award Alpha Kappa Alpha, Chgo., 1995; Harding Found. scholar, 1995-96, Fuller Theological Seminary scholar, 1995-96. Mem. Am. Fedn. Med. Rsch. (trainee investigator award 1994), Am. Assn. Adv. Sci., Am. Counseling Assn., Internat. Assn. Marriage & Family Counselors, Amer. Podiatric Med. Assn., 1998—, Amer. Heart Assn., rsch. counc., 1999—, Amer. Pub health Assn., 1999—, Amer. Diabetes Assn., 1999—. Avocations: basketball, swimming, drawing, acting, modelling. Home: # 307 801 Cherry St Philadelphia PA 19107

EVANGELISTA, ANITA LORETTA, freelance writer, emergency medical technician, nurse; b. L.A., Nov. 9, 1952; d. Carl A. and Etta L. (Erickson) Anderson; m. Nick F. Evangelista, 1979; children: Jamie, Justin. Student, Pepperdine U., 1970-71, U. So. Calif., 1972, S.W. Mo. State U., West Plains and Springfield, 1995—. RN; lic. EMT; cert. clin. hypnotherapist. Asst. to dir. internat. fin. Max Factor, L.A., 1972-73; asst. to 2d mgr. steel dept. Sumitomo Shoji, L.A., 1973-75; freelance writer, 1975—; columnist Mo. Farm Mag., Clark, 1984-87; adminstr. West Plains (Mo.) Coun. on Arts, 1986-91; editor Ranch Dog Trainer mag., West Plains, 1990-92; spkr., lectr. Mid West Hypnosis Conv., Chgo., 1983; cons. film dir. R. Wise, Hollywood, Calif., 1977. Author: Hypnosis-A Journey into the Mind, 1980, Dictionary of Hypnotism, 1991, How to Develop a Low-Cost Family Food Storage System, 1995, How To Live Without Electricity and Like It, 1997, Backyard Meat Production, 1997, How To Survive Moving Back to the Land, 1999; indexer: Tikkum Olam, 1996; contbr. articles to mags., periodicals including Mother Earth News, Sci. Digest, Reason, Chronicles, Backwoods Home, Small Farmers Jour., Practical Farmer of Iowa, Fate, Maine Organic Gardner, Dairy Goat Jour., numerous others. Vol. Ozark Med. Ctr., West Plains, 1995-98. Recipient TZ 1st prize Twilight Zone Mag., 1989, 1st place Fine Arts Heart of the Ozarks Fair, 1989. Mem. Am. Soc. Psychical Rsch., Calif. Profl. Hypnotist Assn. (chpt. pres. L.A. 1976-82), Internat. Assn. Clin. Hypnotherapists, Phi Theta Kappa. E-mail: ale@townsqr.com.

EVANGELISTA, PAULA LEE, public affairs administrator; b. N.Y.C., Sept. 16, 1955; d. Frank Marino and Mary Louise (Denning) E. BA in History and Creative Writing, Carnegie Mellon U., 1977. Mgr. pub. policy and comm. Hoffmann-La Roche Inc., Nutley, N.J., 1986-90, asst. dir., 1990-92, dir. pub. affairs, 1992—. Bd. dirs. Soc. Progressive Supranuclear Palsy, Balt., 1990—; bd. dirs., trustee Boys and Girls Club, Clifton, N.J., 1991-92. Democrat. Roman Catholic. Avocations: golfing, piano, hiking.

EVANKO, PAUL J., commissioner, colonel Pennsylvania state police; b. Gettysburg, Pa., Oct. 20, 1947. BS in Edn., Millersville U.; BS in Police Scis., York Coll. of Pa.; postgrad. studies in Pub. Adminstrn., U. Balt., 1974; grad., FBI Acad., 1987. Enlisted Pa. State Police, Harrisburg, 1970; state trooper Troop H. Pa. State Police, York, 1970-72; corp., officer in charge organized crime task force troop H Pa. State Police, Harrisburg, 1977-84, sgt., supr. organized crime task force, troop H, 1985-86; lieut., cmdr. patrol sect. Troop J Pa. State Police, Lancaster, 1985-86, cmdr. criminal investigation sect. Troop J., 1986-88; capt., dir. drug law enforcement divsn., bur. criminal investigation Pa. Office of Atty. Gen., Harrisburg, 1988-91; major, dir. bur. profl. responsibility Pa. State Police, Harrisburg, 1991-92, colonel, dir. bur. criminal investigation, 1992-95, appointed commr., 1995—; speaker at FBI Leadership Forum, Mid Atlantic Great Lakes Organized Crime Law Enforcement Network, Coalition of Pa. Crime Victims Orgns., various Pa. agencies, veterans orgns., colls., high schs. Mem. Mid Atlantic Govs. Regional Planning Com. on Drugs, Gov.'s Partnership for Safe Children, Pa. Commn. on Crime and Delinquency, Pa. Emergency Mgmt. Coun.; exec. bd. mem. Mcpl. Police Officers Edn. and Tng Commn.; adv. bd. mem. Pa. State Inst. for Non-Lethal Defense Techniques. Recipient Am. Legion award for outstanding police acad. cadet, 1970, Citation for Vice Work, 1975, Outstanding Contbns. award U.S. Dept. Justice Drug Enforcement Adminstrn., 1978, Cert. of award for exceptional activity against organized crime, Daupin County, 1981, Pro Patris award, Sec. Defense, 1997, Humanitarian award, The Chapel of Four Chaplains, 1997, Law Enforcement Commendation medal, Nat. Soc. SAR, 1998, Pa. Meritorious Svc. medal, State of Pa., 1998; named Law Enforcement Officer of Yr., Am. Soc. for Indsl. Security, 1981. Mem. Internat. Assn. Chiefs of Police (chmn. N. Atlantic region state and provincial divsn., liason to nat. alliance state drug enforcement agys., policy bd. mem. police exchange program, guest speaker), Internat. Narcotic Enforcement Officers Assn., Nat. Alliance of State Drug Enforcement Agys., Pa. Narcotic Officers Assn. (founder, past pres.), Pa. Chiefs of Police Assn. Home: 1131 Elizabeth Ct Harrisburg PA 17112 Office: State Police Commr 1800 Elemerton Ave Harrisburg PA 17110

EVANOFF, GEORGE C., retired business executive; b. W. Deer, Pa., June 5, 1931; s. Christ and Luba (Georgieff) E.; m. Mary E. Yelavich, Nov. 21, 1964; 1 son, Michael. BS cum laude, U. Detroit, 1952, MBA, 1956. Engr. Gen. Motors Corp., Detroit, 1953-57; supervisory, mgmt. and exec. positions in sales, marketing, and product devel. Ford Motor Co., Dearborn, Mich., 1957-68; staff v.p. mktg., v.p. corporate planning, v.p. corporate devel. RCA Corp., N.Y.C., 1968-76; with Norton Simon, Inc., Los Angeles and New York, 1977-82; v.p. corp. planning, interim pres. Max Factor & Co., 1977-78; pres. Max Factor Internat., 1979-82; pres., chief exec. officer Cordura Publs., Inc., San Diego, 1984-86; mgmt. cons., 1987-88; pres., chief exec. officer Tago, Inc., Burlingame, Calif., 1989-92; ind. cons., pvt. investor, 1993-96. Served with USAF, 1952-53. Roman Catholic.

EVANOFSKI, BERNARD PETER, Roman Catholic priest; b. Wilkes-Barre, Pa., June 18, 1948; s. Peter Thomas and Margaret Ann (Wilk) E. BA, Wilkes U., 1970; MA, Temple U., 1972; MDiv, Pope John XIII Sem., Weston, Mass., 1986. Cert. sch. psychologist, Pa.; ordained priest, 1986. Psychologist Elwyn (Pa.) Inst., 1971-72, White Haven (Pa.) Ctr., 1972-75, Luzerne Intermediate Unit, Kingston, Pa., 1976-82; asst. pastor St. Mary's Ch., Dickson City, Pa., 1986-92; pastor St. Patrick's Ch., Nicholson, Pa., 1992-96, St. Anthony's Ch., Larksville, Pa., 1996—; auditor Scranton (Pa.) Diocesan Tribunal, 1987—. Pres. Jr. Kosciuszko Assn., Wilkes-Barre, 1976-82. Mem. Polish Am. Congress (rec. sec. 1976-82), KC (2d degree 1997). Democrat. Roman Catholic. Avocations: travel, swimming, fitness. Home and Office: 1 Wilson St Kingston PA 18704-1521

EVANS, ALAN GEORGE, electrical engineer; b. Upland, Pa., June 8, 1942; s. Thomas Leslie and Jennie E.; m. Barbara Lee Kilhefner, June 26, 1965; children: Christopher Alan, Jennifer Lee. BSEE, Widener U., 1964; MSEE, Drexel U., 1967, PhD, 1972. Asst. engr. Phila. Electric Co., 1964-70; computation analyst Material Scis. Corp., Blue Bell, Pa., 1970-72; tchg. asst. Drexel U., Phila., 1965-72; assoc. engr. Calspan Corp., Cheektawaga, N.Y., 1972-74; asst. prof. U.S. Naval Acad., Annapolis, Md., 1983-84; electronic engr. Naval Surface Warfare Ctr., Dahlgren, Va., 1974—; symposium tech. com. Inst. Navigation, Alexandria, Va., 1974—; mem. U.S. Def. Mapping Agy., Arlington, Va., 1986-92, U.S. Nat. Geodetic Survey, Rockville, Md., 1985. Contbr. articles to profl. jours. Sec. Sch. Adv. Coun., LaPlata, Md., 1984-91; asst. leader 4-H, LaPlata, 1982-89; active parent bd. U. Del., 1994-95. Recipient R&D award U.S. Def. Mapping Agy., 1988, Disting. Alumni award Chichester H.S., Pa., 1986, fellowship and teaching assistantship Drexel U., 1965-71. Fellow Internat. Assn. Geodesy (spl. study group 1986—); mem. IEEE, Inst. Navigation (bd. dirs. coun. 1996-97, exec. com. internat. satellite tech. conf. 1996-98), Sigma Xi. Republican. Achievements include patents in field; rsch. in the application of global positioning system satellites in area of relative positioning, in signal multipath, signal processing, receiver devel. and geodetic measurements. Home: 7455 Woodhaven Dr La Plata MD 20646-4008 Office: Naval Surface Warfare Ctr 17320 Dahlgren Rd Dahlgren VA 22448-5150

EVANS, ALFRED LEE, JR., advertising executive; b. Kansas City, Mo., Sept. 16, 1940; s. Alfred Lee and Laura Edith (Redman) E.; m. Jean Perpetua Corcoran, Aug. 29, 1970 (div. Mar. 1994); children: Amanda Corcoran, Cynthia Redman, Cassandra Lee, Nicholas Carpenter; m. Georgiana Coyle Mundy, July 9, 1994. BA, Princeton U., 1962. Account exec. Ted Bates & Co., N.Y.C., 1963-66, Papert Koenig Lois Inc., N.Y.C., 1967-68; v.p. account supr. Lois Holland Callaway, Inc., N.Y.C., 1969-74, v.p. mgmt. supr., 1975, sr. v.p. mgmt. supr., 1976; sr. v.p. mgmt. supr. Norman Craig & Kummel, N.Y.C., 1977-80; sr. v.p. mgmt. supr. Laurence, Charles, Free & Lawson, N.Y.C., 1981-84, 85—, exec. v.p., mem. ops., 1988-95, mem. bd. dirs.; sr. v.p. Partners & Shevack, Inc., N.Y.C., 1995—. Recipient summer travel award Carnegie Found., 1960; scholar Princeton U., 1958-62. Mem. Saltaire Yacht Club (N.Y.). Episcopalian. Avocations: Am. history, tennis, platform tennis. Home: 1530 Palisade Ave Fort Lee NJ 07024-5470 Home (summer): 104 Marine Walk Saltaire Fire Island NY 11781 Office: Partners & Shevack Inc 1211 Avenue Of The Americas New York NY 10036-8701

EVANS, ANTHONY GLYN, materials scientist; b. Porthcawl, Eng., Dec. 4, 1942; came to U.S., 1967; BSc, U. London, Eng., 1964, PhD in Metallurgy, 1967. Ceramics project leader Atomic Energy Rsch. Establishment, N.Y.C., 1967-71, Nat. Bur. Standards, Washington, 1971-74; group leader Rockwell Sci. Ctr., 1974-78; prof. materials sci. and mineral engring. U. Calif., Berkeley, 1978-85, Alcoa prof. and chair materials dept., 1985-91; Alcoa prof. and co-dir. materials high perf. composite ctr. U. Calif., Santa Barbara, 1985-94; Gordon McKay prof. materials engring., divsn. applied sci. Harvard U., Cambridge, Mass., 1994-98; dir. Princeton (N.J.) U. Materials Inst., 1998—; cons. and mem. Materials Rsch. Coun., 1974—; mem. Nat. Materials Adv. Bd., 1976—. Contbr. over 380 articles to profl. jours. Recipient Richard M. Fulrath award 1979, Robert Sosman award 1980, Hobart N. Kraner award, 1986, John Jepson medal 1988, Griffith medal and prize, Inst. of Materials, Eng., 1994; named Van Horne Disting. Lectr., Case Western Reserve U., 1980, Materials Rsch. Lectr., Clyde Disting. Prof., U. Utah, 1984, Materials Rsch. Lectr., Harvard U., 1986, Orton Lectr., 1988, Hon. fellow Internat. Congress Fracture, 1993. Mem. Nat. Acad. Engring., Am. Ceramic Soc. (v.p. 1984—, Ross Coffin Purdy award 1974). Achievements include contributions to knowledge of mechanical properties of brittle materials, particularly fracture of ceramics under conditions of impact, thermal and mechanical stress; failure prediction based on non-destructive evaluation; properties of thin films and multilayer materials. Office: Harvard U Dept Materials Sci 29 Oxford St Cambridge MA 02138-2901*

EVANS, ANTHONY HOWARD, university president; b. Clay County, Ark., Sept. 24, 1936; s. William Raymond and Thelma Fay (Crews) E.; m. Lois Fay Kirkham, Aug. 29, 1959. BA, East Tex. Bapt. Coll., Marshall, 1959; MA, U. Hawaii, 1961; PhD, U. Calif.-Berkeley, 1966. Program officer Peace Corps, Seoul, Korea, 1970-72; chief program planning Peace Corps, Washington, 1972-73, dir. planning office, 1973-75; asst. to pres. Eastern Mich. U., Ypsilanti, 1975-76, exec. v.p., 1976-79, acting pres., 1978-79, provost, v.p. acad. affairs, 1979-82; pres. Calif. State U., San Bernardino, 1982-97; trustee prof. Calif. State U., San Marcos, 1997—. Mem. Orgn. Am. Historians, Phi Kappa Phi. Home: 707 S Live Oak Park Rd Fallbrook CA 92028-3683

EVANS, ARTHUR FORTE, real estate developer; b. Augusta, Ga., Dec. 23, 1957; s. Arthur Forte Jr. and Mary Lou (Nelson) E. Student, Mercer U., 1976-78. Broker Evans Butler Realty, Melbourne, Fla., 1978—; land developer Forte Macaulay Devel. Co. Inc., Melbourne, 1985—; securities broker Sand Dollar Securities, Melbourne, 1988—; founder Metro Devel. Co. Inc., 1993; pres. Harp Holding Co., Inc., TLDC, Inc., Willows II Devel. Co. Inc., Baymeadows Devel. Co. Inc., Saw Grass Devel. Co., Wilson Ridge Devel. Co., Sheridan Lakes Devel. Co., Eagle Lake Devel Co.; bd. dirs. Colonial Bank;. Bd. dirs. Boy Scouts Am. Mem. Melbourne Area Bd. Realtors, Home Builders and Contractors Assn. (bd. dirs.), Melbourne C. of C., Melbourne Hunting and Fishing Club. Republican. Methodist. Avocations: hunting, fishing, sports, theatre, music. Office: Forte Maculay Devel Co Inc 1688 W Hibiscus Blvd Melbourne FL 32901-2631

EVANS, ARTHUR HAINES, JR., educational consultant, researcher; b. Mount Holly, N.J., Apr. 25, 1940; s. Arthur Haines and Betty Ogden (Dougherty) E.; m. Gay Dell Goodwin, Aug. 13, 1967; children: Kristna Jan, Ross Neil. AB cum laude, Princeton U., 1962; MBA, Stanford U., 1964; PhD in Higher Edn., U. Calif., Berkeley, 1970. Cert. cmty. supt., adminstr. and tchr., Calif. Bus. instr. City Coll. San Francisco, 1964-70; assoc. dean instrn. West Hills Coll., Coalinga, Calif., 1970-74; assoc. project dir. Pima C.C., Tucson, 1974-75, asst. to dean, 1975-79, asst. to pres., 1979-91; field faculty No. Ariz. U., Tucson, 1991—; pres. Evans and Assocs., Tucson, 1991—; rsch. cons. Pima County Interfaith Coun., Tucson, 1991-97; rsch. and evaluation coord. Ariz. Interfaith Network, 1998—. Bd. mem. Soc. for Coll. and Univ. Planning, 1977-79, United Way Greater Tucson, 1987-90; pres. Tucson Trade Bur., 1987-90, Tucson Almaty Sister Cities, 1990-92; founding pres. United Way of Ariz., 1989-90; mem. Common Govt. Rels. Coun. for Advancement of Edn., 1990-92. Kellogg fellow U. Calif., Berkeley, 1969. Methodist. Avocations: swimming, bicycling, hiking, traveling. Office: Evans and Assocs PO Box 43693 Tucson AZ 85733-3693

EVANS, AUDREY ELIZABETH, physician, educator; b. York, Eng., Mar. 6, 1925; came to U.S., 1957, naturalized, 1962; d. Leonard Llewellyn and Phyllis Mary (Miller) E. Licentiate Sch. Medicine, Royal Coll. Surgeons, Edinburgh, 1950. Intern Royal Infirmary, Edinburgh, 1950-52; physician tumor therapy Children's Hosp., Boston, 1957-65; instr. pediatrics Harvard U. Med. Sch., 1961-65; asst. prof. pediatric hematologist U. Chgo., 1965-69; prof. pediatrics U. Pa., 1969—; dir. oncology Children's Hosp., Phila., 1969-89. Home: 2010 Spruce St Philadelphia PA 19103-6569 Office: Children's Hosp ARB 902 324 S 34th St Philadelphia PA 19104-4399

EVANS, BARRY CRAIG, financial services company exexutive; b. Cin., Dec. 12, 1944; s. Tracy Warren and Dorothy N. (Burton) E.; m. Judith R. Jacobs, Apr. 28, 1984. BS in Bus., Miami U., Oxford, Ohio, 1967. CLU. Ptnr. Evans & Co., Cin., 1971-81; dir. agt. devel., dir. advanced underwriting Mass. Mut. Life Ins. Co., Cin., 1980-83; br. office mgr. Office Supervisory Jurisdiction Mut. Svc. Corp., Cin., 1982-89, Fahnestock & Co., Inc., Cin., 1991-98; assoc. gen. agt. Cen. Life Assurance Co., Cin., 1989-92; chmn., pres., CEO Evans Fin. Group, Cin., 1983—; pres. Cin. Fin. Cons., Inc., 1980-98; registered prin., br. mgr. Raymond James Fin. Svcs., Inc., 1998—. Apptd. bd. dirs. Cin. State Tech. and C.C., 1995-98; mem. ACS Heritage League; chmn.-bd. dirs. Linton Chamber Music Series, 1998—, Cin. Choral Soc., 1982-84; bd. dirs. Sch. Lay Ministry Ch., 1988-89, co-chmn. fund raising com. bldg. expansion, 1990-91, chmn. bldg. expansion com., 1989-91; mem., Hyde Park Cmty. United Methodist Ch., Ch. coun., co-chmn. Congregational Care Commn.; mem. The Taft Mus. 60th Anniversary Com., 1991-92; mem. exec. com./trustee Am. Cancer Soc., Hamilton County unit, trustee Ohio Divsn.; bd. dirs., chmn. planned and major gifts com.; bd. dirs. Cin. State Tech. and C. of C. Found., 1996-98; trustee Cin. State Found., 1996-98; bd. dirs. Tin Foor Found. Capt. USAF, 1967-71, Vietnam. Decorated Bronze Star, Air Force Commendation medal. Mem. Soc. Fin. Svc. Profls. (pres. Cin. chpt. 1987-88), Chamber Music Am., Am. Coll. CLU/ChFC Golden Key Soc. (benefactur), Internat. Assn. Fin. Planning (pres. Cin. chpt. 1987-88), Nat. Assn. Life Underwriters, Million Dollar Round Table (life), Cin. Estate Planning Coun. (pres. 1988-89), Cin. C. of C., Bankers Club (life, chmn. emeritus bd. govs.), Pres. Club Miami Univ. (Oxford, Ohio), Trout Unltd., Ducks Unltd., Fedn. Fly Fishers (life), Buckeye United Fly Fishers, Ohio Gun Collectors Assn. (life), NRA (life), Fairfield Sportsmen's Assn., Milford Gun Club, Box 13 Assocs. (fire divsn. Cin.). Republican. Avocations: fly fishing, woodworking, cello, skeet shooting, photography. Office: Evans Fin Group 414 Walnut St Ste 1205 Cincinnati OH 45202-3906

EVANS, BARTON, JR., analytical instrument company executive; b. Washington, Dec. 11, 1947; s. Barton and Viola (Gompf) E.; m. Harriet Andrea Neves, Nov. 20, 1983. B.A. in Econ., Claremont McKenna Coll., 1970; B.S. in Engring., Stanford U., 1972, M.S. in Engring., 1972. Sr. engr. Lockheed Missiles and Space Co., Sunnyvale, Calif., 1976-77; sr. engr. Dionex Corp., Sunnyvale, 1977-79, engring. mgr., 1979-81, dir. engring., 1981-83, v.p. engring., 1983-84, v.p. ops., 1984-93, sr. v.p., 1993—. Co-inventor conductivity detector. 1st lt. U.S. Army, 1972-75; col. USAR, 1976—. Mem. ASME, Civil Affairs Assn., PSYOP Assn., Assn. U.S. Army, Res. Officers Assn. Office: Dionex Corp 541 Lakeside Dr Sunnyvale CA 94086-4003*

EVANS, BERNARD WILLIAM, geologist, educator; b. London, July 16, 1934; came to U.S., 1961, naturalized, 1977; s. Albert Edward and Marjorie (Jordan) E.; m. Sheila Campbell Nolan, Nov. 19, 1962. BSc, U. London, 1955; PhD, Oxford U., Eng., 1959. Asst. U. Glasgow, Scotland, 1958-59; departmental demonstrator U. Oxford, 1959-61; asst. research prof. U. Calif., Berkeley, 1961-65; asst. prof. U. Calif., 1965-66, assoc. prof., 1966-69; prof. geology U. Wash., Seattle, 1969—; chmn. dept. geol. scis. U. Wash., 1974-79. Contbr. articles to profl. jours. Recipient U.S. Sr. Scientist award Humboldt Found., Fed. Republic Germany, 1988-89; Fulbright travel award, France, 1995-96. Fellow Geol. Soc. Am., Mineral Soc. Am. (pres. 1993-94, award 1970), Geochem. Soc., Geol. Soc. London, Mineral. Soc. Gt. Britain, Swiss Mineral. Soc. Home: 8001 Sand Point Way NE Apt 55C Seattle WA 98115-6399 Office: U Wash Dept Geol Scis PO Box 351310 Seattle WA 98195-1310

EVANS, BILL (JAMES WILLIAM EVANS), dancer, choreographer, educator, arts administrator; b. Lehi, Utah, Apr. 11, 1940; s. William Ferdinand and Lila (Snape) E.; married, Aug. 27, 1962 (div. 1965); 1 child, Thais. BA in English, U. Utah, 1963, MFA in Modern Dance, 1970; dance student various pvt. dance schs. and studios; cert. in laban and bartenieff, U. Utah, 1997. Apprentice Harkness Ballet Co., N.Y.C., 1966; mem. Chgo. Ballet and Lyric Opera Ballet, 1966-67; teaching asst. dept. ballet and modern dance U. Utah, 1967-68, faculty Virginia Tanner Creative Dance Program, 1968-73, asst. prof. modern dance, 1974-76, dancer, tchr., choreographer, artistic coordinator, mem. Repertory Dance Theatre, 1967-74; artistic dir. Dance Theatre Seattle, 1976-83; artistic dir., resident tchr., choreographer Winnipeg's Contemporary Dancers, Man., Can., 1983-84; assoc. prof., coord. dance program dept. kinesiology Ind. U., Bloomington, 1986-87, 87-88, artistic dir. Ind. Dance Theatre, 1986-88; head dance program dept. theatre and dance U. N.Mex., Albuquerque, 1988-93; prof. dance, 1993—; artistic dir. univ. Contemporary Dance Ensemble U. N.Mex., Albuquerque, 1989-93, dir., founder Univ. Youth Dance Camp, 1990, dir., founder Magnificio Youth Dance Groups, 1991-96; artistic dir. Bill Evans Dance Co., toured U.S., Europe, Mex. 1975-99; Bill Evans Summer Insts. of Dance and Summer Festivals of Dance, Bill Evans Solo Dance Repertory, 1976—, Bill Evans Dance Co. Sch., Seattle; vis. prof. dance div. U. Wash., 1976-81; artistic advisor Fairmount Dance Theatre, Cleve., 1974-75; guest artist in residence Dance Dept., U. Utah; artist in resident Ill. U., Harvard U. Summer Sch., choreographer in residence Repertory Dance Theater; dir., choreographer N.Mex. Repertory Theatre, Santa Fe and Albuquerque; mem. Artists in Edn. Bank, Utah arts council; dance/movement specialist Artist-in-Schs. program Nat. Endowment for Arts; founder, dir. Celebrate Youth Summer Dance Inst., 1993-98; artistic coord. SW Am. Coll. Dance Festival, 1994; guest artist Kala Chhaya Cultural Ctr., India, 1993—; toured Karnataka, Maharastra, India. Free-lance dancer, 1969—, including Berlin Ballet, 1969, Jacob's Pillow Dance Festival, Lee, Mass., 1973, Harvard U., 1973, 74, 90; choreographer over 170 works for various ballet and modern dance cos., 1967—; mem. editl. bd. Dance Connections, 1997. Am. Arts Alliance rep. before House and Senate appropriations coms., 1979. Served as officer U.S. Army, 1963-65. Recipient various choreographic awards, grants and fellowships from Nat. Endowment for Arts, 1972-75, 77-83, Utah Bicentennial Com., 1976, Art Found., Western States Arts Fedn., Wash. Arts Commn., King County Arts Commn., Seattle Arts Commn., Man. Arts Council, Ind. Arts Commn., N.Mex. Arts Div., U. N.Mex. Found., U. N.Mex. Coll. Fine Arts, Ind. U., Multidisciplinary Ventures Fund, U. N.Mex. Rsch. Allocations Com., City of Albuquerque, BRAVO award Albuquerque Arts Alliance, 1997; Guggenheim fellow, 1976-77, Am. Coll. Dance Fest., regional awards, 1986,87, 89-90, nat., 1986, 90; recipient Teaching Plaudit award nat. Dance Assn., 1981, scholar artist, 1997; named adjudicator and guest artist 1st Nat. Ballet Festival Regional Dance Am., 1997-99. Mem. Dancers, Inc. (adv. bd.), Nat. Dance Assn. (chair performance divsn. 1993—), Am. Coll. Dance Festival Assn. (bd. dirs. 1992—, U.S. rep. 1st internat. coll. dance festival Japan 1993). E-mail: beran@unm.edu. Office: U NM Dance Program Ctr for the Arts Dance Program Fine Art Ctr Albuquerque NM 87131

EVANS, BOB OVERTON, electronics executive; b. Grand Island, Nebr., Aug. 19, 1927; s. Walter Bernard and Lillian (Overton) E.; m. Maria Bowman, Nov. 19, 1949; children: Cathleen L., Robert W., David D., Douglas B. B.E.E., Iowa State U., 1949. Electric operating engr. No. Ind. Pub. Service Co., Hammond, 1949-51; with IBM, 1951-84, v.p. devel. Data Systems div., 1962-64, pres. Fed. Systems div., 1965-69, pres. Systems Devel. div., 1970-74, pres. Systems Communication div., 1975-77; v.p. IBM engring., programming and tech., 1977-84; ptnr. Hambrecht and Quist, 1984-88; pres. Vanguard Internat. Semi-conductor Corp., 1995-96; mng. ptnr. Tech. Strategies and Alliances, Menlo Park, Calif., 1989—; chmn. Foothill Research, Inc., 1984-85; pres., CEO Interactive Voice Systems, Monrovia, Calif., 1997-99; chmn. Cambridge Tech. Group, Tysons Corners, Va., 1999—; pres., CEO Ridge Computers Inc., 1986-88; mem. Stark Draper Labs., Inc., Def. Sci. Bd.; mem. area bd. dirs. Md. Nat. Bank; cons. govt. agys.; bd. dirs. Santa Barbara Labs., Integrated CMOS Sys., Inc., V Mark Software, Cullinet Software, Micrognosis, Inc., Athena Sys., Planning Rsch. Corp., Cambridge Rsch. Assocs.; mem. bd. overseers Superconductivity Super Collider, 1991-93. Mem. exec. bd. Nat. Capital Area coun. Boy Scouts Am., 1967-69; trustee Rensselaer Poly. Inst., 1972-84, N.Y. Pub. Libr., 1980-84; mem. elec. engring. vis. com. MIT, Cambridge, 1971-85. Lt. (j.g.) USNR, 1945-46. Recipient Disting. Pub. Svc. award NASA; Disting. Alumni citation Iowa State U., Disting. Achievement citation, 1991; Nat. medal of Tech., 1985; named to Datamation Hall of Fame, 1987. Fellow IEEE (chmn. computer group conf. 1970, Armstrong award 1984), Assn. Computing Machines; mem. Nat. Acad. Engring., Profl. Group Electronic Computers, Nat. Security Indsl. Assn. (trustee), Armed Forces Communications and Electronics Assn. (trustee), Aerospace Industries Assn. (exec. bd.). Presbyterian. (elder). Designed and developed large digital electric computers. Home: 170 Robin Rd Hillsborough CA 94010-6632 Office: Tech Strategies & Alliances B-1 S170 3000 Sand Hill Rd Menlo Park CA 94025-7113

EVANS, BRUCE DWIGHT, lawyer; b. Mt. Hope, W.Va., May 27, 1934; s. M. Albert and Eleanor E. (Fowler) E.; m. Sallie Lee Hazen, Aug. 24, 1957 (div. Jan. 1974); children: Scott C., Leigh F., Randolph D.; m. Doris M. Stritzinger Webster, Sept. 2, 1978. A.B., Princeton U., 1956; LL.B., Harvard U., 1959. Bar: N.Y. 1960, Pa. 1970. Assoc. Debevoise, Plimpton, Lyons & Gates, N.Y.C., 1959-68; ptnr. Reed Smith Shaw & McClay, Pitts., 1969-96. Trustee Ellis Sch., Pitts., 1972-78. Mem. ABA, Pa. Bar Assn., Allegheny County Bar Assn., Rivers Club, Phi Beta Kappa. Republican. Episcopalian. Office: One Oxford Ctr 301 Grant St Ste 1500 Pittsburgh PA 15219-1417

EVANS, BRUCE HASELTON, art museum director; b. Rome, N.Y., Nov. 13, 1939; s. E. Arnold and Joan Sawyer (Haselton) E.; m. Margo Elizabeth Frey, July 14, 1962; children: Barton Haselton, Christopher Andrew. B.A., Amherst Coll., 1961; M.A., NYU, 1964. Asst. curator Dayton (Ohio) Art Inst., 1965-66, curator, 1967-68, chief curator, 1969-72, asst. dir., 1973-74, dir., 1975-91; pres., CEO Mint Mus. Art, Mint Mus. Craft and Design, Charlotte, N.C., 1991—; mem. adv. panels Nat. Endowment for Arts and Humanities, 1973—; v.p. Midwest Museums Conf. Council, 1981; active Dayton River Corridor Design Rev. Com., Historic Architecture Com., Charlotte-Mecklenburg Pub. Art Commn., 1994—. Author: Fifty Treasures of the Dayton Art Institute, 1969, The Paintings of Jean-Leon Gerome, 1972, The Paintings of Edward Edmondson, 1972. Trustee Arts Advs. N.C. Mem. Assn. Art Mus. Dirs. (pres. 1986), Ohio Mus. Assn. (past pres.), Intermus. Conservation Assn. (past pres.), Am. Assn. Museums, Internat. Council Museums. Home: 400 N Church St Charlotte NC 28202-2182 Office: Mint Mus of Art 2730 Randolph Rd Charlotte NC 28207-2012

EVANS, CAROL ANN BUTLER, consultant, lecturer; b. Brenham, Tex., Mar. 4, 1938; d. Ben Thornton Butler and Evelyn Meyer Anderson; m. Jack Guy Courtney, June 30, 1956 (div. 1970); children: Elaine, J. Guy, David, Bruce Courtney; m. J. Warren Evans, Feb. 5, 1988. Student, McNeese State U., Lake Charles, La., 1956-57, Midland (Tex.) Coll., 1971, Am. Inst. Banking, 1970-84. Asst. to pres. San Felipe Bank N.A., Houston, 1977-79; reg. mgr. Gatoil (USA) Inc., Houston, 1979-81; office mgr. Rapada Corp., Houston, 1981-83; mktg. officer Park Tower Nat. Bank, Houston, 1984-85; mktg. dir. First City Bank Med. Ctr., Houston, 1985; asst. to pres. Med Ctr. Bank, Houston, 1985-86; dir. pub. affairs The Doctor's Club of Houston, 1986-87; mgr. The Faculty Club Tex. A&M U., College Station, 1987-90, spl. events coord. The Faculty Club, 1990-94, staff asst. Office of the Commandant, Corps of Cadets, 1994-95; asst. to pres. First Am. Bank, Bryan, Tex., 1995-97; cons. in field; lectr. in field. Author handbook: Essentials of Business Etiquette. Mem. Am. Bus. Women's Assn., Internat. Assn. Bus. Communicators, Assistance League Houston, Bank Mktg. Assn. Houston, Assn. of Faculty Clubs. Republican. Methodist. Avocations: art, music, horseback riding, interior design. Home: 3310 Belmont Cir College Station TX 77845-8210

EVANS, CAROL ROCKWELL, nursing administrator; b. New Orleans, Jan. 8, 1953; d. Daniel Raymond Sr. and Helen (Fischer) Rockwell; divorced; children: Nikki Elizabeth, Mimi Michelle. ADN, La. State Med. Ctr., 1990. RN, La.; cert. ACLS, BLS, cert. case mgr.; lic. life and health ins. agent. Life and health ins. agt. La. Ins. Agts. Assn., New Orleans, 1975-95; dir. case mgmt. and utilization rev. Associated Med. Rev. Svcs., Metairie, La., 1986-95; charge nurse med-surg. telemetry unit Elmwood Med. Ctr., Jefferson, La., 1990—; RN specialist III ICU St. Charles Gen. Hosp., New Orleans, 1993—; dir. med. mgmt. Nat. Health Resources, Inc., Metairie, La., 1995—. Lobby La. Health Care, Baton Rouge, 1991. Mem. ANA, NAFE, Case Mgmt. Soc. Am., Individual Case Mgmt. Assn., Assn. Respiratory Care, New Orleans Continuity Care, La. Managed Healthcare Assn. (Great Nurses award 1997). Republican. Roman Catholic. Avocations: sports, dancing, swimming, traveling, theater. Home: 6316 York St Metairie LA 70003-3557 Office: Managed Care Specialist Inc 3201 Cleary Ave Ste 8 Metairie LA 70002

EVANS, CHARLES ALBERT, microbiology educator; b. Mpls., Feb. 18, 1912; s. Albert Grant and Susan Briery (Thompson) E.; m. Allie Ann Christman, Dec. 22, 1939; children: Nicholas J. (dec.), Susan Ethel, Thomas Charles, Carol Ann. BS, U. Minn., 1935, MD, 1937, PhD, 1943. Diplomate Am. B. Med. Microbiology. NRC fellow U. Rochester, 1941-42; rsch. supr. Minn. State Dept. Conservation, Mpls., 1942-43; asst. prof. dept. bacteriology U. Minn., Mpls., 1942-44, assoc. prof. dept. bacteriology, 1944-46; assoc. dir. Fred Hutchinson Cancer Rsch. Ctr., Seattle, 1971-75; prof. dept. microbiology U. Wash., Seattle, 1946-82, chmn., 1946-70, prof. emeritus, 1982—; mem. nat. cancer coun. USPHS, Bethesda, Md., 1958-59,64-67; chmn. rsch. adv. coun. Am. Cancer Soc., 1967-70. Contbr. over 100 articles to profl. jours. Recipient numerous rsch. grants from NIH and Am. Cancer Soc. Mem. Am. Soc. for Microbiology (hon., pres. 1959-60), Soc. for Infectious Diseases (emeritus), Am. Assn. for Cancer Rsch. (emeritus), Am. Acad. Microbiology (mem. bd. govs. 1959-65, chmn. 1960-61). Avocations: birding, photography. Home: 7739 29th Ave NE Seattle WA 98115-4616 Office: U Wash Sch Medicine Dept Microbiology Seattle WA 98195

EVANS, CHARLES H., federa: judge; b. 1922. BA, U. Ill., 1947, JD, 1948. Pvt. law practice, 1957-62; atty. gen. State of Ill., 1962-76; magistrate judge Ill. Ctrl., Springfield, 1977—. Served with U.S. Army, 1942-45. Office: 124 US Courthouse 600 E Monroe St Springfield IL 62701-1626

EVANS, CHARLES HAWES, JR., immunologist, health science administrator; b. Orange, N.J., Apr. 16, 1940; s. Charles Hawes and Jean Marie (Robinson) E.; m. Nancy Margaret Engel, Aug. 21, 1965; 1 child, Heather Leigh. BS, Union Coll., Schenectady, N.Y., 1962; MD, U. Va., 1969, PhD, 1969. Diplomate Nat. Bd. Med. Examiners. Intern in pediatrics U. Va., Charlottesville, 1969-70, resident in pediat., 1970-71; rsch. assoc. Nat. Cancer Inst., Bethesda, Md., 1971-75, chief tumor biology sect., 1975-98; commd. capt. USPHS, Bethesda, 1971-98; sr. advisor for biomed. and clin. rsch. Nat. Acad. Scis., Washington, 1998—; mem. arts and scis. coun. U. Va., 1987-97, v.p., 1993-97; trustee Suburban Hosp., Bethesda, 1988-97. Contbr., co-contbr. over 120 med. and sci. articles to profl. jours. Recipient John Horsley prize for med. rsch. U. Va., 1982, officers citation USPHS, 1980, commendation medal, 1985, unit commendation, 1992, Outstanding Svc. medal 1996; Sir Henry Wellcome medal and prize Assn. Mil. Surgeons U.S., 1990. Fellow AAAS, Am Inst. Chemists, Am. Acad. Med. Adminstrs.; mem. Am. Assn. for Cancer Rsch., Am. Assn. Immunologists, Am. Coll. Physician Execs., Clin. Immunology Soc. (charter), Azalea Soc. Am. (gov. 1983-89, editor The Azalean Jour. 1983-88, Frederic P. Lee commendation 1984, Disting. Svc. award 1989), Sigma Xi, Alpha Omega Alpha. Democrat. Presbyterian. Avocations: horticulture, piano, philately. Home: 9233 Farnsworth Dr Potomac MD 20854-4504 Office: Nat Acad of Scis FO3080 2101 Constitution Ave NW Washington DC 20418-0007

EVANS, CHARLES WAYNE, II, biologist, researcher; b. Athens, Ohio, Aug. 9, 1929; s. Charles Wayne and Florence Louise (Sheets) Evans Claypool; m. Jo F. Burt, 1948 (div. 1959); children—Charles Wayne III, James Friedrich (dec.), John Burns, Elizabeth Burt; m. Patricia Anne Baker, 1971; children—Debbie Jo, Caralyn Michelle. Student, Tex. A&M U., 1947-51, B.A., 1957, postgrad., 1963-65; postgrad., U. Houston, 1969-70. Seismologist, Universal Seismic Expt., Beaumont, Tex., 1958-65; marine biologist CRI/VIERS, St. Thomas, U.S. Virgin Islands, 1965-71; geologist Dr. C. B. Claypool, Beaumont, 1971-76; research biologist Panthera-Marine-Internat., Ltd., Belize, C.A., Beaumont, 1976-79, pres., chief exec. officer, 1976—; research biologist Synectics, Inc., Las Vegas, 1979-82, bd. dirs., treas., 1979—; research biologist SAC Research Ctr., Beaumont, 1982-88; pres. Jordhammer, Inc., Las Vegas, 1980—; bd. dirs. Ant Fire, Inc., Beaumont, 1985-88, Caribbean World Enterprises, Ltd., New Orleans & Belize, 1987—; pres., dir. rsch. Invicta Corp., 1988—; cons. I.Q. Tech., Houston, 1994-96; cons. Eradicator Corp., Houston, 1994-98. Aire-Mate Inc., Westfield, Ind. Inventor Jordhammer, 1982, Earthfire Injection System, 1988. Sus. mem. Rep. Nat. Com., Washington, 1982—; charter mem. Ellis Island Found., N.Y.C., 1983—; founder, pres. Caribbean Inst. Natural Sci., St. Thomas, 1967-70. Served with N.G., 1945-47. SAC Research Ctr. grantee, 1983, Dr. C. B. Claypool grantee, 1963, 78. Mem. AAAS, Smithsonian Assocs., Am. Mus. Natural History (assoc.), N.Y. Acad. Sci., Internat. Oceanographic Found., World Wildlife Fund. Clubs: Aggie, Century (Tex. A&M U.). Lodge: Lions. Avocations: music; chess; big game fishing.

EVANS, CHARLIE ANDERSON, chemist; b. Columbus, Ga., Dec. 29, 1945; s. James William and Mollie Ree (Carter) E.; m. Phyllis Angela Roberts, Dec. 16, 1967 (div. 1992); children: Timothy Anderson, Laurin Stephen, Paul Thomas. BS, Ga. Inst. Tech., 1968; PhD, U. Ga., 1974. Postdoctoral fellow Centre d'Etudes Nucleaire, Grenoble, France, 1973-74, U. Western Ont., London, 1974-76; applications chemist Varian Assocs., Florham Park, N.J., 1976-80; applications chemist JEOL, Cranford, N.J., 1980-81, mgr. applications lab., 1981-84; scientist Berlex Labs., Cedar Knolls, N.J., 1984-87; sr. prin. scientist Schering-Plough Corp., Bloomfield, N.J., 1987-90, devel. fellow, 1990—; part-time insr. Ga. Inst. Tech., Atlanta, 1967-68; adj. asst. prof. Drew U., Madison, N.J., 1978; adj. prof. Fairleigh Dickinson U., 1988—. Contbr. articles to profl. jours. With U.S. Army, 1969-71. Muscogee Found. scholar, 1964-68; NSF summer fellow, 1967; NDEA Title IV fellow, 1971-73; Fulbright-Hays fellow, 1973-74. Mem. AAAS, Am. Chem. Soc. (chmn. NMR discussion group 1988, 94), N.Y. Acad. Sci., Internat. Soc. Magnetic Resonance. Democrat. Presbyterian. Office: Schering Plough Rsch Inst K15-0450 2015 Galloping Hill Rd Kenilworth NJ 07033-1300

EVANS, CHARLOTTE MORTIMER, communications consultant, writer; b. Newton, N.J., Nov. 26, 1933; d. Karl Otto and Wilhelmina (Otterbach) Pfau; student Douglass Coll., 1952-54; BS, RN, Columbia U. Presbyn. Hosp., 1957, postgrad., 1957-59; postgrad. NYU, 1959-60; MPA, Coll. of Notre Dame, 1979; m. John Atterbury Mortimer, Nov. 20, 1964; children: Meredith Elizabeth, Mandy Leigh; m. G. Robert Evans, Sept. 4, 1982. Spl. assignment nurse Columbia-Presbyn. Med. Center, N.Y.C., 1957-59; med. advt. copywriter Paul Klemtner & Co., N.Y.C., 1959-61, William Douglas McAdams Agy., N.Y.C., 1961-62; account exec. Arndt, Preston, Chapin, Lamb & Keen, N.Y.C., 1962-63; Rocky Mountain corr. Med. World News, Denver, 1963-64; owner Publicite, Denver; gen. mgr. Center Mktg. Assn., Palo Alto, Calif., 1964-66; freelance writer, pub. rels. and mgmt. cons., Woodside, Calif., 1966-85; pres. Communications for Youth, 1979—. Mem. Palo Alto-Stanford Hosp. Aux., 1968-72; pub. rels. assistance Peninsula Children's Ctr., Palo Alto, 1968-73, Triton Mus. Art, San Jose, Calif., 1966-70; chmn. citizens adv. com. San Mateo County Juvenile Social Svcs.; health component Early Childhood Com., Woodside Elem. Sch. Dist.; mem. adv. com. South County Youth and Family Svcs. Program; mem. Statewide Citizens Adv. Com. on Child Abuse and Neglect Ill. Dept. Children and Family Svcs., 1987—; past chair, mem., bd. dirs. ct.-apptd. spl. advocate program CASA-Kane County, 1989—; chair adv. com. to Congressman Dennis Hastert on Family and Child Legis., 1990—; bd. dirs. N.J. Jr. C. of C./UNICEF/African Project, 1960-61; mem. San Mateo County Mental Health Adv. Bd., Friends of Woodside Libr. Bd, 1983-85; mem. Rep. Senatorial Inner Circle, 1982—; vol. Nat. Com. for Prevention Child Abuse and Neglect, 1987—; acting chair, founder Chicagoland Media & Children Com., 1993—; adv. com. Our Children's Place, Kane County, 1995—. Home and Office: PO Box 223380 Carmel CA 93922-3380

EVANS, CHERYL LYNN, elementary school principal; b. Dec. 22, 1956. BS, Okla. State U., 1988, MS, 1998. Tchr. Olive (Okla.) Elem. Sch., 1988-90; tchr. Sunnyside Elem. Sch., Cushing, Okla., 1990-98, prin., 1998—. E-mail: hercules@fullnet.net. Home: 1010 E 11th St Cushing OK 74023

EVANS, COLLEEN MARIE, home health administrator; b. French Camp, Calif., Oct. 17, 1940; d. Leo Roy and Edna Mae (Burgoon) Cornick; m. William A. Evans Jr., Apr. 16, 1966; children: William, Brad, Lori, Donna, Tami. AA in Nursing, Pierce Coll., Woodland Hills, Calif., 1976; Ryan teaching credential, UCLA, 1983; BSN magna cum laude, Calif. State U., Dominguez Hills, Calif., 1989. RN, Calif. Staff nurse pediatrics/oper. rm. Tarzana (Calif.) Regional Med. Ctr., 1976-83; regional dir. nursing Olsten Health Care, L.A., 1988-89; corp. nursing dir. Nursing Svc. Internat., Beverly Hills, Calif., 1990-92; dir. nursing alternative health care Chatsworth, Calif., 1991-92; home health cons. 12 agy. setups, L.A., 1990-94; pres., owner Accountable Home Care Providers, Tarzana, Calif., 1993—. Mem. Assn. Pediatric Oncology Nurses, Home Health Coun. Avocations: fishing, boating, dog showing. Home: 20132 Citronia St Chatsworth CA 91311-5401 Office: Accountable Home Care Providers 19510 Ventura Blvd Ste 208 Tarzana CA 91356-2947

EVANS, DANIEL E., sausage manufacturing and restaurant chain company executive; b. 1936. With Bob Evans Farms Inc., Columbus, Ohio, 1957—, chmn. bd., sec. and CEO, also dir., 1971—. Office: Bob Evans Farms Inc Box 07863 Sta G 3776 S High St Columbus OH 43207-4000*

EVANS, DANIEL FRALEY, college administrator, banker, retail executive; b. Crawfordsville, Ind., Feb. 24, 1922; s. Benjamin C. and Ruth (Fraley) E.; m. Julia Delo Sloan, Oct. 30, 1945; children: Daniel Fraley, David Sloan, Julia Anne. A.B., Wabash Coll., 1943, LL.D., 1976; M.B.A., Harvard U., 1948; LL.D., U. Indpls., 1969. With L.S. Ayres Co., Indpls., 1948-76, treas., 1958-64, exec. v.p., 1964-65, pres., 1965-74, chmn., 1974-76; treas. Wabash Coll., Crawfordsville, Ind., 1975-88; v.p., investment officer Wabash Coll., 1988-92, acting pres., 1992-93; chmn. Midwest Nat. Bank, 1982-84; chmn. Ind. Tax and Financing Policy Commn., 1967-69. Author: It's All Relative, Part I, 1978, It's all Relative, Part II, 1982, Changing from a What to a Who, 1977, At Home In Indiana For 175 Years, A History of Meridian Street Methodist Church, 1996. Mem. Ind. Ann. Conf. Meth. Ch., 1956-87, also mem. commn. on structure; chmn. Indpls. Community Devel. Task Force, 1976, 77; bd. dirs. Ayres Found.; v.p., trustee Meth. Hosp. Ind., pres., 1965-68; trustee Wabash Coll.; chmn. Gov's Com. Utility Future; pres. Oceana Beach Assn., 1989-92. Served as lt. (j.g.) USNR, World War II, PTO. Decorated Bronze Star with 5 clusters; recipient medal of honor U. Evansville, 1970, Alumni award merit Wabash Coll., 1968; Sagamore of Wabash, 1962, 76, 81. Mem. NAACP (life), Ind. Retail Coun. (pres. 1961-64), Ind. Academy, Soc. of Ind. Pioneers, Columbia Club, Meridian Hills Club, Lincoln Hills Club, Phi Beta Kappa (assoc.). Home: 6463 N Illinois St Indianapolis IN 46260-4276 Office: 1010 E 86th St # 44-i Indianapolis IN 46240-1801*

EVANS, DANIEL FRALEY, JR., lawyer; b. Indpls., Apr. 19, 1949; s. Daniel Fraley and Julia (Sloan) E.; m. Marilyn Shultz, Aug. 11, 1973; children: Meredith, Benjamin, Suzannah, Theodore. BA, Ind. U., 1971, JD, 1976. Bar: Ind. 1976, U.S. Dist. Ct. (so. dist.) Ind. 1976, U.S. Ct. Appeals (7th cir.) 1983, U.S. Supreme Ct. 1983. Assoc. Sparrenberger, Duvall, Tabbert & Lalley, Indpls., 1976-77; ptnr. Duvall, Tabbert, Lalley & Newton, Indpls., 1977-81, Bayh, Tabbert & Capehart, Indpls., 1981-85, Baker & Daniels, Indpls., 1985—. Chmn. Ind. Bd. Correction, Indpls., 1976-88, Quayle for Senate Com., 1980, 86, Quayle for v.p. com.; mem. Fed. Jud. Merit Selection Com., Indpls., 1981-88, Adminstrv. Conf. U.S., 1983-88; chmn. Indpls. Dist. Fed. Home Loan Bank Bd., 1987-90, Fed. Housing Fin. Bd., 1990-93; vice chmn. Methodist Health Group, Inc., 1995-96, chmn., 1996—; chmn. Meth. Med. Group Inc., 1996—, Circle Investors, Inc., 1997—; vice chmn. Hudson Inst., Inc., 1996—, Cir. Investors, 1994—. Bd. dirs. Clarian Health Ptnrs. Inc., Indpls. Downtown, Inc., 1992-96, Methodist Hosp. Ind. Mem. Indpls. Bar Assn., Ind. Bar Assn. Republican. Methodist. Clubs: Woodstock, Indpls. Office: Baker & Daniels 300 N Meridian St Ste 2700 Indianapolis IN 46204-1782

EVANS, DANIEL JACKSON, former senator; b. Seattle, Oct. 16, 1925; s. Daniel Lester and Irma (Ide) E.; m. Nancy Ann Bell, June 6, 1959; children: Daniel Jackson, Mark L., Bruce M. B.S. in Civil Engring, U. Wash., 1948, M.S., 1949. Registered profl. engr., Wash. With Assoc. Gen. Contractors, Seattle, 1953-59; cons. civil engr. Seattle, 1949-51; ptnr. Gray & Evans, structural and civil engrs., Seattle, 1961-65; mem. Wash. Ho. of Reps. from, King County, 1956-65; Republican floor leader Wash. Ho. of Reps., 1961-65; gov. State of Wash., State of Wash., 1965-77; pres. Evergreen State Coll., Olympia, 1977-83; mem. U.S. Senate from Wash. State, 1983-89; now involved in environ. work, pub. appearances; cons. Daniel J. Evans & Assocs., Seattle; chmn. Pacific N.W. Electric Power and Conservation Planning Coun., 1981-83; bd. dirs. Puget Sound Energy, Tera Computer Co., Santa Fe, Inc., Flow Internat., Attachmate, Western Wireless Corp. Keynote speaker Rep. Nat. Conv., 1968; chmn. Nat. Gov.'s Conf., 1973-74; chmn. Com. on Policy Options for Global Warming, NAS, 1989-90; regent U. Wash., 1993—. Lt. USNR, 1943-46, 51-53. Recipient Disting. Eagle Scout award, Silver Beaver award, Silver Antelope award Boy Scouts Am., Disting. Citizen award Nat. Mcpl. League, 1977. Congregationalist. Office: 1111 3d Ave Ste 3400 Seattle WA 98101-3299*

EVANS, DANIEL JOSEPH, journalist; b. Phoenixville, Pa., Mar. 31, 1975; s. Gregory William and Kathleen Hickey E. BA, U. Calif., Berkeley, 1998. Webmaster Wellspring Comm., San Diego, 1991-98; photo editor Daily Californian, Berkeley, 1995-98; reporter L.A. Times, 1998—. Mem. Soc. Profl. Journalists, Photographic Excellence, Press photographers Assn. Roman Catholic. Avocations: skiing, photography, acting. Home: 1701 E D St #507 Ontario CA 91764 Office: Our Times/LA Times 430 N vineyard Ave Ste 200 Ontario CA 91764

EVANS, DARRELL J., higher education educator; b. Pocatello, Idaho, Dec. 3, 1937; s. Cedric Coffin and Elsie Christine (Jensen) E.; m. Laurel Bradley, June 13, 1955 (div. Apr. 1962); children: Mark Bradley, Athena Denice; m. Penny L. Deay, Aug. 1963 (div. June 1980); 1 child, Dana Jacqueline; m. Judith Claire Peterson, Feb. 10, 1984 (div. Apr. 1993); m. Leiola Irene Reeder, Aug. 4, 1995 (div. July 1996). AA, San Diego Jr. Coll., 1967; BA, San Diego State Coll., 1969; MA, UCLA, 1970; PhD, U. Idaho, 1997. Cert. tchr. art advanced secondary, Idaho, advanced secondary vocat. specialist, Idaho, C.C. cert., Calif. Asst. art instr. Chula Vista (Calif.) Sch. Dist., summer 1968; dir. arts and crafts Camp Roosevelt, Mountain Center, Calif., summer 1970; art tchr., intern Blackfoot (Idaho) High Sch., 1971-72; chief illustrator-draftsman USN, 1972-84; tech. and art tchr. McCall (Idaho)-Donnelly High Sch., 1984-97; asst. prof. art edn. U. Tex., El Paso, 1997-98; art tchr. Fairfield (Calif.) Suisun Evening Sch., 1973-74; art instr. U. Md.-Naples, Italy, 1975-76; mem. panel Idaho Commn. on Arts, Boise, 1990, 91, 94; owner Evans Design Inc., McCall, Idaho; mem. fine arts framework writing com. Schs. 2000, Idaho State Dept. Edn., 1994; co-chair art 5-12 curriculum writing com. Idaho State Dept. Edn. With USN, 1954-84, ret. 1984. Art Coun. scholar UCLA Art Coun., 1969-70. Mem. Idaho Art Edn. Assn. (pres. 1993-95), Nat. Art Edn. Assn. (chair tech. com. dels. assembly 1995). Avocation: residential archtl. design. Home: 897 Carina Lane Foster City CA 94404-2866

EVANS, DAVID A(LBERT), chemistry educator; b. Washington, D.C., Jan. 11, 1941; s. Albert Edward and Iris (Hill) Evans Yohe; m. Selena Anne Welliver, Dec. 27, 1962; 1 child, Bethan Hill. AB, Oberlin Coll., 1963; PhD, Calif. Inst. Tech., Pasadena, 1967; MA (hon.), Harvard U., Cambridge, 1983. Asst. prof. chemistry UCLA, 1967-72, assoc. prof., 1972-73, prof., 1974; prof. chemistry Calif. Inst. Tech., Pasadena, 1974-83, Harvard U., Cambridge, 1983—; mem. com. on chem. scis. NRC; cons. to pharm. industry; lectr. in field. Contbr. more than 125 articles of profl. jours.; hon. editor Tetrahedron and Tetrahedron Letters, 1981—; mem. editorial adv. bd. Jour. Am. Chem. Soc., 1983—. Recipient Camille and Henry Dreyfus Tchr.-Scholar award Dreyfus Found., 1971-76; Alfred P. Sloan Found. fellow, 1972-74; Disting. Teaching award UCLA Alumni Assn., 1973; Tetra Hedron award, 1998; Prelog Medal, 1999. Mem. Am. Chem. Soc. (award for creative work in synthetic organic chemistry 1982), Nat. Acad. Scis. (award 1984). Home: 39 Pine Hill Ln Concord MA 01742-4414 Office: Harvard U Dept of Chemistry Chemical Biology Dept of Chemistry 12 Oxford St Cambridge MA 02138-2902*

EVANS, DAVID CHARLES, elementary education educator; b. Cleve., Sept. 23, 1945; s. Howard Robert and Verna Eileen (Stark) E.; m. Nancy Ellen Smith, Aug. 10, 1968; children: Charles Ray, James Neal. BS in Edn., Otterbein Coll., Westerville, Ohio, 1967; MEd, Kent State U., 1970. Cert. tchr., elem. prin., Ohio. Tchr. 6th grade Columbus (Ohio) City Schs., 1967; tchr. grades 4-6, team leader Parma (Ohio) City Schs., 1967-77; tchr. 6th grade Southwestern City Schs., Grove City, Ohio, 1978; tchr. grades 5-8 Upper Arlington (Ohio) City Schs., 1978—, also team leader, summer sch. tchr. Recipient Golden Apple Achiever award Ashland Oil, Inc., 1995, 96, others; named to Outstanding Young Men in Am., 1974; Jennings scholar, 1972. Mem. NEA, Ohio Edn. Assn., Upper Arlington Edn. Assn. (pres. 1982-83), Nat. Mid. Sch. Assn., Nat. Coun. Tchrs. English. Home: 4323 Stratton Rd Columbus OH 43220-4371 Office: Upper Arlington City Schs 2100 Arlington Ave Upper Arlington OH 43221

EVANS, DAVID RICHARD, land use administrator; b. Columbus, Ohio, June 18, 1971; s. David Benjamin and Patsie Lois (Henkle) E. BA, Allegheny Coll., 1994; postgrad., U. Pitts., 1996—. Land use adminstr. Twp. of Hamilton, Allison Park, Pa., 1994—. Mem. Am. Planning Assn. Avocations: golf, mountain biking, reading. Office: Twp of Hampton 3101 Mccully Rd Allison Park PA 15101-1331

EVANS, DAVID SHAWN, financial executive; b. West Palm Beach, Fla., Apr. 5, 1965; s. George Arthur and Jeannette (Randall) E.; m. Jeannine Marie Ponton, Aug. 3, 1991; children: Michael Robert, Patrick Randall. Sr. mgr. sales Honda Annapolis, Annapolis, Md., 1989; investment advisor Prudential Securities, Inc., Annapolis, 1989-91, Balt., 1992; investment broker A.G. Edwards & Sons, Annapolis, 1991-92; v.p., mgr. GM divsn. The Scarborough Group, Inc., Annapolis, 1992-98; mng. dir. TeamVest LLC, Charlotte, N.C., 1998—; promotional cons. Kawasaki Motors Corp., U.S.A., Irvine, Calif., 1994—; promotional mgr., racing Wild Goose Brewery, Cambridge, Md., 1995—; pres. Sanitary Pet Products, Inc., Annapolis, 1992—. Author, editor: The Practical Marketing Guide for Novice Inventors, 1993; inventor Kwik Kleen Disposable Pet Dish, 1994, No-Trak Litter Control Device, 1994, Pro-Perch Actuating Lever Mount, 1994. Mem. Am. Motorcyclist Assn. (Motorcycling Unltd. #7). Republican. Avocations: motorcross racing, fitness. E-mail: devans@teamvest.com. Office: TeamVest

LLC 13900 Conlan Cir Charlotte NC 28277 Address: 6700 Red Maple Dr Charlotte NC 28277-2213

EVANS, DENNIS HYDE, chemist, educator; b. Grinnell, Iowa, Mar. 28, 1939; s. Leonard Hyde and Clara Ethel (Parmley) E.; m. Ruth Elizabeth Turnbull, June 28, 1958 (div. July 1986); children: Susan Katherine, John Hyde, Andrew Turnbull; m. Mary Jean Wirth, Aug.2, 1986. B.S., Ottawa U., 1960; A.M., Harvard U., 1961, Ph.D., 1964. Instr. chemistry Harvard U., Cambridge, 1964-66; asst. prof. chemistry U. Wis., Madison, 1966-70, asso. prof., 1970-75, prof., 1975-84, Meloche-Bascom prof. chemistry, 1984-86, chmn. dept., 1977-80, assoc. dean Coll. of Letters and Sci., 1983-86; prof. chemistry U. Del., Newark, 1986—. Contbr. articles to profl. jours. Named Danforth fellow, 1960-64, NIH fellow, 1961-64; recipient C.N. Reilley award Soc. for Electroanalytical Chemistry, 1993. Fellow Electrochem. Soc.; mem. Am. Chem. Soc., Internat. Soc. Electrochemistry, Soc. for Electroanalytical Chemistry (pres. 1993-95). Baptist. Home: 26 E Parkway Pky Elkton MD 21921-2042 Office: U Del Dept Chemistry Newark DE 19716

EVANS, DON A., healthcare company executive; b. Jerome, Ariz., June 22, 1948; s. Rulon Cooper and Berniece (Ensign) E.; m. Susan Dahl, June 3, 1972; children: Emily, Austin, Adrienne, Alan. BS, Ariz. State U., Tempe, 1972; MS, U. Colo., 1974. Asst. adminstr. Nat. Jewish Hosp., Denver, 1974-80; asst. adminstr. LDS Hosp., Salt Lake City, 1980-84, chief operating officer, 1984-88; chief exec. officer Luth. Healthcare Network, Mesa, Ariz., 1988—; adj. prof. U. Minn., 1985-86. Fellow Am. Coll. Healthcare Execs. (regent for Ariz.); mem. Ariz. Hosp. Assn. (bd. dirs., chmn. bd. 1998-99), Rotary. Republican. Office: Lutheran Healthcare Network 500 W 10th Pl Mesa AZ 85201-3216

EVANS, DONALD LEROY, real estate company executive; b. Madison, Wis., Apr. 22, 1933; s. LeRoy E. and Pearl U. Evans. BS, U. Wis., 1959, MS, 1964. Staff appraiser Am. Appraisal Group, Milw., 1959-64; founder, chmn. D.L. Evans, Inc., Madison, 1964—; co-founder U. Wis. Real Estate Alumni Assn., 1979. Dir. U. Wis. Found.; trustee U. Wis. Rsch. Park. Gunnery sgt. U.S. Army, 1953-55, Korea. Mem. Am. Soc. Appraisers (sr.; pres. 1968; Appreciation award 1968), Am. Soc. Real Estate Counselors, Am. Inst. Real Estate Appraisers (pres. 1972; Appreciation award 1972), Madison Bd. Realtors (bd. dirs. 1974-76; Appreciation award 1976). Republican. Lutheran. Lodge: Rotary. Office: D L Evans Co Inc 6409 Odana Rd Madison WI 53719-1125

EVANS, DORINDA, art history educator; b. Wakefield, Mass., Mar. 5, 1944; d. George Jelly and Priscilla (White) E.; 1 adopted child, Antonia Tamsen. BA, Wheaton Coll., Norton, Mass., 1965; MA, U. Pa., 1967; PhD, U. London, 1972. Mus. curator Nat. Gallery Art, Washington, 1967-69; asst. prof. U. Ill., Chgo., 1972-74; vis. curator Phila. Mus. Art, 1974-75; guest curator Nat. Portrait Gallery, Washington, 1975-78; asst. prof. art history Emory U., Atlanta, 1978-84, assoc. prof., 1984-99, prof., 1999—. Author: Benjamin West and His American Students, 1980, Mather Brown, 1982, The Genius of Gilbert Stuart, 1999; contbr. articles to profl. jours. Paul Hamlyn grantee Courtauld Inst. Art, U. London, 1970-71; fellow Samuel H. Kress Found., 1971-72, sr. postdoctoral fellow Smithsonian Instn., 1986-87, Joshua C. Taylor rsch. fellow Nat. Mus. Am. Art, 1991. Office: Emory U Art History Dept Atlanta GA 30322

EVANS, DOUGLAS HAYWARD, lawyer; b. Providence, R.I., July 21, 1950; s. Jerrold Merton and Gladys Jean (Snelgrove) E.; m. Sarah Edwards Cogan, May 28, 1983; children: Anne Morrill, Thomas Taylor Seelye, Elizabeth Hayward. AB, Franklin & Marshall Coll., 1972; JD, Cornell U., 1975. Bar: N.J. 1975, U.S. Dist. Ct. N.J. 1975, N.Y. 1976, U.S. Dist Ct. (so. dist.) N.Y. 1991. Assoc. Windels, Marx, Davies & Ives, N.Y.C., 1975-85; assoc. Sullivan & Cromwell, N.Y.C., 1985-90, spl. counsel, 1990—; faculty NYU Inst. Fed. Taxation, N.Y.C., 1984; counsel, treas., pres. St. David's Soc. State of N.Y., N.Y.C., 1985—; bd. dirs. Friends of Washington Sq. Park, 1989—, Washington Sq. Assn., 1992—. Co-Author: Estate Accounting, 1980, Probate and Estate Administration, 1982, Administration of Estates, 1985, Settling An Estate, 1989; Editor-in-Chief and Co-Author: Probate and Administration of New York Estates, 1995; also articles. Trustee Franklin & Marshall Coll., 1994—, Grace Ch. Sch., N.Y.C., 1997—; mem. Ch. Club of N.Y. Fellow Am. Coll. of Trust and Estate Coun.; mem. ABA, N.J. Bar Assn., N.Y. State Bar Assn. (estate litig. and adminstrn. of trusts and estates com., com. on Cont. Legal Edn.; chmn. 1991-94), N.Y. County Lawyers Assn. (com. for not-for-profit orgns.), Phi Beta Kappa, Phi Delta Phi, Phi Alpha Theta, Pi Gamma Mu. Episcopalian. Home: 43 Fifth Ave New York NY 10003-4368 Office: Sullivan & Cromwell 125 Broad St Fl 28 New York NY 10004-2489

EVANS, DOUGLAS MCCULLOUGH, surgeon, educator; b. Vandergrift, Pa., July 31, 1925; s. Archibald Davis and Helen Irene (McCullough) E.; m. Thelmajean Volkers, Aug. 1, 1959; children: Matthew Kirk, Daniel Scott. Student, Ohio State U., 1943, 46-48; MD, Western Res. U., 1952; postgrad., U. Mich., 1956-58. Diplomate: Am. Bd. Surgery. Resident in surgery Henry Ford Hosp., 1952-57, chief resident in surgery, 1957-58, mem. surgery staff, 1959-60; mem. surgery staff Akron (Ohio) Gen. Hosp., 1960-70; chmn. dept. surgery Akron Gen. Med. Ctr., 1971-90, rsch. cons.; prof. and chmn. surgery emeritus Northeastern Ohio U. Coll. Medicine. Served with AUS, 1943-46. Fellow ACS; mem. AMA, AAAS, Midwest Surg. Soc., Ohio Med. Assn., Soc. Critical Care Medicine, Am. Assn. Cancer Rsch., Akron City Club, Cascade Club. Republican. Presbyterian. Office: 400 Wabash Ave Akron OH 44307-2433*

EVANS, EARL ALISON, JR., biochemist; b. Balt., Mar. 11, 1910; s. Earl Alison and Florence (Lewis) E.; 1 adopted child, David Lasswell. Student, Balt. Poly. Inst., 1922-26; B.Sc., Johns Hopkins, 1931; Ph.D., Columbia, 1936. Research asst. pharmacology Johns Hopkins Med. Sch., 1931-32, asst. lab. endocrine research, 1932-34; univ. fellow biochemistry Columbia, 1934-36; instr. biochemistry U. Chgo., 1937-39, asst. prof., 1939-41, asso. prof. biochemistry, acting chmn. dept., 1941-42; on leave, 1947-48, prof., 1942—; chmn. dept. biochemistry 1942-72; fellow Rockefeller Found. U. Sheffield, Eng., 1939-40; chief sci. officer Am. embassy, London, 1947-48; del. Vatican Acad. Sci., 1948; cons. to sec. state, 1951-53; mem. bd. sci. counselors Nat. Inst. Arthritis and Metabolic Diseases, NIH, 1960-63; mem. div. med. scis. NRC, 1962-65; chmn. postdoctoral fellowships Nat. Acad. Sci.-NRC, 1963-65; mem. divisional com. biol. and med. scis. NSF, 1963-66; Harvey Soc. lectureship, 1942; nat. lectureship Am. Chem. Soc., 1945; Pan Am. lectureship, 1948. Author: Biochemistry of Bacterial Viruses, 1952, (with others) Biological Symposia V, 1941, Symposium on Respiratory Enzymes, 1942; Editor: (with others) Biological Action of the Vitamins, 1942; Contbr. (with others) articles to sci. jours. Adv. bd. Am. Found. Continuing Edn. Fellow All Souls Coll., Oxford U., 1969; Fellow Pierpont Morgan Library; Soc. Scholars Johns Hopkins U.; Recipient Gold Key U. Chgo. Sch. Medicine Alumni Assn. Fellow AAAS; mem. Am. Chem. Soc. (Eli Lilly prize in biol. chemistry 1942), Am. Soc. Biol. Chemists (treas. 1943-44), Biochem. Soc. (Gt. Britain), Am. Soc. Bacteriologists, Asociacion Quimica Argentina, Sigma Xi, Tau Beta Pi. Episcopalian. Clubs: Univ. (Chgo.), Racquet (Chgo.); Travellers (London). Home: 1120 N Lake Shore Dr Chicago IL 60611-1036

EVANS, EDWARD SPENCER, JR., entomologist; b. Woodbury, N.J., Aug. 7, 1943; s. Edward Spencer and Hazel Louise (Flagg) E.; m. Marilyn Dale Kernohan, Aug. 13, 1966 (div. 1981); children: Tracey Lynn, Edward Spencer III; m. Sandra Ruth Ehrhardt, June 9, 1984. BS, Rutgers U., 1965, MS, 1967, PhD, 1975. Cert. entomologist. Asst. wildlife biologist N.J. Div. Fish and Game, Tuckahoe, 1964; grad. asst. dept. entomology Rutgers U., New Brunswick, N.J., 1965-67, 69-73; entomologist U.S. Army Environ. Hygiene Agy., Aberdeen Proving Ground, Md., 1973-76; pesticide coord. U.S. Army Environ. Hygiene Agy., Md., 1976-83, supervisory entomologist, 1983—; chmn. Armed Forces Pest Mgmt. Bd., Washington, 1988-92; adj. asst. prof. Uniformed Svcs. U. Health Scis., Bethesda, Md., 1986—. Co-author: Pesticides, 1991; contbr. articles and tech. reports to profl. jours. Chmn. long range planning com. Bel Air (Md.) United Meth. Ch., 1988, mem. bldg. com., 1990—; coach youth baseball Recreation Coun., Joppatowne, Md., 1980-85. Capt. U.S. Army, 1967-69, Korea. Mem. ASTM (chmn. com. E-35, 1983-89), Am. Mosquito Control Assn., Entomol. Soc. Am., Sigma Xi, Alpha Zeta. Home: 1309 Beckett Ct Bel Air MD 21014-2736 Office: US Army Ctr Health Promotion & Preventive Med Aberdeen Proving Ground MD 21010-5403

EVANS, ELI NACHAMSON, foundation adminstrator; b. Durham, N.C., July 28, 1936; s. Emanuel Joshua and Sara (Nachamson) E.; m. Judith London, Nov. 16, 1981; 1 child, Joshua London. BA, U. N.C., 1958; LLB, Yale U., 1963. Bar: N.C. Asst. to Dr. Eric Goldman, Spl. Cons. Pres. L.B. Johnson White House, Washington, 1964-65; staff dir. to Gov. Terry Sanford Study Am. States, Duke U., Durham, N.C., 1965-67; sr. program exec. Carnegie Corp. N.Y., N.Y.C., 1967-77; pres. Charles H. Revson Found., N.Y.C., 1977—; bd. chair Covenant Found., Chgo., 1995—; mem. Carnegie Commn. on Future of Pub. Broadcasting, N.Y.C., 1977-79, N.C. Task Force on Pub. Telecomm., 1977-79, Commn. on Jewish Edn. in N.Am., N.Y.C., 1989-90, Internat. Commn. of Diaspora Israeli-Rels., N.Y.C., 1995-97; mem. 20th Century Fund Task Force on Pub. Broadcasting, N.Y.C., 1992-93. Author: The Provincials: A Personal History of Jews in the South, 1973, reissued, 1997, Judah P. Benjamin: The Jewish Confederate, 1988 (Book of Yr. 1989), The Lonely Days Were Sundays: Reflections of a Jewish Southerner, 1992. Mem. bd. N.C. State Pub. TV Network, Chapel Hill, 1979-87; mem. Internat. Commn. on Diaspora-Israel Rels., 1995-97. Lt. (j.g.) USN, 1958-60, Japan. Author: The Provincials: A Personal History of Jews in the South, 1973, Judah P. Benjamin: The Jewish Confederate, 1988, The Lonely Days Were Sundays: Reflections of a Jewish Southerner, 1993. Mem. State Bar Assn. N.C., Yale Club. Office: Charles H Revson Found 444 Madison Ave New York NY 10022-6903

EVANS, ELIZABETH ANN WEST, retired realtor; b. Xenia, Ohio, Mar. 28, 1933; d. Millard Stanley and Elizabeth Denver (Johns) West. BA, Ohio U., 1966, MA, 1968. Cert. GRI, 1993. Sec. various orgns., Ohio, 1952-61; tchr. Ohio U., Athens, 1966-67, Zanesville, 1968-72; tchr. Collier County Pub. Schs., Naples, Fla., 1972-77; sales Helen's Hang Ups, Naples, 1978-79; mgr. pvt. practice Wilmington, Ohio, 1979-87; adminstrv. asst. Powell Assocs., Cambridge, Mass., 1987-90; real estate agt. Bill Evans Realty, Inc., Naples, 1989-90, Howard Hanna Real Estate Svcs., Naples, 1991-93, Downing-Frye Realty, Inc., Naples, Fla., 1993-97, Downing-Frye Referral Network Realty Inc., Naples, 1997—. Mem. AAUW, Greater Naples Alumnae Panhellenic (prs. 1984-86), Nat. Soc. DAR (chaplain 1988-90, chmn. Motion Picture, Radio and TV 1992-94, asst. chaplain 1994-96), Naples-Marco Island-Bonita Springs Kappa Alpha Theta Alumnae Club (treas. 1990-92), Phi Beta Kappa, Phi Beta Kappa Assocs., Phi Kappa Phi, Phi Sigma Iota. Republican. Presbyterian. Avocations: book reviews, leading group discussions. Home: 15117 Royal Fern Ct Apt A200 Naples FL 34110-7683

EVANS, ELLIS DALE, psychologist, educator; b. Topeka, Nov. 6, 1934; s. Ellis Meredith and Ruth Alice (Burchinal) E.; m. Cynthia Ann McClure, Dec. 23, 1961; children: Jennifer Ann, Alicia Ruth. MusB in Edn., U. Kans., 1956; MS in Edn, Ind. U., 1962, EdD, 1964. Tchr. Shawnee Mission, Kans., 1957; field rep. Delta Upsilon, 1960-61; research asst., teaching asso. Ind. U., 1961-64; mem. faculty U. Wash., 1964-96, prof. ednl. psychology, 1971-96, chmn. ednl. psychology, 1986-93, prof. emeritus, 1996—; fellow U.S. Office Edn., 1970-71; spl. instr. Shoreline C.C., Seattle, 1973-75; advisor Pacific Marine Rsch. Inst., Ctr. Study Capable Youth, 1972-95; cons. Lakeview Travel and Cruise. Author: Development and Classroom Learning, 1973, Children and Youth: Psychosocial Development, 1973, rev. edit., 1978, Contemporary Influences in Early Childhood Education, 1975, The Transition to Teaching, 1976; cons. editor: Charles E. Merrill Pubs., 1980-87; contbr. over 50 articles to profl. jours. Active local music orgns.; leader E-Sharp Ensembles. Served to capt. USAF, 1957-60. Fellow APA, Am. Psychol. Soc., Am. Assn. Applied Preventive Psychology; mem. Nat. Assn. Edn. Young Children, Am. Fedn. Musicians, Smithsonian Assn., Nat. Trust for Hist. Preservation, Nat. Audubon Soc., Nature Conservancy, Wilderness Soc., Nat. Arbor Day Found., Omicron Delta Kappa, Delta Upsilon (Disting. Alumnus). Home: 19045 46th St NE Seattle WA 98155

EVANS, ERSEL ARTHUR, consulting engineer executive; b. Trenton, Nebr., July 17, 1922; s. Arthur E. and Mattie Agnes (Perkins) E.; m. Patricia A. Powers, Oct. 11, 1945 (div.); children: Debra Lynn (dec.), Paul Arthur; m. Ann Burruss, Aug. 13, 1998. B.A., Reed Coll., Portland, Oreg., 1947; Ph.D., Oreg. State U., 1950. Registered profl. engr., Calif. With Gen. Electric Co., 1951-67; supr. ceramics research and devel. Gen. Electric Co., Hanford, Wash., 1961-64; mgr. plutonium devel. Vallecitos Lab., Pleasanton, Calif., 1964-67; mgr. fuels and materials dept. Battelle Meml. Inst., Richland, Wash., 1967-70; with Westinghouse Electric Corp., 1970-87; v.p. Westinghouse Hanford Co., Richland, 1972-87, v.p., lab. tech. dir., 1985-87, ret., 1987, cons., 1987—; mem. Tech. Assistance Adv. Group for Three Mile Island Recovery, 1981-86; mem. rev. Com. EBR-II, U. Chgo., 1989-91, 94—; mem. Japan Tech. Panel for Nuclear Power, NSF, 1989-90; mem. alt. applications of laser isotope separations tech. com. NRC, 1991-92, separations and tech. study, 1991-95, 96; del. Atlantic Coun. U.S.-Japan Conf. on Global Energy Issues, Maui, 1994, 96. Mem. vis. com. U. Wash. Served with USNR, 1943-45. Recipient Westinghouse Order of Merit; DuPont fellow, 1950-51; recipient Mishima award Am. Nuclear Soc., 1995. Fellow Am. Nuclear Soc. (Spl. Merit award 1964, Spl. Performance award 1980 Fed. Design Achievement award 1991), Am. Inst. Chemists, Am. Soc. Metals, Am. Ceramic Soc.; mem. NAE, Phi Kappa Phi. Patentee in field. Home and Office: Park Row # 21 701 Kettner Blvd San Diego CA 92101-5908 *Inspiration and guidance for my career have often been provided by Justice Oliver Wendell Holmes, "certainty generally is illusion, and repose is not the destiny of man." (Harvard Law Review 1897).*

EVANS, FRANCIS COPE, ecologist; b. Phila., Dec. 2, 1914; s. Edward Wyatt and Jacqueline Pascal (Morris) E.; m. Rachel Worthington Brooks, June 12, 1942; children—Kenneth Richardson, Katharine Cope, Edward Wyatt II, Rachel Howe. B.S., Haverford Coll., 1936; D.Phil. (Rhodes scholar), Oxford U., 1939; Claypole fellow, U. Calif., Berkeley, 1939-40. Research asst. Hooper Found., San Francisco, 1939-41; jr. zoologist U. Calif., Davis, 1941-43; instr., asst. prof. Haverford (Pa.) Coll., 1943-48, acting dean, 1944; asst. prof., assoc. prof. U. Mich., Ann Arbor, 1948-59; prof., assoc. dir. E.S. George Res., 1959-82; prof. emeritus, 1982—. Editor publs.: Mus. Zoology, Ann Arbor, 1968-78; Contbr. sci. articles to profl. jours. Recipient Painton award Cooper Ornithol. Soc., 1963; Guggenheim fellow, 1962-63; Erskine fellow U. Canterbury, Christchurch, N.Z., 1976-77. Fellow AAAS; mem. Ecol. Soc. Am. (pres. 1983, Disting. Service award 1987), Brit. Ecol. Soc., Am. Soc. Naturalists, Soc. for Study Evolution. Quaker. Home: 1050 Wall St Apt 5-d Ann Arbor MI 48105-1981 Office: U Mich 1073 Natural Sci Bldg Ann Arbor MI 48109

EVANS, FRED LYNN, principal; b. Ottawa, Kans., June 10, 1951; s. Fil O. and Margory Lois Evans; m. Linda Y. Karnes, Jan. 2, 1990 (div. Nov. 1975); 1 child, Michelle; m. Sheila Marie Glover, July 5, 1986; children: Sean, Coleman. MusB in Music Edn., Washburn U., 1973; cert. in adminstrn., SD, 1994; M in Music Edn., Kans., 1986. Dir. inst. and choral music United Sch. Dist. #501, Topeka, 1974-75; music cons. sales rep. Hume Music Inc., Topeka, 1975-79; dir. bands United Sch. Dist. #441, Sabetha, Kans., 1980-95; prin. Lexington (Nebr.) Publ. Sch., 1995—; chair strategic planning com., Lexington Pub. Sch., 1997—; spkr., presenter in field. Author: Development and Evaluation of a Clarinet Method For Young Beginning Students, 1985. Pres. Topeka Musical Assn., 1982-87; bd. mem. Ctrl. Nebr. Tech. Fair, Karney, 1996-97, Lexington Area Arts Coun., 1995—, Lexington Cmty. Concert Series, 1995—. Recipient Student Signature In Space award Lockheld Martin Corp., 1997, Bright Site award Bright Site, 1997, Website Sch. 2000 award World Village Safesurf, 1997; Outstanding Young Men of Am., U.S. Jaycees, 1984. Mem. Nat. NAESP named ASCD, Nebr. Coun. Sch. Adminstrn., Nebr. Region IV prin. Achievements include: co-creater electronic grade card, Lexington Pub. Sch. 1995. Avocations: music, performing, writing music, golf, travel. E-Mail: fevans@genie.esu10.k12.ne.us.

EVANS, FREDERICK JOHN, psychologist; b. Wollongong, Australia, Nov. 17, 1937; came to U.S., 1963; s. Frederick John and Phyllis Lurline (Wiffen) E.; m. Barbara Joan Marcelo, June 8, 1968 (div. 1990); children: Christopher Arthur, David Troy, Mark Fredrick, Diana Joy; m. Patricia E. Burns, Nov. 26, 1993; children: Mariefred Joy, Ellen Blessing. B.A. Honors Class I, U. Sydney, Australia, 1959, Ph.D., 1966. Teaching fellow U. Sydney, 1959-63; research psychologist Mass. Mental Health Center, 1963-64; from instr. psychology in psychiatry U. Pa. Sch. Medicine, Phila., 1965-66; to assoc. prof. psychiatry U. Pa. Sch. Medicine, 1972-81, assoc. prof. psychology, 1974-79; sr. research psychologist Unit for Exptl. Psychiatry Inst. of Pa. Hosp., Phila., 1964-79; cons. psychologist pain mgmt. ctr. Med. Ctr. Princeton, N.J., 1998—; mem. cons. staff dept. psychiatry Princeton House, 1998—; vis. fellow psychology Yale U., 1970-71; trustee Inst. Exptl. Psychiatry, Boston, 1970-79; adj. prof. U. Medicine and Dentistry N.J.-Robert Wood Johnson Med. Sch., 1979-88; dir. rsch. divsn. Carrier Found., Belle Mead, N.J., 1979-88; v.p. Tex. Inst. Behavioral Medicine and Neurosci., 1989-96; pres. Pathfinders, Cons. in Human Behavior; dir. Pain Mgmt. Behavioral Medicine Svcs., Reading, Pa.; consulting psychologist The Elms Nursing Home, 1995—, The Back Rehab. Inst., Cranbury, N.J., Hamilton, N.J., 1997—; dir. psychol. svcs. Pain Mgmt. Ctr. The Med. Ctr. at Princeton, 1998—. Adv. editor: Internat. Jour. Clin. and Exptl. Hypnosis, 1968-69, assoc. editor, 1969—; assoc. editor: Am. Jour. Clin. Hypnosis, 1986-91, 95—; cons. editor: Jour. Abnormal Psychology, 1979-87, assoc. editor, 1989-91; co-editor: Functional Disorders of Memory, 1979, Springer Series in Behavior Modification and Behavioral Medicine, 1980-86; contbr. chpts. to textbooks, articles to profl. jours. Served to capt. Australian Army, 1961-63. Fulbright grantee, 1963-66. Fellow AAAS, APA (divsn. 30 program chmn. 1972, sec-treas. 1973-75, pres. 1978-79), Am. Soc. Clin. Hypnosis (chmn. liaison com. 1975-77, 88-89, cert. cons. 1993—), N.J. Pshycol. Soc., Pa. Psychol. Soc., Soc. Clin. and Exptl. Hypnosis (co-chmn. sci. program 1970, chmn. rsch. workshop, 1971, 76, 79, 80, 87-90, sec. 1973-86, co-chmn. publs. com. 1975-77, v.p. 1979-81, pres. 1981-83, chmn. budget com. 1987-89); mem. Am. Pain Soc. (founding dir. 1977-80), Internat. Soc. Hypnosis (sec.-treas. 1973-79, co-chmn. 7th Internat. Congress Hypnosis 1976, vice chmn. bd. dirs. organizing com. 10th Internat. Congress 1985, pres.-elect 1986-88, pres. 1987-91, immediate past pres. 1991-94, chair nominations and election com. 1991-94), Nat. Pain Found. (pres. 1989-92), Royal Soc. Medicine, Internat. Soc. Inner Mental Tng. (v.p. 1993-96).

EVANS, GAREN LEE, laboratory director, regulatory compliance officer; b. Tucson, June 14, 1946; s. Roland Lee and Gertrude Helen (Prouty) E.; m. Theressa Ann Schaefer, Sept. 25, 1965; children: Lois Louise, Garen Lee II, Elaine Diane. Student, U. Wash., Seattle, 1965; BS, U. Ariz., 1973; MRE, SW Bap. Theol. Sem., Ft. Worth, 1973-80; post grad., North Tex. State, Denton, 1984-88. Sr. analytical chemist Skyline Lab., Tucson, 1966-73; sr. process engr. Bell Helicopter, Ft. Worth, 1974-81; chemist, metallurgist Amarillo Mining, Amarillo, Tex., 1982-83; process mgr. Chem. Dynamics, Weatherford, Tex., 1983-85; lab. dir., regulatory compliance officer Andritz Ruthner, Arlington, Tex., 1985—. Inventor, phosphate precipitation of cadmium, 1980, silicate solidification of hazardous waste, 1981. Served with USNR, 1964-71. Mem. TAPPI, Am. Filtration Soc., Am. Chem. Soc. Republican. Baptist. Avocations: church work, farming. Home: 3333 Happy Meadows Dr Alvarado TX 76009-6550

EVANS, GARTH, artist, educator; b. Stockport, Cheshire, Eng., Nov. 23, 1934; came to U.S., 1979; s. Cyril John and Gertrude Veronica (Bayliss) E.; m. Leila Stott Philip; 1 child, Rhys Philip. Student, Manchester Jr. Coll. Art, 1949-51, Manchester Regional Coll. Art, 1955-57; Diploma Fine Art, Univ. Coll., London, 1960. vis. lectr. Cen. Sch. Art, London, 1960-65, Camberwell Sch. Art, London, 1960-69, St. Martin's Sch. Art, London, 1965-79, Chelsea Sch. Art, London, 1978-79, Yale Sch. Art, Yale U., New Haven, 1983, 85, 86; vis. prof. Mpls. Coll. Art and Design, Mpls., 1973; external examiner Maidstone (Kent, Eng.) Coll. Art, 1977-79, Nat. Coll. Art and Design, Dublin, Ireland, 1978, Goldsmiths Coll., U. London, 1978-81; vis. tutor Slade Sch. Fine Art, Univ. Coll., London, 1970-81; vis. artist sculpture dept. Royal Coll. Art, 1970-81; vis. artist Mt. Holyoke Coll., South Hadley, 1979-81, Manchester Poly., 1978-83; assoc. lectr. in sculpture Camberwell Sch. Art, London, 1971-83; faculty N.Y. Studio Sch., N.Y.C., 1988—; condr. numerous lectrs. and workshops; mem. com. for art and design Coun. for Nat. Acad. Awards, 1976-79; mem. fine arts award policy com. Arts Coun. Gt. Britain, 1977-79; mem. fine art adv. panel South Glamorgan Inst. Higher Edn., 1977-79; curator Inst. Contemporary Art, London, 1978, Mpls. Inst. Arts, 1983. One-person shows include Rowan Gallery, London, 1962, 64, 66, 68, 69, 72, 74, 76, 78, 80, Mpls. Inst. of Arts, 1979, Mt. Holyoke Coll. Art Mus., South Hadley, Mass., 1983, Robert Elkon Gallery, N.Y.C., 1983, Tibor De Nagy Gallery, N.Y.C., 1984, Robert Brown Contemporary Art, Washington, 1988, Compass Rose Gallery, Chgo., 1989, Hill Gallery, Birmingham, Mich., 1990, Wrexham Mus. and Art Ctr., Rhyl, Wales, 1991, Rosemary Hall, Wallingford, Conn., 1993, Dana Arts Ctr., Colgate U., Hamilton, N.Y., 1995, Korn Gallery, Drew U., Madison, N.J., 1996, Claudia Carr Gallery, N.Y.C., 1997; exhibited at group shows Air Gallery, London, 1962, Stone Gallery, Newcastle upon Tyne, Eng., 1964, Camden Arts Ctr., London, 1966, Whitechapel Art Gallery, London, 1968, Hayward Gallery, London, 1971, 75, Redfern Gallery, London, 1977, Oporto (Portugal) Sch. Fine Art, 1980, Robert Elkon Gallery, N.Y.C., 1981, Newhouse Gallery, N.Y.C., 1983, John Davis Gallery, Akron, 1986, N.Y. Studio Sch., N.Y.C., 1989, Charles Cowles Gallery, N.Y.C., 1991, PMW Gallery, Stamford, Conn., 1992, Skidmore Coll., Saratoga Springs, N.Y., 1993, Am. Acad. Arts and Letters, N.Y.C., 1996; represented in pub. collections Tate Gallery, London, Welsh Arts Coun., Bklyn. Union Gas, Merthyr Tydfil Art Gallery, Wales, Victoria & Albert Mus., London, Mus. Modern Art, N.Y., Metro. Mus., N.Y., Bklyn. Mus., Joseph H. Hirshhorn Mus., Washington, Nat. Mus. Modern Art, Brazil, Power Gallery Contemporary Art, Sydney, Gulbenkian Found., Lisbon, Portugal, Yale Ctr. brit. Art, New Haven, others; pub. commns. include Ebbw Vale Urban Dist. Coun., Eng., J. Sainsbury Ltd., Maidenhead, Eng., Arts Coun. Gt. Britain; featured in numerous publs. including Arts Rev., The Times, Art & Artists, Guardian. Sr. aircraftsman Royal Air Force, 1952-55. Recipient Sabbatical award Arts Coun. Gt. Britain, 1966, Maj. prize, 1975, Film Bursary award, 1979, Bursary award Greater London Arts Assn., 1978, Pollock-Krasner Found. award, 1996; winner Newcastle Cruddas Park Sculpture Competition, 1961; Brit. Steel Corp. fellow, 1969, John Simon Guggenheim Meml. Found. fellow, 1986; grantee Brit. Coun. Exhbns. Abroad, 1979. Home: 106 N 6th St Brooklyn NY 11211-3002

EVANS, GARY LEE, communications educator and consultant; b. Davison, Mich., June 26, 1938; s. Joe Howard and Annie Annette (Colden) E.; m. Katherine Strand; children: Gary James, Aimee Lynn; stepchildren: John E. Holkeboer, Maja K. Holkeboer. BA, Wayne State U., 1962; MA, U. Mich., 1965, PhD, 1977. Prof. organizational and intercultural communication Eastern Mich. U., Ypsilanti, 1964—; pres. Comm. Rsch. and Tng. Assocs.; cons. Volvo Corp., GM Corp., Ford Motor Car Co., Mich. Pub. Schs. and other ednl. instns.; speaker in field; instr., Davos, Switzerland, 1989; internat. program instr., Australia, New Zealand, Switzerland. Mem. Peace Corps Tng. and Teaching. Named Outstanding Continuing Educator of the Yr., Ea. Mich. U., 1994, Disting. Sr. Tchg. Award, 1998, Disting. Faculty Mem., 1998. Mem. Internat. Communication Assn., Speech Communication assn., Mich. Acad. Sci., Arts and Letters (communication chmn. 1982), Mich. Speech Communication Assn. (communication chmn. 1978—), Golden Key Nat. Honorary Soc., Phi Kappa Phi (pres. 1998—), Delta Sigma Rho, Pi Kappa Delta. Home: 11353 Pleasant Shore Dr Manchester MI 48158-9739 Office: Ea Mich U 121 Quirk Hall Ypsilanti MI 48197-2220

EVANS, GENE M., publishing executive; b. N.Y.C., Dec. 30, 1946; d. Murray and Ruth (Lederer) Weintraub; m. Garry Arthur Evans, May 11, 1974 (div. Feb. 1980). AA in Journalism, Miami (Fla.)-Dade C.C., 1972; BA in English, Fla. Internat. U., 1974. Sales rep. Holt-Saunders Ltd., London, Eng., 1975-79; publs. mgr. Internat. African Inst., London, 1979-81; edtl. dir. Update Publs., London, 1981-83; mng. dir. Excerpta Medica UK, London, 1983-84; pub. dir. Medicom UK and Internat., London, 1984-86; mng. dir. Merit Pub. Internat., Inc., Basingstoke, Hants., Eng., 1986—; pres. Merit Pub. Internat., INc., Coral Springs, Fla., 1992—; adv. cons. Meducom Internat., Guelph, Can., 1992—, Stone & Bender, Basingstoke, 1992—. Avocations: internet, cycling, traveling, reading, aerobics.

EVANS, GERALDINE ANN, academic administrator; b. Zumbrota, Minn., Feb. 24, 1939; d. Wallace William and Elda Ida (Tiedemann) Whipple; m. John Lyle Evans, June 21, 1963; children: John David, Paul William. AA, Rochester Community Coll., 1958; BS, U. Minn., 1960, MA, 1963, PhD, 1968. Cert. tchr., counselor, prin. and supt., Minn. Tchr. Hopkins (Minn.) Pub. Schs., 1960-63; counselor Anoka (Minn.) Pub. Schs., 1963-66; cons. in edn. Mpls., 1966-78; policy analyst Minn. Dept. Edn., St. Paul, 1978-79; dir. personnel Minn. Community Coll. System, St. Paul, 1979-82; pres. Rochester (Minn.) Community Coll., 1982-92; chancellor Minn. C.C. System, St. Paul,

1992-94; exec. dir. Ill. C.C. Bd., Springfield, 1994-96; chancellor San Jose (Calif.) Evergreen C.C. Dist., 1996—. Vice chair, bd. dirs. Wayzata (Minn.) Sch. Bd., 1980-83; bd. dirs. Minn. Tech. Ctr., Rochester, 1991-92; sec.-treas. Coun. North Ctrl. Cmty. and Jr. Colls., 1990-92; moderator Mizpah United Ch. Christ, Hopkins, 1982; mem. Gov.'s Job Tng. Coun., St. Paul, 1983-94, chair, 1992-94; mem. ACE Commn. on Edn. Credit and Credentials, 1992—; mem. Silicon Valley Pvt. Industry Coun., 1997—; mem. Workforce Silicon Valley, 1998—. Winner Rochester C. of C. Athena award, 1990, San Jose YMCA Exec. award, 1998; Inst. Ednl. Leadership fellow, Washington, 1978-79. Mem. Nat. League Nursing (bd. assoc. degree accreditation rev. 1990-93, exec. com. 1993-96), Am. Assn. Cmty. Jr. Colls. (bd. dirs. 1984-87), North Ctrl. Assn. Cmty. and Jr. Colls. (evaluator), C. of C. (com. 1999—), Golden Gate Univ. (bd. trustees 1997—), Rotary. Congregationalist. Avocations: travel, gardening.

EVANS, GREGORY THOMAS, retired commissioner, retired justice; b. McAdam, N.B., Can., June 13, 1913; s. Thomas Vincent and Mary Ellen E.; m. Zita Callon, Oct. 1, 1941; children: Thomas, John, Gregory, Rory, Mary, Kerry, Brendan, Catherine, Erin. BA, St. Joseph's U., 1934; LLB, Osgoode Hall Law Sch., Toronto, 1939, York U., 1991; LL.D., St. Thomas U., Fredericton, N.B., 1963; Ph.D., Université de Moncton, 1964. Bar: Ont. 1939; created Queen's Counsel 1953. Sr. ptnr. firm Evans, Evans, Bragagnolo, Perras & Sullivan, Timmins, Ont., Can., 1939-63; apptd. to Supreme Ct. Ont., 1963, Ct. Appeal, Ont., 1965; apptd. chief justice High Ct., Supreme Ct., Ont., Toronto, 1976-85; vice chmn. Can. Jud. Council, Ottawa, 1981-85; gov. Am. Judges Assn., 1986; commr. Royal Commn. on the Donald Marshall Jr. Prosecution, 1987-90, Commn. on Conflict of Interest, Ont., 1988-95, Integrity Commn., Toronto, 1995-97, Royal Commn. on Compensation for Donald Marshall Jr., 1990; supernumerary judge, 1985-88; treas. Am. Judges Found., 1984-91; commr. Conflict of Interest Northwest Territories, 1992-96; mem. extraordinary challenge com., 1989-94;. Pres. Ont. English Catholic Edn. Assn., 1961. Decorated knight comdr. Order St. Gregory the Great. Mem. Canadian Inst. Advanced Legal Studies (v.p. 1978-79). Roman Catholic.

EVANS, GROSE, former curator, retired educator; b. Columbus, Ohio, Dec. 15, 1916; s. Marshall Blakemore and Elizabeth Theodora (Grose) E.; m. Grace Elizabeth Orvis, Jan. 4, 1946; 1 dau., Grace Elizabeth Grose. B.F.A., Ohio State U., 1938, M.A., 1940; Ph.D., John Hopkins U., 1953. Lectr. Nat. Gallery of Art, Washington, 1946-54; asst. curator ednl. work Nat. Gallery of Art, 1954-58, asso. curator, 1958-60; curator decorative arts Index Am. Design and Extension Service, 1960-70, curator exhbns. and loans, 1970-73, curator decorative arts, 1973, ret., 1973; adj. prof. art history George Washington U., 1973-90, lectr. modern art, 1953-56, professorial lectr. theories of art, 1956-61; guest lectr. baroque and modern art Cath. U. Am., 1948-49; guest lectr. modern art Am. U., 1952-53; curriculum dir. Research in Tchr. Tng. Program U.S. Office Edn., 1966, Arts and Humanities Inst., 1967. Author: Subtle Satire of Magnasco, Gazette des Beaux Arts, 1948, Benjamin West and the Taste of His Times, 1959, Van Gogh, 1968. Home: 2308 Glasgow Rd Alexandria VA 22307-1820

EVANS, H(AROLD) BRADLEY, JR., lawyer; b. Watertown, N.Y., Oct. 12, 1937; s. Harold Bradley Sr. and Kathleen (Whearty) E.; m. Allene Isabel Thompson, July 23, 1967; children: Harold Bradley III, Barrett A., Darryl C. BA, Yale U., 1959; JD, Georgetown U., 1966. Bar: Va. 1966, U.S. Ct. Appeals (4th cir.) 1970, U.S. Supreme Ct. 1977. Law clk. D.C. Ct. Appeals, Washington, 1966-67; assoc. Boothe, Dudley, Koontz, et. al., Fairfax, Va., 1967-69; prin. Evans, Economy & Pickard, Alexandria, Va., 1969-83; owner Hazel & Thomas, P.C., Alexandria, 1983—; trustee U.S. Bankruptcy Panel, 1967-87. Recipient Pro Bono Publico award Va. Supreme Ct., 1993. Fellow Va. Law Found.; mem. Va. State Bar (chmn. com. to reduce litigation costs and delay 1991-94, mem. grievance com. 1979-81, mem. state bar coun. 1983-89, bd. govs. bankruptcy sect. 1998—), Alexandria Bar Assn. (prs. 1981-82), No. Va. Trial Lawyers Assn. (pres. 1974), Walter Chandler Inn of Ct. (master of bench). Republican. Roman Catholic. Avocations: fishing, reading, hiking. Office: Hazel Thomas PO Box 820 510 King St Ste 200 Alexandria VA 22314-3132

EVANS, HAROLD EDWARD, banker; b. Detroit, Apr. 23, 1927; s. Harold J. and Mary Esther (Keenoy) E.; m. Patricia Mae Persons Willy, Mar. 28, 1982; children by previous marriage: D'lorah Ann, M'liss Lorraine, David Keenoy, Craig Edward. BBA, U. Mich., 1950; cert., Bank Adminstrn. Inst., U. Wis., 1968, Stonier Grad. Sch. Banking, Rutgers U., 1975. Auditor Second Nat. Bank Saginaw, Mich., 1952-61, controller, 1961-73, sr. v.p., cashier, sec., chief fin. officer, 1973-92; founder, chmn. art collection, 1976-92, mem. selection com., 1992—; v.p. loan rev. officer Citizens Banking Corp., Flint, Mich., 1986-92; sec.-treas. 2d Nat. Corp., 1973-88, Century Life Ins. Co., Mich., 1973-93; lectr. Robert Perry Sch. Banking, Ctrl. Mich. U. Mem. Saginaw Citizens Coun. for Ctrl. Bus. Dist., 1970-89; mem. adv. bd. Urban Renewal, chmn. econ. base study com., 1954-55; chmn. Downtown Saginaw Beautification Commn., 1968-83, Greater Saginaw Beautification Residential Com., 1965-68, 1988-97; chmn. svcs. Saginaw Valley State U. Humanities Series Com., 1990—; sec., trustee Saginaw Osteo. Hosp., 1960-84; treas., trustee Saginaw Symphony Orch., 1965-72; past trustee Saginaw His. Mus.; treas., dir. United Rehab. Svcs., 1954-65, Temple Theater Arts Assn., 1980-87; fin. officer Saginaw CAP, 1978-84; trustee, treas. Saginaw Valley Dancers, 1977-93; trustee Hartley Nature Ctr. Found., 1987—, Saginaw Hall of Fame, 1989—; mem. adv. bd. Health Source Saginaw, Inc., 1991—, sec. arbrs. bd., 1993, 96, vice chmn., 1997, chmn., 1998; mem. steering com. Cathedral Dist. Renewal, 1990—; mem. com. for advancement Saginaw Valley State U., 1992—, mem. com. Stuart and Vernice Gross History Lit. award, 1996—; mem. com. for advancement Saginaw Area Enrichment Commn., 1992—, Saginaw Twp. Art in Pub. Place Commn., 1991—, Delta Coll. Pub. Radio Fund Raiser Com., 1990-97, Temple Theater Film Selection com., 1998—. With USNR, 1945-46. Recipient Saginaw Arts award Community Enrichment Commn., 1992; nominee Gov's. Art award, 1996. Mem. Saginaw C. of C., Bank Adminstrn. Inst. (life; pres. Ea. Mich. conf. 1955-56, v.p. Mich. chpt. 1958-59), Valley Film Soc. (bd. dirs. 1991—), Tri-County Econ. Club, Econ. Club Detroit, Internat. Torch Club (Saginaw Valley chpt. 1993—), U. Mich. Alumni Club (Saginaw chpt.), Optimists (bd. dirs. Breakfast Club 1960-80, treas. 1961-63, pres. 1970-72), Mich. Women's Hall of Fame (elector 1992-93), Friends Theodore Roethke. Home: 17 Riverside Blvd Saginaw MI 48602-1077 also: 1710 N Charles St Saginaw MI 48602-4848

EVANS, HAROLD J., plant physiologist, biochemist, educator; b. Franklin, Ky., Feb. 19, 1921; s. James H. and Allie (Uhls) E.; m. Elizabeth Dunn, Dec. 14, 1946; children: Heather Mary, Pamela. B.S., U. Ky., 1946, M.S., 1948; Ph.D. (Cook-Vorhees fellow), Rutgers U., 1950. Asst. prof. botany N.C. State U., 1952-54, assoc. prof., 1954-57, prof., 1957-61; postdoctoral fellow Johns Hopkins U., Balt., 1952; prof. plant physiology Oreg. State U., Corvallis, 1961-88, Disting. prof. plant physiology, 1988-90, Disting. prof. plant physiology emeritus, 1990—; dir. Lab. for Nitrogen Fixation, 1978-90; vis. prof. U. Sessex, Eng., 1967; George A. Miller vis. prof. U. Ill., Urbana, 1973; mem. panel for metabolic biology NSF, 1964-68; mem. U.S.-Japan Coop. Sci. Program, 1976. Editl. bd. Biofactors, 1989—; contbr. over 200 articles to profl. jours. Recipient Hoblitzelle Nat. award Tex. Research Found., 1964, Basic Research award Oreg. State U., 1965, NW Sci. award Gov. Oreg., 1967, von Humbolt Found. Sr. Rsch. award, 1991; named Disting. Alumnus U. Ky., 1975; recipient George G. Ferguson Disting. Prof. award and Milton Harris research award Oreg. State U., 1983. Fellow Am. Acad. Microbiology; mem. NAS, Am. Soc. Plant Physiologists (pres. 1971, trustee 1977—, Charles Reid Barnes award 1985), Sigma Xi (award 1968), Phi Kappa Phi. Democrat. Home: 14151 Redwood Ct Lake Oswego OR 97034-2153 Office: Lab for Nitrogen Fixation Rsch Oreg State U Corvallis OR 97331

EVANS, HARRY LAUNIUS, pathology educator; b. Mobile, Ala., June 11, 1948; s. Aurelius A. and Anne (Hathaway) E.; m. Cheryl J. Winfrey, June 6, 1970 (div. Dec. 1990); children: Thomas H., Sarah S. BS, Stetson U., 1970; MD, U. Fla., 1974. Diplomate Am. Bd. Pathology. Resident in pathology Vanderbilt U. Med. Ctr., Nashville, 1974-75; fellow in dermatopathology Mayo Clinic, Rochester, Minn., 1977-78; fellow in pathology U.Tex.-M.D. Anderson Cancer Ctr., Houston, 1975-77, asst. prof. pathology, 1978-82, assoc. prof., 1982-90, prof., 1990—. Contbr. articles to med. jours. Mem. U.S.-Can. Acad. Pathology, Arthur Purdy Stout Soc. Surg. Pathologists. Avocations: mountain climbing, music, crossword puzzles. Office: U Tex-MD Anderson Cancer Ctr Dept Pathology 1515 Holcombe Blvd Houston TX 77030-4009

EVANS, HUGH E., pediatrician; b. N.Y.C., July 6, 1934; s. David and Geraldine (Krebs) E.; m. Ruth L. Orloff, June 5, 1960 (dec. Mar. 1999); children: Margo Lynn, Marc Douglas. A.B. cum laude, Columbia U., 1954; M.D., SUNY Downstate Med. Center, 1958. Intern Johns Hopkins Hosp., Balt., 1958-59; asst. resident Johns Hopkins Hosp., 1959-60; sr. asst. resident NIH, Bethesda, Md., 1960-62; chief resident outpatient dept. NIH, 1962-63; pvt. practice Bellaire, Ohio, 1963-66; assoc. dir. pediatrics Harlem Hosp. Center, N.Y.C., 1966-73; dir. dept. pediatrics Jewish Hosp. and Med. Center, Bklyn., 1973-85; prof. pediatrics U. Medicine and Dentistry of N.J., Newark, 1985—, prof. preventive medicine and community health, 1991—, chmn. dept. pediatrics, 1985-90; dir. dept. pediatrics U. Hosp., Newark, 1985-90, mem. attending staff, 1985—; assoc. clin. prof. pediatrics Columbia U., 1968-73; prof. pediatrics SUNY Downstate Med. Center, Bklyn., 1973-85; cons. Englewood (N.J.) Hosp., Hackensack (N.J.) Hosp.; trustee Bergen-Passiac County Lung Assn., 1973-85. Author: (with Leonard Glass) Perinatal Medicine, 1976, Lung Diseases of Children, 1979, 2d edit., 1985; editor: Hospital Care of Children and Youth, 1986, Jour. Perinatology, 1985—; contbr. articles to profl. jours., chpts. to textbooks. Served to sr. asst. surgeon USPHS, 1960-62. Mem. Soc. Pediat. Rsch., Harvey Soc., Am. Soc. Microbiology, Am. Acad. Pediat. (com. on hosp. care 1982-85, chmn. 1985-88, task force on pediat. AIDS 1987-92), Am. Thoracic Soc., Am. Pediat. Soc., Soc. Exptl. Biology and Medicine, N.Y. Pediat. Soc. (pres. 1982-83), Bklyn. Acad. Pediat. (v.p. 1976, pres. 1977), Infectious Diseases Soc., Med. Soc. N.J. (mem. spl. com. AIDS 1993-95), Alpha Omega Alpha. Home: 165 Serpentine Rd Tenafly NJ 07670-2739 Office: U Medicine and Dentistry NJ MSB-F586 185 S Orange Ave Newark NJ 07103-2757

EVANS, HUGH WILLIAMS, retired mining engineer, consultant; b. Mar. 21, 1924. Cert. engr. of mines, Colo. Sch. of Mines, 1943. Pres. Old Ben Coal Co., Chgo., 1980-84, Enoxy Coal Co., Cin., 1984-85, Union Terminal Assn., Cin., 1986-92; cons. Citizen's Democracy Corp., IESC. E-mail: hevans621@aol.com. Home: 768 Rockway Place Boulder CO 80303-3243

EVANS, JACK, city official; b. Oct. 31, 1953. Student, U. Pa., U. Pitts. Past atty. divs. enforcement SEC, Washington; past co-founder ward 2 Dem. Com., Washington, past chmn. rules and procedures com.; pres. Washington D.C. Dem. Party, 1988; city councilman ward 2 Washington D.C. City Coun., 1991—, chmn. regional auth. com., mem. consumer and regulatory affairs, econ. devel., mem. pub. works and govt. operating coms.; assoc. Baker & Hostetler Law Firm. Mem. Dupont Cir. Adv. Neighborhood Commn., 1988—. *

EVANS, JAMES BREMOND (JIM EVANS), major league baseball umpire; b. Longview, Tex., Nov. 5, 1946; s. Woodrow Wilson and Martha Mae (Wood) E.; m. Duana Cherise Simmons, Feb. 15, 1986; 1 child, Lindsay. AA, Kilgore Jr. Coll., 1966; BS in Edn., U. Tex., 1969. Cert. tchr., Tex. Umpire classification A Fla. State League, 1968; umpire classification AA Tex. League, 1969-70; umpire classification AAA Am. Assn., 1971; umpire maj. league Am. League, 1972—, umpire, crew chief maj. league, 1981—; owner Jim Evans' Acad. of Profl. Umpiring, Kissimmee, Fla., 1989—; umpire internat. Super Series, Am. League-Nat. League All-Stars game, Japan, 1988; condr. umpiring and rules clinic, Japan, 1988. Author: Official Baseball Rules Annotated, 1992, Professional Baseball Rules Index, 1991; creator: (syndicated cartoon strip) Jim Evans' Diamond Challenge, 1991, (animated scoreboard feature) Diamond Challenge, 1992. Umpired World Series games, 1977, 82, 86, 96, Am. League Championship series, 1975, 79, 83, 85, 90, 93, 96, League Divsnl. Series, 1995, 96, All-Star games, 1976, 89. Mem. Maj. League Umpires' Assn. (bd. dirs. 1974-81, v.p. 1982, 83, 86, 87, pres. 1984, 85, 88, 89). Achievements include promotion to maj. league at record age of 23; umpired 7 no-hitters; umpired longest game in maj. league history, 1984; avocations: photography, flying, golf, woodworking. Office: Am League Profl Baseball 350 Park Ave New York NY 10022-6022

EVANS, JAMES BRIAN, geophysics educator; b. Baker City, Oreg., June 25, 1946; s. James Richard and Ruth Mary (Hue) E.; m. Marcia Louise Killam, Aug. 25, 1974; children: Megan Hue, Rebecca Brower, Tristan Isaac. BS cum laude, U. Idaho, 1968; MS in Geophysics, U. Minn., 1975; PhD, MIT, 1978. Postdoctoral assoc. dept. earth, atmos., planetary sci. MIT, Cambridge, 1978-79; asst. prof. dept. geology and geophysics Princeton (N.J.) U., 1980-83; asst. prof. dept. earth, atmos., planetary sci. MIT, Cambridge, 1983-88, assoc. prof. dept. earth, atmos., planetary sci., 1988-93, prof. dept. earth, atmos., planetary sci., 1993—; cons. various indsl. orgns. and govt. panels. Editor: (book; with W. F. Wong) Fault Mechanics and Transport Properties of Rock, 1992; contbr. articles to sci. jours. Lt. USN, 1969-72, Vietnam. Mem. Am. Ceramic Soc., Am. Geophys. Union, Phi Beta Kappa, Sigma Xi. Democrat. Office: MIT 54-718 Cambridge MA 02139-4307

EVANS, JAMES BRUCE, urban planner; b. Troy, Mo., May 26, 1954; s. Jimmie Ray and Sue Ann (Vernatti) E. BA, U. Mo., 1976. From assoc. planner to asst. dir. planning St. Charles County, Mo., 1978-96; spl. projects mgr. City of St. Charles, Mo., 1996—. Mem. Am. Planning Assn. (v.p. Mo. chpt.), St. Charles County Planning Assn. Office: St Charles Dept City Devel 200 N 2nd St Ste 303 Saint Charles MO 63301-2851

EVANS, JAMES E., lawyer; b. 1946. BA, Mich. State U., 1968; JD, Ohio State U., 1970. Bar: Ohio 1971. Assoc. Keating, Muething & Klekamp, 1971-76; v.p., gen. counsel Am. Fin. Corp., Cin., 1976—, now sr. v.p. Office: Am Fin Corp 1 E 4th St Cincinnati OH 45202-3717*

EVANS, JAMES HANDEL, university administrator, architect, educator; b. Bolton, Eng., June 14, 1938; came to U.S., 1965.; s. Arthur Handel and Ellen Bowen (Ramsden) E.; m. Carol L. Mulligan, Sept. 10, 1966; children: Jonathan, Sarah. Diploma of Architecture, U. Manchester, Eng., 1965; MArch., U. Oreg., 1967; postgrad., Cambridge (Eng.) U., 1969-70. Registered architect, Calif., U.K.; cert. NCARB. Assoc. dean. prof. architecture Calif. Poly. State U., San Luis Obispo, 1967-78; prof. art and design San Jose (Calif.) State U., 1979—, assoc. exec. v.p., 1978-81, interim exec. v.p., 1981-82, exec. v.p., 1982-91, interim pres., 1991-92, pres., 1992-95; vice chancellor Calif. State U System, Long Beach, CA, 1995-96; planning pres. Calif. State U. Channel Islands, Ventura; cons. Ibiza Nueva, Ibiza, Spain, 1977-80; vis. prof. Ciudad Universitaria, Madrid, 1977; vis. lectr. Herriott Watt U., Edinburgh, 1970; mem. adv. com. Army Command Staff Coll., Ft. Leavenworth, Kans., 1988. Trustee Good Samaritan Hosp., San Jose, 1987-90; bd. dirs. San Jose Shelter, 1988-90; dir. San Jose C. of C., 1991-94. Sci. Rsch. Coun. fellow Cambridge U., 1969-70. Fellow AIA; mem. Royal Inst. Brit. Architects, Assn. Univ. Architects. Avocation: golf. Office: Calif State Univ Channel Is 1878 S Lewis Rd Camarillo CA 93012-8584

EVANS, JAMES HURLBURT, retired transportation and natural resources executive; b. Lansing, Mich., June 26, 1920; s. James L. and Marie (Hurlburt) E.; m. Mary Johnston Head, 1984; children by previous marriage: Eric B. (dec. 1996), Carol E. Jepperson, Joan E. Madsen. AB, Centre Coll., 1943, DHL (hon.), 1987; JD, U. Chgo., 1948; LLD (hon.), Millikin U., 1978. Bar: Ill. 1949. Atty., loan officer Harris Trust & Savs. Bank, Chgo., 1948-56; sec.-treas. Reuben H. Donnelley Corp., Chgo., 1956-57; v.p., dir. Reuben H. Donnelley Corp. (merged with Dun & Bradstreet 1961), N.Y.C., 1957-62; v.p. fin. Dun & Bradstreet, 1962-65, also bd. dirs.; pres. Seamen's Bank for Savs., N.Y.C., 1965-68, chmn. bd., 1968, trustee, 1965-78; pres. Union Pacific Corp., N.Y.C., 1969-77, chmn., CEO, 1977-85; ret. dir. AT&T, GM Corp., Met. Life Ins. Co., Bristol-Myers, Dun & Bradstreet, Anaconda Corp. Bd. govs. ARC, 1970-76, nat. fund chmn. 1974-76; hon. trustee, former vice chmn. John F. Kennedy Ctr. for Performing Arts; life trustee Nat. Recreation Found., pres. 1971-75, U. Chgo., Ctr. Coll. Ky., Ctrl. Park Conservancy; founding mem. Citizens Adv. Com. on Environ. Quality, 1966-70. Served to lt. USNR, 1943-46; life gov. N.Y. Hosp. Mem. ABA, Bus. Council, Phi Beta Kappa, Omicron Delta Kappa, Delta Kappa Epsilon. Presbyterian. Clubs: Racquet and Tennis, Links, Knickerbocker (N.Y.C.); Metropolitan, Alfalfa (Washington); Maidstone (East Hampton); Bohemian (San Francisco). Office: 375 Park Ave Ste 2005 New York NY 10152-2099

EVANS, JAMES MIGNON, architect; b. Memphis, May 9, 1938; s. Mignon Kemper and Elizabeth Louise (Fulcher) E.; m. Gayle Jean Dupont, Aug. 21, 1965; children: Matthew Moseby, Benjamin Dupont, Bolin Briscoe. BA, Rice U., 1960; MFA in Architecture, Princeton U., 1962. Registered architect, Tenn., Va., Calif., Ariz., N.Y. Intern architect Perkins & Will Ptnrship., Washington, 1965-66; architect Doxiadis Assocs., Washington, 1966-68; architect Gassner Nathan & Browne, Memphis, 1969-70, prin., 1970-87; prin. Nathan/Evans/Taylor, Memphis, 1987-95, Nathan/Evans/Taylor/Coleman/Foster, Memphis, 1995—; mem. bldg. code rev. and adv. bd. Memphis and Shelby Counties, 1980-83; mem. Memphis Heritage Adv. Com., 1980-84. Trustee Grace-St. Luke's Episcopal Sch., Memphis, 1980-86, pres., 1984-85; mem. vestry Grace-St. Luke's Episcopal Ch., 1983-86, 90-93, jr. warden, 1992, 93; bd. dirs. Dismas House, Memphis, 1989-94, pres., 1992, 93. Served with U.S. Army, 1963-65. Lowell M. Palmer fellow, 1961-62; recipient Sylvan award Lumberman's Club of Memphis, 1983, 85, Excellence award Masonry Inst. Tenn., 1980, 89, 91, Energy Design Honor award TVA, 1988. Mem. AIA (treas. 1978, peer reviewer 1987—, Honor award 1978, 94), Tenn. Soc. Architects (bd. dirs. 1977-80, Excellence award 1978, 81, 96, , 97, Honor award 1981, 89, 91), Memphis Inst. Architects (v.p. 1980, pres. 1981), Memphis Rotary. Club: Univ. of Memphis. Avocations: jogging, gardening, reading. Office: Nathan/Evans/Taylor/Coleman/Foster 265 Court Ave Memphis TN 38103-2313

EVANS, JANET, Olympic swimmer; b. Placentia, Calif., Aug. 28, 1971. Degree in comms., U. So. Calif., 1994. 4 time Gold medalist, 400m Freestyle, 800m Individual Medley Seoul Olympic Games, 1988; Gold medalist, 800m Freestyle Barcelona Olympic Games, 1992, Silver medalist, 400m Freestyle, 1992; wubber 40th nat. title-400m Freestyle Phillips 66 Nat. Swimming Championships, Indpls., 1994; competed Atlanta Olympic Games, 1996; swimming coach U. So. Calif. Named U.S. Swimmer of Yr., 1987. Office: US Swimming Inc One Olympic Plaza Colorado Springs CO 80909-5724*

EVANS, JEANETTE MARIE, operating room nurse; b. Detroit, Dec. 1, 1964; d. Edward Francis and Virginia Mary (Schultz) Dolan; m. Peter Haywood Evans, Mar. 21, 1987. BSN, Ga. So. Coll., 1989; student, Auburn U. RN, Ga. Med./surg. nurse Kennestone Hosp., Marietta, Ga., 1989-90, oper. rm. nurse, 1990-91; oper. rm. nurse Commanche County Meml. Hosp., Lawton, Okla., 1992—; nurse CCU St. Vincent's Hosp., Birmingham, Ala., 1992—, evening supr. oper. rm., 1993-98; mgr. oper. rm. Mary Bridge Childrens Hosp: Multicare Med. Ctr., Tacoma, 1998—. Mem. ANA, Assn. Operating Room Nurses (CNOR).

EVANS, JEFFREY ALLEN, lawyer; b. Washington; s. Thomas Jay and Ann Evans. BA in Polit. Sci. with honors, U. Calif., Berkeley, 1992; JD, U. Va., 1997. Intern Select Com. on Narcotics Abuse and Control, Washington, 1987; programmer Montgomery Securities, San Francisco, 1991-92; snowboard instr. Aspen Ski Co., Snowmass, Colo., 1993-94; summer assoc. Freshfields, London, 1995, Davis Polk & Wardwell, N.Y.C., 1996, Covington & Burling, Washington, 1996, O'Melveny & Myers, Newport Beach, Calif., 1997; summer assoc. Wilson Sonsini Goodrich & Rosati, Palo Alto, Calif., 1997, assoc., 1998—; jud. clk. Hon. Raymond A. Jackson U.S. Dist. Ct. for the Ea. Dist. Va., Norfolk, 1997-98; assoc. Wilson Sonsini Goodrich & Rosati, Palo Alto, Calif., 1998—. Mng. editor Va. Jour. Internat. Law, 1995-97; mem. editl. bd. Va. Law Rev., 1996-97. Mem. Phi Delta Phi, Pi Kappa Alpha (Alpha Sigma chpt. sec. 1989-90), Order of the Coif, Order of Omega. Avocations: travel, golf, snowboarding.

EVANS, JIM See EVANS, JAMES BREMOND

EVANS, JO BURT, communications executive, rancher; b. Kimble County, Tex., Dec. 18, 1928; d. John Fred and Sadie (Oliver) Burt; m. Charles Wayne Evans II, Apr. 17, 1949; children: Charles Wayne III, John Burt, Elizabeth Wisart. BA, Mary Hardin-Baylor Coll., 1948; MA, Trinity U., 1967. Owner, mgr. Sta. KMBL, Junction, Tex., 1959-61; real estate broker, Junction, 1965-74; staff economist, adv. on 21st Congl. Dist., polit. campaign Nelson Wolff, 1974-75; asst. mgr., bookkeeper family owned ranches and rent property, Junction, 1948—; gen. mgr. TV Translator Corp., Junction, 1968—, sec.-treas., 1980—. Treas., asst. to coordinator Citizens for Tex., 1972; historian Kimble Hist. Soc.; mem. Com. of Conservation Soc. to Save the Edwards Aquifer, San Antonio, 1973; homecoming chmn. Sesquicentennial Year, Junction; treas., asst. coordinator New Constitution, San Antonio, 1974; legis. chair Hill Country Women, Kimble County, 1990—; cashier Texan Theater. AAUW scholarship named in honor, 1973; named an outstanding Texan, Tex. Senate, 1973. Mem. Nat. Translator Assn., AAUW, Daus. Republic Tex., Tex. Sheriffs Assn., Nat. Cattlewomens Assn., Internat. Platform Assn., Bus. and Profl. Women (pres. 1981-82). Republican. Mem. Unity Ch. Home: PO Box 283 Junction TX 76849-0283 Office: 618 Main St Junction TX 76849-4635

EVANS, JOHN DAVID DANIEL, judge; b. Feb. 5, 1944; m. Valerie Roscoe, 1974; children: Reagan, Quentin Cory, Jonathan. BA, U. Western Ont., 1967; LLB, Windsor Law Sch., 1972. Bar: Ont. 1974. Assoc. W.L.S. trivett, Q.C., Orillia, Ont., 1974, Robert J. Carter, Q.C., Toronto, Ont., 1975-76; ptnr. Evans, Kukurin, Timmins, Ont., 1976-77, Perras, Evans, Kukurin & Huot, Timmins, Ont., 1977-80, Riopelle, Evans, Chornyj and Carr, Timmins, 1980-84; apptd. judge Criminal divsn. Provincial Ct., Ont., 1984-90, apptd. regional sr. jurdge ctrl. east region, 1990—; faculty law St. Clair CC., No. C.C., Laurentian U. Mem. Criminal Lawyers Assn., Can. Bar Assn., Am. Judges Assn. (bd. govs.). Roman Catholic. Avocations: sports, hockey playing. Office: Ont Ct Justice, 3 Dominion St, Bracebridge, ON Canada P1L 2E6

EVANS, JOHN DERBY, telecommunications company executive; b. Detroit, June 3, 1944; s. Edward Steptoe and Florence (Allington) E.; m. Susan Blair Allan, Apr. 7, 1973 (div. Nov. 1986); children: John Derby, Courtenay Boyd. AB, U. Mich., 1966. Pres. Evans Comm. Sys. Inc., Charlottesville, Va., 1970-72; v.p., gen. mgr. Capitol Cablevision Corp., Charleston, W.Va., 1972-76; regional mgr. Am. TV and Comm. Corp., Denver, 1974-76; exec. v.p., COO Arlington (Va.) TeleCom. Corp., 1976-83; pres. Arlington Cable Ptnrs. Ltd., 1983-94, Suburban Cable Ptnrs., Brooklyn Pk., Minn., 1985-89, Hauser Comm., N.Y.C., 1985-94, Evans Telecomm. Co., 1983—; chmn., CEO Waterford Marine Inc., Key West, Fla., 1996—; staff asst. sec. planning and devel. Dept. HEW, Washington, 1976; bd. dirs. Eisenhower World Affairs Inst., strategic planning com., 1997—; vice chmn. bd. dirs. Signature Theater, Inc., Arlington, Va., Cable Satelliter Pub. Affairs Network (C-SPAN), exec. com., 1982-93, 98—, chmn., 1991-93, chmn. fin. com., 1997—; pres. Montgomery Cablevision (LP), Rockville, Md., 1986-94, Washington Metro Cable Club, 1981—; bd. dirs. Falcon Comm. Co., L.A., Falcon Cable TV, 1998—, Sierraware Inc., Sacremento, Calif., 1999—; GBR scientific, 1999—, Sierraware Inc., Sacramento, GBR Sci. Co., Balt.; v.p. North Ctrl. Cable Comm. Co., Roseville, Minn., 1986-92; mng. gen. ptnr. Waterford Farm Partnership, Middleburg, Va., 1993—; Siciliano forum lectr. U. Utah, 1998; future makers lectr. Emory U., 1999. Trustee C-Span Ednl. Found., 1994—, Signature Theater, Arlington; chmn. bd. trustees Evans Found., 1994—; chmn. Cancer/AIDS Rsch. Network, Balt.; mem. steering com. Inst. Human Virology U. Md., Balt.; bd. dirs. Internat. Cancer and AIDS Rsch. Found., Hollings Cancer Ctr., Charleston, S.C.; adv. com. AIDS Rsch. Inst. U. Calif., San Francisco. Mem. Nat. Cable TV Assn. (nat. chmn. awards com. 1981, bd. dirs. 1982—, chmn. govt. rels. com. 1985-86, chmn. elections, bylaws com. 1991-97, mem. regulatory policy com. 1991-95, mem. conv. com. 1999, Pres. award 1979, Vanguard award 1984, convention com. 1998—), Va. Cable Assn. (bd. dirs. 1979—, v.p. 1982, pres. 1983, 84), Asia-Pacific Conf. Sci. and Tech. Leaders (U.S. del. 1996), Fisher Island (Fla.) Club, Caribbean Acad. of Sci. (U.S. del. 10th ann. meeting 1998), Farmington Country Club, Boars Head Sports Club (Charlottesville), Wintergreen (Va.) Sports Club, Washington Golf and Country Club (Arlington), Cable TV Adminstrn., Mktg. Soc. (bd. dirs. 1985). Republican. Episcopalian. Home and Office: Waterford Farm PO Box 1082 Rte 709 Middleburg VA 20118

EVANS, JOHN JOSEPH, management professional, writer; b. St. Louis, Mar. 1, 1940; s. Roy Joseph and Henrietta Frances (Schweizer) E.; BA, Centenary Coll., 1962; postgrad. Syracuse U., 1969, U. Wis., 1971, Harvard Bus. Sch., 1971-73; MBA, Pepperdine U., 1972; children—Todd, Karlyn, Jane, Mark. Pres. Evans & Co., 1966—; adj. prof. Centenary Coll., Golf

Acad. San Diego. Bd. dirs. ARC; trustee Grad. Sch. Sales Mgmt. and Mktg.; pres. La. Real Estate Investment Trust; chmn. bd. dirs. N. La. Mental Health Hosp. Recipient awards United Way, 1965-69, ITVA awards, 1987-88. Mem. Nat. Beer Wholesalers Assn. (adv. dir.), Sales and Mktg. Execs. of Shreveport (pres.), S.W. Sales and Mktg. Execs. Council (pres.), Young Pres. Orgn., Pres.'s Assn. of AMA, Conf. Bd., Aspen Inst., Sales and Mktg. Execs. Internat., Am. Soc. Tng. and Devel., Am. Soc. Personnel Adminstrn., Syracuse U. Grad. Sch. Sales Mgmt. and Mktg. Alumni Assn. (past pres., past trustee), Westlake Village C. of C. (past v.p., bd. dirs.), Shreveport C. of C., Personnel and Indsl. Relations Assn. (vice chmn., bd. dirs.), Harvard Club of San Diego. Home and Office: 9974 Scripps Ranch Blvd # 175 San Diego CA 92131-1825

EVANS, JOHN ROBERT, former university president, physician; b. Toronto, Oct. 1, 1929; s. William Watson and Mary Evelyn Lucille (Thompson) E.; m. Jean Gay Glassco, 1954; children: Derek, Mark and Michael (twins), Gillian, Timothy, Willa. MD, U. Toronto, 1952; DPhil (Rhodes scholar), Oxford U., 1955; LLD (hon.), Dalhousie U., McMaster U., McGill U., 1972, Queen's U., 1974, Wilfred Laurier U., 1975, York U., 1977, U. Toronto, 1980, U. Western Ont., 1982, Yale U., 1978; DSc (hon.), Meml. U., 1973, U. Montreal, 1977, Royal Mil. Coll., 1989; DHL (hon.), Johns Hopkins U., 1978; D Univ. (hon.), U. Ottawa, 1978, U. Limbourg, The Netherlands, 1980. Intern Toronto Gen. Hosp., 1952-53, chief resident physician, 1958-59; practice medicine specializing in cardiology Toronto, 1961-72; assoc. dept. medicine U. Toronto Med. Sch., 1961-65, prof., 1972—, pres. univ., 1972-78, pres. emeritus, 1995—; dir. population, health and nutrition dept. World Bank, Washington, 1979-83; chmn. Allelix Inc., Mississauga, Ont., 1983—; physician Toronto Gen. Hosp., 1961-65; dean Faculty Medicine McMaster U., Hamilton, Ont., 1965-72, v.p. health scis., 1967-72; chmn. Torstar Corp., Toronto, 1993—, Alcan Aluminium Ltd., Montreal, 1995—; bd. dirs. Allelix Inc., Torstar Ltd., Toronto, Alcan Aluminum Ltd., Montreal, MDS Health Group, Toronto, Connaught Labs., Inc., Toronto, Pasteur Merieux Serums and Vaccines, Lyon, France; hon. fellow London Sch. Hygiene and Tropical Medicine, Univ. Coll., Oxford, Eng.; chmn. Can. Found. Innovation, 1997—. Trustee Rockefeller Found., N.Y.C., 1982-95, chmn., 1988-95; chmn. African Med. Rsch. Found., Can., 1986-90; trustee Walter and Duncan Gordon Charitable Found., Toronto, 1991—, chair, 1998—. Decorated companion Order of Can., 1978; Order of Ontario, 1991; Markle scholar, 1960-65; recipient Gairdner Foundation Wightman Award, Gairdner Foundation, 1992. Fellow Royal Soc. Can., Royal Coll. Physicians and Surgeons Can., Royal Coll. Physicians (London); Master ACP. Home: 58 Highland Ave, Toronto, ON Canada M4W 2A3 Office: Torstar Ltd, 1 Yonge St, Toronto, ON Canada M5E 1P9

EVANS, JOHN THOMAS, lawyer; b. N.Y.C., Feb. 28, 1948; s. John Arthur and Dorothy (Reilly) E.; m. Marie Tolnay, June 2, 1979; children—Claire, Grace. B.A., U. Wis., 1970; J.D., Fordham U., 1973. Bar: N.Y. 1974, U.S. Dist. Ct. (so. and ea. dists.) N.Y., U.S. Tax Ct. Asst. dist. atty. N.Y. County, N.Y.C., 1973-79; assoc. Blumenthal & Lynne, N.Y.C., 1979-81; ptnr. Morris & Duffy, N.Y.C., 1982-85, Belair, Klein, Groman & Evans, N.Y.C., 1985—; cons. Vol. Lawyers for Arts, N.Y.C., 1979-84, Hofstra U. Law Sch. Moot Ct. Program, Uniondale, N.Y., 1982; cons., lectr. N.Y.C. Police Dept. Detectives Endowment Assn., 1981—. Author: Arguing Cases Before A Medical Malpractice Law & Strategy; contbr. articles to profl. jours. Recipient Highest award Manhattan Detective Area, N.Y.C., 1979. Mem. N.Y. State Bar Assn., Assn. Bar City of N.Y., N.Y. Criminal Bar Assn. Club: N.Y. Athletic (N.Y.C.). Home: 362 W Broadway New York NY 10013-5303 Office: Belair & Evans 61 Broadway New York NY 10006-2701

EVANS, JOHN VAUGHAN, communications satellite executive, physicist; b. Manchester, Eng., July 5, 1933; came to U.S., 1960; s. Cyril John and Gertrude Veronica (Bayliss) E. BS in Physics, Manchester U., 1954, PhD, 1957. Leverhulme research fellow Jodrell Bank Exptl. Sta., U.K., 1957-60; staff mem. Lincoln Lab., MIT, Lexington, 1960-66, 67-70, assoc. group leader surveillance techniques, 1970-72, group leader, 1972-74, assoc. div. head Aerospace div., 1974-77, asst. dir., 1977-83; dir. Haystack Obs., prof. meteorology MIT, Cambridge, 1980-83; v.p. research and devel. COMSAT Labs., Clarksburg, Md., 1983, v.p., dir., 1983-92, pres., 1992-96; chief tech. officer COMSAT Corp., Bethesda, Md., 1996—; G.A. Miller vis. prof. U. Ill., Urbana, 1966-67; trustee Univ. Corp. for Atmospheric Research, Boulder, Colo., 1980-87. Editor: (with T. Hagfors) Radar Astronomy, 1968; contbr. numerous articles to profl. jours. Served with Brit. Territorial Army, 1951-57. Recipient Appleton prize Royal Soc. London, 1954. Fellow AIAA, IEEE; mem. Nat. Acad. Engring., Am. Geophys. Union, Internat. Astron. Union. Unitarian. Club: Cosmos (Washington). Office: COMSAT Corp 6560 Rock Spring Dr Bethesda MD 20817-1146

EVANS, JUDY ANNE, health center administrator; b. Elmira, N.Y., Mar. 29, 1940; d. Hugh Kenneth and Mary (Faul) Leach; m. Nolly Seymour Evans, Feb. 18, 1965; children: Samantha, Meredydd, Clelia, Nolly III. BS, Cornell U., 1962; MBA, Syracuse U., 1992. Fin. analyst Morgan Guaranty Trust Co., N.Y.C., 1962-66; bus. adminstr. SUNY Health Sci. Ctr., Syracuse, 1983-89, adminstr. dept. pediatrics, 1990-99; adminstr. Biomed. Engring. Inst. Johns Hopkins U., Balt., 1999—. Mem. allocations com. Children Miracle Network, Syracuse, 1990-99; children's hosp. steering com. Crouse Irving/Univ. Hosp., Syracuse, 1990-99; bd. dirs. Syracuse Friends of Chamber Music, 1983-89, Syracuse Camerata, 1982-88; adminstr. Johns Hopkins Biomed. Engring., 1999—. Mem. Assn. Adminstrs. of Acad. Pediatrics. Avocations: sailing, cooking. Home: 912 B Woodson Rd Baltimore MD 21212 Office: 710 Traylor Baltimore MD 21205-2196

EVANS, LANE, congressman; b. Rock Island, Ill., Aug. 4, 1951; s. Lee Herbert and Joycelene (Saylor) E. B.A., Augustana Coll., 1974; J.D., Georgetown U., 1978. Bar: Ill. 1978. Mng. atty. Western Ill. Legal Assistance Found., Rock Island, 1978-79; mem. nat. staff Kennedy for Pres., Washington, 1978-80; atty., ptnr. Community Legal Clinic, Rock Island, Ill., 1981-82; mem. 98th-106th Congresses from 17th Ill. Dist., 1983—; mem. nat. security com., ranking mem. vets. affairs com. Served with USMC, 1969-71. Mem. AmVets, Am. Legion, Marine Corps League, Vietnam Vets Ill. Democrat. Roman Catholic. Office: US Ho of Reps 2335 Rayburn Bldg Washington DC 20515-1317

EVANS, LAWRENCE JACK, JR., lawyer, judge; b. Oakland, Calif., Apr. 4, 1921; s. Lawrence Jack and Eva May (Dickinson) E.; m. Marjorie Hisken, Dec. 23, 1944; children: Daryl S. Kleweno, Richard L., Shirley J. Coursey, Donald B. Diplomate Near East Sch. Theology, Beirut, 1951; MA, Am. U. Beirut, 1951; grad. Command and Gen. Staff Coll., 1960; PhD, Brantridge Forest Sch., Sussex, Eng., 1968; JD, Ariz. State U., 1971; grad. Nat. Jud. Coll., 1974. Bar: Ariz. 1971, U.S. Dist. Ct. Ariz. 1971, U.S. Ct. Claims 1972, U.S. Customs Ct., 1972, U.S. Tax Ct. 1972, U.S. Ct. Customs and Patent Appeals 1972, U.S. Ct. Appeals (9th cir.) 1972, U.S. Supreme Ct. 1975. Enlisted U.S. Navy, 1938-41, U.S. Army, 1942-44, commd. 2d lt. U.S. Army, 1944, advanced through ranks to lt. col., 1962; war plans officer, G-3 Seventh Army, 1960-62, chief, field ops. and tactics divsn., U.S. Army Spl. Forces, 1963, chief spl. techniques divsn., U.S. Army Spl. Forces, 1964, unconventional warfare monitor, U.S. Army Spl. Forces, 1964-65; ops. staff officer J-3 USEUCOM, 1965-68; mem. Airborne Command Post Study Group, Joint Chiefs of Staff, 1967; ret., 1968; mem. faculty Ariz. State U., 1968; sole practice law, cons. on Near and Middle Eastern affairs, Tempe, Ariz., 1971-72, 76—; v.p., dir. Trojan Investment & Devel. Co., Inc., 1972-75; active Ariz. Tax Conf., 1971-75; mem. adminstrv. law com., labor mgmt. rels. com., unauthorized practice of law com. Ariz. State Bar. Author: Legal Aspects of Land Tenure in the Republic of Lebanon, 1951, International Constitutional Law, (with Helen Miller Davis) Electoral Laws and Treaties of the Near and Middle East, 1951; contbr. articles to mags., chpts. to books. Chmn. legal and legis. com. Phoenix Mayor's Com. To Employ Handicapped, 1971-75; active Tempe Leadership Conf., 1971-75; mem. Citizens Against Corruption in Govt., 1976-95; mem. Princeton Coun. on Fgn. and Internat. Studies, 1968; comdr. Ranger Area-Ariz., Ranger Region-West, 1993—. Decorated Silver Star, Legion of Merit, Bronze Star, Purple Heart, Combat Infantryman badge, Master Parachutist badge, Aircrewman badge; named Outstanding Adminstrv. Law Judge for State Service for U.S., 1974; named to U.S. Army Ranger Hall of Fame, 1981. Fellow Coll. of Rites of U.S.A.; mem. Ranger Bns. Assn. World War II (life), Tempe Rep. Mens Club (v.p., bd. dirs. 1971-72), U.S. Army Airborne Ranger Assn. (life), Mil. Order Purple Heart (life), NRA (official referee, life), Masonic Order of the Bath, The Philatethes Soc., Ye Antient and Old Order of Corks, Order of the Secret Monitor, BL (twice past master Thunderbird Lodge # 48 Phoenix, past master Ariz. Rsch. Lodge # 1), Order Ky. Colonels, Sovereign Mil. Order of Temple of Jerusalem (grand avocat pro tem 1993, grand officier 1993), Knight Commdr. Grace Sovereign Mil. Order St. John Jerusalem (Knights Hospitallers), Grand Chpt. Royal Arch Masons Ariz. (grand lectr.), Fraternal Order of Medieval Knighthood, Internat. (sovereign venerable master Ariz. Coll. 1988-93, supreme sovereign grand master 1991), YR (past high priest, past thrice illustrious master, twice eminent past comdr., Knight Templar Cross of Honor, 1988, Orator Order of High Priesthood, Grand Chpt. YRM 1989, pres. Grand Coun. Holy Order of High Priesthood of Ariz. 1996-97, York Rite Mason of Decade, Scottsdale YRB 1989), SR (32, ritual dir.), Chief Adept Ariz. Coll. Socs. Rosicruceana In Civitatibus Foederatis IX Degree, Grand Commandery of Knights Templar of Ariz. (grand insp. gen. 1990-91), Grand Royal Arch Masons Ariz. (grand lectr. 1995-96), Masons (knight U.S.A., Chevalier and Ami du Patriarchate, KCM Ordo Sancti Constantini Magni), Order of Secret Monitor, So. Calif. Rsch. Lodge, Royal Order of Scotland, Comdr. Ranger Area-Ariz. (Ranger Region- West Red 1993), Mil. Order of World Wars (historian, archivist), The Nat. Sojourners Inc., United Assn. (life, local #469 Phoenix), Phi Delta Phi, Delta Theta Phi, Alpha Rho of Theta Chi. Episcopalian. Home: 539 E Erie Dr Tempe AZ 85282-3712

EVANS, LINDA KAY, publishing company executive; b. Tipton, Ind., June 16, 1945; d. Walter K. and Helen S. (Fakes) E. BA in English, Purdue U., 1968. Asst. to mng. editor Random House Pubs., N.Y.C., 1969-71; asst. to dir. editorial svcs. Sch. div. McGraw-Hill Book Co., N.Y.C., 1971-75, mgr. state contracts and inventory dept., 1975-88; bookstore owner, pres. The Literary Bookshop, N.Y.C., 1988-93; prodn. mgr. trade div. Simon & Schuster, N.Y.C., 1994—; pub. cons. for sch. textbooks Prentice-Hall Book Co., Englewood Cliffs, N.J., 1992-93. Recipient Holiday Window Display award to Lit. Bookshop, Greenwich Village C. of C., 1990. Avocations: reading, antique collecting, furniture making, travel. Office: Simon & Schuster Trade Div Ste 383 1230 Avenue Of The Americas Fl Concl New York NY 10020-1586

EVANS, LINDA PERRYMAN, foundation administrator; b. Dallas, Apr. 25, 1950; d. Walter Lewis Perryman Jr. and Betty Lou (Slaughter) Williams; married, 1990. BS, U. Tex., 1972; postgrad., E. Tex. State U., 1975, So. Meth. U., 1976. Press asst. Pres. Ford Com., Washington, 1976; press asst. Connally for Pres. Com., Washington, 1977-79; adminstrv. asst. Am. Enterprise Inst., Washington, 1980-81; staff asst. The White House, Washington, 1981-83; exec. dir. Dallas Welcoming Com., 1984-85; pres. Linda Perryman & Assocs., Dallas, 1985-87; vice chmn. Stern, Nathan & Perryman, Dallas, 1987-90; v.p., dir., trustee Meadows Found., Dallas, 1987-96, pres., COO, 1996—. Active Charter 100, Dallas; bd. dirs. Tex. Bus. Hall of Fame Found., YWCA Dallas, Equest, Dallas Citizens Coun.; mem. Cattle Baron's Ball com. Jr. League of Dallas, mem. Crystal Charity Ball com.; appointee Coll. Opportunity Act Com. Gov. Bill Clements, 1989; mem. Dallas Assembly. Office: Meadows Foundation Inc Wilson Historic Block 3003 Swiss Ave Dallas TX 75204-6049*

EVANS, LISBETH, business networking executive, political party official; b. Clarkton, N.C.; m. James T. Lambie; 3 stepchildren. BS, MBA, Wake Forest U. Tchr.; with Alex. Brown & Sons Inc., Merrill Lynch, Pierce Fenner & Smith; pres. Health Equity Properties; CEO, bd. dirs. BizNexus; CEO, bd. dirs., sole shareholder West 3d St. Mgmt. Co. Chair N.C. Dem. Party; mem. Dem. Nat. Com.; Dem. chair Women's Campaign Fund. Presbyterian. Office: 8 W 3d Ste 400 Winston Salem NC 27101*

EVANS, LOUISE, investor, clinical psychologist, philanthropist; b. San Antonio, Sept. 6; d. Henry Daniel and Adela (Pariser) E.; m. thomas Ross Gambrell, Feb. 23, 1960. BS, Northwestern U., 1949; MS in Clin. Psychology, Purdue U., 1952, PhD in Clin. Psychology, 1955. Lic. Marriage, Family and Child Counselor Calif.; Nat. Register of Health Svc. Providers in Psychology, lic. psychologist, Calif., Am. Bd. Profl. Psychologist N.Y.; diplomate Clin. Psychology, Am. Bd. Profl. Psychology, Am. Bd. Clin. Psychology. Intern clin. psychology Menninger Found. Topeka (Kans.) State Hosp., 1952-53; staff psychologist Kankakee (Ill.) State Hosp., 1954; postdoctoral fellow clin. child psychology Menninger Found. Topeka (Kans.) State Hosp., 1955-56; head staff psychologist Kings County Hosp., Bklyn., 1957-58; dir. psychology Barnes-Renard Hosp., 1959; pvt. practice, 1960-92; cons. Episc. City Diocese, St. Louis, 1959, Fullerton (Calif.) Cmty. Hosp., 1961-81, Martin Luther Hosp., Anaheim, Calif., 1963-70; lectr. in field. Contbr. articles on clin. psychology to profl. jours. Elected to Hall of Fame Ctrl. High Sch., Evansville, Ind., 1966; recipient Svc. award Yuma County (Ariz.) Head Start Program, 1972, Statue of Victory Personality of Yr. award Centro Studi E. Ricerche Delle Nazioni, Italy, 1985, Alumni Merit award Northwestern U. Coll. Arts and Scis., 1997; named Miss Heritage, Heritage Publs., 1965, recipient, first Purdue Alumni Assn. Citizenship Awd. Fellow AAAS, APA (dir. exec. bd. 1976-79), Acad. Clin. Psychology, Am. Assn. Applied and Preventative Psychology, Royal Soc. Health England, Internat. Coun. Psychologists, Am. Orthopsychiat. Assn., Am. Psychol. Soc., World Wide Acad. Scholars of N.Z.; mem. AAUP, Internat. Platform Assn., Am. Pub. Health Assn., N.Y. Acad. Scis., Calif. State Psychol. Assn. (L.A. County chpt., Orange County chpt. founding mem., exec. bd. 1961-62), L.A. Soc. Clin. Psychologists (Orange County chpt. founder, exec. bd. 1963-65, pres. 1964-65), Purdue U. Alumni Assn. (life mem., pres. coun., dean's club pacesetters, citizenship award for contribs. to the mental health field 1975, disting. alumni award 1993, Old Master 1993), Northwestern U. 1851 and Wilson Soc. (coll. arts and scis. Alumni merit award 1997), Ctr. Study Presidency, Soc. Jewelry Historians USA, Alumni Assn. Menninger Sch. Psychiatry, Sigma Xi, Pi Sigma Pi (sec. 1946-47, pres. 1947-48). Achievements include devel. of innovative theories and techniques of clinical practice; acknowledged pioneer in devel. psychology as sci. and profession both nat. and internat., and in marital and family therapy. Office: PO Box 6067 Beverly Hills CA 90212-1067

EVANS, MARGARET ANN, human resources administrator, business owner; b. Great Bend, Kans., Dec. 26, 1947; d. Freddy Florence and Peggy (Hawkins) Green; m. Carl Evans, Aug. 13, 1972; children: Carl Andre, Christopher Dion. B in Psychology, U. Mo., 1971, MPA, 1972. Pers. specialist Met. Jr. Coll., Kansas City, Mo., 1972-73; employee rels. specialist Amoco Oil Co., Kansas City, 1973-74; classification specialist Richards-Gebaur AFB, Mo., 1974-75; employee rels. officer Govt. Employee Hosp. Assn., Kansas City, 1977-84, mgr. pers., 1984-87, dir. human resources, 1987—; mem. pers. com. Sta. KKFI, Kansas City, 1989—; mem. cert. bd. Human Resource Inst., exam devel. dir., 1994-95, sec.-treas., 1995-96. Sec. and v.p. Booster Club, Hickman Mills High Sch., Kansas City, 1989—. Ford Found. fellow U. Mo., 1971; recipient Contbr. of Yr. award Human Resource Mgmt. Assn., 1992, Pres. award 1993, 1995; named One of Kansas City's 100 Most Influential Kansas Citians KC Globe Most Influential African Ams. of Kansas City, 1996. Mem. NAFE, Soc. Human Resources Mgmt. (pers. rsch. com. Kansas City chpt. 1989—, nat. com. 1990—, sec.-treas. Mo. state coun. 1992-93, area IV bd. mem.), Pers. Mgmt. Assn. (co-chmn. coll. rels. 1991), Urban League, NAACP, Links, Inc., ASPA, ASTD, Alpha Kappa Alpha (chair midwestern regional conf., 1996, Outstanding Grad. Soror). Home: 10216 E 96th St Kansas City MO 64134-2309 Office: Govt Employee Hosp Assn 17306 E Us Highway 24 Independence MO 64056-1808

EVANS, MARIWYN, periodical editor. Exec. editor Jour. Property Mgmt., Chgo. Office: Jour Property Mgmt 430 N Michigan Ave Chicago IL 60611-4002*

EVANS, MARK IRA, obstetrician, geneticist; b. Bklyn., May 14, 1952; s. Robert Bernard and Sonia Beatrice (Silverstein) E.; m. Wendy JoAnne Greenwood, Sept. 5, 1981. BS in Psychology, Tufts U., 1973; MD, SUNY, Bklyn., 1978. Diplomate Am. Bd. Ob-Gyn, Am. Bd. Med. Genetics. Resident in ob-gyn U. Chgo., 1978-82; med. genetics fellow NIH, Bethesda, Md., 1982-84; dir. reproductive genetics Hutzel Hosp. Wayne State U., Detroit, 1984—, Charlotte B. Failing prof., chief and chmn. ob-gyn., prof. and chief human genetics, ctr. molecular med. and pathology, 1991-98, dir. Ctr. for Fetal Diagnosis and Therapy, 1985—, dir. human genetics program, 1996—, chmn., chief, 1998—; mem. adv. bd. Ehlrs Danlos Found., L.A., 1986—, Corning Metpath, Quest Diagnostics, Nat. Adv. Bd. on Ethics in Reprodn., Washington; mem. ethics com. Am. Coll. Ob-Gyn., 1987-90, Molecular Medicine and Genetics, Wayne State U. Author: (textbooks) Pretest: Obsterics and Gynecology, 6th rev. edit., 1991, 7th rev. edit., 1995, 8th edit., 1997, (with C.C. Lin) Intrauterine Growth Retardation, 1984, (with others) Fetal Diagnosis Therapy: Science, Ethics and the Law, 1989, Reproductive Risks and Prenatal Diagnosis, 1992, The New Reproductive Genetics, 1993, Maternal Genetic Disease, 1996; (with others) Invasive Outpatient Procedures in Reproductive Medicine, 1997, Principles and Practice of Medical Therapy in Pregnancy, 1998, Study Guide, 1998; contbr. numerous articles to sci. jours. Fellow Am. Coll. Ob-Gyn. (course coordination com. 1996-99), Am. Coll. Med. Genetics (founder); mem. AMA (nat. ultrasound task force 1990-91), Internat. Fetal Medicine Surgery Soc. (pres. 1986-87, 96-97), Am. Soc. Human Genetics, Soc. Gynecol. Investigation, Ctrl. Assn. Ob-Gyn. (bd. dirs. 1998—), Soc. Perinatal Obstetricians, Am. Gynecol. and Obstetrics Soc. Jewish. Home: 4734 Rolling Rdg West Bloomfield MI 48323-3342 Office: Hutzel Hosp Dept Reproductive Genetics 4707 Saint Antoine St Dept Detroit MI 48201-1498

EVANS, MARSHA JO ANNE, nursing administrator; b. Watseka, Ill., Aug. 18, 1951; d. Robert Lewis and Jane Eleanor (Orr) Niles; m. Larry E. Evans, Sept. 16, 1973 (div. Aug. 1997); 1 child, Melinda Joy. BSN, So. Ill. U., 1973. Staff nurse Sevier County Hosp., Sevierville, Tenn., 1973-75; asst. DON Fair Oaks Nursing Home, Edward A. Utlaut Meml. Hosp., Greenville, Ill., 1975-76; insvc. coord., infection control nurse, nursing supr. Fayette County Hosp., Vandalia, Ill., 1976-83, quality assurance coord., 1983-88; infection control coord. St. Anthony's Meml. Hosp., Effingham, Ill., 1988-94, outpatient svcs. rep., 1994-96, home care mgr., 1996-98; utilization mgmt. case mgr. St. John's Hosp., Springfield, Ill., 1998—. Office: St Johns Hosp 800 E Carpenter St Springfield IL 62769

EVANS, MARSHA JOHNSON, former naval officer, non-profit executive; b. Springfield, Ill., Aug. 12, 1947; d. Walter Edward Johnson and Alice Anne (Field) Staffansson; m. Gerard Riendeau Evans, June 30, 1979. AB, Occidental Coll., 1968; MA, Fletcher Sch., 1977, MA in Law & Diplomacy, 1977; postgrad., Nat. War Coll., 1988-89. Commd. ensign USN, 1968, advanced through grades to real admiral, 1993; mideast policy officer Commander-in-Chief, U.S. Naval Forces, Europe, London, 1977-79; spl. asst. to sec. treasury U.S. Treasury Dept., Washington, 1979-80; staff analyst Office of Chief Naval Ops., Washington, 1980-81; dep. dir. Pres. Commn. on White House Fellowships, Washington, 1981-82; exec. officer Recruit Tng. Command, San Diego, 1982-84; commanding officer Naval Tech. Tng. Ctr., San Francisco, 1984-86; battalion officer, sr. lectr. polit. sci. U.S. Naval Acad., Annapolis, Md., 1986-88; chief of staff San Francisco Naval Base, 1989-91, Naval Acad., Annapolis, Md., 1991-92; exec. dir. of the standing com. on mil. and civilian women Dept. of the Navy, 1992-93; comdr. Navy Recruiting Command, Washington, 1993-95; supt. Naval Postgrad. Sch., Monterey, Calif., 1995-97; CEO, nat. exec. dir. Girl Scouts U.S.A., N.Y.C., 1998—; interim dir. George C. Marshall European Ctr. Security Studies, Garmisch Partenkirchen, Germany, 1996-97; nat. exec. dir. Girl Scouts. Am., 1998—. White House fellow, 1979; Chief Naval Ops. scholar, 1976. Mem. Mortar Bd., Phi Beta Kappa. *

EVANS, MARTIN FREDERIC, lawyer; b. Nashville, June 12, 1947; s. Robert Clements and Adelaide Hawkins (Roberts) E.; m. Margaret Carroll Kidder, Apr. 17, 1982. BA, U. Va., 1969; JD, Yale U., 1972. Bar: N.Y. 1973, U.S. Dist. Ct. (so. dist.) N.Y. 1973, U.S. Ct. Appeals (2d cir.) 1974, U.S. Ct. Appeals (D.C. cir.) 1981, U.S. Supreme Ct. 1981, D.C. 1982. Assoc. Debevoise & Plimpton, N.Y.C., 1972-80, ptnr., 1981—; researcher Nat. Commn. for Rev. of Antitrust Laws and Procedure, Washington, 1978. Mem. ABA (sect. for antitrust law), Assn. of Bar of City of N.Y., Phi Beta Kappa. Office: Debevoise & Plimpton 875 3rd Ave Fl 23 New York NY 10022-6256

EVANS, MARY JOHNSTON, corporate director; b. Shawnee, Okla., Feb. 28, 1930; d. Paul Xenophon and Helen Elizabeth (Alford) Johnston; children by previous marriage: Marcy Head Benson, Paul Johnston Head, Eric Talbott Head; m. James H. Evans, 1984. Student, Wellesley Coll., 1947-48, U. Okla., 1949. Dir. Amtrak, 1974-80, vice-chmn., 1975-79; bd. dirs. Household Internat., Inc., Saint-Gobain Corp., The Sun Co., Inc., Baxter Internat. Inc., Delta Air Lines, Inc., Dun and Bradstreet Corp.; mem. adv. bd. Morgan Stanley & Co. Pres. Jr. League Oklahoma City, 1968-69; trustee Nat. Council Crime and Delinquency, 1971-75, Presbyn. Med. Center, Oklahoma City, 1969-75; trustee Brick Presbyn. Ch., 1985-89; bd. dirs. St. Anthony Hosp., 1973-75; bd. visitors U. Pitts. Grad. Sch. Bus., 1978-85; trustee Mary Baldwin Coll., Staunton, Va., 1976-83, Carnegie Hall, 1985-92. Recipient Law Day award-Liberty Bell award Oklahoma Bar Assn., 1971, Disting. Service award U. Okla., 1981; named one of Top 100 Corporate Women Bus. Week mag., 1976; named to Okla. Hall of Fame, 1978. Mem. Conf. Bd. (Sr.), Pi Beta Phi. Presbyterian (elder). Clubs: Colony, River; Maidstone (East Hampton, N.Y.). Address: 920 Fifth Ave New York NY 10021-4160 also: 32 Windmill Ln East Hampton NY 11937-3605

EVANS, MAX JAY, historical society administrator; b. Lehi, Utah, May 11, 1943; s. Karl Robinson and Lucile (Johnson) E.; m. Mary Wheatley, June 16, 1967; children: David Max, Joseph Michael, Katherine Anne, Laura, Emily. BS, U. Utah, 1968; MS, Utah State U., 1971. Archivist LDS Ch. Hist. Dept., Salt Lake City, 1971-75; asst. ch. librarian, archivist Mormon Ch. Hist. Dept., Salt Lake City, 1975-77; dep. state archivist State Hist. Soc. Wis., Madison, 1977-86, library dir., 1986; dir. Utah State Hist. Soc., Salt Lake City, 1986—; acting dir. Utah State Archives, Salt Lake City, 1986-88; archival cons. N.Y. State Archives, Albany, 1981, Wyo Dept. Archives and Hist., Cheyenne, 1982. Co-author: MARC for Archives and Manuscripts: A Compendium of Practice, 1985 (SAA Coker award 1986); articles in field. Trustee Middleton (Wis.) Pub. Libr., 1974-86, Am. West Heritage Found., 1995—; exec. sec. Utah Statehood Centennial Commn., 1988-93, Utah Pioneer Sesquicentennial Celebration Coord. Coun., 1994-98; chair Utah State Rcds. com., 1992—; bd. dirs. Rsch. Librs. Group, 1991-92; coun. mem. Am. Assn. for State and Local History, 1997—. Fellow Soc. Am. Archivists; mem. Utah State Hist. Soc. Mem. LDS Ch. Avocations: cross country and downhill skiing, bicycling, hiking, reading, movies. Office: Utah State Hist Soc 300 Rio Grande St Salt Lake City UT 84101-1106*

EVANS, MICHELLE LEE, lawyer, educator; b. Ft. Sam Houston, Tex., June 22, 1970; d. William H. and Linda Lee (Johnson) E.; m. Richard L. Marryott, Aug. 2, 1996. BS, U. Tex., San Antonio, 1991; JD, St. Mary's U., San Antonio, 1995. Bar: Tex. 1995. Rsch. asst. St. Mary's U. Sch. Law, San Antonio, 1994-95; jud. intern U.S. Dist. Ct., San Antonio, 1995; real estate instr. Am. Coll. Real Estate, San Antonio, 1996-97; instr. Alamo Real Estate Inst., San Antonio, 1997—, Tex. Luth. U., San Antonio, 1997—; paralegal instr. U. Tex., San Antonio, 1997—; prof. San Antonio Coll., 1997—; pvt. practice San Antonio, 1995—; cmty. edn. instr. Northside Ind. Sch. Dist., San Antonio, 1990—. Co-author: Texas Real Estate Contracts, 1999; contbr. articles to profl. jours. Fundraiser March of Dimes, San Antonio, 1991-96. Mem. ABA, Am. Chem. Soc., Real Estate Educators Assn., San Antonio Bar Assn., Greater San Antonio C. of C., San Antonio Women's C. of C., Tex. Real Estate Tchrs. Assn., Phi Delta Phi, Alpha Chi. Office: 11765 West Ave Ste 140 San Antonio TX 78216-2559

EVANS, MYRON WYN, physicist; b. Craigcefnparc, Wales, May 26, 1950; came to U.S., 1986; s. Edward Ivor and Mary (Jones) E.; m. Laura Jean Joseph, Feb. 18, 1988. *Myron's father Edward Ivor Evans was a coalminer, awarded Bronze, Silver and Gold Medals of the Mines Rescue Service. His mother Mary Jones, was a daughter of a coalminer, T. Elim Jones, he was head deacon of Elim Baptist Chapel, composer and conductor. He was self educated, with a Nonconformist Puritan background of miners and hill farmers of the coalmining valleys of South Wales. Entirely Welsh speaking, originating in the Silures, a Celtic nation of Britain, described by the Romans as inhabiting the region, now known as South East Wales.* BSc, Aberystwyth U., Wales, 1971, PhD, 1974, DSc, 1977. Jr. rsch. fellow Wolfson Coll., Oxford, 1975; advanced fellow Sci. and Engring. Rsch. Coun., Aberystwyth, 1978-83; vis. scientist Cornell U., 1989-92, U. Zurich, 1989-90; prof. Alpha Found., Budapest, Hungary, 1995—; dir. Alpha Found. Inst. for Advanced Study, 1998—; nat. com. British Sci. and Engring. Rsch. Coun.; rsch. assoc. Pa. State U., 1992; 1st sci. coord. European Molecular Liquids Group, 1980; sr. assoc. Pa. State U., 1990; sci.-tech. advisor Plaid Cymru, 1991; vis. prof. Trinity Coll., Dublin, 1985, IBM, Kingston, N.Y., 1986,

York U., Toronto, 1995, Indian Statis. Inst., Calcutta, 1995; vis. scientist U. Pisa and Scuala Normale Superiore, 1980, U. Zurich, 1990, Cornell U., 1989, 91. *Mr. Evans, has done over twenty five years of research at the international level in chemistry and physics recorded in about five hundred communications and monographs. He pioneered use of far infra red for analysis of molecular dynamics, and combined the technique with computer simulation and other spectral methods culminating in the formation of the European Molecular Liquids Group. He pioneered the use of computer simulation for non linear optical effects in molecular liquids, the technique of radiation induced fermion resonance and the application of Gauge Theory to electrodynamics.* Editor Modern Nonlinear Optics, 1997, The Enigmatic Photon, 1994-99, five hundred monographs Wiley World Sci. and Kluwer; author: The Enigmatic Photon, 5 vols. 1994-99, Molecular Dynamics, 1982, Classical and Quantum Electrodynamics and the B Field, 1999; contbr. articles to profl. jours. Leverhulme fellow, Humboldt fellow, Brit. Imperial Chem. Industries fellow, 1974, NRC Can. fellow, 1974, Jr. Rsch. fellow Wolfson Coll., Oxford, 1975, Brit. Ramsay Meml. fellow, 1976, IBM fellow; recipient Harrison Meml. prize Royal Soc. Chemistry, London, 1978, Meldola medal, 1979; included in Outstanding People of the Twentieth Century. Fellow Am. Biog. Inst. (life, Key award 1999)), Internat. Biograph. Assn. (Bronze medal 1999); mem. Optical Soc. Am., Am. Inst. Physics, N.Y. Acad. Scis., Sigma Pi Sigma. Republican Nationalist. Avocations: poetry, landscape photography, athletics. Home: 82 Lois Ln Ithaca NY 14850 Office: Alpha Found Inst Physics, 11 Rutafa St, Budapest Hungary

EVANS, NANCY ANN, classics educator; b. Alexandria, Va., July 14, 1963; d. Roy C. and Zoe Ann Evans. BA, Smith Coll., 1985; postgrad., U. Zürich, Switzerland, 1985-86; PhD, Brown U., 1992. Lectr. Brandeis U., Waltham, Mass., 1992-93; vis. asst. prof. Emory U., Atlanta, 1993-94, Smith Coll., Northampton, Mass., 1994-97; asst. prof. Wheaton Coll., Norton, Mass., 1997—. Recipient Newcomb award Woodrow Wilson Found., 1991-92; Fulbright scholar Fulbright Found., Zürich, 1985-86; NEH summer grantee, Princeton, N.J., 1994. Mem. Am. Philol. Assn., Soc. for Bibl. Lit. Jewish. Office: Wheaton Coll PO Box 189 Norton MA 02766

EVANS, NOLLY SEYMOUR, lawyer; b. Augusta, Ga., Sept. 16, 1927; s. Nolly Seymour and Laura (Taylor) E.; m. Judith Anne Leach, Feb. 18, 1965; children: Samantha, Meredydd, Clelia, Nolly. BFA in Music, U. Ga., 1948, MA in English Lit., 1950; LLB, Yale U., 1956; LLD, Yale Law Sch., 1971. Bar: N.Y. 1956. Assoc. firm Milbank, Tweed, Hadley & McCloy, N.Y.C., 1956-64; fin. counsel Amax, Inc., N.Y.C., 1964-70; gen. counsel Gilman Paper Co., N.Y.C., 1970-74; gen. counsel, sec. Crouse-Hinds Co., Syracuse, N.Y., 1976-82; counsel Hancock & Estabrook, Syracuse, N.Y., 1982-83; prin. Nolly S. Evans Law Offices, Syracuse, 1983-93. Served with U.S. Army, 1947-48. Mem. Confrerie des Chevaliers du Tastevin, Grand Officier of Sous Commanderie de Etats-Unis, N.Y., Commanderie de Bordeaux, Le Grand Conseil de Bordeaux, Jurade de St. Emilion, Connetable de Guyenne, Century Club (Syracuse), Royal Over-Seas Club (London), and others. Home: 912-B Woodson Rd Baltimore MD 21212

EVANS, ORINDA D., federal judge; b. Savannah, Ga., Apr. 23, 1943; d. Thomas and Virginia Elizabeth (Grieco) E.; m. Roberts O. Bennett, Apr. 12, 1975; children: Wells Cooper, Elizabeth Thomas. B.A., Duke U., 1965; J.D. with distinction, Emory U., 1968. Bar: Ga. 1968. Assoc. Fisher & Phillips, Altanta, 1968-69; assoc. Alston, Miller & Gaines, Atlanta, 1969-74, ptnr., 1974-79; judge U.S. Dist Ct. (no. dist.) Ga., Atlanta, 1979—; adj. prof. Emory U. Law Sch., 1974-77; counsel Atlanta Crime Commn., 1970-71. Recipient Disting. award BBB, 1972. Mem. Atlanta Bar Assn. (dir. 1979). Democrat. Episcopalian. Office: US Dist Ct 1988 US Courthouse 75 Spring St SW Atlanta GA 30303*

EVANS, PAMELA R., marketing executive; b. Hoisington, Kans., Aug. 25, 1957; d. John Roy and Sarah Mace (Alder) E. BS in Bus., U. Kans., 1980. Sales rep. Home & Automotive Products div. Union Carbide Corp., Seattle, 1981; dist. sales mgr. Home & Automotive Products div. Union Carbide Corp., Syracuse, N.Y., 1981-82; mktg. assoc. Home & Automotive Products div. Union Carbide Corp., Danbury, Conn., 1982-84, assoc. product mgr., 1984; asst. product mgr. Grocery Products div. Ralston Purina, St. Louis, 1984-85, product mgr., 1985-86; product mgr. Eveready Battery Co. subs. Ralston Purina, St. Louis, 1986-88, group dir. mktg., 1988-90; dir. mktg. Consumer Products div. Esselte Pendaflex, 1990-91; dir. new bus. devel. Olympus Am., Inc., Woodbury, NY, 1991-92; v.p. mktg. consumer products group Olympus Am., Woodbury, NY, 1992-95; pres. blueprints, inc., New Hope, Pa., 1995-98, SJI, Inc., St. Louis, 1998—, SJI Fulfillment, Inc., St. Louis, 1998—, SJI Events, St. Louis, 1998—; pres. SJI Cons., St. Louis, 1998—. Bd. advisors Sentry Group, Electri-Cord Mfg. Co. Avocations: music, sports, reading, photography. Office: Ste 3800 One Metropolitan Sq Saint Louis MO 63102-1800

EVANS, PAUL F., protective services official; m. Karen O'Connor; 1 child, Paul III. JD cum laude, Suffolk U., 1978. Police commr. Boston Police Dept., 1994—. Bd. dirs. Police Athletic League, YMCA, City Year. Mem. VFW, Semper Fidelis Soc., Internat. Assn. Chiefs of Police, Police Exec. Rsch. Forum. Office: Office of Police Commr 1 Schroeder Plaza Boston MA 02120-2014

EVANS, PAULINE D., physicist, educator; b. Bklyn., Mar. 24, 1922; d. John A. and Hannah (Brandt) Davidson; m. Melbourne Griffith Evans, Sept. 6, 1950; children: Lynn Janet Evans Hannemann, Brian Griffith. BA, Hofstra Coll., 1942; postgrad., NYU, 1943, 46-47, Cornell U., 1946, Syracuse U., 1947-50. Jr. physicist Signal Corps Ground Signal Svc., Eatontown, N.J., 1942-43; physicist Kellex Corp. (Manhattan Project), N.Y.C., 1944; faculty dept. physics Queens Coll., N.Y.C., 1944-47; teaching asst. Syracuse U., 1947-50; instr. Wheaton Coll., Norton, Mass., 1952; physicist Nat. Bur. Standards, Washington, 1954-55; instr. physics U. Ala., 1955, U. N.Mex., 1955, 57-58; staff mem. Sandia Corp., Albuquerque, 1956-57; physicist Naval Nuclear Ordnance Evaluation Unit, Kirtland AFB, N.Mex., 1958-60; programmer Teaching Machines, Inc., Albuquerque, 1961; mem. faculty dept. physics Coll. St. Joseph on the Rio Grande (name changed to U. Albuquerque 1966), 1961—, assoc. prof., 1965—, chmn. dept., 1961—. Mem. AAUP, Am. Phys. Soc., Am. Assn. Physics Tchrs., Fedn. Am. Scientists, Sigma Pi Sigma, Sigma Delta Epsilon. Achievements include patents on mechanical method of conical scanning (radar), fluorine trap and primary standard for humidity measurement Home: 730 Loma Alta Ct NW Albuquerque NM 87105-1220 Office: U Albuquerque Dept Physics Albuquerque NM 87140

EVANS, PETER KENNETH, advertising executive; b. Brighton, Eng., Apr. 18, 1935; emigrated to Can., 1958; came to U.S., 1968; s. Percy Edward and Doris (McCoy) E.; m. Juana Santana Ramirez, Mar. 31, 1956; children: Luis Miguel, Linda Rosa Del Rocio, Pilar De Los Angeles. Student Varndean Sch., Brighton, 1946-50. Asst. art dir. Grant Advt., Toronto, Ont., Can., 1958-61. creative group head Goodis, Goldberg, Soren, Toronto, Ont., Can., 1961-63; v.p., creative dir. Baker/BBDO, Toronto, 1963-65; creative dir. Kenyon & Eckhardt, Toronto, 1965-67, Mexico City, 1967-68; exec. v.p., creative dir. Vladimir & Evans Inc., Miami, Fla., 1968-71; pres., creative dir. Evans & Ciccarone Inc., Miami, 1971-91; mktg. cons., 1991—; proprietor Peter Evans Pipes, 1994—, cartoonist The Islander News, Key Biscayne, Fla., 1996—, pres. Peter Evans Response Mktg & Adv., 1996—, Peter Evans Creative Svcs., 1997—; instr. advt. Fla. Internat. U., Miami, 1974. Author: Jumpstart Marketing for the New Business Owner, 1993, Treasure Your Teeth, 1998; broadcaster radio reading svc. Sta. WLRN-FM (NPR affiliate), Miami, 1990—; playwright: Ruiz, 1982, Unconscious, 1996, Lost, 1997, Bang, 1998; inventor bed elevator, blind dog head protector, Perfect Wood Carvers Bench, Sander-Expander. Leader, Jr. Achievement, Miami, 1968; asst. leader Boy Scouts Am., Miami, 1970. Served with RAF, 1953-55; ETO. Recipient awards Can. TV Commercials Festival, N.Y. Art Directors Show, Clio awards, Andy awards, 100 Best U.S. TV Commercials, Printing Industry Am. awards, 24 Top U.S. New Product Introductions, Miami Big Mike awards, Miami Addy awards, Fla. State Addy awards, Fla. Press Assn. awards; named 100 Top U.S. Creative Men Ad Day/USA, Art Dir. of Yr. Greater Miami Ad Fedns. Mem. Dramatists Guild, Nat. Wood Carvers Assn., Am. Birding Assn., Nat. Audubon Soc. Anglican. Clubs: NAUI (Miami); Key Biscayne Beach (Fla.), South Fla. Woodcarvers Club. Office: 285 W Mashta Dr Miami FL 33149-2419

EVANS, PETER YOSHIO, ophthalmologist, educator; b. Tokyo, Dec. 19, 1925; came to the U.S., 1957; s. Paul Yuzuru Kawai and Vicki Wichgraf Evans; m. Helga Kemp, Sept. 19, 1953; children: Johannes, Marina, Michael, André, Thomas, Ursula, Christiane. MD, Innsbruck U., 1951. Resident Innsbruck (Austria) and Frankfurt (Germany) Univs., 1951-55; intern Sisters Charity Hosp., Buffalo, N.Y., 1957-58; chief dept. ophthalmology D.C. Gen. Hosp., 1958-63; fellow Georgetown U., Washington, 1958-59, program dir. div. ophthalmology, 1963-69, chmn., 1969-83, prof., 1973-92, prof. emeritus, 1992—; cons. D.C. Columbia Lighthouse for the Blind, 1959-63; sr. cons. D.C. Child and Maternal Welfare Dept., 1961-74; exec. v.p. Joint Commn. Allied Health Pers. in Ophthalmology, St. Paul, 1981-96. Author, producer scientific films; contbr. articles to profl. jours.; editor numerous jours. Recipient Man of Decade award Joint Commn. on Allied Health Pers. in Ophthalmology, 1997. Fellow Am. Acad. Ophthalmology (Disting. Svc. award 1982), Austrian Ophthalm. Soc. (First Fuchs Meml. Lectr. 1975), German Ophthalm. Soc., Am.-Austrian Soc. (pres. 1989-91), Cosmos Club D.C. Lutheran. Avocations: skiing, violin, philately, photography, bridge. Home and Office: 3113 Lewis Pl Falls Church VA 22042-2511

EVANS, RALPH AIKEN, physicist, consultant; b. Oak Park, Ill., Feb. 2, 1924; s. Durward Randall and Hazel Agnes (Aiken) E.; m. Catherine Mary Martin, 1967; children: Paul A., Ann M. BS, Lehigh U., 1944; PhD in Physics, U. Calif.-Berkeley, 1954. Dir. Link-Belt Rsch. Lab., Indpls., 1959-61; rsch. physicist Research Triangle Inst., Durham, N.C., 1961-72, cons., 1972—. Mng. editor IEEE Transactions on Reliability; founding editor Am. Soc. Quality Control Reliability Rev., 1981-86. Ensign USNR, 1944-45. Fellow IEEE, Am. Soc. for Quality. Home and Office: 804 Vickers Ave Durham NC 27701-3143

EVANS, RANDALL DEAN, JR., interior designer; b. Indianola, Miss., Mar. 28, 1970; s. Randall D. and Charlene Grace (Bianca) E. BA in Archtl. Studies, U. Ark., 1993. Assoc. designer Burnett Interiors, Little Rock, 1992-93; designer Legacy Designer Hardware & Interiors, Little Rock, 1993-95; interior designer Malouf Furniture & Interiors, Greenwood, Miss., 1995—; assisting designer Ark. Symphony Orch. Designer House, Little Rock, 1993. Mem. Am. Soc. Interior Designers (assoc., allied). Roman Catholic. Home: 503 E Harding Ave Greenwood MS 38930-3119 Office: Malouf Furniture & Interiors Hwy 82 Bypass Greenwood MS 38930

EVANS, RICHARD JAMES, mechanical engineer; b. Wabash, Ind., Nov. 26, 1960; s. Tommy Lewis E. and Joyce Anne (Leckrone) Wert; children: Matthew Thomas, Kari Lynn, Jenna Marie. BSME, Rose-Hulman Inst. Tech., 1983; MBA with honors, Ind. U., 1993. Registered profl. engr., Ky., Ind.; cert. lighting efficiency profl. Sales engr. Johnson Controls, Inc., Indpls., 1983-90, sales team leader in healthcare mktg., 1990-93; br. mgr. Johnson Controls, Inc., Evansville, Ind., 1993-95, area installation mgr., 1995-98, area svc. mgr., 1998—. Active Sons of Am. Legion, Wabash, 1989—. Energy award U.S. Dept. Energy, 1995. Mem. ASHRAE (pres. ctrl. Ind. chpt. 1991-92, bd. dirs. 1992-93, Presdl. award of Excellence 1992), NSPE, Assn. Energy Engrs. (cert. energy mgr.), Am. Soc. Hosp. Engrs., Ind. Soc. Profl. Engrs. (v.p. ctrl. Ind. chpt. 1997-98, pres. 1998—), Ind. Soc. Hosp. Engrs., Beta Gamma Sigma, Lambda Chi Alpha (housing corp. bd. 1996—). Home: 10478 Magenta Dr Noblesville IN 46060-8398 Office: Johnson Controls Inc 1255 N Senate Ave Indianapolis IN 46202-2200

EVANS, RICHARD LLOYD, financial services company executive; b. Seattle, Oct. 16, 1935; s. Lloyd Herman and Dorleska L. (Rotta) E.; m. Judith Anne Sahlberg, Dec. 20, 1958; children: Dallas J., Douglas L., Daniel A., Marjorie A., Rebecca M. BA in Bus. Adminstrn., U. Wash., 1957. CLU; chartered fin. cons. Agt. Phoenix Mut. Life Ins. Co., Seattle, 1960-69; chmn. R.L. Evans Co. Inc., Seattle, 1969—; mng. prin. Evans Capital Mgmt. Assocs., Seattle; speaker on ins. and fin. planning to numerous orgns., 1975—; adv. Oreas Island Found., 1996—. Mem. exec. bd. Chief Seattle coun. Boy Scouts Am., 1976—; chmn. N.W. Theol. Union, Seattle, 1984-88; chief fin. officer, vice-chmn. San Juan County Pk. Bd., 1996—. Lt. USN, 1957-59. Recipient award of merit Chief Seattle coun. Boy Scouts Am., 1984. Mem. Am. Soc. CLU, Am. Soc. Chartered Fin. Cons., Nat. Assn. Life Underwriters, Wash. State Assn. Life Underwriters (bd. dirs. 1973-79, pres. 1977-78), Seattle Assn. Life Underwriters (v.p. 1972-73), Assn. Advanced Underwriting, Million Dollar Round Table, Estate Planning Coun. Seattle, Rainier Club, Masons, Rotary (dir.). Republican. Presbyterian. Home: 871 Deer Point Rd Olga WA 98279-9702 Office: 600 Stewart St Ste 1210 Seattle WA 98101

EVANS, ROBERT, JR., economics educator; b. Sterling, Colo., Mar. 20, 1932; s. Robert and Mary Louise (Paradise) E.; m. Lois Ellen Herr, Nov. 6, 1955 (dec. 1994); children: Karen E., Robert, Janet K., Thomas W., L. Midori, Laura E., Katherine Joan; m. Marian Elizabeth Grotheer, Dec. 26, 1996. SB, MIT, 1954; PhD (Hillman fellow), U. Chgo., 1959. Asst. prof. indsl. relations MIT, 1959-65; assoc. prof. Brandeis U., Waltham, Mass., 1965-71, prof., 1971—, Atran prof. labor econs., 1975-98, chmn. dept. econs., 1970-72, 73-75, 84-87, dean Coll. Arts and Scis., 1975-81; retired, 1998; vis. prof. Keio U., Tokyo, 1966-67, 72-73, 82-83, 88-89, 94-95; rsch. dir. study on prison industries Can. Corrections Assn., 1968-69. Author: Public Policy Toward Labor, 1965, The Labor Economics of Japan and the United States, 1971, Developing Policies for Public Security and Criminal Justice, 1973. Mem. Acton (Mass.) and Acton Boxborough Regional Sch. Com., 1971-72, 74-82, 84-88, regional chmn., 1972, 79-80, 85-86, town chmn., 1975-77. With U.S. Army, 1955-57. Fulbright Rsch. scholar, Japan, 1982-83, 88-89; Abe fellow, Japan, 1994-95. Mem. Am. Econ. Assn., Indsl. Relations Assn., Assn. Asian Studies. Home: 27 Huntington Rd Milton MA 02186-5311 Office: Brandeis U Dept Econs Waltham MA 02254

EVANS, ROBERT AUGUST, JR., newspaper reporter, editor; b. Hamilton, Ohio, Feb. 21, 1956; s. Robert August and Jayne Anne (Shumar) E.; m. Sheila Reed Evans, May 15, 1979 (dec. Oct. 1995); 1 child, Julia Cary; m. Nancy S. Feigenbaum, Sept. 6, 1998. AB in Philosophy, Coll. William and Mary, 1978; cert. in pub., Harvard U., 1978. Intern Daily News Summary The White House, Washington, 1978; reporter The Times-Herald, Newport News, Va., 1978-83; reporter Daily Press, Newport News, 1983-88, asst. metro editor, 1988-92, sr. reporter, 1992-95, investigative editor, 1995-99, newsgathering editor, 1999—. Recipient Silver gavel ABA, 1993. Mem. Investigative Reporters and Editors Inc. Home: 104 Mirror Lake Dr Williamsburg VA 23188-7017 Office: Daily Press Inc 7505 Warwick Blvd Newport News VA 23607-1500

EVANS, ROBERT GEORGE, JR., retail and mail order executive; b. Wabash, Ind., May 6, 1953; s. Robert George and Helen (Kalb) E.; m. Leisa Marie Napier, June 13, 1987. Student, Ind. U., 1970-74; BSBA, Wesleyan U., 1993. Dir. computer services Ind. U. Northwest Campus, Gary, 1972-75; mgr. configuration planning CNA Ins., Chgo., 1975-79; mgr. tech. support Brylane/Ltd. Inc., Indpls., 1979-85, sr. mgr. tech. svcs., 1985-89; dir. MIS Lane Bryant/Ltd., Inc., Indpls., 1989-91; dir. Brylane/Ltd., Inc., Indpls., 1991-93; v.p. MIS Brylane, LP, Indpls., 1993-97, MIS Brylane, Inc., Indpls., 1997-99; sr. v.p., chief info. officer Brylane Group, 1999—; pres. Tri-Star Consulting, Merrillville, Ind., 1983-86; cons., instr. Ind.-Purdue U. Indpls. Continuing Studies Program, 1980-83. Mem. Major of Indpls. Liaison for County Agys. and Twps., 1991. Republican. Methodist. Avocations: tennis, running, weight training, travel.

EVANS, ROBERT JAMES, architect; b. Alameda, Calif., Apr. 15, 1914; s. Edwin Florence and Idella Mary (Cranna) E.; m. Carol Ann Benton, Sept. 11, 1937; children: Joan Carlson, Ann Blakeman, Marcia Mothorn. A.B., U. Calif., Berkeley, 1935. Registered architect, Calif. Draftsman Wm. C. Hays Architect, San Francisco, 1935-37; draftsman U. Calif., 1937-41, architect, 1941-45, univ. architect, 1945-72, asst. v.p., 1971-72; cons. architect Marshall, Calif., 1973—; asst. to chancellor U. Mich.-Flint, 1972-73; supervising architect U. Calif., Davis, 1942-45, Berkeley, 1948-55; cons. architect campus plan U. Ryukus, Okinawa, 1969; cons. architect campus paln U. N.C., Greensboro, 1979-82; cons. architect campus plan Kabul U., Afghanistan, 1955, U. Hawaii, 1960-62, Salk Inst., San Diego, 1983-84. Founder Tomales Bay Assn., Marshall Calif., 1964. Fellow AIA (emeritus), Assn. Univ. Architects (emeritus, pres. 1955-57). Clubs: Richmond Yacht (treas.) (1961); Inverness Yacht. Address: 18545 Hwy 1 Marshall CA 94940

EVANS, ROBERT SHELDON, manufacturing executive; b. Pitts., 1944. BA in History, U. Pa., 1966; MBA in Fin., Columbia U., 1968. V.p. Evans & Co. Inc., 1971-74; v.p. internat. ops. Crane Co., N.Y.C., 1974-78, sr. v.p., 1978-79, exec. v.p., dir., 1979-84, chmn., chief exec. officer, 1984—, pres., chief ops. officer, 1986-91, 88—; chmn., CEO, bd. dirs. Medusa Corp.; bd. dirs. HBD Industries Inc., Fanstel, Inc. Mem. dean's adv. coun. Columbia Grad. Sch. Bus.; trustee Eaglebrook Sch. Office: Crane Co 100 1st Stamford Pl Stamford CT 06902-6740*

EVANS, ROBERT VINCENT, sales and marketing executive; b. Mobile, Ala., Sept. 21, 1958; s. William Alexander Evans and Katherine Barbara (Doerr) Davidson; m. Debra Marie Winters, July 27, 1984; children: James Vernon, Chelsea Marie. BS in Computer Info. Systems, Regis U., Denver, 1987, BS in Tech. Mgmt., 1987; postgrad. in Mgmt., U. Wash., 1995. Electrician Climax (Colo.) Molybdenum Co., 1978-82; applications engr. Honeywell, Inc., Englewood, Colo., 1982-83, sales engr., 1983-87; systems engr. Apple Computer, Inc., Seattle, 1987-88; regional systems engrng. mgr. Apple Computer, Inc., Portland, Oreg., 1988-96; dist. sales mgr. Apple Computer, Inc., Seattle, 1997—. Author: Anthology of American Poets, 1981. Dir. Operation Lookout, Seattle, 1989; mem. Rep. Nat. Com.; commr. dist. chmn. Boy Scouts Am. Recipient USMC Blues award, Marine Corps Assn. Leatherneck award, 1977, Denver Post Outstanding Svc. award, 1983, N.Y. Zool. Soc. Hon. medal, James West fellowship award, Paul Harris fellowship award, Silver Beaver award Boy Scouts Am., 1998. Mem. Am. Mgmt. Assn., Am. Platform Assn., Mensa, Rotary, Kiwanis. Republican. Mem. Northwest Cmty. Ch. Avocations: reading, church ministry, family activities. Office: Apple Computer Inc PO Box 40355 Bellevue WA 98015-4355

EVANS, ROGER LYNWOOD, scientist, patent liaison; b. Ipswich, Suffolk, Eng., June 25, 1928; came to U.S., 1953; s. Evelyn Jesse and Ethel Jane (Woods) E.; m. Jane Adelaide Baird, Nov. 24, 1954 (div. 1976); children: Robert Malcolm Baird, Roderick Lawrence Woods, Alison Clare; m. Wendy Dorothy Grove, Apr. 11, 1977. *Roger's Welsh grandfather, Thomas Evans, served two successive professional British army careers, in the infantry and chaplains department respectively. His father, Canon Evelyn Jesse Evans, was a chemistry professor who became an ordained missionary and education executive in West Africa (Nigeria). The famous musician, Fela Soande, was one of his students. His American father-in-law, Julian B. Baird, was a member of President Eisenhower's cabinet.* BA in Natural Sci., Oxford (Eng.) U., 1953, MA, 1955, DPhil in Natural Sci., 1958; MS in Inorganic Chemistry, U. Minn., 1955. With chem. and radiopharm. R & D dept. 3M Co., St. Paul., 1958-77, patent liaison, 1977-91; developer intellectual property initiative, tech. devel. dept., 1992-93; cons. 3M, 1993—; originator 3M Richard G. Drew Creativity Award, 1970, program cons., 1995—. *Mr. Evans wanted to return some sort of personal thanks, through action, for American generosity, for the Marshall Plan and the Fulbright Funds. Unconvinced by post-war propaganda about the low quality of America and the Americans, he came to see for himself. Initially perplexed by local reluctance to accept suggestions from a foreigner, he has since enjoyed years of constructive contact with Americans in professional, civic and vocational fields. He is very appreciative of the awards and recognition returned.* Founder, editor Newsletter of the Tech. Forum, 1971-93; inventor, writer, producer series of videos on intellectual property topics. Mem., chmn. Mendota Heights Planning Commn., 1962-68, Sunfish Lake Planning Commn., 1968-84, Dakota County Planning Commn., Minn., 1965-72. 2d lt. Brit. Army, 1946-49, Eng. Anglican. Avocations: photography, amateur opera singer, travel, writing. Home and Office: 9965 Rich Valley Blvd Inver Grove Heights MN 55077-4529

EVANS, RONALD ALLEN, lodging chain executive; b. Louisville, Apr. 5, 1940; s. William Francis and Helen Maxine (Hart) E.; m. Lynne Anne Ingraham, Aug. 25, 1979; children: Nicole Louise, Michele Lynne, Christopher Hart. B.S. in Mgmt., Ariz. State U., 1963. Vice pres. Electronic Data Systems, Dallas, 1969-73; vice pres. First Fed. Savs., Phoenix, 1973-77, Community Fin. Corp., Scottsdale, Ariz., 1977-78; pres. Evans Mgmt. Services, Inc., Phoenix, 1978-84; pres., CEO Best Western Internat., Inc., Phoenix, 1979-98; dean Sch. Hotel and Restaurant Mgmt. No. Ariz. U., Flagstaff, 1998—. Served to lt. USNR, 1963-66. Decorated Bronze Star. Republican. Episcopalian. Lodges: Masons (32 deg.), KT, Shriner. Office: No Ariz U Sch Hotel & Restaurant Mgmt Box 5638 Flagstaff AZ 86011*

EVANS, ROSEMARY HALL, civic worker; b. Lenox, Mass., Mar. 25, 1925; d. Alfred A. and Rosamond (Morse) Hall; m. Richard Morse Colgate, Jan. 1, 1949; children: Jessie Morse, Margaret Auchincloss, Pamela Morse; m. James H. Evans, July 1, 1972 (div. 1984). Trustee Menninger Found., Topeka, Princeton (N.J.) Theol. Sem.; founding mem., life trustee Nat. Recreation and Park Assn., Washington; past dir. Nat. Audubon Soc., N.Y.C.; former collaborator Nat. Park Svc. Mem. Colony Club (N.Y.C.), Tarratine Club (Dark Harbor, Maine), Lenox (Mass.) Club, Profile Club (Sugar Hill, N.J.). Republican. Avocations: walking, gardening, reading, farming, bird watching.

EVANS, ROSEMARY KING (MRS. HOWELL DEXTER EVANS), librarian, educator; b. Forsyth, Ga., Nov. 16, 1924; d. Wiley Gwin and Mary (Goggans) King; B.S., Tift Coll., 1957; librarian's certificate Woman's Coll. of Ga., 1963; M. Library Edn., U. Ga., 1972, postgrad. in library edn., 1975; m. Howell Dexter Evans, June 29, 1945; children—Joseph William, Curtis McKenney. Tchr. elementary sch., Forsyth, Ga., 1946-48, 54-62; librarian Mary Persons High Sch., Forsyth, 1962-73; catalog librarian Tift Coll., Forsyth, 1973-74; head librarian Stratford Acad., Macon, Ga., 1974-77; head librarian, asst. prof. Gordon Jr. Coll., Barnesville, Ga., 1977-87; chmn. regents' acad. com. libraries State Bd. Regents Univ. System of Ga.: Mem. Ga. State Bd. Certification of Librarians. Author: The Christmas Tree Farm, 1989. Spiritual edn. chmn. PTA, 1960-61; mem. Monroe County Hosp. Authority, 1988—, chmn., 1994-98; mem. Monroe County Libr. Bd., 1990—. Named Star Tchr., 1966. Mem. Nat., Ga., Monroe County (sec. 1959-60, v.p. 1961-62, pres. 1962-63) edn. assns., Ga. (dis. pres. 1965), ALA, Southeastern library assns., Ga. Library Assn. Methodist (chmn. local edn. bd. 1964-65, chmn. commn. on Christian vocation 1965—, exec. com., tchr. adult Bible class). Author: Backhome Cuisine, 1984. Home: Evans Rd Smarr GA 31086

EVANS, ROWLAND, JR., columnist, commentator; b. White Marsh, Pa., Apr. 28, 1921; s. Rowl and Elizabeth Wharton (Downs) E.; m. Katherine Winton, June 18, 1949; children: Rowland Winton, Sarah Warren. Grad., Kent Sch., 1939; student, Yale, 1940-41; A.A., George Washington U., 1950. With A.P. Wash. Bureau, 1945-55; mem. staff N.Y. Herald Tribune, 1955-63, syndicated columnist with Robert Novak, 1963—. Roving editor: Readers Digest mag.; co-host on CNN's Evans, Novak, Hunt & Shields; author: (with Robert Novak) Lyndon B. Johnson: The Exercise of Power, 1967, Nixon in the White House: The Frustration of Power, 1971, The Reagan Revolution, 1981. Served with USMCR, 1942-44, Solomon Islands. Office: Ste 1312 1750 Pennsylvania Ave NW Washington DC 20006-4501

EVANS, ROXANNE ROMACK, retired military officer, hospital administrator; b. Idaho Falls, Idaho, Feb. 14, 1952; d. Richard Edward and Anne Elizabeth (Browning) R.; m. Paul Evans. BS, U. Idaho, 1974; postgrad., U. Md., 1979; MHA, Baylor U., 1982. Registered dietitian, Tex., S.C., Va., Okla., Wash. Commd. 2d lt. U.S. Army, 1974, advanced through grades to lt. col., 1990; dietetic intern Brooke Army Med. Ctr., Ft. Sam Houston, Tex., 1974-75; staff dietitian Walter Reed Army Med. Ctr., Washington, 1975-77; chief food service div. Kimbrough Army Hosp., Ft. George G. Meade, Md., 1977-80; adminstrv. resident Tripler Army Med. Ctr., Hawaii, 1981-82, chief clin. dietetics br., 1982-85; chief nutrition care div. Moncrief Army Community Hosp., Ft. Jackson, S.C., 1985-87; chief clin. dietetics div. Nutrition Care Directorate Walter Reed Army Med. Ctr., Washington, 1987-89; chief procurement activity Army Med. Specialist Corps, Dental Corps, Vet. Corp, 1989-92; chief nutrition care divsn. Reynolds Army Community Hosp., Ft. Still, Okla., 1992-93; hosp. adminstrn. Reynolds Army Cmty. Hosp., Fort Sills, Okla., 1993-94; retired U.S. Army, 1994, ret., 1994; health systems cons., 1995, med. svcs. contracting officer, 1996-98. Asst. leader cub scouts Boy Scouts Am., Columbia, S.C., 1985-86. Fellow Am. Dietetic Assn.; mem. Am. Coll. Healthcare Execs. (diplomate). Avocations: cycling, sewing.

EVANS, SARAH NELL, information technology administrator; b. Aug. 22, 1954. MS in Libr. Sci., U. Tex., 1979; MS in Info. Sci., U. Pitts., 1983; MS in Computer Sci., U. N. Tex., 1988. Libr. U. Ga., Athens, 1979-82; dir. acad. computing Austin Coll., Sherman, Tex., 1985—; courseware developer Tex. Instruments, Plano, Tex., 1988-91. E-mail: Westevans@texoma.net. Home: 315 W McGee Sherman TX 75092

EVANS, TERENCE THOMAS, federal judge; b. Milwaukee, Wisc., Mar. 25, 1940; s. Robert Hansen and Jeanette (Walters) E.; m. Joan Marie Witte, July 24, 1965; children: Kelly Elizabeth, Christine Marie, David Rourke. BA, Marquette U., 1962, JD, 1967. Bar: Wis. 1967. Law clk. to justice Wis. Supreme Ct., 1967-68; dist. atty. Milw. County, 1968-70; pvt. practice law Milw., 1970-74; cir. judge State of Wis., 1974-80; judge U.S. Dist. Ct. (ea. dist) Wis., Milw., 1980-95, U.S. Ct. Appeals (7th cir.), 1995—. Mem. ABA, State Bar Wis., Milw. Bar Assn. Roman Catholic. Office: US Courthouse & Federal Bldg 517 E Wisconsin Ave Rm 721 Milwaukee WI 53202-4500*

EVANS, THELMA JEAN MATHIS, internist; b. East St. Louis, Ill., Jan. 29, 1944; d. Clemmie and Catherine (Rose) Mathis; m. Timothy Charles Evans, June 29, 1968; children: Cynthia Marie, Catherine Elizabeth (twins). BS in Zoology with honors, U. Ill., 1967; MD, U. Ill., Chgo., 1969. Intern, then resident U. Ill. Hosp., Chgo., 1969-71, fellow in pulmonary medicine, 1971-73; med. dir., acute care unit Presbyn.-St. Luke's Hosp., Chgo., 1973-75; asst. to dir. emergency svcs. Presbyn.-St. Luke's Hosp., 1975-77; staff physician Health Specialists, S.C., Chgo., 1977-80, AT&T (Western Electric), Cicero, Ill., 1980-85, Health First, Inc., Chgo., 1985-89, Michael Reese Health Plan, Chgo., 1989—; instr., Rush Med. Coll., Chgo., 1973-84; tuberculosis control officer, infectious disease sect. Chgo. Dept. Health, 1976-77. v.p., Com. to Elect Timothy C. Evans, Chgo., 1989. Grantee, Chgo. Lung Assn., 1972-73. Fellow ACP; mem. Am. Soc. Internal Medicine, NAACP, AMA. Democrat. African Methodist Episcopal. Avocations: photography, gardening, collecting thimbles, bells and music boxes. Office: Advocate Health Ctrs 9831 S Western Ave Chicago IL 60643-1740

EVANS, THOMAS EVAN, minister; b. Campinas, Brazil, June 5, 1967; came to U.S., 1968; s. Robert Maxwell and Abigail Ethel Evans; m. Wendy Elizabeth Hoadley, Oct. 14, 1989; 1 child, Elizabeth Josephine. BA, Coll. of William and Mary, 1989; MDiv, Princeton Theol. Sem., 1994. Ordained min. Presbyn. Ch. 1994. Math. tchr. Good Counsel H.S., Silver Spring, Md., 1989-90; assoc. pastor 1st Presbyn. Ch., Idaho Falls, Idaho, 1994-96; head of staff, pastor 1st Presbyn. Ch., Magnolia, Ark., 1996—; chair new ch. devel. com. Presbytery of Pines, Ruston, La., 1996—; mem. Regional Aids Interfaith Network, Magnolia, 1996—, Divsn. Mission Pines Presbytery, Ruston, 1996—; chaplain Trenton (N.J.) State Prison, 1993-94. Bd. dirs. Heart Assn. Columbia County, Ark., 1997—; chairperson Columbia County Ministerial Alliance, 1997—; initiator, mem. steering com. Habitat for Humanity of Columbia County, 1997-98; chairperson Christian Inst., Idaho Falls, 1995-96. Mem. Rotary (chair reader group 1996—), Presbytery of Pines. Avocations: golf, reading, computers, cooking. E-mail: zaphor@guno.com. Home: 6 Edward Cir Magnolia AR 71753 Office: 1st Presbyn Ch 1417 N Jackson Magnolia AR 71753

EVANS, THOMAS PASSMORE, business and product licensing consultant; b. West Grove, Pa., Aug. 19, 1921; s. John and Linda (Zeuner) E.; m. Lenore Jane Knuth, June 21, 1947; children: Paula S., Christina L., Bruce A., Carol L. BS in Elec. Engring., Swarthmore Coll., 1942; M in Engring., Yale U., 1948. Registered profl. engr., Pa. Engr. atomic power divsn. Westinghouse Electric Corp., Pitts., 1948-51; dir. R&D AMF, Inc., N.Y.C., 1951-60; dir. rsch. O.M. Scott & Sons Co., Marysville, Ohio, 1960-62; v.p. R&D W. A. Sheaffer Pen Co., Fort Madison, Iowa, 1962-67; dir. rsch. Mich. Tech. U., Houghton, 1967-80; dir. rsch., mem. faculty Berry Coll., Mt. Berry, Ga., 1980-88; prof. bus. adminstrn. Berry Coll., Mt. Berry, 1980-86. Author, patentee in field. Lt. USN, 1943-46. Mem. IEEE, AAAS. VFW, Am. Forestry Assn., Nat. Defense Industl. Assn., Am. Phys. Soc., Soc. Plastics Engrs., Yale Sci. and Engring. Assn., Nat. Coun. Univ. Rsch. Adminstrs., Air Force Assn., Am. Legion, High Mus. Art, Hunter Mus. Art, Nat. Trust Hist. Preservation, Yale Club of Ga., Sigma Xi, Tau Beta Pi. Home: 1220 Broadrick Dr Apt 1222 Dalton GA 30720-2809

EVANS, THOMAS R., magazine publisher. Pub. U.S. News & World Report, Washington, 1989; pres., editor U.S. News & World Report, N.Y.C., 1989-98; pres. Atlantic Monthly, 1997-98; CEO, pres. GeoCities, Santa Monica, Calif., 1998—. Office: GeoCities 4499 Glen Clove Ave Marina Del Rey CA 90292*

EVANS, THOMAS WILLIAM, lawyer; b. N.Y.C., Dec. 9, 1930; s. William J. and R. Helen (Stenvall) E.; m. Lois deBaun Logan, Dec. 22, 1956; children: Heather, Logan, Paige. BA, Williams Coll., 1952; JD, Columbia U., 1958; EdD, Piedmont Coll., 1993. Bar: N.Y. 1958, U.S. Supreme Ct. 1961. Assoc. Simpson, Thacher & Bartlett, N.Y.C., 1958-64; asst. coun. to spl. state commn. of investigation, spl. dep. asst. N.Y. Atty. Gen., N.Y.C., 1964-65; assoc. Mudge Rose Guthrie Alexander & Ferdon, N.Y.C., 1965-66, ptnr., 1967-93, of counsel, 1993-94; of counsel Andrews & Kurth, Washington, 1995—; founder MENTOR, nat. law-related edn. program for pub. sch. students, 1983. Author: The School in the Home, 1973, Admissions Practices (Center for Public Resources), 1986, Mentors, 1992. Chmn. Nat. Symposium on Partnerships in Edn., 1983-90; chmn. bd. trustees Columbia U. Tchrs. Coll., 1991-98, trustee, 1985—, adj. prof. of ednl. adminstrn., 1992-95; co-chmn. N.Y. Korean Vets. Meml. Commn.; chmn. The Mentor Ctr., L.C., 1998—. With USMC, 1952-54. Mem. ABA, Fed. Bar Coun. (pres. 1989-90, trustee 1981—), Century Assn. Republican. Episcopalian. Home: 10245 Collins Ave Bal Harbour FL 33154-1407 Office: Andrews & Kurth LLP 1701 Pennsylvania Ave NW Washington DC 20006-5805

EVANS, TOMMY NICHOLAS, physician, educator; b. Batesville, Ark., Apr. 12, 1922; s. James Rufus and Carrye Mae (Goatcher) E.; m. Jessica Ray Osment, June 12, 1945; 1 child, Laura Kathreen. A.A., Mars Hill Jr. Coll., 1940; student, Duke U., 1940-41; A.B., Baylor U., 1942; M.D., Vanderbilt U., 1945. Intern U. Mich. Hosp., Ann Arbor, 1945-46; asst. resident ob-gyn U. Mich. Hosp., 1948, resident, 1948-49, jr. clin. instr., 1949-50, sr. clin. instr., 1950-51, instr., 1951-54, asst. prof., 1954-56, assoc. prof., 1956-60, prof., 1960-65; prof. ob-gyn Wayne State U., Detroit, 1965-83; dean Sch. Medicine Wayne State U., 1970-72, dir. C.S. Mott Ctr. Human Growth and Devel., 1973-83; sr. attending physician Hutzel Hosp., 1966-83, chief ob-gyn, 1966-82, vice chief of staff, 1967-70, chief of staff, 1970-74, trustee, 1975-78; mem. teaching, surgeon Harper-Grace Hosps., 1965-83, chief gynecology Harper div., 1970-83, chief ob-gyn, 1975-83; chief gynecology, sr. attending physician Detroit Receiving Hosp., 1965-83; chief gynecology U. Colo., Denver, 1983-89; vice chmn. ob-gyn. U. Colo., 1983-89, prof. emeritus ob-gyn., 1989—; cons. pediatric surgery Children's Hosp.; cons. Sinai Hosp. William Beaumont Hosp., Wayne County Gen. Hosp.; past mem. med. adv. com. Detroit Med. Ctr. Corp. Bd. dirs. Alan Guttmacher Inst. Fellow Am. Assn. Ob-Gyn.; mem. Am. Coll. Obstetricians and Gynecologists (past exec. bd., past pres.), ACS (adv. council ob-gyn credentials com. 1983-85, bd. govs. 1982-86), Am. Fedn. Clin. Research, Am. Fertility Soc., Am. Gynecol. Club (past pres.), Am. Gynecol. Soc. (past pres.), Am. Gynecol. and Obstetrical Soc. (council), AMA, Am. Med. Soc. Vienna, Am. Pub. Health Assn., Am. Soc. Andrology (exec. council), Am. Soc. Study Sterility, Anthony Wayne Soc., Assn. Profs. Ob-Gyn (past chmn. nominating com.), Central Assn. Ob-Gyn (past pres.), Charlie Flowers Ob-Gyn Soc., Chgo. Gynecol. Soc., Continental Gynecol. Soc., Detroit Acad. Medicine, Detroit Cancer Club (past mem. program com.), Engring. Soc. Detroit, Greater Detroit Area Hosp. Council Inc., Internat. Fedn. Ob-Gyn (exec. bd.), Internat. Soc. Advancement Humanistic Studies in Gynecology, Miami Obstet. and Gynecol. Soc., Mich. Assn. Retarded Children, Mich. Cancer Found. (trustee), Mich. Council Study of Abortion, Mich. Soc. Ob-Gyn (past pres.), Mich. State Med. Soc. (past exec. council), Mich. United Cerebral Palsy Assn., Norman Miller Gynecol. Soc. (past pres.), Ob-Gyn Soc. N.Y., Planned Parenthood League, Pan Am. Med. Assn., Royal Soc. Medicine, Soc. Study of Reprodn., Soc. Ob-Gyn of Can., S. Atlantic Assn. Ob-Gyn, numerous others. Republican. Presbyterian. Office: 8146 E Whispering Wind Dr Scottsdale AZ 85255-2840

EVANS, VAN MICHAEL, advertising agency executive, consultant; b. N.Y.C., July 18, 1916; s. Michael James and Catherine (Conte) Livadas; m. Mary Bota, Nov. 8, 1942; children: Stephen, Barbara. BA, NYU, 1938. Sales and editorial positions Social Spectator mag., N.Y.C., 1938-39; account exec. Deutsch & Shea Advt. Agy., N.Y.C., 1940-46, v.p., exec. v.p., 1946-68, pres., 1969-80, chmn. exec. bd., 1981-83; cons. Foote Cone & Belding div. Deutsch Shea & Evans Advt. Agy., N.Y.C., 1983-89; human resources cons. Jupiter, Fla., 1990—; cons. Morality and Media Inc., N.Y.C., 1970-78, Performing Arts Ctr., Palm Beach County, Fla., 1987—, Orthodox Christian Laity, Chgo., 1989—; bd. dirs. Pension and Profit Sharing Fund Am. Assn. Advt. Agys., 1971-73. Editl. cons. The Coming Revolution in Human Resources, 1978; editor: The Complete Job Book, 1980; editor Lamplighter; contbr. articles to publs. Nat. chmn. United Greek Charities, Inc., N.Y.C., 1973-74; adviser Greek Orthodox Youth Council, Inc., 1973-76. Served with Signal Corps U.S. Army, 1942-46. Mem. Solon Culture Soc. (pres. chpt. 1972-74), Ahepa (chaplain Delphi chpt. 1948-52, pub. rels. dir. Fla. chpt. #18 1994—, S.E. coord. affordable housing for the elderly 1995—), Greek Orthodox Am. Leaders. Greek Orthodox. Office: Deutsch Shea & Evans Inc 485 5th Ave New York NY 10017-6104 *My credo for leadership is to foment change...the application of imagination wedded to a quality of restlessness.*

EVANS, VICTOR MILES, retired funeral home, cemetery company executive; b. Hines, Minn., Dec. 8, 1939; s. Miles Byron and Millicent (Owen) E.; m. Joyce M. Dexter, Dec. 17, 1960; children: Terri, Ross, Jana, Stephanie, Anthony. BBA, U. Minn., 1962. CPA, Ill. Staff acct. McGladrey, Hansen, Dunn, Rock Island, Ill., 1962-64; chief fin. officer Roy & E. Roth Co., Rock Island, 1964-69; sr. v.p. Svc. Corp. Internat., Houston, 1969-92, ret., 1993. Republican. Baptist. Avocations: racquetball, skiing.

EVANS, WAYNE LEWIS, lawyer; b. Bluefield, W.Va., Mar. 30, 1954; s. Douglas Evan and Wanda (Shrewsberry) E.; m. Cheryl Jane Richardson, June 28, 1980; children: Lisa Marie, Jason Lloyd. BA summa cum laude, U. N.C., Greensboro, 1976; MS, Radford U., 1978; diploma, Roanoke Police Acad., 1980; JD, Wake Forest U., 1984. Bar: W.Va. 1984, U.S. Dist. Ct. (so. dist.) W.Va. 1984, U.S. Ct. Appeals (4th cir. 1989); cert. Va. Cert. Bds. Zoning Appeals Programs. Probation/parole officer Va. Dept. Corrections, Tazewell, Va., 1976-77; dep. sheriff Roanoke County Sheriff Dept., Salem, Va., 1979-81; summer assoc. Katz Kantor & Perkins, Bluefield, W.Va., 1982; sr. assoc. Katz, Kantor & Perkins, Bluefield, 1985—; summer assoc. Gardner, Moss, Brown & Rocovich, Roanoke, 1983; assoc. Law Office of John H. Shott, Bluefield, 1984-85; v.p., sec. WELD Enterprises, 1989-95; mem. Campaigning With Lee-Civil War Roundtable, Va. Tech., 1994, 95, 96, 97; speaker at seminars. Mem. Bd. Zoning Appeals, Bluefield, 1991—; participant Career Awareness, Mercer County (W.Va.) Schs., 1989, 92; coach Odyssey of the Mind, Tazewell County (Va.) Schs., 1994, 95, 96, 97, judge, 1999; vol. United Way, Mercer and Tazewell Counties, 1989; chmn. com. PTA, Dudley Primary Sch; leader Boy Scouts Am., Bluefield, Va., 1996—; pres. Graham Middle Sch. PTA, Bluefield, 1997—; pres. Graham H.S. Band Boosters, 1999-00. Mem. ATLA, W.Va. Trial Lawyers Assn., Fincastle Country Club, Phi Beta Kappa, Psi Chi, Phi Kappa Phi. Avocations: golf, tennis, Civil War history. Home: 45 College Dr Bluefield VA 24605-1736 Office: Katz Kantor and Perkins 307 Federal St Bluefield WV 24701-3005

EVANS, WILLIAM HALLA, minister; b. Paris, Ky., Nov. 29, 1950; s. James Hughes and Francis (Halla) E.; m. Kathleen Sue Mattingly, Aug. 25, 1973; children: James Anthony, Joshua Halla. BA in Philosophy, U. Ky., 1972; D of Ministry, Lexington Theol. Sem., 1976. Minister Paint Lick (Ky.) Christian Ch., 1970-73, Botland (Ky.) Christian Ch., 1973-76, Crofton (Ky.) Christian Ch., 1976-80, Valley Christian Ch., Valley Station, Ky., 1980-84; assoc. minister Florence (Ky.) Christian Ch., 1984-86; sr. minister First Christian Ch., Pikeville, Ky., 1986-89; computer instr. Clark Mid. Sch., Winchester, Ky., 1990-91; ceo Tek-Dev Computer Svcs., Winchester, 1992-94; dist. tech. coord. Clark County Bd. Edn., 1994—; chmn. Evangelism Com. Christian Ch. in Ky., Lexington, 1984-88; instr. Bellarmine Coll., Louisville, 1991-97; D.T.C., Clark County Schs., 1995—. Cubmaster Council Cub Scouts Am., Pikeville, 1987-89. Democrat. Lodge: Rotary. Avocations: reading, electronics, amateur radio, scouting, computer programming. Home: 3800 Pretty Run Rd Winchester KY 40391-9658

EVANS, WILLIAM LEE, biologist; b. Calvert, Tex., Aug. 28, 1924; s. James Herman and Lilly Australia (O'Neal) E.; m. Lillian Mary Madden, July 30, 1948; children: Kathy A., David C., Susan D. BA with honors, U. Tex., Austin, 1949, MA, 1950, PhD, 1955. Mem. faculty U. Ark., Fayetteville, 1955-89, prof. zoology, 1968-89, prof. emeritus, 1989, chmn. gen. biology, 1967-70; mem. pre-med. com. Fulbright Coll. Arts & Scis., 1982-89, chmn. 1987-89. Author articles, lab. manuals. Capt. AUS, 1942-46, USAF, 1951-52. Decorated Air medal with oak leaf cluster; recipient award for classroom teaching Omicron Delta Kappa, 1959; grantee NSF, 1959-62; grantee NIH, 1960-63; grantee U. Ark. Found., 1979, Fulbright Coll. Arts and Sci., 1982. Mem. Ark. Acad. Sci. (treas. 1972-82, pres. 1984-85), Orthopterists Soc., Am. Philatelic Soc., Am. Numismatic Assn., Phi Beta Kappa, Sigma Xi, Phi Eta Sigma, Phi Kappa Phi. Home and Office: 1916 Albany Ln Fayetteville AR 72704-5382 Also: 9373 Steeple Ct Laurel MD 20723

EVANS, WILLIAM WILL, hospitality executive. Pres., COO Patriot Am. Hospitality, Inc., Dallas. Office: Patriot Am Hospitality 1950 Stemmons Freeway #6001 Dallas TX 75207

EVANS-O'CONNOR, NORMA LEE, secondary school educator, consultant; b. Vanceburg, Ky., Sept. 4, 1952; d. Herbert Martin and Nellie Irene (Parker) E.; 1 child, Karen. AB, Morehead State U., 1975; MEd, Xavier U., 1982. Cert. tchr. Fla., Ky., Tenn., Ohio. Tchr. Forest Hills Sch. Dist., Cin., 1977-83, Osceola County Schs., Kissimmee, Fla., 1983—; chair sch. adv. coun. Osceola H.S. (named Tchr. of Yr. 1995-96, County Social Studies Tchr. of Yr. 1996), activities dir., 1997—; advisor Student Govt., Students Against Drunk Driving, Class of 2000, dept. head social studies; mem. student coun. bd. Nat. Assn. Secondary Sch. Prins., Va., 1990-91; cons. Walt Disney World, Lake Buena Vista, Fla., 1991—; security guard Walt Disney World Co., Lake Buena Vista, 1988—; movie checker Theatrical Entertainment Svcs., L.A., 1990—. Nominated for Nat. Tchrs. Hall of Fame, 1997-98. Mem. NEA, Nat. Assn. Workshop Dirs., Osceola County Tchrs. Orgn., Phi Delta Kappa. Democrat. Roman Catholic. Avocations: basketball, softball, cheerleading. Office: Osceola County Schs 420 S Thacker Ave Kissimmee FL 34741-5963

EVANSON, BARBARA JEAN, middle school education educator; b. Grand Forks, N.D., Aug. 15, 1944; d. Robert John and Jean Elizabeth (Lommen) Gibbons; m. Bruce Carlyle Evanson, Dec. 27, 1965; children: Tracey, John, Kelly. AA, Bismarck State Coll., 1964; BS in Spl. and Elem. Edn., U. N.D., 1966. Tchr. spl. edn. Winship Sch., Grand Forks, 1966-67, Simle Jr. High, Bismarck, 1967-70; tchr. Northridge Elem. Sch., Bismarck, 1980-86, Wachter Middle Sch., Bismarck, 1986—; cons. Dept. Pub. Instrn., Bismarck, 1988—, Chpt. I, Bismark, 1989—, McRel for Drug Free Schs., Denver, 1990-95. Co-founder The Big People, Bismarck, 1978-95; mem. task force Children's Trust Fund, N.D., 1984; senator N.D. Legislature, Bismarck, 1989-94; mem. N.D. Bridges Adv. Bd., 1991-97, DPI English Adv. Com., 1993—; co-facilitator Lead Mid. Sch. for Carnegie, 1994-97; bd. dirs. Caring for Children, 1993-94, N.D. Art Edn.Task Force, 1992-93, N.D. Health Adv. Coun., 1993-94, N.D. Tchr.'s Fund for Retirement, State Investment Bd. 1996—. Recipient Gold Award Bismark Norwest Bank, 1985; named Tchr. of Yr., N.D. Dept. Pub. Instrn., 1989, Legislator of Yr., Children's Caucus, 1991, Outstanding Alumnae, Bismarck State Coll., 1991, Milken Nat. Tchr. of Yr., 1995-96. Mem. N.D. Reading Assn., N.D. Coun. of Tchrs. of English., NEA, N.D. Edn. Assn., Bismarck Edn. Assn. Avocations: clown, walking, reading, travel. Office: Wachter Middle Sch 1107 S 7th St Bismarck ND 58504-6533

EVANSON, ROBERT VERNE, pharmacy educator; b. Hammond, Ind., Nov. 3, 1920; s. Evan and Dorothy (Gordon) E.; m. Helen Louise Wolber, June 29, 1947; children: Yvonne Louise Evanson Nash, Karen Denice Evanson Ivanson. B.S. in Pharmacy, Purdue U., 1947, M.S. in Indsl. Pharmacy, 1949, Ph.D. in Pharmacy Adminstrn., 1953. Apprentice pharmacist Physician's Supply Co., Hammond, 1946; grad. asst. pharmacy Sch. Pharmacy, Purdue U., 1947-48, mem. faculty, 1948—, prof. pharm. adminstrn., 1963-86, head dept., 1966-72; assoc. head dept. pharmacy practice, 1982-86, prof. emeritus, 1986—; cons. in field. Contbr. articles to profl. jours.; contbg. author: Central Pharm. Jour., 1964-72. Served with AUS, 1943-46. Recipient Lederle Faculty award, 1964; award for faculty excellence in pharmacy adminstrn. Nat. Assn. Retail Druggists, 1985. Fellow Am. Found. Pharm. Edn., Am. Pharm. Assn.; mem. Ind. Pharm. Assn., Am. Assn. Coll. Pharmacy (dir., Disting. Educator award 1982), Am. Assn. Coll. Pharmacy Council Faculties (chmn. 1985-86), Acad. Pharm. Scis., Acad. Pharmacy Practice, Soc. Preservation and Encouragement Barbershop Quartet Singing in Am., Sigma Xi. Mem. Fed. Ch. W. Lafayette. Home: 400 Lindberg Ave West Lafayette IN 47906-2032

EVARIST, MILIAN, JR., insurance company executive; Cert. ins. counselor. BA, Pace U., 1982. Pres. Ins. Marketers, Coral Gables, Fla., 1987—. Office: Ins Marketers 141 Almeria Coral Gables FL

EVARTS, CHARLES MCCOLLISTER, orthopaedic surgeon; b. Dunkirk, N.Y., Aug. 16, 1931; s. Charles Melville and Laura (McCollister) E.; m. Nancy Joan Lyons, July 2, 1955; children: Cynthia Ann, Charles Mark, Robert Alan. AB cum laude, Colgate U., 1953; MD, U. Rochester, 1957. Diplomate Am. Bd. Orthopaedic Surgery (pres. 1985-86). Intern Strong Meml. Hosp., 1957-58, resident in orthopaedic surgery, 1961-64; with Cleve. Clinic Found., 1964-74, chmn. dept. orthopaedic surgery, 1970-74; prof., chmn. dept. orthopaedics U. Rochester, 1974-86, Dorris H. Carlson prof., 1975-86, v.p. devel. Med. Ctr., 1985-86; dean Coll. of Medicine, sr. v.p. health affairs Pa. State U., Hershey, 1987—; pres., chief acad. officer Penn State Geisinger Health Sys. Contbr. articles to profl. jours. With USNR, 1959-61. Nat. Found. fellow, 1964. Fellow ACS (gov., chmn. adv. coun. for orthopedics); mem. AMA, NAS, Assn. Am. Med. Colls., Assn. Acad. Health Ctrs. (former chair bd. dirs.), Am. Acad. Orthopaedic Surgeons, Orthopaedic Rsch. Soc., Internat. Knee Soc., Hip Soc. (pres. 1982), Scoliosis Rsch. Soc., Am. Orthopaedic Assn. (pres. 1984-85), Assn. Orthopedic Chmn. (pres. 1982-83), Internat. Hip Soc., Am. Rheumatism Assn., Société Internationale de Chirurgie Orthopedique et de Traumatologie, Continental Orthopaedic Soc., Interurban Orthopaedic Soc., Am. Bd. Orthopaedic Surgery (pres. 1985), Am. Orthopaedic Assn. (pres. 1984), Inst. Medicine, Alpha Omega Alpha.

EVARTS, WILLIAM MAXWELL, JR., lawyer; b. N.Y.C., June 3, 1925; m. Helen Rulison Coleman, Aug. 28, 1948; children: Holly Evarts Bartow, Kate, Alice. AB, Harvard U., 1949, LL.B., 1952. Bar: N.Y. 1953, U.S. Ct. Appeals (2d cir.) 1961, U.S. Dist. Ct. (so. and ea. dists.) N.Y. 1974. Assoc. Winthrop, Stimson, Putnam & Roberts, N.Y.C., 1952-62, ptnr., 1962-97. Bd. dirs. Trust for Pub. Land, San Francisco, United Hosp. Fund, N.Y.C., Scenic Hudson, Poughkeepsie; chmn. distbn. com. N.Y. Community Trust. Sgt. U.S. Army, 1943-46, ETO. Mem. ABA, Assn. of Bar of City of N.Y. Office: Winthrop Stimson Putnam & Roberts 1 Battery Park Plz Fl 31 New York NY 10004-1490

EVATT, PARKER, former state commissioner, former state legislator; b. Greenville, S.C., Aug. 27, 1935; s. H.D. and Ruby (Parker) E.; m. Jane Mangum, Sept. 2, 1960; children—Katherine, Alan. B.S., U. S.C., 1958, M.Criminal Justice, 1978; LL.D. (hon.), Presbyterian Coll., 1977. Exec. dir. Alston Wilkes Soc., Columbia, S.C., 1965-87; mem. S.C. Ho. of Reps., 1975-87; commr. S.C. Dept. Corrections, 1987-95; sr. v.p. Just Care, Inc., 1996—. Mem. adminstrv. bd. Virginia Wingard Meml., United Methodist Ch., del. to gen. conf., 1972, del. to jurisdiction confs., 1972, 76, 80, 84; past lay leader Columbia Meth. Dist. Served with USN, 1958-60. Recipient numerous awards and citations from civic, religious and profl. orgns. Mem. S.C. Youth Workers Assn. (past pres.), Christian Action Council (bd. govs. 1968-71), St. Andrews Jaycees (life), Nat. Assn. Social Workers (named Citizen of Yr. S.C. chpt. 1978), Internat. Halfway Assn. (v.p. 1973-76), Res. Officers Assn. (v.p. Columbia chpt.), Naval Res. Assn. (past pres. Carolina chpt.), Pi Kappa Alpha. Lodge: Rotary.

EVAUL, CHARLEEN MCCLAIN, education educator; b. Huntington, Pa., Dec. 1, 1944; d. Charles Lewis and Eunice C. (Keim) McClain; children: Michael C., Christopher R.; m. Jerome O. Evaul Jr. BS in Edn., Secondary Edn., Math., Millersville U., 1968; cert. in mentally and/or physically handicapped, Kutztown U., 1986; MS in Education, Allentown Coll., 1996. Adult edn. supr. secondary math. Orrville (Ohio) City Schs., 1969-74; substitute tchr. math., sci. Hamburg (Pa.) Area Schs., 1974-76; instructional aide SR/TMR, Reading, Pa., 1976-85; tchr. learning support Conrad Weiser High Sch., Robesonia, Pa., 1985-97; cons. Sci. Rsch. Assocs., Chgo., 1991—; instr. Berks County Intermediate Unit, Reading, 1989—; itinerant tchr., cons. Conrad Weiser S.D., 1997—; adj. prof. Pa. State U.; instr. Learning Inst. St. Joseph's U. Contbr. articles to profl. jours. Recipient Sam Kirk award Pa. Assn. for Learning Disabilities, Annie Sullivan award Pa. Assn. Intermediate Units, Salute to Teaching award Pa. Acad. for Profession of Teaching, Outstanding Educator award Berks County Learning Disabilities Assn. Mem. ASCD, Internat. Soc. Tech. Edn., Pa. Assn. Ednl. Computing & Tech., Coun. Exceptional Children, Assn. Direct Instrn., Phi Delta Kappa. Avocations: flowers, computer bulletin boards, reading. Office: Conrad Weiser HS 347 E Penn Ave Robesonia PA 19551-8900

EVDOKIMOFF, MERRILY WEBER, nursing administrator, community health nurse; b. Pontiac, Mich., July 16, 1945; d. Earl H. and Lillian (Simpson) Weber; m. Victor Evdokimoff, Oct. 14, 1972; children: Justin, Amy. BSN, U. Mich., 1967; MS in Nursing, Boston U., 1984. RN, Mass. Nursing supr. East Seal Home Health Care, Boston, 1985-88; COO Vis. Nurse & Community Health, Inc., Lexington, Mass., 1988-95; home care cons., 1995—; ptnr. V&M Assocs., cons.; chair HING Networking Group. Vol. counselor Serving Health Ins. Needs of Elderly. Shirly Titus scholar U. Mich., 1983. Mem. Mass. Home and Health Assn. (co-chair data com.), Sigma Theta Tau. Home: 130 Depot Rd Harvard MA 01451

EVEILLARD, JEAN-MARIE, financial company executive; b. Poitiers, Poitou, France, Jan. 23, 1940; came to U.S., 1968; s. Hughette (Gautreau); m. Elizabeth Ann Mugar, June 24, 1972; children: Suzanne Marie, Pauline Marie. MBA, Ecole des HEC, Paris, 1962. Security analyst Societé Generale, Paris, 1962-68, Sogen Internat. Fund, N.Y.C., 1968-75; mutual fund portfolio mgr. Societé Generale, Paris, 1975-78; pres. Sogen Internat. Fund, N.Y.C., 1978—. Roman Catholic. Club: Cercle Interallié. Avocation: gardening. Office: Sogen Internat Fund 8th Fl 1221 Avenue Of The Americas New York NY 10020-1001*

EVELETH, EMILY, artist; b. Hartford, Conn., Dec. 13, 1960; d. David Decker and Janet Lee (Pembleton) E.; m. Francis Woodward Penn, May 12, 1984. BA, Smith Coll., 1983; postgrad., Mass. Coll. Art, 1984-86. Mem. acquisition com. Danforth Mus. Art, Framingham, Mass., 1998—; curator mus. show A Painter Selects, 1997. One-woman shows include Harcus Gallery, Boston, 1986, 88, 90, Howard Yezerski Gallery, Boston, 1994, 96, 98, Akus Gallery, East Conn. State U., 1995, Gleason Fine Art, Boothbay Harbor, Maine, 1995, 97, Allan Stone Gallery, N.Y.C., 1996, Danforth Mus. Art, 1997; exhibited in over 35 group shows, Mass., New Eng., N.Y. Painting fellow Nat Endowment for Arts-New Eng. Found. for Arts, Boston, 1994, Art Matters, N.Y.C., 1995, Govt. of France, 1996. Mem. Contemporary Art Support Group (Mass. Fine Arts, Boston). Avocations: gardening, travel, ice skating.

EVELETH, JANET STIDMAN, law association administrator; b. Balt., Sept. 6, 1950; d. John Charles and Edith Janet (Scales) Stidman; m. Donald P. Eveleth, May 11, 1974. BA, Washington Coll., 1972; MS, Johns Hopkins U., 1973. Counselor Office of Mayor, Balt., 1973-75; asst. dir. Gov. Commn. on Children, Balt., 1975-78; lobbyist Balt., 1978-80; comm. specialist Med. Soc., Balt., 1980-81; dir. pub. affairs Mid-Atlantic Food Dealers, Balt., 1981-84; dir. comm. Home Builders Assn., Balt., 1984-87, Md. Bar Assn., Balt., 1987—. Contbr. articles to profl. jours. Recipient Gov. citation State of Md., 1993, Citizen citation City of Balt., 1993. Mem. NAFE, Am. Soc. Profl. Women, Md. Soc. Assn. Execs. (pres. 1992-93), Nat. Assn. Bar Execs. (chmn. pub. rels. sect. 1994-95, achievement award 1995, ABA's E.A. Wally Richter award 1997), Alpha Chi Omega, Pi Lambda Theta. Office: Md Bar Assn 520 W Fayette St Baltimore MD 21201-1781

EVELYN, DOUGLAS EVERETT, museum executive; b. Ossining, N.Y., Sept. 19, 1941; s. Everett Edward and Marie Georgette (Davis) E.; m. Martha Ellen Hutchins MacCornack, Aug. 14, 1965; children: Sarah Ellen, Elizabeth Jane. BA cum laude, Wesleyan U., Middletown, Conn., 1963; PhD, George Washington U., 1997. Staff asst., then adminstrv. asst. to dir.

Am. Assn. Museums, 1963-67; adminstrv. asst. Democratic Nat. Com., 1968; assoc. cons. Monroe Bush & Assocs. (mgmt. cons.), Washington, 1969; various positions to dep. dir. Nat. Portrait Gallery, Smithsonian Instn., Washington, 1969-79; dep. dir. Nat. Mus. Am. History, Smithsonian Instn., Washington, 1979-92, Nat. Mus. Am. Indian, Smithsonian Instn., Washington, 1992—. Co-author: On This Spot: Pinpointing the History of Washington, D.C., 1992. Mem. Am. Assn. Mus. (treas. 1979-82), Cultural Alliance Greater Washington (coun. 1977-84, treas. 1983-84), Am. Assn. State and Local History (coun. 1987-96, v.p. 1990, pres. 1992-94). Home: 2318 King Pl NW Washington DC 20007-1029 Office: Smithsonian Inst Nat Mus Am Indian Washington DC 20560

EVELYN, GWYNETH See VERDON, GWEN

EVEN, FRANCIS ALPHONSE, lawyer; b. Chgo., Sept. 8, 1920; s. George Martin and Cecilia (Neuman) E.; m. Margaret Hope Herrick, Oct. 16, 1945; children: Janet Beth, Dorothy Elizabeth. B.S. in Mech. Engring, U. Ill., 1942; J.D., George Washington U., 1949. Bar: D.C. bar 1949, Ill. bar 1950. Engr. GE, 1945-49; ptnr. Fitch, Even, Tabin & Flannery (patent and trademark law), Chgo., 1952—. Mem. bd. edn., River Forest, Ill., 1963-69; trustee West Suburban Hosp., Oak Park, Ill., 1974-77; mem. adv. bd. Ill. State Hist. Soc., 1997-99. With combat engrs. AUS, 1942-45. Fellow Am. Coll. Trial Lawyers; mem. ABA, Am. Patent Law Assn. (bd. mgrs. 1963-66), Ill. Bar Assn., Chgo. Bar Assn., Patent Law Assn. Chgo. (bd. mgrs. 1972-73, pres. 1984), No. Ill. Ct. Hist. Assn. (pres.), The Lit. Club. Republican. Clubs: Union League (Chgo.); Oak Park (Ill.) Country, River Forest Tennis. Home: 1018 Park Ave River Forest IL 60305-1308 Office: 120 S La Salle St Chicago IL 60603-3403

EVENBECK, SCOTT EDWARD, university official, psychologist; b. Findlay, Ohio, Aug. 14, 1946; s. Benjamin F. and Norma H. (Kelley) E.; m. Elizabeth Ann Jones, Aug. 14, 1970 (div. July 1995); 1 child, Benjamin F. III. AB, Ind. U., 1968; MA, U. N.C., 1971, PhD, 1972. Asst. prof. psychology Ind. U.-Purdue U., Indpls., 1972-76, asst. dean Purdue U. Sch. Sci., 1977-79, assoc. dean, 1979-80, assoc. dir. adminstrv. affairs, assoc. prof. psychology, 1976—, assoc. dir. adminstrv. affairs, 1980-85, dir. continuing studies, 1985—, also assoc. dean Ind. U. Sch. Continuing Studies, 1985-88, assoc. dean of faculties, 1988-90, assoc. vice chancellor, 1990—, dean univ. coll., 1997; bd. dirs. Parent Info. Resource Ctr., 1977-85; exec. v.p. Assn. for Continuing Higher Edn., 1990-93, bd. dirs., 1993—, v.p., 1996—, pres.-elect, 1997, pres., 1998—. Contbr. articles in field to profl. jours. Mem. exec. com., asst. treas., v.p., pres. Am. Lung Assn. Cen. Ind., bd. dirs., 1985—, v.p. 1986; pres. Am. Lung Assn. Ind., 1988; mem. nat. coun. Am. Lung Assn., 1991-94; bd. dirs. Christamore House, 1985—; sec. Indpls.-Searborough Peace Games, 1977-80; mem. bd. Consortium Endowed Episcopal Parishes, 1992—, v.p., 1994-96, pres., 1996—; dep. gen. Episcopal Ch. Convention, 1988, 91, 94, 97, standing commn. on human affairs, 1995-98, standing commn. on domestic mission and evangelism, 1997—; sec. Diocese Indpls., 1995—. USPHS trainee, 1968-72; Arthur R. Metz scholar Ind. U., 1964-68. Mem. APA, Nat. Coun. Univ. Rsch. Adminstrs. (mem. exec. com. 1979-80), Indpls. C. of C. (mem. exec. com. speaker's bur.), Masons. Republican. Episcopalian. Home: 5115 E 74th Pl Indianapolis IN 46250-2529 Office: 815 W Michigan St Indianapolis IN 46202-5199

EVENS, RONALD GENE, radiologist, medical center administrator; b. St. Louis, Sept. 24, 1939; s. Robert and Dorothy (Lupkey) E.; m. Hanna Blunk, Sept. 3, 1960; children: Ronald Jr., Christine, Amanda. BA, Washington U., 1960, MD, 1964, postgrad. in bus. and edn., 1970-71. Intern Barnes Hosp., St. Louis, 1964-65; resident Mallinckrodt Inst. Radiology, St. Louis, 1965-66, 68-70; rsch. assoc. Nat. Heart Inst., 1966-68; asst. prof. radiology, v.p. Washington U. Med. Sch., 1970-71, prof., head dept. radiology, dir., 1971-72, Elizabeth Mallinckrodt prof., head radiology dept., 1972—, prof. med. econs., 1988—; radiologist-in-chief Barnes Hosp., St. Louis, 1971—; radiologist-in-chief Children's Hosp., 1971—, pres., chief exec. officer, 1985-88; vice chancellor fin. Washington U., St. Louis, 1988-91; mem. adv. com. on splty. and geog. distbn. of physicians Inst. Medicine, Nat. Acad. Scis., 1974-76, Hickey lectr., 1976, Carmen lectr. Calif. U., 1985, Kiewit lectr. Eisenhower Med. Ctr., 1986; Hornick lectr. U. Pitts., 1986; ann. orator Can. Radiol. Soc., 1984; Hodes lectr. Jefferson U., 1991—; Smith lectr. Royal Coll. Physicians, Edinburgh, 1992; Seaman lectr. Columbia Presbyn., 1992; dir. Boatmens Bank Inc., Mallinckrodt Group Inc., Right Choice Inc., Blue Choice, Inc.; chmn. bd. Med. Care Group St. Louis, 1980-86. Contbr. over 210 articles to profl. jours. Active Boy Scouts Am., 1975—; elder Glendale Presbyn. Ch., 1971-74, Kirkwood Presbyn. Ch., 1983-86. Served with USPHS, 1966-68. Advance Acad. fellow James Picker Found, 1970; recipient Disting. Svc. award. St. Louis C. of C., 1972; named Disting. Eagle Scout Nat. Coun., 1983. Fellow Am. Coll. Radiology (chair elect 1995, chair bd. chancellors 1996—); mem. AMA (editl. bd. JAMA), Mo. Radiol. Soc. (pres. 1977-78), Soc. Nuclear Medicine (trustee 1971-75), St. Louis Med. Soc., Mo. State Med. Assn., Soc. Chmn. Acad. Radiology Depts. (pres. 1979), Radiol. Soc. N.Am., Assn. Univ. Radiologists (pres. 1988), Am. Roentgen Ray Soc. (pres. 1989), Phi Beta Kappa, Alpha Omega Alpha (Sheard-Sanford award). Office: Washington U Mallinckrodt Inst Radiology 510 S Kingshighway Blvd Saint Louis MO 63110-1016

EVENSEN, ALF JOHN, engineer, researcher, sales executive; b. Marquette, Mich., June 30, 1938; s. Alf and Alice (Edna) E.; m. Judith Lynne Dellinger, June 22, 1979. BS, U. Mich., 1959; MA, Wayne State U., 1966; BA, U. Ala., 1993. System engr. Computer Scis. Internat., Apledoorn, The Netherlands, 1969; project engr. System Devel. Corp., Huntsville, Ala., 1970-81; system engr. electronics div. AVCO Corp., Huntsville, 1981-82; project mgr. Sci. Applications Internat. Corp., Huntsville, 1982-85; staff engr. Teledyne Brown Engring. Corp., Huntsville, 1985-93; prin. rschr. Tech. Masters Inc., Huntsville, Ala., 1994-95; sr. mgmt., tech. staff Systems Devel. Corp., Huntsville, Ala., 1995-97; with Raytheon Systems Co., Huntsville, Ala., 1997-98, Advanced R & D, Huntsville, 1998—. Served to lt. USNR, 1961-68. Mem. IEEE, NRA, Masons, K.T., Royal Order of Scotland, Ancient Arabic Order Nobles Mystic Shrine, Alpha Chi Sigma, Phi Alpha Theta, Phi Iota Sigma. Home: 137 Eldorado Dr Madison AL 35758-7809 Office: Alpine Ind 137 Eldorado Dr Madison AL 35758

EVENSEN, JAY DOUGLAS, newspaper editor; b. DeKalb, Ill., Apr. 17, 1959; s. Glenn Stivers and Anne Berit (Strand) E.; m. Kirsti Elisabet Haneberg, July 16, 1982; children: Daniel, Linnea, Nils, Anders. BA, Brigham Young U., 1983. Reporter/intern UPI, N.Y.C., 1982; sports editor Clinton (Okla.) Daily News, 1983; reporter Las Vegas (Nev.) Review Jour., 1983-86; reporter Deseret News, Salt Lake City, 1986-94, editl. writer, 1994-96, editl. page editor, 1996—; adj. instr. journalism Weber State U., Ogden, Utah, 1988-98. Recipient 3d pl. editl. writing award Assoc. Press, 1994. Mem. Soc. Profl. Journalists (bd. dirs., region 9 dir., 1st pl. feature writing award 1989, 2d pl. column writing award 1995), Nat. Conf. Editl. Writers. Mem. LDS Ch. Home: 9679 Paisley Cir South Jordan UT 84095-9608 Office: Deseret News PO Box 1257 Salt Lake City UT 84110-1257

EVENSON, EDWARD BERNARD, geology educator; b. Milw., Dec. 30, 1942; s. Bernard John and Loraine (Willich) E.; 1 child, Mark John. BS, U. Wis.-Milw., 1965, MS, 1970; PhD, U. Mich., 1972. Sr. rsch. geologist Exxon Rsch. Labs., Houston, 1972-73; asst. to assoc. prof. Lehigh U., Bethlehem, Pa., 1973-85, prof. geology, 1985—; dir. Environ. Sci. and Resource Mgmt. Lehigh U., 1973-95. Contbr. articles to profl. jours. Editor: Tills and Related Deposits, 1983. Fellow Geol. Soc. Am.; mem. Geol. Soc. Argentina, Sigma Xi (treas. 1978—). Republican. Avocation: ice climbing. Home: 18 E Goepp St Bethlehem PA 18018-2818 Office: Lehigh U Earth & Environ Scis Bethlehem PA 18015

EVENSON, ERIC TODD, army officer, public health physician; b. Apr. 17, 1948. BA, Luther Coll., Decorah, Iowa, 1970; MD, Mayo Med. Sch., Rochester, Minn., 1976; MPH, U. Wash., 1986. Commd. U.S. Army, advanced through grades to col.; chief of preventive medicine U.S. Army Alaska, Ft. Wainwright, 1986-89; command surgeon, corp. med. dir. U.S. Army Armament Munition and Chem. Commands, Rock Island, Ill., 1991-93, U.S. Army Materiel Command, Alexandria, Va., 1994-98; occupational health cons. U.S. Army, Falls Ch., Va., 1998—. E-mail: col-eric-evenson@DTSG-amedd.army.mil. Home: 4006 Rainbow Glen Ct Annandale VA 22003-2417

EVENSON, MERLE ARMIN, chemist, educator; b. LaCrosse, Wis., July 27, 1934; s. Ansel Bernard and Gladys Mabel (Nelson) E.; m. Peggy L. Kovats, Oct. 5, 1957; children—David A., Donna L. BS in Chem. Physics and Math., U. Wis., LaCrosse, 1956; MS in Guidance, Madison, 1960, MS in Sci. Edn., 1960, PhD in Analytical Chemistry, 1966. Diplomate Am. Bd. Clin. Chemists, v.p., 1978-81. Tchr. math. and physics St. Croix Falls (Wis.) High Sch., 1956-57; tchr. chemistry Central High Sch., LaCrosse, 1957-59; instr. dept. medicine U. Wis., Madison, 1965-66; asst. prof. U. Wis., 1966-69, asso. prof., 1971-75, prof., 1975—, prof. dept. pathology, 1979—; asst. dir. clin. lab. Univ. Hosps., 1965-66, dir. clin. chemistry lab., 1966-69, dir. toxicology lab., 1971-87; chmn. Gordon Rsch. Conf. on Analytical Chemistry, 1978; vis. lectr. Harvard Med. Sch., 1969-71; mem. staff Peter Bent Brigham Hosp., Boston, 1969-71; cons. on analytical and clin. chemistry to AEC, 1968-93, Am. Chem. Soc., Nat. Bur. Standards, FDA, NIH, study sect. mem. 1968-72, ad hoc memberships, 1973-87. Bd. editors: Chemical Instrumentation, 1973-87, Analytical Chemistry, 1974-77, Jour. Analytical Toxicology, 1976-79, Selected Methods in Clin. Chemistry, 1977-81; editor: Contemporary Topics in Analytical and Clincal Chemistry, 1974-83; contbr. numerous chpts. to books, articles to profl. jours. NIH fellow, 1970-71, NSF, 1959-62; recipient Maurice O. Graff Disting. Alumni award U. Wis., LaCrosse, 1981. Mem. AAAS, Acad. Clin. Lab. Physicians and Scientists, Am. Assn. Clin. Chemists (bd. editors Clin. Chemistry 1970-80, nat. chair pub. rels. com. 1973-78, diplomat 1974, v.p. 1978-81), Am. Chem. Soc. (com. on clin. chemistry 1973-93), Sigma Xi, Kappa Delta Pi. Patentee continuous oil hemoperfusion unit. Office: U Wis 1300 University Ave Madison WI 53706-1510 *As a teacher, the fostering of the development of creativity in people who then make contributions to our society is an exciting process. The most significant professional reward I receive is the observation of the successes of others with whom I have interacted and taught.*

EVENSON, PAUL ARTHUR, physics educator; b. Chgo., Jan. 27, 1946; s. Warren Lawrence and Clemetta Marie (Spanier) E.; m. Karen Lee Sivia, June 22, 1968; children: Mark, Catherine, Elizabeth. BS, U. Chgo., 1967, MS, 1968, PhD, 1972. Rsch. assoc. U. Chgo., 1972-76, sr. rsch. assoc., 1976-83; assoc. prof. Bartol Rsch. Inst., Newark, Del., 1983-90; prof. physics U. Del., Newark, 1990—. Recipient Sr. Rsch. award Alexander von Humboldt Found., 1992; fellowship NATO, 1972. Fellow Am. Phys. Soc.; mem. Am. Geophys. Union, Am. Astron. Soc., Sigma Xi. Republican. Roman Catholic. Avocation: carpentry. Home: 303 Wilson Rd Newark DE 19711-3630 Office: Bartol Rsch Inst Univ Del Newark DE 19716*

EVENSON, ROBERT EUGENE, economics educator; b. Elmore, Minn., July 25, 1934; s. Edven Herbert and Annie Cecelia (O'Toole) E.; m. Bonnie Lee Leak, Dec. 7, 1952 (div. 1959); children: Nancy Lynn, Patsy Ann; m. Judith Joan Ungrodt, June 11, 1967; children: Joseph Robert, Sarah Judith. BA in Bus. Adminstrn., U. Minn., 1961, MSc, 1964; PhD, U. Chgo., 1968. Farmer E.H. Evenson & Son, Minnesota Lake, Minn., 1952-60; asst. prof. U. Minn., Mpls. and St. Paul, 1966-68; vis. asst. prof. So. Meth. U., Dallas, 1968-69; assoc. prof. econs. Yale U., New Haven, 1969-74; assoc. vis. prof. Agrl. Devel. Coun., N.Y.C., 1974-77; prof. Yale U., New Haven, 1977—; cons. World Bank, Washington, 1970—, AID, Washington, 1970—. Author: Agricultural Research and Productivity, 1975, Technology and Income, 1990; editor: Science and Technology: Lessons for Development, 1990. Fellow NSF, 1964. Fellow AAAS; mem. Am. Econ. Assn., Econometric Soc., Am. Agrl. Econs. Assn., Schumpeter Soc. Home: 2 Edgehill Rd New Haven CT 06511-1328 Office: Yale U Econ Growth Ctr 27 Hillhouse Ave New Haven CT 06511-3703

EVENSON, STEVE EARLE, lawyer; b. Reno, Nev., July 6, 1967; s. Phillip Lee E. and Joanne Musselman; m. Jami Delores Fornelli, Jan. 1, 1997; 1 child, Vincent Earle. BA in History, U. Nev., Las Vegas, 1989; JD, U. of the Pacific, 1992. Bar: Nev. Deputy asst. atty., Pioche, Nev., 1992; atty. pvt. practice, Las Vegas, 1993-95; dist. atty. Esmeralda County, Goldfield, Nev., 1995-97; deputy dist. atty. Pershing County, Lovelock, Nev., 1997-99; pvt. practice Lovelock, 1999—. Chair Esmeralda County Rep. Ctrl. Com., 1995-97; mem. So. Nev. Job Tng. Bd., Las Vegas, 1995-97. Mem. Lions, Goldfield C. of C. (pres. 1997), Lovelock C. of C. (pres. 1999—). Avocations: car racing, bike riding. Home: 870 Jamestown Rd Lovelock NV 89419 Office: PO Box 1023 Lovelock NV 89419

EVERBACH, OTTO GEORGE, lawyer; b. New Albany, Ind., Aug. 27, 1938; s. Otto G. and Zelda Marie (Hilt) E.; m. Nancy Lee Stern, June 3, 1961; children: Tracy Ellen, Stephen George. BS, U.S. Mil. Acad., 1960; LLB, U. Va., 1966. Bar: Va. 1967, Ind. 1967, Calif. 1975, Mass. 1978. Counsel CIA, Langley, Va., 1966-67; corp. counsel Bristol-Meyers Co., Evansville, Ind., 1967-74, Alza Corp., Palo Alto, Calif., 1974-75; sec., gen. counsel Am. Optical Corp., Southbridge, Mass., 1976-81; assoc. gen. counsel Warner-Lambert Co., Morris Plains, N.J., 1981-83; v.p. Kimberly-Clark Corp., Neenah, Wis., 1984-86, sr. v.p., gen. counsel, 1986—, sr. v.p. law & govt. affairs, 1988—. Served with U.S. Army, 1960-63. Mem. Am. Bar Assn., Mass. Bar Assn., Ind. Bar Assn., Calif. Bar Assn. Office: Kimberly-Clark Corp DFW Airport Sta PO Box 619100 Dallas TX 75261-9100

EVERDELL, WILLIAM, lawyer; b. N.Y.C., May 29, 1915; s. William and Rosalind (Romeyn) E.; m. Eleanore Darling, July 2, 1940; children—William Romeyn, Coburn Darling, Preston. BA, Williams Coll., 1937; LLB, Yale U., 1940. Bar: N.Y. 1941. Assoc. Debevoise & Plimpton, N.Y.C., 1940-49, ptnr., 1949-85; of counsel Debevoise & Plimpton, 1986-88. Contbr. articles to profl. jours. Trustee Woods Hole Oceanographic Instn., Mass., 1978-86; mem. exec. com., 1981-86, hon. trustee, 1987—; trustee, mem. exec. com. Cold Spring Harbor Lab., N.Y., 1987-93. Served to lt. comdr. USNR, 1942-45, PTO, ATO. Fellow Am. Bar Found.; mem. ABA, Assn. of Bar of City of N.Y. (mem. exec. com. 1960-64), N.Y. State Bar Assn. (chmn. com. corp. law 1971-73). Episcopalian. Club: The Links (gov. 1959-62) (N.Y.C.). Avocations: sailing; golf.

EVERDELL, WILLIAM ROMEYN, humanities educator; b. N.Y.C., June 25, 1941; s. William and Eleanore (Darling) E.; m. Barbara Scott, Dec. 21, 1966; children: Joshua William, Christian Romeyn. AB, Princeton U., 1964; MA, Harvard U., 1965; PhD, NYU, 1971. Asst. English Lycee Arago, Paris, 1963-64; chmn. dept. history St. Ann's Sch., Bklyn., 1972-73, head upper shc., 1973-75, co-chmn. dept. history, 1975-84, dean humanities, 1984—; adj. instr. NYU, N.Y.C., 1984-85, 86, 87, 89; steering com. U.S. history assessment Nat. Assessment Ednl. Progress, 1991-92; rev. panel NEH Tchr. Fellowships, U.S. Dept. Edn. Blue Ribbon Schs., 1992; ednl. testing svc. World History AP Exam. Devel. Com., 1999. Author: The End of Kings, 1983, Christian Apologetics in France, 1987, The First Moderns, 1997; co-author: Rowboats to Rapid Transit, 1974; contbr. articles and poems to profl. jours. and newspapers. With USMC, 1966-68. Recipient Poetry prize Acad. Am. Piets, 1963; Fullbright travel grantee, Paris, 1963; Woodrow Wilson fellow, 1964, 70, NEH fellow, 1985, 90; NEH/Wallace Found. tchr./scholar, 1990-91. Mem. Soc. French Hist. Studies, Internat. Soc. Intellectual History, Nat. Coun. History Edn., Am. Hist. Assn., Orgn. N.Y. Acad. Sci., History Tchrs. (sec. 1987—), East Ctrl. Am. Soc. 18th Century Studies (pres. 1997), Bklyn. Hist. Soc.; New Eng. Soc. Bklyn., Rembrandt Club. Democrat. Episcopalian. Avocation: bicycling. Office: St Ann's Sch 129 Pierrepont St Brooklyn NY 11201-2793

EVERETT, C(HARLES) CURTIS, retired lawyer; b. Omaha, Aug. 9, 1930; s. Charles Edgar and Rosalie (Cook) E.; m. Joan Rose Bader, Sept. 7, 1951; children: Jeffrey, Ellen, Amy, Jennifer. BA cum laude, Beloit Coll., 1952; JD, U. Chgo., 1957. Bar: Ill. 1957. Pvt. practice Chgo., 1957-91; ptnr. Bell, Boyd, Lloyd, Haddad & Burns, 1965-81, successor firm Bell, Boyd & Lloyd, 1981-91; v.p. law, sec., gen. counsel AMRE, Inc., Dallas, 1991-96; v.p. law, sec., gen. counsel, bd. dirs. Am. Remodeling, Inc., Dallas, 1992-96; v.p. Canre Remodelling, Inc., Dallas, 1992-94; v.p., sec. Hans Bader, Cons., Inc., Clearwater, Fla., 1954—, also bd. dirs.; vis. com. U. Chgo. Law Sch., 1986-89; lectr. Ill. Inst. CLE. Mem. editl. bd. U. Chgo. Law Rev., 1956-57; contbr. articles to profl. jours. Chmn. So. Suburban area Beloit Coll. Ford Found. challenge program, 1964-65; pres. The Players, Flossmoor, 1970-71; bd. govs. Lake Shore Dr. Condominium Assn., 1986-91. With AUS, 1952-54. Mem. ABA, Ill. Bar Assn., Chgo. Bar Assn. (mem. securities law com. 1960-91), U. Chgo. Law Sch. Alumni Assn. (dir. 1973-76, pres. Chgo. chpt. 1979-80), Legal Club, Law Club, Monroe Club (bd. govs. 1976-97), Univ. Club Chgo., Order of DeMolay (past master counselor Rock River chpt.), Order of Coif, Sigma Chi, Phi Alpha Delta. Mem. Cmty. Ch. (deacon). Home: 532 Long Reach Dr Salem SC 29676-4214

EVERETT, CHARLES ROOSEVELT, JR., airport executive. BA in Urban Studies, U. Pa., 1984. Transp. planning engr. Gannett Fleming, Inc., Harrisburg, Pa., 1986-88; transp. systems planner II Schimpeler Corradino Assoc., Louisville, 1988-89; project mgr. transp. planning Woolpert Cons., Dayton, Ohio, 1989-91; dir. Syracuse (N.Y.) Met. Transp. Coun., 1991-94; commr. dept. aviation City of Syracuse, 1994—; Bd. dirs. Hancock Field Devel. Corp., Aviation/Aerospace Edn. Found.; presenter in field. Contbr. articles to profl. jours. Maj. N.Y. ANG. Mem. Am. Assn. Airport Execs., N.Y. Airport Mgrs. Assn. (v.p. 1997, pres. 1998, 99), Inst. Transp. Engrs. (trans. planners coun. N.Y. Upstate sect. pres. 1993-94, 96-97, sec. 1995, tech. com., high speed inter-city rail svc. planning 1988-92), Transp. Rsch. Bd., Air Force Res. Office: City of Syracuse Dept Aviation Syracuse Hancock Internat Airport Syracuse NY 13212

EVERETT, CHERYL ANN, music educator, pianist; b. Crawfordsville, Ind., July 7, 1945; d. Howard Dennis and Thelma Louise (Rutledge) P. Student, DePauw U., 1975. Church organist Christian Sci. Ch., Methodist Ch., Presbyn. Ch., Crawfordsvill, Ind., 1958—; celeste player Indpls. Philharmonic Orch., 1994—; accompanist Wabash Coll. Glee Club, Crawfordsville, 1997—; chair Ind. Jr. Festival Nat. Fedn. Music Clubs, 1984-94, Indpls Jr. Festival Nat. Fedn. Music Clubs, 1984-94; performed in recitals and master classes of Internat. Workshops in Italy, Eng., France, Can., Switzerland, 1986-89, with Internat. String Orch. in workshops in Eisenstadt, Austria, 1989; adjudicator Tippecanoe Piano Tchrs. Lafayette, Ind, 1993-97, Logansport (Ind.) Piano Tchrs., 1993-97, Stickley Meml. Competition, South Bend, Ind., 1989. Founder, dir. Presbyn. Artists Concert Series, Crawfordsville, 1991; founder, organizer Montgomery County Multi-keyboard Extavaganza featuring 170 players, Crawfordsville, 1995-97. Chosen 15 times Ideal Lady, Sunshine Soc. Girls, 1977-97. Mem. Indiana Music Tchrs. (chair monster concert 1998), Nat. Music Tchrs., Indpls. Piano Tchrs. (pres. 1986-88), Nat. Guild of Piano Tchrs., Crawfordsville Music Club (pres. 1989), Ind. Fedn. Music Clubs, Nat. Fedn. Music Clubs. Avocations: sewing, needlework, quilting. Home: 207 S Water St Crawfordsville IN 47933-2536

EVERETT, ELBERT KYLE, marketing executive, consultant; b. Knoxville, Tenn., June 17, 1946; s. David Abraham and Lois (Hill) E.; student E. Tenn. U., 1965-67; m. Jane Harville, June 13, 1967; 1 child, Evelyn Anne. Sales rep. Met. Life Ins. Co., Knoxville, 1968-70, Creative Displays, Knoxville, 1970-73; market mgr. central and No. Calif., Nat. Advt. div. 3M Co., Stockton from 1973, dist. mgr. western dist., Fresno, 1984; owner Jane Everett's Country Wholesale Furniture Mfg.; sr. cons. Profl. Practice Systems, Inc., Eastern U.S., 1990—; ptnr. Everett Mgmt. Group, 1990—; advt. cons. athletic dept. U. Pacific, Fresno State U.; lectr. outdoor advt. and mktg. San Joaquin Delta Coll., Fresno City Coll., Fresno State U., W.Va. Optometric Conv., Ind. Optometric Conv.; mgmt. cons. in med. field; lectr. in field. Mayor City of Indian Hills, Ky.; mem. steering com. Jefferson County Governance; mem. subcom. on tourism State of Nev.; cons. Stockton Civic Theater; bd. dirs. Jefferson County League of Cities. Served with AUS, 1964. Recipient cert. of recognition U.S. Treasury Dept., 1977-78, 82-83; recognition award for best design Advt. Age, 1974, 83, Ky. col., 1995; 2 recognition awards Outdoor Advt. Assn. Am., 1973; Cert. of Appreciation United Way, 1978, 81, 82, 83. Mem. U. Pacific Athletic Found., Fresno State Found., Stockton C. of C., Fresno C. of C., Advt. Club Sacramento, Advt. Club Fresno, Internat. Platform Assn., Fresno State Athletic Found., Phi Sigma Kappa. Baptist. Home and Office: 205 S Sherrin Ave Louisville KY 40207-3852

EVERETT, GRAHAM, English language educator, poet, publisher; b. Oceanside, N.Y., Dec. 23, 1947; s. James H. and Jacqueline (Vaughn) E.; m. Elyse Arnow, Dec. 27, 1981; 1 child, Logan James. BA in English, Canisius Coll., 1970; MA in English, SUNY, Stony Brook, 1987, PhD in English, 1994. Pub., editor Street Press, Port Jefferson, N.Y., 1972-92; dir. Backstreet Editions, Inc., Port Jefferson, 1980-86; asst. dir. Poetry Ctr. SUNY, Stony Brook, 1988-91; prof., acad. tutor Adelphi U.; writer in residence N.Y. State Poets in Sch. Program, L.I., 1973-86. Author: (poetry) Strange Coast, 1979, Sunlit Sidewalk, 1985, Minus Green, 1992, Minus Green Plus, 1995; editor: The Doc Fayth Poems, 1998; co-editor: Paumanok Rising, 1980. Mem. MLA, Nat. Coun. Tchrs. English. Office: Street Press PO Box 772 Sound Beach NY 11789-0772

EVERETT, JAMES JOSEPH, lawyer; b. San Antonio, May 7, 1955. BA, St. Mary's U., San Antonio, 1976; JD, Tex. So. U., 1980. Bar: U.S. Dist. Ct. Ariz. 1987, U.S. Tax Ct. 1980, U.S. Ct. Appeals (9th cir.) 1988. Sr. trial atty. IRS, Phoenix, 1980-87; ptnr. Brnilovich & Everett, Phoenix, 1987-89; pvt. practice Law Offices of James J. Everett, Phoenix, 1989—; of counsel Broadbent, Walker & Wales, 1991-95. Mem. ATLA, ABA (bus. and tax sects.), Fed. Bar Assn., Tex. Bar Assn., Ariz. Bar Assn., State Bar Ariz. (cert. tax specialist), Maricopa County Bar Assn., Ariz. Tax Controversy Group, Valley Estate Planners (Phoenix), Ctrl. Ariz. Estate Planners, Ariz. Soc. Boutiques, St. Thomas Moore Soc. (fee arbitration com.). Office: 608 E Missouri Ave Phoenix AZ 85012-1377

EVERETT, JOHN HOWARD, diving business owner, paramedic; b. Beaumont, Tex., Feb. 10, 1948; s. Bennie Earl Everett and Margaret (Weston) Heartfield; m. Kathleen Loraine Savon, May 30, 1983 (div. Mar. 1985); m. Debra Edwinna Haymon, Oct. 31, 1990. Grad., Forest Park High Sch., Beaumont, Tex., 1966; paramedic, Beaumont Emergency Med. Svc., 1983. Svc. technician Bear's Bug Svc., Beaumont, 1966-70; gunsmith Tex. Gunman, Beaumont, 1970-72; owner, pres. Aquaventures Dive Shop, Inc., Beaumont, 1974-91; flight paramedic, Med-Link St. Elizabeth Hosp., Beaumont, 1988—; exam. coord. Nat. Registry of EMTs, Columbus, Ohio, 1984-91. Recipient Underwater Photography award Tex. Gulf Coast Coun. Dive Clubs, 1978. Mem. Profl. Assn. Diving Instrs. (master instr./master dive trainer). Methodist. Avocations: scuba diving, sailing, hunting, photography. Home: 803 N Bowie St Fredericksburg TX 78624-2683 also: 12 Coral Negro, Playa del Carmen Mexico Office: Med-Link Aeromedical Svcs 2830 Calder St Beaumont TX 77702-1809

EVERETT, JOHN PRENTIS, JR., lawyer; b. Shreveport, La., Dec. 17, 1941; s. John Prentis and Doris (Waguespack) E.; m. Mary Jane Spaht, Nov. 5, 1966 (div. 1979); 1 child, John Prentis III; m. Katherine Coghlan, June 25, 1981. BS, La. State U., 1966, JD, 1966. Bar: La. 1966, U.S. Ct. Mil. Appeals 1968, U.S. Supreme Ct. 1970. Ptnr. Kantrow Spaht Weaver & Walter, Baton Rouge, 1970-78; dir. Camp Carmouche Palmer Barsh & Hunter, Lake Charles, La., 1978-90, Carmouche Law Firm, Lake Charles, 1990-95; ptnr. Wright and Everett, L.L.C., Lake Charles, 1995—; pres. Imperial Calcasieu Title Corp. Maj. JAGC, USMC, 1967-70. Fellow Am. Coll. Mortgage Attys., La. Bar Found. (bd. dirs. 1998—); mem. La. Bar Assn. (ho. of dels. 1996—). Home: 4563 Pete Seay Rd Sulphur LA 70665-8264 Office: Wright and Everett LLC 203 W Clarence St Lake Charles LA 70601-5229

EVERETT, JONATHAN JUBAL, lawyer; b. Bellingham, Wash., Sept. 10, 1950; s. John Thomas and Dawn Irene (Speirs) E.; m. Mary Kathryn Penar, May 27, 1973. BA, U. Chgo., 1972; MA, Harvard U., 1975, JD, 1979. Bar: Calif. 1981, Ill. 1982. Law clk. presiding judge U.S. Ct. Appeals (5th cir.), Baton Rouge, 1979-80; assoc. O'Melveny and Myers, L.A., 1980-81, Mayer, Brown and Platt, Chgo., 1982-84; assoc. Skadden, Arps, Slate, Meagher and Flom, Chgo., 1984-87, ptnr., 1987-96; mng. dir. View Group, L.P., Boston, 1996—. Office: View Group LP 186 Lincoln St Ste 300 Boston MA 02111-2403

EVERETT, KAREN JOAN, retired librarian, genealogy educator; b. Cin., Dec. 12, 1926; d. Leonard Kelly and Kletis V. (Wade) Wheatley; m. Wilbur Mason Everett, Sept. 25, 1950; children: Karen, Jan, Jeffrey, Jon, Kathleen, Kerry, Kelly, Shannon. BS in Edn. magna cum laude, U. Cin., 1976, postgrad., 1982-85; postgrad., Coll. Mt. St. Joseph, 1981-86, Xavier U., Cin., 1985-87, U. Cin., 1982-85, Miami U., 1987. Libr. S.W. Local Schs., Harrison, Ohio, 1967-97; dist. media coord. S.W. Local Schs., 1980-97, dist. vol. dir., 1980-97, ret., 1997; instr. genealogy U. Cin., 1998—; tchr. genealogy U. Cin., 1997—; cons. in field; bd. dirs. U. Cin. ILR; lectr. in field. Contbr. articles to profl. jours. Pres. Citizens Adv. Coun., Harrison, Ohio, 1981-84,

88—, Citizens Adv. Coun., 1989; state chmn. supervisory div. Ohio Ednl. Libr./Media Assn.; mem. Ohio Ambulance Licensing Bd., 1991—. Named Woman of the Yr., Cin. Enquirer, 1978, Xi Eta Iota, 1979; named PTA Educator of the Yr., 1981, others. Mem. NEA, Ohio Ednl. Libr./Media Assn. (chair supervisory div. 1990—, bd. dirs. 1993-94), Ohio Edn. Assn., S.W. Local Classroom Tchrs. Assn., Hamilton County Geneal. Soc. (bd. dirs. 1992—). Avocations: flying, travel, genealogy. Office: U Cin PO Box 210146 Cincinnati OH 45221-0146

EVERETT, KAY, councilwoman. City councilwoman City of Detroit. Office: City Coun 1340 City County Bldg Detroit MI 48226*

EVERETT, MARK ALLEN, dermatologist, educator; b. Oklahoma City, May 30, 1928; s. Mark Ruben and Alice (Allen) E.; 1 son, Howard Dean. B.A. in Polit. Sci., U. Okla., 1947, M.D., 1951; USAF intern in pub. health. Intern in pediatrics U. Mich. Med. Sch., 1951, resident in dermatology, 1954-57, instr. dermatology, 1956-57; intern in pub. health Tulane Med. Sch., 1951; mem. faculty U. Okla. Med. Sch., 1959-98, chmn. dept. dermatology, 1964-96, prof. dermatology, head dept., 1967-96, adj. prof. pathology and anatomy, 1975-98, prof., interim head dept. pathology, 1979-84, Regents prof., 1982-98, Regents prof. emeritus, 1998—, chmn. faculty bd., 1974-90; chief staff Okla. Meml. Hosp., 1980-85; vice chmn. bd. Bone and Joint Hosp., Oklahoma City, 1976-85; chmn. Internat. Com. for Dermatopathology, 1980-86; bd. dirs. Am. Bd. Dermatology, 1985-96, pres.-elect, 1994, pres., 1995. Author 200 articles in field, chpts. in books. Pres. Okla. Ballet Soc., 1973, 77-80, Oklahoma City Chamber Orch., 1979-81, Chamber Music Okla., 1989—; pres. bd. trustees Everett Found., 1961—; adv. bd. World Lit. Today, 1970-85, Bizzell Libr. Soc., 1982—; bd. visitors Coll. of Fine Arts, U. Okla., 1990—, Coll. of Arts and Scis., 1996—. With USAF, 1952-54. Recipient Bronze medal U. Okla. Fedn., Mayor's award for Lifetime Contbn. to Arts, Oklahoma City, 1989, Gov.'s Arts award, 1993; grantee Am. Cancer Soc., NIH. Mem. AMA, Am. Acad. Dermatology (chmn. long-range planning coun. 1975-80, dir. 1978-82, chmn. coun. on sci. assembly 1985), Assn. Profs. Dermatology (pres. 1976-78), Am. Soc. Dermatopathology (pres. 1980), Am. Assn. Cancer Rsch., Internat. Acad. Pathology, Am. Dermatol. Assn. (bd. dirs. 1990-95, pres. 1995-96), Am. Soc. Clin. Investigation, Soc. Investigative Dermatology, Radiation Rsch. Soc., Okla. Med. Soc., Coll. Physicians Phila., N.Y. Acad. Scis., N.Mex. Dermatol. Soc., Pacific Dermatol. Assn., South Ctrl. Dermatol. Soc., Austrian Dermatology Soc. (hon.), Polish Dermatology Soc. (hon.), Brit. Assn. Dermatology (hon.), RRC Dermatology RRC Dermapathology, Gourgerot Soc., Sociète Française de Dermatologie (hon.), Phi Beta Kappa. Democrat. Roman Catholic. Club: Lotos (N.Y.C.). Office: U Okla Health Sci Ctr Dept Dermatology 619 NE 13th St Oklahoma City OK 73104-5001*

EVERETT, PAMELA IRENE, legal management company executive, educator; b. L.A., Dec. 31, 1947; d. Richard Weldon and Alta Irene (Tuttle) Bunnell; m. James E. Everett, Sept. 2, 1967 (div. 1973); 1 child, Richard Earl. Cert. Paralegal, Rancho Santiago Coll., Santa Ana, Calif., 1977; BA, Calif. State U.-Long Beach, 1985; MA, U. Redlands, 1988. Owner, mgr. Orange County Paralegal Svc., Santa Ana, 1979-85; pres. Gem Legal Mgmt. Inc., Fullerton, Calif., 1986—; co-owner Bunnell Publs., Fullerton, Calif., 1992-96, The Millennium Network, 1997; instr. Rancho Santiago Coll., 1979—, chmn. adv. bd., 1980-85; instr. Fullerton Coll., 1989—, Rio Hondo Coll., Whittier, Calif., 1992-94; advisor Nat. Paralegal Assn., 1982—, Saddleback Coll., 1985—, North Orange County Regional Occupational Program, Fullerton, 1986—, Fullerton Coll. So. Calif. Coll. Bus. and Law; bd. dirs. Nat. Profl. Legal Assts. Inc., editor PLA News. Author: Legal Secretary Federal Litigation, 1986, Bankruptcy Courts and Procedure, 1987, Going Independent--Business Planning Guide, Fundamentals of Law Office Management, 1994. Republican. Avocation: reading. Office: 406 N Adams Ave Fullerton CA 92832-1605

EVERETT, RALPH BERNARD, lawyer; b. Orangeburg, S.C., June 23, 1951; s. Francis G.S. and Alethia (Hilton) E.; m. Gwendolyn Harris, June 22, 1974. BA, Morehouse Coll., 1973; JD, Duke U., 1976. Bar: N.C. 1977, D.C. 1979. Adminstrv. asst. N.C. Dept. Labor, 1976-77; legis. asst. Office of Sen. Ernest F. Hollings, Washington, 1977-82; minority chief counsel, staff dir. U.S. Senate Com. on Commerce, Sci., Transp., Washington, 1983-87, chief counsel, staff dir., 1987-89; ptnr. Paul, Hastings, Janofsky and Walker, LLP, Washington, 1989—; bd. dirs. Shenandoah Life Ins. Co., Ctr. Nat. Policy, Cumulus Media Inc.; mem. adv. bd. Norfolk So. Corp., 1991—; mem. bd. visitors Duke U. Sch. Law; mem. Pres.'s Bd. Advisors on Historically Black Colls. and Univs.; head U.S. Del. to World Telecomm. Conf., 1998; U.S. amb. to 1998 Internat. Telecomm. Union Plenipotentiary Conf. Former trustee Nat. Urban League, N.Y.C., 1990, 92; senate liaison Clinton/Gore Presdl. Campaign, Washington, 1992; former mem. Congl. Award Found., McLean, Va., 1993—; former mem. Fed. City Coun., Econ. Club Washington. Office: Paul Hastings Janofsky & Walker LLP 10th Fl 1299 Pennsylvania Ave NW Washington DC 20004-2400

EVERETT, RICHARD G., newspaper editor; b. New Brunswick, N.J., Sept. 20, 1950; s. Richard D. and Patricia L. Everett; m. Mary Worth, Aug. 26, 1972; children: Laura, Kathryn. BA in English Lit., Colgate U., 1972. Reporter Daily Advance, Dover, N.J., 1974-77; headline writer The Star-Ledger, Newark, 1977-80, asst. night city editor, 1980-84, asst. city editor, 1984-92, metro editor, 1992-95, asst. mng. editor, 1995-96, mng. editor, 1996—. Office: The Star-Ledger One Star Ledger Plaza Newark NJ 07102-1200

EVERETT, ROBINSON OSCAR, federal judge, law educator; b. Durham, N.C., Mar. 18, 1928; s. Reuben Oscar and Kathrine McDiarmid (Robinson) E.; m. Linda Moore McGregor, Aug. 27, 1966; children: Robinson Oscar Jr., James Douglas McGregor, Lewis Moore. A.B. magna cum laude, Harvard U., 1947, J.D. magna cum laude, 1950; LL.M., Duke U., 1959. Bar: N.C. 1950, D.C. 1954. Mem. faculty Law Sch., Duke U., Durham, N.C., 1950-51, 56—; commr. U.S. Ct. Mil. Appeals, Washington, 1953-55; chief judge U.S. Ct. Mil. Appeals, 1980-90, sr. judge, 1990—; practice law Durham, 1955-80; councilor N.C. State Bar Council, 1978-83; pres., dir. Triangle Telecasters, Durham, 1966-77. Author: Military Justice, 1956; assoc. editor Law and Contemporary Problems, 1950-51, 56-66; contbr. articles to legal jours. Chair, Durham Redevel. Commn., 1959-75. Served as 1st lt. USAF, 1951-53; to col. Res. (ret.). Mem. Am. Law Inst. (life), Conf. Commrs. Uniform State Laws (life), Durham Bar Assn. (pres. 1976-77). Democrat. Presbyterian. Office: US Court of Appeals for Armed Forces 450 E St NW Washington DC 20442-0001 also: Duke U Sch Law Towerview and Science Dr Durham NC 27708*

EVERETT, RONALD EMERSON, government official; b. Columbus, Ohio, Jan. 4, 1937; s. John Carmen and Hermione Alicia (Lensner) E.; BA, Ohio U., 1959; postgrad. Baldwin-Wallace Coll., 1962-63; grad. U.S. Army Command and Gen. Staff Coll., 1978, U.S. Army War Coll., 1984; cert. Inst. Cost Analysis, 1982; cert. profl. estimator; m. Nancy Helen Leibersberger, Aug. 10, 1963; children: Darryl William, Darlene Anne, John Lee (dec.). Reporter, Dun & Bradstreet, Cleve., 1960-66; program analyst Lewis Research Center, NASA, Cleve., 1967-70, contract price analyst and negotiator, 1970-85, chief contract support br., 1985-86; chief space systems br., 1986-96, chief space and grants br., 1996—. Served with inf. U.S. Army, 1960; ret. col. Decorated Legion of Merit, Meritorious Service medal with six oak leaf clusters, Army Commendation medal with oak leaf cluster; cert. cost analyst. Mem. Assn. Govt. Accts., Res. Officer Assn., Internat. Platform Assn., Assn. U.S. Army, Army War Coll. Found. Republican. Presbyterian. Home: 27904 Blossom Blvd North Olmsted OH 44070-1723 Office: 21000 Brookpark Rd Cleveland OH 44135-3127

EVERETT, RUPERT, actor; b. Norfolk, Eng., May 29, 1959. Appeared in movies Princess Daisy, 1983, Another Country, 1984, Dance With A Stranger, 1985, Duet For One, 1986, The Right Hand Man, 1987, Hearts of Fire, 1987, Chronicle of a Death Foretold, 1988, The Comfort of Strangers, 1990, The Madness of King George, 1994, Ready to Wear, 1994, Dunston Checks In, 1996, My Best Friend's Wedding, 1997, A Midsummer Night's Dream, 1998, B. Monkey, 1998, Shakespeare in Love, 1998, The Next Best Thing, 1999, An Ideal Husband, 1999, Inspector Gadget, 1999. Office: ICM 8942 Wilshire Blvd Beverly Hills CA 90211-1934*

EVERETT, TERRY, congressman; b. Dothan, Ala., Feb. 15, 1937. Owner, pres. The Union Springs Herald; mem. 103rd-106th Congresses from 2nd Ala. Dist., Washington, 1992—; mem. nat. security com., agriculture com., and VA com. Office: US Ho of Reps 2312 Rayburn Bldg Washington DC 20515*

EVERETT, THOMAS GREGORY, musician, music educator; b. Phila., Dec. 4, 1944; s. Walter Edgar and Janette Earlene (McFadden) E.; m. Elisabeth G. Everett, June 14, 1984. BS in Music Edn., Ithaca Coll., 1966, MS in Music Edn., 1969. High sch. band dir. Batavia (N.Y.) Pub. Schs., 1968-71; dir. band and jazz program Harvard U., Cambridge, Mass., 1971—; freelance bass trombonist Boston Pops Orch., Boston Ballet and Opera Orch., Portland Symphony, Bolshoi Ballet Orch., Dizzy Gillespie, Phil Wilson, Ray Charles, Tommy and Jimmy Dorsey bands, 1971—; instr. low brass Brown U., Providence, 1976-80; instr. trombone conducting music edn. New Eng. Conservatory, Boston, 1972-81. Author: Annotated Guide to Bass Trombone Literature, 3d edit., 1986; composer Ferowertig Nu, 1969. Vice pres. Little League Baseball, Batavia, 1967-70. Recipient Artisjus award Govt. of Hungary, 1991, Alice T. Bondel award Harvard Band Found., 1996. Mem. Am. Fedn. Musicians, Am. Music Ctr. (commn. 1980), Internat. Trombone Assn. (founder, life, pres., bd. dirs.1972-76, award 1976, workshop award 1986), Internat. Assn. Jazz Educators (life, Outstanding Svc. award 1996), New Eng. Coll. Band Dirs Assn. (pres. 1990-92). Avocations: jazz, collecting rare trombone material, visiting Maine coast, art galleries, baseball. Home: 33 April Ln Lexington MA 02421-8116 Office: Harvard U Band 74 Mount Auburn St Cambridge MA 02138-5051

EVERETT, TOM, actor. MFA, NYU Sch of Arts, London Acad. Music/Drama Arts. Actor: (films) Air Force One, My Fellow Americans, Dances With Wolves, Vaya Con Dios, Best of the Best, The Goodbye Girl, Beverly Hills Cops, Prison, Messenger of Death, Die Hard 2, Earth and the American Dream, Leatherface, Hollywood Vice Squad, others; (Broadway plays) Elizabeth I, Habeas Corpus, Emminent Domain, A Midsummer Night's Dream; numerous Off-Broadway and regional theatre plays; (TV movies) Last Rites, Crash Landing: The Rescue of Flight 232, To Heal A Nation, Gore Vidal's Billy the Kid, Lady Mobster, Double Jeopardy, The Return of Mike Hammer, others; (TV shows) C-16, Pretender, JAG, E.R., Profiler, Picket Fences, Space Above and Beyond, Murder She Wrote, Cheers, LA Law, Hill Street Blues, Cagney and Lacy, Birdland, Newhart, others; songwriter/singer (RCA album): Porchlight On In Oregon; co-author: plays and film scripts. Scholar Jacobs Pillow Dance Festival, Perry Mansfield Dance and Drama Sch.; fellow NYU Sch. of Arts, ITT Internat. Fellowship/Fulbright Competition, London Acad. of Music and Dramatic Arts. Mem. The Actors Studio. Roman Catholic. Avocations: cello, guitar, country-western music.

EVERETT, VIRGINIA SAUERBRUN, counselor; b. Newark, N.J., Mar. 24, 1939; d. Arthur Gordon and Elwyna (Van Alen) Sauerbrun; m. Chandler H. Everett, Sept. 14, 1963 (div. Feb. 1986); children: Chandler P., Alexander U. BA, Coll. Wooster, 1961; MS in Gen. Counseling, Seattle Pacific U., 1990. Cert. chem. dependency counselor I. Counselor South King County Drug & Alcohol Recovery Ctrs., Seattle, 1990—; counselor Seattle Mental Health Inst., 1988-89, King County Perinatal Treatment Program, 1992-93, King County Pub. Health Dept., 1991—. Treas. Pacific N.W. Ballet League, Seattle, 1983; chmn. publicity Seattle Opera Guild, 1984; mem. work com. Washington State Coalition on Women's Substance Abuse Issues, 1990. Mem. ACA, Nat. Assn. Alchoholism and Drug Abuse Counselors, Chem. Dependency Profls. Wash. Republican. Episcopalian. Avocations: hiking, sailing, race walking. Home: 8408 NE 19th Pl Bellevue WA 98004-3236 Office: South King County Recovery Ctrs 15025 4th Ave SW Seattle WA 98166-2301

EVERETT, WARREN SYLVESTER, consultant, former government official; b. Wichita, Kans., Oct. 19, 1910; s. Carl S. and Effie (Barton) E.; m. Ruthmary Francis, June 13, 1935; children: Mary Margaret (Mrs. R.L. Graham), Judith Ann (Mrs. D.L. McKee), Warren Douglas. BA, U. Wichita, 1932; BS, U.S. Mil. Acad., 1935; MS in Engring., Cornell U., 1939; student, Army Engr. Sch., 1939-40, Army Command and Gen. Staff Coll., 1942, Princeton U., 1945, Armed Forces Staff Coll., 1949, Georgetown U., Am. U., 1955, Army War Coll., 1956-57. Registered profl. engr., Wash. Commd. 2d lt. U.S. Army, 1935, advanced through grades to col., 1951; mem. U.S. Presdl. Econ. Missions to Korea, 1952-53; faculty U.S. Army War Coll., 1956-59; dir. U.S. Army Constrn. Agy., France, 1959-61; dist. engr. Vicksburg, Miss., 1961-63; ret., 1963; chief pub. works div. USOM to Vietnam, 1963-65; chief engr. U.S. AID Mission to Nigeria, 1965-66, Vietnam Bur., AID, 1966-67; dir. excess property program AID, 1967-68; cons. Office Emergency Preparedness, Exec. Office Pres., 1968-69; exec. archtl.-engring. firm Saigon, Vietnam, 1969-71; dep. dir. U.S. Property Disposal Agy., Vietnam, 1971-74; dep. dir. Office Planning and Mgmt., chief commodity mgmt. and merchandising divs. Def. Property Disposal Service, Battle Creek, 1974-85; nat. security coord. High Frontier, exec. dir. sci. and engring. adv. bd. Internat. Coalition for Strategic Def. Initiative, Arlington, 1985—; engring. advisor Strategic Def. Initiative Orgn., Washington, 1988-90; mem. Nat. Def. Exec. Res., 1992—. Contbr. articles to profl. jours. Organizer, dir. Nat. Fallout Shelter Survey and Marking Program, 1961; pres. P.T.A., Am. Sch., Tokyo, 1953-54. Decorated Legion of Merit with oak leaf cluster, Korean Ulchi medal with silver star; recipient Korean Disting. Svc. medal, Presdl. citation (Korea), Chuong-My Outstanding Svc. medal (Vietnam), Army Commendation medal. Fellow ASCE (mem. space engring. and constrn. com.), Soc. Am. Mil. Engrs. (past pres. Vicksburg and Saigon); mem. NSPE. Home: 1401 Gower Ct Mc Lean VA 22102-2732 Office: High Frontier 2800 S Shirlington Rd Ste 405A Arlington VA 22206-3608*

EVERETT, WENDY ANN, toy designer; b. East Lansing, Mich., May 6, 1950; d. Donald Franklin and Mary Margaret (Marshall) E. BA in Edn., Fine Arts, Mich. State U., 1972; M in Early Childhood Devel., Fairfield (Conn.) U., 1989. Elem. sch. tchr. Fraser (Mich.) Pub. Schs., 1973-77; creative dir. WFR Ribbon Corp., N.Y.C., 1977-79; pres. Wendy Everett Creations, Westport, Conn., 1979—. Author: The Gift Book, 1986, Active Bulletin Boards, 1979; composer (children's musical) The Vegetable Garden, 1973 (children's TV show) The Dream Makers, 1990; regular guest (TV show) Our Home; contbr. articles to mags.; designer Barbie Doll Fashions, 1983—, Care Bears, Strawberry Shortcake, Cabbage Patch Doll Clothes, Americana Crafts, ET Quilt, ET Wallhanging, 1983, Stenciling Hunt Mfg. Co. Kits, 1979—, Pastime Industries Crafts, 1990, Bath Buddies toy line, 1989—, ednl. toys for Princess Fabrics, N.Y.C., 1992—; painter large acrylic and gold leaf polo paintings; featured artist in Polo Players Mag. and Equine Image Mag. Mem. Cooper Hewitt Mus., Southport Trinity Episc. Ch. Received Artist of Yr. award Greenwich (Conn.) Polo Club, 1998. Mem. Am. Craft Assn., Nat. Arts Club (N.Y.C.), Phi Beta Kappa. Avocations: painting, dancing, golf, classical piano. Home: 1123 Sasco Hill Rd Fairfield CT 06430-6346

EVERETT, WILLIAM JOHNSON, ethics educator, writer; b. Washington, Nov. 18, 1940; s. William Wade Jr. and Elizabeth (Jackson) E.; m. Julie Anne Kaeser, Mar. 27, 1965 (div. Nov. 1981); children: Eric, Aneliese, Elaine; m. Sylvia Johnson, June 12, 1982. BA, Wesleyan U., 1962; BD, Yale U., 1965; PhD, Harvard U., 1970. Prof. theology and social sci. St. Francis Sem., Milw., 1969-84; prof. ethics and ecclesiology Emory U., Atlanta, Ga., 1985-94; prof. Christian social ethics Andover Newton (Mass.) Theol. Sch., 1995—; cons. Luth. World Fedn., Geneva, 1971-77; pres. Assn. Dr. of Ministry Edn., 1990-91. Author: Blessed be the Bond, 1985, God's Federal Republic, 1988, Religion, Federalism, and the Struggle for Public Life, 1997, The Politics of Worship, 1999. Pres. Interchange, Inc., Milw., 1972-74. Recipient Rsch. scholarship Lilly Endowment, 1989-90, Rsch. grant Emory U., 1991-92, Small Grants award Assn. Theol. Schs., 1998. Mem. Soc. Christian Ethics (chair profl. stds. task force, 1997—), Am. Acad. Religion, Soc. Bus. Ethics. Methodist. Avocations: folk singing, woodworking, brewing. E-mail: weverett@ants.edu. Office: Andover Newton Theol Sch 210 Herrick Rd Newton Center MA 02459

EVERETT, WOODROW WILSON, electrical engineer, educator; b. Newton, Miss., Oct. 11, 1937; s. Woodrow Wilson and Katherine (Thrash) E.; m. Cherry Donna Sarff, Aug. 23, 1958; children: Woodrow W., Leanne Everett Traver. B.E.E., George Washington U., 1959; M.S., Cornell U., 1965, Ph.D., 1968. Project engr. Scott Paper Co., 1959, Ithaca (N.Y.) Rsch. Labs., Atlantic Rsch. Corp., 1962-64; postdoctoral program dir. Rome (N.Y.) Air Devel. Ctr., 1964-75; chmn. bd. N.E. Consortium for Engring. Edn., St. Cloud, Fla., 1975—; bd. dirs. Device Assos. Corp. N.Y., Masonwood, Inc., Sunoric Corp., ITG, Inc., Thrash Homestead Corp., The Cherwood Corp. Author works in field. Democratic committeeman, Madison County, N.Y., 1976-79; pres. Village of Groton (N.Y.) Appeals Bd., 1966-69; chmn. Groton Planning Bd., 1968-69. Served with USAF, 1959-62. Fellow IEEE; mem. Air Force Assn. (life), Res. Officers Assn. (life), Am. Soc. Engring. Edn. Club: Rotary. Home: Cherwood-Alligator Lake 6267 S Breeze Rd Saint Cloud FL 34771-9699 Office: 1101 Massachusetts Ave Saint Cloud FL 34769-3733

EVERETTE, MARLENE MILLER, nursing administrator, surgical nurse; b. Columbus, Ohio, Jan. 10, 1951; d. George Clem and Goldie Alberta (Linder) Miller; m. Edwin Lisk Everette Jr., May 21, 1978; 1 child, Kristy Leigh. ADN, Chowan Coll., 1973; BSN, Barton Coll., 1990. RN, N.C.; cert. nurse oper. rm., cert. autotransfusion specialist. Staff nurse surgery N.C. Meml. Hosp., Chapel Hill, 1973-74; open heart surg. nurse VA Hosp., Durham, N.C., 1974-78; staff nurse surgery Nash Gen. Hosp., Rocky Mount, N.C., 1978-80; dir. surg. svcs. Community Hosp. Rocky Mount, 1980-93; oper. rm mgr. Nash Gen. Hosp., Rocky Mount, 1993—. Mem. Assn. Operating Rm. Nurses (women's coun. pres., Tarheels East Perioperative Nurse of Yr. 1997), Eastern N.C. Operating Rm. Nurses (pres.), Sigma Theta Tau.

EVERHART, BRUCE, radio station executive. Sta. mgr. WMBI-AM/FM, Chgo. Home: WMBI-FM 820 N LaSalle St Chicago IL 60610

EVERHART, JUDD, public relations executive. Mgr. pub. rels. Xerox Corp., Stamford, Conn. Office: Xerox Corp PO Box 1600 Stamford CT 06904-1600*

EVERHART, REX, actor, director, photographer; b. Watseka, Ill., June 13, 1920; s. Arthur Mark and Jeanette (Dodson) E.; m. Jill Reardon, Feb. 11, 1944 (div. 1957); m. Claire Violet Richard, Dec. 21, 1962; 1 dau., Degan Jeanette. Student, U. Mo., 1938-40; B.T.A., Pasadena Playhouse, 1942; B.S., NYU, M.A., 1949. Actor films, TV, radio, 25 Broadway or pre-Broadway prodns., TV commls., 1966-67, regional theatres, repertory theatres including 7 seasons Am. Shakespeare Theatre, touring cos., London prodn. of the Odd Couple, 1966-67. Voice Belle's father (animated film) Beauty and the Beast, 1992, Backyard Safari, 1995. Served to 1st lt. USN, 1942-46. Nominated Antoinette Perry (Tony) award, 1978. Mem. Actors' Equity Assn. (councillor 1968-75), Screen Actors' Guild, AFTRA. Democrat. Club: Players (N.Y.C.).

EVERHART, ROBERT PHILLIP (BOBBY WILLIAMS), entertainer, songwriter, recording artist; b. St. Edward, Nebr., June 16, 1936; s. Phillip McClelland and Martha Matilda (Meyer) E.; m. Sheila Dawn Armstrong, Feb. 14, 1992. Student, U. Nebr., 1959-62; A in Radio-TV, Iowa Western Coll., 1971, A in Graphic Arts, 1974; diploma in Journalism, London Sch. Journalism, 1983; spl. studies Mex. Indian culture, U. Okla., 1990—. Disc jockey various stas., Omaha and Juneau, Alaska, 1959-63; songwriter Royal Flair Music, BMI Pub., Walnut, Iowa, 1964—. Host prodr. (TV series) Old Time Country Music, (radio show) Old-Time Music Hour; rec. artist Folkway Records, N.Y.C., 1970—, Smithsonian Inst., Westwood Records, Wales, 1981, Folk Variety Records, Europe, 1980—, Allied Records, The Philippines, OGA Records, Austria, Otro Records, Poland, Prairie Music Records, Unltd. Prodns., internat. concert artist performing traditional Am. country and folk music; curator, owner Pioneer Music Instrument Mus., Am. Country Music Hall of Fame, Am. Old Time Fiddlers Hall of Fame, Capt.'s Quarters Bed & Breakfast, all located in Walnut, Iowa, Lawtell, La., and Vera Cruz, Mex., Oaktree Opera, Anita, Iowa; festival promoter Old-Time Country Music Contest and Pioneer Exposition, 1976—, Am. Traditional Music and Dance Festival, Nat. Traditional Music Performer Awards, 1991—; pres. Nat. Traditional Country Music Assn., Inc., 1982—; regular performer La. Hayride, 1985—; editor: Tradition Country Music Mag., 1980—; author: Clara Bell, 1976, Hart's Bluff, 1977, Listen to the Mockingbird, 1995; (poetry) Silver Bullets, 1979, Savage Trumpet, 1980, Prairie Sunrise, 1982, Snoopy Goes to Mexico, 1983; (TV scripts) The Life of Jimmie Rodgers, 1984, Matecombe Treasure, 1984, The Ghost of Carl Herrmann, 1993, Listen to the Mockingbird, 1998; recs. include: Let's Go, Dream Angel, She Sings Sad Songs, Love to Make Love, Bad Woman Blues, Fishpole John, Time After Time, Street Sleepers, No One Comes Near, Berlin Folksinger Compact Disc release on Otro Records; host (TV) Old Time Country Music, 1990-97. With USN, 1954-59. Named to Profl. Musicians and Entertainers Club Iowa Hall of Fame, 1994, Country Music Showcase Internat. Hall of Fame, 1995; Ky. col., 1995; recipient Lifetime Achievement award World Music Events, Vienna, 1998. Mem. Great Plains Old Time Music Assn., Acad. Country Music, Nat. Bluegrass Assn., Ill. Traditional Country Music Assn., Tri-State Bluegrass Assn., Ky. Cols., Internat. Bluegrass Music Assn., Profl. Musicians Club of Iowa, Midwest Prodrs. Assn. (chmn.), Carribean Club. Democrat. Lutheran. Avocations: scuba diving, traveling. Office: Country Opera House PO Box 492 Anita IA 50020-0492 also: Nat Traditional Country Music Assn PO Box 492 Anita IA 50020-0492

EVERHART, RODNEY LEE, software industry executive; b. Zanesville, Ohio, Sept. 1, 1942; s. James Gray and Levada Marie Everhart; m. Aldena L. Purdy, June 7, 1964; children: Susan Michelle, Deanna Renee. Student in mgmt., U. Ill., 1960-64; student fin. mgmt. program, GE, Louisville, 1967-69. Cost analyst Ford Motor Co., Louisville, 1964-66; mgr. internal audit, ops. analysis, fin. planning GE Co., Louisville, 1966-75; mgr. fin. and adminstrn. GE Co., Ft. Wayne, Ind., 1975-79; mgr. fin. sect. GE Co., Hudson Falls, N.Y., 1979-84; mgr. fin. planning and analysis GE Info. Svcs. Co., Rockville, Md., 1984-85; CFO, v.p. fin. and adminstrn., treasury Sys. and Computer Tech. Corp., Malvern, Pa., 1985-89; v.p. fin. rsch. and adminstrn. Mead DAta Ctrl., Inc., Dayton, Ohio, 1989-92; contr. Mead Corp., Dayton, 1992-93; pres. Lexis-Nexis, Dayton, 1993-95; sr. v.p., cfo fin. admin. Bellcore, Morristown, NJ, 1996-98; pres. edn. sys. divsn. Sys. & Computer Tech. Corp., Malvern, Pa., 1998—. Adv. coun. Sycamore Hosp., Miamisburg, Ohio, 1993-95; bd. trustees WDPR-FM Dayton Pub. Radio, 1992-95; CEO, United Way, Dayton, 1994; bd. overseers Coun. Aid Edn., 1999—. Mem. Am. Arbitration Assn. (bd. dirs. ctrl. sector 1994-95), South Metro Dayton C. of C. (chmn. 1993), N.J. Chamber Music Soc. (bd. trustees 1996—). Office: Systems & Computer Tech Corp 4 Country View Rd Malvern PA 19355-1408

EVERHART, THOMAS EUGENE, retired university president, engineering educator; b. Kansas City, Mo., Feb. 15, 1932; s. William Elliott and Elizabeth Ann (West) E.; m. Doris Arleen Wentz, June 21, 1953; children—Janet Sue, Nancy Jean, David William, John Thomas. AB in Physics magna cum laude, Harvard, 1953; MSc, UCLA, 1955; PhD in Engring., Cambridge U., Eng., 1958. Mem. tech. staff Hughes Research Labs., Culver City, Calif., 1953-55; mem. faculty U. Calif., Berkeley, 1958-78, prof. elec. engring. and computer scis., 1967-78, Miller research prof., 1969-70, chmn. dept., 1972-77; prof. elec. engring., Joseph Silbert dean engring. Cornell U., Ithaca, N.Y., 1979-84; prof. elec. and computer engring., chancellor U. Ill., Urbana-Champaign, 1984-87; prof. elec. engring. and applied physics, pres. Calif. Inst. Tech., Pasadena, 1987-97; pres. emeritus Calif. Inst. Tech., Pasadena, 1997—; fellow scientist Westinghouse Rsch. Labs., Pitts., 1962-63; guest prof. Inst. Applied Physics, U. Tuebingen, Germany, 1966-67, Waseda U., Tokyo, Osaka U., 1974; vis. fellow Clare Hall, Cambridge U., 1975; chmn. Electron, Ion and Photon Beam Symposium, 1977; cons. in field; mem. sci. and ednl. adv. com. Lawrence Berkeley Lab., 1978-85, chmn., 1980-85; mem. sci. adv. com. GM, 1980-89, chmn., 1984-89, bd. dirs., 1989—; bd. dirs. Hewlett Packard Corp., Saint-Gobain Corp., Reveo, Inc., Raytheon Co., Hughes Electronics Co., Elec. Power Rsch. Inst.; tech. adv. com. R.R. Donnelly & Sons, 1981-89; sr. sci. advisor W.M. Keck Found., 1997—; pro-vice chancellor Cambridge U., 1998. Chmn. Sec. of Energy Adv. Bd., 1990-93; bd. dirs. KCET, 1989-97, Corp. for Nat. Rsch. Initiatives, 1990—, Electric Power Rsch. Inst., 1998—; trustee Calif. Inst. Tech., 1998—. Marshall scholar Cambridge U., 1955-58, NSF sr. fellow, 1966-67, Guggenheim fellow, 1974-75. Fellow IEEE, AAAS, ASEE, Royal Acad. Engring.; mem. NAE (ednl. adv. bd. 1984-88, mem. com. 1984-89, chmn. 1988, coun. 1988-94, 96—), Microbeam Analysis Soc. Am., Electron

Microscopy Soc. Am. (coun. 1970-72, pres. 1977), Coun. on Competitiveness (vice-chmn. 1990-96), Assn. Marshall Scholars and Alumni (pres. 1965-68), Athenaeum Club, Sigma Xi, Eta Kappa Nu. Home: PO Box 1639 Santa Barbara CA 93116-1639 Office: Calif Inst Tech Office Pres Emeritus Mail Code 202-31 1200 E California Blvd Pasadena CA 91125-0001

EVERINGHAM, HARRY TOWNER, editor, publisher; b. Memphis, Aug. 14, 1908; s. William Kirby and Ida Pauline (Towner) E.; m. Margaret Sophia Johnson; children: Martha, Barbara, Richard Kirby. Student, Northwestern U., Evanston, Ill., 1936-39, U. Chgo., 1940. Writer, dir. weekly radio drama WREC, Memphis, 1930-33; radio writer, producer Miles Lab., Chgo., Wade Advt. Agy., Chgo., 1934-35; v.p. Sehl Advt. Agy., Chgo., 1936-41; broadcasting Henry C. Lytton & Co., Chgo.; film producer, lectr. Employers Assn., Chgo., 1942; editor, pub. The Fact Finder, 1942—; pub. rels. dir. Ingalls-Shepard Div. Wyman Gordon Co., Harvey, Ill.; editor Forging Ahead Mag., 1942-45. Editor, pub. U.S.A.-Beyond the Crossroads, Chgo., The Am. Patriot, 1959-94; syndicated newspaper columnist, 1960-63. V.p. Greater Chgo. Churchmen, 1946-47; founder Pub. Club Chgo., 1942. Mem. Ariz. Breakfast Club (founder, pres.). Republican. Avocations: teaching, speaking, broadcasting. Office: We the People UNITED Box A Scottsdale AZ 85252

EVERISS, DANA FORD, middle school educator; b. Jacksonville, Fla., Aug. 14, 1935; d. Carroll Patterson and Anne Leone (Austin) Ford; m. Walter Clifford Everiss, Sept. 5, 1959. AB, U. Ga., Athens, 1957; MEd, Kennesaw State Coll., 1989. Cert. tchr., Ga. Tchr. City of Atlanta, 1959-61, Fulton County Bd. Edn., Atlanta, 1951-64, 65—, High Point (N.C.) City Schs., 1964-65; coll. coun. rep. Kennesaw State Coll., 1986-87; lectr. various confs. Co-author: Medieval Mania, 1986. Chmn. bd. dirs. Cherokee County Humane Soc., Canton, Ga., 1975—; Southea. contact for german shepherd rescue; mem. local PTA. Named Master Gardener, 1993. Mem. Nat. Mid. Sch. Assn. (presenter 1987, 88, 89), League Ind. Fulton Educators, So. Order Storytellers, Delta Kappa Gamma. Episcopalian. Avocations: breeding/training German Shepherd dogs, gardening, calligraphy, foreign travel, photography. Home: 1833 Hendon Rd Woodstock GA 30188-1990

EVERITT, JULIE JOY, newspaper reporter; b. St. Clair, Mich., May 6, 1973; d. Mark Alan and Nancy Louise (Wollen) E. BA, Baylor U., 1995. Reporter Waco (Tex.) Tribune-Herald, 1995-99, The Bus. Press, Ft. Worth, 1999—. Vol. Meadowbrook Elem. Sch., Waco, 1996-97; vol. firefighter Woodway Pub. Safety Dept. Mem. Soc. Profl. Journalists. Independent. Avocations: reading, exercise, gardening. Home: 6800 Cumberland Fort Worth TX 76116 Office: Bus Press 314 Main St Ste 300 Fort Worth TX 76102

EVERLY, GEORGE STOTELMYER, JR., psychophysiologist, educator; b. Balt., May 31, 1950; s. George Stotelmyer and Kathleen Webster E.; children: Marideth, George III, Andrea. BS, U. Md., 1972, MA, 1974, PhD, 1978; postdoctoral tng., U. Miami, 1983-85, Harvard U., 1985-86. Lectr. U. Md., College Park, 1975-80; assoc. prof. psychology, dir. psychophysiology lab. Loyola Coll., Balt., 1980-85, prof. psychology, 1985—; dir. psychol. svcs. div. Homewood Hosp. Ctr. Johns Hopkins Health System, Balt., 1990-92; CEO, chmn. bd. dirs. Internat. Critical Incident Stress Found., Balt., 1989-95; chmn. emeritus, 1995—; CEO, Inst. Advanced Studies Crisis and Disaster Mgmt., Balt., 1995—; vis. scholar Harvard U., 1985-87, vis. lectr. medicine Harvard Med. Sch., 1987-88; NGO rep. to UN, 1997—; mem. adj. faculty Johns Hopkins U. Sch. Hygiene and Pub. Health, 1998—;. Author: Occupational Health Promotion, 1985; The Nature and Treatment of the Stress Response, 1981, Psychotraumatology, 1995, Innovations in Disaster and Trauma Psychology, 1995; The Stress Mess Solution, 1980; co-author: Controlling Stress and Tension, 1979; Experiencing Health, 1985; Personality and Its Disorders, 1985, The Assessment of Human Stress, 1987, Clinical Guide to Treatment of the Human Stress Response, 1989; founding and exec. editor Internat. Jour. Emergency MEntal Health, 1999—; rschr., developer The Everly Behavioral Survey, 1982. Recipient cert. of honor Balt. City Police Dept., 1981, Prof.'s medal Weiner U., Lima, Peru, 1997. Fellow Acad. Psychosomatic Medicine, Am. Inst. Stress (trustee); mem. APA, Soc. Behavioral Medicine, Am. Acad. Behavioral Medicine.

EVERLY, JACK, conductor. Grad., Ind. U. Condr. Am. Ballet Theatre, N.Y.C., 1984-87, formerly prin. condr. Conducted shows including Hello, Dolly!, 1978, A Chorus Line, They're Playing Our Song, Showboat, Kismet, Carousel, The Mikado, Hazel Kirk, others; conductor Vancouver Symphony, San Diego Symphony, Lake George Opera Festival, Pacific Symphony, Ravinia Festival; music dir., orchestrator In Performance at the White House; conductor world premiers at Am. Ballet Theatre include Sir Kenneth MacMillan's Requiem, Agnes de Mille's The Informer, Mikhail Baryshnikov's Giselle and Swan Lake. Office: care Kaylord Mgmt Inc 130 W 57th St Ste 86 New York NY 10019*

EVERLY, REBECCA D., lawyer; b. Fairmont, W.Va., Sept. 3, 1973; d. Glenn Alan and Juanita Ann Everly. AB summa cum laude, Duke U., 1995, JD magna dum laude, 1998, LLM, 1998. Bar: N.Y. 1998. Clk. Internat. Human Rights Law Group, Washington, 1997; atty.-advisor U.S. Dept. State Office of Legal Adviser, Washington, 1998—. Contbr. to book: The Integration of Estonians into Non-Estonian Society, 1997. Pro bono atty. Washington Lawyers' Com. for Civil Rights and Urban Affairs, 1999—, Washington Legal Clinic for Homeless, 1999—. Mem. N.Y. Bar Assn., Phi Beta Kappa. Office: US Dept State Office Legal Adviser 2201 C St NW Washington DC 20520

EVERMAN, NANCY LIDTKE, farmer, organization executive; b. Cresco, Iowa, Feb. 28, 1953; d. Paul H. and Donna M. (Stevenson) Lidtke; m. Kenneth F. Everman, July 6, 1973; children: Erica A., Carrie Jo. Grad. in practical nursing, St. Luke's Meth. Sch., Cedar Rapids, Iowa, 1972; BS in Mgmt.-Human Resources with honors, Upper Iowa U., 1996, postgrad., 1997—. Ptnr. family farm Postville, Iowa, 1973—; program planner N.E. Iowa Cmty. Action, Decorah, Iowa, 1984-97; decat coord. Dept. Human Svcs., 1997—; owner, mgr. N.E. Grants, Inc., Fayette, Iowa, 1991-95; cons. IowAccess, Des Moines, 1997; adv. bd. Upper Iowa U., Prairie DuChien (Wis.) Campus, 1996—. Prodr. Iowa Cmty. Action, 1995. Leader 4-H, Iowa State U. Ext., Waukon; bellringer Allamakee Bell Ringers, 1979; mem. found. bd. N.E. Iowa C.C., Calmar, 1995—; vice-chair Iowa Cmty. Action, Des Moines, 1988-97; dir. Big H Fair, Postville, 1986—. Recipient leader award 4-H, 1990. Mem. Iowa Pork Prodrs., Iowa Cattlemen. Lutheran. Avocations: reading, gardening, crafts, antiquing. Home: 370 Pole Line Rd Postville IA 52162-8543 Office: Decat Office PO Box 487 Decorah IA 52101-0487

EVERROAD, JOHN DAVID, lawyer; b. Columbus, Ind., Jan. 6, 1940; s. Henry and Margaret L. (Eckleman) E.; m. Patricia Diane Hayworth, June 10, 1967; children: Andrew Quinn, Matthew Oldham. BA, Vanderbilt U., 1962, JD, 1969. Bar: Ariz. 1970, Calif. 1997. Atty. Fennemore Craig PC, Phoenix, 1969—; mem. panels Nat. Inst. Trial Advocacy programs; lawyer Com. Uniform Jury Standards State of Ariz.; mem. faculty Continuing Edn. Legal Programs. Pres. Parochial Sch. Bd., Phoenix, 1972-78; mem. Christ Luth. Ch., Phoenix, 1969—, sec., 1986, 88-89, pres., 1979-80; bd. dirs. Combined Metro. Phoenix Arts and Scis., 1996-98. With USMC, 1962-66. Fellow ABA, Ariz. Bar Found. (founder), Maricopa County Bar Found. (founder); mem. Am. Bd. Trial Advocates, Maricopa County Bar Assn. (pres. 1992-93), Pima County Bar Assn., Ariz. State Bar Assn. (chmn. edit. bd. Jour., com. revisions uniform jury instructions 1984-89, Disciplinary com. 1984-90), Phi Delta Phi. Republican. Lutheran. Avocations: scuba, skiing, sport fishing, bow hunting. Home: 6625 N 3rd Dr Phoenix AZ 85013-1103 Office: Fennemore Craig PC 3003 N Central Ste 2600 Phoenix AZ 85012-2913

EVERS, GENE, writer; b. Manhattan, N.Y., Mar. 26, 1951; s. Lee Evers and Pauline (Leviton) Stein. AA in Liberal Arts, Nassau C.C., Garden City, N.Y., 1973; BA in Humanities, SUNY, Old Westbury, 1982. Writer L.I. Bus. Rev., Plainview, N.Y., 1978-82; staff Quaker Homecraft, Plainview, 1983-84; ind. writer Manhattan, 1992—; staff Nassau Ctr. for the Developmentally Disabled, Woodbury, N.Y., 1978-84. Author: (movie script) A Christmas Journey, 1997; songwriter A Christmas Song, 1997, Candles of Love, Northern Wind; author of poetry, short stories. Named Disting. Poet of the Yr., Internat. Soc. Poets, Owings Mills, Md., 1997; inductee Hall of Fame, Internat. Soc. Poets, 1996. Mem. Writers Guild, Internat. Platform Assn. Avocations: model trains, weight lifting, studying history, philosophy and literature. Home: 33 Hayden Dr Bethpage NY 11714-4508

EVERSLEY, FREDERICK JOHN, sculptor, engineer; b. Bklyn., Aug. 28, 1941; s. Frederick William and Beatrice Agnes (Syphax) E. B.S.E.E., Carnegie-Mellon U., 1963. One-man shows include Whitney Mus. Am. Art, N.Y.C., 1970, Nat. Acad. Sci., Washington, 1976, 81, L.A. Inst. Contemporary Art, 1976, Santa Barbara Mus., 1976, Newport Harbor Art Mus., 1976, Oakland Mus. Art, 1977, Palm Springs (Calif.) Desert Mus., 1978, AIA, 1981, Va. Mus., 1981, Bacardi Art Gallery, Miami, 1984, Laband Art Gallery, 1985, Loyola Marymount U., L.A., Hokin Gallery, Palm Beach, Fla., 1988, Juda Gallery, London, 1988, Eva Cohen Gallery, Chgo., 1991, Lorenzelli Arte, Milan, 1992, Pavilion of Saudi Arabia, Expo 92, Seville, Spain, 1992; represented in permanent collections Smithsonian Instn., Washington, IRS Nat. Hdqtrs., New Carrollton, Md., Calif. State Coll., L.A., Oakland (Calif.) Art Mus., Milw. Art Center, Whitney Mus. Am. Art, N.Y.C., John Marin Meml. Collection, N.Y.C., U., Kans. Art Gallery, Lawrence, Long Beach (Calif.) Mus. Art, Currier Gallery Art, Manchester, N.H., Taft Mus. Art, Cin., Cranbrook Art Gallery, Bloomfield Hills, Mich., Nat. Acad. Sci., Washington, Nat. Collection Fine Arts, Washington, MIT, Cambridge, Neuberger Mus. Art, Purchase, N.Y., Newport Harbor Art Mus., Newport Beach, Calif., Guggenheim Mus., N.Y.C., Smith Coll. Mus. Art, Northhampton, Mass., Nat. Air and Space Mus., Mus. Contemporary Art, L.A., Palm Springs Desert Mus., Rose Mus. of Art, Brandis U., Boston, Sammlung Goetz, Munich Germany, IRS hdqs., New Carrollton, Md., 1996; artist in residence Nat. Air and Space Mus., Washington, 1977-80. Nat. Endowment Arts grantee, 1972. Mem. L.A. Inst. Contemporary Art, Artworkers Coalition. Address: 1110 Abbot Kinney Blvd Venice CA 90291-3314

EVERSOLE, GREGORY CHARLES, accountant; b. Kalamazoo, Mich., Sept. 23, 1951; s. Charles Gregory and Virginia Mae (Fish) E.; m. Joanne Marion Lucker, July 14, 1978 (div. 1996); 1 child, Elijah. BSBA, Mich. Tech. U., 1983; MBA, Western Mich. U., 1990. Cert. mgmt. acct. Acct. F.P. Rosback Co., St. Joseph, Mich., 1983—; adj. faculty Lake Mich. Coll., Benton Harbor, 1986—, Sienna Heights Coll., Adrian, Mich., 1997—. Mem. Inst. Mgmt. Accts. Avocation: sailing. Office: FP Rosback Co 125 Hawthorne Ave Saint Joseph MI 49085-2636

EVERSOLE, WALTER ROBERT, funeral director; b. Ukiah, Calif., May 25, 1923; s. Edward Anthony and Bess Lea (Gwartney) E.; m. Barbara Louise Ballou, Dec. 16, 1945; children: Ronald Edward, Richard Walter. BMS, San Francisco Coll. Mortuary, 1943. Lic. funeral dir., Calif. Funeral dir. Eversole Mortuary, Ukiah, 1946—; commd. flight officer USAF, 1944, advanced through grades to capt., 1958, ret., 1960; dir. Savs. Bank of Mendo County, Ukiah. Mem. Planning Commn. of Ukiah, 1954, Airport Commn., Ukiah, 1956. Recipient Silver Beaver award Boy Scouts Am., 1968, Outstanding Citizen award Ukiah C. of C., 1987. Mem. VFW, Am. Legion, Calif Funderal Dirs. Assn. (pres. 1947, 85), Redwood Empire Funeral Dirs. Assn., Masons, Elks (exalted ruler 1951), Rotary (pres. 1950-51), 20-30 Club (pres. 1946-48). Republican. Avocations: woodworking, golf, travel. Home: 180 Barbara St Ukiah CA 95482-5416 Office: Eversole Mortuary 141 Low Gap Rd Ukiah CA 95482-3943

EVERSON, DIANE LOUISE, publishing executive; b. Edgerton, Wis., Mar. 27, 1953; d. Harland Everett and Helen Viola (Oliver) E. BS, Carroll Coll., 1975. Co-pub. Edgerton (Wis.) Reporter, 1976—; v.p. Silk Screen Creations, 1981—; bd. dirs. Inland Press. Pub. Career Directors newspaper, 1981—, Directions mag., 1981—, Career Waves Newsletter, 1989—, Coll. and Univs. Directories. Trustee Carroll Coll., 1987—; active ARC, bd. dirs. Badger chpt., pres. local bd., 1997—. Mem. Nat. Newspaper Assn. (regional bd. dirs.), Inland Press Assn. (bd. dirs. 1993—), Madison TEMPO (pres. 1998—). Democrat. Lutheran. Home: 114 Kellog Rd Edgerton WI 53534-9352 Office: Directions Pub 21 N Henry St Edgerton WI 53534-1821

EVERSON, STEVEN LEE, lawyer, real estate executive; b. Philippi, W.Va., June 16, 1950; s. Billie Lee and Mildred Ann (Hill) E.; m. Donna Janine Chmielarz, May 29, 1976; 1 child, Michael. BA in Math. magna cum laude, W. Va. U., 1972; JD, Northwestern U., 1979. Bar: Colo. 1979. Tax sr. acct. Deloitte, Haskins & Sells, Colorado Springs, Colo., 1979-82; v.p., sec., treas. The Schuck Corp., Colorado Springs, 1982—; instr. real estate U. Colo. Bd. dirs., sec., past chmn. Pikes Peak Found. for Mental Health, Colorado Springs, 1986—, Boys and Girls Club of Pikes Peak Region, Colorado Springs, 1987-90; mem. UCCS Exec. Club, Colorado Springs, 1988-90; treas. Steve Schuck for Gov. Com., 1988—; project bus. instr. Jr. Achievement, 1985-87. Capt. USAF, 1972-76. Mem. Phi Beta Kappa. Republican. Mem. Ch. of Christ. Avocations: racquetball, skiing, softball, golf, tennis, vol. coaching youth sports teams. Home: 1450 Lone Scout Lookout Monument CO 80132-8036 Office: Schuck Communities Inc 2 N Cascade Ave Ste 1280 Colorado Springs CO 80903-1631

EVERSULL, JANNA BACON, pediatrics nurse, emergency room nurse; b. Alliance, Nebr., Jan. 2, 1963; d. Richard V. and Betty J. (Anderson) B.; m. Dennis R. Eversull, Feb. 5, 1983 (div.). Licensed Practical Nurse, Nebr. West Coll., 1982; postgrad., San Bernadino Valley Coll., 1989-90. Lic. vocat. nurse, Calif, lic. practical nurse, Nebr. Scrub nurse Box Butte Gen. Hosp., Alliance, Nebr., 1982-85; medication nurse West Nebr. Regional Med. Ctr., Scottsbluff, Nebr., 1985-86; asst. office mgr. William D. Reed, M.D., Inc., San Bernadino, 1986-89; pediatrics nurse, emergency room nurse Loma Linda (Calif.) Community Hosp., 1988—; supr. nursing Inland Empre Cmty. Health Ctr., 1998—. Recipient March of Dimes Scholarship, 1982, Best Geriatric Nurse award, 1982, "We Care" award, 1988, 90, 92, 93, 94, 95. Mem. Nat. Fed. Lic. Practical Nurses.

EVERS-WILLIAMS, MYRLIE, cultural organization administrator; b. Vicksburg, Miss., Mar. 17, 1933; m. Medgar Evers (dec. June 1963); 3 children. Student, Alcorn State U.; BA in Sociology, Pomona Coll., 1968, honorary degree; cert., Simmons Coll.; honorary degree, Medgar Evers Coll., Spelman Coll., Columbia Coll., Chgo., Bennett Coll., Tougaloo Coll. Mem. staff, sec. NAACP; dir. planning Claremont (Calif.) Colls., 1968-70; v.p. advt. & publicity Seligman & Latz, N.Y.C., 1973-75; dir. consumer affairs Atlantic Richfield Co.; commr. Pub. Works Bd., L.A., 1987-95; chairwoman NAACP, 1995-98; civil rights leader, lectr. Author: For Us the Living, 1967; contbg. editor Ladies Home Jour. Candidate for Congress in Calif., 1970; candidate for L.A. City Coun., 1987; head So. Calif. Dem. Women's Divsn.; convener Nat. Women's Polit. Caucus. Named Woman of Yr., Glamour Mag., 1995, Ms. Mag., 1995, one of Women of Yr., Ladies Home Jour., 1996; recipient Mary Church Terrell award Delta Sigma Theta, 1996, Althea T.L. Simmons Social Action award, 1998; recipient Spingarn award, NAACP, Atlanta, 1998; recipient Trumpeter's award, Nat. Consumers League, New Orleans, 1998; named one of 200 most influential women, Vanity Fair mag., Jan. 1999. Office: MEW Assocs Inc 15 SW Colorado Ave Ste 310 Bend OR 97702-1149

EVERT, CHRISTINE MARIE (CHRIS EVERT), retired professional tennis player; b. Ft. Lauderdale, Fla., Dec. 21, 1954; d. James and Colette Evert; m. John Lloyd, Apr. 17, 1979 (div.); m. Andy Mill, July 30, 1988; children: Alexander James, Nicholas Joseph, Colton Jack. Amateur tennis player, until Dec. 1972, profl. tennis player, 1972-89, ret. from tennis, 1989; owner Evert Enterprises/IMG, Boca Raton, Fla., 1989—; Olympics commentator CBS Sports, 1992; commentator NBC Sports tennis events; winner numerous tournaments including U.S. Jr. Championship, 1970, 71, U.S. Open, 1975, 76, 77, 78, 80, 82, Wimbledon Singles, 1974, 76, 81, doubles, 1976, Australian Open, 1982, 84, French Open Singles, 1974, 75, 79, 80, 83, 85, 86, Virginia Slims, 1972, 73, 75, 77, 87, European Women's Open, Geneva, 1987, Eckerd Open, 1987; spl. advisor to U.S. Nat. Tennis Team by U.S. Tennis Assn.; bd. dirs. Internat. Tennis Hall of Fame; trustee Womens Sports Found. Star 3 vols. VCR instrnl. tennis tapes, 1991—; corp. spokesperson and rep., appearing in TV commls. and print advertisements; host and organizer Chris Evert Pro-Celebrity Tennis Classic, 1989, 90, 93, 94, 95, 96. Founder Chris Evert Charities, Inc., Healthy Start. Recipient Lebair Sportsmanship trophy, 1971; named Female Athlete of Yr. AP, 1974, 75, 77, 80, Athlete of Yr. Sports Illustrated, 1976, Greatest Woman Athlete of Last 25 Years Women's Sports Found., 1985, Flo Hyman award Women's Sports Found., 1990, Providencia award Palm Beach County Conv. and Visitors Bur., 1991; named one of Top 10 Romantic People of 1989, Korbel; inducted Madison Sq. Garden Walk of Fame, 1993, inductee, Internat. Tennis Hall of Fame, 1995. Mem. U.S. Lawn Tennis Assn. (Top Women's Singles Player award 1974), Nat. Honor Soc., Fla. Sports Found. (bd. dirs.), Women's Tennis Assn. (pres. 1982-91, exec. com., Sportsmanship award 1979, Player Svc. awards 1981, 86, 87). *

EVERT, SANDRA FLORENCE (WHEELER), medical/surgical nurse; b. Saginaw, Mich., Sept. 18, 1949; d. Charles William and Florence Arlene (Babcock) Wheeler; m. Raymond Clyde Evert, Jan. 20, 1968; children: Christine Michelle, Raymond Clyde II. AD cum laude, Lansing C.C., 1986. Med./surg. staff nurse E.W. Sparrow Hosp., Lansing, Mich., 1986—. Mem. First United Pentecostal Ch. of Grand Ledge, Mich. Mem. Apostolic Ch. Avocations: camping, Bible reading, Christian music, family, church functions. Home: 10 Willard Ct Grand Ledge MI 48837-1356

EVERTON, MARTA VE, retired ophthalmologist; b. Luling, Tex., Nov. 12, 1926; d. T.W. and Nora E. (Eckols) O'Leavy; B.A., Hardin-Simmons U., 1945; M.A., Stanford U., 1947; M.D., Baylor U., 1955; postgrad. N.Y.U.-Bellevue Hosp., 1956-57; m. Robert K. Graham, Oct. 15, 1960; children: Marcia, Christie, Leslie Fox. Intern, Meth. Hosp., Houston, 1955-56; resident in ophthalmology Baylor Affiliated Hosps., Houston, 1956-59; clin. instr. ophthalmology Baylor U., 1959-60; asst. clin. prof. ophthalmology Loma Linda U., 1962-73; practice medicine specializing in ophthalmology, Houston, 1959-60, Pasadena, Calif., 1961-74, Escondido, Calif., 1974-98. Mem. Calif. Med. Assn., Am. Acad. Ophthalmology, Alpha Omega Alpha. Home: 3024 Sycamore Ln Escondido CA 92025-7433

EVERTS, CONNOR, artist; b. Bellingham, Wash., Jan. 24, 1926; s. William Edward and Sophia (Mehan) E.; children: Anon Connor, Meigan Mariko, Geoffrey, Tamura; m. Judith Asa Colman, Dec. 12, 1994. A.A., El Camino Coll., 1950; B.A., U. Wash., 1952. Mem. faculty dept. art Calif. State U., Northridge, 1960-62; mem. faculty dept. art Calif. Inst. Arts, 1962-65, Calif. State U., Long Beach, 1965, San Francisco Art Inst., 1966, U. So. Calif., 1967-69, U. Calif., Riverside, 1972-76; graphics chmn. Cranbrook Acad. Art, Bloomfield Hills, Mich., 1976-81; exchange prof. Prahran Coll. Advanced Studies, Melbourne, Australia; artist in residence Calif. Inst. Tech., 1970-71. One man shows include Pasadena Art Mus., 1960, Michael Walls Gallery, San Francisco, 1967-69, Los Angeles Mcpl. Gallery, 1971, Meckler Gallery, Los Angeles, 1979, World Print Council, 1982, retrospective exhibit, Los Angeles Mus., 1983, Orange County Ctr. for Contemporary Art, 1986, Whatcom Mus. Art, 1987, Print Works Gallery, Chgo., 1988, 90, Ruth Bachofner, L.A., 1986, 89, Dominguez Hills State U., 1989, Joy Emery Gallery, Detroit, 1990, Claremont Gallery, L.A., 1995, Flowers Gallery, London, 1999; exhibited in group shows at Tokyo Biann. Painting Exhbn, 1967, Homage to Lithography, Mus. Modern Art, N.Y.C., 1969, Printmaking, Oskokunst Forening, Oslo, Norway, 1974, Mint Mus., 1987, Kunstsamm-Luggen Der Veste Coburg, 1988; represented in permanent collections, Chgo. Art Inst., Long Beach Mus. Art, Los Angeles County Mus. Art, Milw. Art Mus., Mus. Modern Art, N.Y.C., Pasadena Art Mus., San Francisco Mus. Modern Art, Washington Gallery Modern Art, others. Pres. adv. bd. Los Angeles Mcpl. Gallery, 1968. With USCG, 1946. Mem. AAUP, L.A. Printmaking Soc., Mich. Assn. Printmakers, Artists Equity. Studio: 2351 Sonoma St Torrance CA 90501-3130 *Circumstances, time and place of birth, sex, race, religion, economic status, and the resultant formulative years, determine the rough shape of our lives. But we, above all, are the largest factors in determining the kinds of persons we become. Let it be by conscious choice. If we will be shaped, let it be by ideas and challenge.*

EVETT, PHILIP JOHN, sculptor, educator; b. Swanscombe, Kent, Eng., Feb. 16, 1923; came to U.S., 1954; s. Emanuel John and Ethel May (Jordan) E.; m. Alice Calkins, June 1956 (div. 1968). Cert. Drawing, Cambridge (Eng.) Sch. Art, 1941; student, Belfast Coll. Art, No. Ireland, 1946-48. Prof. sculpture Cambridge Sch. Art, 1949-54, San Antonio Art Inst., 1958-62, Trinity U., San Antonio, 1960-88. Sculpture includes: Mother and Child (1st Sculpture award), 1947, Lannan Perfume (1st prize), 1960, others. Com. mem. San Antonio Fine Arts Commn., 1969-73. Recipient Outstanding Svc. citation San Antonio city Coun., 1973; named San Antonio Artist of the Yr., San Antonio Art League, 1962. Home and Studio: PO Box 1154 Blanco TX 78606-1154

EVIATAR, LYDIA, pediatric neurologist; b. Bucharest, Romania, Apr. 7, 1936; came to U.S., 1966; d. Joseph and Ghitea (Scheinberg) Tamir; m. Abraham Eviatar, Oct. 9, 1956; children: Joseph, Daphne. BSc, Faculte des Scis., Strasbourg, 1954; MD, Hadassah Hebrew U., Jerusalem, 1961. Diplomate Am. Bd. Pediatrics. Intern and resident Tel Hashoner Hosp., Tel Aviv, 1961-65; U.C.P. fellow UCLA, 1966-67, fellow in pediatric neurology, 1967-69; pediatric neurologist Bronx (N.Y.) Lebanon Hosp., 1970-79; resident in neurology Montefiore Hosp. Med. Ctr., Bronx, 1973-75; pediatric neurologist L.I. Jewish Med. Ctr., 1979-86; chief pediatric neurology Schneider Children's Hosp., New Hyde Park, N.Y., 1986—; from assoc. prof. to prof. pediatrics and neurology Albert Einstein Coll. Medicine, Bronx, N.Y., 1989—. Co-author: (with others) Pediatric Neurology, 1988. Grantee Nat. Inst. Neurol. Disease and Blindness, 1970-77, Acad. Cerebral Palsy, 1980-81, Richmond award, 1981; recipient teaching award Am. Acad. Otolaryngology, 1983. Fellow Am. Acad. Pediatrics, Am. Acad. Neurology (cert. neurologist, child neurologist). Office: Schneider Children's Hosp New Hyde Park NY 11042

EVIGAN, GREG, actor, musician; b. South Amboy, N.J., Oct. 14, 1953; m. Pam Serpe; children: Briana, Jason, Vanessa. Actor: (Broadway prodns.) Jesus Christ, Superstar; Grease, (TV shows) A Year at the Top, All That Glitters, B.J. and the Bear, 1979-81, Dallas, 1979, Fame, 1983, Masquerade, 1983-84, My Two Dads, 1987-90, P.S. I Love You, 1991-92, Tek War, 1994-95, Family Rules, 1999, (TV movies) Private Sessions, 1985, Scene of the Crime, 1985, Northstar, 1986, The Lady Forgets, 1989, Lies Before Kisses, 1991; guest star: (TV shows) Barnaby Jones, Murder, She Wrote, Hotel, Matlock, New Mike Hammer, The Hitchiker, Burke's Law, Melrose Place, Pacific Palisades, Crimes of Passion: Nobody Lives Forever, 1998, Earthquake in New York, 1998; films include Stripped to Kill, 1987, Private Road, 1987, Deepstar Six, 1989, Bird In The Hand, 1994, One Of Her Own, 1994, Deadly Family Secrets, 1995, House of the Damned, 1996, Mel, 1999. Address: 5070 Arundel Dr Woodland Hills CA 91364-3602*

EVNIN, ANTHONY BASIL, venture capital investor; b. N.Y.C., Mar. 10, 1941; s. Oscar B. Evnin and Nina (Fradkin) Schick; m. Judith P. Ward, June 9, 1962; children: Luke B., Timothy W. BA, Princeton U., 1962; PhD, MIT, 1966. With Union Carbide Corp., 1966-71, Story Chem., 1971-74; gen. ptnr. Venrock Assocs., N.Y.C., 1974—; bd. dirs. Centocor, Inc., Malvern, Pa., AXYS Pharms., Inc., South San Francisco, Calif., Opta Food Ingredients, Inc., Bedford, Mass., Ribozyme Pharms., Inc., Boulder, Colo., Triangle Pharms. Inc., Durham, N.C. Trustee Princeton U., 1997—, Rockefeller U., 1999—. Office: Venrock Assocs 30 Rockefeller Plz New York NY 10112-0002

EVSLIN, TOM, internet telephone service executive; b. Warner-Robins, Ga., Aug. 28, 1943. AB cum laude, Harvard U., 1965. Owner Solutions, Inc., 1972-91; dir. Microsoft, 1991-94; v.p. AT&T, Bridgewater, N.J., 1994-97; chmn., CEO ITXC Corp., 1997—. Chmn. Policy Com. of The Voice on the Net Coalition. office: ITXC Corp 600 College Rd E Princeton NJ 08540-6636

EWALD, ROBERT FREDERICK, insurance association executive; b. Newark, May 5, 1924; s. Frederick J. and Florence M. (Reiley) E.; m. Jeanine Martinez, Jan. 3, 1976; children: Robert, Steven; children by a previous marriage: William F., John C., George E. BS in Bus. Adminstrn. with spl. honors in Econs., Rutgers U., 1948. Asst. corp. auditor Prudential Ins. Co., Newark, Houston, Chgo., 1948-61; audit mgr. N.Y. Life Ins. Co., N.Y.C., 1962-64; treas. Mass. Gen. Life Ins. Co., Boston, 1965-68; adminstrv. v.p., controller Res. Life Ins. Co., Dallas, 1969-70; pres. Nat. Ben Franklin Life, Chgo., 1971-77; trustee, pres. Rockford (Ill.) Blue Cross Plan, North Cmties. Health Plan, Inc., 1979-82; dir., chmn. audit com. Guaranty Reasurance Corp., 1993-95; exec. dir. Guaranty Sys. Cons. LTD, Guaranty Assn., Chgo. Served with U.S. Army, 1943-46. Fellow Life Mgmt. Inst.; mem. Fin. Execs. Inst., Am. Arbitration Assn., Adminstrv. Mgmt. Soc., Mensa, Nat. Orgn. Life and Health Ins. Guaranty Assn. (emeritus dir., chmn. mems. coun. 1992-95, chmn. exec. com.), VFW. E-mail: zerograv@wwa.com. Home: 12 Wisner St Park Ridge IL 60068-3546

EWALD, WILLIAM BRAGG, JR., author, consultant; b. Chgo., Dec. 8, 1925; s. William Bragg and Mary Ann (Niccolls) E.; m. Mary Cecilia Thedieck, Dec. 6, 1947 (dec. Feb. 1997); children: William Bragg, Charles Ross, Thomas Hart Benton. AB, Washington U., 1946; MA, Harvard U., 1947, PhD, 1951. Instr. English, humanities Harvard U., Cambridge, 1951-54; spl. asst. on White House staff, asst. to Sec. Interior Washington, 1954-61; with IBM, Armonk, 1961-88. Author: The Masks of Jonathan Swift, 1954, The Newsmen of Queen Anne, 1956, Eisenhower the President, 1981, Who Killed Joe McCarthy?, 1984; McCarthyism and Consensus, 1987; asst. to former Pres. Eisenhower in preparation of 2-vol. memoirs, White House Years, 1961-64. Pres. Bruce Mus. Assocs., Greenwich, 1972-73; vestry mem. Christ Ch., Greenwich, 1986-89; bd. dirs. Eisenhower World Affairs Inst., 1984-91. Grantee Am. Philos. Soc., 1952, Harvard Found. Advanced Study and Research, 1952-53; Eisenhower Exchange fellow, 1960. Mem. Judson Welliver Soc., Phi Beta Kappa. Republican. Episcopalian. Clubs: Cosmos (Washington); Round Hill (Greenwich). Home and Office: 3 Dewart Rd Greenwich CT 06830-3418

EWALT, HENRY WARD, lawyer; b. Pitts., July 3, 1940; s. H. Ward and Jane Elizabeth (Stewart) E.; m. Mary Alice Jabsen, June 1, 1968; children: Andrew, Sarah. BA in Polit. Sci. cum laude, Allegheny Coll., 1962; MA in Polit. Sci., U. Mich., 1963, JD, 1966. Bar: U.S. Dist. Ct. (we. dist.) Pa. 1966, Pa. 1967, U.S. Ct. Appeals (3d cir.) 1975, U.S. Supreme Ct. 1984. Field atty. NLRB, Pitts., 1966-71; ptnr. Reding, Blackstone, Rea & Stewart, Pitts., 1971-75; chief labor counsel Allegheny County, Pitts., 1971-87; founder, pres. Brooks & Ewalt, Pitts., 1975-84; ptnr. Tucker Arensberg, P.C., Pitts., 1984-87; assoc., gen. counsel labor and employment law Westinghouse Electric Corp., Pitts., 1987-92; assoc., gen. counsel litigation and employment law CBS Corp., Westinghouse Electric Corp., Pitts., 1993-98; ptnr. Pepper Hamilton, LLP, 1998—; vice-chmn. Allegheny Regional Asset Dist., 1993-96; cons., lectr. in field. Author: Practical Planning - A How to Guide for Solos and Small Law Firms, 1985, Through the Clients Eyes, 1994. Mem. Pitts. City Planning Commn., 1978-82; trustee Children's Home of Pitts., 1976-85; bd. dirs. Zoar Home, Pitts., 1984-88; pres. Perry Hilltop Citizens Coun., Pitts., 1970-76, pres., Depreciation Lands Mus., 1991-93; mem. Hampton Parks and Recreation Bd., 1991-93; chmn., pres. Allegheny Land Trust, 1997—, city theatre, bd. mem., 1997—. Decorated Bronze Star, Purple Heart. Fellow Coll. Law Practice Mgmt.; mem. ABA (chmn. practice mgmt. divsn. econs. of law practice sect. 1986), Fed. Bar Assn. (past pres. Pitts. chpt.). Avocations: outdoor sports, gardening. Home: 4436 Mt Royal Blvd Allison Park PA 15101-2669 Office: Pepper Hamilton LLP 500 Grant Street 50th flr Pittsburgh PA 15219

EWAN, DAVID E., lawyer; b. Camden, N.J., June 23, 1959; s. Eugene H. and Catherine T. (Stannard) E. BA, Dickinson Coll., 1981; JD, Rutgers U., 1991. Bar: N.J. 1991, Pa. 1991, Fla. 1992, Colo. 1994, U.S. Dist. Ct. N.J. 1991, U.S. Ct. Appeals (3d cir.) 1992. Legal intern Camden County Prosecutor, 1989; law clk. U.S. Ct. Appeals (3d cir.), Phila., 1990-91; atty. Begley, McCloskey & Gaskill, Moorestown, N.J., 1991—; sr. adj. prof. paralegal program Burlington County Coll., Pemberton, N.J., 1996—. Home: 400 N Haddon Ave Unit 50 Haddonfield NJ 08033-1731 Office: Begley McCloskey & Gaskill 40 E Main St Moorestown NJ 08057-3068

EWAN, GEORGE THOMSON, physicist, educator; b. Edinburgh, Scotland, May 6, 1927; arrived in Can., 1952; s. Alexander Farmer and Jeannie Young (Taylor) E.; m. Maureen Louise Howard, Aug. 7, 1952; children: Elizabeth Louise, Robert Alexander. BS with 1st class honors, Edinburgh U., 1948, PhD, 1952. Asst. lectr. Edinburgh U., 1950-52; rsch. assoc. McGill U., Montreal, Que., Can., 1952-55; asst. to sr. rsch. officer Atomic Energy of Can., Ltd., Chalk River, 1955-70; prof. physics Queen's U., Kingston, Ont., Can., 1970-94; prof. emeritus, 1994—; head dept. Queen's U., Kingston, Ont., Can., 1974-77; vis. scientist Lawrence Berkeley (Calif.) Lab., 1966. Ford Found. fellow Niels Bohr Inst., Copenhagen, Denmark, 1961-62; Japan Soc. Promotion of Sci. fellow, Tokyo, 1986; recipient Radiation Industry award Am. Nuclear Soc., 1967. Fellow Royal Soc. Can., Royal Soc. Edinburgh, Am. Phys. Soc., Royal Soc. Arts; mem. Can. Assn. Physicists (Gold medal Achievement in Physics 1987). Mem. United Ch. Can. Avocations: golf, walking, reading. Office: Queen's U, Physics Dept, Kingston, ON Canada K7L 3N6

EWART, CLAIRE LYNN, author, illustrator; b. Holland, Mich., June 15, 1958; d. John Adamson Ewart and Caryl Jane (Curtis) Van Houten; m. Thomas Andrew Herr, Aug. 31, 11985; 1 child, Celeste Juliana. Student, Oberlin Coll., 1976-77; BFA, RISD, 1980. Animator, acting art dir. WSJV-TV and Pub. TV, Elkhart and South Bend, Ind., 1977-79; art dir. Computer Creations, South Bend, 1981-85; freelance courtroom illustrator, 1985-92; freelance illustrator Ft. Wayne, 1985-94; freelance author, illustrator Harper Collins, Putnam, Clarion, N.Y.C., 1989—; bd. dirs. Agricor, Marion, Ind. Author: One Cold Night, 1992; illustrator: Time Train, 1991, Sister Yessa's Story, 1992, The Legend of the Persian Carpet, 1993, The Dwarf, The Giant, and the Unicorn, 1996, The Biggest Horse I Ever Did See, 1997; represented in permanent collections. Vol. anti-toxic dump orgns., Ft. Wayne, 1992-93. Recipient ADI awards in computer animation, 1984-85, Women of Achievement in Advt. award Women in Comms., 1985, ADDY Citation of Excellence, 1989, Celibrate Literacy award Internat. Reading Assn., 1992, Woman of Achievement award YWCA, Ft. Wayne, 1996. Mem. Soc. Children's Book Writers and Illustrators, Children's Reading Round Table, Artlink Gallery (mem. panel), Designer/Craftsmen Guild (v.p. 1990-91). Avocations: gardening, hiking.

EWBANK, THOMAS PETERS, lawyer, retired banker; b. Indpls., Dec. 29, 1943; s. William Curtis and Maxine Stuart (Peters) E.; m. Alice Ann Shelton, June 8, 1968; children: William Curtis, Ann Shelton. Student, Stanford U., 1961-62; AB, Ind. U., 1965, JD, 1969. Bar: Ind. 1969, U.S. Tax Ct. 1969, U.S. Dist. Ct. (so. dist.) Ind. 1969, U.S. Supreme Ct. 1974; cert. trust & fin. advisor. Legis. asst. Ind. Legis. Coun., 1966-67; estate and inheritance tax adminstr. mchts. Nat. Bank, Indpls., 1967-69; assoc. Hilgedag, Johnson, Secrest and Murphy, Indpls., 1969-71; asst. gen. counsel Everett I. Brown Co., Indpls., 1971-72; with Mchts. Nat. Bank & Trust Co. (now Nat. City Bank), Indpls., 1972-95; from probate adminstr. to pres. Mechants Capital Mgmt., Inc., Ind., 1990-93; ptnr. Krieg DeVault Alexander & Capehart Law Firm, Indpls., 1995—. Contbr. articles to profl. jours. Asst. treas. Ruckelshaus for U.S. Senator Com., 1968; candidate for Ind. Legislature, 1970, 74; bd. dirs. Noble Found. Ind., 1997—, Indpls. Art Ctr., Ruth Lilly Found., 1997—, Ctr. Philanthropy, Inc. U., Indpls., 1998—, Benjamin Harrison Home Found., 1994—, v.p., 1996-98, pres., 1998—; chmn. adv. com. ARC, 1987—. Fellow Ind. Bar Found. (life patron); mem. Estate Planning Coun. Indpls. (pres. 1982-83), Indpls. Bar Assn., Ind. Bar Assn., Indpls. Bar Found. (treas 1976-81), Blue Key, Meridian Hills Country Club, Masons, Kiwanis (Circle K Internat. trustee 1963-64, pres. 1964-65, chmn. internat. com. 1988-90, George Hixson Diamond fellow, treas. Indpls. club 1980-81, 84-85 designated maj. builder 1983). Republican. Baptist. Home: 1280 Laurelwood Carmel IN 46032 Office: One Indiana Sq Ste 2800 Indianapolis IN 46204-2017

EWELL, A. BEN, JR., lawyer, businessman; b. Elyria, Ohio, Sept. 10, 1941; s. Austin Bert and Mary Rebecca (Thompson) E.; m. Suzanne E.; children: Austin Bert III, Brice Ballantyne, Harrison Dale. BA, Miami U., Oxford, Ohio, 1963; JD, Hasting Coll. Law, U. Calif., San Francisco, 1966. Bar: Calif. 1966, U.S. Dist. Ct. (ea. dist.) Calif. 1967, U.S. Supreme Ct. 1982, U.S. Ct. Appeals (9th cir.) 1967. Pres. A.B. Ewell, Jr., A. Profl. Corp., Fresno, 1984-98, The Clarksfield Co., Inc., Fresno, 1989—; formerly gen. counsel to various water dists. and assn.; gen. counsel, chmn. San Joaquin River Flood Control Assn., 1984-88; CEO Millerton New Town Devel. Co., 1988-94, chmn., 1994-96; mem. task force on prosecution, cts. and law reform Calif. Coun. Criminal Justice, 1971-74; mem. Fresno Bulldog Found., Calif. State U.; mem. San Joaquin Valley Agrl. Water commn., 1979-88; co-chmn. nat. adv. coun. SBA, 1981, 82, mem. 1981-87; bd. dirs. Fresno East Cmty. Ctr., 1971-73; mem. Fresno County Water Adv. Com., 1989, Fresno Cmty. Coun., 1972-73; chmn. various area polit. campaigns and orgns., including Reagan/Bush, 1984, Deukmejian for Gov., 1986; mem. adv. com. St. Agnes Med. Ctr. Found., 1983-89; trustee U. Calif. Med. Edn. Found., 1989-90, Fresno Met. Mus. Art, History and Sci., active, 1989—, mem. adv. coun., 1993-94; bd. dirs. Citizens for Cmty. Enrichment, Fresno, 1990-93; mem. Police Activities League, 1995—, Fresno Conv. and Visitors Bur., 1997—. Mem. Millerton Lake C. of C., Brighton Crest Country Club (pres. 1989-96), Cooper River Country Club, Phi Alpha Delta, Brighton Crest Golf and Country Club, Sigma Nu. Congregationalist. Office: 410 W Fallbrook Ave Ste 102 Fresno CA 93711-6191

EWELL, CHARLES MUSE, health care industry executive, consultant, publisher, educator; b. Richmond, Va., Jan. 12, 1937; s. Charles Muse Sr. and Virginia (Causey) E.; m. Loretta Ann Morris, Feb. 1960 (div. 1967); children—Charles Daniel, Elizabeth Morris; m. Valerie Ann White, Aug. 29, 1984. B.S., M.H.A., Va. Commonwealth U.; Ph.D., U. Wis. Adminstr. for various hosps. in Midwest and East Coast, 1964-74; ptnr. Arthur Young & Co., Los Angeles, 1974-84; pres., chief exec. officer Am. Health Care Systems, San Diego, 1984-86; chmn. The Governance Inst., 1986—. Contbr. articles to profl. jours.; mem. editorial bd. various profl. jours. Chmn. men's bd. L.A. Philharm., 1982-83; bd. dirs. San Diego Symphony, 1986-90, Sharp Meml. Hosp., 1988—. Mem. Am. Hosp. Assn., Valley Club (Sun Valley, Idaho), La Jolla Beach Club, La Jolla Country Club. Republican.

EWELL, MIRANDA JUAN, journalist; b. Beijing, Apr. 25, 1948; d. Vei-Chow and Hsien-fang Yolanda (Sun) J.; m. John Woodruff Ewell Jr., Feb. 20, 1971; children: Emily, David, Jonah. BA summa cum laude, Smith Coll., 1969; postgrad., Princeton U., 1971, U. Calif., Berkeley, 1981-82. Staff writer The Montclarion, Oakland, Calif., 1982-83; with San Jose (Calif.) Mercury News, 1984—, staff writer; now correspondent San Jose (Calif.) Mercury News, San Francisco Bureau, 1990-95; correspondent in bus. San Jose Mercury News, 1997—. Recipient Elsa Knight Thompson award Media Alliance, San Francisco, 1984, George Polk award L.I. U., N.Y., 1989, Heywood Brown award Newspaper Guild, Washington, 1989; Knight fellow Stanford U., 1995. Mem. Asian-Am. Journalists Assn.

EWEN, H.I., physicist; b. Chicopee, Mass., Mar. 5, 1922; s. Arthur and Ruth Frances (Fay) E.; m. Mary Ann Whitney, Feb. 11, 1956; children: Donald, Jim, Bruce, Mark, David, Deborah, Daniel, Rebecca. BA, Amherst Coll., 1943; MA, Harvard U., 1948, PhD, 1951. Mem. faculty Amherst Coll., 1943; co-dir. Harvard Radio Astronomy Program, 1952-58, rsch. assoc. astronomy dept., 1958-65, assoc., 1965-80; v.p. Millitech Corp., South Deerfield, Mass., 1989—; pres. Ewen Knight Corp., Weston, Mass., 1952-88, Ewen Dae Corp., 1958-88, E.K. Assocs., 1993—; sci. advisor to Cin. Electronics Corp. for USAF Air Weather Svc.; mem. Global Solar Radio Telescope Network, 1977-86. Contbg. author: Advances in Microwaves, vol. 5, 1970, Electromagnetic Sensing of the Earth from Satellites, 1967, Geoscience Instrumentation, 1974, also articles; co-discoverer 21 cm interstellar hydrogen line, 1951; remote sensing of atmospheric ozone distribution (resonant line at 102 GHz), 1966. Served to lt. USNR, 1943-46. NRC fellow, 1946-49; recipient svc. award Harvard Coll., 1977. Fellow AAAS (life), IEEE (Morris E. Leeds award 1970), Am. Acad. Arts and Scis.; mem. Am. Astron. Soc. (Tinsley prize 1988), Phi Beta Kappa, Sigma Xi.

EWERS, ANNE, opera company director. Gen. dir. Boston Lyric Opera, 1984-89, Utah Opera, Salt Lake City, 1990—; panelist Nat. Endowment for Arts; freelance stage dir. San Francisco Opera, N.Y.C. Opera, Can. Opera Co., Minn. Opera, Vancouver Opera, numerous others. Dir. nearly fifty opera prodns. including La Giaconda, Un Ballo in Maschera, La Rondine, The Merry Widow, Ring Cycle, Salome, Dialogues des Carmelites, Eugene Onegin; dir. Dame Joan Sutherland's North American Farewell, Dallas Opera. Bd. dirs. Opera Am., 1993—. Office: Utah Opera 50 W 2nd Salt Lake City UT 84101*

EWERS, PATRICIA O'DONNELL, university administrator; b. Chgo., July 22, 1935; d. Patrick Brenden and Johanna Marie (Galvin) O'D.; m. John Leonard Ewers, July 26, 1958; children: John P., Michele M. Ewers DeCesare. BA in English summa cum laude, Mundelein Coll., 1957; MA in English, Loyola U., Chgo., 1958, PhD in English, 1966; LHD (hon.), DePaul U., 1998. Instr. English Mundelein Coll., Chgo., 1964-66; asst. prof. English DePaul U., Chgo., 1966-69, assoc. prof. English, 1969-76, dir. humanities divsn. gen. edn. program, 1969-73, chair dept. English, 1973-76, prof. English, 1976-90, dean Coll. Liberal Arts and Scis., 1976-80, v.p., dean faculties, 1980-90; pres. Pace U., N.Y.C., 1990 ; ptnr. N.Y.C. Ptnrs., 1990—; chmn., mem. North Ctrl. Assn. Accreditation Teams, 1977-90; mem. nat. identification program for women in higher edn. Ill. State Com. for Am. Coun. on Edn., 1983-86; commr.-at-large North Ctrl. Assn. Colls./Schs., 1984-87; mem. com. on study of undergrad. edn. State of Ill. Bd. Higher Edn., 1985-86, 1989-90; mem. Commn. Minorities in Higher Edn., Am. Coun. Edn., 1990-93; mem. N.Y.C. Workforce Devel. Commn., 1993-94; mem. human resources bd. AT&T Corp., Basking Ridge, N.J., 1994-96; mem. adv. coun. on postsecondary edn. State Dept. Edn., 1994-96; mem. adv. com. on telecom., State Edn. Dept., Albany, N.Y., 1995-96. Trustee Riverside (Ill.) Pub. Libr., 1980-86, Cath. Theol. Union, Chgo., 1985-90, sec., 1986-90, NYU Downtown Hosp., 1991-99, Coun. Adult and Exptl. Learning, 1992-95, Our Lady of Mercy Med. Ctr., Bronx, N.Y., 1993—, El Museo del Barrio, N.Y.C., 1994—; trustee Commn. Ind. Colls. and Univs./N.Y. State, 1992—, chair, 1995-96; bd. dirs. Cath. Charities, 1984-90, Com. on Social Svc., 1986-90, subcom. on employer assistance programs, 1986-88, Fortune Brands, 1991—, Phoenix Theatre, 1992-96, Drama League, N.Y.C., 1993-96, Richard Tucker Music Found., 1993—, Westchester County Assn., 1993—, Am. Gen. Life Ins. Co. N.Y., 1996—, U.S. Life Ins. Co. in City of N.Y., 1996—; mem. Chgo. Network, 1986-90; steering com. Assn. Colls. and Univs./N.Y. State Commn. Ind. Colls. and Univs., 1992-96; individual investors adv. com. to bd. dirs. N.Y. Stock Exch., 1994—; mem. commn. on leadership and institutional effectiveness Am. Coun. Edn., Washington; mem. com. econ. devel., N.Y.C., 1996—, citizens budget commn., 1996—. Recipient Outstanding Alumna award Loyola U., Chgo., 1984. Mem. Nat. Assn. Ind. Colls. and Univs. (vice chair bd. dirs. 1997-98, chair bd. dirs. 1998—), Am. Australian Assn. (bd. dirs. 1994—), Regional Plan Assn. (coun. for the region tomorrow 1990-93), Downtown Lower Manhattan Assn., Inc., Westchester Assn. Women Bus. Owners (adv. bd. 1997—), Women's Forum, Inc., Fin. Women's Assn., Econ. Club of N.Y., Univ. Club, Met. Club, St. Andrew's Golf Club, Phi Gamma Mu, Beta Gamma Sigma, Alpha Lambda Delta, Delta Epsilon Sigma. Roman Catholic. Office: Pace U One Pace Plz New York NY 10038

EWERSEN, MARY VIRGINIA, retired educator; b. Van Wert County, Ohio, June 7, 1922; B.S. in Elem. Edn., Bowling Green, 1966, Toledo and Ohio State U.; m. Herbert Ewersen (dec.); 2 cldren. Remedial reading tchr. Port Clinton (Ohio) City Schs., 1966-70, reading tchr. chpt. 1/coord., 1970-94, ret. Cert. tchr. K-12, reading, Ohio.; lyrics writer Hilltop Records. Mem. Internat Reading Assn., Sandusky Choral Soc., Kappa Delta Pi. Author: Keepsakes and Celebrations!, 1997, (activity card set) From Hyperactive to Happy-Active in Limited Spaces, 1979; poet. Home: 1786 S Hickory Grove Rd Port Clinton OH 43452-9637 Office: 431 Portage Dr Port Clinton OH 43452-1724

EWICK, CHARLES RAY, librarian; b. Shelbyville, Ind., Sept. 13, 1937; s. Laurel R. and Loraine Pearl (Tufts) E.; m. Joann Hotchkiss, June 14, 1958; children—David Lee, Jeffrey Allen. B.A., Wabash Coll., 1962; M.A., Ind. U., 1966. Cons. Ind. State Library, Indpls., 1966-68, asst. dir., 1968-72, dir., 1978—; dir. Rolling Prairie Libraries, Decatur, Ill., 1972-78. Mem. ALA, Ind. Library Assn., Phi Beta Mu. Office: Ind State Library 140 N Senate Ave Indianapolis IN 46204-2207*

EWING, ALEXANDER COCHRAN, chancellor; b. N.Y.C., Feb. 25, 1931; s. Thomas and Lucia (Chase) E.; m. Carol Sonne, Feb. 15, 1958 (dec.); children: Alexander, Eric, Caroline; m. Sheila Cobb, Oct. 31, 1970. BA, Yale U., 1953. Bus. mgr., gen. dir. Joffrey Ballet, N.Y.C., 1963-70, assoc. dir., 1990-91; pres. Hillbright Enterprises Inc., Millbrook, N.Y., 1973-90; chancellor N.C. Sch. of the Arts, Winston Salem, 1990—. Home: 28 Cascade Ave Winston Salem NC 27127-2904 Office: NC Sch Arts 1533 S Main St Winston Salem NC 27117-2189

EWING, ANTHONY P., business consultant, lawyer; b. Plainfield, N.J., July 22, 1968; s. Phillips O. Jr. and Lois A. (Mercadante) E.; m. Elda P. Sancho-Mora, Oct. 8, 1993; 1 child, Samantha A. BA, Yale U., 1990; JD, Columbia U., 1995. Bar: N.Y. 1996, N.J. 1996. Program assoc. Internat. League for Human Rights, N.Y.C., 1990-91; English tchr. WorldTeach, Costa Rica, 1991-92; dir. Clark & Weinstock, Inc., N.Y.C., 1995—. Editor-in-chief Columbia Human Rights Law Rev., 1994-95. Mem. Coun. on Fgn. Rels. Office: Clark & Weinstock Inc 52 Vanderbilt Ave New York NY 10017-3808

EWING, BENJAMIN BAUGH, environmental engineering educator, consultant; b. Donna, Tex., Apr. 4, 1924; s. Joshua Fulkerson and Bula Betty (Baugh) E.; m. Elizabeth Malone, Apr. 3, 1947; children: Melissa, Douglas Malone, Frederick Joshua. B.S., U. Tex., Austin, 1944, M.S., 1949; Ph.D., U. Calif. at Berkeley, 1959. Diplomate: Am. Acad. Environ. Engrs. Instr., asst. prof. U. Tex., Austin, 1947-55; assoc. in civil engring., asst. research engr. U. Calif. at Berkeley, 1955-58; assoc. prof., prof. U. Ill., Urbana, 1958-85, prof. emeritus, 1985—, dir. Water Resource Center, 1966-73, dir. Inst. for Environ. Studies, 1972-85, dir. emeritus, 1985—; cons. engr., 1959—. Research and publs. in water quality mgmt. and pollution control, water treatment, wastewater treatment, water resources mgmt. Trustee Urbana and Champaign San. Dist., 1974-80; public mem. Ill. Water Resources Commn., 1975-84. Served to lt. (j.g.) CEC, USNR, 1943-46. Recipient Epstein award dept. civil engring. U. Ill., 1961, Harrison Prescott Eddy award for noteworthy research, 1968. Fellow ASCE; mem. Am. Water Works Assn. (life), Water Environment Fedn. (life), Assn. Environ. Engring. Profs. Emeritus, Internat. Assn. on Water Quality, Rotary. Home: 4374 Cedar Pl Lummi Island WA 98262-8672

EWING, BLAIR GORDON, federal official; b. Kansas City, Mo., Dec. 3, 1933; s. Lynn Moore and Margaret (Blair) E.; m. Barbara F. Thompson, Jan. 3, 1959 (div. Nov. 1991); children: Blair Gordon, Chatham Boyd; m. Martha L. Brockway, April 30, 1994. AB, U. Mo., 1954; postgrad. (Rotary Found. fellow), U. Bonn (Germany), 1957-58; AM, U. Chgo., 1960. Reporter Chgo. City News Bur., 1958-59, UPI, 1959-60, Traffic World Mag., 1960-61; instr. polit. sci. Chgo. City Jr. Coll., 1961-62, SUNY, Binghamton, 1962-67; planning and mgmt. cons. Harold Wise and Assocs., Washington, 1967-69; program analyst Office of Asst. Sec. HEW, Washington, 1969-70; dir. criminal justice planning D.C. Govt., 1970-72; dir. dept. pub. safety Met. Washington Coun. of Govts., 1972-74; dir. planning and evaluation div. U.S. Dept. Justice, Washington, 1974-78; dep. dir. Nat. Inst. Law Enforcement and Criminal Justice, Dept. Justice, 1976—; acting dir., 1977-79; asst. dir. U.S. Office Pers. Mgmt., Washington, 1979-81, dep. dir., 1981-83; sr. exec. U.S. Office Mgmt. and Budget, 1983-86; dir. Mgmt. Improvement, Dept. Def., 1986-98; adj. prof. Law Ctr. Georgetown U., 1971-74. Author: Peace Through Negotiation: The Austrian State Treaty, 1966; contbr. articles to profl. jours. Mem. Montgomery County (Md.) Human Rels. Commn., 1975-76; mem. Montgomery County Bd. Edn., 1976-98, pres., 1982-83, 90-91; elected mem. coun. Montgomery County, Md, 1998. With U.S. Army, 1954-56. Woodrow Wilson fellow, 1956-57; recipient disting. Svc. award Office Pers. Mgmt., 1981, U.S. Dept. Def. Disting. Civilian Svc. award, 1990, Presdl. Rank award Meritorious Sr. Exec., 1990. Mem. Phi Beta Kappa. Democrat. Episcopalian. Home: 3 Park Valley Rd Silver Spring MD 20910-5424 Office: Montgomery County Coun 100 Maryland Ave Rockville MD 20850

EWING, DAVID WALKLEY, magazine editor; b. Grand Rapids, Mich., May 19, 1923; s. Walkley Bailey and Harriet Elissa (Edwards) E.; m. Elizabeth Weld Bennett, Sept. 11, 1948; children: Elizabeth (Mrs. Phillip A. Cook), Bennett, Sarah (Mrs. Paul Carlson), Rebecca. Student, Amherst Coll., 1941-43, Williams Coll., 1943-44; JD, Harvard U., 1949. With Harvard Bus. Rev., Boston, 1949-85; tchr. Harvard U. Bus. Sch., 1966-68, dir. rsch. project, 1986-88. Author: The Managerial Mind, 1964, The Practice of Planning, 1968, The Human Side of Planning, 1969, Freedom Inside the Organization, 1977, Writing for Results: In Business, Government, Science, and the Professions, 1978, Do It My Way or You're Fired, 1983, Justice On the Job, 1989, Inside the Harvard Business School, 1990, other books; editor: Management Thinking, 1961-68. Chmn. Winchester (Mass.) Unitarian Soc., 1973-74. Served with USNR, 1944-46. Home: 195 Cambridge St Winchester MA 01890-2303

EWING, EDGAR LOUIS, artist, educator; b. Hartington, Nebr., Jan. 17, 1913; s. David E. and Laura (Buckendorf) E.; m. Suzanne Peter Giovan, Feb. 12, 1941. Grad., Art Inst. Chgo., 1935; studied, in France, Eng., Italy, 1935-37. Mem. faculty Art Inst. Chgo., 1937-43, U. Mich., Ann Arbor, 1946; asst. prof. fine arts U. So. Calif., 1946-54, assoc. prof., 1954-59, prof., 1959-78, Disting. prof. emeritus, 1978—; Mellon prof. Carnegie-Mellon U., Pitts., 1968-69. One-man shows M.H. DeYoung Meml. Mus. Art, San Francisco, 1948, Long Beach Mus. Art, 1955, Dalzell Hatfield Galleries, Los Angeles, 1954, 56, 58, 61, 63, 65, Hewlett Gallery-Carnegie Mellon U., Pitts., 1969, Nat. Gallery, Athens, Greece, 1973, Los Angeles Mcpl. Art Gallery, 1974, Palm Springs (Calif.) Desert Mus., 1976-77, Fisher Gallery U. So. Calif., 1978; group exhbns. Cin Art Mus., Corcoran Gallery Art, Washington, Denver Art Mus., Dallas Mus. Fine Arts, Fort Worth Art Ctr., Met. Mus., N.Y.C.; represented: San Francisco Mus. Art, Dallas Mus. Fine Arts, Ft. Worth Art Ctr., Met. Mus., N.Y.C., Sao Paulo (Brazil) Mus. Art, Wichita Art Mus., Fisher Gallery, U. So. Calif., 1994. Served with C.E., U.S. Army, 1943-46, PTO. Recipient Aberle Florscheim Meml. prize for Oil Painting, Art Inst. Chgo., 1943, Purchase award for oil painting Los Angeles County Mus. Art, 1952, Samuel Goldwyn award, 1957, Ahmanson Purchase award City of Los Angeles Exhbn., 1962, Disting. Prof. Emeritus award U. So. Calif., 1987; Edward L. Ryerson fellow, 1935; Louis Comfort Tiffany grantee, 1948-49, Jose Drudis Fund grantee, Greece, 1967; named one of 100 Artists-100 Yrs., Art Inst. Chgo., 1980. Mem. AAUP, Nat. Watercolor Soc. (v.p. 1952, pres. 1953). Democrat. Home: 4226 Sea View Ln Los Angeles CA 90065-3350

EWING, ELISABETH ANNE ROONEY, priest; m. James E. Ewing. Student, Mt. San Antonio Coll., 1978. Ordained to ministry Evang. Episcopal Chs., 1998. Pastor, gen. overseers, CEO St. Matthew Living Cathedral, N.Y.C., 1998—; mem. Rand Rsch. Corp.; mem. diplomat cir. L.A. World Affairs Coun. Co-editor: Church History, 1996-98, The Church Visible, 1996-98, George Washington, 1996-98, Life After Death, 1996-98, Bible Lessons, 1996-98; assoc. editor Pinnacle Today Internat. Mag., St. Matthew Publs., St. Matthew Tribune. Mem. Knights of Malta (Dame). Office: St Matthew Cathedral Ste 145 10736 Jefferson Blvd Culver City CA 90230-4969

EWING, FRANK MARION, lumber company executive, industrial land developer; b. Albany, Ga., Apr. 24, 1915; s. Frank Marion and Alpharetta (Tucker) E.; m. Hanna Anderson, June 15, 1935; children: Grace Marit (Mrs. Paul Atherton), Linda Tucker (Mrs. Richard R. Mace), Frances Marion (Mrs. Brian Tennery), Andrew L.; m. Jo Anne Bacon Hilley, Mar. 12, 1964; children: (adopted) Kathleen Melinda, Wayne Edgar; m. Marilyn Hassett Petrie, Mar. 2, 1973. B.A. (Sereno Gaylord scholar), Yale U., 1936. Pres., chmn. bd. Frank M. Ewing Co., Inc., Washington, 1937—, Lumber Distbn. Co., Petersburg, Va., 1942-57; Pres., chmn. bd. Ewing Lumber & Millwork Corp., Beltsville, Md., 1958-71; chmn. bd. Kettler Bros. Inc., Gaithersburg, Md., 1965-88; developer Beltsville Indsl. Center, 1950-89; bd. dirs. Washington Mut. Investors Fund.; mem. industry adv. com. WPB, 1942-46; industry adv. com. to sec. commerce, 1947-50, dep. and later acting asst. sec. def., 1955-56; mem. bd. Met. Washington Bd. Trade, 1957-61. Gen. campaign chmn. Prince Georges Community Chest, 1955; bd. dirs. Childrens Hosp., Washington. Mem. Prince Georges C. of C. (pres. 1956-57). Clubs: Kiwanian (bd. dirs. Prince Georges 1948-52), Mason., Chevy Chase, Metropolitan, Burning Tree (Washington); St. Andrew's Royal and Ancient Golf (Scotland), Tryall Club (Jamaica). Home: 5610 Wisconsin Ave PH 20C Chevy Chase MD 20815-4415 Office: 9624 Stewartown Rd Gaithersburg MD 20886

EWING, GEORGE H., pipeline company executive; b. San Antonio, June 11, 1925; s. Hubert Larkin and Miriam (Galloway) E.; m. Doris Ann Cannan, May 31, 1947; children: Susan J., Beverly A., Bryan G., Mary C. BSCE, Tex. A&M U., 1948. Registered profl. engr., La. Engr. Tex. Eastern Transmission Corp., Houston, 1948-56, chief plans and research div., 1956-64, v.p., chief engr., 1965-75; sr. v.p. gas supply Tex. Eastern Gas Pipeline Co., Houston, 1976-78, pres., CEO, 1979-85; CEO, chmn. bd. Transwestern Pipeline Co., Houston, 1979-85; chmn. bd. Gas Masters, Inc., Houston, 1986—; exec. v.p. Compumasters Internat. Inc., 1988-90; pres. GHE Oil & Gas, Inc., 1988—; pres., CEO Amagosa Pipeline Co., 1987-89; pres. Ewing Cattle Co., 1991—. With USNR, 1943-46, PTO, Submarine

Svc. Mem. ASME (Engring. award 1969), Am. Gas Assn., Tex. Transp. Inst. Presbyterian. Club: Petroleum (Houston), Galveston Country Club. Home: 4154 Pirates Bch Galveston TX 77554-8042

EWING, JACK, communications executive; b. Chgo., Jan. 21, 1945; s. John Cullen and Irene Leone (Roeder) E.; m. Sharon Jean Tomlinson, Oct. 13, 1973. BA in English, Parsons Coll., 1966; MA in English, SUNY, Oswego, 1970. Cert. tchr., N.Y., Mont. Copy chief, pub. svc. dir. Wolf Radio, Syracuse, N.Y., 1970-73; copywriter Silverman and Mower Advt., Syracuse, 1973-74; pres. Mr. E Enterprises, Syracuse, 1974-77; copy chief PJ&L Advt., Syracuse, 1977-80; creative dir. BBW Advt., Boise, Idaho, 1980-82, WRC Advt., Boise, 1986, 92-95; pres. Ewing Concepts and Copy, Boise, 1982-92, 95—. Author: A Freshman's Confessions, 1962, Soft More College Stud, 1963, Freak-out, 1998; editor: Lite 'N Up, 1996; author numerous poems, short stories, articles. Recipient Essay Contest award Syracuse Newspapers, 1973, others. Mem. Log Cabin Lit. Ctr. Avocations: reading, stamp and coin collecting, music, archaeology, cross-country skiing. E-mail: citizenew@aol.com. Office: Ewing Concepts and Copy PO Box 571 Boise ID 83701

EWING, JACK ROBERT, accountant; b. San Francisco, Feb. 14, 1947; s. Robert Maxwell and Blanche Julia (Diak) E.; m. Joan Marie Coughlin Ewing, Nov. 25, 1967; children: Theresa Marie Ewing, Christina Ann Ewing. BS, U. Mo., 1969. CPA. Staff acct. Fox & Co., St. Louis, 1969-70; radio station opr. USAF, Mountain Home, Idaho, 1970-72; internal auditor Air Force Audit Agy., Warren, Wyo., 1972-74; supr. auditor Fox & Co., St. Louis, 1974-79; audit mgr. Erickson, Hunt & Spillman, P.C., Ft. Collins, Colo., 1979-82; stockholder, owner Hunt, Spillman & Ewing, P.C., Ft. Collins, Colo., 1982-93; owner Jack R. Ewing, CPA, 1993—. Mem., pres. Parent Adv. Bd., Beattie Elem. Sch., 1982-83, 86-87; mem. Entrepreneur of Yr. Selection Com., Ft. Collins, Colo., 1989-92, Suicide Resource Ctr. of Larimer County, Ft. Collins, Colo., 1992—, pres., 1998—, bd. dirs.; mem. Leadership Ft. Collins-Class of 1992, State of Colo. Mental Health Planning Coun., 1993—; dir. treas. One West Contemporary Art Ctr., 1989-97—, Ctr. for Diversity in Work Place, 1991—; pres., adv. bd. Larimer County Bd. Mental Health, 1992—; v.p. Colo. Behavioral Healthcare Coun., 1995-97; mem. mental health pro bono project, 1996-97; mem. gov.'s citizen panel on suicide prevention, 1998—. Mem. Am. Inst. CPAs, Colo. Soc. CPAs. Avocations: writing, hiking. Office: 3112 Meadowlark Ave Fort Collins CO 80526-2843

EWING, JAMES E., priest; m. Elisabeth Anne Rooney. Ordained to ministry Evang. Episcopal Chs., 1953. Sr. pastor, gen. overseer St. Matthew Living Cathedral, N.Y.C.; mem. Rand Rsch. Corp.; mem. diplomat cir. L.A. World Affairs Coun.; rsch. bd. dirs. Am. Biog. Inst./Internat. Biog. Ctr. Author, editor: Church History, The Church Visible, George Washington, Life After Death, Bible Lessons. With USAF, 1953-57. Mem. Knights of Malta, Sovereign Order St. John of Jerusalem. Office: St Matthew Cathedral Ste 145 10736 Jefferson Blvd Culver City CA 90230

EWING, JOHN HARWOOD, mathematics educator; b. Bronxville, N.Y., Nov. 25, 1944; s. Robert Edward and Virginia (Harwood) E.; m. Janice Rusche, May 22, 1965; children: Scott Andrew, Jennifer Beth, Amy Sarah. BS, St. Lawrence U., Canton, N.Y., 1966; MS, PhD, Brown U., 1971; DS (hon.), St. Lawrence U., 1996. Instr. Dartmouth Coll., Hanover, N.H., 1971-73; asst. prof., assoc. prof. math. Ind. U., Bloomington, 1973, prof., chmn. dept., 1986-89, 92-95; exec. dir. Am. Math. Soc., Providence, 1995—; Sci. and Engring. rsch. Coun. fellow U. Newcastle, Eng., 1980-81; Sonderforschungsbereicht fellow U. Goettingen, Germany, 1985-86; series editor Springer-Verlag, N.Y.C., 1987-95. Author: Puzzle It Out, 1981; editor: Numbers, 1990, Celebrating 50 Years of Mathematics, 1991, A Century of Mathematics, 1994; editor-in-chief Math. Intelligencer, 1980-86, Am. Math. Monthly, 1992-96; also over 40 articles. Mem. AAAS, Am. Math. Soc., Math. Assn. Am. (Lester R. Ford award 1976, George Polya lectr. 1991-92, Polya award 1996). Episcopalian. Office: Am Math Soc PO Box 6248 Providence RI 02940-6248

EWING, JOSEPH NEFF, JR., lawyer; b. Bryn Mawr, Pa., Nov. 10, 1925; s. Joseph Neff and Anne (Ashton) E.; m. Margaret Converse Howe, Dec. 22, 1951; children: Margaret E. Lloyd, Anne A., Elizabeth M. Peifer,. AB, Princeton U., 1947; JD, U. Pa., 1953. Bar: Pa. 1954, U.S. Tax Ct. 1992, U.S. Supreme Ct. 1978. Assoc. Saul, Ewing, Remick & Saul, Phila., 1953-63, ptnr., 1963-95, of counsel, 1996—; bd. govs. Main Line Health, Inc., 1988-95; bd. trustees The Bryn Mawr Hosp., 1969-96; Bryn Mawr Hosp. Found., 1981-98, Dunwoody Village, Inc., 1997—; trustee Hist. Sugartown, Inc., Malvern, Pa.; chancellor,pres. Clan Ewing in Am. Chmn. Willistown Twp. Planning Commn., Malvern, 1960-69, chmn. bd. suprs., 1970-82, chmn. zoning hearing bd., 1985-95, East Goshen Twp., chmn. Zoning Hearing Bd., 1996—; pres. bd. trustees Embreeville (Pa.) State Hosp., 1965-72, chmn. spl. contacts divsn. Phila. United Fund, 1965-66; mem. hosp. coun. Mental Health Assn., Southeastern Pa., Phila., 1967-68; elder Paoli (Pa.) Presbyn. Ch., 1970-72. Mem. ABA, Phila. Bar Assn. (med.-legal com. 1962-76, chmn. 1971), Am. Acad. Hosp. Attys., Phila. Assn. Def. Counsel (pres. 1973), Nat. Assn. R.R. Trial Counsel, Pa. Soc. Healthcare Attys. (pres. 1975-77), Waynesborough Country Club (v.p. 1965-69), Hershey's Mill Golf Club. Avocations: sailing, photography, gardening, fox hunting, skiing. Home: 1109 Lincoln Dr West Chester PA 19380-5721 Office: Saul Ewing Remick & Saul 1055 Westlakes Dr Berwyn PA 19312-2410

EWING, KEVIN ANDREW, lawyer; b. Washington, May 22, 1966. BA, Yale Coll., 1988; JD, Georgetown U., 1991; LLM, U. Heidelberg, Germany, 1993. Bar: Md., D.C. Lawyer Bracewell & Patterson, L.L.P., Washington, 1992—; internat. interest group coord. Women's Coun. on Energy and the Environ., Washington, 1995—. Vol. Reading for the Blind and Dyslexic, Washington, 1997—. Recipient Hajo Holborn prize Yale Coll. and Fed. Republic Germany, 1988. Mem. ABA. Avocations: speaking German, music, backpacking. Office: Bracewell & Patterson LLP 2000 K St NW Ste 500 Washington DC 20006-1872

EWING, KY PEPPER, JR., lawyer; b. Victoria, Tex., Jan. 7, 1935; s. Ky Pepper and Sallie (Dixon) E.; m. Almuth Rott, Apr. 6, 1963; children: Kenneth Patrick, Kevin Andrew, Kathryn Diana. B.A. cum laude, Baylor U., 1956; LL.B. cum laude, Harvard U., 1959. Bar: D.C. 1959, U.S. Supreme Ct 1963. Assoc. firm Covington & Burling, Washington, 1959-64; partner firm Prather, Seeger, Doolittle, Farmer & Ewing, Washington, 1964-77; dep. asst. atty. gen. antitrust div. Dept. Justice, Washington, 1978-80; ptnr. Vinson & Elkins, Washington, 1980—; dir., sec. Washington Inst. Fgn. Affairs. Co-editor-in-chief: State Antitrust Practice and Statutes, 3 Vols., 1990; mem. antitrust adv. bd. Antitrust and Trade Regulation Report Bur. Nat. Affairs, 1990—; mem. edit. bd. Antitrust Report Matthew Bender & Co., 1993—. Pres. Potomac Valley League, 1977, Carderock Springs Citizens Assn., 1975-78. Fellow Am. Bar Found.; mem. ABA (chmn. legis. com. antitrust sect. 1987-91, coun. antitrust sect. 1991-94, fin. officer antitrust sect. 1994-96, chmn. FTC/Dept. Justice working group 1994-97, mem. ho. of dels. 1996-98, vice chair antitrust sect. 1998—, chair elect 1999—), D.C. Bar Assn., Am. Soc. Internat. Law, Internat. Bar Assn., Met. Club. Democrat. Episcopalian. Home: 8317 Comanche Ct Bethesda MD 20817-4561 Office: Vinson & Elkins 1455 Pennsylvania Ave NW Fl 7 Washington DC 20004-1013

EWING, LYNN MOORE, JR., lawyer; b. Nevada, Mo., Nov. 14, 1930; s. Lynn Moore and Margaret Ray (Blair) E.; m. Peggy Patton Adams, July 10, 1954; children: Margaret Grace, Melissa Lee, Lynn Moore. AB, U. Mo., Columbia, 1952, JD, 1954. Bar: Mo. 1954. Ptnr. Ewing & Hoberock, Nevada, Mo., 1958—; Mem. Mo. Ho. of Reps., 1959-64; mem. Nevada City Coun., 1967-73, mayor, 1969-70, 72-73; mem., Mo. Land Reclamation Commn., 1971-75, Nevada Charter Comm., 1978-79, devel. coun. U. Mo., Columbia, Mo. Acad. of Squires, 1994—; mem. Mo. coord. bd. Higher Edn., 1997—. bd. dirs. Nevada Hosp., 1974-83; bd. dirs., pres. Nev. Area Econ. Devel. Commn., 1985-88; vestryman, sr. warden All Saints Episcopal Ch. Served to 1st lt. USAF, 1954-56. Recipient Legis. award St. Louis Globe-Democrat, 1960, 62; named Citizen of Year, Nevada Rotary Club, 1975. Fellow Am. Bar Found. (life); mem. ABA, Mo. Bar Found. (life), Am. Coll. Trust and Estate Counsel, Am. Coll. Mortgage Attys., Am. Judicature Soc., U.S. League Savs. Assn. (chmn. attys. com. 1977-79), Mo. Bar (adv. com. 1975-84, bd. govs. 1974-78), Vernon County Bar Assn., Jefferson Club (trustee), Nevada Rotary (pres. 1969-70), Nevada Country Club. Democrat. Episcopalian. Home: 146 Country Club Dr Nevada MO 64772-3027 Office: 223 W Cherry St Nevada MO 64772-3361

EWING, MARIA LOUISE, soprano; b. Detroit; m. Sir Peter Hall, 1986 (div.); 1 child: Rebecca. Debut Met. Opera as Cherubino in Marriage of Figaro, 1976, followed by many debuts with major U.S. orchs., opera houses including Chgo. Symphony Orch., Lyric Opera Chgo., Washington Opera, San Francisco Opera, Opera Co. Boston, Santa Fe Opera, Houston Grand Opera, Cologne Opera, L.A. Philharmonic, Phila. Orch., Pitts. Symphony, Cin. Symphony, Met. Opera, L.A. Opera, La Scala, Geneva Opera, Salzburg Festival, Glyndebourne Festivals; European debut La Scala in Pelleas et Melisande; N.Y. Philharmonic debut with Mahler Festival; title role Cenerentola, Geneva Opera, 1981; debut Dorabella in Cosi Fan Tutti, Glyndebourne Festival, Zerlina in Don Giovanni; Covent Garden debut title role in Salome, 1988; appeared as Susanna in Figaro, Lyric Opera, Chgo., 1987, Cosi Fan Tutte, L.A. Opera, 1988, Damnation of Faust, 1988 (rec. Denon Records); summer appearances Ravinia Festival, London's South Bank Festival, Glyndebourne Festival; appeared with Concertgebouw Orch., Amsterdam and Toronto (Ont., Can.) Symphony; recital tour Paris, London, La Scala, Milan, Italy, 1985, Paris, Vienna, Austria, Florence, Italy, 1988; title roles Poppea, Glyndebourne, 1986, Carmen, Met. Opera, 1986, Glyndebourne, 1987, Salome, L.A. Opera, 1986, Chgo., 1988-89, Merry Widow, Lyric Opera Chgo., 1986, Carmen, Covent Garden, 1988, Earls Ct., 1989, Carmen, Tokyo, 1989, Australia, 1990, Covent Garden, 1991-92, Tosca, Seville, 1991, other operatic roles include Blanche in the Dialogues of the Carmelites, Composer in Ariadne auf Naxos; concert, recital appearance with James Levine, N.Y. and Chgo., with Simon Rattle in L.A., Birmingham and Vienna, with Claudio Abbado in Debussy's La Demoiselle Elue at the Barbican, 1986 (Deutsche Gramophon rec. London Symphony Orch. 1986, Grand Prix du Disque award), with Rattle and CBSO in Bluebeard's Castle, 1985, Ravel's Shéhérazade with Phila. Orch. in London and Paris, 1986, 2 BBC Promenade Concerts with Janowski in Nuits d'Eté, 1987, with Abbado in Pulcinella, 1987, with Rattle and City Birmingham Symphony in Strauss' Four Last Songs, 1987, with Andrew Davis and Hessischer Rundfunk, Frankfurt, Ger. Four Last Songs, 1987, also recitals in Paris, Vienna, Florence, Italy, with London Symphony Ravel's Scheherezade, 1987, with London Sinfonietta Weill's Seven Deadly Sins, 1987, with Sir John Pritchard and BBC Symphony in Strauss' Four Last Songs, Royal Festival Hall, 1988, also concerts in Amsterdam and Paris; debut as Tosca, L.A., 1989-90; appeared with Ashkenazy and Royal Philharm. Orch. singing Four Last Songs, 1990, Australian debut, 1990, Salzburg Festival, 1990; performed Salome wih Washington Opera, 1990, BBC Proms with London Symphony Orch., 1990-91, Strauss' Four Last Songs with Michael Tilson Thomas, 1992, Messiaen Poèmes pour Mi in London and Paris with Philharmonia Orch. and Pierre Boulez, 1993, The Trojans with James Levine, Met. Opera, N.Y.C., 1993; recorded Pelleas and Melisande, 1991, Lady Macbeth of Mtzensk (Shostakovich), 1992, Scéhérazade, 1993; performed Madame Butterfly, L.A., 1991-92, Salome, San Francisco Orch., 1992, San Francisco Opera, 1993; performed with L.A. and Berlin Philharmonics at Salzburg and Lucerne festivals, 1992, Lady Macbeth of Mtsensk with Metropolitan Opera, 1994, Conlon Poemes Pour Mi, Carnegie Hall, 1995. E-mail: davidgodfrey@mariaewing.com. Address: Joel E Bloch Artists Mgmt Mitchell-Godfrey Mgmt 48 Grays Inn Rd New York NY 10014*

EWING, PATRICK ALOYSIUS, professional basketball player; b. Kingston, Jamaica, Aug. 5, 1962; m. Rita Ewing; children: Patrick Aloysius, Randi. BFA, Georgetown U., 1985. Basketball player New York Knickerbockers, N.Y.C., 1985—; mem. U.S. Olympic Basketball Teams (received Gold medal), 1984, 92. Named to Sporting News All-Am. 2nd team, 1983-84, Sporting News All-Am. 1st Team, 1985, All-Star team, 1986, 88-93; recipient Naismith award, 1985; named NCAA Disvn. I Most Outstanding Player, 1984, Sporting News Coll. Player of Yr., 1985, NBA Rookie of Yr., 1986, Sporting News Coll. Player of Yr., 1985, All-Defensive 2nd team, 1988, 89, 92, All-NBA 2nd team, 1988, 89, 91, 92, All-NBA 1st team, 1990, NBA All-Star team, 1986-95. Player NCAA divsn. I championship team, 1984; holder NBA Finals series record most blocked shots (30), 1994; cohlder NBA finals single-game record most block shots (8), 1994. Office: NY Knicks Madison Sq Garden 2 Penn Plz New York NY 10121-0091*

EWING, RAYMOND CHARLES, retired ambassador; b. Cleve., Sept. 7, 1936; s. Thomas Davis and Marion (Andrews) E.; m. Jerelyn Patten, Jan. 19, 1962; children: Gregory, Thomas, Joyce, Lillian Patten. BA, Occidental Coll., 1957; MPA, Harvard U., 1970. Joined Fgn. Svc., Dept. State, 1957; various assignments in Washington, Bern, Switzerland, Rome, Lahore, Pakistan, Vienna, Austria, Tokyo, 1957-1977; dir. Office So. European Affairs, Dept. State, Washington, 1977-79; mem. Sr. Seminar, Washington, 1979-80; dep. asst. sec. of state for European affairs, 1980-81; amb. to Cyprus Nicosia, 1981-84; dean Sch. Lang. Studies Fgn. Svc. Inst., Washington, 1985-87; dir. Office Career Devel. and Assignments, Dept. State, 1987-89; amb. to Ghana Accra, 1989-92; chargé d'affaires, a.i. to Tanzania Dar es Salaam, 1992; ret., 1993; mng. editor Mediterranean Quarterly, Washington, 1994—. Mem. Am. Fgn. Svc. Assn., Diplomatic and Consular Officers (ret.). Presbyterian. Avocations: tennis, golf, travel, reading.

EWING, RICHARD EDWARD, mathematics, chemical and petroleum engineering educator; b. Kingsville, Tex., Nov. 24, 1946; s. Floyd Ford and Olivia Clara (Henrichson) E.; m. Rita Louise Williams, Aug. 8, 1970; children: John Edward, Lawrence Alan, Bradley William. BA, U. Tex., 1969, MA, 1972, PhD, 1974; doctorate (hon.), U. Bergen, Norway, 1996. Asst. prof. Oakland U., Rochester, Mich., 1974-77; asst. prof. Ohio State U., Columbus, 1977-80, assoc. prof., 1980-81; sr. rsch. mathematician Mobil R & D Corp., Dallas, 1980-82, assoc. mathematician, 1982-83; prof. math., petroleum and chem. engring. U. Wyo., Laramie, 1983-92, J.E. Warren dist. prof. energy and environ., 1984-92, dir. Enhanced Oil Recovery Inst., 1984-92, dir. Inst. for Sci. Computation, 1986-92, dir. Ctr. for Math. Modeling, 1986-92, Wold Centennial chair in energy, 1991-92; dean Coll. Sci. Tex. A&M U., College Station, 1992—, prof. math. and engring., 1992—, dir. Inst. for Sci. Computation, 1992—, disting. rsch. chair TEES, 1992, dir. Acad. Advanced Telecom. and Learning Techs., 1996—, dir. Acad. Advanced Telecomm. and Lng. Techs., 1996—, Dist. prof. math. and engring., 1998—; chair in sci. computing Mobil Tech. Co., 1999—, Harrison Endowed chair in Sci., 1999—; adj. prof. Rice U., Houston, 1980-84, U. Tex., Houston, 1998—; cons. oil cos., Norway, Mex., France, Bulgaria, Wyo., Tex., Calif., N.Mex., Colo., 1982—; adv. Res. Inst. for Petroleum, Beijing, 1987—; mem. steering com. Ctr. for Fluid Dynamics and Geoscis., Columbia, S.C., 1987—; hon. prof. Shandong (China) U., 1987; adv. bd. Ctr. Sci. Computing, Jyväskylä, Finland, Improved Oil Recovery Ctr., Bergen, Norway, 1990—, Interdisciplinary Ctr. Computational Sci., Heidelberg, Germany, 1992—, Inst. Biosci. Tech., Houston, 1992—, acad. adv. bd. Dow Chem., 1994—; exec. com. Partnership Computational Scis., Oak Ridge Nat. Lab., 1991—; pres. Environ. Modelling and Analysis Corp., 1991—; mem. sci. adv. bd. Inst. for Math. Scis., Alta., Can., 1996—; hon. guest rschr. Wuhan U., China, 1997—; adj. prof. U. Tex., Houston, 1998—; mem. sci. bd. Indsl. Math. Inst., U. S.C., 1999—. Author: The Mathematics of Reservoir Simulation, 1983, Mathematical Modeling in Energy and Environmental Sciences, 1988; contbr. articles to sci. jours., chpts. to books. Cubmaster Boy Scouts Am., Dallas, 1981, Webelos leader, 1982, asst. scoutleader, Laramie, 1984, asst. scoutmaster, College Station, 1995—. Recipient numerous rsch. grants NSF, Dept. Energy, NRC, DOD, oil cos., others, 1978—. Fellow AAAS; mem. Soc. Petroleum Engrs., Soc. Indsl. and Applied Math. (trustee 1986-93), Am. Math. Soc., Math. Assn. Am., Internat. Assn. for Math. and Computers in Simulation, Internat. Assn. Computer Mech. (trustee 1991—), Inst. for Advancement Sci. Computing (trustee 1987-93), Geoscis. Inst. (bd. dirs. 1988-92), N.Y. Acad. Scis., Internat. Computer Club (sci. coun. 1989—). Democrat. Avocations: skiing, tennis, stamp and coin collecting. Home: 2004 Indian Trl College Station TX 77845-5600

EWING, ROBERT CLARK, lawyer; b. Lower Merion, Pa., Nov. 26, 1957; m. Cheralynn Kennedy, Mar. 22, 1986; children: Edward, Jaesun; stepchildren: Kristin, Shannon. BS in Fin., Pa. State U., 1980; JD, Villanova U., 1983. Bar: Pa. 1983, U.S. Dist. Ct. (ea. dist.) Pa. 1985, U.S. Ct. Appeals (3rd cir.) 1987, U.S. Supreme Ct. 1987. Ranger Pa. State Park Svc., 1976-78, Valley Forge Nat. Park, 1979; police officer Ocean City (Md.) Police Dept., 1980-81, Springfield Twp. Delaware County, 1992-99; assoc. Lagoy & Lyons, West Chester, Pa., 1983-86, Ronald H. Silverman, P.C., King of Prussia, Pa., 1986-88, Anthony J. McNulty & Assocs., Media, Pa., 1988-91; pvt. practice Media, Pa., 1991—. Contbr. articles to profl. jours. Mem. Lima (Pa.) Fire Co., 1973—, bd. dirs., 1981-88; mem. Media (Pa.) Fire Co., 1988—; bd. dirs. Hank Nacrelli Scholarship Fund, 1988-97, Delaware County Emergency Health Svcs. Coun., 1986-93; active Delaware County Critical Incident Stress Mgmt. Program, Media, 1987—. Mem. Delaware County Bar Assn., Delaware County Firemen's Assn. Office: 115 N Monroe St PO Box 1468 Media PA 19063-8468

EWING, RUSSELL CHARLES, II, physician; b. Tucson, Aug. 16, 1941; s. Russell Charles and Sue M. (Sawyer) E.; children: John Charles, Susan Lenore. BS, Ariz., 1963; MD, George Washington U., 1967. Diplomate Am. Bd. Family Practice. Intern L.A. County-U. So. Calif. Med. Ctr., L.A., 1967-68; gen. practice in medicine and surgery Yorba Linda and Placentia, Calif., 1970-90, Brea, Calif., 1996-97; mem. staff St. Jude's Hosp., Fullerton, Calif., 1970-98, Placentia Linda Cmty. Hosp., 1972-98; vice chief staff, 1977-78, chief staff, 1978-80, bd. dirs., 1974-81; sec., dir. Yorba Linda Med. Group, Inc., 1974-90; bd. dirs. We. Empire Savs. & Loan Assn., Calif. Bd. dirs. Yorba Linda YMCA, 1973-88, pres., 1973-74, 81. With USN, 1968-70. Fellow Am. Acad. Family Practice; mem. AMA, Am. Coll. Physician Execs., Calif. Med. Assn. (house of dels. 1978-90, 92—, trustee 1990-92), Orange County Med. Assn. (bd. dirs. 1983-90, pres. 1988-89). Republican. Episcopalian. E-mail: rce.md@juno.com. Home and Office: 2400 Natoma Station Dr Apt 286 Folsom CA 95630-8173

EWING, SCOTT EDWIN, physician, psychiatrist, educator, researcher; b. Seattle, July 2, 1956; s. Edwin Stanley Jr. and Mary Alice (Castleman) E.; m. Eileen Smith, June 9, 1990; 1 child, Edwin Stanley III. BS, U. Mich., 1980; DO, Chgo. Coll. Osteo. Medicine, 1989. Diplomate Am. Osteo. Bd. Neurology and Psychiatry; MD, Mass. Resident in psychiatry Mass. Gen. Hosp., Boston, 1991-94; clin. fellow in psychiatry Harvard Med. Sch., Boston, 1991-94; chief resident in psychiatry Mass. Gen. Hosp., Boston, 1993-94; fellow in psychopharmacology Harvard Med. Sch., Boston, 1994-95; psychiatrist in charge short term unit McLean Hosp., Belmont, Mass., 1995-96; instr. in psychiatry Harvard Med. Sch., Boston, 1995—; dir. depression and anxiety disorders outpatient clinic McLean Hosp., Belmont, 1996—; cons. Harvard Pilgrim Health Plan, Boston, 1995—. Contbg. author: (book) Challenges in Psychiatric Treatment: Pharmacologic and Psychosocial Strategies, 1996; patentee in field. Mem. Nat. Trust for Hist. Preservation, Washington, 1995—. Recipient Outstanding Resident award NIMH, 1992, Laughlin fellowship Am. Coll. Psychiatrists, 1993, Dupont-Warren fellowship Harvard Med. Sch. Dept. of Psychiatry, 1994-95, Livingston award, 1995. Mem. AMA, Am. Psychiat. Assn., Am. Osteo. Assn., N.Y. Acad. Scis., Am. Coll. Neuropsychiatrists, Harvard Club of Boston, Harvard Faculty Club, Sigma Sigma Phi. Avocations: creative writing, photography, athletics. Office: McLean Hosp/Harvard Med Sch 115 Mill St Belmont MA 02478-1041

EWING, SIDNEY ALTON, veterinary medical educator, parasitologist; b. Emory University, Ga., Dec. 1, 1934; s. Aubrey Coleman and Grace Eliza (Prickett) E.; m. Margaret Jane Steffens, Aug. 16, 1963; children—Holly Annette, Ann Krull, Leah Grace. BSA, DVM, U. Ga., 1958; MS, U. Wis., 1960; PhD, Okla. State U., 1964. Instr. U. Wis., 1960; mem. faculty Okla. State U. at Stillwater, 1960-65, 68-72, prof., head dept. vet. parasitology, microbiology and public health, 1968-72, 79-84, prof., 1984-91, interim assoc. dean for acad. affairs, 1991-92, Wendell H./Nellie G. Krull endowed prof. vet. parasitology, 1992—; assoc. prof. Kans. State U., 1965-67; prof., head dept. Miss. State U., 1967-68; prof., dean Coll. Vet. Medicine, U. Minn., St. Paul, 1972-78; mem. adv. bd. Morris Animal Found., Denver, 1967-69, cons., 1969-78; mem. animal health com. NRC, 1971-75; mem. adv. panel U.S. Pharmacopeial Conv., 1980-95. Recipient Outstanding Tchr. of Yr. award Okla. State U. Coll. Vet. Medicine, 1970, SmithKline Beecham award for rsch. excellence Okla. State U., 1991, A.M. Mills award for outstanding contbns. to vet. medicine, 1993, Good Neighbor award Radio Sta. WCCO, Mpls.-St. Paul, 1978; commendation Gov. Minn., 1978; named Veterinarian of Yr., State of Okla., 1997. Mem. AAUP, AVMA, Am. Assn. Vet. Parasitologists, Am. Soc. Parasitologists, Am. Vet. History Soc., Am. Soc. Rickettsiology, World Assn. Advancement Vet. Parasitology, Conf. Rsch. Workers in Animal Diseases (coun. 1980-85, v.p. 1983-84, pres. 1984-85), Soc. Vector Ecology, Soc. Tropical Vet. Medicine, Minn. Vet. Med. Assn., Okla. Vet. Med. Assn., N.Y. Acad. Scis., Southwestern Assn. of Parasitologists, Sigma Xi, Phi Kappa Phi, Phi Zeta, Alpha Zeta, Alpha Psi (past nat. pres.), Gamma Sigma Delta, Aghon, Omicron Delta Kappa. Office: Dept Infectious Diseases and Physiology Okla State U Stillwater OK 74078

EWING, SUSAN R., artist, educator; b. Lawrenceville, Ill., 1955. AA in Music, Stephens Coll., 1974; BA in Jewelry, Metalsmithing, Ind. U., 1976, MFA in Jewelry, Metalsmithing, 1980. Head metals program Miami (Ohio) U., 1981—; Please provide your full middle name. One-woman shows include Hans Hansen Sølv, Copenhagen, Denmark; group shows include Aspects Gallery, London, Park Ryu Sook Gallery, Seoul, Korea, Schweizerisches Landesmuseum, Zurich, Switzerland, Cercle Mcpl. Galerie Oféo, Luxembourg, Mus. Kunsthandwerk, Frankfurt, Germany, Deutsches Klingenmuseum, Solingen, Germany, Schmuckmuseum, Pforzheim, Germany, Galerie Matter, Cologne, Germany, Galerie Ende, Cologne, Mathildenhohe Mus., Darmstadt, Germany, Galerie Spectrum, Munich, Germany, Galerie Ventil, Munich, Fortunoff's N.Y.C., Urban BobKat Gallery, N.Y.C., Lever House, N.Y.C., Seventh Regiment Armory, N.Y.C., Am. Craft Mus., N.Y.C.; represented in permanent collections White House. Recipient Dolibois Faculty Devel. award, disting. Lifetime Achievement award Ohio Designer Craftsmen; Summer Rsch. fellow Miami U., Ohio Arts Coun. Individual Artist fellow, 1987, 89, 91, Fulbright grantee, 1997; Rsch. Challenge grantee Ohio State Bd. Regents. Office: Sch Art Fine Arts Dept Miami U Oxford OH 45056

EWING, THOMAS WILLIAM, congressman, lawyer; b. Atlanta, Ill., Sept. 19, 1935; m. Connie Lupo, 1981; children: Jane, Kathryn, Sam, Christine Lupo, John Lupo, Stephanie Lupo. BS, Millikin U., 1957; JD, John Marshall Law Sch., Chgo., 1968. Asst. state atty. Livingston County, 1968-73; ptnr. Satter Ewing Beyer & Spires, Pontiac, Ill., 1969-91; mem. Ill. Ho. of Reps., 1974-91; mem. 102nd, 103rd and 105th-106th Congresses from 15th Ill. Dist., 1991—, mem. sci. com., agr. com., transp. and infrastructure coms.; mem. agr. com. Ill. Ho. Reps., chmn. subcom. on risk mgmt. and specialty crops, subcom. on dept. ops., nutrition and fgn. agr., transp. and infrastructure com., aviation subcom., water resources and environment subcom., joint econ. com., former dep. minority leader, chmn. policy com., house revenue com., 1980, co-chmn. Ill. Econ. and Fiscal Commn., co-chmn. Legis. Space Needs Commn. Rep. precinct committeeman; del. Rep. Nat. Conv., 1980, 84, 88; committeeman 15th Congl. Dist., 1986-93. With U.S. Army, 1958, USAR, 1957-63. Recipient Best Legislator award Nat. Rep. Legislator of the Yr. award, 1982, Ill. Small Businessmen Assn., 1983, 85, 87, Friend of Agr. award Ill. Agrl. Assn., 1985, 87, 89, 91, Legislator of Yr. award Ill. Assn. Homes for the Aging, 1986. Mem. Livingston County Bar Assn., Pontiac C. of C. (past exec. dir., past pres.), Livingston County Farm Bur., Elks, Moose, Masons. Methodist. Home: 310 W Lincoln St Pontiac IL 61764-2511 Office: US Ho of Reps 2417 Rayburn Washington DC 20515-1315*

EWING, WAYNE HILLEY, film producer, director, writer; b. Washington (D.C.), Oct. 25, 1948; s. Frank Marion and Joanne (Bacon) E. BA, Yale Coll., 1970; MA in Communications, U. Tex., 1971. Prin. Wayne Ewing Films, Aspen, Colo., 1972—. Producer, dir. TV spls.: If Elected, 1972, Cowboys, 1974, Copland at 75, 1975, A Journey to Russia, 1983, The Bloods of 'Nam, 1987, Gangs, Cops and Drugs, 1989, The New Hollywood, 1990; producer, dir. TV series: Six Great Ideas with Bill Moyers, 1982; dir. TV spl.: Women Behind Bars, 1988; dir., dir. photography Homicide: Life on the Street, 1993. Office: Wayne Ewing Films PO Box 1751 Aspen CO 81612-1751

EWING, WAYNE TURNER, coal company executive; b. Beech Creek, Ky., Dec. 1, 1933; s. O.E. and Elizabeth E.; m. Jane Gray, June 3, 1960; children—Allyson, Sally. B.A., Georgetown Coll.; M.A., Western Ky. U. With Peabody Coal Co., 1963-85; pres. Peabody Coal Co., St. Louis, 1983-85, Peabody Devel. Co., St. Louis, 1985-90; cons. Peabody Holding Co., St. Louis, 1992-93; sr. v.p. Kerr McGee Corp., Oklahoma City, 1993-96; owner The Ewing Co., Bonita Springs, Fla., 1996—. With U.S. Army, 1955-57.

Mem. Nat. Mining Assn., Ill. Coal Assn., Pelican Nest Country Club. Fax: 941-948-0719.

EWOH, ANDREW IKEH EMMANUEL, political science educator; b. Enugu, Nigeria, Nov. 20, 1959; came to U.S., 1981; s. Lazarus Ngene and Virginia Nnenna (Ani) E.; divorced; children: Tyrone, Emmanuel, Andy, Chelsey. BS in Bus. Adminstrn., U. Southwestern La., 1984; MPA in Pub. Adminstrn., So. U., Baton Rouge, 1986; MA in Polit. Economy, U. Tex., Dallas, 1991, PhD in Polit. Economy, 1993. Grad. intern Office Housing and Tech. Assistance La. Dept. Urban and Community Affairs, Baton Rouge, 1985-86; teaching asst. So. U., Baton Rouge, 1985-86; teaching asst. Sch. Social Scis., U. Tex.-Dallas, Richardson, 1990-92, rsch. asst., 1991, instr., 1993; instr. bus. divsn. Richland Coll., Dallas, 1993; adj. prof. dept. pub. affairs Tex. So. U., Houston, 1986-89, 93; adj. prof. Sch. Bus. and Pub. Adminstrn. U. Houston-Clear Lake, 1994; asst. prof. polit. sci. Prairie View (Tex.) A&M U., 1993—; vis. scholar Iowa Social Sci. Inst., U. Iowa, Iowa City, 1997. Editor in Chief: African Soc. Sci. Review; acting editor Issues in Polit. Economy, 1991-92; contbr. articles to profl. jours. Grad. rsch. fellow Tex. Higher Edn. Coord. Bd., Rsch. Programs Divsn., Austin, Tex., 1990, grad. fellow Minnie K. Patton Scholarship Found., 1991-92, 92-93. Fellow Acad. Polit. Sci.; mem. Am. Soc. Pub. Adminstrn. (mem. Pub. Com.), Assn. for Budgeting and Fin. Mgmt., Am. Acad. Polit. and Social Sci., Am. Polit. Sci. Assn., Ctr. for Study of Presidency, Southwestern Social Sci. Assn. Home: PO Box 691824 Houston TX 77269-1824

EWY, GORDON ALLEN, cardiologist, researcher, educator; b. Brenham, Kans., Aug. 5, 1933; s. Marvin John and Hazel Miller (Allen) E.; m. Priscilla Ruth Weldon; children: Kim Elizabeth, Gordon Stuart, Mark Allen. BA, U. Kans., 1955, MD, 1961. Resident, house officer Georgetown U. Hosp., Washington, 1961-64, cardiology fellow, 1964-65; instr. in medicine Georgetown U., Washington, 1965-68, asst. prof., 1968-69; asst. prof. U. Ariz., Tucson, 1969-70, assoc. prof., 1970-75, prof. medicine, 1975—, chief cardiology, dir. cardiology fellowship program, 1982—, assoc. head dept. medicine, 1986-94, dir. Sarver Heart Ctr., 1991—. Editor: Cardiovascular Drugs and Management of Heart Disease, 1982, 93, Current Cardiovascular Drug Therapy, 1984; author numerous sci. publs.; contbr. numerous revs. to profl. jours., chpts. to books. Lt. (j.g.) USNR, 1955-57. Fellow ACP, Am. Heart Assn. (mem. clin. coun., nat. faculty advanced cardiac life support 1982-84, chmn. nat. programs subcom. 1982, bd. dirs. Ariz. chpt. 1975-82, 84-89, tchg. fellow 1970-75), Am. Coll. Cardiology (chmn. learning ctr. com. 1988-91, trustee 1992-97), Alpha Omega Alpha. Republican. Avocation: travel. Office: Ariz Health Scis Ctr 1501 N Campbell Ave Tucson AZ 85724-0001

EX, TOM, sculptor, gallery owner; b. Traverse City, Mich., June 1, 1948; s. Earl Francis and Margaret (Lipke) E.; m. Sharon Marcel Siver, June 22, 1968 (div. May 1998); children: Seth, Samantha. Student, Western Mich. U., Kalamazoo, 1966-67, Bakersfield (Calif.) C.C., 1973, No. Mich. U., Marquette, 1974-76. Carpenter McGann's Bldg. Supply, Inc., Hancock, Mich., 1976-79; owner Tom Ex Renovating & Restoration, Hubbell, Mich., 1979-87; sculptor Tom Ex Sculpture Studio, Houghton, Mich., 1987—; owner Tosh Gallery, Houghton, 1994—. Pub. commd. white cedar sculptures, 1994, 96, 97; commd. copper and white cedar sculpture Kalamazoo Brewing Co., 1994, 15-ft. white cedar sculpture Guardian of the Waters, Forum for Kalamazoo County, Mich., 1996. Trustee Cmty. Arts Ctr., Hancock, 1996-97; v.p. Houghton Bus. Assn., 1996, chmn. Downtown Improvement com., 1997, bd. dirs., 1998—. With U.S. Army, 1968-71, Korea. Recipient profl. devel. grant Mich. Coun. Arts and Cultural Affairs, 1993, artist in industry grant Mich. Coun. Arts and Cultural Affairs, 1994, Spl. Beautificaiton award City of Houghton, 1996. Mem. Internat. Sculpture Ctr. Avocations: cross country skiing, jogging, mountain biking, weight lifting. Office: Tosh Gallery 315 Shelden Ave Houghton MI 49931-2135

EXLEY, BEN, III, retired pharmaceutical company executive; b. Wheeling, W.Va., Aug. 29, 1911; s. Ben Jr. and Jessie Warfield (Lane) E.; m. Eleanor Wright Drinkard, Oct. 26, 1942; children: Ben IV, Robert Banford, Paul Wright. BS in Pharmacy, W.Va. U., 1934; postgrad., Harvard U., 1943. Lic. pharmacist, W.Va. Salesman Ohio Valley Drug Co., Wheeling, 1934-39, v.p., 1939-50; v.p. Ohio Valley Drug Co./Clarksburg (W.Va.) Drug Co., 1950-77, chmn. bd. dirs., 1977-95; sr. chmn. Ohio Valley Clarksburg div. Ohio Valley-Clarksburg Inc. (A Cardinal Health Co.), 1990-95, ret., 1995; bd. dirs. Fulton Bank and Trust Co., Wheeling. Vice chmn. Wheeling Housing Authority Bd., Wheeling. Served to capt. AUS and USAF, 1942-46. Mem. W.Va. U. Pharmacy Alumni Assn. (pres. 1965-66, Outstanding Alumnus award 1966, Outstanding Service to Sch. Pharmacy 1981, 50 Yrs. Service to Health Profession 1984), Ohio, Ky., Ind. and Mich. Drug Club (past pres.), Ohio-Marshall County Pharmacists Assn. (past pres.), Kappa Kappa Psi, Kappa Psi, Theta Chi. Republican. Presbyterian. Club: Wheeling (W.Va.) Country. Lodges: Masons, Shriners, Rotary (past bd. dirs.). Avocations: golf, skiing. Home: 23 Aaron Way Wheeling WV 26003*

EXLEY, WINSTON WALLACE, middle school educator; b. Clyo, Ga., July 1, 1941; s. Miller Franklin and Marie Amanda Exley; m. Marsha Ann Tatum, 1964 (div. 1977); children: Lisa Star Exley Woods, Winston Wallace; m. Sarah Dianne Phillips Brown, Mar. 27, 1986; children: Mindy D. Brown, S. Angela Brown. AB, Newberry Coll., 1963; MEd in Social Sci., Ga. So. U., 1976. Cert. social sci. tchr., supr., Ga., S.C. Social studies tchr. Effingham County High Sch., Springfield, Ga., 1963-83, supervising tchr., 1967-83; staff, student tchr. supr. program Ga. Southern Univ., 1968-83; head dept. social scis. Effingham County High Sch., Springfield, Ga., 1980-83; social studies tchr. Hilton Head (S.C.) Middle Sch., 1983—; head dept. social studies McCracken Mid. Sch., Hilton Head, 1988—, team leader 7th grade, 1990—; mem. individual/campus tchr. dist. com., mem. incentive pay com. Beaufort (S.C.) County Schs., 1984-89; mem. com. Nat. Geography Bee, State of S.C., 1988-91; advisor Allied Med. Careers Club, Springfield, 1968-76; part time instr. Savannah Area Vocat. Tech. Sch., 1970-83. Author curriculum guide in field. Sunday sch. tchr. Laurel Hill Luth. Ch., Ga., 1966-73. With USAF, 1958-64. Beaufort County Schs. grantee, 1990-91, 91-92. Mem. ASCD, Salsburger Hist. Sco., Coun. Social Sci., Phi Kappa Phi. Democrat. Avocations: farming, boating, guitar, naturalist, writing poetry. Home: 4121 Highway 119 N Clyo GA 31303-3629 Office: Hilton Head Mid Sch Wilborn Rd Hilton Head Island SC 29926

EXNER, ADAM, archbishop; b. Killaly, Sask., Can., Dec. 24, 1928. Ordained priest Roman Catholic Ch., 1957, consecrated bishop, 1974. Bishop of Kamloops B.C., Can., 1974-82; archbishop of Winnipeg Man., Can., 1982-91; archbishop of Vancouver B.C., Can., 1991—. Office: Archdiocese of Vancouver, 150 Robson St, Vancouver, BC Canada V6B 2A7*

EXON, J(OHN) JAMES, former senator; b. Lake Andes, S.D., Aug. 9, 1921; s. John James and Luella (Johns) E.; m. Patricia Ann Pros, Sept. 18, 1943; children: Stephen, Pamela, Candace. Student, U. Omaha, 1939-41; LLD (hon.), Creighton U., 1991, Doane Coll., 1995; LittD (hon.), U. Nebr., 1997. Mgr. Universal Finance Corp., Nebr., 1946-53; pres. Exon's, Inc., Lincoln, Nebr., 1954-71; gov. State of Nebr., 1971-79; mem. U.S. Senate, Nebr., 1979-96; mem. Armed Svcs. Com., ranking Min. mem. of budget com., ranking Min. mem. commerce, sci. and transp. subcom. of consumer affairs, fgn. commerce and tourism. Active state, local, nat. Democratic coms., 1952—; del. Dem. Nat. Conv., 1964, 72, 74, 76, 88, 92; former Dem. nat. committeeman. Served with Signal Corps AUS, 1942-45. Mem. Am. Legion, VFW, Masons (33rd degree), Shriners, Elks, Eagles, Optimist Internat. Home: 1615 Brent Blvd Lincoln NE 68506-1867*

EYERMAN, DAVID JOHN, software engineer; b. Oak Park, Ill., June 14, 1966; s. Thomas Jude and Mary Kathryn (Evans) E.; m. Regan Veasey, Aug. 5, 1995. BS in Computer Sci., Am. U., Washington, 1988, MS in Computer Sci., 1989. Microcomputer project mgr. U.S. Dept. Treasury, Washington, 1987-89; assoc. programmer IBM, Milford, Conn., 1989-90; adv. software engr. IBM, Dallas, 1990-97; tech. cons. Santa Teresa Lab. IBM, San Jose, Calif., 1997—; dir. Thomas J. and Mary Kay Eyerman Found., Chgo., 1992—. Mem. The 500, Inc., Dallas, 1991-97, Voce Forte, The Dallas Opera, 1993-97, Shakespeare Festival of Dallas, 1994-97. Mem. IEEE, Assn. Computing Machinery. Roman Catholic. Avocations: private pilot, cooking, wine. Home: 3649 Copperfield Dr Apt 199 San Jose CA 95136-4056

EYES-PENN, CHIEF PIERCING See TURNBULL, DAVID JOHN

EYLER, JAMES R., judge; b. Westminster, Md., July 13, 1942. AB, U. Md., 1964, LLB magna cum laude, 1967. Bar: Md. 1967, D.C. 1976. Law clk. Ct. Appeals Md., 1967-68; mem. Miles & Stockbridge, Balt., 1968-95; judge Ct. Spl. Appeals Md., Towson, 1995—. Rsch. editor Md. Law Rev., 1966-67. Mem. ABA, Md. State Bar Assn., Bar Assn. Balt. City, Order of Coif. Office: HD Ct of Special Appeals County Cts Bldg Rm M-13 401 Bosley Ave Towson MD 21204-4420*

EYMAN, EARL DUANE, electrical science educator, consultant; b. Canton, Ill., Sept. 24, 1925; s. Arthur Earl and Florence Mabel (Hardin) E.; m. Ruth Margaret Morgan, Apr. 20, 1951; children: Joseph Earl, David James. B.S. in Engring. Physics, U. Ill., 1949, M.S. in Math, 1950, postgrad., 1951-64; postgrad., U. Bradley, 1952-58; Ph.D. in Elec. Engring., U. Colo., 1966. Registered profl. engr., Ill. Scientist Westinghouse Atomic Power Div., Pitts., 1950-51; research engr. Caterpillar Tractor Co., Peoria, Ill., 1951-58, project engr., 1958-66; mem. faculty Bradley U., Peoria, 1952-64; prof. elec. engring. U. Iowa, Iowa City, 1966-92, chmn. elec. engring., 1969-76; cons. Sundstrand Aviation, Denver, 1966, Gould Simulation Systems Div., Melville, N.Y., 1978-81, U.S. Dept. Commerce, Boulder, 1978-92. Author: Modeling Simulation and Control, 1988; contbr. articles to profl. jours. Chmn., mem. Electricians Examining Bd., Iowa City, 1969-74. Served with USNR, 1944-46. Mem. Eta Kappa Nu (mem., pres. internat. bd. 1972-77), Tau Beta Pi, Theta Tau. Avocations: skiing; mountain climbing and hiking. Home: PO Box 3282 Estes Park CO 80517-3282 Office: U Iowa 4400 EB Iowa City IA 52242

EYMAN, RICHARD KENNETH, psychologist, educator; b. Joliet, Ill., Nov. 26, 1931; s. Robert Kennedy and Helen E. (Reick) E.; m. Vivian Kolodziej, Jan. 31, 1959. B.S., U. Ill., Urbana, 1954, M.A., 1955; Ph.D., U. So. Calif., 1966. Diplomate Am. Bd. Profl. Psychology. Personnel research specialist Gen. Motors, South Gate, Calif., 1955-56; asst. research psychologist U.S. Army Def. Human Research Unit, Ft. Bliss, Tex., 1956-58; with Pacific State Hosp., Pomona, Calif., 1958-73; research specialist III Pacific State Hosp., 1967-68; research specialist VA, 1968-73; chief research Pacific State Hosp., 1972-73; asso. research psychologist Pacific State Hosp. research group Neuropsychiat. Inst., UCLA, 1973-75, adj. asso. prof. III, 1975-76, adj. prof., 1976-80, prof.-in-residence, 1980—; research educationist UCLA, 1981; lectr. statistics and edn. U. Calif., Riverside, 1974-81, prof. edn., 1981—; cons. in field. Editorial cons. CHOICE, Assn. Coll. and Research Libraries div. ALA, 1968—, Am. Jour. Mental Deficiency, 1969—, Mental Retardation, 1971—, Hosp. and Community Psychiatry, 1974—, Sci, 1975—, Nature, 1975—; contbr. articles to profl. jours. Bd. dirs. Accreditation Council for Services for Mentally Retarded and Other Devel. Disabled Persons, Washington, 1982—. Served with U.S. Army, 1956-57. Calif. Dept. Mental Hygiene grantee, 1962-64; NIMH grantee, 1964-71; Nat. Inst. Child Health and Human Devel. grantee, 1976-81; Div. Developmental Disabilities Rehab. Services Adminstrn. grantee, 1972-75; Office Econ. Opportunity grantee, 1974-75. Fellow Am. Assn. Mental Deficiency (Research award 1986), Am. Psychol. Assn. (pres. div. 33, 1982-83, Doll award 1997); mem. Am. Acad. Mental Retardation (pres. 1974-75, research adv. bd. 1974—, award 1989), Am. Ednl. Research Assn., Am. Statis. Assn., Psychometric Soc., Western Psychol. Assn., Sigma Xi. Home: 20286 E Lorencita Dr Covina CA 91724-3833 Office: U Calif Sch Edn Riverside CA 92521

EYMAN, ROGER ALLEN, minister; b. Canton, Ill., Mar. 16, 1942; s. Silbert Lionel and Ruth Maxine (Noland) E.; m. Priscilla Ann Baker, Dec. 24, 1979; 1 child, Hans Roger. AA, Orange Coast Coll., Costa Mesa, Calif., 1969; BA in Psychology, Calif. State U., L.A., 1971; MMin, Bethany Theol. Sem., 1975, DMin summa cum laude, 1991. Ordained to ministry Am. Evang. Christian Ch./Gen. Conf., 1983. Missionary Gospel Mission Ch., Liberia, Costa Rica, 1974-76, Wadi Es Sir, Jordan, 1976-79; founder, pastor Ch. of Calvary Grace of Ariz., Tucson, 1984-89, Ch. of Calvary Grace of Alaska, Anchorage, 1989—; ins. claims cons., Anchorage, 1989—. Fellow Internat. Ministerial Fellowship, AECC Gen. Conf., Internat. Chaplains Assn., Alaska Club. Republican. Office: Ch of Calvary Grace Alaska 3107 W Colorado Ave # 241 Colorado Springs CO 80904-2040

EYNON, STEVEN SCOTT, minister; b. Jacksonville, Fla., July 4, 1961; s. John Jerry and Sally Ann (Stevens) E.; m. Lori Lee Hunter, June 25, 1983; children: Christopher, Steven. BA summa cum laude, Fla. Christian Coll., Kissimmee, 1984; MMin, Ky. Christian Coll., 1992. Ordained to ministry Christian Ch., 1984. Min. youth Winter Haven (Fla.) Christian Ch., 1982-84, 1st Christian Ch., Clearwater, Fla., 1985-94; sr. minister Cmty. Christian Ch., Ft. Lauderdale, Fla., 1994—; adj. instr. Fla. Christian Coll., 1988, 90, sec. of trustee, 1996-98; v.p. Fla. Christian Youth Conv., Orlando, 1986; bd. dirs. Christianville Mission, Haiti, 1991-96, chmn. bd. dirs., 1993-94; v.p. Fla. Christian Conv., 1998, pres. 1999. Author: (with others) Ideas, vol. 42, 1987, Good Stuff, vol. 4, 1988. Mem. Nat. Right to Life, Washington, 1983-93; vol. Spl. Olympics, Clearwater, 1985-94; scouting coord. Boy Scouts Am., Clearwater, 1986-94; pres. Fla. Christian Coll. Alumni Assn., Kissimmee, 1987-88, v.p., 1985-87; bd. trustees Fla. Christian Coll., 1995—; pres. South Fla. Minister's Assn., 1997-98. Named Outstanding Young Min., N.Am. Christian Conv., 1989. Mem. Christ in Youth Planning Coun. (advisor 1986-88), Christian Edn. Conf. (dir. 1988), Nat. Eagle Scout Assn. Home: 9590 NW 31st Pl Sunrise FL 33351-7157 Office: Community Christian Ch 155 N Hiatus Rd Fort Lauderdale FL 33325-2526

EYNON, THOMAS GRANT, sociology educator; b. Evanston, Ill. Aug. 10, 1926; s. John and Ruth (Deal) E.; m. Janet Arstingstall, Nov. 24, 1956; children: James Walter, John Robert, Sarah Carolyn. BS in Psychology, Ohio State U., 1953, MA in Anthropology (Scott fellow), 1955, PhD in Criminology and Sociology, 1959. Asst. prof. to assoc. prof. Ohio State U., 1959-68; prof. sociology So. Ill. U., 1968—, dir. grad. studies, 1986-93, dir. undergrad. studies, 1993-96; vis. prof. St. Lawrence U., 1962-70, U. Minn., 1970-75, U. Stockholm, 1972, Nat. U. Ireland, Galway and Dublin, Queens U. Belfast, Oxford U., London Sch. Econs., U. Leeds, 1973, Ill. Inst. Tech. Rsch. Inst., 1974, Niigata Japan, 1991, 92, 93, 96, 97, 98; dir. Social Sci. Rsch. Bur., 1977-79; commr. Ill. Juvenile Justice Commn., 1983-95; mem. Gov.'s Task Force on Prison Crowding, 1983-84, Task Force Released Prisoners, 1988-89. Mem. adv. bd. Ill. Dept. Corrections, 1970-79, chmn., 1979—; chmn. Reading Is Fundamental Program, 1978-87; mem. Gov.'s Task Force Mental Health, 1970-72. Served as naval aviator USNR, 1944-51, PTO, Korea. Decorated Silver Star, Purple Heart, D.F.C.; recipient Sturges Pub. Svc. award, 1998. Methodist. Mem. Midwest Sociol. Soc. (treas. 1987—). Author: Offender Classification in the United States, 1976. Editor Sociol. Quar., 1981-84. Contbr. numerous articles and revs. to profl. jours., chpts. in books. Office: So Ill U Dept Sociology Carbondale IL 62901 *If no one misses me I wasn't there, and if I am remembered let it be for my faith, hope, and charity.**

EYRE, IVAN, artist; b. Tullymet, Sask., Can., Apr. 15, 1935; s. Thomas and Kay E.; m. Brenda Fenske, June 14, 1957; children: Keven, Tyrone. Mem. faculty U. N.D., 1958-59; mem. faculty U. Man., Winnipeg, Can., 1959-92, prof. drawing and painting, 1975-92, head drawing dept., 1974-78, prof. emeritus, 1994—. *A self-styled radical, Eyre has created a distinctive world using the subjects of landscape and the human figure. In 1988 he was the first contemporary painter to have a solo exhibition at the new national gallery in Ottawa, Canada. In 1998, in recognition of his accomplishments, an entire floor of some 5000 square feet in the Pavilion Gallery in Assiniboine Park, Winnipeg, has been devoted to the permanent display of his work. To this newest showcase of art in Manitoba he is donating 5000 of his drawings, paintings, prints and sculptures.* One-man shows include: Montreal Mus. Fine Arts, 1964, Winnipeg Art Gallery, 1964, 66, 74, 82, 88, 92, Fleet Galleries, Winnipeg, 1965, 69, 71, Albert White Galleries, Toronto, 1965, Atelier Vincitore Gallery, Brighton, Eng., 1967, Yellow Door Gallery, Winnipeg, 1966, Mount Allison U., 1968, Mendel Art Gallery, Saskatoon, 1968, Jerrold Morris Gallery, Toronto, 1969, 71, 73, Frankfurter Kunst Kabinett, Frankfurt, Ger., 1973, Burnaby Art Gallery, 1973, McIntosh Gallery, U. W. Ont., 1973, Siemens Werk, Erlangen, Germany, 1974, N.B. Mus., St. John, 1976, Gallery I.I.I., U. Manitoba, 1977, 94, Nat. Gallery Can., Ottawa, 1978, Equinox Gallery, Vancouver, 1978, 81, 82, Robert McLaughlin Gallery, Oshawa, 1980, Mira Godard Gallery, Toronto, 1978, 79, 80, 90, 92, 94, 96, 99, Rodman Hall Arts Centre, St. Catherines, Ont., 1980, Art Gallery Windsor, Ont., 1981, Beaverbrook Art Gallery, Fredericton, N.B., 1981, London (Ont.) Regional Art Gallery, 1981, Sir George Williams Galleries, Montreal, 1981, MacDonald Stewart Art Centre, Guelph, Ont., 1981, Brian Melnychenko Gallery, Winnipeg, 1981, 87, The Ctr. for Inter-Am. Rels. N.Y., 1982, Burlington (Ont.) Art Ctr., 1982, Winnipeg Art Gallery, 1982, Can. Cultural Centre, Paris, 1982, Can. House Gallery, London, Eng., 1982, Talbot Rice Gallery, Edinburgh, Scotland, 1982, The Art Gallery of Greater Victoria, Can., 1973, 82, 99, Evelyn Aimis Fine Art Gallery, Toronto, 1985, 87, The Nat. Gallery of Can., Ottawa, 1988, Ivan Eyre: Personal Mythologies: Images of the Milieu: Figurative Paintings 1957 to 1988 touring Can., Winnipeg Art Gallery, 1989, Nickle Arts Mus., Calgary, 1989, Edmonton Art Gallery, 1989, London (Can.) Regional Art Gallery, 1989; 49th Parallel Gallery, N.Y.C., 1988, Edmonton Art Gallery, 1995, Mackenzie Art Gallery, 1996, Assiniboine Park Pavilion Gallery, 1998; group shows include: London Regional Art Gallery, 1964, Agnes Lefort Gallery, Montreal, 1964, Nat. Gallery, Ottawa, 1965, 67, 74, Yellow Door Gallery, Winnipeg, 1965, Art Gallery of Ont., Toronto, 1968, Montreal Mus. Fine Arts, 1964, 70, 76, Primera Biennial Americana De Artes Graficas, Cali, Columbia, 1971, Art Gallery Ont., 1970, 76, Winnipeg Art Gallery, 1967, 76, 90, 92, 95, Glenbow-Alta. Inst., Calgary, 1976, Vancouver Art Gallery, 1977, Mendel Art Gallery, Saskatoon, 1977, 82, Harbourfront Art Gallery, Toronto, 1977, Edmonton (Alta., Can.) Art Gallery, 1981, Printworld, U.S., 1982, Barcelona, Spain, 1982, Seattle Art Fair, 1987, L.A. Art Fair, 1986, 87, Chgo. Art Fair, 1989, Maison de la Culture Cotes-des-Neiges, Montreal, 1992, Galerie de la Ville Dollard-des-Ormeaux, Que., Can. Coun. Art Bank, 1993, Drabinsky Gallery, Toronto, 1993, Hong Kong Art Fair, 1993, Expo '93, Taejon, South Korea, 1993, Loch and Mayberry Fine Art, Winnipeg, 1997, Mira Godard Gallery, Toronto, 1998, Royal Can. Acad. Arts Prairie Region Exhbn., Winnipeg, 1997, travelling to Regina, 1998, Calgary, 1998, Victoria, 1999; represented in permanent collections, Assiniboine Pk. Pavilion Gallery Art Collection, Winnipeg, Winnipeg Art Gallery, Nat. Gallery, Ottawa, Vancouver Art Gallery, Montreal Mus. Fine Arts, Art Gallery Ont., Toronto. Decorated Queen's Silver Jubilee medal, 1977; recipient Gold medal Acad. of Italy, 1980, Jubilee award U. Man. Alumni, 1982, Outstanding Achievement medal Internat. Biograph. Ctr., 1998; sr. grantee Can. Coun., 1966, 77; Molson prize nominee, 1996. Mem. Royal Can. Acad. Arts. Subject of book Ivan Eyre (Woodcock), 1981; subject of various documentary films. Home: 1098 Des Trappistes St, Winnipeg, MB Canada R3V 1B8

EYRE, PAMELA CATHERINE, retired army officer; b. Chgo., Nov. 3, 1948; d. Francis Thomas and Jane (Burd) E. BA, Ctrl. State U. Okla., 1972; MPA, U. Okla., 1976; postgrad., U. Tex., 1998—. Commd. 2d lt. U.S. Army, 1973, advanced through grades to lt. col., 1991; test and evaluation officer U.S. Army, Ft. Gordon, Ga., 1982-85; R&D coord. U.S. Army, Ft. Monmouth, N.J., 1985-88; with army gen. staff Pentagon U.S. Army, Washington, 1988-91, acquisition policy staff officer Army Secretariat Pentagon, 1991-94, asst. project mgr. Def. Telecom. Svc., 1994-95, test and evaluation officer Army Secretariat Pentagon, 1995-96; ret., 1996. Home: 8222 Summer Place Dr Austin TX 78759

EYRING, HENRY BENNION, bishop; b. Princeton, N.J., May 31, 1933; s. Henry and Mildred (Bennion) E.; m. Kathleen Johnson, July 27, 1962; children: Henry J., Stuart J., Matthew J., John B., Elizabeth, Mary Kathleen. BS, U. Utah, 1955; MBA, Harvard U., 1959, PhD, 1963; D of Humanities (hon.), Brigham Young U., 1985. Asst., then assoc. prof. Stanford U., Palo Alto, Calif., 1962-71; pres. Ricks Coll., Rexburg, Idaho, 1972-77; dep. commr. edn., then commr. LDS Ch., Salt Lake City, 1977-85, presiding bishopric, 1985-92, mem. 1st Quorum of the Seventy, 1992-95, mem. Quorum of the Twelve, 1995—. Author: To Draw Closer to God, 1997; co-author: The Organizational World, 1973. With USAF, 1955-57. Sloan faculty fellow MIT, 1963-64. Avocations: swimming, painting, wood carving. Office: LDS Ch Quorum of the Twelve 47 E South Temple Salt Lake City UT 84150-1005*

EYSTER, MARY ELAINE, hematologist, educator; b. York, Pa., Mar. 21, 1935; d. Charles Gable and Marcia Viola (Schriver) E.; m. Robert E. Dye, Jan. 2, 1965; children: Robert E., Charles. AB, Duke U., 1956, MD, 1960. Intern. N.Y. Hosp.-Cornell Med. Coll., N.Y.C., 1960-61, resident in medicine, 1961-63, fellow in hematology, 1963-66, instr. medicine, 1966-67, asst. prof. medicine, 1967-70; asst. prof. medicine Milton S. Hershey Med. Ctr. Pa. State U., Hershey, 1970-73, assoc. prof. Milton S. Hershey Med. Ctr., 1973-82, prof. Milton S. Hershey Med. Ctr., 1982—, chief hematology divsn., dept. medicine Coll. Medicine, 1973-96; bd. dirs. Hemophilia Ctr. Cen. Pa., 1973—, AIDS Clin. Trials Unit Pa. State U., 1987—; faculty rsch. assoc. Am. Cancer Soc., 1966-71; mem. State Hemophilia Adv. Com, 1973—, chmn., 1977-79, 1988-90; mem. policy bd. Coop. F VII inhibitor study Nat. Heart, Lung and Blood Inst., 1975-79; mem. med. and sci. adv. counc. Nat. Hemophilia Found., 1976-77, 83-89, chmn. med. adv. com. Del. Valley chpt., 1979-82; co-investigator, mem. multi-agy. task force on AIDS HHS, 1982-83; mem. blood products adv. com. FDA, 1985-89; exec. com. NIH-NIAID Clin. Trials, 1988-90; mem. forum on blood safety and availability Inst. of Med., 1993-95. USPHS grantee, 1976-95. Fellow ACP; mem. Pa. Med. Soc., Am. Fedn. Clin. Rsch., World Fedn. Hemophilia, Am. Soc. Hematology, Am. Assn. Blood Banks, Internat. Soc. Thrombosis and Haemostasis, Internat. Soc. Hematology, Pa. Soc. Hematology, Oncology (bd. dirs. 1982-85), Am. Heart Assn. Coun. on Thrombosis, Phi Beta Kappa, Alpha Omega Alpha. Office: Milton S Hershey Med Ctr PO Box 850 Hershey PA 17033-0850

EYTON, JOHN TREVOR, senator, business executive; b. Quebec, Que., Can., July 12, 1934; s. John and Dorothy Isabel (dec.) E.; m. Barbara Jane Montgomery, Feb. 13, 1955; children: Adam Tudor, Christopher Montgomery, Deborah Jane Findlay, Susannah Margaret Belton, Sarah Elizabeth Gould. BA, U. Toronto, Can., 1957, LLB, 1960; LLD, U. Waterloo, 1992. Bar: Ont. 1962, created Queen's Counsel. Read law Tory, Tory, DesLauriers & Binnington, Toronto, Ont., 1960-62, assoc., 1962-67, ptnr., 1967-79; pres., CEO Brascan Ltd., Toronto, 1979-90, chmn., 1990-98; chancellor U. King's Coll., Halifax, N.S., Can., 1996—; sr. group chmn. Edperbrascan Corp., Toronto, 1998—; senator Senate of Can., Ottawa, Ont., Can., 1999—; bd. dirs. Barrick Gold Corp., EdperBrascan Corp., Gen. Motors of Can. Ltd., Gentra Inc., M.A. Hanna Co., Noranda Inc., Coca Cola Enterprises Inc., Trilon Fin. Corp.; chmn. bd. dirs. Can. Sports Hall of Fame; adv. bd. Nestle. Gov. Can. Olympic Found.; exec. com. Brit. N.Am. Com.; mem. Senate Can., 1990—. Decorated Order of Can., 1986. Mem. Upper Can. Law Soc., Can. Bar Assn., Toronto Club, York Club, Caledon Mountain Trout Club, Devil's Pulpit Golf Club (Caledon), The Rideau Club (Ottawa), Royal Palm Yacht and Country Club (Boca Raton). Progressive Conservative. Anglican. Avocations: ski, golf. Home: Tudorcroft RR 2, Caledon, ON Canada L0N 1C0 Office: EdperBrascan Corp, 181 Bay St Ste 4400 PO Box 762, Toronto, ON Canada M5J 2T3

EYUNNI, VIJAY RAGHAVAN, occupational medicine physician; b. Bombay, Apr. 15, 1948; came to U.S., 1974; s. Venkata Sundaram and Sita (Lakshmi) E.; m. Cynthia Rjeanson; children: Sharda, Janram, Neela. MD, Kasturba Med. Sch., Mysore, India, 1972; MPH, U. Minn., 1988. Inter, then resident United Hosp., St. Paul, 1974-76, mem. emergency medicine staff, 1983-88; house resident Diving Redeemer Hosp., South St. Paul, Minn., 1975-76; pvt. practice, South St. Paul, 1976-83; med. dir. Minnetonka, Minn., 1988-98, Minn. Occupl. Health, St. Paul, 1998—; team physician Minn. Twins. Mem. Am. Coll. Occupl. Medicine. Avocations: golf, tennis. Home: 2363 Field Stone Ct Mendota Heights MN 55120 Office: Minn Occupl Health 1661 St Anthony Ave Saint Paul MN 55104

EZAKI-YAMAGUCHI, JOYCE YAYOI, renal dietitian; b. Kingsburg, Calif., Mar. 18, 1947; d. Toshikatsu and Aiko (Ogata) Ezaki; m. Kent Takao Yamaguchi, Oct. 28, 1972; children: Kent Takao, Jr., Toshia Ann. AA, Reedley Coll., 1967; BS in Foods and Nutrition, U. Calif., Davis, 1969. Dietetic intern Henry Ford Hosp., Detroit, 1969-70, staff dietitian, 1970-71; renal dietitian Sutter Meml. Hosp., Sacramento, 1971-72; therapeutic dietitian Mt. Sinai Hosp., Beverly Hills, Calif., 1972-73; clin. dietitian Pacific Hosp., Long Beach, Calif., 1973-77; consulting dietitian Doctor's Hosp., Lakewood, Calif., 1976-77; clin. dietitian Mass. Gen. Hosp., Boston, 1977-78, Winona Meml. Hosp., Indpls., 1978-80; renal dietitian Fresno (Calif.) Community Hosp., 1980—. Author: (computer program) Dialysis Tracker, 1987; author: (with others) Cultural Foods and Renal Diets for the Dietitian, 1988, Standards of Practice Guidlines for the Practice of Clinical Dietetics,

1991. Religious chair Fresno Dharma Sch. Fresno Betsuin Buddhist Temple, 1994—; sec. Japanese Lang., 1997-99. Mem. Nat. Kidney Found. (exec. com. coun. renal nutrition 1992-98, region V rep., nutrition editor, chair patient and pub. edn. com. 1992-93, chair elect comms. chair 1994-95, chair 1995-96, past chair 1997-98, chair nominations com., chair rsch. grant com., Disting. Svc. award 1996), Am. Dietetic Assn. (bd. cert. renal nutrition specialist, renal practice group 1993-98, renal practice group nominating com. chair 1999), No. Calif/No. Nev. chpt. Nat. Kidney Found. (disting. achievement award coun. on renal nutrition 1993, co-chair-elect 1993-94, co-chair 1994-95, co-past chair 1995-96, treas., corr. sec.). Buddhist. Avocations: computers, cross stitch. Office: Cmty Hosps Ctrl Calif Fresno & R Sts Fresno CA 93715-2094

EZARD, GARY CARL, video editor; b. Lancaster, Pa., Apr. 26, 1963; s. Lawrence Allen and Dorothy Jean (Simmons) E. BA in Telecommunications, Pa. State U., 1984. Videographer/editor WTAJ-TV, Altoona, Pa., 1985-88; videotape editor Medstar Communications, Inc., Allentown, Pa., 1988-89; dir. editing svcs. Medstar TV, Inc., Allentown, Pa., 1989-97; sr. editor video resource AT&T, Piscataway, N.J., 1997-98; sr. editor MVI Post, Falls Church, Va., 1998—. Mem. Pa. State Alumni Assn., Pa. State Coll. Communications Alumni Soc. Avocations: golf, Penn State football. Office: MVI Post 6320 Castle Pl Falls Church VA 22044-1903

EZEAMII, HYACINTH CHINEDUM, public administration educator; b. Bukuru, Nigeria, Sept. 8, 1957; came to U.S., 1983, naturalized, 1993; s. Christopher Onuora and Regina Anyankwo (Ajagu) E.; m. Felicia Ngozi Nwambu, Dec. 30, 1991; children: Ikemefuna Hyacinth, Nkemakonam Michelle, Ugochukwu Daniel. BS in Acctg., Shaw U., 1984; MPA in Pub. Fin. Adminstrn., N.C. State U., 1987, EdD in Higher Edn. Adminstrn., Pub. Adminstrn. and Sociology, 1992. Tchr. primary sch. St. Paul's Ctrl. Sch., Achalla, Nigeria, 1974-75; tchr. math. Igwebuike Secondary Sch., Awka, Nigeria, 1976-78; tchr. math., dean studies Nimo (Nigeria) Girls Secondary Sch., 1978-79; adj. asst. prof. pub. adminstrn. program N.C. Ctrl. U., Durham, 1991-93; rsch. and mgmt. cons. Exami Rsch. & Mgmt. Cons. Svcs., Raleigh, N.C., 1993-95; asst. prof. pub. adminstrn. Albany (Ga.) State U., 1995—; vis. asst. prof. Ctr. for Alternative Programs in Edn., Shaw U., Raleigh, 1992-93; mem. S.-E. Regional Seminar on African Studies. Editor, pub. (newsletter) Ekwe Nimo; internat. editor Nimo in Perspective mag. With Biafran Army, 1969-70. Named Ezedioramma I for Ozo title and Oranyelugo I for chieftaincy title Nimo Cmty., Anambra State, Nigeria, 1996. Mem. Am. Assn. Higher Edn., Nat. Congress Black Faculty, Am. Soc. for Pub. Adminstrn., Assn. for Study of Higher Edn., Assn. for Instl. Rsch., Am. Nimo Unions (founder, 1st pres. 1987-96), Nigerian Assn. Rsch. Triangle Area (founder, 1st pres. 1987-88). Avocations: reading, music, dance, organizational affairs, travel. Office: Albany State Univ Dept Hist & Polit Sci PO Box 72304 Albany GA 31708-2304

EZECHUKWU, BONNIE OK., author, educator, counselor, poet, storyteller, multiculturalist, anti-drug and violence speaker; b. Oko, Nigeria, Apr. 30, 1960; s. Gabriel O. and Hannah M. E.; children: Ogochukwu, Chinedu, Amara. BA, Ctrl. State U., Edmond, Okla., 1987; MS, Okla. State U., 1991; BS, Langston U., 1994; DPhil, Union Inst. Coll., 1998. Chmn. Believers Youth and Family Ministries, Stillwater, Okla., 1992—; pres., CEO Youngline Drug Free Assn., Inc., Tulsa, 1993—; pres. U.S.A./African Multicultural Exchange Programs, Okla., 1994—; pres. Parents/Teachers Assn., Stillwater, 1995-97; bd. dirs. Redemption Christian Acad., Balt. Author: (books) Sweet Mother (Ideal Parenting), 1991, When Life Becomes Complex, 1996, Turtle, Father of Wisdom, 1998; (poem) Salute to the King of the Jungle, 1996 (bronze). Bd. dirs. Okla. Fed. Parents, Tulsa, 1994—, World IGBO Congress, Houston, 1994—. Named All-Am. scholar U.S. Achievement Acad., 1994, State of Okla. Man of Yr., 1995, Internat. Poet of Merit, Internat. Soc. Poets, 1996; recipient Congl. Record, U.S. Senate, 1995. Mem. ACA, Internat. Soc. Poets, Nat. Network for Youth, Nat. Assn. Health Svc. Execs., Nat. Assn. Alcoholism and Drug Counselors, Am. Assn. Christian Counselors. Home: 6374 N Denver Ave Tulsa OK 74126-1477 Office: Youngline Drug Free Assn Inc 6374 N Denver Ave Tulsa OK 74126-1477

EZEKOWITZ, MICHAEL DAVID, physician; b. Durban, Natal, South Africa, Jan. 27, 1946; U.S. citizen, 1985; s. Kalman and Lilian (Papilsky) K.; m. Wilma Joan Ezekowitz; children: Lindi Jane, Andrew Joshua. MB ChB, U. Cape Town, 1970; PhD, Imperial Coll., London U., 1976; MA (hon.), Yale U., 1990. Diplomate in internal medicine and cardiology Am. Bd. Internal Medicine. Intern Groote Schuur Hosp., Cape Town, South Africa, 1971-72, sr. house physician in cardiology, 1972; resident U. Nattal, 1972-73; fellow dept. medicine Cardiothoracic Inst., London, 1975-76; fellow divsn. cardiology Johns Hopkins Med. Instn., Balt., 1976-78; from asst. prof. to assoc. prof. medicine U. Okla. Health Sci. Ctr., Oklahoma City, 1978-82; dir. Human Cell Labelling Lab. Yale-New Haven Hosp./West Haven VA Med. Ctr., 1982-90, dir. Cardiovascular Thrombosis Rsch. Lab., 1990-96; attending physician in internalmedicine Yale-New Haven HOsp., 1982—; staff physician incardiology West Haven VA Hosp., 1982—, chief cardiovascular sect., 1990—; prof. medicine (cardiology Yale U. Sch. Medicine, 1990—. Contbr. numerous articles to profl. jours. Fellow Am. Coll. Cardiology, Am. Heart Assn. (coun. on clin. cardiology), Am. Coll. Chest Physicians, Am. Fedn. Clin. Rsch., Royal Coll. Physicians; mem. AAAS, Am. Soc. Echocardiography, Assn. Univ. Cardiologists, Sigma Xi. Office: VA Med Ctr 950 Campbell Ave West Haven CT 06516-2770

EZEKWE, MICHAEL OBI, animal science educator; b. Abatete, Anambra, Nigeria, Nov. 16, 1944; came to U.S., 1972; s. Okudo Ebudike and Ogaobaka (Anyaralu) E.; m. Edith Ifeyinwa Uzodinma, May 18, 1974; children: Obi, Kenechi, Ifemefuna, Chijioke, Nneamaka. BS with honors, U. Nigeria, 1971; MS, Pa. State U., 1974, PhD, 1977. Rsch. scientist Va. State U., Petersburg, 1978—, coord. program, 1993-97; assoc. prof., dir. Swine Devel. Ctr. Alcorn State U., Lorman, Miss., 1997—; cons. in field. Contbr. articles to Jour. Animal Sci., Growth, Devel. and Aging, Va. Jour. Sci., Nutrition Report Internat., Hormone and Metabolic Rsch., Jour. Am. Oil Chemists Soc., Am. Reciprocal Meats Conf. Eucharistic min. St. Joseph's Ch., Petersburg, 1986—, chetechist, 1990—. USDA-CSRS grantee, 1986—. Mem. Am. Soc. Animal Sci., Am. Soc. Nutritional Scis., KC, Sigma Xi, Gamma Sigma Delta. Roman Catholic. Achievements include discovery of usefulness of maternal diabetes in developing fetal pigs; demonstrate the beneficial effects of purslane plant in lowering plasma cholesterol and triglycerides. Office: Alcorn State U Box 1374 1000 Alcorn State U Dr Lorman MS 39096-9400

EZELL, MARGARET PRATHER, information systems executive; b. New Orleans, Aug. 12, 1951; d. Bluford and Mildred Winston (Seab) E. BS, Brigham Young U., 1973; MS, Utah State U., 1975; PhD, Mich. State U., 1982. Asst. prof., extension specialist Coop. Extension Svc., Pa. State U., University Park, 1982-85; So. regional computer coord. Coop. Extension Svc./USDA, Athens, Ga., 1985-88; cons. info. tech. Coop. Extension Svc./USDA, Clemson, S.C., 1988-89; adminstr. info. svcs., ea. region Resolution Trust Corp./FDIC, Atlanta, 1990-93, mgr. database, 1994-96; mgr. info. infrastructure Nat. Inst. of Stds. and Tech., Mfg. Extension Ptnrship., Gaithersburg, Md., 1997—; info. tech. cons., instrnl. designer, Atlanta, Washington, 1989—. Scholar Mich. State U., 1981, Marie Dye scholar, 1981. Mem. Am. Assn. Family and Consumer Scis. (grantee 1983, family econ./home mgmt. sect., pre-conf. local arrangements chmn. 1984-85, mem. nat. electronic tech. com. 1986-89), Ga. Assn. Family and Consumer Scis. (dist. vice chmn. 1986-87), Ctrl. Pa. IBM-PC Assn. (charter, treas. 1983-84), Agrl. Communicators in Edn. (Excellence in Computers award 1989), Assn. Banyan Users Internat. (pres. Atlanta chpt. 1991), World Futures Soc., Epsilon Sigma Phi, Kappa Omicron Nu.

EZELLE, ROBERT EUGENE, diplomat; b. Mattoon, Ill., Dec. 5, 1927; s. Zonner Robert and Nina Leora (Smith) E.; m. Lesly Marion Hopkins, Apr. 30, 1955; children: Robert, Lesley, John, Paul. Student, U. So. Calif., 1947-49, U. Bonn, 1954-56, U. Munich, 1956-57; Ph.D., U. Vienna, 1960; M.S. (Sloan fellow), Stanford Grad. Sch. Bus., 1977; Dr.h.c., Nat. U., 1981. Instr. Bonn, Munich and Vienna, 1954-60; dir. lang. sch., San Mateo, Calif., 1960-61; joined U.S. Fgn. Service, 1961; internat. relations officer State Dept., Washington, 1961-62; staff asst. Fgn. Service Inst., 1962-63; assigned Hong Kong, 1963-65, Bern, Switzerland, 1965-69, Naples, Italy, 1969-72; chief consular affairs sect. Am. Embassy, Bonn, 1972-75; internat. relations officer State Dept., Washington, 1975-76; dep. consul gen. Am. Embassy, London, 1977-80; consul gen. Tijuana, Mex., 1980-84; consul gen. Am. Embassy, Paris, 1984-88, Haiti, 1988-90; cons., internat. trade, 1990—. Served with USAF, 1949-53. Recipient Gold medal City of Paris, 1988. Address: Balmont, 46100 Beduer France

EZELL-GRIM, ANNETTE SCHRAM, business management educator, college official; b. West Frankfort, Ill., June 19, 1940; d. Woodrow C. and Rosa (Franich) Schram; m. John R. Grim, III; BS U. Nev., 1962, MS in Physiology, 1967, postgrad., 1969; EdD in Pub. Adminstrn., Brigham Young U., 1977; children: Michael L., Rona Maria. Mem. staff Washoe Med. Ctr., Reno, 1962; teaching asst. U. Nev., Reno, 1962-63, instr., 1963-64, 1965-67, asst. prof., 1967-71; curriculum specialist U. Nev. Med. Sch., 1971-72, project mgr. Fed. Grant Intercampus Edn. Project, 1969-71, assoc. prof., curriculum specialist rural practitioner program, 1971-73, staff assoc. Mountain States Regional Med. Program, 1974-75; cons. Nev. Dept. Edn., 1975-77; asst. dean acad. affairs U. Utah, Salt Lake City, 1977-80; acting Dean, 1981, dir., prof. doctoral program Edn. Adminstrn.; prof., dept. head Coll. Human Development, Pa. State U., 1982-85; dean Coll. Profl. Studies, prof. bus. adminstrn. U. So. Colo., Pueblo, 1985-87; sr. asst. to pres. Towson State U., Balt., 1987-94, assoc. prof. mgmt. sch. bus., 1994-95; assoc. dean, prof. bus. mgmt. Wor Wic C.C., Salisbury, Md., 1995—; cons. higher edn., TV edn., research methology; adviser to various research, polit. and ednl. bds. Mem. Am. Ednl. Research Assn., AAAS, Am. Acad. Arts and Scis., AAUP, Am. Council on Edn., Am. Assn. Higher Edn., Soc. for Coll. & Univ. Planning, Decision Scis. Inst., Sigma Xi, Phi Kappa Phi, Delta Kappa Gamma. Home: 10 Charlie Dr Bishopville MD 21813 Office: Wor Wic CC 32000 Campus Dr Salisbury MD 21804-1485

EZENWA, JOSEPHINE NWABUOKU, social worker; b. Oct. 20, 1959; d. Igwe Silas O. and H.R.H. Veronica A. Ezenwa; children: Bryan, Brenda, Sean. BA Psychology & Human Svcs. with honors, Fontbonne Coll., St. Louis, 1980; MSW, Washington U., St. Louis, 1981; postgrad., St. Louis U., 1991-93. Rsch. dir. Nat. Benevolent Assn., St. Louis, 1981-89; tchr. University City Sch. Dist., 1989-94; therapist Presbyn. Children's Home, St. Louis, 1994-95; nephrology social worker St. Louis Regional Med. Ctr., 1995-97; founder, chair St. Louis Regional Med. Ctr. Dialysis Support Group, 1995-97; social worker St. Louis U. Hosp., 1997; CEO, pres. BBS Care U.S.A., Inc., St. Louis, 1997—; founder/chair St. Louis Regional Med. Ctr. Dialysis Support Group, 1995-97; chair long range planning com. Washington U.; presenter in field. Mem. NASW, NAFE, Coun. Nephrology Social Workers, Nat. Assn. Forensic Counselors, Nat. Assn. Cognitive Behavioral Therapists, Washington U. Sch. Social Work Alumni Assn. (bd. dirs.), Creve Coeur-Olive C. of C., Lions Club. Avocations: choreography, fashion consulting, event coordinating, design, travel. Home: 8814 Chickasaw Ct Saint Louis MO 63132-2407 Office: St Louis U Hosp 3536 Vista at Grand Saint Louis MO 63110 also: PO Box 12453 Saint Louis MO 63132

EZERSKY, WILLIAM MARTIN, lawyer; b. N.Y.C., Sept. 14, 1951; s. Abraham David and Ada Ezersky; m. Karen Gail Hecht, June 30, 1985. BA in Communications, Philosophy, Queens Coll., 1974; JD, Hofstra U., 1977. Bar: N.Y. 1979, U.S. Dist. Ct. (so. and ea. dists.) N.Y. 1979. Sole practice N.Y.C., 1979—. Mem. ABA. Bar Assn. City N.Y., N.Y. State Trial Lawyers Assn., N.Y. County Trial Lawyers Assn., Queens Bar Assn., Jewish Lawyers Guild. Democrat. Jewish. Lodge: Masons. Avocations: rowing, walking, sailing, tennis, swimming. Office: 3333 New Hyde Park Rd New Hyde Park NY 11042-1205

EZOLD, NANCY O'MARA, lawyer; b. Laconia, N.H., July 21, 1942; d. Francis L. and Edna Mae (Jackson) O'Mara; m. William L. Keenan; children: Christopher E. Ezold, Matthew F. Ezold. BA, U. Maine, 1964; JD, Villanova U., 1980. Bar: Pa. 1980, U.S. Dist. Ct. (ea. dist.) Pa. 1980, U.S. Ct. Appeals (3rd and fed. cirs.) 1982, U.S. Claims Ct. 1989, U.S. Dist. Ct. (mid. dist.) Pa. 1989, U.S. Supreme Ct. 1989, U.S. Dist. Ct. Ariz. 1991. Adminstrv. positions fed., state and local govt. agys., 1964-77; assoc. Kirschner, Walters & Willig, Phila., 1980-81, Phillips & Phelan, Phila., 1981-83, Wolf Block Schorr & Solis-Cohen, Phila., 1983-89, Rosenthal & Ganister, West Chester, Pa., 1990-94; pres., chief counsel BES Environ. Specialists, Larksville, Pa., 1989-90; pvt. practice Bala Cynwyd, Pa., 1994—. Bd. dirs. Women's Law Project, Phila., 1995. Named Feminist of Yr., Feminist Majority Found., 1993. Mem. ATLA, NAFE, Phila. Bar Assn., Nat. Assn. Women Lawyers (pres.' award 1991). Fax #: (610) 660-5595. E-mail: ezoldlaw@msn.com. Office: 401 E City Ave Ste 904 Bala Cynwyd PA 19004-1131

EZRA, DAVID ALAN, federal judge; b. 1947. BBA magna cum laude, St. Mary's U., 1969, JD, 1972. Law clk. Office of Corp. Counsel City and County Honolulu, 1972; mem. firm Greenstein, Cowen & Frey, 1972-73, Anthony, Hoddick, Reinwald & O'Connor, 1973-80, Ezra, O'Connor, Moon & Tam, 1980-88; dist. judge U.S. Dist. Ct., Hawaii, 1988-98, chief judge, 1998—; adj. prof. law Wm. S. Richardson Sch. Law, 1978—; exec. com. 9th cir. Jud. Conf. Co-editor, author: Hwaii Construction Law - What to Do and When, 1987; editor: Hawaii Collection Practices Manual. 1st lt. USAR 1971-77. Daugherty Fund scholar, 1971, San Antonio Bar Assn. Aux. scholar, 1972. Mem. ABA, U.S. Fed. Judges Assn. (bd. dirs., exec. com.), Dist. Judges Assn. (v.p. 9th cir.), Hawaii State Bar, Am. Arbitration Assn., Delta Epsilon Sigma, Phi Delta Phi. Office: US Dist Ct 300 Alamoana Blvd C-400 Honolulu HI 96803

EZRATI, MILTON JOSEPH, investment manager, economist; b. N.Y.C., May 22, 1947; s. Al and Edythe Ezrati; m. Lynda Lamare, July 1970 (div.); m. Susan Arlene Graham, June 19, 1976; 1 child, Isabel Diana. BA in Econs., SUNY, Buffalo, 1969; M Social Sci. in Math. Econs., Birmingham (Eng.) U., 1973. Econ. specialist Citibank, N.Y.C., 1971-73; economist Chase Manhattan Bank, N.Y.C., 1973-77; economist Lionel Edie & Co., N.Y.C., 1977-78, chief economist, 1978-81; chief economist Mfrs. Hanover Investment Corp., N.Y.C., 1981-83, chief economist and strategist, 1983-85, sr. v.p., dir. rsch., 1985-87; chief investment officer Nomura Asset Mgmt., N.Y.C., 1987—. Author: Kawari: How Japan's Economic and Cultural Transformation Will Alter the Balance of Power Among Nations, 1999; contbr. articles to profl. and popular jours. Mem. Am. Econs. Assn., Old Westbury Horseman's Assn. Methodist. Avocations: riding and training horses, skiing. Office: Nomura Asset Mgmt Inc 180 Maiden Ln Fl 26 New York NY 10038-4925

EZSAK, RONALD H., data processing company executive; b. Chgo., Dec. 5, 1956; s. Leonard Leslie and Esther Sarah (Cook) E.; m. Elaine Ezsak, May 29, 1983; children: Jordan, Eden, Noah, Madaline. Degree in Econs., Northwestern U. Pres. Cognitor, Rosemont, Ill.; dir. bus. devel. Intromedia, Rosemont; v.p. internat. Kewill/Metromedia, Foster City, Calif.; dir. strategic mkts. Silvon, Westmont, Ill.; lectr. in field. Mem. MIT Enterprize Forum.

FAAL, EDI M. O., lawyer; b. Gambia, Africa, 1954; came to U.S., 1974; BS, Fla. Internat. U.; Barrister at Law, Mid. Temple Inns Ct., London; JD, Western State U., Fullerton, Calif., 1982. Bar: U.K., Wales, Calif., Ind., U.S. Supreme Ct. Adj. prof. U. So. Calif. Law Ctr., L.A. Named Lawyer of Yr., Langston Bar Assn. L.A., 1994; recipient Pres.'s award L.A. Criminal Cts. Bar Assn., Legal Champion award Ohio Criminal Def. Bar Assn. Office: 221 N Figueroa St Ste 1200 Los Angeles CA 90012-2646

FAATZ, JEANNE RYAN, educational association director; b. Cumberland, Md., July 30, 1941; d. Charles Keith and Myrtle Elizabeth (McIntyre) Ryan; children: Kristin, Susan. BS, U. Ill., 1962; postgrad. (Gates fellow), Harvard U., 1984; MA, U. Colo., Denver, 1985. Instr. Speech Dept. Met. State Coll., Denver, 1985-98; sec. to majority leader Colo. Senate, 1976-78; mem. Colo. Ho. Reps. from Dist. 1, 1978-98; dir. Colo. Sch.-to-Career; asst. majority leader. Past pres. Harvey Pk. (Colo.) Homeowners Assn., S.W. Denver YWCA Adult Edn. Club; S.W. met. coord. UN Children's Fund, 1969-74; mem. bd. mgrs. S.W. Denver YMCA. Home: 2903 S Quitman St Denver CO 80236-2208 Office: State Capitol Denver CO 80203

FABBRI, ANNE R., art museum director, curator; b. Norristown, Pa.; d. Remo and Anna Wild (Butterworth) F.; AB cum laude, Radcliffe Coll.; MA in Art History, Bryn Mawr Coll., 1971; m. Joseph Henry Butera (div.); children—Virginia, Remo, Joseph F. (Jay). Art lectr. Villanova U., Pa., 1971-73, Drexel U., Phila., 1974-76; art critic, art editor The Drummer, Phila., 1976-79; art critic The Bulletin, Phila., 1978-80; dir. Alfred O. Deshong Mus., Widener U., Chester, Pa., 1980-82, The Noyes Mus., Oceanville, N.J., 1982-91; dir. Paley Design Ctr. Phila. Coll. of Textiles and Sci., 1991—; bd. dirs. MUSE Found. for Visual Arts; mem. adv. Italian/Am. Women Artists. Vis. NEH fellow U. Calif.-Berkeley, 1979, Princeton U., 1980. Recipient John Cotton Dana award Mus. N.J. Assn. Mus., 1991. Mem. Am. Assn. Museums, Coll. Art Assn., Internat. Assn. Art Critics. Mem. Am. Assn. Mus., Amici Ctr. for Italian Studies (bd. advisors 1987—), Coll. Art Assn. Home: 642 Valley View Ln Wayne PA 19087-2024 Office: Paley Design Ctr 4200 Henry Ave Philadelphia PA 19144

FABE, DANA ANDERSON, judge; b. Cin., Mar. 29, 1951; d. George and Mary Lawrence (Van Antwerp) F.; m. Randall Gene Simpson, Jan. 1, 1983; 1 child, Amelia Fabe Simpson. B.A., Cornell U., 1973; J.D., Northeastern U., 1976. Bar: Alaska 1977, U.S. Supreme Ct. 1981. Law clk. to justice Alaska Supreme Ct., 1976-77; staff atty. pub. defenders State of Alaska, 1977-81; dir. Alaska Pub. Defender Agy., Anchorage, from 1981; judge Superior Ct., Anchorage; justice Alaska Supreme Ct., Anchorage, 1996—. Named Alumna of Yr., Northeastern Sch. Law, 1983. Mem. Nat. Assn. Women Judges, Alaska Bar Assn., Anchorage Assn. Women Attys. Office: Alaska Supreme Ct 303 K St Fl 5 Anchorage AK 99501-2013

FABENS, ANDREW LAWRIE, III, lawyer; b. Washington, Apr. 8, 1942; s. Andrew Lawrie Jr. and Alicia Gordon (Hail) F.; m. Martha Leigh Leingang, June 24, 1966; children: Andrew Lawrie IV, Jennie Leigh. AB, Yale U., 1964; JD, U. Chgo., 1967. Bar: Ohio 1967. Assoc. Thompson, Hine and Flory, Cleve., 1967-74, ptnr., 1974—, chmn. estate planning and probate area, 1988-94. Contbr. articles on estate planning and related topics to profl. pubis. Pres. Family Health Assn., Cleve., 1978-80, 83-84; trustee A.M. McGregor Home, East Cleveland, Ohio, 1991—, Bascom Little Fund, Cleve., 1985—; vestryman Christ Episcopal Ch., Shaker Heights, Ohio, 1972-77. Fellow Am. Coll. Trust and Estate Counsel; mem. Ohio State Bar Assn. (bd. govs. probate and trust law sect. 1983—, treas. 1997-99, sec. 1999—), Probate Law Jour. Ohio (adv. bd.), Cleve. Bar Assn. (speaker, com. mem. 1976—), Cleve. Skating Club, The Rowfant Club (adv. 1998—), The Novel Club (sec. 1986-88, pres. 1995-97), The Union Club. Home: 2280 Woodmere Dr Cleveland OH 44106-3604 Office: Thompson Hine & Flory LLP 3900 Key Ctr 127 Public Square Cleveland OH 44114-1216

FABER, DAVID ALAN, federal judge; b. Charleston, W.Va., Oct. 21, 1942; s. John Smith and Wilda Elaine (Melton) F.; m. Deborah Ellayne Anderson, Aug. 24, 1968; 1 dau., Katherine Peyton. B.A., W.Va. U., 1964; J.D., Yale U., 1967; LLM, U. Va., 1998. Bar: W.Va. 1967, U.S. Ct. Mil. Appeals 1970, U.S. Supreme Ct. 1974. Assoc. Dayton, Campbell & Love, Charleston, W.Va., 1967-68, Campbell, Love, Woodroe, 1972-74; ptnr. Campbell, Love, Woodroe & Kizer, Charleston, 1974-77, Love, Wise, Robinson & Woodroe, Charleston, 1977-81; U.S. atty. U.S. Dept. Justice, Charleston, 1982-86; ptnr. Spilman, Thomas, Battle & Klostermeyer, Charleston, 1987-91; judge U.S. Dist. Ct. (so. dist.) W.Va., Bluefield, 1991—; counsel to ethics commn. W.Va. State Bar, Charleston, 1974-76. Served to capt. USAF, 1968-72, to col. W.Va. Air N.G., 1978-92. Nat. law scholar Yale Law Sch. New Haven, 1964-65. Mem. W.Va. State Bar, W.Va. Bar Assn., Phi beta Kappa. Republican. Episcopalian. Office: US Dist Ct PO Box 4068 601 Federal St Ste 2303 Bluefield WV 24701-3033*

FABER, DONALD STUART, neurobiology and anatomy educator; b. Buffalo, Mar. 3, 1943; m. Jo Welch, Dec. 27, 1964; children: Eve Susan, Amy Elizabeth. SB, MIT, 1964; PhD, SUNY, 1968. Postdoctoral fellow SUNY, Buffalo, 1968-70; vis. rsch. assoc. Max Planck Inst., Frankfurt, Germany, 1970-72, Lab. Physiology, U. Paris, 1972; asst. prof. U. Cin., 1972-74; rsch. scientist Rsch. Inst. Alcoholism, N.Y. State, Buffalo, 1974-78; assoc. prof. SUNY, Buffalo, 1975-81, prof., 1981-92, dir. divsn. neurobiology, 1978-86; prof. and chmn. dept. neurobiology and anatomy MCP Hahnemann U., Phila., 1992—; Phila. coord. Inst. for Neurosci. Rsch., Allegheny Health, Edn. and Rsch. Found., Pitts., 1993-98; neurosci. investigator Javits NIH, 1988. Editor: Neurobiology of the Mauthner Cell, 1978; contbr. articles to profl. jours. Grass Found. fellow Marine Biol. Lab., Woods Hole, Mass., summer 1969, fellow Claude Bernard Soc., Paris, 1972, fellow Neurosci. Inst., N.Y.C., 1984; exch. scholar Capital Inst. Medicine, Beijing, China, 1986. Mem. Soc. Neurosci. (membership com. 1988-91, fin. com. 1996—), Am. Physiol. Soc. (mem. pubs. com. 1996—), Internat. Brain Rsch. Orgn. (editorial bd Neurosci. 1975—), Biophys. Soc. (editl. bd. Biophys. Jour. 1990-96), N.Y. Acad. Sci. Assn. Neurosci. Dept. and Programs. Office: MCP Hahnemann Univ Neurobiology and Anatomy 3200 Henry Ave Philadelphia PA 19129-1137

FABER, MICHAEL WARREN, lawyer; b. N.Y.C., June 7, 1943; s. Carl Faber and Harriet Ruth Cohen; m. Adele Zolot, Apr. 16, 1975; children: Evan, Jenna. AB, Hunter Coll., 1964; JD, Fordham U., 1967. Bar: N.Y. 1967, D.C. 1972, U.S. Ct. Claims, 1972, U.S. Supreme Ct. 1972, Colo. 1993. Gen. atty. FCC, Washington, 1967-69, trial atty., 1969-71, atty. advisor to Commr. T.J. Houser, 1971; assoc. Peabody, Rivlin, Lambert & Meyers, Washington, 1971-73; ptnr. Peabody, Lambert & Meyers, Washington, 1973-84; ptnr. Reid and Priest, Washington, 1984-93, mem. exec. com., 1986-92; prin. The Faber Group, Cascade, Colo., 1993-94; pres. USA Volleyball Ctrs. LLC, Colorado Springs, Colo., 1995-96; owner The Pantry Restaurant, Green Mountain Falls, Colo., 1996—; cons. White House Office Telecomm. Policy, 1976; chmn. organizing com. Nat. Volleyball League. Bd. dirs. Washington Very Spl. Arts, 1986-93. Mem. N.Y. Bar Assn., D.C. Bar Assn., Fed. Bar Assn., Fed. Communications Bar Assn., Colo. Bar Assn. Office: The Pantry Restaurant Green Mountain Falls CO 80819

FABER, NEIL, advertising executive; b. N.Y.C., May 21, 1938; m. Susan Somer, Jan. 28, 1962; children: Cynthia Farber-Wolf, Amy Farber, Gary Faber. BS, MBA, NYU, 1960. Rsch. analyst Alfred Politz, N.Y.C., 1958-60; eastern sales svc. mgr. ABC, N.Y.C., 1960-63; media supr. Batten, Barton, Durstein & Osborn, N.Y.C., 1964-67; sr. account exec. Wells, Rich, Greene, N.Y.C., 1967-73; v.p., dir. media Della Femina Advt., N.Y.C., 1973-79; founder, pres. Neil Faber Media Inc. Mktg. Media Planning/Buying Co., N.Y.C., 1979—; pres. NexGen Media Worldwide; assoc. prof. mktg. NYU, 1982—; lectr. in field. Developed and introduced new media interactive course at NYU; contbr. articles to profl. jours., consumer mags. Recipient Master Communicator award Advt. Agy., Pa., 1966, Workshop award, L.A., 1989, Seminar award Mktg. Media, 1979-80. Avocations: music, sports. Office: Neil Faber Media Inc 157 W 57th St New York NY 10019-2210

FABER, PETER LEWIS, lawyer; b. N.Y.C., Apr. 29, 1938; s. Alexander W. and Anne L. Faber; m. Joan Schuster, June 14, 1959; children: Michael, Julia, Thomas. AB, Swarthmore Coll., 1960; LLB, Harvard U., 1963. Bar: N.Y. 1964. Assoc. Wiser, Shaw, Freeman, Ickes & Williams, Rochester, N.Y., 1963-65; assoc. Parker, Chapin & Flattau, N.Y.C., 1965-66; ptnr. Harter, Secrest & Emery, Rochester, N.Y., 1966-82; ptnr. Winthrop, Stimson, Putnam & Roberts, N.Y.C., 1982-84, Kaye, Scholer, Fierman, Hays & Handler, N.Y.C., 1984-95, McDermott, Will & Emery, 1995—; mem. adv. com. NYU Ann. Inst. on State & Local Taxation; mem. N.Y. State Coun. on Fiscal and Econ. Priorities, 1991-95. Chmn. Rochester Econ. Devel. Com., 1979-82; pres. Rochester Philharmonic Orch., Inc., 1980-82; bd. dirs. Met. Rochester Devel. Council, Harley Sch., 1978-81; mem. fin. com. Monroe County Dem. Party, 1979-82; active N.Y.C. Partnership. Fellow Am. Bar Found., Am. Coll. Tax Counsel; mem. ABA (chmn. tax sect. 1991-92, vice chmn. 1986-88, chmn.-elect 1990-91, chmn. com. corp. stockholder relationships tax sect. 1980-82, liaison to IRS for North Atlantic region, vice chmn. spl. com. on integration 1979-81, sec. tax sect. 1984-86), N.Y. State Bar Assn. (chmn. sect. taxation 1976-77, exec. com. sect. taxation 1969—), N.Y. C. of C. (chmn. tax. com. 1988—, trustee 1989—, exec. com. 1990—), Monroe County Bar Assn., Am. Law Inst. (tax project adv. group), Rochester Area C. of C. (trustee 1980-82). Contbr. articles to profl. jours. Home: 300 Central Park W New York NY 10024-1513 Office: McDermott Will & Emery 50 Rockefeller Plz New York NY 10020-1605

FABER, SANDRA MOORE, astronomer, educator; b. Boston, Dec. 28, 1944; d. Donald Edwin and Elizabeth Mackenzie (Borwick) Moore; m. Andrew L. Faber, June 9, 1967; children: Robin, Holly. BA, Swarthmore Coll., 1966, DSc (hon.), 1986; PhD, Harvard U., 1972; DSc (hon.), Williams Coll.,

1996. Asst. prof., astronomer Lick Obs., U. Calif., Santa Cruz, 1972-77, assoc. prof., astronomer, 1977-79, prof., astronomer, 1979—; univ. prof. U. Calif., Santa Cruz, 1996—; mem. astronomy adv. panel NSF, 1975-77; vis. prof. Princeton U., 1978, U. Hawaii, 1983, Ariz. State U., 1985; Phillips visitor Haverford Coll., 1982; Feshbach lectr. MIT, Cambridge, Mass., 1990; Darwin lectr. Royal Astron. Soc., 1991; Marker lectr. Pa. State U., 1992; Bunyan lectr. Stanford U., 1992; Tomkins lectr. U. Calif., San Francisco, 1992; Mohler lectr. U. Mich., 1994; mem. Nat. Acad. Astronomy Survey Panel, 1979-81; chmn. vis. com. Space Telescope Sci. Inst., 1983-84; co-chmn. sci. steering com. Keck Obs., 1987-92, leader DEIMOS spectrograph team, 1993—; mem. Wide Field Camera team Hubble Space Telescope, 1985-97, user's com., 1990-92, mem. advanced radial camera selection team, 1995; mem. Calif. Coun. on Sci. and Tech., 1989-94, Nat. Acad. Com. on Astronomy and Astrophysics, 1993-95, Com. on Future Smithsonian Instn., 1994-95; mem. White House Space Sci. Workshop, 1996, Waterman Awards Com., NSF, 1997-99. Assoc. editor: Astrophys. Jour. Letters, 1982-87; editorial bd.: Ann. Revs. Astronomy and Astrophysics, 1982-87; contbr. articles to profl. jours. Trustee Carnegie Instn., Washington, 1985—; bd. dirs. Ann. Revs., Inc., 1989—, SETI Inst., 1997—. Recipient Bart J. Bok prize Harvard U., 1978, Director's Distinguished Lectr. award Livermore Nat. Lab., 1986; NASA Group Achievement award, 1993, DeVaucouleurs medal U. Tex., 1997; Carnegie Lectr. Carnegie Inst. Washington, 1988; NSF fellow, 1966-71; Woodrow Wilson fellow, 1966-71; Alfred P. Sloan fellow, 1977-81; listed among 100 best Am. scientists under 40, Sci. Digest, 1984; Tetelman fellow, Yale U., 1987. Mem. NAS (vice chair adv. panel on cosmotology 1993), Am. Acad. Arts and Scis., Calif. Acad. Scis., 1998—, Am. Astron. Soc. (councilor 1982-84, Dannie Heineman prize 1986), Internat. Astron. Union, Phi Beta Kappa, Sigma Xi. Office: U Calif Lick Obs Santa Cruz CA 95064

FABIAN, JEANNE, entrepreneur, executive recruiter; b. Wilkes Barre, Pa., June 25, 1946; d. Joseph A. and Dorothy (Cannon) F.; m. Christopher Sykes, Sept. 7, 1968 (div. Mar. 1979). BBA, Baruch Coll., N.Y.C., 1969; MBA, Hofstra U., Hempstead, N.Y., 1979; postgrad., N.Y. Coll. Osteo. Medicine, 1998—. CPA, N.Y. Auditor Arthur Andersen & Co., N.Y.C., 1969-73; planning analyst Avon Products, Inc., N.Y.C., 1973-75; fin. analyst Revlon, Inc., N.Y.C., 1975-77; acctg. mgr. Am. Standard, Inc., N.Y.C., 1977-78; sr. fin. analyst Texaco, Inc., Harrison, N.Y., 1979-82; asst. dir. Harper & Row Pubs., Inc., N.Y.C., 1983-86, exec. recruiter, 1986-89; owner Fabian Assocs., Inc., N.Y.C., 1989—. Contbr. articles to profl. jours. Treas., bd. dirs. Stanwix Apts. Corp., Forest Hills, N.Y., 1983—. Mem. AICPA, N.Y. State Soc. CPAs., Golden Key Nat. Hon. Soc. Avocations: real estate investments, international travel, science studies, photography. Office: Fabian Assocs Inc 521 5th Ave Fl 17 New York NY 10175-1799

FABIAN, JOHN MCCREARY, non-profit company executive, former astronaut, former air force officer; b. Goosecreek, Tex., Jan. 28, 1939; s. Felix Monroe and Amy Blanchard (Seip) F.; m. Donna Kay Buboltz, Sept. 18, 1961; children: Michael, Amy. BSME, Wash. State U., 1962; MS in Aerospace Engring., Air Force Inst. Tech., 1964; PhD in Aeronautics and Astronautics, U. Wash., 1974. Commd. officer USAF, 1962, advanced through grades to col.; assoc. prof. USAF Acad., Colorado Springs, Colo., 1974-78; astronaut NASA, Houston, 1978-86, mission specialist Challenger flight 2, 1983; mission specialist Discovery flight, 1985; ret. USAF, 1987; v.p. space sys. ANSER Corp. (Analytic Svcs Inc.), Arlington, Va., 1987-89; exec. v.p. ANSER Corp. (Analytic Svcs. Inc.), Arlington, Va., 1989-91, pres., CEO, 1991—; mem. Presdl. Commn. on Redesign Space Sta., NRC Com. on Space Sta., NASA Adv. Coun. Task Force on Shuttle-MIR Missions; adv. coun. Ga. Tech. Rsch. Inst. Decorated Def. Superior Service medal, Legion of Merit, NASA Space Flight medal, French Legion of Honor, Saudi Arabian King Abdul-Aziz medal, Vietnam Cross of Gallantry. Fellow AIAA, Am. Astronautical Soc.; mem. Assn. Space Explorers (pres. 1990-94), Internat. Astronautical Fedn. (v.p. 1995—), Internat. Acad. Astronautics. Office: Analytic Svc Inc 1215 Jefferson Davis Hwy Arlington VA 22202-4302

FABIAN, LARRY LOUIS, university administrator; b. Aurora, Ill., May 25, 1940; s. Louis and Emma (Mayer) F.; m. Terese Sulikowski, Dec. 1, 1978; children: Christopher, Laura. B.A., Cath. U. Am., 1961, M.A., 1963; Ph.D., Columbia U., 1971. Staff mem. Bur. Intelligence and Research, Dept. State, Washington, 1962; staff mem. Carnegie Endowment for Internat. Peace, N.Y.C., 1964; research staff fgn. policy studies program Brookings Instn., Washington, 1965-71; research asso., co-dir. program on tech. and Am. fgn. policy Brookings Instn., 1971-73; sr. assoc., dir. Middle East program Carnegie Endowment for Internat. Peace, Washington, 1974-77, sec., 1977-94; sr. v.p., COO, Coun. on Fgn. Rels., N.Y.C., 1994-95; v.p. Shorebank Corp., Chgo., 1996-98; deputy commr. Chgo. Dept. Housing, 1998; exec. sec. bd. trustees, exec. dir. N.Y. office Am. U. in Cairo, 1998—; cons. Hudson Inst., N.Y.C., Rockefeller Found. Author: Soldiers without Enemies, 1971, (with others) Regimes for the Ocean, Outer Space and Weather, 1973, Andrew Carnegie's Peace Endowment, 1985; co-editor: Israelis Speak: About Themselves and the Palestinians, 1976. Mem. Coun. on Fgn. Rels., Century Assn. Roman Catholic. Office: Am U in Cairo NY Office 420 5th Ave Fl 3D New York NY 10018-2729

FABIAN, LORI FOLTZ, grant consultant, singer, actress, producer; b. Cairo, Ill., Oct. 8, 1957; d. Alva Ray and Joyce Fay (Pirtle) Foltz; m. Michael Brian Fabian, Nov. 1, 1987; 1 stepchild, Brianne E.; 1 child, Caroline S. B Music Edn. cum laude, Loyola U. New Orleans, 1979, post-grad.; postgrad., Tulane U., U. New Orleans. Prodn. coord. New Orleans Opera, 1982-85; art cons. Hanson Galleries, New Orleans, L.A., Beverly Hills, Calif., 1986-88; prodn. mgr. The Da Camera Soc., L.A., 1989-90; coord. found. funding United Way Greater L.A., 1990-94; pres. Fabian Cons. Inc., Bay St Louis, Miss., 1994—; Sec., bd. dirs. Concert Choir New Orleans, 1985-87, New Life Ctr., Inc., Bay St. Louis, 1996-98; asst. dir. Coast Chorale, Pass Christian, Miss., 1994—; trainer Miss. Ctr. for Non-profits, Jackson, Miss., 1998—; vol. cons. Ctr. for Nonprofit Mgmt., New Orleans, 1998—. Mem. NAFE, Nat. Soc. Fund Raising Execs. Roman Catholic. Avocations: music, theatre. Office: 115 De Montluzin Ave Bay Saint Louis MS 39520

FABIAN, THOMAS ROBERT, superintendent of schools; b. Pottsville, Pa., May 20, 1939; s. Thomas Joseph and Evelyn Dolores (Tobias) F.; m. Dorothy Elizabeth Houterman, Nov. 28, 1963; children: Patricia, Stephen, Catherine. AB, Villanova U., 1962; MEd, Lehigh U., 1965; EdD, Syracuse U., 1978. H.s. prin. Draper Sch. Dist., Schenectady, N.Y., 1970-72; asst. supt. Wauwatosa (Wis.) Sch. Dist., 1983-89; supt. Valders (Wis.) Area Sch. Dist., 1989-99, ret., 1999; vice chmn. Wis. State Adv. Coun. for Tchr. Edn. and Cert. Fellow IDEA, Mott Found. Mem. AASA, NASSP, ASCD, NEA, Wis. Sch. Pub. Rels. Assn. (pres. 1996-97), Wis. Assn. Sch. Dist. Adminstrs., Phi Delta Kappa. Home: 2728 Valley Ave West Bend WI 53095

FABISCH, GALE WARREN, civil engineer; b. Chgo., Sept. 26, 1950; s. Warren Paul and Geraldine Amanda (Zobott) F.; m. Nancy Louise Smith, June 7, 1980; children: Genevieve Marrae, Erika Louise, Paul Hunt. BS in Environ. Engring., So. Ill. U., 1973; postgrad., Ill. Inst. of Tech., 1974-75. Registered profl. engr.; lic. real estate broker. Real estate broker Investments, Chgo., 1975—; asst. civil engr. Met. Water Reclamation Dist. of Greater Chgo., 1973-77, assoc. civil engr., 1977-88, sr. civil engr., 1988—; contract adminstr. Lab. Info. Mgmt. Sys., 1992, Early Warning Monitoring Sys., 1994. Co-author: (computer sys.) Fulton County Data System, 1973, Tax Rate Computer System, 1988, Implementing a Laboratory Information Management System, 1994, Laboratory Information Management System at the Metro Water Reclamation Dist. of Greater Chgo., 1995; project engr. (tech. study) Hanover Park Facility Planning Study, 1975, TARP U-Tube Feasibility Study, 1977. Deacon Edison Park United Ch. of Christ, Chgo., 1982-85, trustee 1997-98. With UNSR, 1970-76. Mem. ASCE, NSPE, Ill. Soc. Profl. Engrs., Water Environment Fedn., Real Estate Bd.-Chgo., Austin-Healey Club-Midwest (pres. 1980-82, treas. 1995-99, svc. award 1982), Glencoe Boat Club (treas. 1981-97), Portage Park C. of C. Avocations: sailing, auto restoration, building restoration, golf, hockey. Office: Metro Water Reclamation Dist of Greater Chgo 100 E Erie St Chicago IL 60611-2829

FABRAY, NANETTE, actress; b. San Diego, Oct. 27; d. Raoul Bernard and Lillian (McGovern) Fabares; m. David Tebet, Oct. 26, 1947 (div. July 1951); m. Ranald MacDougall, 1957 (dec. Dec. 1973); 1 son, Jamie. DHL (hon.), Gallaudet Coll., 1970; DFA (hon.), Md. Coll., 1972; HHD, MacMurray Coll., 1987. Appeared as actress in Broadway shows Let's Face It, 1941, Meet the People, 1941, By Jupiter, 1943, Bloomer Girl, 1944, High Button Shoes, 1947, Arms and the Girls, 1950, Love Life, 1948, Make a Wish, 1951, Mr. President, 1962, Jackpot, 1943, No Hard Feelings, 1973, Applause, 1973-74, Plaza Suite, 1973-74, The Secret Affairs of Mildred Wild, 1977, Bermuda Ave. Triangle, 1997; co-star (with Sid Caesar) on Caesar's Hour, CBS-TV, 1954-56; star: TV series Yes, Yes Nanette, 1961-62; TV spls. Happy Birthday & Goodby, 1974, George M!, 1970; motion pictures include Private Lives of Elizabeth and Essex, 1939, The Bandwagon, 1952, The Happy Ending, 1969, A Child is Born, 1940, Cockeyed Cowboys of Calico County, 1970, That's Entertainment, Part 2, 1976, Harper Valley PTA; TV appearances include: (series) One Day at a Time, CBS-TV; TV appearances include Alice Through the Looking Glass, 1966, Fame Is the Name of the Game, 1966, The Happy Ending, 1969, Cockeyed Cowboys of Calico, 1970, But I Don't Want To Get Married!, 1970, Magic Carpet, 1971, The Couple Takes a Wife, 1972, The Man in the Santa Claus Suit, 1978, Harper Valley P.T.A., 1978; TV guest appearances include The Alcoa Hour, 1955, Laramie, 1959, The Andy Williams Show, 1962, The Mary Tyler Moore Show, 1970, Murder She Wrote, 1984, Coach, 1989. Past bd. dirs. Pres.'s Nat. Adv. Com. on Edn. Deaf, Pres.'s Com. on Employment Handicapped, Muses of Calif. Mus. Found.; mem. Nat. Coun. on Handicapped, 1982—; founding mem. Nat. Captioning Inst. Recipient two Donaldson awards for High Button Shoes, 1947, Tony award for Love Life, 1949, Emmy award as best comedienne, 1955, 56, best supporting performer Caesar's Hour, 1955, Eleanor Roosevelt Humanitarian award, 1964, Human Relations award Anti-Defamation League, 1969, 1st ann. Cogswell award Gallaudet Coll., 1970, Pres.'s Distinguished Service award, 1970; named Woman of Year Radio and TV Editors, 1963, Woman of Year Jewish War Vets. Am., 1969, numerous others. Office: care Macfab Inc 14350 W Sunset Blvd Pacific Palisades CA 90272-3935*

FABRICAND, BURTON PAUL, physicist, educator; b. N.Y.C., Nov. 22, 1923; s. Irving Kermit and Frances (Sobler) F.; m. Heather C. North, Dec. 15, 1972; children by previous marriage: Nicole Diane, Lorraine Stewart. A.B., Columbia U., 1947, A.M., 1949, Ph.D., 1953. Project engr. Philco Corp., Phila., 1952-54; lectr., research asso. U. Pa., 1954-56; sr. research scientist Columbia Hudson Labs., Dobbs Ferry, N.Y., 1957-69; prof. physics Pratt Inst., Bklyn., 1969-92, prof. emeritus, 1992—; mng. ptnr. Fabricand Assocs., 1970—; cons. Moore Sch. Elec. Engring., U. Pa., 1954-60, Indsl. Electronic Hardware Corp., N.Y.C., 1960-64; investment mgr. Beating the Street Fund, 1996—; bd. dirs. Murphey, Marseilles, Smith & Nammack, N.Y.C. Author: Horse Sense: A New and Rigorous Application of Mathematical Methods to Successful Betting at the Track, 1965, Beating the Street, 1969, Horse Sense: Updated and Expanded Edition, 1976, The Science of Winning: A Random Walk on the Road to Riches, 1979, Abolish the Income Tax: A New and Rigorous Inquiry into the Wealth of Nations, 1986, Symmetry in Free Markets in Symmetry—Unifying Human Understanding, 1989, The Science of Winning: A Random Walk Along the Road to Investment Riches, 1996; contbr. numerous articles on atomic and nuclear physics and oceanography. Served U.S. Army, 1942-46. Mem. Am. Phys. Soc., Sigma Xi. Home: 47 Plaza St W Brooklyn NY 11217-3905 Office: PO Box 1107 New Milford CT 06776-1107

FABRICANT, ARTHUR E., lawyer, corporate executive; b. N.Y.C., Aug. 8, 1935; s. Henry and Rita (Wilson) F.; m. Inger Olsson, Nov. 1, 1975; children: Jill, Mary, John, James, Ann. AB, U. St. Andrews, Scotland, 1954, Union Coll., 1956; JD, Harvard U., 1959. Bar: N.Y. 1960. Atty. spl. group organized crime Office U.S. Atty. Gen., 1959-60; mem. firm Abeles & Clark, N.Y.C., 1960-61; v.p. Seligman & Latz Inc., N.Y.C., 1962-67; pres. internat. divsn. Seligman & Latz Inc., London, 1967-84; COO, pres. Seligman & Latz Inc., 1984-85; chmn. Essanelle Holdings, Ltd., Bermuda, 1985-96, Elizabeth Arden, Inc., 1992—; bd. dirs. New England Food Co., 1982-93. Fellow Inst. Dirs.; mem. Royal Wimbledon Golf Club. Home: Old Warren Farm, Wimbledon Common England Office: AE Fabricant & Co, 39 Camp Rd, London SW19 4UR, England

FABRIS, JAMES A., journalist; b. Cleve., Aug. 6, 1938; s. Andrew and Geraldine (Foretic) F.; m. Donna Wilker, Dec. 26, 1960; children—Julia, John, James F., Gerald, Andrew, Fredric. Student, Case Western Res. U., Cleve., 1956-58. Reporter Bklyn.-Parma News, Parma, Ohio, 1954-58; editorial staff Lake County News-Herald, Willoughby, Ohio, 1958-67, Chgo. Daily News, 1967-77; editorial staff Chgo. Sun-Times, 1977-84, dep. mng. editor, 1984-86; mng. editor N.Y. Post, N.Y.C., 1986-89; editorial staff New York Daily News, 1990-92; deputy mng. editor Cleve. Plain Dealer, 1992—. Recipient Marshall Field award Field Enterprises, 1974; Soc. of Publ. Designers award, 1978. Roman Catholic. Home: 20791 Lake Rd Rocky River OH 44116-1335 Office: Cleve Plain Dealer 1801 Superior Ave Cleveland OH 44114-2107

FABRY, PAUL ANDREW, international association executive; b. Budapest, Hungary; came to U.S., 1949, naturalized, 1962; s. Andrew and Ilona (Gombos) F.; m. Louise Hitchcock Fair, May 15, 1958 (div. 1968); children: Lydia Louise, Alexa Fair; m. Angela Andrews Rutledge, May 8, 1971 (div. 1979); m. Elizabeth Adams Garrett, 1988. BA, Godollo Jr. Coll., 1937; PhD, U. Budapest, 1942, JD, 1943. War corr. Central European Press Service, Warsaw, Poland, Berlin, Vienna, Austria, Zurich, Switzerland, Budapest, 1943-44; sec. Fgn. Office, Budapest, 1945; head Prime Minister's Cabinet, Budapest, 1945-46; charge d'affaires of Hungary, Ankara, Turkey, 1946-47; fgn. corr. Istanbul, Turkey, 1948-49; sect. chief Radio Free Europe, N.Y.C., 1950-53; freelance writer, lectr., N.Y.C., 1954; pub. relations adviser E.I. du Pont de Nemours & Co., Wilmington, Del., 1955-62; mng. dir. Internat. House, New Orleans, 1962-85; cons. World Trade Ctr. New Orleans, 1986—. Moderator: Fact and Opinion WYES-TV, 1965-74. Rep. Internat. Red Cross, Vienna-Budapest, 1945-46; adv. bd. Istanbul U., 1948-49, Internat. Econ. Cooperation Com., N.Y.C.; v.p. Cultural Services, Inc., N.Y.C., 1953-54; active United Fund, Wilmington, 1955-60; trustee, mem. exec. com. New Orleans Ednl. TV Found., 1970-75; founder Budapest chpt. Pulitzer Prize Found., 1989—. Served to capt. Royal Hungarian Arty., 1943. Mem. World Trade Ctrs. Assn. (founder, dir. emeritus).

FABRYCKY, WOLTER JOSEPH, engineering educator, author, industrial and systems engineer; b. Springfield, N.Y., Dec. 6, 1932; s. Louis Ludwig and Stephanie (Wadis) F.; m. Luba Swerbilow, 1954; children: David Jon, Kathryn Marie. BS, Wichita State U., 1957; MS, U. Ark., 1958; PhD, Okla. State U., 1962. Instr. indsl. engring. U. Ark., 1957-60; from asst. to assoc. prof. indsl. engring. and mgmt. Okla. State U., 1962-65; from assoc. prof. to prof. indsl. and sys. engring. Va. Poly. Inst. and State U., Blacksburg, 1965-88, John L. Lawrence prof., 1988-95, founding chmn. systems engring., 1969-76, assoc. dean engring., 1970-76, dean rsch. divsn., 1976-81, Lawrence prof. emeritus, sr. rsch. scientist, 1995—; chmn. Acad. Applications Internat., Inc., 1998—. Author: (with G.J. Thuesen and D. Verma) Economic Decision Analysis, 1974, 3d edit., 1998, (with B.S. Blanchard) Systems Engineering and Analysis, 1981, 3d edit., 1998, (with G.J. Thuesen) Engineering Economy, 1950, 8th edit., 1993, (with P.M. Ghare and P.E. Torgersen) Applied Operations Research and Management Science, 1984, (with J. Banks) Procurement and Inventory Systems Analysis, 1987, (with B.S. Blanchard) Life-Cycle Cost and Economic Analysis, 1991; editor: (with J.H. Mize) Prentice-Hall International Series in Industrial and Systems Engineering, 1972—. Recipient Lohmann medal Okla. State U., 1992; Ethyl Corp. doctoral fellow Okla. State U., 1960-62. Fellow AAAS, Inst. Indsl. Engrs. (exec. v.p. 1982-84, trustee, Book of Yr. award 1973, Outstanding Educator award 1990), Internat. Coun. on Sys. Engring. (charter, nat. bd. dirs. 1995-97); mem. Am. Soc. Engring. Edn. (v.p. 1977-78, bd. dirs., Grant award 1995), Ops. Rsch. Soc. Am., Sigma Xi, Alpha Pi Mu (v.p., bd. dirs. 1992—), Sigma Tau. Home: 1200 Lakewood Dr Blacksburg VA 24060-2005 Office: Va Poly Inst and State U 250 New Engring Bldg Blacksburg VA 24061

FABYANSKI, MARY IRENE, nursing administrator; b. Bayonne, N.J., July 14, 1952; d. Edward John and Rose Virginia (Mulhern) F. AAS in Nursing, Felician Coll., Lodi, N.J., 1977; student, Jersey City (N.J.) State Coll., 1970-72. Registered profl. nurse, N.J., 1977. LPN St. Francis Hosp., Jersey City, N.J., 1971-77, registered nurse, 1977-83; registered nurse Children's Specialized Hosp., Mountainside, N.J., 1984-88; asst. dir. nursing Manor Care of Mountainside, N.J., 1988-89; dir. nursing Morrishills Multi-care Ctr., Morristown, N.J., 1989-90; asst. adminstr., dir. nursing Berkeley Hall Nursing Home, Berkeley Heights, N.J., 1990-93; dir. nursing Jewish Home and Rehab. Ctr., Jersey City, N.J., 1993-98, Franciscan Home and Rehab. Ctr., Jersey City, 1998; pres., cons. long term care Quality Care Cons., Union, N.J., 1996-98; dir. ops. Future Care Cons., BHCC, Irvington, N.J., 1998—; bd. adv. Hudson County C.C., Jersey City, N.J., 1996-98. Recipient Award for Excellence Bd. Dirs., Berkeley Hall, Berkeley Heights, 1991, Award of Recognition, Bd. Dirs., Hudson City Coll., Jersey City, 1997, 98. Mem. NAACP, N.J. Long Term Care Nursing Assn., Nat. Assn. Long Term Care. Democrat. Roman Catholic. Home: 147 Jockey Hollow Way Union NJ 07083-4158 Office: Quality Care Consultants 147 Jockey Hollow Way Union NJ 07083-4158

FACCINI, ERNEST CARLO, mechanical engineer; b. Livo, Trento, Italy, May 28, 1949; parents Am. citizens; s. Carlo and Elena Agnes (Pancheri) F.; m. Sharon L. Finisecy; 1 child, Carlo Ernesto. AA, Western Wyo. Community Coll., 1969; BS, U. Wyo., 1972, MS, 1976. Registered profl. engr. Wyo., Md., N.Mex. Engring. technician Laramie (Wyo.) Energy Rsch. Ctr., 1968-71; field engr. Mountain Fuel Supply Co., Rock Springs, Wyo., 1972; research engr. Aberdeen (Md.) Proving Grounds, 1972-73; rsch. asst. mech. engring. U. Wyo., Laramie, 1973-76; engring. asst. Bridger Coal Co., Rock Springs, Wyo., 1973; mech. engr. Naval Explosive Ordnance Disposal Facility, Indian Head, Md., 1976-85; sr. scientist TERA/NMIMT, Socorro, N.Mex., 1986-89; prin. scientist Textron Systems Corp., Wilmington, Mass., 1989—. Contbr. articles to profl. jours.; patentee in field. Mem. ASME (chmn. student sect. 1971-72), TMS, Am. Phys. Soc. Roman Catholic. Achievements include rsch. in ballistics, shaped charge design, explosively formed projectile and explosive effects; also rschr. in fabrication of Ta metal for warhead liners, application of orbital forging to warhead liners, use of powdered metall. techniques to obtain starting material for forging liners, use of end-game analysis, vulnerability lethality analysis codes in the design of warheads, use of reactive/energetic materials and insensitive explosives applications to warheads; patentee in field. Home: 9 Spring Rd Londonderry NH 03053-2912 Office: Textron Def Systems 201 Lowell St Wilmington MA 01887-2969

FACCINTO, VICTOR PAUL, artist, gallery administrator; b. Albany, Calif., Oct. 30, 1945; s. Victor A. and Betty Jean (Smith) Pearson; 1 dau., Denise Michelle. BA in Psychology, Calif. State U.-Sacramento, 1969, MA in Art, 1972. Instr. art Calif. State U., 1972-74; asst. to dir. Nancy Hoffman Gallery, N.Y.C., 1974-78; dir. art gallery Wake Forest U., Winston Salem, 1978—, art faculty, 1983—; founding mem. multi-media performance group Three People, 1990. One-person shows include Mus. Modern Art, N.Y.C., 1975, Collective for Living Cinema, N.Y.C., 1976, Phyllis Kind Gallery, N.Y.C., 1980, 82, 87, N.C. Mus. Art, 1986, Helander Gallery, N.Y.C., 1991, Millennium Film Workshop, N.Y.C., 1996, Cleve. Performance Art Festival, 1998, Southeastern Ctr. for Contemporary Art, N.C., 1999; group shows include Whitney Mus. Am. Art, 1972, 73, 74, Mus. Modern Art, N.Y.C., 1978, Barbara Gladstone Gallery, N.Y.C., 1983, Monique Knowlton Gallery, N.Y.C., 1983, Helander Gallery, Palm Beach, Fla., 1988, 90; represented in permanent collections Mus. Modern Art, N.Y.C., Philip Morris, Inc.; animated film maker: Shameless, 1974. N.Y. CAPS fellow, 1977; N.C. Arts Council fellow, 1982, 86; recipient 1st prize NYU Small Works Competition, 1983. Baptist. E-mail: faccinto@wfu.edu. Home: 1950 Cliffside Dr Pfafftown NC 27040-9507 Office: Wake Forest U PO Box 7232 Winston Salem NC 27109-7232

FACE, WAYNE BRUCE, small business owner; b. Everett, Mass., June 20, 1942; s. Ward Jr. and Margaret Irene (Keil) F.; m. Sharon Lucille Blythe, Mar. 25, 1967; children: Jonathan Jacob, Joseph Matthew. ASA, Bentley Coll., 1962, BSA, 1967; MBA, Pepperdine U., 1975; EdD, Vanderbilt U., 1986. Div. analyst Varian Assocs., Palo Alto, Calif., 1969-71, sr. fin. analyst, 1972-75; acctg. mgr. Veeco Instruments, Sunnyvale, Calif., 1971-72; product line controller Nat. Semiconductor, Santa Clara, Calif., 1975-76; assoc. prof. Hawthorne Coll. of Bus., Antrim, N.H., 1976-86, dept. chmn., 1983-86; owner Learn to Live, Warner, N.H., 1986-88; acctg. mgr. N.H. Correctional Industries, Concord, 1988-91; owner Sharway Gifts, Warner, 1991-93; part-time transp. aide NFI North, Concord, N.H., 1993—. Contbr. to Mensa Rsch. Jour. Advisor Jr. Achievement, Palo Alto, 1971-73; den leader Cub Scouts, Warner, 1990-91; coach Kearsarge Youth Basketball, New London, N.H., 1991-93; bd. dirs. Kearsarge Children's Ctr., Warner, 1987-88. With U.S. Army, 1964-67, Korea. Democrat. Avocations: sports, golf, chess, reading. Home and Office: 45 W Main St Warner NH 03278-4213

FACHES, WILLIAM GEORGE, lawyer; b. Cedar Rapids, Iowa, Feb. 15, 1928; s. George Vlasios and Androniki (Panagopoulos) F.; m. Mary Matzanias, Dec. 6, 1959; children: Andrea Lynn, Allison Lynn. Student, Coe Coll., 1947-48; B.A., U. Iowa, 1951, J.D., 1955. Bar: Iowa 1955, U.S. Supreme Ct. 1971. Mem. firm Reilly & Faches, Cedar Rapids, 1955-67; 1st asst. county atty. Linn County, 1965-67, county atty., 1967-74, probate referee, 1990—; sr. mem. firm Faches, Gloe and Quint, and predecessors, Cedar Rapids, 1967—. Mem. Mayor's Ad Hoc Com. on Alcholism, 1967-68, Linn County Crime Commn., 1971-73, Linn County Bd. Suprs., 1978; pres. Young Democrats, 1960; mem. central com. Linn County Dem. Com., 1956-58, 60-68; bd. dirs. Linn County Assn. Mentally Retarded, 1968-72, Cedar Rapids Teen Club, 1968-74; chmn., mem. bd. 6th Jud. Dist. Iowa Dept. Correctional Services, 1978—; inheritance tax appraiser 6th Jud. Dist., 1980-91; pres. St. John's Hellenic Orthodox Ch., 1981—. Served with Air Corps AUS, 1946-47. Recipient Civil Libertarian award Iowa Civil Liberties Union, 1974, Iowa Gov.'s award for voluntarism, 1986, 90; William G. Faches Ctr. of 6th Jud. Dist. Iowa Dept. Correctional Svcs. named in his honor; named to Linn County Iowa Dem. Party Hall of Fame, 1995. Mem. Iowa, Linn County bar assns., Am. Trial Lawyers Assn., Iowa County Attys. Assn., Nat. Dist. Attys. Assn., Am. Judicature Soc., Criminal Law Assn. Linn County (pres. 1976), Iowa Correctional Services Assn. (Citizen of Yr. award 1980), Am. Legion (trustee Hanford Post 5 1982-89), Phi Alpha Delta. Home: 1901 5th Ave SE Cedar Rapids IA 52403-2710 Office: 318 Paramount Bldg Cedar Rapids IA 52401

FACHNIE, H(UGH) DOUGLAS, film manufacturing company official; b. Windsor, Ont., Can., Sept. 8, 1952; came to U.S., 1957; s. Harold Lennox Fachnie and Mary Jane (Schultz) MacKenzie. B Gen. Studies, U. Mich., 1973. Salesman Quarry, Inc., Ann Arbor, Mich., 1974; store mgr. Quarry, Inc., Ann Arbor and Saginaw, Mich., 1974-77; dist. mgr. Fotomat Corp., San Diego, 1977-80; dir. ops. Fotomat Corp., Wilton, Conn., 1980-81, dir. merchandising, 1981-83; mgr. optical products Fuji Photo Film U.S.A., Inc., N.Y.C., 1983-84; product mgr. consumer film Fuji Photo Film U.S.A., Inc., Elmsford, N.Y., 1984-89, sr. product/packaging mgr. film and one-time use cameras, 1989-94, mktg. mgr. consumer photo, 1995-97; material planning and logistics mgr. Profl. and Photofinishing Markets, Fuji Phot Film USA, Inc., Elmsford, N.Y., 1998—. Mem. AAAS, Photog. Mktg. Assn., Digital Imaging Mktg. Assn., APICS. Republican. Avocations: home maintenance, flying, photography, audiophile, curling. Home: 30 Fleetwood Dr Danbury CT 06810-7010 Office: Fuji Photo Film USA Inc 555 Taxter Rd Elmsford NY 10523-2394

FACKLER, JOHN PAUL, JR., chemistry educator; b. Toledo, July 31, 1934; s. John P. and Ruth (Moehring) F.; m. Naomi Paula Steege, Sept. 2, 1956; children: Katherine G., Cheryl R., Karla S., John M., Dorothy L. Student, MIT, 1952; B.A., Valpraiso U., 1956, D.Sc. (hon.), 1987; Ph.D., MIT, 1960. Jr. chemist Sun Oil Co., 1953-56; teaching asst. MIT, 1956-59, research assoc., 1960; asst. prof. U. Calif., 1960-62, Case Inst. Tech., 1962-64; assoc. prof. chemistry Case Western Res. U., 1964-69, prof., 1970-82, chmn. dept., 1972-77; dean Coll. Sci., Tex. A&M U., 1983-91, Disting. prof. chemistry, 1987—; Wilhelm Manchot Forschung prof. Tech. U., Munich, 1992; vis. prof. U. Calif. at Santa Barbara, 1969; Fulbright lectr. Colombia, 1969; cons. in chemistry Central State U., 1967-69; chmn. Inorganic Synthesis Corp., 1987-90. Author: Symmetry in Coordination Chemistry, 1971; editor: Symmetry in Chemical Theory, 1973, Inorganic Syntheses, Vol. 21, 1982, Modern Inorganic Chemistry Series, Plenum; contbr. articles to profl. jours. Bd. dirs. Luth. Met. Ministry, 1969-72; bd. dirs. Luth. High Sch. Assn., 1974-80, chmn., 1979. NSF summer fellow, 1959; J.S. Guggenheim fellow, 1976; Bye fellow Robinson Coll., U. Cambridge, 1992; recipient Tech. Achievement award Cleve. Tech. Soc., 1971. Fellow AAAS, Am. Inst. Chemists; mem. Am. Chem. Soc. (councilor 1972-73, chmn. elect

1974, chmn. Cleve. sect. 1975, chmn. elect 1978, chmn. inorganic div. 1979, Morley medal Cleve. sect. 1987, Southwest regional award 1990), Gordon Research Conf. (council 1979-82, trustee 1982-89, chmn. 1989), Tex. Acad. Sci. (bd. dirs. 1987-90), Chem. Soc. London, Am. Crystal. Assn., N.Y. Acad. Scis., Sigma Xi, Phi Lambda Upsilon, Phi Delta Theta. Lutheran. Home: 4770 Enchanted Oaks Dr College Station TX 77845-7649 Office: Tex A&M U Chem Dept College Station TX 77842-3012

FACOS, JAMES FRANCIS, English language educator, author; b. Lawrence, Mass., July 28, 1924; s. Chris and Theresa (McAdam) F.; m. Cleo John Chigos, Dec. 1, 1956; children: Theresa-Katina, Elizabeth Joy, Anthony John. AB in English, Bates Coll., Lewiston, Maine, 1949; MA in English, Fla. State U., 1958; DHL, Norwich U., Northfield, Vt., 1989. Instr. Vt. Coll., Montpelier, 1959-72; asst. prof. Norwich U., Northfield, Vt., 1972-73, assoc. prof., 1973-83, prof., 1983-89, prof. emeritus, 1989—. Author: (novel) The Silver Lady, 1972, 95, (poems) Morning's Come Singing, 1981, (plays) A Day of Genesis, 1969, One Daring Fling, 1978; represented in permanent collection 20th Century Archives Mugar Meml. Libr., Boston U. Staff sgt. USAF, 1943-45, ETO. Decorated DFC, Air medal; recipient The Alden award Dramatist's Alliance, Palo Alto, Calif., 1956, Walter Peach award Poetry Soc. Vt., Burlington, 1962, Corinne Davis award Poetry Soc. Vt., Burlington, 1970, Norwich U. Found. award for disting. svc., 1992. Home: 333 Elm St Montpelier VT 05602-2213

FADARISHAN, STEPHEN ROBERT, systems engineer; b. Scranton, Pa., Nov. 24, 1953; s. Steve and Grace Catherine (Mack) F.; m. Ines Fernandez, June 25, 1988. BS in Elec. Engring., Pa. State U., 1982. Lic. gen. radiotelephone operator with ship radar endorsement FCC. Design engr. Locus Inc., State College, Pa., 1982-84, Gen. Instruments, Hatboro, Pa., 1984-86; sr. engr. Norden Systems, Norwalk, Conn., 1986-89; contract software engr. Westinghouse, Balt., 1989-91, Boehringer Mannheim, Indpls., 1991-92; tech. advisor in engring. standards Cummins Engine Co., Columbus, Ind., 1992—; cons. Watermark, Inc., Ft. Wayne, Ind., 1991—. Mem. Homeowners Orgn., Greenwood, Ind., 1993—. Mem. Letters of Commendation, USN, 1975, 77. Mem. IEEE, Assn. for Info. and Image Mgmt., Soc. for Tech. Comm., Eta Kappa Nu. Achievements include development of process and system implementation which converts existing corporate documents for electronic distribution via the corporate intranet web. Avocations: cross-country skiing, reading. Office: Cummins Engine Engring Standards Box 3005 M/C 50111 Columbus IN 47202-3005

FADDA EASTMAN, JULIE SUZANNE, editor; b. Hayward, Calif., May 21, 1967; d. John Stanley Fadda and Sallie Gene Robertson; m. Douglas Eugene Eastman, Aug. 17, 1996. BA in Journalism, San Francisco State U., 1991. Exec. editor Prism mag., San Francisco, 1990-91; contbg. editor The City mag., San Francisco, 1991-92; assoc. editor Emergency mag., Carlsbad, Calif., 1992-94, graphic designer, 1994-95; graphic designer Police mag., Carlsbad, 1994-95; contbg. editor Mus. and More mag., San Diego, 1994-98; mng. editor Software Devel. mag., San Francisco, 1996-99; sr. editor Learn2.com, 1999—. Mem. Soc. Profl. Journalists. Avocations: hiking, skiing, music, writing. E-mail: jeastman@learn2.com.

FADDEN, DELMAR MCLEAN, electrical engineer; b. Seattle, Nov. 10, 1941; s. Gene Scott and Alice Elizabeth (McLean) F.; m. Sandra Myrene Callahan, June 22, 1963; children: Donna McLean, Lawrence Gene. BSEE, U. Wash., 1963, MSEE, 1975. Lic. comml. pilot, Wash. With Boeing Comml. Airplane Co., Seattle, 1969—, chief engr. flight deck, 1988-90, chief engr. 737/757 avonics/flight sys., 1990-96, integration mgr. cabin sys., 1996-98, integration mgr. airplane svcs., 1999—. Contbr. articles to profl. jours. Capt. USAF, 1963-69. Mem. AIAA, IEEE, Human Factors Soc., Soc. Automotive Engrs. (vice chmn. G-10 com. 1981-91, chmn. systems integration task group 1990-96), Mountaineers Found. (pres. 1998—), Am. Alpine Club, Mountaineers Club (pres. 1984-86). Achievements include 2 patents in field. Home: 5011 298th Ave SE Preston WA 98050 Office: Boeing Comml Airplane Co PO Box 3707 Seattle WA 98124-2207

FADELEY, ELEANOR ADELINE, secondary education educator; b. Phila., Aug. 30, 1924; d. Nicholas William and Eleonora (Miceli) Battafarano; m. Herbert John Fadeley, Jr., Feb. 8, 1947; children: Herbert John, Brett Duane, Theresa Jane, Scott Lewis. BS, Drexel U., 1946; postgrad. Sch. Law, Temple U., 1949-51. Exec. trainee Lit Bros., Phila., 1946-67; sec. Hyde-Rakestraw, cotton yarn brokers, Phila., 1947-48; lab. asst. pub. rels. rep. Indsl. By Products & Rsch. Corp., Phila., 1948-51; tchr. Atlantic City Friends Sch., 1957-58; subs. tchr. Troy (N.Y.) Pub. Schs., 1970-71, 78-86; curriculum chmn. Friends of W. Kenneth Doyle Mid. Sch., Troy, 1977-78; English and sci. asst. Friends of W. Kenneth Doyle Middle Sch., 1976-77. Legis. chmn. Samaritan Hosp. Aux., 1975-78, v.p., 1978-79; bd. dirs. Rensselaer County Am. Cancer Soc., 1980-83; chmn. Town of Brunswick Residential Crusade, 1982; vol. Bellevue Maternity Hosp., Niskayuna, N.Y. Mem. AAUW (mem. chmn., pres. br. 1979, sec.-treas. Ea. area interbr. coun. 1981-82, vice-chmn. 1982-83 Troy br., mem. Albany br.), Home Econs. Legis. Monitors, Drexel Alumnae Assn., St. Johns Altar Guild, N.Y. State Gen. Fedn. Women's Clubs (Rensselaer County chmn. 1980-82, internat. chmn. 3d dist., scholarship chmn. 3rd dist. 1994—), Embroiders' Guild Am. Inc. (N.Y. capital dist. chpt.), Panhellenic Alumnae Assn. Schenectady, Panhellenic Garden Club (pres. 1983-84, sec.-treas. 1990-91, v.p. 1994-95), Troy Woman's Club (pres. 1976-78, v.p. 1982-83, 96-98, bd. dirs. 1993-95, 99-2000, vol. Stories Offer Activity Read 1993-95, mem. permanent funds bd. 1995-98, chmn. ann. luncheon 1998), Alpha Sigma Alpha (life). Republican. Episcopalian. Home: 150 Tallmadge Pl Albany NY 12208-1086

FADELY, JAMES PHILIP, admission and financial aid director, educator; b. New Castle, Ind., Jan. 10, 1953; s. Harry Ellison and Viola (Clapp) F.; m. Sally Jane Fehsenfeld, Aug. 16, 1975; children: James Philip Jr., Adele Langsdale. BA, Hanover Coll., 1975; MA, Ind. U., 1977, PhD, 1990. Tchr. Brookstone Sch., Columbus, Ga., 1975-76; tchr., adminstrv. asst. Savannah (Ga.) Country Day Sch., 1979-83; lectr. Ind. U., Indpls., 1984—; tchr., asst. headmaster St. Richard's Sch., Indpls., 1988-90, tchr., 1990-91, dir. admission and fin. aid, tchr., 1991—; bd. dirs. Indpls. br. English-Speaking Union, ; nat. bd. dirs. English-Speaking Union; lectr. Butler U., 1985, U. Indpls., 1995. Author: A Brief History of St. Richard's School, 1960-1995, 1995, Thomas Taggart: Public Servant, Political Boss, 1856-1929, 1997, The Origins of Woodstock Club, 1997; contbr. articles to profl. jours. Dem. nominee 6th Dist. of Ind. for Congress, 1990. Mem. Ind. Assn. Historians, Ind. Hist. Soc. (grant 1991-94), Indpls. Lit. Club, Soc. Ind. Pioneers, Orgn. Am. Historians, Hanover Coll. Alumni Assn. (bd. dirs. 1985-88), Hanover Club Indpls. (bd. dirs. 1988—), Leland (Mich.) Yacht Club, Woodstock Club, Phi Delta Theta. Democrat. Roman Catholic. Avocation: travel. Home: 9146 N Kenwood Dr Indianapolis IN 46260-1400 Office: St Richards Sch 3243 N Meridian St Indianapolis IN 46208-4645

FADEN, LEE JEFFREY, technical advisory service executive; b. Phila., Dec. 18, 1953; s. Myer I. and Thelma A. (Lehrich) F.; m. Susan D. Rosen, Aug. 19, 1978; 3 children. BS in Acctg., Pa. State U., 1976; MBA, Temple U., 1979. Purchasing, advt. and sales exec. Royal Distbrs., Colmar, Pa., 1974-79; co-CEO Tech. Adv. Svc., Inc., Blue Bell, Pa., 1979—. Chmn. troop com. Boy Scouts Am., Dresher, Pa., 1963—; mgr. Horsham (Pa.) Little League, 1991—; coach, mgr. Horsham Soccer Assn., 1994—. Inducted to Chapel of Four Chaplains Phila., 1980. Mem. Assn. Records Mgrs. and Adminsrs. Internat., Am. Fin. Assn., Am. Mgmt. Assn., Greater Phila. C. of C. Avocations: scouts, camping, clay modelling, bicycling, computers. Office: Tech Adv Svc Inc 1166 Dekalb Pike Blue Bell PA 19422-1844

FADEN, RUTH R., medical educator, ethicist, researcher. BA, U. Pa., 1970; MA, U. Chgo., 1971; MPH, U. Calif., Berkeley, 1973, PhD, 1976. Sr. rsch. scholar Kennedy Inst. Ethics, Georgetown U., 1978—; prof. health policy and mgmt. Johns Hopkins U., Balt., 1986—, dir. program in law, ethics & health, 1988—, assoc. Hopkins Population Ctr., Sch. Hygiene & Pub. Health, 1989—, prof., Philip Franklin Wagley chair in biomed. ethics, 1995—, exec. dir. Bioethics Inst., 1995—; chair pres.'s adv. com. on human radiation experiments; chair Adv. Panel on Reproductive Hazards in the Workplace, Office of Tech. Assessment, 1984-85; mem. com. on risk perception and comm. NAS, 1987-88; mem. Panel on Confidentiality and Data Access, Com. on Nat. Stats. and the Social Sci. Rsch. Coun., 1989-91; mem. Alcohol, Drug Abuse, and Mental Health Adminstrn., AIDS Adv. Com., 1990-92; mem. Workshop on Biomed. Ethics in U.S. Pub. Policy, Office of Tech. Assessment, 1992; mem. adv. bd. Finding Common Ground Project: The Reproductive Rights and Needs of Women and the Emerging Conflict in Maternal and Child Health, 1992-93; mem. Adv. Panel on Prospects for Health Tech. Assessment, Office of Tech. Assessment, 1992-93; co-chair Com. on Legal and Ethical Issues Relating to the Inclusion of Women in Clin. Studies, Inst. Medicine, 1992-93; chair Adv. Com. on Human Radiation Experiments, 1994-95. Author: (with T.L. Beauchamp, J. Wallace and L. Walters) Ethical Issues in Social Science Research, 1982, (with T.L. Beauchamp) A History and Theory of Informed Consent, 1986, (with G. Geller, M. Powers) AIDS, Women and the Next Generation, 1991, (with A.C. Mastroianni, D. Federman) Women and Health Research: Ethical and Legal Issues of Including Women in Clinical Studies, vol. I, 1994, (with N. Kass) HIV, AIDS and Childbearing: Public Policy, Private Lives. Fellow APA; mem. APHA, Inst. Medicine, Am. Assn. Bioethics (organizing com.), Forum on Bioethics (co-founder, former chair). Office: Bioethics Inst Hampton House 511 624 N Broadway Baltimore MD 21205-1996*

FADEN-QURESHI, BETSY BRUZZESE, activity director, volunteer coordinator, recreation therapist; b. New Rochelle, N.Y., Jan. 5, 1951; d. Gale (Hafford) Bruzzese; divorced; children: Benjamin Clinton, Carol Edwine; m. Izhar A. Qureshi, 1997. Diploma in musicianship, N.Y. Coll. of Music, 1969; student, Oberlin Conservatory, 1969-71, 74-75; tchr. cert., Diller-Quaile Music Sch., N.Y.C., 1982; BS, Empire State Coll., 1991; MS, Lehman Coll., CUNY, 1994. Cert. activity dir. Nat. Cert. Coun. of Activity Profls., therapeutic recreation specialists Nat. Cert. of Therapeutic Recreation Coun., alcohol substance abuse counsling Westchester Inst. Tng. Psychoanalysis Psychotherapy. Adj. tchr. piano, asst. choir accompanist Rutgers U., New Brunswick, N.J., 1971-73; accompanist dance Douglass Coll., New Brunswick, 1972-73; asst. dir. Roosa Sch. Music, Bklyn., 1979-81; mgr., libr. Brooklyn Heights (N.Y.) Orch., 1982-84; tchr. piano and theory Diller-Quaile Music Sch., 1976-83; dir., founder Adamant (Vt.) Chamber Ensemble Sch. & Camp, 1981-86; activity dir. Waterview Hills Nursing Ctr., Purdys, N.Y., 1990-92; music specialist cons. Wartburg Luth. Home, Mt. Vernon, N.Y., 1992—; dir. activities and vols. Astor Gardens Nursing Home, Bronx, N.Y., 1994-96; supr. recreation therapist outpatient programs Yonkers Gen. Hosp., Greenburgh, N.Y., 1998—. Author: (manual) Making a Difference; compiler, performer: (book and audio tape) The Lullaby Project, 1990; creator, facilitator Musical House Tours, 1982-83. Vol. VA Hosps., Bronx and Montrose, N.Y.; organist, choir dir. Episcopal Ch. of Divine Love, Montrose, 1989-94; organist Trinity Boscobel United Meth. Ch., Buchanan, N.Y., 1996—. Recipient Spl. Project award Vt. Coun. Arts, 1982-85, Nat. Found. Arts, New Eng. Found. Arts. Mem. Nat. Assn. Activity Profls., Westchester Recreation and Parks Soc., Westchester Musicians Guild, Nat. Therapeutic Recreation Soc., Behre Piano Assocs. (past v.p.)., N.Y. State Therapeutic Recreation Assn. Avocations: music and thematic activity programming, collecting lullabyes and earrings, study of multiple personality disorder, collecting donations for the homeless. Home: 6 Arlington Ct Montrose NY 10548-1112

FADER, DANIEL NELSON, English language educator; b. Balt., Jan. 4, 1930; s. Maurice Abraham and Ida Eunice (Browne) F.; m. Martha Alice Agnew, Oct. 8, 1955 (div. 1982); children: Paul Frederick, Lisa Jeanne; m. Christine Verzar, Oct. 15, 1988. B.A., Cornell U., 1952, M.A., 1954; Ph.D., Stanford U., 1963. Research scholar Christ's Coll., Cambridge (Eng.) U., 1955-57; acting instr. Stanford (Calif.) U., 1957-61; instr. U. Mich., Ann Arbor, 1961-63, from asst. prof. to assoc. prof., 1963-73, prof. English lang. and lit., 1973-76, prof. English, chmn. English composition bd., 1976-83, prof. English, 1983-98, prof. emeritus, 1998—; lectr., cons. in field. Author: books including Hooked on Books, 1966, The Naked Children, 1971, 96, Paul and I Discover America, 1975, (with others) New Hooked on Books, 1976; contbr. articles to profl. jours. Served with U.S. Army, 1954-55. Mem. ACLU. Home: PO Box 988 Truro MA 02666

FADER, HENRY CONRAD, lawyer; b. Bronx, Dec. 2, 1946; s. Michael and Ruth (Filler) F.; m. Linda L. Koch, Nov. 23, 1969; children: Melanie, Danielle. AB, U. Rochester, N.Y., 1968; MEd, Temple U., 1970; JD, Syracuse (N.Y.) U., 1973. Bar: Pa. 1973, U.S. Dist. Ct. (ea. dist.) Pa. 1973, N.J. 1988. Ptnr. Fox, Rothschild, O'Brien & Frankel, Phila., 1973-92; ptnr. Schnader, Harrison, Segal & Lewis, Phila., 1992—, chmn. health law dept., 1993—; chmn. Fox Rothchild Health Law Group, 1985-92; bd. dirs PCI Ins., Inc. Bd. dirs., solicitor Eagleville (Pa.) Hosp., 1987—; bd. dirs. Beth Am. Synagogue, Abington, Pa., 1988—, Pa. Info. Hwy. Consortium; chmn. bd. dirs. Intercultural Family Svcs., Inc., 1998—; bd. dirs. Pa. Chamber of Bus. and Industry, 1994—. Mem. ABA, Pa. Bar Assn., Phila. Bar Assn., N.J. Bar Assn. (bd. dirs. corp. law sect. 1989-92), Nat. Assn. Bond Lawyers, Am. Health Lawyers Assn., Soc. Health Law Attys. (bd. dirs. Pa. chpt. 1987-91). Avocations: tennis, reading, gardening, home improvements. Office: Schnader Harrison Segal & Lewis 1600 Market St Ste 3600 Philadelphia PA 19103-7240

FADER, SEYMOUR JEREMIAH, management and engineering consulting company executive; b. N.Y.C., Feb. 9, 1923; s. Louis and Bertha (Stachel) F.; m. Shirley Ruth Sloan, June 26, 1951; children: Susan Deborah, Steven Micah. Student, CCNY, 1938-42; BSEE, U. Pa., 1949, MBA in Indsl. Mgmt., 1950. Mgr. prodn. Bogue Electric Mfg. Co., Paterson, N.J., 1950-56; mgr. planning and control Rowe Mfg. Co., Whippany, N.J., 1956-58; cons., engr. Koor Crafts & Industries, Ltd., Tel Aviv, 1958-59; dir. mfg. ops. ESC Electronics Corp., Palisades Park, N.J., 1959-62; mgr. mfg. Artistic Mfg., Sun Chem. Corp., Carlstadt, N.J., 1962-66; mgr. ops. Fairchild Instrumentation, Fairchild Camera & Instrument Corp., Clifton, N.J., 1966-67; v.p. Graphic Products, Inc., Hackensack, N.J., 1967-69; gen. mgr., v.p. Berkey Tech., Berkey Photo, Inc., Woodside, N.Y., 1969-72; pres. Suste Assocs., Paramus, N.J., 1972—; asst. prof. mgmt. Ramapo Coll., Mahwah, N.J., 1972-75, assoc. prof., 1975-80, prof. mgmt. and indsl. rels., 1980-93, prof. emeritus, 1993—, bd. dirs. Study Abroad programs, 1983-93; program coord. Overseas Program, Southside Va. C.C., 1994-95; adj. prof. mgmt. Grad. Sch. Bus., Fordham U., 1982—; arbitration panelist Better Bus. Bur. of Bergen, Passaic and Rockland Counties, 1983—; program dir. overseas program Coll. Consortium for Study Abroad, 1995—. Author: Fundamentals of Management for First-Line Supervisors, 1974, The Manufacturing Manager, 1975; co-author: Jobmanship, 1979; contbr. articles to profl. jours.; patentee coreless reeler, desk-top copier, photo-copier. Mem. pub. health study N.J. State Assembly Commn. on Conservation, Natural Resources, Air and Water Pollution, 1972-73; commr. Paramus Environ. Commn., 1973-78, vice chmn., 1977-78, chmn. inventory and land use com., 1974-78. With U.S. Army, 1942-45. Mem. Am. Mgmt. Assn. (cert. of achievement 1974), Am. Arbitration Assn. (panelist), Am. Inst. Indsl. Engrs., Soc. Advancement of Mgmt., Nat. Panel Consumer Arbitrators, Am. Prodn. and Inventory Control Soc., Delta Mu Delta. Home and Office: 377 Mckinley Blvd Paramus NJ 07652-4725

FADER, SHIRLEY SLOAN, writer; b. Paterson, N.J.; d. Samuel Louis and Miriam (Marcus) Sloan; m. Seymour J. Fader; children: Susan Deborah, Steven Micah Kimchi. BS, MS, U. Pa. Writer, journalist, author Paramus, N.J.; chmn., coord. ann. writers seminar Bergen C.C., 1973-76. Author: (books) The Princess Who Grew Down, 1968, From Kitchen to Career, 1977, Jobmanship, 1978, Successfully Ever After, 1982 (Brit. edit. 1985), Wait a Minute: You Can Have It All, 1993, paperback edit., 1994; (columns) Jobmanship, People and You, Family Weekly mag., 1971-82, How to Get More From Your Job, Glamour mag., 1978-81, Start Here, Working Woman mag., 1980-88, Work Strategies, Working Mother mag., 1987-88, Women Getting Ahead, Ladies Home Jour., 1980-90, How Would You Handle It, New Idea mag., 1984—, Moving Up, Woman mag., 1989-90, Career Expert "Ask the Experts", Woman's World mag., 1992-95; contbg. editor Family Weekly, 1971-82, Glamour mag., 1978-81, Working Woman mag., 1980-88, Working Mother mag., 1987-88, Ladies Home Jour., 1980-90, Woman mag., 1989-90; contbr. articles on career, relationships and travel to mags. worldwide. Mem. Authors Guild, Am. Soc. Journalists and Authors (moderator ann. writer's conf. 1971-99, nat. v.p. 1976-77, mem.-at-large nat. exec. coun. 1976-78, 83-86, nat. sec., mem. exec. coun. 1995-96), Nat. Press Club, Newswomen of N.Y. Address: 377 McKinley Blvd Paramus NJ 07652-4725

FADIMAN, ANNE, writer, editor; b. N.Y.C., Aug. 7, 1953; d. Clifton and Annalee Whitmore (Jacoby) F.; m. George Howe Colt, Mar. 4, 1989; children: Susannah, Henry. BA, Harvard U., 1975. Contbr. editor Harvard Magazine, Cambridge, Mass., 1973-75; instr. Nat. Outdoor Leadership Sch., Lander, Wyo., 1975-76; columnist Country Journal, Manchester, N.H., 1978-79; asst. sci. editor Life, N.Y.C., 1979-81; columnist Life, 1986-87, staff writer, 1981-88; columnist, editor-at-large Civilization, Washington, 1994-98; editor The Am. Scholar, Washington, 1998—; bd. incorporators Harvard Magazine, Cambridge, Mass., 1985— (bd. dirs., 1985-91). Author: The Spirit Catches You and You Fall Down, 1997. Recipient Nat. Magazine award for Reporting Am. Soc. Magazine Editors, 1987, Gen. Nonfiction award Nat. Book Critics Circle, 1997, Current Interest Nonfiction prize L.A. Times, 1997, Nonfiction prize Anne Rea Jewell Boston Book Rev., 1997; named John S. Knight fellow in Journalism Stanford (Calif.) U., 1991-92. Mem. Phi Beta Kappa (hon.). Address: American Scholar 178 Massachusetts Ave NW Fl 4 Washington DC 20001-1434*

FADIMAN, LOUISE, writer, consultant; b. N.Y.C., May 15, 1929; d. Arthur Robert and Mabel Louise (Scott) Turner; m. Jonathan Rush Fadiman, June 29, 1957; children: Pleasance, Christopher, Matthew, Clarissa. BA magna cum laude, NYU, 1976; cert. profl. achievement MIS, Northeastern U., 1986. Editor, writer Mass. High Tech., Burlington, 1981-83; prodn. editor French, Spanish, English Heinle & Heinle, Boston, 1982-83; sr. tech. writer Computervision, Inc., Bedford, Mass., 1983-85; prin. tech. writer Adage, Inc., Billerica, Mass., 1985-87; sr. tech. writer Alliant Computer, Inc., Littleton, Mass., 1989-91; pres. Litartech Press, Kennebunk, Maine, 1991—; software cons. Internat. Bur. Software Test, 1983-85; cons., book reviewer Prentice Hall, McGraw Hill, 1983-85. Author: From Sea to Sky: Henri Fabre Aviation Pioneer, 1994, The Concord Experience, 1995; contbr. articles to jours. and mags. Lifetime mem. Friends of the Concord Free Pub. Libr., The Concord Mus. Mem. IEEE, U.S. Chess Fedn., N.Y. Acad. Scis. Republican. Episcopalian. Avocations: art gallery owner, goldsmith, artist, photographer.

FADNER, WILLARD LEE, physics educator, researcher; b. Racine, Wis., Aug. 10, 1933; s. Glenn Roland and Evelyn Hannah (Larsen) F.; m. Alice J. Lienhard, June 27, 1959; children: Jenette Marie Dunworth, Peter Willard. BSEE, Purdue U., 1955; MS in Physics, U. Wis., 1962; PhD in Physics, U. Colo., 1971. Project engr. A.C. Electronics, Milw., 1958-62; project asst. U. Wis., Madison, 1962-64; instr. Mankato (Minn.) State U., 1964-68; from rsch. asst. to rsch. assoc. U. Colo., Boulder, 1968-72, instr., 1971-72; from asst. prof. to assoc. prof. U. No. Colo., Greeley, 1972-80, prof., 1980—, chair dept. physics, 1991—; faculty senator U. No. Colo., Greeley, 1991-98; book reviewer, jour. referee in field. Contbr. numerous articles to profl. jours. including Nuclear Physics, Phys. Rev., Physics Letters, Am. Jour. Physics; contbr. photography articles to Shutterbug mag. ElectroOptics Lab. grantee Eastman Kodak, U. No. Colo., 1988, Computer Enhanced Phys. Labs. NSF—Leadership in Lab. Devel. grantee U. No. Colo., 1992-94. Achievements include development on the Generalized Correspondence Principle; work on wave-particle duality for photons; work on educational value of undergraduate research. Avocation: photography. Office: U No Colo Dept Physics Greeley CO 80639

FADUM, RALPH EIGIL, university dean; b. Pitts., July 19, 1912; s. Torgeir Bleken and Mimi (Knudsen) F.; m. Nancy Isabelle Fields, July 19, 1939 (div. 1979); 1 dau., Jane Fields; m. Frances Elaine Lawrence, May 27, 1983. B.S. in Civil Engring, U. Ill., 1935; M.S., Harvard, 1937, S.D., 1941; D.Eng., Purdue U., 1963. Registered profl. engr., N.C. Parttime asst. civil engring. Harvard, 1935-37, instr., 1937-41, faculty instr., 1941- 43; asst. prof. soil mechanics Purdue U., 1943-45, asso. prof., 1945-47, prof., 1947-49; head of civil engring. dept. and prof. of civil engring. N.C. State U., Raleigh, 1949-62; dean of engring. N.C. State U., 1962-78; cons. Dept. Def., U.S. Corps Engrs.; Mem. Army Sci. Bd. Dept. Army, 1959-81; mem. research adv. com. Fed. Hwy. Adminstrn., 1963-70; vice chmn. Army Sci. Adv. Panel, Dept. Army, 1966-70; chmn. adv. group to comdr. gen. Tank Automotive Command, 1967-70. Contbr. articles to profl. jours. Chmn. N.C. Water Control Adv. Council; bd. dirs. Nat. Driving Center, 1973-77; commr. Raleigh Housing Authority, 1962-72; pres. Atlantic Coast Conf., 1966-67, 71-72; v.p. Nat. Collegiate Athletic Assn., 1972-76; Chmn. bd. dirs. N.C. Water Resources Research Inst., U. N.C. Recipient Patriotic Civilian Service award Dept. Army, 1967, Meritorious Civilian Service medal, 1967, Outstanding Civilian Service medal, 1973, 77; Distinguished Civil Engring. Alumnus award U. Ill., 1969. Mem. ASCE (hon. mem. 1978, Outstanding Civil Engr. N.C. award 1971); mem. Nat. Acad. Engring., U.S. Nat. Council Soil Mechanics and Found. Engring., Nat. Soc. Profl. Engrs., N.C. Soc. Engrs. (Outstanding Engring. Achievement award 1971), Raleigh Engrs. Club (Outstanding Engr. award 1977), Am. Soc. Engring. Edn. (hon. mem.; v.p., mem. exec. com. 1973-74, dir.), Sigma Xi, Tau Beta Pi, Chi Epsilon (nat. honor mem.), Phi Kappa Phi, Delta Upsilon. Clubs: Rotary (Raleigh); Carolina Country.

FAERBER, ABIGAIL HOBBS, physician, farm manager; b. Columbus, Ohio, Aug. 30, 1943; d. Theodore Caleb and Olliffe Elizabeth (Litchfield) Hobbs; m. George Oswald Faerber, Feb. 19, 1966; children: Rachel, Peter, George. BA, Ohio Wesleyan U., 1964; MS, U. Ill., 1966; DO, Ohio U., 1985. Bd. cert. in family practice, 1992. Physician, mgr. Dist. Physicians Inc., Columbus, Ohio, 1986-97; adj. clin. faculty Ohio U. Coll. Medicine, Athens, Ohio, 1986-96; physician DH Family Practice VIII, Columbus, Ohio, 1995-96; mgr. Scioto Cliff Farms, Delaware, Ohio, 1995-97; bd. dirs. Nat. Alumni Ohio U., Athens, 1989-92; medicine adv. bd. Ohio U. Coll. Osteo., 1994—. Bd. dirs. Columbus Chamber Music Soc., 1977-83; mem. Beaux Art Columbus Mus. Art, 1971-82. Recipient Cmty. Svc. award Ciba Geigy, 1986. Mem. Am. Osteo. Assn., Ohio Osteo. Assn., Ohio State Med. Assn., Franklin County Med. Soc., (chair of credentials com., 1991-93). Republican. Lutheran. Avocations: sailing, hiking, reading, travel. Home: 7547 Dublin Rd Delaware OH 43015-9237 Office: Dist Physicians Inc 7547 Dublin Rd Delaware OH 43015-9237

FAETH, GERARD MICHAEL, aerospace and mechanical engineering educator, researcher; b. N.Y.C., July 5, 1936; s. Joseph and Helen (Wagner) F.; m. Mary Ann Kordich, Dec. 27, 1959; children: Christine Louise, Lorraine Vera, Elinor Jean. BME, Union Coll., 1958; MS, Pa. State U., 1961, PhD, 1964. Instr. mech. engring. Pa. State U., University Park, 1958-59, research asst., 1959-64, asst. prof., 1964-68, assoc. prof., 1968-74, prof., 1974-85, prof. emeritus, 1985—; Modine prof., head gas dynamics labs. U. Mich., Ann Arbor, 1985—; vis. prof. Air Force Office Sci. Rsch., Washington, 1983-84; cons. GM, Warren, Mich., 1977—, Applied Rsch. Lab., Pa. State U., 1964-85; prof.-in-residence GM Inst., Detroit, 1983. Mem. editorial bd. Combustion Sci. and Tech., 1979—, Ann. Rev. Numerical Fluid Mechanics and Heat Transfer, 1985—, Atomization and Sprays, 1989—, Progress in Energy and Combustion Sci., 1991—, Internat. Jour. Multiphase Flow, 1997—; contbr. numerous articles to profl. jours. Rep. Precinct Chmn. Centre County, Pa., 1977-84; bd. dirs. Eagles Mere (Pa.) Assn., 1982-88, Eagles Mere Park Assn., 1978-85. Recipient Oustanding Engr. Alumnus Awd., 1990, PA State Univ. Alumni Assn. Fellow ASME (tech. editor 1981-84, sr. tech. editor 1985-90, Meml. award heat transfer divsn. 1988), AIAA (Propellants and Combustion award 1993, editor-in-chief 1997—), AAAS; mem. NAE, Combustion Inst. (dep. editor 1984-90, tech. editor 1990-96, bd. dirs. 1990-96), Am. Phys. Soc., Sigma Xi, Pi Tau Sigma, Phi Kappa Phi. Episcopalian. Home: 2665 Overridge Dr Ann Arbor MI 48104-4039 Office: U Mich 3000 FXB Bldg Ann Arbor MI 48109-2140

FAFIAN, JOSEPH, JR., management consultant; b. N.Y.C., Apr., 1939; s. Joseph M. and Mary (Alonso) F.; m. Nathalie Coluccio, Oct. 5, 1963; children: John Joseph, Michael Francis. BA, Bklyn. Coll., 1959. Assoc. actuary U.S. Life Ins. Co., N.Y.C., 1967; 2d v.p. USLIFE Corp., 1967-69, v.p., 1969-72, sr. v.p. ops., 1972-76, exec. v.p. life ins., 1976-77, sr. exec. v.p. life ins., 1977-78; pres., chief exec. officer, dir. U.S. Life, 1978-80; pres., dir. Beneficial Nat. Life Ins. Co., N.Y.C., 1980-82, chmn. bd., CEO, 1982-84; founder, pres., CEO, Fafian and Assocs., Inc., S.I., N.Y., 1984—; dir. Assoc. Madison, pres., COO, 1982-84; acting pres. Maine & Fidelity Life Ins. Co., 1985-86; bd. dirs. Best Meridian Life Ins. Co., Columbian Mut., Columbian Family, Columbia Life. Served with N.G., 1962-67. Fellow Soc. Actuaries; mem. Acad. Actuaries. E-mail: fafian@compuserve.com. Home: 74 Mason St Staten Island NY 10304-3106 Office: 1 Edgewater Plz Ste 304 Staten Island NY 10305-4900 *Guide my actions by three principles: Always be proud of what I am doing; Always seek to improve what I am doing; Always learn more about what I am doing.*

FAGALY, WILLIAM ARTHUR, curator; b. Lawrenceburg, Ind., Mar. 1, 1938; s. William James and Dorothy Rae (Wheeler) F. BA, Ind. U., 1962, MA, 1967. Asst. registrar Art Mus., Ind. U., Bloomington, 1965-66; with New Orleans Mus. Art, 1966—, curator collections, 1967-73, chief curator, 1973-80, asst. dir for art, 1980—, Francoise Billion Richardson curator African art, 1997—; guest curator La. Folk Painting exhibit, Mus. Am. Folk Art, 1973, The 41st Biennial Exhbn. of Contemporary Painting, Corcoran Gallery of Art, Washington, 1989, Arthur Roger Gallery, New Orleans, 1990, Geography of the Body: The Art of Mignon Faget, Contemporary Arts Ctr., 1995, Preacher Art, Phyllis Kind Gallery, N.Y.C., 1997, Watercolor U.S.A., Springfield (Mo.) Art Mus., 1999; mem. adv. panel visual arts and crafts divsn. arts La. Arts Coun., 1978-81, 92; panelist Nat. Endowment Arts GSA Art in Arch. Commn., 1974, 76, 78; guest lectr. S.S. Rotterdam, 1983, H.M.S. Queen Elizabeth II, 1986, Sotheby's, N.Y., 1996; cons. Liberian Pavilion La. World Expn., 1984, Shapes of Power, Belief and Celebration: African Art from New Orleans Collections, 1989, Fritz Bultman: A Retrospective, 1993, Wyo. Art Mus., Laramie, 1995, Oreg. Biennial, Portland Art Mus., 1995, Roots of Am. Jazz: African Mus. Instruments from New Orleans Collections, 1995, He's the Prettiest" A Tribute to Big Chief Allison "Tootie," Montana's Fifty Years of Mardi Gras Indian Suiting; selection panelist McKnight Found. Fellowship Program, Minn. Coll. Arts and Design, Mpls., 1986, So. Arts Fedn., NEA Arts Regional Artists Fellowships, 1990, Adolph and Esther Gottlieb Found. Artist Fellowships, N.Y.C., 1995, Western States Art Fedn./NEA, 1996; bd. dirs. Ctr. for African and African Am. Studies, So. U., New Orleans, 1988—; selection panelist 1984 Visual Arts Fellowships, Wyo. Arts Coun., 1993. Contbr. articles to profl. jours. NEA fellow, 1985, Visual Arts and Media fellow Miss. Arts Commn., 1994, Visual Arts fellow Wyo. Art Coun., 1994; recipient Mayor's Arts award City of New Orleans, 1997, Gov.'s Arts award La. State Arts Coun., 1997, Charles E. Dunbar Jr. Career Svc. award La. Civil Svc. League, 1999. Mem. Am. Assn. Mus. Episcopalian. Fax: (504) 484-6662. E-mail: bfagaly@noma.org. Home: 915 St Philip St New Orleans LA 70116-2407 Office: PO Box 19123 New Orleans LA 70179-0123

FAGAN, A. RUDOLPH, minister; b. Richton, Miss., Jan. 1, 1930; s. Lemuel Thad and Grace Isabell (Smith) F.; m. Florrie Bateman, Feb. 12, 1954; children: Vicki, Max, Myra, Amanda. BA, Howard Coll., 1951; BD, Southwe. Bapt. Theol. Seminary, 1955, MDiv, 1967. Ordained to ministry Bapt. Ch., 1948. Pastor First Bapt. Ch., Boca Grande, Fla., 1948, Kirbyville, Tex., 1952-55, Sebring, Fla., 1955-63, Bradenton, Fla., 1972-74; pastor Delaney St. First Bapt. Ch., Orlando, Fla., 1963-72; pres. Stewardship Commn., Nashville, 1974-94. Author: What the Bible Says About Stewardship, 1994. Avocations: golf, hunting, fishing. Home: 4728 Highway 49 W Springfield TN 37172-5720

FAGAN, ELIZABETH ANN, medical researcher, hepatologist; b. Hampshire, U.K., Sept. 1, 1950; d. Edward Joseph and Elizabeth (Kyca) F. BSc with 1st class honors, London U., 1972; MB, BS, 1975; MSc with distinction, London U., 1982, MD, 1989, diploma in Theology, Assoc. to King's Coll., 1972. Mem. gen. med. staff King's Coll. Hosp., London, 1976; hon. lectr., hon. sr. registrar liver unit King's Coll. Sch. Medicine and Dentistry, London, 1983-86, lectr. in medicine, 1983-90; Wellcome sr. rsch. fellow, hon. sr. lectr. Royal Free Hosp. Sch. Medicine, London, 1991-93, sr. lectr. in medicine divsn. hepatology, 1994-96; sr. lectr. in medicine divsn. hepatology U. Coll. London Med. Sch., 1994-96; hon. cons. gastroenterology (hepatology) U. Coll. London Hosps. NHS Trust, 1994-96; mem. professorial unit in gen. medicine and gastroenterology SHO Hammersmith Hosp., London, 1977; mem. professorial unit in thoracic medicine SHO Brompton Hosp., London, 1977-78; registrar, tutor gen. medicine and gastroenterology Hammersmith Hosp., Royal Postgrad. Med. Sch., London, 1979-81, Wellcome rsch. fellow, hon. registrar, 1981-82; prof. sect. hepatology and pediat. gastroenterology Rush Presbyn. St. Luke's Med. Ctr., Chgo., 1996—; World travelling tutor Tutorial Systems Internat., U.K., 1988; prof. U Gastroenterologists, 1994—. Contbr. numerous articles to profl. publs. Searle fellow, 1971, Wellcome sr. grad. rsch. fellow, 1991-93, Sir Francis Avery Jones molecular biology fellow, 1990-92, Abbott Sr. Rsch. Fellowship, 1994-96. Fellow Royal Coll. Pathologists; mem. Royal Coll. Physicians. Roman Catholic. Avocations: antiques, opera. Home: 1233 W Barry Ave Chicago IL 60657-4209 Office: Rush Presbyn St Luke's Med Ctr 1725 W Harrison St Chicago IL 60612-3828

FAGAN, GARTH, choreographer, artistic director, educator; b. Kingston, Ohio, May 3, 1940; s. S.W. and Louise I. (Walker) F. BA, Wayne State U., 1968; DFA, U. Rochester, N.Y., 1986; LHD, Hobart Coll., 1987, William Smith Coll., 1987; DFA, Nazareth Coll., 1990. From asst. prof. to assoc. prof. SUNY, Brockport, 1972-85, prof., 1985-86, Disting. U. prof., 1986—; artistic dir., founder, pres. Garth Fagan Dance, Rochester, N.Y., 1970—; choreoegapher N.Y. Shakespeare Festival, 1987, The Jamison Project, N.Y., 1988, Dance Theatre of Harlem, N.Y., 1986 (commd.); dir., choreographer Am. Music Theatre Festival, Phila., 1986; panelist, spkr. Nat. Coun. Arts, 1989. Choreographer modern dance including Landscape for 10, 1988, Telling a Story, 1989, Until, By & If, 1990, Griot, New York, 1991. Recipient Arts and Culture award Rochester Black Communicators, 1983, Arts for Greater Rochester Culturla award, 1986, N.Y. State Gov's. Arts award, 1986, Monarch award Nat. Coun. for Culture and Art, 1987, N.Y. Dance and Performance award, 1990, Dance Mag. award, 1990, Program Role model award Learning Through Art Guggenheim Mus. Program, 1992, Tony award for choreography Lion King, 1998; Guggenheim fellow Guggenheim Found., 1988. Mem. Nat. Corp. Fund for Dance, Dance U.S.A. (bd. dirs.), Western State Arts Fedn. (panelist), N.Y. Found. for Arts (bd. dirs.), N.Y. State Coun. on the Arts (dance panelist). Office: Garth Fagan Dance Inc 50 Chestnut St Rochester NY 14604-2318*

FAGAN, JAMES H., state legislator; m. Christine A. Lussier; 6 children. BA, Bridgewater State Coll., 1969; JD, Suffolk U., 1973. Bar: U.S. Dist. Ct. Mass., U.S. Dist. Ct. R.I., U.S. Supreme Ct. Ptnr. Fagan &B Goldrick P.C., Taunton, Mass., chmn. bd. trustees; mem. Mass. Ho. of Reps.; chmn. Com. on Post Audit and Oversight-Mass. Ho. of Reps. Mem. Mass. Com. for Pub. Counsel Svcs., Taunton Boys Club, S.E. Area Coun. of Boys Clubs of Am., taunton Youth; past pres. Oakland Westville Cmty. Ctr. Recipient Cert. of Appreciation for Outstanding Svc. Taunton Coun. on Aging, 1977, Man & Boys award Boys Club, 1987, Bronze Keystone award, 1990. Mem. ATLA, Mass. Bar Assn. (Legis. of Yr. 1996), Bristol County Bar Assn. (Legis. of Yr.), Taunton Bar Assn., Mass. Acad. Trial Lawyers, Mass. Criminal Def. Lawyers Assn., Elks. Address: 46 1/2 Davis St Taunton MA 02780-2115

FAGAN, PETER GAIL, occupational medicine physician; b. Big Spring, Tex., July 25, 1947; s. Joe Gail and Lura Juanita (Allison) F.; m. Susanne Brown, Mar. 18, 1966; children: Pamela Fagan Johnson, Paul Christopher. Md. U. Tex. Southwestern, 1972. Diplomate Am. Bd. Family Practice, Am. Bd. Occupl. Medicine. Physician Buffalo (Wyo.) Clinic, 1974-75, DeLeon (Tex.) Clinic, 1975-76; prof. family practice Tex. Tech. Sch. of Medicine, Amarillo, 1976-78; founder, physician Amarillo Indsl. Health Ctr., 1978-94; co-founder, v.p. Concentra Managed Care (formerly OccuSystems, Inc.), Dallas, 1985—; aviation med. examiner FAA, Washington, 1979—. Dir. Amarillo Bi-City County Health Dept., 1982-94. Fellow Am. Coll. Occupl. and Environ. Medicine. Avocations: outdoor activities. Home: PO Box 488 De Leon TX 76444-0168 Office: OccuSystems Inc West Tower 5080 Spectrum Dr Ste 400 Dallas TX 75001

FAGAN, WILLIAM THOMAS, JR., urologist; b. Rutland, Vt., Sept. 21, 1923; s. William T. Sr. and Irene (Hevey) F.; m. Joy A. Lipman; children from previous marriage: Susan A. Barry, William T. III. BS, U. Vt., 1945, MD, 1948. Diplomate Am. Bd. Urology. Intern Mary Fletcher Hosp., 1948-49; resident Med. Ctr. Hosp. Vt., Burlington, 1949-52, attending physician urology, 1952-86, emeritus attending, 1986—; assoc. prof. U. Vt., Burlington, 1954; chief urology dept. Fanny Allen Hosp., Winooski, Vt., 1956-86; cons. in urology Littleton Hosp., N.H., 1961-92, Cottage Hosp., Woodsville, N.H., 1981-92. Contbr. articles to profl. jours. Decorated Legion of Merit. Fellow ACS; mem. N.Y. Acad. Scis., Am. Urol. Assn., Am. Geriatric Soc., AMA, Royal Soc. Medicine, Assn. Mil. Surgeons U.S. Avocations: skiing, reading. Home and Office: PO Box 1508 Stowe VT 05672-1508

FAGANS, KARL PRESTON, real estate facilities administration executive; b. N.Y.C., Sept. 26, 1942; s. Allen J. and Adrienne L. Fagans; m. Amy D'Lag, Aug. 21, 1965; children: Peter, Douglas, Heather. BS, Clarkson U., 1965; cert. PMD, Harvard Bus. Sch., 1980. Project leader Westvaco Corp., Mechanicville, N.Y., 1965-71; pres. M-7 Papers, Inc., Mechanicville, 1971-72; sr. profl. staff mem. Arthur D. Little, Inc., Cambridge, Mass., 1972-80, v.p., 1984-99; pres. Arthur D. Little Real Estate Corp., Cambridge, 1986-99; pres. bd. dirs. Mass. Coun. Quality, Inc., 1993-94, treas., 1995-96. Chmn. permanent sch. bldg. com. Town of Westford, Mass., 1988—, chmn. fin. com., 1986-88; mem. regional bd. Nat. Alliance Bus. Mem. Internat. Assn. Corp. Real Estate Execs., Indsl. Devel. Rsch. Coun. Office: Fagans & Fagans 110 Kodiak Way #2811 Waltham MA 02451

FAGER, CHARLES ANTHONY, physician, neurosurgeon; b. Nassau, The Bahamas, Jan. 16, 1924; came to U.S., 1924; s. Charles Anthony and Mary Frances (Amoury) F.; m. Margaret Bulkley, May 30, 1947; children: Christopher, Gregory, Mary Louise, Jeffrey. Student, Wagner Coll., 1943; MD, SUNY, 1946. Diplomate Am. Bd. Neurol. Surgery (bd. dirs. 1976-82). Intern Syracuse (N.Y.) U., 1946-47, resident, 1947-48; resident Cushing Gen. Hosp./Lahey Clinic, Burlington, Mass., 1950-53; neurosurgeon Lahey Clinic Med. Ctr., Burlington, 1953—, chmn. dept. neurosurgery, 1963-84, vice chmn., bd. govs., 1973—, chmn. med. practice coun., 1980—, chmn. div. surgery, 1982—, chmn. emeritus, 1984—; trustee Lahey Clinic, 1973—, chmn. coun. dept. chmns., 1965-67, 73-79; exec. com. New Eng. Bapt. Hosp., Boston, 1966-67, 73-78, pres. staff, 1973; vice chmn. med. adminstrv. bd. New Eng. Deaconess Hosp., 1973; Balado Meml. lectr. Argentine Neurosurg. Soc., Buenos Aires, 1972, Teachenor Meml. lectr. Kans. Neurosurg. Soc., Kansas City, 1972, Gardner lectr. Cleve. Clinic, 1986. Author: Atlas of Spinal Surgery, 1989; contbr. numerous articles to profl. jours., chpts. to surg. texts. Capt. USAF, 1948-50. Recipient Alumni Achievement award Wagner Coll., 1972. Mem. ACS (chmn. adv. coun. neurosurgery 1980-82), Am. Assn. Neurol. Surgeons (Lifetime Achievement award AANS/Congress Neurol. Surgeons 1992), Neurosurg. Soc. Am. (pres. 1976-77), New Eng. Neurosurg. Soc. (pres. 1967-68), Boston Soc. Neurology and Psychiatry (pres. 1967-68). Roman Catholic. Avocations: gardening, tennis. Office: Lahey Clinic Med Ctr 41 Mall Rd Burlington MA 01805-0001

FAGER, EVERETT DEAN, minister; b. Redkey, Ind., Apr. 6, 1947; s. Luther Von and Nola Marceil (Elliott) F.; m. Kathy Jo McKean, Mar. 17, 1973 (div. Aug. 1989); children: Holly Renee, Ryan Christopher; m. Janet A. Caskey, June 12, 1993; children: Benjamin Dean, Sarah Ashley; stepchildren: Eric, Mike, Nick Caskey. BA, U. Evansville, 1969; ThM, Boston U., 1972; D of Ministry, Drew U., 1981. Ordained to ministry Meth. Ch. as elder, 1973. Youth and edn. min. First United Meth. Ch., Decatur, Ind., 1972-76, St. Mark's United Meth. Ch., Decatur, 1972-76; min. Albany (Ind.) United Meth. Ch., 1976-82, Osceola (Ind.) United Meth. Ch., 1982-86; sr. pastor Taylor Chapel United Meth. Ch., Ft. Wayne, Ind., 1986-91; assoc. dir. for local ch. ministries North Ind. Conf., 1991-94; ptnr. GROW Ministries, Ft. Wayne, 1983-93; pastor Main St. United Meth. Ch., Peru, Ind., 1994—; chaplain Jaycees, Decatur, 1975-76; mem. area comm. com. United Meth. Ch., 1980-86, conf. comm. chair., 1980-86, 94—; mem. conf. program com. United Meth. Ch., 1984-90; assoc. faculty Bethel Coll., Mishawaka, Ind., 1985-86; chmn. Membership Recruitment Task Force Ch. Builders of Ft. Wayne Dist., 1987-91; mem. com. on Investigation N. Ind. Conf. United Meth. Ch., 1988-91, chair Kokomo dist. com. on superintendency, 1998—; bd. dirs. Assoc. Chs. Allen County, Ft. Wayne, 1988-91. Chmn. Walkathon, Adams County March Dimes, Decatur, 1973-75; mem. Publicity Com. Osceola Days, 1984-86; vice chmn. Osceola Bd. Zoning Appeals, 1985-86; mem. new ch. devel. task force North Ind. U. Meth. Ch., 1989-93; mem. local coord. coun. Gov.'s Task Force for a Drug-Free Ind., 1994—; mem. C.O.M.P.A.S.S., 1995—. Named Outstanding Young Man Am., Jaycees, Decatur, 1975; recipient Ch. Growth awards N. Ind. Conf. United Meth. Ch., 1988. Mem. Peru Min. Assn. (pres. 1995-96), Rotary (Sgt.-at-Arms 1998—). Democrat. Home: 363 W 3rd St Peru IN 46970-1961 *The worst of life is tolerable if one believes that the best is yet to come. The best of life is put in perspective if one believes that the best is yet to come. This is my one overeaching and unconquerable hope: the best is yet to come.*

FAGES, MALCOM I., career officer; m. Shirley Jo Osborn; 1 child, Meredith. BS in Mechanical Engring., Auburn U., 1968; MA in Political Sci., U. Central Fla., 1990. Commd. ensign U.S. Navy, 1968, advanced through grades to rear admiral, 1995—; comdr. Nuclear Field "A" Sch., 1988-91; chief staff Theodore Roosevelt Battle Group, 1993-95; dir. internat. negotiations, 1995-96, comdr. submarine group TWO, 1996—. Decorated Legion of Merit with gold star, Navy Commendation medal with gold star. Office: US Navy Commander Submarine Grp TWO PO Box 100 Groton CT 06349-5100*

FAGG, GEORGE GARDNER, federal judge; b. Eldora, Iowa, Apr. 30, 1934; s. Ned and Arleene (Gardner) F.; m. Jane E. Wood, Aug. 19, 1956; children: Martha, Thomas, Ned, Susan, George, Sarah. BS in Bus. Adminstrn., Drake U., 1956, JD, 1956. Bar: Iowa 1958. Ptnr. Cartwright, Druker, Ryden & Fagg, Marshalltown, Iowa, 1958-72; judge Iowa Dist. Ct., 1972-82; judge U.S. Ct. Appeals (8th cir.), 1982-99, sr. judge, 1999-; mem. faculty Nat. Jud. Coll., 1979. Mem. ABA, Iowa Bar Assn., Order of Coif. Office: US Ct Appeals US Courthouse Annex 110 E Court Ave Rm 455 Des Moines IA 50309*

FAGG, RUSSELL, judge, lawyer; b. Billings, Mont., June 26, 1960; s. Harrison Grover and Darlene (Bohling) F.; m. Karen Barclay, Feb. 15, 1992. BA, Whitman Coll., 1983; JD, U. Mont., 1986; MJS, U. Nev., 1999. Law clerk Mont. Supreme Ct., Helena, Mont., 1986-87; atty. Sandall Law Firm, Billings, Mont., 1987-89; city prosecutor City of Billings, Mont., 1989-91; dep. atty. Yellowstone County, Billings, Mont., 1991-94; mem. Montana State Legislator, Helena, 1991-94; judge State Dist. Ct. (13th dist.) Mont., Billings, 1995—; dir. Midland Empire Pachyderm Club, 1988-94, pres. 1990-91; chmn. judiciary com. House of Reps., 1993-94. Named Outstanding Young Montanan, Mont. Jaycees, 1994. Avocations: hiking, fishing, skiing, reading. Home: 3031 Rimview Dr Billings MT 59102-0955 Office: PO Box 35027 Billings MT 59107-5027

FAGGIN, FEDERICO, electronics executive; b. Vicenza, Italy, Dec. 1, 1941; came to U.S., 1968, naturalized, 1978; s. Giuseppe and Emma (Munari) F.; m. Elvia Sardei, Sept. 2, 1967; children: Marzia, Marc, Eric. Grad., Perito Industriale Instituto A. Rossi, Vicenza, 1960; D.Physics, U. Padua, Italy, 1965. Sect. head Fairchild Camera & Instrument Co., Palo Alto, Calif., 1968-70; dept. mgr. Intel Corp., Santa Clara, Calif., 1970-74; founder, pres. Zilog Inc., Cupertino, Calif., 1974-80; v.p. computer systems group Exxon Enterprises, N.Y.C., 1981; co-founder, pres. Cygnet Technologies, Inc., Sunnyvale, Calif., 1982-86; pres., co founder Synaptics, Inc., San Jose, Calif., 1986—. Recipient Marconi Fellowship award, 1988, W. Wallace McDowell award IEEE Computer Soc., 1994, Kyoto prize, 1997; inducted Nat. Inventor's Hall of Fame, 1996. Developed silicon gate tech. for MOS fabrication, first microprocessor. Office: Synaptics Inc 2702 Orchard Pkwy San Jose CA 95134-2012

FAGIN, CLAIRE MINTZER, nursing educator, administrator; b. N.Y.C.; ž; d. Harry and Mae (Slatin) Mintzer; m. Samuel Fagin, Feb. 17, 1952; children: Joshua, Charles. BS, Wagner Coll., 1948; MA, Tchrs. Coll. Columbia, 1951; PhD, N.Y. U., 1964; DSc (hon.), Lycoming Coll., 1983, Cedar Crest Coll., 1987, U. Rochester, 1987, Med. Coll. Pa., 1989, U. Md., 1993, Wagner Coll., 1993, Loyola U., 1996; DHL, Hunter Coll., 1993; LLD (hon.), U. Pa., 1994; DHL, Rush U., 1996. Staff nurse, clin. instr. Sea View Hosp., S.I., N.Y.; clin. instr. Bellevue Hosp., N.Y.C.; psychiat. nurse cons. Nat. League for Nursing, N.Y.C.; asst. chief psychiat. nursing svc. clin. ctr. NIH; rsch. project coord. dept. psychiatry Children's Hosp., Washington; instr., assoc. prof. psychiat.-mental health nursing NYU, N.Y.C., dir. grad. programs in psychiat. mental health nursing, 1965-69; chmn. nursing dept., prof. Herbert H. Lehman Coll., CUNY, N.Y.C., 1969-77; dir. Health Professions Inst., Montefiore Hosp. and Med. Ctr., 1975-77; Margaret Bond Simon dean sch. of nursing U. Pa., Phila., 1977-92, Leadership chair prof., 1992-96, interim pres., 1993-94, dean emeritus, prof. emeritus, 1996—; project leader Millbank Found.; cons. in health care and orgnl. leadership to state, nat. and internat. coms. and profl. bds.; bd. dirs. Provident Mut. Ins. Co., chmn., 1985-96, mem. exec. com., 1986-97, mem. adv. com., 1996—, mem. audit com., 1978-96; bd. dirs. Solomon Inc., mem. audit com., 1994—, mem. environ. com., 1995-97, mem. corp. contbn., 1995-97; bd. dirs. CMAC, van Ameriggen Found., Vis. Nurse Svc. of N.Y.; mem. compensation com., investment com., bd. dirs. N.Y. Acad. Medicine, chair audit com., 1998—; spkr. at profl. confs., on radio and TV. Contbr. articles to profl. publs. Recipient Achievement award Wagner Coll., 1956, Achievement award Tchrs. Coll., 1975, Disting. Alumna award NYU, 1979, Founders award Sigma Theta Tau, 1981, Hon. Recognition award ANA, 1988, Woman of Courage award Womens Way, 1990, Alumni Merit award U. Pa., 1991, Trustee Coun. Pa. Women First Leadership award, 1991, Caring award Phila. Vis. Nurses Assn., Lillian Wald award, N.Y. Vis. Nurses Assn., 1994, Hildegard Peplau award outstanding contbn. psych-nursing, 1994, Living Legend award Am. Acad. of Nursing, 1998, Pres. medal NYU, 1998; Am. Nurses Found. Disting. scholar, 1984, Disting. Dau. Pa., 1994. Mem. Inst. Medicine of NAS (governing coun. 1981-83, chmn. bd. health promotion and disease prevention 1991-94), Am. Acad. Nursing (governing coun. 1976-78), Am. Orthopsychiat. Assn. (bd. dirs. 1972-75, exec. com. bd. dirs. 1973-75, pres. 1985-86), Nat. League for Nursing (pres. 1991-93). Address: 200 Central Park S Apt 12E New York NY 10019-1415 Office: U Pa Nursing Edu Dept 354 Neb Bldg Philadelphia PA 19104-6096

FAGIN, DAVID KYLE, natural resource company executive; b. Dallas, Apr. 9, 1938; s. Kyle Marshall and Frances Margaret (Gaston) F.; m. Margaret Anne Hazlett, Jan. 24, 1959; children: David Kyle, Scott Edward. BS in Petroleum Engring., U. Okla., 1960; postgrad., Am. Inst. Banking, So. Meth. U. Grad. Sch. Bus. Adminstrn. Registered profl. engr., La., Okla., Tex. Trainee Mobil Oil (formerly Magnolia Petroleum Co.), 1955-56; jr. engr., engr., then partner W.C. Bednar Petroleum Cons., Dallas, 1958-65; petroleum engr. Bank of Am. N.A. (formerly First Nat. Bank Dallas), Dallas, 1965-68; pres. Alamo Petroleum Corp., 1968-82; v.p. Rosario Resources Corp., N.Y.C., 1968-75, exec. v.p., 1975-77; dir. Rosario Resources Corp., 1975-80, pres., 1977-82; v.p. AMAX Inc. (merged with Rosario Resources Corp. 1980), N.Y.C., 1980-82; chmn., dir., pres., chief exec. officer Fagin Exploration Co., Denver, 1982-86; pres., COO, bd. dirs. Homestake Mining Co., San Francisco, 1986-91; CEO Golden Star Resources Ltd., Denver, 1992-96, chmn., 1992-97, also bd. dirs.; chmn., CEO Western Exploration and Devel. Ltd., Denver, 1997—; bd. dirs. several T. Rowe Price mut. funds, Balt., Dayton Mining Co., Vancouver, B.C., Mineral Info. Inst., Miranda Mining Devel., Ltd., 1997—. Bd. dirs. Denver Area coun. Boy Scouts Am.; bd. visitors U. Okla. Sch. Engring., 1995-98; dir. Nat. Mining Hall of Fame and Mus., 1997—. Mem. AIME (chmn. Dallas sect. of Soc. Petroleum Engrs. 1975, chmn. investment fund 1979-82), Soc. Mining, Metallurgy and Exploration (dir. 1996-97), Soc. Petroleum Engrs., Mining and Metall. Soc. Am., Internat. Mining Profls. Soc. (dir., exec. com.). Office: 1700 Lincoln Ste 4710 Denver CO 80203

FAGO, DAVID PAUL, psychologist, educator; b. Warren, Pa., Mar. 14, 1950; s. Paul G. Fago and Billie (Clancy) Foster; m. Susan Goodman, May 25, 1975; children: Nichole Anne, Evan Goodman. AB, Boston Coll., 1971; MA, U. Md., 1973, PhD, 1976. Lic. psychologist, Md. Dir. adult mental health svc. W.Yavapai Guidance Clinic, Prescott, Ariz., 1977-79; faculty Prescott Coll., 1978-82; asst. dir. W.Yavapai Guidance Clinic, Prescott, Ariz., 1979-82; chief rsch. and evaluation VA Ctrl. Office, Washington, 1982-86; cons. Arundel Mental Health Assoc., Annapolis, Md., 1986-92; co-dir. Md. Inst., College Park, 1988—; faculty U. Md., 1996—; adj. faculty mem. dept. psychology Prescott Coll., 1978-82, U. Md., College Park, 1996—. Contbr. articles to profl. jours. Nat. Merit scholar, 1966, Boston Coll. scholar, 1970-71. Mem. APA, Md. Psychol. Assn. Achievements include research on neurodevelopmental factors in sexual aggression in children and adolescents. Avocations: distance running, skiing, hiking. Home: 8212 Queen Annes Dr Silver Spring MD 20910 Office: Md Inst 7307 Baltimore Ave Ste 208 College Park MD 20740-3231

FAGO, GEORGE CLANCY, psychology educator; b. Warren, Pa., July 5, 1943; s. Paul and Billie (Clancy) F.; m. Nancy Ellen Van Buskirk; children: Jennifer Anne, Katharine Emily. AB, Franklin and Marshall Coll., 1965; MS, U. Pitts., 1967, PhD, 1970. Prof. psychology Ursinus Coll., Collegeville, Pa., 1970—. Home: R113 Westridge Pl S Phoenixville PA 19460 Office: Dept Psychology Ursinus Coll Collegeville PA 19460

FAGUNDO, ANA MARIA, creative writing and Spanish literature educator; b. Santa Cruz de Tenerife, Spain, Mar. 13, 1938; came to U.S., 1958; d. Ramón Fagundo and Candelaria Guerra de Fagundo. BA in English and Spanish, U. Redlands, 1962; MA in Spanish, U. Wash., 1964, PhD in Comparative Lit., 1967. Prof. contemporary lit. of Spain and creative writing U. Calif., Riverside, 1967—; vis. lectr. Occidental Coll., Calif., 1967; vis. prof. Stanford U., 1984. Author 9 books of poetry including Invention de la Luz, 1977 (Carbala de Oro Poetry prize Barcelona 1977), Obra Poetica: 1965-90, 1990, Isla En Si, 1992, Antologia, 1994, La Miriada de Los Sonambulos, 1994; founder, editor Alaluz, 1969—. Grantee Creative Arts Inst., 1970-71, Humanities Inst., 1973-74; Summer faculty fellow U. Calif., 1968, 77; Humanities fellow, 1969. Mem. Am. Assn. Tchrs. Spanish and Portuguese, Sociedad Gen. de Autores de Espana. Roman Catholic. Avocations: tennis, jogging, walking. Home: 5110 Caldera Ct Riverside CA 92507-6002 Office: U Calif Spanish Dept Riverside CA 92521

FAHERTY, ROBERT LOUIS, publishing executive; b. St. Louis, Sept. 26, 1939; s. Justin Louis and Elizabeth Veronica (Quigley) F.; m. Claudia C. Hutchison, Jan. 10, 1969; children: Kathleen Marie, Timothy Robert, Mark Robert, Megan Elizabeth, Bridget Justine. BA magna cum laude, Cath. U. Am., 1961, MA, 1962; STL cum laude, Pontifical Gregorian U., Rome, 1966. Editor St. Louis Rev., 1967-69, Ency. Britannica, Chgo., 1969-72; mng. editor sci./Benefic Press Harcourt Brace Jovanovich, Chgo., 1972-73; mng. editor Scholarly Press, Detroit, 1973-75; co-founder, editor-in-chief Reference Publs., Algonac, Mich., 1975-77; editor-in-chief Congl. Budget Office, Washington, 1977-84; dir. Brookings Instn. Press, Washington, 1984—; lectr. Howard U. Book Pub. Inst., 1985-89; mem. adv. com. on pub. and comm. programs U. Va., 1994—, instr., 1995—. Contbr. articles to profl. pubs. Trustee, treas. Ela Area Pub. Libr. Dist., Lake County, Ill., 1973-74; bd. dirs. United Cmty. Ministries, Fairfax County, Va., 1992—, pres., 1995—; chmn. Algonac Recreation Commn., 1976-77; mem. bioethics com. for Mid-Atlantic region Kaiser Permanente HMO, 1989—. Curators' scholar U. Mo., 1957, Basselin Found. scholar Cath. U. Am., 1959. Mem. Assn. Am. Univ. Presses (bd. dirs. 1991-94, 97—. Home: 4303 Mission Ct Alexandria VA 22310-3353 Office: Brookings Instn 1775 Massachusetts Ave NW Washington DC 20036-2188

FAHEY, BARBARA STEWART DOE, public agency administrator; b. Chgo., Aug. 9, 1950; d. William Bethel and Doris (Charn) Doe. BA, U. Colo., 1972; MA, Sangamon State U., 1975. Dir. Wilderness Study Project, Springfield, Ill., 1973-75, Environ. Ctr., Boulder, Colo., 1976-79; natural resource specialist U.S. Bur. Reclamation, Denver, 1977-78; rsch. assoc. Nat. Conf. State Legislatures, Denver, 1979-80; asst. to transp. dir. City of Boulder, 1980-81, project mgr., 1981-85, parking coord., 1985-90, open space planner, 1991-92; interpretive park naturalist Jefferson County, Golden, Colo., 1992, adminstr. Nature Ctr., 1993-95; county dir. Colo. State U. Coop. Extension in Jefferson County, 1995—; vice chmn. Boulder County Energy Adv. Com., Boulder, 1987; bd. mem. County Bd. Rev., Boulder, 1984-86, Historic Boulder, 1991-92. Bd. mem. Colo. Open Space Coun., Denver, 1979-80; mem. Leadership Boulder C. of C., 1986. Named Young Career Woman Colo. Bus. and Profl. Women's Fedn., Denver, 1981; recipient Innovation award Denver Coun. Govts., 1985, State Dir.'s Merit award, 1997. Mem. Nat. Assn. Interpretation, Denver Botanic Gardens, Denver Mus. Natural History, Colo. Native Plant Soc., Boulder Bus. and Profl. Women (treas. 1983-84, v.p. 1987-88, pres. 1989-90, winner speech contest 1985), Sierra Club (bd. mem. Sangamon Valley Group 1973-75). Avocations: cross-country skiing, backpacking, hiking, classical and folk music. Office: 15200 W 6th Ave Ste C Golden CO 80401-5018

FAHEY, CHARLES JOSEPH, priest, gerontology educator; b. Balt., Apr. 13, 1933; s. Charles J. and M. Elizabeth (Kelly) F. AB, St. Bernard's Sem., Rochester, N.Y., 1959, MDiv, 1982; MSW, Catholic U., 1963; LLD, St. Thomas U., Can., 1983; DD (hon.), St. Bernard's Inst., 1985; LLD, D'Youville Coll., 1987, LeMoyne Coll., Syracuse, N.Y., 1993. Ordained priest Roman Catholic Ch., 1959. Asst. pastor St. Vincent Ch., Syracuse, N.Y., 1959-61; asst. dir. Cath. Charities, Syracuse, N.Y., 1961-67, dir., 1967-

79; dir. 3rd Age Ctr. Fordham U., N.Y.C., 1979—, Marie Ward Doty prof. of aging studies, 1980—; crw; chmn. Fed. Council on Aging, 1982; mem. faculty Salzburg Fellow Program, Austria, 1985. Contbr. articles to profl. jours. Fellow Am. Coll. Health Care Adminstrs., Gerontol. Soc., Nat. Acad. Social Ins.; mem. Inst. Medicine of Nat. Acad. Scis., Nat. Assn. Social Workers, Am. Pub. Health Assn., Am. Assn. Homes for Aging (pres. 1976-77), Nat. Conf. Cath. Charities (pres. 1979-81), Cath. Health Assn. (bd. mem.), Am. Fedn. Aging Rsch. (bd. dirs. 1982—), Am. Stroke Assn. (bd. mem. 1983—), N.Y. State Welfare Assn. (pres. 1975), Am. Soc. on Aging (pres.-elect 1990, pres. 1992, 93). Office: Fordham U 3d Age Ctr Bronx NY 10458-9998

FAHEY, HELEN F., prosecutor. Atty. U.S. Dept. Justice, Alexandria, Va., 1993—. Office: US Attys Office 2100 Jamieson Ave Alexandria VA 22314-5702*

FAHEY, HENRY MARTIN, information technology executive; b. Cin., Jan. 27, 1963; s. Richard H. and Gloria A. (Benson) F.; m. Pamela S. Gille, May 23, 1991; children: Jeffrey W. Winton (dec.), Suzy M. Winton. BS in Computer Sci., U. Colo., 1986; MBA, So. Meth. U., 1990. Software engr. Digital Equipment Corp., Colorado Springs, Colo., 1986-89; tech. cons. Digital Equipment Corp., Ft. Worth, 1990-92; network specialist Galderma Labs, Inc., Ft. Worth, 1993-95, mgr. tech. svcs. N.Am., 1995-98; mgr. tech. svcs. ChannelPoint, Inc., Colorado Springs, Colo., 1998—; tech. adv. bd. student work consortium U. Tex., Arlington, 1995-98. Mem. Oracle Applications Users Group, Digital Equipment Computers Users Soc. Republican. Mem. Ch. LDS. Avocations: black belt Taekwondo, downhill skiing, laser tag gaming, scuba diving, martial arts. Home: 2415 Regal View Ct Colorado Springs CO 80919 Office: ChannelPoint Inc Ste 100 5755 Mark Dabling Blvd Colorado Springs CO 80919

FAHEY, JAMES EDWARD, financial executive; b. N.Y.C., May 4, 1953; s. John Michael and Kathleen Rose (Brady) F.; m. Betsy C. Lindberg, Oct. 10, 1993; children: Christiana, James Charles. BBA, Iona Coll., New Rochelle, N.Y., 1975, MBA, 1977. Registered investment advisor. Territory asst. European Am. Bank, N.Y.C., 1978-80; internat. analyst Texaco, Inc., White Plains, N.Y., 1981-83; mgr. internat. treasury Am. Standard Inc., N.Y.C., 1984-88; asst. treas. Perkin Elmer Internat., Inc., 1988-91; sr. mgr. internat. treasury Perkin Elmer Corp., Norwalk, Conn., 1988-91; 1st v.p. investments Salomon Smith Barney, N.Y.C., 1991—. Active Friends of Am. Cancer Soc., N.Y.C., 1986—, Daytop Village Found., 1993—. Mem. Soc. Internat. Treas., Friendly Sons of St. Patrick (N.Y.C.), Rep. Senatorial Inner Circle. Home: 159 Brixton Rd Garden City NY 11530-1418 Office: Salomon Smith Barney 250 Park Ave New York NY 10177-0001

FAHEY, JEFF, actor; b. Buffalo, NY, Nov. 29, 1956. TV appearances include: (series) One Life to Live, 1982-85, The Marshall, 1995, Eye of the Wolf, 1995, Serpant's Lair, 1995, (movies) The Execution of Raymond Graham, 1985, Curiosity Kills, 1990, Parker Kane, 1990, Iran: Days of Crisis, 1991, Sketch Artist, 1991, In the Company of Darkness, 1993, The Hit List, 1993, Blindsided, 1993, Quick, 1994, Virtual Seduction, 1995; film appearances include: Silverado, 1985, Psycho III, 1986, Backfire, 1987, Split Decisions, 1988, Alexander's Treasures, 1989, The Last of the Finest, 1989, Outback, 1989, The Serpent of Death, 1989, True Blood, 1989, Impulse, 1990, White Hunter, Black Heart, 1990, Body Parts, 1991, Iron Maze, 1991, The Lawnmower Man, 1992, Wyatt Earp, 1994, Darkman III: Die Darkman Die, 1996, When Justice Fails, 1997, Lethal Tender, 1997, Catherine's Grove, 1997, Small Time, 1998, No Tomorrow, 1998, Detour, 1998, Time Served, 1998, Spoken in Silence, 1999, Revelation, 1999, Hijack, 1999, The Contract, 1999. *

FAHEY, JOHN LESLIE, immunologist; b. Cleve., Sept. 8, 1924. MS, Wayne State U., 1949; MD, Harvard U., 1951. Intern medicine Columbia-Presbyn. Hosp., N.Y., 1951-52, asst. resident, 1952-53; clin. assoc. Nat. Cancer Inst., NIH, 1953-54, sr. investigator metabolism, 1954-63, chief immunology br., 1964-71; prof. medicine, microbiology and immunology, chmn. dept. Sch. Medicine UCLA, 1971-81; dir. Ctr. Interdisciplinary Rsch. Immunological Diseases UCLA, 1978—. Recipient Abbott Laboratories award Am. Society for Microbiology, 1995. Mem. Assn. Immunologists, Assn. Am. Physicians, Am. Soc. Microbiology, Clin. Immunology Soc. (founding pres.), Clin. Immunology Com. (pres.), Internat. Union Immunological Socs., Am. Assn. Cancer Rsch. Achievements include rsch. in immunology, AIDS, oncology. Office: UCLA Sch Medicine Dept Microbiology & Immunology Factor Bldg 12-262 Los Angeles CA 90095-1747*

FAHEY, JOHN M., JR., book publishing executive. Pres., CEO, chmn. Time Life Inc., Alexandria, Va., 1996; exec. v.p., chair ops. office Nat. Geog. Soc., Washington, 1997—, pres., CEO, 1998—. Office: Nat Geographic Soc 1145 17th St NW Washington DC 20036-4701*

FAHEY, JOSEPH FRANCIS, JR., banker, financial consultant; b. Stamford, Conn., Dec. 19, 1925; s. Joseph Francis and Margaret (Hoffkins) F.; m. June Alice Gleason, July 8, 1950; children: Janice, Jill, Christopher, Colleen, Moira, Kevin, Brian. BA, U. Notre Dame, 1949; postgrad. real estate law, U. Conn., 1951; credit mgmt., Bridgeport U., 1952, Sch. Mortgage Banking, Stanford, 1958, Sch. Mortgage Banking, Northwestern U., 1960, Grad. Sch. Bank Mgmt., Columbia, 1965; LLD (hon.), Sacred Heart U., 1982. With Greenwich Trust Co., Conn., 1947-58; asst. treas. Greenwich Trust Co., 1954-58; asst. v.p. mortgage dept. Nat. Bank & Trust Co., Stamford, 1958-59; v.p. mortgage adminstrn. Nat. Bank & Trust Co., 1959-62; sr. v.p. mortgage dept. State Nat. Bank Conn., Bridgeport, 1962-65; sr. v.p. in charge loan portfolio, chmn. loan com. State Nat. Bank Conn., 1965-74, pres., 1973-82, chmn. bd., 1974-82; chmn. bd. Conn. Bank, 1982-85; pres. CBT Corp., 1982-85; 1st chmn. Southwestern Regional Planning Agy., 1963-64; mem. faculty Am. Inst. Banking, 1964-69; pres. Stamford Devel. Corp., 1967—; dir. Congregate Care Ctrs. of Am., San Diego, 1985-93; pres. St. John's Urban Devel. Corp., 1992—; bd. dirs. Norco, Inc., Ridgefield, Conn., 1989-98. Mem. citizen's adv. com. Ferguson Library, 1964-74; bd. dirs. Citizens Action Council, Stamford, 1965-70, mem. exec. com., 1966-71; regent, treas. St. Mary's Coll., Notre Dame, Ind., 1977-91, BPT Econ. Devel. Council, 1976-78; bd. dirs. Stamford Hosp., 1965-93, treas., 1967-70, v.p., 1970-72, pres., 1972-75, emeritus coun. 1994—; trustee Hartman Theatre, Stamford, 1976-78; bd. dirs. Aspetuck Land Trust, Inc., 1967-71, treas., 1967-71; bd. dirs. Rehab. Center So. Fairfield County, Inc., 1966-70, treas., 1966-70; trustee Fairfield U., 1974-82, mem. adv. council, 1972-74; dir., sec. Bridgeport Econ. Devel. Council, 1976-78; chmn. Stamford Econ. Assistance Corp., 1978-80; trustee Stamford Found., 1982-88, Culpeper Found., Stamford, Conn., 1986-98, St. Camillus Health Found., 1994—; trustee, pres. Rich Found., 1985-89; bd. dirs. Stamford Devel. Fund (now Housing Fund of Lower Fairfield County), 1990-94. Served with AC USNR, 1943-46. Recipient Terrence Cardinal Cooke medal N.Y. Med. Coll., 1991; named Young Man of Yr., Stamford Jr. C. of C., 1961; Stamford Citizen of Yr., 1984. Mem. Conn. Bankers Assn. (pres. 1973-74), Am. Bankers Assn. (nat. conf. commrs. on uniform state laws), Southwestern Area Commerce and Industry Assn. (dir. 1970-71, 75-82), Roasters Club (treas., founding mem.), Landmark Club (gov. 1973-95), Woodway Country Club, The Club at Pelican Bay (Naples, Fla.).

FAHEY, PATRICIA ANNE, editor; b. Methuen, Mass., Aug. 6, 1957; d. Edward James and Evelyn Fay (Benedix) Howard; m. Thomas Francis Fahey, Jr., Mar. 5, 1982; children: Ryan Thomas, Caitlin Elizabeth (dec.), Emily Catherine. AA in Liberal Arts with highest honors, No. Essex Community Coll., Haverhill, Mass., 1977; BA in English magna cum laude, Notre Dame Coll., Manchester, N.H., 1987; MEd in Elem. Edn., Notre Dame Coll., 1995. News reporter Salem (N.H.) Observer, 1975-77, news editor, 1977-78; news corr. Union Leader Corp., Manchester, N.H., 1978-80; lifestyle reporter Union Leader Corp., Manchester, 1980-82, news reporter, 1982-86, copy editor, 1986—; elem. tchr. Concord (N.H.) Sch. Dist., 1994—. Mem. Future Planning Commn., Town of Auburn, N.H., 1983-84; mem. adv. bd. Manchester Assn. Retarded Citizens, 1984-85. Recipient Community Service award Am. Cancer Soc., 1985. Mem. Internat. Reading Assn., Nat. Coun. Tchrs. of Math., Granite State Reading Coun., Concord Edn. Assn., The Newspaper Guild. Congregationalist. Avocations: skiing, travel, photography, interior decorating. Home: 8 Chestnut Pasture Rd Concord NH 03301-7900 Office: 40 Sewalls Falls Rd Concord NH 03301-4649

FAHEY, RICHARD PAUL, lawyer; b. Oakland, Calif., Nov. 2, 1944; s. John Joseph and Helene Goldie (Whetstone) F.; m. Suzanne Dawson, June 8, 1968; children: Eamon, Aaron Chad. AA, Merritt Coll., 1964; BA, San Francisco State U., 1966; JD, Northwestern U., 1971. Bar: N.Mex. 1971, U.S. Dist. Ct. N.Mex. 1972, U.S. Ct. Appeals (10th cir.) 1972, Ohio 1973, U.S. Dist. Ct. (no. and so. dists.) Ohio 1973, U.S. Supreme Court 1975. Vol. Peace Corps, Liberia, 1966-68; atty.-in-charge Dinebeiina Nahiilna Be Agaditahe, Shiprock, N.Mex., 1971-73; asst. atty. gen. State of Ohio, Columbus, 1973-76; ptnr. Fahey & Schraff, 1976-80, Sanford, Fisher, Fahey, Boyland & Schwarzwalder, 1980-84; of counsel Knepper, White, Arter & Hadden, 1984-85; ptnr. Arter & Hadden, 1985—; adj. prof. law Capital U., 1976-86, Ohio State U., 1986-87; chmn. Ohio Oil and Gas Regulatory Rev. Commn., 1986-87; mem. exec. com. Dem. Party, 1996—; mem. charter review com. Columbus City, 1998—. Author: Underground Storage Tanks A Primer of the Federal Regulatory Program, 2nd edit., 1995; contbr. articles to profl. jours. Mem. Charter rev. com. City of Columbus, 1998 Mem. Columbus Pub. Schs. Bd. Edn., 1986-93, pres. 1989; trustee Godman Guild Settlement House, Columbus, 1976-82, Ohio Environ. Council, 1981-83, Downtown Columbus, Inc., 1989, Pilot Dogs, Inc., 1993—; adv. bd. WCBE Pub. Radio. Russell Sage Found. grantee, 1969; mem. bd. dirs. Nat. Audubon Soc. Ohio Chpt., 1999—. Mem. ABA (vice chair Sonreel water quality com. 1993-97), Ohio Bar Assn., N.Mex. Bar Assn., Columbus Bar Assn., Columbus Bar Found. Democrat. Unitarian. Avocations: travel, fishing, reading, jogging, skiing. Home: 449 E Dominion Blvd Columbus OH 43214-2216 Office: Arter & Hadden One Columbus Bldg 10 W Broad St Ste 21 Columbus OH 43215-3418

FAHEY-CAMERON, ROBIN, artist, photographer; b. Bangor, Maine, Mar. 7, 1943; d. Oswald R. and Georgina Marie (Barbin) Fahey; m. Gordon W. vogel, June 27, 1966 (dec. 1993); 1 child, Darren Taggert. BA in Studio Art, U. Minn., 1968; grad., LaJolla Acad. Advt. Arts, Calif., 1984. Tech. dir. The Peppermint Tent, Mpls., 1968; costume designer St. Joseph (Minn.) Coll., 1968-69; copywriter, graphic artist Western Word and Picture Co., Sausalito, Calif., 1984-86; creative dir. 20/20 Catalogue, San Francisco, 1986-89. Author: Games of Deception, 1989, The Inner Door, 1996, Gate Between the Worlds, 1998; recent one-woman exhibits include Images of the Land, photography exhbiit, Alpine, Calif., 1988, The Ancient Land (photography exhibit), Alpine, 1989; represented in group exhibitions Fine Crafts Invitational, Durango, 1991, Photography Invitational, Durango, Colo., 1991, Artists' Invitational, Durango, 1991, Dorango Arts Ctr., 1992, 94, Drawing and Sculpture Show, Durango, 1992, Exhibit Com. Show, Durango, 1993, Heartland, the Art Room, Durango, 1994, Gallery Walk Exhibit, Landscapes, the Art Room, Durango, 1995, Points of View, Four Woman Show, Durango, 1995, Looking with the Heart, Earthdancer Gallery, Alpine, Calif., 1998; mem. exhbn. com. Durango Arts Ctr., 1990-93. Avocation: gardening.

FAHIEN, LEONARD AUGUST, physician, educator; b. St. Louis, July 26, 1934; s. John Henry and Alice Katherine (Schubkegel) F.; m. Rose Marian Burmeister, June 21, 1958; children: Catherine Fahien Reuter, Lisa Fahien Uldrich, James. A.B., Washington U., St. Louis, 1956; M.D., Washington U., 1960. Intern U. Wis., Madison, 1960-61; surgeon NIH, Bethesda, Md., 1964-66; asst. prof. dept. pharmacology U. Wis. Med. Sch., Madison, 1966-69; asso. prof. U. Wis. Med. Sch., 1969-74, prof., 1974—, asso. dean, 1979-83; vis. prof. Inst. Protein Rsch. Osaka U., Japan, 1991; prof. El Julios U. Barcelona (Spain), 1997. Contbr. chpts. to books; contbr. articles to profl. jours. Served with USPHS, 1964-66. Numerous NIH grants, 1966—. Mem. Phi Beta Kappa, Sigma Xi. Lutheran. Home: 3212 Topping Rd Madison WI 53705-1435 Office: 426 S Charter St Madison WI 53715-1626

FAHLBECK, DOUGLAS ALAN, corporate development executive; b. Worcester, Mass., Dec. 27, 1945; s. Robert L. and Evelyn (Drury) F.; m. Jean A. Reardon, Aug. 22, 1970; children: Susan, Lauren. BS in Bus. Adminstrn., Boston U., 1967. Audit mgr. Arthur Andersen & Co., Boston, 1967-76; contr., treas. BTR, Inc., Providence, 1977-81; CFO Textron Fin. Corp., Providence, 1982-95; v.p. mergers and acquisitions Textron Inc., Providence, 1995—. Served as sgt. USMC, 1967-73. Mem. Am. Inst. CPA's., Mass. Soc. CPA's. Avocations: skiing, water skiing.

FAHLE, MANFRED, ophthalmology researcher; b. Duesseldorf, Germany, Dec. 10, 1950; s. Fritz and Helma (Westerfeld) F.; m. Sigrid Henke, Aug. 3, 1979; children: Nora-Katharina, Till Patrick Jacob. Degree in Biology, U. Goettingen, Fed. Republic Germany, 1972; degree in medicine, U. Giessen, Fed. Republic Germany, 1973; diploma in biology, U. Mainz, Fed. Republic Germany, 1975; MD, U. Tuebingen, Fed. Republic Germany, 1977. Fellow Max-Planck Inst. for Biol. Cybernetics, Tuebingen, 1977-81; head electrophysiol. lab. Univ. Eye Clinic, Tuebingen, 1981-88; vis. scientist U. Calif., Berkeley, 1984, MIT, Cambridge, Mass., 1989-90; fellow German Rsch. Coun., Tuebingen, 1990-93; prof. ophthalmology, head sect. visual sci. Univ. Eye Clinic, Tuebingen, 1994-95; head Inst. Brain Rsch. IV human-neurobiology U. Bremen, Germany, 1999—; Wiersma vis. prof. Calif. Inst. Tech., Pasadena, 1996; prof., head dept. optometry & visual sci. City U., London, 1998-99; prof. human neuro-biology U. Bremen, Germany, 1999—. Mem. editl. bd. German Jour. Ophthalmology, 1991-97, Neuroophthalmology, 1993—, Vision Rsch., 1994—. Bd. dirs. Grad. Program Neurobiology, Tuebingen, 1986-91, Drug Rsch. Programme, Tuebingen, 1996-99. Recipient Heisenberg award German Rsch. Coun., 1989, prize von Humboldt/Max-Planck Soc., 1992. Avocations: music, literature, sailing, windsurfing. Home: Bohnenbergerstr 28, D-72076 Tubingen Germany Office: Inst Human Neurobiology, Argonnenstr 3, D 28211 Bremen Germany

FAHLGREN, H(ERBERT) SMOOT, advertising agency executive; b. Parkersburg, W.Va., Aug. 17, 1930; s. C. Herbert and Julia (Smoot) F.; m. Judith Anne Henniger, Dec. 7, 1952; children: Steven, Becky, John. Student, U. Va., 1949-52; BSBA, Marietta Coll., 1952. Chmn. bd. dirs. Fahlgren, Parkersburg, W.Va., 1962—; bd. dirs. United Nat. Bank. Elder 1st Presbyn. Ch., Parkersburg; bd. dirs. West Va. U. Found. Recipient Spirit of Life award, 1998. Mem Am. Assn. Advt. Agys (treas. 1978-79, dir. 1981—), W.Va. Round Table. Home: RR 9 Box 218 Parkersburg WV 26101-9104 Office: PO Box 1628 Rosemar Rd & Seminary Dr Parkersburg WV 26102-1628

FAHMY, IBRAHIM MOUNIR, hotel executive; b. Alexandria, Egypt, July 4, 1943; came to U.S., 1986; s. Ambassador Mounir Ibrahim and Aziza (Kelada) F.; m. Brenda Lee Chenier, Sept. 18, 1970 (div. Jan. 1991); children: Susan Lee, Christine Lynn; m. Ann Marie Jones, Oct. 15, 1995. Certs., St. Mark's Coll., Alexandria, 1949-63; student, U. Alexandria, 1962-63. V.p., gen. mgr. King Edward Hotel, Toronto, Can., 1982-86; sr. v.p. Can. Forte Hotels Inc., N.Y.C., 1986-95; exec. v.p. Forte Hotels Inc., San Diego, Calif., 1986-95; mng. dir. The Carlton, Washington, 1995-99, The Essex House, NY, NY, 1999—; dir. Hotel Assn. Met. Toronto, Ont. Hostelry Inst.; mem. adv. com. Humber Coll. Vol. Kidney Found., Muscular Dystrophy, The Can. Children's Found. Mem. Internat. Wine & Food Soc. Avocations: skiing, English riding, squash, theatre, skeet and sporting clay shooting. Home and Office: The Essex House 160 Central Park South New York NY 10019-1701

FAHN, JAY, commercial bank executive, consultant, art dealer; b. Dallas, Aug. 19, 1949; s. Eli and Marion Fahn. BA, Williams Coll., 1971; PhB, MPhil. in Internat. Relations, Oxford (Eng.) U., 1975. Assoc. Citibank, N.A., N.Y.C. and Nairobi, Kenya, 1976; asst. v.p. Citibank, N.A., Seoul, Republic of Korea, 1981-83; mgr. Citibank, N.A., Ltd., Johannesburg, Republic of South Africa, 1977-79; resident v.p. Citibank Zambia, Ltd., Lusaka, 1979-81; v.p. Citicorp U.S.A., Chgo., 1983-85, First Nat. Bank of Chgo., 1989-91, LaSalle St. Securities, Chgo., 1989-90, Citicorp Investment Bank, Chgo., 1985—; sr. v.p. Hyde Park Bank, Chgo., 1991—; chmn. corp. contbns. com. Citicorp, Chgo., 1985—; prin., pres. Fahn & Assocs., Ltd., Chgo., 1986—; prin., owner Orca Aart Gallery, Chgo., 1987—; vis. lectr. gcopolitics DePaul U., Chgo., 1990—. Author: Chimbuko, 1986; contbr., editorial assoc.: Government by the People, 1971, Edward Kennedy and the Camelot Legacy, 1975. Mem. exec. com. Lincoln Park Zool. Soc., Chgo., 1984-90; nat. youth coord. Nat. Humphrey for Pres. Com., Washington, 1971-72; mem. com. on fgn. affairs Chgo. Coun. Fgn. Rels., 1989. Recipient Oxford U. scholarship, 1973, 74. Mem. Williams Club, Adventurers, Chgo. Zool. Soc. (governing mem. 1993—). Avocations: flying, camping, wildlife, history, scuba. Home: 2650 N Lakeview Ave Apt 2902 Chicago IL 60614-1825 Office: Hyde Park Bank & Trust 1525 E 53rd St Ste 502 Chicago IL 60615-4584

FAHN, STANLEY, neurologist, educator; b. Sacramento, Nov. 6, 1933; s. Ernest and Sylvia (Schumer) F.; m. Charlotte Zmora, June 21, 1958; children: Paul N., James D. BA, U. Calif.-Berkeley, 1955, MD, 1958. Diplomate Am. Bd. Neurology. Resident in neurology Neurol. Inst., N.Y., 1959-62; rsch. assoc. NIH, 1962-65; mem. faculty Columbia U., N.Y.C., 1965-68, prof. neurology, 1973-78, H. Houston Merritt prof., 1978—; mem. faculty U. Pa., Phila., 1968-73; dir. Dystonia Rsch. Ctr., 1981-97; sci. dir. Parkinson's Disease Found., 1979—; chmn. adv. com. peripheral and ctrl. nervous sys. drugs FDA, 1987-89, 91-96. Editor Movement Disorders, 1985-95; assoc. editor Neurology, 1977-87. With USPHS, 1962-65. Grantee NIH, 1974-77, 80-82, 84-91, 94—, 98—. Mem. Am. Acad. Neurology (chair edn. com. 1986-93, v.p. 1993-97, pres.-elect 1999—), Am. Neurol. Assn. (v.p. 1987-88, chair jour. oversight com. 1994-96), Movement Disorder Soc. (pres. 1988-91), Dystonia Med. Rsch. Found. (hon. life, bd. dirs. 1998—). Home: 155 Edgars Ln Hastings on Hudson NY 10706-1107 Office: 710 W 168th St New York NY 10032-2603

FAHNER, TYRONE C., lawyer, former state attorney general; b. Detroit, Nov. 18, 1942; s. Warren George and Alma Fahner; BA, U. Mich., 1965; JD, Wayne State U., 1968; LLM, Northwestern U., 1971; m. Anne Beauchamp, July 2, 1966; children—Margaret, Daniel, Molly. Bar: Mich. 1968, Ill. 1969, Tex. 1984, U.S. Dist. Ct. (ea. dist.) Mich. 1968, U.S. Dist. Ct. (no. dist.) Ill. 1969, U.S. Ct. Appeals (7th cir.) 1969, U.S. Ct. Appeals (5th cir.) 1981. asst. U.S. atty. for No. Dist. Ill., Chgo., 1971-75, dep. chief consumer fraud and civil rights, 1973-74, chief ofcl. corruption, 1974-75; ptnr. Freeman, Rothe, Freeman & Salzman, Chgo., 1975-77; dir. Ill. Dept. Law Enforcement, Springfield, 1977-79; ptnr. Mayer, Brown & Platt, Chgo., 1979-80, 83—; Co-chmn of managmnt comm., Mayer, Brown & Platt, 1998—; atty. gen. State of Ill., Springfield, 1980-83; instr. John Marshall Law Sch., 1973-76, 78-84; pvt. sector rep. UNCTAD; former chmn. Coun. Great Lakes Govs.; chmn. Govs. Adv. Bd. Law Enforcement, 1980-83, Ill. Jud. Inquiry Bd, 1988-92, Chgo., Com. Honest Elections, 1984-92, Com. Internat. Trade and Tourism, Chgo. com. Chgo. Coun. Fgn. Rels. Mem. Toronto sister city com. Chgo. Sister Cities Internat. Program; bd. dirs. Mex.-Am. Legal Defense and Ednl. Fund; mem. corp. adv. com. U. Mich. Coll. Lit., Sci. & The Arts, mem. major gifts com.; Mex.-Am. Legal Def. and Ednl. Fund; mem. William J. Fulbright bd. fgn. scholarships USIA, 1988-93; active Law Sch.'s Com. Visitors Wayne State U., U.S. Info. Agy., Ill. Racing Bd., 1979-80, United Cerbral Palsy, Chgo., 1981-84, Epilepsy Found. Greater Chgo., Evanston Hist. Soc., Bureau Ednl. and Cultural Affairs, 1988-93. Mem. ABA, Am. Coll. Trial Lawyers, Internat. Assn. Gaming Attys., Mich. Bar Assn., Tex. Bar Assn., Chgo. Bar Assn., Law Club Chgo., Am. Inns of Ct. (Chgo. chpt.), Ill. Ambs. (bd. dirs., past pres.), Northwestern U. Sch. Law Alumni Assn. (bd. dirs. 1990-95, chmn. Class 1967 James B. Haddad professorship fundraising com.), Econ. Club of Chgo., Chgo. Club, Chgo. Commonwealth Club, Legal Club Chgo., Am. Effective Law Enforcement (com. cts. and justice), Commercial Club Chgo., U. Mich. Major Gifts com., Just The Beginning Found. Republican. Lutheran. Office: Mayer Brown & Platt 190 S La Salle St Ste 3100 Chicago IL 60603-3441*

FAHNESTOCK, JEAN HOWE, retired civil engineer; b. Pitts., May 22, 1930; d. James Murray and Hazel Margaret (Alberts) F. AA, Stephens, 1950; BS in Civil Engring., Carnegie-Mellon, 1955. Registered profl. engr., Ill., Mich., Iowa. Sr. project mgr. De Leuw, Cather & Co., Chgo., 1955-92; design mgr. De Leuw, Cather & Co., Kuwait, 1978-81, Abu Dhabi, 1981-85, Kennedy Expy. and Elgin-O'Hare Expy., Chgo., 1985-92. Fellow ASCE (life); mem. NSPE, Ill. Soc. Profl. Engrs. (life). Republican. Presbyterian. Avocations: bridge, travel, politics. E-mail: jhf4606@aol.com. Home: 4606 W Bryn Mawr Ave Chicago IL 60646-6632

FAHRBACH, RUTH C., state legislator; b. N.Y.C.. Grad. high sch., N.Y.C. Mem. Dist. 61 Conn. Ho. of Reps., 1981—, minority whip; appropriations com., pub. health com., legis. mgmt. com. Active Windsor Rep. Town Com., Order Women Legislators; v.p. Windsor Bd. Edn., 1979-80. Mem. First Dist. Rep. Womens Club, Fedn. Rep. Women, Civitan Club Windsor (past pres), Nat. Order of Women Legislators, Conn. Order of Women Legislators, Conn. Fedn. of Rep. Women, Nat. Fedn. of Republican Women. Home: 592 Poquonock Ave Windsor CT 06095-2204 Office: Legis Office Bldg Rm 4200 Hartford CT 06106-1591*

FAHRENKOPF, FRANK JOSEPH, JR., lawyer; b. Bklyn., Aug. 28, 1939; s. Frank J. and Rose (Freeman) F.; m. Mary Ethel Bandoni, Aug. 25, 1962; children: Allison Marie, Leslie Ann, Amy Michelle. B.A., U. Nev., 1962; J.D., U. Calif., Berkeley, 1965. Bar: Nev. 1965, D.C. 1983. Assoc. atty. Breen & Young, Reno, Nev., 1965-67; ptnr., atty. Sanford, Sanford, Fahrenkopf & Mousel, Reno, 1967-75, Fahrenkopf, Mortimer, Sourwine, Mousel & Sloane, Reno, 1976-85, Hogan & Harston, Washington, 1985—; pres., CEO Am. Gaming Assn., 1995—; Instr. criminal law U. Nev., 1967-82; panelist reporter Citizens Conf. on Nev. Cts., 1968; mem. Nev. Bd. Bar Examiners, 1971-85; judge pro tem Reno Municipal Ct., 1972-85; mem. faculty Nat. Jud. Coll., Reno, 1974-83; chmn. Coun. for the Future, Nat. Jud. Coll., 1990-94, bd. trustees, 1995—. Chmn. lawyers divsn. United Fund, 1969-70; chmn. Rep. Nat. Com., 1983-89; chmn. Nev. Rep. Com., 1975-83, gen. counsel, 1972-75; No. Nev. co-chmn. Com. for Re-election of Pres., 1972; mem. exec. bd. Nev. Rep. Cen. Com., 1969; nat. committeeman Nev. Young Reps., 1969-73; mem. Rep. Nat. Com., 1975-89; del. Rep. Nat. Conv., 1972, 76, 80, 84, 88; chmn. Western States Rep. Chmn.'s Assn., 1978-83; nat. chmn. Rep. State Chmn.'s Assn., 1981-83; bd. dirs. Nev. Cancer Soc., chmn., 1978-87; bd. dirs. Washoe County Legal Aid Soc., Babe Ruth Baseball League, Nev. Opera Guild, Reno YWCA, Sierra Sage coun. Camp Fire Girls, 1974-76, Nat. Endowment Democracy, 1938-93, Am. Coun. Young Polit. Leaders, 1983-89; co-chmn. Nat. Commn. on Presdl. Debates, 1987—, Commn. on Nat. Polit. Conv., 1989-93; vice chmn. Ctr. Democracy, 1995-98; dep. chmn. Internat. Dem. Union, 1983-98; chmn. Pacific Dem. Union, 1983. With AUS, 1957. Recipient Disting. Service award U.S. Jaycees, 1973, Humanitarian award NCCJ, 1981. Mem. Am. Judicature Soc., Comml. Law League Am., ABA (mem. gov. coun. gen. practice sect., internat. law com., chmn. Coalition for Justice 1993-95), Am. Trial Lawyers Assn., No. Nev. Trial Lawyers Assn. (v.p. 1969), State Bar Nev., Washoe County Bar Assn. (pres. 1973-74), Execs. Assn. Reno (dir. 1973-74), Nat. Assn. Gaming Attys. (v.p. 1981, pres. 1982-83), Barristers Club Nev. (v.p. 1969-73), Alpha Tau Omega. Office: 555 13th St NW Ste 1010 E Washington DC 20004-1109 *I believe each of us as a citizen of this country has an obligation to serve the community, state and nation. The rights of citizens and benefits of citizenship must be balanced by a duty to serve others.*

FAHRINGER, CATHERINE HEWSON, retired savings and loan association executive; b. Phila., Aug. 1, 1922; d. George Francis and Catherine Gertrude (Magee) Hewson; m. Edward F. Fahringer, July 8, 1961 (dec.); 1 child, Francis George Beckett. Grad. diploma, Inst. Fin. Edn., 1965. With Centrust Bank (formerly Dade Savs. and Loan Assn.), Miami, 1958-85, v.p., 1967-74, sr. v.p., 1974-82, sec., 1975-79, head savs. personnel and mktg. divsn., 1979-83, exec. v.p. office of chmn., 1984, dir., 1984-90, co-chmn. audit com. of bd. dirs., 1990; referral assoc. Referral Network Inc. subs. Coldwell Banker, 1990—. Contbr. articles to profl. jours. Trustee United Way of Dade County (Fla.), 1980-87, chmn. audit com. 1982-84, sec. 1976, vice chmn., 1977-78, chmn. bd., 1978-81; mem. adv. coun. Women's Bus. Devel. Ctr., Fla. Internat. U., 1993-95; mem. spl. steering com. Breast Cancer Task Force, Jackson Meml. Hosp., 1991; hon. bd. govs. U. Miami, Soc. for Rsch. in Med. Edn.; trustee South Fla. Blood Svc., Miami, 1979-84, vice chmn., 1980, chmn., 1981-84; trustee Dade County Vocat. Found., 1977-81; trustee Fla. Internat. U. Found., 1976-90; trustee Fla. Internat. U. Found., 1976-90, trustee emeritus, 1990, v.p. bd., 1978-81, pres. 1982-84; bd. dirs. Sta. WPBT-TV, 1984—, founding lifetime dir., 1995, chmn. budget and fin. com., 1986, mem. exec. com. 1985-92, sec. 1987, investment com., 1988-90, vice chmn. 1988-92, mem. fin. com., 1992, chmn. audit and control com., 1994, mem., 1997-98; bd. dirs., mem. nominating com. Girl Scout Coun., Tropical Fla., 1985-89, chmn. 1988-89, mem. long range planning com., 1986-88; citizens oversight com. Dade County Pub. Sch. System, 1986-90, chmn. 1988-90; bd. dirs. New World Sch. of Arts, 1987-90, chmn. devel. com., 1987-90, chair New World Sch. of Arts Gala, 1990; mem. Disaster Relief Com., chair Hurricane Disaster Relief Distbn. Ctr., 1992; mem. fin. com., chmn. capital improvement fund com. Coral Gables Congrl. Ch.; commd. Stephen min., 1995—; mem. grievance com. 11th Jud. Cir. Fla. Bar, 1988-92; bd. trustees United Protestant Appeal, 1994-96; mem. parking adv. bd. City of Coral Gables, 1997-98, bd. of adjustments, 1998—; mem., 3rd v.p. Bush chpt. Women's Cancer Assn. U. Miami, 1997-99, 2nd v.p., 1999—, chmn. meml. fund, 1998—. Named Women of Yr. in fin. Zonta Internat., 1975, amb. Air Def. Arty., U.S. Army Air Def. Command, 1970, Woman of Yr. in Sports, Links Club, 1986; recipient Trail Blazer award Women's Coun. of 100, 1977, Cmty. Headliner award Women in Comm., 1983, Outstanding Citizen of Dade County award 1984, Honors and Recognition award Golden Panthers Club of Fla. Internat. U., 1989, Disting. Svc. and Leadership award Fla. Internat. U., 1991, apprecation New World Sch. of the Arts, 1990, Meritorious Pub. Svc. award Fla. Bar, 1991; hon. BA U. Hard Knocks Alderson-Broaddus Coll., 1987. Mem. Dade Bus. and Profl. Women's Club (past pres. Woman of Yr. 1974), LWV, Inst. Fin. Edn. (life, nat. dir., past pres. Local Greater Miami chpt.), Savs. and Loan Mktg. Soc. South Fla. (past pres.), Savs. and Loan Pers. Soc. South Fla., Internat. Women's Alliance, Fla. Women's Alliance (bd. dirs. 1983-91, pres. 1987-89), Women's Union of Russia (conf. del. 1992), Country Club of Coral Gables (treas. women's golf assn. 1988-89, sec., bd. dirs. 1993, found. trustee 1993, v.p. bd. dir. 1994, pres. 1995, bd. advisor 1996, 97, 98, 99, chmn. bldg. restoration, capital improvement and maintenance com. 1995-99, liaison City of Coral Gables, 1997-99, rear commodore The Fleet 1998, vice commodore 1998, commodore 1999), Links Fla. Internat. U. Club (bd. dirs., sec., v.p. 1992), Greenway Women's Golf Assn. (treas. 1988-89), Biltmore Women's Golf Assn., Greater Miami Women's Golf Assn., Golden Panther Club (bd. dirs. 1988—, v.p. 1991, pres. 1992-94), Fla. Internat. U. Athletics Club. Democrat. *Success is putting forth your full effort and loving what you do. Dreams take time, but you can make them happen if you believe in yourself and in your dreams.*

FAHRLANDER, HENRY WILLIAM, JR., management consultant; b. Hamilton, Ohio, June 24, 1934; s. Henry William and Frances L. (Mitchel) F.; m. Shirley Fontenot, July 16, 1955; children: Henry W. III, Pauline Ann. BSEE, McNeese State U., 1956; cert. indsl. mgmt., So. Meth. U., 1965. Registered profl. engr., Calif.; registered lead auditor; cert. profl. cons. Design engr. Gen. Electric Co., Evendale, Ohio, 1956-60; quality mgr. Gen. Electric Co., St. Petersburg, Fla., 1960-65; quality system evaluation mgr. Tex. Instruments Co., Dallas, 1965-68; quality assurance dir. Recognition Equipment Corp., Dallas, 1968-72; dir. engring. Gen. Computer Systems, Addison, Tex., 1972-75; prin. H.W. Fahrlander & Assocs., Richardson, Tex., 1976—; instr. Dallas County Community Coll., Mesquite, Tex., 1972-78. Contbr. articles to profl. jours. Dir. adv. com. Dallas County Community Coll. Dist. at Richland Coll., 1965-68. Served with USAF, 1952-56, including Korea. Sr. mem. Am. Soc. Quality Control (chmn. Dallas sect. 1971-72, chmn. adminstrv. applications div. Milw. 1976-77, cert. quality engr., reliability engr.). Republican. Roman Catholic. Office: HW Fahrlander & Assocs 640 Downing Dr Richardson TX 75080-6117

FAHRNBRUCH, DALE E., retired state supreme court justice; b. Lincoln, Nebr., Sept. 13, 1924; s. Henry and Bessie M. (Osborne) F.; m. Margaret L. Hunt, July 4, 1952; children: Rebecca Kay Fahrnbruch Braymen, Daniel D. (dec.). AD in Journalism, U. Nebr., 1948, BS in Law, 1950; JD, Creighton U., 1951; LLM, U. Va., 1986. Bar: Nebr. 1951, U.S. Ct. Appeals (8th cir.) 1969. City editor Jour. Newspaper, Lincoln, 1951-52; asst., then dep. county atty. Lancaster County, Lincoln, Nebr., 1952-55; chief dep. county atty. Lancaster County, Lincoln, 1955-59; ptnr. Beynon, Hecht & Fahrnbruch, Lincoln, 1959-73; dist. judge Nebr. Lincoln, 1973-87; justice Nebr. Supreme Ct., Lincoln, 1987-97.

FAHY, JOHN J., lawyer; b. Carlstadt, N.J., Aug. 26, 1954; s. John and Mary (Roche) F.; m. Anne Dixon, Oct. 4, 1985. BS in Acctg., Fairleigh Dickinson U., Rutherford, N.J., 1976, MBA, 1978; JD, Seton Hall U., 1981. Bar: N.J. 1981, U.S. Dist. Ct. N.J. 1981, N.Y. 1982, U.S. Ct. Appeals (3d cir.) 1983; CPA, N.Y.; cert. criminal trial atty. Asst. prosecutor Hudson County, Jersey City, 1982-84; asst. U.S. atty. Office U.S. Atty., Newark, 1984-90; county prosecutor Bergen County, Hackensack, N.J., 1990-95; ptnr. Cole, Schutz, Meisel, Forman & Leonnard, Hackensack, N.J., 1995-96, Waters McPherson McNeill, Secaucus, N.J., 1996—; instr. writing Seton Hall U. sch. law, Newark, 1989-90; commr. N.J. Commn. on Hate Crimes, Trenton, 1992—. Fellow ABA; mem. NAACP, Fed. Bar Assn. (v.p. N.J. sect. 1993—), N.J. Bar Assn., Bergen County Bar Assn., Leadership N.J., Urban League, Seton Hall Law Sch. Alumni Assn. (trustee 1991—), Inns Ct. (barrister 1992—). Democrat. Roman Catholic. Avocations: basketball, golf, reading. Office: Waters McPherson McNeill 300 Lighting Way Secaucus NJ 07094-3695

FAHY, NANCY LEE, food products marketing executive; b. Schenectady, N.Y., Aug. 15, 1946; d. Christopher Mark and Frances (Lee) F.; m. Steven Neil Wohl, June 8, 1945 (div. Apr. 1978). BS cum laude, Miami (Ohio) U., 1968. Educator Palatine (Ill.) Pub. Schs., 1968-70, Glencoe (Ill.) Pub. Schs., 1970-78; sales rep. Keebler Co., Elmhurst, Ill., 1978-80, dist. mgr., 1980-82, account mgr., 1982-83, zone mgr., 1983-85, account mgr., 1985-89; regional mktg. mgr. Keebler Co., Morrow, Ga., 1989—. Vol. Lincoln Park Zool. Soc., Chgo., 1975-78. Mem. Food Products Club, Merchandising Execs. Club (bd. dirs. 1984-85), Grocery Mfgs. Sales Execs. Club (bd. dirs. 1984-85, asst. sec. 1987, treas. 1988, 1st v.p. 1989), Phi Beta Kappa. Avocations: gardening, literature, skiing, antiques. Office: Keebler Co 4751 Best Rd Ste 140 College Park GA 30135

FAIG, KENNETH WALTER, actuary, publisher; b. Cin., Aug. 24, 1948; s. Kenneth Walter and Edith Frances (Kennedy) F.; m. Carol Ann Gaber, May 19, 1979; children: Edith Mary, Walter Gerard. BA, Northwestern U., 1970. Asst. v.p. N.Am. Co. for Life and Health Ins., Chgo., 1973-87; assoc. actuary Allstate Life Ins. Co., Northbrook, Ill., 1987-89; mgr. Polysystems Inc., Chgo., 1989—; pub. books for Moshassuck Press, 1987—. Recipient Spencer L. Kimball award Nat. Assn. Ins. Commrs., 1997. Fellow Soc. Actuaries; mem. Am. Acad. Actuaries, Latin Litury Assn., R.I. Geneal. Soc., Providence Preservation Soc., Foster Preservation Soc. Roman Catholic. Avocations: history of actuarial science, genealogy. Home: 2311 Swainwood Dr Glenview IL 60025-2741

FAIG, WOLFGANG, survey engineer, engineering educator; b. Crailsheim, Germany, Apr. 27, 1939; married; 3 children. Diploma Ing, Techn U. Stuttgart, 1962; Dr Ing, U. Stuttgart, 1969; MScE, U. N.B., 1965. Rsch. assoc. photogrammetry dept. civil engring. U. N.B., 1965, Inst. Applied Geodesy, Stuttgart, Germany, 1966-69; asst. prof. civil engring. U. Ill., Champaign-Urbana, 1970-71; from asst. prof. to assoc. prof. survey and photogrammetry U. N.B., 1971-78, prof. survey engring., 1978—, assoc. dean engring., 1981-90, dean engring., 1990—; chmn. Working Group V-2 Internat. Soc. Photogrammeetry and Remote Sensing, 1972-76, nat. reporter, 1980—; vis. prof. sch. survey U. NSW, Sydney, Australia, 1984-85, Faculty Engring. Survey, Wuhan Tech. U. Survey and Mapping, 1986; active in internat. rels. Nat. Sci. and Engring. Rsch. Coun. Can., 1988-93; commd. Can. Lands Surveyor. Mem. Am. Soc. Photogrammetry and Remote Sensing (Talbert Abrams grand award 1995), Can. Inst. Geomatics, Assn. Profl. Engrs. N.B. (2d v.p. 1994), Assn. N.B. Land Surveyors (hon.). Achievements include rsch. in self-calibration of amateur cameras and their use for precision photogrammetry; modeling of vastly different observables; four-dimensional photogrammetry in deformation studies; digital photogrammetry. Office: U New Brunswick, PO Box 4400, Fredericton, NB Canada E3B 5A3*

FAIGNANT, JOHN PAUL, lawyer, educator; b. Proctor, Vt., Mar. 24, 1953; s. Joseph Paul and Ann (DeBlasio) F.; children: Janelle, Melissa. BA, U. New Haven, 1974; JD, George Mason U., 1978. Bar: Va. 1978, Vt. 1979, U.S. Dist. Ct. Vt. 1979, U.S. Ct. Appeals (4th cir.) 1979, U.S. Supreme Ct. 1992. Assoc. Griffin & Griffin, Rutland, Vt., 1978-79; assoc. Miller, Norton & Cleary, Rutland, 1979-84, ptnr., 1984-87; ptnr. Miller, Cleary and Faignant PC, Rutland, 1987-91, Miller & Faignant, Ltd., Rutland, 1991-97, Miller Faignant & Whelton PC, Rutland, 1997—; adj. prof. Coll. St. Joseph, Rutland, 1982-90. Mem. Rutland Town Fire Dept., 1989—; mem., pres. No. New England Def. Counsel, 1995-96. Mem. Va. Bar Assn., Vt. Bar Assn., Assn. Trial Lawyers Am., Def. Rsch. Inst., Am. Bd. Trial Advocates. Roman Catholic. Avocation: antique trucks. Home: RR 1 Box 3762 Rutland VT 05701-9214 Office: Miller Faignant & Whelton 36 Merchants Row PO Box 6688 Rutland VT 05702-6688

FAIHST, MICHAEL ERNEST, plastics engineer; b. Springville, N.Y., Apr. 30, 1953; s. Ernest J. and Dolores M. (Jaskula) F.; m. Joann M. Smith, July 8, 1978; 1 child, Michelle L. Student, W. Ky. Tech. Coll., West Ky. Tech. Coll. Mechanic Emerling Chevrolet, Boston, N.Y., 1971-73; operator Fisher Price, Holland, N.Y., 1973-74, utility worker, 1974-85, engring. tecnician, 1985-89; plastics process specialist Fisher Price, Murray, Ky., 1989-93; sr. plastics process specialist Fisher Price/Mattel, Murray, Ky., 1993-99; plastics engr./mold designer Fisher-Price/Mattel, Murray, Ky., 1999—. Vol fireman Springville Vol. Fire Co.,1982-90; vol. Ctr. Accessible Living, Murray, 1995—. Recipient Gov.'s Acad. scholarship, W. Ky. Tech. Coll. Mem. Loyal Order of Moose. Avocations: fishing, photography, target shooting. Office: Mattel Murray 307 Poor Farm Rd E Murray KY 42071-7855

FAILING, GEORGE EDGAR, editor, clergyman, educator; b. Kingston, Ont., Can., Nov. 25, 1912; s. Roy Augustus and Nellie (Richardson) F.; m. Phyllis Ogden, Apr. 12, 1939; children: Bunnie Jean, Alice Joy, Lynn Odgen. B.A. magna cum laude, Houghton Coll., 1940, Litt.D., 1960; M.A., Duke U., 1947; D.D., So. Wesleyan U., 1996. Ordained to ministry Wesleyan Meth. Ch., 1938. Pastor in Fillmore, N.Y., 1935-41, Louisville, 1941-44, Marion, Ind., 1953-56; prof. Cen. S.C. Wesleyan Coll., 1944-47; prof. theology Houghton (N.Y.) Coll., 1947-53, dir. pub. relations, 1947-53; editor Sunday Sch. Lit. Wesleyan Meth. Ch., Marion, Ind., 1956-59, Wesleyan Meth., 1959-68; chancellor Satellite Christian Inst., San Diego, 1968-73; prof. Greek and N.T. United Wesleyan Coll., Allentown, Pa., 1973; gen. editor Wesleyan Advocate, Marion, 1973-84. Author: 1 Corinthians, 1963, The Way of Holiness, 1970, Presence, 1977, Secure and Rejoicing, 1980, Did Christ Die for All?, 1980; contbg. author: Ency. World Methodism, 1974; contbg. author, editor: And They Shall Prophesy, 1978, With Open Face, 1983, Way of Wonder, 1983, History of the Wesleyan Ch., 1991, Death Has No Dominion, 1991. Mem. gen. bd. trustees Wesleyan Ch. Am., 1959-68, 74-84; pres. Presence, Inc., 1979—. Recipient Spl. Alumnus award United Wesleyan Coll., 1969, Houghton Coll., 1983. Mem. Soc. Bibl. Lit. and Exegesis, Evang. Press Assn. (pres. 1965-67), Am. Schs. Oriental Research. avocations: photography, travel. Home: PO Box 1867 Easley SC 29641-1867 Office: 102 Fernwood Dr Easley SC 29640-8831

FAILINGER, MARIE ANITA, law educator, editor; b. Battle Creek, Mich., June 29, 1952; d. Conard Frederick and Joan Anita (Lang) F.; children: Joanna, Kristina. BA, Valparaiso U., 1973, JD, 1976; LLM, Yale U., 1983; postgrad., U. Chgo., 1990. Bar: Ind. 1976, U.S. Dist. Ct. (no. dist.) Ind. 1976, U.S. Dist. Ct. (so. dist.) Ind. 1977, U.S. Ct. Appeals (7th cir.) 1979, Minn. 1984, U.S. Supreme Ct. 1980. Prof. of law Hamline U., St. Paul, 1983—, assoc. dean, 1990-93. Editor: Jour. of Law and Religion, 1988—; contbr. articles, book revs. to profl. publs. Mem. Am. Indian Rsch. and Policy Inst., 1993—; sec. Church Innovations Inst.; treas. Luth. Innovations. Mem. Minn. Women Lawyers (bd. dirs. 1989-90), Am. Assn. Law Schs. (chair poverty sect. 1984-88, exec. com. law and religion sect.), Ctrl. Minn. Legal Svcs. Bd., Nat. Equal Justice Libr. (bd. dirs. 1989—). Democrat. Mem. Evang. Luth. Ch. Am. Office: Hamline U Sch Law 1536 Hewitt Ave Saint Paul MN 55104-1284

FAILLA, SOPHIA LYNN, artist, educator; b. Bronx, Oct. 23, 1928; d. Joseph John and Lucy (Iaia) F.; divorced; 1 child, Lynn. Student, Brevard C.C., 1968-75. Asst. designer Vogue Patterns/Conde Nast, Old Greenwich, Conn., 1948-51; owner The Sewing Box, Darien, Conn., 1953-55; draftsman C.B.F., Stamford, Conn., 1957-58; outreach tchr. Brevard (Fla.) C.C., 1969-75; missionary, founder Honduran Christian Crafts, Honduras, 1975-79; owner, founder Fashions of Love, Lompoc, Calif., 1983-89; artist, tchr. Especially for You Gallery, Melbourne, Fla., 1989—. Recipient award of excellence Manhattan Art Internat., cert. of merit Stockholm Internat. Art Show, 1st prize Internat. Art League, 1998; winner 1998 Internat. Art competition (pub. in Art Times). Mem. AAUW, Nat. Mus. Women in Arts. Avocations: teaching, painting, travel, black choir music. Studio: Especially for You Gallery 909 E New Haven Ave # 5-67 Melbourne FL 32901-5478

FAILS, DONNA GAIL, mental health services professional; b. Harlingen, Tex., Apr. 27, 1958; d. Fred R. and L. Beth (Nicholson) F. BS, Phila. Coll. Bible, Langhorne, Pa., 1982; BA in Social Work, Rutgers U., Camden, N.J., 1984, MSW, 1985. Cert. social work mgr., Acad. Social Workers; lic. clin. social worker, N.J. Cmty. resource specialist March of Dimes South Jersey, Mt. Ephraim, N.J., 1982-83; case mgr., liaison Guidance Ctr. Camden County, Cherry Hill, N.J., 1983-84; outpatient coord. CamCare Mental Health Ctr., Blackwood and Cherry Hill, N.J., 1984-86; dir. partial care Comhar Mental Health Ctr., Phila., 1986-87; cons. Callahan Cons. Group, Cherry Hill, 1987-88; dir. mental health svcs., adminstr. mental health svcs. Archway Programs, Inc., Atco, N.J., 1988-94; dir. clin. svcs. Rainbow Healthcare Assocs., Glassboro, N.J., 1994-99; dir. med. day care Camden County Health Svcs. Ctr., Blackwood, N.J., 1999—; chairperson Interagy. Assessment Team of Camden County, 1989-90. Author, cons. Simon for Pres., Cherry Hill, 1988; co-chair statewide tech. assistance team Children's Mental Health Svcs., N.J., 1992-94; mem. stds. com. Children's Assessment and Resource Teams, 1991-94, Children's Interagy. Assessment Coun., 1991-94; mem. exec. com. N.J. Children's Coordinating Coun., 1992-94. Mem. Nat. Assn. Social Workers, Nat. Network for Social Work Mgrs., Inc., N.J. Gerontological Inst. Mem. Free Ch. of Am. Avocations: computers, music, art, reading. Home: 1232 Kohler Ave Deptford NJ 08096-5500 Office: Rainbow Healthcare Assocs 17 Delsea Dr S Glassboro NJ 08028-2620

FAIMAN-SILVA, SANDRA LYNNE, anthropologist; b. Rochester, N.Y., Nov. 12, 1946; d. Milton and Sally Anne (Longmore) Faiman; children: Ishmael Y., Lucas I., Benjamin N. BA in Anthropology, U. Mass., 1968; MA in Am. Studies, U. Minn., 1975; PhD in Anthropology, Boston U., 1984. Asst. prof. anthropology Bridgewater (Mass.) State Coll., 1987-92, assoc. prof. anthropology, 1992-96; full prof., 1996—; chair Acad. Policies Com., Bridgewater State Coll., 1989-92. Contbr. articles to profl. jours. Chair Falmouth (Mass.) Com. for Racial Equality, 1985-88; mem. Cape Codders Against Racism, Cape Cod, Mass., 1991—, Citizens Adv. Com. to the Cape Cod Cancer Study, 1988-91. Doctoral dissertation rsch. grantee NSF, 1980, Fulbright Travel grantee, India, 1990, travel/rsch. grantee Ctr. for Advancement of Rsch. and Teaching, Okla., 1992-93. Mem. Am. Anthropol. Assn., Assn. for Feminist Anthropology, Native Am. Rights Fund, N.E. Anthropol. Assn., Nat. Coun. for Rsch. on Women, Mass. State Coll. Assn. (exec. com. 1990—), Soc. of Lesbian and Gay Anthropologists (co-chair, 1999—), Soc. for Latin Am. Anthropology. Jewish. Avocations: bicycling, camping, travel, woodworking. Office: Dept Sociology/Anthropology Bridgewater State Coll Bridgewater MA 02325

FAIN, CHERYL ANN, translator, editor; b. Providence, May 16, 1953; d. Harry and Pearl (Friedman) F. Student, U. Salzburg, Austria, 1973-74; BA with high distinction, U. R.I., 1975; MA, Monterey Inst. Internat. Studies, 1978, post graduate cert in translation English-German, 1978. Freelance German translator various govt. agys., burs., record co., others, Balt. and Monterey, Calif., 1976—; in-house German and French med. translator Social Security Adminstrn., Balt., 1984-94; German/French translator, asst. to counselor sci. and tech. Embassy of Switzerland, Washington, 1994—; mem. Swiss delegation to the European Space Agy. Internat. Space Sta. Working Group, Washington, D.C. Translator: Perspectives on Mozart, 1978, also various articles and liner notes. Mem. Am. Translators Assn. (accredited for translation from German-English, French-English), Sci. Diplomats' Club of Washington, Phi Kappa Phi. Avocations: international travel, performance in operas, choral concerts and plays. Home: 2401 Calvert St NW Apt 421 Washington DC 20008-2667 Office: Embassy of Switzerland 2900 Cathedral Ave NW Washington DC 20008-3499

FAIN, JAY LINDSEY, brokerage house executive, consultant; b. Ft. Worth, July 16, 1950; s. James Joel Fain and Jeannine Yvonne (Routt) Ashner; m. Beth Jernigan, Oct. 18, 1968 (div. 1997); children: Lisa, Jacob; m. Christine Schroeder, Sept. 5, 1998. BBA, U. Tex., 1974. Cert. fin. planner. Acct. exec. Dallas Coca-Cola Bottling Co., 1968-74; unit sales mgr. Procter & Gamble, Houston, 1974-80; v.p. Morgan Stanley Dean Witter, Houston, Bend (Oreg.), 1981—; speaker in field; panelist hearing bd. N.Y. Stock Exchange, 1987—. Sr. warden St. Cuthbert Episc. Ch., Houston, 1983, 91; mem. fin. com. Episcopal Diocese of Tex. coun.; trustee Bishop Quin Found.; den leader Cub Scouts, troop com. Boy Scouts Am. Mem. Inst. Cert. Fin. Planners, Mt. Bachelor Rotary, Broken Top Club. Episcopalian. Avocations: golf, skiing, bible and church history studies, cooking. Home: 134 SW 17th St Bend OR 97702-1992 Office: Morgan Stanley Dean Witter 777 NW Wall St Bend OR 97701-2712

FAIN, JOEL MAURICE, lawyer; b. Miami Beach, Fla., Dec. 11, 1953; s. William Maurice and Carolyn Genievive (Baggett) F.; m. Moira Joan Slocum, June 15, 1974; children: Hannah Ruth, Dylan Michael, Rachel Joan. BA, Yale U., 1975; JD, U. Conn., 1978. Bar: Conn. 1978, U.S. Dist. Ct. Conn. 1978, U.S. Ct. Appeals (2d cir.) 1989. Assoc. Kahan, Kerensky, Capossela, Levine & Breslau, Vernon, Conn., 1978-83, ptnr., 1984-90; mng. ptnr. Kahan, Kerensky, Capossela, Levine & Breslau, 1990-91; ptnr. Morrison, Mahoney & Miller, Hartford, Conn., 1992—. Chmn. Youth Adv. Bd., Tolland, Conn., 1983-92; chmn. Tolland Town Coun., 1995—. Mem. ABA, Conn. Bar Assn., Tolland County Bar Assn. (pres. 1991-92), Assn. Trial Lawyers Am., Conn. Trial Lawyers Assn., Lions (pres. 1987-88). Democrat. Congregationalist. Home: 76 Tolland Grn Tolland CT 06084-3044 Office: Morrison Mahoney & Miller 100 Pearl St Hartford CT 06103-4506

FAIN, JOHN NICHOLAS, biochemistry educator; b. Jefferson City, Tenn., Aug. 18, 1934; s. Samuel Clark and Virginia Manson (Hunt) F.; m. Ann Duff, June 7, 1958; children: Margaret Ann, John Nicholas Jr., James Clark. BS magna cum laude, Carson-Newman Coll., 1956; PhD in Biochemistry, Emory U., 1960. Research assoc. Emory U., Atlanta, 1960-61; NSF fellow NIH, Bethesda, Md., 1961-62, postdoctoral fellow USPHS, 1962-63; biochemist NIH and Nat. Inst. Arthritis and Metabolic Diseases, Bethesda, 1963-65; asst. prof. Brown U., Providence, 1965-68, assoc. prof., 1968-71, prof., 1971-85, chmn. biochemistry, 1975-85; Van Vleet prof., chmn. U. Tenn., Memphis, 1985—. Contbr. numerous articles to sci. jours. Del. gen. assembly United Presbyn. Ch., Providence, 1972. Recipient Disting. Alumnus award Carson-Newman Coll., 1986; fellow Cambridge U., 1977-78; NIH Fogarty fellow, 1984-85; Macy Faculty scholar, 1977-78. Mem. Am. Soc. Biol. Chemists, Biochem. Soc., Am. Physiol. Soc. Democrat. Office: U Tenn Coll Medicine Dept Biochemistry 800 Madison Ave Memphis TN 38103-3400

FAIN, RICHARD DAVID, cruise line executive; b. Boston, Oct. 9, 1947; s. Morton Edgar and Libby Miriam (Winer) F.; m. Colleen Jo Ferris, July 27, 1969; children: Julie Meredith, Sara Elizabeth, Benjamin Alfred, Jessica Lynn. BS, U. Calif., Berkeley, 1969; MBA, U. Pa., 1972. Mgr. internat. fin. IU Internat. Corp., Phila., 1972-75; joint mng. dir., dir. Gotaas Larsen Shipping Corp., London, Eng., 1975-88; chmn., chief exec. officer Royal Caribbean Cruise Line, Miami, Fla., 1988—; chmn. Internat. Coun. Cruise Lines, Washington, 1993-95; bd. dirs. Assurance Foreningen Gard, SunTrust Bank, Miami, Semi-conductor Packaging Materials, Inc. Chmn. Greater Miami Conf. and Visitors Bur., 1995-97; trustee U. Miami, United Way Miami. Decorated Legion of Honor (France); named ARC Humanitarian of Yr., Dade County, Fla. Mem. Chaine de Rotisseurs. Home: 700 Arvida Pky Miami FL 33156-2325

FAINBERG, ANTHONY, physicist; b. London, Jan. 14, 1944; came to U.S., 1947; s. Benjamin and Elizabeth (Martelli) F.; m. Louise Vasvari (div. 1986); m. Diane August, Sept. 7, 1986. AB, NYU, 1964; PhD, U. Calif., Berkeley, 1969. Physicist INFN U. of Turin, Italy, 1970-72; rsch. prof. Syracuse (N.Y.) U., 1973-78; physicist Brookhaven Nat. Lab., Upton, N.Y., 1978-83; legis. aide Office of Senator Bingaman, Washington, 1983-84; sr. assoc. Office of Tech. Assessment, Washington, 1985-95; dir. Office Policy and Planning for Civil Aviation Security Fed. Aviation Adminstrn., 1996—; fellow Ctr. for Internat. Security & Arms Control, Stanford, 1991-92. Editor: (book) The Energy Source Book, 1991. Fellow Am. Phys. Soc. (mem. panel on pub. affairs 1990-92, 95-96, congl. fellow 1983-84); mem. AAAS. Office: Fed Aviation Adminstrn ACP-1 800 Independence Ave SW Washington DC 20591-0001

FAINGOLD, EDUARDO DANIEL, language and linguistics educator, researcher; b. La Plata, Argentina, Sept. 6, 1958; came to U.S., 1990; s. Enrique and Annie (Turkenich) F.; m. Sonia D. Hocherman; 1 child, Noam. BA in English and French, Hebrew U., Jerusalem, Israel, 1984, MA in English, 1987; PhD in Linguistics, Tel-Aviv U., 1992. Vis. scholar Tech. U. Berlin, 1988-89, UCLA, 1990-92, SUNY, Stony Brook, 1992-95; asst. prof. U. Tulsa (Okla.), 1995—; advisor to UNESCO, 1998; guest prof. Hebrew U. Jerusalem, Israel, 1996. Author: The Case for Fusion: (Jewish) Ladino in the Balkans and the Eastern Turkish Empire, 1989, Child Language, Creolization and Historical Change, 1996; guest editor: S.W. Jour. Linguistics, 1997, mem. editl. bd., 1997—; book rev. editor: Southwest Jour. of Linguistics, 1999-01; contbr. book reviews, articles to profl. jours. Book publ. grantee German Sci. Found., 1996, faculty rsch. grantee U. Tulsa, 1996-99, Salzburg Seimnar grantee, 1999; recipient Fozis Rsch. prize, 1989, Tel-Aviv U. Cultural Doctoral prize, Tel-Aviv, 1991, Teaching award Teaching and Technology, U. Tulsa, 1997. Mem. MLA, Am. Assn. Tchrs. Spanish and Portuguese, Internat. Clin. and Linguistics Assn., Linguistic Assn. S.W., Linguistic Soc. Am., Internat. Linguistic Assn. Office: U Tulsa 600 S College Ave Tulsa OK 74104-3126

FAIR, ANNIE MAY, geological computer specialist; b. Coolidge, Ariz., Sept. 21, 1939; d. Jack C. and Birdie Geneva (Strickland) Cullins; m. Charles Leroy Fair, Sept. 12, 1964; children: Rex Lee Myers, Kathleen Ann, Rebecca Elizabeth. Student, Wichita State U., 1979-81, U. Colo., 1982-84, 94—, Met. State U., Denver, 1983-84. Cert. geol. engr. Pres., bd. dirs. Fresnal Minerals, Inc., Tucson, 1975-80; geol. technician Foxfire Exploration, Inc., Wichita, Kans., 1980-81, Coastal Oil & Gas Corp., Denver, 1981-93; stat. analyst fluid minerals, nat. applications adminstr. Bur. Land Mgmt., Canon City, Colo., 1993—, nat. help desk, 1993—; geol. cons. C.L. Fair & Assocs., Littleton, Colo., 1984-93. Active adv. bd. Masonic-Rainbow Girls-Grand Cross of Color, Denver, 1983-84; vol.- helper United Way Campaign, Denver, 1990, 91; vol. Am. Cancer Soc., Littleton, 1991, 92; art judge Reflections Nat. Art Contest, Denver, 1992, 93, Skyline Elem. Sch., Canon City, 1993. Recipient Grand Cross of Color, Masons-Order Rainbow/Girls, 1957; Music scholar U. No. Ariz., 1957, Ariz. Girls state, 1956. Mem. Am. Assn. Petroleum Geologists, Geol. Soc. Am., Rocky Mountain Assn. Geologists, Computer Oriented Geol. Soc., Alpha Lambda Delta. Avocation: artist. Home: 2853 Melvina St Canon City CO 81212-8837

FAIR, CHARLES MAITLAND, neuroscientist, author; b. N.Y.C., Sept. 18, 1916; s. Charles Maitland Fair and Gertrude Modora (Bryan) Knapp; m. Mary Katherine Ruddy, Feb. 2, 1952 (div. 1980); children: Ellen, Katherine, Charles (dec.); m. Louise Sadler Kiessling, May 5, 1980. Guggenheim fellow Brain Rsch. Inst., UCLA, 1963-64; resident scientist MIT Neuroscis. Rsch. Program, 1964-65; lab. scientist Mass. Gen. Hosp., Boston, 1966-67, MIT, 1967; officer Synax, Somerville, Mass., 1970-72. Author: The Physical Foundations of the Psyche, 1963, The Dying Self, 1969, From the Jaws of Victory, 1971, The New Nonsense, 1974, Memory and Central Nervous Organization, 1988, Cortical Memory Functions, 1992; contbr. articles and revs. to profl. jours. With USNR, 1938. Am. Acad. Arts. and Scis. grantee, 1961. Mem. AAAS, N.Y. Acad. Sci. Democrat. Avocations: jazz, piano, sailing. Home: Jerry Brown Farm 110 Fire Lane 1 Wakefield RI 02879-5460

FAIR, HUDSON RANDOLPH, recording company executive; b. Evanston, Ill., Aug. 15, 1953; s. Harry Joel Jr. and Virginia (Gauntlett F. BS in Speech, Northwestern U., 1976, MA in Speech, 1979. Mktg. rep. Calumet Refining Co., Chgo., 1975-78, Calumet Petro-Chems., Inc., Houston, 1977-78, Stellavox, S.A., Schaumburg, Ill., 1986-87, Nagra Magnetic Recorders, Inc., N.Y.C., 1987-91; pres. Ealing Mobile Recording, Ltd., Chgo., 1981—; music prodr. WFMT Radio, Chgo., 1992—, Ravinia Festival, 1997—; cons. in field. prodr. more than 100 classical albums, 1981—. Speech writer Rep. George Bush Presdl. Campaign, Chgo., 1979-80. Recipient Chorus award for best choral rec., 1989, Deutsche Schallplatten-preis for best chamber music record Juilliard String Quartet, 1998; grantee Ill. Arts Coun., 1982-86, Nat. Endowment for Arts, 1986. Mem. NARAS (bd. govs. 1991-95, 96—, nat. trustee 1993-95), Audio Engring. Soc., Engring. and Rec. Soc. (bd. dirs. 1987—, chmn. 1991-92). Republican. Episcopalian. Avocations: travel, motorcycles, skiing. Office: Ealing Mobile Rec Ltd 4906 N Talman Ave Chicago IL 60625-2722

FAIR, JAMES RUTHERFORD, JR., chemical engineering educator, consultant; b. Charleston, Mo., Oct. 14, 1920; s. James Rutherford and Georgia Irene (Case) F.; m. Merle Innis, Jan. 14, 1950; children: James Rutherford III, Elizabeth, Richard Innis. Student, The Citadel, 1938-40; BS, Ga. Inst.

Tech., 1942; MS, U. Mich., 1949; PhD, U. Tex., 1955; DSc (hon.), Wash. U., 1977; HHD (hon.), Clemson U., 1987. Rsch. engr. Shell Devel. Co., Emeryville, Calif., 1954-56; with Monsanto Co., 1942-52, 56-79; engring. dir. corp. engring. dept. Monsanto Co. (World hdqrs.), St. Louis, 1969-79; McKetta chair chem. engring. U. Tex., Austin, 1979—; dir., v.p. Fractionation Research, Inc., Bartlesville, Okla., 1969-79; pres. James R. Fair Inc., 1981—. Author: North Arkansas Line, 1969, Distillation, 1971, Louisiana and Arkansas, 1997, Distillation, 1998; contbr. numerous articles to profl. publs. Recipient profl. achievement award Chemical Engineering mag., 1968, King award U. Tex., 1987. Fellow AIChE (bd. dirs. 1965-67, Walker award 1973, Practice award 1975, Founders award 1977, Inst. lectr. 1979, Separation Tech. award 1994); mem. NSPE, NAE, Am. Chem. Soc. (Separation Sci. and Tech. award 1993), Am. Soc. Engring. Edn., Faculty Club U. Tex., Headliners Club (Austin), Sigma Nu. Republican. Presbyterian. Home: 2804 Northwood Rd Austin TX 78703-1603 Office: U Tex Dept Chem Engring Separations Rsch Progr Austin TX 78712

FAIR, JAMES STANLEY, hospital administrator; b. Delisle, Sask., Can., May 21, 1933. Bachelors degree, U. Sask., 1955; masters degree, U. Toronto, Ont., Can., 1968. Adminstrv. rschr. Toronto Gen. Hosp., 1967-68; asst. adminstr. Mckellar Gen. Hosp., Ft. William, Ont., 1968-72; dir. diagnostic svcs. Vancouver Gen. Hosp., B.C., Can., 1972-73; acting exec. dir. Gorge Road Hosp., Victoria, B.C., 1984, pub. adminstr., 1984-85; exec. dir. Victoria Gen. Hosp., 1973-84, Guelph (Ont.) Gen. Hosp., 1985-88; pres., CEO Fraser-Burrard Hosp., New Westminster, B.C., 1989-96, Simon Fraser Health Region, New Westminster, B.C., 1995—; regent Am. Coll. Healthcare Execs. Western Can., 1998-99. Contbr. articles to profl. jours. Office: Simon Fraser Health Region, 260 Sherbrooke St, New Westminster, BC Canada V3L 3M2

FAIR, JEAN EVERHARD, education educator; b. Evanston, Ill., July 21, 1917; d. Drury Hampton and Bess Marion (Everhard) F. B.A., U. Ill., 1938; M.A., U. Chgo., 1939, Ph.D., 1953. Tchr. Evanston (Ill.) Twp. High Sch., 1940-48, 1954-58; tchr. U. Minn. High Sch., 1948-49, U. Ill. High Sch., 1951-53; prof. edn. Wayne State U., Detroit, 1958-82, now prof. emeritus; cons. in edn.; cons. in edn.; cons. Mich. Ednl. Goals, Objectives and Assessment in Social Studies; reviewer of position statements for teaching and learning, standards, assessment and other manuscripts for Nat. Coun. Social Studies. Contbr. articles to profl. jours. Mem. Nat. Council for Social Studies (pres. 1972, dir. 1958-61, 73-75), Assn. for Supervision and Curriculum Devel., Social Sci. Edn. Consortium, LWV, Phi Beta Kappa. Mem. United Ch. Christ. Home: 10 Clinton Ln Dearborn MI 48120-1039

FAIR, MARCIA JEANNE HIXSON, retired educational administrator; b. Scobey, Mont.; d. Edward Goodell and Olga Marie (Frederickson) Hixson; m. Donald Harry Mahaffey (div. Aug. 1976); 1 child, Marcia Anne (dec.); m. George Justin Fair, Mar. 26, 1997. BA in English, U. Wash.; MA in Secondary Edn., U. Hawaii, 1967. Cert. secondary and elem. tchr. and adminstr. Tchr. San Lorenzo (Calif.) Sch. Dist., 1958-59; tchr. Castro Valley (Calif.) Sch. Dist., 1959-63, vice prin., 1963-67; vice prin. Sequoia Union High Sch. Dist., Redwood City, Calif., 1967-77, asst. prin., 1977-91, ret., 1991; tchr. trainer Project Impact Sequoia Union Sch. Dist., Redwood City, 1986-91; mem. supr.'s task force for dropout prevention, 1987-91, Sequoia Dist. Goals Commn. (chair subcom. staff devel. 1988); mentor tchr. selection com., 1987-91; mem. Stanford Program Devel. Ctr. Com., 1987-91; chairperson gifted and talented Castro Valley Sch. Dist.; mem. family svcs. bd., San Leandro, Calif. Vol. Am. Cancer Soc., San Mateo, Calif., 1967, Castro Valley, 1965; Sunday sch. tchr. Hope Luth. Ch., San Mateo, 1970-76; chair Carlmont H.S. Site Coun., Belmont, Calif., 1977-91; mem. Nat. Trust for Hist. Preservation. Recipient Life Mem. award Parent, Tchr., Student Assn., Belmont, 1984, Svc. award, 1989, Exemplary Svc award Carlmont High Sch., 1989, 92; named Woman of the Week, Castro Valley, 1967, Outstanding Task Force Chair Adopt A Sch. Program San Mateo (Calif.) County, 1990. Mem. ASCD, AAUW, DAR, Assn. Calif. Sch. Adminstrs. (Project Leadership plaque 1985), Sequoia Dist. Mgmt.Assn. (pres. 1975, treas. 1984-85), Met. Mus. Art, Smithsonian Instn., Libr. of Congress Assocs. (charter), Am. Heritage - The Soc. of Am. Historians, Internat. Platform Assn., Animal Welfare Advocacy, Woodrow Wilson Internat. Ctr. Scholars, Nat. Geographic Soc., Am. Mus. Natural History (charter mem.), Bridle Trails Cmty. Club, Delta Kappa Gamma, Alpha Xi Delta (Order of Rose award 1997). Avocations: oil painting, travel, tap dancing, redecorating, writing poetry. *Personal philosophy: Life is short, so make haste to be kind to one another.*

FAIR, RICHARD BARTON, electronics executive, educator; b. L.A., Sept. 12, 1942; s. Paul Albertus and Emabel (McCollom) F.; m. M. Clare Wilkinson, Sept. 12, 1964; children: Cynthia, Catherine, Peter, Denise. BEE, Duke U., 1964, PhD, 1969; MEE, Pa. State U., 1966. Mem. tech. staff Bell Labs., Reading, Pa., 1969-73, supr., 1973-81; prof. elec. engring. Duke U., Durham, N.C., 1981—; v.p. rsch. programs Microelectronics Ctr. N.C., Research Triangle Park, N.C., 1981-86, v.p. design rsch., 1986-90, chief scientist, 1990-91, v.p. microelectronics, 1991-93; cons. Arnold, White & Durkee, Houston, 1985-90, Richards, Medlock & Andrews, 1992—, Jenner & Block, Chgo., 1994, Wilham, Brinks, Washington, 1994, Jones and Day, 1995—; lectr. in field. Editor: Rapid Thermal Processing, Science and Technology, 1992; contbr. articles to jours. and chpts. to books in field. Named Outstanding Young Elec. Engr. of Yr., Eta Kappa Nu, 1974. Fellow IEEE (Procs. editorial bd. 1988—, assoc. editor Trans. on Electronic Devices 1990-93, editor Procs. 1993—), Electrochem. Soc.; mem. Sigma Xi. Democrat. Episcopalian. Avocations: writing, music, fast cars, venture capital. Home: 3414 Cambridge Dr Durham NC 27707 Office: Dept Elec/ Computer Engring Duke U Box 90291 Durham NC 27708*

FAIRBAIRN, JOYCE, Canadian government official; b. Lethbridge, Alta., Can., Nov. 6, 1939; m. Michael Gillan. BA in English, U. Alta., 1960; B Journalism, Carleton U., 1961. Mem. news staff Ottawa (Ont., Can.) Herald, 1961; mem. staff parliamentary press gallery UPI, Ottawa, 1962-64; mem. staff parliamentary bur. F.P. Publs., 1964-70; legis. asst., sr. legis. advisor Prime Minister of Can. Pierre Elliott Trudeau, 1970-84, comms. coord., 1981-83; mem. Senate for Province of Alta., 1984—, appt. to privy coun., leader govt., 1993-97, minister with spl. responsibility for literacy, 1993—, spl. advisor for literacy, 1997; mem. Spl. Senate Com. on Youth, Senate Standing Coms. on Transp. and Comm., Legal and Constl. Affairs, Fgn. Affairs, Agr. and Forestry; founding mem. standing com. on Aboriginal peoples; vice chair Nat. Liberal Caucus and Western and No. Liberal Caucus, 1984-91; co-chair nat. campaign com. Liberal Party of Can., 1991. Past mem. senate U. Lethbridge. Inducted into Kainai Chieftainship, Blood Nation; hon. lt. col. 18th Air Def. Regt., Royal Can. Army. Office: Can Senate, 571-S Centre Block, Ottawa, ON Canada K1A 0A4*

FAIRBAIRN, URSULA FARRELL, human resources executive; b. Newark, Feb. 5, 1943; d. Henry C. and Clara J. (Ziefle) Otte; m. William Todd Fairbairn III, May 14, 1978; children: W. Todd, Mary. BA, Upsala Coll., 1965; MA in Teaching, Harvard U., 1966. Instr., numerous mktg. positions IBM, N.Y.C., 1966-78; exec. asst. to sec., White House fellow U.S. Treasury Dept., Washington, 1973-74; exec. asst. to chmn. bd., group dir. IBM, Armonk, N.Y., 1978-80, v.p. mgmt. svcs., then v.p. mktg. ops. west, 1980-84, dir. pers. resources, 1984-87, dir. bus. and mgmt. edn., 1987, dir. edn., 1987-89, dir. edn. and mgmt. devel., 1989-90; sr. v.p. human resources Union Pacific Corp., Bethlehem, Pa., 1990-96; exec. v.p. human resources and quality Am. Express Co., N.Y.C., 1996—; bd. dirs. VF Corp., Wyomissing, Pa., Gen. Signal Corp., Stamford, Conn. Contbg. author: Managing Human Resources in the Information Age, 1991. Mem. Com. of 200, Catalyst, N.Y.C. Mem. Bus. Roundtable (chair exec. com. employee rels. com.), Labor Policy Assn. (bd. dirs., mem. exec. com.). Avocations: gardening, art, reading, walking, travel. Office: Am Express Co 200 Vesey St # 51 New York NY 10285-1000*

FAIRBANK, JANE DAVENPORT, editor, civic worker; b. Seattle, Aug. 21, 1918; d. Harold Edwin and Mildred (Foster) Davenport; AB magna cum laude, Whitman Coll., 1939; postgrad. U. Wash., 1940-42; m. William Martin Fairbank, Aug. 16, 1941; children: William Martin, Robert Harold, Richard Dana. Sci. staff mem. Radiation Lab., Mass. Inst. Tech., Cambridge, 1942-45. Chmn. Second Careers for Women, Stanford, Calif., 1970-75; chmn. annual continuing edn. program Whitman Coll. St. Alumni Coll., 1986-96; founding mem. Bay Area Consortium on Ednl. Needs of Women. 1971; mem. Canada Coll. Citizens Adv. Com. for Community Edn., 1968; mem. organizing com. for conf. on frontiers of physics Stanford U., 1982; tchg. asst. U. Wash., 1940-42. Mem. Whitman Coll. Alumni Assn. (bd. dirs. 1986-96), Calif. Congress Parents and Tchrs. (hon. life), Mortar Bd., Phi Beta Kappa. Alpha Chi Omega. Mem. United Ch. of Christ. Mem. Stanford Univ. Women's Club (pres. 1975-76). Editor: Radar Maintenance Manual (2 vols.), 1945; co-editor Near Zero: New Frontiers of Physics, 1988; Second Careers for Women: A View from the San Francisco Peninsula, 1971; Second Careers for Women, vol. II: A View of Seven Fields from the San Francisco Bay Area, 1975. Office: 141 E Floresta Way Menlo Park CA 94028-7530

FAIRBANK, RICHARD, diversified financial services company executive. Chmn., CEO Capital One Finance, Inc., Glen Allen, Va. Office: Capital One Finance Inc 11013 W Broad St Glen Allen VA 23060-5937*

FAIRBANK, ROBERT HAROLD, lawyer; b. Northampton, Mass., Mar. 4, 1948; s. William Martin and Jane (Davenport) F.; m. Gail Lees, Feb. 16, 1992; children: Sarah Julia, David Kivy; stepchildren: Kristin Burdge, Lindsay Burdge. AB in Polit. Sci., Stanford U., 1972; MLS, U. Calif.-Berkeley, 1973; JD, NYU, 1977. Bar: Calif. 1977, U.S. Dist. Ct. (cen. and no. dists.) Calif. 1978, U.S. Dist. Ct. (so. dist.) Calif. 1993. Assoc. Gibson, Dunn & Crutcher, L.A., 1977-84, ptnr., 1985-96; co-founding ptnr. Fairbank & Vincent, 1996—. Author: Effective Pretrial and Trial Motions, 1983, California Practice Guide: Civil Trials and Evidence (The Rutter Group 1993, with yearly updates); mem. editl. bd. NYU Law Rev., 1975-76. Named One of Top 100 Bus. Lawyers in L.A., L.A. Bus. Jour., 1995. Mem. Assn. Bus. Trial Lawyers (co-founder San Francisco and Orange County chpts., bd. govs. 1984-85, treas. 1986-87, sec. 1987-88, v.p. 1988-89, pres. 1989-90), L.A. County Bar Assn. (fed. cts. com. 1983-85), Jud. Coun. Calif. Adv. Com. on Local Rules (subcom. chair on civil trial rules). E-mail: rhf@fvlaw.com. Office: Fairbank & Vincent 11755 Wilshire Blvd Ste 2320 Los Angeles CA 90025-1501

FAIRBANKS, CHARLES F., law educator. Student, Johnson Wales Jr. Coll., Providence, 1968; AA in Bus., Nebr. We. Jr. Coll., Scottsbluff, 1972; BS in Criminal Justice, U. Nebr., Omaha, 1974; MA in Edn., U. Nebr., Kearney, 1994; postgrad., U. Nebr., Lincoln. Dep. sheriff Hall County, Grand Island, Nebr., 1974-79, sheriff, dir. adult correctional facility, 1979-87; dir. adult correctional facility Scotts Bluff County, Gering, Nebr., 1987-94, sheriff, 1987-95; instr. criminal justice We. Nebr. C.C., Scottsbluff, 1995—; presenter in field. Active Boy Scouts Am., Monument Bible Ch., Gering New Horizons. Recipient Outstanding Svc. award United Vets. Grand Island, 1987, Outstanding Loss Prevention award Nebr. Inter-Gov. Risk Mgmt. Assn., 1990, Law Enforcement Cmty. Leadership award U.S. Atty. Dist. Nebr., 1990, Recognition Svc. award Boy Scouts Am., 1990. Phi Theta Kappa Excellence in Edn. award, 1996-97. Mem. Internat. Soc. Crime Prevention Practitioners, Am. Jail Assn., Nat. Assn. Police Planners, Nebr. Sheriff's Assn. (Pres. award 1986), Nebr. Crime Prevention Assn. (Outstanding Support, Guidance and Leadership award 1992), Nebr. Assn. County Officials (Pres. award 1987), Law Enforcement Intelligence Network, We. Intelligence Narcotics Group (grant dir.). Office: 1601 E 27th St Scottsbluff NE 69361-1815

FAIRBANKS, DAVID NATHANIEL FOX, physician, surgeon, educator; b. Ann Arbor, Mich., Mar. 31, 1936; s. Avard Tennyson and Beatrice Maude (Fox) F.; m. Sylvia West, June 17, 1959; children: David W., Lisa Marie, E. Jefferson, Galen J. BS, U. Utah, 1959, MD, 1963. Diplomate Am. Bd. Otolaryngology. Resident in otolaryngology surgery Johns Hopkins Hosp., Balt., 1963-69; grands adminstr. NIH, Bethesda, Md., 1969-71; mem. rotating staff Project HOPE, Kingston, Jamaica, 1971; clin. prof. otolaryngology George Washington U., Washington, 1970—, dir. divsn. otolaryngology, 1976-84; med. bd. Project HOPE, Millwood, Va., 1971—; cons. NIH, Bethesda, Md., 1971—; co-dir. Sleep Disorders Ctr., Sibley Meml. Hosp., Washington D.C., 1994—. Author: Antimicrobial Therapy in Otolaryngolgoy, 1981, 10th edit., 1999, Snoring and Obstructice Sleep Apnea, 1987, 2d edit., 1994; contbr. articles to profl. jours., chpts. to books. Missionary Ch. of Jesus Christ of Latter-day Saints, Calif., 1956-58. With USPHS, 1969-71. Johns Hopkins U. fellow, 1968-69. Fellow ACS, Am. Acad. Otolaryngology (dir. 1983-85), Am. Rhinological Soc., Triol. Soc.; mem AMA, Am. Sleep Disorders Assn., Med. Soc. D.C. (bd. dirs. 1984-86), Met. Ear, Nose and Throat Soc. (pres. 1976), Phi Beta Kappa. Republican. Mem. LDS Ch. Avocations: banjo, folk music, farming, family band. Office: Ear Nose and Throat Med Group 2021 K St NW Ste 210 Washington DC 20006-1003

FAIRBANKS, DOUGLAS ELTON, JR., actor, producer, writer, corporation director; b. N.Y.C., Dec. 9, 1909; s. Douglas Elton and Anna Beth (Sully) F.; m. Lucille LeSueur (Joan Crawford), June 1929 (div. 1933); m. Mary Lee (Epling) Hartford, Apr. 22, 1939 (dec. Sept. 1988); children: Daphne, Victoria, Melissa; m. Vera Shelton, May 30, 1991. Student, Bovée and Collegiate Schs., N.Y.; cadet, Knickerbocker Greys, N.Y., Harvard Mil. Sch., L.A.; student, Pasadena (Calif.) Poly.; pvt. tutoring, London, Paris, L.A.; DFA (hon.), Westminster Coll., 1966, Sr. Churchill fellow; vis. fellow, St. Cross Coll., Oxford U.; M.A. (hon.), Oxford U., 1971; LLD (hon.), Denver U., 1974; fellow, Boston U. Libraries, 1978. Chmn. Dougfair Corp. and subsidiaries, The Fairbanks Co., Calif., 1946, Fairtel Corp., N.Y., 1969, Douglas Fairbanks Ltd., Eng., 1952—, (and asso. cos.), 1952-58; MA (hon.); past pres. Boltons Trading Co., Inc.; also past dir. or cons. several internat. bus. corps., U.S., Europe, Asia; gov. Am. Mus. in Britain; trustee Edwina Mountbatten Trust; mem. exec. com., bd. govs. Royal Shakespeare Theatre, Stratford-on-Avon, Eng.; bd. govs. Ditchley Found., U.K., U.S.; mem. adv. com. Denver Ctr. for Performing Arts; chmn. Internat. Cultural Ctr. for Youth, Jerusalem; lectr. attached Joint Chiefs Staff, Washington, 1971-81. Author: (autobiography) The Salad Days, 1988; (with Richard Schickel) The Fairbanks Album, 1975, A Hell of a War, 1993, also screen plays, articles, polit. essays, short stories; exhibitor paintings and sculpture; began film career, 1923, stage career, 1927; acted in more than 80 films including 3 in French (produced or co-produced 15 in U.S. and U.K.), and about 20 plays U.S., Can., Australia, and U.K.; produced 160 1-act TV plays, 1953-58; films include Stella Dallas, A Woman of Affairs, The Barker, Chances, Union Depot, Little Caesar, Dawn Patrol, The Private Life of Catherine the Great, The Little Accident, The Amateur Gentleman, Accused, Outward Bound, Morning Glory, The Narrow Corner, The Young in Heart, Having Wonderful Time, The Joy of Living, The Prisoner of Zenda, Gunga Din, The Rage of Paris, The Corsican Brothers, Angels Over Broadway, That Lady in Ermine, Sinbad the Sailor, The Exile, The Fighting O'Flynn, State Secret, Ghost Story, others; plays include The Dummy, Toward the Light, Romeo and Juliet, Young Woodley, The Jest, Man in Possession, Saturday's Children, The Winding Stairway, Moonlight Is Silver, My Fair Lady, The Pleasure of His Company, The Secretary Bird, Present Laughter, Out on a Limb; numerous TV and radio plays for CBS, NBC, ABC, CBC, BBC, TV narrations for symphony orchs. throughout U.S. and Europe, various song recordings for Columbia, Caedman, others; organized own prodn. co., Criterion Films Corp., U.K., 1934; subject of biography Knight Errant (by Brian Connell), 1955. Nat. vice-chmn. Com. Defend America by Aiding Allies, 1940-41, Franco-British War Relief Assn., 1939-41; Presdl. envoy for spl. S.Am. mission, 1941; spl. advisor to comdr. 6th Fleet, NATO, 1969-70; U.S. naval del. SEATO Conf., London, 1971; Nat. v.p. Am. Assn. For UN, 1946-63; nat. chmn. Com. for CARE, 1946-50; chmn. Am. Relief for Korea, 1950-53; bd. dirs. United World Coll. Served to capt. USNR, 1941-52, ETO. Decorated Silver Star, Combat Legion of Merit with "v" for valor attachment (U.S.); Knight comdr. Order Brit. Empire; Knight Order St. John of Jerusalem; D.S.C. (U.K.); officer Legion of Honor (mil. and civil); Croix de Guerre with palm (France); Knight comdr. Order George I (Greece); comdr. Order Orange-Nassau (Netherlands); War Cross for Mil. Valor; comdr. Order of Merit; Star of Italian Solidarity (Italy); knight comdr. Order of Merit (Chile); officer Order So. Cross (Brazil); officer Order of the Crown (Belgium); Comdr. Cross Order of Merit (Fed. Rep. Germany); Nat. medal of Korea; Med. for Svc. Murmansk Naval Escort of Convoys (USSR); Hon. Citizen of Korea; others; recipient Gold Medal of Honor VFW, 1966; Armed Forces award, 1972; Am. Image award, 1976; award for contbn. to arts U. Notre Dame, 1971; award for contbn. to world understanding and peace World Affairs Council, Phila., 1978; Spl. award for internat. artistic achievements New Sch. for Social Research, 1978; Nat. Humanitarian award NCCJ, 1979; Nat. Brotherhood award Salvation Army, 1980; Ann. Nat. Vet.'s Day award, 1981; Illustrious Moderns award, 1981; St. Nicholas Soc. Medal of Merit, 1986; Ann. Gold Medal USO, 1985, Spl. Achievement award Varsity Club Internat., 1986, Dist. Pub. Svc. award Navy League, 1995, Shakespeare Globe award, 1995, Dr. Catherine White Achievement award, 1997, Am. Heart Assn.'s Lifetime Achievement in Arts award, 1998; Apptd. spl. post-war missions State Dept. Mem. Coun. Fgn. Rels. (councilor), Brit-Am. Alumni Assn. (pres. 1950-57), Am. Soc. Order St. John Jerusalem (gov. 1970—, dep. vice chancellor), Groupe Navale d'Assaut (hon.), N.Y. Geneal. and Biog. Soc. (hon.), Battalion de Choc (hon.), Assn. des Anciens Combatants (France), Pilgrim's Soc. U.S. (bd. dirs.), Racquet Club (Chgo.), Brook Club, Century Club, Knickerbocker Club (N.Y.C.), Myopia Hunt Club (hon.), Met. Club (Washington), Reading Room (Newport, R.I.), White's Club (London), R.A.C. (London), The Garrick Club (London), Traveller's Club (Paris), Puffin's (Edinburgh). Episcopalian. Avocations: collecting rare books, letters and documents, traveling, sketching.. Home: The Beekman 575 Park Ave New York NY 10021-7332

FAIRBANKS, FRANK BATES, manufacturing company executive; b. Phila., Oct. 23, 1930; s. Frank Bates and Helen (Horix) F.; m. Ellen Wolff, (div. May 1992); children: Krista, Bryan, Linda. BS, MIT, 1952. V.p. Horix Mfg. Co., Pitts., 1957-68; pres. Horix Mfg. Co., 1968-92, chief exec. officer, 1992—. Contbr. articles to profl. jours. Adv. coun. Small Bus. Adminstrn., Pitts., 1986-94; pres. Smaller Mfrs. Coun. Pitts., 1982-83; bd. dirs. Free Enterprise Partnership, Pitts., 1983-97, treas., 1987-94; bd. dirs. Pa. Chamber Bus. and Industry, 1991—. Mem. ASME, Newcomen Soc. U.S., Packaging Machy. Mfrs. Inst., Nat. Assn. Mfrs. (taxation com. 1980—, chmn. 1994-96), Univ. Club, Rotary. Avocation: railroad buff. Office: Horix Mfg Co PO Box 9324 Pittsburgh PA 15225-0324

FAIRBANKS, JONATHAN LEO, museum curator; b. Ann Arbor, Mich., Feb. 19, 1933; s. Avard T. and Beatrice Maude (Fox) F.; m. Louise Ann Eckenbrecht, Feb. 12, 1954; children: Theresa Louise Fairbanks Harris, Hilary-Ann. BFA, U. Utah, 1953; student, Pa. Acad. Fine Arts, 1956-57; MFA, U. Pa., 1957; MA, U. Del., 1961. From curatorial asst. to assoc. curator Winterthur Museum, Del., 1961-71; co-founder Am. Prints Confs., 1970—; Katharine Lane Weems curator Am. Decorative Arts and Sculpture Mus. of Fine Arts Boston, 1971—; adj. lectr. U. Del.; instr. U. Utah Ext., Brigham Young U. Ext., W.Va. U. Ext.; adj. prof. Am. New Eng. studies program Boston U.; trustee Tex. Pioneer Arts Found.; trustee, incorporator Dublin Seminar for Early New Eng. Folklife. Curator exhbns. and catalogues Paul Revere's Boston--1735-1818, New England Begins, The Seventeenth Century; author: American Furniture 1620 to the Present, 1981. Bd. dirs. Revere House, Boston; mem. com. for Preservation White House; pres.. Decorative Arts trust; trustee Forest Hills Cemetery, Longfellow's Wayside Inn, Shirley-Eustis House. Winterthur fellow, 1959-61; recipient Disting. Service award Antiques Monthly, 1983, Robert H. Lord award for excellence in hist. studies. Emmanuel Coll., 1983, medal Excellence Craft, Soc. Arts & Crafts, Boston, 1997. Fellow Pilgrim Soc., Am. Inst. Conservation, Am. crafts Coun. (hon.); mem. Victorian Soc. Am. (past v.p.), Internat. Inst. Conservation, Am. Assn. Mus., Soc. Archtl. Historians, Nat. Trust for Hist. Preservation, Colonial Soc. Mass., Decorative Arts Soc. (v.p. 1978-79, C.F. Montgomery award 1983), Westwood Hist. Soc. (pres. 1978-81), Am. Soc. Interior Designers (hon.), Mass. Hist. Soc., Am. Antiquarian Soc., Colonial Soc., Walpole Soc., St. Botolph Club. Mural executed Hall of Earth History, Acad. Natural Scis., Phila., 1957. Office: Mus Fine Arts 465 Huntington Ave Boston MA 02115-5597*

FAIRBANKS, MARY KATHLEEN, data analyst, researcher; b. Manhattan, Kans., June 4, 1948; d. Everitt Edsel and Mary Catherine (Moran) F. BS, St. Norbert Coll., 1970; postgrad., Calif. Family Study Ctr., 1981-82. Neuropsychology researcher U.S. VA Hosp., Sepulveda, Calif., 1970-76; mgr. print shop Charisma In Missions, City of Industry, Calif., 1976-77; neuropsychology researcher L.A. County Women's Hosp., 1977-79; mem. tech. staff Computer Scis. Corp., Ridgecrest, Calif., 1979-81; systems programmer Calif. State U., Northridge, 1982-84; bus. systems analyst World Vision, Monrovia, Calif., 1984-86; configuration analyst Teledyne System Co., Northridge, 1986-87; applications system analyst Internat. Telephone and Telegraph/Fed. Electric Corp., Altadena, Calif., 1987-88; supr. data analysts OAO Corp., Altadena, 1988—. Co-author, contbr.: Serotonin and Behavior, 1973, Advances in Sleep Research, vol. 1, 1974. Mem. St. Mary's Cath. Cmty. Theatre. Mem. OAO Mgmt. Assn., So. Calif. Application System Users Group, Digital Equipment Computer Users Soc. Roman Catholic. Avocations: photography, reading, music, hiking, camping. Home: 37607 Lasker Ave Palmdale CA 93550-7721 Office: OAO Corp 787 W Woodbury Rd Ste 2 Altadena CA 91001-5388

FAIRBANKS, RICHARD MONROE, broadcasting company executive; b. Indpls., Mar. 27, 1912; s. Richard Monroe and Louise (Hibben) F.; m. Virginia Nicholson Brown, Oct. 26, 1968; children by previous marriage: Anthony Caperton, Richard Monroe, III, Scott Andrew, Charles Hibben (dec.). Grad., Yale U., 1934; LLD (hon.), Butler U., 1985. Pres. Fairbanks Comms. Inc., Indpls., 1947—; bd. dirs. Traffic-copters, Inc.; pres. Fairhill Realty, Indpls., 1990—, Fairwind Aviation, West Palm Beach, 1998. Bd. dirs. Cornelia Cole Fairbanks Found., 1958—, pres., 1968—; bd. corporators Crown Hill Cemetery, Indpls., 1965—; trustee Butler U., 1966—; pres. Richard M. Fairbanks Found., 1987. Lt. commdr. USNR, WWII. Mem. Dramatic Club, Woodstock Club (Indpls.), Key Largo (Fla.) Anglers Club, Ocean Reef Club, Card Sound Golf Club. Home: 22 Snapper Point Dr Key Largo FL 33037 Office: 3071 Continental Dr West Palm Beach FL 33407-3274

FAIRBANKS, RICHARD MONROE, III, lawyer, former ambassador at large; b. Indpls., Feb. 10, 1941; s. Richard Monroe, Jr. and Mary Evans (Caperton) F.; m. Ann Shannon O'Connor, June 13, 1962; children: Woods Alexander, Jonathan Barcroft. A.B., Yale U., 1962; J.D. magna cum laude, Columbia U., 1969. Bar: D.C. Assoc. Arnold & Porter, 1969-71; spl. asst. to adminstr. EPA, 1971; staff asst. Domestic Council, Exec. Office of Pres., White House, 1971-72, assoc. dir. energy, environ. and natural resources, 1972-74; founding ptnr. firm Ruckelshaus, Beveridge & Fairbanks, Washington, 1974-81; asst. sec. congressional relations Dept. State, 1981-82, ambassador, spl. negotiator for Middle East peace process, 1982-83, ambassador-at-large, 1984-85; ptnr. Paul, Hastings, Janofsky & Walker, 1985-88, mng. ptnr., 1990-92, sr. counsel, 1992-94; sr. counsel Ctr. for Strategic and Internat. Studies, Washington, 1992-94, mng. dir. for domestic and internat. issues, 1994—; adj. prof. law Georgetown U., Washington, 1971-72; dir. Fairbanks Broadcasting Co., 1974-81; bd. dirs. SEACOR SMIT Inc., Hercules Inc., GATX Corp.; sr. counselor Am. Enterprise Inst., 1985-90; pres. U.S. nat. com. for Pacific Econ. Coop., 1986-92; internat. chair Pacific Econ. Coop. Coun., 1991-92, U.S. vice chair 1992—; mem. Pres.'s Task Force on U.S. Internat. Broadcasting, 1991. Founder, 1st pres. Washington chpt. Am. Refugee Com., 1978, mem. nat. bd. dirs., 1977-93; trustee Meridian House Internat., 1978-93; mem. com. natural resources Rep. Nat. Com., 1977-80; mem. Pres.'s Citizens Adv. Com. Environ. Quality, 1974-77; bd. visitors Columbia U. Sch. Law. Officer USN, 1962-66. Mem. ABA, D.C. Bar Assn., Coun. Fgn. Rels., Ctr. for Strategic and Internat. Studies (adv. bd. 1989—), Coun. Am. Ambassadors (Bretton Woods com.). Clubs: Anglers, Burning Tree, Ocean Reef, Metropolitan of Washington; Yale (N.Y.C.); Chevy Chase. Office: Ctr Strategic & Internat Studies 1800 K St NW Washington DC 20006-2202

FAIRBANKS, ROBERT ALVIN, lawyer; b. Oklahoma City, July 9, 1944; s. Albert Edward and Lucille Imogene (Scherer) F.; m. Linda Gayle Geer, Aug. 26, 1967; children: Chele Lyn, Kimberly Jo, Robert Alvin II, Michael Albert, Richard Alan, Joseph Alexander. BS in Math., U. Okla., 1967, JD, 1973; MBA, Oklahoma City U., 1970, MCJA, 1975; LLM, Columbia U., 1976; MA, Stanford U., 1984; MEd, Harvard U., 1993. Bar: Okla. 1974, U.S. Dist. Ct. (we. dist.) Okla. 1974, U.S. Ct. Customs and Patent Appeals 1974, U.S. Ct. Mil. Appeals, 1974, U.S. Tax Ct. 1974, U.S. Claims Ct. 1975, U.S. Customs Ct. 1975, U.S. Ct. Appeals (10th cir.) 1975, U.S. Supreme Ct. 1977, U.S. Dist. Ct. (ea. dist.) Okla. 1984, Minn. 1993. Commd. 2d lt. USAF, 1967, advanced through grades to capt., 1970; col. USAFR, 1986; asst. staff judge adv., chief of claims div. Office of Staff Judge Adv., Tinker AFB, Okla., 1974-75; legal asst. to Justice William A. Berry, Okla. Supreme Ct., 1977; pvt. practice Norman, Okla., 1974—; v.p. St. Gregory's U., Shawnee, Okla., 1997—; instr. bus. adminstrn. U. Md. Far East div., Nha Trang, Viet Nam, 1970-71, Rose State Coll., Midwest City, Okla., 1974; rsch. assoc. in law U. Okla., Norman, 1974, spl. lectr., 1974-75, vis. asst. prof., 1976-77, adj. prof. law, 1984—; vis. asst. prof. law Oklahoma City U.,

1977; asst. prof. law U. Ark., Fayetteville, Arks., 1977-81; assoc. prof. law La. State U., Baton Rouge, 1981; rsch. asst. dept. family, community and preventative medicine Stanford (Calif.) Med. Sch., 1981-82; adj. asst. prof. govt. contract law Air Force Inst. Tech., Wright-Patterson AFB, Ohio, 1985—; v.p. St. Gregory's U., Shawnee, Okla.; cons. Cheyenne Tribe, Clinton, Okla., 1977-81, 90, Citizens Band of Pottawatomie Tribe, Shawnee, Okla., 1977-79, Inst. for Devel. of Indian Law, Washington, 1976-81; dir. Native Am. Coll. Prep. Ctr. Bemidji State U., Minn., 1993—. Editor-in-chief Am. Indian Law Rev., 1973; editor Okla. Law Rev., 1971-73; producer, dir.: (with Barbara P. Ettinger) "Aa-Niin" film, 1994; author book revs.; contbr. articles to profl. jours. Mem. bd. control Fayetteville (Ark.) City Hosp., 1977-81; cubmaster Boy Scouts Am., Norman, 1982-83, asst. scoutmaster, Stanford, 1981, scoutmaster, Norman, 1990-91, com. mem., den leader, 1988; softball coach Jr. High Girls League, Fayetteville, 1977-81; mem. adv. bd. Native Am. Prep. Sch., Santa Fe; pres., chmn. bd. Native Am. Coll. Prep. Ctr., Bemidji, Minn.; mem. exec. adv. bd. Aerospace Sci. and Tech. Edn. Ctr. of Okla., Okla. City Univ. U.S. Dept. Edn. fellow Stanford U. Med. Sch.; Charles Evans Hughes fellow Columbia U. Law Sch., 1976; Sequoyah fellow Assn. Am. Indian Affairs, 1975-76; Mellon fellow Harvard U. Sch. Edn., 1993; nominee Pulitzer prize for Disting. Commentary, 1997. Mem. ABA, Okla. Bar Assn., Fed. Bar Assn., Am. Trial Lawyers Assn., Okla. Trial Lawyers Assn., Okla. Indian Bar Assn., Oklahoma County Bar Assn., Assn. Am. Law Schs., N.G. Assn. U.S., Air Force Assn. (life), Res. Officers Assn. (life), Nat. Contract Mgmt. Assn., Soc. Logistics Engrs., Phi Alpha Delta, Phi Delta Epsilon, Phi Delta Kappa. Republican. Roman Catholic. Office: 2212 Westpark Dr Norman OK 73069-4012

FAIRBANKS, RUSSELL NORMAN, law educator, university dean; b. N.Y.C., Oct. 4, 1919; s. Carleton Forrest and Norna (Johnson) F.; m. Rachel France Fain, Apr. 28, 1942; children—Russell Norman, Jonathan, Norna. AB, Harvard U., 1941; LLB, Columbia U., 1952. Bar: D.C. bar 1953, N.J. bar 1975. Commd. 2d lt. U.S. Army, 1941, advanced through grades to lt. col., 1962; chief legal officer U.S.-Japan Procurement Agy., 1955-57; dir. acad. dept. Judge Adv. Gen.'s Sch., Charlottesville, Va., 1960-62; ret., 1962; assoc. dean Columbia U. Law Sch., N.Y.C., 1964-67; prof., dean Sch. Law, Rutgers U., Camden, N.J., 1967-81, provost, prof. emeritus, 1981—; Cons. Congl. Commn. on Govt. Procurement. Mem. policy com., legal services unit Moblzn. for Youth; mem. nat. adv. com. Am. Vets. Com.; Trustee Camden County Legal Services, Inc., N.J. Inst. for Continuing Legal Edn. Decorated Bronze Star. Mem. Assn. Bar City N.Y. Democrat. Club: Harvard (Boston). Home: 729 Signal Light Rd Moorestown NJ 08057-2116 Office: 5th and Penn Sts Camden NJ 08102

FAIRCHILD, DAVID LAWRENCE, philosophy educator; b. Malden, Mass., Feb. 28, 1946; s. Lawrence Wahl and Margaret (Piper) F.; m. Janice Louise Miller, June 29, 1968; 1 child, Emily Meara. B.A., Purdue U., Lafayette, Ind., 1968; M.A., Northwestern U., Evanston, Ill., 1970, Ph.D., 1972. Instr. philosophy Northwestern U., Evanston, Ill., 1970-71; asst. prof. philosophy Purdue U., Fort Wayne, Ind., 1971-76, assoc. prof. philosophy, 1977-88, chmn. dept. philosophy, 1984—; prof. philosophy Purdue U., Fort Wayne, 1988—, St. Francis Coll., Joliet, Ill., 1983—; master tchr. Northrop High Sch., Fort Wayne, Ind., 1983; prof. philosophy Purdue U., Fort Wayne, Ind., 1988—. Author: Logic: A First Course, 1976: Prolegomena to a Methodology, 1979; Toward the Examined Life, 1983, Living the Questions, 1996; review editor Jour. of the Philosophy of Sport, 1970-93; adv. bd. Jour. Gazette Newspaper, 1985-96. Cons. gifted program Fort Wayne Cmty. Schs., 1983-96; bd. dirs. Cmty. Harvest, 1985—. Woodrow Wilson Found. fellow, 1972; NEH fellow, 1975; Danforth Found. fellow, 1979-85; Arts and Scis. disting. lectr., 1999. Mem. Am. Philos. Assn., Philosophic Soc. Study of Sport (Disting. Svc. award 1997), Assn. Informal Logic and Critical Thinking, N.Am. Sociology of Sport Soc. Home: 5219 S Wayne Ave Fort Wayne IN 46807-3122 Office: Dept Philosophy 2101 E Coliseum Blvd Fort Wayne IN 46805-1445

FAIRCHILD, DORCAS SEXTON, English educator; b. Persia, Tenn., June 21, 1938; d. Philip Riley Sr. and Eula Kate (Robinette) Sexton; m. Joe Elmer Fairchild, Apr. 2, 1969. BS, East Tenn. State U., 1960. Cert. secondary English and social studies tchr., Tenn. English tchr. Rogersville (Tenn.) H.S., 1960-80; English tchr. Cherokee Comprehensive H.S., Rogersville, 1980—, chmn. English dept., 1993—; sponsor Beta Club, Rogersville, 1984—, Stock Market Game, Rogersville, 1989—. Sunday sch. tchr. Marion Robinette Meml. Ch., Rogersville, 1975—. Mem. NEA, Tenn. Edn. Assn., Hawkins County Edn. Assn., Nat. Coun. Tchrs. of English, Tenn. Coun. Tchrs. of English, Delta Kappa Gamma (pres. 1972-74). Republican. Avocations: reading, walking, crocheting. Home: 110 Par 3 Cir Rogersville TN 37857-3916 Office: Cherokee Comprehensive HS 2927 Highway 66 S Rogersville TN 37857-5169

FAIRCHILD, HENRY BRANT, III, manufacturing executive; b. Grand Rapids, Mich., May 15, 1945; s. Henry Brant and Leora Mary (Barnaby) F.; m. Marcia Jean Anderson, Jan. 9, 1979; children: Steven May, Timothy May. Student, Miami U., 1963-66; BS, Grand Valley State Coll., 1977. Mgr. Jack Loeks Theatres, Inc., Wyoming, Mich., 1970-77, Commonwealth Theatres, Kansas City, 1977-78; pres. Handy Wacks Corp., Sparta, Mich., 1978—. Mem. Kent County Rep. Com., Grand Rapids 1980-88. Mem. Mfrs. Reps. Am. (mem. adv. council 1985-87), Grand Rapids Econ. Club (dir.), Blytherfield Country Club. Avocations: tennis, boating, collecting classic automobiles. Office: Handy Wacks Corp 100 E Averill St Sparta MI 49345-1516

FAIRCHILD, JAMES LEROY, systems engineer; b. Fort Wayne, Ind., June 18, 1953; s. Robert Eugene, Sr. and Vera Grace (Auld) F.; m. Merri Kay jinnings, Aug. 18, 1973; children: Jennifer Ann, Jeffrey Matthew. BSEE, Ind. Inst. Tech., 1976; MS in Secondary Edn., Ind. U., Ft. Wayne, 1994. Fin. officer Herules Machinery Corp., Ft. Wayne, 1982-84; human factors engr. Magnavox, Ft. Wayne, 1984-91, sys. engr., 1991-95; sr. sys. engr. Magnavox, Denver, 1995-97; sr. human factors engr. Northrop Grumman, Melbourne, Fla., 1997—. Served from 2d lt. to lt. col. USAR, 1976—. Avocations: fly fishing, skiing, cycling, scuba diving. Home: 784 Penguin Ave NE Palm Bay FL 32907-1513 Office: Northrop Grumman Corp 2000 W Nasa Blvd Melbourne FL 32904-2322

FAIRCHILD, JOHN BURR, publisher; b. Newark, Mar. 6, 1927; s. Louis W. and Margaret (Day) F.; m. Jill Lipsky, June 8, 1950; children: John Longin, James Burr, Jill and Stephen L. (twins). B.A., Princeton, 1950. Mem. rsch. dept. J.L. Hudson Co., Detroit, 1950-51; with Fairchild Publs., Inc., N.Y.C., 1951—; pub. Women's Wear Daily, Daily News Record, 1960—, editor in chief corp. publs., 1964-65, pub. dir., 1965-66, pres., 1966-70, chmn. bd., chief exec. officer corp. publs., 1970-97, ret., 1997; exec. v.p., dir. Capital Cities/ABC, Inc., exec. v.p.: Author: The Moonflower Couple, The Fashionable Savages, Chic Savages; editor-at-large W Mag., Women's Wear Daily, 1997. Served with AUS, 1947-48. Decorated chevalier de L'Ordre National de Merite, France; grade de chevalier de la Légion d'Honneur, France, officier des Arts et Lettres, France. Clubs: Travellers (Paris, France), Tir aux Pigeons (Paris, France); Century (N.Y.C.). Office: Fairchild Publs 7 W 34th St New York NY 10001-8100

FAIRCHILD, JOSEPH VIRGIL, JR., accounting educator; b. New Orleans, Nov. 26, 1933; s. Joseph Virgil and Georgiana Malone (Bourgeois) F.; m. Judith Champagne, Aug. 12, 1961; children: Georgianna, Joseph, Benjamin. BS in Geology, La. State U., 1956, MBA, 1963, PhD, 1975. CPA, La. Geologist United Core, Inc., Houston, 1956-57; assoc. acct. Humble Oil & Refining Co., New Orleans, 1963-64; ptnr. L.A. Champagne & Co., Baton Rouge, 1964-69; pvt. practice acctg. Thibodaux, La., 1969—; asst. prof. acctg. Nicholls State U., Thibodaux, 1969-75, assoc. prof., 1975-76, prof., 1976-84, Disting. prof. acctg., 1984—, asst. dean Coll. Bus., 1985-86, dir. grad. bus. studies, 1982-85; rsch. reviewer USAF Bus. Rsch. Mgmt. Ctr., Wright-Patterson AFB, Ohio, 1974-84; cons. Def. Sys. Mgmt. Coll., Ft. Belvoir, Va., 1980-81; faculty senate v.p. govt. com., chmn. dean's search com. Author: (with others) The Acquisition and Distribution of Commercial Products, 1980, 1985-86, 1986-87, 1987-88 and 1988-89 Income Tax Guides for State Legislators; contbr. articles to profl. jours.; actor: (TV, movies) The Kingfish-TNT, Orleans-CBS, Deadman Walking; (plays) South Pacific, Arsenic and Old Lace, Brigadoon, Damn Yankees. Mem. St. Genevieve Sch. Bd., Thibodaux, 1979-83, E.D. White Cath. H.S. Bd., 1985-87, chmn. fin. com., 1985-87; lector St. Genevieve Ch., 1975—, choir, 1989—. 1st lt. USAF, 1957-60, lt. col. USAFR ret. Trueblood Prof. Touche-Ross Found., N.Y.C., 1987. Mem. AICPA, Soc. La. CPA's (lectr. seminars, La.'s Outstanding Acctg. Educator 1994), Am. Acctg. Assn., Nat. Assn. Accts., Nicholls State U. Alumni Assn. (Hon. Alumnus award 1991, Case Educator of Yr. 1994). Roman Catholic. Avocations: flying, skiing, photography, fishing. Home: 412 Plater Dr Thibodaux LA 70301-5616 Office: Nicholls State U Dept Acctg Thibodaux LA 70310

FAIRCHILD, LILLIE MCKEEN, nurse, educator; b. Elizabeth, N.J., Nov. 15, 1935; d. Robert Simpson and Evelyn Irene (Stoyer) McKeen; m. Fred W. Fairchild, Aug. 24, 1957; children: Lynne Fairchild Priest, Robert, Charles. Diploma in Nursing, Westchester Sch. Nursing, Valhalla, N.Y., 1956; BSN, George Mason U., 1981, MSN, 1983. RN, Va. Clinician III-medicine Fairfax Hosp., 1983-85, nursing coord., 1985-88; supervisory clin. nurse Clin. Ctr. NIH, Bethesda, Md., 1988-95, clin. nurse educator, 1995-98, ret., 1998. Mem. George Mason Nursing Alumni, Sigma Theta Tau. Home: 5119 Cherokee Ave Alexandria VA 22312-2004

FAIRCHILD, PHYLLIS ELAINE, school counselor; b. Franklin, La., Feb. 23, 1927; d. Joseph Virgil and Georgiana (Bourgeois) F. BS in Chemistry and Biology, U. Southwestern La., 1946; postgrad., La. State U., 1949-50, MEd in Guidance, 1966. Cert. chemistry, biology, gen. sci., Spanish and social studies tchr., counselor, La. Tchr. sci. St. Mary Parish Sch. Bd., Franklin, 1952-58, counselor, 1977-82; tchr. sci. Am. Dependent Schs., Yokohama, Japan, 1958-60, London, Lakenheath, Eng., 1960-61, Ramey AFB, PR, 1961-62; tchr. sci. Norfolk (Va.) City Schs., 1962-63, Iberville Parish Sch. Bd., Plaquemine, La., 1963-66; tchr. sci., counselor East Baton Rouge Parish Sch. Bd., Baton Rouge, 1966-77; counselor Hanson Sch. Bd., Franklin, 1982-94, 96-98; ret., 1998; mem. adv. com. La. Dept. Edn., Baton Rouge, 1976, 78. Mem. La. Landmarks Soc., Cath. Daugs. Am. (co-chmn. religious litergy 1992-94), Fortnightly Lit. Club (pres. 1982-83), Sigma Delta Pi, Pi Gamma Mu, Kappa Kappa Gamma, Delta Kappa Gamma (chmn. membership, scholarship, profl. affairs, 1971-77, parliamentarian 1996-98). Avocations: reading, walking, piano, writing. Home: 214 Morris St Franklin LA 70538-6127

FAIRCHILD, RAYMOND EUGENE, oil company executive; b. Bowling Green, Ohio, June 25, 1923; s. Ira Ethalbert and Bessie Louise (Gearhart) F.; m. Eleanor Faith Vaughan, Sept. 1, 1973. B.S., Ohio U., 1948; M.S., U. Mo., 1950. Dist. geologist Pan Am. Prodn. Co., Houston, 1950-56; gulf coast div. exploration mgr. Pan Handle Eastern subs., Houston, 1956-72; mayor City of Hunter Creek, Tex., 1967-71; exploration cons. Houston, 1972-73; exploration mgr. A.P. Moller, Copenhagen, 1973-80; v.p. Hunt Oil Co., Dallas, 1980, former sr. v.p. internat. exploration; ret., 1988; pres., dir. Mayfair Petroleum Inc., Mayfair Petroleum Corp., Mayfair Environ. Svcs., 1990—. Alderman, City of Hunter Creek, 1962-67; commr. Spring Br. Fire Dept., 1962. Fellow Geol. Soc. London, Am. Assn. Petroleum Geologists; mem. Petroleum Exploration Soc. Great Britain, Dansk Geologisk Forening, Gulf Coast Assn. Geol. Socs., Houston Geol. Soc., Dallas Geol. Soc., East Tex. Geol. Soc., Assn. Internat. Petroleum Negotiators. Club: Dallas Petroleum. Home and Office: DBA Fairchild Farms RR 6 Box 63866 Winnsboro TX 75494-9790

FAIRCHILD, RAYMOND FRANCIS, lawyer; b. Springfield, Ill., June 29, 1946; s. Francis M. and Estelle G. Fairchild; m. Ann Louise Templeton, Dec. 28, 1968. BA, U. Ill., 1968; JD, Ind. U., 1971. Bar: Ind. 1971, U.S. Dist. Ct. (so. dist.) Ind. 1971, U.S. Ct. Appeals (7th cir.) 1989. Sole practice Indpls., 1971—. Mem. Assn. Trial Lawyers Am., N.Y. State Trial Lawyers Assn., Ind. Trial Lawyers Assn. Club: Manor House, Skyline (Indpls.). Office: 2501 E South St Columbus IN 47201-8637

FAIRCHILD, ROBERT CHARLES, pediatrician; b. Kansas City, Mo., Dec. 22, 1921; s. Charles Clement and Ada Mae (Baker) F.; m. Patricia Louise Russell, May 28, 1964; children—Robert, Nancy, Rex Hartman, Dan Hartman. Student, Kansas City Jr. Coll., 1938-40; B.A., U. Kans., 1942, M.D., 1950. Diplomate Am. Bd. Pediatrics. Intern Kansas City Gen. Hosp., 1950-51; resident in pediatrics U. Kans. Med. Ctr., 1951-53; practice medicine specializing in pediatrics Mission, Kans., 1953-70; dir. area clinics Children's Mercy Hosp., Kansas City, Mo., 1970-74, dir. outpatient services, 1974-88, ret., 1991; prof. pediatrics emeritus U. Mo.-Kansas City Sch. Medicine; mem. adv. com. Assoc. Degree nursing program Johnson County Community Coll. Contbr. articles to med. jours. Served to maj. U.S. Army, 1942-46. Decorated Bronze Star; recipient Physician's Recognition award AMA, 1990; Porter scholar U. Kans. Sch. Medicine, 1950. Mem. AMA, Am. Acad. Pediatrics, Mo. State Med. Assn., Met. Med. Soc. of Kansas City, Greater Kansas City Pediatric Soc., Kansas City S.W. Clin. Soc., Alpha Omega Alpha, Nu Sigma Nu. Presbyterian. Home: 8425 Reinhardt Ln Shawnee Mission KS 66206-1316

FAIRCHILD, SAMUEL WILSON, professional services company executive, former federal agency administrator; b. Ft. Eustis, Va., July 16, 1954; s. Henry Howell and Ruby Mae (Love) F.; m. Linda Elizabeth Doremus, May 17, 1986; children: Elizabeth Christine, Samuel Bruce. BS, BA, Coll. of William and Mary, 1977. Cons. ITT, Inc., Smithfield, Va., 1977; v.p., gen. mgr. P.A., Inc., Hampton, Va., 1977-83; sr. policy advisor Exec. Office of the Pres., Washington, 1983-89; dep. asst. sec. U.S. Dept. Transp., Washington, 1989-91; v.p., sr. fellow Ctr. for Tech. and Pub. Policy Rsch. BDM Internat., Inc., McLean, Va., 1991-94; ptnr. Galland, Kharasch, Morse & Garfinkle, p.c., Washington, 1993—; bd. dirs., mng. dir. GKMG Consulting Svcs., Inc., Schiphol USA, Schiphol China. Author, editor: Moving America, 1989. Active Boy Scouts Am., Irving, Tex., 1972—, mem. World Scout Bur., Geneva, 1972-80, Coun. for Excellence in Govt.; mem. exec. bd. Nat. Capital Area Coun. Boy Scouts Am., 1990—; co-chmn. ARC, Alexandria, Va., 1988-90. Recipient Disting. Alumni award Christopher Newport Coll., 1990; Usry Garland scholar Coll. William and Mary/Christopher Newport Coll., 1975. Mem. Nat. Aviation Assn., Coun. for Excellence in Govt., Aero Club. Presbyterian. Avocations: photography, music. Home: PO Box 341 Brookside NJ 07926-0341 Office: GKMG Consulting 1054 31st St NW Washington DC 20007-4403*

FAIRCHILD, SHARON ELAINE, corrections administrator; b. Little Rock, Sept. 10, 1947; d. Robert Roscoe Fairchild and Mable Tyler Fleming. BA, So. U., Baton Rouge, La., 1972; MS, Tex. So. U., Houston, 1984. Psychologist Mo. Dept. Corrections, St. Louis, 1987-91; corrections supt. Mo. Dept. Corrections, Kansas City, 1991—; mem. criminal justice adv. bd. Penn Valley C.C., Kansas City, Mo., 1997—; bd. dirs. Springfield (Mo.) Pub. TV, 1992-93. Tutor, mentor Youth Friends, North Kansas City Pub. Schs., 1995—. Mem Am. Correctional Assn., Mo. Correctional Assn. (bd. dirs. 1993-95), Nat. Assn. Blacks in Criminal Justice (chair women's task force 1995—, Mary Terrell Church award 1995), Delta Sigma Theta. Methodist. Avocations: reading, skating. Office: Kansas City Cmty Release Ctr 651 Mulberry St Kansas City MO 64101

FAIRCHILD, THOMAS E., federal judge; b. Milw., Dec. 25, 1912; s. Edward Thomas and Helen (Edwards) F.; m. Eleanor E. Dahl, July 24, 1937; children: Edward, Susan, Jennifer, Andrew. Student, Princeton, 1931-33; A.B., Cornell U., 1934; LL.B., U. Wis., 1938. Bar: Wis. 1938. Practiced Portage, Wis., 1938-41, Milw., 1945-48, 53-56; atty. OPA, Chgo., Milw., 1941-45; hearing commr. Chgo. Region, 1945; atty. gen. Wis., 1948-51; U.S. atty. for Western Dist. Wis., 1951-52; justice Supreme Ct. Wis., 1957-66, U.S. Ct. Appeals for 7th Circuit, 1966—. Dem. candidate Senator from Wis., 1950, 52. Mem. ABA, Wis. Bar Assn., Fed. Bar Assn., Milw. Bar Assn., 7th Cir. Bar Assn., Dane County Bar Assn., Am. Judicature Soc., Am. Law Inst., Phi Delta Phi, KP. Democrat. Mem. Unitd Ch. of Christ. Office: US Courthouse Rm 2764 219 S Dearborn St Chicago IL 60604-1702

FAIRCLOTH, DUNCAN MCLAUCHLIN (LAUCH FAIRCLOTH), former senator, businessman, farmer; b. Sampson County, N.C., Jan. 14, 1928; s. James McLaughlin and Mary (Holt) F.; m. Nancy Ann Bryan, May 26, 1967 (div.); 1 child, Anne. Various positions Faircloth Construction, car dealerships, land-clearing, milling, banking, concrete, comml. real estate; farmer Coharie and Faircloth farms; chmn. N.C. Hwy. Commn., 1969-73; sec. N.C. Commerce, 1977-83; U.S. senator from N.C. 103rd Congress, 1993—; mem. Banking Housing & Urban Affairs Com., chmn. subcom. HUD Oversight and Structure; chmn. Environ. & Pub. Works subcom. of Clean Air Wetlands Pvt. Property and Nuclear Safety; appropriations com., sm. bus. com. Republican. Presbyterian. Office: PO Box 496 Clinton NC 28329*

FAIRES, ROSS NORBERT, manufacturing company executive; b. Indpls., July 20, 1934; s. Herbert C. and Thelma (Wood) F.; m. Glady Ann Caley, Dec. 20, 1954; children: Kurt J., Eric S., Jay A. BA, Wabash Coll., 1958; MBA, Ind. U., 1959. Advt. mgr. Cummins Engine Co., Columbus, Ind., 1959-62; pres. Arvin Industries div. Housewares, Columbus, 1962-75, Tibbals Flooring Co., Oneida, Tenn., 1979-91; chmn. Faires Group, Chattanooga, 1991—; bd. dirs. First Am. Nat. Bank, Knoxville, Tenn. Bd. dirs. Knoxville Zoo, Knoxville Mus. Art, Nat. Symphony Orch., Washington, Webb Sch., Knoxville, St. Mary's Hosp. Found., Am. Symphony Orch. League, East Tenn. Comm. Found., Helen Ross McNabb Found.; bd. regents State of Tenn., 1984-91; mem. bd. advisors McCallie Sch. for Boys, Chattanooga; trustee Wabash (Ind.) Coll., Maryville Coll. Mem. Tenn. Bus. Assn. (bd. dirs.), Leadership Knoxville, Cherokee Country Club, Club Le Conte, Blowing Rock Country Club. Republican. Presbyterian. Home and Office: 904 Cherokee Blvd Knoxville TN 37919-7847

FAIREY, CHAD CHRISTOPHER, secondary education educator; b. Titusville, Fla., Mar. 10, 1973; s. John Christopher and Glenda Faye (Perry) F. BS in Social Sci. Edn., Fla. State U., 1995; postgrad., U. Va., 1997. Cert. tchr., Va. Tchr. Hoover Jr. H.S., Indialantic, Fla., 1995; host Walt Disney World Magic Kingdom, Orlando, Fla., 1996; tchr. Astronaut H.S., Titusville, Fla., 1997—; tchr. asst. Astronaut H.S., Titusville, 1997; tchr. Glasgow Middle Sch., Alexandria, Va., 1998—. Democrat. Avocations: sports, creative writing, nostalgia. Home: 4538 Raleigh Ave # 204 Alexandria VA 22304 Office: 4101 Fairfax Pky Alexandria VA 22312

FAIRFIELD-SONN, JAMES WILLED, management educator and consultant; b. Nashua, N.H., Aug. 21, 1948; s. David Alexander and Christine Mary (Fairfield) Sonn; m. Lynn Groark, July 3, 1982; children: Anne Madeline, James Willed, Jr., John Thomas. MS, Cornell U., 1979; MA, Yale U., 1980, MPhil, 1982, PhD, 1985. Mgr. office adminstrn. Hartford Ins. Group, Indpls., 1972-76; asst. prof. mgmt. U. Hartford, West Hartford, Conn., 1982-88, assoc. prof., 1988—, chmn. mgmt. dept., 1987-90, dir. exec. MBA, 1993-95; pres. Fairfield-Sonn Assocs., Centerbrook, Conn., 1981—. Contbr. articles and revs. to profl. jours. Named Outstanding Tchr. of Yr., Barney Sch., 1999; Cornell U. indsl. and labor rels. fellow, 1977-78, Yale U. fellow, 1978-82, Olin fellow, 1981. Mem. Acad. Mgmt., Internat. Personnel Mgmt. Assn., Internat. Coun. for Small Bus., Ea. Acad. Mgmt., Assn. Yale Alumni (chmn. grad. and profl. schs. com. 1982-83). Republican. Congregationalist. Avocations: tennis, travel, gardening. Home and Office: PO Box 1047 Old Lyme CT 06371-0998

FAIRHURST, CHARLES, civil and mining engineering educator; b. Widnes, Lancashire, Eng., Aug. 5, 1929; came to U.S., 1956, naturalized, 1967; s. Richard Lowe and Josephine (Starkey) F.; m. Margaret Ann Lloyd, Sept. 7, 1957; children: Anne Elizabeth Charlet, David Lloyd, Charles Edward, Catherine Mary Kotz, Hugh Richard, John Peter, Margaret Mary. BEng, U. Sheffield, Eng., 1952, PhD, 1955; PhD (hon.), St. Petersburg (Russia) Mining Inst., 1995, Inst. Nat. Poly de Lorraine, France, 1996. Mining engr. trainee Nat. Coal Bd., St. Helens, Eng., 1949-56; research assoc. prof. U. Minn., Mpls., 1956-67; head Sch. Mineral and Metall. Engring. U. Minn., 1967-70, prof. dept. civil and mineral engring., 1970-94, prof. dept. civil engring., 1994-97, head dept., 1972-87, T.W. Bennett Prof. mining engring. and rock mechanics, 1983-97, prof. emeritus, 1997—; pres., sr. engr. Itasca Group Inc., Mpls.; cons. Petrobras, Brazil, Spie. Batignolles, France, Charbonnages de France; chmn. U.S. Com. Rock Mechanics, 1971-74, Waste Isolation pilot Plant Panel NAS/NRC, Carlsbad, N.Mex., 1989-96; chmn. study underground nuclear testing in French Polynesia, Internat. Geomechanics Commn., 1995-98; mem. bd. radioactive waste mgmt. NAS/NRC, 1987-94, vice chmn., 1989-94; adv. prof. Tongji U., Shanghai, 1994. Mem. AIME, ASCE (chmn. rock mechanics com. 1978-80), Internat. Soc. Rock Mechanics (pres. 1991-95), Am. Rock Mechanics Assn. (pres. 1995-97), Am. Underground Constrn. Assn. (pres. 1976-77), Royal Swedish Acad. Engring. Scis. (fgn.), U.S. Nat. Acad. Engring., Sigma Xi. Roman Catholic. Home: 417 5th Ave N South Saint Paul MN 55075-2035 Office: U Minn Dept Civil Engring Minneapolis MN 55455*

FAIRLEIGH, JAMES PARKINSON, music educator; b. St. Joseph, Mo., Aug. 24, 1938; s. William Macdonald and Mable Emily (Parkinson) F.; m. Marlane Alberta Paxson, June 25, 1960; children: William Paxson, Karen Evelyn. MusB, U. Mich., 1960; MusM, U. So. Calif., 1965; PhD, U. Mich., 1973. Instr., asst. prof. Hanover (Ind.) Coll., 1965-75; assoc. prof. R.I. Coll., Providence, 1975-80; prof., head music dept. Jacksonville (Ala.) State U., 1980—; dir. of music First Presbyn. Ch., Anniston, Ala., 1981—; presenter, lectr. at meetings of profl. orgns., 1974-99. Contbr. articles to profl. jours., mags., 1966-95. Served to 1st lt. U.S. Army, 1960-62. Mem. Am. Musicol. Soc., Ala. Music Tchrs. Assn. (cert., treas. 1982-86, 1st v.p. 1986-88, pres. 1988-90), Coll. Music Soc. (southern chpt. exec. bd. 1996-98), Music Tchrs. Nat. Assn. (cert.), Assn. Ala. Coll. Music Adminstrs. (sec., treas. 1985-89, pres. 1989-91), Phi Beta Kappa, Phi Kappa Phi, Pi Kappa Lambda, Phi Eta Sigma, Phi Mu Alpha Sinfonia. Republican. Avocations: waterkiing, swimming, backpacking. Home: 512 Fairway Dr SW Jacksonville AL 36265-3301 Office: Jacksonville State U Dept Music Jacksonville AL 36265

FAIRLEIGH, MARLANE PAXSON, retired business consultant, educator; b. Three Rivers, Mich., Feb. 28, 1939; d. Ronald Edward and Evelyn May (Roth) Paxson; m. James Parkinson Fairleigh, June 25, 1960; children: William Paxson, Karen Evelyn. MusB, U. Mich., 1960; MBA, Jacksonville State U., 1986. Cert. econ. devel. fin. profl. Nat. Devel. Coun. Mem. adj. faculty Providence Coll., 1976-80, R.I. Coll., Providence, 1978-80; grad. asst. news bur. and info. ctr. Jacksonville (Ala.) State U., 1983-84, grad. asst. Coll. Commerce, 1984-85; bus. cons. Jacksonville State U. Small Bus. Devel. Ctr., 1985-96; presenter in field. Contbr. articles to profl. jours.; performed as featured soprano soloist Coll. Music Soc. Internat. Conf., Berlin, 1995, Vienna, 1997. Chair Jacksonville State U. campus United Way Calhoun County, 1986-87; mem. Anniston Mus. Natural History. Mem. Women's Exec. Network, Coll. Music Soc., Sigma Beta Delta. Avocations: vocal performing, water skiing, swimming, hiking. Home: 512 Fairway Dr SW Jacksonville AL 36265-3301

FAIRMAN, JARRETT SYLVESTER, retail company executive; b. Anderson, Ind., Feb. 22, 1939; s. Charles Lawton and Ruth (Rich) F.; m. Delores Rae Anderson, Nov. 13, 1960; children: Adele Suzanne, Jarrett Scott, Angela Christine. BS, Purdue U., 1961. Exec. trainee, div. mgr. Sears, Marion, Ind., 1963-67, mdse. mgr., asst. store mgr., Bloomington, Ind., 1967-69, asst. retail sales mgr. sporting goods, Chgo., 1969-71, territorial mdse. mgr. sporting goods, toys and bus. equipment, Dallas, 1971-78; regional v.p. retail ops. White's Home and Auto Stores, 1978-81; pres. Banner, Hendrik & Grant Co., Inc., Dallas, 1981-86; pres. Rapid Distbg. Co. (subs. Otasco), Tulsa, 1986-88; v.p. devel. Coast-to-Coast Home and Auto, Denver, 1988-89; pres. Fairman and Assocs., Inc., 1989-94; pres., CEO Fairman Properties, Inc., 1994—. Served with U.S. Army, 1961-63. Republican. Lutheran. Home and Office: 2006 Hillcrest Ct Mc Kinney TX 75070-4010

FAIRMAN, JOEL MARTIN, broadcasting executive; b. N.Y.C., Mar. 12, 1929; s. Philip A. and Isabelle (Glackman) Feinberg; m. Claire Martin, Oct. 1, 1959; children: Elizabeth, David, Helen. BA, Amherst Coll., 1952; JD, Yale U., 1955. Assoc. Patterson Belknap & Webb, N.Y.C., 1956-61; asst. to pres., v.p. Gianis & Co., Inc., N.Y.C., 1961-65; sr. v.p. and mng. dir. corp. fin. communications group Prudential-Bache Securities and predecessor firms, N.Y.C., 1965-83; chmn. Faircom Inc., 1984-98; vice chmn. Regent Comms., Inc., 1998—. Home: Bayville Rd Locust Valley NY 11560-2003 Office: Regent Comms Inc 333 Glen Head Rd Old Brookville NY 11545-1947

FAIRWEATHER, EDWIN ARTHUR, electronics company executive; b. London, July 21, 1916; came to U.S., 1967; s. Arthur Henry and Elizabeth (Dawson) F.; m. Joan Barbara Branson, Sept. 14, 1946; children: David Martin, Janet Elizabeth Fairweather Nelson. BSME, London Poly., 1940. Quality engr. Lucas-Rotex, Toronto (Ont., Can.) and Birmingham (Eng.), 1951-58; mfg. engr. Flight Refuelling Co., Dorset, Eng., 1958-62, Spar Aerospace, Toronto, 1962-67, Sperry Flight Systems, Phoenix, 1967-71; engr.

research and devel. Ford Aerospace Co., Palo Alto, Calif., 1971-85; founder, pres., chief engr. Fairweather & Co., Sunnyvale, Calif., 1980—. Patentee in field. Served with RAF, 1940-46. Avocations: sailing, golf. Fax: (408) 773-1613. Home and Office: 1442 S Wolfe Rd Sunnyvale CA 94087-3669

FAIRWEATHER, ROBERT GORDON LEE, lawyer; b. Rothesay, N.B., Can., Mar. 27, 1923; s. Jack H.A.L. and Agnes Charlotte (Mackeen) F.; m. Nancy E. Broughall, June 1, 1946; children—Michael, Wendy, Hugh. B.C.L., U. N.B., 1949, LL.D. (hon.), 1973; LL.D. (hon.), St. Thomas U., 1977, Queens U., 1978, St. Francis Xavier U., 1980, York U., 1993. Called to bar N.B 1949, created Queen's Counsel 1958. Partner firm McKelvey, MacAulay, Machum & Fairweather, St. John, 1957-77; atty. gen. N.B., 1958-60; chief Can. Human Rights Commn., Ottawa, Ont., 1977-87; chmn. Immigration and Refugee Bd., Ottawa, 1987-92. Mem. Legis. Assembly N.B., 1952-62, M.P., 1962-77. Served with Royal Can. Navy, 1941-45. Decorated officer Order of Can.; recipient Outstanding Achievement award of pub. svc. Govt. Can., 1990; Ryerson Poly. U. fellow, 1993. Home: 2865 Rothesay Rd Apt 43, Rothesay, NB Canada E2E 5V1

FAISON, SETH SHEPARD, retired insurance broker; b. N.Y.C., Jan. 18, 1924; s. John Williams and Caroline Goree (Shepard) F.; m. Susan Tyler, Apr. 14, 1956 (dec. 1978); children: Katharine Faison Spencer, Seth Shepard, Sarah, Ann Badger; m. Sara Williams Rose Chew, Mar. 29, 1980; stepchildren: Sara Holten Chew, Katherine Rose Chew, Arthur Duncan Chew. BA with honors and distinction, Wesleyan U., 1947. Personnel mgr. NBC, N.Y.C., 1948-53; div. mgr. Am. Mgmt. Assn., N.Y.C., 1953-58; asst. v.p. Johnson & Higgins, N.Y.C., 1958-68; v.p. Johnson & Higgins, 1968-89. Chmn. Bklyn. Acad. Music, 1966-72, hon. chmn., 1979—; trustee Bklyn. Inst. Arts and Scis., 1963-81, v.p., 1965-71, exec. v.p., 1971-74, vice-chmn., 1974-79, chmn., 1979-81; trustee/gov. Bklyn. Mus. of Art, 1972-91, vice-chmn. 1976-91, trustee 1993—; trustee Bklyn. Hosp., 1963—, v.p. 1968-82, vice-chmn., 1982-93, chmn., 1993—; mem. bd. govs. Hosp. Trustees of N.Y. State, 1992-97, chmn., 1995-97; trustee Poly Prep., 1962-77; bd. dirs. Police Athletic League N.Y., 1957-73, Chelsea Theater Center, 1969-77; regent St. Francis Coll., Bklyn., 1961-70; mem. N.Y.C. Commn. for Cultural Affairs, 1981-91; exec. com. N.Y. and Presbyn. Hosps. Healthcare Network, 1998—. Lt. (j.g.) USNR, 1943-46. Recipient N.Y. State award for Bklyn. Acad. Music (rehab. of 1 of state's most venerable theaters), 1969. Mem. Citizens Union, Huguenot Soc. Am., Heights Casino Club, Rembrandt Club, Ihpetonga Club (Bklyn.), Bellport Bay Yacht Club (N.Y.). Unitarian (deacon). Home: 1 Pierrepont St # 10B Brooklyn NY 11201-3302

FAISON, W. MACK, lawyer; b. Roanoke Rapids, N.C., Oct. 25, 1945. BA, N.C. Ctrl. U., 1966; JD, Harvard U., 1969. Bar: N.Y. 1970, Mich. 1972. Mem. Miller, Canfield, Paddock and Stone, Detroit; mem. local rules adv. com. Ea. Dist. Mich., U.S. Dist. Ct., civil justice reform act adv. com. Mem. ABA, State Bar Mich., Nat. Bar Assn., Detroit Bar Assn., Wolverine Bar Assn., Am. Coll. of Trial Lawyers. Office: Miller Canfield Paddock & Stone 150 W Jefferson Ave Ste 2500 Detroit MI 48226-4429*

FAISS, ROBERT DEAN, lawyer; b. Centralia, Ill., Sept. 19, 1934; s. Wilbur and Theresa Ella (Watts) F.; m. Linda Louise Chambers, Mar. 30, 1991; children: Michael Dean Faiss, Marcy Faiss Ayres, Robert Mitchell Faiss, Philip Grant Faiss, Justin Cooper. *Robert Faiss's grandchildren are Stephanie Jane Faiss, Branden Faiss, Khristopher Robert Faiss, Adelaide Chambers Ayres and Eliza Pennington Ayres. Son Michael Faiss is a regional restaurant manager in California. Daughter Marceline Ayres is an educator in Massachusetts. Son Robert Mitchell Faiss owns an electrical company in Nevada. Sons Philip Faiss and Justin Cooper are involved in the entertainment industry in California.* BA in Journalism, Am. U., 1969, JD, 1972. Bar: Nev. 1972, D.C. 1972, U.S. Dist. Ct. Nev. 1973, U.S. Supreme Ct. 1977, U.S. Ct. Appeals (9th cir.) 1978. City editor Las Vegas (Nev.) Sun, 1957-59; pub. info. officer Nev. Dept. Employment Security, 1959-61; asst. exec. sec. Nev. Gaming Commn., Carson City, 1961-63; exec. asst. to gov. State of Nev., Carson City, 1963-67; staff asst. U.S. Pres. Lyndon B. Johnson, White House, Washington, 1968-69; asst. to exec. dir. U.S. Travel Adminstrn., Washington, 1969-72; ptnr., chmn. adminstrv. law dept. Lionel, Sawyer & Collins, Las Vegas, 1973—; mem. bank secrecy Act Adv. Group U.S. Treasury. Co-author: Legalized Gaming in Nevada, 1961, Nevada Gaming License Guide, 1988, Nevada Gaming Law, 1991, 95, 98. Recipient Bronze medal Dept. Commerce, 1972, Chris Schaller award We Can, Las Vegas, 1995, Lifetime Achievement award Nev. Gaming Attys. Assn., 1997; named One of 100 Most Influential Lawyers in Am. and premier U.S. gaming atty., Nat. Law Jour., 1997. Mem. ABA (chmn. gaming law com. 1985-86), Internat. Assn. Gaming Attys. (founding, pres. 1980), Nev. Gaming Attys. Office: Lionel Sawyer & Collins 300 S 4th St Ste 1700 Las Vegas NV 89101-6053

FAITH, MARSHALL E., grain company executive. CEO The Scoular Grain Co., Omaha. Office: The Scoular Grain Co Scoular Bldg 2027 Dodge St Ste 1 Omaha NE 68102-1234*

FAJANS, JACK, physics educator; b. N.Y., Nov. 17, 1922; s. Harry and Fanny Fajans; m. Eleanor Belfert, Mar. 5, 1944; children—Anita, Joel. B.Chem.Engring., CCNY, 1944; Ph.D., M.I.T., 1950. Engr. Western Electric Co., Kearny, N.J., 1944; group mgr. Sylvania Electric Co., Bayside, N.Y., 1950-53; mem. faculty Stevens Inst. Tech., Hoboken, N.J., 1953—; prof. physics Stevens Inst. Tech., 1953-88, prof. emeritus, 1988—, dean grad. sch., 1974-84; exchange prof. Kabul U., Afghanistan, 1963-65, 67-69; cons. in field, 1956—. Author; patentee in field. Served with AUS, 1944-46. Mem. Am. Phys. Soc., M.I.T. Alumni Assn., CCNY Alumni Assn., Sigma Xi. Home: 1133 Magnolia Rd Teaneck NJ 07666-2745 Office: Dean Grad Sch Stevens Inst Tech Hoboken NJ 07030

FAJANS, STEFAN STANISLAUS, internist, retired educator; b. Munich, Mar. 15, 1918; came to U.S., 1936, naturalized, 1942; s. Kasimir M. and Salomea (Kaplan) F.; m. Ruth Stine, Sept. 6, 1947; children: Peter S., John S. B.S., U. Mich., Ann Arbor, 1938, M.D., 1942. Intern Mount Sinai Hosp., N.Y.C., 1942-43; resident U. Mich., 1947-49, research fellow, 1946-47, 49-51; mem. faculty U. Mich. Med. Sch., 1950—, prof., 1961-88, prof. emeritus, 1988—; chief divsn. endocrinology & metabolism Mich. Diabetes Rsch. and Tng. Ctr., 1973-87, dir., 1977-86; mem. endocrinology study sect. NIH, 1958-62, mem. diabetes and metabolism tng. grants com., 1966-70, mem. nat. diabetes adv. bd., 1987-91; chmn. Am. zone internat. sci. adv. com. Congresses Internat. Diabetes Fedn., 1977-79; Banting meml. lectr., 1978. Contbr. articles med. publns. Mem. career devel. com. VA Med. Rsch. Svc., 1987-91. Officer M.C., AUS, 1943-46. Research fellow in medicine A.C.P., 1949-50; fellow Life Ins. Med. Inst., 1950-51. Mem. Am. Diabetes Assn. (pres. 1971-72, Banting medal 1972, Banting Meml. award 1978), Endocrine Soc. (v.p. 1970-71, council 1967-71, 78-81), ACP (master), Am. Fedn. Clin. Research, Am. Soc. Clin. Investigation, Assn. Am. Physicians, Central Soc. Clin. Research, Nat. Acad. Sci. (sr. mem. inst. med.), Sigma Xi, Alpha Omega Alpha. Home: 2485 Devonshire Rd Ann Arbor MI 48104-2705 Office: Univ Mich Hosp 3920 Taubman Ctr Box 0354 Ann Arbor MI 48109

FAJEN, JOHN HERMAN, minister; b. Stover, Mo., May 26, 1929; s. Otto John and Magdalena Elise (Wittrock) F.; m. Margaret (Peggy) Thompson, June 19, 1955; children: Katherine, Elizabeth, Melanie, Barbara, Pauline. AA, St. Paul's Coll., Concordia, Mo., 1949; BA, Concordia Coll., 1952; diploma in Theology, Concordia Sem., 1955; postgrad., UCLA, 1964-65, 69-70; LHD, Concordia U., 1993. Ordained to ministry Luth. Ch.-Mo. Synod, 1956. Missionary to Nigeria BFMS, Luth. Ch.-Mo. Synod, St. Louis, 1956-80; sec. for pers. Luth. Ch.-Mo. Synod, St. Louis, 1980-87; pastor Trinity Luth. Ch., Glidden, Wis., 1987—; vis. prof. theology Valparaiso U., 1974, Gross Meml. lectr., 1978. Translator Bible; pub. N.T., 1980.

FAKLER, MARY EDITH, English educator; b. Mt. Vernon, N.Y.; d. Charles A. and Kathleen Deierlein; m. Helmut K. Fakler; children: Marè Fakler, Wayne, Kate Collins, Marissa, Heidi. BA in English, SUNY, New Paltz, 1991, MA in English, 1994. Instr. English SUNY, New Paltz, 1992—, Mt. St. Mary Coll., Newburgh, N.Y., 1994—; instr. gifted program Mt. St. Mary Coll., Newburgh, 1996—; creative writing instr. Pine Bush (N.Y.) H.S. E-mail:faklerm@matrix.newpaltz.edu. Home: 150 Plains Rd Walden NY 12586-2443 Office: SUNY CH F104A Mannheim Blvd New Paltz NY 12561

FAKUNDINY, ROBERT HARRY, geologist, educator, consultant; b. Manitowoc, Wis., Feb. 11, 1940; s. Walter P. and Ann (Kakes) F.; m. Anne J. Finch, Jan. 28, 1978. BA in Geology, U. Calif., Riverside, 1962; MA in Geology, U. Tex., 1967, PhD in Geology, 1970. Vol. U.S. Peace Corps., Ghana, West Africa, 1963-65; assoc. scientist and sr. scientist N.Y. State Geol. Survey, Albany, 1970-78, state geologist and chief, 1978—; consulting geologist, Albany, 1967—, adj. asst. prof. SUNY, Albany, 1975-87; cons. to profl. groups, industries and govt. agys. Contbr. articles to profl. jours. Bd. trustees Esquatak Town Hist. Soc., 1983-86; bd. dirs. N.E. Sci. Found., 1988-91; advisor New England River Basins Commn., 1973-75; mem. site selection com. CoCorp, 1978-93; mem. com. on energy resources IOCC, 1978-89, mem. com. on oil and gas info. and data base mgmt., 1989—; chmn. Ian Campbell Award com. Am. Geol. Inst., 1995-96. Hogg fellow U. Tex., 1969; numerous scholarships and grants; chmn. N.Am. Com. on Stratigraphic Nomenclature, 1988. Fellow Geol. Soc. Am. (engring. geology div. mgmt. bd. 1987, chmn. northeast sect. geology and pub. policy com. 1991-97), Geol. Assn. Can., Chartered Geologist Geol. Soc., N.Y. Acad. Scis.; mem. Am. Assn. Petroleum Geologists (George V. Cohee Pub. Svc. award 1997), Am. Geophysical Union, AAAS, Assn. Am. State Geologists (v.p. 1989-90, pres.-elect 1990-91, pres. 1991-92, chmn. low-level radioactive waste com 1980-86, chmn. radon com. 1990-91, earth sci. edn. com. 1993—), Am. Inst. Profl. Geologists (cert., nat. selection com. 1991-95, chmn. nat. selection com. 1993, del. to Soviet Union 1990, nat. sec. 1996-97, John T. Galey Sr. Meml. Pub. Svc. award 1993, Presdl. cert. merit 1994), Nat. Assn. Geology Tchrs., Assn. Earth Sci. Editors, Soc. Exploration Paleontologists and Mineralogists, Assn. Engring. Geologists, Assn. Women Geoscientists, Assn. Geoscientists for Internat. Devel., Multi Agy. Group for Neotechnics in Eatern Can., Buffalo Assn. Profl. Geologists, Ctrl. N.Y. Assn. Profl. Geologists, Nat. Assn. Black Geologists, Geophysicists Hudson-Mohawk Profl. Geologists Assn., N.Y. State Coun. Profl. Geologists (bd. dirs. 1995-97), Sigma Xi, Sigma Gamma Epsilon. Achievements include research in seismic hazard determination, application of glacial studies to environmental issues, geology of low-level radioactive waste disposal, geologic structure of Adirondack Mountains. Home: 3288 River Rd # 9J Rensselaer NY 12144-5121 Office: NY State Geol Survey CEC 3136 ESP Albany NY 12230

FALA, HERMAN C., lawyer; b. Phila., Oct. 15, 1949; s. Herman Anthony and Rose Maria (Iannetti) F.; m. Helen E. Perry, June 26, 1971; 1 child, Danielle. BS summa cum laude, U. Notre Dame, 1971; JD cum laude, Harvard U., 1974. Bar: Pa. 1974, U.S. Dist. Ct. (ea. dist.) Pa. 1974. Assoc. Wolf, Block, Schorr & Solis-Cohen, Phila., 1974-82, ptnr., 1982—; chair real estate dept. Wolf, Block, Schorr & Solis-Cohen. Editor: The Philadelphia Lawyer, 1977—. Bd. dirs. The Wilma Theatre, Phila., 1986—, chmn., 1995-97. Mem. ABA, Pa. Bar Assn., Phila. Bar Assn. (v.p. 1997, chair exec. com. real property sect. 1998), Phi Beta Kappa. Avocations: photography, composing music, travel, cooking, writing. Office: Wolf Block Schorr & Solis-Cohen Packard Bldg 12th Fl Philadelphia PA 19102

FALB, PETER LAWRENCE, mathematician, educator, investment company executive; b. N.Y.C., July 26, 1936; s. Harry and Bertha (Kirschner) F.; m. Karen Forslund, Oct. 9, 1971; children—Hilary, Alison. A.B., Harvard U., 1956, M.A., 1957, Ph.D., 1961. Mem. staff Mass. Inst. Tech. Lincoln Lab., Cambridge, 1960-66; asso. prof. applied math. U. Mich., Ann Arbor, 1966; prof. Brown U., Providence, 1967—; prin., treas. Dane, Falb, Stone & Co., Inc., Boston, 1977—; chmn. Barberry Corp., 1968-85; also dir.; dir. FES Computing Co.; dir. LTCQ, Inc., Toreador Royalty; vis. prof. Lund (Sweden) Inst. Tech., summers 1971, 72, 74, 76, 78; cons. NASA, Bolt, Beranek & Newman Co. Author: (with M. Athans) Optimal Control: An Introduction to the Theory and its Applications, 1966, (with R. Kalman and M. Arbib) Topics in Mathematical System Theory, 1969, (with J. deJong) Some Successive Approximation Methods in Control and Oscillation Theory, 1969; Methods of Algebraic Geometry in Control Theory, Part I: Scalar Linear Systems and Affine Algebraic Geometry, 1989, Methods of Algebraic Geometry in Control Theory, Part II: Multivariable Linear systems and Projective Algebraic Geometry, 1999. Home: 245 Brattle St Cambridge MA 02138-4614 Office: Dane Falb Stone & Co Inc 33 Broad St Ste 7 Boston MA 02109-4215 also: Brown U Box F Providence RI 02912

FALCAO, LINDA PHYLLIS, lawyer, former screenwriter; b. Lisbon, Portugal, June 1, 1960; came to U.S., 1961; d. John Moniz and Phyllis Margaret (Fleming) F.; 1 child, Lauren N. BS in Econs., BA, U. Pa., 1982, JD, 1985. Assoc. Schnader, Harrison, Segal & Lewis, Phila., 1985-86; law clk. Hon. Phyllis W. Beck Superior Ct. Pa., 1986-88, 92; assoc. Dechert, Price & Rhoads, Phila., 1989-92; freelance writer Wynnewood, Pa., 1993-96; shareholder Salmanson and Falcão, LLC, Phila., 1997—. Author: (screenplay) Pattern and Practice, 1993, Millennium, 1996. Presdl. scholar Commn. Presdl. Scholars, Washington, 1978. Mem. Phi Beta Kappa, Beta Gamma Sigma. Office: Salmanson & Falcão 1429 Walnut St Ste 900 Philadelphia PA 19102-3218

FALCI, KENNETH JOSEPH, food and nutrition scientist. BA in Organic Chemistry, Marist Coll., 1968; PhD, Fordham U., 1976. Sr. rsch. chemist Olin Corp., New Haven, Conn., 1976-77; consumer safety officer, food and color additives FDA, Washington, 1977-78, dep. program mgr., 1978-80, supr. petitions control branch, 1980-83, supr. generally recognized as safe branch, 1983-85, supr. consumer safety officer, indirect additives branch, 1985-92, chief regulatory affairs staff, 1991-92; dir. Office of Scientific Analysis and Support, Washington, 1992—; guest speaker various nat. and internat. orgns. Contbr. articles to profl. jours., chpts. in books. Active Sci. and Tech. Commn., Rockville, Md., 1990-93, chmn., 1990-92. Recipient PHS Spl. Recognition award, 1995, Commr.'s Spl. Citation award, 1996, 97. Mem. AOAC, Am. Ch. Soc., Inst. Food Technologists, Sigma Xi. Office: FDA-Center for Food Safety &App Nutr (HFS-700) 330 C St SW Washington DC 20201-0001*

FALCO, EDWARD, writer, English educator; b. L.A., Nov. 25, 1948; s. Joseph and Edith Falco; m. Jane Braley, June 14, 1980 (div. Sept. 1986); 1 child, Susan; m. Lisa Norris, June 19, 1993; 1 stepchild, Will Stauffer-Norris. BS, SUNY, New Paltz, 1971; MA, Syracuse U., 1979. Part-time instr. Enlish Syracuse (N.Y.) U., 1979-84; prof. Va. Tech., Blacksburg, 1984—. Author: (poems) Concert in the Park of Culture, 1984; (short stories) Plato at Scratch Daniel's, 1990, ACID, 1996 (Richard Sullivan prize); (novel) Winter in Florida, 1990. Recipient Emily clark Balch prize Va. Quar. Rev., 1986, Govs. Screenwriting award Va. Film Office, 1991, Pushcart prize Pushcart Press, 1999; Individual Artist grantee Va. Commn. Arts, 1992, 95. Unitarian. Avocation: chess. E-mail: efalco@vt.edu. Office: Va Tech English Dept Blacksburg VA 24061-0112

FALCO, GENNARO ANTHONY, urologist, surgeon; b. Oct. 29, 1953. MD, Creighton U., 1979. Urologist A.O. Fox Hosp., Oneonta, N.Y., 1984—. Fellow Am. Coll. Surgeons. Home: 438 Main St Oneonta NY 13820-2046

FALCO, MARIA JOSEPHINE, political scientist, academic administrator; b. Wildwood, N.J., July 7, 1932; d. John J. and Mafalda M. (Barbieri) F. AB, Immaculata (Pa.) Coll., 1954; student, U. Florence, Italy, 1954-55; MA, Fordham U., 1958; PhD, Bryn Mawr (Pa.) Coll., 1963; postdoctoral rsch. fellow, Yale, 1965-66; mgmt. program, Carnegie-Mellon U., 1983. Instr., then asst. prof. history and polit. sci. Immaculata Coll., Pa., 1957-63; asst. prof. polit. sci. Washington Coll., Chestertown, Md., 1963-64; rsch. asst. Genevieve Blatt; candidate for U.S. Senator from Genevieve Blatt, Pa., 1964-65; asst. prof., then assoc. prof. polit. sci. Le Moyne Coll., Syracuse, N.Y., 1966-73; chmn. polit. sci. dept. Le Moyne Coll., 1967-73; prof. polit. sci. Stockton State Coll., Pomona, N.J., 1973-76; chmn. social and behavioral scis. faculty U. Tulsa, 1976-79; dean Coll. Arts and Scis., Loyola U., New Orleans, 1979-85; prof. polit. sci. Loyola U., New Orleans, 1985-86; v.p. acad. affairs DePauw U., Greencastle, Ind., 1986-88, prof. polit. sci., 1988-93, prof. emerita, 1993—; Participant numerous profl. confs. and convs.; speaker in field; adj. prof. polit. sci. Tulane U., New Orleans, 1996-97. Author: Truth and Meaning in Political Science: An Introduction to Political Inquiry, 1973, Bigotry: Ethnic, Machine and Sexual Politics in a Senatorial Election, 1980; editor: Through the Looking Glass: Epistemology and the Conduct of Political Inquiry: An Anthology, 1979, Feminism and Epistemology: Approaches to Research in Women and Politics, 1987, Feminist Interpretations of Mary Wollstonecraft, 1996; cons. editor Political Parties and the Civic Action Groups; contbr. articles and book revs. to profl. jours. Mem. Mayor's Task Force on Future of New Orleans, 1983-85, Women's Equity Action League, 1979-81, LWV, 1960-63, 82-84; bd. dirs. Inst. for Human Rels., Loyola U., Inst. Human Understanding, New Orleans, 1985-86; pres. Syracuse chpt. New Dem. Coalition, 1970-71; mem. pres.'s coun. Loyola U., New Orleans, 1997—. Fulbright scholar U. Florence, Italy, 1954-55; faculty fellow in state and local politics Nat. Ctr. for Edn. in Politics, 1964. Mem. AAUS, AAUP (v.p. LeMoyne chpt. 1971-72), Womens Caucus Polit. Sci. (pres. 1976, named Mentor of Distinction 1989), Am. Polit. Sci. Assn. (mem. Benjamin Evans Lippincott award com. 1976, chmn. sect. program com. 1975, mem. com. acad. freedom and profl. ethics, chair com. for outstanding conv. paper award women and politics rsch. sect. 1990-91), Midwestern Polit. Sci. Assn. (mem. com. status of women), Northeastern Polit. Sci. Assn., S.W. Polit. Sci. Assn. (outstanding conv. paper com.), Founds. Polit. Theory Group, Common Cause, Great Lakes Coll. Assn. (dean's coun. 1986-88), Assn. Jesuit Colls. and Univs. (dean's coun. 1979-85), Assn. Am. Colls. (coun. for liberal learning 1985-87), Western Polit. Sci. Assn., Ind. Polit. Sci. Assn. (pres., chair 1992-93), Ind. Social Sci. Assn., So. Polit. Sci. Assn. Roman Catholic. Home: 4817 Belle Dr Metairie LA 70006-2274 *Despite the fact that it's difficult being a woman in a man's world, I'm glad I'm a woman.*

FALCON, PATRICIA, educator, health psychologist; b. Ness City, Kans., Apr. 6, 1963; d. Antonio and Dora (Murillo) F.; m. Michael D. Worley, Mar. 17, 1990. BSN, Ft. Hays State U., 1984; MSN, U. Ariz., 1992; PsyD, U. No. Colo., 1998. RN, Kans., Colo., Ariz., Calif., Wash.; cert. oncology nurse; lic. psychologist Colo., N.Mex. Case mgr. home care Tucson Hosp. Home Care, 1984-86; dir. oncology svcs. Redding (Calif.) Med. Ctr., 1986-89; field supr. home care Home Care of So. Ariz., Tucson, 1989-91; nurse clinician bone marrow transplants U. Ariz. Med. Ctr., Tucson, 1991-92; travel nurse acute care Flying Nurses, Dallas, 1992-93; case mgr. home care LHS Home and Cmty. Care, Greeley, Colo., 1993-95; adj. faculty U. No. Colo., Greeley, 1995-97; heal psychologist Acoma-Canoncito-Laguna Hosp., San Fidel, N.Mex., 1997—; cons. Access Tech., San Francisco, 1987-89, Tucson Gen. Hosp., 1990-93, Twilight Manor, Greeley, 1995-96, Gary and Loretta's Bd. and Care, Greeley, 1993-96. Mentor McNair scholar program U. No. Colo., 1995-96. Mem. APA, Am. Counseling Assn., Oncology Nursing Soc. Avocations: photography, sewing, bird watching. Address: 9180 Coors Blvd NW Apt 301 Albuquerque NM 87120-3125

FALCON, RAYMOND JESUS, JR., lawyer; b. N.Y.C., Nov. 17, 1953; s. Raymond J. and Lolin (Lopez) F.; m. Debra Mary Bomeisl, June 4, 1977; children: Victoria Marie, Mark Daniel. BA, Columbia U., 1975; JD, Yale U., 1978. Bar: N.Y. 1979, U.S. Dist. Ct. (so. and ea. dist.) N.Y. 1979, U.S. Ct. Appeals (D.C. and 2d cirs.) 1983, Fla. 1987, N.J. 1988, U.S. Dist. Ct. N.J. 1988. Assoc. Webster and Sheffield, N.Y.C., 1978-82; ptnr. Falcon and Hom, N.Y.C., 1982-85; sr. atty. Degussa Corp., Ridgefield Park, N.J., 1985-88, v.p., sec., gen. counsel, 1989-94; pvt. practice Woodcliff Lake, N.J., 1994-95; ptnr. Falcon & Singer PC, Woodcliff Lake, 1995—. Contbr. articles to profl. jours. Dem. candidate Town Justice, Town of Rye, N.Y., 1983; Dem. jud. del., Westchester, N.Y., 1984-89. Mem. ABA, N.J. State Bar Assn., Fla. Bar Assn., Bergen County Bar Assn., Nat. Acad. Elder Law Attys., Park Ridge Rotary (bd. dirs. 1997—), Columbia Alumni of Westchester County (v.p., bd. dirs. 1983-90, 97—). Home: 582 Colonial Rd River Vale NJ 07675-6107 Office: 172 Broadway River Vale NJ 07675-8077 also: 14 Harwood Ct Scarsdale NY 10583-4120

FALCONE, ALFONSO BENJAMIN, physician and biochemist; b. Bryn Mawr, Pa., July 24; s. B. and Elvira (Galluzzo) F.; m. Patricia J. Lalim, Oct. 22; children: Christopher L., Steven B. AB in Chemistry with distinction, Temple U., 1944, MD with honors, 1947; PhD in Biochemistry, U. Minn., 1954. Diplomate Am. Bd. Internal Medicine subspecialty bd. endocrinology and metabolism. Intern Phila. Gen. Hosp., 1947-48, asst. resident, 1948-49; teaching fellow internal medicine U. Hosps., U. Minn., 1949-51; asst. clin. prof. medicine U. Wis., Madison, 1956-59, assoc. clin. prof., 1959-63, asst. prof. Inst. Enzyme Research, 1963-66, vis. prof., 1966-67; cons. in field; practice in endocrine/metabolic diseases, med.-legal cons. Fresno, Calif., 1968—; active staff mem. Fresno Community Hosp., chmn. dept. medicine, 1973; active staff mem. St. Agnes Hosp., Fresno; hon. staff Univ. Med. Ctr., Fresno; sr. corr. Ettor Majorana Ctr. for Sci. Culture, Erice, Italy. Contbr. articles to profl. jours. with rsch. in mechanisms of energy transduction in biol. sys., mechanism of oxidative phosphorylation, mechanisms of enzyme action, mechanisms of drug action; co-discoverer of phosphate exchange reactions of the mitochondrial ATP Synthetase of Oxidative Phosphorylation, 1953. Served with AUS, 1944-46; served to lt. comdr. M.C., USNR, 1954-56. NIH postdoctoral fellow, 1951-53; NIH research grantee, 1958-68. Fellow ACP; mem. AAAS, Am. Soc. Biochemistry and Molecular Biology, Cen. Soc. Clin. Rsch., Am. Fedn. Clin. Rsch., Am. Chem. Soc., Am. Assn. for Study of Liver Disease, Endocrine Soc., Am. Diabetes Assn., Assn. Acad. Excellence, U. Calif. Fresno Com., Fresno County Assn. for U. Calif. Campus, Archaeol. Inst. Am., Calif. Acad. Medicine, Sigma Xi, Phi Lambda Epsilon. Office: Metabolic and Endocrine Dis 2240 E Illinois Ave Fresno CA 93701-2118

FALCONE, FRANK S., academic administrator; b. Kenosha, Wis., Sept. 26, 1940; s. Frank R. and Theresa (Barca) F.; m. Judith Herbert, Aug. 17, 1963; children: Jennifer, F. Jeffrey. BS, U. WIs., 1963; MA, U. Denver, 1965; PhD, U. Mass., 1973. Prof., provost Ithaca (N.Y.) Coll., 1969-80; v.p., dean Pace U., White Plains, N.Y., 1980-82; exec. v.p. Pace U., Pleasantville, N.Y., 1982-85; pres. Springfield (Mass.) Coll., 1985-93, Carroll Coll., Waukesha, Wis., 1993—. Bd. dirs. Springfield YMCA, 1990-92, Basketball Hall of Fame; bd. visitors Air U., Maxwell AFB, Ala., 1989-90; exec. com. Boy Scouts, 1994—, United Way Exec. Comm., 1994. Mem. Assn. Ind. Colls. and Univs. in Mass. (exec. com. 1987-89, chmn. 1990-91), Assn. Ind. Colls. Mass. (pres. 1990-91), Greater Springfield C. of C. (bd. dirs. 1987-92), Waukesha C. of C. (bd. dirs. 1994—, exec. com. 1995—, v.p. 1995), Wis. Found. for Ind. Colls. (treas. 1995—). Home: 115 S East Ave Waukesha WI 53186-6207 Office: Carroll Coll Office of Pres 100 N East Ave Waukesha WI 53186-3103*

FALCONE, ROBERT EDWARD, surgeon; b. Sulmona, Italy, Apr. 12, 1950; s. Joseph and Sophie (Kosier) F.; 1 child, Melissa. Student, Cleve. State U., 1968-71; BA in Chemistry magna cum laude, Kent (Ohio) State U., 1973; MD cum laude, Ohio State U., 1976, postgrad., 1987-90. Mem. staff and teaching faculty Grant Med. Ctr., Columbus, Ohio, 1981—, dir. trauma svcs., 1985-98, dir. surg. ICU, med. dir. life flight, 1988-95, chmn. dept. surgery, 1989-90, med. co-dir. med flight; v.p. trauma and critical care svcs. Grant/Riverside Med. Ctr. Hosps., 1998—; chmn. Ohio Com. on Trauma, 1994—; chmn. nutritional support com. Riverside Meth. Hosp., Columbus, 1983-84; med. dir. Franklin County Paramedic Sch., Columbus, 1992-95; clin. assoc. prof. Ohio State U. Coll. of Medicine, Columbus, 1985—; surg. product advisor Ethican, Inc., 1984-85, Bd. Cardiosurgery, Inc., 1986-87; lectr. in continuing medicine edn. Merck Sharp and Dohme, Inc., 1986—, Squibb & Sons, Inc., 1989—, Roerig Divsn. Pfizer, Inc., 1994—. Contbr. numerous articles to profl. jours. Fellow ACS, Soc. Critical Care Medicine; mem. Am. Assn. Surgery for Trauma, Pan-Am. Trauma Soc., Soc. Internat. de Chirurgie, Ea. Assn. Surgery for Trauma, Ctrl. Surg. Assn., Alpha Omega Alpha, Sigma Psi. Avocations: music, art, Martial arts. Office: Grant Med Ctr 111 S Grant Ave Columbus OH 43215-4701

FALCONER, JUDITH ANN, public health and occupational therapist, educator; b. Riverside, Ill.; d. Robert John and Marian Ann Falconer; m. E. John Saliba, Feb. 15, 1992. BS in Occupl. Therapy, U. Ill., Chgo., 1975, MPH, 1981, PhD in Pub. Health, 1984. Occupl. therapist Mass. Rehab. Hosp., Boston, 1975-77, Valens (Switzerland) Clinic, 1977-78, London (Eng.) Hosp., 1978-80; tchg. asst. U. Ill., Chgo., 1980-81, rsch. asst., 1981-83; rsch. assoc. Northwestern U., Chgo., 1984-86, rsch. asst. prof., 1986-87, asst. prof., 1987-92, assoc. prof., 1992-96, adj. assoc. prof., 1996—; prof. dept. health scis., dir. occupl. therapy U. Wis., Milw., 1996-98. Mem. editl. bd. Am. Occupl. Therapy Jour., 1988-90, Occupl. Therapy Jour. Rsch., 1989-91, Arthritis Care Rsch., 1990-92, 95-97; editl. bd. assoc. mem. Archives Phys. Medicine and Rehab., 1994—; contbr. articles to profl. jours. Rsch. grantee NIH, 1986-89, 94-96, Arthritis Found., 1986-89, 87-88, 95-96, Robert Wood Johnson Found., 1988-91, rsch. grantee in rehab. VA, 1997—. Mem. APHA, Am. Occupl. Therapy Assn., Assn. Health Svcs. Rsch., Am. Congress Rehab. Medicine, Arthritis Health Prof. (rsch. com. 1989-90, pub. com. 1994-95), Delta Omega.

FALDO, NICK, professional golfer; b. Hertfordshire, Eng., July 18, 1957; m. Gill Faldo; children: Natalie, Matthew, Georgia. Profl. golfer, 1976—; mem. European Ryder Cup Team, 1977, 79, 81, 83, 85, 87, 89, 91, 93, World Cup Team, 1977, 91, Dunhill Cup Team, 1985, 86, 87, 88, 91, Nissan Cup Team, 1986, Kirin Cup Team, 1987, Four Tours Championship Team, 1990. Winner Brit. Open, 1987, 90, 92, Brit. Youths Amateur Championship, 1975, English Amateur Championship, 1975, Colgate PGA Championship, 1978, Brit. PGA Championship, 1978, 80, 81, Car Care Plan Internat., 1984, Spanish Open, 1987, French Open, 1988, Volvo Masters, 1988, Volvo PGA Championship, 1989, Dunhill Brit. Masters, 1989, Peugeot French Open, 1989, Suntory World Match Play, 1989, The Masters, 1989, 90, Irish Open, 1991, Carroll's Irish Open, 1992, 93, Brit. Open, 1992, Scandinavian Masters, 1992, GA European Open, 1992, Toyota World Matchplay, 1992, Johnnie Walker Classic, 1993, Doral/Ryder Open, 1995; named European Rookie of Yr., 1977; recipient MBE award, 1987; leading money winner European Tour, 1983, 92, winner Master Tourn., 1996, Nissan Open, 1997, elected World Golf Hall of Fame, 1997. Office: care IMG 1 Erieview Plz Ste 1300 Cleveland OH 44114-1715*

FALEOMAVAEGA, ENI FA'AUAA HUNKIN, congressman; b. Vailoatai Village, Am. Samoa, Aug. 15, 1943; m. Hinanui Bambridge Cave; children: Temanuata Tuilua'ai, Taualai, Nifae, Vaimoana, Leonne. BA in Polit. Sci. and History, Brigham Young U., 1966; JD, U. Houston, 1972; LLM, U. Calif., Berkeley, 1973. Bar: Am. Samoa, U.S. Supreme Ct. Adminstrv. asst. Am. Samoa del. to Washington, 1973-75; staff counsel to house com. on interior and insular affairs U.S. House of Reps., Washington, 1975-81; dep. atty. gen. Am. Samoa, 1981-84, lt. gov., 1984-89; territorial del. from Am. Samoa U.S. Ho. Reps., 1988; mem. 105th-106th Congresses from Samoa, 1988—; mem. internat. rels. com., resources com. 105th Congress from Samoa; chmn. Gov.'s Task Force for Reorgn. of the Adminstrn., Am. Samoa Adv. Fisheries Council, 1985—, Gov.'s Adv. Com. on Grants Programs, 1985—; mem. nat. lt. gov.'s mission to Egypt, Jordan and Saudi Arabia, South Pacific Leaders Orientation Mission to Paris, 1987; leader Am. Samoa's del. to South Pacific Conf., Noumea New Caledonia, 1987; keynote speaker and leader Am. Samoa's del. to Pacific Trade/Omvestment Conf., 1986. With U.S. Army, 1966-69, including Vietnam, USAR, 1985—. Recipient Alumni Svc. award Brigham Young U., 1979; named Chieftain Faleomavaega, leone Village. Mem. Nat. Conf. of Lt. Govs., Nat. Assn. Secs. of State, Navy League of U.S., VFW, Nat. Am. Indian Prayer Breakfast Group, Lions (charter mem. Pago Pago chpt.), Go for Broke Assn. (life; pres. Samoa chpt.). Office: US Ho of Reps 2422 Rayburn Bldg Washington DC 20515-5201*

FALES, HALIBURTON, II, lawyer; b. N.Y.C., Aug. 7, 1919; s. DeCoursey and Dorothy Mildred (Mitchell) F.; m. Katharine Ladd, Dec. 27, 1941; children: Nancy, Haliburton, Priscilla, Lucy, William E. Ladd. Student, Harvard U., 1938-41; LLB, Columbia U., 1947. Bar: N.Y. 1948, U.S. Supreme Ct. 1957. Assoc. firm White & Case, N.Y.C., 1947-58, ptnr. firm, 1959-88, of counsel, 1988-90, ret. ptnr., 1991—; spl. master Appellate div. 1st dept. N.Y. State Supreme Ct., 1983—, chmn. departmental discipline com., 1991-96, spl. counsel, 1997—. Author: Trying Cases A Life in the Law, 1996; contbr. articles to profl. jours. Trustee, pres. emeritus Pierpont Morgan Libr.; trustee St. Barnabas Hosp., 1949-96, trustee emeritus, 1996—; sr. warden St. Luke's Ch., 1967-93; bd. dirs. Union Theol. Sem., 1986-94; bd. visitors Columbia Law Sch., 1993-98, emeritus, 1998—. Lt. comdr. USNR, 1941-45. Recipient Columbia U. medal, 1994. Fellow Am. Bar Found., N.Y. Bar Found., Inst. Judicial Adminstrn., Am. Coll. Trial Lawyers; mem. ABA, Albert Gallatin Assocs., Am. Judicature Soc., Am. Law Inst. (life), Assn. of Bar of City of N.Y., N.Y. County Lawyers Assn. (William Nelson Cromwell award 1998), N.Y. State Bar Assn. (pres. 1983-84, chair task force on the prof., 1994-96), Assn. of Bar of City of N.Y., Columbia Law Sch. Assn., Inc. (pres. 1991-92), St. Paul's Sch. Alumni Assn. (v.p. 1988-92), Alumni Fedn. Columbia U. Home: 560 Pottersville Rd Gladstone NJ 07934-2046 Office: c/o White & Case 1155 Ave of Americas New York NY 10036-2711

FALES, HENRY MARSHALL, chemist; b. N.Y.C., Feb. 12, 1927; s. Henry Marshall and Cecile Marie (Vatet) F.; m. Caroline Eleanor McCullagh, Dec. 20, 1947; children: Marsha Kent Fales Mazz, Suzanne Kent Fales Palmer, Henry Richard. BSc in Chemistry, Rutgers U., 1948, PhD in Organic Chemistry, 1953. Instr. Rutgers U., New Brunswick, N.J., 1953; rsch. chemist, lab. chief Nat. Heart, Lung and Blood Inst., NIH, Bethesda, Md., 1953—. With USN, 1944-46. Recipient Superior Svc. award U.S. Govt., 1973, 86, Profl. Svc. award Wash. Chpt. of Alpha Chi Sigma. Mem. Am. Chem. Soc., Am. Soc. Mass Spectrometry (mem.-at-large, sec., v.p. programs, pres., past pres.). Avocations: fishing, stained glass. Home: 63 Orchard Way N Potomac MD 20854-6127 Office: NIH Rm 7n318 Bethesda MD 20892

FALETRA, ROBERT, editor. Editor-in-chief Computer Reseller News CMP Media, Inc., Jericho, N.Y.; v.p., editl. dir. CMP Channel Group; editor-in-chief Computer Reseller News. Office: CMP Media Inc 1 Jericho Plz Jericho NY 11753-1680*

FALETTI, TOM, legislative staff member; b. Aug. 1, 1957; m. Sonia Goen, 1980; children: Timothy, Joanna, Luke. BS in Math. Scis., Stanford U., 1979, M Pub. Policy, U. Calif., Berkeley, 1986. Youth min. Holy Rosary Ch., Antioch, Calif., 1979-82; sys. programmer U.S. Steel Corp., Pittsburg, Calif., 1982-84; legis. corr. Office of Rep. Richard J. Durbin, Washington, 1986, legis. asst., 1986-90, legis. dir., 1991-96; legis. dir. Office of Sen. Richard J. Durbin, Washington, 1996—. Office: 364 Russell Senate Office Washington DC 20510

FALEY, R(ICHARD) SCOTT, lawyer; b. Trenton, N.J., Aug. 18, 1947; s. Henry and Winifred (Goeke) F.; m. Josepha Ann Bartlett, Aug. 29, 1970; children: Scott Joseph, Zachary Lorin, Katherine Winifred. BA, Georgetown U., 1969, JD, 1972; LLM, George Washington U., 1975. Bar: D.C. 1973, U.S. Tax Ct. 1973, U.S. Dist. Ct. D.C. 1973, Mont. 1996. Assoc., ptnr. Danzansky, Dickey, Tydings, Quint & Gordon, Washington, 1972-78; prin. R. Scott Faley, P.C., Washington, 1978—; bd. dir. Fed. Employees News Digest, Inc., Fairfax, Va., 1980—; bd. dir., pres. NCC Trout Unltd., 1985—; del. Mid Atlantic Coun. Trout Unltd., 1985—, v.p., 1992—; bd. dirs. Falling Springs Greenway, Inc., Chambersburg, Pa. Inst. for Safety Analysis, Inc., Rockville, Md., 1980-89. Contbr. articles to profl. jours. Mem. instnl. rev. com. Sibley Meml. Hosp., Washington, 1980—. Capt. USAF, 1974. Mem. ABA, FBA, Univ. Club, Boca Bay Pass Club, Alpha Phi Omega, Phi Alpha Delta. Roman Catholic. Home: 25 Primrose St Chevy Chase MD 20815-4228 Office: Ste 401 5100 Wisconsin Ave NW Washington DC 20016-4119

FALEY, ROBERT LAWRENCE, retired instruments company executive; b. Bklyn., Oct. 13, 1927; s. Eric Lawrence and Anna (Makahon) F.; m. Mary Virginia Mumme, May 12, 1950; children: Robert Wayne, Nancy Diane. BS in Chemistry cum laude, St. Mary's U., San Antonio, 1956; postgrad., U. Del., 1958-59. Chemist E.I. Dupont de Nemours & Co., Inc., Wilmington, Del., 1956-60; sales mgr. F&M Sci., Houston, 1960-62; pres. Faley Assocs., Houston, 1962-65; sales mgr. Tech. Inc., Dayton, Ohio, 1965-70; biomed. mktg. mgr. Perkin-Elmer Co., Norwalk, Conn., 1967-69; mktg. dir. Cahn Instruments, L.A., 1970-72; pres. Faley Internat., El Toro, Calif., 1972-93, Status Internat., Las Vegas, Nev., 1993-97; internat. spkr. in field; dir. Whatman Lab. Products Inc., 1981-82, Status Instrument Corp., 1985-87; tech. mktg. cons. Whatman Ltd., Abbott Labs., OCG Tech., Inc., Pacific Biochem., Baker Commodities, Bausch & Lomb Co., Motorola Inc., Whatman Inc., Filtration Scis. Corp., PMC Industries, UVP, Inc., Ericomp, Inc., Data I/O. Contbr. articles on technique of gas chromatography to profl. jours. Mem. adv. com. on sci., tech., energy and water U.S. 48th Congl. Dist., 1985-87. With USMS, 1944-47, 1st lt. USAF, 1948-53. Named Charter mem. Aviation Hall of Fame. Fellow AAAS, Am. Inst. Chemists (life); mem. ASTM, Am. Chem. Soc. (life), Instrument Soc. Am. (life), Inst. Environ. Scis., Aircraft Owners and Pilots Assn., U.S. Power Squadrons, VFW (life), Ret. Officers Assn., Silver Wings Fraternity (life, Golden mem.), Masons, Delta Epsilon Sigma (life). Home: 27850 Espinoza Mission Viejo CA 92692-2156

FALGIANO, VICTOR JOSEPH, electrical engineer, consultant; b. San Francisco, Nov. 25, 1957; s. Victor Anthony and Frances Mary Falgiano; m. Linda Maxine Owens, July 24, 1982; children: Gregory Joseph, Nicholas Rexford. BS in Elec. Engring. Tech. magna cum laude, Cogswell Coll., 1989, BS in Computer Engring. magna cum laude, 1989. Sr. design engr. Amdahl Corp., Sunnyvale, Calif., 1978-93; prin. sys. devel. engr. Nat. Semiconductor Corp., Santa Clara, Calif., 1993-98, engring. mgr. Cyrix divsn., 1998—; mem. steering com. System Design and Integration Conf., Santa Clara, Calif.; mem. acad. adv. com. Cogswell Coll., Cupertino, Calif., 1991; evaluator Accrediting Bd. Engring. and Tech., 1995—. Contbr. articles to profl. publs. Advisor to high sch. students Jr. Achievement. Mem. IEEE (sr.), Assn. Computing Machinery, Internat. Microelectronics and Packaging Soc. Achievements include development of computer program pre-reading children, automobile digital instrumentation, speech recognition user interface for automotive applications, data aquisition circuitry used in mainframe computer power systems, high performance connector system for mainframe computers, developments in commercial/industrial multichip modules and design of personal computer systems. Office: Nat Semicondr Cyrix Divsn/Chipset Engring PO Box 58090 M/S A2-575 2900 Semiconductor Dr Santa Clara CA 95052

FALICK, ABRAHAM JOHNSON, printing company executive; b. Chgo., Oct. 11, 1920; s. Simon Falick and Ellen Martina (Johnson) Sherwood; m. Carolyn Weber, Dec. 11, 1947; 1 child, Leslie Carol Falick Koplof. BA, Ind. U., 1947; MBA, U. Chgo., 1951; MA, UCLA, 1967, PhD, 1970. Cert. pub. planner. Commd. ensign USNR, 1941, advanced through grades to lt. comdr., 1941-46, ret., 1967; mgr. sales/mktg. Webb-Linn Printing Co., Chgo., 1948-56; pres., chief exec. officer Murray and Gee, Inc., Culver City, Calif., 1956-60; planning economist City of Los Angeles, 1967-75; pres., chief exec. officer AJ Falick Assocs., Los Angeles, 1960-67, Navigator Press, Inc., Los Angeles, 1975—; mem., bd. dirs. Navigator Press. Contbr. transp. research articles to profl. jours. Chmn. Coalition Rapid Transit, L.A., 1978—, Friends of Geography UCLA, 1989—; v.p. Westwood Dem. Club, 1988—; chair L.A. Bus./Profl. Dem. Club, 1992—. Mem. Am. Econ. Assn., Am. Planning Assn., Am. Inst. Cert. Planners (counselor 1972-74), Nat. Assn. Bus. Economists (pres. L.A. chpt. 1996-98, bd. mem. L.A. chpt.). Democrat. Jewish. Avocations: photography, bowling, tennis. Office: Navigator Press Inc 516 N Fair Oaks Ave Pasadena CA 91103-3304

FALK, ARMAND ELROY, retired English educator, writer; b. Yankton, S.D., May 16, 1933; s. Robert Leo and Palma Rocelia (Hugelen) F.; m. Ardis Laurene Johnson, July 14, 1956; children: Sean L., Eric B. BA, Concordia Coll., 1955; MA, U. Mont., 1965; PhD, Mich. State U., 1968. Prof. English St. Cloud (Minn.) State U., 1968-96; ret., 1996; sr. lectr. Fulbright Commn., La Cote d'Ivoire, 1985-86, Burkina Faso, 1994-95. Contbr. short stories to profl. publs. Cpl. U.S. Army, 1956-58. Bush Foud. grantee, 1993. Home: 210 3rd St S Apt 102 Saint Cloud MN 56301-4443

FALK, BERNARD HENRY, trade association executive; b. N.Y.C., Sept. 10, 1926; s. Max and Sadie (Orwin) F.; m. Iris G. Tannenbaum, June 13, 1954; children—Cindy, Amy, David. B.E.E., CCNY, 1950; grad. student, Columbia Sch. Bus., 1954. Field engr. RCA, 1950-52; sales engr. Gen. Precision Corp., 1953-56; exec. sec. Nat. Elec. Mfrs. Assn., 1956-65, v.p. govt. rels., 1966-71, pres., 1972-91, vice chmn., 1991-92; chmn. adv. com. elec. goods Dept. Commerce; pres. elect Internat. Electrotech. Commn., 1994-95, pres., 1995—; mem. exec. adv. com. nat. power survey FPC; mem. Bus. Adv. Coun. on Fed. Reports; chmn. liaison com. White House Trade Assn.; bd. dirs. Underwriters Labs., trustee, 1992—; co-chmn. EC 92 com. Dept. Commerce, 1991—. Served with USNR, 1944-46. mem. Am. Nat. Standards Inst. (dir.), Am. Soc. Assn. Execs. (v.p. 1978, dir., chmn. Key industries assn. Council 1985-86), N.Y. State Soc. Assn. Execs. (pres. 1975), U.S. C. of C. (bd. dirs.). Home: 14 Bermuda Lake Dr Palm Beach Gardens FL 33418

FALK, CONRAD ROBERT See CONRAD, ROBERT

FALK, DAVID BENJAMIN, lawyer, professional athletic representative; b. Seaford, N.Y., Aug. 21, 1950; s. Martin and Pearl F.; m. Rhonda Falk; children: Daina, Jocelyn. BA, Syracuse U., 1972; JD, George Washington U., 1975. Bar: D.C. 1975. Assoc. Dell Craighill Fentress & Benton, 1975-83; ptnr. Dell, Benton & Falk, 1983-87; former vice chmn. ProServ, Inc., 1990-92; chmn. Falk Assocs. Mgmt. Enterprises, Washington, 1992—. Mem. D.C. Bar, Bar Assn. D.C. Office: Falk Assocs Mgmt Enterprises 5335 Wisconsin Ave NW Ste 850 Washington DC 20015-2054*

FALK, DIANE M., research director, librarian, editor, writer; b. N.Y.C.; d. Leon H.E. Falk and J. Constance Moorehead (Lilienthal) Stephenson. BA in English and World Lit., Columbia U., 1973, MLS, 1979. Text editor, bibliog. enhancement N.Y. Times Info. Svc., Inc., N.Y.C., 1980—; rsch. libr., documents analyst Atlantis Energy and Minerals, N.Y.C., 1980-81; project coord. for legal dept. GAF Corp., N.Y.C., 1981-82; cataloger Exxon Edn. Found., N.Y.C., 1982; indexer, fact-checker H. W. Wilson & Co., Bronx, N.Y., 1982; bibliog. orgn. The Rockefeller Found., N.Y.C., 1983; info. specialist Harkavy Info. Svc., N.Y.C., 1983, 84, Newsworld Comm., N.Y.C., 1985; dir. rsch., head libr. The World & I Mag., Washington, 1986—; copy editor, rsch. mgr. HSA-UWC, N.Y.C. and Washington, 1974-75, 86; reference asst. Lehman Libr., Columbia U., N.Y.C., 1978; rsch. libr., documents analyst UN Ctr. for Transnational Corps., 1979. Contbr. articles to profl. jours. English and comms. prof., vol. United to Serve Am., Washington Saturday Coll., Howard U., Washington, 1992—; ofcl. tour guide Washington Times Found. and Corp.; conf. coord. Internat. Acad. Arts, Literary, Bus., Legal and Polit. Groups and Issues, 1991—; instr., conf. demonstrator for internet and other knowledge mgmt. tech. rsch. resources. Recipient Corp. award Washington Times Corp., 1997. Mem. ALA, Spl. Librs. Assn., D.C. Libr. Assn., Intellectual Freedom Interest Group (chairperson 1996-97), Rsch. and Reference Interest Group, Women's Fedn. for World Peace (sec. D.C. chpt. 1993), Internat. Leadership Seminars (staff vol. 1991—), Internat. Fedn. for World Peace (signature campaign staff 1990-91, vol. 1990—, acting sec. 1993—), The Prosperity Coun. (editor newsletter 1991). Avocations: photography, arts, travel, writing. E-mail: dmfalk@worldandimag.com, research@worldandimag.com, library@worldandimag.com. Home: 508 Columbia Rd NW Washington DC 20001-2904 Office: The World and I Mag care Libr and Rsch Dept 3600 New York Ave NE Washington DC 20002-1947

FALK, EDGAR ALAN, public relations consulting executive, author; b. Bklyn., Nov. 4, 1932; s. Ralph P. and Lillian (Freud) F. AB, NYU, 1954, postgrad., 1957-59. Pub. rels. asst. Western Electric Co., N.Y.C., 1957-59; dir. pub. rels. Ritter, Sanford, Price & Chalek, N.Y.C., 1959-60; account supr. pub. rels. Batten, Barton, Durstine & Osborn, N.Y.C., 1960-67; group dir. pub. rels. N.W. Ayer & Son, N.Y.C., 1967-73; v.p., dir. pub. rels. div. Cunningham & Walsh, Inc., N.Y.C., 1973-79; dir. communications NBA, 1979-81; pres. Ed Falk Communications, N.Y.C., 1981—; spkr. nat. convs. retailing orgns. Author: 1,001 Ideas To Create Retail Excitement, 1994; contbg. editor, writer for several retail publs. Mem. Kings County Rep. County Com., 1958-61. 1st lt. U.S. Army, 1954-56; lt. col. Res. ret. Recipient Freedoms Found. award, 1971. Mem. Pub. Rels. Soc. Am. (recipient Silver Anvil award 1970, 71, 73), The Author's Guild, Res. Officers Assn., Retired Officers Assn. Home: 301 E 78th St New York NY 10021-1322 Office: Ed Falk Communications 509 Madison Ave Ste 1400 New York NY 10022-5501

FALK, EUGENE HANNES, foreign language educator emeritus; b. Czechoslovakia, Aug. 10, 1913; came to U.S., 1946, naturalized, 1953; s. Herman and Helen (Kircova) F.; m. Ellen Wien, 1938 (div.); children—Ingrid Helen, Ronald Jonathan. Ph.D. in French, Victoria U., Manchester, Eng., 1942; M.A. (hon.), Dartmouth Coll., 1966. Asst., then asst. lectr. German U. Manchester, Eng., 1939-42; master French Alcester (Eng.) Sch., 1943-46; mem. faculty U. Bridgeport, Conn., 1946-53; prof. fgn. langs. U. Bridgeport, 1948-53, chmn. dept. fgn. langs., 1947-53; vis. prof. French U. Minn., 1953-54, mem. faculty, 1954-63, prof. French, 1957-63, chmn. dept. comparative lit., 1956-63, chmn. dept. Romance langs., 1960-63; mem. faculty Dartmouth Coll., 1963-67, chmn. dept. Romance langs., 1964-67, Edward Tuck prof. French, 1964-67; prof. French and comparative lit. U. N.C., 1967-86, chmn. comparative lit., 1972-80, Marcel Bataillon prof. comparative lit., 1973-86, emeritus, 1986—; Fulbright prof., Brazil, 1981. Author: Renunciation as a Tragic Focus, 1954, Types of Thematic Structure, 1967, The Poetics of Roman Ingarden, 1980. Fellow Fund Advancement Edn., 1952-53, Nat. Humanities Center, 1982; decorated chevalier Ordre des Palmes Académiques, France). Mem. MLA, AAUP, Am. Assn. Tchrs. French, Assn. Internat. d'Etudes Francaises, Am. Assn. Comparative Lit., Acad. des Scis., Belles-Lettres and Arts de Lyon (corr.). Home: 348 Wesley Dr Chapel Hill NC 27516-1523

FALK, HEINRICH RICHARD, theater and humanities educator; b. Frankfurt, Germany, May 3, 1939; came to U.S., 1947; s. Heinrich Wilhelm Karl and Janet Elizabeth (Prentice) F.; m. Joyce Duncan, Aug. 14, 1965. BA, Wittenberg U., 1960; PhD, U. So. Calif., 1970. Instr. mgmt. tng. div. Union Bank, L.A., 1963-64; lectr. U. So. Calif., L.A., 1964-67; instr. Chapman Coll., Orange, Calif., 1966-67; prof. Calif. State U., Northridge, 1967—; resident dir. Calif. State U., Madrid, 1986-87; vis. prof. Shanghai Theatre Acad., China, 1993. Editor: Theatre Jour. (book review sect.), 1981-83. Spl. cons. and project writer, Fine Arts and Humanities Framework com., State of Calif., 1967-72. Recipient post-doctoral scholar U. Calif., 1970-72; Younger Humanist fellow, Nat. Endowment Humanities, Madrid, Barcelona, 1972-73, Del Amo Found., Madrid, 1977-78, Asian Cultural Coun., China, 1993, Aston Magma Acad. Nat. Endowment for the Humanities, 1995; grantee Nat. Endowment for the Humanities, 1982. Mem. Internat. Soc. for Eighteenth-Century Studies, Internat. Fed.for Theatre Rsch., Am. Soc. for Theatre Rsch., Am. Soc. Eighteenth-Century Studies, Instituto Feijoo de Estudios del Siglo XVIII, Sociedad Espanola de Estudios del Siglo XVIII. Home: 2726 Cuesta Rd Santa Barbara CA 93105-3708 Office: Calif State U Dept Theatre Northridge CA 91330-8320

FALK, JAMES HARVEY, SR., lawyer; b. Tucson, Aug. 17, 1938; s. George W. and Elsie L. (Higgins) F.; m. Bobbie Jo Vest, July 8, 1960; children: James H. Jr., John Mansfield, Kathryn Colleen. BS, BA, U. Ariz., 1960, LLB, 1965, JD, 1965. Bar: Ariz. 1965, U.S. Dist. Ct. Ariz. 1968, U.S. Dist. Ct. D.C. 1971, U.S. Dist. Ct. Md., 1990, U.S. Ct. Appeals (fed., 4th, 6th and 9th cirs.) 1981, U.S. Ct. Claims 1985, U.S. Supreme Ct. 1972. Counsel El Paso (Tex.) Natural Gas Co., 1965-66, The Anaconda Co., Tucson, 1967-68; ptnr. Waterfall Economidis, Falk & Caldwell, Tucson, 1968-71; staff asst. to pres. Office of the Pres., Washington, 1971-73; assoc. dir. Domestic Coun., The White House, Washington, 1973-76; assoc. Touche Ross & Co., Washington, 1976-78; ptnr. Coffey, McGovern, Noel & Novogroski, Washington, 1978-81, Larkin, Noel & Falk, Washington, 1981-86, Thompson & Mitchell, Washington, 1986-87, McGovern, Noel & Falk, Ltd., Washington, 1987-90, Falk & Causey, Washington, 1991-92; prin. Falk Law Firm, Washington, 1993—; rep. of U.S. Pres. to state and local govts., D.C., U.S. ters., 1974-75, U.S. Govs. Conf., 1974-75, U.S. Conf. Mayors, 1974-75, U.S. Del. Peoples Republic of China, 1974; asst. city prosecutor, city atty., Tucson, 1966-67; chmn. Tucson Transit Authority, 1971-72; apptd. D.C. Bar Jud. Evaluation Com., 1992-95, 95-98. Mem. ABA. Republican. Congregationalist. Home: 9430 Cornwell Farm Rd Great Falls VA 22066-2702 Office: Falk Law Firm 2445 M St NW Washington DC 20037-1435*

FALK, JOAN FRANCES, public relations executive; b. Flushing, N.Y., Jan. 15, 1936; d. Leo Carl Hjalmar and Frances Louise (Masin) F. Cert., Parsons Sch. Design, N.Y.C., 1955; BS, NYU, 1956, MBA, 1958. Assoc. editor Fairchild's Fin. Manual, N.Y.C., 1956-58; editor, costs mgr. Western Printing & Lithographing, N.Y.C., 1958-61; dir. rsch. and costs Grolier, Inc., N.Y.C., 1961-64; budget supr. Ted Bates & Co., N.Y.C., 1965-82; bus. mgr. N.W. Ayer Pub. Rels. (Div. of N.W. Ayer, Inc.), N.Y.C., 1982-95, Diamond Info. Ctr. (Div. of N.W. Ayer, Inc.), N.Y.C., 1992-95, Diamond Info. Ctr. (disvn. of J. Walter Thompson, Inc.), N.Y.C., 1995—. Contbr. photographs to Grolier Internat., 1964, Encyclopedia Brittanica, 1970. Active Broadway Flushing Homeowners; vol. fundraiser pub. broadcast TV, WNET, N.Y.C., WLIW, L.I. Mem. Daus. of Nile (Queen of al Kahbay Temple # 22 1970, supreme temple officer 1980; mem. Pyremus Temple 1994), Order Ea. Star (matron of Bayside Pleiades #737 1962, dist. dep. grand matron 1987), Orgn. Triangles (past queen of Rising Star #69), Nat. Leadership Coun. (Capital award 1991), Bayside H.S. Alumni Assn. (past rec. sec.). Republican. Lutheran. Avocations: photography, gardening. Home: 164-16 32nd Ave Flushing NY 11358-1418 Office: J Walter Thompson Inc 466 Lexington Ave Fl 2 New York NY 10017-3176

FALK, JOHN MANSFIELD, shareholder; b. Tucson, May 6, 1964; s. James Harvey Sr. and Bobbie Jo (Vest) F.; m. Jacqueline Stacey Gray, July 22, 1968; 1 child, John Mansfield Jr. BA with honors, Washington and Lee U., 1986, JD, 1990. Bar: Va. 1991, D.C. 1993, U.S. Ct. Appeals (4th cir.) 1991, U.S. Ct. Appeals (D.C. cir.) 1993, U.S. Dist. Ct. (ea. dist.) Va. 1991, U.S. Dist. Ct. D.C. 1993, U.S. Fed. Ct. Claims 1993, U.S. Tax Ct. 1996, U.S. Supreme Ct. 1997. Asst. to pres. Support Sys. Assoc., Inc., Northport, N.Y., 1986-87; assoc. McGovern, Noel & Falk, Washington, 1990-93, Falk & Causey, Washington, 1993-94; v.p., shareholder The Falk Law Firm, plc, Washington, 1994—; Chmn. contact com., white book revisions com. Washington & Lee U., 1986, student affairs com., 1989-90, sec. Washington alumni chpt., 1992-94, v.p., 1994-95, pres., 1995-98. Bd. dirs. Congl. Award Found., Washington, 1990—, vice-chmn., 1990—. Recipient Congl. award Gold medal U.S. Congress, 1986, Significant Achievement award Sigma Delta Chi, 1990, Frank G. Gillman award Washington and Lee U., 1990, Univ. Svc. award, 1990. Mem. ABA, Fed. Cir. Bar Assn., Va. Bar Assn., D.C. Bar Assn. Episcopalian. Avocations: horse racing, hunting, fishing, tennis. Office: The Falk Law Firm plc 2445 M St NW Ste 260 Washington DC 20037-1435

FALK, JULIA S., linguist, educator; b. Englewood, N.J., Sept. 21, 1941; d. Charles Joseph and Stella Sableski; m. Thomas Heinrich, Jan. 20, 1967; 1 child, Tatiana Prentice. BS, Georgetown U., 1963; MA, U. Wash., 1964, PhD, 1968. Instr. linguistics Mich. State U., East Lansing, 1966-68, asst. prof., 1968-71, assoc. prof., 1971-78, prof., 1978—, asst. dean Coll. of Arts and Letters, 1979-81, assoc. dean Coll. Arts and Letters, 1981-86; cons. on lang. and law, lang. and gender, bias-free communication, East Lansing. Author: Linguistics and Language, 1973, 2d revised edit., 1978; contbr. articles on history of linguistics to profl. jours. Fellow Woodrow Wilson Found., 1963, NDEA Title IV, 1963-66, NSF, 1965; recipient Paul Varg Alumni award for Teaching, 1993. Mem. Linguistic Soc. Am., N.Am. Assn. History of Lang. Scis. (pres.-elect 1999). Home: 2100 Holt Rd Williamston MI 48895-9699 Office: Mich State Univ Dept Linguistics 614 Wells Hall East Lansing MI 48824-1027

FALK, LEE HARRISON, performing arts executive, cartoonist; b. St. Louis; s. Benjamin and Eleanor (Allina) F.; m. Elizabeth Moxley, Dec. 31, 1976; children: Valerie, Diane, Conley. B.A., U. Ill. Pres. Provincetown (Mass.) Acad. of Arts, 1964-72, Truro (Mass.) Center for Arts at Castle Hill, 1979-82. Creator comic strips Mandrake the Magician, 1934—, The Phantom, 1936—; author: (plays) Passionate Congressman, 1945, Winkelberg (with Ben Hecht), 1960, Eris, 1965, Home at Six, 1965, (with Alan Cranston) The Big Story, 1940, (musicals) Mandrake, 1974, (with John LaTouche) Happy Dollar, 1950; prodr., dir. summer theatres, 1940-60;. With Office War Info., Washington, 1942-43; with AUS, 1944-45. Recipient Life-Time Achievement awards: ADAMS, Stockholm, 1986, Lucca, City of Rome, 1984, Inkpot, San Diego, 1989, Haxtur award, Ovieto, Spain, 1989—, Salon award, Barcelona, Spain, 1990 Great Eastern award, N.Y.C. and Goteborg, Sweden, 1990. Mem. Nat. Cartoonist Soc. (Silver T-Square award 1986, Lee Falk Day 1994, St. Louis), Features Coun. (bd. dirs.), Dramatist Guild, Players Club (N.Y.C., bd. dirs., chmn. admissions com. 1991—, lifetime dir. 1998), Century Club (N.Y.C.), Dutch Treat Club (N.Y.C.). Address: PO Box 1207 Truro MA 02666-1207

FALK, MARSHALL ALLEN, retired university dean, physician; b. Chgo., May 23, 1929; s. Ben and Frances (Kamins) F.; m. Marilyn Joyce Levoff, June 15, 1952; children: Gayle Debra, Ben Scott. BS, Bradley U., 1950; MS, U. Ill., 1952; MD, Chgo. Med. Sch., 1956. Diplomate Am. Bd. Psychiatry. Intern Cook County Hosp., Chgo., 1956-57; resident Mt. Sinai Hosp., Chgo., 1964-67; gen. practice medicine Chgo., 1959-64; resident in psychiatry, faculty dept. psychiatry Chgo. Med. Sch., 1964-67, prof., acting chmn. dept. psychiatry, 1973-74, dean, 1974-92, v.p. med. affairs, 1981-82, exec. v.p., 1982-91, dean emeritus, emeritus prof. psychiatry, 1991—; med. dir. London Meml. Hosp., 1971-74; mem. cons. com. to commr. health City of Chgo., 1972-82; mem. Ill. Gov.'s Commn. to Revise Mental Health Code, 1973-77, Chgo. Northside Commn. on Health Planning, 1970-74, Ill. Hosp. Licensing Bd., 1981-91. Contbr. articles to profl. jours. Trustee John F. Kennedy Hosp., Atlanta, 1993-95, cons., 1991-92; trustee Quantum Found. for Health,

Palm Beach, Fla., 1995—; vice chmn. grants com. Quantum Found., 1997—; trustee Finch U./Chgo. Med. Sch., 1998—, chmn. bd. trustees, 1998—. Capt. AUS, 1957-59. Recipient Bd. Trustees award for rsch. Chgo. Med. Sch., 1963, Disting. Alumni award Chgo. Med. Sch., 1976, Alumnus of Yr. award Bradley U., 1990. Fellow Am. Psychiat. Assn., Am. Coll. Psychiatrists; mem. Ill. Coun. Deans (pres. 1981-83), Coun. Free Standing Med. Sch. Deans (bd. dirs. 1984-92, pres. 1989-91), Sigma Xi, Alpha Omega Alpha. *Consistent effort, with an attempt to make decisions based on situations as they occur— with as little prejudgment as possible.*

FALK, MARVIN WILLIAM, historian, bibliographer; b. Wichita, Kans., Jan. 29, 1943; s. Melvin Leroy and Martha Louise (Crew) F.; m. Helen Amanda Widman, June 7, 1969 (div. May 1985); children: Karl, Adelia, Stuart; m. Sylvie Denise Savage, June 21, 1998. BA, U. Minn., 1965; MA, U. Mass., 1966; PhD, U. Iowa, 1976. Arctic bibliographer U. Alaska, Fairbanks, 1975-81, curator rare books, 1981—. Author: Alaska, 1995, (series) Rasmuson Translation Series, 10 vols., 1985—; compiler: Alaskan Maps, 1983. Pres. Fairbanks Sch. Bd., 1985-86. Mem. Alaska Hist. Soc. (pres. 1978-80). Avocation: photography. Home: 865 Gold Pan Rd Fairbanks AK 99712-2041 Office: U Alaska Fairbanks PO Box 756808 Fairbanks AK 99775-6808

FALK, NOEL WESLEY, biology educator, radio and television program host, horticultural consultant; b. Mechanicsburg, Pa., Feb. 1, 1945; s. Leonard A. and Harriet G. (Schuster) F.; children—Deana Lynne, Erin Dawn. B.A., Messiah Coll., 1966; M.Ed., Shippensburg U., 1972; D.Ed., Pa. State U., 1975. Tchr., coach Twillingate Central High Sch., Nfld., Can., 1966-68; prof. natural history, 1998—, dir. Oakes Mus. Natural History, Messiah Coll., Grantham, Pa., 1969-75, asst. prof., 1975-80, assoc. prof. biology, 1980-89, prof. biology, 1989-97, prof. natural history, 1997—, chmn. dept. natural sci., 1980-98; founder, pres. The Plant Doctor Inc., Harrisburg, Pa., 1985—, host The Plant Doctor, WHP-Radio, Harrisburg, 1982—, WHP-TV, Harrisburg, 1989-97. Author: The Plant Doctor's Prescription for a Healthy Garden, 1991; garden writer Ctrl. Pa. Life mag., 1998—; contbr. articles to profl. jours. Bd. dirs. Pa. Wildlife Fedn.; active Hershey Evang. Free Ch. Mem. Am. Ornithologists Union, Am. Soc. Hort. Sci., Garden Writers Assn. Am., Wildlife Soc., Am. Assn. Hort. Scis., Garden Winters Assn Am., Am. Assn. Museums, Assn. Sci. Mus. Dirs., Sigma Xi. Republican. Avocations: bird watching, deer hunting, fishing, gardening, collecting fossils. Home: 1099 Nyes Rd Harrisburg PA 17111-4727 Office: Messiah Coll Grantham PA 17027

FALK, PATRICIA, English language educator; b. N.Y.C., Sept. 16, 1950; d. Moses M. Falk and Lillian Bellin; 1 child, Karen Anna. BA, MA, CUNY, 1976. Mentor Empire State Coll., Old Westbury, N.Y., 1982—; assoc. prof. Nassau C.C., Garden City, N.Y., 1985—; pres., cons. Metasource, Inc., Amityville, N.Y., 1985-99. Author: (book) In the Shape of a Woman, 1995 (Faculty Disting. Achievement award 1996); editor: (book) Sightings: Poems on Discovery, 1999. Mem. L.I. Poetry Collective, 1992-99. Avocations: piano, swimming, yoga, art. Office: Nassau C C 1 Education Dr Garden City NY 11530

FALK, PETER, actor; b. N.Y.C., Sept. 16, 1927; s. Michael and Madeline (Hauser) F.; m. Alyce Mayo, Apr. 17, 1960 (div. 1976); children: Jackie, Catherine; m. Shera Danese, Dec. 1977. B.A., New Sch. Social Research, 1951; M.P.A., Maxwell Sch., Syracuse U., 1953; pupil of, Eva Le Gallienne, 1955, Sanford Meisner, 1957. Theatrical stage appearances include Don Juan, 1956, The Changeling, 1956, The Iceman Cometh, 1956, St. Joan, 1956, Diary of a Scoundrel, 1956, The Lady's Not for Burning, 1957, Purple Dust, 1957, Bonds of Interest, 1956, Comic Strip, 1958, The Passion of Josef D, 1964, The Prisoner of Second Avenue, Light Up the Sky, Glengarry Glen Ross (tour); motion picture appearances include Murder, Inc, 1960, Pocketful of Miracles, 1961, The Balcony, 1962, It's a Mad, Mad, Mad, Mad World, 1963, Italiano Bravo-Gente, 1963, Robin and the 7 Hoods, 1964, The Great Race, 1965, Luv, 1967, Anzio, 1968, Castle Keep, 1969, Machine Gun McCann, 1970, Husbands, 1970, A Woman Under the Influence, 1976, Murder by Death, 1976, Mikey and Nicky, The Brink's Job, 1978, The Cheap Detective, 1978, The In-Laws, 1979, All the Marbles, 1981, Big Trouble, 1986, The Princess Bride, 1987, Vibes, 1988, Wings of Desire, 1988, Cookie, 1989, In the Spirit, Tune in Tomorrow, 1990, The Player, 1992, Faraway, So Close!, 1993, Roommates, 1995, Enemies of Laughter, 1999; numerous TV appearances, 1960— including title role Columbo in NBC Mystery Theater, 1971-78 (Emmy award for best performance 1972), Columbo in ABC Saturday Mystery Movie, 1988, Phoenix and Griffin, Pronto, 1997, Frank Capra's American Dream, 1997, Columbo: A Trace of Murder, 1997, others; TV series Columbo, 1989-90 (Emmy award 1990), also dir. numerous episodes; TV guest appearances include The Twilight Zone, 1959, The Dick Powell Show, 1961, The Larry Sanders Show, others. Recipient Emmy award for TV prodn. The Price of Tomatoes.

FALK, ROBERT BARCLAY, JR., anesthesiologist, educator; b. Lancaster, Pa., July 1, 1945; s. Robert Barclay and Miriam (Neff) F.; m. Carol Anne Gundel, May 30, 1970; 1 child, Juliana Gundel. BA, Franklin and Marshall Coll., 1967; MD, Jefferson Med. Coll., 1971. Diplomate Am. Bd. Anesthesiology. Intern Conemaugh Valley Meml. Hosp., Johnstown, Pa., 1971-72; resident in anesthesiology M.H. Hershey Med. Sch. Hosp., 1974-77; ptnr. Anesthesia Assocs., Lancaster, 1977—, sr. v.p., 1993-94, pres., 1994—; staff anesthesiologist Lancaster Gen. Hosp., 1977—, vice chmn. dept. anesthesiology, 1984-85, chmn., 1985-92; clin. asst. prof. dept. anesthesiology Hershey (Pa.) Med. Sch., 1977—. Contbr. articles to profl. jours. Participant alumni phonathon Franklin and Marshall Coll., 1978-81, vice chmn., 1981, chmn., 1983, mem. alumni admissions com., 1977-79, chmn., 1980-87, chmn. 20th reunion gift com.; mem. Lancaster Regional Alumni Coun., 19987-91, trustee athletic com., 1988-96, 98; mem. Lancaster Area Arts Coun., 1989-91; Sunday sch. tchr. Trinity Luth. Ch., Lancaster, 1977-80; bd. dirs. Lancaster Summer Arts Festival, 1981—, v.p., 1982-84, pres., 1985-90; bd. dirs. Pa. Acad. Music, 1991—, vice-chmn., 1991-92, chmn., 1993—. Lt. M.C., USNR, 1972-74. Mem. Am. Soc. Anesthesiologists, Pa. Soc. Anesthesiologists, Intenat. Anesthesia Rsch. Soc., Pa. Med. Soc., Lancaster Country Club, Hamilton Club (v.p. 1995-97, pres. 1997—), Masons, Shriners, Chaine des Rotisseurs. Republican. Home: 1025 Marietta Ave Lancaster PA 17603-3106 Office: Anesthesia Assocs 133 E Frederick St Lancaster PA 17602-2222

FALK, STEVEN B., newspaper publishing executive. Pres., CEO San Francisco Newspaper Agy. Office: San Francisco Newspaper Agy 925 Mission St San Francisco CA 94103-2905*

FALK, WILLIAM JAMES, lawyer; b. Kew Gardens, N.Y., Aug. 15, 1952; s. Sam and Bertha (Schwartzwald) F.; m. Laurie Jean Dombrowski, June 24, 1973; children: Douglas Charles, Andrew Stephen, Edward Allaire. BS, Ill. Inst. Tech., 1973; JD cum laude, Suffolk U., 1977; LLM in Taxation, Washington U., St. Louis, 1982. Bar: Mass. 1977, Mo. 1981. Trial atty. IRS Office of Dist. Counsel, St. Louis, 1977-81; assoc. Thompson & Mitchell, St. Louis, 1982-83, ptnr., 1984-96; ptnr. Thompson Coburn, St. Louis, 1996—. Contbg. author: Missouri Taxation Law and Practice, 1987; contbr. articles to legal jours. Mem. ABA, Mo. Bar Assn., Bar Assn. Met. St. Louis (chmn. taxation sect. 1992-93, mem. exec. com. 1992-93). Avocations: camping, music. Office: Thompson Coburn 1 Mercantile Ctr Ste 3300 Saint Louis MO 63101-1643

FALKENBERG, WILLIAM STEVENS, architect, contractor; b. Kansas City, Mo., July 21, 1927; s. John Joseph and Maraba Elizabeth (Stevens) F.; m. Janis Patton Hubner, Apr. 13, 1951; children: Ruth Elizabeth, Christopher Joseph, Charles Stevens. BS in Archtl. Engring., U. Colo., 1949. Pres. Falkenberg Constrn. Co., Denver, 1951-71, 74-84, devel. cons., 1984-94; broker Hogan & Stevenson Realty, Denver, 1971-74. Chmn. constrn. Archdiocesan Housing Com., Inc., pres. 1997-98; chmn. restoration 9th Street Hist. Park; chmn. bldg. comm. Four Mile House Hist. Park; chmn. Housing Trust Coun., Denver, 1986-90; chmn. Rocky Mountain Better Bus. Bur., 1965-67; pres. Denver Friends Folk Music, 1966. Lt. (j.g.) USNR, 1945-51. Mem. AIA (bd. dirs. Denver chpt. 1978-81, treas. 1981), Home Builder Assn. Met. Denver, Colo. Hist. Soc. Found. (trustee, sec. 1987-97), Serra Internat. (pres. 1971, dist. gov. 1973), Nat. Assn. Atomic Vets., Colo. Archeol. Soc., Denver Athletic Club, Equestrian Order of Holy Sepulchre, Cactus Club (pres. 1995-98). Home and Office: 430 Marion St Denver CO 80218-3930

FALKENSTEIN, KARIN EDITH, elementary school principal; b. Michigan City, Ind., Feb. 12, 1950; d. Martin Victor and Helen Marion (Hedberg) Sandstrom; m. Charles William Falkenstein Jr., July 13, 1985; 1 stepchild, Amanda Ann. BA in Elem. Edn., Spl. Edn., Mich. State U., 1972, MA in Reading Instrn., 1975. Spl. edn. tchr. Hesperia (Mich.) Pub. Schs., 1972-73; spl. edn. tchr. Buchanan (Mich.) Community Schs., 1973-79, elem. prin. Moccasin Sch., sch. farm coord., 1979-80; elem. prin. Ottawa Sch., Buchanan (Mich.) Community Schs., 1980—; dist. spl. edn. supr., 1980—; gifted and talented coord. Ottawa Sch., Buchanan (Mich.) Community Schs., 1980—, elem. coord., k-12 testing coord. and k-5 curriculum dir., 1993—; instr. Ind. U., South Bend, 1981—; presenter spl. edn. workshops. Mem. Big Bros./Big Sisters of Niles/Buchanan, Inc., 1982-97, v.p., 1985, pres., 1986-87; mem. Mich. State U. Coll. Edn. Alumni Bd., 1982-94, v.p. 1987, pres., 1988; Sun. sch. tchr. First United Meth. Ch., 1982—, bd. trustees, 1986-91, Christian Edn. chairperson, 1988-90; mem. Buchanan Fine Arts Coun., 1987—, treas., 1988-93, sec. 1996-99, pres. 1999—; mem. Hospice Bereavement Care, 1987—; mem. Redbud Ara Ministries LOVE, Inc., 1985-89, pres., 1988-89; bd. dirs. Berrien Coun. for Children, 1987—, mem. edn. com., 1984—; bd. dirs. Four Flags Samaritan Ctr., 1985—, Mich. Gateway Cmty. Found., Buchanan; mem. PTA, 1988—. Recipient Nat. Disting. Prin.'s award, 1989, Mich. Legis. recognition, 1989, Pres.'s award Mich. State U. Coll. Edn. Alumni Assn., 1987, Mich. State U. Nat. Alumni Assn. Svc. award 1995, Golden Nugget award for spl. edn., 1983, Milken Found. Family Educator award, 1993; named Mich. Outstanding Practicing Prin., 1988, Region 5 Prin. award, 1989. Mem. Mich. Elem. and Mid. Sch. Prins. Assn. (membership chair 1984-86, profl. devel. chairperson 1983-84, pres. 1987-88), ASCD, CEC, Tri-County Coun. of Women in Ednl. Adminstrn. (profl. devel. chair 1983-84, pres. 1985-87, historian 1987-92), Spl. Edn. Dirs. and Coords. for Berrien County, Internat. Reading Assn., Mich. Reading Assn., Mich. Alliance for Gifted Edn., Mich. Assn. Learning Disabilities Educators, Mich. State U. Alumni Assn. (nat. bd. v.p. 1992-93, treas. 1991-92, pres. 1993-94, Svc. award 1995), Phi Delta Kappa. Office: Buchanan Community Schs 109 Ottawa St Buchanan MI 49107-1136

FALKER, JOHN RICHARD, investment advisor; b. Detroit, July 15, 1940; s. John Jacob and Helen Katherine (Loeffler) F.; m. Mary Eileen Jacobsen, Nov. 10, 1964; children: Mary Anne, John R. Jr., Peter J. B.A. in English, U. Mich., 1962; M.B.A. in Fin., U. Detroit, 1980. With Chrysler Corp., Detroit, 1964-77; v.p., treas. Chrysler Fin. Corp., 1974-77; treas. Internat. Multifoods Corp., Mpls., 1977-87; founder, co-owner Swenson/Falker Assocs. Inc., Mpls., 1987-95; owner FalkerInvestments, Mpls., 1997—; adj. prof. fin. U. St. Thomas, 1987—. Served to lt. (j.g.) USNR, 1962-64. Mem. Am. Radio Relay League (life). Republican. Roman Catholic.

FALKIE, THOMAS VICTOR, mining engineer, natural resources company executive; b. Mount Carmel, Pa., Sept. 5, 1934; s. Victor J. and Aldona M. Falkie; m. Jean C. Broscius, Nov. 27, 1957; children: Ann, Thomas, Lawrence, Michael, Christine. BS in Mining Engring., Pa. State U., 1956, MS in Mining Engring., 1958, PhD in Mining Engring., 1961. Fellow, research asst. Pa. State U., University Park, 1956-61; various staff and managerial positions Internat. Minerals and Chem. Corp., Skokie, Ill., 1961-69, Bartow, Fla., 1961-69; prof., head mineral engring. dept. Pa. State U., 1969-73; dir. U.S. Bur. Mines Dept. Interior, Washington, 1974-77; pres. Berwind Natural Resources Corp., Phila., 1977; bd. dirs. Berwind Natural Resources Corp.; bd. dirs. Cyprus-Amax Minerals Co.; adj. prof. indsl. engring. U. Fla./U. So. Fla., 1966; cons. UN, 1971-73; chmn. coal task force project ind. study U.S. Govt., 1974; chmn. interagy. task force Fed. Coun. on Sci. and Tech., 1975-76; nat. arbitrator of joint industry health and safety com. of United Mine Workers and Bituminous Coal Operators Assn., 1973; mem. bd. mineral and energy resources NRC, 1982-88; mem. adv. com. mining and mineral resources rsch. Dept. Interior, 1988-94. Contbr. articles to profl. jours. Mem. AIME (hon.), Soc. Mining Engrs. of AIME (disting. mem., bd. dirs. 1971-75, 84-87, v.p. 1977-79, chmn. Phila. sect. 1980-81, pres. 1988, Erskine Ramsay medal 1991), Pa. Coal Assn. (bd. dirs. 1980-90), Nat. Mining Assn. (bd. dirs. 1994—), Am. Coal Found. (chmn. 1993—), Nat. Acad. Engring. (councillor 1994—), Mining and Metall. Soc. Am. (Disting. Alumnus award Penn State U. Mineral Engring. Dept. 1995), Sigma Gamma Epsilon, Tau Beta Pi, Union League Club (Phila.). Republican. Roman Catholic. Home: 347 Echo Valley Ln Newtown Square PA 19073-1619 Office: Berwind Natural Resources Corp 3000 Centre Sq W 1500 Market St Philadelphia PA 19102-2100

FALKINGHAM, DONALD HERBERT, oil company executive; b. Lexington, Ill., Dec. 13, 1918; s. William Bishop and Violet (Ashabran) F.; m. Mary Margaret Chalmers, Aug. 23, 1947 (dec. Nov. 1993); children: Deanna Beth Falkingham Worst, Janis Kay Falkingham Fenwick; m. Joella Hall, May 23, 1998. BS, Mo. Sch. Mines, 1941; Profl. Engr., U. Mo., Rolla, 1973. Registered profl. engr., land surveyor, Wyo. Field engr. Amoco, Rangely, Colo., 1951-53; dist. engr. Amoco Producing Co., Cody, Wyo., 1953-59; div. engr. Amoco Producing Co., Casper, Wyo., 1959-61; dist. supt. Amoco Producing Co., New Orleans, 1961-68; pres. Amoco UK Exploration Co., London, 1968-70, Amoco Iran Oil Co., Tehran, 1970-71; co-chmn. bd. dirs. Pan Am. Iran Oil Co., Teheran, 1970-71; gen. mgr. producing dept. Amoco Internat. Oil Co., Chgo., 1972-77; pres. Amoco Drilling Svcs., Chgo., 1975-77, Oceanwide Constrn. Co., St. Helier, Isle of Jersey, 1977-78; chmn. bd. World Maritime, Bermuda, 1977-78; ptnr., co-owner Falcar Energy Co., Houston, 1978—; mng. dir. hydrocarbon devel. McDermott Inc., Bucharest, Romania, 1994-95; mng. dir. EuroMAC, Sofia, Bulgaria, 1994-95; dist. chmn. Am. Petroleum Inst., 1961; com. mem. Am Bur. Shipping, Bldg. and Classing Offshore Drilling Units, N.Y.C., 1966-68; chmn. exploration and production forum, Oil Industry Internat., London, 1974-77. Pres. bd. trustees, Presbyterian Ch., Cody. Pilot U.S. Army, 1942-45, ETO, maj. ret. Decorated D.F.C., Air medal with oak leaf cluster. Mem. Soc. Petroleum Engrs. (dist. chmn. 1967), Petroleum Club (pres. Casper chpt.), Cody Country Club (pres.), Masons, Shriners. Republican. Avocation: travel. Home: 11515 Barnett Valley Rd Sebastopol CA 95472-9554 Office: Falcar Energy Co PO Box 1323 Montgomery TX 77356-1323

FALKNER, FRANK TARDREW, physician, educator; b. Hale, Eng., Oct. 27, 1918; came to U.S., 1956, naturalized, 1963; s. Ernest and Ethel (Letten) F.; m. June Dixon, Jan. 1948; 2 children. M.D., Cambridge U., 1945. Diplomate: Am. Bd. Clin. Nutrition. Intern London Hosp., 1945; resident Guys Hosp., London, 1947-48, Children's Hosp., Cin., 1948-50; practice medicine specializing in pediatrics U.K. and Paris, 1948-56, Louisville, 1956-70, Yellow Springs, Ohio, 1971-79; chmn. dept. pediatrics U. Louisville, 1963-70; dir. Fels Research Inst., Yellow Springs, 1971-79; Fels prof. pediatrics, prof. obstetrics and gynecology U. Cin. Coll. Medicine, 1971-79; prof. child and family health U. Mich., 1979-81; prof. and chmn. maternal and child health U. Calif., Berkeley, 1981-89; prof. pediatrics U. Calif., San Francisco, 1981-89; prof. emeritus U. Calif., Berkeley, 1989—; San Francisco, 1989—. Editor-in-chief: International Child Health; syndicated columnist on children's and young people's health; contbr. articles to profl. jours. Fellow Am. Acad. Pediatrics, Royal Coll. Physicians, Royal Coll. Pediat. and Child Health; mem. NAS (sr. mem. Inst. Medicine), Am. Pediatric Soc., Société Française de Pédiatrie. Home: 145 Forest Ln Berkeley CA 94708-1519 Office: U Calif Sch Pub Health Maternal and Child Health Berkeley CA 94720

FALKNER, JAMES GEORGE, foundation executive; b. Spokane, Wash., Dec. 24, 1952; s. Albert Andrew and Amanda Rosalia (Reisinger) F.; m. Joleen Rae Ann Brown, June 22, 1974; children: James Jr., Jayson, Jerin, Jarret. BS in Acctg., U. Wash., 1975. CPA, Wash. CPA LeMaster & Daniels, Spokane, 1975-80; treas. Dominican Sisters Spokane, 1980-95; pres. Dominican Outreach Found., Spokane, 1995—; bd. dirs. Dominican Network, Spokane, 1989-98, Dominican Health Svcs., 1989-98, Providence Svcs., Spokane, 1993—, Providence Svcs. Ea. Wash., 1998—; mem. bishop's fin. coun. Diocese of Spokane, 1990-96; mem. investment adv. com. Gonzaga Prep. H.S., 1995—, Spokane Cath. Investment Trust, 1997—, Sinsinawa Dominican Sisters, 1995—. Bd. dirs. sch. bd. St. Mary's Ch., Veradale, Wash., 1986-89, 90, sch. found., 1987—; with acctg. dept. adv. com. Spokane Falls Community Coll., 1989—. Mem. Healthcare Fin. Mgmt. Assn. (bd. dirs. 1982-85), AICPA, Wash. State Soc. CPAs (Spokane Wash. bd. dirs.), Nat. Notary Assn. Avocations: coaching baseball, golf, soccer, carpentry. Office: Dominican Outreach Found 3102 W Fort George Wright Dr Spokane WA 99224-5203

FALKNER, JULIETTE, federal agency administrator; b. Chgo., 1962. BA magna cum laude, Albion Coll., 1985; JD, Washington & Lee U., 1990. Jud. law clk. U.S. Dist. Ct., Washington, Ariz., 1990-93; spl. asst. Dept. of Interior, Washington, 1993-94, dir. office regulatory affairs, 1994-95, dir. office exec. sec., 1995—. Fulbright-Hays scholar U. Saar, Germany, 1985. Office: Dept of Interior 1849 C St NW Washington DC 20240-0002

FALKNER, NOREEN MARGARET, English language educator; b. Dunkirk, N.Y., Apr. 21, 1945; d. Edward John and Marie Catherine (Fern) Roman; m. William Jackson III, Aug. 2, 1974; 1 child, Jessica Hayes. BS in English, Art and Edn., U. Dayton, 1966; MS in English and Drama Edn., SUC, Buffalo, 1971. Cert. tchr. N.Y. 7th and 8th grade lang. arts tchr. Clinton Jr. H.S., Buffalo, 1967; 7th grade English tchr. Amsdell Heights Jr. H.S., Hamburg, N.Y., 1967-68; 10th, 11th, 12th grade English tchr. Frontier Ctrl. H.S., Hamburg, 1968—, English dept. chairperson, 1974-96; prom advisor Frontier Ctrl. H.S., 1968-72, cheerleading advisor, 1969-74, dist. devel. coun., 1983-85, dist. lang. arts com. chairperson, 1981-83, PTSA, 1968—, nat. honor soc. selection com., 1980-96, play dir. and advisor, 1968-74; English dept. chairpersons of Erie County, Buffalo, 1986-96. Co-editor: (cookbook) Great Lake Effects: Buffalo Beyond Winter and Wings, 1997; contbr. articles to The Central Parker. Vol. Jr. League of Buffalo, 1981—; mem. Nat. Coun. of English Tchrs., 1986—, Nardin Parent Coun., Buffalo, 1986—. Mem. Youngstown Yacht Club, Delta Kappa Gamma (Beta chpt.). Democrat. Roman Catholic. Avocations: walking, reading, writing, decorating, knitting. Home: 349 Woodbridge Ave Buffalo NY 14214-1516 Office: Frontier Ctrl High Sch S4432 Bay View Rd Hamburg NY 14075-1335

FALKNER, ROBERT FRANK, lawyer; b. Chgo., Oct. 19, 1940; m. Faith Christian, Oct. 22, 1961; children: Juliette A., Robert F. Jr. BA with honors, Beloit (Wis.) Coll., 1961; JD, Northwestern U., 1965. Labor atty. Clark Equipment Co., 1966-71; labor counsel UOP, 1971-75; corp. dir. personnel rels. Baxter Travenol, Deerfield, Ill., 1975-79; assoc. staff atty. Motorola Inc., Schaumburg, Ill., 1979-80, gen. atty., 1980-84, v.p., gen. atty., 1984-88, corp. v.p., asst. gen. counsel, 1988-93, v.p. asst. gen. counsel, 1993—; bd. advisors to Employment Law Counselor; bd. dirs. Ill. Civil Justice League, Mex.-Am. Legal Defense and Ednl. Fund, Sundial Corp.

FALKOF, MELVIN MILTON, food products executive; b. Boston, June 2, 1919; s. Philip and Esther (Lavine) F.; m. Lucille Beatrice Weintraub, Feb. 6, 1944; children: Ellen Beth Feinberg, Bonnie Dee Blodgett, Moshe Richard, Bradley Benjamin. BS, MIT, 1939; MS, U. Minn., 1941. V.p. Darling Distbg. Corp., N.Y.C., 1946-58; mgr. mdse. Cortland Furniture Mfg. Co., Inc., N.Y.C., 1958-59; dir. Topco Assocs., Inc., Skokie, Ill., 1959-85; vol. exec. Internat. Exec. Svc. Corps, Stamford, Conn., 1987, 88, 95; dir. regional Cairo, Egypt Internat. Exec. Svc. Corps, Stamford, 1989, 90; counselor Svc. Corps Ret. Execs., Chgo., 1990—; chmn. Svc. Corps Ret. Execs., Chgo., 1993-95. Maj. U.S. Army, 1941-46. Mem. MIT Alumni Assn., Boston Latin Sch. Alumni Assn., Phi Lambda Upsilon, Gamma Alpha. Jewish. Avocations: tennis, travel. Home: 1482 Concorde Cir Highland Park IL 60035-3928 Office: Svc Corps Retired Execs 500 W Madison St Chicago IL 60661-2511

FALKOW, STANLEY, microbiologist, educator; b. Albany, N.Y., Jan. 24, 1934; s. Jacob and Mollie (Gingold) F.; children from previous marriage: Lynn Beth, Jill Stuart; m. Lucy Stuart Tompkins, Dec. 3, 1983. BS in Bacteriology cum laude, U. Maine, 1955, DSc (hon), 1979; MS in Biology, Brown U., 1960, PhD, 1961; MD (hon.), U. Umea, Sweden, 1989. Asst. chief dept. bacterial immunity Walter Reed Army Inst. Rsch., Washington, 1963-66; prof. microbiology Med. Sch. Georgetown U., 1966-72; prof. microbiology and medicine U. Wash., Seattle, 1972-81; prof., chmn. dept. med. microbiology Stanford (Calif.) U., 1981-85, prof. microbiology, immunology & medicine, 1981—; Karl H. Beyer vis. prof. U. Wis., 1978-79; Sommer lectr. U. Oreg. Sch. Medicine, 1979, Kinyoun lectr. NIH, 1980; Rubbro orator Australian Soc. Microbiology, 1981; Stanhope Bayne-Jones lectr. Johns Hopkins U., 1982; mem. Recombinant DNA Molecule Com, task force on antibiotics in animal feeds FDA, microbiology test com. Nat. Bd. Med. Examiners. Author: Infectious Multiple Drug Resistance, 1975; editor: Jour. Infection and Immunity, Jour. Infectious Agents and Diseases. Recipient Ehrlich prize, 1981, Becton-Dickinson award in Clin. Microbiology, ASM, 1986, Altemeier medal Surg. Infectious Diseases Soc., 1990; Bristol-Myers Squibb unrestricted infectious disease grantee. Fellow Am. Acad. Microbiology; mem. AAAS, Infectious Disease Soc. Am. (Squibb award 1979), Am. Soc. Microbiology, Genetics Soc. Am., Nat. Acad. Sci., Sigma Xi. E-mail: falkow.edu.com. Office: Stanford U Dept Med Microbiology Stanford CA 94305*

FALKOWSKI, PATRICIA ANN, investment consultant, financial analyst; b. New Brunswick, N.J., Apr. 12, 1947; d. George Francis and Letha Mae Crawford; m. Walter Stanley Falkowski, June 1968; children: Karen Elizabeth, Andrew Walter. BS summa cum laude, Rider Coll., 1969; MBA in Fin., U. Chgo., 1980. Adminstrv. asst. Fed. Home Loan Bank Bd., Washington, 1970-72; analyst corp. fin. SEC, Washington, 1972-73; analyst, sr. analyst Econ. Devel. Adminstrn., Phila., 1974-76; regional analyst FDIC, Chgo., 1977-79; investment analyst Kemper Fin. Cos., Chgo., 1979-81, Harris Trust & Savs., Chgo., 1981-83, Kemper Fin. Corp., Chgo., 1983-88; pvt. practice Winnetka, Ill., 1988-89; chief investment officer, exec. v.p. Fiduciary Mgmt. Assocs., Chgo., 1991-92; pres. Fiduciary Mgmt. Assocs., 1993-98; mng. dir. Chgo. Trust Co., 1998—. Com. chair St. Francis Hosp. Aux., Evanston, Ill., 1989; bd. dirs. Ct. Theater U. Chgo., 1997—. Mem. Fin. Stock Assn. Chgo. (pres. 1988-89), Chgo. Investment Analysts Soc. (com. mem. 1979-89, bd. dirs. 1997—), U. Chgo. Women's Bus. Group (com. co-chmn.). Republican. Roman Catholic. Avocations: jogging, horseback riding, attending plays and concerts. Office: Chgo Trust Co 171 N Clark St Fl 9 Chicago IL 60601-3203

FALL, JOHN ROBERT, management and information technology consultant; b. Rockford, Ill., Sept. 21, 1943; s. Robert Duane and Ruth (Hart) F.; m. Maria Pilar McClintock, Sept. 22, 1990; children: Brian Alexander, Amado Magtoto, Roehl Magtoto. BA, San Diego State U., 1965. Systems engr. IBM, San Diego, 1965-70; v.p. Computer Intelligence Corp., San Diego, 1970-71; dir. corp. devel. Userware Internat., Escondido, Calif., 1972-73; pres. Fall Cons Internat., Inc., San Clemente, Calif., 1974—. Author: Living With a Fast Idiot, 1980. Phone: 632 631-9021. Office: 302 N El Camino Real Ste 200 San Clemente CA 92672-4778 also: Greenhills Comml Ctr, 101-A Landmark Villa I, Kaimito St Valle Verde II, Metro Manila Philippines

FALLACI, ORIANA, writer, journalist; b. Florence, Italy, June 29, 1930; d. Edoardo and Tosca (Cantini) F. Grad., Liceo Classico Galileo Galilei, Italy; student, U. Florence Faculty Medicine, 1946-48; Litt.D. (hon.), Columbia Coll., Chgo., 1977. Editor, spl. corr. Europeo Mag., Milan, Italy, 1958-77; collaborator with major publs. throughout world, including Look mag., 1977-96, Life mag., 1977-96, The Washington Post, 1977-96, N.Y. Times, 1977-96, London Times, 1977-96; writer, 1996—; dir. Rizzoli Pubs. Corp. Author: (novels) Penelope alla guerra, 1962 (pub. as Penelope at War, 1966), Lettera a un bambino mai nato, 1975 (pub. as Letter to a Child Never Born, 1976), Un uomo: romanzo, 1979 (pub. as A Man, 1980; Viareggio prize), In'shallah, 1990 (Hemingway prize 1991, Super Bancarella prize 1991); (nonfiction) I sette peccati di Hollywood, 1958, Il sesso inutile, 1961 (pub. as The Useless sex, 1964), Gli antipatici, 1963 (pub. as The Egoists, 1965), Se il sole muore, 1965 (pub. as If The Sun Dies, 1967), Niente e cosi sia, 1969 (pub. as Nothing, and So Be It, 1972; Bancarella prize 1971), Quel giorno sulla Luna, 1970, Intervista con la Storia, 1974 (pub. as Interview with History, 1976); audio: Oriana Fallaci reads Letter to a Child Never Born, 1993. Recipient St. Vincent award for journalism, 1971, 73. Office: Rizzoli 31 W 57th St Fl 4 New York NY 10019-3496 also: RCS Rizzoli Libri, Via Mecenate 91, 20138 Milan Italy*

FALLAVOLLITA, JAMES A., cardiologist, educator, researcher; b. May 5, 1962. BS in Chemistry and Biology, U. Wash., 1983, MD, 1987. Diplomate Am. Bd. Internal Medicine. Intern and resident internal medicine Strong Meml. Hosp./ U. Rochester, N.Y., 1987-90; rsch./clin. fellow cardiology

SUNY, Buffalo, 1991-94; attending physician/clin. asst., instr. emergency medicine Erie County Med. Ctr., Buffalo, 1990-93; asst. prof. medicine SUNY/ Buffalo Vets. Affairs Med. Ctr., 1994—; chief noninvasive sect. divsn. cardiology Buffalo Vets. Affairs Med. Ctr., 1994—; presenter in field. Manuscript reviewer Jour. Am. Coll. Cardiology, Am. Review Respiratory Disease, Am. Jour. Cardiac Imaging; contbr. articles to profl. jours. John C. Sable Meml. Heart Fund grantee, 1993; summer rsch. fellow Am. Cancer Soc., 1986. Mem. ACP, Am. Heart Assn. (coun. circulation, Clinician Scientist award 1996), Am. Coll. Cardiology (assoc., Young Investigator award 1994). Office: U Buffalo Divsn Cardiology Biomed Rsch Bldg Rm 345 3435 Main St Buffalo NY 14214-3001*

FALLDING, HAROLD JOSEPH, sociology educator; b. Cessnock, New South Wales, Australia, May 3, 1923; s. Frederick and Alice Bessie (Chopping) F.; m. Margaret Hurlstone Hardy, Dec. 18, 1954; children: Marion, Ruth, Helen. Cert. Libr. Sch., Pub. Libr. New South Wales, 1941; BSc, U. Sydney, Australia, 1950, BA, 1951, diploma of edn., 1952, MA with honors, 1955; PhD, Australian Nat. U., 1957. Tchr. h.s. English and history New South Wales Dept. Edn., 1952-53; sr. rsch. fellow in sociology, dept. agrl. econs. U. Sydney, 1956-58; sr. lectr. sociology U. New South Wales, 1959-62; vis. assoc. prof. Grad. Sch., Rutgers U., N.J., 1963-65; prof. U. Waterloo, Ont., Can., 1965-88, disting. prof. emeritus, 1989—. Author: The Sociological Task, 1968, The Sociology of Religion: An Explanation of the Unity and Diversity in Religion, 1974, Drinking, Community and Civilization. The Account of a New Jersey Interview Study, 1974, The Social Process Revisited, 1990; poems Word of the Tangling Fire, 1969, Collected Poetry, 1997. Mem. Clare Hall, U. Cambridge. Fellow Royal Soc. Can.; mem. Am. Sociol. Assn., Can. Inst. Internat. Affairs, Can. Soc. Sociology and Anthropology, Internat. Sociol. Assn., Soc. Sci. Study of Religion, Assn. Sociology of Religion, Social Sci. Fedn. Can. (dir.). Mem. United Ch. Can. Home: 40 Arbordale Walk, Guelph, ON Canada N1G 4X7 Office: Sociology Dept, U Waterloo, Waterloo, ON Canada N2L 3G1 *My life has seemed like a series of arrivals at the same crossroads, compelling me to confirm a decision on priorities made very early, that loyalty to truth comes before achievement. Any achievements have consequently seemed surprises—like spin-offs from giving effect to that loyalty.*

FALLEK, ANDREW MICHAEL, lawyer; b. Bklyn., Aug. 15, 1956; m. Elaine Friedman, June 4, 1984. BA, U. Pa., 1978; JD, Vanderbilt U., 1981. Bar: N.Y. 1982, U.S. Dist. Ct. (so. and ea. dists.) N.Y. 1985, U.S. Ct. Appeals (2d cir.) 1991, U.S. Ct. Appeals (D.C. cir.) 1993. Assoc. Belson, Connolly & Belson, N.Y.C., 1981-84; pvt. practice Bklyn., 1984—. Mem. editl. bd. Bklyn. Barrister. Mem. N.Y. State Bar Assn., Bklyn. Bar Assn. (judiciary com., continuing legal educator com.), Def. Rsch. Inst. Office: 32 Court St Ste 1401 Brooklyn NY 11201-4441

FALLER, DONALD E., marketing and operations executive; b. Jersey City, Mar. 1, 1927; s. Louis John and Gertrude Louise (Hupfield) F.; m. Dolores Adeline Smith, Aug. 28, 1948; children: Mark William, Kyle Lindsay Fernandez, Kimberly Willard, Donald Mark, Krystn Judith, Kelly Bridget Christina Weir. B.S., Mich. State U., 1948. Prodn. mgr. Sealtest Foods Kraft, Detroit, 1958-60, dist. mgr., 1960-67; div. mktg. mgr. Sealtest Foods Kraft, Cleve., 1967-70; v.p. mktg. Citrus Cen. Inc., Orlando, Fla., 1970-78, exec. v.p. mktg. and adminstrn., 1978-83, chief exec. officer, 1980-83; gen. sales mgr. Sunkist Growers Inc., Ontario, Calif., 1984-88, dir. sales, fin. and ops., 1988-90; pres., CEO Trinity Mktg. Cons., Longwood, Fla., 1990—; bd. dirs. Combank Apopka Freedom Savs. & Loan Assn., Winter Park, Fla., Calif.-Ariz. Citrus League. Bd. dirs. Pace Sch., Alamonte Springs, Fla., 1976-82. Mem. Nat. Juice Products Assn. (pres.), Blue Key, Alpha Zeta (pres. 1947-48). Republican. Club: Sweetwater Country (Longwood, Fla.). Office: Trinity Mktg Cons 732 Riverbend Blvd Longwood FL 32779-2349

FALLER, DOROTHY ANDERSON, international agency administrator; b. Chgo., July 6, 1939; d. Albert T. and Lillian G. (Chalbeck) Anderson; student Ill. Wesleyan U., 1956-59; AB, U. Ill., 1959-60; M.S.S.A., Case Western Res. U., 1975. Lic. social worker; m. Adolph Faller, Sept. 5, 1959; children: Carl, Kurt. Child welfare worker Klamath County Pub. Welfare Commn., Klamath Falls, Oreg., 1960-67; social svcs. cons. Ind. State Dept. Pub. Welfare, 1968-72; adminstrv. asst. Berea (Ohio) Children's Home, Berea, 1974; rsch. asst. Case Western Res. U., Sch. Applied Social Scis., 1975, Mandel Sch. Applied Social Scis.; social svcs. supr. Ohio Dept. Pub. Welfare, Cleve., 1975-81; exec. dir. Cleve. Internat. Program, 1981-99; exec. dir. Coun. Internat. Programs USA, 1999—; cons. to Cleve. Found., Am. Sickle Cell Anemia Found., John A. Yankey & Assos.; field instr. Case Western Res. U., 1976-77, lectr., 1981; dir. African Internship Project Substance Abuse Prevention, 1992-95; dir. Ghana Conf., 1995; mem. adv. coun. Mandel Ctr. Non-Profit Orgns., 1995-96, Case Western Res. U., Nat. Network Social Work Mgrs., Nat. Bd. Bd. dirs. West Shore Unitarian Ch., 1978-81, Volgograd Free Speech Forum, 1995—. Mem. Acad. Cert. Social Workers (cert.), Nat. Assn. Social Workers (unit chair state bd., exec. com. nat. bd. dirs. 1985-88, chmn. Internat. Activities Com. of Nat. Bd. 1986-89, program com. 1989—, del. Internat. Fedn. Social Workers, Sweden, 1988, Cleve. unit Social Worker of Yr. 1986, del. from Ohio to del. assembly 1990, conf. chair ann. meeting profession 1993), Natl. Bd., Natl. Network of Social Work Managus, 1995—; Case Western Res. U. Sch. Applied Social Scis. Alumni Assn., Sigma Kappa (pres. 1959), Alpha Lambda Delta (pres. 1956). Unitarian. Editor, contbr. Ohio Children's Budget Project: A Public Policy Study, 1975. Home: 6889 Columbia Rd Olmsted Falls OH 44138-1523 Office: 1700 E 13th St Ste 4se Cleveland OH 44114-3238

FALLER, DOUGLAS V., cancer research scientist, physician. Dir., prof. medicine, biochemistry, pediatrics, microbiology, pathology and lab. medicine, vice chmn. dept. medicine Boston U Cancer Research Ctr., Boston, Mass., 1991—. Office: Boston Univ Cancer Research 80 E Concord St # K-701 Boston MA 02118-2307*

FALLER, RHODA DIANNE GROSSBERG, lawyer; b. N.Y.C., Dec. 21, 1946; d. Benjamin and Marion (Mediasky) Sragg; m. Stanley Grossberg, Apr. 12, 1973 (div. Oct. 1983); children: Joseph Seth, Daniel Benjamin; m. Bernard Martin Faller, May 31, 1987. BS, SUNY, Stony Brook, 1967; MS, Pace U., 1973; JD, N.Y. Law Sch., 1978. Bar: N.Y. 1979, N.J. 1979, U.S. Dist. Ct. N.J. 1979, Fla. 1980, U.S. Dist. Ct. (ea. and so. dists.) N.Y. 1982, Ky. 1996, U.S. Dist. Ct. (e. dist.) Ky. 1997. Assoc. Fuchsberg & Fuchsberg, N.Y.C., 1982-91, DeBlasio & Alton, P.C., N.Y.C., 1991-95, Rhoda Grossberg Faller, Esq., Teaneck, 1995-96, Becker Law Office, Louisville, Ky., 1997—. Mem. Assn. Trial Lawyers Am., Nat. Assn. Women Bus. Owners, Ky. Acad. Trial Attys., Ky. Bar Assn., N.Y. State Trial Lawyers Assn., N.Y. State Bar Assn., Fla. Bar Assn., Louisville Bar Assn., Women Lawyers Assn. Democrat. Jewish. Home: 213 Mockingbird Gardens Dr Louisville KY 40207-5718 Office: Becker Law Office 800 Browns Ln Louisville KY 40207-4009

FALLER, SUSAN GROGAN, lawyer; b. Cin., Mar. 1, 1950; d. William M. and Jane (Eagen) Grogan; m. Kenneth R. Faller, June 8, 1973; children: Susan Elisabeth, Maura Christine, Julie Kathleen. BA, U. Cin., 1972; JD, U. Mich., 1975. Bar: Ohio 1975, Ky. 1989, U.S. Dist. Ct. (so. dist.) Ohio 1975, U.S. Ct. Claims 1982, U.S. Ct. Appeals (6th cir.) 1982, U.S. Supreme Ct. 1982, U.S. Tax Ct. 1984, U.S. Dist. Ct. (ea. dist.) Ky. 1991, U.S. Dist. Ct. (ea. dist.) Ky., 1991. Assoc. Frost & Jacobs, Cin., 1975-82, ptnr. 1982—. Assoc. editor Mich. Law Rev., 1974-75; contbg. author: LDRC 50-State Survey of Media Libel and Privacy Law, 1982—. Bd. dirs. Summit Alumni Coun., Cin., 1983-85; trustee Newman Found., Cin., 1980-86, Catholic Social Svc., Cin., 1984-93, nominating com., 1985-88, sec., 1990; mem. Class XVII Leadership Cin., 1993-94; mem. exec. com., sec. def. counsel sect. Libel Def. Resource Ctr., 1998—; parish coun. St. Monica-St. George Ch., 1997—. Recipient Career Women of Achievement award YWCA, 1990. Mem. ABA (co-editor newsletter media litigation 1993-97), FBA, Ky. Bar Assn., No. Ky. Bar Assn., No. Ky. Women's Bar Assn., Ohio Bar Assn. (bd. govs. litigation sect.), Cin. Bar Assn. (com. mem.), Potter Stewart Inn of Ct., Greater Cin. Women Lawyer's Assn., U. Cin. Alumni Assn., Arts and Scis. Alumni Assn. (bd. gov.'s U. Cin. Coll. 1988—), U. Mich. Alumni Assn., Mortar Bd., Women Entrepreneurs (pres. 1988-89), Leland Yacht Club, Lawyers Club, Coll. Club, Clifton Meadows Club, Phi Beta Kappa, Theta Phi Alpha. Roman Catholic. Home: 5 Belsaw Pl Cincinnati OH 45220-1104 Office: Frost & Jacobs LLP 2500 PNC Ct 201 E 5th St Ste 2500 Cincinnati OH 45202-4182 *Notable cases include: Cin. Bell vs. Gates, libel: Lusby vs. Cin. Mag., libel.*

FALLESEN, ELAINE GERTRUDE, public relations professional; b. Rochester, N.Y., July 22, 1956; d. Robert Frederick and Gertrude Louise Emilie (Rueger) Busse; m. Gary David Fallesen, July 3, 1982; children: Jesse Dane, Hayley Hope. BA, State U. Coll., Geneseo, 1978. Journalist Wolfe Publs., Rochester, N.Y., 1978-80; asst. comty./sch. rels. Greece Cen. Sch. Dist., Rochester, 1980-84; asst. dir. comms., comms. dir., mktg. and comms. dir. Rochester-Monroe County ARC chpt. and Blood Svcs., Rochester region, 1984-93; pub. info. officer Hosp. Consortium of Greater Rochester, 1993-99; asst. dir. devel. Health Assn., Rochester, 1999—; pub. rels. cons. various agys. and orgns., Rochester, 1993—. Bd. dirs., chair pub. rels. com. Rochester Eye and Human Parts Bank, 1994—; chair pub. rels., youth counselor Hope Luth. Ch., Rochester. Mem. Pub. Rels. Soc. Am. (accredited, bd. dirs. 1984-99), Nat. Soc. Fund Raising Execs. Home: 5726 W Wautoma Bch Hilton NY 14468-9126 Office: One Mount Hope Ave Rochester NY 14620

FALLESEN, GARY DAVID, journalist; b. Rochester, N.Y., July 24, 1959; s. Karl David and Mary Lou (Putnam) F.; m. Elaine Gertrude Busse, July 3, 1982; children: Jesse Dane, Hayley Hope. BA, St. John Fisher Coll., Rochester, 1981. Sports clk. Democrat & Chronicle, Rochester, 1979-82, sports writer, 1982-88, sports columnist, 1988-92, sports writer, 1992-96; outdoor writer, 1996—. Contbr. articles to Sporting News, Golf World, Golf Journal, CBS Sportsline, other sports publs. Named Sports Writer of the Yr., N.Y. State Wrestling Coaches Assn., 1984, Rochester Press-Radio Club, 1986, Hon. Mention, N.Y. State AP Writers Contest, 1989, 2nd place column, Profl. Football Writers, 1990, 1st place column Profl. Football Writers, 1991, honorable mention column Profl. Football Writers, 1992, 2nd place enterprise Football Writers Assn., 1995, hon. mention column Football Writers Assn., 1996, N.Y. Newspaper Pub. Assn. award of excellence, 1996-97, 98, hon. mention N.Y. State AP Writers Contest, 1998. Mem. Outdoor Writers Assn. Am. (3d pl. big game hunting, 3d pl. outdoors page 1999), N.Y. State Outdoor Writers Assn., Am. Alpine Club. Lutheran. Avocations: director drama ministry, choir singing, photography, mountain climbing, hiking. Office: Dem & Chronicle 55 Exchange Blvd Rochester NY 14614-2001

FALLET, GEORGE, civil engineer; b. Berlin, Pa., May 18, 1920; s. John and Anna (Hrobak) F.; m. Sybil Lorene DeLoach, Apr. 30, 1949; children: George Michael, Carol Ann, Mary Jane. BCE, Poly. Inst. Bklyn., 1957, MSCE, 1963. Registered profl. engr., N.H., N.Y.; registered land surveyor, N.Y. Asst. engr. Balt. & Ohio R.R., S.I. Rapid Transit Rwy., Staten Island, N.Y., 1946-53; structural designer H.K. Ferguson Co., N.Y.C., 1953-58; civil engr. U.S. Corps Engrs., N.Y.C., 1958-60; structural engr. U.S. Naval Facilities Command, N.Y.C., 1960-68, Fed. GSA, N.Y.C., 1968-85; dep. dir. bldg. dept. City of Nashua, N.H., 1986-89; cons. engr. Nashua, 1989—; mem. subcom. U.S. Com. on Seismic Safety, Washington, 1978-85. Active Community Planning Bd., Staten Island, 1975-81. Recognized for Outstanding Citizenship Borough of Staten Island, 1980. Fellow ASCE (Robert Ridgway award 1957), NSPE (GSA Nat. Engr. of the Yr. 1981), Soc. Am. Mil. Engrs., Chi Epsilon, Tau Beta Pi. Republican. Home: 32 Watersedge Dr Nashua NH 03063-1120 Office: PO Box 3233 Nashua NH 03061-3233

FALLETTA, JO ANN, musician; b. N.Y.C., Feb. 27, 1954; d. John Edward and Mary Lucy (Racioppo) F.; m. Robert Alemany, Aug. 24, 1986. BA in Music, Mannes Coll. Music, N.Y.C., 1976; MA in Music, Juilliard Sch., N.Y.C., 1982; PhD in Musical Arts, Juilliard Sch., 1989; Honorary Doctorate, Marian Coll., Wis., 1988. Music dir. Queens Philharmonic, N.Y.C., 1978-91, Den. Chamber Orch., Colo., 1983-92; assoc. condr. Milw. Symphony, Wis., 1985-88; music dir. Women's Philharmonic, San Francisco, 1986-96; music dir., condr. Long Beach Symphony, Calif., 1989—; music dir. Va. Symphony, Norfolk, 1991—. Stokowski Conducting Competition, Toscanini Conducting award. Office: ICM Artists LTD 40 W 57th St New York NY 10019-4001

FALLETTA, JOHN MATTHEW, pediatrician, educator; b. Arma, Kans., Sept. 3, 1940; s. Matthew John and Norma (Luke) F.; m. Carolyn Ontjes, June 22, 1963; children: Elizabeth, Matthew. AB, U. Kans., 1962, MD, 1966. Diplomate Am. Bd. Pediat., Am. Bd. Hematology-Oncology. Intern in mixed medicine Kans. U. Med. Ctr., Kansas City, 1966-67; surgeon Epidemic Intelligence Svc., Tex. Children's Hosp. USPHS, Houston, 1967-69; asst. instr. pediat. Baylor Coll. Medicine, Houston, 1967-69, resident, 1969-71, chief resident Tex. Children's Hosp., 1971, postdoctoral fellow hematology-oncology, 1971-73, asst. prof. pediat., 1973-76; assoc. prof. Duke U., Durham, N.C., 1976-83, prof., 1984—, chief divsn. hematology-oncology, 1976-94, dir. Clin. Pediat. Lab., 1976-95; chmn. transfusion com. Duke U. Med. Ctr., 1978—, mem. exec. com. med. staff, 1978—, instl. rev. bd. human rsch., 1979—, chmn., 1994—; mem. instl. rev. bd. human rsch. Baylor Coll. Medicine, 1974-76; mem. acad. coun. Duke U., 1982-86, 87-96, 98—, exec. com., 1988, faculty compensation com., 1988—, faculty com. on univ. governance, 1988, trustee-faculty com. to rev. pres., 1989, search com. for pres., 1992; cons. pediat. hematologist-oncologist Charlotte (N.C.) Meml. Hosp., 1978—. Contbr. more than 120 articles to Nature, Am. Jour. Ophthalmology, Pediat., New England Jour. Medicine, Clin. Pediat. Oncology, others. Cons. pediat. hematologist-oncologist Project Hope, Pediatric Inst., Krakow, Poland, 1979—; prin. investigator Pediat. Oncology Group, 1981-95, chmn. epidemiology com., mem. prin. investigator's exec. com., new agts. and pharmacology com.; chmn. prophylactic penicillin study I Nat. Heart, Lung and Blood Inst., NIH, 1982-86, chmn. study II, 1987-95; active Cancer Ctr. Support Rev. Com. Nat. Cancer Inst. NIH, 1986-90, NIH Reviewers Res., 1990—, Cancer Clin. Investigation Rev. Com., 1991-96, chmn., 1995-96; trustee Ronald McDonald Children's Charities, 1986—. Mem. Am. Assn. Cancer Rsch., Am. Acad. Pediat., Am. Pediat. Soc., Am. Soc. Clin. Oncology, So. Soc. Pediat. Rsch. (pres. 1981-82), Soc. Pediat. Rsch., N.C. Pediat. Soc., N.C. Med. Soc., Phi Beta Kappa, Alpha Omega Alpha. Office: Duke U Med Ctr PO Box 2916 Durham NC 27715-2916

FALLIN, BARBARA MOORE, human resources director; b. Paducah, Ky., Nov. 12, 1939; d. James Perry Moore and Margaret Arminta (Winn) Kastner; m. Jon Ball, Jan. 21, 1961 (div. July 1963); m. Ralph Daniel Fallin, May 23, 1965; children: Wade, Cathi, Cindy Pergrim, Danielle. Student, Fla. Christian Coll., 1957-58. Cert. sr. profl. in human resource mgmt. Exec. asst. to contr. The Borden Co., Tampa, Fla., 1958-65; mktg. asst. Martin-Marietta Corp., Shalimar, Fla., 1965-71; asst. to pres. Browning-Marine, Ft. Walton Beach, Fla., 1973; pers. coord. Keltec Fla., Shalimar, 1974-78; pers. mgr. Metric Systems Corp., Ft. Walton Beach, 1979-87, pers. dir., 1987-92; dir. human resources Metric Sys. Corp., Ft. Walton Beach, 1992—; mem. Job Svc. Employer Com., Ft. Walton Beach, 1985—; mem. adv. bd. Bay Area Vocat.-Tech. Ctr., Ft. Walton Beach, 1988-92; mem. adv. bd. Okaloosa Applied Tech. Ctr. Sch. Adv. Coun., 1995-98, chmn., 1997-98; bd. dirs. Pvt. Industry Coun., 1996—, vice chmn., 1998—. First mistress Krewe of Bowlegs, Ft. Walton Beach, 1983-84, first lady to Cap'n Billy Bowlegs XXXII, 1986-87; mem. citizens adv. com. U. West Fla., Pensacola, 1991-97; mem. funds distbn. com. Okaloosa County United Way, 1990-93; mem. BNA's Pers. Policies Forum, 1995-96; mem. Pacesetters fund raiser team Salvation Army Capital Campaign, 1996-97. Mem. NAFE, Soc. Human Resource Mgmt. (Emerald Coast chpt. pres. 1986-88, bd. dirs. 1988-92), Nat. Mgmt. Assn., Ft. Walton Beach C. of C. (hosts com. 1991—), Laureate Gamma Phi (exec. bd. dirs. 1996-97, sec. 1997-98, Valentine queen 1997). Republican. Presbyterian. Avocations: collecting penquins, making scrapbooks. Office: Metric Sys Corp 645 Anchors St NW Fort Walton Beach FL 32548-3803

FALLIN, MARY COPELAND, state official; b. Warrensburg, Mo., Dec. 9, 1954; d. Jospeh Newton and Mary (Duggan) Copeland; m. Joseph Price Fallin, Jr., Nov. 3, 1984; children: Christina, Price. BS, Okla. State U., 1977. Bus. mgr. Okla. Dept. Securities, Oklahoma City, 1979-81; state travel coord. Okla. Dept. of Tourism, Oklahoma City, 1981-82; sales rep. Associated Petroleum, Oklahoma City, 1982-83; mktg. dir. Brian Head (Utah) Hotel & Ski Resort, 1983-84; dir. sales Residence Inn Hotel, Oklahoma City, 1984-87; dist. mgr. Lexington Hotel Suites, Oklahoma City, 1988-90; real estate assoc. Pippin Properties, Inc., Oklahoma City, 1990-94; state rep. Okla. Ho. of Reps., Oklahoma City, 1990-94; lt. gov. State of Okla., Oklahoma City, 1995—; chmn. Nat. Conf. Lt. Govs. Mem., del. Okla. Fedn. Rep. Women; mem. Am. Legis. Exch. Coun., Nat. Conf. State Legislatures. Named Nat. Legislator of the Yr., Okla. Ladies in the News, Guardian of Small Bus. award; named Woman of Yr. Ladies in Comm., 1998, Girl Scouts Am., 1998, Bi-liner award, 1997. Presbyterian. Office: State Capitol Rm 211 Office of Lt Governor Oklahoma City OK 73105

FALLIS, ALBERT MURRAY, microbiology educator; b. Minto Twp., Ont., Can., Jan. 2, 1907; s. William Robert and Martha Melissa (Millen) F.; m. Ada Ruth Bostock, Sept. 21, 1938; children—Alexander Graham, Hugh Murray, Bruce William. B.A., U. Toronto, Ont., 1932, Ph.D., 1937. Research fellow Ont. Research Found., Toronto, 1932-47, dir. parasitology, 1947-66; prof. parasitology U. Toronto, 1952-75, head dept., 1952-72, prof. emeritus, 1975—, assoc. dean Sch. Grad. Studies, 1967-71, mem. governing council, 1972-73; cons. Ont. Rsch. Found., Toronto, 1966-68, WHO, Geneva, 1966, 71; vis. prof. Meml. U. Nfld., 1975-76. Author: Parasites, People and Progress, Historical Recollections, 1993; contbr. articles to profl. jours. Erskine fellow Canterbury U., N.Z., 1975. Fellow Royal Soc. Can.; mem. Am. Soc. Parasitologists (v.p., pres. 1979, emeritus), Can. Soc. Zoologists (hon. mem.), Am. Soc. Tropical Medicine and Hygiene (emeritus), Can. Assn. Adv. Vet. Parasitology (hon. mem.), Wildlife Disease Assn. (emeritus mem.), Royal Can. Inst. (pres. 1955-56, hon. editor 1951-52), Soc. Protozoologists (emeritus), Am. Entomol. Soc. (emeritus), Masons. Avocations: woodworking; photography; gardening; historical research. Home: 4 Greer St, Caledon East, ON Canada L0N 1E0

FALLIS, ALEXANDER GRAHAM, chemistry educator; b. Toronto, Ont., Can., Aug. 20, 1940; s. A. Murray and A. Ruth (Bostock) F.; m. Wanda Lee Wiley, Oct. 7, 1967; children: Graham M., Laura Dawn. BS with honors, U. Toronto, 1963, MA, 1964, Ph.D., 1967. NRC postdoctoral fellow Oxford U., Eng., 1967-69; asst. prof. Meml. U. Nfld., St. John's, Can., 1969-74; assoc. prof. Meml. U. Nfld., St. John's, 1974-78, prof. chemistry, 1978-88; prof. chemistry U. Ottawa, 1988—; chmn. sci. program III, N.Am. Chem. Congress, Toronto, 1984-88; dir. Ottawa Carleton Chemistry Inst., 1990-93. Editor: Can. Jour. Chemistry, 1992-95; mem. editl. bd. Can. Jour. Chemistry, 1984-87; contbr. articles to profl. jours. Recipient Alfred Bader award Can. Soc. Chemistry, 1998. Fellow Chem. Inst. Can. (councillor 1979-82, dir. tech. affairs 1983-84, chmn. bd. dirs. 1984-87, Basic Scis. Rsch. award Ottawa Life Scis. Coun. 1996, Sanders-Matthey award for breast cancer rsch. 1997—), Royal Soc. Chemistry, Nat. Sci. and Engring. Research Council Can. Chemistry (grants com. 1986-88, 90-91); mem. Am. Chem. Soc., The RA Centre Club. Mem. United Ch. of Can. Avocations: photography; squash; reading; outdoor activities. Home: 622 O'Connor St, Ottawa, ON Canada K1S 3R8 Office: U Ottawa, Dept Chemistry, Ottawa, ON Canada K1N 6N5

FALLON, ELDON E., lawyer, educator, judge; b. New Orleans, Feb. 16, 1939; s. Edward and Delia (Koster) F.; m. Cecile Fallon, Sept. 28, 1967. BA, Tulane U., 1960, JD, 1962; LLM, Yale U., 1963. Bar: La. 1962. Assoc. Kierr & Gainsburgh, 1962-66; ptnr. Gainsburgh, Benjamin & Fallon, New Orleans, 1966-95; judge U.S. Dist. Ct., New Orleans, 1995—; adj. prof. Tulane U. Author: Trial Handbook For Louisiana Lawyers, 1981; contbr. articles to profl. jours. Fellow Am. Bar Found., Am. Coll. Trial Lawyers, La. Bar Found. (bd. dirs., pres. 1995-96); mem. La. Bar Assn. (sec. treas. 1984, pres. 1985-86). Office: U.S. Courthouse 500 Camp St New Orleans LA 70130-3313

FALLON, HAROLD JOSEPH, physician, pharmacology and biochemistry educator; b. N.Y.C., Aug. 13, 1931; s. Harold Joseph and Martha A. (Hansen) F.; m. Jo Ann Brouse; children—Thomas, Michael, Elisabeth, John. B.A., Yale U., 1953, M.D., 1957. Diplomate Am. Bd. Internal Medicine. Intern in medicine N.C. Meml. Hosp., Chapel Hill, 1957-58; asst. resident in medicine N.C. Meml. Hosp., 1958-59, chief resident in medicine, 1961-62; clin. assoc. NIH, 1959-61; postdoctoral fellow dept. biochemistry Duke U. Sch. Medicine, 1963-64; asst. prof. medicine U. N.C. Sch. Medicine, Chapel Hill, 1963-71; asst. prof. biochemistry U. N.C. Sch. Medicine, 1966-71, assoc. prof. medicine, 1967-70, chief div. clin. pharmacology, toxicology, environ. health, 1968-74, vice chmn. dept. medicine, 1968-71, assoc. prof. pharmacology, 1969-70, prof. medicine and pharmacology, 1970-74, assoc. prof. biochemistry, 1971-74, acting chmn. dept medicine, 1971-72; William Branch Porter prof. medicine, chmn. dept. medicine Va. Commonwealth U.-Med. Coll. Va., Richmond, 1974-93; dean, Sch. of Med. U. Alabama, Birmingham, 1993-97, assoc. dean grad. med. edn. Sch. Medicine, 1997—; vis. scientist U. Utrecht, Netherlands, 1972-73; mem. numerous med. coms. and councils. Mem. editorial bd. Gastroenterology, Clin. Research, Hepatology; mem. adv. editorial bd. Jour. Lipid Research; mem. editorial com. Jour. Clin. Investigation, 1971-76; contbr. numerous articles to med. jours. Mem. exec. com. YMCA, Richmond, 1984—. Served with USPHS, 1969-62. Recipient Sinsheimer award, 1965-70, Research Career Devel. award, 1968, Burroughs-Wellcome award, 1974, Med. Coll. Va. Deans award, 1981; named Outstanding Affiliate appointee Sch. Basic. Scis., 1984; Yale U. Sch. Medicine research fellow, 1962-63. Fellow ACP (mem. sci. program com. 1982—); mem. Assn. Am. Physicians, Assn. Profs. Medicine (councillor chmn. Va. liaison com. 1982—), Am. Soc. for Clin. Investigation (v.p. 1972-75, councillor 1975-76), So. Soc. for Clin. Investigation (pres. 1976-77, councillor 1971-74), Am. Clin. Climatol. Assn., Am. Fedn. Clin. Research, Am. Gastroenterol. Assn. (mem. governing bd. 1978-82), Am. Liver Found. (bd. dirs. 1981), Am. Assn. for Study Liver Disease (pres. 1979, mem. publ. com. 1983—), Internat. Assn. for Study Liver Disease (councillor 1982-84), Gastroenterology Research Group (sec.-treas. 1973-74, mem. steering com. 1970-74), AAAS, Am. Soc. Pharmacology Exptl. Therapeutics, AMA, also numerous others. Presbyterian. Club: Commonwealth. Home: 4157 Highlands Cir Birmingham AL 35213-2800 Office: U Alabama Med Edn Bldg 1813 6th Ave S Rm 310 Birmingham AL 35233-1920*

FALLON, JOHN GOLDEN, banker; b. Boston, Nov. 2, 1946; s. John Joseph and Marguerite Abbey (Golden) F.; m. Patricia Agnes Simpson, Jan. 16, 1971; children: Elizabeth Martha, John Robert. BA, Boston Coll., 1967; MS in Mgmt., MIT, 1969. Instr. Lowell (Mass.) U., 1968-70; mgr. mktg. info. Shawmut Bank Boston, 1973-78, asst. contr., 1978-82, mgr. treasury dept., 1982; dir. corp. planning Shawmut Corp., Boston, 1983-86, dir. info. sys., 1986-90, dir. credit MIS, 1990, dir. corp. MIS, 1991-93; exec. v.p. Lexington (Mass.) Savs. Bank, 1993-95; exec. v.p., CFO Affiliated Comty. Bancorp, Inc., Waltham, Mass., 1995-98; exec. v.p. Ustrust, Boston, 1998—. V.p., mem. exec. com. Vis. Nurses Assn., Arlington, Mass., 1979-84; bd. dirs. Coop. Elder Svcs., Inc., 1994—; mem. fin. com. Town of Boxborough, Mass., 1986-92, selectman, 1994-96, Boxborough Sch. Com., Acton Boxborough Sch. Com., 1998—; mem. Boxborough Minutemen, 1989—, treas., 1992-94. With USPHS, 1970-73. Mem. Am. Bankers Assn. (mem. exec. com. corp. planning divsn. 1984-86), Mass. Bankers Assn. (chmn. cmty. bank com. 1993-95, chmn. Sys. and tech. Commn., 1998—). Roman Catholic. Office: US TRUST 40 Court St Boston MA 02108-2202

FALLON, L(OUIS) FLEMING, JR., public health consultant, researcher; b. Jersey City, Mar. 21, 1950; s. Louis Fleming and Patricia (Nelson) F. AB in Math. and Psychology, Colby Coll., 1972; MS in Microbiology, Wagner Coll., 1977; MBA in Econs., U. New Haven, 1979; MD, St. George's (Grenada) U., 1984; MPH, Columbia U., 1986. Cert. health officer, N.J., Pa. Bus. rsch. analyst So. New Eng. Telephone Co., New Haven, 1978-80; assoc. A.T. Kearney, Inc., N.Y.C., 1980-81; v.p. Medcon of Am., Chester, N.J., 1984-87; resident in environ. and occupational medicine Columbia U., N.Y.C., 1985-88, lectr. Sch. Pub. Health, 1986-88, asst. prof. clin. pub. health, 1988—; assoc. prof. pub. health Slippery Rock (Pa.) U., 1990-94; epidemiologist Jameson Hosp, Newcastle, Pa., 1994-97; assoc. prof. pub. health adminstrn. Bowling Green (Ohio) U., 1997—; cons. psychologist Psychol. Rsch. Svcs., Cleve., 1973-77; lectr. grad. program St. Joseph's Coll., Windham, Maine, summer 1990, adj. prof., 1990—; cons. in pub. health adminstrn. and occupational medicine, 1988—; presenter in field. Author: The Penultimate Muffin; editor, author: The Management Perspective, 1989; contbr. articles to Brit. Jour. Indsl. Medicine, Jour. Soc. Occupational Medicine, Jour. Perinatal Medicine, New Eng. Jour. Medicine, Indian Jour. Indsl. Medicine, Med. Problems of Performing Artists, HMO Mgmt., also others. Mem. exec. coun. Boy Scouts Am., N.J., Maine, Pa., Ohio, 1986—; pres., mem. Chester (N.J.) Bd. Health, 1987-90; chmn. bd. trustees United Meth. Ch., Gladstone, N.J., 1988-90; mem. Environ. Protection Commn. for Chester Twp., N.J., 1987-90; mem. environ. health adv. com. Maine Bur. Health, Augusta, 1990; exec. bd. Women's Shelter/Rape Crisis Ctr.

Lawrence County.; mem. instnl. rev. bd. protection of human subjects Slippery Rock U.; med. missionary, Bangladesh, 1995, Ukraine, 1997, 99, Bolivia, 1998. Fellow Am. Cancer Inst., 1985-88. Fellow Royal Soc. Medicine (U.K.), Soc. Occupational Medicine (U.K.); mem. APHA, Am. Coll. Occupational Medicine (com. on ethical practice, 1989-92, adv. bd. com. for internat. edn. 1991-93), Am. Coll. Preventive Medicine, Nat. Eagle Scout Assn., Psi Chi. Achievements include establishment of a linkage between noise induced hearing loss and hypertension; creation of personal computer based system linking physicians, hospitals and a state department of health. Office: Bowling Green State U Coll Health and Human Svcs Bowling Green OH 43403

FALLON, PAT, artist, art educator; b. Cartagena, Colombia, Nov. 2, 1939; (parents Am. citizens); d. Carlos Fallon and Maureen (Bryne) Fallon Laird; m. Ronald Patrick Conner, Dec. 26, 1960 (div. June 1976); children: Hadley Kathryn Conner, Kenneth Fallon Conner. *Pat's ancestors include Thomas Fallon, educated by Viscount Chateaubrian at St. Amiens Cathedral School; who arrived in Colombia around 1820 to mine emeralds; his son Diego, poet laureate of Colombia as well as professor of mathematics and music; his son, Diego Jose, and wife, Dona Blanca Convers y Codazzi were Colombian Consul General to the United States. Carlos Fallon, Pat's father, was Chief of Staff of the Colombian Navy and later Captain in the U.S. Air Core. He helped develop the field of Value Engineering in the U.S. Pat's mother, Maureen Bligh Byrne, descends from soldiers in the American Revolution and, sailors in the War of 1812.* BA, Antioch Coll., 1962; BFA, Cleve. Inst. Art, 1980; MFA, Kent State U., 1982. Office mgr. cmty. govt. Antioch Coll., Yellow Springs, Ohio, 1961-62; camp dir. Camp Fire Girls, Dayton, Ohio, 1963-65; tchr. painting Valley Art Ctr., Chagrin Falls, Ohio, 1973-74, Shaker Heights (Ohio) Adult Edn., 1973-77; tchg. asst. Cleve. Inst. Art, 1976-80; grad. asst. art dept. Kent (Ohio) State U., 1980-82; gallery mgr. Kuban Gallery Fine Art, Cleve., 1982-83; gallery dir. Ursuline Coll., Pepper Pike, Ohio, 1983-89, adj. prof. art, 1989-94, assoc. prof., 1994—; coord. N.E. exhibit New Orgn. Visual Arts-NOVA, Cleve., 1974-75; mem. editl. adv. bd. Collegiate Press, 1990-98; presenter in field. One-woman shows include Wasmer Gallery, Ursuline Coll., 1997, In Town Club, Cleve., 1997; exhibited in group shows at Canton (Ohio) Art Inst., 1981, Kuban Galleries, Cleve., 1983, Collector's Gallery, Dayton, 1983, Bonfoey Gallery, Cleve., 1983, Cleve. Inst. Art, 1985-87, Ursuline Coll., 1989, 91, 93, 95, 97, Willoughby (Ohio) Fine Arts Ctr., 1992, Cleve. Mus. Art, 1993, Hallinan Ctr., Case Western Res. U., Cleve., 1995, The Black Box, Cleve., 1996, Cleve. State U., 1996, Valley Art Ctr., Chagrin Falls, Ohio, 1996; represented in permanent collections Coll. Home Econs. Nat. U. Ireland, Sligo; sabbatical year multi-media project exhbns. on homeless; contbr. articles to profl. jours. Vol., advisor art com. N.E. Ohio Coalition for Homeless, Cleve., 1996-97. Fellow Ohio Humanities Coun., 1986-94. Mem. Coll. Arts Assn., Founds. in Art Theory and Edn., Ctr. for Safety in Arts, Amnesty Internat. Democrat. Roman Catholic. Home: 3300 Kenmore Rd Shaker Hts OH 44122-3462 Office: Ursuline Coll 2550 Lander Rd Pepper Pike OH 44124-4318

FALLON, PATRICK R., advertising executive; b. 1946. With Leo Burnett, Chgo., 1967-69; with Stevson & Assocs., Mpls., 1969-76, v.p.; with Martin/Williams Advt., Mpls., 1976-81, v.p.; chmn. bd. dirs. Fallon McElligott, Inc., Mpls., 1981—. Office: Fallon-McElligott Inc 901 Marquette Ave Ste 3200 Minneapolis MN 55402-3205*

FALLON, RAE MARY, psychology educator, early childhood consultant; b. N.Y.C., Apr. 13, 1947; d. Frank J. and Santa A. (Lettera) Taccetta; m. John J. Fallon, 1972; children: Sean, Christopher. BA, CUNY, 1968, MA, 1971; postgrad., Fordham U., 1989—. Cert. N-6 tchr., spl. edn. tchr., N.Y. Elem. tchr. Pub. Sch. 1, Bronx, N.Y., 1968-72; pre-sch. tchr. Valley Nursery Sch., Walden, N.Y., 1972-73; tchr. spl. edn. Orange-Ulster Bd. Coop. Edn. Svcs., Goshen, N.Y., 1973-75, early childhood specialist, 1982-89; instr. edn. Mt. St. Mary Coll., Newburgh, N.Y., 1989-93, asst. prof., 1993—; early childhood cons., Montgomery, N.Y., 1989—; mem. early childhood com. Valley Ctrl. Sch. Sys., Montgomery, 1994. Mem. West Street Sch. Cmty. Sch. Bd., Newburgh, 1990—; mem. early intervention com. Orange County Health Dept., Goshen, 1993—; chmn. program com. Montgomery Rep. Club, 1990-94. Mem. ASCD, Coun. for Exceptional Children, Assn. for Edn. Young Children (regional coord. 1991-92), Kiwanis, Delta Kappa Gamma, Phi Delta Kappa. Roman Catholic. Office: Mt St Mary Coll 330 Powell Ave Newburgh NY 12550-3412

FALLON, RICHARD H., JR., law educator; b. 1952. BA, Yale U., 1975, Oxford U., 1977; JD, Yale U., 1980. Bar: Mass. 1988. Law clk. to Hon. J. Skelly Wright U.S. Ct. Appeals (D.C. cir.), 1980-81; law clk. to Hon. Lewis F. Powell Jr. U.S. Supreme Ct., D.C., 1981-82; asst. prof. Harvard U., Cambridge, 1982-87, prof. law, 1987—; vis. prof. Wash. U., Seattle, spring 1991. Office: Law Sch Griswold 406 Harvard U Cambridge MA 02138*

FALLON, ROBERT THOMAS, English language educator; b. N.Y.C., June 6, 1927; s. John Edward and Winifred (Hanigan) F.; m. Mary Snyder, May 18, 1953 (div. May 1971); children: Frances Fallon Schuster, Robert Thomas Jr. BS, U.S. Mil. Acad., 1949; MA in English, Canisius Coll., 1960; MA in English, Columbia U., 1962, PhD in English, 1965. Commd. 2nd lt. U.S. Army, 1949, advanced through grades to lt. col., 1965, ret., 1970; assoc. prof. English LaSalle U., Phila., 1970-78, prof. English, 1978-95; prof. emeritus, 1995—. Author: Captain or Colonel: The Soldier in Milton's Life and Art, 1984, Milton in Government, 1993, Divided Empire: Milton's Political Imagery, 1995; contbr. articles to profl. publs. NEH fellow, 1990-91; Am. Coun. Learned Socs. grantee-in-aid, 1980. Mem. MLA, Cromwell Assn., Milton Soc. Am. (treas. 1977-86, v.p. 1987, pres. 1988), John Donne Soc. (mem. exec. com. 1991-93). Avocation: tennis. Home: River Rd Lumberville PA 18933

FALLON, STEPHEN MICHAEL, humanities educator; b. Washington, Sept. 18, 1954; s. William Francis and Margaret Mary (Barry) F.; m. Nancy Anne Hungarland, May 30, 1981; children: Samuel, Claire, Daniel. AB in English, Princeton U., 1976; MA in English, McGill U., 1978; PhD in English, U. Va., 1985. Asst. prof. liberal studies U. Notre Dame, 1985-90, assoc. prof. liberal studies, English, 1990—. Author: Milton among the Philosophers, 1991; co-founder great books course for homeless; contbr. essays in books and articles to profl. jours. Fellow Nat. Endowment Humanities, 1988-89, 95-96, Am. Coun. Learned Socs. Mem. Modern Lang. Assn., Milton Soc. Am. (James Holly Hanford award 1991, exec. com. 1990-92), Phi Beta Kappa. Avocations: soccer, bicycling, opera. Office: U Notre Dame 368 Decio Hall Notre Dame IN 46556-5644

FALLON, WILLIAM J., career officer; b. Dec. 30, 1944; m. Mary Elizabeth Trapp; children: Susan, Barbara, William, Christina. BA, Villanova U., 1967; MA in Internat. Studies, Old Dominion. Advanced through grade to vice adm. USN; pilot USS Ranger, 1969; comdr. attack squadron 65 USS Dwight D. Eisenhower, 1984-85; dep. comdr. carrier air wing 8 USS Nimitz; comdr. attack wing 1 Naval Air Sta. Occana, Va., 1989-90; comdr. attack wing 1 USS Theodore Roosevelt, 1991, comdr. carrier group 8, 1995; comdr. Theodore Roosevelt battle group, comdr. Battle Force 6th Fleet; dep. comdr. in chief, chief staff U.S. Atlantic Fleet, 1996—.

FALLOWS, JAMES MACKENZIE, magazine editor; b. Phila., Aug. 2, 1949; s. James Albert and Jean (Mackenzie) F.; m. Deborah Jean Zerad, June 22, 1971; children: Thomas Mackenzie, Tad Andrew. B.A. magna cum laude, Harvard U., 1970; diploma in econ. devel. (Rhodes scholar), Oxford U., 1972. Staff editor Washington Monthly, 1972-74; free-lance mag. writer, 1972-76; assoc. editor Tex. Monthly, 1974-76; chief speech-writer Pres. U.S., Washington, 1977-79; Washington editor Atlantic Monthly, 1979-97; editor U.S. News & World Report, Washington, 1996-98; nat. commentator Pub. Radio, 1987—. Author: National Defense, 1981, More Like Us, 1989, Looking at the Sun: The Rise of the New East Asia Economic and Political System, 1994 ; contbr. articles to numerous mags. and jours. Office: c/o Random House Inc 201 E 50th St New York NY 10022-7703

FALLS, JOSEPH FRANCIS, sportswriter, editor; b. N.Y.C., May 2, 1928; s. Edward and Anna (Zincak) F.; m. Mary Jane Erdei, Oct. 10, 1975; children by previous marriage: Robert, Kathleen, Susan, Janet, Michael. Grad. high sch. Reporter AP, N.Y.C., 1946-56; sports writer Detroit Times, 1956-60; sports editor, sports writer Detroit Free Press, 1960-78; sports writer Detroit News, 1978—, sports editor, 1980—. Author: Man in Motion, 1973, The Detroit Tigers, 1975, The Boston Marathon, 1977, So You Think You're A Die-Hard Tiger Fan, 1986, An Illustrated History, The Detroit Tigers, 1989, Daly Life, 1990. Mem. Baseball Writers Assn. Am., Football Writers Assn. Am., Hockey Writers Assn., Pro Basketball Writers Assn., Golf Writers Assn., U.S. Tennis Writers Assn. Office: Detroit News 615 W Lafayette Blvd Detroit MI 48226-3197*

FALLS, KATHLEENE JOYCE, photographer; b. Detroit, July 3, 1949; d. Edgar John and Acelia Olive (Young) Haley; m. Donald David Falls, June 15, 1974; children: Daniel John, David James. Student, Oakland Community Coll., 1969-73, Winona Sch. Profl. Photography, 1973-80; degree in photography, Winona Sch. Profl. Photography, 1988, 90. Lic. ham radio-technician class. Printer Guardian Photo, Novi, Mich., 1967-69; printer, supr. quality control N.Am. Photo, Livonia, Mich., 1969-76; free lance photographer Livonia, 1969-76; owner, pres. Kathy Falls, Inc., Carleton, Mich., 1976—; instr. digital imaging Monroe County (Mich.) C.C., 1994—; instr. Monroe County Community Coll. Continuing Edn., 1981-83; nat. artisan judge Congl. High Sch. Art Competition, 1985—; owner Picture Perfect, Carleton, 1987; co-owner Haleys Gift Shoppe, Dundee, Mich., 1989; pub. info. officer Am. Radio Relay League, 1998—. Author: (booklet) Emergency Photo-Retouching for Photographers, 1988; editor The Hertzian herald, 1998; contbr. articles to profl. jours.; represented in spl. categories in the Nat. Loan Collection, Profl. Photographers Am., 1980, 81, 83, 87; represented in permanent Collections Monroe County Hist. Mus., Archives Notre Dame; newsletter editor Hertzian Herald. Catechist St. Parick's Ch., Carleton, 1984-87, mem. parish coun., 1998—; active Big Bros. and Big Sisters, Monroe, 1986-87; corr. sec. Monroe Women's Ctr., 1986-88; mem. Amateur Radio Emergency Svc.; bd. dirs. Ladies Ancient Order of Hibernians. Recipient Photographic Craftsman degree, 1989, numerous awards granted by profl. photographic orgns.; editor: Hertzian Herald. Mem. NAFE, Am. Soc. Photographers, Detroit Profl. Photographers Assn. (bd. dirs. 1987—, artisan chmn. 1981-82, Best of Show award 1981, 83), Profl. Photographers Mich. (artisian chair 1982-83, Best of Show award 1976, 81, Artist of Yr. 1980, 91), Profl. Photographers Am. (cert. profl. photog. specialist, photographic specialist degree 1988), Am. Photog. Artisans Guild (coun. mem., bd. dirs. 1987—, pres. 1992, Photog. Artisan degree 1989, Artisan Laurel degree 1991), Monroe County Fine Arts Coun. (pres. 1998-99), Monroe C. of C. (chmn. council women bus. owners), Nat. Orgn. Women Bus. Owners, Profl. Photographers Am. (Photog. Craftsman degree 1990), Monroe County Radio Comms. Assn., Toastmasters, Internat. Club, Ladies Ancient Order of Hibernians (bd. dirs. 1998—), Scarab Club Detroit. Republican. Roman Catholic. Club: Monroe Camera. Avocations: guitar, piano, drawing, travel, camping. Home and Office: 10779 Swan Creek Rd Carleton MI 48117-9324

FALLS, ROBERT ARTHUR, artistic director; b. Springfield, Ill., Mar. 2, 1954; s. Arthur Joseph and Nancy (Stribling) F. BFA, U. Ill., 1976. Artistic dir. Wisdom Bridge Theatre, Chgo., 1977-86, Goodman Theatre, Chgo., 1987—; dir. Pravda (Howard Brenton and David Hare), Guthrie Theater, Mpls., 1989, The Speed Of Darkness (Steve Tesich), Belasco Theatre, N.Y.C., 1991, The Iceman Cometh (Eugene O'Neill), Goodman Theatre, 1990, Abbey Theatre, 1992, Dublin, The Night of the Iguana (Tennessee Williams), Goodman Theatre, 1994, Death of a Salesman, Goodman Theatre, 1998; additional directing credits: Griller, The Young Man from Atlanta, A Touch of the Poet, The Night of the Iguana, The Rose Tatoo, On the Open Road, The Tempest, Three Sisters, Galileo, Landscape of the Body, Book of the Night, Pal Joey. Revivals include: Getting Out, In the Belly of the Beast: Letters from Prison, Of Mice and Men, Wings, Mother Courage and Her Children, Hamlet; directed Am. premieres: Pravda, The Misanthrope, Standing on My Knees, The Food Chain, subUrbia, The Consul and Susannah; Won Tony award for Best Revival, 1999, Death of a Salesman. Office: Goodman Theatre 200 S Columbus Dr Chicago IL 60603-6402*

FALOLA, TOYIN, history educator; b. Jan. 1, 1953; s. James and Grace N. Falola; m. Florence Falola, July 25, 1981; children: Dolapo, Bisola, Toyin. BA, U. Ife, Ile-Ife, Nigeria, 1976, PhD, 1980. Prof. U. Ife, 1977-90, York U., North York, Ont., Can., 1990-91, U. Tex., Austin, 1991—. Author: Decolonization and Development Planning, 1996, Religious Militancy and Self-Assertion, 1997, Violence in Nigeria, 1998; editor African Econ. History, African History and the Diaspora Series. Mem. Am. Hist. Assn., African Studies Assn., Ife Humanities Soc. Office: U Tex Dept History Austin TX 78721

FALOON, WILLIAM WASSELL, physician, educator; b. Pitts., July 6, 1920; s. Joseph Coulter and Martha Louise (Wassell) F.; m. Roberta Jane Emery, Sept. 11, 1948; children: Karen F. Durham, Nancy F. Dodd, William W. BA, Allegheny Coll., 1941; MD, Harvard U., 1944. Diplomate Am. Bd. Internal Medicine; cert. registered arbitrator; ordained as deacon Presbyterian, 1958, elder, 1963. Intern Pa. Hosp., Phila., 1944-45; asst. resident in medicine Albany (N.Y.) Hosp., 1945-46, resident in medicine, 1946-47; rsch. fellow in medicine Harvard Med. Sch., Thorndike Meml. Lab., Boston City Hosp., 1947-48; asst. prof. oncology, instr. medicine Albany Med. Coll., 1948-50; instr. medicine SUNY Coll. Medicine, Syracuse, 1950-51, asst. prof., 1951-56, assoc. prof., 1956-64, prof. medicine, 1964-68; program dir. Adult Clin. Rsch. Ctr., Syracuse, 1965-68; physician-in-chief, dir. clin. rsch. and edn. Santa Barbara (Calif.) Gen.-Cottage Hosps., 1968-69; prof. medicine U. Rochester (N.Y.) Sch. Medicine, 1969-92, emeritus prof. medicine, 1992—; mem. Univ. Senate, 1971-74; mem. staff Strong Meml. Hosp., Rochester; mem. staff Highland Hosp., 1969-90, chief medicine, 1970-80, dir. gastroenterology and nutrition, 1970-86; sr. attending physician The Genesee Hosp., 1990-91. Mem. editl. bd. Am. Jour. Clin. Nutrition, 1970-76; contbr. articles to profl. jours. Bd. mgrs. Camp Dudley YMCA, 1962-67, 69-74, chmn. bd., 1966-67, 71-73; bd. dirs. Onondaga County Met. Health Coun., Syracuse, 1959-61; mem. adv. com. Onondaga County Health Dept., 1966-68; bd. dirs. Am. Liver Found., 1982-92, pres. we. N.Y. chpt., 1982-83. Fellow ACP, Rochester Acad. Medicine (dir. 1979-82); mem. Am. Fedn. Clin. Rsch. (councillor 1956-59), AAAS, Onondaga County Med. Soc. (exec. com. 1964-66), Am. Assn. for Study Liver Disease, Am. Inst. Nutrition, Am. Soc. Clin. Nutrition, Endocrine Soc., Am. Gastroent. Assn., Western Soc. for Clin. Rsch., Med. Soc. Monroe County, Internat. Assn. for Study Liver, Assn. Program Dirs. Internal Medicine (councillor 1978-80), N.Y. State Dept. Health (bd. profl. med. conduct N.Y. State 1986—), Island Profl. Rev. Orgn. (cons. 1991-94), Nat. Health Lawyers Assn. (dispute resolver), Gt. Lakes Interurban (sec. 1977-84), Ea. Gut, Oak Hill Country Club (Rochester). Presbyterian. Home: 4 Whitecliff Dr Pittsford NY 14534-2926

FALSETTI, SHERRY ANN, psychologist, medical educator; b. St. Louis, Oct. 5, 1961; d. Robert A. and Shirley A. (Hluzek) F.; m. Mark Barwick, Oct. 25, 1997; stepchildren: Joshua, Micah, Luke. BA, U. Mo., 1987, MA, 1989; PhD, U. Mo., 1993. Lic. clin. psychologist, S.C. Intern in psychology Med. U. S.C., Charleston, 1991-92; postdoct. fellow Med. U. S.C., 1992-93, instr., 1993-95, asst. prof., 1995—; dir. tng. Nat. Crime Victims Rsch. and Treatment Ctr., Charleston, 1996—. Mem. editl. bd. Cognitive and Behavioral Practice, 1995—; contbr. articles to profl. jours., chpts. to books. Mem. planning com. Cropwalk/Ch. World Svc., Charleston, 1994—; mem. Bread for the World, Charleston and Washington, 1994—. Prin. investigator grantee Nat. Inst. Mental Health, 1996. Mem. APA, Internat. Soc. Traumatic Stress Studies, Assn. Advancement of Behavior Therapy (student rsch. award 1992). Office: Med U SC Dept Psychiatry 171 Ashley Ave Charleston SC 29425-0001

FALSGRAF, WILLIAM WENDELL, lawyer; b. Cleve., Nov. 10, 1933; s. Wendell A. and Catherine J. F.; children: Carl Douglas, Jeffrey Price, Catherine Louise. AB cum laude, Amherst Coll., 1955, LLD (hon.), 1986; JD, Case Western Res. U., 1958. Bar: Ohio 1958, U.S. Supreme Ct. 1972. Ptnr. Baker & Hostetler, Cleve., 1971—. Chmn. vis. com. Case Western Res. U. Law Sch., 1973-76; trustee Case Western Reserve U., 1978-90, chmn. bd. overseers, 1977-78; trustee Cleve. Health Mus., 1975-90, Hirom Coll., 1989—; chmn. bd. trustees Hiram Coll., 1990-99. Recipient Disting. Service award; named Outstanding Young Man of Year Cleve. Jr. C. of C., 1962. Fellow Am. Bar Found., Ohio Bar Found.; mem. ABA (chmn. young lawyers sect. 1966-67, mem. ho. of dels. 1967-68, 70—, bd. govs. 1971-75, pres. 1985-86, bd. dirs. Am. Bar Endowment 1974-84, 87-97), Am. Bar Ins. Plans Cons. (pres. 1991—), Ohio Bar Assn. (mem. coun. of dels. 1968-70), Cleve. Bar Assn. (trustee 1979-82), Amherst Alumni Assn. (pres. N.E. Ohio 1964), Union Club, The Country Club. Home: 616 North St Chagrin Falls OH 44022-2514 Office: Baker & Hostetler LLP 3200 National City Ctr Cleveland OH 44114-3485

FALSTROM, KENNETH EDWARD, lawyer; b. San Luis Obispo, Calif., June 25, 1946; s. William and Irene (Carroll) F.; children: Kenneth Todd, Tricia Karen. BA, UCLA, 1967; JD, U. Calif., Berkeley, 1970. Bar: Calif. 1971, U.S. Dist. Ct. (cen. dist.) Calif. 1977. Rsch. asst. Ctr. Study Dem. Insts., Santa Barbara, Calif., 1971; atty. Law Office Christopher Zayic, Santa Barbara, Calif., 1972; pvt. practice Santa Barbara, Calif., 1973—. Bd. dirs. Hope Sch. Dist. Santa Barbara, 1972-80. Office: 1530 Chapala St Santa Barbara CA 93101-3017

FALTER, ROBERT GARY, correctional health care administrator, educator; b. N.Y.C., Sept. 14, 1945; s. Lawrence Zane and Helen (Smith) F.; m. Kathleen Ann Burrill, July 9, 1982; children: John William Wright III, Jason Michael Wright. AA, St. John's U., Jamaica, N.Y., 1965, BA, 1967; MA, Kean Coll. of N.J., 1973; MBA, Cornell U., 1976; PhD, Walden U., 1993. Cert. correctional health profl. advanced. Adminstrv. resident N.Y. Hosp./Cornell Med. Ctr., N.Y.C., summer 1975; mgr. ophthalmology Hahnemann Med. Coll. & Hosp., Phila., 1976-77; dir. out-patient clinic USPHS Ctr. for Disease Control, Phila., 1977-78; project officer ambulatory care data systems USPHS Div. Hosps. and Clinics, West Hyattsville, Md., 1978-80; assoc. dir. ambulatory care USPHS Hosp., Boston, 1980-81; adminstr. family medicine Sch. of Medicine U. Tenn., Memphis, 1981-82; asst. v.p. customer svc./instnl. benefits Blue Cross/Blue Shield of N.Y., N.Y.C., 1982-86; assoc. v.p. ops. S.I. Hosp., 1986-87; assoc. dir. adminstrv. svcs. divsn. fed. employee occupational health USPHS Region II, N.Y.C., 1988-89; health/resources and svcs. adminstr. Rockville, Md., 1989; materiel mgmt. officer, dep. br. chief, 1989; health care adminstr. individual ready res. USPHS, Rockville, 1989-90, chief program liaison unit, 1990-91, chief budget officer BOP/HSD, 1991-93, chief br. budget and mgmt. support, 1993-99; chief health svcs. officer Office of the Surgeon Gen./Pub. Health Svc., 1995-99; adminstrv. officer Fed. Med. Ctr., Fed. Bur. Prisons, Devens, Ayer, Mass., 1999—; Nat. Health Svcs. Corps rep. to Am. Med. TV, Washington, 1990; instr. Commd. Corps Orientation, Bethesda, Md., 1990-95; chmn. hosp. and med. care adminstrs. Health Svcs. Profl. Adv. Com., 1989-91; co-chmn. centennial symposium planning com. Health Svcs. Officers, 1989; lectr. fiscal mgmt. Christian Bros. U., Memphis, 1982; lectr. health econs. grad. program in health svcs. adminstrn. Salve Regina Coll., Newport, R.I., 1984; mem. assoc. grad. faculty, acad. advisor Ctrl. Mich. U. Coll. of Extended Learning Health Svcs. Adminstrn., 1995—; adj. asst. prof. divsn. nursing rsch. Uniformed Svcs. U. Health Scis. Grad. Sch. Nursing, Bethesda, 1996—;bd. dirs. Nat. Commn. on Correctional Health Care, 1991-94, mem. program com., 1991-92, mem. publs. com., 1991-94, mem. exec. com., 1992-94, mng. editor Jour., 1994-97; adj. asst. prof. preventive medicine and biometrics, Health Svcs. Adminstrn., Uniformed Svcs. U. of Health Scis., Bethesda, 1999—. Bd. dirs. Vis. Nurse Assn. Memphis, Inc., 1982; mem. cmty. adv. bd. Primary Health Care for Srs., Allston-Brighton Med. Care Coalition, Boston, 1981; usher coord. St. Michael's Cath. Ch., Poplar Springs, 1989-91. Capt. USPHS, 1988—. Recipient Capt. Stanley J. Kissel, Jr. award USPHS/Health Svcs. Officer, 1994, Surgeon Gen.'s Exemplary Svc. medal USPHS, 1996, 99. Fellow Am. Coll. Healthcare Execs. (book reviewer Hosp. and Health Svcs. Adminstrn., editl. bd. Healthcare Execs. 1986-88), Am. Acad. Med. Adminstrs. (hon.); mem. Assn. Health Care Adminstrs. Nat. Capital Area, Assn. Mil. Surgeons U.S. (cons., reviewer Mil. Medicine 1989—), Commd. Officers Assn. USPHS (sec. Atlanta chpt. 1978), D.C.-Md.-Va. Hosp. Assn. (chmn. liaison com. 51st ann. conv. 1991), Res. Officers Assn. U.S. (newsletter editor Montgomery County chpt. 1989), Anchor and Caduceus Soc. (charter), KC (warden St. Michael's of Poplar Springs coun. 1990-91, chancelor 1991-92). Avocations: teaching, travel, writing, consulting. Home: 2120 Duvall Rd Woodbine MD 21797-8118 Office: Fed Bur of Prisons DOJ Fed MC POB 880 42 Patton Rd Ayer MA 01432

FALTER, VINCENT EUGENE, retired army officer, consultant; b. Akron, Ohio, Dec. 20, 1932; s Alois S. and Prunella (Scharf) F.; m Anna Marta Stephen, Sept. 6, 1958; children: Vincent Eugene, Laura Diane. B.E., U. Nebr.-Omaha, 1963; grad., Command and Gen. Staff Coll., 1968, U.S. War Coll., 1973; M.P.A., Shippensburg State Coll., 1972. Enlisted U.S. Army, 1953, commd. 2d lt., 1954, advanced through grades to maj. gen., 1981; served with 750th F.A. Bn. U.S. Army, Germany, 1954-57; served with Mortar Battery 2d BG 60th Inf. U.S. Army, 1958-59; served with hdqrs. 1st Cav. Div. U.S. Army, Korea, 1959-60; instr. F.A. Sch. U.S. Army, 1960-63, battery comdg. officer B battery 17th F.A. Bn., 1963-64; asst. G-1, 7th Army U.S. Army, Germany, 1964-66; exec. officer 2d Bn., 13th F.A. Bn. U.S. Army, Vietnam, 1966-67; staff officer Dept. Army Office Dept. Chief of Staff for Ops., Washington, 1968-70; comdg. officer 2d Bn. 19th F.A. U.S. Army, Vietnam, 1970-71; exec. officer F.A. Br. U.S. Army, Washington, 1971-72; sec. F.A. Sch. U.S. Army, 1973-74, comdg. officer 75th F.A Group, 1974-76; dir. nuclear and chem. ops. Dept. Army, Office Dep. Chief of Staff for Ops., Washington, 1977-79; comdg. gen. VII Corps Arty. U.S. Army, Germany, 1979-81; dep. insp. gen. U.S. Army, Washington, 1981-82, with Office Chief of Staff, 1982-83; comdg. gen. Mil Personnel Ctr., 1983-85; dep. dir. ops. Def. Nuclear Agy., Washington, 1985-86, dep. asst. to sec. def. for atomic energy, 1986-88; ret., 1988; founder The Copley Group, nat. security cons., 1988—; mem. NRC/NAS. Decorated Def. D.S.M. with oak leaf cluster, Army D.S.M., Legion of Merit with 2 oak leaf clusters, Bronze Star with 3 oak leaf clusters, Air Medal with 15 oak leaf clusters. Mem. F.A. Assn., Rotary. Roman Catholic. Home: 7914 Colorado Springs Dr Springfield VA 22153-2719 Office: Office Sec Def ATSD (AE) Washington DC 20301

FALUDI, SUSAN C., journalist, scholarly writer. Formerly with West Mag., San Jose, Calif., Mercury News; with San Francisco Bur., Wall St. Jour.; spkr. in field. Author: Backlash: The Undeclared War Against American Women, 1991 (National Book Critics Circle award for general non-fiction 1992); contbr. articles to mags. Recipient Pulitzer Prize for explanatory journalism, 1991. Office: care Sandra Dijkstra Literary Agy 1155 Camino Del Mar Ste 515 Del Mar CA 92014-2605*

FALVEY, PATRICK JOSEPH, lawyer; b. Yonkers, N.Y., June 29, 1927; s. Patrick J. Falvey and Nora Rowley Falvey; m. Eileen Ryan, June 29, 1963; 1 child, Patrick James. Student Iona Coll., 1944-47; JD cum laude, St. John's U., Jamaica, N.Y., 1950. Bar: N.Y. 1951, U.S. Supreme Ct. 1972. Law asst. Port Authority of N.Y. and N.J., 1951, atty., 1951-65, chief condemnation and litigation, 1965-67, asst. gen. counsel, 1967-72, gen. counsel, 1972-91, gen. counsel, asst. exec. dir., 1979-87, dep. exec. dir. 1987-91, spl. counsel, 1991—. With USN, 1945-46. Advisor U.S. del. to UN Com. on Internat. Trade Law, U.S. State Dept. Pvt. Trade Law; advisor to U.S. del. UN diplomatic confs. on treaty on liability of ops. of transport terminals; N.Y. County Lawyers Assn., 1992—. Recipient Howard S. Cullman Disting. Svc. medal Port Authority of N.Y. and N.J., 1982, 91; Loftus award and Trustees' Honoree Iona Coll., 1982. Fellow Am. Bar Found.; mem. ABA (chmn. urban state and local govt. law sect. 1983-84, vice-chmn. model procurement code project 1979—, sect. del. 1987-90), FBA, Airport Operators Coun. Internat. (legal com.), Assn. Bar City N.Y., N.Y. County Lawyers Assn., Nat. Inst. Mcpl. Law Officers, Internat. Assn. Ports and Harbors (hon., legal counsellors com., arbitrator, mediator trade and comml. matters, cons. transp. and trade studies), Woodlawn Comm. Assn. (counsel 1996—). Address: 81 Pondfield Rd #338 Bronxville NY 10708-3818

FALVEY, W(ILLIAM) PATRICK, judge; b. Penn Yan, N.Y., Aug. 31, 1946; s. William Jennings and Thelma Rosetta (Hall) F.; m. Suzanne G. Christensen, Sept. 14, 1968; children: Scott P., Jennifer G. BA, Hobart Coll., 1968; JD, John Marshall Law Sch., 1975; postgrad., U. Nev., 1994. Bar: N.Y. 1976, U.S. Dist. Ct. (we. dist.) N.Y. 1979, U.S. Supreme Ct. 1984. Confidential law clerk N.Y. State Supreme Justice, Penn Yan, 1976-77; atty. Dept. Social Svcs. Yates County, Penn Yan, 1976-77, pvt. practice, 1976-88, asst. pub. defender, 1977-80, acting dist. atty., 1980-81, dist. atty., 1981-88, judge surrogate and family ct., acting Supreme Ct. Justice, 1988—; mem. alternatives to incarceration com. Yates County; mem. Yates County Custody and Visitation Mediation Bd., 1995—; adv. com. Finger Lakes Vol. Lawyer's Svc., Geneva, N.Y., 1989-91; chair bd. trustees Yates County Law Libr.; jud. adv. coun. Seventh Jud. Dist. Mem., sec. Yates County Republican Com., Penn Yan, 1977-81; mem. Yates County Coop. Farm & Craft Market, Penn Yan, 1976-79; bd. dirs. Lit. Vols., Penn Yan, 1979-83; mem., pres. Yates County Profl. & Health Adv. Com., Penn Yan, 1980-88. 1st lt.

U.S. Army, 1969-71, Vietnam. Recipient N.Y. State Conspicuous Svc. Cross, Hon. Hugh R. Carey Gov. N.Y., 1979. Ctr. for Dispute Settlement's Disting. Jurist award, 1996. Mem. Am. Judges Assn., Am. Judicature Soc., Ontario/Yates Magistrates Assn., N.Y. Bar Assn., N.Y. State, County, Family and Surrogate Judges Assn., Yates County Bar Assn. (past pres.), VFW, Am. Legion (post comdr. 1981). Fax: (315) 536-5190. Office: Yates County Cts 108 Court St Penn Yan NY 14527-1102

FALVO, MARK ANTHONY, lawyer; b. Boston, June 11, 1960; s. Carl Albert and Thelma Ann (Evans) F. BA in Polit. Sci., Pa. State U., 1982; JD, Ohio No. U., 1988. Bar: Pa. 1990, U.S. Supreme Ct. 1997; cert. solicitor County Treas.'s Office 1993. Account exec., pub. rels. staff, broadcaster Clearfield (Pa.) Broadcasters, Inc., 1975-82, 91; account exec., pub. rels. staff Ctr. Comm., Inc., State College, Pa., 1982-83, Gilcom Comm., Inc., Altoona, Pa., 1983-84, State College Broadcasters, Inc., 1984-85; pub. rels. mgr. dept. arts and comm. Ohio No. U., Ada, 1985-88; law clk., atty. Ct. Common Pleas of Clearfield County-Pa. 46th Jud. Dist., 1988-93; pvt. practice Clearfield, 1993—; intern Hill, Morgan & Africa, Warren, Pa., summer 1986, Dist. Atty.'s Office Clearfield County, summer 1987; county coord. Clearfield County Statewide Mock Trial Competition, 1989-96; dist. coord. Pa. Statewide Mock Trial Competition, 1991-95, regional coord., 1993-94; dir. Boy Scouts of Am., Law and Law Enforcement Explorers Post, 1992-94; coord. Teen Ct. Program, Clearfield County, 1992—; law clk., atty. Ct. Common Pleas of Clearfield County, Pa., 46th Jud. Dist., 1998—; others. Campaign staff Congressman William F. Clinger, Jr., State College, 1984; bd. dirs., vice-chmn. ARC/Clearfield Chpt., 1989-95; bd. dirs., mem. Am. Cancer Soc./Clearfield County, 1989-93; bd. dirs., treas. Pa. State Alumni Assn., DuBois, 1989-95; vol. Clearfield Sr. Little League Baseball, 1975-82, Clearfield Little League Baseball, 1999—; mem. Clearfield County Crimestoppers, 1998. Recipient Spl. Recognition award Pa. Ho. of Reps., Harrisburg, 1988, Spl. Recognition award Pa. Senate, Harrisburg, 1988, Spl. Recognition award U.S. Congress, 1988, Law Mentoring Program award Conf. of County Bar Leaders, Harrisburg, 1991, Street Law Program award Conf. of County Bar Leaders, Harrisburg, 1991, Outstanding Young Alumni award Pa. State U., DuBois, 1992, Spl. Recognition award Teen Ct. Program Clearfield County, 1996. Mem. ABA (Pub. Svc. award 1990, 91, 98), Pa. Bar Assn., Clearfield County Bar Assn. (v.p. 1998—, rep. under 35 1989-98, chmn. young lawyers divsn. 1989-98, exec. com. 1989—, chmn. Law Day 1989, 90, 91, 92, 97, 98, mem. Law Day com. 1993, 94, 95, 96, 98), Sports, Art and Entertainment Law Com., The Forum on Entertainment and Sports Industries, Clearfield County Pa. Bar Inst. (chmn. CLE 1998—). Democrat. Methodist/Roman Catholic. Avocations: painting, tennis, golf, music, skiing. Home: 7 Bigler Rd Clearfield PA 16830-1762 Office: PO Box 552 211 1/2 E Locust St Clearfield PA 16830-2422

FALVO, ROBERT J., music educator; b. Aug. 27, 1963. MusB, Fredonia (N.Y.) State U., 1985; MusM, Manhattan Sch. Music, 1987, MusD, 1989. Asst. prof. music Appalachian State U., Boone, N.C., 1993—. Home: PO Box 368-DTS Boone NC 28607

FALWELL, JERRY L., clergyman; b. Lynchburg, Va., Aug. 11, 1933; s. Cary H. and Helen V. (Beasley) F.; m. Macel Pate, Apr. 12, 1958; children: Jerry L., Jeannie, Jonathan. BA, Bapt. Bible Coll., Springfield, Mo., 1956; DD (hon.), Tenn. Temple U.; LLD (hon.), Calif. Grad. Sch. Theology, Cen. U., Seoul, Korea. Founder, pastor Thomas Rd. Bapt. Ch., Lynchburg, Va., 1956—; founder Liberty U., Lynchburg, 1971, Moral Majority Inc., 1979-89; chancellor Liberty U., Lynchburg, Va.; Host: (TV show) Old Time Gospel Hour; lectr. in field. Author: Listen, America!, 1980, The Fundamentalist Phenomenon, 1981, Finding Inner Peace and Strength, 1982, When It Hurts Too Much to Cry, 1984, Wisdom for Living, 1984, Stepping Out on Faith, 1984, Champions for God, 1985, If I Should Die Before I Wake, 1986, (autobiography) Strength For the Journey, 1987, New American Family, 1992; co-author: Church Aflame, 1971, Capturing a Town for Christ, 1973. Recipient Clergyman of Yr. award Religious Heritage Am., 1979, Jabotinsky Centennial medal, 1980, Two Hungers award Food for the Hungry Internat., 1981; named Christian Humanitarian of Yr., Food for the Hungry Internat., One of 25 Most Influential People in Am., U.S. News & World Report, 1983; Number One Most Admired Conservative Man Not in Congress Conservative Digest, 1983, 2d Most Admired Man Good Housekeeping, 1982, 84, 86; named to Nat. Religious Broadcasters' Hall of Fame, 1985. Mem. Nat. Assn. Religious Broadcasters (bd. dirs.). Address: PO Box 368 Madison Heights VA 24572-0368 Address: Liberty U 1971 University Blvd Lynchburg VA 24502-2269*

FALZINI, MARK WILLIAM, archivist; b. Trenton, N.J., July 3, 1968; s. Michael Joseph and Barbara Louisa (Kale) F. BA, Trenton State Coll., Ewing, N.J., 1991; MLS, Rutgers U., 1994. Archivist N.J. State Police Mus. and Learning Ctr., West Trenton, 1992—. Mem. MacGregor Pipe Band, 1989—, pipe sgt., 1990—; chmn. history com. Trinity Cathedral, 1996-97; charter mem. U.S. Holocaust Meml. Mus. Mem. Libr. of Congress Assocs., Mid-Atlantic Regional Archives Conf. Anglican Ch. Avocation: bagpiping. Office: New Jersey State Police Museum PO Box 7068 Trenton NJ 08628-0068

FALZONE, JOHN F., association executive; b. Rockford, Ill., May 15, 1942. Founder, pres. Ladies Profl. Bowlers Tour, Rockford, 1980—; bd. dirs. Strike Ten Entertainment. Contbr. articles to profl. jours. Trustee Internat. Bowling Hall of Fame; vol. fundraiser Muscular Dystrophy Soc. Inductee Women's Profl. Bowling Hall of Fame. Mem. Bowling Writers Assn. Am. (dir.). Office: Ladies Professional Bowlers Tour 7171 Cherryvale Blvd Rockford IL 61112*

FALZONE, JOSEPH SAM, retired airlines company crew chief; b. Passaic, N.J., June 20, 1917; s. Ross and Concetta (Miada) F.; m. Anna Rand, June 21, 1947; children: Michael Joseph, Connie R. AAD, Western Air Coll., 1941. Lead field insp. Transworld Airlines, N.Y.C., 1946-83; ret. Author: Particle Physics of the Atom, Vol. I, II, III, 1993; patentee in field. With USN, 1941-43. Recipient Aviation Mechanic citation FAA, 1975. Mem. AAAS, N.Y. Acad. Sci. Roman Catholic. Avocations: astronomy, phys. sci.

FAMIGLIETTI, NANCY ZIMA, computer executive; b. Hartford, Conn., Nov. 10, 1956; d. Jospeh and Angeline (Morello) Zima; m. Arthur R. Famiglietti Jr., May 23, 1981. BA in Math., Computer Sci., Eastern Conn. State Coll., Willimantic, 1978. Sr. programmer analyst Hamilton Standard, Windsor Locks, Conn., 1978-82; system analyst Cigna Corp., Hartford, 1982-83, system designer, 1983-86, lead system designer, 1986-89; system advisor Aetna Life & Casualty Co., Hartford, 1989-93, system adminstr., 1993-94, sr. sys. adminstr., 1994-95, bus. sys. mgr., 1995-98; bus. cons. Hartford Life, Simsbury, Conn., 1998—. Active Windsor (Conn.) Hist. Soc. Mem. Kappa Mu Epsilon. Avocations: reading, walking, crafts, swimming, bicycling. Home: 81 Mcgrath Rd South Windsor CT 06074-1123

FAMMERÉE, RICHARD ARTHUR, poet, composer, performing artist. BA, Beloit Coll. Former chmn. art. dept. The Found., Chgo.; former pres. Chgo. Artists Coalition; former dir. Chgo. Arts Emerging, BHF Atelier, Chgo.; dir. Poetry in Process, 1996—, Nomadica, 1996—. Author: Lessons of Water and Thirst, 1999, poems; editor Lap of Poetica Literary Jour., 1997-98; dir. Poetry and Its Music International, 1999—, Sacred Site, 1999—; co-dir: Linnaeus & Fammerée, 1996—. Avocations: world travel, French studies.

FAMULARO, JOSEPH L., prosecutor; b. Mt. Olivet, Ky., Nov. 6, 1942. BA, Loyola U., New Orleans, 1964; JD, U. Ky., 1967. Clk. to Hon. Mac Swinford U.S. Dist. Ct. Ky.; atty. Ky. Atty. Gen. Office; legal officer Ky. State Police; 1st asst. and U.S. atty. for ea. dist. Ky. Office U.S. Atty., 1977-81; chief dep. atty. gen. Office Atty. Gen. Ky., 1982-86; 1st asst. county atty. Fayette County Attys. Office, 1988-89; commr. pub. safety Lexington Fayette Urban County, Ky., 1990-93; now U.S. atty. for ea. dist. Ky. U.S. Dept. Justice, Lexington. Office: US Atty Ea Dist Ky PO Box 3077 Lexington KY 40588-3077

FAN, HUNG Y., virology educator, consultant; b. Beijing, Oct. 30, 1947; s. Hsu Yun and Li Nien (Bien) F. BS, Purdue U., 1967; PhD, MIT, 1971. Asst. research prof. Salk Inst., San Diego, 1973-81; asst. prof. U. Calif., Irvine, 1981-83, assoc. prof., 1984-88, prof., 1988—, dir. Cancer Rsch. Inst., 1985—, acting dean Sch. Biol. Scis., 1990-91. Contbr. over 120 articles to profl. jours. NIH grantee, 1973—, grant review coms., 1973—; Woodrow Wilson Found. grad. fellow, 1967, Helen Hay Whitney Found. postdoctorate fellow, 1971. Fellow AAAS, Am. Acad. Microbiology; mem. Am. Soc. Microbiology, Am. Soc. Virology, Am. Assn. Cancer Rsch. Avocation: chamber music. Office: U Calif Cancer Rsch Inst Sch Biol Sci Irvine CA 92717

FAN, LINDA C., investment company executive; b. Princeton, N.J., Mar. 22, 1956; d. Chung-Teh and Mook-Lan (Mui) F.; m. William A. Schaefer, Aug. 9, 1985; children: Ralph, Fred, George. AB, Princeton U., 1978; MBA, U. Chgo., 1982. Assoc. Salomon Bros., N.Y.C., 1982-85; assoc. Morgan Stanley & Co., N.Y.C., 1985-87, v.p., 1987-91, prin., 1991—. Office: Morgan Stanley Co Inc 30th Fl 1221 Ave of the Americas New York NY 10020

FAN, TAI-SHEN LIU, dietitian; b. Taichung, Taiwan, Nov. 15, 1950; came to the U.S., 1976; d. Chi-Pei and Ching-Lien Liu; m. Chien-Chung Fan, Feb. 22, 1975; 1 child, Caroline. BA in Social Edn., Nat. Taiwan Normal U., Taipei, 1972; AS in Med. Lab. Tech., Miami (Fla.)-Dade Cmty. Coll., 1980; BS in Nutrition and Med. Dietetics, U. Ill., Chgo., 1986. Lic. dietitian State of Ill. Dept. Profl. Regulation. Counselor, tchr. Ta-Li Girls' Jr. H.S., Taipei, 1972-73, chief counselor, tchr., 1973-76; clin. dietitian Suburban Hosp. and Sanitariam, Hinsdale, Ill., 1986-87, St. Francis Hosp., Evanston, Ill., 1987—. Dean of acads. Chinese Cultural and Ednl. Assn. (CCEA)-Chinese Lang. Sch., Skokie, Ill., 1993-95, rec. sec., 1995-96, asst. prin., dean acads., 1996-97. Cheng-Fu Hsieh Meml. scholar, Taipei, 1971, Yun-Wu Wang scholar, Taipei, 1971. Mem. Am. Dietetic Assn. (registered dietitian), Ill. Dietetic Assn., U. Ill. Alumni Assn., Phi Tau Phi, Phi Theta Kappa. Avocations: reading, cooking. Office: Chinese Cultural Ednl Assn PO Box 4572 7701 N Lincoln Skokie IL 60077

FANCHER, EDWIN CRAWFORD, psychologist, educator; b. Middletown, N.Y., Aug. 29, 1923; s. Frank Dane and Elizabeth (McGarr) F.; m. Vivian Kramer, Nov. 8, 1969; children: Bruce Daniel, Emily Jill. BA, NYU, 1949; MA, $, 1951. Psychologist Linden (N.J.) Mental Hygiene Clinic, 1955-58; co-founder, clin. dir. Cmty. Guidance Svc., N.Y.C., 1958—; pvt. practice psychology, counseling N.Y.C., 1958—; co-founder, dir. Washington Sq. Inst. Psychotherapy and Mental Health, N.Y.C., 1960-70; co-founder, pub. Village Voice, N.Y.C., 1955-74; dir. Orange County Telephone Co., Middletown, N.Y., 1946-60; cons. Plumsock Fund, Indpls., 1974-96, pres. 1985-96. Founder, past chmn. N.Y. Neighborhoods Coun. on Narcotics Addiction. Served with U.S. Army, 1943-46. Decorated Bronze star. Mem. Am. Psychol. Assn., Am. Inst. Psychotherapy and Psychoanalysis, Am. Orthopsychiat. Assn., N.Y. State Psychol. Assn., Coun. Psychoanalytic Assn., N.Y. Freudian Soc. (mem. faculty tng. analyst), Gipsy Trail. Democrat. Home: 40 5th Ave New York NY 10011-8843

FANCHER, MICHAEL REILLY, newspaper editor, newspaper publishing executive; b. Long Beach, Calif., July 13, 1946; s. Eugene Arthur and Ruth Leone (Dickson) F.; m. Nancy Helen Edens, Nov. 3, 1967 (div. 1982); children: Jason Michael, Patrick Reilly; m. 2d Carolyn Elaine Bowers, Mar. 25, 1983; Katherine Claire, Elizabeth Lynn. BA, U. Oreg., 1968; MS, Kans. State U., 1971; MBA, U. Wash., 1986. Reporter, asst. city editor Kansas City Star, Mo., 1970-76, city editor, 1976-78; reporter Seattle Times, 1978-79, night city editor, 1979-80, asst. mng. editor, 1980-81, mng. editor, 1981-86, exec. editor, 1986—, now vice pres., exec. editor, 1989-95; sr. v.p., 1995—; bd. dirs. Blethen Maine Newspapers, Walla Walla Union-Bulletin, Yakima Herald Rep. Ruhl fellow U. Oreg., 1983. Mem. Am. Soc. Newspaper Editors, Soc. Profl. Journalists, Nat. Press Photographers Assn. (Editor of Yr. 1986). Office: Seattle Times Fairview Ave N & John St PO Box 70 Seattle WA 98111-0070

FANELLI, JOSEPH JAMES, retired public affairs executive, consultant; b. Hartford, Conn., Mar. 22, 1924; s. George A.M. and Nicoletta (Lamarra) F.; m. Pirkko Annikki Saarinen, Aug. 30, 1958; children: George Tauno, John Timo, Christina Colette. BS in Fin., Syracuse U., 1949; cert. mgmt., Mich. State U., 1969; MA in Internat. Affairs, Cath. U. Am., 1995. Stockbroker G.H. Walker & Co., N.Y.C. and Hartford, Conn., 1949-51; broker, br. mgr. Schibo Corp., Jersey City and Boston, 1952-55; asst. dir. devel. U. Hartford, 1955-56; spl. asst. U.S. Rep. Edwin H. May Jr., Washington, 1957-58, U.S. Senator Prescott Bush, Washington, 1959-62; asst. mgr., then mgr. pub. affairs dept. U.S. C. of C., Washington, 1963-75; pres. Bus.-Industry Polit. Action Com., Washington, 1975-93. Editor: Enhancing the Image of Business, 1972. Mem. Md. Rep. State Ctrl. Com., Montgomery County, 1970; vol. Cmty. Chest, ARC, Conn. and Md.; active numerous polit. campaigns at local, regional, and state levels, 1956—. Staff Sgt. USAF, 1943-46, PTO. Recipient Legion of Hon. award Chapel of the Four Chaplains, 1980, Scholastic Hon. award Alpha Kappa Psi, 1949. Mem. U.S. C. of C., Nat. Assn. Mfrs. (pub. affairs steering com. 1976—), World Affairs Coun. Washington, Greater Washington Sigma Chi Alumni Assn. (cmty. amb. to France, designee Experiment in Internat. Living 1954, Significant Sig award 1991), D.C. Lions Club (pres. 1984-85, Lion of Yr. 1987, 92), Internat. Club, Univ. Club. Republican. Roman Catholic. Avocations: travel, politics, sports, music, international relations. Home: 11602 Monticello Ave Silver Spring MD 20902-1710

FANELLI, MICHAEL PAUL, music educator; b. Evanston, Ill., Feb. 12, 1943; s. George and Gloria (Del Carlo) F.; m. Carla Jean Saiger, May 28, 1978. BMus, U. Ill., 1968, EdD in Music Edn., 1999; MA in Music History, U. Mo., 1981. Cert. tchr. K-12, Mo., Iowa. Instr. of double bass U. Mo., Columbia, 1968-74; double bass artist-in-residence Stephens Coll., Columbia, 1968-75; profl. double bassist St. Louis Philharmonic, 1975-83; instr. instrumental music Sch. Dist. of the City of Ladue, Mo., 1983-87; instr. of music U. No. Iowa, Cedar Falls, 1987—; instr. of double bass Grinnell (Iowa) Coll., 1996—; founder, music dir. No. Iowa Jr. Orchestra, Cedar Falls, 1990-92; music dir. No. Iowa Youth Orchestra, 1994—; distance learning instr. music iowa Comms. Network, U. No. Iowa, 1995—; adv. bd. Iowa Alliance for Arts Edn., Des Moines, 1994—. Contbr. articles to profl. jours.; contbg. author: American String Teacher, 1997. Double bassist U. Iowa, U.S. State Dept. tour of S.Am., 1964. Microcomputer grantee U. No. Iowa, Cedar Falls, 1989, 92, 95-98. Mem. Iowa String Tchrs. Assn. (pres. 1996-98, Disting. Svc. award 1992, Cert. for Outstanding Contbn. 1996), Iowa Sch. Orchestra Assn. (pres. 1992-96), Am. String Tchrs. Assn. (editl. com. 1997—, Outstanding Contbr. 1995-97), Suzuki Assn. of the Americas (column editor 1992—), Mo. String Tchrs. Assn. (sec.-treas. 1983-87), Kappa Delta Pi. Avocations: Am. art history, photography, fly fishing. Home: 203 Parkgate Rd Cedar Falls IA 50613-1953 Office: Univ No Iowa Price Lab Sch Cedar Falls IA 50613

FANELLI, ROBERT DREW, surgeon; b. Abington, Pa., Dec. 28, 1960; s. Salvatore Michael and Josephine Fanelli; m. Josephine Anne Macri, May 27, 1989. BS magna cum laude, U. Richmond, 1982; MD, Med. Coll. of Pa., 1986. Diplomate Am. Bd. Surgery, Nat. Bd. Med. Examiners; cert. BLS, ACLS, Advanced Trauma Life Support; lic. MD, Mass.; DEA cert.; Mass. Controlled Substance permit. Residency in surgery The Stamford (Conn.) Hosp., 1986-88; integrated residency in gen. surgery Mich. State U., East Lansing, 1988-91; fellow dept. surgery The Mount Sinai Med. Ctr. of Cleve., 1991-92; gen. and laparoendoscopic surgeon Surg. Specialists of Western New Eng., P.C., Pittsfield, Mass., 1992—; surg. dir. New Eng. Pain Diagnosis and Treatment Ctr., Pittsfield, 1996—; surgeon Berkshire Med. Ctr., Pittsfield, 1992—; dir. endoscopic svcs. Hillcrest Hosp., Pittsfield, 1993—; dir. edn. in laparoendoscopic surgery Berkshire Med. Ctr. Residency Program in Surgery, 1996—; asst. prof. surgery U. Mass. Med. Sch.; tchg. assoc. premed. program Williams Coll.; conf. presenter in field. Contbr. articles to profl. publs. Recipient U. Richmond Acad. Honors award, 1980, Va. Inst. for Sci. Rsch. Undergrad. award in Biology, U. Richmond, 1981, John Neasmith Dickinson Meml. Rsch. award in Biology, U. Richmond, 1981, Brownell Found. Resident Rsch. award in Gen. Surgery, McLaren Regional Med. Ctr., 1989, Flint Acad. of Surgery Resident Rsch. award, 1990, Mich. State U. Dept. of Surgery Resident Rsch. award, 1992; named Outstanding Resident Instr. of Yr. in Gen. Surgery, Mich. State U., 1990-91. Fellow ACS; mem. Am. Soc. Gastrointestinal Endoscopy, Soc. Am. Gastrointestinal Endoscopic Surgeons (stds. of practice com.), Am. Neuromodulation Soc., Mass. Med. Soc., Berkshire Dist. Med. Soc., Phi Beta Kappa, Sigma Xi, Gamma Sigma Epsilon, Phi Eta Sigma. Avocations: snow skiing, boating, children's activities, tennis. Office: Surg Specialists Western New Eng 510 North St Ste 202 Pittsfield MA 01201-4111

FANELLI, SEAN A., college president; b. N.Y., Dec. 31, 1937; s. Alphonse and Rose (Siconolfi) F.; m. Marion Ryan, Dec. 27, 1969; children: Elizabeth, Thomas, James. BS, St. Francis Coll., Bklyn., 1966; PhD, Fordham U., 1970. Prof. biology Westchester C.c., Valhalla, N.Y., 1969-72; chmn. dept. biology, sci. Westchester C.c., Valhalla, 1970-72, assoc. dean health sci., 1972-76, dean acad. affairs, 1976-82; pres. Nassau C.C., Garden City, N.Y., 1982—; evaluator, chmn. Middle States Assn., Phila., 1977—; cons. N.J. Dept. Higher Edn., 1977-84. Mem. Westchester County Emergency Med. Svc. Coun., N.Y., 1982-82, Nassau County Criminal Justice Coordinating Coun., N.Y., 1984—; chmn. L.I. Regional coun. High Edn., 1984—, L.I. Regional Adv. Bd. Higher Edn., 1994-95. Recipient Alexander Meiklejohn award for acad. freedom AAUP, 1995, NDEA fellow, 1967-70. Mem. Am. coun. Edn.)comm. ednl. credit and credentials 1992—), Assn. Pres.' of Pub. C.C. (pres. 1985—), AAAS, Order Sons of Italy in Am., Dante Found., Sons of St. Patrick. Avocations: photogray, computers. Office: Nassau Community Coll One Education Dr Garden City NY 11530-6793

FANG, CHENG-SHEN, chemical engineering educator; b. Taipei, Taiwan, Mar. 29, 1936; came to U.S., 1962; s. Hou-Chin and Roumouy Fang; m. Fei-Ying Fang, Oct. 5, 1972. BSChemE, Nat. Taiwan U., Taipei, 1958; MSChemE, U. Houston, 1965, PhD in Chem. Engring., 1968. Registered profl. engr., La. Postdoctoral fellow U. Houston, 1968-69; prof. chem. engring. U. Southwestern La., Lafayette, 1969—; presenter in field. Co-author: Oceanography-Contemporary Reading, 1996; creater (computer software) ChemCalc 2, ChemCalc 3, 1985; contbr. articles to profl. jours. Mem. AIChE, Soc. Petroleum Engrs. Office: U Southwestern La Dept Chem Engring Madison Hall Rex St Lafayette LA 70504

FANG, FRANK FU, physicist, electronics engineer; b. Beijing, Sept. 11, 1930; came to U.S., 1952; s. Chen C. and Roh (Hu) F.; m. Louise T. Hsieh, Aug. 24, 1957; children: Karen, Janis, Eric, Mark. BS, Nat. Taiwan U., Taipei, Republic of China, 1951; MS, U. Notre Dame, 1954; PhD, U. Ill., 1959; DSc (hon.), Nat. Chiao Tung U., Republic of China, 1989. Rsch. specialist Boeing Airplane Co., Seattle, 1959-60; rsch. staff mem. IBM T.J. Watson Rsch. Ctr., Yorktown Heights, N.Y., 1960-93, mgr. semiconductor device physics, 1971-93; ret. IBM T.J. Watson Rsch. Ctr., Yorktown Heights, 1993; adj. prof. physics Brown U., 1986-92; vis. prof. Nat. Taiwan U., 1967-68; vis. sci entist IBM U.K. Lab., 1976-77; Disting. lectr. Nat. Sci. Coun., Republic of China, 1988; vis. scientist, prof. Fraunhofer Inst., Freiburg, Germany, 1990-91; NSC prof. condensed matter physics Nat. Taiwan U., 1994-97. Recipient Disting. Alumnus award Electric and Computer Engring. Alumni Assn., U. Ill., 1989, Achievement award Chinese-Am. Acad. and Profl. Soc., 1989, Humboldt Rsch. award Alexander von Humboldt Found., 1990-91. Fellow IEEE (David Sarnoff award 1987), Am. Phys. Soc. (Oliver E. Buckley prize 1988), Franklin Inst. (John Price Wetherill medal 1981); mem. NAE, Academia Sinica. Home: 1691 Cardinal Ct Yorktown Heights NY 10598-5138 Office: IBM T J Watson Rsch Ctr PO Box 218 Yorktown Heights NY 10598-0218

FANG, LI-ZHI, physicist, educator; b. Beijing, Feb. 12, 1936; came to U.S., 1991; s. Cheng-Pu and Peiji (Shi) F.; m. Shuxian Li, Oct. 6, 1961; children: Ke, Zhe. PhD in Physics, Peking U., 1956; PhD (hon.), Univ. Libre de Bruxelles, 1989, Univ. di Roma, La Sapienza, 1990, Coll. William and Mary, 1991; DSc (hon.), U. Toronto, 1991, York U., Can., 1993; LHD (hon.), U. Wis., River Falls, 1992. Jr. rsch. fellow Inst. Modern Physics, Chinese Acad. Scis., Beijing, 1956-58; asst. prof. U. Sci. and Tech. of China, Beijing, 1958-63, lectr., 1963-77, prof. physics, 1978-87, dir. ctr. for astrophysics, 1980-87, v.p., 1984-87; prof., head of theoretical astrophysics group Beijing Astron. Obs., Chinese Acad. Scis., 1987-89; prof. physics and astronomy U. Ariz., Tucson, 1991—; vis. fellow Academia dei Lincei, Rome, 1979; sr. vis. fellow Inst. Astronomy, Cambridge (Eng.) U., 1979-80, 90; vis. prof. Rsch. Inst. Fundamental Physics, Kyoto U., Japan, 1981-82; vis. fellow physics dept. U. Rome, 1983; assoc. mem. Internat. Ctr. for Theoretical Physics, Trieste, Italy, 1984-89; active Inst. for Advanced Study, Princeton, 1986, 91; vis. prof. dept. physics and astronomy Princeton (N.J.) U., 1991. Author or co-author of 20 books, including Creation of the Universe (with S.X. Li), 1989, Quantum Cosmology (with R. Ruffini), 1987, Bringing Down the Great Wall, 1991; editorial bd. 15 profl. jours., including Internat. Jour. Modern Physics, Modern Physics Letters A, Scienza, Nouvo Comento B.; contbr. more than 200 articles to profl. jours. Decorated officier l'Ordre des Arts et des Lettres (France); recipient numerous scientific awards in China including Nat. award for Sci. and Tech., 1978, Anhui Province award for sci. and tech., 1978, Yunnan Province award for sci. and tech., 1979, Innermongolia Autonomous Region award for sci. and tech., 1980, Chinese Acad. Scis. award, 1982; recipient other awards including First award Internat. Gravity Rsch. Found., 1985, Chinese Dem. Edn. Found. award, 1987, Peace Price of Politiken and Dagens Nyheter, 1989, Robert F. Kennedy Human Rights award, 1989, George Meany Human Rights award, 1990, Evelyn and Louis P. Smith First Amendment award, 1990, Freedom award Internat. Rescue Com., 1991, Human Rights award Internat. League Human Rights, 1991, Sidney Hook Meml. award Nat. Assn. Scholars, 1991, Human Courage award World Pub. Forum, 1993, Andrew Allen Liberty award Fgn. Policy Rsch. Inst., 1993, and numerous others. Mem. Am. Phys. Soc. (vice chair com. Internat. Freedom of Scis. 1993, chair 1994), Am. Astronomical Soc., Internat. Ctr. for Relativistic Astrophysics (mem. coun.), N.Y. Acad. Sci. (award 1988), Internat. Union for Pure and Applied Physics (commn. C19 on Astrophysics, commn. A.2). Achievements include development of theories that the distribution of galaxies might be described by a self-affinity geometry, that the clustering of large redshift quasars is less than that of small redshift quasars, that the topology of the cosmic spacetime is an important remains of the Planck era and the infrared cutoff in the primodial spectrum of density perturbations is probably an evidence of multiply connected topology of the universe, that the phase transitions of vacuum states play an important role in the generation of entropy in the early universe and in the formation of objects with abnormal matter states. Office: U Ariz Dept Physics Tucson AZ 85721

FANG, PEN JENG, engineering executive and consultant; b. Tainan, Taiwan, July 13, 1931; came to U.S., 1958; s. Den Chuang and Wu Tien (Su) F.; m. Elizabeth Meiling Yang, Aug. 4, 1962; children: Kenneth, Terry, Shona. BS, Nat. Taiwan U., 1955; MS, Okla. State U., 1960; PhD, Cornell U., 1966. Registered profl. engr., R.I.; registered structural engr., Ill. Sr. engr. Inar D. Hillman & Assocs., Chgo., 1960-63; sr. rsch. engr. Applied Rsch. Lab., U.S. Steel Corp., Monroeville, Pa., 1965-68; asst. prof. engring. Concordia U. (formerly Sir George Williams U.), Montreal, Que., Can., 1968-70; asst. to assoc. prof. U. R.I., Kingston, 1970-81; mgr. engring. analysis ITT-Grinnell Corp., Providence, 1981-84; pres. Engitek, Inc., Cranston, R.I., 1985—; with Protze Cons. Engrs., Needham Heights, Mass., 1994—, Tangpu EngiTek Arch. and Engring. Co., Shanghai, 1994—; town engr. Town of West Warwick, R.I., 1989-92; exec. com. Promon Engring. Co., Rio de Janeiro, 1975-78, Natron Engring. Co., Rio de Janeiro, 1978-81; dir. Tawan C. of C., New England, 1996—. Contbr. over 20 tech. articles to profl. jours. Vice chmn. bd. dirs. R.I. Assn. Chinese-Ams., Providence, 1978-86; commr. State Fire Safety Bd. Appeal and Rev., Providence, 1988—; mem. R.I. Heritage Commn., Providence, 1988-94; mem. Zoning Bd. Rev., North Kingstown, R.I., 1990-94. Mem. ASCE (structural div., Collingwood prize 1967), Assn. Energy Engrs., Nat. Fire Protection Assn., Am. Concrete Inst. Home: 95 Sedgefield Rd North Kingstown RI 02852-3838 Office: EngiTek Inc 1370 Plainfield St Cranston RI 02920-2549

FANG, ZHAOQIANG, research physicist; b. Ya An, Sichuan, China, Oct. 28, 1939; came to U.S., 1985; s. Zhongdai Fang and Zhijing Zhang; m. Lei Shan; children: Bin Fang, Jing Shan. B in Semiconductor and Solid State Electronics, Tsinghua U., Beijing, China, 1963. Rsch. asst. Inst. Semicondrs. Chinese Acad. Scis., Beijing, 1963-79, rsch. assoc. Inst. Semicondrs., 1979-85; vis. scholar dept. elec. and computer engring. Carnegie Mellon U., Pitts., 1985-89; rsch. physicist, assoc. rsch. prof. dept. physics and Univ. Rsch. Ctr. Wright State U., Dayton, Ohio, 1989—; cons. for mfrs. of III-V compound semicondr. materials. Editor: VLSI Electronics-Micro-Structure Sciences (in Chinese), 1986; contbr. articles to profl. jours. Recipient Nat. Sci. and Tech. Achievement award Nat. Commn. for Sci. and Tech., Beijing, 1985. Mem. Materials Rsch. Soc. Avocations: reading, cooking, table tennis. Office: Wright State U Physics Dept 3640 Col Glenn Hwy Dayton OH 45435

FANGER, DONALD LEE, Slavic language and literature educator; b. Cleve., Dec. 6, 1929; s. Max Leon and Rae (Bercu) F.; m. Margot Taylor, June 18, 1955; children: Steffen, Ross, Katharine. BA, U. Calif., Berkeley, 1951, MA, 1954; PhD, Harvard U., 1962. Mem. faculty Brown U., 1960-66, assoc. prof. Slavic langs. and lit., 1964-66; assoc. prof. Slavic langs., dir. div. Stanford U., 1966-68; prof. Slavic and comparative lit. Harvard U., 1968-98, chmn. dept. Slavic langs and lits., 1973-82, Harry Levin rsch. prof. lit., 1998—; mem. bd. syndics Harvard U. Press, 1968-73. Author: Dostoevsky and Romantic Realism, 1965, The Creation of Nikolai Gogol, 1979; editor: Brown U. Slavic Reprint Series, 1962-66. Mem. program com. Internat. Rsch. and Exchanges Bd., 1968-69, 70-73. With AUS, 1953-55. Guggenheim Found. fellow, 1975-76. Mem. Am. Acad. Arts and Scis., Acad. Lit. Studies, Internat. Comparative Lit. Assn. Home: 74 Putnam St Newton MA 02465-2433 Office: Harvard U Widener Study L Cambridge MA 02138

FANGER, MARK, psychologist, psychotherapist, consultant; b. Boston, Dec. 6, 1943. AB in Polit. Sci., Syracuse U., 1965; EdM in Psychology, Boston State Coll., 1972; EdD in Counseling Psychology, Boston U., 1977; grad. Clin. Consultation Program, Boston Inst. for Psychotherapy, 1984. Lic. psychologist and Family Therapist, Mass., Nat. Register in Psychology; cert. social studies tchr., guidance counselor and dir., Mass.; diplomate Am. Bd. Family Psychology, Am. Acad. Behavioral Medicine. Clin. dir. Milford Assistance Program Community Mental Health Ctr., Milford, Mass., 1971-74; clin. cons. drug treatment program Boston City Hosp., 1975-77; staff psychologist Bay Area Psychiat. Assocs., Burlington, Mass., 1977-80, Suburban Counseling Assocs., Weston, Mass., 1977-80; clin. supr. Whiteman House, Survival, Inc., Quincy, Mass., 1982-84; pvt. practice psychotherapy, Newton Highlands, Mass., 1979—; mem. adj. faculty dept. counseling psychology Boston U., 1976-77, dept. psychology Boston State Coll., 1977-79; mem. adj. faculty Antioch's Inst. Open Edn., Cambridge, Mass., 1979-80; mem. adj. faculty, supr. family therapy Mass. Sch. Profl. Psychology, Newton, 1982-83; group psychotherapy cons. People for People, Inc., Framingham, Mass., 1990-92; mem. faculty group psychotherapy tng. program Northeastern Soc. for Group Psychotherapy, 1991—; presenter in field; condr. workshops. Recipient Svc. of Self award Rotary Club, Franklin, Mass., 1974; grantee Mass. Gen. Hosp., 1975. Fellow Mass. Psychol. Assn.; mem. APA, Am. Group Psychotherapy Assn. (clin. mem.), Am. Mental Health Alliance New Eng. (charter), Internat. Acad. Behavioral Medicine, Counseling and Psychotherapy (diplomate in profl. psychotherapy and behavioral medicine), Psychologists for Social Responsibility, Soc. for Family Therapy and Rsch. (edn. com. 1984-87), Mass. Assn. Marriage and Family Therapy (clin. mem.), N.E. Soc. Study of Multiple Personality and Dissociation, Northeastern Soc. Group Psychotherapy (membership com. 1986-88, program com. 1988-94, faculty tng. program group psychotherapy 1991-99, bd. dirs. 1994-97, 98—, inst. com. 1995-96, chair inst. com. 1996-99, newsletter editor 1999—), Consortium for Psychotherapy, Pi Lambda Theta, Phi Delta Kappa. Office: 4 Hartford St Newton Hlds MA 02461-1553

FANGER, MICHAEL W., medical educator; b. Ft. Wayne, Ind., July 3, 1940. BA in Chemistry and Zoology, Wabash Coll., 1962; PhD in Biochemistry, Yale U., 1967. NIH postdoctoral fellow Nat. Inst. Med. Rsch., London, 1967-68, U. Ill. Med. Sch., Chgo., 1968-70; from asst. prof. to assoc. prof. microbiology Case Western Res. U., Cleve., 1970-81; faculty dept. immunology Middlesex Hosp., London, 1977-78; prof. microbiology and medicine Dartmouth Med. Sch., Lebanon, N.H., 1981—, chmn. dept. microbiology, 1992—, dir. immunology program, 1981-92; dir. immunology program Norris Cotton Cancer Ctr., 1984-92, dir. monoclonal antibody libr., 1984—; cons. Verax Corp., Lebanon, 1982-87, mem. sci. adv. bd., 1984-87; founder Medarex Inc., Annandale, N.J., 1987, dir., 1987—, chmn. sci. adv. bd., cons., 1987—. Contbr. numerous articles to profl. jours.; patentee in field. Mem. Am. Assn. Immunologists. Office: Dartmouth Med Sch Dept Microbiology 1 Medical Center Dr Lebanon NH 03756-0001*

FANGMANN, HEATHER ANN, secondary educator, English; b. Wichita, Kans., Sept. 22, 1973; d. Ronald George and Joice Mary (Fuchs) F. BSE in English, Emporia State U., 1996. Cert. English educator, 5-12. Substitute tchr. USD 394/260, Rose Hill/Derby, Kans., 1996-97; tchr. English USD 490, El Dorado, Kans., 1997—; tchr. Sylvan Learning Ctr., Wichita, 1997-98. Author: (poem) Quivira, 1995. Profl. mem. Assistance League of Wichita, 1995—. English scholar Emporia State U., 1993-96. Mem. Nat. Coun. Tchrs. English. Republican. Avocations: soccer, poetry, running. Home: 512 Adams Ave El Dorado KS 67042-3701

FANN, JAMES ILIN, cardiothoracic surgeon; b. Taipei, Taiwan, May 4, 1961; came to U.S., 1968; s. Charles C.P. and Nancy C.L. Fann; m. Andrea Hutchinson. BS, Northwestern U., 1983, MD with distinction, 1985. Diplomate Am. Bd. Surgery. Resident Stanford (Calif.) U. Med. Ctr., 1985-92; rsch. fellow Stanford U., 1987-89; vascular surgery fellow Stanford U. Med. Ctr., 1992-93, cardiothoracic surgery fellow, 1993-96; clin. asst. prof. cardiothoracic surgery Stanford U. Med. Schs., 1996—; staff cardiovascular surgeon VA, Palo Alto, Calif., 1996—; rsch. asst. Northwestern U., Chgo., 1982-84. Contbr. articles to profl. jours. Nat. Merit scholar, 1979; Carl and Leah McConnell Cardiovascular Rsch. fellow, 1987-89. Mem. AMA, Am. Heart Assn., Am. Coll. Cardiology, Calif. Med. Assn., Alpha Omega Alpha. Roman Catholic. Avocations: bicycling, photography, computers. Office: Stanford U Med Ctr 300 Pasteur Dr Palo Alto CA 94304-2203

FANNING, BARRY HEDGES, lawyer; b. Olney, Tex., Dec. 5, 1950; s. Robert Allen and Carolyn (Parker) F.; m. Rebecca Sue Cobbs, May 24, 1975 (dec. Mar. 1997); m. Sherri Winn Perry, Mar. 6, 1999. B.B.A., Baylor U., 1972, LL.B., 1973. Bar: Tex. 1973, Fla. 1974, U.S. Dist. Ct. (no., ea. we. and so. dists.) Tex. 1974, U.S. Ct. Appeals (5th and 11th cirs.) 1974. Mem. firm Fanning, Harper & Martinson, Dallas, 1974—. Social v.p. Dallas Symphony Orch. Guild, 1975-77; mem. Dallas Regional Young Life Bd., 1977—, fund raising chmn., 1982-84, 86-88, 97—; bd. dirs. Downtown YMCA, 1997—. Mem. ABA (vice chmn. young lawyers com. 1980, pub. rels. com. torts sect.), Baylor U. Student Found. (steering com. 1971-72), Baylor Alumni Assn. (bd. dirs. 1978-82, 95), Tryon Coterie (pres. 1971), Highland Park Forensics Found. (pres. 1993-95), Preston Ctr. Legal Assn. (sec. 1993-94, bd. dirs. 1994-95), Dervish Club, Calyx Club, Dallas Baylor Club (bd. dirs. 1976-84, pres. 1981-82), Christian Men's Club, Phi Eta Sigma, Omicron Kappa Delta, Phi Delta Theta. Baptist. Home: 4213 Greenbrier Dr Dallas TX 75225-6638 Office: Fanning Harper & Martinson 8117 Preston Rd Ste 300 Dallas TX 75225-6375

FANNING, DELVIN SEYMOUR, soil science educator; b. Copenhagen, N.Y., July 13, 1931; s. Clarence Roscoe and Faye Theodora (Hays) F.; m. Mary Christine Balluff, Nov. 22, 1958 (dec. Aug. 1994); children: Michael Christopher, Maurine Faye, Christine Kay; m. Emily Louise Wenzel Manning, Nov. 15, 1997. BS, Cornell U., 1954, MS, 1959; PhD, U. Wis., 1964. Cert. profl. soil scientist. Soil scientist Soil Conservation Svc., USDA, 1954, 59-62; grad. rsch. asst. dept. of soils U. Wis., Madison, 1960-64; from asst. prof. to prof. dept. natural sci. and landscape arch. U. Md., College Park, 1964—; vis. prof. Tech. U. of Munich, Germany, 1971-72, USDA Soil Conservation Svc., Washington, 1986; rsch. assoc. Tex. A&M U., College Station, 1979. Co-author: (with M.C.B. Fanning) Soil: Morphology, Genesis, and Classification, 1989; co-editor Acid Sulfate Weathering, 1982. Bass singer Holy Redeemer Ch. Choir, College Park, Md., 1968—. With U.S. Army, 1954-56. Fellow Am Soc. Agronomy, Soil Sci. Soc. Am. Democrat. Roman Catholic. Achievements include definition, description and naming of processes for sulfide mineral accumulation in soils sulfidization and sulfide mineral oxidation to form sulfuric acid, and reaction of sulfuric acid with soils to form new minerals sulfuricization. Home: 4809 Ravenswood Rd Riverdale MD 20737-1115 Office: U Md Dept Nat Resource Scis and Landscape Arch College Park MD 20742 *Know the earth and live in harmony.*

FANNING, KATHERINE WOODRUFF, editor, journalism educator; b. Chgo., Oct. 18, 1927; d. Frederick William and Katherine Bower (Miller) Woodruff; m. Marshall Field, Jr., May 12, 1950 (div. 1963); children: Frederick Woodruff, Katherine Woodruff Stephen, Barbara Woodruff; m. Lawrence S. Fanning, 1966 (dec. 1971); m. Amos Mathews, Jan. 6, 1984. BA, Smith Coll., 1949; LLD (hon.), Colby Coll., 1979; LittD (hon.), Pine Manor Jr. Coll., 1984; LHD (hon.), Northeastern U., 1984; hon. degree, Harvard U., 1988, Smith Coll., 1988, Babson Coll., 1988, U. Alaska, 1989, Govs. State U., Ill., 1989. With Anchorage Daily News, from 1965, editor, pub., 1972-83; editor The Christian Science Monitor, 1983-88; fall fellow Inst. of Politics Harvard U., Cambridge, Mass., 1989; adj. prof. journalism Boston U., 1991-93; dir. AP, 1988-89, Pulitzer prize bd., 1982-83, Boston Globe Newspaper Co., 1992—; mem. nat. adv. com. Freedom Forum Media Studies Ctr., 1986-97; sr. adv. bd. Joan Shorenstein Ctr., Harvard U.; bd. dirs. Inst. for Global Ethics, Inst. for Journalism Edn., 1989-95. Trustee Kettering Found., Charles Stewart Mott Found.; bd. dirs. Internat. Ctr. Journalists, Boston Pub. Libr. Found. Recipient Elijah Parish Lovejoy award Colby Coll., 1979, Smith Coll. medal, 1980, Mo. medal of Honor, U. Mo. Journalism award, 1980. Mem. Am. Soc. Newspaper Editors (bd. dirs. 1981—, pres. 1987-88), Soc. Profl. Journalists, Coun. Fgn. Rels, Am. Acad. Arts and Scis., St. Botolph Club (Boston), Badminton and Tennis Club (Boston). Home and Office: 330 Beacon St Boston MA 02116-1153

FANNING, RONALD HEATH, architect, engineer; b. Evanston, Ill., Oct. 5, 1935; s. Ralph Richard and Leone Agatha (Heath) F.; m. Jenine Vivian Schnelle, Jan. 9, 1960; children: Anthony Lee, Traycee Anne. BArch, Miami U., Oxford, Ohio, 1959. Registered architect in 24 states; registered profl. engr. in 13 states. Chmn. bd. Fanning/Howey Assocs., Inc., Celina, Ohio, 1959—; mng. ptnr. Manning Partnership, Celina 1978—, FFH Ltd. Partnership, 1986-91. Chmn. Mercer County Young Reps., Celina, 1962-65. Recipient Fred B. Joyner Profl. Achievement award Delta Gamma chpt. Pi Kappa Alpha, 1997. Mem. NSPE, Am. Inst. Architects, Coun. Ednl. Facility Planners Internat. (Great Lakes Midwest regional membership chmn. 1992-97, pres. Great Lakes Midwest region coun. ednl. facility planners internat. 1997-98), Ohio Soc. Profl. Engrs., Ohio Soc. Architects, Soc. Mktg. Profl. Svcs., Fla. Ednl. Facilities Planners Assn., Buckeye Assn. Sch. Adminstrs., Coun. Ednl. Faculty Planners Internat. (membership chmn. 1994-96, dir., 1997—, cert.). Methodist. Avocations: tennis, bowling, golf. Home: 422 Magnolia St Celina OH 45822-1254 Office: Fanning Howey Assoc Inc PO Box 71 Celina OH 45822-0071

FANNING, SHARON, university head basketball coach; b. Chattanooga, Tenn., Dec. 15, 1953. Grad. magna cum laude, U. Tenn., 1975, MS, 1976. Grad. asst. basketball U. Tenn., Chattanooga, 1975-76, head volleyball coach, 1976-78, head basketball coach, 1976-87; head basketball coach U. Ky., 1987-95, Miss. State U., 1995—. Named to Chattanooga Hall of Fame, 1993, All-Am. Coach Am. Women's Sports Fedn., 1984-86, Coach of Yr. So. Conf., 1984, 85. Office: Miss State U Athletic Media Rels PO Box 5308 Mississippi State MS 39762-5308*

FANNING, WANDA GAIL, retired elementary school educator; b. Chattanooga, Dec. 8, 1947; d. O' Knox and Hazel W. (McClendon) F.; stepmother E. Martha (O'Kelley) F. BEd, U. Ten., 1969; MEd, Trinity U., San Antonio, 1982. Elem. tchr. C.Z. Govt., Balboa, 1969-79, Dept. Def. Dependent Schs., Albrook, Panama, 1979-87; tchr. spl. edn. Dept. Def. Dependent Schs., Panama, 1982-84, ednl. prescriptionist, 1987-95; tchr. trainer, drug edn. trainer Dept. Def. Dependent Schs., Panama City, 1987-96, cooperative learning trainer, 1994-96, case mgr., 1995-96; literacy success tchr. Pinellas County (Fla.) Schs., 1988-99. Chmn. fine arts Ishmian Coll. Club, Balboa, 1985, fin. chmn., 1985; mem. Theatre Guild, Ancon, Panama, 1975-96; pres. Diablo Elem. Sch. Adv. Com., 1990-91; mem. orgnl. com. Spl. Games for Spl. People, Panama City, 1983-85. Recipient Just Cause cert. dept. nursing Gorgas Army Hosp., 1990, Spl. Act award Dept. Def. Dependents Sch., 1990. Mem. ASCD, Nat. Coun. Tchrs. Math., Coun. for Exceptional Children (treas. 1987—), Phi Delta Kappa (pres. 1990-91, Kappan of Yr. 1991, 94, v.p. 1991-92, del. 1992, 93), Kappa Delta Pi. Avocations: reading, travel, theater, music. Address: 2255 Grove Valley Ave Palm Harbor FL 34683-3226

FANNING, WILLIAM JAMES, professional baseball team executive, radio and television broadcaster; b. Chgo., Sept. 14, 1927; s. Frank and Gladys Leona (Lighter) F. B.A. in phys. edn., Buena Vista Coll, 1951; M in Phys. Edn., U. Ill., 1961. Profl. baseball player Chgo. Cubs, 1954, 56, 57; player, mgr. Tulsa Oilers, Tex. League, 1958, Dallas Rangers, Am. Assn., 1959-60, Venezuela, Eau Claire Braves, Wis., 1961-62; spl. assignment scout Milw. Braves, 1963-64, asst. gen. mgr., 1964-66; asst. gen. mgr., farm and scouting dir. Atlanta Braves, 1966-67; 1st dir. Major League Scouting Bur., 1967-68; gen. mgr. Montreal Expos., 1968-73, v.p., gen. mgr., 1973-77, v.p. player devel., 1977-81, field mgr., 1981-84, v.p. player devel. and scouting, 1982-86, spl. cons. baseball ops., 1989—; radio and TV broadcaster, 1987-88; spl. cons. baseball ops., 1989-92; major league scout Colo. Rockies, 1993—; radio baseball show CJAD, Montreal. Served with U.S. Army, 1945-47. Methodist. Home and Office: 2303 Place Dynastie, Saint Lazare, PQ Canada J7T 2C9

FANO, UGO, physicist, educator; b. Turin, Italy, July 28, 1912; came to U.S., 1939, naturalized, 1945; s. Gino and Rosa (Cassin) F.; m. Camilla V. Lattes, Feb. 8, 1939; children: Mary, Virginia. Sc.D., U. Turin, 1934; D.Sc. (hon.), Queen's U., Belfast, No. Ireland, 1978, U. Pierre and Marie Curie, Paris, 1979. Lectr., U. Rome, 1937-38; fellow, resident investigator Carnegie Instn. of Washington, 1940-46; cons. ballistician U.S. Army Ordnance, 1944-45; physicist X-ray sect. Nat. Bur. Standards, Washington, 1946-49; chief radiation theory sect. Nat. Bur. Standards, 1949-60, sr. research fellow, 1960-66; prof. Physics Dept. and James Franck Inst., U. Chgo., 1966-82, prof. emeritus, 1982—, chmn. dept., 1972-74; lectr. George Washington U., 1946-47; vis. prof. U. Calif., Berkeley, summer 1958, 68—, Cath. U., Washington, 1963-64. Author: (with G. Racah) Irreducible Tensorial Sets, 1959, (with L. Fano) Basic Physics of Atoms and Molecules, 1959, Physics of Atoms and Molecules, 1972, (with A. R. P. Rau) Atomic Collisions and Spectra, 1986, Symmetries in Quantum Physics, 1996; also articles. Recipient Rockefeller Pub. Svc. award, 1956, Exceptional Svc. award Dept. Commerce, 1957, Stratton award Nat. Bur. Stds., 1963, Davisson-Germer prize Am. Phys. Soc., 1976, Meggers award Optical Soc. Am., 1989, Fermi award U.S. Dept. Energy, 1995. Mem. NAS, Am. Acad. Arts and Scis., Am. Phys. Soc., Radiation Rsch. Soc., Royal Soc. London (fgn. mem.), Acad. Nazionale dei Lincei (Rome). Home: 5801 S Dorchester Ave Chicago IL 60637-1731

FANOS, KATHLEEN HILAIRE, osteopathic physician, podiatrist; b. Bremerhaven, Germany, Aug. 18, 1956; came to U.S., 1957; d. Homer Dantangelo and Ilse Helmar (Ochs) F. AAS in Music, Nassau C.C., Garden City, N.Y., 1976; BS in Music Edn., Hofstra U., 1978, postgrad., 1978-79; D Podiatric Medicine, Coll. Podiatric Med. and Surg., Des Moines, 1987; DO, Coll. Osteo. Med. and Surg., Des Moines, 1994. Diplomate Am. Bd. Internal Medicine. Tchr. music McKenna Jr. H.S. and Eastlake Elem. Sch., Massapequa, N.Y., 1978-79; musician numerous profl. orgns., N.Y., Iowa, 1979—; preceptorship in podiatry Bayshore, N.Y., 1987-88; pvt. practice podiatry Hyde Park, West Roxbury and Brookline, Mass., 1988-91, Des Moines, 1991-92; resident in internal medicine Winthrop U. Hosp., Mineola, N.Y., 1994-97; internist Cmty. Med. Assocs., Jackson, N.J., 1997—; ins. med. examiner Portamedic, Burlington, Mass., 1988-91. Mem. AMA, ACP (assoc.), Am. Bd. Internal Medicine, Am. Soc. Internal. Medicine, Am. Osteo. Assn., Am. Coll. Osteo. Family Physicians, N.Y. State Internal Medicine Soc., Phi Theta Kappa, Pi Kappa Lambda, Sigma Sigma Phi, Phi Delta Epsilon. Avocations: music, tennis, bowling, skiing, travel.

FANSEEN, JAMES FOSTER, lawyer; b. Balt., Feb. 3, 1928; s. Foster Hooker and Lillian (Seguine) F. AB, U. N.C., 1950; JD, U. Md., 1954; grad., Inst. Police Community Relations Mich. State U., 1958. Bar: Md. 1954, D.C. 1968. Magistrate Balt. City Police Ct., 1955-59; assoc. Fanseen & Fanseen, Balt., 1954-62, ptnr., 1962—; commr. FMC, 1967-71, acting chmn., 1969, vice chmn., 1969-71; prof. polit. sci. Community Coll. Balt., 1963-70; spl. asst. to adminstr. NASA, 1981-85; cons. to adminstr. NASA, 1985-88. Active NCCJ, 1965-80; mem. Criminal Justice Commn., 1965-74, pres., 1966-68. Served to maj. USAFR, 1950-69, capt. USNR, 1969-88. Mem. ABA, Md. Bar Assn., Balt. Bar Assn., Trial Judges Assn., Md. Law Enforcement Officers, Gamma Eta Gamma (past pres.), Phi Delta Theta. Republican. Methodist. Clubs: Metropolitan (Washington); Balt. Country; U.S. Naval Acad. Officer and Faculty, Yacht, Power Squadron (Annapolis, Md.). Home: 20 Weems Creek Dr Annapolis MD 21401-1125 Office: 856 Elkridge Landing Rd Linthicum Heights MD 21090-2903

FANSELOW, JULIE RUTH, writer; b. Springfield, Ill., July 26, 1961; d. Byron and Ruth Leona (Neumann) F.; m. Bruce Edward Whiting, Apr. 25, 1992; 1 child, Natalie. BS in Journalism, Ohio U., 1982. Reporter The Salem (Ohio) News, 1982-85; editor The Vindicator, Youngstown, Ohio, 1985-89; reporter The Times-News, Twin Falls, Ohio, 1989-91; pvt. practice writer Twin Falls, 1991—. Author: Traveling the Oregon Trail, 1993, Traveling the Lewis and Clark Trail, 1994, Idaho Off The Beaten Path, 1998, Texas (Lonely Planet), 1999; contbr. articles to nat. publs. Recipient 1st place for mag. writing Idaho Press Club, 1992, 1st place for guidebook Nat. Assn. for Interpretation, 1993. Mem. Am. Soc. Journalists and Authors, Soc. Am. Travel Writers, Lewis and Clark Trail Heritage Found., Oreg.-Calif. Trail Assn. Unitarian-Universalist. Avocations: travel, reading, arts, hiking. Home and Office: Fanselow Comm 1511 9th Ave E Twin Falls ID 83301-6611

FANSHEL, DAVID, social worker; b. N.Y.C., July 29, 1923; s. Hyman and Clara (Kratchman) F.; m. Florence Greenberg, Apr. 10, 1949; children—Ethan Jules, Merrie Lee. B.S.S., CCNY, 1947; M.S., N.Y. Sch. Social Work, 1948; D.S.W. (fellow Russell Sage Found. 1957-59), Columbia U., 1960. Research dir. Family and Children's Service, Pitts., 1955-58; dir. research Child Welfare League Am., 1958-63; mem. faculty Columbia U. Sch. Social Work, 1962—, prof. social work, 1965-93; prof. emeritus, 1993—. Co-author: Therapeutic Discourse, 1977, Children in Foster Care, 1978, Foster Children in Life Course Perspective, 1990, Serving the Urban Poor, 1992. Decorated D.F.C., Air medal. Mem. AAUP, Am. Sociol. Assn., Nat. Assn. Social Workers. Home: 537 Cumberland Ave Teaneck NJ 07666-2650

FANSLER, BRIAN CALDWELL, budget analyst; b. Charlottesville, Va., June 4, 1971; s. Stephen Douglas and Donnetta Fern F. BA, No. Ariz. U., 1993, MPA, 1995. Zoning asst. Beus, Gilbert and Morrill, Phoenix, 1995-96; staff svcs. analyst Calif. Pub. Employee Retirement Sys., Sacramento, 1996-97; budget analyst Calif. Dept. Transp., Sacramento, 1997—. Founder Lincoln Meml. Mus., Washington, 1994. Mem. Am. Soc. Pub. Adminstrs., Calif. State Employees Assn., No. Ariz. U. Alumni Assn. (founder), 20/30 Club. E-mail: bfansler@msn.com. Home: 2407 Larkspur Ln # 208 Sacramento CA 95825

FANT, CLYDE EDWARD, JR., religion educator; b. Marshall, Tex., Nov. 14, 1934; s. Clyde Edward and Margaret (Moos) F.; (div.); children: Brian H., Carol E., Julie A.; m. Cheryl Hammock, Nov. 9, 1984. BA, Baylor U., 1956; BD, Southwestern Bapt. Seminary, Ft. Worth, 1960, ThD, 1964. Ordained to ministry Bapt. Ch., 1956. Pastor First Bapt. Ch., Ruston, La., 1962-66; prof. of preaching Southwestern Bapt. Seminary, Ft. Worth, 1966-75; pastor First Bapt. Ch., Richardson, Tex., 1975-82; pres. Internat. Bapt. Sem., Ruschlikon/Zurich, Switzerland, 1982-83; dean of chapel, prof. religious studies Stetson Univ., Deland, Fla., 1985—; vis. prof. of preaching Div. Sch., Duke U., Durham, N.C., Southeastern Bapt. Sem., Wake Forest, N.C., 1983-84. Author, editor: 20 Centuries of Great Preaching (13 vols.), 1971; author: Preaching for Today, 1977, Bonhoeffer: Worldly Preaching, 1991, The Misunderstood Jesus: Ten Lost Keys to Life, 1996; co-author: An Introduction to the Bible, 1991; editor: Contemporary Christian Trends, 1972; contbg. editor: Pulpit Digest. Recipient Fulbright scholarship, Tubingen, Fed. Republic of Germany, 1956, Venting award/Outstanding Sr., Southwestern Bapt. Sem., 1960. Mem. Am. Acad. Religion, Soc. Bibl. Lit. Democrat. Office: Woodland Blvd Deland FL 32720

FANTA, PAUL EDWARD, chemist, educator; b. Chgo., July 24, 1921; s. Joseph and Marie (Zitnik) F.; m. LaVergne Danek, Sept. 3, 1949; children—David, John. B.S., U. Ill., 1942; Ph.D., U. Rochester, 1946. Postdoctoral research fellow U. Rochester, 1946-47; instr. Harvard, 1947-48; mem. faculty Ill. Inst. Tech., 1948—, prof. chemistry, 1961-84, prof. emeritus, 1984—; exchange scholar Czechoslovak Acad. Sci., Prague, 1963-64, Soviet Acad. Sci., Moscow, 1970-71. Contbr. articles to profl. jours. NSF fellow Imperial Coll., London, Eng., 1956-57. Mem. Am. Chem. Soc., Sigma Xi, Phi Lambda Upsilon. Home: 947 Clinton Ave Oak Park IL 60304-1821 Office: Ill Inst Tech Tech Ctr Chicago IL 60616

FANTACI, JAMES MICHAEL, lawyer; b. Rochester, N.Y., Dec. 23, 1946; s. Anthony John and Shirley (Moose) F.; m. Ellen Louise Steman, Apr. 26, 1969; children: Michael, Matthew. BA, U. Rochester, 1968; JD, U. Va., 1971. Bar: Va. 1971, La. 1972, U.S. Dist. Ct. (ea. dist.) La. Law clk. to Hon. E. Gordon West U.S. Dist. Ct. (ea. and mid. dist.) La., 1971-72; atty. Monroe & Lemann, New Orleans, 1972-84, McGlinchey Stafford, New Orleans, 1984—; mem. The Chamber/New Orleans and the River Region East Jefferson Coun., 1988—; chmn. East Jefferson Coun., 1992; chmn. Area Couns. Coord. Com., 1993; chmn. bd. commrs. Jefferson Parish Econ. Devel. Commn., 1999. Contbr. articles to jours. and legal revs. Mem. ABA (bus. law sect., small bus. com., franchising subcom.), La. Bar Assn., Va. Bar Assn., Jefferson C. of C. Home: 114 Sycamore Dr Metairie LA 70005-4025 Office: McGlinchey Stafford 643 Magazine St New Orleans LA 70130-3477

FANTAZOS, HENRYK MICHAEL, painter, graphic artist; b. Kamionka, Lvov, Poland, Jan. 18, 1944; came to U.S., 1975; s. Antoni and Katarzyna Danuta Ziembicka; 1 child, Jessica. MA, Acad. Fine Arts, Cracow, Poland, 1969. One-man shows include Desa Gallery, Cracow, Poland, 1970, 75, Pegasus Gallery, Zakopane, Poland, 1971, Mus. Teatraine, Cracowq, 1972, Karstadt Gallery, Cologne, Germany, 1973, Gallery of the Sparkasse der Stadt Hagen, Germany, 1974, Koszykowa Gallery, Warsaw, 1975, The Nippon Club, N.Y.C., 1976, Old Warsaw Gallery, Alexandria, Va., 1977, 81, Westlake Gallery, White Plains, N.Y., 1978, French Art Gallery, Gallipolis, Ohio, 1983, Birke Gallery, Marshall U., Huntington, W.Va., 1983, Judge Gallery, Durham, N.C., 1986, 90, McIntosh Gallery, Atlanta, 1987, Lee Scarfone Gallery, U. Tampa, Fla., 1988, Carrboro Art Ctr., N.C., 1988, Hanes Art Ctr., U. N.C., Chapel Hill, 1989, Phila. Art Alliance, 1989, Rockland Art Ctr., Balt., 1989, Dorothy McRae Gallery, Atlanta, 1993, Horace Williams House, Chapel Hill, 1994, Tyndall Gallery, Durham, N.C., 1995, Durham (N.C.) Art Guild, 1996. Recipient numerous art awards including First prize Mannassas (Va.) Art Competition, 1984, Winner Internat. Print Competition San Diego Art Inst., 1994, Best in Show award New Works Exhibition, Raleigh, N.C., 1996; fellow Art Coun. N.C., 1996; grantee Aldegrewer Gesselschaft, West Germany, 1973, Sparkasse der Stadt Hagen, West Germany, 1974, Kosciuszko Found., N.Y., 1976, Artist in Residence, W. Va., 1982-83. Avocations: rose gardening, crystal collecting. Home: 227 West Hill Ave Hillsborough NC 27278

FANTE, RONALD LOUIS, engineering scientist; b. Phila., Oct. 27, 1936; s. Frank Louis and Jeanne Gloria (Bossone) F.; m. Clara Connie Patalano, Apr. 23, 1961; children: Robert, Richard, Karen. BS, U. Pa., 1958; MS, MIT, 1960; PhD, Princeton U., 1964. Sr. scientist AVCO Corp., Wilmington, Mass., 1964-71, Air Force Cambridge Rsch. Labs., Bedford, Mass., 1971-80; asst. v.p. Textron Def. Systems, Wilmington, 1980-87; corp. fellow The MITRE Corp., Bedford, 1988—. Author: Signal Analysis and Estimation, 1988; contbr. numerous articles to jours. in field; mem. editl. bd. Waves in Random Media. Recipient Atwater Kent prize U. Pa., 1958, Dept. Labs. Achievement award USAF, 1974, Marcus O'Day prize USAF, 1975, I Migliori award Pirandello Lyceum, 1989, MITRE Corp. Best Paper prize, 1992, IEEE Disting. Lectr., 1995, 96. Fellow IEEE (editor in chief Transactions 1983-86), Optical Soc. Am.; mem. Electromagnetics Acad., Internat. Union Radio Sci. Roman Catholic. Home: 26 Sherwood Rd Reading MA 01867-3743 Office: MITRE Corp Burlington Rd Bedford MA 01730-1306

FANTINI, SERGIO, physical science researcher, educator; b. Florence, Italy, Sept. 14, 1964; came to U.S., 1993; s. Enio and Luigia Pierina (Scaunich) F.; m. Maria Angela Franceschini, Jan. 8, 1994; 1 child, Lisa Francesca. Diploma, Liceo Statale G.B. Morgagni, Florence, 1983; PhD, U. Florence, 1992. Postdoctoral rsch. assoc. U. Ill., Urbana-Champaign, Ill., 1993-96; vis. lectr. U. Ill., 1995-96, rsch. asst. prof., 1996—; cons. Carl Zeiss, Oberkochen, Germany, 1994, Siemens, Erlangen, Germany, 1997—. Co-inventor photosensor with multiple light sources, 1993, U.S. patent, 1996, determining material concentrations in tissues, 1994, U.S. patent, 1996. Among tchrs. ranked as excellent by their students U. Ill. at Urbana-Champaign, 1996. Avocations: playing piano, tennis, classical music, opera, art. Home: 507A Scovill St Urbana IL 61801-6744 Office: Dept Physics U Ill at Urbana Champaign 1110 W Green St Urbana IL 61801-3003

FANTONE, STEPHEN D., company executive; b. Buffalo, Sept. 4, 1953; m. Elizabeth A. Wayne. SB in Elec. Engring., MIT, 1974, SB in Mgmt., 1974; PhD in Optics, U. Rochester, N.Y., 1979. Sr. prin. engr. Polaroid Corp., Cambridge, Mass., 1978-84; gen. mgr. Frank Cooke, Inc., North Brookfield, Mass., 1981-82; chmn. Benthos, Inc., North Falmouth, Mass., 1997-98; founder, pres. Optikos Corp., Cambridge, Mass., 1984—. Contbr. articles to profl. jours., chpt. to book; patentee in field. Fellow Optical Soc. Am. (treas. 1996—). Office: Optikos 286 Cardinal Medeiros Ave Cambridge MA 02141-1920

FANTOZZI-PACHECO, PEGGY RYONE, environmental planner; b. Providence, Feb. 2, 1948; d. Eugene Baker and Cynthia (Bragg) Ryone; m. Thomas Allen Collins, Jan. 4, 1969 (div. 1985); children: Christin, Cindi; m. Thomas Edward Fantozzi, Mar. 22, 1985 (div. 1989); 1 child, Amy; m. Francis I. Pacheco, Apr. 24, 1997. BA in Earth Scis., Bridgewater State Coll., 1969; MS in Geology, Franklin and Marshall Coll., 1971. Registered sanitarian, Mass. Project mgr. Coastal Zone Mgmt. Grant, Eastham, Mass., 1980-81; geologist, project mgr. BSC Group/Cape Cod, Barnstable Village, Mass., 1982-88; sr. environ. scientist A.M. Wilson Assocs., Osterville, 1988-94, Daylor Consulting Group, Braintree, Mass., 1994-97; instr. earth scis. and geology, prin. environtl. scientist land use permitting Bridgewater (Mass.) State Coll., 1972-74, Cape Cod C.C., West Barnstable, Mass., 1979-82; cons. conservation and health bds. Town of Bourne, Mass., 1984-85; mem., chair State Comm. for the Conservation of Soil, Water and Related Resources, 1996—; mem. Nat. Resources Conservation and Devel. Coun., 1998. Bd. dirs., v.p. Assn. for Preservation of Cape Cod, Orleans, Mass., 1979-85; bd. trustees Cape Cod Mus. Natural History, Brewster, 1982-85; advisor Barnstable County Marine Resources program, 1980-82; chmn. Eastham Conservation Commn., 1978-82, Selectmen's Task Force on Local Pollution, Bourne, 1985-87; del. Barnstable County Water Resources Adv. Coun., 1979-89, Bourne Shore and Harbor Com., 1989-92; rep. Tri-Town Septage treatment Facilities Planning Commn., Eastham, Orleans, citizen's adv. com. groundwater discharge program Mass. Dept. EPA, 1987-88, Surface Water Quality, 1990, 93, Mass. Bays Program Citizen Adv. Steering Com., 1992—; pres. Mass. Assn. Conservation Dists., 1995-98; chair Mass. State Commn. for the Conservation of Soil, Water and Related Resources, 1998—. Grantee USDA-Natural Resources Conservation Svc., 1997-98. Mem. Nat. Assn. Conservation Dists. (dir.), Mass. Health Officers Assn., Mass. Water Works Assn., Monument Beach Civic Assn., Bourne Parents Group. Home: 25 Shore Rd Buzzards Bay MA 02532-5425 Office: Land Use Permitting 25 Shore Rd Bourne MA 02532-5425

FANTRY, JOHN JOSEPH, chemist; b. N.Y.C., Sept. 26, 1921; s. George and Mary (Schwartz) F.; widowed; three children. BS, Mt. St. Mary's Coll., 1944. From rsch. & devel. to direct sales Sun Chem. Corp., N.Y., S.C., 1946-62; gen. mgr., v.p. so. divsn. Roma Chem. Corp./United Merchants & Mfg. Corp., 1962-79; founder, pres., CEO Internat. Cons., Ltd., Greenville, S.C., 1979-90; mktg. mgr., chmn. bd. dirs. Carolina Textile Machinery, Greenville, 1993-96; pres., CEO Internat. Chem. Technologies, Greenville, 1997—. Home: 213 Castellan Dr Greer SC 29650-4253

FANUELE, FRANK JOHN, engineering executive; b. N.Y.C., June 19, 1938. BSEE, Rensselaer Poly. Inst., 1960. Elec. engr. GE, 1960-64; project engr. Fairchild Electrometrics Corp., 1964-69; sys. engring. mgr. Mech. Tech. Inc., 1969-84; tech. sales mgr. Brown & Sharpe Mfg. Co., 1984-86; tech. mktg. mgr. Robotic Vision Sys., 1989; pres. Fanuele Enterprises, Albany, N.Y., 1986—. Achievements include transforming state of the art research and development activities into practical implementation in military, aerospace, automotive sectors and general factory automation. Office: Fanuele Enterprises 256 Partridge St Albany NY 12208-2624

FANWICK, ERNEST, lawyer; b. N.Y.C., Feb. 28, 1926; s. Jacob and Jeanette (Lossof) F.; m. Lee Nathan, Sept. 1, 1951; children: Lewis, Leslie, Eric. BS in Elec. Engring., Pa. State U., 1948; JD, Columbia U., 1951. Bar: N.Y. 1952, Conn. 1988, U.S. Patent Office 1952, U.S. Ct. Appeals (2d cir.) 1952, U.S. Supreme Ct. 1958, U.S. Ct. Appeals (fed. cir.) 1982. Sr. patent atty. ITT Fed. Telephone Labs., Nutley, N.J., 1951-55; div. counsel Avion div. ACF, Paramus, N.J., 1955-57; patent counsel Burndy Corp., Norwalk, Conn., 1957-65, dir. legal dept., 1965-75, gen. counsel, 1975-82, v.p., gen. counsel, sec., 1960-66; mem. faculty Practising Law Inst., N.Y.C., 1964-97; lectr. Conf. Legal Execs., Pa., 1970, 72. Bd. dirs. Aid to Retarded, Stamford, Conn., 1982-87, mem. exec. com., 1997—; bd.dirs. Assn. Jewish Family and Children's Agys., 1992—, Jewish Family Svcs., Stamford, 1989—; alternate mem. Zoning Bd. Appeals, Stamford, 1990-96; active Am. ARbitration Assn.; mem. Arbitration panel N.Y. Stock Exch., Am. Stock Exch., Nat. Assn. Security Dealers. Lt. U.S. Army, 1943-47. Mem. ABA, Conn. Patent Law Assn. (pres. 1966), N.Y. Intellectual Property Law Assn., The Corp. Bar Assn., Am. Intellectual Property Assn., Am. Arbitration Assn., Masons.

FAORO, VICTORIA ANNA, museum director, magazine editor; b. Catskill, N.Y., Aug. 28, 1949; d. Gino John and Mabel Evelyn (Totten) F.; m. Louis Samuel DeLuca, Aug. 17, 1996. BA, SUNY, Albany, 1971, MA, 1974. Cert. English tchr., N.Y. Tchr. English Walton (N.Y.) Ctrl. Schs., 1973-78; project editor Ctr. for Humanities, White Plains, N.Y., 1979-81; artist/quiltmaker Cooperstown, N.Y., 1981-87; adj. instr. SUNY, Oneonta, 1983-89; exec. dir. Upper Catskills Cmty. Coun. on Arts, Oneonta, 1986-89; exec. editor Am. Quilter mag., Paducah, Ky., 1990—; exec. dir. Mus. of Am. Quilter's Soc., Paducah, Ky., 1991-92, 94—; mem. grants review panel/arts in edn. N.Y. State Coun. on Arts, N.Y.C., 1988-90; cons. arts, N.Y., 1986-90; mem. grants review panel Ky. Arts Coun., Frankfort, 1992-94; founding v.p. Paducah Film Soc., 1992-94. Editor over 40 quilting books, 1990-94; contbr. articles to newsletters and mags. Mem. Paducah Rotary Club. Avocations: cooking, quiltmaking, reading. Home: 2026 Jefferson St Paducah KY 42001-7120 Office: Mus Am Quilters Soc 215 Jefferson St Paducah KY 42001-0714

FARABOW, FORD FRANKLIN, JR., lawyer; b. Charlotte, N.C., Jan. 6, 1938; s. Ford Franklin and Louise (Botts) F.; children—Ford Franklin, III, Amy Kathryn, Andrew Leighton. B.S. in Chem. Engring., Clemson U., 1959; J.D. with honors, George Washington U., 1963. Bar: D.C. bar 1965, S.C. bar 1963. With law dept. Swift & Co., Washington, 1959-62; assoc. Nexsen & Pruet, Columbia, S.C., 1962-64; with patent dept. Hercules, Inc., Wilmington, Del., 1964-65; ptnr. Finnegan, Henderson, Farabow, Garrett & Dunner, Washington, 1965—; lectr. to ABA, Am. Patent Law Assn., also others. Contbr. articles to profl. publs. Mem. ABA, S.C. Bar Assn., Am. Judicature Soc., Bar Assn. D.C., Am. Patent Law Assn., U.S. Trademark Assn. (chmn. internat. adv. group), Am. Chem. Soc., Clemson U. Alumni Assn., Giles S. Rich Am. Inns of Ct., Tiger Brotherhood, Order of Coif, Phi Eta Sigma, Delta Theta Phi, Bethesda (Md.) Club (bd. dirs. 1987), TPC Club at Avenel, Touchdown Club, Franklin Sq. Club, Clemson IPTAY. Home: 9107 Belmart Rd Potomac MD 20854-1620 Office: Finnegan Henderson Farabow Garrett & Dunner 1300 I St NW Fl 6-8 Washington DC 20005-3315

FARACE, VIRGINIA KAPES, librarian; b. Hazleton, Pa., July 10, 1945; d. Elmer Bernard and Elizabeth E. (Kuntz) Kapes; m. Frank John Farace, May 9, 1970. BA, Rider U., 1967; MLS, Rutgers U., 1968. Reference and govt. documents librarian Hazleton Area Pub. Libr., 1968-70; libr. dir. Boynton Beach (Fla.) City Libr., 1970—; bldg. cons. Boynton Beach City Libr., 1973-74, 85-89, Palm Springs (Fla.) Pub. Libr., 1976, 86. Editor: (directory) Library Resources in Palm Beach County, 1979; Centennial Book Com. Boynton Beach: The First 100 Years. Chair legis. com. Edn. Alliance, Palm Beach County, 1987-94; mem. strategic planning task force Palm Beach County Sch. Bd., 1990-91; chair job opportunity task force Project Mosaic, Palm Beach County, 1990-93, transition team 1993; chair budget com. Book Fest! A Literary Festival, Palm Beach County, 1990-93, co-chair exhibitors com., 1994-95, chair steering com., 1995-96, chair bd. dirs., 1996-98, dir., 1997—; edn. com. Govs. Initiative for Teens, 1992—, sec., 1993—; adv. coun. Santaluces H.S., 1991—, chair, 1994-98; mem. Congress Mid. Sch. Adv. Coun., 1992—, vice chair, 1997—; mem. Palm Beach County Leadership Class of 1994, mem. pub. issues com., 1995-97; mem. task force Boynton Beach Hist. Schs., Task Force, 1993; mem. cmty. network Palm Beach County Sch. Bd., 1993—, sch. bd. constrn. oversight and rev. com., 1996—, chair pers. and tng. subcom., safe schs. task force; bd. dirs. Boynton Beach Hist. Soc., 1992—, chair by-laws com., 1993, chair nominating com., 1994-95, co-chair Hist. 1913 Schoolhouse Restoration Com., 1994-96; bd. dirs. Boynton Cultural Centre, Inc., 1996—, sec., 1996—. Mem. ALA, AAUW (v.p. Boynton Beach br. 1989—, br. coord. 1995-96, br. pres. 1996—, state strategic planning com. 1990—, chair 1992, Woman of Change award 1991, state conv. planning com. 1992, chair credentials com. 1992, S.E. Fla. cluster rep. state bd. 1994-96, chair state nominating com. 1994-95, bylaws com. 1994-95, state parliamentarian 1996-98, state fin. com. 1998—), Southeastern Libr. Assn., Spl. Libr. Assn., Fla. Pub. Libr. Assn. (pres. 1989-90, chair libr. adminstrn. divsn. 1992-93, parliamentarian 1992-94, legis. com. 1993—, chair adult svcs. divsn. 1994-95, Pres. award for outstanding libr. leadership 1996), Palm Beach County Libr. Assn. (pres. 1979-80, citation for leadership and svc. 1980), Coop. Authority for Libr. Automation (treas. 1984-93, pres. 1993—), Boynton Beach C. of C. (chair edn. com. 1991—, bd. dirs. 1992—, vice chair 1994—, parliamentarian 1993—, chair nominating com. 1994, Outstanding Com. Chair award 1992, Dir. of Yr. 1993, 94, Ann Barrett award for outstanding svc. and leadership to cmty. 1996), Alpha Xi Delta (pres. 1980-84). Roman Catholic. Avocations: reading, counted cross stitch, quilting, jogging, computers. Home: Lake Clarke Shores 1841 Caribbean Rd West Palm Beach FL 33406-8606 Office: Boynton Beach City Libr 208 S Seacrest Blvd Boynton Beach FL 33435-4499

FARACH, RUBEN, city administrator; b. Havana, Cuba, Apr. 13, 1950. Cert. bldg. contractor City Hialeah, Fla., 1973-75, dir. facilities dept., 1975-83, bldg. ofcl., dir. bldg. zoning code enforcement divsn., 1983—. Mem. Bldg. Ofcls. Assn., Bldg. & Zoning Ofcls. Dade County, Latin Buiulders Dade County, Dade County Code & Products Rev. Com. Office: City Hialeah Bldg Dept 501 Palm Ave Hialeah FL 33010-4719*

FARAGE, MICHAEL N., career officer. BSBA, Ctrl. Mich. U., 1970; grad., Squadron Officer Sch., 1974; MBA, U. No. Colo., 1979; grad., Air Command and Staff Coll., 1984, Air War Coll., 1988. Commd. 2d lt. USAF, 1971, advanced through grades to brig. gen., 1997; helicopter pilot 48th Aerospace Rescue Recovery Squadron, Fairchild AFB, Wash., 1972-75, 40th Rescue and Recovery Squadron, Nakhon Phanom Royal AFB, Thailand, 1975; T-37 instr. pilot and flight examiner 35th Flying Tng. Squadron and 64th Flying Tng. Wing, Reese AFB, Tex., 1976-81; plans officer 23d Air Force, Scott AFB, Ill., 1981-83; comdr. detachment 4 40th Aerospace Rescue and Recovery Squadron, Hill AFB, Utah, 1984-86, ops. officer, 1986-87; comdr. detachment 370 Air Force Res. Officer Tng. Corps U. Mass., Amherst, 1988-90; dir. ops. Hdqs. Air Force Res. Officer Tng. Corps, Maxwell AFB, Ala., 1990-92; comdr. 81st Tech. Tng. Group, Keesler AFB, Miss., 1992-94, 58th Spl. Ops. Wing, Kirtland AFB, N.Mex., 1994-97; dep. comdg. gen. Joint Spl. Ops. Command, Ft. Bragg, N.C., 1997—. Office: JSOC-DCG PO Box 70239 Fort Bragg NC 28307

FARAGHAN, GEORGE TELFORD, photographer; b. Phila., July 8, 1926; s. Joseph Telford and Sarah (Earnest) F.; m. Ida Jane Hanley, Dec. 8, 1948; children: Karen, Kurt, Kim, Kyle, Ken. Student, Pa. State U., 1947; grad. comml. photography magna cum laude, Yawn Sch. Photography, Phila., 1949. Printer Thomas Melvin Studio, Phila., 1949-50; printer, asst. Willand Steward Studio, Wilmington, Del., 1950-51; freelance photographer Phila., 1951-52; owner George Faraghan Studio, Phila., 1953—. Inventor spl. camera unit to photograph U.V. photo damage caused by exposure to the sun used in pharm. rsch. With USN, 1944-46, PTO. Recipient 3 George Berry awards, Profl. Photographers Assn. Del. Valley, Phila. Art Dirs. Shows awards, N.Y. Art Dirs. Show Neographics award: photograher 50 Best of Ads of Yr., 1960. Mem. Phila. Art Dir.'s Club (over 100 awards). Republican. Office: 940 N Delaware Ave Philadelphia PA 19123-3111

FARAH, CAESAR ELIE, Middle Eastern and Islamic studies educator; b. Portland, Oreg., Mar. 13, 1929; s. Sam Khalil and Lawrice Farah; m. Irmgard Tenkamp, Dec. 13, 1987; children by previous marriage: Ronald, Christopher, Ramsey, Laurence, Raymond, Alexandra; 1 child, Elizabeth. Student, Internat. Coll. Am. U. Beirut, 1941-46; B.A., Stanford U., 1952; M.A., Princeton U., 1955, Ph.D., 1957. Pub. affairs asst., cultural affairs officer ednl. exchanges USIS, New Delhi, 1957-58, Karachi, Pakistan, 1958; asst. to chief Bur. Cultural Affairs, Washington, 1959; asst. prof. history and Semitic langs. Portland State U., 1959-63; asst. prof. history Calif. State U.-Los Angeles, 1963-64; assoc. prof. Near Eastern studies Ind. U., Bloomington, 1964-69; prof. Middle Eastern and Islamic history U. Minn., Mpls., 1969—, chmn. South Asian and Middle Eastern studies, 1988-91; cons. U.S. Army, 1962-63; vis. prof. Harvard U., summers 1964-65; guest lectr. Fgn. Ministry, Spain, Iraq, Lebanon, Iran, Ministry Higher Edn., Saudi Arabia, Yemen, Turkey, Kuwait, Qatar, Tunisia, Morocco, Syrian Acad. Scis., Acad. Scis., Beijing; vis. scholar Cambridge U., 1974; resource person on Middle East, media and svc. group Minn., 1977—; bd. dirs., chmn. Upper Midwest Consortium for Middle East Outreach, 1980—; vis. prof. Sanaa U., Yemen, 1984, Karl-Franzens U. Austria, 1990, 91, 97-98, Ludwig-Maximilian U., Munich, 1992-93; exec. sec., editor Am. inst. Yemeni Studies, 1982-86; sec.-gen., exec. bd. dirs. Internat. Com. for Pre-Ottoman & Ottoman Studies, 1988—; fellow Rsch. Ctr. Islamic History, Istanbul, 1993, Ctr. Lebanese Studies & St. Anthony Coll., Oxford, Eng., 1994; vis. Fulbright-Hays scholar U. Damascus, 1994. Author: The Addendum in Medieval Arabic Historiography, 1968, Islam: Beliefs and Observances 5th edit., 1994, Eternal Message of Muhammad, 1964, 3d edit., 1981,Tarikh Baghdad li-Ibn-al-Najjar, 1980-83, 3 vols., 2d edit., 1986, al-Ghazali on Abstinence in Islam, 1992, Decision Making in the Ottoman Empire, 1992, The Road to Intervention: Fiscal Policies in Ottoman Mount Lebanon, 1992, The Politics of Interventionism in Ottoman Lebanon, 2 vols., 1999; contbr. over 60 articles and 150 revs. to profl. jours.; editl. bd. Digest of Middle East Studies. Mem. Oreg. Rep. committeeman, 1960-64. Recipient cert. of merit Syrian Ministry Higher Edn.; Fulbright rsch. scholar, 1966-67, 85-86; fellow Am. Coun. Learned Socs., 1953, fellow Am. Rsch. Ctr. in Egypt, 1966-67, Fulbright tng. and rsch. fellow, Germany, 1992-93, Ford Found., 1966, Philos. Soc., 1970-71; Fulbright-Hayes lectr., 1993-94; Dept. State Am. participants program grantee, 1981, 84, 93, grantee Minn. Humanities Commn., 1981, 85, 89, 95, 98, travel to collection grantee NEH, 1989, also others. Mem. Stanford U. Alumni Assn. (leadership recognition award), Stanford Club Minn. (dir., pres. 1979), Am. Oriental Soc., Royal Asiatic Soc. Gt. Britain, Am. Hist. Assn., Middle East Studies Assn. N.Am., Am. Assn. Tchrs. Arabic (exec. bd.), Turkish Studies Assn., Pi Sigma Alpha, Phi Alpha Theta. Greek Orthodox. Club: Princeton. Fax: 612-624-9383. Home: 5125 Blake Rd S Edina MN 55436-1125 Office: Univ Minn 839 Soc Sci Towers Minneapolis MN 55455

FARAH, CYNTHIA WEBER, photographer, publisher; b. Long Island, N.Y., June 2, 1949; d. Andrew John and Aria Emma (Jelnikova) Weber; m. James Clifton Farah, Jan. 12, 1974 (div. 1992); children: Elise, Alexa. BA in Comms., Stanford U., 1971; MA, U. Tex., 1992. Mem. prodn. staff Sta. KDBC-TV, El Paso, Tex., 1971-73; film critic El Paso Times, 1972-77; v.p. Sanders Co. Advtsg., El Paso, 1973-74; freelance photographer El Paso, 1974—; lectr. film studies U. Tex., El Paso, 1995-98; asst. prof. U. Tex., 1998—; pres. CM Pub., El Paso, 1981-89. Author: Literature and Landscape: Writers of the Southwest, 1988, Colors on Desert Walls: The Murals of El Paso, 1997; co-author, photographer: Country Music: A Look at the Men Who've Made It, 1982; film critic St. KTEP, 1993—, Sta. KVIA-TV, 1997—. Bd. dirs. N.Mex. State U. Mus. Adv. Bd., Las Cruces, 1982-90; dir., vice-chmn. Shelter for Battered Women, El Paso, 1981-86; active Jr. League, 1977-90, sustaining mem., 1990—, C.of C. Leadership El Paso Program, 1983-84; mem. El Paso County Hist. Commn., 1984-89, vice chmn., 1986, 87; mem. El Paso County Hist. Alliance, vice chmn., 1986-88; trustee El Paso Cmty. Found., 1984—; mem. adv. bd. El Paso Arts Resources dept., 1987-93, chmn., 1991-93; mem. adv. bd. Tex. Film Alliance, 1991—, Tex. Ctr. for the Book, 1987—; mem. literary adv. panel Tex. Commn. on Arts, 1991-93, media adv. panel, 1997-98; mem. adv. coun. El Paso Bus. Com. for Arts, 1988-90, Harry Ransom Humanities Rsch. Ctr. U. Tex., Austin; mem. tex. Com. Humanities Bd., 1993—; mem. lit. panel Cultural Arts Coun. Houston, 1993; mem. adv. com. Tex. Book Fair, 1996—. Recipient J.C. Penny Golden Rule award, 1989, Vol. Svc. award El Paso Bur. United Way, 1989, Clara Barton Medallion ARC, 1979, Conquistador award City of El Paso, 1991; named Outstanding Active Mem. Jr. League, 1987-88, Outstanding Sustaining Mem., 1993-94; named to El Paso Women's Hall of Fame, 1992. Mem. U. Tex. at El Paso Libr. Assn. (v.p. 1987-88, pres. 1989-91), Modern Lang. Assn., Stanford U. Alumni Assn., Soc. Cinema Studies, Broadcast Film Critics Assn. Episcopalian.

FARAH, FUAD SALIM, dermatologist; b. Haifa, Palestine, 1929. MD, Am. U., Beirut, 1954. Diplomate Am. Bd. Dermatology. Internship Am. U., Beirut, Lebanon, 1954-55; residency Am. U., Beirut, 1955-56; res. internal medicine Am. U., Beirut, Lebanon, 1956-57; fellowship Barnes Hosp., 1957-59; dir. immunology rsch. & tng. ctr. WHO, Beruit, Lebanon, 1970-76; physician SUNY Upstate Med. Ctr., Syracuse, chief sect. dermatology, 1976-99; pvt. practice Syracuse; instr. dept. medicine Am. U., Beirut, 1959-60, asst. prof., 1960-66, assoc. prof., 1966-74, prof., 1976. Fellow Am. Acad. Dermatology; mem. Internat. Soc. of Tropical Medicine, Soc. for Investigative Dermatology. Fax: 315-422-3129. Office: The Hill Med Ctr 1000 E Genesee St Syracuse NY 13210-1892 also: Upstate Med Ctr 750 E Adams St Syracuse NY 13210-2306

FARAH, ROGER, retail company executive. Former chmn., chief exec. officer Rich's, Atlanta, Federated/Allied Merchandising Svcs., N.Y.C.; chmn., CEO, Woolworth Corp. (name changed to Venator Group), N.Y.C., 1994—, also bd. dirs. Office: Venator Group 233 Broadway Fl 3N New York NY 10279-0003*

FARANDA, JOHN PAUL, college administrator; b. Orange, Calif., Feb. 21, 1957; s. Paul L. and Kay S. (Wilson) F. BA cum laude, Claremont McKenna Coll., 1979. Staff liaison L.A. County Bar Assn., 1979-80; spl. programs adminstr. L.A. County Med. Assn., 1980-85; dir. corp. rels. Claremont (Calif.) McKenna Coll., 1985-87, dir. campaign and devel. svcs., 1987-89, dir. devel., 1989-96, assoc. v.p. devel., 1996—. Contbr. articles to profl. jours. Campaign chmn. United Way, Mt. Baldy Region, Ontario, Calif., 1987-90; bd. govs. Faculty Ho. of the Claremont Colls., pres. 1993-95; bd. dirs. Recording for the Blind and Dyslexic, Community Friends of Internat. Students. Recipient Gold award Mt. Baldy United Way, 1988, 91. Mem. L.A. County Bar Assn. (com. on arbitration), Coun. for Advancement and Support of Edn. (USX award 1986), Athletic Club L.A. Avocations: sailing, skiing. Office: Claremont McKenna Coll Bauer Ctr #320 500 E 9th St Claremont CA 91711-5903

FARAONE, TED, public relations executive, consultant; b. Providence, Feb. 21, 1956; s. Raffaele Pietro and Jennie (Landi) F.; m. Teri Dickstein, June 1, 1988. BA, Columbia U., 1978. Publicity dir. Sta. WNYC Radio-TV, N.Y.C., 1979-81; press rep. Sta. WNBC-TV, N.Y.C., 1981-82, Sta. WCBS-TV, N.Y.C., 1982-83; dir. press rels. Sta. WCAU-TV, Phila., 1983-86, Sta. WBBM-TV, Chgo., 1986-87; pres. Faraone Comm., Inc., N.Y.C., 1987-93; vice chmn. Faraone Comm., Inc., 1994, chmn., 1995—. Editor: mag. Sta. WNYC Program Guide, 1979-81. Mem. NATAS (mem. bd. govs. N.Y. chpt. 1993—, sec. 1995-97, v.p. 1997—), NARAS, Acad. of TV Arts and Scis., Internat. Radio and TV Soc., Pub. Rels. Soc. (accredited), Counselors Acad., Writers and Artists for Peace in Mid-East, Eastern Packard Club (dir. 1998—), Friars Club (N.Y.C.), Phi Beta Kappa. Office: Faraone Communications Inc 75 W End Ave New York NY 10023-7853

FARAONE, TERI, public relations executive; b. N.Y.C., July 6, 1953; d. Seymour and Marilyn (Lutsky) Dickstein; m. Ted Faraone, June 1, 1988. BA, Kean Coll. of N.J., Elizabeth, 1979; MA, CUNY, 1996. Asst. mgr. Citicorp, N.Y.C., 1982-88; mgr. Faraone Comms., N.Y.C., 1988-92, dir. acct. svcs., 1990-92, v.p., 1992-94, pres., 1994—. Mem. NATAS. Office: Faraone Communications Inc 75 W End Ave New York NY 10023-7853

FARARO, THOMAS JOHN, sociologist, educator; b. N.Y.C., Feb. 11, 1933; s. Joseph and Anna (Marcello) F.; m. Irmer Johanna Fannasch, Dec. 30, 1955; children: Ramona, Raymond. BA, CCNY, 1959; PhD, Syracuse U., 1963. Asst. prof. sociology Syracuse (N.Y.) U., 1963-64; vis. scholar Stanford (Calif.) U., 1964-67; prof. U. Pitts., 1967—, chmn. dept. sociology, 1980-85. Author: Mathematical Sociology, 1973, Mathematical Sociology, Japanese translation, 1980, The Meaning of General Theoretical Sociology, 1989 (transl. into Japanese 1996); editor: Mathematical Ideas and Sociological Theory, 1984; co-editor Rational Choice Theory, 1992, The Problem of Solidarity, 1998; assoc. editor Jour. Math. Sociology, 1978—; mem. editl. bd. Am. Jour. Sociology, 1977-79, Am. Sociol. Rev., 1980-82, Social Networks, 1978-82, Sociol. Theory, 1988-90, Sociol. Forum, 1989-92. With USAF, 1952-56. Grantee, Social Sci. Rsch. Coun., 1968, NSF, 1969-72. Mem. Am. Sociol. Assn., Internat. Network for Social Network Analysis. Office: U Pitts Dept Sociology 230 S Bouquet St Pittsburgh PA 15213-4015 *I have devoted my intellectual life to the advancement of theoretical sociology by the use of mathematical methods in presenting theories, clarifying and formalizing concepts, representing social processes and social structures, and explaining social phenomena.*

FARB, THOMAS FOREST, financial executive; b. N.Y.C., Oct. 28, 1956; s. Peter and Oriole (Horch) F.; m. Stacy Siana Valhouli, Apr. 29, 1961; children: Peter Forest Valhouli-Farb, Siana Louisa Valhouli-Farb, Andreas John Valhouli-Farb. AB, Harvard U., 1980. Rsch. assoc. Mass. House Ways and Means Com., Boston, 1976-78; asst v.p. Bank of Boston, 1980-83; v.p., CFO and gen. mgr. ea. ops. Symbolics, Inc., Burlington, Mass., 1983-89; sr. v.p., CFO & controller Airfund Corp., Lexington, Mass., 1989-92; v.p. corp. devel., chief fin. officer and treas. Cytyc Corp., Marborough, Mass., 1992-94; exec. v.p., CFO, treas. Interneuron Pharms., Inc., Lexington, Mass., 1994-98; gen. ptnr., CFO Summit Ptnrs., Boston, 1998—; bd. dirs. HNC Software, Inc., San Diego, Redwood Trust, Inc., Mill Valley, Calif., Saf-T-Med. Inc., Barrington, Ill. Mem. Fin. Execs. Inst., Bus. Assocs. Club, Treas. Club Boston, Newcomen Soc. Home: 1228 Lowell Rd Concord MA 01742-5527 Office: Summit Partners 600 Atlantic Ave Fl 28 Boston MA 02210-2211

FARBANISH, THOMAS, sculptor; b. Endicott, N.Y., Mar. 21, 1963. BFA, Rochester Inst. Tech., 1986. Asst. Artpark, Lewiston, N.Y., 1986, Wheaton Village, Millville, N.J., 1989; instr. Golden Glass Sch., Cin., 1990, Corning Bus. Devel. Ctr., 1991; faculty Tyler Sch. Art, Pa., 1991, Urban Glass, N.Y., 1992, Pilchuck Glass Sch., Stanwood, Wash., 1993-94, 97; gaffer Pilchuck Glass Sch., Stanwood, 1996-97; faculty Haystack Sch. Crafts, Maine, 1993, Penland Sch., N.C., 1993, Rochester (N.Y.) Inst. Tech., 1994, 97; tchg. asst. Pilchuck Glass Sch., Stanwood, 1986, 87, 90, Saxe emerging artist in residence, 1988; lectr. in field. One-man and two-man shows include Snyderman Gallery, Phila., 1987, Sarah Squeri Gallery, Cin., 1990, AVA Gallery, Lebanon, N.H., 1992, Artspace, Kohler Art Ctr., Sheboygan, Wis., 1993, Robert L. Kidd Gallery, Birmingham, Mich., 1994, William Traver Gallery, Seattle, 1991, 94, 95, Heller Gallery, N.Y.C., 1995; group shows include Glass Gallery, Bethesda, Md., 1984, 85, Germanow Gallery, Rochester, 1984, Morris Mus., Morristown, N.J., 1985, Upton Hall Galleries, Buffalo, 1985, Courtyard Galleries, Balt., 1986, Huntington (W.Va.) Mus. Art, 1986, Heller Gallery, N.Y.C., 1986, 87, 91, 92, 94, 95, 97, Ward Gallery, 1987, Somerstown Gallery, Somers, N.Y., 1987, Snyderman Gallery, Pa., 1987, Am. Craft Mus., N.Y.C., 1988, So. Alleghenies Mus. Art, Loretto, Pa., 1988, Grohe Gallery, Boston, 1989, Robert L. Kidd Gallery, Birmingham, 1989, 96, William Traver Gallery, Seattle, 1990, 92, 93, Sotheby's, N.Y.C., 1990, Gallery Nakama, Tokyo, 1991, Lehman Gallery, N.Y.C., 1993, Christies, N.Y.C., 1993, Bellevue (Wash.) Art Mus., 1994, Habitat Galleries, Birmingham, 1994, Leedy Voulkos Gallery, Kansas City, Mo., 1995, Philabaum Gallery, Tucson, 1995, Huntsville (Ala.) Mus. Art, 1996; represented in permanent collections Huntsville Mus. Art, Am. Craft Mus., Prescott Collection, Wash., Huntington Mus. Art, Davis Wright and Jones, Wash., Wheaton (N.J.) Mus. Am. Glass, Pilchuck Glass Sch., Wash., Rochester Inst. Tech. Creative Glass Ctr. Am. fellow Wheaton Village, 1985, 90, Visual Artist fellow Nat. Endowment Arts, 1988, 94; Pilchuck Galss Sch. scholar, 1987; Mid Atlantic Arts Found. grantee, 1990. Office: c/o William Traver Gallery 110 Union St Ste 200 Seattle WA 98101

FARBER, BARRY ALAN, psychotherapist, educator; b. Bklyn., Dec. 31, 1947; s. Sol and Nettie Farber; m. April Jill Forrest, Aug. 27, 1972; children: Alissa, David. BA, Queens Coll., 1968; MA, Columbia U., 1970; PhD, Yale U., 1978. Cert. psychologist. Pvt. practice Mamaroneck, N.Y., 1980—; dir. clin. tng. Tchrs. Coll. Columbia U., N.Y.C., 1990—, prof., 1991—, chair dept. counseling and clin. psychology, 1996—. Author: Stress and Burnout in the Human Service Professors, 1983, Crisis in Education, 1991, The Psychology of Carl Rogers, 1996. Prize Tchg. fellow Yale U., 1977; Rsch. grantee Sigma Xi, 1978; grantee Spencer Found., 1982. Mem. APA, N.Y. State Psychol. Assn. Avocations: tennis, softball, book club, 1950-60's rock 'n roll. Office: Columbia U Tchrs Coll 525 W 120th St New York NY 10027

FARBER, BERNARD, sociologist, educator; b. Chgo., Feb. 11, 1922; s. Benjamin and Esther (Axelrod) F.; m. Annette Ruth Shugan, Dec. 21, 1947 (div. 1970); children—Daniel, Michael, Lisa, Jacqueline; m. Rosanna Bodanis, June 10, 1971 (dec. June 1988); 1 dau., Tanya. AB, Roosevelt U., Chgo., 1943; AM, U. Chgo., 1949, PhD, 1953. Research assoc. U. Chgo., 1951-53; asst. prof. Henderson State Tchr. Coll., Arkadelphia, Ark., 1953-54; mem. faculty U. I., 1954-71, prof. sociology, 1964-71; asso. dir. Inst.

Research Exceptional Children, 1967-69; prof. Ariz. State U., 1971-92, prof. emeritus, 1992—, chmn. dept. sociology, 1971-75, 90-92; vis. prof. U. Tex., Austin, 1974-75, U. Ill., Chgo., 1988-95; cons. in field, 1957—. Author: Family: Organization and Interaction, 1964, Mental Retardation: Its Social Context and Social Consequences, 1968, Kinship and Class, 1971, Guardians of Virtue, 1972, Family and Kinship in Modern Society, 1973, Conceptions of Kinship, 1981; editor Sociol. Perspectives, 1985-89; co-editor: Sociological Inquiry, 1997—. Mem. mental retardation research com. Nat. Inst. Child Health and Human Devel., 1971-75. Served with AUS, 1943-46. Recipient E.W. Burgess award Nat. Council on Family Relations, 1975; Disting. Research award Ariz. State U., 1980. Mem. Am. Sociol. Assn. (coun. mem. family sect. 1966-69), Ill. Sociol. Assn. (founding pres. 1965-66), Pacific Sociol. Assn. (pres. 1986-87). Jewish. Home: 7949 E Montebello Ave Scottsdale AZ 85250-6108 Office: Ariz State U Dept Sociology Tempe AZ 85287

FARBER, BERNARD JOHN, lawyer; b. London, Feb. 27, 1948; came to U.S., 1949; s. Solomon and Regina (Wachter) F.; m. Mary Lee Mueller, Feb. 14, 1987; children: Zachary, Anne. BS, U. of State of N.Y., Albany, 1978; JD, Ill. Inst. Tech., 1983. Bar: Ill. 1983, U.S. Dist. Ct. (no. dist.) Ill. 1983, U.S. Ct. Appeals (7th cir.) 1985, U.S. Tax Ct. 1986, U.S. Ct. Mil. Appeals 1986, U.S. Supreme Ct. 1987, U.S. Ct. Appeals (6th cir.) 1988, U.S. Ct. Appeals (4th cir.) 1989, U.S. Ct. Appeals (11th cir.) 1990. Instr. legal writing Chgo.-Kent Law Sch. Ill. Inst. Tech., 1983-85, computer rsch. atty., 1985-86, adj. prof. law, 1987—; legal editor Longman Fin. Svcs., Chgo., 1986-87; rsch. counsel publs. Ams. for Effective Law Enforcement, Chgo., 1987—; instr. Law Scholastic Aptitude Test; preparation course BAR/BRI, Chgo., 1984-88; v.p. Brickton Montessori Sch., Chgo., 1992-93; sec. bd. dirs., 1993-95. Mng. editor: Chgo.-Kent Law Rev., 1981-82, editor-in-chief, 1982-83; co-author: Protective Security Law, 1996; editor: (with others) Dow Jones-Irwin Handbook of Micro Computer Applications in Law, 1987, Illinois Law of Criminal Investigation, 1986; contbr. articles to profl. jours. Elected mem. Local Sch. Coun., Agassiz Elem. Sch., Chgo., 1996—, chmn., 1999—. Mem. ABA, Ill. State Bar Assn., Chgo. Bar Assn., Sci. Fiction Rsch. Assn., Mensa. Avocations: history, computers, science fiction. E-mail: bernfarber@aol.com. Home and Office: 1126 W Wolfram St Rear Chicago IL 60657-4330

FARBER, DONALD CLIFFORD, lawyer, educator; b. Columbus, Nebr., Oct. 19, 1923; s. Charles and Sarah (Epstein) F.; m. Ann Eis, Dec. 28, 1947; children: Seth, Patricia. BS in Law, U. Nebr., 1948, JD, 1950. Bar: N.Y. 1950. Assoc. Newman, Hauser & Teitler, N.Y.C., 1950-58; sole practice N.Y.C., 1958-80; of counsel Conboy, Hewitt, O'Brien & Boardman, N.Y.C., 1980-84; ptnr. Tanner Propp Fersko & Sterner, N.Y.C., 1984-95, Farber & Rich LLP, N.Y.C., 1995-98; of counsel Hartman & Craven LLP, N.Y.C., 1998—; prof. law York U., Toronto, Ont., Can., 1970, 72-73; prof. theatre law Hofstra Law Sch., Hempstead, N.Y., 1974-75; prof. New Sch. for Social Rsch., N.Y.C., 1972—, Hunter Coll., 1978. Author: From Option to Opening, 1968, 4th edit., 1st Limelight edit., 1988, Producing on Broadway, 1969, Actor's Guide: What You Should Know About the Contracts You Sign, 1971, Producing, Financing and Distributing Film, 1973, 2d edit., 1991, The Amazing Story of the Fantasticks: America's Longest Running Play, 1991, Producing Theatre: A Comprehensive Legal and Business Guide, 1981, 3d Limelight edit., 1997, Common Sense Negotiation-The Art of Winning Gracefully, 1996; gen. editor (10 vol. series, author theatre vol.) Entertainment Industry Contracts-Negotiating and Drafting Guide. With AUS, 1941-44, ETO. Mem. Order of Coif, Hon. Law Soc. Fax: (212) 223-0467. Home: 14 E 75th St New York NY 10021-2657 Office: Hartman & Craven LLP 11th Fl 460 Park Ave New York NY 10022-1987

FARBER, EMMANUEL, pathology and biochemistry educator; b. Toronto, Ont., Can., Oct. 19, 1918; s. Morris and Mary (Madorsky) F.; m. Ruth Diamond, Apr. 21, 1942; 1 child, Noami Beth. MD, U. Toronto, 1942; PhD in Biochemistry, U. Calif., 1949; D Medicine and Surgery (hon.), U. Turin, Italy, 1985. Diplomate Am. Bd. Pathology. Intern, then resident in pathology Hamilton (Ont.) Gen. Hosp., 1942-43; fellow in cancer rsch. Am. Cancer Soc. U. Calif., 1947-49, Hektoen Inst. Med. Rsch., Cook County Hosp., Chgo., 1949-50; from instr. to assoc. prof. pathology and biochemistry Tulane U., New Orleans, 1950-59; Am. Cancer Soc. Rsch. prof. Tulane U., 1959-61; prof., chmn. pathology dept. U. Pitts., 1961-70; Am. Cancer Soc. Rsch. prof., sr. investigator Fels Rsch. Inst., Temple U. Sch. Medicine, Phila., 1970-74, prof., dir., 1974-75; prof., chmn. pathology dept. U. Toronto, 1975-85, prof. dept. pathology, dept. biochemistry, 1985; prof. emeritus, 1985—; mem. staff, pathologist-in-chief Toronto Gen. Hosp., 1975-85; chmn. dept. pathology Toronto Western Hosp., 1975-85; prof. dept. pathology and cell biology Jefferson Med. Coll., Phila., 1994—; vis. scientist Toxicology Rsch. Unit Med. Rsch. Coun. Lab., Carshalton, Eng., 1959; vis. prof. Courtauld Inst. Biochemistry. Middlesex Hosp. Med. Sch., London, Eng.,1968-69; vis. prof., lectr. Krakower U. Ill., Chgo., 1989; mem. Surgeon Gen.'s adv. com. on smoking and health, 1962-64; mem. pathology B study sect. NIH, 1962-66, chmn. 1963-66, chem. pathology study sect, 1980-82, metabolic pathology study sect., 1987-89; mem. pathology com. NAS Nat. Rsch. Coun., 1965-66; mem. adv. panel 5 on med. scis. U.S.-Japan coop. sci. program, 1965, panel D Nat. Cancer Inst. Can., 1977-79, panel I com. on food safely and food safety policy NAS, 1978-79; mem. rev. bd. Alachlor Can., 1985-87; mem. sci. adv. bd. Armed Forces Inst. Pathology, 1966-70, Nat. Ctr. Toxicology Rsch., 1973-74; mem. nat. adv. cancer coun. USPHS, 1966-70; mem. com. Cancer Rsch. Tng. Grants Nat. Cancer Inst., 1971-72; mem. bd. sci. overseers Jackson Lab., 1972-81, trustee 1972-74; cons. HEW, 1964-67, St. Michael's Hosp., Toronto, 1976-85, Sunnybrook Med. Centre, Toronto, 1976-85, Wellesley Hosp., 1976-85, Mt. Sinai Hosp., 1976-85, N.Y. Gen. Hosp., 1977-85. Editor: Biochemical Pathology, 1966, The Biochemistry of Disease Series Vols. 1-12, 1971-87, Toxic Liver Injury, 1979, Toxic Injury of the Liver, 1980, Pathogenesis of Liver Diseases, 1987; mem. editorial bd., assoc. editor Cancer Rsch., Teratogenisis Carcinogenesis and Mutagenesis; mem. editorial bd. Oncology News, Internat. Jour. Cancer, Chem. Biological Interactions, Carcinogenesis, Liver, Hepatology, Lab. Investigation; assoc. editor Toxicologic Pathology; contbr. numerous articles to profl. jours. Capt. Med. Corp. Royal Can. Army, 1942-46. Recipient Parke-Davis award Am. Soc. Exptl. Pathology, 1958, Bertha Goldblatt Teplitz Meml. award, 1961, Samuel R. Noble Found. award, 1976, fellow Royal Soc. Can., Eastman Kodak award Nat. Acad. Clin. Biochem., 1986, Founders' award Chem. Industry Inst. Toxicology, 1987, Disting. Pathologist award U.S. and Can. Acad. Pathologists, 1992; named Schofield Meml. lectr. U. Guelph, 1984, Alexander Breslow Meml. lectr. George Washington U., 1986, Robert E. Greenfield lectr. U. Nebr., 1987, Disting. lectr. Roswell Pk. Meml. Inst., 1988; NIH fellow Nat. Cancer Inst., 1969-70. Mem. AAAS, Am. Assn. Cancer Rsch. (GHA Clowes Meml. award 1984, hon. mem. 1995), Am. Assn. Pathologists (Rous-Whipple award 1982), Am. Chem. Soc., Am. Soc. Biochemistry Molecular Biology, Am. Soc. Investigative Pathology (Gold Headed Cane award 1995), Am. Gastroenterol. Assn., Am. Assn. Study Liver Disease, Biochem. Soc., Can. Assn. Pathologists (William Boyd lectr. 1986), Can. Biochem. Soc., Histochem. Soc., Internat. Acad. Pathology (Maude E. Abbott lectr. 1987), Jap. Cancer Assn. (hon.), N.Y. Acad. Scis., Ont. Assn. Pathologists, Ont. Med. Assn., Pathol. Soc. Gt. Britain Ireland (hon.), Soc. Exptl. Biology and Medicine, Soc. Toxicology (U.S. chpt.), Soc. Toxicology Can., Soc. Toxicologic Pathologists (hon.). Office: Jefferson Med Coll Dept Path and Cell Biology Philadelphia PA 19107

FARBER, ERICH A., mechanical engineer. BS in Mech. Engring., U. Mo., 1943, MS in Mech. Engring., 1946; PhD, U. Iowa, 1949. Disting. Svc. prof. EM U. Fla., Gainesville, dir. EM, solar energy and energy conversion lab.; cons. in field; gov. task force, Fla., 1975; adv. U.S. State Dept., 1976—; mem. NSF/NASA Panel, Solar Energy Working Group; established Internat. Tng. Ctr., Tng. in Alt. Techs. Co-author 6 books; contbr. over 600 articles to profl. jours. Apptd. Fla. Energy Com., Task Force to work on Fla.'s energy problems.; mem. U.S./India Coop. Solar Energy Program, 1976; advisor energy problems, The Philippines, Peru, Morocco, others. Recipient Worcester Reed Warner Gold Medal award, Mo. Honor award; decorated Purple Hearts, Silver Star, Battle Field Commn.; charter inductee Solar Hall of Fame, NASA, 1977. Fellow ASME. Office: Univ Fla Solar Energy & Energy Conversion Lab Gainesville FL 32611

FARBER, EUGENE MARK, psoriasis research institute administrator; b. Buffalo, July 24, 1917; s. Simon and Mathilda Farber; m. Ruth Seiffert, Mar. 4, 1944; children: Nancy, Charlotte, Donald. BA, Oberlin (Ohio) Coll., 1939; MD, U. Buffalo, 1943; MS, U. Minn., 1946; DSc, Calif. Coll. Podiatric Medicine, 1973. Clin. asst., prof. dermatology Stanford (Calif.) U., 1949-50, asst. prof. pathology, 1949-50, clin. prof., dir. div. dermatology, 1950-598, prof., chmn. dermatology, 1959-86; pres. Psoriasis Rsch. Inst., Palo Alto, Calif., 1973—; cons. Pacific Med. Ctr., San Francisco, 1982-84; nat. cons. to surgeon gen. USAF, Washington, 1957-64; cons. in dermatology Calif. State Dept. of Pub. Health, Sacramento, 1963-66; hon. prof. Dalian Med. U., People's Republic of China, 1999. Contbr. chpts. to book and articles to profl. jours. Recipient Physician's Recognition award AMA, 1982-85, 83-85, 91-94, Jose Marie Vargas award Cen. U. of Caracas, 1972, Mr. and Mrs. J.B. Taub Internat. Meml. award for Psoriasis Rsch., 1974, Disting. Svc. meda. Bd. Regents Uniformed Svcs. U., 1984, Order of Andres Bello, Banda de Honor, 1984, City of Paris medal, 1991, Most Disting. Alumni award U. Buffalo, 1998, Psoriasis Rsch. award Am. Skin Assn., 1999. Master Am. Acad. Dermatology (bd. dirs. 1957-60, others); mem. Am. Dermatol. Assn. (bd. dirs. 1974, hon. membership com. 1983-87), Assn. of Profs. of Dermatology (exec. bd., sec. 1977-80, pres. 1977-80, chairperson fin. com. 1980), Pacific Dermatology Assn. (bd. dirs. 1965-68, pres.-elect 1979-80, pres. 1980-81), Soc. for Investigative Dermatology (bd. dirs. 1957-62, pres. 1966-67, com. on hon. membership 1979—), Nat. Program for Dermatology, Space Dermatology Found. (v.p. 1986, pres. 1989-90), Chinese Assn. of the Integration of Traditional and Western Medicine (hon. advisor 1997), others. Home: 167 Ramoso Rd Portola Valley CA 94028-7327 Office: Psoriasis Rsch Inst 600 Town And Country Vlg Palo Alto CA 94301-2326*

FARBER, EVAN IRA, librarian; b. N.Y.C., June 30, 1922; s. Meyer M. and Estelle H. (Shapiro) F.; m. Hope Wells Nagle, June 13, 1966; children: Cynthia, Amy, Jo Anna, May Beth; stepchildren: David Nagle, Jeffrey Nagle, Lisa Nagle. AB, U. N.C., 1944, MA, 1953, BLS, 1953; DHL (hon.), St. Lawrence U., 1980, Susquehanna U., 1989, Ind. U., 1996. Instr. polit. sci. U. Mass., Amherst, 1948-49; asst. documents dept. U. N.C. Library, 1951-53; librarian State Tchrs. Coll., Livingston, Ala., 1953-55; chief serials and binding div. Emory U. Library, Ga., 1955-62; head librarian Earlham Coll., Richmond, Ind., 1962-94, coll. libr. emeritus, 1994—; dir. seminar on non-Western studies for coll. librs. Columbia U. Sch. Libr. Sci., summers, 1966, 68-69; cons. Bates Coll., Eckerd Coll., Colo. Coll., Hartwick Coll., Macalester Coll., Maryville Coll., Knox Coll., Ill. Coll., Messiah Coll., Hiram Coll., Centenary Coll., Colby Coll., Ga. State U., Ripon Coll., Hampshire Coll., Reed Coll., Williams Coll., NEH, Lilly Endowment, North Ctrl. Assn., Assn. Am. Colls., Pew Meml. Trust. Author: (with Andreano and Reynolds) Student Economists Handbook, 1967, Classified List of Periodicals for the College Library, 5th edit., 1972; assoc. editor: Southeastern Librarian, 1959-62; asst. editor: Explorations in Entrepreneurial History, 1964-66; co-editor: Earlham Rev., 1965-72; editor: Combined Retrospective Index to Book Revs. in Scholarly Jours., 1886-1974, 1979-83, Combined Retrospective Index to Revs. in Humanities Jours., 1802-1974, 1983-85, (with Ruth Walling) Essays in Honor of Guy R. Lyle; columnist: Choice Mag., 1974-80, Library Issues, 1982-88. Recipient Acad./Rsch. Libr. of the Yr., 1980, B.I. Libr. of Yr. award, 1987. Mem. Assn. Coll. and Rsch. Librs. (pres. 1978-79, bd. dirs. 1989-93), ALA (council 1969-71, 79-83). E-mail: evanf@earlham.edu. Home: 304 SW H St Richmond IN 47374-5243 Office: Earlham Coll Lilly Libr Richmond IN 47374

FARBER, GERALDINE OSSMAN, civic worker; b. Salt Lake City, May 4, 1929; d. Lawrence N. and Janet (Perkins) Ossman; m. John Val Browning, July 19, 1949 (div. June 1964); 1 child, John Allen; m. Seymour M. Farber, June 5, 1973 (dec. 1995). Student, Vassar Coll., 1947-49, U. Liege, Belgium, 1951-53, U. Utah, 1955. Tchrs. aid spl. programs elem. schs. Ogden, Utah, Los Altos and Woodside, Calif., 1962-70; cons. Glasrock Products, Inc., 1979-80. Editor: Teilhard de chardin: In Quest of the Perfection of Man, 1973. Bd. dirs. Am. Field Svc., Ogden, 1960-64, Utah Ballet, Ogden, 1963-64, Christmas Bur., Palo Alto and Los Altos, 1964-66, Jr. League Palo Alto, 1966-69; active Cmty. Com. Internat. Students, Stanford, 1965-67; dir. Ednl. TV Fgn. Student Series, Ogden, 1963-64; bd. dirs. Vol. Bur. No. Santa Clara County, 1965-68, exec. v.p., 1967-68; mem. exec. com. Paul N. McCloskey, Jr. Congl. Campaign, San Mateo, Calif., 1967; vol. parentis in locus, tubercular refugee children Caritas Catholique, Liege, 1952-55; ways and means chmn. San Francisco Ballet Assn. Aux., 1970, pres., 1974-75, trustee assn., 1974-75; co-founder, pres. bd. dirs. Performing Arts Libr. and Mus., 1975-76; bd. dirs. Am. Conservatory Theater, 1975-81; mem. Calif. Pub. Broadcasting Commn., 1975-85; vol., asst. media buyer campaign Supt. Pub. Instrn. Calif., 1970; mem. exec. planning com. and nat. adv. bd. John Muir Med. Film Festival, 1979-91; mem. program com. Kauai Found. Continuing Edn. and Hawaii Med. Assn., 1979-85. Recipient Merit awards City and County San Francisco, Vol. Bur. No. Santa Clara County, commendation Calif. State Senate, 1985. Mem. San Francisco Peninsula Vassar Alumnae Club (pres. 1968-70), Francisca Club. Home and Office: 26303 Esperanza Dr Los Altos CA 94022-2601

FARBER, ISADORE E., psychologist, educator; b. St. Joseph, Mo., May 21, 1917; s. Jacob and Rose (Malkin) F.; m. Billie Frances Gulko, May 5, 1942; children: Ronna Ellen (dec.), Deborah. Student, St. Joseph Jr. Coll., 1934-36; B.A., U. Mo., 1939, M.A., 1940; Ph.D., U. Iowa, 1946. Instr. psychology U. Rochester, 1946-47; asst. prof. to prof. psychology U. Iowa, 1947-64; vis. prof. U. Wis., 1955, Stanford, 1960; research cons. Med. Sch., U. of Okla., 1956-57; prof. psychology U. Ill., Chgo., 1964-84; prof. emeritus U. Ill., 1984—, head dept. psychology, 1964-68, 76-81; vis. prof., sr. Fulbright fellow Hebrew U., Jerusalem, 1971-72. Founding editor Jour. Exptl. Research in Personality, 1965-71; editor Psychology series, Dodd, Mead & Co., 1965-73; cons. editor Jour. Abnormal and Social Psychology, 1955-61, Jour. of Personality, 1955-61, Jour. Abnormal Psychology, 1973-79; contbr. articles to profl. jours. Served with Q.M.C. AUS, 1941-42; to 2d lt. USAAF, 1942-45. Fellow APA, Am. Psychol. Soc.; mem. Midwestern Psychol. Assn. (past pres.), Psychonomic Soc., Midwest Com. for Rational Inquiry, Phi Beta Kappa, Sigma Xi. Jewish. Home: 7912 Church St Morton Grove IL 60053-1628

FARBER, JACKIE, editor; b. Jersey City, Apr. 16, 1927; d. Herman B. and Pauline (Birnbaum) Levine; m. Samuel Farber, June 25, 1950 (div. 1981); children: Thomas Adam, John David; m. 2d Jay Topkis, Sept. 27, 1981. BA, Smith Coll., 1949. Editor Bernard Geis Assocs., N.Y.C., 1963-72; sr. editor Delacorte Press, N.Y.C., 1972-74, exec. editor, 1980-81, editor-in-chief, 1981-89, fiction editor, 1989—; sr. editor William Morrow, N.Y.C., 1974-78, Random House, N.Y.C., 1978-80; fiction editor Delacorte Press div. Bantam Doubleday Dell Pub. Group, 1980-91; v.p., fiction editor Delacorte Press divsn. Bantam Doubleday Dell Pub. Group, 1991—. Mem. Women's Media Group, Columbia Golf and Country Club. Jewish. Home: 155 E 72nd St New York NY 10021-4371 Office: Bantam Doubleday Dell Pub Co 1540 Broadway Ste 9E New York NY 10036-4040

FARBER, JOHN J., chemical company executive; b. Timisoara, Rumania, Aug. 23, 1925; s. Eugene and Magda (Reiter) F.; m. Maya Kleyman, June 28, 1953; children: Sandra, Deborah, Michael, Claudia. MS, U. Cluj, Timisoara, 1948; PhD, Poly. Inst. Bklyn., 1956. Rsch. chemist Sun Chem. Co., N.Y.C., 1951-52; cons. Soc. des Peintures et Vernis Bouvet, Tournus, France, Verneba A.G. Neuallschwill, Basel, Switzerland, Foster Grant Co., Inc., Leominster, Mass., Chemische Fabrik Kalk GmbH, Koln, Kalk, Germany, Asahi Chem. Industry Co., Ltd., Tokyo, 1953-56; chmn. bd., chief exec. officer ICC Industries, Ind., N.Y.C.; chmn. Primex Plastics Corp., Oakland, N.J.; pres. Dover Chem. Corp., Ohio; dir., chmn. Electrochem. Industries (Frutarom) Ltd., Haifa, Israel. Mem. Am. Chem. Soc., Soc. Plastics Industry, Soc. Plastics Engrs., Nat. Petroleum Refiners Assn., Chem. Mfrs. Assn. Office: ICC Industries Inc 460 Park Ave New York NY 10022-1906

FARBER, LILLIAN, retired photography equipment company executive; b. N.Y.C., Aug. 4, 1920; d. Louis and Fannie (Disraeli) Bachrach; m. Leonard L. Farber, Nov. 3, 1940 (div. 1975); children: Lindy Linder, Robert D. (dec.), Peggy, Felicia Gervais. BA, NYU, 1940; MA, Sarah Lawrence Coll., 1966. Co-dir. Upward Bound Sarah Lawrence Coll., Bronxville, N.Y., 1966-70, dean student svcs., 1973-76; v.p., owner Zone VI Studios, Inc., Newfane, Vt., 1976-90, ret., 1990. One-woman photography shows include, Vt., N.Y. V.p. Greenburgh League Women Voters, Hartsdale, N.Y., 1955-63; state com. woman N.Y. State Dem. Com., 1968-70; family adv. Westchester Coun. of Social Agys., White Plains, N.Y., 1970-73; pres. bd. trustees Moore Free Libr., Newfane, 1977-97; chmn. bd. trustees Marlboro (Vt.) Coll., 1992-97, trustee, 1982-97; trustee Vt. Coun. on the Arts, 1992-96; mem. Vt. Bicentennial Commn., 1990-91. Mem. ACLU. Avocation: photography. Home: Maple Hollow PO Box 265 Newfane VT 05345-0265

FARBER, NEAL MARK, biotech executive, molecular biologist; b. N.Y.C., Oct. 23, 1950; s. Sol Z. and Nettie (Handelman) F.; m. Varda E. Farber, Aug. 19, 1973; children: Dani, Arielle. BSc with honors, Hebrew U., Jerusalem, 1973; MA, Columbia U., 1975, PhD, 1979; postgrad., Harvard U., 1979. Rsch. fellow Harvard U., Cambridge, Mass., 1980-82; rsch. scientist Biogen, Inc., Cambridge, 1982, project leader, 1983-85, coord. new projects, 1986-87, mgr. bus. devel., 1988, product mgr., 1989-93; dir. bus. devel. T Cell Scis., Inc., Cambridge, 1993-95; v.p. corp. devel. Cubist Pharm., Inc., Cambridge, 1996; biotech. bus. devel. cons. Collgard Biopharm., Waban, Mass., 1997-98, pres., CEO, 1998—; biotech bus. devel. cons., 1997. Contbr. articles to profl. jours. Pres. SSDS Day Sch., Boston, 1989-91. Recipient Rsch. Svc. award NIH, 1975-78, Hammett award Columbia U., 1979; Helen Hay Whitney Found. fellow, Boston, 1980-82; Wexner Heritage Found. fellow, 1991-93, founding chair CJP Biotech Group, 1994-96. Mem. AAAS, N.Y. Acad. Scis., Licensing Execs. Soc., Sigma Xi. E-mail: farbern@aol.com. Fax: (617) 244-6026. Office: 1860 Beacon St Waban MA 02468

FARBER, ROSANN ALEXANDER, geneticist, educator; b. Charlotte, N.C., Nov. 21, 1944; d. J. Wilson Jr. and June Adell (Childs) Alexander; m. Gerald Lee Farber, July 28, 1966 (div. Jan. 1969); m. Thomas Douglas Petes, July 20, 1973; children: Laura Elizabeth, Diana Christine. AB in Biology, Oberlin Coll., 1966; postgrad., U. Pitts., 1967-68, Albert Einstein Coll. Medicine, 1969; PhD in Genetics, U. Wash., 1973. Diplomate in clin. cytogenetics and clin. molecular genetics Am. Bd. Med. Genetics. Postdoctoral fellow Nat. Inst. for Med. Rsch., London, 1973-75; rsch. assoc. Children's Hosp. Med. Ctr., Boston, 1975-77; from asst. prof. to assoc. prof. U. Chgo., 1977-88; assoc. prof. dept. pathology and lab. medicine, program molecular biology and biotechnology, curriculum genetics and molecular biology U. N.C., Chapel Hill, 1988-97, prof., 1997—; mem. U. N.C. Lineberger Comprehensive Cancer Ctr., 1996—. Contbr. articles to profl. jours. NIH grantee, 1978—. Mem. AAAS, Am. Soc. Human Genetics. Achievements include research in human molecular genetics, somatic cell genetics, cancer genetics. Home: 612 Morgan Creek Rd Chapel Hill NC 27514-4928 Office: U NC CB 7525 Brinkhous-Bullitt Bldg Chapel Hill NC 27599

FARBER, SAUL JOSEPH, physician, educator; b. N.Y.C.; s. Isodor and Mary (Bunim) F.; m. Doris Marcia Balmuth; children—Joshua M., Beth Mina Farber Loewentheil. A.B., NYU, 1938, M.D., 1942; Ph.D. honoris causa, Tel Aviv U., 1983. Diplomate Am. Bd. Internal Medicine. Intern Sinai Hosp., Balt., 1942-43; rsch. resident Goldwarer Meml. Hosp., N.Y.C, 1946-47; resident Bellevue Hosp., N.Y.C, 1947-48; fellow NYU, 1948-49; Instr., asst. prof. medicine NYU, N.Y.C., 1953-62, assoc. prof., 1962-66, prof., chmn. dept. medicine, 1966—, Frederick H. King prof. medicine, 1978—, dean for acad. affairs Sch. Medicine, 1978-98, acting dean Sch. of Medicine, 1963-66, 79-81, 82—, provost, dean sch. medicine, 1987-98, chmn., 1998—; co-chmn. N.Y. State Health Adv. Council, 1975-80; chmn. Com. on Resource Requirements of VA Health Care Systems, NRC, 1974-77; mem. adv. com. on long term care chronic illness Robert Wood Johnson Found., 1979—, co-chmn. clin. nurse scholars adv. com., 1982—; mem. med. adv. bd. Hadassah; mem. adv. com. Harold C. Simmons Arthritis Research Ctr., U. Tex. Health Sci. Ctr., Dallas, 1983-86; organizing chmn. Fed. Council Internal Medicine, 1975, chmn., 1984-85; splty. advisor Naval Med. Command, Washington, 1985-86. Contbr. articles to profl. jours. Recipient Career Scientist award Health Rsch. Coun., N.y.C., 1960-65, Med. Alumni Achievement award NYU Sch. Medicine Alumni Assn., 1966, Gt. Tchr. award NYU Alumni Fedn., 1973, Alumni Assn. Achievement award Washington Sq. Coll. Arts and Sci., NYU, 1978, Alumni Meritorious Svc. award NYU Alumni Fedn., 1984, Wise medal Tel Aviv U., 1990, The Albert Gallatin medal NYU, 1993, The Abraham Flexner award for Disting. Svc. to Med. Edn., 1995. Recipient Career Scientist award Health Rsch. Coun., N.Y.C., 1960-65, Med. Alumni Achievement award NYU Sch. of Medicine Alumni Assn., 1966, Gt. Tchr. award NYU Alumni Fedn., 1973, Alumni Assn. Achievement award Washington Sq. Coll. Arts and Sci., NYU, 1978, Alumni Meritorious Svc. award NYU Alumni Fedn., 1984, Wise medal Tel Aviv U., 1990, The Albert Gallatin medal NYU, 1993. Fellow ACP (master 1975, pres. 1984-85, regent 1978-86, Disting. tchr. award 1986, Alfred Stengal Meml. award 1992); mem. Am. Soc. Internal Medicine (Disting. Internist of Yr. award 1976), Am. Soc. Clin. Investigation (sec.-treas. 1951-60, councillor 1960-63), Assn. Am. Physicians, Interurban Clin. Club, Inst. Medicine Nat. Acad. Scis., Am. Clin. and Climatol. Assn., Am. Physiol. Soc., Assn. Acad. Health Ctrs. (adv. com. 1981—), Sigma Theta Tau (hon.). Office: NYU Sch Medicine 550 1st Ave New York NY 10016-6481*

FARBER, STEVEN GLENN, lawyer; b. Phila., July 20, 1946; s. Isadore Irving and Sylvia (Galperin) F.; children: Jamie, Daniel, Zoey, Avi. BBA, Temple U., 1968, JD, 1972. Bar: Pa. 1972, U.S. Dist. Ct. (ea. dist.) Pa. 1972, U.S. Dist. Ct. Appeals (3d cir.) 1972, N.Mex. 1975, U.S. Dist. Ct. N.Mex. 1975, U.S. Ct. Appeals (10th cir.) 1979, U.S. Supreme Ct. 1980. Asst. defender Pub. Defender Assn. Phila., 1972-74; acting dist. pub. defender State of N.Mex., Santa Fe, 1975-76, asst. atty. gen., 1976-78; pvt. practice Santa Fe, 1978—; mem. N.Mex. Bd. Legal Specialization, 1986-90, chmn., 1991-93. Elected city councilor City of Santa Fe, 1992-96, mem. Santa Fe Mcpl. Home Rule Charter Commn., 1997; bd. dirs. Ptnrs. in Edn., 1997—, Temple Beth Shalom, 1997—, Santa Fe County United Way, 1998—. Mem. Nat. Assn. Criminal Def. Lawyers (vice-chmn. continuing legal edn. com. 1990-91), N.Mex. Lawyers Guild (pres. 1980-81), N.Mex. State Bar Assn. (bd. dirs. criminal law sect. 1980-83, chmn. 1981-82), N.Mex. Criminal Def. Lawyers Assn. (bd. dirs. 1991, treas. 1996), First Jud. Dist. Criminal Def. Lawyers Assn. (sec. 1999). Democrat. Jewish. Office: PO Box 2473 306 Catron St Santa Fe NM 87504-2473

FARBER, VIOLA ANNA, dancer, choreographer, educator; b. Heidelberg, Germany, Feb. 25, 1931; came to U.S., 1938, naturalized, 1944; d. Eduard and Dora (Schmidt) F.; m. Jeffrey Clarke Slayton, June 14, 1971. Student, Am. U., 1949-51, Black Mountain Coll., 1951-52. Dancer Merce Cunningham Dance Co., N.Y.C., 1952-65; instr. dance Adelphi U., N.Y.C., 1959-67, Bennington (Vt.) Coll., 1967-68, NYU, 1971-73; dir., tchr. Viola Farber Dance Studio, N.Y.C., 1969-84; also artistic dir., choreographer, dancer Viola Farber Dance Co., N.Y.C., 1969-86; chair dance dept. Sarah Lawrence Coll., 1988—; artistic dir. Centre National de Danse Contemporaine, Angers, France, 1981-83; guest performer as vampire in Katherine Litz' Dracula; bd. dirs. Found. for the Contemproary Performance Arts; tchr. Am. Dance Festival, Durham, N.C., 1987, ADF, Seoul, Korea, 1990; guest tchr. throughout U.S., Asia and Europe including Holland, Germany, Denmark, others. Choreographer Viola Farber Dance Co., Ballet Theatre Contemparain, Angers, France, Ballet Théâtre Français, Repertory Dance Theatre, Utah, Manhattan Festival Ballet, Nancy Hauser Dance Co., Dance depts. Adelphi, NYU, Ohio State U. and U. Utah, Janet Gillespie and Present Co.; commd. by Heinz Found.; collaborated with Robert Rauschenberg and David Tudor on video tape Brazos River, 1976; choreographed Jeux Chorégraphique for Ballet Théâtre Français de Nancy, 1980, Extemporary Dance co., London, Plymouth, Eng., 1984, London, 1986; performed Centre Poompidou, Paris, 1979; choreographer for Emlyn Claid, London, 1986, Pauline Daniels, London, 1986, Nat. Youth Dance Co., Eng., 1986, New Dance Ensemble, Mpls., 1988; chroeographer Duet for Emmy and Karen, 1989; choregoraphed and performed Au Fil du Temps, Lyon, France, 1989, with Mathilde Monnier Ainsi de Suite, Paris, 1992, Montpellier, 1994, Shipwreck, 1995, choreographed and performed at Joyce Theater, N.Y.C. with Ralph Lemon, 1995; guest tchr. London Contemporary Dance Sch., Richard Alston Dance Company, Centre Nat. de Danse Contemporaine, Angers, France, 1996; tchr. Am. Dance Festival, 1996; choregrapher, performer with Jeff Slayton It's Been a While; guest choreographer USIA auspices with Ce De Ce Dance Co., Setubal, Portugal; choregrapher Dreams of Wind and Dust. Recipient Gold medal with Jeff Slayton, Paris Dance Festival, 1971, awd. French Republic-Ofc. of the Order of Arts and Letters, 1998; Guggenheim fellow, 1983-84; grantee NEA, 1975, 79, NEA, 1976, 81, N.Y. State Coun. on Arts, 1974-79, CAPS, 1974, 78, N.Y. Dept. Cultural Affairs, 1977. Office: Sarah Lawrence Coll Dept of Dance Bronxville NY 10708-5500

FARBERMAN, HAROLD, conductor, composer; b. N.Y.C., Nov. 2, 1930; s. Louis and Lena (Kramer) F.; m. Corinne Curry, June 22, 1958; children: Thea, Lewis. Diploma, Juilliard Sch. Music, 1951; BS, New England Conservatory Music, 1956, MS, 1957. Prin. guest condr. Bournemouth Sinfonietta; founder, dir. Conductors Inst., 1980—; dir. Stokowski Conducting Competition, 1994; prof. conducting Hartt Sch. Author: The Art of Conducting Technique; percussionist, Boston Symphony Orch., 1951-63, condr., New Arts Orch., Boston, 1955-63, guest condr., Royal Philharm. Orch., London, Denver Symphony Orch., BBC Symphony, Victoria (Can.) Philharm., Miami (Fla.) Philharm., N.Y. Philharm., New Philharmonia Orch., London, Orchestre de Lille, France, Stockholm Philharm., Swedish Radio Orch., Danish Radio Orch., Malmö (Sweden) Symphony Orch., Sydney (Australia) Symphony, Melbourne (Australia) Symphony, Perth (Australia) Symphony, Brisbane (Australia) Symphony, London Smyphony Orch., English Chamber Orch., condr., Colorado Springs (Colo.) Philharm., 1967-68, music dir., condr., Oakland Symphony Orch., 1971-79, rec. artist (condr. or composer) for, Columbia, Capitol, Mercury, Vanguard, Cambridge, Serenus, Boston records, rep. U.S. in, Paris Internat. Composition Competition, 1959; Composer symphonies, string quartet, chamber music, operas, jazz.; pioneered recorded works of Charles E. Ives., Michael Haydn. Scholar Juilliard Sch. Music, 1947-51. Mem. Condrs. Guild (founder, bd. dirs. summer inst.), Nat. Assn. Composers and Condrs. Address: 176 E 71st St Fc New York NY 10021-5159

FARCUS, JOSEPH JAY, architect, interior designer; b. McKeesport, Pa., June 17, 1944; s. Howard E. and Fannie (Meyers) F.; m. Jeanne Cohen, Dec. 31, 1983. BArch, U. Fla., 1967. Registered architect, Fla.; cert. Nat. Coun. Archtl. Registration Bds. Designer Morris Lapidus Assocs., Miami Beach, Fla., 1967-77; prin. Joseph Farcus Architect, Miami, Fla., 1977—; featured speaker: Modern Ship Architecture, intl. conf., Natl. Maritime Museum, London, 1996, Pres.' Invitatio Lectr. Royal Instn. Naval Architects, London, 1997; spkr. in field. Published in newspapers and mags. including Hotel and Restaurant Design, Fabrics & Architecture, Travel Weekly, World Cruise Industry Rev., Internat. Cruise & Ferry, Seatrade Rev., Archtl. Record; mem. editl. adv. bd. Internat. Cruise and Ferry Rev., London, 1994; archtl. and interior designer for largest cruise ship ever built, 1996; patentee ship funnel design; design work on ships subject of show Design Mus., London, 1999. Bd. dirs. Am. Jewish Com., Miami, 1991—, Bass Mus. of Art, Miami Beach, 1999. Featured interior architect largest passenger ship ever built Guiness World Book Records, 1998. Mem. Constrn. Specifications Inst. Home and Office: 5285 Pine Tree Dr Miami FL 33140-2109

FARELLA, STEVEN, advertising executive; b. Yonkers, N.Y., Nov. 26, 1955; s. Alfred and Camille (Altomare) F.; m. Ellen Barker, Mar. 22, 1986; children: Christina, David, Steven, Patrick. BS, St. Johns U., N.Y.C., 1977. V.p., assoc. media dir. Benton & Bowles, N.Y.C., 1977-85; sr. v.p., media dir. Armirati & Puris, N.Y.C., 1985-88; exec. v.p., media dir. Wells, Rich, Greene, N.Y.C., 1988-91, Young & Rubicam, N.Y.C., 1991-92; exec. v.p., dir. integrated mktg. and bus. devel. Jordan McGrath Case Ptnrs., Inc., N.Y.C., 1992—; speaker in field. Mem. Advt. Club of N.Y. (pres. bd. dirs. 1994—), Am. Assn. Advt. Agys. (media policy com. 1986—). Avocation: golf. Home: 34 Brundige Dr Goldens Bridge NY 10526-1416 Office: Jordan McGrath Case Ptnrs. Inc 110 5th Ave New York NY 10011-5601

FARENSBACH, MARK AUGUST, banker, real estate executive; b. Teaneck, N.J., June 27, 1969; s. Jan Stubin and Susanna Maria (Aliaga) F. BS, King's Coll., Wilkes-Barre, Pa.; MBA, Columbia U. Mng. dir. Doric Industries, N.Y.C., 1992-97; in bus. devel. Citibank, N.Y.C., 1997—. Home: PO Box 35 Alpine NJ 07620

FARENTHOLD, FRANCES TARLTON, lawyer; b. Corpus Christi, Tex., Oct. 2, 1926; d. Benjamin Dudley and Catherine (Bluntzer) Tarlton; children: Dudley Tarlton, George Edward, Emilie, James Doughterty, Vincent Bluntzer (dec.). AB, Vassar Coll., 1946; JD, U. Tex., 1949; LLD, Hood Coll., 1973, Boston U., 1973, Regis Coll., 1976, Lake Erie Coll., 1979, Elmira Coll., 1981, Coll. Santa Fe, 1985. Bar: Tex. 1949. Pvt. practice 1949-65, 67-76, 80—; mem. Tex. Ho. of Reps., 1968-72; dir. legal aid Nueces County, 1965-67; pres. Wells Coll., Aurora, N.Y., 1976-80; asst. prof. law Tex. So. U., Houston, Thurgood Marshall disting. vis. prof., 1994-95; lawyer; b. Corpus Christi, Tex., Oct. 2, 1926; d. Benjamin Dudley and Catherine (Bluntzer) Tarlton; children: Dudley Tarlton, George Edward, Emilie, James Dougherty, Vincent Bluntzer (dec.). AB, Vassar Coll., 1946; JD, U. Tex., 1949; LLD, Hood Coll., 1973, Boston U., 1973, Regis Coll., 1976, Lake Erie Coll., 1979, Elmira Coll., 1981, Coll. of Santa Fe, 1985. Bar: Tex. 1949. Pvt. practice, 1949-65, 67-76, 80—; mem. Tex. Ho. of Reps., 1968-72; dir. legal aide Nueces County, 1965-67; asst. prof. law Tex. So. U., Houston; pres. Wells Coll., Aurora, N.Y., 1976-80; disting. vis. prof. Thurgood Marshall Tex. So. U., Houston, 1994-95. Mem. Human Relations Com., Corpus Christi, 1963-68, Corpus Christi Citizen's Com. Community Improvement, 1966-68; mem. Tex. adv. com. to U.S. Commn. on Civil Rights, 1968-76; mem. nat. adv. council ACLU; mem. Orgn. for Preservation Unblemished Shoreline, 1964—; Dem. candidate for Gov. of Tex., 1972; del. Dem. Nat. Conv., 1972, 1st woman nominated to be candidate v.p. U.S., 1972; nat. co-chmn. Citizens to Elect McGovern-Shriver, 1972; chmn. Nat. Women's Polit. Caucus, 1973-75; mem. Dem. platform com., 1988; trustee Vassar Coll., 1975-83; bd. dirs. Fund for Constl. Govt., Ctr. for Devel. Policy, 1983—, Mexican Am. Legal Def. and Ednl. Fund, 1980-83; chmn. Inst. for Policy Studies, 1986-91; mem. bd. dirs. Rothko Chapel, 1997—. Recipient Lyndon B. Johnson Woman of Year award, 1973. Mem. State Bar Tex. Mem. Human Rels. Com., Corpus Christi, 1963-68, Corpus Christi Citizens Com. Cmty. Improvement, 1966-68; mem. Tex. adv. com. to U.S. Commn. on Civil Rights, 1968-76; mem. nat. adv. coun. ACLU; mem. Orgn. for Preservation Unblemished Shoreline, 1964—; Dem. candidate for Gov. of Tex., 1972; del. Dem. Nat. Conv., 1972, 1st woman nominated to be candidate v.p. U.S., 1972; nat. co-chair Citizens to elect McGovern-Shriver, 1972; chmn. Nat. Women's Polit. Caucus, 1973-75; mem. Dem. Platform Com., 1988; trustee Vassar Coll., 1975-83; bd. dirs. Fund for Constl. Govt., Ctr. for Devel. Policy, 1983—, Mexican Am. Legal Def. and Ednl. Fund, 198--83; chmn. Inst. for Policy Studies, 1986-91; bd. dirs. Rothko Chapel, 1997—. Recipient Lyndon B. Johnson Woman of Yr. award, 1973, Lifetime Svc. award Dem. Party of Tex., 1998. Mem. State Bar Tex. Office: 2929 Buffalo Speedway Apt 1813 Houston TX 77098-1710

FARENTINO, JAMES, actor; b. Bklyn., Feb. 24, 1938; s. Anthony and Helen (Enrico) F.; m. Elisebeth Ashley, 1961 (div.); m. Michele Lee Dusick, Feb. 20, 1966 (div.); 1 son, David Michael; m. Deborah Mullowney, June, 1985 (div.); m. Stella Farentino, 1994. Ed., Am. Acad. Dramatic Arts. Broadway appearance in Night of the Iguana, 1961; also appeared in: Days and Nights of BeeBee Fenstermaker, 1963, In the Summer House, 1964, One Flew Over the Cuckoo's Nest, 1973, Streetcar Named Desire, 1973, Death of a Salesman, 1975, The Big Knife, Chgo., 1976, The Best Man, Goodbye Charlie, A Thousand Clowns; toured in Calif. Suite, 1978; film appearances include The War Lord, 1964, The Pad (And How to Use It), 1966, Rosie, 1966, Me Natalie, 1968, Story of A Woman, 1968, Storia di Una Donna, 1979, Banning, 1965, Ride to Hangman's Tree, 1965, The Final Countdown, 1980, Dead and Buried, 1982, Her Alibi, 1989, The Spy Within, 1995, Engine Pulver; TV appearances in Death of a Salesman, 1966, Vanished, 1971; series The Bold Ones, 1969-72, John Dos Passos: U.S.A, 1971, Cool Million, 1972, Dynasty, 1982-83, Blue Thunder, 1984, Mary, 1985-86, Julie, 1992; TV movie The Longest Night, 1972, The Family Rico, 1972, The Elevator, 1974, Crossfire, 1975, The Possessed, 1977, Silent Victory: The Kitty O'Neil Story, 1979, Son Rise: A Miracle of Love, Honor Thy Father and Mother, When No One Could Listen, 1992, Miles from Nowhere, 1990, In The Line of Duty: A Cop For The Killing, 1990 , Red Spider, 1988, Who Gets the Friends?, 1988, Picking Up the Pieces, 1985 A Summer to Remember, 1985, The Cradle Will Fall, 1983, License to Kill, 1984, Something So Right, 1982, Kitty O'Neill, Undercover Cop, Wings of Fire, Brothers Rico, The Sound of Anger, That Secret Sunday, 1986, Family Sins, 1987, One Woman's Courage, 1994, Honor Thy Father and Thy Mother: The True Story of the Menendez Murders, 1994, Dazzle, 1995, Scandalous Me: The Jacqueline Susann Story, 1998; spl. Emily, Emily, 1977, Bird Bath ; TV miniseries Jesus of Nazareth, 1977, Eva Peron, 1981, Sins, 1986, Naked Lie, 1989, My Husband is Going to Kill Me, 1993, Dazzle, Uncommon Ground, 1990, Secrets of the Sahara. Named hon. chmn. Ill. Assn. Retarded Citizens. Office: William Morris Agency 151 S El Camino Dr Beverly Hills CA 90212-2775*

FARGHALY, ALI S., educator; b. Alexandria, Egypt, Jan. 15, 1938; came to U.S., 1978; s. Ahmed Sabry and Hafiza Ali F.; m. Zahra El Toukhi, Aug. 22, 1970; children: Samar, Amel, Ahmed. BA, U. Alexandria, Egypt, 1966; MA, U. Leeds, London, 1975; PhD, U. Tex., 1981. Asst. prof. Kuwait U., 1985-89; assoc. prof. Am. U., Cairo, Egypt, 1989-93; prof., chmn. Acad. Arts, Giza, Egypt, 1994-96; instr. fgn. langs. Def. Lang. Inst., Monterey, Calif., 1995-96; sr. lectr. U. Mich., Ann Arbor, 1996—; rsch. assoc. U. Tex., Austin, 1980-81; rsch. linguist Omnitrans Calif., Palo Alto, 1983-84. Contbr. articles to profl. jours. Mem. adv. com. Mid. East Com., Washington, 1998-99. Rsch. grantee Kuwait U., 1985-89, travel grantee Am. U., 1990-93; postdoctoral fellow Brit. Coun., Bath, England, 1982. Mem. Am. Assn. Tchrs. & Instrs., linguistics Soc. Am. Islam. Home: 1580 Franklin St Ann Arbor MI 48103 Office: U Mich Near Eastern Studies Ann Arbor MI 48109

FARGIS, PAUL MCKENNA, publishing consultant, book developer, editor; b. N.Y.C., Mar. 19, 1939; s. George Bertrand and Elizabeth Harlin (McKenna) F.; m. Elizabeth Hackett, Aug. 22, 1964; children: John Hackett, Alison Katherine; m. Dawn Sangrey, Apr. 23, 1977; 1 child, Christopher Sangrey. Student, Cath. U. Am., 1958; B in Social Sci., Fairfield U., 1961; MA (Publs. Tuition scholar), N.Y. U., 1962. Editorial asst. Prentice-Hall, Inc., Englewood Cliffs, N.J., 1961-62; editor Hawthorn Books, Inc., N.Y.C., 1963-67; v.p., editorial dir. Hawthorn Books, Inc., 1967-71; v.p., editor-in-chief Thomas Y. Crowell Co. and Funk & Wagnalls divs. Dun-Donnelley Pub. Corp., N.Y.C., 1971-77; editor-in-chief Apollo Books, N.Y.C., 1972-77; managing dir. Thomas Y. Crowell div. Harper and Row, N.Y.C., 1977-78; pub., editor-in-chief The Stonesong Press div. Grosset & Dunlap, Inc., N.Y.C., 1978-80; founder, pres. and pub. The Stonesong Press, Inc., 1980—; dir., sec. Round Stone Press, Inc., 1990—; mem. adv. bd. Grad. Sch. Corp. and Polit. Communication Fairfield U., 1969-81; pub. arbitrator Am. Arbitration Assn., 1982—. Author: The Consumer's Handbook, 1966, rev. edit., 1974, Company's Coming, 1965; Am. editor: Twentieth Century Ency. Catholicism, 1963-67; editor-in-chief: The New York Public Library Desk Reference, 1989; co-author: Perks and Parachutes, 1997; co-editor: The Big Book of Life's Instructions, 1995; contbr. articles to profl. jours.; patentee in field. Exec. dir. Harrison (N.Y.) Town Recreation Commn., 1970-72; dir. Harrison Town Forum, 1969-73; former bd. dirs. U.S. Cath. Hist. Soc.; past trustee Unitarian Fellowship of No. Westchester. Mem. Am. Book Coun. (bd. dirs. 1987-88), Am. Book Producers Assn. (pres. 1986-87, bd. dir. Charitable Book program 1987-89). Unitarian. Avocations: carpentry, stonework, travel, hiking, sculpture. Office: 11 E 47th St New York NY 10017-1919

FARHAT, CAROL SUE, motion picture company executive; b. Santa Monica, Calif.; d. Annis Abraham Farhat; divorced; 1 child, Michael. Student, Santa Monica Coll., 1967; Assoc. degree, Inst. Audio Rsch., 1976-78; student, Otis Parsons Inst., 1980-84, UCLA, 1984-90; BA in Bus., Music, Antioch U., 1992. Recording studio mgr. The Village Recorder, L.A., 1972-78; audio engr. The Village Recorder Studio, L.A., 1978-79; music adminstr. 20th Century Fox Film Corp., Beverly Hills, Calif., 1980-82, music supr., 1983-86, music dir., 1986-92; supr. internat. music 20th Century Fox Film Corp., Tokyo, 1993; music prodr. Scopus Films, England, 1987-89; songwriter Music Experts Ltd., Santa Monica, Calif., 1989-90; v.p. music 20th Century Fox Film Corp., 1994-95; v.p. TV music and feature Am. Fedn. Musicians advisor 20th Century Fox Music, 1995-99. Author: China Diary, 1992; composer (music book) Children's Songbook, 1991; songwriter (for film) Rockin' Reindeer, 1990; prodr. (soundtrack) Ally McBeal Show (double platinum record award 1998).. Recipient Emmy award contbn. recognition for Simpson TV-show music, 1990, 96, 97, 98. Mem. BMI, NATAs, NARAS, Women in Film, Am. Film Inst., Pacific Composers Forum, Entertainment Industry Counsel. Avocation: classical ballet. Office: 20th Century Fox Film Corp Bldg 222 Rm 8 PO Box 900 Beverly Hills CA 90213-0900

FARHO, JAMES HENRY, JR., mechanical engineer, consultant; b. Omaha, June 28, 1924; s. James Henry and Mary (Mena) F.; m. Dummer Ree Mitchem, Nov. 12, 1946; children: Sandra, Joann, Wayne. BSME, U. Nebr., 1965. Enlisted USN, 1942, advanced through grades to sr. aviation chief machinist, 1942-62, ret., 1962; engr. Exxon Rsch. & Engring. Co., Florham Park, N.J., 1965-66, project engr., 1966-68, sr. project engr., 1968-70, engring. group head, 1970-71, engring. sect. head, 1971-78; sr. staff advisor Exxon Rsch. & Engring. Co., Clinton, N.J., 1978-85; cons. engr. Lighthouse Point, Fla., 1985—; cons. Exxon Prodn. Rsch., Houston, 1985, Swiki Anderson & Assocs., Bryan, Tex., 1986-87, Glaxo Pharms., Research Triangle, N.C., 1988-91. Mem. VFW, Fleet Res. Assn., Am. Legion, Elks, Sigma Xi. Republican. Roman Catholic. Home and Office: 2401 NE 33rd St Lighthouse Point FL 33064

FARICY, JOHN HARTNETT, JR., lawyer; b. Augsburg, Germany, Nov. 5, 1955; came to U.S., 1956; s. John Hartnett and Mary Helen Sarah (Bowe) F. BA, Tulane U., 1977; JD, William Mitchell Coll. Law, St. Paul, 1982. Bar: Minn. 1982, U.S. Dist. Ct. Minn. 1983, U.S. Ct. Appeals (2d cir.) 1987, U.S. Supreme Ct. 1988. Ptnr. Faricy & Roen, P.A., Mpls., 1996—. Mem. Univ. Club of St. Paul. Office: Faricy & Roen PA 150 S 5th St Minneapolis MN 55402-4200

FARICY, RICHARD THOMAS, architect; b. St. Paul, June 1, 1928; s. Roland J. and Clare (Sullivan) F.; m. Carole Murphy, June 24, 1961; children: Althea, Bridget. Registered architect, Minn., Wis., N.D., Colo., N.Mex., Fla., Tex., Okla., Ohio. V.p. The Cerny Assocs., Mpls., 1961-71; exec. v.p. Winsor/Faricy Architects, Inc., St. Paul, 1971-96; founding prin. Symmes Maini McKee Assoc./Winsor Faricy, St. Paul, 1996—; pres. Minn. Archtl. Found., 1986; trustee Am. Mus. Asmat Art, 1995—. Prin. works include: Raughurst Libr., Jamestown, N.C., Warren E. Burger Libr. at William Mitchell Coll. Law, St. Paul, Collier County Courthouse, Naples, Fla., Bandana Sq., St. Paul, Como Park Conservatory Restoration, St. Paul, Earl Brown Heritage Ctr., Brooklyn Center, Minn. Pres. Merrick Community Ctr., St. Paul, 1969; pres. Ramsey County Hist. Soc., 1981-82; chmn. Blue Cross Blue Shield Minn., 1974-77, HMO Minn., 1974-76; bd. dirs. Minn. State Arts Bd., 1988-94, HealthEast Found., 1987—, James J. Hill Reference Libr., 1996—; bd. dirs. Friends St. Paul Pub. Libr., 1986—, pres., 1992-95; trustee Minn. Mus. Art, 1980-86; commr. St. Paul Heritage Preservation Commn., 1986-87; vice chmn. Mounds Midway Found., 1987-91; bd. dirs. sponsor bd. Bapt. Hosp. Fund, 1991—. 1st lt. USAR, 1952-57. Fellow AIA (nat. housing com. 1984-92, trustee AIA Benefit Ins. Trust 1986-89); mem. Minn. Soc. Architects (dir. 1973-77, chair Ins. Trust 1984-86), St. Paul AIA (pres. 1974), St. Paul Athletic Club (pres. 1980), Minn. Club (St. Paul). Home: 2211 St Clair Ave Saint Paul MN 55105-1136 Office: Symmes Maini McKee Assocs Winsor Faricy Architects 801 Nicollet Mall Ste 1600 Minneapolis MN 55402-2530*

FARINA, DENNIS, actor; b. Chgo., Feb. 29, 1944. Appeared in films Thief, 1981, Jo Jo Dancer, Your Life is Calling, 1986, Manhunter Deg, 1986, Midnight Run, 1988, Open Admissions, 1988, The Case of the Hillside Strangler, 1989, Blind Faith, 1990, People Like Us, 1990, Men of Respect, 1991, Serious Money, 1991, Another Blowout, 1993, Striking Distance, 1993, Little Big League, 1994, Get Shorty, 1995, Eddie, 1996, That Old Feeling, 1996, Mod Squad, 1998, Out of Sight, 1998, Saving Private Ryan, 1998, Buddy Faro, 1998, Reindeer Games, 1999; appeared in TV mini-series Bella Maffia, 1997. Office: Geddes Agy 1633 N Halsted St Ste 400 Chicago IL 60614-5517*

FARINA, DONNA MARIE, languages and linguistics educator; b. Elmhurst, Ill., May 23, 1957; d. Charles Joseph and Theresa Rose Farina; m. George Durman, June 29, 1987. Maîtrise de scis. du lang., U. Scis. Humaines, Strasbourg, France, 1981; AM in Linguistics, U. Ill., 1983, PhD in Linguistics, 1991. Rsch. asst. U. Ill., Urbana, 1983-88, vis. postdoctoral rsch. assoc., 1989-91; rschr. Leningrad (Russia) State U., 1988-89; asst. prof. U. Ga., Athens, 1991-92; adj. asst. prof. Lehigh U., Bethlehem, Pa., 1992-93; asst. prof. USAF Acad., Colorado Springs, Colo., 1993-95, New Jersey City U., 1996—; reader Oxford English Dictionary, N.Am. Reading Program, Morristown, N.J., 1989-91; freelance editor Cambridge Univ. Press, N.Y.C., 1995-97, Oxford Univ. Press, Old Saybrook, Conn., 1996—. Editl. asst. (N.Am. book revs.) Lexicographica-International Annual for Lexicography, Tübingen, Germany, 1991—, guest editor vol. 12, 1996; contbr. articles to profl. jours. Fellow for long-term advanced rsch. Internat. Rsch. and Exchs. Bd., Leningrad, 1988-89; Rsch. grantee NEH, U. Ill., Urbana, 1989-91, USAF Acad., U. Ill., Urbana, 1994. Mem. MLA (exec. com. lexicography discussion group 1991-95), AAUW, AAUP, Am. Assn. for Applied Linguistics, Am. Assn. for the Advancement Slavic Studies, Am. Coun. Tchrs. Russian, European Assn. for Lexicography, Dictionary Soc. N.Am., Linguistic Soc. Am., Fulbright Assn.

FARINELLA, PAUL JAMES, retired arts institution executive; b. Trenton, N.J., Sept. 28, 1926; s. Nicholas F. and Grace (Cubberly) F.; m. Margaret Pippitt, May 29, 1948; children: Dianne, Deborah. B.S. in Commerce and Bus. Adminstrn., Rider Coll., 1953. C.P.A., N.J. Pub. acct. Peat, Marwick, Mitchell & Co., Newark, 1953-61; assoc. comptroller U. Rochester, N.Y., 1961-67; v.p. bus. and fin., sec., treas. Ithaca Coll., 1967-76; pres., trustee Munson-Williams-Proctor Inst., Utica, N.Y., 1977-90, sr. advisor to bd., 1990-91. Served with USAAF, 1945-47.

FARINELLI, JEAN L., public relations executive; b. Phila., July 26, 1946; d. Albert J. and Edith M. (Falini) F. BA, Am. U., Washington, 1968; MA, Ohio State U., Columbus, 1969. Asst. pub. relations dir. Dow Jones & Co., Inc., N.Y.C., 1969-71; account exec. Carl Byoir & Assocs., Inc., N.Y.C., 1972-74, v.p., 1974-80, sr. v.p., 1980-82; pres. Tracy-Locke/BBDO Pub. Relations, Dallas, 1982-87; pres. Creamer Dickson Basford, Inc., N.Y.C., 1987-88, chmn., chief exec. officer, 1988-98; pres., chief exec. officer Eurocom Corp. & PR (U.S.), 1991, Corp. Graphics, Inc., 1992; pres. Farinelli Cons. Group, LLC, 1999—; dir. The Cologne Life Reinsurance Co. Recipient PR CaseBook, PR Reporter, N.H., 1984, Silver Spur, Tex. Pub. Rels. Assn., Dallas, 1985, Matrix award Women in Comms., 1993. Mem. Pub. Rels. Soc. Am. (Silver Anvil award 1980-81, 85, Excalibur award Houston chpt. 1985, chmn. 1986, Best of Show Silver Anvil award 1998, Silver Anvil awards chmn. 1987, honors and awards com. chmn. Spring Conf. Counselors Acad. 1989, acad. exec. bd. 1990-91, trustee found.), Women in Comms. (chmn. 1995, dir. 1999—, Matrix award 1993), The Women's Forum, Nat. Investor Rels. Inst., Internat. Pub. Rels. Assn. (pub. rels. seminar), Arthur W. Page Soc. (treas., v.p. adminstrn. and fin., pres.-elect PRSA Found.), Nat. Found. for Infectious Diseases (trustee), The Wisemen. Home: 20 Sutton Pl S Apt 16C New York NY 10022-4165

FARIS, JAMES VANNOY, cardiology educator, hospital executive; b. July 18, 1943; s. Vannoy and Maudeline (Freeman) F.; m. Jacqueline Claire Bexell, July 1, 1978; children: Nathan James, Jamie Lynn, Jenna Claire, Brittany Jean, James Vannoy III, Janessa Marie. AB, Ind. U., 1965, MD, 1968. Diplomate Am. Bd. Internal Medicine, Am. Bd. Cardiology. Intern, resident Ind. U. Med. Ctr., Indpls., 1968-71, asst. prof. medicine, 1976-80, assoc. prof. medicine, radiology, 1980—; chief of staff Richard L. Roudebush VA Med. Ctr., Indpls., 1983-95, chief sect. cardiology, 1995—; asst. dean sch. medicine Ind. U., 1983-95. Maj. U.S. Army, 1971-73, Vietnam. Ind. Heart Assn. grantee. Fellow Am. Coll. Cardiology; mem. AMA, Ind. State Med. Assn., Indpls. Med. Soc. (pres. 1998-99), Alpha Omega Alpha, Alpha Epsilon Delta. Republican. Methodist. Avocations: snow skiing, tennis, water skiing.

FARISON, JAMES BLAIR, electrical biomedical engineer, educator; b. McClure, Ohio, May 26, 1938; s. Blair Albert and Marie Lucille (Ballard) F.; m. Gail Donahue, Mar. 30, 1961; children: Jeffrey James, Mark Donahue. B.S. summa cum laude in Elec. Engring, U. Toledo, 1960; M.S., Stanford U., 1961, Ph.D., 1964. Registered profl. engr., Ohio. Asst. prof. elec. engring. U. Toledo, 1964-67, asso. prof., 1967-74, prof., 1974-95; asst. dean engring., 1969-71; dean engring. U. Toledo, 1971-80, prof. elec. engring. and computer sci., 1995-98; prof. bioengring., 1996-98; prof., chmn. dept. engring. Baylor U., Waco, Tex., 1998—; adj. prof. Med. Coll. Ohio, 1987—. Contbr. articles on control sys. design and image processing to profl. jours. Recipient Outstanding Young Man of 1971 award Toledo Jr. C. of C., 1972, Boss of Year award Limestone chpt. Am. Bus. Women's Assn., 1973, Toledo's Engr. Yr. award, 1984, Outstanding Tchr. award U. Toledo, 1986; named Disting. Alumnus, U. Toledo, 1983. Fellow Ohio Acad. Sci. (Centennial honoree 1991); mem. IEEE (sr. mem., Toledo Elec. Engr. of Yr. 1972, 74, 76), ASME, Nat. Soc. Profl. Engrs., Ohio Soc. Profl. Engrs. (Young Engr. of Yr. 1973, Citation 1983, Outstanding Engring. Educator 1984), Toledo Soc. Profl. Engrs. (Young Engr. of Yr. 1973), Biomed. Engring. Soc., Am. Soc. Engring. Edn., Machine Vision Assn., Soc. Mfg. Engrs., Internat. Soc. Optical Engring., Instrument Soc. Am. (sr.), Blue Key, Sigma Xi, Tau Beta Pi, Pi Mu Epsilon, Phi Kappa Phi, Eta Kappa Nu (Outstanding Young Elec. Engr. 1971). Home: 9613 Old Farm Rd Waco TX 76712-6402 Office: Baylor U PO Box 97356 Waco TX 76798-7356

FARISS, BRUCE LINDSAY, endocrinologist, educator; b. Allisonia, Va., July 22, 1934; s. Alven Pierce and Hetty Jo (Lindsay) F.; BS, Roanoke Coll., 1957; MD, U. Va., 1961; m. Cheryl Louise Tomasie, Jan. 18, 1975; children: Bruce Lindsay, Melissa, Margaret, Susan, Henry, Sarah Jane, Caroline, Adam. Diplomate Am. Bd. Internal Medicine and Am. Bd. Endocrinology. Intern in medicine U. Va. Hosp., 1961-62; commd. capt. M.C. U.S. Army, 1962, advanced through grades to col., 1976; gen. med. officer, Ft. Monroe, Va., 1962-63; resident in internal medicine Brooke Gen. Hosp., Ft. Sam Houston, Tex., 1963-66; fellow in endocrinology U. Calif.-San Francisco, 1966-68; chief, endocrine service Madigan Gen. Hosp., Tacoma, Wash., 1968-71, chief clin. research service, 1968-76, asst. chief dept. medicine, 1972-73, dir. endocrine fellowship program, 1971-76, chief dept. clin. investigation, 1979-85, dir. endocrine-metabolism fellowship tng. program, 1979-85; cons. internal medicine MEDCOM Europe, 1976-79; cons. endocrinology to surgeon gen. U.S. Army, 1979-85; prof. biology dept. Va. Poly. Inst., Blackburg, 1987—. Mem. bd. suprs. Pulaski County, Va., 1988-92, 1992-96, 96—; mem. Pulaski County Planning Commn., 1992-96, 96—, mem. Pulaski County Recreation Com., 1989-93. Decorated Legion of Merit with oak leaf cluster; recipient Meritorious Service award Office of Surgeon Gen. Army, 1977, Roanoke Coll. medal, 1982. Fellow ACP; mem. Southwest Va. Med. Soc., Am. Fedn. Clin. Research, Endocrine Soc. (ednl. com. 1980-83), Am. Diabetes Assn. (trustee 1986-89), So. Med. Assn., N.Y. Acad. Sci., Alpha Omega Alpha. Contbr. articles to med. jours.

FARKAS, ANDREW, library director, educator, writer; b. Budapest, Hungary, Apr. 7, 1936; came to U.S., 1956; s. Miklos and Renee (Schwartz) F. Student, Eötvös Lóránd U. Law, Budapest, 1954-56; BA, Occidental Coll., Los Angeles, 1959; MLS, U. Calif., Berkeley, 1962. Asst. bibliographer U. Calif., Davis, 1962-63, gift and exchange librarian, 1962-65, asst. head acquisitions dept., 1965-67, chief bibliographer, 1966-67; asst. mgr. Walter J. Johnson, Inc., N.Y.C., 1967-70; dir. libraries, prof. library sci. U. North Fla., Jacksonville, 1970—; program com. mem. Fla. Gov.'s Conf. on Librs., Tallahassee, 1978; expert witness IRS, Atlanta, 1981, cons., Washington, 1982; interpretor Howell, Howell, Liles, Braddock, Jacksonville, 1980, Sharp & Gay, 1995. Author, editor: Titta Ruffo: An Anthology, 1984, (with Enrico Caruso Jr.) Enrico Caruso: My Father & My Family, 1990, (with Anna-Lisa Björling) Jussi, 1996; author: (annotated bibliography) Opera and Concert Singers, 1985; editor: (ann. handbook) Librarians Calendar, 1984—, Opera Biographies Series, Great Voices Series, Lawrence Tibbett, Singing Actor, 1989. Mem. Coun. Interinstnl. Planning, Jacksonville, 1983-85. With U.S. Army, 1959-61. Mem. ALA. Avocations: research, creative writing, travel, photography, book and record collecting. E-mail: afarkas@unf.edu. Office: U North Fla 4567 Saint Johns Bluff Rd S Jacksonville FL 32224-2645

FARKAS, CAROL GARNER, nurse, administrator; b. N.Y.C., Apr. 26, 1936; d. Charles Harry and Phyllis (Levine) Schotland; m. Theodore Arthur Garner, 1956 (dec. 1971); children: Charles Hugh Farkas Garner, Judi Beth Garner Farkas, Andrea Lee Garner Farkas Krupen; m. Robin Lewis Farkas, Oct. 17, 1972; adopted children: Bradford Lewis Farkas, Andrew Lawrence Farkas. BSN with distinction, Cornell U., 1976; MPH, Columbia U., 1980. Nursing dir. Am. Inst. Life Threatening Illness and Loss Columbia Presbyn. Med. Ctr., N.Y.C., 1980—; del. white House Conf. Aging, N.Y. State Gov.'s Conf. Aging; mem. N.Y. State Hospice Adv. Group, 1979-81; mem. adv. com. office health mgmt. N.Y. State Dept. Health, 1979-81; mem. select com. financing and licensure, com. legis. edn. Nat. Hospice Orgn., 1980—; vol. adminstr., practitioner in sympton control psychiatry dept. Meml. Sloan-Kettering Cancer Ctr., N.Y.C., 1981-96; mem. Choice in Dying, 1991-92, Nat. Coun. Death and Dying, 1990-91, Soc. Right to Die, 1982-90; co-chair med. student conf. nursing com. Columbia Presbyn., N.Y.C., 1992. Co-editor: Nursing and Thanatology, 1982; contbr. articles to profl. publs., chpt. to book. Bd. mem. N.Y. State Task Force on Life and the Law, 1994-97.

Mem. Sigma Theta Tau. Fax: 307-734-8006. E-mail: rfarkas@inventfund.com. Home: PO Box 9223 485 Indian Springs Dr Jackson Hole WY 83002

FARKAS, DANIEL FREDERICK, food science and technology educator; b. Boston, June 20, 1933; m. Alice Bridgetta Brady, Jan. 25, 1959; children: Brian Emerson, Douglas Frederick. BS, MIT, 1954, MS, 1955, PhD, 1960. Lic. chem. engr., Calif. Commd. U.S. Army, 1954, advanced through grades to major, 1968, ret., 1974; staff scientist Arthur D. Little, Cambridge, Mass., 1960-62; asst. prof. Cornell U. Agrl Expt. Sta., Geneva, N.Y., 1962-66; rsch. leader We. regional rsch. ctr. USDA, Albany, Calif., 1967—; prin. Daniel F. Farkas Assocs., Corvallis, Oreg., 1976—; prof., chair dept. food sci. U. Del., Newark, 1980-87; v.p. process R & D Campbell Soup Co., Camden, N.J., 1987-90; Jacobs-Root prof., head dept. food sci. and tech. Oreg. State U., Corvalis, 1990—. Contbr. more than 50 articles to peer-reviewed sci. and tech. jours. Fellow Inst. Food Technologists (councelor); mem. AICE, Am. Chem. Soc. (profl.), Sigma Xi. Achievements include 5 U.S. patents for centrifugal fluidized bed food drying system, application of ultra-high hydrostatic pressure to food preservation. Office: Oregon State Univ Dept Food Sci & Tech Corvallis OR 97331-6602

FARKAS, JULIUS, chemist; b. Brownsville, Pa., Apr. 9, 1958; s. Julius and Marcella (Stanko) F. BA, Washington and Jefferson Coll., Washington, Pa., 1980; PhD, Pa. State U., University Park, 1985. Tchg./rsch. asst. Washington and Jefferson Coll., 1979-80; lab. technician Stauffer Chem. Co., Washington, 1979-80; tchg./grad. rsch. asst. Pa. State U., University Park, 1980-85; R&D assoc. B.F. Goodrich Co., Brecksville, Ohio, 1985—. Mem. Am. Chem. Soc., Am. Inst. Chemists, Soc. Plastics Engrs. Presbyterian. Office: BF Goodrich Co 9921 Brecksville Rd Brecksville OH 44141-3289

FARKAS, PAUL STEPHEN, gastroenterologist; b. N.Y.C., 1952; s. Benjamin J. and Ellen (Tanner) F.; m. Esta Miriam Cantor, June 24, 1973; children: Melanie Sharon, Joshua David. AB magna cum laude with distinction in psychology, Brandeis U., 1972; MD, Tufts U., 1976. Diplomate Am. Bd. Internal Medicine, Am. Bd. Gastroenterology. Intern Baystate Med. Ctr., Sprinfield, Mass., 1976-77, resident in internal medicine, 1977-79; fellow in gastroenterology Albert Einstein Coll. Medicine, Bronx, N.Y., 1979-81; asst. clin. prof. medicine Tufts U., Boston, 1985—; med. advisor Med. Assist Program Springfield Tech. C.C., 1989—; co-dir. med. edn. Mercy Hosp., Springfield, 1990-95, chmn. dept. gastroenterology, 1995—, dir. libr., 1988-97, mem. exec. com., 1995—, treas. med. staff, 1999—; mem. adv. bd. VNA, Springfield, 1984-88; adj. asst. prof. clin. pharmacology Mass. Coll. Pharmacy, Boston, 1982—. Author: Diagnostic Diagrams Gastroenterology, 1985; contbr. book chpts., articles and revs. in field. Bd. dirs. B'nai Jacob Synagogue, Springfield, 1987-88, Com. for Longmeadow, Mass., 1989, Yeshiva, Longmeadow, 1994—; trustee Mercy Hosp., 1997-98. Fellow ACP; mem. AMA, Am. Coll. Gastroenterology, Am. Gastroent. Assn., Am. Soc. Gastrointestinal Endoscopy, New England Soc. Gastrointestinal Endoscopy. Office: 299 Carew St Springfield MA 01104-2301

FARLEY, ANDREW NEWELL, lawyer; b. Brownsville, Pa., Oct. 31, 1934; s. Andrew Polycarp and Sarah Theresa (Landymore) F.; m. Marta Olha Pisetska, May 5, 1963; children—Andrew Daniel, Mark Landymore. AB, Washington and Jefferson Coll., 1956; MPA, U. Pitts., 1962, JD, 1961; diploma, U.S. Army Command and Gen. Staff Coll., 1972, Indsl. Coll. Armed Forces, 1967; grad., U.S. Army War Coll., 1976. Bar: Pa. 1962, U.S. Supreme Ct. 1965. Assoc. Reed Smith Shaw & McClay, Pitts., 1961-65, ptnr., 1966-91; cons. Pitts., 1992—; bd. dirs. Corp. Devel. USAM Mid-Atlantic and Ohio; mng. dir. USAM-Nat., 1992-95; Am. Arbitration Assn. Nat. Panel Comml. Disputes, 1995—; mediator JAMS-Endispute, 1996—; sec.-treas. Internat. Acad. Mediators, 1996—; lectr. in fed. jurisprudence and adminstrv. law U. Pitts.; adminstrv. asst. Pa. Atty. Gen., 1959; counsel to Pa. Constl. Conv., 1968; mem. Pa. Atty. Gen.'s Task Force on Adminstrn., 1970. Assoc. editor Pitts Legal Jour., 1963— (mem. exec. com.); contbr. articles to profl. jours. Bd. dirs. Ind. Sch. Chmn. Assn., World Affairs Coun., Pitts., Pitts. Opera, 1986-95; sec., bd. dirs. Found. for Calif. U. Pa.,; mem. adv. bd. Western Pa. Advanced Tech. Ctr., Internat. Resuscitation Rsch. Ctr., U. Pitts. Med. Sch., Mon Valley Renaissance; mem. bd. visitors U. Pitts. Grad. Sch. Pub. and Internat. Affairs; trustee Thiel Coll., 1989-95. Brig. gen. U.S. Army. Decorated Meritorious Svc. medals, Dept. Def. and U.S. Army, Army Commendation medals; recipient Gubernatorial citation Commonwealth of Pa., 1978, Omicron Delta Kappa award, 1960; Nat. Def. Transp. Assn. fellow, 1956; named Mon Valley Renaissance MVP, 1987. Mem. Internat. Acad. Mediators (sec.-treas. 1997—), Pa. Bar Assn. (chmn. sect. internat. law, bd. editors, jud. adminstrn. com., statewide computer com. for the cts., alternative dispute resolution com.), Allegheny County Bar Assn. (fee determination com.), Am. Law Inst., Nat. Health Lawyers Assn., Am. Arbitration Assn., Soc. for Profls. in Dispute Resolution, Assn. U.S. Army (pres. Ft. Pitt chpt., pres. Pa.), Sr. Army Res. Comdrs. Assn. (exec. com.), Pitts. Athletic Assn., Duquesne Club, Pa. State Grange, Masons. Home: Gen Del Box 196 Cowansville PA 16218-0196 Office: 942 N Highland Ave Pittsburgh PA 15206-2108

FARLEY, BENJAMIN WIRT, religious studies educator, writer; b. Manila, The Philippines, Aug. 6, 1935; s. Wirt Pamplin and Bessie (Campbell) White F.; m. Alice Anne Gamble; children: John David, Bryan Kirk. AB, Davidson Coll., 1958; BD, Union Theol. Sem., Richmond, Va., 1963, ThM, 1964, PhD, 1976. Ordained to ministry Presbyn. Ch., 1963. Instr. Lees-MacRae Coll., Banner-Elk, N.C., 1973-74; asst. prof. bible, religion, philosophy Erskine Coll., Due West, S.C., 1974-78, assoc. prof., 1978-84, Younts prof., 1985—, chair bible, relgion, philosophy dept., 1978-91. Author: The Hero of St. Lo, 1986, Mercy Road, 1986, The Providence of God, 1988, Corbin's Rubi-Yacht, 1992, In Praise of Virtue, 1994; translator, editor: Calvins Sermons on the Ten Commandments, 1980, Calvin's Treatises Against the Anabaptists and Against the Libertines, 1982; co-translator: Calvin's Ecclesiastical Advice, 1991; contbr. articles to profl. jours. Chair Bi-Racial Com., Franklin, Va., 1967-68, pres. of the Calvin Studies Soc. in America, 1997—. Named Writer of the Season, Nostalgia mag., 1990; Fund for Theol. Edn. fellow, 1970; Thomas Carey Johnson scholar Union Theol. Sem., 1963. Mem. Am. Philos. Assn., Calvin Studies Soc. (pres. 1997—), Coloquium on Calvin Studies, Internat. Calvin Congress, Omicron Delta Kappa. Republican. Avocations: golf, sailing, hunting, fishing, hiking. Office: Erskine Coll PO Box 595 Due West SC 29639-0595

FARLEY, CAROLE, soprano; b. Le Mars, Iowa, Nov. 29, 1946; d. Melvin and Irene (Reid) F.; m. Jose Serebrier, Mar. 29, 1969; 1 dau., Lara Adriana Francesca. MusB, Ind. U., 1968. Fulbright scholar Hochschule für Musik, Munich, 1968-69. (Musician of Month, Musical Am./Hi Fidelity 1977), Am. debut at Town Hall, N.Y.C., 1969, Paris debut, Nat. Orch., 1975, London debut, Royal Philharmonic Soc., 1975, S.Am. debut, Teatro Colon, Philharmonic Orch., Buenos Aires, 1975; soloist with, major Am. and European symphony orchs., 1970—, soloist, Welsh Nat. Opera, 1971, 72, Cologne Opera, 1972-75, Phila. Lyric Opera, 1974, Brussels Opera, 1972, Lyon Opera, 1976, 77, Strasbourg Opera, 1975, Linz Opera, 1969, N.Y.C. Opera, 1976, New Orleans Opera, 1977, Cin. Opera, 1977, Met. Opera Co., N.Y.C., 1977—, Zurich Opera, 1979, Chgo. Lyric Opera, 1981, Can. Opera Co., 1980, Düsseldorf Opera, 1980, 81, 84, Palm Beach Opera, 1982, Theatre Mcpl. Paris, 1983, Theatre Royale dela Monnaie Brussels, 1983, Teatro Regio, Turin, Italy, 1983, Nice Opera (France), 1984, 86, 87, 88, Cologne Opera, 1985, Teatro Comunale, Florence, Italy, 1985, BBC Opera, 1987, TeatroColon, Buenos Aires, 1987, 88, 89, Opera de Montpellier (France), 1988, 94, Theatre des Champs Elysees, Paris, 1988, Helsinki Festival, 1989, Tchaikovsky Opera Arias Pickwick/IMP Records, 1993, Met. Opera Premiere Shostakovich Opera Lady Macbeth of Mzensk, 1994, Theatre Capitole de Toulouse Wozzeck, 1994; on New Zealand Broadcasting Commn. Orchestral Tour, 1986; TV film for ABC Australia La Voix Humaine, also co-producer compact disc and video for BBC, London, 1990; co-producer compact disc and video The Telephone, 1990; recorded compact disc Weill, 1992, Metro. Opera Shostakovich: "Lady Macbeth", 1994, Strausslieder with Czech Philharmonic, 1995, Les Soldats Morts, 1995 (Grand Prix du Disque); recorded for Deutsche Gramophone (Diapason d'or prize 1997), Chandos, CBS, BBC, ASV, RCA, Ricercar and Varese-Sarabande records, London/Decca Records, IMP Masters, Pickwick. Recipient Abiati prize for her role as Lulu, Italy, 1984, Deutsche Schallplatten award for recording Carole Farley Sings French Songs, 1988; named Alumni of Year, U. Ind., 1976. Mem. Am. Guild Mus. Artists. Home: 270 Riverside Dr New York NY 10025-5209 *A young opera singer today has a much greater responsibility than his predecessors 50 years ago. The age of the 200-pound soprano expiring of consumption at the end of La Traviata is a thing of the past. Now we must "look" the part, and be able to act as well as sing.*

FARLEY, CHARLES P., public relations executive; b. Oakland, Calif., Feb. 9, 1950. B Journalism, U. Mo., 1972. With corporate product publicity/store opening promotion Montgomery Ward, Chgo., 1972-75; account supr. Burson-Marsteller, Chgo., 1975-80, assoc. creative dir., 1982, v.p., creative dir., 1982-86, sr. v.p., 1986-88, exec. v.p., creative dir., 1988-89; v.p. Drucilla Handy Co., Chgo., 1980-82; exec. v.p., creative dir. Cohn & Wolfe, Atlanta, 1989-96, vice chmn., chief creative officer, 1993-97, gen. mgr., 1997-98, vice chmn., chief creative officer, 1998—. Recipient Silver Anvil award Pub. Rels. Soc. Am. Office: Cohn & Wolfe 303 Peachtree St NE 26 Fl Atlanta GA 30308-3201*

FARLEY, CLAIRE S., petroleum company executive. Geologist New Orleans exploration and producing divsn. Texaco, 1981, area mgr. for exploration, 1989-92, offshore exploitation mgr., 1992-93; asst. divsn. mgr. ea. region Texaco Exploration and Prodn. Inc., 1993-94, asst. to mgr. office chmn. bd. and CEO, 1994-96; mng. dir., CEO Hydro-Texaco Holdings, Copenhagen, 1996; v.p. Texaco Inc., Lake Charles, La., 1997—; pres. Texaco N.Am. Prodn., Lake Charles, La., 1997—. Office: Texaco Inc 11 Bugby Houston TX 77002*

FARLEY, DANIEL W., utility company executive, lawyer; b. Syracuse, N.Y., Dec. 6, 1955. BS, Clarkson U., 1978; JD, Syracuse U., 1981. Bar: N.Y. 1984. Adminstr. N.Y. State Electric & Gas Co., Binghamton, 1981-86; asst. to sec. N.Y. State Electric and Gas Co., Ithaca, 1986-87, asst. sec., 1987, corp. sec., 1987—, v.p., sec., 1991; sec. Energy East Corp.; v.p., sec., dir. NGE Enterprises, Inc.; sec. Energy East Enterprises Inc., Energy East Solutions, Inc., NYSEG Solutions, Inc., N.H. Gas Corp., Cayuga Energy, Inc., Senaca Lake Storage, Inc., Energy East Telecomms., Inc., So. Vt. Natural Gas Corp.; clk. Xenergy, Inc. Bd. dirs., treas., sec. The NYSEG Found., Inc. Office: NY State Electric & Gas Co PO Box 5224 Binghamton NY 13902-5224

FARLEY, EDWARD RAYMOND, JR., mining and manufacturing company executive; b. S.I., N.Y., Sept. 30, 1918; s. Edward Raymond and Ruth Veronica (Joyce) F.; m. Irene Daly, Feb. 19, 1948; children—Thomas Joyce, Nancy Seaver, Jane Campbell, Edward Raymond III. A.B., Princeton, 1940; J.D., Harvard, 1943. Bar: N.Y. bar 1944. With firm Simpson, Thacher & Bartlett, N.Y.C., 1944-55; v.p. Atlas Corp., N.Y.C., 1956-64; chmn. bd. dirs. Atlas Corp., 1964-87, pres., 1966-87, also chmn. exec. com.; trustee, chmn. exec. com. Lincoln Savs. Bank, Bklyn., 1973-84; dir. Am. Nuclear Energy Council, 1979-89. Active local United Fund; trustee, pres. bd. Lawrenceville Sch., 1970-85; trustee, chmn. bd. Princeton Med. Center, 1976—; assoc. trustee U. Pa., 1988—. Decorated Knight of Malta. Mem. Nat. Football Hall of Fame (pres. Delaware Valley chpt.), Atomic Indsl. Forum, U. Pa. Grad. Sch. Edn. (bd. gov.'s 1988—), Dial Lodge (trustee) Beden's Brook Club (Princeton), Pretty Brook Tennis Club (Princeton), Nassau Club (Princeton), Springdale Golf Club (Princeton). Home: 188 Parkside Dr Princeton NJ 08540-4815 Office: 353 Nassau St Princeton NJ 08540-4623

FARLEY, EUGENE JOSEPH, accountant; b. N.Y.C., Jan. 3, 1950; s. John Joseph and Rita Sara (Johnston) F.; m. Rosaleen Therese Scully, Jan. 10, 1981; children: Sarah, Laura, Patrick. BBA in Acctg., Siena Coll., 1977; MBA in Fin., Russell Sage Coll., 1985. CPA, N.Y. Cost acct. Callanan Industries, S. Bethlehem, N.Y., 1972-75; tax auditor N.Y. State Dept. Taxation and Fin., Albany, 1977-83, EDP auditor, 1983-85, assoc. acct., 1985-89; prin. acct. N.Y. Dept. Taxation & Fin., Albany, 1989-97; asst. chief acct. N.Y. Dept. Taxation & Fin., 1997—. Fund raiser Siena Coll. Alumni Fund; vol. Albany's Tri-Centennial Com., 1986. Mem AICPA, N.Y. State Soc. CPAs, Assn. Govt. Accts. (fin. mgmt. stds. com. 1988-91, Capital chpt. bd. dirs. 1989-93), Inst. Mgmt. Accts. Democrat. Roman Catholic. Avocation: sailing. Home: 9 Middlesex Dr Slingerlands NY 12159-9661 Office: State Office Campus NY Dept Taxation Fin Albany NY 12227

FARLEY, GLEN DAVID, English educator; b. Fort Belvoir, Va., Jan. 16, 1954; s. Glen L. and Rebecca J. Farley; m. Catherine Attilia Angelini, June 23, 1979; children: Dana C., Kevin N., Colin J., Leslie E. BS in Secondary Edn.-English, Bucknell U., 1975; MS in Reading, Duquesne U., 1979. Cert. secondary tchr., reading specialist, Pa. Reading/English tchr. Moon Area Sch. Dist., Moon Twp., Pa., 1976—; dept. head reading Moon Middle Sch., 1998-99. Alumni career adv. bd. Bucknell U., Lewisburg, Pa., 1990—. Democrat. Avocations: fishing, household repair, raising children, student activities director, coaching. Home: 154 Rivercrest Dr Moon Township PA 15108 Office: Moon Area Middle Sch 1407 Beers Sch Rd Moon Township PA 15108

FARLEY, HUGH T., state senator, law educator; b. Watertown, N.Y.; s. Edward A. and Laura Eleanor (Burns) F.; m. Sharon L. Rose, July 3, 1958; children: Susan, Robert, Margaret. BS cum laude, SUNY, 1958; JD, Am. U., 1964. Law prof. Sch. Bus., coord. law area SUNY, Albany, 1965—; mem. N.Y. Senate, 1977—, chmn. com. on aging, 1979-84, com. on environ. conservation, 1985-88, com. on banks, 1989—, select com. on interstate coop., subcom. on librs., majority whip, 1995—; chmn. Coun. State Govts., 1986-87, chmn. ea. region 1984, mem. bd. govs.; mem. exec. com. Nat. Conf. State Legislatures, mem. exec. com. state fed. assembly; del. White House Conf. on Librs., White House Conf. on Aging; del. Rep. Nat. Conv., 1984, 88, 92, 96; univ. sen. mem.-at-large U. Albany, 1971-73. Recipient Nat. Comdrs. award DAV, Cert. of Merit Statewide Sr. Action Coun., Velma K. Moore award for dist. svc. to librs., Most Disting. Alumni award Mohawk Valley C.C., 1974, Disting. Svc. medal U. Albany, 1983, O'Connell award Irish-Am. Legis. Soc., 1983; named Nat. Rep. Legis. of Yr., 1989, Conservation Legis. of Yr., N.Y. State Conservation Coun., 1986. Mem. Nat. Rep. Legislators Assn. (pres. 1985-86), Northeastern Bus. Law Assn. (past pres.). Office: 412 Legislative Office Bldg Albany NY 12247

FARLEY, JAMES NEWTON, manufacturing executive, engineer; b. Hutchinson, Kans., Nov. 8, 1928; s. James N. Farley and Elizabeth (Martin) Sanders; m. Nancy J. Hollabaugh, Apr. 30, 1956; children: Sarah Huskey, Timothy, Barbara, James, Stuart. BSEE, Northwestern U., 1950. Registered profl. engr., Ill. Test engr. GE, Schenectady, N.Y., 1950-51; sales engr. Allen Bradley Co., Milw., 1953-54, Chgo., 1954-60; sales mgr. SpeedFam Corp., Skokie, Ill., 1960-64; pres. SpeedFam Corp., Des Plaines, Ill., 1964-87, chmn. bd. dirs., 1987—; pres., CEO Speedfam Internat. Inc., Des Plaines, 1987-92, CEO, chmn. bd. dirs., 1992-97, chmn. bd. dirs., 1997—; bd. dirs. Lovejoy, Inc., Downers Grove, Ill., Extrude Hone Corp., Irwin, Pa., Berkley Process Control, Richmond, Calif. Bd. dirs. Greater Phoenix Econ. Coun. With U.S. Army, 1951-53. Recipient Alumni Merit award Northwestern U., 1996. Mem. Assn. for Mfg. Tech., Econ. Club Chgo., Oriental Order of Groundhogs. Democrat. Episcopalian. Office: Speedfam Internat Inc 305 N 54th St Chandler AZ 85226-2405

FARLEY, JENNIE TIFFANY TOWLE, industrial and labor relations educator; b. Fanwood, N.J., Nov. 2, 1932; d. Howard Albert and Dorothy Jane (Van Wagner) Towle; m. Donald Thorn Farley Jr., June 16, 1956; children—Claire Hamlin, Anne Tiffany, Peter Towle. BA, Cornell U., 1954, MS, 1969, PhD, 1970. Mem. editorial staff Mademoiselle and Seventeen mags., N.Y.C., 1954-56; freelance writer, Eng., Sweden, Peru, 1956-67; lectr., research assoc., adj. asst. prof. Cornell U., Ithaca, N.Y., 1970-72, dir. women's studies, 1972-76, asst. prof. Sch. Indsl. and Labor Relations, 1976-82, assoc. prof., 1982-89, prof., 1989—, exec. bd. dirs. women's studies program, 1970—; vis. prof. Ctr. for Women Scholars and Research on Women Uppsala U., Sweden, 1985-86; trustee Cornell U., 1988-92. Author: Affirmative Action and the Woman Worker, 1979, Academic Women and Employment Discrimination, 1982; editor: Sex Discrimination in Higher Education, 1982, The Woman in Management, 1983, Women Workers in Fifteen Countries, 1985. Recipient Corinne Galvin award Tompkins County Human Rights Commn., 1987, Unsung Heroine award Cen. N.Y. NOW, 1991. Mem. AAUP, Ithaca AAUW (pres. 1980-82), NOW, Sociologists for Women in Soc., Tompkins County NOW. Club: Cornell Women's of Tompkins County. Home: 711 Triphammer Rd Ithaca NY 14850-2504 Office: Cornell U Sch Indsl & Labor Rels Ithaca NY 14853

FARLEY, JOHN JOSEPH, library science educator emeritus; b. N.Y.C., Mar. 19, 1920; s. John Anthony and Margaret (Green) F.; m. Rita Johnston, Feb. 26, 1944; children—Janet, Eugene, Marian, Joseph, Veronica. B.A., Cath. U., 1940; M.A., Columbia U., 1950, M.S., 1953; Ph.D., NYU, 1964. Tchr., N.Y.C. schs., 1940-50; high sch. librarian Cranford, N.J., 1952-53, W. Hempstead, N.Y., 1953-58; curriculum dir. Sewanhaka Central High Sch. Dist., N.Y., 1958-60; successively asst. prof., asso. prof., chmn. dept. library scis. Queens Coll. of CUNY, 1960-67; vis. prof. library sci. San Jose State Coll., Calif., 1967; prof. library sci. SUNY-Albany, 1967-85, prof. emeritus, 1985—, dean Sch. Library and Info. Sci., 1967-77; cons. in field, 1958—. Author: Introduction to Library Science, 1969, also articles. Served with USAAF, 1943- 46. Recipient Founders Day award N.Y. U., 1964, Pius X medal for disting. service to confraternity Christian doctrine, 1966. Mem. ALA, AAUP, Nat. Council Tchrs. English. Democrat. Roman Catholic. Home: 12 Granada Dr Clifton Park NY 12065-5834

FARLEY, JOHN JOSEPH, III, federal judge; b. Hackensack, N.J., July 30, 1942; s. John Joseph and Patricia (Earle) F.; m. Kathleen Mary Wells, June 27, 1970; children: Maura, Brendan, Thomas, Caitlin. AB in Econs., Holy Cross Coll., 1964; MBA, Columbia, 1966; JD cum laude, Hofstra U., 1973. Bar: N.Y. 1974, D.C. 1975, U.S. Supreme Ct. 1977. Trial atty. torts sect. civil div. U.S. Dept. Justice, Washington, 1973-78, asst. dir. torts br. civil div., 1978-80, dir. torts br. civil div., 1980-89; judge U.S. Ct. of Appeals for Vets. Claims, Washington, 1989—; mem. faculty OPM Exec. Seminar Ctrs., Denver, 1980—; lectr. Atty. Gen.'s Advocacy Inst., Washington, 1976-89, FBI Acad., Quantico, Va., 1978-88. Editor-in-chief Hofstra Law Rev., 1971-73; contbr. articles to profl. jours. Bd. dirs. Amputee Coalition of Am., 1997-98. Served to capt. U.S. Army, 1966-70, Vietnam. Decorated Bronze Star with V device and 3 oak leaf clusters, Purple Heart with oak leaf cluster; recipient Sr. Exec. Service Spl. Achievement award U.S. Dept. Justice, 1984, Civil Div. Spl award U.S. Dept. Justice, 1980; Samuel Bronfman fellow, 1964-65, Dean's award for Disting. Hofstra Law Sch. Alumni, 1995, Disting. Alumni medal Hofstra U. Sch. of Law, 1986. Mem. Fed. Bar Assn. (1st chmn. vets. law sec. 1990-91). Roman Catholic. Avocations: skiing, tennis, bicycling, reading. Office: US Court Of Appeals for Vets Claims 625 Indiana Ave NW Ste 900 Washington DC 20004-2950

FARLEY, JOSEPH MCCONNELL, lawyer; b. Birmingham, Ala., Oct. 6, 1927; s. John G. and Lynne (McConnell) F.; m. Sheila Shirley, Oct. 1, 1958 (dec. July 1978); children: Joseph McConnell, Thomas Gager, Mary Lynne. Student, Birmingham-So. Coll., 1944-45; BSME, Princeton U., 1948; student, Grad. Sch. Commerce and Bus. Adminstrn., U. Ala., 1948-49; LLB, Harvard U., 1952; LHD, Judson Coll., 1974; LLD (hon.), U. Ala.-Birmingham, 1983. Bar: Ala. 1952. Assoc. Martin, Turner, Blakey & Bouldin, Birmingham, 1952-57; ptnr. successor firm Martin, Balch, Bingham & Hawthorne, 1957-65; exec. v.p., dir. Ala. Power Co., 1965-69, pres., dir., 1969-89; v.p. So. Electric Generating Co., 1970-74, pres., dir., 1974-89; exec. v.p. nuclear The So. Co., Birmingham, 1989-90; pres., CEO So. Nuclear Oper. Co., Birmingham, 1990-91, chmn., CEO, 1991-92, also bd. dirs.; exec. v.p., corp. counsel So. Co., 1991-92; of counsel Balch & Bingham, Birmingham, 1993—; bd. dirs. N.A., Torchmark Corp., Waddell & Reed Fin., Inc., Stockham Valve & Fittings Co.; mem. exec. bd. Southeastern Electric Reliability Coun., chmn., 1974-76; bd. dirs. Edison Electric Inst.; bd. dirs. Southeastern Electric Exch., pres., 1984; adv. dir. So. Co., 1992-97; bd. dir. emeritus Am. South Bancorp. Mem. Jefferson County Republican Exec. Com., 1953-65; counsel, mem. Ala. Rep. Com., 1962-65; permanent chmn. Ala. Rep. Conv., 1962; alternate del. Rep. Nat. Conv., 1956; bd. dirs. Ala. Bus. Hall of Fame, Birmingham Area YMCA (hon. dir.); chmn. bd. trustees So. Rsch. Inst.; trustee Tuskegee U.; trustee Children's Hosp. Birmingham, pres. bd. trustees 1983-85; mem. Pres.'s Cabinet U. Ala.-Tuscaloosa; bd. visitors U. Ala. Sch. Commerce, chmn., 1991-93. Served with USNR, 1948; now lt. ret. Mem. NAM (bd. dirs. 1987-92), Ala. Bar Assn., Birmingham Bar Assn., Inst. Nuclear Power Ops. (bd. dirs. 1982-89, chmn. 1987-89), U.S. Coun. for Energy Awareness (bd. dirs. 1985-92), Am. Nuclear Energy Coun. (chmn. bd. dirs. 1987-92), Newcomen Soc. N.Am., Birmingham Country Club, Shoal Creek Club, The Club, Mountain Brook Club, Summit Club, Rotary, Phi Beta Kappa, Kappa Alpha, Tau Beta Pi, Beta Gamma Sigma (hon.). Episcopalian. Home: 3333 Dell Rd Birmingham AL 35223-1319 Office: Balch & Bingham PO Box 306 Birmingham AL 35201-0306

FARLEY, MICHELLE RENAE, secondary school educator; b. Fairmont, W.Va., Apr. 29, 1966; d. Donald Lynn and Mary Ann (McIntire) Fisher; m. Richard W. Farley, Apr. 26, 1991; 1 child, Richard Michael. BA, W.Va. U., 1990. Proofreader Five Star Pub., Sierra Vista, Ariz., 1992-93; recreation specialist Sierra Vista Dept. Parks and Leisure Svc., 1993-94; tchr. English Leesville (La.) H.S., 1996—. Contbr. articles to profl. jours. Sec. Young Dems., Morgantown, W.Va., 1984-86. Mem. Nat. Coun. Tchrs. English, Vernon Fedn. Tchrs. Roman Catholic. Avocations: reading, writing, photography. Office: Leesville High Sch 502 Berry Ave Leesville LA 71446-3599

FARLEY, ROBERT DONALD, lawyer, business executive; b. Oneida, N.Y., Aug. 14, 1941; s. Donald William and Marian Elizabeth (Sawner) F.; m. Jennifer Lynn McCord, Dec. 1, 1967 (div. 1987); 1 son, Jonathan Brett; m. Darilyn Keith, May 20, 1989. B.S., Fordham U., 1962; J.D., Georgetown U., 1965. Bar: D.C. 1966, N.Y. 1971. Assoc. firm Dewey, Ballantine, Bushby, Palmer & Wood, N.Y.C., 1965-66, 69-75; sec., corp. counsel Esterline Corp., Darien, Conn., 1975-77, sec., gen. counsel, 1977-79, v.p., gen. counsel, sec., 1979-87; v.p. The Dyson-Kissner-Moran Corp., N.Y.C., 1987—. Bd. editors: Georgetown Law Jour, 1964-65. Served with JAGC USNR, 1966-69. Mem. ABA, N.Y. State Bar Assn., Rowayton Yacht Club. Office: The Dyson-Kissner-Moran Corp 565 5th Ave New York NY 10017-2413

FARLEY, ROBERT HUGH, police detective, child abuse consultant; b. Chgo., Sept. 12, 1950; s. Hugh John and Dorothy Marie (Kennedy) F. BS in Edn., Chgo. State U., 1970; cert., Northwestern U., 1979, U. So. Calif., 1983, U. Louisville, 1979, 84; MS in Criminal Justice and Corrections, Chgo. State U., 1991. Cert. tchr., Ill. Patrolman Cook County Sheriff's Police Dept., Chgo., 1973-74, tactical officer, 1974-75, detective crimes against children, 1975—; detective Fed. Child Exploitation Strike Force, Chgo., 1988-97, comdr. child exploitation unit, 1997—; instr. cons. office of delinquency prevention U.S. Dept. Justice, 1986—; instr. Ill. Local Law Enforcement Tng. Bd., Springfield, 1984—, Fed. Law Enforcement Tng. Ctr., Glynco, Ga., 1986—, FBI Tng. Acad., Quantico, Va., 1994—, RCMP Tng. Acad., Regina, Alta., Can., 1996—, MVD Inst. Higher Edn., Moscow, 1998—; faculty Nat. Coll. Edn., Evanston, Ill., 1986—, Morain Valley Coll., Palos Hills, Ill., 1985—, Fox Valley Tech. Coll., 1994—. Contbr. articles to profl. jours. Mem. Ill. State Senate Com. on Teen Suicide Prevention, Cook County States Atty.'s Task Force on Sexual Molestation, Ill. Adv. Com. on Child Abuse and Neglect, Cook County Death Rev. Commn., Ill. Atty. Gen.'s Violence to Children Task Force, Cook County Forensic Interviewing Task Force. Recipient Law Enforcement award U. So. Calif., 1985, Superior Pub. Svc. award City of Chgo., 1986, Cook County State's Atty.'s Recognition award, 1988, U.S. Customs Svc. Recognition award, 1987, U.S. Postal Inspector Law Enforcement award, 1994, Am. Profl. Soc. on the Abuse of Children Law Enforcement award, 1995, Sons and Daus. of the Am. Revolution Law Enforcement medal, 1995, Ill. Atty. Gen.'s Law Enforcement award, 1998, Chgo. Crime Commn. Law Enforcement award, 1999; named Police Officer of Yr., Internat. Juvenile Officers Assn., 1991. Mem. Ill. Police Assn. (state exec. bd. 1983—, chmn. 1985—, Law Enforcement award for Bravery 1986), Ill Juvenile Officer Assn., South Suburban Juvenile Officer Assn., Fedn. of Police, Emerald Soc. of Ill., Ill. Art Therapy Assn., Am. Heritage Sertoma, Am. Profl. Soc. on the Abuse of Children, Internat. Soc. for Prevention of Child Abuse, Chgo. Bar Assn. Office: Cook County Sheriffs PD Child Exploitation Unit 1401 Maybrook Dr Maywood IL 60153-2414

FARLEY, ROY C., rehabilitation researcher, educator; b. Dierks, Ark., Feb. 21, 1942; s. Embra and Mildred (Efird) F.; m. Omagene Cowan, May 29, 1969; children: Susanne, Justin. BA, Henderson State U., 1964; MS, Ctrl. Ark. U., 1972; EdD, U. Ark., 1978. Rehab. counselor, adminstr. Ark. Rehab. Svcs., Little Rock, 1967-74; dir., prof. rehab. edn. Ark. Rsch. & Tng. Ctr., Hot Springs, 1974—; condr. over 160 workshops & seminars for rehab. profls. Author, co-author 15 comprehensive tng. packages for rehab. profls. including The Advanced Facilitative Case Management Series, Relationship

Skills for Career Enhancement, Rational Behavior Problem-Solving, Employability Assessment and Planning, Know Thyself: A Strategy for Empowering and Involving Consumers in the Vocational Assessment Process; contbr. over 30 articles to profl. jours., also book chpts., monographs, conf. procs.; presenter 53 papers at confs. & meetings. Home: 117 Village Dr Hot Springs National Park AR 71913-6749 Office: Ark Rsch & Tng Ctr 105 Reserve St Hot Springs National Park AR 71901-4195

FARLEY, SUSAN STRACK, elementary educator; b. Niagara Falls, N.Y., Dec. 20, 1944; d. Charles Napoleon and Mildred May (Rodgers) Strack; m. Daniel Paul Farley, June 27, 1981. BS in Edn., SUNY, Brockport, 1967. Cert. elem. tchr., N.Y. Elem. tchr. Niagara Falls Sch. Dist., 1967-72; elem. tchr. Rochester (N.Y.) City Sch. Dist., 1972—, Learning through English Acad. Program tchr., 1983-89, 94—, mid. sch. acad. lang. specialist, 1989-93; insvc. tchr. Rochester Tchg. Ctr., 1993—. Contbr. articles to profl. jours. Vol. AIDS Rochester, 1996—. State Bilingual Categorical Funding Com. grantee, 1996-97. Mem. N.Y. Geog. Alliance (tchr. cons. 1992—), N.Y. State Social Studies Coun., Rochester Area Social Studies Coun., Rochester Tchrs. Assn. (sch. rep., Journalism award of merit 1997), Rochester Ednl. Assn. for Children and Tchrs. (editor newsletter 1991-94, bd. dirs., past pres.), Coord. Com. for ESOL Resources, Inc. (bd. dirs., past pres.). Democrat. Roman Catholic. Avocations: reading, stitchery, travel, music. Home: 163 Meadowdale Dr Rochester NY 14624-2811

FARLEY, TERRENCE MICHAEL, banker; b. N.Y.C., Mar. 6, 1930; s. Terrence M. and Mary A. (Dundon) F.; m. Audrey E. Churchill, June 8, 1952; children: Elizabeth C., Peter, Matthew. BBA, CCNY, 1955. With Brown Bros. Harriman & Co., N.Y.C., 1951—, ptnr., 1972—, mng. ptnr., 1983-95; bd. trustees Atlantic Mut. Ins. Co.; bd. dirs. Centennial Ins. Co., Atlantic Reinsurance Co. Mem. Univ. Club, Links Club, Echo Lake Country Club (Westfield, N.J.), Wianno Club (Osterville, Mass.). Home: 309 Hillside Ave Westfield NJ 07090-2902 Office: Brown Bros Harriman & Co 59 Wall St New York NY 10005-2808

FARLEY, THOMAS T., lawyer; b. Pueblo, Colo., Nov. 10, 1934; s. John Baron and Mary (Tancred) F.; m. Kathleen Maybelle Murphy, May 14, 1960; children: John, Michael, Kelly, Anne. BS, U. Santa Clara, 1956; LLB, U. Colo., 1959. Bar: Colo. 1959, U.S. Dist. Ct. Colo. 1959, U.S. Ct. Appeals (10th cir.) 1988. Dep. dist. atty. County of Pueblo, 1960-62; pvt. practice Pueblo, 1963-69; ptnr. Phelps, Fonda & Hays, Pueblo, 1970-75, Petersen & Fonda, P.C., Pueblo, 1975—; bd. dirs. Pub. Svc. Co. Colo., Denver, Norwest Pueblo, Norwest Sunset, Found. Health Systems, Inc., Colo. Public Radio. Minority leader Colo. Ho. of Reps., 1967-75; chmn. Colo. Wildlife Commn., 1975-79, Colo. Bd. Agr., 1979-87; bd. regents Santa Clara U., 1987—; commr. Colo. State Fair; trustee Cath. Found. Diocese of Pueblo, Great Outdoors Colo. Trust Fund. Recipient Disting. Svc. award U. So. Colo., 1987, 93, Bd. of Regents, U. Colo., 1993. Mem. ABA, Colo. Bar Assn., Pueblo C. of C. (bd. dirs. 1991-93), Rotary. Democrat. Roman Catholic. Office: Petersen & Fonda PC 650 Thatcher Bldg Pueblo CO 81003

FARLOW, MARTIN RHYS, neurologist, researcher, educator; b. Beech Grove, Ind., Jan. 20, 1953; s. Frank Edward and Evelyn Jean Farlow; m. Diane Sue Fisher; children: Erin Corinne, Nathan Rhys. BA in Psychology, Purdue U., 1975, BS in Math. and Biology, 1975; MD, Ind. U., 1979. Diplomate Am. Bd. Psychiatry and Neurology. Intern in medicine Ind. U. Hosps., Indpls., 1979-80, resident in neurology, 1980-83; asst. prof. neurology Ind. U., Indpls., 1983-89, assoc. prof. neurology, 1989-94, assoc. prof. Univ. Grad. Sch., 1990—, adj. assoc. prof. psychiatry, 1991—, prof. neurology, 1994—, asst. dir. Neuroimmunology Lab., 1983-86, dir. resident postgrad. edn., 1985-96, asst. dir. neurologic ICU, 1987-91, co-dir. Ind. U. Alzheimer's Clinic, 1988—, CORE leader of Nat. Inst. Aging Alzheimer Disease Ctr., 1991—, med. dir. Neurology Outpatient Clinics, 1992-93, vice-chmn. rsch. dept. neurology, 1994—; invited lectr., prof. to numerous hosps., colls., and univs. Contbr. more than 100 articles to profl. jours. including Am. Jour. Radiology, Archives of Neurology, Neurology, Jour. Am. Med. Assn., Brain Rsch. Mem. adv. com. Ctrl. Ind. chpt. Alzheimer Assn.; appointee Ind. Gov.'s Task Force for Alzheimer's Disease and Related Diseases. Grantee Duke U., 1989-95, Parke-Davis Pharm., 1990-93, Am. Health Assistance Found., 1991-92, DuPont-Merck Pharm. Co., 1991-93, Searle Pharm. Co., 1991-94, NIAID, 1992—, Ind. U., 1993-95, Glaxo, Inc., 1993-94, Upjohn Pharms., 1993-97, Montreal Gen. Rsch. Inst., 1993, Internat. Clinic Rsch. Corp., 1994-96, Sandoz Pharm. Co., 1994-96, Miles, Inc., 1994-97, Bayer Corp., 1994-97, Wyeth-Ayerst, 1995-97, Janssen Rsch. Found., 1995-97, Lilly Rsch. Labs., 1995-97, Quintiles, Inc., 1995-98, Warner-Lambert Corp., 1995-98, Somerset Pharms., 1996-97, among others. Fellow Am. Acad. Neurology, Am. Heart Assn. (stroke coun.); mem. AAAS, Ind. Neurol. Soc. (sec. 1988-90, v.p. 1990-92, pres. 1992-94), Ind. Peer Rev. Orgn., Marion County Med. Soc., Ind. State Med. Soc., Am. Soc. for Neurology Investigation, Soc. Neurosci. (Indpls. chpt.), World Fedn. Neurology (rsch. group on dementias) Ctrl. Soc. Neurologic Rsch., N.Y. Acad. Scis., Am. Soc. Exptl. Neurotherapeutics, Am. Neurol. Assn., Phi Beta Kappa. Avocations: backpacking, gardening, art, soccer, antiques. Office: Clin Bldg 541 Clinical Dr Rm 583 Indianapolis IN 46202-5233

FARMAKIDES, JOHN BASIL, lawyer; b. Symi Island (Dodecanese), Italy; s. Basil John and Anna Maria (Zouroudis) F.; m. Maria T. Kambanis, July 12, 1964; children: Basil J., George S. B.S., Case Western Res. U., 1950; J.D. with honors, George Washington U., 1956; LL.M., Georgetown U., 1958. Bar: D.C. 1957, U.S. Supreme Ct. 1958, Va. 1986. Patent examiner U.S. Patent Office, 1955-59; atty. U.S. Air Force, 1960-61; atty. NASA, 1961-70, mem. bd. contract appeals, 1968-70; asst. gen. counsel NSF, 1970-72; mem. NRC appeals bd. AEC (NRC), 1972-75; chmn. bd. contract and patent appeals Energy R&D Adminstrn. Dept. Energy, Washington, 1975-84; ptnr. Whitney & Dempsey, Washington, 1985-88; pres. SunWind Systems, McLean, Va., 1988—; cons. integration and use of sun and wind energy sys.; alt. disputes resolution/hearing officer Arbitration Com., 1986—; mem. Copyright Arbitration Royalty Panels, 1995—; adj. prof. in law Am. U. Law Sch., 1964-72; U.S. del. Internat. Conf. on Govt. Computer Experts, Geneva, 1972; chmn. FCST Subcom. on Legal Aspects of Info Sys., 1969-72; cons. HEW, NSF; chmn. Nat. Conf. on Legal Aspects of Computerized Info. Sys.-FCST, 1969-72; comdg. officer, dir. Joint Army, Navy, Air Force Spl. Analyn Divsn., USAR, 1971-74; mem. U.S. Chinese Workshop on Computerized Info. Sys., NAS, 1972. Contbr. articles to profl. jours. Pres. Cosmos Club Hist. Preservation Found. Recipient letters of appreciation U.S. Army, HEW, NASA, NSF; Exceptional Service medal Dept. Energy. Mem. ABA, Fed. Bar Assn., IEEE, Am. Arbitration Assn., Am. Soc. Pub. Adminstrn., Am. Hellenic Ednl. Progressive Assn., Phi Delta Phi. Clubs: Cosmos, Washington Golf, Nat. Lawyers.

FARMAKIS, GEORGE LEONARD, education educator; b. Clarksburg, W.Va., June 30, 1925; s. Michael and Pipitsa (Roussopoulos) F.; BA, Wayne State U., 1949, MEd, 1950, MA, 1966, PhD, 1971; MA, U. Mich., 1978; postgrad. Columbia U., Yale U., Queens Coll. Tchr., audio-visual aids dir. Roseville (Mich.) Pub. Schs., 1951-57; tchr. Birmingham (Mich.) pub. schs., 1957-61; tchr. Highland Park (Mich.) Pub. Schs., 1961-90; substitute tchr. Grosse Pointe Pub. Schs., 1990—; lectr. Lawrence U., 1990—; lectr. Oakland County C.C., 1990-92; instr. Highland Park C.C., 1966-68, Wayne County C.C., 1969-70; assoc. mem. grad. faculty Coll. Edn. Wayne State U., 1988-89; founder Ford Sch. Math. High Intensity Tutoring Program, 1971; chairperson Highland Park Sch. Dist. Curriculum Coun. and Profl. Staff Devel. Governing Bd., 1979-82; pres. Mich. Coun. Social Studies, 1985-86; founder, dir. Mich. Social Studies Olympiad, 1987; founder, editor Mich. Social Studies Jour., 1986; participant ESEA Title I/Nat. Diffusion Network. Cpl., USNG, 1948-51. Author, translator: Letters of Nicholas Gysis 1842-1901; co-author: Michigan School Finance Curriculum Guide.; contbr. poems to books of poetry, articles to Focus jour. Recipient spl. commendation Office of Edn., 1978, Outstanding Svc. award Nat. Coun. Social Studies 1987, Presdl. award Mich. Coun. Social Studies 1988, 96. Mem. Mich. Assn. Supervision and Curriculum Devel., Am. Hist. Assn., Nat. Council Social Studies (pres. SIG-CASE 1987-88, pres. JESIG, 1988-89), Am. Philol. Assn., Assn. Supervision and Curriculum Devel. (bd. dirs. Mich. 1983-86), Internat. Reading Assn., U. Mich. Alumni Assn., Wayne State U. Coll. Edn. Alumni Assn. (bd. dirs. 1985-86), Mich. Reading Assn., Masons (32 degree), Shriners, Ancient Accepted Scottish Rite, Phi Delta Kappa (Outstanding Educators award 1988). Greek Orthodox Home: 15215 Windmill Dr Macomb MI 48044-4929

FARMAN, ALLAN GEORGE, radiologist, oral pathologist, educator; b. Birmingham, Eng., July 26, 1949; came to the U.S., 1980; s. George (dec.) and Lily (Hewitt) F.; m. Taeko Takemori, May 21, 1996. B Dental Surgery, U. Birmingham, 1971; PhD, U. Stellenbosch, Cape Town, South Africa, 1977, DSc (hon.), 1996; EdS, U. Louisville, 1983, MBA with distinction, 1987. Diplomate Am. Bd. Oral and Maxillofacial Radiology, Japanese Bd. Oral and Maxillofacial Radiology; specialist registration in oral pathology South African Med. and Dental Bd., Ky. Bd. Dentistry. Sr. lectr. oral pathology U. Stellenbosch, Cape Town, 1974-77; head dept. oral biology U. Riyadh, Saudi Arabia, 1978-79; prof., head divsn. radiology and imaging scis. Dental Sch.., U. Louisville, 1980—; clin. prof. dept. diagnostic radiology Med. Sch., U. Louisville, 1990—; cons. Joint Commn. for Dental Bd. Examination, Chgo., 1984-92, NIH, Bethesda, Md., 1990—. Primary author: Oral and Maxillofacial Diagnostic Imaging, 1993; primary editor: Advances in Maxillofacial Imaging, 1997; editor (oral and maxillofacial radiology sect.) Oral Surgery, Oral Medicine, Oral Pathology, Oral Radiology and Endodontics, 1988-95; contbr. articles to profl. jours. CPR instr. Am. Heart Assn., Louisville, 1982—. Mem. Internat. Assn. Dento Maxillofacial Radiology (pres. 1994-97), Internat. Congress and Exposition on Computed Maxillofacial Imaging (initiator, founder, organizer 1995—), Am. Acad. Oral and Maxillofacial Radiology (editor 1988-95), Am. Assn. Dental Schs. (chmn. oral radiology sect. 1988-89). Office: U Louisville Sch Dentistry 501 S Preston St Louisville KY 40202-1701

FARMAN-FARMAIAN, GHAFFAR, investment company executive; b. Tehran, Iran, Jan. 14, 1930; s. Abdol Hossein Mirza and Massoumeh (Tafreshi) F-F.;m. Jahan Aalam, Aug. 5, 1956; children: Massoumeh, Amir Hossein, Ali Reza, Afsar. D.L.C. with honors, Loughborough (Eng.) Coll., 1951; MS, U. Ill., 1953; PhD, U. Calif., Berkeley, 1958. Head power div. Karadj Water & Power Orgn., Tehran, 1961-64; mem. Iranian Nat. Com. on Electro-Tech. Standards, Tehran, 1966-79; pres. Armed Forces Communication & Electronic, Tehran, 1970-71; chmn. IEEE, Tehran, 1972-73; mem. Iranian Nat. Com. on Energy Ministry of Water and Power, Tehran, 1972-79; co-founder, chmn. ASEA Iran Co., Tehran, 1973-79; vice chmn. Bank of Tehran, 1973-79; co-founder, bd. dirs. Tehran Ins. Co., 1975-79; pres. Univest Corp., N.Y.C., 1982—, Astle Properties Inc., Houston, 1989—. Author tech. papers. chmn., bd. trustees Community Sch., Tehran, 1975-79. Recipient 1st prize Inst. Elec. Engrs., 1956, 57, Alfred Nobel prize Am. Inst. Civil Engrs., 1958. Mem. IEEE (life), Armed Forces Communication & Electronic Assn. (life). Avocations: financial planning, tennis, hiking. Office: PO Box 3221, CH-1211 Geneva 3 - Rive, Switzerland

FARMER, CLAUDETTE, collegiate basketball coach; b. Tallahassee, Dec. 26, 1957. BS summa cum laude, Fla. A&M, 1979, MEd, 1983. Cert. tchr. driver edn., phys. edn. K-12, Fla.; cert. basic CPR, first aid. Tchr., coach Rickards H.S., Tallahassee, 1980-90; commr. Fla. Study Commn. on Women's Participation Athletics Fla. Dept. Edn., Tallahassee, 1991; head coach Rattlerettes women's basketball Fla. A&M Univ., Tallahassee, 1990—; asst. coach U.S. Olympic Festival-East Team (Gold medal honors), Denver, 1995; coach various basketball camps; panelist symposium in field. Coaching honors include: NCAA Divsn. One Tournament, 1995, MEAC Tournament finalists, 1997, semi-finalists, 1994-96, 200-89 Girls' Basketball Record (10 seasons) Rickards H.S., 1980-90; named Big Bend Basketball Coach of Yr., Tallahassee Democrat Newspaper, 1987, Big Bend Volleyball Coach of Yr., 1987, Dist. Championship, Girl's Volleyball, 1987; inductee Sports Hall of Fame, Fla. A&M Univ., 1991, others. Mem. Women's Basketball Coaches Assn. (recipient 200 Victory Club award 1990), Black Coaches Assn. (exec. bd. dirs.; Women's Basketball Coach of Yr. 1995), Fla. Assn. for Health, Phys. Edn., Recreation, Dance and Driver Edn., Women's Sports Found., Zonta, Kappa Delta Pi. Avocations: spectator sports, music, photography, fishing. Fax: 850-599-3810. Office: Womens Basketball Office Jake Gaither Athletic Ctr Fla A&M Univ Tallahassee FL 32307

FARMER, CROFTON BERNARD, atmospheric physicist; b. Cardiff, Wales, May 30, 1931; came to U.S., 1967; s. Francis Herbert and Cicely (Arnott) F.; m. Roberta Josephine Stewart, June 20, 1956; (div); children: Louise Josephine, Joanna Cicely, Philippa Bernice, Christopher Llewellyn; m. Christine Louise Conaway, Feb. 29, 1992. B.S., U. London, 1952, Ph.D., 1968. Research physicist EMI Electronics, Ltd., Eng., 1952-60; head infrared research dept. EMI Electronics, Ltd., 1960-62; led sci. expdns. to Bolivian Andes, 1962, 64; sr. research scientist Jet Propulsion Lab., Calif. Inst. Tech., Pasadena, 1967-72; mgr. planetary atmospheres Jet Propulsion Lab., Calif. Inst. Tech., 1972-75; prin. investigator NASA Viking Mars, 1975-77, Shuttle Spacelab, from 1977; vis. prof. divsn. geology and planetary sci. Calif. Inst. Tech., 1978-81; disting. vis. scientist Jet Propulsion Lab., 1989—; mem. subcoms. on planetary atmospheres and stratospheric rsch. NASA; cons., lectr. remote sensing of atmospheres. Contbr. articles on solar-terrestrial spectroscopy and composition of planets' atmospheres to sci. jours. Recipient Exceptional Sci. Achievement medal NASA, 1975, 77, 87, Antarctia Svc. medal, 1987, William T. Pecora award NASA and Dept. Interior, 1996.

FARMER, DEBORAH KIRILUK, marketing professional; b. Richmond, Va., June 6, 1956; d. Curtis Wayne Kiriluk and Lilan Baltz Starford; m. Roger Paul Schatzel, Oct. 1993. Student, J. Sargeant Reynolds Community Coll., 1974-78, Va. Commonwealth U., 1978-79, John Tyler Community Coll., 1986. Paralegal asst. Hunton Willams, Richmond, 1974; coord. office svcs. Va. Housing Devel. Authority, Richmond, 1975-78; dist. adminstr. Lanier Bus. Products, 1978-80; exec. asst. Old Dominion Emergency Med. Svcs. Alliance, Richmond; asst program dir. Sta. WRVA-AM, Richmond, 1981-83; coord. local sales Stas. WRNL-AM and WRXL-FM, Richmond, 1983-84; sr. account exec. Sta. WTVR-FM, Richmond, 1984-85; mgr. nat. sales Sta. WQSF-FM, Richmond, 1985-88; nat. account exec. HNW&H, Atlanta, 1988-89; mgr. local sales Sta. WTKN/WHVE, St. Petersburg, Fla., 1989-90; gen. sales mgr. WFNS-AM, Tampa, Fla., 1990-91; sr. bus. devel. mgr. Staff Leasing Group, Tampa, 1991—; cons. mem., gov. adv. bd. EMS Pub. Info. Edn., Richmond, 1986; bd. dirs. Travelers Aid Soc. Va., 1987-88, sec., mem. exec. commn. Contbr. articles to profl. jours. CPR instr. ARC, Richmond, 1979-87, mem. VOAD com., 1994; emergency med. tech. Manchester Vol. Rescue Squad, Richmond, 1979-86, sec. bd. dirs., 1979-81, pub. rels. officer, 1985-86; dir. disaster relief Tampa Bay Bapt. Assn., 1993—; chair pub. rels. com. FBC Brandon, 1990-94. Am. Bus. Women's Assn. scholar, 1975. Mem. Am. Women in Radio and TV (charter, v.p. 1987-91, pres.). Republican. Baptist.

FARMER, DONALD A(RTHUR), JR., lawyer; b. Wichita, Kans., Apr. 3, 1944; s. Donald Arthur and Ethel Lois (Figge) F.; m. Jane Moran, June 17, 1967; children: Emma Christina, Matthew Todd. AB, Stanford U., 1966, JD, 1969. Bar: Calif. 1970, D.C. 1970. Trial atty. antitrust div. U.S. Dept. Justice, Washington, 1969-74; spl. asst. to head of antitrust div. U.S. Dept. Justice, 1974-77; dir. bur. internat. aviation U.S. CAB, Washington, 1977-79; ptnr. Galland, Kharasch, Calkins & Short, Washington, 1979-81, Beckman & Farmer, Washington, 1981-84, Popham, Haik, Schnobrich & Kaufman, Ltd., Washington, 1984-97, Reed Smith Shaw & McClay, LLP, Washington, 1997—. Mem. ABA, Univ. Club. Washington. Office: Reed Smith Shaw & McClay 1301 K St NW Ste 1100-East Washington DC 20005-3317

FARMER, DWIGHT L., transportation engineer, educator; b. Richmond, Va., Mar. 14, 1951; s. James Alvin Frmer and Virginia (Fulwider) Absher; m. Brenda Sue Miller, Aug. 17, 1974. BSCE, Va. Poly. Inst., 1974; MSCE, Carnegie Mellon U., 1976. Assoc. transp. engr. State of Va., Dept. Transp., Richmond, 1974-78; chief transp. engr. Southeastern Va. Planning Dist. Commn., Norfolk, 1978-90; dep. exec. dir. transp. Hampton Rds. Planning Dist. Commn., Chesapeake, Va., 1990—; adj. assoc. prof. Old Dominion U., Norfolk, 1979—. Contbr. articles to profl. jours. Bd. dirs. Stratford Chase Civic League, Virginia Beach, Va., 1982-90, Sleepy Pt. Estates Civic League, Suffolk, Va., 1992-97. Mem. transp. Rsch. Bd., Inst. Transp. Engrs. Methodist. Avocations: corvette restoration, snow skiing, boating. Office: Hampton Rds Planning Dist Commn 723 Woodlake Dr Chesapeake VA 23320-8909

FARMER, ELAINE FRAZIER, retired state legislator; b. New Castle, Pa., Mar. 14, 1937; d. John R. and Pearle (McLure) Frazier; m. Sterling N. Farmer, Aug. 22, 1959; children: Heather, Drew. BBA, Case Western Reserve U., 1958, MEd, 1964. Employment supr. Stouffer Corp., Cleve., 1958-60; tchr. Lakewood Schs., Cleve., 1960-64; substitute tchr. North Allegheny Schs., Pitts., 1972-77; agt. Howard Hanna Real Estate Services, Pitts., 1977-86, mgr., 1983-86; mem. Pa. Ho. of Reps., Harrisburg, 1986-96; ret., 1996; state dir. Women in Govt. Councilman Town of McCandless, Pa., 1980-86; trustee Northland Libr., Pitts., 1980-85, North Hills Passavant Hosp., 1990-92; liaison McCandless Planning Commn., 1984-86; mem. comty. adv. bd. St. Barnabas Nursing Home, coun. Pitts. Cancer Inst., 1994-96. Mem. Nat. Order Women Legislators, Am. Legis. Exch. Coun., Women in Govt. (state dir.), North Hills C. of C. Republican. Presbyterian. Avocation: golf.

FARMER, GREG, former federal agency administrator. Grad., Fla. Internat. U.; MS, Fla. State U. Exec. dir. Fla. Dem. Party, 1975-79; campaign mgr. Buddy MacKay for U.S. Senate, 1980; govt. liaison Gov. Bob Graham, 1981; chief of staff Congressman Buddy MacKay, 1982-88; dir. govtl. rels. No. Telecom. Inc., 1989-91; sec. Fla. Dept. Commerce; v.p. govt. rels. and internat. trade Nortel Networks, Washington, 1997—; organizer first-ever White House conf. on Travel and Tourism; convenor Western Hemispheric Tourism Ministerial, 1994. Office: Nortel Networks Ste 700 801 Pennsylvania Ave NW Washington DC 20004*

FARMER, GUY OTTO, II, lawyer; b. Washington, Jan. 7, 1941; s. Guy Otto and Rose Marie (Smith) F.; m. Drema Houchins, Jan. 27, 1963; children: Caroline E., Guy Otto III. BS in Polit. Sci., W.Va. U., 1963; JD, U. Va., 1966. Bar: Fla. 1966, U.S. Dist. Ct. (mid. dist.) Fla. 1966, U.S. Ct. Appeals (5th cir.) 1967, U.S. Ct. Appeals (11th cir.) 1970, U.S. Supreme Ct. 1970, U.S. Ct. Appeals (6th cir.) 1991, U.S. Ct. Appeals (2d cir.) 1997. Assoc. to ptnr. Mahoney, Hadlow & Adams, Jacksonville, Fla., 1966-82; ptnr. Smith & Hulsey, Jacksonville, 1982-88, Foley & Lardner, Jacksonville, 1988—. Contbr. articles to profl. jours. Bd. dirs. N.E. Fla. Hospice, Jacksonville, 1987-93, Children's Home Soc., Jacksonville, 1988-91, N.E. Fla. Safety Coun., Jacksonville, 1988—. Fellow Am. Bar Found.; mem. ABA, Fla. Bar Assn., Jscksonville Bar Assn., Def. Rsch. Inst., The River Club, San Jose Country Club (Jacksonville), Ponte Verda Club, Epping Forest Yacht Club. Democrat. Methodist. Avocations: reading, gardening, boating, sports. Home: 4244 San Jose Blvd Jacksonville FL 32207-6343 Office: Foley & Lardner 200 N Laura St Jacksonville FL 32202-3500

FARMER, HIRAM LEANDER, physical education educator; b. Tallahassee, Fla., Aug. 23, 1958; s. Alton Ernest and Betty Geneva (Gainey) F.; m. Yolanda Lavonne Vines, Jan. 15, 1988; children: Gregory Maurice, Grant Malik. BS, Fla. A&M U., 1981. Phys. edn. tchr. MacIntyre Park, Thomasville, Ga., 1981-82; instructional asst. Program for Adolescence Coop. Edn. Sch., Tallahassee, 1982-88, Bond Elem. Sch., Tallahassee, 1988, Leon County Juvenile Detention Ctr., Tallahassee, 1988; phys. edn. tchr. Charles R. Hadley Elem. Sch., Miami, Fla., 1988—, head dept. phys. edn., 1991—, chmn. health and nutrition, 1993-94; 2d v.p. Christian Plan Support Group, 1994-95. Chmn. sports ministry Covenant Missionary Bapt. Ch., Florida City, Fla., 1994—, youth ministry, 1988—, Christian Plan Support Group 2d v.p., 1994—, asst. chmn. bd. trustees; coord. Jump Rope for Heart, Am. Heart Assn., Miami, 1991—. Mem. ASCD, Fla. A&M U. Nat. Alumni Assn., Kappa Alpha Psi. Avocations: exercising, music, sports. Home: 813 SW 5th St Homestead FL 33030-6977 Office: Charles R Hadley Elem Sch 8400 NW 7th St Miami FL 33126-3802

FARMER, JANENE ELIZABETH, artist, educator; b. Albuquerque, Oct. 16, 1946; d. Charles John Watt and Regina M. (Brown) Kruger; m. Michael Hugh Bolton, Apr. 1965 (div.); m. Frank Urban Farmer, May, 1972 (div.). BA in Art, San Diego State U., 1969. Owner, operator Iron Walrus Pottery, 1972-79; designer ceramic and fabric murals, Coronado, Calif., 1979-82; executed commns. for clients in U.S.A., Can., Japan and Mex., 1972—; designer fabric murals and bldg. interiors; environ. artist, painter of rare and endangered animals, Coronado and La Jolla, Calif., 1982—; tchr. Catholic schs., San Diego, 1983-86, Ramona Unified Sch. Dist., 1986—, mentor tchr., 1994-95, 95-96, 97-98; instr. U. Calif., San Diego, 1979-83, 92. Mem. Coronado Arts and Humanities Coun., 1979-81. Grantee Calif. Arts Coun., 1980-81, resident artist U. Calif., San Diego; U. San Diego grad. fellow dept. edn., 1984; tchr. environ. art San Diego Natural History Mus., summer 1996, 97, and San Diego Wild Animal Park, summer, 1996. Mem. edn. adv. com. La Jolla (Calif.) Playhouse, 1996. Mem. Am. Soc. Interior Designers (affiliate). Roman Catholic. Home: 4435 Nobel Dr Apt 35 San Diego CA 92122-1559

FARMER, JOE, municipal official; b. Wilson, N.C., Feb. 11, 1938. BS, SUNY, Oswego, 1960; MS, Hofstra U., 1968. Tchr. Valley Stream (N.Y.) Ctrl. H.S., 1961-68; guidance counselor Freeport (N.Y.) H.S., 1968-70; acing. prin. Roosevelt (N.Y.) Jr./Sr. H.S., 1970-72; prin. Yonkers (N.Y.) Sch., 1973; exec. dir. compliance City of Yonkers, 1986-89, asst. supt., 1989-94, spl. asst. housing, cmty. redevel. affordable housing dept., 1994-98, mayor, 1998—. Mem. Yonkers (N.Y.) City Coun., 1990-92; bd. dirs. Yonkers City Hosp., 1991-95. Office: City Hall 405 Broadway Yonkers NY 10701-4011*

FARMER, MARTHA LOUISE, retired college administrator; b. Cin.; d. William S. and Genevieve (Fye) Farmer. B.A., Wheaton Coll., 1935; postgrad. Wellesley Coll., 1936; M.A., Columbia U., 1937, Ed.D., 1956. Assoc. prof. Manhattanville Coll. Sacred Heart, 1936-43, 46-48; adminstr. dept. student life City Coll., CUNY, 1948-69, prof., coordinator dept. student personnel services, 1969-75, prof. emeritus, 1975—; vis. prof. Grad. Sch. Edn., N.Y. U., 1967-69; cons. student personnel services for adults in higher edn., 1975—. Mem. mgmt. com. Emma Ransom YWCA, N.Y.C., 1958, mem. resident com. 1956-58; mem. jr. high teens com. YWCA, Ridgewood, N.J., 1962-75; mem. N.J. com. U.S. Commn. on Civil Rights; trustee Hispanic Commn. on Alcoholism in N.J. Served as lt. USNR (W), 1943-46. Recipient Bernard Reed award, 1963, 85-86, Winifred Fisher award, 1974. Mem. Am. Coll. Personnel Assn. (program com. 1960-62, mem. com. I, 1963-65, chmn. Com. XIII 1965-67, mem. Com. IV 1968-72), Am. Personnel and Guidance Assn., Assn. U. Evening Colls. (coms. 1961-72), U.S. Assn. Evening Students (chmn. bd. trustees 1970-71, hon. life trustee 1975—), Evening Student Personnel Assn. (pres. 1962-63), Adult Student Personnel Assn. (chmn. bd. trustees 1968-71, hon. life trustee 1975—). Editor: Student Personnel Services For Adults in Higher Education, 1967; Counseling Services for Adults in Higher Education, 1971. Home: 348 Lake St Saddle River NJ 07458-1750

FARMER, MARY BAUDER, small business owner, artist, painter; b. San Diego, Nov. 30, 1953; d. Chester Robert and Dixie (Cook) Bauder; m. L. Michael Dowling, July 1990. BS, Auburn U., 1986; postgrad., Ga. State U., 1992—; ind. study with Joan Snyder. Exec. dir. Birmingham Woman's Med. Clinic, Ala., 1975-80; pres. Beacon Clinic, Montgomery, Ala., 1980-83; ptnr. Hill, Rose and Farmer, Atlanta, 1988-90; owner, mgr. Studio M. Farmer, Atlanta, 1990—; creative dir., pres. Twin Studios, Inc., Atlanta, 1995-97; v.p. Global Interests Inc., 1990—. Author, pub.: The Landlord's Primer for Georgia: A Self-Help Guide for Inexperienced Landlords. Mem. pub. rels. com. Project Open Hand, Ga. Citizens for Arts; mem. Bus. Com. for Arts. Mem. LWV, Ga. Women's Agenda (founder), Omicron Delta Kappa. Democrat. E-mail: www.maryfarmer.com. Office: Studio M Farmer 260 Howard St # 2 Atlanta GA 30313

FARMER, PHILLIP W., company executive; b. 1939. BA, Duke U. Various mgmt. and tech. positions GE, 1962-82; v.p., gen. mgr. govt. support sys. divsn. Harris Corp., Melbourne, Fla., 1982-86, v.p. Palm Bay ops., govt. sys. sector, 1986-88, sr. v.p. sector exec., govt. sys. sector, 1988-89, pres. electronics sys. sector, 1989-91, exec. v.p., 1991, pres., CEO, 1995—, chmn., pres., CEO; bd. dirs. Mfrs. Alliance, Aerospace Industries Assn. Bd. trustees Fla. Inst. Tech. Mem. Bus. Roundtable, Electronic Industries Assn. Office: Harris Corp 1025 W Nasa Blvd Melbourne FL 32919-0002*

FARMER, REBECCA ANNE, educator; b. Norton, Va., July 30, 1952; d. Frank Nelson and Mary Ella (Johnson) F.; m. Carleton Dennis Scully, July 13, 1985. BA in Social Work, U. Ky., 1974, MS in Spl. Edn., 1985. Tchr. Growing Together Presch., Lexington, 1981-84, staff devel. coord., 1984-85; tchr. Fayette County Schs., Lexington, 1985-88; assoc. project dir. early intervention team tng. project Human Devel. Inst., U. Ky., Lexington, 1988-89; family counselor United Cerebral Palsy and Handicapped Children's Assn., Elmira, N.Y., 1990—; adj. clin. assoc. dept. occupational therapy Coll. Allied Health and Nursing, Ea. Ky. U., Richmond, 1983-85; cons. Stephen August Early Intervention Ctr., Cheshire, Conn., 1990-91—, children with phys. disabilities Paceine Sch., Quito, Ecuador; exec. dir. Guilford (Conn.) Aftersch. Program, 1991-92; tech. assistance specialist Ky. systems change project U. Ky. Human Devel. Inst., 1993-97; coord. Project STEPS U. Ky. Human Devel. Inst.; resource specialist Fayette County Pub. Schs., 1998—. Mem. The Assn. for Persons with Severe Handicaps (mem. Ky. exec. bd.), Ptnrs. of Am., Coun. for Exceptional Children. Democrat. Avocations: oil painting, theater, sailing, camping/outdoor recreation, international travel. Home: 26 Mockingbird Valley Rd Winchester KY 40391-2352

FARMER, RICHARD EDWARD, college dean; b. Pawtuckett, R.I., 1951; s. Paul Henry and Ruth Poole Farmer; m. Bonnie Lee Cashin, May 19, 1973; children: Erin Cashin, Paul Henry II. AB, St. Anselm Coll., 1973; MS, U. New Haven, 1974; EdD, Boston U., 1977. Prof. Cape Cod C.C., West Barnstable, Mass., 1974-77, U. New Haven, West Haven, Conn., 1977-89; dean Sacred Heart U., Fairfield, Conn., 1989-97, Providence Coll., 1997—. Author: Law Enforcement and Community Relations, 1976, Stress Management for Police, 1980, Stress Management, 1984. Econ. devel. commr. Town of Madison, Conn., 1982-84, police commr., 1984-88. E-mail: rfarmer@providence.edu. Office: Providence Coll River and Eaton St Providence RI 02918

FARMER, RICHARD GILBERT, physician, foundation administrator, medical advisor, health care consultant; b. Kokomo, Ind., Sept. 29, 1931; s. Oscar Irvin and Elizabeth Jane (Gilbert) F.; m. Janice Mae Schrank, Nov. 29, 1958; children: Amy Lynn, David Richard. Student, Ind. U., 1949-52; M.D., U. Md., 1956; M.S. in Medicine, U. Minn., 1960. Diplomate: Am. Bd. Internal Medicine, Gastroenterology. Fellow in internal medicine Mayo Clinic, Rochester, Minn., 1957-60; mem. staff Cleve. Clinic Found., 1962-91, chmn. dept. gastroenterology, 1972-82, chmn. div. medicine, 1975-91, mem. med. exec. com., 1975-91, bd. govs., 1974-79, mem. exec. com. bd. trustees, 1975-77; sr. med. advisor Bur. for Europe Agy. for Internat. Devel. U.S. Dept. State, Washington, 1992-94; cons. health care Eastern Europe and former Soviet Union, 1994-96; med. dir. Quality Health Internat., Boston, 1997-98; cons. Scandinavian Care, 1998—; clin. prof. medicine (gastroenterology) Georgetown U. Med. Ctr., Washington, 1992—; mem. nat. adv. bd. Nat. Commn. Digestive Diseases, 1977-79; mem. nat. sci. adv. bd. Nat. Found. Ileitis and Colitis, 1973-91; chmn. grants rev. com. Nat. Found. Ileitis and Colitis, 1981-85; mem. Council Subsplty. Socs. in Internal Medicine, 1978-85; mem. com. to assess quality care in Medicare program, GAO and ways and means com. U.S. Ho. of Reps., 1986-89; cons. Am. Medico-Legal Found., Phila., 1996—, Inst. for Health Policy Analysis, Washington, 1996—; med. dir. Eurasian Med. Edn. Program (Russian Fedn.), 1998—. Editor 6 books; contbr. more than 275 articles to sci. jours., in books. Served as lt. comdr. USNR, 1960-62. Recipient Jubilee medal Charles U. of Prague, 1998. Fellow ACP (gov. Ohio 1980-84, health and pub. policy com. 1982-91, chmn. 1986-88, chmn. med. tech. assessment com. 1985-86, regent 1985-91, chmn. clin. practice subcom. 1988-91, del. to AMA 1989-94, Spl. Presdl. citation 1984, master 1993), Am. Coll. Gastroenterology (pres. 1978-79, trustee, exec. com. 1975-80, master 1991); mem. Assn. Program Dirs. in Internal Medicine (founding pres. 1977-79, Founder's award 1993), Inst. Medicine of NAS (life), Am. Gastroent. Assn. (commn. on future 1973-74, tng. and edn. com. 1975-78, chmn. subcom. grad. edn. 1975-78), Interstate Postgrad. Med. Assn. (pres. 1983-84), Internat. Orgn. for Study Inflammatory Bowel Disease (dep. chmn. 1982-86). Democrat. Quaker. Home and Office: 9126 Town Gate Ln Bethesda MD 20817-4111

FARMER, RICHARD T., uniform rental and sales executive; b. Dayton, Ky., Nov. 22, 1934. BBA, Miami U., Ohio, 1956. Chmn. bd. Cintas Corp., Cin. Office: Cintas Corp 6800 Cintas Blvd PO Box 625737 Cincinnati OH 45262-5737*

FARMER, ROBERT LINDSAY, lawyer; b. Portland, Oreg., Sept. 29, 1922; s. Paul C. and Irma (Lindsay) F.; m. Carmen E. Engebretson, Sept. 8, 1943; children: Cort W., Scott L., Eric C. BS, UCLA, 1946; LLB, U. So. Calif., 1949. Bar: Calif. 1949. Since practiced in L.A.; mem. Farmer & Ridley, L.A., 1949—. Trustee Edward James Found., West Dean Estate, Chichester, Eng. Served with AUS, 1943-46. Mem. ABA, Los Angeles County Bar Assn., Order of Coif, Beta Gamma Sigma, Kappa Sigma, Phi Delta Phi, Annandale Golf Club (Pasadena, Calif.). Home: 251 S Orange Grove Blvd Apt 1 Pasadena CA 91105-1766 Office: 444 S Flower St Los Angeles CA 90071-2901

FARMER, SUSAN LAWSON, broadcasting executive, former secretary of state; b. Boston, May 29, 1942; d. Ralph and Margaret (Tyng) Lawson; m. Malcolm Farmer, III, Apr. 6, 1968; children: Heidi Benson, Stephanie Lawson. Student, Garland Jr. Coll., 1960-61, Brown U., 1961-62. Mem. Providence Home Rule Charter Commn., 1979-80; sec. of state State of R.I., Providence, 1983-87; pres., CEO Sta. WSBE-TV, Providence, 1987—; spl. adv. R.I. Family Ct., 1978-83; mem. nat. voting stds. panel Fed. Election Commn. co-chmn. Nat. Voter Edn. Project; mem. electoral coll., 1984; chmn. Gov.'s Com. on Ethics in Govt., 1985-86; mem. teaching facility and adv. panel Internat. Ctr. on Election Law and Adminstrn.; mem. nat. edn. adv. com. Pub. Broadcasting System, 1987-89; trustee Eastern Ednl. TV Network, 1987-95; mem. R.I. Task Force on Tech., 1995—, R.I. Info. Mgmt. Commn., 1997; bd. dirs., mem. exec. com. Program Resources Group, 1993—. Bd. dirs. Justice Resources Corp., Marathon House, Inc., R.I. Council Alcoholism, R.I. Hist. Soc., Planned Parenthood (R.I. chpt.), R.I. Rape Crisis Ctr., The Newport Inst.; mem. Mayor's Task Force on Child Abuse, R.I. Film Commn.; v.p. Miriam Hosp. Found.; mem. adv. com. Women in Polit. and Govtl. Careers Program, U. R.I., 1985—; mem. adv. bd. Com. for Study of Am. Electorate-Ford Found. Project-Efficacy in State Voting Laws, 1986; mem. Commn. to Study Length of Election Process, 1985—; steering com. Nat. Fund for America's Future, Project Vote R.I.; bd. dirs. Dawn for Children Tng. Thru Placement; pres. Channel 36 Found.; bd. dirs. R.I. Anti-Drug Coalition Exec. Com., Nat. Forum for Pub. TV Execs., 1998—. Named Woman of Yr., Nat. Women's Polit. Caucus, 1980. Mem. LWV, NATAS (bd. govs. New Eng. chpt. 1995—), N.E. Assn. Schs. and Colls. (com. on tech. and course instns.), So. Ednl. Comms. Assn. (bd. dirs. 1993-96), R.I. Women's Polit. Caucus (Woman of Yr. 1980), Bus. and Profl. Women (Woman of Yr. 1984), Common Cause, Save the Bay, Providence Preservation Soc., Orgn. State Broadcasting Execs, Agawam Hunt Club, Mill Reef Club (Antigua, West Indies), Nat. Assn. of Ams. Pub. TV Stas. (trustee 1996—), Nat. Acad. TV Arts and Scis. (mem. industry issues adv. com. 1994—, bd. govs. N.E. chpt. 1995—), Nat. Ednl. Telecomms. Assn. (bd. dirs. 1997—, Nat. Forum Pub. TV Execs. (bd. dirs. 1998—). Home: 147 Lloyd Ave Providence RI 02906-1552 Office: Sta WSBE-TV 50 Park Ln Providence RI 02907-3124

FARMER, TERRY D(WAYNE), lawyer; b. Oklahoma City, May 1, 1949; s. Gayle V. and Allene (Edsall) F.; children: Grant L., Tyler M. BA, U. Okla., 1971, JD, 1974. Bar: Okla. 1974, N.Mex. 1975, U.S. Dist. Ct. N.Mex. 1976, U.S. Ct. Claims 1975, U.S. Ct. Appeals (10th cir.) 1977, U.S. Supreme Ct. 1980. Asst. trust officer First Nat. Bank of Albuquerque, 1974-75; assoc. Nordhaus, Moses & Dunn, Albuquerque, 1975-78, ptnr., 1978-80; dir. Moses, Dunn, Farmer & Tuthill, P.C., Albuquerque, 1980—; pres. Albuquerque Lawyers Club, N. Mex., 1982-83. Fellow N.Mex. Bar Found.; mem. N.Mex. Bar Assn. (pres. Young Lawyers div., 1978-79), Okla. Bar Assn., N.Mex. Trial Lawyers. Office: Moses Dunn Farmer & Tuthill PC PO Box 27047 Albuquerque NM 87125-7047

FARMER, THOMAS WOHLSEN, neurologist, educator; b. Lancaster, Pa., Sept. 18, 1914; s. Clarence R. and Laura (Wohlsen) F.; m. Phyllis McCormick, July 19, 1941; children: Pamela Farmer Henderson, Thomas Wohlsen. A.B., Harvard U., 1935, M.D., 1941; M.A., Duke U., 1937; postgrad., U. Copenhagen, 1957-58, U. Calif., San Diego, 1971-72. Diplomate: Am. Bd. Psychiatry and Neurology (dir. 1969—, pres. 1977). Intern Pa. Hosp., Phila., 1941-42; resident Boston City Hosp., 1942-43, Johns Hopkins Hosp., 1943-44, 46-47; mem. staff N.C. Meml. Hosp., Chapel Hill, 1952—; instr. medicine Johns Hopkins U., 1947-48; asst. prof. neurology Southwestern Med. Sch., U. Tex., Dallas, 1948-49; asso. prof. Southwestern Med. Sch., U. Tex., 1949-50, prof., 1950-52, prof. medicine, acting chmn. dept. medicine, 1951-52; prof. neurol. medicine, head div. neurology U. N.C., Chapel Hill, 1952—; Sarah Graham Kenan prof. medicine U. N.C., 1975—. Author: Pediatric Neurology, 1964, 3d edit., 1983, Neurologia Pediatrica, 1972. Served with USNR, 1944-46. Mem. Am. Acad. Neurology (nat. sec. 1955-57), Am. Neurol. Assn., Am. Acad. Neurology, ACP, AMA, Assn. Research Nervous and Mental Diseases, Child Neurology Soc. Home: 1304 Mason Farm Rd Chapel Hill NC 27514-4604 Office: U NC Sch Medicine Clin Scis Bldg Chapel Hill NC 27514

FARMER, WESLEY STEVEN, police officer; b. Albuquerque, Dec. 1, 1950; s. Dewey B. Farmer and Bernice (Willie) Maloch; m. Wendy L. Phillips, Sept. 22, 1992; children: Erica, Alisha, Tara. BA, Calif. Bapt. Coll., 1972; MPA, Calif. State U., San Bernardino, 1989. Police officer San Bernardino (Calif.) Police, 1973-79, police detective, 1979-84, police sgt., 1984-89, police lt., 1989—; adj. faculty Riverside (Calif.) C.C., 1989, 92. Contbr. articles to profl. jours. Mem. Rotary, San Bernardino, 1983-84; bd. dirs. Alliance for Children and Families, Milw., 1995—, bd. chair western region, 1995-99, bd. chair San Bernardino chpt., 1986-96. Mem. ASPA (bd. dirs. 1992-96), Family Svc. Agy. (bd. chair 1993-96, Svc. award 1995). Republican. Avocations: community service, fishing, camping, hiking. Office: San Bernardino Police PO Box 1559 San Bernardino CA 92402-1559

FARNAM, JAFAR, allergist, immunologist, pediatrician; b. Tabriz, Iran, Dec. 18, 1945. MD, Faculty Medicine Tabriz, 1972. Diplomate Am. Bd. Pediatrics, Am. Bd. Allergy and Immunology. Intern U. Ill. Hosp., Chgo., 1977-78; resident in pediatrics Christ Hosp.- Rush U., Oaklawn, 1978-80; fellow in allergy & immunology U. Tex. Med. Br., Galveston, 1980-82; clin. assoc. prof. internal medicine U. Tex. Med. Br.; with Clear Lake Regional Hosp. Mem. Am. Acad. Pediat., Am. Acad. Allergy, Asthma, and Immunology, Am. Coll. Allergy, Asthma, and Immunology, Tex. Med. Assn., Tex. Allergy Soc. Office: Allergy Asthma Ctr 450 Medical Center Blvd Ste 204 Webster TX 77598-4229

FARNAM, WALTER EDWARD, insurance company executive; b. Providence, Nov. 7, 1941; s. Walter Edward, Sr. and Florence Oldfield (Metcalfe) F.; m. Carolyn Ruth Larcom, Sept. 19, 1964; children—Robert and Deborah. BA, Brown U., 1963. Actuarial trainee Aetna Life & Casualty, Hartford, Conn., 1963-69, asst. actuary, 1969-71, assoc. actuary, 1971-72, dir, 1972-76, asst. v.p., 1976-80, v.p., 1980-85; pres., COO Gen. Accident Ins., 1985-91, chmn., CEO, 1991-98; chmn. CUG Ins., 1999—. With U.S. Army, 1963-64. Fellow Casualty Actuarial Soc., mem. Am. Acad. of Actuaries. Republican. Congregationalist. Office: CGU Ins 1 Beacon St Boston MA 02108-3107

FARNAN, JOSEPH JAMES, JR., federal judge; b. Phila., June 15, 1945; s. Joseph James and Philomena (DeLaurentis) F.; m. Patricia Candice Winner, June 28, 1969. BA, King's Coll., (Pa.), 1967; JD, U. Toledo Coll. Law, 1970. Bar: N.J. 1970, Del. 1972. Dir. crime justice program Wilmington Coll., New Castle, Del., 1970-73; pvt. practice law Wilmington, 1973-76; asst. pub. defender State Del., Wilmington, 1973-75; county atty. New Castle County, Wilmington, 1976-79; chief dep. atty. gen. Del. Dept. Justice, Wilmington, 1979-81; U.S. atty. U.S. Dept. Justice, Wilmington, 1981-85; judge U.S. Dist. Ct. Del., Wilmington, 1985—, now chief judge. Mem. ABA, Del. State Bar Assn., N.J. State Bar Assn., Am. Trail Lawyers Assn., Fed. Bar Assn. Republican. Roman Catholic. Office: US Dist Ct Federal Bldg 6325 844 N King St Ste 27 Wilmington DE 19801-3519*

FARNEN, TED WILLIAM, state legislator; b. Mexico, Mo., Sept. 3, 1965; s. John Kevin and Jane Carolyn (Paxson) F. BJ, U. Mo., 1987. Reporter Sedalia (Mo.) Dem., 1987-89; comms. specialist Mo. Senate, Jefferson City, Mo., 1989-94; state rep. Mo. House, Jefferson City, Mo., 1994—; mem. adv. bd. Arthur Ctr., Mexico, 1995—. Mem. Dem. Leadership Coun. Mem. Audrain County Hist. Soc., Boone County Muleskinners, Mo. Alumni Assn., Travelers Protective Assn., Mexico Noon Liions Club. Democrat. Roman Catholic. Home: 13 Wonneman Cir Mexico MO 65265-3140 Office: Mo Ho of Reps State Capitol Jefferson City MO 65101

FARNEY, DENNIS, journalist; b. Mar. 28, 1941; m. Peggy Farney; children: Ryan, Erin. BS in Journalism, U. Kans., 1963, MA in Polit. Sci., 1965. Reporter The Kansas City Star, 1965-66; reporter Dallas bur. Wall St. Jour., 1966-69, editor page 1 desk, 1969-70, feature editor Washington bur., 1970-74, corr. White House, 1974-78, Congl. and nat. polit. reporter, 1978-85, sr. spl. writer, 1985—. Finalist Pulitzer Prize, 1993; recipient Nat. Press Club award. Mem. Phi Beta Kappa. Office: Dow Jones & Co 200 Liberty St Fl 11 New York NY 10281-1099

FARNHAM, ANTHONY EDWARD, English language educator; b. Oakland, Calif., July 2, 1930; s. Willard Edward and Frances Fern (Hicks) F.; m. Frances Anne Larkey, Dec. 28, 1957; children: Allen Nicholas, Timothy John. A.B., U. Calif.-Berkeley, 1951; M.A., Harvard U., 1957, Ph.D., 1964. Instr. English Mt. Holyoke Coll., South Hadley, Mass., 1961-64, asst. prof., 1964-69, assoc. prof., 1969-72, prof., 1972-99, dept. chmn., 1979-85, prof. emeritus, 1999—. Editor: A Sourcebook in the History of English, 1969; author: Statement and Search in the Confessio Amantis, Mediaevalia 16, 1993. Served with M.I. U.S. Army, 1953-56. Mem. MLA, Am. Cath. Hist. Assn., Medieval Acad. Am., Assn. Literary Scholars and Critics, Dante Soc., New Chaucer Soc., Phi Beta Kappa. Roman Catholic. Home: 23 Atwood Rd South Hadley MA 01075-1601 Office: Mt Holyoke Coll Dept English South Hadley MA 01075

FARNHAM, CLAYTON HENSON, lawyer; b. New Brunswick, N.J., Aug. 18, 1938; s. Richard Bayles and Naomi Shropshire (Henson) F.; m. Katharine Gross, Sept. 16, 1967; children: Julia Kernan, Richard Bayles II. BA, U. of the South, 1961; LLB, U. Ga., 1967. Bar: Ga. 1968, U.S. Dist. Ct. (no., so. and mid. dists.) Ga. 1968, U.S. Supreme Ct. 1978, U.S. Dist. Ct. (no. dist.) Miss. 1978, U.S. Ct. Appeals (5th cir., 11th cir.) 1968, (4th cir.) 1980, U.S. Ct. Appeals (8th cir.) 1992. Law clk. to judge U.S. Dist. Ct., Atlanta, 1967-69; from assoc., to ptnr. Swift, Currie, McGhee & Hiers, Atlanta, 1969-82; ptnr. Drew, Eckl & Farnham, Atlanta, 1982—. Contbr. articles to profl. jours. Lt. (j.g.) USNR, 1961-64. Mem. ABA (coun. TIPS sect. 1989-92), Internat. Assn. Def. Counsel (com. chmn. 1987-89), Ansley Golf Club, Lawyer's Club Atlanta, Old War Horse Lawyer's Club. Home: 30 Inman Cir NE Atlanta GA 30309 Office: Drew Eckl & Farnham PO Box 7600 880 W Peachtree St NW Atlanta GA 30309

FARNHAM, SHERMAN BRETT, retired electrical engineer; b. New Haven, June 23, 1912; s. Charles Sherman and Antoinette (Brett) F.; children: Anne Valerie, John Brett. BS, Yale U., 1933, MEE, 1935. Registered profl. elec. engr., N.Y., Mass., N.J. Lab. asst. Yale U., New Haven, 1933-35; test engr. GE, Schenectady, N.Y., 1935-36; design engr. GE, Phila., 1936-37; application engr. GE, Schenectady, 1937-55; engring. mgr. GE, Boston, 1955-66; chief elec. engring. Chas T. Main, Inc., Boston, 1966-80, ret., 1980. Contbr. articles and tech. papers to profl. jours.; patentee in field. Fellow IEEE (chmn. Boston sect. 1962-63, Centennial medal 1984). Republican. Congregationalist. Avocations: travel, gardening. Home: 10 Rivermead Rd Peterborough NH 03458-1701

FARNSWORTH, E(DWARD) ALLAN, lawyer, educator; b. Providence, June 30, 1928; s. Harrison Edward and Gertrude (Romig) F.; m. Patricia Ann Nordstrom, May 30, 1952; children: Jeanne Scott, Karen Ladd, Edward Allan (dec.), Pamela Ann. BS, U. Mich., 1948; MA, Yale U., 1949; JD (Ordronaux prize 1952), Columbia U., 1952; LLD (hon.), Dickenson Law Sch., 1988; Docteur en Droit (hon.), U. Paris, 1988, U. Louvain, 1989. Bar: D.C 1952, N.Y. 1956. Mem. faculty Columbia U., N.Y.C., 1954—, prof. law, 1959—, Alfred McCormack prof. law, 1970—; vis. prof. U. Istanbul, U. Dakar, 1964, U. Paris, 1974-75, 90, 93, Harvard Law S ch., 1970-71, Stetson Coll. Law, 1991, 94, U. Mich., 1994; mem. faculty Salzburg Seminar Am. Law, 1963, Columbia-Leyden-Amsterdam program on Am. law, 1964, 69, 73, 85, San Diego Inst. Internat. and Comparative Law, Paris, 1982, 94, Tulane Summer Inst. Practice, Paris, 1995, 98, 99, Rhodes, 1996, China Ctr. for Am. Law Study, Beijing, 1986; dir. orientation program on Am. law Assn. Am. Law Schs., 1965-68; U.S. rep. UN Commn. on Internat. Trade Law, 1970-81; reporter Restatement of Contracts 2nd, 1971-80; cons. N.Y. State Law Revision Commn., 1956, 58, 59, 61, P.R. comml. code revision, 1988-91; mem. coms. validity and agy. internat. sales contracts Internat. Inst. Unification Pvt. Law, Rome, 1966-72, mem. governing coun., 1978—; mem. adv. com. on pvt. internat. law Sec. of State, 1985-89; spl. counsel city reorgn. N.Y.C. Coun., 1966-68; U.S. del. Vienna Conf. on Internat. Sales Law, 1980, Bucharest and Geneva Conf. on Internat. Agy., 1979, 83. Author: Changing Your Mind: The Law of Regretted Decisions, 1998, An Introduction to the Legal System of the United States, 3d edit., 1993; (with J. Honnold, S. Harris, C. Mooney, and C. Reitz) Cases and Materials on Commercial Law, 5th edit., 1993; (with W.F. Young) Cases and Materials on Contracts, 5th edit., 1995, Cases and Materials on Negotiable Instruments, 4th edit., 1993, Treatise on Contracts, 1982, 3d edit., 1999; (with V. Mozolin) Contract Law in the USSR and the United States, 1987, Farnsworth on Contracts, 3 vols., 1990, 2nd edit., 1998, United States Contract Law, 1992, 2d revised edit, 1999. Capt. USAAF, 1952-54. Fellow British Acad.; mem. ABA (Theberge award for pvt. internat. law 1996), Am. Philos. Soc., Am. Law Inst., Assn. of Bar of City of N.Y. (chmn. com. on fgn. and comparative law 1967-70, chmn. spl. com. on products liability 1979-82), Phi Beta Kappa, Phi Delta Phi. Unitarian. Home: 201 Lincoln St Englewood NJ 07631-3158 Office: Columbia U 435 W 116th St New York NY 10027-7201

FARNSWORTH, ELIZABETH, broadcast journalist; b. Mpls., Dec. 23, 1943; d. H. Bernerd and Jane (Mills) Fink; m. Charles E. Farnsworth, June 20, 1966; children: Jennifer Farnsworth Fellows, Samuel Mills. BA, Middlebury Coll., 1965; MA in History, Stanford U., 1966. Reporter, panelist PBS World Press, KQED, San Francisco, 1975-77; reporter InterNews, Berkeley, Calif., 1977-80; freelance TV and print reporter, San Francisco, 1980-91; fgn. corr. MacNeil/Lehrer News Hour, San Francisco, 1991-95; chief corr., prin. substitute anchor News Hour with Jim Lehrer, Arlington, Va., 1995-97, San Francisco, 1997—; mem. nat. adv. bd. Writers Corps, 1999—, U. Calif. Grad. Sch. Journalism, Berkeley, 1998—. Co-author: El Bloqueo Invisible, 1974; prodr., dir. documentary Thanh's War, 1991 (Cine Golden Eagle award); contbr. articles to various publs. Mem. adv. bd. Berkeley Edn. Found., 1990-95; bd. dirs. Media Alliance, San Francisco, 1985-87, Data Ctr., Oakland, Calif., 1993-95. Recipient Golden Gate award San Francisco Film Festival, 1984, Best Investigative Reporting award No. Calif. Radio, TV News Dirs.' Assn., 1986, Blue Ribbon, Am. Film and Video Festival, 1991. Mem. AFTRA, NATAS, World Affairs Coun. (bd. dirs. 1998—), Pacific Coun. on Internat. Policy. Presbyterian. Avocations: gardening, hiking, writing poetry.

FARNSWORTH, FRANK ALBERT, retired economics educator; s. Frank Adelbert and Lancing Claudine (Miller) F.; m. Ruth Coburn, June 26 1943 (dec. Dec. 1970); children: Frank A., Ruth Farnsworth McDowell, John C.; m. Elizabeth Hoyt Martire, Dec. 26, 1971 (dec. June 1988); children: Elizabeth Martire Cutter, Amy Martire, John Martire. AB in Econs. with honors, Colgate U., 1939; AM, Harvard U., 1946, PhD, 1952. With dept. econs. Colgate U., 1941-87, prof., 1957-87, ret., 1987; dept. chmn., vis. rsch. assoc. Grad. Bus. Sch., Harvard Coll., 1947-48; Fulbright prof. Norwegian Sch. Econs., Bergen, 1954-55; vis. prof. small bus. Wake Forest U., 1975; vis. fellow Massey Coll.-U. Toronto, Ont., Can., 1968; ex-officio mem. Madison County Indsl. Devel. Agy.; bd. dirs. Otter Valley Press, Inc., Tree Farmer, Sureseal Corp.; cons. in field. Mem. AAUP, N.Y. State Econ. Devel. Coun., Masons, Alpha Chi Epsilon, Alpha Delta Phi. Republican. Baptist. Home: 17 E Kendrick Ave Hamilton NY 13346-1311 also: 1119 Wheeler Rd Brandon VT 05733

FARNSWORTH, JOHN SEIBERT, writer; b. Valley Twp., Pa., June 1, 1954; s. F. Dennis and Barbara (Seibert) F.; m. Carol Freer, Aug. 29, 1977. BA, Coll. Santa Fe, 1975; MFA, Antioch U., 1999. Dir. Christian Outdoor Leadership Sch., Denver, 1975-79; dir. dept. youth ministry Cath. Diocese, Phoenix, 1979-81; dir. Nat. N.Y.O. Fedn., Washington, 1981; rep. youth ministries U.S. Cath. Conf., Washington, 1981-84; dir. dept. youth ministru Cath. Diocese, Monterey, Calif., 1984-89; campus min. Santa Catalina Sch., Monterey, Calif., 1989-94; lectr. in field. Author: The Parish Youth Mission, 1979, Issues in Delinquency Prevention, 1984, Implementing the Peace Pastoral, 1985, A Vision Remembered, 1986. Mem. Nat. Assn. Underwater Instrs., Sequoia YAcht Club. Avocations: sailing, scuba diving.

FARNSWORTH, ROBERT LAMBTON, poet, English educator; b. Apr. 8, 1954. BA, Brown U., 1976; MFA, Columbia U., 1979. Writer-in-residence, lectr. Bates Coll., Lewiston, Maine, 1990-99. Author: poems; poetry editor: The Americas Scholar, 1997—; contbr. poems to literary mags. E-mail: rfarnswo@bates.edu.

FARO, PATRICIA BAKER, school psychologist, consultant; b. Greenport, N.Y., Sept. 7, 1939; d. James Addison and Mary Madelyn (Montgomery) Baker; m. Robert Charles Faro, July 21, 1962 (div. Jan. 1989); children: Mary Elisabeth, Rebecca Ann. BA, Alfred U., 1961, MA in Psychology, 1962. Cert. sch. psychologist, N.Y., Mass.; lic. ednl. psychologist, Mass. Sch. psychologist Norfolk (Va.) City Schs., 1962-64, BOCES-Onandaga County, Syracuse, N.Y., 1964-67, Tewksbury (Mass.) Pub. Schs., 1978-84, Woburn (Mass.) Pub. Schs., 1984—; presch. cons. Tewksbury and Woburn, 1980—. Family life coord. Melrose (Mass.) Meth. Ch., 1976-80; parent vol. Melrose H.S. Band, 1981-89; polit. vol. Dukakis Presdl. Campaign, N.H., 1987. Recipient Block Parent award Melrose Police, 1981. Mem. APA (assoc.), NEA, Mass. Schs. Psychologists Assn., Woburn Tchrs. Assn., Kappa Delta Psi. Democrat. Avocations: reading, dancing, sports, needlework. Home: 90 Walton Park Melrose MA 02176-2104 Office: Shamrock Elem Sch Eastern Ave Woburn MA 01801

FARON, FAY CHERYL, private investigator, writer; b. Kansas City, Mo.; d. Albert David and Geraldine Fay (Morgan) F. Student, Glendale (Ariz.) C.C., 1967-68, Ariz. State U., 1968-71, U. Ariz., 1971-72. Lic. pvt. investigator, Calif. Owner Monogramation, San Francisco, 1976-80; assoc. prodr. Sta. KGO-TV, San Francisco, 1980-81, Power/Rector, San Francisco, 1982-83; owner Office in the City, San Francisco, 1982-83, The Rat Dog Dick Detective Agy., San Francisco, 1983—; lectr., guest spkr. San Francisco U., 1984—, San Francisco Assn. Legal Assts., 1984—, Commonwealth Club San Francisco, 1987, Calif. Collectors Coun., San Francisco, 1992—, Book Passage Mystery Writers Conf., 1997-98. Author: A Private Eye's Guide to Collecting a Bad Debt, 1991, Missing Persons, 1997; author/editor: The Instant National Locator Guide, 1991, 2nd edit., 1993, 3rd edit, 1996, Rip-Off, 1998; columnist Ask Rat Dog, 1993—. Co-founder, pres. bd. Elder Angels, San Francisco. Subject of Jack Olsen's book, Hastened to the Grave, 1998. Mem. Nat. Assn. Investigative Specialists, Nat. Assn. Bunco Investigators (asst.), Profls. Against Confidence Crimes (asst.), Sisters in Crime. Avocations: biking, camping, horseback riding, river rafting, travel. Office: The Rat Dog Dick Detective Agy PO Box 470862 San Francisco CA 94147-0862

FARONE, BRIGID ANN, nursing administrator; b. Cleve., Ohio, Dec. 11, 1961; d. Wilfred Patrick and Anna Mae (Pelko) Mannion; m. Gregory Alan Farone, May 2, 1987; 1 child, Alexandria Marie. Diploma, St. Alexis Hosp. Sch. Nursing, 1983; BSN, Ursuline Coll., 1991. Cert. nursing adminstr. Nursing asst. St. Michael Hosp. (formerly St. Alexis Hosp.), Cleve., 1983-84, staff nurse, 1984-85, nurse mgr., 1985-89, mgr. nursing projects/programs, 1989-91, acting asst. dir. nursing, 1990-91, mgr. med.-surg. nursing, 1991-92, dir. nursing, 1992—; clin. instr. nursing Case Western Res. U., 1995—. Mem. NAFE, Nat. League Nursing, Ohio League Nursing (sec./treas. northeast region 1994-95, treas. adminstrs. coun. 1993-95, chair 1995-99, pres. 1999—), Lake Erie Orgn. Nurse Execs. Roman Catholic. Avocations: crocheting, cooking, gardening, reading, family. Office: St Michael Hosp 5163 Broadway Ave Cleveland OH 44127-1593

FAROUDJA, PHILIPPE YVES, television director; b. San Jose, Calif., Feb. 17, 1968; s. Yves Charles and Isabell Emily (O'Brien) F. BA, Wesleyan U., Middletown, Conn., 1990; MFA, UCLA, 1994. Devel. asst. Hanna-Barbera Cartoons, 1994-95, prodr's asst. The Real Adventures of Johny Quest, 1995—; assoc. prodr. What a Cartoon! Cartoon Network, 1996—; Cons. artist Lumysis Corp., Sunnyvale, Calif., 1996. Patentee in field. Mem. Soc. Motion Picture and TV Engrs., Phi Beta Kappa. Avocations: soccer, tennis, skeet shooting, archery, cello. Home: 1437 S Westgate Ave Apt 16 Los Angeles CA 90025-2241

FARQUHAR, JAMES, geochemist, researcher; b. Chgo., Jan. 6, 1965; s. James Douglas and Sue (Wakeman) F.; m. Lisa Joan Tuit, Dec. 31, 1994; children: James Henry. BS, Washington and Lee U., 1987; MSc, U. Chgo., 1990; PhD, U. Alta., Edmonton, Alta., Can., 1995. Fellow Carnegie Instn. Washington, 1995-97; NSF fellow U. Calif., San Diego, 1997—. Contbr. articles to jours. including Nature, Sci., Geochimica and Cosmochimica Acta, Earth and Planetary Sci. Letters. Killam grad. fellow Killam Found.,

Can., 1993-95. Mem. AAAS, Am. Geophys. Union, Mineral. Soc. Am., Geochem. Soc.

FARQUHAR, JOHN WILLIAM, physician, educator; b. Winnipeg, Man., Can., June 13, 1927; came to U.S., 1934; s. John Giles and Marjorie Victoria (Roberts) F.; m. Christine Louise Johnson, July 14, 1968; children: Margaret F., John C.M.; children by previous marriage: Bruce E., Douglas G. A.B., U. Calif., Berkeley, 1949; M.D., U. Calif., San Francisco, 1952. Intern U. Calif. Hosp., San Francisco, 1952-53; resident, 1953-54, 57-58, postdoctoral fellow, 1955-57; resident U. Minn., Mpls., 1954-55; research asso. Rockefeller U., N.Y.C., 1958-62; asst. prof. medicine Stanford (Calif.) U., 1962-66, asso. prof., 1966-73, prof., 1978-97; dir. Stanford Wellness Ctr., 1998—; C.F. Rehnborg prof. in disease prevention Stanford (Calif.) U., 1989—; dir. Stanford Ctr. Research in Disease Prevention, 1973-98; dir. collaborating ctr. for chronic disease prevention WHO, 1985—; prof. health rsch. and policy, 1988—; mem. staff Stanford U. Hosp.; chair Victoria Declaration Implementation com. Author: The American Way of Life Need Not Be Hazardous to Your Health, 1978, 2d edit., 1987, (with Gene Spiller) The Last Puff, 1990, The Victoria Declaration for Heart Health, 1992, How to Reduce Your Risk of Heart Disease, 1994, The Catalonia Declaration: Investing in Heart Health, 1996, Worldwide Efforts to Improve Heart Disease, 1997; contbr. articles to profl. jours. Served with U.S. Army, 1945-46. Recipient James D. Bruce award ACP, 1983, Myrdal prize, 1986, Dana award for Pioneering Achievement in Health, Dana Found., 1990, Nat. Cholesterol award for Pub. Edn., Nat. Cholesterol Edn. Program of NIH, 1991, Rsch. Achievement award Am. Heart Assn., 1992, Order of St. George for Svc. to Autonomous Govt. of Catalonia, 1996. Mem. Inst. Medicine of NAS, Am. Soc. Clin. Investigation, Am. Heart Assn. (coun. epidemiology and prevention), Soc. Behavioral Medicine (pres. 1991-92), Gold Headed Cane Soc., Sigma Xi, Alpha Omega Alpha. Episcopalian. Office: Stanford U Sch of Medicine Ctr Rsch in Disease Prevention 730 Welch Rd Palo Alto CA 94304-1506

FARQUHAR, MARILYN GIST, cell biology and pathology educator; b. Tulare, Calif., July 11, 1928; d. Brooks DeWitt and Alta (Green) Gist; m. John W. Farquhar, June 4, 1952; children: Bruce, Douglas (div. 1968); m. George Palade, June 7, 1970. AB, U. Calif., Berkeley, 1949, MA, 1952, PhD, 1955. Asst. rsch. pathologist Sch. Medicine U. Calif., San Francisco, 1956-58, assoc. rsch. pathologist, 1962-64, assoc. prof., 1964-68, prof. pathology, 1968-70; rsch. assoc. Rockefeller U., N.Y.C., 1958-62, prof. cell biology, 1970-73; prof. cell biology Sch. Medicine Yale U., New Haven, 1973-87, Sterling prof. cell biology and pathology, 1987-90; prof. pathology div. cell molecular medicine U. Calif., San Diego, 1990—, coord. div. cellular and molecular medicine, 1991—. Mem. editorial bd. numerous sci. jours.; contbr. articles to profl. jours. Recipient Career Devel. award NIH, 1968-73, Disting. Sci. medal Electron Microscope Soc., 1987. Mem. NAS, Am. Acad. Arts and Scis., Am. Soc. Cell Biology (pres. 1981-82, E.B. Wilson medal 1987), Am. Assn. Investigative Pathology, Am. Soc. Nephrology (Homer Smith award 1988). Home and Office: U Calif Sch Med 12894 Via Latina Del Mar CA 92014-3730

FARQUHAR, ROBERT MICHAEL, lawyer; b. Chelsea, Mass., Apr. 28, 1954; s. Robert Vociel and Helen Margaret (Stevens) F.; m. Carol Elizabeth Auch, Dec. 16, 1978; children: Stephanie Elizabeth, Andrew Michael. BS, So. Meth. U., 1977, JD, 1980. Bar: Tex. 1980, U.S. Dist. Ct. (no. and ea. dists.) Tex. 1980, U.S. Ct. Appeals (5th and 11th cirs.) 1980, U.S. Supreme Ct. 1990; cert. bus. bankruptcy law Tex. Bd. Legal Specialization. Assoc. Carter Jones MaGee Rudberg Moss & Mayes, Dallas, 1980-82; ptnr. Johnson & Cravens, Dallas, 1982-88; shareholder Winstead Sechrest & Minick, P.C., Dallas, 1988—. Mem. ABA, Dallas Bar Assn. Republican. Episcopalian. Avocations: bicycling, computers. Office: Winstead Sechrest Minick PC 1201 Elm St Ste 5400 Dallas TX 75270-2199

FARQUHAR, ROBIN HUGH, former university president; b. Victoria, B.C., Can., Dec. 1, 1938; s. Hugh Ernest and Jean (MacIntosh) F.; m. Frances Harriet Caswell, July 6, 1963; children: Francine Jean, Katherine Lynn, Susan Ann. B.A. with honors, U. B.C., 1960, M.A., 1964; Ph.D., U. Chgo., 1967; Hon. Diploma in Adult Edn., Red River C.C., 1989. Tchr., counsellor, coach Edward Milne Secondary Sch., Sooke, B.C., 1962-64; assoc. dir., then dep. dir. Univ. Council Ednl. Adminstrn., Columbus, Ohio, 1966-71; chmn. ednl. adminstrn. dept., asst. dir. Ont. Inst. Studies in Edn., Toronto, 1971-76; prof. U. Toronto, 1974-76; prof., dean Coll. Edn., U. Sask., Saskatoon, 1976-81; prof., pres. U. Winnipeg, 1981-89; prof., pres. Carleton U., Ottawa, Ont., 1989-96, prof. pub. adminstrn., 1996—. Author: The Humanities in Preparing Educational Administrators, 1970, Preparing Educational Leaders: A Review of Recent Literature, 1972; editor: Social Science Content for Preparing Educational Leaders, 1973, Educational Administration in Australia and Abroad: Analyses and Challenges, 1975, Canadian and Comparative Educational Administration, 1980, The Canadian School Superintendent, 1989, Advancing Education: School Leadership in Action, 1991; mem. editorial bd. Jour. Edn. Adminstrn., 1973-86. Served with Can. Navy Res., 1956-64. Recipient Edward L. Bernays Found. prize, 1968, Commemorative medal for 125th Anniversary of Confedn. of Can., 1993, Ottawa-Carleton Partnership award of excellence for leadership, 1996, Can. Bur. Internat. Edn. award of Merit, 1998; named Hon. Citizen, City of Winnipeg, 1989; hon. mem. Scouts Can., 1992. Fellow Commonwealth Coun. Ednl. Adminstrn. (former pres.); mem. Can. Bur. Internat. Edn. (former chmn.), Can. Soc. Study Edn. (former pres.), Can. Edn. Assn. (former dir.), InterAm. Soc. for Ednl. Adminstrn. (former dir.), Ottawa-Carleton Econ. Devel. Corp. (former dir.), Ottawa-Carleton Rsch. Inst. (former dir.), Corp. Higher Edn. Forum (former dir.), Nat. Acad. of Sch. Execs. (former dir.).

FARQUHARSON, GORDON MACKAY, lawyer; b. Charlottetown, P.E.I., Can., July 12, 1928; s. Percy Alfred and Rachel Lillian (MacKay) F.; m. Judy Lynne Bridges, Oct. 10, 1980; children: Trevor, Jordan; children by previous marriage: Douglas, Tanyss, Rob, Caryn. B.A., U. Toronto, 1950; LL.B., Osgoode Hall Law Sch., 1954. Bar: Called to Ont. bar 1954; Queen's Counsel 1965. Pvt. practice Toronto, 1954—; ptnr. Lang Michener, 1964—; dir. Valleydene Corp. Ltd., NN Life Ins. Co., Shaw Industries Ltd., Doverhold Investments Ltd., Can. Group Underwriters Inst. co., The commerce Group Ins. Co., The Halifax Inst. Co., The Nordic Inst. Co. Can., Wellington House Co., Western Union Ins. Co.; chmn. bd. dirs. CLC Downsview Inc. Mem. University Club (Toronto), Craigleigh Ski Club, Phi Gamma Delta (pres. 1954). Home: 419 Brunswick Ave, Toronto, ON Canada Office: BCE Pl, 181 Bay St Ste 2500, Toronto, ON Canada M5J 2T7

FARQUHARSON, PATRICE ELLEN, primary school educator; b. West Haven, Conn., Feb. 10, 1956; d. Robert Douglas and Margaret Ellen (Dietle) F. BS in Edn., U. Conn., 1978; MS in Edn., So. Conn. State U., 1984; EdD, Nova Southeastern U., 1995. Cert. tchr., adminstr., Conn. Asst. dir. West Haven (Conn.) Child Devel. Ctr., 1978-82, exec. dir., 1982-96, 97—; edn. cons. dept. pediatrics div. child and family studies U. Conn., 1993-95; mgmt. cons. West Haven Child Devel. Ctr., Inc., 1996—; asst. prof. early childhood, dir. early childhood programs Teikyo-Post U., Waterbury, Conn., 1996—; adj. prof. U. Conn. Inst. Pub. Policy, 1996; cons. early childhood edn., workshop presenter, internat. and New Eng., 1987—; profl. cheerleader The New Eng. Patriots football team, 1980; dir., ptnr. New Eng. Cheerleading Camp, West Haven, 1982-84; cheerleading coach U. New Haven, 1982-90. Conn. Early Childhood Edn. Coun. scholar, 1993-96. Mem. Nat. Assn. Edn. Young Children, Conn. Assn. Edn. Young Children, Coalition for Children, Dirs. Forum, Gov. Adv. Coun. Early Childhood Edn., South Ctrl. Conn. Agy. on Aging (adv. coun.). Avocations: ballet, jazz dancing, horseback riding, reading, traveling. Home: 5 Sunflower Cir West Haven CT 06516-6229 Office: West Haven Child Devel Ctr 201 Noble St West Haven CT 06516-6047

FARR, CAROLE ANNE KLEINRICHERT, retired model, investor; b. Ft. Wayne, Ind., Feb. 11, 1939; d. Russell P. Fairfield and Margaret V. Stark; (div. June 1987); children: Michelle Binzel, Charles K., Ann K., Sheila K. Grad., Bobby Ray Finishing Sch., Ft. Wayne, 1959. Profl. model Wolf & Deshour, Inc., Ft. Wayne, 1958-78; inspector GE, Ft. Wayne, 1979-81, Magnavox Corp., Ft. Wayne, 1982-85; instr. Bankers Dispatch, Ft. Wayne, 1986-89; ind. investor C.K. Investors, Deerfield Beach, Fla., 1989—; swimming tchr. Wawasee H.S., 1986-87. Active Young Reps., Ind., 1977; bd. dirs. Enchanted Hills Playhouse, 1981-83. Mem. Single Sailors South Fla. Roman Catholic. Avocations: sailing, tennis, bridge. Home: 2720 NE 29th St Lighthouse Point FL 33064 Home: 26 Eel River Rd East Falmouth MA 02536

FARR, DONALD EUGENE, engineering scientist; b. Clinton, Iowa, July 1, 1933; s. Kenneth Elroy and Nellie Irene (Bailey) F.; m. Sally Joyce Brauer, Mar. 8, 1954; children: Erika Lyn Farr Leventis, Jolene Karyn Farr Walters. BA in Engring. Psychology, San Diego State U., 1961; MT with honors, Nat. U., 1974; postgrad., Calif. Pacific U., 1976-80. Human factors specialist Bunker Ramo Corp., Canoga Park, Calif., Germany, 1964-69; sr. design specialist Gen. Dynamics, San Diego, 1955-63, 69-76; tech. staff Sandia Nat. Labs., Albuquerque, 1977-80; group supr., sr. tech. advisor The Babcock and Wilcox Co., Lynchburg, Va., 1980-82; dir. human factors sys. Sci. Applications, Inc., Lynchburg, 1982-83; human engring. scientist Lockheed Calif. Co., Burbank, 1983-91; MANPRINT mgr. Teledyne Electronic Sys., Northridge, Calif., 1991-94; human engring. scientist, program mgr. Symvionics, Inc., Pasadena, Calif., 1994—; ergonomics safety cons. govt., industry and academia, 1977—. Contbr. articles to profl. jours. Precinct capt., voter registration vol. Rep. Party, 1963—; lectr., support group Am. Diabetes Assn., L.A., 1993—. With USN, 1952-53. Scholarship USN, 1953; recipient Admiral's award NSIA, 1963. Mem. Human Factors and Ergonomics Soc. (pres. San Diego, L.A. chpt.), Internat. Numismatic Soc. (pres. 1973-75), Am. Nuclear Soc. (human factors chair 1980-82), Am. Legion, NRA Golden Eagles (honor role). Lutheran. Avocations: bridge, numismatics, genealogy, computer graphics, travel. Home: 20054 Avenue Of The Oaks Newhall CA 91321-1361 Office: Symvionics Inc 3280 E Foothill Blvd Ste 200 Pasadena CA 91107-3187

FARR, G(ARDNER) NEIL, lawyer; b. L.A., Jan. 9, 1932; s. Gardner and Elsie M. (Schuster) F.; m. Lorna Jean, Oct. 26, 1957; children: Marshall Clay, Jennifer T., Thomas M. BA, U. Calif., Berkeley, 1957, JD, U. Calif., San Francisco, 1960. Bar: Calif. 1961, U.S. Supreme Ct. 1977. Cert specialist family law Calif. Bd. Specialization, 1980. Dep. dist. atty. Solano County, 1961-66; recreation commr. City of Fairfield, 1964-66; dep. dist. atty. Kern County, 1966-69; ptnr. Young, Wooldridge, Paulden, Self, Farr & Hugie (now Law Offices of Young Wooldridge), Bakersfield, Calif., 1969—; dir. Cen. Calif. Appellate Program, Inc.; judge protem Kern County Superior Ct. Chmn. Kern County Juvenile Justice Commn. With USNR, 1949-53. Mem. ABA, Calif. Bar Assn., Kern County Bar Assn. (pres. 1984, past pres. family law sect.). Fax: (805) 327-1087. Office: Young Wooldridge 1800 30th St Fl 4 Bakersfield CA 93301-1919

FARR, GEORGE F., federal official; b. Oak Park, Ill., Aug. 26, 1936; s. George F. and Evelyn Florence (Eigelberner) F.; m. Judith Banzer, June 30, 1962; 1 child, Alec Winfield. BA, Yale U., 1958, PhD in English, 1970. Asst. prof. English U. Calif., Berkeley, 1963-66, Vassar Coll., Poughkeepsie, N.Y., 1968-76; asst. dir. rsch. programs NEH, Washington, 1976-82, dep. dir. pub. programs, 1982-85, dep. dir. challenge grants, 1985-87, dir. preservations & access programs, 1987—; mem. task force Nat. Inst. Conservation, Nat. Park Svc.; mem. Wenner-Gren Found. Planning Conf.; mem. nat. adv. bd. MLA. Created fed. grant program for cataloging and preserving U.S. newspapers on a state-by-state basis (U.S. Newspaper Program), 1979—, nat. grant programs for the preservation of brittle books and serials, 1989—, for the preservation of material culture collections in museums and hist. socs., 1990—. Vestry mem. St. Mark's Episcopal Ch., Berkeley, 1965-68, St. Alban's Episcopal Ch., Washington, 1980-83. Carnegie Found. Prize Teaching fellow, 1958-59, Wilmarth Lewis Farmington fellow, 1960-61. Mem. Sr. Exec. Svc. of U.S. Avocations: history of art, opera, swimming. Home: 5064 Lowell St NW Washington DC 20016 Office: NEH 1100 Pennsylvania Ave NW Washington DC 20506

FARR, HENRY BARTOW, JR., lawyer; b. N.Y.C., June 16, 1921; s. H. Bartow and Mildred (Blair) F.; m. Mary Elizabeth Roberts, Jan. 22, 1972; children: H. Bartow, Preston Witherspoon, Christopher Blair. B.A. magna cum laude, Princeton U., 1943; LL.B. (Stone scholar), Columbia U., 1948. Bar: U.S. Ct. Appeals (2d Cir.) 1950, U.S. Dist. Ct. 1950. Asso. Sullivan & Cromwell, 1948-53; asst. atty. gen. N.Y. State Crime Commn., 1951-53; asso. Wilkie, Farr & Gallagher, N.Y.C., 1953-58; mng. atty. IBM, N.Y.C., 1959-64, Armonk, N.Y., 1964-65; group counsel data processing group IBM, Harrison, N.Y., 1965-68; v.p., gen. counsel World Trade Corp., N.Y.C., 1968-72; v.p., gen. counsel, sec. World Trade Corp., 1972-74, World Trade Europe, Paris, 1974-77; v.p., gen. counsel Singer Co., N.Y.C., 1977-80; dep. gen. counsel R.J. Reynolds Industries, Inc., Winston-Salem, N.C., 1980-86. Served with USNR, 1943-46. Home: 1020 W Kent Rd Winston Salem NC 27104-1130

FARR, JUDITH BANZER, writer, literature educator; b. N.Y.C., Mar. 13, 1937; d. Russell John and Frances Anna (Wissell) Banzer; m. George F. Farr, Jr., June 30, 1962; 1 child, Alec Winfield. *Judith Farr's father was a professional musician and recording artist, a bassoonist with the NBC Staff and Symphony Orchestras and the Miami Symphony. Her mother studied at Parsons School of Design and was a decorator before marriage. She met her husband George as PhD students at Yale. He is now director of the Division of Preservation & Access at the National Endowment for the Humanities, the office devoted to preserving the nation's material culture: libraries, newspapers, film, artistic and cultural documents. Son Alec, an attorney, is an expert on copyright law and, with his lawyer wife Andrea, the parents of twins, Katherine and Matthew.* BA, Marymount Manhattan Coll., 1957, LHD, 1992; MA, Yale U., 1959, PhD, 1965. Instr. in English Vassar Coll., Poughkeepsie, N.Y., 1961-63; asst. prof. St. Mary's Coll., Moraga, Calif., 1964-68; assoc. prof. SUNY, New Paltz, 1968-77; assoc. prof. Georgetown U., Washington, 1978-90, prof. of English and Am. Lit., 1990-99, prof. emerita, 1999—; vis. assoc. prof. Georgetown U., 1977-78. *Farr was a protege of Marianne Moore and Cleanth Brooks, publishing her first poem at sixteen in a contest Moore sponsored. Her writing career has taken two related directions - in scholarship, and in fiction and poetry. Many recent works - a novel, poems, and criticism - focus on topics concerning classical painting and painters. Thus, she has lectured and given readings at many museums and galleries (e.g. the National Gallery and the National Museum of Women in the Arts) as well as for universities, radio and television.* Author: The Life and Art of Elinor Wylie, 1983, The Passion of Emily Dickinson, 1992, I Never Came to You in White: A Novel, 1996; editor: Twentieth Century Interpretations of Sons and Lovers, 1970, New Century Views: Emily Dickinson, 1995; contbr. articles, poems, short stories to profl. and comml. publs. Am. Philos. Soc. fellow, 1983, Morgan-Porter fellow Yale U., 1960-61; grantee Am. Coun. Learned Socs., 1984, 86, N.Y. State Rsch. FOund., 1974, Georgetown U. Ctr. German Studies, 1992; recipient Alumnae award for Distinction in Arts and Letters, Marymount Manhattan Coll., N.Y.C., 1976, Alpha Sigma Nu Best Book award, 1993. Mem. AAUP, Modern Lang. Assn., Cosmos Club. Avocations: antiques, especially 18th century china, gardening, American painting. Office: Georgetown U 330 New North Hall 37th St and O Washington DC 20057

FARR, LEONARD ALFRED, hospital administrator; b. Pleasant Hill, La., Mar. 19, 1947. BA, La. State U., 1969; MA, Washington U., 1974. Adminstr. resident HCA Wesley Med. Ctr., Wichita, Kans., 1973-74, night adminstr., 1974-75; asst. adminstr. Physicians & Surgeons Hosp., Shreveport, La., 1975, exec. v.p., 1975-76; adminstr. Colo. Springs. (Colo.) Community Hosp., 1976-78; pres., CEO St. Francis Hosp. Systems, Colo. Springs, Colo., 1978-87; COO Penrose-St. Francis Hosp., Colo. Springs, 1987-91, pres., CEO, 1991—; s.r. v.p. United HealthCare, Mpls., 1997; COO ret. and sr. svcs. Am. Assn. Ret. Persons, Mpls., 1997—. Mem. Am. Hosp. Assn. (alternate del., del.), Colo. Hosp. Assn. (chmn. bd.). Office: United Health Group Mail Stop MN008 EZ10 PO Box 1459 Minneapolis MN 55440-1459*

FARR, LONA MAE, non-profit executive, business owner; b. Phila., June 4, 1941; d. Alonzo Schroeder and Lillyan (Nickels) F.; m. Malcolm J. Gross, Aug. 24, 1963 (div. Mar. 1976); children: Andrea Lillyan, Stacey Jane, John Farr; m. David V. Voellinger, Sept. 27, 1981. AB in History and English, Muhlenberg Coll., 1962; MS in Edn., Temple U., 1968; PhD in Philanthropy, Union Inst., 1995. Advanced cert. in fund raising. Tchr. Swain Sch., Allentown, Pa., 1962-63, St. Monica's Sch., Berwyn, Pa., 1963-65, Hebrew Day Sch., Scranton, Pa., 1965-66; pub. rels. assoc. Muhlenberg Coll., Allentown, 1973-75, dir. alumni affairs, 1975-77; dir. devel. and pub. rels. Allentown Coll. St. Frances de Sales, Allentown, 1977-81; dir. pub. rels. Good Shepherd Home, Allentown, 1981-84, dir. devel., 1984-87, group exec., v.p. instnl. devel., 1987-92; v.p. instl. devel. Luth. Home at Topton, Pa., 1992-96; spl. adv. to pres. Luth. Home at Topton, 1996—; prin. Baxter, Farr, Thomas and Weinstein Ltd., 1996—. Prodr. (films) More Than a Name, 1983 (Golden Eagle award 1984), Venture of Faith, 1984 (silver medal N.Y. Film Festival 1985), Spirit of Good Shepherd Day, 1987, Aspects of Topton, 1993 (1st place PANPHA), Topton New Century, 1993 (1st place PANPHA), They Came to Topton, 1994, A Gift of Love, 1995, (video) The Best You Can Be, 1988. Bd. dirs. Muhlenberg Coll.; past bd. dirs. Kids Peace, Allentown Symphony, Baum Sch. Art, Allentown; past bd. dirs. United Way Lehigh Valley; past adviser Lehigh County Human Svcs., Allentown, 1986-91. Recipient Disting. Sales award Sales and Mktg. Execs. Lehigh Valley, 1984, 1st place award in mktg. and pub. rels. Pa. Assn. Nonprofit Homes for Aging, 1994. Mem. Pub. Rels. Soc. Am., Nat. Soc. Hosp. Devel., Nat. Soc. Fund Raising Execs. (past chair cert. bd., vice chair external rels. bd. dirs. 1987—, founding pres. Ea. Pa. chpt. 1986-88, Girl Scout Disting Alumni award, Outstanding Exec. award 1988, Fund Raising Exec. of Yr. 1988), Appalachian Health Care Pub. Rels./Mktg. Assn. (pres. 1987), Ea. Pa. BBB (bd. dirs.), Muhlenberg Coll. Alumni Assn. (pres. 1981-85), Liberty Bell Rotary (Allentown, pres. 1993-94), Quota Club (pres. Allentown 1986-88). Avocations: reading, walking, travel, gourmet cooking. Home and Office: 2238 W Chew St Allentown PA 18104-5548 *To live life to its fullest, endeavor each day to reach out to others in love: open your mind to learn something new, and lead others to do the same. This is living by what I call the Four "L's".*

FARR, MARCIA ELIZABETH, English and Linguistics educator; b. Berkeley, Calif., Mar. 25, 1944; d. Richard Arthur and Mary Margaret (Bollinger) F.; m. David Lee Whiteman, July 30, 1966 (div. July 1981); 1 child, Julianna Downing; m. Michael David Maltz, Dec. 2, 1984; stepchildren: David Selby, Robert Reeves. BA in English, Ohio Wesleyan U., 1965; MA in Linguistics, Am. U., 1970; PhD in Linguistics, Georgetown U., 1976. Sr. rsch. assoc. Nat. Inst. of Edn., Washington, 1976-82; assoc. to full prof. English and linguistics U. Ill., Chgo., 1982—; adv. bd. Ctr. for the Study of Writing, U. Calif., Berkeley, 1986-96. Co-author: Language Diversity and Writing Instruction, 1986; editor: Variation in Writing, 1981; author: (with others) Cultural Performances, 1994, Literacy Across Communities, 1994; editl. bds. jours.; gen. editor rsch. series Hampton Press, Cresskill, N.J., 1992—, Ablex Publs., Norwood, N.J., 1982-92. Rsch. fellow in Mex., Fulbright Found., 1995-96; rsch. grant Spencer Found., 1995-98, 1990-93, 99—, NSF, 1988-90; recipient Mentor Network award Spencer Found., 1995-97. Fellow Am. Anthropol. Assn.; mem. Am. Assn. for Applied Linguistics (exec. com., program chair 1981), Internat. Assessment of Literacy (U.S. nat. com.), Nat. Coun. of Tchrs. of English (commn. on English lang.). Avocations: Mexican folkloric dance, nutritional cooking, mystery novels and films. Office: Dept of English U Ill at Chgo M/C 162 601 S Morgan St Chicago IL 60607-7120

FARR, SAM, congressman; b. Calif., July 4, 1941; m. Shary Baldwin; 1 child, Jessica. BSc Biology, Willamette U., 1963; student, Monterey Inst. Internat. Studies, U. Santa Clara. Vol. Peace Corps, 1963-65; budget analyst, cons. Assembly com. Constl. Amendments; bd. suprs. Monterey (Calif.) County; rep. Calif. State Assembly, 1980-93; mem., regional whip 103d U.S. Congress (now 106th Congress) from 17th Calif. dist., 1993—; mem. agr. com., mem. resources com. 103d U.S. Congress. Named Legislator of Yr. Calif. 9 times. Democrat. Avocations: photography, skiing, fly fishing, Spanish. Office: Ho of Reps 1221 Longworth Bldg Office Bldg Washington DC 20515-0517

FARR, WARREN EARL, artist; b. Ft. Wayne, Ind., Jan. 21, 1949; s. William Dobson and Harriette Lorene (Petersen) F. Student, U. Ky., 1967-69. Draftsman Chgo. Telephone Supply of Paducah, Inc., Ky., 1970-77, Voice/Comm. Coil Co., Paducah, 1977-85; computer programmer Petter Supply Co., Paducah, 1985; software designer, programmer Pebco, Inc., Paducah, 1985. Designer logo Paducah Coop. Ministry, 1980, Habitat for Humanity of Paducah, 1982, Computalk, 1984; designer, programmer 3 entertainment programs for TRS-80 Home Computer; author, artist: Desperate for Love: Poems by An Artist, 1995; one-man shows include Yeiser Art Ctr., Paducah, 1997; exhibited in group shows at Nat. Arts Club, N.Y.C., 1987, Owensboro (Ky.) Mus. Fine Art, 1987, Corcoran Gallery of Art, Washington, 1989, New Harmony (Ind.) Gallery of Contemporary Art, 1990, Cheekwood Mus. Art, Nashville, 1994, New Orleans Mus. Art, 1995, Yeiser Art Ctr.; represented in permanent collections Jackson Purchase Electric Coop., Hilliard and Lyons, Owensboro Nat. Bank, Yeiser Art Ctr., East Tenn. State U., Evansville Mus. Arts and Sci. Treas. Yeiser Art Ctr., Paducah, 1975-76, active artist chmn., 1988-90. Recipient artist fellowships Ky. Arts Coun., Frankfort, 1987, 98, Award of Excellence Huntington (W.Va.) Mus. Art, 1988, So. Arts Fedn., Atlanta, 1990, artist grant Pollock-Krasner Found., N.Y.C., 1992, mus. purchase award Evansville (Ind.) Mus. Art & Sci., 1996. Mem. Am. Numismatic Assn., U.S. Chess Fedn., Poets of Western Rivers, Philosophy Round Table (founder, coord. local discussion group). Avocations: reading, old movies, hiking, jogging, photography. Home: 1018 Davis Ave Paducah KY 42001-7721

FARRAGHER, CLARE M., state legislator; b. Richmond Hill, N.Y., Dec. 11, 1941; m. Liam; children: Irene, Ann Marie, Kathleen, Mary Clare. Student, St. John's U. Mem. N.J. Assembly, Trenton, 1987—; asst. minority whip, 1990-91, dep. spkr., 1989-90, 96—, mem. Legis. Svcs. Commn., 1990-95, vice-chair ins. com., mem. trans. and comm. com., chmn. pub. works dept. and ad hoc recycling com.; mem. Am. Legis. Exch. Coun., 1987—, N.J. chmn., 1990—; mem. Nat. Conf. Ins. Legislators, 1992—, v.p., 1998, pres.-elect, 1999. Former sr. citizen liaison Freehold Twp., committeewoman, 1982-91, police commr., 1984; dep. mayor, 1984, 88, mayor, 1985; mem. Monmouth County Rep. Com., 1978—; treas. Freehold Twp. Rep. Club; mem. exec. com. Rep. Women of 90's. Named Ins. Legislator of Yr., Am. Legis. Exch. Coun., 1995. Mem. Nat. Order Women Legislators, Nat. Coun. Ins. Legislators (v.p.), N.J. Assn. Elected Women Ofcls. (bd. dirs.). Home: 21 Holland Ridge Blvd Freehold NJ 07728-8228 Office: 3rd Fl 400 W Main St Ste 3 Freehold NJ 07728-2539

FARRAKHAN, LOUIS, religious leader; b. N.Y.C., May 11, 1933; changed name from Louis Eugene Wolcott to Louis X, then to Louis Farrakhan; m. Betsy Wolcott; 9 children. Student, Winston-Salem (N.C.) Tchrs. Coll. Formerly leader of Harlem mosque Nation of Islam, N.Y.C., nat. spokesman; founder reorganized orgn. Nation of Islam, 1977. Office: Nation of Islam 7351 S Stony Island Ave Chicago IL 60649*

FARRALL, HAROLD JOHN, retired accountant; b. Harvard, Nebr., Mar. 25, 1918; s. John William and Olive Almira (Frazell) F. BSBA, Nebr. U., 1940. Clerk teletype ctr. Bur. Aeronautics, Washington, 1946-47; cost acct. Bur. Reclamation Br. Office Region 7, Grand Island, Nebr., 1948-53; fin. officer Bur. Reclamation Br. Office Region 7, Ainsworth, Nebr., 1953-54; payroll acct. to supervisory operating acct. Bur. Reclamation Hdqs. Region 7, Denver, Colo., 1955-72; accts. payable supr. Dutton-Lainson Co., Hastings, Nebr., 1974-85; ret., 1985. Author: The Rise and Fall of the United States, 1990, 2d edit., 1998. With U.S. Army, 1941-45. Regents scholarship U. Nebr., 1936. Mem. DAV, VFW, Am. Legion, Ind. order of Odd Fellows, Fed. Govt. Accts. Assn., Mensa. Avocation: big band music.

FARRAND, GEORGE NIXON, JR., marketing professional; b. N.Y.C., Apr. 1, 1936; s. George Nixon and Pauline (Merchant) F.; m. Elyn Marie Hallberg, Aug. 26, 1961; 1 child, Kathryn Elyn (dec. 1985). BSBA, Lehigh U., 1958; postgrad. in bus. adminstrn., NYU, 1962. Advt. and promotions writer Union Carbide Corp., N.Y.C., 1959-62; account exec. McCann-Erickson, Inc., N.Y.C., 1962-63, Vick Chem. Co., N.Y.C., 1963-64; sr. account exec., supr. Grey Advt., Inc., N.Y.C., 1964-65; products mktg. mgr. Hoffmann-LaRoche, Inc., Clifton, N.J., 1965-67; dir. new markets Inmont Corp., N.Y.C., 1967-69; sr. v.p. Bliss/Grunewald, Inc., N.Y.C., 1969-73; pres., chief exec. officer Farrand Mktg. Assoc., Inc., Saddle River, N.J., 1973—, Farrand Enterprises, Saddle River, 1983—. Sgt. U.S. Army, 1959. Mem. Sales Execs. Club N.Y.C., Lehigh U. Alumni Club (past treas. and pres.). Republican. Presbyterian. Avocations: sports, interior decorating, travel, music. FAX: 201-327-1921. Home: 70 Ripplewood Dr Saddle River NJ 07458-1422 Office: Farrand Mktg Assocs Inc Saddle River NJ 07458

FARRAND, WILLIAM RICHARD, geology educator; b. Columbus, Ohio, Apr. 27, 1931; s. Harvey Ashley and Esther Evelyn (Bowman) F.; m.

Claudine Brickmann, Aug. 17, 1962 (div. 1983); children: Frederic Hervé, Anne Marie; m. Carola Hill Stearns, Dec. 6, 1988; 1 child, Michelle Diane. BS in Geology, Ohio State U., 1955, MS in Geology, 1956; PhD, U. Mich., 1960. Rsch. assoc. Lamont Geol. Obs. Columbia U., N.Y., 1960-61, asst. prof., 1961-64; rsch. assoc. in geology U. Mich., Ann Arbor, 1962; postdoctoral rsch. fellow NAS/NRC, Strasbourg, France, 1963-64; asst. prof. geol. scis. U. Mich., Ann Arbor, 1965-67, assoc. prof. geol scis., 1967-74, prof., 1974—, curator analytical collections Mus. Anthropology, 1975—, dir. Exhibit Mus., 1993—; vis. prof. U. Strasbourg, France, 1964-65, Hebrew U., Jerusalem, 1971-72, U. Colo., Boulder, 1983, U. Tex., Austin, 1986; fellow Inst. for Advanced Study, Ind. U., 1985; mem. archaeometry panel NSF, 1989-91; apptd. mem. U.S. Nat. com. Internat. Quaternary Assn., 1989—; sr. fellow Inst. for Study Earth and Man, So. Meth. U., Dallas, 1991—. Mem. governing bd. Radiocarbon; mem. editorial bd. Quaternary Sci. Review, Paleorient, Jour. Archaeological Sci., Review Archaeology, Stratigraphica Archaeologica; contbr. articles and maps to profl jours. With U.S. Army, 1951-53. Fellow AAAS, Geol. Soc. Am. (mem. panel quaternary geology and geomorphology divsn. 1978, vice chmn. archaeological geology divsn, 1979, chmn, 1980, Archaeological Geology award 1986), Ohio Acad. Sci., 1994-96; mem. Am. Quaternary Assn. (sec. 1978-90, program chmn. biennial meeting 1980, pres. 1994-96), Mich. Acad. Sci., Arts and Letters, Internat. Union for Quaternary Rsch. (chmn. working group on Southwest Asia commn. paleoecology early man 1975-83), L'Assn. Francaise pour l'Etude de Quaternaire, Sigma Xi, Phi Beta Kappa. Office: The U Mich-Exhibit Mus 4502 Exhibit Mus 1109 Geddes Ave Ann Arbor MI 48109-1079

FARRAR, ANDREW LOCKETT, agricultural education educator; b. Clarksville, Va., Apr. 5, 1937; s. Albert Adolphus and Elizabeth (Merritt) F.; m. Mavis Ann Wray, June 18, 1960; 1 child, Angela LaVonia. BS, Va. State U., 1960, MS, 1972. Post-profl. tchg. cert. in agr. Sci. tchr. Mecklenburg Sch. Bd., Boydton, Va., 1960-61; agrl. tchr. Pittsylvania County Sch. Bd., Chatham, Va., 1961-84; supr. agr. Va. Dept. Edn., Richmond, 1984-91; chmn. dept. Northside, Gretna Jr. Hi, Gretna, Va., 1967-84; mem. state adv. bd. Future Farmers of Am., Richmond, 1984; chmn. Pittsylvania County Agr. Tchrs., Gretna, 1976; team mem. So. Assn. Accreditation, Richmond, 1984-91; adv. bd. Young Farmers of Va., 1985; chmn. J.R. Thomas New Farmer and New Homemakers of Am. Scholarship Found., Petersburg, Va., 1968—; mem. exec. bd. Va. State Agr. Alumni, Petersburg, 1984—. Contbr. articles to profl. jours. Mem. Councilman Town of Gretna, 1978-84, planning commn., 1978-84; bd. dirs. Pittsylvania County Med. Svc. Ctr., Chatham, Va., 1976-84; deacon Second Bapt. Ch.,, 1984; trustee John Tyler Cmty. Coll., Chester, Va., 1988-96; charter mem. Prince George Econ. Alliance, 1997. Recipient Sound Off for Agr. award Nat. Vocat. Ag. Tchrs., New Orleans, 1980, Disting. Svc. award 1991; inducted into Sports Hall of Fame, Va. State U., 1989;. Mem. Retired Tchrs. Assn. Old Dominion Ag. Tchrs. (state pres. Va. 1969), Dist. D Retired Tchrs. (chmn. 1991-97), Va. Ret. Tchrs., Va. State U. Agr. (awards com. 1985-97, plaque 1994), Petersburg-Prince George (chmn. 1994), NAACP. Democrat. Avocations: growing and exhibiting plants and vegetables, golf. Home: 4329 Prince George Dr Prince George VA 23875-2610

FARRAR, BEVERLY JAYNE, psychologist; b. Albuquerque, N.M., Nov. 6, 1928; d. Jack Murphy and Jane Clark; m. R.L. Farrar, July 1, 1949; 1 child, Dorothy. BA, Southern Methodist U., 1949, MA, 1967; MED, East Texas U., 1972. Tchr. Allen Independent Sch. Dist., Allen, Tex., 1949; instr. Sam Houston State U., Huntsville, Tex., 1949-51; tchr. Houston Ind. Sch. Dist., Houston, Tex., 1951-52, Dallas Ind. Sch. Dist., Dallas, Tex., Houston Ind. Sch. Dist., Houston, Tex., 1953-55, Harlingen Ind. Sch. Dist., Tex., 1957-63; speech pathologist Longview Ind. Sch. Dist., Tex., 1963-69; tchr. Dallas Ind. Sch. Dist., Tex., 1969-71; assoc. Sch. psychologist Richardson Ind. Sch. Dist., Richardson, Tex., 1971-92; ret., 1992. Co-author, Early Childhood Pre-School Screening Test for Richardson Sch., 1973, Handbook For Classroom Management For Richardson Sch., 1980. Mem. Tex. Ret. Tchrs. Assn., Dallas Ret. Tchrs. Assn., Thursday Book Club, Northway Rev. Club, Pi Lambda Theta (pres. Alpha Sigma chpt. 1994-98), Phi Delta Kappa, Delta Kappa Gamma (State Achievement award 1986, S.W. regional rep. to U.S. Forum 1994-96). Republican. Methodist. Avocations: music, reading, sewing. Home: 10220 Mapleridge Dr Dallas TX 75238-2257 *Live today—live Now—Now is 5 minutes; nothing is too hard to handle if you only look at what must be done in the next 5 minutes.*

FARRAR, DONALD KEITH, retired financial executive; b. Indio, Calif., May 18, 1938; s. Keith and Sarah S. (Turner) F.; m. Jo Ann Puttler, Dec. 16, 1961; children: Daniel K., Donald S., Douglas S., Kimberly. BSBA, U. So. Calif., 1960; MBA, Harvard U., 1965. With planning div. Paul Revere Life Ins. Co., Worcester, Mass., 1965, budget supr., 1966, asst. to pres., 1967, asst. sec., 1968-73, v.p. investment, 1969-73; v.p. planning Avco Corp., Greenwich, Conn., 1973-74, sr. v.p., chief acct. officer, 1975-77, exec. v.p., 1978-81, pres., 1981-85, also bd. dirs.; sr. exec. v.p., pres. Avco Ops. Textron Inc., Providence, R.I., 1985-89, sr. exec. v.p. ops., 1985-89; also bd. dirs. Textron Inc., Providence, RI; pres., CEO IMO Industries, Lawrenceville, N.J., 1993-94, chmn., CEO, 1994-97; pvt. investor 1990-93, 98—, retired. With USNR, 1960-63. Home: 39 Governors Ln Princeton NJ 08540-3669 Office: IMO Industries 1009 Lenox Dr Lawrenceville NJ 08648-2313

FARRAR, DONNA BEATRICE, hospital official; b. Ayer, Mass., Feb. 4, 1950; d. Raymond H. and Shirley E. (Perham) F. B Music Edn., U. Mass., 1971; MDiv, Bangor Theol. Sem., 1979; D Ministry, Christian Theol. Sem., 1987; M Family Studies, U. Ky., 1997. Tchr. music Billerica (Mass.) Pub. Schs., 1971-76; chaplain intern various hosps., Bangor, Maine, 1979-80; assoc. pastor Emanuel United Ch., Hales Coriters, Wis., 1980-82; chaplain resident Ind. U & Meth. Hosp., Indpls., 1982-85; assoc. chaplain Ohio State U. Hosp., Columbus, 1985-87; assoc. dir., dir. Ind. U. Med. Ctr., Indpls., 1987-92; dept. dir. U. Ky. Hosps., Lexington, 1992—. Vol. reader Ombudsman Agy., Lexington, 1995. Mem. Am. Assn. Marriage & Family Therapists. Democrat. Mem. Christian Ch. Avocations: reading, felines, dancing, travel, art. Office: U Ky 800 Rose St # H-118 Lexington KY 40536-0001

FARRAR, ELAINE WILLARDSON, artist; b. L.A.; d. Eldon and Gladys Elsie (Larsen) Willardson; children: Steve, Mark, Gregory, JanLeslie, Monty, Susan. BA, Ariz. State U., 1967, MA, 1969, PhD, 1990. Tchr. Camelback Desert Sch., Paradise Valley, Ariz., 1966-69; mem. faculty Yavapai Coll., Prescott, Ariz., 1970-92; chmn. dept. art Yavapai Coll., Prescott, 1973-78, instr. art in watercolor, oil, acrylic painting, intaglio, 1971-92, instr. art relief and monoprints, 1971-92; grad. advisor Prescott Coll. Master of Arts Program, 1993-97. One-man shows include R.P. Moffat's, Scottsdale, Ariz., 1969, Art Ctr., Battle Creek, Mich., 1969, The Woodpeddler, Costa Mesa, Calif., 1979; group show Prescott (Ariz.) Fine Arts Assn., 1982, 84, 86, 89, 90-95, 96, 97, N.Y. Nat. Am. Watercolorists, 1982; Ariz. State U. Women Images Now, 1986, 87, 89, 90-92; works rep. local and stae exhibits, pvt. nat. & internat. collections. Mem., curator Prescott Fine Arts Visual Arts com., 1992-97, mem. exec. com., 1996-98; bd. dirs. Prescott Fine Arts Assn., 1995-98, Friends Y.C. Art Gallery Bd., 1992-97. Mem. Mountain Artists Guild (past pres.), Women's Nat. Mus. (charter Washington chpt.), Kappa Delta Pi. *Through the visual arts many ideas and feelings are expressed that would otherwise be lost to the communication of these thoughts to others—a vital link to understanding...universal as is music and dance!.*

FARRAR, FRANK LEROY, lawyer, former governor; b. Britton, S.D., Apr. 2, 1929; s. Virgil William and Venetia Soule (Taylor) F.; m. Patricia Jean Henley, June 5, 1953; children—Jeanne Marie, Sally Ann, Robert John, Mary Susan, Ann M. B.S., U. S.D., 1951, LL.B., 1953; LL.D., Huron Coll. Bar: S.D. 1953. Practiced law Britton, 1957-63; agt. IRS, 1955-57; judge Marshall County, S.D., 1958, state's atty., 1959-62; atty. gen. State of S.D., 1963-69, gov., 1969-70; ptnr. Farrar & Spiry, Britton, S.D., 1970—; chmn. Cardinal and Gold Ins. Co., Frank L. Farrar & Assocs., Performance Bankers, Inc., Capital, Fulda, Beresford, Wanbay, Sidney, Uptown, Versailles, Glenrock, Wolf Point Bancorps., Inc., NW Investment Inc., Carlton Agy., Inc., 1st Agy. Hasting, Cairo, First, Inc., Peoples Holding Co.; adv. bd. dirs. Citicorp, Correspondent Resources Inc. Past pres. Pheasant council Boy Scouts Am.; past chmn. S.D. March of Dimes; past fund raising chmn. S.D. Mental Health Assn.; bd. dirs. Rural Coalition Am.; chmn. Marshall County Republican Party, 1959; asst. sgt.-at-arms Rep. Nat. Conv., 1960. Served to capt. U.S. Army. Recipient Alumnus Achievement award U. S.D., 1981, named Alumnus of Yr. Sch. Bus., 1979. Mem. S.D. Bar Assn., Ind. Bar Assn., Wash. Bar Assn., S.D. States Attys. Assn. (asst. pres.), Nat. Dist. Attys. Assn., Alpha Tau Omega, Phi Delta Phi. Lodges: Masons, Shriners, Jesters, Lions, Elks, Odd Fellows, Sportsmen. Address: PO Box 936 Britton SD 57430-0936

FARRAR, JAMES MARTIN, chemistry educator; b. Pitts., June 15, 1948; s. Martin W. and Lorraine H. (Williams) F.; m. Kathy June Meyer, Mar. 20, 1971; children: Stacey Elizabeth, Andrew Martin. AB, Washington U., 1970; MS, U. Chgo., 1972, PhD, 1974. Postdoctoral rschr. Lawrence Berkeley (Calif.) Lab., 1974-76; asst. prof. U. Rochester, N.Y., 1976-82, assoc. prof., 1982-86; prof. U. Rochester, 1986—, chair dept. chemistry, 1997—; vis. fellow Joint Inst. Lab. Astrophysics, Boulder, Colo., 1987-88. Mem. editl. bd. J.W. Wiley Pubs., 1992—. Recipient fellowship Alfred P. Sloan, 1981-85. Fellow Am. Phys. Soc.; mem. Am. Chem. Soc. Office: Univ Rochester Dept Chemistry Rochester NY 14627

FARRAR, JOHN T., physician, researcher; b. San Francisco, May 24, 1954; s. Curtis and Eleanor Farrar; m. Shelly Kessler, Oct. 25, 1980; children: Adam, Brian. ScB magna cum laude, Brown U., 1976; MD, U. Rochester, 1981. Diplomate in neurology Am. Bd. Psychiatry and Neurology. Fellow Cold Spring Harbor (N.Y.) Lab., 1978-79; resident in internal medicine Children's Hosp., San Francisco, 1981-83; resident in neurology Cornell Med. Ctr./N.Y. Hosp., N.Y.C., 1984-96, chief resident in neurology, 1986-87; pain fellow, neuro-oncology Meml. Sloan Kettering Cancer Ctr., N.Y.C., 1987-88; lectr. U. Pa., Phila., 1991-93, fellow epidemiology and biostats., 1994—, asst. prof. neurology, 1993-97; adj. asst. prof. epidemiology U. Pa., 1997—, adj. asst. prof. anesthesia, 1997—, clin. assoc. in neurology, 1997—. Office: U Pa 816 Blockley Hall 423 Guardian Dr Philadelphia PA 19104

FARRAR, JOHN THRUSTON, health facility adminstrator; b. St. Louis, June 26, 1920; s. Benedict and Ruth Elizabeth (Gregg) F.; m. Joan Hayward Niedringhaus, May 20, 1947 (div. Feb. 1964); children: John Hayward, Leslie Tweedy; m. Pamela Sedgwick Gibson, May 15, 1966 (div. Mar. 1994); children: Elizabeth Gregg, Anne Dandridge; m. Rowena Kay Bryan, Oct. 28, 1995. AB, Princeton U., 1942; MD, Washington U., St. Louis, 1945. Diplomate Am. Bd. Internal Medicine, Am. Bd. Gastroenterology. Intern St. Louis County Hosp., Clayton, Mo., 1945-46; asst. resident in pathology Boston City Hosp., 1948-49; intern in medicine Mass. Meml. Hosps., Boston, 1949-50, asst. resident in medicine, 1950-51, rsch. assoc. divsn. gastroenterology, 1951-54; instr. medicine Boston U. Sch. Medicine, 1954-55; asst. prof. clin. medicine Cornell U. Coll. Medicine, N.Y.C., 1956-63; assoc. prof. medicine Med. Coll. Va., Richmond, 1963-65, chmn. divsn. gastroenterology, 1963-78, prof. medicine, 1965-92, assoc. dean vets. affairs, 1979-90, prof. emeritus, 1992—; chief gastroenterology sect. med. svc. Vets. Hosp., N.Y.C., 1955-63; assoc. chief of staff rsch. devel. Vets. Affairs Med. Ctr., N.Y.C., 1956-63; cons. gastroenterology McGuire Vets. Affairs Med. Ctr., Richmond, 1963-78, chief of staff, 1979-90; nat. adv. panel nat. program rev. com. VA, 1965-69; adv. com. gastrointestinal drugs FDA, Washington, 1971-74, 77-82, cons., 1976-77; grants rev. com. Nat. Found. Ileitis Colitis, Inc., 1975-79, nat. scientific adv. com. 1975-79; chmn. long range planning com. Nat. digestive Diseases Edn. Info. Clearinghouse, 1983-85, chmn. scientific Evaluation subcom. 1983-85, chmn. exec. com. advisors, 1983-90; mem. steering com. Internat. Conf. Gastrointestinal Motility, 1975-81, chmn. steering com., 1977-79; chmn. Am. Bd. Gastroenterology, 1979-83; mem. bd. govs. Am. Bd. Internal Medicine, 1979-85; first vice-chmn. Coalition Digestive Desease Orgns., 1983-85; pres. Digestive Disease Nat. Coalition (formerly Coalition Digestive Disease Orgns.), 1986-91; rsch. com. Am. Fedn. Aging Rsch., 1983-89; assoc. dep. chief med. dir. Dept. Vets. Affairs, Vets. Affairs Ctrl. Office, Washington, 1990-91, dep. chief med. dir., 1991-93, acting under sec. health, 1993-94, dep. under sec. health, 1994-95; assoc. chief of staff extended care Vets. Affairs med. Ctr., Martinsburg, W.Va., 1995—. Author: (chpts.) Miniaturization, 1961, Modern Trends in Gastroenterology, 1961, Medicine, Essentials of Clinical Practice, 1970, Medical Engineering, 1974, Gastrointestinal Motility, 1971, Scientific Foundations of Gastroenterology, 1980, Tratado De Gastroenterologia Y Hepatologia, 1982, Clinics in Gastroenterology, 1982, Clinical Medicine, 1983, Social Security Practice Guide, 1986, Surgical Management of the Elderly Patient, 1992; editor: Practice of Medicine, Vol. Gastroenterology, 1973-78; mem. editl. bd. Am. Jour. Digestive Diseases, 1959-64, 88—, editor, 1968-76, Gastroenterology, 1964-68, Am. Jour. Med. Electronics, 1962-82; mem. editl. coun. Rendiconti Romani di Gastro-enterologia, 1969-89; contbr. over 55 articles to profl. jours. Bd. trustees Elk Hill Farm for Boys, 1974-80; pres. Goochland Family Svc. Soc., 1975-76, 79-81. Capt. U.S. Army Med. Corps., 1946-48. Mem. ACP (coun. sub-specialty socs. 1985-88, chmn. gastroenterology com. 1985-86, chair Washington 1986, San Francisco 1987), Am. Fedn. Clin. Rsch., Am. Gastroent. Assn. (rsch. com. 1968-71, nat. liaison com. 1971-73, 77-80, treas. 1972-77, chmn. publs. com. 1977-80, gov. bd. 1972-77, 80-89, v.p. 1980-81, pres.-elect. 1981-82, pres. 1982-83, chmn. com. pub. policy and govt. rels. 1986-89, historian, archivist 1986-98), Am. Clin. Climatol. Assn., Am. Liver Found. (bd. dirs. 1986—, chmn. bd. dirs. 1990-94). Home: 113 Falling Creek Cir Williamsburg VA 23185-1482

FARRAR, MARTHA ANN, lay worker, retired gift shop owner; b. Victoria, Tex., July 13, 1943; d. Warrington Siebert and Byrd Lillian Bertha (Dreyer) F. Student, Victoria Coll., 1961-63; cert., Baldwin Bus. Coll., 1964; cert. in nursing, Renger Hosp. Sch. Nursing, 1966. Reporter Zion Luth Ch. Women, Mission Valley, Tex., 1970-76, sec., 1976-78, pres., 1980-82, mem. adult choir, 1957-61, 72-84, Sunday sch. tchr., 1982-93, mem. altar guild, 1990-94; owner Martha' Gift Shoppe, Victoria, 1972-93; mem. Spirit of Zion Choir Zion Luth. Ch., Mission Valley, 1985-94, 97, lay asst. min., 1997-98, mem. Ladies Aid Soc., 1997; mem. Rebecca Cir. Bible Study Group, Mission Valley, 1981-93, pres., 1990-91. Co-organizer, sec. Golden Crescent Mayor's Com. for People With Disabilities, 1994-95, chmn. parade com., 1994-98, treas., 1996-97, pres. 1997-99; owner/operator MicroServ Enterprises, 1996. Democrat. *I believe we could make the world better if we would treat each other like beloved brothers and sisters. We need to treat others with the same respect and compassion we expect from them, without regard for race, color, creed, or behavior. When we do so, mutual love and respect abound and overcome hate and prejudice.*

FARRAR, RICHARD BARTLETT, JR., secondary education educator; b. Penn Yan, N.Y., Apr. 25, 1939; s. Richard B. and Margaret M. (Stevenson) F. BS, Houghton Coll., 1960; MEd, Frostburg (Md.) State U., 1990. Cert. wildlife biologist. Sci. tchr. Hinckley (Maine) Sch., 1960-61, Concord (Mass.) High Sch., 1962-64; program dir. Mass. Audubon Soc., Lincoln, 1964-65; instr. U. Ill., Chgo., 1966-68; chair sci. dept. Woodstock Country Sch., 1968-73; exec. dir. Vt. Inst. Natural Sci., Woodstock, 1971-73, N.J. Audubon Soc., Franklin Lakes, 1974-78; field exec. Nat. Wildlife Fedn., Washington, 1979-81; wildlife biology cons. Washington, 1982-86; lead sci. tchr. Garrett County Bd. Edn., Oakland, Md., 1987-97; adminstr. PPEPTEC High Schs., Tucson, 1997—; rsch. advisor Coastal Facilities Rev. Act, State of N.J., Trenton, 1977-78; mem. State of N.J. Natural Resources Coun., 1978-79; advisor Savage River State Forest Coun., 1991-92; NASA sci. tchr. amb., 1994—. Author: Birds of East-Central Vermont, 1971, The Hungry Snowbird, 1975, The Birds' Woodland, 1976; editor Vt. Natural History mag., 1970-73, N.J. Audubon mag., 1974-78; contbr. articles to popular and sci. publs. Treas. League for Conservation Legis., N.J., 1978; dir. Mid.-Atlantic Naturalist Soc., Md., 1981-82. Recipient Outstanding Biology Tchr. award Nat. Assn. Biology Tchrs., 1971, Conservation award Connecticut River Watershed Coun., 1971, Children's Sci. Book award Children's Libr. Coun., 1975, NSTA, 1976. Mem. Rotary (treas. Friendsville, Md. 1988).

FARRAR, STEPHEN PRESCOTT, glass products manufacturing executive; b. Concord, N.H., Jan. 27, 1944; s. Prescott Samuel and Katherine (Hitchcock) F.; m. Kathleen D. Clark, Dec. 28, 1968 (dec.); children: Sheila E., Stephen Prescott Jr.; m. Rose Marie Bucar, July 4, 1998. BA, Bowdoin Coll., 1965; MSFS, Georgetown U., 1967. Internat. economist U.S. Dept. Commerce, Washington, 1966-72; internat. economist Office of Mngt. and Budget, Washington, 1972-80, chief econ. affairs br. IAD, 1980-86; dir. internat. econ. affairs NSC, Washington, 1986-88, spl. asst. to Pres. and sr. dir. internat. econ. affairs, 1988-89; dep. exec. sec. Econ. Policy Coun., The White House, Washington, 1989-92; spl. asst. to Pres. for Policy Devel. Office of Policy Devel., the White House, Washington, 1989-92; chief of staff Office of the U.S. Trade Rep., Washington, 1992-93; dir. internat. bus. Guardian Industries Corp., Auburn Hills, Mich., 1993—. Republican. Avocations: tennis, running. Office: Guardian Industries Corp 2300 Harmon Rd Auburn Hills MI 48326-1714

FARRAR, THOMAS C., chemist, educator; b. Independence, Kans., Jan. 14, 1933; s. Otis C. and Agnes K. F.; m. Friedemarie L. Farrar, June 22, 1963; children: Michael, Christian, Gisela. BS in Math., Chemistry, Wichita State U., 1954; PhD in Chemistry, U. Ill., 1959. NSF fellow Cambridge U., Eng., 1959-61; prof. chemistry U. Oregon, Eugene, 1961-63; chief, magnetism sect. Nat. Bur. Standards, Washington, 1963-71; dir. R & D Japan Electron Optics Lab., Cranford, N.J., 1971-75; dir. instr. NSF, Washington, 1975-79; prof. chemistry U. Wis., Madison, 1979—; chmn. adv. com. MIT Nat. Magnetics Lab., Cambridge, Mass., 1979-84. Author: Introduction to Pulse NMR Spectros, 1989, Density Matrix Theory, 1995; contbr. over 120 articles to profl. jours. Recipient Silver medal Dept. Commerce, Washington, 1971, Silver medal Nat. Science Found., Washington, 1979. Fellow Wash. Acad. Science; mem. Am. Chem. Soc. (sec.-treas. Wis. sect. 1986-89), Am. Physical Soc. Office: Univ Wis Dept Chemistry 1101 University Ave Madison WI 53706-1322

FARREHI, CYRUS, cardiologist, educator; b. Malayer, Iran, Jan. 26, 1935; s. Mansoor and Nikzad (Agah) F.; m. Z. Jane Christensen, June 6, 1964; children: Peter M., Paul C., Lisa N., Mary M. M.D., U. Tehran, 1958. Diplomate: Am. Bd. Internal Medicine, Am. Bd. Cardiovascular Diseases. Intern Wayne County Gen. Hosp., Eloise, Mich., 1959-60; resident Wayne County Gen. Hosp., 1960-62; fellow in cardiology U. Oreg. Med. Sch., 1962-64; teaching fellow dept. medicine U. Alta., 1964-66; asst. prof. medicine U. Oreg.; also dir. cardiac catherization lab. VA Hosp., Portland, Oreg., 1966-69; chmn. dept. medicine McLaren Gen. Hosp., Flint, Mich., 1971-73; founding dir. cardiovascular diagnostic service McLaren Gen. Hosp., 1973-85; clin. assoc. prof. medicine Mich. State U., 1973-78, clin. prof., 1978—; cons. cardiovascular diseases, Flint, 1969—; bd. dirs. Ind. Practice Assocs., 1979-86, sec., 1979-83; adj. prof. health care, Sch. Health Scis., U. Mich., Flint, 1981-84. Contbr. articles med. jours. Fellow A.C.P., Royal Coll. Physicians and Surgeons of Can., Am. Coll. Cardiology, Clin. Council Am. Heart Assn., Genesee County Med. Soc. (dir. 1980—, pres. 1999—); mem. Detroit Heart Club. Roman Catholic. Home: 8398 Old Plank Rd Grand Blanc MI 48439-2041 Office: 1071 N Ballenger Hwy Flint MI 48504-4487

FARRELL, ANNE VAN NESS, foundation executive; b. Peking, China, July 17, 1935; came to U.S. 1935; d. C. Peter and Virginia (Cheatham) Van Ness; m. E. Robert Farell, June 17, 1955; children: Virginia Farrell Day and Susan Farrell Johnson. BA, U. Wash., 1960. Dir. devel. Seattle Children's Home, 1978-80; exec. v.p. The Seattle Found., 1980-84, pres., CEO, 1984—, dir. WM funds, 1993—; bd. dirs. Washington Mut. Bank, Blue Cross of Wash. and Alaska, Nat. Charities Info. Bur., N.Y.C., 1988—. Author: Puget Soundings, 1989. Regent Seattle U., 1986—; pres. bd. trustees Lakeside Sch., 1992-94; bd. dirs. Nature Conservancy, 1990-95, Ind. Sector, Wash., 1990-95, Girl Scouts U.S., N.Y.C., 1974-83. Recipient Cmty. Svc. award YWCA, Seattle, 1984, Girl Scout of Yr. award, Seattle, 1986. Mem. Pacific N.W. Grantmakers Forum (pres. 1984-85), N.W. Devel. Officers Assn. (pres. 1983-84), Wash. Women's Forum, Seattle, Jr. League, Greater Seattle C. of C., Rotary (pres. Seattle chpt. 1997-98). Republican. Episcopalian. Home: 1616 Lake Washington Blvd Seattle WA 98122-3540 Office: The Seattle Found 425 Pike St Ste 510 Seattle WA 98101-4026

FARRELL, CRAIG, hotel executive; married; 4 children. AD in Transp. and Travel., Coll. of DuPage; BA, DePaul U., Chgo. Dir. travel mktg. Choice Hotels Internat., 1982-84; v.p. travel industry mktg. Days Inns, 1984-90; sr. v.p. worldwide sales Hospitality Franchise Sys., 1990-94; pres., CEO Choice Hotels Can., Inc., Mississauga, Ont., Can., 1994-98; bd. dirs. Can. Tourism Commn., 1998—; planning com. SATH World Congress for Travellers with Disabilities, 1999—. Mem. Tourism Industry Assn. Can. (bd. dirs.), Travel Tourism Rsch. Assn. (pres. S.E. chpt. 1988-90), Can. Profl. Sales Assn., Can. Franchise Assn., Hotel Assn. Can. (bd. dirs.). Fax: (905) 624-7796. E-mail: craigúfarrell@choicehotels.ca. Office: Choice Hotels Can Inc, 5090 Explorer Dr 5th Fl, Mississauga, ON Canada L4W 4T9

FARRELL, EDGAR HENRY, building components manufacturing executive, lawyer; b. N.Y.C., Aug. 31, 1924; s. Edgar Henry and Lillian Sarah (Lancaster) F.; student Tex. A&M U., 1943, Stanford U., 1943-45, George Washington U. Law Sch., 1948-49; J.D., U. Md., 1950; postgrad., Harvard U. Bus. Sch., 1965; m. Mary Louise Whelan, May 3, 1952; children: Brooke Larkin Cragan, Elizabeth Lancaster, Kimberley Hopkins. Exec. sales asst. A.C. Gilbert Co., N.Y.C., 1950; asst. legal counsel U.S. Senate Crime Com., 1951; zone mgr. Life Mag., N.Y.C., 1951-52; account exec. Time Mag., N.Y.C., 1952-55, Phila., 1955-59, Detroit, 1959-62; nat. automotive sales mgr. Worldwide Automotive Products, Detroit, 1962-64, div. sales mgr., 1964-68, sales mgr., 1968; regional mgr. Communications/Research Machines, Inc., Mich., Ohio, 1968; central advt. dir. Petersen Pub. Co., Detroit, 1969; chief exec., officer Internat. Concrete Bldg. Group, London, 1972-79; asst. to pres. Dillon Co., Akron, Ohio, 1979-80; pres. and chief exec. officer Component Bldgs. Group, Woodbury, Conn., 1980-96; v.p. Mktg. Contractors Mkt. Place, Cornwall Bridge, Conn., 1993-96; assoc. pub. Bus. Digest Housatonic Valley Pub. Co., New Milford, Conn., 1996-97; mem. constrn. panel Am. Arbitration Assn., 1992; pres. Motorhome Holidays Internat., Camp Can. Inc., BEK Press, Camp Am., Inc.; housing cons. Saudi Arabia, Nigeria, Sri Lanka. Publicity chmn. Youth for Eisenhower Com., N.Y.C., 1952; trustee Baldwin Library, Birmingham, Mich., 1962-65. Served to lt. U.S. Army, 1945-46, PTO. Recipient Low Cost Housing award Ministry of Housing, Sri Lanka, 1979. Mem. Am. Mktg. Assn., Nat. Assn. Home Builders, Gen. Soc. Mayflower Descendants, Phi Delta Theta, Gamma Eta Gamma, Phi Alpha Sigma. Republican. Episcopalian. Author: Computer Center Construction, 1984, Walls on Wheels, 1993. Home: 1 Woodbury Hl Woodbury CT 06798-2958 Office: Bee Publ Co 5 Church Hill Rd Newtown CT 06470-1605

FARRELL, EDMUND JAMES, retired English language educator, author; b. Butte, Mont., May 17, 1927; s. Bartholomew J. and Lavinia H. (Collins) F.; m. Jo Ann Hayes, Dec. 19, 1964; children: David, Kevin, Sean. A.B., Stanford U., 1950, M.A., 1951; Ph.D., U. Calif., Berkeley, 1969. Chmn. English dept. James Lick H.S., San Jose, Calif., 1954-59; supr. secondary English, U. Calif., Berkeley, 1959-70; adj. prof. English, U. Ill., Urbana, 1973-78; prof. English edn. U. Tex., Austin, 1978-92, prof. emeritus, 1992—; pres. Farrell Ednl. Svcs., Inc., Austin, 1981-97; ret., 1997; participant revision lit. objectives Nat. Assessment of Ednl. Progress, Denver, 1972-73, 78; mem. adv. com. Ctr. for the Book, Libr. of Congress, 1980-86; chmn. adv. com. on English, Coll. Bd., N.Y.C., 1974-79, mem. council acad. affairs, 1978-79; guest lectr. local, state and nat. confs. of English tchrs., 1954—; reader compositions for advanced placement program Rider Coll., Princeton, N.J., 1969, 72-77; pres. Calif. Assn. Tchrs. English, 1962-63. Author: (with others) Exploring Life Through Literature, 1964, Counterpoint in Literature, 1967, Projection in Literature, 1973, Outlooks Through Literature, 1973, Fantasy: Forms of Things Unknown, 1974, Science Fact/Fiction, 1974, Comment, 1976, Myth, Mind and Moment, 1976, I/You, We/They, 1976, Traits and Topics, 1976, Reality in Conflict, 1976, To Be, 1976, Arrangement in Literature, 1979, Purpose in Literature, 1979, Album U.S.A., 1983, Discoveries in Literature, 1985, classic edit., 1989, Patterns in Literature, 1985, classic edit., 1989, Transactions with Literature, 1990, The Perceptive I, 1997. With USN, 1945-46. Fellow Nat. Conf. Rsch. on Lang. and Literacy; mem. Nat. Coun. Tchrs. English (field rep. 1970-71, asst. exec. sec. 1971-73, assoc. exec. dir. 1973-78, chmn. commn. lit. 1979-83; trustees rsch. found. 1983-85; fund for tchg. of English 1993-96, Disting. Svc. award 1982), Tex. Joint Coun. Tchrs. of English (pres. 1986-87, Disting. English Educator award 1989-90, Disting. Lifetime Svc. award 1999). Unitarian. Home: 6500 Sumac Dr Austin TX 78731-4117 Office: U Tex Dept Curriculum and Instrn Austin TX 78712

FARRELL, GREGORY ALAN, biomedical engineer; b. Bklyn., May 12, 1942; s. Edmond William and Edna Florence (Williams) F.; m. Mary Louise Lupiani, Sept. 3, 1966; children: Juliana Eden, Cristina Elizabeth. BSME, Cooper Union, 1964; MS in Biomed. Engring., Columbia U., 1972, postgrad., 1972—. Mech. engr. Gen. Dynamics, San Diego, 1964-65, Rochester, N.Y., 1965-67; rsch. asst. Columbia U. Med. Sch., N.Y.C., 1968-69; instr. pathology N.Y. Med. Coll., 1969-72; rsch. engr. Technicon Instruments Corp., Tarrytown, N.Y., 1972-82; mgr. mech. engring. Baker Instruments

Corp., Allentown, Pa., 1982-84, prin. mech. engr., 1984-86; prin. engr. Nat. Patent Devel. Corp., N.Y.C., 1986-87; project engr. Bayer Diagnostics (formerly Miles Diagnostics) (formerly Technicon Instruments), Tarrytown, 1987-90, new product devel. mgr., 1990—. Patentee in field; contbr. articles to profl. jours. Democrat. Roman Catholic. Achievements include product devel. of several automated clin. hematology and other instruments. Home: 447 Hillcrest Rd Ridgewood NJ 07450-1520 Office: Bayer Diagnostics 511 Benedict Ave Tarrytown NY 10591-5005

FARRELL, HERMAN D., JR., state legislator; married; children: Monique, Herman D. III. Mem. N.Y. State Assembly, 1975—, chmn. ways and means com.; mem. rules com., mem. Black and Puerto Rican Caucus. Del. Dem. Nat. Conv.; chmn. N.Y. County Dem. Com., 1981—, now also vice chmn. exec. com. Address: 2541-55 A Clayton Powell Jr Blvd New York NY 10039

FARRELL, JOHN L., JR., lawyer, business executive; b. N.Y.C., Jan. 24, 1929; s. John Lawrence and Edna (Ziegler) F.; m. Beverly H. Farrell; children: John Lawrence III, Maureen, Jayne, Dianne, Michael. B.A., St. Peters Coll., N.J., 1950; LL.B., St. John's U., 1955; M.B.A., NYU, 1960. Bar: N.Y. 1956. Asst. counsel ACF Industries, Inc., N.Y.C., 1955-61; counsel, sec., asst. to chmn. Knox Glass, Inc., N.Y.C., 1961-68; adminstrv. liaison Williams Cos., Tulsa, 1968-69; cons. on mergers and acquisitions, 1969-71; sr. v.p. law and adminstrn., sec. U.S. Filter Corp., N.Y.C., 1971-82; pres., chief operating officer FRACORP, Tulsa, 1983-84; cons. on mergers, acquisitions and fin. Frates Enterprises, Tulsa, 1984-87; prin. The Morgan Investment Group, Tulsa, 1988—; chmn. exec. com. Diagnetics, Inc., Tulsa, 1989-96. Mem. Ardsley (N.Y.) Sch. Bd., 1965-68. Served to 1st lt. U.S. Army, 1951-53. Republican. Roman Catholic. Home: 2128 E 60th Pl Tulsa OK 74105-7021

FARRELL, JOHN TIMOTHY, hospital administrator; b. St. Louis, Feb. 22, 1947; s. Michael James and Jane Frances (Lautenschlager) F.; m. Martha Anne Paynter, June 4, 1971; children: Kathleen Marie, Margaret Mary, Anne Elizabeth, John Timothy, Mary Ellen. B.A. in Philosophy, Cardinal Glennon Coll., 1969; postgrad., U. Mo., 1969-71; M.H.A., St. Louis U., 1973. Adminstrv. resident St. John's Mercy Med. Center, St. Louis, 1970-72, 73, exec. v.p., chief operating officer, 1979-86; pres., chief exec. officer St. John's Mercy Med. Ctr., St. Louis, 1986-95; pres., chief exec. officer St. John's Mercy Hosp., 1986-95, chmn. bd. trustees, 1991-95; asst. exec. dir. St. Mary's Hosp., Richmond, Va., 1973-74, assoc. exec. dir., 1974-76; adminstr. St. Francis Mercy Hosp., Washington, Mo., 1976-79, exec. v.p., 1979-86; chmn. bd., pres., CEO St. John's Mercy Health Sys., 1986-95; cons. health care St. Louis, 1995-96; v.p. employee benefits Anheuser-Busch Cos., Inc., St. Louis, 1996—; chmn. bd. dirs. Pestalozzi Steel Ins. Co., Ltd., 1996—; adj. faculty mem., designated preceptor Grad. Program in Hosp. and Health Adminstrn., Xavier U., Cin., 1989; pres. Mercy Doctors Bldg., Inc., 1986-93, Mercy Health Ventures, Inc., Edgewood Program, Inc.; mem. health adv. bd. Sisters of Mercy of the Union, Province St. Louis, 1976-79, mem. personnel com., 1978-79; mem. Catholic health care facilities com. Mo. Cath. Conf., Jefferson City, 1976-82, chmn., 1979-82, mem. health affairs task force, 1977-82; mem. adv. com. med. records technician program St. Mary's Coll., O'Fallon, Mo., 1978-79; mem. subcom. on svcs. pediatric tech. adv. group Health Systems Agy., 1978-79; mem. mental health task force St. Louis-Jefferson-Franklin Counties, Devel. Mental Health Facilities, 1977-79; mem. steering subcom. Health Systems Agy. Local Impact Com., 1979; Mercy Physicians Partnership; mem. shared svcs. coun. Sisters of Mercy Health Sys., St. Louis; adj. instr. health care adminstrn. Washington U. Sch. Medicine, St. Louis, 1985—; pres. bd. dirs. Area Rescue Consortium of Hosp., St. Louis, 1988, 91-92, sec., bd. dirs., 1989-94, v.p., treas., 1990; mem. steering com. Greater St. Louis Healthcare Alliance, 1993-95, mem. exec. com., 1993-95, mem. quality measurement com., 1992; cons. com. St. Louis Regional Hosp., 1992-93; program com. Coun. Tchg. Hosps., 1993-94; bd. mgrs. Unity Health Network, 1994-95; bd. dirs. Mercy Med. Group, 1994-95, Packaging Bus. Svcs., Inc., 1996—; trustee Mercy Health Plan, 1994-95. Mem. mgmt. adv. com. Washington (Mo.) Sch. Dist., 1976-79; bd. dirs. St. Francis Mercy Hosp., 1979-82, Mercy Health Conf., 1982-84, Family Planning Coun. St. Louis, 1979-81, mem. personnel com., 1979-81, budget com., 1980; bd. dirs. Mercy Hosp., Mansfield, Mo., 1983-87, St. John's Regional Hosp., Springfield, Mo., 1987-94, Affiliated Hosp. Dialysis Ctr., St. Louis, 1986-95, Midwest Stone Inst., 1987-92; mem. CEO coun., corp. ethics com. Sisters of Mercy Health Systems, St. Louis, 1987-89; pres., bd. dirs. Cath. Outreach Cmty. Program, 1992; bd. dirs. United Way Greater St. Louis, 1995—, chmn. hosp. sect. campaign, 1988, chmn. Health Svcs., 1994, mem. area wide rels. com., 1995-96; bd. dirs., chmn. postgrad. conf. St. Louis U. Alumni; mem. Parish Coun. St. Genevieve DuBois, St. Louis, 1989-92, pres., 1991-92; mem. Brotherhood/Sisterhood dinner com. NCCJ, St. Louis, 1990-94; bd. dirs. James Clinic Mercy Med. Group, Rolla, Mo., 1992-94, chmn. bd. dirs. Cath. Cmty. Svcs., 1992-97; fundraising com. St. Louis County Police and Firefighter Meml., 1993; exec. com. Joint Hosp. Assn. Met. St. Louis and St. Louis Met. Med. Soc., 1991-93; bd. dirs. Priests Mutual Benefits Soc., 1996—. Mem. Am. Coll. Hosp. Adminstrs., Mo. Hosp. Assn. (chmn. bd. trustees 1993, chmn.-elect 1992, past chmn. 1994, trustee 1989, 91-95, chmn. coun. rsch. and policy devel. 1990, chmn. fin. and budget 1991, annual meeting com.), Hosp. Assn. Met. St. Louis (coun. on fin. 1979-81, chmn. environ. svcs. com. 1981-86, mem. coun. mgmt. svcs. 1981-86, physician rels. com. 1987-88, chmn. coun. on pub. policy and issues 1987-88, bd. dirs. 1988-90, sec. 1991, treas. 1992, vice chmn. 1993, chmn. 1994), Midwest Stone Inst. (pres. 1988-92, bd. dirs. 1988-93), St. Louis U. Sch. Pub. Health Alumni Assn. (pres. 1991-92), Shared Resources Enterprise (bd. dirs. 1990, treas. 1991, sec. 1992, vice chmn. bd. dirs. 1993, chmn. 1994), Mental Health Assn. (host Spirit of St. Louis com. 1990), Creve Coeur Squires. Home: 537 Meadow Creek Ln Saint Louis MO 63122-1656

FARRELL, JOSEPH, movie market analyst, producer, entertainment research company executive, writer, sculptor, designer; b. N.Y.C., Sept. 11, 1935; s. John Joseph and Mildred Veronica (Dwyer) F. A.B. summa cum laude, St. John's Coll., 1958; A.M., U. Notre Dame, 1959; J.D., Harvard U., 1965. Bar: N.Y. 1965. With firm Milbank, Tweed, Hadley & McCloy, N.Y.C., 1964-65; exec. assoc. Carnegie Corp. N.Y., 1965-66; exec. v.p., chief oper. officer Am. Council of Arts, 1966-71; cons. Rockefeller Bros. Fund, Spl. Projects, 1966-71; pres. Nat. Research Center of Arts, N.Y.C., 1971-76; exec. v.p. Louis Harris & Assos. (Harris Poll), N.Y.C., 1974-76; vice chmn. Louis Harris & Assocs. (Harris Poll), N.Y.C., 1977; chmn., chief exec. officer Nat. Rsch. Group, Inc., subs. VNU, L.A., London and Tokyo, 1987—; movie market analyst and cons., 1978—; movie exec. producer, 1986—; sculptor, 1958—; designer Farbino Furniture, 1982—. Author, editor: Americans and the Arts, 1973, 75, Museums: USA, 1973, The Cultural Consumer, 1973, The U.S. Arts and Cultural Trend Data System, 1977; screenwriter The Foundation, Second Son, 1990—. Mem. Gov. N.Y. Task Force on Arts, 1975; founder, bd. dirs. Vol. Lawyers for Arts, 1968-76; bd. dirs. Arts and Bus. Coun. N.Y., 1973-76, Aman Folk Ensemble, 1979-82; bd. advisors Actors Studio, 1983-90. Woodrow Wilson fellow, 1958; named among Top 100 Influential People in Hollywood, Premiere mag., 1998. Office: NRG 5900 Wilshire Blvd 29th Flr Los Angeles CA 90036-5013*

FARRELL, JOSEPH CHRISTOPHER, retired mining executive, services executive; b. Boston, Sept. 27, 1935; s. Joseph C. and Ellen G. (Luttrell) F.; children: Christopher, Michael, John. BSEE, Northeastern U., 1958; MBA, Harvard U., 1963. Lic. pvt. pilot. Commd. ens. USN, 1958, advanced through grades to lt. comdr., resigned, 1968; asst. treas. Freeport Indonesia, N.Y.C., 1968-72; treas. Queensland Nickel, Townsville, Australia, 1972-75; v.p. Freeport Minerals, N.Y.C., 1975-78; pres. Freeport Gold, Elko, Nev., 1978-84; exec. v.p., dir. Pittston Co., Greenwich, Conn., 1984-89, pres., COO, 1989-91; chmn., CEO, Pittston Co., Stamford, Conn., 1991-98; ret., 1998; bd. dirs. Aeroquip-Vickers, Inc., Maumee, Ohio, Universal Corp., Richmond, Va.; mem. Northeastern U. Corp., Nev. Commn. Mining and Naturual Resources; trustee Va. Commonwealth U. Sch. Engring.; bd. visitors James Madison U. Mem. AIME, World Coal Inst. (hon. mem.), Harvard Club, The Commonwealth Club Richmond, Sky Club (N.Y.C.), Blind Brook Club, Rotary. Home: 15 Avenue De La Mer Apt 2604 Palm Coast FL 32137-2290

FARRELL, JOSEPH MICHAEL, steamship company executive; b. Yonkers, N.Y., June 7, 1922; s. Joseph Michael and Mary Elizabeth (Powers) F.; m. Cloatta Grace Pennington, Dec. 6, 1946; children: Cloatta M., Anthony J., Christopher J., Janice E. BS Marine Transp., U.S. Mcht. Marine Acad., 1943; postgrad., Columbia U., 1948-50, Fordham U., 1947-48. Commd. ensign, USNR, 1943, advanced through grades to capt., 1960, ret., 1968; mgr. Great Lakes Service, States Marine Lines, 1960-62; European mgr. Bremerhaven, Germany, 1962-65; exec. v.p., Waterman S.S. Corp., Washington, 1965-95; v.p. Hammond Leasing Corp., Mobile, Ala., 1967-89, Waterman S.S. Co. of Del., 1967-89; pres. Waterman Oceanic Corp., 1974-89; sr. v.p. Ctrl. Gulf Lines, 1993-95; v.p. Internat. Shipholding Corp., 1993-95. Recipient Outstanding Profl. Achievement U.S. Merchant Marine Acad., 1968-88. Invested Knight of Malta, 1988. Mem. Propeller Club U.S. (v.p., bd. govs. 1967-68, U.S. Exec. com. 1984-95), Nat. Def. Transp. Assn., Navy League. Clubs: Congressional Country, Univ., George Town (Washington); Siwanoy Country (Bronxville, N.Y.). Home: 3128 Dumbarton Ave NW Washington DC 20007-3308

FARRELL, KELLY JEAN, health and physical education educator; b. Mechanicsburg, Pa., Jan. 10, 1953; d. Eugene S. and Arlene M. (Wiley) Cromer; m. Charles F. Farrell, July 15, 1978 (div. Aug. 1983). BS, Lock Haven State Coll., 1974. Cert. health and phys. edn. tchr., Pa. Health and phys. edn. tchr. Ctrl. Dauphin High Sch., Harrisburg, Pa., 1974—; health and phys. edn. dept. chair Ctrl. Dauphin Sch. Dist., Harrisburg, Pa., 1991—, tennis instr. for C.D. Acad., 1992—; varsity softball coach Ctrl. Dauphin High Sch., Harrisburg, 1975—, varsity girls' basketball coach, 1974-93, varsity field hockey coach, 1977, varsity girls' tennis coach, 1994—, health and phys. edn. curriculum writing coms., 1987, 93-95; softball coach Keystone State Games, 1984-85. Mem. NEA, AAHPERD, Pa. State Edn. Assn., Ctrl. Dauphin Edn. Assn., Pa. State Assn. Health, Phys. Edn., Recreation and Dance, Pa. State Women's Golf Assn. (bd. dirs. Ctrl. Region 1991-93). Avocations: golfing, reading, movies, Pa. State U. football. Home: 210 N 62nd St Harrisburg PA 17111-4327 Office: Central Dauphin High Sch 4600 Locust Ln Harrisburg PA 17109-4498

FARRELL, KENNETH ROYDEN, economist; b. Ont., Can., Jan. 17, 1927; naturalized, 1958; s. William R. and Velma V. (Wood) F.; m. Mary Souter, Sept. 7, 1951; children: Janet, Betty, Deborah, Robert, Patricia, Lisa. BS, U. Toronto, Ont., 1950; MS, Iowa State U., 1955, PhD, 1958. Economist U. Calif., Berkeley, 1957-71; dep. adminstr. USDA, Washington, 1971-77, adminstr., 1977-81; dir. Nat. Ctr., Resources for the Future, Washington, 1981-87; v.p. U. Calif., Oakland, 1987-95, v.p. emeritus, 1995—; economist Nat. Food Commn., Washington, 1965-66, Nat. Productivity Commn., Washington, 1972-73; mem. Presdl. Task Force, Washington, 1982; cons. Robert Nathan Assocs., 1983-84. Contbr. articles to profl. jours.; author (with others) books. Lt. Royal Can. Navy, 1946-48. Fulbright scholar U. Naples (Italy), 1963-64. Fellow AAAS, Am. Agrl. Econs. Assn. (bd. dirs. 1973-76, pres. 1976-77, named for Disting. Pub. Policy Contbn. 1980, 92); mem. Internat. Assn. Agrl. Econs., Commonwealth Club Calif., Phi Kappa Phi, Gamma Sigma Delta. Avocations: golf, gardening, literature. Office: Univ Calif 300 Lakeside Dr Ste 701 Oakland CA 94612-3534

FARRELL, MARGARET DAWSON, lawyer; b. Bellingham, Wash., July 23, 1949; d. Sterling Jacob and Irene (Irving) Hegg; m. David S. Farrell, June 10, 1972; children: Lindsay S., Charles D. BA cum laude, Smith Coll., 1971; postgrad., Georgetown U., 1971-72; JD, U. Cin., 1974. Bar: Ohio 1974, U.S. Dist. Ct. (so. dist.) Ohio 1974, R.I. 1976, U.S. Dist. Ct. R.I. 1976. Assoc. Frost & Jacobs, Cin., 1974-76; assoc., then ptnr. Tillinghast, Collins & Graham, Providence, 1976-81; ptnr. Hinckley, Allen & Snyder, Providence, 1981—; mem. mgmt. com., 1996—; lectr. Bryant Coll., 1979-80; dir., sec. Bank R.I., 1996—. Trustee Women and Infants Hosp., Providence, 1981-96, sec., 1982-96, vice chair, 1996—; trustee Women and Infants Corp., Providence, 1989—, sec., 1989-96, vice chair, 1996—; trustee, sec. Providence Preservation Soc. Revolving Fund, 1982-88; trustee Butler Hosp., 1995—, Hosp. Assn. R.I., 1989—, Care New England Health Sys., 1996—, R.I. Hist. Soc., 1980-85, Gordon Sch., East Providence, R.I., 1990-95; trustee, sec., pres. Found. for Repertory Theatre, R.I., 1978-84; R.I. del. Am. Hosp. Assn. Congress Hosp. Trustees, 1993-98; mem. R.I. Bd. Regents for Elem. and Secondary Edn., 1987-90. Mem. ABA, R.I. Bar Assn. Avocations: sailing, skiing, horseback riding. Office: Hinckley Allen & Snyder 1500 Fleet Ctr Providence RI 02903-2319

FARRELL, MARIAN L., nursing educator; b. Carbondale, Pa., May 8, 1954; d. Nicholas and Louise (Klopfer) Rosler; m. James Farrell; children: Jessica, Dan, Sara, Rebecca. BSN, Coll. Misericordia, 1976, MSN, 1985; MS, Syracuse U., 1992; PhD, Adelphi U., 1992; CRNP, U. Pa., 1999. Staff nurse St. Joseph's Hosp., Carbondale, Pa., 1976-77, Pa. Dept. Health, Scranton, 1977, Clarks Summit (Pa.) State Hosp., 1978; tchr. Lackawanna Vo-Tech., Scranton, 1978-81, Cmty. Med. Sch. Nursing, 1987-87; asst. prof. nursing Marywood Univ., 1987-90; assoc. prof. nursing U. Scranton, 1990—. Mem. ANA, Pa. Nurses Assn., Am. Psychiat. Nurses Assn., Internat. Soc. Psych-Mental Health Nurses. Office: U Scranton P A N Rm 307 Scranton PA 18411

FARRELL, MICHAEL W., state supreme court justice. Grad., U. Notre Dame; MA, Columbia U.; JD, Am. U. Law clerk to Assoc. Judge John P. Moore Md. Ct. Spl. Appeals, 1973; atty. criminal divsn. U.S. Dept. Justice; chief appellate divsn. Office U.S. Atty. D.C., 1982-89; assoc. judge Ct. Appeals, 1989—; chmn. Eng. dept. Georgetown Prep. Sch. Office: Ct Appeals 500 Indiana Ave NW Rm 6000 Washington DC 20001-2131*

FARRELL, MIKE, actor; b. St. Paul, Feb. 6, 1939; s. Michael and Agnes Farrell; m. Judy Hayden, 1963 (div.); children: Michael, Erin; m. Shelley Fabares, 1984. Ed., UCLA, Jeff Corey Workshop, Hollywood. Profl. debut in little theatre prodn. Rain, 1961; motion pictures include: Captain Newman, M.D, 1964, The Americanization of Emily, 1964, The Graduate, 1967, Targets, 1968; numerous TV appearances; regular on TV series Days of Our Lives, NBC-TV, The Interns, CBS-TV, 1970-71, The Man and the City, ABC-TV, 1971-72, M*A*S*H, CBS-TV, 1975-83, The Killers Within, 1995, Superman, 1996, Providence, 1999—; TV spls. include Ladies of the Corridor, PBS, 1975, Child Sexual Abuse, PBS, 1984, JFK, A One-Man Show; TV movies include: The Questor Tapes, The Longest Night, Battered, Sex and the Single Parent, Damien, The Leper Priest, Prime Suspect, 1982, Choices of the Heart, 1983, Memorial Day, 1984, Private Sessions, 1985, Vanishing Act, 1986, A Deadly Silence, 1989, (also co-author) Incident at Dark River, 1990, The Whereabouts of Jenny, 1991, Silent Motive, 1991, Hart to Hart: Old Friends Never Die, 1994, Vows of Deception, 1996, Tangled Web, 1996, Behind the Laughs, 1997, Sins of the Mind, 1997; co-producer motion picture Dominick and Eugene, 1988; dir. M*A*S*H episodes, (TV movie) Run Till You Fall, CBS-TV, 1988; prodr. (films) Memorial Day, 1983, Dominick and Eugene, 1988, Incident at Dark River, 1989, Silent Motive, 1991, Patch Adams, others; dir. M*A*S*H, 1972, Run Till You Fall, 1988; TV guest appearances include Bonanza, 1959, I Dream of Jeannie, 1965, The Monkees, 1966, Ghost Story, 1972, The Six Million Dollar Man, 1974, Murder, She Wrote, 1984, Matlock, 1986, others. Involved in polit. and social causes. Served USMC. Mem. AFTRA, Screen Actors Guild. *

FARRELL, PATRICIA ANN, psychologist, educator; b. N.Y.C., Mar. 11, 1945; d. Joseph Alexander and Pauline (Loth) F. BA, Queens Coll., 1976; MA, NYU, 1978, PhD, 1990. Lic. psychologist, N.J., Fla. Assoc. editor Pubs. Weekly Mag., N.Y.C., 1968-72; editor Bestsellers Mag., N.Y.C., 1972-73; assoc. editor King Features Syndicate, N.Y.C., 1973-78; staff psychologist, intake coord. Mid-Bergen Cmty. Mental Health Ctr., Paramus, N.J., 1978-84; instr. Bergen C.C., Paramus, 1978-94; prof. clin. psychology Prof. Psychology Program (doctoral) Walden U., 1996—, Thomas Edison State Coll.; resident clin. psychology Am. Inst. for Counseling, N.J., 1990-91; cons. Family Counseling Svc. of Ridgewood, N.J., 1984; clin. psychology intern Marlboro (N.J.) Psychiat. Hosp., 1984-85, staff psychologist, 1985-87; rsch. analyst Mt. Sinai Sch. Medicine, 1987-88; account exec., sr. sci. writer Manning, Selvage and Lee, N.Y.C., 1988-90; sr. clin. psychologist, mem. med. staff Greystone Pk (N.J.) Psychiat. Hosp., 1990-96; pvt. practice psychology, Englewood, N.J.; prof. psychology Grad. Sch. Am., 1998—; health sci. editor Time Warner Cable, Channel 10 News, 1995—; med. specialist N.J. Divsn. Disability Determination, 1997—; police surgeon Boro Ft. Lee, N.J., 1998—; psychiatry preceptor U. Medicine and Dentistry N.J. Med. Sch.; cons. pharm. clin. protocols. Guest radio and TV shows including ABC Sports Spl., ABC World News Tonight, Family Talk, Up Front Tonight, Sally Jessy Raphael, Montel Williams, Gordon Elliott Show, Inside Edit., Am. Jour., Fox Cable News, Good Day N.Y., Mark Walberg, Am. After Hours, Dini, The Shirley Show, Camilla Scott, USA Live, Alive and Wellness with Carol Martin, News Talk, Maury Povich, The Carnie Wilson Show, Judge for Yourself TV Show, N.Y.C. 10 O'Clock News, Cosmo, Timeout N.Y., Detroit News, Chgo. Tribune, WPIX-TV, N.Y., UPN 9 News, WWOR-TV News, WNRR-TV, In Your Interest, LTV, Channel 10 News, On Campus, Stá WTTM, WSNJ, WHSI-TV, Last Call, Common Concerns, WHSE-TV; author: (manual) Alzheimer's Disease Assessment Scale test; contbr. book chpt. to Innovations in Clin. Practice: A Source Book, 15th edit., articles to Writer's Digest, Real World, Postgrad. Medicine, newspapers, others. Bd. dirs., chmn. med. liaison com. liaison to dept. psychiatry Bergen Pines County Hosp., Paramus, 1994-95. McDonald's rsch. grantee, 1994-95; recipient Good Citizen award DAR, Sci. award Rotary Club. Fellow Am. Bd. Disability Analysts; mem. APA, Prescribing Psychologists Register, NYU/Bellevue Psychiat. Soc. Avocations: fitness, racquetball, kite-flying. Office: PO Box 1283 Englewood NJ 07632-0283

FARRELL, PEG, magazine publisher. Assoc. pub. Cosmopolitan, N.Y.C.; group dir. for advt. Marie Claire, 1994-95, pub., 1995; pub., v.p. Country Living, N.Y.C., 1997—. Office: Country Living 224 W 57th St New York NY 10019-3212

FARRELL, RICHARD T., human resources administrator; m. Jennifer Farrell; children: Elizabeth, Connor. B in Polit. Sci. magna cum laude, Fla. State U., 1969, M in Govt., 1970. Chief of staff, legis. dir. to U.S. Senator Lawton Chiles, Washington; v.p. govt. affairs Syntex Corp.; sec. Fla. Dept. of Bus. and Profl. Regulation; dir. Human Resources and Adminstrn., Dept. of Energy, Washington, 1998—. With U.S. Army. Nat. Def. Edn. Act fellow, 1970. Office: Human Resources Adminstrn 1000 Independence Ave SW Washington DC 20585-0001

FARRELL, ROBERT JOEL, II, counselor, education therapist, educator, minister; b. Decatur, Ala., May 15, 1965; s. Robert Joel and Amanda Jane (Morrisson) F.; m. Robin Carrie Gosdin, Dec. 8, 1990; children: Revin Joel, Ryan Jordan. BS in Bldg. Sci., Auburn U., 1988; MS in Religion, Ala. Christian Sch., 1990; MEd in Counseling and Psychology, Auburn U., 1992, PhD in Counselor Edn. and Supervision and Ednl. Psychology, 1996. Lic. profl. counselor; nat. cert. counselor. Landscape contractor Farrell Lawns, Oklahoma City, 1977-83; asst. student tchr. Auburn (Ala.) U., 1986-88; intern min. Cen. Ch. of Christ, Anniston, Ala., 1987, Auburn Ch. of Christ, 1989-91; mng. editor Spirit Mag., Auburn, 1988-89; rsch. asst. family and child devel. Auburn U., 1990, tutor, 1990-94; substitute tchr. Auburn City Schs., 1991-94; assoc. prof. counseling, dir. clin. tng. So. Christian U., 1995—, dir. Life Skills Ctr., 1996—; min. of family counseling Hoover Ch. of Christ, 1995-98; adj. prof. Faulkner U., Montgomery, Ala., 1991-95; grad. rsch. asst. Strategic Teams for Rural Intervention Through Drug Edn., 1992-93; doctoral tchg. asst. Auburn U., 1993-95; asst. prodn. mgr. Jour. Rsch. in Childhood Edn., 1993-95; counselor Auburn U., Montgomery, 1994-95; cons. Prison Family Found., Inc., 1996—. Asst. dir. BASIC, Auburn, 1985-90; bd. dirs. Southeastern Drama Workshop, Auburn, 1990; asst. coord. Lee County Ind. Living Ctr., 1991-92; agy. counselor Ala. Coun. Human Rels., Inc., 1992-93; vol. cons. East Ala. Youth for Christ, 1999—; bd. dirs., sec. of bd. Montgomery Mens Ctr., 1994-95; missionary Chs. of Christ; senator Grad. Student Orgn., 1991-92. Mem. ACA, Am. Coll. Pers. Assn., Assn. for Religious and Values in Counseling, Am. Assn. Christian Counselors, Ala. Counseling Assn. (grad. student rep. alternative chpt. VII exec. coun., jour. editor), Ala. Assn. Specialists in Group Work (bd. dirs., sec., chmn. membership com., pres., pres.-elect, newsletter editor), Auburn U. Counseling Assn. (bd. dirs. 1991-95), Am. Coll. Counseling Assn. Avocations: music, writing, reading, sports, travel. Home: 730 Wild Ginger Ln Auburn AL 36830-6050 Office: So Christian U PO Box 240240 Montgomery AL 36124-0240

FARRELL, SHARON ELAINE, real estate broker; b. Boston, Nov. 8, 1941; d. Winston Cushman and Evelyn (Murphy) Lawson; m. James E. Waldron, Oct. 15, 1961 (div. Apr. 1987); children: Peter M., Kathleen M.; m. Richard J. Farrell, May, 1994. AA, Massasoit Community Coll., 1984; grad., Realtors Inst., 1987; BS, Stonehill Coll., 1998. Cert. residential specialist. Adminstrv. asst. Bus. Svcs. Office, Massasoit C.C., Brockton, Mass., 1983-98; assoc. broker Anderson Real Estate, Inc., East Bridgewater, Mass., 1984—. Den mother Cub Scouts Boy Scouts Am., East Bridgewater, 1972-76, den leader, coach, 1976-78; mem. com., 1978-79. Mem. Am. Soc. Notaries (life), Nat. Assn. Realtors, Mass. Assn. Realtors, Nat. Assn. Cert. Residential Specialists, Mass. Assn. Cert. Residential Specialists, Green Key Soc., Beta Xi, Theta Alpha Kappa. Roman Catholic. Avocations: reading, travel. Home: 1725 Washington St East Bridgewater MA 02333-2219 Office: Anderson Real Estate Inc 406 Central St East Bridgewater MA 02333-2020

FARRELL, THOMAS FRANCIS, energy company executive; b. Ft. Buckner, Okinawa, Japan, 1954. BA in Econs., U. Va., 1976, JD, 1979. Ptnr. McGuire Woods Beatle & Booth, 1981-95; sr. v.p., gen. counsel Dominion Resources Inc., Richmond, Va., 1995-97; CEO Va. Power, Richmond, 1995—; sr. v.p. corp. affairs Dominion Resources, Richmond, 1997-99; CEO Dominion Generation, Inc., Richmond, 1999—; Chmn. nominations to the appellate ct. com. State of Va. Mem. Va. Bar Assn. (exec. com., chmn. young lawyers sect.), Va. Law Found. (mem. continuing legal edn. com.). Office: Dominion Generation Inc PO Box 26532 120 Tredegar St Richmond VA 23219*

FARRELL, W. JAMES, manufacturing company executive; b. N.Y.C., 1942. BA, U. Detroit, 1965. Salesman Ill. Tool Wks., Inc., Glenview, Ill., exec. v.p., pres., chmn. bd., chmn. bd., CEO, 1996—. Office: Illinois Tool Wks Inc 3600 W Lake Ave Glenview IL 60025-1215*

FARRELL, WARREN THOMAS, author; b. N.Y.C., June 26, 1943; s. Thomas Edward and Muriel (Levy) F.; m. Ursie Otte Fairbairn, June 19, 1966 (div. 1977). *Grandparents were from Ireland and Italy. Father Thomas Edward Farrell was born in Brooklyn, October 17, 1910. Mother Muriel Levy was born 1918. They raised Warren, Gail, and Wayne in NJ. Thomas Farrell, banker and then accountant at Bendix, was widowed. He met Bendix's librarian, Lydia Merlo, also pianist and church organist. They married and raised Wayne (now deceased). Gail is teacher of both gifted and talented and special education in Allendale, NJ. She, Thomas, and Warren love hiking. Living relatives include Florence Meserole, Ester Marsala and Dottie Rosario, the Flavins and Flavahans in England, and the Burnses in Ireland.* BA in Social Sci., Montclair State U., 1965; MA in Political Sci., U. Calif., L.A., 1966; PhD in Political Sci., NYU, 1974; D. of Humane Letters, Profl. Sch. Psychology, San Diego, 1985. Diplomate Am. Board Sexology; cert. tchr., N.J. adj. asst. prof. Sch. Medicine U. Calif., San Diego, 1986-88; cons. HUD, U.S. Dept. Edn., Bonneville Power, NASA, 1975-98, IBM, Revlon, Ogilvy, Toyota, Beckman Labs., AT&T, Bell Atlantic, 1974-99. *Dr. Farrell was student body president of Midland Park High School, and Student-National Education Association representative to White House Conference on Education, 1965. He was the only man ever elected 3 times to the Board of NOW, NYC. He wrote "The Liberated Man," representing feminist perspectives. Eventually, he felt men's perspectives were neglected. "Why Men Are The Way They Are" and "They Myth of Male Power" articulate men's world-view. "Women Can't hear What Men Don't Say" teaches both sexes to handle personal criticism, explains concept of Lace Curtain, new views on domestic violence, and why Littleton was an outgrowth of neglected boys' feelings.* Author: The Liberated Man, 1975, Why Men Are The Way They Are, 1986, 87, 88, The Myth of Male Power, 1993, 94, Women Can't Hear What Men Don't Say, 1999; contbr. articles to profl. jours; TV appearances include Oprah, Donahue, The Today Show, Larry King Live, ABC World News with Peter Jennings, Crossfire, CBC's Newsworld; TV spls. ABC's 20/20, ABC (Australia), BBC (Britian), CBC (Can.), People Mag., Parade Mag., Japan Times, N.Y. Times, Wall St. Jour., Time, Forbes, Der Speigel, Mac Leans, London Times, So. China Morning Post, others. Recipient Outstanding Contribution award Calif. Assn. Marriage Family Therapists, 1988. Mem. Nat. Coalition Free Men (adv. bd. 1996—, best book 1986), Nat. Congress Fathers & Children (bd. dirs. 1992—, best book 1993), Nat. Org. Women (N.Y.C Chpt. bd. dirs. 1970-73), Children's Rights Council (adv. bd. 1985—), Am. Coalition of Fathers and Children (bd. dirs. 96-98). Unitarian. Avocations: tennis, running. Office: PMB 220 103 N Hwy 101 Encinitas CA 92024-3252

FARRELL, WILLIAM CHRISTOPHER, lobbyist; b. Amsterdam, N.Y., Dec. 30, 1951; s. Francis M. and Margaret (Holmes) F.; m. Mary E. Crowley-Farrell, Sept. 1, 1979; children: Eliza Carolyn, Luke Jeremiah. AB in Polit. Sci., Providence (R.I.) Coll., 1974; MA in Polit. Sci., Rutgers U., New Brunswick, N.J., 1979; student post-grad studies, George Washington U., 1983-87. Social worker Dublin (Ireland) Com., 1980-81; legis. analyst State and Fed. Assocs., Washington, 1981-82; computer mgr. Rep. Gerry Sikorski, 1982; legis. asst. Rep. Bill Richardson, 1982-84; legis. dir. Rep. Tommy Robinson, 1984-89; lobbyist, organizer Nat. Assn. Retired Fed. Employees, 1989—; bd. mem. Action in Montgomery, Montgomery County, 1994—. Mem. Kemp Mill Civic Assn., Silver Spring, Md., 1987—, Montgomery Democrats, Rockville, Md., 1993—, Capital Area Polit. Sci. Assn., Washington, 1993—; player Montgomery United Soccer Team. Fellow Eagleton Inst. of Politics, Rutgers U., New Brunswick, N.J., 1977. Mem. St. Andrew Apostle Parish, Pi Sigma Alpha. Avocations: hiking, biking, rafting, theater, soccer. Office: National Assn Retired Fed Employees 606 N Washington St Alexandria VA 22314-1914

FARRELL, WILLIAM EDGAR, sales executive, infosystems specialist, management consultant; b. Jeanette, Pa., Mar. 13, 1937; s. Arthur Richard and Lelia (Ryder) F.; m. Sara Lynnette Swing, Aug. 20, 1960; children: Wendy J., Tracy L., Rebecca J. BS in Edn., Pa. State U., 1959. Location mgr. IBM Corp., Dover, Del., 1969-72; corp. lobbyist IBM Corp., Washington, 1972-74, planning cons., 1974-78, nat. mktg. mgr., 1978-80, exec. asst., 1980-81; account exec. IBM Corp., Denver, 1981-87, policy exec., 1987-91; pres., CEO Weatherall Co., Inc., Englewood, Colo., 1993-97; CFO, Wide Horizon, Inc., Denver, 1987-92, chmn. bd. trustees, 1989-92; pres. Exec. Mgmt. Cons., 1987—; sec.-treas., bd. dirs. Electronic Shoe Enterprises Inc., 1991-94; mem. Colo. Info. Mgmt. Commn., 1992-95; bd. dirs. Energaire Corp. Founding mem. River Falls Community Assn., Potomac, Md., 1975; first reader First Ch. of Christ Scientist, Chevy Chase, Md., 1976-80; chmn. Amigo's De Ser; bd. dirs. Rocky Mountain Ser, 1991-92. Recipient Outstanding Contbn. award IBM Corp., 1968. Republican. Avocation: flying instrument S.E.L. airplanes.

FARRELL, WILLIAM JOSEPH, university chancellor; b. Milw., Aug. 17, 1936; s. William John and Rita (Taggart) F.; m. Carol Mary Leeming, Aug. 1, 1959; children: William Jr., Charles, Elizabeth. BS summa cum laude, Marquette U., 1958, MBA, 1976; MA, U. Wis., 1959, PhD, 1961; DHL (hon.), St. Anselm's Coll., 1998. Instr. U. Chgo., 1961-63, asst. prof., 1963-68; assoc. prof. Marquette U., Milw., 1968-75, dir. of Found. Support, 1970-75; assoc. v.p. of research U. Iowa, Iowa City, 1975-84; pres. Plymouth (N.H.) State Coll., 1984-92; chancellor Univ. System of N.H., 1992—; vis. prof. U. Calif., Berkeley, 1967-68; trustee Univ. Sys. N.H., 1984—, St. Anselm's Coll., 1992—, chair ednl. policy com., 1995—, mem. exec. com., 1995—, state del. New Eng. Bd. Higher Edn., 1984—, chair N.H. del., 1995—. Co-editor English Literature 1600-1800: A Bibliography of Modern Studies, 1972; editor: (jour.) Renascence: Essays on Values in Literature, 1969-72; contbr. numerous articles to profl. jours. Bd. dirs. N.H. Music Festival, Center Harbor, 1984-93, Bus. and Industry Assn. of N.H., 1998—; mem. N.H. Postsecondary Edn. Commn., 1984—, mem. exec. com., 1988-93, chmn., 1990-92. Woodrow Wilson fellow, 1958, Danforth fellow, 1958. Mem. N.H. Coll. and Univ. Coun. (chmn. 1989-91), Am. Coun. on Edn., Nat. Assn. Sys. Heads, Nat. Assn. State Univs. & Land Grant Colls., State Higher Edn. Exec. Officers, N.H. Bus. and Industry Assn. (bd. dirs. 1998—). Roman Catholic. Home: PO Box 873 17 Denbow Rd Durham NH 03824-3104 Office: Univ System NH Dunlap Ctr 25 Concord Rd Durham NH 03824-6624

FARRELL-LOGAN, VIVIAN, actress; b. N.Y.C.; m. Harvey Lewis, Aug. 5, 1979 (dec. Aug. 1980); m. Tracy Harrison Logan, June 3, 1984 (dec. Sept. 1996). BS in Edn., Syracuse U.; MA in Theatre, NYU. Tchr. elem. sch. Levittown (N.Y.) Schs., 1965-75; tchr. workshops Coll. of Cape Breton, N.S., Can., 1977-79. Appearences include (stage) Gateway Playhouse, Bellport, N.Y., Playhouse 3200, Richmond, Va., Bartke's Dinner Theatre, Tampa, Fla., (film) Impulse; narrator for Nutcracker, Eglevsky Ballet Co. with L.I. Symphony Orch., Nassau Coliseum, Uniondale, N.Y., 1978-79; appeared as The Musical Storyteller, Lincoln Ctr., N.Y.C., Carnegie Recital Hall, N.Y.C., 1978-80, also in various libraries and schs., N.Y. area; performer, 1978—, writer, performer (album) The Musical Storyteller, 1978; author: (children's book) Robert's Tall Friend: A Story of the Fire Island Lighthouse, Island-Metro Publs., Inc., 1987; appearing numerous schs., librs. in Author Narrates Her Book Robert's Tall Friend, 1989—; appearing N.Y.C schs. and on tour in one-woman play Amelia, My Courageous Sister, 1993—. Nassau County (N.Y.) Office Cultural Devel grantee, 1986—, N.Y. State Coun. on the Arts grantee, 1986—. Mem. Actors Equity Assn., SAG, AFTRA, Twelfth Night Club, Ninety-Nines, Alpha Psi Omega, Zeta Phi Eta. Avocations: flying, tennis. Office: PO Box 734 Lindenhurst NY 11757-0734

FARRELLY, BOBBY, writer, producer, director; b. Cumberland, R.I., 1958. Writer, prodr. Outside Providence, 1999; writer, co-prodr. Dumb and Dumber, 1994; exec. prodr., writer, dir. There's Something About Mary, 1998; writer, prodr. dir. Me, Myself and Irene, 1999; writer, dir. Stuck on You, 1999; writer Bushwacked, 1995; dir. Kingpin, 1996. Recipient Screenwriter of Yr. ShoWest Conv., 1999. Office: Creative Artists Agy c/o Adam Kantor 9830 Wilshire Blvd Beverly Hills CA 90212*

FARRELLY, PETER JOHN, screenwriter; b. Phoenixville, Pa., Dec. 17, 1956; s. Robert Leo and Mariann (Neary) F. BA, Providence Coll., 1979; MFA, Columbia U., 1987. Salesman U.S. Lines, Inc., Boston, 1979-81; bartender various libationary locales, Boston, 1981-85; screenwriter Paramount Columbia and Disney Studios, Los Angeles, 1985—. Author Outside Providence, 1988; co-writer (TV spls.) Our Planet Tonight, 1987, Paul Reiser: Out on a Whim, 1987; writer (film) Dumb & Dumber, 1994, Bushwhacked, 1995, There's Something About Mary, 1998; dir. (film) Dumb & Dumber, 1994, Kingpin, 1996, There's Something About Mary, 1998; prodr. There's Something About Mary, 1998, Outside Providence, 1999. Mem. Writers Guild Am. West. Roman Catholic. *

FARRER, LINDSAY AMES, genetic epidemiologist; b. New Brunswick, N.J., May 28, 1958; s. Robert G. and Phyllis Selma (Kushner) F.; m. Anne Marie Swigert, June 28, 1987; children: Jordan Ross, Robert Rogin. BA in Population Genetics, U. N.C., 1981; PhD in Med. Genetics, Ind. U., 1985. Diplomate Am. Bd. Med. Genetics. Postdoctoral fellow Yale U. Sch. of Medicine, Dept. Human Genetics, New Haven, 1985-87; asst. prof. neurology and pub. health Boston U. Sch. of Medicine, 1987-92, assoc. prof. neurology and pub. health, 1992-97; instr. neurology Harvard U. Sch. of Medicine, Boston, 1987—, prof. neurology and pub. health, 1997—, prof. medicine, 1998—; genetic epidemiologist VA Med. Ctr. Hosp., Bedford, Mass., 1997—; chief genetics program Boston U. Sch. Medicine, 1998—; dir. Boston U. Genetic Epidemiology Ctr., 1999—; cons. NIH, Bethesda, Md., 1990—, DNA diagnostic lab. Boston U. Sch. of Medicine, 1991—. Author: (with others) Clinical Neurology of Aging, 1994, Current Protocols of Human Genetics, 1994; mem. editl. bd. Am. Jour. Alzheimer Disease, 1997—; contbr. articles to profl. jours. Active mem. Temple Beth Am, 1987—; mem. Congregation Sha'rei Shalom, 1997—, bd. dirs., 1997—, v.p., 1998—. John H. Edwards fellow Ind. U., 1984-85, Neurosci. fellow Alfred P. Sloan Found., 1991-93; Rsch. grantee Nat. Inst. Neurol. Disease, 1988-93, Nat. Inst. Aging, 1991—. Fellow Am. Coll. Med. Genetics (founding, mem. test and tech. transfer com. 1993—, chair working group ApoE testingin Alzheimer disease 1994—); mem. Am. Soc. Human Genetics, Internat. Genetic Epidemiology Soc., World Fedn. Neurology, Human Genome Orgn. Home: 18 Higley Rd Ashland MA 01721-1783 Office: Boston U Sch Medicine Genetics Program 715 Albany St Boston MA 02118-2307

FARRIMOND, GEORGE FRANCIS, JR., management educator; b. Peerless, Utah, Sept. 23, 1932; s. George Francis and Ruth (Howard) F.; m. Polly Ann Fowler, Mar. 21, 1988; children: George Kenneth, Ronald Kay, Carrie Frances, Holly Jean, Celine Brooke. BS, U. Utah, 1955; MBA, U. Mo., 1968; PhD, Portland State U., 1989. Cert. profl. contracts mgr. Enlisted USAF, 1955, advanced through grades to lt. col., 1971; master navigator USAF, various locations, 1955-71; flight commdr. 360th tactical elec. war squadron USAF, Saigon, Socialist Republic of Vietnam, Vietnam, 1971-72; chief procurement ops. USAF, Wright-Patterson AFB, Ohio, 1972-73, chief pricing ops. div., 1973-76; ret. USAF, 1976; asst. prof. bus. So. Oreg. State Coll., Ashland, 1976-82, assoc. prof., 1982-89, prof., 1989—; cons. small bus., Jackson County, Oreg., 1976-95; cons. Japanese mgmt., Jackson County, 1981-94; facilitated decision making body for econ. devel. in So. Oreg., 1995. Author: (computer program) Spanish Verb Conjugation, 1980, (workbook) Pricing Techniques, 1983. Chmn. Wright-Patterson AFB div United Fund, 1973-76; little league coach various teams, Ark. and Mo., 1963-71; Sunday Sch. tchr. Ch. of Latter-day Saints, various states. Decorated Disting. Flying Cross, 5 Air medals; Minuteman Ednl. scholar Air Force Inst. Tech., 1964, Education with Industry scholar Air Force Inst. Tech., 1970. Mem. Am. Prodn. and Inventory Control Soc. (v.p. edn. com. 1982-84), Prodn. Ops. Mgmt. Soc., Cascade Systems Soc., Air Force Soc., Soc. Japanese Studies, Screenprinting & Graphic Imaging Assn. Internat., Beta Gamma Sigma. Republican. Avocations: oil painting, grandfather clocks, personal computers, reforestation. Home: 550 Carmen Rd Talent OR 97540-9708 Office: So Oreg Univ Sch Bus 1250 Siskiyou Blvd Ashland OR 97520-5010

FARRINGTON, BERTHA LOUISE, nursing administrator; b. Poteet, Tex., Jan. 20, 1937; d. Leonard Gilbert and Janie (Hernandez) Lozano; m. James Charles Farrington, Jan. 30, 1965; children: Mark Hiram, Robert Lee. BSN, Tex. Women's U., 1960; NP, U. Tex., 1984. RN, Tex. Charge nurse emergency rm. Parkland Meml. Hosp., Dallas; head nurse emergency rm./day surgery Bapt. Meml. Hosp., Pensacola, Fla.; asst. dir. health svcs. U. Tex. Southwestern Med. Ctr., Dallas, dir. student health svcs.; mem. instnl. peer rev. com. Wellness and Student Health Com. Office: 5323 Harry Hines Blvd Dallas TX 75235-8861

FARRINGTON, BUFORD LEE, lawyer; b. Kansas City, Mo., July 30, 1947; s. James Spencer and Beverly Jeanne F.; m. Diane M., Aug. 17, 1968; children: Whitney B., Jay B. BS in Pub. Adminstrn., U. Mo., 1969, JD, 1975. Bar: Mo. 1975. Atty., shareholder Paxton, Farrington & Block, P.C., Independence, Mo., 1975-84, Humphrey, Farrington & McClain, P.C., Independence, 1981—. Co-author: Independent Administration. Chmn. election bd. Jackson Co., Independence, 1986-91, mem. Rep. com., Kansas City, 1994—; vice-chmn. Charter Amendment Com., Independence, 1984. Fellow Am. Coll. Trust and Estate Counsel. Republican. Methodist. Office: Humphrey Farrington & McClain 221 West Lexington Ste 400 Independence MO 64050

FARRINGTON, GREGORY C., university administrator; b. Bronxville, N.Y.; m. Jean Farrington, 1 child: Timothy. B in Chemistry, Clarkson U., 1968; AM in Chemistry, Harvard U., 1970, PhD in Chemistry, 1972; degree (hon.), U. Uppsala, Sweden, 1984. Staff sci. GE, Schenectady, N.Y., 1972-79; assoc. prof. materials sci. and engring. U. Pa., 1979-84, prof., 1984, chair dept. materials sci. and engring., 1984-87, dir. Lab. for Rsch. on Structure of Matter, 1987-90, dean Sch. Engring. and Applied Sci., 1990-98; pres. Lehigh U., 1998—; bd. dirs. Mellon Found., Clarkson U., Wharton-SEI Ctr. for Advanced Studies in Mgmt., Moscow State Tech. U., Conv. and Vis. Bur. of Pa., Ben Franklin Partnership, John Scott Award of Pa.; mem. nat. sci. panels. Mem. editorial bd. Chemistry of Materials, Solid State Ionics, MultiVersity; author, editor several books and book chpts.; holds over 24 patents in field. Recipient Cannizzaro Gold medal Italian Chem. Soc., 1999. Mem. NSF, NRC, Carnegie Found., Internat. Soc. for Solid State Ionics (past pres.), Electrochemical Soc. (chair physical electrochemistry com.), Materials Rsch. Soc. (chair young investigator award com., councilor). Office: Lehigh U Alumni Meml Bldg 27 Bethlehem PA 18015 also: Lehigh U Office of Pres and Provost 27 Memorial Dr W Bethlehem PA 18015*

FARRINGTON, HUGH G., wholesale food and retail drug company executive; b. 1945; married. BA, Dartmouth Coll., 1968. With Hannaford Bros., Scarborough, Maine, 1968—, exec. v.p., 1981-84, pres., chief operating officer, 1984-92, pres., CEO, 1992—, dir. Office: Hannaford Bros Co 145 Pleasant Hill Rd Scarborough ME 04074-7118*

FARRINGTON, JERRY S., utility holding company executive; b. Burkburnett, Tex., 1934. B.B.A., North Tex. State U., 1955, M.B.A., 1958. With Tex. Electric Service Co., 1957-60; v.p. Tex. Utilities Co. (parent co.), Dallas, 1970-76, pres., 1983-87, chmn., CEO, 1987-95, chmn., 1995-98; pres. Dallas Power & Light Co., 1976-83; chmn., CEO Tex. Utilities Fuel Co., Tex. Utilities Mining Co., Dallas, 1987-95, chmn. emeritus, 1998—. Office: Tex Utilities Co Energy Plz 1601 Bryan St 41 Fl Dallas TX 75201-3402*

FARRINGTON, THOMAS RICHARD, financial executive, investment advisor; b. Columbus, Ohio, Oct. 10, 1941; s. Robert Alexander and Catherine Ann (Lafferty) F.; m. Saundra Sue Birk, Dec. 9, 1989. BS in Engring., Ariz. State U., Tempe, 1969, postgrad., 1969-71. Fin. systems analyst Motorola, Phoenix, 1971-77; info. systems mgr. McDonnell Douglas, St. Louis, 1977-91; investment rep. Edward D. Jones & Co., St. Louis, 1991-93; pres. Heartland Fin. Svcs. Group, Inc., Cape Girardeau, Mo., 1993—; bd. dirs. Commonwealth Realty, Inc., Cape Girardeau. Served with USAF, 1961-65. Mem. Eta Kappa Nu, Phi Theta Kappa. Republican. Lutheran. Home: 229 Hillview St Cape Girardeau MO 63703-6327 Office: Heartland Fin Svcs Group 121 S Broadview St Cape Girardeau MO 63703-5760

FARRINGTON-HOPF, SUSAN KAY, plumbing and heating contractor; b. Seattle, Dec. 17, 1940; d. Donald Robert and Dorothy May (Graf) Little; m. Edwin Terry Farrington, Sept. 4, 1959 (div. Apr. 1972); children: Cathe T., Jacqueline M.; m. William Desmond Hopf, Nov. 20, 1983. BA cum laude, U.S. Internat. U., 1975, MA, 1976. Program speaker AMR Internat., N.Y.C., 1977-82; pres. Dawson Plumbing & Heating Co., Seattle, 1979—; tng. cons. Fred Sherman, Inc., San Marcos, Calif., 1982—; cons. Pacific S.W. Airlines, San Diego, 1977, Dept. Labor Job Corps, Moses Lake, Wash., 1978. Developer assertive mgmt. workshop, 1976. Mem. Seattle Execs. Assn. (bd. dirs., treas., v.p., pres. 1993—), Nat. Bath and Kitchen Assn., Nat. Assn. Plumbing Heating Cooling Contractors, Women Own Bus. Avocations: skiing, sailing, gardening. Home: 16419 261st Ave SE Issaquah WA 98027-8214 Office: Dawson Plumbing & Heating Co 1522 12th Ave Seattle WA 98122-3908

FARRIS, CLYDE C., lawyer; b. Houston, May 24, 1943. BA, Tex. Tech U., 1966; JD, Washington U., 1973. Bar: Mo. 1973, U.S. Dist. Ct. (ea. dist.) Mo. 1974, U.S. Ct. Appeals (8th cir.) 1976, Ind. 1987, U.S. Supreme Ct. instr. St. Louis U., 1976-77; mem. civil rules com. of the Mo. Supreme Ct., 1989—. Mem. St. Louis Commn. on Crime and Law Enforcement, 1975-77, Kirkwood Rotary Club, City of Kirkwood Tax Increment Financing Commn. Mem. ABA, ATLA. Mo. Bar, Mo. Assn. Trial Attys., Bar Assn. Met. St. Louis, Rotary. Office: Copeland Thompson & Farris PC 231 S Bemiston Ave Ste 1220 Saint Louis MO 63105-1914*

FARRIS, FRANK MITCHELL, JR., retired lawyer; b. Nashville, Sept. 29, 1915; s. Frank M. and Mary (Lellyett) F.; m. Genevieve Baird, June 7, 1941; 1 dau., Genevieve B. B.A., Vanderbilt U., 1937; postgrad. N.Y. Law Sch., 1938-39. Bar: Tenn., 1939, U.S. Tax Ct., 1948, U.S. Supreme Ct., 1968. Conciliation commr. in bankruptcy U.S. Dist. Ct. Middle Dist. Tenn., 1940-42; ptnr. Farris, Warfield & Kanaday, and predecessors, Nashville, 1946-98; gen. counsel, trustee George Peabody Coll. for Tchrs., 1968-79; counsel 3d Nat. Corp., Nashville, Cherokee Equity Corp., Nashville. Commr. Watkins Inst., Nashville, 1953-95; trustee Vanderbilt U., 1979—; chmn. bd. Oak Hill Sch., Nashville, 1968-74, 80-81. Mem. ABA, Tenn. Bar Assn., Nashville Bar Assn. Home: 940 Overton Lea Rd Nashville TN 37220-1503

FARRIS, JEFFERSON DAVIS, university administrator; b. Springdale, Ark., Sept. 30, 1927; s. Jeff D. and Loretta J. (Grunder) F.; m. Patricia Ann Camp, July 31, 1948; children—Rebecca, Elizabeth, Jefferson Davis III. B.S. in Engring, U. Central Ark., 1949; M.A., Peabody Coll., 1950; M.P.H. (USPHS fellow), U. Mich., 1957; Ed.D., U. Ark., 1963; DHL. Sch. of Ozarks, 1981. Tchr. public high sch. Pine Bluff. Ark., 1950-57; dir. public health edn. Ark. Dept. Health, Little Rock, 1957-61; prof. health edn. U. Central Ark., Conway, 1961-86; chmn. dept. health and phys. edn. U. Central Ark., 1961-68, dean, 1968-75, univ. pres., 1975-86; nat. exec. dir. Nat. Assn. Intercollegiate Athletics, Kansas City, Mo., 1986-91; mem. adv. com. Nat. Endowment Humanities; chair U.S. Collegiate Sports Coun., 1988-91. Editor: A Guide for School Health Education, 1956, Handbook for Elementary Physical Education, 1964. Mem. Ark. Gov.'s Council on Youth Fitness; bd. dirs. Conway (Ark.) Meml. Hosp., 1971-86, civilian aide for Ark. to sec. of army, 1979-81. Served with USN, 1946-48. Named Layman of Yr. Ark. Assn. Dentistry for Children, 1970. Mem. Ark. Assn. Deans (pres. 1968-75), Nat. Assn. Intercollegiate Athletics. Methodist. Club: Rotary (pres. local, Paul Harris fellow 1986). Home: 2 Delavaga Cir Hot Springs National Park AR 71909-6009

FARRIS, JEROME, federal judge; b. Birmingham, Ala., Mar. 4, 1930; s. William J. and Elizabeth (White) F.; widower; children: Juli Elizabeth, Janelle Marie. BS, Morehouse Coll., 1951, LLD, 1978; MSW, Atlanta U., 1955; JD, U. Wash., 1958. Bar: Wash. 1958. Mem. Weyer, Roderick, Schroeter and Sterne, Seattle, 1958-59; ptnr. Weyer, Schroeter, Sterne & Farris and successor firms, Seattle, 1959-61, Schroeter & Farris, Seattle, 1961-63, Schroeter, Farris, Bangs & Horowitz, Seattle, 1963-65, Farris, Bangs & Horowitz, Seattle, 1965-69; judge Wash. State Ct. of Appeals, Seattle, 1969-79, U.S. Ct. of Appeals (9th cir.), Seattle, 1979—; lectr. U. Wash. Law Sch. and Sch. of Social Work, 1976—; mem. faculty Nat. Coll. State Judiciary, U. Nev., 1973; adv. bd. Nat. Ctr. for State Cts. Appellate Justice Project, 1978-81; founder First Union Nat. Bank, Seattle, 1965, dir., 1965-69; mem. U.S. Supreme Ct. Jud. Fellows Commn., 1997—; mem. Jud. Conf. Com. on Internat. Jud. Rels., 1997—. Del. The White House Conf. on Children and Youth, 1970; mem. King County (Wash.) Youth Commn., 1969-70; vis. com. U. Wash. Sch. Social Work, 1977-90; mem. King County Mental Health-Mental Retardation Bd., 1967-69; past bd. dirs. Seattle United Way; mem. Tyee Bd. Advisers, U. Wash., 1984—, bd. regents, 1985—, pres., 1990-91; trustee U. Law Sch. Found., 1978-84; mem. vis. com. Harvard Law Sch., 1996—. With Signal Corps, U.S. Army, 1952-53. Recipient Disting. Service award Seattle Jaycees, 1965, Clayton Frost award, 1966. Fellow Am. Bar Found. (sec. of fellows 1998); mem. ABA (exec. com. appellate judges conf. 1978-84, 87—, chmn. conf. 1982-83, del. jud. adminstrn. coun. 1987-88), Wash. Council on Crime and Delinquency (chmn. 1970-72), Am. Bar Found. (bd. dirs. 1987, exec. com. 1989—), State-Fed. Jud. Council of State of Wash. (vice-chmn. 1977-78, chmn. 1983-87), Order of Coif (mem. law rev.), U. Wash. Law Sch. Office: US Ct Appeals 9th Cir 1030 US Courthouse 1010 5th Ave Seattle WA 98104-1130

FARRIS, PAUL LEONARD, agricultural economist; b. Vincennes, Ind., Nov. 10, 1919; s. James David and Fairy Julia (Kahre) F.; m. Rachel Joyce Rutherford, Aug. 16, 1953; children: Nancy, Paul, John, Carl. B.S., Purdue U., 1949; M.S., U. Ill., 1950; Ph.D., Harvard U., 1954. Asst. prof. agrl. econs. Purdue U., West Lafayette, Ind., 1952-56; assoc. prof. Purdue U., 1956-59, prof., 1959-90, prof. emeritus, 1990—, head dept. agrl. econs., 1973-82; agrl. economist Dept. Agr., Washington, 1962; project leader for meat and poultry Nat. Commn. Food Mktg., Washington, 1965-66. Editor: Market Structure Research, 1964, Future Frontiers in Agricultural Marketing Research, 1983; contbr. articles to profl. jours. Served with AUS and USAAF, 1941-46. Fellow Am. Agrl. Econs. Assn.; mem. Am. Econ. Assn. Home: 1510 Woodland Ave West Lafayette IN 47906-2376 Office: Purdue U Dept Agrl Econs West Lafayette IN 47907

FARRIS, ROBERT EARL, transportation consultant, corporate executive; b. Etowah, Tenn., Mar. 7, 1928; s. Garvin B. and Edna Earle (Phillips) F.; m. Dorothy Ann Wright, Oct. 2, 1948; children: Julia Ann Farris Seward, Robert E. Cert., Kennedy Sch. Govt. Harvard U. Asst. sales promotion mgr. Toni div. Gillette Co., Chgo., 1952-60; pres., chief exec. officer Swimco, Inc., Nashville, 1960-81; commr. dept. transp. State of Tenn., Nashville, 1981-86; adminstr. Fed. Hwy. Adminstrn., Washington, 1986-89; v.p. Internat. Road Fedn., 1990—, vice chmn., 1997—; treas. IVHS Am.; vice chmn. Nashville Electric Svc., 1977-81; chmn. Nat. Coun. on Pub. Works, Washington, 1985-86. Chmn. Tenn. Rep. Party, Nashville, 1968, Tenn. Statesman, Nashville, 1984; chpt. chmn. ARC, Nashville, 1975. Recipient resolution of honor Tenn. State Senate, 1986. Mem. NAS (transp. rsch. bd.), Am. Assn. State Hwy. and Transp. Ofcls. (exec. com. 1981—), Kiwanis (pres. 1977-78), Rotary. Avocations: lic. pvt. pilot, golf, travel.

FARRIS, ROBERT HAROLD, JR., artist, educator; b. Lynn, Mass., Mar. 22, 1954; s. Robert Harold Sr. and Helen Louise (Castle) F. Student, Mass. Coll. Art, 1972-73. Assembler Western Electric Co., North Andover, Mass., 1973-74; designer's asst. Star Divsn./London Fog, Lynn, Mass., 1974-77; operator New Eng. Tel., Boston and Salem, Mass., 1977-87; customer svc. rep. Nynex Yellow Pages, Lynn, 1987-91; portrait artist East Boston Courthouse, 1991; artist Am. Embassy, Lima, Peru, 1992; owner Wood End Studio, Lynn, 1991—, tchr., 1995—; ptnr. Saltbox Gallery, Topsfield, Mass., 1994—, v.p., 1999; Contbg. artist WGBH 2 Collection, Boston, 1995—, Christopher Gallery, Cohasset, Mass., 1996—. Inductee Annual Grumbacher Calendar, 1997. Lectr. Greater Lynn Sr. Citizens, 1993; artistic supr. Sterling Cmty. Svcs., Lynn, 1994; fine art donor New Eng. Home for the Deaf, Danvers, Mass., 1996, North Shore Assn. Retarded Citizens, Salem, 1996-97. Recipient 4 Grumbacher Silver medalions Koh-I-Nor Corp., N.J., 1991-98, 3 Grumbacher Gold medallions Koh-I-Nor Corp., N.J., 1997; named to Grumbacher Hall of Fame, Koh-I-Nor Corp., N.J., 1996. Mem. Am. Soc. Classical Realism, Oil Painters Am. (assoc.), Soc. Egg Tempera Painters (artist), North Shore Art Assn. (artist), Lynnfield Art Guild (artist, bd. dirs. 1993, 6 awards 1992-95), Greater Lynn Arts and Crafts Soc. (artist, pres. 1993-94, 16 awards 1991-97). Avocations: antique collecting, gardening, woodworking, traveling. Home and Office: Wood End Studio 188 Chatham St Lynn MA 01902-2221

FARRIS, TRUEMAN EARL, JR., retired newspaper editor; b. Sedalia, Mo., June 2, 1926. PhB in Journalism, Marquette U., Milw., 1948; MA in Polit. Sci., U. Wis.-Milw., 1989. Reporter Milw. Sentinel, 1945-62, asst. city editor, 1962-75, city editor, 1975-77, mng. editor, 1977-89; juror Pulitzer Prizes, 1985-86; mem. dean's coun. Student Publs. Bd., Coll. of Comm., Journalism and Performing Arts, Marquette U., 1987-92; mem. bd. visitors U. Wis., Milw., 1991—; bd. dirs. Wis. Masonic Jour., Newspaper of State Grand Lodge, 1993—. Author series of stories: Japan, 1980. Served with U.S. Army, 1955. Recipient By-Line award Marquette U., 1987; named to Milw. Press Club Media Hall of Fame, 1989. Mem. AP Mng. Editors Assn. (dir. 1980-87, editor ann. reports 1979-85), Milw. Soc. Profl. Journalists (pres. 1982-83), Milw. Press Club (pres. 1968, several reporting awards, editorial writing award 1957, included Media Hall of Fame 1989), Civil War Round Table (sec.), Mil. Order Loyal Legion of U.S. (recorder). Methodist. Avocations: reading, genealogy, Civil War History. Home: 3192 S 80th St Milwaukee WI 53219-3501 Office: Milwaukee Sentinel PO Box 371 Milwaukee WI 53201-0371

FARRIS, VERA KING, college president; b. Atlantic City, July 18, 1940. BA in Biology magna cum laude, Tuskegee Inst., 1959; MS in Zoology, U. Mass., 1962, PhD in Zoology/Parasitology, 1965; LHD (hon.), Marymount Manhattan Coll., 1985; LLD (hon.), Monmouth Coll., West Long Branch, N.J., 1987; DSc honoris causa, Johnson and Wales Coll., 1988. Dean spl. programs, assoc. prof. pathology and biology SUNY, Stony Brook, 1968-72; vice provost acad. affairs, prof. biological sci. SUNY, Brockport, 1973-80; v.p. acad affairs, prof. biological sci. Kean Coll. N.J., Union, 1980-83; pres. Stockton State Coll., Pomona, N.J., 1983—. Contbr. articles to profl. jours. Founding mem. Gov.'s Pride award acad., 1986—, Gov.'s adv. coun. Holocaust Edn. in N.J., 1982—. Recipient Golden Trefoil award, Delaware Valley Coun. Girl Scouts Am., 1987,Chancellors Medal for Exemplary and Extraordinary Svc., U. Mass., 1986, Honor Roll Ednl award Wash. Ctr. for Internships and Acad. Seminars, Commendation for Outstanding Achievement in Edn., N.J. Assembly, 1993, others; named Lifetime Honorary citizen of Atlanta, 1984, N.J. Woman or Yr. N.J. Woman's Mag. Mem. Am. Coun. Edn. (bd. dirs. 1988-91), Coun. Post-Secondary Accreditation (bd. dirs. 1988—), Middle States Assn. Colls. and Secondary Schs. (pres. bd. trustees), Am. Assn. State Colls. and Univs. (nominating com.), N.J. State Bd. Examiners, N.J. State Coll. Pres. (chair 1987-89), B'naiB'rith (life hon.), Cosmos Club (Washington). Home: 300 Shore Rd Linwood NJ 08221-2527 Office: Richard Stockton Coll NJ Office of the President Jimmie Leeds Rd Pomona NJ 08240*

FARRON, ROBERT, physician, family practice; b. N.Y.C., May 17, 1947; s. Irving and Anne (Zavoznick) F.; m. Lorraine Herzberg, May 27, 1972; children: Cory, Eric, Jeffrey. BS, CCNY, 1968; DO, Kansas City Coll. Osteo. Med., 1972. Diplomate Am. Bd. Family Practice, Am. Osteo. Bd. Family Practice. Intern Interboro Gen. Hosp., Bklyn., 1972-73; practice medicine specializing in family practice Far Rockaway, N.Y., 1973—, Valley Stream, N.Y., 1978—; attending physician Peninsula Hosp. Ctr., Far Rockaway, N.Y., 1985—; asst. prof. family practice N.Y. Coll. Osteopathic Medicine. Recipient Physicians Recognition award AMA, 1983, 86, 89, 92, 95, 98. Fellow Am. Acad. Family Physicians; mem. Am. Osteo. Assn., N.Y. Osteo. Soc., Am. Osteo. Coll. Family Practice, Mensa, N.Y. State Med. Soc., Queens County Med. Soc. Avocation: boating. Office: 2240 Mott Ave Far Rockaway NY 11691-3070 also: 201 E Merrick Rd Valley Stream NY 11580-5952

FARROW, JULIE ANNE, retired geriatrics nurse, administrator; b. Columbus, Ohio, Nov. 13, 1941; d. John Edward and Marjorie Elizabeth (Morris) White; m. Gerald D. Farrow, Oct. 14, 1997; children: Kelly Elizabeth, Douglas Kent, Robert Kurt, Steven Michael. Diploma, St. Elizabeth Sch. Nursing, Lafayette, Ind., 1962; student, South Oklahoma City Jr. Coll., 1983. Cert. in intravenous therapy. Adminstr. Alcare Personalized Svcs., Edmond, Okla.; DON, tng. dir. Alpha Nurses, Oklahoma City; DON Bryant Nursing Ctr., Edmond, Westlake Nursing Ctr., Oklahoma City, Stattuck (Okla.) Nursing Ctr.; ret., 1998. Author: Emergency! Faith's Desire, 1999. Home: 4132 Banks Rd Saint Ann MO 63074-1007

FARROW, MARGARET ANN, state legislator; b. Kenosha, Wis., Nov. 28, 1934; d. William Charles and Margaret Ann (Horan) Nemitz; m. John Harvey Farrow, Dec. 29, 1956; children—John, William, Peter, Paul, Mark. Student Rosary Coll., 1952-53; B.S. in Polit. Sci., Marquette U., 1956, postgrad., 1975-77. Tchr., Archiodese of Milw., 1956-57; trustee Elm Grove Village, Wis., 1976-81, pres., 1981-86; mem. Wis. State Assembly, 1986-89, State Senate, 1989—, chair govt. effectiveness, 1998—, mem. com. environment & energy, 1998—, asst. majority leader, 1998—; mem. joint com. on audit, 1995—, mem. joint survey com. on tax exemptions, 1995—, chair Wis. women's coun., 1991—, mem. low level radioactive waste coun., 1991—, mem. com. on land use, 1996, Rep. caucus chair, 1996—, mem. privatization coun., 1995—, mem. coun. on workforce excellence, 1995—, mem. Wis. consumer act rev. com., 1997—, mem. Wis. glass ceiling commn., 1993—. Home: W267 N2825 Woodland Dr Pewaukee WI 53072-4474 Office: Wis State Capitol Senate House Madison WI 53702*

FARROW, ROBERT SCOTT, economist, educator; b. L.A., Dec. 5, 1952; s. Robert Bruce and Eleanor (Dietrich) F.; m. Elaine A. Farrow, July 3, 1988. BA, Whitman Coll., Walla Walla, Wash., 1974; MA, Wash. State U., 1980, PhD, 1983. Rschr. Frank LeRoux Inc., Walla Walla, Wash., 1975-77; economist Coun. on Wage and Price Stability, Exec. Office of the Pres., Washington, 1979, Minerals Mgmt. Svc., U.S. Dept. Interior, Washington, 1985-86; ptnr. West Ten Organic Farm, Walla Walla, Wash., 1975-90; asst. prof. Carnegie Mellon U., Pitts., 1982-89, assoc. prof., 1989-93, dir. ctr. study improvement regulation, prin. rsch. economist, 1999—; sr. economist, assoc. dir. Coun. on Environ. Quality, Exec. Office of Pres., 1990-92; assoc. Dames and Moore, 1994-98; vis. assoc. prof. Pa. State U., 1997-98; cons. Office Tech. Assessment, Coun. on Wage and Price Stability, Harvard Inst. Internat. Devel.; cons., spkr. on offshore oil and gas devel., econ. instruments for environ. policy; mem. sci. com. of outer continental shelf adv. bd. U.S. Dept. Interior, 1990-93; mem. effluent task force EPA, 1994-96; mem. man and biosphere directorate U.S. Dept. State, 1992-95. Author: Managing The Outer Continental Shelf Lands, 1990; contbg. author, rschr.: The Myth of U.S. Agricultural Prosperity, 1976; environ. editor Hist. Statistics of the U.S.; reviewer, contbr. articles to profl. jours. Rev. com. for the aged and disadvantaged United Way, Pitts., 1988-89; trustee Miami Valley Bus. Economists, 1994-95. Lindbergh grant Charles A. Lindbergh Fund, Mpls., 1984; Marine Policy fellow Woods Hole Oceanographic Inst., 1988-89, Sr. fellow, 1998. Mem. Am. Econs. Assn., Assn. Environ. and Resource Econs. (editorial coun., nominating com. 1989-92), Pitts. Athletic Assn., Phi Kappa Phi. Avocation: collecting first edition books. Office: Dept of Engrng and Pub Policy Carnegie Mellon U 5000 Forbes Ave Pittsburgh PA 15213-3815

FARRUG, JAY (EUGENE JOSEPH FARRUG, JR.), technology executive, consultant; b. Hinsdale, Ill., July 17, 1961; s. Eugene Joseph and Dolores (Augustine) F. BS, Ill. State U., 1983. Analyst Motorola Corp., Schaumburg, Ill., 1984-87; cons. Peat, Marwick & Main, Chgo., 87-88, Applied Info., Oak Brook, Ill., 1988-89; v.p. Americom Teledata, Chgo., 1989-90; CEO Interactive Tech. Corp., Oak Brook, 1990—; developer IIT Worldwide Fax/Data Network, 1996—; ptnr. Integrated Internat. Telecomms. LLC, 1996—; bd. dirs. Compuvoice Corp., LLC, Oakbrook; principle of counsel Brandley, McMarie & Seiber, Schaumburg; ptnr. real estate venture firm, 1992—, IIT Worldwide Fax/Data Network. inventor software Windows Computer Telephony. V.p., Bd. dirs. Better Way Found., 1993—. Mem. Data Processing Mgmt. Soc., Ill. State U. Alumni Assn. (bd. dirs. 1992-94), Alpha Tau Omega (v.p. 1984-90, pres. 1990-92, bd. dirs. 1993—). Avocations: boating, skiing, racquetball, sailing, golfing.

FARRUKH, USAMAH OMAR, electrical engineering educator, researcher; b. Beirut, Lebanon, Aug. 24, 1944; came to U.S., 1969; s. Omar Abdullah and Amenah (Helmi) F.; m. Samar M. Hussami, 1980; children: Muna, Omar, Marwa. BSEE, Am. U. Beirut, 1967; PhDEE, U. So. Calif., 1974. Lead analyst Wolf R & D Group, Riverdale, Md., 1975-76; sci. specialist Phoenix Corp., McLean, Va., 1976-77; sci. cons. Applied Sci. and Tech. Inc., Rosslyn, Va., 1978; staff scientist Inst. Atmospheric Optics and Remote Sensing, Hampton, Va., 1978-85; assoc. prof. dept. elec. engring. Hampton U., 1985-93, prof., 1993—; cons. U.S. Army Rsch. Office, 1990-91; summer faculty Dept. Energy, 1995. Contbr. articles to profl. jours. Bd. dirs. Hypohidrotic Ectodermal Dysplasia and Related Disorders Found., Hampton, 1987—. Grantee NASA, 1986-95, U.S. Army Rsch. Lab., 1993-95, Dept. Energy Summer Faculty Subcontract, 1995. Mem. IEEE, Optical Soc. Am. Office: Hampton Univ Olin Engring Bldg Hampton VA 23601

FARSON, RICHARD EVANS, psychologist; b. Chgo., Nov. 16, 1926; s. Duke Mendenhall and Mary Gladys (Clark) F.; m. Elizabeth Lee Grimes, May 21, 1954 (div. 1962); children: Lisa Page, Clark Douglas; m. 2d Dawn Jackson Cooper, Jan. 4, 1964 (div. 1990); children: Joel Andrew, Ashley Dawn, Jeremy Richard. BA, Occidental Coll., 1947, MA, 1951; postgrad., UCLA, 1948-50; PhD, U. Chgo., 1955. Dean Sch. Design Calif. Inst. Arts, Valencia, 1969-73; pres. Esalen Inst., Big Sur and San Francisco, 1973-75; faculty Saybrook Inst., San Francisco, 1975-79; pres. Western Behavioral Scis. Inst., La Jolla, Calif., 1958-68; chmn. bd. Western Behavior Scis. Inst., La Jolla, Calif., 1968-79, pres., 1979—; dir. Internat. Design Conf., Aspen, Colo., 1971—, pres. 1976-80, 94-97. Editor: Science and Human Affairs, 1967; author: Birthrights, 1974, Management of the Absurd: Paradoxes in Leadership, 1996, (with others) The Future of the Family, 1969. Served to lt. j.g. USNR, 1955-57. Ford Found. fellow, Harvard U. Bus. Sch., 1953-54. Mem. Am. Psychol. Assn., Sigma Xi, Psi Chi. Address: 636 Prospect St La Jolla CA 92037-4225

FARST, DON DAVID, zoo director, veterinarian; b. Wadsworth, Ohio, Feb. 25, 1941; s. Walter K. and Ada (Stetler) F.; m. Jan Rae Harber, June 17, 1980; children: Julie K., Jenny Lynn, John David. D.V.M., Ohio State U., 1965. Veterinarian, mammals curator Columbus Zoo, Ohio, 1969-70; assoc. dir. Gladys Porter Zoo, Brownsville, Tex., 1970-74, dir., 1974—. Editor: Jour. Zoo Animal Medicine, 1973-77. Mem. Am. Assn. Zool. Parks and Aquariums (pres. 1979-80, chmn. ethics bd. 1990-91), Am. Assn. Zoo Veterinarians, Internat. Union Dirs. Zool. Home: 640 Edgewater Isle San Benito TX 78586-7614 Office: Gladys Porter Zoo 500 Ringgold St Brownsville TX 78520-7998

FARUKI, CHARLES JOSEPH, lawyer; b. Bay Shore, N.Y., July 3, 1949; s. Mahmud Taji and Rita (Trownsell) F.; m. Nancy Louise Glock, June 5, 1971 (div. Oct. 1995); children: Brian Andrew, Jason Allen, Charles Joseph Jr.; m. Michelle F. Zalar, June 15, 1996. BA summa cum laude, U. Cin., 1971; JD cum laude, Ohio State U., 1973. Bar: Ohio 1974, U.S. Dist. Ct. (no. and so. dists.) Ohio 1975, U.S. Ct. Appeals (9th cir.) 1977, U.S. Tax Ct. 1977, U.S. Supreme Ct. 1977, U.S. Ct. Appeals (6th cir.) 1978, U.S. Dist. Ct. (no. dist.) Tex. 1979, U.S. Dist. Ct. (ea. dist.) Ky. 1982, U.S. Ct. Appeals (D.C. cir.) 1982, U.S. Ct. Customs and Patent Appeals 1982, U.S. Ct. Appeals (4th cir.) 1986, U.S. Ct. Appeals (2d cir.) 1989, U.S. Ct. Appeals (fed. cir.), 1991, U.S. Ct. Appeals (8th cir.) 1997. Assoc. Smith & Schnacke, Dayton, Ohio, 1974-78; ptnr. Smith & Schnacke, Dayton, 1979-89; founder, mng. ptnr. Faruki Gilliam & Ireland, PLL, Dayton, 1989—; Mem. bd. dirs. Smith & Schnacke, Dayton, 1980-88; lectr. various continuing legal edn. programs. Contbr. articles in field. Served to capt. U.S. Army Res., 1971-79. Fellow Am. Bar Found., Am. Coll. Trial Lawyers (complex litigation com.); mem. ABA, Fed. Bar Assn. (officer and exec. com. Dayton chpt. 1988-93, pres. 1991-92), Ohio State Bar Assn. (bd. govs. Antitrust sect. 1992—), Dayton Bar Assn. (officer 1992-94, pres. 1994-95), Def. Rsch. Inst., Human Factors and Ergonomics Soc. (affiliate mem.), Fed. Cir. Bar Assn. Avocation: numismatics. Home: 300 Fairforest Cir Dayton OH 45419-1308 Office: Faruki Gilliam & Ireland PLL 600 Courthouse Plz SW Dayton OH 45402

FARUOLO, EDWARD A., marketing professional. BA in Comm. Arts, Seton Hall U., 1975. Account exec. Tatham-Laird & Kudner Advt./Direct Mktg., N.Y.C., 1977-79; sr. account exec. Warwick Advt., Inc., N.Y.C., 1979-82; v.p., dir. client svcs. Harland, O'Conner, Tine, and White, Inc., Hartford, Conn., 1983-85; mgmt. supr. mktg. svcs. The Travelers Cos., Hartford, Conn., 1985, asst. dir. mktg. svcs., 1986, dir. advt. and promotion, 1986-90; asst. v.p. mktg. comm. CIGNA Cos., Hartford, 1990-93; asst. v.p. corp. mktg. comms. CIGNA Cos., Phila., 1993-99; v.p. corp. mktg. comms. CIGNA Cos., 1999—. Office: CIGNA Corp 900 Cottage Grove Rd Hartford CT 06152-0001*

FARVER, MARY JOAN, building products company executive; b. Nov. 17, 1919; d. Peter Herman and Emma Lucile Kuyper; m. Paul V. Farver, Oct. 12, 1945 (div. 1979); children—Mary Farver Griffith, Charles S., Suzanne. BA, Grinnell Coll., 1941; DFA (hon.), Central Coll., Pella, Iowa, 1988. Sec. Central Nat. Bank, Des Moines, 1941-43; sec. TWA Exec. Office, Washington, 1943-45; chmn. bd. Pella Corp., Pella, Iowa, 1980-92, chmn. emeritus, 1992—. Bd. dirs., mem. exec. com. Central Coll., Pella, 1978—; mem. bd. Iowa Coll. Found., Des Moines, 1984—, Iowa Pub. TV Found., Des Moines, 1983-88. Republican. Mem. Reformed Ch. of Am. Clubs: Pella Garden (pres. 1961). Lodge: P.E.O. Sisterhood (pres. 1962-64). Home: 2609 Spring Grove Ter Colorado Springs CO 80906-3714 Office: Pella Corp 102 Main St Pella IA 50219-2198

FARWATI, ABDUL JALIL, architect, civil engineer; b. Aleppo, Syria, Feb. 26, 1966; s. Bakri and Fatima Farwati. B of Architectural Design, Thomas A. Edison State U., 1994. Civil engring. mgr. USA Engring. Co., Cherry Hill, 1990-93; designer, mgr. Am. Architecture Co., Maclean, 1993-96, master architect, 1996—; sr. projects mgr. Paradox Architecture & Design Co., 1992—. Recipient Best Student award Louver Mus., 1988. Fax: (609) 435-6363. E-mail: alex021966@aol.com. Office: 550 Bilper Ave #5509 Lindenwold NJ 08021

FARWELL, ALBERT EDMOND, retired government official, consultant; b. Providence, June 7, 1915; s. Albert Potter and Elizabeth (Shelmerdine) F.; m. Elizabeth Fuller Thurlow, May 18, 1940 (dec. Apr. 21, 1975); children: Bruce Albert, Christopher James; m. Gertrude Cochran Ridgely, Sept. 9, 1978. AB, Brown U., 1935; MA, U. Ariz., 1937. Various non govtl. positions, 1939-45; exec. dir. Fgn. Trade Found., 1945-46; sr. editor Bur. Nat. Affairs, Washington, 1946-48; chief procedures and publ. br. Dept. Commerce, 1948-49; econ. analyst ECA, Greece, 1949-51; dep. dir. strategic controls div. Dept. Commerce, 1951-52; program analyst MSA, FOA, 1952-54; chief Near East div. FOA, ICA, 1955; chief Program Office Nr. East and So. Asia ICA, 1956-59; spl. asst. to undersec. mut. security Dept. State, 1959-60; dep. dir. AID, Nepal, 1960-65; dir. AID, Costa Rica, 1965-67; dep. dir. AID, Laos, 1967, dir., 1968; assoc. dir. AID, Vietnam, 1968-73; dir. labor relations AID, 1973-74, cons. vector-borne disease control, econ. devel. planning and adminstrn., 1974—; pres. Alphi Assos., 1979—. Recipient Meritorious Service award ICA, 1953, 55, Meritorious Service award Dept. State, 1960; Pub. Safety award Govt. of Costa Rica, 1967; Vietnam Service award AID, 1970; Superior Honor award, 1974; Presdl. Order of Merit; Def. Honor medal; numerous others. Mem. Am. Acad. Polit. and Social Sci., Soc. Labor Relations Profls., Am. Fgn. Service Assn. Address: 13861 N Buccaneer Way Sun City AZ 85351-2735 also: 2831 Oakton Manor Ct Oakton VA 22124-3016

FARWELL, BYRON EDGAR, writer; b. Manchester, Iowa, June 20, 1921; m. Ruth Saxby; children: Joyce, Byron John, Lesley. Student, Ohio State U., 1939-40; A.M., U. Chgo., 1968. Dir. adminstrn. Chrysler Internat., Geneva, 1959-70; archeologist; delivered Anne S.K. Brown Meml. lectr. on mil. history, Brown U., Providence, R.I., 1996. Author: The Man Who Presumed, 1953, 4th edit., paperback, 1989, U.K. edit., 1958, Books on Tape, 1995, Burton: A Biography of Sir Richard Francis Burton, 1964, 75, U.K. edit., 63, 88, 95, Books on Tape, 1994, Prisoners of the Mahdi, 1967, paperback 1971, 89, UK edit., 1967, Books on Tape, 1994, Queen Victoria's Little Wars, 1972, U.S. paperback edit., 1985, 2d edit., 1989, U.K. edit., 1973, Books on Tape, 1994, The Great Anglo-Boer War, 1976, U.K. edit., 1977, paperback edit., 1990, Books on Tape, 1994, Mr. Kipling's Army, 1981, U.K. edit., 1987, Books on Tape, 1994, For Queen and Country, 1981, paperback edit., 1987, Books on Tape, 1994, The Gurkhas, 1984, U.K. paperback edit., 1985, U.S. paperback edit., 1990, Books on Tape, 1994, Eminent Victorian Soldiers, 1985, paperback edit., 1986, U.K. edit., 1988, Books on Tape, 1993, The Great War in Africa, 1914-1918, 1986, UK edit., 1987, U.S. paperback edit., 1989, Books on Tape, 1994, Armies of the Raj, 1989, U.K. edit., 1990, U.S. paperback edit., 1991, Books on Tape, 1994, Ball's Bluff: A Small Battle and its Long Shadow, 1990, Books on Tape, 1994, Stonewall: A Biography of General Thomas Jackson, 1992, paperback edit., 1993, Books on Tape, 1993; Over There: The United States in the Great War, 1916-18, 1999; The Encyclopedia of Nineteenth Century Land Warfare, 1999; contbg. editor: Military History, World War II; contbr. The Reader's Companion to Military History, Oxford Companion to American Military History, 1996; contbr. numerous articles to Colliers Ency., newspapers, revs., mags.; mem. edit. bd. Small Towns Inst.; lectr. in field. Former councilman and mayor, Hillsboro, Va.; hon. mem., bd. dirs. Oatlands of Nat. Trust; former trustee Am. Mil. Inst.; mem. adv. bd. Nat. History Soc. Capt. C.E., U.S. Army, 1940-45, ordnance corps, 1950-53. Fellow Royal Soc. Lit. (U.K.), fell. Royal Geog. Soc. (U.K.). Address: PO Box 3200C Hillsboro VA 20134-1510

FARWELL, ELWIN D., minister, educational consultant; b. Branch County, Mich., May 1, 1919; s. Don J. and Dessa (Clingan) F.; m. Helen Irene Hill, Aug. 23, 1942; children: Don Lucian, Helen Kay, James Lyman, Judith Anne. BS, Mich. State U, 1943, MS, 1947; EdD, U. Calif. at Berkeley, 1959; BD, Pacific Lutheran Theol. Sem., Berkeley, 1959; LLD (hon.), Loras Coll., 1969, Valparaiso U., 1980, Luther Coll., 1986, Dana Coll., 1992; Calif. Luth. U., 1994; LLD (hon.), St. John's U., 1981; LHD (hon.), St. Olaf Coll., 1982. Instr. animal husbandry Mich. State U., 1947-49, asst. prof., 1949-55; cons. point 4 program State Dept. U. Nacional, Colombia, 1952; adminstrv. asst. to chmn. Center Study Higher Edn., U. Calif. at Berkeley, 1956-59; ordained to ministry Luth. Ch., 1958; pastor in Andrew, Iowa, 1959-61; academic dean Calif. Luth. Coll., Thousand Oaks, Calif., 1961-63; pres. Luther Coll., Decorah, Iowa, 1963-82; vis. scholar U. Calif.-Berkeley, 1982; profl. cons., 1983—; pres. Dana Coll., Blair, Nebr., 1985-86; dir. study theol. edn. Luth. Ch. U.S.A., 1984-86; adminstrv. cons. Pacific Luth. Theol. Sem., 1987-88; interim bishop Nebr. Synod Evan. Luth. Ch. in Am., 1990; interim pastor St. Paul Luth. Ch., Monona, Iowa, 1990-91, 97; interim bishop Rocky Mountain Synod Evangel. Luth. Ch. in Am., 1993-94. Author: Livestock Development and Selection, 1951, (with others) Stability of Change, 1964; contbr. articles to profl. jours., encys. Mem. Iowa Gov.'s Com. Conservation Natural Resources, 1964-68, Iowa Gov.'s Commn. Coop. State and Local Govt., 1964-66; mem. Iowa Coordinating Coun. Higher Edn., 1967-70, pres., 1968-69; chmn. Com. Intergovtl. Coop. and Comm., 1964-65, Gov.'s Com. on Govt. Reorgn., 1966, State Adv. Com. on Cmty. and Jr. Coll., 1965-69; mem. exec. com. Iowa Assn. Pvt. Colls. and Univs., 1964-73, 76-78, chmn., 1971-72; chmn. Coun. Coll. Pres.'s Am. Luth. Ch., 1976-77; mem. exec. com. Norwegian-Am. Mus. Assn., 1965-71; chmn. World Brotherhood Found., 1962-77; chmn. Iowa Coll. Found., 1968-69; mem. Iowa Campaign Fin. Disclosure Commn., 1977-91, chmn., 1980-81, 87-89; mem. Iowa Mental Health Adv. Coun., 1978-81, Am. Scandinavian Found.; bd. govs. Calif. Luth. Ednl. Found., 1957-59; bd. dirs. Inst. European Studies, 1977-81; bd. Nat. Luth. Campus Ministry, 1966-69; pres. Luth. Ednl. Conf. N.Am., 1973-74, mem. legis. policy com., 1978-81; counselor Luth. Coun. U.S.A., 1975-79; bd. dirs. Gundersen Med. Found., La Crosse, Wis., 1976-81; bd. regents Dana Coll., 1986-95; trustee Iowa Natural Heritage Found., 1983-92, Iowa Humanities Found., 1992—; bd. dirs. Luth. Social Svc. of Iowa, 1992-95, Winneshiek County Hosp. Found., 1992-97. Capt. U.S. Army, 1943-46, PTO. Decorated Knight's Cross 1st class Order St. Olav, 1975, Knight's Cross 1st class Order No. Star, 1977 (Sweden); recipient Disting. Patriarchs award Mich. State U., 1993. Mem. Ctrl. State Coll. Assn. (dir. 1964-76, chmn. 1967), Nat. Assn. Ind. Colls. and Univs. (bd. dirs. 1977-78), Oneota Golf and Country Club (pres. 1987-89), Rotary, Phi Beta Kappa, Phi Delta Kappa, Alpha Gamma Rho, Alpha Zeta. Home: 504 Locust Rd #3 Decorah IA 52101-1037

FARWELL, HAROLD FREDERICK, JR., English language educator; b. Oak Park, Ill., Apr. 9, 1934; s. Harold Frederick and Dorothy Delma (Cobb) F.; m. Joyce G. Farwell, Feb. 10, 1961; children: Douglas G., Beth Elene, Amy Kathleen, Ellen Claudia. BA, U. Chgo., 1960, MA, 1961; PhD, U. Wis., Madison, 1970. Instr. English Drake U., Des Moines, 1960-61; asst. prof. U. Cin., 1966-70; assoc. prof., prof. Western Carolina U., Cullowhee, N.C., 1970—; dir. English grad. program Western Carolina U., Cullowhee, 1980-90, 97—; ranger U.S. Park Svcs., Great Smokies Nat. Park, 1983. Editor: Smoky Mountain Voices, 1993; reporter Opera News, 1982—; editor, reporter The Arts Jour. With USN, 1956-58. Fulbright sr. lectr., The Phillipines, 1986-87, Indonesia, 1991; rsch. grantee Western Carolina U., 1974, 93, 94, 97; SDIP grantee U. Tex., 1981; China Field Study grantee, 1995, 96; Ctr. for Tchg. Excellence fellow Western Carolina U., 1992-94; fellow East-West Ctr., Honolulu, 1997. Mem. Coll. English Assn., Dictionary Soc. N.Am., South Atlantic Modern Lang. Assn., Southeastern Com. on Linguistics. Avocations: hiking, nature study. Home: PO Box 838 Cullowhee NC 28723-0838

FARWELL, NANCY LARRAINE, public relations executive; b. Sellersville, Pa., May 2, 1944; d. Warren Gregory and Mary Rita (Zaniboni) F. BA, Pa. State U., 1966. Asst. TV rep. H.R. TV Reps., Phila., 1966-68; various positions Hawthorne Advt. Inc., Phila., 1968-73; dir. employee rels. Colonial Penn Group, Inc., Phila., 1973-75, mgr. press rels., 1976-78, mgr. pub. rels., 1978-82; dir. communications Provident Mutual Life Ins. Co., Phila., 1982-83, asst. v.p., communications, 1983-87; pres. Nancy Farwell Assocs., Phila., 1987-90; v.p. Anne Klein & Assocs., Inc., Mt. Laurel, N.J., 1990-92, sr. v.p., 1992-97, sr. v.p., COO, 1998—; Adv. bd. City of Phila. Century IV Tall Ships, 1982. Author: (photo essay) Philadelphia, 1976; contbr. chpt. to home health care marketing book. Founder, co-chair Portico Row Neighborhood Assn., Phila., 1989-92; bd. dirs. Washington Square West Project Area Com., Phila., 1990-92, Boys and Girls Clubs of Metro Phila. Adv. Coun., 1991—; adv. com. Phila. 6th Police Dist., 1990-92. Recipient 2 Gold Quill Phila. chpt. Internat. Assn. Bus. Communicators, 5 Awards of Excellence Life Communicators Assn., Art Dirs. Club of Phila.; named Super Communicator of the 80's Women in Communications, Phila. chpt. Mem. Pub. Rels. Soc. Am. (7 Pepperpot awards, Award of Excellence), Phila. Pub. Rels. Assn., Forum of Exec. Women. Office: Anne Klein & Assocs Inc Three Greentree Ctr Ste 200 Marlton NJ 08053

FARWELL, WALTER MAURICE, vocalist, educator; b. Sidney, Iowa, Mar. 29, 1928; s. Clyde Ross and Erma Leona (Liggett) F. B.Mus.Edn., U. Mo., Kansas City, 1950; MA, U. Iowa, 1953. Vocal music tchr. pub. schs., Fayette, Iowa, 1953-59; head voice tchr. Wartburg Coll., Waverly, Iowa, 1960-61; vocal music tchr. pub. schs., Tipton, Iowa, 1961-67; music educator pub. schs., Davenport, Iowa, 1967-90; choir dir. Meth. Ch., Fayette, Tipton, 1953—; vocal soloist, 1953—; organist Replacement Tng. Ctr., Ft. Bragg, N.C., 1951-52. Author: (4 vols.) History of Fremont County, Iowa, 1968-91; contbr.: Bells of Stony Creek, 1994; editor: Court Records Atchison County, Mo. (pamphlet), 1985; cons. (county history) Thumbprints in time, 1996. Cpl. U.S. Army, 1950-52. Recipient Am. Legion award, 1941. Mem. NEA, Davenport Area Ret. Tchrs. Assn., Fremont County Hist. Soc. (charter), Hacker Creek Pioneer Assn. Methodist. Avocation: historical and genealogical research. Home: 549 E 4th St Tipton IA 52772-1933

FASANELLA, RALPH P., artist; b. Bronx, N.Y., Sept. 10, 1914; s. Joseph and Ginevra (Spagnoletti) F.; m. Matilda Weiss, 1943 (div. 1944); m. Elizabeth Lazorek, July 29, 1950; children: Gina Marie, Ralph Marc. lectr. in field. Co-author: (with Patrick Watson) Fasanella's City, 1973; printings featured in numerous books and mags. Recipient numerous awards. Democrat. Avocations: carpentry, reading. Home: 15 Chester St Ardsley NY 10502

FASANELLA, ROCKO MICHAEL, ophthalmologist; b. Trenton, N.J., Aug. 4, 1916. MD, Yale U., 1943; postgrad. in Ophthalmology, U. Pa., 1946-47, Lancaster Course Ophthalmology, 1947-48. Intern Grace-Comty. Hosp., New Haven, Conn., 1943-44; asst. resident in ophthalmology Grace-Comty. Hosp., New Haven, 1948-49, resident in ophthalmology, 1949-50; rotating intern Mercer Hosp., Trenton, N.J., 1946-47; cons. St. Raphael's Hosp., New Haven, Conn., 1950, Waterbury (Conn.) Hosp., 1950; staff mem. Windham Comty. Meml. Hosp., 1950, instr., 1950-51, chief ophthalmology sect., 1951-61; assoc. clin. prof. ophthalmology Yale U., New Haven, 1961—; cons. Office of Hearings and Appeals, Social Security Adminstrn., Washington;. Editor: (books) Management of Complications in Eye Surgery, 1st edit., 1957, 2d edit., 1965, Eye Surgery-- Innovations and Trends, Pitfalls and Complications, 1977, Modern Advances in Cataract Surgery, Chemical 3onulysis in Cataract Surgery, 1965; contbr. numerous articles to profl. jours. Capt. med. corps Army U.S., 1944-46. Assoc. fellow Ezra Stiles Coll. Fellow AMA (life), Am. Assn. Ophthalmologists and Otolaryngologists; mem. Soc. Francaise d' Ophthal., Soc. Americana de Oft, Pan Am. Ophthal. Found., Glaucoma Soc. Eng., Opthal. Soc., Castroviejo Soc.-Inst. Barraquer-SES (charter), Am. Soc. Ophthalmic, Plastice and Reconstructive Surgery (charter F., Carribean Ophthal. Soc. (founder), Oxford Ophthalmol. Congress, Am. Acad. Ophthalmology and Otolaryngology, Pan. Am. Acad. Ophthalmology and Otolaryngology, Pan Pacific Soc. Ophthalmology, N.Y. Soc. for Clin. Ophthalmology, New Haven Med. Soc., Conn. Med. Soc. Office: 29 Rolling Ridge Rd Orange CT 06477-3002

FASANO, ANTHONY JOHN, marketing consultant; b. San Antonio, Sept. 22, 1947; s. Patrick Joseph and Frances (Greco) F.; m. Leatine Winders, June 21, 1984. AA, Iowa State U., 1968, BS, 1969. Program dir. KDMI-FM, Des Moines, 1966-68; asst. dir. Sta. WHO-TV, Des Moines, 1968-71; advt. assoc. San Antonio Light Newspaper, 1971-75; advt. dir. San Antonio Mag., 1976-77; pres. Anthony J. Fasano & Assocs., San Antonio, 1977-99; dir. mktg. cons. Southwestern Bell Yellow Pages, San Antonio, 1997-98; v.p. account supr. Dialogue Works, 1999; mktg. dir. Environ. Delivery Systems, San Antonio, 1988-90; v.p. prod. devel. Parent Banc, 1990-95, co-developer childrens ednl. product, 1990-95. Account exec. direct mail campaign, Equity III Telephone, 1985, Security Link, 1987-92; account exec. DM program Tie Communication Dealer Co-op., 1987-89; creative dir. campaign The Gun Cleaning System, 1988-90. Vol. Tex. Rep. party, 1979—. Mem. Direct Mktg. Assn. Roman Catholic. Avocations: philately, bicycling, fitness. Office: 433 W Elsmere Pl San Antonio TX 78212-2228

FASCHING, MICHAEL CLOUD, plastic surgeon; b. Mpls., Jan. 21, 1954. BA, St. Thomas U., 1976; MD, Mayo Med. Sch., 1980. Diplomate Am. Bd. Surgery, Am. Bd. Plastic Surgery; certificate added qualification in hand surgery. Intern in gen. surgery Hennnepin County Med. Ctr., 1980-86; resident in plastic surgery Mayo Clinic, Rochester, Minn., 1986-88; pvt. practice, Edina, Minn., 1988—. Office: Midwest Plastic Surgery 6545 France Ave S Ste 240 Edina MN 55435

FASCITELLI, MICHAEL D., real estate executive; m. Beth Fascitelli; children: Nicholas, Matthew, Jack. BS in Indsl. Engring. summa cum laude, U. R.I., 1978; MBA, Harvard U., 1982. Plant mgr. Bristol Myers, 1978-82; assoc., then engagement mgr. McKinsey & Co., Inc., N.Y.C., 1982-85; with real estate dept. Goldman, Sachs & Co., 1985-92, ptnr., 1992-96; pres. Vornado Realty Trust, N.Y.C., 1996—; mem. Real Estate Bd. N.Y.; mem. adv. bd. Wharton Real Estate Ctr. Active Greater N.Y. coun. Boy Scouts Am. Recipient Good Scout award Boy Scouts Am.; James E. West Fellow, 1997. Mem. Urban Land Inst. (trustee), Internat. Coun. Shopping Ctrs., NYU Real Estate Roundtable, Metedeconk Nat. Golf Club, Atlantic Golf Club. Office: Vornado Realty Trust 14th Fl 1330 Ave of the Americas New York NY 10019

FASEL, HERMANN F., aerospace and mechanical engineering educator; b. Schwaebisch Gmuend, Germany, Sept. 8, 1943; s. Karl N. and Maria (Rupp) Fa.; m. Janet L. Fox, June 2, 1972; children: Michael H., Lars B. BS, U. Stuttgart, Germany, 1966, PhD, 1974; MS, U. Kans., 1967. Asst. prof. U. Stuttgart, 1974-78, Heisenberg fellow, 1978-82; vis. assoc. prof. U. Ariz.,

Tucson, 1982-84, prof. aerospace and mech. engring., 1984—. Office: U Ariz Dept Aerospace & Mech Engr Tucson AZ 85718

FASH, MICHAEL WILLIAM, cinematographer, director; b. London, Apr. 29, 1940; came to U.S., 1983; s. Alfred Norris and Katharine (Bell) F.; m. Jane Graham Partridge, Apr. 14, 1972; children: Alexandra, Nicholas, Katharine. Attended, Richmond Art Sch., London, 1959. Dir. of photography B.B.C., London, 1959-69, Thames TV, London, 1969-80. Cinematographer: (TV movies) Naked Civil Servant, 1975 (British Acad. award 1976), The Sun is God, 1975 (British Acad. nomination 1976), The One and Only Phyliss Dixie, 1978 (British Acad. nomination 1978), Bill, 1979 (Emmy for Best Picture 1980), Movie Stars Daughter, 1978 (Emmy for Best Photography 1979), Orpheus Descending, 1990, Sara Plain and Tall, 1993, Christy, 1993, Grace and Glory, 1998, Love Letters, 1998, Double Platinum, 1998; (features) Britannia Hosp., 1981, Betrayal, 1982, The Whales of August, 1986, Entertaining Angels: The Dorothy Day Story, 1996, The Confession, 1997; dir. TV commls. Recipient award British Soc. of Cinematographers, London, 1977. Mem. IATSE, NATAS, Dirs'. Guild Am. Avocations: tennis, skiing, sailing, fly fishing, painting. Home and Office: 415 Mine Hill Rd Fairfield CT 06430-2153

FASH, VICTORIA R., Healthcare company executive. Sr. v.p. bus. strategy Dun & Bradstreet Corp., 1995-96; exec. v.p., CFO Cognizant, 1996—; exec. v.p., chmn., CEO IMS Internat., Westport, Conn., 1999—; bd. dirs. Orion Capital Corp. Office: IMS Health Inc 200 Nyala Farms Rd Westport CT 06880

FASH, WILLIAM LEONARD, retired architecture educator, college dean; b. Pueblo, Colo., Feb. 9, 1931; s. James Leonard and Jewel Dean (Rickman) F.; m. Maria Elena Shaw, June 5, 1982; children: Cameron Shaw, Lauren Victoria; children by previous marriage: Victoria Ruth, William Leonard. B.Arch., Okla. State U., 1958, M.Arch., 1960; postgrad., Royal Acad. Fine Arts, Copenhagen, 1960-61. Asst. prof. U. Ill., Urbana, 1961-64, assoc. prof., 1967-70, prof., 1970-76; assoc. prof. Okla. State U., Stillwater, 1964-66, U. Oreg., Eugene, 1966-67; prof., first dean coll. architecture Ga. Inst. Tech., Atlanta, 1976-92, prof., 1992-93, prof., dean emeritus, 1997—; vis. prof. Chulalongkorn U., Bangkok, Thailand, 1973-74; bd. dirs. Nat. Archtl. Accreditation Bd., 1981-85 (commendation award 1985); mem. edn. com. adv. bd. Nat. Coun. Archtl. Registration Bds., 1982-85; profl. cons. U.S. Navy Trident Submarine Base, Kings Bay, Ga., 1980-89; mem. adv. bd. Atlanta Urban Design Commn.; cons. Atlanta High Mus. Art Bldg. Com., 1982-84. Author, editor monographs. Chmn. tech. adv. com. Gov.'s Commn. State Growth Policy, 1982-83; mem. Mayor's transition team for housing, Atlanta, 1989, Atlanta Symphony New Hall Com., 1991. Recipient awards for design, recognition citations for teaching excellence, 1975, 76; Spl. Recognition cert. Atlanta Coll. Architecture, 1986, Recognition award Indsl. Designers Soc. Am., 1990, Spl. award Atlanta chpt. AIA, 1994; Fulbright-Hays fellow, Copenhagen, 1960-61. Mem. AIA (award juries 1968, 75, 76, 79, spl. recognition award Atlanta chpt. 1994), Assn. Collegiate Schs. Architecture (recognition award 1985), Phi Kappa Phi, Sigma Tau, Pi Mu Epsilon, Alpha Rho Chi, Omicron Delta Kappa. Club: Bent Tree Country (Jasper, Ga.). Home: 2854 Ridgemore Rd NW Atlanta GA 30318-1448

FASI, FRANK FRANCIS, state senator; b. East Hartford, Conn., Aug. 27, 1920. B.S., Trinity Coll., Hartford, 1942. Mem. Hawaii Senate, 1959—; Dem. mayor City and County of Honolulu, 1969-81, Rep. mayor, 1985-94; resigned, 1994; owner Property & Bus., Honolulu, 1995. Mem. Dem. Nat. Com. for Hawaii, 1952-56; del. 2d Constl. Conv., 1968; mem.-at-large Honolulu City Coun., 1965-69. Served to capt. USMCR. Mem. Pacific-Asian Congress Municipalities (founder, past pres., exec. dir.), VFW (former comdr. Hawaii dept.), AFTRA (past v.p.). Office: 401 Waiakamilo Rd Ste 201 Honolulu HI 96817-4955 *Personal philosophy: Moderate/Conservative. I believe in a free enterprise system as the foundation of our economy and in state's rights. I believe that the less government from Washington D.C. the better. I also have a strong belief in Christ Jesus.*

FASICK, ADELE MONGAN, information services consultant; b. N.Y.C., Mar. 18, 1930; d. Stephen Leo and Florence (Geary) Mongan; m. Frank Fasick, Aug. 14, 1955 (div. 1986); children: Pamela, Laura, Julia. BA, Cornell U., 1951; MA, Columbia U., 1954, MSLS, 1956; PhD, Case Western Reserve U., 1970. Libr. N.Y. Pub. Libr., 1955-56, L.I.U., Bklyn., 1956-58; asst. prof. Rosary Coll., River Forest, Ill., 1970-71; prof. U. Toronto, 1971-96, dean Faculty of Libr. and Info. Sci., 1990-95. Author: Managing Children Services in Public Libraries, 1991, 2d edit., 1998, Beauty Who Would Not Spin, 1987; co-author: ChildView, 1987; editor: Lands of Pleasure, 1990; editor International Research Abstracts: Youth Library Services, 1993—. Mem. ALA (com. on accreditation 1990-92), Assn. Libr. Svc. to Children (exec. bd. 1980-84), Assn. Librs. and Info. Sci. Edn. (pres. 1992), Internat. Fedn. Libr. Assn. (sec./treas. sect. on reading 1997—).

FASKE, DONNA See KARAN, DONNA

FASMAN, GERALD DAVID, biochemistry educator; b. Drumheller, Alta., Can., May 28, 1925; came to U.S., 1955, naturalized, 1964; s. Morris and Sarah (Stauffer) F.; m. Jean Schalit, Dec. 27, 1953; children—Michael, Daniel, Jonathan. B.S., U. Alta., 1948; Ph.D., Calif. Inst. Tech., 1952; postgrad., Cambridge (Eng.) U., 1951-53, Eidg. Technische Hochschule, Zurich, Switzerland, 1953-54, Weizmann Inst. Sci., Rehovoth, Israel, 1954-55. Research asst. Children's Cancer Research Found., Children's Med. Center, Boston, 1955-56; research asso. pathology Children's Med. Center and Children's Cancer Research Found., Boston, 1957-61; asst. in pathology Harvard U. Med. Sch., 1957-58, research asso. pathology, 1958-60, research asso. biol. chemistry, 1960-61; lectr. protein chemistry Boston U., 1958-59; asst. head biophys. chemistry lab. Children's Cancer Research Found., Boston, 1959-61; tutor in biochem. sci. Harvard, 1960-62; established investigator Am. Heart Assn., 1961-66; asst. prof. biochemistry Brandeis U., Waltham, Mass., 1961-63, assoc. prof., 1963-67, prof., 1967—, Rosenfield prof. biochemistry, 1971-96, prof. emeritus, 1996—; cons. African Primary Sci. Program, Ednl. Services, Inc., Dar es Salam, Tanzania, 1966, mem. program steering com., Accra, Ghana, 1967, mem. adv. group, 1968-69; mem. sci. adv. com. Am. Cancer Soc., 1979-83; mem. molecular biology adv. panel NSF, 1980-82. Editor: CRC Critical Revs. in Biochemistry, 1972—, Chemtracts, Biochemistry and Molecular Biology, 1990—; adv. bd. Biopolymers, 1975—; editl. bd. Internat. Jour. Peptide and Protein Rsch., 1976-82, Biophys. Jour., 1976-79, Cell Biophysics, 1982—, Jour. Protein Chemistry, 1982—, CRC Critical Revs. in Eukaryotic Gene Expression, 1987—, Letters in Peptide Sci., 1994—. NSF sr. postdoctoral fellow Protein Inst., Osaka (Japan) U. and Weizmann Inst. Sci., 1967-68; Guggenheim fellow, 1974-75, 88-89; research fellow Japan Soc. for Promotion of Sci., 1979. Fellow AAAS, Am. Inst. Chemists; mem. NAS, Am. Chem. Soc., Biophys. Soc., Am. Soc. Biochemistry and Molecular Biology, Royal Soc. Chemistry (London), Nat. Acad. Sci., N.Y. Acad. Sci., Am. Acad. Arts and Scis., Sigma Xi. Home: 69 Kingswood Rd Auburndale MA 02466-1013 Office: Biochemistry Dept Brandeis U Waltham MA 02254*

FASMAN, ZACHARY DEAN, lawyer; b. Chgo., Oct. 27, 1948; s. Irving D. and Lillian V. (Vilatzer) F.; m. Sally Ann Metzger, Aug. 22, 1971; children: Jonathan, Benjamin, Rebecca. BA, Northwestern U., 1969; JD, U. Mich., 1972. Bar: Ill. 1972, D.C. 1977, Supreme Ct. 1977. Assoc., then ptnr. Seyfarth, Shaw et al, Chgo. and Washington, 1972-81; ptnr. Wald, Harkrader et al, Washington, 1981-83, Crowell & Moring, Washington, 1983-88, Paul, Hastings, Janofsky & Walker, Washington, 1988—. Author: Equal Employment Audit Handbook, 1983, Employment Law Compliance Manual, 1988, What Business Must Know About The ADA, 1992. Mem. ABA (labor law sect., ind. rights sect.), Order of Coif. Home: 3908 Highwood Ct NW Washington DC 20007-2132 Office: Paul Hastings Janofsky & Walker 1299 Pennsylvania Ave NW Washington DC 20004-2400

FASS, PETER MICHAEL, lawyer, educator; b. Bklyn., Apr. 11, 1937; s. Irving and Bess (Fordin) F.; m. Deborah K. Orshan, May 6, 1989; 1 child, Olivia Jae; children from previous marriage: Brian Samuel, Lyle Williams. BS in Econs. with honors, U. Pa., 1958; JD cum laude, Harvard U., 1961; LLM, NYU, 1964. Bar: N.Y. 1965; CPA. From assoc. to ptnr. Carro, Spanbock, Fass, Geller, Kaster & Cuiffo, N.Y.C., 1968-86; ptnr. Kaye, Scholer, Fierman, Hayes & Handler, N.Y.C., 1988-95, Battle Fowler LLP, N.Y.C., 1995—; adj. asst. prof. real estate NYU; lectr. Practising Law Inst., N.Y. Law Jour., Instl. mag., Ill. Inst. Continuing Legal Edn.; spl. cons. Calif. Commr. of Corps Real Estate Adv. Com.; mem. ad hoc com. Real Estate Securities and Syndication Inst., chmn. regulatory legis and taxation com., 1975-76; mem., dir. participant/real estate com. NASD, 1991-94. Co-author: Tax Advantaged Securities, 1977—, Real Estate Syndication Handbook, 1985-87, Tax Aspects of Real Estate Investments, 1988, Blue Sky Practice Handbook, 1987—, Real Estate Investment Trusts Handbook, 1987—, S Corporation Handbook, 1985—, Tax Advantaged Securities Handbook, 1979—; contbr. articles to profl. jours. Recipient Haskins award for outstanding achievement in N.Y. State C.P.A.s exam., 1964. Mem. ABA (chmn. real estate investment com., real property, probate and trust sect.), N.Y. State Bar Assn., Am. Inst. CPA's, N.Y. State Soc. CPA's, Pi Lambda Phi, Beta Gamma Sigma, Beta Alpha Psi. Home: 115 Central Park W New York NY 10023-4153 Office: Battle Fowler LLP 75 E 55th St New York NY 10022-3205

FASSEL, DIANE MARY, organizational consultant; b. San Antonio, Sept. 12, 1945; d. Robert Alois and Mary Jane (Stokman) F. BA, Webster U., 1968; MA, Harvard U., 1974; PhD, Union Inst., 1987. Chair English dept. Loretto H.S., Kansas City, Mo., 1968-72; cmty. life coord. Loretto Cmty., Denver, 1974-78; pvt. practice orgnl. cons. Denver, 1978-92, Boulder, Colo., 1994—; v.p. Wilson Schaef Assoc., Boulder, 1992-94; advisor Am. Arbitration Assn., Denver, 1978-84. Author: The Addictive Organization, 1988, Working Ourselves to Death, 1990, Growing Up Divorced, 1991, Organizational Capabilities, 1996. Bd. dirs. St. Mary's Acad., Denver, 1978-86; mem. exec. com. Loretto Cmty., Denver, 1978-82; mediator CDR Assoc., Boulder, 1984. Democrat. Roman Catholic. Avocations: horseback riding, snorkeling, bicycling, movies.

FASSEL, JIM, head coach professional football; b. Anaheim, Calif., Aug. 31, 1949; m. Kitty Fassel; children: John, Brian, Jana, Mike. Collegiate coach various, including Fullerton C.C., Weber State U., Stanford, 1973-83; asst. head coach/offensive coord. Denver Broncos, 1993, 94; quarterback coach Oakland Raiders, 1995; offensive coord., quarterback coach Ariz. Cardinals, 1996; asst. coach N.Y. Giants, 1991-92, head coach, 1997—. Drafted by Chgo. in seventh round of 1972 NFL Draft. Office: NY Giants Giants Stadium East Rutherford NJ 07073*

FASSETT, FRANCES NICHOLAS (KITTY FASSETT), pianist, record producer; b. Louisville, Sept. 15, 1933; d. Charles and Frances (Allen) Nicholas; m. Richard Ashford Lee, Aug. 27, 1955 (div. 1975); children: Frances Lee Davis, Edward Ashford Lee, Maria Catalina Ryan; m. Stephen Bryant Fassett, Dec. 4, 1975 (dec. Mar. 1980). BA with honors, Vassar Coll., 1955; BMus, P.R. Conservatory of Music, San Juan, 1965, MMus, 1966. Founder, dir. Waldo Theatre, Inc., Waldoboro, Maine, 1990—. Office: Waldo Theatre Inc PO Box 587 Waldoboro ME 04572-0587

FASSETT, JOHN D., retired utility executive, consultant; b. East Hampton, N.Y., Jan. 30, 1926; s. Howard J. and Irene (Darby) F.; m. Betty Jean Conrad, Aug. 4, 1947; children—Ellen Joy Fassett Mermin, John D., Lora Jean Fassett Mason. B.A. cum laude, U. Rochester, 1948; J.D. cum laude, Yale U., 1953; LLD (hon.), Ky. Wesleyan Coll., 1999. Law clk. to assoc. justice Stanley F. Reed U.S. Supreme Ct., Washington, 1953-54; assoc. Wiggin & Dana, New Haven, 1954-58, ptnr., 1958-73; v.p., gen. counsel United Illuminating Co., New Haven, 1973, pres., 1974-75, chief exec. officer, 1976-84, chmn. bd., 1985-87. Author: UI—History of an Electric Company, 1991, New Deal Justice: The Life of Stanley Reed of Kentucky, 1994. Served with U.S. Army, 1943-46, 1st lt., 1950-51. Republican. Avocations: tennis, reading, writing. Home: 5108 Brittany Dr S Saint Petersburg FL 33715-1510

FASSETTA, MARY ELIZABETH, nursing educator; b. Rockville Ctr., N.Y., June 22, 1956; d. Frank J. and Jane T. (Buettner) Rudmann; m. Robert S.C. Fassetta, June 12, 1982; children: Melissa, Matthew. BSN, Molloy Coll., 1978; MS, Adelphi U., 1989; postgrad., Columbia U., 1998—. Staff nurse Columbia-Presbyn. Med. Ctr., N.Y.C., 1978-79, Mercy Med. Ctr., Rockville Ctr., 1979-93; asst. prof. Molloy Coll., Rockville Ctr., 1993—; chair grant writing com. dept. nursing Molloy Coll., 1996—; nurse cons., 1999—. Contbr. articles to profl. jours. Recipient 1st prize writing contest Nursing Spectrum, Hempstead, N.Y., 1993. Mem. AAUP, Nurse-Healers Profl. Assocs., Inc., Sigma Theta Tau (faculty advisor 1996—). Roman Catholic. Avocations: photography, sewing, gardening. Office: Molloy Coll 1000 Hempstead Ave Rockville Centre NY 11570-1100

FASSLER, KAREN KAY, human resources specialist; b. Cherokee, Iowa, Jan. 9, 1953; d. Dean Carlyle and Rita Anne (Primus) F.; 1 child, Amanda Martinez. BA, U. Colo., 1975, MPA, 1979. Office supr. U. Colo., Boulder, 1975-80, classification, wage and salary analyst, 1980-86; occupl. specialist, statewide work-life and FMLA coor. State of Colo., Denver, 1986—. Pres. Working Together Found., Denver; mem. staff Colo. Gov.'s First Impressions Task Force, Denver; sec. Boulder Yough Symphony Soc., 1998099; mem. Colo. Pub. Interest Rsch. Group. Mem. NAFE, Am. Compensation Assn., Soc. for Human Resource Mgmt., Internat. Pers. Mgmt. Assn., Greenpeace. Avocations: travel, reading, singing, movies. Fax: 303-866-2458. E-mail: karen.fassler@state.co.us. Office: Human Resource Svcs 1313 Sherman St Rm 122 Denver CO 80203

FASSOULIS, SATIRIS GALAHAD, communications company executive; b. Syracuse, Aug. 19, 1922; s. Peter George and Anastasia P. (Limpert) F. B.A., Syracuse U., 1945. V.p. Commerce Internat. Corp., N.Y.C., 1945-48; pres. Commerce Internat. Corp., 1949-75; chmn. Global Communications Co., N.Y.C., 1976—, Global Def. Products Inc., N.Y.C., 1976—; dir Comml. Exports (Overseas) Ltd., U.K., CIC Internat. Ltd., N.Y.C.; dir. Colombia Technology Corp., Colombia Energy Corp. Mem. U.S. Congl. Adv. Bd.; bd. dirs. Better Life Enterprises for the Blind, Inc. Served to 1st lt., USAAF, 1941-45. Decorated Purple Heart, Air medal with 3 oak leaf clusters, Prisoner of War medal. Mem. N.Y. C. of C., Am. Def. Preparedness Assn., Navy League U.S., Armed Forces Communications and Electronics Assn., U.S. Naval Inat., Air Force Assn., Assn. of U.S. Army, Internat. Platform Assn. Republican. Episcopalian. Clubs: N.Y. Athletic, Order of Ahepa. Home: 20 Waterside Plz New York NY 10010-2612 Office: 38-01 23rd Ave Astoria NY 11105-1903

FAST, DARRELL WAYNE, minister; b. Mountain Lake, Minn., Sept. 5, 1939; s. Henry L. and Anna R. (Rempel) F.; m. Loretta J. Janzen, Aug. 20, 1966; children: Douglas Henry, Larissa Ann. BA, U. Nebr., 1963; BD, Mennonite Biblical Sem., 1966; MTh, Emmanuel Coll., 1977, DMin, 1986. Ordained minister Mennonite Ch., 1970. Mem. conf. staff Gen. Conf. Offices Mennonite Ch., Newton, Kans., 1966-70; pastor Toronto (Ont., Can.) United Mennonite Ch., 1970-86, Bethel Coll. Mennonite Ch., North Newton, Kans., 1986—; moderator Gen. Conf. Mennonite Ch., Newton, 1992—; sec. United Mennonite Chs. of Ont., Toronto, 1972-78. Mem. Leadership Newton, Newton C. of C., 1989; pres. Ministerial Alliance, Newton, 1989-90; mem. exec. com. Man to Man Ont., Toronto, 1972-82; trustee Mennonite Biblican Sem., Elkhart, Ind., 1980-92. Mem. Rotary. Avocations: tennis, chorale singing. Office: Bethel Coll Mennonite Ch 2600 College Ave PO Box 364 North Newton KS 67117-0364

FAST, HOWARD MELVIN, author; b. N.Y.C., Nov. 11, 1914; s. Barney and Ida (Miller) F.; m. Betty Cohen, June 6, 1937; children: Rachel Ann, Jonathan. Student, NAD, 1933. Began writing, 1932, Army film project, 1944; European corr. Esquire and Coronet mags., 1945; mem. staff Office of War Info., 1942-44, chief newswriter, originator Voice of Am., 1982-83. Emmy award for The Ambassador, Benjamin Franklin 1974; author: (novels) Two Valleys, 1932, Strange Yesterday, 1933, The Children, 1936, Place in the City, 1937, Conceived in Liberty, 1939; biography Haym Salomon, 1941; The Romance of a People, 1941; (novel) The Last Frontier, 1941; (biography) Baden Powell, 1941; (novel) Tail Hunter, 1942, The Unvanquished, 1942; (biography) Goethals and the Panama Canal, 1942; The Picture Book History of the Jews, 1942; (novel) Citizen Tom Paine, 1943, Freedom Road, 1944; The Incredible Tito, 1944; The American: A Middle Western Legend, 1946; Never Forget: The Story of the Warsaw Ghetto, 1946; Intellectuals in the Fight for Peace, 1949; Peekskill, U.S.A., 1951; (novel) Spartacus, 1952; The Last Supper, and Other Stories, 1955; The Naked God, 1957; Moses, Prince of Egypt, 1958; The Howard Fast Reader, 1960; The Edge of Tomorrow, 1961; Tony and the Wonderful Door, 1968, The Crossing, 1971; General Zapped an Angel, 1971, Last Frontier, 1971; The Hessian, 1972 (Notable Book citation ALA 1972); My Glorious Brothers, 1972, A Touch of Infinity, 1973, The Art of Zen Meditation, 1977, The Magic Door, 1980, Time and the Riddle: Thirty-One Zen Stories, 1981, The Call of Fife and Drum: Three Novels of the Revolution, 1987, (under name E.V. Cunningham) Sylvia, 1960, Phyllis, 1962, Alice, 1963, Shirley, 1963, Lydia, 1964, Penelope, 1965, Helen, 1966, Margie, 1966, Sally, 1967, Samantha, 1967, Cynthia, 1968, The Assassin Who Gave Up His Gun, 1969, Millie, 1973, The Case of the One Penny Orange, 1977, The Case of the Russian Diplomat, 1978, The Case of the Poisoned Eclairs, 1979, The Case of the Sliding Pool, 1981, The Case of the Kidnapped Angel, 1982, The Case of the Murdered Mackenzie, 1984, The Case of the Angry Actress, 1984, The Wabash Factor, 1986; (as Walter Ericson) Fallen Angel, 1951; (plays) The Hammer, 1950, Thirty Pieces of Silver, 1954, George Washington and the Water Witch, 1956, David and Paula, 1982; Editor: Selected Works of Paine, 1945, Collection of Short Stories: Patrick Henry and the Frigate's Keel, 1945, Best Short Stories of Theodore Dreiser, 1947, Under the Name of Howard Fast, The American (biography of Peter Altgeld, former gov. of Ill.), 1946, Carkton, 1947, My Glorious Brothers, 1948, Departure, 1949, Literature and Reality, 1949, The Proud and the Free, 1950, The Passion of Sacco and Vanzetti, 1953, Silas Timberman, 1954, The Story of Lola Gregg: The Winston Affair, 1959, April Morning, 1961, Power, 1962, The Crossing; (play) Agrippa's Daughter, 1964, The Hill; (drama), 1963, Torquemada, 1966, The Hunter and the Trap, 1967, The Jews, 1968, The Hessians, 1970, The Immigrants, 1977, Second Generation, 1978, The Establishment, 1979, The Legacy, 1981, Max, 1982, The Outsider, (play) The Novelist, 1986, The Immigrant's Daughter; (novel), 1985, (play) Citizen Tom Paine, 1986; (novel) Dinner Party, 1987, The Pledge, 1988, (newspaper column), Greenwich Time, 1981, The Confession of Joe Cullen, 1989, (autobiography) Being Red, 1990, War and Peace, Collection of Essays, 1992, (novel) The Trial of Abigail Goodman, 7 Days in June, The Bridge Builder's Story, 1995, An Independent Woman, 1997, Redemption, 1999; columnist N.Y. Observer, 1989-92, Greenwich Time, 1992—, Stamford Advocate, 1992, Barbara Lavette, 1998. Mem. World Peace Council, 1950-55; Am. Labor Party Congl. candidate 23d Dist., N.Y., 1952. Recipient Breadloaf Literary award, 1937, Schomburg award for race relations, 1944, Literary Lion award N.Y. Public Library, 1945, Newspaper Guild racial equality award, 1947, Jewish Book Council annual award, 1947, Peace Prize USSR, 1954, Secondary Education annual book award, 1962, Emmy award Nat. Acad. TV Arts and Scis., 1976. Mem. Century Club, N.Y.C. Jewish. Office: Care Sterling Lord 65 Bleecker St New York NY 10012-2420

FAST, JULIUS, author, editor; b. N.Y.C., Apr. 17, 1919; s. Barnett Arthur and Ida (Miller) F.; m. Barbara Hewitt Sher, June 8, 1946; children: Jennifer, Melissa, Timothy Hewitt. BA, NYU, 1941. Sr. writer Smith, Kline & French Pharms., Phila., 1955-57; chief dept. med. communications Purdue Fredericks, N.Y.C., 1957-62; feature editor Med. News, 1962-63; sr. editor Med. World News, 1963-64; editor Ob-Gyn Observer, N.Y.C., 1965-75. Author: (mystery novels) Watchful at Night, 1945, Bright Face of Danger, 1946, Walk in Shadow, 1948, Model for Murder, 1956, Street of Fear, 1959, (fiction) What Should We Do About Davey?, 1987, (sci. fiction) League of Grey-Eyed Women, 1970, (nonfiction) Blueprint for Life, 1963, Beatles, 1968, What You Should Know About Sexual Response, 1966, Body Language, 1970, Incompatibility of Men and Women, 1971, You and Your Feet, 1971, The New Sexual Fulfillment, 1972, Bisexual Living, 1974, The Pleasure Book, 1975, Creative Coping, 1976, The Body Language of Sex Power and Aggression, 1977, Psyching Up, 1978, Weather Language, 1979, Talking Between the Lines, 1979, Body Politics, 1980, The Body Book, 1981, Sexual Chemistry, 1983, Ladies Man, 1983, The Omega-3 Breakthrough, 1987, Subtext, 1990, Legal Atlas of the United States, 1996, Courtroom Communication Skills, 1994. Served with AUS, 1942-46. Recipient Mystery Writers Am. award, 1944. Home: 2600 Netherland Ave Apt 1825 Bronx NY 10463-4824

FASTHUBER-GRANDE, TRAUDY, financial services company executive; b. Wels, Austria, July 26, 1950; came to U.S., 1974; d. Franz X. and Friederike (Enzlmuller) Fasthuber; m. John J. Grande, Mar. 27, 1987. Student, U. Vienna, 1973-74; BA, Rutgers U., 1976. CFP; registered investment advisor. Program dir. Alt's Gymnastics, inc., Shrewsbury, N.J., 1974-80; v.p. Tangible Resource Group, Inc., Red Bank, N.J., 1980-81, Grande Fin. Svcs., Inc., Oakhurst, N.J., 1987—; sr. fin. planner Raymond James & Assocs., Inc., Naples, Fla., 1982-85; registered prin. Raymond James Fin. Svcs., Inc., Oakhurst, 1985—; hostess TV program Wall St.-Main St., Naples, 1983-84; guest speaker Am. Heart Assn., Fla., 1984-85; lectr. various women's investment seminars, N.J., 1986—; adminstr. Am. Psychiat. Assn. Mem. Retirement Program, 1990—. Mem. Inst. Cert. Fin. Planners. Avocations: skiing, music, running, travel, swimming. Office: Grande Fin Svcs Inc Ste 7 257 Monmouth Rd Bldg B Oakhurst NJ 07755-1500

FATES, JOSEPH GILBERT, television producer; b. Newark, Sept. 29, 1914; s. Joseph and Dora (Racicot) Faatz; m. Faye Appleberry Smith, Sept. 29, 1946; children—Decia, Amy, Dailey Gilbert. BS, U. Va., 1937. Actor, stage mgr. Broadway legitimate theatre, 1937-40; writer, producer, performer CBS-TV, 1941-50; free-lance TV producer, 1950-53; exec. producer Goodson-Todman Prodns.; v.p. Goodson-Todman Enterprises, Ltd., 1953-86; TV program cons. CTV, Can., BBC, ATV, London Weekend TV and Scottish TV, Gt. Britain, RAI, Italy, Canal Plus, France, Bavarian TV, Germany, TVNZ, New Zealand, Antenna Tres, Spain. Exec. producer: I've Got a Secret, What's My Line?, To Tell the Truth; prodr. Beat the Clock; author: What's My Line?--TV's Most Famous Panel Show, 1978; producer, performer: What's It Worth, CBS TV Quiz, Vanity Fair; producer Faye Emerson Show. Served to lt. USCGR, 1942-46. Mem. Indian Harbor Yacht Club, Harpoon Club, Sigma Nu. Home: Boulder Brook Rd Greenwich CT 06830

FATH, MICHAEL JOHN, pharmaceutical/health care stategic planner; b. Cuyahoga Falls, Ohio, Apr. 1, 1965; s. Michael Albert and Joan Mildred (Schromen) F.; m. Kimberly Marie Quandt, Dec. 30, 1989; children: Kira Marie, Emma Katherine. BA in Microbiology and Chemistry, Miami U., Oxford, Ohio, 1987; MA in Microbiology & Molecular Genetics, Harvard U., 1990, PhD in Microbiology & Molecular Genetics, 1993. Rsch. fellow in molecular genetics U. Chgo., 1993-95; sr. assoc. McKinsey & Co., Inc., Chgo., 1995-98; mgr., Corp. Strategic Planning Abbott Lab., Abbott Park, Ill., 1998—; Contbr. (univ. textbook) Biosphere 2000: Protecting Our Global Environment, 1993. NSF grad. fellow, 1988-91, NSF post-doctoral fellow in plant biology, 1993-95. Mem. AAAS, Am. Soc. for Microbiology, Drum Corps World (staff writer), Chgo. Gargoyle Brass, Prarie Brass Band (bd. dirs.). Roman Catholic. Avocations: brass performance, drum and bugle corps. Office: Abbott Laboratories D-369 AP6D-2 100 Abbott Park Rd Abbott Park IL 60064-3500

FATHAUER, THEODORE FREDERICK, meteorologist; b. Oak Park, Ill., June 5, 1946; s. Arthur Theodore and Helen Ann (Mashek) F.; m. Mary Ann Neesan, Aug. 8, 1981. BA, U. Chgo., 1968. Cert. cons. meteorologist. Rsch. aide USDA No. Dev. Labs., Peoria, Ill., 1966, Cloud Physics Lab., Chgo., 1967; meteorologist Sta. WLW Radio/TV, Cin., 1967-68, Nat. Meteorol. Ctr., Washington, 1968-70, Nat. Weather Svc., Anchorage, 1970-80; meteorologist-in-charge Nat. Weather Svc., Fairbanks, Alaska, 1980-98, lead forecaster, 1998—; instr. U. Alaska, Fairbanks, 1975-76, USCG Aux., Fairbanks and Anchorage, 1974—; specialist in Alaska meteorology. Contbr. chpt to book Denali's West Buttress, 1997, Living With the Coast of Alaska, 1997; contbr. articles to weather mags. and jours. Bd. dirs. Fairbanks Concert Assn., 1988—; bd. dirs. No. Alaska Combined Fed. Campaign, 1996—, campaign chmn., 1996-97; bd. dirs. Friends U. Alaska Mus., 1993—, pres., 1993-95, sec. 1997-98; bd. visitors U. Alaska Fairbanks, 1995—; bd. dirs., sec. Fairbanks Symphony Assn., 1994—; bd. trustees U. Alaska Found., 1997—, mem. coll. fellows, 1993—, exec. com., 1997—, vice chair, 1998—; mem. adv. bd. Salvation Army Fairbanks Corps, 1997—. Recipient Outstanding Performance award Nat. Weather Service, 1972, 76, 83, 85, 86, 89, Fed. Employee of Yr. award, Fed. Exec. Assn., Anchorage, 1978. Fellow Am. Meteorol. Soc. (TV and radio seals of approval), Royal Meteorol. Soc.; mem. AAAS, Am. Geophys. Union, Western Snow Conf., Arctic Inst. N.Am. (exec. sec. U.S. Corp. 1998—), Oceanography Soc., Can. Meteorol. and Oceanographic Soc., Greater Fairbanks C. of C., Am. Sailing Assn. Republican. Lutheran. Avocations: reading, music, skiing, canoeing. Home: PO Box 80210 Fairbanks AK 99708-0210 Office: Nat Weather Svc

Forecast Office Internat Arctic Rsch Ctr U Alaska PO Box 757345 Fairbanks AK 99775-7345

FATT, WILLIAM R., hospitality company executive; b. Toronto, Ont., Can., Mar. 11, 1951. BA in Econs., York U., Toronto. Auditor Thorne Riddell, Toronto, 1973-75; asst. contr. Revenue Properties Co. Ltd., Toronto, 1975-77; acctg. analyst The Consumers Gas Co., Toronto, 1977-78; asst. treas. Hiram Walker Resources, Toronto, 1982-84, v.p., treas., 1984-86; v.p. Morgan Bank of Can., Toronto, 1986-88; treas. Can. Pacific Ltd., Toronto, 1988, v.p., treas., 1988-90, v.p. fin. and acctg., CFO, 1990-94; exec. v.p. and CFO Can. Pacific Ltd., Toronto and Calgary, 1994; chmn., CEO Can. Pacific Hotels Corp., Toronto, 1998—; also bd. dirs.; pres., CEO, trustee Legacy Hotels Real Estate Investment Trust; exec. v.p. Can. Pacific Ltd.; bd. dirs. PanCanadian Petroleum Ltd., Jim Pattison Group Inc., The Corp. of Massey Hall and Roy Thomson Hall, The Consumer's Gas Co. Ltd. Office: Canadian Pacific Hotels 1 University Ave Ste 1400 Toronto ON Canada M5J 2P1

FATTAH, CHAKA, congressman, former state legislator; b. Phila., Nov. 21, 1956; m. Patricia Renfroe; 3 children. Student, Phila. C.C., 1976; M. in Govt., U. Pa., 1986; student, Harvard U. Mem. Pa. Ho. of Reps., 1982-88, Pa. State Senate, 1988-94; congressman, Pa. 2nd Dist. U.S. House Reps., Washington, D.C., 1995—; mem. edn. and the workforce com. U.S. House Reps., mem. govt. reform and oversight com., mem. stds. of ofcl. conduct com. Founder Am. Cities Conf. and Found.; leader task force Child Devel. Initiative, Phila.; founder, convenor Grad. Opportunities Conf., Pa.; chmn. exec. com. Pa. Higher Edn. Assistance Agy.; creator Jobs Project. Recognized nationally for outstanding leadership Time Mag.'s roster of Amer.'s most promising leaders, 1994, Ebony Mag.'s one of 50 Future Leaders, 1984; recipient Pa. Pub. Interest Coalition's State Legislator of Yr. award. Baptist. Office: US House Reps 1205 Longworth Bldg Ofc Bldg Washington DC 20515-3802*

FATUM, RUSS ALLEN, human resources professional, educator; b. Reed City, Mich., Oct. 9, 1964; s. Dennis Charles and Marlene Kay (Swanson) F.; m. Gail M. Loehr, Aug. 9, 1986; children: Alexander, Matthew, Miranda. BS, Ferris State U., Big Rapids, Mich., 1986; MS in Adminstrn., Ctrl. Mich. U., 1993. Mgr. human resources Spartan Corp., White Cloud, Mich., 1986-89, Tower Automotive, Greenville, Mich., 1994-95, ITT Automotive, Walker, Mich., 1995; dir. labor rels. Autodie Inc. Internat., Grand Rapids, Mich., 1993-94; mgr. labor rels. Evart products Textron, Evart, 1995-96; supr. labor rels. Chrysler Motors, Evart, Mich., 1989-93; mgr. human resources Chrysler Motors, Evart, 1996-98; dir. human resources PPG Industries, Evart, 1998—; mem. adv. bd. Ferris State U. Coll. Bus., Big Rapids, Mich., 1992—, mem. dean adv. bd., 1995—; assoc. prof. Baker Coll., Cadillac, Mich., 1996—. Pres. Mecosta-Osceola Human Resources Orgn., Big Rapids, 1991-93, v.p. St. Paul Luth. Ch., Reed City, 1991; mem. adv. bd. Mecosta-Osceola Ind. Sch. Dist., 1995—; bd. dirs .United Way, Big Rapids, 1996—. Mem. Mecosta-Osceola Human Resources Assn., Cadillac Human Resources Assn., Promise Keepers. Republican. Avocations: restoring classic vehicles. Office: Chrysler Motors 6251 S Lowman Rd Evart MI 49631

FATZINGER, JAMES A. S., construction educator, estimator; b. Bethlehem, Pa., Jan. 27, 1926; s. James Andrew and Cora Ellen (Steigerwalt) F.; m. Mary Lois Beckman, June 10, 1972. Student, Pa. State Coll., 1943-44, Moravian Coll., 1957-58, Fullerton Jr. Coll., 1972-73. Journeyman various cos., 1951-72; supr. 3M Co., Montpelier, Ohio, 1966-67; journeyman Endicott Brass Co., Montpelier, 1967; substation operator Pub. Svc. Elec. and Gas Co., Newark, 1959-65; constrn. estimator various cos., 1972—; contractor Calif. and Ariz., 1980-85; constrn. instr. Mesa (Ariz.) C.C., Rio Salado C.C., Mesa, 1974-78, C.C. of So. Nev., Las Vegas, 1978-97, U. Nev., Las Vegas, 1992-97; pres., owner Basic Estimating Ltd., Las Vegas, 1978-99. Author: Basic Estimating for Construction, 1996, Blueprint Reading for Construction, 1997. Trustee Tech. Sch., Fullerton Jr. Coll., 1986-92; scoutmaster Boy Scouts Am., Bethlehem, 1950-60, commr., Huntington Beach, Calif., 1976-77. 1st sgt. U.S. Army, 1944-46, ETO. Mem. Am. Soc. Profl. Estimators (cert., emeritus mem.), Constrn. Specifications Inst. Republican. Avocation: motor home travel, music.

FAUB, KENNETH JAMES, school nurse practitioner; b. Pitts., Sept. 5, 1942; s. Kenneth John and Emma L. (Morgan) F. Diploma, St. John's Gen. Hosp., Pitts., 1970; BSN, Carlow Coll., 1985; MSN in Nursing Edn., Duquesne U., 1995. Cert. ARC disaster nurse, emergency/primary care nurse practitioner, sexually transmitted disease specialist, AIDS educator, sch. nurse practitioner. Charge nurse emergency room St. John's Gen. Hosp., 1970-75; head nurse Family Are Ctr., 1975; nurse practitioner, sexually transmitted disease clinic Allegheny County Health Dept., Pitts., 1976-93; nurse practitioner Pitts. Bd. Pub. Edn., 1989—; pub. speaker on health-related topics. Instr. first aid, CPR and disaster health svcs., ARC; merit badge counselor Boy Scouts Am.; mem. human resource availability list Nat. Red Cross. Mem. Nat. Sch. Nurse Practitioner Assn., Pitts. Sch. Nurse Orgn., Pa. Sch. Nurse Practitioners Orgn., Am. Acad. Nurse Practitioners, St. John's Gen. Hosp. Alumni Assn., Carlow Coll. Alumni Assn., Duquesne U. Alumni Assn., Allegheny U. Nursing Alumni Assn., Allegheny Gen. Hosp. Alumni Assn., Acacia Fraternity, Sigma Theta Tau.

FAUBEL, GERALD LEE, agronomist, golf course superintendent; b. Normal, Ill., Feb. 14, 1941; s. Elmer Joseph and Agnes (Alexander) F.; m. Sally Sue Shook, Feb. 22, 1973; 1 child, Sarah. AAS, Iowa State U., 1963, BS, 1969. Golf course supt. Lawsonia Golf Course, Green Lake, Wis., 1962-63, South Hills Club, Fond du Lac, Wis., 1963-68, Saginaw (Mich.) Country Club, 1969—; pres. Exec. Golf Search, Inc.; dir. Mich. Turfgrass Found., Lansing, 1978-81, sec.-treas., v.p., 1982, pres., 1984. Mem. Parks commn. Saginaw (Mich.) Twp. 1972-78; mem. Valderrama (Spain) Scholarship Com., 1991-95. Mem. Golf Course Supt. Assn. Am. (bd. dirs. 1985-92, sec.-treas. 1988, v.p. 1989, pres. 1990, chmn. historical preservation com. 1998—), U.S. Golf Assn. (green com. 1985—), Mich. Assn. Agr. (exec. sec. 1991-94), Nat. Inst. Golf Mgmt. (bd. regents), Hist. Preservation Golf Course Supt. Assn. Am. (com. mem.), Saginaw Field and Stream Conservation Club (bd. dirs. 1996-99). Republican. Mennonite. Home: 699 Westchester Rd Saginaw MI 48603-6232

FAUCHER, DAVID F., federal judge; b. 1944. Apptd. part-time magistrate judge U.S. Dist. Ct. Hawaii, 1994. Fax: (808) 622-3707. Office: US Courthouse 300 Ala Moana Blvd Honolulu HI 96850-0001

FAUCHEUX, RONALD ANTHONY, publisher, editor; b. New Orleans, July 19, 1950; s. Alvin J. and Janet (Mendoza) F.; divorced; children: Ronald A. Jr., Jonathan. BS in Fgn. Svc., Georgetown U., 1972; JD, La. State U., 1974; PhD, U. New Orleans, 1993. Mem. La. Ho. of Reps., 1976-84; pres. Faucheux & Assoc., New Orleans, 1978-93; La. Sec. of Commerce, 1984-86; dir. Govt. Leadership Inst., New Orleans, 1990—; editor-in-chief Campaigns & Elections mag., Washington, 1993—. Author: The Ringmasters, 1993, The Road to Victory, 1995; host nat. TV show Campaigns and Elections. Mem. Am. Assn. Polit. Cons., Am. Polit. Sci. Assn., La. Bar Assn. Roman Catholic. Office: Campaigns & Elections Mag 1414 22nd St NW Washington DC 20037-1003

FAUCHIER, DAN R(AY), construction management consultant, mediator, arbitrator, educator; b. Blackwell, Okla., Sept. 27, 1946; s. Wallace Munroe and Betty Lou F.; m. Sylvia Stephanie Chan Fauchier, Mar. 15, 1969; 1 child, Angele Calista Fauchier; m. Jonah Keri, 1997. BA cum laude, Southwestern Coll., 1964-68; student, Sch. Theology, Claremont, Calif., 1968-69, Claremont Grad. Sch., 1969-70. Lic. bldg. contractor, Calif. Min. of youth First United Meth. Ch., Winfield, Kans., 1964-68, First Congl. Ch., Riverside, Calif., 1968-69; adminstr. Calif. Youth Authority, Chino and Paso Robles, Calif., 1969-76; tchr. Chaffey Coll., Rancho Cucamonga, Calif., 1971-74; dir. Pacific Fin. Svcs., Beverly Hills, Calif., 1977-81; pres. Littlefields Corp., Santa Maria and Corona de, Calif., 1978-81; cons. Hughes Helicopters, Oasis Oil, Jakarta, Indonesia, 1981; systems designer Teltrans Corp., L.A., 1982-85; project mgr. Pacific Sunset Builders, L.A., 1985-87, DW Devel., Fontana, Calif., 1987-90; owner Fauchier Group Builders, San Diego, Calif., 1988—; pres. Empire Bay Devel. Corp., San Bernardino, Calif., 1991-92; project mgr. White Sys. L.A. Cen. Libr., L.A., 1993; dir. project mgmt. White Sys. divsn. Pinnacle Automation, Inc., San Diego, 1993-95; dir. project mgmt.; dir. design logistics White Systems divsn. Pinnacle Automation, Inc., San Diego, 1995-97; v.p. SDC & Assocs., San Diego and Washington, 1997—; founding dir. Neighborhood Restoration Project, San Bernardino, Calif., 1991-92; consulting project manager White Sys., Inc., Cin. Pub. Libr., 1997, FCC Document Mechanization Project, 1998; instr. U. Calif. San Diego, 1998—; Inst. Constrn. Mgmt., cert. arbitrator Arbitration Works, 1999—. Contbr. cons.: President's Commission on Criminal Justice, 1972; co-author: Consumer Credit, 1984. Deputy Registrar Voters San Bernardino, Calif., 1975; mem. Skid Row Mental Health Adv. Bd., L.A., 1986, Chaffey Coll. Adv. Bd. Rancho Cucamonga, Calif., 1991-95, chmn. Bus. Security Alliance, San Bernardino, Calif., 1992. Named Nat. fellow Woodrow Wilson Fellowship, Princeton, N.J., 1968-69; Grad. scholar State of Calif., Claremont, 1969. Mem. Associated Gen. Contractors (chmn. edn. com.), Am. Subcontractor Assn. (chmn. mktg. com.), Associated Builders and Contractors, Forensics Cons. Assn., Nat. Found. for Dispute Rev. Bds., Self-Realization Fellowship (bd. dirs.), Christmas in April (bd. dirs.), Habitat for Humanity, Internat. Platform Assn., Inst. for Cmty. Econ., Homeless Coalition, People for Ethical Treatment of Animals, Rainforest Alliance. Avocations: painting, photography, writing. Home: 9921 Carmel Mountain Rd San Diego CA 92129-2813 Office: 5703 Oberlin Dr Ste 103 San Diego CA 92121-1743 also: 267 Kentland Blvd Ste 1048 Gaithersburg MD 20878-5446

FAUCI, ANTHONY STEPHEN, health facility administrator, physician; b. Bklyn., Dec. 24, 1940; s. Stephen A. and Eugenia A. Fauci. AB, Coll. of Holy Cross, 1962; MD, Cornell U., 1966; DSc (hon.), Coll. Holy Cross, 1987, Georgetown U., 1990, Hahnemann U., 1990, Mt. Sinai Sch. Medicine, 1990, Universita di Roma, 1990, St. John's U., 1991, Long Island U., 1992, Med. Coll. Wis., 1993, Bard Coll., 1993, Bates Coll., 1993, SUNY, Farmingdale, 1994, U. Conn. Health Ctr, 1994, Duke U., 1995. Diplomate Am. Bd. Internal Medicine, Am. Bd. Allergy and Immunology (bd. dirs. 1984—), Am. Bd. Infectious Diseases. Intern N.Y. Hosp.-Cornell Med. Ctr., 1966-67, asst. resident in medicine, 1967-68, chief resident dept. medicine, 1971-72; clin. assoc. Nat. Inst. Allergy and Infectious Diseases-NIH, Bethesda, Md., 1968-70, sr. staff fellow, 1970-71, sr. investigator, 1972-74, head, clin. physiology sect., 1974-80, dep. clin. dir., 1977-80, chief Lab. Immunoregulation, 1980—, dir. Nat. Inst. Allergy and Infectious Diseases, 1984—; dir. Office of AIDS Rsch., NIH, assoc. dir. NIH for AIDS Rsch., 1988-94; cons. Naval Med. Ctr., Bethesda, 1972—. Contbr. numerous articles to med. jours. Served with USPHS, 1968-96. Recipient meritorious svcs. award USPHS, 1979, Arthur S. Fleming award, 1983, Squibb award Infectious Diseases Soc., 1983, Commrs. spl. citation FDA, 1984, Clemons von Pirquet award Georgetown U. Med. Ctr., 1986, Disting. Clin. Educator award NIH Clin. Ctr., 1988, Leadership award Columbus Citizens Found., Inc., 1988, spl. award for rsch. in AIDS Nat. Hemophilia Fedn., 1989, Lee P. Brown Nat. Pub. Svc. award Nat. Acad. Pub. Adminstrn. and Nat. Soc. for Pub. Adminstrn., 1989, numerous awards Duke U., AMA, Children's Hosp., Nat. med. Ctr., Surgeon Gen., Am. Assn. Physicians for Human Rights, Nat. Health Coun., Nat. Found. Infectious Diseases, Helen Hayes award for med. rsch., 1989, Excellence in Pub. Svc. award Com. for Support of Pub. Svc., 1990, Lifetime Sci. award Inst. Advanced Studies in Immunology and Aging, 1990, Internat. Chiron prize, 1990, Pres. award N.Y. Acad. Sci., 1990, Thomas H. Ham-Louis R. Wasserman award Am. Soc. Hematology, 1992, Dr. Nathan Davis award AMA, 1992, Outstanding Achievement award Howard U., 1992, Humanitarian award Tiro a Segno Fedn., 1993, Cartwright prize Columbia U. Coll. Physicians and Surgeons, 1993, Commr. of Honor award SUNY, Farmingdale, 1994, Theobald Smith award Albany Med. Coll., 1995, Coord. Com. award ABA, 1996, David Rumbough Sci. award Juvenile Diabetes Fedn. Internat., 1996, award Nat. Coun. Internat. Health, 1996, award March of Dimes Fedn., 1996, Ellen Browning Scripps medal Scripps Fedn. Medicine and Rsch., 1996, Md. Gov.'s Citation, 1997, Thomas J. D'Alesandro Jr. award Assoc. Italian Am. Charities, 1997, San Marino Prize for Medicine, 1997, John P. McGovern award Am. Med. Writers Assn., 1997, many others. Fellow AAAS (master), ACP (Richard and Hinda Rosenthal award 1995, John Phillips Meml. award 1997), Am. Med. Writers Assn., Am. Acad. Allergy, Am. Acad. Allergy and Immunology (hon.), N.Y. Acad. Med. (hon. 1991), Am. Acad. Arts and Scis., Am. Acad. Microbiology; mem. AAAS (Westinghouse award 1988), NAS, Am. Fedn. Clin. Rsch., Am. Assn. Immunologists (program chmn. 1982-85, Kober lectr. 1988), Am. Soc. Virology, Am. Soc. Cell Biology, Am. Fedn. Clin. Rsch. (pres. 1980-81), Internat. AIDS Soc., Commd. Officers Assn. USPHS (Pub. Health Leader of Yr. award), Infectious Diseases Soc. Am., Am. Soc. for Clin. Investigation, Assn. of Am. Physicians (recorder 1988-93, councillor 1993—), Inst. Medicine, Royal Danish Acad. Sci. and Letters (fgn.), Royal Acad. Medicine (Spain). Roman Catholic. Avocations: running; tennis. Home: 3012 43rd St NW Washington DC 20016-3547 Office: Nat Inst Allergy & Infectious Diseases 31 Ctr Dr MSC 2520 Bethesda MD 20892-2520*

FAUDE, WILSON HINSDALE, museum director; b. Hartford, Conn., Feb. 20, 1946; s. John Paul and Helen (Hinsdale) F.; m. Janet Bailey, 1985; children: Sarah Hinsdale, Paul Bailey. BA, Hobart Coll., 1969; MA, Trinity Coll., 1975. Curator Mark Twain Meml., Hartford, 1971-78; exec. assoc. to v.p. for devel. U. Hartford, West Hartford, Conn., 1981-85; exec. dir. Old State House, Hartford, 1978-81, 85—; chmn. Conn. Hist. Commn., 1984-96, commr., 1980; commr. Conn. Arts Commn., 1975-83, hon. mem. 350th commn., 1984-86. Author: Renaissance of Mark Twain's House, 1977, The Great Hartford Picture Book, 1985, The Old Photograph Series: Hartford, 1994, vol. II, 1995, vol. III, 1997, Lost Hartford Found River, 1999, (with others) Connecticut Firsts, 1978, 85, Birthplace of Democracy, 1979; contbr. articles to profl. jours. Reader Talking Books for the Blind and Handicapped, Conn. Vol. Svcs., 1986—; mem. faculty Cooperstown Seminars, N.Y., 1979-80, 84-88; bd. dirs. Conn. Equestrian Ctr., 1996, Stowe Ctr., 1996-97, Conn. Women's Hall of Fame, 1996—; trustee Renbrook Sch., West Hartford, 1984-85; hon. trustee Mark Twain House, 1997—; corporator Hartford Art Sch., West Hartford, 1980—; mem. conn. Heritage Task Force, 1980-82. Named Hon. Capt. 1st Co. Gov. Foot Guard, 1979—, Civitan Man of Yr. 1997; recipient 1st prize needlepoint Ea. States Exposition. Mem. Nat. Arts Club, The Century Assn., Mark Twain Meml., Druid Soc., Hartford Club. Episcopalian. Home: 42 Fulton Pl West Hartford CT 06107-1128 Office: Old State House 800 Main St Hartford CT 06103-2399

FAUGHT, HAROLD FRANKLIN, electrical equipment manufacturing company executive; b. Washington, Oct. 16, 1924; s. Robert A.N. and Bessie I. (Towns) F.; m. Kathleen M. Quinn, June 21, 1947; 1 son, Richard H. B.M.E., Cornell U., 1945; M.M.E., U. Pa., 1951; grad. Advanced Mgmt. Program, Harvard U., 1961. Registered profl. engr., Pa. Div. gen. mgr. Westinghouse Electric Corp., 1946-69; sr. asst. postmaster gen. U.S. Postal Service, 1969-73; sr. v.p. Emerson Electric Co., St. Louis, 1973—. Served with USNR, 1943-46. Mem. AIAA. Club: Old Warson Country (St. Louis). Home: 1527 Candish Ln Chesterfield MO 63017-5612 Office: Emerson Electric Co 8000 W Florissant Ave Saint Louis MO 63136-1415

FAUGHT, JOLLY KAY, English language educator; b. Corbin, Ky., Dec. 22, 1954; d. Joshua Pleas and Emma Olive (Patrick) Sharp; m. Kenneth Lyle Faught, June 8, 1974; children: Jessica Ruth, Joshua Paul. BA, Cumberland Coll., 1974; MA, Wright State U., 1988. English tchr. Cumberland (Ky.) H.S., 1982-83; English educator Cumberland Coll., Williamsburg, Ky., 1991—. Mem. Williamsburg PTA, 1991—, sec., 1993-94. Mem. MLA, South Atlantic MLA, Delta Kappa Gamma (Alpha Lambda chpt.). Republican. Baptist. Avocations: reading, counted cross-stitch. Office: Cumberland Coll English Dept 7828 College Station Dr Williamsburg KY 40769-1389

FAUL, GARY LYLE, electrical engineering supervisor; b. Clarksburg, W.Va., Nov. 5, 1939; s. Lyle Joseph and Irene (Hadden) F.; m. Edith Uvenzia Kelly, Nov. 26, 1966. BSEE, AS in Instrumentation and Control, Cleve. State U., 1966; AS in Mktg. Mgmt., ICS, 1969. Lic. FCC 1st class. Engr., project mgr. Bailey Controls, Wickliffe, Ohio, 1962-77; engr. Davey McKee, Independence, Ohio, 1977-78; engr., supr. Ariz. Pub. Svc., Phoenix, 1978—; prin., cons. engr. Advanced Systems Design, Phoenix, 1982—; owner I&C Consulting Firm Advanced Sys. Design. Contbr. tech. papers to jours. Vol. Child Ctr., Phoenix, 1986, Kids Voting, Phoenix, 1992; parade marshall Fiesta Bowl, Phoenix, 1991. With U.S. Army, 1959-65. Mem. Instruments Soc. Am. (ISA E.G. Bailey award). Republican. Office: Ariz Pub Svc Co MS3888 PO Box 53999 2124 W Cheryl Dr Phoenix AZ 85021-1808

FAUL, GEORGE JOHNSON, former college president; b. Santa Ana, Calif., Oct. 11, 1918; s. George William and Esther Francis (Johnson) F.; m. June Patricia Lynch, Dec. 22, 1949; children: Robert M., Alison. Student, Santa Ana Jr. Coll., 1936-38; AB, Stanford U., 1941, MA, 1947, EdD, 1954; HHD (hon.), Monterey Inst. Internat. Studies, 1980. Counselor Visalia Coll., 1947, Stanford U., 1947-48; dir. guidance Coll. of the Sequoias, 1948-50; dean student pers. Contra Costa Coll., 1950-58, pres., 1958-64; pres., supt. Monterey (Calif.) Peninsula Coll., 1964-80, pres. emeritus, 1980—; lectr. U. Calif., Stanford U.; former mem. ednl. adv. bd. Sci. Rsch. Assocs. Mem. exec. com., chmn. Richmond Park and Recreation Commn., 1958-64; pres. Cmty. Welfare Coun., West Contra Costa County, 1960-62; bd. dirs., charter mem. Serviceman's Oppurtunity Coll.; bd. dirs. Monterey Peninsula Cmty. Chest, Cmty. Theatre of Carmel, Bach Festival, Monterey Jazz Festival, Alcoholism Coun. of Monterey Peninsula, USO, Friends of Photography, Monterey History and Art Assn., past pres. Monterey Penisula Mus. of Art, Monterey Peninsula Coll. Found.; v.p. Carmel Heritage, Casa Amesti Found.; bd. govs., treas. Monterey Peninsula Found., mem. adv. bd.; founder, former exec. dir. Monterey County Cultural Commn.; trustee Monterey Peninsula Coll., 1988-91. Lt. cmdr. USNR, 1942-47. Recipient Santa Ana Coll. Alumni Achievement award, 1968. Mem. Stanford U. Alumni Assn. (life), Pacific Biol. Lab. Club, Delta Upsilon. Home: PO Box 4365 Carmel CA 93921-4365

FAUL, JUNE PATRICIA, education specialist; b. Detroit; d. John William and Shirley Olive (Block) Lynch; m. George Johnson Faul, Dec. 22, 1949; Robert M., Alison. BA, U. Calif., Berkeley, 1952. Cert. elem. tchr., Calif. Tchr. Tulare County (Calif.) Schs., 1945-46, Tulare City Schs., 1946-48, Visalia (Calif.) City Schs., 1948-49, Richmond (Calif.) City Schs., 1951-52, Pacific Grove (Calif.) Sch. Dist., 1965-85; designated English teaching specialist State of Calif., 1969—; edn. cons. Leo A. Meyer Assocs., Inc., Hayward, Calif., 1993—; prin. Group Four Assocs.; lectr. Calif. State U., Fresno, 1969, U. Calif., Santa Cruz, 1970. Co-author: The New Older Woman, 1996. Apptd. mem. first human relations commn. City of Richmond, 1962-64; mem. adv. bd. Family Resource Ctr.; founding mem., 1st pres. Monterey (Calif.) Peninsula Child Abuse Prevention Council, 1974; hon. life mem. Calif. PTA; bd. dirs. Carmel Cultural Commn., 1964-67, Harrison Meml. Library, Carmel, Calif., 1978-84; mem. bd. Monterey Peninsula Airport Dist., 1980—. Mem. Am. Assn. Airport Execs., Friends of Hopkins Marine Station (founder, bd. dirs.) Carmel Heritage (founder, bd. dirs.), Monterey NAACP (life), Monterey Mus. Art (life), Monterey Symphony Guild (life). Democrat. Avocation: writing. Home: PO Box 4365 Carmel CA 93921-4365

FAUL, KARENE TARQUIN, art department administrator; b. Pitts., Oct. 16, 1934; d. Nicholas J. and Inez (Iannucci) Tarquin; m. Joseph C. Faul, June 12, 1971; children: Joseph C. Jr., David Thomas. BA, U. Notre Dame, 1966, MA, 1968, MFA, 1970. Cert. tchr. N.Y. Elem. tchr. K-2 St. Luke's Sch., Schenectady, N.Y., 1955-60; art tchr. 9-12 St. John Evangelist H.S., Syracuse, N.Y., 1962-65; printmaking/designer Coll. of St. Rose Art, Albany, 1970—, chairperson art dept., assoc. prof., 1983—; cons. Hudson Valley C.C., Troy, N.Y., 1996, Elmira (N.Y.) Coll., 1997; oral examiner N.Y. State Bur. of Art Edn. Adminstr., 1986. Decoration com. mem. Albany Tricentennial Gala, Albany, 1987; exec. com. Albany Symphony Viennese Ball, 1988; active family fall festival St. Peter's Addiction Ctr., Albany, 1995-97. Mem. N.Y. State Art Tchrs. Assn., Nat. Assn. of Schs. of Art and Design (evaluator, rep. 1984—), Coll. Art Assn., The Ctr. Gallery, Delta Epsilon (Sigma Alpha Chi chpt.). Office: Coll of Saint Rose 432 Western Ave Albany NY 12203-1419

FAULCONER, KAY ANNE, communications executive, dean; b. Shelbyville, Ind., Aug. 19, 1945; d. Clark Jacks and Charlotte (Tindall) Keenan; children: Kevin Lee, Melissa Lynne. BA in English, Calif. State U., Northridge, 1968; MBA, Pepperdine U., 1975, MA in Comm., 1976; EdD in Higher Edn., U. So. Calif., 1993. Pres., Kay Faulconer & Assocs., Oxnard, Calif., 1977—; instr. Oxnard Coll., U. LaVerne, v.p. and instr., 1995—; dean, econ. and cmty. devel., Ventura (Calif.) Coll., 1994—. Former pres., founder Oxnard Friends of Libr.; former exec. bd. Ventura County March of Dimes; mem. PTA; officer, bd. dirs. Oxnard Girls Club. Named Businesswoman of Yr., Ventura Bus. and Profl. Women's Club, 1976; Woman of Achievement, Oxnard Bus. and Profl. Women's Club, 1973, recipient Career Woman award, 1974.Mem. Am. Soc. Tng. and Devel., Am. Assn. Women in Community and Jr. Colls. (Leaders for 80's program), Ventura County Profl. Women's Network. Club: Oxnard Jr. Monday (past pres., hon. life). Home and Office: 1955 La Ramada Dr Camarillo CA 93012-9321

FAULCONER, ROBERT JAMIESON, pathologist, educator; b. Sedlescombe, Sussex, Eng., July 11, 1923; came to U.S., 1925, naturalized, 1932; s. Robert Hoffman and Gladys Alice (Jamieson) F.; m. Virginia Myrl Davis, Aug. 11, 1945; children: Anne Faulconer Hurley, Elizabeth Myrl, Mary Waite, John Edmund. BS, Coll. William and Mary, 1943; MD, Johns Hopkins U., 1947; DSc (hon.), Ea. Va. Med. Sch., 1998. Diplomate Am. Bd. Pathology. Intern Johns Hopkins Hosp., 1948, fellow, 1948-49; resident Presbyn.-U. Pa. Med. Ctr., Phila., 1949-52; pathologist DePaul Hosp., Norfolk, Va., 1954-78; pathologist, dir. labs. DePaul Hosp., 1965-78; clin. prof. pathology Med. Coll. Va., 1972-79; prof. pathology Ea. Va. Med. Sch., 1974-94, chmn., 1978-93, prof. emeritus, 1994—; cons. pathologist U.S. Naval Hosp., Portsmouth, Va., VA Hosp., Hampton, Va., Children;s Hosp., Norfolk, Va. Beach Gen. Hosp. Med. editorial bd. Histology and Histopathology Jour.; contbr. articles on pathology to profl. publs. Pres. Va. div. Am. Cancer Soc., 1963-66, mem. nat. bd. dirs., exec. and sci. rev. coms.; bd. visitors Coll. William and Mary, 1972-76, 79-87, chmn. William and Mary Olde Guarde, 1997-98. With USNR, 1943-46, M.C., U.S. Army, 1952-54. Recipient J. Shelton Horsley award merit Va. div. Am. Cancer Soc., 1966, Alumni medallion Coll. William and Mary, 1985. Fellow AAAS; mem. AMA, Internat. Acad. Pathology, Am. Soc. Clin. Pathologists, Coll. Am. Pathologists, Am. Assn. Anatomists, Am. Soc. Clin. Oncology, Am. Assn. Phys. Anthropologists, Va. Soc. Pathology (pres. 1958-59), Norfolk Acad. Medicine (pres. 1964-65), Am. Assn. History of Medicine, Am. Assn. Pathologists, Assn. Pathology Chmn., Cypher Soc. (Coll. William and Mary), Norfolk Yacht and Country Club, Town Point Club (bd. govs.), Commonwealth Club (Richmond), Sigma Xi. Episcopalian. Home: 1507 Buckingham Ave Norfolk VA 23508-1354 Office: Ea Va Med Sch Med Coll of Hampton Roads PO Box 1980 Norfolk VA 23501-1980

FAULK, MARSHALL WILLIAM, professional football player; b. New Orleans, Feb. 26, 1973. Student, San Diego State U. Running back Indpls. Colts., 1994-99, St. Louis Rams, 1999—. Named to Sporting News Coll. All-Am. 1st Team, 1991-93, NFL Rookie of Year 1994; selected to Pro Bowl, 1994, named outstanding player, 1994. Office: c/o St Louis Rams One Rams Way Bridgeton MO 63045*

FAULK, MICHAEL ANTHONY, lawyer; b. Kingsport, Tenn., Sept. 10, 1953; s. Loy Glade and Rosella E. (Dykes) F.; m. Janet Lynn McLain, Aug. 31, 1974; children: Katherine Lea, Andrew McLain. BS, U. Tenn., 1975; M in Pub. Adminstrn., Memphis State U., 1978, JD, 1979. Bar: U.S. Dist. Ct. (we. dist.) Tenn. 1980, U.S. Dist. Ct. (ea. dist.) Tenn. 1985, U.S. Supreme Ct., 1998. Dep. clk. to presiding justice Shelby County Chancery Ct., Memphis, 1977-79; assoc. Weintraub & Dehart, Memphis, 1980-82; ptnr. Frazier & Faulk, Church Hill, Tenn., 1982-83; sole practice Church Hill, 1983-93; ptnr. Law Offices of Faulk, May & Coup, Church Hill, Tenn., 1993-96; sole practice Church Hill, 1996—; commr. Tenn. Human Rights Commn., Nashville, 1985—, vice chmn. 1988-92; referee Hawkins County Juvenile Ct., Rogersville, Tenn., 1985-96; bd. dirs. Legal Services Inc., Johnson City, Tenn. Bd. dirs. Upper East Tenn. Div. Am. Heart Assn., Blountville, 1984-86. Named one of Outstanding Young Men in Am. U.S. Jaycees, 1977. Mem. ABA, Hawkins County Bar Assn. (pres. 1987-88), Assn. Trial Lawyers Am., Ducks Unltd. (chmn. Holston River chpt. 1984-98). Republican. Baptist. Lodge: Moose. Avocation: outdoors. E-mail: mfaulk@intermediatn.net. Office: 107 E Main Blvd Church Hill TN 37642-3729

FAULK, WARD PAGE, immunologist; b. Ruston, La., Nov. 14, 1937; s. Clarence E. and Louise B. (Page) F.; m. Klára Barabás, 1994; children: Robin, Saskia, Josie, Holly. BS, U. South, 1959; MD, Tulane U., 1964; MRC, Royal Coll. Pathology, 1973, FRC, 1983. NIH fellow Netherlands Red Cross, Amsterdam, 1965-66; fellow Mayo Clinic, Rochester, Minn.,

1966-67, U. Calif. Med. Ctr., San Francisco, 1967-69; mem. staff British Med. Rsch. Coun., London, 1973-76; prof. Med. U. S.C., Charleston, 1976-79; dir. Royal Coll. Surgeons, East Grinstead, England, 1979-81; prof., dir. Purdue U./Meth. Hosp., Indpls., 1986—; vis. prof. faculty medicine U. Nice, France, 1982-84, dept. obstetrics So. Ill. U., Springfield, 1984-85; cons. hematology and oncology Pembury (England) Hosp., 1982-96. Founder, co-editor: Immunological Obstetrics, 1992; contbr. articles to more than 350 publs.; co-editor for 11 jours. Med. officer WHO, Geneva, 1970-73; mem. NATO Advanced Study Group, Cordoba, Spain, 1988, 94, NIH Study Group, Bethesda, Md., 1990. Recipient award Calif. Trudeau Soc., 1965, Metchnikoff medal Bulgarian Acad. Scis., 1971. Fellow Royal Coll. Pathology, Fellow Nat.Inst. of Health; mem. Internat. Soc. for Immunology Reproduction, Am. Soc. Immunology Reproduction (Munksgaard award 1992), Internat. Soc. Heart and Lung Transplantation. Republican. Episcopalian. E-mail: wpfaulk@aol.com. Office: Methodist Hosp 1701 Senate Blvd Indianapolis IN 46202-1299

FAULKENBERRY, VIRGIL THOMAS, retired naval officer, educator; b. Ellington, Mo., Sept. 30, 1928; s. Paul and Lillie Mae (Williams) F.; m. Anna Kate Golemon, Nov. 21, 1952; children: Lauralyn, James, Richard, Kate, Tani, Jennifer. BS Forestry, U. Mo., 1950; MS Human Rels./Mgmt., Golden Gate U., 1987; cert. advanced study, Old Dominion U., 1989, post-grad., 1990. Enlisted USN, 1950, advanced through grades to comdr., 1965; carrier pilot USN/Pacific and Atlantic, 1950-77; dir. tng. Fleet Combat Tng. Ctr. USN, Dam Neck, Va., 1970-77; ret., 1977; tech. engr. Vitro, Silver Spring, Md., 1977-78; naval sci. instr. Tabb (Va.) H.S., 1979-94; mem. curriculum devel. com. staff Chief Naval Edn. and Tng., Pensacola, Fla., 1980-84. Pres. Thalia (Va.) Cmty. Civic League, 1975-76; pres. PTA, Fairfax, Va., 1962-65l cubmaster Boy Scouts Am., Virginia Beach, Va., 1965-67, scoutmaster, 1969-73, Explorer advisor, 1974-77, tng. chair Tidewater coun.; chmn. adminstrv. bd. Thalia United Meth. Ch., Virginia Beach, 1975, chmn. coun. on ministries, 1995, sch. tchr. youth classes; vol. Am. and Judio Christian Outreach Ctr., Virginia Beach, Va. With Mo. N.G., 1944. Recipient Silver Beaver award Boy Scouts Am., 1974, Scouting/Ch. Religious medal Boy Scouts Am., 1996. Avocations: scouting, church, environmental programs, state and national legislative matters.

FAULKNER, BONITA LOUISE, enrichment education educator; b. Erie, Pa., Sept. 5, 1947; d. Albert John and Margaret Anastasia (Gorski) DeLuca; m. Thomas Jay Faulkner, Aug. 30, 1969; children: Sean Thomas, Aaron Michael. BA in Elem. Edn., Mercyhurst Coll., Erie, 1968; MEd, State Pa. Dept. Edn., Erie, 1996. Cert. elem. edn., Pa. Tchr. 3d and 4th grades Erie Sch. Dist., 1968-72, tchr. reading 1st and 2d grades, 1970-72; substitute tchr. Cath. Diocese Erie, Millcreek Twp. Sch. Dist., Erie Sch. Dist., 1980-82; tchr. 3d grade Millcreek Twp. Sch. Dist., Erie, 1983, tchr. gifted program, 1983-86, coord., tchr. schoolwide enrichment program, 1986—; chmn. adv. coun. Millcreek Twp. Sch. Dist., 1991-94, mem. strategic planning com., 1994-95; coord. thrift program Belle Valley Elem. Sch., Erie, 1991-99; presenter in field; emissary to Zibo, China sch. sys. Erie C. of C./Millcreek Twp., 1997. Writer, contbr.: (gifted curriculum) Kindling Individual Devel. in Students, 1983-86, SWEP, 1986-99, Ecol./Futures/Global Curriculum, 1995. Sec. phase IV Montmarc Homeowners Assn., Erie, 1991-97; bd. dirs. Playhouse Wing, Erie, 1972-76; vol. Erie Festival of the Arts, 1984-86. Grantee Presque Isle Rotary, Erie, 1989-97, Erie Area Fund for the Arts, 1996, 97, 99. Mem. AAUW, NEA, Nat. Alliance for the Mentally Ill, Pa. Edn. Assn., Pa. Assn. for Gifted Edn. (spkr. conf. 1991), Nat. Alliance for the Mentally Ill of Erie County, Jr. League. Democrat. Roman Catholic. Avocations: reading, golf, travel, philharmonic, theater. Home: 633 Montroyale Dr Erie PA 16504-2617 Office: Belle Valley Sch Millcreek Twp Sch Dist 5300 Henderson Rd Erie PA 16509-4006

FAULKNER, HENRY, III, automotive executive; b. 1949; m. Susan Price. With Henry Faulkner Inc., Phila., 1970-81; CEO Faulkner Orgn., Trevose, Pa., 1981—. Office: Faulkner/Saturn 4437 E Street Rd Trevose PA 19053-4984*

FAULKNER, JOHN ARTHUR, physiologist, educator; b. Kingston, Ont., Can., Dec. 12, 1923; s. Jack and Winifred (Esdaile) F.; m. Margaret Isabelle Rowntree, Apr. 9, 1955; children: Laura Megan, Melanie Anne. B.A., Queen's U., 1949, B.P.H.E., 1950; M.S., U. Mich., 1956, Ph.D., 1962. Tchr. sci. Glebe Collegiate Inst., Ottawa, Ont., Can., 1952-56; asst. prof. phys. edn. U. Western Ont., 1956-60; asst. prof. edn. U. Mich., 1962-64, assoc. prof. edn., 1964-66, assoc. prof. physiology, 1966-71, prof. physiology, 1971—; rsch. scientist U. Mich. Inst. Gerontology, 1986—, acting dir., 1988-89, assoc. dir. biol. rsch. Inst. Gerontology, 1990—, interim dir., 1997-98. Assoc. editor Jour. Applied Physiology, 1991-93, Basic and Applied Myology, 1990—; contbr. articles on altitude acclimatization, cardiovascular response to swimming and running, skeletal muscles adaptation, mechamism of contraction-induced injury, regeneration of skeletal muscles following transplantation, injury and repair of muscle fibers following plimetric contractions, and contractile properties of muscles in aged rodents, mdxmice, and transgenic mdx mice, to profl. jours. Dir. Nathan Shock Ctr. for Basic Biology of Aging. Served as pilot RCAF, 1942-45, ETO. Burke Aaron Hinsdale scholar, 1962; recipient Glenn Edmonson award U. Mich., Established Investigators award Am. Physiol. Soc., EEP sect., 1998. Mem. Biol. Engring. (founding fellow), Gerontol. Soc. Am., Am. Coll. Sports Medicine (pres. 1971-72, Citation award 1978, Honor award 1992); mem. Biophys. Soc., Nat. Inst. Health (mem. respiration and applied physiology study sect. 1980-84, reviewers res. 1989—). Home: 2200 Navarre Cir Ann Arbor MI 48104-2759 Office: University of Michigan Institute of Gerontology 300 N Ingalls St Ann Arbor MI 48109-2007

FAULKNER, JULIA ELLEN, opera singer; b. St. Louis, Nov. 1, 1957; d. Seldon and Dona Leah (Clark) F.; m. Andrew Bouvet, July 3, 1993. MusB cum laude, Ind. U., 1980, MusM, 1983. Instr. voice No. Ariz. U., Flagstaff, 1984, Iowa State U., 1984-85; solo artist San Francisco Opera Ctr., 1985-86, Wolftrap Opera Co., Vienna, Va., 1986, Bavarian State Opera, Munich, 1987-91, Vienna (Austria) State Opera, 1991-97. Solo performances with opera cos. and theaters at La Scala, Carnegie Hall, N.Y.C., Met. Opera, N.Y.C., L.A. Philharm., San Francisco Philharm., also in Miami Fla., Berlin, Hamburg, Germany, Lyon, Jerusalem, Bordeau, Stockholm, Amsterdam and Genoa; dir. Oklahoma and Old Maid and the Thief, Flagstaff, 1984; rec. artist Elektra, 1990, Der Rosenkavalier, 1991, Rossini, Semiramide, Schumann, Genoveva; recorded Pergolese Stabat Mater Deutsche Grammophone Das Paradis und die Peri, Verdi's Falstaff. Recipient award Met. Opera, N.Y.C., 1985, 3d prize Whitaker Internat. Voice Competition, 1985, Festspiel prize Bavarian State Opera, 1988. Democrat. Office: Met Opera Lincoln Ctr New York NY 10021

FAULKNER, LARRY RAY, chemistry educator, university official; b. Shreveport, La., Nov. 26, 1944; s. James Clifford and Doris Louise (Koch) F.; m. Mary Ann Jordan, Aug. 14, 1965; children: Brian Jordan, Susan Louise. BS, So. Meth. U., 1966; PhD, U. Tex., Austin, 1969. Asst. prof. chemistry Harvard U., Cambridge, Mass., 1969-73; prof. chemistry U. Tex., Austin, 1983-84; asst. prof. U. Ill., Urbana-Champaign, 1973-75, assoc. prof., 1975-79, prof., 1979-83, prof. chemistry, dept. head, 1984-89, dean Coll. Liberal Arts and Sci., 1989-94, provost and vice chancellor acad. affairs, 1994-98; pres. U. Tex., Austin, 1998—; mem. Materials Rsch. Lab., 1978-90. Author: (with A.J. Bard) Electrochemical Methods, 1980; div. editor Jour. Electrochem. Soc., 1975-80; U.S. regional editor Jour. Electroanalytical Chemistry, 1980-85. NSF grad. fellow 1966-69; recipient U.S. Dept. Energy award for Outstanding Sci. Achievement in Material Scis., 1986. Fellow AAAS, Electrochem. Soc. (Edward Weston fellow 1969, Young Author's prize 1976, v.p. 1988-91, pres. 1991-92), Am. Chem. Soc. (award in analytical chemistry 1992), Soc. Electroanalytical Chemistry (Charles N. Reilly award 1998), Phi Beta Kappa (grad. rsch. award Tex. Gamma chpt. 1969-70), Phi Kappa Phi. Home: 5310 Western Hills Dr Austin TX 78731-4822 Office: Office of Pres U Tex at Austin PO Box T Austin TX 78713-8920

FAULKNER, ROBERT LLOYD, advertising executive, graphic designer; b. Chgo., Nov. 8, 1934; s. L. Lester and Agnes Elizabeth (Irons) F.; m. Elizabeth Alice Thomas, June 14, 1958; children: Anne Elizabeth, Lynn Marie, Thomas Robert. BFA in Advt. Design, U. Ill., 1958. Account exec. Brad Sebstad Advt., Chgo., 1966-67; sr. account exec. D'Arcy Advt. Co., Chgo., 1967-70; v.p. Wm. A. Robinson Inc., Northbrook, Ill., 1970-71; nat. mdse. and promotion mgr. James B. Beam Distilling Co., Chgo., 1971-73; v.p. Coord. Advt., Chgo., 1973-77, Grant/Jacoby Inc., Chgo., 1977-79, Kennedy Advt., Chgo., 1979-86; exec. v.p. Kamen/Faulkner Inc., Chgo., 1986-89; pres., owner Bob Faulkner Corporation, Western Springs, Ill., 1989—; course coord., advt. lectr. grad. level advt. courses Northwestern U. and Roosevelt U., Chgo., 1980-85. Author: Learn to Cross Country Ski, 1976; co-author: Cross-Country Skiing for Everybody, 1975. Dir. Western Springs Hist. Soc., 1992-95; mem. Illegitimate Theatre of Western Springs. Recipient numerous advt. awards. Mem. Bus. Mktg. Assn. (Cert. Bus. Communicator), Nat. Ski Patrol (life), Model T Ford Owners Assn., Legend Lake Yacht Club, Sports Car Club Am. Episcopalian. Avocation: fine art painting.

FAULKNER, ROBERT W., federal judge; b. 1938. BA, Quachita Bapt. U., 1960; LLB, U. Ark., 1965. Pvt. practice, 1966-68; atty. magistrate judges divsn. Adminstrv. Office of U.S. Cts., 1988-92; exec. sec. to Gov. Winthrop Rockefeller, 1969-71; commr. Ark. State Claims Commn., 1967-69, chmn., 1969; apptd. magistrate judge ea. dist. U.S. Dist. Ct. Tex., 1993; instr. criminal procedure U. Ark., Little Rock. Mem. Am. Inn of Ct., Ark. Bar Assn. (del. ho. of dels.), Fed. Magistrate Judges Assn. (dir.-at-large), Pulaski County Bar Assn. (pres. 1985-86). Fax: (903) 893-9067. Office: US Courthouse Annex 200 N Travis St Sherman TX 75090-5961

FAULKNER, SEWELL FORD, real estate executive; b. Keene, N.H., Sept. 25, 1924; s. John Charles and Hazel Helen (Ford) F.; AB, Harvard, 1949; MBA, 1951; m. June Dayton Finn, Jan. 10, 1951 (div.); children: Patricia Anne, Bradford William, Sandra Ford, Jonathan Dayton, Winthrop Sewell; m. Constance Mae Durvin, Mar. 15, 1969 (div.); children: Sarah Elizabeth, Elizabeth Jane. Product mgr. Congoleum Nairn, Inc., Kearny, N.J., 1951-55; salesman, broker, chmn., pres. Jack White Co. real estate, Anchorage, 1956-86; chmn. Faulkner, Inc.; chmn. Mem. Anchorage City Council, 1962-65, Greater Anchorage Area Borough Assembly, 1964-65, Anchorage Area Charter Commn., 1969-70. Pres., Alaska World Affairs Council, 1967-68; treas. Alyeska Property Owners, Inc., 1973-75, pres., 1977-78; pres. Downtown Anchorage Assn., 1974-75; mem. Girdwood Bd. Suprs. Served with USAAF, 1943-45. Mem. Anchorage Area C. of C. (dir. 1973-74), Alaska Notch Club. Office: Faulkner Real Estate 604 K St Anchorage AK 99501-3329

FAULKNER, WALTER THOMAS, lawyer; b. New Haven, Sept. 17, 1928; s. Walter Thomas and Alice Marion (McGushin) F.; m. Joan Lee Hills, Mar. 17, 1956; children: John, Andrew, George, Susan. A.B., Providence Coll., 1952; LL.B., Columbia U., 1955. Bar: N.Y. State 1956. Since practiced in N.Y.C.; assoc. firm Rogers, Hoge & Hills, 1959-65, ptnr., 1965-86; ptnr. Kelley Drye & Warren, 1987—; sec. Sterling Drug Inc., 1973-78, Bacardi Corp., 1975-96. Bd. govs. Sound Shore Med. Ctr. Westchester. Served with AUS, 1946-48. Mem. Assn. of Bar of City of N.Y., ABA, N.Y. State Bar Assn., Am. Soc. Corp. Secs. Home: 64 Woodbine Ave Larchmont NY 10538-3525 Office: Kelley Drye & Warren 101 Park Ave New York NY 10178-0002

FAULSTICH, ALBERT JOSEPH, banking consultant; b. New Orleans, May 28, 1910; s. Albert and Mary (Balser) F.; m. Anna Emily Collignon, June 30, 1940; children: Albert Joseph, Richard Charles. *Balthsar Faulstich arrived in Philadelphia, Pennsylvania from Germany, on September 30, 1754 on the ship Ediburgh out of Rotterdam. Albert J. Faulstich, Jr. (BME, AB, MME, PHD) was director of U.S. Navy antisubmarine warfare in the "Cold War" and produced new technologies needed for underwater vehicles Argo and Jason, to discover the Titanic and Bismarck. Richard C. Faulstich (BS, MCS, MS) managed certified public accounting audits of health maintenance organizations, determined eligibility of States for Federal Medicaid grants, and monitored the National Medicaid budget.* Stud. mech. drafting and mathematics, Delgado Coll., New Orleans, 1926-28; stud. structl. drafting and design, Columbia Univ., New York, 1931; BS in Acctg. and Econs, Columbus U., Washington, 1938, M.S. in Acctg. and Finance, 1948; student advanced econs., American U., 1948. With Office Supr. Arch. Pub. Bldg. and Ctrl. Supplies Svcs., Washington, 1930-38; with Treasury Dept., 1939-64, asst. to pers. dir., 1939-42, dir. positions evaluation and job analysis, 1942-43, indsl. relations specialist, 1943-45, dir. salary-wages adminstrn., coord. performance evaluation, also chmn. com. union rels., adminstr. policy and standards of govt. early-age retirement spl. investigative and intelligence agts. from various burs., 1946-60, dir. treas. security programs, 1961, spl. asst. to sec. for mgmt., transition polit. incumbencies, 1961-62, asst. to comptr. currency, managed Currency Bur. and directed issuance and redemption of Fed. Res. currency, 1962-64, coordinator fed. banking, 1964; dir. FDIC, 1965-66, dep. adminstr. nat. banks, 1965-74, asst. dir., 1973-74; treas., mem. Fed. Pers. Coun., 1941; condr. seminars in pub. adminstrn., nat. banking regulation and treas. ops. for reps. China, Japan, Taiwan, Thailand, Vietnam, Philippines, Egypt, Brazil, France, Italy, Romania and Yugoslavia (intermittently) 1948-65; chmn. com. analyze Fed. positions classifications pay plan, 1949; condr. seminars in field, 1948-65; designer basic orgn. structure and established highest level staffing pattern for Econ. Stabilization Agy., 1950; acting dir. pers. mgmt., wage bd. chmn., Treasury Dept., (intermittently) 1953-60, directed equal employment program, 1965-74; composer Pres. Kennedy's Proclamation honoring Centennial of Nat. Banking System, 1963; mem. rev. bd., spl. com. on liquidations, mergers, loans and purchases assets FDIC, 1966-74; cons. Fin. Gen. Bankshares, Inc., 1974-76, for banks and govt., 1976—; dir. Am. Nat. Bank of Md., 1975-77. Author Pres. Kennedy's Proclamation on Centennial Nat. Banking System, 1963. Chmn. compt. currency orgn. for nation-wide campaign for Kennedy Library Fund, 1964. With USMCR, 1935-39; lt. USNR, 1943-46. Decorated Naval Commendation medal, 1946, War Fin. Patriot award, 1946, Cmty. Svc. award, 1964; recipient commendation Treasury Dept., 1962, 3 citations, 1972, Meritorious Svc. award, 1973, Disting. Svc. award 1974, Albert Gallatin award, Am. Flag award, Equal Opportunity award, 1974, citation Internat. Coop. Adminstrn., 1958, Am. Bankers Assn., 1967; Ky. Col. Democrat. Roman Catholic. Home and Office: Waterford in Heartlands 3004 N Ridge Rd Ellicott City MD 21043

FAULSTICH, JAMES R., retired bank executive; b. St. Louis, Dec. 19, 1933; s. Robert C. and Eva D. (Mueller) F.; m. Gretchen Felthouse, July 28, 1956; children: Robert, Julie, Clairann. BS, Ind. U., 1958; JD, U. Chgo., 1961. Dep. legis. counsel State Oreg., Salem, 1961-67, ins. commr., 1967-69, asst. to gov., 1969-71; v.p. industry rels. Nat. Assn. Ind. Insurers, Des Plaines, Ill., 1971-77, dir. rsch., sr. v.p. industry rels., 1977-79; pres., CEO Fed. Home Loan Bank Seattle, 1979-99; bd. dirs. Pentegra. Treas. Bd. of Social Compact, Washington; bd. dirs. Housing Partnership, Seattle, Seattle Ctr. Found.; mem. Higher Edn. Coordinating Bd.; trustee Seattle Opera. Mem. ABA, Am. Judicature Soc., Oreg. Bar Assn., Wash. Athletic Club, Rainier Club, Downtown Seattle Assn., Columbia Tower Club, Rotary. Home: 8101 SE 48th St Mercer Island WA 98040-4301 Office: Fed Home Loan Bank 1501 4th Ave Ste 1900 Seattle WA 98101-1693

FAULWELL, BOND R., government executive; b. Sedalia, Mo., Sept. 24, 1945; s. Bloom R. and Norma Genevieve Bond F.; m. Shirley Kay Middendorf, Mar. 22, 1969; children: Maria Faulwell Mackey, Andrew C. Faulwell. BA, Grinnell Coll., 1967; student, Harvard U., 1968-69; MPA, U. Mo., Kansas City, 1972. Chief personnel mgmt. U.S. GSA, Washington, 1974-75, dir. manpower mgmt., 1975-78, personnel officer, 1978-79, dir. orgn. and mgmt., 1979-81, dir. orgn. and personnel, 1981-83, regional contbr., 1983-86; regional controller U.S. GSA, Kansas City, 1983-86, dep. regional adminstr., 1986—; mem. advisory bd. U. Mo. Sch. Adminstrn., Columbia, 1993-96. Editor Pub. Mgr., 1998—; mem. edtl. bd. Am. Rev. Pub. Adminstrn., 1993—; mem. adv. panel Pub. Mgmt. Rsch. Dirs., 1982. Assoc. coord. Heartland Combined Fed. Campaign, Kansas City, 1994. Mem. ASPA (pres chpt. 1984-85, Pub. Adminstr. of Yr. 1991, chair nat. conf. 1994), Sr. Execs. Assn (pres. chpt. 1989—, charter mem.). Presbyterian. E-mail: bond.faulwell gsa.gov. Office: US GSA 1500 E Bannister Rd Kansas City MO 64113

FAULWELL, GERALD EDWARD, insurance company executive; b. San Francisco, May 13, 1942; s. Albert Jr. and Helen Marie (Thiel) F.; m. Constance Lee Danaher, Aug. 22, 1964 (div. Jan. 1982); children: Jeffrey, Jennifer, Heather, Cullen; m. Marita Girardo Tschirhart, Jan. 30, 1982. Student, Valley Coll., 1960-63; BA, UCLA, 1965. CPA, Tex. Acct. Farmers Group, Inc., L.A., 1966-67, sr. acct., 1967-69, acctg. specialist, 1969-72, acctg. mgr., 1972-78, mgmt. trainee, 1978-79, dir. corp. acctg., 1979-82, v.p. acctg., 1982-87, v.p., treas., 1988-92, v.p. strategic planning and budgets, 1993-95, sr. v.p. strategic planning and budgeting, 1996-97, sr. v.p., cfo, 1998—. Petty officer USN, 1960-64. Mem. AICPA, Tex. State Bd. Pub. Accountancy. Democrat. Roman Catholic. Avocations: golf, bowling. Home: 733 Oldstone Pl Simi Valley CA 93065-5336 Office: Farmers Group Inc 4680 Wilshire Blvd Los Angeles CA 90010-3807

FAUNCE, SARAH CUSHING, former museum curator; b. Tulsa, Aug. 19, 1929; d. George Jr. and Helen Pauline (Colwell) F. BA, Wellesley Coll., 1951; MA, Washington U., St. Louis, 1959; postgrad., Columbia U., 1960-63. Tchr. history Hartridge Sch., Plainfield, N.J., 1954-56; tchr. art Mary C. Wheeler Sch., Providence, 1958-59; instr. art history Barnard Coll., N.Y.C., 1962-64; sec. adv. council art history Columbia U., 1963-70, registrar, curator, 1965-70; curator paintings and sculpture Bklyn. Mus. Art, 1970-98, curator emeritus, project dir. Courbet Catalogue Raisonné project, 1997—; exhbn. cons. Jewish Mus., N.Y.C., 1968-70. Author: Courbet, 1993; exhbn. catalog author: Anne Ryan Collages, 1974, Carl Larsson, 1982; author, editor: Belgian Art 1880-1914, 1980, Courbet Reconsidered, 1988, In the Light of Italy: Corot and Early Plein Air Painting, 1996; editor: Northern Light: Realism and Symbolism in Scandinavian Painting 1880-1910, 1982. Travel grantee Columbia U., 1963. Mem. AAM-ICOM, Coll. Art Assn., Phi Beta Kappa. Democrat. Home: 28 E 92nd St New York NY 10128-0616 Office: Courbet Catalogue Raisonne Project 165B E 82nd St New York NY 10028

FAUNCE, WILLIAM DALE, clinical psychologist, researcher, consultant; b. Lansing, Mich., Dec. 4, 1947; s. Lucius Dale and Wilhelmina (Hall) F. BA, Mich. State U., 1972; MA, Calif. State U., L.A., 1978; PhD in Clin. Psychology, U. So. Calif., 1983. Lic. psychologist, N.C. Psychology intern Brentwood (Calif.) VA, 1981-82; clin. psychologist UCLA Neuropsychiat. Inst., Westwood, Calif., 1983, Coldwater Canyon Hosp., North Hollywood, Calif., 1983-84, So. Peninsula Community Mental Health Ctr., Homer, Alaska, 1984-86; pvt. practice Homer, Alaska, 1986-87; cons. Santa Cruz, Calif., 1987-90; clin. psychologist, program dir. Broughton State Hosp., Morganton, N.C., 1990-92; mem. faculty Appalachian State U., Boone, N.C., 1992-97; pvt. practice cons., 1997—. Co-author: (chpt.) Imagery, 1984; contbr. articles to profl. jours. Fellow NIMH; mem. APA, Union Concerned Scientists. Avocations: creative writing, guitar, travel, foreign languages. Home and Office: PO Box 241 Jonas Ridge NC 28641-0241

FAUNTLEROY, CARMA CECIL, arts administration executive; b. Lynchburg, Va., July 7, 1954. BA in History, Coll. of William & Mary, 1976; MA in Art History, George Washington U., 1985; MBA in Internat. Bus., Rutgers U., 1992. Adminstrv. asst. to dir. divsn. govt. and consumer affairs Electronic Industries Assn., 1976-80; asst. to pres. Internat. Exhbns. Found., Washington, 1980-83; curatorial intern dept. 20th-century art Nat. Gallery Art, Washington, 1984-85; fin. officer The Textile Mus., Washington, 1985-86; dir. coll. galleries and arts mgmt. program Sweet Briar (Va.) Coll., 1986-89; assoc. dir. Jane Voorhees Zimmerli Art Mus., New Brunswick, N.J., 1989-93; exec. dir. Queens (N.Y.) Mus. Art, 1993-98; dir. found. and corp. philanthropy Nat. Trust for Hist. Preservation, Washington, 1998—; grant panelist N.Y. State Coun. on Arts, N.Y.C., 1993; trustee N.J. Assn. Ms., Trenton, 1990-93; project evaluator N.J. Com. for Humanities, New Brunswick, 1990-93; nominating com. Coun. Arts Adminstrs. in Va. Higher Edn., 1988; GOS field reviewer Inst. Mus. Svcs., 1989-90, 93, 99; juror summer exhbns. auction benefit com. Va. Ctr. for Creative Arts, 1988. Author: (catalogue) Japanese Woodblock Prints from the Sweet Briar Collection, 1989; contbr. to mags. and newsletters. Mem. Internat. Coun. Mus., Am. Assn. Mus., Mid-Atlantic Assn. Mus., Nat. Soc.. Fund Raising Execs., The Textile Mus., Coll. Art Assn., ArtTable (bd. dirs. 1995-98), Mus. Trustee Assn. (adv. coun. of dirs. 1996-97). Office: Nat Trust for Hist Preservation 1785 Massachussetts Ave NW Washington DC 20036

FAURE, GUNTER, geology educator; b. Tallinn, Estonia, May 11, 1934; s. Arnulf and Stella (von Harpe) F.; m. Barbara L.L. Goodell, Sept. 5, 1959 (div. Feb. 1985); children: Mary Jennifer, John Eric, Pamela Anne, David Christopher; m. Teresa M. Mensing, June 4, 1988. B.Sc., U. Western Ont., 1957; Ph.D., MIT, 1961; fellow, Sch. Advanced Studies, 1961-62. Asst. prof. geology Ohio State U., 1962-65, assoc. prof., 1965-68, prof., 1968—; field work Antarctica. Author: (with J.L. Powell) Strontium Isotope Geology, 1972, Principles of Isotope Geology, 1977, 2d edit., 1986, Principles and Applications of Geochemistry, 1991, 2d edit., 1998; editor-in-chief Jour. Isotope Geoscience, 1983-88; exec. editor Geochimica et Cosmochimica Acta, 1989-97; assoc. editor Geochimica et Cosmochimica Acta, 1989—; contbr. articles to profl. jours. Recipient univ. gold medal in honours geology U. Western Ont., 1957, disting. teaching award Ohio State U., 1970, 83, Antarctic Service medal, 1976. Fellow Geol. Soc. Am.; mem. Geochem. Soc., Planetary Soc., Meteoritical Soc., Internat. Assn. Geochemistry and Cosmochemistry (v.p. 1992-96, pres. 1996—). E-mail: heath.18@osu.edu. Office: 125 S Oval Mall Columbus OH 43210-1308

FAURER, LOUIS, photographer; b. Phila., Aug. 28, 1916; s. Morris and Sarah F.; 1 son by previous marriage, Mark. Student public schs., Phila. Caricature artist Atlantic City, 1934-37; poster letterer Warner Bros. Theatres, Phila., 1937-42; comml. photographer, 1947-70; vis. prof. U. Va., Charlottesville, 1983-84; lectr. photography seminar Parsons Sch. Design, N.Y.C., 1975-77, New Sch. Social Research, N.Y.C., 1977, SUNY, Purchase, 1978, Stockton (N.J.) State Coll., 1981, U. Md. Art Gallery, College Park, 1981, U. Va., Charlottesville, 1983-84, Cooper Union for Advancement of Sci. and Art, N.Y.C., 1984, thesis class Sch. Visual Arts, N.Y.C., 1985-86; vis. lectr. Yale U., 1983, 85. Contbr. to Harper's Bazaar, Vogue, Life, Time, Fortune, Look mags., Flair (Cowles Publs.), Glamour, Mademoiselle, Seventeen, Elle (Paris), Jardin des Modes (Paris) mags.; one man shows include Marlborough Gallery, N.Y.C., 1977, U. Md. Art Gallery, College Park, 1981, Limelight Gallery, N.Y.C., 1960, Davison Art Ctr., Wesleyan U., Mus. Fine Arts, Houston, 1986, Laurence Miller Gallery, N.Y.C., 1987, Bibliotheque Nationale, Paris, 1990, Howard Greenberg Gallery, N.Y.C., 1990, 93, Victoria and Albert Mus., London, 1991, Ctr. Nat. de la Photographie, Paris, 1992, Sander Gallery, 1992; group exhbns. include Mus. Modern Art, N.Y.C., 1950, 54-78, 84, 85-86, Whitney Mus. Am. Art, N.Y.C., 1978, 83, Light Gallery, N.Y.C., 1978, 86, Quality of Presence, 1978, Fed. Plaza, N.Y.C., 1979, N.Y.C. City Hall, 1979, Westbeth Gallery, N.Y.C., 1980, 90, 19th and 20th Century Photography, Lunn Gallery, Washington, 1980, Am. Children, Mus. Modern Art, N.Y.C., 1981, Ministere de la Culture, Grand Palais, Paris, 1982, Seibu Mus. Am. Art, Tokyo, 1982, N.Y. Cultural Found., N.Y.C., 1983, Mus. Contemporary Art, L.A. and Detroit Inst. of Arts, 1984-85, Corcoran Gallery Art, Washington, 1985, Barbican Centre for Arts, London, 1985, Daniel Wolf Gallery, N.Y.C., 1985, Ministry of Culture, Madrid, 1986, San Francisco Mus. Modern Art, 1986, Nat. Portrait Gallery, London, 1986-87, Nat. Gallery Art, Washington, 1989, The Art Inst. Chgo., 1989, L.A. County Mus. Art, 1989, Worcester (Mass.) Art Mus., 1990, Mus. Fine Arts, Houston, 1986, Kathleen Ewing Gallery, Washington, Bayly Art Mus., U. Va., Charlottesville; represented in permanent collections including Met. Mus. Art, Mus. Modern Art, N.Y.C., Seagram Collection, N.Y.C., N.Y. Pub. Libr. Prints and Photographs Div., New Orleans Mus. Art, Corcoran Gallery, Corcoran Sch. Art, Washington, Bibliotheque Nationale, Paris, Centre National des Arts Plastiques, Paris, Edward Steichen Collection, Mpls. Inst. Arts, Can. Cen. for Architecture, Montreal, Gilmann Paper Co., N.Y.C., Paul Weiss Rifkind Wharton & Garrison, N.Y.C., Davison Art Ctr., Wesleyan U., Kansas City Art Inst., Hallmark Collection, Kansas City, Mo., San Francisco Mus. Modern Art, Australian Nat. Gallery, Canberra, The Chrysler Mus., Norfolk, Va., Mus. Fine Arts, Houston, Cooper Union for Advancement of Sci. and Art, N.Y.C., The Art Inst. Chgo., Balt. Mus. Art, The Consolidated Freightways, Inc. Collection, Palo Alto, Calif., Phila. Mus. Art, Collection Peter MacGill, Bayly Mus., U. Va., Charlottesville, David Ferber, Ferber Greilsheimer Chan & Essner, N.Y.C., Rubin Gorewitz, N.Y.C., Gerd Sander, Cologne, Fed. Republic Germany, U. Pa., Dreyfus Found.; contbr. photographs to Local Color (Truman Capote), 1950, Mag.-Images for Saul Steinberg, 1950, (exbhn.) Smithsonian and Huston Art Collection, 1950, Family of Man, 1965, 100 Years of the American Female, 1967, Aperture, 1978, American Children exhbn. from the Collection Mus. Modern Art, 1981, Contact Theory, 1980, Fall 1980 Photography Courses catalogue New Sch., N.Y.C., 1980; (books) The New York School Photographs 1936-63, Appearances: Fashion Photography Since 1945, 1991, 125 Great Moments of Harper's Bazaar, 1993; subject of book: Photo Poche # 51, 1992, An American Century of Photography: From Dry-Plate to Digital/The Hallmark

Photographic Collection, 1995. Creative Artists Public Service fellow, 1977-78; Nat. Endowment Arts fellow, 1978, 81, 82; John Simon Guggenheim Meml. Found. fellow, 1979-80. Office: c/o Westbeth Group 643 West St Ste H-520 New York NY 10014*

FAURI, ERIC JOSEPH, lawyer; b. Lansing, Mich., Feb. 16, 1942; s. Fedele Fauri and Iris M. Petersen; m. Sherrill Lynn Nurenberg, July 15, 1969; children—Lauren, Nadia, Kirk. B.A., U. Del., 1963; J.D. with distinction, U. Mich., 1966. Bar: Mich. 1967, U.S. Dist. Ct. (ea. dist.) Mich. 1967, U.S. Dist. Ct. (we. dist.) Mich. 1972, U.S. Ct. Appeals (6th cir.) 1974. Assoc. Dykema, Gossett, Spencer, Goodnow & Trigg, Detroit, 1966-71; Parmenter Forsythe, Rude et al, Muskegon, Mich., 1971-73; ptnr. Parmenter, Forsythe, Rude et al, Muskegon, 1973—; Parmenter O'Toole, 1992—. Served to capt. U.S. Army, 1967-68. Mem. ABA, State Bar Mich. Office: Parmenter O'Toole 175 W Apple Ave PO Box 786 Muskegon MI 49443-0786

FAUSEY, NORMAN RAY, soil scientist; b. Fremont, Ohio, Oct. 28, 1938; married; 7 children. BS, Ohio State U., 1962, MS, 1966, PhD in Agronomy, 1975. Soil drainage scientist, project leader USDA, 1967—. Mem. Am. Soc. Agronomy (Hancor Soil and Water Engring. award 1995), Soil Conservation Soc. Am., Am. Soc. Agrl. Engrs., Soil Sci. Soc. Am. Address: 5383 Amy Ln Columbus OH 43235-7302*

FAUST, A. DONOVAN, communications executive; b. Indpls., May 31, 1919; s. Glenn L. and Lela Vivien (Smith) F.; m. Barbara Lou Wilson, Aug. 4, 1951; 1 child, Thomas. Student, Taylor U., 1936-37, Purdue U., 1937-39. Broadcasting performer, producer, exec., 1939-54; gen. mgr. Sta. WJRT-TV, Flint, Mich., 1954-65; with Gen. Electric Broadcasting Co., 1966-82; v.p., gen. mgr. WNGE-TV, Nashville, 1966-70, KOA-TV, Denver, 1970-71; v.p. sta. ops. Gen. Electric Broadcasting Co., 1971-74, pres., 1979-82; v.p., gen. mgr. Gen. Electric Cablevision Corp., Schenectady, 1974-78; pres. Gen. Electric Cablevision Corp., 1979-82; chmn. Evansville Cable TV, Ind.; dir. Tau Epsilon Music, Inc., N.Y.C., Tomorrow Program Syndication, Inc., N.Y.C. Bd. dirs. Com. of Sponsors, Flint Coll. and Cultural Devel., 1958-65, United Way Middle Tenn., 1968-70, 78-84, YMCA, Flint, Mich., 1958-64, Nashville, 1967-70, Denver, 1971-73, Nashville Better Bus. Bur., 1968-70, 78-80, Svc. Corps. of Ret. Execs., Opportunities Industrialization Ctr., 1984-90, Sr. Citizens, Inc., 1986-92, Sr. Citizens Endowment; mem. Mich. Gov.'s Coun. on Traffic Safety, 1962-64, Colo. Gov.'s Task Force on Jobs for Vets., 1972-73. Named Newsmaker of Tomorrow Time Mag.-Pitts. C. of C., 1953. Mem. Nat. Assn. Broadcasters (mem. radio code bd. 1967-70), UHF TV Assn. (v.p., dir. 1953-54), ABC-TV Network Affiliates Assn. (bd. govs. 1966-70), Soc. TV Pioneers. Home: 501 Lynnwood Blvd Nashville TN 37205-3815

FAUST, CHARLES, hotel executive. Chmn. Beck Summit Hotel Mgmt. Group, Boca Raton, Fla., Summit Hotel Mgmt. Co., Ft. Lauderdale, Fla., 1998—. Office: Summit Hotel Mgmt Co 4116 N Ocean Dr Ste 700 Fort Lauderdale FL 33308*

FAUST, JAMES E., church official. Mem. First Presidency, Ch. of Jesus Christ of Latter-day Saints. Office: LDS Church 50 E North Temple Salt Lake City UT 84150-0002

FAUST, MARCUS G., lawyer; b. Salt Lake City, Feb. 23, 1953; s. James E. and Ruth (Wright) F.; m. Susan Jone Hadley, June 23, 1971; children: Nicole, John, Ryan, Justin, Elise. BA cum laude, U. Utah, 1974; JD cum laude, Brigham Young U., 1976. Bar: Utah 1977, D.C. 1980. Staff asst. U.S. Sen. Frank E. Moss, Salt Lake City, 1975-77; legis. counsel U.S. Rep. Gunn McKay, Washington, 1977-80; subcom. counsel Com. on Interior and Insular Affairs, U.S. Ho. Reps., Washington, 1980-81; pvt. practice Washington, 1981—; bd. dirs. Web Bank. Polit. adv. U.S. Sen. Frank E. Moss, Salt Lake City, 1976, U.S. Rep. Gunn McKay, Washington, 1978, '80; nat. fundraiser U.S. Rep. Jim Santini, Washington, 1982;vol. coach Fairfax (Va.) Police Youth Club, 1981—; scoutmaster, troop com. mem. Boy Scouts Am., Oakton, Va., 1986—; trustee So. Va. Coll.; bd. trustees So. Va. Coll., 1997—. Recipient Honor award Nat. Water Resources Assn., Washington, 1982; named one of Capitol's Top 25 Lobbyists, Washington Bus. Jour. Mem. Utah State Bar Assn., D.C. Bar, J. Reuben Clark Law Soc. (chmn. Mid-Atlantic chpt.), Clark Law Soc. (vice chair mid-Atlantic chpt.). Mormon. Avocations: golf, soccer, basketball, skiing, church services. Home: 10232 Martinhoe Dr Vienna VA 22181-5367 Office: 332 Constitution Ave NE Washington DC 20002-5922

FAUST, MARILYN B., middle school principal. Prin. Little Oak Mid. Sch., Slidell, La., 1983—. Recipient Elem. Sch. Recognition award U.S. Dept. Edn., 1989-90. Office: Little Oak Mid Sch 59241 Rebel Dr Slidell LA 70461-3713*

FAUST, NAOMI FLOWE, education educator, poet; b. Salisbury, N.C.; d. Christopher Leroy and Ada Luella (Graham) Flowe; AB, Bennett Coll.; MA, U. Mich., 1945; PhD, N.Y. U., 1963; m. Roy Malcolm Faust, Aug. 16, 1948. Elem. tchr. Pub. Schs. Gaffney (S.C.); tchr. English, French, phys. edn. Atkins High Sch., Winston-Salem; instr. English, Bennett Coll. and So. U., Scotlandville, La., 1944-46; prof. English, Morgan State Coll., Balt., 1946-48; tchr. English, Greensboro (N.C.) Pub. Schs., 1948-51, N.Y.C. Pub. Schs., 1954-63; prof. edn. Queens Coll. of City U. N.Y., Flushing, 1964-82; lectr. in field; writer, lectr., poetry readings, 1982—. Named Tchr.-Author of 1979, Tchr.-Writer; cert. of Merit for poem Cooper Hill Writers Conf., 1970; Achievement award L.I. br. AAUW, 1985; named Internat. Eminent Poet, Internat. Poets Acad. Mem. AAUP, Nat. Coun. Tchrs. English, Nat. Women's Book Assn., Nat. Assn. Univ. Women (L.I. br.), World Poetry Soc. Intercontinental, N.Y. Poetry Forum, NAACP, United Negro Coll. Fund, Alpha Kappa Alpha, Alpha Kappa Mu, Alpha Epsilon. Author: Discipline and the Classroom Teacher, 1977; (poetry) Speaking in Verse, 1974, All Beautiful Things, 1983, And I Travel by Rhythms and Words, 1990; contbr. poetry to jours. Home: 11201 175th St Jamaica NY 11433-4135

FAUSTINO, PETER J., school psychologist; b. Bronx, Jan. 10, 1973; s. Ismael C. P. and Janice A. Faustino; m. Cynthia Faustino, Apr. 19, 1997. BA in Psychology, Marist Coll., 1995, MA in Comty./Counseling Psychology, 1996, cert. advanced grad. study sch. psych., 1997. Cert. sch. psychologist, N.Y. state. Sch. psychologist A. MacArthur Barr Mid. Sch., Nanuet, N.Y., 1997—; grad. asst. Marist Coll., Poughkeepsie, N.Y., 1995-96; presenter AAAS Nat. Conf., 1995. Mem. Nat. Assn. Sch. Psychologists (mem. conf. com. 1997, presenter symposium 1998), N.Y. Assn. Sch. Psychologists, Psi Chi, Alpha Chi, Alpha Phi Delta. Fax: (914) 624-3138. Home: 42 Park Pl Harrison NY 10528-2904 Office: A MacArthur Barr Mid Sch 143 Church St Nanuet NY 10954-3030

FAUTH, JOHN J., venture capitalist. Chmn., dir., pres., CEO Churchill Capital, Inc., Mpls. Office: Churchill Capital Inc 333 S 7th St Ste 2400 Minneapolis MN 55402-2435*

FAUVER, JOHN WILLIAM, mayor, retired business executive; b. Detroit, Dec. 11, 1921; s. John Newton and Margaret Burns (Schofield) F.; children: John, Johanna, Jeffrey; m. Irene Byerlein. B.S.M.E., U. Mich., 1943. With J.N. Fauver Co., Madison Heights, Mich., from 1946; now ret. chmn., chief exec. officer. J.N. Fauver Co.; bd. dirs. N.B.D. Trust co. of Fla., N.A., Beaumont Hosp. Found. Mayor City of Bloomfield Hills, Mich., 1976-77, 81—, city commr., 1972—; trustee Cranbrook Schs., 1970-80; pres. Boys and Girls Clubs of S.E. Mich., 1972, bd. dirs. Capt. AUS, 1942-46. Mem. Nat. Indsl. Distbrs. Assn. (pres. 1979-80), Fluid Power Ednl. Found. (trustee), Johns Island Country Club, Bloomfield Hills Country Club, Orchard Lake Country Club, Rotary (past pres. Detroit chpt.). Republican. Presbyterian. Home: 3475 Bloomfield Club Dr Bloomfield Hills MI 48301-2102

FAUX, JEFF (GEOFFREY PETER FAUX), economist, writer; b. N.Y.C., June 18, 1936; s. George Frederick and Caroline Pauline (Goyanovic) F.; m. Mary Ruth Robbins, June 11, 1957 (div. Dec. 1983); children: Thomas Geoffrey, George Frederick. AB, Queens Coll., 1959; postgrad., George Wash. U., 1963-65, Harvard U., 1971-72; HHD (hon.), U. New Eng., 1983. Economist Dept. Commerce, Washington, 1962, Dept. Labor, Washington, 1963-65, Dept. State, Washington, 1965-67; dir. econ. devel. divsn. Office Econ. Opportunity, Washington, 1967-70; fellow Inst. Politics Harvard U., Cambridge, Mass., 1970-71, dir. Ctr. for Cmty. Econ. Devel., 1972; co-dir. Nat. Ctr. for Econ. Alternatives, Washington, 1973-84; dir. Project on Indsl. Policy, Washington, 1984-85; pres. Econ. Policy Inst., Washington, 1985—; mem. adv. bd. The Am. Prospect, Boston, 1990—, Ctr. for Pub. Integrity, Washington, 1991—; mem. U.S. Nat. Adv. Cmty. Econ. Opportunity, Washington, 1977-81; chair New Eng. Housing Devel. Corp., Boston, 1972-75. Author: New Hope for Inner City, 1971, The Party's Not Over, 1996; co-author: Star Spangled Hustle, 1972, Rebuilding America, 1984; co-editor: Reckoning Prosperity, 1996; mem. editl. bd. Dissent, 1989—. Mem. Planning Bd., Whitefield, Maine, 1977-79; bd. dirs. Rural Am., Washington, 1974-78; chair Com. for Utility Rate Return, Augusta, 1977-81, Cmty. on Maine Economy, Augusta, 1976-80. Recipient Weinberg award Wayne State U., 1991; fellow Harvard U., 1970-71. Democrat. Office: Econ Policy Inst 1660 L St NW Washington DC 20036-5603*

FAVALORA, JOHN CLEMENT, bishop; b. New Orleans, Dec. 5, 1935; s. Felix J. and Leona M. (Stevens) F. BA in Philosophy and History, Notre Dame Sem., New Orleans, 1958; STL, Pontifical Gregorian U., Rome, 1962; MEd, Tulane U., 1969. Ordained priest, Roman Cath. Ch., 1962. Asst. pastor St. Theresa of the Child Jesus Ch., New Orleans, 1962-70; sec. to archbishop Archdiocese of New Orleans, 1963-65, vice chancellor, 1963-65; vice rector St. John Prep., New Orleans, 1964-67, prin., 1968-71; dir. Office of Permanent Diaconate, New Orleans, 1971-74; adminstrv. asst. Notre Dame Sem., New Orleans, 1971-73, rector-pres., 1981-86; pastor St. Angela Merici Ch., Metairie, La., 1973-79; dir. Office of Vocations, New Orleans, 1979-81; bishop Diocese of Alexandria, La., 1986-89, Diocese of St. Petersburg, Fla., 1989-94; archbishop Diocese of Miami, 1994—; ecclesiastical notary Archdiocese of New Orleans, 1962-64, pro-synodal judge, 1973-79; dean East Jefferson Deanery, New Orleans, 1974-77; vicar Pastoral Planning, New Orleans, 1976-81; chmn. Permanent Diaconate Adv. Com., New Orleans, 1984; consultor Archdiocese of New Orleans, 1984-86. Office: Archdiocese of Miami Pastoral Ctr 9401 Biscayne Blvd Miami Shores FL 33138*

FAVARO, MARY KAYE ASPERHEIM (MRS. BIAGINO PHILIP FAVARO), pediatrician; b. Edgerton, Wis., Sept. 30, 1934; d. Harold Wilbur and Genevieve Catherine (Hyland) Asperheim; m. Biagino Philip Favaro, May 31, 1969; children: Justin Peter, Gina Sue. BS, U. Wis., 1956; MS, St. Louis Coll. Pharmacy, 1965; MD, U. Wis., 1969. Instr. pharmacology St. Louis U. and St. Mary's Hosp. Sch. Practical Nurses, 1959-64; staff pharmacist U. Hosps., Madison, Wis., 1964-65; intern Albany (N.Y.) Med. Center, 1969-70; resident, 1970-71; resident in pediatrics U. S.C., Charleston, 1971-72, asst. prof. pediatrics, 1973-75; pvt. practice pediatrics, 1974—. Author: Pharmacology, an Introductory Text, 1992; The Pharmacologic Basis of Patient Care, 1985. Mem. A.M.A., Am. Med. Women's Assn. Roman Catholic. Home: 1407 Southwood Dr Surfside Beach SC 29575 Office: 5390 Dorchester Rd Charleston SC 29418-5652

FAVOR, KEVIN ELI, psychology educator; b. Pitts., Sept. 30, 1953; s. Homer Eli and Henrietta Teressa (Strong) F.; m. Leda Anne Fuller, Aug. 1, 1981; 1 child, Trevor Eli. BA, Towson State U., 1977; MA, Washington U., St. Louis, 1978; PhD, U. Ill., 1987. Lic. psychologist, Pa.; cert. of proficiency in treatment of alcohol and other psychoactive substance use disorders; diplomate Am. Bd. Psychol. Spltys. with forensic splty. in psychol. assessment, evaluation and testing. Pre-doctoral psychology intern Provident Hosp., Inc., Balt., 1983-84; mgmt. analyst Morgan State U., Balt., 1984-87; psychol. assoc. Johns Hopkins Health Plan, Balt., 1987-89; cons. psychologist Lincoln U., Pa., 1989—, asst. prof. psychology, 1989—, enrollment planning, student life, 1995-96, interim assoc. v.p., 1996—, assoc. prof., 1997—, dean campus life, 1997-99; EEO working group mem., Pa. Dept. Edn., Harrisburg, 1996—; program evaluator Lincoln's Family Life ctr., 1994—; evaluation cons. Circle of Care Pediatric AIDS, Phila., 1990-94; adv. bd. Collegiate Press Editl. Adv. Bd., 1994—. Mem. Prescribing Psychologist's Register, 1995—, NAACP, 1993—, Urban League, 1990—. Mem. Am. Psychol. Assn., Assn. Black Psychologists, Am. Ednl. Rsch. Assn., Pa. Psychol. Assn., Delaware Valley Assn. Black Psychologists (chair student concerns com.). Democrat. Baptist. Avocations: swimming, tenor saxophone, clarinet, jazz music. Home: 1803 Sparks Dr Forest Hill MD 21050-2645 Office: Lincoln U Dean of Student Life Lincoln University PA 19352

FAVOR, LESLI JOANNA, writer, researcher; b. Dallas, Apr. 29, 1970; d. John Lewis and Linda June Frost; m. Stephen L. Favor, July 21, 1990. BA in English, U. Tex., Arlington, 1992; MA in English, U. North Tex., 1993, PhD in English, 1995. Writing tutor U. Tex., Arlington, 1991-92; grad. tchg. fellow U. North Tex., Denton, 1992-95, adj. prof. English, 1996; asst. prof. English Sul Ross State U.-Rio Grande Coll., Eagle Pass, Tex., 1996-98; coord. liberal arts Higher Rsch. Orgn., Austin, Tex., 1998—; freelance writer, editor, rschr. Austin, Tex., 1998—. Author: Sex, Drugs, and Rock & Roll: Women as Casualties of Culture, 1998; book reviewer: (by Christine Froula) Modernism's Body: Sex, Culture, and Joyce, 1998; contbr. articles to profl. jours. Recipient Mary Patchell Grad. award U. North Tex., 1995, Craig B. Raupe scholarship U. North Tex., 1997, Faculty Rsch. Enhancement grant Sul Ross State U., 1998. Mem. MLA, South Ctrl. Modern Lang. (session coord. spl. session 1998), Popular Culture Assn., Semiotic Soc. Am. Avocations: reading fiction, creative writing, E-mailing friends, lifting weights, walking. E-mail: lfavor@corridor.com. and lfavor@higher-research.org. Home: #1308 12320 Alameda Trace Cir. Austin TX 78727

FAVOR-HAMILTON, SUZANNE MARIE, track and field athlete, Olympian; b. Stevens Point, Wis., Aug. 8, 1968; m. Mark Hamilton, May 1991. BS, U. Wis., 1991. Track and field athlete Nike. Winner 4 indoor NCAA mile titles, 4 outdoor 1,500m titles; winner 9 NCAA titles and 21 individual Big Ten championships, 6 time nat. champaion; 2 time Olympian. Am. Record Holder in 1,000m 1995 and indoor 800m, 1999. Office: USA Track and Field PO Box 120 Indianapolis IN 46206-0120

FAVORITE, FELIX, oceanographer; b. Quincy, Mass., Mar. 18, 1925; s. Felix Christian and Irene Vibert (Doyle) F.; m. Betty Lou Donnelly, Nov. 2, 1951; children: Lee H., Kim C., Kit C., Felix Scott. BS, Mass. Maritime Acad., 1950; postgrad., Boston U., 1949-50; BS, U. Wash., 1956, MS, 1966; PhD, Oreg. State U., 1968. Research oceanographer U. Wash., 1957; dir. oceanographic research Bur. Comml. Fisheries Biol. Lab., Seattle, 1957-70; program mgr. oceanography Nat. Marine Fisheries Service, Seattle, 1971-75, resource ecology studies coordinator, 1977-80; prin. investigator Outer Continental Shelf Environ. Assessment Program, 1976-78; expert in oceanography Internat. No. Pacific Fisheries Commn., 1959-72; oceanographic cons., 1981—. Served to lt. comdr. USNR, 1947-48, 50-53. Recipient Silver medal Dept. Commerce, 1973. Mem. Sigma Xi. Club: Sheridan Beach Community of Seattle (trustee 1960-61). Home: 16103 41st Ave NE Lake Forest Park WA 98155-6725

FAVRE, BRETT LORENZO, professional football player; m., 1 child, Brittany. Quarterback Atlanta Falcons, 1991-92, Green Bay Packers, 1992—; first team all-pro Assoc. Press, 1995; MVP, East-West Shrine Game, All-American Bowl. Named to Pro Bowl Team, 1992, 93, 95, 96; named NFL MVP 1995. Office: Green Bay Packers PO Box 10628 Green Bay WI 54307-0628*

FAVRE, GREGORY, publishing executive; b. New Orleans, Apr. 19, 1935; m. Beatrice Favre; children: Monica Kauppinen, Jeff. Asst. sports editor Atlanta Jour.; mng. editor Dayton Daily News; editor Palm Beach (Fla.) Post; news dir. Sta. WPLG-TV, Miami; editor Corpus Christi Caller-Times; mng. editor Chgo. Daily News, Chgo. Sun-Times; exec. editor Sacramento Bee, 1984-98; v.p. news The McClatchy Co., Sacramento, 1989—; bd. dirs. Found. for Am. Comms., Inter Am. Press Assn., membership chmn. Bd. visitors Medill Sch. Journalism, Northwestern U., U. Calif., Berkeley, Sch. Journalism, U. Calif.-Davis Med. Sch.; bd. advisors Pacific Coast Ctr. of Freedom Forum. Named News Exec. of Yr., Calif. Press Assn., 1992, Silver Em award U. Miss., 1996, Catalyst award Nat. Assn. Minority Media Execs., 1997. Mem. Am. Soc. Newspaper Editors (past pres., past chmn. program com., readership com., journalism edn. com., future of newspapers com.), Calif. Soc. Newspaper Editors (past pres.). Office: The McClatchy Co 2100 Q St Sacramento CA 95816-6816

FAVREAU, SUSAN DEBRA, management consultant; b. Cleve., Dec. 15, 1955; d. Donald Francis and Helen Patricia (Rafferty) F. Cert., N.Y. State Police Acad., 1974; student, Cornell U., 1984, SUNY, 1986. Comms. specialist N.Y. State Police, Loudonville, 1974-87, comms. specialist div. hdqrs., 1987-98; mgmt. cons., sec.-treas., dir. Don Favreau Assocs., Inc., Clifton Park, N.Y., 1983-86, v.p., 1986—; comms. specialist divsn. hdqrs. N.Y. State Police, Albany, 1987-98, sys. support specialist divsn. hdqrs., 1998—; adj. faculty Internat. Assn. Chiefs of Police; NYSPIN coord. FBI/Nat. Crime Info. Ctr. cert. program, 1986—. Author: Teamwork in the Telecommunication Center, 1986, One More Time: How to be a Mature and Successful Telecommunications Manager, 1987, Law Enforcement Terminal Security, 1991; also NYSPIN cert. manuals. Recipient Dirs. commendation N.Y. State Police Acad., 1977, commendation N.Y. State Police, 1978, Supt.'s commendation, 1986. Mem. NAFE, N.Y. State Civil Svc. Assn., Emergency Communicators Profl. Assn. (adv. bd.), Colonie Police Benevolent Assn. (hon.), Am. Soc. Law Enforcement Trainers, Assoc. Pub. Safety Communications Officers (planning commn. Atlantic chpt. 1991, registration chair ann. NE conf. 1991), N.Y. State Troopers Police Benevolent Assn. (hon.), Nat. Bus. Women Am., Internat. Assn. Chiefs Police, Am. Horse Shows Assn., Am. Soc. Law Enforcement Trainers, Capital Dist. Hunter/Jumper Coun. Republican. Roman Catholic. Avocations: equestrienne, target shooting, reading, sewing. Home: 60 Tallow Wood Dr Clifton Park NY 12065 Office: Hdqrs NY State Police State Office Bldg Campus Bldg # 22 Albany NY 12226

FAVROT, HENRI MORTIMER, JR., architect, real estate developer; b. New Orleans, Apr. 23, 1930; s. Henri Mortimer and Helen Rebecca (Parkhurst) F.; m. Kathleen Loker Gibbons, Sept. 16, 1956; children: James P., Kathleen Favrot VanHorn, T. Semmes, Caroline. BArch, Tulane U., 1953; MArch, Harvard U., 1957. Lic. architect, La., Miss. Architect Favrot, Reed, Mathes & Bergman, New Orleans, 1955-56, Curtis & Davis, New Orleans, 1957-58; ptnr. Favrot & Grimball, New Orleans, 1958-62; pvt. practice architecture New Orleans, 1962-64; ptnr. Mathes, Bergman, Favrot & Assocs., New Orleans, 1964-69, Favrot & Shane, Metairie, La., 1969—; chmn. La. Architects Selection Bd., Baton Rouge, 1976, 97. Prin. works include: Parktowne Townhouses, 1971 (Design Honor award La. Architects Assn.), Favrot & Shane Office Bldg., 1982 (Design Honor award New Orleans chpt. AIA). Mem. City Planning Commn., New Orleans, 1970-84, chmn., 1976, 77; commr. La. Housing Commn., Baton Rouge, 1985-86; bd. dirs. Met. Area Com., New Orleans, 1985-98, New Orleans Mus. Art, 1985-91, v.p., 1986-87; bd. dirs. Preservation Resource Ctr. of New Orleans, 1988-96, pres., 1994-96; mem. bd. adminstr. Tulane U., 1986—. Recipient Outstanding Alumnus award Tulane U. Sch. Architecture, 1985, named Tulane U. Alumni Vol. of the Yr., 1997. Mem. AIA (pres. New Orleans chpt. 1982), La. Architects Assn. (pres. 1984), New Orleans Apt. Assn. (pres. 1980), So. Yacht Club, New Orleans Lawn Tennis Club, Boston Club, La. Club, Stratford Club. Republican. Roman Catholic. Avocations: tennis, sailing, fishing, hunting. Home: 1400 State St New Orleans LA 70118-6047

FAW, MELVIN LEE, retired physician; b. Kansas City, Mo., Dec. 4, 1925; s. Floyd Butler and Ivalee Muriel (Harvey) F.; m. Anna Margaret Rose, July 17, 1948; children—Linda, Gary, David, Nancy. Student, U. Kans., 1943-44, Baylor U., 1945; BS magna cum laude, Washburn U., 1948; MD, Washington U., St. Louis, 1951. Diplomate Am. Bd. Internal Medicine. Intern Washington U. Service St. Louis City Hosp., 1951-52; asst. in medicine Washington U. Sch. Medicine, St. Louis, 1951-54; resident in internal medicine Washington U. Service St. Louis City Hosp., 1952-54, U. Kans. Hosp., Kansas City, 1954-55; practice medicine specializing in internal medicine and cardiology Welborn Clinic, Evansville, Ind., 1955-87, mng. ptnr., 1965-78; pres. med. staff Welborn Hosp., 1980, chief medicine, 1958-64, dir. cardiovascular services, 1981-87; mem. So. Ind. Health Service Agy., 1976-80. Served with Inf. AUS, 1944-45. Decorated Bronze Star medal with V device oak leaf cluster, Purple Heart, Combat Infantryman Badge; recipient Disting. Service award U. Evansville, 1980. Fellow Am. Coll. Chest Physicians; mem. ACP, Am. Soc. Internal Medicine, AMA, Ind. Med. Assn., Vanderburgh County Med. Soc., Phi Kappa Phi. Methodist. Home: 2400 E Chandler Ave Evansville IN 47714-2421 Office: Welborn Clinic 421 Chestnut St Evansville IN 47713-1297

FAWBUSH, ANDREW JACKSON, lawyer; b. Miami, Fla., Oct. 7, 1946; s. Andrew T. Fawbush; m. Melinda Wheeley, Dec. 18, 1982; children: Andrew J. Jr., Tyler S., Karin J., Michelle L. BSBA in Acctg., U. Fla., 1972, JD, 1974. Bar: Fla. 1975. Assoc. Smith & Hulsey, Jacksonville, Fla., 1975-80; ptnr. Smith & Hulsey, Jacksonville, 1980-88, LeBoeuf, Lamb, Greene & MacRae, Jacksonville, 1988—; chmn. employee benefits dept. LeBoeuf Lamb Greene & MacRae, Jacksonville, 1993-95. Contbg. author The Tax Lawyer. Bd. dirs. YMCA, Jacksonville, 1981-83; bd. dirs., past pres. Employee Benefits Coun. N.E. Fla.; bd. dirs., exec. com. Gator Boosters, Inc.; trustee, tchr. Cert. Employee Benefits Specialists, U. North Fla., 1982-88; bd. dirs. U. Fla. Found., 1993. With U.S. Army, 1968-70. Mem. ABA, Fla. Bar Assn. (spkr. employee benefit sect. 1983-88), D.C. Bar Assn., N.Y. Bar Assn., U. Fla. Alumni Assn. (bd. dirs. 1987-98, pres. 1994), Jacksonville C. of C. (gen. counsel, sports coun.). Office: LeBoeuf Lamb Greene MacRae 50 N Laura St Ste 2800 Jacksonville FL 32202-3634

FAWCETT, CHRISTOPHER BABCOCK, civil engineer, construction and water resources company executive; b. N.Y.C., Dec. 17, 1951; s. George Gifford Fawcett Jr. and Andi Adams Emerson; m. Nina Beth Williamson, June 20, 1986 (div. Aug. 1993); 1 child, Kyle Christopher Adams. Student, U. Okla., 1969-72, Concordia U., Montreal, Que., Can., 1979-81; BS, Clarkson U., 1984. Lic. civil engr.; registered civil engr., N.Y. Owner C.B.F. Handyman Co., N.Y.C., 1974-77; v.p., gen. mgr. Fawcett & Fawcett, Inc., N.Y.C., 1977-84; project mgr. U.S. Army Corps Engrs., N.Y.C., 1985-86; asst. project mgr. N. Kruger Constrn., Inc., Locust Valley, N.Y., 1986-87; project mgr., engr. Finch, Pruyn & Co., Inc., Glens Falls, N.Y., 1987-98; propr. Caton Hill Enterprises, 1992—. Founder, chmn. Tri-County Nat. Engrs. Week and Nat. Jr. H.S. Mathcounts Competition programs, Glens Falls, 1987-98; founding sponsor Challenger Ctr. for Space Sci. Edn. Mem. NSPE, ASCE, TAPPI, Am. Welding Soc., Paper Industry Mgmt. Assn., Am. Concrete Inst., Nat. Space Soc. (charter), Engrs. for Edn., Assn. State Dam Safety Ofcls., Constrn. Specifications Inst., Order of Engr., Cousteau Soc., Greenpeace. Avocation: scuba diving. Office: Caton Hill Enterprises 14 Lake Ave Glens Falls NY 12801-2229

FAWCETT, DON WAYNE, anatomist; b. Springdale, Iowa, Mar. 14, 1917; s. Carlos J. and Mabel (Kennedy) F.; m. Dorothy Marie Secrest, 1941; children: Robert S., Mary Elaine, Donna, Joseph. AB cum laude, Harvard, 1938, MD, 1942; DSc (hon.), U. Siena, Italy, 1974, N.Y. Med. Coll., 1975, U. Chgo., 1977, U. Cordoba, Argentina, 1978; MD (hon.), U. Heidelberg, Germany, 1977; DVM (hon.), Justus Liebig U., Giessen-Lahn, Germany, 1977; DSc (hon.), Georgetown U., 1987, U. Rome, 1997. Intern surgery Mass. Gen Hosp., Boston, 1942-43; instr. anatomy Harvard Med. Sch., 1946-48, asso. anatomy, 1948-51, asst. prof. anatomy, 1951-55, Hersey prof. anatomy, 1958-80, James Stillman prof. comparative anatomy, 1962-80, sr. asso. dean preclin. affairs, 1975-77; prof. anatomy Cornell Med. Coll., 1955-58; scientist Internat. Lab. Research on Animal Diseases, Nairobi, Kenya, 1980-85. Author: The Cell, 1966, 2d edit., 1981, Textbook of Histology, 1968, 10th edit., 1975, 11th edit., 1986, 12th edit., 1993. Served as capt. M.C. AUS, 1943-46; bn. surgeon A.A.A. John and Mary Markle scholar med. sci., 1949-54; recipient Lederle Med. Faculty award, 1954. Fellow Am. Acad. Arts and Sci., Nat. Acad. Sci. U.S., Royal Microscopical Soc. (hon.); mem. AAAS, N.Y. Acad. Sci., Am. Assn. Anatomists (pres. 1964- 65, Henry Gray award 1983, Centennial medal 1987), N.Y. Soc. Electron Microscopists (pres. 1957-58), Histochem. Soc., Tissue Culture Assn. (v.p. 1954-55), Soc. Exptl. Biology and Medicine, Assn. Anatomy Chairmen (pres. 1973-74), Am. Soc. Zoologists, Am. Soc. Mammalogists, Electron Microscope Soc. Am. (Disting. Scientist award in Life Scis. 1989), Soc. Study Devel. and Growth, Harvey Soc., Am. Soc. Cell Biology (pres. 1961-62), Argentine Nat. Acad. Sci., Anat. Soc. So. Africa (hon.), Japanese Anat. Soc. (hon.), Anat. Soc. Australia and N.Z. (hon.), Japanese Electron Microscope Soc., Internat. Fedn. Soc. Electron Microscopy (pres. 1976-78), Am. Soc. Andrology (pres. 1977-78), Soc. Study Reprodn. (Carl Hartman award 1985), Mexican (hon.), Canadian (hon.) Assn. Anatomists. Address: 1224 Lincoln Rd Missoula MT 59802-3041

FAWCETT, JAMES DAVIDSON, herpetologist, educator; b. New Plymouth, N.Z., Jan. 10, 1933; s. James and Edna Lola (Catterick) F.; B.Sc., U. N.Z., 1960; M.Sc., U. Auckland (N.Z.), 1964; Ph.D., U. Colo., 1975; m. Georgene Ellen Tyler, Dec. 21, 1968. Head dept. biology Kings Coll., Auckland, 1960; grad. demonstrator dept. zoology U. Auckland, 1961-62, sr. demonstrator, 1963-64; grad. asst. U. Colo., 1969-72; instr. biology U. Nebr., Omaha, 1972-75, asst. prof., 1975-81, asso. prof., 1981—. Recipient Great Tchr. award U. Nebr., 1981. Mem. Royal Soc. N.Z., N.Z. Assn. Scientists, Am. Soc. Zoologists, Soc. Systematic Zoology, Herpetologists League, Brit. Soc. Herpetologists, AAAS, Nebr. Herpetological Soc. (pres. 1979-80), Sigma Xi (pres. Omaha chpt. 1980-81), Phi Sigma. Contbr. articles to profl. jours. Home: 309 S 56th St Omaha NE 68132-3413 Office: U Nebr Biology Dept Omaha NE 68182

FAWCETT, JOHN SCOTT, real estate developer; b. Pitts., Nov. 5, 1937; s. William Hagen and Mary Jane (Wise) F.; m. Anne Elizabeth Mitchell, Dec. 30, 161; children: Holly Anne, John Scott II (dec.). BS, Ohio State U., 1959. Dist. dealer rep. Shell Oil Co., San Diego, 1962-66; dist. real estate rep. Shell Oil, Phoenix, 1967-69; region real estate rep. Shell Oil, San Francisco, 1970-71; head office land investments rep. Shell Oil, Houston, 1972-75; pres., CEO Marinita Devel. Co., Newport Beach, Calif., 1976—; lectr. in land devel. related fields. With U.S. Army, 1960-61. Named Ky. Col., Gov. Ky., 1996. Mem. Internat. Platform Assn., Internat. Coun. Shopping Ctrs., Internat. Right of Way Assn., Internat. Inst. Valuers, Inst. Bus. Appraisers, Nat. Assn. Rev. Appraisers and Mortgage Underwriters, Am. Assn. Cert. Appraisers, Urban Land Inst., Nat. Assn. Real Estate Execs. (pres. L.A. chpt. 1975), Calif. Lic. Contractors Assn., Bldg. Industry Assn., U.S. C. of C., Town Hall of Calif., Ohio State U. Alumni Assn., Toastmasters (pres. Scottsdale Ariz. club 1968, pres. Hospitality T club 1964), U. Athletic Club, Phi Kappa Tau. Republican. Roman Catholic. Avocations: antiques, tennis, skiing. Home: 8739 Hudson River Cir Fountain Valley CA 92708 Office: Marinita Devel Co 3835 Birch St Newport Beach CA 92660-2600

FAWCETT, JOHN THOMAS, archivist; b. West Branch, Iowa, Nov. 27, 1943; s. Floyd Thomas and Mary Helen (Miller) F.; m. Sharon Atchison, July 25, 1971 (div. 1993); children: Allen, Katherine. BA, U. Iowa, 1966; MA, U. Tex., 1978. Archivist, mus. tech. Herbert Hoover Libr., West Branch, Iowa, 1962-67; asst. acting dir., exec. dir. Herbert Hoover Libr. and Assn., West Branch, Iowa, 1983-87; archivist Office Presdl. Librs., Washington, 1967-68, supervisory and acting dir., 1978-83, asst. archivist, 1987-95; mil. aide to President of U.S. Exec. Office, Austin, Tex., 1968-70; supervisory archivist Lyndon B. Johnson Libr., Austin, 1970-78; pres. John T. Fawcett and Assocs., Inc., Washington, 1995—. Mem. exec. bd. Boy Scouts Am., 1984-87. Mem. Masons, Kiwanis (pres. 1985).

FAWCETT, JOY LYNN, soccer player; b. Inglewood, Calif., Feb. 8, 1968; m. Walter Fawcett; children: Katelyn Rose, Carli. Degree in phys. edn., U. Calif., Berkeley, 1990. Women's soccer coach UCLA, 1993-97; mem. U.S. Nat. Women's Soccer Team, 1987—, including 1991 World Cup, China, 1995 FIFA World Cup, Sweden, 1994 CONCACAF Qualifying Championship, Montreal, U.S. Olympic Festival, Denver, 1995, FIFA Women's World Cup, Sweden, 1995, gold medal U.S. Olympic team, 1996; mem. Ajax of Manhattan Beach Club Soccer Team (champions U.S. Women's Amateur Nat. Cup 1992, 93). Named to U. Calif. Berkeley Hall of Fame, 1997; 3-time All-Am., 1987-89; selected Most Valuable Player So. Calif., L.A. Times, 1987. Office: US Soccer Fedn 1801-1811 S Prairie Ave Chicago IL 60616*

FAWCETT, LESLIE CLARENCE, JR., accountant; b. Ft. Davis, Tex., May 12, 1920; s. Leslie Clarence and Estelle Virginia (Bloys) F. Student, San Antonio Jr. Coll., 1938-41, St. Mary's U., San Antonio, 1947-48; BBA, U. Tex., 1949, MBA, 1951. CPA, Tex. Jr. acct. Fred E. Pflughaupt & Co., San Antonio, 1951-52, sr. acct., 1953-59, ptnr., from 1960, now ret. With Signal Corps, U.S. Army, 1942-45. Mem. AICPA, Tex. Soc. CPA's. Presbyterian. Home: 428 Hammond Ave San Antonio TX 78210-3035

FAWCETT, MARIE ANN FORMANEK (MRS. ROSCOE KENT FAWCETT), civic leader; b. Mpls., Mar. 6, 1914; d. Peter Paul and Mary (Stepanek) Formanek; m. Roscoe Kent Fawcett, Mar. 16, 1935; children: Roscoe Kent, Peter Formanek, Roger Knowlton II, Stephen Hart. Grad. high sch., Mpls.; cert., Harvard U., 1976-83. Chmn. of vols. Merry Go Round Club House and Mews, Greenwich, Conn., 1949-92, trustee, 1948-90, v.p., bd. dirs., 1949—, corr. sec., 1992—, chmn. entertainment, 1970-90; bd. dirs., vol. chmn., corr. sec. Nathaniel Witherell Hosp., Greenwich, 1952—, chmn. vols., 1956-89, corr. sec. aux. bd., 1956-94; bd. dirs., corr. sec. Nathaniel Witherell Auxiliary Hosp., 1952—; chmn. vols. Greenwich Hosp., 1953-54; dist. chmn. ARC, Community Chest, Mental Health, 1946-50; vol. mentally retarded children Milbank Sch., Greenwich, 1958-92. Bd. dirs. Cerebral Palsy, Greenwich Symphony, 1956—, Greenwich Symphony Guild, 1956—, Putnam Indianfield Sch.; bd. dirs., corr. sec. Merry Go Round Mews, 1949—; bd. dirs. Multiple Sclerosis Soc., 1948—, v.p., 1970, corr. sec., 1958—; active drives for ARC, Community Chest, Leukemia, Muscular Dystrophy, Mental Health, Mentally Retarded Children Milbank Sch.; bd. dirs. Merry-Go-Round News for the Elderly, 1948—, Nathaniel Whitherell Hosp. for Elderly, 1952—, Greenwich Symphony Guild, 1956—, Travel Club Greenwich, 1982—; participating mem. Huxley Inst. Biosocial Rsch.; mem. polo com. Susan Cancer Fund, Pegasus Therapeutic Riding and Rusk Inst. Rehab. Medicine. Named Woman of Year, Soroptimist Club, 1967; recipient Community Svc. award United Cerebral Palsy Assn. Fairfield County, 1972, Fund Drive award Cerebral Palsy, 1970, citations for 36 yrs. outstanding vol. svcs. Nathaniel Witherell Hosp. Aux., Conn. Dept. Health, 1977. Mem. Internat. Platform Assn., The Woman's Club of Greenwich, Travel Club of Greenwich (corr. sec., bd. dirs. 1982—). Address: 4452 Portland Ave S Minneapolis MN 55407-3548

FAWCETT, SHERWOOD LUTHER, research laboratory executive; b. Youngstown, Ohio, Dec. 25, 1919; s. Luther T. and Clara (Sherwood) F.; m. Martha L. Simcox, Feb. 28, 1953; children: Paul, Judith, Tom. BS, Ohio State U., 1941; MS, Case Inst. Tech., 1948, PhD, 1950; hon. degrees, Ohio State U., Gonzaga U., Whitman Coll., Otterbein Coll., Detroit Inst. Tech., Ohio Dominican Coll. Registered profl. engr., Ohio. Mem. staff Columbus Labs. Battelle Meml. Inst., 1950-64, mgr. physics dept., 1959-64; dir. Pacific Northwest Labs., Richland, Wash., 1964-67; trustee Battelle Meml. Inst., Columbus, Ohio, 1968-92, exec. v.p., 1967-68, CEO, 1968-84, pres., 1968-80, chmn., 1981-84, chmn. bd. trustees, 1985-87; assoc. trustee Columbus, Ohio, 1987-94; chmn. bd. dirs. Transmet Corp. Served with the USNR, 1941-46. Decorated Bronze Star; recipient Washington award Western Soc. Engrs., 1989. Mem. AIME, NSPE, Am. Phys. Soc., Am. Nuclear Soc., Am. Phys. Soc., Sigma Xi, Tau Beta Pi, Delta Chi, Sigma Pi Sigma. Home: 2820 Margate Rd Columbus OH 43221-3062 Office: Transmet Corp 4290 Perimeter Dr Columbus OH 43228-1036

FAWELL, BEVERLY JEAN, state legislator; b. Oak Park, Ill., Sept. 17, 1930. BA, Elmhurst Coll., 1970; postgrad., No. Ill. U., 1974. Mem. Ill. Ho. of Reps., Springfield, 1981-83; mem. Ill. Senate, Springfield, 1983—, chair Rep. policy com., transp. com., mem. appropriations com., revenue com. Republican. Office: 213 W Wesley St Ste 105 Wheaton IL 60187-5135*

FAWELL, HARRIS W., lawyer former congressman; b. West Chicago, Ill., Mar. 25, 1929; m. Ruth Johnson, 1954; children: Richard, Jane, John. Student, Naperville North Central Coll., 1949; LL.D., Chgo. Kent Coll. Law, 1952. Ptnr. Fawell, James & Brooks, Naperville, Ill., 1954-84; mem. Ill. Senate, Springfield, 1963-77; gen. counsel Ill. Assn. Park Dists., 1977-84; mem. 99th-105th Congresses from 13th Ill. dist., 1985-98; of counsel James, Gustafson & Thompson, 1999—; mem. Edn. and the Workforce Com., chmn. subcom. on employer-employee rels.; mem. House Sci. Com. Office: 1001 E Chicago Ave Ste 103 Naperville IL 60540*

FAWKS, DAVID ROBERT, psychiatric clinical nurse specialist; b. Moline, Ill., Sept. 13, 1962; s. David Edward and Lois Lovetta (Moore) F.; m. Kay Joanne Psaltis, Apr. 29, 1988; children: Gina Elizabeth, Johnathan David. BSN, Olivet Nazarene U., Kankakee, Ill., 1986; MSN, Andrews U., Berrien Springs, Mich., 1997. ARNP, Fla.; cert. HIV counselor, CPR Instr. Psychiat. nurse Sarasota (Fla.) Meml. Hosp., 1990—. Bd. dirs. Luth. Ministries Adv. Coun. Mem. Southwest Coast Coun. for Advanced Nursing Practice), Mental Health Task Force of the Sarasota Health and Human Svcs. Planning Coun. Republican. Nazarene. Avocations: camping, boating, fishing, bicycling. Home: 5783 Vanderipe Rd Sarasota FL 34241-9597 Office: Sarasota Meml Hosp 1650 S Osprey Ave Sarasota FL 34239-2928

FAWLEY, JOHN JONES, retired banker; b. Phila., Oct. 1, 1921; s. James L. and Edna (Jones) F.; m. Ann Kemp, Jan. 8, 1944; children: Jo Ann (Mrs. Richard High), Christine, James K. BS in Econs, U. Pa., 1948; grad., Rutgers U., 1957. With First Pa. Bank, Phila., 1948-69; sr. v.p. First Pa. Bank, 1968-69; pres., dir. United Va. Bank/First & Citizens Nat. Bank, Alexandria, Va., 1969-72; exec. v.p. Indsl. Valley Bank, Phila., 1973-83, Dauphin Deposit Bank, Harrisburg, Pa., 1983-87; lectr. Comml. Lending Sch., U. Okla., 1969. former trustee Hahnemann U.; past pres. Presbyn. Ch. With AUS, 1942-45. Mem. Robert Morris Assocs. (nat. pres. 1972-73), Masons. Presbyterian. Home: Brittany Pointe Estates #2214 1001 Valley Ford Rd Lansdale PA 19446 also: 4550 Pinebrook Cir Apt 401 Bradenton FL 34209-8017

FAWSETT, PATRICIA COMBS, federal judge; b. 1943. BA, U. Fla., 1965, MAT, 1966, JD, 1973. Pvt. practice law Akerman, Senterfitt & Edison, Orlando, Fla., 1973-86; commr. 9th Cir. Jud. Nominating Commn, 1973-75, Greater Orlando Crime Prevention Assn., 1983-86; judge U.S. Dist. Ct. (mid. dist.) Fla., Orlando, 1986—. Trustee Loch Haven Art Ctr., Inc., Orlando, 1980-84; commr. Orlando Housing Authority, 1976-80, Winter Park (Fla.) Sidewalk Festival, 1973-75; bd. dirs. Greater Orlando Area C. of C., 1982-85. Mem. ABA (trial lawyers sect., real estate probate sect.), Am. Judicaturs Soc., Assn. Trial Lawyers Am., Fla. Bar Found. (bd. dirs. grants com.), Commn. on Access to Cts., Fla. Coun. Bar Assn. Pres.'s (pres., bd. dirs. 9th cir. grievance com.) Osceola County Bar Assn., Fla. Bar (bd. govs. 1983-86, budget com., disciplinary rev. com., integration rule and bylaws com., com. on access to legal system, bd. of cert., designation and advt., jud. adminstrn., selection and tenure com., jud. nominating procedures com., pub. rels. com., ann. meeting com., appellate rules com., spl. com. on judiciary-trial lawyer rels., chairperson midyr. conv. com., bd. dirs. trial lawyers sect.), Orange County Bar Assn. (exec. coun. 1977-83, pres. 1981-82, trustee Legal Aid Soc. 1977-81), Order of Coif, Phi Beta Kappa. Office: US Dist Ct Federal Bldg 80 N Hughey Ave Ste 611 Orlando FL 32801-2224*

FAXON, ALICIA CRAIG, art educator; b. N.Y.C., July 27, 1931; d. William Donald and Clara Alicia (Harnecker) Craig; m. Richard Bremer Faxon, Feb. 21, 1953; children: Richard Paul, Thomas Hardwick. AB, Vassar Coll., 1952; MA, Radcliffe Coll., 1953, Boston U., 1971; PhD, Boston U., 1979; DHL (hon.), Simmons Coll., 1998. Lectr. New Eng. Sch. Art and Design, Boston, 1974-77; acting dir. Danforth Mus., Framingham, Mass., 1977; teaching assoc. Boston U. Sch. for Art, 1978-79; vis. lectr. Simmons Coll., Boston, 1979-80, asst. prof. art, 1980-86, assoc. prof., 1986-91, chmn. dept. art and music, 1987-93, prof. art, 1991-93, alumnae endowed chair, 1992-93; lectr. Sch. for Lifelong Learning, Harvard U., Cambridge, Mass., 1978-80; program chmn. Women's Studies Adv. Bd., 1982-84; R.I. editor Art New Eng., 1994-99. Author: Catalog Raisonné of Prints of J.-L. Forain, 1982, Pilgrims and Pioneers, 1987, Dante Gabriel Rossetti, 1989; co-editor (with Susan Casteras) Pre-Raphaelite Art in its European Context, 1995; mem. editl. bd. Woman's Art Jour., 1989—. Mem. acquisitions com. Danforth Mus., 1974-89, trustee, 1975-77. Recipient Nan award for art criticism Art New Eng., 1987; grantee Nat. Endowment for Arts, 1982, Simmons Coll., 1984, NEH, 1989, 92. Mem. Coll. Art Assn. (chmn. preRaphaelite session 1990), Women's Caucus for Art (program co-chmn. 1986-88), Victorian Soc., 19th Century Art Historians Group, Vassar Coll. Alumnae Assn. Democrat. Episcopalian. Avocations: travel, writing.

FAXON, BRAD, professional golfer; b. Oceanport, NJ, Aug. 1, 1961; m. Bonnie Faxon (div.); children: Melanie, Emily, Sophie Lee. B in Econs., Furman U., 1983. Member PGA, professional golfer, 1983-. Co-sponsor Billy Andrade/Brad Faxon Charities for Children, 1991—; co-host CVS Charity Classic, 1999. Winner Provident Classic, 1986, Buick Open, 1991, New England Classic, 1992, The International, 1992, Heineken Australian Open, 1993, Freeport-McDermott Classic, 1997. Ranked 7th on PGA tour, 1992; mem. (nat. teams) Walker Cup, 1983, Ryder Cup, 1995, 97, Dunhill Cup, 1997, (PGA tour charity team) JCPenney Classic, 1999. Home: 144 Westminster St Providence RI 02903-2216*

FAXON, JACK, headmaster; b. Detroit, June 9, 1936; s. Morris Faxon and Pauline Krimsky. BS in Edn., Wayne State U., 1956, MEd, 1958; MA in History, U. Mich., 1963. Tchr. Detroit Pub. Schs., 1956-64; founder, headmaster Internat. Sch., Farmington Hill, Mich., 1968—; corp. dir. Cellex Bioscis. Corp. Inc., Mpls., 1988—; dir. Quest Biotech. Inc., Detroit, 1986—. Paintings exhibited in group shows at Wayne State U. (Arts award 1978), U. Mich., 1981; dancer The Nutcracker Ballet, Detroit Symphony Orch./Dance Detroit, 1979, 88-96, Sleeping Beauty, Mich. Opera Theater, 1994, Romeo and Juliet, 1996; singer Die Fledermaus, Naughty Marietta, Mich. Opera Theater, 1976, 77, 78, 79, 94. Elected del. to Mich. Constnl. Conv., State of Mich., Lansing, 1961-62, elected rep. to State Ho. of Reps., Lansing, 1964-70, elected senator, Lansing, 1970-94; pres. pro tem Mich. Senate, Lansing, 1977-83; bd. dirs. Anti Defamation League, Friends of African Art, Detroit, 1987-91, Friends of Asian Art, Detroit Inst. Arts, 1984-91, Russian Am. Studio Theater, 1991—; trustee Mich. Libr., Lansing, 1976-87, Harlem Sch. of the Arts, Inc., N.Y.C.; mem. Edn. Commn. of State, Denver, 1975-85, Mich. Hist. Soc., 1981-89, Mus. African Art, N.Y.C., 1993—; mem. com. on Jewish elderly svcs. Detroit Jewish Cmty. Coun. Recipient 1st pl. award Mich. Watercolor Soc., 1978, Citation of Merit, Wayne County Coun. on Smoking Health, 1981; Eagleton fellow Rutgers U., 1966. Mem. Founder Soc. Detroit Inst. Arts (life), Mus. African Art (N.Y.C.), Pres.'s Club (U. Mich.). Democrat. Avocations: ballet, performance art in opera, theater, painting, art. Office: The Internat Sch 28555 Middlebelt Rd Farmington Hills MI 48334

FAXON, THOMAS BAKER, lawyer; b. Des Moines, Oct. 15, 1924; s. Ralph Henry and Prue (Baker) F.; m. Virginia Webb Johnson, Sept. 8, 1949; children: Rebecca Webb Osgood, Thomas Baker Jr. BA, Princeton U., 1949; LLB, Harvard U., 1952. Bar: Colo. 1953. Asst. prof., asst. dir. Inst. Govt. U. N.C., Chapel Hill, 1952-53; assoc. Pershing, Bosworth, Dick & Dawson, Denver, 1953-57; ptnr. Dawson, Nagel, Sherman & Howard, Denver, 1957-84; of counsel Sherman & Howard, Denver, 1984-92; bd. trustees Colo. Legal Aid Found., Denver, 1984-91. Bd. dirs. Urban League Colo., Denver, 1964-67, Colo. chpt. UN Assn. of U.S.A., 1980-81, Recording for the Blind Colo., 1988-94; pres. bd. trustees 1st Unitarian Ch., Denver, 1960; mem. Denver Equality of Edn. Com., 1969. USAAF, 1943-46. Mem. Harvard Law Sch. Assn. Colo. (pres. 1968), Cactus Club Denver. Democrat. Address: 830 Race St Denver CO 80206-3734

FAY, ABBOTT EASTMAN, history educator; b. Scottsbluff, Nebr., July 19, 1926; s. Abbott Eastman and Ethel (Lambert) F.; m. Joan D. Richardson, Nov. 26, 1953; children: Rand, Diana, Collin. Grad., Scottsbluff (Nebr.) Jr. Coll.; BA, Colo. State Coll., 1949, MA, 1953; postgrad., U. Denver, 1961-63; cert. advanced study, Western State U., 1963. Tchr. Leadville (Colo.) Pub. Schs., 1950-52, elem. prin., 1952-54; prin. Leadville Jr. H.S., 1954-55; pub. info. dir., instr. history Mesa Coll., Grand Junction, Colo., 1955-64; asst. prof. history Western State Coll., Gunnison, Colo., 1964-76, assoc. prof. history, 1976-82, assoc. prof. emeritus, 1982—; adj. faculty Adams State Coll., Alamosa, Colo., Mesa State Coll., Grand Junction, Colo., 1989—; propr. Mountaintop Books, Paonia, Colo.; bd. dirs. Colo. Assoc. Univ. Press; dir. hist. tours; columnist Valley Chronicle, Paonia, Best Years Beacon, Grand Junction, Guide Lines, Denver, The Historian, Fruita, Colo., Grand Mesa Byway News, Delta, Colo., Agewave: Get Up & Go!, Mpls.; profl. speaker in field; cons. Colo. Welcome Ctr., 1997—. Author: Mountain Academia, 1968, Writing Good History Research Papers, 1980, Ski Tracks in the Rockies, 1984, Famous Coloradans, 1990, I Never Knew That About Colorado, 1993; playwright: Thunder Mountain Lives Tonight!; contbr. articles to profl. jours.; freelance writer popular mags. Founder, coord. Nat. Energy Conservation Challenge; travel cons. Colo. State Welcome Ctr., 1997—; project reviewer NEH, Colo. Hist. Soc.; steering com. West Elk Scenic & Historic Byway, Colo., 1994—; founder Leadville (Colo.) Assembly, pres., 1953-54; mem. Advs. of Lifelong Learning, 1994—. Named Top Prof. Western State Coll., 1969, 70, 71; fellow Hamline U. Inst. Asian Studies, 1975, 79; recipient Colo. Ind. Pubs. award, 1998. Mem. Western Writers Am., Rocky Mountain Social Sci. Assn. (sec. 1961-63), Am. Hist. Assn., Assn. Asian Studies, Western History Assn., Western State Coll. Alumni Assn. (pres. 1971-73), Internat. Platform Assn. Profl. Guides Assn. Am. (cert.), Rocky Mountain Guides Assn., Colo. Antiquarian Booksellers Assn., Am. Legion (Outstanding Historian award 1981), Phi Alpha Theta, Phi Kappa Delta, Delta Kappa Pi. Home: 1156 Bookcliff Ave Apt 4 Grand Junction CO 81501-8198

FAY, CAROLYN M., education marketing business owner; b. Cambridge, Ohio, June 15, 1958; d. Frederick Russell and Lillian Marianna Mbiad; m. Michael Elliott Fay, Oct. 22, 1988. BA in Mass Comm., U. South Fla., 1984. Mktg. dir. Specialty Restaurants Corp., Clearwater, Fla., 1984-85; account exec. Landers & Ptnrs. Advt., St. Petersburg, Fla., 1986-87; mktg. mgr. Patchington Fashions, Inc., Clearwater, 1987-90; sr. project mgr. Modern Talking Picture Svc., St. Petersburg, 1990-92; pres., owner MarketingWorks Edn. Sys., Inc., Safety Harbor, Fla., 1992—. Creative dir., editor tchg. materials for various Fortune cos. programs; co-author, creative dir., editor tchg. materials Am. Egg Bd., 1991—. Recipient Excellence for Creation of Client Direct Mktg. award Fla. Dir. Mktg. Assn., 1994, 95, 98, Merit award Chgo. Nat. Agri-Mktg. Assn., Internat. Assn. Bus. Communicators, 1994, 96, What's New in Home Econs. Healthy Living award, 1996, 98, Prodn. Excellence award Consol. Papers, 1995-96, Judges award Printing Industry Fla., 1996, Nat. Mature Market Media award (2), 1998, S.E. Regional Silver Quill award of Excellence IABC, 1998. Mem. Exec. Women in Sales and Mktg. (pub. rels. chair 1990), Nat. Agri-Mktg. Assn., Fla. Dir. Mktg. Assn., Pinellas County (Fla.) Home Econ. Tchrs. Assn., Pub. Rels. Com. Democrat. Avocation: travel. Office: PO Box 273 Safety Harbor FL 34695-0273

FAY, CHRISTOPHER WAYNE, mechanical engineer, consultant; b. N.Y.C., Mar. 9, 1955; s. John Henry and Marie (Erickson) F.; m. Elizabeth Brownfield, Mar. 5, 1983; children: Abigail, John, Patrick, Dana. BS in Nautical Sci., Maine Maritime Acad., 1976. Profl. engr., Wash., Alaska; lic. Master 1600 GTand Third Mate Unltd., USCG. Officer U.S. Merchant Marines, various locations, 1976-80; mech. engr. JJ Henry Co., Alexandria, Va., 1980-83, GD Quincy Shipyard, Quincy, Mass., 1983-85, Lockheed Shipbuilding, Seattle, 1985-87; pvt. practice cons. Seattle, 1987-89; mech. engr. Boeing, Seattle, 1989—. Contbr. articles to profl. pubs. including Marine Transactions, ASNE Jour., Am. Forests. Sch. vol. Seattle Pub. Schs., 1991—. Mem. ASME. Am. Soc. Naval Engrs., Soc. Naval Architects & Marine Engrs. Home: 7037 18th Ave NE Seattle WA 98115-5742

FAY, CONNER MARTINDALE, management consultant; b. Chillicothe, Mo., May 9, 1929; s. Vernon Martindale and Corinne (Conner) F.; m. Evelyn Caffey Buford, Dec. 2, 1961; children: Leslie Conner Francesca, Buford Martindale Edoardo, David Curtis Anselmo. BA, Yale U., 1951; MBA cum laude, Harvard U., 1953. Brand mgr. Procter & Gamble Co., Cin., 1956-62; mktg. mgr. Procter & Gamble Co. Italia, Rome, 1962-69; sr. v.p. Clairol Inc., N.Y.C., 1970-89; mgmt. cons., 1989—. Bd. fgn. parishes Am. Episcopal Ch., N.Y., 1977—, pres., 1989—; bd. fgn. parishes St. Paul's Ch., Rome, 1977—, pres., 1989—; bd. fgn. parishes St. James Ch., Florence, Italy, 1977—, pres., 1989—; vice chmn. St. Stephen's Sch., Rome, 1980-94; trustee Samuel and Lois Silberman Fund of N.Y. Cmty. Trust, 1993—; sr. warden St. Mary the Virgin Episcopal Ch., Chappaqua, N.Y., 1982-83, 91-93; chmn. coun. of advisors Hunter Sch. Social Work, CUNY, 1985-97; mem. univ. coun. and com. on devel. and alumni affairs Yale U., 1996-98; chmn. of agts. Yale Alumni Fund, 1982-86, reunion gift chmn., 1991, vice chmn., 1994-96, chmn., 1996-98; bd. dirs. Katonah Mus. Art, 1995—. Mem. Am. Indsl. Health Coun. (bd. dirs. 1979-91, chmn. 1988-89), Yale Glee Club Assocs. (pres. 1979-81, treas. 1996—), Yale Club. Republican. Avocation: music.

FAY, DAVID B., sports association executive; b. N.Y.C., Oct. 12, 1950; s. Peter Donald and Sarah (McGrath) F.; m. Joan Margaret Mcananey, June 2, 1979; children: Katherine, Mary Elizabeth. BA, Colgate U., 1972. Communications dir. Met. Golf. Assn., N.Y.C., 1975-78; tournament rels. mgr. U.S. Golf Assn., Far Hills, N.J., 1978-81, dir. rules and program devel., 1981-87, asst. exec. dir., 1987-89, exec. dir., 1989—; joint sec. World Amateur Golf Coun., 1991—. Office: USGA Golf House PO Box 708 Far Hills NJ 07931-0708*

FAY, HELYN, college counselor; b. Fontana, Calif., Sept. 9, 1950; d. James R. Sammon and Patricia J. (Burton) Murarik; m. Ronald E. Fay, Sept. 4, 1971; children: Emily, Timothy. BA in English cum laude, Pasadena Coll., 1972; MS in Counseling with distinction, Calif. Poly. State U., 1991. Tchr. elem. sch. Hickman Mills Sch. Dist., Kansas City, Mo., 1972-75; tchr. asst. Cuesta C.C., San Luis Obispo, Calif., 1984-88; sch. counselor San Luis Coastal Unified Dist., San Luis Obispo, 1990-95; marriage, family and child counselor intern in pvt. practice Barry Martin, Los Osos, Calif., 1992-95; counselor Pt. Loma Nazarene Coll., San Diego, 1995—; mem. human devel. adv. com. Cuesta Coll., San Luis Obispo, 1993-95; chair eating behavior profl team Pt. Loma Nazarene Coll., San Diego, 1995—. Mem. Am. Assn. of Christian Counselors, Am. Coll. Counselors Assn., Am. Counseling Assn., Calif. Assn. of Marriage & Family Therapists (Clinton E. Phillips scholar 1990), Phi Delta Lambda. Office: Pt Loma Nazarene Coll 3900 Lomaland Dr San Diego CA 92106-2810

FAY, JAMES ALAN, mechanical engineering educator; b. Southold, N.Y., Nov. 1, 1923; s. William Joseph, Jr. and Margaret (Keenan) F.; m. Agatha Marie Kelly, Jan. 12, 1946; children: David Anthony, Mark Bernard, Colin Michael, Jamie Martin, Peter Robert, Michele Marie. B.S., Webb Inst. Naval Architecture, 1944; M.S., MIT, 1947; Ph.D., Cornell U., 1951. Research engr. Lima-Hamilton Corp., 1947-49; asst. prof. engring. mechanics Cornell U., 1951-55; mem. faculty MIT, 1955-89, prof. mech. engring., 1960-89, prof. emeritus, 1989—; cons. to govt. and industry; mem. NRC Environ. Studies Bd., 1973-78, 80-83. Author: Molecular Thermodynamics, 1965, Introduction to Fluid Mechanics, 1994; also articles. Chmn. Boston Air Pollution Commn., 1969-72, Mass. Port Authority, 1972-77; bd. dirs. Union Concerned Scientists, 1978—, Conservation Law Found., 1984-94. Served with USNR, 1942-46. Overseas fellow Churchill Coll., Cambridge U., 1980; Fulbright lectr., India, 1990. Fellow Am. Acad. Arts and Scis., Am. Phys. Soc. (exec. com. div. fluid dynamics 1964-67), AAAS, AIAA (chmn. plasmadynamics com. 1966-68); mem. NAE, ASME, Air and Waste Mgmt. Assn., Sigma Xi. Home: 36 Spruce Hill Rd Weston MA 02493-2134 Office: MIT Rm 3-258 Cambridge MA 02139-4307

FAY, JULIE, writer; b. Balt., Dec. 5, 1951; d. Dudley Holland and Jean (Preston) F.; m. Laszlo Ery, Dec. 27, 1986 (div. Feb. 1990); m.Henry James Stindt, Feb. 27, 1993; 1 child, Zoe Jean. BA, U. Conn., 1974; MA, Ariz. State U., 1977; MFA, U. Ariz., 1979. Assoc. prof. East Carolina U., Greenville, N.C., 1999—; dir. Writers Reading Series Ea. N.C., 1993—. Author: In Every Mirror, 1985, Portraits of Women, 1991, The Woman Behind You, 1998. N.C. Arts Coun. fellow. Office: East Carolina U Dept English Greenville NC 27858

FAY, SISTER MAUREEN A., university president. BA in English magna cum laude, Siena Heights Coll., 1960; MA in English, U. Detroit, 1966; PhD, U. Chgo., 1976. Tchr. English, speech, moderator student newspaper, student council St. Paul High Sch., Grosse Pointe, Mich., 1960-64; chairperson English dept., dir. student dramatics, moderator student pubs. Dominican High Sch., Detroit, 1964-69; co-dir. Cath. student ctr. Adrian (Mich.) Coll., 1969-71; instr. English Siena Heights Coll., Adrian, 1969-71; evaluators inst. criminal justice execs. U. Chgo., 1971-73; instr. English U. Ill., Chgo., 1971-74; dir. evaluation sch. new learning DePaul U., Chgo., 1974-75; fellow in acad. adminstrn. Saint Xavier Coll., Chgo., 1975-76, dean. grad. studies, 1979-83, dean continuing edn., 1976-83; asst. prof. No. Ill. U., Dekalb, 1980-83; pres. Mercy Coll. Detroit, 1983-90, U. Detroit Mercy, 1990—; v.p. VAUT Corp, bd. dirs. four inner city high schs., Archdiocese Chgo.; mem. exec. com. Assn. Mercy Colls.; adv. com. Adult Learning Svcs., The Coll. Bd., Met. Affairs Corp. of Detroit and S.E. Mich., cons. Nat. Assn. for Religious Women, 1974-75, North Cen. Assn. Colls. and Schs., evaluator commn. on higher edn.; trustee Rosary Coll., River Forest, Ill., New Detroit, Inc., 1993; emeritus mem. div. bd. Mercy Hosps. and Health Svcs. of Detroit; bd. dirs. Nat. Bank of Detroit., Detroit Econ. Growth Corp., 1992; mem. Nat. Commn. Ind. Higher Edn.; commr. North Centrl Assocs., Commn. on Instns. of Higher Edn., 1993. Asst. editor: (book rev.): Adult Education, A Journal of Research and Theory, 1971-74. Bd. dirs. United Way SE Mich., 1991, Assn. Catholic Colls. and Univs., 1992;

Steering com. Metro Detroit GIVES; exec. com., edn. task force Detroit Strategic Planning com., 1987; trustee Mich. Opera Theatre; bd. dirs. Greater Detroit Interfaith Round Table Nat. Conf. Christians and Jews, Inc., The Detroit Symphony; mem. Nat. Bipartisan Commn. on Ind. Higher Edn. in U.S., 1993. Mem. Am. Assn. Higher Edn., North Cen. Assn. (cons., evaluator commn. on higher edn.), Nat. Assn. Ind. Colls. and Univs. (bd. dirs.), Assn. Ind. Colls. and Univs. of Mich. (exec. com., chairperson), Am. Assn. Cath. Colls. and Univs., AAUW, Pi Lambda Theta. Office: U Detroit Mercy Office Pres PO Box 19900 4001 W McNichols Rd Detroit MI 48219-0900*

FAY, MICHAEL LEO, lawyer; b. Springfield, Mass., Oct. 3, 1949; s. Joseph L. and Marie A. (Wilson) F.; m. Christine B. Miller, Sept. 8, 1979; children: Matthew, Kathryn, Christopher. BA summa cum laude, Dartmouth Coll., 1971; postgrad., Oxford (Eng.) U., 1972; JD, Harvard U., 1975. Bar: Mass. 1975, U.S. Tax Ct. 1992. Assoc. Hale & Dorr, Boston, 1975-80, jr. ptnr., 1980-85, sr. ptnr., 1985—; chmn. trusts and estates dept.; bd. dirs. Family Firm Inst., 1993—; lectr. Mass. Continuing Legal Edn., Boston, 1984—. Overseer Aquinas House/Cath. Students Ctr. Dartmouth Coll., Hanover, N.H., 1984—; sec. Dartmouth Ednl. Assn., Boston, 1984—, Dartmouth Club Greater Boston, 1984—; mem. corp. Tenacre Country Day Sch., Wellesley Hills, Mass., 1992—. Fellow Am. Coll. Trust and Estate Counsel; mem. ABA, Mass. Bar Assn., Boston Bar Assn. Republican. Roman Catholic. Office: Hale and Dorr 60 State St Boston MA 02109-1816

FAY, NANCY ELIZABETH, nurse; b. Fulton, N.Y., May 10, 1943; d. Harold and Jean (Junker) Sant; m. Ronald George Fay, July 30, 1966; stepchildren: Rory Patrick, Ronald George Jr. RN, Genesee Hosp., Rochester, N.Y., 1964. Cert. gerentology nurse practitioner; cert. physician's asst., cert. diabetes eductor, N.Y. Head maternity nurse St. Luke's Hosp., Utica, N.Y., 1975-78; diabetes clinician St. Luke's Hosp., Utica, 1978-82, co-dir. diabetes out-patient clinic, 1980-82; nurse practitioner, physician's asst., cert. diabetes educator Slocum Dickson Med. Group, Utica, 1982-88; gerontol. nurse practitioner, physicians's asst., diabetes educator Masonic Home, Utica, 1988—; diabetes educator Upstate N.Y. Spl. Profl. Program Eli Lilly and Co., 1988—. Chair ann. Gerontol. Tchg. Day, Masonic Home, 1988—, N.Y. State Physicians Diabetes Tchg. Day A.D.A., 1983-90. Recipient Extra Mile award St. Luke's Hosp., 1979, Outstanding Citizenship award Am. Legion, Utica, 1982; Diabetes rsch. grantee Diabetes Project, Ctr. Disease Control Utica, 1980-82, 21st Ann. Scroll award Ctrl. N.Y. Acad. Medicine. Fellow Acad. Medicine Ctrl. N.Y.; mem. Am. Diabetes Assn. (pres. Utica chpt. 1983-85, Outstanding Vo. of Yr. 1978, bd. dirs. N.Y. State affiliate 1983-95, 1st v.p. 1986-87, Program award 1985-86, profl. edn. chmn. 1983-92, chair patient and pub. edn. Upstate Affiliate, 1987-92, 1st v.p. 1988-89, applicant nat. com. patient and pub. and profl. edn. 1988-89, pres.-elect N.Y. State Affiliate 1987-89, pres. 1990-92, immediate past pres. 1992-94, Spl. Svc. award N.Y. Upstate Affiliate 1994), Am. Acad. Physician's Assts., Am. Assn. Diabetes Educators, Womens Health Edn. Referral Svs. St. Luke's Hosp. (bd. dirs. 1987—), N.Y. State Coalition Nurse Practitioners. Republican. Methodist. Avocations: doll collecting, dancing, poetry, bike riding. Home: Valley Rd PO Box 910 Oriskany NY 13424-0710 Office: Masonic Home 2150 Bleecker St Utica NY 13501-1788

FAY, PETER THORP, federal judge; b. Rochester, N.Y., Jan. 18, 1929; s. Lester Thorp and Jane (Baumler) F.; m. Claudia Pat Zimmerman, Oct. 1, 1958; children: Michael Thorp, William, Darcy. B.A., Rollins Coll., 1951, LL.D., 1971; J.D., U. Fla., 1956; LL.D., Biscayne Coll., 1975. Bar: Fla. 1956, U.S. Supreme Ct. 1961. Ptnr. firm Nichols, Gaither Green, Frates & Beckham, Miami, Fla., 1956-61, Frates, Fay, Floyd & Pearson (and predecessors), Miami, 1961-70; prof. Fla. Jr. Bar Practical Legal Inst., 1959-65; judge U.S. Dist. Ct. for So. Fla., Miami, 1970-76, U.S. Ct. Appeals (5th cir.), 1976-81; judge U.S. Ct. Appeals (11th cir.), 1981-94, sr. judge, 1994—; lectr. Fla. Bar Legal Inst., 1959—; faculty Fed. Jud. Center, Washington, 1974-94; mem. Jud. Conf. Com. for Implementation Criminal Justice Act, 1974-82, Adv. Com. on Codes of Conduct, 1980-87, Adv. Com. on Appellate Rules, 1987-90; co-chmn. Nat. Jud. Coun. for State and Fed. Cts., 1990—. Mem. Orange Bowl Com., 1974—; dist. collector United Fund, 1957-70; mem. adminstrv. bd. St. Thomas U., 1970—; trustee U. Miami, Fla., 1989—; mem., supr. Ind. Counsel, 1994—. With USAF, 1951-53. Mem. Law Sci. Acad., Fla. Acad. Trial Attys., Am., Fla., Dade County, John Marshall (past pres.) bar assns., Fla. Council of 100, U. Fla. Alumni Assn. (dir.), Miami C. of C., Medico Legal Inst., Order of Coif, Phi Delta Phi (past pres.), Omicron Delta Kappa (past pres.), Pi Gamma Mu (past pres.), Phi Kappa Phi, Phi Delta Theta (past sec.). Republican. Roman Catholic. Clubs: Wildcat Cliffs (N.C.); Snapper Creek Lakes (Miami), Coral Oaks (Miami), Miami. Office: US Ct Appeals 11th Cir 99 NE 4th St Rm 1255 Miami FL 33132-2140*

FAY, PETER WARD, history educator; b. Paris, France, Dec. 3, 1924; s. Willis Ward and Joan (Peters) F.; m. Phyllis Ford, 1950 (div. 1955); 1 dau., Jennifer; m. Mariette Robertson, Dec. 21, 1957; children: Todor, Lisa, Jonathan, Benjamin. B.A., Harvard U., 1947, Ph.D., 1954; B.A., Oxford U., 1949. Instr. Williams Coll., 1951-55; asst. prof. history Calif. Inst. Tech., 1955-60, assoc. prof., 1960-70; prof. history Calif. Inst. Tech., Pasadena, Calif., 1970-97; prof. emeritus Calif. Inst. Tech., Pasadena, 1997—. Author: Opium War 1840-42, 1975, The Forgotten Army: India's Armed Struggle for Independence, 1942-45, 1993. Served with AUS, 1943-46. Rhodes scholar, 1947. Mem. Am. Hist. Assn., Assn. for Asian Studies. Democrat. Club: Signet Soc. Home: 590 Auburn Ave Sierra Madre CA 91024-1158 Office: Calif Inst Tech # 228-77 Pasadena CA 91125

FAY, REGAN JOSEPH, lawyer; b. Cleve., Sept. 19, 1948; s. Robert J. and Loretta Ann (Regan) F.; married; children: John, Mary, Matthew, Jessica, Samantha. BS in Chem. Engring., MIT, 1970; JD with honors, George Washington U., 1974. Bar: Ohio 1974, U.S. Dist. Ct. (no. dist.) Ohio 1974, U.S. Patent Office 1973, U.S. Ct. Appeals (fed. cir.) 1974, U.S. Ct. Appeals (9th cir.) 1975, U.S. Dist. Ct. (ea. dist.) Wis. 1976, U.S. Dist. Ct. (no. dist.) Tex. 1986, U.S. Supreme Ct. 1988. Patent examiner U.S. Patent and Trademark Office, Washington, 1970-72; law clk. to presiding justice U.S. Ct. Customs and Patent Appeals, Washington, 1973-75; assoc. Yount & Tarolli, Cleve., 1975-79; assoc., then ptnr. Jones, Day, Reavis & Pogue, Cleve., 1979—; lectr. patent and trademark law Case Western Res. U., Cleve., 1976-86. Mem. Cleve. Intellectual Property Law Assn (pres. 1996-97). Republican. Roman Catholic. Avocation: skiing. Office: Jones Day Reavis & Pogue 901 Lakeside Ave E Cleveland OH 44114-1116

FAY, RICHARD JAMES, mechanical engineer, executive, educator; b. St. Joseph, Mo., Apr. 26, 1935; s. Frank James and Marie Jewell (Senger) F.; m. Marilyn Louise Kelsey, Dec. 22, 1962; BSME, U. Denver, 1959, MSME, 1970. Registered profl. engr., Colo., Nebr. Design engr. Denver Fire Clay Co., 1957-60; design, project engr. Silver Engring. Works, 1960-63; research engr., lectr. mech. engring. U. Denver, 1963-74, asst. prof. Colo. Sch. of Mines, 1974-75, founder, pres. Fay Engring. Corp., 1971—. Served with Colo. N.G., 1962. Mem. Soc. Automotive Engrs. (past chmn. Colo. sect.), ASME (past chmn. Colo. sect., past regional v.p.), La Societe des Ingenieurs de L'Automobile (France). Contbr. articles to profl. jours.; patentee in field. Office: 5201 E 48th Ave Denver CO 80216-5316

FAY, ROBERT CLINTON, chemist, educator; b. Kenosha, Wis., Mar. 14, 1936; s. Clinton Edward and Selma (Lenz) F.; m. Carol Lee Baker, Aug. 25, 1960. A.B., Oberlin Coll., 1957; postgrad., Wheaton Coll., 1957-58; M.S., U. Ill., 1960, Ph.D., 1962. Teaching fellow Wheaton (Ill.) Coll., 1957-58; teaching asst. U. Ill., Urbana, 1958-59; inorganic chemist Nat. Bur. Standards, Washington, summers 1957-60; asst. prof. chemistry Cornell U., Ithaca, N.Y., 1962-68; assoc. prof. Cornell U., 1968-75, prof., 1975—; vis. prof. chemistry Harvard U., Cambridge, Mass., 1990-91, contract prof. U. Bologna, Italy, 1992. Co-author: (text) Chemistry, 1995, 98; contbr. articles to profl. jours. NSF fellow, 1960-62; NSF faculty fellow U. East Anglia, U. Sussex, Eng., 1969-70; Sci. and Engring. Research Council vis. fellow and NATO/Heineman sr. fellow Oxford (Eng.) U., 1982-83; NSF grantee, 1964-80; recipient Clark Disting. Teaching award Cornell U., 1980. Mem. Am. Chem. Soc., Royal Soc. Chem. (London), Am. Crystallographic Assn., Am. Sci. Affiliation, Sigma Xi, Phi Kappa Phi, Phi Beta Kappa, Phi Lambda Upsilon, Pi Mu Epsilon. Home: 318 Eastwood Ave Ithaca NY 14850-6202 Office: Cornell Univ Dept Chemistry/Chem Biology Baker Lab Ithaca NY 14853

FAY, ROBERT JESSE, lawyer; b. Cleve., Apr. 9, 1920; s. Horace Byron and Florence (Keating) F.; m. Ann Regan, Sept. 24, 1948 (div.); children: Regan, Laura, Karen, Michael, Molly, Ford, Genny. BS, MIT, 1942; JD, Case Western Res. U., 1948. Bar: Ohio 1948, D.C. 1964. Patent examiner U.S. Patent Office, Washington, 1948-49; since practiced in Cleve.; ptnr. Fay and Sharpe, Cleve., to 1992; pvt. practice Cleve., 1992—; pres. Gridiron Steel Co.; adj. prof. law Case Western Res. Sch. Law, 1960-75. Mem. Lakewood (Ohio) Planning Commn., 1961-70. With AUS, 1942-46. Mem. IEEE, AAAS, ABA, Ohio Bar Assn., Cleve. Bar Assn., Cuyahoga County Bar Assn. (pres. 1989-90), Cleve. Athletic Club, Rotary (trustee Cleve. club). Home: 12700 Lake Ave Apt 402 Cleveland OH 44107-1547

FAY, ROWAN HAMILTON, minister; b. Wells, N.Y., Apr. 10, 1943; s. Orrin Lewis and Dorothy Francis (Posson) F.; m. Judith Ann Smith, Sept. 8, 1962; children: Scott, Yolanda, Vicki, Ramona. Assoc. Constrn. Engring., Hudson Valley Community Coll., 1961-62, 62-63; grad., Hobe Sound Bible Coll. Draftsman Parker Dodge Assn., Renselaer, N.Y., 1961-62; trainee Niagara Mohawk Power, Albany, N.Y., 1962-63; salesman Albany (N.Y.) Lumber, 1963-65, Abele Tractor & Equipment, Albany, 1965-71; sales mgr. Vermeer of N.Y., Castleton, 1971-73, Contractor Sales, Albany, 1970-73; owner Spectra Physics of N.Y., Averill Park, 1972-73; pastor Pilgrim Holiness Ch., East Worcester, N.Y., 1973-79, Marcy, N.Y., 1979-93, Binghamton, N.Y., 1993—. Bd. dirs. Appalachian Youth Camp, Roxbury, Pa., 1986-92, Love Inc., Utica, N.Y., 1991-92; chmn. Inter-Ch. Bus. Convs., 1988—. Mem. Internat. Pin Collectors Club (pres. 1980—, publ. newsletter 1980—). Avocation; collecting Olympic memorabilia. Home: 602 Chenango St Binghamton NY 13901-2029 Office: Pilgrim Holiness Ch 604 Chenango St Binghamton NY 13901-2029

FAY, TERRENCE MICHAEL, lawyer; b. Cleve., Feb. 25, 1953; s. J. Francis and Alice Wilsona (Porter) F.; m. Beverly Ann Luciow, Feb. 25, 1983; children: Robert Michael, Katherine Elizabeth. BA cum laude, Baldwin Wallace Coll., 1974, BS cum laude, 1975; JD, Ohio State U., 1978. Bar: Ohio 1978, U.S. Dist. Ct. (no. dist.) Ohio 1983, U.S. Dist. Ct. (so. dist.) Ohio 1987, U.S. Ct. Appeals (6th cir.) 1987, U.S. Dist. Ct. (no. dist.) Ind. 1992, U.S. Dist. Ct. (ea. dist.) Mich. 1993. Law clk. for chief adminstrv. law judge Ohio Power Siting Commn., Columbus, 1977-78; asst. atty. gen. environ. sect. Ohio Atty. Gen.'s Office, Columbus, 1978-87, chief civil atty., 1988-89; sr. assoc. Smith & Schnacke, L.P.A., Columbus, 1988-89; sr. assoc. Benesch, Friedlander, Coplan & Aronoff, Columbus, 1990-91, 92, ptnr., 1992—; chair hiring com., 1995-97. Bd. dirs. Hucksters, Inc., Columbus, 1990. Abrahms scholar, 1975; recipient Book award Lawyers Coop., Inc., 1978, Ohio Gov.'s Spl. Recognition award, 1988. Mem. Phi Alpha Theta, Omicron Delta Kappa, Pi Kappa Delta, Psi Chi. Office: Benesch Friedlander Coplan Aronoff 200 Public Sq Cleveland OH 44114-2301 also: 88 E Broad St Ste 900 Columbus OH 43215-3550

FAY, THOMAS A., philosopher, educator; b. Utica, N.Y., July 18, 1927; s. Thomas A. and Theresa A. (Miller) F.; m. Evelyn C. DaCorta, Apr. 6, 1984. B.A., Cath. U. Am., 1952; M.A., U. Laval, Quebec, 1963; Ph.D., Fordham U., 1970. Asst. prof. philosophy St. Bernard Coll., 1963-64; mem. faculty St. John's U., Jamaica, N.Y., 1967—, prof. philosophy, 1977—; chmn. dept. philosophy St John's U., Jamaica, N.Y., 1974-80; vis. prof. Drew U., 1969. Author: Heidegger: The Critique of Logic, 1977, And Smoking Flax Shall He Not Quench: Reflections on New Testament Themes, 1979; mem. editorial bd. Guidebook for Publishing Philosophy, 1977, 2d edit., 1986; contbr. articles to profl. jours.. Served with U.S. Army, 1945-46. Mem. Am. Cath. Philos. Assn. (pres. Met. chpt. 1975-81, exec. council 1976-79), Internat. Thomistic Soc. (v.p.), Internat. Soc. Metaphysics, Am. Philos. Assn., Medieval Acad. Am. Home: 20 Melody Ln Kings Park NY 11754-5026 Office: St Johns U Philosophy Dept Jamaica NY 11439

FAY, TONI GEORGETTE, communications executive; b. N.Y.C., Apr. 25, 1947; d. George E. and Allie C. (Smith) Fay. BA, Duquesne U., Pitts., 1968; MSW (NIMH fellow 1970-72), U. Pitts., 1972, MEd, 1973; cert. Yale U. Drug Dependence Inst., 1973. Caseworker, N.Y.C. Dept. Welfare, 1968-70; regional commr. Gov. Pa. Coun. Drugs and Alcohol, 1973-76; dir. social services Pitts. Drug Abuse Ctr., 1972-73; dir. planning and devel. Nat. Council Negro Women, 1977-79; exec. v.p. D. Parke Gibson Assocs., 1979-82; mgr. community relations Time Inc. (name now Time-Warner Inc.), N.Y.C., 1982-83, dir. corp. community rels. and affirmative action Time Warner, Inc., 1983-93; v.p., corp. officer, Time Warner, Inc. 1993—. Bd. dirs. UNICEF, Congressional Black Caucas Found.,, NAACP Legal Def. Fund. Bd., Franklin and Eleanor Inst.; apptd. bd. advs. Nat. Inst. Literacy, 1996—. Named Woman of Yr., Pitts. YWCA, 1975, N.Y. Women's Forum; recipient Twin award YWCA of USA, 1987; named one 100 Top Women in Bus., Dollars and Sense Mag., 1986. Bd. dirs. Exec. Leadership Coun., U.S. Com. for UNICEF (v.p.), Congl. Black Caucus Found., Alpha Kappa Alpha, Office: Time Warner Bldg 75 Rockefeller Plz New York NY 10019-6990

FAY, WILLIAM MICHAEL, federal judge; b. Pittston, Pa., 1915; s. William Morris and Carolyn (Runner) F.; m. Jean Burke, 1945; 1 son, W. Michael. Student, Georgetown U., 1939; LL.B., Cath. U. Am., 1942. Bar: D.C. 1942. Asst. counsel atomic energy com. U.S. Senate, 1946; exec. asst. U.S. Senator McMahon, 1946-48; with Chief Counsel's Office, IRS, 1948-57; asst. head Appeals and Civil Divsn. IRS, 1948-57; dist. counsel IRS, Washington, 1958-61; judge U.S. Tax Ct., 1961—, sr. judge. Lt. comdr. USNR, 1942-45. Named Man of Yr., Friendly Sons St. Patrick of Greater Pittston, 1983. Mem. Am. Bar Assn., Bar Assn. D.C. Office: US Tax Ct 400 2nd St NW Washington DC 20217*

FAYNE, GWENDOLYN DAVIS, air force officer, English educator; b. Toledo, Dec. 8, 1951; d. Robert Louis and Marietta Beatrice (Sautter) Davis; m. Barry Dennis Fayne, Jan. 6, 1979; children: Ashleigh Elizabeth, Zachary Alexandur-John. BFA, So. Meth. U., 1972; MEd, U. North Tex., 1978; MA, U. Denver, 1987. Cert. tchr., Tex., Ala. Substitute tchr. Toledo and Dallas, 1972-73; film dir. Channel 39 Christian Broadcasting Network, Dallas, 1973-75; engr., air operator Channel 40 Trinity Broadcasting Network, Tustin, Calif., 1978; commd. 2d lt. USAF, 1978, advanced through grades to maj., 1989, ret., 1995; mgr. western area Hdqrs. USAFR Officers Tng. Corp., Norton AFB, Calif., 1979-81; chief tng. systems support Hdqrs. Air Force Manpower Pers. Pentagon, Washington, 1981-84; pers. policies officer J1, Orgn. of Joint Chiefs of Staff Pentagon, Washington, 1984-85; asst. prof. English, dir. forensics USAF Acad., Colorado Springs, Colo., 1987-92; adj. faculty mem. dept. English Auburn U., Montgomery, Ala., 1994-95; adj. faculty mem. dept. arts and scis. Troy State U., Montgomery, 1994-96; dir. Bullock County HS Learning Ctr., Union Springs, Ala., 1995-96; tech. and acad. tchr. Ctr. for Advanced Tech. Booker T. Washington Magnet H.S., Montgomery, 1996; tchr. speech and English, Mountain Brook H.S., Birmingham, Ala., 1997-98; tchr. humanities Joseph Bruno Montessori Acad., Birmingham, 1998—; assoc. editor Airpower Jour., Maxwell AFB, Ala., 1992-94, mil. doctrine analyst, 1994-95; chmn. mil. affairs Jr. Officer's Coun., Norton AFB, 1981; invited spkr. in field; chmn. program devel. com. for nat. orgn. Cross Exam. Debate Assn., 1990-91. Contbr. articles to profl. jours. Teacher, mem. choir, soloist various chs., 1973; chair publicity com. Birthright, Inc., Woodbridge, Va., 1983. Named Command Jr. Officer of Yr., Hdqrs. USAFR Officers Tng. Corps, 1979. Mem. Nat. Parliamentary Debate Assn. (co-founder, editor Parliamentary Debate jour. 1992-95), Phi Upsilon Omicron. Avocations: reading, antiques, sight-seeing, family. Home: 3833 Asbury Pl Birmingham AL 35243 Office: Bruno's Montessori Acad 5509 Timber Hill Rd Birmingham AL 35242

FAY-SCHMIDT, PATRICIA ANN, paralegal; b. Waukegan, Ill., Dec. 25, 1941; d. John William and Agnes Alice (Semerad) Fay; m. Dennis A. Schmidt, Nov. 3, 1962 (div. Dec. 1987); children: Kristin Fay Schmidt, John Andrew Schmidt. Student, L.A. Pierce Coll., 1959-60, U. San Jose, 1960-62, Western State U. of Law, Fullerton, Calif., 1991-92. Cert. legal asst., Calif. Paralegal Rasner & Rasner, Costa Mesa, Calif., 1979-82; paralegal, adminstr. Law Offices of Manuel Ortega, Santa Ana, Calif., 1982-92; sabbatical, 1992-94; mem. editorial adv. bd. James Pub. Co., Costa Mesa, 1984-88. Contbg. author: Journal of the Citizen Ambassador Paralegal Delegation to the Soviet Union, 1990. Treas., Republican Women, Tustin, Calif., 1990-91; past regent, 1st vice regent, 2d vice regent NSDAR, Tustin, 1967—; docent Richard M. Nixon Libr. and Birthplace, 1993—, bd. dirs. Docent Guild, 1994—; docent Orange County Courthouse Mus., 1992-94. Mem. Orange County Paralegal Assn. (hospitality chair 1985-87). Roman Catholic. Avocations: theater, dance. E-mail: gabriellex@pacbel.net. Home: 13571 Hewes Ave Santa Ana CA 92705-2215

FAZAL, SHEIKH, photographer; b. N.Y.C., 1965. BA, Princeton U., 1987. Exhbns. include Photographic Resource Ctr., Boston, 1994, Opsis Gallery, N.Y.C., 1994, PaceWildensteinMacGill, N.Y.C., 1995, 98, Schneider Gallery, Chgo., 1996, Internat. Ctr. Photography, N.Y.C., 1996, Diggs Gallery, Winston-Salem (N.C.) State U., 1997, Schneider Gallery, Chgo., 1998, Sprengel Mus., Hannover, Germany, 1998, others; represented in permanent collections. Recipient Infinity award Internat. Ctr. Photography, 1995, Ferguson award Friends of Photography, 1995, Ruttenberg award Friends of Photography, 1995, Mother Jones Internat. Documentary award, 1995, Leica Medal of Excellence, 1995; Fulbright fellow in the arts, Kenya, 1992; photography fellow N.J. State Coun. on Arts, 1994; photography fellow NEA, 1994. Fax: 212-759-8964. Office: care Pace Wilden Stein MacGill 32 East 57th St New York NY 10022

FAZIO, ANTHONY LEE, investment company executive; b. Wheeling, W.Va., Jan. 27, 1937; s. Frank G. and Julia Louise (DeFillipo) F.; m. Faye Elizabeth Kelly, Sept. 3, 1964; children: Tracey Lee, Kelly Ann. BSEE, W.Va. U., 1959. Registered investment advisor, investment mgmt. cons., bus. mgmt. cons.; cert. fin. planner. With computer div. RCA, 1964-72, mgr. product mktg., 1970-71, mgr. systems planning, 1971-72; dir. bus. and product planning Univac, 1972-73, dir. product mktg. and bus./product planning N.Am., 1973-75, regional mgr., 1975-77; v.p. sales Sycor, Inc., Ann Arbor, Mich., 1977-78; v.p. sales No. Telecom Systems Corp., 1978-79, v.p. mktg., 1979-80; pres. Gibbs Irwin Investments Co., 1981-83; product procurement and due diligence officer Midland Mgmt. Corp., 1983-86; pres. Fazio Investments, Inc., 1986—. With U.S. Army, 1959-61. Mem. Inst. Cert. Fin. Planners, Minn. Soc. Inst. Cert. Fin. Planners (pres.-elect, bd. dirs.), Tau Beta Pi, Eta Kappa Nu. Republican. Home and Office: 4770 Regents Walk Ste 100 Excelsior MN 55331-9209

FAZIO, PETER VICTOR, JR., lawyer; b. Chgo., Jan. 22, 1940; s. Peter Victor and Marie Rose (LaMantia) F.; m. Patti Ann Campbell, Jan. 3, 1966; children: Patti-Marie, Catherine, Peter. AB, Holy Cross Coll., Worcester, Mass., 1961; JD, U. Mich., 1964. Bar: Ill. 1964, D.C. 1981, Ind. 1993, U.S. Dist. Ct. (no. dist.) Ill. 1965, U.S. Ct. Appeals (7th cir.) 1972, U.S. Supreme Ct. 1977, U.S. Ct. Appeals (D.C. cir.) 1988. Assoc. Schiff, Hardin & Waite, Chgo., 1964-70, ptnr., 1970-82, 84—; exec. v.p. Internat. Capital Equipment, Chgo., 1982-83, also dir., 1982-85, sec., 1982-87; bd. dirs. Planmetrics Inc., Chgo., 1984-92, Chgo. Lawyers Commn. for Civil Rights Under Law, 1976-82, co-chmn., 1978-80; bd. dirs. Seton Health Corp. No. Ill., Chgo 1987-90, vice chmn., 1989-90. Trustee Barat Coll., Lake Forest, Ill., 1977-82; bd. dirs. St. Joseph Hosp., Chgo., 1990-95, mem. exec. adv. bd. 1984-89, chmn., 1986-89; vice chmn. bd. dirs. Cath. Health Ptnrs., 1995—; dir. exec. com. Ill. Coalition, 1994—, Northwest Ind. Forum, 1994-98. Mem. ABA (mem. coun. 1991-94, vice-chmn. sect. pub. utlity, transp. and comm. law), Ill. State Bar Assn., Chgo. Bar Assn., Fed. Bar Assn., Fed. Energy Bar Assn., Edison Electric Inst. (vice chmn. legal com., chmn. legal exec. adv. com.), Am. Gas Assn. (mem. legal com.), Am. Soc. Corp. Secs., Met. Club (Chgo.), Econ. Club of Chgo., Commercial Club of Chgo. Office: Schiff Hardin & Waite 6600 Sears Tower 233 S Wacker Dr Chicago IL 60606-6473

FAZIO, SERGIO, medical educator, researcher. MD in Medicine summa cum laude, U. Rome, 1983; PhD in Molecular Biology, U. Siena, Italy, 1989. Intern and resident in internal medicine U. Rome, Italy, 1983-86; resident svc. of emergency medicine Gen. Hosp. Udine, Italy, 1984-85; fellow in metabolism dept. medicine Univ. Hosp. U. Rome, 1986-88; postdoctoral fellow Gladstone Inst. Cardiovasc. Disease, San Francisco, 1988-91, staff rsch. investigator, 1991-93; rsch. fellow Cardiovasc. Rsch. Inst. U. Calif., San Francisco, 1988-93; asst. prof. medicine and pathology, dir. lipid lab. Vanderbilt U., Nashville, 1993—. Ad hoc reviewer Jour. Biol. Chemistry, Biochimica Biophysica Acta, Lipids, Arteriosclerosis and Thrombosis, Jour. of Lipid Rsch., Diabetes; contbr. to articles to profl. jours. Recipient Pilot Project and Young Investigator award CNRU, Established Investigatorship award Am. Heart Assn., 1996; grant-in-aid Am. Heart Assn., 1995; Joe C. Davies Found. scholar. Fellow Am. Heart Assn. (mem. coun. on arteriosclerosis); mem. Am. Fedn. for Clin. Rsch. Office: Vanderbilt U Sch Medicine Divsn Endocrinology 715 MRB II 2220 Pierce Ave Nashville TN 37232-6303*

FAZIO, TOM, design firm executive, golf course designer; b. Norristown, Pa., 1945; married; 6 children. Landscape designer intern George Fazio, ptnr.; prin., pres. Fazio Golf Course Designers, Inc., Jupiter, Fla., 1990—; cons. architect major golf tournaments including U.S. Open, Duluth, Ga., 1974, Tulsa, Okla., 1977, Toledo, 1979, P.G.A. Championship, Rochester, N.Y., 1980, Duluth, 1991, Toledo, 1986, Palm Beach Gardens, Fla., 1987, U.s. Amateur Championship, Jupiter, Fla., 1987, U.S. Open Championship, Rochester, 1989. Prin. works include Edgewood Tahoe Country Club, Lake Tahoe, Nev., Jupiter Hills Club, Jupiter, Fla., Am. Great Gorge Resort, McAfee, N.Y., Cariari Internat. Club, San Jose, Costa Rica, Pinehurst (N.C.) # 6, Golf Club Okla., Tulsa, Windstar Country Club, Naples, Fla., The Vintage Club, Indian Wells, Calif., Shadow Creek, Las Vegas, Emerald Dunes, West Palm Beach, Fla., Karsten Creek-Okla. State U., Stillwater, The Quarry, La Quinta, Calif., The Champions Club at Summerfield, Stuart, Fla., Glen Oaks, Des Moines, Iowa, Wade Hampton Golf Club. Cashiers, N.C., Black Diamond Ranch, Lecanto, Fla., Caves Valley Golf Club, Balt., Pelican Hill, Newport Beach, Calif., numerous others. Active Boys and Girls Club. Named Favorite Present-Day Designer of Golf Courses, Golf Digest, 1991, 93. Office: Fazio Golf Course Designers Inc 17755 SE Federal Hwy Jupiter FL 33469-1792 also: 8675 W 96th St Ste 204 Overland Park KS 66212-3382 also: 109 S Main St Hendersonville NC 28792-5083*

FAZIO, VIC, former congressman; b. Winchester, Mass., Oct. 11, 1942; m. Judy Kern; children: Dana Fazio, Anne Fazio (dec.), Kevin Kern, Kristie Kern. BA, Union Coll., Schenectady, 1965; postgrad., Calif. State U., Sacramento. Journalist, founder Calif. Jour.; congl. and legis. cons., 1966-75; mem. Calif. State Assembly, 1975-78; mem. 96th -103rd Congresses from Calif. 3rd Dist., 1979-98; former chmn. Dem. Congl. Campaign Com.; chmn. Dem. caucus, house steering policy com.; mem. legis. br. appropriations subcom., ranking mem. appropriations subcom. energy and water; mem. Ho. budget com. 97th-100th Congress; majority whip-at-large 96th-105th Congress; also co-chmn. Fed. Govt. Svcs. Task Force 96th-101st Congresses, former chmn. bipartisan com. on ethics; mem. approriations com. 105th Congress; former mem. Sacramento County Charter and Planning Commns. Bd. dirs. Asthma Allergy Found., Jr. Statesman, Nat. Italian-Am. Found. Coro Found. fellow; named Solar Congressman of Yr. Mem. Air Force Assn. Address: 2224 N Kentucky St Arlington VA 22205-3221*

FAZIO, VICTOR WARREN, physician, colon and rectal surgeon; b. Sydney, Australia, Feb. 2, 1940; came to U.S., 1971; s. Victor Warren and Kathleen Eleanor (Hills) F.; m. Carolyn Kisandra Sawyer, Dec. 2, 1961; children: Victor, Jane, David. MB, BChir, U. Sydney, 1965, MS (hon.), 1997. Diplomate Am. Bd. Colon and Rectal Surgery (pres. 1991-92). Intern and resident St. Vincent's Hosp., Sydney, 1965-67, surgical registrar, 1969-71; lectr. anatomy U. NSW Med. Sch., Sydney, 1967; surg. registrar Repatriation Gen. Hosp., Concord, Australia, 1968; gen. surgeon Australian Surg. Team, Bien Hoa, Vietnam, 1971; fellow gen. surgery Lahey Clinic, Boston, 1972; fellow colorectal surgery Cleve. Clinic, 1973, staff surgeon colorectal surgery, 1974, chmn. dept. colon and rectal surgery, vice chmn. divsn. surgery, 1975—; bd. govs. Cleve. Clinic Found., 1990-95, exec. mem. bd. trustees, 1994-95. Author 320 manuscripts and book chpts.; editor: Current Therapy in Colon and Rectal Surgery, 1989; editor-in-chief Diseases of Colon and Rectum, 1997—. Fellow ACS, Royal Australian Coll. Surgeons, Am. Soc. Colon and Rectal Surgery (pres. 1995-96); mem. Soc. Pelvic Surgeons (exec. com. 1980), Soc. for Surgery Alimentary Tract, Ctrl. Surg. Assn., James IV Assn. Surgeons, Ohio Valley Soc. Colon and Rectal Surgeons (past pres.). Roman Catholic. Avocations: naval history, sailing. Home: 17414 S Woodland Rd Cleveland OH 44120-1761 Office: Cleve Clinic 9500 Euclid Ave Cleveland OH 44195-0001*

FEAGIN, EUGENE LLOYD, pastor; b. Hendersonville, NC, July 19, 1950; s. Eugene Lloyd and Martha (Hodges) F.; m. Anna Johnson, July 3, 1972; children: James Eugene, Travis Lee, Melissa Ann. BA, U. S.C., 1972, MEd,

1976; MDiv, Candler Sch. Theology, 1981. Ordained to ministry Methodist Ch., 1984. Pastor Fingerville (S.C.) United Meth. Ch., 1974-79, Saxon United Meth. Ch., Spartanburg, S.C., 1979-85, Cherokee Springs United Meth. Ch., Spartanburg, 1982-85, Sharon (S.C.) United Meth. Ch., 1985-91, Aldersgate United Meth. Ch., Inman, S.C., 1991-95; Heath Springs (S.C.) United Meth. Ch., 1995—; dir. communications, Spartanburg United Meth. Dist., 1982-85; bd. dirs., Pastoral Counseling Svc., Spartanburg, 1982-85; cluster leader, York/Clover United Meth. Cluster, S.C., 1986-91. Firefighter Sharon Vol. Fire Dept., 1986-91; mem. Schs./Community Team, York, 1990-91. Mem. Western York Ministerial Assn. (pres. 1989-90), Rotary (pres. Inman chpt. 1994-95, pres. Kershaw chpt. 1996-97). Home: PO Box 36 Heath Springs SC 29058-0036 Office: 201 S Main St Heath Springs SC 29058

FEAGLES, GERALD FRANKLIN, marketing executive; b. Kansas City, Kans., Dec. 8, 1934; s. George Joseph and Florence Ada (Johnson) F.; m. Eleanor Jean Holder, Aug. 31, 1957; 1 child, Gerald Franklin II. Student, Kansas City Jr. Coll., 1953-55. Mktg. and sales rep. Sears Roebuck and Co., Kansas City, 1963-70; br. mgr. SunarHauserman, Overland Park, Kans., 1970-86; mgr. bus. devel. govt. svcs. group The Austin Co., Kansas City, 1986-91; mgr. mktg.-indsl. divsn. Black & Veatch Architects & Engrs., Kansas City, 1991-93; mgr. ctrl. region Va. Metal Industries Inc., Orange, Va., 1994-96; mgr. bus. devel.-ctrl. region The Austin Co. Engrs. and Constructors, Kansas City, 1996—. Com. chmn. Boy Scouts of Am. Kansas City, 1973. Mem. Kansas City C. of C., Constrn. Specifications Inst., Prodrs. Coun., Internat. Facility Mgmt. Assn., Assoc. Gen. Contractors, Soc. Am. Mil. Engrs.

FEARING, WILLIAM KELLY, art educator, artist; b. Fordyce, Ark., Oct. 18, 1918; s. George David and Frankie (Kelly) F. BA, La. Tech. U., 1941; MA, Columbia U., 1950. Classroom tchr. Windfield Pub. Schs., La., La., 1942-43; prodn. illustrator Consolidated Vultee Aircraft, Fort Worth, 1943-45; prof. art Tex. Wesleyan Coll., Fort Worth, 1945-47; prof. art U. Tex., Austin, 1947-87, Ashbel Smith prof., 1983—, Ashbel Smith prof. emeritus, 1987—. Author: (with C.I. Martin and E. Beard) Our Expanding Vision, 1960, The Creative Eye, 1969, 2d edit., 1979; (with E. Beard, N. Krevitsky, C.I. Martin) Art and the Creative Teacher, 1971 (with E.L. Mayton, B. Francis, E. Beard) Helping Children See Art and Make Art, 1982; (with E.L. Mayton and R. Brooks) The Way or Art Inner Vision Outer Expression, 1986; guest editor Tex. Quar.: Creativity and the Human Spirit, vol. XVI, 1978. One-man shows include El Paso Mus. Art, Esther Bear Gallery, Santa Barbara, 1964, Gallery Visual Arts, La. Tech. U., Ruston, 1966, U. Tex. Art Mus., Austin, 1967, Fort Worth Art Ctr., 1969, Witte Meml. Mus., San Antonio, 1969, U. Tex. Art Mus., Austin, 1974, Mary Moore Gallery, La Jolla, 1975, Mary Moffett Gallery, La. Tech. U., Ruston, 1976, DuBose Gallery, Houston, 1977, L and L Gallery, Longview, 1975, 78, Retrospective Spencer Gallery, Fine Arts Ctr., U. Ark.-Monticello, 1981, Mary Moffett Gallery, Sch. Art and Architecture, La. Tech. U., Ruston, 1981, Old Jail Art Ctr., Albany, Tex., 1985, Marion Koogler McNay Art Mus., San Antonio, 1986, Valley House Gallery, Dallas, 1992, 96, Robinson Galleries, Houston, 1995, Flatbed Press and Gallery, Austin, 1995, 97; exhibited in group shows at Carnegie Inst., Pitts., 1955, Pa. Acad. Art, Phila., 1954-56, Carnegie Inst., Pitts., 1956-57, Mus. Fine Arts, Houston, 1956-57, Dallas Mus. Fine Art, 1956-57, Munson-Williams-Proctor Inst., Utica, 1956-57, Edwin Hewitt Gallery, N.Y.C., 1957, Dallas Mus. Fine Art, 1958, Am. Fedn. Art, 1958, Mus. Fine Arts, Little Rock, 1961, Colorado Springs Art Ctr., 1961, 63 Philbrook Art Ctr., Tulsa, 1963, Fort Worth Art Ctr., 1963, U. Ill., Urbana, 1955, 59, 63, Denver Art. Mus., 1963, U. Ariz. and Ark Art Ctr., 1964-65, N.Y. World's Fair, Tex. Pavillion, 1964, Tex. Pavillion Hemistair, San Antonio, 1968, Tex. Tech U. Mus. Art, Lubbock, 1978, U. Tex.-Austin, 1979, Art Gallery Sch. Art and Architecture, La. Tech. U. Ruston, 1984, Jack S. Blanton Mus. Art (formerly Archer M. Huntington Art Gallery), U. Tex.-Austin, 1963-82, 83-91, 92-98, Longview Mus. and Arts Ctr., Tex., 1962, 63, 75, 85, 90, 91, Amarillo Art Ctr., Tex., 1988, Dallas Mus. Fine Arts, 1991, Robinson Galleries, Houston, 1993, 94, 96, 97, 98, 99, Valley House Gallery, Dallas, 1994-99, Flatbed Press and Gallery, Austin, 1996, 97, 98, 99, Ga. Art Mus., U. Ga., Athens, 1997, Marion Koogler McNay Art Mus., San Antonio, 1997, 98, 99, Mus. of Big Bend, Sul Ross State U., Alpine, Tex., 1998, Nancy Wilson Scanlon Gallery, Helms Fine Art Ctr., Austin, 1999. Mem. Nat. Soc. Lit.. and Arts, Tex. Art Edn. Assn., Phi Kappa Phi. Home: 914 Calithea Rd Austin TX 78746-2716

FEARON, JEFFREY ARCHER, surgeon; b. N.Y.C., Aug. 19, 1953; s. Robert Archer and Mary Galarneau Fearon; m. Regen Horchow, June 19, 1998. BA, Brown U., 1975; postgrad., Columbia U., 1975-77; MD, U. Cin., 1981. Diplomate Am. Bd. Surgery, Am. Bd. Plastic Surgery. Gen. surg. resident Deaconess/Harvard Surg. Svc., Harvard Med. Sch., Boston, 1981-87; plastic surg. resident Mass. Gen. Hosp., Harvard Med. Sch., Boston, 1987-89; craniofacial fellow Childrens Hosp. Phila., U. Pa., 1989-90; dir. Craniofacial Ctr. Med. City Dallas, 1990—; clin. instr. in plastic surgery U. Tex. Southwestern Med. Sch., Dallas, 1994—. Contbr. chpt. to book and articles to profl. jours. Fellow ACS, Am. Acad. Pediat.; mem. Internat. Soc. Craniofacial Surgeons, Childrens Craniofacial Assn. (adv. bd., chmn. 1996-98). Achievements include patent pending for bone distraction device. Avocation: sculpting. E-mail: cranio f@aol.com. Office: Ste C700 7777 Forest Ln Dallas TX 75230

FEARRINGTON, ANN PEYTON, writer, illustrator, newspaper reporter, portraitist; b. Winston-Salem, N.C., Aug. 25, 1945; d. James Cornelius Pass Fearrington and Florence Moore (McCanless-Fearrington) Blackwood; m. Hege Hill Russ, Sept. 1967 (div. 1984); children: James Pass Fearrington Russ, Joseph Peyton Fearrington Russ; m. Vance Edwin Cox, Jr., June 17, 1985; 1 stepson, Charles Jonathan Cox. BA in Secondary Edn. and English, U. N.C., 1967; MS in Life Scis., Botany & Horticulture, N.C. State U., 1972. Mid. sch. tchr. Wake County Sch. Sys., Raleigh, 1967-71; landscape designer pvt. practice N.Y.C., Winston-Salem, N.C., 1972-83; corr. Raleigh News & Observer, 1993—; writer/artist-in-residence Raleigh-Wake County Pub. Schs., 1997—. Author, illustrator: Christmas Lights, 1996, Little Green Book-18 Keys to Your Child's Reading Success, 1998, Up in the Air, Junior Birdmen, 1998. Sch. libr. vol. Wake County Sch. Sys., Raleigh, 1985—; Sunday Sch. tchr. Highland United Meth. Ch., Raleigh, 1986—. Mem. Soc. Children's Book Writers & Illustrators, Raleigh Racquet Club. Avocations: gardening, reading, sketching.

FEARS, JESSE RUFUS, historian, educator, academic dean; b. Atlanta, Ga., Mar. 7, 1945; s. Emory Binford Fears; m. Charlene Louise Bauer, July 6, 19 66; children: Laura Elizabeth, Jesse Rufus IV. BA summa cum laude, Emory U., 1966; MA, Harvard U., 1967, PhD, 1971. Asst. prof. classical langs. Tulane U., New Orleans, 1971-72; asst. prof. history Indiana U., Bloomington, 1972-75, assoc. prof. history, 1975-80, prof. history, 1980-86; prof., chair classical studies Boston U., 1986-90, assoc. dean Coll. Liberal Arts, 1987-89, dir. humanities found., 1988-90; dean Coll. Arts and Scis. U. Okla., Norman, 1990-92, prof. Classics, 1990—, G.T. and Libby Blankenship prof. history of liberty, 1992—, dir. Ctr. for History of Liberty, 1992—. *Jesse Rufus Fears was chosen in 1981 as the first Distinguished Faculty ResearchLecturer at Indiana University. He was named by the students as the Outstanding Professor at Indiana University in 1983. Fears has received awards for teaching excellence on 14 occasions and in 1996 and 1999, he was named Professor of the Year at the University of Oklahoma.* Author: Princeps A Diis Electus, 1977, (monographs) The Cult of Jupiter, 1981, The Theology of Victory, 1981, The Cult of Virtues, 1981; editor: (3 vols.) Selected Writings/Lord Acton, 1985-88; contbr. chpts. to books, numerous articles to profl. jours. Bd. dirs. Okla. Sch. Sci./Math., Oklahoma City, 1990—. Danforth fellow Danforth Found., 1966-71; fellow Am. Acad. in Rome, 1969-71, Guggenheim Found., 1976-77, Howard Found., 1977-78, Alexander Von Humboldt, 1977-78, 80-81, Ctr. for History of Freedom, Wash. U., 1989-90; grantee Am. Philos. Soc., 1972, 79, NEH, 1974, Am. Coun. Learned Soc., 1979, Woodrow Wilson, 1983, Kerr Found., 1994, 99. Mem. AAUP, Am. Philol. Assn., Classical Assn. Middle West and South, Archaeol. Inst. of Am., Phi Beta Kappa, Golden Key Nat. Honor Soc. Office: U Okla Dept Classics Ctr History of Liberty Kaufman Hall Norman OK 73019

FEATHER, WILLIAM L., corporate lawyer. BA, U Tex. Austin, 1969, JD, 1972. Bar: Tex. 1972, D.C. 1975, Ill. 1977. Gen. coun. Continental Can. Co., 1978-81; sr. coun. Wickes Co., Inc., 1981-82; sr. coun. Household Internat., Inc., 1982-86; sr. coun. Baxter Internat., Inc., 1986-95; asst. gen. counsel, 1995-96, assoc. gen. counsel; sr. v.p., sec., gen. counsel Allegiance Corp., McGaw Pk., Ill., 1996—. Office: Allegiance Corp 1430 Waukegan Rd Mc Gaw Park IL 60085-6726

FEATHERLY, HENRY FREDERICK, lawyer; b. Stillwater, Okla., Aug. 10, 1930; s. Henry Ira and Lucy Anne (Borsch) F.; m. Dorcas Diane Rowley, July 19, 1952; children—Henry Frederick, Charles Alan. B.S., Okla. State U., Stillwater, 1952; LL.B., Okla. U., Norman, 1957. Bar: Okla. 1957, U.S. Dist. Ct. (we. and ea. dists.) Okla. 1957, U.S. Ct. Appeals (10th cir.) 1958. Assoc. Pierce, Mock & Duncan, Oklahoma City, 1957-63; ptnr. Chiles & Featherly, Oklahoma City, 1963-64; sole practice, Oklahoma City, 1964-66; ptnr. Lamun, Mock, Featherly, Baer & Timberlake, Oklahoma City, 1966-85; ptnr. Lamun, Mock, Featherly, Kuehling & Cunningham, Oklahoma City, 1986—. Mem. commrs. staff Dan Beard Dist. council Boy Scouts Am., 1966-89, Last Frontier council; trustee Heritage Hall Sch., Oklahoma City, 1974-77. Mem. ABA, Okla. Bar Assn., Oklahoma County Bar Assn., Am. Trial Lawyers Assn., Okla. Trial Lawyers Assn., Okla. Assn. Def. Counsel, Am. Judicature Soc. Republican. Methodist. Lodge: Lions (pres. 1970-71, 83-84). Home: 2433 NW 46th St Oklahoma City OK 73112-8307

FEATHERMAN, SANDRA, university president, political science educator; b. Phila., Apr. 14, 1934; d. Albert N. and Rebe (Burd) Green; m. Bernard Featherman, Mar. 29, 1958; children: Andrew Charles, John James. BA, U. Pa., 1955, MA, 1978, PhD, 1978. Asst. prof. dept. polit. sci. Temple U., Phila., 1978-84, assoc. prof., 1984-91, asst. to pres., 1986-89, pres. faculty senate, 1985-86, dir. Ctr. for Pub. Policy, 1986-91; vice chancellor acad. adminstrn., prof. polit. sci. U. Minn., Duluth, 1991-95; pres. U. New Eng., Biddeford, Maine, 1995—. Author: Jews, Blacks and Ethnics, 1979; contbr. articles to profl. jours. Bd. dirs. Citizens Com. Pub. Edn. in Phila., 1977-89, pres., 1979-81; pres. Pa. Fedn. Community Coll.; trustee C.C. Phila., 1970-92, chmn. bd. trustees, 1984-86; life trustee, v.p. Samuel Fels Found., 1978—; bd. dirs. United Way SE Pa., 1977-89, United Way Pa., 1981-84, Maine Civil Liberties Union, 1995-97, U. New Eng., Gulf of Maine Aquarium; pres. Girls Clubs Am., Phila., 1971-73, mem. nat. bd., 1971-74; mem. Pa. Coun. on Arts, 1979-83; nat. bd. dirs. Women and Founds.-Corp. Philanthropy, 1986-91; v.p. Jewish Community Rels. Coun., 1982-89; speaker Commonwealth of Pa. Humanities Coun., 1988, 90, 91; bd. govs., mem. exec. com. Am. Assn. Colls. Osteopathic Medicine; bd. dirs. Kennebec Girl Scout Coun. Recipient Brooks Graves award Pa. Polit. Sci. Assn., 1982, City of Phila. Community Svc. award, 1984, Women's Achievement award YWCA, 1989, Adminstr. of Yr. award Minn. Women in Higher Edn., 1994. Mem. AAUW (bd. dirs. Phila. chpt. 1975-78, 80-91, pres. 1984-86, nat. chair internat. fellowships panel 1987-91, Outstanding Woman award 1986, nat. bd. dirs. 1993—), Am. Polit. Sci. Assn., Maine Ind. Colls. Assn. (pres. 1998—), Greater Portland Alliance Colls. and Univs. (pres. 1997—). Office: U New Eng Hills Beach Rd Biddeford ME 04005-9526

FEATHERSTONE, BRUCE ALAN, lawyer; b. Detroit, Mar. 2, 1953; s. Ronald A. and Lois R. (Bosshart) F.; children: Leigh Allison, Edward Alan. BA cum laude with distinction in Econs., Yale U., 1974; JD magna cum laude, U. Mich., 1977. Bar: Ill. 1977, Colo. 1983, U.S. Dist. Ct. (no. dist.) Ill. 1978, U.S. Dist. Ct. Colo. 1983, U.S. Ct. Appeals (5th cir.) 1980, U.S. Ct. Appeals (7th cir.) 1981, U.S. Ct. Appeals (10th cir.) 1983, U.S. Ct. Appeals (9th cir.) 1991, U.S. Supreme Ct. 1984. Assoc. Kirkland & Ellis, Denver, 1977-83, ptnr., 1983-96; ptnr. Featherstone & Shea, LLP, Denver, 1996—. Articles editor U. Mich. Law Rev., 1976-77. Mem. ABA (litigation sect.), Colo. Bar Assn., Denver Bar Assn., Order of Coif. Avocations: swimming, biking, running. Home: 725 Saint Paul St Denver CO 80206-3912 also: PO Box 1467 Denver CO 80201-1467 Office: Featherstone & Shea LLP 600-17th St Ste 2500 Denver CO 80202-5402*

FEAVER, DOUGLAS DAVID, retired university dean, classics educator; b. Toronto, Ont., Can., May 14, 1921; came to U.S., 1948; s. Charles John and Margaret Adeline (Brett) F.; m. Margaret Ruth Seaman, June 10, 1950; children: David, John, Paul, Ruth, Peter. BA, U. Toronto, 1948; MA, Johns Hopkins U., 1949, PhD, 1951; postgrad., Am. Sch. Classical Studies, 1951-52. Instr. Yale U., New Haven, 1952-56; mem. faculty Lehigh U., Bethlehem, Pa., 1956—, prof. classics, 1966-84; internat. dean emeritus Coll. Humanities and Internat. Studies, Univ. of the Nations, Kailua, Kona, Hawaii, 1985-94; dean Coll. Humanities and Internat. Studies, Univ. of the Nations, Kailua, Kona, Hawaii, 1994-98; dean emeritus Coll. Humanities and Internat. Studies, Univ. of the Nations, Kailua, Hawaii, 1998—; jr. fellow Ctr. Hellenic Studies, 1967-68; ann. research prof. Am. Sch. Classical Studies, 1976-77; dir. Humanities Perspectives on Tech., 1972-75; cons. in field. Author: El mundo en que vivio Jesus, 1972; contbr. articles to profl. jours. Served with RCAF, 1940-45. NEH scholar, 1971-84; cons. NEH, 1975—. Presbyterian. Office: Univ of the Nations 75-5851 Kuakini Hwy Kailua Kona HI 96740-2199

FEAVER, GEORGE ARTHUR, political science educator; b. Hamilton, Ont., Canada, May 12, 1937; came to U.S., July 4, 1967; s. Harold Lorne and Doris Davies (Senior) F.; m. Nancy Alice Poynter, June 12, 1963 (div. 1978); m. Ruth Helene Tubbesing, Mar. 8, 1986 (div. 1991); children: Catherine Fergusson, Noah George, Anthea Jane. B.A. with Honors, U. B.C., 1959; Ph.D., London Sch. of Econs., 1962. Asst. prof. Mt. Holyoke Coll., South Hadley, Mass., 1962-65; lectr., research assoc. London Sch. Econs. and Univ. Coll., London, 1965-67; assoc. prof. Georgetown U., Washington, 1967-68, Emory U., Atlanta, 1968-71; assoc. prof. U.B.C., Vancouver, B.C., Canada, 1971-74, prof., 1974—; vis. fellow Australian Nat. U., Canberra, 1987. Author: From Status to Contract, 1969; editor: Beatrice Webb's Our Partnership, 1975; editor: The Webbs in Asia: The 1911-12 Travel Diary, 1992; co-editor: Lives, Liberties and the Public Good, 1987; contbr. articles to profl. jours., books. Fellow Canada Council, 1970-71, 74-75, Am. Council Learned Socs., 1974-75, Social Scis. and Humanities Research Council of Canada, 1981-82, 86-91. Mem. Can. Polit. Sci. Assn., Am. Polit. Sci. Assn., Am. Soc. for Polit. and Legal Philosophy, Conf. for Study of Polit. Thought, Inst. Internat. de philosophie politique. Club: Travellers' (London). Avocations: hiking and wine appreciation. Home: 4776 W 7th Ave, Vancouver, BC Canada V6T 1C6 Office: Univ British Columbia, Dept Polit Sci, Vancouver, BC Canada V6T 1Z1

FEAZELL, JOHNNY RAY, physicians assistant; b. Springfield, Mo., July 18, 1945; s. Raymond Maurice and Rosemary (Bunting) F.; m. Jeannie Feazell, July 30, 1966; children: Johnna, Jonathan. BS in Criminal Justice, Drury Coll., 1980. Police officer Springfield Mo. Police Dept., 1969-72; physician's asst. Bur. of Prison's, Springfield, 1972—. Pres. Parkview Legion Baseball, Springfield, 1990-94, Springfield Cath. Baseball Assn., 1995—; coach varsity baseball, Hurley, Mo., 1997, jr. high sch. basketball, Hurley, 1998. Home: 1002 W Portland St Springfield MO 65807-1946 Office: Bur of Prisons US Med Ctr Fed Prisoners 1900 W Sunshine St Springfield MO 65807-2240

FEBO, NILDA LUZ, pediatrics and psychiatric-mental health nurse; b. Rio Piedras, P.R., Feb. 26, 1947; d. José Febo Febo and Petra Pastrana Diaz; children: Annette K. Cancel, Melissa S. Stepherson. Diploma, Meth. Hosp. Sch. Nursing, Bklyn., 1971; student, Empire State Labor Coll., N.Y.C., 1975-76, Hunter Coll., 1976-77; BSN, U. P.R., Rio Piedras, 1984. RN, N.Y., P.R.; cert. in gen. nursing practice. Pub. health nurse N.Y.C. Dept. Health and Rubella Project, 1971-77; office nurse, physician's asst. Dr. Vargas, Carolina, P.R., 1977-78; staff nurse med. and psychiat. ICU VA Hosp., San Juan, P.R., 1978-88; staff nurse pediatrics unit Mt. Sinai Hosp., N.Y.C., 1988-92; prof. practical nursing San Juan, P.R., 1993-96; multidisciplinary nurse United Health Care Plans of P.R. Nurse Line, 1996—. With USAF, 1966-67. Mem. N.Y. State Nurses Assn., P.R. Nurse's Assn. Home: RR 9 Box 1568 San Juan PR 00926-9713

FEBRES-SANTIAGO, SAMUEL F., university chancellor. BA in Secondary Edn.-Hispanic Studies, Inter Am. U. P.R.; MA in Spanish-Am. Literature, Temple U., MEd in Curriculum and Instrn.; MA in Sch. Mgmt., U. P.R.; postgrad., Harvard U.; EdD in Adminstrn. of Edn1. Instns., Seton Hall U. Chancellor Guayama Campus, Interam. U. P.R., 1989—. Recipient Disting. Alumni award Inter Am. U. Mem. Am. Assn. Higher Edn., Hispanic Assn. Colls. & Univs., Mid. State Assn. Colls. & Univs., Lions (pres. edn. com., bd. dirs.), Phi Delta Kappa. E-mail: sffebre@ns.inter.edu. Office: InterAm U PR Guayama Campus PO Box 10004 Guayama PR 00785-4004*

FECHER, VINCENT JOHN, priest; b. Wilmette, Ill., Feb. 10, 1924; s. Joseph Martin and Emilia Cecilia (Siemer) F. D. Ch. History, Gregoriana, Rome, 1954; MA in Philosophy, Cath. U. Am., 1960; PhD, Angelicum, Rome, 1974; MA in Gerontology, Trinity U., San Antonio, 1981. Ordained priest Roman Cath. Ch., 1950. Sem. prof. Divine Word Sem., Techny, Ill., 1954-59, Manila, Philippines, 1959-64; sec. gen. Soc. of Divine Word, Rome, 1968-74; parish priest San Antonio Archdiocese, 1974—; pastor Sacred Heart Cath. Ch., Uvalde, Tex., 1980-92, St. John the Evangelist Ch., Hondo, Tex., 1995-99; dean Uvalde deanery Diocese of San Antonio, 1980-86; sec. Diocesan Presbyteral Coun., 1980-86. Author: German National Parishes, 1955, Error, Deception, Incomplete Truth, 1974, Religion and Aging, 1982, The Lord and I, 1990, Man, Woman, and God, 1993; contbr. articles to profl. publs. Mem. adv. coun. Tex. Dept. Human Svcs., Austin, 1984-88; mem. Uvalde Arts Coun. Mem. Nat. Fedn. Priests' Coun. (Tex. rep. 1980s), Hondo C. of C., KC, Knights of Holy Sepulcher, Lions. Home: 8520 Cross Mountain Trail San Antonio TX 78255

FECHNER, ROY FREDRIC, mathematics educator; b. Bklyn., Feb. 12, 1954; s. Paul Fredric and Lillian Victoria (Dannevig) F. AA in Liberal Arts, Kingsborough C.C., 1974; BS in Phys. Edn., U. Ala., 1977, BS in Edn., 1979, MA in Secondary Edn., 1988. Cert. tchr. in math. and history. Social studies instr. Tuscaloosa Christian Sch., 1979-80; math. instr. Jackson (Ala.) Acad., 1983-84, So. Acad., Greensboro, Ala., 1984-85, Douglas County H.S., Douglasville, Ga., 1985-86; tutor, night mgr. U. Ala. Ctr. for Tchg. and Learning, Tuscaloosa, 1987-89; math. instr. U. Ala., Tuscaloosa, 1988-91, 96—, Tuscaloosa City Schs., 1992-95, Shelton State C.C., Tuscaloosa, 1993-95, Pickens Acad., Carrollton, Ala., 1995-96; lectr. in field. Mem. Rep. Nat. com., Washington, 1996, 99; mem. Campus Crusade for Christ, Tuscaloosa, 1974-80, 89-92, Reformed U. Fellowship, Tuscaloosa, 1989-92. Recipient Saffold Hall Svc. award, 1978; Named Outstanding Tchr. Program Future, 1994. Mem. Ala. Alumni Assn., Christian Faculty Fellowship, Coll. Studies Inst., Christian Leadership Ministries. Republican. Avocations: running, swimming, reading, sports, sports card collecting. Home: 3715 3rd Ave E Apt A-36 Tuscaloosa AL 35405-3124 Office: Math Dept U Ala PO Box 870350 Tuscaloosa AL 35487

FECHT, LORENE, surgical nurse; b. Keokuk, Iowa, July 13, 1949; d. Alvin and Norma Ruth (Jenkins) Fink; m. Herb Fecht, June 29, 1969; children: Kristie, Tiffanie, Lindsay, Lacey. Diploma, Burlington (Iowa) Med. Ctr., 1970; student, Robert Morris Coll., Carthage, Ill., Carl Sandburg Coll., Carthage, Southeastern Community Coll. Cert. BCLS, ACLS, cert. nurse in operating rm. Physician's asst. Carthage; supr. RR, Cen. Supply; surgery supr. Meml. Hosp., Carthage, staff nurse in med.-surg. CCU; head nurse ambulatory surgery recovery rm. Keokuk Area Hosp., dir. surg. svcs., 1992—. Mem. Am. Soc. Past Anesth. Nurses, Soc. Gastrointestinal Nurses Am., Assn. Oper. Rm. Nurses (chpt. pres., vice chmn.), Iowa Orgn. Nurse Leaders. Office: Keokuk Area Hosp 1600 Morgan St Keokuk IA 52632-3497

FECHTEL, VINCENT JOHN, legal administrator; b. Leesburg, Fla., Aug. 10, 1936; s. Vincent John and Annie Jo (Hayman) F.; m. Dixie Davenport, Feb. 1992; children: John, Katherine, Elizabeth D., MaryKatherine. BSBA, U. Fla., 1959. Mem. Fla. Ho. of Reps., 1972-78, Fla. Senate, 1978-80; parole commr. U.S. Dept. Justice, Chevy Chase, Md., 1983-96. Served with USNR and Fla. Nat. Guard. Mem. Alpha Tau Omega. Republican. Roman Catholic. Home: 1101 S 9th St Leesburg FL 34748-6843

FECHTOR, STEVE, advertising executive. With Lowe Marschalk, N.Y.C.; creative dir. Lowe Marschalk, Cleve., DMB & B, St. Louis; exec. creative dir. Buntin Group, Nashville, HMS Ptnrs., Colombus, Ohio; bd. dirs. Lowe Marschalk. Recipient numerous advertising awards including One Show awards, ADDYs, London Internat. Festivals, N.Y. Internat. Festivals, Mercury awards, Art Dirs. Annual, British D&AD awards; named ADWEEK's Midwest Copywriter of Yr., 1987. Office: HMS Ptnrs 250 Civic Center Dr Columbus OH 43215

FECK, LUKE MATTHEW, utility executive; b. Cin., Aug. 15, 1935; s. John Franz and Mercedes Caroline (Rielag) F.; m. Gail Ann Schutte, Aug. 12, 1961; children: Lisa, Mara, Paul. BA, U. Cin., 1957. Copyboy Cin. Enquirer, 1956, reporter, TV editor, columnist, 1957-64, asst. features editor, 1969-70, mag. editor, 1970, news editor, 1971-73, mng. editor, 1974-75, exec. editor, 1975, editor, 1976-80; editor Columbus Dispatch, 1980-89; sr. v.p. corp. comms. Am. Electric Power, Columbus, 1990—; pres. Ackerman and Feck Press, Inc., 1964-69, Feicke Web, Inc., 1974-75. Chairperson Met. Human Svcs. Commn.; bd. dirs. Thurber House. 1st lt. AUS, 1957-59. Mem. Pub. Rels. Soc. Am., Edison Electric Inst., Lit. Club Cin., Capital Club, Lakes Golf and Country Club, Torch Club of Columbus, Sigma Delta Chi (pres. chpt.), Phi Kappa Theta. Home: 6880 Worthington Rd Westerville OH 43082-9491 Office: Am Electric Power 1 Riverside Plz Columbus OH 43215-2355

FECTEAU, ROSEMARY LOUISE, educational administrator, educator, consultant; b. Niagara, Wis., Aug. 7, 1930; d. Andrew Raymond and Julianna Agnes (Wodenka) Waitrovich; m. Jack Richard Fecteau Sr. (dec. Dec. 1994), June 12, 1954; children: Michele, Julienne, Gervaise, Jack Jr., Andrew, Anne-Marie. BA with high distinction, U. R.I., 1974; MS in Edn., U. Maine, 1976; MS in Ednl. Adminstrn., U. So. Maine, 1979; postgrad., Columbia Pacific U., 1997—. Cert. supt. schs. K-12. Sec. A.O. Smith Corp., Milw., 1949-54, Judge Irving W. Smith, Niagara, 1954-55; asst. tchr. Regional Resource Rm., Yarmouth, Maine, 1974-75; prin. Breakwater Sch., Cape Elizabeth, Maine, 1975-78; tchr. grades 6-8 Wells (Maine) Jr. H.S., 1978-79; dir. spl. svcs. Maine Sch. Adminstrv. Dist. 75, Bowdoin, Bowdoinham, Harpswell, Topsham, Maine, 1979-84; ednl. cons. various states, 1984—; owner Serendipity Acres Sheep Farm; secondary handicapped task force State Dept. Edn., Augusta, 1980-81; chairperson nat. insvc. network U. Ind., Topsham, Maine, 1981-84. Mem. Friends of the Royal River, Friends of Prince Meml. Libr., Maine Spl. Edn. Rev. Team; founder Project Co-Step and Project S.E.A.R.C.H.; mem. focus group Casco Bay Estuary Project Maine; brownie leader, girl scout cons. Girl Scouts Am., Erie, Pa., 1965-66; dir. women's Cursillo Movement, Erie, 1967; co-chair publicity St. Vincent Hosp., Erie, 1966-67; chairperson conservation commn. Town of North Yarmouth, 1987; del. Maine Dem. Conv., 1986. Mem. AAUW, LWV, U. So. Maine Alumni Assn., The Muskie Club, North Yarmouth Hist. Soc., Maine Organic Farmer and Gardener Assn., Maine Assn. Supervision and Curriculum Devel., Consumers for Affordable Health Care, Union of Concerned Scientists. Avocations: music, arts, nutrition, physical fitness. Home: Serendipity Acres 140 W Pownal Rd North Yarmouth ME 04097-6819

FECZKO, WILLIAM ALBERT, radiologist; b. Homestead, Pa., May 27, 1937; s. Albert George and Rosalia Melania (Toth) F.; m. Margaret Ann Cloonan, July 8, 1961; children: Margaret Christine, William Martin. AB, St. Vincent Coll., Latrobe, Pa., 1959; MD, U. Pitts., 1963. Diplomate Am. Bd. Radiology. V.p. Almar Radiologists, Inc., Pitts., 1975-93, pres., 1993—; assoc. dir. St. Francis Med. Ctr., Dept. Diagnostic Radiology, Pitts., 1978-86; dir. radiology residence prog. St. Francis Med. Ctr., Pitts., 1980-86; med. dir. Imaging Ctr., Pitts., 1986—; pres. Imaging Ctr. Inc., 1986—; v.p. med. staff St. Francis Med. Ctr., 1988, pres., 1989, bd. dirs., chmn. exec. com., 1990. Contbr. articles to profl. jours. Capt. USAF, 1965-67. Fellow Am. Coll. Radiology; mem. Pitts. Roentgen Soc. (treas. 1984-85), Pa. Radiologic Soc. (bd. dirs. 1985-88), AMA, Allegheny County Med. Soc., Pa. Med. Soc., Radiol. Soc. N.Am., Am. Inst. Ultrasound in Medicine, Am. Roentgen Ray Soc. Republican. Roman Catholic. Avocations: golf, fishing, cross country skiing, photography. Home: 217 Highland Rd Pittsburgh PA 15238-2136 Office: Imaging Ctr 4221 Penn Ave # 102G Pittsburgh PA 15224-1389

FEDAK, BARBARA KINGRY, technical center administrator; b. Hazleton, Pa., Feb. 7, 1939; d. Marvin Frederick and Ruth Anna (Wheeler) Siebel; m. Raymond F. Fedak, Mar. 27, 1993; children: Sean M., James Goldey. BA, Trenton State Coll., 1961; MEd, Lesley Coll., Cambridge, Mass., 1986. Registered respiratory therapist. Dept. dir. North Platte (Nebr.) Community Hosp., 1974-75; newborn coord. Children's Hosp., Denver, 1975-79; edn. coord. Rose Med. Ctr., Denver, 1979-81; program dir. respiratory tech. program Pickens Tech., Aurora, Colo., 1981-86; mktg. rep. Foster Med. Corp., Denver, 1986-87; staff therapist Porter Meml. Hosp., Denver, 1987-88; dir., br. mgr. Pediatric Svcs. Am., Denver, 1988-90; dir. clin. edn. Pickens

Tech., Aurora, Colo., 1991—, divsn. chair health occupations, 1991—; site evaluator Joint Rev. Com. for Respiratory Therapy Edn., Euless, Tex. Co-editor: AARC Record. Met. coun. mem. Am. Lung Assn., 1987-91. Mem. Am. Assn. Respiratory Care (edn. sect. program com. 1992—, abstract rev. com. 1993-96, alt. del. AARC Ho. Dels., 1997-98, del. 1999—), Colo. Soc. Respiratory Care (dir. at large 1983-86, 90-92, sec. 1980-81, program com. 1982-92), Colo. Assn. Respiratory Educators (chair 1991-96), Lambda Beta (faculty). Methodist. Avocations: reading, mountain biking, golf, singing, piano playing. Home: 11478 S Marlborough Dr Parker CO 80138-7318 Office: Pickens Tech 500 Airport Blvd Aurora CO 80011-9307

FEDDER, NORMAN J., theatre educator, playwright; b. N.Y.C., Jan. 26, 1934; s. Abraham Herbert and Harriet Dorothy (Solomon) F.; m. Deborah Pincus, Nov. 24, 1955; children: Jordan Michael, Tamar Beth Fedder Katz. Student, Johns Hopkins U., 1950-52; BA, Bklyn. Coll./CUNY, 1955; MA, Columbia U., 1956; PhD, NYU, 1962. Registered drama therapist; bd. cert. trainer. Asst. prof. English Trenton (N.J.) State Coll., 1960-61; assoc. prof. English Indiana U. of Pa., 1961-64, Fla. Atlantic U., Boca Raton, 1964-67; assoc. prof. drama U. Ariz., Tucson, 1967-70; Disting. prof. theatre Kans. State U., Manhattan, 1970—; founder, dir. Israel Theatre Program, Tel Aviv. Author: (teleplay) We Can Make Our Lives Sublime, 1970, (plays) The Betrayal, 1978, Out of the Depths, 1998, (musical play) The Buck Stops Here!, 1983. Mem. Nat. Assn. for Drama Therapy (bd. mem. 1990—), Assn. for Jewish Theatre (founding). Democrat. Jewish. Avocations: swimming, walking. Office: Kans State U Theatre Program Nichols 129 Manhattan KS 66506

FEDDERS, JOHN MICHAEL, lawyer; b. Covington, Ky., Oct. 21, 1941; s. Aloysius Henry and Mary Margaret (Schmidt) F.; m. Barbara E. Baxter; children: Luke D., Mark A., Matthew C., Andrew M., Peter J. B.A. in Journalism, Marquette U., 1963; LL.B., Cath. U. Am., 1966. Bar: N.Y. 1967, D.C. 1967. Assoc. Cadwalader, Wickersham & Taft, N.Y.C., 1966-71; exec. v.p. Gulf Life Holding Co., Dallas, 1971-73; with firm Arnold & Porter, Washington, 1973-81; ptnr., 1975-81; dir. Div. of Enforcement, SEC, 1981-85; ptnr. Miller, Cassidy, Larroca & Lewin, 1985-87; sole practice Washington, 1987—; lectr. corp. securities and fin. Contbr. articles to legal jours. Recipient Service award Marquette U., 1977, Achievement award Cath. U. Am. Alumni Assn., 1982, Chmn.'s award for excellence SEC, 1982, Supervisory Excellence award, SEC, 1983. Mem. ABA, Assn. Bar City N.Y., Sigma Delta Chi, Phi Alpha Delta. Republican. Roman Catholic. Office: 1742 N St NW Washington DC 20036-2907

FEDER, ALLAN APPEL, management executive, consultant; b. Chgo., Aug. 6, 1931; s. Tobias M. and Belle (Appel) F.; m. Joan Feldman, Nov. 19, 1961; children: Steven, Michael, Lisa, Valerie. B.S., Syracuse U., 1952; M.B.A., U. Pa., 1953. With Topps Chewing Gum, Inc., Duryea, Pa., 1965-70; gen. ops. mgr., v.p. mfg. Life Savers subs. Squibb Corp., N.Y.C., 1970-72, exec. v.p. Dobbs Life Savers subs., 1972-73; pres. Dobbs Houses, Inc., Memphis, 1973-76; pres. mfg. group Gt. Atlantic & Pacific Tea Co. Inc., Montvale, N.J., 1976-82, also corp. sr. exec. v.p. and dir.; mgmt. cons., 1982—; pres., CEO Vitarroz Corp., 1988-96, dir., 1988—, vice chmn., CEO, 1996—; bd. dirs. Edward Don & Co., The Topps Co. Bd. dirs. Fla. West Coast Symphony Orch.; bd. dirs., v.p. Sarasota-Manatee Jewish Fedn. Home and Office: 3959 Boca Pointe Dr Sarasota FL 34238-5507

FEDER, ARTHUR A., lawyer; b. N.Y.C., Mar. 23, 1927; s. Leo and Bertha (Franklin) F.; m. Ruth Musicant, Sept. 4, 1949; children: Gwen Lisabeth, Leslie Margaret, Andrew Michael. BA, Columbia Coll., 1949; LLB, Columbia U., 1951. Bar: N.Y. 1951. Assoc. Fulton Walter & Halley, 1951-53; rsch. asst. Am. Law Inst. Fed. Income, Estate and Gift Tax Project, 1953-54; assoc., ptnr. Roberts & Holland, N.Y.C., 1954-66; ptnr. Willkie, Farr & Gallagher, N.Y.C., 1966-69; ptnr. Fried, Frank, Harris, Shriver & Jacobson, N.Y.C., 1970-94, of counsel, 1994—; sr. adv. to exec. com. Herzog, Heine, Geduld Inc., 1996—; lectr. in law Columbia U., 1961-63; lectr. Am. Law Inst., NYU Inst. on Fed. Taxation, Practicing Law Inst., various profl. groups. Editor Columbia Law Rev., 1949-51; contbr. articles to profl. jours. With USN, 1945-46. Fellow Am. Coll. Tax Counsel; mem. ABA (taxation sect., chmn. com. on real property tax problems 1964-66, com. on legis. drafting 1968-84), Assn. of Bar of City of N.Y. (various coms.), N.Y. State Bar Assn. (taxation sect., co-chmn. various coms. 1982-86, sec. 1987-88, 2d vice chmn. 1988-89, vice chmn. 1989-90, chmn. 1990-91), Internat. Fiscal Assn. (coun. U.S.A. br. 1984-91), Am. Law Inst. (tax adv. group fed. income tax project), Univ. Club, Phi Beta Kappa. Democrat. E-mail: afeder@herzog.com. Fax: 201-418-5293. Home: 25 W 81st St New York NY 10024-6023 Office: Herzog Heine Geduld Inc 525 Washington Blvd Jersey City NJ 07310-1690

FEDER, DONALD ALBERT, syndicated columnist; b. Troy, N.Y., Nov. 25, 1946; s. Harold Samuel and Esther Ruth (Whitman) F.; m. Andrea Helen Mills, Aug. 5, 1973; children: Helena, Anna, Jonathan, Aaron. BA cum laude, Boston U., 1969, JD, 1972. Bar: N.Y. 1973, Mass. 1976. Assoc. Pozefsky, Tocci & Pozefsky, Gloversville, N.Y., 1973-76; exec. dir. Citizens for Ltd. Taxation, Boston, 1976-79, Second Amendment Found., Bellevue, Wash., 1979-81, WEEI-NewsRadio, Boston, 1983-84; editor, pub. On Principle, Longmeadow, Mass., 1981-83; columnist, editorial writer Boston Herald, 1984—. Author: A Jewish Conservative Looks at Pagan America, 1992, Who's Afraid of the Religious Right?, 1996. Recipient 1st prize writing award AMY Found., 1992, Internat. Comm. award, Republic of China, 1998. Mem. Internat. Churhill Soc., Theodore Roosevelt Assn., Calvin Coolidge Meml. Found. Jewish. Avocations: history, gardening, hiking. Office: Boston Herald 1 Herald St Boston MA 02118-2200

FEDER, HARRY SIMON, bank executive; b. N.Y.C., Aug. 20, 1953; s. Morris Louis and Lucy (Kraus) F.; m. Gilli Bortman, Mar. 1, 1977; children: Jean Ella, Laura Ann. BA in Econs., NYU, 1974; MBA in Internat. Fin., Syracuse U., 1976. Credit analyst Israel Discount Bank of N.Y., N.Y.C., 1977-78, with domestic lending, 1978-79, with internat. lending, 1979-81, asst. v.p. corr. banking, 1981-85, v.p. treasury, 1986-94; 1st v.p. treasury, 1995-96; mgr. corr. banking and treasury Israel Discount Bank of N.Y., N.Y.C., 1996—. Avocations: collecting stamps and coins, travel. Home: 66 Dora Ln New Rochelle NY 10804-1006 Office: Israel Discount Bank NY 511 5th Ave Rm 1003 New York NY 10017-4997

FEDER, JOHN NATHAN, molecular biologist; b. Bklyn., June 28, 1955; s. John Jacob and Doris Marie (Mahoney) F. BA, Calif. State U., Chico, 1977, MA, 1980; PhD, Stanford U., 1990. Lectr. Calif. State U., 1980; rsch. asst. Stanford U., 1980-84, tchg. asst., 1987; postdoctoral fellow U. Calif., San Francisco, 1990-93; sr. scientist Progenitor, Menlo Park, Calif., 1993-99; sr. rsch. scientist Bristol-Myers Squibb, Princeton, N.J., 1999—. Contbr. articles to profl. pubs. Fellow Am. Cancer Soc., 1990, NIH, 1990. Achievements include patents for hereditary hemochromatosis gene, methods to diagnosis and treat iron overload diseases. Home: 277 Dutchtown Zion Rd Bellemead NJ 08502 Office: Bristol Myers Squibb Pharm Rsch Inst Princeton NJ 08543-5400

FEDER, ROBERT, lawyer; b. N.Y.C., Nov. 29, 1930; s. Benjamin and Bertha (Bloodstein) F.; m. Marjorie Feder, Dec. 3, 1950; children: Susan E., Judith D., Benjamin D., Jessica R., Abigail M. BA cum laude, CCNY, 1953; LLB, Columbia U., 1953. Bar: N.Y. 1953, U.S. Tax Ct. 1956, U.S. Dist. Ct. (so. dist.) N.Y. 1973. V.p., gen. counsel Presdl. Realty Corp., White Plains, N.Y., 1953-71; ptnr. Cuddy & Feder & Worby, White Plains, 1971—; bd. dirs. Westchester County (N.Y.) Legal Aid Soc., 1972—, pres., 1974-78; adj. prof. sch. bus. Columbia U., 1988-89; bd. dirs. Presdl. Realty Corp. (Amex), Interplex Industries, Inc., Healthstar Network, Inc. Pres., White Plains Community Action Program, 1967-69; bd. dirs. White Plains Hosp. Ctr., 1978—, also sec., treas., chmn. 1992-97; commr. White Plains Housing Authority, 1984—; trustee SUNY-Purchase Coll. Found., 1988—, vice-chmn., 1995—; adj. prof. Pace U. Law Sch., 1985-87. Mem. ABA, N.Y. State Bar Assn., White Plains Bar Assn., Westchester County Bar Assn., Am. Coll. Real Estate Lawyers. Home: 9 Oxford Rd White Plains NY 10605-3602 Office: Cuddy & Feder & Worby 90 Maple Ave White Plains NY 10601-5105

FEDER, ROBERT, television and radio columnist; b. Chgo., May 17, 1956; s. Harold J. and Selma (Reisberg) F.; m. Janet Gail Elkins, June 16, 1985; 1 child, Emily Jacklyn. BS in Journalism, Northwestern U., 1978. Reporter, news editor Lerner Newspapers, Chgo., 1974-78, mng. editor, 1978-80; reporter Chgo. Sun-Times, 1980-83, TV/radio columnist, 1983—. Project cons. (TV documentary) Radio Faces, 1989; contbr. (spl. report) Ency. Britannica, 1983, World Book Ency., 1996. Recipient Page One award Chgo. Newspaper Guild, 1976. Mem. Soc. Profl. Journalists, Chgo. Headline Club, Chgo. Newspaper Guild, Northwestern Club of Chgo., Skokie Hist. Soc. Office: Chgo Sun-Times 401 N Wabash Ave Chicago IL 60611-5642

FEDER, ROBERT ELLIOT, psychiatrist; b. Detroit, July 8, 1951; s. Norman W. and Helen (Kadushin) F.; m. Marsha Susan Cooper; children: Daniel, Elana. BS with high honors, U. Mich., 1972; MD, U. Wash., 1977. Diplomate Am. Bd. Med. Examiners, Am. Bd. Psychiatry and Neurology. Resident in psychiatry Yale U., New Haven, 1981; assoc. psychiatrist Elmcrest Psychiat. Inst., Portland, Conn., 1980-81; med. dir. inpatient psychiatry Beverly (Mass.) Hosp., 1981-83; chief psychiatrist Matthew Thornton Health Plan, Nashua, N.H., 1983-86; courtesy staff Nashua Meml. Hosp., 1983—, St. Joseph's Hosp., Nashua, 1984—; attending staff Cath. Med. Ctr., Manchester, N.H., 1988—; med. dir. Psychiatric Inst. Cath. Med. Ctr., Manchester, N.H., 1995—; dir. outpatient svcs. Charter Brookside Hosp., Nashua, 1986-95; assoc. med. dir. Brookside Hosp., Nashua, 1993-95; pvt. practice psychiatry Manchester, 1995—; chmn. dept. psychiatry Nashua Meml. Hosp., 1988-93, chmn. credentials com., 1991-93. Contbr. articles in psychiatry to profl. jours. Recipient Exemplary Psychiatrist award Nat. Alliance for Mentally Ill, 1992, 94. Fellow Am. Psychiat. Assn.; mem. AMA, Am. Assn. Gen. Hosp. Psychiatrists, Physicians for Social Responsibility, N.H. Psychiat. Soc. (pres. 1995-96, chmn. pub. affairs 1985-95, mem. exec. com. 1985—, N.H. rep. to Am. Psychiat. Assn. assembly 1996—), Am. Psychiat. Assn. Arts Assn. (sec.-treas. 1985-87), Phi Beta Kappa, Phi Eta Sigma. Democrat. Avocations: hiking, skiing, computer art, stained glass, music. Office: 100 Mcgregor St Manchester NH 03102-3709

FEDER, SAUL E., lawyer; b. Bklyn., Oct. 8, 1943; s. Joseph Robert and Toby Feder; m. Marcia Carrie Weinblatt, Feb. 25, 1968; children: Howard Avram, Fayge Miriam, Tamar Miriam, Michael Elon, David Ben-Zion Aaron, Alexandra Rachel, Evan Daniel. BS, NYU, 1965; JD, Bklyn. Law Sch., 1968. Bar: N.Y. 1969, U.S. Ct. Appeals (2d cir.) 1969, U.S. Ct. Claims 1970, U.S. Customs Ct. 1972, U.S. Supreme Ct. 1972, U.S. Ct. Customs and Patent Appeals 1974. Mng. lawyer Queens Legal Services, Jamaica, N.Y., 1970-71; ptnr. Previte-Glasser-Feder & Farber, Jackson Heights, N.Y., 1972-73, Hein-Waters-Klein & Feder, Far Rockaway, N.Y., 1973-78, Regosin-Edwards-Stone & Feder, N.Y.C., 1979—; spl. investigator Bur. Election Frauds, Atty. Gen.'s Office, N.Y.C., 1976-77, spl. dep. atty. gen., 1969-70; arbitrator, consumer counsel small claims div. Civil Ct. City of N.Y., 1974—. Pres. Young Israel Briarwood, Queens, N.Y., 1978; chmn. polit. affairs com. Young Israel Staten Island, 1985—; rep. candidate State of N.Y. Assembly, Queens, 1976; chmn. Stat Pac Polit. Action Com., Young Israel Staten Island Pub. Affairs Com. Mem. N.Y. Bar Assn., Queens County Bar Assn. Nassau County Bar Assn., Am. Judges Assn., N.Y. Trial Lawyers Assn., Richmond County Bar Assn., Com. on Law and Pub. Affairs, Internat. Acad. Law & Sci., Am. Jud. Soc., Soc. Med. Jurisprudence, Am. Arbitration Assn. Republican. Home: 259 Ardmore Ave Staten Island NY 10314-4349 Office: Regosin Edwards Stone & Feder 225 Broadway Rm 515 New York NY 10007-3059

FEDERICI, WILLIAM VITO, newspaper reporter; b. Bklyn., June 22, 1931; s. Theodore and Margaret (DeMaio) F.; m. Arlene Ann McAuliffe, Oct. 1, 1955 (dec.); children: William Theodore, Robert Gerard. Student, Hofstra Coll., 1949-50, St. John's U., 1954-56. With N.Y. Daily News, 1950—, nat. corr., until 1965, spl. reporter, 1965-72, asst. city editor in charge investigations, 1975-79, Bklyn. editor, 1979—; dir. spl. projects Office Spl. State Prosecutor, N.Y.C., 1972-75; exec. dir. corp. affairs Bklyn. Union Gas Co., 1987—. Author series on child abuse which initiated N.Y. laws to protect children, 1969. Served with USN, 1950-54, Korea. Recipient several journalism awards, including George Polk award Long Island U., 1970, Sigma Delta Chi award for met. reporting, 1975.

FEDERING, ERIC K., congressional communications director, motion picture preservationist, lecturer; b. Bronx, N.Y., Feb. 10, 1960; s. Abraham M. and Eileen (Katz) F. BA with Distinction, George Washington U., 1982. Aide U.S. Dept. State, Washington, 1979-81; founder, dir. motion picture restoration effort MAD WORLD Campaign, Washington, 1982-91; press sec., speechwriter for mem. of congress Rep. Norman Y. Mineta, Washington, 1987-93; supr. press information ctr. Dem. Nat. Conv., N.Y.C., 1992; mgr. press info. ctr. ops. Dem. Nat. Conv., Chgo., 1996; dir. comm. Pub. Works and Transp. Com. U.S. Ho. of Reps., Washington, 1993-94, Dem. dir. comm. Transp. and Infrastructure Com., 1994-97; press sec. Senator Joseph I. Lieberman, Washington, 1997-99; dir. bus. pub. policy KPMG LLP, 1999—; freelance writer, 1982-87; contract writer Larsen-Pomada Lit. Agts., San Francisco, 1984-96, Farber Literacy Agy., N.Y., 1996—; advisor media and motion pictures The Lincoln Theatre Found., Washington, 1989-90; lectr. U. Queensland, Australia, Bond U., Australia, Australian Ctr. Am. Studies, East-West Ctr. Hawaii, 1992, U. Western Australia, Edith Cowan U., Australia, Curtin U., Australia, U. Melbourne, Australia, La Trobe U., Australia, Victoria U., Australia, U.S. Consulate, Melbourne, 1993, U.S. Consulate, Sydney, U.S. Embassy, Canberra, Finders U. So. Australia, 1995; mem. Com. for Econ. Devel. of Australia U. Tasmania, Australian Inst. of Internat. Affairs, James Cook U., 1996, Monash U. Australia, U.S.-Australia Bus. and Trade Coun., Com. for Econ. Devel. of Australia, Flinders U. So. Australia, 1998; congl. liaison to Smithsonian Instn. Bd. Regents, 1995. Press sec. to nat. co-chair Dukakis-Bentsen Presdl. Campaign, Washington, 1988. Recipient Commendation for Outstanding Achievement by Sec. of State, 1981. Mem. Phi Beta Kappa. Democrat. Avocations: sound recordings, motion pictures, theater restoration, photography.

FEDERMAN, ARTHUR, federal judge; b. 1951. Bankruptcy judge U.S. Bankruptcy Ct. (we. dist.) Mo., Kansas City, 1989—; adj. instr. U. Mo., Kansas City. Office: 903 US Courthouse 811 Grand Blvd Kansas City MO 64106-1904

FEDERMAN, DANIEL DAVID, medical educator, educational administrator, endocrinologist; b. N.Y.C., Apr. 16, 1928; m. Elizabeth Buckley; children: Lise, Carolyn. BA, Harvard U., 1949, MD, 1953. Diplomate Am. Bd. Internal Medicine. Instr. to prof. Harvard Med. Sch., Boston, 1961-72, prof. medicine and dean for students and alumni, 1977-92, Carl W. Walter prof. medicine and med. edn., dean med. edn., 1992—; chmn. medicine Stanford Med. Sch., Palo Alto, Calif., 1972-77; Carl W. Walter prof. medicine, med. edn., dean med. edn., 1992—. Author: med. textbook Abnormal Sexual Development, 1967; editor: med. textbook Scientific American Medicine. Master ACP (pres. Phila. 1982-83). Home: 1 Evergreen Way Belmont MA 02478-2127 Office: Harvard Med Sch Office of Dean 25 Shattuck St Boston MA 02115-6027*

FEDERMAN, RAYMOND, novelist, English and comparative literature educator; b. Paris, May 15, 1928; came to U.S., 1948, naturalized, 1953; s. Simon and Marguerite (Epstein) F.; m. Erica Hubscher, Sept. 13, 1960; 1 child, Simone Juliette. B.A., Columbia U., 1957; M.A., UCLA, 1958, Ph.D., 1963. Asst. prof. U. Calif.-Santa Barbara, 1959-64; assoc. prof. SUNY-Buffalo, 1964-68, prof. English and comparative lit., 1968—, Disting. Faculty prof., 1990—, Melodia E. Jones prof., 1994; vis. prof. U. Montreal, Que., Can., 1969-70, Hebrew U. Jerusalem, 1982-83. Author: Double Or Nothing, 1971 (Frances Steloff prize 1971), Take It or Leave It, 1976, The Voice in the Closet, 1979, The Twofold Vibration, 1982; Smiles on Washington Square, 1985 (Am. Book award 1986), To Whom It May Concern, 1990, Now Then, 1991, Critifiction, 1993, The Supreme Indecision of The Writer, 1996, La Fourrure de Ma Tante Rachel, 1996, Loose Shoes, 1999. Served with U.S. Army, 1951-54, Korea. Guggenheim fellow, 1966-67; Camargo Found. fellow, Cassis, France, 1977; Fulbright fellow, Israel, 1982-83; Nat. Endowment for Arts fellow, 1985. Mem. Samuel Beckett Soc. (life hon. trustee), PEN Am. Ctr., Fiction Collective (co.-dir. 1978-81), Phi Beta Kappa. Democrat. Jewish. Club: Bernardo Heights Country Club (San Diego). Avocations: golf, tennis, jazz. Office: SUNY Dept English Clemens Hall Buffalo NY 14260

FEDERS, SID, journalist, television producer; b. Pitts., Apr. 7, 1941; s. Jerome and Jean Federbusch; m. Susan B. Karp, Aug. 7, 1966; children: Stephen, Penny. BA in Journalism, Duquesne U., 1962. Assignment editor, prodr. CBS News, Washington, 1969-74, foreign editor, 1974-78, prodr. Sunday Morning with Charles Kuralt, 1978-79, prodr. writer NBC Nightly News, NBC Mag. with David Brinkly, Prime Time, 1979-84, sr. prodr., dir., writer numerous prime time specials, weekly newsmags., 1985-87, exec. prodr., dir. writer, 1988—; pres., exec. prodr. Sid Feders Prodns., Inc., 1992—. With U.S. Army, 1963-64. Recipient Emmy award, George Foster Peabody award, Dupont award. Mem. Dirs. Guild of Am., Writers Guild of Am. Office: Sid Feders Prodns Inc 209 E 56th St Fl 4 New York NY 10022-3705

FEDORJAKA, KATHY, university basketball coach; b. Groton, Conn.; m. Frank Fedorjaka; 1 child, Matthew Ryan. BA in English, Fairfield U., 1990; MS in Edn., Bucknell U., 1992. Asst coach Bucknell U., 1992-93, head coach, 1997—; head coach Conn. Coll., 1993-94, Bloomsburg Coll., 1994-97; head coach women's basketball Bucknell U., Lewisburg, Pa., 1997—. Office: Bucknell Univ Womens Basketball Office Davis Gym Lewisburg PA 17837*

FEDOROCHKO, WILLIAM, JR., retired army officer, policy analyst; b. Bayonne, N.J., Sept. 6, 1940; s. William and Helen (Dinis) F.; m. Sandra L. Clements, Dec. 10, 1966; 1 child, Sharon. BA in Econs., Washington and Jefferson Coll., 1962; MA in Econs., U. Pitts., 1971. Commd. 2d lt. U.S. Army, 1962, advanced through grades to brig. gen., 1989; platoon leader, staff officer 14th Armored Cav. Rgt., Fed. Republic Germany, 1962-64; staff officer Dept. Army, Washington, 1973-76; comdr. 1st Armored Div. Materiel Mgmt. Ctr., 501st Supply and Transport Bn., Fed. Republic Germany, 1976-80; student Def. Systems Mgmt. Coll., 1980, Indsl. Coll. Armed Forces, 1981; spl. asst. for joint activities Office of Comdr., Army Materiel Command, Alexandria, Va., 1981-83; chief acquisition and support program analysis div. Office Chief of Staff Army, Washington, 1983-84; comdr. 13th Support Command, Ft. Hood, Tex., 1984-87; spl. asst. Office Under Sec. Def. for Acquisition, Washington, 1987-88, dep. dir. program integration, 1988-90; dep. dir. force structure and resources Joint Staff, J-8, Washington, 1990-93; ret., 1993; sr. policy analyst RAND, Washington, 1993-94; sr. fellow Logistics Mgmt. Inst., McLean, Va., 1994—. Decorated Legion of Merit with 4 oak leaf clusters, Def. D.S.M. with oak leaf cluster. Mem. Assn. U.S. Army, Assn. Quartermasters. Baptist. Avocations: golf, tennis. Home: 11404 Stonewall Jackson Dr Spotsylvania VA 22553-4607 Office: Logistics Mgmt Inst 2000 Corporate Rdg Mc Lean VA 22102-7805*

FEDOROFF, NINA VSEVOLOD, research scientist, consultant, educator; b. Cleve., Apr. 9, 1942; d. Vsevolod N. and Olga S. (Snegireff) Stacy; m. T. Patrick Gaganidze, June 18, 1966 (div. 1978); children: Natasha, Kyr; m. M. Broyles, 1990 (div. 1997). B.S., Syracuse U., 1966; Ph.D., Rockefeller U., 1972. Asst. mgr. transl. bur. Biol. Abstracts, Phila., 1962-63; flutist Syracuse (N.Y.) Symphony Orch., 1964-66; acting asst. prof. UCLA, 1972-74; postdoctoral fellow UCLA and Carnegie Inst. Washington, Los Angeles and Balt., 1974-78; staff scientist Carnegie Inst. Washington, Balt., 1978-95; dir., biotechnol. inst. Pa. State U., 1995—, Willaman prof. of life scis., 1995—; dir. Life Scis. Consortium, Pa. State U., 1996—; prof. dept. biology John Hopkins U., 1979-95; mem. devel. biology panel NSF, Washington, 1979-80; sci. adv. panel Office of Tech. Assessment, Congress, Washington, 1979-80; recombinant DNA adv. com. NIH, Bethesda, Md., 1980-84; sci. adv. com. Japanese Human Frontier Sci., 1988; sci adv. com. Competitive Rsch. Grants Office, USDA; mem. commn. on life scis., basic biology bd. NRC, NAS, 1984-90; bd. dirs. Genetics Soc. Am.; mem. bd. overseers Harvard U., 1988-91; trustee BIOSIS, Phila., 1990-96; mem. NAS Coun., 1991-94; dir. Internat. Sci. Found., 1992-93; mem. adv. com. Directorate for Biol. Scis., 1994-97; chmn., bd. dirs. Sigma-Aldrich Corp., 1996. Editor: Gene, 1981-84; editor, bd. rev. editors Sci., 1985; mem. sci. adv. bd. The Plant Jour., 1991—; editor Perspectives in Biology and Medicine, 1991—, Procs. Nat. Acad. Sci., 1996—; book editor various publs.; contbr. chpts. to books, articles to profl. jours. Recipient merit award NIH, 1990; grantee NSF and USDA, 1979-84, NIH, 1984—, NSF, 1992—, NASA, 1997—. Mem. AAAS, NAS (editor procs. 1995—), Am. Acad. Arts and Scis., Phi Beta Kappa (vis. scholar 1984-85), Sigma Xi (McGovern Sci. and Soc. medal 1997). Avocations: chamber music, gardening, skiing, tennis, flying. Home: 2398 Shagbark Ct State College PA 16803-3367 Office: Biotechnol Inst Pa State U University Park PA 16802

FEDOROV, SERGEI, hockey player; b. Pskov, Russia, Dec. 13, 1969. Forward Detroit Red Wings. Recipient ice hockey Silver medal Olympic Games, Nagano, Japan, 1998. Avocations: golfing, boating, travel. Office: Detroit Red Wings 600 Civic Center Dr Detroit MI 48226-4419*

FEE, WILLARD EDWARD, JR., otolaryngologist; b. Portchester, N.Y., June 10, 1943; s. Willard E. and Jane Frances (Cromwell) F.; m. Caroline Fee, June 13, 1965; children: Heather, Adam. BS cum laude, U. San Francisco, 1965; MD magna cum laude, U. Colo., 1969. Intern Harbor Gen. Hosp., Torrance, Calif., 1969-70; resident in gen. surgery Wadsworth VA Hosp., L.A., 1970-71; resident in head and neck surgery UCLA Sch. Medicine, 1971-74; asst. prof. Stanford (Calif.) U. Med. Ctr., 1974-80, assoc. prof., chmn., 1980-86, prof. chmn. in otolaryngology, 1986—, Edward C. & Amy H. Sewall prof., 1996—; dir. Am. Bd. of Otolaryngology, Houston, 1985—; chmn. med. sch. faculty senate Stanford U., 1992-94. Editl. bd. Archives in Otolaryngology, Chgo., 1984-95; contbr. numerous articles to profl. jours. Mem. Collegium ORLAS-US (chmn. 1995—), Paul H. Ward Soc., Inc. (pres. 1988-89), Am. Soc. Head and Neck Surgery (pres. 1989-90), Am. Acad. Otolaryngology and Head and Neck Surgery, Calif. Soc. Otolaryngology (pres. 1995—), Alpha Omega Alpha. Home: 27299 Ursula Ln Los Altos CA 94022-3222 Office: Stanford Univ Med Ctr Divn Otolaryngology Edwards R135 300 Pasteur Stanford CA 94305-5328

FEELEY, HENRY JOSEPH, JR. (HANK FEELEY), artist, former advertising agency executive; b. Cambridge, Mass., July 9, 1940; s. Henry Joseph and Florence Patricia (O'Connor) F.; m. Mary Diane Dudenhoefer, May 14, 1966; children: Kathleen Anne, Mary Patricia, Henry Joseph III, James Brian. BA, Coll. Holy Cross, 1963; postgrad., Northwestern U., 1966, Sch. Art Inst. Chgo., 1994; PMD, Harvard U., 1976. With Leo Burnett Co., Inc., Chgo., 1965—, v.p., 1973-76, sr. v.p., 1976-82, exec. v.p., 1982—, vice chmn. bd. dirs., 1985-86; chmn., chief exec. officer Leo Burnett Internat., 1986-92; vice chmn. Leo Burnett, Inc., 1992-93, cons., 1993—. Bd. dirs. Oxbow Sch. Art, Mich., Allendale Sch., Chgo., Am. Ireland Fund, Jr. Achievement, Chgo., Loyola Acad., Chgo.; mem. Irish Fellowship Chgo., 1982—. Lt. USN, 1963-65. Mem. Chgo. Yacht Club, Bob O'Link Golf Club, Johns Island Club (Vero Beach, Fla.), Skokie (Ill.) Country Club. Republican. Roman Catholic. Home: 1501 N State Pkwy Chicago IL 60610-1676

FEELEY, JOHN PAUL, retired paper company executive; b. Akron, Ohio, July 17, 1918; s. John Joseph and Pauline (Wallace) F.; m. Patricia; children: Joanne, Suzanne. B.S. in Bus. Adminstrn, U. Akron, 1941. Civilian with Dept. of Navy, 1946-56; chief Navy Mgmt. Office, Pentagon, 1955-56; sec.-treas. Am. Colortype Corp., 1956-57; treas. Rapid Am. Corp., 1958-59; asst. controller Remington Rand Co., 1960-62; v.p., dir. APS Paper Corp., 1963-64; v.p., dir. Allied Paper Inc., Kalamazoo, 1964-72, sr. v.p., 1972-84. Served to lt. comdr. USNR, World War II. Home: 3619 57th Avenue Dr W Bradenton FL 34210-3522

FEELEY, MALCOLM M., law educator, political scientist; b. North Conway, N.H., Nov. 28, 1942; s. John Aloysius and Mildred (McCollum) F.; divorced; children: Jacob, Miriam, Amin. B.A., Austin Coll., 1964; M.A., U. Minn., 1966, Ph.D., 1969. Asst. prof. NYU, N.Y.C., 1968-72; fellow, lectr. Yale U., New Haven, Conn., 1972-77; prof. U. Wis.-Madison, 1977-84; prof. law U. Calif.-Berkeley, 1984—; v.p. Silbert-Feeley Assn., New Haven, 1975-83; editorial advisor Longman Inc., N.Y.C., 1979—. Author: The Process is the Punishment, 1979, The Policy Dilemma, 1981, Court Reform on Trial, 1983, Judicial Policy - Making, 1998; Editor: American Constitutional Law, 1985, Judicial Policy Making, 1998. Recipient Silver Gavel award ABA, 1980, cert. merit ABA, 1984; Hubert Humphrey fellow U. Minn., 1968. Mem. Law and Soc. Assn. (trustee 1975-80), Am. Polit. Sci. Assn. Democrat. Jewish. Avocations: canoeing; hiking; reading. Office: U Calif Sch Law Boalt Hall Ctr Study Law Society Berkeley CA 94720

FEEMAN, JAMES FREDERIC, chemist, consultant; b. June 1, 1922; s. Edwin L. and Florence A. (Wenrich) F.; m. June Permilla Zartman, Apr. 12, 1947; children: James Frederic, Jane Elizabeth, Joan Ann, John Harry. BS,

Muhlenberg Coll., 1945; MS, Lehigh U., 1947, PhD in Chemistry, 1949. Rsch. assoc. Ohio State U. Rsch. Found., Columbus, 1949-50, Althouse Chem. Co., Reading, Pa., 1950-54; rsch. assoc. Crompton & Knowles Corp., Reading, 1954-68, asst. dir. rsch., 1972-74, dir. rsch., 1974-80, v.p. R&D, 1980-86, sr. scientist, 1986-89; cons. Lawrence Livermore Nat. Lab., 1989-93, Lexmark Internat. Inc., 1990—. Holder 35 patents in field; author: (with others) The Chemistry of Synthetic Dyes, Vol. VIII, 1978; contbr. articles to sci. jours.; rschr. on textile, paper, jet dyes for computer printer, laser dyes, leather dyes; inventor first neutral dyeing series of dyes for nylon having outstanding properties. Instr. CD, 1955-65; dir. Reading-Berks Sci. Fair, 1955-70. With Signal Corps, U.S. Army, 1942-46, ETO, PTO. Muhlenberg Coll. scholar, 1940-43; Lehigh U. fellow, 1947-49. Fellow AAAS, Am. Inst. Chemists; mem. Am. Chem. Soc. (sect. chair 1967-68, nat. councillor 1973-75), Am. Assn. Textile Chemists and Colorists, N.Y. Acad. Scis., Reading Chemists Club, Torch Club (pres. 1977-78, sec. 1987—), Rotary (West Reading-Wyomissing), Sigma Xi. Republican. Lutheran. Avocations: art, woodworking, photography. Home and Office: 6 Oriole Dr Reading PA 19610-2841

FEENANE, SISTER MARY ALICE, principal. Prin. Gwynedd Mercy Acad., Gwynedd Valley, Pa., 1981—. Recipient Blue Ribbon Sch. award, 1990-91. Office: Gwynedd Mercy Acad Sumneytown Pike Gwynedd Valley PA 19437

FEENEY, DON JOSEPH, JR., psychologist; b. Greenville, N.C., Jan. 17, 1948; s. Don Joseph Sr. and Louise (Saieed) F.; 1 child, Kelly Lynn. BA, Colgate U., 1971; MA, Gov.'s State U., 1973; PhD, Loyola U., Chgo., 1979. Registered psychologist, Ill., Ind.; cert. addictions counselor. Clin. dir. Champaign (Ill.) Coun. on Alcoholism, 1976-79; pvt. practice psychology, hypnotherapy, family services Downers Grove, Ill., 1979—; pvt. practice psychology, hypnotherapy and family svcs. Dangerous Drugs Com., Chgo., 1979-80; psychologist Tri-City Mental Health Ctr., East Chicago, Ind., 1980-82; psychologist alcohol treatment program Christ Hosp., Oak Lawn, Ill., 1982—; cons. Cons. Psychol. Svcs. PC, Downers Grove, Ill., 1985—; ceo Cons. Psychol. Svcs. PC, Downers Grove, 1998—; chmn. adv. coun. on alcoholism Govs. State U., University Park, Ill., 1979-82; devel., presenter self-hypnosis and wellness programs on smoking, weight control and chem. abuse. Author: Entrancing Relationships: Exploring the Hypnotic Framework of Addictive Relationships, 1999; contbr. articles to profl. jours.; guest cons. to nat. talk shows, Oprah Winfrey, Jerry Springer, Jenny Jones, others. Loyola U. fellow, 1976. Mem. APA, Ill. Psychol. Assn. Roman Catholic. Avocations: chess, tennis, weightlifting, jogging, reading. Office: Cons Psychol Svcs PC 6900 Main St Ste 54 Downers Grove IL 60516-3455

FEENEY, FLOYD FULTON, legal educator; b. Franklin, Ind., Sept. 26, 1933; s. Burla L. and Ona Marie (McMillin) F.; m. Peggy Ann Ballard, June 15, 1956; children: Elizabeth, Linda. B.S. in History with honors, Davidson Coll., 1955; LL.B., NYU, 1960. Bar: N.C. 1960, D.C. 1961. Law clk. U.S. Supreme Ct., 1961-62; spl. asst. to solicitor Dept. Labor, 1962-63; dep. spl. counsel Pres.'s Com. on Equal Employment Opportunity, 1963; asst. dir. Pres.'s Crime Commn., 1966-67; spl. asst. to adminstr. AID, 1963-68; prof. law U. Calif.-Davis, 1968—; mem. Calif. Atty. Gen.'s Research Adv. Council, 1985-90; cons. Nat. Ctr. for State Cts., Nat. Inst. Justice, Brit. Home Office. Author: The Police and Pretrial Release, 1982, (with Roger Baron) Juvenile Diversion Through Family Counseling, 1976, (with Dill and Weir) Arrests Without Conviction, 1983, (with Philip Dubois) Lawmaking with Initiative, 1998. Served to 1st lt. U.S. Army, 1956-58. Fulbright scholar, 1995-96; recipient Pepperdine award, 1978. Mem. ABA, Am. Assn. Law Schs., Am. Law Inst., D.C. Bar Assn., N.C. Bar Assn., Assn. for Criminal Justice Research Calif. Home: 1228 Colby Dr Davis CA 95616-1719 Office: U Calif Sch Law Davis CA 95616

FEENEY, JOAN N., judge. BA in French and Govt., Conn. Coll., 1975; MA, Amherst Coll.; JD, Suffolk Univ. Law Sch., 1978. Law clk. to Judge Harold Lavien U.S. Bankruptcy Ct. Mass., 1978-79, law clk. to Judge James N. Gabriel, 1978-79, 82-86; assoc. Feeney & Freeley, Boston, 1979-82; assoc., then ptnr. Hanify & King P.C., Boston, 1986-92; bankruptcy judge U.S. Bankruptcy Ct. Mass., Boston, 1992—; mem. Suffolk Univ. Law Review, 1976-78; editor Suffolk Transnational Journal, 1977-78, Suffolk Voluntary Defenders, 1977-78, Volunteer Lawyer's Project. Mem. Mass. Assn. of Women Lawyers. Office: Thomas O'Neill Federal Bldg 10 Causeway St Rm 1101 Boston MA 02222-1009

FEENEY, JOHN ROBERT, banker; b. Newark, Feb. 26, 1950; s. P. John and Elizabeth (Podda) F.; m. Judi Tomkowit, June 22, 1974; children—Michael, Ryan, Mark. B.S., U. Del., 1972; M.B.A., Seton Hall U., 1977. Asst. sec., also various other positions Irving Trust Co., N.Y.C., 1972-76; asst. sec., mgr. profit planning Irving Bank Corp., N.Y.C., 1976-78; controller, v.p. Ocean County Nat. Bank, Point Pleasant, N.J., 1978-81; controller, sr. v.p. Ocean County Nat. Bank, 1981-83; sr. v.p., CFO, The Summit Bancorporation, N.J., 1983-85, exec. v.p., CFO, 1985-93, sr. exec. v.p., CFO, 1994-96; exec. v.p. Summit Bancorp, N.J., 1996—. Republican. Roman Catholic. Avocations: surfing, basketball, golf. Home: 249 Williamsburg Dr Shrewsbury NJ 07702-4564 Office: Summit Bancorp 301 Carnegie Ctr Princeton NJ 08540-6227

FEENEY, LYNDA JEAN, secondary education educator; b. Boston, June 6, 1966; d. William B. and Jean Marie (Walsh) F. BS, Springfield Coll., 1988; MEd, Lesley Coll., 1990. Educator Fairfax County Pub. Sch., Springfield, Va., 1990-96, Malden (Mass.) Pub. Sch., 1996—. Mem. ASCD, Coun. for Exceptional Children (presenter). Office: Malden Middle Sch 77 Salem St Malden MA 02148-5228

FEENEY, MARK, newspaper editor; b. Winchester, Mass., July 28, 1957; s. Henry Patrick and Agnes Patricia (Carney) F.; m. Claire Silvers; 1 child, William. BA, Harvard U., 1979. Researcher The Boston Globe, 1979, data base mgr., 1980, asst. book editor, 1982, book editor, 1993-94, editor Focus sect., 1991; staff writer Boston Globe Mag., 1993-94, editor Focus sect., 1994-95, staff reporter, 1995—. Contbr. articles to The New Republic, Commonweal, Washington Monthly, L.A. Times, other publs. Mem. Nat. Book Critics Circle (v.p. 1986-89). Democrat. Roman Catholic. Home: 26 Mead St Cambridge MA 02140-2014 Office: The Boston Globe 135 Morrissey Blvd Boston MA 02125-3338

FEENEY, MARY KATHERINE O'SHEA, retired public health nurse; b. Niagara Falls, N.Y., July 10, 1934; d. James T. and Mary Elizabeth (Woodside) O'Shea; m. Gerald E. Feeney, Apr. 27, 1957; children: Patricia, Elizabeth, Susan, Kathleen. BSN, Niagara U., 1956; MS in Mgmt., SUNY, Binghamton, 1981. RN, N.Y.; hypnotherapist; Assessment Modified Reflexology for Nurses. Pub. health nurse Herkimer County (N.Y.) Pub. Health Nursing Svc.; ret.; past coord. Herkimer County Long Term Health Care; bd. dirs. Oneida/Herkimer Coalition for Tobacco Control. Home: 146 State Route 169 Little Falls NY 13365-5017

FEENEY, ROBERT EARL, research biochemist; b. Oak Park, Ill., Aug. 30, 1913; s. Bernard Cyril and Loreda (McKee) F.; m. Mary Alice Waller, Dec. 3, 1954; children: Jane, Elizabeth. Student, Rochester (Minn.) Jr. Coll., 1932-33; BS in Chemistry, Northwestern U., 1938; MS in Biochemistry, U. Wis., 1939, PhD in Biochemistry, 1942. Diplomate Am. Bd. Nutrition. Rsch. assoc. Harvard U. Med. Sch., Boston, 1942-43; rsch. biochemist USDA Lab., Albany, Calif., 1946-53; prof. chemistry U. Nebr., Lincoln, 1953-60; prof. dept. food sci. and tech. U. Calif., Davis, 1960-84, prof. emeritus, rsch. biochemist, 1984—, interim dir. protein structure lab., 1990-91; bd. dirs. Creative Chemistry Cons., Davis. Author: (with Richard Allison) Evolutionary Biochemistry of Proteins, 1969, (with Gary Means) Chemical Modification of Proteins, 1971, Professor On the Ice, 1974, Polar Journeys, 1998, The Role of Food and Nutrition in Early Exploration, 1998; editor: (with John Whitaker) Protein Tailoring for Food and Medical Uses, 1986. Capt. wound rsch. team M.C., U.S. Army, 1943-46. Recipient Superior Svc. award USDA, 1953, ; Feeney Peak, Antarctica named in his honor U.S. Bd. on Geog. Names, 1968. Mem. Am. Chem. Soc. (chmn. div. agrl. and food chemistry, 1978-79, award for disting. svc. in agrl. and food chemistry, 1978), Am. Soc. for Biochemistry and Molecular Biology, Inst. of Food Technologists, Explorers Club. Democrat. Avocations: polar sci., polar exploration author. Home: 780 Elmwood Dr Davis CA 95616-3517 Office: U Calif Dept Food Sci and Tech Cruess Hall Davis CA 95616

FEENY, MARGARET A., English language educator, real estate agent; b. Phila., Nov. 14, 1943; d. John J. and Catherine (Coll) O'Connell; m. William S. Feeny, Feb. 8, 1969; children: Norah Catherine, Edwin Joseph, Catherine O'Connell. BA, Chestnut Hill Coll., 1965; postgrad., various univs. Cert. English tchr., Pa. Elem. tchr. Norwood Acad., Phila.; jr. H.S. English tchr. Colonial Sch. Dist., Plymouth Meeting, Pa.; real estate agt. Century 21 Gallagher Scanlon, Blue Bell, Pa.; English tchr. East Norriton Mid. Sch., Norristown, Pa., Roosevelt Annex of Norristown Area H.S., Norristown, Pa., Eisenhower Mid. Sch., Norristown, Pa., Norristown Area H.S.; faculty sponsor YES-Youth Vol. at Norristown Area H.S., 1996—. Mem. St. Titus Roman Cath. Ch., Norristown, Hist. Soc. Montqom County, Norristown, 1985-92, Preservation N.C., 1996—. Recipient grant NEH, 1986, 89. Mem. Edn. Assn. Norristown Area (union rep. 1985-90, 96—). Democrat. Avocations: reading, travel, handcrafts, lampmaking, sewing. Office: Norristown Area HS 1900 Eagle Dr Norristown PA 19403-2700

FEERICK, JOHN DAVID, dean, lawyer; b. N.Y.C., July 12, 1936; s. John D. and Mary J. F.; m. Emalie Platt, Aug. 25, 1962; children: Maureen, Margaret, Jean, Rosemary, John, William. B.S., Fordham U., 1958, LL.B., 1961; hon. degree, Coll. New Rochelle, 1991. Bar: N.Y. 1961. Assoc. Skadden, Arps, Slate, Meagher & Flom, N.Y.C., 1961-68; partner Skadden, Arps, Slate, Meagher & Flom, 1968-82; dean Fordham U. Sch. Law, 1982—. Author: From Failing Hands: The Story of Presidential Succession, 1965, The 25th Amendment, 1976; co-author: The Vice Presidents of the United States, 1967, NLRB Representation Elections-Law, Practice and Procedure, 1980; also articles; editor-in-chief Fordham Law Rev., 1960-61. Chmn. N.Y. State Commn. Govt. Integrity, 1987-90. Recipient Eugene J. Keefe award Fordham U. Law Sch., 1975, 85, spl. award Fordham U. Law Rev. Assn., 1977. Fellow Am. Bar Found.; mem. ABA (chmn. spl. com. election law and voter participation 1976-79, spl. award 1966), N.Y. State Bar Assn. (chmn. com. fed. constrn. 1979-83, exec. com. 1985-87), Assn. Bar City N.Y. (v.p. 1986-87, pres. 1992-94), Am. Arbitration Assn. (chair exec. com. 1995, chair Fund for Modern Cts. 1995—), Fordham U. Law Sch. Alumni Assn. (dir. 1972—, medal of achievement 1980), Phi Beta Kappa. *

FEES, NANCY FARDELIUS, special education educator; b. Santa Monica, Calif., Mar. 25, 1950; d. Carl August and Dodi Emma (Hedenschau) Fardelius; m. Paul Rodger Fees, June 4, 1971; children: Evelyn Wyoming, Nelson August. BS, Mills Coll., 1971; MA in Edn., Idaho State U., 1975. Cert. tchr., Calif., Idaho, Wyo., R.I. Specialist curriculum mgmt. Barrington (R.I.) High Sch., 1975-81; coordinator learning skills ctr. Northwest Community Coll., Powell, Wyo., 1982-84, instr., 1985—; pres. Children's Resource Ctr., 1985-89, bd. dirs., 1983-89, 91—. Editor (with others) The Great Entertainer, 1984. Vol. Buffalo Bill Hist. Ctr., Cody, Wyo., 1981—; mem. Centennial Com., Cody, 1983; mem. parent's adv. com. Livingston Sch., 1989-92, chmn., 1991-92; dir. Christian Edn. Christ Episcopal Ch., 1995—. Mem. Council Exceptional Children, Assn. Children with Learning Disabilities, Council Adminstrs. of Spl. Edn. Democrat. Episcopalian. Home: 1718 Wyoming Ave Cody WY 82414-3320

FEFFER, GERALD ALAN, lawyer; b. Washington, Apr. 24, 1942; s. Louis Charles and Elsie (Glick) F.; children: Andrew, John, Keith. BA with honors, Lehigh U., 1964; JD, U. Va., 1967. Bar: N.Y. 1968, D.C. 1980. Assoc. Mudge, Rose, Guthrie & Alexander, N.Y.C., 1967-71; asst. U.S. atty. So. Dist. N.Y., 1971-76, asst. chief criminal div., 1975-76; ptnr. Kostelanetz & Ritholz, N.Y.C., 1976-79; dep. asst. atty. gen. tax div. Dept. Justice, Washington, 1979-81; ptnr. Steptoe & Johnson, Washington, 1981-86, Williams & Connolly, Washington, 1986—. Mem. editl. bd. Busniess Crimes Bulletin: Compliance and Litigation, Health Care Fraud and Abuse Newsletter; contbr. articles to profl. jours. Fellow Am. Coll. Tax Counsel, Am. Coll. Trial Lawyers; mem. ABA (criminal justice litigation and taxation sects.), Nat. Inst. on Criminal Tax Fraud (chmn.), Nat. Assn. Criminal Def. Lawyers. Home: 3000 Garrison St NW Washington DC 20008-1032 Office: Williams & Connolly 725 12th St NW Washington DC 20005-5901

FEFFERMAN, CHARLES LOUIS, mathematics educator; b. Washington, Apr. 18, 1949; s. Arthur Stanley and Liselott Ruth (Stern) F.; m. Julie Anne Albert, Feb. 1975; children: Nina Heidi, Elaine Marie. BS, U. Md., 1966, hon. doctorate, 1979; PhD, Princeton U., 1969; hon. doctorate, Knox Coll., 1981, Bar-Ilan U., Israel, 1985, U. Madrid (Autonoma), 1990. Instr. math. Princeton (N.J.) U., 1969-70, prof. math., 1974-97, grad. dir. dept. math., 1997-99; mem. faculty U. Chgo., 1970-74, prof. math., 1971-74; dept. chmn. Princeton (N.J.) U., 1999—. Author research papers. Recipient Salem prize for outstanding work in fourier analysis by young mathematician, 1978, Alan T. Waterman award, 1978, Fields medal Internat. Cong. Mathematicians, 1978, 84. Mem. Nat. Acad. Scis., Am. Math. Soc., Am. Acad. Arts and Scis. Home: 234 Clover Ln Princeton NJ 08540-4051 Office: Princeton U Math Dept 1102 Fine Hall Washington Rd Princeton NJ 08544*

FEFFERMAN, HILBERT, lawyer, government official; b. N.Y.C., June 5, 1913; s. Jacob and Sarah F.; m. Helen Libby Relkin, June 16, 1940. BS, NYU, 1934; LLB, Harvard U., 1937. Bar: N.Y. 1938, U.S. Supreme Ct. 1953. Pvt. practice N.Y.C., 1938-41; atty. U.S. Housing and Home Fin. Agy., Washington, 1941-59, asst. gen. counsel for legislation, 1960-62, assoc. gen. counsel for ops., 1962-67; chief legislative counsel HUD, Washington, 1967-72; cons. Housing and Devel. Legislation, Bethesda, Md., 1973—; lectr., vis. prof. city planning MIT, Cambridge, Mass., 1973-76. Contbr. articles to profl. jours. Recipient Disting. Svc. award HUD, 1968. Home and Office: 5661 Bent Branch Rd Bethesda MD 20816-1049

FEGAN, JEFFREY P., airport executive. BS in Geography, Frostburg U.; M in City Planning, Ga. Inst. Tech.; advanced airport mgmt. course, Internat. Aviation Mgmt. Tng. Inst., Montreal. Aviation cons., 1978-83; noise abatement officer Westchester County Airport, N.Y., 1983-84; chief planner Dallas/Ft. Worth Internat. Airport Bd., 1984, asst. dir., dir. planning and engring., 1989-93, dep. exec. dir. fin. and adminstrn., 1993-94, exec. dir., chief adminstr., exec. officer, 1994—. Mem. Airports Coun. Internat.-NA Environ. Affairs Com., Internat. Civil Airports Assn.-Passenger Facilitation World Com., Am. Assn. Airport Execs., Am. Planning Assn., Am. Inst. Cert. Planners. Office: DFW Int'l Airport Adminstrn PO Drawer 619428 Dallas TX 75261-4928*

FEGAN, MARTINA KRINER, secondary education educator; b. Chambersburg, Pa., Aug. 27, 1950; d. Robert Eugene and Betty Lou (Dixon) Kriner; m. Larry Frank Witmer, June 27, 1971; children: Jennifer Elizabeth, Annisa Caroline, Mary Rebecca; m. James Elwood Fegan Jr. BS in Edn., Pa. State U., 1971. Cert. tchr., Pa., Masters equivalency cert. English tchr. Abington (Pa.) Jr. H.S., 1972-74, Greencastle (Pa.) Sch. Dist., 1974-75; regional sales mgr. Creative Expressions, Chambersburg, Pa., 1977-86; asst. exec. dir. Greater Chambersburg C. of C., 1986-91; English tchr. Tuscarora Sch. Dist., Mercersburg, Pa., 1993—; adv. bd. mem. Pa. State U. Monto Alto, 1990-91. Mem. Pa. Holocaust Edn. Task Force, 1998—. Recipient Athena award, C. of C., 1990, Outstanding English Educator award Pa. Coun. Tchrs. English and Lang. Arts, 1997; tchg. grantee Lifetouch, 1996-97. Mem. Nat. Coun. Tchrs. English, Pa. Coun. Tchrs. English, Tuscarora Ednl. Found. (chmn. bd. 1996-97). Presbyterian. Avocations: needlework, travel, reading, antiques. Office: James Buchanan High Sch 4773 Fort Loudon Rd Mercersburg PA 17236-9698

FEGELY, EUGENE LEROY, retired humanities educator; b. Allentown, Pa., Dec. 10, 1930; s. Leroy Tracy and Viola Eliza (Sterner) F.; m. Margaret Ann Maconaghy, Sept. 18, 1954; children: Barbara, Laura, Hugh. BS in Edn., Temple U., Phila., 1956, MS in Edn., 1960. Cert. prin., tchr., edn. specialist. Tchr. Bucks County C.C., Newtown, Pa., 1970-78; instr. Craven C. C., New Bern, N.C., 1988—; stage mgr., actor Bucks County Playhouse, New Hope, Pa., 1984-86, various dinner theaters, Pa., N.Y., N.J., N.C., 1984—; asst. to producer-dir. Worthy is the Lamb, Swansboro, N.C., 1988; pres. Imagers, Inc., Langhorne, Pa., 1984-90; cons., advisor various ednl. assns., schs., Pa., N.J., N.C., 1970—. Author: Best of the Least, 1973; editor: Temple PDK, 1960-70, Rebel Rouser, 1995—; N.C. editor SERA Jour., 1990—; contbr. articles to profl. jours. Recipient Citation, Pa. Ho. of Reps., Harrisburg, 1987. Mem. NEA (life), Actors Equity, Pa. State Edn. Assn. (life, pres. 1967-68, Plaque 1968), Phi Delta Kappa (life, area coord. 1970-78, plaque 1978). Republican. Methodist. Avocations: amateur radio, photography, golf, barbershop quartet singing. Home: 115 Randomwood Ln New Bern NC 28562-9556 Office: PO Box 13311 New Bern NC 28561-3311

FEGLEY, KENNETH ALLEN, systems engineering educator; b. Mont Clare, Pa., Feb. 14, 1923; s. Henry Stanley and Bertha (Malone) F.; m. Virginia Ruth Weaver, Sept. 1, 1951; children: Alan Donald, John David, Paul Andrew. BSEE, U. Pa., 1947, MSEE, 1950, PhD, 1955. Instr. Moore Sch. Elec. Engring., U. Pa., Phila., 1947-53, assoc., 1953-55, asst. prof., 1955-58, assoc. prof., 1958-66, prof. elec. engring., 1966-72; prof. sys. engring. U. Pa., Phila., 1972-90, chmn. dept. sys. engring., 1972-75, chmn. dept. sys., 1986-93, Joseph Moore prof. sys., 1990-93, Joseph Moore prof. emeritus sys., 1993—; cons. U.S. Army, Phila., Dover, N.J., 1955-85, USN, Phila., 1970-86. Contbr. numerous articles to tech. jours. and chpts. to books. With USN, 1944-46. Fellow IEEE, AAAS; mem. Am. Soc. Engring. Edn., Masons, AAUP, Sigma Xi, Eta Kappa Nu, Tau Beta Pi, Sigma Tau. Republican. Presbyterian. Office: U Pa Dept Systems Engring Philadelphia PA 19104-6315

FEHER, STEVE JOSEPH KENT, design engineer, research developer; b. Honolulu, Mar. 29, 1950; s. Joseph and Lillian Elizabeth (Waller) F. Ptnr., chief engr. Charger Hawaii, Honolulu, 1975-77, Transitron, Honolulu, 1977-84, EVR, Inc., Honolulu, 1985-88; chmn., chief engr. Feher Design, Inc., Honolulu, 1985—; proprietor Feher Rsch. Co., 1991—. Patents for variable temperature seat, mattress and blanket. Mem. Soc. Automotive Engrs. (treas. Honolulu chpt. 1977-78). Republican. Avocations: cars, cooking, the environ. Home and Office: Feher Design Ste 1505 1 Keahole Pl Apt 1505 Honolulu HI 96825-3421

FEHLBERG, ROBERT ERICK, architect; b. Kalispell, Mont., Apr. 28, 1926; s. Otto Albert Erick and Mary Grace (Nelson) F.; m. LaDonna Karen Rognlie, May 31, 1953; children: Kolby J., Kenje A., Kurt E., Klee J. B.S. in Architecture, Mont. State U., 1951. Architect in tng. with Gehres D. Weed Architect, Kalispell, 1952-55; partner Weed & Fehlberg Architects, Kalispell, 1955-57; pvt. practice Kalispell, 1957-58; with Cushing Terrell Assos., Billings, Mont., 1958-72; partner Cushing Terrell Assos., 1960-72; v.p. CTA Architects Engrs., Inc., Billings, 1973-87; ptnr. Collaborative Design Architects, Oakland, Calif., 1987-91, Robert Fehlberg Architects, Pleasanton, Calif., 1991—. Bd. dirs. Yellowstone Art Center Found., 1965-84, 1st pres., 1965; bd. dirs. Mont. Inst. Arts Found., 1976-86, pres., 1976-80, treas., 1980-86. Served with AUS, 1944-46. Recipient (with wife) Gov.'s award for arts, 1983. Fellow AIA (pres. Mont. 1965, nat. dir. 1971-74), Mont. Inst. Arts (pres. 1963-64); mem. Prodn. Systems for Architects and Engrs. (dir. 1971-74, chmn. 1974), East Bay AIA. Home: 7566 Rosedale Ct Pleasanton CA 94588-3762 also: PO Box 2431 Sitka AK 99835-2431

FEHLE, FRANK RUDOLF, finance educator; b. Koblenz, Germany, Dec. 24, 1968; came to the U.S., 1992; s. Hans-Jochen Fehle and Christine (Doetsch) Loeffler. Diploma, WHU, Koblenz, 1994; MBA, U. Tex. Austin, 1994, postgrad. Mktg. asst. Lucas Automotive GmbH, Koblenz, 1990; jr. underwriter Assicurazioni Generali SpA, Trieste, Italy, 1991; cons. McKinsey & Co., Inc., Frankfurt, Germany, 1993, 95-98; tchg. asst. U. Tex. Austin, 1994-96, asst. instr., 1996—; adj. prof. St. Mary's U., San Antonio, 1997—; asst. prof. U. S.C., 1999—; cons. Lola Wright Found., Georgetown, Tex., 1996—; examiner German Am. C. of C., Austin, 1996. Contbr. articles to profl. jours. Lt. Corps Engrs. Germany, 1988-90. Mem. Internat. Assn. Fin. Engrs., Am. Fin. Assn., Fin. Mgmt. Assn., Phi Kappa Phi. Roman Catholic. Avocations: art history, sports, travel. Fax: 512 471-5073. E-mail: ffehle@mail.utexas.edu. Home: 16415 Pemelm Dr San Antonio TX 78240-5617 Office: Dept Finance B6600 Univ Tex Austin Austin TX 78712

FEHLER, POLLY DIANE, neonatal nurse, educator; b. Harvard, Ill., Jan. 6, 1946; d. Arthur William and Charlotte (Stewart) Eggert; m. Gene L. Fehler, Dec. 26, 1964; children: Timothy, Andrew. AS, summa cum laude, Kishwaukee Coll., 1974; BSN, magna cum laude, No. Ill. U., DeKalb, 1977, MSN, summa cum laude, 1980. Cert. BLS, neonatal resuscitation instr. Ob-gyn. staff nurse Kishwaukee Hosp., 1977; community health nurse DeKalb County Health Dept., 1977-79; grad. teaching asst. No. Ill. Univ., 1978-80; adj. maternity instr. Auburn Univ., Montgomery, Ala., 1980-81; maternal/newborn nurse USAF Regional Hosp. Maxwell, Montgomery, Ala., 1980-81, nurse internship coord., 1981-83; edn. coord. USAF Hosp., Bergstrom, Austin, Tex., 1983-87; neonatal ICU & transport RN St. Mary's Hosp., Athens, Ga., 1988-90; nursing instr. Tri-County Tech. Coll., Pendleton, S.C., 1990-97, dept. head nursing program, 1998—; EMT, course lectr. U. Tex., Austin, 1984-86; counselor, vol. Hospice, 1984-87; sec., v.p. Shared Resources for Nurses, Austin, 1984-87, high blood pressure instr.-trainer, 1986-87, home health staff nurse Interim Health Care, Anderson, S.C., 1991-94; expert witness St. Mary's Hosp., Athens, 1991-92; coord. NCLEX rev. course Health Edn. Systems, Inc., 1993-96; lectr. on interculturalism in nursing, 1993—; mem. adv. bd. Tri-County Student Competencies, 1990—, mem. advising team, 1995—, mini grant sel. com., 1992-93, 95-97, com. chmn., 1996-97. Nursing-textbook reviewer Addison Wesley Pubs., 1993-99, Mosby Yearbook, 1995-99, Saunders Publisher, 1999—. Nurse, med. evaluator Mass Casualty Exercises, Austin, 1984-87; tchr., sec. United Meth. Chs., Ill., Ala., Ga., S.C., 1970—; mem. alumni bd. No. Ill. Alumni, DeKalb, 1979-80; mem. Malta Dist. Bd. Edn., 1979-80; judge Austin Sch. Dist. Sci. and Math. Fair, Austin, 1983-84; S.C. Gov.'s Guardian ad Litem Vol., 1995-99; vol. Oconee County Healthy Visions Task Force, 1996-98, S.C. Good Health Appeal Coll. Campaign Mgr., 1996, Oconee County Humane Soc., 1996—; mem. adv. coun. Oconee Kid's Health, 1997-99, Planning Work Force (1998—), Institutional Development Com., 1998—, mem. SC Nurses Assn. Continuing Edn. Approval Com. (1998—), SC Maternal Child Health Counc., 1999—. Capt. USAF, 1980-88. Decorated USAF Commendation medal with oak leaf cluster; recipient Sr. Nursing Class of Tri-County Tech. Coll. Instr. of the Yr. award, 1992, Nat. Inst. for Staff and Orgnl. Devel. Excellence award, 1995; Duke Power grantee Alliance 2020, 1997-98. Mem. ANA, S.C. Nurses Assn., S.C. Assn. Perinatal Nurses, S.C. Tech. Edn. Assn., Nursing Faculty Orgn. (v.p. 1991-94, pres. 1998—), United Meth. Women (pres. 1998-99), S.C. Internat. Ednl. Consortium, S.C. Colleagues in Caring, S.C. Nursing Deans and Dirs., Sigma Theta Tau, Lambda Chi Nu. Meth. Avocations: reading, swimming, hiking, writing. Home: 106 Laurel Ln Seneca SC 29678-2705 Office: Tri-County Tech Coll PO Box 587 Pendleton SC 29670-0587

FEHR, DONALD M., baseball union executive; m. Stephanie Fehr; 4 children. Grad., U. Mo. Past law clerk to Hon. Elmo Hunter U.S. Dist. Ct. Mo.; former atty. Jolley, Moran, Walsh, Hager and Gordon, Kansas City, Mo.; gen. counsel Major League Baseball Players Assn., 1977-83, exec. dir., gen. counsel, 1983—. Office: Major League Baseball Players Assn 12 E 49th St Fl 24 New York NY 10017-1028

FEHR, GREGORY PARIS, marketing and distribution company executive; b. Urbana, Ill., Nov. 10, 1943; s. Orval Joachim and Cuba Lucile (Paris) F.; m. Sharon Louise Burba, Jan. 21, 1965 (div. Jan. 1975); children: Kristina K., Gregory Tyson Howard; m. Kathleen Lorretta Meyers, Aug. 10, 1990. BS in Indsl. Engring., Okla. U., 1967; MBA, Drake U., 1977. Registered profl. mech. engr. Iowa, Okla., Ala.; cert. corrosion technologist. From engr. to sr. project engr. Fisher Controls Co., Marshalltown, Iowa, 1967-77; fgn. liaison GE, Portland, Maine, 1977-79; gen. mgr. Arabian Am. Oil Co., Dhahran, Saudi Arabia, 1979-81; v.p. Oil Tech. Svcs., Houston, 1981-85; mgr. materials engring. Standard Oil Prodn. Co., Houston, 1985-86; mgr. nuclear products Wyle Labs., Huntsville, Ala., 1986-88; sr. materials engr. Sci. Applications Internat., Las Vegas, Nev., 1988-96; prin. GPF Mktg. and Distbn., Las Vegas, 1988-96; sr. project mgr. Converse Cons. S.W., Inc., Las Vegas, 1996—; cons. task groups Am. Petroleum Inst., 1983-86, Electric Power Rsch. Inst., San Mateo, Calif., 1986-89; chmn. employee adv. coun. Sci. Applications Internat., Las Vegas, 1992. Contbr. articles and tech. papers to profl. jours. Pres. Marshalltown Tennis Assn., 1972-73; head swim coach YMCA/YWCA, Marshalltown, 1973-74; mem. adv. bd. Marshalltown C.C., 1975. Mem. NSPE, ASME, Nat. Assn. Corrosion Engrs., Am. Petroleum Inst., Am. Soc. Nondestructive Testing. Avocations: skiing, scuba diving, sailing, photography.

FEHR, J. WILL, newspaper editor; b. Long Beach, Calif., Mar. 8, 1926; s. John and Evelyn (James) F.; m. Cynthia Moore, Sept. 4, 1951; children—Michael John, Martha Ann. B.A. in English, U. Utah, 1951. City editor Salt Lake City Tribune, 1964-80, mng. editor, 1980-81, editor, 1981-91. Served to 1st lt. USAF, 1951-53. Mem. Am. Soc. Newspaper Editors, Sigma Chi. Home: 468 13th Ave Salt Lake City UT 84103-3229 Office: Salt Lake City Tribune 143 S Main St Salt Lake City UT 84111-1924

FEHR, KENNETH MANBECK, retired computer systems company executive; b. Schuylkill Haven, Pa., Feb. 21, 1928; s. Theodore E. and Eva (Manbeck) F.; m. Jean Alice Greenawalt, June 28, 1952; children: K. Craig, Karen Jean, K. Todd. BS, Pa. State U., 1951; MBA, U. Pitts., 1953. With U.S. Steel Corp., 1951-62, div. controller, 1962; controller Interlake Steel Corp., Chgo., 1962-68; v.p. fin. Hallicrafters Co., 1968-71, E.W. Bliss Co., Salem, Ohio, 1971-74; treas. Alliance Machine Co., Ohio, 1974-86; pres. I.M.S. Corp., Hudson, Ohio, 1986-90, Fehr & Greenawalt Investments, Salem, Ohio, 1990—; dir. Fegreen Inc.; night sch. tchr. U. Pitts., 1956-57. Mem. Salem Preservation Soc., Trumbull Preservation Alliance, Salem Hist. Soc.; trustee Save Our Salem, Inc.; treas. Salem Renaissance. With USNR, 1945-46. Mem. Fin. Execs. Inst., Nat. Assn. Accts., Salem-Golf Club, Masons, Kiwanis (chpt. pres.). Home and Office: 725 S Lincoln Ave Salem OH 44460-3709

FEHR, LOLA MAE, nursing association director; b. Hastings, Nebr., Sept. 29, 1936; d. Leland R. and Edith (Wunderlich) Gaymon; m. Harry E. Fehr, Aug. 15, 1972; children: Dawn, Cheryl, Michael. RN, St. Luke's Hosp., Denver, 1958; BSN magna cum laude, U. Denver, 1959; MS, U. Colo., Boulder, 1975. Dir. staff devel. Weld County Gen. Hosp., Greeley, Colo., 1972-76; dir. nursing Weld County Gen. Hosp., 1976-80; exec. dir. Colo. Nurses Assn., Denver, 1980-89; dir. membership Assn. Oper. Rm. Nurses, Inc., Denver, 1989-90, exec. dir., 1990-99; dir. AORN Found., Denver, 1999—. Editor Colo. Nurse, 1980-89. Recipient U. Colo. Alumni award, Colo. Nurses Assn. Profl. Nurse of the Yr. award. Mem. Am. Acad. Nursing, Nat. Assn. Parliamentarians, Am. Soc. Assn. Execs., Colo. Nurses Assn., Sigma Theta Tau.

FEHRENBACH, T(HEODORE) R(EED), author, businessman; b. San Benito, Tex., Jan. 12, 1925; s. T. R. and Rose Mardel (Wentz) F.; m. Lillian Breetz, Aug. 22, 1951. BA magna cum laude, Princeton U., 1947. Field supr. Travelers Ins. Co., San Antonio, 1954-56; owner ind. ins. agy., San Antonio, 1956-69; mng. trustee Fehrenbach Trusts, 1970—; pres. Royal Poinciana Corp., San Antonio, 1971-92. Author: This Kind of War, 1963; This Kind of Peace, 1966; Lone Star (PBS TV series 1985-86), 1968; Fire and Blood, 1973; Comanches, 1974; Seven Keys to Texas, 1983; Texas: A Salute from Above, 1985, others; contbr. numerous articles, stories to mags., U.S., fgn. periodicals. Mem., Tex. 2000 Commn., 1981-82; chmn. Tex. Hist. Commn., 1987-91. Served to 1st lt. AUS, 1943-46, to lt. col., 1950-53. Recipient Freedoms Found. award, 1965; Evelyn Oppenheimer award, 1968; citations Tex. Ho. of Reps., 1969, 73, Tex. Legislature, 1977; T.R. Fehrenbach Book awards created in his honor Tex. Hist. Commn., 1986; named Disting. Citizen, San Antonio, 1973; Knight of San Jacinto. Fellow Tex. State Hist. Assn. ; mem. Philos. Soc. Tex., Authors Guild, Sci. Fiction Writers Am., Conopus Club, Argyle Club, Torch Club, Princeton Club, Garden of the Gods Club (Colo.). Republican. Episcopalian. Home: 131 Mary D Ave San Antonio TX 78209-5667 Office: 5108 Broadway St # San San Antonio TX 78209-5728

FEHSENFELD, MARTHA DOW, writer, editor; b. Cambridge, Mass.; d. Winthrop Griffin Dow and Ann Merrill Fair; m. William Tarun Fehsenfeld, Oct. 12, 1963 (div. Aug. 1970). BA, Bennington Coll., 1953; MA, U. N.C., 1956. Instr. drama Bennett Jr. Coll., Millbrook, N.Y., 1960-62; tchg. asst. drama and speech U. Ill., Champaign-Urbana, 1963; rsch. assoc. Emory U. Grad. Sch., Atlanta, 1990—, editor Correspondence of Samuel Beckett, 1990—; exec. bd. mem. Alan Schneider Meml. Found., N.Y.C.; adv. bd. Sam Beckett Internat. Found., Reading, Eng. Co-author: Beckett in Route, 1988; actor cmty. theatre. Grantee NEH, 1985-89, 91-97, 92-99. Mem. MLA, SAMLA, AETA, S.B. Soc., Harold Pinter Soc., Soc. Authors. Democrat. Episcopalian. Avocations: theatre, books, sports. E-mail: mfehsen@emory.edu. Office: The Correspondence Samuel Beckett Grad Sch Emory Univ 202 Administration Atlanta GA 30322

FEI, JAMES ROBERT, engineer; b. Tucson, May 24, 1947; s. Robert Fleming and Barbara Jean (Dukes) F.; m. Patricia Christine Wilson, Aug. 24, 1968; children: Robert Fleming, Christina Kalani. BSME, U. So. Calif., 1969; MS in Ocean Engring., U. Hawaii, 1973. Registered profl. engr., S.C., La., Tex., Ga., Va., N.H. Design engr. USN, Mare Island, Calif., 1969-70; project mgr. Pearl Harbor (Hawaii) Shipyard, 1970-73; mech. systems engr. Submarine Maintenance Monitoring Systems Office Dept. of the Navy, Washington, 1973-76; chmn., chief exec. officer Life Cycle Engring., Inc., Charleston, S.C., 1977—; bd. dirs., adv. bd. Nat. Bank of S.C., 1985-92; mem. adv. coun. St. Francis Hosp., 1992-95; mem. pres.'s adv. coun. Med. U. S.C., Charleston, 1995-96; mem. Cold War Submarine Meml. Found., exec. com., bd. Mem. SCSPE, NSPE, ASME, Navy League. Republican. Avocations: golf, boating. Office: Life Cycle Engring Inc 4360 Corporate Rd Ste 100 North Charleston SC 29405-7445

FEIBEL, FREDERICK ARTHUR, financial consultant; b. Chgo., Oct. 27, 1942; s. Fred and Emma Feibel; BSEE, Purdue U., 1964; MBA, Northwestern U., 1970; m. Marlene Ruth Edwards, Aug. 7, 1965; 1 son, Frederick Curtis. Project engr. Johnson Controls Corp., Milw., 1964-69; sr. mgmt. cons. Arthur Andersen & Co., Chgo., 1970-76; rep. pension fund evaluation A.G. Becker Securities Co., Chgo. 1976-77; spl. agt. Northwestern Mut. Life Ins. Co., Milw., 1977-82; pres. F.A. Feibel Fin. Assocs., Northbrook, Ill., 1982—. Chmn., Village of Northbrook Bicentennial Commn., 1975-76, Boy Scouts Am. Troop 67, 1990—, chmn.; v.p., Northbrook Civic Found., 1977, pres., 1978, also bd. dirs., life mem.; pres. Northbrook Hist. Soc., 1977, also bd. dirs.; deacon Northfield Cmty. Ch., 1978-81, 95— asst. treas. 1986—. Recipient Disting. Svc. award State of Ill., 1976, Northbrook Civic Found., 1983, Civic Svc. award Northbrook B'nai B'rith, 1981-82, Disting. Svc. award Northbrook Civic Found., 1989; Vol. Initiative of Pvt. Sector Recognition award, Northbrook C. of C. and Industry, 1985, Vol. Appreciation award Northbrook Park Dist., 1987; named Northbrook Rotary Man of Yr., 1978-79, Hall of Fame Ill. Festival Assn., 1992; Mem. Am. Soc. CLU & ChFC, Greater North Shore Estate Planning Coun., Eta Kappa Nu, Tau Beta Pi. Home: 1342 Hillside Rd Northbrook IL 60062-4613 Office: FA Feibel Fin Assocs PO Box 355 Northbrook IL 60065-0355

FEIDELSON, MARC, advertising executive; b. N.Y.C., Aug. 20, 1939; s. Robert and Ceil (Robbins) F.; m. Linda Sarnoff, June 11, 1964; children—Lee, Pamela. B.S. in Bus. Adminstrn., Boston U., 1961; M.A. in Psychology, CUNY, 1966. Media research analyst CBS-TV, N.Y.C., 1964-65; sr. media research analyst Ted Bates Advt., N.Y.C., 1966-67; media research dir. Benton & Bowles Advt., N.Y.C., 1967-70; media mgr. RCA Corp., N.Y.C., 1970-72; dir. advt. services Hunt-Wesson Foods, Fullerton, Calif., 1973-79; sr. v.p., media dir. Dailey & Assocs. Advt., Los Angeles, 1979—; guest lectr. UCLA. Mem. Hollywood Radio and TV Soc., Los Angeles Media Dirs. Council (pres. 1981-82). Jewish. Guest editor Media Decisions mag., Apr. 1983. Office: Dailey & Assocs 8687 Melrose Ave West Hollywood CA 90069-5701

FEIDER, GARY JOSEPH, newspaper editor; b. Sheboygan, Wis., Apr. 24, 1953; s. Joseph Nicholas and Elaine Sylvina (Schueller) F. BA, U. Wis., 1975. Editor, gen. mgr. The Sounder, Random Lake, Wis., 1975—; editor Dancers' Dateline, Random Lake, 1992—. Roman Catholic. Avocation: competitive ballroom dancing. Home: W3672 County Road K Cedar Grove WI 53013-1478

FEIERSTEIN, MARK BARRY, diplomat; b. N.Y.C., June 19, 1963; s. Saul and Rita Carol (Goldberg) F.; m. Itzel del Carmen Sclopis, June 27, 1991; 1 child, Bianca Pilar. BA, Tufts U., 1987; MA, Fletcher Sch. Law & Diplomacy, Medford, Mass., 1987. Lyndon Baines Johnson intern U.S. Rep. Stewart McKinney, Washington, 1984; copy editor Hartford (Conn.) Courant, 1985; reporter Mexico City News, 1985-86; dep. western fin. dir. Dukakis for President Campaign, Boston, 1987; dir. Latin Am. programs Nat. Dem. Inst. Internat. Affairs, Washington, 1987-93; spl. asst. to U.S. amb. OAS, State Dept., Washington, 1993-97; sr. adviser elections AID, Washington, 1997—. Editor, reporter Trumbull (Conn.) Times, summrs, 1981-83. Mem. Toastmasters Internat. (club pres. 1996-97, area gov. 1997-98, 1st pl. area humorous speech contest 1995). Democrat. Jewish. Avocations: playing with my daughter, reading history, tennis, baseball, racquetball. Home: 8608 Battailles Ct Annandale VA 22003-3608 Office: USAID Ctr Democracy Rm 3-10/051 Ronald Reagon Bldg Washington DC 20523

FEIFFER, JULES, cartoonist, writer, playwright; b. N.Y.C., Jan. 26, 1929; s. David and Rhoda (Davis) F.; m. Judith Sheftel, Sept. 17, 1961 (div. 1983); 1 child, Kate; m. Jennifer Allen, Sept. 11, 1983; children: Halley, Julie. Student, Art Students League, N.Y.C., 1946, Pratt Inst., N.Y.C., 1947-48, 49-51. Asst. to syndicated cartoonist Will Eisner, 1946-51; co-chmn. maj. funds com. Yaddo Corp.; writer-in-residence Northwestern U., Evanston, Ill., Medill Sch. Journalism, 1996; sr. fellow New Arts Journalism Program, Columbia U., 1998; writers program prof. Southampton U., 1999. Cartoonist, author: syndicated Sunday page Clifford, 1949-51; engaged in various art jobs, 1953-56; contbg. cartoonist: Village Voice, N.Y.C., 1956—; cartoons pub. weekly in London (Eng.) Observer, 1958-66, 72-82; regularly in Playboy Mag., 1959—, New Yorker, 1993—, New Statesman & Society, 1994—; cartoons nationally syndicated U.S., 1959—; illustrator The Phantom Tollbooth, 1961; author: (books) Sick, Sick, Sick, 1958, Passionella and other stories, 1959, The Explainers, 1961, Boy, Girl, Boy, Girl, 1962, Hold Me, 1962, Harry, The Rat With Women, 1963, Pictures at a Prosecution, 1971, Feiffer on Nixon: The Cartoon Presidency, 1974, Ackroyd, 1977, (children's novel) The Man in the Ceiling, 1993; mus. revue The Explainers, 1961; Feiffer's Album, 1963, The Unexpurgated Memoirs of Bernard Mergendeiler, 1965, The Great Comic Book Heroes, 1965, Feiffer's Marriage Manual, 1967; (plays) Crawling Arnold, 1961, Little Murders, 1967 (Best Fgn. Play of Yr., Obie award, Outer Circle Drama Critics award), Feiffer on Civil Rights, 1967, God Bless, 1968, O Calcutta, 1969 (contbr. revue), The White House Murder Case, 1970, Knock-Knock, 1976, Grownups, 1981, A Think Piece, 1982, Carnal Knowledge, 1988, Anthony Rose, 1989, Elliot Loves, 1990, Jules' Blues, 1999; screenplays Little Murders, 1971, Carnal Knowledge, 1971, Popeye, 1980, I Want to Go Home, 1989 (Best Screenplay Venice Film Festival 1989); revue Hold Me!, 1977, Urban Blight, 1989; cartoon novel Tantrum, 1979; (non-fiction) Jules Feiffer's America: From Eisenhower to Reagan, 1982, Marriage is An Invasion of Privacy, 1984, Feiffer's Children, 1986, Ronald Reagan In Movie-America, 1988, Feiffer The Collected Works Vol. 1, 2, 3, 1989, 90; childrens novel The Man in the Ceiling, 1994, A Barrel of Laughs, A Vale of Tears, 1995, Meanwhile..., 1997, I Lost My Bear, 1998, Bark, George, 1999. Served with AUS, 1951-53. Recipient Acad. award for animated cartoon, Munro 1961, spl. George Polk Meml. award 1962, Obie award, 1969, Outer Circle Drama Critics award 1969, 70; Pulitzer prize for editorial cartooning, 1986. Mem. AAAL, Authors Guild (life), Dramatists Guild (coun., pres. found. 1982-83), P.E.N., Writers Guild Am.

FEIG, STEPHEN ARTHUR, pediatrics educator, hematologist, oncologist; b. N.Y.C., Dec. 24, 1937; s. Irving L. and Janet (Oppenheimer) F.; m. Judith Bergman, Aug. 28, 1960; children: Laura, Daniel, Andrew. AB in Biology, Princeton U., 1959; MD, Columbia U., 1963. Diplomate Am. Bd. Pediatrics, Am. Bd. Hematology-Oncology. Intern Mt. Sinai Hosp., N.Y.C., 1963-64, resident in pediatrics, 1964-66; hematology fellow Children's Hosp. Med. Ctr., Boston, 1968-71, assoc. in medicine, 1971-72; asst. prof. pediatrics UCLA, 1972-77, chief div. hematology and oncology, sch. medicine, 1977—, assoc. prof., 1977-82, prof., 1982—, exec. vice chmn. dept. pediatrics sch. mediicne, 1994—; cons. Olive View Med. Ctr., Van Nuys, Calif., 1973—, Valley Med. Ctr., Fresno, Calif., 1973—, Sunrise Hosp. dept. pediatrics, Las Vegas, Nev., 1980—; med. advisory com. Los Angeles chpt. Leukemia Soc. Am., 1978—; bd. trustees, 1984—; bd. dirs. Camp Ronald McDonald for Good Times; active numerous other pediatric hosp. and med. sch. coms. Reviewer Am. Jour. Pediatric Hematology/Oncology, Blood, Jour. Clin. Investigation, Pediatrics, Pediatric Rsch., Am. Jour. Diseases of Children, Jour. Pediatrics; contbr. articles to profl. jours.; editl. bd. Jour. Pediat. Hematology & Oncology, Stem Cells. Served with USNR, 1966-68. Mem. Am. Soc. Hematology, Soc. Pediatric Research, Am. Pediatric Soc., Internat. Soc. Exptl. Hematology, Am. Assn. Cancer Research. Jewish. Avocation: native arts. Office: UCLA Sch Medicine Dept Pediatrics 10833 Le Conte Ave Los Angeles CA 90095-3075

FEIGELSON, PHILIP, biochemist, educator; b. N.Y.C., Apr. 20, 1925; s. David and Rose (Venitsky) F.; m. Muriel Horowitz, Mar. 30, 1947; children—Janet Lauren, Eric Dennis. B.S., Queens Coll., 1947; M.S., Syracuse U., 1948; Ph.D., U. Wis., 1951. Asst. prof. biochemistry Antioch Coll., Yellow Springs, Ohio, 1951-54; rsch. assoc. Fels Rsch. Inst., 1951-54; asst. prof. Coll. Phys. and Surg., Columbia U., N.Y.C., 1954-61, assoc. prof. biochemistry, 1961-70, prof. biochemistry, 1970-98, assoc. dean, 1987-98, asst. v.p., 1987-98; ret., 1998; Mem. study sect. pharmacology USPHS, 1966-70. Mem. editorial bd. Cancer Research, 1973-76, Jour. Biol. Chemistry, 1977-82, Molecular Endocrinology, 1989-92. Fellow AAAS, N.Y. Acad. Scis. (bd. govs. 1970-82, chmn. awards com. 1974-85, pres. 1975), World Acad. Arts and Sci.; mem. Am. Soc. Biol. Chemists, Am. Assn. Cancer Rsch., Harvey Soc. Home: 265 Tenafly Rd Tenafly NJ 07670-2529

FEIGEN, BRENDA S., literary manager, lawyer, motion picture producer; b. Chgo., July 7, 1944; d. Arthur Paul Feigen and Shirley (Bierman) Feigen Kadison; children: Alexis Feigen Fasteau. BA in Math. cum laude, Vassar Coll., 1966; JD, Harvard U., 1969. Bar: Mass. 1970, N.Y. 1971. Chief analyst Boston Redevel. Authority, 1969; assoc. firm Rosenman, Colin, Kaye, Petschek, Freund & Emil, N.Y.C., 1970; pvt. practice N.Y.C., 1971—; founder, coordinating dir. Women's Action Alliance, N.Y.C., 1970-72; co-founder Ms. Mag., 1971; dir. Nat. Women's Rights project ACLU, N.Y.C., 1972-74; ptnr. firm Fasteau and Feigen, N.Y.C., 1974-80; assoc. firm Hess, Segall, Guterman, Pelz & Steiner, N.Y.C., 1980-81; atty., motion picture agt. William Morris Agy., N.Y.C., 1982-87; pres. Brenda Feigen Prodns., N.Y.C., L.A., 1987-97; ptnr. Baxter/Feigen Prodns., 1919-92, Berton & Feigen, Beverly Hills, 1992-94; of counsel Berton & Donaldson, Beverly Hills, 1994-96; pres. Feigen/Parrent Lit. Mgmt., Bel Air, Calif., 1995—; co-pres. Reel Life Women Prodn. Co., Bel Air, 1996—; adj. instr. law Coll. New Rochelle, 1976; prof. UCLA Ext., 1990; guest spkr., panelist numerous confs., seminars; panelist Harvard Law Sch. seminar, 1999, Yale Law Sch. seminar, 1999, Calif. Lawyers for Arts, 1999; co-chair Practicing Law Inst. Seminars on Entertainment Law, 1987, 88, Harvard Law and Harvard Bus. Schs. Entertainment Law Conf., 1999, Vassar Coll. Symposium on Entertainment Industry, 1998; practicing Law Inst., 1987, 88; bd. dirs. Calif. Lawyers for the Arts, 1996—; panelist AFI/Cinetex Conf., 1990, SAG Women's Conf., 1990, Show Coalition, L.A., 1990-92; emerita mem. bd. dirs. Women's Action Alliance. Film prodr. Orion Pictures (film) NAVY SEALS, 1990; contbr. chpt. to book and articles to mags. Mem. adv. bd. Working Women United, nat. adv. bd. Take Our Daus. to Work, 1993—; bd. dirs. Film Forum, 1986-90, Calif. Lawyers for the Arts, 1996—; mem. Pen Ctr. USA West, 1996—, Authors' Guild, 1996—, Harvard Com. Entertainment, Sports and Cyberspace Law, 1997—; candidate for N.Y. State Senate, 1978. Hon. Pres.'s fellow Columbia U., 1977, 78; participant Exec. Seminar, Aspen Inst., 1979. Mem. NOW (nat. legis. v.p., bd. dirs. 1970-71), Show Coalition (bd. govs. 1990-92), N.Y. Women in Film (bd. dirs. 1985-86), Women's Action Alliance (co-founder, dir.), Nat. Women's Polit. Caucus (co-founder, nat. adv. com.). Democrat. Office: 10158 Hollow Glen Cir Los Angeles CA 90077-2112

FEIGEN, RICHARD L., art dealer; b. Chgo., Aug. 8, 1930; s. Arthur P. and Shirley (Bierman) F.; m. Sandra Elizabeth Canning Walker, Feb. 23, 1966 (div. 1978); children: Philippa Canning, Richard Wood Bliss; m. Margaret Langan Culver, Sept. 12, 1998. B.A., Yale U., 1952; M.B.A., Harvard U., 1954. Asst. treas. Beneficial Standard Life Ins. Co., Los Angeles, 1955-56; mem. N.Y. Stock Exchange, 1956-57; pres., dir. Richard L. Feigen & Co., Inc., N.Y.C. and London, 1957—; mem. com. works fine art N.Y. State Office Bldg., Harlem; lectr. in field. Contbr. articles to art publs. Candidate, del. Dem. Nat. Conv., 1972; trustee John Jay Homestead Assn., Katonah, N.Y., 1979-90, Lincoln U., Pa., 1988-92; trustee, mem. pres.'s coun. U. South Fla. Fellow Mpls. Soc. Fine Arts, Met. Mus. Art, Art Inst. Chgo.; mem. Art Dealers Assn. Am. (bd. dirs. 1972-76, 97—), Harvard Bus. Sch. Assn., Arts Club, Casino Club, Tavern Club of Chgo. Home: Cantitoe House Cantitoe Rd Katonah NY 10536-9718 also: 950 N Michigan Ave Chicago IL 60611-4500 Office: 49 E 68th St New York NY 10021-5012

FEIGENBAUM, ABRAHAM SAMUEL, nutritional biochemist; b. N.Y.C., Mar. 11, 1929; s. Benjamin and Pearl Feigenbaum; m. Hannah Devries, Aug. 17, 1952; children: Benjamin, Josef, Miriam. BS, Rutgers U., 1951, MS, 1959, PhD, 1962. Chemist E.R. Squibb, New Brunswick, N.J., 1954-57; rsch. asst. Rutgers U., New Brunswick, N.J., 1957-61; rsch. scientist, chief neuroendocrinology N.J. Bur. Rsch. in Neurology and Psychiatry, Skillman, 1961-73; dir. clin. nutrition, dir. clin. coordination Warren-Teed Pharm./Adria Labs., Inc., Columbus, Ohio, 1973-81; clin. project dir., dir. rsch. Pharm. Rsch. Inst., sub. Akzo, Columbus, Ohio, 1981-94; dir. clin. devel. Organon, Inc., West Orange, N.J., 1981-94; ret., 1994; guest lectr. in nutrition Hahnemann Med. Coll., Phila., 1977-80. Mem. Bd. Edn., Highland Park, N.J., 1969-73, pres., 1970-72, v.p., 1972-73. NSF fellow, 1961. Mem. Am. Inst. Nutrition, Am. Chem. Soc., Soc. Exptl. Biology and Medicine. Home: 209 N 4th Ave Highland Park NJ 08904-2723

FEIGENBAUM, ARMAND VALLIN, systems engineer, systems equipment executive; b. N.Y.C., Apr. 6, 1920; s. S. Frederick and Hilda (Vallin) F. BS, Union Coll., 1942, DSc (hon.), 1992; MS, MIT, 1948, PhD, 1951; LHD (hon.), U. Mass., 1996. Engr. test program GE, Schenectady, 1942-45; factory tng. course GE, 1945-47, sales engr., 1947-48; supr. tng. mfg. personnel GE, Lynn, Mass., 1948-50; asst. to gen. mgr. aircraft gas turbine divsn. GE, Cin., 1950-52; mgr. aircraft nuclear propulsion dept. GE, N.Y.C., 1952; co. mgr. quality control GE, 1956, co.-wide mgr. mfg. ops. and quality control, 1958-68; pres., CEO Gen. Systems Co., Inc., Pittsfield, Mass., 1968—; Nat. Acad. Engring. U.S., 1992—; mem. bd. overseers Malcolm Baldridge Nat. Quality Program, Washington, D.C., 1988-91; pres. Internat. Acad. for Quality, 1966-79, chmn. bd. dirs., 1979—; adv. group U.S. Army, 1966—; lectr. MIT, U. Cin., Union Coll., U. Pa. Author: Quality Control-Principles and Practice, 1951, Total Quality Control-Engineering and Management, 1961, Management Programming, 1980, The Organization Process, 1980, Total Quality Control, 3d edit., 1983, Total Quality Control, 40th Anniversary edit., 1991; contbr. articles to profl. jours. Chmn. inst. adminstrn., mgmt. coun. Union Coll., 1963—. Recipient Founders medal, 1977, medaille Georges Borel, Republic of France, 1988, Disting. Svc. award Nat. Inst. for Engring., Mgmt. and Sys., 1991, Disting. Leadership award Quality and Productivity Mgmt. Assn., 1993, Ishikawa/Harrington medal Asia-Pacific Quality Orgn., 1996; Armand V. Feigenbaum Mass. Quality award established by Gov. Mass., 1992, Singapore's Ngee Ann Polytechnic inaugurated the ann. Dr. A.V. Feigenbaum Gold medal award for outstanding quality assurance engring. grad., 1994; fellow World Acad. Productivity Sci., 1993; Armand V. and Donald S. Feigenbaum Hall named in his honor Union Coll., 1996, Armand and Donald Feigenbaum Disting. Professorship named in his honor U. Mass. Med. Sch., 1998. Fellow Am. Soc. Quality Control (pres. 1961-63, chmn. bd. 1963-64, Edwards medal 1966, Lancaster medal 1982, hon. mem. 1986, Feigenbaum award established 1999), World Acad. Productivity Sci.; mem. IEEE (life), NSPE (Disting. Svc. award 1991), ASME (life), AAAS (hon.), Nat. Security Indsl. Assn. (nat. award merit 1965), Inst. Math. Stats., Acad. Polit. and Social Scis., Am. Econ. Assn., Soc. Advancement Mgmt., Indsl. Rels. Rsch. Soc., Coun. Internat. Progress in Mgmt. (chmn. bd. 1968-70), China Assn. Quality Control (hon. advisor), Argentine Inst. Quality (hon.), Philippines Soc. for Quality Control (hon.). Home: 123 Ann Dr Pittsfield MA 01201-8405 Office: Berkshire Common South St Pittsfield MA 01201-6123

FEIGENBAUM, EDWARD ALBERT, computer science educator; b. Weehawken, N.J., Jan. 20, 1936; s. Fred J. and Sara Rachman; m. H. Penny Nii, 1975; children: Janet Denise, Carol Leonora, Sheri Bryant, Karin Bryant. BEE, Carnegie Inst. Tech., 1956, Ph.D. in Indsl. Adminstrn., 1960. From asst. prof. to assoc. prof. bus. adminstrn. U. Calif., Berkeley, 1960-64; from assoc. prof. computer sci. to prof. Stanford U., 1965—, prin. investigator heuristic programming project, 1965—, dir. Computation Ctr., 1965-68, chmn. dept. computer sci., 1976-81, Kumagai prof. computer sci., 1991—; pres. Intelli Genetics Inc., 1980-81; chmn., dir. Teknowledge, Inc., 1981-82; mem. tech. adv. bd. Intelli Genetics Inc., 1983-86; dir. IntelliCorp, 1984-90; chief scientist USAF, 1994-97; Kumagoi prof. computer sci. Stanford (Calif.) U., 1997—; cons. to industry, 1957—; mem. computer and biomath. scis. study sect. NIH, 1968-72, mem. adv. com. on artificial intelligence in medicine, 1974—; mem. Math. Social Sci. Bd., 1975-78; computer sci. adv. com. NSF, 1977-80; mem. Internat. Joint Coun. on Artificial Intellignece, 1973-83; bd. dirs. Design Power Ind. Author: (with others) Information Processing Language V Manual, 1961, (with P. McCorduck) The Fifth Generation; author: (with R. Lindsay, B. Buchanan, J. Lederberg) Applications of Artificial Intelligence to Organic Chemistry: the Dendral Program; Editor: (with J. Feldman) Computers and Thought, 1963, (with A. Barr and P. Cohen) Handbook of Artificial Intelligence, 1981, 82, 89, (with Pamela McCorduck and H. Penny Nii) The Rise of the Expert Company: How Visionary Companies are using Artificial Intelligence to Achieve Higher Productivity and Profits; mem. editorial bd.: Jour. Artificial Intelligence, 1970—. Fulbright scholar, 1959-60; Feigenbaum medal established in his honor World Congress on Expert Systems, 1991. Fellow AAAI, AAAS, Am. Coll. Med. Informatics, Am. Inst. Med. and Biol. Engring.; mem. Nat. Acad. Engring., Assn. Computing Machinery (nat. coun. 1966-68, chmn. spl. interest group on biol. applications 1973-76, A.M. Turing award 1994), Am. Assn. Artificial Intelligence (pres. 1980-81), Cognitive Sci. Soc. (coun. 1979-82), Sigma Xi, Tau Beta Pi, Eta Kappa Nu, Pi Delta Epsilon. Home: 1017 Cathcart Way Palo Alto CA 94305-1048 Office: Stanford U Knowledge Systems Lab Gates Computer Sci Rm 227 Stanford CA 94305-9020*

FEIGENBAUM, EDWARD D., legal editor, publisher, consultant; b. Rochester, N.Y., Mar. 16, 1958; s. Samuel and Norma Feigenbaum; m. Ann Elizabeth Andrews, Aug. 6, 1983; children: Edward Andrews, Breanna Layne. BA with honors, Ind. U., 1978, MBA, JD, 1982. Bar: Ind. 1983, U.S. Dist. Ct. (no. and so. dists.) Ind. 1983. Sr. staff assoc. Inst. for Rsch. in Pub. Safety, Bloomington, Ind., 1977-83; dir. legal affairs Coun. State Govts., Lexington, Ky., 1983-87; legal counsel, dir. mktg. Hudson Inst., Indpls., 1987-89; editor, pub. Ind. Legislative Insight, Indpls., 1989—, Ind. Gaming Insight, Indpls., 1993—, Ind. Edn. Insight, Indpls., 1997—; researcher D.T. Skelton Svc. Assocs. Inc., Bloomington, 1983-88. Contbr. numerous articles to profl. jours. Chmn. City of Bloomington Environ. Quality & Conservation Commn., 1982, mem. Redistricting Com., 1982-83, City of Noblesville (Ind.) Planning Commn., 1989-96; co-chair election sub-com. of urban, state and local govt. law govt. ops. com. 1994-96. Mem. ABA (vice chmn. com. election law adminstrv. law sect. 1984-90), Coun. on Govtl. Ethics Laws (steering com. 1987-90), Am. Polit. Sci. Assn., Midwest Polit. Sci. Assn., Ind. State Bar Assn. (chair govtl. practice sect. 1991-92), Columbia Club. Avocation: collecting polit. memorabilia. Home: 5537 Salem Dr N Carmel IN 46033-8582 Office: INGroup PO Box 383 Noblesville IN 46061-0383

FEIGENBAUM, HARVEY, cardiologist, educator; b. East Chicago, Ind., Nov. 20, 1933; s. Julius and Tillie (Sol) F.; m. Phyllis M. Cohn, Oct. 20, 1957; children: Steven, Thomas, Lyle. AB, Ind. U., 1955, MD, 1958. Diplomate Am. Bd. Internal Medicine. Intern Phila. Gen. Hosp., 1958-59; resident Ind. U. Med. Ctr., Indpls., 1959-61, cardiology fellow, 1961-62; instr. Ind. U. Sch. Medicine, Indpls., 1962-64, asst. prof., 1964-67, assoc. prof., 1967-71, prof., 1971-80, Disting. prof., 1980—; rsch. assoc. Krannert Inst. Cardiology, Indpls., 1962-73, sr. rsch. assoc., 1973—. Author: Echocardiography, 5th edit., 1994; editor: Jour. Am. Soc. Echocardiography; mem. editorial bd. Am. Jour. Medicine, Circulation, Cardiology, Jour. Am. Coll. Cardiology, Am. Heart Jour.; contbr. articles to profl. jours. Bd. dirs. Regenstrief Found. for Delivery Health Care. Fellow ACP, Am. Coll. Cardiology; mem. Am. Soc. for Clin. Investigation, Assn. Am. Physicians, Am. Soc. Echocardiography (pres. 1975-78, editor jour.), Am. Heart Assn. (coun. on clin. cardiology), Am. Inst. Ultrasound in Medicine (dir. 1969-72), Cen. Soc. for Clin. Rsch., Phi Beta Kappa, Alpha Omega Alpha. Jewish. Office: Univ Hosp Rm 5420 550 N University Blvd Indianapolis IN 46202-5250

FEIGHT, THEODORE J., financial planner; b. Alma, Mich., Oct. 18, 1946; s. William T. Feight and Wilma (Richardson) Recker; m. Kathleen Lischkge, June 13, 1969; children: Jay David, Richard Thomas, James Daryl, Brian Lynn. BS, Western Mich. U., Kalamazoo, 1972. Cert. fin. planner, divorce planner. Dist. mgr. Clark Oil, Milw., 1972-73; fin. planner Mut. Benefit Life Ins. Co., Lansing, Mich., 1973-78, Creative Fin. Design, Lansing, 1978—; mem. Inst. CFP Registry, Denver, 1991—; bd. dirs., treas. Commemorative Bucks of Mich., Inc. Ghost writer book on fin. planning, 1984. Bd. dirs. The Adoption Cradle, Battle Creek, Mich., 1988—. With U.S. Army, 1967-68, Viet Nam. Decorated DSM, Air medal, 2 Bronze Stars. Mem. Internat. Assn. Fin. Planners, Internat. Bd. CFPs, Inst. CFPs, Mich. State Assn. Life Underwriters (Nat. Pub. Svc. award 1980), Lansing Assn. Life Underwriters (bd. dirs. 1978-79), Rotary Internat. (bd. dirs. 1979-81). Avocations: hunting, golf, karate, cars, computers. Home and Office: Creative Fin Design 2112 Tulane Dr Lansing MI 48912-3546

FEIGIN, RALPH DAVID, medical school president, pediatrician, educator; b. N.Y.C., Apr. 3, 1938; s. Jack Bernard and Dorothy Phyllis (Strauss) F.; m. Judith Sue Zobel, June 26, 1960; children: Susan M., Michael E., Debra F. AB, Columbia U., 1958; MD, Boston U., 1962. Diplomate Am. Bd. Pediatrics, sub bd. for infectious diseases. Pediatric intern Boston City Hosp., 1962-63; pediatric resident Boston City Hosp. and Mass. Gen. Hosp., 1963-65; teaching fellow pediatrics Harvard U. Med. Sch., 1964-65; rschr. U.S. Army Rsch. Inst. Infectious Diseases, Frederick, Md., 1965-67; chief resident children's svc. Mass. Gen. Hosp., 1967-68; from instructor to prof. pediatrics Washington U. Med. Sch., St. Louis, 1968-77; dir. divsn. infectious diseases dept. pediatrics Washington U. Med. Sch., 1973-77; prof. pediatrics, chmn. dept. Coll. Medicine Baylor U., Houston, 1977—, disting. svc. prof., 1990—; sr. v.p. Baylor Coll. Medicine, Houston, 1992-95, dean med. edn., 1994-95, pres. and CEO, 1996—; physician-in-chief Tex. Children's Hosp., 1977—, exec. v.p., 1987-89; chief pediatric svc. Harris County Hosp. Dist., 1977—; pediatrician-in-chief Methodist Hosp., 1980—; mem. adv. ad hoc study group on spl. infectious disease problems U.S. Army Med. R & D Command, 1974-83; vis. prof., cons. in field; pres. Pediatric Rsch. Found., 1982—. Co-editor: Nutrition and the Developing Nervous System, 1975, Textbook of Pediatric Infectious Diseases, 1981, 4th edit., 1997, Roundsmanship, 1989-93, Practices and Principles of Pediatrics, 1989, 2nd edit., 1993; mem. editorial bd. Pediatrics, 1978-90, consulting editor, 1993-94, assoc. editor, 1994—; mem. editorial bd. Jour. Pediatric Infectious Diseases; assoc. editor Jour. Infectious Diseases, 1984-88; editor-in-chief Seminars in Pediatric Infectious Diseases, 1990—; contbr. articles to med. jours., chpts. to books. With M.C., USAR, 1965-67. Recipient Rsch. Career Devel. award USPHS, 1970, Founders Day award Washington U. Med. Sch., 1977, Sr. Class Outstanding Tchr. award Baylor Coll. Medicine, 1978, 80, 81, 82, 83, 84, 85, 86, Minnie Stevens Piper Professorial award, 1984, John McGovern Outstanding Clin. Faculty award Baylor Coll. Medicine, 1986, 94, Disting. Alumnus award Boston U. Sch. of Medicine, 1989, Joseph St. Geme Jr. Leadership award in Pediatrics, Fedn. Pediatric Orgns., 1995, Disting. Faculty award Alumni Assn., Baylor Coll. of Medicine, 1994; named to Baylor Coll. Medicine Outstanding Tchr. Hall of Fame, 1984; Alumni Tchg. scholar Washington U. Med. Sch., 1975, Amer. Acad. Pediatrics Med. Educ. Lifetime Ach. Award. Fellow AAAS, Am. Microbiology; mem. AMA, Am. Pediatric Soc. (pres. 1997-98), Am. Acad. Pediat., Infectious Diseases Soc. Am., Pediatric Infectious Disease Soc. (Disting. Physician award 1996), Inst. Medicine of NAS, N.Y. Acad. Scis., Tex. Med. Assn., Tex. Pediatric Soc., Harris County Med. Soc., Houston Pediatric Soc., Soc. Pediatric Rsch. (pres. 1982-83), Assn. Med. Sch. Pediatric Dept. Chairpersons (pres. 1991-93). Office: Baylor Coll Medicine Office of President One Baylor Plz Houston TX 77030-3411*

FEIGL, DOROTHY MARIE, chemistry educator, university official; b. Evanston, Ill., Feb. 25, 1938; d. Francis Philip and Marie Agnes (Jacques) F. B.S., Loyola U., Chgo., 1961; Ph.D., Stanford U., 1966; postdoctoral fellow, N.C. State U., 1965-66. Asst. prof. chemistry St. Mary's Coll., Notre Dame, Ind., 1966-69; assoc. prof. St. Mary's Coll., 1969-75, prof., 1975—, chmn. dept. chemistry and physics, 1977-85, bd. regents, 1976-82, acting v.p., dean faculty, 1985-87, v.p., dean faculty, 1987-99. Author: (with John Hill and Erwin Boschmann) General Organic and Biological Chemistry, 1991, (with John Hill and Stuart Baum) Chemistry and Life, 1997; contbr. articles to chem. jours., chpts. to texts. Recipient Spes Unica award St. Mary's Coll., 1973, Maria Pieta award, 1977. Mem. Am. Chem. Soc., Royal Soc. Chemistry, Internat. Union Pure and Applied Chemistry, Am. Assn. Higher Edn., Am. Conf. Acad. Deans, Sigma Xi, Iota Sigma Pi. Democrat. Roman Catholic. Office: Dean Faculty Saint Mary's College Notre Dame IN 46556

FEIKENS, JOHN, federal judge; b. Clifton, N.J., Dec. 3, 1917; s. Sipke and Corine (Wisse) F.; m. Henriette Dorothy Schulthouse, Nov. 4, 1939; children: Jon, Susan Corine, Barbara Edith, Julie Anne, Robert H. A.B., Calvin Coll., Grand Rapids, Mich., 1938; J.D., U. Mich., 1941; LL.D., U. Detroit, 1979, Detroit Coll. Law, 1981. Bar: Mich. 1942. Gen. practice law Detroit; dist. judge Ea. Dist. Mich., Detroit, 1960-61, 70-79, chief judge, 1979-86, sr. judge, 1986—; past co-chmn. Mich. Civil Rights Commn.; past chmn. Rep. State Central Com.; past mem. Rep. Nat. Com.; mem. com. visitors U. Mich. Law Sch. Past bd. trustees Calvin Coll. Fellow Am. Coll. Trial Lawyers; mem. ABA, Detroit Bar Assn. (dir. 1962, past pres.), State Bar Mich. (commr. 1965-71), U. Mich. Club (com. visitors). Office: US Dist Ct 851 Theodore Levin US Ct 231 W Lafayette Blvd Detroit MI 48226-2702

FEIL, LINDA MAE, tax preparer; b. Dallas, Oreg., Apr. 9, 1948; d. Fred Henry and Ruth Irene (Hoffman) F. AA, West Valley Community Coll., 1975; student, Golden Gate U. Ctr. for Tax Studies, 1975, Menlo Coll. Sch. Bus. Adminstrn., 1978. Enrolled agt. IRS; cert. in fed. taxation. Income tax preparer, office mgr. H & R Block, Inc., Santa Clara, Calif., 1972-74, asst. area mgr., 1974-76; propr. L.M. Feil Tax Service, Santa Clara, 1976-80; ptnr. Tennyson Tax Service, Santa Clara, 1980-81; owner McKeany-Feil Tax Service, San Jose, Calif., 1981-83; owner Feil Tax Service, San Jose, 1983-90, Richmond, Calif., 1990-96, Vallejo, Calif., 1996—. Mem. Nat. Soc. Pub. Accts., Nat. Assn. Enrolled Agts. (chpt. sec. 1981-83, chpt. v.p. 1983-84), Mission Soc. Enrolled Agts. (pres. 1984-85, Enrolled Agt. of Yr. 1985), Calif. Soc. Enrolled Agts. (bd. dirs. 1985-86). Office: Feil Tax Svc 824 Foothill Dr Vallejo CA 94591-3697

FEILER, MICHAEL BENJAMIN, lawyer; b. Miami, Fla., Nov. 23, 1964; s. Barton C. and Linda Q. (Goldman) F.; m. Anna Marie Prozzillo, Mar. 30, 1990. BS in Polit. Sci., Fla. State U., 1987; JD with honors, U. Fla., 1992. Bar: Fla. 1996, U.S. Dist. Ct. Fla. 1997, U.S. Ct. Appeals (11th cir.) 1997. Atty. High, Stack, Lazenby, Palahach, Platt & Feiler, Coral Gables, Fla., 1993—; dir. Eric Stack Meml. Found., Melbourne, Fla., 1996—. Best Buddies citizen Best Buddies Internat., Miami, 1993—, celebration of friendship com., 1997. Mem. ABA, Assn. Trial Lawyers Am., Acad. Fla. Trial Lawyers, Dade County Trial Lawyers Assn., Dade County Bar Assn., Coral Gables Bar Assn. Jewish. Avocation: golf. Office: High Stack Lazenby Platt & Feiler 3929 Ponce De Leon Blvd Coral Gables FL 33134-7323

FEIMAN, THOMAS E., investment manager; b. Canton, Ohio, Dec. 21, 1940; s. Daniel Thaviu and Adrienne (Silver) F.; m. Marilyn Judith Miller, June 26, 1966; children: Sheri, Michael. BS in Econs., U. Pa., 1962; MBA, Northwestern U., 1963. CPA, Calif. Staff acct. Arthur Young & Co., L.A., 1963-66; field auditor IRS, L.A., 1966-68; pvt. practice acctg. Thomas Feiman, C.P.A., L.A., 1968-69; ptnr. Wideman & Feiman, C.P.A.s, L.A., 1969-74; pres. Wideman, Feiman, Levy, Sapin & Ko, L.A., 1974-93; investment mgr., v.p. Schroder Wertheim & Co., Inc., 1993-96; CFO Spinal Home Health Systems, Inc. L.A., 1983-85; fin. cons., v.p. Merrill Lynch, 1996—; pres., dir. Urol. Scis. Rsch. Found., 1993—; sr. instr. UCLA Extension, 1967-84. Trustee Temple Israel of Hollywood, Calif., 1981-83, treas., 1983-84. Recipient cert. of award IRS, 1967. Mem. AICPA, Calif. Soc. CPAs. Republican. Jewish. Clubs: Northwestern Bus. Sc. Calif. (pres. 1977-80), Northwestern Alumni of So. Calif. (trustee 1977-92, treas. 1977-90) (L.A.). Office: Merrill Lynch Ste 1600 2121 Avenue of One Stars Century City CA 90067

FEIN, BERNARD, investments executive; b. N.Y.C., Jan. 15, 1908; s. Samuel and Anna (Fine) F.; m. Elaine Schneir, Dec. 26, 1948; children—Kathy Joyce, Lawrence Seth, Susan, Adam, David. LLB, St. Lawrence U., 1929. Bar: N.Y. 1931. Pvt. practice law N.Y.C., 1931-41; pres., chmn. bd. United Indsl. Corp., N.Y.C., N.Y.C; dir. AAI Corp., Balt. Home: 80 Garden Rd Scarsdale NY 10583-2108 Office: United Indsl Corp 570 Lexington Ave New York NY 10022

FEIN, IRVING ASHLEY, television and motion picture executive; b. Bklyn., Jan. 21, 1911; s. Harry and Fannie (Milstein) F.; m. Florence Kohn, Dec. 25, 1941 (dec.); children: Michael Anthony, Patricia Ann; m. Marion Shepard Schechter, June 21, 1969. Student, U. Balt., 1928-29, U. Wis., 1930-32; LL.B., St. Lawrence U., 1936. Publicity and advt. dept. Warner Bros., N.Y.C., 1933-36; dir. exploitation and radio West Coast studios, 1936; asst. publicity dir. Samuel Goldwyn, 1941; dir. exploitation and radio Columbia Pictures, Hollywood, 1942; publicity, advt. dir. Amusement Enterprises, Inc., 1947; with CBS, Inc., 1948-56; dir. exploitation CBS, Inc., Hollywood, 1950; dir. publicity and exploitation CBS Radio, Hollywood, 1951-53; dir. pub. relations CBS Radio, 1953-55; v.p. sales promotion, advt. and press info. CBS Radio, N.Y.C., 1955-56; pres. J & M Prodns., Inc., Beverly Hills, Calif., 1956-65; exec. v.p. J.B. Prodns., 1965-75; producer Jack Benny Programs, 1958-74; pres. TV Prodn. Co. Producer: George Burns TV spls., 1975-96, (films) Just You and Me Kid, Oh God! You Devil, Eighteen Again; author: Jack Benny: An Intimate Biography, 1976. Recipient Emmy award, 1961. Home: 1100 Alta Loma Rd Los Angeles CA 90069-2455

FEIN, LEONA MOSS, artist; b. N.Y.C., Apr. 6, 1930; d. Leo and Pauline (Binnick) Moss; m. Harris Abraham Fein, May 25, 1952 (dec. Oct. 25, 1988); children: Ellen Beth Fein Shapiro, Scott Martin, Eric Bruce. BA in Studio Art, Queens Coll., 1980. Instr. The Craft Students League, N.Y.C., 1972-87; owner Leona M. Fein Ltd., Queens, N.Y., 1982—; lectr. Met. Mus. of Art, N.Y.C., 1970-80; cons., tchr. N.Y. Coun. Arts, N.Y.C., Elder Craftsman, N.Y.C. One-woman show Queens Coll., N.Y.C., 1981; gallery show Nabisco Internat. and more, 1986; artist-in-residence Queens Mus., N.Y.C.; represented in collection of Pres. Bill Clinton. Mem. Nat. Assn. Women Artists, Nat. Guild Decoupeurs, Guild Judaic Artists. Avocation: travel. Home and Office: 125 Knickerbocker Rd Plainview NY 11803-2629

FEIN, LINDA ANN, nurse anesthetist, consultant; b. Cin., Dec. 10, 1949; d. Joseph and Elizabeth P. (Kannady) Stofle; m. Thomas Paul Fein, Dec. 11, 1971. Nursing diploma, Miami Valley Hosp. Sch. Nursing, Dayton, Ohio, 1971, Wright State U., Dayton, 1969; postgrad. U. Cin. Med. Ctr., 1978. Nursing asst. Miami Valley Hosp., Dayton, 1969-71; staff nurse operating room Cin. Children's Hosp. and Med. Ctr., 1971, 73, Peninsula Hosp., Burlingame, Calif., 1972-73; staff nurse operating room and emergency room Doctors Hosp., San Diego, 1972; staff nurse emergency room Ohio State U. Hosps., Columbus, 1973-75, head nurse operating room, 1975-76; staff nurse anesthetist Bethesda Hosps., Cin., 1978-86; staff nurse anesthetist Mercy Hosp. of Fairfield, Cin., 1986-95; locum tenens anesthetist Good Samaritan Hosp., Dayton, Ohio, 1993—; staff nurse, anesthetist Fort Hamilton-Hughes Hosp., Hamilton, Ohio, 1995—. childbirth educator psychoprophylactic method, 1975—; critical care nursing cons. Med. Communicators & Assocs., Salt Lake City, 1985-89; ind. nursing cons., 1989—; co-owner Exec. Shops, Cin., 1982-85; speaker in field. Mem. search com. Cin. Gen. Hosp. Sch. of Anesthesia for Nurses, 1981-82; bd. dirs. YWCA, 1988-91, Children's Diagnostic Ctr., 1989-95, pres. bd. dirs., 1994, Planned Parenthood, 1992-95. Recipient Recognition of Profl. Excellence, First Nurse Anesthesia Faculty Assocs., 1982, Florence Nightengale awards, 1995. Mem. Miami Valley Hosp. Sch. of Nursing Alumni Assn., Cin. Gen. Hosp. Sch. Anesthesia for Nurses Alumni Assn., Nurse Anesthetists of Greater Cin., Ohio Assn. Nurse Anesthetists, Am. Assn. Nurse Anesthetists, Am. Assn. Operating Room Nurses, Am. Assn. Critical Care Nurses, Nat. Registry of Cert. Nurses in Advanced Practice (cert.), Ohio Coaliation of Nurses with Specialty Cert., Am. Soc. Critical Care Medicine, Am. Trauma Soc., NAFE, Altrusa Internat. (officer 1985-92). Republican. Methodist. Lodge: Eastern Star. Avocations: antiques, gourmet cooking, African violets, roses, swimming. Home: 650 History Bridge Ln Hamilton OH 45013-3659

FEIN, RASHI, health sciences educator; b. N.Y.C., Feb. 6, 1926; s. Isaac M. and Clara(Wertheim) F.; m. Ruth Judith Breslau, June 19, 1949; children: Alan, Michael, Karen, Bena (dec.). Student, Bridgeport Jr. Coll., 1942-43; B.A., Johns Hopkins U., 1948, Ph.D., 1956; LittD (hon.), SUNY, 1996. Mem. staff Pres.'s Commn. on Health Needs, 1952; from lectr. to asso. prof. U. N.C., 1952-61; statistician Bur. of Census, 1958-59; sr. staff Pres.'s Council Econ. Advisers, 1961-63; sr. fellow Brookings Inst., 1963-68; prof. Harvard U., 1968—; Heath Clark lectr. London Sch. Hygiene and Tropical Medicine, 1980; chmn. med. assistance adv. council to sec. HEW, 1967-69; mem. adv. com. research and devel. Social Security Adminstrn., 1968-71; mem. Nat. Manpower Policy Task Force, 1967-79, Office Tech. Assessment, Health Adv. Panel., 1981-86; mem. spl. med. adv. group VA, 1987-91; mem. nat. adv. rsch. resources coun. NIH, 1995-99; chair nat. adv. com. Robert Wood Johnson Found. Scholars in Health Policy Rsch. Program; bd. dirs. Ctr. for Child Health Rsch., Am. Acad. Pediat. Author: Economics of Mental Illness, 1958, The Doctor Shortage: An Economic Diagnosis, 1967, (with Gerald Weber) Financing Medical Education: An Analysis of Alternative Policies and Mechanisms, 1971, (with Charles Lewis and David Mechanic) A Right to Health: The Problem of Access to Primary Medical Care, 1976, Alcohol in America: The Price We Pay, 1984, Medical Care, Medical Costs: The Search for a Health Insurance Policy, 1986, 89. Bd. overseers Beth Israel Deconess Med. Ctr., Boston; trustee Hebrew Rehab. Home for Aged, Boston; bd. dirs. Harvard Cmty. Health Plan Found., 1980-87, Harvard-Radcliffe Hillel; mem. tech. bd. Millbank Meml. Fund, 1975-78, 86-90, bd. dirs., 1987-90. Recipient John M. Russell award for advancement knowledge in medicine, 1971; Fellow Inst. History Medicine Johns Hopkins, 1951-52; traveling fellow WHO, 1971. Mem. APHA, AAUP, Inst. Medicine of NAS, Nat. Acad. Social Ins., Am. Econ. Assn., Am. Adv. Coun. World Orgn. for Ednl. Resources and Tech. Tng. Union. Jewish. Office: Harvard U Sch Medicine Dept Social Medicine 641 Huntington Ave 2d Fl Boston MA 02115-6019

FEIN, ROGER GARY, lawyer; b. St. Louis, Mar. 12, 1940; s. Albert and Fanny (Levinson) F.; m. Susanne M. Cohen, Dec. 18, 1965; children: David I., Lisa J. Student Washington U., St. Louis, 1959, NYU, 1960; BS, UCLA, 1962; JD, Northwestern U., 1965; MBA, Am. U., 1967. Bar: Ill. 1965, U.S. Dist. Ct. (no. dist.) Ill. 1968, U.S. Ct. Appeals (7th cir.) 1968, U.S. Supreme Ct. 1970. Atty. div. corp. fin. SEC, Washington, 1965-67; ptnr. Arvey, Hodes, Costello & Burman, Chgo., 1967-91, Wildman, Harrold, Allen and Dixon, Chgo., 1992—, co-chair Corp., Securities and Tax Practice Group; mem. Securities Adv. Com. to Sec. State Ill., 1973—, chmn., 1973-79, 87-93, vice chmn., 1983-87, chmn. emeritus, 1994—; spl. asst. atty. gen. State of Ill., 1974-83, 85—; spl. asst. state's atty. Cook County, Ill., 1989-90; mem. Appeal Bd., Ill. Law Enforcement Commn., 1980-83; mem. lawyer's adv. bd. So. Ill. Law Jour., 1980-83; mem. adv. bd. securities regulation and law report Bur. Nat. Affairs Inc., 1985—; lectr., author on land trust financing, consumer credit and securities law. Mem. Bd. Edn., Sch. Dist. No. 29, Northfield, Ill., 1977-83, pres., 1981-83; mem. Pub. Vehicle Ops. Citizens Adv. coun., City Chgo., 1985-86; mem. Chgo. regional bd. Anti-Defamation League of B'nai B'rith, 1975-91, vice chmn. 1980-88, mem. exec. com. Greater Chgo./Upper Midwest Region, 1996—; chmn. lawyers' com. for ann. telethon Muscular Dystrophy Assn., 1983; past bd. dirs. Jewish Nat. Fund., Am. Friends Hebrew U., Northfield Community Fund. Stalwart fellow, 1997; recipient Sec. State Ill. Pub. Svc. award, 1976, Citation of Merit, WAIT Radio, 1976, Sunset Ridge Sch. Community Svc. award, 1984; City of Chgo. Citizen's award 1986. Fellow Am. Bar Found. Ill. Bar Found. (bd. dirs. 1978-88, v.p. 1982-84, pres. 1984-86, chmn. Fellows 1983-84, chmn., past pres. adv. com. 1988-90, Cert. of Appreciation 1985, 86, Stalwart fellow, 1997), Chgo. Bar Found.; mem. Decalogue Soc. Lawyers, ABA (state regulation of securities com. 1982—, Ill. liaison of com., ho. of dels. 1981-85, chmn. subcom. liaison with securities adminstrs. and NASD 1998—), Ill. State Bar Assn. (bd. govs. 1976-80, del. assembly 1976-88, sec. 1977-78, cert. of appreciation 1980, 88, chmn. Bench and Bar com. 1982-83, chmn. Bench and Bar sect. coun. 1983-84, chmn. bar elections supervision com. 1986-87, chmn. assembly com. on hearings 1987-88, mem. com. on jud. appointments 1987-90), Chgo. Bar Assn. (mem. task force delivery legal svcs. 1978-80, cert. of appreciation 1976, chmn. land trusts com. 1978-79, chmn. consumer credit com. 1977-78, chmn. state securities law subcom. 1977-79), Northwestern U. Sch. of Law Alumni Assn. (dir.), Standard Club, Legal Club Chgo., Tau Epsilon Phi, Alpha Kappa Psi, Phi Delta Phi (named one of leading Ill. attys.). Office: Wildman Harrold Allen & Dixon 225 W Wacker Dr Ste 3000 Chicago IL 60606-1224

FEIN, RONNIE, writer, journalist; b. N.Y.C., June 5, 1943; d. William and Lily (Hoffman) Vail; m. Edward Fein, Nov. 15, 1969; children: Meredith, Gillian. BA, Northwestern U., 1964; LLB, NYU, 1967. Atty. Chadbourne, Parke, Whiteside & Wolff, N.Y.C., 1967-70, Rosenman, Colin, N.Y.C., 1970-71; dir. Ronnie Fein Sch. Creative Cooking, Stamford, Conn., 1971—; freelance demonstrator cooking, dept. stores various locations, 1971—; journalist Stamford Trader, 1980-81, The Advertiser, New Canaan, 1981-98, Times-Mirror newspapers, 1984—, Consumer's Digest Mag., 1989—, Darien Times, 1993—, Newsday, 1995—, Hersam-Acorn newspapers, 1997-98, Consumers Digest, 1989—, Westport Mag., 1999—, L.A. Times Syndicate, 1999—, Westport Mag., 1999—, Greenwich Mag., 1999—; talk show host WNLK, Norwalk, Conn., 1984. Author: The Complete Idiot's Guide to Cooking Basics, 1995, 2d edit. 1997. Alumni admissions dir. Fairfield County, Northwestern U., Evanston, Ill., 1985-98. Fellow Conn. Womens Culinary Alliance (charter, newsletter co-chmn. 1988-89, pres. 1996-97). Home: 438 Hunting Ridge Rd Stamford CT 06903-2123

FEIN, RUSS STUART, financial executive; b. Queens, N.Y., Mar. 29, 1963; s. Arthur and Judith L. (Greenberg) F.; m. Marjorie Ellen Glazer, June 20, 1987; children: Hannah Laurel, SaraJane Sussman, Jake Logan. BA in Managerial Econs. with honors, Union Coll., 1985; MBA in Fin./Acctg., U. Chgo., 1987. Sr. assoc. Mergers and Acquisitions dept. Jefferies & Co., N.Y.C., 1987-91; sr. assoc., prin. Providence Capital, N.Y.C., 1991; mng. dir. FH Capital Advisors, N.Y.C., 1992-96; exec. v.p. fin., COO Specialty Retail Group, Westport, Conn., 1992-96; exec. v.p. United Studios of Self Def., North Haven, Conn., 1996—. Mem. Omicron Delta Epsilon. Avocation: martial arts. Home: 75 Maplevale Dr Woodbridge CT 06525-1116 Office: United Studios of Self Def 33 Bernhard Rd North Haven CT 06473-3906

FEIN, SEYMOUR HOWARD, pharmaceutical executive; b. N.Y.C., Oct. 28, 1948; s. Abner and Beatrice (Wolkoff) F.; m. Mary Louise Orizzonto, Apr. 1, 1979; children: Jessica Ann, David Thomas, Renee Elizabeth, Jonathan Parker. BA, U. Pa., 1970; MD, N.Y. Med. Coll., 1974. Intern Dartmouth-Hitchcock Med. Ctr., Hanover, N.H., 1974-75; resident in internal medicine Dartmouth-Hitchcock Med. Ctr., Hanover, 1975-77; fellow in hematology, oncology Beth Israel Hosp., Harvard Med. Sch., Boston, 1977-80; instr. medicine Harvard Med. Sch., Boston, 1979-80; sr. rsch. physician Hoffmann-LaRoche, Nutley, N.J., 1980-83; dir. med. rsch. Miles Pharmaceuticals, West Haven, Conn., 1983-86, Rorer Pharmaceuticals, Fort Washington, Pa., 1986-87; v.p. med. rsch. Greenwich Pharmaceuticals, Fort Washington, 1987-88; dir. clin. rsch. and devel. Anaquest, Murray Hill, N.J., 1988-92; v.p. clin. rsch. and biostats. Oxford Rsch. Internat. Corp., Clifton, N.J., 1992-94; pres. Fein Consulting and Rsch. Svcs., New Canaan, Conn., 1994—; chmn. ChiRhoClin Inc., 1996—. Mem. Am. Soc. Clin. Oncology, N.Y. Acad. Scis., AAAS. Republican. Jewish. Avocations: reading, cooking, tennis, gardening, travel.

FEIN, THOMAS PAUL, software support specialist; b. Cin., Jan. 13, 1946; s. Harold Robert and Virginia May (Gray) F.; m. Linda Ann Stofle, Dec. 11, 1971. Student, Ohio State U., 1964-67, BBA, 1976. Programmer The Ohio Casualty Group, Hamilton, 1976, Am. Laundry Machinery, Cin., 1976; programmer/analyst Automated Data Systems, Cin., 1976-78, Savs. and Loan Data Corp., Cin., 1978-81; programmer/analyst Champion Internat. Corp., Hamilton, 1981-85, data security adminstr., 1985-89, pers. computer software analyst, 1990—. Bd. dirs. St. Raphael Social Svc. Agy., Inc. Mem. Cin. Personal Computer Users Group, Ohio State U. Alumni Assn. (life). Republican. Methodist. Lodges: Masons (local trustee 1982-97, sec.-treas. 1982-97, chmn. scholarship com. 1983-86), Order of Eastern Star. Avocations: sports, electronics, antiques, gardening, volunteering. Home: 650 History Bridge Ln Hamilton OH 45013-3659 Office: Champion Internat Corp 101 Knightsbridge Dr Hamilton OH 45011-3166

FEINBAUM, GEORGE, internist, endocrinologist; b. Samarkand, Uzbekistan, July 31, 1945; came to the U.S., 1965, naturalized, 1972; s. Joseph and Cyrla (Szoken) F.: 1 son, Livius. Student, Med. Acad. Wroclaw, Poland, 1963-65, Queens Coll., 1966-70; MD, Albert Einstein Coll. Medicine, 1973. Diplomate Am. Bd. Internal Medicine. Intern Met. Hosp. Ctr., N.Y.C., 1973-74, resident in internal medicine, 1974-76, fellow in endocrinology and metabolism, 1976-77; pvt. practice in internal medicine and endocrinology Bklyn., 1977—; asst. in medicine Brookdale Hosp. Med. Ctr., Bklyn. Fellow ACP; mem. Kings County Med. Soc., N.Y. Acad. Scis., Mensa. Office: 3245 Nostrand Ave Brooklyn NY 11229-3716 also: 934 Manhattan Ave Brooklyn NY 11222-5915

FEINBERG, DAVID ERWIN, publishing company executive; b. Mpls., 1922. Grad., U. Minn., 1948. Chmn., chief exec. officer EMC Corp., St. Paul; sec. bd. dirs., v.p. Paradigm Pub., Inc.; dir. Digital Excellence, Inc. Home: 111 Kellogg Blvd E Saint Paul MN 55101-1237 Office: EMC Corp 875 Montreal Way Saint Paul MN 55102-4245

FEINBERG, DENNIS LOWELL, dermatologist; b. Bridgeport, Conn., June 10, 1951. AB, Cornell U., 1973; MD, SUNY, Syracuse, 1976. Diplomat Nat. Bd. Med. Examiners, Am. Bd. Internal Medicine, Am. Bd. Dermatology. Intern U. Miami (Fla.) Affiliated Hosps., 1976-77, resident, 1977-78; resident Johns Hopkins Med. Inst., Balt., 1978-80; dermatologist pvt. practice, Washington, 1981, Stratford, Conn., 1981—; assoc. attending Bridgeport Hosp., 1981—; attending St. Vincent's Med. Ctr., Bridgeport, 1981—, cons. Milford (Conn.) Hosp., 1982—; asst. clin. prof. Yale U. Sch. Medicine, New HAven, Conn., 1985—. Fellow Am. Acad. Dermatology; mem. AMA, Am. Coll. Physicians, New Eng. Dermatological Soc., Conn. State Med. Soc., Fairfield County Med. Assn., Greater Bridgeport Med. Assn., Syracuse Med. Alumni Assn. Office: 2875 Main St Stratford CT 06614-4937

FEINBERG, GLENDA JOYCE, restaurant chain executive; b. Louisville, Feb. 8, 1948; d. Harold and Winnie Esther (McIntosh) F.; divorced; 1 child, Anthony John. Student, Purdue U., 1967-68, Ind. U., 1977-79. Cert. in restaurant and personnel mgmt. Beverage mgr. Don Ce Sar Beach Hotel, St. Petersburg Beach, Fla., 1979-80; catering dir. Best Western-Skyway Inn, St. Petersburg, Fla., 1980-83; gen. mgr. Village, Inc., St. Petersburg Beach, 1983-86; banquet mgr. Tradewinds Resort Hotel, St. Petersburg Beach, 1986-87; exec. mgr. Ponderosa, Inc., Clearwater, Fla., 1987-90; food and beverage dir. Days Inn Island Beach Resort, St. Petersburg Beach, 1990-92; owner, mgmt. cons., pvt. caterer G.F. Sans Inc., 1992—. Bd. dirs. AIDS Coalitions Pinellas, 1990. Mem. NOW, World Wildlife Fedn., Nat. Geog. Soc., Greenpeace, Amnesty Internat., Environ. Def. Fund, Nat. Audubon Soc., Nat. Arbor Day Found. Democrat.

FEINBERG, HERBERT, apparel and beverage executive; b. N.Y.C., June 20, 1926; s. Harry Feinberg and Dorothy (Hurwitz) Goldstein; m. Audrey Frank, Sept. 15, 1948 (div. Mar. 1972); children: Michael, Mark, Harry; m. Barbara Mays Jones, May 25, 1972 (div. June 1989); 1 child, Candice; m. Sandi Ann Gold, June 1989; 1 child, Tara. BS, U. Ill., 1949. Owner, v.p. Monsieur Henri Wines Ltd., N.Y.C., 1949-72; owner, pres. Hudson Valley Wine Village, Highland, N.Y., 1972—; owner, CEO I. Appel Corp., N.Y.C., 1976—, also chmn. bd.; owner, pres. Regent Champagne Cellars, Highland, N.Y., 1988. With USAF, 1944-46. Republican. Jewish. Avocations: tennis, boating.

FEINBERG, IRWIN L., retired manufacturing company executive; b. Bklyn., Mar. 4, 1916; s. Philip F. and Rose (Meyers) F.; m. Helen Kadison, Dec. 3, 1944; children: Marjorie, Phyllis. B.S., NYU, 1936. Sr. ptnr. Feinberg & Kadison, N.Y.C., 1947-94; exec. v.p., dir. Mallory Randall Corp., N.Y.C., 1971-76; pres., chief exec. officer, dir. Mallory Randall Corp., 1976-92, Savoy Industries Inc., 1984-92; chmn. bd. Robert Bruce Industries Inc., 1984-91. Mem. AICPA, N.Y. State Soc. CPAs, NYU Alumni Assn. Clubs: NYU, B'nai B'rith. Home: 16625 Powells Cove Blvd Apt 17D Whitestone NY 11357-1522*

FEINBERG, KENNETH ROY, lawyer, law educator; b. Brockton, Mass., Oct. 23, 1945; s. Martin B. and Dorothy (Rubenstein) F.; m. Diane Shaff, June 29, 1975; children: Michael, Leslie, Andrew. BA cum laude, U. Mass., 1967; JD, NYU, 1970. Bar: N.Y. 1971, D.C. 1977, Mass. 1980. Asst. U.S. atty. So. Dist. N.Y., 1972-75; gen. csl. subcom. on adminstrv. practice and procedure Com. on Judiciary, U.S. Senate, 1975-77, spl. counsel, 1979-80; adminstrv. asst. Senator Edward M. Kennedy, 1977-79; mng. ptnr. Kaye, Scholer, Fierman, Hays & Handler, Washington, 1980-92; ptnr. The Feinberg Group, Washington, 1993—; adj. prof. law Georgetown U. Law Ctr., 1979—. Trustee Dalkon Shield Claimants Trust; active Presdl. Adv. Commn. Human Radiation Experiments, Presdl. Commn. Catastrophic Nuclear Accidents, 1989-90, Carnegie Commn. Task Force Sci. and Tech. in Judicial and Regulatory Decision Making, 1989-93, Nat. Judicial Panel, Ctr. Pub. Resources, Marine Spill Response Corp. Named one of 27 Future Leaders of Am. Major Firms, The Am. Lawyer, 1986, one of 100 Most Influential Lawyers in Am., Nat. Law Jour. Mem. Am. Arbitration Assn., Bar Assn. City N.Y., Bar Assn. D.C., Mass. Bar Assn. Home: 5200 Edgemoor Ln Bethesda MD 20814-2342 Office: The Feinberg Group 1120 20th St NW Ste 740S Washington DC 20036-3441*

FEINBERG, LAWRENCE BERNARD, university dean, psychologist; b. Bklyn., June 2, 1940; s. Robert Erwin and Geraldine F.; m. Lynn J. Feinberg; children: Ronald, Nancy, Jillian. B.A., U. Buffalo, 1961; M.S.,

SUNY, Buffalo, 1963, Ph.D., 1966. Lic. psychologist, Calif. cert. rehab. counselor. Lectr. dept. counselor edn. SUNY, Buffalo, 1965-66; prof. spl. edn. and rehab. Syracuse U., 1966-77, dir. rehab. edn., 1967-77; prof. counselor edn. San Diego State U., 1977—, adj. prof. public health, 1981-96, assoc. dean grad. div. and research, 1977-98, acting dean Coll. Edn., 1984-85, acting dean grad. div. and research, 1986-87, exec. dir internat. programs, 1988-98, assoc. v.p. for rsch. and tech., 1998—; cons. psychologist VA Hosp., Syracuse, 1970-77; cons. Rehab. Services Adminstrn., HEW, Washington, 1976-77, Nat. Inst. Handicapped Research, U.S. Dept. Edn., 1982; chmn. Nat. Commn. Accreditation of Rehab. Edn., 1974-76; bd. dirs. Nat. Commn. Rehab. Counselor Cert., 1973-77. Author: (with others) Rehabilitation and Poverty: Bridging the Gap, 1969, Rehabilitation in the Inner City, 1970, Education for the Rehabilitation Services, 1974; cons. editor 6 profl. jours.; contbr. articles to profl. jours. Recipient 20 fed. grants, 4 nat. profl. service awards. Fellow Am. Psychol. Assn. (treas. div. rehab. psychology 1980-83, pres. div. rehab. psychology 1984-85), Am. Psychol. Soc.; mem. Am. Rehab. Counseling Assn. (pres. 1973, dir. 1980-83), Am. Personnel and Guidance Assn. (dir. 1974), N.Y. State Rehab. Counseling Assn. (pres. 1970), Council Rehab. Counselor Educators (regional dir. 1969-71), Phi Beta Delta (pres. Delta chpt. 1987-89). Home: 5021 Bluff Pl El Cajon CA 92020-8212 Office: San Diego State U Grad Div And Rsch San Diego CA 92182

FEINBERG, MARY STANLEY, judge. AB, Mt. Holyoke Coll., 1970; JD, Univ. of Va., 1973. Bar: W. Va., U.S. Dist. Ct. (so. dist.) W. Va., U.S. Ct. Appeals (4th cir.). Atty. Columbia Gas Transmission Corp., 1973-76; law clk. to Judge Dennis R. Knapp, 1976-77; asst. U.S. atty. Charleston, W. Va., 1977-92; magistrate judge U.S. Dist. Ct. (so. dist.) W. Va., Bluefield, W. Va., 1992—. Mem. Am. Bar Assn., W. Va. Bar Assn., Kanawha County Bar Assn. Office: US Courthouse PO Box 4190 Bluefield WV 24701-1990

FEINBERG, MORTIMER ROBERT, psychologist, educator; b. N.Y.C., Aug. 26, 1922; s. Max and Frieda (Siegel) F.; m. Gloria Granditer, June 22, 1947; children: Stuart Andrew, E. Todd. BS, CCNY, 1944; MS, Ind. U., 1945; PhD, NYU, 1950; D in Aviation (hon.), Embry-Riddle Aero. U., 1996. Diplomate Am. Bd. Examiners in Indsl. Psychology. Instr. psychology N.Y. U., 1945-50; chief psychologist Research Inst. Am., 1953-58; prof. psychology Bernard M. Baruch Coll., City U., 1958—, acting chmn. dept. psychology, 1969-70, dir. advanced mgmt., asst. dean, 1974-80; prof. emeritus, 1980—; pres. BFS Psychol. Assos., 1960-74, chmn., 1974—; bd. dirs. Senses Internat.; prin. lectr. Am. Mgmt. Assn., lectr. Young Pres.'s Orgn.; indsl. psychology cons. psychiatry div. Mt. Sinai Hosp.; rsch. adviser City of N.Y. Exec. Tng. Program, 1959-61; lectr. orgnl. behavior Beijing Mgmt. Assn., 1985. Pub.: Interaction; author: (with D. Fryer) Developing People in Industry, 1956, Effective Psychology for Managers, 1965, New Psychology for Managing People, (with G. Feinberg and J. Tarrant) Leavetaking, 1978, (with R. Dempewolff) Corporate Bigamy, (with J. Tarrant) Why Smart People Do Dumb Things; contbr. to Wall St. Jour., Reader's Digest; dir. Corp. Ethics audio program for Simon & Schuster. Fellow Am. Psychol. Assn., AAAS, Yale Club, N.Y. Sales Execs. (dir. 1974-85), Esquire Reporting (dir. 1993—). Clubs: Yale, N.Y. Sales Execs. (dir. 1974-85). Home: 34 Brook Ln Cortlandt Mnr NY 10567-6502 Office: BFS Psychol Assocs 666 5th Ave New York NY 10103

FEINBERG, NORMAN MAURICE, real estate executive; b. Bklyn., Nov. 28, 1934; s. Harry and Beatrice (Soroca) F.; m. Arline S. Itzkoff, Nov. 26, 1960; children: Mitchell, David. BS, NYU, 1956. Exec. Columbia Pictures Corp., N.Y.C., 1956-62; pres. Gateside Corp., Rye, N.Y., 1965—; owner, gen. ptnr. 27 companies, Rye; bd. dirs. St. Marys Rehab. Ctr. for Children. Arbitrator Am. Arbitration Assn., N.Y.C.; trustee, vice-chmn. Bklyn. Museum; bd. dirs. Assn. for Mentally Ill Children, Scarborough, N.Y, bd. dirs. St. Mary's Rehab. Ctr. for Children. Mem. World Pres. Orgn., Young Pres. Orgn. (chmn.), Chief Execs. Officers. Avocations: art collecting, skiing, tennis, travel, languages. Home: 188 E 76th St New York NY 10021 Office: Gateside Corp 555 Theodore Fremd Ave Rye NY 10580-1437

FEINBERG, PAUL H., lawyer; b. Yonkers, N.Y., Nov. 24, 1938. AB, U. Pa., 1960; LLB cum laude, Harvard U., 1963; LLM, NYU, 1970. Bar: N.Y. 1965, Ohio 1979. Asst. gen. counsel The Ford Found., 1971-77; ptnr. Baker & Hostetler LLP, Cleve.; speaker in field. Contbr. articles to profl. jours. Mem. ABA (mem. sect. taxation, mem. tax exempt orgns. com., co-chair subcom. non C3 organs. 1993-94, co-chair subcom. pvt. founds. 1995—), N.Y. State Bar Assn., Ohio State Bar Assn., Cleve. Bar Assn. (treas. 1996-99). Office: Baker & Hostetler LLP 3200 Nat City Ctr 1900 E 9th St Ste 3200 Cleveland OH 44114-3475

FEINBERG, RICHARD, anthropologist, educator; b. Norfolk, Va., Nov. 4, 1947; s. Isadore and Rose Selma (Hartmann) F.; m. Nancy Ellen Grim, Apr. 15, 1978; children: Joseph Grim-Feinberg, Kate Grim-Feinberg. AB, U. Calif., Berkeley, 1969; MA, U. Chgo., 1971, PhD, 1974. Asst. prof. anthropology Kent (Ohio) State U., 1974-80, assoc. prof., 1980-86, prof., 1986—; mem. editorial bd. Kent State U. Press, 1990-93; chair Kent State U. Faculty Senate, 1997-98; pres. Kent Rsch. Group, 1997-98. Author: Anuta: Social Structure of a Polynesian Island, 1981, Polynesian Seafaring and Navigation, 1988; editor: Politics of Culture in the Pacific Islands, 1995, Seafaring in the Contemporary Pacific Islands, 1995, Leadership and Change in the Western Pacific, 1996, Oral Traditions of Anuta, 1998. Kent State Rsch. Coun. grantee, 1983, 88; Wenner-Gren Found. grantee, 1991. Fellow Am. Anthrop. Assn., Assn. for Social Anthropology in Oceania (newsletter editor 1986-90); mem. Polynesian Soc., Am. Ethnological Soc., Ctrl. States Anthrop. Soc. (bull. editor 1994-98). Avocations: camping, white water kayaking, scuba diving, folk music, running. Office: Kent State U Dept Anthropology Kent OH 44242

FEINBERG, RICHARD ALAN, clinical psychologist; b. Oakland, Calif., Aug. 12, 1947; s. Jack and Raechel Sacks (Hoff) F. BA, Calif. State U.-Hayward, 1969; MA in Clin. Psychology, Mich. State U., 1972, PhD, 1979; Nat. Register of Health Service Providers in Psychology, 1980. Instr., Merritt Coll., Oakland, 1975-76; clin. psychologist Highland Gen. Hosp., Oakland, 1976-79; asso. Lafayette Center Counseling and Edn., 1978-79; clin. psychologist Tri-City Mental Health Center, Fremont, Calif., 1979-81, dir., 1981-86; pvt. practice clin. psychology, 1976—; participant profl. conf. USPHS fellow, 1969-71. Mem. Am. Psychol. Assn., Calif. Psychol. Assn. Jewish. Office: 38950 Blacow Rd Ste D Fremont CA 94536-7379

FEINBERG, ROBERT EDWARD, advertising agency executive, writer; b. N.Y.C., May 16, 1935; s. Alfred and Esther (Krutick) F.; m. Frances Greenfield, Sept. 1962 (div. 1980); children: Bradford, Karen; m. Jane Laurie Scheckter, Apr. 1980. AB, Hunter Coll., 1956. Publicist Bernstein Kornzweig, N.Y.C., 1956-59; pub. dir. William Morris Agy., N.Y.C., 1959-64; v.p., creative dir. Kameny Assocs., N.Y.C., 1964-68; copy group head J. Walter Thompson, N.Y.C., 1968-72; v.p., creative dir. William Esty Co., N.Y.C., 1972-77; exec. v.p. creative dir. Bozell and Jacobs, Los Angeles, 1977-82; exec. v.p., creative dir. Bozell, Jacobs, Kenyon & Eckhardt, N.Y.C., 1982-89; chief creative officer worldwide Grey Direct Mktg. Group, N.Y.C., 1989—. Author: (motion pictures) The American Way, 1962, Caribbean Celebration, 1980, (play) Everybody Else, 1976, Blitz, 1986; writer (TV series) Mork & Mindy, 1978, Adventures of Sheriff Lobo, 1979, Out of the Blue, 1978, Working Stiffs, 1989; contbr. articles Playboy mag., 1958. Recipient Internat. Broadcast award Hollywood Radio and TV Soc., 1966, 86, 87, Belding award Los Angeles Advt. Club, 1978, Clio awards, 1979, 80, 85, 86, 87, 88, 89, 90, Mobius award Chgo. Internat. Film Festival, 1986, Internat. Film and TV Festival award N.Y. Market Radio Advertisers, 1986 87, Creativity '87 award Art Direction mag., 1987, Andy award N.Y. Advt. Club, 1987, Effie award Am. Mktg. Assn., 1986, 88, 90. Mem. Writers Guild of Am., Direct Mktg. Club of N.Y. Avocations: travel; collecting vintage photographs, contemporary art. Office: Grey Direct Internat 875 3rd Ave Fl 9 New York NY 10022-6286

FEINBERG, ROBERT I(RA), lawyer; b. Boston, Jan. 6, 1956; s. Philip I. and Evelyn Helene (Hurvitz) F.; m. Lisa Michelle Palmer, Aug. 18, 1991; children: Perry, Justin. BA magna cum laude, Brown U., 1978; JD, U. Pa., 1981. Bar: Mass. 1982, Fla. 1985. Assoc. Parker, Coulter, Daley & White, Boston, 1981-83; ptnr. Feinberg and Alban, P.C., Brookline and Boston, Mass., 1984—; v.p. MVP Assocs., Brookline, 1980-87. Author: Jewish Voting Patterns in America, 1978. Active Anti-Defamation League, Boston, 1987—. Mem. Mass. Acad. Trial Attys. (lectr., mem. bd. govs. 1991—), Mass. Bar Assn., Boston Bar Assn., Nat. Polit. Action Com. (Washington). Jewish. Avocations: baseball, politics. Home: 1650 Commonwealth Ave West Newton MA 02465-2821 Office: Feinberg & Alban PC 141 Tremont St Boston MA 02111-1209

FEINBERG, ROBERT S., plastics manufacturing company executive, marketing consultant; b. Newark, May 14, 1934; s. Clarence Jacob and Sabina (Zorn) F.; BA in English, BS in Chemistry, Trinity Coll., Hartford, Conn., 1955; MBA in Mktg., Fairleigh Dickinson U., 1966; advt. diploma Assn. Indsl. Advt., 1967, advt. diploma N.Y. Inst. Advt., 1967; Pres., Trebor Assocs. and Trebor Plastics Co., Teaneck, N.J., 1961—; mktg. cons. computer software Zettler Softwear Co., Burroughs Corp.; sr. council Yankelovich, Skelly and White, Inc.; cons. Greenwich Assocs.; co-chmn., ptnr. Edgeroy Co., Inc., Ridgefield and Palisades Park, N.J., 1973—; co-chmn., ptnr. LeMont Sales Co., Teaneck, 1973—; cons. plastic formulations W.R. Grace, Endicott Johnson, Brown Shoe Co., U.S. Shoe Co., Ciba, Uniroyal. Mem. Soc. Plastics Engrs. (sr.), Sporting Goods Mfrs. Assn., Sell Overseas Am., U.S. Profl. Tennis Assn., Bergen County Tennis League (v.p.). Club: Ahdeek Tennis. Author: Olympia Shoe Co., 1966; co-inventor Edgeroy Ball Press (Internat. Tennis Hall of Fame, Newport, R.I.); patentee in polymer and mech. engring. fields. Home: PO Box 273 Teaneck NJ 07666-0273

FEINBERG, SHELDON NORMAN, pediatrician; b. N.Y.C., Mar. 16, 1930; m. MaryEllen Wisker, Jan. 2, 1988; children: Lynn Ann, Bette Joan, Barbara Ellen, Paul Howard, John Joseph. MD, N.Y. Med. Coll., 1955. Diplomate Am. Bd. Pediat. Intern Bronx Mcpl. Hosp. Ctr., N.Y.C., 1955-56; resident Met. Hosp., N.Y.C., 1956-57; fellow pediatrics N.Y. Med. Coll., 1959-60; pediat. staff Passack Valley Hosp., Westwood, N.J., 1960-82; emergency physician various hosps., 1982-85; pediat. staff Hackensack (N.J.) U. Med. Ctr., 1985—; clin. asst. prof. pediat. U. Med. & Dentistry N.J., Newark, 1985—. Inventor infant scale guard, simple stool stain. Maj. USAF med. corps., 1957-59. Honor award Bergen County Med. Soc., 1965. Fellow Am. Acad. Pediat.; mem. AMA, N.J. Pediat. Soc. (pres. 1989-91, Honor award 1991). Home: 125 N Country Rd Mount Sinai NY 11766-1503

FEINBERG, WILFRED, federal judge; b. N.Y.C., June 22, 1920; s. Jac and Eva (Wolin) F.; m. Shirley Marcus, June 23, 1946; children: Susan Stelk, Jack Feinberg, Jessica Twedt. BA, Columbia U., 1940, LLB, 1946, LLD (hon.), 1985; LLD (hon.), Syracuse U., 1985, Bklyn. Law Sch., 1998. Bar: N.Y. 1947. Law clk. Hon. James P. McGranery U.S. Dist. Ct. (ea. dist.) Pa., 1947-49; assoc. Kaye, Scholer, Fierman & Hays, N.Y.C., 1949-53; ptnr. McGoldrick, Dannett, Horowitz & Golub, N.Y.C., 1953-61; dep. supt. N.Y. State Banking Dept., N.Y.C., 1958; judge U.S. Dist Ct. (so. dist.), N.Y.C., N.Y., 1961-66; judge U.S. Ct. Appeals (2nd cir.), N.Y.C., N.Y., 1966—, chief judge, 1980-88, sr. judge, 1991—; mem. U.S. Jud. Conf. U.S., 1980-88, chmn. exec. com., 1987-88, mem. Devitt award com., 1989, 90, mem. long-range planning com., 1991-96; Madison lectr. NYU Law Sch., 1983; Sonnett lectr. Fordham U. Law Sch., 1984; Inaugural Howard Kaplan Meml. lectr. Hofstra U. Law Sch., 1986; The Future of Justice lectr. Inst. of Comparative Law, Chuo U., Japan, 1991. Editor-in-chief Columbia Law Rev, 1946; contbr. to profl. jours. and mags. With AUS, 1942-45. Recipient Learned Hand medal for excellence in fed. jurisprudence, 1982, Gold medal, award for disting. svc. in the law N.Y. State Bar Assn., 1990, medal for excellence Columbia Law Alumni Assn., 1990, Pursuit of Justice award Internat. Assn. Jewish Lawyers and Jurists, 1993, Disting. Pub. Svc. award N.Y. County Lawyers Assn., 1994, Edward Weinfeld award N.Y. County Lawyers Assn., 1995; Ann. Wilfred Feinberg Prize named in his honor for best student work at Columbia Law Sch. related to fed. cts., 1998. Mem. ABA, Assn. of Bar of City of N.Y., N.Y. County Lawyers Assn., Am. Judicature Soc., Am. Law Inst., Phi Beta Kappa. Office: US Ct Appeals 2nd Cir Room 2004 US Court House Foley Sq New York NY 10007-1501

FEINDEL, WILLIAM HOWARD, neurosurgeon, consultant; b. Bridgewater, N.S., Can., July 12, 1918; s. Robert Ronald Feindel and Annie Swansburg; m. Dorothy Faith Roswell Lyman, July 28, 1945; children: Christopher, Alexander, Patricia, Janet, Michael, Anna. BA, Acadia U., Can., 1939, DSc (hon.), 1963; MSc, Dalhousie U., Can., 1942; MD, CM, McGill U., Can., 1945, DSc (hon.), 1984; DPhil in Neuroanatomy, Oxford U., Eng., 1949; LLD (hon.), Mt. Allison U., 1983, U. Sask., Can., 1986. Diplomate Am. Bd. Neurol. Surgery; licentiate Med. Coun. Can. Rsch. asst. Montreal (Can.) Neurol. Inst., 1942-44, fellow in neuropathology, 1944-45, dir. neuro-isotope lab., 1959-88, dir. inst., 1972-84; dir. gen., dir. profl. svcs. Montreal Neurol. Hosp., 1972-84; rsch. asst., demonstrator in anatomy Oxford U., Eng., 1946-49; demonstrator in neurosurgery McGill U., 1951-52, lectr. neurosurgery, 1952-55, William Cone prof. neurosurgery, 1959-88, chmn. dept. neurology and neurosurgery, 1972-77, dir. Cone lab. neurosurg. rsch., 1959-88; assoc. prof. surgery U. Sask., 1955-56, prof. surgery, 1956-59; coord. rsch. in positron emission tomography Montreal Neurol. Inst. and Hosp., 1975-84, dir. brain imaging ctr., 1984-87, dir. neuro history project, 1987—; chancellor Acadia U., 1991-96, chancellor emeritus, hon. gov., 1996—; prin. investigator brain tumor project NIH, Bethesda, Md., 1986-89, co-investigator rsch., 1989—, mem.-reviewer neurol. disorders program project rev., 1983-88, external reviewer spl. programs, 1989-95; lectr. dept. history medicine and sci. U. B.C., 1976-78; neurol. cons. St. Paul's and City Hosps., Saskatoon, sask., 1955-59; cons. neurosurgeon Royal Victoria Hosp. and Catherine Booth Hos., Montreal, 1959-79, Sherbrooke (Que.) Gen. Hosp., 1964-85, Montreal Gen. Hosp., 1978—; cons. Champlain Valley Physicians Hosp., Plattsburgh, N.Y., 1973-85; neurosurgeon-in-chief Montreal Neurol. Hosp., 1961-72, sr. neurosurgeon, 1985—; neurologist and neurosurgeon-in-chief Royal Victoria Hosp., 1971-85, cons. neurosurgeon, 1985—; mem. sci. com. Found. for Study Ctrl. and Peripheral Nervous Sys., Geneva,1983—; mem. expert panel on neurology WHO and Pan-Am. Health Orgn., 1976-94, cons. in neuroscis., 1996—. Author more than 450 articles on epilepsy, neurosurgery, brain imaging and history of medicine; editor: Memory, Learning and Language—The Physical Basis of Mind, 1960, The Anatomy of the Brain and Nerves by Doctor Thomas Willis, tercentenary edit., 1965; co-editor: Dynamics of Brain Edema, 1976, Brain Imaging and Metabolism, 1985. Mem. bd. curators Osler Libr., McGill U., 1963—, curator Penfield Archive, 1976—, hon. assoc. libr. Osler Libr., 1964-65, hon. libr., 1996—; bd. govs. Acadia U., 1981-89, mem. exec. com., 1984-86. Decorated officer Order of Can., 1982; Rhodes scholar Merton Coll. Oxford U., 1939; recipient Neilson award Hannah Inst. History Medicine, 1997. Fellow ACS, Royal Coll. Physicians and Surgeons Can., Royal Soc. Can.; mem. Am. Assn. Neurol. Surgeons, Am. Acad. Neurol. Surgeons (pres. 1976), Am. Neurol. Assn. (v.p. 1976), Am. Epilepsy Soc. (J. Kiffin Penry award 1998), Am. Soc. Neurol. Surgeons, Can. Neurosurg. Soc. (pres. 1968), Montreal Medico-Chirurg. Soc. (pres. 1974), Osler Soc. McGill U. (pres. 1945, hon. pres. 1985-88, 90-97), James McGill Soc. (pres. 1997), Acad. Mexicana Cirugia (hon.), Am. Osler Soc., Osler Club London (hon.), Univ. Club Montreal, Faculty Club McGill U., Indoor Tennis Club, Alpha Omega Alpha. Anglican. Avocations: medical history, travel, music, book-binding, Maya culture. Office: Montreal Neurol Inst, 3801 University St # 110, Montreal, PQ Canada H3A 2B4

FEINDLER, JOAN LA GARDE, foreign language educator; b. N.Y.C., Oct. 5, 1929; d. Francis Harry and Marie La Garde (Engleke) Scantlebury; m. Klaus Stefan Feindler, Oct. 20, 1952; children: Eva, Alexa. BA, Mt. Holyoke Coll., 1950; MA, Columbia U., 1959. Cert. supr. secondary edn., N.Y. Tchr. L'Ecole Normale d'Institutrices, Rouen, France, 1950-51, Berkeley Inst., Bklyn., 1954-56, German Am. Sch. Assn., Ridgewood, N.Y., 1981-86; master tchr. French Grad. Sch. Harvard U., Cambridge, Mass., 1966, supr., 1967; instr. SUNY, Stony Brook, 1968-69, Columbia U., N.Y.C., 1973-74; tchr. French and Latin The Wheatley Sch., Old Westbury, N.Y., 1957-96, curriculum assoc., 1963-96; ret., 1996; demo tchr. U. Colo., Boulder, 1961, Hollins Coll., Va., 1962; bd. dirs. Northeast Conf. on Teaching Fgn. Langs., 1968-74; campus prin. Am. Inst. Fgn. Study at Schloss Nordkirchen, Germany, 1969; tchr. French Fgn. Study League Summer Program, Strasbourg, France, 1971; dean Scholastic Internat. Summer Program, 1973-75; supr. Sch. Exch. Program of Counc. on Internat. Ednl. Exch., France and Switzerland, 1978, 81, 83-84; fgn. lang. cons. various sch. dists., 1975-90. Recipient Palmes Academiques award Govt. of France, Paris, 1986. Mem. Am. Assn. Tchrs. French (pres. Nassau County chpt. 1971-74), N.Y. State Assn. Fgn. Lang. Tchrs. (Disting. Fgn. Lang. Tchr. 1988), Classical Assn. of the Empire State, L.I. Lang. Tchrs., Fgn. Lang. Assn. Chairmen and Suprs. (L.I. chpt., Morel award 1991), Phi Beta Kappa. Methodist. Avocations: crossword puzzles, substitute teaching. Home: 31 Beaumont Dr Melville NY 11747-3415

FEINEN, CYNTHIA LUCILLE, pediatric nurse; b. Pt. Pleasant, N.J., May 16, 1965; d. Lawrence Joseph and Lucille Carol F. Diploma in Nursing, Ann May Sch. Nursing. RN, N.J.; cert. pediatric advanced life support, BLS, ICC-PICC cen. cathether. Pediatric nurse Jersey Shore Med., Neptune, N.J., 1986—, Good Samaritan Hosp., West Palm Beach, Fla., 1990-91; nurse supr. Kimberely Quality Care, Eatontown, N.J., 1991-93; pediatric nurse cons. div. youth and family svcs. State of N.J., Asbury Park, 1993—, spl. home provider tng., foster parent tng.; owner Kidz First Consulting. Author: Task Sheet; co-author: (matrix) Medically Fragile, 1993, (guide) Medically Fragile, 1993; pub. Child Abuse: A Quick Reference, 1998. Mem. Perinatal Health Consortium, Monmouth County, 1993. Mem. ANA (cert. in pediatrics), N.J. League Nursing. Home: PO Box 762 Howell NJ 07731-0762

FEINER, ARLENE MARIE, librarian, researcher, consultant; b. Spring Green, Wis., Mar. 23, 1937; d. Herman Joseph and Cecelia Margaret (Meixelsperger) F. BA in History, Alverno Coll., 1959; MA in Libr. Sci., Rosary Coll., 1971; MA in Orgnl. Devel., Loyola U., Chgo., 1985. Gen. office worker USIA, Washington, 1959-60; adminstrv. sec. Nat. Coun. Cath. Women, Washington, 1960-62; asst. libr. Munich campus, U. Md., Fed. Republic Germany, 1962-64; preliminary cataloger, 1st editor MARC Pilot Project, Libr. of Congress, Washington, 1965-67; head libr. Acad. of the Holy Cross, Kensington, Md., 1967-70, Jesuit Sch. of Theology Libr., Chgo., 1971-79, coord. serial activities; women's studies bibliographer, Loyola U., Chgo., 1979-86; tech. svcs., collection devel. cons. DuPage Libr. System, 1986-91; contract adminstr. Wabash Nat. Fin., Arlington Heights, Ill., 1992—. Editor: (bibliography) Current Serials, 1980-85; compiler: (bibliography) Guide to Women's Studies Sources, 1985; author of poems; contbr. articles to profl. jours. Bd. dirs. Women's World Ctr., Chgo., 1985-88. Assn. of Theol. Schs. in U.S. and Can. grantee, 1976. Mem. ALA, Nat. Mus. Women in Arts, C.G. Jung Inst. Chgo. Roman Catholic. Avocations: poetry, hiking, music. Home: 336 W Wellington Ave Apt 2102 Chicago IL 60657-5614

FEINER, AVA SOPHIA, public affairs and management consultant, economist; b. Bklyn., Feb. 13, 1950; d. Ignace and Lola (Pasternak) F.; m. Clifford Douglas Stromberg, June 25, 1972; children: Kimberly Greta, Eric George. BA summa cum laude, Yale U., 1971; MA, Harvard U., 1974, PhD in Govt., 1978. Legis. asst. to U.S. Senator Bill Bradley, Washington, 1979-82; dir. internat. trade policy U.S. C. of C., Washington, 1982-83, mgr. internat. policy dept., 1983-85; corp. program dir. IBM, Washington, 1985-87, corp. dir. pub. affairs, trade and investment, 1987; pres. Feiner Pub. Affairs Cons., Washington, 1988—; co-founder, dir. Washington Alive! Inc., 1989-90; pres. Washington Networks, 1990—; teaching fellow Harvard U., Cambridge, Mass., 1972-74; lectr. nat. and internat. politics and econs., 1978—; bd. dirs., World Trade Forum, Washington, 1987-89. Co-author: American Excellence in A World Economy, 1987; contbr. articles on econs., trade, fgn. policy to various publs. Del. to Atlantic Coun. Young Leadership Program, Wis. and Can., 1978, 80, Aspen Inst. Exec. Seminar, 1982, Germany-U.S. Young Leadership Conf., San Francisco, 1982, Harbor Sch. Bd., 1992-93; co-chair Holton-Arms Sch. Silent Auction, 1995-96; mem. adv. com. Cmty. Homeowners, 1999—. Fgn. Policy fellow Brookings Instn., 1975-76, guest scholar, 1976-77; Carnegie Endowment for Internat. Peace fellow, 1975-76. Mem. Coun. Fgn. Rels. (task force on women 1988-91, term membership com. 1988-91, internat. affairs fellows com. 1991-95, Washington program adv. com. 1995-98), Trade Policy Forum, Phi Beta Kappa. Avocations: photography, karate, swimming, bicycling, tennis.

FEINER, ROBERT FRANKLIN, petroleum and mechanical engineer; b. Boston, Jan. 26, 1969; s. Maxwell and Zipora (Kreisler) F. BSE, Tulane U., 1991; MBA, U. Tex., Austin, 1997. Engr.-in-tng., Tex. Drilling engr. ARCO Oil & Gas, Houston, LaFayette, La., 1991-93; applications engr. Camco, Houston, 1994, exec. sales rep., 1995; summer intern. fin. analyst Nabors Industries, Houston, 1996; mgmt. cons. Ernst & Young, Dallas, 1997-99, Dell Computer, Austin, 1999—. Contbr. articles to Petroleum Engr. Internat.; opinions editor Tex. Bus. Weekly, 1995-96. Vol. United Way, LaFayette, 1991-93, Dallas, 1997-98; vol. U.S. Presdl. Election, New Orleans, 1988, Amnesty Internat., 1991-96, Tulane Alumni Admissions, 1991-96; dir. Grad. Bus. Network, Dallas, 1998; del. Tex. Senatorial Dist. Party Conv., 1998. Mem. ASME, NSPE, Am. Assn. Drilling Engrs. (industry com. 1994), Soc. Petroleum Engrs. Home: # 3402 800 W 38th St Austin TX 78705

FEINGLASS, NEIL GORDON, anesthesiologist; b. Miami, Fla., 1957. MD, Vanderbilt U., 1983. Resident in anesthesiology U. Fla. Coll. Medicine, Gainesville, 1983-86, fellow in critical care medicine, 1986-87; fellow in cardiac anesthesia Tex. Heart Inst., 1986; cons. anesthesiologist/critical care medicine Mayo Clinic, Rochester, Minn., 1990—, chief of cardiac anesthesia, head intraoperative echo svc., 1995—, dir. anesthesia info. svcs.; asst. prof. Mayo Grad. Sch. Medicine. Fellow Am. Coll. Chest Physicians; mem. AMA, Am. Bd. Echocardiography, Am. Surg. Assn., Minn. Med. Assn., Minn. Surg. Assn., Am. Lung Assn. (regional bd. dirs. 1999—), ZVMS. Office: Mayo Clinic Jacksonville 4500 San Pablo Rd S Jacksonville FL 32224-1865

FEINGLOS, SUSAN JEAN, library director; b. Montreal, Que., Can., Apr. 23, 1949; d. Ralph and Beryl Goldman; m. Mark Neil Feinglos. BA with honors in Art History, McGill U., Montreal, 1970, MLS, 1972. Reference libr., cataloger Cote St Luc (Que.) Pub. Libr., 1971-72; cataloger, libr. cons. Reader's Digest Assn. (Can.) Ltd., Montreal, 1972; asst. med. libr. Montreal Children's Hosp., 1972-73; libr., ref. libr. Duke Ctr. for Study Aging-Human Devel., Duke U., Durham, N.C., 1973-76, sr. fellow, 1975—; reference libr. Duke U. Med. Ctr. Libr., 1976-80, coord. interlibr. loan, 1978-80, coord. online svcs., 1980-91, acting dir., 1991-92, dir., 1992—; reviewer Annals Internal Medicine, 1986—; mem. user adv. bd. and tech. svcs. com. Bibliographic Retrieval Svcs., 1984-87; mem. user adv. bd. Excerpta Medica, 1985-87; tech. resource person Nat. Libr. Medicine, 1981-83; presenter in field. Author: MEDLINE: A Basic Guide to Searching, 1985 (transl. into Japanese 1991); contbr. articles to profl. jours. Grantee Integrated Acad. Info. Mgmt. Svcs., 1991-95. Mem. Med. Libr. Assn. (cert., instr. continuing edn. 1983—, nominating com. 1994, liaison to credentialling com. Mid-Atlantic chpt. 1992—, books panel com. 1997-2000, Janet Doe lectureship award com. 1996-97), Acad. Health Info. Profls. (disting.), Assn. Health Scis. Libr. Dirs. (libr. info. mgmt. tech. com. 1993—), Spl. Librs. Assn. (recruitment com. N.C. chpt.. 1976-77, cons. com. 1977-78), Microcomputer Users Group for Librs. in N.C., Assn. N.C. Health and Sci. Librs. (chmn. nominating com. 1987-88), Triangle Rsch. Librs. Network (governing bd.). Home: 20 Scott Pl Durham NC 27705-5719 Office: Duke U Med Ctr Med Libr Durham NC 27710

FEINGOLD, BENJAMIN S., broadcast executive. BA, Brandeis U.; MA, London Sch. Econs.; JD, U. Calif., San Francisco. With Kaye, Scholer, Fierman, Hays & Handler, N.Y.C.; corp. counsel, securities lawyer Sony Pictures Entertainment, 1988, v.p. entertainment transactions, 1989, sr. v.p. corp. devel.; pres. Sony Pictures Entertainment Columbia TriStar Home Video, Culver City, Calif., 1994—. Office: Sony Pictures Entertainment Columbia Tristar Home Video 10202 Washington Blvd Culver City CA 90232-3119*

FEINGOLD, DANIEL LEON, anesthesiologist; b. Boston, May 19, 1958; s. Macey Gerson and Hélène Sultana (Benlolo) F. BS with distinction, U. Ill., Chgo., 1980; MD, U. Health Scis., Chgo. Med. Sch., 1984. Intern Weiss Meml. Hosp., Chgo., 1984-85; resident in anesthesiology U. Ill. Hosps. and Clinics, Chgo., 1986-89; anesthesiologist Hosp. Anesthesia Group, Chgo., 1989—. Contbr. articles to profl. publs. Mem. AMA, AAAS, Am. Soc. Anesthesiologists, Ill. State Med. Soc. Home: PO Box 577429 Chicago IL 60657-7429 Office: PO Box 25678 Chicago IL 60625-0678

FEINGOLD, DAVID SIDNEY, microbiology educator; b. Chelsea, Mass., Nov. 15, 1922; s. Louis Edward and Miriam (Young) F.; m. Batia Babette Haber, Nov. 15, 1949; children: Oded, Anat, Michele. B.S., MIT, 1944; Ph.D., Hebrew U., Jerusalem, Israel, 1956. Chemist Lucidol Corp., Buffalo,

1944; jr. research biochemist U. Calif. at Berkeley, 1957-60; asst. prof. biology U. Pitts., 1960-62, asso. prof., 1962-65, prof., 1965—; prof. microbiology Sch. Medicine, 1966-93, prof. emeritus molecular genetics and biochemistry, 1993—. Contbr. articles to profl. jours. Served with USNR, 1944-46. Recipient State of Israel prize in natural sci., 1957, Career Devel. award NIH, 1965-75. Fellow Infectious Disease Soc. Am.; mem. Internat. Endotoxin Soc., Am. Soc. for Biochemistry and Molecular Biology. Home: 6420 Bartlett St Pittsburgh PA 15217-1832

FEINGOLD, RUSSELL DANA, U.S. senator, lawyer; b. Janesville, Wis., Mar. 2, 1953; s. Leon and Sylvia (Binstock) F.; m. Susan Levine, Aug. 21, 1977; children: Jessica, Ellen; m. Mary Speerschneider, Jan. 20, 1991; stepchildren: Sam, Ted. B.A. with honors, U. Wis.-Madison, 1975; postgrad. Magdalen Coll., Oxford U., 1975-77; J.D. with honors, Harvard U., 1979. Bar: Wis. 1979. Assoc., Foley & Lardner, Madison, 1979-82, LaFollette, Sinykin, Anderson & Munson, Madison, 1983-85, Goldman & Feingold, 1985-88; mem. Wis. Senate, 1983-92, U.S. senator from Wis., 1993—, mem. aging com., budget com., fgn. rels. com., judiciary com., senate Dem. policy com. Wis. Honors scholar, 1971; Rhodes scholar, 1975. Mem. Phi Beta Kappa. Democrat. Jewish. Office: US Senate 716 Hart Senate Office Bldg Washington DC 20510 Office: US Senators Office 8383 Greenway Blvd Middleton WI 53562-3506

FEINGOLD, S. NORMAN, psychologist; b. Worcester, Mass., Feb. 2, 1914; s. William and Aida (Salit) F.; m. Marie Goodman, Mar. 24, 1947; children: Elizabeth Anne, Margaret Ellen, Deborah Carol, Marilyn Nancy. AB, Ind. U., 1937; MA, Clark U., 1940; EdD, Boston U., 1948; LLD, Edward Waters Coll., Saints Coll. Dir. vocat. service, also ednl. and vocat. dir. Hecht. Neighborhood House, Boston, 1940-43; exec. dir. Boston Jewish Vocat. Service and Work Adjustment Center, 1946-58; nat. dir. B'nai B'rith Career and Counseling Services, Washington, 1958-80; pres. Nat. Career and Counseling Services, 1980—, pvt. practice, 1980—; exec. adviser Rehab. Services, Boston, 1953-58; dir. ednl. and vocat. workshop United Cerebral Palsy of Greater Boston, Inc., 1957-58; cons. to Scholarships, Fellowships and Loans News Service, Social Security Adminstrn., 1962—; instr., spl. lectr. Boston U., 1951-58; profl. lectr. Am. U. Rehab. Counseling Adv. Panel, 1963-65; mem. Am. Bd. Counseling Services, 1962-65, 70—. Author: It Pays to Advertise, 1975, Occupations and Careers, 1969, The Vocational Expert in the Social Security Disability Program, 1969, A Counselor's Handbook, 1972, Counseling for Careers in the 80's, 1979, Whither Counseling, 1981, Making It on Your Own, rev., 1991, A Guide to Financial Success, 1981, rev., 1985, Emerging Careers: New Occupations for the Year Two Thousand and Beyond, 1983, The Professional and Trade Association Job Finder, 1983, Getting Ahead: A Woman's Guide to Career Success, 1983, Scholarships, Fellowships and Loans, Vol. 8, 1987, New Emerging Careers: Today, Tomorrow, and in the 21st Century, 1988, Futuristic Exercises: A Work Book for Emerging Lifestyles and Careers in the 21st Century and Beyond, 1989, Where the Jobs Are: A Comprehensive Directory of 1200 Journals Listing Career Opportunities, 1989, The Complete Job and Career Handbook: 101 Ways to Get from Here to There, 1993; past editor Counselors Information Service. Chmn. Gov.'s Council on Aging, 1956-58, Washington Bus.-Industry Group, 1963-64; mem. Pres.'s Com. on Employment Handicapped, 1950—; mem. adv. com. Nat. Health Council; mem. Nat. Home Study Accrediting Commn.; chmn. human relations com. Dept. Agr. Grad. Sch.; mem. profl. adv. bd. Epilepsy Found. Served from pvt. to 1st lt. AUS, 1943-46, ETO and PTO. Recipient Community Service award B'nai B'rith, 1957, Brotherhood and Americanization award, 1958, Eminent Career award Nat. Capital Personnel and Guidance Assn. Fellow Am. Psychol. Assn.; mem. Greater Boston Personnel and Guidance Assn. (pres. 1952-53), Am. Personnel and Guidance Assn. (pres. 1974-75), Mass., Eastern psychol. assns., Nat. Vocat. Guidance Assn. (pres. 1968-69), Am. Assn. Adult Edn., Am. Assn. Marriage and Family Counselors (clin.), Internat. Coun. Psychologists, Nat. Press Club, Nat. Rehab. Assn., Torch Club, New Century Club (bd. dirs. 1954-58), Phi Delta Kappa. Home: 1801 E Jefferson St # 442 Rockville MD 20852-4057 *Any success I may have attained is because of conscientiousness, a love of life, a high energy level, a supportive family, close friends, and being an optimist by temperament and conviction. I believe in people and the tremendous potential of all people. To me, everyone is a Very Important Person, who can make a contribution. My premise is that our most precious resource is people, and everything we do individually or collectively now or in the future depends on that conviction and acting accordingly.*

FEINHANDLER, EDWARD SANFORD, writer, photographer, art dealer, sports mentor, consultant, educator; b. Elko, Nev., Jan. 13, 1948; s. Samuel and Sylvia (Manus) F. BA, U. Nev., 1972; EED in Elem. Edn., Sierra Nevada Coll., 1997. Supr. underprivileged Washoe County Extension Program, Reno, 1970-71; sports editor, writer Sagebrush Campus newspaper, Reno, 1971-72; internal salesman, mgr. Trigon Corp., Sparks, Nev., 1975-88; owner, operator Art Internat. Gallery Extraordinaire, Reno, 1981—; tennis dir. City of Sparks, 1991-93, Cmty. Edn. Program, Sparks, 1994, Sparks YMCA, 1995-96; with nat. news Top Ten radio interviews, U.S. and Can., 1978-79; freelance writer and photographer; pres. No. Nev. H.S. Tennis Assn., 1996. Contbr. articles to newspapers and mags.; extra in various movies; TV interviewee AM Chgo., AM L.A., 1979, Afternoon Exchange, Cleve., 1979, To Tell the Truth, 1975, Reno Tonight TV show, 1989, Fox Across America TV show, 1989, Wheel of Fortune, 1995. Player, coach Summer Volleyball League, Reno, 1982-85; tennis coach Cmty. Svc. Ctr., Reno, 1986-88, 94; founder softball event Make-A-Wish Found., Reno, 1985-99; active U. Nev. Journalism Dept., 1985-93, UNR Children's Svcs., Reno, 1986-88; basketball coach Little Flower Cath. Sch., 1987-89; head coach girls varsity tennis team Bishop Manogue H.S., 1989-91; coach boys varsity tennis Sparks H.S., 1993-97, spl. olympics, 1989, girls jr. varsity basketball, 1989-90; active Ptnrs. in Edn., 1988-99, Jr. Achievement, 1989-94, Animal Welfare Inst., Statue of Liberty Found., 1984-98, No. Nev. Cancer Coun., United Blood Svcs., Arthritis Found., Cancer Soc., Sta. KNPB, Ret. Sr. Citizens, Reno Fire Dept. Christmas Basket Delivery, 1991-98, Sierra Arts Found.; vol. free tennis lessons, 1993-99; fundraiser H.L.A. Testing United Blood Svcs., 1991-98; founder, dir. No. Nev. Youth Opportunistic Tennis program, 1997-99. Sgt. U.S. Army, 1968-69, Vietnam. Winner Ugly Man contest No. Nev. Bone Marrow Program, 1991-98, ind. category Ugly Bartender contest Multiple Sclerosis, 1989-90, UNR Ugly Man, 1967, 70, 71, 72; Sparks Tennis Club singles, doubles, and mixed doubles Champion B/C divsn., 1994, STC Singles B Champion, Mixed B Doubles Champion, 1995, STC Ladder B Singles Men's Champion, 1996, 97, 3rd Ann. STC B Doubles Champion, 1996; recipient numerous tennis, billiards, volleyball and bowling awards including 1st pl. C divsn. NNCC Tennis Tournament, 1991, RTC C Mixed Doubles Champion, 1992, Sparks Recreation Open Doubles Champion, 1993; world record holder nosedarts and squint, 1972—; recipient Cmty. Svc. award United Blood Svcs., 1995, Svc. Above Self award Rotary Internat., 1995, Joeil Vowell Charity Softball award Make-A-Wish Found., 1997, 98, Cmty. Safety award Associated Builders and Contractors, 1997, Spl. Thank You award Pine Mid. Sch. Students Concerned with Quick Thinking and Gt. Effort, 1997, Angel award Washoe County Sch. Dist., 1997. Mem. DAV, Orthodox Jewish Union. Democrat. Avocations: bowling, tennis, basketball, baseball, volleyball. Office: Art Internat Gallery Extraordinaire PO Box 13405 Reno NV 89507-3405

FEININGER, THEODORE LUX, artist; b. Berlin, June 11, 1910; s. Charles Lyonel and Julia (Lilienfeld) F.; m. Patricia Randall, Dec. 17, 1954; children: Lucas, Conrad, Charles. Grad., Bauhaus, Dessau, Germany, 1929. Instr. Sarah Lawrence Coll., 1950-52; lectr. drawing and painting Harvard U., 1953-62; instr. drawing and painting Boston Fine Arts Mus. Sch., 1962-75. Author: Lyonel Feininger: City at the Edge of the World, 1965, Photographs of the 20s and 30s (illustrated catalogue), 1980; exhbns. include Am. Realists and Magic Realists, Mus. Modern Art, N.Y.C., 1943, Revolution and Tradition in Modern Am. Art, Bklyn. Mus., 1951, Whitney Mus. Am. Art Ann., N.Y.C., 1951, Am. Painters, MIT, 1954, Retrospective, Busch-Reisinger Mus., 1962, Wheaton Coll., 1973, Wamsutta Club, New Bedford, Mass., 1974, Prakapas Gallery, N.Y.C., 1980, Sacramento St. Gallery, Cambridge, Mass., 1982, Gallery on the Green, Lexington, Mass., 1986, 88, 90, 92, Achim Moeller Fine Art, N.Y.C., 1954-94, Staatliche Galerie Moritzburg Halle, Saale, Germany, 1998; represented in permanent collections Mus. Modern Art, N.Y.C., Busch-Reisinger Mus. and Fogg Art Mus., Harvard U., Altonaer Mus., Hamburg, Germany, Schleswig-Holstein Landes Mus., Mus. Folkwang, Essen, Germany, Bauhaus Mus., Weimar, Germany, Getty Mus., Calif., Met. Mus., N.Y., L.A. County Mus., Stedelijk Mus., Amsterdam, Guggenheim Mus., N.Y. With U.S. Army, 1942-45. Mem. Westport Art Group. Democrat. Address: 22 Arlington St Cambridge MA 02140-2713 *The practice and teaching of art has shown me that I must seek progress on the basis of understanding and assimilating tradition: that every individual incorporates both revolutionary and conservative tendencies; and that the task of the individual lies in assessing and acting upon his findings, his own proportionate share of these two conflicting trends. I am Society, and Society cannot do without me.*

FEINN, BARBARA ANN, economist; b. Waterbury, Conn., Feb. 16, 1925; d. David Harris and Dora (Brandvein) F.; m. Steven L. Wissig, Jan. 10, 1991. AB magna cum laude, Smith Coll., 1946; MA (univ. scholar), Yale U., 1947, PhD (univ. fellow), 1952; cert., Oxford (Eng.) U., 1949. Rsch. economist First Nat. City Bank, N.Y.C., 1953-54; assoc. economist Office Messrs. Rockefeller, N.Y.C., 1954-61; asst. to dir. N.Y. State Office for Regional Devel., N.Y.C., 1961-62; cons. economist Nelson A. Rockefeller, N.Y.C., 1963-64; pvt. cons., 1965-68; sr. coun. economist N.Y. State Coun. Econ. Advisers, N.Y.C., 1969-72; chief economist Office S.C. Gov., Columbia, 1972-74, State of S.C., 1974-92; mem. bd. econ. advisors, 1976-88, sec. bd. econ. advisors, 1986-88, exec. dir. bd. econ. advisors, 1988-92, econ. cons., 1993—; adj. prof. bus. adminstrn. U. S.C., Columbia, 1972-74; ofcl. participant White House Conf. on Balanced Nat. Growth and Econ. Devel., 1978; del. meetings on nat. balanced growth Nat. Govs. Assn., Leesburg, Va., 1977; mem. S.C. Gov.'s Task Force on the Economy, 1980-84; mem. productivity measurement com. S.C. Coun. on Productivity, 1981-84. Dir. Smith Coll. Alumnae Fund Program, N.Y.C., 1965-66, mem. spl. gifts com., 1971, class v.p., 1986-91, class treas., 1991-96, 96—; del. assembly Assn. Yale Alumni, 1983-86, 91-94. Recipient Wilbur Lucius Cross medal Yale U., 1987. Mem. Am. Econ. Assn., Nat. Assn. Bus. Econs., Downtown Economists Luncheon Group, Carolinas Econ. Assn., Phi Beta Kappa. Clubs: Yale (N.Y.C. and cen. S.C.); Summit, Wildewood (Columbia, S.C.), Woodcreek (Columbia), The Faculty (Columbia), Smith Coll. (Columbia). Contbr. articles to profl. jours. Home: 50 Mallet Hill Ct Columbia SC 29223-3126

FEINSILVER, STEVEN HENRY, physician, educator; b. N.Y.C., Oct. 27, 1952; s. Albert S. and Mildred C. (Weissman) F.; m. Margaret Caldwell Hall, July 4, 1982; children: Joseph, Samuel. ScB, Brown U., 1974, MD, 1977. Diplomate Am. Bd. Internal Medicine, sub-bds. pulmonary diseases and critical care medicine; cert. in sleep medicine; diplomate Nat. Bd. Med. Examiners; lic. physician, Mass., R.I., N.Y. Resident in internal medicine Univ. Hosp.-Boston U. Med. Ctr., 1977-80; fellow in pulmonary medicine Stanford U. Med. Ctr., 1980-82; from instr. to asst. prof. medicine Brown U., Providence, 1982-86; asst. prof. medicine SUNY, Stony Brook, 1986-92, assoc. prof., 1992—; mem. med. staff, dir. Pulmonary Function Lab. Winthrop-Univ. Hosp., Mineola, N.Y., 1986-94, dir. Sleep Disorders Ctr., 1986-97; dir. divsn. of pulmonary medicine North Shore U. Hosp., Manhasset, N.Y., 1997—. Author textbook; contbr. articles to profl. jours. Pres. bd. dirs. Harbor Day Care Ctrs., New Hyde Park, N.Y., 1991-94; asst. scoutmaster Troop 10 Boy Scouts Am. Fellow ACP, Am. Coll. Chest Physicians (nat. adv. com. on cardiopulmonary sleep disorders 1990, Nat. chair sec. of Sleep Disorders, ACCP, 1994-98), Am. Sleep Disorders Assn. (bd. dirs. 1998—); mem. Am. Thoracic Soc., Clin. Sleep Soc., N.Y. State Med. Soc., N.Y. Trudeau Soc., L.I. Pulmonary Soc. (sec.-treas.), Steppingstone Sailing Club (commodore 1993-95), Knickerbocker Yacht Club, Sigma Xi. Office: North Shore U Hosp 300 Community Dr Manhasset NY 11030-3801

FEINSTEIN, ALAN SHAWN, writer, financial adviser; b. Boston, June 25, 1931; s. Louis and Lillian Edith (Pector) F.; m. Pratarnporn Chiemwichit, June 2, 1963; children—Ari Jason, Richard Justin, Leila Jane. BS, Boston U., 1952; MS, Boston State Coll., 1956; PhD (hon.), Johnson and Wales U., 1994, Providence Coll., 1996; hon. degree, New Eng. Tech., Roger Williams U.; hon. doctorate, R.I. Coll., Salve Regina U. Tchr. pub. schs., Mass. and R.I., 1956-57; founder English Sch., Bangkok, Thailand, 1965; writer syndicated column The Treasure Chest, 1968-85; writer syndicated feature My America, 1971-85; lectr. in field; originator Citizenship Ctr., R.I. Internat. Inst., 1996—. Author: Triumph, 1960, Folk Tales from Siam, 1969, Folk Tales from Persia, 1971, Folk Tales from Portugal, 1972, Making Your Money Grow, 1972, How To Make Money, 1976, How To Secure Your Financial Future, 1978, The Vanishing Treasure, 1980, The Key To Riches, 1982, (newsletters) The Insiders Report, The Wealth Maker; subject of book The Four Treasures of Alan Shawn Feinstein. Founder World Hunger Ctr., Brown U., Youth World Hunger Brigade, 1991, supports numerous food pantries and soup kitchens throughout U.S.; chmn. Cranston Crime Stoppers, 1982—; founder Inst. of Pub. Svc. at Providence Coll.; established pub. svc. programs in numerous pub. and pvt. high schs. and elem. schs., R.I. and in over 500 elem. schs. nationwide; founder Louis Feinstein-Horatio Alger Humanitarian Award, Enriching Am. Program, 1996, Lillian Feinstein Child Care and Child Devel. Ctr., Lillian Feinstein Literacy Ctr., Louis Feinstein Legal Svcs. Ctr. at Roger Williams U., scholarship fund to memorialize people whose lives are tragically cut short; chmn. Rhode Islanders for Hunger Free State, 1997. Recipient 1st Humanitarian award City of Cranston, Red Cross Humanitarian award, 1994, Disting. Svc. award Am. Hist. Soc., 1994, Hope award KC, 1996, Citizen of Yr. award March of Dimes, 1996, Pres.'s medal Brown U., 1996, R.I. Coll.; founder $3,000,000 scholarship endowment fund for entering coll. students committed to pub. svc.; named first U.S. pub. high sch. with pub. svc. as core named in his honor; named to R.I. Hall of Fame, 1995; Tufts U. Internat. Famine Ctr. named in his honor, also Central Falls and Providence elem. schs., R.I. Coll. Edn., Roger Williams Coll. Arts and Sci., Johnson and Wales Grad. Sch., Coll. Cont. Edn. U. R.I., Burriville Boy Scout Camp, Citizenship Ctr. at R.I. Internat. Inst. named in his honor. Jewish. Home and Office: 41 Alhambra Ctr Cranston RI 02905-3416

FEINSTEIN, ALLEN LEWIS, lawyer; b. N.Y.C., Apr. 18, 1929; s. Jacob and Kate (Goldberg) F.; m. Charlesa Joan Wolfe, Dec. 14, 1957. AB, CCNY, 1949; LLB, Columbia U., 1952. Bar: N.Y. 1952, U.S. Supreme Ct. 1958, Ariz. 1960, U.S. Dist. Ct. Ariz. 1960, U.S. Ct. Appeals (9th cir.) 1960. Assoc. Proskauer Rose Goetz & Mendelsohn, N.Y.C., 1955-59; law clk. to justice Supreme Ct. Ariz., Phoenix, 1959-61, 1st adminstrv. dir., 1961-64; pvt. practice law Phoenix, 1964-72, 1995—; ptnr. Daughton Feinstein & Wilson, Phoenix, 1972-86; sr. ptnr. Rawlins, Burrus, Lewkowitz & Feinstein, P.C., Phoenix, 1986-95; mem. Phoenix Housing Code Com., 1968; vice-chmn. adv. com. State Legislative com. on Medicaid; mem. Phoenix Charter Review Com., 1969; mem. exec. com. Phoenix Sister City Commn., 1973-75. Author: First, Second and Third Reports of Courts of Arizona, 1962, 63, 64. Bd. dirs. Meml. Hosp. Phoenix, chmn., 1973-76, Community Coun., 1970-76, Ariz. Jewish Hist. Soc.; chmn. Meml. Hosp. Found., 1980-82; bd. dirs., chmn. coun. trustees, mem. exec. com. Ariz. Hosp. Assn., 1981-87, chmn. 1986-87, Ariz. del. to nat. conf. governing bds.; chmn. PMH Health Resources, Inc., 1983-89, Ariz. Voluntary Hosp. Fedn., 1984-88; chmn. Phoenix chpt. Am. Jewish Com., 1989-91. 2d lt. USAF, 1952-53. Mem. Ariz. Bar Assn., Maricopa County Bar Assn., State Bar Ariz. (chmn. com. civil practice and procedure 1971-74, chmn. long-range com. 1980, peer rev. com., sole practitioner com. sect., alternate dispute resolution sects., mentor-mentee com.), Univ. Club Phoenix (pres. 1971-72), Phi Beta Kappa, Phi Delta Phi. Democrat. Jewish. Address: 2110 Encanto Dr SW Phoenix AZ 85007-1526

FEINSTEIN, ALVAN RICHARD, physician, educator; b. Phila., Dec. 4, 1925; s. Joel B. and Bella (Ukasz) F. BS, U. Chgo., 1947, MS in Math., 1948, MD, 1952; MA (hon.), Yale U., 1969; ScD (hon.), McGill U., Montreal, Que., Can., 1997. Intern, then resident Yale-New Haven Hosp., 1952-54; research fellow Rockefeller Inst., 1954-55; resident Columbia-Presbyn. Med. Center, N.Y.C., 1955-56; clin. dir. Irvington House, N.Y.C., 1956-62; instr., then asst. prof. N.Y. U. Sch. Medicine, 1956-62; chief clin. pharmacology VA Hosp., West Haven, Conn., 1962-64; chief clin. biostatistics VA Hosp., 1964-74; mem. faculty Sch. Medicine, Yale U., 1962—, prof. medicine and epidemiology, 1969—, dir. clin. scholar program, 1974—, Sterling prof., 1991—; chief Eastern Research Support Ctr. VA, 1967-74; pres. New Haven area chpt. Assn. Computing Machinery, 1968-69. Author: Clinical Judgment, 1967, Clinical Biostatistics, 1977, Clinical Epidemiology, 1985, Clinimetrics, 1987, Multivariable Analysis, 1996; editor Jour. Clin. Epidemiology; contbr. articles to profl. jours. Served with AUS, 1944-46. Recipient Francis G. Blake award for outstanding teaching Yale Med. Sch., J. Allyn Taylor Internat. prize, awards Soc. for Gen. Internal Medicine, U. Chgo., Ludwig Heilmyer Soc. (Europe), Gairdner Found. Internat. award 1993 (Can.), Oscar B. Hunter Meml. award, Am. Soc. Clin. Pharmacology and Therapeutics, 1999. Master ACP (disting. tchr. award); mem. AMA, Assn. Am. Physicians, Am. Soc. Clin. Investigation, Am. Epidemiol. Soc., Inst. Medicine, Am. Bd. Internal Medicine, Am. Fedn. Med. Research, Am. Soc. Clin. Pharmacology Therapeutics, Am. Statis. Assn., Assn. Computing Machinery, Biometric Soc., Am. Assn. History Medicine, Alpha Omega Alpha. Home: 18 Rockland Park Branford CT 06405-4720 Office: Yale U Sch Medicine 333 Cedar St New Haven CT 06510-3289

FEINSTEIN, DIANNE, senator; b. San Francisco, June 22, 1933; d. Leon and Betty (Rosenburg) Goldman; m. Bertram Feinstein, Nov. 11, 1962 (dec.); 1 child, Katherine Anne; m. Richard C. Blum, Jan. 20, 1980. BA History, Stanford U., 1955; LLB (hon.), Golden Gate U., 1977; D Pub. Adminstrn. (hon.), U. Manila, 1981; D Pub. Service (hon.), U. Santa Clara, 1981; JD (hon.), Antioch U., 1983, Mills Coll., 1985; LHD (hon.), U. San Francisco, 1988. Fellow Coro Found., San Francisco, 1955-56; with Calif. Women's Bd. Terms and Parole, 1960-66; mem. Mayor's com. on crime, chmn. adv. com. Adult Detention, 1967-69; mem. Bd. Suprs., San Francisco, 1970-78, pres., 1970-71, 74-75, 78; mayor City of San Francisco, 1978-88; mem. U.S. Senate from Calif., Washington, 1992—; mem. exec. com. U.S. Conf. of Mayors, 1983-88; Dem. nominee for Gov. of Calif., 1990; mem. Nat. Com. on U.S.-China Rels., mem. judiciary com., rules and adminstrn senate Dem. Policy Com.; fgn. rels. com. Mem. Bay Area Conservation and Devel. Commn., 1973-78; mem. Senate Fgn. Rels. Com. Recipient Woman of Achievement award Bus. and Profl. Women's Clubs San Francisco, 1970, Disting. Woman award San Francisco Examiner, 1970, Coro Found. award, 1979, Coro Leadership award, 1988, Pres. medal U. Calif., San Francisco, 1988, Scopus award Am. Friends Hebrew U., 1981, Brotherhood/Sisterhood award NCCJ, 1986, Comdr.'s award U.S. Army, 1986, French Legion of Honor, 1984, Disting. Civilian award USN, 1987; named Number One Mayor All-Pro City Mgmt. Team City and State Mag., 1987. Mem. Trilateral Commn., Japan Soc. of No. Calif. (pres. 1988-89), Inter-Am. Dialogue, Nat. Com. on U.S.-China Rels. Office: US Senate 331 Hart Senate Office Bldg Washington DC 20510-0504

FEINSTEIN, FRED IRA, lawyer; b. Chgo., Apr. 6, 1945; s. Bernard and Beatrice (Mines) F.; m. Judy Cutler, Aug. 25, 1968; children: Karen, Donald. BSC, DePaul U., 1967, JD, 1970. Bar: Ill. 1970, U.S. Supreme Ct. 1977. Ptnr. McDermott, Will & Emery, Chgo., 1976—; lectr. in field. Pres., Skokie/Evanston (Ill.) Action Council, 1981-84; bd. dirs. Temple Judea Mizpah, Skokie, 1982-84, Deborah Goldfine Meml. Cancer Research, 1968—, YMCA of Chgo., 1985—. Mem. Ill. Bar Assn., Am. Coll. Real Estate Lawyers, Union League, Blue Key, Beta Gamma Sigma, Beta Alpha Psi, Pi Gamma Mu, Lambda Alpha. Contbr. articles to profl. jours. Office: McDermott Will & Emery 227 W Monroe St Ste 3100 Chicago IL 60606-5096

FEINSTEIN, FREDERICK LEE, lawyer; b. N.Y.C., June 27, 1947; s. Alan and Mary (Kotick) F.; m. Karen E. Collins, Sept. 13, 1981; children: Emma Collins, Samuel Collins. BS, Swarthmore Coll., 1969; JD, Rutgers U., Newark, 1974. Bar: N.Y. 1975. Tchr. N.Y.C. Pub. Schs., 1969-71; staff dir., chief counsel labor-mgmt. rels. subcom. U.S. Ho. of Reps., Washington, 1977-94; field atty. NLRB, Winston-Salem, N.C., 1975-77; gen. counsel NLRB, Washington, 1994—. Pres. Takoma Park (Md.) Elem. Sch. PTA, 1991-93; coach Takoma Park Soccer, 1995—. Mem. ABA. Avocations: music, playing in cajun band with wife. Home: 7114 Sycamore Ave Takoma Park MD 20912-4639 Office: NLRB 1099 14th St NW Rm 10100 Washington DC 20045-2001

FEINSTEIN, MARION FINKE, artistic director, dance instructor; b. Nov. 7, 1925; d. Charles and Anne (Krein) Finke; m. Seymour Feinstein, Apr. 2, 1944; children: Sandi, Sheree, Lori. Degree in sec. sci., U. S.C., 1944; student, Joffrey Ballet, N.Y.C., Am. Ballet Theatre, N.Y.C.; studied with Alvin Ailey, N.Y.C. Instr. dance Recreation Dept., Columbia, S.C., 1945; instr. ballet Furman Basketball Team, Greenville, S.C., 1950-55; instr. jazz U. S.C., Spartanburg, 1986-87; dance dir. Carolina Youth Dance Theatre, Spartanburg, 1980—; tchr. various pageant winners and profl. dancers, including Miss Black Am., Miss World, Miss Am. finalist, Miss Dance Am., 1972, Jr. Miss Dance of S.C., Miss Dance of S.C., 1993, 94, 96, 97. Mem. USO troupe, Spartanburg, 1942-44; choreographer Spartanburg Little Theatre, 1955-62, Miss Spartanburg Pageant, 1963-72. Recipient Resolution award S.C. Ho. Reps. and Senate, 1988, Cert. Performance Appreciation, City New Orleans, Resolution of Appreciation award Spartanburg County Council, S.C., Cert. Performance Appreciation N.Y.C. com. for entertainment at the Statue of Liberty, Fund Raising award March of Dimes; students performed in opening ceremonies at 1996 Olympic Games, Atlanta. Mem. Dance Educators Am. (regional dir.), Dance Masters Am., So. Coun. Dancemasters (v.p.), Cecchetti Coun. Am., Bus. and Profl. Women, Hadassah Club (Spartanburg), B'nai Israel Sisterhood Orgn. Democrat. Jewish. Office: Miss Marion's Sch Dance 1206 Reidville Rd Spartanburg SC 29306-3930

FEINSTEIN, MARTIN, performing arts consultant, art director; b. N.Y.C., Apr. 12, 1921. BSS, CCNY, 1942; MA, Wayne State U., 1943; MusD (hon.), Cath. U. Am., 1980, Shenandoah Coll. & Conservatory, 1983; LHD (hon.), Am. U., 1991; DFA, U. Md., 1995. Publicity dir. Hurok Concerts, N.Y.C., 1945-50, v.p., 1950-71; vis. prof. Yale U., New Haven, 1971-73; exec. dir. performing arts John F. Kennedy Ctr., Washington, 1972-80; pres., CEO Nat. Symphony, Kennedy Ctr., Washington, 1980-81; gen. dir. Washington Opera, 1980-95, cons., 1995—; sr. cons. U. Md. Performing Arts Ctr., College Park, 1995-98, artistic dir., 1998—. Decorated commendatore Republic of Italy; cross of officer Order Arts and Letters (France); Grand Decoration of Honor for Svcs. (Austria), officer Order of Merit (Germany); recipient medal Nat. Soc. Lit. and the Arts, 1977, award of Contbns. in Field of Dance Am. Assn. Dance Cos., 1979, Townsend Harris medal CCNY, 1977, John Cranko medal, Stuttgart, 1979, Myrtle Wreath award Washington Hadassah, 1982, Amphion award Memphis Symphony, 1983. Office: 7816 Laurel Leaf Dr Potomac MD 20854-1768

FEINSTEIN, ROBERT P., dermatologist; b. N.Y.C., July 31, 1941; s. Jerome and May (Wolpin) F.; m. Diane Marla Gutstein, Oct. 25, 1969; children: Steven, Michelle, Suzanne, Gary, Lori. AB in Biology, NYU, 1963, MD, 1967. Diplomate Am. Bd. Dermatology. Intern Kings County Hosp. Ctr., Bklyn., N.Y., 1967-68; resident in dermatology Columbia U. Dept. Dermatology, N.Y.C., 1968-71; assoc. clin. prof. Columbia U. Dept. Dermatology; chief of dermatology, innoculations and phys. exams. Navy Regional Med. Clinic, Washington, 1971-73; pvt. practice in dermatology Mineola and Smithtown, N.Y., 1973—. Author: (book) Dermatology, 1975, (monograph) Rosacea, 1998; contbr. articles to profl. jours. Lt cmmdr. USNR, 1971-73. Fellow Am. Acad. Dermatology (mem. exec. com. of adv. bd., managed care com.), Am. Soc. for Dermatologic Surgery; mem. AMA, N.Y. State Soc. of Dermatology (pres. 1997—), L.I. Dermatology Soc. (pres. 1996-98), Suffolk County Dermatology Soc. (pres. 1982-84), Atlantic Dermatology Soc. (bd. dirs. 1995); N.Y. State Med. Soc. (health care delivery sys.). Avocation: golf. Office: Dermedx 173 Mineola Blvd Mineola NY 11501-2526 also: 222 E Middle Country Rd Smithtown NY 11787-2871

FEINSTEIN, ROCHELLE, artist, educator. BFA, Pratt Inst., 1975; MFA, U. Minn., 1978. Represented by Max Protetch Gallery, N.Y.C.; tchr. Bennington Coll., 1979-94; assoc. prof. painting, printmaking Yale U., 1994—; participant pub. arts project CETA/N.Y. Artists Program, 1978-79. Represented in permanent collection Mus. Modern Art. Nat. Endowment Arts grantee, 1990, Joan Mitchell Found. grantee, 1994; John Simon Guggenheim Meml. Found. fellow, 1996. Office: Yale U Sch Art Arch Bldg Rm 303 180 York St 3rd Fl New Haven CT 06520

FEINSTEIN, SASCHA, English language educator; b. N.Y.C., Mar. 13, 1963; s. Samuel L. and Anita (Askild) F.; m. Marleni Rajakrishnan, June 3, 1989; children: Kiran Anders, Divia Anita. BA, U. Rochester, 1985; MFA, Ind. U., 1990, PhD, 1993. Assoc. prof. English Lycoming Coll., Williamsport, Pa., 1995—. Author: Jazz Poetry, 1997, A Biographic Guide to Jazz poetry, 1998; co-editor: The Jazz Poetry Anthology, 1991, The Second Set, 1996; editor-in-chief Brilliant Corners: A Jour. of Jazz and Lit., 1996—. Mem. Phi Kappa Phi, Phi Beta Kappa. Office: Lycoming Coll 700 College Pl Williamsport PA 17701-5157

FEINSTEIN, STEPHEN MICHAEL, lawyer; b. Stamford, Conn., Jan. 19, 1959; s. Norton Perry and Phyllis Marilyn (Fabel) F.; m. Bonnie Helene Litsky, Aug. 27, 1989; children: Shayna Justine, Maxwell Benjamin, Sydney Ilana. BA, U. Conn., 1981; JD, Quinnipiac Coll., 1984. Bar: Conn. 1984, U.S. Dist. Ct. Conn. 1985. Assoc. Feinstein & Hermann, Norwalk, Conn., 1984-91; ptnr. Feinstein & Hermann, P.C., Norwalk, Conn., 1991—; instr. Conn. Inst. Paralegal Studies, Stamford, 1994—; bd. dirs. Conn. State Law Libr. Adv. Com., Hartford, Conn., 1993—. Chmn. adult adv. bd. B'nai B'rith Youth Orgn., New Haven, 1994-96. Mem. Assn. Trial Lawyers Am., Conn. Bar Assn., Conn. Trial Lawyers Assn., Friends of Stamford Law Libr. (pres. 1992-94, v.p. 1994). Republican. Jewish. Home: 21 Ludlow Mnr Norwalk CT 06855-2010 Office: Feinstein and Hermann PC 5 Myrtle St Norwalk CT 06855-1315

FEINSTEIN, TIKVAH, writer, editor, publisher; b. Pitts., Mar. 27, 1944; d. Rudolph and Ruth (Gregg) Dobsch; m. Marshall Feinstein, Oct. 23, 1966 (div. July 1976); 1 child, Marsha Lynn. Assoc. in Biol. Sci., C.C. Allegheny County, 1980; BA in English Writing, U. Pitts., 1982. Lic. pracitical nurse. Reporter, writer Beaver County Times, 1982-96; dir. Taproot Writer's Workshop Inc., 1984—; editor/pub. Taproot Lit. Review, 1985—; bd. dirs. United Israel World Union, N.Y.C.; founder/pub. Taproot Press Pub. Co., Ambridge, Pa., 1995; health aide Hopewell (Pa.) Elem. Sch., 1993—; presenter, tchr., vol. Geneva Coll., 1998; dir. writing Laughlin Meml., 1986; workshop vol. libr. Ambridge, 1998—. Author: Inanna of Tianat, 1997, Don't Ever Tell, 1998. Mem. steering com. Cmty. Outreach, Hopewell Area Sch. Dist.; mem. Dem. Com., Washington, 1994—. Jewish. Avocations: music, art, reading prehistorical and scientific research. Office: Taproot Press PO Box 204 Ambridge PA 15003-0204

FEINTUCH, HENRY PHILIP, public relations executive; b. Bklyn.. BA, Bklyn. Coll. TV and Radio, 1976. Anchorperson, reporter Stas. WMTR and WDHA-FM, N.J.; news editor Sta. WCBS-TV, N.Y.C.; pub. rels. sr. acct. exec. Paul Kaufman Assocs., N.Y.C., Booke and Co., N.Y.C.; dir. corp. comm. Ring Group N.Am., N.Y.C., 1985-86; mng. ptnr. KCSA Pub. Rels., N.Y.C., 1987—. Office: KCSA Pub Rels 800 2nd Ave New York NY 10017-4709*

FEIR, DOROTHY JEAN, entomologist, physiologist, educator; b. St. Louis, Jan. 29, 1929; d. Alex R. and Lillian (Smith) F. B.S., U. Mich., 1950; M.S., U. Wyo., 1956; Ph.D., U. Wis., 1960. Instr. biology U. Buffalo, 1960-61; mem. faculty St. Louis U., 1961—, prof. biology, 1967-99, prof. biology emeritus, 1999—; mem. tropical medicine and parasitology study sect. NIH, 1980-84. Editor Environ. Entomology, 1977-84; mem. editl. bd. Jour. Med. Entomology, 1995-99, chair editl. bd., 1999. Fellow Entomol. Soc. Am. (hon., pres. 1989, Riley Achievement award north ctrl. br. 1993), Mo. Acad. Sci. (v.p. 1987-88, pres.-elect 1988-89, pres. 1989-90, Most Disting. Scientist award 1995); mem. AAAS, Am. Physiol. Soc., N.Y. Acad. Scis., Phi Beta Kappa, Sigma Xi.

FEIRSON, STEVEN B., lawyer; b. Bklyn., June 6, 1950; s. Aaron M. and Gertrude F. BA, U. Pa., 1972; JD, U. Chgo., 1975. Bar: Pa. 1975, U.S. Dist. Ct. (ea. dist.) Pa. 1975, U.S. Ct. Appeals (3d cir.) 1976, U.S. Ct. Appeals (2d cir.) 1990, U.S. Ct. Appeals (9th cir.) 1990, U.S. Ct. Appeals (8th cir.) 1992, U.S. Ct. Appeals (6th cir.) 1994, U.S. Supreme Ct. 1980, U.S. Dist. Ct. (ea. dist.) Mich. 1996. Assoc. Dechert, Price & Rhoads, Phila., 1975-83, ptnr., 1983—. Mem. Phila. Bar Assn. Office: Dechert Price & Rhoads 4000 Bell Atlantic Tower 1717 Arch St Ste 3 Philadelphia PA 19103-2793

FEISEL, LYLE DEAN, university dean, electrical engineering educator; b. Tama, Iowa, Oct. 16, 1935; s. Clyde Edward and Clara Maria (Ehlers) F.; m. Dorothy Evelyn Stadsvold, June 15, 1957; children: Patricia, Margaret, Kenneth. BSEE, Iowa State U., 1961, MSEE, 1963, PhDEE, 1964. Registered profl. engr., S.D. Engr. Honeywell, Mpls., 1961-62; staff engr. IBM Corp., Poughkeepsie, N.Y., 1963, Burlington, Vt., 1967; mem. faculty of elec. engring. S.D. Sch. of Mines, Rapid City, 1964-83, head elec. engring. dept., 1975-83; dean Watson Sch. SUNY, Binghamton, 1983—; vis. prof. Cheng Kung U., Tainan, Taiwan, 1969-70; rsch. engr. Northrop Corp., L.A., 1974; Wachmeister prof. engring. Va. Mil. Inst., 1982; mem. engring. accreditation commn. Accreditation Bd. Engring. and Tech., 1987-92, bd. dirs., 1992-97. Recipient profl. achievement citation Iowa State U., 1984, Ednl. Achievement award N.Y. State Soc. Profl. Engrs., 1989; Nat. Def. fellow, 1961-64. Fellow IEEE (pres. edn. soc. 1978-79, Meritorious Svc. award, Ben Dasher award 1983, Centennial medal 1984, Ronald J. Schmitz award 1989), Am. Soc. Engring. Edn. (bd. dirs. 1982-83, 94-95, 96—, pres. 1997-98); mem. S.D. Renewable Energy Assn. (pres. 1979-81). Democrat. Lutheran. Office: SUNY Watson Sch PO Box 6000 Binghamton NY 13902-6000

FEISS, GEORGE JAMES, III, financial services company executive; b. Cleve., June 24, 1950; s. George James Jr. and Bettie (Kalish) F.; m. Susan Margaret Cassel, May 30, 1981; children: Kalish Ilana Cassel-Feiss, Nika Catherine Cassel-Feiss. BA in Social Studies, Antioch Coll., 1973; MBA in Internat. Fin., Am. Grad. Sch. Internat. Mgmt., Phoenix, 1975. Registered investment advisor, Wash.; CFP Coll. Fin. Planning, Denver. Ptnr. Healthcare Cons., Seattle, 1976-80; pres. M2 Inc., Seattle, 1980—; CFO, bd. dirs. Vivid Image Co., San Diego, Calif., 1994—; cons. Sta. KRAB, Seattle, 1988-89, Zion Christian Acad., Seattle, 1990—. Author: Mind Therapies/Body Therapies, 1979, Hope & Death in Exile - The Economics and Politics of Cancer in the United States, 1981. Bd. dirs. B'nai Brith, Seattle, 1988-91; mem. fin. com. Univ. Child Devel. Sch., Seattle, 1989—; mem. social action com. Am. Jewish Com., Seattle, 1992. Mem. Eastside Estate Planning Coun., Inst. for CFPs, Social Investment Forum, Social Venture Network. Avocations: sailing, skiing, travel, writing, sculpture. Home: 603 38th Ave Seattle WA 98122-6423 Office: M2 Inc 1932 1st Ave Ste 614 Seattle WA 98101-2447

FEISS, HUGH BERNARD, priest, religious educator; b. Lakeview, Oreg., May 8, 1939; s. Sherman H. and Margaret I. (Furlong) F. Licentiate in Sacred Theology, Cath. U. Am., 1967, Lic. in Philosophy, 1972; STD, Anselmianum, Rome, 1976; MA, U. Iowa, Iowa City, 1987. Ordained priest Roman Cath. Ch., 1966. Asst. dean of men Mt. Angel Seminary, St. Benedict, Oreg., 1967-72, prof. philosophy, 1967-74, prof. humanities and theology, 1976-96; dir. Mt. Angel Abbey Libr., St. Benedict, 1987-96. Translator: Works of Pierre de Celle, 1988, Supplement to Life of Marie d'Oignies, 1986, Hildegard of Bingen, Explanation of the Rule of Benedict, 1990, Life of Holy Hildegard, 1996; contbr. articles to profl. jours. Mem. Am. Acad. Religion, Am. Benedictine Acad., Cath. Theol. Soc. Am., Am. Cath. Philos. Assn. E-mail: hughf@magiclink.com. Home and Office: Ascension Priory 541 E 100 S Jerome ID 83338-5655

FEIST, EDWARD JOSEPH, secondary education educator; b. Denver, June 8, 1947; s. Edward J. and Jean (Nielsen) G.; m. Ricki Lynn Hetts, Aug. 15, 1970; children: Trevor, Trent. BA in Speech Arts, Colo. State U., 1970; MA in Theater Arts, Univ. No. Colo., 1972; EdD, Univ. Colo., 1987. Tchr. Estes Park (Colo.) Jr./Sr. H.S., 1970-72, Littleton (Colo.) H.S., 1972—. Coach soccer Littleton Soccer Assn., 1980-83, Cherry Creek Soccer Assn., 1983-90. Avocations: stamp collecting. Home: 7358 S Spruce St Englewood CO 80112-1752 Office: Littleton High Sch 199 E Littleton Blvd Littleton CO 80121-1106

FEIST, GENE, theater director; b. N.Y.C., Jan. 16, 1923; s. Henry and Hattie (Fishbein) F.; m. Kathe Snyder (Elizabeth Owens), Feb. 10, 1957; children: Nicole, Gena. B.F.A., Carnegie Mellon U., 1951; M.A., N.Y. U., 1952. Artistic dir., founding dir. Roundabout Theater Co., Inc., N.Y.C., 1965—; artistic dir. Roundabout Conservatory and Ensemble, N.Y.C., 1980-95; founder Fourth Street Theatre, N.Y.C.; lectr., cons. Staged prodns. John Houseman Theatre, Cherry Lane Theatre, East End Theatre, Actors' Studio; author: (plays) James Joyce's Dublin, 1975, Jocasta and Oedipus, 1970, also others; adapted plays for stage, including Ibsen's The Master Builder, Chekhov's Uncle Vanya, Pirandello's Naked, also others. Mem. Dramatists Guild Am., Soc. Stage Dirs. and Choreographers, League Am. Theaters and Producers, Internat. Theatre Inst., League Resident Theatres. Office: 351 W 24th St Apt 17F New York NY 10011-1510

FEIST, LES, conusmer products company executive; b. Memphis, Tenn., Apr. 24, 1943; s. Herbert B. and Betty B. F.; m. Bobbye W. Feist, Jan. 24, 1943; children: Samuel Edward, Tamara, Danielle, Stephen. BA, Vanderbilt U., 1965; MBA, Cornell U., 1967. Product mgr. Keller Mfg. Co., Corydon, Ind., 1970-72; pres. RH/Bobbie Brooks, Cleve., 1972-79; COO NMI/Norton Simon, N.Y.C., 1980; pres. Remington Products, Bridgeport, Conn., 1981-90; CEO Lifesavers Internat., Ridgefield, Conn., 1991—; also bd. dirs. Lifesavers Internat., Ridgefield, 1997—; bd. dirs. Westen Sales, Ripley, Tenn., ICR Internat., N.Y.C. Recipient Fulbright grant U.S. Dept. State, Trinidad & Tobago, 1968-69. Avocations: scuba diving, private pilot. E-mail: leeawe@aol.com. Home: 16 Copper Beech Ridgefield CT 08977 Office: Lifesavers Internat 380 Lexington Ave New York NY 10017

FEIT, GLENN M., lawyer; b. Elizabeth, N.J., Oct. 16, 1929; s. Charles Theodore and Beatrice (Esther) F.; m. Rona F. Gottlieb, June 14, 1953 (div. 1974); children: Glenn M., John Paul, Adam Gibbs (dec.); m. Barberi Platt Paull. BS in Econ., U. Pa., 1951; JD magna cum laude, Harvard U., 1957. Bar: N.Y. 1958, U.S. Dist. Ct. (2d dist.) 1959). Assoc. Cravath, Swaine & Moore, N.Y.C., 1957-64; ptnr. London, Buttenwieser & Chalif, N.Y.C., 1965-70, Feit & Ahrens, N.Y.C., 1970-88, Feit & Shor, N.Y.C., 1988-89, Proskauer Rose LLP, N.Y.C., 1989—; bd. dirs. C&D Techs., Inc., Blue Bell, Pa., Blair Industries, Inc., Scott City, Mo.; sec. Charterhouse Group Internat., Inc., N.Y.C. Mem. editl. bd. Harvard Law Rev., 1955-57. Bd. dirs. Friends of the IDF, N.Y.C. Lt. USN, 1951-54. Mem. ABA, Assn. Bar City N.Y., Aircraft Owners and Pilots Assn., Exptl. Aircraft Assn., Tailhook Assn., Harvard Club, Seaplane Pilots Assn. Office: Proskauer Rose LLP 1585 Broadway New York NY 10036-8200

FEIT, MICHAEL, controller; b. Tarnopol, Poland, Sept. 8, 1928; came to U.S., 1949; s. Henryk and Anna (Taube) F.; m. Irene Mischel, Mar. 17, 1956; children: Elizabeth, Susan. BS cum laude, NYU, 1955, postgrad., 1956-57; postgrad., Boston U., 1958-59. CPA, Ma., Pa., Ill. Mgr. cost acctg. Microwave & Powertube div. Raytheon Co., Waltham, Mass., 1957-59; sr. cons. Price Waterhouse & Co., Boston, 1959-64; mgr. MIS Scott Paper Co., Phila., 1964-68; dir. MIS Admiral Corp., Chgo., 1968-70; contr. Superior Tea & Coffee Co., Chgo., 1971-76; contr., CFO Ride Corp., Chgo., 1977-78; contr. Bd. of Edn. City of Chgo., 1978-81; interim CFO Bd. of Edn. City of Chgo., 1980-81; contr., CFO The Lambs, Inc., Libertyville, Ill., 1981—. Mem. AICPA, Mass. Soc. CPAs (Silver medal 1961), Ill. Assn. Rehab. Facilities. Home: 1240 Park Ave W Highland Park IL 60035-2264 Office: The Lambs Inc PO Box 520 Libertyville IL 60048-0520

FEITLOWITZ, MARGUERITE, writer, literary translator; b. Hagerstown, Md., July 14, 1953; d. Robert Daniel and Virginia (Giancola) F.; m. David L. Anderson, Feb. 19, 1984. Student, U. Dijon, France, 1974; BA, Colgate U., 1975. Precpetor expository writing program Harvard U., Cambridge, Mass., 1993-99. Author: A Lexicon of Terror: Argentina and the Legacies of Torture, 1998; editor, translator: Information for Foreigners: Three Plays by Griselda Gambaro, 1992; translator: Theatre Pieces: An Anthology by Liliane Atlan, 1985; contbr. article to profl. jours. Mary Ingram Bunting fellow, 1992-93; Fulbright scholar, Argentina, 1990, 98-99; grantee Marion and Jasper Whiting award, Boston, 1995. Mem. Authors Guild, Am. Literary Translators Assn., Latin Am. Studies Assn., Amnesty Internat. Democrat. Jewish.

FEITO, JOSE, architect; b. Havana, Cuba, Jan. 30, 1929; came to U.S., 1961; s. Jose and Hermina (Mayo) F.; m. Bertha A. Abascal, Oct. 7, 1995; children: Patricia Maria, Maria Esther, Jose Alfonso, Sergio P. (dec.). MArch, U. Havana, 1954. Registered architect, Fla. Prin. J. Feito Architects, Havana, 1954-60; assoc. J. DeHaro Architects, Madrid, 1960-61; ptnr. Ferendino et al, Miami, Fla., 1966-79; prin. F&F Architects and Planners, Miami, 1979-80, F&F Fraga and Feito Architects, Miami, 1980—; pres. Professio Inc., Miami, 1983-84. Bd. dirs. Dade Co. Shoreline Com., 1986—; chmn. Gov.'s com. for Handicapped, Miami, 1973-75; trustee United Way, Miami, 1979-84. Recipient Meritorious Svcs. citation Gov.'s Com. for Handicapped, 1975. Fellow AIA (pres. Miami South chpt. 1977, Honor award 1985); mem. Fla. Assn. AIA (bd. dirs. 1978, Excellence award 1985), Interam. Businessmen's Assn. (pres. 1978-80), Cuba Soc. Architects (Gold medal 1957), Cuban Mus. Arts and Culture (founder), Greater Miami C. of C. (mem. bd. govs. 1978-83), Miami Symphony (bd. dirs.). Republican. Roman Catholic. Avocations: history, tennis, sailing. Office: F&F Fraga & Feito Architects 3900 NW 79th Ave Ste 219 Miami FL 33166-6546

FEJER, T. WILLIAM, pianist, composer, architect, furniture designer; b. L.A., Sept. 18, 1940; s. Andrew A. and Edith (Behal) F.; divorced; children: Tony (Stephen), Andrew. BS in Architecture, Ill. Inst. Tech., 1964, MS, 1967. Exhibit designer 20th century Art Inst. Chgo., 1962-67; archtl. draftsman Mies Van de Rohe, Chgo., 1964-66; design architect Skidmore, Owings & Merrill, Chgo., 1966-68; mng. dir. Evanston (Ill.) Art Ctr., 1970-72; instr. architecture Ill. Inst. Tech., Chgo., 1967-74; nat. designer, advt. mgr. Plastofilm, Chgo., 1974-84; staff pianist, creative dir. Design Prodns., Chgo., 1984-87, Nordstrom, Schaumburg, Ill., 1994—; CEO Live From Chgo., 1968—; co-dir., chief composer Anderson/Fejer Musicals, Round Lake, Ill., 1996—; ofcl. pianist Boy Scouts Am., Chgo., 1990—; entertainment coord. Internat. Press Club Chgo., 1992-96; theme composer Little City Found., Chgo., 1992. Designer contemporary furniture; composer: (musical comedy) Menage A Trois, 1997. Spl. occasion pianist Unitarian Ch., Chgo., 1987—; vol. entertainment chair Woodfield Area Charitable Orgn., Schaumburg, 1994—. Recipient Outstanding Archtl. Design award Women's Archtl. League, 1963. Mem. Internat. Press Club Chgo. (cartoonist), Phi Gamma Delta. Avocations: art collecting, photography, skiing, sailing, golf. Office: Live From Chgo 161 Nasa Cir Round Lake IL 60073-2844

FEKETE, GEORGE OTTO, judge, lawyer, pharmacist; b. Budapest, Hungary; s. Bela and Ilona (Meer) F.; m. Amy Zheng; children: Jacqueline Kim, Jeanette Lee. BS in Psychology, Wayne State U., 1960; PhD, U. So. Calif., 1965; postgrad. in psychology, Calif. State U., Long Beach; JD, Pepperdine U., 1973. Bar: Calif. 1973, U.S. Dist. Ct. (so. dist.) Calif. 1973, U.S. Supreme Ct. 1980, U.S. Dist Ct. (no. dist.) Calif. 1986. Chief pharmacist Hylo Drug Co., Huntington Beach, Calif., 1970; pres. G.O. Fekete Law Corp., Anaheim, Calif., 1973-86; lead trial lawyer Melvin Belli Law Offices, San Francisco, 1986-88; ind. trial specialist, superior ct. apptd. arbitrator San Francisco and Bay Area, 1988—; judge pro tem. Served to maj. USAF, 1954-59. Mem. ABA, Assn. Trial Lawyers Am., Calif. Trial Lawyers Assn. (legis. com. 1976-78), Orange County Trial Lawyers Assn (bd. dirs. 1977).

FEKETY, ROBERT, physician, educator; b. Pitts., June 29, 1929; s. Francis Robert and Grace (McShaffery) F.; m. Nancy Jane Baker, June 24, 1954; children: Susan Elizabeth, Sally Jane. AB, Wesleyan U., 1951; MD, Yale U., 1955. Instr. dept. medicine Johns Hopkins U., Balt., 1960-64, asst. prof., 1960-67; assoc. prof. medicine U. Mich., Ann Arbor, 1967-71, chief div. infectious diseases, 1967-95, prof. medicine, 1971-95, prof. medicine emeritus, 1995—; prof. epidemiology, 1987-95; active emeritus prof. medicine U. Mich., Ann Arbor, 1995—. Sr. asst. surgeon USPHS, 1956-58. Fellow ACP, Infectious Diseases Soc. Am. (councillor). Roman Catholic. E-mail: rfekety@umich.edu. Fax: 734-747-9965. Home: 812 Berkshire Rd Ann Arbor MI 48104-2631 Office: Univ Mich Hosp 3116 Taubman Ctr Ann Arbor MI 48109

FELBINGER, CLAIRE LOUISE, adult education educator, administrator; b. Joliet, Ill., Jan. 9, 1956; d. Thomas C. and Mary Ann F.; m. Richard John Martin Jr., May 27, 1978 (div. Mar. 1980); m. Richard Donnelly Bingham, Oct. 23, 1982. BA in Polit. Sci., Pub. Adminstrn., Augustana Coll., Rock Island, Ill., 1977; MA in Polit. Sci., U. Wis., Milw., 1979, PhD in Polit. Sci., 1986. Rsch. asst. NSF, Washington, 1981-82; asst. prof., rsch. assoc. No. Ill. U., DeKalb, 1986-88; acad. coord., asst. prof. Cleve. State U., 1988-92, dir., assoc. prof., 1992-98; editor pub. works mgmt., policy Sage Publs., Thousand Oaks, Calif., 1995—; chmn., assoc. prof. Am. U., Washington, 1998—; rsch. asst., U. Wis., Milw., 1978-85; bd. dirs. Accreditation Bd. Engring. Tech., Balt., 1998. Author: Evaluation in Practice, 1989; editor Pub. Works Mgmt. Policy, 1995—. Bd. dirs. St. Clair-Superior Coalition, Cleve., 1992-98, Pub. Works Hist. Soc., 1995—. Mem. NAS (bd. infastructure and the constructed environment), ASPA (chpt. pres. N.E. office, nat. coun. 1996-98), Am. Pub. Works Assn. (Excellence Edn. award 1993), Sect. Women Pub. Adminstrn. (bd. dirs. 1995—), Pi Alpha Alpha (v.p. 1997—). Avocations: traveling, fly fishing, gourmet cooking. E-mail: claire@american.edu. Home: 4200 Mass Ave NW #913 Washington DC 20016 Office: Am U 4400 Mass Ave NW Ward 322 Washington DC 20016

FELCH, WILLIAM CAMPBELL, internist, editor; b. Lakewood, Ohio, Nov. 14, 1920; s. Don Harold Willison and Beth (Campbell) F.; m. Nancy Cook Dean, Aug. 4, 1945; children: Patricia, William Campbell, Robert Dean. B.A., Princeton U., 1942; M.D., Columbia U., 1945. Diplomate: Nat. Bd. Med. Examiners, Am. Bd. Internal Medicine. Intern St. Luke's Hosp., N.Y.C., 1945-46, resident in internal medicine, 1948-51; pvt. practice specializing in internal medicine Rye, N.Y., 1951-88; chief staff United Hosp., Port Chester, N.Y., 1975-77; med. dir. Osborn Home, Rye, N.Y., 1979-88; exec. v.p. Alliance for Continuing Med. Edn., 1978-91. Author: Aspiration and Achievement, 1981, Decade of Decision, 1989, Vision for the Future, 1992, The Secrets of Good Patient Care, Thoughts on Medicine for the 21st Century, 1996, Alliance for Continuing Medical Education: The First 20 Years, 1996; editor: The Internist, 1975-86, ACME Almanac, 1978-91, Journal of Continuing Education in the Health Professions, 1992-95; co-editor: Continuing Med. Edn.: A Primer, 2d edit., 1991. Trustee N.Y. Med. Coll., Valhalla, 1971-73. Served to capt. U.S. Army, 1946-48. Recipient award of merit N.Y. State Soc. Internal Medicine, 1976, Disting. Svc. award Alliance for Continuing Med. Edn., Founder's medal, 1995; named Internist of Distinction Internal Medicine Soc. N.Y. County, 1973. Mem. ACP, Alliance for Continuing Med. Edn. (exec. v.p. 1978-91), Am. Soc. Internal Medicine (pres. 1973-74), Inst. of Medicine of Nat. Acad. Scis., AMA (chmn. council on legislation 1977-79). Republican. Home: 26337 Carmelo St Carmel CA 93923-9133

FELD, ALAN DAVID, lawyer; b. Dallas, Nov. 13, 1936; s. Henry R. and Rose (Scissors) F.; m. Anne Sanger, June 1, 1957; children: Alan David, Elizabeth S., John L. B.A., So. Methodist U., 1957, LL.B., 1960. Bar: Tex. 1960. Since practiced in Dallas; from ptnr. to chmn. bd. Akin, Gump, Hauer, Strauss & Feld, Dallas, 1960-96, sr. exec. ptnr., 1996—; lectr. Southwestern U. Med. Sch.; chmn. Tex. State Securities Bd.; bd. dirs. Clear Channel Comms., Inc., Ctr. Point Properties, Inc. Contbr. articles to legal jours. Bd. trustees Brandeis U., AMR Advantage Funds; bd. dirs. Dallas Day Nursery Assn., Timberlawn Found., Dallas Symphony Orch. Mem. Am., Tex., D.C., Dallas bar assns., Salesmanship Club, Dallas Club, Royal Oaks Country Club, Phi Delta Phi. Home: 4235 Bordeaux Ave Dallas TX 75205-3717 Office: Akin Gump Strauss Hauer & Feld 1700 Pacific Ave Ste 4100 Dallas TX 75201-4675

FELD, CAROLE LESLIE, marketing executive; b. L.A., Nov. 12, 1955; d. Harold Brenman and Phyllis Pearl (Fishman) F.; m. David C. Levy; 1 child, Alexander Wolf Levy. BA, U. Calif., Berkeley, 1979; MBA, U. So. Calif., 1982. Mgr. rsch. Columbia Pictures, L.A., 1982-83; dir. promotion and field pub. Tri-Star Pictures, N.Y.C., 1983-86; dir. promotion and retention mktg. Home Box Office, N.Y.C., 1987-92; v.p. promotion and advt. Pub. Broadcasting Svc., Washington, 1992-97, sr. v.p. advt., promotion and corp. communications, 1995-99, sr. v.p. comms. and brand mgmt., 1999—; bd. dirs. Promax Internat.; cons. New Sch. Beacons in Jazz Program, N.Y.C., 1990—. Named one of Mktgs. Top 100 Advertising Age, 1995. Mem. Am. Film Inst., Nat. Acad. TV Arts and Scis. Avocations: skiing, travel, art, fishing.

FELD, DONALD H., network consultant; b. Marshalltown, Iowa, Mar. 12, 1945; s. Donald C. and Wanda L. (Morgan) F.; m. Ruth L. Hensley, Aug. 29, 1965; children: Donald O., Derrick H. BSEE, Iowa State U., 1968; ME in Indsl. Engring./Ops. Rsch., U. Fla., 1975. Commd. 2d lt. USAF, 1968-94, advanced through grades to col., 1989; comdr. 95th Reconnaissance Squadron USAF, RAF Alconbury, U.K., 1985-87; chief tactical sys. divsn. USAF Ctr. for Studies and Analysis, Pentagon, Washington, 1987-90, dir. resources directorate, 1990-91; chief flying tng. divsn. Air Edn. and Tng. Command, Randolph AFB, Tex., 1991-94; ret.; v.p. Commonwealth Cons. Corp., Arlington, Va., 1994-96; network cons. Make Systems, Inc., Mountain View, Calif., 1996—. Decorated DFC with 1 oak leaf cluster, Air Medal with 10 oak leaf clusters, Legion of Merit. Mem. IEEE, Air Force Assn. Avocations: water and snow skiing, computers, camping, golf, antique restoration. Office: Make Systems Inc 201 San Antonio Ct Mountain View CA 94040 Office: Make Systems Inc 1 Waters Park Dr Ste 250 San Mateo CA 94403*

FELD, ELIOT, dancer, choreographer; b. Bklyn., July 5, 1942; s. Benjamin Noah and Alice (Posner) F. Student, High Sch. Performing Arts, N.Y.C., 1954-58; DFA (hon.), Juilliard Sch., 1991. Debut as child prince in: The Nutcracker, N.Y.C. Ballet, 1954; mem. cast: West Side Story, 1958; danced with cos. of Donald McKayle, Sophie Maslow, Pearl Lang, Mary Anthony, 1954-59; with co.: I Can Get It for You Wholesale, 1962, Fiddler on the Roof; began dancing with Am. Ballet Theatre, 1963, later resident choreographer; solo dance appearances in: Les Noces, Wind in the Mountains, Dark Elegies, Fancy Free, Billy the Kid, Helen of Troy, Giselle; founder Am. Ballet Co., 1968, subsequently prin. dancer, mgr., chief choreographer, 1969-71; with Bklyn. Acad. Music two seasons, guest choreographer, Am. Ballet Theatre, Royal Danish Ballet, Nat. Ballet of Can., N.Y.C. Ballet, various others; founder, artistic dir., chief choreographer Feld Ballets/N.Y., 1974; founder New Ballet Sch., 1978, Kids Dance, 1994, Ballet Tech, 1996; prin. founder The Joyce Theater, 1982, The Lawrence A. Wien Ctr. Dance and Theater, 1986; choreographed: Harbinger, 1967, At Midnight, 1967, Meadowlark, 1968, Intermezzo, 1969, Cortege Burlesque, 1969, Pagan Spring, 1969, Early Songs, 1970, Cortege Parisien, 1970, Consort, 1970, A Poem Forgotten, 1970, Romance, 1971, Theatre, 1971, The Gods Amused, 1971, A Soldier's Tale, 1971, Eccentrique, 1971, Winters Court, 1972, Jive, 1973, Sephardic Song, 1974, Tzaddik, 1974, The Real McCoy, 1974, Mazurka, 1975, Excursions, 1975, Impromptu, 1976, Variations on 'America', 1977, A Footstep of Air, 1977, Santa Fe Saga, 1978, La Vida, 1978, Danzon Cubano, 1978, Half-Time, 1978, Papillon, 1979, Circa, 1980, Anatomic Balm, 1980, Scenes, 1980, Play Bach, 1981, Song of Norway, 1981, Over the Pavement, 1982, Straw Hearts, 1983, Summer's Lease, 1983, Three Dances, 1983, Adieu, 1984, The Jig Is Up, 1984, Moon Skate, 1984, Intermezzo No. 2, 1985, Against the Sky, 1985, The Grand Canon, 1985, Aurora I, 1985, Aurora II, 1985, Medium: Rare, 1985, Echo, 1986, Bent Planes, 1986, Skara Brae, 1986, Embraced Waltzes, 1987, A Dance for Two, 1987, Shadow's Breath, 1987, Petipa Notwithstanding, 1988, Kore, 1988, The Unanswered Question, 1988, Asia, 1988, Love Song Waltzes, 1988, Ah Scarlatti, 1989, Mother Nature, 1989, Contra Pose, 1990, Charmed Lives, 1990, Ion, 1990, Fauna, 1990, Common Ground, 1991, Savage Glance, 1991, Clave, 1991, Evoe, 1991, Endsong, 1991, Wolfgang Strategies, 1992, To the Naked Eye, 1992, Hello Fancy, 1992, Frets and Women, 1992, Hadji, 1992, Blooms Wake, 1993, The Relative Disposition of the Parts, 1993, Doo Dah Day, 1993, MRI, 1993, Doghead & Godcatchers, 1994, 23 Skidoo, 1994, Gnossiennes, 1994, Ogive, 1994, Chi, 1994, Ludwig Gambits, 1995, Tongue and Groove, 1995, Meshugana Dance, 1996, Paean, 1996, Paper Tiger, 1996, Shuffle, 1996, Industry, 1996, Evening Chant, 1996, Jukebox, 1997, Re:X, 1997, Yo Shakespeare, 1997, Joggers, 1997, Umbra Rumba, 1997, Yo Johann, 1997, The Last Sonata, 1997, Simon Sez, 1998, Cherokee Rose, 1999, Mendig, 1999, Felix: the ballet, 1999, Apple Pie, 1999. Recipient Dance Mag. award, 1990. Office: Ballet Tech 890 Broadway Fl 8 New York NY 10003-1211

FELD, HARVEY JOEL, pathologist; b. St. Petersburg, Fla., Mar. 16, 1949; s. Harold and Mona Feld; m. Karen Wendy Markman, June 2, 1973; children: Howard, Shari. BS in Chemistry, U. Fla., 1971, postgrad., 1971-73; MD, U. East Coll. Medicine, Manila, 1977. Diplomate Am. Bd. Pathology. Clin. clerkship L.I. Coll. Hosp., Bklyn., 1978; resident in pathology Mt. Sinai Sch. Medicine, N.Y.C., 1978-82; fellow in cytopathology MD. Anderson Cancer Ctr., Houston, 1982-83; pathologist Pasco Cmty. Hosp. (formerly Dade City (Fla.) Hosp.), 1983—, East Pasco Med. Ctr., Zephyrhills, Fla., 1983—; sec./treas. med. staff East Pasco Med. Ctr., 1991. Contbr. articles to profl. jorus. Trustee, treas. Suncoast chpt. Leukemia Soc.; trustee Chesed Shel Emes of Greater Tampa; chmn. med. adv. com. Mus. of Sci. and Industry, Tampa; program sponsor "Cornerstones of the Cmty.: the Jewish Presence in Ybor City", Ybor City Mus., Tampa, 1999. Recipient Ralph Colp award for journalistic excellence Mt. Sinai Jour. Medicine, 1982-83, Brooks Bros. Man of Yr. award Leukemia Soc., 1995. Fellow Coll. Am. Pathologists, Am. Soc. Clin. Pathologists; mem. Am. Pathology Found., Fla. Soc. Pathology, So. Med. Assn., Philippine Med. Soc. (West Coast chpt.,

Sunsine & Scholarship com.), Tampa Palms Country Club. Jewish. Avocations: rock collecting, reading. Home: 16111 Ancroft Ct Tampa FL 33647-1041 Office: Pasco Cmty Hosp (Lab) 13100 Fort King Rd Dade City FL 33525-5294

FELD, JOSEPH, construction executive; b. N.Y.C., June 25, 1919; s. Morris David and Gussie (London) F.; m. Doris Rabinor, Apr. 10, 1948 (dec.); 1 child, Elaine Susan. Student, CCNY, 1946-47. Builder housing, apt. projects L.I., N.Y.C., N.J., 1948-54; pres. Kohl and Feld, Inc., builder housing devels., Rockland County, N.Y., 1955-57, Feld Constrn. Corp., New City, N.Y., 1957—, Birchland Constrn. Corp., 1957-70, Ramapo Towers, Inc., 1963-83; vice-chmn. People's Nat. Bank Rockland County, Monsey, N.Y., 1974-85. Mem. Clarkstown Bldg. Code Com., 1959; mem. indsl. devel. adv. com. Rockland County Bd. Suprs., 1969-71; chmn. housing adv. coun. Rockland County Legislature, 1976-86; chmn. Housing Task Force, 1979-80; mem., past pres. Men's Club; mem. Rockland County coun. Jewish War Vets., past commdr. New City post. Staff sgt. AUS, 1941-45. Mem. Rockland County Assn., Inc. (former bd. dir.), Rockland County Home Builders Assn. (past pres., bd. dirs., chmn. rental housing com.), Nat. Assn. Home Builders (past bd. dirs., mem. rental housing com.), N.Y. State Assn. Home Builders (past dir., mem. rental housing com.), Rockland County Apt. Owners Assn. (pres., bd. dirs. 1971-94), Rockland County Bd. Realtors, N.Y. State Assn. Realtors (past dirs.), Masons, Lions (local pres. 1959-60, zone chmn. 1961-62), B'nai B'rith. Home: 3821 Environ Blvd Apt 501 Fort Lauderdale FL 33319-4218

FELD, KAREN IRMA, columnist, journalist, broadcaster, public speaker; b. Washington, Aug. 23; d. Irvin and Adele Ruth (Schwartz) F. BA, Am. U., 1969. Columnist, reporter Roll Call Newspaper, Washington, 1969-74; nat. pub. rels. coord. Ringling Bros./Barnum & Bailey Circus, Washington, 1971-74; publicist Twentieth Century Fox, L.A., 1974-75; pub. rels. account exec. Harshe, Rotman & Druck, L.A., 1975; freelance writer, broadcaster, 1970—; corr. People mag., Washington, 1980-85; adj. instr. Kent State U. Pol. Campaign Mgmt. Inst., 1981; broadcaster Voice of Am., 1984; columnist, contbg. editor Capitol Hill mag., Washington, 1980-89; columnist Washington Times, 1986-87, Universal Press Syndicate, 1988-89, Creators Syndicate, 1989-90; syndicated columnist Capital Connections, 1990—; Prodigy polit. columnist, 1990-93; radio/TV commentator syndicated radio segment Radio America, 1993—; syndicated columnist Nat. Post, 1998—; lectr. in field, 1990—. Contbr. articles to Parade mag., People mag., Money mag., Time mag., Vogue mag., George, USA Weekend, Family Circle, Others. Recipient Health Journalism award Am. Chiropractic Assn., 1991. Mem. AFTRA/SAG, Nat. Fedn. Press Women (Excellence in Journalism awards 1984-99), Women in Comms., Capital Press Women (v.p. 1985-91, Excellence in Journalism awards 1984-99, Entrepreneur/Communicator of Yr. award 1995), Am. Soc. Journalists and Authors, Nat. Press Club, Capitol Hill Club, Woodmont Country Club (Rockville, Md.), U.S. Senate Press Gallery, White House Corr. Assn., Sigma Delta Chi. Jewish. Office: 1698 32nd St NW Washington DC 20007-2969

FELD, KENNETH, performing company executive; married; 3 children. BS, Boston U., 1970. Prodr. Siegfried & Roy, Las Vegas, Nev., 1980-81; pres., CEO Feld Entertainment Inc./Ringling Bros. and Barnum & Bailey, worldwide, 1984—; creator with the Walt Disney Co. Walt Disney's World on Ice, The Wizard of Oz on Ice, 1995; founder Ringling Bros. and Barnum & Bailey Clown Coll.; foundng ptnr. Pachyderm Entertainment. Broadway prodns. include Big, Fool Moon, Largely New York, Barnum; prodr. (TV spl) George Lucas' Super Live Advneture. Trustee Boston Coll. Named one of 25 Most Influential Names inthe World of Figure Skating Internat. Figure Skating mag. Office: Feld Entertainment Barnum & Bailey Combined Shows Inc 8607 Westwood Center Dr Vienna VA 22182-7506*

FELD, KENNETH J., entertainment executive; b. Washington, 1947; married; 3 children. BS, Boston U., 1970. Chmn., CEO Feld Entertainment, Inc., Vienna, Va., 1971—; founder Ringling Bros. and Barnum & Bailey Clown Coll., Ringling Bros. and Barnum & Bailey Ctr. Elephant Conservation. Prodr.: Ringling Bros. and Barnum & Bailey, Walt Disney's World On Ice, The Wizard of Oz on Ice, Starlight Express, (Broadway plays) Big, Fool Moon, Largely New York, Barnum, (TV spls.) George Lucas's Super Live Adventure, Siegfreid & Roy, MADhattan, Las Vegas. Bd. trustees Boston U., endowed Sch. Mgmt.'s Feld Family Career Opportunity Ctr. Office: Feld Entertainment Inc 8607 Westwood Center Dr Vienna VA 22182-7506*

FELD, MARJORIE NAN, history educator; b. Harrisburg, Pa., Mar. 10, 1971; d. Arthur Michael and Rosalind Ilene (Sperling) F.; m. Michael Fein, Oct. 10, 1999. BA in History and Judaic Studies, SUNY, Binghamton, 1993; MA, Brandeis U., Waltham, Mass., 1995, postgrad., 1995—. Rsch. asst. SUNY, Binghamton, 1991-94; environ. project coord. Henry St. Settlement, N.Y.C., 1993; rsch. asst. Brandeis U., Waltham, 1994-96; instr. Urban Scholars Program, Boston, 1996, 97, 98; bd. dirs. Radical Tchr. jour. Contbr. articles to profl. jours. Pres. Coll. Democrats, SUNY, Binghamton, 1991-93. Recipient Crown fellowship Brandeis U., Waltham, 1994-98. Jewish. Avocation: swimming, reading. Home: 28 Hamilton Rd Somerville MA 02144-1532

FELD, MICHAEL STEPHEN, physics educator; b. N.Y.C., Nov. 11, 1940; s. Albert and Lillian R. Norwalk; m. Frances Aschheim, Mar. 2, 1980; children: David A., Jonathan R., Alexandra A. SB in Humanities and Sci., MIT, 1963, SM in Physics, 1963; Ph.D. in Physics, M.I.T., 1967. Postdoctoral fellow MIT, Cambridge, 1967-68, asst. prof., 1968-73, assoc. prof., 1973-79, prof. physics, 1979—, dir. George R. Harrison Spectroscopy Lab., 1976—, dir. Laser Research Ctr., 1979—; dir. Laser Biomed. Research Ctr., 1985—. Co-editor: Fundamental and Applied Laser Physics, 1973, Coherent Nonlinear Optics, 1980. Alfred P. Sloan rsch. fellow, 1973; recipient Disting. Svc. award MIT Minority Cmty., 1980, Gordon Y. Billard award, 1982, Thomas award Spectrochimica Acta, 1991, Vinci d'Excellence, France, 1995. Fellow AAAS, Am. Optical Soc., Am. Phys. Soc., Am. Soc. Laser Medicine and Surgery (bd. dirs.), Sigma Xi. Home: 56 Hinckley Rd Newton MA 02168 Office: MIT George R Harrison Spectroscopy Lab 77 Massachusetts Ave Cambridge MA 02139-4307

FELD, THOMAS ROBERT, academic administrator; b. Carroll, Iowa, Sept. 30, 1944; s. Edward Martin and Elaine (Wirtz) F.; m. Donna Jean Jorstad, June 1, 1968; children: Jacqueline Joan, William Jay. BA, Loras Coll., 1966; MA, No. Ill. U., 1969; PhD, Purdue U., 1972. Instr. Loras Coll., Dubuque, Iowa, 1966-70; v.p. Lea Coll., Albert Lea, Minn., 1972-73; v.p. Cen. Meth. Coll., Fayette, Mo., 1973-76, acting pres., 1976-77; pres. Mt. Mercy Coll., Cedar Rapids, Iowa, 1977—; bd. dirs. Assn. Mercy Colls., Washington, D.C., Norwest Bank. Bd. dirs. Iowa Coll. Found., Des Moines, 1977—, chmn., 1988-89; bd. dirs. Assn. Retarded Citizens, Cedar Rapids, 1979-85. Recipient Poetry award Am. mag., 1966, Teaching award Purdue U., 1971, Outstanding Fundraiser award Nat. Soc. Fundraising Execs., 1996; named Outstanding Young Dem. of Iowa, State Dems., 1965, knight Order Holy Sepulchre, 1992, Knight Comdr., 1996. Mem. CMC Colls. Assn. (bd. dirs., pres. 1979-80, 84-85, 88-89), Iowa Coordinating Coun. Postsecondary Edn. (chmn. bd. dirs. 1985-86), Assn. Mercy Colls. (exec. com. 1985—, bd. dirs.), Nat. Assn. Intercollegiate Athletics (chmn. bd. dirs. 1986-89, 94—, Hall of Fame 1996), Iowa Assn. Ind. Colls. and Univs. (chmn. bd. dirs. 1984-85), Nat. Assn. Ind. Colls. and Univs. (bd. dirs. 1990-93), Rotary (bd. dirs. 1993-97, pres. 1995—). Democrat. Roman Catholic. Avocations: golfing, fishing, poetry. Home: 4404 Hickory Wind Ln Marion IA 52302-9600 Office: Mt Mercy Coll Office of Pres Cedar Rapids IA 52402

FELDBERG, CHESTER BEN, banker, lawyer; b. N.Y.C., Dec. 16, 1939; s. William and Janet (Mesh) F.; m. Lynn Lea Uebelhack, Sept. 17, 1963; children: Gregory Howard, Suzanne. A.B., Union Coll., Schenectady, 1960; LL.B., Harvard, 1963. Bar: N.Y. bar 1963. Atty. Fed. Res. Bank of N.Y., N.Y.C., 1964-68; asst. counsel Fed. Res. Bank of N.Y., 1968-73, sec., 1969-73, v.p., 1975-83, sr. v.p., 1984-89, exec. v.p., 1989—; sec. bd. govs. Fed. Res. System, 1973-74. Office: Fed Res Bank NY 33 Liberty St New York NY 10045-1003

FELDBERG, MEYER, university dean; b. Johannesburg, South Africa, Mar. 17, 1942; s. Leon and Sarah (Kretzmer) F.; m. Barbara Erlick, Aug. 9, 1965; children: Lewis Robert, Ilana. B.A., Witwatersrand U., Johannesburg, 1962; M.B.A., Columbia U., 1965; Ph.D., Cape Town (South Africa) U., 1969. Product mgr. B.F. Goodrich Co., Akron, Ohio, 1965-67; dean Grad. Sch. Bus., U. Cape Town, 1968-79; assoc. dean J.L. Kellogg Sch. Mgmt., Northwestern U., Evanston, Ill., 1979-81; prof., dean Sch. Bus., Tulane U., New Orleans, 1981-86; pres. Ill. Inst. Tech., Chgo., 1986-89, chmn. bd. govs. Rsch. Inst.; dean Grad. Sch. Bus. Columbia U., N.Y.C., 1989—; bd. dirs. Federated Dept. Stores, PaineWebber Fund, Revlon, Inc., Primedia Inc.; vis. prof. MIT, 1974, Cranfield Inst. Tech., 1970, 76. Author: Organizational Behaviour: Text and Cases, 1975; contbr. articles to profl. jours. Named Jaycee Young Man of Yr., 1972. Mem. Internat. House (New Orleans), Univ. Club (N.Y.C. and Chgo.), Econ. Club (N.Y.C. and Chgo.). Office: Columbia U Grad Sch Bus 3022 Broadway New York NY 10027-6945

FELDBERG, MICHAEL SVETKEY, lawyer; b. Boston, May 21, 1951; s. Sumner Lee Feldberg and Eunice (Svetkey) Cohen; m. Ruth Lazarus, Sept. 23, 1978; children: Rachel, Jesse, Ben. BA, Harvard U., 1973, JD, 1977. Bar: N.Y. 1978, U.S. Dist. Ct. (ea. and so. dists.) N.Y. 1978, U.S. Ct. Appeals (2d cir.) 1983, U.S. Supreme Ct. 1994. Assoc. Orans, Elsen, Polstein & Naftalis, N.Y.C., 1977-80; asst. U.S. atty. So. Dist. of N.Y., N.Y.C., 1981-84; ptnr. Shea & Gould, N.Y.C., 1985-91, Schulte Roth & Zabel, N.Y.C., 1991—. Bd. dirs. 92d St. YMCA, N.Y.C., Child Devel. Rsch., N.Y.C., 1988—. Mem. Assn. Bar City N.Y. (criminal law com., com. on the judiciary, com. on profl. responsibility). Office: Schulte Roth & Zabel 900 3rd Ave Fl 19 New York NY 10022-4774

FELDBERG, SUMNER LEE, retired retail company executive; b. Boston, June 19, 1924; s. Morris and Anna (Marnoy) F.; married; children: Michael S., Ellen R.; stepchildren: Mollye S., Beth, James. BA, Harvard, 1947, MBA, 1949. With New England Trading Corp., 1949-56; treas. Zayre Corp., 1956-73, sr. v.p., 1965-68, exec. v.p., 1969-73, chmn. bd., 1973-87; chmn. exec. com. Zayre Corp. (name now TJX Cos., Inc.), 1987-89; chmn. bd. Waban Corp., 1989-96, TJX Cos., Inc., Framingham, Mass., 1989-95. Trustee Beth Israel Hosp., Combined Jewish Philanthropies of Greater Boston. Served to 1st lt. USAAF, 1943-46. Office: 770 Cochituate Rd Framingham MA 01701-9175 Office: PO Box 9175 Framingham MA 01701-9175

FELDBUSCH, MICHAEL F., engineering company executive; b. Evansville, Ind., Aug. 26, 1951; s. Ronald Farrell and Rita Carolyn (Snodgrass) F.; m. Lisa Ann McDowell, Feb. 14, 1986. AAS in architecture, ITT Tech. Inst., Indpls., 1971. Cert. profl. land surveyor, Ind., Ky., Fla., Ill., Tex., Ohio, Tenn. Engr. Lake States Engring., Chgo., 1974, Mayfair Constrn., Detroit, 1975; surveyor Warrick County Planning Commn., Boonville, Ind., 1976, Warrick County, Boonville, 1977-85; CEO AES/U.S. Surveyor Engring., Newburgh, Ind., 1978—; pres. Warrick County Planning Commn., 1978, 85; chief surveyor Warrick County, 1985—; mem. Examinations for Profl. Surveyors com. Nat. Soc. Examiners Engrs. Surveyors; pro-tem law judge Bd. of Registrations for Land Surveyors. Del. Ind. Dems., Indpls., 1978, 82, 86; sec. Newburgh Youth Sports Assn., 1980-81; apptd. by gov. Evan Bayh to Ind. State Bd. Registration For Profl. Engrs. and Land Surveyors, 1990. Served with USAR, 1971-77. Recipient Edward Gesser Jr. Meml. award Newburgh Youth Sports Assn., 1986; named one of Outstanding Young Men Am., 1980, 81, 83-85. Mem. NSPE, Ind. Soc. Prof. Land Surveyors, County Surveyors Assn., Am. Congress on Surveying, Nat. Soc. Prof. Surveyors, Ind. Jaycees (Top 40 award, 1979). Lodge: Lions. Avocations: boating, camping. Home: 9911 Powers Dr Newburgh IN 47630-8866 Office: AES US Surveyor Engring 605 State St Newburgh IN 47630-1299

FELDCAMP, LARRY BERNARD, lawyer; b. Hannibal, Mo., Nov. 24, 1938; s. Bernard Ernest and Mildred Elizabeth (Lehenbauer) F.; m. Irma Elaine Dahse, Mar. 13, 1964; children: David Allen, Michael Neal. BS in Chem. Engring., U. Mo., 1961; JD, U. Tex., 1967. Bar: Tex. 1967, U.S. Dist. Ct. (so. dist.) Tex. 1968, U.S. Ct. Appeals (5th cir.) 1970, U.S. Supreme Ct. 1973. Chem. engr. Union Carbide Corp., Texas City, Tex., 1963-65; ptnr. Baker & Botts, Houston, 1967—; gen. counsel Tex. Chem. Coun., Austin, 1981-92; mem. U.S. EPA Clean Air Act Adv. Com., 1991—. Chmn. Houston Area Oxidant Study Steering Com., 1978-80, Greater Houston Partnership/Greater Houston C. of C., Clean Air Coordinating Coun., 1990-95; pres. Woodlands Med. Ctr. Inc., Tex., 1978-88; mem. Houston-Galveston Area Coun. Govts. Air Quality Planning Com., 1988—, Mayor's Environ. Com., Houston, 1992—; chmn. bd. dirs. Houston-Galveston Area Emission Reduction Credit Orgn., 1994—; co-chair pub. adv. com. State of Tex. Environ. Priorities Project, 1993—. Served to 1st lt. U.S. Army, 1961-63. Mem. ABA, Tex. Bar Assn. (chmn. environ. sect. 1989-90), Houston C. of C. (chmn. environ. com. 1976-78), Tex. Ozone Task Force (chmn. 1987-90), Order of Coif, Phi Delta Phi, Omicron Delta Kappa, Tau Beta Pi. Presbyterian. Home: 3501 Georgetown St Houston TX 77005-2911*

FELDE, MARTIN LEE, advertising agency executive, accountant; b. Milw., Feb. 26, 1951; s. Walter Henry and Arline B. (Bergmann) F.; m. Virginia Rose Schlesing, Aug. 9, 1975; children—Erin, David. B.B.A., U. Wis., 1972. C.P.A., Wis. Staff auditor Arthur Andersen & Co., Milw., 1972-74; controller Page-Schwessinger, Milw., 1974-78; fin. adminstr. Bozell & Jacobs, Milw., 1978-79; controller Hoffman York, Milw., 1979-82, v.p., controller, 1982-83, v.p. fin., 1983-89; exec. v.p. Directory Data Mgmt., Inc., Milw., 1989-90; pres. Directory Data Mgmt./Telephone Mktg. Programs, Milw., 1990-91, divsn. CFO TMP Worldwide, Milw., 1991-93, corp. v.p. fin., 1993—. Mem. Am. Inst. C.P.A.s, Wis. Inst. C.P.A.s. Home: 17550 Senlac Ln Brookfield WI 53045-1312 Office: TMP Worldwide Inc 9045 N Deerwood Dr Milwaukee WI 53223-2437

FELDER, MYRNA, lawyer; b. N.Y.C., Apr. 19, 1941. BA magna cum laude, Brown U., 1961; JD cum laude, NYU, 1971. Bar: N.Y. 1971, U.S. Dist. Ct. (so. and ea. dists.) N.Y. 1974, U.S. Ct. Appeals (2nd cir.) 1977, U.S. Supreme Ct. 1978. Ptnr. Raoul Lionel Felder P.C., N.Y.C., 1972—; lawyer; b. N.Y.C., Apr. 19, 1941. B.A. magna cum laude, Brown U., 1961; J.D. cum laude, N.Y.U., 1971. Bar: N.Y. 1971, U.S. dist. ct. (so. and ea. dists.) N.Y. 1974, U.S. Ct. Apls. (2d cir.), 1977, U.S. Sup. Ct. 1978. ptnr. Raoul Lionel Felder, P.C., N.Y.C., 1972—; lectr., cons. in field. Mem. N.Y. State Civil Practice Adv. Com., chair subcom. Matrimonial Procedures, 1983—. Editor-in-chief The Matrimonial Strategist, 1985-89; bimonthly columnist New York Law Journal; contbr. chpts. to books. Mem. ABA, N.Y. State Bar Assn. (chair cts. of appellate jurisdiction com., 1988-92), Assn. Bar City N.Y., Women's Bar Assn. State N.Y. (dir. 1980-85, chmn. com. on matrimonial law 1984-85, pres. 1986-87), N.Y. Women's Bar Assn. (pres. 1976-77), Order of Coif, Phi Beta Kappa. Editor-in-chief: The Matrimonial Strategist, 1985-89; bimonthly columnist New York Law Jour.; contbr. chpts. to books. Mem. ABA, N.Y. State Bar Assn. (chair cts. of appellate jursidiction com. 1988-92), Assn. Bar City of N.Y., Women's Bar Assn., State N.Y. (dir. 1980-85, chmn. com. on matrimonial law 1984-85, pres. 1986-87), N.Y. Women's Bar Assn. (pres. 1976-77), Order of the Coif, Phi Beta Kappa. Home: 60 Sutton Pl S # 19AS New York NY 10022-4168 Office: Raoul Lionel Felder PC 437 Madison Ave New York NY 10022-7001

FELDER, RAOUL LIONEL, lawyer; b. N.Y.C., May 13, 1934; s. Morris and Millie (Goldstein) F.; m. Myrna Felder, May 26, 1963; children: Rachel, James. BA, NYU, 1955; JD, NYU, Switzerland, 1959; postgrad., U. Bern, Switzerland, 1955-56; hon. degree of fellow in jurisprudence, Oxford U., 1995. Bar: N.Y. 1959, U.S. Dist. Ct. (so. and ea. dists.) N.Y. 1962, U.S. Ct. Appeals (2d cir.) 1962, U.S. Supreme Ct. 1970. Pvt. practice N.Y.C., 1959-61, 64—; asst. U.S. atty., 1961-64; mem. faculty Practicing Law Inst., 1979, Marymount Coll., 1982—, Ethical Culture Sch., 1981, 82; moderator Nat. Conf. on Child Abuse, 1989; apptd. to N.Y.C. Cultural Affairs Adv. Commn., 1995—, State Commn. on Child Abuse, 1996. Author: Divorce: The Way Things Are, Not the Way Things Should Be, 1971, Lawyers Practical Handbook to the New Divorce Law, 1981, Raoul Felder's Encyclopedia of Matrimonial Clauses, 1990, updated, 1991—, Getting Away with Murder, 1996, Restaurant Guide to Los Angeles and New York, 1996, Survival Guide to New York, 1997; columnist Fame mag., 1988-92, Am. Women Mag., 1994, N.Y. Daily News Sundays, 1995; contbr. articles on law to profl. jours. and N.Y. Times; editorials to Newsweek mag., Harper's Bazaar mag., Newsday newspaper, N.Y. Post, The Guardian (London), Penthouse mag., Cosmopolitan mag., N.Y. Times; commentator Cable News Network, 1989, BBC World Wide, 1994, 95, 97, Crossing the Line, 1997-99, The Felder Report, 1998-99; guest commentator Court TV, 1992, bd. advisors, 1992-95, editl. contr.; (documentary) Survival Guide to New York, 1998; host (TV series) Metrolaw, 1995—. Chmn. Nat. Kidney Found. Auction, also N.Y. Fund; chmn. Dinner Jerusalem Reclamation Project; grand marshall U.S.A. Day Washington, Israel Day Parade, N.Y.C.; bd. dirs. Big Apple Greeters, Cop Care, Hosp. Audiences Inc., Nat. Kidney Found. Named Man of Yr. Bklyn. Sch. for Spl. Children, Met. Geriatric Ctr., Shield Inst., 1997; recipient Defender of Jerusalem medal, 1990, Crimebusters award Take Back N.Y., 1996. Mem. ABA (judge nat. finals client counseling competition), Assn. of Bar of City of N.Y. (spl. com. matrimonial law 1975-77), N.Y. State Trial Lawyers Assn. (past chmn. matrimonial law 1974-75), Am. Arbitration Assn., N.Y. Women's Bar Assn., Minion of the Stars (chmn. bd. 1993). Home: 60 Sutton Pl S New York NY 10022-4168 Office: 437 Madison Ave New York NY 10022-7001

FELDER, RICHARD BRUCE, pipeline safety administrator; m. Deborah Slater; children: Jon, Jeff. BA in Govt., Cornell U.; JD, NYU, 1972. Instr. regulatory mgmt. U. Wis., 1976-95; v.p. govt. affairs Transamerica Interway, Washington, 1980-81; ptnr. Arnall, Golden & Gregory, Washington, 1981-87; mgr. trucking and R.R. programs Interstate Commerce Commn., 1988-95; assoc. adminstr. pipeline safety Rsch. and Spl. Programs Adminstrn. Dept. of Transp., Washington, 1995—; mem. exec. program faculty Northwestern U. Transp. Ctr., 1995—. Office: Dept of Transp Pipeline Safety 400 7th St SW Washington DC 20590-0003

FELDERMAN, ROBERT JOHN, real estate appraiser, realtor; b. Dubuque, Sept. 13, 1955; s. John Laverne and Janet Barbara (Soppe) F.; m. Nancy J. Said, Apr. 12, 1986; children: Jacob Robert, Jamie Rae. BS in Aviation Mgmt., U. Dubuque, 1988. Cert. rescue diver Profl. Assn. Divers Internat. Realtor, appraiser Continental Realty, Dubuque, 1982—; advisor Nat. Edn. Ctr. for Agrl. Safety, Peosta, Iowa, 1997—. Contbr. articles to various publs. Commn., co-chmn. Environ. Stewardship, Dubuque, 1992-95; co-chmn. Dubuque County Compensation Bd., 1995-98; sec., bd. dirs. Dubuque Main Street, Ltd., 1995-98. Lt. col. Army N.G., 1975-99. Mem. Army Aviation Assn. Am., Iowa Assn. Master Appraisers (adviser 1987-90), Iowa N.G. Officers Assn (pres. 1996), Am. Legion. Roman Catholic. Avocations: running, golf, travel, flying, computers. Home: 1980 Marion St Dubuque IA 52003-7136 Office: Continental Realty Felderman Appraisals 1399 Jackson St Dubuque IA 52001-5046

FELDERSTEIN, STEVEN HOWARD, lawyer; b. Rochester, N.Y., Oct. 28, 1946; s. Lester and Ruth (Tatelbaum) F.; m. Sandra Lynn Goldman, Aug. 26, 1969; 1 child, Janis. BA, SUNY, 1968; JD, U. Calif., San Francisco, 1973. Bar: Calif. Law clk. U.S. Dist. Ct., Sacramento, 1973-75; ptnr. Felderstein Rosenberg & McManes, Sacramento, 1978-86, Diepenbrock, Wulff, Plant & Hanmegan, Sacramento, 1986-98, Felderstein Willoughby & Pascuzzi LLP, Sacramento, 1999—. Contbr. articles to profl. jours. Bd. trustees Jewish Fedn. Sacramento Region, 1990-95. Mem. Calif. Bar Assn. (uniform comml. code com. bus. sect. 1983-85), Calif. Continuing Edn. of Bar (lectr. 1987—), Practicing Law Inst. (lectr. 1995—), Am. Coll. Bankruptcy, Calif. Bankruptcy Forum (v.p. 1998, pres. 1998-99). Office: Felderstein Willoughby & Pascuzzi LLP 400 Capitol Mall Ste 1450 Sacramento CA 95814

FELDHAUS, STEPHEN MARTIN, lawyer; b. Lawrenceburg, Tenn., Jan. 12, 1945; s. Lawrence Bernard and Margaret Martha (Holthouse) F.; m. Allis Rennie, Aug. 18, 1968 (div. Dec. 1980); 1 child, Rennie Elizabeth; m. Marcia Virginia Hughes, Dec. 30, 1980; stepchildren: Matthew Rankin FitzSimmons, Ryan Ford FitzSimmons. AB, U. Notre Dame, 1967; JD, Stanford U., 1973. Bar: Tex. 1973, D.C. 1984, U.S. Tax Ct. Law clk. to Hon. Eugene A. Wright U.S. Ct. Appeals (9th cir.), Seattle, 1972-73; assoc. Fulbright & Jaworski, Houston, 1973-76; assoc. Fulbright & Jaworski, London, 1976-79, ptnr., 1979-81; ptnr. Fulbright & Jaworski, Washington, 1981—; bd. dirs. Foundation, Vaduz, Liechtenstein. Bd. dirs. D.C. Downtown Partnership, Washington, 1988-92;. Mem. ABA, Internat. Bar Assn., Internat. Fiscal Assn., D.C. Bar, MIT Enterprise Forum Washington-Balt., City Club of Washington. Democrat. Avocations: tennis, skiing, chess, reading. Office: Fulbright & Jaworski 801 Pennsylvania Ave NW Fl 3-5 Washington DC 20004-2623

FELDMAN, ALBERT JOSEPH, lawyer; b. Phila., June 30, 1929; s. Martin and Mildred (Baum) F.; m. Ellen M. Jonas, Aug. 15, 1954; children—Rachel A., David J., Emily L. A.B. cum laude, Harvard U., 1950; LL.B. cum laude, U. Pa., 1953. Bar: Pa. Assoc. Wolf, Block, Schorr & Solis-Cohen, Phila., 1956-62, ptnr., 1963-73, sr. ptnr., 1974-93, chmn. exec. com., 1975, 78, 81, of counsel, 1993—. Contbr. to Legal Aspects of Certification and Accreditation, 1983. Assoc. trustee U. Pa.; mem. bd. advisors U. Pa. Cancer Ctr. Served to 1st lt. JACG, U.S. Army, 1954-56. Mem. ABA, Nat. Assn. Bond Lawyers, Phila. Bar Assn., Pa. Bar Assn., Harvard Alumni Assn. (regional dir. 1988-91), Harvard Club (pres. 1985-87), Philmont Country Club, Ballen Isles Country Club. Office: Wolf Block Schorr and Solis-Cohen 12th Fl Packard Bldg 1650 Arch St 22nd Fl Philadelphia PA 19103

FELDMAN, ALLAN ROY, corporate development and marketing executive; b. Chgo., June 2, 1945; s. Michael and Sophie (Grossman) F.; m. Micki McCabe, Sept. 21, 1984. BS, Roosevelt U., 1968; postgrad., U. Louvain, Belgium, 1969-71; MBA, U. Chgo. Asst. to dir. gen. Rank-Xerox, S.A., Brussels, Belgium, 1969-71; dir. new bus. ventures graphic sys. group Rockwell Internat. Corp., Chgo., 1971-73, dir. mktg., consumer ops., 1973-75, gen. mgr. microwave oven divsn., 1975-78; group v.p. Chromalloy Am. Corp., N.Y.C., 1978-80; mng. ptnr. Mktg. Trademark Cons., N.Y.C., 1980-85; CEO, pres. Leveraged Mktg. Corp. Am., N.Y.C., 1986—; bd. dirs. Alimansky Venture Group, Inc., N.Y.C., ITC Integrated Sys., Inc., N.Y.C., Growthtech Corp., N.Y.C., Indsl. Computer Corp., Farmington, Conn.; guest lectr. Columbia U.; spkr. trademark licensing and brand bldg., orgns. including Internat. Trademark Assn. and Licensing Execs. Soc., various U.S. and European confs. Bd. dirs. Riverside Fund, N.Y.C., 329108 Owners Corp., N.Y.C., 1993. Avocations: helicopter flying, master carpenter, photography, motorcycle riding. Office: Leveraged Mktg Corp 156 W 56th St New York NY 10019-3800

FELDMAN, ARLENE BUTLER, aviation industry executive. BA cum laude in Polit. Sci., U. Colo., 1975; JD, Temple U. Sch. Law, 1978. Supervising atty. U.S. Railway Assn., Phila., 1977-82; dir. divsn. aeronautics N.J. Dept. Transp., Trenton, 1982-84; from acting dir. to dep. dir. tech. ctr. FAA, Atlantic City, N.J., 1984-86; dep. dir. Western-Pacific region Exec. Sch. FAA, L.A., 1986-87, dep. dir. Western-Pacific region, 1986-87; regional adminstr. N.Eng. Region FAA, Burlington, Mass., 1988-94, exec. sch., 1986-87; eastern regional adminstr. FAA, Jamaica, N.Y., 1994—; panelist, guest spkr. Women in Aviation Conf., 1992, 93; vice-chair N.Y. Fed. Exec. Bd.; chairperson regional airport sys. planning adv. com. Delaware Valley Regional Planning Commn.; founder rotorcraft R&D forum FAA. Chairwoman Boston Federal Exec. Bd. Saving Bond, 1993; mem. adv. bd. U. So. Calif. Recipient Presdl. Meritorius Rank award Sr. Exec. Svc., Disting. Svc. award N.J. Aviation Hall of Fame, Amelia Earhart medal; inducted N.J. Aviation Hall of Fame, 1997. Mem. ABA, Ninety-Nines Internat. Orgn. (Earhart medal), Lawyer/Pilot Bar Assn., Air Traffic Control Assn. (dir., exec. bd., conf. panel moderator 1993, 91, spkr. 1993, chmn. bd. 1996, chmn. elect 1997), Am. Assn. Airport Execs., Am. Assn. State Hwy. and Transp. Ofcls., Am. Helicopter Soc., Helicopter Assn. Internat. (hon.), Nat. Assn. State Aviation Ofcls., Nat. Coun. Women in Aviation Aerospce, Internat. Aviation Women's Assn., Profl. Women Contrs., Inc. (1st hon. mem.), Wings Club N.Y.C. (bd. govs. 1996), Pi Sigma Alpha. Office: FAA Fed Bldg # 111 JFK Internat Airport Jamaica NY 11430*

FELDMAN, ARTHUR EDWARD, urologist; b. Phila., Pa., July 9, 1946; s. Herman and Elayne (Rhodes) F.; m. June 22, 1981; children: Brad, Elyse, Todd. BS, Muhlenberg Coll., AllentownPa., 1968; MD, Temple U., 1972. Urology resident Temple U., 1974-77; ptnr. Somerset Urol. Assocs., Bridgewater, N.J., 1977—. Contbr. articles to profl. jours. Fellow ACS; mem. Am. Urol. Assn., Med. Soc. N.J. Avocations: swimming, music, aerobics. Office: Somerset Urol Assocs PA 201 Union Ave Bridgewater NJ 08807-3002

FELDMAN, BRUCE ALAN, psychiatrist; b. St. Louis, Apr. 21, 1959; s. Jerome Stanley and Arlene (Greenberg) F.; m. Kathryn Matilda Estill, May 25, 1990. BA in Biology, U. Mo., Kansas City, 1982, MD, 1985. Diplomate Nat. Bd. Med. Examiners, Am. Bd. Psychiatry and Neurology, added qualifications geriatric psychiatry. Resident in psychiatry So. Ill. U., Springfield, 1986-89, adminstrv. chief resident, 1988, chief resident in geriat. psychiatry, 1989; pvt. practice Psychiat. Assocs., Springfield, 1990—; resident cons. psychiatrist Alzheimers Ctr. for Decatur, Ill., 1989, Alzheimers Ctr. and Memory Disorders Ctr., Springfield, 1989; cons. psychiatrist Taylorville (Ill.) Mental Health Ctr., 1990—, Country View Living Ctr., Decatur, 1990-96, Jacksonville Terr. Nursing Home, 1990-98, Walnut Ridge N.H., 1992-96, Taylorville Terrace, N.H., 1995—, Prairie Rose, N.H., 1995—, Morganview Terrace, N.H., 1995-97, Briarbrook Living Ctr., 1995—, Eisenhower Terrace Living Ctr., 1995-96, Springfield Mental Health Ctr., 1992-96, Prairie Village, N.H., 1997—, Macon County Resources, 1998—; hosp. affiliate Drs. Hosp., 1990—, Meml. Med. Ctr., 1990—, St. Johns Hosp., 1990—, St. Vincent Meml. Hosp., 1990—, Passavant Hosp., 1990—; mem. utilization rev. com. Drs. Hosp., 1990-91, St. Johns Hosp., 1994—, pharm. and therapeutics com., 1992-96; ltd. ptnr., owner Drs. Hosp., Springfield, 1990-94, Wentville, Mo., 1991-96; bd. dirs. Ind. Physicians Network, Springfield, 1995—; contbr. THA clin. studies SIU Alzheimers Clinic, 1989, Prosom Clin. Study, 1992; treas. Psychiat. Assn. Ctrl. Ill., 1997—. Mem. Jewish Fedn., Springfield, Ill., Temple Israel Synagogue, Springfield; exec. prodr., dir. Miss K.C. Pageant, 1981; mem. Nat. Rep. Congress com., 1988—, Rep. Nat. Candidate Trust, 1992—, Rep. Inner Circle, 1993-96, Rep. Nat. Com., 1994—, Crescent Counties Found. for Med. Care, 1993-96. Named to Rep. Nat. Hall of Honor, 1992; recipient Rep. Congl. Order of Liberty, 1993, Rep. Senatorial Medal of Freedom, 1994, RNC Citation of Leadership, 1996. Mem. AMA, Am. Psychiat. Assn., N.Y. Acad. Scis. (life), So. Med. Assn., Am. Assn. for Geriatric Psychiatry, U.S. Senatorial Club, Bnai Brith (Emes chpt., former exec. bd. mem.), Delta Chi (past pres. Kansas City chpt. 1979, nat. v.p., chpt. advisor 1981-82, Alumnus of Yr. Kansas City chpt. 1982). Republican. Avocations: reading, politics, sports, stamps, travel. Office: Psychiat Assocs 1124 S 6th St Springfield IL 62703-2406

FELDMAN, BRUCE ALLEN, otolaryngologist; b. Washington, Mar. 22, 1941; s. Irvin and Miriam Thelma (Rothstein) F.; m. Sharon Lee Pearlman, Dec. 25, 1966; children: Kathryn Ellen, Michael Aaron. AB, Dartmouth Coll., 1962, B Med. Sci., 1963; MD, Harvard U., 1965. Diplomate Am. Bd. Otolaryngology. Intern Hosp. of U. Pa., Phila., 1965-66, resident in surgery, 1966-67; resident in otolaryngology Mass. Eye and Ear Infirmary-Harvard U., Boston, 1967-70; pvt. practice Washington, 1972—; clin. prof. surgery (otolaryngology), pediatrics/hlth. care George Washington U., Washington, 1990—; clin. prof. otolaryngology Georgetown U. Sch. Medicine, Washington, 1995—; pres. med. staff Children's Hosp. Nat. Med. Ctr., Washington, 1994-96; bd. dirs. Children's Hosp., 1997—. Contbr. articles to med. jours., chpt. to book. Lt. comdr. M.C., USNR, 1970-72. Mosby scholar, 1963; recipient Physician's Recognition award Children's Hosp. Washington, 1991. Fellow ACS, Am. Laryngol., Rhinol. and Otol. Soc. (Mosher award 1981), Am. Acad. Pediatrics; mem. AMA, Med. Soc. D.C., Jacobi Med. Soc. (pres. 1986-87), Washington Met. Ear, Nose and Throat Soc. (pres. 1978-79), Woodmont Country Club (Rockville, Md.), Phi Beta Kappa, Alpha Omega Alpha, Phi Delta Epsilon (pres. grad. club 1979-80). Jewish. Office: 1145 19th St Washington DC 20036

FELDMAN, BURTON GORDON, printing company executive; b. Chgo., Dec. 19, 1911; s. Maurice J. and Goldye (Gordon) F.; m. Dorothy Straus, Dec. 28, 1942 (dec. 1969); children: Roger, Susan. B.S., Northwestern U., 1933. Group copy chief Foote, Cone & Belding, Chgo., 1942-46; v.p. charge Chgo. office Buchanan & Co., 1946-48; exec. v.p. Gordon Best/Post, Keyes, 1948-59; pres. Burton G. Feldman, Inc., 1959-68; chmn. bd. Feldman & Assocs. Advt., Inc., Chgo., 1968-74; pres. Instant Printing Corp., Chgo., 1972—; pres. Phoenix Electric Co., Chgo., 1963-68, chmn. bd., 1968-84, dir., 1963-88; v.p. mktg., dir. Cummins Tool Corp., 1977-84. Pres. James Gordon Found., 1962—; bd. fellows Brandeis U., 1981—, v.p., 1981-83; v.p., bd. dirs. Chgo. Chamber Orch. Assn., 1982-86; bd. dirs. Burton Gordon Feldman Pub. Policy Award Endowment; bd. dirs. Gordon Ctr. for Pub. Policy Research. Mem. Brandeis Roundtables Assn. (chmn. 1988-90), Pi Lambda Phi, Sigma Delta Chi. Clubs: Columbia Yacht, Arts of Chgo, Brandeis U. of Chgo. (pres. 1980-84). Address: Gordon Foundation 3100 Lexington Ln Glenview IL 60025-5938

FELDMAN, CLARICE ROCHELLE, lawyer; b. Milw., Dec. 2, 1941; d. Harry and Beatrice (Hiken) Wagan; m. Howard J. Feldman, July 11, 1965; 1 child, David Lewis. B.S., U. Wis., 1963, LL.B., 1965. Bar: Wis. 1965, D.C. 1969, Md. 1984. Appellate atty. NLRB, Washington, 1965-69; co-counsel to Joseph A. Yablonski, Washington, 1969; atty. Washington research project Clark Coll., 1970-72; asso. gen. counsel United Mine Workers Am., Washington, 1972-74; partner Becker, Channell, Becker & Feldman, Washington, 1974-76, Becker & Feldman, 1976-77; gen. counsel Ams. for Energy Independence, Washington, 1978-80; atty. Office of Spl. Investigations, Dept. Justice, 1980-84; pvt. practice law Washington, 1984-98. Trustee Washington Internat. Sch., 1987-98; advisor Assn. Union Democracy. Mem. Wis., D.C., Md. bar assns. Democrat. Jewish. Home: 4455 29th St NW Washington DC 20008-2307

FELDMAN, DEBORAH KARPOFF, nursing education consultant; b. Boston, Jan. 25, 1943; m. Samuel Feldman, 1961. AS, Miss. State Coll. for Women, 1973; BSN, Miss. U. for Women, 1975; M of Nursing, U. Miss., Jackson, 1976. Staff nurse, relief charge nurse Golden Triangle Regional Med. Ctr., Columbus, Miss., 1973-75; asst. prof. Sch. Nursing Miss. U. for Women, Columbus, 1975-77, Calif. State U., Chico, 1978; asst. prof., asst. dir. Sierra Coll., Rocklin, Calif., 1978-79; asst. prof. Coppin State Coll., Balt., 1979-80; nursing edn. cons. Md. Bd. Nursing, Balt., 1980—; cons. Allied Health programs Md. Higher Edn. Commn., Annapolis, 1989—. Contbg. author: (monograph) Collaboration for Articulation, 1987; editor: (newsletter) Communicator Board of Nursing Newsletter, 1986—. Presenter Am. Cancer Soc., Columbus, 1978-79; tchr. Hebrew sch. Temple Bnai Israel, Columbus, 1970-76; chair funds campaign Am. Cancer Soc., Balt., 1982; campaign worker Reelection of State Sen., Reisterstown, Md., 1994. Higher edn. scholar Miss. State Bd. Trustees of Instns. of Higher Learning, 1974-76, Harriet Hatcher scholar Miss. Nursing Assn. Dist. 17, 1973. Mem. Md. Nurses Assn., Md. League Nursing, Nat. Coun. State Bd. Nursing (chair com. to evaluate implementation of computer adaptive testing, mem. adminstr. of exam. com. 1989-94, com. on nominations 1996, exam. com. 1996—), Sigma Theta Tau. Office: Md Bd Nursing 4140 Patterson Ave Baltimore MD 21215-2254

FELDMAN, EDMUND BURKE, art critic; b. Bayonne, N.J., May 6, 1924; s. Lucian Theodore and Bertha (Seldin) F.; m. Lailah G. Link, Mar. 15, 1953; children: Eva Jeanne, Jessica Marion. B.F.A., Syracuse U., 1949; M.A., UCLA, 1951; Ed.D., Columbia U., 1953. Curator painting and sculpture Newark Mus., 1953; assoc. prof. art Livingston (Ala.) State U., 1953-56, Carnegie Inst. Tech., 1956-60; head art div. State U. Coll., New Paltz, N.Y., 1960-66; vis. prof. art Ohio State U., 1966; prof. art U. Ga., Athens, 1966-91, Alumni Found. disting. prof. art, 1973-91, prof. emeritus, 1991—; vis. prof. aesthetic edn. U. Calif., Berkeley, 1974; bd. govs. Pitts. Plan for Art, 1964-66; mem. U.S. Office Edn., Art TV Project, Whitney Mus., 1967, Ednl. Testing Svc., N.Y.C., 1969-70, Coll. Entrance Exam Bd., Princeton, N.J., 1969-70, Nat. Instructional TV Ctr., Bloomington, Ind., 1969-71; editorial cons. art Prentice-Hall, Inc. (arts and humanities Canfield Press subs. Harper & Row); advisor Ga. Coun. for arts, 1973-74, Nat. Faculty for Arts and Humanities, 1986; cons. J. Paul Getty Trust, 1981-85. Author: Art as Image and Idea, 1967, Varieties of Visual Experience, 1971, 4th edit., 1992, The Artist, 1982, 2d edit., 1994, Thinking About Art, 1985, Practical Art Criticism, 1993, Philosophy of Art Education, 1995; editor Art Bull., Ea. Arts Assn., 1957-60, Art in American Institutions, 1970; mem. editorial bd. Rev. Rsch. in Visual Arts Edn., 1975-77; mem. editorial adv. bd. Jour. Aesthetic Edn., 1976-80; chmn. editorial bd. Ga. Rev., 1977. Served with USAAF, 1942-46. Recipient Roswell Hill prize in painting Syracuse U., 1948. Fellow Nat. Art Edn. Assn. (pres. 1981-83, Disting. 1984), Royal Soc. Arts; mem. Coll. Art Assn., U.S. Soc. for Edn. Through Art, Tau Sigma Delta, Kappa Delta Pi, Kappa Pi, Phi Kappa Phi. Jewish. Home: 140 Chinquapin Pl Athens GA 30605-3314 Office: U Ga Sch Art Athens GA 30602

FELDMAN, ELAINE BOSSAK, medical nutritionist, educator; b. N.Y.C., Dec. 9, 1926; d. Solomon and Frances Helen (Fania) Nevler Bossak; m. Herman Black, Dec. 23, 1951 (div. 1957); 1 child, Mitchell Evan; m. Daniel S. Feldman, July 19, 1957; children: Susan, Daniel S. Jr. AB magna cum laude, NYU, 1945, MS, 1948, MD, 1951. Diplomate Am. Bd. Internal Medicine, Nat. Bd. Med. Examiners; cert. in Clin. Nutrition. Rotating intern Mt. Sinai Hosp., N.Y.C., 1951-52, resident in pathology, 1952, asst. resident, 1953, fellow in medicine, resident in metabolism, 1954-55, rsch. asst. in medicine, 1955-58, clin. asst. physician Diabetes Clinic, 1957; asst. vis. physician Kings County Hosp., Bklyn., 1958-66, assoc. vis. physician, 1966-72; asst. attending physician Maimonides Hosp., Bklyn., 1960-68; spl. fellow USPHS Dept. of Physiol. Chemistry U. of Lund, Sweden, 1964-65; attending physician Eugene Talmadge Meml. Hosp., Augusta, Ga., 1972-92; attending physician Univ. Hosp., Augusta, 1972-92, cons., 1973; prof. medicine Med. Coll. Ga., Augusta, 1972-92, prof. emeritus, 1992—, chief sect. of nutrition, 1977-92, chief emeritus, 1992—, acting chief sect. of metabolic/endocrine disease, 1980-81, prof. physiology and endocrinology, 1988-92, prof. emeritus physiology and endocrinology, 1992—; instr. medicine SUNY Downstate Med. Ctr., 1957-59, asst. prof. medicine, 1959-68, assoc. prof. medicine, 1968-72; tchg. fellow dept. zoology U. Wis. Grad. Sch., 1945-46, dept. biology NYU Grad. Sch., 1946-47; cons. N.Y.-N.J. Regional Ctr. for Clin. Nutrition Edn., 1983-92; vis. prof. and Harvey lectr. Northeastern Ohio Sch. Medicine, Youngstown, 1985; cons., vis. prof. U. Nev. Sch. Medicine (NCI grant), 1989-94; mem. nat. adv. com. nutrition fellowship program Nat. Med. Fellowship Inc., 1988-95; dir. Ga. Inst. Human Nutrition, 1978-92, dir. emeritus, 1992—; dir. Clin. Nutrition Rsch. Unit, 1980-86; mem. med. nutrition curriculum initiative adv. bd. U. N.C., Chapel Hill, 1992—; advisor ednl. materials Am. Inst. Cancer Rsch., 1997—. Author: Essentials of Clinical Nutrition, 1988; (with others) Conference on Biological Activities of Steroids in Relation to Cancer, 1969, Nicotinic Acid, 1964, The Menopausal Syndrome, 1974, Hyperlipidemia, Medcom Special Studies, 1974, Medcom Famous Teaching in Modern Medicine, 1979, Harrison's Principles of Internal Medicine, 1980, Health Promotion: Principles and Clinical Applications, 1982, The Encyclopedic Handbook of Alcoholism, 1982, The Climacteric in Perspective, 1986, Selenium in Biology and Medicine, Part A., 1987, Medicine for the Practicing Physician, 1988, Clinical Chemistry of Laboratory Animals, 1989, Ency. Human Biology, 1991, Laboratory Medicine: The Selection and Interpretation of Clinical Laboratory Studies, 1993, Modern Nutrition in Health and Diseases, 1994, Nutrition Assessment-A Comprehensive Guide for Planning Intervention, 1995, The Women's Complete Healthbook, 1995, The American Medical Women's Association Guide to Nutrition and Wellness, 1996; editor: Nutrition and Cardiovascular Disease, 1976, Nutrition in the Middle and Later Years, 1983 (paperback edit. 1986), Nutrition and Heart Disease, 1983; mem. editorial adv. bd. Contemporary Issues in Clin. Nutrition, 1980-92; mem. editorial bd. Am. Jour. Clin. Nutrition, 1983-91, 92-98, Jour. Clin. Endocrinology and Metabolism, 1984-88, MidPoint: Counseling Women through Menopause, 1984-85, Jour. Nutrition, 1985-89; cons. editor Jour. Am. Coll. Nutrition, 1982-94; mem. editorial bd. Complementary Med. for the Physician, 1996—; contbg. editor Nutrition Rev., 1997—; mem. editl. bd. Nutrition Today, 1999—; reviewer Jour. Lipid Rsch., Biochm. Pharmacology, Sci., The Physiologist, Jour. Am. Acad. Dermatology, Israel Jour. Med. Scis., N.Y. State Jour. Medicine, Jour. of Nutrition Edn., Jour. Am. Dietetic Assn., Am. Jour. Medicine, Am. Jour. Med. Sci., So. Med. Jour., Jour. AMA; author 160 published articles in field, numerous abstracts and presentations. Mem. tech. adv. com. for sci. and edn. Rsch. Grants Program, Human Nutrition Grants Peer Panel, USDA, 1982, mem. bd. sci. counselors human nutrition; Community Svc. Block Grant Discretionary Program Panel; vice chmn. Urban and Rural Econ. Devel. Panel, Dept. HHS, 1982, grant reviewer, 1983; mem ad hoc and spl. rev. coms. and groups NIH, 1979-93, mem. nutrition study sect., 1976-80; mem. Rev. Panel Nat. Nutrition Objectives, Life Scis. Rev. Office, Fed. Am. Socs. Exptl. Biology, 1985-86; mem. subcom. Women's Health Trial Nat. Cancer Inst., 1987, mem. bd. sci. counselors cancer prevention and control program, 1990-94; mem. adv. com. Clin. Nutrition Rsch. Unit, U. Ala., 1986-94, Ga. Nutrition Steering Com., 1974-75, Ctrl. Savannah River Area Nutrition Project Coun. 1974-75, ednl. adv. com. Health Central, 1980; mem. geriatrics and gerontology rev. com. Nat. Inst. on Aging, 1986-90; breast cancer initiative peer rev. Dept. of Def., 1997, 98. N.Y. Heart Assn. rsch. fellow, 1955-57. Fellow Am. Heart Assn. Coun. on Atherosclerosis (nominating com. 1978, chmn. nominating com., mem. exec. com. 1979-80, Spl. Recognition award 1995), Am. Inst. Nutrition (grad. nutrition edn. com. 1980-83, 89-93); mem. Am. Coll. Nutrition (chmn. com. pub. affairs), Am. Soc. for Clin. Nutrition (com. on nutrition edn. 1982, chmn. subcom. on nutrition edn. in med. schs. 1983-84, chmn. com. on med./dental residency edn., 1985-87, com. on subsplty. tng. 1988-92, nominating com. 1982, 90, chair nominating com. 1994, com. on clin. practice issues in health and disease 1989-92, Nat. Dairy Coun. award 1991, rep. coun. acad. socs. 1990-96, membership com. 1996—, chair 1999), Fedn. Am. Socs. Exptl. Biology. Am. Oil Chemists Soc., Am. Physiol. Soc., Endocrine Soc., Soc. Exptl. Biology and Medicine, So. Soc. Clin. Investigation, Am. Diabetes Assn., Am. Fedn. Clin. Rsch., Am. Gastroent. Assn., AMA (Joseph B. Goldberger award 1990), Am. Med. Women's Assn. (profl. resources com. 1975-76, med. edn. and rsch. fund com. 1976-79, chmn. 1978-90, chmn. student liaison subcom. of membership com. 1981-84, pres. Br. 51, Augusta 1977-80, treas. 1980—, Calcium Nutrition Edn. award 1991, CSRA Girl Scout Women of Excellence award 1994), Am. Soc. Parenteral and Enteral Nutrition, Am. Heart Assn. (Ga. affiliate, nutrition com., chmn. sci. session for nutritionists, 1978, chmn. nutrition com. 1979-90, mem. long range planning com. 1980-81, rsch. com. 1980-83, bd. dirs. 1987-90, profl. edn. task force, 1988-89), Richmond Country Med. Assn., Augusta Opera Assn. (bd. dirs. 1973—, recording sec. 1973-74, pres. 1974-75, coord. audience devel. 1975-77, at-large exec. com. 1994-96, chair nominating com. 1994-96, corr. sec. 1998-99, 1st v.p. 1999—), Augusta Sailing Club (women's com. 1973), Greater Augusta Arts Coun. (Arts Festival Collage 1982 chmn. promotion and publicity com., Festival coms. 1983-86, 89-93, 95, 96, 98, bd. dirs. 1984-94), Gertrude Herbert Inst. Art (bd. dirs. 1987-92), Authors Club Augusta, Philomathic Club (sec. 1999—), Phi Beta Kappa, Sigma Xi (chpt. sec. 1982-83, pres. elect 1983-84, pres. 1984-85), Alpha Omega Alpha. Avocations: opera, wine tasting, travel. Home: 2123 Cumming Rd Augusta GA 30904-4333

FELDMAN, ERIC ADAM, law educator, academic administrator; b. N.Y.C., Oct. 18, 1959; s. Saul and Gloria F.; m. Stephanie Cecile Cridelose, June 20, 1997. Student, U. Leeds, 1979-80; BA in History and Philosophy of Sci. cum laude, Vassar Coll., 1982; JD, U. Calif., Berkeley, 1989, PhD in Jurisprudence and Social Policy, 1994; student, Nichibei Kaiwa Gakkuen, Tokyo, 1990-91. Bar: Calif. 1989. Rsch. asst. Hastings Ctr., N.Y.C., 1982-84; tchg. asst. Sch. Journalism Columbia U., N.Y.C., 1984; vis. fellow biomed. ethics Mitsubishi-Kasei Inst. Life Scis., Japan, 1984-85; assoc. LeBoeuf, Lamb, Leiby & MacRae, San Francisco, 1989; fgn. rsch. scholar Inst. Social Scis. U. Tokyo, 1990-91, rsch. scholar faculty law internat. ctr. comparative law and politics, 1991-93; health policy rsch. scholar Instn. Social and Policy Studies Yale U., vis. fellow Sch. Law, 1994-96; assoc. dir. Inst. Law and Soc. NYU, 1996—; cons. Toyota Found., Tokyo, 1993-95, World Health Orgn., 1995-96; vis. prof. Inst. D'Etudes Politiques de Paris, 1999; mem. organizing com. 1999 Law and Soc. Assn. Grad. Student Workshop; prin. investigator various profl. projects; organizer, cons., participant AIDS prevention: bldg. U.S./Japan cooperation and exchange project, 1994-96; chair various profl. meetings; presenter in field. Co-author: AIDS in the Industrial Democracies: Passion, Politics, and Policies, 1992, German transl., 1993, Containing Health Care Costs in Japan, 1996, Comparing Legal Cultures, 1997; guest editor Jour. AIDS and Human Retrovirology, 1997; mem. editl. bd. Law and Soc. Rev., 1998—; contbr. articles to profl. jours.; book reviewer in field; reviewer numerous manuscripts. Vol. Tenderloin Housing Clinic, San Francisco, 1987; bd. dirs. Village Acad. Charter Sch., New Haven, 1997-98. Recipient award U.S.-Japan Culture Ctr. Essay Contest, 1988; Fulbright Grad. Rsch. fellow Japan-U.S. Ednl. Commn./IIE, 1989-93; Toyota Found. Rsch. fellow, 1990; Dissertation grantee Social Sci. Rsch. Coun., Joint Com. Japanese Studies, 1991; Rsch. fellow Japan Soc. Promotion Sci., 1992; Doctoral Dissertation Improvement grantee NSF, 1993; Robert Wood Johnson Found. scholar, 1994-96; Abe fellow Social Sci. Rsch. Coun., Am. Coun. Learned Socs. and Ctr. Global Partnership, 1998—; Stephen Charney Vladeck Jr. Faculty fellow NYU, 1999. Mem. Law and Soc. Assn., Assn. Asian Studies, Japan Policy Rsch. Inst., The Hastings Ctr. Fax: 212-995-4034. E-mail: eric.feldman@nyu.edu. Home: 14 Washington Dr # 4A New York NY 10003 Office: Inst Law and Soc NYU 249 Sullivan St New York NY 10012-1079

FELDMAN, FRANCES LOMAS, educator, consultant; b. Phila., Dec. 3, 1912; d. Harry and Dora (Hoffman) Lomas; m. Albert George Feldman, Mar. 16, 1935 (dec. Dec. 1975); 1 child, Dona Feldman Munker. BA, U. So. Calif., 1934, MSW, 1940; cert., U. Chgo., 1953. Social worker State Relief Adminstrn., L.A., 1934-39; dir. Housing Authority, L.A., 1940-41, Family Svc. L.A., 1941-43, L.A. County Bur. Pub. Assistance, L.A., 1943-50, Jewish Family & Cmty. Svc., Chgo., 1950-53; prof. U. So. Calif. Sch. Social Work, L.A., 1954-82; cons. in field. Author: Family in Money World, 1957, Family Social Welfare: Helping Troubled Families, 1967, Evolution of Professional Social Work, 1996, Work and Cancer, 1976, 78, 82, Rural Alaska Services, 1973. Mem. NASW, Phi Kappa Phi. Avocations: travel, music, writing. Home: 765 S San Rafael Ave Pasadena CA 91105-2326 Office: U Southern California Los Angeles CA 90089-0411

FELDMAN, FRANKLIN, lawyer, printmaker; b. N.Y.C., Nov. 12, 1927; s. Reuben and Anne (Schulman) F.; m. Naomi Goldstein, June 3, 1956; children: Sarah, Eve, Jacob. BA, NYU, 1948; LLB, Columbia U., 1951. Bar: N.Y. 1952. Mem. office Gen. Counsel, USAF, Dept. Def., Washington, 1951-53; atty. office gen. counsel to gov. State of N.Y., Albany, 1954; assoc. Stroock & Stroock & Lavan, N.Y.C., 1955-64, ptnr., 1965-88, counsel, 1989—; cons. Temp. N.Y. Commn. on Constl. Conv., 1967; lectr. in law Columbia Law Sch., 1979—. Editor-in-chief Columbia U. Law Rev., 1950-51; author: (with Stephen E. Weil) Art Works: Law, Policy and Practice, 1974, Art Law, 1986 (Best Law Book Published in 1986, Scribes); contbr. articles to profl. jours. Trustee Am. Jewish Hist. Soc., Waltham, Mass., 1987-96. 1st lt., USAF, 1951-53. Yaddo Fellow, Saratoga Springs, 1983. Fellow Am. Bar Found.; mem. NAD (adv. bd.), N.Y. State Bar Assn., Assn. of Bar of City of N.Y. (chmn. art com. 1968-71), Internat. Found. Art Rsch. (pres. 1971-76, bd. dirs. 1976-96), Internat. Art Loss Register, Ltd., Soc. Am. Graphic Artists, Century Assn., Pvt. Art Dealers Assn., Inc. (counsel, dir. 1993—), Grolier Club. Jewish. Home: 15 W 81st St New York NY 10024-6022 Office: Stroock & Stroock & Lavan 180 Maiden Ln New York NY 10038-4925

FELDMAN, GARY MARC, nutritionist, consultant; b. Bklyn., Dec. 3, 1953; m. Debra Lynn Bieler, Sept. 21, 1984. Diploma in Sci. of Nutritional Cons., Am. Nutrition Cons. Assn., 1986. Pres. Steps In Health, Ltd., Douglaston, N.Y., 1986-88, Margate, Fla., 1988-90, Nesconset, N.Y., 1990—; educator for children in sci. of food and nutritional supplementation. Developer: Steps in Health Ltd.'s Catalogue of Vegetarian Name-Brand Nutritional Supplements and Health Products; author nutrition newsletter. Vol. listen to children program Mental Health Assn. and Vol. Program Broward County (Fla.) Pub. Schs., 1989; arbitration participant Better Bus. Bur. South Fla., 1989-90. Mem. AAAS, Am. Nutrition Cons. Assn., Life Extension Found., Pub. Citizen Health Rsch. Group, People for Ethical Treatment of Animals, Doris Day Animal League, Humane Soc. Broward County, Ctr. for Sci. in the Pub. Interest, Internat. Platform Assn., N.Y. State Sheriffs Assn., L.I. Assn. Inc., Herb Rsch. Found., Vegetarian Resource Group, N.Am. Vegetarian Soc., Nutritionists Health Am. (nutrition edn. program com.), Ctr. Sci. Pub. Interest (edn. com.), Feingold Assn., U.S. Co-op Am. Bus. Network, N.Y. Acad. Scis. Avocations: reading and data collection in health field, bodybuilding. Office: PO Box 23-1182 Great Neck NY 11023-0182

FELDMAN, GORDON, physics educator; b. Windsor, Ont., Can., Dec. 6, 1928; s. Henry and Veta Feldman; m. Janet Mary Robson, Mar. 23, 1968; children: Leonard Carl, Joanna Mary, Matthew John. B.A., U. Toronto, Ont., 1950, M.A., 1951; Ph.D., U. Birmingham, Eng., 1953. Research assoc. U. Birmingham, 1953-55; mem. Inst. Advanced Study, Princeton, N.J., 1955-56; research assoc. U. Wis., Madison, 1956-57; asst. prof. to assoc. prof. physics Johns Hopkins U., Balt., 1957-64; prof. Johns Hopkins U., 1964—; vis. prof. Imperial Coll., London, 1968-69, 74-75; Royal Soc. guest research fellow Cambridge U., 1984-85. Contbr. numerous articles to profl. jours. Raymond Priestly fellow; Guggenheim fellow, 1962-63. Home: 4832 Keswick Rd Baltimore MD 21210-2338 Office: Johns Hopkins U Baltimore MD 21218

FELDMAN, H. LARRY, lawyer; b. Tyler, Tex., Apr. 18, 1941; s. Henry and Bess (Booken) F.; m. Janice Kay Asner, June 26, 1960; children—Joseph, Katherine. B.A., U. Okla., 1963; J.D., So. Methodist U., 1966. Bar: Tex. 1966, U.S. Dist. Ct. (no. dist.) Tex. 1969, U.S. Sup. Ct. 1976. Adj. prof. law U. Dallas, 1967-68; mem. dept. tax Peat, Marwick & Mitchell, 1968-69; atty. Marks, Time & Aranson, 1970; ptnr. Feldman, O'Donnell & Neil, Dallas, 1971; sole practice, Dallas, 1971—. Mem. Assn. Trial Lawyers Am., Tex. Trial Lawyers Assn., Phi Alpha Delta. Jewish. Office: 8300 Douglas Ave Fl 8 Dallas TX 75225-5603

FELDMAN, IRVING, poet; b. Bklyn., Sept. 22, 1928; m. Carmen Alvarez del Olmo, 1955; 1 son, Fernando R. Ed., CCNY, Columbia U. Formerly prof. English U. P.R., Rio Piedras, Kenyon Coll., Gambier, O.; disting. prof. English State U. N.Y., Buffalo, 1964—. Author: Works and Days, 1961, The Pripet Marshes, 1965, Magic Papers, 1970, Lost Originals, 1972, Leaping Clear, 1976, New and Selected Poems, 1979, Teach Me, Dear ister, 1983, All of Us Here, 1986, The Life and Letters, 1994; contbr. to periodicals. Recipient poetry prize Jewish Book Coun. Am., 1962, award Nat. Inst. and AAAL, 1973; Ingram Merrill Found. grantee, 1963, N.Y. State Creative Artists Pub. Svc. grantee, 1980; Guggenheim fellow, 1973, Acad. Am. Poets fellow, 1986, MacArthur fellow, 1992; grantee Nat. Endowment for the Arts, 1987. Home: 309 Bryant St Buffalo NY 14222-1941 Office: SUNY Dept English Buffalo NY 14260

FELDMAN, JAY NEWMAN, lawyer, telecommunications executive; b. N.Y.C., Nov. 11, 1936; s. Morris Kenneth and Della (Newman) F.; m. Nancy Tobias, Dec. 7, 1963; children—Nina Cheryl, Karen Elise. AB with high honors in History magna cum laude, Colgate U., 1958; J.D., Harvard U., 1961. Bar: N.Y. 1962, U.S. Dist. Ct. (so. and ea. dists.) N.Y. 1962. Assoc. Jacobs Persinger and Parker, N.Y.C., 1961-68; sec., treas., gen. counsel Lynch Corp., N.Y.C., 1968-69; counsel Allied Artists Industries, Inc., N.Y.C., 1970-80, sec., 1970-76, v.p., 1975-76, v.p. adminstrn., 1976-77, group v.p., 1977-80, dir., 1973-80; sec. Allied Artists Pictures Corp., 1973-74, dir., 1974-80; v.p., sec., dir. Allied Artists Video Corp., 1978-80; resident counsel Lorimar Prodns., Inc., N.Y.C., 1980-83; gen. corp. atty. NYNEX Corp., White Plains, N.Y., 1983-94; sec. NYNEX Devel. Co., White Plains, N.Y., 1984-87, NYNEX Internat. Co., White Plains, N.Y., 1985-87, Data Group Corp., White Plains, N.Y., 1985-87, NYNEX Info. Solutions Group Inc., White Plains, N.Y., 1987, NYNEX Sci. & Tech., Inc., White Plains, N.Y., 1991, NYNEX Venture Co., White Plains, N.Y., 1992-94; sec., counsel, dir. PSP, Inc., 1970-76; sec., dir. D. Kaltman & Co., Inc., 1970-79, v.p., 1977-79; sec., dir. Vitabath, Inc., 1970-72, Apollo Motor Homes, Inc., 1970-80, v.p., 1977-80; sec., dir. Westwood Import Co., Inc., 1972-79, v.p., 1977-79; sec., dir. Paul-Marshall Products Inc., 1972-75, Adstat Co., 1972-74; v.p., dir. Palmland Fashions, Inc., 1971-78; mem. com. on criminal cts. Legal Aid Soc., 1969-72. Trustee Temple Beth Israel, Port Washington, N.Y., 1981-83, 87-89, rec. sec., 1983-85, fin. sec., 1985-87. Mem. ABA, N.Y. State Bar Assn., Am. Law Inst., Corp. Bar Assn. Westchester-Fairfield (co-chmn. SEC corp. and fin. com. 1989-90, bd. dirs. 1991-93, chmn. major program com. 1991, co-chmn. 1992-93), Phi Beta Kappa. Home: 61 Roger Dr Port Washington NY 11050-2527 *Dare to be different - the path to success is the road least travelled.*

FELDMAN, JEROME IRA, lawyer, patent development executive; b. N.Y.C., July 17, 1928; s. George and Tanya (Rubenstein) F.; m. Terry Jean Harmon, Oct. 23, 1964; children: Rebecca Page, Michael Dana, Kyra Joelle, Sarah Allison. BA, Ind. U., 1949; LLB, NYU, 1951, JD, 1951, PhD (hon.), 1990. Bar: N.Y. 1951. Ptnr. Feldman & Pollak, N.Y.C., 1953-60; pres., CEO GP Strategies Corp., N.Y.C., 1959—, also bd. dirs.; chmn., bd. dirs. Global Simulation and Engring. Sys. Inc. Former pres., exec. com. New Eng. Colls. Fund.; trustee No. Westchester Hosp. Mem. N.Y. State Bar Assn. Office: GP Strategies Corp 9 W 57th St Ste 4170 New York NY 10019-2701

FELDMAN, JEROME MYRON, physician; b. Chgo., July 27, 1935; s. Louis and Marian (Swichkow) F.; m. Carol Bish; children: Karen Joy, Ellen Deborah, Mark Steven. B.S., Northwestern U., 1957, M.D. with distinction, 1961. Diplomate: Am. Bd. Internal Medicine. Mem. faculty Duke U. Med. Sch., 1968—, prof. medicine, 1972—, dir. diabetes clinic, 1972-80; assoc. dir. diabetes sect. Regional Med. Program N.C., 1967-70; clin. investigator Durham VA Hosp., 1971-74, chief endocrinology service, 1971—. Editor Jour. Clin. Endocrinology and Metabolism, 1983-89; contbr. articles to med.

jours., chpts. to books. Served as officer M.C. USAR, 1965-67. Fellow A.C.P.; mem. Am. Diabetes Assn., Endocrine Soc., Am. Fedn. Clin. Research, So. Sugar Club, N.C. Diabetes Assn. (pres. 1973-74), Phi Beta Kappa, Sigma Xi, Alpha Omega Alpha. Home: 2744 Sevier St Durham NC 27705-5745 Office: Duke Univ Med Ctr PO Box 2963 Durham NC 27715-2963

FELDMAN, JOEL MARTIN, magistrate judge; b. Atlanta, Jan. 2, 1941; s. Louis Aaron and Rosalie (Bach) F.; m. Debora A. Kirkpatrick; children: Lawrence A., Allison R. AB in Law, Emory U., 1962, JD, 1964. Bar: Ga. 1963, U.S. Dist. Ct. (no. dist.) Ga. 1963, U.S. Ct. Mil. Appeals 1964, U.S. Ct. Appeals (5th cir.) 1963, U.S. Ct. Appeals (11th cir.) 1981, U.S. Supreme Ct. 1967. Asst. legis. counsel Gen. Assembly Ga., Atlanta, 1964-66; asst. atty. gen. State of Ga., Atlanta, 1966-68; asst. dist. atty. Atlanta Jud. Cir., 1968-72, 74; legis. asst., legal counsel Sen. Sam Nunn of Ga., 1973-74; magistrate U.S. Dist. Ct. (no. dist.) Ga., Atlanta, 1974—; cert. mil. judge Naval-Marine Corps Trial Judiciary, 1982-92. Former chmn. North Fulton Citizens Mental Health Adv. Coun.; pres. Temple Sinai Synagogue, Atlanta, 1994-96; chmn. Met. Atlanta 50th Ann. WWII Commemorative Cmty. With USAFR, 1964, capt. USNR, 1964-92. Mem. Fed. Bar Assn., State Bar Ga., Atlanta Bar Assn., Naval League U.S. (pres. Atlanta coun. 1985-86), Naval Res. Assn. (pres. 6th Dist. 1982-83), Nat. Coun. U.S. Magistrates (dir. 11th cir. 1982-83), Atlanta Lawyers Club, Navy League (Atlanta dir., pres.), Naval Order (Atlanta pres., dir.), Assn. Naval Aviation. Office: 1619 US Courthouse 75 Spring St SW Atlanta GA 30303-3309

FELDMAN, JOEL SHALOM, mathematician; b. Ottawa, Ont., Can., June 14, 1949; s. Keiva and Anna (Ain) F. BS, U. Toronto, Ont., 1970; AM, Harvard U., 1971, PhD, 1974. Rsch. fellow Harvard U., Cambridge, Mass., 1974-75; Moore instr. MIT, Cambridge, 1975-77; prof. U. B.C., Vancouver, Can., 1977—. Assoc. editor Revs. Math. Physics, 1988—, Can. Jour. Math., 1994-98, Can. Math. Bull., 1994-98, Math Phys. EJ, 1995—; contbr. articles to profl. jours. Recipient Killam Rsch. prize U. B.C., 1988; Woodrow Wilson fellow, 1970. Fellow Royal Soc. Can. (John L. Synge award, Aisenstadt chair 1999-2000). Office: U BC, Dept Math, Vancouver, BC Canada V6T 1Z2

FELDMAN, LEONID ARIEL, rabbi; b. Kishinev, Moldavia, Russia, May 3, 1953; came to U.S. 1980; s. Moisey and Rebekkah (Aronova) F.; m. Melissa Kim Weinstein, Apr. 29, 1990; 2 children, Mikha Adam, Liat Hava. MS in Physics, Kishinev Pedagogical Inst., Russia, 1975; MA in Edn., Hebrew U., 1979; LittB in Jewish Studies, U. Judaism, L.A., 1984; MA, Jewish Theol. Sem., N.Y.C., 1987; postgrad., U. Miami, 1991—. Ordained rabbi, 1987. Dir. Russian dept. Bur. of Jewish Edn., L.A., 1981-84; faculty Wexner Heritage Found., N.Y.C., 1986-91, CLAL-Nat. Jewish Ctr. for Learning & Leadership, N.Y.C., 1986—; rabbi Temple Emanu-El, Palm Beach, Fla., 1988—; pres. Ami-Da Inst., Palm Beach, Fla., Children of Abraham Inst., Palm Beach, 1999—; vis. rabbi Jewish Cultural Assn., Kishinev, summer 1990; nat. bd. dirs. Union of Coun. for Soviet Jews, Washington, 1986—; scholar-in-residene Gen. Assn. of Coun. Jewish Fedns., San Francisco, 1990; keynote speaker Masorti Assn., London, 1987; lectr. in field; radio broadcaster to Russia, Voice of Am., 1985-86; mem. Rabbinic Cabinet of United Jewish Appeal, 1989—; pres. Palm Beach County Bd. Rabbis, 1992-94; vis. prof. Jewish U. of Moscow, 1996, Jewish Theol. Sem., N.Y.C., 1999—. *Leonid Feldman is the Senior Rabbi of Temple Emanu-El in Palm Beach, Florida, and is the first and only Soviet-born Conservative Rabbi. He is also the president of the Ami-Da Institute for training Russian Jewish leaders in America. In 1996 he was a visiting professor at the Jewish University of Moscow. Rabbi Feldman has lectured in thirty-seven states and sixteen countries. He is currently on the faculty of the National Jewish Center for Learning and Leadership (CLAL). He has also served as a scholar for the Brandeis-Bardin Institute in California and as Director of Education for Soviet Emigres in Italy.* Contbr. articles to profl. jours. Internat. bd. govs. Jewish U. Moscow, 1997—. Recipient Gates of Jerusalem medal State of Israel Bonds, 1990, Rabbinic Leadership award Coun. Jewish Fedns., 1990, Rabbi Simon Greenberg Rabbinic Leadership award Jewish Theol. Sem., 1994, Tree of Life award Jewish Nat. Fund, 1996, Jerusalem 3000 award State of Israel Bonds, 1996; fellow Shma Mag., 1984-85; hon. fellow Bar-Ilan U., Israel, 1991. Mem. Rabbinical Assembly, Assn. of New Ams. (exec. com. 1990-94), Jewish Fedn. of Plam Beach County (bd. dirs.). Office: Temple Emanu-El 190 N County Rd Palm Beach FL 33480-3740 *Ever since my childhood I have often asked myself two questions: "What will I say to myself in the last five minutes of my life?" and "What will people say at my funeral?" It gives me a perspective and an optimistic impetus to do more in my life.*

FELDMAN, MARK B., lawyer; b. Rochester, N.Y., Oct. 3, 1935; s. Edward P. and Grace (Relin) F.; m. Marcia Smith, Nov. 23, 1963; children: Ilana, Rachel. A.B., Wesleyan U., 1957; LL.B., Harvard U., 1960. Bar: N.Y. 1961, D.C. 1974. Assoc. Kaye, Scholer, Fierman, Hays & Handler, N.Y.C., 1960-65; with Office Legal Adviser, Dept. State, 1965-81, dep. legal adviser, 1974-81, acting legal adviser, 1981; of counsel Donovan, Leisure, Newton & Irvine, Washington, 1981-84, ptnr., 1984-87; mem. Feith & Zell, P.C., 1988—; adj. prof. law Georgetown U., 1982-89. Mem. ABA, Coun. Fgn. Rels., Am. Soc. Internat. Law. Address: 4010 48th St NW Washington DC 20016-2318

FELDMAN, MARTIN L. C., federal judge; b. St. Louis, Jan. 28, 1934; s. Joseph and Zelma (Bosse) F.; m. Melanie Pulitzer, Nov. 26, 1958; children: Jennifer Pulitzer, Martin L.C. Jr. B.A., Tulane U., 1955, J.D., 1957. Bar: La., Mo. 1957. Law clk. to Hon. J.M. Wisdom, U.S. Ct. Appeals, 1958-59; assoc. Bronfin, Heller, Feldman & Steinberg, New Orleans, 1959-60; ptnr. Bronfin, Heller, Feldman & Steinberg, 1960-83; judge U.S. Dist. Ct., New Orleans, 1983—; trustee, former chmn. Sta. WYES-TV; spl. counsel to Gov. of La., 1979-83. Contbr. articles to profl. jours. Former nat. sec. Anti-Defamation League; former pres. bd. mgrs. Touro Infirmary; bd. dirs. Public Broadcasting Service. Mem. ABA (chair nat. conf. of fed. trial judges 1996-97), La. Bar Assn. (chmn. law reform com. 1981-82), Mo. Bar Assn., Am. Law Inst., Order of Coif. Republican. Jewish. Home: 12 Rosa Park New Orleans LA 70115-5044 Office: US Dist Ct Chambers of Judge Feldman 500 Camp St New Orleans LA 70130-3313

FELDMAN, MARVIN HERSCHEL, financial consultant; b. East Liverpool, Ohio, Dec. 1, 1945; s. Ben and Freda (Zaremberg) F.; m. Vicki Jo Smith, Mar. 18, 1967; children: Terri Nicole, Barbi Lynn. BS, Ohio State U., 1967. CLU, chartered fin. cons. Agt. N.Y. Life Ins. Co., Columbus, Ohio, 1967-69, 74—, asst. mgr., 1969-74; ptnr. Feldman Agy., East Liverpool, 1974—; corp. sec., v.p. Fremar Corp., East Liverpool, 1974—; pres. Fremar Mgmt. Co., Youngstown, 1975-89, Fremar Fin. Group, East Liverpool, 1983—; mng. exec. Royal Alliance Assocs., Inc., East Liverpool, 1983—; founder, bd. dirs. 1st Nat. Community Bank, East Liverpool, Ohio, 1987—; mem., sec. agt. adv. coun. N.Y. Life, N.Y.C., 1985-86; internat. speaker in field. Contbr. articles to profl. jours. Chmn. United Jewish Appeal, East Liverpool, 1976—, v.p., sec. Temple Beth Shalom, East Liverpool; mem. Econ. Devel. Com., East Liverpool; bd. dirs. East Liverpool City Hosp., 1992-97, chmn., 1998. Mem. Nat. Assn. Life Underwriters, Am. Soc. Fin. Svc. Profls., Internat. Assn. Fin. Planners, Assn. Advanced Life Underwriters, Million Dollar Round Table (life, v.p. divsn. 1985-86, ann. meeting chmn. 1998, exec. com. 1998—), Top of the Table (bd. dirs. 1982-87, chmn. 1985-86). Republican. Avocations: golf, reading, sports car racing, boating. Office: The Feldman Agy PO Box 30 16569 Saint Clair Ave East Liverpool OH 43920-9123

FELDMAN, MAX, insurance executive; b. Newark, Jan. 24, 1935; s. Daniel J. and E. Ruth (Fast) F.; m. Bernita Braha, June 14, 1959; children: Alan, Renee. BBA cum laude, U. Miami, Coral Gables, Fla., 1956; MA, Western Mich. U., 1958. Ins. agt. The Feldman Agy., Bloomfield, N.J., 1958—; owner Rotisserie baseball team. Sec. Congregation Ahawas Achim B'nai Jacob and David, West Orange, N.J., 1963-93, dir. emeritus 1993—, pres. Men's Club, 1970-80; chmn. Israel Bond Campaign, West Orange, 1971-80; mem. West Orange Dem. Com., 1974-82. Master sgt. USAR, 1952-59, Korea. Mem. Profl. Ins. Agts., Ind. Ins. Agts., N.J. Ins. Brokers Assn., N.J. U. Miami Alumni Assn. (pres. 1972-74), West Orange Current Affairs Club, Huntington Lakes Tennis Club, B'nai B'rith. Avocations: tennis, travel, reading, golf. Home: 10 Wessman Dr West Orange NJ 07052-2809 Office: The Feldman Agy Inc PO Box 1069 1246 Broad St Bloomfield NJ 07003-3031

FELDMAN, MYER, lawyer; b. Phila., June 1917; s. Israel and Bella (Kurland) F.; m. Adrienne Arsht, Sept. 28, 1980; children by previous marriage: Jane Margaret, James Alan. Student, Girard Coll., Phila., 1922-31; B.S. in Econs., U. Pa., 1935, LL.B. (fellow 1938-39), 1938. Bar: Pa. 1938, D.C. 1965, U.S. Supreme Ct. 1965. Pvt. practice Phila. and D.C., 1939-42, 65—; spl. counsel, exec. asst. to chmn. SEC, 1946-54; mem. counsel armed svcs. com. U.S. Senate, 1954-55, counsel banking and currency commn., 1955-57; legis. asst. to Senator John F. Kennedy, 1958-61; dep. spl. counsel to Presidents Kennedy and Johnson, 1961-64; counsel to Pres. Johnson, 1964-65; founder, ptnr. Ginsburg Feldman & Bress, Washington, 1965-98; pres. Ardman Broadcasting Corp., 1992—; pres. S.W. Fla. Broadcasting, KEFCO Apparel Corp.; lectr. law U. Pa., 1941-42; prof. law Am. U., 1955-56; pres. Radio Assocs., Inc., 1959-81; dir. Music Fair Group, Inc.; chmn. bd. Fin. Satellite Corp.; partner Key Stas., 1960-79; chmn. bd. Speer Publs., 1972-77, Capital Gazette Press, Inc., 1972-77, Bay Publs., 1972-77; dir. Flying Tiger Line, Inc., 1966-82, Nat. Savs. & Trust Co., Flame Hope, Inc., Media and Art Services, Inc., WSSH, Inc., Internat. Fusion Energy Systems Co., Inc., WLLH Broadcasters, WLAM Broadcasters, Capitol Broadcasting Inc., Lazare Kaplan, Inc., Totalbank Corp. (chmn. bd., chief exec officer), Trade Nat. Bank. Author: Standard Pennsylvania Practice, 4 vols., 1958; prodr. various broadway musicals and plays; prodr. Am. Forum TV show; contbr. articles to profl. jours. Pres. N.Y. Art Festival, Inc., 1972-80; del. Democratic Nat. Conv., 1968; pres. McGovern for Pres. Com., 1971-72; vice chmn. Congl. Leadership for Future, 1970; finance chmn. Bayh for Pres. Com., 1975-76; bd. dirs. Weitzman Inst., 1963-84, Spl. Olympics, Inc.; trustee Eleanor Roosevelt Meml. Found., 1963—, Jewish Publ. Soc., 1966-78, Declaration of Independence, House and Library, 1965-75; bd. dirs. Henry M. Jackson Found., 1984-92, trustee; mem. exec. com. Hollings for Pres. Com., 1984; bd. dirs. John F. Kennedy Library, 1983—; bd. overseers V.I. U., 1962—; dir. U. Minn. Freeman Ctr., 1991—. Served with USAAF, 1942-46. Mem. U. Pa. Law Alumni Assn. Washington (pres. 1952-58), Potomac Tennis Club, Tau Epsilon Rho (pres. 1938). Office: 10608 Stapleford Hall Dr Potomac MD 20854-4447 *Using your sense of humor will diffuse any problem.*

FELDMAN, MYRNA LEE, elementary education educator; b. Cin., July 18, 1936; d. Lawrence Raymond and Lee Ann (Hanson) Roll; m. Gilbert Maurice Feldman, Sept. 8, 1962; children: Edith Lee, Elisabeth Lee Feldman Higgins. BS in Edn., U. Cin., 1958, MA in Adminstrn. and Supervision, 1963. Administr. kindergarten USN Schs., Yokosuka, Japan, 1966, classroom tchr., 1965-66; classroom tchr. Cin. Sch. System, 1958-62, Cook County Sch. System, Waukegan, Ill., 1962-63, Monroe County Sch. System, Key West, Fla., 1963-65, Pine Crest Prep. Sch., Ft. Lauderdale, Fla., 1971—; drama club dir. Pine Crest Sch., Ft. Lauderdale, 1986—, shell club sponsor, 1986-90, acad. games coach, 1987—, dir. Actors' Frat, 1989—. Author: poetry, 1988, 91, multiplication facts program Blast-Off, 1991. Pres. Broward Shell Club, Pompano Beach, Fla., 1987-89. Recipient $1000 anonymous donor award Pine Crest Sch., 1987; named Outstanding Tchr. Pompano C. of C., Pompano Beach, 1989. Mem. ASCD, Nat. Coun. Tchrs. of Math., Delta Kappa Gamma. Republican. Presbyterian. Avocations: drama, music, reading, writing, crafts. Office: Pine Crest Sch 1501 NE 62nd St Fort Lauderdale FL 33334-5199

FELDMAN, NANCY JANE, health organization executive; b. Green Bay, Wis., July 6, 1946; d. Benjamin J. and Ellen M. Naze; m. Robert P. Feldman, Aug. 24, 1968; 1 child, Sara J. BA, U. Wis., 1969, MS, 1974. Supr. EPSDT program Minn. Dept. Human Svcs., St. Paul, 1974-80, supr. healthcare programs, 1980-84; team leader human resources budget Minn. Dept. Fin., St. Paul, 1984-87; asst. commr. Minn. Dept. Health, St. Paul, 1987-91; team leader CORE program Minn. Dept. Adminstrn., St. Paul, 1991-93; dir. state pub. programs Medica, Allina Health Sys., Mpls., 1993-95; CEO UCare Minn., St. Paul, 1995—; chair Minn. Coun. Health Plans, Mpls., 1997—; bd. dirs. Health Edn. Rsch. Found., St. Paul, 1996—. Bd. dirs. Vols. Am. Health Svcs., Mpls., 1994—; bd. dirs. Ctr. for Victims of Torture, 1997—. Mem. Women's Health Leadership Trust. Avocations: distance swimming, bicycling, travel. Home: 4124 Burton Ln Minneapolis MN 55406-3638 Office: UCare Minn 2550 University Ave W Ste 201 Saint Paul MN 55114-1052*

FELDMAN, RICHARD DAVID, health commissioner. BA in Psychology phi beta kappa, Ind. U., 1972, MD, 1977. Diplomate Am. Bd. Family Practice; Lic. physician, Indiana. Resident Ind. U. Sch. Med., Indpls., 1977; resident St. Francis Hosp., Beech Grove, Ind., 1977-80, pvt. practice, 1981—; pvt. practice Family Physicians of Carmel, Ind., 1980-81; asst. prof. Family Med., Ind. U., 1981—; cons. in field; lectr. in field. Contbr. articles to profl. jours. Pres. Golden Hill Neighborhood Assn., 1988-90, 1995-97; founder Indpls. Totem Pole Reconstruction Project Eiteljorg Mus., 1990-96; mem. O'Bannon Ind. Gubinatorial Campaign (health care policy com. 1996); bd. dirs. Ind. State Med. Assn. Political Action Com., 1996, Golden Hill Neighborhood Assn., 1986—, United Northwest Neighborhood Day Care Ctr., Indpls.; pres. Ethnographic Art Soc. Indpls., 1983—. Rsch. grantee Mead-Johnson Nutritional Div., 1982, St. Joseph County Cancer Soc., 1982. Fellow Am. Acad. Family Physicians (Ind. chpt. Rsch. award 1980, A. Alan Fischer award 1994, Pres. award 1995, Distinguished Pub. Svc. award 1997); mem. AMA, Nat. Assn. Family Practice Residency Dirs., Soc. Tchrs. Family Med., Ind. State Med. Assn., Marion County Med. Soc., Assn. Ind. Dirs. Med. Edn. Office: Indiana State Dept Health 2 N Meridian St Indianapolis IN 46204-3003 also: St Francis Family Practice Residency 1500 Albany St # 807 Beech Grove IN 46107-1555

FELDMAN, ROBERT C., public relations executive; b. N.Y.C., Oct. 22, 1956. BA, Syracuse U., 1978. Gen. mgr. Sta. WPNR-FM Utica Coll. Syracuse U., 1976-78; from asst. acct. exec. to sr. v.p., group mgr. Burson-Marsteller, 1978-88; exec. v.p. Ketchum Pub. Rels., N.Y.C., 1988-98; pres., CEO Ketchum Pub. Rels., 1998—. Office: GCI GROUP INC 777 3rd Ave New York NY 10017-1401*

FELDMAN, ROBERT ELLIOT, investment company executive; b. Pitts., Nov. 9, 1955; s. Paul Harvey and Sally Iris (Weissberg) Nussbaum; m. Cynthia Kay Stauff, Sept. 8, 1985; children: Hannah, Lily, Emery. BBA, Emory U., 1977; postgrad., Carnegie Mellon U., 1997. Owner, creator Shadyside Balcony Inc., Pitts., 1980—, Hotlicks, Pitts., 1985—; v.p. Advest, Inc., Pitts., 1993—. mem. program steering com. Leadership Pitts., 1997; bd. dirs. Cystic Fibrosis Found., 1993—, Emmerling House Restoration Com., Pitts., 1996; mem. Allegheny Conf., Pitts., 1996; pres. Israel Bonds Fin. Com., 1996—; mem. Allegheny Regional Asset Dist. Adv. Bd., 1999. Mem. Internat. Assn. Fin. Planners, Pitts. High Tech. Coun., CFOs Network (mem. adv. bd. 1996-97), Pitts. C. of C. Democrat. Jewish. Office: Advest Inc 3400 One Oxford Ctr Pittsburgh PA 15219

FELDMAN, ROBERT GEORGE, neurologist, medical educator; b. Cin., Apr. 27, 1933; s. Jacob and Katie (Green) F.; m. Gail Poliner, Dec. 25, 1960; children—John, Elise. B.A., U. Cin., 1954, M.D., 1958. Diplomate Am. Bd. Psychiatry and Neurology, Am. Bd. Electroencephalography. Research asst. pharmacology U. Cin., 1949-54; jr. pharmacologist William S. Merrell Co., Reading, Ohio, 1951-56; fellow Nat. Assn. Mental Health, UCLA, 1957; intern Los Angeles County Hosp., 1958-59; resident neurology Yale-New Haven Med. Center, 1959-63, W. Haven VA Hosp., 1961; fellow metabolic diseases Yale Med. Sch., 1961-62; USPHS spl. fellow, 1962-63; practice medicine, specializing in neurology Boston, 1963—; neurologist-in-chief Boston Med. Ctr. (formerly Univ. Hosp., Boston City Hosp.), 1969—; co-investigator Environ. Hazards Ctr., Boston VA Med. Ctr., 1995—; chief neurology VA Med. Ctr., Boston, 1968-97; mem. staff Beth Israel Hosp.; vis. fellow Montreal (Can.) Neurol. Inst., 1962, Mayo Clinic and Found., Rochester, Minn., 1962; asso. electroencephalographer Yale-New Haven Med. Center, 1962-63; mem. faculty Harvard Med. Sch., 1963—, lectr., 1968—; lectr. Sch. Public Health, 1978—; mem. faculty Boston U. Sch. Medicine, 1963—, prof. neurology, 1970—, chmn. dept., 1969—, prof. pharmacology, 1977—; prof. environ. health Boston U. Sch. Pub. Health chief neurology services Boston VA hosps., 1968-97; mem. nat field adv. group Neurology VA, 1972-75; mem. sci. council Com. to Combat Huntington's Disease, 1972-75; chmn. Zone 1 Profl. Standards Rev. Orgn., 1973-78; mem. profl. adv. bd. Epilepsy Found., 1976-85; mem. council sci. advisors Nat. Inst. Occupational Safety and Health, 1984-90. Editor-in-chief Jour. Club Neurology, 1982-85; contbg. editor Am. Jour. Indsl. Medicine, 1980—; mem. editl. bd. Jour. Clin. Neuropharmacology, 1986—, editor sect. on neurotoxicology, 1996—; mem. editl. bd. Jour. Occupl. Rehab., 1991—, Neurology Forum, 1990-95, others; author book; editor 3 books; contbr. articles and abstracts to profl. jours. Bd. dirs. Postgrad. Med. Inst., 1973; bd. dirs. Norfolk County Med. Soc.; v.p. Mass. Med. Soc., 1973. Recipient Robbins award for excellence in teaching, 1987, Metcalf award for excellence in teaching, 1995. Fellow Am. Acad. Neurology (councillor 1979-84, v.p. 1989-91), Royal Acad. Medicine; mem. Am. Epilepsy Soc. (v.p. 1989—), Am. Assn. Electromyography and Electrodiagnosis (cert.), Am. Assn. Univ. Profs. Neurology, Boston Soc. Psychiatry and Neurology (pres. 1972-73), Am. Acad. Toxicology, Am. Neurol. Assn. (2d v.p. 1992-93), Eastern EEG Soc., Am. Med. EEG Assn., Am. Heart Assn. (fellow stroke coun.), AMA, Mass. Med. Soc., APHA, Assn. Am. Med. Colls. (rep. to coun. of acad. socs. 1991-96), Am. Parkinson Disease Assn. Ctr. Advanced Rsch. (dir. 1993—), Boston U. Med. Ctr. Med. Dental Staff (pres. 1994-95). Home: 74 Rita Rd Braintree MA 02184-3904 Office: 80 E Concord St Boston MA 02118-2307

FELDMAN, ROBERT HARRY, health psychology educator; b. Bklyn., Feb. 10, 1943. PhD, Syracuse U., 1974. Asst. prof. psychology SUNY Coll. at Utica/Rome, 1974-77; postdoctoral fellow in health psychology U. Conn. Med.-Dental Sch., 1977-78; asst. prof. Johns Hopkins U., Balt., 1978-79; asst. prof. dept. health edn. U. Md., College Park, 1979-84, assoc. prof., 1984-90, prof., 1990—. Author: Occupational Health Behavior, 1985. Grantee Adminstrn. on Aging, 1989. Office: U Md Dept Health Edn College Park MD 20742

FELDMAN, ROGER BRUCE, government official; b. Bklyn., Sept. 21, 1939; s. Jacob and Rose (Doodlesack) F.; m. Gilda Weinstock, June 19, 1960; children—Hadley, Scott, Mitchell. A.B., Brown U., 1960; postgrad., NYU Grad. Sch. Pub. Adminstrn., 1962-64. Mgmt. intern USIA, Washington, 1964-65, budget officer, 1965-70, chief programming, planning, 1970-73; dir. budget and fin. U.S. Consumer Product Safety Commn., Washington, 1973-74, dir., adminstrn., 1974-75; dep. dir. office budget Dept. State, Washington, 1975-76, dir. budget, 1976-78, dep. asst. sec. budget and fin., 1978-79, comptroller, 1979-89, cons. fin. and mgmt. systems, 1989—. Pres.'s award of Meritorious Exec., 1981, 87, Pres.'s award of Disting. Exec., 1986, Joint Fin. Mgmt. Improvement Program Scantlebury award, 1984. Mem. Assn. Gov. Accts. (chmn. nat. awards com.), U.S. Chief Fin. Officers Counc., Internat. Consortium on Fin. Mgmt. Home: 23096 Via Stel Boca Raton FL 33433-3930 Office: PO Box 84 Grantham NH 03753-0084

FELDMAN, ROGER DAVID, lawyer; b. N.Y.C., Apr. 7, 1943; s. Louis and Dora (Goldsmith) F.; m. Gail Steg, May 31, 1969; children: Rebecca, Seth. AB, Brown U., 1962; LLB, Yale U.; MBA, Harvard U. Bar: N.Y. 1966, D.C. 1977. Ops. rsch. analyst Office Asst. Sec. Def., Washington, 1967-68; staff asst. Office of Pres. U. S., Washington, 1968-69; assoc. LeBoeuf Lamb Leiby & MacRae, 1969-75; ptnr. Le Boeuf Lamb Leiby & MacRae, 1977-83; dep. asst. adminstr. FEA, Washington, 1975-77; mng. ptnr. project fin. group Nixon Hargrave Devans & Doyle, Washington, 1983-89; head ptnr. project fin. group McDermott Will & Emery, Washington, 1989-97; chair project fin. group Bingham Dana LLP, 1997—; mem. fin. adv. bd. EPA, 1989-92; bd. dirs. R.J. Rudden & Assocs. Inc., Bingham Consulting Group, LLC, Cogeneration Inst., pub.-pvt. venture divsn. Am. Road and Transp. Builders, 1991-93, N.E. Energy and Commerce Assn.; pres. Nat. Coun. for Pub. & Pvt. Partnerships, 1983-98, chair, 1998—; mem. bd. advisors Inst. Gas Tech., Infrastructure Fin. *Roger Feldman is a leading advisor on techniques for projects and structured financing of energy and infrastructure projects and services. The Project Finance Group which he chairs is active throughout the U.S. and internationally in structuring, negotiating, and providing the legal framework for the finance of infrastructure, electric power, water, transportation, and facilities.* Author: (with others) Infrastructure Finance: Tools for the Future, 1988, Public-Private Ventures in Transportation, 1990, Comprehensive Guide to Water and Wastewater Finance, 1991, Privatization of Public Utilities, 1995, Privatization, 1995; mem. bd. editors Yale Law Jour., 1964-65, Jour. Project Fin., 1995—, Constrn. Bus. Rev., 1992—; Washington editor Cogeneration and Power Marketing Monthly Letter, 1987—, Mcht. Power Monthly, 1998—, Strategic Planning for Energy and the Environment, 1992— (Author of the Yr. 1998); contbr. articles to profl. jours. Mem. ABA (chmn. energy law com. 1980-83, alt. energy sources com. 1981-84, 86-90, chmn. environ. values com. 1983-89, com. on privatization 1985-90, chmn. energy fin. 1990-91), Fed. Energy Bar Assn. (chmn. cogeneration com. 1981-82), Nat. Coun. for Pub.-Pvt. Partnerships (Outstanding Contbn. to Privatization award), N.Y. Bar Assn., D.C. Bar Assn. (chair internat. fin. and investment com. 1998—), Assn. Energy Engrs. (Cogeneration Profl. of Yr. 1990), Phi Beta Kappa. Office: Bingham Dana LLP 1200 19th St NW Ste 400 Washington DC 20036-2427

FELDMAN, ROGER LAWRENCE, artist, educator; b. Spokane, Wash., Nov. 19, 1949; s. Marvin Lawrence and Mary Elizabeth (Shafer) F.; m. Astrid Lunde, Dec. 16, 1972; children: Kirsten B., Kyle Lawrence. BA in Art Edn., U. Wash., 1972; postgrad., Fuller Theol. Sem., Pasadena, Calif., 1972-73, Regent Coll., Vancouver, B.C., 1974; MFA in Sculpture, Claremont Grad. Sch., 1977. Teaching asst. Claremont (Calif.) Grad. Sch.; assoc. prof. art Biola U., La Mirada, Calif., 1989—; adj. instr. Seattle Pacific U., 1979, 80, 82, 83, Linfield Coll., 1978, Edmonds C.C., 1978-80, Shoreline C.C., 1978; guest artist and lectr. One-man shows include Art Ctr. Gallery, Seattle Pacific U., 1977, 83, 84, Linfield Coll., McMinnville, Oreg., 1979, Blackfish Gallery, Portland, 1982, Lynn McAllister Gallery, Seattle, 1986, Biola U., 1989, 93, Coll. Gallery, La. Coll., Pineville, 1990, Gallery W, Sacramento, 1991, 96, Aughinbaugh Gallery, Grantham, Pa., 1992, Riverside Art Mus., 1994, Azusa Pacific U., 1995, Cornerstone '96, Bushnell, Ill., 1996, Davison Gallery, Roberts Wesleyan Coll., Rochester, N.Y., 1997; group shows include Pasadena Artist's Concern Gallery, 1976, Libra Gallery, Claremont, 1977, Renshaw Gallery, McMinnville, 1978, Cheney Cowles Mus., Spokane, 1979, 80, 83, Lynn McAllister Gallery, Seattle, 1985, Bumbershoot, Seattle, 1985, 86, West Bend (Wis.) Gallery, 1992, L.A. Mcpl. Satellite Gallery, 1993, Greenbelt 93, Northamptonshire, Eng., 1993, Claremont Sch. Theology, 1994, Queens Coll. Cambridge U., Eng., 1994, Jr. Arts Ctr. Gallery, Barnsdall Park, L.A., 1994, Bade Mus. Pacific Sch. of Religion, Berkeley, Calif., 1995, Cen. Arts Collective, Tucson, 1995, L.A. Mcpl. Gallery Barnsdall Art Park, 1996, Reconstructive Gallery Santa Ana, Ct., 1997, Guggenheim Gallery, Chapman U., Orange, Calif., 1997, Weaver Art Gallery, Bethel Coll., Mishawaka, Ind., 1998; comms. include Renton Vocat. Tech. Inst., 1987-89, East Hill Cmty. Ctr., Gresham, Oreg., 1979; contbr. articles to profl. jours. Recipient King County Arts Commn. Individual Artist Project award, Seattle, 1988, Natl. Endowment for the Arts Individual Artist fellowship in Sculpture, 1986, David Gaiser award for sculpture Cheney Cowles Mus., 1980, Disting. Award for Harborview Med. Ctr. "Viewpoint", Soc. for Tech. Comm., 1987, Design award for "Seafirst News", Internat. Assn. Bus. Comm., 1987, Pace Setter award, 1987, others; individual artist sculpture grantee Nat. Endowment for Arts, 1986, Connemara Sculpture grante, 1990, Biola U., 1991. Office: Biola Univ 13800 Biola Ave La Mirada CA 90639-0001*

FELDMAN, RONALD, art gallery director; b. N.Y.C., Apr. 25, 1938; s. Irving E. and Judith (Solon) F.; m. Frayda Beth Futterman, Sept. 14, 1963; children: Mark Allen, Andrew Jay, Julie Mara. BA, Syracuse U., 1959; JD, NYU, 1962. Atty., ptnr. Helfand, Traub, Lesser, N.Y.C., 1963-70; adj. prof. Brown U., Providence, R.I., 1991; pres. Ronald Feldman Fine Arts Inc., N.Y.C., 1971—; bd. dirs. Exit Art, N.Y.C.; chair Merchandisers Alliance Corp., 1968-70; adv. bd. Franklin Furnace, N.Y.C., 1980—; panelist NEA, Washington, 1980, 82. Co-publisher Andy Warhol Prints, 1989; contbr. articles to books, profl. jours. Adv. bd. Columbia U. Rsch. Ctr. Arts and Culture, N.Y.C., 1985; chair New Mus. Annual Benefit, 1989; co-chair Artists for Freedom of Expression, 1990-92; majority trust Dem. Senatorial Campaign com., 1993; mng. trustee Dem. Nat. Com., 1990—. Mem. ABA, Art Dealers Assn. Am. (bd. dirs. 1991—, v.p.), Nat. Coun. on Arts, People for the Am. Way (bd. dirs.), N.Y. State Bar Assn., Social Venture Network, Bus. for Social Responsibility. Office: Ronald Feldman Arts Inc 31 Mercer St New York NY 10013-2541

FELDMAN, RONALD ARTHUR, social work educator, researcher; b. Buffalo, Jan. 17, 1938; s. David Jacob and Clara (Spector) F.; m. Dina Cohen Feinstein, Dec. 23, 1962; children: Daniel, Deborah, Darrah. BA, U.

Buffalo, 1960; MSW, U. Mich., 1963, PhD, 1966. Cert., Acad. Cert. Social Workers. Asst. prof. U. Calif., Berkeley, 1966-68; Fulbright lectr. Social Services Acad., Ankara, Turkey, 1968-69; assoc. prof. Washington U. Sch. Social Work, St. Louis, 1969-72, prof., 1972-86, acting dean, 1973-74; dir. Ctr. for Study of Youth Devel., Boys Town, Nebr., 1974-78, Ctr. for Adolescent Mental Health, St. Louis, 1983-87; assoc. dean Columbia U. Sch. Social Work, N.Y.C., 1985-86, prof., dean, 1986—, Ruth Harris Ottman Centennial prof., 1995—; cons. NIMH, Rockville, Md., 1980-91; bd. dirs. Ednl. Inst., Jewish Bd. Family and Children's Svcs., N.Y.C., 1986—, William T. Grant Found., Bd. Behavior and Mental Disorders, Inst. Medicine. Sr. author: Contemporary Approaches to Group Treatment, 1975, The St. Louis Conundrum: The Effective Treatment of Antisocial Youths, 1983, Children at Risk: In the Web of Parental Mental Illness, 1987; sr. editor: Advances in Adolescent Mental Health, vols. 1-4, 1986—. Citizen leader Clayton (Mo.) Bd. Edn., 1981-82; mem. profl. rev. bd. Mo. Dept. Mental Health, Jefferson City, 1981-86; trustee Wm. T. Grant Found., 1993—. Recipient Disting. Faculty award Washington U., St. Louis, 1984; research grantee NIMH, Rockville, Md., 1970-75, 80-84, Office of Human Devel. Services, Washington, 1983-87. Fellow NASW, Soc. for Rsch. in Child Devel.; mem. Coun. on Social Work Edn. (bd. dirs. 1992-95), Am. Sociol. Assn., Internat. Assn. Child and Adolescent Psychiatry and Allied Professions (v.p. 1995—). Avocations: swimming, tennis. Office: Columbia U Sch Social Work 622 W 113th St New York NY 10025-7982

FELDMAN, SAMUEL MITCHELL, neuroscientist, educator; b. Phila., Sept. 26, 1933; s. Boris and Fannie B. (Shrager) F.; children—Lee Stephen, David Saul. B.A., U. Pa., 1954; M.A., Northwestern U., 1955; Ph.D., McGill U., 1959. Fellow in physiology U. Wash., Seattle, 1958-60; from instr. to asso. prof. physiology Albert Einstein Coll. Medicine, 1960-71; prof. psychology N.Y. U., 1971—, head dept., 1972-76, prof. neuroscience, 1988—, dir. grad. studies neural sci., 1989—; mem. psychol. sci. study sect. NIMH, 1968-72, chmn., 1970-72, mem. biol. sci. tng. grant rev. com., 1977-83; cons. in field. Contbr. articles to profl. jours. Fellow USPHS, 1958-60; recipient Career award, 1969-71, research grantee, 1963—. Mem. Eastern Psychol. Assn., Am. Physiol. Soc., Soc. Neurosci., Sigma Xi. Home: 37 Washington Sq W New York NY 10011-9181 Office: New York Univ Ctr for Neural Science New York NY 10003

FELDMAN, SANDRA, labor union administration; b. N.Y.C.; m. Arthur Barnes. M in English Lit., NYU. Tchr. Pub. Sch. 34, Manhattan, N.Y.; field rep. United Fedn. Tchrs., 1966, exec. dir., sec., 1983-86; pres. United Fedn. Tchrs., N.Y.C., 1986-97, Am. Fedn. Tchrs., 1997—; exec. com. Edn. Internat.; exec. coun. AFL-CIO, 1997—. active Coun. on Competitiveness, Internat. Rescue Com., Freedom House, A. Philip Randolph Inst., Jewish Labor Com., Coalition Labor Union Women, Nat. Coun. Ams. to Prevent Handgun Violence, N.Y. Urban League, Women's Forum, Women's Commn. on Refugee Children, NAACP-N.Y. chpt.; co-chair Child Labor Coalition; nat. bd. mem. Profl. Tchg. Stds.; chair AFL-CIO Com. on Social Policy; mem. U.S. com. UNICEF;. Named one of N.Y.C. 75 Most Influential Women, Crain's New York Bus. Avocations: collecting African art, jazz, reading. Office: Am Fedn Tchrs 555 New Jersey Ave NW Washington DC 20001-2029*

FELDMAN, SCOTT M., lawyer; b. N.Y.C., July 31, 1942; s. Abe and Lilian F.; m. Susan Lauer, July 13, 1968; children: James W., Mark A. BA, Amherst Coll., 1964; JD, Harvard U., 1967. Bar: NY 1968, Ill. 1978. Instr. UCLA Law Sch. 1967-68; lt. Judge Advocate Gen's. Corp. U.S. Navy, Washington, 1968-71; assoc. Sullivan & Cromwell, N.Y.C., 1971-77; ptnr. Winston & Strawn, Chgo., 1978—. Trustee Village of Glencoe, Ill., 1983-91. Mem. ABA, Chgo. Bar Assn., Assn. Bar City N.Y., Amherst Alumni Assn. E-mail: sfeldman@winston.com. Office: Winston & Strawn 35 W Wacker Dr Ste 4200 Chicago IL 60601-1695

FELDMAN, STANLEY GEORGE, state supreme court justice; b. N.Y.C., N.Y., Mar. 9, 1933; s. Meyer and Esther Betty (Golden) F.; m. Norma Arambula; 1 dau., Elizabeth L. Student, U. Calif., Los Angeles, 1950-51; LL.B., U. Ariz., 1956. Bar: Ariz. 1956. Practiced in Tucson, 1956-81; ptnr. Miller, Pitt & Feldman, 1968-81; justice Ariz. Supreme Ct., Phoenix, 1982—, chief justice, 1992-97; lectr. Coll. Law, U. Ariz., 1965-76, adj. prof., 1976-81. Bd. dirs. Tucson Jewish Community Council. Mem. ABA, Am. Bd. Trial Advocates (past pres. So. Ariz. chpt.), Ariz. Bar Assn. (pres. 1974-75, bd. govs. 1967-76), Pima County Bar Assn. (past pres.), Am. Trial Lawyers Assn. (dir. chpt. 1967-76). Democrat. Jewish. Office: Ariz Supreme Ct 1501 W Washington St Phoenix AZ 85007-3231

FELDMAN, STEPHEN, academic administrator; b. N.Y.C., Sept. 11, 1944; s. Harry and Mae (Morris) F.; m. Constance M. Lerudis, June 1, 1969; children—Jennifer Dawn, Timothy Richard. BBA, CCNY, 1966, MBA, 1968, PhD (fellow), 1971. Chmn. dept. banking, fin. and investments Hofstra U., Hempstead, N.Y., 1969-77, assoc. prof., 1974-77; dean Ancell Sch. of bus. Western Conn. State U., Danbury, 1977-81, pres., 1981-92; pres. Nova Southeastern U., Ft. Lauderdale, Fla., 1992-94; v.p. real estate Ethan Allen Inc., Danbury, 1995-96; v.p. univ. rels., devel. Calif. State U., Long Beach, 1996-99; pres. Astronaut Meml. Found., Long Beach, 1999—; bd. dirs. Ethan Allen Inc., Sci. Horizons Inc.; cons. IBM, N.Y. Telephone Co. Editor: Credit Unions, 1974, Handbook of Wealth Management, 1977, Smarter Money, 1985; contbr. articles to profl. jours. Trustee Danbury Hosp., United Way. Mem. Am. Assn. State Colls. and Univs. (chmn. corp. coll. rels.), Greater Ft. Lauderdale C. of C. Office: Astronaut Meml Found Ctr Space Kennedy Space Ctr Mail Code AMF Long Beach CA 32899*

FELDMAN, WALTER SIDNEY, artist, educator; b. Lynn, Mass., Mar. 23, 1925; s. Hyman and Fradel (Gordon) F.; m. Barbara Rose, June 4, 1950; children—Steven, Mark. B.F.A., Yale U., 1950, M.F.A., 1951; studied with, Willem de Kooning, 1950-51; M.A. (hon.), Brown U., 1953. Instr. painting Yale U., 1951-53; mem. faculty dept. art Brown U., 1953—, prof., 1961—, John Hay prof. bibliography, 1993—, chmn. studio div., 1973—; founder Ziggurat Press, 1985—; dir. Brown/Ziggurat Press, 1990—; vis. prof. Harvard U., 1968, U. Calif., Riverside; artist-in-residence Dartmouth Coll., 1978; cons. Providence Lithography Co.; artist-in-residence Rutgers Ctr. for Innovative Printmaking, 1993. One-man shows include Kruaushaar Galleries, N.Y.C., 1958, 61, 63, Obelisk Gallery, Boston, 1965-66, 67, Inst. Contemporary Arts, London, 1967-68, Bristol Mus., 1975, Hopkins Ctr., Dartmouth Coll., 1978; group shows include Mus. Modern Art, 1954, 55, Bklyn. Mus., 1957-58, 60, Corcoran Gallery, Washington, 1959, Butler Inst. Am. Art, Youngstown, Ohio, 1960, Harvard U. Carpenter Ctr. for Visual Arts, 1963, Lowe Art Ctr., Syracuse, 1964, Inst. Contemporary Art, Boston, 1961, 66; represented in permanent collections at Brown U., Fogg Mus., L.A. County Mus., Met. Mus. Art, Mus. Modern Art, Phoenix Art Mus., Princeton U., Yale U. Art Gallery, Lehigh U. Art Collection, U. Mass., Mex.-Am. Inst., U. Florence, Italy, Folger Shakespeare Libr., Washington, Fuller Mus., Brockton, Mass., Victoria and Albert Mus., London and others. Served with U.S. Army, 1943-46. Decorated Purple Heart, Combat Inf. Badge; Alice Kimball English fellow Yale U., 1950, Fulbright fellow, Italy, 1956-57; Eliza Howard fellow Mex., 1961; recipient Gov.'s award for arts, 1980. Home: 107 Benevolent St Providence RI 02906-3154 Office: Brown U 64 College St Providence RI 02912-9021

FELDMANN, JUDITH GAIL, language professional, educator; b. Grenova, N.D., Feb. 10, 1938; d. Jule and Evelyn (Hagen) F.; children: Robert, Carole Elizabeth. BA magna cum laude, Minot State Tchrs. Coll., 1962; MA, Mich. State U., 1971; postgrad, U. Oslo, 1980, U. London, 1982, 85; postgrad., Western Mich. U., 1987, Eastern Mich. U., 1992-93, Harvard U., 1994. Cert. tchr., secondary adminstrn., Mich. English tchr. Minot Pub. Schs., N.D., 1961; english tchr. Charlotte Pub. Schs., Mich., 1962; grad. asst. instr. Mich. State Univ., East Lansing, Mich., 1963; reading specialist, English educator Jackson (Mich.) Pub. Schs., 1964-95; English educator Jackson, 1964-99. Mem. Internat. Reading Assn., Mich. Reading Assn. (presenter Grand Rapids 1995), Assn. for Supervision and Curriculum Devl., Jackson Edn. Assn. (v.p.). Home: 2791 Brookside Blvd Jackson MI 49203-5532

FELDMANN, SHIRLEY CLARK, psychology educator; b. Niagara Falls, N.Y., Apr. 14, 1929; d. Franklin T. and Mildred L. (Payne) Clark; m. Robert Feldmann, June, 1952 (dec.); m. Horace S. Bush (dec.). BA, Barnard Coll., 1951; MA, Columbia U., 1952, PhD, 1961. Asst. prof. edn. SUNY, Fredonia, 1958-60; asst. research prof. psychiatry N.Y. Med. Coll., N.Y.C., 1960-63; prof. sch. edn. City Coll., CUNY, N.Y.C., 1963-98; prof., PhD program in ednl. psychology CUNY Grad. Sch., N.Y.C., 1974-98, exec. officer, 1976-85; ret., 1998. Contbr. articles to prof. jours. Mem. Am. Psychol. Assn., Internat. Reading Assn., Am. Ednl. Research Assn. Home: 11 Cedar Lake Rd Chester CT 06412-1009

FELDSTEIN, CHARLES ROBERT, fund raising consultant; b. Chgo., Nov. 9, 1922; s. Herman and Fannie (Frank) F.; m. Janice Josephson, Sept. 6, 1948; children: James Frank, Frances Emily, Thomas Mark. MA, U. Chgo., 1944. Dir. devel. U. Chgo., 1948-53; pres. C.R. Feldstein & Co., Chgo., 1953-88, chmn. bd., 1988—; pres. Charles Frank & Co. Antiquarians, Chgo., 1970—. Bd. dirs. Scholarship & Guidance, Chgo., United Charities, Chgo., Ragdale Found., Lake Forest. Mem. Am. Assn. Fund Raising Counsel (chmn. 1982-83), Cliff Dwellers, Mid-Day. Home: 680 N Lake Shore Dr Chicago IL 60611-4402 Office: 737 N Michigan Ave Chicago IL 60611-4402

FELDSTEIN, JOSHUA, educational administrator; b. Russia, Apr. 12, 1921; came to U.S., 1939, naturalized, 1944; s. Cemach and Fania B. Feldstein; B.S., Delaware Valley Coll., Doylestown, Pa., 1952; M.S., Rutgers U., 1956, Ph.D., 1962; m. Miriam Myzel, Dec. 24, 1944; children: Theodore Lee, Daniel Ethan. Instr. horticulture Delaware Valley Coll., 1952-56, asst. prof., 1956-60, assoc. prof., 1960-65, prof. horticulture, from 1965, dept. chmn., 1959-69, chmn. plant sci. div., 1966-73, assoc. dean, 1969-73, dean, 1973-75, pres. Delaware Valley Coll. Sci. and Agr., 1975-87, pres. emeritus, 1987—, interim pres., 1995-97; coord. nat. tchg. fellowships, student fin. aid, chmn. admissions, curriculum, athletics, student affairs, acad. standard coms. Accorded Legion of Honor membership by Chapel of Four Chaplains, Phila., 1974; recipient award Pa. Future Farmers Am., 1980. Mem. Am. Soc. Hort. Sci. (L.M. Ware Disting. Teaching award), Am. Inst. Biol. Scis., Eastern Assn. Coll. Deans and Advs. to Students, Soil Conservation Soc. Am., Pa. Assn. Colls. and Univs., Commn. of Ind. Colls. and Univs. Jewish. Author (with N.F. Childers): Effect of Irrigation on Fruit Size and Yield of Peaches in Pennsylvania, 1957; Peach Irrigation in a Humid Region, 1964; Effects of Irrigation on Peaches in Pennsylvania, 1965.

FELDSTEIN, KATHLEEN FOLEY, economist, consultant; b. Boston, Feb. 3, 1941; d. Charles Joseph and Eleanor (Croxon) Foley; m. Martin Feldstein, June 19, 1965; children: Margaret, Janet. BA, Radcliffe Coll., 1962; PhD, MIT, 1977. Pres. Econs. Studies, Inc., Belmont, Mass., 1987—; bd. dirs. Bank Am. Corp., Ionics Corp., John Hancock Mut. Life Ins. Co., Knight-Ridder, Bell South Corp. Contbr. articles to nat. and internat. newspapers. Corp. mem. Winsor Sch., Boston, 1985-97, Simmons Coll., Boston, 1986-96; bd. overseers Mus. Fine Arts, Boston, 1990-92, trustee, 1992—, treas., 1998; trustee Com. for Econ. Devel., 1990—, McLean Hosp., 1993—. Home: 147 Clifton St Belmont MA 02478-2603 Office: Econs Studies Inc 147 Clifton St Belmont MA 02478-2603

FELDSTEIN, MARTIN STUART, economist, educator; b. N.Y.C., Nov. 25, 1939; s. Meyer and Esther (Gevarter) F.; m. Kathleen Foley, June 19, 1965; children—Margaret, Janet. AB summa cum laude, Harvard U., 1961; MA, Oxford U., 1964, DPhil, 1967; LLD (hon.), Rochester U., 1984, Marquette U., 1985. Research fellow Nuffield Coll., Oxford U., 1964-65, ofcl. fellow, 1965-67, lectr. pub. fin., 1965-67; asst. prof. econs. Harvard U., 1967-68, assoc. prof., 1968-69, prof., 1969—; George F. Baker prof. Harvard U., 1984—; pres. Nat. Bur. Econ. Research, 1977-82, 84—; chmn. Council Econ. Advisers, 1982-84; gov. Am. Stock Exch., 1991-94; bd. dirs. TRW, Am. Internat. Group, JP Morgan, Columbia/HCA. Bd. contbrs. Wall St. Jour. Fellow Am. Acad. Arts and Scis., Econometric Soc. (coun. 1977-82), Nat. Assn. Bus. Economists, Am. Philos. Soc., Nuffield Coll. (hon.), Brit. Acad. (corr. fellow); mem. Am. Econ. Assn. (John Bates Clark medal 1977, exec. com. 1980-82, v.p. 1988), Corp. Mass. Gen. Hosp., Austrian Acad. Scis. (fgn.), Inst. Medicine Nat. Acad. Scis., Coun. on Fgn. Rels. (bd. dirs. 1998—), Trilateral Commn. (exec. com. 1987—), Phi Beta Kappa. Home: 147 Clifton St Belmont MA 02478-2603 Office: Nat Bur Econ Rsch Inc 1050 Massachusetts Ave Cambridge MA 02138-5317

FELDSTEIN, PAUL JOSEPH, management educator; b. N.Y.C., Oct. 4, 1933; s. Nathan and Sarah Feldstein; m. Anna Martha Lee, Dec. 24, 1968; children: Julie, Jennifer. BA in Econs., CCNY, 1955; MBA in Fin., U. Chgo., 1957, PhD in Econs., 1961. Dir. divsn. rsch. Am. Hosp. Assn., Chgo., 1961-64; prof. Sch. Pub. Health U. Mich., Ann Arbor, 1964-87; prof. Grad. Sch. Mgmt. U. Calif., Irvine, 1987—; trustee Sutter Health, Sacramento, 1988—. Author: Health Care Economics, 5th rev. 1998, Health Policy Issues: An Economic Perspective on Health Reform, 2nd edit., 1999, The Politics of Health Legislation, 2nd edit., 1996; contbr. articles to profl. jours. 1st lt. inf. U.S. Army, 1955-57. Mem. Am. Econs. Assn. Avocations: jogging, biking. E-mail: pfeldste@uci.edu. Office: U Calif Grad Sch Mgmt Irvine CA 92697

FELDT, GLENDA DIANE, educational administrator; b. Mobile, Ala., Sept. 15, 1950; d. William and Thelma G. (Sullivan) Sanderson; m. Fitzhugh M. Nuckols, 1969 (div. 1979); children: Thomas F., William L.; m. Everett R. Feldt, Jr., July 26, 1980; 1 child, Everett R., III. Student, Radford Coll., 1967-69; BA, Averett Coll., 1974; M of Pub. Adminstrn., Old Dominion U., 1981; EdD in Ednl. Leadership, Nova U., Ft. Lauderdale, Fla., 1993. Cert. tchr. voct. edn., adminstr., sociology, evaluator, work adjustment specialist, sch. supt., Va. Welfare eligibility technician Danville (Va.) Social Svc. Bur., 1971-73, social worker I, 1973-74; counselor, evaluator Fred T. Hatcher Ctr., Danville, 1974-75; vocat. evaluator Va. Dept. Vocat. Rehab., Danville, 1975-78; vocat. evaluator Va. Beach City Pub. Schs., 1978-80, work adjustment specialist, 1980-87; program leader vocat. spl. needs Norfolk (Va.) Pub. Schs., 1987-93; asst. prin. Bayside High Sch., Virginia Beach, Va., 1993-94; prin. New Horizons Regional Edn. Ctr., Newport News, Va., 1994-97, Franklin (Va.) H.S., 1997—; project dir. Tidewater (Va.) Regional Nursing Articulation Project, 1988-90; cons. Johnson & Wales U., Norfolk, 1992-93; project dir. High Schs. that Work So. Regional Edn. Bd., 1993-94; presenter numerous confs. Presenter Coun for Exceptional Children, Boston, 1985, Nashville, 1987, Albuquerque, 1993; keynote speaker W. Va. Tech. prep. health occupations, Charleston, 1991. Bd. dirs Goodwill Industries, Danville, 1977-78; pres. PTA, 1977-78. Mem. NEA, ASCD, Nat. Assn. Secondary Sch. Prins., Va. Edn. Assn., Am. Vocat. Edn. Assn. (bd. dirs. Va. 1987-93, 96), Nat. Assn. Vocat. Edn. Spl. Needs Pers., Va. Assn. Vocat. Spl. Needs Pers. (pres. 1983-85, Va. Tchr. of Yr. 1986, Va. Adminstr. Yr. 1993), Jr. League Hampton Rds., Va. Women's Network, Exch. Club of York, Franklin Rotary Club. Baptist. Avocations: reading, crafts, walking, bicycling. Home: 405 Marlbank Dr Yorktown VA 23692-4306 Office: Franklin High Sch 310 Crescent Dr Franklin VA 23851-2341

FELDT, GLORIA A., social service administrator; b. Temple, Tex., Apr. 13, 1942; m. Alex Barbanell; 3 children; 3 stepchildren. BA in Sociology and Speech with honors, U. Tex. Permian Basin, 1974; postgrad., Ariz. State U., Western Behavioral Scis. Inst., La Jolla, Calif. Broadcast operator Sta. KOIP-FM, Odessa, Tex., 1965-67; substitute tchr. Ector County Ind. Sch. Dist., Odessa, Tex., 1967-68; tchr., spl. projects dir. head start Greater Opportunities of the Permian Basin, Odessa, Tex., 1968-73; exec. dir. Planned Parenthood of West Tex., Odessa, 1974-78; exec. dir., CEO Planned Parenthood Ctrl. and Northern Ariz., Phoenix, 1978-96; pres.-elect Planned Parenthood Fedn. Am., Planned Parenthood Action Fund, N.Y.C., 1996—; also bd. dirs. Planned Parenthood Fedn. Am.; mem. steering com. Pro-Choice Ariz.; founder Planned Parenthood Fedn. Am. Leadership Inst.; cons. in leadership and strategic planning for non-profit orgns. Spkr. in field. Mem. exec. bd. Ariz. Affordable Health Care Found.; bd. dirs. Pro-Choice Resource Ctr., Hospice of the Valley; mem. cmty. adv. bd. Jr. League of Phoenix; mem. adv. bd. UN Assn.; charter mem. Ariz. Women's Town Hall; active Charter 100, World Affairs Coun., Ariz. Acad. Town Halls. Recipient Women of Achievement award, 1987, Ruth Green award Nat. Exec. Dirs. Coun., 1990, award Women Helping Women, 1989, 94, Golden Apple award Sun City chpt. NOW, 1995, City of Phoenix Martin Luther King, Jr. Living the Dream award City of Phoenix Human Rels. Commn., 1996. Mem. APHA, Nat. Family Planning and Reproductive Health Assn., Ariz. Pub. Health Assn. Office: Planned Parenthood Fedn Am 810 7th Ave New York NY 10019-5818*

FELDT, LEONARD SAMUEL, university educator and administrator; b. Long Branch, N.J., Nov. 2, 1925; s. Harry and Bessie (Doris) F.; m. Natalie Ruth Fischer, Aug. 29, 1954; children: Sarah Feldt Roach, Daniel C. BS in Edn., Rutgers U., 1950, MEd, 1951; PhD, U. Iowa, 1954. From asst. prof. to prof. U. Iowa, Iowa City, 1954-94; prof. emeritus, 1994; dir. testing programs U. Iowa, Iowa City, 1981-94, Lindquist prof. ednl. measurement, 1981-94; pres. Iowa Measurement Rsch. Found., Iowa City, 1978—; editor standardized tests Iowa Tests Ednl. Devel., 1960—. With U.S. Army, 1943-46. Recipient Disting. Svc. award Rutgers U., 1999. Mem. Am. Ednl. Rsch. Assn. (E.F. Lindquist award 1995), Nat. Coun. on Measurement in Edn. (Career Contriutions award 1994), Am. Statis. Assn., Inst. Math. Stats., Psychometric Soc., Phi Beta Kappa, Sigma Xi. Avocation: golf. Home: 810 Willow St Iowa City IA 52245-5438 Office: Univ Iowa Lindquist Ctr Iowa City IA 52242

FELDT, ROBERT HEWITT, pediatric cardiologist, educator; b. Chgo., Aug. 3, 1934; s. Robert Hewitt and Frances (Swanson) F.; m. Barbara Ann Fritz, Aug. 17, 1957; children: Christine, Susan, Kathryn. B.S., U. Wis., 1956; M.D., Marquette U., 1960; M.S., U. Minn., 1965. Diplomate: Am. Bd. Pediatrics, Am. Bd. Pediatric Cardiology. Intern Miller Hosp., St. Paul, 1960-61; resident in pediatrics cardiology Mayo Found., Rochester, Minn., 1961-65; cons. pediatrics Mayo Clinic, Rochester, Minn., 1966—, chmn. dept. pediatrics, 1980-85, prof. pediatrics; mem. Am. Bd. Pediatrics; chmn. sci. coun. Am. Heart Assn. Author numerous sci. articles, book chpts., monographs. Fellow Am. Acad. Pediatrics, Am. Cardiology Coll.; mem. Minn. Heart Assn. (pres. 1982), Midwest Soc. Pediatric Research, Am. Pediatric Soc. Congregationalist. Home: 1804 Walden Ln SW Rochester MN 55902-0903 Office: Mayo Clinic Dept Pediatrics 200 1st St SW Rochester MN 55905-0002

FELGAR, RAYMOND E(UGENE), pathologist, medical educator; b. Mt. Pleasant, Pa., Mar. 2, 1963; s. Samuel Hurst and Anna June (Stull) F. BS in Microbiology with honors, Pa. State U., 1985; PhD in Pathology, U. Pitts., 1990, MD, 1992. Diplomate Am. Bd. Pathology in Anatomic and Clin. Pathology. Resident in anatomic and clin. pathology U. Pa. Med. Ctr., Phila., 1992-96; fellow in hematopathology dept. pathology Vanderbilt U., Nashville, 1996-98; dir. hematopathology and clin. flow cytometry Hahnemann Hosp., Phila., 1998; asst. prof. dept. pathology and lab medicine MCP-Hahnemann Sch. Medicine, Phila., 1998; dir. clin. flow cytometry lab., hematopathologist and co-dir. hematopathology Strong Meml. Hosp., Rochester, N.Y., 1998—; asst. prof. Dept. Pathology & Lab. Medicine U. Rochester Sch. Medicine & Dentistry, 1998—. Contbr. articles to profl. jours., chpt. to book. NIH med. scientist tng. fellow, 1987-92. Mem. AMA, Pa. Med. Soc., Phila. County Med. Soc., Coll. Am. Pathologists, Am. Soc. Clin. Pathologists, Am. Soc. Hematology, U.S. and Can. Acad. Pathology, Soc. for Hematopathology, European Soc. for Hematopathology, Pa. State Alumni Assn., Phi Beta Kappa.

FELGRAN, STEVEN DAVID, economist; b. N.Y.C., July 1, 1953; s. Howard H. and Ilse H. (Sturm) F.; m. Hilary Ann Macht, June 13, 1999. BA, U. Pa., 1975; MA in Econs., Yale U., 1978, MPhil in Econs., 1978, PhD in Econs., 1982. Analyst Congl. Budget Office, Washington, 1975-76; cons. Arthur D. Little, Inc., Cambridge, Mass., 1981-83; economist Fed. Res. Bank of Boston, 1983-89; prof. Coll. Bus. Adminstrn. Northeastern U., Boston, 1989-93; sr. mgr. Economic Cons. Svcs./KPMG, N.Y.C., 1993-97, ptnr., 1997—. Contbr. numerous articles to profl. jours., mags. and newspapers. Mem. ABA, Am. Econ. Assn., Phi Beta Kappa. Avocations: theater, musical comedy, historic preservation and restoration, Civil War era, travel. Office: KMPG 345 Park Ave Fl 35 New York NY 10154-0004

FELHOFER, MARYLOUISE KATHERINE, nursing administrator; b. Milw., June 30, 1952; d. Charles Walter and Tillie Elizabeth (Hrymnak) Tomasicyk; m. Paul Robert Felhofer, Aug. 12, 1977. BSN, Alverno Coll., Milw., 1974; MS in Nursing Adminstrn., U. Md., Balt., 1991. RN, Md.; cert. profl. in healthcare quality. Commd. ensign USN, 1972, advanced through grades to capt., 1997; staff and charge nurse Naval Regional Med. Ctr., Orlando, Fla., 1974-77; instr., adminstrv. officer Naval Officer Indoctrination Sch., Newport, R.I., 1977-81; charge nurse, relief dept. head, supr. Naval Hosp., Great Lakes, Ill., 1981-86; head command quality assurance dept. Naval Hosp., Guam, 1986-89; head command quality assessment dept. Nat. Naval Med. Ctr., Bethesda, Md., 1991-93; head orgnl. performance improvement customer support br. Navy Bur. Medicine and Surgery, 1994-95, head tricare quality br., 1995-96; dir. nursing adminstrv. matters, quality mgmt. specialist Office of Naval Med. Insp. Gen., 1996-99; head clin. ops. Mil. Med. Support Office, 1999—; U.S. Navy Medicine fellow Joint Commn. on Accreditation of Healthcare Orgns., 1993-94. Decorated Navy Commendation medals (3), Navy Meritorious Svc. medal; recipient various awards. Mem. Nat. Assn. for Healthcare Quality, Assn. Mil. Surgeons U.S., Navy Nurse Corps Assn., Nurses Alumnae Assn. U. Md., Sigma Theta Tau, Delta Epsilon Sigma, Kappa Gamma Pi, Phi Kappa Phi. Avocations: reading, cooking, gardening, traveling.

FELICE, NICHOLAS R., state legislator; b. Passaic, N.J., Feb. 5, 1927; s. Paul D. and Maria (Martini) F.; children: Paul T., John A., Robert N. BS, Fairleigh Dickinson U., 1976. Council mem. Fairlawn, N.J., 1967-73, dep. mayor, then mayor, 1973-75; assembly mem. dist. 40 N.J. State Assembly, 1982—; asst. majority leader N.J. State Assembly, 1986-89, asst. minority leader, 1990-91, dep. speaker, 1992-93, assembly spkr. pro tempore, 1996—, vice chmn. health & human svc. com., 1986—, select com. on drug & substance abuse, solid waste mgmt. com., energy & natural resources coms., Alzheimer's Disease study com., Nat. Conf. State Legis. Internat. Trade Com.; v.p., chief engr. Smith-Meeker Engr. Co., N.Y.C. Trustee Bergen C.C., 1980-82; bd. dirs. Fair Lawn Mental Health Ctr.; vol. Am. Cancer Soc. Mem. Rotary, K. of C. (trustee 1973-76), Bergen County Rep. Mayor's Assn., VFW. Address: 4-02 Fair Lawn Ave Fair Lawn NJ 07410-1221*

FELICETTI, DANIEL A., academic administrator, educator; b. N.Y.C., Apr. 25, 1942; s. Ernest and Rose (DiAdamo) F.; m. Barbara D'Antonio, July 13, 1969. BA in Polit. Sci., Hunter Coll., 1963; MA in Polit. Sci., NYU, 1966, PhD in Polit. Sci., 1971. From asst. to assoc. prof. Fairfield (Conn.) U., 1967-77, chmn. dept. politics, 1973-76, spl. asst. to pres., 1977; acad. v.p., acad. dean Wheeling (W.Va.) Coll., 1977-80; sr. v.p. for acad. affairs Coll. New Rochelle, N.Y., 1980-81, Southeastern U., Washington, 1982-84; v.p. acad. affairs U. Detroit, 1984-89; pres. Marian Coll., Indpls., 1989—; participant Am. Coun. on Edn., Washington, 1976-77, vis. assoc., 1984-85; intern Inst. for Ednl. Mgmt. program Harvard U., 1981; cons. Coun. for Ind. Colls., Washington, 1986. Trustee Am. Heart Assn., Mich.; bd. dirs. Am. Heart Assn., Ind., Mental Health Assn. Marion County, Econ. Club Indpls., Coun. Ind. Colls.; mem. health and substance abuse com. New Detroit, Inc., 1986-89; mem. Greater Indpls. Progress Com.; mem. Pub. Safety Task Force Ind.; mem. Colls. Ind. Found.; mem. Indpls. delegation to Pres.'s Summit for Am.'s Future, 1997. Trustee Am. Heart Assn., Mich.; bd. dirs. Am. Heart Assn., Ind., Mental Health Assn. Marion County, Econ. Club Indpls., Coun. Ind. Colls.; mem. health and substance abuse com. New Detroit, Inc., 1986-89; mem. Greater Indpls. Progress Coml; mem. Pub. Safety Task Force Ind.; mem. Colls. Ind. Found. Named to Hunter Coll. Hall of Fame, Hunter Coll. Alumni Assn., 1986; recipient Cert. of Recognition Sen. Lugar, 1994; Lilly Found. vis. faculty fellow Yale U., 1975; named Sagamore of the Wabash Gov. of Ind., 1990. Mem. Indpls. Athletic Club, Rotary, Alpha Sigma Nu (hon.), Beta Gamma Sigma (hon.). Democrat. Roman Catholic. Avocations: baseball, reading, antiques. Office: Marian Coll 3200 Cold Spring Rd Indianapolis IN 46222-1960*

FELICIANO, JOSÉ, entertainer; b. Larez, P.R., Sept. 10, 1945; s. Jose and Hortencia (Garcia) F.; m. Susan Feliciano; children: Melissa, Jonathan. P-res. Feliciano Enterprises. Folk singer in Greenwich Village, N.Y.C., 1962, rec. artist for EMI Records; TV appearances Feliciano—Very Special, 1969, Monsanto Night Presents Jose Feliciano, 1972, Statue of Liberty Celebration, 1984, over 100 others; has performed with major symphonies worldwide; composer some of own material including: Affirmation, Rain, Chico and the Man, Feliz Navidad, Ay Carino, Como tu Quieres; composer: guitar concerto Concerto de Paulinho, Mozartean Influence. Recipient 6 Grammy awards, including award in 1990, 11 Grammy nominations, Best Folk Guitarist award Guitar Player Mag. 1973, Best Pop Guitarist award 1973-77; 40 Gold albums; star in his name implanted on Hollywood Blvd., 1987. José Feliciano Sch. Performing Arts, East Harlem, N.Y., dedicated in his honor,

1987. Address: care Thomas Cassidy Inc 11761 E Speedway Blvd Tucson AZ 85748-2017 *The greatest tragedy for many so-called handicapped people is that they let others convince them that there are limits to what they can accomplish. It's just not so.**

FELIX, KELVIN EDWARD, archbishop; b. Roseau, Dominica, Feb. 15, 1933; s. Edward Mosley and Melanie (Cadette) F. Student, Sem. St. John Vianney, Trinidad and Tobago, 1951-56; diploma in adult edn., St. Francis Xavier U., N.S., Can., 1963, LLD (hon.), 1986; MA in Sociology and Anthropology, U. Notre Dame, 1967; postgrad., U. Bradford, Eng., 1967-70. Ordained priest Roman Cath. Ch., 1956. Assoc. pastor Roman Cath. Ch., Dominica, 1956-62; lectr., tutor U. West Indies and Sem., Trinidad and Tobago, 1970-72; assoc. gen. sec. Caribbean Conf. Chs., Trinidad and Tobago, 1975-81; archbishop of Castries St. Lucia, 1981—; cons. Pontifical Coun. for the Family, Roman Cath. Ch., Rome, 1988. Granted OBE by Queen Elizabeth II, 1992, COR UNUM by Holy Father John Paul II, 1994-99. Fax: 758-452-3697. E-mail: archbishop@candw.lc. Office: Archdiocese of Castries, PO Box 267, Castries Saint Lucia

FELIX, PATRICIA JEAN, steel company purchasing professional; b. Baptistown, N.J., Dec. 13, 1941; d. Dmitri and Rosalia (Hryckowian) F. Student, Pratt Inst., 1960-61, Moravian Coll., Bethlehem, Pa., 1961-63. Cert. purchasing mgr. Pricing analyst Riegel Paper Corp., N.Y.C., 1966-69; placement mgr. Gardner Assocs., N.Y.C., 1969-72; buyer Bethlehem Steel Corp., 1973-78, buyer exempt, 1978-84, sr. buyer, 1984, purchasing supr., 1984-94, mem. raw materials team, 1994-97, sr. sourcing specialist, 1997—. Sec. coun. St. Nicholas Russian Orthodox Ch., Bethlehem, 1982-85, mem. coun., 1985-91, mem. bldg. com., 1992-93, 97, mem. icon com., 1996-97; mem. bldg. com. 1998— Bethlehem-Tondabayashi Sister City Commn., 1988-91, sec., 1989-90, chmn., 1991-93. Mem. Nat. Assn. Purchasing Mgrs. Home: 1721 Millard St Bethlehem PA 18017-5142 Office: 1170 8th Ave Bethlehem PA 18016-7600

FELIX, RICHARD E., academic administrator. Pres. Azusa (Calif.) Pacific U. Office: Azusa Pacific U Office of President 901 E Alosta Ave Azusa CA 91702-2769*

FELIX, TED MARK, accountant; b. Bklyn., Apr. 23, 1947; s. Jack and Shirley (Starr) F.; m. Vicki Jane Robin, Dec. 23, 1967; children: Randi Sue, Jennifer Lynn. BS in Acctg., L.I. U., 1968, MBA in Fin., 1976. CPA, N.J., N.Y. Sr. auditor KPMG Peat Marwick, N.Y.C., 1968-71, 75-80; mgr. tech. standards Clarence Rainess & Co., N.Y.C., 1971-75; ptnr. Trien, Rosenberg, Felix, Rosenberg, Barr & Weinberg, N.Y.C., Morristown, 1980-95, Lazar Levine & Felix LLP, N.Y.C. and Roseland, N.J., 1995—; adj. prof. acctg. Ocean County Coll., Toms River, N.J., 1976-79, Rutgers U., New Brunswick, N.J., 1981-83; bd. dirs. Internat. Group Acctg. Firm, N.Y.C., London, Hong Kong. Contbr. articles to profl. jours. Bd. dirs. JCC of Metrowest, Whippany, N.J., 1989—, v.p., 1992—. Mem. AICPA (dir. quality control rev. divsn. 1975-80, numerous coms.), N.Y. Soc. CPAs (numerous coms.), N.J. Soc. CPAs (v.p. 1993-94, trustee 1989-90, numerous coms.), B'nai B'rith (pres. West Morris 1987-89, bd. govs. dist. 3, 1988-92, treas. No. N.J. coun. 1989-90, v.p. 1990-92, internat. bd. govs. 1998—, v.p. Tri-State region 1997—). Avocations: personal computers, first day covers, model railroading. Home: 10 Springhill Rd Randolph NJ 07869-4313 Office: Lazar Levine & Felix LLP 350 5th Ave New York NY 10118-0110

FELKER, G(EORGE) STEPHEN, textile company executive; b. Bronxville, N.Y., Dec. 15, 1951; s. George W. and Lella (Burnett) F.; m. Christine Klekner, Nov. 30, 1974; children: George Stephen, Emily Tichenor. BA, U. Va., 1974. Supr. mfg. Avondale Mills, Inc., Sylacauga, Ala., 1974, sales rep., N.Y.C., 1975-77; v.p. mktg. Walton Monroe Mills, Inc., Monroe, Ga., 1977-79, exec. v.p., 1979-80, pres., chief exec. officer, now also chmn., from 1980—; also bd. dirs.; pres., chief exec. officer, bd. dirs. Dacotah Mills, Inc., Lexington, N.C., 1984-89; chmn. bd., CEO Avondale, Inc., Monroe, Ga., Avondale Mills, Inc., Sylacauga, Ala.; bd. dirs. Wacharia Bank Ga., Monroe, also chmn., pres., Signal Thread Co., Inc., Nat. Cotton Coun., Am. Textile Mfrs. Inst., Textile Edn. Found., Atlanta. Pres. Walton County Hist. Soc., Monroe, 1980; bd. dirs. Va. Episcopal Sch. Mem. Nat. Assn. Mfrs. (bd. dirs. 1982-85), Ga. Textile Mfrs. Assn. (bd. dirs.), Walton County C. of C. (bd. dirs. 1980-83), Phi Psi. Club: Commerce (Atlanta). Home: 800 Belle Meade Rd Monroe GA 30655-2034 Office: Avondale Mills PO Box 1109 506 S Broad St Monroe GA 30655-2172*

FELKNOR, BRUCE LESTER, editorial consultant, writer; b. Oak Park, Ill., Aug. 18, 1921; s. Audley Rhea and Harriet (Lester) F.; m. Joanne Sweeney, Feb. 8, 1942 (div. Jan. 1952); 1 child, Susan Harriet Felknor Pickard; m. Edith G. Johnson, Mar. 1, 1952; children: Sarah Anne, Bruce Lester II. Student, U. Wis., 1939-41. Reporter Dunn County News, Menomonie, Wis., 1937-39; freight brakeman Pa. R.R., N.Y.C., 1941; asst. yardmaster Pa. R.R., 1942; prodn. coordinator Hwy. Trailer Co., Edgerton, Wis., 1943; radio officer U.S. Maritime Service, 1944-45; flight radio officer Air Transport Command, 1945; mem. pub. relations dept. Am. Airlines, 1945; writer pub. relations dept. ITT, 1946; Southeast regional pub. relations dir. Ford Motor Co., Chester, Pa., 1946-48; free lance pub. relations N.Y.C., 1948-49; pub. relations exec. Foote, Cone & Belding, Inc., N.Y.C., 1950-53; v.p. Market Relations Network, N.Y.C., 1954-55; exec. dir. Fair Campaign Practices Com., Inc., N.Y.C., 1956-66; asst. to William Benton (chmn. and pub. Ency. Brit.), 1966-70; dir. mktg. info. internat. div. (Ency. Brit.), 1970-73, dir. advt. and promotion, 1973, dir. pub. info., 1974-76, exec. editor, 1977-83; dir. yearbooks Ency. Brit., 1983-85; editorial cons., 1985—; vis. lectr. Hamilton Coll., 1966, 75, 82. Author: Fair Play in Politics, 1960, State-by-State Smear Study, 1956, You Are They, 1964, (with C.P. Taft) Prejudice & Politics, 1960, Dirty Politics, 1966, reprinted, 1975, (with Frank Jonas et al) Political Dynamiting, 1970, How to Look Things Up and Find Things Out, 1988, Political Mischief: Smear, Sabotage, and Reform in U.S. Elections, 1992, The Highland Park Presbyterian Church: A History 1871-1996, 1996 (Robert Lee Stowe award 1997), The U.S. Merchant Marine at War 1775-1945, 1998; editor: The U.S. Government: How and Why it Works, 1978; also various newspaper, jour. and yearbook articles on politics; contbg. editor (with Clifton Fadiman) The Treasury of the Encyclopaedia Britannica, 1992; contbr. Encyclopedia of the American Presidency, 1993. Chmn. Citizens Com. for Sch. Centralization in Armonk, N.Y., 1957-61; bd. dirs., mem. exec. com. Fair Campaign Practices Com.; mem. nat. adv. bd. Amigos de las Americas, 1982-89, Am. U., Washington, 1982—; mem. Ill. Literacy Coun., 1984-86; mem. bd. advisors, acad. adv. coun. Nat. Strategy Forum, 1987—; mem. bd. edn. Lake Forest (Ill.) H.S. Dist., 1989-93. Mem. Am. Legion, Am. Mcht. Marine Vets., Navy League, Am. Polit. Sci. Assn., Authors League Am., Authors Guild, Soc. Midwest Authors, Tavern Club (Chgo., Bonifex Maximus award 1995), Dutch Treat Club (N.Y.C.). Republican. Presbyn. (ruling elder, chmn. com. religion and race Presbytery Hudson River 1963-67, mem. nat. council on ch. and soc. 1966-72). Home and Office: 509 Trinity Ct Evanston IL 60201 *Man's greatest gifts are empathy and the ability to penetrate balderdash.*

FELL, FREDERICK VICTOR, publisher; b. Bklyn., May 21, 1910; s. Samuel and Victoria (Greenhut) F.; m. Selma Shampain, May 18, 1975; children: Linda Fell Firestein, Nancy. Student, NYU, 1928-31; LLB, Bklyn. Law Sch., 1935. Pres. Frederick Fell Pubs., N.Y.C., 1943-81; prin. Frederick Fell & Assocs., Inc., Literary Agts., Hollywood, Fla., 1981—. Author: (pseudonym Vic Fredericks) Crackers in Bed, 1953, More for Doctors Only, 1953, Just Married, 1958, For Golfers Only, 1964, Wit and Wisdom of Presidents, 1966, others; editor and publisher: The Hillcrest Hotline, 1993—. Trustee Long Beach (N.Y.) Library, 1948-50; councilman City of Long Beach, 1950-54, pres. city council, 1950-52; pres. Long Beach Hosp. Club, 1949, 59; chmn. book pubs. div. crusades N.Y.C. div. Am. Cancer Soc., 1977-81. Mem. Assn. Am. Pubs., Am. Booksellers Assn., Book Group South Fla. Democrat. Jewish. Clubs: Hillcrest Country, Hollywood (Fla.). Home: 3800 Hillcrest Dr Apt 1120 Hollywood FL 33021-7940

FELL, JAMES F., lawyer; b. Toledo, Ohio, Nov. 18, 1944; s. George H. Fell and Bibianne C. (Hebert) Franklin; children from a previous marriage: Jennifer A., Brian F.; m. Betty L. Wenzel, May 23, 1981. BA, U. Notre Dame, 1966; JD, Ohio State U., 1969. Bar: N.Y. 1970, Calif. 1972, Idaho 1978, Wash. 1981, Oreg. 1984, U.S. Ct. Appeals (9th cir.) 1983, U.S. Dist. Ct. Idaho 1978. Assoc. Breed, Abbott & Morgan, N.Y.C., 1969-72; ptnr. McKenna & Fitting, L.A., 1972-78; atty. Office Atty. Gen., State of Idaho, Boise, 1978-79; dir. policy and administrn. Idaho Pub. Utilities Commn., Boise, 1979-81; gen. counsel, dep. dir. Northwest Power Planning Coun., Portland, Oreg., 1981-84; ptnr. Stoel Rives LLP, Portland, 1984—. Mem. ABA (pub. utility law sect.), Oreg. State Bar (exec. com. pub. utility law sect.). Office: Stoel Rives LLP 900 SW 5th Ave Ste 2600 Portland OR 97204-1232

FELL, JENNIFER ANNE, writer; b. Columbus, Ohio, Nov. 6, 1968; d. James Frederick Fell and Mary Elizabeth Kelly McColl. BA in English, Santa Clara U., 1990. Pub. rels. asst. de Saisset Mus., Santa Clara, Calif., 1987-90; tech. writer Rational Software Corp., Santa Clara, 1990-94; sr. tech. writer ParcPlace-Digitalk, Inc., Sunnyvale, Calif. and Austin Tex., 1994-97; mem. tech. staff Neometron, Austin, Tex., 1997; tech. writer Expert Support, Mountain View, Calif., 1997—. Vol. Planned Parenthood, Calif. and Idaho, 1993-96. Mem. NOW, NARAL, Planned Parenthood, Soc. for Tech. Comm., Alpha Sigma Nu, Sigma Tau Delta, Phi Sigma Tau. Avocations: electric bass, dogs, poker, softball.

FELL, SAMUEL KENNEDY (KEN FELL), infosystems executive; b. Wilmington, Del., Oct. 6, 1944; s. S. Kennedy and Anna Elizabeth (Alford) F.; m. Diana Marie Dickson, May 8, 1965; children: Melissa Ann, Michael Kennedy. BSBA, Oklahoma City U., 1983; postgrad. in bus., John F. Kennedy U.; grad. exec. mgmt. program, Duke U., 1991. Mgmt./data processing sys. designer/implementor Gen. Motors Corp., Detroit and Oklahoma City, 1967-81; v.p. info. systems Totco Divsn. Baker Internat., Norman, Okla., 1981-85; v.p. computer info. Cleve. Pneumatic subs. Pneumo Abex Corp. div. IC Industries, 1985-88; sr. dir. systems devel. Sprint, Kansas City, Mo., 1988-95; sr. v.p. product devel., exec. bd. mem. SynQuest, Inc., A Warburg Pincus Co., 1995—. Mem. Data Processing Mgrs. Assn., Oracle Users Group, Am. Prodn. and Inventory Control Soc., Soc. Info. Mgrs. Office: SynQuest Inc 855 Route 146 Ste 150 Clifton Park NY 12065-3837

FELLEGI, IVAN PETER, statistician; b. Szeged, Hungary, June 22, 1935; immigrated to Can., 1957; s. Andor and Barbara (Partos) F.; m. Marika Gulyas, Dec. 27, 1958; children—Nicolette Katherine, Vivien Susan. BSc, U. Budapest, Hungary, 1956; MSc, Carleton U., Ont., Can., 1958, PhD, 1961; PhD (hon.), Simon Fraser U., 1995; LLD (hon.), McMaster U., 1997. With Statistics Can., Ottawa, Ont., 1957—, asst. chief statistician, 1973-84, dep. chief statistician, 1984-85, chief statistician of Can., 1985—. Contbr. articles to profl. jours. Bd. govs. Carleton U., 1989—, chmn. bd. govs., 1995-97; chair Conf. European Statisticians, 1993-97. Recipient Order of Can., 1992, Robert Schuman medal European Cmty., 1997. Fellow AAAS, Am. Statis. Assn., Royal Statis. Soc. (hon.); mem. Internat. Statis. Inst. (hon., pres. 1987-89), Statis. Soc. Can. (pres. 1982), Internat. Assn. Survey Statisticians (pres. 1985-87). Home: 16 Larchwood Ave, Ottawa, ON Canada K1Y 2E3 Office: Statistics Canada, RH Coats Bldg Tunney's Pasture, Ottawa, ON Canada K1A 0T6

FELLENSTEIN, CORA ELLEN MULLIKIN, retired credit union executive; b. Edwardsville, Ill., June 2, 1930; d. Russell K. and Elberta Mable (Rheude) Mullikin; m. Charles Frederick Fellenstein, Feb. 24, 1951; children: Keith David, Kimberly Diane. Student, Cmty. Coll., 1980-83. Teller, loan officer, office mgr. Credit Union of Johnson County, Lenexa, Kans., 1976-84, 1st. v.p., supr. lending, collection and Mastercard depts., 1984-86, exec. v.p., 1987-94. Author: Moore Family History, 1987. Precinct committeewoman Johnson County Reps., Olathe, Kans., 1976-92; vol. Cerebral Palsey, 1957-66, Olathe Cmty. Hops., 1976-92, Shawnee Mission (Kans.) Med. Ctr., 1986-90, Caring For Others, Amigos Los Ninos de Mexico, 1996-99. Mem. NAFE, Internat. Assn. Credit Card Investigators, Internat. Credit Assn., Kans. Credit Assn., Credit Profls. (dir. 1983-92, Exec. of Yr. Johnson county chpt.), DAR (treas. 1966-86), Daus. Am. Colonists (treas. 1976-86), Friends of Historic Mahaffie Farmstead, Soroptimist Internat., Beta Sigma Pi. Mem. Christian Ch. Avocations: genealogy, camping, travel. Home: 800 FM 495 # 689 Alamo TX 78516-9780

FELLER, BENJAMIN E., actuary; b. Bronx, N.Y., Mar. 4, 1947; s. Morris and Beatrice (Wolff) F.; m. Debra May Morane, June 1973 (div. 1983); children: Amy; m. Sue Ann Kaufman, Sept. 23, 1984; children: Meredith; stepchildren: Stefanie McCoy, Alison McCoy. BS in Math., Clarkson U., Potsdam, N.Y., 1968; MA in Math., Ind. U., 1971. Enrolled actuary. Actuarial asst. U.S. Life Ins. Co., N.Y.C., 1971-75; assoc. actuary The Wyatt Co., Washington, 1975-76; cons. actuary Buck Cons., N.Y.C., 1976-85; ptnr. Chernoff Diamond & Co., Williston Park, N.Y., 1985-92; pres. Pension Rev. Svcs., Plainview, N.Y., 1992—. Fellow Soc. Actuaries; mem. Am. Soc. Pension Actuaries, Am. Acad. Actuaries. Republican. Jewish. Home: 10 Allison Dr Old Bethpage NY 11804-1602 Office: Pension Rev Svcs 45 Executive Dr Plainview NY 11803-1737

FELLER, DAVID E., law educator, arbitrator; b. 1916. AB, Harvard U., 1938, LLB, 1941. Bar: Mass. 1941, D.C. 1942. Lectr. law and econs. U. Chgo., 1941-42; atty. U.S. Dept. Justice, Washington, 1946-48; law clk. U.S. Supreme Ct., 1948-49; assoc. gen. counsel CIO, Washington, 1949-53, United Steelworkers, Washington, 1949-60; gen. counsel ind. union dept. AFL-CIO, Washington, 1961-66, United Steelworkers, 1961-65; ptnr. Goldberg Feller & Bredhoff, Washington, 1955-60, Feller, Bredhoff & Anker, 1961-65, Feller & Anker, 1965-67; John H. Boalt prof. emeritus U. Calif.-Berkeley Sch. Law. Editor Harvard Law Rev. Bd. dirs. NAACP Legal Def. and Edn. Fund, 1960-97; pres. Council Univ. Calif. Faculty Assns., 1973-89. Mem. Nat. Acad. Arbitrators (v.p. 1985-87, pres. 1992-93), Fed. Mediation and Conciliation Service Roster of Arbitrators, ABA (sec. labor law sect. 1972-73), Phi Beta Kappa. Home: 728 Santa Barbara Rd Berkeley CA 94707-2005 Office: U Calif Sch of Law Boalt Hall Berkeley CA 94720-7200

FELLER, IRWIN, think-tank executive, economics educator. BBA in Econs., CUNY, 1959; PhD in Econs., U. Minn., 1966. Prof. dept. econs. Pa. State U., University Park, 1973—, dir. inst. policy rsch. and evaluation, 1977—, dir. grad. sch. pub. policy and adminstrn., 1993—, dir. Inst. for Policy Rsch. and Evaluation; cons. Carnegie Commn. Sci., Tech., and Govt., Cleveland Found., Ford Found., Hilton Found., Nat. Conf. State Legislatures, Nat. Govs.' Assn., NSF, Pres.'s Office Sci. and Tech. Policy, U.S. Gen. Acctg. Office, U.S. Dept. Edn., U.S. Dept. Energy, pres.'s office U. Calif., chancellor's office U. Md. System, others; presenter in field. Author: (with others) Dynamics of Industrial Location, 1975, Productivity and Public Policy, 1984, Policy for Agriculture Research, 1987, Government Innovation Policy: Design, Implementation, Evaluation, 1988, Growth Policy in the Age of High Technology: The Role of Regions and States, 1990, Technology and Competitiveness, 1992, University and Research: The United Kingdom and the United States, 1992, Industrial Policy for Agriculture in the Global Economy, 1993; author: Universities and State Governments, 1986; contbr. articles to profl. jours. Grantee Appalachian Regional Commn., USDA, Bell Telephone Co. Pa. Mem. AAAS (mem. com. sci., engrng. and pub. policy 1991-93, 93—), Am. Econ. Assn., Nat. Coun. Advancement Rsch. (mem. conf. com. 1991—), Econ. History Assn., Assn. Pub. Policy Analysis and Mgmt. Office: Pa State U Inst Policy Rsch Evaluation N253 Burrowes Bldg University Park PA 16802*

FELLER, JEROME, federal judge; b. 1941. BA, Yeshiva Coll., 1962; LLB, N.Y. Law Sch., 1966. Bar: N.Y. Legal editor West Pub. Co., 1965-69; trial atty. SEC, N.Y.C., 1969-74, br. chief, 1974-79, asst. regional adminstr., 1979-85; bankruptcy judge for ea. dist. N.Y., U.S. Bankruptcy Ct., Bklyn., 1985—. Office: US Bankruptcy Ct 75 Clinton St Brooklyn NY 11201-4201

FELLER, LLOYD HARRIS, lawyer; b. New Brunswick, N.J., Aug. 27, 1942; s. Alexander and Freda (Kaminsky) F.; m. Susan Sydney Weinberg, Aug. 6, 1967; children: Jennifer, Andrew. BS in Econs., U. Pa., 1964; LLB, NYU, 1967. Bar: N.Y. 1967, D.C. 1980. Assoc. Rubin, Wachtel, Baum & Levin, 1967-70; trial atty. organized crime sect., divsn. enforcement SEC, Washington, 1970-72, legal asst. Commr. A. Sydney Herlong, Jr., 1972-73, legal asst. Commr. A.A. Sommer, Jr., 1973-76; chief counsel Office of the Chief Acct., 1976-77; assoc. dir. divsn. market regulation Office of Market Structure and Trading Practices, 1977-79, of counsel, 1979-81; ptnr. Morgan, Lewis & Bockius LLP, Washington, 1981-99, mem. governing bd., 1996-99, mem. exec. com., 1998-99, mem. allocations com., 1999—; sr. v.p., co-gen. counsel Wit Capital Group, N.Y.C., 1999—. Home: 419 S Lee St Alexandria VA 22314-3815 Office: Wit Capital Group 826 Broadway New York NY 10003

FELLER, MIMI, newspaper publishing executive. BA cum laude, Creighton U.; JD, Georgetown U. Asst. dir. congl. rels. Gen. Svcs. Adminstrn., 1975-77; legis. asst. Environ. and Pub. Works Com. U.S. Senate, 1977-81; from legis. dir. to Washington chief of staff Sen. John Chafee (Rep.), R.I., 1981-83; dep. asst. sec. legis. affairs U.S. Dept. Treasury, 1983-85; from v.p. govt. rels. to sr. v.p. Gannett Co., 1985—; bd. advisors Nat. Ct. Apptd. Spl. Advocates Assn. Bd. dirs. Creighton U.; trustee Marymount U. Recipient Disting. Alumnus award Creighton U., 1987. Office: Gannett Co Inc 1100 Wilson Blvd Ste 2100 Arlington VA 22209-2299

FELLER, RALPH PAUL, dentist, educator; b. Quincy, Mass., Aug. 31, 1934; s. Paul Frederich and Frances Elizabeth (Hubert) F.; children: Lynne Anne Feller Grenier, Paul Herbert, Wendy Elizabeth. BS, Tufts U., 1956, DMD, 1964; MS, U. Tex., Houston, 1975; MPH, Loma Linda U., 1981. Asst. prof. Harvard U., Boston, 1965-71; assoc. prof. U. Tex. Med. Br., Houston, 1971-75; clin. investigator VA Med. Ctr., Houston, 1971-75; chief dental svc. VA Med. Ctr., Lyons, N.J., 1975-77, Loma Linda, Calif., 1977-95; assoc. prof. Fairleigh Dickinson U., Hackensack, N.J., 1975-77; prof., dir. clin. rsch. ctr. Loma Linda U. Sch. Dentistry, 1995—; cons. Johnson & Johnson, East Windsor, N.J., 1980-85, Oral-B Labs., Inc., Redwood City, Calif., 1986-92, Richardson-Vicks, Shelton, Conn., 1988-92, Colgate-Polmolive Co., Piscataway, N.J., 1988—. Contbr. articles to profl. jours. Col. USAR, 1960-95, ret. Mem. ADA (Achievement award 1995), Internat. Assn. Dental Rsch. (numerous offices 1964—), am. Coll. Prosthodontists, Am. Assn. Dental Schs., Calif. Dental Assn., Assn. Mil. Surgeons U.S., Rotary. Avocations: boating, golf. E-mail: rpfeller@aol.com. Fax: (909) 478-4328. Home: 30832 Alta Mira Dr Redlands CA 92373-7402 Office: Loma Linda U Sch Dentistry Loma Linda CA 92350

FELLER, ROBERT, counselor; b. L.A., Mar. 1, 1949; m. Linda Feller, Apr. 3, 1993. BA, UCLA, 1968; MA, Mt. St. Mary's Coll., L.A., 1983. Elem. and adult edn. tchr. L.A. Unified Sch. Dist., 1980-90; tchr. Alisal Union Sch. Dist., Salinas, Calif., 1991-95; bilingual Spanish counselor Family Svc. Agy., Salinas, Calif., 1995—; bilingual Spanish parent educator Salinas Adult Sch., 1996—; wellness staff mem. Salinas YMCA. Author: A Cool River, 1995 (Steinbeck award 1995), Lantern Eyes-A Tribute to Henry Miller, 1995, Driver Beware/David and Goliath-The Ultimate DUI Story, 1995, P'Tui! and Other Stories, 1996, Leafwriter, a screen play, Success Journal, an autobiography. Mem. Steinbeck Toastmasters (past pres. Salinas), Elks,. Avocations: swimming, creative writing. Office: Family Svc Agy of Monterey County 433 Salinas St Salinas CA 93901-7852

FELLER, ROBERT LIVINGSTON, chemist, art conservation scientist; b. Newark, Dec. 27, 1919; s. William Henry and Edna (Buckelew) F.; m. Ruth M. Johnston, Mar. 31, 1975. A.B., Dartmouth Coll., 1941; M.S., Rutgers U., 1943, Ph.D., 1950. Sr. fellow Nat. Gallery Art Research Project, Mellon Inst., Pitts., 1950-76; dir. Research Ctr. on Materials of Artist and Conservator, Carnegie-Mellon Rsch. Inst., Pitts., 1976-88, dir. emeritus, 1988—; vis. scientist Conservation Ctr., Inst. Fine Arts, NYU, 1961; pres. Nat. Conservation Adv. Council, 1975-79. Co-author: On Picture Varnishes and their Solvents, 2d rev. edit., 1985, Evaluation of Cellulose Ethers for Conservation, 1990, Accelerated Aging: Photochemical and Thermal Aspects, 1994; editor: Artists' Pigments: A Handbook of Their History and Characteristics, Vol. I, 1986. Served with USN, 1944-46. Recipient Coll. Art Assn.-Nat. Inst. for Conservation Joint award, 1992. Fellow Internat. Inst. Conservation Hist. and Artistic Works (hon.), Am. Inst. Conservation Hist. and Artistic Works (hon.), Illuminating Engring. Soc.; mem. AAAS, Am. Chem. Soc. (Pittsburgh award 1983), Internat. Coun. Museums (pres. conservation com. 1969-78), Fedn. Socs. Coatings Tech., Inter-Soc. Color Coun., Am. Inst. Conservation. Clubs: Cosmos (Washington); Univ. (Pitts.). Research on deterioration of varnishes, paper, pigments and dyes used by artists. Office: Carnegie Mellon U Carnegie Mellon Rsch Inst 700 Technology Dr Pittsburgh PA 15219-3124

FELLER, ROBERT WILLIAM ANDREW, baseball team public relations executive, retired baseball player; b. Van Meter, Iowa, Nov. 3, 1918; s. William and Lena (Forrett) F.; m. Anne Morris Gilliland, Oct. 1, 1974. Pub. rels. exec. Cleveland Indians Baseball Team, 1936-56; played first major league game Cleve. vs. St. Louis Browns, 1936; pitched 3 no-hitters Cleve. vs. Chgo., 1940, Cleve. vs. N.Y., 1946, Cleve. vs. Detroit, 1951; member 9 all-star teams. Author: (book) Strikeout Story, 1947, How to Pitch, 1948, Now Pitching Bob Feller, 1990. CPO USNavy, 1941-45, PTO. Inducted to Baseball Hall of Fame, Cooperstown, N.Y., 1962; named Greatest Living Right-Hand Pitcher Profl. Baseball Centennial Celebration, 1969. Republican. Episcopalian. Avocation: restoring Caterpiller tractors. Fax: 440-423-3248.

FELLER, WILLIAM FRANK, surgery educator; b. St. Paul, Nov. 2, 1925; s. William and Eva Caroline (Nordstrom) F.; m. Margareta Elizabeth Helm, Sept. 5, 1964; children: William Frank III, Elizabeth Suzanne. BA magna cum laude, U. Minn., 1948, BS, 1952, MD, 1954, PhD, 1962. Diplomate Am. Bd. Surgery. Intern U. Minn., Mpls., 1954-55; asst. prof. Georgetown U., Washington, 1964-69, assoc. prof., 1969-92; ret.; ret., 1992. Contbr. articles to profl. jours. Warden St. John's Episc. Ch., Chevy Chase, Md., 1975-76. Recipient St. George's medal Am. Cancer Soc., 1987. Mem. AAAS, ACS, Am. Assn. Cancer Rsch., Am. Scandinavian Found. (chpt. pres. 1969-71), Med. Soc. D.C., Am. Cancer Soc. (D.C. divsn. pres. 1984-85, St. George's medal 1987), Washington Acad. Medicine, Washington Acad. Surgery (pres. 1982-83), Cosmos Club (Washington). Achievements include 2 patents for Cancer Detection Methods. Home: 7028 Barkwater Ct Bethesda MD 20817-4402

FELLER, WINTHROP BRUCE, physicist; b. Cleve., Nov. 1, 1950; s. Robert William and Virginia Adele (Winther) F.; m. Lydia M. Conca, Aug. 14, 1988; 1 child, Daniel James. SB, MIT, 1974; postgrad., Yale U., 1974-75. Lectr. in physics and astronomy Northwestern U., Evanston, Ill., 1977-83; scientist Galileo Electro-Optics Corp., Sturbridge, Mass., 1984-85, sr. scientist, 1985-90, assoc., 1990—; v.p., chief scientist Nova Sci., Inc., 1993—; prin. Emission Sys., L.L.C. Contbr. articles to profl. jours. Recipient R&D 100 award R&D mag., 1989; grantee NASA, ARPA, NIH, NSF, Dept. Energy, Dept. Def., Dept. Commerce. Mem. AAAS, Am. Phys. Soc., Am. Philos. Assn., Optical Soc. Am., Soc. Photo-Optical Instrumentation Engrs. (session co-chmn. detector conf.), Fedn. Am. Scientists, Union Concerned Scientists. Achievements include patents in microchannel plate field; development of low noise, conductively cooled, neutron-, hard x-, and gamma ray sensitive microchannel plate detectors, lobstereye x-ray telescope optics, digital readout systems, electron-beam lithography sources, x-ray lithography optics, mammography imaging, quantum computing, x-ray and neutron focusing microchannel lens, others; research on detectors for EUV and x-ray astronomy, space plasma detectors, mass analysis of biomolecules, and the philosophy of science. Home: 50 Shanda Ln Tolland CT 06084-3951 Office: Nova Sci Inc P.O. Box 928 Sturbridge MA 01566-1281

FELLERS, FREDERICK PAUL, librarian; b. Dayton, Ohio, Feb. 4, 1947; s. Paul William and Lois Irene (Eby) F. BA in German, Wright State U., 1969; MLS, Kent State U., 1976. Libr. Indpls.-Marion County Pub. Libr., Indpls., 1977—; bd. dirs. Rouen Chamber Ensemble, Indpls., 1991-94. Author: Discographies of Commercial Recordings, The Cleveland Orchestra, 1924-77, Cincinnati Symphony Orchestra, 1917-77, 1978, The Metropolitan Opera on Record, 1984. With U.S. Air Force, 1969-73. Mem. Assn. for Recorded Sound Collections, Met. Opera Guild, The Kipling Soc., Masons (master lodge 477, Ohio). Avocations: collector records, books, music scores; piano player. Home: 5124 Norwaldo Ave Indianapolis IN 46205-1342 Office: Indpls Marion County Libr PO Box 211 Indianapolis IN 46206-0211

FELLERS, RHONDA GAY, lawyer; b. Gainesville, Tex., July 20, 1955; d. James Norman and Gaytha Ann (Sanders) F.; m. Bruce C. Hinton, Oct. 15, 1981 (div. Oct. 1985). BA, U. Tex., 1977, JD, 1980; LLM in Taxation, U. Denver, 1987. Bar: Tex. 1981, Colo. 1981, U.S. Dist. Ct. (no. dist.) Tex. 1982, U.S. Dist. Ct. Colo. 1985, U.S. Tax Ct. 1985, U.S. Ct. Appeals (5th cir.) 1986, U.S. Ct. Appeals (10th cir.) 1989, U.S. Supreme Ct. 1993, U.S. Ct. Claims 1993. Assoc. Walters & Assocs., Lubbock, Tex., 1981-83; gen. counsel Security Nat. Bank, Lubbock, 1983; sole practice Lubbock, 1983-87; assoc. Melvin Coffee & Assocs., P.C., Denver, 1984-85, 87-90; atty. adviser U.S. Tax Ct., Washington, 1990-94; pvt. practice Pinehurst, Tex., 1994-98;

with Arthur Andersen LLP, Houston, 1998—. Mem. ABA, State Bar Tex., Colo. Bar Assn., Houston Bar Assn. Avocations: golf, tennis, photography.

FELLHAUER, DAVID E., bishop; b. Kansas City, Mo., Aug. 19, 1939. Student, Pontifical Coll. Josephinum; D in Canon Law, PhD, St. Paul U., Ottawa, Can. Ordained priest Roman Cath. Ch., 1965. Former prof. Holy Trinity Sem., Dallas; judicial vicar Diocese of Dallas, until 1990; bishop of Victoria Tex., 1990—; bd. govs. Canon Law Soc. Am. Recipient Role of Law award Canon Law Soc., 1998. Office: PO Box 4070 Victoria TX 77903-4070*

FELLIN, OCTAVIA ANTOINETTE, retired librarian; b. Santa Monica, Calif.; d. Otto P. and Librada (Montoya) F. Student U. N.Mex., 1937-39; BA, U. Denver, 1941; BA in L.S., Dominican U., River Forest, Ill., 1942. Asst. libr., instr. libr. sci. St. Mary-of-Woods Coll., Terre Haute, Ind., 1942-44; libr. U.S. Army, Bruns Gen. Hosp., Santa Fe, 1944-46, Gallup (N.Mex.) Pub. Libr., 1947-90; post libr. Camp McQuaide, Calif., 1947; freelance writer mags., newspapers, 1950—; libr. cons.; N.Mex. del. White House Pre-Conf. on Librs. & Info. Svcs., 1978; dir. Nat. Libr. Week for N.Mex., 1959. Chmn. Red Mesa Art Ctr., 1984-88; pres. Gallup Area Arts Coun., 1988; mem. Western Health Found. Century Com., 1988, Gallup Multi-Model Cultural Com., 1988-95; v.p., publicity dir. Gallup Cmty. Concerts Assn., 1957-78, 85-95; organizer Gt. Decision Discussion groups, 1963-85; co-organizer, v.p. chair fund raising com. Gallup Pub. Radio Com., 1989-95; mem. McKinley County Recycling Com., 1990—; mem. local art selection com. N.Mex. Art Dirs., 1990; mem. Gallup St. Naming Com., 1958-59, Aging Com., 1964-68; chmn. Gallup Mus. Indian Arts and Crafts, 1964-78; mem. Eccles. Conciliation and Arbitration Bd., Province of Santa Fe, 1974; mem. publicity com. Gallup Inter-Tribal Indian Ceremonial Assn., 1966-68; mem. Gov's. Com. 100 on Aging, 1967-70; mem. U. N.Mex.-Gallup Campus Cmty. Edn. Adv. Coun., 1981-82; N.Mex. organizing chmn. Rehoboth McKinley Christian Hosp. Aux., pres., 1983, chmn. aux. scholarship com., 1989—, chmn. cmty. edn. loan selection com. 1990—, bd. dirs., corr. sec., 1991-94; mem. N.Mex. Libr. Adv. Coun., 1971-75, vice chmn., 1974-75; chmn. adv. com. Gallup Sr. Citizens, 1971-73; mem. steering com. Gallup Diocese Bicentennial, 1975-78, chmn. hist. com., 1975; chmn. Trick or Treat for UNICEF, Gallup, 1972-77, Artists Coop, 1985-89; chmn. pledge campaign Rancho del Nino San Huberto, Empalme, Mex., 1975-80; active Nat. Cath. Social Justice Lobby; bd. dirs. Gallup Opera Guild, 1970-74; bd. dirs., sec., co-organizer Gallup Area Arts Council, 1970-78; mem. N.Mex. Humanities Council, 1979, Gallup Centennial Com., 1980-81; mem. Cathedral Parish Council, 1980-83, v.p., 1981, century com. Western Health Found., 1988-89; active N.Mex. Diamond Jubilee/U.S. Constn. Bicentennial Gallup Com., 1986-87, N.Mex. Gallup Campus 25 Silver Anniversary Com., 1994. Recipient Dorothy Canfield Fisher $1,000 Libr. award, 1961, Outstanding Community Service award for mus. service Gallup C. of C., 1969, 70, Outstanding Citizen award, 1974, Benemerenti medal Pope Paul VI, 1977, Celebrate Literary award Gallup Internat. Reading 8 Assn., 1983-84, Woman of Distinction award Soroptimists, 1985, N.Mex. Disting. Pub. Svc. award, 1987, finalist Gov's award Outstanding N.Mex. Women, 1988, Edgar L. Hewett award Hist. Soc. N.Mex., 1992; Octavia Fellin Pub. Libr. named in her honor, 1990. Mem. ALA, N.Mex. Library Assn. (hon. life, v.p., sec., chmn. hist. materials com. 1964-66, salary and tenure com., nat. coordinator N.Mex. legislative com., chmn. com. to extend library services 1969-73, Librar. of Yr. award 1975, chmn. local and regional history roundtable 1978, Community Achievement award 1983, Lifetime Membership award 1994), AAUW (v.p., co-organizer Gallup br., N.Mex. nominating com. 1967-68, chmn. fellowships and centennial fund Gallup br., chmn. com. on women), Plateau Scis. Soc., N.Mex. Folklore Soc. (v.p. 1964-65, pres. 1965-66), N.Mex. Hist. Soc. (dir. 1979-85), Gallup Hist. Soc., Gallup Film Soc. (co-organizer, v.p. 1950-58), LWV (v.p. 1953-56), NAACP, Pax Christi U.S.A., Women's Ordination Conf. Network, Call to Action Nat. Ch. Renewal Org., Gallup C. of C. (organizing chmn. women's div. 1972, v.p. 1972-73), N.Mex. Women's Polit. Caucus, N.Mex. Mcpl. League (pres. libr.'s div. 1979), Alpha Delta Kappa (hon.). Roman Catholic (Cathedral Guild, Confraternity Christian Doctrine Bd. 1962-64, Cursillo in Christianity Movement, mem. of U.S. Cath. Bishop's Adv. Council 1969-74; corr. sec. Latin Am. Mission Program 1972-75, sec. Diocese of Gallup Pastoral Council 1972-73, corr. sec. liturgical commn. Diocese of Gallup 1977). Author: Yahweh the Voice that Beautifies the Land, A Chronicle of Mileposts A Brief History of the University of New Mexico, Gallup Campus. Home and Office: 513 E Mesa Ave Gallup NM 87301-6021

FELLINGHAM, WARREN LUTHER, JR., retired banker; b. Chgo., Dec. 28, 1934; s. Warren Luther and Dorothy Eaton (Park) F.; m. Judith Cutler, Sept. 14, 1962; children: Warren III, Margo, Victoria. AB, Dartmouth Coll., 1956; MBA, Northwestern U., 1968. Cert. bank compliance officer. Auditing asst. The Northern Trust Co., Chgo., 1956-61, asst. cashier, 1962-71, 2d v.p., 1972-77, v.p., 1978-96, consumer compliance officer, 1988-96; pres. Chicagoland Compliance Assn., 1988-96. Village pres., mayor Village of Golf, Ill., 1981-85, village trustee, clk., 1973-81; bd. dirs. United Way of Glenview-Golf, 1983-92; unit commr. N.E. Ill. coun. Boy Scouts Am., 1996—; treas. Glenview Area Hist. Soc., 1998—. Recipient Dist. award of Merit, 1989, N.E. Ill. Coun. Boy Scouts of Am., 1989, William H. Spurgeon III award, 1998. Mem. Glenview Area Hist. Soc. (treas. 1998—), Dartmouth Club Chgo., Order of Arrow. Avocation: bicycling. Home: 37 Overlook Dr Golf IL 60029

FELLNER, ERIC, film producer. Prodr. (films) Sid & Nancy, 1986, Straight to Hell, 1987, Pascali's Island, 1988, The Rachel Papers, 1989, Hidden Agenda, 1990, A Kiss Before Dying, 1991, Liebestraum, 1991, Year of the Gun, 1991, Wild West, 1992, Romeo is Bleeding, 1993, No Worries, 1993, The Hawke, 1993, Posse, 1993, Four Weddings and a Funeral, 1994, The Hudsucker Proxy, 1994, Loch Ness, 1995, Panther, 1995, French Kiss, 1995, Moonlight & Valantino, 1995, Fargo, 1996, Bean, 1997, The Matchmaker, 1997, The Borrowers, 1997, The Hi-Lo Country, 1998, Elizabeth, 1998 (Alexander Korda Awd, ALFS Awd, 1999), The Big Lebowski, 1998, What Rats Won't Do, 1998, Notting Hill, 1999, Solo, 1999, Plunkett & MacCleane, 1999. Office: Working Title Films 9333 Wilshire Blvd Beverly Hills CA 90210*

FELLNER, MICHAEL JOSEPH, government executive, educator; b. St. Paul, Minn., Aug. 10, 1949; s. Joseph George and Carol Marie (Bovy) F.; m. Carol Lois Archer, Oct. 14, 1972; children: Christopher Michael, Kimberly Ann. BS in Edn., U. Minn., Mpls., 1971; postgrad., U. Wis., La Crosse, 1972. Cert. Dept. Def. acquisition profl. Secondary sch. educator La Crescent (Minn.) Sch. Dist., 1971-72; contract price analyst Def. Contract Adminstrn. Svcs., Mpls., 1977-84, adminstrv. contracting officer, 1984-86, div. adminstrv. contracting officer, 1986—; mem. Dept. Def. Acqusition Corp.; mem. bd. advisors U. St. Thomas, St. Paul, 1988—. Mem. Jaycees, Richfield, Minn., 1978-79; coach St. Peter's Sch., Richfield, Minn., 1982-88; chmn. St. Peter's Ch., Richfield, 1983-84; CPR instr. ARC, Mpls., 1984-85; active Habitat for Humanity Blitz Build, Mpls., 1998. Named Civil Servant of Yr., Fed. Exec. Bd., Twin Cities, Minn., 1982, Disting. Employee of Yr., DCASR St. Louis, 1983. Fellow Nat. Contract Mgmt. Assn. (cert. profl. contract mgr. 1991, chmn. Mentor com., sec. 1982-83, treas. 1985-86, v.p. 1986-87); mem. Minn. Street Rod Assn. Republican. Roman Catholic. Avocation: antique vehicle restoration. Home: 1796 Valley Ridge Pl Chanhassen MN 55317-8416 Office: Def Contract Mgmt Command Twin Cities 3001 Metro Dr Bloomington MN 55425-1573

FELLOWS, ALICE COMBS, artist; b. Atlanta, Sept. 14, 1935; d. Andrew Grafton III and Wilhelmina Drummond (Jackson) Combs; m. Robert Ellis Fellows Jr., Aug. 20, 1957 (div. 1978); children: Ariadne Elisabeth Fellows-Mannion, Kara Suzanne. BFA, Syracuse U., 1957; M in Clin. Psychology, Antioch U., 1992. guest artist Yaddo, Saratoga Springs, N.Y., 1991; artist-in-residence Dorland Colony, Temecula, Calif., 1983; guest lectr. psychology seminar UCLA, 1990. Exhibited works in numerous group and one-woman shows including L.A. Mcpl. Art Gallery, C.O.L.A. Fellows Exhbn., 1998, El Camino Coll., 1997, Hunsaker-Schlesinger Gallery, 1996, The Armory Ctr. at Pasadena, 1996, Barnsdall Mcpl. Gallery, 1995, Claremont Grad. Sch. Gallery, 1991, Saxon-Lee Gallery, L.A., 1989, Santa Monica Coll. Gallery Art, 1988, J. Rosenthal Gallery, Chgo., 1986, The Biennial at the Hirshhorn Mus. and Sculpture Garden, Washington, 1986, Kirk de Gooyer Gallery, L.A., 1984, 85, many others; works represented in numerous collections including The Norton Collection, Santa Monica, Broad Found., Santa Monica, Mint Mus., Charlotte, N.C., N.C. Mus. Raleigh, N.C., Security Pacific Corp., L.A., others. Arts commr. City of Santa Monica Arts Commn., 1995-99; mem. artists adv. bd. L.A. Mcpl. Art Gallery at Bransdall, 1998—. Grantee Dale Chihuly grant for Srs. Making Art Workshops, 1996; painting fellow Western States Arts Fedn./NEA, 1990, Getty Trust, 1990, NEA, 1991, City of L.A. Individual Artist's fellow, 1998. Home and Studio: 656 Copeland Ct Santa Monica CA 90405-4416

FELLOWS, DIANA POTENZANO, educational administrator; b. N.Y.C., Aug. 29, 1939; d. Paul John and Frances (Castrovinci) P.; m. William Thomas Fellows, June 16, 1962; children: Paul Warren, Joan Fellows Madden. BA, St. Joseph's Coll., 1960; MA, Fordham U., 1963, Coll. St. Joseph, Rutland, Vt., 1979. Cert. guidance, early childhood, spl. edn. tchr., Vt., N.Y. Tchr. N.Y.C. Pub. Schs., 1960-68; guidance counselor Rutland Pub. Schs., 1968-86, Colchester (Vt.) H.S., 1986-88; dir. guidance Otter Valley Union H.S., Brandon, Vt., 1988-91, Burr & Burton Sem., Manchester, Vt., 1991-94, Colchester Sch. Dist., 1994—; grant writer Rutland N.E. Supervisory Union; bd. dirs. Rutland County Parent/Child Ctr.; presenter in field. Author: School-to-Work Resource Guide, 1997, Crisis Manual, 1997, Workbase Learning Manual, 1998. Vol. Dismiss House of Vt., Rutland, 1988—, Rutland Regional Med. Ctr., 1972-90; mem. Cmty. Choir of Rutland, 1976—; organizer teen vol. program Rutland Hosp., 1972; organizer Rutland County Parent/Child Ctr., 1983; organizer literacy vol. program Otter Valley Union H.S., 1989; bd. dirs. Vt. State Hugh O'Brian Youth Leadership Found., 1993, Lake Champlain Sch.-to-Work Collaborative; crisis intervention specialist Rutland Cen. Supervisory Union; drug/alcohol coord. Colchester Sch. Dist.; edn. specialist Vt. Student Assistance Corp. Grantee in field, 1985-92; named Vt. Counselor of Yr., State Orgn., 1983; recipient Cert. of Merit, Rutland N.E. Supervisory Union, 1989, Lake Champlain Regional Sch. to Work award, 1997. Mem. ACA, New Eng. Conf. for Counseling and Devel. (bd. dirs. 1986—, co-chair Vt. chpt. 1990, bd. dirs. 1990-92), Vt. Assn. Counselors (treas. 1984-86), Vt. Counseling Assn. (membership chair, treas. 1996—), Manchester C. of C. (bd. dirs.), Rotary. Roman Catholic. Avocations: china painting, Chinese caligraphy. Home: 25 Howard Aver Rutland VT 05701 Office: Colchester Sch Dist Blakley Rd Colchester VT 05446

FELLOWS, ESTHER ELIZABETH, musician, music educator; b. Miami, Ariz., Nov. 5, 1952; d. John Wilmont and Flora Elizabeth (Eyestone) Walker; m. James Michael Fellows, Aug. 20, 1976; children: Joy Christine, Rachel Lindsay, Daniel Matthew, Jessica Grace. B in Music Edn., U. Colo., 1975. Co-dir. Children's Piano Lab. U. Colo., Boulder, 1975-76; instr. So. Calif. Conservatory Music, Sun City, 1976-78; pvt. instr. Ft. Lauderdale, 1978-84; instr. Ft. Lauderdale Christian Sch., 1981-83; sect. violinist Okla. Sinfonia/Tulsa Ballet, 1984—, Bartlesville (Okla.) Symphony, 1990—; pvt. instr. Broken Arrow, Okla., 1984—; pvt. instr. Ft. Lauderdale, 1978-84. Mem. Music Tchrs. Nat. Assn. (cert. piano, violin and viola), Suzuki Assn. Am., Hyechka Music Club Tulsa, Tulsa Accredited Music Tchrs. Assn. (chair scholarship com.). Avocations: biking. Home: 19821 S Harvard Ave Mounds OK 74047

FELLOWS, HENRY DAVID, JR., lawyer; b. N.Y.C., Dec. 17, 1954; s. Henry D. Sr. and Mary (Stecko) F.; m. Pam Neal Fellows, May 15, 1982; children: Christopher, Suzanne, Thomas. BSBA, Bucknell U., 1975; JD, Georgetown U., 1978. Bar: Ga. 1978, U.S. Dist. Ct. (no. dist.) Ga. 1978, U.S. Ct. Appeals (11th cir.) 1978, U.S. Supreme Ct. 1997. Law clk. to hon. judge Charles A. Moye Jr. U.S. Dist. Ct. (no. dist.) Ga., Atlanta, 1978-80; assoc. Hurt, Richardson, Garner, Todd & Cadenhead, Atlanta, 1981-87, ptnr., 1987-92; ptnr. Fellows, Johnson & LaBriola, LLP (and predecessor firm), Atlanta, 1993—. Mem. ABA, Ga. Bar Assn., Atlanta Bar Assn. (chmn. ct. com. 1992-98), Lawyers Club of Atlanta. Avocations: tennis, piano. Office: Fellows Johnson & LaBriola LLP Peachtree Ctr # 2300 South 225 Peachtree St NE Atlanta GA 30303-1701

FELLOWS, JERRY KENNETH, lawyer; b. Madison, Wis., Mar. 19, 1946; s. Forrest Garner and Virginia (Witte) F.; m. Patricia Lynn Graves, June 28, 1970; children: Jonathon, Aaron, Daniel. BA in Econs., U. Wis., 1968; JD, U. Minn., 1971. Bar: U.S. Dist. Ct. (no. dist.) Ill. 1971. Ptnr. McDermott, Will & Emery, Chgo., 1971—; speaker Bur. Nat. Affairs, Washington, 1985—. Contbr. articles to profl. jours. Bd. dirs. Midwest Benefits Coun., 1998. Mem. U. Minn. Law Alumni Assn. (bd. visitors), Gamma Eta Gamma. Avocations: coaching track, basketball, baseball. Home: 4541 Middaugh Ave Downers Grove IL 60515-2761 Office: McDermott Will & Emery 227 W Monroe St Ste 3100 Chicago IL 60606-5096*

FELLOWS, MARILYN KINDER, elementary education educator; b. Louisville, July 21, 1952; d. Clyde White and Violet (Nicklies) Kinder; m. Steven Anthony Fellows, Jan 5, 1973; children: Suzann Renee, Amber Marie. BA in Edn., U. Ky., 1974; MS in Edn., U. Louisville, 1978; MS in Counseling, Ind. U. S.E., 1991. Tchr. profoundly handicapped Jefferson County Pub. Schs., Louisville, 1975-77; tchr. learning disabled Greater Clark County Schs., Jeffersonville, Ind., 1977; tchr. 1st grade Greater Clark County Schs., 1977-78; tchr. learning disabled Greater Clark County Schs., 1978-92; coord. spl. needs students Jonathan Jennings/Greater Clark County Schs., 1992-94; 1st grad. tchr., 1994—; chmn. performance based accreditation team Charlestown, Ind., 1988-89, team leader, 1998-99. Leader 4-H, New Wash., Ind. 1989—. Recipient recognition Ind. Dept. Edn., Indpls., 1990, Teacher Excellence award Louisville Courrier Jour. and WHAS-TV, 1992; grantee Greater Clark County Schs., 1989, 90, 99. Mem. ASCD, Internat. Reading Assn., Ind. State Tch. Assn. (presentor 1978). Assn. Supervision Curriculum Devel., Phi Dela Kappa. Avocations: reading, swimming, waterskiing. Home: 7013 Taflinger Rd RR 1 Nabb IN 47147-9801 Office: Jonathan Jennnings Elem 603 Market St Charlestown IN 47111-1973

FELLOWS, ROBERT ELLIS, medical educator, medical scientist; b. Syracuse, N.Y., Aug. 4, 1933; s. Robert Ellis and Clara (Talmadge) F.; m. Karlen Kiger, July 2, 1983; children—Kara, Ari. A.B., Hamilton Coll., 1955; M.D., C.M., McGill U., 1959; Ph.D., Duke U., 1969. Intern N.Y. Hosp., N.Y.C., 1959-60; asst. resident N.Y. Hosp., 1960-61, Royal Victoria Hosp., Montreal, Que., Can., 1961-62; asst. prof. dept. medicine Duke U., Durham, N.C., 1966-76; asst. prof. dept. physiology and pharmacology Duke U., 1966-70, assoc. prof. dept. physiology and pharmacology, asso. dir. med. scientist tng. program, 1970-76; prof., chmn. dept. physiology and biophysics U. Iowa Coll. Medicine, dir. med. sci. tng. program, 1976-97, dir. physician sci. program, 1984-88, dir. neurosci. program, 1984-88; mem. Nat. Pituitary Agy. Adv. Bd.; mem. NIH Population Rsch. Com., 1981-86, VA Career Devel. Rev. Com., 1985-88; cons. NIH, NSF March of Dimes. Mem. editorial bd.: Endocrinology, Am. Jour. Physiology. Mem. AAAS, Am. Chem. Soc., Am. Fedn. Clin. Research, Am. Physiol. Soc., Am. Soc. Biol. Chemists, Am. Soc. Cell Biology, Assn. Chairmen Depts. Physiology, Biochem. Soc., Biophys. Soc., Endocrine Soc., Internat. Soc. Neuroendocrinology, N.Y. Acad. Scis., Soc. for Neurosci., Tissue Culture Assn., Assn. Neuroscience Depts. and Programs (pres. 1995-96), Sigma Xi, Alpha Omega Alpha. Home: 135 Pentire Cir Iowa City IA 52245 Office: 5-660 Bowen Sci Bldg Iowa City IA 52242

FELLOWS, WARD JAY, philosophy educator, minister; b. Chgo., Dec. 6, 1913; s. Norman Jay and Milfred (Myers) F.; m. Ada Louise Johnson, Sept. 18, 1937; children: Milfred L. Fellows Goodall, Catherine C. Fellows Smith, Ward J. Jr. BA, Cornell U., 1936; MDiv, Union Theol. Sem., 1939, STM, 1946, PhD, 1988; MA in Philosophy, U. Calif., Berkeley, 1964. Ordained to ministry Congregational Ch./United Ch. of Christ, 1939. Minister various Congl. chs., 1939-62; prof. in world religions and philosophy of religion Coll. San Mateo (Calif.), 1968-83, prof. emeritus, 1988—; vis. scholar Harvard U. Ctr. for Study of World Religions, Cambridge, Mass., 1982. Author: Religions East and West, 1979, 2d rev. edit., 1998. Chaplain USAAF, 1942-45, ETO. Mem. AAUP, Am. Acad. Religion, Alumni of Deep Springs and Telluride Assn. Democrat. Home: 1139 Parrott Dr San Mateo CA 94402-3626 *There is a struggle between God's good and the evil in the world. The great religions—in spite of their imperfections—help people to stay on God's side.*

FELMAN, MARC DAVID, air force officer; b. Biloxi, Miss., June 19, 1954; s. Harold Arnold and Vivian Kathryn (Knox) F.; m. Pamela Adams, Feb. 29, 1992; 1 child, Marc David. BS in History, USAF Acad., 1976; MS in Systems Mgmt., U. So. Calif., 1982; postgrad., U. Ala., 1990-91; MS in Air Power Art and Sci., USAF Sch. Adv. Airpower Study. Commd. 2d lt. USAF, 1976; advanced through grades to col. USAF, 1996; pilot 909th Air Refueling Squadron, Kadena Air Base, Japan, 1978-80, aircraft commander, 1980-82; flight comdr. 9llth Air Refueling Squadron, Goldsboro, N.C., 1983-85; current ops. planner 68th Air Refueling Wing, Goldsboro, 1985-88, flight examiner, 1988-89; assigned to Air U. faculty Air Command Staff Coll., Montgomery, Ala., 1989-91; 1st class Air Force Sch. for Advanced Airpower Studies, Maxwell AFB, Ala., 1991-92; comdr. 911th Air Refueling Squadron, Goldsboro, N.C., 1992-94; squadron comdr. 711th Air Refueling Squadron, Goldsboro, 1994; strategic planner, strategy divsn. Office Joint Chiefs of Staff, Washington, 1995-97; comdr. 34th Ops. Group, USAF Acad., Colo., 1997-98; Harvard Internat. fellow Weatherhead Ctr. for Internat. Affairs, Harvard U., Cambridge, Mass., 1998-99; asst. dep. chief of staff for plans and policy NATO AirSouth, 1999—. Decorated DFC; recipient Mackay trophy USAF and Nat. Aeros. Assn., 1986, Kalberer trophy SAC, 1986, Jabara trophy USAF Acad., 1988. Mem. Air Force Assn., Daedalians, Am. Legion, USAF Acad. Assn. of Grads., Phi Sigma Alpha. Avocations: music, reading, soccer, golf. Home: 165 Fayerweather St # 1 Cambridge MA 02138-1242 Office: Harvard U Ctr for Internat Affairs 1737 Cambridge St Rm 417 Cambridge MA 02138-3016

FELPER, DAVID MICHAEL, lawyer; b. Springfield, Mass., Dec. 17, 1954; s. Lawrence Allen and Edith Charlotte (Flesher) F.; m. Kimberlee White, May 19, 1979; children: Andrew Martin, Evan Matthew, Scott Tyler. BA in Polit. Sci., George Washington U., 1976; JD cum laude, Western New Eng. Coll., 1980. Bar: Mass. 1980, U.S. Dist. Ct. Mass. 1981, U.S. Ct. Appeals (1st cir.) 1987. Assoc. Michelman & Feinstein, Springfield, 1980-82; asst. regional counsel Dept. Social Services, Commonweatlh of Mass., Springfield, 1982-83; labor relations counsel Sprague Electric Co., Lexington, Mass., 1983-87; assoc. Bowditch & Dewey, Framingham, Mass., 1987-92; ptnr. Bowditch & Dewey, Framingham, 1992—; lectr. various human resource orgns. throughout U.S., 1984—; pres. Valley Tech. Ednl. Found. Inc., 1998—; corporator Milford-Whitinsville Regional Hosp. Bd. dirs. United Way of Tri-County, Hopedale Youth Baseball Assn. Inc.; fin. com. Town of Hopedale. Mem. Mass. Bar Assn. (labor law com., labor and employment sect. coun.), Worcester County Bar Assn. (labor and employment law com.), Blackstone Valley C. of C. (dir.). Avocations: golf, running, reading. Office: Bowditch & Dewey PO Box 9320 Framingham MA 01701-9320

FELS, NICHOLAS WOLFF, lawyer; b. White Plains, N.Y., Mar. 19, 1943; s. Lawrence P. and Fredericka (Gaines) F.; m. Susan T. McEwan, Dec. 28, 1968; 1 child, Sarah. BA, Harvard U., 1964; MA, U. Calif., Berkeley, 1965; LLB, Harvard U., 1968. Bar: N.Y. 1968, Calif. 1970, U.S. Dist. Ct. (cen. dist.) Calif. 1970, D.C. 1971, U.S. Dist. Ct. D.C. 1971, U.S. Ct. Appeals (10th cir.) 1976, U.S. Ct. Appeals (D.C. cir.) 1977, U.S. Supreme Ct. 1978, U.S. Ct. Appeals (4th cir.) 1979, U.S. Ct. Appeals (8th cir.) 1981, U.S. Ct. Appeals (5th cir.) 1982. Law clk. to Hon. John Minor Wisdom U.S. Ct. Appeals, New Orleans, 1968-69; atty. OEO Legal Services, Los Angeles, 1969-70; assoc. Covington & Burling, Washington, 1970-76, ptnr., 1976—; mem. Nat. Com. on U.S.-China Relations, N.Y.C., 1982—. Contbr. articles to profl. jours. Mem. Fed. Energy Bar Assn., D.C. Appleseed Ctr. (bd. dirs. 1994—, pres. 1996—). Home: 3534 Edmunds St NW Washington DC 20007-1431 Office: Covington & Burling PO Box 7566 1201 Pennsylvania Ave NW Washington DC 20044-7566

FELS, ROBERT ALAN, psychotherapist; b. Phila., Apr. 24, 1954; s. Joseph and Lenore F. BS, Pa. State U., 1974; MA, John F. Kennedy U., 1980; MS, Miami Inst. of Psychology, 1998. Lic. marriage and family therapist; cert. by the Biofeedback Cert. Inst. of Am. Probation officer Broward County Probation, Ft. Lauderdale, Fla., 1979; family counselor Child Protective Svcs., State of Fla., Plantation, Fla., 1981-84; psychotherapist Jewish Family Svc., Boca Raton, Fla., 1984-88, Ctr. for Psychol. Svcs., Boca Raton, 1987-90; dir. biofeedback svcs. Lake Hosp., Lake Worth, Fla., 1990-92; pvt. practice psychotherapy Boca Raton, Fla., 1990—; facilitator Stop Smoking Clinic, Am. Cancer Soc., Boca Raton, 1987-93. Fellow Am. Bd. Vocational Experts, Am. Acad Pain Mgmt.; mem. Am. Assn. for Marriage and Family Therapy, Assn. for Applied Psychophysiology and Biofeedback. Jewish. Avocations: eastern philosophy and practice. Office: 20423 State Road 7 Ste 231 Boca Raton FL 33498-6797

FELSEN, LEOPOLD B., engineering educator. DEE, Polytechnic Inst. Bklyn., 1952; D (hon.), Tech. U. Denmark, 1979. Prof. Polytechnic Inst. N.Y., 1961-78, dean engring., 1975-78, inst. prof., 1978-85; prof. Polytechnic U., 1985-94, Dept. Aerospace & Mech. Engring., Boston U.; vis. disting. prof. Northeastern U., 1991-94; vis. lectr. Soviet Acad. Sci., 1967, 71, 88; fellow Guggenheim Meml. fellow, 1973-73; vis. mem. Faculty Math & Physics Charles U., Prague, 1984; vis. Sackler fellow Tel Aviv U., 1985; vis. scholar Acoust Inst., Academia Sinica, Beijing, 1985; vis. prof. Nat. Defense Acad., Japan, 1985. Recipient citation Sigma Xi, Van der Pol Gold medal Internat. Union Radio Science IEEE, 1975, Heinrich Hertz medal, 1991. Fellow IEEE, Internat. Union Radio Science, Optical Soc. Am., Acoustic Soc. Am.; mem. Nat. Acad. Engring. Home: Brook House 33 Pond Ave Brookline MA 02445-7128

FELSENFELD, GARY, government official, scientist; b. N.Y.C., Nov. 18, 1929; (married), 1956; 3 children. A.B., Harvard, 1951; Ph.D. in Chemistry (NSF fellow), Calif. Inst. Tech., 1955; postgrad. (NSF fellow), Oxford (Eng.) U., 1954-55. Officer NIH, USPHS, HEW, 1955-58; chief phys. chemistry sect., lab. molecular biology Nat. Inst. Diabetes, Digestive and Kidney Diseases, 1961—; asst. prof. biophysics U. Pitts., 1958-61; cons. NIMH, 1958-61; vis. prof. Harvard, 1963; Merck disting. lectr. Rutgers U., 1977. Mem. editorial bd.: Jour. Biol. Chemistry, 1965-70, Jour. Molecular Biology, 1967-73, Biophys. Chemistry, 1973-76, Biopolymers, 1975-77, Ann. Rev. of Biochemistry, 1975-80, Quar. Rev. of Biophysics, 1975-88, Cell, 1979-95, Jour. Molecular and Cellular Biology, 1980-84, Development, 1992, Genes to Cells, 1996—. Recipient Merck award Am. Soc. Biol. Chemists, 1987, Disting. Presdl. Rank award U.S. Govt., 1988. Fellow AAAS; mem. Am. Chem. Soc., Am. Biophys. Soc., Am. Assn. Biol. Chemists, Nat. Acad. Scis., Am. Acad. Arts and Scis. Office: Nat Inst Diabetes Digestive and Kidney Diseases Lab Molecular Biology Bethesda MD 20892*

FELSENSTEIN, FRANK ARJEH, educator; b. London, July 28, 1944; came to U.S., 1998; s. Ernest Maurice and Vera Lotte F.; m. Carole Alison Jaffe, Dec. 22, 1985; children: Kenny, Joanna. BA with honors, U. Leeds, England, 1966, PhD, 1971. Asst. lectr. English U. Geneva, Switzerland, 1968-70; lectr. English U. Leeds, England, 1971-86, sr. lectr. English, 1986-96, reader 18th century studies, 1996-98; vis. prof. English Vanderbilt U., Nashville, 1989-90, YEshiva U., N.Y.C., 1998—, Drew U., Madison, N.J., 1998—. Author: Anti-Semitic Stereotypes, 1995; editor: Travels Through France and Italy, 1979, A Practical Treatise to Flowers, 1985. Mem. Am. Soc. 18th Century Studies. Jewish. Avocations: antiquarian books and prints. Home: 8 Manor Dr Morristown NJ 07960-2611

FELSENTHAL, GERALD, physiatrist, educator; b. N.Y.C., Aug. 27, 1941; s. Richard and Fay (Braunspiegel) F.; m. Diane Shretter, June 6, 1964; children: David, Steven, Suzann. BA, NYU, 1963; MD, Albany Med. Coll., 1967. Diplomate Am. Bd. Phys. Medicine and Rehab., Am. Bd. Electrodiagnostic Medicine. Rotating intern USPHS Hosp., Seattle, 1967-68; resident in phys. medicine and rehab. Bronx Mcpl. Hosp. Ctr., Albert Einstein Coll. Medicine, 1970-73; assoc. physiatrist Sinai Hosp., Balt., 1973-76, assoc. chief, 1976-86, chief dept. rehab. medicine, 1986—; head div. rehab. medicine Levindale Hebrew Geriatric Ctr. and Hosp., Balt., 1983—; dir. residency tng. prog. in phys. medicine and rehab. Sinai Hosp.-Johns Hopkins U., 1986—; assoc. prof. U. Md. Coll. Medicine, Balt., 1987-92, prof., 1992—; assoc. prof. Johns Hopkins U. Sch. Medicine, 1989—. Editor of book Rehab of Aging and Elderly Patient and articles to profl. jours. Surgeon USPHS, 1967-70. Mem. Phys. Medicine and Rehab (residency review com. 1990, vice chmn. 1994, chmn. 1996—), Am. Bd. Phys. Medicine and Rehab. (bd. dirs. 1993—, treas. 1998), Am. Assn. Electrodiagnostic Medicine (bd. dirs. 1990-93), AMA, Am. Geriat Soc., Am. Acad. Phys. Med. and Rehab., Assn. Acad. Physiatrists. Avocation: horticulture. Office: Sinai Hosp Dept Rehab Med 2401 W Belvedere Ave Baltimore MD 21215-5216

FELSENTHAL, STEVEN ALTUS, lawyer; b. Chgo., May 21, 1949; s. Jerome and Eve (Altus) F.; m. Carol Judith Greenberg, June 14, 1970; children: Rebecca Elizabeth, Julia Alison, Daniel Louis Altus. AB, U. Ill.,

1971; JD, Harvard U., 1974. Bar: Ill. 1974, U.S. Dist. Ct. (no. dist.) Ill. 1974, U.S. Ct. Claims 1975, U.S. Tax Ct. 1975, U.S. Ct. Appeals (7th cir.) 1981. Assoc. Levenfeld, Kanter, Baskes & Lippitz Chgo., 1974-78, ptnr. Levenfeld & Kanter, Chgo., 1978-80; ptnr. Levenfeld, Eisenberg, Janger, Glassberg & Lippitz, Chgo., 1980-84; sr. ptnr. Sugar, Friedberg & Felsenthal, Chgo., 1984—; lectr. Kent Coll. Law, Ill. Inst. Tech., Chgo., 1978-80. Mem. ABA, Ill. State Bar Assn., Chgo. Bar Assn., Chgo. Coun. Lawyers, Harvard Law Soc. Ill., Phi Beta Kappa. Clubs: Standard, Harvard (Chgo.). Office: Sugar Friedberg & Felsenthal 30 N La Salle St Ste 2600 Chicago IL 60602-2506

FELSTED, CARLA MARTINDELL, librarian, travel writer; b. Barksdale Field, La., June 21, 1947; d. David Aldenderfer Martindell and Dorthe (Hetland) Horton; m. Robert Earl Luna, Aug. 24, 1968, (div. 1972); m. Hugh Herbert Felsted, Nov. 2, 1974. BA in English, So. Meth. U., 1968, MA in History, 1974; MLS, Tex. Woman's U., 1978. Cert. secondary tchr., Tex.; cert. learning resources specialist, Tex. Tchr. Bishop Lynch High Sch., Dallas, 1968-72, Lake Highlands Jr. High Sch., Richardson, Tex., 1973-75; instr. Richland Coll., Richardson, Tex., 1973-76; library asst. So. Meth. U., Dallas, 1977-78; librarian Tracy-Locke Advt., Dallas, 1978-79; corp. librarian Am. Airlines, Inc., Ft. Worth, 1979-84; research librarian McKinsey & Co., Dallas, 1984-85; reference librarian St. Edward's U., Austin, Tex., 1985—, assoc. prof., 1994—; ptnr. Southwind Info. Svcs. and Southwind Bed-Breakfast, Wimberley, Tex., 1985-92; bd. dirs. Women's S.W. Fed. Credit Union, 1978-81. Editor, compiler: Youth and Alcohol Abuse, 1986; co-editor Mexican Meanderings, 1991—; contbr. to Frommer's travel guides, 1991-96. Mem. adv. bd. Sch. Libr. and Info. Scis., Tex. Women's U., Denton, 1982-84; mem. curriculum com. Wimberley Ind. Sch. Dist., 1986; bd. dirs. Hays-Caldwell Coun. on Alcohol and Drug Abuse, San Marcos, Tex., 1986-88, Inst. Cultures for Wimberley Valley, 1989-91, Tex. Alliance Human Needs, 1992-96; co-capt. Tex. Team Survivor, Danskin Triathlon, 1998—; vol. Breast Cancer Resource Ctr., 1998—. Grantee St. Edward's U., 1986-89, 96. Mem. ALA, Tex. Libr. Assn. (dist. program com., membership com. 1986-88, Tex.-Mex. rels. com. 1992—), Wimberley C. of C. (bd. dirs. 1987-88). Unitarian. Avocations: regional and ethnic cooking, physical fitness, art history, travel. Home: PO Box 33057 Austin TX 78764-0057

FELTEAU, ANNE L., patient care consultant; b. Benton Harbor, Mich., Mar. 16, 1942; d. Frank and Anne (Figlus) Graziano; m. Leonel Felteau, Aug. 31, 1963; children: Leonel, Wesley, Douglas. Diploma in nursing, Meml. Hosp., South Bend, Ind., 1963; BBA, Mercer U., 1984; MBA, Ga. Coll., 1986. RN, Ga., Mich.; C.N.A.A., C.H.E. and NMCC cert. Staffing mgr. Med. Ctr. of Cen. Ga., Macon, 1980-85; project coord. nursing info. systems Gwinnett Hosp. System, Lawrenceville, Ga., 1986-88; product mgr., nursing info. systems, nurse cons. SunHealth Corp., Atlanta, 1988-90; program mgr. nursing svcs. HBO & Co., Atlanta, 1990-92; dir. bus. affairs, nursing Grady Health System, Atlanta, 1992—. Mem. ANA, Am. Soc. Higher Edn., Am. Coll. Healthcare Execs., Am. Orgn. Nurse Execs., Healthcare Info. Mgmt. Systems Soc., Ga. Nurses Assn., Ga. Orgn. Nurse Execs., Healthcare Fin. Mgmt. Assn., Sigma Theta Tau. Home: 116 Olde Marietta Ct Marietta GA 30060-1365

FELTENSTEIN, HARRY DAVID, JR., chemical executive; b. St. Joseph, Mo., Nov. 6, 1920; s. Harry David and Isabel (Rosenbaum) F.; m. Rosalie Goldstein, Jan. 18, 1945 (dec. Sept. 1977); children: Andrew, Martha; m. Carmen Arechabala Fernandez, Aug. 24, 1979; 1 son, Henry. *Mr. Feltenstein son, Andrew, received his BA from Harvard and his PhD from Yale. He is currently a Professor of Economics at Virginia Tech and a consultant to World Bank, International Monetary Fund and Asia Development Bank. His daughter, Martha, received her BA in 1975 from Princeton and her M. Phil. in 1977 from the London School of African and Oriental Studies, University of London. She received her JD in 1981 from Columbia Law School. She is currently a partner at Skadden, Arps, Slate, Meagher & Flom.* B.S., Harvard U., 1942. Engaged in book pub., 1946-50; with Merrill Lynch, Pierce, Fenner & Smith, 1951-57, Lithium Corp., Am. Inc., N.Y.C., 1957-69; financial v.p., treas. Lithium Corp., Am. Inc., 1957-58, exec. v.p., treas., 1958-60, pres., treas., 1960-69; pres., dir. Beryllium Metals & Chems. Corp., 1962-69, Gt. Salt Lake Minerals and Chems. Corp., 1967-69; exec. v.p., dir. Gulf Resources & Chem. Corp., 1967-69; pres., bd. dirs. Fuel Mgmt. Corp., Washington, 1970-94, chmn., 1995—; pres., bd. dirs. Internat. Wine Investors, Ltd., 1972-86, Wildenstein & Co., 1972-74; European rep. C & K Coal Co. div. Gulf Resources & Chem. Corp., 1981-82; cons. to Spanish govt. cos., 1990—. Served with USNR, 1942-46. Address: Calle Lerez 4, Madrid 2, Spain

FELTER, EDWIN LESTER, JR., judge; b. Washington, Aug. 11, 1941; s. Edwin L. Felter and Bertha (Peters) Brekke; m. Yoko Yamauchi-Koito, Dec. 26, 1969. BA, U. Tex., 1964; JD, Cath. U. of Am., 1967. Bar: Colo. 1970, U.S. Dist. Ct. Colo. 1970, U.S. Ct. Appeals (10th cir.) 1971, U.S. Supreme Ct. 1973, U.S. Tax Ct. 1979, U.S. Ct. Claims 1979, U.S. Ct. Internat. Trade 1979. Dep. pub. defender State of Colo., Ft. Collins, 1971-75; asst. atty. gen. Office of the Atty. Gen., Denver, 1975-80; state adminstrv. law judge Colo. Divsn. of Adminstrv. Hearings, Denver, 1980-83, chief adminstrv. law judge, 1983—; disciplinary prosecutor Supreme Ct. Grievance Com., 1975-78. Contbg. editor Internat. Franchising, 1970. Mem. Colo. State Mgmt. Cert. Steering Com., 1983-86; No. Colo. Criminal Justice Planning Coun., Ft. Collins, 1973-75; bd. dirs., vice chmn. The Point Cmty. Crisis Ctr., Ft. Collins, 1971-73; mem. Denver County Dem. Party Steering Com., 1978-79, chmn. 12th legis. dist., 1978-79; bd. dirs., pres. Denver Internat. Program, 1989-90. Mem. ABA, Nat. Conf. Adminstrv. Law Judges (vice chmn.), Colo. Bar Assn. (chmn. grievance policy com. 1991-94, interprofl. com. 1995—), Arapahoe County Bar Assn., Nat. Assn. Adminstrv. Law Judges (pres. Colo. chpt. 1982-84, Nat. Fellowship winner 1994), Am. Inns of Ct. (master level 1996—). Office: Colo Divsn Adminstrv Hearings 1120 Lincoln St Ste 1400 Denver CO 80203-2140

FELTER, JOHN KENNETH, lawyer; b. Monmouth, N.J., May 9, 1950; s. Joseph Harold and Rosanne (Bautz) F. BA magna cum laude, MA in Econs., Boston Coll., 1972; JD cum laude, Harvard U., 1975. Bar: Mass. 1975, U.S. Dist. Ct. Mass. 1976, U.S. Ct. Appeals (1st cir.) 1977, U.S. Supreme Ct. 1982, U.S. Tax Ct. 1993. Assoc. Goodwin, Procter & Hoar, Boston, 1975-83, ptnr., 1983—; spl. asst. gen. Commonwealth of Mass., 1982-84, 94-95; spl. counsel Town of Plymouth, Mass., Town of Salisbury, Mass., Town of Edgartown, Mass.; spl. outside counsel City of Boston, 1990-92; mem. devel. com. Greater Boston Legal Svcs., 1982—, bd. dirs., 1980—, mem. exec. com., 1989-93; mem. faculty Mass. Continuing Legal Edn., Inc., Boston. Mem. adv. com. The Boston Plan for Excellence in Pub. Schs.; mem. elem. edn. com. Blue Ribbon Commn. on Cmty. Learning Ctrs.; VIP panelist Easter Seals Telethon, Boston, 1978-79. Fellow Mass. Bar Found.; mem. ABA (litigation sect., gen. practice sect., mem. personal rights litigation com. environ. law sect., mem. ABA-Am. Law Inst. com. on continuing edn.), Am. Arbitration Assn. (comml. arbitrator), Mass. Bar Assn. (co-chmn. edn. com. pub. law sect.), Boston Bar Assn. (bd. dirs. law firm resources project 1985—, mem. coll. and univ. law com. 1986—, chmn. fed. rules com. litigation sect. 1994), Greater Boston C. of C. (mem. edn. com., mem. health care com.). Office: Goodwin Procter & Hoar Exchange Pl 53 State St Boston MA 02109-2803*

FELTHEIMER, JON, entertainment company executive. Pres. Columbia Tristar TV; exec. v.p. Sony Pictures Entertainment Inc. Office: Sony Pictures Entertainment Inc 10202 Washington Blvd Culver City CA 90232-3119*

FELTON, CYNTHIA, educational administrator; b. Chgo., Apr. 1, 1950; d. Robert Lee Felton Sr. and Julia Mae (Cheton) Felton-Phillips. BA, Northeastern, 1970; MEd, National Coll., 1984; MA, DePaul U., 1988; PhD, Loyola U., Chgo., 1992. Cert. tchr, adminstrv., Ill. Tchr. Chgo. Pub. Schs., 1971-86, adminstr., 1986-89, asst. prin., 1989-92, prin., 1992—; dir. Chgo. Acad. for Sch. Leadership, 1997—. Mem. ASCD, Nat. Staff Devel. Coun., Nat. Coun. Tchrs. Math, Nat. Coun. Suprs. Math, Ill. Coun. Tchrs. Math (bd. dirs. 1992-95). Office: Chgo Acad Sch Leadership 221 N Lasalle St Chicago IL 60601-1206

FELTON, GORDON H., retired publishing executive; b. New Virginia, Iowa, Nov. 20, 1925; s. Elmer Harold and Velda Ann (Frederick) F.; m. Elizabeth Lanza, July 22, 1961. BA, Rollins Coll., Winter Park, Fla., 1946; MA, U. Denver, 1951, U. D.C., 1987. Asst. to v.p. Look mag., N.Y.C., 1960-64; bus. mgr. Cowles Communications Books Co., N.Y.C., 1965-67; v.p. Cambridge Book Co., N.Y.C., 1968-70; gen. mgr. publs. NEA, Washington, 1971-91, ret., 1991. Served with AUS, 1950-52. Home: 4615 N Park Ave Chevy Chase MD 20815-4509

FELTON, GUY PAGE, III, website publisher, consultant; b. Spartanburg, S.C., May 21, 1937; s. Guy Page II and Winnie Nell (Thomas) F. BS in Edn, SUNY, Oneonta, 1961. CEO Guy P. Felton & Assocs., Reno, 1983-86, Resume Cons. Internat., Reno, 1986-90, Career Cons. Internat., Reno, 1990-96, Webitor Internet U.S.A., Reno, Nev., 1996—. Pub. Internet Mag., 1996—; pub. cons. for book Sonic Boom vs. The American Way, 1987, Airspace Blues, 1989; columnist on govtl. affairs The Daily Sparks Tribune, 1992-93. Mem. charter com. City of Reno, 1994; candidate for mayor Reno, Nev., 1995.

FELTON, JEAN SPENCER, physician; b. Oakland, Calif., Apr. 27, 1911; s. Herman and Tess (Davidson) F.; m. Janet E. Birnbaum, June 27, 1937 (dec.); children: Gary, Keith, Robin; m. Suzanne E. Colvin, Sept. 2, 1990. AB, Stanford U., 1931, MD, 1935. Diplomate: Am. Bd. Preventive Medicine, Am. Bd. Indsl. Hygiene. Intern Mt. Zion Hosp., San Francisco, 1934-35; resident in surgery Mt. Zion Hosp., 1935-36, Dante Hosp., San Francisco, 1936-38; practice medicine San Francisco, 1938-40; guest lectr. indsl. sociology U. Tenn. at Knoxville, 1946-53; med. dir. Oak Ridge Nat. Lab., 1946-53; cons. dept. medicine, prof. dept. preventive medicine, pub. health U. Okla. Med. Sch., 1953-58; cons. indsl. hygiene Okla. State Dept. Health, 1953-58; past cons. VA, St. Louis area; prof. occupational health U. Calif. Schs. Medicine and Pub. Health, Los Angeles, 1958-68; dir. occupational health service Dept. Personnel, County Los Angeles, 1968-74; med. dir. occupational health Naval Regional Med. Center, Long Beach, Calif., 1974-78; clin. prof. community medicine U. So. Calif., 1968-82, clin. prof. emeritus, 1982—; clin. prof. medicine U. Calif., Irvine, 1975—; cons. occupational health NASA, USN, VA, AEC, USPHS, Social Security Adminstrn., 1955-62; Fellow through Distinction faculty occupational medicine Royal Coll. Physicians, London, 1997—. Author: (with A. H. Katz) Health and Community, 1965, Man, Medicine, and Work, 1965, Occupational Medical Management, 1990; bd. dirs. Excerpta Medica, Sect. XXXV, The Netherlands; mem. editl. panel Occupational Medicine, London, 1994—; contbr. articles to med. jours. Past mem. youth svc. com. Oak Ridge Welfare Coun., 1946-53; past mem. Tenn. Commn. on Childen, Welfare Svcs. Dept.; chmn., mem. adv. bd. Oak Ridge; past mem. Gov.'s Com. on Utilization Physically Handicapped Pres.'s Com. on Employment People with Disabilities, 1947-94. Lt. col. M.C., 1940-46. Decorated Army Commendation Ribbon, 1946; recipient Citation for Excellence in Med. Authorship by Am. Assn. Indsl. Physicians and Surgeons, 1948; Knudsen award Indsl. Med. Assn., 1968; Physician of Yr. award Calif. Gov.'s Com. on Employment of Handicapped, 1979; Physician of Yr. award Pres.'s Com. on Employment of Handicapped, 1979. Fellow Am. Coll. Preventive Medicine (pres. 1966-67), Am. Acad. Occupational Medicine, Am. Occupational Med. Assn. (Meritorious Svc. award 1965, Health Achievement in Industry award 1983), Am. Pub. Health Assn., Collegium Ramazzini (coun. of fellows 1994—); mem. AMA (sec., vice chmn. sect. preventive and indsl. medicine and pub. health 1949-53, chmn. sect. 1953), Am. Indsl. Hygiene Assn., Nat. Rehab. Assn. So. Calif. (dir.), So. Calif. Ind. Hygiene Assn. (past pres.), Am. Coll. Occupational Medicine (Robert A. Kehoe award 1989), New Eng. Occupational Med. Assn. (Harriet F. Hardy award 1989), Soc. Occupational Medicine (hon.). Unitarian. Prepared standard operating procedure of U.S. Army indsl. med. program at San Francisco Port of Embarkation (adopted by the U.S. Army Chief of Transp. for use by all Ports of Embarkation). Home: PO Box 246 45150 Cypress Dr Mendocino CA 95460-9796 Office: U Calif Dept Medicine Nelson Rsch Ctr Bldg Med Sci Complex Irvine CA 92717 *Irrespective of the occupation or professional ladder one ascends, skills in basic written and spoken communication are mandatory. It is essential in this period of frequent misquotation by overeager media that one's ideas are correctly conveyed and that one's feelings are accurately transmitted.*

FELTON, JULE WIMBERLY, JR., lawyer; b. Macon, Ga., July 22, 1932; s. Jule Wimberly and Mary Julia (Sasnett) F.; m. Kate Gillis, May 15, 1965; children—Jule Wimberly III, Mary Katherine, Laura Borden. Student, Emory U., Atlanta, 1949-50; A.B., U. Ga., Athens, 1954, LL.B, 1955. Bar: Ga. 1954. Assoc. Hansell & Post, Atlanta, 1955-59, mng. ptnr., 1959-89; sr. of counsel Jones Day Reavis & Pogue, Atlanta, 1989-92; ptnr. Ford & Felton, 1993-95, Proctor, Felton & Atkinson, Atlanta, 1995-96, Proctor, Felton & Chambers, Atlanta, 1996-99; of counsel Peterson & Harris, Atlanta, 1999—. Mem. Ga. Gen. Assembly, Atlanta, 1969-72; mem. ofcl. bd. dirs. Northside United Meth. Ch., Atlanta, 1974-85, 88; mem. U. Ga. Bd. Visitors, 1986, 87, 91, chmn., 1987-88, 93-94. 1st lt. JAGC, U.S. Army, 1955-56. Fellow Am. Bar Found.; mem. ABA, Ga. Bar Assn. (pres. 1973-74), Nat. Conf. Bar Pres., Am. Coll. Trial Lawyers, Ga. Bar Found., Am. Judicature Soc., U. Ga. Law Sch. Assn. (pres. 1984-85), Lawyers Club Atlanta, Old War Horse Lawyers Club (pres. Atlanta chpt. 1983), Piedmont Driving Club, Capital City Club. Avocations: piano; golf; boating. Home: 1061 Arbor Trce NE # 34 Atlanta GA 30319-5381 Office: Peterson & Harris Lennox Towers Ste 1725 3400 Pete St Rd Atlanta GA 30326*

FELTON, NORMAN FRANCIS, motion picture producer; b. London, Apr. 29, 1913; came to U.S., 1929, naturalized, 1939; s. John Thomas and Gertrude Anne (Francis) F.; m. Aline Stotts, Sept. 15, 1940 (dec. Apr. 1996); children: Julie Anne, John Christopher, Aline Elizabeth. BFA, U. Iowa, 1939, MA, 1940. Dir., St. Paul Civic Theatre, 1940-41, Saginaw (Mich.) Civic Theatre, 1941-42, prodr., NBC Radio, Chgo., 1944-48, exec. prodr. ctrl. divsn., NBC TV, 1948-50; dir.: Robert Montgomery TV dramatic series, 1950-54; writer, dir. TV dramas, N.Y.C., 1950-56; prodr.: Studio One, CBS-TV, 1957-59; exec. prodr., CBS West Coast, 1959-60; dir. TV programs, 1960-61, TV films, Metro-Goldwyn-Mayer, 1961—; pres., Arena Prodns., 1961—; developed TV series: The Psychiatrist; also produced: (features) To Trap a Spy, 1964; features The Spy With My Face, 1965, One Spy Too Many, 1966, The Spy in the Green Hat, 1966, The Karate Killers, 1967, The Helicopter Spies, 1967, How to Steal the World, 1968, God Bless the Children, 1970; exec. prodr.: TV series The Psychiatrist, 1971, Baffled, The Man from U.N.C.L.E., 1972; TV feature Hawkins on Murder, 1973; prodr.: TV film Babe, 1975, Executive Suite, 1976, And Your Name is Jonah, 1979. Bd. dirs. Nat. Coalition to Abolish Death Penalty, Death Penalty Focus, Inc.; estab. Felton Media Scholars Program, Ctr. for Media Literacy. Recipient Emmy award for TV direction, 1953, Sylvania award for Directing Achievement, 1952, 56, 76, 79, Christopher award, 1954, 56, 75, 79, TV Guide Gold medal, 1952, TV Guide award 1963, 64, Aline and Norman Felton Commitment to Justice award, 1997; others; Norman Felton Prodr. of Yr. award named in his honor Prodrs. Guild Am. Mem. Prodrs. Guild Am. (past pres.), Caucus Prodrs., Writers and Dirs. Am. (co-chmn.).

FELTON, SAMUEL PAGE, biochemist; b. Petersburg, Va., Sept. 7, 1919; s. Samuel S. and Pearl (Williams) F.; m. Helen Florence Martin, Dec. 31, 1955; 1 child, Samuel Page. Degree in pharmacy, U.S. Army, San Francisco, 1942; BS in Chemistry, U. Wash., 1951, postgrad., 1954. Chief technician U. Wash., Seattle, 1952-59, research assoc., 1959-62, sr. research assoc., 1976—, dir. cen. facilities lab. anesthesiology, 1969-73, dir. water quality lab., 1973-83, dir. biochem. lab. sch. of Fisheries, 1983-85; emeritus, micro-nutrition, rsch. and health in salmonids Sch. Fisheries, U. Wash., Seattle, 1985—; asst. mem., asst. to dir. div. biochemistry Scripps Clinic and Research Found., La Jolla, Calif., 1962-66; asst. biochemist Children's Orthopedic Hosp., Seattle, 1966-68; vis. scientist Va. Inst. Marine Scis. at Coll. William and Mary, Williamsburg, 1985. Mem. bd. of adjustments City of Edmonds, Wash., Shoreline Mgmt. Commn., Snohomish County, Wash. Served to sgt. MC, U.S. Army 1941-45. Fellow Am. Inst. Chemists; mem. Am. Chem. Soc., Am. Inst. Fishery Research Biologists, N.Y. Acad. of Scis., Soc. Exptl. Biology and Medicine. Avocations: sailing, music, travel. Office: U Wash Fisheries Rsch & Teaching PO Box 355100 Seattle WA 98195-5100

FELTON, WARREN LOCKER, II, surgeon; b. Bartlesville, Okla., Oct. 25, 1925; s. Warren Locker and Elizabeth (Keller) F.; m. Judith Ann Mead, July 25, 1969; children: Warren Locker, III, Susan Elizabeth Felton Skove, Richard John Conrad, Alecia Ann Felton George, Christina Jane. B.S., Washington U., St. Louis, 1949, M.D., 1949. Diplomate: Am. Bd. Surgery, Am. Bd. Thoracic Surgery. Intern, then resident in surgery and instr. Yale-New Haven Med. Center, 1949-56; practice medicine specializing in thoracic and vascular surgery Oklahoma City, 1958-86; med. dir. Okla. Found. for Peer Rev. Inc., Oklahoma City, 1986-91; mem. staff Mercy Health Center, St. Anthony Hosp., Baptist Med. Center; clin. prof. U. Okla. Med. Sch. Contbr. articles to med. jours. Bd. dirs. Travelers Aid Soc., Oklahoma City, 1961-64; mem. U. Okla. Assocs., 1980; bd. dirs. City Health Dept., Oklahoma City, 1987-96; mayor Nichols Hills, Okla., 1993-94, 96-97, 99—. Served with USN, 1943-45, with M.C., U.S. Army, 1956-58. Mem. AMA, A.C.S., Am. Thoracic Soc., Am. Assn. Thoracic Surgery, Soc. Thoracic Surgeons, Southwestern Surg. Congress, Sigma Xi, Alpha Omega Alpha. Episcopalian. Club: Oklahoma City Golf and Country. Home: 1612 Dorchester Dr Oklahoma City OK 73120-1205

FELTS, MARGARET DAVIS, librarian, bibliographer; b. Walla Walla, Wash., Jan. 26, 1917; d. Schuyler Ernest and Blanche Marie (Fischer) Davis; m. Wells Carter Felts, June 20, 1940 (div. 1966); children: Carol Margaret, Thomas William, Helen Elizabeth. StaBA, Stanford U., 1938; MLS, U. Calif., Berkeley, 1965. Libr. Mills Coll., Oakland, Calif., 1965-68; libr., bibliographer U. Calif., Santa Cruz, 1968-85; ret. Author: Archives of the South Pacific Commission and Related Papers, 1971; contbr. to Catalog of the South Pacific Collection, 1978; Selection of Library Materials for Area Studies, 1990, Part IV: The South Pacific: Polynesia, Micronesia, Melanesia, 1990.

FELTS, WILLIAM ROBERT, JR., physician; b. Judsonia, Ark., Apr. 24, 1923; s. Wylie Robert and Willie Etidorpha (Lewis) F.; m. Jeanne E. Kennedy, Feb. 17, 1954 (div. 1971); children: William R. III, Thomas Wylie, Samuel Clay, Melissa Jeanne; m. Lila Mitchell Dudley, Feb. 14, 1987 (dec. Feb., 1993). BS, U. Ark., 1944, MD, 1946. Intern Garfield Meml. Hosp., Washington, 1946-47; resident in medicine Gallinger Mcpl. Hosp., Washington, 1949-51; resident in medicine George Washington U. Hosp., 1951-53, trainee in rehab. (rheumatology), 1955-57; asst. chief arthritis rsch. unit VA Hosp., Washington, 1953-54, adj. asst. chief, 1954-58, chief, 1958-62; cons. in rheumatology U.S. Naval Hosp., Bethesda, Md., 1959-70; mem. faculty dept. medicine George Washington U., instr., 1957-59, asst. prof., 1959-62, assoc. prof., 1962-80, prof., 1980-93, prof. emeritus, 1993—, dir. divsn. rheumatology, 1970-79, mem. univ. faculty senate exec. com., 1991-93; mem. Nat. Commn. on Arthritis and Related Musculoskeletal Diseases, 1975-76, Nat. Arthritis adv. bd., 1977-80, 90-93, nat. com. on health policy Project Hope, 1977, steering com. Health Policy Agenda for Am. People, 1982-87, Nat. Com. Vital and Health Stats., 1983-87, 88-91; mem. adv. com. on disabilities White House Conf. on Aging, 1995; mem. D.C. Health Planning Adv. Com., 1969-72, WHO Task Force on Rheumatology in Developing Countries, 1982, 84; mem. U.S. del. to 10th Revision Conf. Internat. Classification of Diseases; chmn. med. adv. com. D.C. chpt. Arthritis Found., 1963-85, vice chmn. of chpt. bd. dirs., 1983-94, chmn., 1992-96; bd. dirs. Symposium on Computer Applications in Med. Care, 1980-88, pres.-elect, 1982-83, pres., 1983-84; cons. health affairs and mem. profl. adv. bd. Control Data Corp., 1976-83, Nat. Ctr. for Health Stats., 1991-93. Author articles in field, especially med. socioecons.; mem. editorial adv. bd., cons. internal medicine Current Procedural Terminology, 3d edit., 1972-73; editorial adv. bd. Internal Medicine News, 1976-93. Bd. dirs. Nat. Capital Med. Found., 1979-84, pres., 1980-81. Served with AUS, 1947-49. Recipient Disting. Svc. award AMA, 1996. Master Am. Coll. Rheumatology, 1992; fellow Am. Coll. Med. Informatics; mem. Nat. Acads. of Practice (pres. 1993-96), Nat. Acad. Practice in Medicine (chmn. 1991-93), Am. Soc. Internal Medicine (dir. 1968-78, pres. 1976-77), AMA (mem. coun. on legis. 1980-90, chmn. 1985-87, chmn. editl. adv. panel CPT-4 1980-92), Inst. Medicine of NAS, D.C. Med. Soc. (chmn. legis. com. 1972-76, 76-78), D.C. Soc. Internal Medicine (mem. exec. coun. 1975-78), So. Med. Assn. (sec. sect. internal medicine 1978-79, vice-chmn. 1979-80, chmn. 1980-81, assoc. councilor 1979-81, 85-86), Rheumatism Soc. D.C. (pres. 1963-64), Internat. League Against Rheumatism (chmn. subcom. on classification and nomenclature 1982-94, mem. epidemiology com. 1989-93), Med. Assn. South Africa (lectr. 1995, 96), Alpha Epsilon Delta, Phi Chi, Kappa Sigma. Republican. Baptist. Home and Office: 1492 Hampton Hill Cir Mc Lean VA 22101-6016*

FEMMINELLA, CHARLES JOSEPH, JR., real estate appraiser, tax assessor, broker; b. Bklyn., Aug. 10, 1938; s. Charles J. and Rose L. Femminella; m. Mary Ann DeCaro, Sept. 11, 1965; children: Cindy L., Christy J. BS, Fairleigh Dickinson U., 1966. Cert. gen. real estate appraiser, tax assessor, N.J. Pres. Cert. Valuations, Inc., Randolph, N.J., 1974—; advisor Tax. Ct. N.J., 1995—; instr. real estate Rutgers U.; expert witness real estate affairs; cert. green acres, farm, condemnation, right of way, development rights and local property tax appraiser; lectr., cons. in field. Author: Real Property Appraisal, 1974 (Presdl. Citation 1978, 95). Pres. Randolph Rep. Club, 1980, Pla. 447 Condominium Assn., 1986—, also bd. dirs. Cpl. USMC, 1958-64. Named to Hon. Order of Ky. Cols. Mem. Soc. Profl. Assessors, Pocono Forestry Assn., Randolph C. of C. (v.p., dir. 1972), Am. Legion, Marine Corps League. Lodge: Kiwanis, KC. Avocation: real estate teaching, development and investing. Office: Cert Valuations 447 Rt 10 St 8 Randolph NJ 07869

FENCHEL, GERD H(ERMAN), psychoanalyst; b. Berlin, Mar. 29, 1926; arrived in U.S., 1940; s. Erich Otto and Rosa (Goldschmidt) F.; children: Karen Fenchel Spiler, Erich; m. Leslie Spitz, June 30, 1991. BSS, CCNY, 1949, MS in Edn., 1950; PhD, NYU, 1959; cert., Washington Sq. Inst., 1970. Cert. psychologist, N.Y., Pa. Pvt. practice psychoanalysis N.Y.C., 1949—; asst. dean Alfred Adler Inst., N.Y.C., 1955-73; psychotherapist, supr. and dir. group psychotherapy L.I. Cons. Ctr., Forest Hills, N.Y., 1953-60; mem. faculty Inst. for Analytic Psychotherapy, N.J., 1960-71; exec. dir., dean Washington Sq. Inst., N.Y.C., 1960—. Co-author: Development of Ego and Emergence of the Self in Group Psychotherapy, 1979; editor: Psychoanalysis at 100, 1994, The Mother-Daughter Relationship, 1998; contbr. articles to profl. jours. Fellow Coun. Psychoanalysts and Psychotherapists (pres. 1966-67), Am. Group Psychotherapy Assn., Pa. Psychol. Assn.; mem. APA. Avocations: travel, stamps, photography. Office: Washington Sq Inst 41 E 11th St Fl 4 New York NY 10003-4678

FENDLER, JANOS HUGO, chemistry educator; b. Budapest, Hungary, Aug. 12, 1937; came to U.S., 1964; s. Janos and Vilma (Csiky) F.; m. Eleanor Johnson, june 15, 1965 (div. 1975); children: Michael, Lisa; m. Ann Fendler, Feb. 15, 1976 (div. 1997); children: Peter, Monika; m. Eliza Hutter, Sept. 15, 1997; children: Veronika Isabelle, David Viktor. BSc, U. Leicester, Eng., 1960; Diploma in Radiochemistry, Leicester Coll. Tech., 1961; PhD, U. London, 1964, DSc, 1978. Postdoctoral fellow U. Calif., Santa Barbara, 1965-66; fellow Mellon Inst., Pitts., 1966-70; assoc. prof. chemistry Tex. A&M U., College Station, 1970-75, prof., 1975-81; prof. chemistry Clarkson Coll., Potsdam, N.Y., 1982-85; disting. prof. chemistry, dir. Ctr. Membrane Engring. & Sci. Syracuse U., 1985-97; disting. Camp prof. chemistry Clarkson U., 1997—; adj. prof. U. Montreal, 1967-94; indsl. cons., vis. prof., Japan, 1975, Switzerland, 1979, Sweden, 1981, France, 1985, Germany, 1992, Israel, 1997. Author: Catalysts in Micellar and Macromolecular Systems, 1975, Membrane Mimetic Chemistry, 1982, Membrane Mimetic Approach to Advanced Materials, 1994; rsch., numerous publs. in field; mem. editl. bd. Jour. Organic Chemistry, 1978-82, jour. Colloid and Interface Sci., 1981-87, Langmuir, 1985-87, Bull. Chem. Soc. France, 1986-92, Magyar Kèmiai Folyoirat, 1992—, Advanced Materials, 1994—, Chemistry of Materials, 1997—. Recipient Sr. Humboldt Rsch. award, 1992. Mem. Am. Chem. Soc. (Kendall award 1982), Royal Chem. Soc., Internat. Assn. Colloid and Interface Scientists. E-mail: feudler@clarkson.edu. Home: 608 Swan St Potsdam NY 13676-1147 Office: Clarkson U Ctr Adv Material Processing Box 5814 Potsdam NY 13699

FENDLER, OSCAR, lawyer; b. Blytheville, Ark., Mar. 22, 1909; s. Alfred and Rae (Sattler) F.; m. Patricia Shane, Oct. 26, 1946; children: Tilden P. Wright III (stepson), Frances Shane. B.A., U. Ark., 1930; LL.B., Harvard, 1933. Bar: Ark. bar 1933. Practice in Blytheville, 1933-41, 46—; spl. justice Ark. Supreme Ct., 1965; Mem. Ark. Jud. Council, 1959- 60; pres. Conf. Local Bar Assn., 1958-60; pres. bd. dirs. Ark. Law Rev., 1961-67; mem. Ark. Bd. Pardons and Paroles, 1970-71. Mem. Miss. County Democratic Central Com., 1948—. Served with USNR, 1941-45. Fellow Am. Coll. Trust and Estate Counsel, Am. Bar Found.; mem. ABA (chmn. gen. practice sect. 1966-67, mem. council sect. gen. practice 1964—, ho. dels. 1968-80, mem. com. edn. about Communism 1966-70, com. legal aid and indigent defendants 1970-73, chmn. com. law lists 1973-76, Founders award 1992), Ark. Bar Assn. (chmn. exec. com. 1956-57, pres. 1962-63), Am. Judicature

Soc. (dir. 1964-68), Scribes, Nat. Conf. Bar Presidents (exec. council 1963-65), Blytheville C. of C. (past v.p., dir.), Navy League, Am. Legion. Club: Blytheville Rotary (past pres.). Home: 1062 Hearn St Blytheville AR 72315-2659 Office: 104 N 6th St Blytheville AR 72315-3315

FENDLEY-HERBERT, DEBI LYNN, artist, art educator; b. Arkadelphia, Ark., Sept. 7, 1964; d. Ruben R. and Peggy L. Fendley; m. Jay Andrew Herbert, Aug. 12, 1995. BSE in Art, Henderson State U., 1987, MSE in Art, 1989, MSE in English, 1996. Art tchr. Gurdon (Ark.) Pub. Schs., 1987-95; adj. instr. English Henderson State U., Arkadelphia, 1996-98; adj. instr. art Ouachita Bapt. U., Arkadelphia, 1998-99; state del. exhbn. Nat. Mus. Arts, Washington, 1992; bd. dirs. Bridge Found. Children, Arkadelphia. Artist (book) A Personal Statement: Arkansas Women in the Arts, 1991; illustrator (mag.) Chin Chit Chat, 1997, 98; staff writer Christian Min., 1996-97. Mem. Clark County Humane Soc., Arkadelphia, 1995-99. Mem. Nat. Art Edn. Assn., Ark. Art Edn. Assn., Coll. Art Assn., Japanese Chin Club Am., Saline County Kennel Club Ark. (pub. edn. coord., puppy kindergarten instr.). Baptist. Avocations: dog training, photography, writing, vocal performance. E-mail: puparooh@aol.com. Home: 2704 Mockingbird Ln Arkadelphia AR 71923

FENDRICH, ROGER PAUL, lawyer; b. Newark, Dec. 27, 1943; s. Howard and Elsie (Zahler) F.; m. Renee Madeleine Obestein, July 10, 1965; children: Howard Joseph, Alexander Daniel. AB, U. Miami, Coral Gables, Fla., 1965; PhD, U. Tex., 1971; JD, Yale U., 1980. Bar: D.C. 1980, U.S. Ct. Appeals (D.C. cir.) 1981, U.S. Supreme Ct. 1987, U.S. Ct. Appeals (4th cir.) 1987, U.S. Ct. Appeals (9th cir.) 1991, U.S. Ct. Appeals (3rd cir.) 1992, U.S. Ct. Appeals (2nd cir.) 1993. Assoc. prof. Beloit (Wis.) Coll., 1969-77; acting asst. gen. counsel Yale U., New Haven, 1980; assoc. Hughes, Hubbard & Reed, Washington, 1980-88; ptnr. Arnold & Porter, Washington, 1988—; spl. master U.S. Dist. Ct., New Haven, 1985; barrister Am. Inns Ct., Washington, 1985-88; cons. Fed. Cts. Study Com., Washington, 1989-90. Contbg. author The Individual and Society, 1978; contbr. philosophy articles to profl. jours. Spl. master U.S. Dist. Ct. Conn., New Haven, 1985; barrister Am. Inns Ct., Washington, 1985-88. Woodrow Wilson fellow, 1966; NEH rsch. grantee, 1976, 77. Mem. ABA, D.C. Bar Assn. Office: Arnold & Porter 555 12th St NW Washington DC 20004-1206

FENDRICK, ALAN BURTON, retired advertising executive; b. Bronx, N.Y., Mar. 22, 1933; s. Louis and Esther (Silberberg) F.; m. Beverly R. Schoenfeld, June 12, 1960; children: Sarah Fendrick Shifrin, Lisa Rubinstein. AB with honors in Econs, Columbia U., 1954; MBA, Harvard U., 1958. Asst. sales mgr. splty. divsn. Hankins Container Co., 1958-60; mgr. bus. adminstrn., ops. and engring. NBC, 1960-67; exec. v.p., sec., treas. Grey Advt. Inc., N.Y.C., 1967-89, exec. v.p., chmn. fin. com., 1990-93. Trustee Woodlands H.S. Scholarship Fund, Greenburgh, N.Y., pres., 1977-78; trustee Jewish Child Care Assn. N.Y., 1985-97, hon. trustee, 1997—; trustee SAG Producers Pension and Health Plans, 1993—; mem. sch. bd. Mt. Plesant Cottage Sch., 1985-99; bd. dirs. Columbia Coll. Alumni Assn., 1989-96. With AUS, 1954-56. Mem. Am. Assn. Advt. Agys. (chmn. com. on fiscal control 1979-81), Advt. Agy. Fin. Mgmt. Group (chmn. exec. com. 1980-82, pres. 1982-84), Exec. Svc. Corps of Manasota, Otis Woodlands Club Inc. (bd. dirs. 1985-89, treas. 1984-88), Columbia U. Alumni Club of Sarasota (pres. 1997—). Jewish (trustee temple). E-mail: bevalam711@aol.com. Home: 5880 Midnight Pass Rd Sarasota FL 34242-2184

FENECH, JOSEPH CHARLES, lawyer; b. London, May 28, 1950; came to U.S., 1953; s. Carmel John and Elizabeth Frances (Borg) F.; m. Cynthia A. Rennie, June 14, 1980 (div. 1998); children: Paul C., Peter J., Elizabeth F. BA with honors, Mich. State U., 1972; JD, U. Mich., 1975. Bar: Mich. 1975, U.S. Dist. Ct. (ea. dist.) Mich. 1975, U.S. Ct. Appeals (6th cir.) 1977, Ill. 1980, U.S. Dist. Ct. (no. dist.) Ill. 1980, U.S. Dist. Ct. (ctrl. dist.) Ill. 1993, U.S. Dist. Ct. (ea. dist.) Wis. 1993, U.S. Ct. Appeals (7th cir.) 1980, U.S. Supreme Ct. 1993, U.S. Tax Ct. 1993. Law clk. Washtenaw Cir. Ct., Ann Arbor, Mich., 1975-76; asst. atty. gen. State of Mich., Detroit, 1976-80; labor rels. counsel McDonald's Corp., Oak Brook, Ill., 1980-82, sr. internat. atty., 1982-84; sr. mem. Fenech & Assoc., Oak Brook, Ill., 1985—. Contbr. articles to profl. jours. Bd. dirs. Cath. Charities Diocese of Joliet, Ill.; active Family Focus, Mich., 1979-80, Internat. Found. Employee Benefit Plans, Brookfield, Wis., 1980-83, Chmns. Club Ctrl.; mem. bd. govs. DuPage Hosp., Ctrl. DuPage Hosp. Tree Life, Ctrl., Glen Oaks Med. Ctr., Tree of Life, Rep. Campaign Coun., 1995; supt. adv. com. Naperville Cmty. Sch. Dist. 203; improvement com. Mill St. Sch., Naperville; charter mem. Marklund Children's Home Endowment; bd. govs. Ctrl. DuPage Hosp. Named Regents scholar U. Mich., 1973, 74, 75; Trustees scholar Mich. State U., 1969-72. Mem. ABA, Ill. State Bar Assn., Mich. Bar assn., DuPage Estate Planning Coun., U. Mich. Lawyers Club, Ill. Bankers Assn., Ill. Mortgage Bankers Assn., Internat. Platform Assn. Am. Hosp. Assn. (sr. mem.), Am. Acad. Healthcare Attys. (sr. mem.). Office: Fenech & Pachulski PC 1 Lincoln Ctr Ste 840 Oakbrook Terrace IL 60181-4265

FENG, GEN-SHENG, medical educator, researcher; b. Sept. 8, 1961. BSc in Biology, Hangzhou U., China, 1981; MSc in Immunology, 2d Med. Sch. of Army, Shanghai, China, 1984; PhD in Molecular Biology, Ind. U., 1990. Rsch. assoc. in molecular genetics 2d Med. Sch. of Army, Shanghai, China, 1985-86; assoc. instr. dept. biology Ind. U., Bloomington, 1987-90; postdoctoral fellow in molecular biology U. Toronto, 1990-94; with Rsch. Inst. The Hosp. for Sick Children, Toronto, 1990-91, Rsch. Inst. Mt. Sinai Hosp., Toronto, 1991-94; asst. prof. dept. biochemistry and molecular biology, dept. med. and molecular genetics, asst. mem. Walther Oncology Ctr. Ind. U., Indpls., 1994—. Ad hoc reviewer Jour. Biol. Chemistry, Jour. Cell Sci., Oncogene, Leukemia; contbr. articles to profl. jours.; reviewer of rsch. grants Internat. Human Frontier Sci. Program, 1994, 95, U.S. Vets. Affairs Med. Rsch. Sys., 1996; spkr. in field. Recipient Silver prize for Achievement of Health Sci. and Tech., China, 1986, Carrie E. Wolff award Am. Heart Assn. Ind. Affiliate, Inc., 1995. Mem. AAAS, Am. Diabetes Assn. (career devel. award 1995—), Am. Soc. Microbiology, Soc. Chinese Biologists Am. Office: Ind U Sch Medicine Dept Biochemistry and Molecular Biology 1044 W Walnut St Rm 302 Indianapolis IN 46202-5126*

FENG, TSE-YUN, computer engineer, educator; b. Hangchow, China, Feb. 26, 1928; s. Shih-ching and Lin Shao; m. Elaine Hu, Jan. 28, 1965; children: Wu-chun, Wu-chi, Wu-che, Wu-chang. B.S., Nat. Taiwan U., 1950; M.S., Okla. State U., 1957; Ph.D., U. Mich., 1967. Asst. engr. Taiwan Power Co., 1950-56; sr. designer Ebasco Services, N.Y.C., 1957-60; teaching fellow U. Mich., 1962-65, research asst., 1965-66, asst. research engr., 1966, research asso., 1967; asst. prof. elec. and computer engring. Syracuse U., 1967-71, asso. prof., 1971-75; prof. elec. and computer engring. Wayne State U., Detroit, 1975-79; prof. computer sci. Wright State U., Dayton, Ohio, 1979-80; chmn. dept. Wright State U., 1979-80; prof. computer and info. sci. Ohio State U., 1980-84; Binder prof. computer engring. Pa State U., University Park, 1984—; dir. computer engring. program Pa State U., 1984-88; program dir. NSF, Arlington, Va., 1993—; cons. Transidyne Gen., Syracuse U., Pattern Analysis and Recognition Corp., N.Y. State Bd. Edn.; chmn. Internat. Conf. on Parallel Processing, 1975—, Internat. Conf. on Computers and Applications, 1983-87; dir. N.E. Consortium for Engring. Edn., 1976—; participant U.S. Technol. Policy Conf., 1978; leader del. U.S. Sr. Experts to China, 1985; cons. USAF. Contbr. numerous articles to others: patentee in field. Fellow Assn. Computing Machinery, IEEE (chmn. computer soc. standards com. 1974-78, mem. numerous other coms., presiding officer computer soc. governing bd. 1979-80, computer soc. disting. visitor 1973-78, pres. 1979-80, chmn. nominations com. 1981-83, chmn. disting. visitors program, 1987-93, Best Paper award 1975, Honor Roll award 1978, Spl. award 1981, Centennial medal 1984, Richard E. Merwin Disting. Service award 1985, Meritorious Service award, 1986, mem. del. to Chinese Electronics Soc. 1978, leader del. 1980, del. to Popov Soc. Congress, USSR 1978, editor-in-chief Trans. on Computers 1982-86, Trans. on Parallel and Distributed Systems, 1989—, Tech. Achievement award and Outstanding Contbn. award, 1991); mem. Am. Fedn. Info. Processing Socs. (dir. 1979-80, 82-87, nominating com. 1979-80, 83-85, chmn. publs. com. 1984-86, exec. com. 1986-87, mem. numerous other coms.), Am. Nat. Standards Inst. (info. systems standards mgmt. bd. 1974-78), Sagamore Computer Conf. (chmn., editor proc. 1972-75), Pa. State Engring. Soc. (Outstanding Rsch. award 1989), Internat. Assn. Computers and Comms. (pres. 1995—), Hon. Order of Ky. Cols., Sigma Xi, Phi Kappa Phi, Tau Beta Pi, Eta Kappa Nu, Phi Tau Phi. Home: 319 Christopher Ln State College PA 16803-1261 Office: U Pa Dept Computer Sci & Engring Pond Lab University Park PA 16802

FENG, WILLIAM CHING-LIH, cardiothoracic surgeon; b. Shanghai, Dec. 23, 1950; came to U.S., 1970; BS in Biology cum laude, Tulane U., 1974; DSc in Microbiology, Harvard U., 1979; MD, Brown U., 1982. Diplomate Am. Bd. Surgery, Am. Bd. Thoracic Surgery. Gen. surg. resident med. ctr. U. Ala., Birmingham, 1982-87, chief resident, 1987; thoracic and cardiovascular resident R.I. Hosp., Providence, 1987-89, chief resident, 1989, surgeon divsn. cardiothoracic surgery dept. surgery, 1989—, dir. cardiac surg. ICU, 1992—; clin. asst. prof. surgery sch. medicine Brown U., 1990—; presenter in field. Contbr. articles to profl. jours. Fellow ACS, Am. Coll. Chest Physicians; mem. AMA, R.I. Med. Soc., Providence Med. Soc., Soc. Thoracic Surgeons. Office: CVT Surgical Group Inc 2 Dudley St Ste 470 Providence RI 02905 also: RI Hosp 593 Eddy St Providence RI 02903-4923

FENG, XIANGDONG SHAWN, chemist; b. Lingling, Hunan, China, July 27, 1956; came to the U.S., 1982; s. Hui Feng and Yuying Jiang; m. Meiling Gong, Dec. 26, 1984; children: Melinda G., Stephanie G. BS, Hunan Normal U., Changsha, Hunan, China, 1978; MS, Cath. U. Am., 1984, PhD, 1988. Lectr. Hunan Normal U., Changsha, 1978-82; rsch. asst., tchg. asst. Cath. U. Am., Washington, 1982-88; postdoctoral fellow Vitreous State Lab., Washington, 1988-89, rsch. scientist, 1989-91; chemist Argonne Nat. Lab., Chgo., 1991-94; sr. rsch. scientist project mgr. Pacific N.W. Nat. Lab., Richland, Wash., 1995-97, staff scientist, project mgr., 1997-98; Glass Core Tech. chair, rsch. assoc. Ferro Corp., 1998—; mem. tech. program organizing com. Am. Nuclear Soc., La Grange Park, Ill., 1996. Contbr. chpts. to books and articles to profl. jours.; patentee in field. Named Hon. Prof., Human Normal U., 1995, China Inst. Atomic Energy, Beijing, 1995; recipient Outstanding Performance award Pacific N.W. Nat. Lab., 1997, Materials Sci. award U.S. Dept. Engry, 1998, Alumni Outstanding Achievement award in sci. Cath. U. Am., 1998; grantee Dept. Energy, Washington, 1992—. Mem. Am. Ceramic Soc. (symposium chair for tech. meetings 1989—, fed. liaison com. 1996—), Am. Chem. Soc., Materials Rsch. Soc. (tech. program com. 1995, Finalist of 1998 Discover Award for Tech. Innovation. Achievements include development of specialty glass/ceramics; development of thermodynamic models based on glass structure for the prediction of glass properties from composition; development of advanced composite and polymeric materials for water purification and recycle, catalysis, drug delivery, and industrial coatings and applications. Avocations: jogging, table tennis, swimming, bicycling, computers. Office: 8300 E Pleasant Valley Rd Independence WA 44131

FENGLER, JOHN PETER, television producer, director, advertising executive; b. Leipzig, Germany, Dec. 29, 1928; came to U.S., 1939; naturalized, 1952; m. Jessica M. Atkins, Dec. 7, 1961; 1 child, John Mark. BA in Radio and TV, NYU, 1952. Producer, dir. NBC, N.Y.C., 1950-58; exec. producer N.W. Ayer Co., N.Y.C., 1958-65; dir., exec. producer radio and TV dept. Doyle, Dane, Bernbach, 1965-70, Kurtz and Symon Inc., N.Y.C., 1970-73; v.p., dir. comml. prodn. dept., exec. producer D'Arcy-MacManus & Masius, N.Y.C., 1974-75; pres. U.S. TV Co., N.Y.C., 1975-90, Boca Raton, Fla., 1990-94. With U.S. Army, 1950-52. Mem. NATAS (Emmy award best children's program 1957, 58). Office: 6309 NW 25th Way Boca Raton FL 33496-3624

FENICHEL, GERALD MERVIN, neurologist, educator; b. N.Y.C., May 11, 1935; s. Max I. and Sarah M. Fenichel; m. Barbara Ellen Ross, June 8, 1958; children—Amy Beth, Eric Ross, Adam Seth. A.B., Johns Hopkins U., 1955; M.D., Yale U., 1959. Diplomate Am. Bd. Neurology and Psychiatry. Intern in surgery Strong Meml. Hosp., Rochester, N.Y., 1959-60; research in neuropathology Nat. Inst. Neurol. Diseases and Stroke, Bethesda, Md., 1960-66; resident in neurology Nat. Inst. Neurol. Diseases and Stroke, Bethesda, 1961-63; instr. neurology George Washington U., 1964-67; asst. prof. Children's Hosp., Washington, 1967-69; prof., chmn. dept. neurology Vanderbilt U., Nashville, 1969—; dir. Jerry Lewis Neuromuscular Ctr., Nashville. Author: Neonatal Neurology; contbr. articles to profl. jours. Fellow Am. Acad. Neurology; mem. AMA, Am. Neurol. Assn., Child Neurology Soc. (pres. 1973-74), So. Clin. Neurol. Soc. (councilor 1984). Avocation: tennis. Office: Vanderbilt U Dept Neurology 2100 Pierce Ave Nashville TN 37212-3162*

FENICHEL, RICHARD LEE, retired biochemist; b. N.Y.C., July 23, 1925; s. Irving and Dorothy (Rothchild) F.; student Bucknell U., 1941-43; AB, N.Y. U., 1947; MS, Poly. Inst. Bklyn., 1951; PhD, Wayne U., 1956; widowed; children: Gladys, Marilyn. Commonwealth fellow for research Poly. Inst. Bklyn., 1948-50; biochemist med. dept. Chrysler Corp., Highland Park, Mich., 1951-54; grad. teaching asst. Wayne U. Med. Sch., 1954-56; investigator Aviation Med. Acceleration Lab., Johnsville, Pa., 1957-59; group leader Ortho Research Found., Raritan, N.J., 1959-63; sr. rsch. fellow biochemistry and pharmocology Wyeth-Ayerst Labs., Princeton, N.J., 1963-95. Served with U.S. Army, 1943-45. Recipient Angus McClean Research award Wayne U., 1956, Superior Accomplishment award USN Med. Lab., 1966; Legion of Honor, Chapel of Four Chaplains, 1982. Mem. Am. Chem. Soc., N.Y. Acad. Sci., AAAS, Am. Soc. Biol. Chemists, Sigma Xi. Contbr. numerous articles to profl. jours.; patentee in field. Home: 1637 Oakwood Dr Apt S119 Narberth PA 19072-1005

FENICHELL, STEPHEN CLARK, writer; b. N.Y.C., Apr. 22, 1956; s. Stephen Sidney and Lois Elizabeth (Forde) F.; m. Carol Goodstein, Mar. 4, 1995; children: Loisa Anna, Aaron Forde. AB, Harvard U., 1977. Author: Daughters at Risk: A Personal Des History, 1980, Other Peoples Money, 1985, Plastic: The Making of a Synthetic Century, 1996, (with Mark Mobius) Passport to Profits, 1999. Home: 523 Hudson St Apt 2rs New York NY 10014-6119

FENIGER, JEROME ROLAND, JR., broadcasting executive; b. Peoria, Ill., June 16, 1927; s. Jerome Rol and Marie Dorothy (Miller) F.; m. Marian Laura Schwartz, June 24, 1951; children: Robin Jean, Bruce David. B.A., U. Iowa, 1948; postgrad., Columbia U., 1948, N.Y. U., 1949-50; D.Bus. Sc. (hon.), St. John's U., 1984. Advt. account exec. Biow Co., N.Y.C., 1949-50; chief advt. time buyer Cunningham & Walsh, N.Y.C., 1950-51, v.p., 1954-60; sales exec. CBS, N.Y.C., 1952-54; exec. Cowles Communications Co., N.Y.C., 1960-65; v.p. Grey Advt. Inc., N.Y.C., 1965-70; pres. Horizons Communications Corp., N.Y.C., 1970-83; mng. dir. Sta. Reps. Assn., Inc., N.Y.C., 1983—; dir., mem. exec. com. Advt. Council, 1984—; pres. Louise Wise Svcs., 1986-89; mem. pvt. sector commn. USIA/Voice of Am. Trustee Columbia Grammar and Prep Sch., 1965-77, treas., 1970-77; bd. dirs. UJA Fedn. on Domestic Affairs. Mem. Internat. Radio and TV Soc. (pres. 1975-77), Friars Club, Dutch Treat Club, Yale Club of N.Y.C. Democrat. Home: 16 W 77th St New York NY 10024-5126

FENIMORE, GEORGE WILEY, management consultant; b. Bertrand, Mo., 1921. BBA in Fin., Northwestern U., 1941; LLB, Harvard U., 1947; JD, UCLA, 1955; LLD (hon.), Southwestern U., 1992. Bar: Mich. 1948. Asst. to dir. planning Ford Motor Co., Dearborn, Mich., 1947-48; exec. to v.p. and gen. mgr. Hughes Aircraft Co., Culver City, Calif., 1948-53; adminstrv. mgr. tech. products Packard Bell Electronics Co., 1954-55; with TRW, Inc., Los Angeles, 1955-64; v.p., gen. mgr. TRW Internat., Los Angeles, 1959-64; v.p. internat. ops. Bunker Ramo Corp., Los Angeles, 1964-65; dir. public relations, then corp. sec. Litton Industries, Inc., Beverly Hills, Calif., 1965-73, v.p., corp. sec., 1973-81, sr. v.p., corp. sec., 1981-86, mgmt. cons., 1986—; sr. v.p. Peck Jones Constrn., Beverly Hills; trustee, past chmn. bd. Southwestern U. Sch. Law; mem. Calif. Tchrs. Retirement Bd. bd. dirs. Children's Bur. L.A., Child Shelter Homes a Rescue Effort, Multiple Sclerosis Soc.; sec. French Found. for Alzheimer's Rsch.; mem. Calif. Fair Polit. Practices Comm., 1986-91; mem. United Way Emergency Food Sys. Study Task Force; elder, chmn. fin. com. Westwood Presbyn. Ch.; trustee Sheldon Jackson Coll., Sitka, Alaska; bd. govs. Western Los Angeles County coun. Boy Scouts Am.; mem. Beverly Hills Mayor's Econ. Adv. Com. Maj. USAAF, WWII. Recipient Citizen of Yr. award Beverly Hills Lions Club, 1976, Spirit Honoree Beverly Hills Edn. Found., 1986, Beverly Hills YMCA, 1988, Brentwood/San Vicente C. of C., 1987, Hon. Citizen award Beverly Hills City Coun., 1986, Guardian Angel award Child S.H.A.R.E., 1989, Highest award for Lifetime Svc. to Cmty., Key to City of Beverly Hills, 1990, State Gold award Calif. Tchrs. Assn., 1993. Mem. Am. Soc. Corp. Secs. (dir., past nat. dir., past pres. Los Angeles Group), Beverly Hills C. of C. (past pres., Citizen of Yr. award 1979, chmn. edn. com., bd. dirs., David Orgell Meml. award 1990), Hemet Fed. Savs. and Loan Assn. (bd. dirs.), Mandeville Canyon Assn. (past pres.), Bar Assn. Mich., L.A. Country Club, Rotary (past pres. Beverly Hills chpt., Paul Harris fellow, William C. Ackerman trophy 1986), Shriners. Presbyterian. Office: 360 N Crescent Dr Beverly Hills CA 90210-4802

FENINGER, CLAUDE, industry management services company executive; b. Cairo, Jan. 15, 1926; came to U.S., 1960; s. Paul and Therese (DeRogatis) F.; m. Jill Ellis, Nov. 26, 1986; children from previous marriage: Paul Gordon, Eric. Student, Lausanne (Switzerland) Sch. Hotel Mgmt., 1948, Am. U., Cairo, 1945, Lincoln Sch., Cairo, 1943, Lycee Francais, Cairo, 1935. With Hilton Internat., 1955-67; product line mgr. ITT, 1967-68; pres. Sheraton Internat., 1968-74; chmn. bd., chief exec. officer Omni Internat. Hotels, Inc., Atlanta, 1974-80; pres. Aramark Internat., Phila., 1980—; cons. in field, 1960—; dir. VS Services, Can., Traulsen Refrigeration Co., N.Y.C. Mem. Am. Mgmt. Assn., Am. Hotel Assn. Home: 2045 Yellow Springs Rd Malvern PA 19355-8702 Office: Aramark Corp ARA Svcs Inc 1101 Market St Ste 45 Philadelphia PA 19107-2988

FENN, ORMON WILLIAM, JR., furniture company executive; b. Tyler, Tex., Mar. 13, 1927; s. Ormon William and Madonna (Muphree) F.; m. Lucille Adrianne Kelley; children: Andrea Lee, Miles Linton, Kelly Sue, Michael Thomas. Student U. Minn., 1945, Okla. U., 1945, Imperial U., 1946; BS Yale U., 1949. Asst. dist. mgr. Armsrong Cork Co., Lancaster, Pa., 1949-59, asst. gen. sales mgr., 1959-70; vice pres., gen. sales mgr. Thomasville (N.C.) Furniture Industries, Inc., 1970-74, sr. v.p., gen. sales mgr., 1974-77; exec. v.p. sales and mktg. Stanley Furniture Co. Mead Corp., Stanleytown, Va., 1977-78, pres., 1978-79; pres. CEO Stanley Furniture Co., 1979-82; vice chmn. LADD Furniture Co., High Point, N.C., 1982-92, dir., 1982-98; chmn. emeritus N.C. furnishings export coun. N.C. Dept. Commerce, High Point, 1993-95; chmn. N.C. Home Furnishing Coun., 1995-97; chmn./CEO Caliber Components Inc., 1998; past chmn. bd. govs. Western Mdse. Mart, San Francisco; past chmn. market adv. bd. High Point So. Furniture Market Center; past dir. N.C. Furniture Export Office; past chmn. Internat. Home Furnishings Mktg. Assn.; past bd. dirs. Furniture Info. Coun.; past bd. dirs./exec. com. Home Furnishing Coun.; bd. dirs. Am. Furniture Mfrs. Hall of Fame; apptd. by Gov. of N.C. to nat. adv. bd. HandMade in Am. Active adv. bd. Bryan Sch. Bus. and Econs., U. N.C., Greensboro. Served to 1st lt. U.S. Army, 1944-52, PTO. Recipient The Order of the Long Leaf Pine award (Ala.) Gov. Hunt (N.C. highest civilian honor), 1995. Mem. String and Splinter Club (past bd. dirs.). Episcopalian. Avocations: golf, hunting, physical fitness. Home: 510 Emerywood Dr High Point NC 27262-2812 Office: Caliber Components Inc PO Box 35032 Greensboro NC 27425-5032

FENN, PETER HUNTINGTON, political consultant, media producer, educator; b. Boston, Dec. 12, 1947; s. Dan Huntington and Nancy Ruland (Ring) F.; m. Alison Hulett Seale, Sept. 6, 1974; children: Kristina, Dan. BA, Macalester Coll., 1970; MA, U. So. Calif., 1972. Sr. rsch. analyst Westinghouse Corp., Washington, 1972-74; prof. staff mem. U.S. Senate Intelligence Com., Washington, 1974-75; exec. asst., chief staff Sen. Frank Church, Washington, 1976-81; exec. dir. Dems. for 80's, Washington, 1981-83; exec. dir., founder Ctr. Responsive Politics, Washington, 1983-84; pres. Fenn & King Comm., Washington, 1984—. Contbr. Campaigns & Elections mag., 1991, 96, 97. Bd. trustees Macalester Coll., St. Paul, Minn., 1996—, pres. alumni assn., 1994-96, bd. dirs. alumni assn., 1990-96; bd. dirs. Coun. Econ. Priorities, N.Y.C., 1985-91. Mem. Am. Assn. Polit. Cons. (4 Telly awards 1997, 2 Pollie awards 1996). Unitarian. Avocations: baseball, golf. Home: 3347 Tennyson St NW Washington DC 20015-2442 Office: Fenn & King Comms 2715 M St NW Ste 150 Washington DC 20007-3636

FENN, RAYMOND WOLCOTT, JR., retired metallurgical engineer; b. Torrington, Conn., Feb. 4, 1922; s. Raymond W. and Josephine (Mueller) F.; m. Beatrice Myra Christian, Jan. 19, 1946; children—Carol Louise, Ralph Christian. B.Metall. Engring., Rensselaer Poly. Inst., 1943; M.Engring., Yale, 1947, D.Engring., 1949. Registered profl. engr., Calif. Metall. engr. Gen. Electric Co., West Lynn, Mass., 1943-44; supr. testing lab., chief testing and instrumentation sect. Metall. Lab., Dow Chem. Co., Midland, Mich., 1949-61; cons. scientist, sr. mem. research lab., mgr. materials and prodn. systems engring., mgr. mfg. research, mgr. material and process control ctr. Lockheed Missiles & Space Co., Sunnyvale, Calif., 1961-87; bd. dirs. Rancho San Antonio Retirement Housing Corp., Cupertino, Calif. Contbr. articles to profl. jours. Served with USNR, 1944-46. Fellow Am. Soc. Metals (trustee 1969-71, chmn., mem. exec. com. Santa Clara Valley chpt. 1966-69); mem. Am. Soc. Testing Materials (dir. 1966-69, R.E. Templin award 1961), Am. Inst. Mining and Metall. Engrs., Research Soc. Am., Am. Welding Soc., Soc. Mfg. Engrs., Soc. for Advancement of Material and Process Engring. (chmn. No. Calif. chpt. 1973-74, nat. dir. 1974-76, 2d v.p. 1976-77, 1st v.p. 1977-78, pres. 1978-79), Nat. Mgmt. Assn., Sigma Xi. Home: The Forum 522F 23500 Cristo Rey Dr Cupertino CA 95014-6503

FENN, SANDRA ANN, programmer, analyst; b. Sugar Land, Tex., Oct. 31, 1953; d. William Charles and Helen Maxine (Kyle) F.; m. Jimmie Dan Watts, May 21, 1973 (div. June 1988); children: Gabriel Nathaniel Watts, Lindsay Nichelle Garza. AA in Gen. Studies summa cum laude, Alvin (Tex.) C.C., 1994; student, U. Houston, 1994—. Shampoo asst. LaVonne's Salon of Beauty, Houston, 1972-73; coding clk. Prudential Ins. Co., Houston, 1974-75; word processing operator MacGregor Med. Assn., Houston, 1983-85; computer applications analyst Computer Scis. Corp., Houston, 1987-92; program support adminstr. Sci. Applications Internat. Corp., Houston, 1992-95, programmer/analyst, 1995—; software developer astronaut office Johnson Space Ctr., 1998—. Mem. Am. Bus. Women's Assn. (newsletter chair, 1999 Woman of Excellence), Phi Theta Kappa. Avocations: horseback riding, camping, biking, volleyball, reading. Home: 1516 Bay Area Blvd Apt M6 Houston TX 77058-2114 Office: Sci Applications Internat Corp 2200 Space Park Dr Houston TX 77058-3677

FENN, SHERILYN, actress; b. Detroit, Feb. 1, 1965. TV series: Twin Peaks, 1990 (Emmy award nomination best supporting actress in a drama series), (TV mini-series) A Season in Purgatory, 1996; TV movies Silence of the Heart, 1984, Dillinger, 1991, Spring Awakening, 1994, Liz: The Elizabeth Taylor Story, 1995, The Assasination File, 1996; TV specials Divided We Stand, 1988, A Family Again, 1988; film appearances The Wild Life, 1984, Just One of the Guys, 1985, Out of Control, 1985, Thrashin', 1986, The Wraith, 1986, Zombie High, 1987, Two Moon Junction, 1988, Crime Zone, 1988, True Blood, 1989, Wild at Heart, 1990, Backstreet Dreams, 1990, Meridian: Kiss of the Beast, 1990, Ruby, 1992, Desire and Hell at Sunset Motel, 1992, Diary of a Hitman, 1992, Of Mice and Men, 1992, Twin Peaks: Fire Walk With Me, 1992, Three of Hearts, 1993, Boxing Helena, 1993, Fatal Instinct, 1993, Just Write, 1997, Lovelife, 1997, Darkness Falls, 1998, Outside Ozona, 1998, Cement, 1999, others. *

FENNEL, PETER J., SR., retired anesthesiologist; b. Alexandria, La., Nov. 28, 1928; s. Lawrence Sr. and Ruth (Carnahan) F.; m. Ruth Kettenring, Dec. 31, 1965; children: Peter J. Jr., Tracy E. BA, Bowdoin Coll., 1948; MD, Cornell U., 1952. Diplomate Am. Bd. Anesthesiology. Intern Maine Med. Ctr., 1952-53, resident, 1953-54; resident Meml. Ctr. for Cancer, 1956-57; staff Meml. Hosp., N.Y.C., 1956-57, Touro Infirmary, New Orleans, 1959-65, Lafayette (La.) Gen. Hosp., 1966-68, Sunrise Hosp., Las Vegas, 1968—. Lt. comdr. USN, 1954-56. Mem. Am. Soc. Anesthesia. Republican. Home: 1820 Dolce Dr Las Vegas NV 89134-6150

FENNELL, CHRISTINE ELIZABETH, healthcare system executive; b. Providence, July 14, 1948; d. Edmond John and Geraldine Mary (Goodenough) F. BS cum laude, Nat. Coll. Denver, 1983. Activity dir. Turtle Creek Convalescent Centre, Ft. Wayne, Ind., 1974-76; co-owner, operator Trail Ridge Welding, Estes Park, Colo., 1976-77; accounts mgr. Mayfair Women's Clinic, Denver, 1977-80; asst. adminstr. Ob-Gyn. Assocs., Aurora, Colo., 1980-82; admissions supr. St. Anthony Hosp. Sys., Denver, 1982-86; adminstr. Parkside Lodge of Colo., Thornton, 1986-89; ops./fin. mgr. Colo. Biodyne, Inc., Denver, 1989-90; adminstr. Kimberly Quality Care, Denver, 1990-93; br. mgr. Preferred Home Health Care, Inc., Lafayette, Ind., 1993-95; regional ops. dir. Arcadia Health Svcs., Inc., Southfield, 1995—; part-time instr. Nat. Coll., Denver, 1983-84. Contbr. articles to profl. jours. Bd. dirs. S.W. Denver Community Mental Health Svcs., 1986. Mem. Denver Bus. Women's Network (pres. 1986-87), Colo. Coun. Hosp. Admitting Mgrs.

(v.p. 1985-86), Rotary Club. Avocations: target shooting, horseback riding, tennis. Office: Arcadia Health Svcs Inc 26777 Central Park Blvd Southfield MI 48076-4162

FENNELL, DIANE MARIE, marketing executive, process engineer; b. Panama, Iowa, Dec. 11, 1944; d. Urban William and Marcella Mae (Leytham) Schechinger; m. Leonard E. Fennell, Aug. 19, 1967; children: David, Denise, Mark. BS, Creighton U., Omaha, 1966. Process engr. Tex. Instruments, Richardson, 1974-79; sr. process engr. Signetics Corp., Santa Clara, Calif., 1979-82; demo lab. mgr. Airco Temescal, Berkeley, Calif., 1982-84; field process engr. Applied Materials, Santa Clara, 1984-87; mgr. product mktg. Lam Rsch., Fremont, Calif., 1987-90; dir. sales and mktg. Ion & Plasma Equipment, Fremont, Calif., 1990-91; pres. FAI, Half Moon Bay, Calif., 1990-96; v.p. mktg. Tegal Corp., Petaluma, Calif., 1997—; founder, coord. chmn. Plasma Etch User's Group, Santa Clara, 1984-87; tchr. computer course Adult Edn., Half Moon Bay, Calif., 1982-83. Founder, bd. dirs. Birth to Three program Mental Retardation Ctr., Denison, Tex., 1974-75; fund raiser local sch. band, Half Moon Bay, 1981-89; community rep. local sch. bd., Half Moon Bay, 1982-83. Mem. Am. Vacuum Soc., Soc. Photo Instrumnentation Engrs., Soc. Women Engrs., Material Rsch. Soc. Avocations: hiking, reading, gardening. Home: 441 Alameda Ave Half Moon Bay CA 94019-5337

FENNELL, RICHARD ARTHUR, artist; b. Ridgeland, S.C., Mar. 24, 1947; s. Joseph Edward and Mary Elizabeth (Jenkins) F.; m. Dorothy Hooper, Aug. 6, 1977; 1 child, Sarah Katherine. BFA, E. Carolina U., 1977; MFA, U. N.C., Greensboro, 1982. part-time instr. U. N.C., Greensboro, 1987-88, Alamance C.C. Solo shows include Gilliam and Peden Art Gallery, 1989, Somerhill Gallery, Chapel Hill, 1990, 93, 96, 99, Hodges Taylor Gallery, Charlotte, 1991, 94, 97, 99, Cmty. Arts Coun., Goldsboro, N.C., 1991, Marita Gilliam, Inc., Gallery, Raleigh, 1992, Elon Coll., N.C., 1992, Greenville Mus. Art, 1993-94, Green Hill Ctr. for N.C. Art, 1995, others; group shows include erl Originals, Inc., Winston-Salem, 1995, fayetteville (N.C.) Mus. Art, 1995, Marita Gilliam Gallery, Raleigh, 1994, Somerhill Gallery, 1994, Weatherspoon Gallery of Art, 1987, 86, Hickory Mus. Art, 1986, others; works in permanent collections at N.C. Mus. Art, Raleigh, Montgomery (Ala.) Mus. Fine Art, U. N.C., Chapel Hill, Duke U., Durham, N.C., Alamance Art Soc., Graham, N.C., East Carolina U., Elon Coll., Ctr. for Creative Leadership, Greensboro; corp. collections include Miller Breweries Corp., Phillip Morris Co., N.Y.C., No. Telecom, R.J. Reynolds, Winston-Salem, IBM, Raleigh, Dillard Paper Co., Greensboro, Interstate Securities, Charlotte, Coca-Cola Ent., Atlanta, Glaxo Pharm., Washington, Reagan Bldg., Inst. of Free Enterprise, Washington, others. Mayor-pro-tem Town of Whitsett, N.C., 1991-93, councilman, 1993-97. Recipient numerous purchase awards, best-in-show awards. Home and Office: 816 Hwy 61 Whitsett NC 27377

FENNELL ROBBINS, SALLY, writer; b. Greensburg, Pa., Feb. 17, 1950; d. Clifford Seanor and Charlotte Louise (Hoffman) Fennell; m. John W. Robbins, Sept. 22, 1984. BS in Journalism, cum laude, Ohio U., 1972; MA in Journalism, magna cum laude, Marshall U., 1974. Intern, reporter Tribune-Rev., Greensburg, Pa., 1972; prodn. asst. Harper's Bazaar, N.Y.C., 1972; reporter UPI, Birmingham, Ala., 1972-73; reporter, dept. editor Home Furnishings Daily, Fairchild Pubs., N.Y.C., 1974-77; account exec. supr., client svc. mgr., v.p. Burson-Marsteller, N.Y.C., 1977-83; group mgr., v.p. pub. rels. div. Ketchum Communications, 1983-84; freelance writer, editor, 1984-89; dir. retail communications Deloitte & Touche Retail Svcs. Group, N.Y., 1989-93; writer and author, 1993—. grad. teaching asst. Sch. Journalism/Reporting, Marshall U., Huntington, W.Va., 1973-74. Home and Office: 237 E 20th St New York NY 10003-1805

FENNELLY, JANE COREY, lawyer; b. N.Y.C., Dec. 12, 1942; d. Joseph and Josephine (Corey) F. BA, Cornell U., 1964; MLS, UCLA, 1968; JD, Loyola U., L.A., 1974. Bar: Calif. 1974, U.S. Dist. Ct. (ctrl. and so. dists.) Calif. 1974, U.S. Dist. Ct. (ea. dist.) Calif. 1977, U.S. Dist. Ct. (no. dist.) Calif. 1980, N.Y. 1982, Colo. 1993, Ariz. 1995. Ptnr. Graham & James, 1976-83; with legal dept. Bank of Am., L.A., 1973-76, Wyman, Bautzer, Kuchel & Silbert, L.A., 1983-87, Dennis, Shafer, Fennelly & Creim (merged with Bronson & McKinnon), L.A., 1987-96; with Squire, Sanders & Dempsey, Phoenix, 1996-98, Fennelly & Assocs., Phoenix, 1998—. Mem. ABA, N.Y. State Bar Assn., Am. Bankruptcy Inst., Calif. Bankruptcy Forum, L.A. County Bar Assn. (bd. dirs., mem. exec. com. comml. law and bankruptcy sect. 1989-92), Fin. Lawyers Conf. (pres. bd. dirs. 1983-84, mem. bd. govs. 1984—). Home: 10241 E Palo Brea Dr Scottsdale AZ 85262-2929 Office: Fennelly & Assocs PMB 612 Ste D-8 34522 N Scottsdale Rd Scottsdale AZ 85262

FENNELLY, WILLIAM, basketball coach; b. Davenport, Iowa., May 14, 1957; m. Deborah fennelly; children: Billy, Steven. BBA and Econs., William Penn Coll., 1979. Women's basketball coach William Penn Coll., Fresno State U., Notre Dame (Ind.) U.; head women's basketball coach U. Toledo, Ohio, Iowa State U., Ames, 1995—. Office: Iowa State Univ Jacobson Athletic Bldg 1800 S 4th St Ames IA 50011*

FENNEMA, BETTY JANE, nurse; b. Chgo., Nov. 21, 1942; d. William Louis and Dorothy Helen (Swanson) Bertz; m. Eugene Raymond Fennema, Apr. 10, 1965; children: Paul Brett, Craig William. BS, Coll. St. Francis, Joliet, Ill., 1979; postgrad., Roseland Community Hosp. Sch., Chgo., 1964. Cert. childbirth educator, CPR instr., trainer, perinatal bereavement counselor, lactation educator, instr. infant massage. Staff nurse nursery St. Francis Hosp., Blue Island, Ill., 1964-67, asst. nurse nursery, 1967-75, head nurse post partum, 1975-80, coordinator edn., 1980-90; dir. Riverside Women and Family Ctr. Riverside Med. Ctr., Kankakee, Ill., 1990-93; staff devel. specialist, coord. perinatal edn. St. Joseph Med. Ctr., Joliet, Ill., 1993—. Mem. NAACOG, Am. Soc. Psychoprophylaxis Obstetrics, Lamaze, Internat. Childbirth Edn. Assn., Coun. Childbirth Edn. Specialists. Avocations: oil painting, reading, gardening, needlework.

FENNEMA, OWEN RICHARD, food chemistry educator; b. Hinsdale, Ill., Jan. 23, 1929; s. Nick and Fern Alma (First) F.; m. Ann Elizabeth Hammer, Aug. 22, 1948; children: Linda Gail, Karen Elizabeth, Peter Scott. BS, Kans. State U., 1950; MS, U. Wis., 1951, PhD, 1960; PhD of Agrl. and Environ. Scis. (hon.), Wageningen Agrl. U., The Netherlands, 1993. Project leader for research and devel Pillsbury Co., Mpls., 1953-57; asst. prof. food sci. dept. U. Wis., Madison, 1960-64, assoc. prof., 1964-69, prof., 1969-96, chmn. dept., 1977-81, interim chmn. Dept. Landscape Architecture, 1994-96, prof. emeritus, 1996—; cons. Grand Metropolitan, Mpls., 1979—; pub. mem. Internat. Life Scis. Inst.-Nutrition Found., 1987-90; mem. food adv. com. U.S. FDA, 1995-99. Author: Low Temperature Preservation of Foods, 1973; editor: Principles of Food Science, 2 vols., 1976, Proteins at Low Temperatures, 1979, Food Chemistry, 3d edit., 1996; mem. editl. bd. Cryobiology, 1966-82, Internat. Jour. Food Sci. and Nutrition, Jour. Food Sci., 1975-77, scientific editor, 1999—, Jour. Food Processing Preservation, 1977—, Jour. Food Biochemistry, 1977-80, Nutrition Rsch. Newsletter, 1983-98, Acta Alimentaria (Budapest, Hungary), 1990-98, South African Jour. Food Sci. and Nutrition, 1991—; sci. editor Jour. Food Sci., 1999—. Served to 2d lt. U.S. Army, 1951-53. Recipient Excellence in Teaching award U. Wis., Madison, 1977; Fulbright disting. lectr., Spain, 1992. Fellow Am. Chem. Soc. (Agrl. and Food Chemistry Divsn. award 1995), Inst. Food Technologists (pres. 1982-83, treas. 1994-99, Excellence in Tchg. award 1978, Carl R. Fellers award 1988, Nicholas Appert award 1988); mem. Am. Soc. Nutritional Sci., Am. Soc. Landscape Archts. (Wis. chpt. award Merit), Internat. Union Food Sci. and Tech. (del. 1983-88, exec. com. 1988-99, v.p. 1992-95). Fax: 608-262-6872. E-mail: ofennema@facstaff.wisc.edu. Home: 5010 Lake Mendota Dr Madison WI 53705-1305 Office: U Wis 1605 Linden Dr Madison WI 53706-1519

FENNER, PETER DAVID, communications executive; b. Newark, Apr. 18, 1936; s. John David and Janice (Gleason) F.; m. Nancy Carroll Royce, Aug. 1958; children: Guy David, Karl Gleason, James Andrew. BS in Indsl. Engring., Lehigh U., 1958; MSBA, MIT, 1975. Field engr. Factory Mut.Engring., Montclair, N.J., 1958-61; progressive assignments in pricing, engring., data processing, software devel, product planning Western Electric Co., Inc., N.J., N.Y., Mo., Colo., Calif., Mass., 1961-82; regional v.p. AT&T Network Systems, Balt. and Bethesda, Md., 1982-85, v.p. product planning, Morristown, 1986-88, pres. Transmission Systems, 1989-92; mgmt. cons., 1993-95; pres., CEO COM 21, Milpitas, Calif., 1996—; bd. dirs. Cornet Internat., Stroudsburg, Pa.; bd. advisors Metricom, Inc., Los Gatos, Calif.; bd. advisors Applied Biononics, San Rafael, Calif. Sloan fellow MIT, Cambridge, 1974-75. Mem. Westhampton Yacht Squadron. Avocations: sailing, skiing, golfing, tennis. Home: 215 Hanna Way Menlo Park CA 94025-3583 Office: Com 21 750 Tasman Dr Milpitas CA 95035-7456

FENNER, SUZAN ELLEN, lawyer; b. Grand Junction, Colo., Dec. 5, 1947; d. Harry J. and Louise (Bain) Shaw; m. Michael Lee Riddle, Apr. 24, 1969 (div. Feb. 1976); m. Peter R. Fenner, Nov. 24, 1978; children: Laura Elizabeth, Adam Kyle. BA, Tex. Tech U., 1969, JD, 1971. Bar: Tex. 1972, U.S. Dist. Ct. (no. dist.) Tex. 1972. Assoc. Smith & Baker, Lubbock, Tex., 1971-72; law clk. to presiding judge U.S. Dist. Ct., Dallas, 1972-73; assoc. Gardere & Wynne, L.L.P., Dallas, 1973-78, ptnr., 1978—; also mem. ptnrs. bd. Gardere & Wynne, L.L.P., 1991-94; chair retirement com., 1990—, chair recruiting com. 1992-94, mem. ptnrs. compensation com., 1999—; bd. dirs. Tex. Lawyers Ins. Exch., 1985—; bd. dirs. S.W. Benefits Assn. (formerly S.W. Pension Conf.), 1987-92, pres. 1990-91. Bd. dirs. East Dallas Devel. Ctr., 1982-91; Lone Star coun. Camp Fire Boys and Girls, Inc., 1995—; v.p. outdoor programs, 1996-98, pres.-elect, 1997, pres., 1998—; bd. dirs. Episcopal Ch. Women, del. to triennial nat. conv., 1994, 97; bd. dirs. Episcopal Ch. Women, Diocese of Dallas, 1992—, pres., 1996—, del. ann. conv., 1992-93, 97, asst. chancellor, 1994—, exec. coun., 1995—; pres. Episcopal Ch. Women for Episcopal Ch. of Ascension, 1992, bd. dirs., 1992-94. Mem. ABA, Tex. Bar Assn. (chmn. bar. jour. com. 1982-88), Dallas Bar Assn. (treas. employee benefits com. 1998, sec. 1999), Dallas Bus. League (pres. 1986), 500 Club. Episcopalian. Avocation: sailing. Home: 600 Goodwin Dr Richardson TX 75081-5603 Office: Gardere & Wynne LLP 1601 Elm St Ste 3000 Dallas TX 75201-4761

FENNESSEY, PAUL VINCENT, pediatrics and pharmacology, educator, research administrator; b. Oklahoma City, Oct. 3, 1942; m. Susan Blackwell; children—Shirley, Karl, Shaun. B.S. in Chemistry, U. Okla., 1964; Ph.D. in Organic Analytical Chemistry, MIT, 1968. Research asst. U. Okla., Norman, 1963-64; predoctoral fellow MIT, Cambridge, 1964-69; asst. prof. pediatrics and pharmacology U. Colo. Health Sci. Ctr., Denver, 1975-81, co-dir. mass spectral ctr. 1980, assoc. prof. pediatrics and pharmacology, 1981-90, prof. ped. and pharmacology, 1990—, vice chair pediat., 1991—. Contbr. articles to profl. jours. Asst. program scientist Viking Project, Martin Marietta Corp., Denver, 1969-72, program scientist, 1972-74. Recipient NSF Undergrad. Research award, 1963-64; Merck award in Organic Chemistry, 1963; Woodrow Wilson Nat. fellow, 1964-65; NIH fellow, 1964-68. Mem. Am. Chem. Soc., Am. Soc. Mass Spectometry, Nat. Acad. Clin. Biochemists, Soc. Inherited Metabolic Diseases, Am. Assn. Clin. Chemistry, AAAS, Am. Soc. Pharmacology and Exptl. Therapeutics, Internat. Soc. Study Xenobiotics, Sigma Xi. Home: 13009 S Parker Ave Pine CO 80470-9617 Office: U Colo Health Sci Ctr 4200 E 9th Ave # C232 Denver CO 80220-3706

FENNESSY, JOHN JAMES, radiologist, educator; b. Clonmel, Ireland, Mar. 8, 1933; s. John and Ann (McCarthy) F.; m. Ann M. O'Sullivan, Aug. 20, 1960; children—Deirdre, Conor, Sean, Emer, Rona, Nial, Ruairi. M.B., B.Ch., BAO, Univ. Coll., Dublin, Ireland, 1958. Assoc. prof. U. Chgo., 1971-74, prof., 1974—, chief chest and gastrointestinal radiology, 1971-73, acting chief diagnostic radiology, 1973-74, chmn. dept. radiology, 1974-84, assoc. chair edn., 1990—. Fellow Royal Coll. Surgeons Ireland (hon.), Am. Coll. Radiology; mem. Am. Assn. Univ. Radiologists, Chgo. Radiol. Soc., Thoracic Radiology Soc., Radiology Soc. N.Am., Am. Gastroent. Soc., Fleischner Soc., Irish Am. Cultural Inst., County Tipperary Hist. Soc., Sigma Xi, Alpha Omega Alpha. Republican. Roman Catholic. Office: U Chgo Dept Radiology 5841 S Maryland Ave Chicago IL 60637-1463

FENNING, LISA HILL, federal judge; b. Chgo., Feb. 22, 1952; d. Ivan Byron and Joan (Hennigar) Hill; m. Alan Mark Fenning, Apr. 3, 1977; 4 children. BA with honors, Wellesley Coll., 1971; JD, Yale U., 1974. Bar: Ill. 1975, Calif. 1979, U.S. Dist. Ct. (no. dist.) Ill., U.S. Dist. Ct. (no., ea., so. & cen. dists.) Calif., U.S. Ct. Appeals (6th, 7th & 9th cirs.), U.S. Supreme Ct. 1989. Law clk. U.S. Ct. Appeals 7th cir., Chgo., 1974-75; assoc. Jenner and Block, Chgo., 1975-77, O'Melveny and Myers, L.A., 1977-85; judge U.S. Bankruptcy Ct. Cen. Dist. Calif., L.A., 1985—; bd. govs. Nat. Conf. Bankruptcy Judges, 1989-92; pres. Nat. Conf. of Women's Bar Assns., N.C., 1987-88, pres.-elect, 1986-87, v.p., 1985-86, bd. dirs.; lectr., program coord. in field; bd. govs. Nat. Conf. Bankruptcy Judges Endowment for Edn., 1992—, Am. Bankruptcy Inst., 1994-97; mem., bd. advisors Nat. Jud. Edn. Program to Promote Equality for Women and Men in the Cts., 1994—. Mem., bd. advisors: Lawyer Hiring & Training Report, 1985-87; contbr. articles to profl. jours. Durant scholar Wellesley Coll., 1971; named one of Am's. 100 Most Important Women Ladies Home Jour., 1988, one of L.A.'s 50 Most Powerful Women Lawyers, L.A. Bus. Jour., 1998. Fellow Am. Bar Found., Am. Coll. Bankruptcy (bd. regents 1995-98); mem. ABA (standing com. on fed. jud. improvements 1995-98, mem. commn. on women in the profession 1987-91, Women's Caucus 1987—, Individual Rights and Responsibilities sect. 1984—, bus. law sect. 1986—, bus. bankruptcy com.), Nat. Assn. Women Judges (nat. task force gender bias in the cts. 1986-87, 93-94), Nat. Conf. Bankruptcy Judges (chair endowment edn. bd.), Am. Bankruptcy Inst. (nominating com. 1994-95, bd. steering com. statis. project 1994-96), Calif. State Bar Assn. (chair com. on women in law 1986-87), Women Lawyers' Assn. L.A. (ex officio mem., bd. dirs., chmn., founder com. on status of women lawyers 1984-85, officer nominating com. 1986, founder, mem. Do-It-Yourself Mentor Network 1986-96), Phi Beta Kappa. Democrat. Office: US Bankruptcy Ct 255 E Temple St Rm 1682 Los Angeles CA 90012-3334

FENNO, RICHARD FRANCIS, JR., political science educator; b. Winchester, Mass., Dec. 12, 1926; s. Richard Francis and Mary Brooks (Tredennick) F.; m. Nancy Davidson, Sept. 10, 1948; children: Mark Richard, Craig Pierce. Student, Williams Coll., 1944-46; AB, Amherst Coll., 1948, LLD (hon.), 1986; PhD, Harvard U., 1956; LHD (hon.), Union Coll., 1989. Instr. govt. Wheaton (Mass.) Coll., 1951-53; instr. polit. sci. Amherst Coll., 1953-56, asst. prof., 1956-57; mem. faculty U. Rochester, N.Y., 1957—; prof. U. Rochester, 1964—, Don Alonzo Watson prof. polit. sci., 1971-78, William R. Kenan prof. polit. sci., 1978—, Disting. Univ. prof., 1985—. Author: The President's Cabinet, 1959, The Power of the Purse, 1966, Congressmen in Committees, 1973, Home Style: U.S. House Members in Their Districts, 1978 (Woodrow Wilson Found. award 1979, D.B. Hardeman prize 1980), (with F. Munger) National Politics and Federal Aid to Education, 1962, The Making of a Senator: Dan Quayle, 1989, The Presidential Odyssey of John Glenn, 1990, Watching Politicians, 1990, The Emergence of a Senate Leader: Pete Domenici and the Reagan Budget, 1991, Learning to Legislate: The Senate Education of Arlen Specter, 1991, When Incumbency Fails: The Senate Career of Mark Andrews, 1992; editor: The Yalta Conf., 1956, 73, Senators on the Campaign Trail: The Politics of Representation, 1996, Learning to Govern: An Institutional View of the 104th Congress, 1997. Served with USNR, 1944-46. Social Sci. Research Council fellow, 1960-61; Rockefeller Found. fellow, 1963-64; Ford fellow, 1971-72; Guggenheim fellow, 1976-77; Russell Sage Found. grantee, 1978, 80-85. Mem. Am. Polit. Sci. Assn. (council 1971-73, v.p. 1975-76, pres. 1984-85), Nat. Acad. Scis., Social Sci. Research Council (dir. 1973-75), Am. Acad. Arts and Scis., Am. Philos. Soc., Phi Beta Kappa. Home: 108 Farm Brook Dr Rochester NY 14625-1519

FENOGLIO-PREISER, CECILIA METTLER, pathologist, educator; b. N.Y.C., Nov. 28, 1943; d. Frederick Albert and Cecilia Charlotte (Asper) Mettler; m. John Fenoglio Jr., May 27, 1967 (div. 1977); children: Timothy, Johanna, Andreas, Nicholas; m. Wolfgang F.E. Preiser, Feb. 16, 1985. BS, Coll. St. Elizabeth, 1965; MD, Georgetown U., 1969. Diplomate Am. Bd. Pathology. Intern Presbyn. Hosp., N.Y.C., 1969-70; dir. Central Tissue Facility Columbia-Presbyn. Med. Ctr., N.Y.C., 1976-83; co-dir. div. surg. pathology Presbyn. Hosp., N.Y.C., 1978-82; div. div. surg. pathology Presbyn. Hosp., 1982-83; dir. Electron Microscop. Lab. Internat. Inst. Human Reprodn., 1978-85; assoc. prof. pathology Coll. Physicians and Surgeons, Columbia U., 1981-82, prof., 1982-83, attending pathologist, 1982-83; dir. lab. services Albuquerque VA Med. Ctr., 1983-90; prof. pathology U. N.Mex. Sch. Medicine, Albuquerque, 1983-90, also vice-chmn. dept. pathology; MacKenzie prof., chmn. dept. pathology and lab. medicine U. Cin. Sch. Medicine, 1990—. Author: General Pathology, 1983, Gastrointestinal Pathology, An Atlas and Text, 1989, 2nd edit., 1999, Tumors of the Large and Small Intestine, 1990; editor: Advances in Pathobiology Cell Membranes, 1988-92, Advances in Pathobiology: Aging and Neoplasia, 1976, Progress in Surgical Pathology, vols. I-XIV, 1980-87, Advances in Pathology, vols. I-V, 1988-89. Grantee NIH, 1973, 79-82, 94-87, 85-94, Cancer Rsch. Ctr., 1975-83, Population Coun., 1977-83, Nat. Ileitis and Colitis Found., 1979-80, Am. Cancer Soc., 1987-94. Mem. NSABP (sci. adv. bd.), AAAS (life), U.S. and Can. Acad. Pathology (edn. com. 1980-85, com. 1984-87, exec. com. 1987-91, v.p. 1987, pres.-elect 1988, pres. 1989), Internat. Acad. Pathology (N.Am. v.p. 1990-94, pres. 1996-98, exec. com. 1990), Am. Assn. Pathologists, N.Y. Acad. Sci., N.Y. Acad. Medicine, Fedn. Am. Scientists for Exptl. Biology, Gastrointestinal Pathologist Group (founding mem. edn. com. 1983-85, sec.-treas. 1993-96, pres.-elect 1996, pres. 1997), S.W. Oncology Group (chmn. GI tumor biology com., chmn. pathology com.), Arthur Purdy Stout Soc. (coun. 1987-90). Office: U Cin Sch Medicine 231 Bethesda Ave Cincinnati OH 45229-2827

FENSELAU, CATHERINE CLARKE, chemistry educator; b. York, Nebr., Apr. 15, 1939; d. Lee Keckley and Muriel (Thomas) Clarke; m. Allan Herman Fenselau, 1962 (div. 1980); children: Andrew Clarke, Thomas Stewart; m. Robert James Cotter, 1984. AB, Bryn Mawr Coll., 1961; PhD, Stanford U., 1965. Research scientist U. Calif.-Berkeley, 1965-67; instr. to prof. Johns Hopkins U., Balt., 1967-87; prof., chmn. dept. chemistry and biochemistry U. Md., Balt. County, 1987-98; prof., chmn. dept. chemistry and biochemistry U. Md., College Park, 1998—; cons. NIH, NSF, U.S. Dept. Agr., U.S. Army, FDA, others. Editor Biomed. Environ. Mass Spectrometry, 1973-89; assoc. editor Analytical Chemistry, 1990—; contbr. articles to profl. jours. Mem. Am. Soc. Mass Spectrometry (pres.), Am. Chem. Soc. (Garvan medal 1985, Md. Chemist award Md. sect. 1989), AAAS, Am. Soc. Pharmacology and Exptl. Therapeutics. Office: U Md Dept Chemistry/Biochemistry College Park MD 20742-2021

FENSIN, DANIEL, diversified financial service company executive; b. 1943. BS in Acctg., DePaul U., 1965. Ptnr. Topel, Forman & Co., 1965-74; ceo, mng. ptnr. Blackman Kallick Bartelstein, L.L.P., Chgo., 1974—. Office: Blackman Kallick Bartelstein 300 S Riverside Plz Ste 660 Chicago IL 60606-6616*

FENSKE, EDWARD CHARLES, special education educator, consultant; b. West Palm Beach, Fla., Oct. 28, 1949; s. Edward and Frances (Frankenberger) F.; m. Susan Louise Schaeffer, Dec. 29, 1971; children: Joanna S., Melissa S. BS, U.S. Mil. Acad., 1971; MA, Trenton State Coll., 1976, EdS, 1981. Cert. tchr. handicapped, tchr. cons. learning disabilities, prin.-supr., N.J. Tchr. aide Carolyn Stokes Day Nursery, Trenton, N.J., 1974-75; child therapist Princeton (N.J.) Child Devel. Inst., 1975-76, head tchr., 1976-77, edn. program coord., 1977-95, dir. edn. programs, 1995—. Contbr. articles to profl jours.; mem. edit. rev. bd. Edn. and Treatment Children Jour., 1983. Pres. Sherbrooke II Civic League, Trenton, 1990, Ewing Girls Softall Assn., 1998. 1st Lt. U.S. Army, 1971-74. Mem. Coun. Exceptional Children, Autism Soc. Am. (Mercer County chpt.), Assn. for Behavior Analysis, Kappa Delta Pi. Fax: (609) 924-4119. E-mail: njpcdi@earthlink.net. Office: Princeton Child Devel Inst 300 Cold Soil Rd Princeton NJ 08540-2002

FENSKE, JERALD ALLAN, minister; b. Wausau, Wis., Sept. 29, 1960; s. Martin W. and Whynona B. (Ramthun) F.; m. Kay A. Lang, Aug. 17, 1985; children: Kiersten, Deena. BA, Lakeland Coll., 1983; MDiv, United Theol. Sem. of the Twin Cities, 1988. Ordained to ministry United Ch. of Christ, 1991. Pastor Congl. Ch. of Excelsior United Ch. of Christ, Excelsior, Minn., 1998—. Mem. Excelsior Masons, Western Clergy Cluster United Ch. of Christ, Excelsior Ministerial Assoc., Minn. Conf. United Ch. of Christ Nominating Com. Mem. Lakeland Coll. Alumni Assn. (Zeta Chi chpt.). Home: 17411 Creek Ridge Pass Minnetonka MN 55345 Office: Congl Ch of Excelsior United Ch of Christ 471 Third St Excelsior MN 55331

FENSTER, CRAIG MICHAEL, actuary; b. N.Y.C., Jan. 5, 1964; s. Harvey Leonard and Edy Lou (Gelfand) F. AB, Columbia U., 1986; MBA, Trinity Coll., U. Dublin, 1999—. Actuarial trainee Am. Internat. Group, N.Y.C., 1986, actuarial assoc., 1986-91, sr. actuarial analyst, 1991-92; actuarial analyst Ctr. Re, 1992-95, asst. vice pres., 1995-99. Mem. exec. com. Varsity C Club of Columbia U., track chmn., 1988—; asst. scoutmaster Troop 1 Roseland (N.J.) Boy Scouts Am., 1982-86, Everybody Wins Power Lunch Reader, 1996-99, Greater NY Counc., BSA (Boy Scouts of Amer.), vice chair, 1997-99. James P. Gorman Meml. scholar West Essex Regional High Sch., 1982. Mem. Nat. Eagle Scout Assn., Old Guard of Camp Glen Gray, Phi Epsilon Pi (v.p. 1986). Avocations: skiing, running.

FENSTER, HERBERT LAWRENCE, lawyer; b. N.Y.C., Mar. 29, 1935; s. Oscar Samuel and Bessie Estelle (Schafran) F.; m. Gail Frances Meier, Apr. 18, 1964; children—Christopher Lawrence, Jennifer Gail, Jonathan Adam; m. Jane Porter Elam Allen, Dec. 31, 1993. A.B., U. Pa., 1957, M.A., 1958; J.D., U. Va., 1961. Bar: Va. 1961, D.C. 1962, U.S. Supreme Ct. 1967, Colo., 1993. Assoc., Sellers, Conner & Cuneo, Washington, 1961-66, ptnr., 1967-78, sr. ptnr., 1978-80; sr. ptnr. McKenna, Conner & Cuneo, 1980-90, McKenna & Cuneo, 1990—. Author treatise Anti Deficiency Act, ABA, 1979. Litigation counsel Reagan-Bush Campaign Com., Washington, 1980-83, pres.'s pvt. sector survey Grace Commn., 1982—; bd. dirs. Nat. Chamber Litigation Ctr., Washington, 1983—; bd. dirs. Keewaydin Found., Middlebury Vermont, 1982—, also trustee, corp. dir. Fenster Assn. Trial Lawyers Am.; mem. ABA, Fed. Bar Assn., D.C. Bar Assn., Am. Law Inst. Republican. Episcopalian. Clubs: Metropolitan, University. Home: 845 6th St Boulder CO 80302-7418 Office: McKenna & Cuneo 815 Connecticut Ave NW Washington DC 20006-4004 also: 370 17th St Denver CO 80202-1370

FENSTER, ROBERT DAVID, lawyer; b. N.Y.C., Sept. 25, 1946; s. Alfred Howard and Esther (Eisenberg) F.; m. Janet Lynne Shanes, July 27, 1969; children: Lori Beth, Eric Steven. BA, Queens Coll., 1968; JD, Bklyn. Law Sch., 1973. Bar: N.Y. 1974, U.S. Dist. Ct. (so. and ea. dists.) N.Y. 1974, U.S. Supreme Ct. 1977. Investigator, prosecutor N.Y. Stock Exchange, N.Y.C., 1972-73; assoc. various law firms, Rockland County, N.Y., 1973-80; ptnr. Fenster & Weiss, New City, 1980—; bd. dirs. Brit. Pub. Corp., various other corps. Advisor Clarkstown Youth Ct., New City, N.Y., 1982; bd. dirs. Legal Aid Soc., Rockland County, 1974-78, Nyack Hosp. Found., Good Samaritan Hosp. Found. Mem. ABA, N.Y. State Bar Assn., Rockland County Bar Assn., Am. Arbitration Assn. (arbitrator). Office: Fenster & Weiss 337 N Main St Ste 11 New City NY 10956-4310

FENSTERSTOCK, BLAIR COURTNEY, lawyer; b. N.Y.C., Aug. 20, 1950; s. Nathaniel and Gertrude (Isaacson) F.: children: Michael Bayard, Evan Steele, Laurel Sage. AB summa cum laude, Bowdoin Coll., 1972; JD, Columbia U., 1975. Bar: Ind., N.Y. 1976, U.S. Dist. Ct. (so., ea. and no. dists.) N.Y., U.S. Ct. Appeals (2d cir.), U.S. Customs Ct., U.S. Ct. Internat. Trade, U.S. Supreme Ct. Assoc. Simpson, Thacher & Bartlett, N.Y.C., 1975-79, Dewey, Ballantine, Bushby, Palmer & Wood, N.Y.C., 1979-83; v.p., assoc. gen. counsel, asst. sec. Reliance Group Holdings, Inc., N.Y.C., 1983-91; sr. v.p., gen. counsel, sec. Frank B. Hall & Co., Inc., 1987-92; ptnr. Sutherland, Asbill & Brennan, 1993-95, Brock, Fensterstock, Silverstein & McAuliffe, LLC, N.Y.C., 1995-98, Fensterstock & Ptnrs., LLP, N.Y.C., 1998—; mem. bd. visitors Columbia U. Sch. Law, 1988—. Bd. dirs. Safety Nat. Casualty Corp., 1990-93. Harlan Fiske Stone scholar Columbia U., 1975. Mem. ABA, N.Y. State Bar Assn., Assn. Bar City N.Y., Coun. N.Y. Law Assocs. (bd. dirs. 1979-82), Lawyers Com. for Internat. Human Rights (bd. dirs. 1979-80), Am. Arbitration Assn. (panel of arbitrators), Internat. Peace Acad. (sec. 1977-79), Univ. Club (N.Y.C.), Aspetuck Valley Country Club (Weston, Conn.) (bd. govs. 1993-97), Palmas del Mar Country Club, Phi Beta Kappa. Republican. Jewish. Home: 799 Park Ave New York NY 10021-3275 Office: Fensterstock & Ptnrs LLP 30 Wall St New York NY 10005-2201

FENTON, ARNOLD N., obstetrician, gynecologist, educator; b. N.Y.C., 1921. MD, Columbia U., 1944. Intern Lenox Hill Hosp., N.Y.C., 1944-45; asst. resident ob-gyn Presbyn. Hosp., N.Y.C., 1945-46, 48-50, fellow gynecol. pathology, asst. ob-gyn, 1949-50; fellow gynecol. pathology Columbia U. Coll. Physicians and Surgeons, N.Y.C., 1949-50, lectr. ob-gyn, 1951—; resident in gynecology Mt. Sinai Hosp., N.Y.C., 1950-51; prof. Cornell U., N.Y.C., 1975—, vice chmn. ob-gyn, 1980—, Edie and Marvin H. Schur Disting. prof. ob-gyn, 1986—. Lt. (j.g.) M.C., USNR, 1947-48. Fellow

ACS, Am. Coll. Ob-Gyns; mem. AMA. Office: North Shore U Hosp 300 Community Dr Manhasset NY 11030-3801

FENTON, CLIFTON LUCIEN, investment banker; b. Bryan, Ohio, May 11, 1943; s. Gibson Lucien and Elizabeth (Newcomer) F.; m. Judith Todd Wallis, June 23, 1973; children: Gregory, Eric, Alyssa. AB, Princeton U., 1965; JD, Ohio State U., 1968; MBA, Columbia U., 1970. Bar: Ohio 1968. Assoc. Bank N.Y., N.Y.C., 1970-72, Morgan Guaranty Trust Co., N.Y.C., 1972; v.p. Kidder, Peabody, N.Y.C., 1972-84; mng. dir. Prudential-Bache Securities, N.Y.C., 1984-89; v.p., nat. mgr. John Nuveen & Co., Chgo., 1989-95, v.p. and mgr. Investment Banking Divsn., 1995—. Bd. trustees Ravinnia Festival; mem. Winnetka (Ill.) Bible Ch. Mem. Bond Club N.Y., Met. Club (N.Y.C.), Princeton Club (N.Y.C.), Univ. Club Chgo. Avocations: water and snow skiing, sailing, piano. Home: 808 Sunset Rd Winnetka IL 60093-3850 Office: John Nuveen & Co Inc 333 W Wacker Dr Ste 3200 Chicago IL 60606-1286

FENTON, COLIN PATRICK, investment banker; b. Boulder, Colo., Dec. 13, 1970; s. Francis Michael and Karen Leslie (Rohlf) F. BA in History, Princeton U., 1993; MS in Internat. Polit. Economy, Georgetown U., Washington, 1995. Registered rep. N.Y. Stock Exch. Rsch. asst. Amb. Chester A. Crocker, Washington, 1994-95; global metals economist and strategist Goldman, Sachs & Co., N.Y.C., 1996—. Contbr. articles to profl. jours. Mentor Everybody Wins Found., N.Y.C., 1996—. Avocations: reading, science and technology, Africa, short-story writing, golf. Office: Goldman Sachs & Co 1 New York Plz Fl 46 New York NY 10004-1901

FENTON, DONALD MASON, retired oil company executive; b. L.A., May 23, 1929; s. Charles Youdan and Dorothy (Mason) F.; m. Margaret M. Keehler, Apr. 24, 1953; children: James Michael, Douglas Charles. BS, U. Calif., L.A., 1952, PhD, 1958. Chemist Rohm and Haas Co., Phila., 1958-61; sr. rsch. chemist Union Oil Co., Brea, Calif., 1962-67, rsch. assoc., 1967-72, sr. rsch. assoc., 1972-82, mgr. planning and devel., 1982-85; mgr. new tech. devel. Unocal, Brea, 1985-92; cons. AMSCO, 1967-73; co-founder, 1st chmn. Petroleum Environ. Rsch. Forum; chmn. bd. dirs. Calif. Engring. Found., 1991-92. With U.S. Army, 1953-55. Inventor in field. Fellow Am. Inst. Chemists, Alpha Chi Sigma; mem. Am. Chem. Soc. Achievements include more than 100 patents in field; co-invention of unisulf process. Home: 2861 E Alden Pl Anaheim CA 92806-4401

FENTON, LAWRENCE JULES, pediatric educator; b. Chgo., June 1, 1940; s. Arthur S. Fenton and Dorothy (Schochet) Wade; m. Gayle Ann Yeager, Apr. 10, 1965; children: Lori Ann, Scott L. BS, U. Mich., 1962; MD, U. Cin., 1966. Diplomate Am. Bd. Pediatrics, Sub-bd. Neonatal and Perinatal Medicine. Intern U. Cin. Med. Ctr., 1966-67, jr. and sr. resident, 1967-69, chief pediatric resident, 1969-70, fellow neonatal, perinatal medicine, 1972-74; asst. prof. pediatrics U. Ariz. Health Scis. Ctr., Tucson, 1974-78; assoc. prof. pediatrics U. S.D. Sch. Medicine, Sioux Falls, 1978-84, head sect. of neonatal, perinatal medicine, 1979-88, prof. pediatrics, 1984—, chmn. dept. pediatrics, 1988—; dir. newborn intensive care unit Sioux Valley Hosp., 1980-88; chmn. pharmacy and therapeutics com. Sioux Valley Hosp., 1992-97, bd. dirs., 1997—. Contbr. articles to med. jours.; author: (with others) Current Therapy in Neonatal and Perinatal Medicine, 1989, Conn's Current Therapy, 1989, 90. Chmn. rsch. funding group Am. Heart Assn., Dakota Affiliate, 1986-88; mem. allocations com. Childrn's Miracle Network Telethon, Sioux Falls, 1986-87; bd. dirs. Childrens Miracle Network, 1996-99; chmn. Health Svcs. Adv. Com., State of S.D., 1991-93. Maj. U.S. Army, 1970-72. Rsch. grantee Nat. Inst. Child Health and Human Devel., Tucson, Sioux Falls, 1976-79, Am. Heart Assn., Sioux Falls, 1984; recipient Army Commendation medal, 1991-93, Pioneer award S.D. Perinatal Assn., 1993; inductee Hall of Honor Children's Hosp. U. Cin. MEd. Ctr., 1993. Fellow Am. Acad. Pediatrics; mem. Society for Pediatric Rsch., Midwest Soc. for Pediatric Rsch., Assn. Med. Sch. Pediatric Dept. Chmn., S.D. States Med. Assn. Avocations: water skiing, boating, hiking, cross country skiing, classical music. Office: U SD Sch Medicine Dept Pediatrics 1100 S Euclid Ave Dept Of Sioux Falls SD 57105-0411

FENTON, LEWIS LOWRY, lawyer; b. Palo Alto, Calif., Aug. 20, 1925; s. Norman and Jessie (Chase) F.; m. Gloria J. Palmieri, Aug. 21, 1978; children: Lewis Lowry, Juanita F. Donnelly, Daniel Norman, Pamela Chase. B.A., Stanford U., 1948, LL.B., 1950. Bar: Calif. 1950, U.S. Dist. Ct. (no. dist.) Calif. Atty. Calif. Dept. Pub. Works, 1950-52; chmn., bd. dirs. Hoge, Fenton, Jones & Appel, Inc., Monterey, San Luis Obispo and San Jose, 1952-93; counsel Fenton & Keller, P.C., Monterey, 1993—, Hoge, Fenton, Jones & Appel, Inc., San Jose, 1993—; bd. dirs. 1st Nat. Bank Monterey County, 1984— (chmn. 1987-90). Mem. bldg. com. Community Hosp. Monterey Peninsula, Carmel, 1961-62; found. dir. Monterey Jazz Festival, 1958; past bd. dirs. Monterey Peninsula Coll., pres. 1971-72, Monterey Inst. Fgn. Studies; past pres. and bd. dirs. York Sch., Monterey, Calif., 1960-74, chmn. bd., 1992—; bd. dirs. Monterey Bay Aquarium, Community Found. Monterey County, chmn., 1998—; bd. visitors Stanford Law Sch. Served to 2d lt. USAAF, 1942-46. Fellow Am. Coll. Trial Lawyers, Internat. Acad. Trial Lawyers; mem. ABA, Calif. Bar Assn., Santa Clara Bar Assn., Monterey County Bar Assn. (pres. 1963, 1st Chief Justice Gibson award), Assn. Def. Counsel (pres. 1969), Nat. Bd. Trial Advocacy, Nat. Assn. R.R. Counsel, Internat. Assn. Def. Counsel, Def. Research Inst., Am. Judicature Soc., Am. Acad. Hosp. Attys., Am. Bd. Trial Advs. (adv.), Stanford U. Alumni Assn. (pres. 1966-67), Calif. Med. Legal Nat. Health Lawyers Assn. Episcopalian (vestryman, sr. warden 1956-58). Clubs: Cypress Point, Old Capital, Pacheco, Pacific Union. Home and Office: PO Box 791 Monterey CA 93942-0791

FENTON, MARJORIE, university official, consultant; b. Warren, Ohio, Feb. 7, 1935; d. Leland Reed and Elma Arlene Titus; m. Harold W. Fenton, June 11, 1955 (div. Sept. 1984); children: Brian, Amy. BS in Edn., Kent State U., 1985, M in Edn. Adminstrn., 1988. Treas. Champion Local Sch. Dist., Warren, 1967-80, Trumbull County Joint Vocat. Sch. Dist., Warren, 1980-89; pres., cons. Sch. Mgmt. Svcs., Inc., Worthington, Ohio, 1989—; coord. Ashland U., Ohio, 1989—; cons. Ohio Dept. Edn., Columbus, 1980-84, 89—, Kemper Securities, Inc., 1993-94; trustee Champion Cmty. Sr. Housing, Inc., Warren, 1982-90, Trimble & Julian, Inc., 1996—. Mem. Trumbull County Bd. Edn., Warren, 1968-93. Recipient Exemplary Service to Edn. award Champion Local Schs., Warren, 1980. Mem. Ohio Assn. Sch. Bus. Ofcls. (state pres. 1979-80, state legis. chmn. 1980-89, Pres.'s Disting. Svc. award 1984, Recognition Outstanding Svc. 1985), Assn. Sch. Bus. Ofcls. Internat. (chair profl. devel. rsch. com.), Ohio Sch. Bds. Assn., Phi Delta Kappa. Avocations: travel, reading.

FENTON, NOEL JOHN, venture capitalist; b. New Haven, May 24, 1938; s. Arnold Alexander and Carla (Mathiasen) F.; m. Sarah Jane Hamilton, Aug. 14, 1965; children: Wendy, Devon, Peter, Lance. B.S., Cornell U., 1959; M.B.A., Stanford U., 1963. Research asst. Stanford (Calif.) U., 1963-64; v.p. Mail Systems Corp., Redwood City, Calif., 1964-66; v.p., gen. mgr. products div. Acurex Corp., Mountain View, Calif., 1966-72, pres., chief exec. officer, dir., 1972-83; pres., chief exec. officer, dir. Covalent Systems Corp., Sunnyvale, Calif., 1983-86; mng. gen. ptnr. Trinity Ventures Ltd., 1986—; bd. dirs. Requisite Tech., Inc., Decision.ism, Inc., Enterprise Network Sys., Inc., LoopNet, Inc., SciQuest, Inc. Chmn. adv. coun. resource Ctr. for Women, chmn. bd. dirs. 1987-88; mem. San Jose Econ. Devel. Task Force, 1983, Young Pres.'s Orgn., 1976-88, Pres. Reagan's Bus. Adv. Panel; mem. World Pres.'s Orgn., 1988—, dir., 1994—. Lt. (j.g.) USN, 1959-61. Mem. Am. Electronics Assn. (chmn. 1978-79, dir. 1976-80), Santa Clara County Mfrs. Group (dir. 1980-83), Chief Execs. Orgn., Stanford Bus. Sch. Alumni Assn. (pres. 1976-77, dir. 1971-76), Stanford Alumni Assn. (exec. bd. 1985-89). Republican. Episcopalian. Home: 247 Mapache Dr Portola Vally CA 94028-7354 Office: Trinity Ventures Bldg 1 3000 Sand Hill Rd Ste 240 Menlo Park CA 94025-7113

FENTON, ROBERT EARL, electrical engineering educator; b. Bklyn., Sept. 30, 1933; s. Theodore Andrew and Evelyn Virginia (Brent) F.; m. Alice Earlyn Gray, Dec. 13, 1934; children: Douglas Earl, Andrea Leigh. BEE, Ohio State U., 1957, MEE, 1960, PhD in Electrical Engring., 1965. Registered profl. engr., Ohio. Engr. rsch. N. Am. Aviation, Columbus, Ohio, 1957; instr. electric engring. Ohio State U., Columbus, 1960-65, prof., 1965-95, prof. emeritus, 1995—; cons. Gen. Motors Transp. Systems Div., Warren, Mich., 1974-80, Battelle Meml. Inst., Columbus, Ohio, 1991-93. Inventor kinesthetic-tactile display; contbr. articles to profl. jours. Capt. USAF, 1957-60. Recipient Outstanding Tchr. award Eta Kappa Nu, 1963, Neil Armstrong award Ohio Soc. Profl. Engrs., 1971, Pioneering Rsch. award Nat. Automated Hwy. Systems Consortium, 1997. Fellow IEEE, Radio Club of Am. (Significant Achievement award IVHS Ohio, 1993), IEEE Vehicular Tech. Soc. (pres. 1985-87, v.p. 1983-85, treas. 1981-83, prize paper 1980, Stuart F. Meyer Meml. award 1998); mem. Sigma Xi. Avocations: bicycling, swimming, classical music. Home: 2177 Oakmount Rd Columbus OH 43221-1229 Office: Ohio State Univ Dept Elec Engring 2015 Neil Ave Dept Elec Columbus OH 43210-1210

FENTON, ROBERT LEONARD, lawyer; b. Detroit, Sept. 14, 1929; s. Ben B. and Stella Frances (Saffir) F.; children: Robert L. Jr., Cynthia R. AB, Syracuse U., 1952; LLB, U. Mich., 1955. Bar: Mich. 1955. Asso. Marks, Levi, Thill & Wiseman, Detroit, 1955-60; ptnr. Fenton, Nederlander, Tracy & Dodge, Detroit, 1960-85; pvt. practice Detroit, 1985—; adj. prof. U. Mich. Law Sch.; lectr. Flint and Lansing Real Estate Bds., 1966-68; spl. counsel Detroit Fire Dept., 1975—, Mich. Motion Picture and TV Commn., 1978-82; producer Universal Studios, Calif., 1983-86, 20th Century Fox, 1986-87; guest lectr. U. Mich. Law Sch., 1998; presenter entertainment law seminar, U. Mich., Apr. 1998, writer's workshop Holland Am. Cruise Lines, Feb. 1999. Author: (novels) Black Tie Only, 1990, Blue Orchids, 1992, Royal Invitation, 1995; producer NBC movie of week Double Standard, 1988, Woman on the Ledge, 1993. Treas. Oakland County Dem. Com., 1960-64; mem. Dem. State Fin. Com., 1966-69, Nat. Fin. Com., 1962-74, Dem. Pres.'s Club, 1962-74; fin. adviser to Mayor Roman S. Gribbs, 1969-73, Mayor Coleman A. Young, 1974-94; chmn. State of Mich. Film and TV Commn.; bd. dirs. Detroit Bicentennial Commn., Rivers and Harbour Congress of U.S.; mem. adv. bd. NAACP, U. Mich. Pres.'s Club. Served with USAF, 1950-52. Recipient Distinguished Pub. Service medal City of Detroit, 1973; named Man of the 60's City of Detroit, 1964; decorated Order of St. Johns of Jerusalem, 1980. Mem. ABA, Mich., Detroit bar assns., Econs. Club, Acad. Magical Arts, Soc. Preservation Variety Arts, Franklin Hills Country Club, Variety Club of Detroit (bd. dirs.), Variety Clubs Internat., Recess Club (Detroit), St. James Club (L.A., N.Y.C., London, Paris), Mt. Kenya Safari Club (Nairobi), Masons, Shriners. Office: Village Park Bldg 31800 Northwestern Hwy Ste 390 Farmington Hills MI 48334

FENTON, THOMAS CONNER, lawyer; b. Cin., Feb. 9, 1954; S. William Conner and Virginia (Rawnsley) F.; m. Karen Lois Haswell, Oct. 20, 1979; children: Margaret Lois, Rebecca Conner, Robert Ellis. BA, Centre Coll., 1976; JD, Ohio State U., 1979. Bar: Ky. 1979, U.S. Dist. Ct. (we. dist.) Ky. 1979, U.S. Ct. Appeals (D.C. cir.) 1981, U.S. Dist. Ct. (ea. dist.) Ky. 1985, U.S. Ct. Appeals (6th cir.) 1986. Assoc. Greenebaum, Treitz, Brown & Marshall, Louisville, 1979-85, ptnr., 1985-88; v.p., counsel Nat. City Bank Ky., Louisville, 1989-93; counsel Nat. City Corp., Cleve., 1989-93; v.p. human resources Nat. City Processing Co., Louisville, 1993-95; of counsel Morgan & Pottinger PSC, Louisville, 1996—; lectr. Ohio Bankers Assn. Sch. of Human Resources Adminstrn., 1989-91. Author: Affirmative Action Relevant to Bankers, 1996. Bd. dirs. Elder Serve Inc., Louisville, 1983-91, 95—, sec. 1984-86, v.p., 1986-87, pres., 1987-90; bd. dirs. Louisville Youth Choir, Inc., 1996—, chmn., 1997—. Mem. Ky. Bar Assn. (chmn. labor rels. law sect. 1981-83), Louisville Bar Assn. Methodist. Home: 11003 Fox Moore Ct Louisville KY 40223-5531 Office: Morgan & Pottinger PSC 601 W Main St Louisville KY 40202-2976

FENTON, THOMAS E., JR., federal judge. Apptd. part-time magistrate judge U.S. Dist. Ct. Alaska, 1991. Fax: (907) 456-2615. Office: 324 US Fed Bldg/Courthouse 101 12th Ave Fairbanks AK 99701-6236

FENTON, THOMAS TRAIL, journalist; b. Balt., Apr. 8, 1930; s. Matthew Clark and Beatrice (Trail) F.; m. Simone France Marie Lopes-Curval, Jan. 10, 1959; children: Ariane France, Thomas Trail. A.B., Dartmouth Coll., 1952; PhD (hon.), U. Balt., 1999. Mem. staff Balt. Sun, 1961-70, chief Rome bur., 1966-68, chief Paris bur., 1968-70; reporter-producer Rome bur. CBS News, 1970-73, corr. Tel Aviv bur., 1973-77, corr. Paris bur., 1977-79; chief European corr. CBS News, London, 1979-94, Moscow, 1994-96, London, 1996—. Notable assignments include 1967 Middle East War, 1968 Paris Peace Talks, 1971 Indo-Pakistan War, 1973 Middle East War, 1979 takeover of the Am. Embassy in Tehran, 1985 Geneva Summit, 1989-90 Revolution in Ea. Europe, 1990 Gulf Crisis, Moscow Coup, 1991, Collapse of Communism and the Soviet Union, German Nationalism, 1992, War in Former Yugoslavia, 1992, War in Chechnya, 1995, 1991 Persian Gulf War, Balkans War, 1999, many others; mem. CBS News Team reporting on death and funeral of Princess Diana, in 1997. Served with USN, 1952-61. Recipient Overseas Press Club awards for articles from Paris, 1968, for coverage Indo-Pakistan War, 1971, Mid. East War, 1973, Sadat visit to Jerusalem, 1977, Mountbatten funeral, 1980, hunger in Africa, 1981, radio documentary series, 1992, Emmy awards NATAS for bombing of Marines in Beirut, 1983, for assassination in Indira Gandhi, 1984, 2 Emmy awards for death of Princess Diana, 1998, DuPont award, 1990, Weintal award Georgetown U. Mem. Soc. the Cin., Internat. Inst. Strategic Studies, Royal Inst. Def. Studies, Assn. Am. Corrs. London, Fgn. Assn. de la Presse Presdl. Paris. Office: care Fgn Desk CBS News 524 W 57th St New York NY 10019-2902

FENTON, WENDELL, lawyer; b. Yonkers, N.Y., May 8, 1939; s. Martin and Katharine (Douglas) F.; m. Jeannie Hobart Woolston, Sept. 9, 1967; children: Joshua W., Nicholas W., Lewis D. BA, Yale U., 1961; postgrad., Oxford U., Eng., 1961-62; LLB, Harvard U., 1965. Bar: N.Y. 1966, Del. 1971. Assoc. Debevoise & Plimpton, N.Y.C., 1965-66, Sullivan & Cromwell, N.Y.C., 1966-71; assoc. Richards, Layton & Finger, Wilmington, Del., 1971, ptnr., 1972—; trustee Kalmer Pooled Investment Trust, 1998—; adj. prof. Widener U. Sch. Law, 1993-94. Sec., trustee Winston Churchill Found. U.S., N.Y.C., 1970—; trustee Del. League for Planned Parenthood, Wilmington, 1971-79, pres., 1973-76, chmn., 1976-78; trustee Brandywine Conservancy, Chadds Ford, Pa., 1972—, pres., 1976-78, 81-83, 88—; trustee, pres. World Affairs Coun. Wilmington, 1978—; trustee St. Mark's Sch., Southborough, Mass., 1990-93. Mem. ABA (fed. regulation securities 1979—), Del. Bar Assn. (corp. law. coun. 1991-94). Office: Richards Layton & Finger PO Box 551 1 Rodney Sq Wilmington DE 19801-3305

FENWICK, JAMES H(ENRY), editor; b. South Shields, Eng., Mar. 17, 1937; came to U.S., 1965; s. James Henry and Ellen (Tinmouth) F.; m. Suzanne Helene Hatch, Jan. 27, 1968. BA, Oxford U., Eng., 1960. Freelance lectr., writer, 1960-65; assoc. editor Playboy mag., Chgo., 1965-71; planning and features editor Radio Times, BBC, London, 1971-77; U.S. rep. Radio Times, BBC, N.Y.C., 1978-87; sr. editor Modern Maturity mag., Lakewood, Calif., 1987-90, exec. editor, 1990-91, editor, 1991-98, cons. editor, 1998—. Office: Age Wave Comm 2000 Powell Rd Emeryville CA 94608

FENZL, TERRY EARLE, lawyer; b. Milw., Mar. 19, 1945; s. Earle A. and Elaine A. (Chandler) F.; m. Barbara Louise Pool, June 24, 1967; children: Allison, Andrew, Ashley. BBA, U. Wis., 1966; JD, U. Mich., 1969. Bar: Ariz. 1970, U.S. Dist. Ct. Ariz. 1970, U.S. Ct. Claims 1970, U.S. Ct. Appeals (9th cir.) 1973, U.S. Supreme Ct. 1973, U.S. Dist. Ct. (no. dist.) Calif. 1983. Assoc. Brown & Bain, P.A. and predecessor firms, Phoenix, 1969-74, ptnr., 1975—. Mem. ABA, Ariz. State Bar Assn., Maricopa County Bar Assn., Ariz. Town Hall. Democrat. Mem. United Ch. of Christ. Home: 6610 N Central Ave Phoenix AZ 85012-1014 Office: Brown & Bain PA PO Box 400 Phoenix AZ 85001-0400

FEOLA, DAVID CRAIG, secondary school administrator; b. Akron, Ohio, Oct. 14, 1954; s. Thomas and Mary (Koci) F. BA in Edn., U. Akron, 1976, MA in Edn., 1979, PhD, 1999. Tchr. math. Akron Pub. Schs., 1976-86, asst. prin., 1986-95; asst. prin. Revere H.S., Richfield, Ohio, 1995—; part-time prof. U. Akron, 1997—; math./computer cons. Associates: Programs for Learning, Akron, 1991—. Interviewer People to People, Akron, 1994—; vol. for homeless Gennesaret, Inc., Akron, 1997. Named Top Asst. Prin., Akron Edn. Assn., 1995. Mem. ASCD, Nat. Assn. Secondary Sch. Prins., Ohio Assn. Secondary Sch. Prins., Akron Adminstrs. Assn. (treas. 1986-95), Akron City Club, Pi Lambda Theta. Democrat. Congregationalist. Avocations: travel, computers, woodworking, reading, outdoor sports. Home: 1864 Gless Ave Akron OH 44301-3238 Office: Revere High Sch 3420 Everett Rd Richfield OH 44286-9712

FEOLA, LOUIS, broadcast executive. Pres. MCA/Universal Home Video, Inc., North Hollywood, Calif., 1983-98, Universal Family & Home Entertainment Prodn., North Hollywood, 1998—. Office: Universal Family & Home Entertainment Prodn 70 Universal City Plz North Hollywood CA 91608-1011*

FERAN, RUSSELL G., sales executive; b. New Orleans, Oct. 1, 1948; s. Fred and Jean (Zyslina) F.; m. Phyllis Sobel, 1973; 1 child, Leslie. BS in Indsl. Engring., La. State U., 1973. Cert. audio cons.; cert. technician Nat. Assn. Bus. and Ednl. Radio. Engr. South Cen. Bell. Telephone Co., New Orleans, 1973-75; SMIA mgr. Tandy Corp., Fort Worth, 1975-87; regional sales mg. Internat. Union Police Assns., Alexandria, Va., 1987-93; regional mgr. S.W. Pub., Phoenix, 1993—; bd. dirs. Book Rack Metairie, La., Crohn's & Colitis Found. Am.; cons. Vietnam Vets. Am., Washington, 1987—; arbitrator Better Bus. Bur. New Orleans, 1984-90. With USMC, 1967-70. Mem. Am. Philatelic Soc., Vietnam Vets. Am., Patrolman's Assn. New Orleans (hon. life 1988), Westside Amateur Radio Club (pres. 1983-85), JWV-USA (post # 580), Am. Radio Relay League (DCXX award 1971), Delta DX Assn., B'nai B'rith (pres. lodge # 182 1986-88, 93-95, v.p. New Orleans coun. 1990-92). Avocations: philately, amateur radio (W5RGF; ex-WA5OXK). Home: 101 Fairway Dr New Orleans LA 70124-1016 Office: RGF Enterprises Inc 2305 Metairie Rd Metairie LA 70001-5533

FERARES, KENNETH, automobile executive; b. Bklyn., Jan. 29, 1957; s. William Harry and Elsie Marion (Millard) F.; m. Rosanne Misiti, Oct. 11, 1981; children: Jessica Lee, Michael Kenneth, Gina Michelle. Grad. high sch., Bayside, N.Y. Parts salesman Ed DiBenedetto Imports, Great Neck, N.Y., 1981-82, Penn Toyota, Roslyn, N.Y., 1982-83; mgr. Wantagh (N.Y.) Mitsubishi, 1983-88, Hassett Lincoln Mercury, Wantagh, 1988-91, Manhasset (N.Y.) Mitsubishi, 1991-96, Valley Stream (N.Y.) Mitsubishi, 1996—. Recipient parts excellence award Mitsubishi Motor Sales Am., 1986-88, 91—. Mem. Mem. Mitsubishi Motors Excellence Soc., Metro N.Y. Parts and Svc. Mgrs. Guild (treas. 1991, pres. 1992-93, v.p. 1996—). Republican. Office: Valley Stream Mitsubishi 700 W Merrick Rd Valley Stream NY 11580-4825

FERBEL, THOMAS, physics educator, physicist; b. Radom, Poland, Dec. 12, 1937; came to U.S., 1949, naturalized, 1955; s. Joseph and Natalie (Gotfryd) F.; m. Barbara G. Goolnick, Apr. 20, 1963; children: Natalie, Peter Jordan. B.S., Queens Coll., 1959; M.S., Yale U., 1960, Ph.D., 1963. Research staff physicist Yale U., New Haven, 1963-65; asst. prof. physics U. Rochester, N.Y., 1965-69, assoc. prof., 1969-73, prof., 1973—, assoc. dean grad. studies, 1989-91; sci. assoc. CERN, Geneva, 1980-81; vis. scientist cen. design group Superconducing Supercollider, Lawrence-Berkeley Lab., U. Calif., 1988-89; mem. program adv. com. Stanford Linear Accelerator Ctr., Calif., 1974-76, Brookhaven Lab., Upton, N.Y., 1981-84; exec. com. Users' Orgn. of Brookhaven Lab., 1972-74; exec. com. Fermi Nat. Accelerator Lab., 1973-75, chmn., 1986-87; sci. dir. Biennial Advanced Study Inst. on High Energy Physics, St. Croix. Author: (with A. Das) Introduction to Nuclear and Particle Physics, 1993; editor: Techniques and Concepts of High Energy Physics I, 1981, II, 1983, III, 1985, IV, 1987, V, 1990, VI, 1992, VII, 1994, VIII, 1995, IX, 1997, Silicon Detectors in High Energy Physics, 1982, Experimental Techniques in High Energy and Nuclear Physics, 1991; mem. editl. bd. Phys. Rev., 1978-80, Zeitschrift fur Physik, 1981-85, Internat. Jour. Modern Physics, 1995—. Alfred P. Sloan fellow, 1970, John S. Guggenheim fellow, 1971; recipient Alexander von Humboldt prize, 1995. Fellow Am. Phys. Soc. (sec.-treas. div. particles and fields 1983-85, chmn. com. on internat. freedom of scientists 1990—). Office: U Rochester Dept Physics Rochester NY 14627

FERBER, LAURENCE ROBERT, television producer; b. Mt. Vernon, N.Y., Mar. 27, 1947; s. Harry and Doris (Zinovoy) F.; m. Marcia Bellak, Dec. 23, 1979. BA in Drama and Liberal Arts, Northeastern U., 1970. Prodr. KHJ-TV, L.A., 1974-78; assoc. prodr. Mike Douglas Show, L.A., 1978-80; supervising prodr. Hour Mag., L.A., 1980-89; exec. prodr. Joan Rivers Show/Tribune, N.Y.C., 1990-94, Dennis Miller Show/Tribune, L.A., 1993, Lifetime TV, N.Y.C., 1995-96, Pat Bullard, N.Y.C., 1996-97, God Squad Cable, N.Y.C., 1998-99. Vol. Jewish Fedn., N.Y.C., 1995. Recipient Emmy award nomination NATAS, 1974, 92. Home and Office: 25 Central Park W New York NY 10023-7253

FERBER, LINDA S., museum curator; b. May 17, 1944. BA cum laude, Barnard Coll., 1966; MA, Columbia U., 1968, PhD in Art History, 1980. Curator Am. painting and sculpture The Bklyn. Mus., 1980-97, Andrew W. Mellon curator Am. painting and sculpture, 1982-97,, 1997—. Author: William Trost Richards (1833-1905): American Landscape and Marine Painter, 1980, Tokens of a Friendship: Miniature Watercolors by William T. Richards, 1982, (with others) The New Path: Ruskin and the American Pre-Raphaelites, 1985, Never at Fault: The Drawings of William T. Richards, 1986, (with others) Albert Bierstadt: Art and Enterprise, 1991, (with others) Masters of Color and Light: Homer, Sargent and the American Watercolor Movement, 1998; also articles on 19th and 20th century Am. art history. Wyeth Endowment for Am. Art fellow, 1976-77. Mem. Coll. Art Assn., Am. Assn. Mus., Am. Studies Assn., Century Assn., Phi Beta Kappa. Office: Brooklyn Mus 200 Eastern Pky Brooklyn NY 11238-6052

FERBER, NORMAN ALAN, retail executive; b. N.Y.C., Aug. 25, 1948; m. Rosine Abergel; children: Robert, Lauren, Richard. Student, L.I. U., 1965-68. Buyer, mdse. mgr. Atherton Industries, N.Y.C., 1976-79; v.p., mdse. mgr. Raxton Corp., N.Y.C., 1979-82; v.p. Fashion World, N.Y.C., 1982; v.p merchandising, mktg. and distbn. Ross Stores Inc., Newark, Calif., 1982-87, pres., COO, 1987-88, pres., CEO, 1988-93; chmn., CEO Ross Stores Inc., Newark, 1993-96, chmn., 1996—. Home: 1455 Edgewood Dr Palo Alto CA 94301-3118 Office: Ross Stores Inc PO Box 728 8333 Central Ave Newark CA 94560-3440

FERBER, ROBERT RUDOLF, physics researcher, educator; b. June 11, 1935; s. Rudolf F. and Elizabeth J. (Robertson) F.; m. Eileen Merhaut, July 25, 1964; children: Robert Rudolf, Lynne C. BSEE, U. Pitts., 1958; MSEE, Carnegie-Mellon U., 1966, PhD in Semiconductor Physics, 1967. Registered profl. engr., Pa. Mgr. engring. dept. WRS Motion Picture Labs., Pitts., 1954-58, sec., 1959-76, v.p., 1976-79; sr. engr. Westinghouse Rsch. Labs., Pitts., 1956-67; mgr. nuclear effects group Westinghouse Elec. Corp., Pitts., 1967-71; mgr. adv. engr. energy projects Westinghouse Elec. Corp., East Pittsburgh, 1971-77; photovoltaic materials and collector rsch. mgr. Jet Propulsion Lab., Pasadena, Calif., 1977-85, SP100 Project contract tech. mgr., 1985-90, asst. project mgr. Spaceborne Imaging Radar, 1990-95, Earth Observing Sys. microwave limb sounder radiometer mgr., 1995—; v.p. Executaire Inc., Pitts., 1960-64; pres. Tele-Cam Inc., Pitts., 1960-78. Editor: Transactions of the 9th World Energy Conf. 1974, Digest of the 9th World Energy Conf., 1974. Contbr. articles to profl. jours.; patentee in field. Mem. Franklin Regional Sch. Dist. Bd., Murrysville, Pa., 1975-77. Fellow Buhl Found., 1965-66, NDEA, 1976-77. Mem. IEEE (sr.), ASME (chmn. 1986 Solar Energy divsn. conf.). Republican. Lutheran. Home: 5314 Alta Canyada Rd La Canada Flintridge CA 91011-1606 Office: Jet Propulsion Lab 4800 Oak Grove Dr Pasadena CA 91109-8001

FERBER, SAMUEL, publishing executive; b. N.Y.C., June 6, 1920; s. Isidore and Sadie (Irgang) F.; m. Beatrice Ruth Ziman, June 18, 1944; children: Bruce Joseph, Joel David. B.B.A., CCNY, 1941; postgrad., Columbia U., 1946-48. Promotion dir. Nat. Advt. Service, Inc., N.Y.C., 1946-50, Boys' Life mag., N.Y.C., 1950-52; promotion dir. Esquire mag., N.Y.C., 1952-58; advt. mgr. Esquire mag., 1959-65, sr. v.p., assoc. pub., 1965-70, advt. dir., 1970-74, pub., 1974-76; co-dir. Esquire mag. (Bus. and the Arts awards program), 1966-74; dir. Esquire mag. (Corp. Social Responsibility awards program), 1972-75; sr. v.p., prin. Altman, Stoller, Weiss Advt., 1976-80, exec. v.p., 1980-82; v.p. Nadler & Larimer Advt., 1982-84; owner Sam Ferber, Pub. Cons., 1984—; mem. faculty econs. and advt. Latin Am. Inst., N.Y.C., 1946-49; lectr. on mag. pub. at various colls. and univs.; mem. bd. advisors Alliance Resident Theatres, N.Y.C., 1987—. Mem. Leader Gt. Books Discussion Group, Bd. Art/N.Y. Served with Adj. Gen.'s Dept. AUS, 1942-46. Home and Office: 17 Solar Ln Albertson NY 11507-1118 *I have always subscribed to the philosophy of my former colleague, Arnold Gingrich, that one should "never leave well enough alone". When things are progressing smoothly is the precise moment to plan the evolutionary change that insures progress and vitality. In my time, I have* *seen pillars of industry and publishing fall by the wayside because their emphasis has been on self-preservation rather than innovation.*

FERDERBER-HERSONSKI, BORIS CONSTANTIN, process engineer; b. Craiova, Romania, May 17, 1943; came to U.S., 1980; s. Boris Modest and Anetta (Mihail) F.; m. Alexandra Ionescu; children: Boris Constantin Jr., Alexandru Vlad. MS in Process Engring.; Poly. Inst., Bucharest, Romania, 1968; diploma fgn. trade, Romanian U., Bucharest, 1975; BA, Cornell U.; BS, Rutgers U.; MA. Registered profl. engr., Romania; engr.-in-tng., N.J. Plant engr. Pham. Complex, Bucharest, 1968-69, plant mgr., 1969-73; prin. engr. Indsl. Export Import, Bucharest, 1973-75, fgn. trade diplomate, 1975-80; sr. process engr. Foster Wheeler Corp., Livingston, N.J., 1980-85; projects mgr. CPC Internat./Best Foods, Fairfield, N.J., 1985-91; sr. process engr., project mgr., engring. mgr. Aqualytics, Inc., Morristown, N.J., 1991-99; engr., mgr. Ameridia, Tokuyama, Eurodia, Japan, France, 1999—; founder, pres. B.F.H. Design Corp., 1984—. Inventor in field. Mem. Rep. Nat. Com., Washington, 1981. Mem. AIChE, Instrument Soc. Am., Am. Rowing Assn. Avocations: electronic applications, water and snow skiing.

FEREBEE, STEPHEN SCOTT, JR., architect; b. Detroit, July 30, 1921; s. Stephen Scott and Caroline (Cheatham) F.; m. Mary Elizabeth Cooper, July 7, 1945; children: Scott III, John, Caroline. B.Archtl. Engring., N.C. State U., 1948; D. Fine Arts (hon.), U. N.C., Charlotte, 1992. Job capt. A.G. Odell, Jr. & Assocs. (Architects), Charlotte, N.C., 1948-53; partner Higgins & Ferebee (Architects), Charlotte, 1953-59, Ferebee & Walters (Architects), 1959-64; pres. Ferebee, Walters & Assos. (Architects/Planners), Charlotte, 1964-86; chmn., chief exec. officer FWA Group (Architects & Planners), Charlotte, 1987-90; dir. AIA Found., Washington, 1986-87, Prodn. Systems for Architects and Engrs., Inc., Washington, 1969-71, 77-78, Republic Bank & Trust Co., Charlotte, 1971-91, John Crosland Co., Charlotte, 1973-83. Prin. projects include Hickory Ridge Mall, Memphis, Tenn., 1981, Tech. Center for Union Carbide Agrl. Products Co., Inc, Research Triangle Park, N.C., 1982, Sch. Vet. Medicine, N.C. State U., Raleigh, 1983, Charlotte Conv. Ctr., 1994, Coll. Architecture bldg., U. N.C., Charlotte, 1990. Pres. N.C. Design Found., 1966-68, 78-79; bd. dirs. United Comty. Svcs., Charlotte, 1977-82, Opera Carolina, Charlotte, 1988-91, bd. dirs. Meth. Home, Charlotte, 1995—, Habitat for Humanity, Charlotte, 1999—. Capt. 101st Airborne Divsn. AUS, 1942-46; maj. gen. Res.; ret.). Decorated D.S.M., Bronze Star, Purple Heart; Croix de Guerre, France and Belgium; recipient Deitrick medal AIA N.C., 1995. Fellow AIA (pres. N.C. 1964, chmn. commn. profl. practice 1971, nat. pres. 1973, chancellor Coll. of Fellows 1987), Internat. Union Architects (council 1975-81), Royal Archtl. Inst. Can. (hon. fellow); mem. Mex. Soc. Architects (hon.), Charlotte C. of C. (v.p. 1975-76, bd. dirs. 1989-91), N.C. State U. Alumni Assn. (pres. 1980-81), Rotary (pres. Charlotte East 1997-98), Phi Kappa Phi. Methodist (past chmn. ofcl. bd.). Home: 5334 Sandtrap Ln Charlotte NC 28226-7978

FERENCE, HELEN MARIE, nursing consultant; b. Ohio, Sept. 1, 1946; d. Emery and Josephine Leona (Terlecki) F.; m. William Verill Nick. Diploma, Youngstown (Ohio) Hosp. Assn., 1967; BS, Youngstown U., 1970; MS, Ohio State U., 1972; PhD, NYU, N.Y.C., 1979. Cert. advanced cardiac life support; cert. nursing sci. Cons., pres. Nursing Cons. and Rsch., Pebble Beach, Calif., 1972—; dir. rsch. and programs Sigma Theta Tau, Indpls., 1986-88; dir. clin. evaluation, rsch. and nursing standards Mt. Sinai Hosp., N.Y.C., 1986-88; asst. prof. Ohio State U., Columbus, 1972-80; cons. Battelle Meml. Inst., Columbus, 1972-81, VA, Chillicothe, Ohio, 1975-80; asst. prof. NYU, 1979-80; cons. McGraw-Hill, Monterey, Calif., 1981-85; bd. dirs. Mt. Sinai Hosp., N.Y., 1986-88. Editor Notes on Nursing Sci., 1986—. Bd. dirs. Monterey Health Inst. Recipient Laureate: Nightingale Prize, 1991. Fellow Nightingale Soc. (bd. dirs.); mem. Sigma Theta Tau. Home: PO Box 862 Pebble Beach CA 93953-0862

FERENCHAK, SUZANNE MARY, counselor; b. Plainfield, N.J., Oct. 22, 1966; d. Andrew John and Sondra Ann (Austin) F. BA in Sociology, William Paterson U., 1988; MA in Counselor Edn., Kean U., 1992. Residential social worker St. Agatha Home, Nanuet, N.Y., 1992-94; asst. dir. Blassberg Adult Home, Lake Carmel, N.Y., 1994-95; counselor N.J. Dept. Pers. Employee Adv. Svc., Trenton, 1995—. Vol. at Soc. for Prevention of Cruelty to Animals. Mem. ACA. Avocations: traveling, horseback riding, yoga. Home: PO Box 8452 Piscataway NJ 08855-8005 Office: NJ Dept Pers Employee Adv Svc CN32O Trenton NJ 08625

FERENCZ, BRADLEY, judge; b. Queens, N.Y.; s. Murray Eugene and Regina Lorrain (Ingelberg) F.; m. Dulce Rodrequez, July 8, 1984; children: Margot Melissa Ferencz, Alexander Mikel Ferencz. BA, Ohio State U., 1969; JD, Rutgers U., 1971, postgrad., 1976-78. Bar: N.J. 1972, U.S. Dist. Ct. N.J. 1972, U.S. Supreme Ct. 1977, U.S. Ct. Appeals (3d cir.) 1980. Staff legal svcs. Middlesex County, N.J., 1972-76; pvt. practice Woodbridge, Highland Pk., N.J., 1976-80; supr. litigation Office Pub. Defender, Middlesex, 1979-84, 1st asst. dep., 1984-86, dir., 1986—; apptd. superior ct. judge Middlesex County, 1997—; adj. prof. Rutgers U., 1985-89. Trustee Middlesex County Bar Found., 1993—, Middlesex County Legal Svcs., 1981—, N.J. State Bar Found., scholarship com., fellowship com., mock trial com.; adv. com. mem. Puerto Rican Assn. Human Devel., 1993—, Middlesex County Coll. Divsn. Social Scis. and Humanities, 1991—. Mem. Nat. Assn. Criminal Def. Lawyers, N.J. State Bar Assn. (trustee criminal sect.), N.J. Assn. Criminal Def. Lawyers, Middlesex County Bar Assn. (pres. 1990-91, pres. elect 1989-90, 1st v.p. 1988-89, 2d v.p. 1987-88, sec. 1986-87, treas. 1985-87, trustee 1985-87, publicity and pub. rels. com., criminal practice com.), Assn. County Bar Pres., New Brunswick Bar Assn. Office: Middlesex County Court House 1 Kennedy Sq New Brunswick NJ 08901-1952

FERENCZ, CHARLOTTE, pediatrician, epidemiology and preventive medicine educator; b. Budapest, Hungary, Oct. 28, 1921; came to U.S., 1954; d. Paul Ferencz and Livia deFekete. BSc, McGill U., 1944, MD, CM, 1945; MPH, Johns Hopkins U., 1970. Cert. pediatrics Royal Coll. Physicians and Surgeons, Can., pediatric cardiology Am. Bd. Pediatrics. Demonstrator McGill U., Montreal, 1952-54; asst. prof. pediatrics Johns Hopkins U., Balt., 1954-58, U. Cin., 1959-60; asst. prof. SUNY, Buffalo, 1960-66, assoc. prof., 1966-73; assoc. prof. epidemiology and preventive medicine U. Md. Sch. Medicine, Balt., 1973-74, prof., 1974-98, prof. pediatrics, 1985—, prof. emeritus, 1998—; Prin. investigator population based study Etiology of Congenital Heart Disease, 1981-89; mem. epidemiology and disease control study sect. NIH, 1984-88; pres. Delta Omage Alpha chpt. Pub. Health Soc., 1990-92. Recipient M.E.S. Abbott scholarship McGill U., 1943-45, M.E.R.I.T. award Nat. Heart, Lung & Blood Inst., 1987, Fogarty Internat. Ctr. Health Sci. Exchange award NIH, 1988, Helen B. Taussig award Am. Heart Assn. Md. Affiliate, 1991, Achievement award Univ. Ctr. Life Scis., Balt., 1993. Fellow Am. Acad. Pediatrics (Spl. Achievement award Md. chpt. 1994), Am. Coll. Cardiology; mem. Teratology Soc. Democrat. Office: U Md Sch Medicine 660 W Redwood St Baltimore MD 21201-1541

FERENCZ, ROBERT ARNOLD, lawyer; b. Chgo., Sept. 10, 1946; s. Albert and Frances (Reiss) F.; m. Marla J. Miller, May 20, 1973; children: Joseph, Ira. BS in Acctg., U. Ill., 1968; JD magna cum laude, U. Mich., 1973. Bar: Ill. 1973. From assoc. to ptnr. Sidley & Austin, Chgo., 1973—. Mem. ABA, Ill. Bar Assn., Chgo. Bar Assn. Office: Sidley & Austin 1 First Natl Plz Chicago IL 60603-2003

FERET, ADAM EDWARD, JR., dentist; b. Newark, Mar. 5, 1942; s. Adam Edward and Bronislawa Anne (Szorc) F. BA (athletic scholar), Seton Hall U., 1963; DMD, U. Medicine & Dentistry of N.J., 1967. Pvt. practice Westfield, N.J., 1972—. With USNR, 1967-70. Fellow Am. Acad. Gen. Dentistry; mem. ADA, N.J. Dental Assn., L.D. Pankey Study Club, Soc. Oral Physiology and Occlusion, Quest Study Club, Internat. Coll. Oral Implantologists, Am. Soc. Oral Implantology, Central Dental Soc., Balloon Fedn. Am., Polish-Am. Guardian Soc., Polish Falcons of Am., Copernicus Soc. Am., Toastmasters, Psi Omega. Roman Catholic. Home and Office: 440 E Broad St Westfield NJ 07090-2124

FERGENSON, ARTHUR FRIEND, lawyer; b. N.Y.C., Dec. 9, 1947; s. A. Leon and Constance Elinor (Friend) F.; m. Jeannette Emma Festa, Nov. 23, 1974; children: Leah F., Nina E. Festa, Micah F. AB, Dartmouth Coll., 1969; JD, Yale U., 1972. Bar: N.Y. 1973, U.S. Dist. Ct. (so. dist.) N.Y. 1973, D.C. 1975, U.S. Ct. Appeals (2d cir.) 1975, U.S. Dist. Ct. Md. 1984, U.S. Ct. Appeals (4th cir.) 1984, Md. 1985, U.S. Supreme Ct. 1986. Law clk to Hon. Thomas P. Griesa U.S. Dist. Ct., N.Y.C., 1972-73; law clk. to U.S. Chief Justice Warren E. Burger U.S. Supreme Ct., Washington, 1973-74; atty. Covington & Burling, Washington, 1974-76; asst. prof. Ind. U. Sch. Law, Bloomington, 1976-79; assoc. prof. U. Md. Sch. Law, Balt., 1979-81; gen. counsel Action Agency, Washington, 1981-82; cons. Nat. Inst. Justice, Washington, 1982-83; asst. U.S. atty. U.S. Atty.'s Office, Balt., 1983-85; ptnr., of counsel Weinberg and Green, Balt., 1985-95; of counsel Ballard Spahr Andrews & Ingersoll, Balt., 1995—; mem. adv. coun. Atlantic Legal Found., Inc., 1997—. Trustee Center Stage, Balt., 1988—. Republican. Jewish. Avocations: theater, film, politics, political theory. Home: 507 Edgevale Rd Baltimore MD 21210-1901 Office: Ballard Spahr Andrews & Ingersoll LLP 300 E Lombard St 19 Flr Baltimore MD 21202-3219

FERGUS, GARY SCOTT, lawyer; b. Racine, Wis., Apr. 20, 1954; s. Russell Malcolm and Phyl Rose (Muratore) F.; m. Isabelle Sabina Beekman, Sept. 28, 1985; children: Mary Marckwald Beekman Fergus, Kirkpatrick Russell Beekman Fergus. SB, Stanford U., 1976; JD, U. Wis., 1979; LLM, NYU, 1981. Bar: Wis. 1979, Calif. 1980. Assoc. Brobeck, Phleger & Harrison, San Francisco, 1980-86, ptnr., 1986—, mng. ptnr. products liability, ins. coverage, environ. and antitrust/appellat practices, 1996—, mgr. product liability/ins. coverage, environ. and antitrust, 1996—. Arch. computerized case mgmt. sys. Vol. San Francisco Leadership. Mem. ABA. Home: 3024 Washington St San Francisco CA 94115-1618 Office: Brobeck Phleger & Harrison 1 Market Plz Ste 341 San Francisco CA 94105-1193

FERGUSON, ARLEN GARY, human resources specialist; b. Houston, Oct. 11, 1941; s. Olever S. and Vivian B. (Burnett) F.; m. Gayle Tate, June 19, 1971; 1 child, April Lynn. BBA, Southwestern U., 1963; MBA, U. Tex., 1965. Sr. adminstrv. officer Chubb Group Inst. Cos., N.Y.C., 1966-72; compensation cons. McKee, Carter & Stewart, Inc., Houston, 1972-76; sr. exec. compensation cons. William M. Mercer, Inc., Houston, 1976-77, mng. dir. exec. compensation, 1982-85; prin. exec. compensation cons. Booz, Allen & Hamilton, Inc., Houston, 1977-81, Sibson & Co., Inc., Houston, 1986-87; sr. v.p. human resources Am. Gen. Corp., Houston, 1987-88; prin. exec. compensation cons. Watson Wyatt & Co., Houston, 1989—; human resources roundtable Cox Bus. Sch., Dallas, 1992-98. Mem. vestry St. Martin's Episcopal Ch., Houston, 1984-86, chmn. every mem. canvass, 1986; chmn. long range planning com. Ch. Transfiguration, Dallas, 1990-91; chmn. bd. trustees Parish Day Sch., 1993-94. With U.S. Coast Guard Res., 1966-71. Mem. Houston Compensation Assn., Alumni Assn. Southwestern U. (pres. 1982-84), Forest Club (pres. 1983-85), River Oaks Breakfast Club (v.p. 1981-82), Kappa Alpha Order (Disting. Alumnus award 1994). Avocations: tennis, skiing, fishing. Office: Watson Wyatt & Co 1301 McKinney St Ste 3000 Houston TX 77010-3033

FERGUSON, BARBARA, legislative staff member; m. Kevin Ferguson. Adminstrv. asst. to chief clk. State of Ky. Senate, Frankfort, 1978-88, asst. clk., 1988-99, chief clk., 1999—. Fax: 502-564-0456. E-mail: bferguson@mail.irc.state.ky.us. Home: 1185 Bridgeport Benson Frankfort KY 40601 Office: Ky Senate Capitol Ave Rm 323 Frankfort KY 40601

FERGUSON, BRADFORD LEE, lawyer; b. Ottumwa, Iowa, May 29, 1947; s. G. Wendell and Virginia Sue (Baker) F. BA, Drake U., 1969; JD, Harvard U., 1972. Bar: Minn. 1972, Ill. 1980. Assoc. Dorsey, Marquart, Windhorst, West & Halladay, Mpls., 1972-75; legis. asst. Senator Walter F. Mondale, Washington, 1975-77; spl. asst. to asst. sec. tax policy U.S. Treasury Dept., Washington, 1977-78, assoc. tax legis. counsel, 1978-80; ptnr. Hopkins & Sutter, Chgo., 1980-96, Sidley & Austin, Chgo., 1996—; mem. planning com. fed. tax conf. U. Chgo. Law Sch. Fellow Am. Coll. Tax Counsel; mem. ABA (taxation sect., chair com. formation tax policy 1991-93, mem. coun. 1994-97), Chgo. Bar Assn., Nat. Tax Assn. (bd. dirs. 1994-97). Office: Sidley & Austin One First National Plz Chicago IL 60603

FERGUSON, CHARLES AUSTIN, retired newspaper editor; b. New Orleans, Mar. 16, 1937; s. Austin and Josephine Hayes (Gessner) F.; m. Jane Pugh, Dec. 21, 1961; children: Elizabeth Hayes, Caroline Pugh. B.A., Tulane U., 1958, LL.B., 1961; DLitt (hon.), Dillard U., New Orleans, 1996. Bar: La. bar 1961. From reporter to editor States-Item, New Orleans, 1961-80; editor Times-Picayune/States-Item, New Orleans, 1980-90; anchor TV program City Desk, New Orleans, 1971-78. Trustee Dillard U., New Orleans, 1972—, chmn. exec. com., 1978—, chmn. bd. trustees, 1992—; trustee Inst. Politics, Loyola U., New Orleans, 1968-75, pres., 1971-75; co-chmn. Louis Armstrong Meml. Park Com., New Orleans, 1971-79. Recipient Torch of Liberty award Anti-Defamation League of B'nai B'rith, 1981; Nieman fellow, 1965-66. Mem. La. Bar Assn. Club: New Orleans Lawn Tennis. Home: 1448 Joseph St New Orleans LA 70115-4263

FERGUSON, CHRISTINE C., lawyer, state agency administrator; b. East Lansing, Mich., Oct. 28, 1958; d. George and Claire Ferguson; m. Fred Glomb; 1 child, Gregory. BA, U. Mich., 1980; JD, Am. U., 1986. Staff asst. Hon. John H. Chafee, U.S. Senate, Washington, 1981-88, legis. dir., 1988-92, dep. chief of staff, 1992-94; dir. R.I. Dept. Human Svcs., 1995—. Recipient awards Nat. Assn Community Health Care Ctrs., Nat. Downs Syndrome Congress, Nat. Family Planning and Reproductive Health Assn., Sec. Health and Human Svcs.; named one of 100 Most Influential Attys., Nat. Law Jour., 1994. Avocations: sailing, outdoor sports. Office: Dept Human Svcs 600 New London Ave Cranston RI 02920-3024

FERGUSON, CRAIG, actor; b. Glasgow, Scotland. Actor (tv series) The Ferguson Theory, 1994, Freakazoid!, 1995, Maybe This Time, 1995, The Drew Carey Show, 1996—, (film) Modern Vampyres, 1999, The Big Tease, 1999; writer (film): The Tease, 1999; tv guest appearances include: Red Dwarf, 1988, Chelmsford 123, 1988, Have I Got News for You, 1991, The Brain Drain, 1993, Almost Perfect, 1995; co-writer, co-prodr., actor: Je M'Appelle Crawford; comedian, comic actor in one-man shows, U.K.; writer (screenplay): All American Man, (with others) Saving Grace, The Ferguson Theory. Office: Warner Bros Television Domestic 4001 N Olive Ave Burbank CA 91522*

FERGUSON, DAVID ROBERT, energy research manager; b. Atlanta, Dec. 26, 1949; s. Robert H. and Elizabeth (Whatley) F.; m. Marilyn Shuptrine, Dec. 13, 1970; children: Mary Elizabeth, Michelle Lynn. BBA in Mktg., Ga. State U., 1973. Mgr. market research Standard Fed. Savs., Atlanta, 1973-77; mgr. new constrn. First Union Nat. Bank, Charlotte, N.C., 1977-82; mgr. constrn. div. Cen. Carolina Bank, Durham, N.C., 1982-86; mgr. residential and comml. program Alternative Energy Corp., Research Triangle Park, N.C., 1986-93, dir. comml. market rsch., 1994-97; sr. facility mgr. Faison Assocs., Atlanta, 1997-99; gen. mgr. Carter & Assocs./Regions Bank Properties, Gainesville, Ga., 1999—. Mem. AIA, Am. Mktg. Assn., Illuminating Engring. Soc., Bldg. Owners and Mgrs. Assn. Carolinas (pres. N.C.-S.C.-W.Va. chpt. 1990, bd. dirs. So. region 1990-92), Bldg. Owners and Mgrs. Assn. Atlanta, Internat. Ground Source Heat Pump Assn., Kiwanis, Charles M. Setzer Lodge. Democrat. Methodist. Avocations: water skiing, music. Home: 1163 Colony Creek Ct Lawrenceville GA 30043-7079 Office: Careter & Assocs Regions Bank Properties PO Box 937 Gainesville GA 30503

FERGUSON, DONALD GUFFEY, radiologist; b. Hewton, Pa., July 19, 1923; s. Rutherford Hayes and Beylah Cristabel (Guffey) F.; m. Anne Benedict Gallagher, MAr. 4, 1961. BS, U. Pitts., 1944, MD, 1946. Diplomate Am. Bd. Radiology, Am. Bd. Nuclear Medicine. Intern S. Side Hosp., Pitts., 1946-47; resident in radiology and radiation therapy Meml. Sloan-Kettering, N.Y.C., 1950-52; staff radiologist Thomas Jefferson U. Hosp., Phila., 1952-55; attending radiologist Mercy Hosp., Pitts., 1955-57; sr. staff S. Side Hosp., Pitts., 1957—, St. Clair Meml. Hosp., Pitts., 1957—; clin. asst. prof. radiology U. Pitts., 1956—. With M.C., U.S. Army, 1948-50. Am. Cancer Soc. fellow. Fellow Am. Coll. Radiology (dist. councilor 1972-78, pres. Pa. chpt. 1979-80); mem. Soc. Nuclear Medicine (chpt. pres. 1957-58), Pitts. Roentgen Soc. (pres. 1967-68), Am. Med. Assn. (ho. of dels. 1987—), Pa. Med. Soc. (pres. 1992-93), Radiol. Soc. N.Am., Am. Roentgen Ray Soc., Orgn. State Med. Assn. Pres. (pres. 1998-99), Allegheny County Med. Soc., Masons. Presbyterian. Home: Hidden Valley Rd Canonsburg PA 15317 Office: 1000 Bower Hill Rd Pittsburgh PA 15243-1873

FERGUSON, DONALD JOHN, surgeon, educator; b. Mpls., Nov. 19, 1916; s. Donald Nivison and Arline (Folsom) F.; m. Lillian Elizabeth Mack, June 26, 1943; children—Anne Elizabeth, Donald John, Merrill James. B.S., Yale, 1939; M.D., U. Minn., 1943, M.S. in Physiology, 1951, Ph. D. in Surgery, 1951. Intern, then resident U. Minn. Hosp., 1947-52; asst. prof. surgery U. Minn., 1952-54, assoc. prof., 1954-56, prof., 1956-60; prof. surgery U. Chgo., 1960-87, prof. emeritus, 1987—. Contbr. articles in field. Served to capt. M.C. AUS, 1943-46. Mem. ACS, Am. Surg. Assn., Soc. U. Surgeons. Home: The Mather 1615 Hinman Ave Evanston IL 60201 Office: U Chgo Med Ctr 5841 S Maryland Ave Chicago IL 60637-1463

FERGUSON, DOUGLAS EDWARD, financial executive; b. Bronx, N.Y., Apr. 21, 1940; s. Lawrence and Claire (Billingheimer) F.; m. Cynthia L. Kords, Jan. 29, 1966; children: Elisabeth, Keith, Jonathan. AB, Columbia Coll., 1962. Chartered fin. analyst. Security analyst Heritage Securities/Nat. Securities and Rsch. Corp., N.Y.C., 1963-68; asst. v.p. John W. Bristol & Co., Inc., N.Y.C., 1968-74; v.p. Van Cleef, Jordan & Wood, Inc., N.Y.C., 1974-75; portfolio mgr. Trustees of Columbia U., N.Y.C., 1975-76; mgr. investment svcs. Trascott, Alyson, Craig, Inc., Teaneck, N.J., 1977-84; v.p. portfolio mgmt. Swiss Bank Corp., N.Y.C., 1984-88; pres. Ferguson Investment Cons., Inc., Sleepy Hollow, N.Y., 1988—. Contbr. articles to profl. jours. and newspaper. Pres. Westchester ARC, 1991-95; mem. Estate Planning Coun., Westchester County. Mem. N.Y. Soc. Security Analsyts. Home and Office: Ferguson Investment Cons 528 Bellwood Ave Sleepy Hollow NY 10591-1336

FERGUSON, EARL WILSON, cardiologist, physiologist, medical executive; b. Lebanon, Pa., Aug. 29, 1943; s. Warren Earl and Norma Laura (Wilson) F.; m. Sun Hye Paik, May 1, 1998; children: Steven Mark, Matthew Earl, Erin Lee. BA in Chemistry, Baylor U., 1965; MD, PhD in Physiology, U. Tex., Galveston, 1970. Diplomate Am. Bd. Internal Medicine, Cardiovascular Disease, Am. Bd. Preventive Medicine, Am. Bd. Med. Mgmt. Grad. teaching asst. dept. physiology U. Tex. Med. Br., Galveston, 1967-70, intern medicine, 1970-71; resident medicine, then fellow cardiology Duke U. Med. Ctr., Durham, N.C., 1971-75, mem. assoc. faculty dept. medicine, 1974-75; research assoc. cardiology VA Hosp., Durham, 1974-75; commd. lt. USAF, 1966, advanced through grades to col., 1984-95; staff cardiologist, dir. coronary care Wilford Hall USAF Med. Ctr., Lackland AFB, Tex., 1975-76, chief cardiology, dir. cardiology tng. program, 1983-84; asst. prof. biochemistry, medicine and mil. medicine Uniformed Svcs. U. Health Scis., Bethesda, Md., 1976-80, assoc. prof. physiology, medicine and mil. medicine, 1980-84, asst. comdt., 1977-82, mem. faculty senate, 1979-80, adj. prof. physiology, 1984-93; dir. hosp. services USAF Med. Ctr., Scott AFB, Ill., 1984-86; comdr. USAF Hosp., Little Rock AFB, Ark., 1986-88; dep. command surgeon Mil. Airlift Command, Scott AFB, 1988-90; comdr. USAF Med. Ctr., Wiesbaden, Germany, 1990-93; dir. Aerospace Medicine and Occupl. Health NASA, Washington, 1993-96; cons. to surgeon gen. for cardiology, medicine and physiology USAF, 1980-95; cons. N.J. State Police, 1984-88, Ind. Atty. Gen.'s Office, 1985-87, NASA, 1997—; mem. life scis. subcom. NASA, 1989-93, interagency working group on telemedicine, 1994-96; adj. assoc. prof. preventive medicine Uniformed Svcs. U. Health Scis., Bethesda, 1993-96; physician So. Sierra Med. Clinic, Ridgecrest, Calif., 1996—; advisor House/Senate Com. on telemedicine and health care, 1994-96; corp. bd. Ridgecrest Regional Hosp., 1997—, bd. dirs.; bd. dirs. Calif. Telemedicine/Telehealth Ctr.; mem. Indian Wells Valley Cmty. Health Coun., Developing Rural Integrated Sys., 1997—. Contbr. articles to profl. jours. Rsch. grantee VA, 1974-75, Dept. Def., 1976-82, NASA, 1982-84; Cardiovascular Health fellow Health Forum/Am. Hosp. Assn., 1999—. Fellow Am. Coll. Cardiology (bd. govs. 1985-88), ACP, Soc. Air Force Physicians (bd. govs. 1982-85, v.p. 1987-88), Am. Coll. Preventive Medicine; mem. Am. Physiol. Soc., Am. Coll. Execs. Medicine, Am. Heart Assn. Unitarian. Avocation: physical fitness activities, flying.

FERGUSON, EMMET FEWELL, JR., surgeon; b. DeSoto, Ga., Mar. 28, 1921; s. Emmet Fewell Sr. and Emma Ruth (Smith) F.; Edith Geraldine Strozier, Nov. 26, 1954; children: Berrylin, Joann, Virginia, Fran, Emmet III. Student, U. Ga., 1938-40; MS in Zoology with honors, US Naval Acad., 1943; MD, Med. Coll. Ga., 1950. Diplomate Am. Bd. Surgery, Am. Bd. Colon-Rectal Surgery. Rsch. assoc. U.S. Naval Hosp., St. Albans, N.Y., 1950-51; surg. resident U. Fla., Jacksonville, 1951-53, 54-55, U. Ala., Brimingham, 1953-54; pvt. practice Jacksonville, 1955-93; pres. staff Meth. Hosp., Jacksonville, 1958-60, U. Hosp., Jacksonville, 1972-73; chief colon rectal surgery Bapt., Meth., and St. Vincents Hosps.; clin. prof. surgery coll. medicine U. Fla., 1960-93; mem. med. missions to Honduras, Costa Rica, Nicaragua, Ecuador; del., speaker Pan Am. Med. Meeting, Buenos Aires, 1967; mem. adv. com. coll. medicine U. Fla., Gainesville, 1976-82; chmn. bd. dirs. N.E. Fla. Health Svc. Agy., 1980-83; mem. Statewide Health Coun., 1980-89, chair, 1980-82. Author: Commonly Memorized Verse, 1991, The Five Most Important Numbers in our World, 1995, Guide to the Major and Minor Springs of Florida, 1997; contbr. articles to profl. jours. Del., speaker from Jax C. of C. to Internat. Exhbn., Moscow, 1959; tchr. Sunday sch. Riverside Bapt. Ch., 1955—, deacon, 1960, 90; del. from Am. Cancer Soc. to Internat. Cancer Soc., Tokyo, 1966; mem. United Way Bd., Jacksonville, 1970-80, chmn. profl. divsn., 1980; chmn. Fla. host com. Pres. Carter's Inauguration, Washington, 1977; life mem. Jacksonville Hist. Soc., pres., 1986-88; mem. Jacksonville Indigent Care Com.; bd. regents Nat. Libr. Medicine, Washington, 1977-81; founder bd. dirs. Bapt. Towers, 1970—; trustee, pres. bd. trustees Riverside Bapt. Day Sch., 1971-75; trustee health sci. ctr. libr. U. Fla., 1972-93; trustee Bartram Sch., 1974-84, pres., 1976-77; mem. exec. com., mem. office state commn. rsch., profl. svc. Am. Cancer Soc. With USN, 1940-46, 50-51, capt. M.C. res. Decorated Am. Def. medal, Naval Res. medal; recipient Disting. Svc. award Fla. divsn. Am. Cancer Soc., Tampa, 1972, 75, Silver Beaver award Boy Scouts Am., 1986, Emmet Ferguson award U. Fla. Health Sci. Ctr. Fellow ACS (pres. Fla. chpt. 1968), Am. Soc. Surgery Alimentary Tract, Am. Soc. Colon Rectal Surgeons, Piedmont Soc. Colon Rectal Surgeons (pres. 1996-97), Fla. Soc. Colon Rectal Surgeons (pres. 1972-74, 76-78); mem. AMA, Fla. Med. Assn. (life), So. Med. Assn., Southeastern Surg. Congress (Best Motion Picture award 1975), Duval County Med. Soc. (life, editor bull. 1970-73, pres. 1975-76), Navy League (life, pres. Jacksonville coun. 1983-84, Commendation award 1984), Sons Confederate Vets., Rotary (bd. dirs. 1978-80, chmn. com. polio plus 1987-88, Commendation award 1989), St. John's Dinner Club (pres. 1975-78, Commendation award 1978), Fla. Yacht Club (life), River Club. Democrat. Avocations: hunting, fishing, tennis, sailing, sculpture.

FERGUSON, ERIK TILLMAN, transportation consultant; b. Seattle, Apr. 3, 1957; s. Charles Harvey and Alice Eloise (Storaasli) F.; m. Elaine Ana Samayoa, May 17, 1985 (div. Oct. 1996); children: Britnay Alexandra, Erik Tillman II. BA in History, U. So. Calif., L.A., 1979; PhD., U. So. Calif., 1988; M.C.R.P., Harvard U., 1982. Community planner Transp. Systems Ctr., Cambridge, Mass., 1982-84; projects specialist Commuter Transp. Svcs., L.A., 1984-86; assoc. planner Orange County Transit Dist., Garden Grove, Calif., 1986-88; asst. prof. Ga. Inst. Tech., Atlanta, 1988-95. Editor newsletter/jour. Transp. Planning, 1990-94; mem. editl. bd. Jour. Planning Edn. and Rsch., 1991-94. Mem. Task force on Regionally Important Resources, State of Ga., 1990. German Marshall Fund scholar, 1982-83, Nat. Merit scholar, 1974; Fed. Transit Adminstrn. grantee, 1991, 92, 94, 95; Lilly Found. Tchg. fellow, 1990-91; recipient Rsch. Practitioner award Western Govtl. Rsch. Assn., 1988. Mem. Am. Planning Assn. (chair transp. planning divsn. 1993-94, chair divsn. coun. 1994-96), Transp. Rsch. Bd., Assn. for Commuter Transp. (bd. dirs. 1990-94), Inst. Transp. Engrs., Travel Demand Mgmt. Coun. (steering com. 1995—). Home: 3301 Ashford Gables Dr Dunwoody GA 30338-6762 Office: PO Box 888729 Atlanta GA 30356-0729

FERGUSON, GARY L., public relations executive; b. Okarche, Okla., Sept. 17, 1949; s. Jack J. Ferguson and Joan C. (Hauser) Long; m. Georgia A. Keller, Jan. 20, 1975 (div. Nov. 1994); 1 child, Laura J. BA in English, Met. State Coll., Denver, 1980; MA in Comm., U. No. Colo., 1992. Dir. pub. rels. Assoc. Builders and Contrs., Denver, 1981-83; pres. Ferguson Comm., Inc., Littleton, Colo., 1983-88; mng. editor MacGuide Mag., Lakewood, Colo., 1988-89; sr. adminstr. pub. affairs Ball Aerospace and Technologies, Broomfield, Colo., 1989-94; journalism instr. Colo. State U., Ft. Collins, 1994-95; sr. rep., pub. rels. Storage Tech. Corp., Louisville, Colo., 1995—. Author: (book of poetry) Excavating Camelot, 1979. Mem. Pub. Rels. Soc. Am. (chair employee comm. sect. 1999, Gold Pick for feature/news writing 1991, Gold Pick Award of Merit for feature writing 1992, Silver Pick award for feature writing 1993, Silver Pick award for mag./periodicals 1994), Soc. Profl. Journalists (pres. Colo. chpt. 1992-93, 94-95, dir.-at-large 1993-94, 96-97, v.p. membership 1991-92, sec. 1990-91, Circle of Excellence award), Clan Fergusson Soc. N.Am. Office: Storage Technology Corp 2270 S 88th St Louisville CO 80028-0001

FERGUSON, GARY WARREN, retired public relations executive; b. Stockton, Kans., May 5, 1925; s. Richard and Nelle (McBee) F.; m. Doris Drisler, Oct. 2, 1948; children: Arthur Richard, Frances (Mrs. Gregory H. Gebhart), Robert Warren, Scott William. A.B., Yale U., 1946; M.S. in Journalism, Columbia U., 1948. Reporter Providence Jour. Bull., 1948-49, Richmond (Va.) News Leader, 1949-52; reporter St. Louis Post-Dispatch, 1954-55, spl. writer, 1955-60; counselor Fleishman-Hillard, Inc., St. Louis, 1961-62; sr. partner Fleishman-Hillard, Inc., 1962-71; pres. Gary Ferguson Assocs., Inc. pub. relations/mktg. communications, 1971-93; vice chmn. Dorf and Stanton Communications, Inc., 1988-93; 1st v.p. St. Louis Newspaper Guild, 1959-60; editorial cons., 1993-99. Mem. founding bd. Greater St. Louis Coun. Alcoholism, 1965, pres., 1966-69; pres. mental Health Assn., St. Louis, 1980-81; trustee World Affairs Coun. St. Louis, 1990-95. Recipient Bishop's award Episcopal Diocese Mo., 1965. Mem. Soc Profl. Journalists. Home: 130 Plant Ave Saint Louis MO 63119-3028

FERGUSON, GERALD PAUL, lawyer; b. Teaneck, N.J., Oct. 17, 1951; s. James Richard and Ilene Veronica (Meyer) F.; m. Nancy Ivers, Aug. 20, 1977; 1 child, James Ralph. BA, Fairleigh Dickinson U., 1974; JD, Capital U., 1979. Bar: Ohio 1979, U.S. Dist. Ct. (so. dist.) Ohio 1980, U.S. Ct. Appeals (6th cir.) 1986, U.S. Supreme Ct. 1990. Ptnr. Vorys, Sater, Seymour and Pease, Columbus, 1979—; mem. rules adv. com. Ohio Supreme Ct., Columbus, 1993. Mem. ABA (litigation sect., mem. trial evidence subcom. 1985-86), Ohio State Bar Assn. (mem. jud. adv. and legal reform com., unauthorized practice law com. 1985-90), Columbus Bar Assn. (chmn. juror subcom. 1979-86). Republican. Roman Catholic. Avocations: tennis, golf, fishing. Office: Vorys Sater Seymour & Pease 52 E Gay St Columbus OH 43215-3161

FERGUSON, GLENN WALKER, consultant, writer, lecturer; b. Syracuse, N.Y., Jan. 28, 1929; s. Forrest Erwin and Mabel Gertrude (Walker) F.; m. Patricia Lou Head, June 22, 1950; children: Bruce Walker, Sherry Lynn, Scott Sherwood. B.A., Cornell U., 1950, M.B.A., 1951; student, U. Santo Tomas, Manila, 1952-53, U. Chgo. Law Sch., 1955-56; J.D., U. Pitts., 1957; D.S. (hon.), Worcester Poly. Inst., 1973; LL.D. (hon.), Sacred Heart U., 1974; DHL (hon.), Am. U. Paris, 1995. Staff asso. Govtl. Affairs Inst., Washington, 1954-55; asst. editor, asst. sec.-treas. Am. Judicature Soc., Chgo., 1955-56; asst. to chancellor and asst. dean Grad. Sch. Pub. Affairs, U. Pitts., 1956-60; with McKinsey & Co. (mgmt. cons.), Washington, 1960-61; with Peace Corps, 1961-64, dir. Thailand, 1961-63; asso. dir. Peace Corps, Washington, 1963-64; dir. Vols. in Service to Am., Washington, 1964-66; U.S. ambassador to Kenya, 1966-69; pres. Clark U., 1970-73, U. Conn., 1973-78, Radio Free Europe/Radio Liberty, Munich, Ger., 1978-82, Lincoln Ctr. Performing Arts, N.Y.C., 1983-84, Equity for Africa, 1985-92, The Am. U. of Paris, 1992-95; cons. govt. agys., 1959-64, TV moderator fgn. affairs, Pitts., 1957-60; USIS lectr. India, Sudan, Uruguay, Argentina, 1984-92; vis. prof. fgn. policy Conn. Coll., U. R.I., 1990-91; cons. Internat. Exec. Svc. Corps., Uruguay, 1992. Contbr. articles to profl. jours. Human rights commr. City of Worcester, 1971-72; trustee Cornell U., 1972-76, former mem. corp. bds.; mem. French-Am. Commn. for Ednl. Exch., 1992-95. 1st lt. USAF, 1951-53, Korea. Recipient Arthur S. Flemming award, 1968; Asso. fellow Timothy Dwight Coll., Yale U. Mem. ABA, Fed. Bar Assn., Coun. Fgn. Rels., Fgn. Policy Assn. (bd. dirs. 1974-83), Coun. Am. Ambs. (bd. dirs. 1996—), Nat. Press Club, Century Assn., Phi Beta Kappa, Psi Upsilon, Phi Delta Phi. Address: 1060 Governor Dempsey Dr Santa Fe NM 87501-1078

FERGUSON, HARLEY ROBERT, service company executive; b. Windsor, Ont., Can., Aug. 13, 1936; U.S. citizen; s. Robert Clifford and Ruby Mills (Chase) F.; m. Ruth Elizabeth Mann, 1956 (div. 1970); children: Keith, Elizabeth, Kevin, Kent; m. Joyce Elizabeth Bradley, 1972; children: Harley Robert Jr., William, John, Ian. Student U. Western Ont., London, 1955-56, U. Windsor (Ont.), 1957-58; BSc, Carleton U., Ottawa, Ont., 1968, PhD, 1999. Cert. in data processing. Sys. analyst Ford Motor Co., Windsor, 1956-59; various positions Govt. of Can., Ottawa, 1959-70; dir. data processing Canfarm, Guelph, Ont., 1970-76; dir. support svcs. Bell Can., Toronto Ont., 1976-77; dir. bus. sys. Bell No. Software Rsch., Toronto, 1977-80; v.p. info. services ALLTEL Corp. (formerly Mid-Continent Telephone Corp.), Hudson, Ohio, 1980-85; sr. v.p. mgmt. info. svcs. Kelly Svcs., Inc., Troy, Mich., 1985-94; v.p. mgmt. info. svcs. O/E Systems, Inc., Troy, Mich., 1994-95; sr. v.p., chief info. officer Butler Internat., Montvale, N.J., 1995—; bd. dirs. VIM (Internat. Control Data Users Group), 1973-75; guest lectr. MBA program U. Mich. 2d lt. Can. Army, 1955-56. Mem. Soc. for Info. Mgmt. (1st v.p.), Info. Systems Exec. Forum. Lutheran. Home: 111 Green Terrace Way West Milford NJ 07480-2713

FERGUSON, HENRY, international management consultant; b. Schenectady, May 31, 1927; s. Charles Vaughan and Harriet Esther (Rankin) F.; m. Joan Alice Metzger, July 18, 1953; children: Jean Rankin Gerbini, Cynthia Harriet Waldman, Henry Closson, Margaret Susan Ferguson Corrigan. AB, Union Coll., 1950; AM, Harvard U., 1954, PhD, 1958. With Conn. Gen. Life Ins. Co., Hartford, 1950-53; lectr., asst. prof., assoc. prof. history, chmn. Non-Western studies com. Union Coll., Schenectady, 1957-69; dir. Ednl. Resources Ctr. N.Y. State Dept. Edn., 1967-69, dir. Ctr. for Internat. Programs, 1979-85; spl. lectr. Trinity Coll., Hartford, 1969-72; pres., dir. InterCulture Assocs., Inc., Thompson, Conn., 1969-79; pres. Henry Ferguson Internat., Inc., 1985-90, Transnational Bus. Devel. Corp., Albany, 1990—; faculty specialist SUNY, Albany, 1985-88; bd. dirs. Indus Inc., Milw. Author: (with Joan M. Ferguson) Village Life Study Kit Guide and Village Life Study Kit, 1970, Changing Africa, a Guide, 1973, Manual for Multicultural and Ethnic Studies, 1977; (with N. Abramowitz) Opportnities for Interprofessional Collaboration, 1980, Manual for Multicultural Education, 1987, Tomorrow's Global Executive, 1988, Corporate Leadership in a Global Age, 1991, Globalistics: The Art and Science of Building a Profitable Transnational Business, 2d edit., 1995, Globalistics: Building Your Transnational Business Career, 1994, Globalize! Essays on Business in a Global Age, 1998; editor: Handbook on Human Rights and Citizenship, 1981, Ferguson Fortnightly, 1979, Cross Cultural Currents, 1980, Global Business Observer, 1989. Trustee Freedom Forum, Schenectady, 1963-66; citizen del. White House Conf. on Library and Info. Services, 1979; pres. Internat. Center of Capital Region, 1981-82, pres. world trade coun., 1988-90. Bus. With USN, 1945-46. Sr. fellow Oriental studies Columbia U., 1960-61, N.Y. State Bd. Regents sr. fellow in Non-Western studies, 1965-66; Fulbright Research grant Osmania U., India, 1961, Fulbright Sr. Research grant, 1966-67. Mem. Ft. Orange Club. Episcopalian. Home: Chestnut Hill N Albany NY 12211 Office: 5 Chestnut Hill Rd N Loudonville NY 12211-1606

FERGUSON, HUGH W., III, lawyer; b. Dallas, Dec. 12, 1943. Student, Westminster Coll.; BA, U. Tex., 1965, JD with honors, 1968. Bar: Tex. 1968. Briefing atty. to Hon. Joe Greenhill Supreme Ct. Tex., 1968-69; mem. Jenkens & Gilchrist, Dallas. Assoc. editor Tex. Law Rev., 1966-68. Mem. ABA, State Bar Tex., Dallas Bar Assn., Order of Coif. Office: Jenkens & Gilchrist 1445 Ross Ave Ste 3200 Dallas TX 75202-2799*

FERGUSON, JAMES CLARKE, mathematician, algorithmist; b. Spokane, Wash., June 23, 1938; s. James Forsythe and Dorothy Eileen (Dillon) F. MS in Math., U. Wash., 1963; PhD in Math., U. N.Mex., 1984. Sci. programmer Boeing, Seattle, 1960-64; staff mem. GE Tech. Mil. Planning Office, Santa Barbara, Calif., 1964-66; mathematician TRW, Inc., Redondo Beach, Calif., 1966-71, Teledyne-Ryan Aero., San Diego, 1971-77; staff mem. Los Alamos (N.Mex.) Nat. Lab., 1977-85; sr. scientist Tektronix, Beaverton, Oreg., 1985-87, BBN Systems and Techs. Corp., Bellevue, Wash., 1987-92; with Point Control, Eugene, 1993-94, Camax Mfg. Technologies, Eugene, 1994-95; mathematician SDRC/Camax, Eugene, 1995—; cons. in field, 1975-87. Co-author: Key Works in Geometric Modeling, 1991, Fundamental Developments of Computer Aided Geometric Modeling, 1992; contbr. articles to profl. jours. Recipient advanced study fellowship, Los Alamos Nat. Lab., 1981. Mem. Assn. Computing Machinery, Soc. Indsl. and Applied Math. Achievements include introduction of parametric curve and surface techniques into computer aided geometric design field; complete classification of parametric planar cubics; application of parametric curve techniques to problem of shape preservation.

FERGUSON, JAMES EDWARD, II, obstetrician, gynecologist; b. Glendale, Calif., Oct. 25, 1951; m. Lynn Corpening, June 21, 1975; children: James Edward III, David Gregory, Joshua Scott. Student, USCG Acad., 1969-71; AB in History, Marquette U., 1973; MD, Wake Forest U., 1977. Diplomate Nat. Bd. Med. Examiners, Am. Bd. Ob-Gyn., Am. Bd. Maternal and Fetal Medicine. Intern USPHS Hosp., San Francisco, 1977-78; resident ob/gyn Stanford (Calif.) U. Sch. Medicine, 1978-80, postdoctoral fellow ob/gyn, 1982-84, asst. prof. ob/gyn, 1984-87, chief divsn. maternal-fetal medicine dept. ob/gyn., 1985-87, dir. prenatal diagnosis program dept. ob/gyn., 1986-87; chief resident Wake Forest U. Bowman Gray Sch. Medicine, Winston-Salem, N.C., 1980-81, mem. clin. faculty, 1981-82; pvt. practice Pollak, Zammit, Ferguson, MD, P.C., Winston-Salem, 1981-82; asst. prof. ob/gyn. U. Va. Sch. Medicine, Charlottesville, 1987-90, assoc. prof. depts. ob/gyn. and radiology, 1990-91, assoc. prof. dept. ob/gyn., assoc. prof. dept. radiology, 1991-96, dir. prenatal diagnosis and treatment unit dept. ob/gyn., 1989—, dir. divsn. maternal-fetal medicine dept. ob/gyn., 1990—, John Nokes prof. ob/gyn., 1996—; prof. dept. radiology U. Va. Sch. Medicine, 1996—; med. dir. perinatal svcs. U. Va. Hosp., Charlottesville, 1990-96, med. dir. women's svcs., 1997—; attending staff mem. U. Va. Hosp., 1987—, Va. Bapt. Hosp., 1996—, Stanford U. Hosp., 1982-87, Forsyth Meml. Hosp., Winston-Salem, 1981-82, Med. Park Hosp., Winston-Salem, 1981-82; assoc. staff mem. Va. Bapt. Hosp., Lynchburg, 1992-96, Santa Clara Valley Med. Ctr., San Jose, Calif., 1982-87; cons. Mid-Coastal Calif. Perinatal Outreach Program, Stanford U., 1982-87, San Joaquin Gen. Hosp., Stockton, Calif., 1985-87, Va. Bapt. Hosp., Lynchburg, 1992—; fellow Project Hope, maternal-fetal medicine program, Krakow, Poland, 1987, 89, others; mem. numerous coms. in field. Editl. referee Am. Jour. Ob-Gyn., Ob-Gyn. Jour., Clin. Chemistry Jour., Am. Jour. Human Genetics, Am. Jour. Perinatology, Jour. Reproduction, Fertility and Devel., Jour. Maternal-Fetal Medicine; obstet. editl. cons. Perinatal Continuing Edn. Program, 1991—; contbr. articles to profl. jours., chpts. to books in field. Hon. chmn. March of Dimes Walkathon, U. Va. Health Scis. Ctr., 1990; active task force on smoking and pregnancy, Am. Lung Assn. of Santa Clara-San Benito Counties, 1983; active First Presbyn. Ch., Charlottesville; coach Soccer Orgn. Charlottesville-Albemarle; bd. dirs. Ednam Forest Owners Assn., Inc., 1993-96; vol. physician Camp Va., Goshen. Recipient numerous grants in field, including Dept. Mental Health, Retardation and Substance Abuse, Commonwealth of Va., 1992-93, Perinatal Nurse Liaison Contract, 1991-92, others. Fellow ACOG (examiner for specialty oral bds. 1995—, mem. health care partnerships adv. com. to DMAS Va. sect. 1995); mem. AAAS, Am. Gynecol. and Obstets. Soc., Am. Physiol. Soc., Am. Inst. Ultrasound in Medicine (sr.), Internat. Cytokine Soc., South Atlantic Assn. Ob-Gyn., Soc. Gynecologic Investigation, Soc. Perinatal Obstetricians (bd. dirs. 1996—), Frank Lock Soc., Assn. Profs. Ob-Gyn., So. Ob-Gyn. Seminar, Va. Ob-Gyn. Soc., U. Va. Residents' Soc. (hon.), N.C. Ob-Gyn. Soc. (hon.), Phi Beta Kappa, Phi Alpha Theta. Achievements include research in prenatal diagnostic techniques, prostaglandins and cervical compliance, fetal-pelvic disproportion, preterm labor, control of parathyroid hormone-related protein (PTHrP) secretion in myometrial and human umbilical vein endothelial (HUVEC) cells in culture, expression of PTHrP and its receptor in human myometrium in pregnancies complicated by preterm labor, expression of PTHrP and its receptor in placental and umbilical vessels in pregnancies complicated by pregnancy-induced hypertension. Office: U Va Sch Medicine Div Maternal and Fetal Medicine PO Box 387 Charlottesville VA 22902-0387

FERGUSON, JAMES JOSEPH, JR., physician, academic administrator, researcher; b. Glen Cove, N.Y., Feb. 1, 1926; s. James Joseph and Elizabeth Marie Ferguson; m. Martha Randolph Saunders, Nov. 29, 1952; children: James Joseph III, William L., Nancy G. Yoh, Katherine E. BA, U. Rochester, 1946, MD, 1950. Intern, resident medicine Mass. Gen. Hosp., Boston, 1950-55; research fellow Case Western Res. U., Cleve., 1956-59; faculty U. Pa., Phila., 1959-89; assoc. dean Sch. Medicine U. Pa., 1975-86; spl. expert Nat. Libr. Medicine, Bethesda, Md., 1986-93. Served with USNR, 1943-45, 52-55. Markle fellow, 1960-65; recipient NIH research career devel. award, 1965, grantee, 1963-80. Mem. ACP, Soc. Clin. Investigation, Endocrine Soc., Merion Cricket Club, Woods Hole (Mass.) Golf Club, Chevy Chase Club. Home: 5600 Wisconsin Ave Apt 1607 Chevy Chase MD 20815-4413

FERGUSON, JAMES PETER, distilling company executive; b. Landis, Sask., Can., Aug. 12, 1937; s. James and Gertrude (Schmit) F.; m. Patricia Woodruff, Aug. 27, 1960; children—James, Carolyn. Chartered Acct., McGill U., 1971. Mgr. Clarkson Gordon, Montreal, Que., Can., 1965-73; lectr. McGill U., Montreal, Que., Can., 1970-72; contr. CI Power Ltd., Montreal, Que., Can., 1973-74; mgr. taxation Hiram Walker-Gooderham & Worts Ltd., Windsor, Ont., Can., 1974-79, treas., v.p., chief fin. officer, 1979-82, sr. v.p., treas., chief fin. officer, 1982-88; exec. v.p., corp. devel. dir. Hiram Walker-Allied Vintners, 1988-90, exec. v.p., chmn. Latin Am. and So. Europe sector, 1990-92; pres. Latin Am., corp. devel. dir. Allied Domecq Spirits and Wine (The Hiram Walker Group), 1992-95, corp. strategy dir., 1995-97; ret., 1998; bd. dirs. Pedro Demecq S.A., Spain, Corby Distilleries Ltd., Montreal. Chmn. Met. Gen. Hosp., Windsor, Ont., 1979-80. Capt. Can. Air Force, 1956-65. Mem. Inst. Chartered Accts., Order Chartered Accts. Que. Club: Essex Golf, Renaissance. Home: 6470 Riverside Dr E, Windsor, ON Canada N8S 1B9 Office: Allied Domecq Spirits/Wine PO Box 33006 Detroit MI 48232-5006

FERGUSON, JO MCCOWN, lawyer; b. Central City, Ky., Apr. 5, 1915; s. Jo Marvin and Willie Mae (Cain) F.; m. Margarita Hauser, July 12, 1947; children—Rita, Diane, Jo Frances. A.B., U. Ky., 1937, LL.B., 1939. Bar: Ky. 1938. Practiced in Central City, 1939-42; asst. atty. gen. Ky., 1948-56; atty. gen., 1956-60, commr. econ. security, 1960-61; partner firm Harper, Ferguson & Davis.; mcpl. bd. counsel, 1961—. Chmn. Gov.'s Com. on Constl. Revision, 1961-62; chmn. Gov.'s Task Force on Fin., 1976-77; pres. Ky. Hist. Soc., 1988-90; chief Property Control br. Mil. Govt., Bavaria, 1946-47. Capt. AUS, 1944-47, ETO. Decorated Brigadier d'Honneur 3eme Regiment Anjou, French Army. Mem. ABA, Ky. Bar Assn., VFW, So. Attys. Gen. (chmn. 1957-58). Democrat. Episcopalian. Home: 403 Duff Ln Louisville KY 40207-1524 Office: 1730 Meidinger Tower Louisville KY 40202-3445

FERGUSON, JOHN BARCLAY, biology educator; b. Balt., July 5, 1947; s. John Miller and Helen (Sucro) F.; m. Jane Hough, June 28, 1970 (div. 1987); children: Hallam H., Gillian D.; m. Valeri J. Thomson, July 1, 1988; 1 child, Samantha T. BS, Brown U., 1969; PhD, Yale U., 1973. Asst. prof. Bard Coll., Annandale, N.Y., 1977-83, assoc. prof., 1983-92, prof., 1992—, health professions advisor, 1985—. Contbr. to Microsoft Encarta 97 CD-ROM, 1 book and articles to profl. jours. Bd. trustees Ch. St. John Evangelist, Barrytown, N.Y., 1988—. NIH Postdoctoral fellow, 1974-76. Mem. AAAS, Am. Soc. Microbiology, N.Y. Acad. Scis., Sigma Xi. Home: RR 3 Box 305 Red Hook NY 12571-9425 Office: Bard Coll Dept Biology Annandale On Hudson NY 12504

FERGUSON, JOHN DUNCAN, medical researcher; b. Saskatoon, Sask., Can., Aug. 20, 1929; s. George Alexander and Urdine (LeValley) F.; m. Tamara van den Bergh, Sept. 12, 1958. MA, U. Toronto, Ont., Can., 1956; PhD, Columbia U., 1966. Project dir. Bur. Applied Social Rsch., Columbia U., N.Y.C., 1958-64; asst. prof. Northeastern U., Boston, 1966-68; from assoc. prof. to prof. U. Windsor, Ont., 1968—; mem. assoc. med. staff Harper Hosp., Detroit, 1982—. Author reports in field. Grantee Ont. Cmty. and Social Svcs. Ministry, 1991-93. Presbyterian. Home: 1516 Iroquois Ave Detroit MI 48214-2747 Office: U Windsor, Windsor, ON Canada N9B 3P4

FERGUSON, JOHN LEWIS, state historian; b. Nashville, Ark., Mar. 1, 1926; s. Clarence Walter and Nannye Nell (McCrary) F.; m. Oris Brandon, June 9, 1956; children—Clay Walt, Ora Lee. B.A., Henderson State Tchrs. Coll., 1950; M.A., U. Ark., 1952; Ph.D., Tulane U., 1960. Head dept. social studies Conway Bapt. Coll., Ark., 1952-58; asst. prof. history Ark. Poly. Coll., Russellville, 1958-60; state historian Ark. History Commn., Little Rock, 1960—. Editor: Arkansas and the Civil War, 1965; author: Arkansas Lives, 1965; co-author: Historic Arkansas, 1966. Baptist. Home: 12 Pilot Point Pl Little Rock AR 72205-2856 Office: Ark History Commn 1 Capitol Mall Little Rock AR 72201-1049

FERGUSON, JOHN MARSHALL, retired federal magistrate judge; b. Marion, Ill., Oct. 14, 1921; s. John Marshall and Vessie (Widdows) F.; m. Jeanne Harmon, Sept. 23, 1950; children: Marcia Ferguson Velde, Mark Harmon, John Scott, Mary Sue. Student, So. Ill. U., 1939-41, S.E. Mo. Tchrs. Coll., 1941; LLB, JD, Washington U., St. Louis, 1948. Bar: Ill. 1949, U.S. Ct. Appeals (7th cir.) 1956, U.S. Supreme Ct. 1960. Asst. mgr. I.W. Rogers Theaters, Inc., Anna, Ill., 1934-42; atty. U.S. Fidelity & Guaranty Co., St. Louis, 1948-51; assoc. Baker, Kagy & Wagner, East St. Louis, Ill., 1951-56; ptnr. Baker, Kagy & Wagner, 1956-59, Wagner, Ferguson, Bertrand & Baker, East St. Louis and Belleville, Ill., 1959-72; magistrate judge U.S. Dist. Ct. (so. dist.) Ill., 1990-94; pres. bd. Arch Aircraft, Inc., 1966-68; disciplinary commr. Ill. Supreme Ct., 1957-90, mem. joint com. on revision disciplinary rules, 1972-74; mem. hearing bd. Ill. Registration and Disciplinary Commn., 1974-90; pres. 1st Dist. Fedn. Bar Assns. Precinct committeeman Stookey Twp., St. Clair County (Ill.) Republican Com., 1958-62; Bd. dirs., v.p. East St. Louis chpt. ARC. Capt. AUS, 1942-45. Mem. ABA, Ill. Bar Assn. (prof. responsibility com. 1975-86, chmn. 1983-84), St. Clair County Bar Assn., 7th Fed. Cir. Bar Assn. (bd. govs.), East St. Louis City Club (pres. 1960-61), Ill. Club (govs., pres. 1966-67), East St. Louis City Club (pres. 1960-61), Ill. Club (gov. pres. 1966-67), St. Clair Country Club (Belleville, pres. 1972-73), Masons, Elks, Delta Theta Phi. Home: 12 Oak Knoll Belleville IL 62223-1817

FERGUSON, JOHN PATRICK, medical center executive; b. Weehawken, N.J., Jan. 22, 1949; s. Donald George and Margaret (Rienzo) F.; m. Gene Marie Promersperger, Jan. 16, 1971; children: Adam, David, Kate. BS in Econs., St. Peter's Coll., 1970; MBA in Hosp. Adminstrn., George Washington U., 1973. Sr. v.p. St. Vincent's Hosp., N.Y.C., 1972-81; v.p. ops. Hackensack (N.J.) Med. Ctr., 1981-85, sr. v.p., 1985, acting pres., chief exec. officer, 1985-86, pres., chief exec. officer, 1986—; mem. adj. faculty New Sch. for Social Rsch. Grad. Sch. Mgmt. and Urban Professions, N.Y.C., 1978-84; pres. Met. Health Adminstrs., N.Y.C., 1977-78; vice chmn. bd. trustees Univ. Health Sys., Trenton, N.J., 1988-90; rep. to coun. on tchg. hosps. Assn. Am. Med. Coll., 1994-97; abstract presenter China-U.S. Conf. on Managing Hosps. in 1990s; bd. dirs. Commerce Bank/North. Bd. govs. Ramapo Coll. Found., 1993—; trustee Univ. HealthCare Corp., 1994—, Molly Found. for Diabetes Rsch., 1995—; mem. exec. bd. Bergen coun. Boy Scouts am., 1993-97; commr. Econ. Devel. Commn. of City of Hackensack, 1996—; founding mem. Bergen County Econ. Devel. Corp., 1996—. Recipient Man of Yr. award Tomorrow's Children's Fund, 1989, Medallion award Bergen C.C., 1993, Disting. Cmty. Health Svc. award Bergen County Bd. of Chosen Freeholders, 1996; named Man of Yr. Nat. Burn Victim Found., 1994; named One of Top 12 Up and Coming Healthcare Execs., Modern Healthcare mag., One of 50 People to Watch for the 1990's, N.J. Bus. Jour., Citizen of Yr., Meadowlands Regional C. of C., 1993, Humanitarian of Yr., Make A Wish Found., 1996; named disting. citizen of N.J. Ramapo Coll. Found., 1998; recipient pres.'s award N.J. State Nurses Assn., 1999. Fellow Am. Coll. Healthcare Execs. (regent, gov. dist. II 1994-99); mem. Am. Hosp. Assn., Cath. Hosp. Assn., Am. Heart Assn. (pres. Mid-Bergen div. 1992-93, bd. dirs. 1993-94), Commerce and Industry Assn. N.J. (bd. dirs. 1996—, Chmn.'s award for Outstanding Leadership 1997), Am. Fedn. for Aging Rsch. (bd. dirs. 1997—), Met. Health Adminstrn. Assn. (Distinction award 1997). Office: Hackensack U Med Ctr 30 Prospect Ave Hackensack NJ 07601

FERGUSON, JULIE ANN, physical education educator; b. Maquoketa, Iowa, June 19, 1958; d. Donald Hayes and Bonnie Lea (Bullock) Maxey; m. John Stephen Ferguson, Aug. 10, 1985; children: Dawn Ann, John Ryan, John Scott. BS in Edn., U. Mo., 1980; MS in Athletic Adminstrn., U. Ill., 1982. Cert. tchr. Mo. Sub. tchr. Ritenour Dist., St. Louis, 1978-80; asst. women's basketball coach U. Ill., Champaign, 1980-82, instr. phys. edn., 1981-82, adminstrv. asst. Athletic Assn., 1982-83; dir. championships, supr. officials Big Eight Conf., Kansas City, Mo., 1983-90; instr. phys. edn., head volleyball and girls basketball coach Lee's Summit (Mo.) Sch. Dist., 1990—; speaker, clin. coord. Fellowship Christian Athletes, Kansas City, 1986; selection com. U. Mo., Kansas City, 1987, 88; scholar athlete Kansas City Star, 1989; coach, tour adminstr. Athletes in Action Basketball Team to China and Far East, 1984; tour adminstr. Big Eight Conf. Basketball Tour to Czechoslovakia, 1990. Deacon Lee's Summit Christian Ch., 1990--. Mem. (life) U. Mo. Columbia Alumni Assn., U. Ill. Alumni Assn., Women's Basketball Coaches Assn., Am. Volleyball Coaches Assn., Coun. Collegiate Women Athletic Adminstrs., Fellowship Christian Athletes (Tchr. of Yr. finalist 1997). Avocations: horseback riding, cross stitch, sports, family. Home: 4151 SE Paddock Cir Lees Summit MO 64082-4926

FERGUSON, KATHRYN CUCCIA, judge; b. New Brunswick, N.J.. BA, Rutgers Coll., N.J., 1980; JD, Rutgers Sch. of Law, N.J., 1983. Law clk. to Judge Judith H. Wizmur U.S. Bankruptcy Ct. (N.J. dist.), 1985-86; atty. Markowitz & Zindler, 1986-93; judge U.S. Bankruptcy Ct. (N.J. dist.), 3rd circuit, Trenton, 1993—. Office: US Post Office & Courthouse 402 E State St Trenton NJ 08608-1507

FERGUSON, KINGSLEY GEORGE, psychologist; b. Newcastle-on-Tyne, Eng., Apr. 13, 1921; emigrated to Can., 1927; s. William George and Isobel (Finnegan) F. B.A. in English and French, U. Western Ont., 1943; M.A. in Psychology, U. Toronto, 1951, Ph.D., 1956. Diplomate Am. Bd. Profl. Psychology. Staff psychologist Sunnybrook Vets. Hosp., Toronto, Ont., Can., 1949-50; chief psychologist Westminster Vets. Hosp., London, Ont., Can., 1950-61, Montreal Gen. Hosp., Que., Can., 1961-68; psychologist-in-chief Clarke Inst. Psychiatry, Toronto, 1968-86; chmn. Ont. Bd. Examiners in Psychology, Toronto, 1972-77. Served to lt. Can. Navy, 1942-45. Fellow Can. Psychol. Assn.; mem. Am. Psychol. Assn., Ont. Psychol. Assn. (pres. 1959-60). E-mail: kingsley@interlog.com. Address: 694 Sammon Ave, Toronto, ON Canada M4C 2E4

FERGUSON, LARRY EMMETT, educational administrator; b. Coolridge, W.Va., Oct. 19, 1934; s. Clarence Emmett and Marjorie Evelyn (Ransom) F.; m. Lynne Alice Jackson, May 17, 1957 (div. May 1975); children: David (dec.), Karen J. Ramsey; m. Alma Jeanette (Jeanne) Mitchell, Oct. 24, 1975; stepchildren: Dona Williamson, Patti Rae, Terri Musa-Jones, Ron Musa. AAS, Clark Coll., Vancouver, Wash., 1977; BS in Psychology and Elem. Edn., Portland State U., 1979, postgrad., 1979-91. Cert. continuing tchr., Wash. Customer engr. RCA Svc. Co., Portland, Oreg., 1975-77; tchr. Ft. Simcoe Job Corps, White Swan, Wash., 1982-89; mgr. Life Skills Tng. Inst., Vancouver, Wash., 1990—. Bd. dirs. Slocum Theatre Group, Vancouver, Wash., 1982; loaned exec. Consolidated Fed. Campaign, Yakima, Wash., 1988. Master sgt. USAF, 1954-75. Mem. Internat. Order Foresters, Non-Commd. Officers Assn., Am. Legion. Mem. Disciples of Christ. Avocations: community theatre, travel. Office: Life Skills Tng Inst 1920 Broadway St Vancouver WA 98663-3325

FERGUSON, LEONARD PRICE (BEAR FERGUSON), advertising executive, consultant; b. Bryan, Tex., Mar. 23, 1951; s. Thomas Morgan and Grace Evelyn (Barnett) F.; m. Kathleen Ann Winter, Feb. 15, 1986; children: Hillary Annette, Carissa Marie. BBA, Tex. A&M U., 1973; MS in Communications, U. Ill., 1975. Field supr. Agri-Systems Tex., Inc., Bryan, Tex., 1966-69; mgr., sales rep. Wang Labs., Inc., Beaumont and Houston, Tex., 1973-75; account exec. Leo Burnett Advt., Inc., Chgo., 1976-79, Clinton E. Frank Advt., Chgo., 1979-80; v.p., supr. account group Ogilvy & Mather Advt., Inc., Houston, 1980-84; co-founder, mgr. sales ops. Nat. Recycling Corp., Houston, 1984-85; sr. v.p., mgmt. supr., stockholder Eisaman, Johns & Laws Advt., Houston, 1985-95; exec. v.p. Lois/EJL, Houston, 1996-97, Chgo., 1997-99; exec. v.p. Fogarty Klein 312, Chgo., 1999—; pres. Pathfinder Cons., Houston, 1980—. Inventor glass crusher, recycling system. Chmn. Houstonians on Watch Program, Braeburn Glen and Houston, Tex., 1982-84. Grantee U. Ill., 1969, 73, Sam Houston U., 1970. Mem. Am. Advt. Agy. Assn. (affiliate), Direct Mail Mktg. Assn. (affiliate), Advt. Research Found. (affiliate). Methodist. Avocations: golf, music, landscaping, wildlife, travel. Home: 1215 Redfield Rd Naperville IL 60563-0440 Office: Fogarty Klein 312 divsn Lois/USA-NY 111 E Wacker Ste 500 Chicago IL 60563

FERGUSON, LEWIS LEROY, senior correspondent; b. Ponca City, Okla., Jan. 9, 1934; s. Luther LeRoy and Henrietta Marie (Mueller) F.; m. Sue Ann Thomson, June 5, 1958; children: John Michael, Diane Marie. BA in Journalism, U. Okla., 1956, MA in Journalism, 1964. Sports and wire editor Ponca City (Okla.) News, 1958-60; newsman The AP, Okla. City, 1960, Sioux Falls, S.D., 1960-62; night editor, sports editor The AP, Mpls., 1962-68; sports editor The AP, Kans. City, Mo., 1968-70; corr. in charge The AP, Topeka, 1970—; trustee Karl Menninger Lecture Series, 1982—, pres., 1988. Cons. on cameras in the courtroom Kans. Supreme Ct., Topeka, 1987-88. Capt. USAR, 1957-64. Recipient Outstanding Journalism Grad. award Sigma Delta Chi, U. Okla., 1956, AP Staffer of Yr. award Kans. City Star, 1992, Kans. Justice award Kans. Supreme Ct., 1993, Disting. Alumnus award Herbert Journalism Sch., U. Okla., 1996; featured in 1984 promotional film "One of a Kind" narrated by former NBC anchor John Chanselor. Mem. William Allen White Found. (trustee 1987—), Kans. Bar Assn. (Bar-Media com. mem. 1994—). Lutheran. Avocations: internet, statistics, fishing. Office: The Associated Press 616 SE Jefferson St Topeka KS 66607-1137

FERGUSON, MARGARET ANN, tax consultant; b. Steuben County, Ind., Mar. 24, 1933; d. Leo C. and Ruth Virginia (Engle) Wolf; m. Billy Hugh Ferguson, Feb. 15, 1955 (dec. Oct. 1971); children: Theresa Ruth, Scott Earl, Wade Leo, Luke, Angela, Cynthia, Brenda. AA in Psychology/Social Svs., Palomar Coll., San Marcos, Calif., 1977; BA in Behavioral Sci., Nat. U., Vista, Calif., 1980. Enrolled agt. Office mgr., adminstr. asst. Better Bus. Bur., San Diego, 1979-82; tax technician IRS, Oceanside, Calif., 1982-84, problem resolution tax specialist, 1985-87, revenue agt., 1987-90; pvt. cons. Vista, Calif., 1991—; instr. adult edn. Vista Unified Sch. Dist., 1990—; mem. adv. com. of nat. cemetery sys. Dept. Vet. Affairs, 1991-98, adv. coun. IRS, 1999—. Mem. AAUW (treas.), Calif. Assn. Ind. Accts., Calif. Soc. Enrolled Agts. (dir. Palomar chpt. 1993-95, 1st v.p. 1998—), Inland Soc. Tax Cons., Assn. Homebased Bus., Gold Star Wives Am., Inc. (regional pres. 1989-90, chpt. pres. 1992-93, 96-97, nat. pres. 1993-95). Avocations: lace making, needle work, gardening, writing. Home and Office: 1161 Tower Dr Vista CA 92083-7144

FERGUSON, MARGARET GENEVA, author, publisher, real estate broker; d. James B. and Dollie (McCloud) F. Student, Kansas City Jr. Coll., 1949, YMCA Real Estate Inst., 1960, Bryant and Stratton Bus. Coll., 1962, Ill. Inst. Tech., 1969, 70, 72. pub. spkr. Sec. Cook County Grand Jury, 1979; acting mgr. internal svc. dept. Xerox Corp., 1985-86; tutor reading and math., 1988; host Black Image Prodn. Cable 19, 1989; interviewed on various TV shows, including PM Mag., 1983; active pub. rels. newspapers, Chgo., Detroit, Kansas City, St. Louis, 1970-91; conductor workshops in field; participant Pan Meth. Pilgrimage to Eng., 1984, World Meth. Conf., Nairobi, Kenya, 1986. Author, pub.: The History of St. Paul CME Church 1907-1988, 1989, Books in Print, 1989-90, This Is Your Life Dr. Owens, 1991. Co-treas. fund raiser Citizens for Mayor Harold Washington, Chgo., 1987; treas. St. Paul Mortgage Fund, 1984; vol. Am. Cancer Soc., Salvation Army, Lighthouse for the Blind, 1982, Dem. Nat. Conv., 1996; dist. pres. Christian Methodist Episcopal Ch. Nat. Women's League, 1980-86, nat. fin. sec., 1980-92; officer St. Paul Christian Methodist Episcopal Ch., 1983—; v.p. lay ministry, 1987-92, pres. 1992—; 2d v.p. Ann. Conf. Lay Ministry, 1996—; sec. Christian Methodist Episcopal Long Range Planning Commn., 1982-86; mem. Chgo. State Street Women's Coun.; judge, Chgo. City Elections Bur., 1997, 98. Recipient History Writing award Christian Meth. Episcopal Ch., 1990, Gold Coaster Kiwanis Club award, 1983, Black on Black Love award, 1988; named to Cultural Citizens Found. Hall of Fame, 1990, Vol. of Yr. Chgo. Lighthouse, 1982, 1st Lady award V-103FM, 1991, Citizens award, 1994, Key to City, Ft. Smith, Ark., 1992, Bishop's award C.M.E. Ch., 1996. Mem. NAACP, Nat. Coun. Negro Women, People United to Serve Humanity (prison ministry award 1991, Fred Davis award 1994, Steward of Yr. award 1999), Chgo. Bd. Realtors, S.W. Suburban Bd. Realtors, Hyde Park Co-op Soc. (bd. dirs. 1994-95), Internat. Platform Assn., Am. Assn. Ret. Persons (55 Alive instr. 1996—), DuSable Mus., Lambda Kappa Mu. Home: 727 E 60th St Apt 808 Chicago IL 60637-2592

FERGUSON, MARK HARMON, banker, lawyer; b. St. Louis, Dec. 9, 1953; s. John M. and Jeanne (Harmon) F.; m. Nancy Colleen Ogg, May 19, 1984; children: Claire E., Sara C. BA, U. Ill., 1975, JD, 1978. Bar: Ill. 1978. Assoc. Brown, Hay & Stephens, Springfield, Ill., 1978-83, ptnr., 1983-86; sr. v.p., CFO, Firstbank Ill. Co., Springfield, 1986-87, exec. v.p., 1987-88, pres., COO, 1988-89, pres., CEO, 1989—, chmn., 1990-98, also bd. dirs.; chmn., pres., CEO Mercantile Bank Ill., Springfield, 1998—; bd. dirs. MII, Inc., Lincoln, Ill.; bd. dirs. Meml. Health Sys., Inc., Springfield, chmn., 1995-97. Bd. dirs. Springfield Theatre Guild, 1980-83, So. Ill. U. Found., 1989—, Springfield Art Assn., 1990-91, U. Ill. Found., 1996—; mem. devel. adv. coun. So. Ill. U. Sch. Medicine, Springfield, 1988—; mem. cabinet Sangamon County chpt. United Way, 1989; trustee Ill. Coll., Jacksonville, 1993—; mem. bd. edn. Sch. Dist. #186, SPringfield, 1997—. Mem. Ill. Bar Assn., Sangamon County Bar Assn., Ill. Bankers Assn. (bd. dirs. 1993-97).Am. Bus. Club (bd. dirs. Springfield 1985). Republican. Roman Catholic. Home: 1920 Wiggins Ave Springfield IL 62704-3337 Office: Mercantile Bank Ill 205 S 5th St Apt 900 Springfield IL 62701-1406

FERGUSON, MICHAEL JOHN, electronics and communications educator; b. Toronto, Ont., Can., May 7, 1941; s. John Albert and Dorothy (Bracewell) F.; m. Virginia Louise Boardman, June 15, 1969; 1 child, Margaret Elizabeth. BASc, U. Toronto, 1962; MS, Calif. Inst. Tech., 1963; PhD, Stanford U., 1966. Engrng. specialist Ford Aerospace Co., Palo Alto, Calif., 1966-68; prof. McGill U., Montreal, Que., Can., 1968-76; rsch. assoc., mgr. Aloha system U. Hawaii, Honolulu, 1974-76; rsch. scholar Internat. Inst. Applied Systems Analysis, Laxenburg, Austria, 1976-78; mgr. systems analysis Bell Northern Rsch., Montreal, Que., 1978-82; Cyrille Duquet prof. communication software INRS-Telecommunications, Verdun, Que., 1985-98. Fellow IEEE; mem. Assn. for Computer Machinery (chmn. spl. interest group on communications 1985-87), Tex User Group (bd. dirs. 1991-96), Sigma Xi. Avocation: bicycle touring. Home: 4336 King Edward Ave, Montreal, PQ Canada H4B 2H5 Office: INRS-Telecommunications, 16 Place du Commerce, Verdun, PQ Canada H3E 1H6

FERGUSON, MILTON CARR, JR., lawyer; b. Washington, Feb. 10, 1931; s. Milton Carr and Gladys (Emery) F.; m. Marian Evelyn Nelson, Aug. 21, 1954; children: Laura, Sharon, Marcia, Sandra. B.A., Cornell U., 1952; LL.B., 1954; LL.M., N.Y. U., 1960. Bar: N.Y. State 1954. Trial atty. tax div. Dept. Justice, Washington, 1954-60; asst. atty. gen. Dept. Justice, 1977-81; asst. prof. law U. Iowa, 1960-62; assoc. prof. N.Y.U., 1962-65; prof. N.Y. U., 1965-77; vis. prof. law Stanford (Calif.) U., 1972-73; of counsel Wachtell, Lipton, Rosen & Katz, N.Y.C., 1969-76; ptnr. Davis Polk & Wardwell, N.Y.C., 1981—; spl. cons. to Treasury Dept., Commonwealth P.R., 1974. Author: (with others) Federal Income Taxation Legislation in Perspective, 1965, Federal Income Taxation of Estates and Beneficiaries, 1970, 2d edit., 1994. Trustee NYU Law Ctr. Found., Lewis and Clark Coll. Mem. ABA (chmn. tax sect. 1993-94), N.Y. State Bar Assn., Soc. Illustrators. Home: 32 Washington Sq W New York NY 10011-9156 Office: Davis Polk & Wardwell 450 Lexington Ave New York NY 10017-3911

FERGUSON, PAMELA ANDERSON, mathematics educator, educational administrator; b. Berwyn, Ill., May 5, 1943; d. Clarence Oscar and Ruth Anne (Stroner) Anderson; m. Donald Roger Ferguson, Dec. 18, 1965; children: Keith, Amanda. BA, Wellesley Coll., 1965; MS, U. Chgo., 1966, PhD, 1969. Asst. prof. Northwestern U., Evanston, Ill., 1969-70, U. Miami, Coral Gables, Fla., 1972-77; assoc. prof. U. Miami, 1978-81, prof. math., 1981-91, dir. honors program, 1985-87, assoc. provost, dean Grad. Sch., 1987-91; pres. Grinnell Coll., Iowa, 1991-97, prof. math., 1991—; mem. Nat. Sci. Bd., 1998-2004. Contbr. over 50 articles to refereed jours. Mem. Iowa Rsch. Coun., 1993-97. NSF grantee. Mem. Am. Math. Soc., Am. Women in Math., Wellesley Club, Sigma Xi, Phi Beta Kappa, Omicron Delta Chi. Lutheran. Avocations: hiking, reading, skiing. Office: Grinnell Coll Dept Math PO Box 805 Grinnell IA 50112-0805

FERGUSON, PIETE JACKSON, home health nurse; b. New Orleans, Nov. 29, 1960; d. Clyde Allison and Lillian (Petersen) Jackson; m. Jim M. Ferguson Sr., June 5, 1982; children: Jim M. Jr., Charles Benjamin. Diploma, Touro Infirmary, New Orleans, 1981; student, Our Lady of Holy Cross Coll., New Orleans, 1978-79, U. New Orleans, 1979-81. RN; cert. generalist ANCC; cert. gen. nursing practice, AACN. Staff nurse med.-surg. Touro Infirmary, 1981-82, nurse emergency rm., 1982-84; nurse ICU and critical care unit Alvin C. York Med. Ctr., Murfreesboro, Tenn., 1984-85; staff nurse emergency rm. So. Hills Med. Ctr., Nashville, 1985-90; rheumatology nurse Arthritis and Joint Replacement Ctr., Vanderbilt U. Med. Ctr., Nashville, 1990-92; home health nurse Mid. Tenn. Med. Ctr., Murfreesboro, 1992-93, VIP Home Health & Rehab., Murfreesboro, 1993-94; with Century Home Health, Murfreesboro, Tenn., 1994-95, Willow Brook Home Health, 1995—. Mem. ANA, La. State Nurses Assn. Home: 10095 Taylor Rd Rockvale TN 37153-4210

FERGUSON, R. NEIL, computer systems consultant; b. Dallas, June 22, 1952; s. Roy and Hellon Ferguson; m. L. Jean Ferguson, Aug. 12, 1977; 1 child, Rheachel Claire. BA in Psychology, U. Tex., 1976; grad., Winfield Sch. Race Driving, 1984. Systems engr. EDS, Dallas, 1976-77; systems programmer Collins Radio/Rockwell Internat., Richardson, Tex., 1977-78; systems programmer/analyst Moore Bus. Systems, Denton, Tex., 1978-79; supr., computer graphics Atlantic Richfield Co., Dallas, 1979-85; software engrng. specialist E-Systems, Inc., Garland, Tex., 1986-90; dir. product mgmt., graphics and database systems MPSI, Inc., Irving, Tex., 1990-92; pvt. practice computer cons. Lewisville, Tex., 1990—; owner Computer Sys. Svc. & Cons. Co.; tech. program dir. Internat. Microcomputer Exposition, Dallas, 1978. Vol. computer sys. adminstr. Trinity Presbyn. Ch. Recipient Golden Eagle award Am. Acad. Achievement, Tymshare award Tymshare Corp., Panasonic Sci. Achievement award Matsushita Electric Corp. of Am. and Jr. Engrng. Tech. Soc., NASA award, Dallas County Med. Soc. award, 1st Place award in math. and computers 21st Internat. Sci. Fair; featured in Grolier's Sci. Ency. supplement, 1967; named Regional Class Champion, Sports Car Club of Am. Mem. Assn. for Computing Machinery, Spl. Interest Group on Computer Graphics, Am. Congress Surveying and Mapping, Am. Soc. Photogrammetry and Remote Sensing. Avocations: exotic sportscar restoration, stamp collecting, scale model car construction, wrist and pocket watch collecting and restoration. Home and Office: 1097 Holly Ln Lewisville TX 75067-5711

FERGUSON, RICHARD L., educational administrator. Pres. Am. Coll. Testing Program, Iowa City. Office: Am Coll Testing Program Instl Srvcs 2201 N Dodge St Iowa City IA 52243-0168*

FERGUSON, ROBERT, financial services executive, educator, writer; b. N.Y.C., Nov. 24, 1937; s. Lawrence and Claire (Billingheimer) F.; m. Catherine Latil, July 7, 1961 (div. Dec. 1982); children: Anne, Alice, Magali, Jose; m. Magali Vigo, Apr. 26, 1991. BA, Columbia U., 1959; M of Philosophy, NYU, 1983, PhD, 1987. V.p. Bradford Trust Co., N.Y.C., 1977-78, Coll. Retirement Equities Fund, N.Y.C., 1978-82; exec. v.p. Leland O'Brien Rubinstein Assocs., L.A., 1982-91; pres. Axiomatic Systems, N.Y.C., 1986—; vice chmn. SuperShare Svcs., L.A., 1989-91; assoc. prof. fin. Fordham U. Sch. Bus., N.Y.C., 1991-98; bd. dirs. SuperShare Svcs. Corp.; assoc. editor Fin. Analysts Jour., 1974—; mem. adv. bd. Jour. Performance Measurement; adj. assoc. prof. fin. Columbia U. Sch. Bus., 1987-90. Contbr. articles to profl. jours. With USAR. Mem. Fin. Analysts Fedn. (Graham & Dodd award 1961, 78, 80), Investment Tech. Assn. (chmn. bd. 1975), Inst. for Quantitative Research in Fin. (chmn. 1974-75). Avocation: aviation. Office: 417 Riverside Dr Apt 8A New York NY 10025-7932

FERGUSON, ROBERT BURY, mineralogy educator; b. Cambridge, Ont., Can., Feb. 5, 1920; s. Alexander Galt and Harriet Henrietta (Bury) F.; m. Margaret Irene Warren, Dec. 29, 1948; children: Evelyn Bury, Robert Warren, Marion Galt. B.A., U. Toronto, 1942, M.A., 1943, Ph.D., 1948. Asst. prof. mineralogy U. Man. (Can.), Winnipeg, 1947-50; assoc. prof. U. Man, Winnipeg, Can., 1951-59; prof. U. Man.(Can.), Winnipeg, 1959-85, disting. prof., 1983; prof. emeritus U. Man.(Can.), 1985—. Fellow Royal Soc. Can., Mineral Soc. Am.; mem. Mineral Soc. Great Britain, Mineral Assn. Can. (Hawley award 1981). New Democratic Party. Unitarian. Home: 184 Wildwood Park, Winnipeg, MB Canada R3T 0E2 Office: U Man, Dept Geol Scis, Winnipeg, MB Canada R3T 2N2

FERGUSON, ROBERT HARRY MUNRO, lawyer; b. N.Y.C., Oct. 10, 1937; s. Robert Munro and Frances (Hand) F.; m. Kirk Palmer, Sept. 21, 1960; children: Robert, Martha Taft-Ferguson. BA, Yale U., 1959; LLB, Harvard U, 1964. Bar: N.Y. 1965. Assoc. Dewey Ballantine et al., N.Y.C., 1964-71; assoc. Patterson Belknap Webb & Tyler, N.Y.C., 1971-72, ptnr., 1972-96, of counsel, 1997—. Contbr. articles to profl. jours. Bd. dirs. John B. Pierce Lab., New Haven, Conn., 1979—, Fannie and John Hertz Found., Livermore, Calif., 1990—. 1st lt. U.S. Army, 1959-61. Mem. ABA (tax sect., mem. com. on tax exempt orgns., vice chair 1997-99, chmn. 1999—), Bedford Golf and Tennis Club. Democrat. Avocation: golf. Office: Patterson Belknap LLP 1133 Avenue Of The Americas New York NY 10036-6710

FERGUSON, RONALD EUGENE, reinsurance company executive; b. Chgo., Jan. 16, 1942; s. William Eugene and Elizabeth (Hahnneman) F.; m. Carol Jean Chapp, Dec. 27, 1964; children: Brian, Kristin. BA, Blackburn Coll., 1963; MA, U. Mich., 1965. Statistician Lumbermans Mut. Casualty Co., Long Grove, Ill., 1965-69; actuary Gen. Reins. Corp., Greenwich, Conn., 1969-70, asst. v.p. 1972-74, v.p., 1974-77, sr. v.p., 1977-82, exec. v.p., 1982, dir., 1983, chmn., 1985—, CEO, bd. dirs.; v.p., group exec. Gen. Re Corp., Stamford, 1981, pres., chief operating officer, 1983-87, chmn., pres., chief exec. officer, 1987—; bd. dirs. Gen. Signal Corp., Colgate-Palmolive Co., Ins. Inst. Am., ISO, Inc. Contbr. articles to profl. jours. Served with USPHS, 1966-68. Fellow Casualty Actuarial Soc. (bd. dirs. 1978-81); mem. Am. Acad. Actuaries (dir. 1981—). Congregationalist. Clubs: Patterson. Office: Gen Re Corp Financial Ctr PO Box 10351 Stamford CT 06904-2351

FERGUSON, RONALD MORRIS, surgeon, educator; b. Milaca, Minn., Nov. 12, 1945; children: Melissa, Jason, Meredith. BS, Augsburg Coll., 1967; MD, Washington U., St. Louis, 1971; PhD, U. Minn., 1982. Diplomate Am. Bd. Surgery. Dir. transplantation VA Med. Ctr., Mpls., 1980-82; assoc. prof. surgery Ohio State U., Columbus, 1982-88, prof. surgery, 1988—, chmn. dept. surgery, transplant, 1993-99, chief divsn. transplant, 1999—; asst. prof. surgery U. Minn. Health Sci. Ctr., Mpls., 1980-82; med. dir. Lifeline of Ohio Organ Procurement, Columbus, 1985—. Mem. Am. Coll. Surgeons, Am. Soc. Transplant Surgeons, Soc. Univ. Surgeons (pres. 1988), Transplantation Soc. (v.p. 1992—). Office: Ohio State U 362 Means Hall 1654 Upham Dr Columbus OH 43210-1250*

FERGUSON, RONALD THOMAS, writer; b. N.Y.C., May 3, 1933; s. Thomas Robert and Eleanor Lillian (Jonasson) F.; m. Faith Ann Casebolt, Dec. 28, 1964; children: Elizabeth, Karen, Thomas. BA in History and French, SUNY, Albany, 1954; MA in European History, Pa. State U., 1961; PhD in European and Asian History, U. Minn., 1970. Temp. instr. history Pa. State U., University Park, 1957-59; head dept. history Atlantic Highlands (N.J.) H.S., 1958-59; instr. history Ithaca (N.Y.) Coll., 1961-63; sr. tchg. asst., supr. history 1-2-3 program U. Minn., Mpls., 1963-65; acting assoc. prof. history U. Hawaii Manoa, Honolulu, 1966-69; prof. history Indiana (Pa.) U., 1969-88; writer Indiana, Pa., 1988—. *Created the first film course in the catalog of any American University, " The Film as Cultural, Intellectual, and Social History", (undergraduate and graduate), 1973-82. Shichinin No Samurai (The Seven Samurai), 1954, was the basic film, with Yojimbo, and other fiction films and literature. At present he is working on the television program Babylon 5.* Author: Blood and Fire: Contribution Policies of French Armies in Germany, 1667-1715, 1970. With U.S. Army, 1955-57. Fulbright rsch. scholar French Army Archives, 1965-66. Mem. Aircraft Owners and Pilots Assn., Air Force Assn. (life), USN Inst., Polit. Sci. Assn. Lutheran. Avocations: locksmith, French-German-Swedish linguist. Office: PO Box 207 Indiana PA 15701-0207

FERGUSON, SANFORD BARNETT, lawyer; b. Boston, Feb. 3, 1947; s. Albert Barnett and Louise (Enequist) F.; children: Andrew, Robert, Gavin; m. Kelly Ann Westhoff. BA, Dartmouth Coll., 1970; MA, Oxford U., Eng., 1972; JD, Yale U., 1975. Bar: Pa. 1975, U.S. Dist. Ct. (we. dist.) Pa., U.S. Tax Ct., U.S. Ct. Appeals (3d cir.) 1975. Ptnr. Kirkpatrick & Lockhart, L.L.P., Pitts., 1981—; bd. dirs. Avalon Holdings, Inc., Innovation Works, Inc., Solutions Cons., Inc. Bd. dirs., chmn. United Way of Allegheny County; trustee, pres. Scaife Family Found. Mem. ABA, Pa. Bar Assn., Allegheny County Bar Assn., Am. Law Inst., Duquesne Club, Fox Chapel Golf Club. Presbyterian. Office: Kirkpatrick & Lockhart LLP 1500 Oliver Building Pittsburgh PA 15222-2312

FERGUSON, SUSAN KATHARINE STOVER, nurse, psychotherapist, consultant; b. Warsaw, Ind., Mar. 11, 1944; d. Robert Eugene and Barbara Louise (Swaney) Stover; m. Philip Charles Ferguson, Oct. 2, 1965 (div.); children: Scott Duane, Shawn Alaine, Erin Kirsten. Diploma in nursing, Meth. Hosp., 1966; BA in Psychology, Purdue U., 1988; MSW, Smith Coll., 1991; advanced cert. in Psychoanalytic Psychotherapy, Psychoanalytic Psychotherapy Ctr., 1993-94. Staff nurse, health hazard appraiser Meth. Hosp. of Ind., Indpls., 1966-68; staff nurse USPHS, Bethel, Alaska, 1968-70; instr. childbirth preparation Wabash, Ind., 1973-83; nurse Family Physicians Associated, Wabash, 1976-83; rsch. asst. Purdue U., Ft. Wayne, Ind., 1986-88; staff nurse, self-awareness seminar coord. Charter Beacon Hosp., Ft. Wayne, Ind., 1988-89; intern clin. social work Clifford Beers Guidance Ctr., New Haven, Conn., 1990-91; psychiat. nurse Yale-New Haven Hosp., 1990-91; pvt. practice Citadel Psychiat. Clinic, Ft. Wayne, Ind., 1991-93; dir. social svcs. Charter Northridge Behavioral Health sys., Raleigh, N.C., 1993-94; dir. social svcs., clinician adult psychiatry Charter Northridge Hosp., Raleigh, 1993-94; pvt. practice Raleigh, 1993—. Bd. dirs. Hoosiers for Safety Belts, Indpls., 1987-88, Ind. Med. Pol. Action Com., Indpls., 1986-87; coordinator, founder Safe Start Infant Safety Seat Loan Program, Wabash, 1981-87; participant in leadership devel. com. Wabash County C. of C., 1983; workshop leader Wabash County Hosp. Stop Smoking Program, 1982-83. Mem. Charles F. Menniger Soc., N.C. Psychoanalytic Soc., Kappa Kappa Kappa. Republican. Office: Atlantic Behavioral Health Systems Inc 2501 Atrium Dr Ste 400 Raleigh NC 27607-6452

FERGUSON, SUZANNE CAROL, English educator; b. East Stroudsburg, Pa., Aug. 13, 1939; d. Edwin Roy and Edna Mabel (Reeves) Butts; m. James H. Ferguson, May 29, 1960 (dec. Mar. 1989); 1 child, Cynthia Katherine. AA, Va. Intermont Coll., 1958; BA, Converse Coll., 1960; MA, Vanderbilt U., 1961; PhD, Stanford U., 1966. Asst. prof. English U. Calif., Santa Barbara, 1966-71; assoc. prof. Ohio State U., Columbus, 1971-83; prof. chmn. dept. English Wayne State U., Detroit, 1983-89; Samuel B. and Virginia C. Knight prof. humanities Case Western U., Cleveland, 1998—, dean humanities, arts and social scis., 1989-93, chair English dept., 1996—; vis. assoc. prof. Kenyon Coll., Gambier, Ohio, 1976; cons., evaluator North Ctrl. Assn. Schs. and Colls., 1992—, review panelist, 1994-98. Author: The Poetry of Randall Jarrell, 1971; editor: Critical Essays on Randall Jarrell, 1983; co-editor: Literature and the Visual Arts in Contemporary Soc., 1985; contbr. articles on fiction and poetry to profl. jours. Trustee Erich Katz Meml. Fund, N.Y.C., 1983-88; bd. dirs. Apollo's Fire, The Cleveland Baroque Orch., 1991—, founding pres., 1991-92, pres., 1994-95; trustee Nat. History Day, 1990-93. Woodrow Wilson fellow, 1960-61; Stanford U. Wilson fellow, 1965-66. Mem. MLA, Am. Lit. Assn., Midwest Modern Lang. Assn., Soc. for the Study of the Short Story, Assn. for Study of Am. Indian Lit., Am. Recorder Soc. (bd. dirs. 1980-88). Democrat. Avocations: performing early music. Home: 2 Bratenahl Pl Apt 2D Cleveland OH 44108-1167

FERGUSON, THOMAS, federal agency administrator; b. Trenton, N.J.; married; two children. BA in Econs., Lafayette Coll.; MPA, U. So. Calif. Assoc. dir. mgmt., dir. Securities Tech. Inst. Bur. of Engraving and Printing/Dept. of Treasury, Washington, 1974-97, dep. dir., 1997—. Office: Office of Director Bur of Engraving & Printing 14th & C Streets SW Washington DC 20228*

FERGUSON, THOMAS CROOKS, lawyer; b. Nov. 27, 1933; s. Thomas C. and Grace (Crooks) F.; children: Leslie Mead, Ian Thomas. AB, Vanderbilt U., 1955, JD, 1959; cert., Hague Acad. Internat. Law, 1958; postgrad., Kenney Sch. Govt., Harvard U., 1985. Bar: Ill. 1960, Ky. 1961, D.C. 1993. Bd. mem. Mead Johnson Found., 1960-70; mktg. mgr. Pharmaseal Labs., 1962-75; pres. Atlantic Salvage Corp., 1975-78, Brevard Marina, 1977-82; dir. Eastern Caribbean Peace Corps, 1982-84; dep. commr. Immigration and Naturalization Service Dept. Justice, 1984-87; U.S. amb. to Brunei Darussalam, 1987-89; pres. Airscan Internat., Indialantic, Fla., 1989-91; pvt. practice Washington, 1991—. With U.S. Army, 1955-56. Recipient Comdr.'s medal for civilian svc. Grenada, 1983. Mem. ABA, Fed. Bar Assn. Clubs: Offshore Cruising of Calif., Eau Gallie Yacht. Avocations: sailing, tennis, diving. Home: 6781 Linford Ln Jacksonville FL 32217-2660 Office: 336 S Carolina Ave SE Washington DC 20003-4223

FERGUSON, THOMAS GEORGE, retired healthcare advertising agency executive; b. Newark, Oct. 14, 1941; s. George Francis and Dorothy Marie (Stinson) F.; m. Roberta Chiaviello, Jan. 27, 1967; children: Thomas, Jr., Michael, Cathleen, Margaret. BS in Bus. Mgmt., Fairleigh Dickinson U., 1965. Product mgr. Bard-Parker div. Becton Dickinson & Co., Lincoln Park, N.J., 1965-70; acct. exec. L.W. Frolich, Inc., 1970-71; v.p., acct. group supr. Sudler & Hennessey, Inc., N.Y.C., 1971-74; chmn., pres. Thomas G. Ferguson Assocs., Inc., Parsippany, N.J., 1974—; chmn. Ferguson Common Health USA. Mem. Hemophilia Assn. N.J., 1981-98, ret., 1998; bd. dirs. Tri-County Scholarship Fund, Paterson, N.J., 1982—; pres., bd. trustees Epilepsy Found. N.J., Trenton, 1982—; past pres., bd. mem. Delbarton Sch. Fathers & Friends, Morristown, N.J. Served with USNG, 1971. Recipient Humanitarian award Hemophilia Assn. N.J., 1985, Disting. Svc. award Epilepsy Found. N.J., 1987. Mem. Pharm. Advt. Club, Pharm. Mfrs. Assn., Midwest Pharm. Advt. Club, Nat. Wholesale Druggists' Assn., Bus. Publication Audits, Fairleigh Dickinson U. Alumni Assn. Republican. Roman Catholic. Clubs: Morris County Golf (bd. dirs. 1975—), Baltusrol Golf. Avocation: golf. Office: Ferguson Common Health USA 30 Lanidex Plz W Parsippany NJ 07054-2717*

FERGUSON, THOMAS GLEN, internist; b. Chgo., Nov. 7, 1947; s. Thomas Glen and Mildred C. (Barrios) F.; m. Susan Ann Brumfield, Jan. 23, 1971; children: Nancy, Sarah. BS, Northwestern State U., Natchitoches, La., 1969, MS, 1970; MD, U. Tenn. Ctr. for Health Scis., 1974. Diplomate Am. Bd. Internal Medicine and Critical Care Medicine; cert. spl. competency in electrocardiography Am. Coll. Cardiology, spl. competency in echocardiography Am. Soc. Echocardiography. Chief of medicine, dir. critical care, noninvasive cardiol. S. La. Med. Assocs. and Leonard J. Chabert Med. Ctr., Houma, La., 1978—; med. dir. Leonard J. Chabert Med. Ctr., Houma, 1997; CEO and med. dir. S. La. Med. Assocs., 1997, also bd. dirs., 1978—. Contbg. author (book) Proceedings of the International Vascular Surgical Soc., 1993; also articles to profl. jours. Cons. La. State Legislature, Baton Rouge, Dept. Health and Hosps., State of La., Baton Rouge; participant Downtown on Bayou Festival Com., Houma, La., 1995—. Recipient Commendation VA, Memphis, 1978, Tchr. of Yr. award Alton Ochsner Med. Found., New Orleans, 1982, Best Drs. in Am. award, 1998. Fellow ACP, Am. Coll. Critical Care (Pres. award 1997); mem. AMA, Am. Soc. Echocardiography, Soc. Critical Care Medicine, La. State Med. Soc., Terrebone Parish Med. Soc., Houma C. of C., Alpha Omega Alpha. Avocations: bus., travel, fin., sports, music. Home: 1 Dandra Cir Houma LA 70360-6002 Office: S La Med Assocs 1978 Industrial Blvd Houma LA 70363-7055

FERGUSON, WARREN JOHN, federal judge; b. Eureka, Nev., Oct. 31, 1920; s. Ralph and Marian (Damele) F.; m. E. Laura Keyes, June 5, 1948; children: Faye F., Warren John, Teresa M., Peter J. B.A., U. Nev., 1942; LL.B., U. So. Calif., 1949; LL.D. (hon.), Western State U., San Fernando Valley Coll. Law. Bar: Calif. 1950. Mem. firm Ferguson & Judge, Fullerton, Calif., 1950-59; city atty. for cities of Buena Park, Placentia, La Puente, Baldwin Park, Santa Fe Springs, Walnut and Rosemead, Calif., 1953-59; mcpl. ct. judge Anaheim, Calif., 1959-60; judge Superior Ct., Santa Ana, Calif., 1961-66, Juvenile Ct., 1963-64, Appellate Dept., 1965-66; U.S. dist. judge Los Angeles, 1966-79; judge U.S. Circuit Ct. (9th cir.), Los Angeles, 1979-86; sr. judge U.S. Ct. Appeals (9th cir.), Santa Ana, 1986—; faculty Fed. Jud. Ctr., Practising Law Inst., U. Iowa Coll. Law, N.Y. Law Jour.; assoc. prof. psychiatry (law) Sch. Medicine, U. So. Calif.; assoc. prof. Loyola Law Sch. Served with AUS, 1942-46. Decorated Bronze Star. Mem. Phi Kappa Phi, Theta Chi. Democrat. Roman Catholic. Office: US Courthouse 411 W Fourth St Ste 10080 Santa Ana CA 92701 *Having been born and raised in Nevada, I have adopted an old prospector's philosophy: "Live today; look every man in the eye; and tell the rest of the world to go to hell."*

FERGUSON, WHITWORTH, III, consulting company executive; b. Buffalo, Aug. 16, 1954; s. Whitworth Jr. and Elizabeth (Rice) F.; m. Mary Barstow, May 30, 1981 (div. 1993). BA in Econs., St. Lawrence U., Canton, N.Y., 1976; MBA in Fin., U. Pa., 1978; JD, Cornell U., 1981; MDiv, Princeton U., 1999. Bar: Ill. 1981, N.Y. 1983. Assoc. McDermott, Will & Emery, Chgo., 1981-82, Damon & Morey, Buffalo, 1982-84; officer fin. planning Key Trust Co., Buffalo, 1984-86; pres. Alpine Sports, Ltd., Williamsville, N.Y., 1986-90, Buffalo Consulting Co., Buffalo, 1990-94; editor The Economist Intelligence Unit, N.Y.C., 1994-96; cons. The Wharton Sch., 1996—; mng. dir. The NORAM Group, Ltd., Buffalo, 1990-94. Bd. dirs. Senecare Corp., 1983-88; bd. dirs. YMCA Greater Buffalo, 1985-94, vice chmn., 1988-90; ho. of dels. United Way Buffalo and Erie County, 1984-94; chmn. campaign for creativity Creative Edn. Found.; advisor ctr. entrepreneurial leadership Sch. Mgmt., SUNY, Buffalo, 1991-94; dir. Western N.Y. Venture Assn., 1991-94; mem. Westminster Presbyn. Trustees, 1989-91, chmn. stewardship, 1989, v.p., 1990, pres., 1991, ruling elder, 1992; advisor Ctr. for Entrepreneurship, Canisius Coll., 1992-94; active Brick Presbyn. Ch. Mem. ABA, Brick Presbyn. Ch.

FERGUSON, WILLIAM MCDONALD, retired lawyer, rancher, author, banker, former state official; b. Wellington, Kans., Dec. 2, 1917; s. William McDonald and May (Deems) F.; m. Harriet Shelden, Sept. 12, 1939; children—Joan, William McDonald III. A.B., U. Kans., 1938; LL.B., Harvard U., 1941. Bar: Kans. 1946. City atty. Wellington, 1948-57; gen. practice law, 1948-73; atty. gen. Kans., 1961-65; pres. Security State Bank, Wellington, 1958-74, chmn. bd., 1974-85, chmn. emeritus, 1985—; co-mgr. Ferguson Ranch, Ferguson Cattle Co., 1965—, Spur Cattle Co., 1980-96; pres. Ferguson Ranch, Inc., 1993—. Author: (with John Q. Royce) Maya Ruins of Mexico in Color, 1977, Maya Ruins in Central America in Color, 1984, (with Arthur H. Rohn) Anasazi Ruins of the Southwest, 1986, Mesoamerica's Ancient Cities, 1990, Anasazi of Mesa Verde and the Four Corners, 1996. Mem. Kans. Ho. of Reps. 69th Dist., 1949-57. Served to lt. (s.g.) USNR, 1942-46. Mem. ABA (ho. dels. 1961-62), Kans. Bar Assn. (exec. council 1952-61, v.p. 1961, pres. 1963), Am. Legion, Sigma Alpha Epsilon. Republican. Lodge: Elks. Home: 123 N Jefferson Ave Wellington KS 67152-3813

FERGUSON KENNEDY, BARBARA BROWNELL, journalist; b. Essex, Conn., June 27, 1951; d. Edward John Joseph and Virginia (Gearhart) F.; m. Eugene Timothy Kennedy, June 1, 1993. AA, Colo. Women's Coll., 1971; BA, U. Minn., 1974; postgrad., Sorbonne U., 1975-77. Tech. rschr. UNESCO, Paris, 1980-82; mng. editor, co-owner Internat. Mideast Tourist & Bus. Mag., Paris, 1984-88; corr. Saudi Gazette Newspaper, Paris, 1987-88, London, 1988-90; bur. chief Saudi Gazette Newspaper, Washington, 1990-98; Washington corr. Arab News, Arlington, Va., 1998—; spkr. in field. Contbr. articles to profl. jours. Lay minister All Souls Episcopal Ch., Washington, 1992—. Recipient Tihama Pub. Co. award for journalistic excellence, Jeddah, Saudi Arabia, 1988, Outstanding Support award U.S. Intelligence and Threat Analysis Ctr. Pentagon, 1990. Mem. Nat. Press Club (chair internat. corrs. com.), Overseas Writers Assn., Fgn. Corrs. Assn. (v.p. 1990-96) Fgn. Press Assn., London Assn. de la Presse Etrangere (bd. dirs. 1985-88), Women's Fgn. Policy Group, Washington, Anglo-Am. Press Assn., Paris, DAR, Soc. of Profl. Journalists, Sigma Delta Chi, Alpha Phi. Independent. Avocation: horseback riding. Office: Arab News 1535 N Taylor St Arlington VA 22207-3132

FERGUSON-RAYPORT, SHIRLEY MARTHA, psychiatrist; b. Syracuse, N.Y., Mar. 9, 1923; married; three children. AB magna cum laude, Syracuse U., 1945, MD magna cum laude, 1947; Diploma in Psychiatry, McGill U., Montreal, Can., 1955. Diplomate Am. Bd. Psychiatry and Neurology, Nat. Bd. Med. Exaaminers; lic. MD, N.Y., Calif., Ohio. Rotating intern Jewish Hosp., Bklyn., 1947-48; intern in surgery and gynecology N.Y. Infirmary, N.Y.C., 1948-49, asst. resident in obstetrics, 1949-50; asst. resident in medicine and neurology Goldwater Meml. Hosp., N.Y.C., 1950-51; resident in neuropsychiatry U.S. VA Hosp., Lexington, Ky., 1951-53; sr. asst. resident Allan Meml. Inst. Psychiatry, Montreal, Can., 1953-54; rsch. fellow various univs. and insts., 1954-55, 57-58; spl. postdoctoral fellow Tng. & Rsch. Neurol. Scis Albert Einstein Coll. of Medicine, N.Y.C., 1963-65; rsch. assoc. Dept. Neurol. Surgery and Neurology Columbia U., N.Y.C., 1958-60; rsch. assoc. psychiatry Dept. Neurol. Surgery Albert Einstein Coll. Medicine, N.Y.C., 1960-65; assoc. prof. psychiatry Med. Coll. Ohio, Toledo, 1969-84, assoc. prof. neuroscis., head behavioral neurology, 1976-84, head sect. neuropsychiatry Dept. Psychiatry, 1982-93, prof. psychiatry and neurol. surgery, 1984-93, prof. emerita ofpsychiatry, 1993—; presenter in field. Contbr. numerous articles to profl. jours. and chpts. in books. Fellow Am. Psychiat. Assn. (life); mem. Am. Epilepsy Soc., Soc. Biol. Psychiatry, N.W. Ohio Psychiat. Assn. (pres. 1980-82, exec. com. 1982-83), Acad. Medicine of Toledo and Lucas County (cmty. health com. 1981-92), Ohio State Med. Assn., Ohio Psychiat. Assn. (membership com. 1980-83, cmty. mental health com. 1980-86, chairperson cmty mental health com. 1982-83, long range planning com. 1981-86, pub. mental health com. 1986—, liaison com. 1989-92, sec. 1991-93), Internat. Assn. for Study of Pain, Assn. Acad. Psychiatry, Am. Med. Women's Assn., Internat. Neuropsychol. Soc., Behavioral Neurology Soc., Am. Neuropsychiat. Soc., Sigma Xi, Lucas County Mental Health Bd. (adult svc. com. 1991-92). Office: Med Coll of Ohio Dept of Psychiatry Toledo OH 43614-5809

FERGUSSON, FRANCES DALY, college president, educator; b. Boston, Oct. 3, 1944; d. Francis Joseph and Alice (Storrow) Daly. BA, Wellesley Coll., 1965; MA, Harvard U., 1966, PhD, 1973. Asst. prof. Newton Coll., Mass., 1969-75; assoc. prof. U. Mass., Boston, 1974-82, asst. chancellor, 1980-82; provost, prof. Bucknell U., Lewisburg, Pa., 1982-86; pres. Vassar Coll., Poughkeepsie, N.Y., 1986—; bd. dirs. Marine Midland Bank, Ctrl. Hudson Gas and Electric Corp. Trustee Mayo Found., 1988—, chair, 1998—; trustee Ford Found., 1989—, Historic Hudson, 1989-99. Recipient Founder's award Soc. Archtl. Historians, 1973, Eleanor Rossevelt at Val-Kill medal, 1998. Avocation: piano. Office: Vassar Coll PO Box 1 Poughkeepsie NY 12604-0001

FERHOLT, J. DEBORAH LOTT, pediatrician; b. New Rochelle, N.Y., Aug. 27, 1942; d. Sidney and Rose (Rubin) Lott; m. Julian Ferholt, June 19, 1963; children: Beth, Sarah. BS in Biology, U. Rochester, 1963, MD, 1967. Diplomate Am. Bd. Pediatrics. From instr. to assoc. prof. Yale Sch. Nursing, New Haven, Conn., 1969-90, lectr., 1990—, clin. assoc. prof. pediatrics, 1987—; pvt. practice pediatrics New Haven, Conn., 1982—. Author: (book) Health Assessment of Children, 1980 (Best Pediatric Book award 1981). Fellow Am. Acad. Pediatrics (mem. com. daycare State of Conn.). Office: 303 Whitney Ave New Haven CT 06511-7204*

FERIA, BERNABE FRANCIS, linguist; b. Chgo., July 2, 1949; s. Bernabe Famanily and Gertrude Elizabeth Feria. BA, U. Chgo., 1971, Oxford (Eng.) U., 1973; MA, Oxford (Eng.) U., 1977, PhD, 1977. Dist. pedagogical dir. Berlitz Internat., Chgo., 1977-89, nat. pedagogical dir. U.S. and Can., 1989-94; dir. curriculum worldwide Berlitz Internat., Princeton, N.J., 1995—. George M. Pullman scholar Pullman Found., Chgo., 1967-71, English Speaking Union fellow, London, 1971-73. Mem. Oxford Cambridge U. Club, Oxford Soc. Avocations: theatre, music, writing, travel. Office: Berlitz Internat 293 Wall St Princeton NJ 08540-1519

FERILLO, CHARLES TRAYNOR, JR., public relations executive; b. Charleston, S.C., Nov. 2, 1945; s. Charles Traynor and Mae Girard (Mathewes) F.; children: Joseph Todd, Margaret Amelia, Aden Casey; m. Julia Blanding Holman Ferillo, Dec. 11, 1993. BA, Coll. of Charleston, 1972. Accredited in pub. rels. Legis. asst. S.C. House of Reps., Columbia, 1973-74, exec. dir. Office of Rsch. and Personnel, 1974-82; deputy lt. gov. State of S.C., Columbia, 1982-86; pres. pvt. practice, Columbia, S.C., 1987—. mem., bd. dirs. Habitat for Humanity of Ctrl. S.C., Columbia, 1992-95, City Yr. of Columbia, S.C., 1993-97, Planned Parenthood of Ctrl. S.C., 1991-95; vice chmn. United Way of the Midlands, Columbia, S.C., 1994; mem. adv. bd. McKissick Mus., 1997-99. Sgt. U.S. Army, 1967-69, Vietnam. Mem. Pub. Rels. Soc. Am. Democrat. Avocations: travel, antiques, gardening. Home: 1938 College St Columbia SC 29201-3922 Office: Ferillo & Assocs Inc 1945 Blossom St Columbia SC 29205-2217

FERINO, CHRISTOPHER KENNETH, computer information scientist; b. Chgo., May 25, 1961; s. Natale Ferino and Carol Marie Anderson; m. Anita Louise Vanderhoof, Oct. 19, 1985; children: Anthony Natale, Kenneth Allen. Student computer sci., acctg., Elgin Community Coll., 1978; student computer sci., McHenry County Coll., 1985. Cons. Lachman Assn., Inc., Westmont, Ill., 1979-80; AS/RS operator W.W. Grainger, Niles, Ill., 1980-82; mem. computer staff Paddock Publs., Arlington Heights, Ill., 1982-84; data processing coord. Power Systems, Schaumburg, Ill., 1984-85; dir. tech. svcs. Follett Software Co., Crystal Lake, Ill., 1985-88; tech. editor MacGuide mag., 1988-89; pres. CKF Assoc., 1989—; cons. faculty Boston MacWorld Expn., 1988, 90, San Francisco, 1988, 89, 92, 93, 94. Avocations: computers, numismatics, personal finance, optical media, emerging technology CD/ROM.

FERKENHOFF, ROBERT J., retail executive; b. Kansas City, Mo., Aug. 17, 1942; s. John Michael and Eileen Marie (Owens) F.; m. Patricia Lee Venneman, Oct. 1, 1966; children: Jennifer, Deborah, Carrie. BA, Benedictine Coll., Atchison, Kans., 1964. Staff asst. Sears Mdse. Group, Chgo., 1972-73, nat. mgr. retail inventory mgmt., 1973-74, group mgr. retail systems, 1974-77, group retail mdse. mgr., 1977-79, nat. retail mktg. mgr., 1979-81, asst. dir. strategic planning, 1981-84, nat. mgr. bus. planning, 1984-88; v.p. data processing and info. svcs. Sears Canada, Toronto, 1988-89; v.p. info. svcs. Sears Mdse. Group, Chgo., 1989-93; v.p. CIO SPS Payment Systems, RIverwoods, Ill., 1993-98; judge Retail Innovation Tech. Award, 1991-92; bd. dirs. Voluntary Interindustry Coun. Standards, 1989-93, Nat. Retail Fed. Info. Svcs., N.Y.C., 1989-93, Chgo. Rsch. and Planning Group, 1991—. Chmn. Sears United Fund, Chgo., 1991. Recipient Retail Innovation Tech. award Chain Store Age and DEC, 1990. Republican. Roman Catholic. Avocations: gardening, golf, biking. Office: SPS Payment Systems 2500 Lake Cook Rd Riverwoods IL 60015-3851

FERKINGSTAD, SUSANNE M., cosmetics executive; b. Red Wing, Minn., Aug. 19, 1955; m. Steve Ferkingstad, Oct. 19, 1991. Diploma Cosmetology, Ritter St. Paul Coll., 1974; grad., Bruno's, 1978. Instr. Ritter's St. Paul Coll., 1974-75; asst. mgr., mgr. Scot Lewis Inc., Bloomington, Minn., 1975-79; edn. dir. My Kind of Place, St. Paul, 1979-80; pres., co-owner Someone's Looking (formerly Charpentier's Inc.), St. Paul, 1980-86, owner, 1986—; styles dir. women's sect. Minn. Cosmetology Edn. Com. Fundraiser, chairperson Battered Women's Shelter, St. Paul, 1984, Children's Home Soc., St. Paul, 1985; vol. St. Paul Food Shelves Food Dr., 1985, 88; vol., model United Arts Fashion Show, 1986; vol. fundraiser pub. TV Action Auction, Ronald McDonald House, Food Shelf Drives Someone's Looking, St. Paul, MS Walkathon, 1988. Recipient numerous hairstyling awards. Mem. Nat. Cosmetologists Assn., Minn. Hairdressers and Cosmetologists Assn., St. Paul Cosmetologists Assn. (dir. 1981-83, pres. 1983-85), Hair Am., Minn. Hair Fashion Com. Avocations: singing, cross country skiing, traveling. Home: 3111 Drew Ave N Robbinsdale MN 55422-3247 Office: Someone's Looking Inc 141 4th St E Ste 125 Saint Paul MN 55101-1620

FERLAND, E. JAMES, electric utility executive; b. Boston, Mar. 19, 1942; s. Ernest James and Muriel (Cassell) F.; m. Eileen Kay Patridge, Mar. 9, 1964; children: E. James, Elizabeth Denise. BS in Mech. Engring., U. Maine, 1964; MBA, U. New Haven, 1979; postgrad. in program mgmt. devel., Harvard U. Grad. Sch. Bus. Adminstrn. Electric utility engr. HELCO, New London, Conn., 1964-67; supt. nuclear ops. NNECO, Waterford, Conn., 1967-78; dir. rate regulation N.E. Utilities, Berlin, Conn., 1978-79, v.p., CFO, 1980-83, pres., COO, 1983-86; chmn., pres., CEO Pub. Svc. Enterprise Group Inc., Newark, 1986—; chmn., CEO Pub. Svc. Electric and Gas Co., 1986—; also bd. dirs. all Pub. Svc. Enterprise Group subs.; bd. dirs. HSB Group, Foster Wheeler Corp. Office: Pub Svc Enterprise Group Inc 80 Park Plz # 4B Newark NJ 07102-4194

FERLINGHETTI, LAWRENCE, poet; b. Yonkers, N.Y., 1919; s. Charles and Clemence (Mendes-Monsanto) F.; children: Julie, Lorenzo. AB, U. N.C.; MA, Columbia U.; M.A., Doctorat de l'Université, mention très honorable, Sorbonne, 1950. Founder (with Peter D. Martin), first all paperbound bookstore in U.S., City Lights Books, San Francisco, City Lights Rev., firm also publishes works of modern poets and writers; widely traveled poetry reader, also painter; participant (with Allen Ginsberg), Pan Am. cultural conf., U. Concepcion, Chile, 1960; participant, One World Poetry Festival, Amsterdam, 1981, Internat. Poetry Festival of Rome, 1979-85, World Congress of Poets, Florence, Italy, 1986; author: poetry Pictures of the Gone World, 1955, A Coney Island of the Mind, 1958, Starting from San Francisco, 1961, The Secret Meaning of Things, Open Eye, Open Heart, 1973, Who Are We Now?, 1976, Landscapes of Living and Dying, 1979, Endless Life: Selected Poems, 1981, Over All the Obscene Boundaries, 1984, These Are My Rivers: New and Selected Poems, 1955-1993, 1993; novel Her, 1960, Routines; plays Back Roads to Far Places; (poetry) A Far Rockaway of the Heart, 1997; poetry and prose jour. Northwest Ecolog, 1978, (with Nancy J. Peters) Literary San Francisco: A Pictorial History, 1980; Seven Days in Nicaragua Libre, 1984, novel Love in the Days of Rage, 1988; performed in literary events Winter Olympic Games, Calgary, 1988; one-man exhbns., paintings: Butler Inst. Am. Art, Youngstown, Ohio, 1993, Retrospective Painting Exhbn. Palazzo delle Esposizioni, Rome, 1996. Lt. comdr. USNR, World War II, Normandy. A San Francisco street named in his honor, 1994; recipient poetry prize City of Rome, 1993. Address: City Lights Bookstore 261 Columbus Ave San Francisco CA 94133-4519

FERLITA, ROSS, municipal government official; b. 1937. B of Architecture, U. Fla., 1963. Sr. planner Hillsborough City and County, Tampa, Fla., 1967-71; dir. Landscape Design Assocs., Tampa, 1971-73; dep. dir. City of Tampa, 1974-79, dir. of Parks Dept., 1979—. Office: City of Tampa 7525 Norths Blvd Tampa FL 33604*

FERLITA, THERESA ANN, clinical social worker; b. Pinar del Rio, Cuba, Sept. 8, 1944; came to U.S., 1945; d. Sam Marion and Maria (Garcia-Collia) F. AB in Sociology, Spalding Coll., Louisville, 1966; MS in Social Work, U. Louisville, 1972. Lic. clin. social worker, Fla. Various positions, 1966-70; sr. resource program developer Children's Bd. Hillsborough County, Tampa, Fla., 1990-92; supr. homefinding unit Ky. Dept. Child Welfare, Louisville, 1972-73; foster care worker Fla. Dept. Health and Rehabilitative Svcs., Tampa, 1974; homemaker supr. Family Counseling Ctr., Clearwater, Fla., 1974; sr. social worker, mem. intake team London Borough of Newham Social Svcs., 1976; clin. social worker Alcoholism Svcs. Hillsborough Community Mental Health Ctr., Tampa, 1977-78; clin. social worker The Children's Home, Inc., Tampa, 1978-80; case coord., coord. tng. and edn., supr. teen mother program The Child Abuse Coun., Inc., Tampa, 1980-90, clin. supr. Rainbow Family Learning Ctrs., 1989-90; pvt. practice family therapy, adults abused as children, 1991; social worker med.-surg. and trauma Tampa (Fla.) Gen. Hosp., 1992-95; mgr. family svcs. Hillsborough County Headstart Dept., Tampa, 1995-96; clin. social worker St. Joseph's Hosp. Home Health Svcs., 1996—; adj. instr. Hillsborough C.C., Tampa, 1988; cons. The Spring Battered Spouse Shelter, Tampa, 1984; coord. Parents Anonymous Children's Group, Tampa, 1980-85; mem. state health adv. com. Redlands Christian Migrant Assn., Immokalee, Fla., 1982—; mem. policy coun. Hillsborough County Headstart, Tampa, 1986-89; mem. Cmty. Action Bd., Hillsborough County. Editor, compiler manuals for child abuse and neglect investigations, 1986, 87. Pres. Fair Oaks Condominium Assn., Tampa, 1990-91; past pres. Child Abuse Com., Fla., Inc.; bd. dirs., v.p. Centro Tampa, 1989-90. Mem. NASW (sec. Tampa Bay unit 1981-83, vice-chmn. 1990-91, Social Worker of Yr. award 1988, sec. Fla. chpt. 1986-88, del. assembly 1986-91), Acad. Cert. Social Workers, Nat. Network Social Work Mgrs. Democrat. Roman Catholic. Avocation: gardening. Home: 3810 N Oak Dr Unit N-31 Tampa FL 33611-2540 Office: St Joseph's Hosp Home Health Svcs Ste 320 2727 W Dr Martin Luther King Jr Blvd Tampa FL 33607

FERM, DAVID G., magazine publisher. BS in Mktg., Loyola U. With Chgo. Tribune, 1969-80, dir. Eastern div. advt. sales, mktg., circulation dir., 1977-80; dir. mktg. N.Y. Times, 1980-82; group v.p. N.Y. Times Mag. Group, 1982; exec. v.p., gen. mgr. Family Circle Mag., 1982; now pub. Golf Digest Mag., Trumbull, Conn.; pub. Bus. Week, N.Y.C. Office: Business Week/McGraw-Hill Companies Inc Ste 2518 40th Fl 1221 Ave of the Americas New York NY 10020-1001*

FERM, ROBERT LIVINGSTON, religion educator; b. Wooster, Ohio, Jan. 2, 1931; s. Vergilius Ture Anselm and Nellie Agnette (Nelson) F.; m. Fleur Kinney, June 28, 1952 (dec. 1968); children: Eric, Alison; m. Sonja Olson. BA, Coll. Wooster, 1952; BD, Yale U., 1955, MA, 1956, PhD, 1958. From instr. to assoc. prof. religion Pomona Coll., Claremont, Calif., 1958-67, prof., 1967-69, acting chmn. dept. religion, 1960-63, chmn. dept. religion, 1963-69; prof., chmn. dept. religion Middlebury (Vt.) Coll., 1969-94, Pardon E. Tillinghast prof. religion, 1988—. Author: Jonathan Edwards The Younger 1745-1801: A Colonial Pastor, 1976, Piety, Purity Plenty: Images of Protestantism in America, 1991; editor Readings in the History of Christian Thought, 1964, Issues in American Protestantism, 1969. Mem. Am. Acad. Religion. Presbyterian. Office: Middlebury Coll Dept Religion Middlebury VT 05753

FERM, VERGIL HARKNESS, anatomist, embryologist; b. West Haven, Conn., Sept. 13, 1924; s. Vergilius T.A. and Nellie (Nelson) F.; m. Ruth Eleanor Rowe, June 5, 1948; children—Daniel W., David V., Judith N., Susan C. A.B., Coll. Wooster, 1946; M.D., Western Res. U., 1948; M.S., U. Wis., 1950, Ph.D., 1955; M.A. (hon.), Dartmouth, 1967. Asst. prof. Ind. U., 1955-57; asso. prof. U. Fla., 1957-61; asso. prof. pathology Dartmouth Med. Sch., Hanover, N.H., 1961-66, prof. anatomy and embryology, 1966-94, also chmn. dept. anatomy.; cons. on environ. effects of heavy metals. Mem. Am. Assn. Anatomists, Am. Soc. Human Genetics, Teratology Soc. Exptl. Pathology, Phi Beta Kappa, Sigma Xi. Research, publs. on environ. and genetic factors causing birth defects. Home: 202 Dogford Rd Etna NH 03750-4307

FERMANIS, ERNEST GEORGE, urologic surgeon; b. N.Y.C., May 15, 1944; s. George Anastasios and Georgia Martha Fermanis; m. Pauline Angelique Papageorgopoulos, Feb. 20, 1982; children: Nicole Elaine, Alexis Georgette. *Mother, Contessa Georgia Martha Mylona Bourbon-Morossini, was daughter of Count Alexander Mylona-Bourbon-Morossini. Her great grandmother was first cousin to Louis XVI of France and widow to Count Morrossini of Venice. Married to the Greek, Mavromihalis after Count Morrossini's death in Greece. Great grandmother fled France during the French revolution in the early 1800s. She lived almost all of her life in Greece and died there at age 92. She was influential in the Northern Greek Wars of Independence.* BS cum laude, CUNY, 1966; MA cum laude, Columbia U., 1969; MD, Vanderbilt U., 1974. Diplomate Am. Bd. Urology, Nat. Bd. Med. Examiners. Urologic surgeon Atlanta, 1982—. Columbia U. scholar, 1966-69. Mem. AMA, AMA Southeastern Sect., Am. Urol. Assn., Am. Urol. Assn. Southeastern Sect., Ga. Urol. Assn., Med. Assn. Ga., Atlanta Urol. Assn., Med. Assn. Atlanta, Lions Club. Greek Orthodox. Avocations: reading, pets, swimming, fishing.

FERMIN, JOHN ENRIQUEZ, investor; b. San Francisco, July 14, 1954; s. James Monterey and Conchita (Enriquez) F.; m. Mary Fermin, July 1988 (div. July 1997). BA in Polit. Sci., Antioch Coll., Yellow Springs, Ohio, 1974. Polit. campaign mgmt./fundraising cert. U. Calif., Davis, 1994. Mgr. Stereotown/Genco, Des Moines, 1974-76; v.p. mktg. Beveridge Loudspeakers, Santa Barbara, Calif., 1977-80; pres., owner Audio Directions, San Diego, 1981-83; pres., owner, editor Media Directions, San Diego, 1984; nat. sales mgr. Counterpoint Electronics, Carlsbad, Calif., 1988-93; sales assoc. Circuit City/Good Guys, Emeryville, Calif., 1994-95; dir. Satellite Direct, Albuquerque, 1996-97; pvt. investor, 1998—. Contbr. articles to profl. jours. Dir. Earth Day Coalition, Albuquerque, 1996-98; cmty. activist, strategist Dem. Party, Albuquerque, 1996-98. Democrat. Roman Catholic. Home: 3345 Espanola #1 NE Albuquerque NM 87108

FERN, ALAN MAXWELL, art historian, museum director; b. Detroit, Oct. 19, 1930; s. Martin and Rose F.; m. Lois Ann Karbel, Mar. 17, 1957. A.B., U. Chgo., 1950, M.A., 1954, Ph.D., 1960; Fulbright scholar, Courtauld Inst., U. London, 1954-55. Asst., instr., asst. prof. humanities The Coll., U. Chgo., 1952-61; asst. curator prints and photographs div. Library of Congress, Washington, 1961; curator fine prints Library of Congress, 1962-64, asst. chief, 1964-73, chief, 1973-76, dir. research dept., 1976-78, dir. spl. collections, 1978-82; dir. Nat. Portrait Gallery, 1982—. Author: A Note on the Eragny Press, 1957, (with others) Art Nouveau, 1960, (with M. Constantine) Word and Image, 1968, Leonard Baskin, 1970, (with M. Constantine) Revolutionary Soviet Film Posters, 1974; introductory essay Lasansky: Printmaker, 1975, Eichenberg, The Wood and the Graver, 1977, People and Power, 1985, Arnold Newman's Americans, 1992, (with H. Wright) Prints at the Smithsonian, 1996; contbr. articles to profl. jours. Bd. dirs. Smart Mus. Art, Chgo. Decorated chevalier Ordre de la Couronne (Belgium); Ordre des Arts et Lettres (France); comdr. Royal Order of Polar Star (Sweden). Mem. Print Coun. Am. (past pres.), Coll. Art Assn. Am., Am. Antiquarian Soc., AIA (hon.), Double Crown Club (hon.), Cosmos Club (Washington), Grolier Club (N.Y.C.). Home: 3605 Raymond St Chevy Chase MD 20815-4151 Office: Nat Portrait Gallery F St at 8th St NW Washington DC 20560

FERN, EMMA ELSIE, state agency administrator; b. Columbus, Ohio, July 22, 1927; d. Frederick and Wilhelmina (Boxheimer) Brauler; m. Joseph S. Fern, Mar. 31, 1956. AA in Criminal Justice, Miami-Dade C.C., 1975. Adminstrv. asst. Lucayan Beach Hotel, Bahamas, 1956-68, Loew's Hotels, Miami Beach, Fla., 1968-70; intelligence analyst Metro-Dade Police Dept., Miami, Fla., 1970-78; crime intelligence analyst supr. Fla. Dept. Law Enforcement, Miami, 1978—. Recipient award Fla. Dept. Law Enforcement for disting. contbn. to criminal justice, 1984, U.S. Dept. Justice award for pub. svc. Mem. Internat. Assn. Law Enforcement Intelligence Analysts (charter, pres. 1990-96), Internat. Assn. Chiefs of Police, Police Investigative Ops. Com., Soc. of Cert. Criminal Analysts (bd. govs.). Home: 1365 NW 192nd Ter Miami FL 33169-3442 Office: Fla Dept Law Enforcement 7265 NW 25th St Miami FL 33122-1707

FERNALD, HAROLD ALLEN, publishing executive; b. Haverhill, Mass., June 1, 1932; s. Harold Allen and Leona Swan (Horton) F.; m. Sally Camilla Carroll, June 23, 1956; children: Robert Arthur, Melissa Anne, Thomas Allen. BA in Psychology, U. Maine, 1954; MBA, NYU, 1964. Trainee Nat. Shawmut Bank, Boston, 1954-55; sales Carter's Ink Co., Cambridge, Mass., 1955-56; sect. chief Western Electric Co., Andover, Mass., 1956-60; buyer Western Electric Co., N.Y.C., 1960-64; corp. devel. Holt Rinehart & Winston, N.Y.C., 1964-66, pers. dir., 1966-68, mgr. adminstrn., 1968-70; v.p. adminstrn. CBS, Inc. Pub. Group, 1970-77, v.p., gen. mgr. coll. pub. div., 1971-77; pub. Down East mag., Fly Rod and Reel mag., Fly Tackle Dealer Mag., Shooting Sportsman Mag., Fishing Tackle Trade News; pres. Down East Enterprise, Inc., Camden, Maine, 1977—, Twin City Printery, Inc., Lewiston, Maine, 1978-80, Fernald-Spahn Enterprise, Inc., Rockport, Maine, 1978-80; pres., treas. Hanson Energy Products, Inc., Newcastle, Maine, 1981-85; co-chmn., treas. Global Info. Inc., N.Y.C., 1987-95; pub., CEO Fishing Tackle Trade News, 1995-99; bd. dirs. John Wiley & Sons., Inc., N.Y.C., United Publs., Inc., Wayfarer Marine, Foreside Co., Inc., Sun Jour., Inc., U. Maine Press. Vice chmn. Maine Gov.'s Coun. Vacation Travel, 1979-81; bd. dirs. N.E. Health Found., 1982-89, 91—; bd. dirs. U. Maine-Orono Devel. Found., 1982—, vice chair, 1991, chmn., 1992-93; mem. U. Maine Pres.'s Coun., 1995-97, bd. visitors, 1998—; bd. dirs. Maine Cmty. Found., 1989—, Bay Chamber Concerts, Inc., 1981-85, U. Maine Alumni Coun.; v.p. Farnsworth Mus., 1985-88, pres., 1988-93; chair Knox County Fund, 1996—, Expansion Arts Fund, 1995—; mem. Maine Gov.'s Bus. Adv. Com., 1985-86; mem. Maine Tourism Commn., 1981-89; pres. 1st Congl. Ch., Camden, 1985-86; dir. The Camden Conf., 1987-92. Mem. Assn. Am. Pubs., Internat. Regional Mag. Assn. (dir., pres. 1988-89), Camden-Rockport C. of C. (dir. 1977-85), Alpha Tau Omega, Sigma Mu Sigma. Club: Camden Outing (dir. 1979). Lodge: Masons, Rotary (Camden pres. 1986).

FERNANDES, CARLA MICHELLE, advertising assistant; b. Jan. 10, 1976. BA in Journalism, Hofstra U., 1997. Advt. asst. Bon Appétit Mag., N.Y.C., 1998—. Office: 2167 Poe Ave East Meadow NY 11554

FERNANDES, JEANNE MARY, human resource administrator; b. Nairobi, Kenya, May 21, 1948; came to U.S., 1984; d. John Joseph and Joan Bertha (Correya) Athaide; m. Leonard Maurice Fernandes, Oct. 17, 1970; children: Donna Michelle, Nigel Leonard. Royal Soc. arts Diploma, Kenya Poly., 1965. Sec. East African Community, Nairobi, Kenya, 1966-67; exec. sec. East African Airways, Nairobi, 1968-69; adminstrv. asst. to M.D. Cadbury Schweppes, Nairobi, 1969-73; exec. sec. Pfizer Africa Middle East M.C., Nairobi, 1973-79, pers. adminstr., 1979-84; internat. pers. specialist Pfizer, Inc., N.Y.C., 1984-87, sr. pers. assoc., 1987-91, assoc. pers. mgr., 1991-92, pers. mgr., 1992-98, dir. employee resources and comms., 1999—. Mem. NAFE, Am. Fedn. Police, Am. Mgmt. Assn., N.Y. Personnel Mgmt.

Assn., Nat. Fgn. Trade Coun. (immigration com.). Roman Catholic. Avocations: music, dancing, reading. Home: 27 Ballaro Dr Huntington CT 06484-2424 Office: Pfizer Pharmaceuticals 42nd St New York NY 10017

FERNANDES, RICHARD LOUIS, retired advertising firm executive, author, publisher; b. Bklyn., Jan. 4, 1931; s. Louis and Rose (Conarello) F.; m. Adele N. Faverzani, May 25, 1957; children: Laura Ann, Gregory Richard, Donna Marie, Diane Rose. BBA, Bernard Baruch Sch. Bus., CCNY, 1956. Sr. v.p. Albert Frank-Guenther Law Inc., N.Y.C., 1956-77, Charles Barker/Ayer Fin., N.Y.C., 1977-81; v.p. N.W. Ayer, N.Y.C., 1980-81, Doremus & Co., N.Y.C., 1981-96, ret. 1996; chmn., pres. Ferde Enterprises Inc., N.Y.C., 1960-86. Author, pub. 4 books on fin. advt. and direct response. Served with USN, 1951-55. Mem. Fin. Communications Soc. (past pres.), Holy Name Soc. (past pres.), Am. Legion (past vice. comdr.). Roman Catholic. Home: 54 Eltinge St Staten Island NY 10304-1425

FERNÁNDEZ, ALBERTO ANTONIO, security professional; b. Santiago de Cuba, Oriente, Cuba, May 21, 1945; came to the U.S., 1962; s. Carlos and Lydia (Sotera) F.; m. Alexis Quesada, July 19, 1968 (div. July 1984); children: Gyselle, Alexander; m. Rebeca Perez, Sept. 7, 1984; 1 child, Yanelle. Computer programmer, Fla. Computer Coll., 1968; police officer, Metro Dade Police Acad., 1970; AA, Miami (Fla.) Dade C.C., 1973; BS in Criminology, Fla. Internat. U., 1994; drug enforcement spl. agt., DEA Spl. Tng. Sch., 1977. Lic. pvt. investigator, Fla. Police officer Metro Dade Police, Miami, 1969-75; spl. agt. Drug Enforcement Adminstrn., 1976-88; ret., 1988; chief security advisor A.P.A. Internat. Airline, Miami, 1995-96, Faucett Internat. Airline, Miami, 1995-96, Servivensa Internat. Airline, Miami, 1996. Author (movie script) The Challenge, 1993, (screenplay) Between Two Worlds, 1997. Recipient Recognition award for fighting against drugs Dominican Govt., 1987, Outstanding Law Enforcement award U.S. Dept. Justice, 1988; named Police Officer of Yr., Kiwanis Club, Miami, 1971. Mem. Assn. Former Fed. Narcotic Agts., Fla. Internat. U. Alumni. Avocation: reading.

FERNANDEZ, AURELIO, sales executive. BSEE, U. Fla.; MBA, Fla. Atlantic U. Various mgmt. and sales positions VLSI Tech. Inc., Intel Corp., Digital Equipment Corp.; sr. v.p. worldwide sales IC Works, Inc., EXAR Corp.; v.p. worldwide sales Broadcom Corp., Irvine, Calif. Office: Broadcom Corp 16215 Alton Pkwy Irvine CA 92618

FERNANDEZ, CARMEN LUCY, biologist, mental health counselor; b. Dallas, Nov. 19, 1969; d. Guillermo and Lucille (Mestres) F. AA, Miami Dade C.C., Miami, Fla., 1993; BS in Biology, Fla. Internat. U., Miami, 1995; MA in Psychology, St. Thomas U., Miami, 1997. Youth group counselor St. Brendan Cath. Ch., Miami, 1986-90; spare parts clk. Am. Dade Hosp. Supply, Miami, 1987-89; lab. asst. Baxter-Travenol Diagnostics, Miami, 1989-90; scientist I Baxter Healthcare, Miami, 1990-91; product coord. Dade Internat., Miami, 1991-94, scientist, assoc., 1995—; vol. mental health counselor New Horizons Mental Health Ctr., Miami, 1997—; vol. youth counselor J.R. Lee Project Sch., Miami, 1995. Honors cert. Phi Theta Kappa, 1993, Golden Key, 1995, Sigma Chi Iota, 1997. Mem. ACA, Assn. Am. Coll. Women. Roman Catholic. Avocations: reading, sewing, biking, swimming, volunteer work for various organizations.

FERNANDEZ, DENNIS SUNGA, lawyer, electrical engineer, entrepreneur; b. Manila, June 3, 1961; came to U.S., 1972; s. Gil Conui and Imelda Sunga (Miller) F.; m. Irene Y. Hu, Aug. 26, 1989; children: Megan H., Jared R. BSEE, Northwestern U., 1983; JD, Suffolk U., 1989. Bar: Mass. 1989, U.S. Dist. Ct. Mass. 1989, D.C. 1990, U.S. Ct. Appeals (Fed. cir.) 1990, Calif. 1991. Engr. NCR, Ft. Collins, Colo., 1983-84; product mgr. Digital Equipment Corp., Hudson, Mass., 1984-86; program mgr. Raytheon, Andover, Mass., 1986-88; engr. Racal, Westford, Mass., 1988-89; assoc. Nutter, McClennen & Fish, Boston, 1989-91, Fenwick & West, Palo Alto, Calif., 1991-94; v.p. Walden Internat. Investment Group, San Francisco, 1995-96, Singapore Techs./Vertex Mgmt., 1996-97, Neo Paradigm Labs., Inc., 1997-98; ptnr. Dennis & Irene Fernandez LLP, 1998—. Contbr. articles to profl. jours. Mem. IEEE, Sci. and Tech. Adv. Coun. (dir.).

FERNANDEZ, FERDINAND FRANCIS, federal judge; b. 1937. BS, U. So. Calif., 1958, JD, 1963; LLM, Harvard U., 1963. Bar: Calif. 1963, U.S. Dist. Ct. (cen. dist.) Calif. 1963, U.S. Ct. Appeals (9th cir.) 1963, U.S. Supreme Ct. 1967. Elec. engr. Hughes Aircraft Co., Culver City, Calif., 1958-62; law clk. to dist. judge U.S. Dist. Ct. (cen. dist.) Calif., 1963-64; pvt. practice law Allard, Shelton & O'Connor, Pomona, Calif., 1964-80; judge Calif. Superior Ct. San Bernardino County, Calif., 1980-85, U.S. Dist. Ct. (cen. dist.) Calif., L.A., 1985-89, U.S. Ct. Appeals (9th cir.), L.A., 1989—; Lester Roth lectr. U. So. Calif. Law Sch., 1992. Contbr. articles to profl. jours. Vice chmn. City of La Verne Commn. on Environ. Quality, 1971-73; chmn. City of Claremont Environ. Quality Bd., 1972-73; bd. trustees Pomona Coll., 1990—. Fellow Am. Coll. Trust and Estate Counsel; mem. ABA, State Bar of Calif. (fed. cts. com. 1966-69, ad hoc com. on attachments 1971-85, chmn. com. on adminstrn. of justice 1976-77, exec. com. taxation sect. 1977-80, spl. com. on mandatory fee arbitration 1978-79), Calif. Judges Assn. (chmn. juvenile cts. com. 1983-84, faculty mem. Calif. Jud. Coll. 1982-83, faculty mem. jurisprudence and humanities course 1983-85), Hispanic Nat. Bar Assn., L.A. County Bar Assn. (bull. com. 1974-75), San Bernardino County Bar Assn., Pomona Valley Bar Assn. (co-editor Newsletter 1970-72, trustee 1971-78, sec.-treas. 1973-74, 2d v.p. 1974-75, 1st v.p. 1975-76, pres. 1976-77), Estate Planning Coun. Pomona Valley (sec. 1966-76), Order of Coif, Phi Kappa Phi, Tau Beta Pi. Office: US Ct Appeals 9th Cir 125 S Grand Ave Ste 602 Pasadena CA 91105-1621

FERNANDEZ, FERNANDO LAWRENCE, aeronautical engineer, research company executive; b. N.Y.C., Dec. 31, 1938; s. Fernando and Luz Esther (Fortuno) F.; m. Carmen Dorothy Mays, Aug. 26, 1962; children: Lisa Marie, Christopher John. BSME, Stevens Inst. Tech., 1960, MS in Applied Mechanics, 1961; PhD in Aeronautics, Calif. Inst. Tech., 1969. Engr. Lockheed Missiles & Space Co., Sunnyvale, Calif., 1961-63; div. mgr. The Aerospace Corp., El Segundo, Calif., 1963-72; program mgr. R & D Assocs., Santa Monica, Calif., 1972-75; v.p. Phys. Dynamics, Inc., San Diego, 1975-76; pres. Arete Assocs., San Diego, 1976-93, AETC Inc., San Diego, 1994-98; dir. Def. Advanced Rsch. Projects Agy., Arlington, Va., 1998—; mem. Chief Naval Ops. Exec. Panel, Washington, 1983—. Editor Jour. AIAA, 1970; contbr. articles to Fluid Mechanics. Office: DARPA 3701 N Fairfax Dr Ste 983 Arlington VA 22203-1714*

FERNANDEZ, GIGI, professional tennis player; b. San Juan, Puerto Rico, Feb. 22, 1964; came to U.S.; d. Tuto F. Winner grand slam title U.S. Open, 1988, winner doubles championship, 1988, 90; winner doubles championship French Open, 1991; winner nine major doubles titles, 1992-94, winner gold olympic medal in doubles, 1992. Named Puerto Rican Female Athlete of Yr., 1988. Ranked 1st with White in doubles, 1989, with Navratilova in doubles, 1990. Office: USTA 70 W Red Oak Ln White Plains NY 10604-3602*

FERNANDEZ, GISELLE, newscaster, journalist. Former student, Sacramento State U. Past journalist Pueblo, Colo.; past anchor WCIX-TV, Miami; past anchor Today (weekend edit.), NBC Nightly News (Sunday edit.) NBC-TV, now co-host Access Hollywood; guest anchor CBS This Morning, CBS Evening News, CBS Weekend News; contbr. (TV) Eye On America, CBS Sunday Morning News, Face the Nation, 48 Hours. Recipient 5 Emmy awards. Avocations: hiking, running. Office: Skinny Hippo Prodns 1305 N Beverly Dr Beverly Hills CA 90210*

FERNANDEZ, HAPPY CRAVEN (GLADYS FERNANDEZ), city council member; b. Scranton, Pa., Mar. 3, 1939; d. Orvin William and Florence (Waite) Craven; m. Richard Ritter Fernandez, June 10, 1961; children: John Ritter, David Craven, Richard William. BA, Wellesley Coll., 1961; MA in Teaching, Harvard U., 1962; MA, U. Pa., Phila., 1970; EdD, Temple U., 1984. Social studies tchr. various pub. schs., 1961-64; from vis. asst. prof. to prof. Sch. Social Adminstrn. Temple U., Phila., 1974-93; exec. dir. Parents Union for Pub. Sch., Phila., 1980-82; dir. The Child Care and Family Policy Inst., Phila., 1988-92; city councilwoman Phila., 1992—; cons. Nat. Com. for Citizens in Edn., Columbia, Md., 1982-87, Phila. Youth Study Ctr., 1988-90; commr. Phila. Gas Commn., 1992-97; trustee Edn. Law Ctr., Phila., 1983—; bd. dirs. Pa. Academy of Fine Arts, Philadelphia, 1996—, Cultural Fund, 1996—; Chair, Select Committee of Buisness Taxes, 1992—; Chair, Select Committee on Land Reuse, 1997—; pres. Delaware Valley Child Care Coun., 1988-90. Author: Parents Organizing to Improve Schools, 1976, The Child Advocacy Handbook, 1980, Elder Care and Child Care Policies of Philadelphia Area Businesses, 1991. Chair bd. dirs. Am. for Dem. Action, Phila., 1980-92; chair Children's Coalition, 1982-86; bd. dirs. Phila. Citizens for Children and Youth, 1986-93; del. Dem. Nat. Conv., Atlanta, 1988, N.Y.C., 1992, Chicago, 1996. Recipient Women in Edn. award Womens Way, 1989, Pub. Citizen of Yr. award NASW, 1991, Local Elected Ofcl. award Pa. Citizens for Better Librs., 1993, Pub. Svc. award Homeowners Assn. Phila., 1994; named Outstanding Adv., Health Promotions Coun., 1994; Wellesley Coll. scholar, 1961. Fellow Nat. Assn. Orthopsychiatry; mem. Parents Union for Pub. Schs. (founder, chair 1972-75, 78-80). Mem. United Church of Christ. Avocations: tennis, gardening. Home: 3400 Baring St Philadelphia PA 19104-2076 Office: Phila City Coun City Hall # 484 Philadelphia PA 19107-3201

FERNANDEZ, HENRY A., lawyer, consultant; b. Bklyn., Dec. 5, 1949; s. Henry and Pura (Perez) F. BA Sociology, St. John's U., 1971; student, Empire State Military Acad. Army Reserve Nat. Guard, Peekskill, N.Y., 1972-73; JD, Bklyn. Law Sch., 1977. Bar: N.Y. 1978, U.S. Dist. Ct. (so. and ea. dists.) N.Y. 1978, U.S. Dist. Ct. (no. dist.) N.Y. 1981. Supr. Hornblower & Weeks Hemphill-Noyes, 1967-72; ednl. counselor, devel. exec. Aspira of N.Y. and Am., Inc., 1972-74; field placement counselor Bur. Coop. Edn. N.Y.C. Bd. Edn., 1974-75; dir. Coll. Adapter Program Higher Edn. Devel. Fund, 1975-77; vis. atty., grad. honors fellow Puerto Rican Legal Defense and Edn. Fund Inc., 1977-79; staff atty. Williamsburg Legal Svcs., 1979-81; asst. counsel N.Y. State Office Mental Health, 1981-86; dir. adminstrn. Capital Dist. Psych. Ctr., 1986-88; dir. Bur. Investigation and Audit N.Y. State Office Mental Health, 1988; state rev. officer N.Y. State Edn. Dept., 1990-93; dep. commr. U. State N.Y., 1988-93; pres., CEO Assn. of Univ. Programs in Health Adminstrn., Arlington, Va., 1993-98; mng. dir. KPMG/Peat Marwick LLP, Atlanta, Ga., 1998—; bd. dirs., pres. Coun. Licensure Enforcement & Regulation, program com., fin. com. 1989, vice chair fin. com. 1989-90, pres.-elect 1991-92, treas. 1991-92, pres. 1992-93; nat. bd. cert. Occpl. Therapy, 1994—. Mem. N.Y. State Coun. Grad. Med. Edn., 1990-93; bd. dirs. N.Y. State Divsn. Youth Independent rev. bd., 1977-88, Legal Aid Soc. Northeastern N.Y., chair labor rels. com., exec., policy, nomination com., 1984-89. Recipient Disting. Svc. Citation N.Y. State Chiropractic Assn., 1991, Presdl. Citation Assn. Architects, AIA, 1991; Hispanic Health Leadership fellow Nat. Coalition Hispanic Health and Human Svc. Orgns., Kellogg Found., 1990-91; DeGray Meml. scholar St. John's U., 1967-71; Bklyn. Law Sch. scholar, 1973-77. Fellow N.Y. Acad. Medicine, N.Y. State Bar Found.; mem. N.Y. State Bar Assn. (chair com. Minorities in Profession 1990-94, Labor and Employment law sect. 1982-92, com. Mental and Phys. Disabilities 1986-88, com. atty. professionalis 1989-92, Action Unit 4 1993-94), Puerto Rican Bar Assn. (Capital dist. chpt. pres. 1986-88), N.Y. Health Careers (adv. coun.), Coun. State Govs. (exec. com. 1992-93, VA bd. nursing home adminstrn. 1993-97), Coalition Hispanic Health Human Svc. Orgn. (sec., bd. dirs. 1994—), AIHA, Inst. for Diversity. Home: 211 Colonial Homes Dr NW Atlanta GA 30309-1262 Office: KPMG/Peat Marwick LLP 303 Peachtree St NE Ste 2000 Atlanta GA 30308-3244

FERNANDEZ, ISABEL LIDIA, human resources specialist; b. Miami, Fla., Jan. 23, 1964; d. Rafael Juvencio and Lidia Rafaela (Morin) Fernandez. BBA, Fla. Internat. U., Miami, 1984, MS in Hospitality Mgmt., 1990. Diversity and human resources cons., Miami, 1984—; asst. dir. human resources Turnberry Isle Yacht & Country Club, Miami, 1985-87; dir. personnel Sheraton River House, Miami, 1987-88; program dir. hospitality mgmt. programs Miami-Dade Community Coll., 1988-89; dir. human resources Doubletree Hotel, Miami, 1989-91, Sky Chefs, Miami, 1991-93; tng. cons. Barnett Banks Inc., Miami, 1993-98; dir. diversity svcs. IGI Internat., Inc., North Miami, Fla., 1998; ptnr., dir. Workplace Pntrs. Inc., Miami, 1998—. Editor newspaper The Sunblazer, 1983-84; contbr. articles to profl. jours. Founder, pres. South Fla. Diversity Coun. Mem. ASTD, Soc. for Human Resources Mgmt. Republican. Lutheran. Avocations: opera, theater, art, language. Home: 8510 NW 3d Ln Apt 501 Miami FL 33126-3857

FERNANDEZ, JOSE WALFREDO, lawyer; b. Cienfuegos, Cuba, Sept. 19, 1955; came to U.S., 1967; s. Jose Rigoberto and Flora (Gomez) F.; m. Andrea Gabor, June 22, 1985. BA, Dartmouth Coll., 1977; JD, Columbia U., 1980. Bar: N.Y. 1981, N.J. 1981, U.S. Dist. Ct. (so. dist.) N.Y. 1981, U.S. Dist. Ct. N.J. 1981. Assoc. Curtis, Mallet, Prevost, Colt & Mosle, N.Y.C., 1981-84; assoc. Baker & McKenzie, N.Y.C., 1984-89, ptnr., 1989-96; ptnr. O'Melveny & Myers, L.L.P., N.Y.C., 1996—; adj. prof. N.Y. Law Sch., 1984-87. Contbr. articles to profl. jours. Bd. dirs. Ballet Hispanico, Ceiba Prodns., WBGO-FM Newark Pub. Radio. Mem. ABA (com. Inter-Am. law 1985—, Ctrl. Am. task force 1985-92, presdl. commn. L.Am. 1986-91), N.Y.C. Bar Assn. (com. fgn. and comparative law, chmn. Inter-A m. affairs com. 1996-98), U.S.-Spain C. of C. (bd. dirs. 1999), Brazilian-U.S. C. of C. (bd. dirs. 1994-99). Avocations: sports, non-fiction writing, travel. Home: 508 E 87th St New York NY 10128-7602 Office: O'Melveny & Myers LLP Citicorp Ctr 153 E 53rd St Fl 53D New York NY 10022-4611

FERNANDEZ, JOSEPH ANTHONY, educational administrator; b. 1935. BA in Edn., U. Miami, 1963; MEd, Fla. Atlantic U., 1970; EdD, Nova U., 1985; HHD (hon.), Marymount Manhattan Coll., N.Y.C., 1990, Bank St. Coll. Edn., N.Y.C., 1990, CUNY, 1990; LHD, CUNY, 1990, Bank Street Coll. Edn., 1990. Former tchr. math., former supt. Dade County Pub. Schs., Miami; chancellor N.Y.C. Pub. Schs., 1990-93; pres., CEO Sch. Improvement Svcs., Inc., Winter Park, Fla., 1993-95. Pres. Coun. of the Great City Schs., Washington. Office: Joseph Fernandez & Assocs Inc 4392 Live Oak Blvd Palm Harbor FL 34685-4021

FERNANDEZ, KATHLEEN M., cultural organization administrator; b. Dayton, Ohio, Oct. 8, 1949; d. Norbert Katzen and Yenema Vermeda (Bermingham) F.; m. James Robert Hillibish, Oct. 1, 1977. BA, Otterbein Coll., 1971. Edn. asst. Ohio Hist. Soc., Columbus, 1971, vol. coord., 1971-74; interpretive specialist Ohio Hist. Soc., Zoar, 1975-88, site mgr., 1988—. Bd. dirs., newsletter editor Ohio & Erie Canal Corridor Coalition, Akron, 1989—. Mem. Am. Assn. State & Local History, Nat. Trust Hist. Preservation, Zoar Cmty. Assn., Communal Studies Assn. (pres. 1981, editor newsletter 1981-86, bd. dirs. 1995—). Office: Zoar Village State Meml 221 W 3d St Zoar OH 44697

FERNANDEZ, LINDA FLAWN, entrepreneur, social worker; b. Tampa, Fla., Sept. 14, 1943; d. Frank and Rose (D'Amico) F.; 1 child, Marci. B.S., U. South Fla., 1965; M.S., U. Nev., 1976. Social worker Hillsborough County, Tampa, Fla., 1965-67; parole officer adult div. Fla. Parole Commn., Tampa, 1967-69; dir. social services Sunrise Hosp., Las Vegas, Nev., 1969-78; ind. real estate investor, Fla. and Nev., 1965—; pres. Las Vegas Color Separations, Inc., 1978—, Las Vegas Typesetting, Inc., 1983—; LMR Enterprises, Inc., Las Vegas, 1984—; sec.-treas. Sierra Color Graphics, Inc., Las Vegas, 1983—. Founder, organizer Human Relations, pet mascots for elderly; team ofcl. girls' softball, 1985; mem. Clark County Citizens Com. Efficiency and Cost Reduction, 1991; vice-chmn. Citizens Com. Efficiency and Cost Reduction, 1992. Recipient numerous awards Ad Club Fedn. Mem. Las Vegas C. of C. (congl. com.) Women's Las Vegas C. of C., Ad Club Fedn., Citizens for Pvt. Enterprise, U.S. C. of C. Avocations: tennis; water skiing. Office: 3351 S Highland Dr Ste 210 Las Vegas NV 89109-3430

FERNANDEZ, LISA, softball player; b. Long Beach, Calif., Feb. 27, 1971. Grad., UCLA, 1997. Winner Silver medal Super Classic, Columbus, Ga., 1997; mem. Calif. Commotion Amateur Softball Assn. Recipient Gold medal Pan Am. Games, 1991, ISF Women's World CHampionship, 1990, 94, Women's World Challenger Cup, 1992, Intercontinental Cup, 1993, South Pacific Classic, 1994, Superball Classic, 1995, Atlanta Olympics, 1996, Honda award, 1991-93; named All-Am. Amateur Softball Assn., Sports Woman of Yr., 1991-92. Office: USA Softball 2801 NE 50th St Oklahoma City OK 73111-7203 also: TPS Hdqs care Lisa Fernandez PO Box 35700 Louisville KY 40232-5700*

FERNANDEZ, MARTIN ANDREW, secondary school educator; b. Gary, Ind., Dec. 5, 1969; s. Luther Fritz and Martha June (Yingling) F. BA in Edn., Olivet Nazarene U., Kankakee, Ill., 1992. Cert. tchr. English/Spanish, Ind. From server to mgr. Wingfield's Restaurant, Chesterton, Ind., 1988-95; custodian Duneland Cmty. Ch., Chesterton, 1991-97; tchr. North Newton H.S., Morocco, Ind., 1993—; vacation bible sch. leader Duneland Ch. of Nazarene, Chesterton, 1993-95; drama dir., sr. class sponsor, N. Newton H.S., Morocco, 1994—, retention com. mem. 1995-96. Hon. mem. FFA, N. Newton H.S., 1996. Mem. Nat. Coun. Tchrs. of English, Ind. State Tchrs. Assn. (rep. 1993—). Republican. Avocations: golf, tennis, reading, acting, jigsaw puzzles. Home: 841 E 250 N Morocco IN 47963-8231 Office: North Newton HS 1641 W 250 N # North Morocco IN 47963-8267

FERNANDEZ, MARY JOE, professional tennis player; b. Dominican Republic, Aug. 19, 1971; d. Jose and Sylvia F. 3rd ranked woman USTA; winner women's doubles (with Patty Fendick) Australia Open, 1991; gold medalist women's doubles Olympic Games, Barcelona, Spain, 1992, Atlanta, 1996; winner (with Davenport) French Open doubles Paris, 1996; mem. winning U.S. Fed Cup Team Atlantic City, N.J., 1996. Ranked # 8 World Tennis Assn. Tour, 1995, # 1 USA Women, 1995. *

FERNANDEZ, MIGUEL ANGEL, process safety, design engineer, energy consultant; b. Habana, Cuba, Oct. 30, 1939; came to U.S., 1957; s. Miguel Angel and Olga Eulalia (Rodriguez) F.; m. Barbara Frances LeGette, Jan. 7, 1967; children: Michael Anthony, Mark Angel, Stephen Hartley. B in Chem. Engring., Ga. Tech., 1962, MS in Chem. Engring., 1963, postgrad. in engring., 1965. Engr. E.I. DuPont, Richmond, Va., 1965-66; devel. group leader Phillips Fibers Corp., Greenville, S.C., 1966-80; mgr. energy and process engring. J P Stevens & Co., Greenville, S.C., 1980-83; mgr. industry and energy program S.C. Energy Rsch. & Devel. Ctr., Clemson, S.C., 1983-85; cons. M.A. Fernandez & Assocs., Greenville, 1985—; sr. process design engr. Fluor Daniel, Greenville, 1987-93; sr. process safety engr. JBF Assocs., Knoxville, 1994-96; cons. Process Safety Internat., Greenville, S.C., 1996—; process design specialist Lockwood Greene, Spartanburg, S.C., 1997—; cons. S.C. Energy Office, Columbia, 1985—. Patentee in field. Vice pres. Parents-Tchrs.-Student Assn., Eastside High Sch., Greenville, S.C., 1987-88; pres. Foxcroft Cmty., 1992. Mem. Am. Inst. Chem. Engrs. Avocations: tennis, camping, sports coaching, choir. Home: 3 Foxcroft Rd Greenville SC 29615-3711

FERNANDEZ, RAMONA ESTHER, adult education educator; b. Elizabeth, N.J., Nov. 26, 1947; d. Domingo Fernandez and Irene Czertan. BA, SUNY, Old Westbury, 1970; MA, U. Ariz., 1973; PhD, U. Calif., Santa Cruz, 1995. Prof. Sacramento City Coll., 1975-97; asst. prof. Mich. State U., E. Lansing, 1998-99. Co-author: From Mouse to Mermaid: The Politics of Film, Gender, and Culture, 1995; author: Imagining Literacy, 1999. Fellow Ford Found., 1989-95, Smithsonian Instn., 1992-94. E-mail: fernan47@pilot.msu.edu. Office: Mich State U Am Thought and Lang East Lansing MI 48824

FERNANDEZ, RENÉ, aerospace engineer; b. Havana, Cuba, Oct. 2, 1961; came to U.S., 1967; s. Ramon and Emma (Fumero) F. Student, Broward Community Coll., Ft. Lauderdale, Fla., 1979-80; BS in Engring., Case Western Res. U., 1986, MSc in Engring., 1993, postgrad., 1993—. Registered profl. engr., Ohio. Rsch. fellow Univ. Space Rsch. Assn., Cleve., 1986; grad. teaching asst. Case Western Res. U., Cleve., 1986-87; rsch. engr. NASA Lewis Rsch. Ctr., Cleve., 1987—; mem. speaker's bur. NASA Lewis Rsch. Ctr., 1988—; sci. fair judge Ohio Acad. Sci., Columbus, Ohio, 1988, 90. 2d lt. CAP. Mem. AIAA (chmn. No. Ohio sect. 1991-92, dep. dir. for young mem. programs region III), ASTM, ASME, AAAS, IEEE, Optical Soc. Am., Aircraft Owners & Pilots Assn., Soc. Photo-optical Instrumentation Engrs., Ohio Acad. Sci., NASA Ski Club, NASA Karate Club. Roman Catholic. Avocations: scuba diving, skiing, dancing, astronomy, flying. Office: NASA Lewis Rsch Ctr 21000 Brookpark Rd Cleveland OH 44135-3191

FERNANDEZ, RICARDO R., university administrator; b. Santurce, P.R., Dec. 11, 1940; s. Ricardo F. and Margarita (Marchese) F.; m. Patricia M. Kleczka, Aug. 7, 1965; children: Ricardo F., Amanda M., Daniel E., David R., Jose M. BA, Marquette U., 1962, MA, 1965; MA, Princeton U., 1967, PhD, 1970. Asst. prof. Marquette U., Milw., 1968-70; asst. prof. U. Wis., Milw., 1970-78, assoc. prof., 1978-90, prof., 1990; pres. CUNY Herbert H. Lehman Coll., Bronx, 1990—; pres. Nat. Assn. Bilingual Edn., 1980-81; fellow ACE, 1981-82. Co-author: Reducing the Risk, 1989, Effective Desegregation Strategies, 1983, IEM, 1992. Bd. dirs. P.R. Legal Def. and Edn. Fund. Recipient Faculty Disting. Svc. award U. Wis., 1984. Mem. Hispanic Assn. of Colls. and Univs. (bd. dirs.). Office: CUNY Herbert H Lehman Coll 250 Bedford Park Blvd W Bronx NY 10468-1527*

FERNANDEZ, TONY (OCTAVIO ANTONIO CASTRO FERNANDEZ), baseball player; b. San Pedro de Macoris, Dominican Republic, June 30, 1962; m. Clara F.; children: Joel, Jonathan, Abraham. Baseball player Toronto Blue Jays, 1979-90, 93-94, San Diego Padres, 1990-92, N.Y. Mets, 1992-93, Cin. Reds, 1994; player N.Y. Yankees, 1995, Cleve. Indians, 1997, Toronto Blue Jaus, 1997—; mem. Am. League All-Star Team, 1986-87, 89; mem. Nat. League All-Star Team, 1992; recipient Gold Glove award, 1986-89. Office: Toronto Blue Jays, One Blue Jays Way Ste 3200, Toronto, ON Canada M5V 1J1*

FERNÁNDEZ-COLL, FRED, microbiologist, food technology laboratory director; b. San Juan, P.R., Sept. 14, 1952; s. Roberto and Lila (Coll) F. BS in Biology cum laude, U. P.R., 1974; MS in Food Sci. and Tech., Va. Polytech. Inst. and State U., 1979; postgrad., Purdue U., 1985. Rsch. asst. food tech. lab. agrl. exptl. sta. U. P.R., San Juan, 1974-82, asst. food microbiologist, 1982-88; prof. microbiology U. P.R., Rio Piedras, 1984-88, prof. food hygiene animal health tech. program Med. Scis. Campus, 1984-93; tech. dir. food tech. lab. agrl. exptl. sta. U. P.R., San Juan, 1987—, assoc. food microbiologist, 1988-94, food microbiologist, 1994—; prof. microbiology Bayamon Cen. U., 1980, Met. Campus Interam. U., 1980-89, Turabo U., 1989-91; prof. indsl. microbiology World U., Hato Rey Campus, 1980-83. Contbr. articles to profl. jours. Mem. Am. Soc. Microbiology, P.R. Assn. Food Sci. and Tech., P.R. Soc. Microbiologists, P.R. Soc. Agrl. Scis., Inst. Food Technologists, Internat. Assn. Milk, Food and Environ. Sanitarians. Office: U PR Food Tech Lab PO Box 21360 San Juan PR 00928-1360

FERNANDEZ-POL, BLANCA DORA, psychiatrist, researcher; b. Buenos Aires, Mar. 5, 1932; came to U.S., 1967; d. Balbino Fernandez and Maria Remedios van Pol. MD, U. Buenos Aires, 1958. Diplomate Am. Bd. Psychiatry and Neurology. Intern N.Y. Polyclinic Med. Sch., 1967-68; resident in psychiatry UCLA/Brentwood Hosp., 1968-69, NYU/Bellevue Hosp., 1969-71; gen. practitioner Hosp. Espanol, Buenos Aires, 1959-62; forensic psychiatrist Criminoloy Inst., Buenos Aires, 1963-65; clin. attending psychiatrist Bellevue Psychiat. Hosp., N.Y.C., 1971-75; pvt. practice St. Petersburg, Fla., 1976-78; chief psychiat. svcs. USAF Hosp. Yokota, Tokyo, 1980, USAF Hosp., Homestead, Fla., 1981; chief continuing treatment program dept. psychiatry Bronx-Lebanon Hosp., Bronx, 1983—; prof. psychology U. Moran, Buenos Aires, 1962-67; asst. prof. psychiatry N.Y. Med. Coll., N.Y.C., 1972-74; clin. asst. prof. psychiatry Albert Einstein Coll. Medicine, Bronx, 1982—. Contbr. articles to profl. jours. Maj. USAF, 1978-81. Mem. Am. Psychiat. Assn., N.Y. Acad. Scis., Am. Acad. Psychiatrists in Alcoholism and Addictions, Res. Officers Assn. U.S., Assn. Mil. Surgeons U.S. Avocations: travel, painting, sculpture. Home: PO Box 21644 Brooklyn NY 11202-1644 Office: Bronx Lebanon Hosp 1285 Fulton Ave Bronx NY 10456-3401

FERNÁNDEZ-V., JUAN RAMON, university chancellor; b. San Juan, P.R., Aug. 9, 1936; s. Ramon Fernández-Serrano and Elena Velazquez; m. Norah Moran, 1960 (div. 1967); children: Lynnette, Yasmin; m. Sonia M. Ramirez de Fernández, Aug. 12, 1971 (div. 1992); 1 child, Juan Ernesto. BS, U. P.R., 1957, M in Pub. Adminstrn., 1963; PhD, CUNY, 1978; D honoris causa, U. Nacional, Piura, Peru, 1987. Adminstrv. tech. II Dept. Labor, San Juan, 1960; asst. to dir., lectr. Sch. Pub. Adminstrn., U. P.R., Rio Piedras Campus, 1961-64, asst. prof., 1969-72, 79-80, assoc. prof., 1980-85, prof., 1984, also chancellor, 1985-92; acad. senator faculty of social scis. U. P.R., 1983-85, mem. univ. bd., rep. Rio Piedras Campus Acad. Senate, 1984-85; spl. asst. to Gov. of P.R., 1965-68; prof. Bklyn. Coll., CUNY, 1973-76; prof. sch. of pub. affairs Baruch Coll., CUNY, 1994—; vis. assoc. rschr. Bildner Ctr. CUNY Grad. Sch., 1993-95; participant Fifth Ann. Conf. Caribbean Studies Assn., Curacao, 1980 and ann. meeting, 1981, seminar P.R. Planning Bd., 1979, symposium P.R. Found. for the Humanities, 1979, panel discussion Inst. Policy Scis. Ctr. for Study of State Policy, Duke U., 1981, seminar for grad. students Grad. Sch. Edn., Harvard U., 1981, Fifth Hispanic-Am. Conf., U. Mich., Ann Arbor, 1983, other confs., seminars; lectr. in field, 1975—; cons. Tchr.'s Assn., Hato Rey, P.R., 1984; hon. prof. U. Iberoamericana Sto. Do., Dominican Republic; lectr., bd. dirs. Ralph Bunche Inst. on the UN, 1986; vis. scholar, Bildner Ctr. for Western Hemisphere Studies, CUNY, 1993, adv. to the pres., Interam. U. P.R., 1996-97. Contbr. chpts. to books and articles to profl. jours. Mem. Puerto Rico's delegation to UNESCO World Conf. on Higher Edn., Paris, 1998; del. to Internat. Sem. on Evaluation and Accreditation Models for Higher Edn. Instns. in Latin Am. and the Caribbean/sponsored by IESALC-UNESCO, San Juan, 1999. Named Most Disting. Grad. Class 1953, Cen. High Sch. P.R.; Ford Found. grantee, 1981; recipient Disting. Alumni award CUNY, 1988. Mem. Acad. Arts, History and Archeology of P.R., Acad. for the Humanities and Scis., Caribbean Studies Assn.

FERNANDO, J. ANICETUS P., manufacturing executive; b. Colombo, Sri Lanka, Apr. 17, 1959; came to U.S., 1977; s. Patrick and Mary (Silva) F.; m. Sabrina J. Fernando, June 22, 1985; 1 child, Jeremy Malcolm Patrick. BA, Pacific Western, 1993; MBA, Western Mich. U., 1997. Dir. Crossland, Portland, 1978-85; v.p. Pacific Corp., Portland, 1985-89, Whirlpool, Benton Harbor, 1989-97. Home: 1212 Forest Hills Dr Southlake TX 76092 Office: Whirlpool 750 Monte Rd Benton Harbor MI 49022-2600

FERNBACH, LOUISE OFTEDAL, physician, educator; b. Fargo, N.D., Dec. 24; d. Sverre and Agnes Lenore (Halland) Oftedal; children: Bertram, Olinda, David, Pamela, Theodore; m. Alfred Philip Fernbach. BA, Wellesley (Mass.) Coll.; MD, George Washington U. Gen. practice medicine and obstets. Fishersville, Va., 1954-59; psychiatry resident UCLA, 1960; psychiatry fellow Johns Hopkins U., Balt., 1972; dir. mental health U. Fla., Gainesville, 1961-64, U. Ariz., Tucson, 1965-68; asst. prof. psychiatry Sch. Medicine Johns Hopkins U., Balt., 1972-74; dir. Washington Acupuncture Ctr., 1974-81; dir. Orthomolecular Med. Ctr. Linus Pauling Inst., Palo Alto, Calif., 1981-85; pvt. practice Charlottesville, Va., 1985—; lectr. Physicians for Social Responsibility, 1980—. Author: Acupuncture in Medical Practice, 1980. Fellow Am. Geriat. Soc.; mem. AMA, Am. Med. Women's Assn. (Va. state dir. 1991—, Cmty. Svc. award 1994), Am. Psychiat. Assn. Unitarian. Avocation: tennis, cooking, painting, writing, golf, swimming. Office: 11 Orchard Rd Charlottesville VA 22903-4728

FERNBACH, STEPHEN ALTON, pediatrician; b. N.Y.C., Oct. 22, 1944. BA summa cum laude, Amherst Coll., 1965; MD, Harvard U., 1969. Diplomate Am. Bd. Pediatrics, Am. Bd. Perinatal Neonatal Medicine. Intern in medicine U. Chgo., 1969-70; resident in pediatrics U. Calif., San Francisco, 1970-72; fellow in neonatology Stanford U., 1972-73; chief of newborn svc. Letterman Army Med. Ctr., 1973-75, Kaiser-Permeanente Med. Ctr., Santa Clara, 1975—; med. advisor to state coun. March of Dimes, 1986-88; med. adv. bd. Calif. Children's Svc., 1987-89; mem. Calif. PRAMS adv. bd. Editl. bd. Jour. Perinatology; editor Newsletter of NAACP, 1985-91; contbr. numerous articles to profl. jours. Fellow Am. Acad. Pediatrics (chmn. fetus and newborn com. chpt. 1 dist IX 1979-87, treas. 1985-87, pres. 1987-89), Calif. Perinatal Assn. (v.p. 1984-86, pres. elect 1986-87, pres. 1987-88, editor newsletter 1980-87), Calif. Med. Assn. (sec. pediatric scientific adv. com. 1987-88), Nat. Perinatal Assn. (bd. dirs. 1993-96), Phi Beta Kappa, Sigma Xi. Home: 900 Kiely Blvd Santa Clara CA 95051-5329

FERNELIUS, NILS CONARD, physicist; b. Columbus, Ohio, Nov. 10, 1934; s. Willis Conard and Anna Naomi (Baker) F. AB, Harvard U., 1956; student, Oxford (Eng.) U., 1956-57; MS, U. Ill., 1959, PhD, 1966. Rsch. assoc. dept. physics U. Ill., Urbana, 1966-67; asst. physicist Materials Sci. Divsn., Argonne, Ill., 1968-71; v.p. Rsch. Cons., Oak Ridge, Tenn., 1971-72; Nat. Rsch. Coun. sr. fellow Aerospace Rsch. Lab., Wright-Patterson AFB, Ohio, 1973-75; vis. scientist Universal Energy Sys., Dayton, Ohio, 1975-76; physicist U. Dayton Rsch. Inst., 1977-82; Nat. Rsch. Coun. sr. rsch. assoc. Materials Lab., Wright-Patterson AFB, 1982-85; vis. scientist Systran Corp., Dayton, 1985, 87-88; physicist Stolle Corp., Sidney, Ohio, 1985-86, Materials Directorate AF Rsch. Lab., Wright-Patterson AFB, 1988—. Contbr. articles to profl. jours. NSF fellow, 1959-62. Mem. IEEE, SPIE, Optical Soc. Am., Am. Phys. Soc. (life), Am. Assn. Physics Tchrs., Am. Vacuum Soc., Soc. Applied Spectroscopy (George Rappoport Meml. award 1995), Materials Rsch. Soc., Sigma Xi. Avocations: genealogy, stamp collecting, travel, photography. Home: 1528 Sussex Rd Troy OH 45373-2446 Office: AFRL/MLPO Materials Directorate Air Force Rsch Lab Wright Patterson AFB OH 45433

FERNER, DAVID CHARLES, non-profit management and development consultant; b. Rochester, N.Y., Mar. 14, 1933; s. John Theodore and Dorothy Flora (Seel) F.; m. Ursula Milda Thieme, Sept. 6, 1958. BA, Amherst Coll., 1955; MEd, U. Rochester, 1957; postgrad., Columbia U., 1961. Dir. student activities U. Rochester, N.Y., 1956-58; asst. to provost Tchrs. Coll. Columbia U., N.Y.C., 1959-60; asst. dir. devel. St. Lawrence U., Canton, N.Y., 1961-62; dir. devel. Sarah Lawrence Coll., Bronxville, N.Y., 1962-66; cons., v.p. Frantzreb & Pray Assocs., Inc., N.Y.C., 1966-72; v.p., sec. Frantzreb & Pray Assocs., Inc., Arlington, Va., 1972-75; pres. Frantzreb, Pray, Ferner & Thompson, Inc., Arlington, 1975-77, David C. Ferner & Assocs., Annandale, Va., 1977-80; v.p., dir. devel. Minn. Orchestral Assn., Mpls., 1980-87; mng. ptnr. Currie, Ferner, Scarpetta & DeVries, Mpls., 1987—. Contbr. articles to profl. publs. Bd. dirs. Madeline Island Mus. Camp, Nat. Soc. Fundraising Execs. Minn. chpt. Amherst Coll. scholar, 1951-55. Mem. Nat. Soc. Fundraising Execs. (bd. dirs. Minn. chpt. 1995-97), Nat. Com. Planned Giving, Coun. for Advancement and Support of Edn., Am. Symphony Orch. League, Opera Am. Home: 245 Wekiva Cv Destin FL 32541-4763 Office: Currie Ferner Scarpetta & DeVries 401 2nd Ave S Ste 1012 Minneapolis MN 55401-2310

FERNG, DOUGLAS MING-HAW, infosystems executive; b. Anshan, Peoples Republic of China, Feb. 27, 1945; came to U.S., 1968; s. Jau-Tarng and Hwei-In (Chu) F.; m. Gloria K. Chao, Oct. 28, 1972; children: Jennifer, Albert. BS, Nat. Taiwan U., Taipei, 1967; M in Forestry, Yale U., 1970; MBA, U. Wash., Seattle, 1979. Sci. programmer Weyerhaeuser Co., Federal Way, Wash., 1970-72, computer analyst, 1972-77, forest economist, 1977-79; mgr. silvicultural econs. Champion Internat., Stamford, Conn., 1979-80, mgr. resource econs., 1980-83; mgr. bus. systems Champion Internat., Hamilton, Ohio, 1983-87, mgr. paper applications, 1987-93; dir. bus. info. svcs. Champion Internat., Hamilton, 1993-96, dir. info. tech., 1996—. Served as 2d lt. Taiwan Army, 1967-68. Fellow Yale Univ., 1968-70. Mem. Paper Industry Mgmt. Assn., Assn. System Mgmt., Cin. Chinese Assn., Chinese Assn. of Fairfield County (v.p. 1981-83). Club: Cin. Yale. Avocation: photography. Office: Champion Internat 101 Knightsbridge Dr Hamilton OH 45011-3166

FERNIE, JOHN DONALD, astronomer, educator; b. Pretoria, South Africa, Nov. 13, 1933; emigrated to Can., 1961, naturalized, 1967; s. John Fernie and Nell (Beattie) F.; m. Yvonne Anne Chaney, Dec. 23, 1955; children: Kimberly Jan, Robyn Andrea. BSc, U. Cape Town, 1953, BSc with Honors, 1954, MSc, 1955; PhD, Ind. U., 1958. Lectr. physics, astronomy U. Cape Town, 1958-61; asst. prof. astronomy U. Toronto, Ont., Can., 1961-64, asso. prof., 1964-67, prof., 1967-96, prof. emeritus, chmn. dept., 1978-88, 93-94; dir. David Dunlap Obs., 1978-88, 93-94. Author: Variable Stars in Globular Clusters and Related Systems, 1973, The Whisper and the Vision, 1976; contbr. articles to profl. jours. Fellow Royal Soc. Can.; mem. Internat. Astron. Union, Can. Astron. Soc., Am. Astron. Soc. Office: U Toronto David Dunlap Obs, Box 360, Richmond Hill, ON Canada L4C 4Y6

FERNOUS, LOUIS FERDINAND, JR., consumer products company executive; b. Bklyn., Dec. 26, 1938; s. Louis F. and Adelaide (Rohsen) F.; m. Eileen Mary Blenn, Apr. 25, 1964; children: Danielle Fernous Ingeri, Louis F. III, Guy Edward. AAS in Indsl. Rels., CUNY, 1960; BA in Bus., Adelphi U., 1976. Various positions sales dept. and supervisory positions Am. Tobacco Co. subs. Fortune Brands, Inc., Old Greenwich, Conn., 1957-81; sec. Fortune Brands, Inc., 1981—, v.p., 1988—; chmn. Sacia Expo '92, Stamford, Conn., 1992—. Vol. disaster svcs. ARC, Southwestern Conn., 1990—; mem. fin. com. Holy Family Ch., Fairfield, Conn. With USAR, 1961-67, mem. N.Y. State Guard Res. Named to Acad. of Distinction, Adelphi U., 1985. Mem. Am. Soc. Corp. Secs. (corp. practices and non-profit com.), Internat. Soc. Meeting Planners (registered), KC (4th degree). Republican. Home: 93 Windsor Rd Fairfield CT 06430-3421 Office: Fortune Brands Inc PO Box 811 1700 E Putnam Ave Old Greenwich CT 06870-1321

FERNSLER, JOHN PAUL, lawyer; b. Lebanon, Pa., Dec. 24, 1940; s. K. Paul and Elizabeth M. (Snyder) F.; m. Christine Joan Chester, July 31, 1965; children: Euan, Scott. AB, Dickinson Coll., 1962; JD, U. Mich., 1965. Bar: Pa. 1965, U.S. Dist. Ct. (ea. and we. dists.) Pa., U.S. Ct. Appeals (3d cir.). Assoc. Snyder, Balmer & Kershner, Reading, Pa., 1965-66; dep. atty. gen. Commonweatlh of Pa., Harrisburg, 1968-70; chief counsel HUD, Pitts., 1970-81; ptnr. Reed Smith Shaw & McClay, Pitts., 1981-97; corp. counsel Weis Markets, Inc., Sunbury, Pa., 1997—; lectr., spl. cons. Mortgage Bankers Assn., 1985-92; solicitor Mt. Lebanon Parking Authority, 1990-91; mem. Mt. Lebanon Commn., 1992-96, pres. 1993; bd. mem., treas. Med./Rescue Team South Authority, 1995-97. Contbr. articles to profl. jours. Mem. Mt. Lebanon Zoning Hearing Bd., 1981-88, sec., 1981-82, chmn., 1983-88; bd. dirs., counsel Coun. for Luth. Campus Ministry in Gt. Pitts., 1979-82; chmn. Mt. Lebanon Rep. Com., 1990-92. Decorated Commendation medal; recipient Spl. Cert. Pa. Dept Community Affairs, 1970. Mem. ABA (urban state and local law sect. coun. 1984-87), Pa. Bar Assn., Allegheny County Bar Assn. (real property sect., chmn., 1988), Am. Coll. Real Estate Lawyers (elected). Republican. Episcopalian. Avocations: bicycling, walking, photography. Home: 20 Brown St Lewisburg PA 17837-2104 Office: Weis Markets Inc 1000 S 2nd St # Sunbury PA 17801-3399

FERO, LESTER K., aerospace engineer, consultant; b. Beaver Dams, N.Y., Feb. 28, 1919; s. Ray L. and Bertha (Kniffin) F.; m. Margery G. Wilde, Sept. 11, 1944; children: Gregory G. (dec.), Leslie Kay. BS in Aerospace Engring., U. Mich., 1940. Structures engr. Curtiss-Wright, Buffalo, 1940-46; v.p. Dansaire Corp., Dansville, N.Y., 1946-47; chief structural engr. Bell Aircraft, Niagara Falls, N.Y., 1947-56; program mgr. Martin Co., Balt., 1956-63, NASA Hdqrs., Washington, 1963-70; staff asst. NASC/Exec. Office of Pres., Washington, 1970-72; dir. space transp. plans NASA Hdqrs., Washington, 1972-82; pres., chief engr. Fero Enterprises, Inc., Bowie, Md., 1984-87, Loudon, Tenn., 1987—; guest lectr. U. Mich., Ann Arbor, 1953. Pres. Community Assn., Lutherville, Md., 1960. Recipient Achievement awards NASA, 1969, 75, 82. Assoc. fellow AIAA (chmn. Balt. sect. 1961).

FEROZ, EHSAN HABIB, accounting educator, researcher, writer; b. Chittagong, Bangladesh, Jan. 9, 1952; came to U.S., 1979, permanent resident, 1983, naturalized, 1990; s. Mohammad Obaidul and Sabera (Begum) Hakim; m. Kishwar Sultana Beg, Oct. 16, 1982; children: Rubens, Jonas, Amran. BA with honours, U. Dacca, 1972, MA, 1974; MA, Carleton U., 1978; PhD, U. Chgo., 1982. Cert. fraud examiner; cert. govt. fin. mgr. Asst. prof. acctg. SUNY, Buffalo, 1983-86; asst. prof. acctg. CUNY, Baruch, 1986-89; vis. asst. prof. acctg. Carlson Sch. of Mgmt. U. Minn., 1989-91, assoc. prof. acctg., assoc. mem. grad. faculty, 1991-93, prof. acctg., assoc. mem. grad. faculty, 1993—; invited guest Ctr. For Internat. Studies, MIT, 1979; disting. faculty mentor U. Minn., 1990, 91; faculty mentor sch. bus. and econs., mem. honors and awards com., dean's tsearch com., outcome measures com., student behavior judiciary com., libr. policy com. U. Minn., Duluth, 1991—, spl. project assoc. of vice-chancellor for acad. adminstrn., spring, 1995; invited presenter Jour. Acctg. Rsch. Conf., 1991; invited nominator Seidman Disting. Award in Polit. Economy, 1991, 92. Contbr. numerous articles to profl. jours., including Advances in Acctg., Acctg. Horizons, Australian Jour. Mgmt., Acctg. Orgns. and Soc., Acctg. Rev., Jour. Acctg. Rsch., Jour. Bus. Fin. and Acctg., Pub. Adminstrn. Quarterly, Fin. Accountability and Mgmt., Jour. Acctg. Abstracts, IEE Transactions on Neural Networks, Encyclopedic Dictionary of Acctg.; mem. editl. bd. Internat. Jour. Acctg., Internat. Jour. Acctg. and Bus. Soc., Rsch. in Govtl. and Non Profit Acctg. Bd. dirs. Duluth Children's Mus., 1996—; mem. affirmative action rev. com. Minn. Edn. Assn., 1996-98. Mem. Assn. Govt. Accts., Assn. Cert. Fraud Examiners, Acad. Internat. Bus., Am. Acctg. Assn. (rsch. com. GNP sect. 1982—, fin. com. 1992), Minn. Coun. Acctg. Educators. Avocations: walking, swimming, classical music. Office: U Minn-Dept Acctg 125 Sch Bus and Econs 10 University Dr Duluth MN 55812-2403

FERRA, DENNIS J., telecommunications company executive. Sr. v.p. Alltel Corp, Little Rock. Office: Alltel Corp One Allied Dr Little Rock AR 72202*

FERRALL, VICTOR EUGENE, JR., college administrator, lawyer; b. Urbana, Ill., July 31, 1936; s. Victor Eugene and Lucile Elizabeth (Hill) F.; m. Suzanne Elizabeth Lilly (div. 1985); children: Christopher Key, David Hill, Katherine Elizabeth; m. Linda K. Smith, 1987. AB, Oberlin Coll, 1956; student law, Harvard U., 1956-57; MA in Econs., Yale U., 1958, LLB, 1960. Bar: D.C. 1961, U.S. Supreme Ct. 1981. Atty. U.S. Dept. Justice, Washington, 1960-61; asst. to staff dir. antitrust and monopoly subcom. U.S. Senate, Washington, 1961-63; assoc. then ptnr. Koteen & Burt, Washington, 1963-75; ptnr. Jones, Day, Reavis & Pogue, Washington, 1975-79, Crowell & Moring, Washington, 1979-91; pres. Beloit (Wis.) Coll., 1991—. Contbr. articles to profl. jours.; editor: Yearbook of Broadcasting Articles (anthology edition), 1980. Trustee Olivet (Mich.) Coll., 1979-81. Mem. ABA, D.C. Bar Assn., Wis. Bar Assn., Nat. Assn. Ind. Colls. and Univs. (bd. dirs. 1993—). Democrat. Episcopalian. Home: 709 College St Beloit WI 53511-5571 Office: Beloit Coll 700 College St Beloit WI 53511-5596*

FERRAND, JEAN C., oil company executive; b. Lyon, France, Feb. 10, 1930; s. Jean A. and Andree (Desire) F.; m. Bayote Odette, Feb. 20, 1960 (dec. Sept. 1994); children—Jean Pascal, Isabelle, Patrick. Engr.'s degree, Ecole de L'Air France, 1952; research asst., Calif. Inst. Tech., 1958-59, advanced mgmt. program Harvard Bus. Sch., 1970-71. Geophysicist in France and Africa for Compagnie Generale de Geophysique, 1955-58; mgr. Compagnie Reynolds de Geophysique, Algeria, 1959-61; adviser to Australian Govt. with French Inst. Petroleum, 1961-63; geophysicist Australia; then chief geophysicist, asst. to exploration mgr. New Zealand for local subsidiaries Societe Nationale des Petroles d'Aquitaine, 1963-65; exec. v.p., dir. Aquitaine Oil Corp., 1965-73; v.p., dir. First Bus. Computing Corp., 1969-73; gen. mgr. internat. ops. Tex. Eastern Transmission Corp., Houston, 1973-74; pres. J.C. Ferrand & Assocs., Houston, 1974—, Kemerton Energy Cy., Inc., 1976-86; mng. venturer Francamer Cy, 1986-93; v.p., dir. Compagnie des Petroles Transcontinental (S.A.), France, 1974-76. Served as officer French Army, 1951-55. Mem. European Assn. Exploration Geophysicists, Soc. Exploration Geophysicists, Am. Assn. Petroleum Geologists, Ind. Petroleum Assn. Am., Harvard Alumni Assn. Home: 13046 Trail Hollow Dr Houston TX 77079-3740

FERRAND, LOUIS GEORGE, lawyer; b. East Grand Rapids, Mich., Apr. 12, 1942; s. Louis George and Margaret Louise (LaBour) F.; m. Mary Eleanore Braseth, Oct. 25, 1969; children: Anne Elizabeth, Gregory Louis, Jacqueline Louise. BA, Alma Coll., 1964; JD, U. Mich., 1971. Bar: Mich. 1971, D.C. 1974, U.S. Supreme Ct. Pres., co-founder Cornerstone Project, Inc., Bklyn., 1966; vol. Peace Corps., Dominican Republic, 1966-68, trainer, 1968; dir. manpower programs Grand Rapids CAP, Mich., 1969-70; trial atty. Dept. Justice, Washington, 1971-76; counsel for civil rights Dept. Labor, Washington, 1976-81, dep. assoc. solicitor for civil rights, 1981-87, dep. assoc. solicitor for mine safety and health, 1987-88; of counsel Newman & Newell, 1988-89; of counsel Orgn. of Am. States, 1989—, sr. atty., 1990-94, prin. atty., 1994—. Bd. dirs. Ayuda, Inc., 1988—, Parklawn Recreation Assn., Alexandria, Va., 1982-84, No. Va. Meml. Soc., 1991-95, Arlington Retirement Housing Corp., 1988-93; chmn. social responsibilities com. Unitarian Ch., Arlington, Va., 1981, co-chmn. capital fund dr., 1993-94; co-founder, bd. dirs. Fondo Quisqueya Found., Inc., 1993—, treas., 1992—; co-founder, bd. dirs. Friends of Williamsburg Rowing, Inc., 1993-97, treas. 1993-95; leader cub scout pack George Washington dist. Boy Scouts Am., 1984-86; basketball coach Recreational League, 1983-89; trustee Unitarian Ch. of Arlington, 1984-87, chmn. bd. trustees, 1986-87; bd. dirs. T.C. Williams H.S. Track Boosters, 1992-97, treas. 1992-95, co-pres. 1995-96; bd. dirs. MOASIS Found., 1997—, I-A Bar Found., 1995—. Mem. Fed. Bar Found. (adv. 1994—), Fed. Bar Assn. (bd. dirs. D.C. chpt. 1986—, officer 1988-94, pres. 1993-94, nat. cir. officer 1993-97, nat. coun. mem. 1993—, chair fed. career svc. divsn. 1996—, co-chmn. nat. conv. com. 1989), D.C. Bar Assn., Mich. Bar Assn., Inter-Am. Bar Assn. (asst. sec. 1989-91, co-chmn. labor law sect. 1986-91, asst. treas. 1993-94, sec. gen. 1995—, mem. exec. com. 1995—, coun. mem. 1995—), Fed. Am. Inns of Ct. (charter mem., master 1989—, program chmn., counselor, pres. elect 1998-99, pres. 1999—). Avocations: reading, tennis, swimming, bike riding, travel. Office: Orgn of Am States Office Sec Gen Gen Legal Svcs Washington DC 20006

FERRANTE, JOAN MARGUERITE, English and comparative literature educator; b. N.Y.C., Nov. 11, 1936; d. Nicholas Henry and Josephine (Pisacane) F.; m. R. Carey McIntosh. Student, Brearley Sch., 1950-54, Radcliffe Coll., 1954-55; B.A., Barnard Coll., 1958; M.A., Columbia U., 1959, Ph.D., 1963. Asst. prof. English and comparative lit. Columbia U., N.Y.C., 1966-70; assoc. prof. Columbia U., 1970-74, prof. English and comparative lit., 1974—, chmn. English and comparative lit., 1988-91, dir. Ctr. for Italian Studies, 1977-80; lectr. modern langs. Swarthmore (Pa.) Coll., 1968; lectr. medieval studies Fordham U., N.Y.C., 1976; Andrew Mellon prof. humanities Tulane U., 1984. Author: The Conflict of Love and Honor, 1973, Guillaume d'Orange, Four Twelfth Century Epics, 1974, Woman as Image in Medieval Literature from the Twelfth Century to Dante, 1975, (with Robert Hanning) The Lais of Marie de France, 1978, The Political Vision of the Divine Comedy, 1984, To the Glory of Her Sex: Women's Roles in the Composition of Medieval Texts, 1997; editor: (with George Economou) In Pursuit of Perfection, Courtly Love in Medieval Literature, 1975, (with Robert Hanning) The Challenge of the Medieval Text, 1985; mem. adv. bd. Speculum, 1975-78; cons. editor Records of Civilization, Columbia U. Press, 1975—. Am. Council Learned Socs. fellow, 1969-70; NEH fellow, 1980-81. Fellow Medieval Acad. Am. (councillor, 2d v.p. 1998-99); mem. Dante Soc. Am. (councillor, v.p. 1978-83, pres. 1985-91), MLA (exec. coun. 1986-90), Internat. Arthurian Soc., Internat. Courtly Lit. Soc., Phi Beta Kappa (senator 1979-97, v.p. 1988-91, pres. 1991-94). Office: Columbia U 616 Philosophy Hall New York NY 10027*

FERRANTE, OLIVIA ANN, retired educator, consultant; b. Revere, Mass., Nov. 9, 1948; d. Guy and Mary Carmella (Prizio) F. BA, Regis Coll., 1970; MEd, Boston Coll., 1971, postgrad., 1977-81; postgrad., Middlebury Coll., 1974, Lesley Coll., 1982. Cert. history tchr., tchr. of blind. Chmn. Braille dept. Nat. Braille Press, Boston, 1971-74; tchr. of visually impaired, spl. needs dept. Revere H.S., 1974-92; Steven J. Rich scholarship com., 1993—; cons. Revere PTA, 1984—. Contbr. articles to profl. jours. Vol. Morgan Meml., Boston, 1983—, tchr. braille, 1993—, tchr. literacy program, 1993—; mem. Revere Com. for Handicapped Affairs, 1985—, Everett (Mass.) Chorus, 1974-76, Adult Music Ministry, 1989, Revere First Com., 1993, publicist; soloist Revere Music Makers, 1977-79; mem. partnership com. Internat. Year Disabled, 1980-81; mem. adult choir Immaculate Conception Ch., 1966—, lectr., 1995—, cantor, 1997; publicist Revere Commn. on Disabilities, 1985—, Revere Hist. Commn., 1996—, Cath. Daus., SHARE, 1995—, A Woman's Concern, 1996; mem. adv. bd. Mass. Commn. of Blind, 1988—, governing bd. on ind. living, 1989; access monitor Mass. Orgn. on Disability, 1988—; mem. adv. bd. Radio Reading Svc. for Blind, 1989; mentor Nat. Braille Literacy Project, 1992, Braille Lib., 1995—; mem. Friends of the Sick Children's Trust, 1992; vol. Birthright, 1992, ProLife Office, 1992; active Arts Coun. Coop, 1992—; mentor Vision Found., 1993—; friend Wang Ctr., 1993—, Boston Pub. Garden and Common, 1993—, Boston Pops, 1992—; mem. mobility adv. bd. Mass. Com. for Blind, 1994—; mem. Historic Mass., 1994—, Cath. League, 1994—; friend Paul Revere House, 1994—; mem. Peregrine Fund, 1994—, Ctr. for Marine Preservation, 1994—; sponsor Rite of Cath. Initiation for Adults, 1995—; publicist Next Door Theater Group, 1996; mem. access task force Revere Pub. Libr., 1996; mem. Revere 2000 Com., 1998-99. Mem. NEA, Internat. Soc. for Endangered Cats, Mass. Tchrs. Assn. Revere Tchrs. Assn., Nat. Space Soc., Nat. Cath. Assn. for Persons with Visual Impairment, Cath. Daus. of Am. (publicist), Soc. Bl. Kateri Tekakwitha, 1997, Friends of Revere Pub. Libr., Friends of Librs. for Blind, Friends of Boston Symphony Orch., Nat. Writers Union, Amnesty Internat., Soc. Creative Anachronism, Women Affirming Life, Michael Crawford Internat. Fan Assn., Revere Soc. for Cultural and Hist. Preservation (publicist, life mem., v.p. 1998—, chmn. grants com. 1998, 2000 com., 1998), Chelsea Hist. Soc., Mass. Aviation Hist. Soc., Brian Boitano Fan Club. Roman Catholic. Avocations: travel, music, swimming, ice skating, crafts. Home: 115 Reservoir Ave Revere MA 02151-5825 Office: Revere High Sch Spl Needs Dept 101 School St Revere MA 02151-3099

FERRANTI, THOMAS, JR., lawyer; b. Bklyn., Mar. 14, 1969; s. Thomas and Janet Rose (Giordano) F.; m. Renee Esposito, July 11, 1998. BA, St. John's U., N.Y.C., 1991, JD, 1994. Bar: N.Y. 1995, N.J. 1995, D.C. 1995. Dietary aide S.I. (N.Y.) U. Hosp., 1987-1993; intern Dept. of Investigation, N.Y.C., 1990, Justice Finnegan, N.Y. State Supreme Ct., Queens, 1990; legal intern Macy's Northeast, N.Y.C., 1991, N.Y.C. Coun., S.I., 1992; intern Supreme Ct. trial divsn. Richmond County Dist. Atty., S.I., 1993-94; tchr. law Monsignor Farrell H.S., S.I., 1994-95; pvt. practice, S.I., 1995—; lawyer, witness Criminal Trial Inst., St. John's U., 1991-94, Civil Trial Inst., 1991-94; tutor, counselor Student Network Accessing Counselor Program, 1991-94; fire fighter N.Y.C. Fire Dept., 1993—. Gen. mgr., pres. Sta. WMOC, S.I., 1989-91. St. John's U. scholar, 1988-91. Mem. ABA, N.Y. State Bar Assn., Nat. Italian-Am. Bar Assn., Golden Key, Lambda Kappa Phi, Kappa Gamma Pi, Iota Alpha Sigma (pres. 1990-91). Roman Catholic. Avocations: aquarium hobbyist, weight training, science fiction, coin collecting, travel. Fax: 718-948-5000. Home: 99 Pitney Ave Staten Island NY 10309 Office: 11 Sunfield Ave Staten Island NY 10312

FERRARA, ABEL, film director; b. Bronx, May 12, 1952; m. Nancy Ferrara; children: Endira, Lucy. Student, Rockland C.C. Dir. (films) Driller Killer, 1979, Ms. 45, 1981, Fear City, 1985, China Girl, 1987, Cat Chaser, 1989, King of New York, 1990, Bad Lieutenant, 1992 (Ind. Spirit award nomination for best dir. Ind. Feature Project/West 1993), Body Snatchers, 1993, Dangerous Game, 1993, The Addiction, 1995, The Funeral, 1996, California, 1996, The Blackout, 1997, New Rose Motel, 1998; dir. (tv) The Gladiator, 1986, Crime Story, 1986, The Loner, 1988, Subway Stories, 1998, various episodes Miami Vice; screenplay writer (with Zoe Tamarlaine Lund) Bad Lieutenant, 1992, Dangerous Game, 1993; appeared in films Driller Killer, 1979, Ms. 45, 1981. *

FERRARA, DONNA, state legislator. Rep. Dist. 15 N.Y. State Assembly. Office: NY Assembly Legis Office Bldg Rm 322 Albany NY 12224*

FERRARA, KATHERINE JUNE, executive television producer; b. Lancaster, Pa., Nov. 26, 1972; d. Raymond Michael and June Madeline Ferrara. BA in Broadcast Journalism, Fla. So. Coll., 1993. Cmty. news reporter Sarasota-Herald-Tribune, 1994-95; prodr., sr. prodr. SNN Channel 6, Sarasota, 1995-97; exec. prodr. Ctrl. Fla. News 13, Orlando, 1997—. Mem. NAFE, Soc. of Profl. Journalists. Office: Ctrl Fla News 13 64 E Concord St Orlando FL 32801

FERRARA, PETER JOSEPH, federal official, lawyer, author, educator; b. N.Y.C., Apr. 26, 1955; s. Joseph B. and Betty (San Filippo) F.; 1 child, Peter Joseph Jr. BA, Harvard U., 1976, JD, 1979. Bar: N.Y. 1980, D.C. 1984. Assoc. firm Cravath, Swaine & Moore, N.Y.C., 1979-81; spl. asst. to asst. sec. for policy devel. and research HUD, Washington, 1981-82; mem. sr. staff White House Office Policy Devel., Washington, 1982-83; of counsel Shaw Pittman, Potts & Trowbridge, 1983-92; assoc. prof. George Mason Sch. Law, 1987-91; assoc. dep. atty. gen. U.S. Justice Dept., Washington, 1992-93; sr. fellow Heritage Found., 1993-94, Nat. Ctr. for Policy Analysis, Washington, 1994-95; gen. counsel and chief economist American for Tax Reform, Washington, 1995—; sr. fellow CATO Inst., Washington, 1988-91; dir. Legal Svcs. Corp., 1984. Author: Social Security: The Inherent Contradiction, 1980, (with others) Enterprise Zones Sourcebook, 1981, Social Security: The Family Security Plan, 1982, Social Security: Averting the Crisis, 1982, Religion and the Constitution, 1983, (with others) Mandate for Leadership II, 1984, (with others) Beyond the Status Quo: Policy Proposals for America, 1985, Social Security: Prospects for Real Reform, 1985, (with others) The Political Economy of Privatization, 1987, (with others) The Third Generation, 1987, (with others) The Judges' War, 1987, (with others) Mandate for Leadership III, 1988, (with others) An American Vision, 1988, (with others) A New Deal for Social Security, 1998; editor and co-author: Free the Mail: Ending the Postal Monopoly, 1990, The Choctaw Revolution: Lessons for Federal Indian Policy, 1998; contbr. articles to profl. jours. John M. Olin Disting. fellow Heritage Found., 1987-88. Republican. Office: 1320 18th St NW Washington DC 20036-1811

FERRARA, RALPH C., lawyer; b. Gloversville, N.Y., June 16, 1945; s. Rufus Ferrara and Clara F. Riccitiello. BSBA, Georgetown U., 1967; JD, U. Cin., 1970; LLM in Corp. Law summa cum laude, George Washington U., 1972. Bar: D.C. 1970, U.S. Ct. Appeals, U.S. Supreme Ct.; cert. ind. assessor Ins. Marketplace Stds. Assn. Profl. asst. to law librarian Nat. Law Ctr., Washington, 1970-72; mem. faculty George Washington U. Nat. Law Ctr.; atty. Div. of Enforcement, SEC, Washington, 1971-72, trial atty. Div. Trading and Markets, 1972-73, spl. counsel to Chief Enforcement atty., 1973-74, supervisory trial atty., 1974-75, spl. counsel to chmn. SEC, 1975, asst. gen. counsel, 1975-76, exec. asst. to legal counsel, 1976-77, exec. asst., 1977-78, gen. counsel, 1978-81; ptnr. Debevoise & Plimpton, Washington, 1981—. co-chmn. PLI Ann. Inst. on Securities Law, 1994-98; bd. advisor The Ctr. for Corp. Law, U. Cin. Coll. Law, 1995—; bd. visitors U. Cin. Coll. Law, 1995—. Author: Takeovers II: A Strategist's Manual for Business Combinations in the 1990s, 1993, Shareholder Derivative Litigation: Beseiging the Board, 1995, Ferrara on Insider Trading and the Wall, 1995. Served in USAR. Recipient John L. Sayler award, Am. Jurisprudence award, Judge Alfred Mack award. Mem. ABA (sect. on corp., banking bus. law, planning rev. com., fed. regulation of securities com.), Fed. Bar Assn. (mem. exec. council securities law com., nat. council, gen. counsels' com.), Southwestern Legal Found. (adv. com.). Contbr. numerous articles on topics related to fed. securities laws to profl. jours. Office: Debevoise & Plimpton 555 13th St NW Ste 1100E Washington DC 20004-1163 also: Debevoise & Plimpton 875 3rd Ave New York NY 10022-6225

FERRARA, STEVEN, educational researcher, test developer; b. Boston, May 8, 1951; s. Stanley S. and Ruth V. (Robinson) F.; m. Linda Blauer, June 19, 1976; children: Rachel, Samuel. BA in English, U. Mass., 1973; MEd in Spl. Edn., Boston State Coll., 1978; EdS in Program Evaluation, Stanford U., 1984, PhD in Ednl. Psychology, 1989. Tchr. Head Start, 1974-75; resource room tchr. learning disabled h.s. students Quincy and Barnstable, Mass., 1975-80; chief of measurement, stats., evaluation Md. Dept. Edn., Balt., 1985-91, dir. assessment, 1991-97; dir. rsch. and psychometrics Am. Inst. Rsch., Washington, 1997-98, mng. rsch. assoc., 1998—; instr. gen. ednl. devel. Cape Cod C.C., 1979-80; course instr. Stanford U. Sch. Edn., 1985, Johns Hopkins U., 1986-89, U. Md., College Park, 1989, Western Md. Coll., 1990-91; trainer and cons. on test devel. and assessment issues to local sch. systems, states, testing orgns., univs. in U.S. and Taiwan; presenter in field. Mem. editl. bd. Applied Measurement in Edn., Ednl. Measurement: Issues and Practice; contbr. articles to ednl. jours. Mem. ASCD, Am. Ednl. Rsch. Assn., Md. Assessment Group, Nat. Coun. on Measurement in Edn. (bd. dirs. 1995-98). Office: Am Inst Rsch Ctr for Ednl Assessment 1000 Thomas Jefferson St NW Washington DC 20007-3835*

FERRARA-LOVE, ROSEANN, nurse; b. Pitts., Mar. 6, 1955; d. Joseph James and Rose Ann (McGraw) Ferrara; m. Paul A. Love, Oct. 30, 1982. AS in Nursing, Community Coll. Allegheny, 1975; BS in Nursing, Carlow Coll., 1984; MSN, Duquesne U., 1996, postgrad. cert. in Nursing Edn., 1998. RN, Pa.; cert. post anesthesia nurse, perianesthesia nurse, ACLS instr., BCLS instr. Staff nurse Allegheny Gen. Hosp., Pitts., Divine Providence Hosp., Pitts., Mercy Hosp., Pitts., Montefiore U. Hosp., Pitts., U. Pitts. Med. Ctr. at Montefiore; nursing supr. Mercy Providence Hosp./Pitts. Mercy Health Sys.; mem. clin. faculty Duquesne U. Sch. Nursing, Pitts. Sect. editor Jour. Post Anesthesia Nursing; contbr. chpt. to book. Mem. Am. Soc. Peri Anesthesia Nurses (bd. dirs. 1992-95), Pa. Assn. Peri Anesthesia Nurses (bd. dirs. 1992-95), W.Va. Soc. Peri Anesthesia Nurses (newsletter editor, componet sec. 1997-98), Sigma Theta Tau. Home: 1240 Success St Pittsburgh PA 15212-2960

FERRARA-SHERRY, DONNA LAYNE, education educator; b. Trenton, N.J., Aug. 19, 1946; d. Joseph and Rita Marie (Cerra) F.; m. Peter P. Barsczeski Jr., July 20, 1968 (div. Sept. 1974); 1 child, Lisa Ayn; m. James John Sherry, Jan. 20, 1980; 1 child, James John Joseph; stepchildren: Jennifer, Kimberly. BA, Manhattanville Coll., 1968, MA in Teaching,' 1973; profl. diploma, L.I. U., 1985; PhD, NYU, 1992. Cert. English and social studies tchr., N.Y. Tchr. Holy Rosary Sch., Port Chester, N.Y., 1968; adminstrv. asst. for curriculum coord. Blind Brook High Sch., Port Chester, 1973—; English tchr. Rye (N.Y.) Country Day Sch., 1973-75; English tchr. Hampton Bays (N.Y.) Jr. and Sr. High Schs., 1975-87, English coord., 1985-87, dist. curriculum coord., 1987-89; asst. dir. Southampton (N.Y.)-Hampton Boys Tchr. Ctr., 1986-89; coord. curriculum planning rsch. and evaluation Suffolk Dist. 2 BOCES, Patchogue, N.Y., 1989; prof. edn. L.I. U., Southampton, 1993—, outcomes assessment coord., 1995-99; exec. dir. Smith-Layne Ednl. Cons. Svc., Hampton Bays, N.Y., 1988—; assoc. Shared Edn. Decisions Assocs., 1992—. Mem. Community Awareness Program, Hampton Bays; mem. facilities planning com. Hampton Bays Schs., 1987-88, co-chair AIDS adv. com., 1988-89; mem. steering com. Shared Decision Making Dist., 1993. Mem. ASCD, Am. Ednl. Rsch. Assn., Spl. Edn. Parent Tchrs. Assn., NYU Adminstr.'s Roundtable (com.), Kappa Delta Pi, Phi Delta Kappa, Delta Kappa Gamma. Roman Catholic. Achievements include research in school reform, decentralization, autonomy, school indicators, evaluation, staff development, shared decision making, leadership. Office: LIU Southampton 239 Montauk Hwy Southampton NY 11968

FERRARI, DAVID GUY, auditor; b. Scottsbluff, Nebr., Jan. 12, 1944; s. Guy C. and Waunita E. (Bailey) F.; m. Kay Cooper, May 29, 1966; children: Brian S., Justin D. BSBA, U. Wyo., 1966, MS in Bus. Adminstrn., 1971. Fin. dir. Wyo. Dept. Edn., Cheyenne, 1967-71; budget analyst State of Wyo., Cheyenne, 1971-73, state budge dir., 1973-75, dep. state auditor, 1975-87; cons. Cheyenne, 1987-90; state auditor State of Wyo., Cheyenne, 1991-99. Author, cons.: Wyoming 1988-A Study of Revenues and Expenditures, 1988, A Study in State Government Efficiency, 1989, Accountability and Efficiency in State Government, 1990, The Final Report on Accountability and Efficiency in State Government, 1991. Elected state ofcl. Rep. Party, Cheyenne, 1991—. Mem. Rotary (hon.). Avocations: reading, writing, boating, drawing, sports. Office: State Auditors Office PO Box 2072 Cheyenne WY 82003-2072

FERRARI, DENNIS M., secondary education educator. Tchr. Burlington (Vt.) High Sch. Recipient Tchr. Excellence award Internat. Tech. Edn. Assn., 1992. Office: Burlington High Sch 52 Institute Rd Burlington VT 05401-2721*

FERRARI, MERCEDES V, secondary education educator. English tchr. Milford (Del.) High Sch. Named Del. State English Tchr. of Yr., 1992. Office: Milford High School 1019 N Walnut St Milford DE 19963-1201*

FERRARI, MICHAEL RICHARD, JR., university administrator; b. Monongahela, Pa., May 12, 1940; s. Michael Richard and Lillian Ann (Cristina) F.; m. Janice Bjurstrom, Sept. 5, 1964; children: Elizabeth Anne, Michael, III. BA, Mich. State U., 1962, MA, 1963, DBA (Ford Found. fellow), 1968; D of Pub. Svc. (hon.), Bowling Green State U., 1991. Asst. to dean men U. Cin., 1965-66; asst. to dir. residence life, resident hall head advisor Mich. State U., 1966-68; acting chmn. dept. adminstrv. scis. Kent (Ohio) State U., 1970-71; mem. adminstrv. staff Bowling Green (Ohio) State U., 1971-73, v.p. resource planning, 1973-78, provost, exec. v.p., 1978-81, interim pres., 1981-82; vis. scholar U. Mich., 1982-83; prof. mgmt., provost Wright State U., Dayton, 1983-85; pres. Drake U., Des Moines, 1985-98; chancellor Tex. Christian U., Ft. Worth, 1998—; bd. dirs. Pier One Imports, Irish Life of N.Am.; mgmt. cons., 1968—. Author: Profiles of American College Presidents, 1970, Measuring the Quality of Universities, 1970, National Study of Student Personnel Manpower Planning, 1972. Research fellow Am. Coll. Testing Program, 1970. Mem. Acad. Mgmt., Omicron Delta Kappa, Phi Kappa Phi, Beta Gamma Sigma, Pi Gamma Mu, Alpha Tau Omega. Episcopalian. Office: Tex Christian Univ 2800 S University Dr Fort Worth TX 76129-2800

FERRARI, ROBERT JOSEPH, business educator, former banker; b. Bklyn., Dec. 3, 1936; m. Patricia A. Cantalupo, Sept. 6, 1958; children—Robert Joseph, James G., Judith A., Thomas A. B.S. in Econs. Villanova U., 1958; M.B.A., N.Y. U., 1962; grad. certificate, Brown U., 1969, Henry George Sch. Social Sci., 1961; D.Sc., London Inst., 1973. With arbitrace dept. Goodbody & Co., 1957-60; bank audito Fed. Reserve Bank, N.Y.C., 1960-65; v.p. fin. Am. Savings Bank, N.Y.C., 1965-81; prof., chair dept. econs. and bus. Marymount Coll., Tarrytown, N.Y., 1981—; Cons. LaCorte Agy., Inc., 1963-65; adj. lectr. C.W. Post Coll., 1963-65; adj. lectr. econs. N.Y. U., 1968-81; adj. prof. Mercy Coll., 1976—, N.Y. Inst. Tech., 1976—. Vice pres. Better Bklyn. Com.; v.p., bd. dirs. Kensington Flatbush Preservation Assn.; treas. Boy Scouts Am. Mem. Flatbush/Flatlands Republican Assn., Am. Econ. Assn., Am. Finance Assn., Am. Statis. Assn., Nat. Assn. Bus. Economists, Nat. Economists Club, N.Y. State, Met. econ. assns., Am. Acad. Polit. and Social Sci. Club: University (N.Y.C.). Home: 222 Martling Ave Apt 6J Tarrytown NY 10591-4724 Office: Marymount Coll 100 Marymount Ave Tarrytown NY 10591-3704

FERRARO, BETTY ANN, corporate administrator, state senator; b. Newport, Vt., Mar. 3, 1925; d. Clarence John and Mauretta Rowena (Potter) Morse; m. Dominic Thomas Ferraro, Oct. 8, 1964; children: Deborah, David, Susan, Barbara. Student, Mary Hitchcock Hosp. Sch. Nursing, Coll. St. Joseph, Rutland, Vt. Exec. sec. to asst. treas. Ctrl. Vt. Pub. Svc. Corp., Rutland, 1943-44; sec. to dean N.Y. Med. Coll., N.Y.C., 1944-46; model G. Fox Co., Hartford, Conn., 1947; corp. sec., office mgr. John Russell Corp., Rutland, 1970-80; exec. dir. Rutland Area Coordinated Child Care Com., Washington, 1977-79; adminstrv. asst. Hilinex of Vt., Rutland, 1981-83; owner Classic Connection Gift Shop, Rutland, 1983-87; adminstr. Vicon Recovery Sys., Inc., Rutland, 1987-90; owner, operator nursery sch., 1973-77; mgr. Day Care Ctr., 1978-80; alderman City of Rutland, 1984-86; resource dir. Rutland City, Vt. Emergency Mgmt. Team for State of Vt., 1984-90; mem. Cmty. Devel. Commn., 1986; lectr. St. Peter's Parish, Rutland. Chmn. Rutland City Rep. Com., 1991-93; state committeewoman State Rep. Com., 1991—, rep.; rep. Rutland County Rep. Com.; state del. Rep. Nat. Conv., 1992; Rep. campaign coord. State of Vt., 1997-98; mem. Vt. Ho. Reps., 1990-92; mem. Vt. Senate, 1992-94, 95-97; mem. jud. nominating bd. Human Resource Investment Coun., 1995-96, Vt. Student Assistance Corp. Bd.; mem. Amtrak Study Commn., 1995-96; bd. dirs. Vt. Physicians Coun., 1997—, Coll. St. Joseph, 1996—, Marble Valley Transit, 1996—; mem. adv. bd. Paramount Theatre, 1997—; campaign coord. Vt. Rep. Party, 1998—. Fleming Inst. fellow, 1995. Mem. Nat. Assn. Women in Constrn. (chatered, past pres.), Ruthland County Rep. Women (founder, elected Women of the Year, Green Mt. Coun. of Boy Scouts, cert. award, U. Vt.). Republican. Roman Catholic. Avocation: flower arranging. Home and Office: Condo 17 155 Dorr Dr Rutland VT 05701-3811

FERRARO, F. RICHARD, psychologist, educator; b. Amsterdam, N.Y., Sept. 7, 1959; s. Richard and Mary (Palma) F. BA, SUNY, Potsdam, 1982; MA, U. Kans., 1989, PhD, 1989. Postdoctoral fellow psychology dept. Washington U., St. Louis, 1989-92; from asst. prof. to assoc. prof. psychology U. N.D., Grand Forks, 1992—. Mem. APA, Nat. Acad. Neuropsychology, Psychonomic Soc. Office: U ND Dept Psychology Grand Forks ND 58202-8380

FERRARO, GERALDINE ANNE, lawyer, former congresswoman; b. Newburgh, N.Y., Aug. 26, 1935; d. Dominick and Antonetta L. (Corrieri) F.; m. John Zaccaro, 1960; children: Donna, John, Laura. B.A., Marymount Manhattan Coll., 1956, hon. degree, 1982; J.D., Fordham U., 1960; postgrad., N.Y. U. Law Sch., 1978, hon. degree, 1984; hon. degree, Hunter Coll., 1985, Plattsburgh Coll., 1985, Coll. Boca Raton, 1989, Va. State U., 1989, Muhlenberg Coll., 1990, Briarcliffe Coll. for Bus., 1990, Potsdam Coll., 1991. Bar: N.Y. 1961, U.S. Supreme Ct. 1978. Pvt. practice, N.Y.C., 1961-74; asst. dist. atty. Queens County, N.Y., 1974-78; chief spl. victims bur., 1977-78; mem. 96th-98th Congresses from 9th N.Y. Dist.; sec. House Democratic Caucus; first woman vice presdl. nominee on Democratic ticket, 1984; fellow Harvard Inst. of Politics, Cambridge, Mass., 1988; mng. ptnr. Keck Mahin Cate & Koether, N.Y., 1993-94; pvt. practice N.Y.C., 1995—; appointed Amb. to UN Human Rights Commn., 1994, 95; guest moderator CNN TV program Crossfire, co-host, 1996-97. Author: Ferraro, My Story, 1985, Changing History: Women, Power, and Politics, 1993. Chmn. Dem. Platform Com., 1984; bd. dirs. N.Y. Easter Seal Soc.; Dem. candidate U.S. Senate, 1992, 98; U.S. President Clinton's appointee to UN Human Rights Commn. Conf., Geneva, 1993, World Conf., Vienna, Austria, 1993, 4th World Conf. on Women, 1995; bd. dirs. Fordham Law Sch. Bd. Visitors, Nat. Italian Am. Found.; bd. advocates Planned Parenthood Fedn. Am.; bd. advisors Nat. Breast Cancer rsch. Fund., Pension Rights Ctr. Mem. Queens County Bar Assn., Queens County Women's Bar Assn. (past pres.), Nat. Dem. Inst. for Internat. Affairs (bd. dirs.), Coun. Fgn. Rels., Internat. Inst. Women's Polit. Leadership (former pres.). Roman Catholic. *

FERRARO, JOHN, city official; b. Los Angeles County, May 14, 1924; s. Dominico and Lucia Ferraro; m. Margaret Ferraro, 1982; 1 child, Luckey. BS, U. So. Calif., 1948; LLD, Southestern U., 1981. Mem. L.A. Police Commn., 1953-66, pres., three terms; city councilman 4th dist. L.A. City Coun., 1966—, pres. Pro-Tempore, 1975-77, pres., 1977-81, 87—, chmn. intergovtl. rels. com., vice chmn. rules and election com., mem. com. energy and natural resources com., mem. ad hoc com. on devel. reform; pres. Meml. Coliseum Commn.; mem. sanitation dist. Los Angeles County; mem. interagy. AWMD implementation & so. Calif. water coms. Bd. dirs. L.A. Museum Contemporary Art, Wilshire YMCA, Gene Autry Western Heritage Museum. With USN. Named All-Am Football Player, U. So. Calif., 1944, Citizen of Yr. L.A. Marathon, 1996; named to Nat. Football Found. Hall of Fame, 1974, U. So. Calif. Hall of Fame, 1995; recipient Heritage award L.A. City Assn., 1992. Mem. League of Calif. cities (bd. dirs.), Ind. Cities Assn. (alt., past pres.), So. Calif. Assn. Govts., Rotary. Roman Catholic. *

FERRARO, JOHN FRANCIS, business executive, financier; b. N.Y.C., Jan. 3, 1934; s. John Anthony and Angelina Figliola; children: Elizabeth Ann, John Robert, Laura Marie, Rosemary. B.S.I.E. with honors and distinction, NYU, 1962. With United Technologies Corp., Windsor Locks, Conn., 1962-66; sr. project engr. United Techs. Corp., Windsor Locks, Conn., 1962-64, chief research and devel. promotion, 1964-66; founding ptnr. P.M.C. Corp., 1966-78; chmn. bd., chief exec. officer Thermodynetics, Inc.; pres. Spectrum Inc., 1966—, also dir.; pres. Pioneer Capital Corp.; bd. dirs. Turbotec Products, Inc., Xtec Corp., Am. Interactive Media, Inc., Fidelity First Fin. Corp. Contbr. numerous articles on bus., fin. and stock market to fin. publs., 1966-81; contbg. editor: Handbook of Wealth Management, 1977. Chmn. Congl. Com. for Appointees to USAF Acad., 1980; commr. Devel. Agy., Enfield, Conn., 1981; trustee Suffield (Conn.) Acad., 1980-93, chair budget and fin. com., 1987-92; trustee Birth Right, Conn., 1970-80; mem. exec. com. Holy Family Retreat League, 1984-88; mem. Gov.'s Task Force for Mfg. State of Conn., 1989-91; mem. bd. advisors St. Joseph's Residence, Conn., 1991—; trustee Western New Eng. Coll., 1997—. 1st lt. USAF, 1954-58. Decorated Meritorious Service medal. Mem. Psi Upsilon, Suffield Country Club. Home: 86 Berkshire Ave Southwick MA 01077-9642 Office: 651 Day Hill Rd Windsor CT 06095-1719

FERRARO, MARGARET LOUISE (PEG FERRARO), educator; b. Apr. 9, 1939. BS in Edn., Kutstown State U., 1961. Tchr. Abington (Pa.) Sch. Dist., 1961-64, Nazareth (Pa.) Area Sch. Dist., 1978—. Chmn. zoning bd. Upper Nazareth Twp., 1970, sec. planning commn., 1968, treas., 1986, 1st woman elected to bd. suprs., 1986; bd. dirs., chair edn. com. Lehigh Valley Chamber Orch., 1982—; 1st Rep. woman elected countywide Northampton County Coun., 1989-97; chmn. Northampton County Rep. Com., 1998—. Recipient Nazareth Area H.S. Disting. Alumni award, 1994. Republican. Home: 339 Schoeneck Ave Nazareth PA 18064

FERRARO, RAY, hockey player; b. Trail, B.C., Can., Aug. 23, 1964. Hockey player Hartford Whalers Nat. Hockey League, 1985-91, hockey player N.Y. Islanders, 1991-96, hockey player L.A. Kings, 1996—; played All-Star Game, 1992. Office: LA Kings Gt Western Forum 3900 W Manchester Blvd PO Box 10 Inglewood CA 90308-2200*

FERRARO, ROBERT, customer service executive. BS, U. Nev., Reno, 1957, MS, 1959. Asst. county agt. U. Nev., Fallon, 1959-63, Lovelock, 1963-70; mgr. electrocytic sys. Pacific Engring. and Prodn. of Nev., Henderson, 1970-85; mgr. Pepcon sys. Pepcon Sys. Inc., Las Vegas, Nev., 1985-96; mgr. customer rels. Ampac, Las Vegas, 1996—. Pres. boulder City (Nev.) Mus. and Hist. Assn., 1980—. Address: Boulder City/Hoover Dam Mus PO Box 60516 Boulder City NV 89006-0516

FERRARONE, TERESA LANE, educational consultant; b. New Rochelle, N.Y., July 4, 1945; d. John William and Anne Gayne L.; m. Edward J. Ferrarone Jr., Oct. 4, 1967; children: Edward III, John B., James D. BA, Newton Coll., 1967; MA, Fairfield U., 1974. Tchr. Phila. Pub. Schs., 1967-68, Framingham (Mass.) Pub. Schs., 1968-72; tchr. Katonah (N.Y.) - Lewisboro Pub. Schs., 1972-85, coord. enrichment programs, 1985—; ednl. cons. Mamaroneck Pub. Schs., Mamaroneck, N.Y., 1998—, Bethel (Conn.) Pub. Schs., 1996—. Author: Sleuth, An Enrichment Program, 1974, Thinking As A Skill, 1986. Mem. ASCD, Larchmont Yacht Club, Ocean Reef Club. Fax: 914-834-1380. Home: PO Box 154 29 Donbrook Rd Pound Ridge NY 10576 Office: Katonah Lewisboro Schs Katonah NY 10536

FERRAZ, FRANCISCO MARCONI, neurological surgeon; b. Floresta, Pernambuco, Brazil, Aug. 14, 1951; came to U.S., 1976. Student, Colegio Nobrega, Recife-Brazil, 1967-69; MD, Faculdade de Medicine da Universidade Federal de Pernambuco-Brazil, 1975. Diplomate Am. Bd. Neurol. Surgery, 1987. Intern, Jamaica Hosp., N.Y.C., 1976-77; resident Georgetown U. Med. Ctr. and Affiliated Hosps., Washington, 1977-82; pvt. practice medicine specializing in neurol. surgery, Washington, 1982—; staff Georgetown U. Hosp., 1982—, Arlington Hosp., 1982—; chief divsn. neurosurgery, faculty clin. instr. Georgetown U. Sch. Medicine, 1982—; faculty clin. assoc. prof. George Washington Sch. Medicine, 1994—; cons. in field. Contbr. articles to profl. jours. Fellow ACS, Internat. Coll. Surgeons; mem. AMA, Am. Assn. Neurol. Surgeons, Pan Am. Med. Soc., D.C. Med. Soc., Arlington Med. Soc., Neurosurg. Soc. of D.C., Washington Acad. Neurosurgery, Congress of Neurol. Surgery. Home: 1004 Utterback Store Rd Great Falls VA 22066-1527 Office: 611 S Carlin Springs Rd Ste 105 Arlington VA 22204-1061

FERRE, ANTONIO LUIS, newspaper publisher; b. Ponce, P.R., Feb. 6, 1934; s. Luis A. and Lorenza (Ramirez de Arellano) F.; m. Luisa Rangel, Feb. 23, 1963; children: Maria Luisa, Antonio Luis, Luis Alberto, Maria Eugenia, Maria Lorenza. AB magna cum laude, Amherst Coll., 1955, PhD in Humanities (hon.), 1995; MBA, Harvard U., 1957; student, Inst. for Sr. Mgmt. and Govt. Execs., Dartmouth Coll.; PhD in Comm. Sci. (hon.), U. Turabo, 1992; HHD (hon.), Amherst Coll., 1994. Chmn Puerto Rican Cement Co.; vice chmn. Banco Popular; pres., editor El Nuevo Dia, 1968—; chmn. P.R. Conservation Trust. Author: (essays) Un Alto en el Camino; Pan, Paz y Palabra; also numerous newspaper editorials. Pres. P.R. Coun. on Higher Edn., 1966-68, Gov.'s Adv. Coun., 1968-72; mem. Gov.'s Labor Adv. Coun., 1975; pres. Com. for Econ Devel. P.R.; vice chmn. Ponce Mus. Art. With U.S. Army, 1958. Recipient Presdl. citation, 1976. Mem. P.R. Mfrs. Assn. (pres. 1965-66), Am. Mgmt. Assn. (President's Assn. 1963—), Coun. of Fgn. Rels., Inter-Am. Dialogue, P.R. C. of C., Dorado Beach and Golf Club, Bankers Club P.R., Club Deportivo de Ponce, Phi Beta Kappa. Roman Catholic.

FERREE, CAROLYN RUTH, radiation oncologist, educator; b. Liberty, N.C., Jan. 29, 1944; d. Numer Floyd and Mary Isabel (Glass) Black; m. Bill K. Ferree, Aug. 17, 1968 (div. 1980). DSc (hon.), U. N.C., Greensboro, 1998, BA, 1966, DSc (hon.), 1998; MD, Bowman Gray Coll., Winston-Salem, 1970. Diplomate Am. Bd. Radiation Oncology. Intern medicine N.C. Bapt. Hosp., Winston-Salem, 1970-71, resident in radiation oncology, 1971-74; instr. radiation oncology Bowman Gray Sch. Medicine, Winston-Salem, 1974-75, asst. prof., 1975-80, assoc. prof., 1980-87, prof., 1987—. Contbr. articles to profl. jours. Mem., v.p. County Bd. of Pub. Health, Winston-Salem, 1985-92; bd. dirs. U. N.C.-Greensboro Excellence Found., 1988-94; med. dir. Forsyth County chpt. Am. Cancer Soc., 1975-90. Recipient Disting. Svc. award U. N.C.-G Alumni, 1997; named Disting. Woman of N.C. in Professions, Gov.'s award, 1998. Fellow Am. Coll. Radiology; mem. AMA (N.C. del. to AMA), Pediat. Oncology Group (radiotherapy coord.), N.C. Med. Soc. (2d v.p. 1990-91, sec.-treas. 1991-95, pres.-elect 1996, pres. 1997), Am. Soc. Therapeutic Radiologists Orgn. Office: Bowman Gray Sch Medicine Med Center Blvd Winston Salem NC 27157

FERREE, DAVID CURTIS, horticultural researcher; b. Lock Haven, Pa., Feb. 9, 1943; s. George H. and Ruth O. (McClain) F.; m. Sandra J. Corman, Aug. 31, 1968; children: Curtis P., Thomas A. BS, Pa. State U., 1965; MS, U. Md., 1968, PhD, 1969. From asst. to assoc. prof. Ohio State U., Wooster, 1971-81, prof., 1981—. Contbr. numerous articles to profl. jours. Capt. U.S. Army, 1969-71. Recipient sr. scientist disting. rsch. award Ohio Agrl. Rsch. and Devel. Ctr., 1997, Disting. Svc. award Fruit Growers Soc., 1998. Fellow Am. Soc. Hort. Sci. (assoc. editor 1983-86, v.p. 1988-89, J.H. Gourley award 1982, Stark award 1983), Am. Pomological Soc. (editor), Internat. Dwarf Fruit Tree Assn. (Disting. Rschr. award 1989), Gamma Sigma Delta (Rsch. award 1981). Lutheran. Office: Ohio Agrl R & D Ctr Dept Horticulture Crop Sci Wooster OH 44691

FERREE, JOHN NEWTON, JR., fundraising specialist, consultant; b. Wadesboro, N.C., Nov. 21, 1946; s. John Newton and Mary Cleo (Tice) F.; m. Ginger Ann Rogers, June 6, 1969 (div. 1991); m. Patricia Gayle Kruger, Nov. 19, 1994. AA, Bluefield (Va.) Coll., 1966; BA, Baylor U., 1968; JD, Samford U., 1975. Bar: Ala. Contr. Aetna Life Ins. Co., Seattle, 1972; atty. Ferree & Armstrong, Alabaster, Ala., 1975-82; exec. dir. Northwest Bapt. Found., Portland, Oreg., 1982-84; asst. v.p. Harris Trust Co. of Ariz., Scottsdale, 1984; v.p. Bapt. Found. of Ariz., Phoenix, 1985-89; dir. planned giving Phoenix Children's Hosp., 1989-91; pres. Scottsdale (Ariz.) Healthcare Found., 1991—; bd. dir. Nat. Com. Planned Giving, 1994-96; bd. dirs. FBI Citizen's Acad. Found., v.p. 1994-96, 98, Charitable Accord, v.p., 1996-98; instr. Cannon Sch. Found. Mgmt., 1995—; adj. prof. Ariz. State U., 1998—; cons. in field. Named Ariz. Profl. Fundraiser of Yr., 1996. Mem. Nat. Soc. Fund Raising Execs. (pres. 1990), Planned Giving Roundtable of Ariz. (pres. 1992, 97), Assn. for Healthcare Philanthropy. Republican. Baptist. Office: Scottsdale Healthcare Found Ste 121 10001 E 92nd St Scottsdale AZ 85258-4530

FERREIRA, ARMANDO THOMAS, sculptor, educator; b. Charleston, W.Va., Jan. 8, 1932; s. Maximiliano and Placeres (Sanchez) F.; children—Lisa, Teresa. Student, Chouinard Art Inst., 1949-50, Long Beach City Coll., 1950-53; B.A., UCLA, 1954, M.A., 1956. Asst. prof. art Mt. St. Mary's Coll., 1956-57; mem. faculty dept. art Calif. State U., Long Beach, 1957—, prof., 1967—, chmn. dept. art, 1971-77, assoc. dean Sch. Fine Arts, acting dean Coll. Arts; lectr., cons. on art adminstrn. to art schs. and universities, Brazilian Ministry Edn. One man shows include, Pasadena Mus., 1959, Long Beach Mus., 1959, 69, Eccles Mus., 1967, Clay and Fiber Gallery, Taos, 1972, group shows include, Los Angeles County Art Mus., 1958, 66, Wichita Art Mus., 1959, Everson Mus., 1960, 66, San Diego Mus. Fine Arts, 1969, 73, Fairtree Gallery, N.Y.C., 1971, 74, Los Angeles Inst. Contemporary Art, 1977, Utah Art Mus., 1978, Bowers Mus., Santa Ana, Calif., 1980, No. Ill. U., 1986, Beckstrand Gallery, Palos Verdes (Calif.) Art Ctr., 1987, U. Madrid, 1993; permanent collections include Utah Mus. Art, Wichita Art Mus., State of Calif. Collection; vis. artist, U. N.D., 1974, exhibited widely abroad including, Poland, Portugal, Morocco, Spain, France, Austria, Germany. Fulbright lectr. Brazil, 1981. Fellow Nat. Assn. Schs. Art and Design (dir.); mem. Internat. Video Network (dir.), Assn. Calif. State Univ. Profs. *I suppose much of my own life has been shaped by my experience as a first generation American. What modest success I may have had in my work is considerably due to that sense of ambition with which immigrant parents imbue their children. My vision as an artist is also shaped by the strong sense of Spanish culture that was part of my upbringing.*

FERREIRA, DANIEL ALVES, secondary education Spanish language educator; b. Lisbon, Portugal, Feb. 24, 1944; came to U.S., 1959, naturalized, 1963; s. Manuel and Lourdes (Alves) F.; m. Cheryl R. Jann, July 1, 1978; children: Jeffrey, Douglas, Peter. BA, U. Ill., 1966, MEd, 1970; Diploma Superior, U. Salamanca, Spain, 1994. Cert. tchr., Ill. Tchr. Homewood-Flossmoor (Ill.) High Sch., 1966—; boys and girls Soccer Coach at Homewood-Flossmoor (Ill.). Bd. dirs. Grace Migrant Day Care Ctr., Park Forest, Ill., 1971-80. Named Chgo. Area Tchr. of Yr., U. Chgo., 1985. Mem. Am. Assn. Tchrs. of Spanish and Portuguese, Ill. High Sch. Soccer Coaches Assn., Nat. Soccer Coaches Assn. Am., Ill. Edn. Assn., NEA, Homewood-Flossmoor Edn. Orgn. (pres. 1981-82), Phi Delta Kappa. Avocations: soccer, golf. Home: 21343 Ginger Ln Frankfort IL 60423-9428 Office: Homewood Flossmoor High Sch 999 Kedzie Ave Flossmoor IL 60422-2248

FERREIRA, JO ANN JEANETTE CHANOUX, time-definite transportation industry executive; b. Dec. 3, 1943; d. John W. and June B. Chanoux;

m. G. Dodge Ferreira, Apr. 21, 1979 (div. Dec. 1993). BS, Purdue U., 1965, MS, 1969. With sys. devel. rsch. IBM, San Jose, Calif., 1965-67; asst. dir. mgmt. info. sys. edn. Union Carbide Corp., N.Y.C., 1969; mgmt. cons. Touche Ross & Co., N.Y.C., 1974-75; dir. corp. devel. strategy cons. A.T. Kearney-Mgmt. Cons., Chgo., 1975-83; dir. Computer Devel. Ctr. United Airlines, 1983-88; pres. WSG Designs Inc., Northbrook, Ill., 1988-92, Accorde-Moraine Cons., Inc., 1992-93; gen. mgr. acoustic rsch. divsn. Internat. Jensen, Inc., Lincolnshire, Ill., 1993—, v.p. bus. plans and export ops., 1994—; mng. dir. market planning and analysis FDX holding co. for Fed Ex, RPS; lectr. Purdue U., 1969, 73-74; guest lectr. Northwestern U., 1981; gen. mgr. acoustic rsch. divsn., exec. asst. to pres. Internat. Jensen, Inc., 1993-98, mng. dir. strategic market planning and analysis FDX Corp. (parent co. Fed. Express Co.), Memphis; spkr. in field. Contbr. articles to profl. publs. NSF fellow, 1969. Mem. Inst. Mgmt. Cons. (cert. mgmt. cons.), am. Arbitration Assn., Japan Am. soc., Phi Kappa Phi.

FERREIRA, JOSE, JR., consumer products company executive; b. Naugatuck, Conn., Apr. 21, 1956; s. Jose Sr. and Rose (Soares) F.; m. Nancy Possiel, Aug. 10, 1980; children: Matthew Charles, Justin Paul, Todd Lucas. BS in Acctg., Cen. Conn. U., 1978; MBA in Fin., Fordham U., 1982. Acct. Marcade Group, N.J., 1978-79, mgr. acctg., 1979-80; product cost analyst Avon Products Inc., N.Y.C., 1980, planning analyst, 1980-81, sr. planning analyst, 1981-82, mgr. planning Latin Am., 1982-83, group mgr. fin. Latin Am., 1983-84, dir. fin. Latin Am., 1984-86, contr. internat. div., 1986-88, v.p. fin. and ops., internat. div., 1988-89; v.p. fin. Worldwide Direct Sales Group, 1989, corp. v.p., fin. adminstrn., gen. mgr. home office, 1989-90; area v.p. Ams. region, 1990-93; chmn. bd., pres. Avon Spain, 1993-94; pres. Avon Iberia (Portugal and Spain), 1994-95; exec. v.p., pres. Avon, Asia Pacific, 1995-98; exec. v.p., pres. Europe, Asia and Africa Avon, 1999—; v.p. bd. dirs. Talbot Perkins Children's Svcs., N.Y.C., 1991-93. Mem. Chimney Hill Owners Assn., Inc., Vt., 1988—. Mem. Direct Sales Assn., Japan Soc., various C of C. Avocations: sailing, skiing, cycling. Office: Avon Products Inc 1345 Avenue Of The Americas New York NY 10019-5374

FERREIRA, LINDA DOREEN, long term, acute care and rehabilitation nurse; b. Elmhurst, Ill., Apr. 10, 1948; d. Louis S. and Clarice J. (Passey) Grupe; m. Arthur M. Ferreira, Nov. 26, 1979; children: Scott Allen, Curtis Paul. ADN, U. Hawaii, Hilo, 1983. LPN, Hawaii, RN, Hawaii, Alaska, Nev.; cert. gerontological nurse; cert. rehab. nurse. Nurse mgr. long term care, supr. Kona Hosp., Kealakekua, Hawaii, 1986-88; dir. long term care South Peninsula Hosp., Homer, Alaska, 1988; evening supr. Our Lady of Compassion Care Ctr., Anchorage, 1989-91; Alaska Psychiat. Inst., Anchorage, 1991-92; dir. nursing svc. Hillhaven-Kona Health Care Ctr., Kailua-Kona, Hawaii, 1993-95; evening charge nurse Fairbanks Meml. Hosp./Denali Ctr., Fairbanks, Alaska, 1995-97; subacute mgr. Washoe Progressive Care Ctr., Sparks, Nev., 1998; nurse mgr. Health South Rehab. Hosp., Reno, 1998-99; coord. restorative care program I.H.S. Physicians Hosp. Extended Care, Reno, 1999—. Mem. ANA, Assn. Rehab. Nurses, Nat. Assn. Dirs. Nursing Adminstrn., Nat. Gerontol. Nurses Assn., Nev. Nurses Asn.

FERRELL, CONCHATA GALEN, actress, acting teacher and coach; b. Charleston, W.Va., Mar. 28, 1943; d. Luther Martin and Mescal Loraine (George) F.; m. Arnold A. Anderson; 1 dau., Samantha. Student, W.Va. U., 1961-64, Marshall U., 1967-68. N.Y. theater appearances The Hot L Baltimore, 1973, The Sea Horse, 1973-74 (OBIE award and Drama Desk award 1974), Battle of Angels, 1975; appeared in: Los Angeles plays Getting Out, 1978, Here Wait, 1980, Picnic, 1986; appeared in TV series: The Hot L Baltimore, 1975, B.J. and the Bear, 1979, McClain's Law, 1981, E.R., 1984, A Peaceable Kingdom, 1989, L.A. Law, 1991, Hearts Afire, 1993-94, Townies, 1996, Teen Angel, 1997; appeared in movies: Network, 1975, Dangerous Hero, 1975, Heartland, 1981, Where the River Runs Black, 1986, For Keeps,1987, Mystic Pizza, 1987, Witches of Eastwick, 1987, Chains of Gold, 1990, Edward Sissorhands, 1990, Family Prayers, 1993, True Romance, 1993, Samurai Cowboy, 1993, Heaven and Earth, 1993, Freeway, 1995, Touch, 1996, My Fellow Americans, 1996; appeared in TV movies: A Girl Called Hatter Fox, 1977, A Death in Canaan, 1977, The Orchard Children, 1978, Before and After, 1979, Bliss, 1979, Reunion, 1980, The Rideout Case, 1980, The Great Gilley Hopkins, 1981, Life of the Party, 1982, Emergency Room, 1983, Nadia, 1984, Miss Lonely Hearts, 1985, Samaritan, 1986, Northbeach and Rawhide, 1986, Picnic, 1986, Eye on the Sparrow, 1987, Runaway Ralph, 1987, Goodbye Miss Liberty (Disney Channel), 1988, Running Mates, 1990, Deadly Intentions, Again, 1990, Back Field in Motion, 1991, 120 Volt Miracle, 1992, Forget Me Not, 1996, Sweetdreams, 1996. Recipient Wrangler award Nat. Cowboy Hall of Fame, 1981, Most Promising Newcomer award Theatre World, 1974, Emmy award nomination, 1991-92. Mem. AFTRA, ACLU, NOW, Actors Equity Assn., Screen Actors Guild, Women in Films. Democrat. Office: Paradigm 10100 Santa Monica Blvd Los Angeles CA 90067-4003

FERRELL, JOHN FREDERICK, advertising executive; b. Waterloo, Iowa, Dec. 1, 1942; s. Dwight R. and Beth I. F.; m. Barbara M. Ferrell, Sept. 14, 1975; 1 child, Joanna Beth. BS in Communications, U. Ill., 1964. Copywriter Leo Burnett Co., Chgo., 1964-67; copywriter Young & Rubicam, N.Y.C., 1967-69, copy supr., 1969-70, creative supr., 1970-74, v.p., assoc. creative dir., 1974-80, sr. v.p., group creative dir., 1980-84, exec. v.p., creative dir., 1984-88; exec. v.p., chief creative officer Hill Holliday/N.Y., 1989-92; pres., chief creative officer FERRELLCALVILLO Comm. Inc., N.Y.C., 1992—. Office: Ferrellcalvillo Comm Inc 250 Park Ave S New York NY 10003-1402

FERRELL, LYNN DUWAYNE, county official; b. Fairfield, Iowa, June 27, 1951; s. James Latimer and Alice Marie (Kane) F.; m. Linda K. Roberts, Mar. 30, 1984. BA, U. Iowa, 1973; MA, Rutgers U., 1974. State-local rels. assoc. U.S. Adv. Commn. on Intergovernmental Rels., Washington, 1974-77; asst. project dir. ABA, Washington, 1977-80; project dir. Nat. Assn. Counties, Washington, 1980-82; dir. Human Svcs. Coordinating Bd. United Way Ctrl. Iowa, Des Moines, 1982-84; exec. dir. Polk County Health Svcs., Des Moines, 1984—; bd. dirs. Area Comprehensive Evaluation Svcs., Des Moines, 1985—, Nat. Assn. of Counties, 1992-94; pres. Nat. Assn. County Behavioral Health Dirs., 1992-94; mem. intergovtl. adv. group Substance Abuse and Mental Health Svcs. Adminstrn., 1993. Vol. United Way, Des Moines, 1986—; mem. Iowa Spl. Olympics Outreach Com., Des Moines, 1987-88. Avocations: travel, reading. Office: Polk County Health Svcs 218 6th Ave Ste 1000 Des Moines IA 50309-4006

FERRELL, MARK STEPHEN, flight nurse; b. Fayetteville, Ark., Nov. 24, 1968; s. Vance Harold and Cherie Camille (Eller) F. ASN, Motlow Coll., Tullahoma, Tenn., 1989; EMT, Valencia Coll., Orlando, Fla., 1991. RN, Tenn., Calif.; CCRN; CEN; cert. flight RN, ACLS instr., pediatric advanced life support instr., neonatal resuscitation program instr., trauma nursing core course, emergency nursing pediatric course, BLS, advanced burn life support; lic. paramedic, Calif. Staff nurse ICU Fla. Hosp., Orlando, 1989-91; staff nurse emergency dept. Orlando (Fla.) Regional Med. Ctr., 1991-92; flight nurse Travelor Rapid City (S.D.) Regional Hosp. Life Flight, 1992; staff nurse Travelor U. Calif.-Davis Med. Ctr., Sacramento, 1992-93; flight nurse St. Joseph's Care Flight, Lexington, Ky., 1993-94, Stanford (Calif.) U. Hosp., 1994—; mem. protocol com. sTanford Life Flight, 1994—. Mem. AACN, Emergency Nurses Assn., Nat. Flight Nurse Assn. Seventh-Day Adventist. Avocations: camping, skiing, mountain biking, rock climbing, hiking. Home: 325M Sharon Park Dr # 604 Menlo Park CA 94025-6845 Office: Stanford Life Flight 300 Pasteur Dr Palo Alto CA 94304-2203

FERRELL, MILTON MORGAN, JR., lawyer; b. Coral Gables, Fla., Nov. 6, 1951; s. Milton M. and Annie (Blanche) Bradley; m. Lori R. Sanders, May 22, 1982; children: Milton Morgan III, Whitney Connolly. BA, Mercer U., 1973, JD, 1975. Bar: Fla. 1975. Asst. state's atty. State's Atty.'s Office, Miami, 1975-77; ptnr. Ferrell & Ferrell, Miami, 1977-84; sole practice Miami, 1985-87; ptnr. Ferrell & Williams, P.A., Miami, 1987-90, Ferrell & Fertel, P.A., Miami, 1990-98, Ferrell Schultz Carter & Fertel P.A., 1999—. Trustee Mus. Sci. and Space Transit Planetarium, 1977-82; mem. Ambs. of Mercy, Mercy Hosp. Found., Inc., 1985-94; trustee, mem. legal com., chair com. U. Miami Project to Cure Paralysis, 1985-94; bd. trustees Eaglebrook Sch., 1995-98, Robinson Charitable Found., 1993—. Fellow Nat. Assn. Criminal Def. Lawyers, Am. Bd. Criminal Lawyers (bd. govs. 1981-82, sec. 1983-84, v.p. 1984-86, pres. 1987-88); mem. ABA (grantee 1975), Fla. Bar Assn. (jury instrns. com. 1987-88, chmn. grievance com. 11-L 1989-91), Dade County Bar Assn. (bd. dirs. 1977-80), mem. Performing Arts Ctr. Found. Greater Miami, Bath Club (bd. govs. 1992-95), Miami Club, Banker's Club, Cat Cay Yacht Club, Inc. (bd. dirs. 1997—, treas. 1998-99), Indian Creek County Club, LaGorce County Club, Fisher Island Club. Home: Bay Point 4511 Lake Rd Miami FL 33137-3372 Office: Ferrell Schultz Carter & Fertel PA 201 S Biscayne Blvd Ste 1920 Miami FL 33131-4329

FERRELL, PAUL CLEVELAND, author; b. Morehouse, Mo., Aug. 17, 1943; s. Sherman Gentry and Virginia Irene (Brawley) F.; m. Wanda Darlene Jones, Nov. 27, 1963. Student, Mineral Area Jr. Coll., Flat River, Mo., 1965-66, U. Mo., S.E. Mo. State U. Registered technologist Am. Radiol. Soc. Head radiology dept. Madison Meml. Hosp., Fredericktown, Mo., 1965-66; ambulance attendant Pub. Emergency Svc., Sikeston, Mo., 1970-73; tchr. math. Sikeston Pub. Schs., 1978-80, vocat. instr., 1980-85; ghost writer Sikeston, 1981-84; author Bloomfield, Mo., 1985—; mem. adv. bds. Vocat. Edn., Sikeston, 1980-85; lectr. in math., health and philosophy. Author: Diet and the Cardiovascular Condition, 1995, The Utopian Cause, 1996, Night Reader I, 1997, Night Reader II, 1997, Morehouse Missouri, 1997, vol. 2, 1998, Night Reader III, 1998, others; ghost writer, editor: The Headlee Anthology, 1984; author cultural newsletter The Plow and the Stars, 1992-93; inventor game Choice and Chance, 1992. Served with USN, 1966-70, Vietnam. Mem. Am. Registry Radiol. Technologists. Avocations: local history, visual and performing arts. Office: The Plow and the Stars 21212 County Road 510 Bloomfield MO 63825-8500

FERRELL, ROBERT CRAIG, computational physicist, consultant; b. Washington, Nov. 21, 1960. BA in Physics, Cornell U., 1984; PhD in Physics, U. Calif., Santa Barbara, 1989. Rschr. U. Calif., Santa Barbara, 1985-90; prin. scientist Thinking Machines Corp., Cambridge, Mass., 1990-95, CPC Assocs., Brookline, Mass., 1995—; vis. scientist MIT, Cambridge, 1995—. Office: CPC Assocs 2 Still St Brookline MA 02446-3444

FERRELL, ROBERT HUGH, historian, educator; b. Cleve., May 8, 1921; s. Ernest Henry and Edna Lulu (Rentsch) F.; m. Lila Esther Sprout, Sept. 8, 1956; 1 dau., Carolyn Irene. BS in Edn., Bowling Green State U., 1946, BA, 1947, LLD (hon.), 1971; MA, Yale U., 1948, PhD, 1951. Intelligence analyst U.S. Air Force, 1951-52; lectr. in history Mich. State U., 1952-53; asst. prof. history Ind. U., 1953-58, asso. prof., 1958-61, prof., 1961-74, Disting. prof., 1974-88, emeritus, 1988—; vis. prof. Yale U., 1955-56, Am. U. at Cairo, 1958-59, U. Conn., 1964-65, Cath. U. Louvain, Belgium, 1969-70, Naval War Coll., 1974-75, U.S. Mil. Acad., 1987-88. Author: Peace in Their Time, 1952, American Diplomacy in the Great Depression, 1957, American Diplomacy: A History, 1959, 2d rev. edit., 1987, Frank B. Kellogg and Henry L. Stimson, 1963, (with M.G. Baxter and J.E. Wiltz) Teaching of American History in High Schools, 1964, George C. Marshall, 1966 (with R.B. Morris and W. Greenleaf) America: A History of the People, 1971, (with others) Unfinished Century, 1973, Harry S. Truman and the Modern American Presidency, 1983, Truman: A Centenary Remembrance, 1984, Woodrow Wilson and World War I, 1985, Harry S. Truman: His Life on the Family Farms, 1991, Ill-Advised, 1992, Choosing Truman: The Democratic Convention of 1944, 1994, Harry S. Truman: A Life, 1994, The Strange Deaths of President Harding, 1996, The Dying President: Franklin D. Roosevelt, 1998, The Presidency of Calvin Coolidge, 1998, Truman and Pendergast, 1999, ; editor: Off the Record: The Private Papers of Harry S Truman, 1980, The Autobiography of Harry S. Truman, 1980, The Eisenhower Diaries, 1981, Dear Bess: The Letters from Harry to Bess Truman, 1983, Banners in the Air: The Eighth Ohio Volunteers and the Spanish-American War, 1988, Monterrey is Ours!, 1990; Truman in the White House: The Diary of Eben Ayers, 1991 (with L.E. Wikander) Grace Coolidge: An Autobiography, 1992, Holding the Line: The Third Tennessee Infantry 1861-64, 1994; (with Samuel Flagg Bemis) American Secretaries of State and Their Diplomacy. 10 vols., 1963-85, Truman and the Bomb, 1996, (with Joan Hoff) Dictionary of American History Supplement, 2 vols., 1996, FDR's Quiet Confidant: The Autobiography of Frank C. Walker, 1997, The Kansas City Investigation, 1999. Served with USAAF, 1942-45. Mem. Soc. Historians Am. Fgn. Relations. Home: 512 S Hawthorne Dr Bloomington IN 47401-5024 Office: Dept History Ind U Bloomington IN 47405

FERREN, JOHN MAXWELL, lawyer; b. Kansas City, Mo., July 21, 1937; s. Jack Maxwell and Elizabeth Anne (Hansen) F.; m. Ann Elizabeth Speidel, Sept. 4, 1961 (div.); children: Andrew John, Peter Maxwell; m. Linda Jane Finkelstein, June 17, 1994. AB magna cum laude, Harvard U., 1959, LLB, 1962. Bar: Ill. 1962, Mass. 1967, D.C. 1970. Assoc. Kirkland, Ellis, Hodson, Chaffetz & Masters, Chgo., 1962-66; dir. Neighborhood Law Office Program, Harvard U. Law Sch., Cambridge, Mass., 1966-68; teaching fellow, dir. Neighborhood Law Office Program, Harvard Law Sch. (Legal Svcs. Program), Cambridge, 1968-69, lectr. law, dir., 1969-70; ptnr. Hogan & Hartson, Washington, 1970-77; assoc. judge D.C. Ct. Appeals, 1977-97, Corp. Counsel, Washington, 1997—; mem. disciplinary bd. D.C. Ct. Appeals, 1972-76; mem. exec. com., bd. dirs. Council on Legal Edn. for Profl. Responsibility, 1970-80; exec. com. Washington Lawyers Com. for Civil Rights Under Law, 1970-77. Contbr. articles to profl. jours. Treas., bd. dirs. Firman Neighborhood House, Chgo., 1964-66; legis. subcom. on consumer credit Chgo. Commn. on Human Rels. Com. on New Residents, 1964-66; bd. dirs. Frederick B. Abramson Meml. Found., 1991-97, People's Devel. Corp., Washington, 1970-74, George A. Wiley Meml. Fund, 1974-84, Nat. Resource Ctr. for Consumers of Legal Svcs., 1973-77, Ctr. for Law and Edn., Cambridge, Mass., 1989-94; originator, chmn. Neighborhood Legal Advice Clinics, Ch. Fedn. Greater Chgo., 1964-66; exec. com. of legal adv. com. Nat. Com. Against Discrimination in Housing, 1974-77; steering com. Nat. Prison Project of ACLU Found., 1975-77. Fellow Am. Bar Found.; mem. ABA (Commn. on Nat. Inst. Justice 1972-80, mem. consortium on legal svcs. and pub. 1972-73, 76-79, chmn. 1979-82, chmn. spl. com. on pub. interest practice 1976-78), Am. Law Inst., Phi Beta Kappa. Presbyterian. Office: Office of the Corp Counsel 441 4th St NW # 1060N Washington DC 20001-2714

FERRENDELLI, JAMES ANTHONY, neurologist, educator; b. Trinidad, Colo., Dec. 5, 1936; s. Alex and Edna Ferrendelli; children—Elisabeth, Cynthia, Michael. AB cum laude in Chemistry, U. Colo., Boulder, 1958; M.D., U. Colo., Denver, 1962. Diplomate Am. Bd. Psychiatry and Neurology. Intern U. Ky. Med. Ctr., 1962-63; resident in neurology Cleve. Met. Gen. Hosp., 1965-68; research fellow in neurochemistry Washington U. Sch. Medicine, St. Louis, 1968-70, asst. prof. neurology and pharmacology, 1970-74, assoc. prof., 1974-77, prof., 1977-95, Seay prof. clin. neuropharmacology in neurology, 1977-95; prof., chmn. dept. neurology, prof. pharmacology U. Tex., Houston, 1995—, Kraft-Eidmann prof., 1995—. Contbr. numerous articles to profl. jours. Served to capt. M.C., U.S. Army, 1963-65. Recipient rsch. career devel. award USPHS, 1971-76, Founders Day award Washington U., 1981, Disting. Tchr. award, 1993, 94, Disting. Prof. of Yr. award, 1993, NIH grantee, 1971—. Mem. Am. Acad. Neurology, Am. Neurol. Assn., Am. Soc. for Pharmacology and Exptl. Therapeutics (Epilepsy award 1981), Am. Epilepsy Soc. (Lennox lectr. 1991, pres. 1995). Avocation: fly-fishing. Office: U Tex-Houston Med Sch Dept Neurology 6431 Fannin St Ste 7044 Houston TX 77030-1501

FERRER, MIGUEL ANTONIO, brokerage firm and investment bank executive; b. Ithaca, N.Y., May 18, 1938; s. Miguel and Conchita (Bolivar) F.; m. Suzan Nudelman, Aug. 1962 (div. 1973); children: Miguel Antonio, Ilena Christine; m. Lizette Gratacos, Sept. 4, 1980; children: Alejandro Miguel, Augusto Miguel. BA, Cornell U., 1959, MBA, 1961. Account exec. Merrill Lynch Pierce Fenner Smith, San Juan, P.R., 1961-65; br. mgr. Eastman Dillon Union Securities, San Juan, 1965-71, ptnr., 1971-73; sr. v.p. Blyth Eastman Dillon & Co., Inc., San Juan, 1973-80, PaineWebber Inc., San Juan, 1980—; pres., CEO PaineWebber Inc. of P.R., Hato Rey, 1983—; chmn. PaineWebber Latin Am., 1993-98; pres., CEO PaineWebber Trust Co. of P.R., 1997—; bd. dirs. P.R. Investors Tax Free Fund; dir. consultive bd. U. P.R., Rio Piedras, 1989-92; mem. governing bd. P.R. Strategy Project. Bd. dirs. P.R. Aqueducts and Sewer Authority, San Juan, 1986-88, P.R. Pub. Broadcasting Corp., 1990-92, P.R. Mus. Architecture, San Juan; Rafael Hernández Colon Found., 1993, U. P.R. Found., 1995; pres. fund raising ARC, Rio Piedras, 1990-91; bd. dirs., treas. Casa del Libro, San Juan; founding dir. Found. Friends of P.R. Acad. of Spanish Lang., 1996—. Recipient Top Mgmt. award in fin. Sales and Mktg. Execs. Assn., 1980. Mem. Securities Industry Assn. (founding mem., bd. dirs., past pres.), P.R. Fin. Analysts Assn. (founding mem., past pres.), Banker's Club. Avocation: gymnasiums, art collecting, philanthropy. Home: K-22 St Villa Caparra Guaynabo PR 00966 Office: PaineWebber Inc PR American International Plz Penthouse Fl Hato Rey PR 00918

FERRERA, ARTHUR ROCCO, food distribution company executive; b. Boston, Feb. 1, 1916; s. James F. and Mary (Mangini) F.; m. Mildred Grace Rugg, Sept. 9, 1944; children: Kenneth Grant, James Howard. A.B., Harvard U., 1938. Co-founder James Ferrera & Sons, Inc., 1945—, pres., 1945-57, chmn. bd., 1957-89, chmn. emeritus, cons., 1989—; chmn. emeritus, cons. James Ferrera & Sons, Inc.; dir. Commonwealth Bank of Boston, 1966-70; past dir. Romi Foods, Toronto; chmn. food div. CD, Mass., 1966. Served with AUS, 1942-46; to lt. col. USAFR (ret.). Name to Mass. Food Assn. Hall of Fame, 1993. Mem. New Eng. Wholesale Food Distbrs. Assn. (dir., past pres.), Nazareth Food Assn. (dir.), Mass. Food Assn. (Hall of Fame 1993), DAV (life). Republican. Roman Catholic. Club: Officers (Bedford, Mass.). Home: 5 Longfellow Rd Winchester MA 01890-2209 Office: 135 Will Dr Canton MA 02021-3710

FERRERI, MICHAEL VICTOR, optometrist; b. Park Ridge, Ill., May 15, 1967; s. Samuel Joseph and Dolores Jean (Liebich) F.; children: Christopher, Anthony. BS in Biol. Scis., U. Calif., Irvine, 1989; OD, So. Calif. Coll. Optometry, 1993. Cert. therapeutic optometrist, Calif., Tex. Extern Ctr. for the Partially Sighted, Santa Monica, Calif., 1992-93; pvt. practice, Long Beach, Calif., 1993—; assoc. optometrist Antelope Mall Vision Ctr., Palmdale, Calif., 1995-99; color vision analysis cons. Dept. Health and Human Svcs., Long Beach, 1994-97; participating doctor Vision USA, Long Beach, 1995—. Contbr. articles to profl. jours. Mem. Rep. Nat. Com., 1991—; v.p. congregation Grace Luth. Ch., Long Beach, 1996-99, also elder. Recipient Corning Low Vision award Corning Optics, Anaheim, Calif., 1993, Vision Therapy Enhancement cert. So. Calif. Coll. Optometry, Fullerton, 1993, appreciation cert. for outstanding contbns. to Save Your Vision Week, U.S. Senate, 1997, gov.'s letter of commendation for organizing coloring and essay contest for sch. children State of Calif., 1997, appreciation certificate Calif. Optometric Assn., 1998. Mem. Am. Optometric Assn. (contact lens sect.), Calif. Optometric Assn., Fellowship of Christian Optometrists, Optometric Ext. Program (clin. assoc.), Rio Hondo Optometric Soc. (treas. 1997-99). Avocations: camping, golfing, watersports. Home: PO Box 2573 Guasti CA 91743-2573 Office: Los Altos Med Ctr 1777 N Bellflower Blvd Ste 109 Long Beach CA 90815-4013

FERRETTI, KEVIN MICHAEL, human resource director; b. Fairfax, Va., Feb. 18, 1972; s. Michael Joseph and Eleanor Jean (Raymond) F. BA in English Comms. and Secondary Edn., York Coll. of Pa., 1994. Corp. trainer Old Line Plastics, Inc., Forest Hill, Md., 1995-96, human resource dir., 1996—. Pres. Theatre Therese, Balt., 1995-97. Mem. Soc. Human Resource Mgmt., Susquehanna Human Resource Assn. Republican. Roman Catholic. Avocations: acting, singing, hiking, reading. Office: Old Line Plastics Inc PO Box 295 Forest Hill MD 21050-0295

FERRICK, THOMAS JEROME, JR., journalist; b. Phila., Jan. 14, 1949; s. Thomas Jerome and Dolores (Sprows) F.; m. Sharon A. Sexton, Sept. 10, 1977; children: Thomas Joseph, Cormac James. Student, Temple U., 1970. Reporter UPI, Phila. and Harrisburg, 1971-76; reporter, editor Phila. Inquirer, 1976—. Recipient George Polk award for investigative reporting, 1979, Roy Howard award for pub. svc., 1979, AP Mng. Editors award for pub. svc., 1979, Disting. Grand prize Nat. Edn. Writers Assn., 1981, Disting. Grand prize 1994, World Hunger Media award 1989, Award Nat. Assn. of Black Journalists, 1990. Office: Phila Inquirer 400 N Broad St Philadelphia PA 19130-4099

FERRIER, JOSEPH JOHN, atmospheric physicist; b. Weehawken, N.J., Jan. 28, 1959; s. Henry Pierre and Josephine (Logalbo) F. BS, Columbia U., 1980; MS, NYU, 1983. Sci. programmer Sigma Data Svcs. Corp., N.Y.C., 1980-81; programmer/analyst M/A-Com Info. Systems, Inc., N.Y.C., 1981-86; atmospheric physicist, planetary group mgr. Centel Fed. Svcs. Corp., N.Y.C., 1986-89, Hughes Aircraft Co., N.Y.C., 1989-94; atmospheric physicist, planetary group mgr., interdisciplinary group mgr. S.S.A.I., N.Y.C., 1994—. Mem. AAAS. Office: NASA/GISS 2880 Broadway New York NY 10025-7886

FERRIER, RICHARD BROOKS, architecture educator, architect; b. Ft. Worth, Mar. 29, 1944; s. Samuel Foster and Opal Birtha (Brooks) F.; m. Lynna Gail Elmore Mindlin; 1 child, Sean Brooks. BA, Tex. Tech U., 1968; MA in Art, U. Dallas, Irvine, Tex., 1973. With planning dept. City of Lubbock, Tex., 1962-63; with Atcheson, Atkinson and Cartwright: Architects, Lubbock, 1963-65, Engring. Assocs., Lubbock, 1966-68; mem. faculty U. Tex., Arlington, 1968—, prof. architecture, assoc. dean, 1980—; prin. Richard B. Ferrier, AIA, architect, Arlington, 1982-91, Firm X Richard B. Ferrier, FAIA, architect, Arlington, 1991—; with Ralph Kelman, architects, Dallas, 1969-70; assoc. William S. Austin, Architect, Arlington, 1976-80; with Comm. Cons., Arlington, 1970-82; mem. architecture adv. bd. Dallas County C.C., 1983-88; architecture critic Ft. Worth Star Telegram, 1989; numerous lecturers in field, including Rice U. Sch. Architecture, Houston, 1970, St. Thomas More Inst., Ft. Worth-Dallas, 1987, U. Houston, 1988, U. Dallas, 1988, Dallas Mus. Art, 1990; juror in field. Contbr. articles and revs. to profl. jours.; prin. works include 1st Bapt. Ch. Chapel, Crosbyton, Tex., 1965, Golf and Country Club, Rule, Tex., 1966, Seagraves (Tex.) H.S., 1967, Episcopal Pastoral Ctr., Ft. Worth, 1977, student housing project 22 units, Arlington, 1982, also numerous pvt. residences; exhibited in numerous group shows, 1968—, including Dallas Mus. Art, 1991, Arlington Mus. Art, 1992, 93, 94, Tex. Fine Arts Assn., Austin, 1992, Archtl. Gallery, Chgo., 1994. Named Alumni of Yr., Tex. Tech U. Coll. Architecture, 1993; recipient numerous awards Am. Soc. Architecture Perspectivists, 1986—, 12 awards Tex. Architect Graphics Competition, 1988—, amateur animated film award Cannes Internat. Film Festival, 1973. Mem. AIA (elected to Coll. Fellows 1993, recipient 8 Dallas design awards 1991-96, 46 Dallas graphic awards 1980—, including 14 honor awards); mem. Tex. Tech U. Coll. Architecture Alumni Assn. (bd. dirs. 1989-92). Democrat. Episcopalian. Home: 1628 Connally Ter Arlington TX 76010-4516 Office: U Tex Sch Arch Box 19108 Arlington TX 76019

FERRIN, MARSHALL SIMS, telecommunications executive; b. Millington, Tenn., Feb. 6, 1950; s. Robert Wheatley and Janis (Sims) F.; m. Margaret Jarvis, 1987; 1 child, Theodore Wheatley. BA, Am. U., 1972, MA, 1978. Rural indsl. officer Ministry of Commerce Industry U.S. Peace Corps, Molepolole, Botswana, 1979-81; mng. dir. Botswana Craft Mktg. Co., Gaborone, 1982-84; mgmt. trainee Pier One Imports, Rockville, Md., 1985; exhibits coord. Returned Peace Corps Vols., Washington, 1986; commodities procurement advisor U.S. AID, Kampala, Uganda, 1987-89; dir. internat. bus. devel. George Mason U., Fairfax, Va., 1990-95; v.p. mktg. Global Com Internat., San Antonio, 1996-97; dir. internat. bus. devel. George Mason U., Fairfax, Va., 1998—. Author play: The Tragedy of King Richard III, 1972. Mem. Adv. Neighborhood Commn., Washington, 1978-79. Mem. Free Trade Alliance, San Antonio C. of C., Am. Soc. Travel Agts. Avocations: skiing, theater, piano. Home: 20410 Settlers Vly San Antonio TX 78258-3147

FERRINI, JAMES THOMAS, lawyer; b. Chgo., Jan. 14, 1938; s. John B. and Julia (Marre) F.; m. Jeanne Marie Fontana, June 8, 1963; children: Anthony, Mary Caren, Emily, Joseph, Danielle. JD, Loyola U., 1963. Bar: U.S. Supreme Ct. 1963, U.S. Ct. Appeals (7th cir.) 1967, U.S. Ct. Appeals (8th cir.) 1969, U.S. Ct. Appeals (3d cir.) 1975, U.S. Ct. Appeals (6th cir.) 1982, U.S. Ct. Appeals (10th cir.) 1984, U.S. Ct. Appeals (4th cir.) 1987, U.S. Ct. Appeals (9th cir.) 1989. Sr. ptnr. Clausen Miller Gorman Caffrey & Witous, P.C., Chgo., 1963—; mem. pattern jury instructions Ill. Supreme Ct. Commn., Chgo., 1978-94. Contbr. articles to profl. jours. Mem. Mary Seat of Wisdom Parish, Park Ridge. Fellow Am. Acad. Appellate Lawyers; mem. ABA, Ill. Bar Assn., Chgo. Bar Assn. (chmn. civil practice com.), Ill. Assn. Def. Trial Counsel, Appellate Lawyers Assn. (pres. Chgo. chpt. 1978, 79), Justinian Soc. Roman Catholic. Avocations: handball, sailing, skiing, cooking. Office: Clausen Miller PC 10 S La Salle St Ste 1600 Chicago IL 60603-1098

FERRIS, DONALD WILLIAM, JR., lawyer; b. Terre Haute, Ind., Jan. 18, 1951; s. Donald W. and Margaret L. (Rademaker) F.; m. Heidi L. Salter, May 28, 1995. BA, U. Notre Dame, 1973; JD, U. Mich., 1976. Bar: Mich. 1976, U.S. Dist. Ct. (ea. dist.) Mich. 1980, U.S. Dist. Ct. (we. dist.) Mich. 1988, U.S. Ct. Appeals (6th cir.) 1982, U.S. Supreme Ct., 1987. Sr. asst. pub. defender Washtenaw County Pub. Defender, Ann Arbor, 1976-80; pvt. practice Ann Arbor, 1980-95; ptnr. Ferris & Salter, P.C., Ann Arbor, 1995—; instr. Washtenaw C.C., Ann Arbor, 1980-84. Mem. ATLA, Nat. Assn. Criminal Def. Lawyers, Washtenaw Trial Lawyers Assn. (pres. 1996-97), Criminal Def. Lawyers of Washtenaw County (pres. 1994-96), Washtenaw County Bar Assn. (chmn. criminal sect. 1986-90), Mich. Trial Lawyers Assn. (adv. bd. 1996-97). Democrat. Avocations: golf, travel. Office: Ferris & Salter PC 4158 Washtenaw Ave Ann Arbor MI 48108

FERRIS, ERNEST JOSEPH, radiology educator; b. Adams, Mass., Nov. 17, 1932; m. Alice Manchester, May 28, 1960; children: Susan, Paul, Kathryn, Donald. B.S. cum laude, Coll. of Holy Cross, 1954; M.D., Tufts U., 1958. Diplomate Am. Bd. Radiology, Am. Bd. Vascular and Interventional Radiology. Intern Boston City Hosp., 1958-59, resident in radiology, 1961-64; resident in medicine Boston VA Hosp., 1959-60; prof. radiology Boston U. Sch. Medicine, 1968-76; assoc. prof. radiology Tufts U. Sch. Medicine, Boston, 1967-68, lectr., 1970; clin. instr. radiology Harvard U., Boston, 1970; prof., chmn. dept. radiology U. Ark. Med. Sci., Little Rock, 1977—; trustee U. Ark. Med. Sci., Little Rock, 1982-83; rep. AMA residency rev. com. for radiology. Fellow Am. Coll. Radiology (program chmn. Ark. chpt. 1980-83), Am. Coll. Chest Physicians, Am. Soc. Lasers in Medicine and Surgery, Soc. Lasers in Medicine, Soc. Cardiovascular Intervention Radiology; mem. Am. Roentgen Ray Soc. (lectr., com. participant 1981-83), Radiol. Soc. N.Am. (com. participant, bd. dirs. 1988-96, pres.-elect 1995, pres. 1995-96), Soc. Chmn. Acad. Radiology Depts. (exec. com. 1983—, sec.-treas. 1985—, pres. 1987-88), Little Rock Club, Alpha Omega Alpha. Home: 13241 Rivercrest Dr Little Rock AR 72212-1452 Office: U Ark Med Scis Dept Radiology 4301 W Markham St Little Rock AR 72205-7101

FERRIS, FREDERICK JOSEPH, gerontologist, social worker; b. Troy, N.Y., June 2, 1920; s. John and Amelia (Deeb) F.; m. Ellen J. Walsh, June 12, 1965. BA cum laude, SUNY, Albany, 1942; MS, Columbia U., 1949, DSW, 1968. Head social studies dept. Heatly H.S., Green Island, N.Y., 1946-47; sec. info. svc. Greater N.Y. Fund, N.Y.C., 1949-51; exec. sec. N. Met. div. United Community Svcs., Boston, 1951-53, mem. rsch. div. com., 1953-57; dir. community orgn., asst. prof. Boston Coll. Sch. Social Work, 1953-57; dean, prof. Nat. Cath. Sch. Social Svc. Cath. U. Am., Washington, 1960-69, mem. adv. com. Gerontology Conf., 1985-91; with AARP-Nat. Ret. Tchrs. Assn., Washington, coord. White House Conf. on Aging, 1970-72; dir. planning and rsch. dept. and adminstr. Andrus Found., 1970-86; adv. assoc. prof. Fordham U. Sch. Social Svc., 1957-60; lectr. Adelphi U., Rutgers U., 1959-60; social planning cons. Am. Found. for Blind, 1958-59; proposal reviewer NSF; cons. Inst. Community Studies, United Way Am., 1970, Psychiat. Inst. Found.; del. White House Conf. on Aging, 1971, resource person, 1981; tech. rev. panel Nat. Coun. on Aging; mem. commn. on svcs. to aging Archdiocese of Washington, 1971-76; vice chmn. Joint Legis. Com., Boston, 1954-57. Book reviewer Social Thought. Mem. exec. com. Nat. Vol. Orgns. for Ind. Living for the Aging, 1972-74, 77-82; mem. commn. on aging Cath. Charities U.S.A., 1972—, chmn., 1978-84; bd. dirs. Social Svc. Exch., Boston, 1955-57, Child Welfare League Am., 1966-70, Cath. Internat. Union Social Svc., 1967-72, Christ Child Soc. Washington, 1967-73; treas., bd. dirs. Nat. Conf. Cath. Charities, 1971-74; bd. dirs. Associated Cath. Charities, Archdiocese of Washington, 1976-83; chmn. Washington com. 13th Internat. Conf. Schs. Social Work, 1965-66; active Montgomery County Commn. on Aging, 1987, mem. pub. policy com., 1st and 2d vice chmn., 1988-92, mem. exec. com., planning com., chmn., 1992-93, nominating com., chmn. econ. security com., 1988-90; mem. Am. Task Force for Lebanon; mem. parish coun. Ch. of the Annunciation, Washington, 1968-70, chair ch. and comty. com., chair task force on self-study, chair nominating com., mem. nominating com., mem. task force for self-study; bd. dirs. Montgomery County Dept. Social Svcs., 1994—. Capt. U.S. Army, 1942-46, maj. Res. Recipient Lasker Doctoral fellowship Columbia U., 1957-58, Pres.'s Centennial medal Cath. U. of Am., 1988, Outstanding Citizenship award Albany County LWV, 1942. Mem. Nat. Assn. Social Workers (chpt. treas. 1956-57, task force on svcs. to aging 1973-75), Mass. Conf. Social Work (dir., chmn. nominating com. 1956-57), Alumni Assn. Columbia U. Sch. Social Work (chpt. chmn. 1954-55, dir. 1956-59), United Comty. Funds and Couns. Am. (nat. adv. com. health and welfare svcs. 1955-57, coun. planning execs. 1957-59), Nat. Assn. Hearing and Speech Agy. (nat. tng. adv. com. 1963-70), Acad. Cert. Social Workers, Coun. Social Work Edn. (deans adv. com. fed. welfare agys. 1962-64, 66-68, ho. of dels. 1977-86, adv. bd. gerontol. content in social work edn. 1983-86), So. Gerontol. Soc. (dir. 1981-86), Am. Soc. on Aging, Assn. Gerontology in Higher Edn. (com. interorganizational rels., program com., Disting. Svc. Recognition award 1995), Gerontol. Soc., John Carroll Soc., Univ. Club Washington. Home: 5101 River Rd Bethesda MD 20816-1512

FERRIS, GEORGE MALLETTE, JR., investment banker; b. Washington, Mar. 11, 1927; s. George Mallette and Charlotte (Hamilton) F.; m. Nancy Strouce, Jan. 25, 1964; children: George Mallette III, Willard Bradley, Kimberly Anne, David Hamilton. BS in Engring. magna cum laude, Princeton U., 1948; MBA, Harvard U., 1950. Chmn. Ferris, Baker Watts, Inc., Washington, 1971—; bd. dirs. Entron Industries, N. Va. Tech. Coun., Internat. Exec. Svcs. Corps; commr. Md. Aviation Commn.; mem. exec. com. Fed. City Coun.; vice chmn. bd. dirs. Nat. Mus. Am. History; past bd. govs. N.Y. Stock Exch.; past chmn. Pres.'s Commn. on Mgmt. Aid Programs. Past gen. campaign chmn. United Givers Fund, 1966; past gen. chmn. sustaining fund drive Nat. Symphony Orch.; mem. Pres.'s Task Force Internat. Pvt. Enterprise; past chmn. investment adv. bd. AID. Recipient Princeton in Nation's Svc. award, Washingtonian award Jaycees, Order Red Triangel award YMCA Greater Washington, Silver Beaver award Boy Scouts Am. Mem. Washington Soc. Investment Analysts (past pres.), No. Va. Roundtable, Harvard Bus. Sch. Club Washington (past pres.), Met. Club, Chevy Chase Club (Md.), Burning Tree Club (Md.), The Ctr. Club (Balt.), Econ. Club of Washington (bd. dirs.), Phi Beta Kappa, Tau Beta Phi. Home: 5601 Kirkside Dr Bethesda MD 20815-7113 Office: Ferris Baker Watts Inc 1700 Pennsylvania Ave NW Washington DC 20006-4721

FERRIS, JAMES LEONARD, academic administrator; b. Bellingham, Wash., Jan. 15, 1944; s. Gerald Durward and Esther Evelyn (Larson) F.; m. Virginia Marie Dowde, June 23, 1972; children: Eric, Heidi. BSChemE, U. Wash., 1966; MS in Pulp and Paper Sci., Lawrence U., Appleton, Wis., 1969, PhD in Pulp and Paper Sci., 1974; Advanced Mgmt. Program, Harvard Bus. Sch., 1992. Mill engr. Weyerhaeuser Paper Co., Everett, Wash., 1966-67, scientist R & D dept., 1974-75; mgr. tech. svcs. pulp div. Weyerhaeuser Paper Co., Tacoma, 1975-80, dir. R & D, 1980-85, mgr. mfg. pulp div., 1985-88, v.p. rsch., 1988-96; pres. Inst. Paper Sci. and Tech., Atlanta, 1996—; trustee Ga. Tech. Rsch. Corp., 1996—; dir. Tech. Assn. of Pulp and Paper Industry, 1997—; dir. Atlanta Consortium for Higher Edn., 1998—. Lt. (j.g.) USN, 1970-72, Vietnam. Mem. TAPPI. Office: Inst Paper Sci and Tech 500 10th St NW Atlanta GA 30318-5794

FERRIS, JAMES PETER, chemist, educator; b. Nyack, N.Y., July 25, 1932; s. Richard B. and Mabel G. (Collier) F.; m. Joan E. Herrlich, Sept. 3, 1955 (div. 1985); children—Alison R., Laura J.; m. Susan Shipherd, Mar. 7, 1992. B.S., U. Pa., 1954; Ph.D., Ind. U., 1958. Postdoctoral researcher MIT, 1958-59; asst. prof. Fla. State U., 1959-64; research assoc. Salk Inst., 1964-67; assoc. prof. chemistry Rensselaer Poly. Inst., Troy, N.Y., 1967-73, prof., 1973-97, chmn. dept. chemistry, 1980-83, rsch. prof., 1997—; dir. N.Y. Ctr. for the Study of the Origins of Life, a NASA NSCORT, 1998—; vis. prof. Lab. Organic Chemistry, Swiss Fed. Inst. Tech., Zurich, 1985-86, Salk Inst., 1995; mem. life scis. adv. com. NASA, 1987-88, chair adv. panel on exobiology, 1995—; mem. task force on life scis. of space sci. bd. NRC, 1984-86, mem. space studies bd., 1990-94, past vice chair subcommn. F3 com. space rsch., sci. com. oceanic rsch. working group on hydrothermal sys., 1989-92; mem. panel on exobiology Am. Inst. Biol. Scis., 1984-90. Mem. editl. bd. Biosystems. Recipient Career Devel. award USPHS, 1969-74; NRC fellow, 1976. Fellow AAAS; mem. Am. Chem. Soc., Internat. Soc. for Study Origins of Life (treas. 1980-89, editor Origins Life and Evolution of Biosphere 1982—, pres. 1993-96, Oparin medal 1996), Clay Minerals Soc., Inter-Am. Photochem. Soc. Home: 10 Saddle Hill Rd Wynantskill NY 12198-7616 Office: Rensselaer Poly Inst Dept Chemistry Troy NY 12180

FERRIS, KATHERINE ANN, civic worker; b. Kankakee, Ill., Oct. 19, 1939; d. Sanford Brownell Jr. and Katherine Elizabeth (Troup) White; m. David Whitney Ferris, Nov. 14, 1959 (dec. Oct. 1983); children: Katherine Nancy, Benjamin Burr, Susanna Jane. AA, Kankakee (Ill.) C.C., 1982. Author of poems, essays, stories and letters. vol. First Presbyn. Ch., Kankakee, 1959-74, St. Patricks Grade Sch., Kankakee, 1969-75, Asbury United Meth. Ch., Kankakee, 1974-87; vol., sec., office aid Hist. Soc., Kankakee, 1974-78; vol., office aid St. Peters Episcopal Ch., Carson City, Nev., 1990-94; vol., cashier thrift shop Sr. Citizen Ctr., Carson City, 1991-94; vol., clk. Child and Family Svcs., Carson City, 1992-93; docent vol. Nev. State Mus., Carson City, 1993-94; vol., sec., typist Geneal. Soc., Kankakee; vol. Symphony and Youth Symphony, Kankakee, Christian Women and Couples, Kankakee, Little Theater and Youth Kankakee Valley Theatre; active St. Pauls Episcopal, Kankakee. Recipient 1st place Poets and Patrons, Inc., Chgo., 1982, 2d place Poets and Patrons, Inc., Chgo., 1982, award of appreciation McGraw-Hill Book Co., N.Y.C., 1984, award of poetic excellence Sparrowgrass Poetry Forum, 1994, Editors Excellence 1st place Creative Arts and Sci. Ent., Abilene, Tex., 1996. Mem. LWV, New Eng. Hist. Geneal. Soc. Avocations: family activities, writing.

FERRIS, MICHELLE L., women's health nurse; b. Springfield, Mass., Aug. 13, 1953; d. Henry and Elsie L. (Bissonnette) Marotte; m. Carl M. Ferris, May 20, 1988; children: Elsa Louise, Mariel Amelia, Spencer Emil. Diploma, St. Luke's Sch. Nursing, Pittsfield, Mass., 1974; student, Calif. State U., Northridge. Charge nurse New Eng. Bapt. Hosp., Boston, Riverside Hosp., North Hollywood, Calif., Valley Presbyn. Hosp., Van Nuys, Calif.; clin. II nurse labor and delivery Hartford (Conn.) Hosp.; case mgr. Metra Health Managed Care Ins.; RN, clin. investigator ctrl. office fraud and abuse dept. United Health Care Ins. Co.; cons. United Health Care Ins. Co., Pelham, Ala., 1998—; part time tchr. child birth classes; participated nursing grand rounds eizemengers syndrome Hartford Hosp., 1983. 2d lt. USAF, 1975-77. Home: 115 Emerald Lake Dr Pelham AL 35124

FERRIS, PAUL WAYNE, JR., religious studies educator; b. Sycamore, Ill., Mar. 25, 1944; s. Paul Wayne Sr. and Isabel Sarah Ferris; m. Lois Anne Fransen, June 19, 1965; children: Paul Wayne III, Heide Lynne, Jeremy Tyler Fransen. MA, Trinity Evangel. Div. Sch., 1969, MDiv, 1971; PhD, Dropsie Coll. Hebrew/Cognate, 1985. Prof. Moody Bible Inst., Chgo., 1968-71; pastor Emmanuel Bapt. Ch., Willow Grove, Pa., 1971-75; prof. Columbia (S.C.) Bibl. Sem., 1975-92; pres. Prairie Bible Coll., Three Hills, Alta., Can., 1992-98, Prairie Grad. Sch., Calgary, Alta., 1992-98; prof. Bethel Theol. Sem., St. Paul, 1998—; vis. prof. Trinity Evangel. Divinity Sch., Deerfield, Ill., 1971, Jerusalem U. Coll., 1986-91; dir. Ch. Advancement Resources, Columbia, 1985-92, Jerusalem U. Coll., 1976-92, 97-98; assoc. chaplain Lexington County Hosp., West Columbia, S.C., 1976-92. Author: (book) Genre of Communal Lament, 1992; contbr. articles to profl. jours., Anchor Bible Dictionary, Wyciffe Bible Ency. Named one of Outstanding Young Men of Am., Jaycees, 1976. Fellow Inst. for Bibl. Rsch.; mem. Soc. Bibl. Lit., Nat. Assn. Profs. of Hebrew, Evangel. Theol. Soc., Evang. Miss. Soc. Southern Baptist. Avocations: photography, traveling, graphics, woodworking. E-mail: pferris@bethel.edu. Home: 1822 Tioga Blvd New Brighton MN 55112 Office: Bethel Theol Sem 3949 Bethel Dr Saint Paul MN 55112

FERRIS, ROBERT ALBERT, lawyer, venture capitalist; b. N.Y.C., May 11, 1942; s. Albert Gerard and Helen Elizabeth (Jones) F.; m. Evelyn T. Jarvis; children: Robert C., Kathleen J. AB, Boston Coll., 1963; JD, Fordham U., 1966; grad. Advanced Mgmt. Program, Harvard U., 1974. Bar: N.Y. 1967, Calif. 1973. Assoc. Carter Ledyard & Milburn, N.Y.C., 1966-71; v.p., sec., gen. counsel Arcata Corp., Menlo Park, Calif., 1972-82; ptnr. Sequoia Assocs., Menlo Park, 1982-98; mng. dir. Caxton-Iseman Capital Inc., N.Y.C., 1998—; bd. dirs. Newell Mfg. Co., Anteon Corp., Clayton Group, Inc., Golden Valley Produce, LLC, Newell Indsl. Corp. Served with AUS, 1966-67. Home: 77 Elena Ave Atherton CA 94027-4025

FERRIS, ROBERT EDMUND, lawyer; b. Chgo., May 22, 1918; s. Edmund H. and Rose M. (Collins) F.; m. Jane H. Conybear, June 7, 1941; children: Robert E., John F., Kathy J. A.B., U. Ill., 1939, J.D., 1941. Bar: Ill. 1941, Fla. 1946. Mem. firm McCune, Hiaasen, Crum, Ferris & Gardner and predecessor firms, Ft. Lauderdale, Fla., 1947-88; of counsel Gustafson, Stephens, Ferris, Forman & Hall, P.A., Ft. Lauderdale, 1989-94; ret., 1994. Author: Cooperative Apartments Florida Real Property Practice II. Mem. Bd. Pub. Instrn. Broward County, 1955-58, chmn., 1958; founding bd. trustees Nova U.; chmn. Planning and Zoning Bd. Plantation, Fla., 1953-68; chmn. bd. trustees Broward Community Coll., 1959-71; pres. emeritus bd. visitors U. Ill. Coll. Law, 1989-90; mem. U. Ill. Pres.' coun., U. Ill. Found. With AUS, 1941-46; lt. col. Res. (ret.). Mem. ABA, Fla. Bar Assn., Broward County Bar Assn., Lauderdale Yacht Club, Ft. Lauderdale Country Club, Kappa Delta Rho. Baptist. Home: 120 N Bel Air Dr Plantation FL 33317-2567

FERRIS, ROGER PATRICK, architect; b. Buffalo, Jan. 3, 1952; s. Herbert Parkhill and Dolores (Murphy) F.; m. Yvonne DeHaas, May 20, 1995. BA, La Salle Coll., 1974; postgrad. Columbia U. Grad. Sch. Architecture and Planning, 1977-78; M in Design Harvard U. Grad. Sch. Design, 1982. Registered arch., Conn., N.Y., Mass., Vt., Maine, N.H., Ill., Tex., N.Mex., Washington, Va., N.C., Pa., R.I., N.J., Fla.; cert. Nat. Coun. Archtl. Registration Bds. Arch. Victor Christ-Janer & Assocs., New Canaan, Conn., 1974-78; prin. Landworks Assocs., Southport, Conn., 1978-80, Ferris Franzen Assoc., Southport, 1980-82, Ferris Architects, Westport, Conn., 1982—. Co-editor: Architectural Practices in the Nineties, 1996. Recipient Progressive Architecture Citation award 1991, Outstanding Design award James Beard Found., 1997; Loeb fellow in advanced environ. design Grad. Sch. Design Harvard U., 1991, 92. Mem. Am. Planning Assn., Conn. Soc. Archs. (Award of Merit), AIA (cert., New England Regional Award of Excellence in Architecture, 1985, 94, 96, 97, Builders Nat. Design and Planning award 1988, 90-92, 94, 98, Design Award Conn. Am. Inst. Architects 1985-86, 89, 93-94, 96-98), Nat. Trust for Hist. Preservation, Conn. Trust for Hist. Preservation (Conn. Preservation Design award 1994). Office: Ferris Architects 90 Post Rd E Westport CT 06880-3409

FERRIS, RONALD CURRY, bishop; b. Toronto, Ont., Can., July 2, 1945; s. Herald Bland and Marjorie May (Curry) F.; m. Janet Agnes Waller, Aug. 14, 1965; children: Elisa, Jill, Matthew, Jenny, Rani, Jonathan. Grad., Toronto Tchrs. Coll., 1965; BA, U. Western Ont., London, 1970; MDiv, Huron Coll., London, 1973, DD (hon.), 1982; DMin, Pacific Sch. of Religion, Calif., 1995; STD (hon.), Thorneloe U., 1995. Ordained to ministry Anglican Ch., 1970. Tchr. Pape Ave. Sch., Toronto, 1965-66; prin. Carcross Elem. Sch., Y.T., 1966-68; incumbent St. Luke's Ch., Old Crow, Y.T., 1970-72; rector St. Stephen's Ch., London, Ont., 1973-81; bishop Diocese of Yukon, Whitehorse, 1981-95, Diocese of Algoma, Sault Sainte Marie, Can., 1995—. Author: (poems) A Wing and a Prayer, 1990. E-mail: diocese-ofalgoma@on.aibn.com. Home: 134 Simpson St, Sault Sainte Marie, ON Canada P6A 3V4 Office: Diocese of Algoma, Box 1168, Sault Sainte Marie, ON Canada P6A 5N7

FERRIS, THEODORE VINCENT, chemical engineer, consulting technologist; b. Rochester, N.Y., Apr. 26, 1919; s. Theodore Clodoveo and Lucille T. (Pucci) F.; m. Doris Donaghue, June 26, 1943; children: William, Donald, Jean, Peter, Kathleen. BSChemE, MIT, 1941, MS in Chem. Engring. Practice, 1942. Registered profl. engr., Mass. Process engr. Allied Chem. Corp., Buffalo, 1942; devel. engr. GE Plastics, Pittsfield, Mass., 1943-44; process engr. Aspinook Corp., Lawrence, Mass., 1946-48; chief engr. Dehydrating Process Co., Boston, 1949-54; project engr., cons. Monsanto Co., Springfield, Mass., 1954-85; adj. prof. mech. engring. Western New England Coll., Springfield, 1986; cons. Ferris Tech. Svcs., Longmeadow, Mass., 1985—. Contbr. articles to profl. jours. Coach Little League, Longmeadow, 1955-65; cubmaster Boy Scouts Am., Longmeadow, 1955-65; co-author, mem. Bldg. Code Com., Longmeadow, 1955-56; chmn. Regional MIT Ednl. Coun., 1987—. Lt. USN Ordnance, 1944-46. Mem. Am. Inst. Chem. Engrs. (chmn. west mass. sect. 1958), Assn. Cons. Chemists and Chem. Engrs., MIT Club of Conn. Valley (treas. 1987—). Roman Catholic. Achievements include 10 patents for organic chemical processing and distillation; development of spray drying processes for resin emulsions including equipment design; computerized process simulations of chemical manufacturing; design of rupture disks for formaldehyde converters and emergency relief systems for a variety of chemical plant vessels; research on more efficient removal of methanol from formalin. Home and Office: 136 Lynnwood Dr Longmeadow MA 01106-2014

FERRIS, VIOLETTE IRENE, nursing educator; b. Mt. Holly, N.J., July 12, 1947; d. Charles R. and Violet F. (Brown) Gale; m. Seymour B. Ferris, Sept. 9, 1967; children: Dawn M., Gale I, Denise L., Charles S. RN, Trenton State Coll., 1968; BS in Health Care Adminstrn., St. Joseph Coll., Windham, Maine, 1988; edn. cert. nursing instr., Glassboro State Coll., 1988; D of Naturopathy, Clayton Sch. Natural Healing, 1994; DD, Univ. Life Ch., 1994; PhD, Am. Inst. Theology, 1995. Cert. administering sodium/bicarbonate to high risk infants, gentle therapeutic massage, edn. health occupations, health unit coord.; cert. health occupations tchr., N.J.; registered reflexologist, Internat. Inst. Reflexology; victim advocate cert. 1996; adv. victim advocate cert. 1997. Charge nurse, staff nurse Toms River Hosp., N.J., 1968-70; med. charge nurse Burlington County Meml. Hosp., Mt. Holly, N.J., 1970-77; agy. nurse Upjohn Health Care, Marlton, N.J., 1973-75; charge nurse, supr. Jewish Geriatric, Cherry Hill, N.J., 1981-83; agy. nurse Med Staff, Cherry Hill, 1980-83; LPN instr. Burlington County Vo Tech., Medford, N.J., 1985-92; curriculum developer Burlington County Inst. Tech., Westampton, N.J., 1992-94; health occupation instr. Burlington County Inst. Tech., Medford, 1994—; instr. Nat. Cert. Licensing Exam-Practical Nurse Rev. Student Practical Nurse Assn., Maplewood, N.J., 1986-88. Author: Decubitus Prevention/Care, 1985, Biological and Physical Science Abstracts, 1995-97. Organizer, pres. MADD of Burlington County, N.J., 1995—, state treas., 1998—. Mem. Am. Assn. Med. Assts., Nat. Assn. Health Unit Coords. (cert. health unit coord.). Avocations: knitting, crocheting, crafts, reading, antique/classical cars. Office: Burlington County Inst Tech Adult Edn Divsn 10 Hawkin Rd Medford NJ 08055-9412

FERRIS, VIRGINIA ROGERS, nematologist, educator; b. Abilene, Kans.; d. Ames P. and Virginia (Lucas) Rogers; m. John M. Ferris, June 20, 1953; children: Jeffrey Ames, Susan Virginia. Student, U. Kans., 1945-46; B.A. (Durant scholar), Wellesley Coll., 1949; M.S., Cornell U., 1952, Ph.D. (NSF fellow, Horton-Hallowell fellow), 1954. Teaching asst. plant pathology Cornell U., 1949-52, asst. prof. (1st woman prof. in dept.), 1954-55; cons. nematology West Lafayette, Ind., 1956-65; asst. prof. nematology, entomology Purdue U., 1965-70, asso. prof., 1970-74, prof., 1974—, asst. dean Grad. Sch., 1971-75, asst. provost, 1976-79; cons. NSF, 1979-82, 85, 88. Asso. editor Nematology News Letter, 1963-66, Jour. Nematology, 1974-76; contbr. articles to sci. jours. Recipient H.B. Schleman Gold medal, 1973, Outstanding Faculty award Assn. Women Students, 1977, Alumnae Achievement award Wellesley Coll., 1988. Fellow Soc. Nematologists, Ind. Acad. Sci.; mem. Am. Phytopath. Soc., N.Y. Acad. Sci., Helminthological Soc. Washington, Soc. Systematic Zoology (council 1978-81), Hennig Soc. (council 1981-85), Entomol. Soc. Am., Soc. Nematologists (sec. 1965-68, v.p. 1968-69, pres. 1969-70), European Soc. Nematologists, Assn. Systematics Collections (dir. 1975-76, 78-81), AAAS, Am. Inst. Biol. Sci., Phi Beta Kappa (senator United chpts. 1979-97), Phi Beta Kappa Assocs., Sigma Xi, Mortar Bd. (hon.), Phi Kappa Phi, Kappa Kappa Gamma, Sigma Delta Epsilon, Gamma Sigma Delta (hon.). Home: 2237 Delaware Dr West Lafayette IN 47906-1917 Office: Purdue U Dept Entomology West Lafayette IN 47907

FERRIS, WILLIAM MICHAEL, lawyer; b. Jackson, Mich., May 1, 1948; s. Franklyn C. and Betty J. (Dickerson) F.; m. Cynthia L. Muffitt, June 26, 1970 (div.); 1 child, Christina M.; m. Kathleen S. Santacroce, Mar. 21, 1987; stepchildren: Michael W. Santacroce, Megan D. Santacroce. BS with distinction, U.S. Naval Acad., 1970; JD summa cum laude, U. Balt., 1978, LLM in Taxation, 1994. Commd. ensign USN, 1970, advanced through grades to lt., 1974, resigned active duty, 1977; staff atty. Md. Legis., Annapolis, 1977-78, 80-81; assoc. Semmes, Bowen & Semmes, Balt., 1978-80; ptnr. Ferris & Robin, Annapolis, 1981-83, Krause & Ferris, Annapolis, 1983-87, Michaelson, Krause & Ferris, PA, Annapolis, 1987-91, Krause & Ferris, Annapolis, 1991—; adj. faculty Anne Arundel C.C., 1988—, U. Balt. Sch. Law, 1997—. Author: Maryland Style Manual for Statutory Law, 1985; article supr. Md. Annotated Code, 1981-84. Elder Woods Meml. Presbyn. Ch., Severna Park, Md., 1980—; chmn. Com. to rev. Anne Arundel County Code, Annapolis, 1985-86; temporary zoning hearing officer, Anne Arundel County, Annapolis, 1984-87; hearing officer Anne Arundel County Bd. Edn., Annapolis, 1990—; pres. Md. Bd. Dental Examiners, Balt., 1987-88; mem. inquiry com. Md. Atty. Grievance Commn., 1987—; ; mem. Md. Commn. on Jud. Disabilities, 1995—; treas. Bay Hills Cmty. Assn., 1990-96. Comdr. USNR, 1984-91, ret. Mem. ABA, Md. State Bar Assn., Maritime Law Assn., Anne Arundel County Bar Assn. Republican. Avocations: golfing, running, tennis. Home: 606 Bay Green Dr Arnold MD 21012-2009 Office: Krause & Ferris 196 Duke Of Gloucester St Annapolis MD 21401-2515

FERRIS, WILLIAM REYNOLDS, folklore educator; b. Vicksburg, Miss., Feb. 5, 1942; s. William Reynolds and Shelby Gibbs (Flowers) F.; 1 child, Virginia Louise. BA, Davidson (N.C.) Coll., 1964; MA in English, Northwestern U., 1965; MA in Folklore, U. Pa., 1967, PhD in Folklore, 1969. Asst. prof. English Jackson State U., 1970-72; assoc. prof. Am. and Afro-Am. Studies Yale U., 1972-79; prof. anthropology U. Miss., University, 1979-97; chmn. Nat. Endowment for Humanities, Washington, 1997—; dir. Ctr. for Study So. Culture, U. Miss., Oxford, 1979—; nat. advisor U. Pa. Black Lit. Ctr., Phila., 1989—; mem. history and memory group DuBois Inst., Harvard U., Cambridge, Mass., 1987—; vis. fellow Stanford U. Humanities Ctr., Palo Alto, Calif., 1989-90. Author: Local Color, 1982, Blues from the Delta, 1984; editor Afro-Am. Folk Arts and Crafts, 1983; co-editor Ency. of Southern Culture, 1989, You Live and Learn, And Then You Die and Forget It All, Ray Lum's Tales of Horses, Mules, and Men, 1992. Decorated chevalier des arts et des lettres (France), 1985, Officer in Order of Arts and Letters, 1994; named Disting. Alumnus, Rotary Found., 1989, One of Top 10 Tchrs. in Nation, Rolling Stone, 1991. Mem. Am. Folklore Soc. (exec. bd. 1987—), Am. Studies Assn. (nat. coun. 1991). Home: PO Box 40339 Washington DC 20016-0339 Office: NEH 1100 Pennsylvania Ave NW Washington DC 20004-2501

FERRISS, ABBOTT LAMOYNE, sociology educator emeritus; b. Jonestown, Miss., Jan. 31, 1915; s. Alfred William Overby and Grace Chiles (Mitchell) F.; m. Ruth Elizabeth Sparks, Dec. 21, 1940; children—John Abbott, William Thomas. B.J., U. Mo., 1937; M.A., U. N.C., 1943, Ph.D., 1950. Asst. prof. sociology Vanderbilt U., 1949-51; research social scientist Human Resources Research Inst., Air U., 1951-54; chief unit effectiveness br. Air Force Personnel and Tng. Res. Ctr., 1954-57; chief health survey br. Bur. of Census, 1957-59; supervisory survey statistician Outdoor Recreation Resources Rev. Commn., 1959-62; asst. study dir. NSF, 1962-67; research sociologist Russell Sage Found., 1967-70; prof. sociology Emory U., 1970-82, prof. emeritus, 1982—, chmn. dept., 1970-76; lectr. George Washington U., 1958-59, U. Md., 1959-61, No. Va. Ctr. of U. Va., 1960-70; guest prof. ZUMA, Mannheim, Fed. Republic Germany, 1989. Served with USAAF, 1943-46; CBI. NSF grantee, 1976-78. FellowInternat. Soc. Quality of Life Studies (disting. scholar award 1997); mem. Am. Sociol. Soc., Sociol. Research Assn., So. Sociol. Soc. (pres. 1986-87, editor The So. Sociologist 1981-84), Population Assn. Am. (sec.-treas. 1968-71, editor PAAAffairs), Ga. Sociol. Assn. (cert. of merit 1989), D.C. Sociol. Soc. (sec.-treas. 1965-68, pres. 1969-70, Stuart Rice award 1984), Midsouth Sociol. Assn., Internat. Sociol. Assn. Democrat. Episcopalian. Club: Cosmos, 70 (Washington). Author: National Recreation Survey, 1962; Indicators of Trends in the Status of American Women, 1971; Indicators of Change in the American Family, 1970; Indicators of Trends in American Education, 1969; Attitudes of Far Eastern Air Force Personnel Toward Natives, 1953; editor: Research and the 1970 Census, 1971; (with J.C. Glidwell) Reducing Traffic Accidents by Use of Group Discussions-Decision: An a Priori Evaluation, 1957; editor, pub. SINET (Social Indicators Network News), 1984-95, editor emeritus, 1995—; editor So. Sociologist, 1981-84; assoc. editor Social Forces, 1976-79; editor PAA Affairs, 1968-71, SINET Selections, Social Rsch. Indicators, 1990—; mem. editorial bd. Social Indicators Research, 1980—. Home: 1273 Oxford Rd NE Atlanta GA 30306-2426

FERRISS, JOHN ALDEN III, medical educator; b. Erie, Pa., Sept. 7, 1951; s. John Alden Jr. and Helen Ritchie (Collison) F.; m. Mary Elizabeth Maloney, June 20, 1981; children: Katherine, John IV, Elizabeth. BS in Biology, Nasson Coll., Springvale, Maine, 1973; MD in Medicine, Thomas

Jefferson U., Phila., 1977. Diplomate Am. Bd. Internal Medicine, Rheumatology, 1986. Battalion surgeon 2d Battalion, 12th Marine Regiment, Okinawa, Japan, 1978-79; chief primary care clinic U.S. Navy Hosp., Groton, Conn., 1980-82; cons. in rheumatology Cen. Vt. Hosp., Montpelier, 1986-88; asst. prof. medicine Pa. State U., Hershey, 1988-94, assoc. prof. medicine, acting chief of rheumatology, 1994-96, chief rheumatology, 1996-99. Vice chmn. Ctrl. Pa. chpt. Arthritis Found., Camp Hill, 1995-97, chmn., 1997-98; treas. Ch. of the Redeemer, Hershey, 1995; deacon United ch. of Christ. Comdr. USNR, 1978-91. Fellow ACP, Am. Coll. Rheumatology; mem. Am. Fedn. for Clin. Rsch. Office: Pa State U Coll Medicine 500 University Dr Hershey PA 17033-2360

FERRIS-WAKS, ARLENE SUSAN, financial analyst; b. N.Y.C., Apr. 4, 1954; d. Jack Charles and Marcia (Berman) Ferris; m. Robert Gilman Waks, Sept. 20, 1981; 1 child, Jason Lowell. BA cum laude, SUNY, Buffalo, 1977; M. of Libr. and Info. Sci., CUNY, 1981. Rsch. analyst Zimmerman & Assocs., Washington, 1981-83; sr. mkt. analyst Am. Stock Exch., N.Y.C., 1983-84; prin. mkt. analyst N.Y. Stock Exch., N.Y.C., 1984-97; sr. compliance officer J.W. Genesis Securities Corp., Boca Raton, Fla., 1996—; lectr./demonstrator N.Y. Stock Exch., 1989-96. Home: 8741 Wiles Rd Apt 304 Coral Springs FL 33067-1860 Office: 980 N Federal Hwy Boca Raton FL 33432-2708

FERRITER, EDWARD CHADWICK, naval officer; b. Washington, July 24, 1947; s. John Baker and Julia Ellen (Turner) F.; m. Patricia Eileen Laque, Nov. 28, 1975; children: John Laqua, Edward Andrew. BA in English, U. Va., 1970; MS in Oceanography, Naval Postgrad. Sch., Monterey, Calif., 1981; MA in Nat. Security & Strategic Studies, Naval War Coll., Newport, R.I., 1990; MA in Internat. Rels., Salve Regina U., Newport, 1990. Commd. ensign USN, 1973, advanced through grades to capt., 1994; ops. officer Patrol Squadron Five, Naval Air Sta., Jacksonville, Fla., 1985-87; battle group ops. officer Patrol Wings Atlantic Fleet, Naval Air Sta., Brunswick, Maine, 1987-89; comdg. officer Fleet Composite Squadron 6, Naval Air Sta., Norfolk, Va., 1990-92; sr. naval officer Air Land Sea Application Ctr., Langley AFB, Va., 1992-95; dir. Unmanned Aerial Vehicle Divsn. Def. Airborne Reconnaissance Office, Pentagon, Washington, 1995-97; staff Comdr. Naval Air Force, Norfolk, Va., 1997—. Editor Air Land Sea Bull., 1992-94. Dir. Running Man Cmty. Assn., Yorktown, Va., 1993-95; pres. Youth Baseball League, Brunswick, Maine, 1989. Decorated Navy Commendation medal, Meritorious Svc. medal, Def. Meritorious Svc. medal, Def. Superior Svc. medal. Avocations: scuba, boating, skiing, hiking, running. Office: Comdr Naval Air Force US Atlantic Fleet 1279 Franklin St Norfolk VA 23511-2406*

FERRITER, JOHN PIERCE, diplomat; b. Boston, Jan. 26, 1938; s. John Clement and Anna Belle (O'Brien) F.; m. Daniela Calvino, Mar. 17, 1970. B.A., Queens Coll., CUNY, 1960; LL.B., Fordham U., 1963; M.P.A., Harvard U., 1973. Bar: N.Y. Fgn. service officer Dept. State, 1964, ambassador to Djibouti, 1985-87, dep. asst. sec. energy and resources policy, 1987-89; chmn. standing group on long-term coop. Internat. Energy Agy., Paris, 1981-83, 87-89, dep. exec. dir., 1989—. Served with USMCR, 1957-62. Office: International Energy Agency, 9 rue de la Federation, 75739 Paris Cedex 15, France

FERRITOR, DANIEL E., educator; b. Kansas City, Mo., Nov. 8, 1939; m. Patricia Jean Ferritor; children: Kimberly Ann, Kristin Marie, Sean Patrick. BA, Rockhurst Coll., 1962; MA, Washington U., St. Louis, 1967, PhD, 1969. Tchr. grade sch. Raytown, Mo., 1962-64; program assoc., asst. dir. Nat. Program on Early Childhood Edn., 1970-71; asst. program dir. CEMREL Inc., St. Ann, Mo., 1969-70, assoc. dir. instrnl. systems program, 1970-71; asst. prof. sociology U. Ark., Fayetteville, 1967-68, assoc. prof., 1973-79, prof., 1979-85, chmn. dept., 1973-85, vice chancellor for acad. affairs, provost, 1985-86, chancellor, 1986-97, prof., 1997—. Author: (with Robert L. Hamblin, D. Buckholdt, M. Kozloff and L. Blackwell) The Humanization Processes, 1971; contbr. articles to profl. jours. Office: Dept Sociology Social Work Criminal Justice U Ark Office of Chancellor Fayetteville AR 72701*

FERRO, ELIZABETH KRAMS, lawyer; b. Cheverly, Md., Oct. 14, 1948; d. Harry Francis and Jeanne Elizabeth (Edwards) Krams; children: Stephen Christopher, Elizabeth Juliet, Alexander Eli; m. Jose M. Ferro, Oct. 7, 1994. BS magna cum laude, U. Md., 1977; JD, George Washington U., 1982. Bar: D.C. 1983. Adminstr. Raleigh Stores Corp., Washington, 1973-83; atty. Lansfam Mgmt. Corp., Balt., 1983—, corp. sec., 1986—. V.p., dir. Sidney Lansburgh III Found., 1989—; bd. dirs. Debel Foods Corp., Elizabeth, N.J., 1986. Mem. ABA, D.C. Bar Assn., Alpha Sigma Lambda, Phi Kappa Phi. Roman Catholic. Home: 10210 Riggs Rd Hyattsville MD 20783-1213 Office: Lansfam Mgmt Corp 300 E Lombard St Ste 1900 Baltimore MD 21202-6739

FERRO, WALTER, artist; b. N.Y.C., Oct. 6, 1925; s. Joseph Salvador and Mary Elizabeth (Potezna) F.; m. Lore Gausmann, Sept. 20, 1966; children—Elizabeth, Paula. Certificate, Bklyn. Mus. Art Sch., 1952. Art cons. One-man exhbns. include Wakefield Gallery, N.Y.C., 1960, Dominican Coll., Racine, Wis., 1962, Kings Coll., Briarcliff, N.Y., 1967, Hiram Malle Meml. Library, Pound Ridge, N.Y., 1988, Gallery L 9, Oberursel, Fed. Republic Germany, 1991; group exhbns. include Bklyn. Mus., 1953, U. Okla., 1959, Jersey City Mus., 1966, Phila. Mus., 1966; represented in permanent collections Met. Mus. Art, Nat. Mus. Am. Art, Smithsonian Instn. Served with USNR, 1942-44. Recipient Kenneth Hayes Miller Meml. award Audubon Artists, 1953; Kate W. Arms Meml. award Soc. Am. Graphic Artists, 1959; Guggenheim fellow, 1972. Address: PO Box 304 Pound Ridge NY 10576-0304

FERRUA, PIETRO MICHELE STEFANO, foreign language educator, writer; b. San Remo, Italy, Sept. 18, 1930; came to U.S., 1969; s. Libero and Anita Libera (Taggiasco) F.; m. Diana Jane Lobo Filho, June 24, 1957; children: Anna Piera, Franco Dorian. MA, U. Geneva, Switzerland, 1957, Cath. Pentifical U., Rio de Janeiro, 1966; postgrad., U. Fed., Rio de Janeiro, 1969; PhD, U. Oreg., 1973. Prof. Italian Ecole Internat., Geneva, 1958-62; prof. French Alliance Française, Rio de Janeiro, 1964-69; asst. prof. French Pontifícia U. Cath., Rio de Janeiro, 1966-68; lectr. Italian U. Gámafilho, Rio de Janeiro, 1968-69; asst. prof. Portuguese Portland (Oreg.) State U., 1970-73; prof. French Lewis and Clark Coll., Portland, 1970-87; prof. emeritus Lewis and Clark Coll., 1987—; cons. Nat. Endowment for the Humanities; chmn. Luso-Brazilian sect. 24th Pacific N.W. Conf. on Fgn. Lang; sec. workshop 8th INternat. Congress Comparative Lit., Budapest, 1976. Author: Gli Anarchici nella Rivoluzione Messicana: Praxedis G. Guerrero, 1976, Eros Chez Thanatos, 1979, Avanguardia Cinematografica Lettrista, 1984, Appunti Sul Cinema Nero Americano, 1987, Italo Calvino A San Remo, 1992, INI Art USA, Individual Expressions within the International Group, Espressioni individuali in seno al gruppo internazionale, 1996, L'Obiezione di Conscienza Anarchica in Italia, 1997, Conversations About Letterism, 1998. Founder Ctr. Internat. de Rsch. sur L'Anarchisme, Ctr. Brasileiro de Estudos Internats. Recipient Cittadino Benemerito, Municipality of San Remo, Italy, 1984; Chmn. grantee Oreg. Com. for the Humanities, Portland, 1983, Travel grantee Am. Coun. Learned Socs., 1979. Mem. Am. Assn. Tchrs. of French, Am. Assn. Tchrs. of Italian, Am. Assn. Tchrs. of Spanish and Portuguese, Internat. Assn. Comparative Lit., Romanian Study Group, Latin Am. Studies Assn. Avocation: multimedia creations. Office: Lewis and Clark Coll Palatine Hill Rd Portland OR 97219

FERRY, DAVID KEANE, electrical engineering educator; b. San Antonio, Oct. 25, 1940; s. Joseph Jules and Elizabeth (Keane) F. m. Darleen Heitkamp; Aug. 25, 1962; children: Lara Annette, Linda Renee. BSEE, Tex. Tech U., 1962, MSEE, 1963; PhD, U. Tex., 1966. Lectr. U. Tex., Austin, 1966; postdoctoral fellow U. Vienna, Austria, 1966-67; asst. prof., then assoc. prof. Tex. Tech U., Lubbock, 1967-73; sci. officer Office Naval Rsch., Arlington, Va., 1973-77; prof., head elec. engring. Colo. State U., Ft. Collins, 1977-83; Regent's prof., dir. Ctr. for Solid State Electronics Rsch. Ariz. State U., Tempe, 1983-89, Regent's prof., chair elec. computing engring., 1989-92, Regent's prof., 1992—; mem. microelectronics panel NRC, Washington, 1977-79; mem. materials rsch. coun. Def. Advanced Rsch. Projects Agy., Arlington, 1982-98; mem. supercomputer adv. group NSF, Washington, 1984-87. Author: (with D. R. Fannin) Physical Electronics, 1971; (with L. A. Akers and E. W. Greeneich) Ultra Large Scale Integrated Microelectronics, 1988, Semiconductors, 1991, (with R.O. Grondin) Physics of Submicron Devices, 1991, Quantum Mechanics, 1995, (with S.M. Goodnick) Transport in Nanostructures, 1997; over 525 pub. sci. articles; editor: GaAs Technology, 1985, GaAs Technology II, 1989; (with J. R. Barker and C. Jacoboni) Physics of Nonlinear Transport in Semiconductors, 1979, (with J.R. Barker and C. Jacoboni) Granular Nonelectronics, 1991, (with C. Jacoboni) Quantum Transport in Semiconductors, 1992, (with C. Jacoboni, A.P. Jauho, H.L. Grubin) Quantum Transport in Ultrasmall Devices, 1995; patentee in field. Fellow IEEE (Cledo Brunetti prize for advancements in nanosci. 1999), Am. Phys. Soc.; mem. Sigma Xi. Avocations: photography, skiing. Office: Ariz State U Elec Dept Tempe AZ 85287

FERRY, JAMES ALLEN, physicist, electrostatics company executive; b. Roxbury, Wis., Sept. 9, 1937; s. Darwin J. and Eleanor J. (Irwin) F.; m. Karen A. Greenwood, Feb. 8, 1964; children: Thomas E., Jennifer J. BS in Physics, U. Wis., 1959, MS in Physics, 1962, PhD in Physics, 1965. Research assoc. U. Wis., Madison, 1965-66; exec. v.p., chief operating officer Nat. Electrostatics Corp., Middleton, Wis., 1967-95; pres., CEO, chmn. bd. Nat. Electrostatics Corp., Middleton, 1995—. Patentee in field. Mem. Am. Phys. Soc. Home: 6810 Forest Glade Ct Middleton WI 53562-1711 Office: Nat Electrostatics Corp Graber Rd PO Box 620310 Middleton WI 53562-0310

FERRY, JOAN EVANS, school counselor; b. Summit, N.J., Aug. 20, 1941; d. John Stiger and Margaret Darling (Evans) F. BS, U. Pa., 1964; EdM, Temple U., 1967; postgrad., Villanova U., 1981. Cert. elem. sch. tchr., elem. sch. counselor. Indsl. photographer Bucksco Mfg. Co., Inc., Quakertown, Pa., 1958-59; math. and German tutor St. Lawrence U., Canton, N.Y., 1959-61; research asst. U. Pa., Phila., 1963; tchr. elem. sch. Pennridge Schs., Perkasie, Pa., 1964-74, 75-77, elem. sch. counselor, 1981—; pvt. practice counselor, real estate partnership Perkasie, 1981—; chair child study team Perkasie Elem. Sch., 1988-94; tutor math., German, St. Lawrence U., Canton, N.Y., 1959-61; supervisory tchr. East Stroudsburg U., Pennridge Schs., 1971-74; research asst. U. Pa., Phila., 1963; mem. acad. coms. for Pennridge Schs.; adj. faculty Bucks County Community Coll., 1983—; instr. Am. Inst. Banking, 1982—; notary pub., 1986—; mcpl. auditor, sec. bd. auditors, 1984-90, mcpl. auditor 1990—, chmn. bd. auditors 1990—; cons. in field. Author (with others) Life-Time Sports for the College Student: A Behavioral Objective Approach, 1971, 3d rev. edit. 1978, Elementary Social Studies as a Learning System, 1976. Vol. elem. sch. counselor Perkasie, 1979-80; mem. Hilltown Civic Assn., 1965-70, 92—; exec. com. chairperson Hilltown PTO, 1965-73; soloist Good Shepherd Episcopal Ch. Choir, Hilltown, 1964-77; steering com. Perkasie Sch., 1989-95; poll watcher, 1993; med. vol. Olympics, Atlanta, 1996; vol. Dublin Ambulance Squad, 1996—, House Rabbit Soc., Chadds Ford, Pa., 1998—; mem. Dublin Vol. Fire and Ambulance Co.; mem. prin.'s round table Perkasie (Pa.) Sch., 1997; vol. House Rabbit Soc. Southeastern Pa./Del. Foster Home and Sanctuary, Chadds Ford, Pa., 1998—. NSF grantee, Washington, 1972-73, Philanthropic Edn. Orgn. grantee, Doylestown, Pa., 1982; recipient Judith Netzky Meml. Fellowship award B'nai B'rith, Phila., 1979; Durning scholar Delta Delta Delta, Arlington, Tex., 1981, Am. Mgmt. Assns. scholar, N.Y.C., 1983, Statesman's award World Inst. Achievement, 1989, Achievement award Women's Inner Circle, 1990, Golden Acad. award for lifetime achievement, 1991; named to Internat. Tennis Hall of Fame, 2000 Notable Am. Women Hall of Fame, 1989, Cmty. Leaders of Am. Hall of Fame, 1990, Internat. Book of Honor Hall Of Fame, 1990, Internat. Bus. & Profl. Women's Hall of Fame, 1994, Lifetime Achievement Acad. Humane Soc. of U.S., Internat. Honor Soc. In Edn., Certificate of appreciation in recognition and acknowledgement for outstanding service and dedication as a member of the 1996 Atlanta Olympics Med. Team, 1997, Certs. of Appreciation Spring Mountain Ski Patrol, 1997, ARC, 1986. Fellow Internat. Biog. Assn.; mem. AAUW, NEA, NAFE, Humane Soc. U.S., World Inst. Achievement, Pa. State Edn. Assn. (polit. action com. for edn., chair Pennridge Schs. 1986—, del. leadership conf. 1987, 89), Pennridge Edn. Assn. (faculty rep. 1986-88, exec. coun. 1986—, negotiations resource com. 1987-89, 1990-93, steering com. Perkasie Sch. 1989-95, chairperson Child Study Team, 1988-94, Instructional Support Team, 1992—, selection com. for asst. supt. Pennridge Schs. 1993, selection com. for prin. Perkasie Sch. 1994, prin. round table 1997—), Am. Inst. Banking (chairperson 1987), U.S. Tennis Assn. (hon. life), Pa. and Mid. States Tennis Assn. (hon. life), U.S. Profl. Tennis Registry, Mid. States Profl. Tennis Registry, Women's Internat. Tennis Assn., Nat. Ski Patrol (Svc. Recognition award 1994, award outstanding svc. and dedication as a mem. of the 1996 Olympics med. team Atlanta., 1997), Spring Mountain Ski Patrol (Outstanding Aux. 1993, MOM Dedication award 1995, Outstanding Svc. and Dedication award 1996, 98, certificate of appreciation, 1997), Pa. Elected Women's Assn., Bucks County Assn. Twp. Ofcls., Bucks County Sch. Counselors Assn., Pa. Sch. Counselors Assn., Pa. Assn. Notaries, Am. Soc. Notaries, Internat. Fedn. Univ. Women, Internat. Platform Assn., World Inst. Achievement, Am. Biog. Inst. Rsch. Assn. (rsch. bd. advisors, bd. govs. 1989—), World Inst. of Achievement, Lifetime Achievement Acad., Rails-to-Trails Conservancy, World Wildlife Fund, Bucks County Sch. Counselors Assn., Highpoint Athletic Club, Pennridge Cmty. Rep. Club. (recording sec. 1986-91, publicity chmn. 1991-92, Pen care chmn. 1992—), Assn. Tennis Profls. Tour Tennis Ptnrs., Sierra Club, The Nature Conservancy, Nat. Wildlife Fedn., John Wayne Found., Mediterranean Club, Nockamixon Boat Club, Peace Valley Yacht Club, Kappa Delta Pi. Episcopalian. Avocations: archery, flying, music, parasailing, photography. Home: 834 Rickert Rd Perkasie PA 18944-2661 Office: Pennridge Schs 601 N 7th St Perkasie PA 18944-1507

FERRY, JOHN DOUGLASS, retired chemist, educator; b. Dawson, Can., May 4, 1912; s. Douglass Hewitt and Eudora (Bundy) F.; m. Barbara Norton Mott, Mar. 25, 1944; children—Phyllis Leigh, John Mott. A.B., Stanford U., 1932, Ph.D., 1935; student, U. London, 1932-34. Pvt. asst. Hopkins Marine Sta., Stanford, Calif., 1935-36; instr. biochem. scis. Harvard U., 1936-38; mem. Soc. Fellows, 1938-41; assoc. chemist Woods Hole Oceanographic Inst., 1941-45; research assoc. Harvard U., Cambridge, Mass., 1942-45; asst. prof. chemistry U. Wis., 1946, assoc. prof., 1946-47, prof., 1947-82, prof. emeritus, 1982—, Farrington Daniels Research prof., 1973-82, chmn. dept., 1959-67; chmn. Internat. Com. on Rheology, 1963-68; vis. lectr. Kyoto U., Japan, 1968, Ecole d'Ete, U. Grenoble, France, 1973. Author: Viscoelastic Properties of Polymers, 1961, 2d edit., 1970, 3d edit., 1980; coeditor: Fortschritte der Hochpolymeren Forschung, 1958-85. Recipient Eli Lilly award Am. Chem. Soc., 1946, Bingham medal Soc. Rheology, 1953, Kendall Co. award Am. Chem. Soc., 1960, Witco award, 1974, Colwyn medal Instn. Rubber Industry, U.K., 1972, Tech. award Internat. Inst. Synthetic Rubber Producers, 1977. Fellow Am. Phys. Soc. (high polymer physics prize 1966), Am. Acad. Arts and Scis.; mem. Nat. Acad. Sci., NAE, Am. Chem. Soc. (Goodyear medal Rubber div. 1981, Polymer div. award 1984), Am. Soc. Biol. Chemists, Soc. Rheology (pres. 1961-63), Internat. Soc. Hematology, d'Honneur Groupe Francais Rheologie, Soc. Rheology Japan (hon.), Phi Beta Kappa, Sigma Xi, Phi Lambda Upsilon, Alpha Chi Sigma. Lodge: Rotary. Home: 5015 Sheboygan Ave Madison WI 53705-2825

FERRY, MILES YEOMAN, state official; b. Brigham City, Utah, Sept. 22, 1932; s. John Yeoman and Alta (Cheney) F.; m. Suzanne Call, May 19, 1952; children: John, Jane Ferry Stewart, Ben, Helen, Sue Ferry Thorpe. BS, Utah State U., 1954. Rancher Corinne, Utah, 1952; pres. J.Y. Ferry & Son, Inc.; mem. Utah Ho. of Reps., 1965-66; mem. Utah Senate, 1967-84, minority whip, 1975-76, minority leader, 1977-78, pres. senate, 1979-84; mem. presdl. advisor commn. on intergovtl. affairs, 1984; mem. governing bd. Council State Govts., 1983-84; v.p. Legis./Exec. Consulting Firm, 1994—; chmn. Corinne Cemetery Dist., 1989—. Pres. Brigham Jr. C. of C., 1956-61, Nat. Conf. of State Legislators, 1984, v.p., 1982, pres.-elect, 1983, pres., 1984; v.p. Utah Jr. C. of C., 1960-61; nat. dir. Utah Jaycees, 1961-62; pres. Farm Bur. Box Elder County, 1958-59; food and agr. commr. USDA, commr. agr. State of Utah, 1985-93. Recipient award of merit Boy Scouts Am., 1976, Alumnusi of Yr. award Utah State U., 1981, award of merit Utah Vocat. Assn., 1981, Friend of Agr. award Utah Farm Bur., 1988, Cert. Appreciation USDA, 1988, Contbn. to Agr. award Utah-Idaho Farmers Union, 1989, Disting. Svc. award Utah State U., 1993, 94; named Outstanding Young Man of Yr., Brigham City Jr. C. of C., 1957, Outstanding Nat. Dir. U.S. Jaycees, 1963, Outstanding Young Man in Utah, Utah Jr. C. of C., 1961, Outstanding Young Farmer, 1958, One of 3 Outstanding Young Men of Utah, 1962, Rep. Legislator of Yr., 1984, One of 10 Outstanding Legislators of Yr., 1984. Mem. SAR, Sons Utah Pioneers, Gov.'s Cabinet, Utah Commn. Agr., Fed. Rsch. Com., Nat. Assn. State Depts. Agr. (bd. dirs. 1989), Western Assn. of State Depts. of Agr. (v.p. 1990-91, pres. 1991-92), Western U.S. Agr. Trade Assn. (sec. treas- elect 1987-88, pres. 1989-90), Utah Cattlemen's Assn., Nat. Golden Spike Assn. (dir. 1958—), Phi Kappa Phi, Pi Kappa Alpha. Republican. Address: 815 N 6800 W Corinne UT 84307-9737

FERRY, RICHARD MICHAEL, executive search firm executive; b. Ravenna, Ohio, Sept. 26, 1937; s. John D. and Margaret M. (Jeney) F.; m. Maude M. Hillman, Apr. 14, 1956; children: Richard A., Margaret L., Charles Michael, David W., Dianne E., Ann Marie. BS, Kent State U., 1959. CPA. Cons. staff Peat, Marwick, Mitchell, Los Angeles, 1965-69, ptnr., 1969; chmn., co-founder Korn/Ferry Internat., Los Angeles, 1969—; bd. dirs. Mellon/1st Bus. Bank, L.A., Avery Dennison, Pasadena, Calif., Dole Food Co., Calif., Pacific Life Ins. Co., Newport Beach, Calif. Trustee Calif. Inst. Tech., L.A., St. John's Health Ctr., Santa Monica, Calif.; bd. dirs. Cath. Charities, L.A., Calif. Cmty. Found., Hugh O'Brien Youth Leadership. Republican. Roman Catholic. Office: Korn/Ferry Internat 1800 Century Park E Ste 900 Los Angeles CA 90067-1512

FERSHTMAN, JULIE ILENE, lawyer; b. Detroit, Apr. 3, 1961; d. Sidney and Judith Joyce (Stoll) F.; m. Robert S. Bick, Mar. 4, 1990. Student, Mich. State U., 1979-81, James Madison Coll., 1979-81; BA in Philosophy and Polit. Sci., Emory U., 1983, JD, 1986. Bar: Mich. 1986, U.S. Dist. Ct. (ea. dist.) Mich. 1986, U.S. Ct. Appeals (6th cir.) 1987, U.S. Dist. Ct. (we. dist.) Mich. 1993. Assoc. Miller, Canfield, Paddock and Stone, Detroit, 1986-89; assoc. Miro, Miro & Weiner P.C., Bloomfield Hills, Mich., 1989-92; pvt. practice, Bingham Farms, Mich., 1992—; adj. prof. Schoolcraft Coll., Livonia, Mich., 1994—; lectr. in field. Author: Equine Law & Horse Sense, 1996; contbr. article to Barrister Mag. Bd. dirs. Franklin Cmty. Assn., 1989-92, sec., 1991-92; mem. Franklin Planning Commn., 1993-94. Recipient Nat. Ptnr. in Safety award Assn. for Horsemanship Safety and Edn., 1997, Outstanding Achievement award Am. Riding Instrs. Assn., 1998; named one of Crain's Detroit Bus. "40 Bus. Leaders Under 40", 1996. Mem. ABA (planning bd. litigation sect. young lawyers divsn., honoree Barrister mag., 1995, FBA (courthouse tours com. Detroit chpt., featured in Barrister mag. in 21 Young Lawyers Leading US and the 21st Century 1995), State Bar Mich. (exec. coun. young lawyers sect. 1989—, sec. -treas. bd. commrs. 1991-93, vice chmn. 1993-94, chmn. elect 1994-95, chmn. 1995-96, professionalism com. 1997—, grievance com. 1997—, structure and governance com. 1997—, rep. assy. 1997—), Oakland County Bar Assn. (prof. com. 1995—, Inns of Ct. com. 1995—, chair 1998—), Markel Equestrian Safety Bd., Women Lawyers Assn., Mich. Soc. Coll. Journalists, Phi Alpha Delta, Omicron Delta Kappa, Phi Sigma Tau, Pi Sigma Alpha. Avocations: horse showing, writing, music, art. Home: 31700 Briarcliff Rd Franklin MI 48025-1273 Office: 30700 Telegraph Rd Ste 3475 Bingham Farms MI 48025-4527

FERSON, LU ANN, medical and surgical nurse; b. Girard, Kans., June 12, 1935; d. Sammy M. and Lilly H. (Coury) F. Diploma, St. John's Sch. Nursing, Joplin, Mo., 1961; BSN, Mo. So. State Coll., 1990; postgrad., U. Mo., Kansas City, 1998—. Staff nurse operating room St. John's Hosp., Joplin, Mo., 1961-62; pvt. duty nurse N.Y. State Registry, L.I., 1964-68; psychiat. therapist Ansonia, Conn., 1969-72; staff nurse surg. dept. Waterbury (Conn.) Hosp., 1972-76; staff nurse urology dept. St. John's Med. Ctr., Joplin, 1976-79; IV nurse Danbury (Conn.) Hosp., 1980-85, McCune Brooks Hosp., 1986-88, HMSS, Inc., Lenexa, Kans., 1989-90; clin. coord. IV therapy home care dept. Mt. Carmel Hosp., Pitts., Kans., 1990-95; IV specialist, nurse mgr. Joplin (Mo.) Home Therapeutics, 1995-96; IV nurse Homebound Med., Joplin, 1996—; clin. instr. for practical nursing McCune Brooks Hosp., Mt. Carmel Hosp.; lectr. in field. With USN, 1962-64. Mem. ANA, Intravenous Nurses Soc., Nursing Honor Soc. of Mo. So. State Coll. Home: 603 S Monroe Ave Joplin MO 64801-3272

FERSON, SCOTT MELBOURNE, public relations executive; b. Medford, Mass., Dec. 8, 1961; s. Wayne Melbourne and Barbara Mary Ellen (Smith) F.; m. Lucy Jennifer Pullen, June 30, 1990; children: Andrew Melbourne, Cate Lovisa. BA, U. Mass., 1985. Dir. econ. devel. Congressman Chet Atkins, Lowell, Mass., 1985-87; town adminstr. Town of Westford (Mass.), 1988-90; press sec. Sen. Edward M. Kennedy, Boston, 1990-95; sr. v.p. McDermott O'Neill & Assocs., Boston, 1995—. Democrat. Unitarian. Home: 83 School St Belmont MA 02478-3012 Office: McDermott O'Neill & Assocs 1 Beacon St Ste 1600 Boston MA 02108-3106

FERST, WALTER B., lawyer; b. Jan. 3, 1951. Student, Washington U.; BA, U. Pa., 1972; JD, Emory U., 1975. Bar: Pa. 1975. Mem. Mesirov Gelman Jaffe Cramer & Jamieson, Phila.; instr. real estate and estate adminstrn. Pa. State U., 1978-80; lectr. Banking Law Inst., N.Y.C. and Chgo., 1989-90; spkr. S. Jersey Nursing Home Adminstrs. Assn., 1994. Chmn. bd. trustees Hillel Greater Phila. Recipient Am. Jurisprudence Estates award. Office: Mesirov Gelman Jaffe Cramer & Jamieson 1735 Market St Philadelphia PA 19103-7598*

FERSTENFELD, JULIAN ERWIN, internist, educator; b. Des Moines, Sept. 5, 1941; m. Sharon Rukas, Mar. 8, 1975; children: Megan Ann, Adam Justin. B.A., U. Iowa, 1963, M.D., 1966. Intern Milwaukee County Gen. Hosp., Milw., 1966-67, resident in internal medicine, 1969-71, fellow in infectious diseases, 1972-73; instr. internal medicine Med. Coll. Wis., Milw., 1974-75, asst. prof. medicine, 1975-78, asst. clin. prof. medicine and family practice, 1978-83, assoc. clin. prof. family practice and medicine, 1983—, internal medicine dir. Waukesha family practice residency, 1978—; practice medicine specializing in infectious diseases, Milw., 1974—; mem. staff Waukesha Meml. Hosp. (Wis.), West Allis Meml. Hosp. (Wis.), Elmbrook Meml. Hosp., Brookfield, Wis., Froedtert Meml. Hosp., Milw. Served as capt. M.C., U.S. Army, 1967-69; Korea. Fellow ACP; mem. Wis. Thoracic Soc., Am. Fedn. Clin. Research, Phi Beta Kappa. Contbr. articles, abstracts to profl. jours.

FERTEL, RUTH U., restaurant owner; b. 1927. Pres. Ruth's Chris Steak House, New Orleans, 1965-97, chmn., founder, 1997—. Office: 711 N Broad St New Orleans LA 70119-4206*

FERTIG, HOWARD, publisher, editor; b. N.Y.C.; s. Benjamin and Rose (Mallman) F.; m. Ellen C. Bandler (div. 1993); children: Paul, Daniel. B.A., NYU. Book reviewer Village Voice, N.Y.C., 1956-57; editor Queens Post, N.Y.C., 1957-60; asst. editor Commentary mag., N.Y.C., 1960; editor Alfred A. Knopf, Inc., N.Y.C., 1961-62; chief editor Univ. Library Paperbacks, Grosset & Dunlap, Inc., N.Y.C., 1962-65; pres., editor-in-chief Howard Fertig, Inc., N.Y.C., 1966—. Mem. MLA, P.E.N., Am. Hist. Assn., Friends of Columbia Library. Home: 49 E 10th St New York NY 10003-6153 Office: Howard Fertig Inc 80 E 11th St New York NY 10003-6000

FERTIG-DYKES, SUSAN BEATRICE, communications executive, human resourses professional; b. Panay, The Philippines, Jan. 9, 1944; d. Claude Edward and B. Laverne (Shockley) Fertig; m. George Middleton Dykes III, Sept. 18, 1965; children: George M. Dykes IV, Dirk Fertig Dykson. BA in Comm., U. Mo., 1982. Freelance writer, dir. producer Kansas City, Mo., 1981-83; dir. pub. svc. Sta. KSHB-TV, Kansas City, Mo., 1982-83; dir. broadcast svc. VA, Washington, 1983-86; pres., CEO Victoria Prodns., Ltd., Alexandria, Va., 1986-89; dir. media info. Bicentennial Presdl. Inaugural com., Washington, 1988-89; resume review Office Presdl. Personnel The White House, Washington, 1989; dir. policy, spl. projects Office Human Resources & Adminstrn. Dept. Vets. Affairs, Washington, 1989; dir. pub., visual comm. USDA, Washington, 1989-93; pres., CEO Fertig Comms., Alexandria, Croatia, 1993-96; CEO, bd. dirs. Fertig & Assocs. Internat., Zagreb, Croatia, 1993-96; dir. Inst. Cultural Affairs: Bosnia & Herzegovina, Sarajevo, 1996-97; internat. bd. dirs. ICA Internat., Brussels, 1994-98; mgr., pub. rels., human resource devel., civil soc. initiatives World Vision Internat., Bosnia and Herzegovina, 1997-99; internat. recruiter World Vision Internat., Washington, 1999—; dir. Inst. Cultural Affairs Internat. Belgium, Zagreb, 1993-96; chmn. Philippine Festival Commn., Washington, 1992, 1st v.p. 1994, pres.-elect, 1995; pres.-elect, chmn. Internat. Gold Screen Film/Video Competition, Nat. Assn. Govt. Communicators, 1994; talent, script cons., writer/prodr. Hrvatska Radio-Televizija, 1994-96; script cons. Jadran Film, Zagreb, 1994-96; dep. head ICA observer delegation to UN Internat. Conf. on Women, Beijing, 1995; participant numerous confs.; presenter in field. Ofcl. U.S. observer XVI Internat. Film Competition, Berlin, 1990; judge XVII Internat. Film Competition, Berlin, 1992, Internat. Contest Agrarian Cinema & Video, Zaragosa, 1992; judge Golden Eagle awards Coun. Internat. Non-Theatrical Events (CINE), 1992—, adv. coun., 1993—; judge Festival Internat. du Court Metrages de Mons, Belgium, 1994. Active Christ Ch., Alexandria, Va., 1983—; chmn. coord. George Bush for Pres., Alexandria, 1987-88; surrogate speaker women's groups Bush/Quayle and Victory 88, Washington; campaign tours N.H. primaries, 1988; mem. Pres.'s Club Rep. Nat. Com., Washington, 1984; bd. dirs. Found. for Aid to the Philippines, 1991-92. Mem. NATAS, Assn. Philippine Am. Women (pres. 1991-93), Women in Film & Video, Fed. City Rep. Women, Filipino-Am. Rep. Coun., Philippine Heritage Fedn., Rep. Nat. Com. (life). Episcopalian. E-mail: sfertig@worldvision.org. Fax: 202-547-0973/703-751-7626. Home: 205 S Yoakum Pky Apt 1021 Alexandria VA 22304-3826 Office: World Vision US 220 I St NE Washington DC 71000

FERYO, CATHERINE M. LESCOSKY, home health nurse, educator; b. Pottsville, Pa., Feb. 12, 1962; d. George A. Jr. and Helen F. (Novitsky) L. Diploma, Nursing Sch. Wilmington (Del.), 1982; student, Immaculata (Pa.) Coll. Cert. med.-surg. nurse, BCLS, CPR instr. Med.-surg. staff nurse Pottstown Meml. Med. Ctr., 1983-87, clin. coord., 1987-90; home health nurse Pottstown Vis. Nurse Assn., 1990-98, 1990-98; home health nurse Phoenixville (Pa.) Cmty. Vis. Nurse Svc., 1995-98, U. Penn Care at Home Nursing Svcs., Phoenixville, 1998—.

FERZACCA, WILLIAM, education educator, consultant; b. Iron Mountain, Mich., Apr. 26, 1927; s. William Olando and Santina Maria (Bruno) F.; m. Suzanne Rogers, Sept. 19, 1953 (dec. 1997); children: Steven, Matthew, Laurie; m. Ruth Hopewell, Jan. 30, 1999. BA, Mich. State U., 1950, MA, 1957. Cert. Am. Bd. Med. Therapists. Desk clk. Huron Hotel, Ypsilanti, Mich., 1948-50; asst. mgr. in tng. Hotel LaSalle, South Bend, Ind., 1950-52; swing and asst. chef Midland (Mich.) Country Club, 1952-54; head tchr. Harding Day Nursery, Kalamazoo, 1954; group tchr. Nursery Found., St. Louis, 1954-56, Mich. State Faculty Nursery Sch., East Lansing, Mich., 1956-57; dir. Jewish Community Ctr., St. Louis, 1957-59, nat. cons. for headstart, 1960-63; tchr. Child Guidance Clinic, St. Louis, 1959-65; pres., ednl. and child devel. cons. Learning Cons., Inc., Clayton, Mo., 1963-98; ret., 1998; child devel. cons. Affton (Mo.) Lindbergh Early Childhood, 1992-98, Edgewood children's Ctr., Webster Groves, Mo., 1965-98, Clayton Pub. Schs., 1967-78, Mehlville (Mo.) Pub. Schs. Early Childhood, 1975-98; tchr. evaluation and assessment of learning environment, com. early childhood Mo. Dept. Elem. and Secondary Edn., 1989—; mem. adj. faculty St. Louis U. Sch. Social Work, 1993-96, St. Louis C.C. Meramel Campus, 1993-96; masters of teaching program Webster U., 1992-95. Chair St. Louis County Family Svcs. Commn., 1985-94; reviewer Human Studies Com., St. Louis, 1986-94; bd. dirs. Nursery Found., St. Louis, 1987-89, Therapeutic Intervention Pre-sch., Ctr. for Holistic Health, 1992; mem. mental health disaster team ARC, Task Force Sudden Infant Death Syndrome Devel. Brochure; docent St. Louis Repertory Theater, 1998. With USN, 1945-47. Mem. Am. Bd. Psychotherapists, Am. Ortho-Psychiat. Assn., St. Louis Assn. Early Childhood Edn. (pres. 1957-58), Mo. Assn. Children with Learning Disabilities (bd. dirs. 1986-89), Kappa Delta Phi. Democrat. Avocations: harness racing, reading, gardening, jazz music, acting. Home: 260 Lake Coweta Trl Newnan GA 30263-5917

FESHBACH, HERMAN, physicist, educator; b. N.Y.C., Feb. 2, 1917; s. David and Ida (Lapiner) F.; m. Sylvia Harris, Jan. 28, 1940; children: Carolyn Barbara, Theodore Philip, Mark Frederick. B.S., CCNY, 1937; Ph.D., MIT, 1942; DSc, Lowell Tech. Inst., 1975. Tutor CCNY, 1937-38; instr. MIT, Cambridge, 1941-45, asst. prof., 1945-47, assoc. prof., 1947-55, prof., 1955-87, Cecil and Ida Green prof. physics, 1976-83, inst. prof., 1983-87, inst. prof. emeritus, 1987—, dir. Ctr. for Theoretical Physics, 1967-73, head dept. physics, 1973-83; cons. AEC; chmn. nuclear sci. adv. com. of Dept. Energy and NSF, 1979-82. Author: (with P.M. Morse) Methods of Theoretical Physics, 1953, (with A. deShalit) Theoretical Nuclear Physics, Nuclear Structure, 1974, Theoretical Nuclear Physics: Nuclear Reactions, 1992; editor: Annals of Physics, Contemporary Concepts in Physics; contbr. articles to sci. jours. Trustee Associated Univs. Inc., 1974-87, 1990-96, hon. trustee, 1996—. John Simon Guggenheim Meml. Found. fellow 1954-55; Ford fellow CERN, Geneva, Switzerland, 1962-63; recipient Harris medal CCNY, 1977, Nat. Medal of Sci., 1987. Mem. Am. Phys. Soc. (chmn. div. nuclear physics 1970-71, divisional councillor 1974-78, exec. com. 1974-78, chmn. panel on pub. affairs 1976-78, v.p. 1979-80, pres. 1980-81, Bonner prize 1973), Nat. Acad. Scis., NRC, Am. Acad. Arts and Scis. (v.p. Class I 1973-76, pres. 1982-86), AAAS (chmn. physics sect. 1987-88), Internat. Union Pure and Applied Physics (chmn. nuclear physics sect. 1984-90). Home: 5 Sedgwick Rd Cambridge MA 02138-2037 Office: MIT 77 Massachusetts Ave Cambridge MA 02139-4307

FESHBACH, MURRAY, demographer, educator; b. N.Y.C., Aug. 8, 1929; s. Benjamin and Lilly (Harfenist) F.; m. Muriel Joan Schreiner, Dec. 30, 1956; children: Michael Lee, David Steven. AB in History, Syracuse U., 1950; MA in History, Columbia U., 1951; Ph.D. in Econs., Am. U., 1974. Rsch. asst. Nat. Bur. Econ. Rsch., N.Y.C., 1955-56; economist U.S. Bur. Census, Washington, 1957-67, chief USSR population, employment, rsch. and devel. br., 1967-81; sr. rsch. scholar Georgetown U., Washington, 1981-84, rsch. prof. demography, 1984—; bd. dirs Internat. Rsch. and Exchanges Bd., program com., 1975-94; cons. Rand Corp., Santa Monica, Calif., 1981-90, U.S. Dept. Def., 1981-90, U.S. Dept. State 1982-83, NSF, 1987, World Bank, 1992-93, Health Found. of Russia, 1992, Russian Winter Campaign, 1992; sr. advisor CH2M Hill on Environ. Policy and Tech. in Russia; vis. prof. Columbia U., N.Y.C., 1983-84; Sovietologist-in-residence Office of Sec. Gen., NATO, Brussels, 1986-87; internat. adv. bd. Fernand Braudel Inst. World Econs., Sao Paulo, Brazil; disting. vis. lectr. U.S. Dept. State. Author: Ecological Disaster: Cleaning Up the Hidden Legacy of the Soviet Regime, 1995; (with Alfred Friendly Jr.) Ecocide in the USSR: Health and Nature Under Siege, 1992; editor-in-chief Environmental and Health Atlas of Russia, 1995; editor National Security Issues in the USSR, workshop held at NATO, Nov. 6-7, 1986, Brussels, Dordrecht, Nijhoff, 1987; contbr. articles to profl. jours. Mem. Coun. on Fgn. Rels. Served to sgt. U.S. Army, 1951-55. Recipient Silver medal Dept. Commerce, Washington, 1979; Woodrow Wilson Internat. Ctr. for Scholars fellow Smithsonian Instn., 1979. Mem. Assn. Comparative Econ. Studies (pres. 1985), Am. Assn. for Advancement of Slavic Studies (pres. Washington chpt. 1974-78, bd. dirs. 1979-82, v.p. 1984-85; nat. pres. 1985-86), Internat. Union for Sci. Study of Population, Internat. Inst. Strategic Studies, Ctr. for Strategic and Internat. Studies (adv. coun.). Democrat. Jewish. Club: Cosmos (Washington). Home: 11403 Fairoak Dr Silver Spring MD 20902-3136 Office: Georgetown U Sch Fgn Svc Ctr Eurasian Russian Study Washington DC 20057-1214

FESKOE, GAFFNEY JON, investment banker, management consultant; b. N.Y.C., Feb. 21, 1949; s. George Jon and Mary Margaret (Gaffney) F.; children: Gregory, Alexandra, Julia, Elizabeth. BS, Boston Coll., 1971; MBA, Fordham U., 1976. With Mfrs. Hanover Trust, N.Y.C., 1971-75; asst. treas. European-Am. Bank, N.Y.C., 1975-77; asst. v.p. Citibank, N.A., N.Y.C., 1977-80; asst treas. U.S. Filter Corp., N.Y.C., 1980-82; v.p. Bank of N.Y., N.Y.C., 1982-84; cons. Arthur D. Little, Inc., N.Y.C., 1986-88; exec. v.p. Madison One Group, N.Y.C., 1988-93; mng. ptnr. Horton Group Internat., N.Y.C., 1994-95; pres. Gaffney J. Feskoe & Assocs., LLC; ptnr. Handy Ptnrs., Inc., N.Y.C.; advisor Fed. Bus. Devel. Bank of Can.; mem. Balt. Exch., London. Trustee Yale Libr. Assocs., 1983—; mem. Darien (Conn.) Cable TV and Comm. Commn., 1985-87; mem. steering com. Friends of Yale Ctr. for Brit. Art; mem. London Libr. Mem. Bibliog. Soc. (London), Bibliog. Soc. Am., Boston Athenaeum (propr.), Champlain Soc. (Can.), Can. Soc. N.Y., Club of Odd Vols. (Boston). Roman Catholic. Office: 380 Lexington Ave New York NY 10168

FESLER, DAVID RICHARD, foundation director; b. Mpls., Sept. 21, 1928; s. John K. and Elsie Lampert Fesler; m. Elizabeth P.; children: Dael R., Nancy K., Janet C. B.B.A. with distinction, U. Minn., 1950. Pres. Lampert Yards, Inc., 1950-79; pres. Liberty State Bank, St. Paul, 1952-82, chmn. bd., 1982-85; treas. Mason City Builders Supply Co., Inc., 1972-85, The Sussel Co., Inc., 1975-79; pres. Wim Co., St. Paul, 1952-79, Liberty Agy., Inc., 1952-75; profl. vol. various orgns., 1960—. past pres., bd. dirs. Stout U. Found., Menomonie, Wis.; past bd. dirs., mem. fin. com., mem. exec. com. Shattuck St. Mary's Sch., Faribault, Minn., Inver Grove Heights (Minn.) Planning Commn., Indianhead coun. Boy Scouts Am., St. Croix Valley coun. Girl Scouts U.S., St. Paul Area YMCA, Family Svc. St. Paul Area, Edgcumbe Presbyn. Ch., Presbyn. Homes Minn., St. Paul Tech. Coll. Trust, U. Minn. Found., The Works, Mpls., Lyngblomston Found., Depot Found., Duluth, Minn., Minn. Planned Giving Coun.; sec. Minn. Natural Resources Found. Office: 1573 Selby Ave Ste 246 Saint Paul MN 55104-6328

FESSENDEN, STEPHEN FRANCIS, anesthesiologist; b. Tampa, Fla., Feb. 25, 1945; s. Price dela Vergne and Francis (Prescott) F.; m. Cristine Minotti, June 19, 1965; children: Rebecca Louise, John Michael, Carol Frances, Peter Xavier, Joseph Vincent. Student, St. Leo Coll., 1963-64; BA, U. S. Fla., 1967; MD, U. Fla., 1971. Diplomate Am. Bd. Anesthesiology. Resident in anesthesiology U. Fla., Gainesville, 1971-74; ptnr. Punches Molina Jaffe & Rosway, Ft. Pierce, Fla., 1976-81; pvt. practice Lakeland (Fla.) Regional Med. Ctr., 1981-92; ptnr. Anesthesia Pain Mgmt., Lakeland, 1993—. Maj. U.S. Army, 1974-76. Fellow Am. Coll. Anesthesiology; mem. AMA, Polk County Med. Assn. (chmn. pub. health com. 1996—), Fla. Med. Assn., Fla. Soc. Anesthesiologists, Am. Soc. Anesthesiologist, Am. Soc. Regional Anesthesia. Roman Catholic. Avocations: traveling, scuba diving, flying. Office: Anesthesia Pain Mgmt Cons 1429 Lakeland Hills Blvd Lakeland FL 33805-3206

FESSLER, PATRICIA LOU, retired library and media coordinator; b. Chgo., Dec. 1; d. Eugene Rickert and Dorothy May McKeen; m. Kermit John Fessler, June 23, 1951; children: Barbara, Peter, James. BA, Cornell Coll., 1950; MS, Chgo. State U., 1970. Cert. tchr., supr., Ill. Tchr. phys. edn. Harlan (Iowa) Pub. Schs., 1950-51, Blue Island Community High Sch. Dist. # 218, Oak Lawn, Ill., 1960-63, 67-70; coord. library, media A.B. Shepard High Sch., Oak Lawn, Ill., 1971-93; ret.; mem. adv. coun. Grad. Sch. Libr. Scis. U. Ill., Champaign, 1977-80; mem. libr./media adv. coun. State Bd. Edn., Springfield, Ill., 1980-83. Deacon Palos Park (Ill.) Presbyn. Ch., 1991-93. Named as one of Those Who Excel Ill., State Bd. Edn., 1987. Mem. AAUW (ednl. found. honoree 1992), Assn. for Ednl. Comms. and Tech. (bd. dirs. 1981-84, Spl. Svc. plaque 1989, bd. trustees 1984—, found. sec. 1988—), Ill. Ednl. Comms. and Tech. (pres. 1977-78, 80-82, Disting. Svc. award 1982-84, Meritorious Svc. award A.V. Am. 1983). Avocations: reading, knitting, needlework, golf, watching sports.

FESSLER, RAYMOND R., metallurgical engineering consultant; b. St. Nazianz, Wis., May 6, 1939. BS, Carnegie Inst. Tech., 1961; PhD in Metallurgy, MIT, 1965. Staff mem. Batelle Columbus Divsn., 1965-68, assoc. mgr. ferrous metallurgy sect., 1968-77, mgr. phys. metallurgy sect., 1977-82, assoc. dir. programs corp. tech. devel., 1982-83, mgr. transp. and structure dept., 1983-85, mgr. advanced materials dept., 1985-86; dir. basic indsl. rsch. lab. Northwestern U., Evanston, Ill., 1987-96; prin. cons. BIZTEC Cons., Inc., Evanston, Ill., 1997—. Fellow Am. Soc. Metals Internat. Achievements include research in physical metallurgy of steels, high temperature alloys and nonferrous metals; fracture toughness; metal physics; optical and electron metallography; advanced ceramics; process and physical metallurgy; polymers; corrosion; electrochemistry; mechanics. Address: 820 Roslyn Ter Evanston IL 60201-1724

FESTA, JO ANN V., nursing educator; b. Bklyn., Oct. 10, 1950; d. Lambert and Joan (Saxton) Schmidt; m. Robert Daniel Festa, July 22, 1972; children: Jillian L., Raymond S., Jeanine T. AAS, Nassau Community Coll.; BS, SUNY, Stonybrook; MS and PhD, Adelphi U., 1986; postgrad., SUNY at Stony Brook. RN, N.Y.; CPR instr.; cert. PRI assessment; cert. med.-surg. nurse. Staff nurse med.-surg., pediatrics Nassau County Med. Ctr., East Meadow, N.Y.; head nurse Brunswick Hosp., Amityville, N.Y.; instr. continuing edn. program Farmingdale Coll.; instr. Adelphi U., Garden City, N.Y.; prof. nursing Nassau Community Coll., Garden City, N.Y.; cons. home health care. Contbr.: Mosby's Comprehensive Review Nursing; content editor Mosby's Assesstest, Mosby's Calculation Drugs and Solutions. Mem. Am. Heart Assn., La Leche League, Sigma Theta Tau. Office: Nassau CC 1 Education Dr Garden City NY 11530-6719

FESTA, ROGER REGINALD, chemist, educator; b. Norwalk, Conn., Sept. 6, 1950; s. Reginald and Rosemary (Chappa) F. BA in Biology and Chemistry magna cum laude, St. Michael's Coll., 1972; MA in Agr., U. Vt., 1979; cert. in Adminstrn., Fairfield U., 1981; PhD in Edn., U. Conn., 1982. Tchr. Cen. Cath. High Sch., Norwalk, 1975-79, Brien McMahon High Sch., Norwalk, 1979-82; asst. prof. chemistry Truman State U. (formerly N.E. Mo. State U.), Kirksville, 1983-89, dir. Chem. Comm. Devel. Ctr., 1983-90, assoc. prof., 1989-97, prof., 1997—, coach men's volleyball, 1991—, dean frats., 1991-92; adj. prof. U. Conn., 1983. Author: National Curriculum Development Programming for Teachers of High School Chemistry, 1981, Fairfield County High School Chemistry Curriculum Handbook, 1982. Sec. Diocese Bridgeport (Conn.) Edn. Assn., 1978-79, sci. cons. schs. office, 1979, exec. adminstr., 1979; bd. dirs. Norwalk Community Services Agy., 1980-81. Named one of Ten Outstanding Young Men of Mo., Mo. Jaycees, 1986. Fellow Am. Inst. Chemists (pub. edn. com. 1980-83, edn. editor The Chemist Jour. 1981-95, mem. editl. bd. The Chemist 1986-91, bd. dirs. 1982—, chmn. nat. meetings com. 1982-91, 94-95, history com. 1982—, archivist 1983—, sec. 1991-93, pres.-elect 1994-95, pres. 1996-97); mem. Am. Chem. Soc. (founding editor The Fairfield Chemist 1978-79, assoc. editor Jour. Chem. Edn. 1980-89, vice chmn. edn. com. Western Conn. sect. 1979-81, chmn. elect Mark Twain sect. 1985, chmn. 1986, exec. bd. 1984-95, program chair 1984-95), St. Louis Inst. Chemists (founder 1984, pres. 1985-87, sec.-treas. 1987—), Acad. Sci. St. Louis, Assn. Frat. Advisors, Coll. Frat. Editors' Assn., Kirksville Jaycees (bd. dirs. 1983-86, sec. 1984-85, chair ret. sr. vols. com. 1985-87), Order of Omega, Delta Epsilon Sigma, Alpha Chi Sigma (assoc. editor The Hexagon 1984—), Sigma Phi Epsilon (bd. govs. 1994—, advisor Truman State U. chpt. 1991—). Democrat. Roman Catholic. Home: 114 E Mcpherson St Kirksville MO 63501-3570 Office: Truman State U 100 E Normal Ave SH202 Kirksville MO 63501-4221

FESTINGER, RICHARD, music educator, composer; b. Newton, Mass., Mar. 1, 1948; s. Leon and Mary (Ballou) F.; m. Karen Cummings Rosenak; stepchildren: Jacob Rosenak, Max Rosenak. Student, Stanford U., 1965-68, Berklee Coll. Music, 1970-72; BM magna cum laude, San Francisco State U., 1976; MA in Music, U. Calif., Berkeley, 1978, PhD in Music, 1983; post-grad., Calif. State U., Hayward, 1984-85, Calif. State U., San Jose, 1985, Stanford U., 1985-86, 91. Lectr. music theory U. Calif., Berkeley, 1982-83, Davis, 1989-90; assoc. prof. music San Francisco State U., 1990-94, assoc. prof., 1994—, dir. theory and composition, dir. Electronic Music Studio, 1992—; asst. conductor U. Calif. Symphony Orch., 1980-82; vis. asst. prof. music Dartmouth Coll., 1984; rsch. affiliate Ctr. for Computer Rsch. Music and Acoustics, Stanford U., vis. prof., 1996, 97; founding mem., artistic dir. music ensemble EARPLAY, San Francisco; resident Edward Macdowell Colony, 1983, 85; music panelist New England Found. for Arts, 1983, dir., Composition program, Summer Arts Festival, Calif. State U., 1996, 97. Recordings and publs. include Triptych for unaccompanied flute, Live at Pangaea Improvisations, vols. I and II, Impromptu for clarinet and piano, 1991, Triptych for solo flute, 1991, Two Little Piano Pieces, 1992, Septet, 1994, A Serenede for Six, 1995, Piano Variations, 1995, Trionometry, 1997, Twinning, 1997, String Quartet, 1997, A Serenade for Six, 1998. Recipient George Ladd Grand Prix de Paris, 1978, Nicolo di Lorenzo prize, 1981, Roslyn Schneider Eisner award, 1982, Prometheus Orch. Composition Competition award, 1982, Walter Hinrichsen award Am. Acad. Arts and Letters, 1993; Composition Assistance grantee Am. Music Ctr., 1982, Regents fellow U. Calif., 1976; Meet the Composer grantee, 1984, 91, Rsch. and Profl. Devel. grantee San Francisco State U., 1991, 93-94, Alfred Hertz Meml. fellow, 1977, Edward MacDowell Colony Norlin/MacDowell fellow, 1982, Wellesley Composers Conf. fellow, 1993, June in Buffalo Conf. fellow, 1994; Jerome Found. commn., 1990, San Francisco Contemporary Music Players commn., 1992, N.Y. New Music Ensemble commn., 1993, Alexander String Quartet commn., 1994, Fromm Found. commn., 1995, City Winds commn., 1996, Laurel Trio commn., 1997, Koussevitzky Music Found. commn., 1997, Left Coast Ensemble commn., 1998, Calif. Assn. Profl. Music Tchrs. commn., U. Calif. Davis commn. Office: San Francisco State U 1600 Holloway Ave San Francisco CA 94132-1722*

FETISOV, SLAVA, hockey coach, former professional hockey player; b. Moscow, May 20, 1958. Selected 12th round NHL entry draft Montreal Canadiens, 1978; selected 8th round NHL entry draft N.J. Devils, 1983, def., 1989-95; traded Detroit Red Wings, 1995-98; asst. coach NJ Devils, 1998—; mem. USSR Olympic Hockey teams, 1980 (silver medal), 1984 (gold medal), 1988 (gold medal); named to Soviet League All-Star team 1977-78, 81-88. Recipient Golden Stick award 1983-84, 87-88, 88-89; recipient Soviet Player of Yr. award, 1981-82, 85-86. Office: c/o NJ Devils PO Box 504 East Rutherford NJ 07073*

FETKOVICH, JOHN G., physics educator; b. Aliquippa, Pa., June 9, 1931; s. Michael and Anna (Klacik) F.; m. Anna Marie Argenziana, Dec. 13, 1958; children: Anne Marie, John G. BS, Carnegie Mellon U., 1953, MS, 1955, PhD, 1959. From postdoctoral rschr. to prof. physics Carnegie Mellon U., Pitts., 1959—; vis. scientist Argonne (Ill.) Nat. Lab., 1970-71, Rutherford High Energy Lab., England, 1971-72; spl. asst. to pres. acad. affairs Carnegie Mellon U., 1990-98, assoc. head physics dept., 1990-95. Fellow Am. Phys. Soc.; mem. AAAS, Penn Arts Assn., Pitts. Soc. Artists, Pitts. Ctr. Arts, Sigma Xi, Phi Kappa Phi. Avocations: furniture design and construction, art. Home: 113 Yorkshire Dr Pittsburgh PA 15238-2417 Office: Dept Physics Carnegie Mellon U Pittsburgh PA 15213

FETLER, ANDREW, author, educator; b. Riga, Latvia, July 24, 1925; came to U.S., 1939, naturalized, 1944; s. Basil Andreyevitch and Barbara (Kovalevski) Fetler-Malof; m. Carol J. McMahon, Aug. 29, 1960; 1 son, Jonathan. Student, U. Chgo., 1946-48; B.A., Loyola U., Chgo., 1959; M.F.A., U. Iowa, 1964. Tchr. Master Fine Arts Program in English, U. Mass., Amherst, 1964-89. Author: The Travelers, 1965, To Byzantium, 1976, Norton Anthology of Short Fiction, 5th edit., 1994; contbr. fiction to lit. quars. Served with AUS, 1944-46. Recipient grants for fiction writing Iowa Industries, 1962-63; grantee Mass. Arts and Humanities Found., 1976, Nat. Endowment for Arts, 1976-77, 83-84, Guggenheim Found., 1978-79; recipient O. Henry awards, 1977, 84.

FETLER, PAUL, composer; b. Phila., Feb. 17, 1920; s. William Basil and Barbara (Kovalerski) Fetler-Malof; m. Ruth Regina Pahl, Aug. 13, 1947; children: Sylvia, Daniel, Beatrix. MusB, Northwestern U., 1943; MusM, Yale U., 1948; PhD, U. Minn., 1956. From instr. to prof. music theory and composition U. Minn., Mpls., 1948—; vis. composer, condr. and lectr. various colls. and univs. Composer Contrasts for orch., 1958, Soundings for orch., 1962, Jubilate Deo for voices and brass, 1963, Te Deum for mixed voices, 1963, Four Symphonies, 1948-67, Cantus Tristis for orch., 1964; opera Sturge Maclean, 1965, A Contemporary Psalm for chorus, organ and percussion, 1968, Cycles for percussion and piano, 1970, The Words From the Cross for mixed voices, 1971, First Violin Concerto, 1971, Dialogue for flute and guitar, 1973, Lamentations for chorus, narrator, percussion and flute, 1974, Three Venetian Scenes for guitar, 1974, Dream of Shalom for mixed voices, 1975, Songs of the Night for voices, narrator and flute, 1976, Three Poems by Walt Whitman for narrator and orch., 1975, Pastoral Suite for piano trio, 1976, Celebration for orch., 1976, Three Impressions for guitar and orch., 1977, Five Piano Games, 1977, Sing Alleluia, 1978, Song of the Forest Bird for voices and chamber orch., 1978, Six Songs of Autumn for guitar, 1979, Second Violin Concerto, 1980, Missa de Angelis for three choirs, orch., organ and handbells, 1980, Serenade for chamber orch., 1981, Rhapsody for violin and piano, 1982 ; song cycle The Garden of Love for voice and orch., 1983, Piano Concerto, 1984; Capriccio for chamber orch., 1985; Frolic for Flute, Winds and Strings, 1986, Three Excursions, A Concerto for Percussion, Piano and Orchestra, 1987, String Quartet, 1989, Toccata for Organ, 1990, Twelve Sacred Hymn Settings, 1993, Divertimento for Flute and Strings, 1994, December Stillness for Flute, Harp and Voices, 1994, Suite for Woodwind Trio, 1995, Up the Dome of Heaven, Three Pieces for Mixed Voices and Flute, 1996; The Raven for basso, clarinet, percussion and string, 1998. Served with AUS, 1943-45. Recipient Guggenheim awards, 1953, 60, Soc. for Publ. Am. Music award, 1953, Yale U. Alumni Assn. cert. of merit, 1975, NEA award, 1975, 77, 87; Ford Found. grantee, 1958. Mem. ASCAP (ann. award 1962—), Sigma Alpha Iota (nat. arts assoc.). Home: 174 Golden Gate Pt Apt 32 Sarasota FL 34236-6602 Office: U Minn 100 Ferguson Hall Minneapolis MN 55455 *Ultimately there is no way to explain a new work of art if it does not explain itself.*

FETNER, ROBERT HENRY, radiation biologist; b. Savannah, Ga., Feb. 22, 1922; s. William Westcott and Lucille Fedora (Goodrich) F.; m. Mary Carolyn Guiney, July 8, 1972; 1 dau., Amber. B.S., U. Miami, Fla., 1950, M.S., 1952; Ph.D., Emory U., 1955. Mem. faculty Ga. Inst. Tech., Atlanta, 1955—; prof. radiation biology Ga. Inst. Tech., 1963—; dir. Ga. Inst. Tech. (Sch. Biology), 1964-70; cons. in field. Contbr. articles in field to profl. jours. Served with AUS, 1942-45. Decorated Combat Inf. badge. Mem. Ga. Acad. Sci. (editor bull. 1960-64), Sigma Xi, Phi Kappa Phi. Presbyterian. Patentee computer digitizer. Address: 2219 Walker Dr Lawrenceville GA 30043-2473 *My most rewarding career experience has been as a participant in the search for knowledge in science.*

FETNER, SUZANNE, small business owner; b. Fowlerville, Mich., May 4, 1929; d. Clayton Charles and Ferne Marie (Abbey) Fenton; m. William Clyde Peters, June 1950 (div. Aug. 1971); children: Randall Ray, Gregory Kim, Melinda Jane Peters Jones, Kelly Sue Peters Raymond; m. Eugene Macelee Fetner, Apr. 10, 1977. BS, Ea. Mich. U., 1967. Cert. early childhood edn., Fla. Tchr. kindergarten Fowlerville (Mich.) Pub. Schs., 1949-50, Horsebrook Sch., Lansing, Mich., 1950-51, Grand Ledge (Mich.) Pub. Schs., 1951-52, Manchester (Mich.) Pub. Schs., 1952-56, Holy Trinity Episcopal Sch., Melbourne, Fla., 1967-72; owner, tchr. Country Adventure, Inc., Melbourne, 1973-77; owner, dir. Woodlake Wonderland, Inc., Palm Bay, Fla., 1978-89, Country Beginnings, Inc., Palm Bay, 1985-93; mem. Presch. Adminstrv. Cons., Palm Bay, 1985-96; mem. adv. bd. Dist. Interagy. Coun. for Early Childhood Svcs., Brevard County, 1990-96, South Brevard H.S. Child Care, Melbourne, 1980-93. Author: (booklet) Stepping Stones, 1984. Founder, coord. Read to Your Child Week, Melbourne, Palm Bay, 1978-92. Named Unforgettable Lady of 80's Soroptomist Club, Melbourne, 1989. Mem. Nat. Assn. Child Care Profls., Brevard Assn. Children Under Six (pres. 1981-82), Fla. Assn. Children Under Six, So. Assn. Children Under Six. Republican. Methodist. Home and Office: 567 Birch St West Melbourne FL 32904-2541

FETRIDGE, BONNIE-JEAN CLARK (MRS. WILLIAM HARRISON FETRIDGE), civic volunteer; b. Chgo., Feb. 3, 1915; d. Sheldon and Bonnie (Carrington) Clark; m. William Harrison Fetridge, June 27, 1941; children: Blakely (Mrs. Harvey H. Bundy III), Clark Worthington. Student, Girls Latin Sch., Chgo., The Masters Sch., Dobbs Ferry, N.Y., Finch Coll., N.Y.C. Bd. dirs. region VII com. Girl Scouts U.S.A., 1939-43, nat. program com., 1966-69, nat. adv. bd., 1972-85, internat. commr.'s adv. panel, 1973-76, Nat. Juliette Low Birthplace Com., 1966-69; bd. dirs. Girl Scouts Chgo., 1936-51, 59-69, sec., 1936-38, v.p., 1946-49, 61-65, chmn. Juliette Low world friendship com., 1959-67, 71-72; mem. Friends Our Cabana Com. World Assn. Girl Guides and Girl Scouts, Cuernavaca, Mexico, 1969—, vice chmn., 1982-87; founder, pres. Olave Baden-Powell Soc. of World Assn. Girl Guides and Girl Scouts, London, 1984-93, bd. dirs., 1984—, hon. assoc., 1987; asst. sec. Dartnell Corp, Chgo., 1981-91, sec., 1991-98, bd. dirs. 1989-98; vice chmn. Dartnell Found., 1990—; bd. dirs. Jr. League of Chgo., 1937-40, Vis. Nurse Assn. Chgo., 1951-58, 61-63, asst. treas., 1962-63; women's bd. dirs. Children's meml. Hosp., 1946-50; v.p. parents coun. Latin Sch., 1952-54, bd. dirs. alumni assn., 1964-69; Fidelitas Soc., 1979, 96; mem. women's bd. U.S.O., 1965-75, treas., 1969-71, v.p., 1971-73; mem. women's svc. bd. Chgo. Area coun. Boy Scouts Am., 1964-70, mem. nat. exploring com., 1973-76; staff aide and ARC Motor Corps, World War II. Recipient Citation of Merit Sta. WAIT, Chgo., 1971, Juliette Low World Friendship medal Girl Scouts U.S.A., 1989; 1st recipient Medal of Recognition World Assn.Girl Guides and Girl Scouts, London, 1993; Baden-Powell fellow World Scout Found., Geneva, 1983. Mem. Nat. Soc. Colonial Dames Am. (life, Ill. bd. mgrs. 1962-65, 69-76, 78-82, v.p. 1970-72, corr. sec. 1978-80, 1st v.p. 1980-84, state chmn. geneal. info. svcs. com. 1972-76, corr. sec. 1978-80, hist. activities com. 1979-83, mus. house com. 1980-83, house gov. 1981-82), Chgo. Dobbs Alumnae Assn. (past pres.), Nat. Soc. DAR, Conn. Soc. Genealogists, New Eng. Hist. Geneal. Soc., N.Y. Geneal. and Biog. Soc., Newberry Libr. Assocs., Chgo. Hist. Soc. (life), Casino Club, The Racquet Club Chgo., Onwentsia Club, Union League Club. Republican. Episcopalian. Home: 1100 Pembridge Dr Apt 215 Lake Forest IL 60045-4215

FETRIDGE, CLARK WORTHINGTON, publisher; b. Chgo., Nov. 6, 1946; s. William Harrison and Bonnie-Jean (Clark) F.; m. Jean Hamilton Huebner, Apr. 19, 1980; children: Clark Worthington II, William Hamilton. BA, Lake Forest Coll., 1969; MBA, Boston Coll., 1971. Money market specialist Continental Ill. Nat. Bank, Chgo., 1971-73; with Dartnell Corp., Chgo., 1973-98; sr. v.p. Dartnell Corp., 1977-78; pres., CEO Dartnell

Corp., Chgo., 1978-98; chmn. bd., CEO Dartnell Corp., 1995-98, The Ravenswood Corp., 1998—. Author: Office Administration Handbook, 1975. Trustee Lake Forest Coll., 1977-85, 91-95, Jacques Holinger Meml. Found., 1983-95; pres. Dartnell Found., 1989—; trustee Latin Sch. Chgo., 1990-94; internat. commr. Boy Scouts Am., 1992-95, mem. nat. exec. bd., 1986-96, mem. internat. com., mem. Chgo. coun.; pres. U.S. Found. Internat. Scouting 1991-95; chmn. 1200 Club Ill., 1975-84; Rep. candidate for Congress, 1972; del. Rep. Nat. Conv., 1976; bd. dirs. Rep. Fund of Ill.; mem. pres.'s coun. Mus. Sci. and Industry, Chgo., 1986-94. Mem. Ill. Mfrs. Assn. (bd. dirs. 1990-96), Latin Sch. Chgo. Alumni Assn., St. Andrews Soc. (bd. dirs. 1994-97, 98—), Nat. Eagle Scout Assn. (chmn. 1985-88), Chgo. Pres. Orgn. (bd. dirs. 1998—), Tau Kappa Epsilon. Republican. Episcopalian. Fax: (773) 878-9491. Office: Ravenswood Corp 4660 N Ravenswood Ave Chicago IL 60640-4595

FETROW, GEORGE LAWRENCE, retired roadway engineering executive; b. Newberrytown, Pa., Mar. 22, 1935; s. John Gilbert and Laura Matilda (King) F.; m. Mary Ann Millar, Nov. 24, 1963; children: Karen, Jackie, George Jr. AS, York Jr. Coll., 1960. Cert. profl. land surveyor, Pa. Draftsman, surveyor Capitol Engring. Inc., Dillsburg, Pa., 1960-65; draftsman, designer Bachart-Horn, York, Pa., 1965-69; designer Pa. Turnpike Commn., Harrisburg, 1969-76, civil engr. II specifications, 1976-86, contract mgmt. supr., 1986-89, plans engr., 1989-96, roadway engring. mgr., 1996-97; ret., 1997. Chmn. coun. St. Paul's United Meth. Ch., Etters, Pa., 1993-97, chmn. fin. com., 1997—. With U.S. Army, 1955-58. Avocations: raising honey bees, master gardening, photography, travel by R.V., music directing.

FETSCHER, PAUL GEORGE WILLIAM, brokerage house executive; b. Bklyn., Dec. 21, 1945; s. William Paul Albert and Marion Beatrice (Darragh) F.; m. Eileen Melia. BS in CE, The Citadel, 1967. Cert. leasing specialist Internat. Coun. Shopping Ctrs. Owner/operator The Waterwheel Resort, Summerville, S.C., 1968; civil engr. Raymond Internat., N.Y.C., 1968-69; real estate rep. Fotomat Corp., LaJolla, Calif., 1969-70; real estate broker Newmark & Co., N.Y.C., 1970-71; v.p. Cushman & Wakefield, N.Y.C., 1971-80; pres. Great Am. Brokerage, N.Y.C., 1981—; bd. dirs. Protel Communications; guest lectr. NYU, Adelphi U.; instr. The Learning Annex, N.Y.C.; bd. dirs. Price/Costco; program com. Urban Land Inst., N.Y. Dist. Contbr. articles to various publs.; guest columnist for Nation's Restaurant News. Chmn. mem. svcs. com. Vanderbilt YMCA, bd. dirs. 1989-93; vol. Games for the Disabled Spl. Olympics, Nassau County, N.Y., 1986-89. Holds record running time from Providence to Boston. Competitor in over 230 marathons; number of races run exceeds 1,400; 1st American to run a marathon in USSR, 1982, East Germany, 1990; Nat. Champion 50km run. Mem. Internat. Coun. Shopping Ctrs. (pub. speaker, cert. leasing specialist), Real Estate Bd. N.Y., S.W. Conn. Comml. and Investment Coun. (v.p. 1973-89), Internat. Coun. Shopping Ctrs. (mem. program com., cert. leasing specialist, mem. steering com.), Nat. Bd. of Realtors, Nat. Assn. Real Estate Bds. (cert. comml. investment mem.). Avocations: track and field, long distance running. Fax: (212) 557-7272. E-mail: gtamerican@aol.com. Home: 516 W Beech St Long Beach NY 11561-3010 Office: Gt Am Brokerage 630 3d Ave Fl 15th Fl New York NY 10017-6705

FETTER, ALEXANDER LEES, theoretical physicist, educator; b. Phila., May 16, 1937; s. Ferdinand and Elizabeth Lean Fields (Head) F.; m. Jean Holmes, Aug. 4, 1962 (div. Dec. 1994); children: Anne Lindsay, Andrew James. AB, Williams Coll., 1958; BA, Balliol Coll., Oxford U., 1960; PhD, Harvard U., 1963. Miller rsch. fellow U. Calif., Berkeley, 1963-65; mem. faculty dept. physics Stanford U., 1965—, prof., 1974—, chmn. dept. physics, 1985-90, assoc. chmn. dept. physics, 1998—, asso. dean undergrad. studies, 1976-79, assoc. dean humanities and sci., 1990-93, dir. Hansen Exptl. Physics Lab., 1996-97; vis. prof. Cambridge U., 1970-71; Nordita vis. prof. Tech. U., Helsinki, Finland, 1976. Author: (with J.D. Walecka) Quantum Theory of Many Particle Systems, 1971, Theoretical Mechanics of Particles and Continua, 1980. Alumni trustee Williams Coll., 1974-79. Rhodes scholar, 1958-60; NSF fellow, 1960-63; Sloan Found. fellow, 1968-72; Recipient W.J. Gores award for excellence in teaching Stanford U., 1974. Fellow Am. Physics Soc. (chmn. div. condensed matter physics 1991), AAAS; mem. Sigma Xi. Home: 904 Mears Ct Palo Alto CA 94305-1029 Office: Stanford U Physics Dept Stanford CA 94305-4060

FETTER, RICHARD ELWOOD, retired industrial company executive; b. Lewisburg, Pa., Feb. 25, 1923; s. Elwood M. and Emily (Rogers) F.; m. Mary Virginia Gabriel, June 22, 1947; 1 dau., Molly Elizabeth. BS in Commerce and Fin., Bucknell U., 1947. With Gen. Electric Co., 1947-64; fin. mgr. indsl. heating dept. Gen. Electric Co., Shelbyville, Ind., 1954-64; controller F.W. Dodge Co. div. McGraw- Hill, Inc., 1964-65, v.p., 1965-67; financial v.p., treas. Standard & Poor's Corp., 1967-70; v.p. fin., adminstr. Research-Cottrell, Inc., Bedminster, 1970-75; v.p. fin., sec.-treas. Debron Corp., St. Ann, Mo., 1975-81; v.p. fin. Fasco Industries, Inc., Boca Raton, Fla., 1981-88, ret., 1988. Mem. fin. adv. com. Chatham Twp., 1971-74; Bd. dirs. Shelby County United Fund, 1963-64. Served with USAAF, 1945-47. Decorated Air medal. Mem. Fin. Execs. Inst., Phi Gamma Delta, Omicron Delta Kappa. Presbyn. (trustee 1960-63). Clubs: Rotarian (Shelbyville) (dir. 1960-61); Boca Raton Hotel and Club (Boca Raton, Fla.). Home: 5637 Cameo Dr N Boca Raton FL 33433-5322

FETTER, ROBERT BARCLAY, retired administrative sciences educator; b. Berwyn, Ill., May 6, 1924; s. Russell M. and Dorothy (Dupuis) F.; m. Audrey Louise Lillard, Feb. 7, 1951; children: Sarah Anne, Robert Alan, Martha Sue. B.S., Va. Poly. Inst., 1947; M.B.A., Ind. U., 1949, D.B.A., 1952; M.A. (hon.), Yale U., 1963. Instr., asst. prof. Ind. U., 1949-53; asst. prof. Mass. Inst. Tech., 1953-58; asso. prof. Yale U., 1958-63, prof. adminstrv. scis., 1963-86, Harold H. Hines Jr. prof. health care mgmt., 1986-89, chmn. adminstrv. scis., 1969-72; dir. Health Systems Mgmt. Group, Sch. Orgn. and Mgmt., 1976-89, Instn. Social and Policy Studies, 1969-89; cons. Rand Corp., 1963-71, E.I. duPont de Nemours & Co., Inc., 1960-72, McKinsey & Co., Inc., 1960-89, 3M, 1990-97; cons. editor R.D. Irwin, Inc., Homewood, Ill., 1960-90, WHO, 1972-73; v.p. Puter Assocs., Inc., 1971-77, chmn., 1977-82; v.p., dir. Health Systems Internat. Inc., 1982-90; dir. Dead River Co., 1984-94. Served with USNR, 1944-46. Recipient Baxter Found. prize Assn. Univ. Programs in Health Adminstrn., 1992; Ford Found. fellow, 1964. Fellow Acad. of Mgmt., Decision Scis. Inst.; mem. Ops. Research Soc. Am., Inst. Mgmt. Scis. (Franz Edelman prize 1990). Home: # 305 8795 W Orchid Island Cir Vero Beach FL 32963-9552

FETTER, WILLIAM ALLAN, computer graphics executive; b. Independence, Mo., Mar. 14, 1928; s. William Herbert and Edna Katherine (Werner) F.; m. Darlene Glea Wyss, Aug. 20, 1950 (div. 1962); 1 child, William Arnold (dec.); m. Barbara Ann Shaffer, Dec. 21, 1963; children: Brant Shaffer, Elena Katherine (twins). Student, Kansas City Jr. Coll., 1945-46, Kansas City U., 1948-49; BFA, U. Ill., 1952. Supr. computer graphics The Boeing Co., Wichita, Kans. and Seattle, 1959-69; v.p. Graphcomp. Scis., Newport, Calif., 1969-70; chmn. design dept., lectr. So. Ill. U., Carbondale, 1970-77; pres. So. Ill. Rsch. and Corp. Office (SIROCO), Carbondale, Ill., 1977—; also bd. dirs. So. Ill. Rsch. and Corp. Office (SIROCO), Bellevue, Redmond, Wash.; owner ORIGIN, Bellevue, Redmond, 1982—; presenter 3D conf. U. Tokyo, 1992; spkr. in field. Author: Human figures for Designers by Computer, 1983, Computer Graphics in Communication, 1964; author (TV program) Computer Graphics, The Accurate Eye, 1975; exhibited in show Mus. Modern Art, N.Y.C., 1976; patentee in field. Bd. dirs. Com. on Handicapped, Park Forest, Ill., 1957-58, Master Resources Council Internat., Seattle, 1980—; mem. UNESCO TACT Task Force, Washington, 1975-85. With U.S. Army, 1946-48; 2nd lt. USAFR, 1952-57. Recipient Cert. Merit Internat. Graphic Design, 1967, Letter Commendation USAF, Boeing Airplane Co., 1962, Bronze Medal Nat. Soc. Art Dirs., 1963. Fellow AIAA (assoc.); mem. Internat. Design Conf. (presenter 1976, 78), Soc. Info. Display, Indsl. Designers Soc. Am., N.W. Human Factors Soc., Mus. Modern Art Club, Alfa Romeo Owner's Club.

FETTERLY, LYNN LAWRENCE, real estate broker, developer; b. Ogdensburg, N.Y., Oct. 21, 1947; s. Keith C. and Florence E. Fetterly; m. Melody Bulriss, July 23, 1971; children: Kim Marie, Adam Lynn. AAS, Canton (N.Y.) Coll., 1967; BS, SUNY, Albany, 1969; MA, U. Detroit, 1972; cert. in mgmt., U. So. Calif., L.A., 1984. Auditor Arthur Andersen & Co., Rochester, N.Y., 1969-70; asst. v.p. Security Pacific Nat. Bank, L.A., 1972-75, Security Pacific Corp., L.A., 1976-77, Citibank, N.A., Rochester, 1977-81; v.p. regional mgr. Security Pacific Nat. Bank, N.Y.C., 1981-84; pres., CEO Security Pacific EuroFinance, Inc., London, 1984-88; vice chmn. Security Pacific Fin. Svcs. Sys., Inc., San Diego, 1988-90; pres., COO Security Pacific Fin. Svcs. System, Inc., San Diego, 1991-92; ind. real estate broker/developer, 1993—. With USAR, 1969-75. Mem. Dayton Valley Country Club. Republican. Presbyterian. Avocations: golf, tennis.

FETTERMAN, ALAN ROY, equipment sales executive; b. Shamokin, Pa., Sept. 8, 1958; s. LeRoy J. and Lorraine J. (Mirarchi) F. A in Am. Studies, Bucks County C.C., Newtown, Pa., 1997; student, U. Pa., Phila. Oil painter, sculptor Doylestown, Pa.; equipment sales exec. Opdyke Inc., Hatfield, Pa., 1983—. One-man show at Bianco Gallery, 1997, 98, 99; group exhbn. U.S. Artists, Phila. 1990, others throughout Europe and Brazil. Mem., chmn. Doylestown Boro Shade Tree Commn., 1990-97; mem. Bucks County Planning Commn., Doylestown, 1996—, James Michener Art Mus., 1997—, Woodmere Art Mus., 1996—; co-founder, bd. dirs. children's charity Doylestown Lahaska Ironman, 1985—; mem. Doylestown Hist. and Archtl. Rev. Bd., 1998—. With USAF N.G., 1980-84. Honoree membership for travel to Brazil, Rotary Internat., 1996. Mem. Doylestown Art League, Phila. Sketch Club, Salmagundi Club (N.Y.C.). Avocations: triathlons, fishing, guitar. Home: 284 N Main St Doylestown PA 18901-3732 Office: Opoyke Inc 3123 Bethlehem Pike Hatfield PA 19440-1315

FETTERMAN, ANNABELLE, packing company executive. Ceo. Lundy Packing Co., Clinton, N.C. Office: Lundy Packing Co PO Box 49 Clinton NC 28329-0049*

FETTEROLL, EUGENE CARL, JR., human resources professional; b. Hartford, Conn., Mar. 8, 1935; s. Eugene Carl and Gladys Marion (Crilley) F.; m. Barbara Ann Meeker, June 15, 1957; children: Eugene Carl III, Douglas Alan, Steven Joseph, Gary Michael. BA, U. Conn., 1957; MEd, Suffolk U., 1973. Supt. cumstomer svc., mgr. personnel svcs., dir. tng. Boston Gas Co., 1957-76; dir. Ea. Enterprises, Boston, 1977-81; dir. Associated Industries of Mass., Boston, 1981-87, v.p. human resources, 1987-89; pres. Fetteroll Assocs., South Portland, Mass., 1989—; tng. cons. Associated Industries of Mass., Boston. Author: Growing Teams, 1993; editor: Trainer's Resource, 1989. Vol. United Way, Mass. and R.I., 1965—; vice chmn. bd. trustees Medfield (Mass.) Pub. Libr., 1966-70; chmn. Sch. Land Acquisition Com., Medfield, 1963-65; bd. dirs. Growth Opportunity Alliance Lawrence/Quality Productivity Competitiveness, Salem, N.H. Mem. ASTD (pres. Mass. chpt. 1972-73, Bay Colonies chpt. 1981-82, mem. nat. ethics com. 1986—, Torch award 1979), Mass. Coalition for Adult Edn., Mass. Arms Collectors. Republican. Roman Catholic. Avocations: collecting antique powder flasks, photography, travel. Fax: 207-741-9031. Home and Office: Fetteroll Assocs PO Box 2887 South Portland ME 04116

FETTERS, DORIS ANN, retired secondary education educator; b. Bklyn.; d. John Joseph and Loreta Gertrude (Stratford) F. BA, Calif. State Coll., L.A., 1952. Cert. gen. secondary tchr. Tchr. Temple City (Calif.) H.S., 1954-55, L.A. City Schs., 1955-56; vice consul 3d sec. of embassy Dept. of State, Washington, 1957-60; tchr. U. Rafael Landivar, Guatemala, 1960-63, L.A. Unified Schs., 1964-90. Mem. Am. Fedn. Tchrs., United Tchrs. L.A. Democrat. Roman Catholic. Avocations: gardening, arts and crafts, reading.

FETTERS, J. MICHAEL, museum administrator. BA in Govt., Coll. of William and Mary, 1986. Account coord. Hannaford Co., 1987-88, account exec., 1988-89, office adminstr., 1989; pub. affairs specialist Nat. Air and Space Mus., Smithsonian Instn., Washington, 1989-92, dir. office pub. affairs, 1992—. Office: Nat Air & Space Mus 6th St and Independence SW Washington DC 20560

FETTERS, NORMAN CRAIG, II, banker; b. Pitts., Aug. 27, 1942; s. Karl Leroy and Hazel (Lower) F.; m. Linda Wood, Aug. 14, 1965; children—Eric Craig, Kevin Edward, Brian Allan. A.B., Westminster Coll., 1964; M.B.A., U. Pitts., 1965. Various positions to v.p. Security Pacific Nat. Bank, Los Angeles, 1965-66, 69-74, v.p., 1974-82; sr. v.p. Security Pacific Bank Washington, Seattle, 1982-92, SeaFirst Bank, Seattle, 1992-93; sr. v.p., dir. Security Pacific Savs. Bank, Seattle, 1993-94; v.p. Key Bank of Wash., Seattle, 1994-96, sr. v.p., 1996—. Served to lt. U.S. Army, 1966-69. Mem. Robert Morris Assocs., Lions Club (pres. 1988-89). Presbyterian (elder). Avocations: cross-country skiing, travel, hiking. Office: Key Bank of Washington PO Box 11500 Tacoma WA 98411-5500

FETTIG, JOHN MICHAEL, fund raising executive; b. Cin., Dec. 1, 1945; s. Fred and Katherine (Dennis) F.; m. June Ann Hancock, Aug. 21, 1966; children: Aaron, Pamela. BA, Hanover (Ind.) Coll., 1967. Cert. fund raising exec. Dir. devel. Spl. Olympics Nebr., Omaha, 1992—. Mem. Nat. Soc. of Fund Raising Execs. (Nebr. chpt., v.p. edn.), Rotary (pres. 1996-97, asst. dist. gov. 1998—). Presbyterian. Office: Spl Olympics Nebr 8801 F St Omaha NE 68127

FETZER, EDWARD FRANK, transportation company executive; b. Kossuth, Wis., Jan. 29, 1940; s. Frank J. and Nora Ann (Holsen) F.; m. Cheryl Jean Saler, Jan. 6, 1968; children: Kristine, Karen, Eric, Mark. Grad. high school, Mishicot, Wis., 1957. Relief clk. Soo Line R.R., Manitowoc, Wis., 1957-63; rate clk. Soo Line R.R., Neenah, Wis., 1963-66; staff asst. Menasha Corp., Neenah, 1966-68; traffic coord. Menasha Corp., Anaheim, Calif., 1968-73; asst. traffic mgr. Menasha Corp., Neenah, 1973-76, traffic analyst, 1976-78, corp. traffic mgr., 1986-99; pres. Menasha Transport Inc., Neenah, 1986-99. Mem. Project Bus., Jr. Achievement, Neenah, Wis., 1987-88. With U.S. Army, 1963-65. Mem. Transp. Devel. Assn., Wis. Motor Carrier Assn., Wis. Paper and Pulp Mfrs.' Transp. Assn. Inc., Delta Nu Alpha. Republican. Roman Catholic.

FETZER, MARK STEPHEN, lawyer; b. Louisville, Oct. 10, 1950; s. Sherrill Lee and Betty Ann (Meyer) F.; m. Pamela Ferrell, May 8, 1982; children: Martha Meyer, John Mark. Student, Purdue U., 1968-70; BA, U. Ky., 1973; JD, U. Denver, 1976. Bar: Colo. 1979, U.S. Dist. Ct. Colo. 1979. Sr. landman Minerals Svc. Co., Grand Junction, Colo., 1976-79; mgr. land & pub. affairs Marline Oil Corp., Danville, Va., 1980-85; mgr. R.R., utility & govtl. acquisition Dallas Area Rapid Transit, 1986-88; environ. counsel Cura, Inc., Dallas, 1989-91; dir., environ. counsel Terra-Mar, Inc., Dallas, 1991-92; environ. counsel Infodata Systems, Inc., Falls Church, Va., 1992-94; project mgr. Walcoff & Assocs., Inc., Fairfax, Va., 1994; sr. regulatory analyst Ecology and Environment, Inc., Idaho Falls, Idaho, 1995—. Mem. ABA, Colo. Bar Assn., Rocky Mountain Mineral Law Found., Air and Waste Mgmt. Assn. Evangelist. Avocation: bicycling.

FEUER, CY, motion picture and theatrical producer, director; b. N.Y.C., Jan. 15, 1911; s. Herman and Ann (Abrams) F.; m. Posy Greenberg, Jan. 20, 1946; children: Robert, Jed. Student, Inst. Mus. Art Julliard Found., 1928-32. Head music dept. Republic Pictures, 1938-42, 45-47; partner Feuer and Martin Prodns., N.Y.C., 1947—; mgr.-dir. San Francisco Civic Light Opera Assn., 1975-80; Pres. The League of Am. Theatres and Producers, 1989—. Theatrical prodns. include Where's Charley, 1948, Guys and Dolls, 1950, Can-Can, 1953, The Boy Friend, 1954, Silk Stockings, 1955, Whoop-Up, 1958, How To Succeed in Business Without Really Trying, 1961 (Pulitzer prize for drama), Little Me, 1962, Skyscraper, 1965, Walking Happy, 1966, The Goodbye People, 1968, The Act, 1977; producer: motion pictures Cabaret, 1972 (winner 8 Acad. awards), Piaf, 1975, Chorus Line, 1985. Inducted into the Theater Hall of Fame, 1994. Office: Feuer and Martin 630 Park Ave New York NY 10021-6544

FEUER, HENRY, chemist, educator; b. Stanislau, Austria, Apr. 4, 1912; came to U.S., 1941, naturalized, 1946; s. Jacob and Julia (Tindel) F.; m. Paula Berger, Jan. 19, 1946. M.S., U. Vienna, Austria, 1934, Ph.D., 1936. Postdoctoral fellow U. Paris, France, 1939; with dept. chemistry Purdue U., Lafayette, Ind., 1943-79; prof. chemistry Purdue U., 1961-79, prof. emeritus, 1979—; vis. prof. Hebrew U., Jerusalem, Israel, 1964, Indian Inst. Tech., Kanpur, India, 1971, Peking (China) Inst. Tech., 1979. Pres., contbr. Organic Electronic Spectral Data, Inc., 1962—; mng. editor Organic Nitro Chemistry Series, 1982—; mem. adv. bd. Turkish Jour. Chemistry; mem. editl. bd. Chimica Acta Turcica. Fellow AAAS; mem. Am. Chem. Soc., Chem. Soc., Sigma Xi, Phi Lambda Upsilon. Research, publs. in organic nitrogen compounds; discovered new methods for syntheses nitro compounds, cyclic hydrazides; research on mechanism of these reactions. Home: 726 Princess Dr West Lafayette IN 47906-2036 Office: Purdue U Dept Chemistry Lafayette IN 47907

FEUER, MICHAEL, office products superstore executive. Chmn., CEO OfficeMax, Shaker Heights, Ohio. Office: OfficeMax 3605 Warrensville Center Rd Shaker Heights OH 44122*

FEUERHERM, KURT KARL, artist, educator; b. Mar. 22, 1925; s. Erich Max and Erna Martha (Koenig) F.; divorced; children: Karl, Lisa, Eric. BFA, U. Buffalo, 1950; MFA, Cranbrook Acad. Art, Bloomfield Hills, Mich., 1951; fellow, Yale U., 1952. Instr. in painting Rochester (N.Y.) Inst. Technology, 1953-54, Meml. Art Gallery, Rochester, 1955-71; asst. prof. U. Rochester, 1956-71; conservator ICA Lab Oberlin (Ohio) Coll., 1972; assoc. prof. Monroe Conn. Coll., Rochester, 1972-73, Empire State Coll., Rochester, 1973-87; instr. internat. program Polimoda, Firenze, Italy, 1995-97; owner Guttenberg's Book Store, Rochester, 1983-86, Kurt Feuerherm Bookseller, Rochester, 1986-88, Hopper's, Rochester, 1980-83; vis. prof. painting Rochester Inst. Technology, 1976-85, mentor Empire State Coll., 1973-85; adj. faculty Monroe C.C., 1973-75; vis. prof. painting U. Wash., Seattle, 1969, numerous others.; judge for various local art exhibits; demonstrator painting techniques at various confs. Group shows include Meml. Art Gallery Lending and Sales Gallery, Rochester, 1960-86, Arena Exhbn., M.A.G., Rochester, 1974-93, Syracuse (N.Y.) State Fair, 1957-62, Everson Mus. of Art, Syracuse, 1957-70, Chautaugua (N.Y.) Exhibit Am. Art, 1969, others; one-man shows include Malton Gallery, Cin., 1978, 81, 82, Oxford Gallery, Rochester, 1974, 76, 78, 80, 83, 87, 90, East-West Gallery, Victor, N.Y., 1997, others: represented by Oxford Gallery, Secrest Gallery, No. Turo, Mass., Swainsborough Gallery, Wellfleet, Mass., Turtle Gallery, Deer Isle, Maine, others; several archtl. commns. With U.S. Army, 1943-45, ETO. Recipient scholarships Cranbrook Acad. Art, 1950-51, Norfolk Art Sch., 1950, Yale U., 1951-52, numerous painting prizes including Lillian Fairchild award U. Rochester, 1958, Henri Projansky award Rochester Finger Lakes Exhbn., 1969; represented in corp. collections including Lincoln First Bank, Rochester, Gannett Newspapers, Rochester, The Norry Corp., Rochester, Marine Midland Bank, Rochester, Security Trust Bank, Rochester, Rochester Savs. Bank, Cen. Trust Bank, Rochester, others. Home: 42 Wilmer St Rochester NY 14607-3130

FEUERLEIN, WILLY JOHN ARTHUR, economist, educator; b. Zurich, Switzerland, May 8, 1911; came to U.S., 1933, naturalized, 1940; s. Gustave Otto and Kate Elizabeth (Dickes) F.; m. Margaret Elizabeth Gammons, Apr. 11, 1942 (dec. Dec. 1990); 1 child, Elizabeth. A.B., George Washington U., 1935, M.A., 1935; Ph.D., Yale U., 1939; LL.D. (hon.), Fla. Atlantic U., 1983. Statistician Fed. Res. Bank of N.Y., 1940-42; economist Fgn. Econ. Adminstrn., Washington, 1942-44; fgn. trade specialist E. I. du Pont de Nemours & Co., Wilmington, Del., 1944-50; lectr. econs. and bus. adminstrn. Temple U., 1946-47, U. Del., 1947-49; mem. U.S. Econ. and Financial Mission to Peru, 1949-50; cons. UN and Internat. Monetary Fund, 1950-52; head UN Tech. Assistance Mission to El Salvador, 1952-56; vis. prof. econs. U. Fla., 1956-57; indsl.-economist ICA, U.S. Ops. Mission, Karachi, Pakistan, 1957-62; asst. dir. for devel. Office Brazil Affairs, AID State Dept., Washington, 1962-65; prof. econs. Fla. Atlantic U., Boca Raton, 1965-81, prof. emeritus, 1981—, chmn. dept., 1974-81, Rockefeller research fellow, 1938-39. Author: (with Hannan) Dollars in Latin America, 1940; also; UN publ., articles profl. jours. Mem. Fla. Atlantic U. Found., Atlantic Econ. Soc. Home: 6035 S Verde Trl Apt 111J Boca Raton FL 33433-4430 Office: Fla Atlantic U Dept Econs Boca Raton FL 33431

FEUERSTEIN, ALAN RICKY, lawyer, consultant; b. Buffalo, Oct. 24, 1950; s. Aaron Irving and Doris Jean (Davis) F.; m. June, 1973 (div. Jan. 1984); children: Marni Lauren, Jami Lynn; m. Susan T. Skop, Dec. 31, 1986; children: Christopher Borkowski, Philip Borkowski. BS cum laude, SUNY, Buffalo, 1974; LLB, U. Toledo, 1977. Bar: N.Y. 1978, Territorial and Dist. Ct. V.I. 1989, U.S. Supreme Ct. 1991, Fed. Ct. Puerto Rico 1993. Assoc. Law Offices of Salvatore Martoche, Buffalo, 1977-79; ptnr. Martoche & Feuerstein, Buffalo, 1979-81; lectr. Erie County Cen. Police Svcs. Acad., Buffalo, 1981-82; pvt. practice Buffalo, 1981-93; ptnr. Feuerstein & Santapia, Buffalo, 1993-94; prin. Law Offices of Alan R. Feuerstein, Buffalo, 1994-97; ptnr. Feuerstein & Smith, LLP, Buffalo, 1998—; lectr. Daemen Coll. Consortium, Buffalo, 1980-81; cons. in field. Mem. Erie County Reps., Buffalo, 1979—. Mem. Niagara Club, St.Thomas Yacht Club, The Buffalo Launch Club, Confrérie de la Châne des Rôtisseurs (chevalier). Republican. Jewish. Office: 17 St Louis Pl Buffalo NY 14202-1502 also: Woods & Woods 1 Comptroller Plz San Juan PR 00917 also: PO Box 502008 Saint Thomas VI 00805-2008

FEUERSTEIN, BERNARD A., lawyer; b. Bklyn., Aug. 17, 1928; s. Emil and Rae (Diamond) F.; m. Irene A. Marcus, Apr. 3, 1955; children: Susan, Barbara, Steven. AB, NYU, 1946, LLM, 1956; JD cum laude, Harvard U., 1949. Bar: NY 1950. Tchg. fellow U. Chgo. Law Sch., 1949-50; asst. dist. atty. New York County, N.Y.C., 1951; from assoc. to ptnr. Scribner & Miller, N.Y.C., 1953-62; ptnr. various law firms, N.Y.C., 1962-80, Baer, Marks & Upham LLC, N.Y.C., 1980—; dir., sec. Dale Carnegie & Assocs., Inc., Garden City, N.Y., 1978—. Trustee, counsel Ctr. Preventive Psychiatry, White Plains, N.Y., 1978-97, World Edn. Svcs., N.Y.C., 1992-95. 1st lt. U.S. Army, 1951-53. Mem. ABA, Assn. Bar N.Y.C. Office: Baer Marks & Upham LLP 805 3rd Ave New York NY 10022-7513

FEUERSTEIN, DONALD MARTIN, lawyer; b. Chgo., May 30, 1937; s. Morris Martin and Pauline Jean (Zagel) F.; m. Dorothy Rosalind Sokolsky, June 3, 1962 (dec. Mar. 1978); children: Eliza Carol, Anthony David; m. Summer Donna Berben, May 25, 1987; 1 child, Ashley Paul. BA magna cum laude, Yale U., 1959; JD magna cum laude, Harvard U., 1962. Bar: N.Y. 1962. Assoc. firm Cleary, Gottlieb, Steen & Hamilton, N.Y.C., 1962-63; law clk. to U.S. dist. judge N.Y.C., 1963-65; assoc. firm Saxe, Bacon & Bolan, N.Y.C., 1965; asst. gen. counsel, chief counsel instl. investor study SEC, Washington, 1966-71; ptnr., counsel Salomon Bros., N.Y.C., 1971-81, mng. dir., sec., 1981-91; exec. v.p., chief legal officer Salomon, Inc., 1991; spl. asst. U.S. Dept. Edn., Washington, 1993-94, sr. advisor, 1994—; spl. cons. Intersch. Group, N.Y.C., 1991-93. Editor Harvard Law Rev., 1960-62; mem. editl. adv. bd. Securities Regulation Law Jour., 1973-90; bd. editors Nat. Law Jour., 1978-90. Mem. vis. com. Northwestern U. Law Sch., 1975-78; bd. dirs. 1st All Children;s Theatre, 1976-85, chmn., 1976-82; mem. long-range planning and capital campaign coms. Brearley Sch., N.Y.C., 1981-83; mem. adv. bd. Solomon R. Guggenheim Mus., N.Y.C., 1984-91, chmn. bus. com., 1988-91, mem. internat. coun., 1991—; bd. dirs. Arts and Bus. Coun., 1980-85, v.p., 1985-88; trustee, v.p., mem. exec. com. Dalton Sch., 1983-89, 90-93; mem. dean's adv. coun. Harvard U. Law Sch., 1988-95, mem. steering com. and capital campaign, 1991-95; mem. com. on univ. resources Harvard U., 1988—; mem. vis. com. Harvard Grad. Sch. Edn., 1993-99; mem. tech. adv. coun., 1996—; chmn. tech. com. Georgetown Day Sch., 1997—, trustee, 1997—. Mem. ABA, Phi Beta Kappa, Pi Sigma Alpha. Home: 6430 Bradley Blvd Bethesda MD 20817-3246 Office: US Dept Edn Office Dep Sec FOB-6 Rm 7W213 400 Maryland Ave SW Washington DC 20202

FEUERSTEIN, HERBERT, food company executive; b. Vienna, Austria, Dec. 22, 1927; came to U.S., 1947, naturalized, 1953; s. David and Eva (Seif) F.; m. Regina Katz, June 10, 1956; children: Robert Allen, Lisa Ann. Student, Gymnasium, Berne, Switzerland, 1942-47; postgrad., CUNY, 1948-50. With Mondial Co., Inc., N.Y.C., 1948-60, sr. ptnr., 1960-64; chmn., pres. Rema Foods Inc., N.Y.C., 1964—; v.p., gen. mgr. imports Universal Foods Corp., Carlstadt, N.J., 1980-85; v.p., gen. mgr. commodities Universal Foods Corp., Teaneck, N.J., 1985-88; chmn., pres. Am. Pistachio Comm. Corp., 1990—; chmn. bd. On-Line Data Software, Pearl River, N.Y., 1986—, Source Atlantique. Pres. Jewish Cmty. Ctr. of Ft. Lee, N.J., 1982-95; chmn. bd. Israeli Bond Orgn., 1982-95. Mem. Assn. Food Industry (chmn. bd. 1995-97). Jewish. Home: 1530 Palisade Ave Apt 28F Fort Lee NJ 07024-5419 Office: Rema Foods 140 Sylvan Ave Englewood Cliffs NJ 07632

FEUERSTEIN, HOWARD M., lawyer; b. Memphis, Sept. 16, 1939; s. Leon and Lillian (Kapell) F.; m. Tamra Lynn Saperstein, May 19, 1968; children:

Laurie, Leon. BA, Vanderbilt U., 1961, JD, 1963. Bar: Tenn. 1963, Oreg. 1965. Law clk. to justice U.S. Ct. Appeals (5th cir.), Montgomery, Ala., 1963-64; teaching fellow Stanford U., 1964-65; assoc. Davies, Biggs et al (now Stoel Rives LLP), Portland, Oreg., 1965-71; ptnr. Stoel Rives LLP, Portland, 1971—; mem. Oreg. Gov.'s Task Force on Land Devel. Law, 1974; bd. realtors Condominium Study Com., Oreg., 1975-76. Editor-in-chief Vanderbilt Law Rev., 1962-63. Trustee Congregation Beth Israel, Portland, 1977-83; bd. dirs. Jewish Family & Child Service, Portland, 1975-81, Young Musicians and Artists Inc., 1991-96. Recipient Founder's medal Vanderbilt Law Sch., 1963. Mem. ABA, Oreg. State Bar, Multnomah County Bar Assn. (pres. real property com. 1976), Community Assn. Inst. (bd. dirs. Oreg. chpt. 1980-86), Am. Coll. Real Estate Lawyers. Office: Stoel Rives LLP Ste 2600 900 SW 5th Ave Portland OR 97204-1232

FEUERSTEIN, MARTIN, state legislator; b. Laconia, N.H., July 31, 1924; m. Pauline Feuerstein; 3 children. BS, U. N.H., 1948, U.S. Merchant Marine Acad., 1948; MEd, Plymouth State Coll., 1970. Elem. sch. prin., ret.; dir. Adult Basic Edn., Franklin, N.H., 1971—; city councilman Franklin, N.H., 1969-78, mayor, 1983; rep. dist. 13 N.H. Ho. of Reps., Franklin, 1991—; mem. health human svcs. com. N.H. Ho. of Reps.; mem. resources, recreation, and devel. coms., N.H. Ho. of Reps. Mem. Meridian Lodge No. 60. Address: 801 Central St Franklin NH 03235-2026

FEUERSTEIN, PAUL BRUCK, social services agency executive; b. Jersey City, Dec. 22, 1947; s. Charles Philip and Helen Lydia (Bruck) F.; m. Kathleen Olivia Pasco, May 30, 1970 (div. June 1979); children: Kristin, John Mark; m. Rebecca Ruth Eddy, Sept. 15, 1979; 1 child, Martha. BA in Philosophy, Concordia Sr. Coll., 1969; MA in Comm., NYU, 1971; M of Sacred Theology, Gen. Theol. Seminary, N.Y.C., 1973; MSW, Hunter Sch. Social Work, 1982; grad. Inst. Non-Profit Mgmt., Columbia U., 1997. Cert. social worker, N.Y.; ordained Episcopal priest. Mem. youth team Diocese of N.Y. Region II, 1973-74; asst. St. Mary's Episcopal Ch., Chappaqua, N.Y., 1973-74; assoc. rector Ch. of Holy Trinity, N.Y.C., 1974-76; assoc. chaplain St. Albans Sch., Washington, 1976-77; assoc. dir. Project Outward Bound Fedn. of Handicapped, N.Y.C., 1978-80; pres., CEO Barrier Free Living, N.Y.C., 1981—; founder, first chairperson N.Y.C. Coalition on Housing for People with Disabilities, 1979-81; mem. exec. com. Fedn. Mental Health Mental Retardation and Alcoholism Agy., N.Y.C., 1993—; mem. N.Y.C. Domestic Violence Task Force, 1993—, Traumatic Brain Injury Housing Task Force, 1994-97, N.Y.C. Medicaid Managed Care Task Force, 1995—; bd. dirs. Coalition of Vol. Mental Health Agys., N.Y.C., 1995—, Integrated Behavioral Health Sys., 1996—, Citywide Behavioral Network, 1998—. Author: Women and Children with Disabilities and Domestic Violence, 1997. Mem. Manhattan Borough Pres. Adv. Com. on Persons with Disabilities, 1987—; priest assoc. Ch. of the Holy Trinity, 1978—; bd. dirs. Open Congregation, 1990—; mem. Episcopal Diocese of N.Y. Commn. on Ministry with Persons with Disabilities. Fellow Brookdale Ctr. on Aging, Am. Orthopsychiat. Assn.; mem. Harlem Yacht Club. Avocations: sailing, model boat building, hiking, cross country skiing, painting. E-mail: pbfbflnyc@aol.com. Home: 431 E 118th St New York NY 10035-4318 Office: Barrier Free Living 270 E 2nd St New York NY 10009-7815

FEUERWERKER, ALBERT, history educator; b. Cleve., Nov. 6, 1927; s. Martin and Gizella (Feuerwerker) F.; m. Yi-tsi Mei, June 11, 1955; children: Alison, Paul. AB, Harvard U., 1950, PhD, 1957. Lectr. history U. Toronto, Ont., Can., 1955-58; rsch. fellow Harvard U., Cambridge, Mass., 1958-60; assoc. prof. history U. Mich., Ann Arbor, 1960-63, prof., 1963-96, chmn. dept., 1984-87; dir. U. Mich. Ctr. for Chinese Studies, Ann Arbor, 1961-67, 72-83; A.M. and H.P. Bentley prof. of history U. Mich., Ann Arbor, 1986-96, prof. emeritus, 1996—; dir. d'études École des Hautes Etudes en Scis. Sociales, Paris, 1981; vis. scholar Acad. Social Scis., Shanghai, China, 1981, 88, Sichuan U., Chengdu, China, 1988; joint com. on contemporary China, Social Sci. Research Council-Am. Council Learned Socs., 1966-78, 80-83, chmn., 1970-75; mem. com. on scholarly comm. with the People's Republic of China, Nat. Acad. Scis.-Social Sci. Rsch. Coun.-Am. Council Learned Socs., 1971-78, 81-83, vice-chmn., 1975-78. Author: China's Early Industrialization, 1958, History in Communist China, 1968, The Chinese Economy 1870-1911, 1969, Rebellion in 19th Century China, 1975, The Foreign Establishment in China, 1976, Economic Trends in the Republic of China, 1977, Chinese Social and Economic History from the Song to 1900, 1982, Studies in the Economic History of Late Imperial China, 1996, The Chinese Economy, 1870-1949, 1996; co-editor: Cambridge History of China, vol. 13, 1986; mem. editl. bd. Am. Hist. Rev., 1970-75, The China Quar., 1967-91, Comparative Studies in Soc. and History, 1964—. Served with AUS, 1946-47. Fellow NEH, 1971-72, Social Sci. Research Council-Am. Council of Learned Socs., 1962-63, Guggenheim Found., 1987-88. Fellow AAAS; mem. Assn. for Asian Studies (v.p. 1990, pres. 1991), Nat. Com. on U.S.-China Rels. Home: 1224 Ardmoor Ave Ann Arbor MI 48103-5346 Office: U Mich Ctr for Chinese Studies 1080 S University Ave Ste 3668 Ann Arbor MI 48109-1107

FEUERZEIG, HENRY LOUIS, lawyer; b. Chgo., Dec. 12, 1938; s. Samuel Alexander Feuerzeig and Esther Fleeger; m. Penny Zweigenhaft, Apr. 8, 1967; children: Paul Lawrence, Darcy Elizabeth. B.S., U. Wis., 1962; J.D., George Washington U., 1970. Bar: D.C., V.I., Fla., Md. Reporter various newspapers Dubuque, Iowa, Chgo., Madison, Wis., Cin. and Washington, 1962-64, 65-67; assoc. Sachs, Greenebaum, Frohlich & Tayler, Washington, 1970-72; asst. atty. gen. V.I. Dept. Law, St. Thomas, 1972-73, chief civil and adminstrv. law div., 1973-74, 1st asst. atty. gen., 1974; ptnr. Feuerzeig & Zebedee, St. Thomas, 1974-76; judge Territorial Ct. V.I., St. Thomas, 1977-87; del., chmn. jud. powers and functions com. 4th V.I. Constl. Conv., 1981; ptnr. Dudley, Topper and Feuerzeig, St. Thomas, 1987—; mem. supervisory bd. V.I. Law Enforcement Planning Commn., 1978-87, Juvenile Justice and Delinquency Prevention, 1988—; mem. V.I. Juvenile Code Revision Task Force, 1978-83, V.I. Criminal Code Revision Task Force, 1978-87. Mem. Montgomery County (Md.) Dem. State Ctrl. Com., 1970-72; mem. V.I. Indsl. Devel. Commn., 1976; bd. dirs. Environ. Studies Program, St. Thomas, 1977-80, United Way, 1986-92; bd. reps. Hebrew Congregation of St. Thomas, 1983-90, 96—, co-chair Bicentennial Campaign com., 1993-97; trustee Antilles Sch., St. Thomas, 1983-91; mem. adv. coun. Youth Multi-Svc. Ctr., 1989-94; dir. Cmty. Found. of V.I., 1992—, pres., 1993-94. Sigma Delta Chi scholar, 1962; Congressional fellow Am. Polit. Sci. Assn., 1964-65. Mem. ABA (mem. lawyers conf. jud. performance and conduct com. 1984—), D.C. Bar Assn., Fla. Bar Assn., V.I. Bar Assn. (pres. 1976), Am. Law Inst. (cons. group for principles of family dissolution, 1992—, cons. group for restatement of law governing lawyers, 1992—), Am. Judicature Soc., Assn. Trial Lawyers Am., Order of Coif, Sigma Delta Chi, Phi Delta Phi. Jewish. Lodges: Rotary, Harmonic Lodge No. 356, E.C. Office: Dudley Topper and Feuerzeig 1A Frederiksberg Gade PO Box 756 Charlotte Amalie VI 00804-0756 Home: PO Box 9547 Saint Thomas VI 00801-2547

FEUILLE, RICHARD HARLAN, lawyer; b. Mexico City, Mexico, June 10, 1920; s. Frank and Margaret (Levy) F.; m. Louann Johnston Hoover, Oct. 20, 1948; children: Louann H., Richard H., Robert R., Joseph L. (dec.), James M., Patrick F. (dec.), Margaret J. B.A., U. Va., 1947, LL.B., 1948; JD, 1970. Bar: Tex. 1948. Assoc. Jones, Hardie, Grambling & Howell, El Paso, Tex., 1948-53; ptnr. Hardie, Grambling, Sims & Feuille, El Paso, 1953-57; sr. ptnr. Scott, Hulse, Marshall & Feuille, El Paso, 1957—; bd. dirs. El Paso Nat. Bank (now known as Chase Bank of Tex., N.A.), 1964-93. Active United Fund El Paso, 1963—, founder, v.p. trust fund, 1969—, pres., 1968, 75—, bd. dirs., 1966-72; pres. El Paso Cmty. Concert Assn., 1961-67; mem. adv. coun. U. Tex. at El Paso, 1968—, mem. exec. com., 1968-70; bd. dirs. Providence Meml. Hosp., 1986-92; bd. dirs. St. Clement's Episcopal Parish Sch., El Paso, pres., 1993-95; trustee YWCA, El Paso; bd. dirs. El Paso Cmty. Found., 1980—, pres., 1983-84. Served to maj. USAAF, 1941-46, PTO. Decorated bronze star. Mem. ABA (estate and gift tax com.), El Paso County Bar Assn. (pres. 1972-73), Tex. Bar Assn., Greater El Paso Tennis Assn. (bd. dirs.), Rotary Club of El Paso, Order Coif, Phi Beta Kappa, Omicron Delta Kappa. Episcopalian (vestryman, sr. warden). Clubs: Coronado Country (El Paso), El Paso Tennis (El Paso) (pres. 1973). Home: 1021 Broadmoor Dr El Paso TX 79912-2003 Office: Scott Hulse Marshall & Feuille 201 East Main Dr 1100 Chase Tower El Paso TX 79901

FEULNER, EDWIN JOHN, JR., research foundation executive; b. Chgo., Aug. 12, 1941; s. Edwin John and Helen J. (Franzen) F.; m. Linda C. Leventhal, Mar. 8, 1969; children: Edwin John III, Emily V. BS, Regis Coll., 1963; MBA, U. Pa., 1964; PhD, U. Edinburgh, 1981; hon. degree, Nichols Coll., 1981, Universidad Francisco Marroquin, Guatemala City, 1982, Hanyang U., Seoul, Korea, 1982, Bellevue Coll., Nebr., 1987, Gonzaga U., 1992, Grove City Coll., 1994. Richard Weaver fellow London Sch. Econs., 1965; pub. affairs fellow Hoover Instn., 1965-67; rsch. analyst Rep. Conf. U.S. Ho. of Reps., 1968-69; confidential asst. to sec. def. Melvin Laird, 1969-70; campaign mgr. Crane for Congress Com., 1972; adminstrv. asst. to U.S. Congressman Philip M. Crane, 1970-74; exec. dir. Rep. Study Com., Ho. of Reps., 1974-77; pres. Heritage Found., Washington, 1977—; chmn. Inst. European Def. and Strategic Studies, 1977-96; U.S. adv. com. pub. diplomacy USIA, 1982-94, chmn., 1982-91; trustee Sequoia Nat. Bank; nat. adv. bd. Ctr. for Edn. and Rsch. in Free Enterprise, Tex. A&M U.; Disting. fellow mobilization concepts Devel. Ctr. Nat. Def. U., 1983-89; mem. Pres.'s Commn. on White House Fellows, 1981-83, mem. Exec. Com. of the Presdl. Transition, 1980-81; mem. U.S. Delegation to IMF/World Bank, 1974-76; mem. Carlucci Commn. on Fgn. Assistance, 1983; pub. del. UN 2d Spl. Session on Disarmament, 1982; mem. U.S. Commn. Improving Effectiveness of UN, 1989-93; White House cons. on domestic policy, 1987; mem. adv. com. Am. Polit. Channel, 1994-96; vice-chmn. Nat. Commn. on Econ. Growth and Tax Reform, 1995-96, Congrl. Policy Adv. Bd., 1997—. Author: Congress and the New International Economic Order, 1976, Looking Back, 1981, Conservatives Stalk the House, 1983, The March of Freedom, 1998; contbr. articles to profl. jours., newspapers, chpts. to books. Trustee Lehrman Inst., 1981-90, Sarah Scaife Found., 1988—, St. James Sch., 1990-98, Sequoia Nat. Bank, 1987—, Regis U., 1991—, Internat. Rep. Inst., 1995—, Acton Inst., 1995—; vice-chmn. bd. Aequus Inst., 1989—, Intercollegiate Studies Inst., 1979—, chmn., 1989-93; vice-chmn. bd. dirs. Roe Found.; mem. exec. com. Coun. Nat. Policy; trustee Am. Coun. Germany, N.Y., 1982-92; Found. Francisco Marroquin; trustee Inst. Rsch. Econs. Taxation, 1980-87; chmn. Citizens for Am. Edn. Found., 1985-89; vice chmn., trustee Manhattan Inst. Policy Studies, 1977-86; mem. coun. acad. advisors Bryce Harlow Found.; bd. visitors George Mason U., 1996—. Recipient Washington award Freedom Found., 1979, 80, Disting. Alumni award Regis U., 1985, Superior Pub. Svc. award Dept. of Navy, 1987, Presdl. Citizens medal, 1989, Dir.'s Svc. award USIA, 1992, Thomas Jefferson Servant Leadership award Coun. Nat. Policy, 1996, Free Enterprise Man of Yr., Tex. A&M U., 1985, Man of Yr., Wharton Sch., 1993; decorated Order of Brilliant Star with Grand Cordon, Rep. of China. Mem. Am. Econs. Assn., Internat. Inst. Strategic Studies, U.S. Strategic Inst., Inst. d'Etudes Politques, Phila. Soc. (treas. 1964-79, pres. 1982-83), Mont Pelerin Soc. (treas. 1979-96, pres. 1996-98), Internat. Com. of the G.K. Chesterton Soc. (chmn. 1989-92), Belle Haven Country Club, Union League (N.Y.C.), Met. Club, Reform Club (London), Bohemian Club (San Francisco), Knights of Malta, Alpha Kappa Psi. Republican. Roman Catholic. Office: The Heritage Found 214 Massachusetts Ave NE Washington DC 20002-4958

FEUREY, CLAUDIA PACKER, not-for-profit executive; b. Pt. Hueneme, Calif., Apr. 24, 1949; d. Benjamin Ray and Phyllis Laura (McGrath) Packer; m. John J. Feurey Jr.; children: Matthew, Sarah, Nicholas. BA, Barnard Coll., 1970. V.p. comm. and corp. affairs Com. for Econ. Devel., N.Y.C., 1976—. Contbr: Wall St. Journal on Management, Successful Training Strategies. Mem. Pub. Rels. Soc. Am. (exec. bd. dirs.). Republican. Presbyterian. Office: Com for Econ Devel 477 Madison Ave New York NY 10022-5802*

FEUSS, LINDA ANNE UPSALL, lawyer; b. White Plains, N.Y., Dec. 9, 1956; d. Herbert Charles and Edna May (Hart) Upsall; m. Charles E. Feuss, Aug. 16, 1980; children: Charles Herbert, Anne Hart. BA, Colgate U., 1978; JD, Emory U., 1981. Bar: Ga. 1981, S.C. 1981. Assoc. Rainey, Britton, Gibbes & Clarkson, Greenville, S.C., 1981-83; counsel Siemens Energy & Automation, Atlanta, 1983-91; counsel Siemens Corp., Atlanta, 1991-93, sr. counsel, 1993-94, assoc. gen. counsel, 1994-98; v.p., gen. counsel Pillsbury Co., 1998—; rep. law coun. II Mfr.'s Alliance, Washington, 1995-98; rep. law com. Nat. Elec. Mfr.'s Assn., Washington, 1995-98. Bd. dirs. Am. Heart Assn., Greenville, 1981-83; mem. leadership com. Woodruff Arts Ctr. Campaign, Atlanta, 1985-90; vol. High Mus. Art, Atlanta, 1993—, Ga. 100 Mentor Exch., 1998. Mem. ABA, Am. Corp. Coun. Assn. (dir. Ga. chpt. 1995-98, v.p. Ga. chpt. 1996, pres. 1997), State Bar Ga., S.C. Bar, Atlanta Bar Assn., Colgate Club Atlanta (pres. 1986-88, bd. dirs. 1989—). Office: Pillsbury Co MS 19F3 200 S 6th St Minneapolis MN 55402-1464*

FEVURLY, KEITH ROBERT, educational administrator; b. Leavenworth, Kans., Oct. 30, 1951; s. James R. Fevurly and Anne (McDade) Barrett; m. Peggy L. Vosburg, Aug. 4, 1978; children: Rebecca Dawn, Grant Robert. BA in Polit. Sci., U. Kans., 1973; JD, Washburn U. of Topeka Sch. Law, 1976; postgrad., U. Mo. Sch. Law, 1984; MBA, Regis U., 1988; LLM, U. Denver, 1992. Bar: Kans. 1977, Colo. 1986; cert. fin. planner. Sole practice Leavenworth, 1977; atty. estate and gift tax IRS, Wichita and Salina, Kans., Austin, Tex., 1977-83; atty., acad. assoc. Coll. for Fin. Planning, Denver, 1984-91, program dir., 1991-95, v.p. edn., 1995-98; COO U. St. Augustine (Fla.) for Health Scis., 1998—; adj. prof. taxation Met. State Coll., Denver; adj. faculty in retirement planning and estate planning Coll. Fin. Planning. Contbg. author tng. modules, articles on tax mgmt., estate planning. Mem. Colo. Bar Assn., Toastmasters Internat., Rotary Internat., Delta Theta Phi, Pi Sigma Alpha. Republican. Presbyterian. Avocations: softball, racquetball. Home: 505 Hoot Owl Ct Saint Augustine FL 32084 Office: U St Augustine for Health Scis 1 University Blvd Saint Augustine FL 32086

FEWELL, CHARLES KENNETH, JR., lawyer; b. Washington, Jan. 26, 1943; s. Charles Kenneth and Mary Amanda (Hunt) F.; m. Christine Baker Huff, Jan. 23, 1971; children: Anna Catherine, John Maenner. BA magna cum laude, Dartmouth Coll., 1964; JD, Harvard U., 1967. Bar: N.Y. 1968, U.S. Dist. Ct. (so. dist.) N.Y. 1970, U.S. Ct. Appeals (2d cir.) 1975. Law clk. U.S. Dist. Ct. (so. dist.) N.Y., N.Y.C., 1967-68; assoc. White & Case, N.Y.C., 1968-75; v.p., counsel Nat. Westminster Bank, N.Y.C., 1975-80; sr. counsel, sr. v.p. Deutsche Bank AG, N.Y.C., 1980-92; chief counsel, mng. dir. Deutsche Bank N.Am., 1992-97; ptnr. Eaton & Van Winkle, N.Y.C., 1998—; bd. dirs. Deutsche Bank Trust Co., Deutsche Fin. Svcs. Can. Corp.; v.p., sec. Deutsche Bank Fin., Inc., N.Y.C., 1980-97. Mem. ABA (banking com. 1980—, co-chair internat. banking and fin. com. 1995-98), Inst. International. Bankers (legis. and regulatory com. 1988-97), German Am. Law Assn. (dir. 1982—), N.Y. State Bar Assn. (internat. banking and securities markets 1987—, internat. employment law 1992—), Assn. Bar City N.Y. (banking law sect. 1992-95), Phi Beta Kappa. E-mail: cfewell@evw.com. Office: Eaton & Van Winkle Three Park Ave New York NY 10016-2078

FEWELL, CHRISTINE HUFF, psychoanalyst, alcohol counselor; b. Ancon, Canal Zone, Oct. 12, 1942; d. Maenner B. and Antoinette (Baker) Huff; m. Charles K. Fewell, Jr., Jan. 23, 1971; children: Anna C., John M. BA, Antioch Coll., Yellow Springs, Ohio, 1965; MSW, U. Chgo., 1967; student, NYU Sch. Social Work, 1999. Cert. social worker; cert. psychoanalyst; credentialed alcohol and substance abuse counselor. Social worker Ill. Children's Home and Aid Soc., Chgo., 1967-68, Bronx (N.Y.) State Hosp., 1968-70; field work instr. Columbia Sch. Social Work, 1973-75; social worker in alcoholism treatment ctr. St. Lukes/Roosevelt Hosp., N.Y.C., 1970-75; pvt. practice Hastings-on-Hudson, 1976—, N.Y.C., 1976—; alcoholism disability com. Ctrl. Westchester Area Mental Health Com. Westchester Dept. Cmty. Mental Health, 1981—; mem., chair N.Y. State Bd. Social Work, 1993—; adj. prof. NYU Sch. Social Work, 1995—; faculty advisor NYU Sch. of Social Work, 1996—. Editor: Social Work Treatment of Alcoholism 1984, Pychosocial Issues in the Treatment of Alcoholism, 1985, Alcoholism Treatment Quar., 1986; editorial adv. bd. Social Casework, 1978; contbr. articles to profl. jours. Mem. NASW (N.Y.C. chpt. alcoholism com. 1971—, chairperson 1975, 98-99, editl. com. 1978-86, peer consultation com. for impaired social workers chairperson 1976—, cons. Com. on Inquiry), Internat. Psychoanalytical Assn., Inst. for Psychoanalytical Tng. and Rsch. (libr.), Acad. Cert. Social Workers (diplomate), N.Y. State Soc. Clin. Social Workers (Westchester chpt. fellow 1981—, referral com. 1983-86), Employee Assistance Profls. Assn. (N.Y. and mid-Hudson chpt. 1983—). Home: 4 Nichols Dr Hastings Hdsn NY 10706-3525 Office: 1651 3rd Ave Ste 201 New York NY 10128-3679

FEY, JOHN THEODORE, retired insurance company executive; b. Hopewell, Va., Mar. 10, 1917; s. Raymond B. and Ruth (Fultz) F.; m. Jane K. Gerber, Apr. 5, 1947 (dec.); 1 child, John Theodore; m. Deborah F. Fitzgerald, Dec. 6, 1986. Student, Washington and Lee U., 1935-37, LL.D., 1978; LL.B., U. Md., 1940; M.B.A., Harvard U., 1942; J.S.D., Yale U., 1952; LL.D., Middlebury Coll., Alma Coll., 1961, U. Vt., 1967, Washington and Lee U., 1980, St. Augustine Coll., 1981. Bar: Md. 1940, D.C. 1953, Vt. 1959, N.Y. 1977. County atty. Md., 1947-49; faculty Law Sch., George Washington U., 1949-53, dean, 1953-56, professorial lectr., 1956; clk. Supreme Ct. U.S., 1956-58; pres. U. Vt., 1958-64, U. Wyo., 1964-66; pres. Nat. Life Ins. Co., 1966-74, also dir., 1966-74; chmn. bd. Equitable Life Assurance Soc. U.S., N.Y.C., 1974-82, Nat. Westminster Bank U.S.A., N.Y.C., 1982-85, Fidelity Union Life Ins. Co., Dallas, 1982-85; bd. dirs. Sara Lee Corp., Certain-Teed Co., Norton Corp.; chmn. bd. dirs. Saint-Gobain Corp.; mem. Md. Legislature, 1946-50. Trustee Getty Mus., Malibu, Calif., 1979-92. Served to col. USMCR, 1942-46. Mem. Am. Coll. Life Underwriters, Order of Coif. Home: PO Box 4529 Tubac AZ 85646-4529

FEZZEY, MIKE, radio station executive. Pres., gen. mgr. WJR-AM, Detroit, 1994—. Office: WJR-AM 2100 Fisher Bldg Detroit MI 48202*

FFOWCS WILLIAMS, JOHN EIRWYN, acoustical engineer; b. Wales, May 25, 1935; 3 children. BSc, U. Southampton, PhD in Engring.; MA, Cambridge U., DSc. Sr. rsch. fellow divsn. aerodyns. Nat. Physics Lab., 1960-62; sr. scientist Bolt, Beranek & Newman Inc., 1962-64; reader applied math.-Rolls Royce prof. theoretical acoustics Imperial Coll. Sci. and Tech., 1964-69; Rank prof. engring. acoustics Cambridge U., 1972—; professorial fellow Emmanuel Coll., Cambridge, 1972—, master, 1997—; chmn. panel Concorde noise, 1965, Topexpress Ltd., Cambridge, 1978-89; gov. Felsted Sch., 1979-93; vis. prof. Sch. Ctrl. Lyon, Melbourne U., Mass. Inst. Tech., Harvard U., Stanford U. Recipient Aero. Acoustics medal Am. Inst. Aeros. and Astronautics, 1977, Siver medal Acoustical Soc. France, 1989, Per Bruel Gold medal for noise control and acoustics ASME, 1997. Fellow Royal Acad. Engrs., Royal Soc. Arts, Acoustical Soc. Am., Royal Aero. Soc., Inst. Acoustics (Rayleigh medal 1984), Inst. Physics; mem. AAAS (fgn. hon. mem.), Nat. Acad. Engrs. (fgn. assoc.), Inst. Noise Control Engrs. Office: Cambridge U, Trumpington St, Cambridge 1PZ ZZ, England

FIALA, DAVID MARCUS, lawyer; b. Cleve., Aug. 1, 1946; s. Frank J. and Anna Mae (Phillips) F. BBA, U. Cin., 1969; JD, Chase Coll., No. Ky. State U., 1974. Bar: Ohio 1974, U.S. Dist. Ct. (so. dist.) Ohio 1974, U.S. Tax Ct. 1974. Assoc. Benesch, Friedlander, Coplan and Aronoff, Cin., 1974-78, ptnr., 1979-92; ptnr. Rice & Fiala, 1992-94, sole practice, Cin., 1995—. lectr. Southwestern Ohio Tax Inst., 1978-79, 88, Cin. Bar Assn. Estate Planning Inst., 1989. Bd. dirs. Elkhorn Collieries. Trustee, sec. Sta. WCET-TV, Cin., 1983-87, auction chmn., 1979, chmn. 1987-90, trustee emeritus, 1990—; trustee Jr. Achievement Greater Cin., 1979-93, 99—, Mental Health Svcs. West, 1974-83, Contemporary Dance theatre, 1974-80. Mem. ABA, Ohio State Bar Assn., Cin. Bar Assn. (lectr. estate planning inst. 1989), Am. Culinary Fedn. Cin. (trustee 1985-90), Cincinnatus Assn.

FIALKA, JOHN JOSEPH, journalist; b. New Ulm, Minn., 1938. BA, Loras Coll., 1960; MS in Journalism, Columbia U., 1962; JD, Georgetown U., 1965. Legis. aide Nat. Petroleum Refiners Assn., 1962-65; reporter Sun, Balt., 1965-67, Washington Star, 1967-81; nat. security reporter Wall St. Jour., N.Y.C., 1981-97, energy and environment reporter, 1997—. Office: Wall St Jour Ste 800 1025 Connecticut Ave NW Washington DC 20036-5419*

FIALKOV, HERMAN, investment banker; b. Bklyn., Mar. 23, 1922; s. Isidore and Pearl (Heinish) F.; m. Elaine Dampf, Nov. 25, 1942; children: Carol Fran, Jay Michael. Student, CCNY, 1938-41; B.Adminstrv. Engring., NYU, 1951. Engr. Emerson Radio Corp., 1941-47, MBS, 1947-49, Tele-Tone Radio Corp., 1949-51; chief engr. Radio Receptor Co., 1951-54; pres. Gen. Transistor Corp. (merged with Gen. Instrument Corp. 1960), 1954-60; v.p., dir. Gen. Instrument Corp., 1960-67, sr. v.p., 1967-68; partner Geiger & Fialkov, 1968-78, Venture Capital Investments, 1978—; bd. dirs. Primus Telecom., Inc., Globecomm Systems, Inc., Perlucid Corp. Trustee Adelphi U., Garden City, 1959-70, Poly. U. N.Y., Heinish Found. Served with AUS, 1943-46. Decorated Bronze Star with oak leaf cluster; Conspicuous Service Cross N.Y. Mem. IEEE, Am. Technion Soc. (dir.), Tau Beta Pi, Alpha Pi Mu. Home: 1 Kensington Gate Great Neck NY 11021-1202 Office: 500 N Broadway Ste 144 Jericho NY 11753-2111

FIBICH, HOWARD RAYMOND, retired newspaper editor; b. Oak Park, Ill., Jan. 6, 1932; s. Raymond Clarence and Vivian (Barrie) F.; m. Carrol Jean Anderson, June 5, 1954; children: Linda, Steven, Barbara. B.S., Northwestern U., 1954, M.S., 1955; postgrad., Columbia U., 1966. Reporter Kokomo (Ind.) Tribune, 1955-56; copy editor Milw. Jour., 1956-64, telegraph editor, 1964, asst. news editor, 1964-67, news editor, 1967-84, asst. mng. editor, 1984-86, dep. mng. editor, 1986-93; ret., 1994; freelance writer, 1959-63; chmn. Mid-Am. Press Inst.; producer, host Jazz for the Quiet Hours, WYMS, Milw. Bd. dirs. Friends of WYMS. Named Milw. Media Hall of Fame, 1994. Mem. Mid.-Am. Press Inst. (bd. dirs. 1976-86, chmn. 1980-81), Wis. History Found., AP Mng. Editors Assn. (new tech. com.), Milw. Press Club, Kappa Tau Alpha. Home: 2537 N Swan Blvd Wauwatosa WI 53226-1844

FIBIGER, JOHN ANDREW, life insurance company executive; b. Copenhagen, Apr. 27, 1932; came to U.S., 1934, naturalized, 1953; s. Borge Rottboll and Ruth Elizabeth (Wadmond) F.; m. Barbara Mae Stuart, June 22, 1956; children: Karen Ruth McCarthy, Katherine Louise. B.A., U. Minn., 1953, M.A., 1954; postgrad., U. Wis. With Lincoln Nat. Life Ins. Co., Ft. Wayne, Ind., 1956-57; with Bankers Life Ins. Co. Nebr., Lincoln, 1959-73; sr. v.p. group Bankers Life Ins. Co. Nebr., 1972-73; with New Eng. Mut. Life Ins. Co., Boston, 1973-89; vice chmn., pres., chief operating officer New Eng. Mut. Life Ins. Co., 1981-89; with Transam Life Cos., 1991-94; exec. v.p., CFO, then pres. Transamerica Occidental Life Ins. Co., L.A., 1994-95, chmn., 1995-97; past vice chmn. Actuarial Bd. for Counseling and Discipline; bd. dirs. Transamerica Life Can., Transamerica Life N.Y., Conning Corp. Life trustee, past chmn. Mus. Sci., Boston, 1989-91; past overseer New Eng. Med. Ctr.; bd. dirs. Menninger Found., L.A. Chamber Orch.; past chmn. Menninger Fund; bd. dirs., vice-chmn. U. So. Calif. Sch. Gerontology; pres. Andrus Inst.; dir. L.A. Chamber Orch.; past trustee Calif. Mus. Sci. and Industry. Fellow Soc. Actuaries (past bd. dirs.); mem. Nat. Acad. Social Ins. (founding mem.), Am. Acad. Actuaries (past pres.), Assn. Calif. Life Cos. (past bd. chmn.).

FICCA, STEPHEN A., federal agency administrator. Assoc. dir., dir. rsch. svcs. office rsch. svcs NIH Dept. Health and Human Svcs., Bethesda. Office: NIH 9000 Rockville Pike Bldg 1 Bethesda MD 20892-0003*

FICCAGLIA, LESLIE M., psychologist, portrait artist; b. Huntington, N.Y., Oct. 3, 1943; d. Sewall M. and L. Lillian (Bartok) Pastor; m. Anthony W. Ficcaglia, Nov. 4, 1968; children: Jeremy Clinton, Linnet Kyung. BA in Psychology, NYU, 1965; MA in Psychology, Western Wash. U., Bellingham, 1971; student, Rowan Coll., Glassboro, N.J., 1984. Cert. sch. psychologist. Clin. psychologist Eastern Diagnostic and Evaluation Ctr., Phila., 1968; staff clin. psychologist Vineland (N.J.) State Sch., 1970-74; staff psychologist Cumberland County Hosp., Hopewell Twp., N.J., 1974-81; sch. psychologist Downe Twp. Bd. Edn., Newport, N.J., 1981—; grantswriter Downe Twp. Bd. Edn., Newport, 1990—; portrait artist Minnamuska Creek Studio, Port Elizabeth, N.J., 1995—. Developer website; author newspaper articles, booklet "What's This ADD?". Mem. Maurice River Twp. Planning Bd., 1979-98, chair, 1990-98; mem. Cumberland County Planning Bd., Bridgeton, N.J., 1982—, vice chair, 1988—; mem. N.J. State Pinelands Commn., New Lisbon, 1996—; trustee Assn. N.J. Environ. Commns., Mendham, 1995—; trustee Citizens United to Protect the Maurice River and Its Tributaries, 1999—; mem. Del. Bayshore adv. bd. Nature Conservancy, 1998—. Recipient Outstanding Svc. award Cumberland County Bd. Freeholders, 1991. Mem. N.J. Planning Ofcls., Nat. Assn. Sch. Psychologists, Phi Delta Kappa. Avocations: land use planning, environmental issues. Home: Minnamuska Creek Farm and Studio Port Elizabeth NJ 08348-0027

FICHENBERG, ROBERT GORDON, newspaper editor, consultant; b. Phila., Jan. 1, 1920; s. Samuel Harrison and Katherine (Gordon) F.; m. Ruth Pollard, Sept. 14, 1947; children: Ruth Ann, Kathryn Leigh. B.S., Syracuse U., 1940. City editor Adirondack Daily Enterprise, Saranac Lake, N.Y.,

1940-42; reporter, copy editor, asst. city editor Binghamton (N.Y.) Press, 1942-57; mng. editor Knickerbocker News, Albany, N.Y., 1957-66; exec. editor Knickerbocker News, 1966-78; chief Washington bur. Newhouse Newspapers, editor Newhouse News Svc., 1979-91; writer, cons. Nat. Dist. Attys. Assn., Washington, 1991—; bd. dirs. Nat. Press Found. Served to 1st lt. Signal Corps AUS, 1942-46; to capt. U.S. Army, 1951-52. Mem. Am. Soc. Newspaper Editors, N.Y. State Soc. Newspaper Editors (pres.), AP Mng. Editors Assn., White House Corrs. Assn., N.Y. State AP Assn. (past pres.), Soc. Profl. Journalists, Nat. Press Club, Army and Navy Club, Fed. City Club, Univ. Club Washington, Gridiron Club (Washington). Home: 1605 Mason Hill Dr Alexandria VA 22307-1930 Office: Nat Dist Attys Assn 99 Canal Center Plz Ste 510 Alexandria VA 22314-1588

FICHTEL, RUDOLPH ROBERT, retired association executive; b. N.Y.C., Dec. 12, 1915; s. Paul Gotthard and Helen (Szapka) F.; m. Elsie E. Terebesy, Dec. 24, 1942; children: Nancy Lynn, Robert Paul, Richard John. B.B.A. cum laude, Coll. City N.Y., 1938; cert., Am. Inst. Banking, 1941; diploma fin. pub. relations, Northwestern U., 1950; M.B.A., NYU, 1951; diploma banking, Rutgers U. Stonier Grad. Sch. Banking, 1954. Tchr. N.Y.C. Pub. Schs., 1938-39; adminstr. East River Savs. Bank, 1939-42; dir. pub. relations, editor, asst. sec. Savs. Banks Assn. N.Y. State, 1945-53; dir. pub. relations council, savs. and mortgage div. Am. Bankers Assn., N.Y.C. and Washington, 1953-64; nat. dir. Am. Inst. Banking, 1964-78; regional v.p. United Student Aid Funds, Inc., N.Y.C., 1978-87; mem. lender relations com. Higher Edn. Loan Programs; mem. faculty Am. Inst. Banking, Stonier Grad. Sch. Banking; contbg. editor Am. Inst. Banking textbooks; speaker. Contbr. articles to profl. jours. Vol. tutor Literacy Program, N.Y.C.; income tax counsellor Am. Assn. Retired Persons. Served to capt. AUS, 1942-45, ETO. Recipient highest award citation Internat. Council Indsl. Editors, 1948, Dr. Marcus Nadler award for excellence in finance; N.Y. U., 1951. Mem. Beta Gamma Sigma. Home: 65-19 170th St Flushing NY 11365-1949 *Success in my life has been the result of hard work, continuing search for knowledge, constant effort to understand and relate to people, and total dedication to excellence in full partnership with a loving family.*

FICHTER, DAVID HARRY, conservationist, environmentalist; b. Englewood, N.J., Jan. 18, 1941; s. Harry Charles and Mary Louise (Kay) F. BS, Ariz. State U., 1966; BFT, Am. Grad. Sch. Internat. Mgmt., 1967. Dir. environ. affairs Chgo. Bridge & Iron Co., Plainfield, Ill., 1967—. Elected commr. Oak Brook (Ill.) Park Dist., 1995—, pres. 1998, dir., 1994-99; pres. Mayslake Landmark Conservancy, 1994-99. Mem. Sigma Lambda Chi. Home: 3804 Washington St Oak Brook IL 60523-2749 Office: Chgo Bridge & Iron Co 1501 N Division St Plainfield IL 60544-8984

FICHTNER, MARGARIA, journalist; b. Lakeland, Fla., May 4, 1944; d. August Albert and Margaret Louise (Kelly) F. BA, Fla. So. Coll., 1966. Book editor Miami Herald. Recipient First Place criticism award Am. Assn. Sunday and Feature Editors, 1996, First Place criticism award Fla. Soc. Newspaper Editors, 1997. Office: The Miami Herald Pub Co One Herald Plz Miami FL 33132-1693

FICK, E(ARL) DEAN, insurance executive; b. Holstein, Iowa, July 9, 1944; s. Earl Frederick and Donna Belle (Schmidt) F.; m. Barbara Jean Robinson, Sept. 4, 1966; children: Bryan Dean, Anthony Wayne. BS, Iowa State U., 1967; MBA, U. Iowa, 1990. CPCU. Adjuster Grinnell (Iowa) Mut. Reins. Co., 1967-70, claims supr., 1970-72, tel. claims supr., 1972-75, regional claims mgr., 1975-78, asst. claims mgr., 1978-82, claims mgr., 1982-85, v.p. claims, 1985-87, sr. v.p. claims, 1987-91; v.p. chief claims officer United Fire Group, Cedar Rapids, Iowa, 1991; bd. dirs. Iowa Ins. Guaranty Assn., St. Luke's Health Care Found.; mem. Nat. Assn. Ind. Insurers Claims Com., Des Plaines, Ill., 1985-91; mem. Iowa Claims Exec. Coun., Des Moines, 1982—, pres., 1986. Del. Poweshiek County Rep. Conv., Montezuma, Iowa, 1978, 82, 88, Rep. State Conv., Cedar Rapids, 1978; bd. dirs. Fire and Police Pension Bds., Grinnell, 1985-91, Town and Gown Fund Drive, Grinnell, 1991. Mem. Ctrl. Claim Execs. Assn. (exec. com. 1995-2001, pres. 1998-99), Grinnell Country Club (past bd. dirs., v.p. 1991), Rotary. Republican. Lutheran. Avocations: golf, hunting, trap and skeet shooting. Office: United Fire & Casualty Co 118 2nd Ave SE Cedar Rapids IA 52401-1253

FICK, GARY WARREN, agronomy educator, forage crops researcher; b. O'Neill, Nebr., July 10, 1943; s. Walter Henry and Doris Marie (Parks) F.; m. Mae Ellen Ruddell, June 29, 1969; children—Joseph, David, Charles. B.S., U. Nebr., 1965; diploma Agr. Sci., Massey U., 1968; Ph.D., U. Calif., 1971. Asst. prof. Cornell U., Ithaca, N.Y., 1971-76, assoc. prof., 1976-84, prof., 1984—; acting chair dept. soil crop and atmospheric scis., 1993, 95; teaching leader soil crop and atmospheric scis. Cornell U., Ithaca, N.Y., 1994—; vis. scientist Lincoln Coll., N.Z., 1977-78; assoc. editor Agronomy Jour., 1978-81. Assoc. editor Jour. of Prodn. Agr., 1987-93; mem. editl. bd. Jour. of Sustainable Agr., 1996—; contbr. articles to profl. jours. and monographs. Fellow Crop Sci. Soc. Am., Am. Soc. Agronomy (tchg. award N.E. br. 1991); mem. Coun. for Agrl. Sci. and Tech., Internat. Assoc. Plant Taxonomy, Am. Forage and Grassland Coun. (Merit cert. 1989), N.Y. Forage and Grassland Coun., Gamma Sigma Delta (Cornell pres. 1992-93, Chancellor's tchg. award 1995). Office: Cornell U Dept Soil Crop and Atmospheric Scis Ithaca NY 14853

FICKENSCHER, GERALD H., chemicals company executive; b. Buenos Aires, Argentina, 1943. Graduate, Cath. U. Argentina, Buenos Aires, 1967; Post-Graduate, Cath. U. Argentina, 1970. V.p., cfo Uniroyal Chem. Corp., Middlebury, Conn.; v.p.-Europe Crompton & Knowles, Stamford, Conn. *Key member of Uniroyal Chemical Corporation's Management Led LBO. Executive with broad international and mergers and acquisition experience. Member of and active in Financial Executives Institute, corporate boards and non profit organizations.* Office: Crompton & Knowles 1 Station Pl Stamford CT 06902-6800 Home: 3200 Park Ave Apt 6B-1 Bridgeport CT 06604-1142

FICKETT, EDWARD HALE, architect, planner, arbitrator; b. L.A., 1923; s. George Edward and Marguerite (Hale) F.; m. Joyce Helen Steinberg, Apr. 8, 1982. BArch, U. So. Calif., grad. studies in engrng. and archaeology; M in City Planning, MIT, MArch. Registered architect, 50 states. Pvt. practice architecture L.A., 1950—; archtl. advisor to Pres. Dwight D. Eisenhower, 1957-60; cons. to Federal Govt. on Housing; archtl. commr. City of Beverly Hills, Calif., 1977-86, chmn. Archtl. Commn., 1979-82; guest lectr., vis. prof. UCLA, U. Calif., Berkeley, MIT, Stanford U., U. So. Calif., U. Fla., Calif. Poly. State U.-San Luis Obispo, Rensselaer Poly. Inst., N.Y., U. Chgo.; speaker in field; arbitrator Nat. Panel Arbitrators, 1961—, Am. Arbitration Assn., 1963—. Archtl. works include L.A. Harbor Cargo and Passenger Terminals, San Pedro, Sands Hotel, Las Vegas, Nev., La Costa Resort and Condominiums, Carlsbad, Calif., Las Cruces Resort Hotel, La Paz, Mex., Hacienda Hotel, Cabo San Lucas, Mex., Bistro Gardens Restaurant, Beverly Hills, Calif., Univ. High Sch., L.A., master plans for Edwards AFB, Calif., Norton AFB, Calif., Murphy Canyon Heights Naval Base, Calif., L.A. City Hall Hist. and Seismic Renovation, Nethercutt Antique Car Mus., others; architect comml. devels., master planned communities, office bldgs., restaurants, resorts, hotels, homes, condominiums, shopping ctrs., air force bases, naval bases, schs., renovation of hist. bldgs., historic & seismic rehab, designed over 40,000 homes. Mem. Gov. Pat Brown's Housing Bd. for Calif. Lt. comdr. Sea Bees, USN. Recipient Merit of Honor award by Pres. of U.S., L.A. Conservancy Preservation Arch. award, 1999, L.A., National Progressive Architecture Design awards, city beautification awards from L.A., Beverly Hills, Reno, Seattle, numerous Nat. Assn. Home Builders awards, Sunset Magazine and House and Home awards, Nat. Assn. Home Builders awards, Los Angeles Conservancy Archtl. Design Award, 1999, Nat. Hist. Monuments Archtl. Design Award, 1999, Housing Hall of Fame, others. Fellow AIA (First Honor award, numerous merit awards, nat. com. for bldg. industry, chmn. 1962-72, bd. dirs. So. Calif. chpt. 1958-62, pres. Calif. chpt. 1962, featured speaker nat. convs., lectr., developed and participated in AIA Univ. Lecture series), Nat. Assn. Home Builders (speaker nat. convs.), Calif. Coun. Architects (sec. 1960), Am. Archtl. Found. Octagon Soc., U. So. Calif. Archtl. Guild (charter). Avocations: tennis, golf. Fax: 323-939-8060. Office: 7421 Beverly Blvd Los Angeles CA 90036-2703

FICKINGER, WAYNE JOSEPH, communications executive; b. Belleville, Ill., June 23, 1926; s. Joseph and Grace (Belton) F.; m. Joan Mary Foley, June 16, 1951; children: Michael, Joan, Jan, Ellen, Steven. BA, U. Ill., 1949; MS, Northwestern U., 1950. Overnight editor United Press, Chgo., 1950-51; spl. project writer Sears-Roebuck & Co., Chgo., 1951-53; account exec. Calkins & Holden Advt. Agy., Chgo., 1953-56; account supr. Foote, Cone & Belding Advt. Agy., Chgo., N.Y.C., 1956-63; sr. v.p. J. Walter Thompson Co., Chgo., 1963-72; exec. v.p., dir. U.S. Western div. J. Walter Thompson Co., 1972-75, pres. N.Am. divsn., 1975-78; pres., chief operating officer J. Walter Thompson Co. Worldwide, 1978-79; pres. JWT Group, Inc., 1979-82, trustee retirement fund, dir., mem. exec. com., 1980-82; mng. dir. Spencer Stuart & Assocs., 1982-83; vice chmn., dir. Bozell, Jacobs, Kenyon & Eckhardt Inc., Chgo., 1984-89; pres. Mid-Am. Com., Chgo., 1989-93; exec. v.p., dir. Monroe Comm. Corp., 1992—; v.p., dir. Adams Comm., 1994—; advisory bd. Phase One, Susidiary, Cyberoffice Tech., 1993—; bd. dirs. Alford Group, Inc., Frankel & Assocs. Fundraising cons. Nat. Mental Health Assn., 1970; communications counselor Cook County (Ill.) Rep. Orgn., 1970; bd. dirs. Off-the-Street Club, Chgo., 1974-77, Mundelein Coll., 1985-91, United Cerebral Palsy, 1986, Chgo. Conv. and Tourists Bur., 1986-90, Columbia Coll., Chgo., 1990-95; chmn. Chgo. Funding Statue of Liberty, 1986, March of Dimes, 1987, Mayor's Chgo. Tourism Com., 1990-92; mem. steering com. El Valor, 1997-98. With USNR, 1943-46. Recipient Five-Year Meritorious Service award A.R.C., 1963, Service award Mental Health Assn., 1970. Mem. Am. Assn. Advt. Agys., Council on Fgn. Relations (Chgo. com.), Sigma Delta Chi, Alpha Delta Sigma. Clubs: Exmoor Country (Highland Park, Ill.); N.Y. Athletic; Mid-Am. (Chgo.), Internat. (Chgo.). Office: 350 S Beverly Dr Ste 300 Beverly Hills CA 90212-4817

FICKLER, ARLENE, lawyer; b. Phila., Apr. 21, 1951. BA cum laude, U. Pa., 1971, JD cum laude, 1974. Bar: Pa. 1974, D.C. 1980, U.S. Supreme Ct. 1989. Ptnr. Hoyle Morris & Kerr LLP, Phila.; staff atty. Commn. on Revision of Fed. Ct. Appellate System, 1974-75; exec. asst. Bicentennial Com. Jud. Conf. of U.S., 1975-76. Comment editor U. Pa. Law Rev., 1973-74; contbr. articles to law jours. Pres. U. Pa. Law Sch. Alumni Bd. Mgrs., 1997-99; trustee Jewish Fedn. of Greater Phila., 1981-88, 89-93, 94-98, 99—, Phila. Bar Found., 1993-98, Jewish Cmty. Ctrs. of Phila., 1997—, asst. treas., 1999—; pres. HIAS Immigration Svcs. Phila., 1998—, treas., 1999—; pres. Jewish Cmty. Rels. Coun. Greater Phila., 1983-94, 98—; mem. United Jewish Appeal Nat. Young Women's Leadership Cabinet, 1982-87; v.p. Phila. chpt. Am. Jewish Congress, 1995—. Recipient Mrs. Isidor Kohn Young Leadership award Jewish Fedn. Greater Phila. Mem. ABA, Am. Law Inst., Am. Bar Found., Pa. Bar Assn., D.C. Bar, Phila. Bar Assn. (chmn. fed. cts. com. 1992), Fed. Bar Coun. of Second Cir. Office: Hoyle Morris & Kerr LLP 1650 Market St Ste 1 Philadelphia PA 19103-7397

FICKLING, WILLIAM ARTHUR, JR., health care manager; b. Macon, Ga., July 23, 1932; s. William Arthur and Claudia Darden (Foster) F.; m. Neva Jane Langley, Dec. 30, 1954; children: William Arthur III, Jane Dru, Julia Claudia, Roy Hampton. BS cum laude, Auburn U., 1954. Exec. v.p. Fickling & Walker, Inc., Macon, 1954-74; chmn. bd. dirs., chief exec. officer Charter Med. Corp., Macon, 1969-85, pres., chmn. bd. dirs., 1985-93; chmn. bd. Beech St. Corp., Macon, 1986—; bd. dirs. Ga. Power Co., Riverside Ford. Trustee Wesleyan Coll., Macon, Auburn Univ. Found.; mem. adv. bd. Med. Coll. Ga. Mem. Macon Bd. Realtors, Kappa Alpha, Delta Sigma Phi, Phi Kappa Phi. Methodist. Home: 6300 Rivoli Dr Macon GA 31210-1459 Office: Beech St Corp PO Box 307 Macon GA 31202-0307*

FICKS, F. LAWRENCE, communications executive; b. Denver, Apr. 4, 1930; s. Herman and Roselee (Pearl) F.; m. Carlyn Scheff, 1952 (div. 1970); m. Shola Lewis, Nov. 10, 1979; children: Robin, Georgia, Randi. BS, Pa. State U., 1951, MS, 1952. Commd. 2d lt. U.S. Army, 1953, advanced through grades to capt., 1963; col. USAR, 1963-83, ret., 1983; engr. AVCO, Lawrence, Mass., 1963-65; sr. engr., project mgr. MacDonald, St. Louis, 1965-67; founder, prin. F.L. Ficks Assocs., 1967-70; with Bell Labs. and AT&T, various locations, 1970-84; dir. Bellcore, Livingston, N.J., 1984-93; founder, prin. Digital Workers Inc., 1993—; adj. prof. U. Md., Frankfurt, Germany, 1958-60, Newark Coll. Engring., 1968-75. Contbr. articles to profl. jours. Decorated Legion of Merit. Home: 4 Bongart Dr West Orange NJ 07052-2143

FIDDICK, PAUL WILLIAM, broadcasting company executive; b. St. Joseph, Mo., Nov. 20, 1949; s. Lowell Duane and Betty Jean (Manring) F.; m. Julie Hanna Lorms, July 31, 1983; children: Lea Elizabeth, Hanna Manring. BJ, U. Mo., 1971. Account exec. Sta. KCMO-KFMU, Kansas City, Mo., 1971-72; account exec. Sta. WEZW, Milw., 1972-74, dir. sales mktg., 1974-76, v.p., gen. mgr., 1976-81; sr. v.p. Multimedia Broadcasting Co., Milw., 1981; pres. Multimedia Radio, Cin., 1982-86, Radio Group, Heritage Communications, Inc., Des Moines, 1986-87, Radio Group, Heritage Media Corp., Dallas, 1987-98; mgmt. cons., Dallas, 1998—; dir., vice chmn. RadioWave Comm., Inc., Schaumburg, Ill., 1998—, acting pres., 1999—; chmn. Radio Advt. Bur., N.Y.C., 1993-94; mem. acad. staff U. Wis., Milw., 1978-81. Elder Westminster Presbyn. Ch., Dallas, 1997—. Named one of 40 Most Powerful People in Radio, Radio Ink Mag., 1996, Fifth Estater, Broadcasting Mag., 1990, Up and Coming Radio Exec. of Yr., Radio Only mag., 1983, recipient Pub.'s Profile, Radio and Records mag., 1998. Mem. Phi Eta Sigma, Kappa Tau Alpha.

FIDDLER, BARBARA DILLOW, sales and marketing professional; b. Decatur, Ill., Sept. 2, 1940; s. N. Eugene and Ruth (Kirchhoff) Dillow; children: John Eugene, Thomas Crawford. BA, U. Vt., 1963. Grad. registrar Troy State U., European div., Wiesbaden, W. Ger., 1977-79; adminstrv. asst. Mt. Mansfield Co. Mktg. Dept., Stowe, Vt., 1980-84; asst. dir. promotions and advt. Rossignol Ski Co., Tennis div., Williston, Vt., 1984-85; project mgr. Birch Hill Devel. Co., Stowe, 1985-86; asst. to dir. of devel. Johnson State Coll., Johnson, Vt., 1986-89; asst. dir. devel. The Trustees of Reservations, Beverly, Mass., 1989-91; adminstr. Epsilon Inc., Burlington, Mass., 1991-94; group sales mgr. Topnotch at Stowe, Vt., 1994-98; bd. dirs., v.p. Robert Alden Ellsworth Trust, Johnson, Vt., 1991—. Trustee Fund for Johnson (Vt.) State Coll.; bd. dirs. United Way of Lamoille County, Hyde Park, 1988-92, 95—, pres., 1998—; mem. Stowe (Vt.) Planning Commn., 1988-92; bd. dirs., chmn. fin. and fundraising com. Johnson Friends of Arts, 1986-88; regional trustee Vt. Symphony Orch., 1995—. Mem. Women in Devel. in Greater Boston, Lamoille Valley C. of C. (bd. dirs.). Republican. Episcopalian. Avocations: skiing, knitting, reading, creative cooking. Home and Office: 227 Upper Baird Rd Stowe VT 05672-4203

FIDLER, CAROL ANN, accountant; b. Sharon, Pa., Apr. 28, 1942; d. Thomas Daniel and E. Geraldine (Boyer) Bracken; m. Michael Lawrence Fidler, Aug. 23, 1969 (div. 1991); 1 child, Michael Lawrence Jr. Diploma, Akron City Hosp. Sch. Nursing, 1963; BS in Chemistry, Kent State U., 1967; MS in Preventive Medicine, Ohio State U., 1972, MBA, 1979. CPA, Ohio; RN, Ohio; cert. valuation analyst, Nat. Assn. Cert. Valuation Analysts. Rsch. assoc. dept. preventive medicine Ohio State U., Columbus, Ohio, 1969-70; dir. Riverside Meth. Hosp. Sch. Nursing, Columbus, 1973-77; dir. nursing devel. Ohio Hosp. Assn., Columbus, 1977-79; sr. bus. analyst Borden Inc.-Chem. Divsn., Columbus, 1979-81; fin. adminstr. Bank One, Columbus N.A., 1981-84; pres. Northwest Tax Svc., Columbus, 1984-86; sr. cons. Peat, Marwick, Mitchell, Columbus, 1985-86; pvt. practice Columbus, 1986-90; controller The Wood Co's., Columbus, 1987-88; co-owner Clem & Fidler CPAs, 1991-94; owner Carol A. Fidler & Assocs., CPAs, Columbus, 1994-97; with Whalen & Co., CPAs, Columbus, 1997—; instr. Newton Becker CPA Rev., Columbus, 1988-90; dir., treas. Donovan Prodns. Inc., Columbus, 1989—; bd. dirs. Dominican Home Health Agy., 1995—, treas., 1997-99, pres., 1999—. Vol. Arthritis Assn., Columbus, 1978-84; treas. Northside Child and Family Devel. Ctr., Columbus, 1987-95, bd. dirs., 1986-97. Mem. Ohio Soc. CPAs (chair MAP com. Columbus chpt. 1991-93, mem. MAP com. 1992-96, Cert. award 1986, Silver medal 1986), Inst. Mgmt. Accts. (dir. member attendance Columbus chpt. 1988-89, dir. tech. programs 1989-90, dir. student and acad. affairs 1990-91, dir. CMA program 1991-93, treas. 1993-95, lead instr. CMA rev. course 1991-94), Planning Forum (pres. Columbus chpt. 1986-87, v.p. fin. com. 1985-86, v.p. programs 1984-85, dir. 1987-90). Republican. Home: 4138 Winfield Rd Columbus OH 43220-4606

FIEBACH, H. ROBERT, lawyer; b. Paterson, N.J., June 7, 1939; s. Michael M. and Silvia Irene (Nadler) F.; m. Elizabeth D. Carlton, Mar. 17, 1984; children: Michael, Emma; children by previous marriage: Jonathan, Rachel. B.S., U. Pa., 1961, LL.B. cum laude, 1964. Bar: Pa. 1965, U.S. Supreme Ct. 1971. Law clk. to Chief Judge Biggs U.S. Ct. Appeals for 3d Cir., 1964-65; assoc. Wolf, Block, Schorr and Solis-Cohen, Phila., 1965-71, ptnr., 1971-79, sr. ptnr., 1979-95; sr. mem. Cozen & O'Connor, Phila., 1995—; permanent mem. U.S. Jud. Conf. for 3d cir., 1967—; mem. Pa. Supreme Ct. Adv. Com. on Appellate Rules, 1987-93, Commn. on Jud. Elections, 1997—; arbitrator, mediator U.S. Dist. Ct. (ea. dist.) Pa., Am. Arbitration Assn., 1966—; bd. dirs. Pa. Capital Case Resource Ctr. Contbg. author: Business and Commercial Litigation in the Federal Courts, 1998; rsch. editor U. Pa. Law Rev., 1964-65; contbr. articles to legal jours. Past mem. Phila. adv. bd. Anti-Defamation League of B'nai Brith, Greater Phila. Regional Commn. on Law and Social Action, Am. Jewish Congress; bd. dirs. Greater Phila. chpt. ACLU, past chmn. criminal justice and police practices com.; past bd. dirs. Pa. chpt. ACLU. Fellow Am. Coll. Trial Lawyers; mem. ABA (bd. govs. 1997—, Ho. of Dels., pres. nat. caucus state bar assns. 1994-95, chmn. standing com. on lawyers profl. liability 1994-95, past chmn. jud. performance and conduct com., jud. adminstrn. divsn., 1989-91, litig. sect., 1988 midyear meeting host com.), Pa. Bar Assn. (pres.-elect 1992-93, pres. 1993-94, bd. govs. 1987-95, ho. of dels. 1983—, Pa. Bar Trust 1996—, past vice chmn. jud. selection com., past chmn. jud. retention election com. 1980-83, chmn. com. on profl. liability 1984-87, past chmn. polit. action com. for merit retention of judges 1980-83, Spl. Achievement award 1986), Phila. Bar Assn. (bd. govs. 1983-87, past chmn. fed. cts. com., past vice chmn. arbitration com., past mem. spl. com. to study appellate cts., past chmn. spl. com. on ins. 1983-84, civil jud. procedures com., spkr. various panels), Pa. Bar Inst. (bd. dirs. 1984-90), Defender Assn. Phila. (bd. dirs.), Am. Judicature Soc. (state membership chmn. 1988), Phila. Trial Lawyers Assn. (past chmn. bus. litig. com., bd. dirs. 1989-90), Soc. of Fellows, Am. Bar Found., Order of Coif (past dir. U. Pa. chpt.). Home: 301 Delancey St Philadelphia PA 19106-4208 Office: Cozen & O'Conner 1900 Market St Fl 3 Philadelphia PA 19103-3572

FIEDEROWICZ, WALTER MICHAEL, lawyer; b. Hartford, Conn., Aug. 23, 1946; s. Michael and Sylvia Christine (Ramunno) F.; m. Gerry Prattson, June 1, 1968; children: Michael, Catherine. B.A., Yale U., 1968; J.D. (DuPont fellow), U. Va., 1971. Bar: Conn. 1971, U.S. Supreme Ct. 1977. Mem. firm Cummings & Lockwood, Stamford, Conn., 1971-76, ptnr. firm, 1979-88, of counsel, 1989-91; pres. Covenant Mut. Ins. Co., Hartford, 1985-92; White House fellow U.S. Dept. Justice, Washington, 1976-77; spl. asst. to Atty. Gen., Dept. Justice, Washington, 1976-77; assoc. dep. Atty. Gen., 1977-79; bd. dirs. Photronics, Inc., First Albany Corp., Compensation Value Alliance, Hematech, Cyagra; chmn. CDT Corp., Meacock Capital. Mem. editorial bd.: Va. Law Review, 1969-71. Mem. grad. council Loomis-Chaffee Sch. Bd. Mem. ABA, Conn. Bar Assn., Order of the Coif, Hartford Golf Club, Citrus Club, Univ. Club. Roman Catholic. Home: 39 Painter Hill Rd Woodbury CT 06798-1517

FIEDLER, HAROLD JOSEPH, electrical engineer, consultant; b. Detroit, Apr. 29, 1924; s. Oscar Emil and Frances (Majczak) F.; m. Ruth Irene Ciesielski, Aug. 20, 1949; children: Charles Steven, Susan Allison Fiedler Gobat, James Brian. BEE, U. Detroit, 1951. Application engr. GE, Schenectady, N.Y., 1951-67, sr. application engr., 1967-70, mgr. system automation operation, communication and control, 1970-73, sr. application engr., 1973-86, cons. elec. utility communication and control, 1986—; chmn. automated distbn. systems GE Task Force, 1980-81; expert advisor Conference Internationale des Grands Reseaux Electriques Study Com. 35, Schenectady, 1973-92. Co-author: EPRI RP3158-1 HVDC Handbook, 1991-92; contbr. over 35 tech. articles on electric utility application to profl. jours., 1952-86. Pres., bd. dirs. Mohawk Opportunities in Mental Health, Inc., Schenectady, 1990-94, fund distbn. com. United Way, 1988-96; fin. officer sect. II Marriage Encounter, Schenectady, 1987-89. 1st class petty officer USN, 1943-46, PTO. Recipient prize paper AIEE Power Div., 1957. Fellow IEEE (chmn. Schenectady sect. 1961-62, chmn. power system communication com. 1965-67, mem. adminstrv. com. 1978-82, Centennial medal 1983); mem. NSPE (registered profl. engr.), IEEE Power Engring. Soc. (chmn. chpts. dept. 1972-82), Mayfield Yacht Club (open class racing 1980-81), Eta Kappa Nu, Tau Beta Pi. Republican. Roman Catholic. Avocations: sailing, photography, electronics. Home: 22 Beechwood Dr Ballston Lake NY 12019-2650

FIEDLER, KATHY LOU, library media specialist; b. Allentown, Pa., May 14, 1957; d. Charles William and Mary Lou (Zwoyer) Lutter; m. James Joseph Fiedler, Dec. 15, 1979; children: Kristen Leah, Meredith Kay, Gregory Steven, Andrew James. BS in Edn., Bloomsburg U., 1979; MLS, Kutztown U., 1986. Cert. in elem. edn. K-8, Pa.; libr. sci. K-12, Pa. Tchr. 5th grade Northwestern Lehigh Sch. Dist., New Tripoli, Pa., 1979-82, elem. libr., 1982-92, mid. sch. libr., 1992—; prof. of libr. sci. Kutztown (Pa.) U., 1997—; cooperating libr. media specialist for student tchrs. Kutztown U., 1992—. Mem. ch. coun. Zion Lehigh Evang. Luth. Ch., Alburtis, Pa., 1991-95, pres. ch. coun., 1992-94. Recipient Literacy award Colonial Pa. Assn. Reading Educators, 1995. Mem. Pa. State Libr.'s Assn., Pa. br. Nat. Coun. Tchrs. English (libr. liaison 1996—). Republican. Lutheran. Avocations: jogging, reading, playing piano, needlework. Home: 8711 Summit Ct Fogelsville PA 18051-2047 Office: Northwestern Lehigh Mid Sch 6636 Northwest Rd New Tripoli PA 18066-2006

FIEDLER, LAWRENCE ELLIOT, real estate investment company executive; b. N.Y.C., Sept. 30, 1938; s. Charles and Polly F.; m. Paula Kassover, June 18, 1969; 1 child, Meridith. BS, Syracuse U., 1959; JD, NYU, 1963, LLM, 1965. Bar: N.Y. 1963; CPA, N.Y. Staff acct. various acctg. firms, N.Y.C., 1959-64; assoc. atty. Forsythe McGovern, N.Y.C., 1964-66; asst. to the mayor City of New York, 1966-67; v.p. New Dimensions & Edn., Inc., N.Y.C., 1967-69; CEO Childcraft Edn. Corp., N.Y.C., 1969-71; investment banker, cons. Merkin and Co., N.Y.C., 1971-73; pres. JRM Devel. Enterprises, Inc. and affiliates, N.Y.C., 1973—; adj. prof. NYU Real Estate Inst., N.Y.C., 1979—; profl. devel. cons. Chem. Bank, N.Y.C., 1993; co-chmn. NYU Real Estate Capital Markets Confs., 1997, 98, 99; litigation cons. on investor/promoter disputes and land lessor/lessee valuation disputes. Mem. editorial bd. Real Estate Rev., 1993—; contbr. articles to profl. jours. Served with A.N.G., N.Y., 1963-66. Mem. Internat. Coun. Shopping Ctrs., Urban Land Inst., Am. Arbitration Assn. (comml. arbitrator). Office: JRM Devel Enterprises Inc 156 W 56th St Ste 1101 New York NY 10019-3800

FIEDLER, LESLIE AARON, English educator, actor, author; b. Newark, Mar. 8, 1917; s. Jacob J. and Lillian (Rosenstrauch) F.; m. Margaret Ann Shipley, Oct. 7, 1939 (div. 1972); children: Kurt, Eric, Michael, Deborah, Jenny, Miriam; m. Sally Andersen, 1973; stepchildren: Soren Andersen, Eric Charles Andersen. BA, NYU, 1938; MA, U. Wis., 1939, PhD, 1941; postgrad., Harvard U., 1946-47. Mem. faculty U. Mont., 1941-64, from instr. to assoc. prof. English, 1941-53, prof., 1953-64, chmn. dept. English, 1954-56; prof. SUNY, Buffalo, 1965—; vis. prof. U. Rome, 1951-52, U. Bologna and Ca Foscari U., Italy, 1952-53, Princeton (N.J.) U., 1956-57, Athens U., 1961-62, U. Sussex, Eng., 1967-68, U. Paris, 1970-71; jr. fellow Ind. U. Sch. Letters, 1951—; assoc. Calhoun fellow Yale U., New Haven, 1969—. Author: (with others) Leaves of Grass: 100 Years After, 1955, An End to Innocence, 1955, The Art of the Essay, 1959, rev. edit., 1969, The Image of the Jew in American Fiction, 1959, Love and Death in the American Novel, 1960, rev. edit., 1966, No. In Thunder, 1960; (with J. Vinocur) The Continuing Debate, 1964; Waiting for the End, 1964, Back to China, 1965, Waiting for the End, 1964, Back to China, 1965; (with others) The Girl in the Black Raincoat, 1966; The Last Jew in America, 1966, The Return of the Vanishing American, 1967, Nude Croquet and Other Stories, 1969, Being Busted, 1970, Collected Essays, 1971, The Stranger in Shakespeare, 1972, The Messengers Will Come No More, 1974, In Dreams Awake, 1975, Freaks, 1977, A Fiedler Reader, 1977, The Inadvertent Epic, 1979, Olaf Stapledon, 1982, What Was Literature?, 1982, Fiedler on the Roof, 1991, Love and Death in the American Novel, 1993, Freaks, 1993, (collected essays) Stranger in a Strange Land, 1994, Tyranny of the Normal, 1996; (short stories) Pull Down Vanity, 1962; (novel) The Second Stone, 1963; (film) When I Am King; editor: (with others) Master of Ballantrae, 1951; (with S. Weil) Waiting for God, 1952; Poems of Whitman, 1959; (with Arthur Zeiger) O Brave New World, 1967; assoc. editor: Ramparts, 1959-65; contbg. editor: Am. Judaism; lit. editor: Running Man, 1967-69; contbr. short stories, poems and articles to jours. U.S. and abroad. Lt. (j.g.) USNR, 1942-46. Rockefeller fellow in humanities, 1946-47, Fulbright fellow, 1951-53, Kenyon rev. fellow in criticism, 1956-57, Guggenheim fellow, 1970-71; recipient Furioso prize for Poetry, 1951, Nat. Inst. Arts and Letters award, 1957, grant-in-aid Am. Coun. Learned Socs., 1960, 61; Christian Gauss lectr., 1956; recipient Ivan Sandroff award for lifetime contbn. to Am. arts and letters Nat. Book Critic Cir., 1998. Mem. MLA (Hubbell medal),

AAUP, English Inst., Am. Acad. and Inst. Arts and Letters (dept. lit.), Dante Soc. Am., PEN, Phi Beta Kappa. Office: SUNY Buffalo Dept English Clemens Hall Buffalo NY 14260 Address: 154 Morris Ave Buffalo NY 14214-1610

FIEDLER, PATRICK JAMES, circuit court judge; b. Milw., July 24, 1953; s. James P. and Georgette M. (Baltus) F.; m. Sandra M. Manka, July 21, 1979; children: Sean, Erin. BBA in Fin., U. Wis., Milw., 1977; JD, Marquette U., 1980. Bar: Wis. 1980, U.S. Dist. Ct. (we. and ea. dists.) Wis. 1980, U.S. Ct. Appeals (7th cir.) 1987. Asst. dist. atty. Office of Dist. Atty., Waukesha, Wis., 1980-84; atty. Runkel, Runkel & Ansay, Port Washington, Wis., 1984-85, Hamilton, Mueller & Fiedler, S.C., Dodgeville, Wis., 1985-87; U.S. atty. U.S. Dept. Justice, Madison, Wis., 1987-91; sec. Wis. Dept. Corrections, Madison, 1991-93; cir. ct. judge Dane County, Madison, 1993—. Active Rep. Party of Dane County, Madison, 1988-93. Mem. State Bar of Wis., Dane County Bar Assn., Kiwanis. Roman Catholic. Avocations: sports, reading. Office: Circuit Court Rm 316 210 Martin Luther King Jr Blvd Madison WI 53709-0001

FIEDLER, ROBERT MAX, management consultant; b. Midland, Mich., June 19, 1945; s. Edward Louis and Lenora Margaret Fiedler; m. Carol Ann Raddatz, Nov. 28, 1981; children: Katy, Christa. BS in Packaging Sci., Mich. State U., 1967, MS in Packaging Sci., 1971, MBA, 1971. Grad. rsch. asst. Mich. State U., East Lansing, 1969-71; div. mgr. MTS Systems Corp., Mpls., 1971-80; cons. Robert Fiedler & Assocs., Mpls., 1980—; adj. prof. dept. engring. U. Minn., Mpls., 1990; mem. adv. bd. ad-hoc com. on packaging U. Minn., 1985—; seminar lectr. in field, Brazil, Mex., China, Italy, The Netherlands, Tunisia. Contbg. editor: Fundamentals of Packaging Dynamics, 1985; editor: Distribution Packaging Technology, 1995, The Best of Transpack, 1966; contbr. articles to profl. jours. Lt. USNR, 1967-69. Recipient Diamond Wing award U.S. Parachute Assn., 1974. Fellow ASTM (chmn. subcom. 1986-95, divsn. chmn. 1995—), Inst. Packaging Profls. (cert. profl. in packaging, past chmn. cons. coun., chmn. tech. com. 1993-97, v.p. coun. of specialists 1997—, Mem. of Yr. 1997). Office: PO Box 24405 Minneapolis MN 55424-0405

FIEL, MAXINE LUCILLE, journalist, behavioral analyst, lecturer; b. N.Y.C.; d. William Jack and Rowena (Burton) Stempel; m. David H. Fiel; children: Meredith Susan, Lisa Beth. Student in psychology and humanities, NYU. Nat. columnist, contbg. editor Mademoiselle Mag., N.Y.C., 1972—; nat. columnist Womens World, Englewood, N.J., 1979-89; contbg. editor Overseas Promotions, N.Y.C., 1979—; articles and features editor Japanese Overseas Press, 1976—; feature editor N.Y. Now, N.Y.C., 1980-91; contbg. editor Woman's World mag., 1979-89, Bella mag., Eng., 1987-89; nat. columnist First mag. for women, 1989-91; founder Starcast Astrological Svcs., Floral Park, N.Y., 1993—; cons. legal profession jury selection, 1984—; mktg. cons. Imperial Enterprises, Tokyo and Princeton, N.J., 1983—; cons. spokesperson Rowland Co., N.Y.C., 1972-81, Allied Chem. Co., N.Y.C., 1972-75; lectr., cons. Atlanta and Fla. Bar Assns., 1986—; creator Touch Game Parker Bros., Salem, Mass., 1971-76; behavior analyst and communications advisor multi-nat. bus. corps.; cons. Chesebrough-Ponds, Footwear Coun., Grand Marnier Liquor; founder Starcast Astrological Svcs., 1993. Pioneer field of polit. body lang., 1969; author: Lovescopes, 1998; contbr. articles to News Am., L.A. Times, Newhouse News Svc., Newspaper Entertainment Assocs., King Features, Borderland Mag.; TV appearances on morning and afternoon shows, including A Current Affair, The Regis Philbin Show, Eyewitness News, Cable News Network, Tonight Show, Today Show, Good Morning Am., Joan Rivers Show, Jenny Jones, Entertainment Tonight, Hard Copy, Inside Edition, BBC Breakfast Show, Good Morning Japan, many others; appeared in daily segment Good Morning Japan; columnist I'M Mag. Japan, 1997—; own daily TV show on Nippon Network, Japan, 1989—. Active Sister Cities, Tokyo and N.Y.C.; charter mem. Elem. Sch. Cultural Exchange, Toyko and N.Y.C., Ctr. Environ. Edn.; bd. dirs. Periwinkle Prodns. Anti-Drug Abuse, N.Y.C. Recipient Achievement award field behavioral sci. and photojournalism, Tokyo, 1974, Outstanding Rsch. award field psychology of gesture, Tokyo, 1976, Outstanding Achievement award Internat. Conf. Soc. Para-Psychology, 1974-75; honored guest at award dinner for involvement and support in the merging of Eye Rsch. Inst. Boston and Harvard Med. Sch., 1991. Mem. AFTRA, Internat. Found. Behavioral Rsch. (past v.p.), Nat. Writers Assn. (profl.), Authors Guild, Authors League, World Wildlife Fund, Whale Protection Fund, Cousteau Soc., Nature Conservancy, Greenpeace, People for Ethical Treatment Animals, Humane Assn. U.S., Guiding Eyes for Blind, Braille Camps for Blind Children, Save the Children, Lotos Club (N.Y.C.), East End Yacht Club (Freeport, N.Y.). Office: 338 Northern Blvd Ste 3 Great Neck NY 11021-4808

FIELD, ALEXANDER JAMES, economics educator; b. Boston, Apr. 17, 1949; s. Mark George and Anne (Murray) F.; m. Valerie Nan Wolk, Aug. 8, 1982; children: James Alexander, Emily Elena. AB, Harvard U., 1970; MS, London Sch. Econs., 1971; PhD, U. Calif., Berkeley, 1974. Asst. prof. econs. Stanford (Calif.) U., 1974-82; assoc. prof. Santa Clara (Calif.) U., 1982-88, acad. v.p., 1986-87, prof., chmn. dept. econs., 1988-93, assoc. dean Leavey Sch. Bus. and Adminstrn., 1993-96, dean, 1996-97, Michel and Mary Orradre prof. econs., 1992—; mem. bd. trustees Santa Clara U., 1988-91. Author: Educational Reform and Manufacturing Development in Mid-Nineteenth Century Massachusetts, 1989; author, editor: The Future of Economics, 1995; assoc. editor Jour. Econ. Lit., 1981-98, 99—; editor Rsch. in Econ. History, 1993—; mem. editl. bd. Explorations in Econ. History, 1983-89. Recipient Nevins prize Columbia U., 1975; NSF rsch. grantee, 1989. Mem. Phi Beta Kappa, Beta Gamma Sigma. Home: 3762 Redwood Cir Palo Alto CA 94306-4255 Office: Santa Clara Univ Dept Econs Santa Clara CA 95053

FIELD, ANDREA BEAR, lawyer; b. New London, Conn., Nov. 30, 1949; d Geurson Donald and Lorraine (Solomon) Silverberg; m. Thornton Withers Field, May 17, 1984; children: Benjamin, Geoffrey. Student, Wellesley Coll., 1967-69; BA, Yale U., 1971; JD, U. Va., 1974. Bar: Va. 1974, D.C. 1978, U.S. Ct. Appeals (3d, 4th, 5th, 7th, 8th and D.C. cirs.). Assoc. Hunton & Williams, Washington and Richmond, Va., 1974-81; ptnr. Hunton & Williams, Washington, 1981—. Mem. ABA (chair sect. natural resources, energy and environ. law 1989-90, coun. 1984-87, 90-91, chair com. air quality 1982-84, vice chair teleconf. com. 1990—, environ. controls bus. law sect. 1990-91, vice chair com. environ. law, real property, probate and trust law sect. 1990-91; chair standing com. on natural conf. groups 1993-94, nat. conf. lawyers and scientists 1990-93, sect. ad hoc com. nat. insts. 1989-90, coun. sect. sci. and tech. 1991-92). Office: Hunton & Williams Ste 9000 2000 Pennsylvania Ave NW Washington DC 20006-1812

FIELD, ARTHUR NORMAN, lawyer; b. N.Y.C., Sept. 28, 1935; s. Harry and Rose (Lemberg) F.; m. Doris Helen Rabbiner, Sept. 1, 1957; children: Michael, Karen. BBA, CCNY, 1955; LLB, Harvard U., 1958. Bar: N.Y. 1959, Fla. 1975. Assoc. Shearman & Sterling, N.Y.C., 1959-68, ptnr., 1968—; bd. dirs. Sunset Realty Corp., Punta Gorda, Fla. Author: (with R. Ryan) Legal Opinions in Corporate Transactions, 1995; editor: (with M. Moskin) N.Y. and Delaware Business Organizations, 1997. Chmn., bd. dirs. Community Action for Legal Svcs., 1972-77; bd. dirs. Brookdale Found., 1983—, Wave Hill Inc., N.Y.C., 1968-80, Washington Square Legal Svcs., 1979-95; trustee Ramapo Trust, 1983—. Fellow Am. Bar Found., N.Y. Bar Found., N.Y. County Lawyers Assn. (pres. 1990-92); mem. ABA (ho. of dels. 1990-92), N.Y. State Bar Assn. (v.p. 1992-97), Assn. of Bar of City of N.Y., Am. Law Inst.

FIELD, BARRY ELLIOT, internist, gastroenterologist; b. Hartford, Conn., Apr. 21, 1947; s. Arnold and Selma (Nechrich) F.; m. Julie Farr, Jan. 6, 1991; children: Rachel Elizabeth, Hannah Margaret. B.A. (scholar), Harvard U., 1968; M.D., Albert Einstein Coll. Medicine, 1972. Intern in pediatrics Montefiore Hosp., Bronx, N.Y., 1972-73; intern medicine Met. Hosp., N.Y.C., 1973-74, resident in medicine, 1974-76; fellow in gastroenterology Harbor Gen. Hosp., Torrance, Calif., 1976-78; practice medicine specializing in internal medicine and gastroenterology, N. Tarrytown, N.Y., 1978—; dir. medicine Phelps Meml. Hosp., N. Tarrytown, N.Y. Mem. Am. Gastroenterol. Assn., Alpha Omega Alpha. Office: 777 N Broadway Ste 305 Tarrytown NY 10591-1040

FIELD, CHARLES TWIST, artist, art educator; b. Van Nuys, Calif., Oct. 17, 1936; s. Edward Winter and Enid (Twist) F.; m. Germaine E., Dec. 27, 1961; children: Michele, Caroline, Mark Charles. BA, Stanford U., 1958; MFA, U. Wash., 1965. Instr. art Western Ill. U., Macomb, 1965-67; asst. prof. art U. Tex., Austin, 1967-72; assoc. prof. art U. N.Mex., Albuquerque, 1972-74; prof. divsn. visual arts U. Tex., San Antonio, 1974—. Capt. USAF, 1958-62. Ballinglen Arts Found. fellow, 1999—. Roman Catholic. Home: 10562 Rocking M Trl Helotes TX 78023-4034 Office: U Tex Divsn Visual Arts 6900 N Loop 1604 W San Antonio TX 78249-1130

FIELD, CURTIS LINCOLN, church elder, library director; b. Troy, N.Y., Oct. 29, 1949; s. Harold Lincoln and Barbara Elizabeth (Atherton) F.; m. Linda Eastman, June 25, 1994; two children: Margaret Doris, Susannah Atherton. AB in Polit. Sci., Grove City (Pa.) Coll., 1971; MLS, SUNY, Albany, 1979. Deacon Madison Ave. Presbyn. Ch., N.Y.C., 1986-92, elder, 1993—; libr. dir. Can. Consulate Gen., N.Y.C., 1985—. Capt. USAF, 1972-75. Mem. Spl. Libr. Assn., Beta Phi Mu. Home: 201 W 92nd St Apt 6I New York NY 10025-7437 Office: Canadian Consulate Gen 1251 Avenue Of The Americas New York NY 10020-1104

FIELD, DANIEL, history educator; b. Boston, July 26, 1938; s. Richard Hinckley and Caroline (Crosby) F.; m. Harriet Beecher, June 26, 1959; children: Richard Henry, Jonathan Beecher. BA, Harvard U., 1959, MA, 1962, PhD, 1968. Lectr. Harvard U., Cambridge, Mass., 1968-70; asst. prof. Barnard Coll., N.Y.C., 1970-76; prof. Syracuse (N.Y.) U., 1976—; vis. prof. Harvard U., Cambridge, 1981-82; Fulbright lectr. Moscow State U., 1996. Author: The End of Serfdom, 1976, Rebels in the Name of the Tsar, 1988; editor: Quantitative Studies in Agrarian History, 1993; editor Russian Rev., 1982-89. Fulbright Hays fellow U.S. Govt., 1964, 78, 81, Sr. fellow Harriman Inst., Columbia U., N.Y.C., 1990-91. Fellow Davis Ctr. for Russian Studies-Harvard U. Democrat. Office: Syracuse Univ Dept History 145 Eggers Hall Syracuse NY 13244

FIELD, DAVID ELLIS, lawyer; b. Washington, Feb. 3, 1953; s. Ellis Arrington and Phyllis Martina (Anderson) F. BA, U. Va., 1975, MEd, 1976; JD, George Mason U., 1983. Bar: Va. 1983, D.C. 1990, Md. 1991, U.S. Dist. Ct. (ea. dist.) Va. 1984, U.S. Ct. Appeals (4th cir.) 1985. Assoc. Law Offices Alphonse Audet, Fairfax, Va., 1984; asst. commonwealth's atty. Office of Fairfax County, Va., 1984-87; assoc. Miller & Bucholtz, P.C., Reston, Va., 1987-89, Falcone & Rosenfeld, Ltd., Fairfax, 1989, Lewis, Dack, Paradiso, O'Connor & Good, Wasington, 1989-91, Deckelbaum, Ogens & Fischer, Wasington, 1991-92; atty. Alan S. Toppelberg & Assocs., Washington, 1992-94; ptnr. Field & Cram, Fairfax, Va., 1994-98; pvt. practice Fairfax, Va., 1998—; asst. city atty. City of Fairfax, 1988-89. Mem. Am. Arbitration Assn., Va. Coll. Criminal Def. Attys., Fairfax Bar Assn., Delta Theta Pi. Democrat. Presbyterian. Office: Law Office David E Field P C Ste B6 10605 Judicial Dr Fairfax VA 22030

FIELD, ELLEN, marketing professional; b. Marlinton, W.Va., Dec. 26, 1952; d. George S. and Vivienne W. Sharp; m. John A. Field, May 7, 1977 (div.); children: Margaret Elaine, George William Butler. BS, W.Va. U., 1974; MA, Coll. Grad. Studies, 1976. Rsch. assoc. Nat. Gov.'s Assn., Washington, 1978-80; mem. presdl. pers. Reagan-Bush Transition Team, Washington, 1980; vice chmn. McLean (Va.) Cmty. Ctr., 1987-90; spl. asst. Office Drug Control Policy, Washington, 1990-93; vol. coord., dir. spl. events Tom Davis Campaign, Springfield, Va., 1994-95; exec. dir. McLean (Va.) C. of C., 1995-98; field dir. Bobbie Kilberg for Lt. Gov., McLean, 1993, George Allen for Gov., McLean, 1993; legis. dir. Congressman Tom Davis, Washington, 1995. Author: Governing the American States, 1978; editor: Governor's Policy Initiatives, 1980, Reflections on Being Governor, 1981. Treas. Dranesville Rep. Party, McLean, 1994-98, mem. Fairfax County Rep. Commn., 1994—; mem. Greater McLean Republican Women's Club, 1983—, pres., 1987. Mem. Nat. Fedn. Rep. Women, Va. Fedn. Rep. Women (exec. com. decision strategies, chmn. pub. affairs). Presbyn.

FIELD, GEORGE BROOKS, theoretical astrophysicist; b. Providence, R.I., Oct. 25, 1929; s. Winthrop Brooks and Pauline (Woodworth) F.; m. Sylvia Farrior Smith, June 23, 1956 (div. Oct. 1979); children: Christopher Lyman, Natasha Suzanne; m. Susan Alice Gebhart, Feb. 26, 1981. BS in Physics, MIT, 1951; PhD in Astronomy, Princeton U., 1955. Asst. prof., then assoc. prof. astronomy Princeton U., 1957-65; vis. prof. Calif. Inst. Tech., 1964; prof. astronomy U. Calif., Berkeley, 1965-72; chmn. dept. U. Calif., 1970-71; prof. astronomy Harvard U., 1972—; sr. physicist Smithsonian Astrophys. Obs., 1982—; Phillips visitor Haverford (Pa.) Coll., 1965, 71; vis. prof. Cambridge (Eng.) U., 1969; Willson prof. applied astronomy, dir. Harvard Coll. Obs., 1973-82; dir. Smithsonian Astrophys. Obs., 1973-82, now physicist; lectr. Ecole d'Ete de Physique Theorique, Les Houches, France, 1974; mem. Nat. Commn. on Space, 1985-86; mem. study group NRC-Space Sci. Bd.; chmn. NAS-NRC Com. Astronomy Survey Commn., 1978-82. Recipient Disting. Pub. Svc. medal NASA, 1977, 1986, Joseph Henry medal Smithsonian Inst., 1983; Guggenheim fellow, 1960-61. Fellow AAAS, Am. Phys. Soc.; mem. NAS, Am. Acad. Arts and Scis., Am. Astron. Soc., Astron. Soc. Pacific, Internat. Astron. Union, Explorers Club, Harvard Club N.Y., Sigma Xi. Office: Harvard-Smithsonian Ctr for Astrophysics 60 Garden St Cambridge MA 02138-1516*

FIELD, HENRY AUGUSTUS, JR., lawyer; b. Wisconsin Dells, Wis., July 8, 1928; s. Henry A. and Georgia (Coakley) F.; m. Patricia Ann Young, Nov. 30, 1957 (dec. 1980); children: Mary Patricia (dec. 1992), Thomas Gerard, Susan Therese (Mrs. Thomas Hempel); m. Molly Kelly Martin, Apr. 13, 1985. Student, Western Mich. Coll., 1946-47; PhD, Marquette U., 1950; LLB (cum laude), U. Wis., 1952. Bar: Wis. 1952, U.S. Dist. Ct. (we. dist.) Wis. 1952, U.S. Ct. Appeals (7th cir.) 1957, U.S. Supreme Ct. 1980. Asst. U.S. atty. Western Dist. of Wis., 1956-57; assoc. Roberts, Boardman, Suhr, Bjork & Curry, 1957-62; jr. ptnr. Roberts, Boardman, Suhr & Curry, 1962-70; ptnr. Boardman, Suhr, Curry & Field, Madison, Wis., 1970—, chmn. exec. com., 1985-95; mem. Wis. Jud. Council, 1974-79. Dir. Family Service Soc., 1969-75, treas., 1971-72, pres., 1973-74; trustee Dane County Bar Pro Bono Trust Found., 1995—. Served with C.I.C., AUS, 1952-55. Fellow Am. Coll. Trial Lawyers (state chmn. 1982-83), Am. Bar Found.; mem. ABA (Wis. chmn. legis. com. 1975-76), 7th Fed. Circuit Bar Assn., Wis. Bar Assn. (chmn. litigation sect. 1971-72), Milw. and Dane County Bar Assn. (pres. 1971-72), Phi Delta Phi, Sigma Tau Delta, Order of Coif. Republican. Roman Catholic. Club: Madison. Home: 3310 Valley Creek Cir Middleton WI 53562-1988 Office: Boardman Suhr Curry & Field 1 S Pinckney St Madison WI 53703-2892

FIELD, HERMANN HAVILAND, architect, educator, author; b. Zurich, Switzerland, Apr. 13, 1910; s. Herbert Haviland and Nina (Eschwege) F.; m. Kate Margaret Thornycroft, June 14, 1940; children: Hugh, Alan, Alison. BA cum laude, Harvard U., 1933; postgrad., Harvard Grad. Sch. Design, Cambridge, 1932-34; diploma in architecture, Swiss Fed. Poly. Inst., Zurich, 1936. Resident architect Roche Products Ltd., Welwyn Garden City, Eng., 1936-38; field rep. Czech Refugee Trust Fund, Poland and Eng., 1939-40; site planner Tuttle, Seelye, Place & Raymond, N.Y.C., 1941-45; dir. research Raymond & Rado, Architects, N.Y.C., 1945-47; dir. bldg. plans Case Western Res. U., Cleve., 1947-49; victim of kidnapping in Cold War incident, secretly held in Polish prison cellar Miedzeszyn, 1949-54; preparation of prison novels London, 1955, Boston, 1956-60; dir. planning office Tufts-New England Med. Ctr., Boston, 1961-72; founder, dir. grad. program in urban, social and environ. policy, prof. environ. planning Tufts U., Medford, Mass., 1972-78, prof. emeritus polit. sci., 1978—. Author: (with Stanislaw Mierzenski) Angry Harvest, 1958, German, Swedish, English, Polish edits., 1958-62, also cons. on film, 1984, Duck Lane, 1961, (with Frank Thibodeau) Sustaining Tomorrow, 1984, 2d edit., 1985, (with Kate Field) Departure Delayed, German and Polish edits., 1996, 97; contbg. author: Problems of Pediatric Hospital Design, 1965, Evaluation of Hospital Design, 1982, Environment and Cognition, 1973; contbr. articles to profl. jours. Chmn. planning bd. Shirley, Mass., 1984-86, 89-93, vice-chmn., 1986-89; active Devens Enterprise Commn., 1995—, Hist. Dist. Commn., Shirley, 1973-88, Conservation Commn., Shirley, 1970-83, Cambridge, 1975-81; dir. Nashua River Watershed Assn., Fitchburg, Mass., 1981-85, Coolidge Ctr. Environ. Leadership, Cambridge, 1983-89; del. Internat. Conf. Sustainable Devel., Ottawa, 1986; v.p., dir. Mass. Assn. Conservation Commn., Medford, 1976-85. Recipient Environ. Leadership award New Eng. Environ. Network, 1987, Conservation award Nashua River Watershed Assn., 1988, Lifetime Preservation award Mass. Hist. Commn., 1990, Quality of Life award N.E. Regional Coun., AIA, 1993. Fellow AIA; mem. Am. Assn. Univ. Profs., Am. Inst. Cert. Planners (charter 1978—), Boston Soc. Architects (dir. 1968-70, sec. 1970-74), Boston Archtl. Ctr., Internat. Union Conservation Nature (planning commn. 1978—), Sierra Club, Appalachian Mountain (Boston) Club. Avocations: managing wildlife sanctuary, writing autobiographical manuscript. Home and Office: Valley Farm 110 Center Rd Shirley MA 01464-2106

FIELD, JAMES BERNARD, internist, educator; b. Fort Wayne, Ind., May 28, 1926; s. Abraham and Clara (Ridner) F.; m. Dorothy Spivey, Sept. 25, 1954; children—Carolyn, Nancy, Douglas, Susan. Student, Harvard Coll., 1946-47; M.D. cum laude, Harvard Med. Sch., 1951. Diplomate: Am. Bd. Internal Medicine. Intern internal medicine Mass. Gen. Hosp., Boston, 1951-52; asst. resident internal medicine Mass. Gen. Hosp., 1952-53, resident internal medicine, 1953-54; practice medicine specializing in endocrinology Pitts., 1962-78, Houston, 1978-89; med. officer USPHS, Nat. Inst. Arthritis and Metabolic Diseases, Bethesda, Md., 1954, sr. asst. surgeon, 1954-58, sr. investigator, 1958-60, surgeon, 1958-60, sr. surgeon, 1960-61; asst. in medicine diabetic dept. Kings Coll. Hosp., London, 1957-58; med. officer Nat. Inst. Metabolic Disease, Bethesda, Md., 1961-62; head div. endocrinology and metabolism U. Pitts. Sch. Medicine, 1962-78, assoc. prof. medicine, 1962-66, prof. medicine, 1966-78, dir. clin. research unit, 1962-78; Rutherford prof. medicine Baylor Coll. Medicine, Houston, 1978-89, head div. endocrinology and metabolism, 1978-87; vis. prof. dept. exptl. medicine Univ. Coll. Med. Sch., London, 1985-86; dir. Diabetes and Endocrinology Research Ctr., Baylor Coll Medicine, 1980-89; med. adv. bd. Nat. Pituitary Agy., 1967-69; research collaborator Brookhaven Nat. Lab., 1972-85; mem. nat. diabetes adv. bd. HEW, 1977-85, chmn., 1982-85; mem. endocrinology study sect. USPHS, 1965-69, chmn., 1968-69, endocrinology and metabolism tng. grant com., 1970-74, gen. clin. research center rev. com., 1976-79; mem. panel clin. scis. com. study nat. needs biomed. and behavioral rsch. pers. Nat Rsch. Coun., 1976-80; mem. VA merit rev. com. on endocrinology and metabolism, 1982-85; lectr. medicine Harvard Med. Sch., 1992—; mem. honors com. Harvard Med. Sch., 1993—. Contbr. numerous articles on research studies in endocrinology to profl. jours.; assoc. editor: Metabolism, 1959-69; editor-in-chief, 1969—; editor: Jour. Cylic Nucleotide Research, 1974-79; mem. editorial bd.: Clin. Research, 1965, Postaglandins, 1968-72; contbng. editor: Clin. Thyroidology, 1988—. Bd. dirs. Gen. Clin. Research Centers, 1977-79. Served with U.S. Army, 1944-45. Decorated Purple Heart, Bronze Star; recipient Van Meter prize award Am. Goiter Assn., 1961, Prize Boylston Soc., 1951. Mem. Assn. Am. Physicians, Endocrine Soc. (mem. coun. 1972-75, internat. liaison com. 1972-75, mem. pub. affairs com. 1972-75, mem. awards com. 1972-75, chmn. 1974-75, nominating com. 1982-84, chmn. 1984), Am. Diabetes Assn. (dir. 1968-74, vice chmn. com. on rsch. 1972-73, chmn. com. rsch. 1975-77, mem. established investigative rev. bd. 1975-77, Eli Lilly award 1958), Am. Fedn. Clin. Rsch., Am. Clin. and Climatol. Assn., Am. Physiology Soc., Am. Soc. Clin. Investigation, Mass. Med. Soc. (chmn. com. on ret. physicians 1993—, Prize 1951), Moseley, Warren, Whitman, Richardson Com., Harvard Med. Sch., Quechee Lakes Club, Belmont Hill Club, Harvard Med. Alumni Assn., (treas. 1997), Alpha Omega Alpha. Club: Sea Pines Racquet (Hilton Head, S.C.). Home: 241 Perkins St Apt I101 Boston MA 02130-4046

FIELD, JEFFREY FREDERIC, designer; b. Los Angeles, July 6, 1954; s. Norman and Gertrude Clara (Ellman) F.; m. Susan Marie Merrin, Jan. 8, 1978. BA in Art, Calif. State U., Northridge, 1977, MA in Art, 1980. Cert. indsl. plastics tchr., Calif. Designer Fundamental Products Co., N. Hollywood, Calif., 1972-82; designer/model maker The Stansbury Co., Beverly Hills, Calif., 1982-84; mech. engr. Vector Electronic Co., Sylmar, Calif., 1984-87; pres., prin. Jeffrey Field Design Inc., Camarillo, Calif., 1987—; cons. MiniMed Techs., Sylmar, 1987—, Best Time Inc., Leander, Tex., 1987—, Spectrum Design, Granada Hills, Calif., 1987—, Raycom Systems Inc., Boulder, Colo., 1988-89, Alfred E. Mann Found. for Sci. Rsch., Sylmar, 1988—, Atomic Elements, L.A., E-O Products, Laguna Hills, Calif., Autogenics, Newbury Park, Calif., 1990—, Pacesetter Systems, Sylmar, 1990—, Baxter Healthcare Corp., Pharmaseal Div., Valencia, Calif., 1990—, Surgidev Corp., Goleta, Calif., 1990—, Sensor Medics Inc., Yorba Linda, Calif., 1997—, Percusurge Inc., Sunnyvale, Calif., 1996—, Whittader Safety Systems, Simi Valley, Calif., 1998—, Howard Leight Ind., San Diego, Calif., 1996—, Indsl. Strength Eyewear/Grafix Mktg. Group, Manhattan Beach & Campbell, Calif., 1991—. Democrat. Jewish. Avocations: bicycle riding, backpacking, cartooning, reading. Home and Office: 3061 Vista Grande Camarillo CA 93012-8893

FIELD, JOHN LOUIS, architect; b. Mpls., Jan. 18, 1930; s. Harold David and Gladys Ruth (Jacobs) F.; m. Carol Helen Hart, July 23, 1961; children: Matthew Hart, Alison Ellen. BA, Yale U., 1952, MArch, 1955. Individual practice architecture San Francisco, 1959-68; v.p. firm Bull, Field, Volkmann, Stockwell, Architects, San Francisco, 1968-83; ptnr. Field/Gruzen, Architects, San Francisco, 1983-86, Field Paoli Architects, San Francisco, 1986—; guest lectr. Stanford, 1970; chmn. archtl. council San Francisco Mus. Art. 1969-71; mem. San Francisco Bay Conservation and Devel. Commn., Design Rev. Bd., 1980-84; founding chmn. San Francisco Bay Architects Review, 1977-80. Co-author, producer, dir.: film Cities for People (Broadcast Media award 1975, Golden Gate award San Francisco Internat. Film Festival 1975, Ohio State award 1976); film The Urban Preserve (Calif. Council AIA Commendation of excellence 1982); co-design architect: design for New Alaska Capital City (winner design competition). Recipient Archtl. Record award, 1961, 1972; AIA, Sunset mag. awards, 1962, 64, 69; No. Calif. AIA awards, 1967, 82; Calif. Council AIA award, 1982; certificate excellence Calif. Gov.'s Design awards, 1966; Homes for Better Living awards, 1962, 66, 69, 71, 77; Albert J. Evers award, 1974, Best Bldg. award Napa (Calif.) C. of C., 1987, Design award Internat. Council Shopping Ctrs., 1988, Stores of Excellence award Nat. Mall Monitor, 1989, 92, 93, Pacific Coast Builders Gold Nugget award, 1989, 91, Urban Design award Calif. Coun. AIA, 1991, 93. Fellow AIA (com. on design); mem. Nat. Coun. Archtl. Registration Bds., Urban Land Inst. (Design award 1995), Yale Club, Lambda Alpha. Office: Field Paoli Architects 1045 Sansome St Ste 206 San Francisco CA 94111-1315*

FIELD, JOSEPH MYRON, broadcast executive; b. Phila., Jan. 11, 1932; s. Sylvan Hector and Hannah (Worobe) F.; m. Marie Helene Felber, June 28, 1959; children: David Jonathan, Nancy Elizabeth. BA, U. Pa., 1952; LLB, Yale U., 1955. Bar: Conn. 1955, N.Y. 1957, Pa. 1961. Law clk. U.S. Ct. Appeals for 2d Cir., N.Y.C., 1955-56; assoc. Roberts & Holland, N.Y.C., 1956-59; asst. U.S. atty. for so. dist. N.Y., U.S. Dept. Justice, N.Y.C., 1959-61; assoc. Meltzer & Schiffrin, Phila., 1961-65; pvt. practice Phila., 1965-69; founder, CEO, chmn. bd. Entercom Comm. Corp., Phila., 1968—. Editor Yale Law Jour., 1953-55. Violinist, asst. concertmaster New Haven Symphony Orch., 1952-53; trustee West Park Hosp., Phila., 1964-87, pres. bd. trustees, 1972-75; bd. dirs. Jewish Employment and Vocat. Svc., Phila., 1990—, Curtis Inst. Music, Phila., 1994—, Settlement Music Sch. Ctrl. Bd., 1995—, Am. Interfaith Inst., 1997—, Liberty Mus., 1998—, Phila. Chamber Music Soc., 1998—. Mem. Phila. Bar Assn., Nat. Assn. Broadcasters (steering com. 1990-91, moderator, speaker nat. conv. 1991, radio bd. dirs. 1992-96). Office: Entercom 401 E City Ave Ste 409 Bala Cynwyd PA 19004-1121

FIELD, JULIA ALLEN, futurist, strategist; b. Boston, Jan. 5, 1937; d. Howard Locke and Julia Wright (Field) Allen. BA cum laude, Harvard U. 1960, Harvard Grad. Sch. Design, 1964-65; postgrad. Pius XII Grad. Art Inst., Florence, Italy, 1961; postgrad. Walden U. Inst. for Advanced Studies, 1983-89. Cons. to archtl. and environ. firms, 1964-69; cons. Forestry Dept. of Simla (India), 1969-70; founder, v.p. Black Grove, Inc., Miami, Fla., 1970-80; founder, pres. Amazonia 2000, Bogotá, Colombia, 1970-72; leader Task Force Amazonia 2000, DAINCO, 1977-78; elected pres. Foundation Amazonia 2000 in Gen. Assembly, Leticia, Colombia, 1979—; pres. Acad. Arts and Scis. of the Ams., Miami, Fla., 1979—; mem. Presdl. Adv. Com. on tech. devel. Group of Yr. 2000, Colombia, 1971-74; mem. Man and Biosphere Com. UNESCO, Colombia, 1972-78; mem. Task Force on Colonization Report to President of Colombia, 1973; cons. Amazon Unified Command, Republic of Colombia 1981-86; hon. nat. insp. resources and environment Republic of Colombia, 1982—; bd. visitors Duke U. Primate Ctr., 1979-82; prin. speaker various seminars, congresses. Mem. City of Miami Bicentennial com., 1975-76; coord. Cmty. of Man Task Force, Miami, 1975-76; mem. Blueprint for Miami 2000, 1982-85; adv. Tech. Jour., Delhi,

India, 1985-86; participant Only One Earth Forum, UN Environ. Programme/Rene Dubos Ctr., N.Y.C., 1987, 15 Internat. Human Unity Conf., New Delhi, 1988; founder Amacayacu National Park, Amazonia, Colombia, 1975; creator, builder with other scientists Villa Ciencia, Rio Cotuhé, Colombia, 1975; signed Third Amazon World Model Accord for Amazonia 2000 with IGAC and DAINCO, Colombia, 1988-93. Author: Amazonia 2000, 1978, Amazonia as a World Model, 1972. Fellow Royal Geog. Soc. (London); mem. Internat. Assn. Hydrogen Energy, UN Assn. U.S., Friends of the Earth, The Friends of Worldwatch, EarthJustice Legal Def. Fund.

FIELD, KAREN ANN (KAREN ANN SCHAFFNER), real estate broker; b. New Haven, Jan. 27, 1936; d. Abraham Terry and Ida (Smith) Rogovin; m. Barry S. Crown, 1954 (div. 1969); children: Laurie Jayne, Donna Lynn, Bruce Alan, Bradley David; m. Michael Lehmann Field, 1969 (div. 1977); m. Ronald E. Schaffner, April 1998. Student Vassar Coll., 1953-54, Harrington Inst. Interior Design, 1973-74, Roosevelt U., 1987—. Cert. residential specialist. Owner Karen Field Interiors, Chgo., 1970-86, Karen Field & Assocs. Realtors, Chgo., 1980-81; pres., ptnr. Field-Pels & Assocs. Realtors, Chgo., 1981-86; with top sales volume Sudler-Marling, Inc., 1989; sales broker Koenig & Strey, Inc., Chgo., 1992—; elected to Pres.'s Club, Koenig & Strey, Inc., 1996. Mem. Women's Coun. Camp Henry Horner, Chgo., 1960; bd. dirs., treas. Winnetka Pub. Sch. Nursery (Ill.), 1961-63; pres. Jr. Aux. U. Chgo. Cancer Rsch. Found., 1960-66, mem. exec. com. woman's bd., 1965-66; bd. dirs., sec. United Charities, Chgo., 1966-68, Victory Gardens Theatre, Chgo., 1979; co-founder, pres. Re-Entry Ctr., Wilmette, Ill., 1978-80; mem. br. Child Abuse Svcs., Chgo., 1981-89, Stop AIDS Real Estate Div., 1988, AIDS Walkathon Com., 1990; bd. dirs. The Chicago Ctr. for Self-Taught Art, 1993-96. Recipient Servian award Jr. Aux. of U. Chgo. Cancer Rsch. Found., 1966, Margarite Wolf award Women's Bd., U. Chgo. Cancer Rsch. Found., 1967, Founder's award, 1997, WAIT Woman of Day. Mem. Internat. Real Estate Fedn. (chmn. membership Chgo. chpt. 1994, bd. dirs. 1996), Chgo. Real Estate Bd., Chgo. Assn. Realtors, Chgo. Coun. Fgn. Rels., English Speaking Union (jr. bd. 1958-59), Carlton Club, Art Inst. Chgo., Field Mus., Union League Club, Presidents Club, Founders Club. Office: Koenig & Strey Inc 900 N Michigan Ave Chicago IL 60611-1542

FIELD, LARRY, paper company executive. CEO Field Container, Elk Grove Village, Ill. Office: Field Container 1500 Nicholas Blvd Elk Grove Village IL 60007-5575*

FIELD, LYMAN, lawyer; b. Kansas City, Mo., Oct. 6, 1914; s. Russell and Gertrude (Brown) F.; 1 dau. by previous marriage, Kathleen; m. Jo Ann Straube, Apr. 10, 1965; 1 dau., Jennifer Ann. A.B., U. Kans., 1936; LL.B., Harvard U., 1939. Bar: Mo. 1939. Since practiced in Kansas City; partner Field, Gentry & Benjamin, P.C.; spl. commr. Supreme Ct. Mo., 1953-54. Founding bd. dirs. Greater Kansas City Mental Health Found., 1950-58; pres. Council Social Agys., Kansas City, Mo., 1951-55; gen. chmn. Citizens Regional Planning Council of Greater Kansas City, 1949-53; chmn. Mayor's Mcpl. Services Commn., 1951-53; pres. Bd. Police Commrs., Kansas City, Mo., 1957-61; mem. Mo. State Council on Arts, 1965-75, chmn., 1966-73; chmn. N.Am. Assembly State and Provincial Art Agencies, 1968-70; co-chmn. Midwest Regional Assembly on Future of Performing Arts, 1979; participant 46th Am. Assembly on Art Mus., Arden House, N.Y., 67th Am. Assembly on Arts and Pub. Policy, Arden House; Mem. Mo. Humanities Coun., 1996—; mem. and chmn. Thomas Hart Benton Homestead Meml. Adv. Commn. Mo., 1975—; trustee Thomas Hart Benton and Rita P. Benton testamentary trusts; trustee, v.p. Kansas City Philharm. Orch. Assn., 1961-71; trustee Samuel H. Kress Found., N.Y.C., Conservatory of Music of Kansas. City; bd. dirs. Cross Found., Kansas City Soc. Western Art, Mid-Am. Arts Alliance, Mo. Inst. for Justice, Mo. Repertory Theater; mem. adv. com. Cockefair Chair of Continuing Edn., U. Mo., Kansas City; trustee, bd. dirs. Kansas City Art Inst., 1969-74; mem. Soc. of Fellows, Nelson-Atkins Art Mus., The Univ. Assocs. of U. Mo.-Kansas City, adv. bd. Spencer Mus. Art, U. Kansas. Served from pvt. to maj. USMCR, 1942-46, PTO. Decorated Bronze Star medal; recipient Mo. Arts award, 1989. Fellow Am. Coll. Trial Lawyers; mem. ABA, Mo. Bar Assn., Kansas City Bar Assn., Am. Judicature Soc., Internat. Assn. Ins. Counsel, Lawyers Assn. Kansas City, Kansas City Country Club, Univ. Club, Carriage Club, River Club, Beta Theta Pi. Home: 5815 State Line Rd Kansas City MO 64113-1151 Office: Field Gentry & Benjamin PC 210 Plaza West Bldg 4600 Madison Ave Kansas City MO 64112-1277

FIELD, MARSHALL, business executive; b. Charlottesville, Va., May 13, 1941; s. Marshall IV and Joanne (Bass) F.; m. Joan Best Connelly, Sept. 5, 1964 (div. 1969); 1 child, Marshall; m. Jamee Beckwith Jacobs, Aug. 19, 1972; children: Jamee Christine, Stephanie Caroline, Abigail Beckwith. BA, Harvard Coll., 1963. With N.Y. Herald Tribune, 1964-65; pub. Chgo. Sun-Times, 1969-80, Chgo. Daily News, 1969-78; dir. Field Enterprises, Inc., Chgo., 1965-84; dir., mem. exec. com. Field Enterprises, Inc., 1965-84, chmn. bd., 1972-84; chmn. bd. The Field Corp., 1984—; chmn. bd. Cabot, Cabot & Forbes, 1984—, chmn. exec. com., 1985-89, sr. dir., chief exec. officer, 1989—; pub. World Book-Childcraft Internat. Inc., 1973-78, dir., 1965-80. Bd. trustees Art Inst. Chgo., Chgo. Pub. Libr. Found., Rush-Presbyn.-St. Lukes Med. Ctr.; vice-chmn. bd. trustees Field Mus. Natural History; bd. dirs. First Nat. Bank Chgo., 1970-85, Field Found. Ill., Lincoln Park Zool. Soc., World Wildlife Fedn., Atlantic Salmon Assn.; adv. bd. Brookfield Zoo; active Chgo. Orchestral Assn. Mem. Nature Conservancy, River Club, Chgo. Club, Comml. Club, Harvard Club, Racquet Club, Onwentsia Club, Jupiter Island Club, Shore Acres Club. Office: 225 W Wacker Dr Ste 1500 Chicago IL 60606-1229

FIELD, MICHAEL, gastroenterologist; b. London, July 20, 1933; came to U.S., 1938; m. Linda Seidel; children: John, Ezra, Ben. AB, U. Chgo., 1953; MD, Boston U., 1959. Diplomate Am. Bd. Internal Medicine. Intern, asst. resident Cleve. Met. Gen. Hosp., 1959-61, sr. asst. resident, 1963-64; clin. assoc. Nat. Cancer Inst., Medicine Br., 1961-63; rsch. fellow in biophysics Harvard Med. Sch., 1964-66; rsch. fellow in gastroenterology Beth Israel Hosp., 1966-68, instr. to assoc. prof., 1968-77; prof. Pritzker Sch. Medicine, U. Chgo., 1977-84; prof., dir. divsn. gastroenterology Coll. Physicians and Surgeons, Columbia U., 1984—; bd. trustee, exec. mem. Mt. Desert Island Biol. Lab., 1982-84; ad hoc mem. several NIH study sections, Cystic Fibrosis Found., 1977—; dir. NIH tng. program gastroenterology Coll. Physicians and Surgeons, Columbia U., 1985-88, mem. faculty coun., 1985-88, mem. com. appointments and promotions, 1989-92, mem. exec. com. Inst. Human Nutrition, 1989—. Editl. bd. Am. Jour. Physiology, 1985-90, Gastroenterology, 1978-82; editl. com. Jour. Clin. Investigation, 1976-79; coeditor: Secretory Diarrhea, Am. Physiol. Soc., 1980, Intestinal Absorption and Secretion, vol. IV, Handbook of Physiology, 1991; editor: Diarrheal Diseases, 1991; contbr. numerous articles, editls., reviews and reports to profl. jours. With USPHS, 1961-63. Recipient Hoffman-LaRoche award, 1980, King Faisal Internat. prize, 1984, Disting. Achievement award Am. Gastroent. Assn., 1984; Norman Frankel Vis. scholar U. Chgo., 1996. Mem. Am. Physiol. Soc., Am. Gastroent. Assn. (nominating com. 1985, dist. achievement award com. 1985-86, 91-92, 94-95, chmn. 1993-94; William Beaumont prize com. 1987-88, chmn. 1991-92; Dist. award 1984), Am. Soc. Clin. Investigation, Assn. Am. Physicians, Gastroenterology Rsch. Group (steering com. 1978-86, chmn. 1984-86. Office: Columbia Presbyn Med Ctr PS10 508 PO Box 83 630 W 168th St New York NY 10032-3702

FIELD, NOEL MACDONALD, JR., lawyer; b. Providence, May 15, 1934; s. Noel Macdonald and Ellen DeWolf (Preston) F.; m. Phyllis Campbell, Nov. 10, 1962; children: Ellen, Noel III, Campbell, Margaret. AB, Brown U., 1956; LLB, Harvard U., 1961. Bar: R.I. 1962. Ptnr. Hinckley, Allen & Snyder and predecessors, Providence, 1961—. Former v.p. and sec. bd. dirs. U.S. Yacht Racing Union, Newport, R.I.; former trustee Rocky Hill Sch., Providence Country Day Sch.; asst. clk. vice chair, bd. overseers Lincoln Sch., Providence; bd. dirs., former mem. Arthritis Found. (Southern New Eng. chpt.). Fellow Am. Coll. Trust and Estate Counsel (state chmn. 1986-91). Avocations: sailing, bicycle riding. Office: Hinckley Allen & Snyder 1500 Fleet Ctr Providence RI 02903-2319

FIELD, RICHARD ALBERT, sales and marketing professional; b. Bangor, Maine, June 10, 1944; s. Harold A. and Aida A. (Martini) F.; m. Judith P. Wescott, Aug. 12, 1967; children: Susan M., Robert C. BS in Chem. Engring., U. Maine, 1967. Sales staff Heyden Newport Divsn. Tenneco, Pensacola, Fla., 1967-69; sales and mktg. staff Nalco Chem., Oakbrook, Ill., 1969-84, Searle, Skokie, Ill., 1984-93, Quality Chems., Kenilworth, Ill., 1993-94, ChemSource & Svcs., N.Y.C., 1995—. Home: 591 Old Kings Hwy West Barnstable MA 02668-1128

FIELD, RICHARD CLARK, lawyer; b. Stanford, Calif., July 13, 1940; s. John and Sally Field; m. Barbara Faith Butler, May 22, 1967 (dec. Apr. 1984); 1 child, Amanda Katherine; m. Eva Sara Halbreich, Dec. 1, 1985. BA, U. Calif., Riverside, 1962; JD, Harvard U., 1965. Bar: Calif. 1966, U.S. Supreme Ct., 1971, U.S. Ct. Appeals (9th cir.) 1979. Assoc. Thompson & Colegate, Riverside, 1965-69; ptnr. Adams, Duque & Hazeltine, Los Angeles, 1970-89, mem. mgmt. com., 1981-84, chmn. litigation dept., 1985-89; ptnr. Cadwalader, Wickersham & Taft, Los Angeles, 1989-97, McCutchen, Doyle, Brown & Enersen, LLP, Los Angeles, 1997—. Bd. dirs. ARC, L.A., 1984-93, 97—. Mem. ABA (litigation, torts and ins. practice sects., bus. torts com., products, gen. liability and consumer law com.), Los Angeles County Bar Assn. (trial lawyers sect.), Assn. Bus. Trial Lawyers (bd. govs. 1978-82), Am. Arbitration Assn. (comml. arbitration panel). Episcopalian. Office: McCutchen Doyle Brown & Enersen LLP 355 S Grand Ave Ste 4400 Los Angeles CA 90071-1560

FIELD, ROBERT EDWARD, lawyer; b. Chgo., Aug. 21, 1945; s. Robert Edward and Florence Elizabeth (Aiken) F.; m. Jenny Lee Hill, Aug. 5, 1967; children: Jennifer Kay, Kimberly Anne, Amanda Brooke. BA, Ill. Wesleyan U., 1967; MA, Northwestern U., 1969, JD, 1973. Bar: Ill. 1973, U.S. Dist. Ct. (no. dist.) Ill. 1974, U.S. Supreme Ct. 1979. Exec. dir. Winnetka Youth Orgn., Ill., 1969-73; assoc. Seyfarth, Shaw, Fairweather & Geraldson, Chgo., 1973-79, ptnr., 1979-93; ptnr. Field, Golan & Swiger, Chgo., 1993—; bd. dirs. Gt. Lakes Fin. Resources, Matteson, Ill., 1983—, vice chmn., 1988-91, chmn. 1991—; bd. dirs. Chgo. chpt. Ill. Wesleyan U. Assocs.; chmn. bd. dirs. 1st Nat. Bank of Blue Island, 1989—, Bank of Homewood, 1988—; bd. dirs. Winchester Mfg. Co., Wood Dale, Ill., Ludell Mfg. Co., Milw.; dir. Comml. Resources Corp., Naperville, Ill., 1984-93; dir., sec. Ellis Corp., Itasca, Ill., 1980—; chmn. bd. dirs. Cmty. Bank of Homewood-Flossmoor, Ill., 1983-92, Bank of Matteson, Ill., 1992—; mem. State Banking Bd. Ill., 1993-97. Bd. dirs. Ctr. for New Beginnings, 1997—, Family Svc. Ctrs. Cook County, Matteson, 1979—, treas., 1981-82, pres. 1986-88, chmn., 1988-93; pres. Lakes of Olympia Condominium Assn., 1987-89; trustee Village of Olympia Fields, Ill., 1981-89, pres., 1991-97; trustee Ill. Wesleyan U., 1990—, treas. 1994—; bd. dirs. Northwestern U. Sch Law Alumni Assn., 1990-94. Mem. ABA, Ill. Bar Assn., Am. Bankers Assn., Ill. Bankers Assn., United Meth. Bar Assn. (v.p. Chgo. chpt. 1989), Chgo. Bar Assn., Bankers Club of Chgo., Union League Club Chgo., Calumet Country Club. Home: 3424 Parthenon Way Olympia Fields IL 60461-1321 Office: Field Golan & Swiger 3 1st Nat Plz Ste 1500 Chicago IL 60602

FIELD, SALLY, actress; b. Pasadena, Calif., Nov. 6, 1946; m. Steve Craig, Sept. 1968 (div. 1975); children: Peter, Eli; m. Alan Greisman, Dec. 1984 (div. 1994); 1 son, Samuel. Student, Actor's Studio, 1973-75. Starred in TV series Gidget, 1965, The Flying Nun, 1967-69, The Girl With Something Extra, 1973; film appearances include The Way West, 1967, Stay Hungry, 1976, Heroes, 1977, Smokey and the Bandit, 1977, Hooper, 1978, The End, 1978, Norma Rae, 1979 (Cannes Film Festival Best Actress award 1979, Acad. award 1980), Beyond the Poseidon Adventure, 1979, Smokey and the Bandit II, 1980, Back Roads, 1981, Absence of Malice, 1981, Kiss Me Goodbye, 1982, Places in the Heart, 1984 (Acad. award for best actress 1984), Murphy's Romance (also exec. producer), 1985, Surrender, 1987, Punchline, 1987 (also prodr.), Steel Magnolias, 1989, Soapdish, 1991, Not Without My Daughter, 1991, Homeward Bound: The Incredible Journey, 1993 (voice only), Mrs. Doubtfire, 1993, Forrest Gump, 1994; TV movies include Maybe I'll Come Home In the Spring, 1971, Marriage: Year One, 1971, Home for the Holidays, 1972, Bridges, 1976, Sybil, 1976 (Emmy award 1977), A Woman of Independent Means, 1994; prodr. Dying Young, 1991, Eye for an Eye, 1995, Homeward Bound II: Lost in San Francisco, 1996, Merry Christmas George Bailey, 1997, From The Earth to the Moon, 1998. *

FIELD, TED (FREDERICK FIELD), film and record industry executive; b. Chgo.; s. Marshall Field IV and Katherine W. Fanning; 6 children. Student, U. Chgo., Pomona Coll. Former race car driver; founder, chmn. Interscope Communications; co-chmn. Interscope, Geffen, A&M Records; former co-owner Field Enterprises, Chgo.; owner Panavision, 1985-87. Co-producer (films) Critical Condition, 1987, Outrageous Fortune, 1987, Three Men and a Baby, 1987, Revenge of the Nerds II, 1987, Cocktail, 1988, The Seventh Sign, 1988, An Innocent Man, 1989; co-exec. producer (films) Bill and Ted's Excellent Adventure, 1989, Renegades, 1989; producer Revenge of the Nerds, 1984, Turk 182, 1985, Three Men and a Little Lady, Class Action, Jumanji, 1995, Mr. Holland's Opus, 1996, Runaway Bride, 1999; exec. producer The First Power, 1990, Bird on a Wire, 1990, What Dreams May Come, 1998, Very Bad Things, 1998; exec. producer Hand That Rocks The Cradle, 1992; co-exec. producer (TV films) The Father Clements Story, Everybody's Baby: The Rescue of Jessica McClure, A Mother's Courage. Avocations: chess, martial arts. Office: Interscope Communications 10900 Wilshire Blvd # 1400 Los Angeles CA 90024-6581*

FIELD, THOMAS HAROLD, software engineer; b. Flint, Mich., May 13, 1951; s. Harold Franklin and Evelyn Agnus (DeHate) F.; m. Sharon Deborah Patronis, Dec. 11, 1982 (div. April 1999); 1 child, Gabriel. BSEE, U. Mich., Dearborn, 1973; MS in Computer Sci., Fla. Inst. Tech., 1986. Sr. field engr. Gen. Dynamics Def. Systems, Pittsfield, Mass., 1974—. Mem. IEEE, Assn. for Computing Machinery. Roman Catholic. Avocations: photography, gardening, woodworking. Office: General Dynamics Def Sys PO Box 246 Cape Canaveral FL 32920-0246 Address: PO Box 320405 Cocoa Beach FL 32932-0405

FIELD, THOMAS LEE, business executive, politician; b. Grosse Pointe Farms, Mich., Sept. 17, 1950; s. Earl Leroy and Gertrude Mary (Gunn) F.; m. Elaine Anita Jay, Nov. 21, 1969 (div. 1974); 1 child, Eric Charles; m. Donna Mae Hansen, May 15, 1981; children: Kristen Marie, Devin Patrick, Michael Hansen. Cert. real estate brokerage mgr., one and two family building insp., environ. insp. Sales rep. Olga Rashid Real Estate, Detroit, 1969-71; broker G. M. Field State Wide Real Estate, Inc., St. Clair Shores, Mich., 1971—, appraiser, 1975-85; bldg. insp. The House Insps., Inc., St. Clair Shores, 1985—. Author: Home Time '92, 1992, Home Time '93, 1993. Commr. Macomb County Bd. Commrs., Mt. Clemens, Mich., 1980-82, Macomb County Planning Commn., Mt. Clemens, 1983; trustee Comprehensive Health Planning Coun. S.E. Mich., Detroit, 1981-85, Nat. Assn. Counties Aging Program, 1982; pres. East Detroit Homeowners Assn., 1985-88; chmn. East Detroit Tax Assessment Bd., 1986-88. Recipient Bd. Resolution for Outstanding Svc. award Macomb County Bd. Commrs., 1982, Meritorious Svc. award Comprehensive Health Planning Coun. S.E. Mich., 1985. Mem. Nat. Assn. Realtors Brokerage Coun., Am. Soc. Home Insps., Bldg. Officials and Code Adminstrs. Internat., Environ. Assessment Assn., Builders Assn. S.E. Mich., Macomb County Bd. Realtors (bd. dirs. 1984-87, Meritorious Svc. award 1987), East Detroit C. of C. (bd. dirs. 1985-86). Republican. Mem. Unity Ch. Avocations: walking, racquetball, pool, golf, billiards. Home: 22759 Piper Ave Eastpointe MI 48021-1731 Office: G M Field State Wide Real Estate Inc 22029 Oconnor St Saint Clair Shores MI 48080-2045

FIELDEN, C. FRANKLIN, III, early childhood education consultant; b. Gulfport, Miss., Aug. 4, 1946; s. C. Franklin and Georgia (Freeman) F.; children: Christopher Michaux (dec.), Robert Michaux, Jonathan Dutton. Student, Claremont Men's Coll., 1964-65; AB, Colo. Coll., 1970; MS, George Peabody Coll. Tchrs., 1976, EdS, 1979. Tutor Proyecto El Guacio, San Sebastian, P.R., 1967-68; asst. tchr. GET-SET Project, Colorado Springs, Colo., 1969-70, co-tchr., 1970-75, asst. dir., 1972-75; tutor Early Childhood Edn. Project, Nashville, 1975-76; pub. policy intern Donner-Belmont Child Care Ctr., Nashville, 1976-77; asst. to urban min. Nashville Presbytery, 1977; intern to prin. Steele Elem. Sch., Colorado Springs, 1977-78, tchr., 1978-86; resource person Office Gifted and Talented Edn. Colorado Springs Pub. Schs., 1986-87; tchr. Columbia Elem. Sch., Colorado Springs, 1987-92; tchr., pre-sch. team coord. Helen Hunt Elem. Sch., Colorado Springs, 1992-93; validator Nat. Acad. Early Childhood Programs, 1992—, mentor, 1994—, commr., 1996—; cons. Colo. Dept. Edn., Denver, 1993-96, sr. cons., 1996—, state coord. Even Start Family Literacy Program, 1997—; lectr. Arapahoe C.C., Littleton, Colo., 1981-82; instr. Met. State Coll., Denver, 1981; cons. Jubail Human Resources Devel. Inst., Saudi Arabia, 1982; mem. governing bd. GET-SET Project, 1969-79, 91-93. Mem. ad hoc bd. trustees Tenn. United Meth. Agy. on Children and Youth, 1976-77; mem. So. Regional Edn. Bd. Task Force on Parent-Caregiver Relationships, 1976-77; mem. day care com. Colo. Commn. Children and Their Families, 1981-82; mem. Nashville Children's Issues Task Force, 1976-77, Tenn. United Meth. Task Force on Children and Youth, 1976-77, Citizens' Goals Leadership Tng., 1986-87, Child Abuse Task Force, 4th Jud. Dist., 1986-87, FIRST IMPRESSIONS (Colo. Govs. Early Childhood Initiative) Task Force, 1987-88; mem. El Paso County Placement Alternatives Commn., 1990-96; mem. proposal rev. team Colo. Dept. Edn., 1992—; co-chair City/County Child Care Task Force, 1991-92; charter mem. City/County Early Childhood Care and Edn. Commn., 1993-96; mem. bd. dirs. Colo. Office of Resource and Referral Agys., 1996-99. Recipient Arts/Bus./Edn. award, 1983, Innovative Tchg. award, 1984; fellow NIMH, 1976. Mem. ASCD, Nat. Assn. Edn. Young Children (founding mem. primary caucus 1992—, co-chair Western States Leadership Network 1993, Membership Action Group grantee 1993, mem. panel profl. ethics in early childhood edn. 1993-97), Colo. Assn. Edn. Young Children (legis. com. 1979-84, governing bd. 1980-84, 85-86, 89-95, exec. com. 1980-84, 93, sec. 1980-84, rsch. conf. chmn. 1982, tuition awards com. 1983-86, chmn. tuition awards com. 1985-86, pub. policy com. 1989-96, treas. 1993, primary grades conf. chmn. 1994), Nat. Assn. Early Childhood Specialists in State Depts. of Edn. (v.p. 1997—), Pikes Peak Assn. Edn. Young Children, Huguenot Soc. Great Britain and Ireland, Nat. Trust Hist. Preservation, Phi Delta Kappa. Presbyterian. Home: PO Box 7766 Colorado Springs CO 80933-7766 Office: 201 E Colfax Ave Denver CO 80203-1704

FIELDER, CECIL GRANT, professional baseball player; b. L.A., Sept. 21, 1963; m. Stacey Granger; child, Prince. Student, U. Nev., Las Vegas. Baseball player Kansas City Royals, 1982-83, Toronto Blue Jays, Can., 1983-88, Hanshin (Japan) Tigers, 1988-90, Detroit Tigers, 1990-96, N.Y. Yankees, 1996-97, Anaheim Angels, 1998—; player Venezuelan League in off-season. Player Am. League All-Star Team, 1990-91, 93, All-Star Team Sporting News, 1990-91; named twice Am. League Player of Week, Am. League Player of Month, Am. League Player of Yr. Sporting News, 1990; recipient Silver Slugger award, 1990, 91; ranked 1st in Am. League for home runs, 1990-91, 1st in Am. League for runs batted in, 1990-92. Office: Anaheim Angels 2000 Gene Autry Way Anaheim CA 92806-6100*

FIELDER, CHARLES ROBERT, oil industry executive; b. Lubbock, Tex., Mar. 9, 1943; s. Clarence Daniel and Ola Marie (Sewell) F.; m. Mary Ruth Wills, May 31, 1964; 1 child, Sara Elizabeth. B.B.A., Tex. Tech. U., 1965, M.S. in Acctg., 1972. C.P.A., Tex. Staff acct. Peat, Marwick, Mitchell & Co., Dallas, 1965-66, Arthur Andersen & Co., Dallas, 1968-69; treasury acct. Halliburton Co., Dallas, 1969-71, treasury supr., 1971-72, asst. treas., 1972-78, treas., 1978-89, v.p., treas., 1990-96; ret. Halliburton Co., 1997. Mem. AICPA, Fin. Execs. Inst., Tex. Soc. CPAs, Phi Eta Sigma, Beta Alpha Psi, Beta Gamma Sigma, Phi Kappa Phi. Republican. Mem. Ch. of Christ. Office: 6757 Arapaho Rd Ste 711 Dallas TX 75248-4073

FIELDER, DOROTHY SCOTT, postmaster; b. Detroit, Apr. 20, 1943; d. William Lacy and Gertrude Elizabeth (Coddington) Davis; m. Douglas Stratton Fielder, July 13, 1968; 1 child, William Todd. AB, Randolph-Macon Woman's Coll., 1965; MA, Kent State U., 1968. Lab. instr. Mary Baldwin Coll., Staunton, Va., 1965-66, Hartwick Coll., Oneonta, N.Y., 1969-70; rsch. and teaching asst. Kent (Ohio) State U., 1966-68; high sch. tchr. biology Fairfax County Pub. Schs., Va., 1968-69; postal clk. U.S. Postal Svc., Maryland, N.Y., 1978-80, rural carrier, 1980-81; postmaster U.S. Postal Svc., Schenevus, N.Y., 1981—; coord. Benjamin Franklin Stamp Club, U.S. Postal Svc., Albany, N.Y., 1982-93. Author: Pictorial History of the Town of Maryland, N.Y., 1990, Otsego County Postal History, 1994, (with others) Time Once Past Never Returns, 1996. Vice chmn. Maryland Planning Bd., 1989-93, chmn., 1993—. Recipient Otsego County Local History award, 1995. Mem. AAUW, Nat. Assn. Postmasters U.S., Town of Md. Hist. Assn. (pres. 1982—), Tri-County Postmasters Assn. (pres. 1990-94), Empire State Postal History Soc., Am. Philatelic Soc., Rotary. Methodist. Avocations: stamp collecting, gardening, local history, photography. Home: 112 Stevens Rd Maryland NY 12116-3302 Office: US Postal Svc 62 Main St Schenevus NY 12155-2009

FIELDER, MARYANN, artist, consultant; b. Linton, Ind., Mar. 19, 1946; d. Everett M. Fielder and Florence Evalyn Mitchell; children: Bartholomew, Robin; m. Mark Steven Schroeder, June 20, 1982. BFA, U. Calif., Davis, 1983. Asst. dir. Hockaday Ctr. for Arts, Kalispell, Mont., 1989-96; peer cons. Mont. Arts Coun., Helena, 1995-98, arts profl., 1999—; arts coord. Arts Eureka, Mont., 1999—; arts instr. The Studio, Whitefish, Mont., 1997-98. Represented in permanent collection at Hockaday Ctr. for Arts, Kalispell, 1996. Visual arts fellow Mont. Arts Coun., 1991-92; recipient Purchase award Walla Walla (Wash.) C.c., 1980-81. Avocations: travel, golf, tennis. Fax: (406) 862-2190. E-mail: mfielder@digisys.net. Home: 436 W 7th St Whitefish MT 59937 Office: Fielder Studio 434 W 7th St Whitefish MT 59937

FIELDING, ALLEN FRED, oral and maxillofacial surgeon, educator; b. Paterson, N.J., Jan. 22, 1943; s. Fred W. and Emily Claire (Boehm) F. B.S., Fairleigh Dickinson U., 1959, D.M.D., 1963; postgrad. in oral surgery, N.Y. U., 1965-66. Diplomate Am. Bd. Oral and Maxillofacial Surgery (adv. bd. 1983-86). Intern in oral surgery Roosevelt Hosp., N.Y.C., 1966-67; resident in oral surgery Phila. Gen. Hosp., 1967-69; practice dentistry specializing in oral-maxillo facial surgery Phila., 1969—; prof., chmn. dept. oral and maxillofacial surgery Temple U., Phila., 1983-88; staff prof., chief dept. oral and maxillofacial surgery univ. hosp. Temple U., 1982-87; cons. VA Hosp., Wilmington, Del.; staff St. Christopher's Hosp. for Children, Phila., Northeastern Hosp.; staff, chief div. oral and Maxillofacial surgery Epics. Hosp.; sect. chief oral and maxillofacial surgery Quakertown (Pa.) Hosp., Lawndale Hosp., Phila.; cons. Gt. Lakes Naval Hosp., Ill., Brandywine Hosp.; lectr. in field. Contbr. articles to profl. jours. Mem. Chapel of Four Chaplains, Valley Forge, Pa. Served to capt. USAF, 1963-65. Fellow Am. Dental Soc. Anesthesiology, Royal Soc. Health, Am. Soc. Oral and Maxillofacial Surgeons, World Affairs Coun. (Phila. chpt.), Am. Coll. Dentistry (editor local chpt.), Am. Assn. Oral Maxillofacial Surgeons, Am. Coll. of Oral Maxillofacial Surgeons, Internat. Assn. Oral Maxillofacial Surgery; mem. AAUP, ADA, Pa. Dental Soc., Phila. County Dental Soc., Assn. Mil. Surgeons, Am. Assn. Dental Schs., Pa. Soc. Oral Surgeons, Del. Valley Soc. Oral Surgeons (com. resident tng. 1973-85, exec. com., pres. 1985), Am. Assn. Hosp. Dentists (sec.-treas. Del. County chpt. 1972-74, v.p. 1974, pres. 1976), Great Lakes Soc. Oral Maxillofacial Surgeons, Mid-Atlantic Soc. Oral Maxillofacial Surgeons, Temple U. Oral Surgery Honor Soc. (advisor), Pa. Soc. Oral and Maxillofacial Surgeons (exec. com., govt. affairs com., pres. 1995-96), Coll. Physicians and Surgeons Phila., Dental Assts. Nat. Bd. (adv. bd.), Internat. Assn. Oral Implantologists, Del. Valley Acad. Osseointegration, Pierre Fauchard Soc. (elected mem.), Omicron Kappa Upsilon (pres. 1985, Temple chpt.). Home: 1203 Rodman St Philadelphia PA 19147-1129 Office: 3223 N Broad St Philadelphia PA 19140-5007 also: 3043 Kensington Ave Philadelphia PA 19134-2415 also: 435 Exton Commons Exton PA 19341-2451

FIELDING, FRED FISHER, lawyer; b. Phila., Mar. 21, 1939; s. Fred P. and Ruth Marie (Fisher) F.; m. J. Maria Dugger, Oct. 21, 1967; children: Adam Garrett, Alexandra Caroline. AB, Gettysburg Coll., 1961; LL.B, JD, U. Va., 1964; LittD (hon.), U. Detroit, 1986, Pepperdine U., 1986. Bar: Pa. 1965, D.C. 1974. Assoc. Morgan, Lewis & Bockius, Phila., 1964-65, 67-70; ptnr. Morgan, Lewis & Bockius, Washington, 1974-81; asst. counsel to Pres. of U.S. The White House, Washington, 1970-72, dep. counsel, 1972-74, counsel to Pres. of U.S., 1981-86; ptnr. Wiley, Rein & Fielding, Washington, 1986—; pres. Gilmore Broadcasting Corp., 1988-90; mem. Jud. Conf. D.C. Cir. Ct., 1976—; mem. internat. adv. bd. Credit Internat. Bank, 1990—; bd. dirs. Gilmore Broadcasting Corp., Coun. for Excellence in Govt.; spl. counsel Adminstrv. Conf. U.S., 1982-86, pub. mem., 1987-94, chmn. spl. com. on ethics in govt., 1988-92, com. on regulation, 1992-94; presdl. appointment to panel arbitrators Internat. Ctr. for Settlement Investment Disputes, 1987-95. Mem. Commn. on White House Fellowships, 1981-86, Pres.'s Commn. for German-Am. Tricentennial, 1983-84; mem. presdl. del. to observe Philippine presdl. elections, 1986, pres.'s personal rep. Australia/Am. Friendship Week,

1986; spl. counsel to Rep. vice presdl. campaign, 1988, sr. legal advisor Bush-Quayle campaign, 1992; conflict-of-interest counsel Office of Pres.-Elect, 1980; gen. counsel 50th presdl. inaugural, 1984-85; dep. dir. presdl. transition, 1988-89; mem. Pres.'s Commn. on Fed. Ethics Law Reform, 1989; U.S. designated arbitrator Arbitration Tribunal on U.S.-U.K. Air Treaty Dispute, 1989-94, Sec. of Transp. Task Force on Air Disaster Victims, 1996-98; mem. bd. visitors Sch. Law Pepperdine U., 1989-92; bd. dirs. Coun. for Excellence in Govt., 1989-95; bd. fellows Gettysburg Coll., 1992—, also trustee; bd. dirs. USAir Shuttle, 1992—, Ethics Resource Ctr., 1993; sec.-treas., bd. dirs. Arlington Va. Hosp. Found., 1994—; mem. commn. on selection fed. judges U. Va. Miller Ctr., 1994-97; bd. dirs. Washington Scholarship Fund, 1994-97, Ctr. Democracy, 1995-98, vice-chmn. 1996-97, chmn., 1997. Served to capt. AUS, 1965-67. John McKee Found. fellow. Mem. ABA (standing com. on fed. judiciary), Fed. Bar Assn., D.C. Bar Assn. (bd. govs. 1996-98), Pa. Bar Assn., Am. Arbitration Assn. (nat. panel), Lawyer's Club of Washington, Fed. City Club, Washington Golf and Country Club, 1925 F Street Club, Univ. Club, Phi Gamma Delta, Pi Delta Epsilon, Omicron Delta Kappa, Pi Lambda Sigma, Phi Delta Phi. Republican. Lutheran. Office: Wiley Rein & Fielding 1776 K St NW Washington DC 20006-2304

FIELDING, HOWARD WILLIAM, newspaper editor, columnist; b. Teaneck, N.J., Apr. 14, 1955; s. Alfred William and Virginia Fielding; m. Barbara Jeanne Hampton; 3 children. AB in English cum laude, Dartmouth Coll., 1977. Editor, columnist Waterbury (Conn.) Rep.-Am., 1985—. Office: Waterbury Republican-American 389 Meadow St Waterbury CT 06702-1808

FIELDING, JONATHAN E., pediatrician; b. Oct. 4, 1942. BA, Williams Coll., 1964; MA, MD, Harvard Coll., 1969, MPH, 1971; MBA, U. Pa., 1977. Diplomate Am. Bd. Pediats., Am. Bd. Preventive Medicine. Josiah Macy fellow Harvard U., Cambridge, Mass., 1969; intern, resident Boston Children's Hosp., 1969-71; fellow Harvard U., Boston, 1971; resident in pediats. Georgetown U. Med. Ctr., Washington, 1971-72, prin. med. svcs. nat. officer Job Corps, 1971-73; commr. pub. health Commonwealth of Mass., 1975-79; prof. health svcs. & pediats. UCLA, 1979—; dir. pub. health L.A. County, 1997—; spl. asst. to dir. Bur. Cmty. Health Svcs. Health Svcs. & Mental Health Adminstrn. HEW, 1971-73; co-dir. Ctr. Health Enhancement Edn. & Rsch., 1979-84; co-dir. Ctr. for Healthier Children, Families & Cmtys., 1985—; lectr. Harvard U., Boston, 1973-75, Boston U., 1975-79, Brandeis U., 1975-79, Northwestern U., 1975-79; vis. lectr. UCLA, 1977; rsch. assoc. Urban Rsch. Ctr. Hunter Coll. CUNY, 1978; vis. prof. Nordic Sch. Pub. Health, Sweden, 1980, 83, 93. editor: Ann. Revs. Pub. Health, 1995—; asst. editor Mercy-Rosenau Pub. Health and Preventive Medicine 1992-98, 14th edit. Fellow Assn. Health Svcs.: mem. NAS Inst. Medicine, Am. Acad. Pediats., Am. Assn. Pub. Health Physicians, Am. Med. Peer Rev. Assn., Am. Pub. Health Assn., Assn. Health Svcs. Medicine, Am. Heart Assn., Am. Coll. Preventive Medicine (pres. 1997—). Office: UCLA Sch Pub Health Ctr Health Sci 61-253A Los Angeles CA 90095

FIELDING, MARALYN JOY, principal, consultant; b. Bronx, N.Y., Oct. 19, 1940; d. David and Sylvia (Kassof) Lowy; m. Stuart Fielding, Aug. 26, 1962; children: Kimberly, Bradford. BA, Queens Coll., 1962; MA, Fairleigh Dickinson, 1983. Cert. elem. edn., tchr. of handicapped, learning disabilities tchr./cons., supervision/principal. Elem. tchr. Chillum (Md.) Elem. Sch., 1962-64, Alfred I. DuPont Elem. Sch., Wilmington, Del., 1964-66; supplemental instr. Alfred Vail Elem. Sch., Morris Plains, N.J., 1974-83; spl. edn. principal Hackensack (N.J.) Med. Ctr., Little Red Sch. House, 1983-95; principal Allegro Sch., Cedar Knolls, N.J., 1995-97; dir., principal Banyon Sch., North Caldwell, N.J., 1997—; edn. adv. bd. Coll. St. Elizabeth, Convent Station, N.J., 1995—; cons. pvt. practice, Mt. Freedom, N.J., 1985-95. Trustee Banyon Sch., North Caldwell, N.J., 1997—. Mem. Assn. Learning Cons., Assn. Supervision and Curriculum Devel., Assn. Schs. and Agencies for Handicapped. Avocations: music, art, boating, travel, reading. Home: 16 Bromleigh Way Morris Plains NJ 07950-1642

FIELDING, STUART, psychopharmacologist; b. Bronx, N.Y., Oct. 31, 1939; s. Harry and Ethel (Weisberg) Feinblatt; m. Maralyn J. Lowy, Aug. 26, 1962; children: Kimberly Ellen, Bradford Scott. BA, Monmouth Coll., 1962; MS, Howard U., 1964; PhD, U. Del., 1968. Mgr. psychopharmacology rsch. Ciba-Geigy Corp., Summit, N.J., 1967-75; assoc. dir. pharmacology Hoechst-Roussel Pharms., Inc., Somerville, N.J., 1975-76, assoc. dir. biol. sci., mgr. pharmacology, 1977-84, dir. pharmacology, 1984-86, dir. biol. rsch., 1987-89; v.p. R & D, dir. Interneuron Pharms., Inc., Lexington, Mass., 1989-92; chmn., CEO Bio-Enhancement Systems Corp., Morris Plaines, N.J., 1992—. Editor: (book) Psychopharmacology of Clonidine, 1981, (book series) Industrial Pharmacology: A Monograph Series, 1974-79, (jour.) Drug Devel. Rsch., 1980-92; contbr. articles to profl. publs. Fellow Am. Psychol. Assn.; mem. Am. Chem. Soc., Am. Soc. Pharmacology and Exptl. Therapeutics, Soc. Neurosci. Home and Office: 16 Bromleigh Way Morris Plains NJ 07950-1642

FIELDS, ANITA, dean; b. Amarillo, Tex., Oct. 29, 1940; d. Dera and Mamie Maureen (Craig) Bates; 1 child, William Kyle. Grad. nursing, Jefferson Davis Hosp., 1962; BSN, Tex. Christian U., 1966; MSN, Northwestern State U. La., 1974; PhD, Tex. Women's U., 1980. C.E. coord., asst. prof. Northwestern State U., Shreveport; prof., dean McNeese State U., Lake Charles, La.; gov.'s appointee Southwest La. Hosp. Dist. Commn., 1989-91, chmn., 1989-91. Mem. allocations com. and loaned exec. United Way, 1991-92, Am. Heart Assn., Am. Cancer Soc., ARC. Recipient Ben Taub award, 1962, Ann Magnussen award ARC, 1977. Mem. ANA (del.), La. Nurses Assn. (past pres. and 1st v.p., spl. recognition award 1993), Lake Charles Dist. Nurses Assn. (bd. dirs., Nurse of Yr. award 1972, 80), Nat. League Nursing (agy. mem.), Sigma Theta Tau (Image of Nursing award 1993), Delta Kappa Gamma, Phi Kappa Phi. E-mail: afields@usunwired.net. Fax: (318) 475-5924. Home: 1915 Alvin St Lake Charles LA 70601-5835

FIELDS, ANTHONY LINDSAY AUSTIN, health facility administrator, oncologist, educator; b. St. Michael, Barbados, Oct. 21, 1943; arrived in Can., 1968; s. Vernon Bruce and Marjorie (Pilgrim) F.; m. Patricia Jane Stewart, Aug. 5, 1967. MA, U. Cambridge, 1969; MD, U. Alta., 1974. Diplomate Am. Bd. Internal Medicine. Sr. specialist Cross Cancer Inst., Edmonton, Alta., Can., 1980-85, dir. dept. medicine, 1985-88, dir., 1988—; asst. prof. medicine U. Alta., Edmonton, 1980-84, assoc. prof., 1984-98, prof., 1998—, dir. divsn. med. oncology, 1985-89, dir. divsn. oncology, 1988-93. Fellow ACP (gov. Alta. chpt.), Royal Coll. Physicians and Surgeons Can. (specialist cert. med. oncology, internal medicine); mem. Can. Assn. Med. Oncologists (pres. 1994-96), Am. Soc. Clin. Oncology, Am. Fedn. Clin. Rsch., Can. Soc. for Clin. Investigation, Can. Med. Assn. Avocation: photography. Office: Cross Cancer Inst, 11560 University Ave, Edmonton, AB Canada T6G 1Z2

FIELDS, ARNOLD, military officer; b. Early Branch, S.C.; m. Charlotte T. Skidmore. BS in Agr., MA in Mgmt.; grad., Amphibious Warfare Sch., USMC Command and Staff Coll., U.S. Army War Coll. Commd. 2nd lt. USMC, 1969, advanced through grades to brig. gen.; recruit series comdr., then asst. dir. drill instr. sch. USMC Recruit Depot, Parris Island, S.C., 1972-74; instr. Edn. Ctr. USMC Devel. and Edn. Command, Quantico, Va., 1974-77; inf. co. comdr. 3rd Marine Divsn., 1978-79; officer in charge dist. contact team 6th Marine Corps Dist., 1979; commdg. officer USMC Recruiting Sta., Orlando, Fla., Co. B, Marine Security Guard Bn.; asst. dep. chief of staff, readiness 2nd Marine Divsn., 1989; commdg. officer USMC Support Activity, Kansas City, Mo., 1991; comdr. USMC Hdqrs. Command, Camp Fuji, Japan; chief evaluation and analysis divsn. Operational Plans and Interoperability Directorate, Washington; comdr. forward hdqrs. element, insp. gen. U.S. Ctrl. Command, MacDill AFB, Fla. Decorated Bronze Star with Combat V. Office: USAF US Central Command MacDill AFB FL 33621*

FIELDS, BERTRAM HARRIS, lawyer; b. Los Angeles, Mar. 31, 1929; s. H. Maxwell and Mildred Arlyn (Ruben) F.; m. Lydia Ellen Minevitch, Oct. 22, 1960 (dec. Sept. 1986); 1 child, James Eldar, m. Barbara Guggenheim, Feb. 21, 1991. B.A., UCLA, 1949; J.D. magna cum laude, Harvard U., 1952. Bar: Calif. 1953. Practiced in Los Angeles, 1955—; assoc. firm Shearer, Fields, Rohner & Shearer, and predecessor firms, 1955-57, mem. firm, 1957-82; ptnr. Greenberg, Glusker, Fields, Claman & Machtinger, 1982—. Author: (as D. Kincaid) The Sunset Bomber, 1986, The Lawyer's Tale, 1992, (as B. Fields) Royal Blood Richard III and the Mystery of the Princes, 1998; mem. bd. editors: Harvard Law Rev., 1953-55. Bd. dirs. U. So. Calif. Annenberg Sch. Comm. 1st. lt. USAF, 1953-55, Korea. Mem. ABA, L.A. County Bar Assn., Coun. Fgn. Rels. Subject of profiles Calif. Mag., Nov. 1987, Avenue Mag., Mar. 1989, Am. Film Mag., Dec. 1989, Vanity Fair Mag., Dec. 1993, Harvard Law Sch. Bull., spring 1998. Office: Greenberg Glusker Fields Claman & Machtinger Ste 2000 1900 Avenue Of The Stars Los Angeles CA 90067-4590

FIELDS, C. VIRGINIA, city councilwoman; b. Birmingham, Ala., Aug. 4, 1946; d. Peter and Lucille (Chappel) Clark; div. BA, Knoxville Coll., 1967; MSW, Ind. U., 1969; grad., NYU. Chair Cmty. Bd. 10, 1981-83; dist. leader 70th AD, Part C; city councilwoman Dist. 9, N.Y.C., 1990-97; boro pres. Manhattan, N.Y., 1997—; mem. land use, zoning, stds., ethics, youth svcs., health, fin. coms. N.Y.C. Coun. Mem. N.Y. State Coun. Black Elected Dems., N.Y.C. Coun. Black and Hispanic Caucus, Harlem Urban Devel. Corp., N.Y. Urban League, Manhattan, Black Leadership Commn. on AIDS; bd. dirs. Morningside Daycare and Headstart Program. Mem. Ea. Star, Alpha Kappa Alpha. Office: Mcpl Bldg 1 Centre St Fl 19 New York NY 10007-1602*

FIELDS, CLEO, state senator; b. Nov. 22, 1962; m. Debra Horton; 1 child, Cleo Brandon. BA, Southern U., 1984, JD, 1987. Mem. La. State Senate from Dist. 14, 1987-92, 97—, 103d-104th Congresses from 4th La. Dist., 1993-96. Founder Young Adults for Positive Action. Named Outstanding Young Men in Am., 1987. Democrat. Baptist. *

FIELDS, DENNIS H., state legislator; b. North Troy, Vt., May 2, 1945; divorced; 1 child. Mem. N.H. Ho. of Reps., Manchester, 1983—; mem. pub. protection, vet. affairs, and state-fed. rels. coms., N.H. Ho. of Reps. With USN, 1964-71. Mem. VFW (nat. dep. chief of staff 1981-82, membership co-chmn. 1981-83), Jaycees (dir., recruiter Hall of Fame 1980, co-chmn.). Republican. Address: State House 107 N Main St Concord NH 03301*

FIELDS, DOUGLAS PHILIP, building supply and home furnishings wholesale company executive; b. Jersey City, May 19, 1942; s. M. Emanuel and Priscilla (Wagner) F.; m. Paulette Susan Titko, Dec. 15, 1970 (div. Feb. 1990); children: Douglas Philip, Priscilla Wagner, Jessica Elizabeth; m. Maureen Virginia Hanmer, June 12, 1993; 1 child, Jacob Wagner. BS summa cum laude, Fordham U., 1964; MBA with distinction, Harvard U., 1966. Investment analyst Lehman Bros., N.Y.C., 1966-67; asst. to pres. Talley Industries Inc., Mesa, Ariz., 1967-69; CEO, pres. TDA Industries Inc., N.Y.C., 1969—; founder Unimet Corp., N.Y.C., 1970-73; pres., chmn. Westcalind Corp., R.I., 1971-87; CEO Acqueren, Inc., 1995-98; chmn. bd. TDA Industries, Inc., N.Y.C., 1970—, Westco Corp., Boston, 1970-79, Cooper Flooring Internat., Inc., Miami, Fla., 1972-98, Eagle Supply, Inc., Tampa, Fla., 1973—, CEO JEH/Eagle Supply Inc., Dallas, 1997—; CEO MSI/Eagle Supply Inc., Dallas, 1998—, Eagle Supply Group, N.Y.C., 1996—; chmn. Norhtea Plastics, Inc., N.Y., 1986-98; cons. U.S. Office Edn., 1973-74, Fed. Energy Adminstrn., 1974-75. Outside dir. NYU Grad. Sch. Bus., Mgmt. Decision Lab., 1973-78; mem. N.Y. State adv. com. U.S. Civil Rights Commn., 1974-85; bd. dirs. YMHA-YWHA of So. Westchester, Mt. Vernon, N.Y., 1981-92, Associated YMHA-YWHA of N.Y.C., Inc., 1989-91. Mem. Chief Execs. Orgn., Met. Pres. Orgn., World Pres. Orgn. Clubs: Harvard of N.Y.C, Harvard of Fairfield County (Conn.), Harvard Bus. Sch. of N.Y.C; Midtown Tennis (N.Y.C.) (pres. 1969—).

FIELDS, EDDIE, women's collegiate basketball coach; b. New Orleans, May 2, 1954; m. Annazette McCane; children: Troy, Brianna Lynne. BA in Elem. Edn., U. Okla., 1985. Player Harlem Globetrotters, 1978-83; head coach jr. varsity basketball Acad. Ctrl., Tulsa, 1985-86; asst. coach men's basketball South Plains Coll., Levelland, Tex., 1986-89, Drake U., 1989-92; head women's basketball Murray (Ky.) State Coll., 1992—. Avocation: golf. Office: Murray State Coll Women's Athletic Dept Stewart Stadium Carr Health Bldg Murray KY 42071*

FIELDS, FREDDIE, producer, agent; b. Ferndale, N.Y., July 12, 1923; s. John Jacob and Jeanette (Sewal) F.; m. Polly Bergen; children: Kathy, P.K., Peter; m. Corinna Tsopei (Miss Universe 1968); children: Andrew, Steven, Paris. V.p. MCA Inc., N.Y., 1946-59; pres. Freddie Fields Assocs., N.Y., 1959-60; founder, pres., chief exec. officer Creative Mgmt. Assocs. Inc., Internat. Creative Mgmt. Agy., Los Angeles and worldwide, 1960-75; pres., chief exec. officer Freddie Fields Prodns., Los Angeles and N.Y.C., 1975-78; pres., chief operating officer MGM Film Co., Los Angeles, 1980-81; pres. worldwide prodn. MGM/UA Entertainment, Los Angeles, 1981-84; pres., chief exec. officer The Fields Orgn., Los Angeles, 1984—; chmn. programming Network Event Theatre, 1995. Prodr.: (films) Looking for Mr. Goodbar, American Gigolo, Citizens Band, Victory, Fever Pitch, Poltergeist II, Lipstick, Crimes of the Heart, Millenium, Glory; executive prodr.: The Montel Williams Show. Recipient Creativity awards, 1970, 71, 72, Soc. Illustrators awards, 1969, 70, 71. *

FIELDS, HARRIET LEONA, writer; b. Davenport, Iowa, June 18, 1916; d. Harrison M. and Antoinette C. (Hoenes) Beery; m. Clyde Garland Fields, Oct. 25, 1941 (dec.); children: Douglas Clyde, Diana Lynn Fields Sell. Student, Principia Coll., 1942. Puppeteer Adrian, Mich., 1937-42; woman's/ch. editor Daily Telegram, Adrian, 1957-72; editor Maple City Reporter, Adrian, 1972-74, Vo-Tec Topics, Adrian, 1974-79; author Little Red Sch., 1976 Schs. Today, Adrian, 1974-78; editor Access, Adrian, 1974-89; corrd. Mich. Christian Adv., 1989—. Contbr. articles to profl. jours. Active 1st Ch. of Christian Scientist, Adrian, 1955—. Named Woman of Yr., Bus. and Profl. Women's Club, 1974. Mem. Nat. Fedn. Press Women (Mich. br.), Adrian Women's Club (pres. 1995-97, Woman of Yr. 1992), Adrian Drama Club (past pres.). Republican. Avocation: reading. Home: 537 Dennis St Adrian MI 49221-3333

FIELDS, JACK MILTON, JR., former congressman; b. Humble, Tex., Feb. 3, 1952; s. Jack Milton and Jessie Faye F.; m. Lynn Hughes, July 1, 1988. BA, Baylor U., 1974, JD, 1977. Bar: Tex. Pvt. practice Humble, Tex., 1977-79; v.p. Rosewood Meml. Park Cemetery, 1977-79; mem. 97th-104th Congresses from 8th Tex. dist., Washington, 1981-96; mem. energy and commerce com., mem. merchant marine and fisheries com.; CEO, pres. Twenty-First Century Group, Inc., Washington, 1996—, Texana Global Inc., 1997—. Republican. Baptist. Lodge: Masons. Office: Texana Global Inc 8810 Will Clayton Pkwy Humble TX 77338-5822 also: Twenty-First Century Group Inc East Tower 1301 K St NW Ste 1050 Washington DC 20005-3317 also: 2602 Old Humble Rd Humble TX 77396-2286*

FIELDS, L. MARC, producer, director, writer, educator; b. Champaign-Urbana, Ill., Sept. 9, 1955; s. Armond and Rona Marcia Fields; m. Nancy Reed Spencer. AB summa cum laude, Princeton U., 1977; MFA with honors, NYU, 1984. Freelance prodr., writer N.J. and N.Y., 1984—; asst. prof. screenwriting Inst. Grad. Film and TV NYU, N.Y.C., 1990-93, assoc. chair, 1992-93; series prodr. State of the Arts N.J. Pub. TV, Trenton, 1994—; adj. prof. screenwriting The New Sch., N.Y.C., 1987-90; cons. Vaudeville USA TV documentary, Am. Masters, PBS, 1997, Red, Hot, and Blue, Nat. Mus. Am. History, Smithsonian, 1996. Co-author: From the Bowery to Broadway: Lew Fields and the Roots of American Popular Theater, 1993 (Kurt Weill prize, 1995, Barnard Hewitt award for theatre rsch. 1994); prodr., writer, dir.: (TV documentary) New Stage for a City, 1997 (Regional Emmy nominee Outstanding Documentary 1998), (TV documentary) From Gulag to Glasnost, 1996 (Ea. Ednl. Network Cultural Programming award 1997); script writer: (TV documentary series) Broadway: The American Musical, 1998—; contbr. articles to profl. publs. Mem. NATAS (bd. govs. Phila. chpt. 1997—, Emmy Outstanding Mag. Format Show 1997, Emmy Outstanding Programming Feature 1995, Emmy Outstanding Talk Show 1996), Phi Beta Kappa. Democrat. E-mail: marcfields@mindspring.com. Office: NJN Pub TV 25 S Stockton St Trenton NJ 08611

FIELDS, LENNON, engineer; b. Mar. 6, 1958. Engr., NYU, New York. Vice pres. Four SeasonInsulation, NY; mech. engr. Eng. Amer. Constr., NY. Home: 484 W 43rd St #35B New York NY 10036

FIELDS, LEO, former jewelry company executive, investor; b. Wichita Falls, Tex., 1928; married. Student, U. Tex. With Zale Corp., Irving, Tex., 1942-87; pres. Fine Jewelers Guild div. Zale Corp., Irving, Tex., 1965-69; v.p. jewelry mdse. dir. Zale Corp., Irving, Tex., 1969-81, vice chmn., 1981-83, also bd. dirs.; co-chmn., investment advisor Weisberg & Fields, Inc.; bd. dirs. CBL & Assocs. Properties Inc.; mem. DiamondTrade.com., LLC. Trustee M.B. and Edna Zale Found.; pres. Dallas Home for the Jewish Aged Found.

FIELDS, LINDA JEAN, library director; b. St. Paul, Feb. 10, 1947; d. Vernon George and Harriet Marie Giossi; m. William Frazer, Mar. 29, 1966 (div.); children: William Vernon, Robert Allen; m. James A. Fields, Nov. 30, 1985. AA, Southwestern C.C., Chula Vista, Calif., 1974, AS, 1975; BA in Geography, San Diego State U., 1977, MA, 1981. Grad. asst. San Diego State U., 1977-79; instr. Southwestern Coll., Chula Vista, 1979, Grossmont Coll., El Cajon, Calif., 1980, U.S. Army, Yuma, Ariz., 1984-85; libr. Richfield (Utah) Pub. Libr., 1994—; spkr. Christian Women's Club, El Cajon, Calif., 1991-93. Mem. Utah Libr. Assn. Avocations: weaving, spinning, basket weaving. Email: lfields@inter.state.lib.ut.us. Office: Richfield Pub Libr 83 E Center St Richfield UT 84701

FIELDS, PAUL ROBERT, retired research nuclear chemist, consultant; b. Chgo., Feb. 4, 1919; s. Alexander and Anna (Greene) F.; m. Bernice White, Jan. 3, 1943; children: Marlene Frances, Rita Norine, Donald Brian. BS, U. Chgo., 1941. Chemist TVA, Wilson Dam, Ala., 1941-43, Metall. Lab. U. Chgo., 1943-45, Standard Oil Co., Whiting, Ind., 1945-46; with Argonne Nat. Lab., Ill., 1946—, dir. Chemistry Div., 1971-81, dir. Sci. Support Div., 1982—; assoc. lab. dir. Argonne Nat. Lab., 1981-82; cons. Simon & Schuster, Cleve., 1982—. Author, editor: Laboratory Experiments in Heavy Element Chemistry, 1955, Lanthanide-Actinide Chemistry, 1967, Cleaning our Environment, 1978; contbr. articles in field to profl. jours.; co-discoverer 3 new elements; patentee in field. Fellow AAAS, Am. Nuclear Soc.; mem. Am. Chem. Soc. (recipient Nuclear Applications in Chemistry award 1970), Am. Phys. Soc., Phi Beta Kappa. Office: Argonne Nat Lab 9700 Cass Ave Argonne IL 60439-4803

FIELDS, ROBERT MEDDIN, lawyer; b. Savannah, Ga., Sept. 9, 1953; s. Maurice and Phyllis (Meddin) Fields; m. Robyn Elleen, Apr. 12, 1981; 1 child, Michael Benjamin. BA, Duke U., 1975; JD, Cornell U., 1978; LLM, Georgetown U., 1982. Bar: Ga. 1979, N.J. 1980, Conn. 1983, D.C. 1986. Tax law specialist IRS, Washington, 1979-82; assoc. Reid & Riege, P.C., Washington, 1982-84, Winthrop, Stimson, Putnam & Roberts, N.Y.C., 1984—. Mem. ABA (employee benefits com.). Office: Winthrop Stimson et al 40 Wall St New York NY 10005-2301

FIELDS, SAMUEL PRESTON, JR., lay worker; b. Sparta, Mo., Oct. 2, 1918; s. Samuel Preston Sr. and Ada (Mallory) F.; m. Anna Elizabeth Yandell, June 6, 1971. On farm tng., vocat. schooling, Rogersville, Mo., 1946-50. Bible class tchr. Church of Christ, Fordland, Mo., 1948—, treas., 1960-65, sec.-treas., 1983—; trustee Ch. of Christ, Fordland, 1980—; retired farmer, woodworker. Contbr. poems to publs.; inventor no-fall bath aid, 1976. Bd. dirs. Fordland Farmers Exch., 1964-67; v.p. Fordland Cemetery Bd., 1983-95, pres., 1995—. Sgt. 1st c. U.S. Army, 1942-46, ETO. Named Farmer of Yr. Kiwanis Club, Springfield, Mo., 1951. Mem. VFW, Nat. Soc. Sons Am. Revolution, Springfield (treas. 1991), Ozarks Geneal. Soc., Springfield, Am. Legion, Springfield. Home: RR 1 Box 169 Fordland MO 65652-9424 *In a day and time when no one seems willing to take responsibility for anything, we need to remember that God always has, and still does, hold men responsible for their actions.*

FIELDS, STUART HOWARD, labor relations specialist; b. Chgo., Dec. 15, 1943; s. Albert B. and Cecelia (Kessler) F.; m. Birgit Willeke, Dec. 5, 1971; children: Jessica N., Jascha D. BS, UCLA, 1965; MS, U. Calif., Northridge, 1968. Cert. tchr. and instr., Calif. Labor relations specialist Hughes Tool Co., Culver City, Calif., 1970, Dept. of the Navy, Point Mugu, Calif., 1971-76; employee relations specialist Agricl. Rsch. Svc., Hyattsville, Md., 1976-81; labor relations specialist Agricl. Rsch. Svc., 1981-84, Pub. Health Svc., Rockville, Md., 1985-86; employee relations specialist Def. Nuclear Agy., Bethesda, Md., 1986-88, Consumer Product Safety Commn., Bethesda, 1988-89, U.S. Dept. Commerce, Washington, 1989-97; sr. paralegal Gagliardo & Zipin, Attys. at Law, Silver Spring, Md., 1997—; labor rels. specialist IRS, Washington, 1997—; presdl. classroom instr.; cons. in field. Author: Requirements for Top Positions in Personnel Administration, 1968. Lt. U.S. Army, 1968-70. Mem. Soc. Fed. Labor Relations Profls., Jewish Community Ctr., Mensa. Democrat. Avocations: classical music, coin collecting, tax law, basketball. Home: 9449 Reach Rd Potomac MD 20854-2853 Office: IRS 1111 Constitution Ave NW Washington DC 20224-0001

FIELDS, SUZANNE BREGMAN, syndicated columnist; b. Washington, Mar. 7, 1936; d. Samuel Holiday and Sadie (Hurwitz) Bregman; m. Theodore Martin Fields, June 16, 1957; children: Alexandra, Miriamne, Tobias. BA, George Washington U., 1957, MA, 1964; PhD, Cath. U., 1970. Freelance writer Washington, 1965-71; editor Innovations Mag., Washington, 1971-79; columnist Vogue mag., Washington, 1982; author Like Father, Like Daughter (Little Brown), 1983; columnist Washington Times, 1984—; syndicated columnist L.A. Times Syndicate, Washington, 1988—; TV commentator, regular panelist CNN & Co. Mem. Phi Beta Kappa. Jewish. Home: 1934 Biltmore St NW Washington DC 20009-1510 Office: The Washington Times 3600 New York Ave NE Washington DC 20002-1996

FIELDS, THEODORE, consulting medical radiation physicist; b. Chgo., Jan. 23, 1922; s. Samuel and Jean (Golber) F.; m. Audrey H. Engerman, June 24, 1945 (dec. 1981); children—Brad, Scott, Gary; m. Evie Levy, Nov. 28, 1985. B.S., U. Chgo., 1942; M.S., DePaul U., 1953. Pres. Health Physics Assocs., Northbrook, Ill., 1961-90; pres. Isotope Measurements Lab., Northbrook, Ill., 1969-87, Fields, Griffith, Hubbard & Broadbent Inc., Glencoe, Ill., 1969-94; lectr. radiology Rush Med. Sch., 1988-94, ret., 1998; adj. assoc. prof. radiology, U. Miami, 1992-97. Author: Treatment of Toxic Goiter with Radioactive Iodine, 1953, Clinical Use of Radioisotopes, 1957, 61; contbr. articles to profl. jours.; patentee in field. Served with USAAF, 1945-46. Recipient Disting. Alumni award DePaul U., 1989. Fellow Am. Coll. Radiology, Am. Pub. Health Soc.; mem. IEEE, Radiol. Soc. N.Am., Am. Phys. Soc., Health Physics Soc., Am. Assn. Physicists in Medicine, Am. Bd. Med. Physicists (cert.), Am. Bd. Health Physics (cert.), Am. Bd. Radiology (cert.), Sigma Xi. Home: 11570 Losano Dr Boynton Beach FL 33437-1926 Office: PO Box 3781 Boynton Beach FL 33424-3781

FIELDS, VALERIE DARALICE, journalist; b. Farmerville, La., Apr. 29, 1965; d. Elvadus and Mamie Marie (Harrison) F.; m. Clarence Edward Hill, Jr. BA in Liberal Studies, So. U. and A&M Coll., 1987; postgrad., Robert Maynard Inst. Jour. Edn, 1993. Billing acct. rep. Sprint, Atlanta, 1987-88; reporter Daily Comml., Leesburg, Fla., 1988-90; urban affairs writer Ft. Worth Star-Telegram N.E., Bedford, Tex., 1990-94; advt. acct. rep. Ft. Worth Star-Telegram, 1994-95, religion writer, 1995-96; sr. writer, religion editor Arlington (Tex.) Morning News, 1996—; media cons. One Church, One Child, Ft. Worth, 1997. Mem. Leadership Arlington, 1997; co-chmn. Urban H.S. Journalism Workshop, Dallas, 1996. Named Journalist of Yr., Duborma Liberian Women's Orgn., 1997. Mem. Nat. Assn. Black Journalists, Dallas-Ft. Worth Assn. Black Communicators (exec. bd. 1992-97), Soc. Profl. Journalists, Delta Sigma Theta. Democrat. Baptist. Home: 2407 Forest Oaks Cir Apt 235 Arlington TX 76006-6055 Office: Arlington Morning News 1112 E Copeland Rd Ste 400 Arlington TX 76011-4913

FIELDS, WENDY LYNN, lawyer; b. N.Y.C., Sept. 22, 1946; d. Sidney and Helen (Silverstein) F. BA, George Washington U., 1968, JD, 1976. Bar: D.C. 1976. Assoc. Arent, Fox, Kintner, Plotkin & Kahn, Washington, 1976-78; ptnr. Weissbard & Fields, Washington, 1978-83, Wilkes, Artis, Hedrick & Lane, Washington, 1983-86, Foley & Lardner, Washington, 1986-97, Katten Muchin & Zavis, Washington, 1997—. Mem. George Washington Law Rev., 1973-75. Mem. D.C. Bar. Assn. Office: Katten Muchin & Zavis Ste 700E 1025 Thomas Jefferson St NW Washington DC 20007-5214

FIELDS, WILLIAM ALBERT, lawyer; b. Parkersburg, W.Va., Mar. 30, 1939; s. Jack Lyons and Grace (Kelley) F.; m. Prudence Brandt Adams, June 26, 1964. B.S. magna cum laude, Ohio State U., 1961; postgrad., Harvard Law Sch., 1961-64. Bar: Ohio bar 1964. Since practiced in Marietta, city prosecutor, 1964-65; acting Judge Marietta Mcpl. Ct.; dir. elections Washington County, 1967-74; profl. bass-baritone soloist.; bd. dirs. Bank One, Marietta, N.A. Chmn. Washington County Heart Assn., 1965-67; county chmn. Am. Cancer Soc., 1967; mem. dist. exec. com. Boy Scouts Am., 1967-74; Treas. County Republican Exec. Com., 1966—; county chmn. Nixon for Pres., 1968, Saxbe for Senator, 1968; Trustee YMCA, Salvation Army; pres. bd. trustees Washington State Community Coll., Marietta; exec. com., trustee Coll. Adminstrv. Scis., Ohio State U.; trustee Appalachian Bible Inst., Bradley, W.Va., 1974-77, Marietta Meml. Hosp. Recipient Wall St. Jour. award, 1961; named Outstanding Young Man of Marietta, 1968, Outstanding Citizen of Marietta, 1992. Fellow Am. Coll. Trust and Estate Counsel; mem. Ohio Bar Assn. (chmn., bd. govs., probate and trust law sect.), Washington County Bar Assn., Marietta Area C. of C. (v.p., trustee), Am. Mensa, Sigma Chi, Beta Gamma Sigma. Clubs: Rotarian (pres. 1970-71), Marietta Country (trustee). Home: 129 Hillcrest Dr Marietta OH 45750-9321 Office: 217 2nd St Marietta OH 45750-2916 *Without the light of Christ, all is darkness and vain machination.*

FIELEKE, NORMAN SIEGFRIED, economist, educator; b. Kankakee, Ill., Aug. 22, 1932; s. Lessly and Catharine M. (Nicholson) F.; m. Carol A. Curtiss, June 16, 1962 (div. Dec. 1985); children: Andrew, Eric, Michael. BA summa cum laude, Amherst Coll., 1954; AM, Harvard U., 1955; PhD, 1969. Economist, budget examiner Office Mgmt. and Budget, Washington, 1959-64; industry economist Office U.S. Trade Rep., Exec. Office Pres., 1964-65; v.p., economist Fed. Res. Bank of Boston, 1967-97; dir. econ. rsch. U.S. Internat. Trade Commn., Washington, 1980; cons. IMF, Washington, 1993; adj. prof. Boston U., 1975-76, Brandeis U., 1988-90, Duke U., Durham, N.C., 1998-99. Author: The Welfare Effects of Controls over Capital Exports from the United States, 1971, The International Economy under Stress, 1988; contbr. articles to profl. jours. Lt. USAF, 1955-57. Littauer fellow, NSF fellow Harvard U., 1969. Home: 101 Dundalk Dr Chapel Hill NC 27514-6583

FIELO, MURIEL BRYANT, space engineer, interior designer; b. Bklyn., Dec. 11, 1921; d. Harry and Minnie (Dick) Bryant; m. Julius Fielo, June 17; 1 child, Michael Kenneth. Student, CCNY, 1938-41, Rutgers U., 1965-69; cert. N.Y. Sch. Interior Design, 1970. Gen. mgr. Fidelity Discount Corp., Irvington, N.J., adv. supr. Lincoln Loan Cos., Essex County, N.J., 1941-49; interior designer Alex Fielo Interior Decorators, Newark, 1942-49, prin., 1949-69, owner, 1969—; designer, cons. space engr. MUDGE Interior Design Studios, East Orange, N.J., 1969—. Mem. adv. panel Interior Design Mag, 1977—. Essex County freeholder clk. Bd. Freeholders, 1972-76; commr. East Orange Bus. Devel. Authority, 1977-86; mem. U.S. adv. coun. SBA-Region II, 1980-81; active LWV, 1950-55; organizer, 1st pres. South Orange chpt. Women's Am. ORT, 1952-54, mem. nat. speakers bur., 1952-65, parliamentarian No. N.J. coun., 1955-65; pres. Amity chpt. B'nai B'rith, Newark, 1946-48, v.p. No. N.J. coun., 1948-49, various nat. and state positions, 1948-80; mem. nat. com. on sect. fund raising Nat. Coun. Jewish Women, 1979-81, nat. tour. chmn., 1979-81; trustee cmty. svcs. coun. Oranges and Maplewood, United Way of Essex and West Hudson, 1981-83; bd. dirs. East Orange Central Ave. Mall Assn., 1979-83, chmn. new voter registration drive East Orange 2d Ward, 1955—, entire city, 1969; pres. East Orange Dem. Club, 1957-58, campaign coord. for Dem. mayoral candidate, 1969, calendar coord. Essex County Dem. Party, 1970-76; mem. N.J. Bipartisan Coalition for Women's Appts., 1981—. Named Outstanding Entrepreneur of 1984 N.J. Gov., Outstanding Orgn. Pres. Kean Coll. Profl. Women's Assn., 1985, Wonder Woman of 1986, Bus. Jour. of N.J., One of 8 Women to Watch in 1987 Jersey Woman Mag., 1987; also recipient various awards for civic svc.; named Bus. Person of Yr. East Orange C. of C., 1988. Mem. Internat. Soc. Interior Designers (bd. dir. 1981-85), Nat. Home Fashions League (N.J. membership chmn. N.Y. chpt. 1981-82), Interior Design Soc., Internat. Interior Design Assn. (charter mem.), N.J. Assn. Women Bus. Owners (state bd. 1979-82), Women Entrepreneurs N.J. (pres. 1981-85, chief exec. officer 1987—), N.J. Home Furnishings Assn. (bd. dirs. 1981-84, 86—), Constrn. Specifications Inst., N.J. Soc. AIA (profl. affiliate), Guild Designer Woodworkers, Women Bus. Ownership Ednl. Coalition (N.J. State pres. 1985-87, chief exec. officer 1987—, mem. steering com. interior designers for licensing in N.Y. 1985—), East Orange C. of C. (bd. dir. 1977—, v.p. 1981-85), Bus. and Profl. Women's Club of Oranges (bd. dir. 1958-66). Jewish. Fax: 973-673-6612. Home and Office: Mudge Interior Design Studio 185 S Clinton St East Orange NJ 07018-3039

FIENBERG, STEPHEN ELLIOTT, statistician; b. Toronto, Ont., Can., Nov. 27, 1942; came to U.S., 1964; B.S., U. Toronto, 1964; A.M., Harvard U., 1965, Ph.D., 1968. Asst. prof. dept. stats. and theoretical biology U. Chgo., 1968-72; asso. prof. dept. applied stats. U. Minn., St. Paul, 1972-76, prof., 1976-80, chmn. dept., 1972-78; prof. dept. stats. and social sci. Carnegie Mellon U., Pitts., 1980-85; Maurice Falk prof. Carnegie-Mellon U., Pitts., 1985-91, head dept. stats., 1981-84, dean Coll. Humanities and Social Scis., 1987-91; vice pres. acad. affairs York U., Toronto, 1991-93; chmn. com. on nat. stats. NRC, 1981-87; Maurice Falk prof. dept. stats Carnegie Mellon U., Pitts., 1992-97, Maurice Falk univ. prof., 1997—. Author: (with others) Discrete Multivariate Analysis: Theory and Practice, 1975, Analysis of Cross-classified Categorical Data, 1977, 2d edit., 1980, (with others) Beginning Statistics with Data Analysis, 1983, (with M. Anderson) Who Counts? The Politics of Census-Taking in Contemporary America, 1999; editor: (with A. Zellner) Studies in Bayesian Econometrics and Statistics, 1975, (with D.V. Hinkley) R.A. Fisher: An Appreciation, 1980, (with A.J. Reiss, Jr.) Indicators of Crime and Criminal Justice: Quantitative Studies, 1980, (with others) Sharing Research Data, 1985, (with W. Mason) Cohort Analysis in Social Research, 1985, (with A.C. Atkinson) A Celebration of Statistics, 1985, (with others) Statistics and the Law, 1986, The Evolving Role of Statistical Assessments as Evidence in the Courts, 1989, (with others) A Statistical Model: Frederick Mosteller's Contributions to Statistics, Science and Public Policy, 1990, (with M. M. Meyer) Assessing Evaluation Studies: The Case of Bilingual Education Strategies, 1992, (with others) Intelligence, Genes, and Success: Scientists Respond to The Bell Curve, 1997; editor: Jour. Am. Statistics Assn., 1977-79, Chance, 1987-92. Recipient Pres. award Com. Pres. Statis. Socs., 1982. Fellow AAAS, Am. Statis. Assn. (v.p. 1986-88), Inst. Math. Stats. (pres. 1998-99), Internat. Soc. Bayesian Analysis (pres.1996-97), Royal Statis. Soc.; mem. Nat. Acad. Sci. (elected), Biometric Soc., Internat. Statis. Inst., Psychometric Soc., Statis. Soc. Can. Office: Carnegie Mellon U Dept Stats Pittsburgh PA 15213

FIENNES, RALPH NATHANIEL, actor; b. Suffolk, Eng., Dec. 22, 1962; s. Mark and Jini Fiennes; m. Alex Kingston, 1993 (div. 1997). Student, Chelsea Coll. Art and Design, Royal Acad. Dramatic Art. Actor (theatre prodns.) with Royal Shakespeare Co., Broadway debut in Hamlet, 1995 (Tony award Lead Actor in a Play), Ivanov, 1997; (TV films) Prime Suspect, 1991, A Dangerous Man: Lawrence After Arabia, 1992, Wuthering Heights, 1992, The Baby of Macon, (films) Schindler's List, 1993 (Academy award nomination best supporting actor 1993, New York Film Critics Circle award best supporting actor 1993), Quiz Show, 1994, Strange Days, 1995, The English Patient, 1996 (Academy award nominee, Golden Globe award nominee), Oscar & Lucinda, 1997, The Avengers, 1997; prodr., actor Eugene Onegin, 1998, Taste of Sunshine, 1999, End of the Affair, 1999; voice Prince of Egypt, 1998. *

FIER, ELIHU, lawyer; b. N.Y.C., Mar. 25, 1931; s. Charles H. and Helen N. (Nadel) F.; m. Jane Lee Saltser, Jan. 10, 1956 (dec. Jan. 1964); children—Jennifer, Michael; m. Dorothy Elaine Broman, Sept. 25, 1977; children—Paige, Carlyn. B.A., Dartmouth Coll., 1952; LL.B., Harvard U., 1958. Bar: N.Y. 1959, U.S. Dist. Ct. (so. and ea. dists.) N.Y. 1960 U.S. Tax Ct. 1961, U.S. Ct. Appeals (2d cir.) 1961, Fla. 1997. Ptnr. Weil, Gotshal & Manges, N.Y.C., 1969-80, Morgan, Lewis & Bockius, N.Y.C., 1980-83; ptnr. Finley, Kumble, Wagner, Heine, Underberg, Manley & Casey, Beverly Hills, Calif., 1983-88, N.Y.C., 1983-88; of counsel Pryor, Cashman, Sherman & Flynn, N.Y.C., 1988-93, Blum & Fier P.C., N.Y.C., 1993-97, Gillespie & Allison, P.A., Boca Raton, Fla., 1995-97, Blum & Fier LLP, Boca Raton, 1998—; adj. assoc. prof. NYU, N.Y.C., 1969-76; lectr. N.Y. Law Jour., Law and Bus., Practicing Law Inst. Served to lt. (j.g.) USNR, 1952-60. Mem. ABA (com. creditors' rights in real estate financing 1983—), Assn. Bar City N.Y., N.Y. Bar Assn. Home: 2121 N Ocean Blvd Apt 403W Boca Raton FL 33431-7877 Office: 505 Park Ave New York NY 10022-1106

FIERHELLER, GEORGE ALFRED, corporate director; b. Toronto, Apr. 26, 1933; s. Harold Parsons and Ruth Hathaway (Bauld) F.; m. Glenna E. Fletcher, Apr. 17, 1957; children: Vicki Elaine, Lori Ann. BA, U. Toronto, 1955; LLD, Concordia U. With IBM, Toronto, 1955-58, account mgr., 1962-65, mktg. mgr., 1966-68; founder, pres. Sys. Dimensions Ltd., Ottawa, Ont., 1968-79; pres., CEO Rogers Cable TV Broadcasting Co. Ltd., Vancouver, B.C., Can., 1979-85, Cantel Inc., Toronto, 1985-90; chmn., CEO Roger Cantel Mobile, Inc., 1990-93; vice chair Rogers Comm., Inc., Toronto, 1993-96; pres. Four Halls Inc., Toronto, 1997—; bd. dirs. Extendicare Inc., Rogers Cantel Inc., GBC N.Am. Fund Inc., Proctor andRedfern Ltd., Nexsys Commtech Internat., Telesys. Internat. Wireless, N.V., Sierra Sys.; pres. Bd. of Trade of Met. Toronto, 1996-97. Contbr. articles to profl. jours. Gen. chmn. United Appeal Campaign, Ottawa, 1972; chmn. campaign Carleton U., 1975-77, also chmn. bd. govs., 1977-79; mem. adv. com. Norman Paterson Sch. Internat. Affairs; bd. dirs., v.p. United Way Ottawa, 1975-79 (United Way of Can. highest award 1998); Opera Ottawa, 1970-71; trustee, mem. exec. com. Nat. Arts Ctr., 1973-79; trustee Royal Ottawa Hosp., 1978-79, Vancouver Gen. Hosp. Found., 1981-85; mem. Vancouver Centennial Commn., 1983-84; bd. govs. Simon Fraser U., Vancouver, 1981-84; chmn. United Way Vancouver, 1981; chmn. B.C. Coun. of 80's, 1980-83; chair United Way Met. Toronto, 1994-96, chmn. gen. campaign, 1991; chmn. Vision 2000, 1990-91; trustee Sunnybrook Hosp. Found., 1993—, McMichael Can. Art Collection, 1993—; chair Trinity Coll. Campaign, 1996—. Recipient Award of Merit, City of Toronto, 1991, Award of Excellence, Can. Wireless Ind. Assn., 1996; named to Can. Info. Tech. Hall of Fame, 1998. Mem. Can. Info. Processing Soc. (pres. 1970-71), World Pres. Orgn., Chief Execs. Orgn., Can. Assn. Data Processing Svc. Orgns., Assn. Cert. Computer Profls. (founding com.), Can. Ctr. for Philanthropy (bd. dirs. 1987-91), Bus. Coun. on Nat. Issues, Cellular Telecom. Industry Assn. (bd. dirs. 1986-94), Smart Toronto (chmn. 1996), Greater Toronto Mktg. Alliance (chair 1997—), Vancouver Club, Rideau Club, Granite Club, Nat. Club, Ont. Club, Rosedale Golf Club. Home: 24 Pearwood Crescent, Toronto, ON Canada M3B 2C2 Office: Four Halls Inc, 121 King St W Ste 2525, Toronto, ON Canada M5H 3T9

FIERING, STEVEN, medical educator; b. Aug. 28, 1951. BS in Geology with distinction, U. Mich., 1975; BS in Microbiology, Eastern Mich. U., 1985; PhD in Genetics, Stanford U., 1990. Ptnr. food processing bus. Soy Plant, Ann Arbor, Mich., 1975-83; teaching asst. microbiology Eastern Mich. U., 1982-84, lectr. microbiology, 1985; teaching asst. Med. Sch. Stanford U., 1986-89; rsch. group leader AFRC Ctr. Genome Rsch. U. Edinburgh, Scotland, 1990-91; postdoctoral fellow Hutchinson Cancer Rsch. Ctr., Seattle, 1991-96; asst. prof. microbiology dept. Dartmouth Med. Sch., Lebanon, N.H., 1997—. Contbr. articles to profl. jours. Scholar Am. Soc. Hematology, 1995. Mem. AAAS. Office: Dartmouth-Hitchcock Med Ctr 6 W Borwell Lebanon NH 03756*

FIERKE, THOMAS GARNER, lawyer; b. Boone, Iowa, Nov. 12, 1948; s. Norman Garner and Mary Margaret (Mullen) F.; m. Susan Marie Butler, July 17, 1976 (div. Mar. 1983); m. Debra Lynn Clayton, Sept. 17, 1988; children: Veronica Helen, Caroline Margaret. BSMetE, Iowa State U., 1971; JD, U. Minn., 1974; LLM, Boston U., 1978. Bar: Ill. 1974, U.S. Dist. Ct. Mass. 1976, U.S. Dist. Ct. (no. dist.) Ill. 1976, U.S. Ct. Appeals (1st cir.) 1976, U.S. Tax Ct. 1978, U.S. Supreme Ct. 1978, Mass. 1980, N.Y. 1981, U.S. Ct. Appeals (fed. cir.) 1989. Commd. 2nd lt. U.S. Army, 1971, advanced through grades to capt., resigned, 1980; trial ct. prosecutor Ft. Devens, Mass., 1974-77; group judge adv. 10th Spl. Forces Group, 1975-78; chief adminstrv. law sect. Ft. Devens, 1977-78; chief legal counsel, contracting officer U.S. Def. Rep., Am. Embassy, Tehran, Iran, 1979; chief adminstrv. law Ft. Devens, 1979-80; judge adv. gen. corps, 1974-80; atty., advisor Army Materiel Command, 1980-82; mgr. contracts policy and review Martin Marietta Michoud Aerospace, Martin Marietta Corp., New Orleans, 1982; gen. counsel Lockheed Martin Manned Space Sys., Lockheed Martin Corp., New Orleans, 1984—; apptd. to La. Gov.'s Mil. Adv. Commn., 1991—; bd. dirs. La. Orgn. for Jud. Excellence, 1988—; mem. La. state com. Employer Support of Guard and Res., 1988—, regional ombudsman, 1989-92, dep. state ombudsman, 1992-94, state ombudsman, 1994—, chmn. New Orleans sect., 1992-94. Col. USAR, 1995. Recipient Most Valuable Employer Support for the Guard and Res. award, NASA Pub. Svc. medal, 1992, La. Cross Merit award State of La., 1994, 4 Outstanding Vol. Svc. medals Dept. Def., 1994, 96, 97, Legion of Merit, 1998. Mem. Am. Corp. Counsel Assn. (bd. dirs. New Orleans chpt. 1987—, v.p. 1989-90), Internat. Assn. Def. Counsel. Republican. Episcopalian. Avocations: snow skiing, reading, running. Office: Lockheed Martin Michoud Space Sys PO Box 29304 New Orleans LA 70189-0304

FIERMAN, GERALD SHEA, electrical distribution company executive; b. Wilkes-Barre, Pa., Dec. 14, 1924; s. Abe and Mary (Jacobs) F.; m. Bernice Perloff, June 12, 1949; children: Robert Alan, Lawrence David, Daniel John. AB in Liberal Arts, Pa. State U., 1948. Pres. Shea Realty Corp., Wilkes-Barre, 1959—, Barre Realty Corp., Wilkes-Barre, 1955—, Chase Wholesale Elec. Supply, Stroudsburg, Pa., 1960—, Tomberg Elec. Supply Co., Wilkes-Barre, 1954—, ANESCO, Kingston, Pa., 1949—, L&R Elec. Supply Co., Scranton, Pa., 1987—, Effco Inc., Scranton, 1987—. Chmn. United Jewish Campaign, Wilkes-Barre, 1963; pres. Jewish Fedn. Wyoming Valley, Pa., 1971-74; active Temple Israel, Wilkes-Barre. Served with 82d Airborne Divsn., AUS, 1942-46. Decorated Purple Heart. Mem. Masons, Westmoreland Club Wilkes-Barre, Jockey Club Miami, Huntsville Golf Club, Valley Tennis Club, Keystone Consistory, Williams Island Club (Miami). Home: 76 James St Kingston PA 18704-4730 Office: 517 Pierce St Kingston PA 18704-5731

FIERMAN, RONALD S., advertising agency executive; b. Cleve., July 14, 1950; s. Morris and Miriam Fierman; m. Elaine F. Fierman, June 17, 1972; children: Amy, David. BS, Miami U., Oxford, Ohio, 1972; MBA, Loyola U., Chgo. Staff acct. Arthur Andersen & Co., Chgo., 1972-77; controller Don Tennant Co., Chgo., 1977-86; chief fin. officer Warwick Advt. Inc., N.Y.C., 1986—. Office: Warwick Baker O'Neill 100 Avenue Of The Americas New York NY 10013-1689*

FIERO, PETRA SCHUG, language professional educator; b. Oberwinkling, Bavaria, Germany, June 4, 1962; came to U.S., 1985; d. Alfred and Edda (Baarmann) Schug; m. David Brian Fiero, May 25, 1989. BA, U. Regensburg, Germany, 1984; MA, U. Nebr., 1989, PhD, 1994. Tchg. asst., lectr. U. Nebr., Lincoln, 1985-94; asst. prof. German and Spanish Western Wash. U., Bellingham, 1995—. Author: Schreiben gegen Schweigen: Grenzerfahrungen in Jean Amérys autobiographischem Werk, 1997. Mem. Am. Assn. Tchrs. Germans, Modern Lang. Assn., Pacific NW Coun. Fgn. Langs., Wash. Assn. Fgn. Lang. Tchrs., Delta Phi Alpha. Avocations: playing piano, reading. Home: 655 W Horton Way Apt 140 Bellingham WA 98226-7346 Office: Western Washington Univ Dept Modern Classical Lang HU 241 Bellingham WA 98225

FIERROS, RUTH VICTORIA, retired secondary school educator; b. McRoberts, Ky., Mar. 29, 1920; d. Willie A. and Harriet (Wright) Cornett; m. Jose Fernando Fierros, Nov. 22, 1945 (dec.); children: Cedric Joseph, Philip Alonso, Stephen Michael. BA in English, Berea Coll., 1942; MA in English and Edn., Tex. A&I U., 1954. Cert. tchr., Tex. Tchr. Jenkins Ind. Schs., McRoberts, 1942-43, Laredo (Tex.) Ind. Schs., 1951-87; ret., 1987. Editor: Class '42 Yearbook, 1982, 87, 92; author: Upon the Easel of My Heart, 1982, Love's Collage of Rose Petals, 1996; co-author: The Berea Experience of Class of '42, 1997; contbr. poems to anthologies. Chairperson 50th, 55th, 58th, and 60th anniversary reunions Berea Coll. Class of 1942; pres.Tuesday Music & Literature, 1986-88. With USN, 1943-46. Recipient Tchr. Excellence award U. Tex., 1987, Golden Apple award Alpha Delta Kappa, 1987, Golden Poet award, 1988, Cert. of Citation State of Tex. Ho. of Reps., 1987, Armed Forces award, 1988, Leadership award, 1988; inducted into edn. area Laredo Hall of Fame, 1998. Mem. AAUW (charter, 1st v.p. 1966-68), NEA, Gifted and Talented Assn., Nat. Coun. Tchrs. English, Tex. State Tchrs. Assn., So. Poetry Assn. (Critics Choice award), Nat. Libr. of Poetry, Webb County Unit Ret. Tchrs. Assn. (2d v.p. 1994-95), Charles T. Morgan Soc., Internat. Soc. Poets (Disting. mem.), Delta Kappa Gamma (pres. 1966-68), Internat. Poetry Assn. Democrat. Roman Catholic. Avocations: church choir, writing poetry, reading, walking, collecting dolls and figurines. Home: 1801 Fremont St Laredo TX 78043-2606

FIERS, JOHN ROBERT, business executive, police chaplain; b. Lafayette, Ind., Dec. 3, 1961; s. John Ludwig and Virginia Lee Fiers; m. Marlene Ann Hughes, July 30, 1993; 1 child, Amber Lynn. BS in Mgmt., Purdue U., 1983; MBA, Ind. Wesleyan U., 1990; degree, Inst. Fin. Edn., Chgo., 1988; DDiv (hon.), World Christianship, Fresno, Calif., 1997. Ordained to ministry World Christianship Ministries. Sr. loan officer First Fed. Savs. Bank, Lafayette, 1984-91; v.p. Tippecanoe Title Svcs., Lafayette, 1991-93; pastor Romney (Ind.) United Meth. Ch., 1991-93; assoc. pastor Trinity United Meth. Ch., Lafayette, 1993-94; pres. First Mortgage of Ind., Indpls., 1994-97; chaplain Marion County Sheriff's Dept., Indpls., 1997—; corp. treas. Electro Painters, Inc., Indpls., 1997—; mem. pres.'s bd. U. Indpls., 1994-95; mem. lenders bd. State Student Assistance Commn., Indpls., 1987-90; treas. Ind. Student Lenders Assn., Indpls., 1989-90. Festival fin. mgr. Downtown Bus. Ctr., Lafayette, 1988-93, Greater Lafayette C. of C., 1988-93. Mem. York Rite, Pi Sigma Alpha. Republican. Avocations: reading, current events. Email: JRFPM@Indy.net. Home: 8632 Mariesi Dr Indianapolis IN 46278 Office: Electro Painters Inc 8533 Zionsville Rd Indianapolis IN 46268

FIERSTEIN, HARVEY FORBES, playwright, actor; b. Bklyn., June 6, 1954; s. Irving and Jacqueline Harriet (Gilbert) F. Acting debut in Andy Warhol's Pork, N.Y.C., 1971; author: (plays) In Search of the Cobra Jewels, 1973, Freaky Pussy, 1975, Flatbush Tosca, 1976, Cannibals Just Don't Know Better, 1978, Spookhouse, 1984, Safe Sex, 1987, Forget Him, 1988; (book of musical) La Cage Aux Folles, 1983 (Tony award best book of musical 1984, Tony award best musical 1984, L.A. Drama Critics Circle award 1984, Dramatists Guild award 1984), (with Peter Allen and Charles Suppon) Legs Diamond, 1989; author and star: The International Stud, 1978, Fugue in a Nursery, 1979 (Villager award 1980), Widows and Children First!, 1979, (all three one-acts compiled into) Torch Song Trilogy, 1981 (Obie award 1982), (on Broadway), 1982 (Tony award best play 1982, Tony award best actor 1982, Drama Desk award best play 1982, Drama Desk award best actor 1982, George Oppenheimer-Newsday Playwrighting award 1982, Theatre World award 1983), (in London's West End), 1985 (Olivier Best Play award nominee 1985); screenwriter and star: Torch Song Trilogy, 1988, Tidy Endings, 1988 (ACE award best dramatic special 1988, ACE award writing 1988); actor: (off-Broadway) The Haunted Host, 1991, (films) Garbo Talks, 1984, The Harvest, 1992, Mrs. Doubtfire, 1993, White Lies, 1993, Bullets Over Broadway, 1994, Dr. Jekyl and Ms. Hyde, 1995, The Celluloid Closet, 1996, Independence Day, 1996, Everything Relative, 1996, Kull The Conqueror, 1997, Safe Men, 1998, Legend of Mulan, 1998; (TV guest star appearances) Miami Vice, 1985, The Simpsons, Murder She Wrote, 1992, Cheers, 1992 (Emmy award nomination 1992), (narrator) The Times of Harvey Milk, (Sesame Street spl guest star) Elmo Saves Christmas, 1996, (spl. project) Am. Film Inst. TV or Not TV (Guest star HBO) Larry Sanders Show, 1996; audio CD This Is Not Going to Be Pretty, 1995, (Live Performance Plump Record) 1996. Recipient Theater World award for Broadway debut, 1983, Fund for Human Dignity award, 1983. Avocations: AIDS activist, gay rights activist, painting, gardening, cooking. Office: c/o AGF Inc 30 W 21st St Fl 7 New York NY 10010-6905*

FIES, JAMES DAVID, elementary education educator; b. Chgo., May 19, 1950; s. Arthur Herbert Sr. and Ruth Paulina (Rehm) F.; m. Ruth Elaine Carlson, June 24, 1972; children: Samuel Jacob, Sarah Rae. BA, Purdue U., 1972, MS, 1975. Cert. elem. edn. tchr., Ind. Tchr. math. Morton Elem./Mid. Sch., Hammond, Ind., 1972-82, Eggers Elem./Mid. Sch., Hammond, 1982-88; tchr. math. Gavit Jr./Sr. High Sch., Hammond, 1988—, interim asst. prin., 1992; dept. chair Eggers Mid. Sch., 1983-86. Bldg. union rep. Hammond Tchrs. Fedn. Local 394, 1981-87; trustee Trinity Luth. Ch., Hammond, 1976-82, 86-87, bd. fin., 1993—. Mem. Nat. Coun. Tchrs. of Maths., Hammond Tchrs. Fedn., Am. Fedn. of Tchrs. Avocations: traveling, fishing, family activities. Home: 544 Hickory Ln Munster IN 46321-2409

FIES, RUTH ELAINE, media specialist; b. Hammond, Ind., Oct. 13, 1949; d. Raymond O. and Elmyra C. (Papageorge) Carlson; m. James. D. Fies, June 24, 1972; children: Samuel Jacob, Sarah Rae. BA in edn., Purdue U., 1971, MS, 1974. Cert. elem. educator, ednl. media profl. K-12, Ind. Tchr. 5th grade Highland (Ind.) Sch. Dist., 1971-72; media specialist Cook County Sch. Dist. #149, Dolton, Ill., 1972-78, George Rogers Clark Middle/H.S., 1991—. Mem. Trinity Luth. Ch. Mem. Hammond Tchrs. Fedn., Delta Kappa Gamma Soc. Internat. Avocations: crafts, needlework, travel, family activities. Home: 544 Hickory Ln Munster IN 46321-2409 Office: George Rogers Clark Sch 1921 Davis Ave Whiting IN 46394-1820

FIETSAM, ROBERT CHARLES, accountant; b. Belleville, Ill., Oct. 18, 1927; s. Celsus J. and Viola (Ehret) F.; BS, U. Ill., 1955; m. Miriam Runkwitz, Apr. 12, 1952; children: Robert C., Guy P., Nancy A., Lisa R. CPA, Mo., Ill. Claims adjuster Ely & Walker Dry Goods, St. Louis, 1947-48; acct. Price Waterhouse & Co., 1949-54; staff acct. J.W. Boyle & Co., East St. Louis, 1955-59; owner R.C. Fietsam, CPA's, Belleville, Ill., 1959-68; mng. ptnr. R.C. Fietsam & Co. CPA's, 1969—. Mem. Belle-Scott Com., 1979—; bd. dirs., pres. Belleville Center, Inc., 1980-81; mem. Ill. Pub. Accts. Registration Com., 1985-87; bd. dirs. Meml. Hosp., 1982-85, Meml. Found., Inc., 1986-91, Bellville Hosp. Golf Classic, mem., 1983-91, chmn., 1986-91, Ill. Bd. Examiners, 1994—, vice chair, 1997-98, chair 1998-99. council v.p., pres. St. Paul United Ch. of Christ., 1969-73. With USAF, 1951-53. Mem. AICPAs (coun. 1981-84, 85-90), Ill. CPA Soc. (pres. south chpt. 1972-73, Mr. Southern Chpt. award 1976, state bd. dirs. 1979-81, sr. v.p. 1987-88, pres. 1988-89, bd. dirs. 1989-90, hon. mem. 1992, ICPAC PAC 1979-92, chmn. PAC 1989-92, Pub. Svc. award 1982-83), Nat. Assn. State Bds. Accountancy (del.), Mo. Soc. CPA's, U. Ill. Greater Belleville Illini Club (past pres.), Belleville C. of C. (pres. 1973-74), Belleville Jr. C. of C. (life, Key Man award 1959-60, Outstanding Citizen award 1976), Belleville Econ. Progress, Inc. (Ambassadors 1973—), U. of Ill. Found. (St. Louis Accountancy Com. 1991—), U. Ill. Alumni Assn. (life), Lambda Chi Alpha Alumnae Assn., St. Clair Country Club. Optimists (life, Belleville Chpt. pres. 1979-80, Disting. Pres. award 1979-80, Optimist of Yr. Belleville, 1977, Ill. Dist. 1980), Elks. Home: 23 Persimmon Rdg Belleville IL 62223-3946 Office: 325 W Main St Belleville IL 62220-1505

FIFE, BETTY H., librarian; b. Indpls., Mar. 31, 1925; d. Otho Cova and Mae Craddock (Paxton) Hay; m. James A. Fife, Aug. 30, 1945; children: Andrew, Marlie, John, Laurie. BS, Boston U., 1967, MS, 1969; student, Northeastern U. Classroom tchr., libr. Town of Hanover (Mass.); elem. libr. Town of Newburgh (N.Y.). Fellow Northeastern U. Mem. NCTE. Home: 174 Cedar Acres Rd Marshfield MA 02050-6036 Office: PO Box 115 Vails Gate NY 12584-0115

FIFE, EDWARD H., landscape architecture educator; b. Mass., Oct. 18, 1942; s. Edwin Kenneth and Yvonne Barbara (Bartlett) F.; children: Sarah Rodman and Mike Malcolm. BS in Landscape Architecture, R.I. Sch. Design, Providence, 1965; M in Landscape Architecture, Harvard U., 1967. Registered landscape architect, Ont. Designer Sasaki, Strong Assoc., Toronto, Ont., Can., 1964-66; asst. prof. landscape architecture Ohio State U., Columbus, 1967-69; asst. prof. landscape architecture U. of Toronto, 1969-73, assoc. prof., 1973—, asst. chmn., 1983-85, chmn. program in landscape architecture, 1985-89, 92-96, dir. Ctr. for Landscape Rsch., 1987-89; prin. E. H. Fife Landscape Architecture, Toronto, 1979—; mem. roster vis. educators Landscape Archtl. Accreditation Bd., 1986-96. Bd. dirs. Koffler Gallery, Toronto, 1986-95, Landscape Architecture Can. Found., 1987-88, 94—; mem. adv. com. Restoration of Monserrate Park, Portugal, 1988-90; mem. sci. and edn. com. Royal Bot. Garden, 1988-91, mem. property com., 1991-93; mem. acad. bd. governing coun. U. Tornoto, 1988-89. Fellow Can. Soc. Landscape Architects; mem. Internat. Fedn. Landscape Architects, Can. Soc. Landscape Architects (roster vis. educators), Ont. Assn. Landscape Architects (pres. 1987-88, bd. dirs. 1983-89). Avocations: painting, organic farming, canoeing, hiking. E-mail: fife@clr.utoronto.ca Fax: (416) 971-2094. Home: 269 Waverley Rd, Toronto, ON Canada M4L 3T5

FIFE, JONATHAN DONALD, higher education educator; b. Washington, Nov. 9, 1941; s. G. Donald and Marie (Wall) F.; m. Janice McKenna, Aug. 10, 1968 (div.); children: Patrick McKenna, Timothy Kingston, Brendan Martin; m. Ann Ferren, 1996. BBA, U. Mass., 1965; MS, SUNY, Albany, 1970; postgrad, U. Cin., 1965-67; EdD, Pa. State U., 1975. Asst. dir. student activities State U. Coll., Buffalo, 1967-69; rsch. asst. Pa. State U. Ctr.

for Study Higher Edn., State College, 1970-72; assoc. dir. ERIC Clearinghouse on Higher Edn., George Washington U., Washington, 1972-77, dir., 1977-98, prof. edn., 1977-98; dir. Ctr. on Quality Leadership and Adminstrn. in Edn., Va. Poly. Inst. and State U., Blacksburg, 1998—, also vis. prof., 1998—; edn. pilot team evaluator Malcolm Baldridge Nat. Quality Award, 1994, sr. evaluator, 1995-96, bd. examiners, sr. examiner, 1996-97. Mng. editor Rev. Higher Edn., 1980-86; cons. editor Change, 1981—. Bd. dirs. Nat. Ctr. for Higher Ednl. Mgmt. Systems, Boulder, 1980-82; cons. Rosenberg Commn., Md., 1975; pres., Wheaton Sq. East Condominium, Wheaton, Md., 1973-78. Mem. Assn. Study Higher Edn. (exec. sec. treas. 1978-87), Am. Ednl. Rsch. Assn. (sec. treas. spl. interest group postsecondary edn. 1977-81), Higher Edn. Group Washington (sec. 1979-81, v.p., 1997-98, pres. 1998-99), Assn. Instl. Rsch., Phi Kappa Phi. Avocations: tennis, golf, boating.

FIFE, WILLIAM FRANKLIN, retired drug company executive; b. Buffalo, W.Va., Nov. 6, 1921; s. Alfred Charles and Grace (Pitchford) F.; children: Scott Franklin, Susan Elizabeth, Cindy Francine. AB, Berea Coll., 1949; MS, U. Wis., 1950. Operating mgr. McKesson & Robbins, Chgo. and Kansas City, Mo., 1950-56, Cleve. Wholesale Drug Co., 1956-58; with Owens, Minor & Bodeker, Inc., 1958-91; pres., exec. v.p., sr. v.p. Owens & Minor, Inc., Richmond, Va., 1981-87, chief oper. officer, 1987-91, exec. v.p., 1989-91, ret., 1991—, now cons., bd. dirs.emeritus, 1998—. Capt. C.E. U.S. Army, 1942-46. Home: 507 Gaskins Rd S Richmond VA 23233-5709 Office: Owens & Minor Inc 4800 Cox Rd Glen Allen VA 23060-6294

FIFE, WILMER KRAFFT, chemistry educator; b. Wellsville, Ohio, Oct. 19, 1933; s. Wilmer George and Lourene Elizabeth (Krafft) F.; m. Betsy Louise Jones, Dec. 26, 1959; children: Kimberly, Julia, Steven. B.Sc. in Chemistry, Case Inst. Tech., 1955; Ph.D. in Organic Chemistry, Ohio State U., 1960. Applications chemist Monsanto Chem. Co., Dayton, Ohio, summers 1955, 57; instr. Muskingum (Ohio) Coll., 1959-60, asst. prof., 1960-64, asso. prof., 1964-70, prof., 1970-71, chmn. dept. chemistry, 1966-71; prof. chemistry Ind. U.-Purdue U. at Indpls., 1971—, chmn. dept., 1971-80. NIH postdoctoral fellow Harvard U., 1965-66; NIH postdoctoral fellow Columbia U., 1968-69; NSF fellow, 1955-56; Sinclair Oil Co. fellow, 1958-59; DuPont fellow, 1960; Danforth assoc., 1969—; others. Mem. Am. Chem. Soc., AAAS, Sigma Xi, Tau Beta Pi, Phi Lambda Upsilon. Home: 7102 Dean Rd Indianapolis IN 46240-3626 Office: IUPUI Chemistry 402 N Blackford St Indianapolis IN 46202-3217

FIFER CANBY, SUSAN MELINDA, library administrator; b. Stockton, Calif., Jan. 23, 1948; d. Reginald Dekovan and Shirley Rae (Canaday) Fifer; m. Thomas Yellott Canby, Oct. 9, 1982. BS, U. Nebr., 1970; MLS, U. Md., 1974. Curriculum libr. Nat. Geog. Soc., Washington, 1975-81, asst. libr., 1981-83, dir. libr., 1983-94, dir. libr. & indexing, 1994-99, dir. librs., 1999—; mem. OCLC User-Coun., Dublin, Ohio, 1997—; literacy tutor. Bd. dirs. tech. com. D.C. Coun. Govts., 1985-88, D.C. Libr. Coun., 1997—, Capital Area Libr. Network, 1989-95, 98—, chair, 1994-95. Mem. ALA (John Cotton Dana award 1985, 89), Spl. Librs. Assn. (chmn. geography and map divsn. 1978, 85, joint spring workshop 1990, 97, chmn. publs. com. 1993-94), D.C. Libr. Assn. (pres. 1991-92, v.p. 1990-91, sec. 1981-83, Disting. Svc. award 1993), Assn. Am. Geographers, Hort. Soc. Sandy Spring, Delta Delta Delta. Avocations: gardening, reading. Home: 6855 Haviland Mill Rd Clarksville MD 21029-1308 Office: Nat Geog Soc Library 1145 17th St NW Washington DC 20036-4701

FIFIELD, WILLIAM O., lawyer; b. Crown Point, Ind., May 25, 1946. BS with honors, Purdue U., 1968; JD cum laude, Harvard U., 1971. Bar: Ill. 1971, Tex. 1998. Assoc. Sidley & Austin, Dallas, 1971-77, ptnr., 1977—, mng. ptnr., 1996—; bd. dirs. Kimberly-Clark Corp. Office: Sidley & Austin 717 N Harwood St Ste 3400 Dallas TX 75201-6538

FIFLIS, TED JAMES, lawyer, educator; b. Chgo., Feb. 20, 1933; s. James P. and Christine (Karakitsos) F.; m. Vasilike Pantelakos, July 3, 1955; children: Christina Eason, Antonia Fowler, Andreanna Lawson. BS, Northwestern U., 1954; LLB, Harvard U., 1957. Bar: Ill. 1957, Colo. 1975, U.S. Supreme Ct. 1984. Pvt. practice law Chgo., 1957-65; mem. faculty U. Colo. Law Sch., Boulder, 1965—; prof. U. Colo. Law Sch., 1968—; vis. prof. NYU, 1968, U. Calif., Davis, 1973, U. Chgo., 1976, U. Va., 1979, Duke U., 1980, Georgetown U., 1982, U. Pa., 1983, Am. U., 1983, Harvard U., 1988; Lehmann Disting. vis. prof. Washington U., 1991; cons. Rice U. Author: (with Homer Kripke, Paul Foster) Accounting for Business Lawyers, 1970, 3rd edit., 1984, Accounting Issues for Lawyers, 1991; editor-in-chief Corp. Law Rev., 1977-88; contbr. articles to profl. jours. Mem. ABA, Am. Assn. Law Schs. (past chmn. bus. law sect.), Colo. Bar Assn. (mem. coun. sect. of corp., banking and bus. law 1974-75), Am. Law Inst., Colo. Assn. Corp. Counsel (pres. 1998—). Greek Orthodox. Home: 1340 Bluebell Ave Boulder CO 80302-7832 Office: Univ of Colo Law Sch Boulder CO 80309

FIGA, PHILLIP SAM, lawyer; b. Chgo., July 27, 1951; s. Leon and Sarah Figa; m. Candace Cole, Aug. 19, 1973; children: Benjamin Todd, Elizabeth Dawn. BA, Northwestern U., 1973; JD, Cornell U., 1976. Bar: Colo. 1976, U.S. Dist. Ct. Colo. 1976, U.S. Ct. Appeals (10th cir.) 1980, U.S. Supreme Ct. 1980. Assoc. Sherman & Howard, Denver, 1976-80; ptnr. Burns & Figa, P.C., Denver, 1980-90, pres., 1988-90; pres., shareholder Burns, Figa & Will, P.C., Englewood, Colo., 1991—; instr. U. Denver Law Sch., 1984, 86, Nat. Inst. Trial Advocacy, Rocky Mountain Region, 1992, 94; bd. dirs. Colo. Lawyers Com., Denver, 1984-89, vice chair 1987-88, treas. 1988-89; mem. model rules of profl. conduct, com. on group legal svcs. and advt. Colo. Supreme Ct., 1987-92; mem. U.S. Dist. Ct. Justice Reform Act. Adv. Com., 1994-97; active Colo. Commn. on Jud. Discipline, 1995—. Articles editor Cornell Internat. Law Rev., 1975-76; contbr. articles to legal jours. Bd. dirs. B'nai B'rith Anti-Defamation League, 1984—, regional bd. chair, 1996-98; trustee Rose Med. Ctr., 1987-95, exec. com., 1990-95, AMC Cancer Rsch. Ctr., 1993-95; co-chmn. Civil Rights Com., 1988-90. Evans scholar, 1969-73. Fellow Internat. Soc. Barristers, Am. Bar Found., Colo. Bar Found. (trustee 1999—); mem. ABA (standing com. on profl. discipline 1997—), Am. Judicature Soc., Colo. Bar Assn. (mem. ethics com. 1978-93, chair ethics com. 1984-85, bd. govs. 1986-88, 89-91, pres. 1995-96), Denver Bar Assn., Arapahoe County Bar Assn., Phi Beta Kappa, Phi Eta Sigma. Home: 9928 E Ida Ave Greenwood Village CO 80111-3743 Office: Burns Figa & Will PC Plaza Tower One Ste 1030 6400 S Fiddlers Green Cir Englewood CO 80111

FIGANIAK, LAURA MARY ANN, poet, executive assistant; b. Phila., Aug. 20, 1959; d. John Emanuel and Laura Antoinette (Nowakowska) F.; m. Dr. Anthony Farole, Oct. 18, 1997. Adminstrv. asst. Berger & Co. Real Estate, Phila., 1977-84, Thomas Jefferson U., Phila., 1986-94, J & H Marsh & McLenna, Phila., 1994—, Triton PCS, Inc., Malvern, Pa., 1998—; mem. Meeting Planners Internat., Phila., 1986—. Contbr. poetry to jours., 1994—. Mem. Am. Poet Soc., Poetry Soc. Am., Phila. Art Mus. Roman Catholic. Avocations: baking, gardening, dogs, writing, travel. Home: PO Box 646 Valley Forge PA 19482-0646 Office: Triton PCS Inc 375 Technology Dr Malvern PA 19355

FIGG-CURRIER, CINDY, professional golfer; b. Mount Pleasant, Mich., Feb. 23, 1960; 1 child, Kaitland Elizabeth. Degree in mktg., 1982. Golfer LPGA, 1984—; winner State Farm Rail Classic, 1997. 1 LPGA career hole-in-one. Office: c/o LPGA 100 International Golf Dr Daytona Beach FL 32124-1082*

FIGGE, FREDERICK HENRY, JR., retired publishing executive; b. Chgo., Apr. 8, 1934; s. Frederick H. and Theodora M. (Hosto) F.; m. Beverly J. Menz, June 20, 1956; children: Dora, Ann, Jane, Fred C. B.S., U. Ill., 1956. CPA, Ill. With Arthur Young & Co. (C.P.A.s), Chgo., 1958-64; controller Ency. Brit., Inc., Chgo., 1964-74, v.p., treas., 1974-85, sr. vp., 1985-86, exec. v.p., 1986-93, ret., 1993. Past. treas. Direct Selling Ednl., Found., past bd. dirs.; past bd. dirs. Coll. Commerce, U. Ill. With USNR, 1956-58. Mem. Beta Theta Pi, Beta Gamma Sigma. Democrat. Congregationalist. Clubs: LaGrange Country; Chgo. Athletic. Home: 220 S Collier Blvd Apt 702 Marco Island FL 34145-4800

FIGGIS, MIKE, film director; b. Carlisle, Cumbria, Eng., June 9, 1949; arrived in Eng., 1957; Mem. band Gas Board; mem. exptl. theater group The People Show, 1970's. Dir. films, music Stormy Monday, 1988, Internal Affairs, Liebestraum, Mr. Jones, Leaving Las Vegas, The Browning Version, 1994, One Night Stand, 1997, Flamenco Women, 1997, Miss Julie, 1999, The Loss of Sexual Innocence, 1999, (TV) The House, 1994; prodr. films Redheugh, Slow Fade, Animals of the City, The House. *

FIGGS, LINDA SUE, educational administrator; b. Westhope, N.D., Dec. 19, 1946; d. Clifford James and Ethel Grace (Geise) Drake; m. Tom R. Figgs, Dec. 27, 1969. Student, Minot State U., 1964-66; B.Music Edn., U. Kans., 1968, M.Music Edn., 1972, EdD, 1978; postgrad., U. del Valle de Mex., 1996, Habla Hispana Lang. Inst. San Miguel de Allende, Guanajuato, Mex., 1997. Cert. secondary music tchr., ednl. adminstr., Kans., Iowa, Nebr., N.D. Music tchr. Jefferson County N. High Sch., Winchester, Kans., 1968-76, 89-91, supr. student tchrs., 1970-75; rsch. asst. to assoc. dean of edn. U. Kans., Lawrence; prin. McKinley Elem., Liberal, Kans., 1992-95, Maynard Elem., Emporia, Kans., 1995-96, Stanton Street Early Childhood Ctr., 1995-96; gen. dir. Academia Cultural de Espanol, San Miguel de Allende, Mex., 1997—; rsch. asst. Sch. Edn., U. Kans., Lawrence, 1977; piano tchr. Toon Shop, Atchison, Kans., Leavenworth, Kans.; music tchr. Little Flower Sch., Minot, N.D., Effingham, Kans.; mgr. music store, Effingham; sec. humanities Minot State U.; counselor Internat. Music Camp, Dunseith, N.D., Midwestern Music and Art Camp, Lawrence; summer counselor, unit leader Nat. Music Camp, Interlochen, Mich.; sponsor 5th grade Positive Peer Group; mem. edn. adv. panel TeleKansas Alliance; mem. U.S. D.480 Action Team Mem., McKinley Action Team Mem.; reader adv. bd. S.W. Daily Times; chmn. rural residency coordinating team Chamber Music Am. and NEA; mem. tech. com. for Unified Sch. Dist. 480 and McKinley Quality Performance Accreditation Team; elem. adminstrn. rep. Stakeholders Com., Sch. Site Coun., strategic planning teams Unified Sch. Dist. 480, McKinley preassessment team, 504 team, intensive assistance team, skunk works, supervision, stakeholders, McKinley Drug Team; bd. dirs., patron, docent Baker Arts Ctr.; coord. ESL and migrant summer sch.; coord. for Unified Sch. Dist. 253 Migrant/ESL program, 1995—; 1st grade prin. rep. for Supt.'s Curriculum Coun. for Sci., elem. prin. rep. sci. com. Singer, pianist, dir. San Miguel Chorale; contbr. articles to profl. publs. Bd. dirs. Am. Youth Symphony Band and Orch., Nebr., 1970-76; music dir. United Meth. Ch., Atchison, 1988-92; mem. choir United Meth. Ch., Liberal, 1992-95; choir dir. 1st Christian Ch., Liberal, 1995, McKinley Elem. PTA, S.W. Kans. Humane soc.; bd. dirs. Cmty. Concert, 1994-95; vol. Mid Am. Air Mus.; mem. 500 Club, Leadership Liberal, 1995, Leadership Emporia, 1996, Maynard Elem. PTO, Maynard Elem. Sch. Site Coun., Flint Hills Humane Soc., SOS, Emporia Arts Coun., Emporia Area Friends of the Zoo. Mem. ASCD, NEA, AAUW (edn. and scholarship com.), Nat. Assn. Elem. Sch. Prins., United Sch. Adminstrs., Kans. Assn. Sch. Adminstrs., Kans. ASCD, Kans. Assn. Elem. Sch. Prins., Kans. Edn. Assn., Nat. Mid. Sch. Assn., Kans. Assn. Mid Level Edn., Kans. Reading Assn., Knas. Reading Coun., Profl. Devel. Coun. (co-pres., insvc. com.), U. Kans. Alumni Assn. (life), S.W. Symphony Soc. (pres. 1993-95), Assn. Cmty. Art Agys. Kans., Emporia Area C. of C. (bus. edn. com.), Sigma Alpha Iota, Pi Kappa Lambda, Phi Delta Kappa. Presbyterian. Avocations: reading, walking, piano performance, computers, stained glass. Mailing Address: 1007 Dickinson Rd Effingham KS 66023-5130

FIGLAR, ANITA WISE, banker; b. Camas, Wash., Oct. 7, 1950; d. William Hulon and Mary Wise (Adkisson) Ward; m. Richard Bould Figlar, Aug. 7, 1976; children: Richard Bould II, David Wise. Student, U. Wash., 1968-70; BA in Intercultural Studies, Ramapo Coll., 1974. Mktg. coord. power and control ops. Gen. Cable Corp., Union, N.J., 1975-76, mktg. analyst power and control ops., 1976-78; various positions Potters Industries, Inc., Hasbrouck Heights, N.J., 1971-75; with highway safety programs dept. Potters Industries, Inc., Parsippany, N.J., 1981-82, mgr. highway safety programs dept., 1982-84, mgr. bus. devel., 1985-86, industry mgr. Highway Products div., 1986-89; with customer svc. United Jersey Bank, Hackensack, N.J., 1989; fin. svc. rep. United Jersey Bank, 1989-90, asst. br. mgr., bank officer, 1990-91; bank officer retail sales United Jersey Bank, Hackensack, N.J., 1991-92, bank officer retail sales mgr., 1992-94; v.p., mgr. retail sales Summit Bank (formerly United Jersey Bank), Hackensack, N.J., 1994-97, market mgr., 1997-98; sr. regional mgr. Summit Bank (formerly United Jersey Bank), New Canaan, Conn., 1998—. Contbr. articles to many profl. and govtl. publs.

FIGLEY, MELVIN MORGAN, radiologist, physician, educator; b. Toledo, Dec. 5, 1920; s. Karl Dean and Margaret (Morgan) F.; m. Margaret Jane Harris, Mar. 16, 1946; children: Karl Porter, Joseph Dean, Mark Thompson. Student, Dartmouth, 1938-41; MD magna cum laude (John Harvard fellow), Harvard, 1944. Diplomate: Am. Bd. Radiology (trustee 1967-72). Intern, then resident internal medicine Western Res. U., 1944-46; resident radiology U. Mich., 1948-51, instr., asst. prof., asso. prof. radiology, 1950-58; practice specializing in radiology Seattle, 1958-86; prof. radiology, chmn. dept. U. Wash., 1958-78, prof. radiology and medicine, 1979-85, emeritus prof. radiology and medicine, 1986—; mem. radiation study sect. NIH, 1963-67; mem. com. on radiology Nat. Acad. Scis.-NRC, 1964-69, chmn., 1968-69. Editor: Am. Jour. Roentgenology, 1976-85; contbr. articles profl. jours. Bd. dirs. James Picker Found., 1970-80. Served to capt. M.C. AUS, 1946-48. John and Mary R. Markle scholar, 1952-57. Fellow Am. Coll. Radiology (Gold medal 1987), Royal Coll. Radiologists (hon., London), Royal Australian Coll. Radiologists (hon.); mem. Royal Soc. Medicine (hon.), Assn. Univ. Radiologists (pres. 1966, Gold medal 1983), Am. Roentgen Ray Soc. (exec. council 1970-88, pres. 1983-84, Gold medal 1986), N. Am. Soc. Cardiac Radiology (pres. 1974), Fleischer Soc. (pres. 1986-87), Radiol. Soc. N.Am. (Gold medal 1986), AMA, Boylston Med. Soc., Wash. Heart Assn. (past trustee), Soc. Chmn. Acad. Radiology Depts. (exec. council 1969-71), Phi Beta Kappa, Sigma Xi, Alpha Omega Alpha, Sigma Alpha Epsilon. Episcopalian. Home: PO Box 859 Grantham NH 03753-0859 Office: U Wash Dept Radiology Seattle WA 98195

FIGLIN, ROBERT ALAN, physician, hematologist, oncologist; b. Phila., June 22, 1949; s. Jack and Helen Figlin; 1 child, Jonathan B. BA in Chemistry, Temple U., 1970, postgrad., 1972; MD, Med. Coll. Pa., 1976. Diplomate Am. Bd. Internal Medicine, sub-bd. Med. Oncology; diplomate Nat. Bd. Med. Examiners; lic. physician, Calif. Med. intern, resident in medicine Cedars-Sinai Med. Ctr., L.A., 1976-79, chief resident in medicine, 1979-80; fellow in hematology-oncology UCLA, 1980-82, asst. prof. medicine Sch. Medicine, 1982-88, assoc. prof. Sch. Medicine, 1988-94, prof. medicine Sch. Medicine, 1994—, chmn. instnl. rev. bd., human rsch. policy bd., 1998—; dir. Bowyer Oncology Ctr., dir. outpatient clin. rsch. unit Jonsson Comprehensive Cancer Ctr., 1990-92, dir. clin. rsch. unit, 1993-98; med. dir. thoracic oncology program Jonsson Comprehensive Cancer Ctr., 1994—, genito uninary program, 1994—, solid tumor program, 1997—; prin. investigator UCLA S.W. Oncology Group, 1992—; sci. founder UroGeneSys, 1996—. Editor Interferons in Cytokines, 1988-90, Kidney Cancer Jour., 1993-94; affiliate editor Current Clin. Trials, 1992-96; mem. editorial bd. UCLA Cancer Trials Newsletter, 1990-96, Seminars on Oncology-Kidney Cancer, 1995, Cancer Therapeutics, 1997, Cancer Biotherapy and Radio Pharms., 1997; author articles and revs. Mem. med. adv. bd. Nat. Kidney Cancer Assn., 1993—; FDA cons., 1990-92. Recipient numerous awards. Fellow ACP; mem. Am. Soc. Clin. Oncology, Am. Fedn. Clin. Rsch., Am. Assn. for Cancer Rsch., Soc. for Biologic Therapy (chmn. ann. scientific meeting 1997, pres. cancer panel 1997, S.W. Oncology Group, Assn. Subsplty. Profs., Internat. Assn. for Study of Lung Cancer. Office: UCLA 10945 Le Conte Ave Ste 2333 Los Angeles CA 90024-2828

FIGNAR, EUGENE MICHAEL, financial company executive, lawyer; b. Hazleton, Pa.; s. Basil W. and Helen (Hannock) F.; m. Rosemary Casey. BBA, King's Coll., Wilkes-Barre, Pa., 1967; JD, Duquesne U., 1972. Bar: Pa. 1972, U.S. Dist. Ct. (we. dist.) Pa. 1972, Conn. 1988, N.Y. 1998; lic. real estate broker, N.Y., Conn. Counsel Westinghouse Electric Corp., Pitts., 1972-80; asst. gen. counsel Champion Internat. Corp., Stamford, Conn., 1980-81; v.p., gen. counsel, sec. Merrill Lynch Realty, Stamford, Conn., 1981-82; v.p., gen. counsel, sec. Merrill Lynch Mortgage, Stamford, Conn., 1982-84, v.p. quality, product devel., 1985-88, also bd. dirs.; sr. v.p., sr. lending officer The Bank Mart, Bridgeport, Conn., 1988-90; pres., CEO TDS Fin., Inc., Stamford, 1990—. Mem. bus. adv. coun. King's Coll., Wilkes-Barre, 1985—; mem. bus. adv. coun. Norwalk C.C., 1996—; bd. dirs. Ea. Fairfield County United Way, 1988-94; bd. dirs., vice chmn. Bridgeport Regional Counsel for Homeless, 1989-94. Sgt. U.S. Army, 1969-71. Mem. Am. Arbitration Assn., Real Estate Fin. Assn., N.Y. State Bar Assn., West End Yacht Club, Old Greenwich Yacht Club. Democrat. Catholic. Avocations: sailing, bicycling, model railroading, gardening. Home and Office: 21 West End Ave Old Greenwich CT 06870-1611 Office: TDS Fin Inc 2001 W Main St Stamford CT 06902-4501

FIJALKOWSKI, ISABELLE, professional basketball player; b. May 23, 1972; d. Tadeusz and Leokadia Fijalkowski. Student, U. Colo., 1995, U. d'Orleans, 1997—. Basketball player Euroleague, 1996-97; forward Cleveland Rockers, (WNBA), 1997—. Office: Cleveland Rockers Gund Arena One Center Ct Cleveland OH 44115*

FIKE, EDWARD LAKE, newspaper editor; b. Delmar, Md., Mar. 31, 1920; s. Claudius Edwin and Rosa Lake (Pegram) F.; m. Rosa Amanda Drake, Apr. 1, 1952; children: Rosa, Evelyn, Amy, Melinda. BA, Duke U., 1941; postgrad., U. Cin., 1941-42. Editor, co-pub. Nelsonville (Ohio) Tribune, 1945-48; dir. bur. pub. info. Duke U., Durham, N.C., 1948-52; mem. U.S. del. N. Atlantic Council, Paris, 1952-53; assoc. editor Rocky Mount (N.C.) Evening Telegram, 1953-57; editor, pub. Fike Newspapers, Lewistown and Glendive, Mont., 1957-62; also Fike Newspapers, Wilmington and Tujunga, Calif., 1957-68; assoc. editor Richmond (Va.) News Leader, 1968-70; dir. news and editorial analysis Copley Newspapers, 1970-77; editor editorial pages San Diego Union, 1977-90; lectr. journalism San Diego State U., San Diego Evening Coll. Parole commr. San Diego County, 1993-94, pres. adv. coun. San Diego State U., 1988-93; bd. dirs. Grossmont Hosp. Found., Armed Svcs. YMCA. Lt. USNR, 1942-45. Recipient George Washington award Freedoms Found., 1969-71, 73, 78, Editorial Writing awards N.C. Press Assn., 1954-55, Va. Press Assn., 1969, Calif. Newspaper Pubs. Assn., 1969, 80; Hoover Inst. Media fellow Stanford U., 1990-91. Mem. Omicron Delta Kappa. Republican. Methodist. Home: 17369 Plaza Maria San Diego CA 92128-2251

FIKRIG, EROL, rheumatologist, medical educator; b. Dec. 15, 1959. BA in Chemistry cum laude, Cornell U., 1981, MD, 1985. Diplomate Am. Bd. Internal Medicine, Am. Bd. Infectious Diseases. Resident in internal medicine Vanderbilt U. Hosp., 1985-88; fellow in infectious diseases and immunobiology Yale U., 1988-92, assoc. rsch. scientist in immunobiology, 1992, asst. prof. medicine sect. of rheumatology, 1992-96, assoc. prof. medicine sect. of rheumatology, 1996—. Contbr. articles to profl. jours.; ad hoc reviewer NIH study sect. Bacteriology and Mycology I, 1994; spkr. in field. Recipient Young Investigator award Nat. Found. Infectious Disease, 1991, award in vaccine devel. Infectious Disease Soc. Am., 1992, Young Investigator award Am. Heart Assn., 1993, Investigator award Arthritis Found., 1993, Apollo Kinsley award State of Conn., 1993, NIH First award, 1994, Goodyear award State of Conn., 1994, Established Investigator award Am. Heart Assn., 1996; NIH Clin. Investigation fellow, 1990, Daland fellow Am. Philos. Soc., 1990; pew scholar, 1993. Mem. Phi Beta Kappa. Office: Yale U Sch Medicine Dept Rheumatology 333 Cedar St Dept New Haven CT 06520*

FIKS, ARSEN PHILLIP, physician, researcher; b. Odessa, Ukraine, Apr. 23, 1930; came to U.S., 1978; s. Phillip G. and Klara M. (Kolkin) F.; m. Eva Bubis, Sept. 16, 1951 (div. Sept. 1979); 1 child, Vitaly; m. Irina Bozilenko, June 20, 1984; 1 stepchild, Marina. MD, Odessa Med. Sch., 1952, PhD, 1972. Pathologist, dept. chief pathomorphology State Oncology Hosp., Odessa, USSR, 1956-77; sr. pathologist Ill. Inst. Tech. Rsch. Inst., Chgo., 1979-84; rsch. assoc. cytology U. Chgo., 1989-92; sr. cytotechnologist Roshe BioMed. Labs., Northbrook, Ill., 1989-92; cytotechnologist MatPath, Inc., Wood Dale, Ill., 1992—; pathologist Kiev Radio-Oncology Inst., 1960-61, Moscow Oncology Ctr., 1964, Leningrad Inst. Oncology, 1968, The Armed Forces Inst. Pathology, Washington, 1980, U. Chgo., 1986; rschr. in pathology, oncology, the history of medicine and biology, cosmobiology, history of scis., and self-experimentation. Contbr. more than 100 articles to profl. jours. including Archives Pathology, Clin. Surg., Problems Oncology, Urology, Breast Cancer Rsch. and Treatment, among others. Recipient Highest Category Pathologist award State Pub. Health Office, 1969. Mem. Internat. Soc. for Chronobiology, Internat. Acad. Cytology, Internat. Acad. Pathology, Am. Assn. for Cancer Rsch. Avocation: classical music. Home: 360 E Randolph St Apt 1108 Chicago IL 60601-7333

FILATOV, VICTOR SIMEONOVICH, investment professional; b. Norwalk, Conn., Nov. 3, 1951; s. Simon and Sonia Filatov; children: Jason, Michael. BA in Math. summa cum laude, Clark U., 1975; MA in Econs., U. Pa., 1977. Economist UN Diesa, N.Y.C., 1979-80; project mgr. of Project Link U. Pa., Phila., 1980-82; v.p., sr. internat. economist Morgan Guaranty Trust Co., N.Y.C., 1982-87; v.p., head of internat. fin. analysis J.P. Morgan Securities, N.Y.C., 1987-92; v.p. and head of fixed income rsch. & bond index derivatives J.P. Morgan Securities, London, 1992-93; pres. Smith Barney Global Capital Mgmt. Inc., London, 1993-98; COO SSB Citi Asset Mgmt., 1998—; v.p., dir. Smith Barney World Funds, N.Y.C., 1993—; bd. dirs. J.P. Morgan Commodity Index, N.Y.C., Salomon Smith Barney Asset Mgmt. Australia, Ltd.; cons. Japanese Econ. Planning Agy., Tokyo, 1982. Author: (with others) Festschrift for Lawrence R. Klein, 1982; contbr. chpts. to books and articles to profl. jours. Econ. rsch. fellowship U. Pa., 1976-78. Mem Phi Beta Kappa. Avocations: classic British sports cars, skiing, baseball, golf. Office: 388 Greenwich St New York NY 10013-2339

FILBY, PERCY WILLIAM, library consultant; b. Cambridge, Eng., Dec. 10, 1911; came to U.S., 1957, naturalized, 1960; s. William Lusher and Florence Ada (Stanton) F.; m. Nancie Elizabeth Giddens (div. 1957); children: Ann Veronica Filby Chesworth, Jane Vanessa Johnson, Roderick, Guy; m. Vera Ruth Weakliem, 1957. Student, Cambridge U. Librarian Cambridge U., 1930-37, dir. sci. library, 1937-40; sec. to Sir James Frazer, 1934-39; crytographer, head German Dip. sect. Bletchley, 1940-45; sr. researcher, archivist Brit. Fgn. Office, 1946-57; asst. dir. Peabody Inst., Balt., 1957-65; librarian, asst. dir. Md. Hist. Soc., Balt., 1965-72; dir. Md. Hist. Soc., 1972-78, ret., 1978; library cons., 1978—; cons. on rare books, calligraphy; appraiser rare books and manuscripts. Author: Cambridge Papers, 1936, Calligraphy and Handwriting in America, 1710-1962, 1963, (with others) Two Thousand Years of Calligraphy, 1965, American and British Genealogy and Heraldry, 1970, 3d edit., 1983, supplement, 1986, (with others) Star Spangled Books, 1972, Who's Who in Genealogy and Heraldry, 1981, 2d edit., 1990, Passenger Lists Bibliography, 1538-1900, 1981, 2d edit., 1988, (with others) Passenger and Immigration Lists Index, 13 vols., 1981, 82, supplements, 1983—, Philadelphia Naturalizations, 1982, Bibliography of American County Histories, 1985, 2d printing 1987, Directory of American and Canadian Libraries with Genealogy and Local History Collections, 1988, (with others) Germans to America, 1850—, vols. 1-50, Italians to America, 1880-87, vols. 1-11. Mem. Ellis Island Restoration Commn. Served to capt. Intelligence Corps. Brit. Army, 1940-46, cryptographer, Bletchley, Eng., 1940-46. Recipient Genealogy award RASD History Sect., 1993. Fellow Soc. Genealogists (London), Nat. Geneal. Soc., Manuscript Soc. (pres. 1976-78); mem. ALA (Mudge citation for disting. reference librarianship 1989), Spl. Libraries Assn. (pres. Balt. chpt. 1961-62), Soc. Scribes (v.p.), Soc. for Italic Handwriting, Soc. Am. Archivists, Typophiles, Balt. Bibliophiles (pres. 1963-65, 89-91), Am. Antiquarian Soc., Bibliog. Soc. Am. (coun. 1978-82), Grolier Club (N.Y.C.). Home: PO Box 413 Savage MD 20763-0413 *It has been partly luck sent to Bletchley as a cryptographer during WWII, where as head of the German Diplomatic Section, all German codes were broken.*

FILENER, MILLARD LEE, wholesale and retail distribution company executive; b. Delta, Colo., May 4, 1946; s. Millard Otis and Rosie Everetta F.; m. Connie Sue Einspahr; children: Kimberly, Weslee. BA in Acctg., Western State Coll., Gunnison, Colo., 1972. Mgmt. trainee Am. Parts Syss., Denver, 1972-76; ops. mgr. Am. Parts Syss., Portland, Oreg., 1976; sales mgr. Am. Parts Syss., Portland, 1977; corp. parts mgr. Howard-Cooper Corp., Portland, 1977-79; sales mgr. Mark VII Data Syss., Portland, 1980; dist. mgr. Valley Refuse Removal BFI, Grand Junction, Colo., 1981-82; co-owner, bd. dirs. Superior Trash Co., Montrose, Colo., 1981-84; distrbn. mgr. Meta Syss. Inc., Gladstone, Oreg., 1984-87; pres. Meta Syss. Inc., Gladstone, 1987-91, The Distbn. Group, 1991—; bus. cons., 1991—, Resource Metabolics, 1993—; bd. dirs. The Distribution Group, Resource Metabolics Inc.; pres. Sierra Sales Corp., 1997—, bd. dirs.; computer cons. City of Palisade, Colo., 1981; pres. Resource Metabolics Inc., 1993—; mem. standards com. Natural Products Quality Assurance Alliance. Designed software various bus. applications, 1974—. Mem. West. Colo. Health Facilities Review Bd., Grand Junction, 1982; bd. dirs. Metabolic Health Orgn., Portland, Oreg., 1985-91. With U.S. Army, 1965-67. Mem. Nat.

Natural Foods Assn. Avocations: flying, business startups. Office: The Distribution Group Inc PO Box 567 Beavercreek OR 97004-0567

FILER, EMILY SYMINGTON HARKINS, social services administrator; b. Balt., May 12, 1936; d. Frank Fife and Grace (Cover) Symington; m. George Archer Harkins, June 21, 1958 (div. 1982); children: Montgomery Fox, Emily Harrison (dec. Apr. 1978); m. Robert Hoagland Filer, June 24, 1989. Degree, Villa Julie Med. Sec. Sch., Balt., 1955. Cert. vol. adminstr. Registrar Johns Hopkins Hosp., Balt., 1955-57, sec. hearing and speech ctr., 1957-58; pres. Distaff Wives, San Francisco, Boston, 1958-63; v.p., bd. dirs. The Planning Council, Tidewater, Va., 1969-78; pres. Jr. League of Norfolk (Va.)-Virginia Beach, 1972-74; founder, coord. Lee's Friends, Norfolk, 1978-86, exec. dir., 1986—; chmn. Tidewater dist. Va. Council Soc. Welfare, 1985-87, Va. Council Social Welfare, 1988; bd. dirs. Va. Wesleyan Coll., Norfolk, 1979—, Olde Huntersville Devel., Norfolk, 1985-87; mem. Glennan Geriat. Clerkship Faculty Ea. Va. Med. Sch., 1996—; nat. cons., trainer, vis. instr. Norfolk State U., Old Dominion U., Regent U., Tidewater C.C., Va. Wesleyan Coll. Lic. pastoral caregiver, lay reader The Ch. of Good Shepherd, 1992—, instr. adult Sunday sch., 1998; bd. dirs., exec. com. Westminster Canterbury of Virginia Beach, 1992—, exec. com. sec., 1993—; mem. Mayor's Commn. on Aging, 1996—, vice chair, 1997—; trustee Va. Wesleyan Coll.; mem., past pres. Tidewater dist. Va. Coun. on Social Welfare; steering com. Hampton Rds. Leadership Prayer Luncheon, 1999. Named Gt. Citizen of Hampton Roads, 1987, Va. Vol. Adminstr. of Yr., Internat. Assn. for Vol. Adminstrn. Va. affiliates, 1992; recipient Women in Transition award YWCA of South Hampton Roads, 1989, Spl. award Outstanding Profl. Women of Hampton Roads, 1989, Disting. Merit citation NCCJ, 1992, Outstanding Cmty. Svc. award Delta Sigma Theta Norfolk Alumae chpt., 1997, Pub. Citizen of Yr. award NASW, 1999. Mem. Internat. Assn. for Vol. Adminstrs. (cert. liaison, region IV 1986, profl. devel. liaison assn. 1987-88, region IV 1987-88, 93-94, recertification chair 1990-92, exec. planning com. Internat. Conf. on Vol. Adminstrn. 1997), Colonial Va. Assn. for Vol. Adminstrs. (dep. sec. 1986-87, pres. 1987-89), Tidewater Cancer Network (assoc. 1986), Nat. Hospice Orgn. (profl.), Va. Assn. for Hospice Orgn. (assoc.), Jr. League of Norfolk-Va. Beach (hon., sustainer, past pres., 1st Outstanding Sustainer award 1981), Assn. for Jr. Leagues Internat. (Disting. Vol. Centennial Cookbook profile 1996). Episcopalian. Avocations: reading, walking, gardening, cooking. Office: Lees Friends 618 Stockley Gdns Norfolk VA 23507-2017

FILERMAN, GARY LEWIS, health education executive; b. Mpls., Nov. 16, 1936; s. Joseph H. and Bonnie (Kobrin) F.; m. Jane Harding, Sept. 15, 1962; children: Amy Beth, Joseph Harding, Suzanne Louise. B.A., U. Minn., 1959, M.Health Adminstrn. (Phillips Found. fellow 1959-60), 1961, M.A. (W.K. Kellogg fellow 1961-64), 1963, Ph.D. (Milbank travel grantee 1964, Orgn. Am. States fellow 1964), 1970. Adminstrv. resident Johns Hopkins Hosp., 1961-62; acting dir. Minn. Hosp. Assn., 1965; pres. Assn. Univ. Programs in Health Adminstrn., Washington, 1965-93; exec. sec. Accrediting Commn. Edn. Health Services Adminstrn., 1968-80; assoc. dir. PEW Health Professions Commn., Washington, 1993-95; dir. Madison Info. Techs., Chgo., 1995—; dir. David A. Winston Fellowship, 1986—, pres., 1998—; mem. faculty George Washington U., chmn., prof. dept health mgmt. aand policy, 1998—; guest scholar Brookings Instn., 1962; sr. health advisor Aca. Ednl. Devel., 1998—; cons. in field. Author: A Futute of Consequence, 1989;, editor Jour. Health Adminstrn. Edn., 1982-93; author articles in field.; mem. editorial bds. profl. jours. Mem. nat. health professions adv. coun. HHS, 1983-87, coun. agy for health care policy and rsch., 1990-92; bd. dirs. Am. Refugee Commn., Fairfax Audubon, 1989-93, Am. Internat. Health Alliance; chmn. Planned Parenthood Metro Washington, 1990-91, bd. dirs. 1989-92. Recipient Silver medal Leuven (Belgium) U., 1972, Disting. Contbn. award Assn. U. Programs Health Adminstrn., 1979, Outstanding Achievement award Regents of U. Minn., 1982, Outstanding Achievement award Ohio State U., 1992. Fellow APHA, Am. Acad. Med. Adminstrn. (hon.), hon. alumni, Univ. Chgo.,1992, diplomate Am. Coll. of Health Care Execs., 1990—; mem. Royal Soc. Health, Assn. Am. Med. Colls., Assn. Health Svcs. Rsch., Cosmos Club (Washington), Phi Beta Kappa. Home: 1322 Banquo Ct Mc Lean VA 22102-2707

FILERMAN, MICHAEL HERMAN, television producer; b. Chgo., May 4, 1938; s. Arthur Joseph and Anne Leah (Greenfield) F. B.S. in Communications, U. Ill., 1960. Gen. program dir. Sta. WGN-TV, Chgo., 1962-67; gen. program dir., dir. daytime programs CBS TV Network, N.Y.C., 1967-72; dir. series devel. Paramount TV, 1972-74; v.p. series devel. Lorimar Prodns., 1976-83; with 20th Century Fox, 1983-85, NBC Prodns., 1985-88. Exec. prodr. Knots Landing, Falcon Crest, Flamingo Road, Secrets of Midland Heights, King's Crossing, Sisters, John Grisham's The Client, Four Corners; M.O.W. exec. prodr. Christmas Eve, Peyton Place: The Next Generation, A Letter to Three Wives, Assault and Matrimony, The Child Saver, Take My Daughters, Please, Turn Back the Clock, Coins in the Fountain, The Story Lady, The Return of Eliot Ness, Roommates, Deadly Family Secrets, Once You Meet a Stranger, Knots Landing: Back to the Cul-de-Sac; theatrical prodr.: 24th Day, I Love You!, You're Perfect!, Now Change!.

FILES, MARK WILLARD, business and financial consultant; b. Bartlesville, Okla., Dec. 5, 1941; s. Francis Marion and Alice Wade (Webb) F.; m. Elizabeth Kay Maltby; children: Patrick, Jennifer Leigh. BBA, U. Okla., 1963, MA, 1964, postgrad. Stanford U. CPA, Okla., La. From asst. acct. to ptnr. Peat, Marwick, Mitchell & Co., Tulsa, 1964-80; vice chmn., dir. Braeloch Holdings, Inc., Covington, La., 1980-93; ptnr. Graham Ptnrs. Fin. Cons. and Investments, Covington, 1993—. Exxon Corp. fellow U. Okla., 1964. Trustee Christ Episc. Sch., Covington, 1993—, Ctr. for Devel. and Learning. Mem. AICPA, Okla. Soc. CPAs (chmn. ethics com. 1975-76), La. Soc. CPAs, Am. Petroleum Inst., Beau Chene Golf and Racquet Club (Mandeville, La.), Phi Eta Sigma, Beta Gamma Sigma, Pi Kappa Alpha. Republican. Episcopalian. Home: 40 Green Hills Dr Covington LA 70435-8417 Office: Graham Ptnrs 5000 Highway 190 Ste A-1 Covington LA 70433-4950

FILI-KRUSHEL, PATRICIA, broadcast executive. Pres. ABC TV, Century City, Calif. Office: ABC Inc 2040 Ave of the Stars Century City CA 90067*

FILIMONOV, MIKHAIL ANATOLYEVITCH, investment company executive; b. Odessa, Ukraine, Oct. 26, 1956; came to the U.S., 1971; s. Anatoly M. and Ludmila G. (Yankelevitch) F.; m. Lena Vayman (div.); 1 child, Alexandra K. AAS, N.Y. Tech. Coll., 1982; BS, Baruch Coll., 1983. V.p. Arnhold & S. Bleichroder, N.Y.C., 1983, Cresvale Internat., London and N.Y.C., 1984; 1st v.p. Quadrex Securities, N.Y.C., 1985-87; v.p. Baring Securities, N.Y.C., 1987-90; first v.p. London Investment Trust Am., Inc., N.Y.C., 1990-92; chmn., chief investment officer, CEO Alexandra Investment Mgmt. (formerly Hermes Capital Mgmt.), N.Y.C., 1992—; bd. dirs. Alexandra Global Investment Fund, Brit. Virgin Islands. Republican. Office: Alexadra Investment Mgmt 237 Park Ave Fl 9 New York NY 10017-3140

FILIPIC, MATTHEW VICTOR, state official; b. Cleve., Oct. 12, 1945; s. Henry M. and Norma (Grady) F.; m. Louise Hutter Filipic, Mar. 16, 1974; children: Kristen, Katherine, Anne. AB in History, John Carroll U., 1967; MA in Polit. Sci., Ohio State U., 1975, PhD in Polit. Sci., 1977. CPA, Ohio. Budget analyst, sr. analyst, dep. dir., asst. dir. Office Budget and Mgmt., State of Ohio, Columbus, 1977-82; legis. budget officer Ohio Gen. Assembly, Columbus, 1983-85; dir. budgets Ohio Bd. Regents, Columbus, 1985-89, vice chancellor adminstrn., 1990-98, sr. vice chancellor, 1998—. Bd. dirs. Ohio Tuition Trust Authority, Columbus, 1991—, Ohio Higher Edn. Facilities Commn., Columbus, 1993—. Lt. (j.g.) USNR, 1968-71. Recipient Elijah Watts Sells award AICPA, Columbus, 1984. Mem. Am. Soc. for Pub. Adminstrn. (pres. Ctrl. Ohio chpt. 1987), Assn. for study of Higher Edn. Home: 250 Fairlawn Dr Columbus OH 43214-2711 Office: Ohio Bd Regents 30 E Broad St Columbus OH 43266-0417

FILIPOS, XENIA ELIZABETH LYCHOS, political scientist; b. Bloomsburg, Pa.; d. Anastassios A. and Victoria (Palaiologos) Lychos; m. Michael Filipos; children: John, Anastassios, Elizabeth, Gregory, David. *Father Anastassios A. Lychos left Lemnos, Greece in 1900 for the U.S. At age 17, he purchased a Good Humor ice cream truck franchise, and, in 1915 at age 26, opened The Candyland, a candy store. In 1926, he opened the Martha Washington Hotel Beer Garden and Restaurant in Bloomsburg, Pennsylvania. His wife, Victoria Palaiologos, was born in 1900 in Lemnos, Greece. She was a direct decendant of Constantine Palaiologos, the last emperor of the Byzantine Empire. She came to the U.S. in 1909. She was an amateur artist and an accomplished musician. She studied both piano and violin at Bloomsburg University.* BA, Moravian Coll., 1995. Pro se litigant appeal divorce case U.S. Supreme Ct., 1994—. Contbr. articles to profl. jours. Mem. Trinity Ch. Home: 822 Center St Bethlehem PA 18018-2837

FILIPOWICZ, HALINA, literature educator; b. Moscow, Feb. 7, 1947; came to U.S., 1974; d. Antoni and Kazimiera (Kurtiak) F. MA, Warsaw U., 1969; PhD, U. Kans., 1979. Prof. U. Wis., Madison, 1982—. Author: A Laboratory of Impure Forms: The Plays of Tadeusz Rozewicz, 1991, Eugene O'Neill, 1975; guest editor Slavic and East European Jour., 1989, 99, Renascence, 1995; editl. bd. Slavic and East European Jour., 1989-93, 99—, Periphery: Jour. Polish Affairs, 1997-99. Fellowship Nat. Endowment for Humanities, 1992-93, Bunting Inst., Radcliffe Coll., 1984-86, Am. Coun. of Learned Socs., 1981-82, 88-89. Mem. MLA, Am. Assn. of Tchrs. of Slavic and East European Langs., Am. Assn. for the Advancement of Slavic Studies. Office: U Wis Dept of Slavic Lit 1220 Linden Dr Madison WI 53706-1525

FILIPPINE, EDWARD LOUIS, federal judge; b. 1930. A.B., St. Louis U., 1951, J.D., 1957. Bar: Mo. 1957. Pvt. practice law St. Louis, 1957-77; spl. asst. atty. gen. State of Mo., 1963-64; chief judge U.S. Dist. Ct. (ea. dist.) Mo., St. Louis, 1977-95, sr. judge, 1995—, 1995—. Served with USAF, 1951-53. Mem. ABA, Mo. Bar Assn., Bar Assn. Met. St. Louis, St. Louis County Bar Assn., Lawyers Assn. of St. Louis. Office: US Dist Ct 1114 Market St Rm #329 Saint Louis MO 63101-2043*

FILIPS, NICHOLAS JOSEPH, management consultant; b. Garrett, Ind., June 10, 1925; s. John and Elizabeth (Grigore) F.; children by previous marriage: Steven, Mary Beth, Fred John; m. Kathryn V. McDowell, Apr. 6, 1982. Student, U. Detroit, 1942-45, Ind. U., 1945-47; BS in Biology, Am. U., 1948; postgrad., Ind. U., 1979. V.p., mgr. Wayne Pharmacal Supply Co., Ft. Wayne, Ind., 1949-67, pres., chmn. div. Bendway, Inc., South Bend, Ind., 1955-67; v.p., gen. mgr. Karel First-Aid Supply Co., Chgo., 1967-71; pres., gen. mgr. Amedic Surg. Supply Co., Miami, 1971-78; pres., chief exec. officer Med. Supply Co., Inc., Jacksonville, Fla., 1978-81; pres., chmn. bd. KNF Med. Enterprises, Inc., Jacksonville, 1985—; cons. Wholesale Distbrs. Contbr. articles to profl. jours. Benefactor numerous non-profit hosps. and clinics, Colombia, S.Am. Recipient Am. Legion Leadership award, 1939; named Cons. and Mktg. Dir. of Yr. Retiree Skills, Inc., Tucson, 1990. Mem. Am. Surg. Trade Assn. (Distinctive Svc. award 1960), Lions, Fla. Sheriffs Assn. Democrat. Roman Catholic. Office: Health Distbrs Mgmt and Cons Co Ltd PO Box 331245 Atlantic Beach FL 32233

FILKINS, PETER JOEL, English language educator; b. Pittsfield, Mass., Jan. 7, 1958; s. Ronald Cooper and Bernice Beatrice (Mongue) F.; m. Susan Kay Roeper, May 20, 1989; children: Malina, Isabel. BA cum laude, Williams Coll., 1980; MFA, Columbia U., 1983. Instr. English North Adams (Mass.) State Coll., 1986, 87-88; assoc. prof. English Simon's Rock Coll., Great Barrington, Mass., 1988—; vis. instr. English Hiram (Ohio) Coll., 1986-87. Author: What She Knew, 1998; asst editor: Parnassus: Poetry Interview, 1981-83; translator: Songs in Flight - Collected Poems of Ingeborg Bachmann, 1994; transl. Leonardo's Hands, by Alois Hotschnig, 1999, The Book of Franza and Requiem for Fanny Goldmann, by Ingeborg Bachmann, 1999. Fulbright grantee, 1983-84. Mem. Am. Lit. Translators, Associated Writing Programs, Poetry Soc. Am. Home: PO Box 34 Williamstown MA 01267-0034 Office: Simons Rock Coll Bard 84 Alford Rd Great Barrington MA 01230-1559

FILLBROOK, THOMAS GEORGE, telephone company executive; b. Detroit, Jan. 3, 1949; s. John Moyle and Marie Evelyn (Pelto) F. BA, Wayne State U., 1970. Cert. tchr., Mich. Substitute tchr. Van Dyke Pub. Schs., Warren, Mich., 1971-73; mgr. Ameron, Okemos, Mich., 1973-74; salesman F&E Check Protector, Detroit, 1974-76; ops. mgr. Loss Prevention Inc., Royal Oak, Mich., 1976-78; svc. rep. Ameritech, Southfield, Mich., 1979—; actor/clown Clowning Around Entertainment, Romeo, Mich., 1958—; actor Holy Cow Show, WGPR Channel 62, Detroit, 1988; dir. Winter Magic, Harron Cable, Rome, 1991. Polit. and hist. columnist, polit. editor Mill Creek View Newspaper, Washington; mem. City of Hope 1994 Com. Mem. Reg. Nat. Com., Washington, Founders Soc., Detroit Inst. Arts. Recipient commendation Macomb County Bd. Commrs., 1991, 1st Place Clown Costume Competition and Group Act award Mich. State Fair and Exposition, 1995, Top Individual Fund Raiser City of Hope, 1997, 98. Mem. Internat. Platform Assn., Finnish Ctr. Assn., Detroit Zool. Soc., Citizens Against Government Waste (charter), Elks (chmn. 1985). Episcopalian. Avocation: poetry. Home: 54723 Shelby Rd Shelby Township MI 48316-1441

FILLER, MARY ANN, librarian; b. Altoona, Pa., Aug. 6, 1940; d. James Arthur and Mary DeLellis (Hopple) Sides; m. Richard Anthony Filler; children: Tracy Anne, Christopher Anthony. BS in Med. Tech., St. Francis Coll., 1962; MLS, U. Pitts., 1968; postgrad., Shippensburg U., 1975-77. Cert. med. tech. Rsch. asst. U. Pitts. Med. Sch. of Pub. Health, 1963-68; asst. tech. asst. program Pa. State U., 1968-70; asst. librarian Sheperstown (W.Va.) U., 1971-72; sr. reference librarian Pa. State U., Middletown, 1979-86; mgr. info. ctr. Armstrong World Ind., Inc., Lancaster, Pa., 1986—. Author: Acid Rain: A Pennsylvania Problem?, 1983. Mem. AAAS, Spl. Librs. Assn. (bus. mgr. 1987-88, nominating com. 1989, dir. 1990), Beta Phi Mu. Democrat. Roman Catholic. Home: 127 Maple Ave Hershey PA 17033-1547 Office: Armstrong World Industries 2500 Columbia Ave Lancaster PA 17603-4117

FILLER, RONALD HOWARD, lawyer; b. St. Louis, Apr. 11, 1948; s. Leon Isaac and Jeanette Frances (Sanofsky) F.; m. Paula; children: Stephen Paul, Lindsay Ann. BS, U. Ill., 1970; JD, George Washington U., 1973; LLM in Taxation, Georgetown U., 1976. BAr: D.C. 1973, Ill. 1976, N.Y. 1993. Atty. SEC, Washington, 1973-76; assoc. Abramson & Fox, Chgo., 1976-77; assoc. counsel Conti Cmty. Svc., Chgo., 1977-78, dir. mgmt. accounts, 1978-80; mng. ptnr. Filler Zaner & Assocs., Chgo., 1980-85; ptnr. Vedder, Price, Kaufman & Kammholz, Chgo., 1985-93, corp. practice leader, 1989-91, mem. exec. com., 1991-93; dir. futures adminstrn. Lehman Bros, Inc., 1993—; dir. Commodities Law Inst., Ill. Inst. Tech./Chgo-Kent Law Sch., 1978-97, adj. prof. law, 1977-93, bd. overseers, 1982-97; lectr. Commodities Ednl. Inst., 1977-89; adj. prof. law Bklyn. Law Sch., 1994-96. Contbr. articles to jours. and futures mags. Named one of top 315 lawyers State of Ill., 1991. Mem. ABA (chmn. sub futures commn. mchts. 1986—), Nat. Futures Assn. (bd. dirs. 1984-87), Am. Arbitration Assn. (arbitrator), Mid Am. Commodity Exch. (bd. dirs. 1984-86), Chgo. Bar Assn. (chmn. commodities law com. 1981-82, vice chmn. fin. and legal svcs. com. 1988-89, co-vice chmn. large law firm com. 1991-92), Nat. Assn. Futures Traders Assn., Futures Industry Assn. (bd. dirs. 1990-92, exec. com. Chgo. divsn. 1986-88, exec. com. Law and Comp. divsn. 1985-90, 92—, sec. 1995-98, pres. 1998—), N.Y. State Bar Assn., Ill. State Bar Assn. Democrat. Jewish. Fax: 212 526-6193. E-mail: RFiller@LEHMAN.com. Home: 54 Collinwood Rd Maplewood NJ 07040-1038 Office: Lehman Bros Inc Am Exp Tower 3 World Fin Ctr 8th Fl New York NY 10285

FILLEY, CHRISTOPHER MARK, neurologist; b. Saranac Lake, N.Y., July 31, 1951; s. Giles Franklin and Mary Brown (Klinefelter) F. BA, Williams Coll., 1973; MD, Johns Hopkins U., 1979. Diplomate Am. Bd. Psychiatry and Neurology. Intern U. Conn., Farmington, 1979-80; resident in neurology U. Colo., Denver, 1980-83; behavioral neurology fellow Boston U., 1983-84; from instr. to asst. prof. neurology U. Colo. Sch. Medicine, Denver, 1984-91, assoc. prof. neurology, 1991-97, prof. neurology, 1997—; prin. investigator studies in Alzheimers Disease NIH, Bethesda, Md., 1991-94. Author: Neurobehavioral Anatomy, 1995, Best Doctors in America, 1996-97, 1998-99; contbr. articles to profl. jours. Health com. Denver Found., 1995-98. Mem. Am. Acad. Neurology, Am. Neurol. Assn., Internat. Neuropsychol. Soc., Behavioral Neurology Soc., Colo. Soc. Clin. Neurologists. Avocations: piano, hiking, reading, guitar, skiing. Office: Univ Colo Behavioral Neurology Sect 4200 E 9th Ave Denver CO 80220-3700

FILLEY, WARREN VERNON, allergist, immunologist; b. Topeka, Kans., Oct. 27, 1950. MD, U. Kans. Sch. Medicine, 1976. Diplomate Am. Bd. Allergy & Immunology, Am. Bd. Internal Medicine. Intern U. Okla., 1976-77, resident in internal medicine, 1977-79; fellow allergy & immunology Mayo Clin., Rochester, 1979-81; with Presby. Hosp., Okla. City; clin. asst. prof. medicine U. Okla. Mem. ACP, ACAAI, AAAAI, OSMA. Office: Okla Allergy and Asthma Clinic 750 NE 13th St Oklahoma City OK 73104-5051

FILLICARO, BARBARA JEAN, business owner, consultant; b. Chgo.; d. Frank and Lillian (Kosach) F. Student, DePaul U., 1974-78, BA in Bus. Mgmt., 1978; desktop publishing cert., Coll. of DuPage, 1992; MA in Comm. and Tng., Govs. State U., 1999. Exec. sec. Continental Bank, Chgo., 1962-68; supr. secretarial svcs. Morton Quality Products, Chgo., 1968-71; adminstrv. asst. Libby, McNeill & Libby, Chgo., 1971-76, purchasing agt., 1976-78; mktg. rep. TRW Fin. Sys., Orlando, Fla., 1978-82; dist. sales rep. Streamline Industries, N.Y.C., 1982-84; office automation specialist Microage Computer Stores, Lombard, Ill., 1984-86; applications software trainer, cons. Fillicaro & Assocs., Lombard, 1986—; mem. faculty Coll. of Du Page, Glen Ellyn, Ill., 1988—; mem. adj. faculty Coll. of Lake County, Ill., 1996—; multimedia tech. specialist St. Augustine Coll., Chgo., 1993-95, tech. mgr. 1995-96; charter mem., chmn. advocacy com. DuPage County Women's Bus. Coun., 1992; spkr. Multimedia '95, Orlando. Mem. Art Inst., Chgo., 1975-78. Mem. Chgo. Orgn. Data Tng. Educators (membership chair 1992-93, treas., registrar for Lake Michigan data trainers conf. 1992), Am. Mgmt. Assn., Women in Mgmt. (bd. dirs., program chmn. 1986-88), Am. Assn. Individual Investors, Assn. for Devel. of Desktop Pub. Technique, DePaul U. Alumni Coun., Zonta Internat. (charter mem., treas. 1979-80), Internat. Interactive Comm. Soc., Internat. Soc. for Performance Improvement (Cispi Chgo. chpt. 1999—). Avocations: antiques, collectibles, dancing, cooking, theater. Home and Office: 7226 W Crain Niles IL 60714

FILLIOS, LOUIS CHARLES, retired science educator; b. Boston, July 1, 1923; s. Charles Louis and Pagona (Kefalas) F.; m. Iphigenia Loomis, June 15, 1947; children: Despena, Diana, Hilary. AB, Harvard, 1948, MS, 1953, ScD, 1956. Rsch. assoc., then assoc. Harvard U., 1956-60; asst. prof. physiol. chemistry MIT, 1961-64, assoc. prof., 1964-66; assoc. rsch. prof. biochemistry and pathology Boston U. Sch. Medicine, 1966-68, prof. biochemistry, 1970-94; dir. div. basic sci. Boston U. Sch. Medicine (Sch. Grad. Dentistry), 1970-75, chmn. dept. nutritional scis., 1973-94; prof. emeritus Boston U., 1994—; chmn. Mass. Task Force Nutrition and Aging, 1970-71; cons. Mass. Office of Elder Affairs, 1971-73; co-chmn. nutrition sect. White House Conf. Aging, 1971-72; cons. VA, Bedford, Mass., 1982-87; mem. pres.'s adv. council Hellenic Coll., 1968-73. Author numerous research articles fields biochemistry, pathology and nutrition; contbr. sci. and profl. jours. 1st lt. USAAF, 1943-45. Decorated DFC, Air Medal with 3 oak leaf clusters (7 battle stars); recipient Outstanding Educator of Am. award Boston U., 1972, Spl. Honor, 1995. Fellow AAAS, Am. Heart Assn. (established investigator 1961-66); mem. Am. Inst. Nutrition (chmn. fellow award com. 1978-81), Am. Soc. for Nutritional Scis., Sigma Xi (Harvard chpt.), Omicron Kappa Upsilon (hon.). Home: 19 Eliot Rd Lexington MA 02421-5630

FILLIUS, MILTON FRANKLIN, JR., food products company executive; b. N.Y., Nov. 17, 1922; s. Milton Franklin and Georgiana (Bergh) F.; m. Nelma Chauncey, May 11, 1996; children by previous marriage: Julie, Karen, Anthony, Donald. BA, Hamilton Coll., 1946; JD, U. Mich., 1949; LHD (hon.), Hamilton Coll., 1996. Bar: Calif. 1950, U.S. Supreme Ct. 1950. Adminstrv. asst. to banker in San Diego, 1949-51; treas., gen. mgr. Nat. Steel and Shipbldg. Co., San Diego, 1951-56; exec. v.p., gen. mgr. Nat. Steel and Shipbldg. Co., 1956-62; exec. v.p. Westgate-Calif. Corp., 1962-65; chmn. Vita-Pakt Citrus Products Co., 1966-90. Mem. State Bar of Calif., San Diego C. of C. (pres. 1962-64), Theta Delta Chi, Phi Alpha Delta. Home: 18163 Viceroy Dr San Diego CA 92128-1302 Office: Vita-Pakt Citrus Products Co PO Box 309 Covina CA 91723-0309

FILLMAN, G. ALLAN, priest, educator; b. Defiance, Ohio, Sept. 17, 1951; s. William Henry and Mary Monica (Justinger) F. BA in Am. Studies, Pontifical Coll. Josephinum, Worthington, Ohio, 1973, MA in Theology, 1977; MA in English, U. Toledo, 1989. Ordained as priest Roman Cath. Ch. Assoc. pastor St. Wendelin Ch., Forstoria, Ohio, 1977-82, Blessed Sacrament Ch., Toledo, 1982-89; chmn. religion dept. Calvert H.S., Tiffin, Ohio, 1989—; chaplain St. Francis Motherhouse, Tiffin, 1989—; mem. family counseling bd. Tiffin Family Counseling, 1991-97.

FILLMORE, LAURA, publisher. Pres. Online BookStore, Rockport, Mass. Office: Online BookStore 37J Whistlestop Mall Rockport MA 01966-1437

FILLMORE, PETER ARTHUR, mathematician, educator; b. Moncton, N.B., Can., Oct. 28, 1936; s. Henry Arthur and Jeanne Margaret (Archibald) F.; m. Anne Ellen Garvock, Aug. 6, 1960; children: Jennifer Anne, Julia Margaret, Peter Alexander. B.Sc., Dalhousie U., 1957; M.A., U. Minn., 1960, Ph.D., 1962. Instr. U. Chgo., 1962-64; asst. prof. math. Ind. U., 1964-67, assoc. prof., 1967-71, prof., 1971-72; vis. assoc. prof. U. Toronto, Can., 1970-71; prof. math. Dalhousie U., Halifax, N.S., Can., 1972—, Killam sr. fellow, 1972-73; Killam rsch. prof. Dalhousie U., Halifax, N.S., 1973-78; chmn. dept. math., stats. and computer sci. Dalhousie U., Halifax, N.S., Can., 1987-91; sr. vis. fellow U. Edinburgh, 1977; mem. Math. Scis. Rsch. Inst., Berkeley, Calif., 1984-85, Fields Inst. Rsch. Math. Sci., 1994-95; vis. prof. U. Copenhagen, 1990. Author: Notes on Operator Theory, 1970, A User's Guide to Operator Algebras, 1996; mem. editl. bd. Jour. Integral Equations and Operator Theory, C.R. Math. Rep. Acad. Soc. Can.; contbr. articles to profl. jours. Fellow Royal Soc. Can.; mem. Can. Math. Soc. (council 1973-75, 77-79, v.p. 1975-77, pres. 1994-96), Am. Math. Soc. (council 1982-84). Office: Dalhousie U, Math Dept, Halifax, NS Canada B3H 3J5

FILLOY, BEVERLEE ANN HOWE, clinical social worker; b. Ogden, Utah, Mar. 11, 1926; d. Albert Herman Howe and Bernice Anna (Ewing) Howe Routt; m. Jose Antonio Filloy-Alvarez, Feb. 4, 1945 (dec. 1988); children: Richard Anthony, Emily Ann. BA with honors, U. Calif., Berkeley, 1947, MSW, 1954; PhD, Calif. Inst. Clin. Social Work, Berkeley, 1980. Bd. cert. diplomate clin. social work, sex therapist, clin. supr. Social caseworker Family Svc. Agy., Sacramento, Calif., 1959-63; cons. Stanford Lathrop Meml. Home, Sacramento, 1964-69; cons., supr. Arnold Homes for Children, Sacramento, 1968-71; pvt. practice social work Sacramento, 1963—; faculty Calif. Soc. Clin. Social Work, Sacramento, 1979—, Calif. State U., Sacramento, 1956-58, 90; sec. Nat. Registry Providers of Health Care in Clin. Social Work, 1983-85, bd. dirs., 1980-86, treas. Nat. Fedn. for Socs. for Clin. Social Work, 1981-86. Founder, bd. Planned Parenthood of Sacramento, 1964. Fellow Calif. Soc. for Clin. Social Work (pres. 1983-85, bd. dirs. 1969-87, Mem. of Yr. award 1990), Calif. Inst. for Clin. Social Worker (bd. trustees, sec.-treas. 1976-88, v.p. 1989-94); mem. ACLU, Soc. for Sci. Study Sex, Amnesty Internat., Older Women's League, Am. Assn. Sex. Educators, Counselors, Therapists, Phi Beta Kappa. Democrat. Avocations: traveling, swimming, gardening, theater, entertaining. Office: 3009 O St # 2 Sacramento CA 95816-6516

FILMON, GARY ALBERT, Canadian provincial premier, civil engineer; b. Winnipeg, Man., Can., Aug. 24, 1942; s. Albert and Anastasia (Doskocz) F.; m. Janice Clare Wainwright, 1963; children—Allison, David, Gregg, Susanna. B.Sc. in Civil Engring., U. Man., 1964, M.Sc., 1967. Registered profl. engr. Municipal design engr. Underwood McLellan and Assocs., Winnipeg, 1964-67, br. mgr., Brandon, Man., 1967-69; v.p. Success Bus. Coll., Winnipeg, 1969-71, pres., 1971-81. City councillor Queenston Ward, City of Winnipeg, 1975-77, Crescent Heights Ward, City of Winnipeg, 1977-79; mem. legis. assembly River Heights Constituency, Man., 1979-81, Tuxedo Constituency, Man., 1981—, minister consumer and corp. affairs and environment Man. Govt., 1981, leader of the opposition, 1983-88, premier of Manitoba, 1988—; chmn. com. of works and ops. City of Winnipeg, 1977-79. Recipient award of merit B'nai B'rith Can., 1991; honored for many yrs. of svc. to Jewish cmty. Man.-Sask. region Jewish Nat. Fund Can., 1996. Mem. Assn. Profl. Engrs. (Province of Man.), Assn. Can. Career Colls. (pres. 1974-75), U. Man. Alumni Assn. (pres. 1974-75). Mem. Progressive Conservative Party. Anglican. Office: Man Legis Assembly, Legislature Bldg Rm 204, Winnipeg, MB Canada R3C OV8

FILNER, BOB, congressman; b. Pitts., Sept. 4, 1942; m. Jane Merrill; children: Erin, Adam. BA in Chemistry, Cornell U., 1963; MA in History, U. Del., 1969; PhD in History, Cornell U., 1973. Prof. history San Diego State U., 1970-92; legis. asst. Senator Hubert Humphrey, 1974, Congressman Don Fraser, 1975; spl. asst. Congressman Jim Bates, 1984; city councilman 8th dist. City of San Diego, 1987-92, dep. mayor, 1992; mem. 103rd Congress (now 106th Congress) from 50th Calif. dist., 1993—. Pres. San Diego Bd. Edn., 1982, mem.-elect 1979-83; chmn. San Diego Schs. of the Future Commn., 1986-87. Democrat. Office: US Ho of Reps 2463 Rayburn HOB Washington DC 20515-0550

FILO, DAVID, computer communications executive; b. Moss Bluff, La.. Co-founder, chief yahoo Yahoo!, Santa Clara, Calif., 1994—. Office: Yahoo Inc 3420 Central Expy Ste 201 Santa Clara CA 95051-0703*

FILOMENO, LINDA JEAN HARVEY, elementary education educator. Tchr. in language, culture William D'Abate Elem. Sch., Providence. Named R.I. State Tchr. of Yr., 1993, 94; recipient Milken Family Educator award, 1995. Office: William D Abate Elem Sch 650 Prairie Ave Providence RI 02905*

FILOR, ANNA MAY, secondary education educator; b. N.Y.C., Apr. 12, 1941; d. Hugo and Ann Theresa (Hombrose) Mileo; m. Stephen Wilson Filor, Dec. 20, 1969; children: Daniel Post, John-Hugo. BS, NYU, 1963; MS, SUNY, New Paltz, 1968, cert. for advanced study, 1989. Cert. sch. adminstr. and supr., sch. dist. adminstr., N.Y. Tchr. Dover Jr.-Sr. High Sch., Dover Plains, N.Y., 1963-68; tchr. Poughkeepsie (N.Y.) High Sch., 1968—, dept. chmn., 1977—; adj. lectr. Dutchess Community Coll., 1973-85. Contbr. articles to profl. jours. and newsletters; author and editor of monographs. Sr. warden, vestrywoman, lay reader, Small Blessings shop St. Paul's Ch., Poughkeepsie; congrl. dist. coord. We the People program, N.Y. Grantee NDEA, NSF, NEH, NYSCOH. Mem. ASCD, N.Y. State Social Studies Supervisory Assn. (bd. dirs. 1985-91, sec. 1986-88), Nat. Coun. for Social Studies, Mid. States Coun. Social Studies (bd. dirs. 1987-96), Hudson Valley Coun. Econ. Edn. (chmn. 1975-85), N.Y. State Coun. Social Studies (bd. dirs. 1985-87), Mid Hudson Social Studies Coun. (pres. 1983-87), N.Y. State Coun. Edn. Assns., Delta Kappa Gamma (v.p. 1986-88, 90-94, pres. 1994-96), Phi Delta Kappa. Democrat. Episcopalian. Home: 46 Durocher Ter Poughkeepsie NY 12603-6407

FILOSA, GARY FAIRMONT RANDOLPH V., II, multimedia executive, financier, writer; b. Wilder, Vt., Feb. 22, 1931; s. Gary F.R. de Marco de Viana and Rosaline M. (Falzarano) Filosa; m. Catherine Moray Stewart (dec.); children: Marc Christian Bazire de Villadon III, Gary Fairmont Randolph de Viana III. Grad., Mt. Hermon Sch., 1950; PhB, U. Chgo., 1954; BA, U. Americas, Mex., 1967; MA, Calif. Western U., 1968; PhD, U.S. Internat. U., 1970. Sports reporter Claremont Daily Eagle, Rutland Herald, Vt. Informer, 1947-52; pub. The Chicagoan, 1952-54; account exec., editor house publs. Robertson, Buckley & Gotsch, Inc., Chgo., 1953-54; account exec. Fuller, Smith & Ross, Inc., N.Y.C., 1955; prodr./host Weekend KCET Channel 13, N.Y.C., 1955-67; editor Apparel Arts mag. (now Gentlemen's Quar.), Esquire, Inc., N.Y.C., 1955-56; chmn. bd., CEO, pres. Filosa Publs. Internat., N.Y.C., 1956-63; pub. Teenage, Rustic Rhythm, Teen Life, Mystery Digest, Top Talent, Rock & Roll Roundup, Celebrities, Stardust, Personalities, Campus monthly mags.; pres., chmn. bd. Teenarama Records, Inc., N.Y.C., 1956-62; chmn. bd., pres. Produciones Mexicanes Internationales (S.A.), Mexico City, 1957-68; assoc. pub. Laundromatic Age, N.Y.C., 1958-59; ptnr. of Warner LeRoy purchase of Broadway plays for Hollywood films, N.Y.C., 1958-61; pres. Montclair Sch., 1958-60, Pacific Registry, Inc., L.A., 1959-61; exec. prodr. Desilu Studios, Inc., Hollywood, Calif., 1959-61; exec. asst. to Benjamin A. Javits, 1961-62; propr. Gino's of Hollywood, 1961-70; dean adminstrn. Postgrad. Ctr. for Mental Health, N.Y.C., 1962-64; chmn. bd., CEO Filosa Films Internat., Beverly Hills, Calif., 1962—; chmn. bd., pres. Filosa Films Internat., Honolulu, 1996-98; pres. Amateur Athletes Internat., Iowa City, Iowa, 1996—; chmn. bd., pres. Cinematografica Americana Internationale (S.A.), Mexico City, 1964-74; pres. Casa Filosa Corp., Palm Beach, Fla., 1982-87; dir. Community Savings, North Palm Beach, Fla., 1982-87; v.p. acad. affairs World Acad., San Francisco, 1967-68; asst. to provost Calif. Western U., San Diego, 1968-69; assoc. prof. philosophy Art Coll., San Francisoc, 1969-70; v.p. acad. affairs, dean of faculty Internat. Inst., Phoenix, 1968-73; chmn. bd. dirs., pres. Universite Universelle, 1970-73; bd. dirs., v.p. acad. affairs, dean Summer Sch., Internat. C.C., L.A., 1970-72; chmn. bd., pres. Social Directory Calif., 1967-75, Am. Assn. Social Registries, L.A., 1970-76; pres. Social Directory U.S., N.Y.C., 1974-76; pres. Herbert Hoover Forum, Iowa City, 1996—; chmn. bd. dirs. Internat. Soc. Social Registers, Paris, 1974—; surfing coach U. Calif. at Irvine, 1975-77; instr. history Coastline C.C., Fountain Valley, Calif., 1976-77; v.p. Xerox-Systemic, 1979-80; CEO Internat. Surfing League, Palm Beach, 1987-95; pres., CEO Filosa Harrop Internat., Phoenix, 1987-89; pres. Amateur Athletes Internat., Iowa City, 1996—; nationally syndicated columnist Conservations with Am., 1997—. Editor: Sci. Digest, 1961-62; composer: (lyrics) The Night Discovers Love, 1952, That Certain Something, 1953, Bolero of Love, 1956; author: (stage play) Let Me Call Ethel, 1955, The Bisexual, 1961, Technology Enters 21st Century, 1966, (mus.) Feather Light, 1966, No Public Funds for Nonpublic Schools, 1968, Creative Function of the College President, 1969, The Surfers Almanac, 1977, The Filosa Newsletter, 1986-92, The Sexual Continuum, 1990, Traveltalk, 1991, God's Own Prince, 1995, Holy Hawaii, 1996, (biography) A Plague on Paradise, 1994, (TV series) Danny Thomas Show, 1963, Surfing USA, 1977, Payne of Florida, 1985, Honolulu, 1991, The Gym, 1992, Sales Pitch, 1992, 810 Ocean Avenue, 1992, One Feather, 1992, Conversations with America, 1989, All American Beach Party, 1989; contbr. numerous articles, editorials, to profl. jours., newspapers, and encys., including Life, Look, Sci. Digest, Ency. of Sports, World Book Ency., New York Times, Cedar Rapids Gazete, L.A. Times, others. Trustee Univ. of the Ams., Pueblo, Mex., 1986—; candidate for L.A. City Coun., 1959; chmn. Educators for Re-election of Ivy Baker Pirest, 1970; mem. So. Calif. Com. for Olympic Games, 1077-84. With AUS, 1954-55. Recipient DAR Citizenship awrd, 1959, Silver Conquistador award Am. Assn. Social Registers, 1970, Ambassador's Cup U. Ams., 1967, resolution Calif. State Legis., 1977, Duke Kahanamoku Classic surfing trophy, 1977, gold pendant Japan Surfing Assn., 1978, Father of Olympic Surfing award Internat. Athletic Union, 1995, Father of Surfing trophy Amateur Athletes Internat., 1997; inducted into Rock & Roll Mus. & Hall of Fame, Cleve., 1995. Mem. NAACP, NCAA (bd. dels. 1977-82), AAU (gov. 1978-82), Am. Acad. Motion Picture Arts and Scis., Internat. Surfing Com., U.S. Surfing Com. (founder, pres. 1960—), Internat. Surfing League (founder, pres. 1988—), Internat. Surfing Fedn. (pres. 1960—), Am. Assn. UN, Authors League, Authors Guild, Alumni Assn. U. Ams. (pres. 1967-70), Surf Club of the Palm Beaches (pres. 1983-94), Sierra Club, Surfing Hui of Hawaii, Internat. Soc. Bibliotherapists (Paris, pres. 1997—), The Corybantes (Berlin) (pres. 1998—), Commonwealth Club (San Francisco), Town Hall (L.A.), Calif. Club (L.A.), Sigma Omicron Lambda (founder, pres. 1965-92). Republican. Episcopalian. Home: Box 2883 Palm Beach FL 33480 Office: PO Box 299 Beverly Hills CA 90213-0299

FILPI, ROBERT ALAN, lawyer; b. Chgo., Oct. 8, 1945; s. John Andrew and Eunice Lorraine (Taylor) F.; m. Janice Elizabeth Crusoe, June 24, 1967; children—Jennifer Anne, Christopher Alan, Emily Elizabeth. B.A. in History, magna cum laude, Harvard U., 1967; J.D., Northwestern U., 1970. Bar: Ill. 1970, U.S. Dist. Ct. (no. dist.) Ill. 1971, U.S. Ct. Appeals, 7th cir. 1971, U.S. Supreme Ct. 1975. Asst. U.S. atty. No. Dist. Ill., Chgo., 1971-75; dep. chief U.S. atty. No. Dist. Ill., Civil Div., Chgo., 1975-76; ptnr. Stack & Filpi, Chgo., 1976—. Assoc. editor Jour. Criminal Law, Criminology and Police Sci., 1969-70. Coach, Spring Lake Sports League, Lincolnshire, Ill., 1984-91; mem. Village of Lincolnshire Plan Commn., 1984-94. Recipient Hyde prize Northwestern U. Sch. Law, 1967. Mem. Chgo. Bar Assn. Clubs: Union League, Harvard. Office: 140 S Dearborn St Ste 411 Chicago IL 60603-5298

FILSON, RONALD COULTER, architect, educator, college dean; b. Chardon, Ohio, Dec. 11, 1946; s. Clifford Coulter and Mae Alice (Foster) F.; m. Susan Virginia Saward, Dec. 14, 1973 (div. May 1996); children: Timothy Coulter, Lily Virginia. Diploma, Am. Acad. in Rome, 1970; B.Arch., Yale U., 1970. Registered arch., Calif., La., Mass., Ohio, Miss., Nat. Coun. Archtl. Registration Bds. Architect Atelier d'Etudes, Ghardaia, Algeria, 1971-73; asst. prof., asst. dean Sch. of Architecture UCLA, 1974-80; dean sch. architecture Tulane U., New Orleans, 1980-92, prof. sch. architecture, 1980—; prin. Ronald Filson, FAIA, Architects, New Orleans. Prin. works include Piazza d'Italia, New Orleans, 1978 (award 1976), Eola Hotel, 1980, Lee House, 1984, Hyatt Hotel, Poydras Plaza, 1987-88, Nat. Pk. Svc. Edn. Ctr., Nat. D-Day Mus., Trump Casino, L.A. Artists Guild, Natchez Visitors Ctr. Pres. Friends of the Schnidler House, L.A., 1978-80; bd. dirs. New Orleans Arts Coun., 1980-93, pres., 1989-92, Contemporary Arts Ctr., New Orleans, 1980-84, New Orleans Planning Commn., 1985-87. Recipient design citations Progressive Architecture mag., 1969, 76, Rome prize Am. Acad. in Rome, 1969. Fellow AIA (Design awards 1980, 81, 85, 87, 89, 92, 94, 98, 99, Richardson medal 1992); mem. AIA La. (pres. 1998), New Orleans AIA (pres. 1994), Yale Alumni Assn. La. (pres. 1992-94), So. Yacht Club, New Orleans Lawn Tennis Club (bd. govs. 1998—). Avocations: sailing; watercolors. Office: 531 Wilkinson St New Orleans LA 70130-2129

FILSTON, HOWARD CHURCH, pediatric surgeon, educator; b. N.Y.C., Dec. 29, 1935; s. Howard Samuel and Marion (Church) F.; m. Nancy Lee Jameson, June 3, 1961; children: Scott Jameson (dec.), Timothy Howard, Megan Lee Johnson. AB, Harvard U., 1958; MD, Case Western Res. U., 1962. Diplomat Am. Bd. Med. Examiners. Intern in gen. surgery Univ. Hosps., Cleve., 1962-63, asst. resident in gen. surgery, 1963-64, 66-68, chief resident, 1968-69; asst. chief resident pediatric surgery Children's Hosp. Phila., 1969-70; instr. pediatric surgery U. Pa. Sch. of Medicine, Phila., 1969-71; chief resident pediatric surgery U. Pa. Sch. of Medicine, 1970-71; asst. prof. pediatric surgery Case Western Res. U. Hosp., Cleve., 1971-76; assoc. prof. pediatric surgery and pediatrics Duke U. Med. Ctr., Durham, N.C., 1976-82, chief pediatric surgery, 1976-90, prof. pediatric surgery and pediatrics, 1982-90; prof. pediatric surgery and pediatrics U. Tenn. Med. Ctr., Knoxville, 1990—, chief pediatric surgery, 1990—, vice chmn. dept. surgery, 1992—; specialist site visitor, pediatric surgery, Accreditation Coun. Grad. Med. Edn., 1982-90, 1995—. Author: Surgical Problems in Children, 1982; author: (with others) The Surgical Neonate, 1978, rev. 1985; assoc. editor, Jour. Pediatric Surgery, 1985—; mem. editorial bd. Pediatrics, 1990-97; contbr. articles to profl. jours. Bd. dirs. Pediatric Family Ctr. of N.C. (Ronald McDonald House), Durham, 1980-90, Surgeon Gen.'s Workshop on Drunk Driving, chmn. Citizens Adv. Panel, 1988; mem. exec. bd. Met. Drug Commn., Knoxville, 1993—, v.p., 1997-99, pres. 1999—, chair DUI task force, 1994—. Served to capt. U.S. Army, 1964-66. Nat. scholar Harvard U., 1954-58. Fellow ACS (gov. 1992-98), Am. Acad. Pediatrics (surg., exec. com. 1984-91, chmn. 1989-90), Am. Pediatric Surg. Assn. (edn. com. 1984-90, sec., bd. govs. 1994-97), Am. Surg. Assn., So. Surg. Assn.; mem. Alpha Omega Alpha. Republican. Presbyterian. Avocations: family activities, water sports, sailing. Fax: (423) 544-6898. Office: Univ of Tenn Med Ctr Dept Surgery Box U-11 1924 Alcoa Hwy Knoxville TN 37920-1511

FILTER, E. MARGIE, business equipment manufacturing executive; b. Teaneck, N.J., Sept. 19, 1940. BA in Econs., CCNY, 1966. Security analyst Morgan Guaranty Trust Co. N.Y., 1966-70; sr. tech. analyst G.A. Saxton & Co., N.Y.C., 1970-73; mgr. Xerox Corp., Stamford, Conn., 1973-79, dir. investor rels., 1979-84, v.p., corp. sec., 1984—, treas., 1990—; bd. dirs. Baker Hughes, Inc., Houston, Briggs & Stratton, Milw. Chmn. bd. trustees Wells Colls., Aurora, N.Y., 1990—; bd. dirs. United Way Tri-State, N.Y.C., 1989-93, Westport-Weston (Conn.) United Way, 1989-93. Recipient Graham & Dodd award Fin. Analysts Fedn., N.Y.C., 1971; named to Acad. of Women Achievers YWCA of N.Y.C., 1981. Mem. Fin. Execs. Inst. (com. on corp. fin. 1994—), Investor Rels. Assn. of N.Y. (pres. 1984-85), Nat. Investor Rels. Inst., Nat. Assn. Corp. Treas., Am. Soc. Corp. Secs., Fin. Women Assn. of N.Y., The Conf. Bd. - Coun. of Corp. Treasurers. Office: Xerox Corp 800 Long Ridge Rd Stamford CT 06902-1288

FINA, PAUL JOSEPH, lawyer; b. Chgo., Mar. 1, 1959; s. Paul Emil and Vera Christiane (Mutzbauer) F.; m. Robyn Leann Hughes, May 24, 1986; 1 child, Paul George. BA in Econs., U. Ill., 1982, MA, 1983; JD, DePaul U., Chgo., 1987. Bar: Ill. 1988, U.S. Dist. Ct. (no. dist.) Ill. 1990, U.S. Ct. Appeals (7th cir.) 1990, U.S. Supreme Ct. 1991. Assoc. Haskin, Taylor & McDonough, Wheaton, Ill., 1988-90, Komessar & Wintroub, Chgo., 1990-94; pvt. practice Law Office of Paul J. Fina, Chgo., 1994—; mem. bus. faculty Coll. of DuPage, Glen Ellyn, Ill., 1986—, Aurora (Ill.) U., 1997—. Gen. counsel Housing Helpers, Inc., Riverside, Ill., 1991—. DePaul law grantee, 1985. Mem. ABA, Ill. BAr Assn., Assn. Trial Lawyers Am., DuPage County Bar Assn. (civil practice com.), Phi Alpha Delta. Roman Catholic. Avocations: music performance, athletics. Home: 101 Red Fox Run Montgomery IL 60538-2914 Office: 30 N La Salle St Ste 1530 Chicago IL 60602-2503

FINAISH, FATHI ALI, aeronautical engineering educator; b. Tripoli, Libya, July 22, 1954; came to U.S., 1981; s. Ali Finaish and Zuhra (Lamin) Mahfud; m. Deborah Lynn Demijohn, Dec. 28, 1984. BS in Aero. Engring., U. Al-Fateh, Tripoli, 1978; MS in Aerospace Engring., U. Colo., 1984, PhD in Aerospace Engring., 1987. Lic. pvt. pilot; FAA airframe and power plant cert. mechanic. Rsch. asst. U. Colo., Boulder, 1984-87, adj. asst. prof., 1987-88; asst. prof. aero. engring. U. Mo., Rolla, 1988-94, assoc. prof., 1994—; airworthiness engr. Dept. Civil Aviation, Tripoli, 1979-81; ground sch. instr. Tripoli Flight Ctr., 1980-81; rsch. fellow Naval Under Water Systems Ctr., Newport, R.I., 1991, NASA Langley Rsch. Ctr., Hampton, Va., 1992; lectr. various univs.; advisor Licking High Sch., St. James High Sch.; summer rsch. fellow U.S. Navy-Am. Soc. Engring. Edn., 1991, NASA-Am. Soc. Engring. Edn., 1992. Contbr. articles to profl. jours. Head coach Rolla Soccer Club, asst. to soccer head coach, 1997-99. Grantee U. Mo., Rolla, 1988-92, U. Mo. Systems, 1991-92, U. Mo. Rsch. Bd., 1994-95, Office Naval Rsch., 1991, NASA, 1993-95, Precision Environ. Sys., 1995-96, Ctr. Indoor Rsch., 1998—, ASHRAE, 1999—. Fellow AIAA (assoc., Outstanding Tchr. award U. Mo. chpt. 1993); mem. ASEE, ASHRAE (grantee 1992-93, 99). Achievements include development of several ednl. computer codes and courses in aerospace engring.; design and bldg. an exptl. system that generates and visualizes impulsive and accelerating motions and other unsteady airflow histories; designed and developed several wind tunnels for steady and unsteady aerodynamic testing at the University of Missouri-Rolla. Office: U Mo Dept Mech Engring Rolla MO 65401

FINAMORE, DANIEL ROBERT, museum curator; b. Binghamton, N.Y., Aug. 21, 1961; s. Richard E. and Judith M. (Goldstein) F. AB, Vassar Coll., 1983; MA, Boston U., 1987, PhD in Archaeology, 1994. Project archaeologist Franklin Delano Roosevelt Nat. Historic Site, Hyde Park, N.Y., 1987; field dir. Historic Travellers' Rest, Nashville, 1988; asst. curator maritime history Peabody Mus., Salem, Mass., 1988-91, assoc. curator Maritime History, 1991-92, acting curator maritime history, 1992-93, Russell W. Knight curator maritime arts and history, 1993—; mem. faculty Sch. for Field Studies, Cambridge, Mass., 1986; dir. Belize Hist. Archaeol. Survey, 1990-94; mem. faculty Summer Inst. Local History, Salem Coll., 1993; faculty Mass. Bay Marine Studies Consortium, 1995—; monitor, advisor State Atty. Gen.'s Office Consumer Affairs, 1993; mem. adv. com. Spring Point Maritime Mus., South Portland, Maine, 1993-94; cons. Issembert Prodns., 1993, No. Lights Prodns., 1993-94; dir. Coun. Am. Maritime Mus., 1997—; presenter in field. Arts editor Am. Neptune. Grantee Sigma Xi., 1988, NSF, 1990; Alice M. Brennan Humanities scholar Humanities Found., 1989. Mem. Coun. Am. Maritime Mus. (nominating, exec. and fellowship coms.), Soc. for Hist. Archaeology (cou n. underwater archaeology), Soc. for Am. Archaeology (award 1996), Soc. for Post-Medieval Archaeology, Coun. on Northeast Hist. Archaeology, Am. Ceramic Circle, Salem Marine Soc. (hon.), Newburyport Maritime Soc. (trustee 1998—). Office: Peabody Essex Mus E India Sq Salem MA 01970*

FINAN, ELLEN CRANSTON, secondary education educator, consultant; b. Worcester, Mass., June 26, 1951; d. Thomas Matthew and Maureen Ann (Moulton) F. BA, U. San Francisco, 1973; MA, U. Calif., Riverside, 1978. ESL specialist U.S. Peace Corps, Finote Selam, Ethiopia, 1974-75; English instr. U. Redlands, Calif., 1977-79; mentor tchr. Jurupa Unified Sch. Dist., Riverside, 1979—; teaching supr. U. Calif., Riverside, 1993—; tech. writer Callan Assocs., San Francisco, 1973-74, Wilshire Assocs., Santa Monica, Calif., 1976-77; English instr. U. Pa., Phila., 1979; writing cons. Inland Area Writing Project U. Calif., Riverside, 1980—; tchr., coordinator U. Calif., Riverside, 1982. Author: Prickley Pear, 1981, CAP Attack Handbook, 1987. NEH fellow, 1985, 92; Squaw Valley Community of Writers scholar, 1981, Carnegie Mellon fellow, 1987, NEH Inst. fellow, 1993, 97. Mem. Nat. Council English Tchrs., Assn. Supervision and Curriculum Devel., Alpha Sigma Nu, Phi Delta Kappa. Democrat. Avocations: writing, travel. Home: 22440 Mountain View Rd Moreno Valley CA 92557-2655 Office: Jurupa Unified Schs 4250 Opal St Riverside CA 92509-7251

FINBERG, BARBARA DENNING, nonprofit executive; b. Pueblo, Colo., Feb. 26, 1929; d. Rufus Raymond and Velma Aileen (Hopper) Denning; m. Alan R. Finberg, June 21, 1953 (dec. 1995). BA, Stanford U., 1949; MA, Am. U. Beirut, Lebanon, 1951. Intern U.S. Dept. State, Washington, 1949-50, fgn. affairs officer, Tech Coop. Adminstrn., 1952-53; program specialist, area chief Inst. Internat. Edn., N.Y.C., 1953-59; editorial assoc., program officer Carnegie Corp. N.Y., N.Y.C., 1959-80, v.p. program, 1980-88, exec. v.p., 1988-97; v.p. MEM Assocs., Inc., 1997—; vis. fellow Woodrow Wilson Nat. Fellowship Found., 1998—. Trustee Stanford U., 1976-86, v.p. bd. dirs., 1982-85, vis. com. Stanford U. Librs., 1984-90, 93-96, chmn., 1986-88; nat. adv. panel Inst. for Rsch. on Women and Gender, 1991—, Humanities and Scis. Coun., 1996—; trustee N.Y. Found., 1979-91, vice chmn. bd. dirs., 1983-85, chmn., 1985-89; mem. accreditation com. Assn. Am. Law Schs., 1986-88; adv. com. Henry A. Murray Rsch. Ctr. for Study of Lives, Radcliffe Coll., 1986-97; bd. dirs. The Hole in the Wall Gang Fund, Inc., 1987—, Investor Responsibility Rsch. Ctr. Inc., 1989-97, vice chmn. bd. dirs., 1992-94, Ind. Sector, 1990—, chmn. mgmt. com., 1994-96, chmn. bd., 1996-98, Consortium for Advancement of Pvt. Higher Edn., 1992; bd. dirs. Bard Musical Festival, 1995—; mem. adv. com. to govtl. studies program Brookings Instn., 1996—; bd. dirs. High/Scope Ednl. Rsch. Found., 1998—; mem. Human Rights Watch, Europe and Ctrl. Asia and Children's Rights Divsn. Steering Com., 1996—; bd. dirs. U. Cape Town (South Africa) Fund, 1997—. Recipient Women of Vision award N.Y. Women's Found., 1995, John Dewey award for disting. pub. svc. Bard Coll., 1998; Rotary Found. fellow, 1950-51. Mem. Soc. for Rsch. in Child Devel., Coun. on Fgn. Rels. Club: Cosmopolitan of N.Y. Home: 165 E 72nd St Apt 19L New York NY 10021-4351 Office: MEM Assocs Inc 521 5th Ave Rm 1801 New York NY 10175-0088

FINBERG, JAMES MICHAEL, lawyer; b. Balt., Sept. 6, 1958; s. Laurence and Harriet (Levinson) F.; m. Marian D. Keeler, June 28, 1986. BA, Brown U., 1980; JD, U. Chgo., 1983. Bar: Calif. 1984, U.S. Dist. Ct. (no. dist.) Calif. 1984, U.S. Dist. Ct. (ea. dist.) Calif. 1987, U.S. Ct. Appeals (9th and fed. cirs.) 1987, U.S. Dist. Ct. Hawaii, 1988, U.S. Supreme Ct. 1994. Law clk. to assoc. justice Mich. Supreme Ct., 1983-84; assoc. Feldman, Waldman and Kline, San Francisco, 1984-87, Morrison and Foerster, 1987-90; ptnr. Lieff, Cabraser, Heimann & Bernstein, L.L.P., San Francisco, 1991—; adv. com. local rules for securities cases U.S. Dist. Ct., Calif., 1996; lawyer rep. to 9th Cir. Jud. Conf., 1998—. Exec. editor U. Chgo. Law Rev., 1982-83. Mem. ABA (chmn. securities subcom. class and derivative action com. 1998—), ACLU (bd. dirs. No. Calif. chpt. 1995), Bar Assn. San Francisco (bd. dirs. 1999—, jud. evaluation com. 1994, bd. dirs. 1998—), Calif. Bar Assn. (mem. standing com. on legal svcs. to poor 1990-94, vice-chmn. 1993-94), Lawyers Com. for Civil Rights of San Francisco Bay Area (bd. dirs. 1992-98, fin. chmn. 1992-95, sec. 1996, co-chmn. 1997-98). Office: Lieff Cabraser Heimann & Bernstein LL 275 Battery St Fl 30 San Francisco CA 94111-3305

FINBERG, LAURENCE, pediatrician, educator, dean; b. Chgo., May 20, 1923; s. Joseph and Anne (Malkow) F.; m. Harriet Levinson, June 17, 1945 (dec. Jan. 1994); children: Robert, Jeanne, James; m. Joann Quane, Mar. 17, 1995. BS, U. Chgo., 1944, MD, 1946. Diplomate: Am. Bd. Pediatrics (examiner 1969-94, bd. dirs. 1974-79, 82-88 , pres. 1978, chmn. 1987). Intern U. Chgo. Clinics, 1946-47; asst. resident pediatrics Balt. City Hosps., 1949-50, resident in pediat., 1950-51; practice medicine specializing in pediat. Balt., 1951-63, N.Y.C., 1963—; asst. chief pediatrician Balt. City Hosps., 1951-61, dir. pediatric out-patient dept., 1951-63, dir. premature nursery, 1951-59, assoc. chief pediatrics, 1961-63; pediatrician Harriet Lane Home, 1951-63; chmn. dept. pediatrics Montefiore Hosp. and Med. Center, Bronx, N.Y., 1963-80, prof., 1995—; chmn. dept. pediatrics SUNY Health Sci. Ctr., Bklyn., 1982-95, prof. pediatrics, 1982-95, prof. emeritus, 1995—, dean, 1988-91; prof. clin. pediat. U. Calif., San Francisco, 1995—, Stanford U. Sch. Med., 1997—; instr. pediatrics Johns Hopkins U., 1951-56; asst. prof., 1956-63; prof. pediatrics Albert Einstein Coll. Medicine, Yeshiva U., Bronx, 1963-82, chmn., 1968-80; cons. in field; mem. pediatric adv. com. N.Y.C. Dept. Health, 1970-94. Mem. editl. bd. Jour. Pediat., 1973-83, Am. Jour. Diseases of Children, 1984-94, named changed to Archives of Pediat. and Adolescent Medicine, 1994—, editor nutrition sect., 1995—. Served with USPHS, 1947-49. Recipient Bela Schick medal, 1992, Nutrition award Am. Acad. Pediatrics, 1992. Mem. AAAS, AMA (Goldberger Clin. Nutrition award 1993), Am. Pediatric Soc., Soc. Pediatric Research, Am. Acad. Pediatrics (com. on environ. hazards 1968-83, chmn. 1979-83, com. nutrition 1983-89—, chmn. 1984-89), Am. Coll. Nutrition, Am. Soc. for Nutritional Scis., Nat. Cholesterol Edn. Program Coordinating Com. (panel on children and adolescents 1989-93), Ambulatory Pediatric Assn., Am. Soc. Clin. Nutrition, Am. Fedn. Clin. Research, Sociedad Peruana de Pediatria, Sociedad Dominica De Peditria, Harvey Soc., N.Y. Acad. Medicine (past chmn. pediatric sec.), Phi Beta Kappa, Sigma Xi, Alpha Omega Alpha. Research in electrolyte physiology. Home: 152 Lombard St Apt 602 San Francisco CA 94111-1134

FINCH, ANNIE R(IDLEY) C(RANE), poet; b. New Rochelle, N.Y., Oct. 31, 1956; d. Henry Leroy and Margaret (Rockwell) Finch; m. Glen Brand, Dec. 6, 1985; children: Julian Hughan Finch-Brand, Althea Crane Finch-Brand. BA, Yale U., 1979; MA, U. Houston, 1986; PhD, Stanford U., 1991. Lectr. New Coll., San Francisco, 1991; asst. prof. U. No. Iowa, Cedar Falls, 1992-95; asst. prof. Miami U., Oxford, Ohio, 1995-98, assoc. prof., 1999—. Author: The Encyclopedia of Scotland, 1982, The Ghost of Meter, 1993, Catching the Mermother, 1996, Eve, 1997; editor: A Formal Feeling Comes, 1994, After New Formalism, 1999; co-editor: An Exaltation of Forms, 1999. Recipient Sparrow Sonnet award, 1993; nominated for Pushcart prize, 1994, 96, 97. Mem. MLA, Acad. Am. Poets, Poetry Soc. Am., Emily Dickinson Internat. Soc. Avocations: painting, camping, guitar, yoga. Office: Miami U Dept English Oxford OH 45056

FINCH, C. HERBERT, retired archivist, library administrator, historian; b. Boise City, Okla., Nov. 8, 1931; s. Cloyd Herbert and Gladys Erma (Fellows) F.; m. Joyce Ongelene Hamilton, May 23, 1954 (dec.); children: Douglas Hamilton, Philip Andrew, Diana Ruth; m. Elsie Thorp Freeman, Aug. 2, 1992. BA, Okla. Bapt. U., 1953; BD, So. Bapt. Theol. Sem., Louisville, 1957; MA, U.Ky., Lexington, 1959, PhD, 1965. Field rep. U. Ky., Lexington, 1961-64; assoc. archivist Cornell U., Ithaca, N.Y., 1964-67, archivist, 1967-72, asst. Univ. librarian, 1972-96, lectr., 1972-80; mem. adv. coun. Nat. Archives, Washington, 1975-81, N.Y. State Hist. Records, Albany, 1976-85; cons. archives and libraries; cons. John A. Woods Appraisers, South Windsor, Conn. Author: Charter Day: Cornell University Centennial, 1965; Guide to Manuscripts - Charles Abrams: Papers & Files, 1975; contbr. articles to profl. jours. Fellow Soc. Am. Archivists. Democrat. Baptist. Home: 904 Coddington Rd Ithaca NY 14850-6022

FINCH, CALEB ELLICOTT, neurobiologist, educator; b. London, July 4, 1939; came to U.S., 1939; s. Benjamin F. and Faith (Stratton) Campbell; m. Doris Nossamen, Oct. 11, 1975; stepsons: Michael, Alec Tsongas. BS, Yale U., 1961; PhD, Rockefeller U., 1969. Guest investigator Rockefeller U., N.Y.C., 1969-70; asst. prof. Cornell U. Med. Coll., N.Y.C., 1970-72; asst. prof. biology, gerontology U. So. Calif., L.A., 1972-75, assoc. prof., 1975-78, prof., 1978—, ARCO and William Kieschnick prof. neurobiology of aging, 1985—, Univ. prof., 1989—. Mem. editl. bd. Jour. Gerontology, 1979-86, Neurobiology of Aging, 1982—, Synapse, 1992—, Exp. Gerontol., 1997—; contbr. more than 350 articles to profl. jours.; author: Longevity, Senescence and the Genome, 1990, Aging: A Natural History, 1995, (with T. Kirkwood) Chance, Development and Aging, 1999. HIN rsch. grantee, 1972—; recipient Brookdale award, 1985, Allied Signal Inc. award Achievement in Biomed. Aging, 1988, Rsch. award Alzheimer's Assn. L.A., 1989, Cherkin award UCLA, 1991, Am. Aging Assn. award, 1994, Sandoz Premier prize Internat. Assn. Gerontology, 1995. Recipient Allied Signal Inc. award Achievement in Biomed. Aging, 1988, Rsch. award Alzheimer's Assn. L.A., 1989, Am. Aging Assn., 1994, Cherkin award UCLA, 1991, Sandoz Premier prize IAG, 1996, prize for longevity rsch. IPSEN Found., 1996, award for leadership in comms. IASIA, 1996, Irving Wright award AFAR, 1999; NIH rsch. grantee, 1972—. Fellow AAAS, Gerontol. Soc. Am. (chmn. biology sect. 1992-93, Robert W. Kleemeier award 1984); mem. Neurosci. Soc., Endocrine Soc., Neuroendocrine Soc., Psychoneuroendocrine Soc., Iron Mountain String Band (fiddler 1963—). Home: 2144 Crescent Dr Altadena

CA 91001-2112 Office: U So Calif Gerontology Ctr University Park Los Angeles CA 90007

FINCH, CAROL ANNE, former secondary education educator; b. N.Y.C., Oct. 22, 1942; d. William George and Anna Frances (O'Connell) Simpson; m. Aug. 1, 1970 (div.); children: Robert A., James J. BA, William Paterson Coll., 1964, MA, 1968. Cert. English, reading and learning disabilities tchr., N.J. Tchr. Bridgewater-Raritan (N.J.) Sch. Dist., 1964-67, Ramsey (N.J.) Bd. of Edn., 1967-71; office mgr. Maywood (N.J.) Pub. Libr., 1985-86; tchr. Teaneck (N.J.) Bd. of Edn., 1987-88, Passaic County Tech. & Vocat. High Sch., Wayne, N.J., 1988-91, Elizabeth (N.J.) Bd. Edn., 1991-93; collections asst. Party Rental, Teterboro, N.J., 1994-98; adminstrv. asst. Randy Hangers, LLC, East Rutherford, N.J., 1998, Bryant Staffing, Emerson, N.J., 1999—. Mem. NEA, Internat. Reading Assn., N.J. Edn. Assn., N.J. Reading Assn. Avocations: reading, crocheting, ceramics, crewel work. Home: 279 Clark St Apt A15 Hackensack NJ 07601-1062 Office: Bryant Staffing 466 Old Hook Rd Emerson NJ 07630

FINCH, EDWARD RIDLEY, JR., lawyer, diplomat, author, lecturer; b. Westhampton Beach, N.Y., Aug. 31, 1919. AB with Atwater honors, Princeton U., 1941; JD, NYU, 1947; LLD (hon.), Mo. Valley Coll., 1963; DSc (hon.), Cumberland Coll., 1985. Bar: N.Y. 1948, U.S. Supreme Ct. 1953, D.C. 1978, Fla. 1980, Pa. 1992. Ptnr. Finch & Schaefler, N.Y.C., 1950-85; of counsel Le Boeuf, Lamb, Leiby & MacRae, N.Y.C., 1986-88; commr. City of N.Y., 1955-58; v.p. gen. counsel, dir. St. Giles Found., 1994—, Am. Internat. Petroleum Corp., 1988-92; U.S. del. 4th UN Congress, Geneva, 1970, 5th UN Congress, Japan, 1975; U.S. spl. ambassador to Panama, 1972; legal advisor, mem. U.S. Del. Unispace, 1982, Vienna, 1982; lectr. in field. Author: Holes in Your Pockets, 3rd edit., Astro Business-A Guide to Commerce and Law of Outer Space, Judicial Politics; contbr. articles to legal and sci. jours. Pres., bd. dirs. St. Nicholas Soc. N.Y., 1948—; past pres. N.Y. Inst. Spl. Edn., 1950—; bd. govs. Nat. Space Soc., 1984—; mem. faculty adv. com. dept. politics Princeton U.; treas. Jessie Ridley Found., N.Y.C., Finch Trusts; pres. Adams Meml. Fund Inc.; trustee St. Andrew's Dune Ch., Southampton, Cathedral of St. John the Divine, 1989-92; bd. dirs. Am. Found. Cancer Rsch.; life trustee Met. Mus. of Art, N.Y.C.; trustee Whittell Trust. Col. JAG, USAFR, 1941-72. Decorated U.S. Legion of Merit with oak leaf cluster; order Brit. Empire; Knight Order St. John; officer French Legion of Honor, Disting. Eagle Scout, Coun. of Am. Ambassadors. Fellow Am. Bar Found. (chmn. aerospace coun. sect. sci. and tech 1986-92); mem. ABA (ho. of dels. 1971-72, chmn. corp. lawyers sr. lawyer divsn., chmn. aerospace law divsn. internat. law sect.1973-79), AIAA (sr.), Fed. Bar Assn., Inter-Am. Bar Assn. (Hallgartern telecommunications award 1991), N.Y. State Bar Assn. (internat. law and practice sec., chmn. arms control and nat. security com.), Pa. Bar Assn., Fla. Bar Assn., Assn., Bar City of N.Y., Internat. Bar Assn., Judge Advs. Assn. U.S. (past pres.), Am. Law Inst., Am. Judicature Soc. (sr.), Internat. Astronautical Acad. (full elected mem.), Internat. Inst. Space Law (Lifetim Disting. Svc. award 1997), Am. Arbitration Assn. (panelist), Univ. Clubs of Wash. and N.Y., Union League Club, Union Club, Princeton Club (bd. govs. 1982—), L.I. Club, Bathing Corp. of Southampton, Westhampton Country Club. Fax: 212-327-0593. Office: 862 Park Ave New York NY 10021-1806

FINCH, EVELYN VORISE, financial planner; b. Marietta, Ohio, Jan. 20, 1930; d. Richard Raymon Juantzee (deceased) and Oreatha Fay (Carnes) Metcalf; m. Herman Frederick Ahrens, May 13, 1948 (div. Nov. 1957); children: Erick K.F., Hilda Kate (dec.), Nicole Schwartz; m. James Derwood Finch, June 29, 1973 (dec. Oct. 1993). BS in Music Edn., Concord Coll., 1961; student, Northeastern U., 1990. Registered health underwriter Northeastern U., Boston. Music tchr. Prince George's County (Md.) pub. schs., 1961-72; pvt. piano tchr. Washington, 1961-73; china and crystal sales rep. Quality Products Co., Washington, 1973-80; ins. agt. Mut. of Omaha Cos., Washington, 1980-92, Memphis, 1992-94; pvt. practice fin. planner Alamo, Tenn., 1994—; mem. internat. mktg. and investments divsn. Tri-Ocean Internat., LLC, Emeryville, Calif., 1995—. Supporting mem. Nat. Mus. Women in the Arts, Washington, 1990—, Women's Philharm., San Francisco, 1993—. Mem. NAFE, AAUW (br. pres. 1994-96, Tenn. chair ednl. found. 1996-98, mem. Nat. Diversity Resource Team 1997—) Nat. Assn. Health Underwriters (registered health underwriter), Internat. Assn. for Fin. Planning, Nat. Boating Fedn. (pres. 1985), Potomac River Yacht Clubs Assn. (legis. chair 1978-87), Chesapeake Bay Yacht Clubs Assn. (commodore 1982), Prince George's Yacht Club (commodore 1978), Pi Mu, Kappa Delta Pi. Home and Office: Finch Fin Svcs 208 Finch Rd Alamo TN 38001-5923

FINCH, FRANK HERSCHEL, JR., lawyer; b. Mpls., Mar. 13, 1933; s. Frank H. and Louise A. (Henry) F.; m. Margaret Lee Samuel, June 13, 1953; children: Frank H. III, Lani D.L. BA, Harvard U., 1953; LLB, Harvard U. Law Sch., 1959. Bar: Conn. 1959, U.S. Supreme Ct. 1967. Assoc. Howd & Lavieri, Winsted, Conn., 1959-61; ptnr. Howd, Lavieri & Finch, Winsted, 1961—; pros. atty. Conn. Cir. Ct., 1961-78; adv. bd. Conn. Bank and Trust Co., 1976—; bd. dirs. Northwest Conn. Health Corp. Chmn., bd. dirs. Winsted Meml. Hosp., 1975-77; chmn. personnel com. Town of Barkhamsted, Conn., 1984—; mem. regional adv. coun. N.W. Conn. C.C.; vice-chmn. bd. trustees N.W. Conn. YMCA. Lt. USNR, 1953-59. Mem. ABA, Conn. Bar Assn. (chmn. standing com. on admissions 1978—, bd. govs. 1985—), Litchfield County Bar Assn. (pres. 1974-76, grievance com. 1982-86, state trial referee 1984—), Am. Arbitration Assn. (arbitrator 1975—), Nat. Assn. Dist. Attys., N.W. Conn. C. of C. (bd. dirs. 1978—, chmn. 1980-81, sec. 1985-89, v.p. 1989—). Club: University (exec. com. 1985—), Rotary (pres. Winsted club 1967-68). Office: Howd Lavieri & Finch PO Box 1080 682 Main St Winsted CT 06098-1515*

FINCH, JANET MITCHELL, academic administrator; b. Nashville, June 4, 1950; d. James W. and Helen A. (Ardis) Mitchell; m. Harold William Finch, Aug. 6, 1977; children: Harold W. II, Toria Janette. BA in Math., Tenn. State U., 1972, MEd, 1978; EdD, Vanderbilt U., 1985. Cost analyst gen. parts div. Ford Motor Co., Plymouth, Mich., 1972; quality control analyst glass div. Ford Motor Co., Nashville, 1973-74; project engr. Procter & Gamble Mfg. Co., Greenville, N.C., 1974-75; system engr. Procter & Gamble Mfg. Co., Jackson, Tenn., 1975-77; edn. specialist Nashville State Tech. Inst., 1977-80, dir. spl. svcs., 1980-81, asst. dean gen. studies, 1981-86; dean acad. affairs Motlow State C.C., Tullahoma, Tenn., 1988-91, exec. asst. to pres., 1991—; asst. to vice chancellor acad. affairs C.C. System Office, Lexington, Ky., 1986; acting v.p. adminstrn. Mid. Tenn. State U., Nashville, 1987; dept. head devel. studies Nashville State Tech. Inst., 1980-85. Active YWCA, Nashville, 1987-88; bd. dirs. Jackson Transit Authority, 1976-77; pres. Temple Acad. Parent Tchr. Orgn., Nashville, 1986-87; sec. Temple Daycare Parent Tchr. Orgn., Nashville, 1985-86. Am. Coun. on Edn. fellow, 1986; named Leader of the 80's Fund for Improving Postsecondary Edn., 1985, one of Outstanding Young Women Am., 1985, 86. Mem. Phi Theta Kappa. Avocations: church music, spectator sports. Home: 221 Rising Sun Ter Old Hickory TN 37138-2128 Office: Metropolitan Community Coll 601 James R Thompson Blvd East Saint Louis IL 62201-1129

FINCH, RAYMOND LAWRENCE, judge; b. Christiansted, St. Croix, V.I., Oct. 4, 1940; s. Wilfred Christopher and Beryl Elaine (Bough) F.; m. Anne Marie Mohammed, May 8, 1996; children—Allison, Mark, Jennifer. A.B., Howard U., 1962, J.D., 1965. Bar: V.I. 1971, Third Circuit Ct. of Appeals 1976. Law clk. Judge's Municipal Ct. of V.I., 1965-66; partner firm Hodge, Sheen, Finch & Ross, Christiansted, 1970-75; judge Territorial Ct. of V.I., Charlotte Amalie, 1975-86, Ct. of Appeals, V.I., Charlotte Amalie, 1986-94, U.S. Dist. Ct. of V.I., 1994—; instr. Grad. div., Coll. of V.I., Am. Inst. Banking, 1976—. Bd. dirs. Boy Scouts Am., Boys Club Am. Served to capt. U.S. Army, 1966-69. Decorated Army Commendation medal, Bronze Star medal. Mem. Am. Judges Assn., Am., Nat. bar assns., Internat. Assn. Chiefs of Police. Democrat. Lutheran. Office: PO Box 24051 Christiansted VI 00824-0051

FINCH, ROBERT JONATHAN, communications engineering consultant; b. Chgo., Sept. 21, 1955; s. Herman Manuel and Frances (Gutlow) F.; m. Gayle Deborah Falk, Mar. 28, 1991; children: Layla Michelle, Grant Dillon. BA in Broadcast Mgmt., U. So. Calif., 1977. Engr.-in-charge LFI Prodns., Inc., Lafayette, Ind., 1990-92; comm. engring. cons., L.A., 1978-90, Lafayette, 1992—. Developer: ABC Hollywood's 1st satellite video-tape ctr., Saudi Arabia's 1st color TV studio, 1st digitally based pub. transponder in 2-way radio svc. in continental U.S., 1st large volume, pub. access and radio accessed computer database in U.S.; contbr. articles to publs. Mem. Tippecanoe Amateur Radio Assn. (trustee), Hollywood (Calif.) Magic Castle, Pasadena Casting Club (instr.). Avocations: fly fishing, close-up magic. Home: 7530 Ridgeview Ln Lafayette IN 47905-9795

FINCH, ROGERS BURTON, association management consultant; b. Broadalbin, N.Y., Apr. 16, 1920; s. Cecil Clement and Olga Ulrika (Lofgren) F.; m. Barbara Ellen Hine, Jan. 3, 1942; children: David Rogers, John Richard, Steven Alan, Kathryn Ann, Elizabeth Gale. B.S., Mass. Inst. Tech., 1941, M.S., 1947, Sc.D., 1950. Prof. Mass. Inst. Tech., 1946-53; dir. U.S. Fgn. Aid Mission, Rangoon, Burma, 1953-54; dir. research Rensselaer Poly. Inst., Troy, N.Y., 1954-61; v.p. planning Rensselaer Poly. Inst., 1963-72; dir. univ. relations Peace Corps, Washington, 1961-63; exec. dir. ASME, N.Y.C., 1972-81; cons., 1987—; exec. v.p. Illuminating Engineering Soc. N.Am., 1982-87. Contbr. articles profl. jours. Served to maj. AUS, 1941-46; to brig. gen. U.S. Army Res.; ret. 1975. Decorated Army Commendation medal, Legion of Merit. Fellow ASME (life), AAAS; mem. Am. Soc. Assn. Execs. (life), Am. Soc. Engring. Edn. (life), Council Engring. and Sci. Soc. Execs. (emeritus past pres.), Illuminating Engring. Soc. N.Am., Sigma Xi, Tau Beta Pi. Home: 12 Sherwood Rd Little Silver NJ 07739-1309

FINCH, SHEILA, writer, author science fiction; b. London; 3 children. Postgrad., Ind. U. Faculty creative writing El Camino Coll., Torrance, Calif. Author: Infinity's Web (Crompton Crook/Stephen Tall award 1985), 1985, Triad, 1986, The Garden of the Shaped, 1987, Shaper's Legacy, 1988, Shaping the Dawn, 1989, The Falcon and the Falconer, 1997. Winner 1998 Nebula award for novella: Reading the Bones. Avocations: travel, Tai Chi, hiking, 4-wheeling in the desert. Office: c/o Avon Books The Hearst Corp 1350 Ave of the Americas New York NY 10019*

FINCH, THOMAS WESLEY, corrosion engineer; b. Alhambra, Calif., Dec. 17, 1946; s. Charles Phillip and Marian Louisa (Bushey) F.; m. Jinx L. Heath, Apr. 1979. Student Colo. Sch. Mines, 1964-68. Assayer, prospector Raymond P. Heon, Inc., Idaho Springs, Colo., 1968; corrosion engr. Cathodic Protection Service, Denver, 1973-80, area mgr., Lafayette, La., 1980-81; area mgr. Corrintec/USA, Farmington, N.Mex., 1981-83; dist. mgr. Cathodic Protection Services Co., Farmington, 1983-98 . Served with C.E., U.S. Army, 1968-72. Mem. Nat. Assn. Corrosion Engrs., Soc. Am. Mil. Engrs., U.S. Ski Assn., Am. Security Council (nat. adv. bd. 1978—), Kappa Sigma. Republican. Lutheran. Home and Office: 2404 Municipal Dr Farmington NM 87401-3942

FINCHER, CAMERON LANE, education educator; b. Douglas County, Ga., Nov. 4, 1926; s. Andrew Jackson and Ada (Swafford) F.; m. Mary Frances Cutts, June 15, 1957; children: Marcel Andriette, Matthew Donnellan, Ada Amanda, Melissa Lane. B.C.S., Ga. State U., 1950; M.A., U. Minn., 1951; Ph.D., Ohio State U., 1956. Lic. psychologist, Ga. Dir. testing and counseling Ga. State U., Atlanta, 1956-65; assoc. dir. Inst. Higher Edn., U. Ga., Athens, 1965-69; dir. Inst. Inst. Higher Edn., U. Ga., 1969—, prof. higher edn. and psychology, 1965—, Regents prof. higher edn. and psychology, 1981—; cons. various indsl. and comml. cos., also state governing bds. colls. and univs., La., S.C., Ala., Tenn.; mem. Gov.'s Com. on Postsecondary Edn., Ga., 1978-83; mem. rsch. panel So. Edn. Found., 1978-86. Author: A Preface to Psychology, 1972, Challenge of Reform in Higher Education, 1991, Historical Development of the University System of Georgia, 1991; contbg. columnist: Athens Banner-Herald, 1970—; editor: Planning Imperatives for the 1990s, 1989, Assessing Institutional Effectiveness in Higher Education, 1989, Defining and Assessing Quality, 1994; contbg. editor Rsch. in Higher Edn., 1978—; contbr. articles to profl. jours. Served with USNR, 1944-46. Recipient Disting. Achievement in Public Service medallion U. Ga., 1980, Ben W. Gibson award So. Regional Council, Coll. Bd., 1982; Ga. Ho. of Reps. and Senate Resolution recognizing contbns. to higher edn. and State of Ga., 1986, Abraham Baldwin award U. Ga. Alumni Assn., 1991. Mem. APA, Ga. Assn. Instnl. Rsch., Planning, Assessment and Quality (1st recipient Cameron Lane Fincher outstanding svc. award 1997), Assn. Study of Higher Edn. (Howard Bowen Disting. Career award 1991), So. Assn. Instl. Rsch. (James R. Montgomery award 1991), Am. Assn. Higher Edn., Assn. Instnl. Rsch. (Disting. Mem. 1983, Outstanding Svc. award 1980, AIR/Suslow award, 1995), So. Assn. Instnl. Rsch. (disting.), Alpha Kappa Psi, Phi Delta Kappa, Golden Key. Office: U Ga Inst Higher Edn Candler Hall Athens GA 30602

FINCHER, DAVID, film director; b. Calif., 1963. Dir. videos for Paula Abdul, Aerosmith, Madonna, Michael Jackson, Rolling Stones, Wallflowers; dir.:(films) Alien 3, 1992, Seven, 1995, The Game, 1997, The Fight Club, 1999, Rendezvous with Rama, 1999. *

FINCK, KEVIN WILLIAM, lawyer; b. Whittier, Calif., Dec. 14, 1954; s. William Albert and Ester (Gutbub) F.; m. Kathleen A. Miller, Oct. 7, 1989. BA in History, U. Calif., Santa Barbara, 1977; JD, U. Calif., San Francisco, 1980. Bar: Calif. 1980. lectr. Internat. Bar Assn., Learning Annex. Author: California Corporation Start Up Package and Minute Book, 1982, 9th edit., 1998; contbr. articles to various profl. jours. Avocations: hiking, golf, skiing. Office: Ste 1670 Two Embarcadero Ctr San Francisco CA 94111

FINCKE, GARY W., educator; b. Pitts., July 7, 1945; s. William A. and Ruth L. Lang F.; m. Elizabeth L. Locker, Aug. 17, 1968; children: Derek, Shannon, Aaron. BA, Thiel Coll., 1967; MA, Miami U., 1969; PhD, Kent State U., 1974. Tchr. English Freedom (Pa.) Area Schs., 1968-69; instr. English Pa. State U., Monaca, 1969-75; chair English dept. LeRoy (N.Y.) Ctrl. Sch., 1975-80; prof. English Susquehanna U., Sellinsgrove, Pa., 1980—; coach men's tennis Susquehanna U., Sellinsgrove, &, 1980—; instr. fiction Pa. Govs. Sch. Arts, 1984; cons. in field. Author of poems. Dir. Ea. Region Pa. Act 101 Program, Harrisburg, 1987-89. Recipient Best Hokin prize Poetry Mag., 1991, Pushcart prize, 1996, PEN Fiction prize, 1984; Artist fellow Pa. Coun. Arts, 1982, 85, 87, 91, 95. Mem. Associated Writing Programs. Avocations: tennis, golf, music, pool. Office: Susquehanna U Dept English Selinsgrove PA 17870

FINDER, ROBERT ANDREW, pharmaceutical company executive; b. Washington, Mo., Apr. 27, 1947; s. Richard Joseph and Jeanette Mary (Graser) F.; m. Sheryl Jean Johnson, Feb. 6, 1971. B in Chem. Engring., U. Detroit, 1970. Process engr. Monsanto-J.F. Queeny Plant, St. Louis, 1970-71, prodn. supr., 1975-79, project mgr., 1980-81; engring. supt. Monsanto-Trenton (Mich.) Plant, 1981-82; mng. dir. Monsanto Chems. Thailand, Ltd., Bangkok, 1982-85, dir., 1985-89, 1985-89; chmn. bd., mng. dir. Rhone-Poulenc Thai Industries Ltd., Bangpoo Samutprakarn, Thailand, 1989-91; dir. mfg. Rhone-Poulenc Inc., Princeton, N.J., 1992-93; v.p. mfg. and process tech. Ecogen, Inc., Langhorne, Pa., 1993-95; v.p. ops. Purepac Pharm. (Faulding, Inc.), Elizabeth, N.J., 1993—; mem. pres's. cabinet U. Detroit, 1988—. Life mem. World Wild Life Fund, Bangkok, 1988—. Lt. U.S. Army, 1971-74. Mem. AIChE, Am. Philatelic Soc., Bangkok Sports Club. Office: Purepac Pharm (Faulding Inc) 200 Elmora Ave Ste 2 Elizabeth NJ 07202-1191

FINDLAY, GLEN MARSHALL, agrologist; b. Shoal Lake, Man., Can., July 15, 1940; s. Marshall Fredrick and Verna Bernice (Cochrane) F.; m. Katherine Elizabeth Kennedy, Oct. 7, 1957; children: Carole, Keith, Gary, Jill. BS with honors, U. Man., Winnipeg, 1963, MS, 1964; PhD, U. Ill., 1968. Post doctoral fellow Nat. Rsch. Coun., Ottawa, Ont., Can., 1968-70; assoc. prof. agrology U. Man., Winnipeg, 1970-77; mem. for Virden Man. Legis. Assembly, 1986-90, mem. for Springfield, 1990—; min. agr. Man. Legis. Assembly, Winnipeg, 1988-93, min. highways and transp., 1993—; pres. Edgehill Farms Ltd., Shoal Lake, 1977—; bd. dirs. KAP; cons. Herbicide Complaint Com., Man., 1984-86. Coach ringette, baseball, soccer, minor and sr. hockey, Ill., Man., 1965-84; founding mem. Shoal Lake Rink Complex Com., 1981-84. Fellow NAS; mem. Man. Inst. Agrologists, Can. Grains Coun., Shoal Lake Agrl. Soc. (pres. 1983-84). Progressive Conservative. Mem. United Ch. Avocations: hockey, curling, family activities, writing. Home: PO Box 429, Shoal Lake, MB Canada R0J 1Z0 Office: Man Legis Assembly, Legislature Bldg, Winnipeg, MB Canada R3C 0V8

FINDLAY, MICHAEL ALISTAIR, auction house executive, poet; b. Innellan, Scotland, May 13, 1945; came to U.S., 1964; s. Robert John Findlay and Mary Beatrice (Duffy) Collins; m. Naomi Sims, Aug. 4, 1973 (div. Jan. 1990); 1 child, John P. BA, York U., Toronto, Ont., Can., 1963. V.p., dir. exhbns. Richard L. Feigen and Co., Ltd., N.Y.C., L.A., Chgo., 1964-70; founder, owner, dir. J.H. Duffy and Sons, Ltd., N.Y.C., 1970-77; dir. William Beadleston Gallery, N.Y.C., 1977-84; sr. v.p., sr. dir. Christie, Manson and Woods, N.Y.C., 1984-94, sr. dir., 1994-97, internat. dir., 1997—; lectr. Moore Coll. Art, Phila., 1970-80; find arts advisor N.Y.C. Parks Dept., 1979-84; mem. art adv. panel GSA, N.Y.C., 1985; keynote spkr. Oxford U. Alumnae Assn., N.Y.C., Rotary Clubs Internat., Taipei, Taiwan, Credit Suisse, Singapore, Young Pres.'s Orgn., N.Y.C., 1993-96; sr. faculty Christie's Edn., 1994—; bd. dirs. Christie's Internat. Contbr. poetry and articles on art criticism to Arts, Artnews, mags. Bd. dirs. Peacemaker Found., Inc., Santa Fe, 1975—, Lacoste Sch. Arts, Vaucluse, France; hon. sec., v.p. for grants Brit. Sch. and Univs. Found., Inc., N.Y.C., 1975-85, bd. dirs., 1985—; trustee Parrish Mus., Southampton, N.Y., 1993—; mem. adv. coun. Shanghai Mus., adv. coun. for Warren Arts, Shanghai Mus. China, 1996. Mem. Amnesty Internat. Roman Catholic. Office: Christies Internat 20 Rockefeller Ctr New York NY 10019

FINDLEY, DELPHA YODER, retired public health nurse; b. Falls City, Nebr., Mar. 6, 1930; d. Ralph A. and Marguerite (Prior) Brackhahn; m. James E. Findley, Jan. 30, 1988; children: Kimberly Yoder Goff, Steven Amos Yoder. Diploma, Mo. Meth. Sch. Nursing, St. Joseph, 1950. RN, Nebr., Mo. Missionary sch. nurse and tchr. Meth. Bd. Missions, Iquique, Chile, 1957-61; dir. nurses Northview Care Center Nursing Home, Falls City, 1973-75; dir. nurses, asst. adminstr. Community Hosp. Inc., Falls City, 1975-88; pub. health nurse Clinton County Health Dept., Plattsburg, Mo., 1988-91; ret., 1991. Recipient Dist. V Nursing Leadership award Nebr. Orgn. Nurse Execs., 1986. Home: 8485 SE Highway 33 Osborn MO 64474-9148

FINDLEY, DON AARON, manufacturing company executive; b. Gadsden, Ala., June 11, 1926; s. Royal Guy and Hattie Elizabeth (Walden) F.; m. Mary Elizabeth Abernathy, Oct. 22, 1947; children—Elizabeth Jane Findley Dever, David Walden. B.S., Auburn U., 1950. Acct. Buckeye Cellulose Corp. Augusta, Ga., 1950-51; acct. Tenn. Eastman Co., Kingsport, 1951-59, gen. supr. standard cost and analysis dept., 1959-64, gen. mgmt. staff, 1964-67, asst. comptroller, 1971-73, comptroller, 1975-79, v.p. fin. and adminstrn., 1979-88; mng. dir. Ectona Fibres Ltd., Cumberland, Eng., 1967-71; asst. comptroller Eastman Chem. Products, Eastman Chem. Internat. Ltd., Kingsport, 1971-73, comptroller, 1975-79, v.p. fin. and adminstrn., 1979-88; asst. comptroller Eastman Chem. Internat. Co., Kingsport, 1971-73, comptroller, 1975-79; comptroller Holston Def. Corp.; asst. v.p. Ark. Eastman Co., Carolina Eastman Co., Tex. Eastman Co.; dir. 1st Am. Nat. Bank, Kingsport. Bd. dirs. Holston Valley Hosp. and Med. Ctr., Kingsport, 1978-90, treas., 1978-83; dir. United Way of Kingsport, 1994-97. Recipient Achievment award Ala. Soc. C.P.A.s, 1950, Outstanding Acctg. Alumnus award Auburn U., 1981. Fellow Inst. Dirs. (U.K.); mem. Nat. Assn. Accts. (pres. East Tenn. chpt. 1963-64), Tenn. Mfrs. and Taxpayers Assn. (bd. dirs. 1978-86), Delta Sigma Pi, Phi Kappa Phi, Beta Alpha Psi, Greater Kingsport C. of C. (bd. dirs. 1975-77). Republican. Methodist. Club: Ridgefields Country (Kingsport) (bd. dirs. 1984-86). Avocations: photography; coin collecting; gardening; golfing. Home: 524 Lakewood Rd Kingsport TN 37660-3420

FINDLEY, JOHN SIDNEY, dentist; b. Bryan, Tex., Oct. 3, 1942; s. Sidney Albert and Leila Mae (Reading) F.; m. Patricia Ann Reep, June 10, 1967 (div. 1977); children: John Brett, Sidney Alan; m. 2nd Judith Ann Smith, May 22, 1981. Student USAF Acad., 1961-62, N. Tex. State U., 1963-65; DDS, Baylor U. Coll. Dentistry, 1970, Pvt. practice , Plano, Tex., 1970—; bd. dirs. Fin. Svcs. Inc. Contbr. articles to profl. jours. Formerly bd. dirs. Plano YMCA, United Way of Plano, Park Bd. City of Plano, Charter Rev. Commn. City of Plano; pres. Colleagues of the Plano Police, City of Plano; chmn. advancement com. North Trail Dist. Boy Scouts Am.; campaign chmn. Plano YMCA Fund Dr., 1978; councilman City of Cross Rds., Tex., 1988-89, mayor, 1992-94; chmn. bd. trustees Oak Grove United Meth. Ch.; gen. chmn. Dallas Midwinter Dental Clinic. Recipient Cert. of Recognition Am. Acad. Dental Radiology, 1970; Paul Harris fellow Rotary Internat., 1979. Fellow Am. Coll. of Dentists, Internat. Coll. Dentists; mem. ADA, Tex. Dental Assn. (pres. elect, 1996, pres. 1997-98, chmn. coun. govt. affairs, Pres. award 1994, 95), Dallas County Dental Soc. (bd. dirs., editor DDS News, gen. chmn. Dallas Mid-winter Dental Clinic 1992, pres.-elect 1992-93, pres. 1994, dentist of yr. 1995), Acad. Gen. Dentistry, Rotary (Plano, bd. dirs., pres. 1977-78). Methodist. Home: 3800 S Potter Shop Rd Aubrey TX 76227-2587 Office: 1410 14th St Plano TX 75074-6359

FINDLEY, MILLA JEAN, nutritionist; b. Dallas, Aug. 14, 1934; d. Houston Henry and Juanita Imogene (Lisenbe) Shaw; m. Jack Stacy, may 29, 1952; children: Jere, David. Diploma, Rutherford Bus. Sch., Dallas, 1959; student, Mountain View C.C., El Centro C.C., Cedar Valley C.C. File clk. Texaco Oil Co., Dallas, 1952-53; sales assoc. Toys R Us and Sears, Dallas, 1970s; nutrition specialist Cedar Hill Ind. Sch. Dist., Tex., 1983-87, Duncanville Ind. Sch. Dist., Tex., 1996—. Active cradle roll Cedar Hill Ch. of Christ, 1996. Recipient nutrition award Tex. Sch. Food Svcs. Assocs., Lewisville Ind. Sch. Dist., 1987. Mem. NAFE, Assn. Tex. Profl. Educators. Avocations: foods, grandchildren, church, parks, books. Home: 510 Meadow Ridge Dr Cedar Hill TX 75104-1977

FINDLEY, PAUL, former congressman, author, educator; b. Jacksonville, Ill., June 23, 1921; s. Joseph S. and Florence Mary (Nichols) F.; m. Lucille Gemme; children: Craig Jon, Diane Lillian. AB, Ill. Coll., 1943, LLD, 1972; LHD (hon.), Lindenwood Coll., 1969, Lincoln U., 1988, MacMurray Coll., 1997; LLD, Sana'a U., Yemen, 1997. Mem. 87th-97th Congresses from 20th Ill. dist., mem. Fgn. Affairs com., mem. Agr. com.; chmn. factfinding mission to Paris, 1965; chmn. Rep. NATO Task Force, 1965-68; chmn. com. to investigate internat. problems caused by agrl. support policies Ditchley (Eng.) Conf., 1973; del. N. Atlantic Assembly, 1965-70, 72-79, Munich Conf. German Rels., 1969-71; Ditchley Conf. Atlantic Trade, 1967, European Parliament, 1974-76; mem. 7th Congl. Del. to People's Republic China, 1975; chmn. Ill. Trade Mission to, USSR, 1972, People's Republic of China, 1978; mem. internat. food and agrl. devel. bd. AID, 1983-94; vis. prof. MacMurray Coll., 1994—. Author: Abraham Lincoln: The Crucible of Congress, The Federal Farm Fable, They Dare to Speak Out: People and Institutions Confront Israel's Lobby, Deliberate Deceptions: Facing the Facts About the U.S.-Israel Relationships; contbr. numerous articles on fgn. policy and agr. to periodicals. Chmn. Human Rels. Com., Jacksonville; trustee emeritus Ill. Coll.; lectr. leadership program UN Leadership Acad., Amman, Jordan, 1987-88; chmn. Coun. for the Nat. Interest, 1989—. Served to lt. (j.g.) USNR, WWII. Named laureate Lincoln Acad., 1980; decorated Grand Cross Order of Merit Fed. Republic of Ger.; recipient Outstanding Svc. to Agr. citation So. Ill. U., Kefauver award for promoting Fedn. of Atlantic Nations; Hon. Am. Farmer degree FFA, Outstanding Achievmeent award FFA Alumni Assn., citation Nat. Assn. State Univs. and Lnd-Grant Colls., EAFORD Humanitarian award, 1986, Alex Odeh Human Rights award Am. Arab Anti-Discrimination Com., 1992, Disting. Svc. award Assn. for Internat. Agr. and Rural Development, 1995. Mem. Assn. to Unite Democracies (bd. dirs.), Am. Legion, Phi Beta Kappa. Republican. Presbyterian. Home and Office: 1040 W College Ave Jacksonville IL 62650-2306

FINDLEY, TROY R., state legislator, bank officer; b. Lawrence, Kans., July 11, 1964; s. Paul Wayne and Virginia Lee (Coffman) F.; m. Jennifer Ann Sharp, Aug. 30, 1997. BS in Polit. Sci., U. Kans., 1990. Asst. mgr. Food Barn, Inc., Overland Park, Kans., 1989-92; county out reach dir. Kans. Dems., Topeka, 1992-95; mem. Kans. Legislature, Topeka, 1995—; customer svc. rep. UMB Bank, Lawrence, 1997—. Bd. dirs. Big Bros./Big Sisters, Lawrence, 1992-93, mem. adv. bd., 1994—; mem. Horizon 2020 Edn. Task Group, Lawrence, 1993; bd. dirs. Prairie Renaissance, Lawrence, 1995—, ARC Douglas County, Lawrence, 1998—. Home: 1316 Crosswind Ct Apt 1 Lawrence KS 66046-5469 Office: Kans Statehouse 300 SW 10th Ave Rm 272W Topeka KS 66612-1504

FINDLEY, WILLIAM NICHOLS, mechanical engineering educator; b. Mankato, Minn., Feb. 12, 1914; s. Joseph Stillwell and Florence Mary

(Nichols) F.; m. Ruth Woolsey, Aug. 31, 1939; 1 dau., Elizabeth Jo. A.B., Ill. Coll., 1936, D.Sc., 1970; B.S.E. in Math. and Mech. Engring, U. Mich., 1937; M.S. (McMullen scholar), Cornell U., 1939. Instr. engring. George Washington U., 1938-39; instr. engring. U. Ill., 1939-42, assoc., 1942-43, asst. prof., 1943-47, assoc. prof., 1947-54; prof. engring. Brown U., 1954-84, prof. engring. emeritus, 1984—; dir. Central Facility for Mech. Testing, 1965-68; mem. sci. adv. council Picatinny Arsenal, Dover, N.J., 1951-62; cons. Lawrence Livermore Lab., 1962-78; lectr. Colloquium on Fatigue, Stockholm, Sweden, 1955, Internat. Union of Theoretical and Applied Mechanics, Cracow, Poland, 1990; Mem. organizing com. Joint Internat. Conf. on Creep, 1963; mem. panels on rapid deformation and on European creep practice. Author: (with J. Lai, K. Onaran) Nonlinear Creep and Relaxation of Viscoelastic Materials, 1976, 2d edit., 1989; cons. editor: Bull. Mech. Engring. Edn; contbr. articles to tech. jours., chpts. in books. Recipient prize for paper Soc. Plastics Engrs., 1949, 50; Office Naval Rsch.-AIAA rsch. scholar in naval structural mechanics, 1978. Fellow ASME (life); mem. ASTM (Charles B. Dudley medal 1945, Richard L. Templin award 1953, 64), Am. Soc. Engring. Edn., Acad. Mechanics, Soc. Exptl. Stress Analysis, Soc. Rheology, Atlantic Union Com., R.I. Watercolor Soc., Sigma Xi, Phi Kappa Phi, Tau Beta Pi. Home: 35 Mayfair Dr Rumford RI 02916-1827

FINDORFF, ROBERT LEWIS, retired air filtration equipment company executive; b. Mpls., Apr. 15, 1929; s. Hugo Clarence and Elfriede Louise (Schade) F.; m. Jocelyn J. Curtis, June 20, 1953; children—Robert H., Jean, Paul, Laura, Mary, Karl, John. BBA, U. Minn., 1952, MBA, 1956; JD magna cum laude, William Mitchell Coll. Law, 1962. Bar: Minn. bar 1962. Trust accounting mgr. No. Trust Co., Chgo., 1953-54; personnel mgr. purchasing dir. Donaldson Co., Inc., Mpls., 1955-62; plant mgr., v.p. mfg., v.p., gen. mgr. then sr. v.p. Donaldson Co., Inc., 1965-94; assoc. firm Oppenheimer, Hodgeson, Brown, Wolf & Leach, St. Paul, 1962-64; instr. property law William Mitchell Coll. Law, 1981-89. Trustee William Mitchell Coll. Law, 1981-89. Served with AUS, 1947-48; USAF, 1962-68. Recipient Minn. State Bar Scholarship award 1962. Mem. Svc. Corp. Ret. Execs. Roman Catholic. Home: 6812 Paiute Dr Minneapolis MN 55439-1033

FINE, ANNE, author; b. Leicester, Eng., Dec. 7, 1947; d. Brian and Eileen Mary (Baker) Laker; m. Kit Fine, Aug. 3, 1968 (div. 1991); children: Ione, Cordelia. BA with honors, U. Warwick, Eng., 1968. Tchr. Cardinal Wiseman Secondary Sch., Coventry, U.K., 1968-69; info. officer Oxfam, Oxford, England, 1969-71; tchr. Saughton Prison, Edinburgh, Scotland, 1971-72. Author: (children's fiction) The Summer-House Loon, 1978, The Other Darker Ned, 1979, The Stone Menagerie, 1980, Round Behind the Ice House, 1981, The Granny Project, 1983, Scaredy-Cat, 1984, Anneli the Art Hater, 1986, Madame Doubtfire, 1987, Crummy Mummy an Me, 1987, A Pack of Liars, 1988, Goggle-Eyes, 1989, Bill's New Frock, 1989, The Book of the Banshee, 1991, Flour Babies, 1992, Step By Wicked Step, 1995, The Tulip Touch, 1996, Charm School, 1999, others; (adult fiction) The Killjoy, 1986, Taking the Devil's Advice, 1990, In Cold Domain, 1994, Telling Liddy, 1998. Recipient children's lit. award The Guardian, 1990, Carnegie medal Brit. Libr. Assn., 1990, 93, Whitbread children's novel award, 1993, 96; named Children's Author of Yr., Brit. Book Awards, 1990, 93. Avocations: reading, walking. Office: David Higham Assocs, 5-8 Lower John St Golden Sq, London W1R 4HA, England

FINE, ARTHUR I., philosopher; b. Lowell, Mass., Nov. 11, 1937; s. David Fine and Rae (Silverberg) Mintz; m. Helene S. Feldberg, June 16, 1957 (div. May 1980); children: Dana S., Sharon D.; m. Micky Forbes, July 11, 1980. Student, Harvard U., 1955-56; BS, U. Chgo., 1958; MS, Ill. Inst. Tech., 1960; PhD, U. Chgo., 1963. Asst. prof. math and philosophy Ill. Inst. Tech., Chgo., 1961-63; asst. prof. philosophy U. Ill., Urbana, 1963-65; assoc. prof. philosophy Cornell U., Ithaca, N.Y., 1967-71, prof. philosophy, 1971-72; prof. philosophy U. Ill., Chgo., 1972-82; prof. philosophy Northwestern U., Evanston, Ill., 1982-85, John Evans prof. philosophy, 1985—; mem. nat. com. Internat. Union History and Philosophy of Sci. Nat. Acad. Sci., 1973-77; mem. adv. panel History and Philosophy of Sci. Nat. Sci. Found., 1975-77, 87-88, 92-93. Author: The Shaky Game, 1986, 2d edit., 1996; co-editor: Philosophical Review, 1969-71; editor: (with others) PSA: 1986, 88, 90, vols. I and II; subject editor: Philosophy of Science Routledge Encyclopedia of Philosophy, 1993-98; contbr. articles to profl. jours. NSF fellow, 1966-67; NSF grantee 1968, 73, 78, 80, 89; sr. fellow NEH, 1974-75; Guggenheim fellow, 1982-83; fellow Ctr. Advanced Study in Behavioral Scis. Stanford, 1985-86; vis. fellow Dibner Inst., MIT, 1996. Mem. Philosophy of Sci. Assn. (pres. 1986-88), Am. Philos. Assn. (ctrl. divsn. pres. 1997-98). Office: Northwestern U Grad Sch-Philosophy Dept Evanston IL 60208

FINE, A(RTHUR) KENNETH, lawyer; b. N.Y.C., June 29, 1937; s. Aaron Harry and Rose (Levin) F.; m. Ellen Marie Jensen, July 11, 1964; children: Craig Jensen, Ricki-Barie, Desiree-Ellen. AB, Hunter Coll., 1959; JD, Columbia U., 1963; CLU, Coll. Ins., 1973; diploma, Command and Gen. Staff Coll., 1978. Bar: N.Y. 1974; registered rep. and limited prin. Nat. Assn. Securities Dealers, Inc. Joined U.S. Army N.G., 1955, advanced through grades to maj., 1973, ret., 1980; cons. U.S. Life Ins. Co., N.Y.C., 1970-74, atty., 1975-78, asst. gen. counsel, 1978; asst. counsel USLIFE Corp., N.Y.C., 1978-79, assoc. counsel, 1979-93; v.p., counsel Western Res. Life Assurance Co. Ohio, Clearwater, Fla. Mem. ABA, Am. Soc. CLU and ChFC (Suncoast chpt.), N.Y. State Bar Assn., NG Assn. U.S., Militia Assn. N.Y. (chmn. vet. officers com. 1981-90), Am. Legion (7th regt. post), Ret. Officers Club St. Petersburg, Fla. Republican. Lutheran. Home: 5953 36th Ave N Saint Petersburg FL 33710-1835 Office: Western Res Life Assurance Co of Ohio PO Box 5068 Clearwater FL 33758-5068

FINE, AUBREY HOWARD, educator; b. Montreal, Que., Can., May 15, 1955; s. Morris and Fanny Betty (Shuster) F.; m. Nya Marie Daniels, Aug. 27, 1978; children: Sean David, Corey Ryan. BA, Concordia U., Montreal, 1977; MEd, U. South Ala., 1978; EdD, U. Cin., 1982. lic. psychologist, Calif.; cert. sch. psychologist. Project dir., cons. Que. Assn. for Children with Learning Disabilities, Laval, Que., Can., 1974-77; dir. learning disability and aging program Mobile (Ala.) Jewish Ctr., 1977-78; dir. normalization project Cin. Ctr. for Developmental Disabilities, 1980-82; psychologist Our Lady of Lourdes, Cin., 1981-82; lic. psychologist/dir. Children's Diagnostic Svcs., Claremont, Calif., 1986—; prof. Calif. State Poly. U., Pomona, 1982—; cons. psychologist Charter Oak Schs., Covina, Calif., 1989-93. Author: Total Sports Experience for Kids, 1997, Therapeutic Recreation and Exceptional Children, 1996, Behavior Management and Parenting Children, 1989; assoc. cons. editor Jour. Developmental Disabilities, 1993—; cons. editor Mental Retardation, 1988—; editor Living and Learning with Attention Deficit Disorder, 1992—. Profl. advisor San Gabriel Valley Assn. for Children with Attention Deficit Disorder, 1992-97, Pomona Valley Learning Disability Assn., 1985—; bd. dirs. Temple Sholom, Ontario, 1988-92, San Gabriel Valley Regional Ctr. for Developmental Disabilities, Covina, 1989-91. Named Educator of the Yr., Learning Disability Assn. of Calif., 1989. Fellow Am. Assn. Mental Retardation (pres. region II 1992-94, Outstanding Leadership award 1994), Prescribing Psychologist Register (diplomate, bd. cert.); mem. APA, Acad. on Mental Retardation (mem.-at-large of bd. 1988-97). Avocations: racquetball, playing saxaphone, hockey, sports collecting. Office: Calif State Poly Univ 3801 W Temple Ave Pomona CA 91768-2557

FINE, BARRY KENNETH, lawyer; b. N.Y.C., May 15, 1938; s. Harry Harold and Ann (Elkind) F.; m. Rho Joy Stengel, Sept. 3, 1965; children: Scott Jefferson, Jill Ashley. BS, SUNY Empire State Coll., 1986; JD, Touro Coll., 1990. Jr. civil engr. N.Y.C. Transit Authority, 1957-58; pres. Active Industries (formerl Active Steel Drum Co.), L.I., N.Y., 1958-93; founder, pres. Glass Tint Svcs., Inc., L.I., N.Y., 1985-93; founding ptnr. Fine Hummel, Huntington, N.Y., 1990—. Patentee in field. Project bus. cons. Queens Jr. Achievement, Queens, N.Y., 1984-88. With USAR, 1957-63. Mem. ABA, Suffolk County Bar Assn. (former co-chair Environ. law com., lectr., environ. law writer Suffolk Lawyer), Nassau County Bar Assn., N.Y. State Bar Assn., Masons (past master). Republican. Jewish. Avocations: boating, cabinetmaking, gardening. Office: Fine Hummel PC 7 High St Huntington NY 11743-3417

FINE, CHARLES LEON, lawyer; b. Waukegan, Ill., Jan. 30, 1932; s. David M. and Henrietta (Goodman) F.; m. Penny J. Haines, Aug. 30, 1958; children: Karen L., Andrew H. BS, U. Wis., 1955; LLB, JD, Am. U., 1961. Bar: Mich. 1962, Ariz. 1981, U.S. Supreme Ct. 1971. Newscaster, news editor WKOW Radio and TV, Madison, Wis., 1953-58; editor, writer U.S. Bur. Pub. Roads, Washington, 1958-61; trial, staff atty. U.S. NLRB, Washington, Detroit, 1961-63; atty, assoc. Griffith & Griffith law firm, Detroit, 1963-69; atty., ptnr. Clark, Hardy, Lewis & Fine, Detroit, Birminghan, 1969-81; assoc. prof. law U. Detroit Sch. Law, 1976-80; ptnr. O'Connor, Cavanagh, et al, Phoenix, 1981-96, Streich Lang, 1996—; cons. Met. Detoit Bur. Sch. Studies, 1970-80, Employer's Assn. Detroit, 1970-80. Assoc. editor Washington Coll. Law Rev., 1960; co-editor, author: Ariz. Employment Law Handbook, 1994; contbr. articles to legal jours. and chpts. to books. mem. Ariz. Supreme Ct. Commn. on Minorities, 1996—; pres. Meadowlake Homeowners Assn., Birmingham, Mich., 1972-73; bd. dirs. Sch. Law Inst., Detroit, 1976-77; atty., advisor Gov.'s Office, Mich., 1979-80; cons. Cmty. Legal Svcs., Phoenix, 1986—. 1st lt. U.S. Army, 1955-57. Recipient Best Advocate award Nat. Moot Ct. Competition, Washington, 1960, Order of Barristers award Nat. Honor Soc., 1978; scholarship fund in his name U. Detroit Sch. of Law, 1979. Fellow Coll. Labor and Employment Lawyers; mem. Ariz. Bar Assn., Mich. Bar Assn., Am. Arbitration Assn. (arbitrator, employment arbitration panelist 1995—), Am. Employment Law Coun., Ariz. Insl. Rels. Assn. Avocations: badminton, hiking, swimming, reading. Home: 9041 N 33rd Way Phoenix AZ 85028-4968 Office: Streich Lang 2 N Central Ave Fl 2 Phoenix AZ 85004-2391

FINE, DEBORAH JANE, researcher, author; b. Boston, May 16, 1942; d. Irving Horace and Muriel (Baer) F. BA, UCLA, 1965; MLS, Simmons Coll., 1967. Researcher Paramount Studios, Hollywood, Calif., 1968-69, Zoetrope Studios, L.A., 1972-77; dir. rsch. Lucasfilm Ltd., San Rafael, Calif., 1978-95; freelance work, 1995—. Researcher (film) Godfather, Part II, 1974, Apocalypse Now, 1979, More American Graffiti, 1979, Return of The Jedi, 1983, Raiders of the Lost Ark, 1981, Indiana Jones and the Temple of Doom, 1984, Willow, 1987, Tucker, 1988, Indiana Jones and the Lost Crusade, 1989, (TV series) The Young Indiana Jones Chronicles, 1992—, Sphere, 1996; producer's asst. (film) The Black Stallion, 1979; author: SW Chronicles, 1996. Mem. Acad. Motion Picture Arts and Sci.

FINE, HOWARD ALAN, travel industry executive; b. N.Y.C., Dec. 21, 1941; s. William and Shirley (German) F.; m. Ingvelde Rathkamp, Dec. 20, 1970. BS, NYU, 1961, MBA, 1964. Internat. sales mgr. Pfaff, A.G., Fed. Republic of West Germany, 1964-67; regional sales dir. Brit. Transport Hotels, London, Eng., 1967-70; dir. internat. mktg. Sonesta Internat. Hotels, N.Y.C., 1970-71; dir. Pacific mktg. Trusthouse Forte Hotels, Los Angeles, 1971-74; dir. Atlantic area and Latin Am. mktg. Trusthouse Forte Hotels, N.Y.C, 1974-75, v.p. sales and mktg., 1975-78, exec. v.p., 1978-81; pres. Norwegian Am. Cruise Line, N.Y.C, 1981-83; pres., chief exec. officer Costa Cruise Line, Miami, Fla., 1983-87; chmn., chief exec. officer Tourism Devel. Internat., Miami, 1987—; bd. dirs. Bahamas Devel. Found., Nassau, Traveling Times, Los Angeles; speaker, presenter Young Pres.'s Orgn, World Pres.'s Orgn., 1987—. Contbr. articles to profl. jours. Mem. mayors adv. bd. City of Los Angeles, 1972-74; mem. senatorial commn. Rep. Senatorial Inner Circle, Washington, 1984—, Presdl. task force to Pres. Bush, 1989—; bd. dirs. Calif. Dept. Agr. Wine Bd., 1974-75, Ptnrs. for Liveable Places, Washington, 1978-83, NYU Ctr. for Study of Foodservice, 1978-83, Fla. Crime Prevention Commn., 1984—, Boys Town of Italy, 1986—. Served to capt. USAR, 1961-66. Named Hon. Order Ky. Cols., 1986; named Man of Yr. Am. Jaycees, 1983, Man of Yr. Internat. Hotel Industry, 1980; recipient Disting. Marker of Yr. Sales and Mktg. Mgmt. Mag., 1979, Christopher Columbus award Nat. Columbus Day Com., 1986, Spirit of Life Humanitarian award City of Hope, 1987; numerous hotel and travel industry awards and citations from fgn. govts., 1972-87. Fellow Inst. Cert. Travel Agts.; mem. Young Pres.'s Orgn. (chmn. 1978—), World Pres.'s Orgn., Hotelier of the World Com. (bd. dirs. 1978—), Italian C. of C. (bd. dirs. 1975—), Brit. C. of C. (bd. dirs. 1975—), Norwegian C. of C. (bd. dirs. 1975—), South African C. of C. (bd. dirs. 1975—), Greater Ft. Lauderdale C. of C. (bd. govs. 1986—), NYU Alumni Fedn., Sigma Alpha Mu, NYU Club (N.Y.C.), 110 Tower Club (bd. dirs. 1987—), Harbor Beach Club (bd. dirs. 1987—). Clubs: NYU (N.Y.C.); 110 Tower (bd. dirs. 1987—), Harbor Beach (Ft. Lauderdale) (bd. dirs. 1987—). Avocations: boating, travel, gardening, photography, flying. Office: Tourism Devel Internat PO Box 22323 Fort Lauderdale FL 33335-2323

FINE, J. DAVID, lawyer; b. N.Y.C., Jan. 30, 1951; s. Phillip and Irma (Miller) F.; m. Judith Lynn McMillan, June 6, 1984. BSFS, Georgetown U., 1970; LLB, McGill U., Montreal, Que., 1973, BCL, 1974; LLM, Columbia U., 1978. Bar: We. Australia, 1987, High Ct. Australia, 1987, Oreg., 1992, U.S. Dist. Ct. Oreg., 1994. Asst. prof. U. Melbourne, Australia, 1974-76; clin. instr. Osgoode Hall Law Sch., Toronto, Ont., Can., 1976-77; Jervey fellow comp. law Columbia U., N.Y.C., 1977-79; assoc. prof. Loyola U., New Orleans, 1979-84, Macquarie U., Sydney, Australia, 1984-86; prof. U. Western Australia, Perth, 1986-91; pvt. practice Ashland, Oreg., 1992—; traffic safety commr., City of Ashland, 1997-99. contbr. articles to profl. jours. City councilman City of Ashland, 1999—. Mem. Internat. Trademark Assn., So. Oreg. Internat. Trade Coun. (charter mem.), Oreg. State Bar Assn. (continuing legal edn. com. 1995-98), Jackson County Bar Assn. (sec. 1999), Ashland Gun Club. Jewish. Avocations: reading, shooting, cooking, fly fishing. Home: 735 Frances Lane Ashland OR 97520-0166 Office: 50 3rd St PO Box 66 Ashland OR 97520-0166

FINE, J(AMES) ALLEN, insurance company executive; b. Albemarle, N.C., May 2, 1934; s. Samuel Lee and Ocie (Loflin) F.; m. Marie Nan Morris, Sept. 1, 1957 (dec. Apr. 1989); children: James A(llen), William Morris. Student Pfeiffer Coll., 1957-58; BS, U. N.C., 1961, MBA, 1965. Sr. accountant Haskins & Sells, CPAs Charlotte, N.C., 1961-62, Watson, Penry, & Morgan, Asheboro, N.C., 1962-64; instr. U. N.C., Chapel Hill, 1964-65; asst. prof. Pfeiffer Coll., Misenheimer, N.C., 1965-66; treas., v.p. adminstrn. Nat. Lab. for Higher Edn. (formerly Regional Edn. Lab. Carolinas and Va.), Durham, N.C., 1966-72; organizer, CEO, treas., dir. Investors Title Ins. Co., Inc., Chapel Hill, 1972—; CEO, treas., dir. Investors Title Ins. Co., Inc., Columbia, S.C., 1973—; pres., dir. Investors Title Co., Inc., Chapel Hill, 1976—; developer Carolina Forest Subdiv., Chapel Hill, 1970-78, Springhill Forest subdiv., Chapel Hill, 1977-80, Stoneycreek subdiv., 1978—; lectr. accounting U. N.C., Chapel Hill, 1967-70. Area officer ann. alumni giving U. N.C., Chapel Hill, 1968-69, 71-73, 75—. With USN, 1953-57. Recipient Haskins & Sells Found. award for excellence in accounting, 1961; N.C. Assn. CPAs award for most outstanding accounting student U. N.C., 1961. Mem. Am. Inst. CPA's, N.C. Assn. CPAs, Am. Accounting Assn., Am. Land Title Assn. (research com. 1983—, membership com. 1984-85, exec. com. underwriters sect. 1986, recruitment, retention subcom., 1985), Nat. Assn. Ins. Commrs. (liaison com. 1987-88, 1994—), U. N.C. Nat. Devel. Com. 1994—, CEDAR Bus. Mgrs. (chmn. nat. exec. com. 1971), Phi Beta Kappa, Beta Gamma Sigma (treas. 1961). Home: 112 Carolina First Chapel Hill NC 27516-9033 Office: 121 N Columbia St Chapel Hill NC 27514-3502

FINE, JAMES STEPHEN, physician; b. St. Paul, June 14, 1946; s. Ralph Irving and Beverlee Lois (Rockler) F.; m. Meredith Ann Blehert, June 20, 1970; children: Zachary, Esther, Gabriel. BA in Math., U. Minn., 1968, MD, 1972, MS in Biometry, Health Info. Systems, 1977. Intern in medicine St. Paul-Ramsey Hosp., 1972-73; residency U. Minn., Mpls., 1973-77; assoc. prof., dir. info. and specimen processing div. U. Wash. Hosp., Seattle, 1977-94, chmn. lab. medicine, 1994—. Mem. Am. Assn. Clin. Chemistry, Acad. Clin. Lab. Physicians and Scientists, Computer Soc. of IEEE, Am. Med. Informatics Assn., Wash. State Med. Assn., King County Med. Soc. Office: U Wash Hosp Box 357110 1959 NE Pacific Ave NW 120 Seattle WA 98195

FINE, MARJORIE LYNN, lawyer; b. Bklyn., Aug. 14, 1950; d. Percy and Sylvia (Bernstein) F.; m. John Kent Markley, May 6, 1979; children: Jessica Paige Markley, Laura Anne Markley. BA, Smith Coll., 1972; JD, U. Calif., 1977. Bar: Calif. 1977. Assoc. to ptnr. Donahue Gallagher Woods & Woods, Oakland, Calif., 1977-87; sr. counsel Bank of Am., San Francisco, 1987-89; assoc., gen. counsel Shaklee Corp., San Francisco, 1989-90; gen. counsel, v.p. Shaklee U.S., Inc., San Francisco, 1990-94, Shaklee U.S., Shaklee Technica, 1995-99, Shaklee U.S., Shaklee Technica, and YS Pharma, Inc., 1999—; judge pro tem Oakland Piedmont Emeryville Mcpl. Ct., 1982-89; fee arbitrator Alameda Co. Bar Assn., 1980-87. Mem. ABA, Calif. Bar Assn., Calif. Employment Law Coun. (bd. dirs. 1993—). Jewish. Office: Shaklee Corp 444 Market St Ste 3400 San Francisco CA 94111-5334

FINE, MICHAEL JOSEPH, publishing company executive; b. N.Y.C., Jan. 30, 1937; s. William and Rosa F.; m. Marlene Rosen, Apr. 4, 1959; children: Anton Adeus, Kaethe Elizabeth. Student, U. Fla., 1953-54; BA, Bklyn. Coll., 1957; postgrad., State U. Iowa, 1959-60. Propr. Paper Place Bookstore, Iowa City, 1960-63; v.p. Paperback Affiliates, Inc., N.Y.C., 1963-74; mgr., co-owner The Paperback Forum Bookstore, N.Y.C.; mgr. The Manhattanville Book Forum, Manhattanville Coll., Purchase, N.Y.; asst. to pres. Simon & Schuster, Inc., N.Y.C., 1964-65; v.p. Assoc. Ednl. Svcs. Simon & Schuster, Inc., 1966; assoc. dir. Washington Square Press Simon & Schuster, Inc., N.Y.C., 1967-69, mem. editorial bd., 1968; founder, pub. trade paperback div. Simon & Schuster Clarion Books, N.Y.C., 1967-69; founder, exec. v.p. Bookthrift, Inc., 1971-78; pres. Bookthrift, Inc. div. Simon & Schuster, 1978-81; sr. v.p., exec. com. mem. Ingram Book Co., Nashville, 1981-83; pres., chief exec. officer Ingram Ventures, Inc., N.Y.C., 1981-83; chief exec. officer Feeling Fine Programs, Inc., 1984-86; co-founder, pres. Lynx Communications, Inc., N.Y.C., 1987-90; founder, pres. Fine Creative Media, Inc., N.Y.C., 1991—; pub. MJF Books. Contbr. articles to profl. jours. Past chmn. bd. dirs. St. Michaels Montessori Sch., N.Y.C.; bd. dirs. Morningside Area Alliance, Inc., 1974-83. Mem. N.Y. Acad. Scis. (mem. publs. com. 1984-88), Nat. Arts Club. Office: Fine Comm MJF Books Two Lincoln Sq 60 W 66th St New York NY 10023-6214 *The older I become the more I am struck by how uniquely independent each of us is, one from the other and, at the same time, how urgently connected we all are, one to each other. To publish is to navigate the time and the space between the two ...*

FINE, MILTON, hotel company executive, lawyer; b. Pitts., May 18, 1926; s. Samuel and Ida (Krimsky) F.; m. Sara Mariam Fogel, June 15, 1952 (div. 1971); children: Carolyn Francis Fine Friedman, Sibyl Ann Fine King, David Jeremy; m. Sheila Dianne Cook, Nov. 24, 1989. BA magna cum laude, U. Pitts., 1949, JD, 1950. Bar: Pa. 1951. Pvt. practice, 1951-55; ptnr. Fine, Perlow & Stone, Pitts., 1955-75; co-chmn. Interstate Hotels Corp., Pitts., 1960-88, chmn., CEO, 1988-96, chmn. bd. dirs., 1996-98; chmn. FCC Hotel Devel. Corp., 1998—; mem. adv. bd. Greenwich St. Capital Ptnrs., Inc., 1996—. Lifetime trustee Carnegie Inst., Pitts., 1983—; chmn. bd. dirs. Carnegie Mus. Art, 1992—: trustee U. Pitts., 1997—; mem. bd. dirs. Warhol Mus., Pitts., 1989—. Recipient Bicentennial Medallion of Distinction, U. Pitts., 1987, Cultural award Pitts. Ctr. for the Arts, 1995. Mem. Pa. Bar Assn., Duquesne Club. Republican. Jewish. Avocations: golf, collecting contemporary art. Office: Interstate Hotels Corp Foster Plz 10 680 Andersen Dr Pittsburgh PA 15220-2700 *With all the unexpected turns in my life, the thing which has been most predictable has been change. What remains constant is the need to be flexible and resilient, the need to take advantage of change rather than being overwhelmed by it, and, most importantly, the need to remain a student throughout one's life.*

FINE, MORRIS EUGENE, materials engineer, educator; b. Jamestown, N.D., Apr. 12, 1918; s. Louis and Sophie (Berrington) F.; m. Mildred Eleanor Glazer, Aug. 13, 1950; children: Susan Elaine, Amy Lynn. B.Metall. Engring. with distinction, U. Minn., 1940, M.S., 1942, Ph.D., 1943. Instr. U. Minn., 1942-43; mem. tech. staff Bell Telephone Labs., Murray Hill, N.J., 1946-54; prof. emeritus Northwestern U., Evanston, Ill., 1954—, prof., chmn. dept. metallurgy Tech. Inst., 1955-57; chmn. dept. materials sci. Northwestern U., 1958-60, prof. and chmn. materials research center, 1960-64, Walter P. Murphy prof. materials sci., 1963-89, tech. inst. prof., 1985-89, dir. Am. Iron and Steel Inst. steel resource ctr., 1986-93, assoc. dean grad. studies and research Tech. Inst., 1973-85, prof. emeritus, 1989, mem. grad. faculty, 1989—; vis. prof. dept. materials sci. Stanford U., 1967-68; JSPS vis. scholar, Japan, 1979; chmn., vis. prof. materials sci. and engring. U. Tex., Austin, 1984-95; assoc. engr. Manhattan Project, U. Chgo. and Los Alamos, N.Mex., WWII; mem. materials adv. bd. NAS, 1963-68; mem. com. geol. and materials scis. NRC, 1979-82; chmn. adv. bd. program on modular methods for tchg. materials Pa. State U., 1973-77; chmn. vis. com. metallurgy and materials Sci. and Materials Rsch. Ctr., Lehigh U., 1965-75; mem. vis. com. Lawrence Berkeley Lab., 1978-81, chmn., 1981, mem. vis. com. Ames Dept. Energy Lab., 1976-80, Materials Rsch. Ctr., Pa. State U., 1988-91, Colo. Sch. Mines, 1991-96; chmn., organizer numerous confs. in field. Author numerous tech. and sci. articles on mech. properties of metals and ceramics, fatigue of metals, phase transformations, high temperature alloys, and other subjects.; author: Introduction to Phase Transformation in Condensed Systems. Recipient Gilbert Speich award Iron and Steel Soc., 1993; named Chicagoan of Year in Sci., 1961. Fellow Am. Phys. Soc., Japan Soc. Metals (hon.), Am. Soc. Metals (chpt. chmn. 1963, Campbell lectr. 1979, chmn. seminar com. 1979, hon. mem. com. 1993-96, gold medal 1986), Metall Soc. of AIME (chmn. inst. metals div. 1966-68, bd. dirs. 1968-71, bd. dirs. inst. 1972-75, mem. Bardeen gold medals com. 1992-96, chmn. 1995-96, Methewson gold medal for rsch. 1981, James Douglas gold medal 1982, Educator award 1993, hon. mem.), Am. Ceramic Soc. (keynote lectr. electronic materials div. 1972); mem. NAE (astronautics space engring. bd. 1973-77, membership com. 1974-79, chmn. 1977-78, mem. membership adv. com. 1991-94), Scripta Met et Mat (Outstanding Paper award 1991), The Metals, Materials, Minerals Soc. (inst. metals lecture and R.F. Mehl gold medal 1996), Sigma Xi, Tau Beta Pi, Alpha Sigma Mu, Sigma Alpha Sigma. Home: 1101 Manor Dr Wilmette IL 60091-1026 Office: Dept Materials Sci and Engring Northwestern U Evanston IL 60208

FINE, PAM, newspaper editor. Mng. editor Mpls. Star Tribune. Office: Star Tribune 425 Portland Ave Minneapolis MN 55488*

FINE, ROGER SETH, pharmaceutical executive, lawyer; b. Bklyn., Sept. 22, 1942; s. Jack F. and Mildred (Perlmutter) F.; m. Rebecca Gold, June 14, 1964; children: David, Adam. BA, Columbia Coll., 1963; LLB, NYU, 1966. Bar: N.Y. 1966, U.S. Dist. Ct. (so. dist.) N.Y. 1967, U.S. Ct. Appeals (2d cir.) 1967. Assoc. Cahill, Gordon & Reindel, N.Y.C., 1966-74; gen. atty. Johnson & Johnson, New Brunswick, N.J., 1974-78; asst. gen. counsel Johnson & Johnson, New Brunswick, 1978-84, assoc. gen. counsel, 1984-91, v.p. adminstrn., mem. exec. com., 1991-95, v.p., gen. counsel, mem. exec. com., 1996—. Mem. ABA. Home: 26 Brook Dr Milltown NJ 08850-1932 Office: Johnson & Johnson 1 Johnson & Johnson Plz New Brunswick NJ 08933*

FINE, SAMUEL, biomedical engineering educator, consultant; b. Baranowiczach, Poland, Jan. 21, 1925; came to U.S., 1950; s. Abraham and Rose (Perlin) F. B.Applied Sci., U. Toronto, 1946, MD, 1957; SM, MIT, 1953. Registered profl. engr., Ont., Can. Intern, E.G. Meyer Hosp., Buffalo, 1957-58; mem. staff rsch. lab. electronics MIT, Cambridge, 1951-53; biomed. engr. NIH, Bethesda, Md., 1958-59; rsch. assoc., assoc. in medicine Brookhaven Nat. Lab., Upton, N.Y., 1959-61; assoc. prof. elec. engring. Northeastern U., Boston, 1961-64; prof. biomed. engring., 1964—, chmn. dept., 1966-88, dir. biomed. engring., 1988—; Klein lectr., 1969; cons. Mass. Dept. Pub. Health, 1966-80; cons. NIH, 1975-85; mem. exptl. cardiovascular scis. study sect. NIH, 1978-81; mem. Z136 com. Am. Nat. Stds. Inst., N.Y., 1972-80; mem. U.S. adv. group tech. com. Internat. Electrotech. Commn., 1973-78; dir. Advanced Tech. Publs., Newton, Mass., 1968-81, Biometrics, Cambridge, 1968-72. Pres. New Eng. chpt. U. Toronto Alumni, 1968; mem. adv. bd. New Eng. Intercollegiate Sailing, Cambridge, 1981-90, Combined Jewish Philanthropies Team, Boston, 1983—; trustee New England Coll. Optometry, 1975-80; cons. Inst. Svcs. Edn., Washington, 1970-75. Served as cadet Royal Can. Elec. and Mech. Engrs., 1945. Grantee NIH, NSF, U.S. Army, U.S. Air Force; recipient Am. Soc. Laser Medicine and Surgery award, 1986. Mem. IEE (program com. N.E. region 1965-66, chmn. engring. in medicine and biology Boston chpt. 1969, prog. com. electro 1993-95), Laser Industry Assn. (founding dir. 1967-71), Soc. Exptl. Pathology, Sigma Xi, Tau Beta Pi, Eta Kappa Nu, Phi Kappa Phi, Zeta Beta Tau (Disting. Service award 1984, faculty advisor). Jewish. Home: 16 Ware St Cambridge MA 02138-4034 Office: Northeastern U 360 Huntington Ave Boston MA 02115-5000

FINE, WILLIAM IRWIN, real estate developer; b. St. Paul, May 26, 1928; s. Adolph and Ida (Cohen) F.; m. Bianca M. Fine, Apr. 10, 1994. BLS, U. Minn., 1949, LLB, 1950. Bar: Minn. 1950, Tex. 1950. Asst. dist. atty. Dallas County, 1950-52; judge adv. gen. USAF, Keesler AFB, Miss., 1952-53; ptnr., founder Fine, Simon & Schneider, Mpls., 1953-69; pres., co-founder Fine Properties Corp., Chgo., 1969-71; mng. gen. ptnr., co-founder Fine Assocs., Mpls., 1972—; co-founder VISTA Sci., Inc., 1991, DYUAR, Inc., 1992; advisor Inst. Tech. U. Minn., Mpls., 1987—. Trustee Sci. Mus. Minn., St. Paul, 1989-94; co-founder/co-chmn. Theoretical Physics Inst. U. Minn.,

1987; charter mem. indsl. liaison com. Materials Rsch. Lab. U. Chgo., 1993-97. Mem. AAAS, Am. Inst. Physics. Office: Fine Assocs 1916 IDS Ctr Minneapolis MN 55402

FINEBERG, HARVEY VERNON, university official, physician, educator; b. Pitts., Sept. 15, 1945; s. Saul and Miriam (Pearl) F.; m. Mary Elizabeth Wilson, May 16, 1975;. A.B., Harvard U., 1967, M.D., 1972, M.P.P., 1972, Ph.D., 1980. Intern Beth Israel Hosp., Boston, 1972-73; asst. prof. Sch. Pub. Health, Harvard U., Boston, 1973-78, assoc. prof., 1978-81, prof., 1981—, dean Sch. Pub. Health, 1984-97; provost Harvard U., Cambridge, Mass., 1997—; physician East Boston Health Ctr., 1974-76, Harvard Street Health Ctr., 1976-84. Co-author: Clinical Decision Analysis, 1980, The Epidemic That Never Was, 1983. Trustee Newton Wellesley Hosp., Mass., 1981-86; study sect. chmn. Nat. Ctr. Health Services Research, Rockville, Md., 1982-85; active Pub. Health Council, Mass., 1976-79; bd. dirs. Am. Found. AIDS Rsch., 1986-97. Jr. fellow Harvard U., 1974-75; Mellon fellow, 1976. Mem. Inst. Medicine, Nat. Acad. Scis., Soc. Med. Decision Making (pres. 1980-81). Jewish. Home: 23 Craigie St Cambridge MA 02138-3403 Office: Harvard U Massachusetts Hall Cambridge MA 02138*

FINEFROCK, JAMES ALAN, editor; b. Bellefontaine, Ohio, May 4, 1947; s. Richard Harvey and Mary Jane (Smith) F.; m. Diane Curtis, 1981; children: Jessica, John. AB, Princeton U., 1969. Reporter, editor San Francisco Examiner, 1972-82, head investigative team, 1982-87, met. editor, 1987-89, opinion editor, 1989-91, editl. pages editor, 1991—. Recipient Silver Gavel, ABA, 1986, 87, Best Story award Investigative Reporters and Editors, 1986, Mark Twain award AP, 1979; fellow Journalists in Europe, Paris, 1974-75. Office: San Francisco Examiner 110 5th St San Francisco CA 94103-2918

FINEGAN, COLE, lawyer; b. Tulsa, Oct. 1, 1956; s. Philip Cole and Margaret (Hudson) F.; m. Robin Fudge, Dec. 29, 1984; children: Jordan Nicole, Ryan Andrew. BA in English, U. Notre Dame, Ind., 1978; JD, Georgetown U., 1987. Legis. asst., adminstrv. asst. Ctrl. Dist.-1st Dist. Okla., Tulsa and Washington, 1978-87; assoc. Brownstein Hyatt Farber & Strickland, Denver, 1987-91, shareholder, 1993—; dir. Office Policy and Initiatives Gov. State of Colo., Denver, 1991-93. Staff mem. The Tax Lawyer, 1984-86. Bd. mem. Greater Denver Corp., 1993-96, State Bd. of Agr., 1997—, I Have A Dream Found.; bd. trustees State Colls. Colo., 1993-97; bd. mem. Auvaria Higher Edn. Commn., 1993-95. Democrat. Roman Catholic. Home: 1934 Forest Pkwy Denver CO 80220-1337 Office: Brownstein Hyatt Farber & Strickland 410 17th St Fl 22 Denver CO 80202-4402

FINEGOLD, MAURICE NATHAN, architect; b. Providence, Sept. 6, 1932; s. Samuel R. and Ruth (Marks) F.; m. Muriel Ann Savitz, Apr. 30, 1964; 1 child by previous marriage, Jordan; children by present marriage: Daniel Warren, Jonathan Eric, Michael Andrew. AB, Harvard Coll., 1954; MArch, Harvard U., 1958. Lic. architect. Mass., Maine, Vt., R.I., Nebr., Minn., Tex., N.J., Ohio, Tenn., Conn., Wis. Prin. Maurice N. Finegold & Assocs., AIA, Architect, Boston, 1964-69; ptnr. Finegold & Bullis, Architects, Boston, 1969-74; prin. Notter Finegold & Alexander, Boston, 1974-92; pres. Finegold Alexander & Assocs., Inc., Boston, 1992—; chair Mass. Bd. of Registration of Architects, Boston, 1989-91. Bd. dirs. Downtown North Assn., Boston, 1990—; mem. design com. New Eng. Holocaust Meml. Com., Boston, 1990; chair presdl. search com. Boston Archtl. Ctr., 199091, 96—, bd. dirs., 1994—, vice chair bd., 1995—; mem. Nat. Trust for Hist. Preservation, League Hist. Am. Theaters, 1990—, Am. Lib. Assn. Sgt. U.S. Army, 1958-64. Fellow AIA (N.E. regional coun., Mass. Hist. Commn award, Gov.'s award, Nat. Honor award, Design award, numerous others), mem. Boston Soc. Architects (chmn. several coms. 1961—), Soc. Coll. and Univ. Planning. Democrat. Jewish. Avocations: sailing, skiing, travel. Office: Finegold Alexander & Assocs Inc 77 N Washington St Boston MA 02114-1908*

FINEGOLD, SYDNEY MARTIN, microbiology educator; b. N.Y.C., Aug. 12, 1921; s. Samuel Joseph and Jennie (Stein) F.; m. Mary Louise Saunders, Feb. 8, 1947 (dec. June 1994); children: Joseph, Patricia, Michael; m. Gloria Weiss, Feb. 18, 1996. A.B., UCLA, 1943; M.D., U. Tex., 1949. Diplomate: Am. Bd. Med. Microbiology (mem. bd. 1979-85), Am. Bd. Internal Medicine. Intern USPHS, Galveston, Tex., 1949-50; fellow in medicine U. Minn. Med. Sch., 1950-52, research fellow, 1951-52; resident medicine Wadsworth Hosp., VA Ctr., Los Angeles, 1953-54; instr. medicine U. Calif. Med. Ctr., Los Angeles, 1955-57, asst. clin. prof., 1957-59, asst. prof., 1959-62, assoc. prof., 1962-68, prof., 1968—, prof. microbiology and immunology, 1983—; chief chest and infectious disease sect. Wadsworth Hosp., 1957-61, chief infectious disease sect., 1961-86, assoc. chief staff for research and devel., 1986-92; staff physician infectious disease sect. VA Med. Ctr., L.A., 1992—; mem. pulmonary disease research program com. VA, 1961-62, infectious disease research program com., 1961-65, merit rev. bd. (infectious diseases), 1972-74, med. research program specialist, 1974-76, adv. com. on infectious disease, 1974-87; mem. NRC-Nat. Acad. Sci. Drug Efficacy Study Group, 1966-69; mem. subcom. on gram-negative anaerobic bacilli Internat. Com. on Nomenclature Bacteria, 1966—, chmn., 1972-78; mem. adv. panel U.S. Pharmacopoeia, 1970-75; chmn. working group on anaerobic susceptibility test methods Nat. Commn. Clin. Lab. Standards, 1987-97. Mem. editl. bd. Calif. Medicine, 1966-73, Applied Microbiology, 1973-74, Western Jour. Medicine, 1974-77, Am. Rev. Respiratory Disease, 1974-76, Jour. Clin. Microbiology, 1975-85, Infection, 1976—, Jour. Infectious Disease, 1979-82, 84-85, Antimicrobial Agts. Chemotherapy, 1980-89, Diagnostic Microbiology and Infectious Diseases, 1982-90; editor Revs. of Infectious Diseases, 1990-91, Clin. Infectious Diseases, 1992—; sect. editor: infectious diseases vols. Clin. Medicine, 1978-82, Microbiol. Ecology in Health and Disease, 1987-90; assoc. editor, consulting editor Anaerobe, 1994—. editor-in-chief, 1998—. Vice chmn. UCLA Acad. Senate, 1986-87, chair, 1987-88. Served with USMCR; Served with USNR, 1943-46; to 1st. lt. AUS, 1952-53. Co-recipient V.A. Williams S. Middleton award for biomed. rsch.; recipient Profl. Achievement award UCLA, 1987, Mayo Soley award Western Soc. Clin. Investigation, 1988, Disting. Alumnus award U. Tex. Med. Br., 1988, UCLA Med. Alumni Assn. Med. Scis. award, 1990, Hoechst Roussel award Am. Soc. Microbiology, 1992, medal Helsinki U., Finland, 1995, Lifetime Achievement award Infectious Disease Assn., 1995. Master ACP; fellow APHA, AAAS, Am. Acad. Microbiology, Infectious Diseases Soc. Am. (councilor 1976-79, pres.-elect 1980-81, pres. 1981-82, exec. com. 1980-83, Bristol award 1987); mem. Assn. Am. Physicians, Am. Soc. Microbiology (chmn. subcom. on taxonomy of Bacteroidaceae 1971-74), Am. Thoracic Soc., Western Soc. Clin. Rsch., Western Assn. Physicians, Wadsworth Med. Alumni Assn. (past pres.), Anaerobe Soc. of the Ams. (interim pres. 1992-94, pres. 1994-96), Soc. Intestinal Microbiology Ecology and Disease (interim pres. 1982-83, pres. 1983-87), Va. Soc. Physician in Infectious Diseases (pres. 1986-88), Am. Fedn. Clin. Rsch., Sigma Xi, Alpha Omega Alpha. Democrat. Jewish. Home: 11715 Folkstone Ln Los Angeles CA 90077-1311 Office: Infectious Disease Sect VA Med Ctr Wilshire & Sawtelle Blvds Los Angeles CA 90073*

FINELSEN, LIBBI JUNE, lawyer; b. Encino, Calif., Apr. 14, 1968. BA in Polit. Sci. summa cum laude, U. Nev., 1990; JD magna cum laude, Lewis and Clark Coll., 1993. Bar: Oreg. 1993, D.C. 1996, U.S. Ct. Appeals (9th, 11th and D.C. cirs.) 1996. Jud. law clk. Gen. Svcs. Bd. Contract Appeals, Washington, 1993-94; assoc. McAleese & Assocs. P.C., McLean, Va., 1994-96; atty. U.S. Dept. Agr., Washington, 1996—. V.p. edn. Hadassah Young Profls. Group, Washington, 1998-99; mem. hospitality com. Kesher Israel Synagogue, Washington. Mem. ABA, Phi Alpha Delta, Phi Kappa Phi. Avocations: cooking, handicrafts, travel, art exhibitions. Office: USDA Office of Gen Counsel Mail Stop 1418 1400 Independence Ave SW Washington DC 20250-1418

FINEMAN, HOWARD DAVID, political correspondent; b. Pitts., Nov. 17, 1948; s. Charles Morton and Jean (Lederman) F.; m. Amy Lee Nathan, Apr. 21, 1984; children: Meredith Claire, Nicholas Lowell. AB, Colgate U., 1971; MS, Columbia U., 1973; JD, U. Louisville, 1980. Reporter The Courier-Journal, Louisville, 1973-79; correspondent Newsweek, Washington, 1980-84, chief polit. corrs., 1984—, dep. bur. chief, 1994—, sr. editor, 1996—; panelist "Washington Week in Review" PBS, Arlington, Va., 1982-95, "Capital Gang Sunday", CNN, Washington, 1995-98; contbr. MSNBC, CNBC, Fox News Network, 1996-98; news analyst NBC, 1998—. Recipient Front Page award N.Y. Newspaper Guild, 1983, Silver Gavel award ABA, 1990, Nat. mag. award 1983, 92, Pulitzer Traveling fellowship Columbia U., 1976, Watson fellowship Thomas J. Watson Found., 1971. Office: Newsweek Ste 1220 1750 Pennsylvania Ave NW Washington DC 20006-4578

FINEMAN, MARTHA ALBERTSON, law educator; b. Phila., May 27, 1943; d. Jonathan Yerkes and Martha Lillian (Boyes) Albertson; children: Martha Ann, Amy Lynn, Benjamin Hayim, Jonathan Wesley. BA, Temple U., 1971; JD, U. Chgo., 1975. Bar: Ill. 1975. Law clk. to Hon. Luther M. Swygert U.S. Ct. Appeals (7th cir.), 1975-76; from asst. to assoc. prof. law U. Wis., Madison, 1976-86, prof., 1987-91; Maurice T. Moore prof. law Columbia U., N.Y.C., 1991-99; Dorothea S. Clark prof. Feminist Jurisprudence Cornell U. Sch. Law, Ithaca, N.Y., 1999—; dir. family law and policy program U. Wis. Law Sch. Inst. Legal Studies, 1978-90, dir. Feminism and Legal Theory project, 1984—; vis. prof. Columbia U., 1990-91. Author: (with others) The Politics of Child Custody Decisionmaking, 1989, Child Advocacy, 1990, Lawyering and Its Limits, 1991, Symbolism, Language and Politics, 1992; co-editor, author: (with others) At Boundaries of Law: Feminism and Legal Theory, 1990, The Public Nature of Private Violence, 1994, Mothers In Law, 1995, Feminism, Media and the Law, 1997; author: The Illusion of Equality: The Rhetoric and Reality of Divorce Reform, 1991, The Neutered Mother, The Sexual Family and Other Twentieth Century Tragedies, 1995; contbr. book revs. and articles to profl. jours. Mueller fellow Franklin and Marshall Coll., 1992. Mem. Law and Soc. Assn. (Hurst prize com. 1988-89, exec. com. 1988-90, 93-96, Kalven prize com. 1990-91, recipient Kalven prize 1999). Unitarian. Avocations: painting, creative writing. Office: Cornell U Sch Law Myron Taylor Hall Ithaca NY 14853

FINERAN, DIANA LOU, association administrator; b. Rice Lake, Wis., Dec. 25, 1945; d. Earl Orin and Leona May (Steltzner) Frommader; m. John James Fineran, III, Apr. 28, 1979. Grad. high sch., Rice Lake. Tel. operator Wis. Tel. Co., Rice Lake, 1964-69; svc. rep. Gen. Tel. Co., Rice Lake, 1969-79, Dallas, Tex., 1979-80; founder, sec., treas. The Traditional Cat Assn. Inc., Jonesborough, Tenn., 1987-92, Alpharetta, Ga., 1992-96, Battle Ground, Wash., 1996—. Contbr. articles to mags. Leader 4-H, Jonesborough, 1990. Lutheran. Avocations: animal training, sewing, outdoor activities. Home and Office: Traditional Cat Assn Inc 18509 NE 279th St Battle Ground WA 98604-9717

FINERTY, MARTIN JOSEPH, JR., military officer, researcher, association management executive; b. Wilmington, Del., July 22, 1936; s. Martin Joseph and Jane Morris (McClenaghan) F.; m. Joan Eddleman, Dec. 3, 1960; children: Nancy Jane, Laura Tourison. BSE, U.S. Naval Acad., 1959; MS in Phys. Oceanography, U. Miami, Coral Gables, Fla., 1966; MS in Indsl. Mgmt., Coll. of the Armed Forces, 1979. Commd. ensign USN, 1959, advanced though grades to capt., 1985; head, polar programs Office of Oceanographer of Navy, Alexanrdria, Va., 1975-76; spl. asst. submarines Office of Asst. Sec. of Navy, Washington, 1976-77; spl. asst. ocean environ. Office of Chief of Naval Ops., Washington, 1977-78; commdg. officer Naval Polar Oceanography Ctr., Washington, 1982-85; program officer NAS, Washington, 1985-87; asst. dir. rsch. ASME, Washington, 1987-88; exec. dir. Marine Tech. Soc., Washington, 1988-99; sr. cons. editor Compass Publs., Arlington, Va., 1999—; expert in ocean and hydro survey ops., polar programs and assn. mgmt. Author/editor tech. publs. Fellow Marine Tech. Soc.; mem. AAAS, Assn. of U.S. Naval Acad. Class of 1959 (sec. 1971-74), The Army Navy Club. Lodge: Masons. Avocations: reading, gardening. Home: 1841 Northbridge Ln Annapolis MD 21401-6576 Office: Marine Tech Soc 1828 L St NW Ste 906 Washington DC 20036-5104

FINES, GERALD D., federal judge; b. 1940. BS, Eastern Ill. U., 1965, MS, 1967; JD, U. Ky., 1970. Bar: Ill., D.C., U.S. Claims Ct., U.S. Supreme Ct. Dep. dir., acting dir. U.S. Atty.'s Office U.S. Dept. Justice, 1970-76; U.S. atty. Ctrl. Dist. Ill., 1977-86; with firm Giffin, Winning, Linder, Cohen & Bodewes, 1987; bankruptcy judge Ill. Cts., Danville, 1987—; instr. comml. law Eastern Ill. U., 1966-67. Cpl. U.S. Army, 1958-60. Mem. Ill. Bar Assn., Ky. Bar Assn. Office: 201 N Vermilion St Rm 127 Danville IL 61832-4733

FINESILVER, ALAN GEORGE, rheumatologist; b. Hartford, Conn., Sept. 4, 1942; s. Merrill Joseph and Bernice Ruth (Kamerman) F.; m. Cynthia Ann Philbrook, Sept. 8, 1973; children: Matthew Phillip, Elizabeth Ann. AB, U. Rochester, 1964; MD, Yale U., 1968. Diplomate Nat. Bd. Med. Examiners, Am. Bd. Internal Medicine. Intern in surgery Beth Israel Hosp., Boston, 1968-69; fellow in radiation therapy Yale-New Haven Hosp., 1969-70; resident in internal medicine U. Mich. Med. Ctr., Ann Arbor, 1972-75; primary care physician Community Health Care Plan, New Haven, 1975-78; fellow in rheumatology U. Mo. Med. Ctr., Columbia, 1978-81, instr. medicine, 1981-82; rheumatologist Green Bay (Wis.) Clinic, 1982—. Lt. comdr. USN, 1970-72. Fellow Am. Coll. Rheumatology; mem. ACP, AMA, Am. Soc. Internal Medicine. Avocations: sport fishing, tennis, photography. Office: Green Bay Clinic 123 N Military Ave Green Bay WI 54303-3299

FINESTONE, SHEILA, Canadian government official; b. Montreal, Que., Can., Jan. 28, 1927; d. Monroe and Minnie Abbey; m. Alan Finestone, June 9, 1947; children: David, Peter, Maxwell, Stephen. BS in Edn., McGill U. M.P. to Ho. of Commons for Mount Royal, 1984, 88, 93—, critic for commn. and culture, 1985-93, sec. of state for multiculturalism and the status of women, 1993-96. Mem. Nat. Coun. Jewish Women; hon. gov. Jewish Gen. Hosp. Mem. Orgn. Rehab. and Tng. Liberal. Office: House of Commons, Rm 533 Confederation Bldg, 111 Wellington St, Ottawa, ON Canada K1A 0A6*

FINGARETTE, HERBERT, philosopher, educator; b. Bklyn., Jan. 20, 1921; m. Leslie J. Swabacker, Jan. 23, 1945; 1 dau., Ann Hasse. B.A., UCLA, 1947, Ph.D., 1949; LHD, St. Bonaventure U., 1993. Mem. faculty U. Calif.-Santa Barbara, 1948—, Phi Beta Kappa Romanell prof. philosophy, 1983—; William James lectr. religion Harvard U., 1971; W.T. Jones lectr. philosophy Pomona Coll., 1974; Evans-Wentz lectr. Oriental religions Stanford U., 1977; Gramlich lectr. human nature Dartmouth Coll., 1978; cons. NEH; Raphael Demos lectr. Vanderbilt U., 1985; Disting. tchr. U. Calif.-Santa Barbara, 1985, faculty research lectr., 1977. Author: The Self in Transformation, 1963, On Responsibility, 1967, Self Deception, 1969, Confucius: The Secular as Sacred, 1972, The Meaning of Criminal Insanity, 1972, Mental Disabilities and Criminals Responsibility, 1979, Heavy Drinking: The Myth of Alcoholism as a Disease, 1988, Rules, Rituals, and Responsibility: Essays Dedicated to Herbert Fingarette, 1991, Death: Philosophical Soundings, 1996. Washington and Lee U. Lewis law scholar, 1980; fellow NEH, NIMH, Walter Meyer Law Research Inst., Battelle Research Ctr., Addiction Research Ctr., Inst. Psychiatry, London; fellow Ctr. for Advanced Studies in Behavioral Sci., Stanford, 1985-86. Mem. Am. Philos. Assn. (pres. Pacific div. 1977-78). Home: 1507 APS Santa Barbara CA 93103 Office: U Calif Dept Philosophy Santa Barbara CA 93106

FINGER, HAROLD B., energy, space, nuclear energy, urban affairs and government management consultant; b. N.Y., Feb. 18, 1924; s. Beny and Anna (Perlmutter) F.; m. Arlene Karsch, June 11, 1949; children: Barbara Lynn Korengold, Elyse Sue Camozzo, Sandra Ruth Ciccarelli. BME, CCNY, 1944; MS in Aero Engring., Case Inst. Tech., 1950. With NASA and predecessor NACA, 1944-69; mgr. AEC-NASA Space Nuc. Propulsion Office, 1960-67; dir. nuc. sys. NASA, 1958-64, dir. space power and nuclear sys., 1964-67; dir. space nuc. sys. divsn. AEC, 1965-67; assoc. adminstr. for orgn. and mgmt. NASA, 1967-69; asst. sec. for rsch. and tech. HUD, 1969-72; mgr. electric utility enging. oper. GE, Schenectedy, N.Y., 1972-74; gen. mgr. Ctr. for Energy Sys. GE, Washington, 1972-80; staff exec. Power Sys. Strategic Planning and Devel., Fairfield, Conn., 1980-83; pres., CEO U.S. Com. for Energy Awareness, Washington, 1983-87, U.S. Coun. for Energy Awareness, Washington, 1987-91; cons. energy, space, nuc. energy, urban affairs, govt. mgmt. Potomac, Md., 1991—. Recipient Manley Meml. award Soc. Automotive Engrs., 1958. Fellow Nat. Acad. Pub. Adminstrn., AIAA (James H. Wyld Propulsion award 1968, assoc.); mem. AIA (hon.), AAAS, Am. Soc. Pub. Adminstrn., Am. Nuc. Soc., Nat. Housing Conf. (bd. dirs.), NASA Alumni League (pres.), Cosmos Club.

FINGER, IRIS DALE ABRAMS, elementary school educator; b. Ironton, Ohio, Jan. 22, 1939; d. Frank Abrams and Pearl (Moore) Schwab; m. Robert James Roderick Sr., July 20, 1957 (div. Nov. 1971); children: Robert James Roderick Jr., Elizabeth Ann Roderick Travis; m. Henry Waterman Bromley Jr., May 14, 1972 (div. June 1987); child: Henry Waterman Bromley III; m. Grover Cleveland Finger III, Apr. 1, 1989. Degree in early childhood and elem. edn., U. South Fla.; degree in design, Jackson Coll., Honolulu. Cert. middle sch. math. tchr.; cert. TESOL. Children's libr. Ft. Myers (Fla.) Pub. Libr., 1955-57; workmen's compensation payroll adminstr. San Diego, 1964-66; permanent substitute tchr. Sigsbee Elem. Sch., Key West, Fla., 1968-70; part-time libr. Danielson (Conn.) Libr., 1970-71; residential design Bateman Homes, Leigh Acres, Fla., 1971-72; structural steel designer So. Machine and Steel, Ft. Myers, 1972-73; dir. Ft. Myers Bus. Coll., 1973-77; structural prestress concrete designer Southland Prestress, Dean Steel and Kirby MaCumber Steel, 1977-83; tchr. Lee County Sch. Bd., Ft. Myers, 1983—, team leader, math. coach, 1983, 94-95; with Bonita Spring Mid. Sch., 1994-96, equity coord., 1995-96. Pres. PTA, Key West, 1966-68, Fla. Art League, Ft. Myers, 1984-86; dir. Ft. Myers Bus. Coll., 1973-77; hosp. nurse ARC, 1964-66; med. evac for Vietnam wounded Philippine Islands Subic Hosp. Recipient Pres. Regan Achievement award NEA, 1976, Pres. Johnson People to People award and plank award for sch. constrn. at San Meguel, the Philippines, 1960. Mem. NEA, Fla. Tchrs. Profession, Tchrs. Assn. Lee County, Rep. Assembly, Fla. Math. Coun., Lee County Math. Coun., Pioneer Club Ft. Myers, Navy Wives and Navy Relief Soc., VFW Aux., Am. Legion, Alpha Delta Kappa. Republican. Methodist. Avocations: arts and crafts, reading, vacationing at the beach, family socials, swimming. Home: PO Box 7068 Naples FL 34101-7068 Office: Bonita Springs Mid Sch Terry St Bonita Springs FL 30000

FINGER, SEYMOUR MAXWELL, political science educator, former ambassador; b. N.Y.C., Apr. 30, 1915; s. Samuel and Bella (Spiegel) F.; widowed; m. Annette S. Baslaw, June 12, 1988; 1 child, Mark. B.S., Ohio U., 1935; postgrad., U. Cin., 1942, Littauer Sch. Pub. Affairs, Harvard U., 1953-54. Branch mgr. Photo Reflex Studios, Inc., 1935-37, 1938-40, regional supr., 1940-43, asst. to v.p., 1945-46; tchr. O'Keefe Jr. High Sch., 1937-38; vice consul Am. Consulate, Stuttgart, Fed. Republic of Germany, 1946-49; 2d sec. Am. Embassy, Paris, 1949-51; 2d sec., econ. officer Am. legation Budapest, Hungary, 1951-53; econ. def. officer Am. Embassy, Rome, 1954-55; 1st sec. Vientane, Laos, 1955-56; sr. econ. adv. U.S. Mission to UN, 1956-65; min. counselor of mission to UN, 1965-67; ambassador, sr. adviser to permanent rep. U.S. Mission to UN, 1967-71; prof. govt. and internat. orgn. CUNY, Coll. of S.I., 1971-85; prof. polit. sci. Grad. Sch. CUNY, 1973-85, prof. emeritus, 1985—, adj. prof., 1986—; dir. Ralph Bunche Inst. on UN, 1973-85, dir. emeritus, 1985—; adj. prof. NYU, 1986—; exec. dir. Nat. Com. on Am. Fgn. Policy, 1986-88; vis. prof. Georgetown U., Washington, 1993; sr. adviser policy studies UN Assn. of U.S.A., N.Y.C., 1971-73; mem. U.S. del. to UN Gen. Assembly, 11th-25th sessions, chmn. security council com. on sanctions in, Rhodesia; mem. UN com. on contbrs.; spl. cons. to Brookings Instn., 1964; mem. Task Force for Nuclear Test Ban. Author: People, Politics and Bureaucracy in the Making of Foreign Policy, 1980, American Ambassadors at the UN, 1987, Bending with the Winds: Kurt Waldheim and the UN, 1990; editor: (with others) The New World Balance and Peace in the Middle East, 1975, Terrorism: Interdisciplinary Perspectives, 1978, U.S. Policy in International Institutions, 1978, American Jewry and the Holocaust, 1984; contbr. articles to nat. newspapers, mags. and jours. Bd. dirs. Travel Program for Fgn. Diplomats, South Nassau Communities Hosp., 1973-74. Served as staff sgt. AUS, 1943-45. Mem. Coun. on Fgn. Rels., Inst. for Mediterranean Affairs (pres. 1971—), Am. Soc. Internat. Law, Commn. for Study Orgn. Peace, Phi Beta Kappa, Kappa Delta Pi. Office: 33 W 42nd St New York NY 10036-8003

FINGERHUT, MARILYN ANN, federal agency administrator; b. Bklyn., Oct. 3, 1940; d. Robert Vincent and Marion (Carroll) F.; m. David W. Haartz, May 14, 1988; children: Margot, D. Bradley. BS in Cell Biology, Coll. of St. Elizabeth, Convent Station, N.J., 1964; PhD in Cell Biology, Cath. U. Am., 1970; MS in Occupational Health, Harvard U., Boston, 1981. Tchr. elem. schs., Jersey City, 1961-62, East Orange, N.J., 1964-65; instr. Coll. of St. Elizabeth, 1970-71; rsch. assoc. N.J. Coll. Medicine and Dentistry, Newark, 1971-72; asst. prof. to assoc. prof. St. Peter's Coll., Jersey City, 1973-80; researcher St. Joseph Med. Ctr., Paterson, N.J., 1977-80; predoctoral fellow USPHS, 1966-69, commd. capt., 1989; epidemiologist Nat. Inst. for Occupational Safety and Health, Cin., 1981-88, br. chief, 1988-94; sr. scientist office of dir. Nat. Inst. for Occupational Safety and Health, Washington, 1994-95, asst. dir. ops., 1995-96, chief staff, 1996—. Contbr. articles to sci. jours. Founding mem. Women's R&D Ctr., Cin., 1987-95. Recipient commendation medal USPHS, 1989, 92. Mem. APHA, Soc. for Epidemiologic Rsch. Democrat. Roman Catholic. Office: Nat Inst Occupl Safety Hlth 200 Independence Ave SW Rm 715H Washington DC 20201-0004

FINGERMAN, MILTON, biologist, educator; b. Boston, May 21, 1928; s. Irving and Rose Lillian (Goodman) F.; children: Stephen Whitsell, David Clay; m. Maria Esperanza Espinosa, Dec. 17, 1994. BS, Boston Coll., 1948; MS, Northwestern U., 1949, PhD, 1952. Instr. Tulane U., New Orleans, 1954-56, asst. prof., 1956-60, assoc. prof., 1960-63, prof. dept. ecology, evolution and organismal biology, 1963—, chmn. dept., 1990—; chmn. dept. ecology, evolution and organismal biology Tulane U., 1990-99; mem. univ. senate Tulane U., 1995-96, pres.'s faculty adv. com., 1995-96; instr. invertebrate zoology Marine Biol. Lab., Woods Hole, Mass., 1958-60; Petrie chair vis. prof. Technion, Haifa, Israel, 1986; mem. adv. panel for regulatory biology NSF, 1966-69; mem. com. on marine invertebrates Inst. Lab. Animal Resources of NRC, 1976-81; cons. Food and Agr. Orgn. of UN, Cochin, India, 1986, U.S. Office Naval Rsch. project on biofouling, Goa and Aurangabad, India, 1990-97, Inst. Wood Sci. & Tech., Bangalore, India, 1997—; Ming Yu vis. scholar Chinese U. Hong Kong, 1997. Author: The Control of Chromatophores, 1963, Animal Diversity, 1969; assoc. editor Jour. Crustacean Biology, 1980-85, Pigment Cell Rsch., 1986-91; mem. editorial bd. Physiol. Zoology, 1976-84, Trends in Life Scis., 1986—, Indian Jour. Invertebrate Zoology and Aquatic Biology, 1989, 1998—; co-editor Recent Advance in Marine Biotech., 1997—. Served with U.S. Army, 1952-54. NSF grantee, 1956-85; named to Hon. Order Ky. Cols. Fellow AAAS; mem. Am. Inst. Biol. Scis., Am. Soc. Zoologists (exec. com. 1981-95, mng. editor Am. Zoologist 1981-95), Sigma Xi (pres. chpt. 1972-73), Delta DX Assoc. (pres. 1983-84, 96-97). Democrat. Jewish. Avocation: amateur radio. Home: 1730 Broadway St New Orleans LA 70118-5304 Office: Tulane U Dept Ecol-Evol-Orgn Biology New Orleans LA 70118-5698

FINGERS, ROLAND GLEN, retired baseball player; b. Steubenville, Ohio, Aug. 25, 1946. Baseball player Oakland (Calif.) Athletics, 1968-1976, San Diego Padres, 1977-1980, Milw. Brewers, 1981-84; mem. sports adv. bd. Acubid.com, 1999—; staff player McHenry Metals Golf Corp., 1998—. Named to Baseball Hall of Fame, 1992; recipient Am. League Fireman of Yr. award, 1981, Nat. League Fireman of. Yr. award, 1977, 78, 80, Cy Young award, 1981; mem. World Series Champions, 1972, 73, 74. *

FINGERSON, LEROY MALVIN, engineering executive, mechanical engineer; b. Rochester, Minn., July 1, 1932; s. Malvin Ferdinand and Corolla Racelia (Sundet) F.; m. Ruth Anne Johnson, Nov. 26, 1960; children: Mark, Karin, Laura. BSME, U. Minn., 1954, MSME, 1955, PhDME, 1961. Chmn. bd. TSI, Inc., St. Paul, 1961-98, CEO, 1961-97, ret., 1998, chmn. emeritus. Contbr. articles to profl. jours. Mem. Nat. Acad. Engring. Lutheran.

FINK, AARON, artist; b. Boston, 1955. Skowhegan Sch. Painting, 1976; BFA, Md. Inst. Coll. of Art, 1977; MFA, Yale U. Sch. of Art, 1979. One man shows include Galerie Barbara Farber, Amsterdam, The Netherlands, 1981, 82, 85, 87, 91, 94, Alpha Gallery, Boston, 1981, 83, 85, 87, 91, 92, 93, 95, 97,David Beitzel Gallery, N.Y.C., 1988, 90, 93, 95, 97, Magidson Fine Art, Aspen, Colo., 1994, Jaffe Baker Blau Gallery, Ft. Collins, Colo., 1994, Rockford (Ill.) Art Mus., 1995-96, Alpha Gallery, Boca Raton, Fla., 1995, Hatton Gallery Colo. State U., and numerous others; exhibited in group shows at Mus. Fine Arts, Boston, 1994, Olga Dollar Gallery, San Francisco, 1994, Galerie Mourlot, Boston, 1994, Karl Drerup Fine Arts Gallery, Plymouth, N.H., 1994, Art Complex Mus., Duxbury, Mass., 1997, and numerous others; represented in numerous pub. and pvt. collections. Recipient Skowhegan Scholarship award, Md. Inst. Coll. Art, 1976; grantee NEA, 1982, 1987; artists fellow Mass. Coun. Arts and Humanities, 1984. Home: 63 Maverick Sq Boston MA 02128-2312

FINK, CONRAD CHARLES, journalism educator, communications consultant; b. Marquette, Mich., Sept. 16, 1932; s. Donald Ellsworth and Mary Ruth (Fox) F.; m. Sue Carol Henry, Sept. 4, 1954; children: Karen Sue,

Conrad Stephan. B.S., U. Wis., 1954. Reporter Bloomington (Ill.) Daily Pantagraph, 1956-57; various positions to night city editor AP, Chgo., 1957-60; writer fgn. desk AP, 1961, fgn. corr. Tokyo Bur., 1961-64; bur. chief South Asia AP, New Delhi, India, 1964-67; dir. AP-Dow Jones Econ. Report, London, 1967-70; asst. to pres. AP, N.Y.C., 1970; v.p. AP, 1971-77, sec., 1974-77; 1st v.p., dir. Wide World Photos, Inc.; v.p. Press Assn., Inc.; v.p., dir. AP (Can.), Ltd.; sec., dir. N.Y.C. News Assn., Inc., 1974-77; exec. v.p. adminstrn., dir. Park Broadcasting, Inc., Ithaca, N.Y., 1977-81, Park Newspapers, Inc., 1977-81; disting. lectr. U. Ga. Sch. Journalism, Athens, 1982, prof. newspaper mgmt., 1983—; dir. James M. Cox Jr. Inst. for Newspaper Mgmt. Studies, Athens, 1990—, William S. Morris prof. newspaper strategy and mgmt., 1995—; sr. fellow U. Ga., 1996—. Author: Strategic Newspaper Management, 1988, Media Ethics, 1988, Inside the Media, 1990, Introduction to Professional Newswriting, 1992, Introduction to Magazine Writing, 1993, Writing Opinion for Impact, 1999. Served to 1st lt. USMCR, 1954-56. Recipient Disting. Service award U. Wis., 1969. Home: 116 S Stratford Dr Athens GA 30605-3024 also: Alta Vista Farm RR 2 Box 90 Cherry Valley NY 13320-9718 Office: U Ga Sch Journalism Athens GA 30602

FINK, DANIEL JULIEN, management consultant; b. Jersey City, Dec. 13, 1926; s. Joseph and Dorothy (Weisberger) F.; m. Tobie E. Weiss, June 24, 1951; children: Kenneth Wayne, Betsy Ilene, Karen Patrice. BS, MIT, 1948, MS, 1949. Registered profl. engr., Mass. Aeromechanics engr. Cornell Aero. Lab., 1948; chief aircraft dynamics Bell Aircraft Corp., Buffalo, 1949-52; v.p. Allied Rsch. Assos., Inc., Concord, Mass., 1952-63; asst. dir. def. rsch. and engring. (def. systems) Dept. Def., 1963-65, dep. dir. def. rsch. and engring. (strategic and space systems), 1965-67; with Gen. Electric Co., 1967-82, v.p., gen. mgr. space div., 1969-77; v.p., group exec. aerospace group Gen. Electric Co., Phila., 1977-79; sr. v.p. corp. planning and devel. Gen. Electric Co., Fairfield, Conn., 1979-82; pres. D.J. Fink Assocs., Inc., 1982—; bd. dirs. Titan Corp., Orbital Scis. Corp., Magellan Corp; def. sci. bd. Dept Def., 1968-72, sr. cons., 1979-98; nat. indsl. adv. coun. Opportunities Industrialization Ctrs., 1977-79; sci. adv. panel Dept. Army, 1971-74; adv. coun. NASA, 1978-79, chmn. adv. coun., 1982-88; corp. vis. dept. aero. and astronautics MIT, 1972-82, Sloan Sch., 1982-85; chmn. dept. adv. bd. dept. mech. engring. Rensselaer Poly. Inst., 1981-84; mem. Vice Pres.'s Space Policy Adv. bd., 1992. Patentee vibration isolation, weapon systems mgmt., aerospace mgmt. and corp. planning. Recipient Disting. Pub. Svc. award Dept. Def., 1967, NASA Disting. Svc. medal, 1986, NASA medal for Outstanding Leadership, 1988; Collier trophy, 1974. Hon. fellow AIAA (pres. 1974-75, von Karman lectr. 1980); fellow AAAS; mem. NAE (chmn. space applications bd. 1976-81, chmn. telecomms. and computer applications bd. 1984-87, chmn. com. on U.S.-Japan linkages in transport aircraft 1993, chmn. com. on space facilities 1994), Cosmos Club. Office: 8016 Matterhorn Ct Potomac MD 20854-4058

FINK, EDWARD MURRAY, lawyer, educator; b. N.Y.C., Mar. 11, 1934; s. Nathaniel and Elsa Charlotte (Lenrow) F.; divorced; children: Jeffrey Neil, Andrea Sue; m. Rita Toby Cohen, Aug. 11, 1985. BS in Chemistry, CCNY, 1955; JD, Georgetown U., 1959. Bar: D.C. 1960, U.S. Dist. Ct. D.C. 1960, U.S. Ct. Appeals (D.C. cir.) 1960, N.Y. 1962, N.J. 1970, U.S. Dist. Ct. N.J. 1970, U.S. Patent and Trademark Office 1960. Patent examiner U.S. Patent Office, Washington, 1955-60; atty. Bell Labs., Murray Hill, N.J., 1960-83, Bell Comm. Rsch. Inc., Livingston, N.J., 1984-91, Edward M. Fink, P.A., Edison, N.J., 1991—; adj. prof. torts, bus. law and civil litigation Middlesex County Coll., Edison, N.J., 1980—; adj. prof. partnerships and corps, contract law Montclair State U., Upper Montclair, N.J., 1984—. Mem. ABA, Am. Intellectual Property Assn., N.J. Patent Law Assn., N.J. State Bar Assn., Middlesex County Bar Assn., D.C. Bar Assn., N.Y. State Bar Assn. Democrat. Jewish. Home and Office: 51 Jamaica St Edison NJ 08820-3726

FINK, ELOISE BRADLEY, educator, writer, editor; b. Decatur, Ill., Mar. 13, 1927; d. Keith and Eileen Bradley; m. John Fink, Aug. 8, 1949 (div.); children: Sara, Joel, Alison. BA in English with honors, U. Ill., 1949; student, Colo. Coll., 1951. Cert. tchr., Ill. Tchr. English, social studies Paxton, Decatur and Arlington Heights, Ill., 1949-56; freelance Scott Foresman, Ency. Brit. and SRA, 1956-80; dir. pub. rels. Rehab. Inst. Chgo., 1980-82; instr. creative writing and poetry Loyola U., Water Tower campus, Chgo., 1983-90; artist-in-residence Ill. Arts Coun., 1984-93; facilitator workshops in poetry, fiction and nonfiction New Trier Extension, 1974—; founder, editor, pres. Thorntree Press, Winnetka, Ill., 1985—. Author: The Girl in the Empty Nightgown, 1986, Lincoln and the Prairie After, 1999. Recipient Friends of Lit. award (2), Gwendolyn Brooks award for Twenty Significant Ill. Poets; Breadloaf Writing Conf. fellow, 1986. Mem. Acad. Am. Poets, Poetry Soc. Am. Home: 547 Hawthorn Ln Winnetka IL 60093-4148

FINK, JEROLD ALBERT, lawyer; b. Dayton, Ohio, July 16, 1941; s. Albert Otto and Marjorie Carolyn (Scheidt) F.; m. Mary Jo McHone, Dec. 31, 1961 (div. July 1978); children: Marjorie, Kathryn, Erick; m. 2d, Deborah Lynn Bailey, Dec. 25, 1980 (div. Oct. 1986); 1 child, Justin. AB, Duke U., 1963, LLB, 1966. Bar: Ohio 1966. Assoc. Taft, Stettinius & Hollister, Cin., 1966-73, ptnr., 1973—; bd. dirs. The Wm. Powell Co., Cin., 1974—, Great Trails Broadcasting Co., Cin., 1974-79. Co-author: (with Judy Cohn) Power Defensive Carding, 1988, (with Joe Lutz) The American Forcing Minor Bidding System, 1995. Pres. Cin. Musical Festival Assn., 1978-79; trustee Cin. Playhouse, 1976-95, New Life Youth Svcs., Cin., 1971—. Republican. Presbyterian. Office: 1800 Star Bank Ctr 425 Walnut St Cincinnati OH 45202-3923

FINK, JOEL CHARLES, dermatologist, retired; b. Lebanon, Pa., June 29, 1922; s. Isadore Harry and Rose (Cohn) F.; m. Selma Florence Fink, Dec. 28, 1946 (dec. Dec. 1979); children: Ellen, Myles, Janet, Bruce, Paul; m. Carol Kaplan, Aug. 31, 1980. BS, U. Ala., 1943; MD, U. Md., 1947. Diplomate Am. Bd. Dermatology. Intern Walter Reed Army Hosp., Washington, 1947-48, resident, 1948-50; resident Brooke Army Hosp., San Antonio, 1952-53; pvt. practice, Smithtown, N.Y., 1955-82, Phoenix, 1982-98. Maj. M.C., U.S. Army, 1950-54. Fellow Am. Acad. Dermatology; mem. Phoenix Dermatology Soc. (pres. 1987—), Southwestern Dermatology Soc. Republican. Avocations: gardening, travel, reading. Home: 9760 E San Salvador Dr Scottsdale AZ 85258-5621

FINK, JOHN FRANCIS, retired newspaper editor, columnist, writer; b. Ft. Wayne, Ind., Dec. 17, 1931; s. Francis Anthony and Helen Elizabeth (Hartman) F.; m. Marie Therese Waldron, May 31, 1955; children: Regina Marie, Barbara Ann, Robert Paul, Stephen Lawrence, Therese Rose, David Francis, John Noll. B.A., U. Notre Dame, 1953. Assoc. editor Our Sunday Visitor, Religious Pub. Co., Huntington, Ind., 1956-68; editor Family Digest, 1956-67, mktg. mgr., 1967-72, exec. v.p., 1972-76, pres., 1976-82, pub., 1982-84; chmn. Noll Printing Co., 1978-84; editor in chief The Criterion, Indpls., 1984-96, ret., 1996; columnist The Criterion, 1984—, The Indpls. Star, 1997—; bd. dirs. Center for Applied Research in the Apostolate, 1978-85, Internat. Cath. Orgns. Center, 1979-85; mem. Cath. Com. for White House Conf. on Families, 1980; mem. communications com. U.S. Cath. Conf., 1981-84. Author: Moments in Catholic History, 1992, Traveling With Jesus in the Holy Land, 1998, The Mission and Future of the Catholic Press, 1998, Married Saints, 1999. Chmn. United Fund Drive, 1963; pres. United Way of Huntington County, 1973-74, bd. dirs., 1971-74; bd. dirs. YMCA, Huntington, 1966-78, Cath. Journalism Scholarship Fund, Founds. and Donors Interested in Cath. Activities, 1977-84; trustee Huntington Coll., 1978-81; bd. dirs. Huntington Coll. Found., 1977-84, pres. bd., 1978-81; bd. dirs. Huntington Med. Meml. Found., 1978-84. Served as 1st lt. USAF, 1954-56. Decorated knight of Malta, knight of Holy Sepulchre; recipient Disting. Svc. award Huntington Jaycees, 1960; named Chief of Flint Springs Tribe, 1971, St. Francis de Sales award Cath. Press Assn., 1981, award of yr. Notre Dame Club of Indpls., 1994. Mem. Internat. Fedn. Cath. Press Assn. (v.p. 1974-80, pres. 1980-86), Internat. Cath. Union of the Press (hon., coun. and bur. mem. 1974-86), Cath. Press Assn. (pres. 1973-75, dir. 1965-75, hon. 1997—), Indpls. Serra Club (pres. 1995-96).

FINK, JOSEPH ALLEN, lawyer; b. Lexington, Ky., Oct. 4, 1942; s. Allen Medford and Margaret Ruth (Draper) F.; children: Alexander Mentzer, Justin McGranahan. Student, Wayne State U., 1960-61; BA, Oberlin Coll., 1964; JD, Duke U., 1967. Bar: Mich. 1968, U.S. Dist Ct. (ea. dist.) Mich. 1968, U.S. Dist. Ct. (we. dist.) Mich. 1974, U.S. Ct. Appeals (6th cir.) 1987, U.S. Supreme Ct. 1998. Assoc. Dickinson, Wright, McKean & Cudlip, Detroit, 1972-75, Lansing, Mich., 1968-75; ptnr. Dickinson Wright PLLC, Lansing, 1976—; instr. U.S. Internat. U. Grad. Sch. Bus., San Diego, 1971; adj. prof. trial advocacy Thomas M. Cooley Law Sch., Lansing, 1984-85; mem. com. on local rules U.S. Dist. Cts., 1985; chmn. trial experience subcom. U.S. Dist. Ct. (we. dist.) Mich., 1981. Contbg. author: Construction Litigation, 1979, Legal Considerations in Managing Problem Employees, 1988, Michigan Civil Procedure During Trial, 2d edit., 1989; contbr. articles to profl. jours. Bd. dirs. Lansing 2000 Inc., 1985-92; bd. trustees Olivet (Mich.) Coll., 1985-94; mem. bd. advisors Mich. State U. Press, 1993-96. Lt. JAGC, USNR, 1968-72. Fellow Mich. State Bar Found.; mem. Fed. Bar Assn., State Bar of Mich. (chmn. local disciplinary com. 1983—, mem. com. for U.S. Cts. 1984), Mich. Def. Trial Counsel Assn. Episcopalian. Avocations: writing, reading, golf. Home: 1356 Hickory Island Dr Haslett MI 48840-8944 Office: Dickinson Wright PLLC 215 S Washington Sq Ste 200 Lansing MI 48933-1816

FINK, JOSEPH RICHARD, college president; b. Newark, Mar. 20, 1940; s. Joseph Richard and Jean (Chorazy) F.; m. Donna Gibson, 1965 (div. 1986); children: Michael, Taryn; m. Christine Gaudenzi, oct. 4, 1992; children: Madison, Joseph. AB, Rider U., 1961; PhD in Am. History, Rutgers U., 1971; DLitt (hon.), Rider U., 1982, Coll. of Misericordia, 1992, Golden Gate U., 1994. Asst. then assoc. prof history Immaculata (Pa.) Coll., 1964-72, adminstrv. asst. to pres., 1969-72; dean of Arts & Scis. City Colls. Chgo., 1972-74; pres. Raritan Valley Coll., Somerville, N.J., 1974-79, Coll. Misericordia, Dallas, 1979-88, Dominican Coll., San Rafael, Calif., 1988—; pres. Regional Planning Coun. Higher Edn., Region 3/Northeastern Pa., 1986-88. Mem. exec. com. Philharm. Soc. Northeastern Pa., 1986-89; bd. dirs. Marin Symphony, 1989—, San Francisco Ballet, 1994-97, Ind. Coll. No. Calif., 1992—, Marin Forum, 1991—, Guide Dogs for the Blind, 1994-97; bd. dirs. Am. Land Conservancy, 1995—, exec. com.; mem. campaign cabinet United Way San Francisco, 1990; bd. dirs. North Bay Coun., 1993—, chmn., 1996, exec. com. Mem. Nat. Assn. Ind. Colls. and Univs. (secretariat 1986), Nat. Assn. Intercollegiate Athletics (pres.'s adv. coun. 1986), Am. Coun. on Higher Edn. (commn. leadership devel. higher edn. 1978-82, commn. on internat. edn. 1993-96, acad. adminstrn. fellow 1974-75), Assn. Mercy Colls. (pres. 1985-87, exec. com. 1981-87), Coun. for Ind. Colls. (bd. dirs. 1989-92), Am. Hist. Assn., World Affairs Coun. No. Calif. (bd. dirs. 1990-96), Commonwealth Club Calif. (quar. chmn. 1989, chmn. Marin County chpt. 1989—, bd. dirs. 1992—, exec. com. 1997—). Home: 900 Green St San Francisco CA 94133-3600 Office: Dominican Coll of San Rafael 50 Acacia Ave San Rafael CA 94901-2230

FINK, KRISTIN DANIELSON, secondary education educator; b. Camden, N.J., Sept. 23, 1951; d. Ralph J. and Marguerite J. (Bickerstaff) Danielson; m. Garl L. Fink, Nov. 23, 1976; children; Karl Tony, Tracy Denise, Brittany Mar. BA in English, U. Utah, 1973, MA in Edn., 1979. Cert. secondary edn. tchr., Utah; endorsements in English, theatre, speech, reading, journalism and gifted/talented edn. Tchr. Kearns (Utah) Jr. H.S., 1973-85, Hunter Jr. High, West Valley City, Utah, 1986-93; tchr. English Olympus H.S., Salt Lake City, 1993-95; character edn. specialist Utah State Office Edn., Salt Lake City, 1995—; adj. instr. U. Utah, 1993-94, U. So. U., 1998—; chair dept. performing arts Kearns Jr. H.S., 1978-80, 83-85; chair dept. performing arts Hunter Jr. H.S., 1987-93; grad. com. adv. Westminster Coll., 1979; dir. Hunter Acting Co., 1985-93; attended White House Conf. on Character, 1996-98; bd. dirs. Character Edn. Partnership; presenter in field. Lead tchr. Cmty. of Caring; cons. Joseph P. Kennedy Found.; peer leadership team advisor Olympus H.S., 1993-95; mem. Gov.'s Commn. on Centennial Values, 1996. Named Tchr. of Yr., Hunter PTA, WVC, 1988; recipient Granite Dist. Employees Ptnrs. in Edn. Outstanding Svc. award, 1989-90, 1st Pl. award Best Jr. H.S. Newspaper in the State of Utah, Utah Press Assn., 1990, Holladay Rotary Club Svc. award, 1994, Excel Outstanding Educator award, 1995, Gov.'s Friends to Families award, Utah, 1998. Avocations: reading, travel, music. Home: 5179 Danshill Cir Salt Lake City UT 84118-2274 Office: Utah State Office Edn 250 E 500 S Salt Lake City UT 84111-3204

FINK, LOIS MARIE, art historian; b. Michigan City, Ind., Dec. 30, 1927; d. George Edward and Marie Helen (Hensz) F. B.A., Capital U., 1951; M.A., U. Chgo., 1955, Ph.D., 1970; H.H.D. (hon.), Capital U., 1982. Instr. Lenoir Rhyne Coll., Hickory, N.C., 1955-56; instr. Midland Coll., Fremont, Nebr., 1956-58; asst. prof. Roosevelt U., Chgo., 1958-70; curator Nat. Mus. of Am. Art, Smithsonian Instn., Washington, 1970-93; curator emeritus, 1993—; adv. com. Washington area Archives Am. Art, 1979—; mem. nat. adv. com. Brauer Mus. Art Valparaiso (Ind.) U., 1992—. Co-author: Academy: The Academic Tradition in American Art, 1975; contbg. author: Elizabeth Nourse: A Salon Career, 1983; author: American Art at the Nineteenth-Century Paris Salons, 1990; contbr. articles to profl. jours. Fellow The Soc. for the Arts, Religion, and Contemporary Culture; mem. Coll. Art Assn., Am. Studies Assn. Home: 10401 Grosvenor Pl Apt 1306 Rockville MD 20852-4640 Office: Nat Mus of Am Art Smithsonian Instn Washington DC 20560

FINK, MATTHEW POLLACK, trade association executive, lawyer; b. N.Y.C., Jan. 8, 1941; s. Harry L. and Helen (Pollack) F.; m. Ellanor Thompson Stengel, June 22, 1945; children: Emily Pollack, Owen Thompson, Nina Pepper. BA summa cum laude, Brown U., 1962; LLB cum laude, Harvard U., 1965. Asst. gen. counsel Investment Co. Inst., Washington, 1971-77, gen. coun., 1977-82, sr. v.p., 1982-91, pres., 1991—; dir. Am. Coun. for Capital Formation; prin. Coun. of Excellence for Govt.; past mem. Dept. Commerce Industry Sector Adv. Com. on Svcs., SEC Emerging Markets Adv. Com. With U.S. Army, 1967-68. Mem. Fed. Bar Assn., Investment Co. Com. (past chmn.), Met. Club. Office: Investment Co Inst 1401 H St NW # 1200 Washington DC 20005-2110

FINK, NORMAN STILES, lawyer, educational administrator, fundraising consultant; b. Easton, Pa., Aug. 13, 1926; s. Herman and Yetta (Hyman) F.; m. Helen Mullen, Sept. 1, 1956; children: Hayden Michael, Patricia Carol. AB, Dartmouth Coll., 1947; JD, Harvard U., 1950. Bar: N.Y. 1951, U.S. Dist. Ct. (ea. and so. dists.) N.Y. 1954, U.S. Supreme Ct. 1964. Mem. legal staff Remington Rand, Inc., N.Y.C., Washington, 1949-54; ptnr. Lans & Fink, N.Y.C., 1954-68; counsel devel. program U. Pa., Phila., 1969-80; v.p. devel. and univ. rels. Brandeis U., Waltham, Mass., 1980-81; dep. v.p. devel., alumni rels., assoc. gen. counsel devel. Columbia U., N.Y.C., 1981-89; sr. counsel John Grenzebach & Assocs., Inc., Chgo., 1989-91; cons. v.p. Engle Consulting Group, Inc., Chgo. Editor: Deferred Giving Handbook, 1977; author: (with Howard C. Metzler) The Costs and Benefits of Deferred Giving, 1982. V.p. Am. Australian Studies Found.; mem. bd. vis. Brevard (N.C.) Coll., 1995—, life trustee, 1999, Warren Wilson Coll., 1997—. With U.S. Army, 1945-46. Recipient Alice Beeman award for excellence in devel. writing Coun. Advancement and Support of Edn., 1984; Lilly Endowment grantee, 1979-80. Mem. ABA (mem. com. on exempt orgns. sect. taxation and com. estate planning and drafting, charitable givint), Coun. Advancement and support of Edn. (various coms.), Am. Arbitration Assn. (panelist), Assn. of Bar of City of N.Y.C. (com. on tax-exempt orgns. 1987-90), Dartmouth Lawyers Assn., Harvard Law Sch. Assn., Nat. Soc. Fund Raising Execs (Contbn. to Knowledge award 1985), Harvard Club Western N.C. Democrat. Jewish.

FINK, RAYMOND, medical educator; b. N.Y.C., Apr. 21, 1927; s. William and Yetta (Rales) F.; m. Ruth Ursula Gebhard, May 28, 1961 (div. 1982); children: William D., David S.; m. Louise Berenson, Jan. 27, 1983. BBA, CCNY, 1947; MA, U. Denver, 1949; PhD, Cornell U., 1956. Statistician Opinion Rsch. Ctr. U. Denver, 1949; survey statistician U.S. Bur. Census, Suitland, Md., 1949-50, 56; rsch. assoc. human resources rsch. George Washington U., Washington, 1952-53; rsch. assoc. Bur. Social Sci. Rsch., Washington, 1957-60; assoc. dir. drinking practices study Calif. State Dept. Pub. Health, Berkeley, 1960-62; v.p. rsch. and stats. Health Ins. Plan Greater N.Y., N.Y.C., 1962-78; prof. community and preventive medicine N.Y. Med. Coll., Valhalla, 1978—, dir. health policy mgmt., 1982-90, dir. health svcs. rsch., 1990—; chmn. social sci.a dv. com. Planned Parenthood Fedn. Am., N.Y.C., 1966-71; chair task force on HMOs Nat. Inst. Mental Health, Rockville, Md., 1971-72. Contbr. articles to med. and sci. jours. Trustee Health Svcs. Improvement Fund, N.Y.C., 1986—. Sgt. U.S. Army, 1950-52. Grantee Nat. Inst. Mental Health, 1968-72, Nat. Cancer Inst., 1972-78, Social Sci. Rsch. Coun., 1982-83, Robert Wood Johnson Found., 1990-94. Mem. APHA, Am. Assn. Public Opinion Rsch. (co-editor 1968-69), Med. and Health Rsch. Assn. (chair 1975—), Assn. for Health Svcs. Rsch., World Assn. for Pub. Opinon Rsch., Herman Biggs Soc. (pres. 1994—). Jewish. Office: NY Med Coll Grad Sch Health Sci Munger Pavillion Valhalla NY 10595 also: Medical Health Rsch Assn of NYC 40 Worth St Rm 720 New York NY 10013-2904

FINK, RICHARD DAVID, chemist, educator; b. N.Y.C., July 14, 1936; s. Merwin Jesse and Claudia (Lowenthal) F.; m. Alice Christine Hovenden, Sept. 8, 1961; children: Rebecca Elisabeth, Johanna Hovenden. AB, Harvard U., 1958; PhD, MIT, 1962; MA (hon.), Amherst Coll., 1971; LHD (hon.), Doshisha U., Kyoto, 1988. NSF fellow in chemistry Yale U., 1962-63; NIH fellow, 1963-64; asst. prof. chemistry Amherst (Mass.) Coll., 1964-67, assoc. prof., 1967-71, prof., 1971—, Mellon prof., 1977-80, chmn. dept., 1970-73, 79-82, dean of faculty, 1983-88; vis. prof. U. London, 1972-73, 76-77, 96-97, 99—, U. Kans., 1980; vis. scholar U.S. Army War Coll., 1992, MIT, 1988-90, 93-95; cons. Edn. Assocs., Inc. Contbr. articles to profl. jours. NSF fellow U. London, 1968-69, Sloan Found. fellow, 1970-74; Dreyfus Found. tchr.-scholar prize, 1971; NSF Profl. Devel. award, 1979. Mem. Am. Phys. Soc., Am. Chem. Soc., AAAS, Sigma Xi. Home: 30 Orchard St Amherst MA 01002-2516 Office: Amherst Coll Amherst MA 01002

FINK, RICHARD H., manufacturing company executive. Sr. v.p. govt. and pub. affairs Koch Industries, Wichita, Kans., to 1997, exec. v.p., 1997—. Office: Koch Industries 4111 E 37th St N Wichita KS 67220-3298*

FINK, ROBERT RUSSELL, music theorist, former university dean; b. Belding, Mich., Jan. 31, 1933; s. Russell Foster and Frances (Thornton) F.; m. Ruth Joan Bauerle, June 19, 1955; children: Denise Lyn, Daniel Robert. B.Mus., Mich. State U., 1955, M.Mus., 1956, Ph.D., 1965. Instr. music SUNY, Fredonia, 1956-57; instr. Western Mich. U., Kalamazoo, 1957-62, asst. prof., 1962-66, assoc. prof., 1966-71, prof., 1971-78, chmn. dept. music, 1972-78; dean Coll. Music U. Colo., Boulder, 1978-93; retired, 1994; prin. horn Kalamazoo Symphony Orch., 1957-67; accreditation examiner Nat. Assn. Schs. Music, Reston, Va., 1973-92, grad. commr., 1981-89, chmn. grad. commn., 1987-89, assoc. chmn. accreditation commn., 1990-91, chmn., 1992. Author: Directory of Michigan Composers, 1972, The Language of 20th Century Music, 1975; composer: Modal Suite, 1959, Four Modes for Winds, 1967, Songs for High School Chorus, 1967; contbr. articles to profl. jours. Bd. dirs. Kalamazoo Symnphony Orch., 1974-78, Boulder Bach Festival, 1983-90. Mem. Coll. Music Soc., Soc. Music Theory, Mich. Orch. Assn. (pres.), Phi Mu Alpha Sinfonia (province gov.), Pi Kappa Lambda. Home: 643 Furman Way Boulder CO 80303-5614

FINK, ROBERT STEVEN, lawyer, writer, educator; b. Bklyn., Dec. 7, 1943; s. Samuel Miles and Helen Leah (bogen) F.; m. Abby Deutsch, Mar. 20, 1980; children: Juliet Leah, Robin Rachel. Diploma, U. Vienna, 1962; BA, Bklyn. Coll., 1965; JD, NYU, 1968, LLM, 1973. Bar: N.Y. 1969, U.S. Dist. Ct. (so. and ea. dists.) N.Y. 1970, U.S. Tax Ct. 1970, U.S. Ct. Appeals (2d cir.) 1970, U.S. Supreme Ct. 1972, U.S. Dist. Ct. (we. dist.) N.Y. 1975, U.S. Ct. Claims 1984, U.S. Dist. Ct. (no. dist.) N.Y. 1985, U.S. Ct. Appeals (fed. cir.) 1990, U.S. Ct. Internat. Trade 1998. Assoc. Kostelanetz & Ritholz, N.Y.C., 1968-75, ptnr., 1975-87; ptnr. Kostelantez, Ritholz, Tigue and Fink, N.Y.C., 1987-94, Kostelanetz & Fink, N.Y.C., 1994—; lectr. in field; expert witness IRS; mem. adv. com. tax divsn. Dept. Justice; chmn. IRS/Bar Liaison Com. N.E. Region, 1996-99; adj. prof. law NYU. Author: Tax Fraud: Audits, Investigations, Prosecutions, 2 vols., 1980, 18th rev. edit., 1999; co-author: How to Defend Yourself Against the IRS, 1985, You Can Protect Yourself from the IRS, 1987, 2d rev. edit., 1988; dept. editor Jour. of Taxation; contbr. numerous articles in field to profl. jours. Fellow Am. Coll. Tax Counsel; mem. ABA (chmn. com. civil and criminal tax penalties 1983-85, chmn. task force for revision of tax penalties 1982), N.Y. State Bar Assn. (chmn. com. criminal and civil tax penalties 1982-85, 88-90, chmn. compliance and unreported income 1985-87, chmn. commodities and fin. futures 1987-88, chmn. com. compliance and penalties 1991-93, chmn. com. compliance practice and proceduce 1993—, mem. house of dels. 1995-97), Fed. Bar Assn., N.Y. County Lawyers Assn. (chmn. com. taxation 1988-92, 969-7, bd. dirs. 1989-95), Assn. of Bar of City of N.Y., Am. Arbitration Assn. (arbitrator). Office: Kostelanetz & Fink 530 5th Ave New York NY 10036

FINK, THOMAS MICHAEL, lawyer; b. Huntington, Ind., Oct. 6, 1947; s. Francis Anthony and Helen Elizabeth (Hartman) F.; m. Sheila Ann Jeffers, Aug. 11, 1973; children: Mark, Matthew, Megan. BBA, U. Notre Dame, 1970; JD, Northwestern U., 1973. Bar: Ind. 1973, U.S. Dist. Ct. (no. dist.) Ind. 1973. Assoc. Barrett & McNagny, Ft. Wayne, Ind., 1973-78, ptnr., 1979—; speaker Estate Planning Coun., Ft. Wayne, 1987—. Pres. Bishop Luers H.S. Bd. Edn., Ft. Wayne, 1992-93; bd. dirs. Ft. Wayne Cmty. Found. Bus. Edn. Fund, 1990—; bd. dirs., treas. Planned Giving Coun. N.E. Ind., 1995—. Mem. Ft. Wayne Country Club, Notre Dame Club of Ft. Wayne, Beta Gamma Sigma. Roman Catholic. Avocations: coaching basketball, golf, tennis, travel. Home: 1302 Sunset Dr Fort Wayne IN 46807-2952 Office: Barrett & McNagny 215 E Berry St Fort Wayne IN 46802-2705

FINK, TRACEY MARKS, chiropractor; b. N.Y.C., Nov. 3, 1968; d. Martin Ira and Joan (Marks) F. BA, Skidmore Coll., 1991; D Chiropractic, Logan Coll. Chiropractic, 1996. Chiropractic asst. Union Sq. Chiropractic, N.Y.C., 1991-93; chiropractor Ctr. for Integrated Health, St. Louis, 1997—. Fellow Internat. Chiropractic Assn., Am. Chiropractic Assn., Internat. Coll. Applied Kinesiology, Periclean Soc., Phi Beta Kappa. Avocations: biking, mountain climbing, skiing, ice climbing, rollerblading, meditation. Office: Ctr for Integrated Health 7700 Clayton Rd Ste 304 Saint Louis MO 63117

FINKBEINER, CARLTON S. (CARTY FINKBEINER), mayor; b. Toledo, 1939. BA, Dennison U. Tchr., football coach Maumee Valley Country Day Sch., St. Francis De Sales H.S., U. Toledo; city councilman City of Toledo, vice-mayor, mayor, 1994—; founder Toledo's Cmty.-Oriented Drug Enforcement program; co-sponsor City-wide Curfew; chair Coun.'s Housing, Neighborhood Revitalization and Natural Resources Com., Toledo; mem. Econ. Opportunity Planning Assn. of Greater Toledo, Presidential Scholars Commn., U.S. Small Bus. Adminstrn. Adv. Commn. Northeastern and Northwestern Ohio, Internat. Gt. Lakes St. Lawrence Mayors Conf. Appointed to the Presidential Scholars Commission by President Gerald Ford, 1975. Office: Office of the Mayor/City Coun One Goverment Ctr Ste 2200 Toledo OH 43604*

FINKE, LEONDA FROEHLICH, sculptor; b. N.Y.C.; d. Herman and Evelyn (Praeger) Froehlich; m. Arnold I. Finke; children: David, Erica, Rachel. Student, Art Students League, N.Y.C., 1945. Instr. large bronze figure sculpture and samll art medals Roslyn, N.Y., 1969-95; academician NAD, 1994—. Works in permanent collections including Smithsonian Nat. Portrait Gallery (portrait of Georgia O'Keefe), Brit. Mus., Century Assn., Chrysler Mus., The Butler Inst. Am. Art, Bates Coll. Mus. Art; commd. works include 3 life-size bronzes for park in Altlanta, Max Som medal for Albert Einstein Med. Coll., 1991, Brit. Art Med. Soc. commn. of Virginia Woolf medal, 1989, Royal Philharm. Orch. commn. for medal, 1995; exhibited medals FIDEM, Helsinki, 1990, Brit. Mus., London, 1992; slide talk FIDEM, London, 1992. Recipient medal of Honor Nat. Assn. Women Artists, 1972, Alex Ettl award for sculpture NAD, 1990, J. Sanford Saltus award for Signal Achievement in the Art of the medal Am. Numismatic Soc., 1997. Fellow Nat. Sculpture Soc. (sec. 1987—, Gold medal 1989, Bas Relief award 1991, Maurice Hexter award 1992, Agop Agapoff award 1993, Silver medal and John Cavanaugh prize 1994), Sculptors Guild, N.Y. Soc. Women Artist (sculptors guild exhbn. in Kyoto, Japan 1993), Medallic Sculpture Assn., Audubon Artists (pres. 1984-85, medal of honor 1979). Jewish. Home: 10 The Locusts Roslyn NY 11576-1724

FINKE, ROBERT FORGE, lawyer; b. Chgo., Mar. 11, 1941; s. Robert Frank and Helen Theodora (Forge) F. AB, U. Mich., 1963; JD, Harvard U., 1966. Bar: Ill. 1966, U.S. Dist. Ct. (no. dist.) Ill. 1966, U.S. Ct. Appeals (4th and 6th cirs.) 1982, U.S. Ct. Appeals (7th cir.) 1966, U.S. Ct. Appeals (9th cir.) 1980, U.S. Supreme Ct. 1970. Law clk., 1966-67; assoc. firm Mayer, Brown & Platt, Chgo., 1967-71, ptnr., 1972—. Bd. dirs. Lyric Opera Guild; assoc. Rush Presbyterian St. Luke's Med. Ctr. Mem. ABA (sects. litigation, antitrust, legal edn. and admissions to the bar, vice chmn. 1974-75, bus. law sect.), Law Club Chgo., Legal Club Chgo., Univ. Club, Econ. Club. Office: Mayer Brown & Platt 190 S La Salle St Ste 3100 Chicago IL 60603-3441

FINKEL, ADAM, government agency administrator; b. Phila., Apr. 24, 1959; m. Joanne E. Booth. AB in Biology, Harvard U., 1979, M in Pub. Policy, 1984, ScD in Environ. Health Scis., 1987. Fellow Ctr. for Risk Mgmt./Resources for the Future, 1987-94, dir. rational risk reduction program, 1987-94; sr. fellow Cecil and Ida Green Ctr. Study of Sci. and Soc. U. Tex., Dallas, 1995; dir. health standards programs OSHA, Washington, 1995—; advisor Universo Veintiuno, Mexico City, 1985; mem. com. on risk assessment for hazardous air pollutants, 1991-94. Co-editor: Worst Things First? The Debate over Risk-Based National Environmental Priorities; formerly editor-in-chief Hazardous Materials Intelligence Report; author more than 35 articles on risk assessment and mgmt.; profl. singer and choral condr. Mem. Risk Assessment and Policy Assn. (pres.-elect). Office: Dept of Labor Health Standards Programs 200 Constitution Ave NW Washington DC 20210-0002

FINKEL, BERNARD, public relations, communications and association management consultant, radio host; b. Chgo., Nov. 12, 1926; s. Isadore and Sarah (Goldzweig) F.; m. Muriel Horwitz, Dec. 23, 1951; children: Phillip Stuart, Calvin Mandel, Norman Terry. Student, Hebrew Theol. Coll., Chgo., 1939-44, Ill. Inst. Tech., Chgo., 1944-45, U. Ill., Chgo., 1947-48; BS in Journalism, U. Ill., 1951. Reporter, rewriter Peacock Newspapers, Chgo., 1949, Defender Newspapers, Chgo., 1951, Chgo. North Side Newspapers, 1952; asst. dir. pub. rels. Combined Jewish Appeal-Jewish Fedn. Met. Chgo., 1953; mng. editor Electric Appliance Svc. News, Chgo., 1954-57; asst. account exec. Burlingame-Grossman Advt., Chgo., 1957; account exec. Glassner & Assocs., Pub. Rels., Chgo., 1958-61; pub. rels. cons. Bernard Finkel Comm., Chgo., 1961—; dir. devel. and pub. rels. Japanese Am. Svc. Com., 1981-89; nat. dir. comm. and donor rels. Little Bros.-Friends of the Elderly, Chgo., 1989-90; owner, prodr., host weekly radio show Jewish Cmty. Hour, Sta. WONX-AM, Evanston, Ill. Author: Life and the World, 1947. Mem. pub. rels. and youth commns. Village of Skokie, 1964-65; v.p., coach Boys Baseball, Skokie, 1963-67; mem. adv. bd., chmn. pub. rels. Chgo. Area Career Conf., 1961-62; pres. Acad. Assocs. of Ida Crown Jewish Acad., Chgo., 1973-75; v.p. Hillel Torah North Suburban Day Sch., 1965-66, Congregation Or Torah, Skokie, 1970-71; bd. dirs. Skokie Valley Traditional Synagogue, 1987—. With U.S. Army, 1945-46. Recipient award for pub. svc. Jewish Cmty. Hour, 1978, Chgo. Rabbinical Coun., Chgo. Bd. Rabbis, Coun. Traditional and Orthodox Synagogues of Greater Chgo., Midwest Region of Nat. Fedn. Jewish Men's Clubs, Israel Aliyah Ctr. of World Zionist Orgn., Religious Zionists of Chgo., B'nai B'rith Lodge of Survivors of Nazi Holocaust, others. Mem. Nat. Soc. Fund-Raising Execs., Pub. Rels. Soc. Am., Social Svc. Communicators, Publicity Club Chgo. (profl. achievement awards). Home and Office: 3300 Capitol St Skokie IL 60076-2402

FINKEL, DONALD, poet; b. N.Y.C., Oct. 21, 1929; s. Saul A. and Meta (Rosenthal) F.; m. Constance Urdang, Aug. 14, 1956; children: Elizabeth Antonia, Thomas Noah, Amy Mariah. B.S., Columbia U., 1952, M.A., 1953. Poet-in-residence Washington U., St. Louis, 1965-91; cons. prosody Random House Dictionary. Author: The Clothing's New Emperor, 1959, Simeon, 1964, A Joyful Noise, 1966, Answer Back, 1968, The Garbage Wars, 1970, Adequate Earth, 1972, A Mote in Heaven's Eye, 1975, Endurance and Going Under, 1978, What Manner of Beast, 1981, The Detachable Man, 1984, The Wake of the Electron, 1987, Selected Shorter Poems, 1987, A Splintered Mirror: Chinese Poetry from the Democracy Movement, 1991, Beyond Despair, 1994, A Question of Seeing, 1998. Recipient Theodore Roethke Meml. award, 1974, Morton Dauwen Zabel award, 1980, Dictionary of Literary Biography award, 1994; Guggenheim fellow, 1966; grantee Ingram Merrill Found., 1972; grantee Nat. Endowment for Arts, 1973. Mem. Cave Rsch. Found., Phi Beta Kappa. Address: 2051 Park Ave Saint Louis MO 63104-2553

FINKEL, EUGENE JAY, lawyer; b. Phila., June 21, 1931. BA, Swarthmore (Pa.) Coll., 1952; MA, George Washington U., 1961, JD, 1965. Bar: U.S. Dist. Ct. D.C. 1966, U.S. Ct. Appeals (D.C. cir.) 1972, U.S. Supreme Ct. 1980. Various positions U.S. Dept. Treasury, Washington, 1952-74; dep. dir. Office Internat. Fin. Policy Coordination and Ops., Washington, 1963-67; dir. Office Latin Am., Washington, 1967-70, Multilateral Instns. Program Office, 1970-74, Developing Nations Fin., 1974-75; asst. exec. sec. World Bank-IMF Devel. Com., 1975-77; alt. U.S. exec. dir. Inter-Am. Devel. Bank, Washington, 1977-81; ptnr. Porter Wright Morris & Arthur, Washington, 1981—. Lt. comdr. USNR ret. Office: Porter Wright et al 1667 K St NW Washington DC 20006-1605

FINKEL, GERALD MICHAEL, lawyer; b. N.Y.C., July 29, 1941; s. Abraham B. and Elizabeth B. (Michaels) F.; m. Beverly Lynne Jaffee, Aug. 26, 1962; children: Bruce Daniel, Judith Michelle. B.A., NYU, 1962; J.D., U. S.C., 1970. Bar: S.C. 1970, U.S. Dist. Ct. S.C. 1970, U.S. Ct. Appeals (4th cir.) 1973, U.S. Supreme Ct. 1973, D.C. 1973. Prin. Finkel & Altman, L.L.C. and predecessor firm, Columbia, S.C., 1970—; adj. prof. trial advocacy and ins. law U. S.C.; mem. faculty fed. trial practice AM. Law Inst., ABA; lectr. S.C. Bar, S.C. Trial Lawyers Assn., Richland County Bar and Profl. Insts.; instr. S.C. Dept. Pub. Safety/Criminal Justice Acad.; spl. judge Richland County Family Ct., 1974-78, Ct. Gen. Sessions 5th Jud. Cir., 1976. Author: (with Ralph C. McCullough II) A Guide to South Carolina Torts, 1st edit., 1981, 2d edit., 1986, 3d edit., 1990, 4th edit., 1995, (with Elizabeth Rhodes) South Carolina Legal and Business Forms, Vols. 1 and 3, 1997. Hearing officer S.C. Dept. Health and Environ. Control, 1979-82; mem. S.C. Appellate Def. Commn., 1982-83, Gov.'s Sentencing Guidelines Commn., 1982-83. Served to capt. U.S. Army, 1962-67. Recipient Outstanding Alumni cert. Phi Alpha Delta, 1972. Mem. ABA, S.C. Bar Assn. (bd. govs. 1985-88, profl. responsibility com. and ethics adv. com.), Richland County Bar Assn., Assn. Trial Lawyers Am., Am. Law Inst. (consultative group for restatement of the law 3d unfair competition), S.C. Trial Lawyers Assn. (exec. bd. 1978-81, pres. 1982-83), Phi Alpha Delta (dist. justice 1976-78). Democrat. Jewish. Home: 156 Pelzer Dr Summerville SC 29483 Office: Finkel & Altman 1201 Main St Ste 1800 Columbia SC 29201-3294

FINKEL, MARION JUDITH, physician, pharmaceutical company administrator; b. N.Y.C., Nov. 2, 1929; d. Israel and Bella (Stillman) F.; premed. student L.I. U., 1945-48; M.D. (Howard Sloan Meml. scholar), Chgo. Med. Sch., 1952; m. Simon V. Manson, Sept. 12, 1954. Intern, Jersey City Med. Center, 1952-53; resident in internal medicine Bellevue Hosp., N.Y.C., 1954-56; med. editor Merck and Co., 1957-61; pvt. practice specializing in internal medicine, N.Y.C., 1956-57, N.J., 1961-63; with FDA, 1963-85, dir. div. metabolic and endocrine drugs, 1966-70, dep. dir. bur. drugs, 1970-71, 72-74, dir. office new drug eval., 1971-72, 74-82, dir. office orphan products devel., 1982-85; exec. dir. research and devel. Berlex Labs., Inc., 1985-88, v.p. drug registration and regulatory affairs Sandoz Pharms., Inc., 1988-94, v.p. corp. regulatory compliance, 1994-95, cons. regulatory affairs, clin. rsch. and devel., 1995—. Recipient award of merit FDA, 1974; Superior Service award USPHS, 1976, 84; Fed. Woman's award Fed. Govt., 1976, Meritorious Exec. award, 1980; named Disting. Alumnus, Chgo. Med. Sch., 1977, L.I. U., 1980. Mem. Am. Soc. Clin. Pharmacology and Therapeutics, Drug Info. Assn. Contbr. chpts., numerous articles to profl. publs. Office: 21 Squirrel Run Morristown NJ 07960-6411

FINKEL, SANFORD NORMAN, lawyer; b. Troy, N.Y., Oct. 19, 1946; s. Max and Mildred (Fares) F.; m. Amy Lynn Gordon, Oct. 13, 1974 (div. July 1984); children: Marcy Jennifer, Melanie Gordon. BA, SUNY, Buffalo, 1968; JD, Union U., 1974. Bar: N.Y. 1975, U.S. Dist. Ct. (no. dist.) N.Y. 1975. Tchr. sci. Enlarged City Sch. Dist. of Troy, N.Y., 1968-71; pvt. practice Troy, 1975—; counsel to dem. study group N.Y. State Assembly, Albany, 1977-78; instr. paralegal studies Jr. Coll. Albany divsn. Russell Sage Coll., 1977-81; dep. corp. counsel City of Troy, 1990-94. Mem. Rensselaer County Bar Assn. Avocations: reading, numismatics, philately, travel. Home: 19 Capitol Pl Rensselaer NY 12144-9658 Office: 68 2nd St Troy NY 12180-3932

FINKELSTEIN, ALLEN LEWIS, lawyer; b. N.Y.C., Mar. 19, 1943; s. David and Ella (Miller) F.; m. Judith Elaine Stutman, June 20, 1964 (div. Mar. 1980); children: Jill, Jennifer; m. Shelley Gail Barone, June 15, 1980; 1 child, Amanda. BS, NYU, 1964; JD, Bklyn. Law Sch., 1967; MBA, L.I. U., 1969. Bar: N.Y. 1968, U.S. Dist. Ct. (ea. and so. dists.) N.Y. 1973, U.S. Ct. Appeals (2d cir.) 1973, U.S. Supreme Ct. 1976, U.S. Tax Ct. 1979. Ptnr. Finkelstein, Bruckman, Wohl, Most & Rothman, N.Y.C., 1974-97; sr. ptnr. Pressman Finkelstein, N.Y.C., 1997-99; ptnr. Schwarzfeld Ganfer & Shore, N.Y.C., 1999—; asst. prof. L.I. U., N.Y.C., 1969-73, adj. assoc. prof., 1973-74; bd. dirs. Amotrophic Laterial Sclerosis Assn. Mem. ABA (bus. law and family law sect.), N.Y. State Bar Assn., Assn. of Bar of City of N.Y., Queens County Bar Assn. Jewish. Lodge: Masons. Home: 425 E 63rd St New York NY 10021-7804 Office: Schwarzfeld Ganfer & Shore 360 Lexington Ave New York NY 10017

FINKELSTEIN, BARBARA, education educator; b. Bklyn., Mar. 22, 1937; d. Joseph and Helene (Gutter) Eisenberg; m. James D. Finkelstein; children: Donna Ilene, Laura Helene. BA, Barnard Coll., 1959; MA, Columbia U., 1960, EdD, 1970. Asst. prof. U. Md., College Park, 1970-74, assoc. prof., 1974-83, dir. Internat. Ctr. for Study of Edn., Policy and Human Values, 1979—, mem. East Asian com., 1980—, prof. edn., 1983—; dir. Mid-Atlantic Region Japan-in-the-Schs. Program, 1985—, Ctr. for Study of Edn. Policy and Human Values, 1979—, Nat. Intercultural Edn. Leadership Inst. Author, editor: Regulated Children, Liberated Children, 1979 (Critic's Choice award 1981), Governing the Young: Teacher Behavior in Primary Schools in Nineteenth-Century United States, 1988, Experiencing Education and Culture inJapan: Transcending Stereotypes, 1990, Discovering Culture in Education: An Approach to Program Design and Evaluation; editor Reflective History series Tchrs. Coll. Press; exec. editor Pedagogica historica, Jour. Edn. Policy; contbr. articles to profl. jours. Grantee U.S.-Japan Found., 1985-88; NEH fellow, 1976-77, fellow U. of Tokyo, 1992. Mem. Am. Ednl. Studies Assn. (pres. 1979-82), History of Edn. Soc. (bd. dirs. 1980-82, v.p. 1998, pres. 1998-99), Am. Ednl. Rsch. Assn. (v.p. 1989—). Home: 3916 Garrison St NW Washington DC 20016-4220 Office: U Md Dept Edn Policy College Park MD 20742

FINKELSTEIN, BERNARD, lawyer; b. N.Y.C., Jan. 21, 1930; s. Irving and Sadie (Katz) F.; m. Adele S. Levine, June 29, 1952; children: Sharon Ann, Marcia Lyn. BA, NYU, 1951; LLB, Yale U., 1954. Bar: N.Y. 1954, D.C. 1970. Assoc. Paul, Weiss, Rifkind, Wharton & Garrison, N.Y.C., 1956-64, ptnr., 1965-95, of counsel, 1996—; mem. wills and trusts adv. com. Practicing Law Inst. Trustee, mem. Altman Found., N.Y.C., 1985—. Named one of the Best Lawyers in N.Y., N.Y. Mag., 1995. Fellow Am. Coll. of Trust and Estate Counsel (estate and gift tax com. 1987-93); mem. ABA (com. on pre-death planning, probate and trust div. of sect. on real property, probate and trust law 1985-88), N.Y. State Bar Assn. (chmn. gift and tax com. of tax sect. 1978-80), Assn. of Bar of City of N.Y. (trusts, estate and surrogate's ct. com. 1986-89), N.Y. Bar Found., Yale Law Sch. Assn. (exec. com. 1983-86), Phi Beta Kappa, Phi Alpha Delta, Order of Coif. Club: Elmwood Country (White Plains, N.Y.). Home: 1 Tory Ln Scarsdale NY 10583-2314 Office: Paul Weiss Rifkind Wharton & Garrison Rm 202 1285 Avenue Of The Americas Fl 21 New York NY 10019-6028

FINKELSTEIN, DAVID RITZ, physicist, educator, consultant; b. N.Y.C., July 19, 1929; s. Isidore and Esther (Rubinstein) F.; m. Helene Cooper, 1948 (div.); children: Daniel, Beth, Eve; m. Shlomit Ritz, 1981; 1 child, Aria. B.S., CCNY, 1949; Ph.D., MIT, 1953. Asst., then assoc. prof. physics Stevens Inst. Tech., 1954-60; assoc. prof. Yeshiva U., then prof., chmn., dean, 1960-79; prof. physics Ga. Inst. Tech., 1979—; vis. prof. Tougaloo Coll., 1965, Hebrew U. Jerusalem, 1974. Author: Quantum Relativity, 1996; editor Internat. Jour. Theoretical Physics; editl. bd. mem. Jour. Math. Physics, 1991-93. Co-chmn. Miss. Project Parents Com., 1965. Ford Found. fellow, 1958; NSF grantee, 1954-96. Fellow Lindisfarne Assn.; mem. AAAS, Am. Phys. Soc., Internat. Quantum Structures Assn. (sec. 1990-93). Jewish. Research in high energy physics, quanta space-time, topological physics, gravity, quantum logic, Clifford-algebraic quantum network dynamics. Office: Ga Inst Tech Physics Dept Atlanta GA 30332-0430

FINKELSTEIN, EDWARD SYDNEY, department store executive; b. New Rochelle, N.Y., Mar. 30, 1925; s. Maurice and Eva (Levine) F.; m. Myra Schuss, Aug. 13, 1950; children: Mitchell, Daniel, Robert. B.A., Harvard U., 1946, M.B.A., 1948; DCS (hon.), N.Y.U., 1988. Successively trainee, buyer mdse. adminstr. Macy's, N.Y.C., 1948-62; sr. v.p., dir. merchandising Macy's, N.J., 1962-67, exec. v.p., merchandising and sales promotion, 1967-69; pres. Macy's, Calif., 1969-74; pres., chmn., chief exec. officer Macy's, New York, 1974-80; chmn., chief exec. officer R.H. Macy & Co. Inc., 1980-92; dir. R.H. Macy, Inc., 1971-92; chmn. bd. Finkelstein Assocs., N.Y.C., 1992-97; chmn., CEO CWT Specialty Stores, Inc. d/b/a/ Cherry & Webb, N.Y.C., 1997—; mem. adv. bd. Yale Sch. Mgmt., 1984-89. Mem. nat. adv. coun. Cystic Fibrosis Found., 1975-80, trustee, 1977-80, hon. trustee, 1980—; mem. adv. bd. Harvard Bus. Sch., 1983-91. With USN, 1943-46. Mem. Harvard Club. Jewish. Office: Cherry & Webb 1430 Broadway Rm 308 New York NY 10018-3308

FINKELSTEIN, JAMES ARTHUR, management consultant; b. N.Y.C., Dec. 6, 1952; s. Harold Nathan and Lilyan (Crystal) F.; m. Lynn Marie Gould, Mar. 24, 1984; children: Matthew, Brett. BA, Trinity Coll., Hartford, Conn., 1974; MBA, U. Pa., 1976. Cons. Towers, Perrin, Forster & Crosby, Boston, 1976-78; mgr. compensation Pepsi-Cola Co., Purchase, N.Y., 1978-80; mgr. employee info. systems Am. Can. Co., Greenwich, Conn., 1980; mgr. bus. analysis Emery Airfreight, Wilton, Conn., 1980-81; v.p. Meidinger, Inc., Balt., 1981-83; prin. The Wyatt Co., San Diego, 1983-88; pres., chief exec. officer W. F. Corroon, San Francisco, 1988-95; chmn., CEO FutureSense, Inc., Larkspur, Calif., 1995—; founder TallyUp Software, 1996—; dir. En Wisen, Inc., 1996-98; ptnr. Arthur Andersen LLP, San Francisco, 1997-99, Larkspur, Calif., 1999—; mem. regional adv. bd. Mchts. and Mfrs. Assn., San Diego, 1986-88; instr. U. Calif., San Diego, 1984-88. Mem. camp com. State YMCA of Mass. and R.I., Framingham, 1982-86; pres. Torrey Pines Child Care Consortium, La Jolla, Calif., 1987-88; vice chmn. La Jolla YMCA, 1986-88; chmn. fin. com. YMCA, San Francisco, 1992-95, vice chmn., 1993-95, chmn., 1995—; bd. dirs. San Domenico Sch., 1994—; bd. trustees World Affairs Coun., 1998—. Avocations: music, sports, camping. Home: 17 Bracken Ct San Rafael CA 94901-1587 Office: Arthur Andersen LLP Ste 211 101 Larkspur Landing Cir Larkspur CA 94939

FINKELSTEIN, JAMES DAVID, physician; b. N.Y.C., Oct. 16, 1933; s. Harry and Sylvia Z. (Bernstein) F.; m. Barbara Joan Eisenberg, Dec. 12, 1959; children—Donna Ilene, Laura Helene. A.B., Harvard U., 1954; M.D., Columbia U., 1958. Diplomate Am. Bd. Internal Medicine. Intern, resident in medicine Presbyn. Hosp., N.Y.C., 1958-61; fellow in gastroenterology Columbia U., N.Y.C., 1961-63. Chief med. service VA Med. Ctr., Washington, 1979—, chief gastroenterology, 1970-79, assoc. chief staff for research, 1975-79, med. investigator, 1970-75, clin. investigator, 1965-68, chief biochemistry research lab., 1965—; cons. Children's Hosp., Washington, 1968-85; prof. medicine George Washington U., 1969—; clin. prof. medicine Georgetown U., 1981—; prof. medicine Howard U., Washington, 1983—; mem. Nutrition Study sect. NIH, 1972-78. Contbr. articles biochemistry and nutrition of methionine to profl. jours. Served as surgeon USPHS, 1963-65. Recipient F.P. Gay Research award Columbia U., N.Y.C., 1956; Arthur S. Fleming award Jr. C. of C., Washington, 1971; NIH grantee, 1966-95. Mem. Am. Soc. for Clin. Investigation, Am. Gastroent. Assn., Assn. of Am. Physicians, Am. Inst. Nutrition, Am. Soc. Clin. Nutrition, Am. Fedn. Clin. Research. Club: Harvard. Office: VA Med Ctr 50 Irving St NW Washington DC 20422-0001

FINKELSTEIN, LOUIS, retired art educator; b. Mar. 24, 1923; s. Abraham Leonard Finkelstein and Belle (Schiff) Finson; m. Gretna Mary Campbell, May 28, 1947; children: Martha, Henry; m. Jane Stout Culp, Nov. 8, 1989. Cert., Cooper Union, 1947; DFA honoris causa, Md. Inst. Coll. of Art, 1999. Instr. Bklyn. Mus. Art Sch., 1950-56; assoc. prof. Phila. Coll. Art, 1958-62; asst. prof. Yale U., New Haven, Conn.; prof. art Queens Coll., Flushing, N.Y., 1964-90; artist-in-residence Dartmouth Coll., 1995. 1st lt. USAAF, 1942-46. Recipient B. Altman prize NAD, 1989, 95, Carnegie prize, 1997; PTO Fulbright fellow, 1982-83, NEA fellow, 1983. Home: PO Box 89 Stillwater NJ 07875-0089

FINKELSTEIN, RICHARD ALAN, microbiologist; b. N.Y.C., Mar. 5, 1930; s. Frank and Sylvia (Lemkin) F.; m. Helen Rosenberg, Nov. 30, 1952; children: Sheri, Mark, Laurie; m. Mary Boesman, June 20, 1976; 1 dau., Sarina Nicole. B.S., U. Okla., 1950; M.A., U. Tex., Austin, 1952, Ph.D., 1955. Teaching fellow, research scientist U. Tex., Austin, 1950-55; fellow, instr. U. Tex. Southwestern Med. Sch., Dallas, 1955-58; chief bioassay sect. Walter Reed Army Inst. Research, Washington, 1958-64; dep. chief, chief dept. bacteriology and mycology U.S. Army Med. Component, SEATO Med. Research Lab., Bangkok, Thailand, 1964-67; assoc. prof. dept. microbiology U. Tex. Southwestern Med. Sch., Dallas, 1967-73; prof. U. Tex. Southwestern Med. Sch., 1973-79; prof., chmn. dept. microbiology Sch. Medicine U. Mo., Columbia, 1979-93, Curators' prof., 1990—; Millsap Disting. Prof., 1985—; mem. Nat. Com. for Coordination Cholera Rsch., Ministry for Pub. Health, Bangkok, 1965-67; cons. WHO, 1970—, commdg. gen. U.S. Army Med. R&D Command, 1975-79, Schwarz-Mann Labs., 1974-79, ICN Biomeds., 1979—, Wyeth-Ayerst, 1992—, Amgen, 1992, Molecular Pharms., 1993—; Microbiolog. and Infectious Diseases Rsch. Com. Nat. Inst. Allergy and Infectious Diseases, NIH, 1994-98; vis. assoc. prof. U. Med. Scis., Bangkok, 1965-67; vis. prof. U. Chgo., Med. Sch., 1977; vis. scientist Japanese Sci. Coun., 1976, Ciba-Geigy lectr. Waksman Inst., Rutgers U., 1975; vis. lectr. Nat. Sci. Coun., Taipei, Taiwan, 1995, others. Contbr. articles on cholera, enterotoxins, gonorrhea, and role of iron in host-parasite interactions to profl. jours. Recipient Robert Koch prize Bonn, Fed. Republic Germany, 1976; Chancellor's award for outstanding faculty rsch. in biol. scis. U. Mo.-Columbia, 1985, Sigma Xi Rsch. award U. Mo.-Columbia, 1986. Fellow Am Acad. Microbiology (bd. govs. 1990-93), Am. Soc. for Microbiology (pres. Tex. br. 1974-75, hon. Tex. br. divsn. councilor, chmn. program com. 1979-82, sec.-treas. Mo. br. 1985-87, v.p. 1987-89, pres. 1989-91, councillor, 1991-92, coun. policy com. 1992-95, Disting. Svc. award 1998), Am. Assn. Immunologists, Infectious Diseases Soc. of Am., Soc. Gen. Microbiology, Pathol. Soc. Gt. Britain and Ireland, Sigma Xi. Achievements include first purification of cholera enterotoxin; first purification of heat-labile enterotoxin from Escherichia coli; patent for living attenuated candidate cholera vaccine. Home: 3861 S Forest Acres Dr Columbia MO 65203-8608 Office: U Mo-Columbia Sch Medicine Dept Molecular Microbiol Columbia MO 65212

FINKELSTEIN, SEYMOUR, business consultant; b. N.Y.C., July 14, 1923; s. Morris and Anna (Landin) F.; m. Hermine Yuder, June 19, 1948 (dec. Aug. 1989); children: Andrew, Charles, Robert, Adam. BS in Econs., U. Pa., 1946; student Wharton Sch., Univ. of Pa. Supr. Glemby Internat., N.Y.C., 1946-53, mktg. exec., 1953-58, account exec., 1958-62, v.p., 1962-64, pres., 1964-89, chmn., 1989-90. Cons. in field, mem. adv. bd. Inst. Contemporary Art, 1988—; trustee U. Pa., 1980-85, bd. dirs. Am. Crafts Mus., N.Y.C.; mem. Pres.'s Council U. Pa. Lt. USAAF, 1943-45. Mem. Air Force Assn., Am. Numismatics Assn. (life), Chief Execs. Orgn., Met. Pres.'s Orgn., Scarsdale Hist. Soc., Am. Numismatics Soc., World Presidents Org. Clubs: Fairview Country (Greenwich, Conn.) (mem. bd. 1982-84), City Athletic Club (N.Y.C.), U. Pa. Club. N.Y. Republican. Jewish. Avocations: numismatics, tennis, music, art.

FINKENBINE, ROY EUGENE, history educator; b. Sidney, Ohio, Sept. 9, 1953; s. Richard Roy and Joy Evelyn (Miller) F.; m. Barbara Therese Emley, July 31, 1982; children: Michael, Daniel, Lorah, Sarah. BS in Social Studies, Taylor U., 1975; MA in History, No. Ariz. U., 1976; PhD in Am. Culture, Bowling Green State U., 1982. Adminstrv. asst. grants and spl. projects River Corridor Project Shelby County, Sidney, Ohio, 1977-78; from asst. editor to assoc. editor Black Abolitionist Papers Project/Fla. State U., Tallahassee, 1981-91; asst. prof. history Hampton (Va.) U., 1992-96; asst. prof. history U. Detroit Mercy, 1996-98, assoc. prof. history and African-Am. studies, 1998—, dir. Black Abolitionist Archives; vis. asst. prof. history Murray (Ky.) State U., 1991-92; assoc. editor Am. Nat. Biography, 1990-98. Author: (with C. Peter Ripley et al) Witness for Freedom: African American Voices on Race, Slavery, and Emancipation, 1993, The Black Abolitionist Papers, 1830-1865, 1985-92, Sources of the African-American Past, 1997; contbr. articles to profl. jours. Grantee Fla. State U., 1986-88, 91, Rockefeller Archive Ctr., 1983; Bowling Green State U. Dissertation fellow, 1980-81, Teaching fellow Bowling Green State U., 1978-80, Nat. Hist. Publ. and Records Commn. fellow, 1981-82; Victorian Soc. in Am. scholar, 1979; Princeton U. fellow, 1986. Mem. Am. Hist. Assn., Orgn. Am. Historians, Assn. for the Study Afro-Am. Life and History, Phi Kappa Phi. Democrat. Lutheran. Home: 30850 Puritan Livonia MI 48154-3253 Office: U Detroit Mercy History Dept 4001 W McNichols Rd Detroit MI 48219

FINKLE, JEFFREY ALAN, professional association executive; b. Newark, Ohio, Apr. 22, 1954; s. Richard James and Margery (Orr) F.; m. Diane Elizabeth Letchford, Aug. 20, 1983 (div. July 1989). BSc cum laude, Ohio U., 1976; postgrad., Ohio State U., 1978-80. Legis. dir. Ohio Rep. Party, Columbus, 1976-78; legis. liason Ohio Dept. Mental Health, Columbus, 1978-80; mktg. dir. Systems 80, Bethesda, Md., 1980-81; exec. asst. HUD, Washington, 1981-83, dep. asst. sec., 1983-86; pres., CEO Nat. Council for Urban Econ. Devel., Washington, 1986—; mem. adv. com., Ohio U. Inst. for Local Govt. Adminstrn. and Rural Devel., 1986—. Bd. dirs., pres. Bollinger Found., 1989—, Arlington County Va. Econ. Devel. Corp., D.C. Mktg. Ctr. Mem. Housing Rehab. Assn. (bd. dirs. 1986-90), Nat. Assn. Ind. Living Ctrs. (nat. adv. bd. 1987-89, treas. 1995—), Sr. Living Choices (bd. dirs. 1991—), Ohio U. Alumni Assn. (past pres. Washington chpt., past bd. dirs. nat. assn.). Republican. Roman Catholic. Avocations: golf, geneology. Office: Nat Coun for Urban Econ Devel 1730 K St NW Ste 700 Washington DC 20006-3834

FINKS, ROBERT MELVIN, paleontologist, educator; b. Portland, Maine, May 12, 1927; s. Abraham Joseph and Sarah (Bendette) F. B.S. magna cum laude, Queens Coll., 1947; M.A., Columbia U., 1954, Ph.D., 1959. Lectr. Bklyn. Coll., 1955-58, instr., 1959-61; lectr. Queens Coll., CUNY, 1961-62, asst. prof., 1962-65, acting chmn., 1963-64, assoc. prof. geology, 1966-70, prof., 1971—; geologist U.S. Geol. Survey, 1952-54, 63—; research assoc. Am. Mus. Natural History, 1961-77, Smithsonian Instn., 1968—; doctoral faculty CUNY, 1983—; cons. in field. Author: Late Paleozoic Sponge Faunas of the Texas Region, 1960; Editor: Guidebook to Field Excursions, 1968; Contbr. articles profl. jours. Queens Coll. Scholar, 1947. Fellow AAAS, Geol. Soc. Am., Explorers Club; mem. AAUP, Paleontol. Soc. (vice chmn. Northeastern sect. 1977-78, chmn. 1978-79), Paleontol. Assn. Britain, Soc. Econ. Paleontologists and Mineralogists, Internat. Palaeontol. Assn., Geol. Soc. Vt. (charter mem.), Planetary Soc. (charter), Phi Beta Kappa (v.p. Sigma chpt. N.Y. 1993-95, pres. 1995-99), Golden Key (hon.), Sigma Xi (exec. sec. Queens Coll. chpt. 1982-85), Golden Key Nat. Hon. Soc. (hon.). Office: Queens Coll CUNY Sch Earth and Environ Scis Flushing NY 11367 *Be humble in studying nature.*

FINLAY, JAMES CAMPBELL, retired museum director; b. Russell, Man., Can., June 12, 1931; s. William Hugh and Grace Muriel F.; m. Audrey Joy Barton, June 18, 1955; children: Barton Brett, Warren Hugh, Rhonda Marie. BSc, Brandon U., 1952; MSc in Zoology, U. Alta., 1968. Geophysicist Frontier Geophys. Ltd., Alta., 1952-53; geologist, then dist. geologist Shell Can., Ltd., 1954-64; chief park naturalist and biologist Elk Island (Can.) Nat. Park, 1965-67; dir. hist. devel. and archives, dir. hist. and sci. service, dir. Nature Center, dir. interpretation and recreation City of Edmonton, Alta., 1967-92; founder Fedn. Alta. Naturalists, 1969. Author: A Nature Guide to Alberta, Bird Finding Guide to Canada; (with Joy Finlay) Ocean to Alpine-A British Columbia Nature Guide, A Guide to Alberta Parks. Recipient Order of the Bighorn, Govt. of Atla., 1987, Heritage award Environment Can., 1990, Loran Goulden award Fedn. Alta Naturalists, 1991, Can. 125th Anniversary award, 1993; named to Edmonton Hist. Hall of Fame, 1976. Mem. Can. Mus. Assn. (pres. 1976-78), Alta. Mus. Assn. (founding mem., past pres.), Am. Mus. Assn. (past council), Am. Ornithol. Union. Home: 270 Trevlac Pl, RR 3, Victoria, BC Canada V8X 3X1 *I will walk but once on this earth. In this short time I hope to help my fellow man come to a greater awareness, appreciation and understanding of the world environment of which we are very much a part. I am trying to ensure that our descendants have a fit planet on which to live.*

FINLAY, JOHN BAIRD, government official; b. Santo Domingo, Dominican Republic, Jan. 29, 1929. BA, U. Toronto, Ont., Can., 1952; MEd, U. Western Ont., 1974. Tchr. Upper Can. Coll., Ottawa, 1952-54; tchr. high sch., 1955-64; asst. sec. Ont. Secondary Sch. Tchrs. Fedn., 1964-67; vice prin. Oxford County Bd. Edn., 1967-70; prin. O.C.B.E., 1970-77, supt. schs., 1977-88; ret., 1988; adr. parliament House of Commons, Ottawa, 1993—. Office:

House of Commons, Rm 331 Confederation Bldg, Ottawa, ON Canada K1A 0A6

FINLAY, ROBERT DEREK, food company executive; b. U.K., May 16, 1932; s. William Templeton and Phyllis F.; m. Una Ann Grant, June 30, 1956; children: Fiona, Rory, James. B.A. with honors in Law and Econs, Cambridge (Eng.) U., 1955, M.A., 1959. With Mobil Oil Co. Ltd., U.K., 1955-61; assoc. McKinsey & Co., Inc., 1961-67, prin., 1967-71, dir., 1971-79; mng. dir. H.J. Heinz Co. Ltd., U.K., 1979-81; sr. v.p. corp. devel. world hdqs. H.J. Heinz Co., Pitts., 1981-93, chief fin. officer world hdqrs., 1989-92, sr. v.p. corp. devel., area v.p., 1992-93; chmn. Dawson Internat., 1995-98. Mem. London com. Scottish Coun. Devel. and Industry, 1979—; trustee Mercy Hosp., Pitts., 1983-93; bd. dirs. Pitts. Symphony Soc., 1989-92, U.S.-China Bus. Coun., 1984-92, Pitts. Pub. Theater, 1988-92. Capt. Gordon Highlanders, 1950-61. Fellow Inst. Dirs.; mem. Inst. Mktg., Highland Brigade Club, Leander Club, Annabel's, Caledonian Club, Three Rivers Rowing Assn. (gov.).

FINLAY, TERENCE EDWARD, bishop; s. Terence John and Sarah (McBryan) F.; m. Alice-Jean Cracknell, 1962; 2 daus. BA, U. We. Ont., London; BTh, Huron Coll., London, Ont.; MA, U. Cambridge, Eng.; DD (jure dignitatis), Huron Coll., 1987. Ordained deacon Anglican Ch., 1961, priest, 1962. Dean of residence Renison Coll., Waterloo, Can.; incumbent All Saints, Waterloo, 1964-66, St. Aidan's, London, Can., 1966-68; rector St. John the Evangelist, London, 1968-78; archdeacon of Brant, 1978-82; incumbent Grace Ch., Brantford, Can., 1978-82, St. Clement's, Eglinton, Toronto, Can., 1982-86; suffragan bishop Diocese of Toronto, 1986, coadjutor bishop, 1987; bishop Diocese of Toronto, Toronto, 1989—. Avocations: music, skiing, travel. Office: Diocese of Toronto, 135 Adelaide St E, Toronto, ON Canada M5C 1L8

FINLAYSON, BRUCE ALAN, chemical engineering educator; b. Waterloo, Iowa, July 18, 1939; s. Rodney Alan and Donna Elizabeth (Gilbert) F.; m. Patricia Lynn Hills, June 9, 1961; children: Mark, Catherine, Christine. BA, Rice U., 1961, MS, 1963; PhD, U. Minn., 1965. Asst. prof. to assoc. prof. U. Wash., Seattle, 1967-77, prof. dept. chem. engrng. and applied math., 1977-82, Rehnberg prof. dept. chem. engrng., 1983—, chmn. dept. chem. engrng., 1989-98; vis. prof. Univ. Coll., Swansea, Wales, U.K., 1975-76, Denmark Tekniske Hojskole, Lyngby, 1976, Universidad Nacional del Sur, Bahia Blanca, Argentina, 1980; Gulf vis. prof. Carnegie Mellon U., 1986; trustee Computer Aids to Chem. Engrng. Edn., Austin, Tex., 1980-92; mem. bd. on chem. sci. and tech. NRC, 1990-92. Mem. editorial bd. Internat. Jour. Numerical Methods in Fluids, Swansea, 1980—, Numerical Heat Transfer, 1981—, Numerical Methods for Partial Differential Equations, 1984—, Chem. Engrng. Edn., 1991—; author: The Method of Weighted Residuals and Variational Principles, 1972, Nonlinear Analysis in Chemical Engineering, 1980, Numerical Methods for Problems with Moving Prints, 1992. Lt. USNR, 1965-67. Mem. AIChE (CAST divsn. programming 1981-85, William H. Walker award 1983, bd. dirs. CAST divsn. 1984-86, vice chmn. 1987-88, chmn. 1989, bd. dirs. 1992-94, editorial bd. 1985-91, v.p. 1999), Am. Chem. Soc., Am. Soc. Engrng. Edn. (dir. Summer Sch. for Chem. Engrng. Faculty), Soc. Indsl. and Applied Math., Soc. Rheology, Nat. Acad. Engrng. Home: 6315 22nd Ave NE Seattle WA 98115-6919 Office: U Wash Dept Chem Engrng PO Box 351750 Seattle WA 98195-1750

FINLAYSON, JOHN SYLVESTER, biochemist; b. Phila., Sept. 19, 1933; s. Alexander Smeillie and Anna Eva (Sylvester) F.; m. Rasma Irēne Bramane; children: Mark Lars, Siglinda Erika Finlayson Beyeler. BA summa cum laude, Marietta Coll., 1953; MS, U. Wis., 1955, PhD, 1957. Rsch. fellow Inst. Radiophysics, Stockholm, Sweden, 1957-58; biochemist NIH, Bethesda, Md., 1958-72; rsch. chemist FDA, Bethesda, 1972-75, chief Lab. Plasma Derivatives, 1975-86, chief Lab. Hepatitis, 1986-89, chief Lab. Hemostasis & Thrombosis, 1988-89, acting dir. divsn. hematology, 1990-92, assoc. dir. sci. office blood rsch. and review, 1993—; vis. prof., scientist Protein Rsch. Inst., Osaka, Japan, 1976; lectr. in biochemistry Found. Advanced Edn. in Sci., Bethesda, 1961-76, 86-96. Author: Basic Biochemical Calculations, 1969; co-editor: Immunoglobulins, 1980; contbr. numerous articles to sci. jours. With USPHS, 1958-61. Mem. Internat. Soc. Thrombosis and Haemostasis (charter), Soc. Exptl. Biology and Medicine, Sr. Biomed. Rsch. Svc. Office: FDA Ctr Biol Eval & Rsch 1401 Rockville Pike Rockville MD 20852-1448

FINLEY, CHUCK (CHARLES EDWARD FINLEY), baseball player; b. Monroe, La., Nov. 26, 1962. Student, N.E. La. U., Monroe. Pitcher Anaheim Angels (formerly Calif. Angels), 1986—. Mem. Calif. Angels Am. League West Divsn. Champions, 1986; selected to Am. League All Star Team, 1989-90, 95-96; named to The Sporting News All-Star Team, 1989-90. Office: Anaheim Angels 2000 Gene Autry Way Anaheim CA 92806-6100*

FINLEY, GARY ROGER, financial company executive; b. Gays, Ill., June 3, 1940; s. Fred Forrest and Dena Maxine (Jeffris) F.; m. Ardeth Kay Clawson, June 12, 1960; children: Deborah Finley Fisher, Shari Finley Swiger. AB, Lincoln (Ill.) Christian Coll., 1964; MA, Lincoln Christian Sem., 1971. Lic. commodities broker, securities broker. Ministry work Christian Ch. of Christ, Cen. and Western Ill., 1959-74; personnel counselor Jamar Personnel, Rock Island, Ill., 1974-75; sales and dept. mgr. Commodity Trend Svc., Davenport, Iowa, 1975-79; co-founder, co-owner Valley Commodities, Orion, Ill., 1979-83; sales rep. FGL Commodity Svcs., West Des Moines, Iowa, 1983-85; commodity pool operator pvt. practice, Orion, 1979-89; commodity broker, equity raiser Farmers Commodities Corp., Inc., West Des Moines, Iowa, 1987-93; pres. FCC Investments, Inc. and FCC Ultra, Inc., West Des Moines, 1990-93, also bd. dirs.; v.p., treas. The Com-Pac Corp., Davenport, Iowa, 1989-94; founder, pres. Finley Fin. Svcs., Inc., Gays, Ill., 1993—; owner, pres. Value Fuel, Inc., Gays, Ill., 1995—. Dir., assoc. Nat. Ch. Growth Rsch. Ctr., Washington, 1992—; elder Orion Christian Ch., 1986-91; v.p. Prayerhouse Warehouse Ministry, Des Moines, 1992—; chaplain Heartland Christian Village, Neoga, Ill., 1998. Avocations: ministry, fishing, art, music, bldg. constrn. Home and Office: Finley Fin Svcs Inc RR 1 Box 17 Gays IL 61928-9700

FINLEY, GEORGE ALVIN, III, wholesale executive; b. Aurora, Ill., Apr. 25, 1938; s. George Alvin, II, and Sally Ann (Lord) F.; m. Sue Sellors, June 20, 1962 (dec. 1995); m. Phyllis Ann Finley; children: Valerie, George Alvin IV. BBA, So. Meth. U., 1962; postgrad. Coll. Grad. Program, Ford Motor Co., 1963. Rep. for Europe Finco Internat., 1959-61; trainee Ford Motor Co., Dearborn, Mich., 1962-63; v.p. mktg. Internat. Motor Cars, Oakland, Calif., 1963-64; Sequoia Lincoln lease mgr. Internat. Motor Cars, Oakland, 1965; regional mgr. Behlen Mfg. Co., Dallas, 1965-67; pres. C C Distbrs., Corpus Christi, Tex., 1967—; guest instr. Sch. Bus., So. Meth. U., pres., 1986-91, Nueces River Authority, 1975—; bd. dirs. Contract Svcs. Assn. Am. Sec. Bd. Washington, MD Anderson Hosp. U. Tex., Curistus-Spohn Health Sys., McDonald Obs., U. Tex., exec. com.; mem. Del Mar Coll. Pres.' Coun. Mem. Tex. Wholesale Hardware Assn. (pres. 1991-92), Nat. Assn. Wholesalers, Am. Supply Assn., Wholesale Distbrs. Assn. (bd. dirs. 1994—), Impact Industries Inc. (chmn. bd. Sandwich, Ill. 1986-93), Nat. Retail Hardware Assn., Internat. Hardware Distbrs., Rotary Internat., State Bar of Tex. (grievance com. 1995—), Phi Delta Theta. Democrat. Methodist. Achievements include assisted in design, engrng., production, mktg. Apollo Automobile, 1963-64. Home: 3360 Ocean Dr Corpus Christi TX 78411-1457 Office: PO Box 9153 210 Mcbride Ln Corpus Christi TX 78408-2338

FINLEY, GLENNA, author; b. Puyallup, Wash., June 12, 1925; d. John Ford and Gladys De Ferris (Winters) F.; m. Donald MacLeod Witte, May 19, 1951; 1 child, Duncan MacLeod. B.A. cum laude, Stanford U., 1945. Producer internat. div. NBC, 1945-49; film librarian March of Time, 1949; with news bur. Life Mag., 1950; publicity and radio writer Seattle, 1950-51; freelance writer, 1951-57; contract writer New Am. Library Inc., N.Y.C., 1970—. Author numerous books including Master of Love, 1978, Beware My Heart, 1978, The Marriage Merger, 1978, Wildfire of Love, 1979, Timed for Love, 1979, Love's Temptation, 1979, Stateroom for Two, 1980, Affairs of Love, 1980, A Business Affair, 1983, Wanted for Love, 1983, A Weekend for Love, 1984, Love's Waiting Game, 1985, A Touch of Love, 1985, Diamonds for My Love, 1986, Secret of Love, 1987, The Marrying Kind, 1988, Island Rendezvous, 1990, Stowaway for Love, 1992, The Temporary Bride, 1993. Named Matrix Table Woman of Achievement, 1976. Republican. Anglican. Club: Women's Univ. (Seattle). Home: 9718 Fairway Ridge Rd Charlotte NC 28277-8759 *I have always made a point of writing pleasant books that "turn out right"- believing that after readers have opened their wallets to purchase a book all suffering should cease.*

FINLEY, HAROLD MARSHALL, investment banker; b. McConnelsville, Ohio, Feb. 24, 1916; s. Harry Marshall and Kate (Cotton) F.; m. Jean Rowley, Sept. 19, 1943; 1 child, Robert W. BS cum laude, Northwestern U., 1933; BD cum laude, Chgo. Theol. Sem., 1944; postgrad., U. Chgo., 1949; LLD, Lincoln Meml. U., 1975; DHL, Lakeland Coll., 1990; LLD, Lewis U., 1995; DHL, Muskingum Coll., 1997. Vice pres. Chgo. Title and Trust Co., 1963-76; sr. v.p. Burton J. Vincent, Chesley & Co., Chgo., 1976-84, Prescott, Ball & Turben, Chgo., 1984-92, Kemper Securities, 1992-94; 1st v.p. Howe Barnes Investments, Chgo., 1994—. Author: Everybody's Guide to the Stock Market, 1956, 59, 65, 68, The Logical Approach to Successful Investing, 1971; columnist Market Trends, Chgo. Today, 1961-74, Chgo. Tribune, 1974-81. Trustee Chgo. Boys and Girls Club; active Lockport Twp. H.S. Bd. Edn., 1961-64; trustee Alice Lloyd Coll., Chgo. Theol. Sem., Kobe Coll., Lewis U.; trustee Lincoln Meml. U., chmn., 1981—; trustee Scholl Coll. Podiatric Medicine, 1986-96, Sci. and Arts Acad., 1994—; treas. Ill. Humane Soc., 1986—. Mem. Investment Analysts Soc. Chgo., Chartered Fin. Analysts, Transp. Securities Club Chgo., Delta Sigma Pi. Congregationalist. Clubs: Univ. (Chgo.), Rotary (Chgo.) (pres. 1978-79). Home: 535 Tonelli Trl Lockport IL 60441-3344 Office: 135 S La Salle St Ste 1500 Chicago IL 60603-4201 *I have had a wide range of experiences and have enjoyed them all. I find each day and each person interesting and am continually thankful for the health to enjoy them.*

FINLEY, JACK DWIGHT, investments and consultation executive; b. Lawrence County, Ind., Aug. 7, 1927; s. Paul and Esther Irene (Keithley) F.; m. Beverly Janice Burpee, June 11, 1949; children: Janice Blair, Jennifer Brooke Finley Nichols, Jena Blake. BS, U.S. Mil. Acad., 1949; MSEE, U. Ill., 1953; LittD (hon.), Westbrook Coll., 1996. Commd. 2d lt. USAF, 1949, advanced through grades to capt., 1955, resigned, 1956; mem. tech. staff Ramo-Wooldridge Corp., L.A., 1956-60; v.p. R&D Data Corp., Dayton, Ohio, 1960-68; v.p., tech. dir., chmn. bd. dirs., founder EIKONIX Corp., Bedford, Mass., 1968-86, cons. investments, dir. svcs., 1986—; cons. Ramo-Wooldridge, 1960-61; vis. lectr. Rochester (N.Y.) Inst. Tech., 1966-68; bd. dirs. Quipp, Inc., Miami, Fla., chmn., 1995—. Contbr. articles to profl. jours.; patentee in field. Trustee Westbrook Coll., Portland, Maine, 1987-96, vice chmn. bd., 1988-90, chmn. bd., 1990-95; trustee U. New Eng., 1996-97, trustee emeritus, 1998. Fellow Soc. Photo Optical Instrumentation Engrs.; mem. IEEE (life sr. mem.), AIAA, Missile Range and Space Pioneers (life charter mem.), Am. Soc. Photogrammetry and Remote Sensing (emeritus), U. Ill. Alumni Assn., Assn. Grads. U.S. Mil. Acad., Eta Kappa Nu, Nashawtuc Country Club, Wyndemere Country Club. Home and Office: 338 Edgemere Way N Naples FL 34105-7105 also: 30 Washington Dr Acton MA 01720-3122

FINLEY, JULIE HAMM, political party official. Chairperson D.C. Republican Party. Office: DC Republican Party 3221 Woodland Dr NW Washington DC 20008-3548*

FINLEY, KAREN, actress; b. 1956. Writer, illustrator Shock Treatment, 1990, Enough Is Enough: Weekly Meditations for Living Dysfunctionally, 1993; performer The Constant State of Desire, 1987, We Keep Our Victims Ready, 1990, A Certain Level of Denial, 1992; author Living It Up: Humorous Adventures In Hyperdomesticity. Office: care City Lights Books Inc 261 Columbus Ave San Francisco CA 94133*

FINLEY, KATHERINE MANDUSIC, professional society administrator; b. Mansfield, Ohio, Nov. 8, 1954; d. Sam and Ann Julia (Konves) Mandusic; m. Edwin D. McDonell, Aug. 18, 1979 (div. Dec. 1994); m. Jeffrey A. Finley, June 12, 1999. BA, Ohio Wesleyan U.; MA in History and Mus. Studies, Case Western Res.; MBA, Ind. U. Rschr. Conner Prairie Mus., Fishers, Ind., 1978-82; exec. dir./rsch. historian Ind. Med. History Mus./Ind. Hist. Soc., Indpls., 1982-91; asst. dir. for comm. and mktg. Ind. U. Ctr. on Philanthropy, 1991-93; exec. dir. Roller Skating Assn. Internat., Indpls., 1993—. Author: The Journals of William A. Lindsay, 1989; contbg. editor The Encyclopedia of Indianapolis, 1994; contbr. articles to profl. jours. Pres. Altrusa Internat. of Indpls., 1995-97, treas., 1998—; bd. dirs. Nat. Mus. of Roller Skating, Lincoln, 1994—; bd. dirs. Ind. Soc. of Assn. Exec. Found., 1996—, chair edn. com., 1997-98. Mem. Am. Soc. of Assn. Execs. (cert.), Nat. Soc. of Fund Raising Execs. (cert.), Am. Mktg. Assn., Toastmasters (v.p. edn. 1998—), Beta Gamma Sigma, Sigma Iota Epsilon, Phi Beta Kappa. Avocations: reading, walking, gourmet cooking, traveling. Office: Roller Skating Assn 6905 Corporate Dr Indianapolis IN 46278-1927

FINLEY, LEWIS MERREN, financial consultant; b. Reubens, Idaho, Nov. 29, 1929; s. John Emory and Charlotte (Priest) F.; m. Virginia Ruth Spousta, Feb. 23, 1957; children: Ellen Annette, Charlotte Louise. Student pub. schs., Spokane. With Household Fin. Co., Portland, Oreg. and Seattle, 1953-56, Doug Gerow Fin., Portland, 1956-61; pres. Family Fin. Planners Inc., Portland, 1961—; assoc. broker Peoples Choice Realty, Inc., Milwaukie, Oreg., 1977-82, Lewis M. Finley, Real Estate Broker, Inc., 1982—; standing trustee Chpt. 13, Fed. Bankruptcy Ct., Dist. of Oreg., 1979. Author: The Complete Guide to Getting Yourself Out of Debt, 1975. With U.S. Army, 1951-53. Mem. Oreg. Assn. Credit Counselors (past pres.), N.W. Assn. Credit Counselors (past treas.), Am. Assn. Credit Counselors (v.p. 1982-85), Authors Guild, Nat. Assn. Realtors, Masons (past master), Shriners. Republican. Methodist. Home: 3015 SE Riviere Dr Portland OR 97267-5548 Office: 2154 NE Broadway St Ste 120 Portland OR 97232-1561

FINLEY, MADISON K., dean; b. Aug. 17, 1951. BA cum laude, Union Coll., 1972; MA, Coll. St. Rose, 1975. Mgr. Computer Ctr. Tandy Corp., Albany, N.Y., 1980; regional edn. coord. Tandy Corp., Poughkeepsie, N.Y., 1981-82; assoc. prof. computer info. sys. Dutchess C.C., Poughkeepsie, 1982-92, assoc. dean acad. affairs, 1993—. E-mail: finley@sunydutchess.edu. Office: 69 Poplar Ave Pine Plains NY 12567

FINLEY, MARGARET MAVIS, retired elementary school educator; b. Jackson, Mich., Dec. 2, 1927; d. Allen Aaron and Minnie Mavis (Graham) Lincoln; m. Duane Douglas Finley, Aug. 23, 1952; 1 child, Linda Louise. BS, Ea. Mich. U., 1960; postgrad., Pepperdine U., 1968-72. Cert. tchr., Mich., Calif. Tchr. Jackson Sch. Dist., 1960-67, Pomona (Calif.) Sch. Dist., 1967-88; vol. proofreader Calif. Assn. Ind. Bus., Inc. Contbr. poetry and articles to profl. jours. Mem. AAUW, Calif. Ret. Tchrs. Assn. Avocations: writing, reading, hiking, travel, theater. Home: 1072 Cypress Point Dr Banning CA 92220-5404

FINLEY, MICHAEL, national park administrator; m. Lillie Eiteneier, June 1969; children: Devon Maranne, Laura Christine. BS in Biology, So. Oreg. State U., 1970, postgrad. in environ. edn. Various positions in field to supt. Assateague Island Nat. Seashore, Berlin, Md., 1981-83; assoc. regional dir. for mgmt. and opers. Alaska Region, Anchorage, 1983-86; supt. Everglades Nat. Park, Homestead, Fla., 1986-89, Yosemite Nat. Park, Calif., 1989-94; acting assoc. dir., opers. Yellowstone Nat. Park, Wyo., 1994, supt., 1994—; mem. coun. Bahamas Nat. Trust, Nassau; mem. gov.'s task force Everglades Expansion Project, Fla.; mem. Dade County Well Field Commn., Miami, Yosemite Regional Transport Com.; rep. to Loxahatchee Wild and Scenic River Adv. Coun.; bd. mem. Zapovednicks Environ. Edn. Ctr., Moscow. Sgt. U.S. Army Res. Recipient Disting. Pub. Svc. award Am. Rivers, 1996, Meritorious Svc. award Dept. of Interior, 1995, Conservationist of the Yr. award Everglades Coalition, 1990, Conservation award Tropical Audubon Soc., 1989, Pub. Svc. award for Environmental Protection, Sierra Club, 1988; named Conservationist of the Yr., Fla. Audubon, 1988, others. Mem. Assn. Nat. Park Rangers (pres., bd. dirs.). Office: Mammoth Hot Spring Park Hdqrs PO Box 148 Yellowstone Park WY 82190

FINLEY, PHILIP BRUCE, retired state adjutant general; b. White City, Kans., Mar. 25, 1930; s. Marshall Arthur and Zelma Rena (Krenkle) F.; m. Jacqueline Lou Thomas, May 23, 1952; children: Jeffrey Allen, Robin Lyn. BS, Kans. State U., 1951, MS, 1954. Commd. U.S. Army, 1951, advanced through grades to maj. gen., 1988; served in Kans. N.G., 1967-84; served with Res. Norton, Kans., 1954-67; high sch. tchr. Bird City, Kans., 1954-55, Norton, Kans., 1955-67; extension agt. Decatur County Agr. Extension Council, Oberlin, Kans., 1967-72; rural devel. specialist Kans. State U. Area Office, Colby, 1972-74; N.W. Area dir. Kansas State U. Agrl. Extension, Colby, 1974-86, assoc. head, 1986—; adjutant-gen. State of Kans., Topeka, 1987-90; retired, 1990. Mem. N.W. Kans. Planning and Devel. Group, Hill City, 1972-74, "Future Kans." Planning Commn., Topeka, 1985-86. Mem. 7th Div. Assn., VFW, Am. Legion, Phi Delta Kappa, Epsilon Sigma Phi. Republican. Methodist. Avocations: game bird hunting, horsemanship, beekeeping, automobile mechanics. Home: 685 S Court Ave Colby KS 67701-3411*

FINLEY, ROBERT COE, III, interventional cardiologist, consultant, educator; b. Aurora, Ill., July 14, 1947; s. Robert Coe Jr. and Elizabeth Lorraine (Winkenweder) F.; m. Celia Ann Oberg; children: Robert IV, Timothy, Rebecca; stepchildren: Erik, Jacquelyn. BS magna cum laude, U. Ill., 1970, postgrad., 1970-72; MD, Loyola U, Chicago, 1976. Diplomate Am. Bd. Med. Examiners, Am. Bd. Internal Medicine, Am. Bd. Cardiovasc. Disease. Resident internal medicine Loyola U. Med. Ctr., Maywood, Ill., 1976-79, cardiology fellow, 1979-81, attending physician, asst. prof. medicine, 1981-83, clin. asst. prof., 1983—; physician, ptnr. Suburban Cardiologist, Hinsdale, Ill., 1983—; dir. founder Cardiac Rehab. Ctr., Maywood, 1982-83; dir., founder cardiac catherization lab. Hinsdale Hosp., 1984-91, dir. coronary angioplasty program, founder, 1989-91, dir., founder outpatient inotropic support program, 1989-91, chmn. cardiac catheterization com., 1984—, chmn. dept. medicine, 1996-97. Co-founder, co-dir. Men's Bible Group, Riverside Presbyn. Ch., 1983-85; physician vol. advanced cardiac life support tag com. Chgo. Heart Assn., 1988-91; physician vol. Cmty. Nurse Assn., La Grange, Ill., 1995—. Commendation for Caring and Bravery City Woodstock, Ill., 1983; Edmund Janes James scholar U. Ill., 1966-70. Fellow Am. Coll. Cardiology, Soc. Cardiac Angiography and Interventions, Am. Coll. Chest Physicians; mem. Alpha Sigma Nu. Avocations: martial arts, snow and water skiing, hiking, bicycling. Home: 136 Circle Ridge Dr Burr Ridge IL 60521-8379 Office: Suburban Cardiologist 333 Chestnut St Hinsdale IL 60521-3247

FINLEY, ROBERT VAN EATON, minister; b. Charlottesville, Va., May 2, 1922; s. William Walter and Melissa (Hoover) F.; m. Ethel Drummond, Dec. 23, 1949; children: Deborah Ann, Ruth Ellen. BA, U. Va., 1944; postgrad., U. Chgo. Div. Sch., 1946-47; LittD, Houghton Coll., 1952. Ordained to ministry Bapt. Ch., 1957. Evangelist Youth for Christ Internat., Chgo., 1945-46, Inter-Varsity Christian Fellowship, Chgo., 1945-46, overseas, 1948-51; pastor Evnag. Free Ch., Richmond, Calif., 1951-52; minister to fgn. students 10th Presbyn. Ch., Phila., 1952-55; founder, gen. dir. Christian Aid Mission, Charlottesville, 1953-70, chmn., CEO, 1970—; founder, gen. dir. Overseas Students Mission, Ft. Eire, Ont., Can., 1954-68; pres. Overseas Students Mission, Ft. Eire, 1969-85; pastor Temple Bapt. Ch., Washington, 1965-66; founder, pres. Christian Aid Mission Can., 1985-88, chmn. bd. dirs., 1989—; pres. Bharat Evang. Fellowship, Washington, 1973-87; chmn., bd. dirs. Internat. Congress Indigenous Missions, Harrisburg, Pa., 1988—. Editor Conquest for Christ, 1954-74, Christian Mission mag., 1974—. Founder, pres. Internat. Students, Inc., Colorado Springs, Colo., 1952-67, chmn., 1968-70. Mem. Assn. Christian Ministries to Internats. (bd. dirs. 1995—), Omicron Delta Kappa. Office: Christian Aid Mission PO Box 9037 Charlottesville VA 22906-9037 also: Christian Aid Mission, 201 Stanton St, Fort Erie, ON Canada L2A 3N8 *To indulge myself, beyond actual need, with the benefits of material wealth leaves me the poorer. But when my surplus resources are used to uplift those who lack opportunity, I am enriched.*

FINLEY, SARA CREWS, medical geneticist, educator; b. Lineville, Ala., Feb. 26, 1930; m. Wayne H. Finley; children: Randall Wayne, Sara Jane. B.S. in Biology, U. Ala., 1951, M.D., 1955. Diplomate Am. Bd. Med. Genetics; cert. clin. geneticist; cert. clin. cytogeneticist. Intern Lloyd Noland Hosp., Fairfield, Ala., 1955-56; NIH fellow in pediatrics U. Ala. Med. Sch., Birmingham, 1956-60; NIH trainee in med. genetics Inst. Med. Genetics, U. Uppsala, Sweden, 1961-62; mem. faculty U. Ala. Med. Sch., 1960-96, co-dir. lab. med. genetics, 1966-96, prof. pediatrics, 1975-96, occupant Wayne H. and Sara Crews Finley chair med. genetics, 1986-96, prof. emeritus, 1996—; Disting. Faculty lectr. Med. Ctr., U. Ala. at Birmingham, 1983; mem. staff Univ. U. Ala. Hosp., Children's Hosp. Ala.; mem. ad hoc com. genetic counseling Children's Bur., HEW, 1966; mem. ad hoc rev. panel for genetic disease and sickle cell testing and counseling programs, 1980; mem. genetic diseases program objective rev. panel Bur. Maternal and Child Health and Resources Div., HHS, 1989, mem. adv. group on lab. quality assurance, 1989; Birmingham bd. dirs. Compass Bank. Author papers on clin. cytogenetics, human congenital malformations, human growth and devel. Mem. White House Conf. Health, 1965; mem. rsch. manpower rev. com. Nat. Cancer Inst., 1977-81; mem. Sickle Cell Disease Adv. Com., NIH, 1983-87; chairperson physician's campaign bd. dirs. United Way, 1993-95. Recipient Disting. Alumna award U. Ala. Sch. Medicine Alumni Assn., 1989, Med. award Ala. Assn. for Retarded Children, 1969, Turlington award Planned Parenthood of Ala., 1982, Nat. Outstanding Alumnae award Zeta Tau Alpha, 1992, Disting. Alumna award U. Ala. Nat. Alumni Assn., 1994; co-recipient Will Holmes award Children's Aid Soc. Birmingham, 1999; named Top Ten Women in Birmingham, 1989, Top 31 Most Outstanding Alumnae U. Ala., Tuscaloosa, 1993. Fellow AMA (founding), Am. Coll. Med. Genetics; mem. Am. Soc. Human Genetics, Am. Fedn. Clin. Rsch., Soc. Exptl. Biology and Medicine, N.Y. Acad. Scis., So. Soc. Pediatric Rsch., Med. Assn. Ala., Ala. Assn. Retarded Children (Ann. Med. award 1969), Ala. Acad. Sci., Jefferson County Med. Soc. (pres. 1990), Jefferson County Pediatric Soc., The Harrison Soc., Rotary Club of Birmingham, Phi Beta Kappa, Sigma Xi, Alpha Omega Alpha, Alpha Epsilon Delta, Omicron Delta Kappa, Phi Kappa Phi, Zeta Tau Alpha. Home: 3412 Brookwood Rd Birmingham AL 35223-2023 Office: U Ala UAB Station Birmingham AL 35294

FINLEY, SARAH MAUDE MERRITT, social worker; b. Atlanta, Nov. 19, 1946; d. Genius and Willie Maude (Wright) Merritt; m. Craig Wayne Finley, Aug. 10, 1968; children: Craig Wayne Jr., Jarret Lee. *Sarah's son, Craig Jr., is a certified technical instructor with the New Horizons Computer Learning Center, a division of Appletree Technologies, Inc. He received a scientific diploma from Riverside Military Academy in 1988, and received a Bachelor of Arts degree from Morehouse College in 1993. He was commissioned second Lieutenant in the United States Army Reserves, Corps. of Engineers, in 1993. He currently is a Certified Network Engineer. Her son Jarret, is a Sophomore at Morehouse College. Sarah's husband Craig, is a decorated Vietnam Veteran, and a retired Lieutenant Colonel of the United States Army Reserve.* BA, Spelman Coll., 1968; postgrad., Atlanta U., 1968-69. Job placement advisor Marsh Draughton Bus. Coll., Atlanta, 1971-72; child attendant Fulton County Juvenile Ct., Atlanta, 1972; social worker Fulton County Dept. Family and Children Svcs., Atlanta, 1972—, casework supr., 1976-98, Title VI customer svc. coord. Ctrl. City/North Area office, 1990-98; RTD Fulton County Govt., 1996—; outreach counselor Right Way Home Project N.W. Area Office, 1998—; supr. Count on Me video Ga. Dept. Human Resources, 1987. *In 1998, Sarah composed a manual for the Right Way Home Project. She has also added a new section to the manual on financial accountability.* Vol. coord. family support program Family Support Group of Atlanta Detachment of 2d Army Maneuver Tng. Commd.; vol. family support com. 87th Maneuver Area Command (now 4th Brigade, 87th Divsn.), 1991-93; del. Ft. McPherson (Ga.) Army Family Symposium, 1992, 3d ann. worldwide USAR Family Support Conf., St. Louis, 1992. Mem. Am. Pub. Human Svcs. Assn., Ga. County Welfare Assn., Ga. Conf. on Social Welfare, Nat. Assn. Counties, Nat. Alumnae Assn. Spelman Coll., Fulton County Ret. Employees Assn., Womens Aux. Ga. VFW, Atlanta Urban League. Baptist. Avocations: poetry, reading, volunteer work, stress mgmt. Office: Fulton County Dept Family and Children Svcs 1249 Bankhead Ave NW Atlanta GA 30318-6657

FINLEY, SKIP, media consultant, communications executive; b. Ann Arbor, Mich., July 23, 1948; s. Ewell W. and Mildred Virginia (Johnson) F.; m. Karen Michele Woolard, May 6, 1971; children: Kharma I., R. Kristin. *Skip Finley's father (deceased) received his undergraduate degree in engineering from Howard University, and his Masters of Engineering from the University of Michigan and went on to form one of the world's largest Black owned consulting engineering firms. Ewell W. Finley & Associates, a New York city based company, played significant roles in the structural design of Atlanta's Hartsfield Airport, the Harlem State Office Building, the Schomberg Cultural Center, the Throgs Neck bridge and the Martin Luther*

King, Jr. Center for Cultural Change. He was a leading integrationist in the 1950's to 1970's who worked closely in the areas of education. Student, Northeastern U., 1966-71. Owner Skifin Gallery, Boston, 1970-71; floor dir. Sta. WHDH-TV, Boston, 1971; floor mgr., asst. dir., producer Sta. WSBK TV, Boston, 1971-72; account exec. Sta. WRKO-AM, Boston, 1972-73; account mgr. Humphrey, Browning, MacDougall Advt., Boston, 1973-74; sales mgr. Sta. WAMO-AM-FM Sheridan Broadcasting Corp., 1974-75, gen. mgr. Sta. WAMO-AM-FM, 1975-76; v.p. radio div. Sheridan Broadcasting Corp., Pitts., 1976-77; dir. of sales Sheridan Broadcasting Network, 1977-79, exec. v.p., gen. mgr., 1979-81, pres., 1981-82; gen. ptnr. Sta. KEZO AM-FM, Omaha, 1983-88, Sta. KDAB-FM, Salt Lake City and Ogden, Utah, 1985-90; pres., gen. mgr. Sta. WKYS-FM, Washington, 1988-95; pres., CEO, Albimar Communications, Washington, 1982-95; CEO, COO Am. Urban Radio Networks, Pitts., 1995-98; pres., CEO Answers, Solutions, 1999—. *Skip Finley has worked in television, radio, advertising, and network radio since 1971 in radio sales, management and ownership. He has had responsibilities with 18 radio stations in 12 U.S. markets and owned four in Omaha, Salt Lake City and Washington D.C. Since 1987 he has served on the Board of Directors of the Carter Broadcast Group that owns KPRT-AM/KPRS-FM, founded by Andrew Skip Carter (deceased) in 1949. KPRT was the second and is the longest continuously black owned radio station in America. Mr. Finley is presently a radio consultant who developed a radio manager's Executive Development system, Answers, Solutions.* Contbr. numerous articles on media-related subjects to various publs. Testimony to House subcom. on Communications, 1977, Congl. Black Caucus, 1990; mem. bd. overseers, trustee Vineyard Open Land Found. Recipient Excellence in Media award Nat. Assn. Media Women, 1981, Communicator of Yr. award Washington Area Media Orgn., 1982, New Horizons award D.C. Gen. Hosp., Washington, 1990, Advocacy in Edn. award D.C. Pub. Schs., Washington, 1990, Radio Wayne award as best overall broadcaster Radio Ink Mag., 1994. Mem. Nat. Assn. Black Owned Broadcasters (bd. dirs. 1977-95), Radio Advt. Bur. (bd. dirs. 1990—, chair 1997-98), Nat. Assn. Broadcasters (bd. dirs., vice chair radio bd. 1990-94), Nat. Thespian Soc., The Advt. Coun., Inc. (bd. dirs. 1998—), Martha's Vineyard Rod and Gun Club, Lowes Island Golf Club (founding adv. bd. govs. 1992-97). Avocations: computers, model trains, shooting, automobiles, boating. Fax: 508-696-8692. E-mail: Abe-Lackman@aol.com. Office: Answers Solutions 4370 Argyle Terr NW Washington DC 20011

FINMAN, TED, lawyer, educator; b. San Francisco, Feb. 10, 1931; s. Samuel and Dora (Weinberg) F.; m. Susan F. Heifetz, Jan. 2, 1950; children—Rona Irene, Terry Janette. B.A., U. Chgo., 1950; LL.B., Stanford U., 1954. Bar: Calif. 1955, U.S. Ct. Appeals (9th cir.) 1955. Pvt. practice law, 1954-59; asst. prof. law U. N.Mex. Law Sch., 1959-62; vis. asso. prof. Rutgers U. Law Sch., 1962-63; mem. faculty U. Wis., Madison, 1963—; prof. law U. Wis., 1966—, Bascom Prof. Law, 1986—. Co-author: The Lawyer in Modern Society, 2d edit, 1976; contbr. articles to legal jours. Research grantee U. Wis.; Research grantee Am. Bar Found. Mem. Calif. Bar Assn., Order of Coif. Democrat. Jewish. Office: U Wis Law Sch Madison WI 53706

FINN, ALBERT FRANK, JR., physician; b. Huntington, N.Y., Sept. 30, 1956; s. Albert F. and Margaret F. (May) F.; m. Anna M. Cannella, July 19, 1982; children: Anastasia, Alexandria, Abigail. BS cum laude, St. John's U., 1980; MD cum laude, SUNY, Syracuse, 1984. Diplomate Am. Bd. Internal Medicine, Am. Bd. Pathology, Am. Bd. Allergy and Immunology. Intern gen. medicine SUNY, Stony Brook, 1984-85, resident clin. pathology, 1985-88, resident internal medicine, 1988-89, allergy and clin. immunology fellow, 1989-91, clin. assoc. instr., 1985-91, cons. divsn. lab. medicine Med. Ctr., 1988-91, clin. asst. prof. medicine, 1991-92, head sect. on allergy, 1991-92; clin. assoc. prof. medicine, microbiology and immunology Med. U. S.C., Charleston, 1992—; adj. asst. prof. St. John's U., N.Y.C., 1991-92. Contbr. articles to profl. jours. Mem. com. on advance cardiac life support Am. Heart Assn., Nassau County, N.Y., 1988-92; mem. Am. Lung Assn., S.C., 1992—, pres. Coastal br. Mem. ACP (bd. rev. course allergy and immunology sect. 1992), Am. Acad. Allergy and Immunology (task force 1994), Am. Soc. Clin. Pathology (course dir. lyme borreliosis 1989-92), S.C. Soc. Allergy & Immunology (pres. 1998—), Dorchester County Med. Soc. (pres. 1997-98), Rho Chi (pres.), Alpha Omega Alpha. Avocations: fishing, antique collecting, boating, skiing. Office: Allergy & Asthma Ctrs of Charleston PA 9165 University Blvd Charleston SC 29406-9120

FINN, BRENDAN PETER, school psychologist; b. Somerville, Mass., Oct. 31, 1960; s. Brendan Augustus and Edith Marjorie (Goggin) F.; m. Carolyn Heising, July 9, 1988 (div. Dec. 1997); 1 child, Peter. BS magna cum laude, Northeastern U., 1990, MEd, 1993, cert. advanced grad. study, 1993. Cert. sch. psychologist, Mass., Iowa. Warehouse asst. mgr. Harvard Coop. Soc., Cambridge, Mass., 1979-93; sch. psychologist Heartland Area Edn. Agy., Johnston, Iowa, 1993—; presenter in field. Mem. Nat. Assn. Sch. Psychologists, Iowa Sch. Psychologists Assn., Phi Kappa Phi. Roman Catholic. Avocations: music, sports, reading. Home: 1503 Grand Ave Ames IA 50010-5350 Office: Heartland Area Edn Agy # 11 511 S 17th St Ames IA 50010

FINN, CHESTER EVANS, lawyer; b. Dayton, Ohio, July 13, 1918; s. Samuel Lawrence and Lillian Rose (Evans) F.; m. Phyllis Muriel Kessel, Apr. 29, 1942 (dec. Oct. 30, 1987); children: Chester E. Jr., Natalie K., Samuel J.; m. Theodora K. Wilks, Sept. 18, 1988. BA, Yale U., 1940; LLB, Harvard U., 1946. Bar: Ohio 1947, U.S. Dist. Ct. (so. dist.) Ohio 1949, U.S. Ct. Claims 1949, U.S. Ct. Appeals (6th cir.) 1966, U.S. Supreme Ct. 1975, U.S. Ct. Internat. Trade 1984. Assoc. Estabrook, Finn & McKee, Dayton, 1947-53, ptnr., 1953-83; ptnr. Porter, Wright, Morris & Arthur, Dayton, 1983-92, of counsel, 1992—. Pres. Dayton United Way, 1969; trustee various civic groups. Lt. USNR, 1942-45, PTO. Mem. ABA, Ohio Bar Assn., Dayton Bar Assn. (pres. 1969), Moraine Country Club, Moss Creek Golf Club, Dayton Bicycle Club. Avocations: golfing, traveling. Home: 23 Cedar Ln Hilton Head Isle SC 27726 Office: Porter Wright Morris & Arthur PO Box 1805 1 S Main St Dayton OH 45401

FINN, DAVID, public relations company executive, artist; b. N.Y.C., Aug. 30, 1921; s. Jonathan and Sadie (Borgenicht) F.; m. Laura Zeisler, Oct. 20, 1945; children: Kathy, Dena, Peter, Amy. BS, CCNY, 1943. Co-founder Ruder Finn, Inc., N.Y.C., 1948, pres., 1956-68, chmn. bd., chief exec. officer, 1968—, also bd. dirs.; adj. assoc. prof. NYU. One-man show New Sch. for Social Research, N.Y.C.; exhibited in group shows at Nat. Acad., Washington, Met. Mus. Art, N.Y.C., Boston Mus. Art, L'Orangerie, Paris, Andrew Crispo Gallery, N.Y.C., Westchester County Ctr., others; author: Public Relations and Management, 1956, The Corporate Oligarch, 1969; photographer: (books) Embrace of Life, 1969, As the Eye Moves, 1970, Donatello: Prophet of Modern Vision, 1973, Henry Moore Sculpture and Environment, 1976, Michelangelo's Three Pietas, 1975, Oceanic Images, 1978, The Florence Baptistry Doors, 1980, Sculpture at Storm King, 1980, Busch-Reisinger Museum, 1980, Canova, Giambologna, Donatello, Cellini, David by the Hand of Michelangelo, In the Mountains of Japan, others; contbr. articles and chpts. to profl. jours. and art publs.; editor-in-chief Sculpture Rev. mag. Bd. dirs. Inst. Advanced Studies in Humanities, MacDowell Colony, Inst. for Future, Artists for Environment Found., Internat. Ctr. Photography, Am. Coll. Switzerland, Jewish Theol. Sem. Am.; mem. adv. coun. NEH; treas. Bus. Com. for Arts. Served to 1st lt. A.C. AUS, 1944. Mem. AAAS, Am. Fedn. Arts, Am. Inst. Graphic Arts (past dir.), Internat. Pub. Relations Assn., Kappa Tau Alpha (hon.). Office: Ruder Finn Inc 301 E 57th St New York NY 10022-2900*

FINN, EDWIN A., JR., publishing executive. BA in English and Polit. Sci., Tufts U.; MA in Internat. Banking and Fin., Columbia U. Asst. mng. editor Blackstone Valley Tribune, 1970s; mng. editor Southbridge (Mass.) Daily News, 1970s; nat. copyreader The Wall St. Jour., N.Y.C., 1980-81, editor fgn. desk, 1981-84, banking and fin. reporter Dallas bur., 1984-85; sr. editor internat. bus. and fin. Forbes Mag., 1986-89, asst. mng. editor, 1989-90; editor Am. Banker, 1990-92; mng. editor Barron's, The Dow Jones Bus. and Fin. Weekly, N.Y.C., 1993-95, editor, 1995—, pres., 1998. Office: Barron's 200 Liberty St New York NY 10281-0083*

FINN, FRANCES MARY, biochemistry researcher; b. Pitts., May 6, 1937; d. Stephen B. and Geraldine H. (Weber) F.; m. Klaus Hofmann, Feb. 26, 1965. BS in Chemistry, U. Pitts., 1959, MS in Biochemistry, 1961, PhD in Biochemistry, 1964. Asst. rsch. prof. biochemistry U. Pitts., 1969-73, assoc. rsch. prof., 1973-80, assoc. prof. medicine, 1980-88, prof., 1988—. Mem. Am. Chem. Soc., Endocrine Soc., Am. Soc. for Biochemistry and Molecular Biology, Am. Peptide Soc., Protein Soc. Home: 1467 Mohican Dr Pittsburgh PA 15228-1613 Office: U Pitts Protein Rsch Lab 3550 Terrace St Pittsburgh PA 15261-0076

FINN, GARY, educator, entrepreneur; b. Worcester, Mass., Apr. 2, 1961; s. Stanley M. and Lois I. (Solomon) F. ALB, Harvard U., 1988, ALM, 1994; postgrad., The Union Inst., 1996—. Milieu therapist Human Resource Inst., Brookline, Mass., 1988-89; sales assoc. New England Realty, Brookline, 1984-90; pres. Competitive Edge Enterprise, Cambridge, Mass., 1990—; pres., broker Starbridge Real Estate, Cambridge, 1995—. With U.S. Navy, 1978-82. Mem. APA., Am. Philos. Assn., Assn. for Advancement of Philosophy and Psychiatry, Soc. Ind. Scholars, Am. Soc. Spkrs. and Authors. Home and Office: PO Box 1671 Framingham MA 01701-1671

FINN, GERARD, federal government official; b. Inkerman, N.B., Can., Oct. 22, 1947; s. James and Elisabeth (Robichaud) F.; m. Linda O'Rourke, June 5, 1971. BA, U. Moncton, N.B., 1968; MA in History, Ottawa (Ont., Can.) U., 1971; Doctorat, U. Sorbonne, Paris, 1974. Prof. Moncton U., 1970-71; parliamentary intern Parliament of Can., Ottawa, 1974-75; historian Parks Can., Ottawa, 1975-78; dir. rsch. Parks Can., Calgary, Alta., 1978-81; regional dir. Commr. of Ofcl. Lang., Edmonton, Alta., 1981-84; dir. policy/program Can. Sec. of State, Ottawa, 1984-89; asst. dep. min. Govt. of N.B., Fredericton, 1989-90; dir. program/policy Treasury Bd. Secretariat, Ottawa, 1990-96; dir. gen. policies Commr. of Ofcl. Langs., Ottawa, 1997—. Scholar French Govt., 1971-74, Can. Polit. Sci. Assn., 1974-75. Roman Catholic. Home: 68 Atholl Doune, Aylmer, PQ Canada J9J 1B8 Office: Office of Commr, 344 Slater St, Ottawa, ON Canada K1A 0T8

FINN, JACK, press secretary; b. Denver, Apr. 16, 1966. BA, Calif. State U., North Ridge, 1989. Press sec. Office of Gov. of Nev., Carson city, 1999—. Office: Press Sec Office of the Gov Capitol Complex Carson City NV 89701

FINN, MARY RALPHE, artist; b. St. Paul, Nov. 13, 1933; d. Wendell W. and Rose Marie (Arendt) Ralphe; m. H. Roger Finn, June 15, 1957; children: Mark W., Shelly, Scott R. BS, U. Ark., 1955; MS, U. Iowa, 1957. Workshop demonstrator and cons. in field. Exhibited in solo shows at Art Mart Gallery, 1973, 76, Brown's Gallery, Boise, 1977, 80, 85, 89, 94, St. Lukes Regional Med. Ctr., Boise, 1982, Piper Jaffray Hopwood, Boise, 1979, 85, St. Alphonsus Med. Ctr., Boise, 1981, 90, Bank of Idaho, Boise, 1975, 79, Morrison Knudsen, Boise, 1978; group shows include Browns Galleries, 1975-98, St. Lukes Regional Med. Ctr., 1976-90, Idaho State Capitol, 1978, Idaho Watercolor Soc., 1987, St. Alphonsus Hosp., 1990, Albertson Coll. Idaho, 1988-98, Boise State U., 1991; represented in permanent collections Morrison-Knudsen Corp., West One Bancorp, 1st Security Bank Idaho, Inc., St. Lukes Regional Med. Ctr., 1st Interstate Bank, Am.-Hydro Corp. Mem. Boise Art Mus., Phi Upsilon Omicron, Zeta Tau Alpha, Omicron Nu.

FINN, PETER, public relations executive; b. N.Y.C., Mar. 31, 1954; s. David and Laura (Zeisler) F.; m. Sarah Duncan; children: Noah J., Emily M. BA, Brown U., 1976; MA, Columbia U., 1977. Researcher Research & Forecasts Inc., N.Y.C., 1977-79, dir. ops., 1979-81, chmn., 1981-84; chmn. fin. com. Ruder-Finn, Inc. (formerly Ruder, Finn & Rotman, Inc.), N.Y.C., 1984—, CFO, 1985-94, exec. v.p., 1986-87, chmn. exec. com., 1988—. Office: Ruder-Finn Inc 301 E 57th St New York NY 10022-2900*

FINN, PETER MICHAEL, television production executive; b. Milton, Mass., Feb. 19, 1936; s. Matthew Charles and Mary Germaine (Ireland) F.; m. Judith Mary Barry, Sept. 7, 1957 (div. Aug. 1996); children: Pamela Ann, Mary Kathryn, Matthew Ireland; m. Debra Jo McGraw, Oct. 18, 1997. A.B., Holy Cross Coll., 1956; M.B.A., George Washington U., 1962; A.M.P., Harvard U., 1980. Account exec. J. Walter Thompson Co., N.Y.C., 1962-64; account supr. J. Walter Thompson Co., 1966-67; account exec. Foote Cone & Belding, N.Y.C., 1964-66; v.p., account supr. Foote Cone & Belding, 1967-68, Doyle Dane Bernbach, N.Y.C., 1968-70; sr. v.p., dir. F.W. Free, N.Y.C., 1970-74; pres. Henderson Advt., Greenville, S.C., 1974-80, Bozell & Jacobs, Dallas, 1980-85; also dir. Bozell & Jacobs; sr. ptnr., div. pres. Whittle Communications, Knoxville, Tenn., 1985-92; pres., CEO Peter Matthew Prodns., Dallas, 1992—. Mem. Greater Greenville Planning Council, 1976-79, Dallas Citizens Council. Served to lt. USNR, 1957-62. Mem. Am. Assn. Advt. Agys. (bd. govs.), Am. Advt. Fedn., Am. Mktg. Assn. Office: Peter Matthew Prodns 3131 Mckinney Ave Ste 825 Dallas TX 75204-2466

FINN, ROBERT, writer, lecturer, broadcaster; b. Boston, July 13, 1930; s. Edward Anthony and E. Caroline (Seifert) F.; m. Mary Pacana, Oct. 12, 1957; children: Laurence, Elaine. BA, Boston U., 1952. Staff reporter, music-drama critic New Bedford (Mass.) Standard-Times, 1956-59, Akron (Ohio) Beacon Jour., 1959-64; music critic Cleve. Plain Dealer, 1964-92; mem. guest faculty Rockefeller Found. project for tng. music critics, 1965, 66. Contbr. to Opera News mag., Am. Record Guide. Served with AUS, 1953-56. Co-recipient ASCAP-Deems Taylor award for, 1972, 74, 78, 80. Mem. Music Critics Assn. (exec. bd. 1975-83, v.p. 1983-85, pres. 1985-89). Roman Catholic. Home: 1211 Blanchester Rd Cleveland OH 44124-1325

FINN, STEPHEN MARTIN, producer; b. Indpls., June 21, 1949; s. Martin Joseph and Theresa Diane (Mervar) F.; children: Shawn Marie, Stephanie Michelle, Rhyan Linthicum, Raimie Catherine (dec.). Pres. Equinox Systems, Grand Rapids, Mich., 1975-77, Solstice, 1978—. Photographer Equitable Gallery, N.Y.C., 1978; contbr. articles profl. mags. Recipient Kinsa award Kodak Internat., N.Y.C., 1978. Mem. Am. Film Inst., Profl. Photographers Am., Aircraft Owners and Pilots Assn., Mensa, Fla. Motion Picture Theater Assn. Home: PO Box 129 Lake Helen FL 32744-0129

FINN, TERRENCE M., lawyer; b. Mpls., Feb. 13, 1948. BA, Yale U., 1970; JD, U. Pa., 1973. Bar: R.I. 1973, U.S. Dist. Ct. R.I. 1973, U.S. Ct. Appeals (1st. cir.) 1982, Mass. 1984. Mng. ptnr. Edwards & Angell, Boston. Mem. R.I. Bar Assn., Mass. Bar Assn., Fla. Bar. Office: Edwards & Angell 101 Federal St Fl 23 Boston MA 02110-1810

FINNBERG, ELAINE AGNES, psychologist, editor; b. Bklyn., Mar. 2, 1948; d. Benjamin and Agnes Montgomery (Evans) F.; m. Rodney Lee Herndon, Mar. 1, 1981; 1 child, Andrew Marshal. BA in Psychology, L.I. U., 1969; MA in Psychology, New Sch. for Social Rsch., 1973; PhD in Psychology, Calif. Sch. Profl. Psychology, 1981. Diplomate Am. Bd. Forensic Examiners, Am. Bd. Forensic Medicine, Am. Bd. Med. Psychotherapists and Psychodiagnosticians, Am. Bd. Disability Analysts, Am. Bd. Psychol. Specialties, Prescribing Psychologists Register; lic. psychologist, Calif. Rsch. asst. in med. sociology Cornell U. Med. Coll., N.Y.C., 1969-70; med. abstractor USV Pharm. Corp., Tuckahoe, N.Y., 1970-71, Coun. for Tobacco Rsch., N.Y.C., 1971-77; editor, writer Found. of Thanatology Columbia U., N.Y.C., 1971-76, cons. family studies program cancer ctr. Coll. Physicians &Surgeons, 1973-74; dir. grief psychology and bereavement counseling San Francisco Coll. Mortuary Scis., 1977-81; rsch. assoc. dept. epidemiology and internat. health U. Calif., San Francisco, 1979-81, asst. clin. prof. dept. family and cmty. medicine, 1985-93, assoc. clin. prof., dept. family and cmty. medicine, 1993—; active med. staff Natividad Med. Ctr., Salinas, Calif., 1984—, chief psychologist, 1984-96; prof. adv. coun. Am. Bd. Disability Analysts; asst. chief psychiatry svc. Natividad Med. Ctr., 1985-96, acting chief psychiatry, 1988-89, vice-chair medicine dept., 1991-93, sec.-treas. med. staff, 1992-94; cons. med. staff Salinas Valley Meml. Hosp., 1991—, Mee Meml. Hosp., 1996-97; dir. tng. Monterey Psychiat. Health Facility, 1996-97, chief clin. staff, 1996-97; expert cons. Calif. Bd. Psychology. Editor: The California Psychologist, 1988-95; editor Jour. of Thanatology, 1972-76, Cathexis, 1976-81. Govs. adv. bd. Agnews Devel. Ctr., San Jose, Calif., 1988-96, chair, 1989-91, 94-95. Fellow Prescribing Psychologists Register (diplomate); mem. APA, Nat. Register Health Svc. Providers in Psychology, Calif. Psychol. Assn. (Disting. Svc. award 1989), Soc. Behavioral Medicine, Mid-Coast Psychol. Assn. (sec. 1985, treas. 1986, pres. 1987, Disting. Svc. to Psychology award 1993), Forensic Mental Health Assn. Calif., Western Psychol. Assn., Assn. Advancement Behavior Therapy, Am. Med. Writers Assn., Assn. Treatment Sexual Abuses, Soc. for Personality Assessment, Internat. Rorschach. Soc., Internat. Soc. Police Surgeons, Internat. Soc. of Police Surgeons.

FINNEGAN, CYRIL VINCENT, retired university dean, zoology educator; b. Dover, N.H., July 17, 1922; emigrated to Can., 1958; s. Cyril Vincent and Hilda A. (McClintock) F.; children: Maureen A., Patrick S., Cathaleen C., Kevin S., Eileen D., Gormlaith R., Michaeleen S., Mairead B., Conal E. BS., Bates Coll., Lewiston, Maine, 1946; M.S., U. Notre Dame, 1948, Ph.D., 1951. From instr. to asst. prof. St. Louis U., 1952-56; asst. prof. U. Notre Dame, South Bend, Ind., 1956-58; from asst. prof. to prof. zoology U. B.C., Vancouver, 1958-88, emeritus, 1988—, assoc. dean sci., 1972-79, dean sci., 1979-85, dean emeritus, 1988—; assoc. acad. v.p., 1986-88. Contbr. articles to sci. jours. Served to sgt F.A. and C.E. AUS, 1942-45, NATOUSA, CBI. Postdoctoral research fellow NIH, 1952-53; Killum sr. fellow, 1968-69. Mem. Soc. Devel. Biology, Can. Soc. Cell Biology, Tissue Culture Assn., Internat. Soc. Develop. Biology, Sigma Xi. Roman Catholic. Office: U BC Dept Zoology, Faculty of Science, Vancouver, BC Canada V6T 1Z4

FINNEGAN, JAMES JOHN, JR., editor, publisher; b. Chgo., Dec. 21, 1948; s. James John and Carmen Maria (Carrasquillo Badillo) F.; m. Joan Karen Quinlan, June 26, 1971; children: James III, Erin, Byron. BA, De Paul U., 1973. Editor, asst. dir. Ill. Inst. Tech., Chgo., 1974-76; gen. mgr. Scroll Studio, Inc., Chgo., 1976-78; pres. Scribes, Inc., Riverside, Ill., 1978—; founder, editor, pub. The Landmark newspaper, Riverside, 1985-96. Bd. dirs. Riverside Arts Coun., 1986—, Riverside Little League, 1986-87, IHM High Sch., Westchester, Ill., 1986-88; commr. Riverside Hist. Commn., 1989-93; chmn. St. Mary Elem. Sch. Bd., Riverside, 1990-91; mem. Riverside Strategic Planning Task Force Com., 1995-98. Mem. Frederick Law Olmstead Soc. (bd. dirs. 1987-94), Exec. Club of Chgo., Riverside Swim Club. Avocations: basketball, swimming, writing. Office: Scribes Inc 45 W 83d St Burr Ridge IL 60521

FINNEGAN, NEAL FRANCIS, banker; b. Boston, Mar. 28, 1938; s. Neal Francis and Mary Theresa (McNeil) F.; children: Theresa, Lynn, Neal, Wayne. BS, Northeastern U., 1961; MBA, Babson Coll., 1969. With Shawmut Bank of Boston, 1961-80, sr. v.p. in charge of OIC comml. banking, 1977-80; pres., chief exec. officer Worcester Bancorp Inc., Mass., 1980-82; chmn., chief exec. officer Worcester County Nat. Bank, 1980-82; sr. exec. v.p. Shawmut Corp., Boston, 1982-83, vice-chmn., 1983-86, dir., 1982-86; exec. v.p. Shawmut Bank of Boston, N.A., 1983-86; pres., chief operating officer, dir. Bowery Savs. Bank, N.Y.C., 1986-88; exec. v.p. Bankers Trust Co., N.Y.C., 1988-93; pres., CEO UST Corp., Boston, 1993—, US Trust Bank, Boston. Dir. Met. Boston Housing Ptnrship.; trustee Northeastern U., Boston, 1989, vice chmn. exec. com.; bd. trustees Cath. Charities, Mass. chpt. Multiple Schlerosis Soc., vice-chmn.; bd. trustees Mus. of Sci.; chmn. bd. trustees Northeastern U., Boston, 1998; chmn. Mass. Comty. and Banking Coun.; mem. Mass. Bus. Roundtable; trustee WGBH. Office: UST Corp 40 Court St Boston MA 02108-2202

FINNEGAN, PHILIP, journalist; b. Omaha, 1953. Student, Carleton Coll., 1976; MA in History, Stanford U., 1977; MA in Econs., Am. U., 1991. North African corr. Time mag., 1983-85; C.Am. corr. U.S. News & World Report, 1985-86; indsl. and trade issues writer McGraw-Hill Newsletters, 1986-88; staff writer Def. News, Springfield, Va., 1988—. Office: Def News 6883 Commercial Dr Springfield VA 22151-4202*

FINNEGAN, SARA ANNE (SARA LYCETT), publisher; b. Balt., Aug. 1, 1939; d. Lawrence Winfield and Rosina Elva (Huber) F.; m. Isaac C. Lycett, Jr., Aug. 31, 1974. BA, Sweet Briar Coll., 1961; MLA, Johns Hopkins U., 1965; exec. program, U. Va. Grad. Sch. Bus., 1977. Tchr., chmn. history dept. Hannah More Acad., Reisterstown, Md., 1961-65; redactor Williams & Wilkins Co., Balt., 1965-66, asst. head redactory, 1966-71, editor book div., 1971-75, assoc. editor-in-chief, 1975-77, v.p., editor-in-chief, 1977-81, pres. book div., 1981-88, group pres., 1988-94; editor Kalends, 1973-78, 89-92; exec. sponsor jour. Histochemistry and Cytochemistry, 1973-77; dir. Passano Found., 1979-91. Trustee St. Timothy's Sch., Stevenson, Md., 1974-83; mem. adv. bd. Balt. Ind. Schs. Scholarship Fund, 1977-81, mem. adv. coun. grad. study Coll. Notre Dame of Md., 1983; bd. overseers Sweet Briar Coll., 1987-88, bd. dirs. 1988—, chmn.-elect, 1994, chmn., 1995—; mem. bd. mgrs. The Woman's Indsl. Exch., Balt., 1997—, v.p., 1998—; docent The Walters Art Gallery, 1994—. Mem. Assn. Am. Pubs. (exec. coun. profl. and scholarly pub. div. 1984-85), Internat. Sci., Tech. and Med. Pubs. Assn. (group exec. 1986-93, chmn.-elect 1988, chmn. 1989-92). Republican. Lutheran.

FINNELL, MICHAEL HARTMAN, corporate executive; b. L.A., Jan. 27, 1927; s. Jules Bertram and Maribel Hartman (Schumacher) F.; m. Grace Vogel, Sept. 11, 1954 (div. June 1964); children: Lesley Finnell Blanchard, Carter Hartman, Hunter Vogel. Student, Asheville (N.C.) Sch., 1939-44; BA, U. Toronto, 1950; MBA, Harvard U., 1952; HHD (hon.), Capital U., Columbus, Ohio, 1980. Sec.-treas. Triad Oil Co. Ltd., 1952-62, v.p., dir., 1962-65; pres. Devon-Palmer Oils Ltd., 1963-65; v.p., dir. Can. Hydrocarbons, Ltd., 1967-71, pres., 1971-72. Trustee Capital U., Columbus, 1982-94; life trustee Columbus Mus. of Art; pres. Tamarack Corp., 1978—, Montreal River Internat. Silver Mines, 1972—. Mem. Calif. Club (L.A.), Annandale Golf Club (Pasadena, Calif.), Ranchmen's Club, Calgary Petroleum Club, Calgary Golf and Country Club, La Grulla Gun Club (Baja, Calif.), Nantucket (Mass.) Yacht Club, Delta Upsilon (v.p. 1949-50). Home: 724 Holladay Rd Pasadena CA 91106-4115 Office: Tamarack Corp 135 N Los Robles Ave Ste 240 Pasadena CA 91101-4503

FINNERTY, FRANCES MARTIN, medical administrator; b. Asheville, N.C., Dec. 23, 1936; d. Robert James and Elizabeth Howerton (Babbitt) Martin; m. Richard Phillip Caputo, Sept. 23, 1961 (div. 1974); m. Frank A. Finnerty Jr., July 26, 1975; children: Jonathan, Robert, Richard. Student, Mary Washington Coll., 1954-55, Croft Coll., 1955-57. Dist. mgr. Bus. Census Dept. Commerce, Suitland, Md., 1969-71; program coord. Georgetown U. D.C. Gen. Hosp., Washington, 1972-76; clin. mgr. Hypertension Ctr. Washington, 1976-82; project dir. PharmaKinetic Clin. Rsch. Labs., Balt., 1983; dir. mktg. Classic Glass, Alexandra, Va., 1984-86; office adminstr. Frank A. Finnerty Jr., M.D., Washington, 1987—; cons. U.S. Census, U.S. Army, The Pentagon, Washington, 1969-70; cons. mapping ops. U.S. Census, Prince Georges County, Md., 1970; cons. paramedics pers. Merck Sharpe & Dohme, West Point, Pa., 1974. Contbr. articles to profl. jours. Recipient Cmty. Svc. award Dist. of Columbia, 1980. Mem. Am. Art League (Disting. Artist award 1993), Nat. Assn. Women in Arts, Dist. Med. Soc. Wives. Avocations: artist, landscape artist, reading. Home: 519 E Front St New Bern NC 28560-4952

FINNERTY, JOHN DUDLEY, investment banker, financial educator; b. Glen Ridge, N.J., Apr. 23, 1949; s. John Patrick and Patricia (Conover) F.; m. Christine Watt, Dec. 29, 1973 (div. Jan. 1987); m. Louise Hoppe, May 21, 1988; 1 child, William Patrick Taylor. AB, Williams Coll., 1967-71; BA, U. Cambridge (Eng.), 1971-73, MA, 1977; PhD, Naval Postgrad. Sch., 1977. Adj. prof. Naval Postgrad. Sch., Monterey, Calif., 1973-77; sr. assoc. Morgan Stanley and Co. Inc., N.Y.C., 1977-82; v.p. Lazard Frères and Co., N.Y.C., 1982-86; exec. v.p., CFO Coll. Savs. Bank, Princeton, N.J., 1986-89, also bd. dirs.; gen. ptnr. McFarland Dewey & Co., N.Y.C., 1989-95; dir. Houlihan Lokey Howard & Zukin, N.Y.C., 1995-97; ptnr. Pricewaterhouse Coopers LLP, N.Y.C., 1997—; adj. prof. Fordham U., N.Y.C., 1987-89, prof., 1989—. Author: Bond Refunding Analysis, 1984, Corporate Financial Analysis, 1986, Financial Manager's Guide, 1988, Principles of Finance with Corporate Applications, 1991, Yearbook of Fixed Income Investing, 1995, Project Financing, 1996, Corporate Financial Management, 1997, Principles of Financial Management, 1998; assoc. editor Jour. of Corp. Fin., 1987-89, Fin. Mgmt., 1982-93, mem. adv. bd. Jour. Portfolio Mgmt., 1990—, editorial bd. Jour. Fin. Engring., 1992—; patentee Restructuring Debt Obligations, 1987, 88, Funding a Future Liability of Uncertain Cost, 1988, Insuring the Funding of a Future Liability of Uncertain Cost, 1989; editor: Financial Management, 1993—. Co-chmn. fund-raising in N.J. for Williams Coll., 3d Century Campaign, 1990-93. Lt. USNR, 1973-77. Recipient Marshall Commn. Scholarship, London, 1971. Mem. Fin. Mgmt. Assn. (bd. dirs. 1984-86, 91—), Am. Fin. Assn., Western Fin. Assn., Fixed Income Analysts Soc. (program chmn. 1989-90, v.p. 1990-91, pres. 1991-92, bd. dirs. 1990-92), Williams Club (N.Y.C.), Spring Lake Bath and Tennis Club (N.J.). Republican. Roman Catholic. Avocations: coin collecting. Home: 400 Park Ave Rye NY 10580-1213

FINNERTY, JOSEPH GREGORY, JR., lawyer; b. Balt., Jan. 25, 1937; s. Joseph G. Sr. and Sara V. (Porter) F.; children: Sara F. Kelly, Joseph G. III, Alice Ann Martin, Thomas P., Kathleen F. Curtis, Eileen F. McCoy, Bridget P.; m. Deborah A. Barrett, Oct. 20, 1989. BS in Physics, Loyola Coll., Balt., 1958; postgrad., Cornell U., 1958-59; JD, U. Md., 1963. Bar: Md. 1963, D.C. 1981, N.Y. 1993. Law clk. Supreme Bench Balt. City, 1960-63; assoc. Piper & Marbury, Balt., 1963-66; ptnr. Gallagher, Evelius & Finnerty, Balt., 1966-72; gen. counsel The Ryland Group, Columbia, Md., 1972; ptnr. Piper & Marbury, Balt., 1972-97, N.Y.C., 1997—; mem. standing com. Rules of Practice & Procedure of Md., 1991-94. Exec. dir. Md. Cath. Conf., 1967-70; bd. dirs. Liquor License Commrs. Balt. City, 1968-70. 2d lt. US Army, 1959. Fellow Am. Coll. Trial Lawyers, Am. Bar Found.; mem. ABA, Md. State Bar Assn., N.Y. State Bar Assn., D.C. Bar Assn., Order of Coif. Avocation: farming. Home: 300 E 56th St Apt 32C New York NY 10022-4143 Office: Piper & Marbury LLP 1251 Avenue Of The Americas New York NY 10020-1104

FINNERTY, LOUISE HOPPE, beverage and food company executive; b. Alexandria, Va., Jan. 19, 1949; d. William G. and Ruth A. (Ehren) Hoppe; m. John D. Finnerty, May 21, 1988; 1 child, William Patrick Taylor. BA, Va. Commonwealth U., 1971; postgrad., Am. U., 1972-73. Staff asst. to Dr. Henry Kissinger NSC, Washington, 1971-73; adminstrv. asst. Nat. Petroleum Coun., Washington, 1973-75; profl. staff mem. Senate Armed Svc. Com., Washington, 1976-81; spl. asst. Office Legis. Affairs, U.S. Dept. State, Washington, 1981-84, dep. asst. sec. of state, 1984-88; mgr. govt. affairs PepsiCo, Inc., Purchase, N.Y., 1988-91; dir. govt. affairs PepsiCo Foods and Beverages Internat., Somers, N.Y., 1991-95; v.p. internat. govt. affairs PepsiCo., Inc., Purchase, N.Y., 1995—. Mem. Nat. Fgn. Trade Coun. (bd. dirs. 1991—), Spring Lake Bath and Tennis Club. Republican. Lutheran. Avocations: reading; gardening; cooking. Home: 400 Park Ave Rye NY 10580-1213 also: 506 2nd Ave Spring Lake NJ 07762-1107 Office: PepsiCo Inc 700 Anderson Hill Rd Purchase NY 10577-1444

FINNEY, CLIFTON DONALD, publishing executive; b. Dubuque, Iowa, Apr. 7, 1941; s. Clifton Monroe and Violet Irene (Snyder) F.; m. Kazuko Akiyama, Aug. 17, 1968; 1 child, Ann. BA in Chemistry, Austin Coll., 1964; PhD in Phys. Chemistry, Kans. State U., 1970. Postdoctoral fellow U. Toronto, Ont., Can., 1969-71; asst. prof. chemistry Drake U., Des Moines, 1971-75; pres. Natural Dynamics, Des Moines and Houston, 1975-86, Golf Physics Co., Baton Rouge, 1986-94, DeerStats, Houston and Baton Rouge, 1996—; assoc. Ames (Iowa) Lab., U.S. AEC, 1971-75; instr. computer sci. U. Houston, 1984-86. Contbr. articles to Phys. Chemistry, Sci., Computers and Edn. Recipient energy rsch. grant Iowa Energy Policy Coun., 1975, USERDA, 1976. Mem. Am. Chem. Soc., N.Y. Acad. Scis. Achievements include patents in Inertial Weighting Systems for Golf Clubheads and a Superventuri Power Source. Address: 17732 Glen Knoll Ave Baton Rouge LA 70817

FINNEY, ERNEST ADOLPHUS, JR., state supreme court chief justice; b. Smithfield, Va., Mar. 23, 1931; s. Ernest A. Sr. and Collen (Godwin) F.; m. Frances Davenport, Aug. 20, 1955; children: Ernest A. III, Lynn Carol (Nikky) Finney, Jerry Leo. BA, Claflin Coll., 1952; JD, S.C. State U., 1954, LHD (hon.), 1996; HHD (hon.), Claflin Coll., 1977; LLD, U. S.C., 1991, The Citadel, 1995, Johnson C. Smith U., 1995, Morris Coll., 1996; LHD (hon.), Coll. of Charleston, 1995; LLD, Morris Coll., 1996. Bar: S.C. 1954, U.S. Dist. Ct. S.C. 1957, U.S. Ct. Appeals (4th cir.) 1964. Pvt. practice law Conway, S.C., 1954-60, Sumter, S.C., 1960-66; with Finney and Gray, Attys. at Law, Sumter, 1966-76; mem. S.C. Ho. of Reps., Columbia, 1973-76; judge S.C. Cir. Ct., Columbia, 1976-85; assoc. justice S.C. Supreme Ct., Columbia, 1985-94, chief justice, 1994—. Chmn. S.C. Legis. Black Caucus, Columbia, 1973-75; chmn. bd. dirs. Buena Vista Devel. Corp., Sumter, 1967—; mem. S.C. State Elections Commn., Columbia, 1968-72; trustee Claflin Coll., Orangeburg, S.C., 1986—, chmn. bd. trustees, 1987-95; sch. law minority adv. com. U. S.C., 1988—. Recipient Disting. Alumni of Yr. award Nat. Assn. Equal Opportunity Edn., 1986, Achievement award C. of C., Sumter, 1986, Presdl. Citation Morris Coll., Sumter, 1986, Wiley A. Branton award NBA, 1998, Afro Am. Achievement award Turner Broadcasting Sys., 1998; named 1987 Citizen of Yr. Charleston (S.C.) Med. Soc., 1987; inductee Nat. Black Coll. Alumni Hall of Fame, 1988. Mem. ABA, Am. Judges Assn., Am. Law Inst. (bd. dirs.), Conf. Chief Justices (bd. dirs.), Sumter County Bar, S.C. Bar, Assn. Trial Lawyers Am., Nat. Bar Assn. (appellate com.), S.C. Trial Lawyers Assn. (hon.), Masons, Shriners. Methodist. Avocations: reading, fishing, golf. Home: 24 Runnymede Blvd Sumter SC 29153-8742 Office: SC Supreme Ct PO Box 11330 Columbia SC 29211-1330 Office: PO Box 1309 Sumter SC 29151-1309

FINNEY, GRAHAM STANLEY, management consultant; b. Greenwich, Conn., Sept. 6, 1930; s. William Stanley and Sarah Margaret (Boswell) F.; m. Katharine Pillsbury Becker, June 22, 1957; children: Sarah Boswell Finney Johnston, Martha Becker, Samuel Warner, Garrett Stevens. Student, Washington and Lee U., 1948-49; BA, Yale U., 1952; MPA, Harvard U., 1954. Planning dir. City of Portland, Maine, 1957-60; asst. exec. dir. Phila. City Planning Commn., 1961-65; exec. dir. Phila. Coun. for Cmty. Advancement, 1965-66; dep. supt. schs. Phila., 1966-69; commr. addiction svcs. agy. City of N.Y.; mng. ptnr. Greater Phila. Partnership, 1975-76; dir. Phila. Partnership, 1973-75; pres. Corp. for Pub./Pvt. Ventures, Phila., 1977-80; sr. ptnr. The Conservation Co., Phila., 1980-87, pres., 1988-95; mgmt. cons.; pres. 21st Century League, 1997—; bd. dirs. Replication and Program Sys., Inc., 1993—, Exec. Svc. Corp. Delaware Valley; trustee Seybert Instn., Phila., 1978; mem. Union Benevolent Assn. Author: Administering Catastrophe, 1975; (with others) Philadelphia: 1776-2076, 1975. Served with U.S. Army, 1954-56. Recipient The Phila. award, 1998. Mem. Yale Club (N.Y.C.). Democrat. Presbyterian. Avocations: gardening, tennis. Home: 615 W Hortter St Philadelphia PA 19119-3650

FINNEY, LEE, negotiator, social worker; b. Balt., Feb. 25, 1943; d. E. William and Mildred Lee (Refo) Carr; m. James Nathaniel Finney, Feb. 25, 1967 (div. Aug. 1970); 1 child, Karen Elizabeth. Student, Sweet Briar Coll., 1961-63; BA in Govt., George Washington U., 1965; MS in Counseling, Calif. State U., Hayward, 1986. Caseworker N.Y.C. Welfare Dept., 1966-68; probation officer N.Y.C. Probation Dept., 1968-74; dep. probation officer Alameda County Probation Dept., Oakland, Calif., 1974-78, child welfare social worker, 1979-80; children's svcs. social worker Contra Costa County Dept. Social Svcs., Richmond, Calif., 1980-87; social work supr. Contra Costa County Dept. Social Svcs., Antioch, Calif., 1987-88; dir. staff devel. Contra Costa County Dept. Social Svcs., Martinez, Calif., 1989-90; pay equity analyst Contra Costa County Pers. Dept., Martinez, 1988-89; labor rels. cons. Indsl. Employers and Distributors Assn., Emeryville, Calif., 1990—; instr. edn. psychology dept. Calif. State U., Hayward, 1987-89; mem. exec. bd. Contra Costa Ctrl. Labor Coun., Martinez, 1987-89; no. v.p., chief negotiator Svc. Employees Internat. Union Local 535, Oakland, 1983-88; chair Coalition for Children and Families, Richmond, Calif., 1986-88. Author booklet: First Steps to Identifying Sex and Race Based Inequities in a workplace: A Guide to Achieving Pay Equity, 1989. Bd. dirs. YWCA, Contra Costa County, 1989-91; pres., acting dir. Comparable Worth Project, Inc., Oakland, 1984-87; mem. Adv. Com. on Employment and Econ. Status for Women Contra Costa, 1984-89, chair, 1987-89. Recipient Cmty. Svc. award Vocare Found., 1976, Golden Nike award Emeryville Bus. and Profl. Women, 1986, Woman of Yr. award Todos Santos Bus. and Profl. Women, 1989, Women Who Have Made a Difference award Coalition of Labor Union Women, 1989. Democrat. Avocations: sailing, travel, natural history. Home: 6 Commodore Dr # C336 Emeryville CA 94608-1649 Office: IDEA 2200 Powell St Ste 1000 Emeryville CA 94608-1869

FINNEY, MICHAEL J., publishing executive; b. Peoria, Ill., Oct. 2, 1942. BA in English, Bradley U., 1966. Gen. mgr. Print Graphics, Inc.; co-owner, editor Prophetstown (Ill.) Echo; city editor then editor Beloit (Wis.) Daily News, 1969-74; sr. editor various Knight-Ridder papers, 1975-80; mng. editor Bradenton Herald, Duluth Herald, News Tribune; exec. editor Grand Forks Herald; mng. editor Mpls. Star, 1981-82; dep. mng. editor Mpls. Star Tribune, 1982-89; mng. editor Rocky Mountain News, 1989-90; exec. editor Omaha World-Herald, 1991-98; pres., CEO World Media Co., Omaha, 1998—. Mem. Am. Soc. Newspaper Editors (former chmn. literacy com., contbr. to bull., mem. reporter com., journalism values com.). Address: 9415 Davenport St Omaha NE 68114 Office: World Media Co 1334 Dodge St Omaha NE 68102

FINNEY, WILLIAM K., police chief; b. St. Paul, Nov. 28, 1948. BA, Mankato State U., 1970. Patrolman through granks to chief of police St. Paul Police Dept., 1971-92, chief of police, 1992—. Office: St Paul Police Dept 100 11th St E Ste 1 Saint Paul MN 55101-2296*

FINNIE, IAIN, mechanical engineer, educator; b. Hong Kong, July 18, 1928; s. John and Jessie Ferguson (Mackenzie) F.; m. Joan Elizabeth Roth, July 28, 1969; 1 dau., Shauna. B.S. with honors, U. Glasgow, 1949; M.S., MIT, 1951, M.E., 1952, Sc.D., 1954; D.Sc. (hon.), U. Glasgow, 1974. With Shell Devel. Co., 1954-61, engr., to 1961; mem. faculty dept. mech. engring. U. Calif., Berkeley, 1961—; prof. U. Calif., 1963—; vis. prof. Cath. U. Chile, 1965, Ecole Polytechnique, Lausanne, Switzerland, 1976, 87. Author: Creep of Engineering Materials, 1959; contbr. articles to profl. jours. Guggenheim Found. fellow, 1967-68. Mem. Nat. Acad. Engring., ASME (hon., Nadai award 1982). Home: 2901 Avalon Ave Berkeley CA 94705-1401 Office: U Calif 6179 Etcheverry Berkeley CA 94720

FINNIE, WILLIAM C., consulting company executive, educator; b. Lexington, Ky., Feb. 19, 1944; s. Thomas C. and Evelyn (Warren) F.; m. Glenda Lewis, July 1, 1967; children: John W., Stephen L. BS in Engring., Washington U., St. Louis, 1966; PhD in Ops. Rsch., U. Pa., 1970. Dir. strategic planning Anheuser-Busch, St. Louis, 1970-91; pres. The Finnie Group, St. Louis, 1991—; prof. mktg. Washington U., 1978—; bd. dirs. Strategic Leadership Forum, St. Louis, 1992—, chair publs. com., 1994-95; mem. adv. bd. TSI Graphics, St. Louis, 1992—. Author: Hands-On Strategy, 1994; exec. editor newsletter The Real World Strategist, 1994-95; editor-in-chief mag. Strategy and Leadership, 1995-96; columnist Mktg. Trends, 1991—. Trustee, fin. chair Kirkwood (Mo.) United Meth. Ch., 1991-97. Named Tchr. of Yr., Olin Sch. Bus./Washington U., 1995, Exec. of Yr., Profl. Secs. Internat., 1995. Mem. Assn. for Corp. Growth (v.p. comm. 1994—), Am. Mktg. Assn., Sunset Country Club, Tau Beta Pi. Methodist. Home: 12501 Glencroft Dr Saint Louis MO 63128-2513 Office: Grace & Co PC 3117 S Big Bend Blvd Saint Louis MO 63143

FINNIGAN, JOSEPH TOWNSEND, public relations executive; b. Springfield, Ill., Aug. 26, 1944; s. Joseph Thomas and Mary Frances (McCarthy) F.; m. Kathleen Burke, July 2, 1966; children: Matthew, Brendan, Patrick. A.B., Marquette U., 1966. With Fleishman-Hillard, 1972—, v.p., 1975-77, ptnr., 1975—; exec. v.p. Fleishman-Hillard, St. Louis, 1977—, part-time cons., 1998—. Bd. dirs. St. Louis Better Bus. Found. Mem. Pub. Rels. Soc. Am., Sigma Delta Chi. Roman Catholic. Clubs: Sunset Country, Island Bay Yacht, St. Louis Press, Mo. Athletic. Home: 12415 Ballas Trails Dr Saint Louis MO 63122-2145*

FINNIGAN, ROBERT EMMET, business owner; b. Buffalo, May 27, 1927; s. Charles M. and Marie F. (Jacobs) F.; m. Bette E. van Horn, Apr. 1, 1950; children: Michael, Patrick, Robert E. Jr., Joan, Shawn, Thomas, Matthew. BS, U.S. Naval Acad., 1949; MS, U. Ill., 1954, PhD, 1957. Commd. lt. USAF, 1949, advanced through grades to capt., 1954; sr. scientist Livermore Lab., U. Calif., 1959, U. Calif. Lawrence Livermore Lab., 1957-62; sr. rsch. scientist Stanford Rsch. Inst., Menlo Park, Calif., 1962-63; dir. Electronic Assocs. Inc., Palo Alto, Calif., 1963-67; founder, vice chmn., sr. v.p. Finnigan Corp., San Jose, Calif., 1967-92, vice chmn. emeritus, cons., 1992—; cons. Thermo Instrument Sys., Santa Fe, 1992—; mem. panel NAS, Washington, 1986-89; bd. dirs. Strategic Diagnostics, Inc., Newark, Del., Thermo Spectra Corp., Waltham, Mass.; advisor to Environ. Tech. Fund, Hambrecht and Quist, San Francisco. Author: Identification and Analysis of Organic Pollutants in Water, 1976, Advances in Identification and Analysis of Organic Pollutants in Water, 1981. Chmn., co-founder U.S. Nat. Working Group on Pollution, Internat. Orgn. for Legal Metrology, Washington, 1982-87. Recipient Alumni Honor award Coll. of Engring., U. Ill., 1980; named Pioneer in Analytical Instrumentation-Mass Spectrometry, Soc. for Analytical Chemists of Pitts., 1994, Pitts. Conf. on Analytical Chemistry, 1994, Instrumentation Hall of Fame, Pitts., 1999. Mem. IEEE (sr.), Am. Soc. for Mass Spectrometry (bd. dirs.), Am. Electronic Assn. (bd. dirs. 1982-84, 87, chmn., co-founder environ. and occupational health com.). Avocations: wine, hiking, snowshoeing. Home: 125 Los Altos Ave Los Altos CA 94022-2125 Office: Finnigan Corp 355 River Oaks Pkwy San Jose CA 95134-1991

FINO, MARIE GEORGETTE KECK, retired real estate broker; b. Greenville, Pa., Jan. 30, 1923; d. Harvey I. and Winifred L. (Fuller) Keck; m. Alex F. Fino, Sept. 27, 1947; children: Timothy A., Jeffrey J. Cert. in real estate, Pa. State U., 1980; grad., Realtors Inst., Harrisburg, Pa., 1981. RN, Pa.; lic. real estate broker, Pa. Broker, owner 305 Realty, North Warren, Pa., 1983-96; instr. Pa. State U., 1985-96, ret., 1996; treas. Warren County Bd. Realtors, 1981-84, v.p., 1984-86, pres., 1988. Patentee fuel storage vent. Treas. Northwestern Pa. Regional Planning Commn., 1985-92, exec. com., 1988-92, treas., 1991; bd. dirs. Warren County Devel. Assn., Warren County Crime Stoppers, 1989-96. Named Woman of Yr. in Bus. and Industry, County of Warren, 1986, Citizen Amb. to China, 1994. Mem. Nat. Assn. Realtors, Pa. Assn. Realtors (bd. dirs. 1984-88, vice-chair comml.-indsl. com. 1984-88, bd. dirs. 1992-93), Soc. Indsl. and Office Realtors (nat. bd. dirs. 1992-95, dist. v.p. 1993-95), Warren County C. of C., Philomel Club (bd. dirs. 1978-80), Conewango Valley Country Club (Warren), Conewango Valley Kennel Club. Republican. Roman Catholic. Avocations: golf, bridge, showing and breeding Maltese dogs.

FINSTAD, SUZANNE ELAINE, writer, producer, lawyer; b. Mpls., Sept. 14, 1955; d. Harold Martin and Elaine Lois (Strom) F. Student, U. Tex., 1973-74; BA in French, U. Houston, 1976, JD, 1980; postgrad., London Sch. Econs., 1980, U. Grenoble, France, 1979. Bar: Tex. 1981. Legal asst. Butler & Binion, Houston, 1976-78, law clk., 1978-81, assoc., 1982; spl. counsel Ad Litem in the Estate of Howard Hughes Jr., Houston, 1981; mng. ptnr. Finstad & Assoc., Houston, 1990—. Author: Heir Not Apparent, 1984 (Frank Wardlaw award 1984), Ulterior Motives, 1987, Child Bride, 1997, Sleeping With the Devil, 1991, co-prodr. (TV), 1997; collaborator Queen Noor biography; screenwriter, exec. prodr.: (feature film) Elvis' Child Bride, 1999. Named to Order of Barons, Bates Coll. Law, 1979-80. Mem. Order of Barons. Office: Joel Gotler Renaissance Agy 9220 W Sunset Blvd West Hollywood CA 90069-3501

FINSTER, BRENT EDWIN, public safety communications administrator; b. Sept. 13, 1958; s. Arno C. and Barbara E. Finster. Student, U. Colo., 1976-77, AIMS C.C., 1986-88. Asst. store mr. Radio Shack-Tandy Corp., Boulder, Colo., 1976-77; store mgr. Radio Shack-Tandy Corp., Laramie, Wyo., 1977-79, Lakewood, Colo., 1977-79; patrol dispatcher Colo. State Patrol, Eagle, 1979-80; dispatcher Boulder County Sheriff, Boulder, 1980-85, comms. supr., 1986-88; mktg. mgr. DPZ Systems, Boulder, 1988; comms. dir. Pitkin County Sheriff, Aspen, Colo., 1989—; fire chief Lyons (Colo.) Fire Protection Dist., 1983-89; cert. peace officer Peace Officer Stds. Bd., Denver, 1993—. Co-author: Public Safety Communications Standard Operating Procedure Manual, 1986; mem. editl. bd. Radio Resource Mag., Denver, 1991—. Mem. Assn. Pub. Safety Comms. Ofcls. (Colo. pres. 1991-92, rep. exec. coun. 1997—), Nat. Emergency Number Assn. (Colo. v.p. 1995-98). Avocations: travel, bowling, RF monitoring, amateur radio, ATV's. Office: Aspen-Pitkin County Comms 506 E Main St Dept C Aspen CO 81611-2923

FINSTER, DIANE L. STELTEN, secondary educator, media specialist, home economics educator; b. St. Cloud, Minn., Sept. 11, 1953; d. George Henry and Theresa Lucy (Becker) Stelten; m. Jon Gregory Dane, Aug., 1976 (dec. Oct. 1981); m. James Robert Finster, June 1, 1985 (div. Feb. 1993); children: James Andrew, Nicholas William. BS in Home Econs., U. Wis. at Stout, Menomonie, 1975, MS in Ednl. Media; MS in Ednl. Media, U. Wis., LaCrosse, 1987. Cert. in vocat. and gen. home econs. edn., ednl. media specialist, Wis., Minn. With Hagerty Catering, Chgo., Tri-R Vending, Chgo.; instr. home econs. Blair (Wis.) Pub. Schs.; edn. media specialist Brillion (Wis.) Pub. Schs.; home econs. dept. head Blair-Taylor Pub. Schs., Blair, Wis., 1980-87; libr. media specialist Brillon Pub. Schs., 1987-88; dist. libr., audio/visual coord. Pardeeville (Wis.) Pub. Schs., 1989-90; dist. media dir. St. Croix Falls (Wis.) Pub. Schs., 1990—. Contbr. articles to profl. jours. Coach Spl. Olympics, Blair, 1980-87; homemaking divsn. chairperson Cheese Festival, Blair, 1980-87; mem. adv. bd. Com. Tech., Vocat. Adult Edn., Blair, 1980-87, Sch. Evaluation Consortium, Blair, 1980-87, St. Croix Falls Pub. Libr., 1990—; with Boy Scouts of Am.; vol. CRA-Battered Women, Children's Shelter, hosp. aux.; soccer coach River Valley Soccer Club. Mem. AAUW, ALA, Am. Home Econs. Assn., Wis. Ednl. Media Assn., Wis. Libr. Assn., Wis. Assn. Sch. Librs., Phi Upsilon Omicron. Avocations: travel, outdoor sports, gourmet cooking, sketching, reading. Home: PO Box 182 Dresser WI 54009 Office: St Croix Falls High Sch PO Box 130 Saint Croix Falls WI 54024-0130

FINSTER, JAMES ROBERT, library media specialist; b. Milw., Sept. 29, 1947; s. Milton Robert Finster and Eleonore B. (Worgull) Helvey; children: James Andrew, Nicholas William. BS in Edn., Dr. Martin Luther Coll., 1971; BS in Resource Mgmt., U. Wis., Stevens Point, 1976; MS in Edn. Media, U. Wis., LaCrosse, 1987. Cert. libr. media specialist, Wis., Minn. Ski instr. various ski clubs, resorts, Wis. and Colo., 1971-99, 84-85; elem. tchr. pvt. and pub. schs. Wis., 1971-73, 78-81; teaching asst. U. Wis., Stevens Point, 1975; park ranger Nat. Park Svc., various locations, 1976-77; ski. sch. dir. Whitecap Mountain, Montreal, Wis., 1982-83, Coffee Mill Ski Area, Wabasha, Minn., 1983-84; grad. asst. U. Wis., LaCrosse, 1986-87; libr. media specialist Chilton (Wis.) High Sch., 1987-93; libr. media specialist K-12 Rib Lake (Wis.) Pub. Schs., 1993-94, Elcho (Wis.) Pub. Sch., 1994-96; ski instr. Trollhaugen, 1997—. Mem. Wis. Ednl. Media Assn. Republican. Lutheran. Avocations: downhill skiing, travel, sports, games, music. Home: 200 Seminole Ave Lot 78 Osceola WI 54020-8076

FINUCANE, ANNE M., communications and marketing executive; married; 4 children. BA with honors, U. N.H. Pub. info. officer Mayor of City of Boston; dir. creative svcs. Sta. WBZ-TV, Boston; head creative svcs. Hill, Holliday, Connors, Cosmopulos, Inc., Boston, dir. account mgmt., dir. corp. devel.; prin. Anne Finucane Mktg. and Telecomm., Boston; sr. v.p., dir. corp. mktg. and comm. Fleet Fin. Group, Boston, 1995—; bd. dirs. Internat. Ctr. for Journalists. Bd. dirs. Urban Improv, Emerson Coll., New Eng. Coun., Mass. Women's Forum; co-chmn. tech. divsn. United Way of Mass. Bay Campaign, 1995, 96; mem. adv. coun. Children's Defense Fund, Washington, Conservation Law Found. Fax: 617-346-4740. Office: Fleet Fin Group Corp Mktg & Comm One Federal St Boston MA 02110

FINZEN, BRUCE ARTHUR, lawyer; b. Mpls., Mar. 11, 1947; s. Floyd Arthur and Lorraine Jeannette (Offerdahl) F.; m. Julianna Margaret Ryan, July 12, 1975; children: Margaret, Sara, Stephanie. BA, U. Minn., 1970; JD, U. Kans., 1973. Bar: Minn. 1973, U.S. Dist. Ct. Minn. 1973, Calif. 1988, U.S. Ct. Appeals (8th cir.) 1973, U.S. Ct. Appeals (7th cir.) 1983, U.S. Ct. Appeals (2d cir.) 1986, U.S. Ct. Appeals (4th cir.) 1994, U.S. Ct. Appeals (9th cir.) 1994, U.S. Supreme Ct. 1996. Law clk. to presiding justice Minn. Supreme Ct., St. Paul, 1973-74; assoc. Robins, Kaplan, Miller & Ciresi, Mpls., 1974-79; ptnr. Robins, Kaplan, Miller & Ciresi LLP, Mpls., 1979—. Bd. dirs. Union Gospel Mission, St. Paul, 1983-89; sec. bd. dirs. Boys and Girls Clubs St. Paul, 1984-91; trustee House of Hope Presbyn. Ch., 1988-94. Mem. ABA, Minn. Bar Assn., Assn. Trial Lawyers Am., Minn. Trial Lawyers Assn., Consumer Attys. Calif., Assn. Pers. Injury Lawyers, Internat. Bar Assn. Avocations: hunting, fishing. Office: Robins Kaplan Miller & Ciresi LLP 2800 LaSalle Plz 800 Lasalle Ave Ste 2800 Minneapolis MN 55402-2015

FIOCK, SHARI LEE, event planner, entrepreneur, publishing executive; b. Weed, Calif., Oct. 25, 1941; d. Webster Bruce and Olevia May (Pruett) F.; m. June 6, 1966 (div. 1974); children: Webster Clinton Pfingsten, Sterling Curtis. Cert., Art Instrn. Sch., Mpls., 1964. Copywriter Darron Assocs., Eugene, Oreg., 1964-66; staff artist Oreg. Holidays, Springfield, 1966-69, 1971; co-owner, designer Artre Enterprises, Eugene, 1969-74; design entrepreneur Shari & Assocs., Yreka, Calif., 1974—; cons., devel. sec. Cascade World Four Season Resort, Siskiyou County, Calif., 1980-86; owner Coyote pub., 1991—; part-time adminstrv. asst., coord. regional catalog Gt. Northern Corp., U.S. Dept. Commerce and Econ. Devel., 1994-96; local cons., proposed geothermal powerplant CalEnergy Co., Inc., 1998—. Designer 5 ton chain saw sculpture, Oreg. Beaver, 1967; illustrator; Holiday Fun Book, 1978; author, illustrator: Family Reunions and Clan Gatherings, 1991, Blue Goose Legend, 1995, rev. edit., 1998; co-creator Klamath Nat. Forest Interpretive Mus., 1979-91; editor: Choo and Moo Cookbook, 1998. Residential capt. united Way, Eugene, 1972; rschr. Beaver Ofcl. State Animal, Eugene, 1965-71; counselor Boy Scouts Am., 1983-91. Mem. Siskiyou Writers Club (pres., founder 1986—). Avocations: family activities, outdoor recreation, travel, theater, music. Home: 406 Walters Ln # 1854 Yreka CA 96097

FIONDELLA, ROBERT WILLIAM, insurance company executive; b. Bristol, Conn., May 19, 1942; s. Sisto William and Theresa (Nestico) F.; m. Carolyn Brozinski; children: Robert J., Jeffrey. A.B., Providence Coll., 1964; J.D., U. Conn., 1968. Computer programmer-analyst Travelers Ins. Co., Hartford, Conn., 1965; atty. Danaher, Lewis, Tamoney, Hartford, Conn., 1968-69; atty. law dept. Phoenix Mutual Ins. Co., Hartford, Conn., 1969-72, asst. counsel, officer, 1972-74, assoc. counsel, 1974-75, investment counsel, 1975-77, 2d v.p., counsel, 1977, v.p., gen. counsel, 1978-81, sr. v.p.-gen. counsel, 1981-83, exec. v.p. individual ins., 1983-87, pres., 1987-89, bd. dirs., pres., COO, 1989-92, pres., prin. oper. officer, 1992-94; chmn. bd., pres., CEO Phoenix HomeLife Mutual Ins. Co., Hartford, Conn., 1994—; bd. dirs., pres. PML Internat. Ins Ltd., Phoenix Investment Ptnrs. Ltd; bd. dirs. Life Ins. Coun. N.Y., The Advest Group, Phoenix Investment Ptnrs. Ltd., PXRE (formerly Phoenix Reins.), Phoenix Equity Planning Corp., Am. Phoenix; bd. dirs., pres. Phoenix Am. Life Ins. Co.; bd. dirs., chmn. bd. dirs. Phoenix Charter Oak Trust; bd. dirs. St. Francis Hosp. and Med. Ctr. Chmn. ea. regional fundraising Little League Ctr., Bristol; mem. Britol City Coun., 1969-71, Bristol Urban Renewal Commn., 1971-76; mem. steering com. Mayor Peter's Hartford AmeriCorps, 1995—; chmn. Bristol Retirement Bd., 1978-83; coach Edgewood Little League, Bristol, 1984-85; bd. dirs. St. Francis Hosp. and Med. Ctr., 1992—, Spl. Olympics World Summer Games, 1995—, Spl. Olympics Internat., 1996—, Barnes Group Inc., 1997—; mem. cabinet Conn. Children's Ctr. Campaign for Our Children, 1995—; mem. adv. bd. WKND Greater Hartford Initiative; co-chmn. Cmty. Cancer Ctr. Bldg. Fund, Johnson Meml. Mem. Conn. Bar Assn., Conn. Bus. and Industry Assn. (bd. dirs.), Greater Hartford C. of C. (bd. dirs., chmn. 1997—). Home: 29 Summerberry Cir Bristol CT 06010-2957 Office: Phoenix Home Life Mutual Ins Co One American Row Hartford CT 06115-2520

FIORA, NANCY, federal judge. Apptd. magistrate judge U.S. Dist. Ct. Ariz., 1987. Fax: (520) 620-7193. Office: 416 US Courthosue 55 E Broadway Blvd Tucson AZ 85701-1719

FIORE, JAMES LOUIS, JR., public accountant, educator, professional speaker, trainer consultant; b. Jersey City, Oct. 7, 1935; s. James Louis and Rose (Perrotta) F.; m. Alberta W. Pope, July 21, 1957; children: Carolyn Leigh, James Louis III, Toni Lynn. BS in Acctg. and Statistics, Seton Hall U., 1957; MBA, We. Colo. U., 1972; PhD, Calif. We. U., 1979. Lic. acct. Pa., N.J. Field auditor State of N.J., Trenton, 1958-60; supr. internal auditing Ronson Corp., Woodbridge, N.J., 1960-64; surp. gen. acctg. Electronic Assocs., West Long Branch, N.J., 1964-65; pvt. practice acctg., 1965—; pres. Bucks County Rsch. Inst., Inc., 1972-79; mem. adj. faculty Alletown Coll. St. Francis de Sales, Center Valley, Pa., 1979-81, Pa. Coll. Chriopractic, 1986-94, Holy Family Coll., Phila., 1995. Author: (with others) Shareholder Loans, The National Public Accountant, 1988, Fiancial Problems and Your Profession, 1989, Non-Absorption of Nitrofurazone from the Urethra in Men, 1976, Comparative Bioavailability of Doxycycline, 1974; contbr. articles to profl. jours. Bd. dirs. Brick Twp. (N.J.) Scholarship Found., 1963-67; mem. adv. coun. Inst. for Accts., Pa. State U.; trustee Pa. Coll. Chiropractic, 1986-94; founder Cath. Acad. Sci. in U.S.A., Washington. Lt. U.S. Army, 1957. Named Jayce of Yr., 1962; recipient Legion of Honor, Chapel of Four Chaplains, 1979. Mem. Assn. Cert. Fraud Examiners, Pa. Soc. Pub. Accts., Nat. Soc. Pub. Accts., N.J. Assn. Pub. Accts., Calif. We. U. Alumni Assn., We. Colo. U. Alumni Assn., Seton Hall U. Alumni Assn. (Crest and Centrury Clubs), Royal Arch Mason (chpt. 270 Pa.), Masons (ancient accpeted Scottish rite, Harmony coun. # 70, royal and select master Masons Phila.), Ancient Order Nobles Mystic Shrine, Crescent Temple, Egypt Temple, Mercer Lodge (# 50 F. & AM, Trenton, N.J.), Knights Templar (Mizpah Commandry 60). Home: 265 Thompson Mill Rd Newtown PA 18940-3105

FIORE, JOSEPH ALBERT, artist; b. Cleve., Feb. 3, 1925; s. Salvatore Emmanuel and Gemma Marie (Cominelli) F.; m. Mary Falconer Fitton, Oct. 10, 1952; children—Thomas, Susanna. Student, Black Mountain Coll., 1946-48, 49, San Francisco Sch. Art Inst., 1948-49. Instr. painting, drawing Black Mountain (N.C.) Coll., 1949-56, chmn. art dept., 1951-56; free lance designer N.Y.C., 1958-61; instr. painting Phila. Coll. Art, 1962-70, Md. Inst. Coll. Art, Balt., 1970-75; instr. landscape painting Nat. Acad. Design, N.Y.C., 1979, Parson's Sch. Design Summer Program, Dordogne, France, 1980; vis. artist-critic Artists for Environment Found., Walpack Center, N.J., 1972-83, Vt. Studio Sch., Johnson, Vt., 1987. One-man shows include Ten-Thirty Gallery, Cleve., 1944, 48, 50, Gallerie Parnass, Wuppertal, Germany, 1955, Round Top Ctr. for Arts, Damariscotta, Maine, 1997, Cathedral of St. John the Divine, N.Y.C., 1997, Black Mountain Coll. Mus. and Arts Ctr. at Zone One Contemporary, Asheville, N.C., 1995-96, Staempfli Gallery, N.Y.C., 1960, Robert Schoelkopf Gallery, N.Y.C., 1965, 69, Green Mountain Gallery, N.Y.C., 1973, John Bernard Myers Gallery, N.Y.C., 1974, Fischbach Gallery, N.Y.C., 1977, 81, Caldbeck Gallery, Rockland, Maine, 1988, Le Va-Tout Gallery, Waldboro, Maine, 1991; exhibited in group shows Stable Gallery, N.Y.C., 1954, 55, Whitney Mus. Am. Art, 1959, U. Ill., Urbana, 1961, Am. Fedn. Art Travelling Exhbn., 1964, Corcoran Gallery Art, Washington, 1975, State Mus., Augusta, 1976, Cape Split Place, Addison, Maine, 1977, Am. Acad. Arts and Letters, N.Y.C., 1981, Landmark Gallery, N.Y.C., 1981, Jersey City Mus., 1982, Farnsworth Mus., Rockland, Maine, 1983, Artist's Choice Mus., 1983, Black Mountain Connection, Gilliam and Peden Gallery, Raleigh, 1987, Black Mountain Coll., Blum Art Inst., Bard Coll., N.Y.C., 1987, N.C. State Mus., Raleigh, 1987, Grey Art Ctr., NYU, 1987, Snyder Fine Arts, N.Y.C., 1992, Station Gallery, Katonah, N.Y., 1992, Anita Shapolsky Gallery, N.Y.C., 1997, numerous others; represented in permanent collections Whitney Mus. Am. Art, N.Y.C., N.C. State Mus. Art, Raleigh, Corcoran Gallery, Art, Washington, Colby Art Mus., Waterville, Maine, Weatherspoon Gallery, Greensboro, N.C., NAD, N.Y., Chase Manhattan Collection, N.Y.C., Asheville Mus. of Art, N.C., Black Mountain Coll. Mus. and Art Ctr., Housatonic Mus. Art, Bridgeport, Conn. Served with AUS, 1943-46. Recipient prize for painting San Francisco Mus. Ann., 1949, 1st prize Met. Young Artists 1st Ann. Nat. Arts Club, N.Y.C., 1958; Artists for Environment Found. residence grantee, 1976; Nettie Marie Jones fellow Ctr. Music, Drama and Art, Lake Placid, N.Y., 1983, purchase award Am. Acad. Arts and Letters, 1998. Mem. NAD (cert. of merit 168th Ann. Exhbn. 1993, Edwin Palmer Meml. prize), Artists Equity Assn. N.Y., Nature Conservancy, Maine Audubon Soc., Natural Resources Coun. Maine. Home: 414 N Mountain Rd Jefferson ME 04348-3855

FIORE, LOIS FRANCES, editor, artist; b. Newport, R.I., Aug. 27, 1945; d. Louis Wesley and Frances Mary F. BA, So. Conn. State U., 1967; MA, Columbia U., N.Y.C., 1972. Asst. to curator Nieman Found. Journalism Harvard U., Cambridge, Mass., 1973-93; asst. editor Nieman Reports Nieman Found., Cambridge, 1993—. Mem. Brickbottom Artist Assn. E-mail: lfiore@harvard.edu. Office: Nieman Reports 1 Francis Ave Cambridge MA 02138

FIORE, MERCIA V., author; b. Belvidere, Ill., Jan. 21, 1934; d. Erwin August and Lily Susan (Koertge) Balgemann; m. Frank Joseph Fiore, June 23, 1957; children: Gina Lilanne Gabriel, Debra Rose Coconate, Michele Mercia Holman. Student, Wright Jr. Coll., Chgo., So. Ill. U., 1952. Lic. real estate broker, Ill. With Presley Tour, 1956; columnist Times Newspapers, Chgo., 1988, Oak Brook (Ill.) Gazette, 1993; vocalist, entertainer Fiore Duo, Elmwood Park, Ill., 1993—. Author: The Lady Behind the Light, 1985, Life is a Baseball Game, 1987, My Heroes, 1994; lyricist (songs) Dear Mama and Papa, 1986, America - The best Place, 1990; contbr. articles to profl. jours. Organizer concers for flood benefits, Vietnam vets. Home: 2119 N 78th Ave Elmwood Park IL 60707-3022

FIORE, MICHELE MERCIA, reporter; b. Chgo., June 3, 1970; d. Frank Joseph Fiore and Mercia Vimay Balgemann; m. Lawrence, Aug. 31, 1996; 1 child, Hana. AA, Triton C.C., River Grove, Ill., 1990; BA, No. Ill. U., 1992. Radio news anchor, reporter Sta. WDZ/WDZQ, Decatur, Ill., 1992-93, Sta. WKRS/WXLC, Waukegan, Ill., 1993-96; radio news anchor Sta. WMAQ, Chgo., 1995-97; news bur. chief Met. Networks, Chgo., 1996-97; news reporter Sta. WDJT-TV, Milw., 1997—; voice over talent Conversational Voice, Gurnee, Ill., 1996—. Recipient George Cushing award Chgo. Dental Soc., 1995. Avocations: piano, aerobics, weightlifting, sledding.

FIORE, NICHOLAS FRANCIS, specialty metals and materials company executive; b. Pitts., Sept. 24, 1939; s. William H. and Margaret (Scinto) F.; m. Sylvia M. Chinque, Aug. 13, 1960; children: Maria L., Nicholas F., Kristin M., Anthony T. BS, Carnegie-Mellon U., 1960, MS, 1963, PhD, 1964. Asst. prof. metall. engring. and materials sci. U. Notre Dame (Ind.), 1966-69, prof., 1969-81, chmn. dept., 1969-72, 80-81; v.p. Cabot Corp., Boston, 1982-89; mng. dir. materials and applied physics Arthur D. Little Inc., Cambridge, Mass., 1989-90; v.p. Carpenter Tech. Corp., 1990-93, sr. v.p., 1993—; vis. scientist Argonne Nat. Labs. (Ill.), 1974-75. Co-author: Binding of Solute to Dislocations, 1967; Hydrogen Related Embrittlement of High Temperature Materials, 1975; trustee Albright Coll. Editor: (with B.J. Berkowitz) Advanced Techniques for Characterizing Hydrogen in Metals, 1982. Contbr. articles to profl. jours. Chmn. adv. bd. Primary Day Sch. Inc.; mem. sci. and tech. edn. com. New Eng. Council. Served to capt. U.S. Army, 1964-66. Fellow Am. Soc. Metals (trustee); mem. AIME, Alpha Sigma Mu. Office: Carpenter Tech PO Box 14662 Reading PA 19612-4662

FIORE, PETER AMADEUS, English educator, clergy; b. Sept. 8, 1927. MA in English, Catholic U., Washington, 1955; PhD in English, U. London, Eng., 1961. Entered Franciscan Order, 1950; ordained priest, 1955. Dean of arts Siena Coll., Loudonville, N.Y., 1966-91; chair English dept. Siena Coll., Loudonville, 1962-67, 75-85, prof. English, 1971-85, prof. English, comm., 1996—. E-mail: fiore@siena.edu. Office: Siena Coll 515 Loudon Rd Loudonville NY 12211-1459

FIORELLI, KAREN LYNN, nurse; b. Milw., Jan. 8, 1954; d. Enzo and Lydia Ann (Naspini) Fiorelli; children: Anthony P., Jack R. BS in Nursing, U. Wis., Milw., 1978. RN, Wis. Nursing asst. St. Luke's Hosp., Milw., 1974-75, nursing unit sec., 1975-79, staff nurse IV, orthopedics, 1979-85, chmn. unit based quality assurance, 1984-85; employee health supervisor Aurora Health Care Inc., Milw., 1986-91; sr. quality mgmt. coord., 1991—. Roman Catholic. Avocations: music, art, theatre, sports. Home: 14132 Waters Way New Berlin WI 53151-4563 Office: St Luke's Med Ctr PO Box 2901 2900 W Oklahoma Ave Milwaukee WI 53215-4330

FIORENTINO, CARMINE, lawyer; b. Bklyn., Sept. 11, 1932; s. Pasquale and Lucy (Coppola) F. LL.B., Blackstone Sch. Law, Chgo., 1954, John Marshall Law Sch., Atlanta, 1957. Bar: Ga., D.C., U.S. Supreme Ct., U.S. Dist. Ct. D.C., U.S. Ct. Appeals (2d cir.), U.S. Dist. Ct. (no. dist.) Ga., U.S. Ct. Appeals (5th cir.), U.S. Ct. Claims. Mem. N.Y. State Workmen's Compensation Bd., N.Y. State Dept. Labor, 1950-53; ct. reporter, hearing stenographer N.Y. State Com. State Counsel and Attys., 1953; public relations sec. Indsl. Home for Blind, Bklyn., 1953-55; legal stenographer, researcher, law clk., Atlanta, 1955, 57-59; sec. import-export firm, Atlanta, 1956; sole practice, Atlanta, 1959-63, 73—; atty., advisor, trial atty. HUD, Atlanta and Washington, also legal counsel Peachtree Fed. Credit Union, 1963-74; acting dir. Elmira (N.Y.) Disaster Field Office, HUD, 1973; former candidate U.S. Adminstrv. Law Judge. Recipient State of Victory World Culture prize. Mem. Smithsonian Instn., pres., dir., gen. counsel The Hexagon Corp., Republican Nat. Com., Rep. Presdl. Task Force, Nat. Hist. Soc.; Inducted into Rep. Presdl. Legion Merit, 1993; Life Dynamics fellow; mem. Atlanta Hist. Soc., Atlanta Bot. Gardens, Am. Mus. Natural History, Mus. Heritage Soc. Mem. ABA, Fed. Bar Assn., Atlanta Bar Assn., Decatur-DeKalb Bar Assn., Am. Judicature Soc., Old War Horse Lawyers Club, Assn. Trial Lawyers Am., AAAS, Internat. Platform Soc., Nat. Audubon Soc. Presbyterian. Clubs: Toastmasters, Gaslight, Sierra. Writer non-fiction and poetry; composer songs and hymns. Home and Office: 4717 Roswell Rd NE Apt R4 Atlanta GA 30342-2915

FIORENTINO, LINDA, actress; b. Phila., Mar. 9, 1960. Student, Rosemont Coll., 1980, Cir. on Sq. Theatre Sch. Appeared in films Vision Quest, 1985, Gotcha!, 1985, After Hours, 1985, The Moderns, 1988, Queens Logic, 1991, Shout, 1991, Wildfire, 1992, Chain of Desire, 1993, The Desperate Trail, 1994, The Last Seduction, 1994, Bodily Harm, Jade, 1995, Unforgettable, The Split, 1997, Men in Black, 1997, Kicked in the Head, 1997, Dogma, 1999, Ordinary Decent Criminal, 1999, Where the Money Is, 1999; appeared in TV movies The Neon Empire, 1989, The Last Game, 1992, Action on Impulse, 1993, Beyond the Law, 1994, The Last Seduction, 1994; TV guest appearances Alfred Hitchcock Presents, 1985. Mem. Cir. in Sq. Performing Workshops.

FIORENTINO, THOMAS MARTIN, transportation executive, lawyer; b. Washington, Aug. 4, 1959; s. Thomas Martin Sr. and Julia (Bray) F.; m. Mary Ann Hammer, June 12, 1983; children: Sara Elizabeth, Caroline McKay, Thomas Martin III. BA, U. Fla., 1980; JD, Mercer U., 1983. Bar: Fla. 1984. Claims rep. Seaboard System R.R., Evansville, Ind., 1983-84; claims atty. Seaboard System R.R., Jacksonville, Fla., 1984-86; dir. risk mgmt. CSX Corp., Jacksonville, 1986-87; asst. to pres. CSX Tech., Jacksonville, 1987-89; chief of staff Fed. R.R. Adminstrn., 1989-90; counselor to dep. sec. of transp. Office of the Sec., Dept. Transp., Washington, 1990-91; asst. v.p. pub. affairs CSX Transp., Jacksonville, 1991-94, v.p. govt. affairs, 1994-95, v.p. corp. comms. and pub. affairs, 1995—. Mem. bd. visitors The Bolles Sch., 1990-96; bd. dirs. St. Mark's Episcopal Day Sch., 1992-94, Theatreworks, 1992-95, Boys and Girls Clubs of N.E. Fla., 1992-95, Mus. Sci. and History, 1993-96, Jacksonville Urban League, 1993-95, I.M. Sultzbacher Ctr. for the Homeless, 1994-95, Gov. Coun. Sustainable Devel., 1996-97, Children's Home Soc. of Jacksonville, 1996-98, James Madison Inst., 1997—, Fla. Theatre, 1997-99, Ronald McDonald House, 1998—; chmn. Bapt. Health Sys. Found., 1992—. Mem. Fla. Bar Assn., Fla. C. of C., Jacksonville C. of C., First Coast Mfrs. Assn., The Capital Hill Club, River Club, Marsh Landing Country Club, The Lodge and Bath Club (Ponte Vedra Beach), Phi Delta Phi, Fla. C. of C. (bd. trustees 1996—), Jacksonville C. of C. (bd. trustees 1995-96). Republican. Presbyterian. Avocation: golf, tennis. Home: 140 Indian Hammock Ln Ponte Vedra Beach FL 32082-2155

FIORENZA, FRANCIS P., religion educator; b. Bklyn., Feb. 27, 1941; married, 1967; 1 child. AB, St. Mary's U., 1961, STB, 1963; ThD, U. Münster, Fed. Republic of Germany, 1972. Asst. prof. theology U. Notre Dame, Ind., 1971-77, Villanova (Pa.) U., 1977-79; assoc. prof. theology Cath. U. Am., Washington, 1979-87; now Charles Chauncey Stillman prof. Roman Cath. theol. studies Harvard U., Cambridge, Mass.; vis. scholar Union Theol. Sem., N.Y.C., 1974-75; vis. prof. Yale U., 1995. Author: Critical Social Theory and Christology, 1975, Political Theology as Foundational Theology, 1977, Religion und Politik, Christliche Glaube, 1982; translator: Schleiermacher: Open Letters on the Glaubenslehre, 1981, Foundational Theology: Jesus and Church, 1984; editor: Systematic Theology, Roman Catholic Perspectives, 2 vols., 1991; co-editor: (with Don Browning) Habermas, Modernity and Public Theology, 1992, Handbook of Catholic Theology, 1995; contbr. articles to religious jours. Fellow Div., U. Chgo., 1978-79; rsch. fellow Am. Assn. Theol. Schs., 1982-83, 89. Mem. Am. Acad. Religion, Cath. Theol. Soc. Am. (pres. 1985-86), Soc. Values Higher Edn., Coll. Theol. Soc., Hegel Soc. Office: Harvard U Div Sch 45 Francis Ave Cambridge MA 02138-1911

FIORENZA, JOSEPH A., bishop; b. Beaumont, Tex., Jan. 25, 1931. Student, St. Mary's Dem., LaPorte, Tex. Ordained priest Roman Catholic Ch., 1954, consecrated bishop, 1979. Bishop Diocese of San Angelo, Tex., 1979-85, Diocese of Galveston-Houston, Tex., 1985—. Office: Roman Cath Ch 1700 San Jacinto St Houston TX 77002-8216*

FIORETTI, MICHAEL D., lawyer; b. Phila., Mar. 25, 1946; s. Michael R. and Mafalda (Fala) F. BS, St. Joseph's U., Phila., 1967; JD, Villanova U., 1972. Bar: Pa. 1972, N.J. 1981. Sr. ptnr. Law Offices of Michael D. Fioretti, Phila., 1972—; sole propietor Law Offices of Michael D. Fioretti, Cherry Hill, N.J., 1981—. Author: Divorce Rules and Practice Manual. With U.S. Army, 1968-70, Vietnam. Roman Catholic. Office: Bourse Bldg Ste 790 111 S Independence Mall E Philadelphia PA 19106-2515 also: 1765 Springdale Rd Cherry Hill NJ 08003-2177

FIORI, FRANK ANTHONY, land use planner, historic preservation consultant; b. Brunswick, Maine, Mar. 7, 1950; s. Andrew and Rejane Maxine (Fournier) F.; m. Linda Charlotte Hill, Aug. 13, 1977 (div. June 1986); m. Jane Drummond, June 27, 1986; children: Kellene, Scotlund, Heather, Jared, Brodey. BA in Polit. Sci., St. Michael's Coll., Winooski, Vt., 1973; MS in Historic Preservation, U. Oreg., 1983. Mill mgr., foreman Marriner Lumber Co., Brunswick, 1974-76; carpenter self employed, Pocatello, Idaho, 1976-81; adj. faculty Idaho State U., Pocatello, 1979-81, lectr., 1984-86; cons. planner City of Pocatello, 1983-86; project mgr. Pelletier & Flanagan, Brunswick, 1986-87; dir. planning and codes Town of Topsham, Maine, 1987-98; sr. planner City North Las Vegas, 1998—; cons. Preservation Svcs., Monmouth, Maine, 1983-98. Trustee, pres. Pejepscot Hist. Soc., Brunswick, 1989-95; trustee, sec. Maine Preservation, Portland, 1992-98; trustee, treas. Monmouth San. Dist., 1995-98. Mem. Am. Inst. Cert. Planners, Am. Planning Assn. (sec. No. New Eng. chpt. 1990, 98), Maine Assn. Planners. Home: 7640 Little Valley Ave Las Vegas NV 89147-8506 Office: City of North Las Vegas 2266 Civic Center Dr North Las Vegas NV 89030

FIORI, PAMELA, publishing executive, magazine editor; b. Newark, Feb. 26, 1944; d. Edward and Rita Marie (Rascati) F.; m. Colton Givner. B.A. cum laude, Jersey City State Coll., 1966. Tchr. English Gov. Livingston High Sch., Berkeley Heights, N.J., 1966-67; assoc. editor Holiday Mag., N.Y.C., 1968-71; assoc. editor Travel & Leisure Mag., N.Y.C., 1971-74, sr. editor, 1974-75, editor-in-chief, 1975-80; editor-in-chief, exec. v.p. Am. Express Pub. Corp. (Travel & Leisure/Food & Wine), N.Y.C., 1980-89, editorial dir., exec. v.p., 1989-93; editor-in-chief Town & Country, N.Y.C., 1993—. Contbr. articles to periodicals; columnist: Window Seat, 1976-89. Bd. dirs. Jazz at Lincoln Ctr., East Side Houses Settlement. Recipient Chevalier de l'Ordre du Merite, 1985, Melva C. Pederson award for disting. travel journalism Am. Soc. Travel Afts., 1992, Outstanding Woman of the 90s award Found. for Neurosurg. Rsch., 1994, Bus. award Nat. Italian Am. Found., 1996. Mem. Am. Soc. Mag. Editors, Century Assn. Office: Town & Country 1700 Broadway New York NY 10019-5905

FIORILLA, JOHN LEOPOLDO, lawyer; b. Paterson, N.J., July 1, 1965; s. Giovanni and Maria Giuseppa (Mazzara) F. BS, Seton Hall U., 1987; JD, U. Pitts., 1990; LLM in Internat. Legal Studies, NYU, 1999. Bar: N.J. 1990, N.Y. 1991, D.C. 1991, U.S. Dist. Ct. (so. and ea. dists.) N.Y. 1991, U.S. Dist. Ct. N.J.1990, U.S. Ct. Appeals (3rd, 9th, D.C. and fed. cirs.) 1991, U.S. Supreme Ct. 1995; master lic. USCG. Assoc. Sullivan & Cromwell, N.Y.C., London, 1990-94; prin., gen. counsel Elysium Group Inc., N.Y.C., 1994—; of counsel Studio Legale Vassalli, Milan, Italy, 1994—, Studio Legale Associato Caffie & Maroncelli, Milan, Italy, 1994—; bd. dirs. Elysium Group Inc., Elysium Group U.S. Holdings Inc., Elysium Boca Raton Inc., Elysium Dialysis Ctr. Inc.; assoc. Brosio, Casati & Assocs., Milan, 1992-93; legal adviser to the nunciature, permanent observer Mission of the Holy See to the UN, 1997—, mem. Holy See Del. to the Gen. Assembly and other UN bodies, 1997—. Mem. parish coun. St. John the Evangelist Ch., N.Y.C., 1996-98; mem. new com. steering com. Am. Assn. Royal Acad. Trust, 1998—; mem. standing com. Young Friends Save Venice, Inc., 1998—. Decorated Knight Equistrian Order Holy Sepulcher of Jerusalem, Sovereign Mil. Hospitaller Order St. John of Jerusalem Aux. Mem. ABA, Am. Soc. Internat. Law, Assn. of Bar of City of N.Y. (com. on internat. law), Internat. Bar Assn., N.Y. County Lawyers Assn., N.Y. State Bar Assn., Met. Club, Econ. Club N.Y. Roman Catholic. Home: 430 E 57th St New York NY 10022-3061 Office: Elysium Group Inc 230 Park Ave New York NY 10169-0005

FIORILLO, JOHN A(NTHONY), health care executive; b. N.Y.C., Jan. 20, 1943; s. John Albert and Matilda (Marotti) F.; m. Anita Daves Pitney, Dec. 6, 1969; 1 child, Alexandra. AB, NYU, 1963; AM, Brown U., 1965; post-grad., CUNY, 1972-74. Planning officer OEO, Washington, 1964-66; exec. asst. to commr. N.Y.C. Health and Hosps. Design, 1966-69; sr. cons. Peat Marwick Mitchell and Co., N.Y.C., 1968-72; pres. Policy Planning Inc., N.Y.C., 1972-77; asst. v.p. Columbia U., N.Y.C., 1977-81; mng. dir. Am. Health Found., N.Y.C., 1981-82; pres. The Health Strategy Group, Inc., N.Y.C., 1982—; mem. cons. NIH, Bethesda, Md., 1979-86; founding dir. People's Med. Soc., Emmaus, Pa., 1982-84. Author: (with others) Art Work, No Commercial Value, 1972; contbr. articles to profl. jours., chpts. in book. Mem. White House Task Force on Peace Corps., Washington, 1969, N.Y.C. Task Force on Employee Health Benefits, 1974-75; mem. advance team Sen. Robert Kennedy, 1964; asst. campaign dir. Congressman Jonathan Bingham, N.Y.C., 1964; bd. trustees Daytop Village Found., 1986—; bd. dirs. The Shaker Mus., 1995-98, N.Y. Assn. for Ambulatory Care, 1997—. With USCG, 1965. Brown U. fellow, 1963-64. Avocations: tennis, photography, modern jazz. Home: 275 Central Park W New York NY 10024-3015 Office: The Health Strategy Group Inc 920 Broadway # 1401 New York NY 10010*

FIORINI, JOHN E., III, lawyer; b. Sayre, Pa., Oct. 3, 1946; s. John Eugene and Jewel Eleanor (Lang) F; m. Gail Kathryn Driscoll, Mar. 29, 1969; children: Cara Rose, John Carl, Michael James. BS, Georgetown U., 1968; JD, U. Pa., 1971. Bar. D.C. Ptnr. Pepper & Corazzini, Washington, 1976-86, Heron, Burchette, et al., Washington, 1986-89, Gardner, Carton & Douglas, Washington, 1990—. Mem. Phi Beta Kappa. Home: 2281 Marginella Dr Reston VA 20191-1106 Office: Gardner Carton & Douglas 1301 K St NW Ste 900E Washington DC 20005-3370*

FIORINO, ANTHONY SAVERIO (TONY EITAN), research analyst; b. Bronxville, N.Y., Nov. 27, 1967; s. Francis Michael and Frances Rosemary (Campisi) F.; m. Deborah Alexandra Goldberg, May 23, 1994; 1 child, Shoshana Elian. BS in Biology, MIT, 1989; MS in Molecular Pharmacology, Yeshiva U., 1993, PhD in Molecular Pharmacology, 1995, MD, 1996. Intern internal medicine U. Pa., Phila., 1996-97, resident dermatology, 1997-98; rsch. analyst Paramount Capital, N.Y.C., 1998—; assoc. JP Morgan Securities, N.Y.C., 1998—. Contbr. articles to Annals Internal Medicine, Brain Rsch., Ob-gyn., In Vitro, Cell Biology Internat., Leukemia. Treas., bd. dirds. Albert Einstein Synagogue, Bronx, N.Y., 1992-96. Mem. AMA, N.Y. Acad. Scis., Alpha Omega Alpha, Phi Beta Kappa, Sigma Xi. Jewish. Achievements include cloning a cell line useful in studying liver development. Avocations: medical ethics, Jewish law and texts. Office: JP Morgan Securities 60 Wall St Fl 48 New York NY 10005-2836

FIORINO, JOHN WAYNE, podiatrist; b. Charleroi, Pa., Sept. 30, 1946; s. Anthony Raymond and Mary Louise (Caramela) F.; m. Susan K. Bonnett, May 2, 1984; children—Jennifer, Jessica, Lauren, Michael. Student Nassau Coll., 1969-70; B.A. in Biology, U. Buffalo, 1972; Dr. Podiatric Medicine, Ohio Coll. Podiatric Medicine, 1978. Surg. Res., MESA Gen. Hosp., 1978-79, Bd. cert. primary podiatric medicine Am. Podiatric Med. Specialties Bd. Salesman, E. J. Korvettes, Carle Place, N.Y., 1962-65; orderly Nassau Hosp., Mineola, N.Y., 1965-66; operating room technician-trainee heart-lung machine L.I. Jewish-Hillside Med. Center, New Hyde Park, N.Y., 1967-69; pharmacy technician Feinmel's Pharmacy, Roslyn Heights, N.Y., 1969-70; mgr., asst. buyer Fortunoffs, Westbury, N.Y., 1972-73; bd. certified perfusionist L.I. Jewish-Hillside Med. Center, New Hyde Park, N.Y., 1973-74; clin. instr. cardiopulmonary tech. Stony Brook (N.Y.) Univ., 1973-74; operating room technician Cleve. Met. Hosp., 1975; lab. technician Univ. Hosp., Cleve., 1976-78; surg. resident Mesa Gen. Hosp., 1978-79; staff podiatrist, 1979—; pvt. practice podiatry, Mesa, 1979—; staff podiatrist Sacaton (Ariz.) Hosp., 1979—, Mesa Gen. Hosp., 1979, Valley Luth. Hosp., Mesa, 1985, Chandler Community Hosp., 1985, Desert Samaritan Hosp., Mesa, 1986, podiatrist U.S. Govt. Nat. Inst., Sacaton, 1980-87, Indian Health Services, Sacaton, 1980-87; cons. staff Phoenix Indian Med. Ctr., 1985. Served with USN, 1966-67. Mem. Am. Podiatry Assn., Ariz. Podiatry Assn. (treas. 1984-86), Acad. Ambulatory Foot Surgery, Am. Coll. Foot Surgeons (assoc.), Mut. Assn. Profls., Am. Acad. Pain Mgmt. (cert.), Pi Delta, Alpha Gamma Kappa. Home: 2624 W Upland Dr Chandler AZ 85224-7870 Office: 5520 E Main St Mesa AZ 85205-8793

FIORITO, EDWARD GERALD, lawyer; b. Irvington, N.J., Oct. 20, 1936; s. Edward and Emma (DePascale) F.; m. Charlotte H. Longo; children—Jeanne C., Kathryn M., Thomas E., Lynn M., Patricia A. BSEE, Rutgers U., 1958; JD, Georgetown U., 1963. Bar: U.S. Patent and Trademark Office 1960, Va. 1963, N.Y. 1964, Mich. 1970, Ohio 1975, Tex. 1984. Patent staff atty. IBM, Armonk, N.Y., 1958-69; v.p. patent and comml. relations Energy Conversion Devices, Troy, Mich., 1969-71; mng. patent prosecution Burroughs Corp., Detroit, 1971-75; gen. patent counsel B.F. Goodrich Corp., Akron, Ohio, 1975-83; dir. patents and licensing Dresser Industries, Inc., Dallas, 1983-93; alt. mem. Dept. Commerce Adv. Commn. on Patent Law Reform, 1991-92; spl. master, arbitrator, neutral evaluator, expert providing opinion testimony in intellectual property litigation, 1986—; U.S. del. to World Intellectual Property Orgn. Diplomatic Conf., 1991. Bd. dirs. Akron's House Extending Aid on Drugs, 1976. Mem. ABA (chmn. sci. and tech. sect. 1984-85, vice chair intellectual property law sect.), IEEE, Tex. Bar Assn. (chmn. intellectual property law sect. 1990-91), Internat. Assn. for Protection Indsl. Property (exec. bd. 1989—), Assn. Corp. Patent Counsel (exec. com. 1982-84), Tau Beta Pi. Roman Catholic. Avocations: music, running. *Those of you who have received gifts in great abundance at the beginning of your journey here, should remember to use them before your journey ends in the service of your creator who gave them to you.*

FIRCHOW, EVELYN SCHERABON, German educator, author; b. Vienna, Austria; came to U.S., 1951, naturalized, 1964; d. Raimund and Hildegard (Nickl) Scherabon; m. Peter E. Firchow, 1969; children: Felicity (dec. 1988), Pamina. BA, U. Tex., 1956; MA, U. Man., 1957; PhD, Harvard U., 1963. Instr. coll. math. Balmoral Hall Sch., Winnipeg, Man., Can., 1953-55; teaching fellow in German Harvard U., Cambridge, Mass., 1957-58, 61-62; lectr. German U. Md. in Munich, 1961; instr. German U. Wis., Madison, 1962-63, asst. prof., 1963-65; assoc. prof. German U. Minn., Mpls., 1965-69, prof. German and Germanic philology, 1969—; vis. prof. U. Fla., Gainesville, 1973; Fulbright research prof. Iceland, 1980, 94; vis. research prof. Nat. Cheng Kung U., Tainan, Taiwan, 1982-83; permanent vis. prof. Jilin U., Changchun, People's Republic of China, 1987—; vis. prof. U. Graz, Austria, 1989, 91, U. Vienna, Austria, 1995, U. Bonn, 1996. Editor: (under name E.S. Coleman) Taylor Starck-Festschrift, 1964, Stimmen aus dem Stundenglas, 1968, (under name E.S. Firchow) Studies by Einar Haugen, 1972, Studies for Einar Haugen, 1972, Was Deutsche lesen, 1973, Deutung und Bedeutung, 1973, Bibliotheca Germanica, Modern Scandinavian Lit. in Translation, (with Kaaren Grimstad), Elucidarius in Old Norse Translation, 1989, The Old Norse Elucidarius: Original Text and English Translation, 1992, Notker der Deutsche von St. Gallen: De Interpretatione, 1995, Categoriae, 2 Vols., 1996, De Nuptiis Philologiae et Mercurii, 2 Vols., 1999; translator: Einhard: Vita Caroli Magni, Das Leben Karls des Grossen, 1968, 84, 95, Einhard: Vita Caroli Magni, The Life of Charlemagne, 1972, 85, Icelandic Short Stories, 1974, 87, (with P.E. Firchow) East German Short Stories, 1979, (with P.E. Firchow) Alois Brandstetter, The Abbey, 1998; dir., editor Computer Clearing-House Project for German and Medieval Scandinavian; contbr. articles and book revs. to profl. jours. Fulbright scholar Tex., 1951-52; fellow Alexander von Humboldt-Stiftung, Munich, 1960-61, Tuebingen, 1974, Marburg, 1981, Goettingen, 1985, Tokyo, 1991, Marburg and Berlin, 1993, Fulbright fellow, Iceland, 1967-68, 80, 94, Austrian Govt., 1977, NEH, 1980-81, Am. Inst. Indian Studies, 1988, BUSH fellow, 1989, Thor Thors fellow, 1994; elected hon. mem. Multilingual Rsch. Ctr., Brussels, 1986. Mem. AAUP, MLA (chmn. div. German lit. to 1700 1979-80, 93-96, vice chmn. pedagogical seminar for Germanic philology 1979-86, 91-93, chair 1994), Medieval Acad. Am., Soc. German-Am. Studies (chair Linguistics I 1992), Internat. Comparative Lit. Assn., Soc. for Advancement Scandinavian Studies (chmn. Germanic philology 1979, text editing 1980, linguistics 1984, computers and Old Norse 1985), Assn. for Lang. and Linguistic Computing (founding mem.), Am. Comparative Lit. Assn., Midwest Modern Lang. Assn. (chmn. German I 1965-66, chmn. Scandinavian 1979), Internationale Vereinigung der Germanisten, Am. Assn. Tchrs. German, Modern Humanities Rsch. Assn., Mediävisten Verband, Soc. for Germanic Philology, Österreichische Germanisten-Gesellschaft. Office: U Minn Dept German Minneapolis MN 55455

FIRCHOW, PETER EDGERLY, language professional, educator, author; b. Needham, Mass., Dec. 16, 1937; s. Paul Karl August and Marta Loria (Montenegro) F.; m. Evelyn Maria Scherabon Coleman, Sept. 18, 1969; 1 dau., Pamina Maria Scherabon. B.A., Harvard Coll., 1959; postgrad., U. Vienna, Austria, 1959-60; M.A., Harvard U., 1961; Ph.D., U. Wis., 1965. Asst. prof. English U. Mich., 1965-67; asst. prof. English and comparative lit. U. Minn., Mpls., 1967-69; assoc. prof. U. Minn., 1969-73, prof., 1973—, chmn. Comparative Lit. Program, 1972-78; disting. vis. prof. Nat. Cheng Kung U., Taiwan, 1982-83, Jilin U., Peoples Republic China, 1987, U. Munich, Germany, 1988, U. Graz, Austria, 1989; Fulbright prof. U. Bonn,

Germany, 1995-96. Author: Friedrich Schlegel's Lucinde and the Fragments, 1971, Aldous Huxley, Satirist and Novelist, 1972, The Writer's Place: Interviews on the Literary Situation in Contemporary Britain, 1974; (with E.S. Firchow) East German Short Stories: An Introductory Anthology, 1979; The End of Utopia: A Study of Huxley's Brave New World, 1984; The Death of the German Cousin: Variations on a Literary Stereotype, 1986; translator (with Firchow) The Abbey (Alois Brandstetter), 1998; contbr. articles on modern lit. subjects to profl. jours. Fellow Inst. Advanced Studies in Humanities, Edinburgh, 1977. Mem. MLA, Midwest Modern Lang. Assn. (v.p. 1977, pres. 1978), Am. Comparative Lit. Assn., Coll. English Assn. Home: 135 Birnamwood Dr Burnsville MN 55337-6814 Office: U Minn Dept English 310D Lind Hall 207 Church St SE Minneapolis MN 55455-0134

FIREBAUGH, FRANCILLE MALOCH, university official; b. El Dorado, Ark., July 15, 1933; d. Delton Verdis and Dorothy Lucille (Measeles) Maloch; m. John David Firebaugh, Dec. 28, 1970. BS, U. Ark., 1955; MS, U. Tenn., 1956; PhD, Cornell U., 1962. Instr. U. Tex., Austin, 1956-58; asst. prof. home econs. Ohio State U., Columbus, 1962-65, assoc. prof., 1965-69, prof., 1969-88; dir. Sch. Home Econs., 1973-82; acting v.p. agrl. adminstrn., exec. dean of agr., home econs., natural resources, 1982-83; assoc. provost Office Acad. Affairs, 1983-84; vice provost for internat. affairs, 1984-88, acting provost, v.p. acad. affairs, 1985-86; dean coll. human ecology Cornell U., Ithaca, N.Y., 1988-99; bd. dirs. Midland Life Ins., 1984—; mem. joint com. on agrl. research and devel. Bd. Internat. Food and Agr., 1982-87. Author: Home Management: Context and Concepts, 1975, Family Resource Management, 1981, 88. Bd. dirs. Columbus Council on World Affairs, 1987-88, Boyce Thompson Inst. for Plant Rsch., 1991-97; moderator First Baptist Ch., 1981-83; bd. dirs. Cayuga Med. Ctr., 1992—, Panamerican Agr. Sch., Zamorano, Honduras, 1994—, Kendal at Ithaca, 1995—; Families and Work Inst., N.Y.C., 1995—. Mem. Nat. Coun. Family Rels., AAAS, Am. Home Econs. Found. (bd. dirs. 1987-90), Am. Assn. of Family and Consumer Scis., Ohio State U. Faculty Club (pres. 1988), Assn. Women in Devel. (sec. 1988-89), Sigma Xi, Sigma Delta Epsilon, Kappa Omicron Nu, Phi Upsilon Omicron, Gamma Sigma Delta, Phi Kappa Phi, Epsilon Sigma Phi. Office: Cornell U Coll Human Ecology Office of the Dean Martha Van Rensselaer Hall Ithaca NY 14853

FIREHOCK, BARBARA A., interior designer; b. Alexandria, Va., Feb. 2, 1944; d. George W. Jr. and Geraldine Tinsley (Wallin) Sickler; m. Scott Walton Ripley, Dec. 27, 1966 (div.); m. Raymond B. Firehock, Jr.; 1 child, Christopher Francis. BA, U. N. Tex., 1966; postgrad., U. Md., 1976-77. Owner Walnut Hill Interiors, LaPlata, Md., 1981—; instr. in interior design Charles County C.C., LaPlata, 1990; site supr./interior design internship U. Md., College Park, 1992; mem. program com. Matawoman Creek Arts Ctr., Charles County, Md., 1995-96; fundraiser The Gallery Com. of Charles County, 1988-94; interior designer Fredericksburg Area Svc. League Decorator Showhouse, 1997—, So. Md. Decorator Showhouse, 1998. Design work featured in Town and Country, 1997, Community Carousel Weekly Show/Prestige Cable, Fredericksburg, The Maryland Independent, 1991, The Maryland House and Garden Pilgrimage, 1995, 96, Traditional Home, 1999. Spl. events chair Charles County Garden Club of Md.; chair Christ Ch. Concert Series, LaPlata, 1995. Named Woman of Yr. Bus. and Profl. Women, Charles County, 1982. Mem. ASID, Interior Design Soc. (pres. Md. chpt.), Nat. Trust for Hist. Preservation (design assoc.), AAUW (pres., v.p., cultural chair Charles County chpt.), Chi Omega (rush info. chair for So. Md. 1993-98). Democrat. Episcopalian. Avocations: horseback riding, gardening, needlework, genealogy. Office: Walnut Hill Interiors PO Box 1451 La Plata MD 20646-1451

FIREMAN, PAUL B., footwear and apparel company executive; b. Cambridge, Mass., Feb. 14, 1944. Student, Boston U. Pres., chmn., CEO Reebok Internat. Ltd., Stoughton, Mass. Founder The Reebok Found. Honored by Human Rights Law Group; recipient numerous industry awards. Office: Reebok Internat Ltd 100 Technology Center Dr Stoughton MA 02072-4705

FIREMAN, PHILIP, pediatrician, allergist, immunologist, medical association executive; b. Pitts., 1932. MD, U. Chgo., 1957. Diplomate Am. Bd. Allergy and Immunology. Intern Phila. Gen. Hosp., 1957-58; resident in pediatrics Children's Hosp., Pitts., 1958-60, resident pediatrician, 1964—; fellow in allergy and immunology NIH, Bethesda, Md., 1960-62; fellow allergist, immunologist Harvard Children's Hosp., Boston, 1962-64; prof. pediatrics, internal medicine U. Pitts. Med. Sch. Office: Children's Hosp 3705 5th Ave Pittsburgh PA 15213-2583

FIRESIDE, HARVEY FRANCIS, political scientist, educator; b. Vienna, Austria, Dec. 28, 1929; came to U.S., 1940, naturalized, 1945; s. Norbert and Frances F.; m. Bryna Joan Levenberg, Dec. 12, 1959; children—Leela Ruth, Douglas Leonard, Daniel Ephraim. B.A. magna cum laude, Harvard U., 1952, M.A., 1955; Ph.D., New Sch. Social Research, 1968. Info. specialist AEC, 1957-58; editor Palmerton Publishing Co., N.Y.C., 1959-60, Am. Cyanamid Co., N.Y.C., 1960-61, Fgn. Policy Assn., N.Y.C., 1961-62; freelance editor, 1962-64; asst. prof. polit. sci. N.Y. Inst. Tech., 1964-68; Charles A. Dana prof. politics Ithaca (N.Y.) Coll., 1968-96, prof. emeritus, 1998; cons. in field. Author: Icon and Swastika: The Russian Orthodox Church under Nazi and Soviet Control, 1971, Soviet Psychoprisons, 1979, Brown vs Board of Education, 1994, Young People from Bosnia Talk About War, 1996, Plessy vs. Ferguson, 1997, The Fifth Amendment, 1998, New York Times vs. Sullivan, 1999; also articles. Group leader Amnesty Internat., Ithaca, 1973-80; co-chmn. Socialist Studies Com., Ithaca, 1977-83, Working Group Against Psychiat. Abuse, 1980-83; bd. dirs. Tompkins County chpt. ACLU, 1968-71, Ithaca Sanctuary Com., 1986-92, Tompkins County Mental Health Assn., 1986-89, 93-95, pres., 1995-96; bd. dirs. Com. on U.S.-Latin Am. Rels., 1990-92, Hillel Found., Ithaca Coll., 1991-93; coord. The Border Fund, 1989—, Bosnian Student Project, 1994—; Citizenship Project, 1997—. Recipient Tompkins County Human Rights award, 1992, 98; Harvard U. Russian Rsch. Ctr. fellow, summers 1975, 80; fellow Harvard U. Ukrainian Rsch. Inst., summer 1976; fellow Cornell U. Inst. for European Studies, 1995-98, Peace Studies Program, 1998—; grantee N.Y. Dept. Edn., 1965; vis. scholar Russian Inst., Columbia U., 1966; Nat. Endowment Humanities fellow, summer, 1983, 94. Mem. Am. Polit. Sci. Assn. Democrat. Jewish. Home: 202 Eastwood Ave Ithaca NY 14850-6239 Office: 322 N Aurora St Ithaca NY 14850-4202

FIRESTEIN, CECILY BARTH, artist; b. N.Y.C., Apr. 25, 1933; d. Sidney Monte and Esther (Schwartz) Barth; m. Stephen Kern Firestein; children: Conrad Elliot, Lesley Adam. BA, Adelphi U., 1953; MA, NYU, 1955, cert. in advanced study, 1958; cert., N.Y. Sch. of Interior Design, 1964. Cert. elem. tchr., N.Y. Art tchr., cons. Union Free Schs. Dist. #24, Valley Stream, N.Y., 1953-60; printmaker Phoenix Gallery, Valley Stream, 1962—; interior designer Firestein Interiors, Valley Stream, 1964—; instr., lectr. Mus. of the City of N.Y., 1978, The New Sch., N.Y.C., 1979, 80; tchr. Cooper Hewitt Mus., N.Y.C., 1980, South St. Seaport Mus., N.Y.C., 1981, Parson's Sch. Design, N.Y.C., 1982, U. S.C., Columbia, 1989; freelance writer N.Y. Daily News Detroit News, 1977; with Montclair State U., N.J., 1993, U. S.C.; art critic Art Speak, N.Y.C., 1983-91, Manhattan Arts Internat. mag. 1992, 93, Conn. Graphic Art Ctr.; cons. Miami (Fla.) Preservation League, 1980, Tarrytown (N.Y.) Hist. Soc., 1979; instr., lectr. Fordham U., N.Y., 1972, Bronx Mus. History, 1974-77, The New Sch., 1977-83. Author: Making Paper & Fabric Rubbings, 1999; represented in permanent collections Corcoran Gallery of Art, Washington, Cin. Mus. Art, N.Y. Pub. Libr., Yale U. Art Gallery Mus., Newark Mus., Columbia (S.C.) Art Mus., Rose Art Mus., Mass. Art Mus., Fla. Internat. U., Del. Art Mus., Wilmington, Skirball Mus., L.A., So. St. Seaport Mus., B'nai Brith Klutznik Nat. Jewish Mus., Washington, Freud Mus., London, Freud Mus., Vienna; solo exhibitor at 20 galleries and mus.; author: Rubbing Craft, 1977. Recipient Artist-in-residence award Bronx Mus. of History; grant N.Y. State Council on the Arts, 1974. Mem. N.Y. Soc. Women Artists, Nat. Assn. Women Artists, Art Students League, Phoenix Gallery (pres. 1990—), Brandeis Club, Kappa Delta Pi, Pi Lambda Theta. Democrat. Jewish. Avocation: buying and selling antique jewelry.

FIRESTONE, EVAN RICHARD, art educator, art historian; b. Richmond, Va., Nov. 21, 1940; s. Abner Morton and Ruth Selma (Gloven) F.; m. Gail Cynthia Cotter, Sept. 6, 1970; children: Hillary, Erin. BA in Art, History, Kent State U., 1962; MA in Art History, U. Wis., 1965, PhD in Art History, 1971. Instr. to assoc. prof., chair art history dept. U. Mass. Dartmouth (formerly Southeastern Mass. U.), 1968-77; assoc. prof. to prof., chair art dept. Western Carolina U., Cullowhee, N.C., 1977-83; prof., chair dept. art and design Iowa State U., Ames, 1983-90; dir. Sch. Art U. Ga., Athens, 1990-97, prof., 1990—; mem. bd. officers Founds. in Art: Theory and Edn., 1979-83; trustee Asheville (N.C.) Art Mus., 1982-83, Octagon Ctr. for Arts, Ames, 1984-90, pres. bd., 1989-90; adv. bd. Ga. Mus. Art, 1990-97. Contbr. numerous articles to profl. publs.; exhibiton catalogues. Recipient Throne-Aldrich award State Hist. Soc. Iowa, 1992; Marc. B. Rojtman European Study fellow, London, 1965-66, Samuel H. Kress Found. fellow, U. Wis., 1966-67. Mem. Coll. Art Assn. *

FIRESTONE, JUANITA MARLIES, sociology educator; b. Wurzburg, Germany, Jan. 30, 1947; d. Harrison and Marlies (Breit) Gillette; m. Kenneth Todd Firestone, Aug. 31, 1968 (div. Oct. 1993); children: Jason Dean, Krystillin Elisabeth. BS in Sociology cum laude, Black Hills State U., 1979; MA in Sociology, U. Tex., 1982, PhD in Sociology, 1984. Office mgr. Silver Wings Aviation, Rapid City, S.D., 1975-76; pub. rels. mgr. Pacer Mining Co., Custer, S.D., 1976-79; lectr. sociology U. Tex., Austin, 1980-87; asst. prof. sociology U. Tex., San Antonio, 1987-94, assoc. prof., 1994—; cons. in field; attendee Nat. Security Forum, 1994; mem. Chancellor's Faculty Adv. Coun., U. Tex. Sys., 1994-96; testimony U.S. Congress Black Polit. Caucus, 1996. Contbr. articles to profl. jours. Mem. spkrs. bur. Rape Crisis Ctr., Austin and San Antonio, 1984-94; bd. dirs. AIDS Found., San Antonio, 1992; coord. workshop Expanding Your Horizons, San Antonio, 1992-96; mem. Task Force on Crime and Violence, San Antonio, 1990. Recipient Rsch. award U. Tex. Sys., Austin, 1991, 95, 98; Congrl. fellow, Washington, 1983. Mem. Internat. Sociol. Assn., Am. Sociol. Assn., S.W. Soc. Social Sci. (pres. women's caucus 1994-95), Golden Key (faculty advisor 1990-96), Inter Univ. Consortium Armed Forces and Soc. (bd. dirs. 1998—), Alpha Kappa Delta. Avocations: swimming, skiing, water skiing, reading. Office: U Tex at San Antonio Divsn Social and Policy Sci San Antonio TX 78249

FIRESTONE, MARSHA L., economic organization executive; b. Mobile, Ala., May 13, 1943; d. Albert and Ida (Bernstein) Sidel; m. Monroe Firestone, June 30, 1968; children: Justin, Daren. BA, Sophie Newcomb, 1965; MA, Tchrs. Coll., 1966; PhD, Columbia U., 1972. Exec. dir. ORT, N.Y.C., 1984-86; pres. Phillip Colls., N.Y.C., 1986-90; v.p. tng. AWED, N.Y.C., 1990-95; v.p. Women Inc., N.Y.C., 1995-98; exec. dir. Women's Econ. Summit, N.Y.C., 1998—; v.p. N.Y. Women's Agenda, N.Y.C., 1997-99. Co-author: Busy Woman's Guide to Successful Self-Employment, 1996. Benefit chair New Alternatives for Children, N.Y.C., 1995; v.p. 55 East End Corp., N.Y.C., 1996-99. Mem. Internat. Women's Forum. Avocations: golf, theater, traveling. Office: Womens Econ Summit 335 Madison Ave Fl 4 New York NY 10017-4605

FIRESTONE, MORTON H., business management executive; b. Chgo., Feb. 4, 1935; s. William and Lillian (Kliot) F.; m. Roberta (Bobbie) Schwartz, Feb. 3, 1957; children—Jeffrey, Scott, Dan. BS, U. Calif., Davis, 1957; MBA, U. So. Calif., 1971. V.p. Security Pacific Nat. Bank, Los Angeles, 1957-77; chmn. bd., chief fin. officer, corp. sec. Elixir Industries, 1977-87, also dir.; pres. Garden Ins., 1978-87, Club Wholesale Concepts, Inc., 1986-87; chmn. bd., chief exec. officer Rondure Industries, 1987-90; pres. Lin Mor Corp., Woodland Hills, Calif., 1990—; bd. dirs. Robert Burns & Sons, Inc. Past chmn. Los Angeles-Eilat Sister City Com. Mem. Fin. Execs. Inst., Beta Gamma Sigma. Lodges: Optimist (past pres. Hollywood), Kiwanis (past pres. West Hollywood). Office: Lin Mor Corp 21130 Costanso St Ste 1 Woodland Hills CA 91364-2053

FIRESTONE, RICHARD FRANCIS, chemistry educator; b. Canton, Ohio, June 18, 1926; s. Lester Ellis and Elizabeth Mary (Corkran) F.; m. Olwen Margaret Huskins, Aug. 21, 1954; children—William, Mark, Robert. A.B., Oberlin Coll., 1950; Ph.D., U. Wis., 1954. Resident research assoc. Argonne Nat. Lab., Ill., 1954-56; asst. prof. chemistry Western Res. U., Cleve., 1956-60; assoc. prof. chemistry Ohio State U., Columbus, 1961-66, prof., 1967-94; prof. emeritus, 1994—. Served with USNR, 1944-46. Fellow AAAS; mem. Am. Chem. Soc., Am. Phys. Soc. Address: 120 W 18th Ave Columbus OH 43210-1106

FIRESTONE, ROY, sportscaster; b. Miami Beach, Fla., Dec. 8, 1953; s. Bernard and Regina Firestone; m. Midori Firestone, 1987; 2 children. Diploma in Mass Communications, U. Miami, 1974. Sports reporter Sta. WTVJ-TV, Miami, Fla., 1973-75, Sta. WPLG-TV, Miami, 1975-77; sports reporter, anchor Sta. KCBS-TV, Los Angeles, 1977-85, color analyst, football telecasts, 1978-79; host Mazda SportsLook ESPN, 1980-97, play-by-play football announcer, 1987—. Host (syndicated TV show) Sports Comedy Around the World, Up Close Prime Time, Up Close, 1991-95, SportsLook, 1980-90, Into the Night, 1992; halftime commentator ESPN, 1988; play-by-play commentator NFL, 1987; appeared in movies Jerry Maguire, The Scout; comedy appearances include Late Night with David Letterman, The Tonight Show, Nightline, others. Recipient 4 L.A. Emmy awards Acad. TV Arts and Scis., Excellence in Sports Broadcast Journalism award Northeastern U., 1990, 2 Golden Mike awards, Best Sportscast award L.A. Press Club, 1981; named Best Program Interviewer, CableACE awards, 1996, Best Sports Host, 1986, 88, 91. Office: PO Box 56927 Sherman Oaks CA 91413*

FIRESTONE, SHEILA MEYEROWITZ, retired gifted and talented education educator; b. Bronx, N.Y., Dec. 20, 1941; d. Boris and Bella Meyerowitz; m. Bruce Firestone, Oct. 1, 1961; children: Wayne, Evan. AA, Miami-Dade Community Coll., North Miami, Fla., 1969; BA in Edn., Fla. Atlantic U., 1972; MS in Spl. Edn., Fla. Internat. U., 1973. Cert. learning disabilities, elem., gifted, early childhood, emotionally disturbed, Fla. Tchr. to gifted Highland Oaks Elem. Sch., North Miami Beach, Fla., 1973-98; ret., 1998; chairperson Dade County Very Spl. Arts Festival, 1989-93. Composer: Premiere - Psalm 117, Because I Love, South Florida Youth Symphony, 1994. Mem. choir Temple Sinai, North Miami Beach, 1979-92; state evaluator Future Problem Solving, 1989-96; creative writing supt. Dade County Youth Fair, 1982-87; founder "Songs for a New Day; pub. teaching curriculum and leadership/citizenship tng. thematic music and interdisciplinary whole lang. learning units, 1990; mem. choir Aventura Turnberry Jewish Ctr., 1993. Named Master Tchr., State of Fla., 1985; recipient Very Spl. Arts Honor award Dade County Bd. Pub. Instns., 1990, 1st pl. Jim Harbin Fame award Fla. Media Educators, 1994, Tchr. of Note, Young Patronesses of the Opera, 1996; Freedom Found. grantee, summers, 1983, 84, 87, 90, Nancy Givens Instrnl. grantee, Fla. Coun. Exceptional Children, 1995, Javitts grant Nat. Evaluator F.P.S., 1992-93, grantee Dade Pub. Edn. Fund Impact II Adapter, 1994. Mem. ASCAP Coun. for Exceptional Children (various offices 1963-97, chpt. pres. 1988, Fla. Exceptional Tchr. of Yr. finalist 1989, Chpt. 121 Dade County Exceptional Student Tchr. of Yr. award 1989, Highland Oaks Elem. Sch. Tchr. of Yr. 1990), Sigma Alpha Iota (patroness 1996—, chairperson patroness chpt. U. Miami 1998-99). Democrat. Avocations: studying and composing music.

FIRIMITA, FLORIN ION, artist, educator, curator; b. Bucharest, Romania, July 30, 1965; came to the U.S., 1990; s. Ion and Anica (Manu) F. AA magna cum laude, Naugatuck Valley Coll., 1995; BS summa cum laude, Ctrl. Conn. State U., 1997. Cert. art edn. grades K-12. Asst. stage designer Nat. Theatre of Opera and Ballet, Bucharest, 1986-90, prodn. mgr., 1988-90; curator, mem. adv. bd. Gallery on the Green, Canton, Conn., 1996—; artist-tchr. Middlebury (Conn.) Elem. Sch., 1997—; mgr., owner Fif Studio, Winchester, Conn., 1995—. Works exhibited at various group and solo shows York Sq. Gallery, New Haven, 1994, Miss Porter's Sch., Farmington, Conn., 1995, Pat Steier Gallery, Litchfield, Conn., 1995, Emporium Gallery, Mystic, Conn., 1996; represented in various pvt. and pub. collections; author of essays and short stories. Vis. artist and educator Vol. Outreach Program, New Britain, Conn., 1997. Recipient Honorable mention Nat. Arts Program, Hartford, Conn., 1992, Nat. prize for lit. NYU, Suffern, 1994. Mem. NEA, Conn. Edn. Assn., Washington Art Assn., Canton Art Guild. Avocations: classical music, jazz, travel, reading. Home: 155 Smith Hill Rd Winchester CT 06098

FIRMIN, MICHAEL WAYNE, counselor educator; b. New Orleans, July 28, 1961; s. Lloyd John and Betty L. (Shepherd) F.; m. Karen Sue Tuttle, Aug. 4, 1984; children: Ruth, Sarah. BA, Calvary Bible Coll., 1983, MA, 1985; MS, Bob Jones U., 1987, PhD, 1988; MA, Marywood U., 1992; postgrad., Syracuse U., 1992—. Nat. cert. counselor. Dir. counseling svcs. Bapt. Bible Coll. of Pa., Clarks Summit, 1988-98, assoc. prof., 1988-98, chmn. divsn. grad. studies, 1995-97; assoc. prof. psychology Cedarville (Ohio) Coll., 1998—; cons. for psychol. svcs. Assn. Bapts. for World Evangelism, Harrisburg, 1991-94; clin. assessment cons. Keystone City Residence, 1994—. Pastor Faith Fellowship Bapt. Ch., Danbury, Conn., 1991-94. Mem. Psi Chi. Republican. Home: 84 Elms St Cedarville OH 45314-8513 Office: Cedarville Coll PO Box 601 Cedarville OH 45314-0601

FIROOZABADY, EBRAHIM, plant scientist; b. Kangavar, Iran, Mar. 1, 1952; came to U.S., 1976; s. Khosrow and Tavous (Gharloghi) F.; m. Nickoo Tavassoli, Oct. 2, 1976; children: Amy, Yasmin, Navid. BS, U. Tehran, Iran, 1975; MS, U. Calif., Davis, 1978, PhD, 1982. Postdoctoral assoc. U. Nebr., Lincoln, 1982-84; rsch. scientist Agrigenetics, Madison, Wis., 1984-86, sr. rsch. scientist, 1986-88; prof. U. N.Mex., Las cruces, 1989; group rsch. scientist DNA Plant Tech., Oakland, Calif., 1989-93, prin. rsch. scientist, 1993—. Contbr. chpts. to books, numerous articles to profl. jours. Mem. Soc. for In Vitro Biology (plant divsn. v.p. 1994-96, symposium chmn. congress 1991—, plant program com. 1990—). Achievements include research in genetic engineering of different crop plants including pineapple, carnation, rose, banana, papaya, chrysanthemum, cotton, tomato, sunflower, alfalfa and tobacco; production of new cultivars by genetic engineering; inventor/patentee in field. Avocations: gardening, camping, skiing. Office: DNA Plant Tech 6701 San Pablo Ave Ste B Oakland CA 94608-1275

FIRST, CRAIG PATRICK, composer, educator; b. Harrisburg, Pa., Mar. 16, 1960; s. William E. and Jeanette J. (Capalbo) F.; m. Jean Ann Harris, June 22, 1990; children: Craig Francis, Caroline Lauren. BMus, Am. Conservatory Music, 1982; MMus, Northwestern U., 1983, DMus, 1990. Instr. Am. Conservatory Music, Chgo., 1983-84; lectr. Northwestern U., Evanston, Ill., 1990-95; assoc. prof. U. Ala., Tuscaloosa, 1995—; artistic dir. Chgo. 20th Century Music Ensemble, Chgo., 1992—. Composer: (piano trio) Intimate Voices, 1986, (League Composers award 1989), (violin, piano) Black Sun, 1990, Nat. Assn. Composers USA award 1990), (mandolin, tape) Tantrum, 1992, (World Music Days award 1998), String Quartet, 1996 (Octavo Concurso Internat. Musical Composition Spain 1997). Recipient Astral Composition award Nat. Found. Advancement Arts, Miami, 1998. Mem. ASCAP, Nat. Assn. Composers, Soc. Composers Inc., Coll. Music Soc.

FIRST, HARRY, law educator; b. 1945. BA, U. Pa., 1966, JD, 1969. Bar: Pa. 1969, N.Y. 1979. Law clk. to justice Supreme Ct. Pa., 1969-70; atty. U.S. Dept. Justice, Washington, 1970-72; asst. prof. U. Toledo Coll. Law, 1972-76; vis. assoc. prof. NYU Law Sch., N.Y.C., 1976-77, assoc. prof., 1977-79, prof., 1979—; counsel Loeb & Loeb, N.Y.C. and Los Angeles. Mem. editorial bd.: Pa. Law Rev. Mem. Pa. Law Rev., Order of Coif, Phi Beta Kappa. Office: NYU Law Sch 40 Washington Sq S New York NY 10012-1099*

FIRST, TINA LINCER, writer; b. Bklyn., June 8, 1955; d. Maxwell J. and Laura (Siwek) Lincer. BA in English, Art magna cum laude, SUNY, Albany, 1976. Features writer, reporter The Times Record, Troy, N.Y., 1976-81; freelance writer various newspapers and mags., 1981—; sr. writer Sawchuk, Brown Assocs., Albany, 1992—; dance critic The Albany Times Union, 1981-87; assoc. editor The Pub. Sector-Civil Svc. Employees Assn., Albany, 1981-85; editor-in-chief The Adv.-NEA, Albany, 1985-86; mng. editor The Voice-United Univ. Professions, Albany, 1987-90; sec./exec. bd. Women's Press Club N.Y. State, Albany, 1991-92. Author: (guidebooks) Dutchess County: The New Business Frontier, 1994, Your Business, 1995, (screenplay) Herschel, 1997. Panelist Arts Decentralization Panel of N.Y. State Coun. on the Arts, Albany, 1986-89. Recipient Internat. Labor Comm. awards Internat. Labor Comm. Assn., 1981, 87, 88, 95, 98, Second Place award for brochures and Third Place award for documentary Hudson Valley Area Mktg. Assn., 1994, Honorable Mentions, Writer's Digest Mag., 1996, 97, 98. Mem. Hudson Valley Writers Guild. Democrat. Avocations: drawing, painting, dancing, skiing. Office: Sawchuk Brown Assocs 41 State St Ste 500 Albany NY 12207-2869

FIRST, WESLEY, publishing company executive; b. Erie, Pa., Feb. 18, 1920; s. Orson John and Pearle (Unger) F.; m. Margaret Elizabeth Whittlesey, Apr. 3, 1943 (div. June 1967); 1 child, Michael; m. Dianne Jones, Dec. 1975 (div. Sept. 1981); m. Suzanne Lavenas, Jan. 9, 1982. Student, U. Mich., 1937-40; BS, Columbia U., 1958; MA, New Sch. for Social Research, 1963. Reporter Erie Dispatch, 1943-47, asst. city editor, 1947-48, asst. to editor, 1948-50; with N.Y. World-Telegram and Sun, N.Y.C., 1950-63; successively copyreader, night news editor N.Y. World-Telegram and Sun, 1950-57, asst. mng. editor, 1957-60, mng. editor, 1960-63; prof. journalism Ohio State U., 1963-65; dir. univ. relations Columbia, N.Y.C., 1965-67; asst. to pres. Sarah Lawrence Coll., 1967-68, Juilliard School, N.Y.C., 1968-69; editor Travel Weekly, 1969-76; editor-in-chief Psychology Today, 1976-77; staff v.p. editorial Ziff-Davis Pub. Co., 1977-82, cons., 1982—; guest lectr. newspaper design and makeup Fordham U.; instr. journalism Finch Coll., N.Y.C.; Rep. to newspaper design and makeup seminar Am. Press Inst., 1957. Editor: Columbia Remembered, University on the Heights. With USAAF, 1944-46. Woodrow Wilson Fellow, 1959. Mem. U. Mich. Alumni Assn., Columbia U. Alumni Assn., Phi Beta Kappa, Kappa Tau Alpha, Sigma Delta Chi. Clubs: Overseas Press, Silurians. Home: Montauk Manor 236 Edgemere St Apt 413 Montauk NY 11954-5249 *Believe in miracles, then make them happen.*

FIRSTENBERG, DONALD ELLIOTT, chemist; b. New Brunswick, N.J., Sept. 13, 1946; s. Seymour Sidney and Mae (Hamelsky) F.; m. Ilene Lois Sager, Aug. 11, 1968 (div. 1982); children: Michael Harrison, Sheri Hope. BS, Rutgers U., 1968; MS, U. Fla., 1971, PhD, 1975. Vis. asst. prof. Rutgers U., New Brunswick, 1975-78; group leader Reed & Carnrick, Kenilworth, N.J., 1978-83; biochemical specialist Boyle-Midway, Cranford, N.J., 1983-86; sect. head Miles Lab., Bedford Park, Ill., 1986-88; group leader L'Oreal, Clark, N.J., 1988-95; sr. chemist Amerchol, Inc., Edison, N.J., 1995—. contbr. rsch. papers to profl. jours.; patentee in field. Capt. USAF, 1975-77. Mem. Soc. Cosmetic Chemists. Avocations: golf, tennis. Home: 32 Sherborne St Somerset NJ 08873-4642 Office: Amerchol Inc 136 Talmadge Rd Edison NJ 08817-2852

FIRSTENBERG, JEAN PICKER, film institute executive; b. N.Y.C., Mar. 13, 1936; d. Eugene and Sylvia (Moses) Picker; m. Paul Firstenberg, Aug. 9, 1956 (div. July 1980); children—Debra, Douglas. BS summa cum laude, Boston U., 1958. Asst. producer Altman Prodns., Washington, 1965-66; media advisor J. Walter Thompson, N.Y.C., 1969-72; asst. for spl. projects Princeton (N.J.) U., 1972-74, dir. publs., 1974-76; program officer Markle Found., N.Y.C., 1976-80; dir., CEO Am. Film Inst., L.A., Washington, 1980—; bd. dirs. Trans-Lux Corp.; former chmn. nat. adv. bd. Peabody Broadcasting Awards; bd. dirs. Trans-Lux Corp. Former trustee Boston U.; mem. adv. bd. Will Rogers Inst., N.Y.C.; chmn., bd. advisors Film Dept. N.C. Sch. of Arts. Recipient Alumni award for disting. service to profession Boston U., 1982; seminar and prodn. chairs at directing workshop for women named in her honor Am. Film Inst., 1986. Mem. Women in Film (Crystal award 1990), Trusteeship for Betterment of Women, Acad. Motion Picture Arts and Scis. Office: Am Film Inst 2021 N Western Ave PO Box 27999 Los Angeles CA 90027-0999*

FIRSTENBERG, SAMUEL, film director; b. Poland, Mar. 13, 1950; came to U.S., 1971; s. Ariehleib and Rivka (Rechtman) F.; m. Iris Rubinstein; children: Noga, Ayelet, Gaili. BA, Columbia Coll., Los Angeles, 1974; MA, Loyola Marymount U., 1980; hon. doctorate, Columbia Coll., 1988. Freelance film dir. L.A., 1980—. Dir. feature films One More Chance, 1982, Revenge of the Ninja, 1983, The Domination, 1983, Electric Boogaloo, 1984, American Ninja, 1985, Avenging Force, 1986, American Ninja II, 1987, Riverband, 1989, The Day We Met, 1990, Delta Force III, 1991, The American Samurai, 1992, Cyborgcop, 1993, Blood Warriors, 1994, Cyborg Soldier, 1995, Operation Delta Force, 1996, McLinsey's Island, 1997, Motel Blue, 1998. Recipient Silver plaque Chgo. Film Festival, 1982. Jewish.

FIRSTER, D. JAMES, small business owner; b. Franklin, Pa., Jan. 6, 1953; s. Ronald Wayne and Dorothy Lucille (Parker) F.; m. Susan Jean Erno, Oct. 11, 1980; 1 child, Allison Lee. BS in Edn., Pa. State U., 1975. Cert. elem. tchr., Pa. Dir. activities Eldercare Gardens Nursing Home, Charlottesville,

Va., 1980-84; ops. coord. Springmoor Care Retirement Cmty., Raleigh, N.C., 1984-86; exec. dir. Push, Inc., Morganton, N.C., 1986-89; exec. dir., gen. mgr. U. Village, Charlottesville, Va., 1989-96; owner First Fine Art Assoc., Charlottesville, Va., 1996—; COO Anderson Bus. Environ., Charlottesville, Va., 1997—; cons. Eldercare Corp. Office, Charlottesville, 1982-84. Contbr. articles to popular mags. Bd. dirs. Thomas Jefferson Health Coun., Charlottesville, 1997—; treas. Northwestern Va. Health Sys. Agy., Charlottesville, 1997—; bd. dirs., sec. Jordon Devel. Bd., Charlottesville, 1989-92; participant, task force mem. Govs. Commn. for the Family, Raleigh, 1988; invited spkr. Congl. Task Force on Behalf of ADA Legislation, 1989. Recipient Cert. Appreciation award Va. Health Care Assn., 1981-84, Am. Heart Assn., 1981, ARC, 1981, Outstanding Svc. award Am. Cancer Soc., 1982-84. Mem. Am. Assn. Homes & Svcs. for the Aging, Pa. State Alumni Assn., Pi Kappa Phi (Cert. Appreciation 1989), Elks (trustee lodge #389, swim team com. chmn. 1997, meet dir. 1994-97). Unitarian. Avocations: travel, swimming, reading, music, photography.

FIRTH, EVERETT JOSEPH, timpanist; b. Winchester, Mass., June 2, 1930; s. Everett Emanuel and Rosemary (Scandura) F.; m. Olga Kwasniak, June 22, 1960; children—Kelly Victoria, Tracy Kimberly. Mus.B. with distinction, 1952. Faculty head New Eng. Conservatory, 1950—; mem. faculty Berkshire Music Center, 1956—; pres., CEO Vic Firth Inc. (mfr. and distbr. worldwide drum sticks and mallets); CEO Vic Firth Mfg. parent co. Banton Precision Wood Turning of Newport Maine. Solo timpanist, Boston Symphony Orch., 1952—, Boston Pops Orch., 1952—, with, Boston Symphony Chamber Players; Recs. with, RCA Victor, Mercury, Columbia, Cambridge, Deutsche Grammophon. Mem. ASCAP, Phi Kappa Lambda, Phi Mu Alpha Sinfonia. Home: 3 Pinewood Rd Dover MA 02030-2521 Office: Vic Firth Inc 65 Commerce Way Dedham MA 02026-2953

FISCALINI, FRANK, city councilman. BS, U. Santa Clara, 1948; MA, Stanford U., 1950; PhD, U. No. Colo., 1976. City councilman Dist. 6 San Jose City Coun., Calif., vice mayor, 1999—; pres., CEO, Alezian Bros. Hosp., San Jose, 1982-86,. Exec. dir. St. Joseph Cathedral Restoration, Diocese San Jose, 1986-88; cons. Sch. Planning Ctr. With AUS, 1943-46. Recipient City of Hope Golden Torch award, Award of Honor Am. Assn. Coll. Baseball Coaches, 1973, Ignatian award Santa Clara U. Alumni Assn., Brotherhood award Nat. Conf. Christians and Jews, Disting. Citizen award Kiwanis, San Jose, Legacy medal San Jose Hosp. Found., Courage award Children's Discovery Mus., 1984; Frank Fiscalini Internat. Swim Ctr. named in his honor, 1979; inducted into U. Santa Clara Hall of Fame, 1982. Office: 801 N 1st St Rm 600 San Jose CA 95110-1704*

FISCH, CHARLES, physician, educator; b. Nesterov (Zolkiew), Poland, May 11, 1921; s. Leon and Janette (Deutscher) F.; m. June Spiegal, May 23, 1943; children: Jonathan, Gary, Bruce. AB, Ind. U., 1942, MD, 1944; MD (hon.), U. Utrecht, The Netherlands, 1983. Diplomate Am. Bd. Internal Medicine, Am. Bd. Cardiovasc. Medicine (mem. 1977-82). Intern St. Vincent's Hosp., Indpls., 1945; resident in internal medicine VA Hosp., Indpls., 1948-50; fellow gastroenterology Marion County Gen. Hosp., Indpls., 1950-51; fellow in cardiology Marion County Gen. Hosp., 1951-53; asst. prof. medicine Ind. U. Med. Sch., 1953-59, assoc. prof., 1959-63, prof., 1963—, disting. prof., 1975, dir. cardiovasc. divsn., 1963-90, disting. prof. emeritus, 1990—; dir. Krannert Inst. Cardiology, 1953-90; mem. cardio-renal adv. com. HEW-FDA, 1973-77, 79—; Connor lectr. Am. Heart Assn., 1980; chmn. manpower rev. com. Nat. Heart, Lung and Blood Inst., 1985-89; Charles Fisch chair in cardiology Ind. U. Author: Electrocardiography of Arrythmias, 1989; co-editor Digitalis, 1969, Cardiac Electrophysiology and Arrythmias, 1991; contbr. articles to med. jours.; mem. editorial bd. Am. Heart Jour., 1967—, Am. Jour. Electrocardiology, 1967—, Coeur et Medicine Interne, 1970—, Am. Jour. Medicine, 1973—, Circulation, 1977—, Am. Jour. Cardiology, 1967—; assoc. editor Am. Jour. Cardiology, 1977—. Capt. M.C. AUS, 1946-48. Recipient James Herrick award Am. Heart Assn. Fellow ACP, Am. Coll. Cardiology (pres. 1975-77, dir., chmn. publ. com. 1988-94, Gifted Tchr. award 1993), World Congress Cardiology (v.p. 1986); mem. Am. Fedn. Clin. Rsch., Ctrl. Soc. Clin. Rsch., Am. Physiol. Soc., Assn. Univ. Cardiologists, Assn. Am. Physicians, N.Am. Soc. for Pacing and Electrophysiology (Dist. Tchr. award 1994). Home: 7901 Morningside Dr Indianapolis IN 46240-2526 Office: Ind U Med Ctr Krannert Inst Card 1111 W 10th St Indianapolis IN 46202-4800

FISCH, NATHANIEL JOSEPH, physicist; b. Montreal, Quebec, Can., Dec. 29, 1950; s. Mandel and Helene (Greenfield) F.; m. Tobe Michelle Mann, Aug. 12, 1984; children: Jacob, Benjamin, Adam. BS, MIT, 1972, MS, 1975, PhD, 1978. Researcher Princeton (N.J.) Plasma Physics Lab., 1978-91, assoc. dir. for acad. affairs, 1993—; dir. program in plasma physics Princeton U., 1991—, prof. astrophys. scis., 1991—; cons. Exxon Rsch. and Engring., Clinton, N.J., 1981-86; vis. scientist IBM, Yorktown Heights, N.Y., 1986. Recipient fellowship Guggenheim Found., 1985, 1992 APS award for Excellence in Plasma Physics, Am. Phys. Soc., 1992. Fellow Am. Phys. Soc. (vice chair divsn. of plasma physics 1996, chair-elect 1997, chair 1998). Achievements include patents in new ways to produce current in plasmas. Office: Princeton U Forrestal Campus PO Box 451 Princeton NJ 08543-0451

FISCH, ROBERT OTTO, medical educator; b. Budapest, Hungary, June 12, 1925; came to U.S., 1957.; s. Zoltan and Irene (Manheim) F.; divorced; 1 dau., Rebecca A. Med. diploma, U. Budapest, 1951; study art, Acad. Fine Arts, Budapest, 1943, Mpls. Coll. Arts and Design, 1970-76. Gen. practice medicine Hungary, 1951-55, pub. health officer, 1955; pediatrician Hosp. for Premature Children, Budapest, 1956; intern Christ Hosp., Jersey City, 1957-58; intern pediatrics U. Minn. Hosps., 1958-59, researcher, 1959-60, research fellow, 1961; instr. U. Minn. Sch. Medicine, 1961-63, asst. prof., 1963-72, assoc. prof., 1972-79, prof., 1979—, dir. phenylketonuric clinic, 1961-97. Author: Respiratory Diseases; PKU, Child Development (Best Cover Minn. Med. 1975), Light from the Yellow Star: A Lesson of Love from the Holocaust, 1994; contbr. articles to profl. jours.; exhibited art works in various one-man and group shows. Mem. Soc. Pediatric Rsch., Am. Physician Art Assn. (1st prize 1990, numerous others). Office: U Minn Mayo Hosp PO Box 384 Minneapolis MN 55455

FISCH, WILLIAM BALES, lawyer, educator; b. Cleve., May 11, 1936; s. Max Harold and Ruth Alice (Bales) F.; m. Janice Heston McPherson, Sept. 2, 1961 (dec. 1987); m. Suzanne Fischer Good, June 19, 1993 (dec. 1998); children: Katherine Emily, Stephen McPherson. AB, Harvard Coll., 1957; LLB, U. Ill., 1960; M.Comparative Law (univ. fgn. law fellow), U. Chgo., 1962; JUD, U. Freiburg, Germany, 1972. Bar: Ill. 1961, Mo. 1982. Assoc. firm Kirkland & Ellis, Chgo., 1962-65; asst. prof. law U. N.D., 1965-68, assoc. prof., 1968-70; assoc. prof. U. Mo., Columbia, 1970-74; prof. U. Mo., 1974—, Isador Loeb prof. law, 1977—. Author: Die Vorteilsausgleichung im amerikanischen und deutschen Recht, 1974; co-author: Problems, Cases and Materials on Professional Responsibility, 1985, 2d edit., 1995; bd. editors: Am. Jour. Comparative Law; contbr. articles, revs. to law jours. Alexander von Humboldt-Stiftung Rsch. fellow, 1968-69, 89-90; Fulbright-Hays Rsch. scholar Hamburg, Germany, 1980-81, 89-90; Max Planck Soc. Rsch. fellow, Hamburg, 1992. Mem. ABA, AAUP, Am. Law Inst. Office: U Mo Law Sch Columbia MO 65211

FISCHBACH, CHARLES PETER, railway executive consultant, lawyer, arbitrator, mediator; b. N.Y.C., Apr. 3, 1939; s. Howard C. and Pauline Lillian (Wasserman) F.; BS, U. Wis., 1960, JD, 1967; MA, Rutgers U., 1962; m. Paula Rae Steinhorn, July 15, 1973. Bar: Wis. 1967, U.S. Supreme Ct. 1974. Pvt. practice, Madison, Wis., 1967-68; labor rels. rsch.analyst and cons., N.Y.C., 1968-70; asst. to exec. officer labor rels. and personnel N.Y.C. Transit Authority, N.Y.C., 1970; labor rels. rsch. analyst, N.Y.C., 1970-72; exec. dir. Classified Mcpl. Employees Assn. Balt. City, 1972-74; labor rels. cons./arbitrator, Balt., 1974-77; dir. labor rels., chief labor rels. officer Chgo., Rock Island and Pacific R.R. Co., 1977-81, dir. personnel and employee rels., Chgo., 1981-84; dir. adminstrn. and human resources Chgo. Pacific Corp., 1984-85; arbitrator, mediator, 1985—; v.p. Rock Island Improvement Co., 1984-85; dir. Peoria and Bureau Valley R.R. Co.; lectr. Am. Mgtm. Assn., Am. Arbitration Assn. Collective Bargaining Inst. Mem. pub. sector labor relations conf. bd. U. Md., 1973-77, Ill. Econ. Bd., 1988-90; mem. landlord-tenant law study commn., State of Md., 1976-77; mem. govs. commn. on sci. and tech. State of Ill., 1990-98; advisor Balt. City Charter Revision Commn., 1974-75, Balt. City Commn. on Aging, 1973-74; mem. Chgo. Workforce Bd., City of Chgo., 1999—; mem. coll. edn. adv. coun. Roosevelt U., 1990-93; mem. Chgo. postal customer adv. coun. U.S. Postal Svc., 1994-95. Recipient Am. Jurisprudence prize in corp. law Joint Pubs. of Annotated Reports System, 1966; cert. for encouragement of vol. dispute settlement procedures Am. Arbitration Assn., 1981-84; named hon. fellow Harry S. Truman Library Inst., 1976, ABA., Mem. Nat. Hist. Soc., State Bar Wis., Am. Arbitration Assn. (labor employment and comml. panel arbitrators, chair Chgo. labor adv. com. 1998—), Fed. Mediation and Conciliation Svc. Roster of Arbitrators, Nat. Mediation Bd. Register of Arbitrators, Ill. Pub. Employee Arbitration Mediation Panel, Nat. Assn. R.R. Referees (Regional v.p.), Indsl. Relations Rsch. Assn., Soc. Profls. in Dispute Resolution, Ill. Bd. Edn. Panel of Hearing Officers, Social Security Adminstrn./Am. Fedn. Govt. Employees Arbitration Panel, United Airlines and Internat. Assn. Machinists and Aerospace Workers Am. (mem. sys. bd. adjustment), Am. Found. Automation and Employment, Wis. Alumni Assn., Rutgers Alumni Assn., Statue of Liberty-Ellis Island Found. (charter), Soc. Am. Baseball Rsch. Contbg. editor: The Railway Labor Act, 1995; contbr. articles on labor relations and arbitration to profl. jours. Avocations: collecting commemorative coin series and first day medallic covers, reading, baseball history and research, art.

FISCHBACH, GERALD D., neurobiology educator; b. New Rochelle, N.Y., Nov. 15, 1938; children: Elissa, Peter, Neal, Mark. AB, Colgate U., 1960; MD, Cornell U., 1965; MA (hon.), Harvard U., 1978. Intern U. Washington Hosp., Seattle, 1965-66; sr. surgeon, Pub. Health Svc., Lab. of Neurophysiology, Nat. Inst. Neurol. Diseases and Stroke NIH, Bethesda, Md., 1966-69; fellow Behavioral Biology Br. Nat. Inst. Child Health, 1969-73; assoc. prof. pharmacology Harvard Med. Sch., Boston, 1978-81, prof., 1978-81; Nathan Marsh Pusey prof. neurobiology, chair dept. neurobiology Harvard Med. Sch., Mass. Gen. Hosp., Boston, 1990-98; Edison prof. neurobiology, chmn. dept. anatomy and neurobiology Washington U. Sch. Med., St. Louis, 1981-90; dir. Neurol. Disorders and Stroke NIH, Bethesda, Md., 1998—; mem. exec. com. Program in Cell and Devel. Biology, Harvard Med. Sch., 1974-81; nonresident tutor Leverett House, Harvard Coll., 1974-77; clk. of corp. Marine Biol. Lab., Woods Hole, Mass, 1978-81, trustee, 1982—, exec. com., 1984-89; master Fuller Albright Acad. Soc., Harvard Med. Sch., 1979-81, faculty coun., 1980-81; chmn. Gordon Conf. on Molecular Pharmacology, 1983; dir. Ctr. for Cellular and Molecular Neurobiology, Washington U. Sch. of Med., 1983-90, dir. Jacob Javits Ctr. for Excellence in Neurosci., 1985-90, dir. Ctr. for Higher Brain Function, 1988-90, mem. Med. Ctr. Bd., 1989-90; dir. Neurosci. Ctr., Mass. Gen. Hosp., 1990—; mem. adv. bd. Nat. Spinal Cord Injury Assn., 1978—, Neurology B Study Sect., NIH, 1978-80, Alfred P. Sloan Found., 1984-89, Dept. Biology Adv. Coun., Princeton U., 1984-88, Fidia Rsch. Found., 1986—, McKnight Neurosci. Rsch. Awards Rev. Com., 1986—, Howard Hughes Med. Inst., 1988—, SUNY Health Sci. Ctr. at Bklyn, 1988—, Helen Hay Whitney Found., 1991, Children's Hosp., Boston, 1991; vis. prof. Dept. Pharmacology U. Calif. at San Francisco, 1978; lectr. Disting. Lecture Series in Pharmacology, U. Md. Sch. Medicine, 1978, 25th Ann. Bishop Lecture, Washington U. Sch. Medicine, 1980, Disting. Lecture Series, Dept. Zoology, U. Tex., 1981; invited speaker 5th Ann. Meeting European Neurosci. Assn., 1981 ; Alden Spencer lectr. Coll. Physicians and Surgeons, Columbia, U., 1981, Stephen W. Kuffler lectr. Harvard Med. Sch., 1990, numerous others; assoc. Neurosci. Rsch. Program, k1981—. Editor Jour. Cell Biolog, 1985-86; assoc. editor Devel. Biology, 1974-78, Jour. Neurophysiology, 1975-81, 1989—, Jour. Neurobiology, 1986—; corr. editor Proc. Royal Soc., Series B, London, 1989—; contbr. articles to profl. jours. Recipient Polk award Cornell U., 1965, Mathilde Solowey award Found. for Advanced Edn. in the Scis., NIH, 1975, W. Alden Spencer award Coll. Physicians and Surgeons, Columbia U., 1981; N.Y.State Regents scholar, 1956-60, N.Y. State med. scholar, Cornell U., 1962-65; Salk Inst. non-resident fellow, 1990. Mem. Soc. for Neurosci. (llth ann. lectr., pres.-elect 1982-83, pres. 1983-84), Soc. Gen. Physiologists, Am. Soc. Cell Biology, Phi Beta Kappa. Office: Natl Inst of Neurological Disorders and Stroke NIH Bldg 31 Rm 8A 52 31 Center Dr Bethesda MD 20892-2540*

FISCHBARG, ZULEMA F., pediatrician, educator; b. Buenos Aires, Mar. 22, 1937; came to U.S., 1962; d. Naun and Esther (Pollner) Fridman; m. Jorge Fischbarg; children: Gabriel Julian, Victor Ernesto. MD, U. Buenos Aires, 1960. Pediatric intern Children's Hosp., Louisville, 1962-63, resident in pediatrics, 1963, chief resident in pediatrics, 1964; fellow hematology Michael Reese Med. Ctr., Chgo., 1964-66, Presbyn. St. Lukes Hosp., Chgo., 1966-67; fellow pediatric hematology Children's Meml. Hosp., Chgo., 1967-68; asst. clin. pediatrician U. Chgo., 1968-69; instr. in pediatrics Cornell U. Med. Sch., N.Y.C., 1970-72, asst. prof. in pediatrics, 1972-76, assoc. prof. pediatrics, 1978—; assoc. attending pediatrician Flushing Hosp. Me.d Ctr., N.Y. Hosp., Queens, 1978—; attending in pediatrics St. John's Hosp./Cath. Med. Ctr., N.Y.C.; med. specialist, sch. physician Bur. of Sch. Children and Adolescent Health, N.Y.C., 1994—; instr. in medicine Ill. U., Chgo., 1967-68; assoc. attending pediatrician, N.Y. Hosp., N.Y.C., 1972—. Fellow Am. Acad. Pediatrics. Democrat. Jewish. Home: 175 E 62nd St # 6D New York NY 10021-7626 Office: 37-51 72d St Jackson Heights NY 11372

FISCHBEIN, CHARLES ALAN, pediatrician; b. Newark, June 5, 1945; s. Martin and Naomi (Litzky) F.; m. Ellen Ruth Niemtzow, Aug. 10, 1969; children: Melissa Paige, Neil Todd. BA in Biology, Case Western Reserve U., 1966; MD, SUNY, Buffalo, 1970. Diplomate Am. Bd. Pediatrics. Resident in pediatrics Children's Hosp. Med. Ctr., Cin., 1970-72; fellow in pediatric cardiology Children's Hosp. Med. Ctr., Boston, 1972-74; pvt. practice pediatrics, 1974—; pres. Pediatric Assocs. of Conn., Waterbury, 1982—; asst. clin. prof. U. Conn. Med. Sch., Farmington, Conn., 1974—, Yale U. Sch. Medicine, New Haven, Conn., 1974—; acting co-chief dept. pediatrics St. Mary's Hosp., Waterbury, Conn., 1995-97. Fellow Am. Acad. Pediatrics; mem. AMA, Am. Coll. Sports Medicine. Avocation: mountain biking. Office: Pediatric Assocs Conn PC 160 Robbins St Waterbury CT 06708-2652

FISCHEL, DANIEL NORMAN, publishing consultant; b. Bklyn., Apr. 13, 1922; s. Joseph Louis and Liza (Herman) F.; m. Maxine Friedman, May 9, 1943; children: Anne, Jonathan, Lisa. B.A., N. Y. U., 1943. Mng. editor Am. Water Works Assn., N.Y.C., 1946-55; editor Dodge Books, N.Y.C., 1955-61; with McGraw-Hill Book Co., N.Y.C., 1962-78; v.p., gen. mgr. profl. and reference books div. McGraw-Hill Book Co., 1970-78; pres. Elsevier North-Holland, Inc., N.Y.C., 1978-81, Gordon & Breach Sci. Pubs., N.Y.C., 1982-85; pub. cons., 1981—; Mem. exec. com. tech., sci. and med. div. Am. Assn. Pubs., 1972-78, 79-81. Author: A Practical Guide to Writing and Publishing Professional Books: Business, Technical, Scientific, Scholarly, 1984. Served with AUS, 1943-45. Home and Office: 2200 N Central Rd Fort Lee NJ 07024-7557

FISCHEL, DAVID, astrophysicist, remote sensing specialist; b. DuBois, Pa., Sept. 12, 1936; s. Leonard and Elizabeth Mae (Brown) F.; m. Constance Jean Newham, June 11, 1960; children: Valerie Dawn, Walter David, Brenda Jill. ScB in Physics, Brown U., 1958; MA, Ind. U., 1960, PhD in Astrophysics, 1963. Astrophysicist NASA Ames Research Center, Moffett Field, Calif., 1963-65; astrophysicist Lab. for Astronomy and Solar Physics NASA Goddard Space Flight Center, Greenbelt, Md., 1965-79, earth resources system scientist, info. processing divsn., 1979-84; project mgr. Systems and Applied Scis. Corp., 1984-85; sr. systems engr. image processing Earth Observation Satellite Co., 1985-89, chief scientist, 1989-96; cons., 1996-97, 99—; chief scientist SGT Inc., 1997-99; co-organizer Internat. Conf. in Stellar Pulsation, 1974, 78. Vol. Boy Scouts Am., 1964-87, with Balt. Area council, 1975-87; chmn. Columbia (Md.) Coop. Ministry Refugee Resettlement Com., 1975-82; elder First Presbyn. Ch. of Howard Country; vice-chmn., bd. dirs. Musical Arts Internat., Inc., 1998—. Mem. IEEE, AIAA (former chair Balt. chpt.), COSPAR (assoc.), Soc. Photo-optical Instrumentation Engrs., IAF Commn. on Remote Sensing, Internat. Astron. Union, Sigma Xi. Research and publs. in field.

FISCHEL, EDWARD ELLIOT, physician, educator; b. N.Y.C., July 29, 1920; s. Joseph L. and Lisa (Herman) F.; m. Pauline Dunieff, Dec. 26, 1943; children—Robert, Janet. B.A., Columbia U., 1941, M.D., 1944, Sc.D. in Medicine, 1948. Diplomate: Am. Bd. Internal Medicine. Intern Presbyn. Hosp., N.Y.C., 1944-45; asst. resident medicine Presbyn. Hosp., 1945-46; asst. in medicine Columbia U. Coll. Physicians and Surgeons, N.Y.C., 1947-50; asso. medicine Columbia U. Coll. Physicians and Surgeons, 1950-55, assoc. clin. prof. medicine, 1969-72, lectr. medicine, 1972-87; practice medicine specializing in internal medicine and rheumatology; asst. physician Presbyn. Hosp., N.Y.C., 1947-55; asso. clin. prof. medicine Albert Einstein Coll. Medicine, Yeshiva U., N.Y.C., 1957-69; prof. medicine Albert Einstein Coll. Medicine, Yeshiva U., 1972-80, vis. prof. medicine, 1980-81; dir. dept. medicine Bronx-Lebanon Hosp. Center, Bronx, N.Y., 1954-80; chief dept. medicine Mt. Sinai Hosp., Hartford, Conn. and prof. medicine U. Conn., 1980-83; chief of staff VA Med. Ctr., Northport, N.Y., 1983-91; prof. medicine, assoc. dean vet. affairs SUNY, Stony Brook, 1983-91, prof. medicine emeritus, 1991—; mem. exec. com. Health Rsch. Coun. City N.Y., 1966-75, chmn. allergy and infectious disease panel, 1968-75; mem. N.Y. State Coun. on Grad. Med. Edn., 1991-94. Recipient Disting. Svc. award The Arthritis Found., 1978, Silver Medallion Bicentennial Awd., Columbia Univ., Coll. of Physicians, 1967. Fellow ACP, AAAS (past mem. coun.), N.Y. Acad. Medicine (past v.p., trustee 1972-80, plaque 1981); mem. Am. Soc. Clin. Investigation, Am. Assn. Immunologists, Am. Coll. Rheumatology (past pres.), Assn. Am. Med. Colls., Infectious Diseases Soc., Harvey Soc., Soc. Exptl. Biology and Medicine, Am.Fedn. Clin. Rsch., AMA, Bronx County Med. Soc., Am. Heart Assn. (past mem. rsch. com.), N.Y. TB and Health Assn. (past dir.), Phi Beta Kappa, Alpha Omega Alpha. Home: 220 Little Neck Rd Centerport NY 11721-1145

FISCHEL, WILLIAM ALAN, economics educator; b. Bethlehem, Pa., Apr. 10, 1945; s. John Jacob and Lois T. (Yerger) F.; m. Janice M. Goldberg, Aug. 5, 1973; 1 child, Joshua. BA, Amherst Coll., 1967; PhD, Princeton U., 1973. Prof. Dartmouth Coll., Hanover, N.H., 1973—; vis. assoc. prof. U. Calif., Davis, 1980-81; vis. prof. U. Calif., Santa Barbara, 1985-86, U. Wash., Seattle, 1998-99; adj. prof. Vt. Law Sch., South Royalton, 1985, 87-92. Author: Economics of Zoning Laws, 1985, Regulatory Takings, 1995; mem. editorial bd. Land Econs. Jour., 1984—, Ea. Econ. Jour., 1992—. Mem. Zoning Bd., Town of Hanover, N.H., 1987-97, chmn., 1993-97. Olin fellow U. Calif., Berkeley, 1991-92. Mem. N.H. Jud. Coun., Phi Beta Kappa, Psi Upsilon. Home: 2 Read Rd Hanover NH 03755-1909 Office: Dartmouth Coll Dept Of Econs Hanover NH 03755

FISCHELL, ROBERT ELLENTUCH, physicist; b. N.Y.C., Feb. 10, 1929; s. Philip and Julia (Ellentuch) F.; m. Marian Standard; children: David R., Tim A., Scott J.S. BSMechE cum laude, Duke U., 1951; MS in Physics, U. Md., 1953, ScD (hon.), 1996. Physicist U.S. Naval Ordnance Lab., Silver Spring, Md., 1951-56; prin. staff engr. Emerson Rsch. Labs., Silver Spring, 1956-60; various staff positions Applied Physics Lab., Johns Hopkins U., Laurel, Md., 1959-97, prin. profl. physicist, 1962—, chief engr. space dept., 1972-80, chief tech. transfer space dept., 1978-88; pres., chmn. bd. MedInnovations, Inc., Dayton, Md., 1988-90, MedInTec, Inc., Dayton, Md., 1990—; chmn. bd., v.p. R & D Cathco, Inc.; chmn. bd. IsoStent, Inc., Dayton, Md., 1993—, NeuroPace, Inc., Dayton, 1997—; expert witness Brown and Bain, Palo Alto, Calif., 1992-93; rsch. assoc. in medicine Johns Hopkins U. Sch. Medicine, 1983—, Yale U. Sch. Medicine, 1988—; mem. exec. panel Chief of Naval Ops., Washington, 1983-87; expert witness Fish and Neave, N.Y.C., 1986-92; field reviewer for orphan products FDA, 1984-90; mem. rsch. com. Md. affiliate Am. Heart Assn., 1985-87; mem. tech. com. on space guidance and control, AIAA, 1972-75, chmn. nat. conf., 1973; mem. space com. Internat. Fedn. Automatic Control, 1970-75; mem., chmn. photovoltaic specialities com. IEEE, 1959-72. Author 49 tech. publs.; assoc. editor AIAA Jour. Spacecraft and Rockets, 1972-75; holder 74 U.S. patents in field of biomed. engring. devices and spacecraft. Bd. vis. U. Md., 1997—. Recipient Tech. Achievement award ASME, 1962, Outstanding Young Engr. award Washington Capitol Area, 1963, awards for most significant inventions Indsl. Rsch. mag., 1967, 70, 73, Inventor of Yr. award Intellectual Property Owners Assn., 1984, Gold medal for contbn. to aerospace sci. and tech. N.Y. Acad. Sci., 1987; NASA awards include Exceptional Engring. for MAGSAT satellite, 1980, Individual Achievement for human tissue stimulator, 1982, Exceptional Engring. medal, 1984, Space Act prize, 1984, Disting. Engring. Alumnus award Duke U., 1992; named Disting. Citizen of Yr. "M" Club U. Md., 1984; inducted into Space Technology Hall of Fame U.S. Space Found., 1988. Mem. NAE, Internat. Soc. for Artificial Organs, N.Y. Acad. Scis., Phi Beta Kappa, Tau Beta Pi, Pi Mu Epsilon, Sigma Pi Sigma, Pi Tau Sigma, Beta Omega Sigma. Avocations: tennis, sailing. Office: MedInTec Inc 14600 Viburnum Dr Dayton MD 21036-1247

FISCHER, AARON JACK, accountant; b. Chgo., Feb. 6, 1947; s. Ralph Hyman and Florence Idel (Kaufman) F.; m. Robin Gail Cole, Jan. 23, 1972; children: Amy Lauren, Michael Kenneth. BS in Commerce, DePaul U., 1969. CPA, Ill.; diplomate Am. Bd. Forensic Accts., Am. Bd. Forensic Examiners. Staff acct. BDO Seidman, Chgo., 1969-79, ptnr., 1979-86, tech. dir. acctg., auditing sec midwest regional, 1986-89; ptnr. Drobny and Fischer CPA, Crystal Lake, Ill., 1990—. Bd. dirs. Young Men's Jewish Coun., 1978-79. Mem. AICPA, Ill. Soc. CPA (acctg. principles com. 1978-80, ethics com. 1980-82), Am. Coll. Forensic Examiners, Twin Orchard Country Club. Home: 2243 Elm Ridge Dr Northbrook IL 60062-6507*

FISCHER, A(LBERT) ALAN, family physician; b. Indpls., June 30, 1928; 4 children. MD, Ind. U., 1952. Diplomate Am. Bd. Family Practice. Intern St. Vincent Hosp., Indpls., 1952-53; pvt. practice, 1953-70; dir. family practice residency program St. Vincent Hosp., Indpls., 1969-75; prof. family medicine, chmn. dept. Ind. U., Indpls., 1974-90; med. dir. Lakeview Manor, Indpls., 1970—; pvt. practice family medicine, 1953—. Mem. AMA, Inst. Medicine-NAS (mem. nat. joint practicing commn.), Am. Acad. Family Physicians (v.p. 1971-72, cert. mem. Am. Bd. Family Practice). *

FISCHER, ALFRED GEORGE, geology educator; b. Rothenburg, Germany, Dec. 10, 1920; came to U.S., 1935; s. George Erwin and Thea (Freise) F.; m. Winnifred Varney, Aug. 26, 1939; children: Joseph Fred, George William, Lenore Ruth Fischer Walsh. Student, Northwestern Coll., Watertown, Wis., 1935-37; BA, U. Wis., 1939, MA, 1941; PhD, Columbia U., 1950. Instr. Va. Poly. Inst. and State U., Blacksburg, 1941-43; geologist Stanolind Oil & Gas Co., Kans. and Fla., 1943-46; instr. U. Rochester, N.Y., 1947-48; from instr. to asst. prof. U. Kans., Lawrence, 1948-51; sr. geologist Internat. Petroleum, Peru, 1951-56; prof. geology Princeton (N.J.) U., 1956-84, U. So. Calif., Los Angeles, 1984—. Co-Author: Invertebrate Fossils, 1952, The Permian Reef Complex, 1953, Electron Micrographs of Limestone, 1967; editor: Petroleum and Global Tectonics, 1975. Recipient Verrill medal Yale U., Geol. Soc. London (hon. Lyell medal) 1992. Fellow Geol. Soc. Am. (Penrose medal 1993), Geol. Soc. London (hon., Lyell medal 1992), Soc. Econ. Paleontologists (hon., Twenhofel medal); mem. AAAS, NAS, Am. Assn. Petroleum Geologists, Paleontol. Soc. (medal 1995), German Geol. Soc. (Leopold van Buch medal), Geol. Union (Gustav Steinmann medal 1992), Mainz Acad. Sci. Lit. (corr.), Lincei Acad. Rome (fgn.), Sigma Xi. Home: 1736 Perch St San Pedro CA 90732-4218 Office: U So Calif Dept Earth Scis Univ Park Los Angeles CA 90089-0741

FISCHER, CARL, graphic designer, photographer; b. N.Y.C., May 3, 1924; s. Joseph Albert and Irma (Schwerin) F.; m. Marilyn Wolf, Oct. 30, 1949; children—Kim Alison Lloyd George, Douglas James, Kenneth Lee. BFA, Cooper Union Sch. Art, 1948; Destgrad., Ctrl. St. Martins Coll. Art & Design, London, 1952. Designer Columbia Records, 1948, Look mag., 1949-51; asst. art dir. William H. Weintraub & Co., 1952-54; art dir. Sudler & Hennessey, 1954-56, Grey Advt., 1956-58; owner Carl Fischer Photography Inc., N.Y.C., 1960—; vis. instr. art Cooper Union; TV, film dir.; William A. Reedy Meml. lectr. Rochester Inst. Tech. Exhibited Mus. Modern Art, 1965, Whitney Mus. Am. Art, 1974; represented in permanent collections, Met. Mus. Art, Rose Art Mus., Amherst, Mass., Internat. Ctr. of Photography, N.Y.C., Internat. Mus. Photography at George Eastman House, Rochester; contbg. editorial photographer various mags. including London Observer, London Sunday Times, Time, Life, Fortune, Esquire, New York. Served with AUS, 1942-45, PTO. Fulbright grantee, 1951; Recipient Profl. Achievement citation Cooper Union, 1966, St. Gaudens medal, 1969, Mark Twain Jour. award, 1971. Mem. Dirs. Guild, Art Dirs. Club (Gold medal 1960, Silver medal 1975, past pres.), Am. Inst. Graphic Arts, Am. Soc. Media Photographers, Advt. Photographers N.Y, Century Assn. Office: 121 E 83rd St New York NY 10028-0821

FISCHER, CARL G., anesthesiologist; b. Cin., Dec. 4, 1937; s. Carl G. and Dorotha W. F.; m. Joyce D. BS, U. Cin., 1960; MD, U. Rochester, 1965. Diplomate anesthesia. Intern Christ Hosp., Cin., 1965-66; resident Yale U. Hosp., New Haven, 1969-71; fellow in pediat. anesthesia/ICU Pitts. Children's Hosp., 1971-72, staff anesthesiologist, asst. prof., 1972-77; staff anesthesiologist, from assoc. prof. to prof. U. Cin./Cin. Children's Hosp., 1977—; dir. anesthesia Shriners Burns Inst., Cin., 1989—. Lt. USN, 1967-69. Mem. Am. Soc. Anesthesia, Am. Acad. Pediatrics, Soc. Pediat. Anthesiology. Office: Shriners Burns Hosp 3229 Burnet Ave Cincinnati OH 45229-3018

FISCHER, CARL R., hospital executive. MSN, SUNY; MS in Health and Pub. Adminstrn. Program, Yale U. CEO Med. Coll. Va. Hosps., 1986; founder Univ. Health Sys. Consortium, Chgo. Office: 401 N 12th St Richmond VA 23219

FISCHER, CARL ROBERT, health care facility administrator; b. Rahway, N.J., Nov. 15, 1939; s. Robert Carlton and Elsie Marie (Wolfarth) F.; m. Lynn Elaine Ekstrand, Mar. 12, 1966; children: Kristen, Leslie, Meredith, Kelly. B.S. in Nursing, Wagner Coll., 1964; M.S., SUNY-Buffalo, 1966; M.P.H., Yale U., 1968. With Yale-New Haven Hosp., 1968-77, assoc. dir., 1975-77; exec. assoc. adminstr. U. Cin. Med. Ctr., 1977-80; exec. dir. clin. programs U. Ark. for Med. Scis., Little Rock, 1980-86; assoc. v.p. health scis., CEO Med. Coll. of Va. Hosps., Richmond, 1986—; active Univ. Hosps., Richmond, 1986—; bd. dirs. Univ. Health Systems Consortium, 1986—, exec. com. 1994—, chmn. bd. dirs. 1997-98, chmn. supply and svcs. divsn., 1988-89, 95-96; bd. dirs. Novations; mem. exec. com. NAPH, 1999. Mem. Am. Assn. Med. Colls., Am. Hosp. Assn., Va. Hosp. Assn. (bd. dirs. 1986-91, 99, chmn. coun. on adminstrn. and health planning 1988, coun. on assn. devel. 1987-88, physician liaison com. 1989-90, chmn. ctrl. Va. regional planning coun. 1997—), Ctrl. Va. Health Planning Agy. (pres. 1991-93, 97—). Lutheran. Office: Med Coll Va Hosps Va Commonwealth U PO Box 980510 Richmond VA 23298-0510

FISCHER, CLARE, composer; b. Durand, Mich., Oct. 22, 1928; s. Cecil Harold and Luella Blanche (Roussin) F.; children: Lee Clare, Brent Sean Cecil, Tahlia Georgienne Marguerite Bianca; m. Donna Van Ringelesteyn. MusB in Music Composition and Theory, Mich. St. U., 1952, MusM, 1955. Arranger albums for Donald Byrd, George Shearing, Dizzy Gilespie, The Hi-lo's, Singers Unlimited, Cal Tjader, João Gilberto, Charles Lloyd, Chaka Khan, Prince, Michael Jackson, Robert Palmer, Paul McCartney, Paula Abdul, Earl Klugh, The Jacksons, most recent albums: Lembranças and Just Me- Solo Piano Excursions on Concord Records, Memento on Discovery, Rockin' in Rhythm on JVC Records, The Latin Side, Clare Fischer's Jazz Corps; arranger movies for Prince; composer orchestral The Duke, Sweé Pea and Me, Tahlia, Sonatine for Clarinet and Piano, Time-piece and numerous others.

FISCHER, CRAIG LELAND, physician; b. Bklyn., Feb. 17, 1937; s. Emil Carl and Ruth Barbara (Minarcik) F.; m. Sandra Lucile Canfield, Feb. 17, 1962; children: Craig L. Jr., Emil Lewis, Lisa Anne. BS, Kans. State U., 1958; MD, U. Kans., 1962. Diplomate Nat. Bd. Med. Examiners, Am. Bd. Family Practice; cert. anatomic and clin. pathology, nuclear medicine. Intern in anatomic pathology Kansas U. Med. Ctr., 1962-63, resident in anatomic pathology, 1963-64, rsch. fellow in nuclear medicine, 1965-66; resident in clin. pathology, Meth. Hosp. Baylor U. Coll. Medicine, 1967-68; rsch. med. officer Manned Spacecraft Ctr., NASA, Houston, 1965-68, pathologist, chief clin. labs., 1968-71, chief med. ops., 1980-82; assoc. dir. labs. to dir. labs. Eisenhower Med. Ctr., Rancho Mirage, Calif., 1971-78, dir. nuclear med., 1975-78; gen. practice medicine Palm Desert, Calif., 1978-80; dir. labs. J.F. Kennedy Hosp., Indio, Calif., 1982-99; gen. practice medicine Indio, Calif., 1982-99; dir. post grad. edn. J.F. Kennedy Hosp., 1982-92; dir. Fischer and Yao Cons. Pathologists, Indio, 1987-89; pres. Fischer Assocs., Cons. in Pathology, Indio, 1989-95; ptnr. Fischer and Starke Assocs., Indio, 1995-99; aviation med. examiner FAA, 1991-99; asst. dir. space medicine NASA Johnson Space Ctr., 1999—; asst. clin. prof. U. Calif., Irvine, 1986-99; mem. sci. adv. bd. Dept. Air Force, Washington, 1986-90, NAE, NRC; mem. Air Force Studies Bd., Washington, 1987-93; mem. aerospace med. adv. com. Office Space Scis. and Applications, NASA Hdqrs., Washington, 1988-93, chmn. operational medicine discipline working group, Life Scis. Directorate, 1988-92, mem. Shuttle-Mir Joint Sci. Working Group, 1993-94, mem. Adv. Coun. Task Force on the Shuttle-Mir Rendezvous and Docking Missions, 1995; mem. Mir Sci. Program Rev. Panel, 1993-98; mem. Internat. Space Sta. Task Force (Stafford Commn.), 1998—. Contbr. numerous articles to profl. jours. Capt. USAR, 1964-66, hon. discharge, 1966; lt. col. USAFR, 1983-97, hon. discharge, 1997. Recipient Group Achievement award NASA Manned Spacecraft Ctr., 1966, 69, 70, Group Achievement award Gemini support team NASA Manned Spacecraft Ctr., Apollo 7 Flight Ops. Team award NASA Manned Spacecraft Ctr., 1969, Sustained Superior Achievement award NASA Manned Spacecraft Ctr., 1969, Superior Achievement award, 1969, Skylab Group Achievement award NASA Johnson Space Ctr., 1974, Presdl. medal of Freedom Apollo 13 Mission Ops. Team, 1970, Group Achievement award NASA Space Shuttle Launch and Ops. Team NASA Manned Spacecraft Ctr., 1982, Meritorious Civilian Svc. award Dept. of Air Force, 1990. Fellow Coll. Am. Pathologists, Am. Soc. Clin. Pathologists (CCE Commr.'s medal 1989), Am. Pub. Health Assn.; mem. Aerospace Med. Assn., Calif. Soc. Pathologists, Riverside County Med. Assn. (councilor 1984-89, pres.-elect 1989-90, pres. 1990-91, alternate delegate 1991-96, councilor 1996-99, Outstanding Contbn. to Medicine award 1996), Calif. Med. Assn., Palm Springs Acad. Medicine (pres. 1988-89). Republican. Avocations: sailing, tennis, flying. Home: 4402 N Pine Brook Way Houston TX 77059 Office: NASA Johnson Space Ctr Houston TX 77058

FISCHER, DALE SUSAN, judge; b. East Orange, N.J., Oct. 17, 1951; d. Edward L. and Audrey (Tenner) F. Student, Dickinson Coll., 1969-70; BA magna cum laude, U. So. Fla., 1977; JD, Harvard U., 1980. Bar: Calif. 1980. Ptnr. Kindel & Anderson L.L.P., L.A., 1980-96; spl. counsel Heller Ehrman White & McAuliffe, L.A., 1996-97; judge L.A. Mcpl. Ct., 1997; faculty Nat. Inst. Trial Advocacy; lawyer in classroom Constl. Rights Found.; moderator, panelist How to Win Your Case with Depositions. Mem. Nat. Assn. Women Judges, Am. Judicature Soc., Calif. Assn. Judges, L.A. Complex Litigation Inn of Ct. (past pres.). Office: LA Mcpl Ct Supervising Judge 5925 Hollywood Blvd Hollywood CA 90028

FISCHER, DANIEL EDWARD, psychiatrist; b. New Haven, Apr. 22, 1945; s. Alexander and Miriam (Kramer) F.; m. Linda Lee Bradford, June 12, 1969; children: Meredith Tara, Alexis Anne. BA, Boston U., 1969, MD, 1969; JD, Coll. William and Mary, 1986. Bar: Va. 1986, U.S. Dist. Ct. (ea. dist.) Va. 1986, U.S. Ct. Appeals (4th cir.) 1986. Intern in medicine Baylor Affiliated Hosps., Houston, 1969-70; resident in psychiatry Washington U. Sch. Medicine, St. Louis, 1970-73; practice medicine specializing in psychiatry Virginia Beach, Va., 1975—; chmn. dept. psychiatry DePaul Hosp., Norfolk, Va., 1978-79, Bayside Hosp., Virginia Beach, 1980-81, 88-89, 1990-91; assoc. med. dir. adult in-patient svcs. rapid stabilization unit Tidewater Psychiat. Inst., Norfolk, 1989-94; med. dir. Norfolk (Va.) Psychiat. Ctr., 1995-96. Contbr. articles to profl. jours.; patentee in field. Bd. dirs. Tidewater Pastoral Counseling Svc., Norfolk, 1976—, Kempsville Conservative Synagogue, Virginia Beach, 1982-86, Beth Chavarim, 1987-90; pres. Am. Investment Mgmt. Svcs., Inc., Virginia Beach, 1987-98. Served as maj. U.S. Army, 1973-75. Decorated Army Commendation medal. Fellow Acad. Psychosomatic Medicine, Am. Psychiat. Assn., Am. Coll. Forensic Examiners; mem. AMA, Va. Med. Soc., Va. Psychiat. Assn., Virginia Beach Med. Soc., Tidewater Acad. Psychiatry. Democrat. Jewish. Avocation: Stamp Collecting. Office: 621 Lynnhaven Pky Ste 366 Virginia Beach VA 23452-7300

FISCHER, DAVID CHARLES, lawyer; b. Columbia, S.C., Oct. 10, 1952; s. Emeric and Bernice (Cooper) F.; m. Vicki Joyce Stoller, Nov. 9, 1985; children: Adam, Jeremy. BA, Vanderbilt U., 1975; JD, Coll. William & Mary, 1978. Bar: Mich. 1978, N.Y. 1980. Lawyer GM, Detroit, 1978-79, N.Y.C., 1979-80; assoc. Finley Kumble Wagner Heine Underberg & Casey, N.Y.C., 1980-82, Burns Summit Rovins & Feldesman, N.Y.C., 1982-86; ptnr. Summit Rovins & Feldesman, N.Y.C., 1986-90, Loeb & Loeb, LLP, N.Y.C., 1990—.

FISCHER, DAVID J., mayor; b. Evanston, Ill., July 24, 1933; m. Margo Fischer; children: Susan, David, James, Allison. BA in Bus. Adminstrn., Duke U., 1955. Chartered mcpl. fin. advisor, mcpl. bond dealer, 1958-90; pres., owner Fischer Johnson, Inc., 1977-86; mayor City of St. Petersburg, Fla.; pres. Fla. Mcpl. Bond Coun., 1982-83, mem., 1975-90. Vice mayor St. Petersburg City Coun., 1978-79, mem., 1975-79; pres. Lakewood H.S. Parent Coun., 1973-74; chmn. Environ. Devel. Commn., 1972-75, Bayfront Ctr. Found. and Adv. Coun., 1989, mem., 1989-91; chmn. United Way Allocations and Admissions Com., 1967, treas., 1968-70; co-chmn. Cmty. Alliance, 1970-71; chmn. bd. trustees Eckerd Coll., 1985-87, mem. bd. trustees, 1979—. Served to capt. USAF, 1956-58. Recipient Leadership award St. Petersburg Alumni Assn., 1979, Disting. Citizen award U. So. Fla., 1994. Dist. committeeman Nat. Assn. Securities Dealers, 1980-83; pres. C. of C., 1982 (Outstanding Contbns. to Community award 1986). Office: Office of Mayor PO Box 2842 Saint Petersburg FL 33731-2842*

FISCHER, DAVID JON, lawyer; b. Danville, Ill., July 27, 1952; s. Oscar Ralph and Sarah Pauline (Pomerantz) F. BA, U. Miami, 1974, JD, 1977. Bar: Fla. 1977, Iowa 1978, (mid. dist.) Fla. 1993, U.S. Ct. Appeals (8th cir.) 1978, U.S. Ct. Appeals (D.C. cir.) 1979, U.S. Ct. Appeals (llth cir.) 1984, U.S. Tax Ct. 1987, Ga. 1989, U.S. Dist. Ct. (no. dist.) Ga. 1990, U.S. Supreme Ct. 1990, U.S. Dist. Ct. (mid. dist.) Fla., 1993. Atty. Iowa Dept. Social Svcs., Des Moines, 1978; assoc. Parrish & Del Gallo P.C., Des Moines, 1978-79, Donald M. Murtha & Assocs., Washington, 1979-80; assoc. editor Lawyers Coop. Pub. Co., Washington, 1980-82; pvt. practice law Washington, 1982-83, Des Moines, 1983-84, Atlanta, 1984-93; pvt. practice Tampa, Fla., 1993; asst. dist. legal counsel Fla. Dept. Health and Rehab. Svcs., Largo, 1993-95; pvt. practice law Atlanta, 1995—; part-time atty. Fla. Dept. of Children and Families, 1996—; prof. John Marshall Law Sch., Atlanta, 1986-88; instr. legal studies program dept. ins. and risk mgmt. Ga. State U., 1988-93, instr. aviation adminstrn. program Coll. Pub. and Urban Affairs, 1989-93; apptd. gen. counsel Techwerks, Inc., Mo., 1990-92; instr. Bridge the Gap seminar, Inst. CLE in Ga., 1993; presenter State of Fla. Dept. Health and Rehabilitative Svcs. Dist. Legal Counsel Workshop, 1994, 96, 97; spkr. Clearwater Bar Assn., 1993, 94, 95. Author: The Aeronaut's Law Handbook, 1986, (with others) Georgia Corporate Practice Forms for the Small Business Attorney, 1992; contbg. editor Balloon Life mag., 1986-96; editor: (suppl.) Georgia Corporate Forms, 1993—, Florida Criminal Sentencing, 1997—. Vol. liaison Atlanta Com. for the Olympic Games, 1991-92. Mem. ABA (sect. com. 1980-82), Fed. Bar Assn., Iowa Bar Assn., State Bar Ga., Atlanta Bar Assn., Fla. Bar Assn., D.C. Bar Assn., Polk County Bar Assn., Pros. Attys. Coun. Ga. (tech. editor Computer Crime Jour.), U. of Miami Alumni Assn., Balloon Fedn. Am. (chmn. com. 1986-91), Carolinas Balloon Assn., Ga. Balloon Assn. (chmn. com. 1985-90), Chesapeake Balloon Assn., Great Ea. Balloon Assn., Alpha Epsilon Pi (hon., faculty advisor). Jewish. Avocations: hot air balloon pilot, writing, competetive sports.

FISCHER, DAVID SEYMOUR, internist, consultant; b. Bklyn., May 13, 1930; s. Simon and Charolotte Fischer; m. Iris Liquerman, June 1, 1958; children: Karen, Louise, Francie. AB, Williams Coll., 1951; MD, Harvard U., 1955. Diplomate Am. Bd. Internal Medicine, Am. Bd. Med. Oncology, Am. Bd. Hematology. Intern, Kings County Hosp., 1955-56; resident U. Utah, 1956-57, Montefiore Hosp., Bronx, N.Y., 1957-58; fellow U. Washington, Seattle, 1958-59, Yale U., 1962-64; attending physician Yale New Haven Hosp; emeritus attending physician, Hosp. St. Raphael; cons. Milford Hosp., Conn., 1970—, VA Hosp., West Haven, Conn., 1974—, Yale Comprehensive Cancer Ctr., New Haven, 1978—; clin. prof. medicine Yale U. Author: Cancer Chemotherapy Handbook, 5th edit., 1997, Follow-Up of Cancer, 4th edit. 1996; also articles; editor, author: Cancer Therapy, 1982. Pres., Conn. div. Am. Cancer Soc., 1981; pres. med. staff Hosp. St. Raphael, New Haven, 1980; pres. med. adv. bd. Jewish Home for Aged, 1983-85; med. adv. bd. Leukemia Soc. South Cen. Conn., 1984—; pres. Congregation Bikur Cholim Sheveth Achim, 1983-85; pres. Hebrew Congregation of Woodmont, 1995—. Capt. U.S. Army, 1959-61. Recipient Harris award Yale New Haven Hosp., 1974; Bronze medal Am. Cancer Soc., 1982. Fellow ACP; mem. AMA, Am. Soc. Hematology, Am. Soc. Clin. Oncology (chmn. pub. issues), Am. Fedn. Clin. Rsch., Am. Soc. Internal Medicine, Conn. State Med. Soc., Conn. Oncology Assn. (pres. 1979-80), New Haven County Med. Soc., New Haven Med. Assn. (pres. 1990-91). Jewish. Office: 37 Hilldale Ct Milford CT 06460-7706

FISCHER, DENNIS JAMES, government official; b. N.Y.C., Aug. 15, 1939. B in Math., Vanderilt U., 1961; M in Fin. Mgmt., George Washington U., 1969. With HEW, 1970-86, fin. mgmt. officer, exec. officer health care Financing Adminstrn., HHS; assoc. dir. policy and mgmt. U.S. Mint, Treasury Dept., 1984-86; dep. asst. sec. fin., dep. CFO HHS, 1986-92; CFO Gen. Svcs. Adminstrn., 1992-97; commr. Fed. Tech. Svc. Gen. Svcs. Adminstrn., Falls Church, Va., 1997—; rep. Joint Fin. Mgmt. Improvement Program Steering Com., 1993-98, Cost Acctg. Stds. Bd., 1994-98; sec.-treas. Fed. CFO Coun., 1994-97; mem. Gen. Acctg. Office Govtl. Auditing Stds. Adv. Coun., 1996-98. Home: 2727 Duke St #814 Alexandria VA 22314 Office: US Gen Svcs Adminstrn 7799 Leesburg Pike Ste 210N Falls Church VA 22043-2413

FISCHER, DUNCAN KINNEAR, neurosurgeon; b. Chapel Hill, N.C., Sept. 14, 1957; s. Newton Duchan and Janet (Jordan) F.; m. Anne Holmes Billington, Sept. 10, 1983; children: Luke, Kent, Duncan II. AB, Princeton U., 1979; MPhil, Yale U., 1982, MD, PhD, 1986. Cert. in neurosurgery. Intern in surgery Baylor Coll. Medicine Affiliated Hosps., Houston, 1986-87, resident in neurosurgery, 1987-92; rsch. assoc. Baylor U., Houston, 1988-92; neurosurgeon San Angelo (Tex.) Cmty. Med. Ctr. and Neurosci. Ctr., 1992—. Contbr. numerous articles to profl. publs. Fellow ACS; mem. Harvey Cushing Soc., Am. Assn. Neurol. Surgeons, Sigma Xi. Republican. Episcopalian. Office: 3515 Executive Dr San Angelo TX 76904-6883

FISCHER, EDMOND HENRI, biochemistry educator; b. Shanghai, Republic of China, Apr. 6, 1920; came to U.S., 1953; s. Oscar and Renée (Tapernoux) F.; m. Beverley B. Bullock. Lic. es Sciences Chimiques et Biologiques, U. Geneva, 1943, Diplome d'Ingenieur Chimiste, 1944, PhD, 1947; D (hon.), U. Montpellier, France, 1985, U. Basel, Switzerland, 1988, Med. Coll. of Ohio, 1993, Ind. U., 1993, U. Bochum, Germany, 1994. Pvt. docent biochemistry U. Geneva, 1950-53; research assoc. biology Calif. Inst. Tech., Pasadena, 1953; asst. prof. biochemistry U. Wash., Seattle, 1953-56, assoc. prof., 1956-61, prof., 1961-90, prof. emeritus, 1990—; mem. exec. com. Pacific Slope Biochem. Conf., 1958-59, pres., 1975; mem. biochemistry study sect. NIH, 1959-64, symposium co-chmn. Battelle Seattle Rsch. Ctr., 1970, 73, 78; mem. sci. adv. bd. Biozentrum, U. Basel, Switzerland, 1982-86; mem. sci. adv. bd. Friedrich Miescher Inst., Ciba-Geigy, Basel, 1976-84, chmn., 1981-84; mem. bd. sci. govs. Scripps Rsch. Inst., La Jolla, Calif., 1987—, Basel Inst. for Immunology, 1996—; bd. govs. Weizmann Inst. Sci., Rehovot, Israel, 1997—. Contbr. numerous articles to sci. jours. Mem. sci. council on basic sci. Am. Heart Assn., 1977-80, sci. adv. com. Muscular Dystrophy Assn., 1980-88. Recipient Lederle Med. Faculty award, 1956-59, Guggenheim Found. award, 1963-64, Disting. Lectr. award U. Wash., 1983, Laureate Passano Found. award, 1988, Steven C. Beering award, 1991, Nobel prize in Physiology or Medicine, 1992. Fellow Am. Acad. Arts and Scis.; mem. NAS, AAAS, AAUP, Am. Soc. Biol. Chemists (coun. 1989-93), Am. Chem. Soc. (adv. bd. biochemistry divsn. 1962, exec. com. divsn. biology 1969-72, monograph adv. bd. 1971-73, editl. adv. bd. Biochemistry, 1961-66, assoc. editor 1966-91), Swiss Chem. Soc. (Werner medal), Spanish Royal Acad. Scis. (fgn. assoc.), Venice Inst. Sci., Arts and Letters (fgn. assoc.), Japanese Biochem. Soc. (hon.). Achievements include cellular regulation by phosphorylation/dephosphorylation cycle. Office: U Washington Med Sch Box 357350 Seattle WA 98195-7350

FISCHER, ERIC ROBERT, lawyer, educator; b. N.Y.C., Aug. 22, 1945; s. Maurice and Pauline (Pilcer) F.; m. Anita Ellen Cohen, July 31, 1977; children: Joshua, Lauren. BA, U. Pa., 1967; MBA, JD, Stanford U., 1971; LLM in Taxation, Boston U., 1982. Bar: N.Y. 1975, Mass. 1977. Assoc. Fried, Frank, Harris, Shriver & Jacobson, N.Y.C., 1971-76; v.p., asst. gen. counsel, asst. sec. First Nat. Bank of Boston, 1976-86; exec. v.p., gen. counsel, corp. sec. UST Corp., Boston, 1986—; lectr. on law Boston U. Law Sch., 1984—. Trustee Boston Lyric Opera, Inc., 1989—; bd. dirs. Boston Area Youth Soccer, 1989-90, Spirit of Mass. Boys Soccer Club, 1991-97. Mem. ABA (banking law com., vice chmn. cmty. banking subcom., banking law com.), Bank Capital Markets Assn. (chmn. banking law subcom. 1984-90), UN Assn. Boston (treas. 1978-91), New Eng. Legal Found. (bd. dirs. 1990-92). Jewish. Home: 205 Waban Ave Waban MA 02468-2101 Office: UST Corp 40 Court St Boston MA 02108-2202 *The pursuit of an objective which you believe is meaningful and constructive (whether you are right or wrong) gives definition to your life and allows you to accept your own limitations.*

FISCHER, ERNST OTTO, chemist, educator; b. Munich, Germany, Nov. 10, 1918; s. Karl T. and Valentine (Danzer) F. Diplom, Munich Tech. U., 1949, Dr. rer. nat., 1952, Habilitation, 1954, Dr. rer. nat. h.c., 1972, D.Sc.h.c., 1975, Dr. rer. nat. h.c., 1977, Dr.h.c., 1983. Assoc. prof. inorganic chemistry U. Munich, 1957, prof., 1959; prof. inorganic chemistry inst. Munich Inst. Tech., 1964—. Author: (with H. Werner) Metall-pi-Komplexe mit di- und oligoolefinischen Liganden, 1963; transl. Complexes with di- and oligo-olefinic Ligands, 1966; Contbr. (with H. Werner) numerous articles in field to profl. jours. Recipient ann. prize Göttingen Acad. Scis., 1957, Alfred Stock Meml. prize Soc. German Chemists, 1959, Nobel Prize in Chemistry, 1973; Am. Chem. Soc. Centennial fellow, 1976. Mem. Bavarian Acad. Scis., Soc. German Chemists, German Acad. Scis. Leopoldina, Austrian Acad. Scis. (corr.), Accademia Nazionale dei Lincei, Italy (fgn.), Acad. Scis. Göttingen (corr.), Am. Acad. Arts and Scis. (fgn., hon.), Chem. Soc. (hon.). Spl. research in organometallic chemistry: metal pi complexes of arenes, olefins, carbene and carbyne complexes with metals, ferrocene type sandwich compounds, metal carbonyls. Home: 16 Sohnckestrasse, D-81479 Munich Germany Office: Chemistry Inst, Lichtenbergstrasse 4, D-85747 Garching Germany

FISCHER, FRED WALTER, physicist, engineer, educator; b. Zwickau, Germany, June 26, 1922; s. Fritz and Louiska (Richter) F.; m. Yongja Kim, Oct. 1, 1970. BS in Mech. Engring., Columbia U., 1949, MS, 1950; MS in Physics, U. Wash., 1957; D in Elec. Engring., Tech. U. Munich, 1966. Analyst Boeing Co., Seattle, Munich, Bonn, Germany, 1950-84; cons. Boeing Co., Seattle, Munich, Bonn, 1984-88; owner Fischer Cons.; instr. physics, math., and engring. North Seattle Community Coll., 1973-93. Author: Analysis for Physics and Engineering, 1982, Renaissance Mathematics, 1992. First v.p. Wedgwood Cmty. Coun.; mem. Wedgwood Elem. Sch. Site Coun., Eckstein Med. Sch. Site Coun. With AUS, 1943-46. Boeing shcolar Max Planck Inst. Plasma Physics, 1964-65. Mem. AAAS, N.Y. Acad. Sci., Mercedes Benz Club (bd. dirs.), Sigma Xi (life). Office: North Seattle CC 9600 College Way N Seattle WA 98103-3514

FISCHER, JENNIFER WELSH, English educator; b. Canton, Ohio, Apr. 9, 1970; d. Danny Howard and Omeda Ellen (Hedges) Welsh; m. David Joseph Fischer, May 31, 1997. BA in Edn., U. Akron, 1992, MEd, 1995. Cert. tchr., Ohio, S.C. Rsch. asst. KKR & Assocs., Inc., Canton, 1993-94; English tchr. Wagener-Salley (S.C.) H.S., 1994-96; rsch. asst. U. Akron, Ohio, 1996—; tutor Plain Local Sch. Dist., Canton, 1996—. Active Stark County Young Dems., Canton, 1996-97. Mem. Nat. Coun. for Tchrs. English, Am. Ednl. Rsch. Assn., Student Assn. Grads. in Edn., Pi Lambda Theta. Avocations: golf, reading, gardening. Home: 2605 # 4 Williamsburg Ln Canton OH 44708 Office: U Akron Akron OH 44325

FISCHER, JOEL, social work educator; b. Chgo., Apr. 22, 1939; s. Sam and Ruth (Feiges) F.; m. Renee H. Furuyama; children: Lisa, Nicole. BS, U. Ill., 1961, MSW, 1964; D in Social Welfare, U. Calif., Berkeley, 1970. Prof. sch. social work U. Hawaii, Honolulu, 1970—; vis. prof. George Warren Brown Sch. Social Work, Washington U., St. Louis, 1977, U. Wis. Sch. Social Welfare, Milw., 1978-79, U. Natal, South Africa, 1982, U. Hong Kong, 1986; cons. various orgns. and univs. Author: (with Harvey L. Gochros) Planned Behavior Change: Behavior Modification in Social Work, 1973, Handbook of Behavior Therapy with Sexual Problems, vol. I, 1977, vol. II, 1977, Analyzing Research, 1975, Interpersonal Helping: Emerging Approaches for Social Work Practice, 1973, The Effectiveness of Social Casework, 1976, (with D. Sanders and O. Kurrem) Fundamentals of Social Work Practice, 1982, Effective Casework Practice: An Eclectic Approach, 1978, (with H. Gochros) Treat Yourself to a Better Sex Life, 1980, (with H. Gochros and J. Gochros) Helping the Sexually Oppressed, 1985, (with Martin Bloom) Evaluating Practice: Guidlines for the Helping Professional, 1982, (with Kevin Corcoran) Measures for Clinical Practice, 1987, (with Daniel Sanders) Visions for the Future: Social Work and Pacific-Asian Perspectives, 1988, (with Martin Bloom and John Orme) Evaluating Practice, 2nd edit., 1995, (with Kevin Corcoran) Measures for Clinical Practice, 2nd edit., vol. 1, 1994, Couples, Children, Families, vol. 2, 1999, Adults, 1994, East-West Connections: Social Work Practice Traditions and Change, 1992, (with Martin Bloom and John Orme) Evaluating Practice, 3d edit., 1999, (with Martin Bloom and John Orme) Teacher's Manual for Evaluating Practice, 1999; (with Kevin Corcoran) Measures for Clinical practice, 2d edit, vol. 1, 1999; mem. editl. bd. 12 profl. jours.; contbr. over 150 articles, revs., chpts. and papers to profl. jours. With U.S. Army, 1958. Mem. Hawaii Com. for Africa, Nat. Assn. Social Workers, Coun. Social Work Edn., Acad. Cert. Social Workers, Nat. Conf. Social Welfare, AAUP, Unity Organizing Com., Hawaii People's Legis. Coalition, Bertha Reynold Soc. Democrat. E-mail: jfischer@hawaii.edu. Home: 1371-4 Hunakai St Honolulu HI 96816-5501 Office: U Hawaii 2500 Campus Rd Honolulu HI 96822-2217

FISCHER, JOHN JULES, clergy member, theology educator, writer; b. Budapest, Hungary, May 27, 1946; came to U.S., 1949; s. George S. and Marianne (Komlos) F.; m. Patrice Eloise Pavka, June 4, 1972; children: Eve, Seth. BS in Bibl. Studies, Phila Coll. Bible, 1970; MS in Comm., Temple U., 1970; MA in New Testament, Trinity Internat. U., 1972; B Judaic Studies, Spertus Coll. Judaica, 1978; PhD in Edn., U. So. Fla., 1987; ThD in Judaic Studies, Calif. Grad. Sch. Theology, 1989. Ordained by Union of Messianic Jewish Congregations, 1988. Dir. tng. Am. Messianic Fellowship, Chgo., 1973-74; v.p. The Watchmen Assn., Highland Park, Ill., 1975-78;; rabbi Congregation B'nai Maccabim, Highland Park, Ill., 1975-81; v.p. B'rit Shalom, Highland Park, 1978-81; dep. sec. N.Am. Internat. Messianic Jewish Alliance, Palm Harbor, Fla., 1981-84; rabbi Congregation Ohr Chadash, Clearwater, Fla., 1982—; exec. dir. Menorah Ministries, Palm Harbor, 1984—; v.p. acad. affairs St. Petersburg (Fla.) Theol. Sem., 1994—; mem. vis. faculty Trinity Evangelical Div. Sch., Deerfield, Ill., 1975-81; v.p. Union Messianic Jewish Congregations, Washington, 1978-81; mem. exec. com. Internat. Messianic Jewish Alliance, Va. Beach, Va., 1994—; adv. bd. King of Kings Coll., Jerusalem, 1996—. Author: The Olive Tree Connection, 1983, Siddur for Messianic Jews, 1988, Messianic Svcs. for Festivals Holy Days, 1992. Dem. precinct com. man, Lake County, Ill., 1979-81. Mem. Am. Assn. Messianic Jewish Believers (pres. 1996—), Messianic Jewish Alliance Am. (treas. 1977-79), Messianic Jewish Alliance Chgo. (pres. 1974-78), Assn. Messianic Believers (pres. 1994—). Avocations: baseball, reading, playing games, tennis, physical fitness. Office: Menorah Ministries PO Box 669 Palm Harbor FL 34682-0669

FISCHER, KATHERINE MARY, English educator; b. Milw., Jan. 5, 1951; d. Norman John and Mary Patricia (Mack) F.; m. Jerome Anthony Enzler, Oct. 6, 1973; children: Rebekah, Jason, James, Elizabeth, Andrew. BA, Clarke Coll., 1973; MA, Loras Coll., 1984; MFA in Creative Nonfiction and Poetry, Goddard Coll., 1998. Tchr. Ctrl. Alternative, Dubuque, Iowa, 1971-73, Immaculate Conception, Clarksdale, Miss., 1974-75, Hempstead H.S., Dubuque, 1975-80; tchr., dept. chair Wahlert H.S., Dubuque, 1980-89; English tchr., writing lab. dir. Clarke Coll., Dubuque, 1989—; developer, presenter Writing the Right Way!, Dubuque, 1989-97; advisor, cons. NAACP, Dubuque, 1991-96; exhibit writer, presenter Western Village, Imiachi City, Japan, 1996-97. Author: Computers and Composition, 1996, Situating Portfolios, 1997, Electronic Communication Across the Curriculum, 1998; author of poetry. Mem. Birthright, Dubuque, 1980-97; mem., writer Com. for Peace and Justice, Dubuque, 1989-97. Named Popular Demand Presenter, U. Scotland, St. Andrew, 1996; Title III tchg. grantee Fed. Govt., 1994, 95, 96, 97, 98. Mem. Nat. Coun. Tchrs. English, Am. Poetry Soc., Hist. Soc. (writer), Wis. Poetry Assn., Iowa Poetry Assn. Avocations: running, boating, camping, knitting, dancing. Office: Clarke Coll PO Box 1569 Dubuque IA 52004-1569

FISCHER, KEITH C., nuclear medicine physician, radiology educator; b. Bklyn., Aug. 7, 1945. BA magna cum laude, Oberlin Coll., 1967; MD, Johns Hopkins Med. Sch., 1971. Diplomate Am. Bd. Nuclear Medicine, Am. Bd. Radiology, Nat. Bd. Med. Examiners. Resident in internal medicine Parkland Meml. Hosp., Dallas, 1971-72; resident in diagnostic radiology Mass. Gen. Hosp., Boston, 1972-75; fellow in nuclear medicine Harvard Joint Nuclear Medicine Program, Boston, 1975-76, chief resident in nuclear medicine, 1976-77; asst. clin. prof. radiology Washington U. Sch. of Medicine, St. Louis, 1977-94, assoc. prof. radiology, 1994—; dir. divsn.

nuclear medicine Jewish Hosp. St. Louis, Washington U. Sch. of Medicine, 1977-94; staff physician divsn. nuclear medicine St. Louis Children's Hosp., 1994—, Barnes-Jewish Hosp., St. Louis, 1994—; mem. cancer com., radiation safety com., radioactive drug rsch. com. Washington U.; mem. cancer com. The Jewish Hosp., 1988-95, med. staff coun., 1989-92. Contbr. articles to profl. jours., chpts. to books. Mem. Am. Coll. Radiology, Am. Coll. Nuclear Physicians, Am. Soc. Nuclear Cardiology (founding), Soc. Nuclear Medicine (trustee Missouri Valley chpt.), Cardiovascular Coun., Phi Beta Kappa. Home: # 1 Lenox Pl Saint Louis MO 63108 Office: Barnes-Jewish Hosp Divsn Nuclear Medicine Mallinckrodt Inst Radiology 216 S Kingshighway Blvd Saint Louis MO 63110

FISCHER, KURT WALTER, education educator; b. Balt., June 9, 1943; s. Kurt Wilhelm and Irmgaard-Louise (Funke) F.; m. Sandra Pipp (div.); 1 child, Seth; m. Jane Haltiwanger, Dec. 7, 1986; children: Johanna, Lukas, Kara. BA in Psychology summa cum laude, Yale U., 1965; MA in Soc. Rels., Harvard U., 1968, PhD in Soc. Rels., 1971. Asst. prof. Univ. Denver, 1972-78, assoc. prof., 1978-85, prof., 1985-87; prof. edn. Harvard U., Cambridge, Mass., 1986—, chair human devel., 1989-92, 94-95; vis. scholar Univ. Geneva, 1978-79; vis. prof. U. Pa., Phila., 1985-86; master lectr. U. Groningen, The Netherlands, 1996. Author: Cognitive Development, 1981, Levels and Transitions in Cognitive Development, 1983; co-author: (with P. Shaver and A. Lazerson) Psychology Today: An Introduction, 2d and 3d edits., 1972, 75; co-author: Human Development from Conception to Adolescence, 1984, Development in Context, 1993, Human Behavior and the Developing Brain, 1994, Self Conscious Emotions, 1995, Development and Vulnerability in Close Relationships, 1996; contbr. articles to profl. jours. Fellow James McKeen Cattell Fund, 1985-86, Ctr. for Advanced Study, Palo Alto, Calif., 1992-93; grantee Carnegie Found., Nat. Inst. Child Health and Devel., 1994—, Sloan Found., Spencer Found., Rose Found., 1995—. Mem. Jean Piaget Soc. (pres. 1988-91), Phi Beta Kappa, Sigma Xi. Home: 29 Vincent Ave Belmont MA 02478-4418 Office: Harvard U Human Devel Grad Sch Edn Cambridge MA 02138

FISCHER, LAWRENCE JOSEPH, toxicologist, educator; b. Chgo., Sept. 2, 1937; s. Lawrence J. and Virginia H. (Dieker) F.; m. Elizabeth Ann Dunphy, Oct. 24, 1964; children—Julie Ann, Pamela Jean, Karen Sue. B.Sc., U. Ill.-Chgo., 1959, M.S., 1961; Ph.D., U. Calif.-San Francisco, 1965. NIH postdoctoral fellow St. Mary's Hosp. Med. Sch., London, 1965-66; sr. research pharmacologist Merck Sharp and Dohme, West Point, Pa., 1966-68; asst. prof. pharmacology U. Iowa, Iowa City, 1969-73, assoc. prof., 1974-76, prof., 1976-85; prof., dir. Inst. for Environ. Toxicology Mich. State U., East Lansing, Mich., 1985—; cons. FDA Bur. Vet. Medicine, 1974-77; mem. bd. scientific counselors div. of cancer Etiology Nat. Cancer Inst., 1986-92. Mem. editorial adv. bd. Jour. Pharmacology and Exptl. Therapeutics, Toxicology and Applied Pharmacology, Drug Metabolism Revs. Recipient Faculty Scholar award Josiah Macy Found., U. Geneva, 1976. Mem. Am. Soc. for Pharmacology and Exptl. Therapeutics, Soc. Toxicology, AAAS, Soc. for Environ. Toxicology and Chemistry. Avocations: hunting upland birds, tennis. Home: 11630 Center Rd Bath MI 48808-9431 Office: Mich State U Inst for Environ Toxicology C231 Holden Hall East Lansing MI 48824

FISCHER, LEROY HENRY, historian, educator; b. Hoffman, Ill., May 19, 1917; s. Andrew LeRoy and Effie (Risby) F.; m. Martha Gwendolyn Anderson, June 20, 1948; children: Barbara Ann, James LeRoy, John Andrew. B.A., U. Ill., 1939, M.A., 1940, Ph.D., 1943; postgrad., Columbia U., 1941. Grad. asst. history U. Ill., 1940-43; asst. prof. history Ithaca (N.Y.) Coll., 1946; asst. prof. history Okla. State U. at Stillwater, 1946-49, assoc. prof. history, 1949-60, prof. history, 1960-73, Oppenheim Regents prof. history, 1973-78, Oppenheim prof. history, 1978-84, Oppenheim prof. emeritus, 1984—; exec. sec. honors program, 1959-61. Author: Lincoln's Gadfly, Adam Gurowski, 1964; (with Muriel H. Wright) Civil War Sites in Oklahoma, 1967, The Civil War Era in Indian Territory, 1974, The Western States in the Civil War, 1975, Territorial Governors of Oklahoma, 1975, The Western Territories in the Civil War, 1977, Civil War Battles in the West, 1981, Oklahoma's Governors 1907-1979, 3 vols., 1981-85, Oklahoma State University Historic Old Central, 1988; co-author: A History of Governance at Oklahoma State University, 1992; editor: The History of the Oklahoma State University Centennial Histories Project, 1993; contbr. articles to profl. jours. Vice chmn. Honey Springs Battlefield Park Commn., 1968-92, Okla. Civil War Centennial Commn., 1958-65; chmn. Old Ctrl. com. Okla. State U., 1971-98; mem. Okla. State Hist. Preservation Rev. Commn., 1978—, vice chmn., 1978-81, chmn., 1981-83, 97—; bd. dirs. Nat. Indian Hall of Fame, 1969—, YMCA, 1951-54, 83-85; bd. dirs. Assocs. Western History Collections, U. Okla., 1981—, pres., 1989-90; bd. dirs. Stillwater Mus. Assn., 1987-93, pres., 1990-91; mem. Okla. Chisholm Trail Centennial Commn., 1967-68; bd. dirs. Friends of Honey Springs Battlefield Park, 1991—, pres., 1994-97, sec. 1997—. With Signal Corps, AUS, 1943-45. Recipient Lit. award Loyal Legion U.S., 1963; named tchr. of Yr., Okla. State U.-Okla. Edn. Assn., 1969; inducted in Okla. Historians Hall of Fame, 1995, Centralia (Ill.) Hall of Fame, 1997. Mem. Am. Hist. Assn., Southern Hist. Assn., Western History Assn., Am. Assn. State and Local History, AAUP, Okla. Heritage Assn. (Disting. Svc. award 1989), Okla. Hist. Soc. (bd. dirs. 1966—, treas. 1984-87), Ill. Hist. Soc., Orgn. Am. Historians, Omicron Delta Kappa, Pi Gamma Mu, Phi Alpha Theta, Alpha Kappa Lambda. Methodist (chmn. various coms. 1946—, adminstrv. bd. 1950-77, chmn. 1976-77, lay leader 1970-71). Home: 1010 W Cantwell Ave Stillwater OK 74075-4603

FISCHER, LINDA MARIE, nursing educator; b. Paterson, N.J., Sept. 26, 1959; d. William Jr. and Marie (Bilz) F. BSN cum laude, Coll. Misericordia, 1981; MSN magna cum laude, Bloomsburg U., 1996. RN, Pa.; BLS instr.; CCRN-R. Staff nurse cardiac ICU Geisinger Med. Ctr., Danville, Pa., 1981-90, clin. nurse II cardiac ICU, 1987-90, clin. instr. cardiac ICU and cardiovasc. spl. care unit, 1990—; chair adv. group profl. pers. case record rev. subcom. Columbia-Montour Home Health/Vis. Nurses Assn., Inc. Contbr. articles to profl. jours. Active Montour-Riverside chpt. Am. Heart Assn., 1989-92. Mem. AACN, Sigma Theta Tau (nominating com. Theta Zeta chpt. 1995-97, 97—).

FISCHER, MARK ALAN, lawyer, law educator; b. Evanston, Ill., Sept. 28, 1950; s. Lee Earle and Zelda (Dlugo) F. BA magna cum laude, Emerson Coll., 1975; JD, Boston Coll., 1980. Bar: Mass. 1980, U.S. Dist. Ct. Mass. 1980, U.S. Ct. Appeals (1st cir.) Mass. 1985. Sole practice Cambridge, Mass., 1980-83; mem. Cohen & Burg, Boston, 1983-86; ptnr. Wolf, Greenfield & Sacks, Boston, 1986-96, Palmer & Dodge, Boston, 1996—; co-chair Pub. & Entertainment Group, Intellectual Property Group; lectr. copyright and trademark law Boston Coll. Law Sch., 1985-87, entertainment law New Eng. Sch. Law, Boston, 1983-93; assoc. prof. music law Berklee Coll. of Music, 1989-90, 94-95, lectr. intellectual property Northeastern Sch. Law, Boston, 1986; mem. adj. faculty advanced copyright law Suffolk U., 1999—. Contbr. articles to profl. jours.; columnist New Eng. Entertainment Digest, 1982-90; co-editor: Perle & Williams on Publishing Law, (3rd edit.). Mem. ABA, Mass. Bar Assn., Boston Patent Law Assn. (chmn. copyright law com., 1985-96), Copyright Soc. U.S.A. (trustee 1997—), Copyright Soc. New Eng. (co-founder). Office: Palmer & Dodge 1 Beacon St Ste 22 Boston MA 02108-3190

FISCHER, MARY E., special education educator; b. Kansas City, Mo., July 7, 1948; d. Tom Earl and Sue Turner (Fitts) Walker; m. Timothy Montgomery Fischer, Sept. 4, 1971; children: Ethan David, Elizabeth Louise. AB, U. Mo., 1971; MSE, Cen. Mo. State U., Warrensburg, 1981; PhD, U. Wash., 1997. Occupl. therapy asst. Children's Therapy Ctr., 1971-73, tchr., 1976-78, psychometrist, 1978-79; program coord. United Cerebral Palsy, Camp Wonderland, Lake of the Ozarks, Mo., 1983; developmental presch. tchr. Children's Therapy Ctr., 1979-84, 75-76; project assoc. Early Childhood Follow Along Study, U. Wash., 1985-87; rsch. assoc. U. Wash., 1987-88; project assoc. Rsch. and Evaluation Network, U. Wash., 1989; project mgr. ChildFind project, Child Devel./Mental Retardation Ctr., Seattle, 1989-90; project coord. N.W. Insvc. Coop. for Transdisciplinary Teams U. Wash., Seattle, 1990-93; project coord. Choices, 1992-95; coord. Wash. Statewide Sys. Change Project, 1993-94; regional dir. Ctr. for Supportive Edn., Seattle, 1994-97; elem./early childhood spl. edn. coord. Olympic Ednl. Svc. Dist. 114, Bremerton, Wash., 1997—. Contbr. articles to profl. jours. Mem. ASCD, Nat. Assn. Edn. Young Children, Coun. for Exceptional Children, The Assn. for Persons with Severe Handicaps, Wash. Assn. for Persons with Severe Handicaps, Wash. State Staff Devel. Assn., Phi Kappa Phi, Pi Lambda Theta (named Outstanding mem. 1990). Avocations: singing, camping. Home: 3539 NE 113th St Seattle WA 98125-5739

FISCHER, MARY ELIZABETH, library director; b. Buffalo, N.D., Feb. 14, 1935; d. Patrick Francis and Elizabeth Sarah (Laufenberg) Killoran; m. Clair Arthur Fischer, Sep. 27, 1952 (dec. Aug. 1967); children: Judith, Barbara, Veronica, Theresa, Ruth, Raymond, Linda, Rudolph; m. Donald Edward Anderson, Apr. 17, 1995. BS in Edn. summa cum laude, Valley City (N.D) State U., 1978. Librn. Valley City Barnes County Pub. Libr., 1978-88, libr. dir., 1988—, ADA promotor, 1990—; instrumental in completion of handicapped-accessible to VCBC Pub. Libr., 1997, instrumental in providing internet access to libr. users and collection automnation. Columnist Valley City Times Record, 1978—; contbr. poetry to anthologies, stories to collections. Active St. Catherine's Ch., Valley City, 1970-79; 4H leader Hobart Honeydews (5 yr. leadership pin 1975), Valley City, 1960-79; active local PTA, 1960-79; club and orgn. spkr.; active bible study, prayer groups; mem. Friends of the Libr. (facilitator, 1988—). Recipient various poetry awards, 1990—, Universal Access award Mayor's Com. on Employment of People with Disabilities, 1999. Mem. N.D. Libr. Assn. Democrat. Roman Catholic. Avocations: reading, bird watching, gardening, cooking, handicrafts. Home: 3420 113th Ave SE Valley City ND 58072-9430 Office: Valley City Barnes County Libr 410 Central Ave N Valley City ND 58072-2949

FISCHER, MICHAEL JOHN, computer science educator; b. Ann Arbor, Mich., Apr. 20, 1942; s. Carl Hahn and Kathleen (Kirkpatrick) F.; m. Alice Edna Waltz, June 1, 1963; children: Edward Michael, Robert Patrick, David Frederick. BS, U. Mich., 1963; MA (NSF fellow), Harvard U., 1965, PhD, 1968. Teaching fellow Harvard U., 1965-67; asst. prof. computer sci. Carnegie-Mellon U., 1968-69; asst. prof. math. MIT, 1969-73, assoc. prof. elec. engring., 1973-75; prof. computer sci. U. Wash., 1975-81, dir. Computer Sci. Lab., 1976-79; prof. computer sci. Yale U., New Haven, 1981—, dir. grad. studies in computer sci., 1992—; program chmn. 17th IEEE Symposium on Founds. Computer Sci., 1976, 11th Assn. Computing Machinery Symposium on Theory Computing, 1979, Assn. Computing Machinery Symposium on Principles of Distributed Computing, 1982; sr. vis. fellow U. Warwick, Coventry, Eng., summer 1972; vis. assoc. prof. U. Toronto, spring, 1974; gastprofessor U. Frankfurt, Germany, summer 1974, ETH, Zurich, summer 1975; vis. scientist U. Saarbrücken, Germany, fall 1988; mem. adv. com. for math. and computer scis NSF, 1978-81; mem. com. on recommendations for U.S. Army Basic Sci. Research, 1978-81; cons. Xerox Palo Alto Research Ctr., 1982; co-organizer Oberwolfach Confs. on Math. Methods of VSLI and Distributed Computing, 1983, 87, 91; bd. dirs. Computing Rsch. Assn., 1988-91, founding mem. subcom. on status women in computer sci., 1990-93; chmn. internat. sci. adv. bd. Max-Planck-Inst. for Informatik, Saarbrücken, 1993—. Grantee NSF, 1974-92. Fellow Assn. Computing Machinery (sec.-treas. spl. interest group on programming langs. 1971-73, local arrangements chmn. conf. 1973); mem. Am. Math. Soc., Soc. Indsl. and Applied Math., European Assn. Theoretical Computer Sci., Yale Figure Skating Club (pres. 1989-91, 97—), Phi Beta Kappa, Phi Kappa Phi. Office: Yale U Dept Computer Sci PO Box 208285 New Haven CT 06520-8285

FISCHER, MICHAEL LUDWIG, environmental executive; b. Dubuque, Iowa, May 29, 1940; s. Carl Michael and Therese Marie (Stadler) F.; m. Jane Pughe Rogers; children: Christina Marie, Steven Michael. BA in Polit. Sci., Santa Clara U., 1964; M in City and Regional Planning, U. Calif., Berkeley, 1967; grad. exec. program in environ. mgmt., Harvard U., 1980. Planner City of Mountain View, Calif., 1960-65; assoc. Bay Area Govts., 1966-67; planner County of San Mateo, Calif., 1967-69; assoc. dir. San Francisco Planning and Urban Rsch. Assn., nonprofit civc orgn., 1969-73; exec. dir. North Cen. region Calif. Coastal Zone Conservation Commn., San Rafael, 1973-76; chief dep. dir. Gov.'s Office Planning and Rsch., Sacramento, 1976-78; exec. dir. Calif. Coastal Commn., San Francisco, 1978-85; sr. assoc. Sedway Cooke Assocs., environ. cons., San Francisco, 1985-87; exec. dir. Sierra Club, San Francisco, 1987-93; resident fellow John F. Kennedy Sch. Govt., Inst. Politics, Harvard U., Cambridge, Mass., 1993; sr. cons. Natural Resources Def. Coun., San Francisco, 1993-95; exec. officer Calif. Coastal Conservancy, Oakland, 1994-97; program officer environ. William & Flora Hewlett Found., Menlo Park, Calif., 1997—; lectr. dept. city and regional planning U. Calif., Berkeley, 1984; chairperson environ. com. adv. coun. Calvert Social Investment Fund, 1989—; mem. Harvard Commn. Global Change Info. Policy, 1993—; mem. com. on impact of maritime facility devel. NAS/NRC, 1975-78; mem. nat sea grant review panel Nat. Oceanic and Atmospheric Adminstrn., 1998—. Co-author Calif. state plan, An Urban Strategy for Calif., 1978, Building a New Municipal Railway, 1973, Oral History, Coastal Commn. Yrs., 1973-85, Oral History, Sierra Club Yrs., 1987-93; author intro. Ansel Adams: Yosemite, 1995; contbr. papers to profl. publs. Recipient Life Achievement award Assn. Environ. Profls., 1986, Disting. Leadership award, Am. Soc. Pub. Adminstrn., 1987, Outstanding Nat. Leadership award Coastal States Orgn., 1990, Exemplary Pub. Svc. award San Francisco Bay Conservation and Devel. Commn., 1997, Spl. Recognition award Calif. State Legis., 1998. Mem. Nat. Resources Def. Coun., 1000 Friends of Fla., Calif. Planning and Conservation League (bd. dirs. 1970-76), Alliance Ethnic and Environ. Orgn. (founding bd. dirs. 1991-93), The Oceanic Soc. (bd. dirs. 1983-88), Sierra Club, Friends of the Earth (bd. dirs. 1988-94), League for Coastal Protection, Save San Francisco Bay Assn., Am. Youth Hostels, Inc. (bd. dirs. 1985-87), Yosemite Restoration Trust (bd. dirs. 1990-97), Lambda Alpha. Office: William & Flora Hewlett Found 525 Middlefield Rd Menlo Park CA 94025-3460

FISCHER, PATRICIA ANN, middle school educator; b. Cleve., Apr. 11, 1951; d. Norman Stanley and Teresa (Domagalski) Michaels; m. David Leland Stroh, June 1, 1973 (div. June 1977); m. Lawrence Joseph Fischer, June 14, 1986. BA in Edn., Ohio No. U., 1973; MBA in Edn., Mt. St. Joseph Coll., Cin., 1986; postgrad., Miami U., Oxford, Ohio, 1985—, Ohio State U., 1988. Cert. K-8 tchr., 7-12 history tchr., Ohio. Mid. sch. tchr. St. Gerard Sch., Lima, Ohio, 1973-79, Our Lady of Rosary Sch., Cin., 1980-89; mid. sch. tchr. Little Flower Sch., Cin., 1989—, coord. sci., 1989—. Recipient award Project Bus., Cin., 1986, 87, 88, 89, 98, 99 Civic Achievement award Burger King Corp., Cin., 1990, 91, 92, Sci. Tchr. award NSTA, 1993, 20-Yr. award for Cath. educator Diocese of Cin., 1994. Mem. Nat. Cath. Edn. Assn., Ohio Edn. Assn., European Am. Study Ctr. Alumni Assn., Order Ea. Star, Alpha Omicron Pi. Roman Catholic. Avocations: painting, travel, needlework, reading. Home: 5450 Cecilia Ct Cincinnati OH 45247-7508 Office: Little Flower School 5555 Little Flower Ave Cincinnati OH 45239-6898

FISCHER, PATRICK CARL, computer scientist, retired educator; b. St. Louis, Dec. 3, 1935; s. Carl Hahn and Kathleen (Kirkpatrick) F.; m. Linda Loomis, Dec. 22, 1956 (div. Jan 1967); 1 child, Carl; m. Charlotte Froese, Apr. 2, 1967; 1 child, Carolyn. B.S., U. Mich., 1957; M.B.A., 1958; Ph.D. (Woodrow Wilson fellow, NSF fellow), Mass. Inst. Tech., 1962. Asst. prof. Harvard U., Cambridge, Mass., 1962-65; assoc. prof., Cornell U., Ithaca, N.Y., 1965-68; vis. assoc. prof. U. B.C., 1967-68; prof. computer sci. U. Waterloo, Ont., Can., 1968-74; chmn. dept. applied analysis and computer sci. U. Waterloo, 1972-74; prof. dept. computer sci. Pa. State U., State College, 1974-79; head dept. Pa. State U., 1974-78; prof. dept. computer sci. Vanderbilt U., Nashville, 1980-98, chmn. dept., 1980-95; prof. emeritus Vanderbilt U., 1998—; mem. computing and info. sci. grant selection com. Nat. Research Council Can., 1973-76; vis. prof. U. Calif., Berkeley, 1986, Ga. Tech., 1987. Editor in chief: spl. publs. Assn. Computing Machinery, 1971-88; assoc. editor: Jour. Computer and System Scis. 1968-74; editor, 1974-99, SIAM Jour. on Computing, 1974-84; mem. editorial bd.: Jour. Computer Lang. 1974-98; contbr. profl. jours. database theory. Research grantee, 1964-66, 66-68, 79-81, 82-84; Nat. Research Council Can. grantee, 1968-75. Fellow Soc. Actuaries; mem. Assn. Computing Machinery (founder, chmn. spl. interest group automata and computability theory 1968-73), IEEE, IEEE Computer Soc., Sigma Xi, Phi Beta Kappa, Phi Kappa Phi, Beta Gamma Sigma. Home: 221 Burlington Pl Nashville TN 37215-1859 Office: Vanderbilt U PO Box 1679B Nashville TN 37235

FISCHER, R. M., sculptor; b. N.Y.C., Mar. 21, 1947; s. Bernard and Alva (Sherman) F.; m. Patti Paige, June 22, 1986; 1 child, Dena Paige. BA, L.I. U., 1971; MFA, San Francisco Art Inst., 1973. Numerous one-man shows, including Musee Ville Toulon, France, 1984, Whitney Mus. Am. Art, N.Y.C., 1984, Inst. Contemporary Art, Boston, 1985, Jay Gorney Modern Art, N.Y.C., 1989, Donald Young Gallery, Chgo., 1988, Sidney Janis Gallery, N.Y.C., 1991, Deitch Projects, N.Y.C., 1998; exhibited in numerous group shows, including Mus. Modern Art, 1984, Whitney Mus. Am. Art, 1985, 88, 91, Aldrich Mus. Contemporary Art, 1988, Vienna (Austria) Seccession, 1990; represented in permanent collections Cin. Art Mus., Whitney Mus. Modern Art., Mus. Modern Art, Dallas Mus. Art, Mass. State House, Boston, Carnegie Mus. Fine Arts, Pitts., Fundacao de Serrales Found., Oporto, Portugal, Kansas City Convention Ctr., Cleve. Gateway Plaza; permanent pub. artworks include Battery Park City, N.Y., Mass. State House, Boston. Studio: 12 Warren St New York NY 10007-2238

FISCHER, RICHARD LAWRENCE, metal products executive; b. Pitts., Oct. 22, 1936; s. Francis William and Catherine Ellen (Haggerty) F.; m. Virginia Mae Fullerton, Aug. 19, 1961; children—Richard F., Lynn A., Laura A., Greg L. A.B. in Econs., U. Pitts., 1958, J.D. in Law, 1961; LL.M. in Internat. Law, Georgetown U., 1965. Bar: Pa. 1963, D.C. 1963. Spl. agt. FBI, Washington, 1961-65; atty. Aluminum Co. Am., Pitts., 1965-69, gen. atty., 1969-72, internat. counsel, 1973-74, asst. gen. counsel, 1975-82, gen. mgr. Brazilian project, 1980-82, v.p., dep. gen. counsel, 1982-83, v.p., gen. counsel, 1984, sr. v.p., gen. counsel, 1984-85, sr. v.p. corp. affairs, gen. counsel, 1985-86, sr. v.p. devel., corp. affairs and gen. counsel, 1986-90, sr. v.p. corp. devel., gen. counsel, 1990-91; exec. v.p., chmn's counsel Aluminum Co. Am. (name changed to ALCOA), Pitts., 1991—. Bd. dirs. Alcoa Found., Pitts., 1984—, U. Pitts. Med. Ctr. Sys., 1995—; trustee U. Pitts., 1995—. Mem. ABA, Allegheny County Bar Assn., Pa. Bar Assn. Clubs: Duquesne, Oakmont Country. Office: ALCOA 201 Isabella St at 7th St Bridge Pittsburgh PA 15212-5858*

FISCHER, RICHARD SAMUEL, lawyer; b. Buffalo, July 31, 1937; s. Richard D. and Isabel B. (Van Dorn) F.; m. Malinda Berry, June 3, 1960; children: Richard B., Van D. A.B., Harvard U., 1959, J.D., 1963. Bar: N.Y. 1963. Law clk N.Y. Ct. Appeals, Albany, 1963-65; assoc. Nixon, Hargrave, Devans & Doyle, Rochester, N.Y., 1965-71, ptnr., 1972-95, mem. policy com., 1991-95, head Rochester office, 1992-95; mem. faculty Okla. State U., Stillwater, 1997—. Past chair, trustee Highland Hosp.; past pres. Harley Sch.; past bd. dirs. Rochester Area Hosp. Corp., Primary Mental Health Project. Mem. ABA, N.Y. State Bar Assn. (past chmn. com. ins. programs and retirement plans), Monroe County Bar Assn., NYU Inst. Fed. Taxation (adv. com.), Okla. Bar Assn. Club: Genessee Valley, Country Club of Rochester (N.Y.), Stillwater Country Club, Karsten Creek Golf Club. Office: PO Box 1897 Stillwater OK 74076-1897

FISCHER, ROBERT ANDREW, computer executive; b. St. Louis, Jan. 3, 1937; s. Erwin G. and Minnie (Van Berg) F.; m. Annabelle Cole, Sept. 12, 1959; children: Douglas, Robert Jr., Gregg, Holly, Nancy. BSBA, Washington U., 1959. Ind. dir. ins./other mgmt. positions IBM Corp., Armonk, N.Y., 1961-79; sr. v.p. Dun & Bradstreet Computing Svcs., Wilton, Conn., 1979-82; chief exec. officer McDonnell Douglas Info. Systems Group, St. Louis, 1982-86; pres. Prime Computer CAD/CAM, Natick, Mass., 1986-88, Computervision Corp., Bedford, Mass., 1988-90; sr. v.p. SDRC Corp., Milford, Ohio, 1991-94; v.p. Pol. Mgmt. Sys. Corp., Columbia, S.C., 1995—; chmn. Occupational Health Safety Inc., Natick, 1988-89. Capt. USAR, 1959-61. Mem. St. Louis Club, Bellerive Country Club (St. Louis), Alpha Kappa Psi. Office: Pol Mgmt Sys Corp PO Box 10 Columbia SC 29202-0010*

FISCHER, ROBERT BLANCHARD, university administrator, researcher; b. Hartford, Conn., Oct. 24, 1920; s. Charles Albert and Matilda (Nylen) F.; m. Mary Ellen Mitchell, June 29, 1946; children: Lois, Marcia, Philip, Vivian, Valerie. BS, Wheaton Coll., 1942; PhD, U. Ill., 1946. Rsch. chemist U.S. Army Atomic Bomb Project, Chgo., 1944-46; instr. chemistry U. Ill., Urbana, 1946-48; prof. chemistry Indiana U., Bloomington, 1948-63; dean sch. of sci. Calif. State U.-Dominguez Hills, Carson, 1963-79, dean emeritus, 1979—; provost, sr. v.p. Biola U., La Mirada, Calif., 1979-88, disting. prof., 1988-89, provost, disting. prof. emeritus, 1989—; research assoc. Calif. Inst. Tech., Pasadena, 1959-60; cons. in field. Contbr. articles to profl. jours. Fellow AAAS, Am. Sci. Affiliation (nat. pres. 1965-66); mem. Am. Chem. Soc. (sect. and region chmn.). Republican. Avocations: theology, amateur radio, sports. Home: 30238 Via Victoria Palos Verdes Estates CA 90275

FISCHER, ROBERT EDWARD, meteorologist; b. Bethlehem, Pa., Aug. 4, 1943; s. Frederic Philip and Muriel Winifred (Johnson) F. BS cum laude, U. Utah, 1966; MS, Colo. State U., 1969. Meteorologist Nat. Weather Svc., Fairbanks, Alaska, 1973—. Contbr. articles to profl. jours. Vol. classical music program prodr. Sta. KUAC-FM, Fairbanks. Recipient Nat. Oceanic and Atmospheric Adminstrn. Unit citation, 1989. Fellow Royal Meteorol. Soc.; mem. Am. Meteorol. Soc. (Charles L. Mitchell award 1985), Nat. Weather Assn. (Outstanding Operational Performance award 1987), Assn. Lunar and Planetary Observers, Am. Assn. Variable Star Observers, Royal Astron. Soc. Can., Sigma Xi, Phi Kappa Phi. Avocations: running, photography, astronomy, bird watching. Home: PO Box 82210 Fairbanks AK 99708-2210 Office: Nat Weather Service Forecast Office 101 12th Ave Unit 12 Fairbanks AK 99701-6237

FISCHER, ROBERT LEE, engineering executive, educator; b. Huntington, W.Va., Feb. 4, 1947; s. Charles Lee and Frances Louise (Pennington) F.; m. Mona Lynn Reeser, Oct. 27, 1966; children: Robert Lee Jr., Amy Lynn, Cory Brandon. Cert. in electronics tech., Huntington East Vocat. Tech., 1965; BA in Physics and Gen. Sci., Marshall U., 1970, MS in Vocat. Tech. Edn., 1976; PhD in Elec. Engring., Kennedy-Western U., 1993. Registered profl. electrical engr.; lic master electrician; cert. plant engr. Electrical engr. J.F. & M. Co., Huntington, 1970-71; electronics prodn. supr. polan ind. div. Wollensak, Inc., Huntington, 1971-72; electrical maintenance supr. ACF Industries, Inc., Huntington, 1972-76, electrical maintenance supt., 1976-78, sr. maintenance engr., 1978-80, plant engr., 1980-84, mgr. plant, prodn. and tooling engring., 1984-85; engr., prin. cons. Fischer Tech. Svcs., Huntington, 1979—; electrical, instrumentation and utilities mgr. Calgon Carbon Corp., Catlettsburg, Ky., 1985-93, maintenance mgr., 1993-94, maintenance svcs. mgr., 1994—; robotics instr. Marshall U. Community and Tech. Coll., Huntington, 1986—; instrumentation and control engring. curriculum adv. com. Shawnee State U., Portsmouth, Ohio, 1985—. patentee electronic height control device, robot safety mechanism. Elected to West Jr. High Sch. Hall of Fame, Huntington, 1988; recipient Sr.-Under Black Belt-Open 3d Place award United Fighting Arts Fedn. Nat. Karate Tournament, 1984; named W.Va. ambassador of sci. and engring. among all people, 1982. Mem. NSPE, W.Va. Soc. Profl. Engrs., W.Va. Acad. Sci., Ohio Valley Astron. Soc., Am. Radio Relay League, Six Meter Internat. Radio Club. Democrat. Avocations: ham radio, martial arts, amateur astronomy. Home: 3606 Route 75 Huntington WV 25704-9012 Office: Calgon Carbon Corp PO Box 664 Catlettsburg KY 41129-0664

FISCHER, ROBERTA JANE, accountant; b. Whitefish Bay, Wis., Feb. 5, 1959; d. Joseph R. and Margaret A. (LaRussa) Damiano; m. Jeffery S. Fischer, Oct. 22, 1983; children: Quinn, Anthony. BS in Acctg., Marquette U., 1981; MBA, U. Wis., 1997. Cost acct. Badger Meter, Milw., 1981-84; acct. Ampco Metal, Milw., 1984-85; corp. contr., treas. Hein Werner Corp., Waukesha, Wis., 1985-96; exec. v.p., CFO Design House, Inc., Germantown, Wis., 1996—. Mem. Fin. Exec. Inst., Inst. Mgmt. Acct. (cert.). Office: Design House Inc 11691 River Ln Germantown WI 53022

FISCHER, ROGER ADRIAN, retired history educator; b. Mpls., May 8, 1939; s. Roger Adrian and Dorothy Jane (Campbell) F.; m. Susan Phyllis Carlson, Oct. 27, 1962; children: Brian Campbell, David Peter, Timothy Lincoln. BA, U. Minn., 1960, MA, 1963; PhD, Tulane U., 1967. Asst. prof. history Sam Houston State U., Huntsville, Tex., 1967-69; assoc. prof. history S.W. Mo. State U., Springfield, 1969-72; prof. history U. Minn., Duluth, 1972-99. Author: The Segregation Struggle in Louisiana, 1862-1877, 1974 (L. Kemper Williams prize 1975), American Political Ribbons and Ribbon Badges, 1825-1981, 1985, Tippecanoe and Trinkets, Too: Material Culture in American Presidential Campaigns, 1828-1984, 1989, Them Damned Pictures: Explorations in American Political Cartoon Art, 1996; contbr. articles to profl. jours. Mem. state cen. com. Minn. Dem. Farmer-Labor Party, 1976-78. Named Outstanding Am. Educator, 1972; named to Honorable Order of Ky. Cols., 1987. Mem. Am. Studies Assn., Am. Culture Assn. (Carl Bode award 1988), Popular Culture Assn. Republican. Roman Catholic. Avocations: political Americana, tropical fish. Home: 612 N 34th Ave E Duluth MN 55804-1755

FISCHER, STANLEY, economist, educator; b. Lusaka, Zambia, Oct. 15, 1943; came to U.S., 1966, naturalized, 1976; s. Philip and Ann (Kopelowitz) F.; m. Rhoda Keet, Dec. 12, 1965; children: Michael Adam, David Benjamin, Jonathan Phillip. BSc, London Sch. Econs., 1965, MSc, 1966; PhD, MIT, 1969. Fellow U. Chgo., 1969-70, asst. prof. econs., 1970-73; assoc. prof. MIT, 1973-77, prof., 1977—, Killian prof., 1992-94; chief economist, v.p. devel. econs. World Bank, 1988-90; 1st dep. mgr. dir. IMF, 1994—; vis. sr. lectr. Hebrew U. Jerusalem, 1972; fellow Ctr. for Advanced Studies Hebrew U., 1976-77; vis. fellow Hoover Instn., Stanford U., 1981-82; cons. on Israeli economy Dept. State, 1984-87, 91-94; cons. IMF, 1991-92. Author: Indexing Inflation and Economic Policy, 1986, (with R. Dornbusch and R. Schmalensee) Economics, 1988, (with O. Blanchard) Lectures in Macroeconomics, 1989, (with R. Dornbusch and R. Startz) Macroeconomics, 7th edit., 1998; editor Nat. Bur. Econ. Rsch. Macroecons. Ann., 1986-94; contbr. articles to profl. jours. Guggenheim fellow. Fellow Econometric Soc.; mem. Am. Acad. Arts and Scis., Coun. on Fgn. Rels. Office: 12-300 F IMF Washington DC 20431

FISCHER, ZOE ANN, real estate and property marketing company executive, real estate consultant; b. L.A., Aug. 26, 1939; d. George and Marguerite (Carrasco) Routsos; m. Douglas Clare Fischer, Aug. 6, 1960 (div. 1970); children: Brent Sean Cecil, Tahlia Georgienne Marguerite Bianca. BFA in Design, UCLA, 1964. Pres. Zoe Antiques, Beverly Hills, Calif., 1973—; v.p. Harleigh Sandler Real Estate Corp. (now Prudential-Jon Douglas), 1980-81; exec. v.p. Coast to Coast Real Estate & Land Devel. Corp., Century City, Calif., 1981-83; pres. New Market Devel., Inc., Beverly Hills, 1983—; dir. mktg. Mirabella, L.A., 1983, Autumn Pointe, L.A., 1983-84, Desert Hills, Antelope Valley, Calif., 1984-85; cons. Lowe Corp., L.A., 1985. Designer interior and exterior archtl. enhancements and remodelling; designed album cover for Clare Fischer Orch. (Grammy award nomination 1962). Soprano Roger Wagner Choir, UCLA, 1963-64. Mem. UCLA Alumni Assn. Democrat. Roman Catholic. Avocations: skiing, designing jewelry, interior, landscape and new home design, antique collecting.

FISCHETTI, MICHAEL, public administration educator, arbitrator; b. Bklyn., Sept. 3, 1940; s. Michael A. and Marion T. (Verona) F.; m. Renate M. Winkler, Dec. 26, 1966; children: Peter N., Flori. BA, U. Md., 1965, MA, 1967, PhD, 1979; MPA, Am. U., 1971. Asst. to city mgr. City of Greenbelt, Md., 1966-67; rsch. assoc. Nat. League of Cities, Washington, 1967-68; div. dir. U.S. Dept. of Treasury, Washington, 1976-77; prof. and dir. Community Rsch. Svc. Montgomery Coll., Rockville, Md., 1968—, internat. edn. fellow, 1998-99; cons. Montgomery County Govt., Rockville, 1986-89, Pension Benefit Guarantee Corp., 1988-92. Editor Public Admin. Review, 1976-77, Public Admin. Quarterly, 1977-86. V.p. Montgomery County Coun. PTA's, 1985-87. With U.S. Army, 1959-62. Recipient Mayor's Citation for Pub. Svc, Mayor's Office, City of Balt., 1975, Pres.'s Citation for Outstanding Merit, pres. City Coun., City of Balt., 1975. Mem. Am. Soc. Pub. Adminstrn.(nat. coun. 1976-78), Am. Arbitration Assn., Soc. Prof.'s in Dispute Resolution, Soc. Fed. Labor Relations Prof.'s, Indsl. Rels. Rsch. Assn. Roman Catholic. Avocation: swimming, softball. Home: 10624 Great Arbor Dr Potomac MD 20854-4219

FISCHETTI, MICHAEL JOSEPH, accounting educator; b. Bklyn., Sept. 20, 1939; s. Anthony Joseph and Nicolina Rose (Marchitello) F.; m. Carlotta Theresa Cannarili, Sept. 25, 1960; children: Christine, Doreen, Clorissa, Diana. BBA, Pace U., 1968, MBA, 1970. CPA, N.Y. Audit mgr. Arthur Young & Co., N.Y.C., 1973-77; prin. Arthur Young & Co., Reston, Va., 1978-81; sr. mgr. Friedman & Fuller, Rockville, Md., 1982-86, Hoffman & Dykes, Vienna, Va., 1987-91; asst. dir. U.S. Gen. Acctg. Office, Washington, 1991—; lectr. U. Md., Marymount U. Pace U. teaching fellow, 1967. Mem. AICPAs (chair computer edn. subcom. 1973-74), Christian Businessmen's Com. (chair 1988-91). Avocations: swimming, running, Bible study. Office: US Gen Acctg Office 441 G St NW Washington DC 20548-0001

FISCHHOFF, BARUCH, psychologist, educator; b. Detroit, Apr. 21, 1946; s. Henry and Shirley (Levine) F.; m. Andrea Marks, Dec. 22, 1968; children: Maya, Ilya, Noam. BS in Math., Wayne State U., 1967; MA in Psychology, Hebrew U., Jerusalem, 1972, PhD in Psychology, 1975. Rsch. assoc. Oreg. Rsch. Inst., Eugene, 1974-76, Decision Rsch., Eugene, 1976-85, Applied Psychology Unit Med. Rsch. Coun., Cambridge, Eng., 1981-82, Eugene Rsch. Inst., 1985-87; prof. Carnegie-Mellon U., Pitts., 1987—, Univ. prof., 1998—; vis. prof. U. Stockholm, 1982-83; mem. panels NRC; cons. in field. Author: Acceptable Risk, 1981; mem. editl. bd. Jour. Risk Uncertainty, Jour. Exptl. Psychology: Applied, Risk, others; contbr. numerous articles to profl. jours. Mem. Eugene Commn. on Rights of Women, 1975-81; pres. Eugene Human Rights Coun., 1979-81. Fellow APA (Disting. Sci. award 1981, psychology in Pub. Interest award 1991), Soc. for Risk Analysis (Disting. Achievement award 1991), Soc. Judgment and Decision-Making (mem. coun. 1988-91, pres. 1990-91), Inst. Medicine, Phi Beta Kappa. Home: 1437 Denniston Ave Pittsburgh PA 15217-1332 Office: Carnegie Mellon U Dept Engrng & Pub Policy Pittsburgh PA 15213-3890

FISCHLER, ABRAHAM SAUL, education educator, retired university president; b. Bklyn., Jan. 21, 1928; s. Morris and Esther P. Fischler; m. Shirley Balter, Apr. 9, 1949; children: Bruce Evan, Michael Alan, Lori Faye. BS in Soc. Sci., CUNY, 1951; MA in Sci. Edn., NYU, 1952; EdD, Columbia U., 1959; DSc (hon.), N.Y. Inst. Tech., 1981; LLD (hon.), Nova U., 1992. Sci. tchr., supr. Ossining (N.Y.) Pub. Schs., 1952-58; instr. Columbia U., N.Y.C., 1958-59; asst. prof. edn. Harvard U. Grad. Sch., Cambridge, Mass., 1959-62; assoc. prof. then prof. edn. U. Calif., Berkeley, 1962-66; dean grad. studies Nova U., Ft. Lauderdale, Fla., 1966-70, James Donn prof., 1966—, exec. v.p., 1969-70, pres., 1970-92; pres. emeritus, univ. prof., 1992—; mem. Broward County Sch. Bd., 1994-98, chair, 1996-97; visiting prof. nat. and internat. univs., 1963-65; cons. numerous sch. dists., Calif., 1962-67; advisor ednl. pubs.; mem. bus.-edn. adv. com. Alameda-Contra Costa Counties, Calif.; mem. Calif. Elem. Sci. Adv. Com., Sacramento; mem. Overseas Tchrs. Examining Team, Berkeley; bd. dirs. Cardio-Metrics, Inc., Inst. Learning Techs., Inc., Hollywood (Fla.) Fed. Savs. & Loan Assn., Hollywood Med. Ctr.; chair Broward Workforce Devel. Bd., Aquagenix, Sun Globe. Author: Modern Science, Grades 7,8,9, 1963; (with others) Science: A Modern Approach, 1966, Modern Science, 1967, Modern Elementary Science: Grades 1 through 8, 1971, Nova U.'s Three National Doctoral Degree Programs: An Analysis and Formative Evaluation, 1977; contbr. numerous articles to profl. jours., author monograph and research reports. Pres. United Way Broward County (Fla.), 1984-85, bd. dirs., 1973—, chmn. budget com., 1976-81; chmn. Broward County Overall Econ. Devel. Com., 1980-88, Broward Edn. and Tng. Coun., 1989—; pres. S.E. Fla. Holocaust Meml. Ctr., 1985-87, Temple Beth El, Hollywood, 1988-90; adv. bd. Leadership Broward; mem. 17th Jud. Nominating Commn., Broward County, 1982-86, Ft. Lauderdale Mus. Art, Fla. Philharm., Broward County Crime Commn., Broward Workshop Edn. Task Force, Town of Davie, Fla. Econ. and Indsl. Devel. Bd.; bd. dirs. Hollywood (Fla.) Med. Ctr., 1982—, chmn. bd. dirs., 1985—; pres. Health Care Rsch. and Edn. Found., 1988-89, United Ways Fla., 1990-91; bd. govs. Fla. Bar, 1991-95, Fla. Bar Found., 1996—. With USN. Recipient Outstanding Mgmt. and Leadership award Sales and Mktg. Execs., Ft. Lauderdale, 1978, Leader of Yr. award Leadership Broward, 1991, Humanitarian of Yr. award E.A.S.E. Found., 1991, Disting. Educator award Assn. Ind. Schs. Fla., 1992, Tree of Life award Jewish Nat. Fund, 1993, Spirit of Broward award, 1994, Lifetime Achievement award Urban League, 1994; named Broward Educator of Yr., Women's Am. ORT, 1997, Disting. Pub. Svc. award ADL, 1998; DuPont fellow UCLA, 1958, Sci. Manpower fellow Columbia U., 1958-59. Fellow AAAS, Phi Delta Kappa; mem. ASCD, NSTA, Assn. for Edn. Tchrs. Sci. (past pres.), Nat. Assn. Research in Sci. Teaching, Soc. Advancement Edn., Soc. Research Adminstrs., Am. Assn. Higher Edn., Nat. Council Univ. Research Adminstrs., Com. of 100, Hollywood, Hundred Club Broward County (pres. 1985-86), Cosmos Club (Washington), 110 Tower Club, Kappa Delta Pi. Avocations: running, golf, travel. Office: Nova U Office of PresEmeritus College Ave Fort Lauderdale FL 33314-7796

FISCHLER, SHIRLEY BALTER, retired lawyer; b. Oct. 9, 1926; d. David and Rose (Shapiro) Balter; m. Abraham Saul Fischler, Apr. 9, 1949; children: Bruce Evan, Michael Alan, Lori Faye. BA, Bklyn. Coll., 1947, MA, 1951; JD, Nova U., 1977. Bar: Fla. 1977, D.C. 1980, U.S. Ct. Appeals (D.C. cir.) 1980. Tchr. N.Y.C. Bd. Edn., 1948-50, Richmond (Calif.) Pub. Schs., 1965-66; assoc. Panza, Maurer, Maynard, Platow & Neel, Ft. Lauderdale, Fla., 1977-95; pro bono atty. Broward Lawyers Care, 1982-86. V.p. Gold Cir. Nova Southeastern U., 1995-97, treas., 1997—; bd. govs. Nova U. Law Ctr., 1982-99; mem. Commn. on Status of Women, Broward County, Fla., 1982-87, vice chair, 1983-84, Entourage, Broward Ctr. for Performing Arts. Mem. Fla. Bar Assn., D.C. Bar Assn., Broward County Bar Assn., Bklyn. Coll. Alumni Assn. (sec.-treas. So. Fla. chpt. 1997—), Close Encounters with Music (bd. dirs. 1998—). Home: 5000 Taylor St Hollywood FL 33021-5839

FISCHLER, STEVEN ALAN, film producer; b. Bklyn., July 24, 1949; s. Samuel and Michelle Louise (Rubin) F.; m. Erika Davidson Gottfried, Aug. 6, 1953; 1 child, Sophia-Celine Fischler-Gottfried. BFA, NYU, N.Y.C., 1971. Co-founder, prodr., dir. Pacific St. Films, Hastings-on-Hudson, N.Y., 1969—; exec. prodr. Pacific St. Prodrs. Group, Hastings-on-Hudson, 1980—. Filmmaker, co-prodr., co-dir.: (with Joel Sucher) Red Squad, 1971, Frame-up! The Imprisonment of Martin Sostre, 1972, Free Voice of Labor: The Jewish Anarchists, 1980, Anarchism in America, 1981, I Promise To Remember: Frankie Lymon and the Teenagers, 1983, Man's Best Friends, 1984, Blue Helmets: The Story of U.N. Peacekeeping, 1990, Martin Scorsese Directs, 1990, Jessica Lange: It's Only Make-Believe, 1991, Oliver Stone: Inside/Out, 1992, In Search of Peace, 1995, Sidney Lumet: An American Director, 1996, The Warrior Tradition. Recipient Guggenheim fellowship in film, N.Y.C., 1978, N.Y. State CAPS fellowship, 1974, 77, Grand prize Nat. Student's Assn. Film Festival, N.Y. Emmy The Lincoln-Douglas Debates, 1993, Grand prizes Nat. Students Assn. Film Festival, 1970, Mannheim Film Festival, 1974, 1st prize Urban Focus Film Festival, 1975, John Grierson award for social documentaries, 1975, Village Voice Vanguard award, 1975, Blue Ribbon, Am. Film Festival, 1981, Silver Plaque, Chgo. Film Festival, 1982, Cert. fo Appreciation Humane Soc., 1984, CEBA award for excellence in comm., 1984, Red Ribbon Am. Film Festival, 1984, 91, Paul Robeson award Newark Film Festival, 1985, CINE Golden Eagle, 1985, 93, N.Y. Emmy award Best Mag. Program, 1988. Jewish. Avocations: woodworking, cooking, history of Anarchism. Office: Pacific St Films 579 Broadway St Hastings On Hudson NY 10706

FISCHMAN, BERNARD D., lawyer; b. N.Y.C., Feb. 26, 1915; s. Isidor and Rose Josephine F.; m. Hilda Schlang, June 10, 1937; children: Judith Fischman Johnson, Robert W. Student CCNY, 1931-33, Yeshiva U., 1931-34; LLB, NYU, 1936. Ptnr. Shea & Gould, N.Y.C., 1950-94; of counsel Le Boeuf, Lamb, Greene & MacRae, N.Y.C., 1994—. bd. dirs. Lechters, Inc., Apple Bank for Savs., N.Y. Water Svc. Corp. Mem. privacy com. ACLU, N.Y.C.; bd. govs. High Point Hosp.; adv. bd. CUNY Law Sch. at Queens Coll. Fellow Am. Orthopsychiat Assn. (atty.); mem. Century Assn. (N.Y.C.). Home: 115 Central Park W New York NY 10023-4153 Office: Le Boeuf Lamb Greene & MacRae 125 W 55th St New York NY 10019-5369

FISCHMAN, BURTON LLOYD, communications educator, management consultant; b. Newark, Nov. 19, 1930; s. Harry and Anna (Blackstone) F.; m. Rhoda Chorney, June 7, 1959; children: Gail, Helene. BS, Curry Coll., 1958; MA, Seton Hall U., 1960; PhD, U. Conn., 1971. Prof. communications Bryant Coll., Smithfield, R.I., 1966—; cons. to more than 100 different businesses, govtl. agys. and profl. assns., 1970—. Author: New Directions in Public Speaking, 1972, Business Report Writing, 1975, Developing Leadership, 1976. With U.S. Army, 1951-53, Korea. Recipient Disting. Faculty award Alumni of Bryant Coll., 1984, Youth Svcs. award B'nai B'rith, 1990, Maasim Touim (Doerof Good Deeds) award Nat. Fedn. Jewish Men's Clubs, 1993. Office: Bryant Coll 1150 Douglas Pike Smithfield RI 02917-1291

FISCHMAR, RICHARD MAYER, resort executive, financial consultant; b. N.Y.C., Apr. 11, 1938; s. John B. and Sylvia (Moosnick) F.; m. Sandra P. Fensin, July 3, 1967; children: Brian, Laura. BS, U. Ill., 1959, MA, 1962. CPA, Ill. Sr. auditor L.K.H.&H., Chgo., 1962-66; contr. Lake States Engr., Park Ridge, Ill., 1966-68, New Communities Enterprises, Park Forest South, Ill., 1968-70; dep. dir. Ill. Drug Abuse Program, Chgo., 1970-71; dir. internal audit Ill. Dept. Labor, Chgo., 1971-73; contr. Ill. Dept. Employment Security, Chgo., 1973-78, D.L. Pattis Real Estate, Lincolnwood, Ill., 1978-86, Goodman Realty Group, Inc., Chgo., 1986-90, Harold J. Carlson, Rosemont, Ill., 1990-92; CFO L.J. Sheridan & Co., Chgo., Ill., 1992-94, Am. Resorts Internat., Oakbrook, Ill., 1994—; guest lectr. Mich. State U., Gov.'s State U. Author: (booklet) Bibliography of Management Services, 1972; contbr. articles to profl. jours. Mem. Ill. Soc. CPAs (real estate com., mgmt. adv. svcs. and constrn. com., entertainment and leisure industries coms.).

FISCHOFF, EPHRAIM, humanities educator, sociologist, social worker; b. N.Y.C., Oct. 2, 1904; s. Aaron and Betty (Gunsberg) F.; m. Marion Judson, Dec. 28, 1943; children: Aronel, Gabriel and Raphael (twins), Michael, Bettina, Daniel. AB, CCNY, 1924; MHL, Jewish Inst. Religion, 1928; DSocial Sci., New Sch. Social Research, 1942; DD, Hebrew Union Coll., 1982. Ordained rabbi, 1928. Ministry, religious edn. group work, 1928-42; lectr. sociology Pa. State U., 1935-36; lectr. Jewish Tchrs. Sem., N.Y., 1937-42; editorial cons. World Jewish Congress, 1941-45; lectr. New Sch. Social Research, N.Y.C., 1942-51, Hunter Coll. (CCNY), 1942-46; asst. editor Jour. Legal and Polit. Sci., 1943-45; acting exec. dir. Conf. Jewish Relations, 1946; head dept. sociology Am. Internat. Coll., Springfield, Mass., 1946-54; lectr. Hartford Sem. Found., 1953-54; dir. B'nai B'rith Hillel Found. (U. Calif.-Berkeley), 1954-55, B'nai B'rith Hillel Found. (Yale U.), 1955-58; prof. humanities and social sci., dir. honors program Lynchburg Coll., Va., 1960-69; prof. sociology, anthropology and Am. Studies U. Wis.-Stevens Point, 1969-76; prof. social welfare Sangamon State U., Springfield, Ill., 1976, univ. prof. humanities, 1977-83; prof. emeritus Sangamon State U., 1983—; vis. prof. Hollins Coll. U. Va., 1965-67, Sir George Williams U. Montreal, 1970; lectr. So. Ill. Sch. Medicine, 1979-81, lectr., sr. cons., vis. prof. in med. humanities, 1982-84; clin. prof. dept. internal medicine, vis. prof.dept. surgery, 1984—; lectr. in humanities Lincoln Library, Springfield, Ill., 1978-90. Author: William Beaumont, Elizabeth Blackwell, Oliver Wendell Holmes, Sir William Osler, Pearson Mus. Monograph Series, 1981-82; trans., editor: (M. Hirschfeld) Sexual History of the World War; translator: (Max Weber) Sociology of Religion, 1963; contbr.: Great Thinkers of the Twentieth Century, 1963, Contemporary Jewish Thought, A Reader, 1963, Economy and Society, 1968; contbr., dept. editor: Encyclopaedia Judaica, 1967-68; editorial cons. From War to Peace Series, Inst. Jewish Affairs, World Jewish Congress, 1944-48. Mem. exec. bd. ARC; mem. exec. bd. Pres.'s Com. Physically Handicapped, NCCJ; active Park Ridge Ctr. Fellow Am. Sociol. Assn. Fellow Soc. for Applied Anthropology; mem. Nat. Assn. Social Workers (charter mem.), Acad. Cert. Social Workers, Am. Philos. Assn., Am. Studies Assn., Am. Acad. Polit. and Social Scis., Central Conf. Am. Rabbis, Soc. for Pschol. Study Social Issues; mem. Hist. Sci. Soc., Am. Soc. for History of Medicine, Soc. Sci. Study Religion, Am. Acad. Religion, Soc. Health Human Values, Hastings Ctr., Gerontol. Soc. Am., Am. Jewish Hist. Soc., Jewish Law Assn., Abraham Lincoln Assn., Société Européenne de Culture, Internat. Sociol. Assn., Soc. for Lit. and Sci., Ill. State Hist. Soc., Nat. Humanities Faculty, H.G. Wells Soc., Assn. for Sociology Religion, Amnesty Internat., Alpha Omega Alpha (hon.). Lodge: B'nai Brith. Office: So Ill U Sch Medicine Dept Internal Medicine 801 N Rutledge St Springfield IL 62702-4910

FISCHOFF, GARY CHARLES, lawyer; b. Manhasset, N.Y., Nov. 23, 1954; s. Harold and Ann (Yablon) F.; m. Linda Lee Sacca, Nov. 22, 1985; 1 child, Lisa Frances. BA, U. Buffalo, 1976; JD, St. John's U., Jamaica, N.Y., 1983. Bar: N.J. 1983, U.S. Dist. Ct. N.J. 1983, N.Y. 1984, U.S. Dist. Ct. (so. and ea. dists.) N.Y. 1985, U.S. Dist. Ct. (no. and we. dist.) N.Y., U.S. Ct. Appeals (2d cir.) 1988. Asst. treas. IAP, Inc., Lyndhurst, N.J., 1980-82; assoc. Hannoch Weisman, Roseland, N.J., 1983-85; ptnr. Fischoff Gelberg & Director, Garden City, N.Y., 1985-96, Fischoff & Assocs., Garden City, 1996—; lectr. seminar Nat. Bus. Inst., Westbury, N.Y., 1990, 91, Practicing Law Inst., 1992, 93, N.Y. State Bar Assn., 1995. Rep. Greentree Homeowners Assn., Northport, N.Y., 1988-89; trustee Suffolk County Vanderbilt Mus., 1994—, corp. sec., 1995-97, treas. 1997-99, 1st v.p., 1999—. Mem. Am. Bankruptcy Bd. Cert. (cert. bus. bankruptcy and consumer bankruptcy), N.Y. State Bar Assn. (real property sect., seminar lectr. 1995, Practicing Law Inst., continuing legal edn. lectr. 1992, 93), Nassau County Bar Assn. (mem. bankruptcy com., jud. liaison 1988-89). Jewish. Avocation: bicycling. Office: Fischoff & Assocs 600 Old Country Rd Garden City NY 11530-2001

FISCINA, ELIZABETH GLADYS, former hotel industry administrator; b. Kew Gardens, N.Y., Mar. 27, 1944; d. Elizabeth C. Gaddis; m. Peter J. Fiscina (dec.); children: Vincent P. Musac, Elizabeth D. Musac Metz. Grad., L.I. Beauty Sch., Hempstead, N.Y., 1978. Lic. hairdresser. Cosmetologist, 1978; adminstrv. asst. I.W. Industries, Melville, N.Y., 1983-85; exec. housekeeper Woodcrest Club, Syosset, N.Y., 1986-87; head housekeeper Seawanhaka Corinthian Yacht Club, Centre Island, N.Y., 1987-88; exec. housekeeper Royal Inn Motor Lodge, Manhasset, N.Y., 1989-92, housekeeping mgr., 1992-98.

FISETTE, SCOTT MICHAEL, golf course designer; b. Orange, Tex., May 17, 1963; s. Roderick John and Addie Faye (Byrnes) F.; divorced; 1 child, Shane Roderick. BS in Landscape Architecture, Tex. A&M U., 1985. Registered landscape architect, Tex., Hawaii, Commonwealth of No. Mariana Islands. Project architect Dick Nugent Assocs., Long Grove, Ill., 1985-90; prin., pres. Fisette Golf Designs, Kaneohe, Hawaii, 1991—. Mem. Golf Course Supts. Assn. Am., Am. Soc. Landscape Architects, Nat. Golf Found., Hawaii Turf Grass Assn. (bd. dirs. 1991-96), Donald Ross Soc. Avocations: golf, fishing, water skiing, softball. Office: Fisette Golf Designs PO Box 1433 Kaneohe HI 96744-1433

FISH, A. JOE, federal judge; b. L.A., Nov. 12, 1942; s. John Allen and Mary Magdalene (Martin) F.; m. Betty Fish, Jan. 23, 1971; children: Abigail, Stephen. B.A., Yale U., 1965, LL.B., 1968. Bar: Tex. Assoc. firm McKenzie & Baer, Dallas, 1968-80; judge Tex. Dist. Ct., 1980-81; assoc. judge Tex. Appeals Ct., 1981-83; judge U.S. Dist Ct. (no. dist.) Tex., Dallas, 1983—. Mem. ABA, State Bar Assn. Tex., Dallas Bar Assn. Office: US District Court US Courthouse 1100 Commerce St Ste 15d6L Dallas TX 75242-1027*

FISH, ANDREW JOSEPH, JR., electrical engineering educator, researcher; b. New Haven, Aug. 15, 1944; s. Andrew Joseph and Katherine Pauline (Frey) F.; m. Paula Jean Boisclaré, June 21, 1985; 1 child, Ashley Marie. B.S.E.E., Worcester Poly. Inst., 1966; M.S.E.E., U. Iowa, 1973; M.S. in Math., St. Mary U., San Antonio, 1974; Ph.D., U. Conn., 1981. Asst. prof. elec. engrng. U. Hartford, West Hartford, Conn., 1979-84, Western New Eng. Coll., Springfield, Mass., 1984-87; assoc. prof. elec. engrng. U. New Haven, 1987—, chmn. Dept. of Elec. Engrng., 1992-94, Dept. Elec. and Computer Engrng., 1993—; co-chmn. nonlinear systems group Am. Control Conf., 1980. Contbr. articles to profl. publs. Gate keeper West Suffield Grange, 1982; Fellow Yale U., 1982-83. Mem. IEEE (co-chmn. large scale and nonlinear systems group 22d Conf. on Decision and Control, ASME. Research on modeling, analysis, control of nonlinear systems, particularly Hybrid Analog-Digital Systems.

FISH, BARBARA, psychiatrist, educator; b. N.Y.C., July 31, 1920; d. Edward R. and Ida (Citrin) F.; m. Max Saltzman, Dec. 12, 1953; children: Mark, Ruth Saltzman Deutsch. *Her early interest in science was encouraged by her engineer father. In her 13 formative years at the Ethical Culture Fieldston schools, teachers helped to develop the self-confidence that every child needs to fulfill their own unique potential. Later she was inspired by the insights of her child psychiatry professor, Dr. Loretta Bender. But she never could have accomplished what she has, without the patient encouragement of the most supportive husband a dedicated career woman could ever have.* B.A. summa cum laude, Barnard Coll., Columbia U., 1942; M.D., NYU, 1945. Diplomate Am. Bd. Psychiatry and Neurology, Am. Bd. child psychiatry. Intern Bellevue Hosp., N.Y.C., 1945-47, resident in pediatrics, 1948-49, resident in psychiatry, 1949-52; resident in pediatrics N.Y. Hosp., N.Y.C., 1947-48; practice medicine specializing in child psychiatry N.Y.C., 1952-65; instr. psychiatry Med. Coll Cornell U., N.Y.C., 1955-60; instr. pediatrics Cornell U., 1955-56, asst. prof. clin. pediatrics, 1956-60; child psychiatrist dept. pediatrics N.Y. Hosp.-Cornell Med. Center, 1955-60; mem. faculty William A. White Inst. Psychoanalysis, N.Y.C., 1957-66; assoc. prof. psychiatry sch. medicine N.Y. U., N.Y.C., 1960-70; prof. N.Y. U., 1970-72, adj. prof., 1972—, dir. child psychiatry med. ctr., 1960-72; prof. psychiatry and behavioral sci. UCLA, 1972-89, Della Martin prof. psychiatry and behavioral sci., 1989-91, Della Martin prof. psychiatry and behavioral sci. emeritus, 1991—; mem. advisory com. mental health services for children N.Y.C. Community Mental Health Bd., 1963-72; mem. profl. advisory com. on children N.Y. State Dept. Mental Hygiene, 1966-72; mem. com. cert. child psychiatry Am. Bd. Psychiatry and Neurology, 1969-77; mem. clin. program projects research rev. com. NIMH, 1976-78. *She is widely known for her research on the antecedents of schizophrenia. Her study of infants of schizophrenic mothers, from birth to age 30, was the first such prospective study. It is also unique and made psychiatric history, as it is the only one in which subjects were followed from birth and for so long. It identified a disorganization of early neurological development, or "pandysmaturation", that predicted which individuals would develop schizotypal (schizophrenic-like) traits as adults. Her findings shed light on the neuroanatomical abnormalities recently found in adult schizophrenics, which most scientists now believe point to an early neurodevelopmental disorder.* Contbr. articles on the antecedents of schizophrenia and other severe mental disorders, and on the psychiat. diagnosis and treatment of children; mem. editorial bd.: Jour. Am. Acad. Child Psychiatry, 1966-71, Jour. Autism and Childhood Schizophrenia, 1971-74, Child Devel. Abstracts and Bibliography, 1974-82, Archives Gen. Psychiatry, 1975-84. Recipient Woman of Sci. award UCLA, 1978; NIMH grantee, 1961-72, 78-88, Harriett A. Ames Charitable Trust grantee, 1961-66, William T. Grant Found. grantee, 1977-83, Scottish Rite schizophrenia rsch. grantee, 1979-87. Fellow Am. Psychiat. Assn. (Agnes McGavin award 1987), Am. Acad. Child Psychiatry, Am. Coll. Neuropsychopharmacology (charter); mem. Am. Psychopath. Assn. (v.p. 1967-68), Assn. for Research in Nervous and Mental Diseases, Soc. Research in Child Devel., Psychiat. Research Soc. Home: 16428 Sloan Dr Los Angeles CA 90049-1157 Office: UCLA Neuropsychiat Inst 760 Westwood Plz Los Angeles CA 90095-8353

FISH, BARBARA JOAN, investor, small business owner; b. Seattle, June 12, 1936; d. George Francis Linehan and Maureece Shirley (Frederick) McCullough; m. Ralph Edwin Fish, July 14, 1956 (dec. Nov. 1986). Grad. high sch., Portland, Oreg. Owner Sea and Sand R.V. Park, Depoe Bay, Oreg., 1977—; real estate investor State of Oreg. Active St. Augustine's Ch. Mem. Lincoln City C. of C., Depoe Bay C. of C., Oreg. Sheriff's Assn. (hon.). Republican. Roman Catholic. Avocations: R.V. traveling, gardening. Home and Office: Sea and Sand RV Park 4985 N Highway 101 Depoe Bay OR 97341-9740

FISH, CHESTER BOARDMAN, JR., retired publishing consultant, writer; b. Worcester, Mass., June 30, 1925; s. Chester Boardman and Mary Elizabeth (Sheehan) F.; m. Claire Margaret Commo, Sept. 10, 1948; children: Craig Michael, Scott Kevin, Maribeth Ann, Andrea Dawn, Brian John. B.A., Syracuse U., 1950, M.A., 1952. Asst. editor Boys' Life mag., N.Y.C., 1951-53; assoc. editor Sports Afield mag., N.Y.C., 1953-55; copy chief Am. Home mag., N.Y.C., 1955-57; assoc. editor Outdoor Life mag., N.Y.C., 1957-63, article editor, 1963-67, mng. editor, 1967-73, editor in chief, 1973-76; sr. editor David McKay Co., Inc. book pubs., N.Y.C., 1976-80, Charles Scribner's Sons (pubs.), N.Y.C., 1980-81; pub. cons. The Competitive Edge, Greenlawn, N.Y., 1981-83; editorial dir. Stackpole Books, Harrisburg, Pa., 1983-85, exec. v.p., 1986-89; exec. v.p. Stackpole Inc., Harrisburg, Pa., 1989-90; pub. Harness Horse mag., Harrisburg, 1989-91; pub. cons. and freelance writer Carlisle, Pa., 1990-94. Served with USNR, 1943-46, PTO. mem. Outdoor Writers Assn. Am., Carlindian Barbershop Chorus. Republican. Roman Catholic. Home: 709 Sutton Dr Carlisle PA 17013-3546

FISH, DAVID CARLTON, architect; b. Oceanside, Calif., Oct. 25, 1956; s. David and Agnes Lois (Noe) F.; m. Jamey Louise Burris, Mar. 14, 1980; children: Celeste Nicole, Jessica J., Carlton Neyle. AA, Mira Costa Coll., Oceanside, 1976; BArch, Calif. Poly. U., San Luis Obispo, 1983. Registered architect, Kans., Mo.; cert. Nat. Coun. Archtl. Registration Bds. Architect Seidler Owsley Assocs., Pittsburg, Kans., 1984-87, Architects Workshop, Pittsburg, 1990—; assoc. prof. constrn. engrng. tech. Pitts. State U., 1993-95. Mem. Pittsburg Community Child Care Learning Ctr., 1985. Mem. AIA, Nat. Trust for Hist. Preservation, Kans. Soc. Architects. Democrat. Office: Architects Workshop 110 W 6th St Pittsburg KS 66762-3804

FISH, DAVID EARL, insurance company executive; b. Port Jervis, N.Y., Sept. 22, 1936; s. William Earl and Elizabeth Dorthea (Schleer) F.; m. Patricia Ann Reilly, June 14, 1958 (dec.); children: Nancy S., Susan L., Brian D. BSBA, Muhlenberg Coll., 1958. Claims adjuster Liberty Mut. Ins., East Orange, N.J., 1961-65; claims supr. Liberty Mut. Ins., Pitts., 1966-68; claims examiner Liberty Mut. Ins., Boston, 1969-70; claims mgr. Liberty Mut. Ins., Buffalo, Syracuse, Balt., Phila., 1971-80; asst. divsn. claims mgr. Liberty Mut. Ins., Phila., 1980-81; asst. v.p. Liberty Mut. Ins., Chgo., 1981-86, divsn. claims mgr., asst. v.p., 1986-87; v.p. Liberty Mut. Ins., Boston, 1988-94, sr. v.p., 1994—; bd. dirs. Arbitration Forums, Tampa, Fla., Nat. Ins. Crime Bur., Palos Hills, Ill. Avocations: golf, spectator sports. Home: 13 Chandler Dr East Sandwich MA 02537-1729 Office: Liberty Mut Ins Co Riverside Office Park 13 Riverside Rd Weston MA 02493-2249

FISH, ELIZABETH ANN, physical education educator; b. Bryn Mawr, Pa., June 24, 1964; d. George David and Elizabeth (Eby) F. BS in Health and Phys. Edn., U. Del., 1987; MS in Health Edn., Saint Joseph's U., Phila., 1990. Coord. life issues, dept. head phys. edn. Springside Sch., Phila., 1987—; coach Eastern Field Hockey Camp, Pottstown, Pa., 1983-93, Pvt. I's All-Star Field Hockey Team, Pa., 1990. Mem. Am. Alliance for Health, Phys. Edn., Recreation and Dance, U.S. Field Hockey Assn., Pa. Assn. for Health, Phys. Edn., Recreation and Dance, Phi Kappa Phi, Kappa Delta Pi. Avocations: woodworking, gardening, fitness, golf. Home: 279 Deerfield Ct New Hope PA 18938-1076 Office: Springside Sch 8000 Cherokee St Philadelphia PA 19118-4135

FISH, HILDA JEAN BARKER, library director; b. New Hill, N.C., Aug. 12, 1938; d. John Hollie and Vila Belle (Melton) Barker; m. James Lloyd Fish, July 7, 1961; children: Rheth Alexander, Hollie Ann. BS, East Carolina U., 1960; MS in Edn., N.C. Agrl. and Tech. U., 1979; MLS, U. N.C., Greensboro, 1990. Cert. librarian, N.C. Bus. tchr. Contentnea H.S., Kinston, N.C., 1960-61; math. tchr. Great Bridge (Va.) Jr. H.S., 1961-62; spl. edn. tchr. Craddock Jr. H.S., Portsmouth, Va., 1962-63; sec. Dan River Mills, Danville, Va., 1963-64; bus. tchr. Bartlett Yancey H.S., Yanceyville, N.C., 1964-67, Rockingham C.C., Wentwork, N.C., 1967-72; dir. vols. Annie Penn Meml. Hosp., Reidsville, N.C., 1973-78; librarian Caswell County Schs., Yanceyville, 1978-87; bibliographer Elem. Sch. Libr. Collection, Greensboro, 1987-89; reference librarian Franklin County Libr., Louisburg, N.C., 1991, libr. dir., 1991—. Contbr. video revs. to Libr. Jour. Treas. Franklin County Partnership for Children, Louisburg, 1984—. Avocations: sewing, crafts. E-mail: Hfish@ncsl.dcr.state.nc.us. Office: Franklin County Libr 906 N Main St Louisburg NC 27549

FISH, HOWARD MATH, aerospace industry executive; b. Melrose, Minn., Aug. 1, 1923; s. Nathaniel and Louise Magaret (Gaetz) F.; m. Jamie Katherine Tom, May 15, 1948; 1 child, Howard Math Jr. Student, Air Command and Staff Coll., 1954; MBA, U. Chgo., 1957; postgrad., Armed Forces Staff Coll., 1960, Air War Coll., Montgomery, Ala., 1964; MAIA, George Washington U., 1964. Enlisted USAF, 1942, commd. 2d lt., 1944, capt., 1950, col., 1965, advance through grades to lt. gen., 1974, retired, 1979; deputy asst. sec. defense internat. security affairs Dept. Defense, Washington; asst. vice chief of staff USAF, Washington; chmn. U.S. Mil. Delegation to UN; v.p. internat. LTV Aerospace and Defense Co., 1980-82, Loral Corp., 1992-96; sr. advisor Internat. Lockheed-Martin Vought Sys., Dallas, La., 1996—; mem. Def. Policy Adv. Com. on Trade, Washington, 1987-94; chmn. Am. League for Exports and Security Assistance, Washington, 1986-94, Wash. Inst. Fgn. Affairs, 1996—. Decorated Def. DSM, Air Force DSM, Legion of Merit, DFC, Air medal, Purple Heart, POW medal. Mem. Am. Def. Preparedness Assn. (chmn. internat. div. 1984-94), Army Navy Club, Air Force Assn., Washington Inst. Fgn. Affairs, Beta Gamma Sigma. Roman Catholic. Avocations: tennis, fishing. Home: RR 2 Box 32 Thorndale TX 76577-9517 also: 1233 Capilano Dr Shreveport LA 71106-8286

FISH, JACOB, civil engineer, educator; b. Vilnius, Lithuania, Oct. 4, 1956; came to U.S., 1986; s. David and Gutia (Shmukler) F.; m. Ora Kogan, July 12, 1985; children: Efrat, Adam. BS, Technion, Haifa, Israel, 1982, MS, 1984; PhD, Northwestern U., Evanston, Ill., 1989. Registered profl. engr., N.Y., Israel. Structural engr. Bikshpan-Consulting, Tel Aviv, 1982-84; rsch. engr. Israel Aircraft Industries, Lod, Israel, 1984-86; rsch. asst. Northwestern U., 1986-89; asst. prof. Rensselaer Poly. Inst., Troy, N.Y., 1989-94, assoc. prof., 1994-98, prof., 1998—; prof. civil, mech. and aerospace engring. and info. tech. Rensselaer Poly. Inst., Troy, 1998—; cons. Lockheed Missiles, Palo Alto, Calif., 1990-91, ANSYS Software House, Pitts., 1991-92, EHRC Software House, Troy, Mich., 1995—, N.Y. Dept. Law, Albany, 1995. Editor-in-chief U.S. Assn. Computational Mechs. Bull., 1993—, Internat. Jour. for Computational Civil and Structural Engring, Internat. Jour. of Civil and Structural Engring., 1998—; contbr. over 60 articles to profl. jours. Recipient Presdl. award NSF, 1991, Best Paper award AIAA/Structural Dynamics and Materials, 1993, Young Investigator award USACM, 1994, Best Paper award ASME, 1995. Home: 7 Burton Ln Loudonville NY 12211-1472 Office: Rensselaer Poly Inst Troy NY 12180

FISH, JAMES HENRY, library director; b. Leominster, Mass., Feb. 21, 1947; s. Danny Mack and Doris Grace (Harvey) F. BA, U. Mass., 1968; MLS, Ind. U., 1971; MBA, Anna Maria Coll., Paxton, Mass., 1979. Dir. librs. Levi Heywood Meml. Libr., Gardner, Mass., 1971-72; dir. Leominster Public Libr., 1972-77, Robbins Libr., Arlington, Mass., 1977-80; state librarian Mass. State Libr., Boston, 1980-82; dir. Springfield City Libr. (Mass.), 1982-90; city librarian San Jose (Calif.) Pub. Libr., 1990-96; dir. Balt. County (Md.) Pub. Libr., 1996—. Author libr. reports and cons. projects, community analysis, planning and evaluation. Bd. dirs. United Fund Leominster, 1974-76, Vis. Nurses Assn. Leominster, 1974-76, Leominster chpt. ARC, 1975-77, Santa Clara Valley YMCA, 1991-94; chmn. Leominster Bicentennial Com., 1975-76. With U.S. Army, 1969-71. Decorated Commendation medal; recipient Disting. Service award Arlington C. of C., 1979. Mem. ALA, Pub. Libr. Assn. (New Standards Task Force 1986-87, adv. com. chmn. Pub. Libr. Data Svc., mem. conf. program com., 1988-90, 90-91, mem. nominating com. 1993, mem. common concerns com. 1994, mem. ptnrs. program 1994, mem. exec. bd. 1998, mem. issues and concerns steering com. 1998), Calif. Libr. Assn. (mem. com. 1993-96, conf. planning com. 1994-95, chair local arrangements com. 1994-95), Urban Librs. Coun. (symposium planning com. chair 1998, steering com. 1994-97, video tng. project 1994-97, strategic dirs. com., bd. dirs. OCLC adv. com. pub. librs. 1998), Beta Phi Mu. Office: Balt County Pub Libr 320 York Rd Towson MD 21204-5121

FISH, JAMES STUART, college dean, advertising consultant; b. Mt. Pleasant, Iowa, Sept. 8, 1915; s. Don Ellsworth Fish and Belle (Osborn) Thompson; m. Dorothea Merritt, Nov. 3, 1941 (dec. 1993); children: James Stuart, Richard Merritt (dec.), Nancy Osborn Payne; m. Candace Anderson, June 10, 1995. B.A., U. Minn., 1937; postgrad., Northwestern U., 1938. With advt. dept. Gen. Mills, Inc., Mpls., 1938-76, sr. v.p., 1976-79; pres. Ad-Ventures in Wayzata, Minn., 1979—; dean grad. programs in bus. communications Coll. St. Thomas, St. Paul, 1983-86, dean emeritus; dir. N.W. Teleprodns., Mpls.; chmn. cmty. adv. bd. KTCA, 1979-91. Bd. dirs. Wayzata Crime Prevention Coalition, 1980—, pres., 1989; pres. Mpls. People to People Internat., 1988—; bd. dirs. People to People Internat., 1989-96; bd. dirs., mem. exec. com. Better Bus. Bur. Minn., 1980-93; bd. dirs. Nat. Retiree Vol. Ctr., 1989—, vice chmn., 1995—; chmn. Founders Club, Am. Advt. Mus., Portland, Ore., 1990-92, emeritus bd. mem., 1998; mem. nat. adv. coun. C.M. Russell Mus., Great Falls, Mont., 1994—. Recipient Disting. Alumni award U. Minn., 1984, Outstanding Achievement award, 1984, St. Thomas Aquinas medallion Coll. of St. Thomas, 1986, Torch of Truth award BBB, Minn., 1996, Oustanding Leadership award, Mpls. People to People Internat., 1998. Fellow Am. Acad. Advt. (Disting. Svc. award 1984); mem. Am. Advt. Fedn. (Hall of Fame award 1985, Bart Cummings award 1995), Advt. Fedn. Am. (chmn. 1959-60), Advt. Fedn. Minn. (pres. 1959-60, Silver medal 1963), Wayzata C. of C. (Citizen of Yr. 1985), Wayzata Hist. Soc. (pres., bd. dirs. 1982—), Wayzata Country Club (pres. 1958-59). Republican. Congregationalist. Avocations: boating, graphics, travel, sketching. Home: 19005 12th Ave N Minneapolis MN 55447-2517 Office: Adventures in Wayzata 19005 12th Ave N Plymouth MN 55447-2517 *Died July 3, 1998.*

FISH, JANET ISOBEL, artist; b. Boston, May 18, 1938; d. Peter and Florence (Voorhees) F. BA, Smith Coll., 1960; postgrad., Skowhegan (Maine) Art Sch., summer 1961; BFA, MFA, Yale U., 1963. Represented by D.C. Moore Gallery, N.Y.C. One-woman shows D.C. Moore Gallery, N.Y.C., John Szoke Graphics, Inc., also others; represented in permanent collections Whitney Mus. Am. Art, N.Y.C., Met. Mus. Art, N.Y.C., Cleve. Mus. Art, Dallas Mus. Fine Arts, Am. Fedn. Arts, Am. Acad. Inst. Arts and Letters, Art Inst. Chgo., Nat. Gallery, Kansas City (Mo.) Art Inst., Albright-Knox Gallery, Buffalo, N.Y., Newark Mus., Mpls. Mus. of Art, Nat. Gallery of Victoria, Melbourne, Australia, Okla. Art Ctr., Powers Inst., Sydney, Australia, Colby Coll., Waterville, Maine, N.Y. Mus. of Fine Arts, Houston Art Ctr., RISD, Providence, Mus. Art, Providence, Va. Mus. Fine Arts, Richmond, Yale U., New Haven, Smith Coll. Mus. Art, Northampton, Mass., Albrecht Art Mus., St. Joseph, Mo., Kansas City (Kans.) Art Inst., Milw. Art Mus., Hunter Mus. Art, Chattanooga. Bd. govs. Skowhegan Sch. Painting and Sculpture, Marie Walsh Sharpe Art Found. Recipient Harris award Chgo. Bienale award, 1974, Outstanding Woman Artist award Aspen Mus., 1992, Am. Acad. of Arts and Letters award, 1994; MacDowell fellow, 1968, 69, 72; Yale scholar, Australian Coun. for Arts grantee, 1975. Mem. Am. Acad. and Inst. of Arts and Letters (assoc.).

FISH, MARY MARTHA, economics educator; b. Albert Lea, Minn., July 17, 1930; d. Charles H. and Olga (Stennes) Thomassen; m. Donald C. Fish, Oct. 1954 (dec.); children: Jill S., Lynn M., Jason M. B.B.A., U. Minn., 1951; M.B.A. in Econs, Tex. Tech. Coll., 1957; Ph.D. (AAUW fellow 1960), U. Okla., 1963. Statis. asst. Iowa Bd. Control, 1951-53; pub. health analyst State of Calif., 1953-54; analytical statistician 46th Med. Gen. Lab., U.S. Army Forces, Tokyo, 1954-57; instr. econs. and bus. Odessa (Tex.) Coll., 1957-58; asst. prof., then assoc. prof. West Tex. State U., 1961-66; prof. econs. U. Ala., 1966—; Fulbright lectr. U. Liberia, 1974-75, Gambian Govt., 1978-79; cons. in field. Co-author: Convicts, Codes and Contraband, 1974; contbr. articles to profl. jours. Grantee U. Ala., 1967-68, 87-89, Dept. Labor, 1978-79; Fulbright rsch. fellow, Taiwan, 1995; Phifer Faculty Scholar, 1998. Mem. Am. Econ. Assn., So. Econ. Assn. Mem. Baha'i faith. Home: 1405 High Forest Dr N Tuscaloosa AL 35406-2153 Office: U Ala Culverhouse Comm Bus Econ & Fin Dept PO Box 870224 Tuscaloosa AL 35487-0154

FISH, MICHAEL, psychologist; b. Montreal, Que., Can., May 2, 1953; came to U.S., 1978; s. Gerald and Resi Fish; m. Diane Clement, 1979 (div. June 1985); m. Renée J. Greene, Mar. 29, 1986; children: Brandon, Gilah. BA, McGill U., Montreal, 1977; PhD, East Tex. State U., Commerce, 1985. Clin. dir. Lippman Shelter, Ft. Lauderdale, Fla., 1984-85; supervising psychologist Children's Psychiat. Ctr., Miami, Fla., 1985-90; pvt. practice Ft. Lauderdale, 1986—; supervising psychologist Parent Resource Ctr., Miami, 1990-91; guest lectr. Nova Southeastern Osteo. Sch. Medicine, Ft. Lauderdale, 1997—; mem. adv. bd. C.H.A.D.D., Plantation, Fla., 1984; chmn. quality control The Retreat Hosp., Sunrise, Fla., 1990-91. Contbr. articles to profl. jours. Mem. APA. Avocation: photography. Office: 274 S University Dr Plantation FL 33324

FISH, MICHELE LOYD, retailer; b. Belleville, Ill., Jan. 5, 1952; d. Delmer Edward and Patricia Ann (Marshall) Munie; m. Robert Wendelin Fish, May 25, 1973 (div. Feb. 1981). BS cum laude, U. Mo., 1973. Asst. buyer Famous-Barr, St. Louis, 1974-75, dept. mgr., 1975-76, buyer, 1976-81, store mgr., 1981-82; buyer Venture Stores, St. Louis, 1982-84, divsn. merchandise mgr., 1984-85, divsn. v.p., 1985-93; sr. v.p. Roman Co., St. Louis, 1993-94; sr. dir. frame buying LensCrafters, Cin., 1995; market rep. May Co., St. Louis, 1995-98, divisional merchandise mgr., 1998—; adv. bd. dept. textile and apparel mgmt. U. Mo., Columbia, 1987, chair, 1988-90. Spl. venue mgr. Athlete's Village, U.S. Olympic Festival, 1994; dir. AMC Cancer Rsch. Ctr., 1986-96, also v.p., sec.; chair gifts Women's Event, 1988-94, chair gifts golf tournament, 1989-93, co-chair St. Louis Walks for Women, 1994, Together a Day of Caring, 1995, co-chair women's event, 1997, co-chair workout women, 1997—; vol. Reach to Recovery, 1992-94; vol. coord. First Night St. Louis, 1994-96, bd. dirs. 1996—; bd. dirs. Talking Tapes for the Blind, 1996—. Recipient Torch of Liberty award Anti-Defamation League, 1990, Citation of Merit, U. Mo., 1992. Republican. Roman Catholic. Avocations: aerobic exercise, reading, gardening, home decorating. Home: 82 E Sherwood Dr Saint Louis MO 63114-5717

FISH, PAUL WARING, lawyer; b. Ligonier, Pa., Apr. 12, 1933; s. Edmund R. and Catherine (McGuiggan) F.; m. Jacquelyn A. Shea, Sept. 19, 1959; children: Charles M., Edmund J., Catherine G., John H., Jacquelyn A. B.S. in Elec. Engring, Cath. U. Am., 1959, M.E.E., 1961; LL.B., George Washington U., 1965. Bar: D.C. 1965, N.Y. 1966, Mich. 1967, Wis. 1976, Ill. 1983, Pa. 1993. Patent agt., atty. Xerox Corp., Rochester, N.Y., 1965-66; patent atty., asst. dir. patent div. Burroughs Corp., Detroit, 1969; dir. patents Burroughs Corp., to 1976; asst. gen. counsel Jos. Schlitz Brewing Co., Milw., 1976-79; v.p., gen. counsel., sec. Jos. Schlitz Brewing Co., 1979-83; v.p., gen. counsel. Comdisco, Inc., Rosemont, IL, 1983-86, sr. v.p., gen. counsel, 1986-91; cons. Comdisco, Inc., Rosemont, Ill., 1991-93; of counsel Mason, Fenwick and Lawrence, Washington, 1992-94, Christie, Parker & Hale, Pasadena, Calif., 1994-97, Rader, Fishman & Grauer, Bloomfield Hills, Mich., 1997—; mem. adj. faculty Cath. U. Am. Columbus Sch. of Law. Bd. regents Cath. U. Am., 1985—, bd. visitors, 1998—. With USN, 1951-55. Mem. Am. Intellectual Property Law Assn., D.C. Bar Assn., Pa. Bar Assn., Wis. Bar Assn., Ill. Bar Assn., Mich. Bar Assn. Roman Catholic. E-mail: fish@westol.com. and pwf@raderfishman.com. Fax: 724-593-6250. Home and Office: PO Box 239 Jones Mills PA 15646-0239

FISH, STANLEY EUGENE, university dean, English educator; b. Providence, Apr. 19, 1938; s. Max and Ida Dorothy (Weinberg) F.; m. Adrienne A. Aaron, Aug. 23, 1959 (div. 1980); 1 dau., Susan.; m. Jane Parry Tompkins, Aug. 7, 1982. B.A., U. Pa., 1959; M.A., Yale U., 1960, Ph.D., 1962. Instr. U. Calif., Berkeley, 1962-63, asst. prof., 1963-67, assoc. prof., 1967-69, prof., 1969-74; Kenan prof. English and Humanities Johns Hopkins U., Balt., 1978-85, chmn. dept., 1983-85; Arts and Sci. Disting. prof. English and prof. law Duke U., Durham, N.C., 1985-98, chmn. dept., 1986-92; exec. dir. Duke U. Press, Durham, 1994-98; dean U. Ill. Coll. Liberal Arts and Scis., Chgo., 1999—. Author: John Skelton's Poetry, 1965, Surprised by Sin: The Reader in Paradise Lost, 1967, 97 (Hanford Book award 1998), Seventeenth Century Prose: Modern Essays in Criticism, 1971, Self-Consuming Artifacts, 1972, The Living Temple: George Herbert and Catechizing, 1978, Is There a Text in This Class?, 1980, Doing What Comes Naturally, 1989, There's No Such Thing as Free Speech...And It's a Good Thing Too, 1994 (PEN/Spielvogel-Diamonstein award 1994), Professional Correctness: Literary Studies and Political Change, 1995; mem. editl. bd. Milton Studies, Milton Quar. Recipient 2d place, Explicator prize, 1968; Am. Council Learned Socs. fellow, 1966; Guggenheim fellow, 1969. Mem. MLA, Am. Acad. Arts and Scis., Milton Soc. (hon. scholar 1991), Spenser Soc. Office: U Ill Chgo LAS Dean's Office M/C 228 601 S Morgan St Chicago IL 60607-7104

FISH, THOMAS EDWARD, English language and literature educator; b. Redbud, Ill., Aug. 1, 1952; s. Edward Charles and H. Grace (Thomas) F.; m. Kathryn Jane Griffith, Nov. 17, 1979; children: Dana Rose, Sally Kathryn. BA, Iowa State U., Ames, 1974; MA, U. Kans., 1976, MPhil, 1979, PhD, 1981. Asst. instr. in English U. Kans., Lawrence, 1974-81, staff mem. communications resource ctr., 1978, 80; adj. asst. prof. English Iowa State U., 1981-84; asst. prof. English Cumberland Coll., Williamsburg, Ky., 1984-86, assoc. prof. English, 1986-96, prof. English, 1996—. Self-study editor SACS, 1992-95. Elder Corbin (Ky.) Presbyn. Ch., 1986, 90-92. Lilly grantee Cumberland Coll., 1990, named Prof. for Excellence in Teaching, 1990; tchg. grantee Cumberland Coll., 1998; faculty-student rsch. grantee Appalachian Coll. Assn., 1999. Mem. Modern Lang. Assn., Nat. Coun. Tchrs. of English, Popular Culture Assn., Browning Inst., South Atlantic Modern Lang. Assn., Phi Beta Kappa, Phi Kappa Phi. Democrat. Home: 260 Brush Arbor Rd Williamsburg KY 40769-1717 Office: 7193 College Station Dr Williamsburg KY 40769-1382

FISHBAUGH, CAROLE SUE, secondary school educator; b. Newark, Ohio, Mar. 11, 1938; d. Lawrence William Baird and Thelma Irene (Kennon) Baird-Thogmartin; m. Emerson LaVerna Fishbaugh, Sept. 11, 1961. BS in Edn., Ohio U., 1962; postgrad., Ohio State U., 1963-65, U. North Fla., 1985—, Jacksonville U., 1994. Cert. elem., K-12 reading tchr., K-12 tchr. mentally retarded, Fla. Elem. tchr. Greenfield (Ohio) Exempted Village Schs., 1958-60; elem. tchr. Newark Pub. Schs., 1960-61, tchr. mentally retarded, 1961-62. 63-65; tchr. mentally retarded Alexandria (Va.) Pub. Schs., 1962-63; vice prin. Lincoln Jr. High Sch., Newark, 1964-65; tchr. reading Nassau County Pub. Schs., Fernandina Beach, Fla., 1986-93; contact person reading dept. Fernandina Beach Mid. Sch., 1990-93, mem. sch. adv. coun., 1991—, contact person for alternative edn., chair dept. alternative edn., 1993-94, chair sch. improvement adv. coun., 1994-96, tchr. varied exceptionalities, 1994—, ESE dept. chair, 1996-98, mem. dist. team, 1994-96; mem. grant com. Fernandina Beach Mid. Sch., 1992-98, mem. tech. com. Mem. ch. and soc. com., organizer drug abuse fight Meml. United Meth. Ch., Fernandina Beach, 1987; mem. adminstrv. coun. Meth. Children's Home Soc. for United Meth. Ch., 1987-98; mem. Fernandina Beach Task Force to Fight Crime, 1992-96; dist. rep. Sch. Adv. Coun., 1994-96; vol., mem. adv. coun. Quality Health Nursing Home, Fernandina Beach, 1996—. Mem. ASCD, Nat. Mid. Sch. Assn., Fla. League Mid. Schs., Nassau Tchrs. Assn. (sch. rep. 1987-90, treas. 1988-90, rep. on sch. improvement 1992, sec. 1994, treas. 1995-98), Nat. Alzheimers Assn. Democrat. Avocations: travel, volunteering in national parks, birdwatching, photography, music, swimming. Office: Fernandina Beach Mid Sch 315 Citrona Dr Fernandina Beach FL 32034-2716

FISHBEIN, PETER MELVIN, lawyer; b. N.Y.C., June 20, 1934; s. Arthur L. and Lotta (Chary) F.; m. Bette Klinghoffer, June 16, 1957; children: Stephen, Bruce, Gregory. BA magna cum laude, Dartmouth Coll., 1955; JD, Harvard U., 1958. Bar: N.Y. 1959, U.S. Supreme Ct. 1973. Note editor Harvard Law Rev., Cambridge, Mass., 1956-58; law clk. to Justice William J. Brennan, Jr. U.S. Supreme Ct., Washington, 1958-59; dep. sec. gen. Internat. Peace Corps., Washington, 1962-64; ptnr. Kaye, Scholer, Fierman Hays & Handler, N.Y.C., 1967—, mng. ptnr., 1984-91; chief counsel N.Y. State Constl. Conv., Albany, 1967; mem. Presdl. Commn. to Nominate Candidates for Fed. Ct. of Appeals, N.Y.C., 1980; adj. prof. constl. law NYU Law Sch., 1970-84. Contbr. articles to profl. jours. Trustee Goddard Coll., 1967-75, Fedn. Jewish Philanthropies, N.Y.C., 1975-81, Citizen's Budget Commn.; mem. N.Y. State Gov.'s Bd. Pub. Disclosure, Albany, 1975-77; bd. dirs. Health Care Chaplaincy, 1993—, Brennan Ctr. for Justice, 1995—; mem. legal and ethics com. Whitney Mus.; mgr. Justice Arthur J. Goldberg's Campaign for Gov., 1970. Recipient Disting. Cmty. Svc. award Brandels U., Jurisprudence award Am. Ort. Fellow Am. Coll. Trial Lawyers, Am. Bar Found.; mem. ABA, Assn. of Bar of City of N.Y., Harvard Club (N.Y.), Beach Point Club (bd. govs. 1981-86), Phi Beta Kappa. Home: 101 Woodlands Rd Harrison NY 10528-1423 Office: Kaye Scholer Fierman Hayes & Handler 425 Park Ave New York NY 10022-3506*

FISHBERG, GERARD, lawyer; b. Bronx, N.Y., May 23, 1946; s. Alfred and Sarah (Goldberg) F.; m. Eileen Taubman, Dec. 23, 1972; children: David, Dana. BA, Hofstra U., 1968; JD, St. John's U., Bklyn., 1971. Bar: N.Y. 1972, U.S. Dist. Ct. (ea. and so. dists.) N.Y. 1973, U.S. Ct. Appeals (2d cir.) 1975, U.S. Supreme Ct. 1976. Assoc. Cullen & Dykman, Garden City, N.Y., 1972-79, ptnr., 1980—. Assoc. editor St. John's U. Law Rev., 1970-71. Mem. legis. com. N.Y. Conf. of Mayors and Mcpl. Ofcls., Albany, 1976—; bd. dirs. Am. Heart Assn. L.I. region, 1995—, treas. 1997-98, exec. com., 1997—, vice chair, 1998—. Capt. USAR, 1968-77. St. Thomas Moore scholar St. John's U. Sch. Law, 1969-71. Mem. N.Y. State Bar Assn. (mcpl. law and labor law sects., sec. 1985-87, 1st vice chmn. 1989-91, chmn. 1991-93, mem. ho. of dels. 1993-95, mem. exec. com. 1978—), Nassau County Bar Assn. (chmn. mcpl. law com. 1981-83, 85-87, chmn. labor law com. 1991-92), Garden City C. of C., Rotary (bd. dirs. 1988-94, treas. 1990-91, pres. 1992-93), Rotacare (bd. dirs. 1992—, pres. 1993—). Jewish. Home: 1 Bucknell Dr Plainview NY 11803-1801 Office: Cullen & Dykman 100 Quontin Roosevelt Bvld Garden City NY 11530

FISHBURN, KAY MAURINE, nurse; b. Kearney, Nebr., Nov. 1, 1939; d. Kenneth Charles and Maurine Estelle (Neustrom) Kauer; m. Charles Wylie Fishburn, Nov. 21, 1962; children: Jeffrey Scott, Ann Charlotte Klein. Diploma in nursing, Henry Ford Hosp., 1960; BSN with honors, U. Wis., Milw., 1974. Nurse Henry Ford Hosp., Detroit, 1960-61, U. Colo. Med. Ctr., Denver, 1961-63, Wayne County Gen. Hosp., Eloise, Mich., 1964; faculty asst. U. Wis., Milw., 1974-75; pvt. practice occupational health nursing New Berlin, Wis., 1974—. Founder, nat. coord. Citizens for Debt-Free Am., New Berlin, 1983—; amb. at large VFW Post #5716, 1988. Recipient Community Svc. award Todays Girls/Tomorrows Women, 1992. Mem. Am. Nurses's Assn., Milw. Dist. Nurses Assn. (Nursing Svc. award 1984). Methodist. Home: 2550 S Sunnyslope Rd New Berlin WI 53151-3076

FISHBURNE, BENJAMIN P., III, lawyer; b. South Bend, Ind., Nov. 14, 1943; s. Benjamin Postell and Peggy (Gahan) F.; m. Edith E., Aug. 5, 1983. BA cum laude, U. Notre Dame, 1965; JD, U. Va., 1968. Bar: Va. 1968, U.S. Ct. Mil. Appeals 1968, U.S. Army Ct. Mil. Rev. 1968, D.C. 1972. Capt. Judge Advocate gen's. corps. US Army, 1968-72; atty. Surrey & Morse, Washington, 1968; ptnr. Surrey & Morse, 1975; mng. ptnr. Surrey & Morse, Washington, 1981-84; ptnr. Jones, Day, Reavis & Pogue, 1986, ptnr.-in-charge Hong Kong office, 1986-91, ptnr., 1991-93; ptnr. Winston & Strawn, Washington, 1993—; gen. counsel. Nat. Coun. U.S.-China Trade, 1981-87, assoc. coun. 1987-89, chmn. legal com. 1994—; mem. nat. coun. U.S.-China Trade Investment Delegation to China, 1986; alt. mem. U. Assn's. Nat. Policy panel study U.S.-China Rels., 1979; spkr. in field. Contbr. articles to profl. jours. Co-chmn. Am. C. of C. Hong Kong legal com., 1990, mem. bd. govs., 1991; mem. bd. advisors Johns Hopkins Nanjing Ctr., 1986-97. Mem. ABA (mem. Mid. East law com. internat. sect. 1979-81), Am. Arbitration Assn. (mem. China-U.S. Conciliation Ctr. adv. com. 1993—, mem. spl. corp. com. East-West trade arbitration 1973-79), Chartered Inst. Arbitrators (assoc.), Order of Coif. Home: 5535 Nevada Ave NW Washington DC 20015-1768 Office: Winston & Strawn 1400 L St NW Ste 800 Washington DC 20005-3508

FISHBURNE, JOHN INGRAM, JR., obstetrician-gynecologist, educator; b. Charleston, S.C., Aug. 18, 1937; m. Jean Crawford, June 10, 1971; children: John Ingram III, Barron Crawford, Virginia Heyward. AB, Princeton U., 1959; MD, Med. Coll. S.C., 1963. Diplomate Am. Bd. Ob-Gyn. (sub. specialty maternal-fetal medicine). Surg. intern Duke U. Hosp., Durham, N.C., 1963-64; resident in ob-gyn. U. N.C., Chapel Hill, 1966-70, resident in anesthesiology, 1970-72, instr. dept. ob-gyn., 1970-71, asst. prof., 1971-74, assoc. prof., 1974-75, asst. prof. dept. anesthesiology, 1972-75; assoc. prof. dept. ob-gyn. Bowman Gray Sch. Medicine, Wake Forest U., Winston-Salem, N.C., 1975-78, prof., 1978-83, assoc. prof. anesthesiology, dept. anesthesiology, 1975-83; prof., chmn. dept. ob-gyn. U. Okla. Health Scis. Ctr., Oklahoma City, 1983-97, adj. prof. dept. anesthesiology, 1983-97, chmn. search com. for chair pathology dept., 1987-88, chmn. search com. for chair family medicine dept., 1993-94; chmn., residency program dir. dept ob-gyn. Maricopa Med. Ctr., Phoenix, 1997—; dir. maternal-fetal medicine dept. ob-gyn. Forsyth Meml. Hosp., Winston-Salem, 1977-83; vis. prof. U. W.I., Kingston, Jamaica, 1973-74, African-Health Tng. Instns. Project Nairobi, Kenya, 1975; cons. devel. mission U.S. AID, Dacca, Bangladesh, 1980, Assn. Vol. Surg. Contraception World Fedn. Health Agys., Manila, 1984, Singapore, 1986, Zhordania Inst., Tbilisi, Republic of Georgia, 1992, 93, 97, Ivanovo, Russia, 1994, Almaty, Kazakhstan, 1994, St. Petersburg, Russia, 1995, Khojand, Tahjikistan, 1995, Odessa, Ukraine, 1995, Chechenov, Moldova, 1996, L'viv Ukraine; oral examiner Am. Bd. Ob-Gyn, 1980—; chmn. Gov.'s Task Force on Perinatal Care, 1984-86; mem. steering com. Robert Wood Johnson Healthy Futures of Okla., 1988-92; trustee Am. Assn. for Gynecologic Laparascopists, 1980-81; presenter numerous sci. papers and lectures local, nat. and internat. profl. meetings. Author: (with others) The Prostaglandins, 1972, Endocrine-Metabolic Drugs, 1974, Gynecologic Laparoscopy: Principles and Techniques, 1974, Laparoscopy, 1977, Endoscopy in Gynecology, 1978, Clinics in Perinatology, 1982, Obstetric Anesthesia, 1982, Clinical and Diagnostic Procedures Obstetrics and Gyncecology, Part B, 1984, Advances in Clinical Obstetrics and Gynecology, Medical Economics Books, 1985, Clinical Obstetrics, 1987, Danforth's Obstetrics and Gynecology, 1994, 98, Bonica's Obstetric Analgesia and Anesthesia, 1995; contbr. update series Am. Coll. Obstetricians and Gynecologists; editorial bd. Obstetrics and Gynceology, 1985-89; author self instructional programs in field; contbr. numerous articles to profl. jours. Capt. USAFR, 1964-66. Clin. fellow Am. Cancer Soc. U. N.C., 1968-69, clin. fellow obstet. anesthesia Pub. Health Svc. U. Hosps. Case Western Res. U.,

1969; tng. rsch. grantee NIH Med. U. S.C., 1961-62. Fellow ACOG (spl. interest rep. for obstet. anesthesia 1974-78, learning resources commn. 1981-82, mem. personal rev. of learning in ob-gyn. task force for obstetrics 1981-82, chair obs. IV, 1996-98, chair edn. commn. 1996-98, chair residency rev. com. ob/gyn. Accreditation Coun. for Grad. Med. Edn. 1994-97, vice chair coun. of residency rev. com. chairs 1996, chair accreditation coun. for grad. med. edn. coun. res. rev. com. chairs, 1997-98), Am. Coll. Anesthesiologists (assoc. examiner 1974); mem. Am. Soc. Anesthesiologists, Maternal & Fetal Medicine Soc. (rep. liaison com. ob.-gyn. 1983-89, bd. dirs. 1981-84), S. Atlantic Assn. Obstetricians and Gynecologists (assoc.), Perinatal Rsch. Soc., Oklahoma City Ob-Gyn. Soc., Okla. County Med. Soc., Okla. Anesthesia Soc., Internat. Soc. Advancement Humanistic Studies in Medicine, Cen. Assn. Obstetricians and Gynecologists, Continental Gynecol. Soc., So. Med. Assn., Am. Gynecol. and Obstet. Soc., Med. Alumni Assn., Med. U. S.C. (Disting. Alumnus award 1989), Alpha Omega Alpha. Episcopalian. Home: 7060 N Hillside Dr Paradise Valley AZ 85253-2813 Office: Maricopa Med Ctr Dept Ob-Gyn 2601 E Roosevelt St Dept Ob Phoenix AZ 85008-4973

FISHBURNE, LAURENCE, III, actor; b. Augusta, Ga., July 30, 1961; s. Laurence John Jr. and Hattie Bell Crawford F.; m. Majna Mass Fishburn, July 1, 1985; children: Langston Issa, Montana Isis. Appearances include (theatre) Section D, 1975, Eden, 1976, Short Eyes, 1984, Loose Ends, 1988, Urban Blight, 1988, Two Trains Running, 1992 (Best Featured Actor Tony award 1992), (films) Cornbread, Earl and Me, 1975, Apocalypse Now, 1979, Fast Break, 1979, Willie and Phil, 1980, Death Wish II, 1982, Rumble Fish, 1983, The Cotton Club, 1984, The Color Purple, 1985, Band of the Hand, 1986, Quicksilver, 1986, Gardens of Stone, 1987, A Nightmare on Elm Street 3: Dream Warriors, 1987, School Daze, 1988, Red Heat, 1988, King of New York, 1990, Cadence, 1991, Class Action, 1991, Boyz N the Hood, 1991, Deep Cover, 1992, What's Love Got To Do With It, 1993 (Academy award nominee, Best Actor, 1993), Searching For Bobby Fischer, 1993, Higher Learning, 1995, Bad Company, 1995, Just Cause, 1995, Fled, 1996, Hoodlum, 1997, Event Horizon, 1997, Hoodlum, 1997, Welcome to Hollywood, 1998, Once In the Life, 1999, The Matrix, 1999, (TV movies) A Rumor of War, 1980, I Take These Men, 1983, 1983, The Father Clements Story, 1987, Decoration Day,,1990, Miss Ever's Boys, 1997, Always Outnumbered, 1998; prodr. Miss Evers' Boys, 1997, Hoodlum, 1997, Always Outnumbered, 1998, Once In the Life, 1999 (also dir., writer); TV guest appearances M*A*S*H, 1972, Hill Street Blues, 1981, Miami Vice, 1984, Spenser: For Hire, 1985, The Equalizer, 1985. Office: Paradigm 10100 Santa Monica Blvd Fl 25 Los Angeles CA 90067-4003*

FISHE, GERALD RAYMOND AYLMER, engineering executive; b. Farnham Royal, Eng., Feb. 22, 1926; s. Daniel Hamilton and Dorothy Vida (Norton) F.; m. Patricia Ann Roach, Aug. 18, 1949; children: Martha Vida Bindshedler, Raymond Patrick Hamilton, G. Keith Hamilton. BS in Mech. Engring., Duke U., 1949. Registered profl. engr. Fla., Ga., Iowa (inactive Ala., Mo., Tenn. W.Va.). Project engr. E.I. DuPont de Nemours & Co., Martinsville, Va., 1952-58; architect's staff engr. So. Ill. U., Carbondale, 1958-63; sec. Adair Brady & Fishe, Inc., Lake Worth, Fla., 1965-66; chief engr. Gamble Pownall & Gilroy, Ft. Lauderdale, Fla., 1963-65; cons. forensic engr. Ft. Lauderdale, 1966—; Pres. Fishe and Kleeman, Inc., Ft. Lauderdale, 1974-85, Fidelity Inspection & Svc. Co., Ft. Lauderdale, 1983-91, Farletot Found., Inc., Ft. Lauderdale, 1985-91. Patentee in field. With U.S. Army, 1944-45. Fellow Internat. Inst. Forensic Engring. Scis., Nat. Acad. Forensic Engrs., Am. Acad. Forensic Scis. (chmn. engring. sect. 1988-89, bd. dirs. 1990-93); mem. ASHRAE, Constrn. Specification Inst., Nat. Fire Protection Assn. Republican. Episcopalian. Home: 2031 SW 36th Ave Fort Lauderdale FL 33312-4208 Office: GRA Fishe Cons Engr PO Box 478 Fort Lauderdale FL 33302-6470

FISHEL, ANDREW S., director, federal; b. Apr. 7, 1948; married, 1969. BA, Am. U., 1969; EdD of Am. Politics and Edn., Columbia U., 1974; MEd, Am. U., 1970. Legis. planning coord. U.S. Dept. HEW, Washington; mgmt. dir. Office for Civil Rights U.S. Dept. Edn., Washington; dir. fin. and resource mgmt. EEOC, Washington, 1982-89; mng. dir. FCC, Washington, 1989—. Co-author: (with Jan Pottker) Sex Bias in the Schools: The Research Evidence, 1977, National Politics and Sex Discrimination in Schools, 1996. Recipient Quality Improvement Prototype award OMB, 1987, Outstanding Mgr. award ASTD, 1992, Disting. Svc. medal FCC, 1992. Office: Fed Comm Commn 445 12th St SW Washington DC 20036-3507

FISHEL, PETER LIVINGSTON, accounting business executive; b. Chgo., Apr. 25, 1935; s. Philip W. and Dorothy B. (Livingston) F.; m. Donna Swift, Dec. 17, 1961; children: Pamela Leslie Fishel Saccocio, Patricia Jane Fishel Baquadano, Françoise Suzanne. BS, U. Pa., 1959. CPA, Pa., Fla. Agt.-in-charge investigation and civil rights div. Commonwealth of Pa. Dept. Justice, 1961-62; contr. Internat. Playtex Corp., 1962-70, BVD Knitwear, 1970-71; corp. contr. BVD Co., Inc., N.Y.C., 1971-73; v.p. fin. BVD Co., Inc. (BVD div.), N.Y.C., 1973; chief fin. officer Colebrook Mills, div. Bobbie Brooks, Inc., Hialeah, Fla., 1973-77; owner Gen. Bus. Services, 1978-86, regional dir. S.E. Fla., 1982-86; pvt. practice acctg., 1987—; mem. adv. com. Oceanmark Fed. Savs. & Loan, 1983-88. Mem. citizens adv. com. Met. Dade Police, Miami, Fla., 1981—, treas., 1985—; mem. fin. com. Metro-Dade Pig Bowl, 1985; mem. Andover Civic Assn., 1973—, v.p., 1986-91; mem. NMB Pride, 1989-93, bd. dirs., 1991-93; mem. Aventura Mktg. Coun., 1991—; bd. dirs. Dade Alumni Club, U. Pa., 1991—; mem., treas. Coalition for the Improvement of N.W. Dade, 1996—. With M.P. U.S. Army, 1954-56. Mem. AICPA, Pa. Inst. CPAs, Fla. Inst. CPAs, Nat. Assn. Tax Practitioners, Mensa, N. Dade C. of C. (bd. dirs. 1978-97, v.p., Businessman of Yr. 1990, Mem. of Month, 1987, 91), N. Miami Beach C. of C. Home: 1041 NW 203rd St Miami FL 33169-2308 Office: 2396 NE 172nd St Miami FL 33160

FISHER, ALAN HALL, guidebook writer; b. Evanston, Ill., July 16, 1945; s. Howard Taylor and Marion Ethel (Hall) F.; m. Margaret Ellen Williams, July 3, 1974; children: Ellen Williams, Howard Williams. BA, Harvard U., 1967; JD, Boston U., 1977. Bar: Md. 1977. English tchr. Trinity-Pawling (N.Y.) Sch., 1967-68, Acton (Mass.)-Boxborough H.S., 1968-70; rsch. asst. Harvard U., Grad. Sch. Design, Cambridge, Mass., 1971-72; assoc. Venable, Baetjer and Howard, Balt., 1977-80; guidebook writer Balt., 1980—. Author: Country Walks Near Boston, 1976, 86, Country Walks Near Baltimore, 1981, 88, 93, Country Walks Near Philadelphia, 1983, 94, Country Walks Near Washington, 1984, 96, Country Walks Near Chicago, 1987, Day Trips in Delmarva, 1992, 98. Home and Office: 1430 Park Ave Baltimore MD 21217-4230

FISHER, ALAN WASHBURN, historian, educator; b. Columbus, Ohio, Nov. 23, 1939; s. Sydney Nettleton and Elizabeth E. (Scipio) F.; m. Carol L. Garrett, Aug. 24, 1963; children: Elizabeth, Ann Christy, Garrett. BA, DePauw U., 1961; MA, Columbia U., 1964, PhD, 1967. Instr. history Mich. State U., East Lansing, 1966-67, asst. prof., 1967-70, assoc. prof., 1970-78, prof. Russian and Turkish history, 1978—, assoc. dean grad. studies and research, Coll. Arts and Letters, 1987-89, dir. Ctr. for Integrative Studies in Arts and Humanities, 1989-97. Author: Russian Annexation of the Crimea, 1772-1783, 1970, The Crimean Tatars, 1978, revised edit., 1987, Ottoman Studies Directory, I, 1979, II, 1981, III, 1983, Between Russians, Ottomans, and Turks: Crimea and Crimean Tatars, 1999. Am. Rsch. Inst. in Turkey fellow, 1969, 73, 76; Am. Coun. Learned Socs. grantee, 1976-77. Fellow Royal Hist. Soc., Turkish Hist. Assn. (corr.), Am. Rsch. Inst. Turkey (mem. bd. dels. 1990—, v.p. 1995—), Mid. East Studies Assn., Turkish Studies Assn. (pres. 1982-84, editor bull. 1984-87), Inst. Turkish Studies (dir., sec./treas. 1995-97, chmn. 1997—). Office: Mich State U Dept History 301 Morrill Hall East Lansing MI 48824-1036

FISHER, ALLAN CAMPBELL, railway executive; b. Westerly, R.I., Aug. 9, 1943; s. Arthur Chester and Norma Jean (Campbell) F.; m. Ellen Tryon Roop, June 14, 1969; children: Bradford Booth, Katherine Thayer. BA in Econs., St. Lawrence U., 1965; MS in Transp., Northwestern U., 1970. Rsch. economist Gen. Motors Rsch. Labs., Warren, Mich., 1969; mgmt. trainee Penn Cen., 1970, asst. trainmaster, Chgo., 1970-71, trainmaster, Toledo, 1971-72, terminal trainmaster, Elkhart, Ind., 1972, trainmaster, Cleve., 1972-74, asst. terminal supt., Cleve., 1974, terminal supt., Balt., 1974-75, asst. divsn. supt. Chesapeake divsn., Balt., 1975-76, terminal supt. Conrail, Conway, Pa., 1976, divsn. supt. N.J. divsn., Elizabethport, 1977, Lehigh divsn., Bethlehem, Pa., 1978, regional supt. ops. improvement Cen. region, Pitts., 1978-80, dir. budget control, 1980-82, regional supt. indsl. engring. So. region, Indpls., 1982-83, system dir. operating rules, Phila., 1983—. Served with U.S. Army, 1966-67, Vietnam. Decorated Bronze Star medal; Urban Transp. fellow, 1969. Mem. NAS (com. mem. Transp. Rsch. Bd.), Women's Transp. Seminar (Phila. chpt.), Transp. Rsch. Forum, Internat. Assn. Oper. Officers, Am. Inst. Indsl. Engrs. (sr.), Assn. Am. R.R.'s (chmn., oper. rules com., chmn. transport nuclear waste com.), Oper. Rules Assn. (chmn.), Norac Rules Adv. Com. (chmn.), Mayflower Descendents (life), Phila. Boys Choir and Men's Chorale (bd. dirs., Man of Yr. 1987, 89-91, 98), Masons, Sigma Chi (life). Unitarian. Home: 215 Poplar Ave Wayne PA 19087-3503 Office: 2001 Market St # 14D Philadelphia PA 19101-1414

FISHER, ALLAN MICHAEL, government official, educator; b. Bklyn., Apr. 9, 1955; m. Wendy Ellen Aronson, Nov. 11, 1979; children: Daniel Brian, Nicole Meredith. BBA, Baruch Coll., 1976; MPA, Am. U., 1988; PhD, Walden U., Mpls., 1993; diploma, Nat. Def. U., Washington, 1994; MS, Syracuse U., 1996. Cert. info. resource mgr., computing profl., sys. profl., office automation profl., govt. fin. mgr. Sr. auditor GSA, Washington, 1979-82; supervisory sys. acct. USDA, Washington, 1982-85; mgr. U.S. Dept. Treasury, Washington, 1985-91; auditor U.S. Dept. Def., Washington, 1977-79; asst. insp. gen. U.S. Dept. Def., Ft. Meade, Md., 1991-96, dir. tactical programs, 1996-97; asst ins. gen. U.S. Dept. Commerce, Washington, 1997—; adj. prof. George Mason U., Fairfax, Va., 1994-96, Hood Coll., Frederick, Md., 1996-97, U. Md., 1999—. Contbr. articles to profl. jours. Mem. coun. Montgomery County (Md.) Fiscal Affairs Com., 1984-86; coach Gaithersburg (Md.) Sports Assn., 1994—. Recipient Disting. Svc. award Montgomery County Coun., 1986. Mem. Nat. Assn. Hispanic Fed. Execs., Assn. Govt. Accts., Assn. Inst. for Cert. Computer Profls., Key Exec. Program Alumni Assn., Maxwell D.C. Alumni Assn., Syracuse U. Alumni Club Washington.

FISHER, ANDREW, management consultant; b. Richmond, Va., Dec. 17, 1920; s. Marion Nimmo and Sarah Randolph (Talcott) F.; m. Cornelia Johnson, Oct. 10, 1942; children: Peter R., Carolyn, Andrew R. B.A., Amherst Coll., 1943; M.B.A., Harvard U., 1947; D.Sc. (h.c.), Albany Med. Coll. Dir. indsl. relations Internat. Braid Co., Providence, 1947; with N.Y. Times, 1947-71, v.p., 1963-70, exec. v.p., 1971; mgm. cons., 1972-76; chmn., pres., pub. News Jour. Co., 1976-78; mgmt. cons. Trustee emeritus Albany Med. Coll. Capt. AUS, 1943-46. Mem. Moorings Club. Home: 1780 Cedar Ln Vero Beach FL 32963-2621

FISHER, ANDREW, IV, newswriter, television producer; b. Richmond, Va., Jan. 15, 1944; s. Andrew III and Dorothy Dale (Crannis) F.; m. Sharon Mary Cozza, Aug. 16, 1969. BA, Columbia U., 1965. News anchor Sta. WIP Radio, Phila., 1965, investigative reporter, 1968-69; writer, editor WNEW News, N.Y.C., 1969-74; overnight news anchor Sta. WNEW-AM, N.Y.C., 1974-79; morning news anchor Sta. WNEW-FM, N.Y.C., 1979-81; radio news corr. NBC News, N.Y.C., 1981-89, prin. news writer Today Show, 1990—; adj. prof. journalism Columbia U., N.Y.C., 1989-90; guest lectr. Rutgers U., New Brunswick, N.J., 1984, NYU, 1978, 80. Network radio anchor Winter Olympics, Calgary, 1988, Summer Olympics, Seoul, 1988; host/prodr. Andy Fisher Reporting on Religion, 1986-89, Catch of the Day, 1985-88; corr. The Source Report, 1981-88; contbr. Marketplace, Am. Pub. Radio, 1989, More Holy Humor, 1997, Dick Clark's American Bandstand: An Anniversary Celebration of Music and Dance, 1997; reporter/prodr. Sunday News Closeup, 1969-79; consulting editor Joyful Noiseletter, Kalamazoo, Mich., 1988—. Founding patron Flying Boat Mus., Foynes, Ireland, 1990—; lectr. St. Catherine of Siena Ch., Mountain Lakes, N.J., 1995—; mem. various coms. Episcopal Diocese, Newark, 1982-87; lay reader Ch. of Saviour, Denville, N.J., 1982-87; clk. vestry St. Peter's Ch., Morristown, N.J., 1979; mem. Denville Hist. Soc. Recipient Headliner Reporting award Nat. Headliners Club, 1985, Media award Am. Women in Radio & TV, 1985, Media award N.Y. State Bar Assn., 1985, Gold medal Internat. Radio Festival, 1989. Mem. Am. Fedn. TV & Radio Artists, Actors Fund (life), Boston Street Railway Assn., Fellowship Merry Christians (bd. dirs.), N.Y.C. Transit Mus. (sustaining), N.Y. Acad. Scis., Writers Guild Am., Indian Lake Cmty. Club, Albany Acad. Alumni Assn., Ancient Order of Hibernians, N.Y. Acad. Scis. Roman Catholic. Office: NBC News 30 Rockefeller Plz Rm 300S New York NY 10112-0002

FISHER, ANN BAILEN, lawyer; b. N.Y.C., Oct. 15, 1951; d. Eliot and Elise (Thompson) Bailen; m. John C. Fisher, Apr. 6, 1980. BA magna cum laude, Radcliffe Coll., 1973; JD, Harvard U., 1976. Bar: N.Y. 1977. Assoc. Sullivan & Cromwell, N.Y.C., 1976-80, 82-84, ptnr., 1984—; assoc. Sullivan & Cromwell, Paris, 1980-82. Mem. ABA, N.Y. State Bar Assn. Episcopalian. Clubs: Cosmopolitan, Harvard (N.Y.C.). Office: Sullivan & Cromwell 125 Broad St Fl 28 New York NY 10004-2489

FISHER, ARON BAER, physiology and medicine educator; b. Phila., Apr. 20, 1936; m. Joan C. Fisher, 1957; children: Marc L., Steven A., Eric R., Mara E. BS in Chemistry summa cum laude, Dickinson Coll., 1956; MD, U. Pa., 1960. Diplomate Am. Bd. Internal Medicine; diplomate Nat. Bd. Med. Examiners. Intern and resident in medicine U. Hosps., Cleve., 1960-61, 64-65; resident in pulmonary medicine Hosp. U. Pa., 1965-66; fellow dept. physiology U. Pa., 1966-68, assoc. in medicine, assoc. in physiology, 1968-70, from asst. prof. to assoc. prof. medicine, 1970-80, prof. medicine, 1980—, from asst. prof. to assoc. prof. physiology, 1970-1980, prof. physiology, 1980—, prof. environmental medicine, 1986—; staff physician VA Hosp., Phila., 1968-73, clin. investigator, 1973-76, cons. in pulmonary medicine, 1976-82; mem. med. staff Hosp. U. Pa., 1976—, dir. hyperbaric medicine clin. practice, 1985—; dir. Inst. Environ. Medicine U. Pa., 1985—; mem. Am. Heart Assn. student rsch. fellowship adv. com. U. Pa., 1983-97, mem. diabetes ctr. adv. com., 1985—, mem. teaching awards com., 1989-92, chmn. animal care com. 1982-84, 87-89, chmn. com. for animal facility planning, 1985-86, chmn. transgenic mouse facility com., 1989, chmn. instnl. animal care and use com., 1989-92, mem. bioengring. grad. group, 1988—, chmn. biochemistry grad. group rev. com., 1989-90, others, supr. grad. students; fellow dept. biophysics and phys. chemistry U. Pa., 1971-72; mem. study sect. Pa. Coal Worker's Respiratory Disease Program, 1976-78; mem. cardiovascular study sect. A NIH, 1979-81, mem. respiratory and applied physiology sect., 1981-83; mem. adv. panel U.S. Army Med. R&D Command, 1980-85; mem. VA Merit rev. com. for respiration, 1998—. Editor: (with others) Handbook of Physiology: The Respiratory System (Section 3), vol. 1, 1980-85; mem. editorial bd. Exptl. Lung Rsch. 1979-88, Am. Rev. Respiratory Diseases, 1981-87, Jour. Applied Physiology, 1984-87, Am. Jour. Physiology, 1988—; guest editor Symposium on Lung Surfactant Apoproteins, 1984; contbr. numerous articles and revs. to profl. jours., chpts. to books. With USPHS, 1958, 59-61; capt. MC USAR, 1961-65. Grantee NIH, 1986-91, 1988—; recipient Clin. Investigator award VA Res. Svc., 1973-76, Established Investigator award Am. Heart Assn., 1977-82, Christian R. and Mary F. Lindback Found. award for Disting. Teaching, 1984. Mem. AAAS, ACP, Am. Physiol. Soc. (chmn. respiration dinner 1991, councillor respiratory sect. 1991-95), Am. Thoracic Soc. (sec. assembly on structure, function and metabolism 1973-74, chmn. 1981, sec. sect. on pulmonary circulation 1979, councillor ea. sect. 1973-77, chmn. ann. meeting program com. 1976, pres. 1983), Am. Fedn. Clin. Rsch., Am. Soc. Clin. Investigation, Am. Heart Assn. (cardiopulmonary coun.), Am. Soc. Cell Biology, Undersea and Hyperbaric Med. Soc., Oxygen Soc., Aerospace Med. Assn., John Morgan Soc. U. Pa., Laennec Soc. Phila., Pa. Thoracic Soc. (chmn. rsch. com. 1985-87), Phi Beta Kappa, Alpha Omega Alpha. Achievements include co-determination that lung lamellar bodies maintain an acidic internal pH, that phospholipids co-isolated with rat surfactant protein-C account for the apparent protein-enhanced uptake of liposomes into lung granular pneumocytes, that secretogues for lung surfactant increase lung uptake of alveolar phospholipids, that cAMP increases synthesis of surfactant-associated protein A by perfused rat lung; research on secretory granule calcium loss after isolation of rat alveolar type II cells, on alveolar uptake of lipid and protein components of surfactant, on oxygen-dependent peroxidation during lung ischemia, on choline transport by lung epithelium, and on role of acidic compartment in synthesis of disaturated phosphatidylcholine by rat granular pneumocytes; isolation and molecular cloning of a new calcium-independent phospholipase A2. Home: 239 E Gowen Ave Philadelphia PA 19119-1021 Office: U Pa Inst Environ Medicine One John Morgan Bldg 36th St and Hamilton Walk Philadelphia PA 19104-6068

FISHER, ARTHUR, magazine editor; b. N.Y.C., Mar. 10, 1931; s. Abraham G. and Sadie (Gold) F.; m. Liliane E. Kowarsky, Aug. 18, 1951; 1 child, Anthony E. BA, NYU, 1951. Sr. rsch. aide NYU, 1954-56; mng. editor Dodge Books, 1957-62, Sci. World & Sr. Sci., 1962-68; sci. and tech. editor Popular Sci., N.Y.C., 1969-94, exec. editor, 1994-96, sci. editor emeritus, 1996—. Author: The Healthy Heart, 1981; co-author: (with Ernest V. Heyn) Century of Wonders, 1972, Fire of Genius, 1976; contbr. articles to mags. Recipient citations for excellence in sci. writing Deadline Club, 1973, 74, Claude Bernard Sci. Journalism award Nat. Soc. Med. Rsch., 1978, Sci. Writing award Am. Heart Assn., 1981, Am. Inst. of Phys. Sci. Writing award, 1985, Sci. Writing award AAAS, 1986, Grady-Stack Sci. Writing award Am. Chem. Soc., 1988, Writing award Ednl. Writers Assn., 1993, Journalism award Engring. Found., 1997. Mem. Nat. Assn. Sci. Writers, Coun. for Advancement of Sci. Writing (bd. dirs. 1989—). Home: 120 Cabrini Blvd New York NY 10033-3438

FISHER, BARRY ALAN JOEL, protective services official; b. N.Y.C., Sept. 11, 1944; s. George and Pearl (Newman) F.; m. Susan Joan Saperstein, Dec. 29, 1968; children: David, Michael. BS, CCNY, 1966; MS, Purdue U., 1969; MBA, Calif. State U., Northridge, 1973. With criminalistics lab. L.A. County Sheriff's Dept., 1969-79, chief sheriff's criminalistics lab., 1979-86, dir. Sci. Svcs. Bur., 1986—; lectr. U. Calif., L.A.; adj. lectr. Calif. State U., 1996. Fellow Am. Acad. Forensic Scis. (co-chmn. local arrangements com. 1981, chmn., sec. criminalistics sect. program 1981-82, sec., chmn. 1982-83, chmn. local arrangements com. 1991, chmn. sect. 1995—, pres.-elect 1997, pres. 1998-99); mem. Am. Soc. Crime Lab. Dirs. (chmn. forensic sci. ops. and program com. 1982-86, bd. dirs. 1986-89, pres. 1988-89, editor newsletter 1989-90), Forensic Sci. Found. (bd. dirs. 1985—, sec. 1988—), Forensic Sci. Soc., Internat. Assn. of Identification, Internat. Assn. Chiefs of Police, Internat. Assn. Forensic Scis. (pres. 1996-99). Republican. Jewish. Avocations: computers, reading, photography. E-mail: bajfisher@earthlink.net. Office: LA County Sheriffs Crime Lab 2020 Beverly Blvd Los Angeles CA 90057-2404

FISHER, BART STEVEN, lawyer, educator, investment banker; b. St. Louis, Feb. 16, 1943; s. Irvin and Orene (Moskow) F.; m. Margaret Cottony, Mar. 1, 1969; 1 child, Ross Alan. AB, Washington U., 1963; MA, Johns Hopkins Sch. Advanced Internat. Studies, 1967, PhD, 1970; JD, Harvard U., 1972. Bar: D.C. 1972. Assoc. Patton, Boggs & Blow, Washington, 1972-78, ptnr., 1978-94; ptnr. Arent Fox Kintner Plotkin & Kahn, Washington, 1994-95; mng. ptnr. Capital House, LLC, 1995—; of counsel Porter, Wright, Morris & Arthur, 1996—; adj. prof. internat. rels. Georgetown U. Sch. Fgn. Svc., Washington, 1974-82, 97; profl. lectr. internat. rels. Johns Hopkins U. Sch. Advanced Internat. Studies, 1993—, George Mason U., 1991, 93; bd. dirs., CitX Corp., exec. br. Webcasting Corp. Author: The International Coffee Agreement, 1972, (with John H. Barton) International Trade and Investment: Regulating International Business, 1986; editor: Regulating the Multinational Enterprise, 1983, Barter in the World Economy, 1985. Pres. Aplastic Anemia Found. Am. Inc., Balt., 1983-92, pres. emeritus, 1993; bd. dirs. Nat. Marrow Donor Program, Marrow Found., Aplastic Anemia Found., The Inst. at Mars Hill Coll.; program com. Georgetown Leadership Sem., Washington, 1981—; pres. Capital Baseball, Inc.; ex-officio bd. govs. Internat. Practice sect. Bar Va.; participating mem. Pres. Coun. on Year 2000 Conversion. Recipient Dean's Cert. Appreciation Georgetown U. Sch. Fgn. Svc., Washington, 1984. Mem. ABA, Internat. Bar Assn., Am. Soc. Internat. Law (rapporteur, panel trade policy and insts. 1974-77), Va. State Bar (bd. govs. internat. law sect.), Wash. Fgn. Law Soc., Parkville Post Am. Legion, Great Falls Swim and Tennis Club Va. Jewish. Home: 9009 Potomac Forest Dr Great Falls VA 22066-4110 Office: Porter Wright Morris & Arthur 1667 K St NW Ste 1100 Washington DC 20006-1660

FISHER, BENJAMIN CHATBURN, lawyer; b. Coos Bay, Oreg., Feb. 6, 1923; s. Benjamin S. and Catherine Selina (Chatburn) F.; m. Jean L. Whiting, June 30, 1951; children: John, Richard, Robert. AB with honors, U. Ill., 1948; JD magna cum laude, Harvard U., 1951. Bar: D.C. 1951. Law clk. to Judge Learned Hand, 2d cir., N.Y.C., 1951-52; mem. firm Fisher, Wayland, Cooper, Leader & Zaragoza, Washington, 1952—; mem. edn. appeal bd. U.S. Office Edn., 1973-83; mem. Adminstrv. Con. U.S., 1970-76; U.S. del. Plenipotentiary Conf. Internat. Telecomm. Union, Nice, France, 1989, Geneva, 1992, Kyoto, Japan, 1994, Mpls., 1998; mem. U.S. del. World Radio Conf., Torremolinos, Spain, 1992, Geneva, 1995, 97; mem. nat. com. radio comm. sect., 1989—; chmn. bd. dirs. Ctr. Adminstrv. Justice, Washington, 1972-77; gen. counsel Commn. Population Growth and Am. Future, 1970-72. Bd. dirs., v.p. Boys and Girls Clubs of Greater Washington, 1990—; bd. govs. Sigma Chi Found., 1991—. Mem. ABA (chmn. sect. adminstrv. law 1968-69, mem. ho. of dels. 1970-72, 73-75), Fed. Commn. Bar Assn. (pres. 1967-68), D.C. Bar Assn., Am. Law Inst., Soc. Satellite Profls. (chmn. 1983-85, bd. dirs. 1986-93, gen. counsel 1993—), Rotary (bd. dirs. Washington Club 1980-85, pres. 1983-84), Phi Beta Kappa, Phi Kappa Phi. Home: 5118 Cammack Dr Bethesda MD 20816-2902 Office: 2001 Pennsylvania Ave NW Washington DC 20006-1850

FISHER, BENNETT LAWSON, investment executive; b. Greenwich, Conn., Nov. 25, 1942; s. Bennett and Elsie (Lawson) F.; m. Susan Huntington, Sept. 20, 1969; children: Louisa H., James B. BA, Yale U., 1966. Investment officer Fiduciary Trust Internat., N.Y.C., 1968-69, v.p., 1969-84, sr. v.p., 1984—. Trustee, chmn. investment com. Pomfret (Conn.) Sch., 1974—. Mem. Inst. for the Advancement of Health (trustee, treas. 1985-90). Republican. Office: Fiduciary Trust Co Internat 2 World Trade Ctr New York NY 10048

FISHER, BERNARD, surgeon, educator; b. Pitts., Aug. 23, 1918; s. Reuben and Anna (Miller) F.; m. Shirley Kruman, June 5, 1947; children: Beth, Joseph, Louisa. BS, U. Pitts., 1940, MD, 1943; DSc (hon.), Mt. Sinai Sch. Medicine, CUNY, 1986. Diplomate Am. Bd. Surgery. Intern Mercy Hosp., Pitts., 1943-44, resident in surgery, 1944-48; fellow in surg. research, resident in gen. surgery Harrison Dept. Dept. Surg. Research U. Pa., Phila., 1950-52; fellow London Postgrad. Med. Sch. Hammersmith Hosp., 1955-56; tchg. fellow in pathology U. Pitts., 1944-45, 1945-47, assoc. prof., 1956-59, prof. surgery, 1959-86, Disting. Svc. prof., 1986—; med. surg. staff Presbyn.-Univ. Hosp., 1953-98; Univ. prof. Allegheny U. Health Scis., 1998—; mem. cons. staff Children's Hosp., Pitts., Magee-Women's Hosp., VA Hosp., Pitts.; chmn. Nat. Surg. Adjuvant Breast and Bowel Project, 1967-94, sci. dir., 1995—; chmn. Adjuvant Therapy Ctr., 1973-94, Breast Care and Diagnostic Ctr., 1980-93, Pitts. Cancer Inst., 1985—, Comprehensive Breast Care Ctr., 1992—; mem. spl. del. to China, 1977; mem. President's Cancer Panel, 1979-82, Nat. Cancer Adv. Bd., 1986-92, Inst. Medicine of NAS. Mem. edit. bd. Transplantation, 1966-71, Cancer, 1969-73, 75, Year Book of Cancer, 1973-85, Internat. Jour. Radiation Oncology Biology Physics, 1975-78, Cancer Clin. Trials, 1977, Invasion and Metastasis, 1981-85, Cancer Metastasis Revs., 1981-85, Jour. Clin. Oncology, 1982-87, Internat. Jour. Breast and Mammary Pathology, 1982-84, Cancer Rsch., 1976, Seminars in Oncology, 1979, Breast Cancer Rsch. and Treatment, 1980, 92—, Clin. and Exptl. Metastasis, 1980-94, Breast Diseases: Yr. Book Quar., 1989-95, Annals Surg. Oncology, 1993-96, Internat. Jour. Oncology, 1993-94, Advances in Oncology, 1992—, Breast Disease: Internat. Jour., 1993—, Cancer Jour., 1994—, Internat. Jour. Cancer, 1994—, European Jour. Cancer, 1995-97; contbr. over 500 articles to med. jours. Recipient Man of yr. award in medicine Pitts. Jr. C. of C., 1966, Philip Hench Disting. Alumnus award U. Pitts. Sch. Medicine, 1976, McGraw medal Detroit surg. Assn., 1978, Lucy Wortham James Clin. Rsch. award, 1981, Heath Meml. award, 1982, Joseph H. Morton Meml. award, 1983, Julia Hudson Freund Meml. award, 1983, Albert Lasker Med. rsch. award, 1985, Hammer Cancer prize 1988, Am. Cancer Soc. Medal of Honor, 1986, Milken Med. Found. Ctr. Rsch. award, 1989, Assn. Commn. Cancer Ctrs. award, 1990, Chancellors Dist. Rsch. award U. Pitts., 1992, Nat. Health Couns. Med. Rsch. award, 1992, Brinker Internat. Breast Cancer award 1992, Durham N.C. City of Medicine award, 1992, Dr. Josef Steiner Cancer Rsch. prize, 1992, GM Cancer Rsch. Found. Kettering prize, 1993, Susan Komen Found. Sci. Distinction award, 1988, Bristol-Myers Squib award, 1993, James Ewing Lectr. award SSO, 1993, Gottlieb Meml. award, 1993, Sheen award, 1993, Claude Jacquillet award, 1995, Lifetime Achievement award in Breast Cancer Rsch., Senologic Internat. Soc., 1996; Markle scholar in med. sci. John and Mary Markle Found., 1953-58; Alpha Omega Alpha, 1989, Fisher Breast Cancer lectureship established in his honor U. Pitts., 1989. Fellow AAAS; mem. AAUP, ACS, Assn. Cancer Edn., Am. Assn. Cancer Research (bd. dirs.), Am. Soc. Clin. Oncology (pres. 1992-93, bd. dirs., Karnofsky award 1980), Am.

Physiol. Soc., Assn. Am. Med. Colls., Cell Kinetic Soc., Am. Surg. Assn. (v.p. 1996), N.Y. Acad. Scis., Soc. Surg. Oncology, Soc. Univ. Surgeons, Am. Socs. for Exptl. Biology, Pa. Med. Soc., Allegheny County Med. Soc. (Man of Yr. award 1983), Pitts. Acad. Medicine, Pitts. Surg. Soc. (pres. 1979), Peruvian Acad. Surgery (hon.), Italian Surg. Research Assn., Assn. Italiana per la Divulgaxione Sci. della Cancerologia Clinica, Internat. Assn. Breast Cancer Research, Am. Italian Fedn. Cancer Research, Phi Beta Kappa. Office: Allegheny U of Health Scis 4 Allegheny Ctr Ste 602 Pittsburgh PA 15212-5234*

FISHER, BRUCE DAVID, elementary school educator; b. Long Beach, Calif., Dec. 24, 1949; s. Oran Wilfred and Irene (May) F.; m. Mindi Beth Evans, Aug. 15, 1976; 1 child, Jenny Allison Viola. BA, Humboldt State U., 1975, standard elem. credential, 1976, learning handicapped credential, 1977. Instrnl. svcs. specialist Blue Lake (Calif.) Elem. Sch.; resource specialist Fortuna (Calif.) Union Sch. Dist., tchr. 3d grade, tchr. 5th grade, 1988—; prof. Humboldt State U., 1996—; sci. cons. Pitsco, 1995; cons. Newton's Apple, 1995-97, NASA, 1995; site leader tchr., cons., 1998-99, curriculum writer Calif. Sci. Internet, 1995-97; cons. U.S. Forest Svc., 1999; mem. J.P.L./NASA/Johns Hopkins U. Core Curriculum Devel. Team Project KidSat and CASOE; mem. ednl. adv. bd. Calif. Dairy Coun., 1998-99, advisor, 1998; rep. Calif. Tech. Assistance Project, 1998; mem. Calif. Ski Industry and U.S. Forest Svc. Vice chmn. Tchrs. Edn. and Cmty. Helpers, Arcata, Calif., 1990—; v.p. Sequoia Pk. Zool. Soc., Eureka, 1989-90, chmn. Whale Fair, 1989—; mem. selection com. Christa McAuliffe Fellowship; bd. dirs. Redwood Environ. Edn. Fair, Eureka, 1990—, Family Wellness Project, 1991; apptd. to Calif. Curriculum and Supplemental Materials Commn.; commr. Calif. Curriculum Commn., 1992-95; chairperson math. assessment Calif. Dept. Edn., 1995; cons. PITSCO Sci., 1995, NASA/JPL, 1995-97; mem. NASA/JPL and Johns Hopkins U. CORE Curriculum Devel. Team, 1995-96; lead tchr. KidSat and CASDE projects Calif. Sci. Internat. Site. Named Calif. Tchr. of Yr. Dept. Edn., 1991, Favorite Tchrs. ABC-TV, 1991, Humboldt County Tchr. of Yr., 1991; recipient Leadership Excellence award Calif. Assn. Sci. Specialists, 1990, Masonic Meritorious Svc. award for Pub. Edn., 1991, Profl. Best Leadership award Learning Mag., Oldsmobile Corp., and Mich. State U., 1991, Nat. Educator award Miliken Found. Calif. State Dept. Edn., 1991, NASA/NSTA Newest award, 1993, Newton's Apple Multimedia Inst., 1995, Lifetime Achievement award Humboldt County Bd. Edn., 1996. Mem. Calif. Tchrs. Assn., Calif. Sci. Tchrs. Assn., Calif. Assn. Health, Phys. Edn., Recreation, and Dance. Democrat. Avocations: whale watching, curriculum development, photography, sports, aviation, travel. Home: 4810 14th St Arcata CA 95519-9778 Office: Fortuna Elem Sch 843 L St Fortuna CA 95540-1997

FISHER, CALVIN DAVID, food manufacturing company executive; b. Nerstrand, Minn., June 10, 1926; s. Edward and Sadie (Wolf) F.; m. Patricia Vivian Capriotti, July 28, 1950; children: Cynthia, Nancy Joann, Michael. BS, U. Minn., 1950. Dairy specialist U.S. Dept. Agr., Mpls., 1950-54; chemist and dairy specialist U.S. Dept. Agr., Omaha, 1954-58; with Roberts Dairy Co., Omaha, 1958-80; sr. v.p., chief operating officer Roberts Dairy Co., 1967-70, pres., chief exec. officer, 1970-80, owner, chief exec. officer, 1975-80; owner, chief exec. officer Fisher Foods Ltd., Lincoln, Nebr., 1980—; pres., dir. Master Dairies, Indpls., 1968-80; bd. dirs. Internat. Assn. Ice Cream Mfrs. Milk Industry Found., 1973-80. Bd. dirs., v.p. Omaha Safety Council, 1981; bd. dirs. Arthritis Found., 1972-81; mem. adv. council SBA; bd. dirs. Nebr. State Patrol Found., 1990—. With USN, 1944-47. Mem. Omaha C. of C. (pres.'s coun. 1976, 78), Internat. Food Scientists Assn., Inst. Food Tech., Nat. Ind. Dairies Assn., Rotary, Univ. Club (Lincoln), Firethorn Country Club. Republican. Methodist. Patentee spray-dried ice cream mix, pasteurized egg products. Home: University Towers 128 N 13th St Ste 1001 Lincoln NE 68508-1501 Office: Fisher Foods Ltd 220 S 20th St Lincoln NE 68510-1007

FISHER, CARRIE FRANCES, actress, writer; b. Beverly Hills, CA, Oct. 21, 1956; d. Eddie Fisher and Debbie Reynolds; m. Paul Simon, 1983 (div. 1984); 1 child, Billie Catherine. Ed. high sch., Beverly Hills, Calif.; student, London Cen. Sch. Speech and Drama. Mem. chorus in Broadway musical Irene, 1972, also in Broadway prodn. Censored Scenes from King Kong; appeared in films Shampoo, 1975, Star Wars, 1977, Mr. Mike's Mondo Video, 1979, The Blues Brothers, 1980, The Empire Strikes Back, 1980, Under the Rainbow, 1981, Return of the Jedi, 1983, Garbo Talks, 1984, The Man with One Red Shoe, 1985, Hannah and Her Sisters, 1986, Hollywood Vice Squad, 1986, Amazon Women on the Moon, 1987, Appointment With Death, 1988, When Harry Met Sally..., 1989, The 'Burbs, 1989, Loverboy, 1989, She's Back, 1989, Sibling Rivalry, 1990, Drop Dead Fred, 1991, Soapdish, 1991, This Is My Life, 1992, Austin Powers: International Man Of Mystery, 1997; TV movies include Come Back, Little Sheba, (spl.) 1977, Leave Yesterday Behind, 1978, Liberty, Sunday Drive, 1986, Sweet Revenge, 1990; TV series Leaving L.A., 1997; author: Postcards from the Edge, 1987, (also screenplay, 1990), Surrender the Pink, 1990, Delusions of Grandma, 1994. *

FISHER, CHAMPE ANDREWS, lawyer; b. Brockton, Mass., Aug. 22, 1928; s. Frederick G. and Genevieve M. (Clark) F.; m. Patricia Helms, Apr. 16, 1951; children: Candace, Champe Andrews, Sarah, Karen. BA, Yale U., 1950; JDS, Harvard U., 1955. Bar: Mass. 1955. Assoc. Ropes & Gray, Boston, 1955-67, ptnr., 1967-97, of counsel, 1997—. Trustee West Suburban YMCA. Served to capt. USMC, 1950-55. Mem. ABA, Boston Bar Assn., Brae Burn Country Club, Downtown Club (bd. govs.). Republican. Congregationalist. Home: 43 Prince St Newton MA 02465-2610 Office: Ropes & Gray 1 International Pl Boston MA 02110-2602*

FISHER, CHARLES HAROLD, chemistry educator, researcher; b. Hiawatha, W.Va., Nov. 20, 1906; s. Lawrence D. and Mary (Akers) F.; m. Elizabeth Dye, Nov. 4, 1933 (dec. 1967); m. Lois Carlin, July 1968 (dec. June 1990); m. Elizabeth Snyder Kiser, Nov. 29, 1991. BS in Chemistry, Roanoke Coll., 1928, ScD (hon.), 1963; MS in Chemistry, U. Ill., 1929, PhD, 1932; DSc (hon.), Tulane U., 1953. Tchg. asst. in chemistry U. Ill., Urbana, 1928-32; instr. Harvard U., 1932-35; rsch. group leader U.S. Bur. Mines, Pitts., 1935-40; head carbohydrate divsn. Ea. Regional Rsch. Ctr. USDA, 1940-50; dir. So. mktg. and nutrition rsch. div. So. Regional Rsch. Ctr., USDA, New Orleans, 1950-72; adj. rsch. prof. Roanoke Coll., Salem, Va., 1972-99, resigned, 1999; established The Elizabeth Snyder Fisher Scholarship, Roanoke Coll., 1992. Co-author: Profiles of Eminent American Chemists, 1988; contbr. over 200 articles to profl. jours. Co-inventor 72 patents. Pres. New Orleans Sci. Fair, 1967-69; bd. dirs. Salem Hist. Soc., 1982-85, Salem Ednl. Found., 1991—; established Lawrence D. and Mary A. Fisher Scholarship Roanoke Coll., 1978, Lois Carlin Fisher Scholarship, 1991. Recipient So. Chemists award, 1956, Herty medal, 1959, Chem. Pioneer award Am. Inst. Chemists, 1966; named Polymer Science Pioneer, 1981, Roanoke Coll. medal, 1996; named to Hall of Fame, Salem Ednl. Found., 1996; The Charles H. Fisher Lecture established in his honor Roanoke Coll., 1990. Mem. AAAS, Am. Inst. Chemists (hon., pres. 1962-63, chmn. bd. dirs., Presdl. citation of merit, 1986), Oil Chem. Soc., Am. Chem. Soc. (dir. region IV 1969-71), Chemurgic Coun. (dir.), Am. Assn. Textile Chemists and Colorists, Hidden Valley Country Club (Salem, Va.), Cosmos Club (Washington), Internat. House, Round Table Club (New Orleans); Chemists Club (N.Y.C.). Achievements include co-invention of acrylic rubber. *I have worked hard as a physical scientist and research administrator because research is fun and offers the best way of benefiting humankind.*

FISHER, CHARLES PAGE, JR., consulting geotechnical engineer; b. Richmond, Va., Sept. 24, 1921; s. Charles Page and Annie Laura (Wright) F.; m. Joyce Mayo Ison, Dec. 23, 1972. B.S.C.E., U. Va., 1949; S.M., Harvard U., 1950; Ph.D., N.C. State U., 1962. Registered profl. engr., Md., Va., N.C., S.C., Tenn. Instr. to assoc. prof. civil engring. N.C. State U., Raleigh, 1955-69; pres. Geotech. Engring. Co., Research Triangle Park, N.C., 1963-78; prin. C. Page Fisher Cons. Engr., Durham, N.C., 1978—; corp. sec. Troxler Electronics Labs., Research Triangle Park, N.C., 1961—. Served with USN, 1941-45. Fellow Am. Cons. Engrs. Council, ASCE; mem. ASTM, Nat. Soc. Profl. Engrs., Am. Arbitration Assn., Internat. Soc. Soil Mechanics and Found. Engring., Cons. Engrs. Council N.C. Address: 2534 1/2 Chapel Hill Rd Durham NC 27707-1463 Office: PO Box 51968 Durham NC 27717-1968

FISHER, CHARLES WORLEY, editor; b. Phila., July 30, 1917; s. Charles Worley and Emily (Kohler) F.; m. Mary McCain Wilcox, Nov. 28, 1941; children: Linda Fisher Eveland, Mary Emily Fisher Vigna, Charles Worley Jr., Anthony Hay, Lisa McCain Fisher Brown. Grad., Mercersburg Acad., 1935; student, Haverford Coll., 1936-40. ETO 9th Infantry Div., 1942-45; div. spl. svc. officer, 1945; With Benton & Bowles, Inc., N.Y.C., 1946-65; dir. daytime radio programs, 1948-52, dir. TV programs, 1951-56. Producer: (TV shows) As the World Turns, 1956-60, The Edge of Night, 1960-65, Another World, 1965, Hidden Faces, 1970; editor: Hagerstown (Md.) Town & Country Almanack, 1973—; co-author, dir.: (motion picture) Washington Crossing the Delaware, 1967; co-producer: Taconic Music Theatre, Manchester, Vt., 1988-89; freelance theatrical dir., audio-visual cons. TV cons. Trenton (N.J.) Bd. Edn., 1972-81; advisor Friends of Hildene, Manchester, Vt., 1985-89; actor Oldcastle Theatre Co., Bennington, Vt., 1987-88, Williamstown Theatre Festival, 1993, 94, 95, 97; performing arts chair So. Vt. art Ctr., Manchester, 1989-93. Home: 132 Trout Run Arlington VT 05250-8862 Office: Gruber Almanack Co PO Box 609 Hagerstown MD 21741-0609 *How many of us have missed a golden opportunity because we lacked the courage to attempt what we believed was the impossible and consequently never achieved our highest level of ability?.*

FISHER, CHESTER LEWIS, JR., retired lawyer; b. Maplewood, N.J., May 30, 1911; s. Chester Lewis and Katherine Barton (Riddle) F.; m. Grace Annette Tainsh, Nov. 23, 1943; children: Chester Lewis III, Jane Alison Swiggett. Grad., Mercersburg Acad., 1929; A.B., Princeton U., 1933; J.D., Cornell U., 1936. Bar: N.Y. 1937, P.I. 1945, N.J. 1947, U.S. Supreme Ct 1972. Instr. phys. edn. Cornell U., 1933-36; practiced law N.Y.C., 1936-39; atty. Met. Life Ins. Co., 1939-57, asst. v.p., asst. to pres. and chmn., 1957-60, 3d v.p., 1960-63, 2d v.p., 1963-65, v.p., 1965-76. Village trustee Briarcliff Manor, N.Y., 1969-71, mayor, 1971-77. Served from 1st lt. to col. USAAF, 1940-46. Decorated Legion of Merit. Mem. Assn. Life Ins. Counsel (past pres.), SAR. Episcopalian. Home: 5622 Boatwright Cir Williamsburg VA 23185-3799

FISHER, CHRISTINE S., music educator. BA cum laude, Pembroke State U., 1975; M in Music Edn., U. S.C., 1980. Tchr. 10-12 Dillon H.S., 1975-78; K-6 music tchr., band tchr. McKenzie, Timrod, Bonaire & TansBay Elem., 1978-84; tchr. 7-8 Southside Mid. Sch., 1984-97; 7-8 grade band tchr. Southside Mis. Sch., 1998—. Clarinet Florence Symph. Orch., bd. dirs.; bd. dirs. Cmty. Concert Assn., S.C. Arts Alliance; chairperson Pee Dee Tchr. Forum. Named S.C. Tchr. of Yr., 1998, State Honor Roll Tchr. 1993; recipient numerous grants. Mem. Palmetto State Tchrs. Assn., Music Educators Nat. Conf., S.C. Music Educators Assn., S.C. Band Dirs. Assn., Pi Beta Mu. Avocations: playing clarinet, traveling. Home: 1918 Effies Ln Florence SC 29505

FISHER, CLARKSON SHERMAN, JR., judge; b. Red Bank, N.J., Nov. 29, 1952; s. Clarkson Sherman and Mae Shannon (Hoffmann) F.; m. Carolyn Ann Sullivan, Aug. 27, 1977; children: Clarkson Sherman III, Caylan S., Cilloran S. BA, Villanova (Pa.) U., 1974; JD, Seton Hall U., 1977. Bar: U.S. Dist. Ct. N.J. 1977, N.J. 1978, U.S. Ct. Appeals (3d cir.) 1979, U.S. Ct. Appeals (2d and 5th cirs.) 1983, U.S. Supreme Ct. 1983, N.Y. 1984, U.S. Dist. Ct. (so. and ea. dists.) N.Y., 1984, U.S. Ct. Appeals (4th cir.) 1984. Law clk. N.J. Superior Ct., Newark, 1977-78; assoc. Robinson, Wayne & Greenberg, Newark, 1978-82; assoc. Evans, Koelzer, Osborne & Kreizman, Red Bank, 1982-85, ptnr., 1985-86; ptnr. Ober, Kaler, Grimes & Shriver, Edison, N.J., 1986-93; judge Superior Ct. N.J., Freehold, 1993-97; presiding judge Superior Ct. Chancery Divsn., Freehold, 1997—. Mem. ABA, N.J. Bar Assn., Maritime Law Assn. Democrat. Roman Catholic. Home: 116 Bridgewaters Dr Oceanport NJ 07757-1316 Office: Monmouth County Court Freehold NJ 07728

FISHER, D. MICHAEL, state attorney general; b. Pitts., Nov. 7, 1944; s. C. Francis and Dolores (Darby) F.; m. Carol Hudak, Aug. 9, 1973; children: Michelle Lynn, Brett Michael. AB, Georgetown U., 1966; JD, Georgetown Law Ctr., 1969. Bar: Pa. 1970. Asst. dist. atty. Allegheny County, Pitts., 1970-74; rep. Pa. Ho. of Reps., Harrisburg, 1974-80; mem. Pa. Senate, Harrisburg, 1980-96; ptnr. Houston Harbaugh, Pitts., from 1984; atty. gen. Commonwealth of Pa., Harrisburg, 1997—; chmn. House Subcom. on Crime and Corrections, 1979-80, Senate Environ. Resources & Energy, 1981-90, Senate Majority Policy Com., 1988-90, Senate Rep. Caucus, 1992—; vice-chmn. Senate Jud. Com., 1981-90; elected Majority Whip, 1990. Author numerous reports. Rep. candidate for lt. gov. Pa., 1986; mem. Pa. Gov.'s Energy Coun., 1981-86, Pa. Energy Devel. Authority, 1984-86, Environ. Quality Bd., 1980-90, Pa. Commn. on Crime and Delinquency, 1979—; del. Rep. Nat. Conv., 1988, 92. Named Man of Yr. Upper St. Clair Rep. Club, 1980, Outstanding Young Man Am., 1977-79, Man of Yr. Vector's Law & Govt., 1991. Mem. Pa. Bar Assn., Elks, Am. Legion, Bethel Park Chamber, Rotary. Roman Catholic. Avocations: golf, hockey, football. Office: Atty Gen Strawberry Sq 16th fl Harrisburg PA 17120*

FISHER, DALE DUNBAR, animal scientist, dairy nutritionist; b. Lewisburg, Pa., Feb. 13, 1945; s. Glenn Murray and Elsie May (Bryson) F.; divorced; children: Elsie Maria, Maria Vanessa. *Daughter Elsie Maria Fisher, Bachelor in Economics degree 1995 University of Costa Rica (UCR), is currently employed as the Credit Manager of Banco Bantec CQ, S.A. Daughter Maria Vanessa Fisher, Law and Notary Public degree 1996 UCR and Specialist in Agrarian and Environmental Law degree 1998 UCR, is currently presiding as the regional judge, Agrarian Tribunal of the Costa Rican Judicial Power, Ciudad Quesada. Both daughters have previously completed the advanced oral and written English curriculum of the American-Costa Rican Cultural Center, San Jose. Since birth, the two daughters have held dual U.S./Costa Rican citizenship.* BS in Animal Sci., Pa. State U., 1967, MS in Animal Industry, 1978, PhD in Animal Industry, 1980. Cert. nutrition specialist; lic. dietitian-nutritionist, N.Y. Vol. animal husbandry Peace Corps, Ciudad Quesada, Costa Rica, 1967-71; area animal husbandry-pasture specialist Costa Rican Ministry of Agr., Ciudad Quesada, 1971-73; vis. scientist Internat. Ctr. for Tropical Agr., Cali, Colombia, 1973-75; animal nutritionist Co-op. Feed Dealers, Inc., Chenango Bridge, N.Y., 1981—. Contbr. articles to profl. jours. Eva B. and G. Weidman Groff Meml. scholar Pa. State U., 1979. Mem. Am. Soc. Animal Sci., Am. Dairy Sci. Assn., Am. Soc. Agronomy, Am. Acad. Vet. Nutrition, N.Y. Acad. Scis., Am. Coll. Nutrition, Sigma Xi, Phi Kappa Phi, Gamma Sigma Delta. Democrat. Avocations: jogging, reading. Home: 578 Chenango St Binghamton NY 13901-2134 Office: Coop Feed Dealers Inc PO Box 670 Chenango Bridge NY 13745-0610

FISHER, DALE JOHN, chemist, instrumentation and medical diagnostic device investigator; b. Omro, Wis., June 4, 1925; m. Ruth J. Laird, Apr. 27, 1957; 1 dau., Shelley Dale. B.S., U. Wis., Oshkosh, 1947; Ph.D. (Univ. fellow), Ind. U., 1951. Staff mem. Inst. Paper Chemistry, Appleton, Wis., summer 1945; chemist City of Oshkosh, Wis., summers 1946-48; chemist ionic analyses group Oak Ridge Nat. Lab., 1951-52, group leader analytical instrumentation group, 1952-72, mem. dir.'s staff, 1972-73; physicist (nuclear medicine) VA Hosp., Gainesville, Fla., 1973-74; tech. dir. nuclear medicine VA Hosp., 1974-76; grad. studies faculty U. Fla., Gainesville, 1974-76; physicist FDA, 1976-91, physicist div. in vitro diagnostic device standards, 1976-83, physicist Office Sci. and Tech., div. life scis., health scis. br., 1983-91; ret., 1991. Recipient Disting. Alumni award U. Wis., Oshkosh, 1982. Mem. Am. Chem. Soc. (nat. award chem. instrumentation), ASTM, Sigma Xi, Phi Lambda Upsilon. Design and new applications of instrument systems and methods for analysis, process monitoring and research; creation electronic and mechanical designs and administration of research. Patentee in field. Research with computer-based nuclear medicine imaging instrumentation for the improvement of patient care. Development of med. device standards and performance requirements. Establish sci. basis for med. diagnostic and clin. lab. instruments. Improve safety and effectiveness of medical devices through toxicology and statistics research. Home: 6319 Golden Hook Columbia MD 21044-3710

FISHER, DARRYL, information services company executive. COO bus. info. svcs. Lexis-Nexis, Miamisburg, Ohio, until 1998; pres., CEO Reed Tech. Info. Svcs., Horsham, Pa., 1998—. Office: Reed Tech Info Svcs 1 Progress Dr Horsham PA 19044*

FISHER, DAVID BRUCE, land development executive; b. Glen Cove, N.Y., Oct. 22, 1954; s. David James and Margaret Virginia (Peters) F.; m. Janice Katherine Patterson, Oct. 25, 1980; children: Courtney Elizabeth, David Robert. BA in Geology, Susquehanna U., 1976; M in Cmty. Planning, U. Cin., 1979. Lic. profl. planner, N.J. Dir. environ. affairs and planning N.J. Builders Assn., Plainsboro, 1979-81, 83-87; project planner Ernst, Ernst & Lissenden, Toms River, N.J., 1981-83; v.p. forward planning N.J. div. Leisure Tech., Inc., Lakewood, N.J., 1987-91; dir. regulatory affairs, prin. planner Ernst, Ernst & Lissenden, Toms River, 1991-92; v.p. devel. Sammis Co./Gale & Wentworth, Florham Park, N.J., 1992-93; v.p. land devel. Matzel & Mumford Orgn., Hazlet, N.J., 1993—. Chmn. N.J. Clean Water Coun., Trenton, 1985-89; mem. Citizen Com. of Permit Coord., Trenton, 1986-97; mem. N.J. Dept. Wetlands Adv. Com., Trenton, 1987—; coach Toms River Soccer Assn., 1989-95; mem. vestry St. Raphael's Episcopal Ch., Brick, N.J., 1989-93; officer N.J. Shore Builders Assn., 1993—, pres., 1998—. Recipient Bus. Watch award Bus. Jour. N.J., Vol. 5, No. 5, 1988. Mem. Am. Planning Assn. (chartered), Am. Inst. Cert. Planners, N.J. Builders Assn. (bd. dirs. 1997—). Avocations: skiing, tennis, soccer. Office: Matzel & Mumford Orgn 100 Village Ct Hazlet NJ 07730-1546

FISHER, DEENA KAYE, social studies education, administrator; b. Elk City, Okla., Dec. 20, 1950; d. Earl Dean and Rosa Lee (Stone) Music; m. Mike Fleck, May 29, 1970 (div. June 1988); children: DeeAnna Michelle, Carrie Denise, William Michael; m. Tom Fisher, Nov. 13, 1993; 1 stepchild, Eleni. BA in Edn.-Social Sci., Southwestern Okla. State U., 1979, MEd in Social Sci., 1983, MEd in Sch. Counseling, 1987; postgrad., U. Okla., 1980. Instr. in social sci. Cordell (Okla.) H.S., 1979-85; instr. in social sci. El Reno (Okla.) C.C., 1985-88, Upward Bound guidance and career counselor, instr., 1987-89; instr. Am. History Yukon (Okla.) H.S., 1986-87; instr. polit. sci. and Am. history Southwestern Okla. State U., 1987-89; chair dept. Am. history, instr. Am. govt. Woodward (Okla.) H.S., 1989-96; instr. social studies Northwestern Okla. State U., Alva, 1989—; dir. Woodward campus Northwestern Okla. State U., 1996—. Author ednl. materials in field. Del. Dem. Nat. Conv., Okla. Dem. Party, Chgo., 1996; law day coord. Okla. Bar Assn., Woodward, 1990-96; regional coord. Citizen Bee, Tulsa World, 1994-97; panelist U.S. History Nat. Assessment of Ednl. Progress, St. Louis, 1994. Recipient Outstanding Am. History Tchr. award Okla. Soc. DAR, 1993, Tchr. of Yr. award Okla. Supreme Ct., 1992; Bill of Rights Edn. Collaborative grantee, 1991. Mem. Nat. Coun. for Social Studies (ho. dels., co-chmn. resolution com. 1996), Okla. Social Studies Suprs.' Assn. (membership bd. 1997), Okla. Coun. for Social Studies (del.-at-large 1996, pres. 1994-96), Woodward Edn. Assn. (pres. 1996), Woodward C. of C. (mem. edn. com. 1997), Delta Kappa Gamma (pres. Psi chpt. 1996-98). Mem. Christian Ch. (Disciples of Christ). Avocations: reading, chess. Home: 3308 Bent Creek Dr Woodward OK 73801-6931 Office: Northwestern Okla State U Woodward Campus PO Box 1046 Woodward OK 73802-1046

FISHER, DELBERT ARTHUR, physician, educator; b. Placerville, Calif., Aug. 12, 1928; s. Arthur Lloyd and Thelma (Johnson) F.; m. Beverly Carne Fisher, Jan. 28, 1951; children: David Arthur, Thomas Martin, Mary Kathryn. BA, U. Calif., Berkeley, 1950; MD, U. Calif., San Francisco, 1953. Diplomate Am. Bd. Pediat. (examiner 1971-80, mem. subcom. on pediat. endocrinology 1976-79). Intern, resident in pediat. U. Calif. Med. Ctr., San Francisco, 1953-55; resident in pediat. U. Oreg. Hosp., Portland, 1957-58; from asst. prof. to assoc. prof. pediat. Med. Sch. U. Ark., Little Rock, 1960-67, prof. pediat., 1967-68; prof. pediat. UCLA, 1968-73, prof. pediat. and medicine Med. Sch., 1973-91, prof. emeritus, 1991—; chief, pediat. endocrinology Harbor-UCLA Med. Ctr., 1968-75, rsch. prof. devel. and perinatal biology, 1975-85, chmn. pediat., 1985-89, sr. scientist Rsch. and Edn. Inst., 1991—; dir. Walter Martin Rsch. Ctr., 1986-91; pres. Nichols Inst. Reference Labs, San Juan Capistrano, Calif., 1991-93; pres. acad. assocs., chief sci. officer Nichols Inst., San Juan Capistrano, Calif., 1993-94; pres. acad. assocs., chief sci. officer Quest Diagnostics-Nichols Inst., San Juan Capistrano, Calif., 1994-97, sr. sci. officer, 1997-98, chief sci. officer, 1999—; cons. genetic disease sect. Calif. Dept. Health Svcs., 1978-98; cons. genetic disease sect. Calif. Dept. Dept. Health Svcs., 1978—; mem. organizing com. Internat. Conf. Newborn Thyroid Screening, 1977-88. Co-editor: Pediatric Thyroidology, 1985, 7 other books; editor-in-chief Jour. Clin. Endocrinology and Metabolism, 1978-83, Pediat. Rsch., 1984-89; contbr. chpts. to numerous books, over 500 articles to profl. jours. Capt. M.C., USAF, 1955-57. Recipient Career Devel. award NIH, 1964-68. Mem. Inst. Medicine NAS, Am. Acad. Pediat. (Borden award 1981), Soc. Pediat. Rsch. (v.p. 1973-74), Am. Pediat. Soc. (pres. 1992-93), Endocrine Soc. (pres. 1983-84, Williams Leadership award 1998)), Am. Thyroid Assn. (pres. 1988-89), Am. Soc. Clin. Investigation, Assn. Am. Physicians, Lawson Wilkins Pediatric Endocrine Soc. (pres. 1982-83), Western Soc. Pediat. Rsch. (pres. 1983-84), Phi Beta Kappa, Alpha Omega Alpha. Home: 24582 Santa Clara Ave Dana Point CA 92629-3031 Office: Quest Diagnostics-Nichols Inst 33608 Ortega Hwy San Juan Capistrano CA 92675-2042

FISHER, DENISE BUTTERFIELD, marketing executive; b. San Diego; d. Wyartt Grant and Therese Marie (Hoffman) Butterfield; m. Paul Elliott Fisher, June 15, 1985 (div. Dec. 1997). BS, Old Dominion U., 1978; MA, U. Va., 1984. Cert. Mktg. Prof. Environ. planner Rappahannock Area Devel. Commn., Fredericksburg, Va., 1978-80; grants coord. Va. State Water Control Bd., Richmond, 1980-81, project mgr., 1981-83; mgmt. analyst City of Newport News, Va., 1984-88; intergovtl. rels. mgr. City of Newport News, 1988-91; mktg. mgr. Malcolm Pirnie, Inc., Newport News, 1991—, assoc., 1997—; cons. Va. State Water Control Bd., Virginia Beach, 1984. Contbr. articles to profl. jours. Chmn. United Way Campaign, Newport News, 1985, 86, 87; v.p. North Suffolk Cir. Children's Hosp. of King's Daus., Suffolk, Va., 1989, 90; mem. Va. Choral Soc., 1998—; trustee Peninsula Fine Arts Ctr., 1999—. Recipient Betty Crocker Homemaker of Am. award Gen. Mills, 1972; tuition scholar Old Dominion U., 1973, Wallerstein scholar Va. Mcpl. League, U. Va., 1983. Mem. Internat. City Mgmt. Assn., Soc. Mktg. Profl. Svcs., Am. Soc. Pub. Adminstrn. (pres. Hampton Rds. chpt. 1992), Va. Choral Soc. Avocations: cooking, dance, antiques, certified Reiki practitioner. Office: Malcolm Pirnie Inc 11832 Rock Landing Rd Ste 400 Newport News VA 23606-4278

FISHER, DON CARLTON, toxicologist; b. May 13, 1954. BS, Okla. State U., 1985; MD, U. Okla., Tulsa, 1979; MS, U. Ariz., 1984. Diplomate Am. Bd. Preventive Medicine, Am. Bd. Toxicology. Intern family practice U. Okla., 1980-82; resident in family practice and occupl. medicine U. Ariz., 1982-84; med. dir. health venture St. Joseph Hosp., Tacoma, 1985-87, Presbyn. Occupl. Health Network, Albuquerque, 1987-98; pvt. practice toxicology and occupl. diseases, Albuquerque, 1998—; asst. clin. prof. toxicology U. N.Mex. E-mail: fishertox@earthlink.net. Office: 6001 Marble NE Ste 13 Albuquerque NM 87110

FISHER, DONALD G., casual apparel chain stores executive; b. 1928; married. B.S., U. Calif., 1950. With M. Fisher & Son, 1950-57; former ptnr. Fisher Property Investment Co.; co-founder, pres. The Gap Stores Inc., San Bruno, Calif., dir., now chmn., founder, 1996—. Office: The Gap Stores 1 Harrison St San Francisco CA 94105-1602

FISHER, DONALD WAYNE, medical association executive; b. Pitts., Mar. 2, 1946; s. David H.W. and Jean K. F.; children by previous marriage—Kimberly Elizabeth, Jeffrey Wayne. A.A., Hinds Jr. Coll., 1966; B.S. in Biology and Chemistry, Millsaps Coll., 1968; M.S. in Anatomy, U. Miss., 1970, Ph.D. in Anatomy, 1973; postgrad. in assn. mgmt., U. Md., 1977-79. Cert. assn. exec. Instr. dept. chemistry and biology Hinds Jr. Coll., Raymond, Miss., 1968-74; instr. dept. anatomy U. Miss. Sch. Medicine, Jackson, 1973-74; co-dir. and exec. officer physician asst. program U. Miss. Sch. Medicine, 1972-74; asst. professorial lectr. George Washington U. Sch. Medicine, 1974—; exec. dir. Assn. Physician Asst. Programs, Arlington, Va., 1974-80, Am. Acad. Physician Assts., Arlington, 1974-80; CEO, Am. Med. Group Assn., Alexandria, Va., 1980—; pres., CEO, Am. Group Practice Corp., Inc., 1989, treas. polit. action com., 1980—; mem. Nat. Commn. on Allied Health Edn., 1977-80; mem. adv. com. for tng., devel. and utilization of physician extenders Systems Scis., Inc., 1975-80; pres. Am. Acad. Physician Assts. Ednl. and Rsch. Found., 1977-80; sec., treas. Am. Group Practice Found., 1980—; mem. Am. Express Health Care Faculty, 1985-88. Robert Wood Johnson Found. grantee, 1973-80. Mem. Am. Soc. Assn. Execs. (govt. rels. com. 1980—), Assn. Am. Med. Colls., AAAS, Am. Internat. Health Alliance (bd. dirs. 1992—, treas. 1995—), Greater Washington

Soc. Assn. Execs., Fairfax County Hosp. Assn., Arlington (Va.) C. of C. Home: 3814 Ivanhoe Ln Alexandria VA 22310-2170 Office: Am Med Group Assn 1422 Duke St Alexandria VA 22314-3403

FISHER, DONALD WIENER, lawyer; b. Sandusky, Ohio, Jan. 27, 1923; s. Albert Livingston and Orpha (Wiener) F.; m. Jeanne Marie Bolan, Oct. 4, 1952; children: Sarah Jeanne Fisher Schmitt, Laura Laskey Fisher Pories (dec.), John Bolan, Andrew Donald, Martha Emily. B.S., Ohio State U., 1947, J.D., 1949. Bar: Ohio 1949, D.C. 1970. Practiced in Toledo, 1949-95; ret., 1995; of counsel Sheet Metal Workers Internat. Assn., 1951-95. Served with AUS, 1943-45, PTO. Mem. D.C. Bar Assn., Toledo Bar Assn. Home: 2926 Talmadge Rd Toledo OH 43606-2251

FISHER, EARL MONTY, utilities executive; b. Chgo., June 26, 1938; s. Harry George and Fannie (Feinberg) F.; m. Joyce Leah Bender, Mar. 14, 1959 (div. Dec. 1978); children: Jan Carol, Wendy Robin; m. Teri Jean Janssen, Jan. 27, 1979. Student, La. Trade Tech. Coll., 1961. Apprentice and journeyman Comfort Air Refrigeration Corp., L.A., 1955-64; contractor Bonanza Air Conditioning and Refrigeration Corp., Van Nuys, Calif., 1964—. Bd. dirs. Hidden Hills (Calif.) Homeowners Assn., 1982-84, vice chmn., v.p., 1990; chmn. Hidden Hills Rds. Com., 1984-85, Hidden Hills Gate Ops. Commn., 1988-91; commr. emergency svcs. City of Hidden Hills, 1986—; pres. Hidden Hills Cmty. Assn., 1991-93; mem. Hidden Hills City Coun., 1994, 99—; mayor City of Hidden Hills, 1996-98. Mem. Air Conditioning Sheet Metal Assn. (vice chmn. 1994-96, dir. 1996—). Democrat. Avocations: scale model aircraft, horses. Office: Bonanza Air Conditioning Heating & Refrigeration Co 7653 Burnet Ave Van Nuys CA 91405-1081

FISHER, EDWARD ABRAHAM, cardiologist, educator; b. Honolulu, Apr. 30, 1958; s. Hyman Wendell and Rosalie (Joseph) F.; m. Vivian Degenszejn, Mar. 27, 1993; children: Rebecca, Alexander. BA in Econs., U. Va., 1980; MD, Ea. Va. Med. Sch., 1984. Diplomate Nat. Bd. Med. Examiners, Am. Bd. Internal Medicine, Am. Bd. Cardiovascular Disease; lic. physician, N.Y. Intern Lenox Hill Hosp., N.Y.C., 1984-85, resident, 1985-87, adj. attending physician dept. medicine, 1987—; cardiology fellow Mt. Sinai Med. Ctr., N.Y.C., 1987-89, cardiology rsch. fellow, 1989-90, clin. asst. dept. medicine, 1990, asst. dir. echocardiography dept. medicine divsn. cardiology, 1990—; asst. attending Mt. Sinai Sch. Medicine, N.Y.C., 1990-92, asst. clin. prof., 1992-97, assoc. clin. prof., assoc. attending, 1997—. Co-author: Effects of Estrogen and Progesterone on Blood Vessels, 1991, Restrictive Cardiomyopathy, 1996, Native Aortic Valve Endocarditis, 1996; author numerous articles concerning transthoracic and transesophageal echocardiography. Fellow ACP, Am. Coll. Cardiology, Am. Heart Assn. Avocation: marathon running. Office: 941 Park Ave New York NY 10028-0318 also: Mt Sinai Med Ctr Cardiovascular Inst #1030 1 Gustave L Levy Pl New York NY 10029-6500

FISHER, ELLEN ROOP, librarian, educator; b. Washington, Dec. 16, 1944; d. Robert Wendell and Katherine (Booth) Roop; m. Allan Campbell Fisher, June 14, 1969; children: Bradford Booth, Katherine Thayer. BA, Smith Coll., Northampton, Mass., 1966; MA, U. Chgo., 1974. Cert. library sci. edn., Pa. Rsch. asst. Indsl. Rels. Ctr. Library, U. Chgo., 1967-68; asst. sys. libr. U. Chgo. Libraries, 1968-71; reference asst. Toledo (Ohio) Pub. Libr., 1972; libr. Cleve. Orch. Chorus Library, 1973-74; reference libr. Harford County Library Sys., Bel Air, Md., 1975; computer tchr. Lawrence Twp. Sch. Dist., Indpls., 1982-84; music tchr. Hegvik Sch. of Music, Wayne, Pa., 1984-86; libr. Edn. Resource Ctr., Cabrini Coll., Wayne, 1986-87; libr. Radnor Twp. Sch. Dist., Wayne, 1987-94, head libr., 1994—. Author: Sources and Nature of Errors in Transcribing Bibliographic Data into Machine Readable Form, 1974; co-author: The University of Chicago Bibliographic Data Processing System, 1970. Singer, Vox, The Renaissance Consort, Radnor, 1991—, Amadeus Ensemble, Radnor, 1991—. La Verne Noyes scholar U Chgo., 1966. Mem. ALA, Am. Assn. Sch. Librs., Am. Recorder Soc., Pa. Sch. Librs. Assn. Unitarian Universalist. Avocation: travel. Home: 215 Poplar Ave Wayne PA 19087-3503 Office: Radnor HS 130 King Of Prussia Rd Radnor PA 19087-5234

FISHER, ESTELLE MAUDE, artist; b. Battle Creek, Mich., Feb. 14, 1913; d. Clyde and Mabel (Blake) Clinefelter; m. Charles Fisher, Jan. 16, 1935; children: Charles, Norman, Virginia. Libr. asst. Coldwater (Mich.) Pub. Libr., 1966-68. Exhbns. include Mich. Art Exhibit, South Bend, Ind., 1987, U. Mich., 1962. Home: 111 Elm St Coldwater MI 49036-2037

FISHER, EUGENE, marketing executive; b. Sept. 30, 1927; s. Morris and Sarah (Edelstein) F.; m. Joline Cobb, July 28, 1956 (dec.); children: Robin Downing, Amy Homer, Douglas; m. Penny Blanchard, Dec. 18, 1988. PhB, U. Chgo., 1945, MBA, 1948. With Brunswick Corp., Lake Forest, Ill., 1955-95; dir. mktg. planning bowling divsn. Brunswick Corp., Lake Forest, 1965-72, dir. corp. mktg. rsch., 1972-87, corp. mktg. dir., 1987-95; pres. Fisher Mktg. Intelligence, Inc., 1982—; guest lectr. in field. Mng. editor Profile Mag., 1988-98; prodr. Chgo. Maritime Festival, 1988-91, Brunswick 150th Anniversary Exhbn., 1995, Chgo. Cultural Ctr. Mem. civic planning com. Ill. State Hist. Soc., 1994—; mem. U. Chgo. Class of 1945 reunion com., 50th reunion dinner chmn., 1995; bd. dirs 2626 Lakeview Condominium Assn., 1995—, pres. 1996—. Mem. Am. Mktg. Assn., Chgo. Maritime Soc. (bd. dirs. 1991-95), Nat. Bowling Coun. (mktg. com. 1975-83), Phi Sigma Delta. Fax: 773-281-0822. Home and Office: Apt 4103 2626 N Lakeview Ave Chicago IL 60614-1832

FISHER, FENIMORE, business development consultant; b. N.Y.C., 1926; s. Benn and Sadie (Cohan) F.; m. Marcia Obler, Nov. 9, 1952; children: Bennett G., Alan L., Karen Soo. BS in Physics, Columbia U., 1951; MBA, U. Pa. 1952. Staff physicist USN Research Lab., Phila., 1951-52; ops. mgr., chief engr. instrument div. Thomas A. Edison Industries, West Orange, N.J., 1952-60; pres. Analogue Controls Inc., Hicksville, N.Y., 1960-67; corp. v.p. IMC Magnetics Corp., Jericho, N.Y., 1967-77, pres., chief exec. officer, 1977-89, also bd. dirs.; chmn. bd. Hansen Mfg. Co. Inc., Princeton Ind., IMC Ariz. Div., Tempe, IMC Fla. Div., Miami Lakes, IMC Tenn. Div., Camden, IMC Tex. Div., Mexia, IMC Western Div., Cerritos, Calif., New Eng. Alloys Inc., Lawrence, Mass., Pacific Propeller Inc., Kent Washington, Universal Magnetics Corp., Cerritos, 1989—; exec. v.p. Synergy Gas Corp., 1989-93; bus. devel. cons., 1993-96; v.p. bus. and fin. Dowling Coll., Oakdale, N.Y., 1996—. Contbr. numerous articles on bus. econs., tech. edn., relation with the Far East. Bd. dirs. L.I. Philharm., West Suffolk YM & YWHA, United Way L.I.; chmn. L.I. Forum for Tech., Suffolk Community Planning Council, Old Westbury Coll. Found.; trustee Dowling Coll. Served to 1st lt. U.S. Army, 1944-46, PTO. Mem. Am. Phys. Soc. Am. Def. Preparedness Assn. Clubs: Pine Hollow Country (East Norwich, N.Y.), Indian Hills Country Club (East Northport, N.Y.). Office: 4 Chatham Pl Dix Hills NY 11746-5412

FISHER, FRANCES, actress; b. Milford-on-Sea, Eng., May 11, 1952; d. William I. and Olga (Moen) F.; 1 child, Francesca Ruth Fisher-Eastwood. Student, Lee Strasberg, Stella Adler, Marilyn Fried, Sandra Seacat, HB Studios. Appearances include (film) Can She Bake a Cherry Pie?, Tough Guys Don't Dance, Patty Hearst, Lost Angels, Pink Cadillac, Welcome Home Roxy Carmichael, L.A. Story, Unforgiven, Baby Fever, The Stars Fell on Henrietta, Female Perversions, Striptease, Wild America, Titanic, (TV) Elysian Fields, Sudie & Simpson, Cold Sassy Tree, Promises to Keep, Lucy & Desi: Before the Laughter, Devlin, Crime and Punishment, Praying Mantis, Attack of the 50 Foot Woman, The Other Mother, Strange Luck, (theater) Cat on a Hot Tin Roof, Hay Fever, The Chain, Desire Under the Elems, Still Life, Ruffian on the Stair, A Midsummer Night's Dream, Hunchback of Notre Dame, Orpheus Descending, The Hitchhikers, Crackwalker, Fool for Love, Three More Sleepless Nights, Jammed, The Big Tease, 1999, True Crime, 1999. Mem. Actors Studio. Home and Office: PO Box 645 Pacific Palisades CA 90272-0645*

FISHER, FRANKLIN MARVIN, economist; b. N.Y.C., Dec. 13, 1934; s. Mitchell Salem and Esther (Oshiver) F.; m. Ellen Jo Paradise, June 22, 1958; children—Abraham Samuel, Abigail Sarah, Naomi Leah. A.B. summa cum laude, Harvard U., 1956, M.A., 1957, Ph.D., 1960. Asst. prof. econs. U. Chgo., 1959-60; asst. prof. econs. MIT, 1960-62, assoc. prof., 1962-65, prof., 1965—; chair Mid. East Water Project, 1992—; cons. various law firms; dir. cons. Charles River Assocs., Inc., chmn. bd. 1997—; bd. mem. Nat. Bur. Econ. Rsch., 1990—, exec. com., 1992—. Editor: Econometrica, 1968-77. Trustee Combined Jewish Philanthropies, Boston, 1975—, bd. mgrs., 1979-92; trustee Beth Israel Hosp., Boston, 1979-97; chmn. faculty adv. cabinet United Jewish Appeal, 1975-77; bd. govs. Tel Aviv U., 1976-92; bd. dirs. New Israel Fund, 1983—, treas., 1984-96, pres. 1996-99; pres. Boston Friends of Peace Now, 1984-85, N.E. region Am. Jewish Congress, 1993-95; chmn. steering com. N.Am. Friends of Peace Now, 1986-88, bd. dirs., treas., 1988-91. NSF fellow, 1962-63; Ford Found. Faculty Research fellow, 1966-67; Guggenheim fellow, 1981-82; Erksine fellow U. Canterbury, N.Z., 1983. Fellow Econometric Soc. (council 1972-76, v.p. 1977-78, pres. 1979), Am. Acad. Arts and Scis.; mem. Am. Econ. Assn. (John Bates Clark medal 1973). Home: 130 Mt Auburn St Cambridge MA 02138-5757 Office: MIT 50 Memorial Dr # E52 359 Cambridge MA 02142-1347

FISHER, FREDERICK HENDRICK, oceanographer emeritus; b. Aberdeen, Wash., Dec. 30, 1926; s. Sam (Sverre) and Astrid K. Fisher; m. Julie Gay Saund, June 17, 1955 (dec. 1993); children: Bruce Allen, Mark Edward, Keith Russell, Glen Michael; m. Shirley Mercedes Lippert, Oct. 10, 1994. BS, U. Wash., 1949, PhD, 1957. Tchg. asst. U. Wash., 1949-53; rsch. asst. UCLA, 1954-55; grad. rsch. physicist Marine Phys. Lab., Scripps Inst. Oceanography, 1955-57, rsch. physicist, rsch. oceanographer, 1958-91, assoc. dir., 1975-87, dep. dir., 1987-93, acting assoc. dir., 1993-94, rsch. oceanographer emeritus, 1997—; rsch. fellow acoustics Harvard U., 1957-58; dir. rsch. Havens Industries, San Diego, 1963-64; prof., chmn. dept. physics U. R.I., Kingston, 1970-71; mem. governing bd. Am. Inst. Physics, 1984-90. Mem. San Diego County Dem. Ctrl. Com., 1956-57, 60-62. Midshipman U.S. Naval Acad., 1945-47, with USNR, 1945. NCAA nat. tennis doubles champion, 1949; named to U. Wash. Athletic Hall of Fame, 1989; recipient Disting. Svc. award IEEE Oceanic Engring. Soc., 1991, Disting. Tech. Achievement award, 1996. Fellow Acoustical Soc. Am. (assoc. editor jour. 1969-76, v.p. 1980-81, pres. 1983-84, Am.'s Finest Acousticians award San Diego chpt. 1997); mem. IEEE (sr., editor Jour. Oceanic Engring. 1988-91), Marine Tech. Soc., Am. Geophys. Union, Acoustic Soc. Am., The Oceanographic Soc., Seattle Tennis Club. Achievements include co-designer and project scientist ocean research platform FLIP, 355' long manned spar buoy with 300' draft in vertical position, 1960-62. Home: 5034 Park West Ave San Diego CA 92117-1046

FISHER, GAIL FEIMSTER, government official; d. Maurice Blake and Sarah Estelle (Abell) Feimster; m. Eugene Joseph Fisher, Dec. 2, 1950 (dec.); children: Laurence Eugene, Robert Maurice. BA, U. Md., 1949, MA, 1951; PhD, U. N.C., 1976. Rsch. analyst Bur. of State Svcs., Dept. HHS, 1956-66; chief evaluation officer Bur. Health Svcs., Dept. HHS, 1966-68; planning officer Nat. Ctr. Health Stats.-Ctr. for Disease Control-Dept. HHS, Rockville, Md., 1968-93; assoc. dir. Nat. Ctr. Health Stats.-Ctr. for Disease Control-Dept. HHS, Hyattsville, Md., 1973-98; cons. epidemiologist, 1998—. Contbr. rsch. reports to profl. jours. and presentations. Avocation: antique vehicle restoration and preservation. Office: DHHS-CDC-Nat Ctr Hlth Stats PO Box 234 9685 Johnstontown Rd La Plata MD 20646

FISHER, GARY ALAN, publishing executive; b. Akron, Ohio, Apr. 4, 1951; s. Paul McCray and Betty Elaine F.; m. Helen Louise Barr, Feb. 10, 1985. A.B. in History, Princeton U., 1973. Founder, pub. Courselector, Princeton, N.J. and Boston, 1973-75; bus. mgr. CBS Spl. Interest Mags., N.Y.C., 1976-78, dir. bus. ops., 1979; pub. Am. Photographer Mag., N.Y.C., 1980-84; CEO Fisher & Co., Inc., N.Y.C., 1984—; pres. One World Enterprises Ltd., Hong Kong, 1995—; bd. dirs. Marble Vision. Mem. Marble Collegiate Ch. Office: Fisher & Co Global Mktg Svcs 470 Park Ave S New York NY 10016-6819

FISHER, GENE JORDAN, retired chemical company executive; b. Quitman, Miss., Mar. 26, 1931; s. Ira R. and Gertrude (Jordan) F.; m. Christine Ann Hodges, May 28, 1954; children—Denise, Darrell. B.S., U. Tex., 1952. From research chemist to sr. research chemist Celanese Chem. Co., Corpus Christi, Tex., 1952-59, group leader, 1959-67, research mgr., 1967-77, dir. research, 1977-83, tech. dir., 1983-85, ret., 1985; tech. and mgmt. cons., 1985—. Contbr. articles to profl. jours. Baptist. Patentee in field. Home: PO Box 1944 Rockwall TX 75087-2044

FISHER, GENE LAWRENCE, financial executive; b. Chillicothe, Ill., Nov. 15, 1929; s. Lawrence Hubert and Alyce Anne (Niggemeyer) F.; m. Sandra Kay Burns, Sept. 19, 1959; children—Kyle Butler, Kelley Anne. B.S., U. Ill., 1957. Staff acct. Inland Container Corp., Indpls., 1957-63, mgr. corp. acctg., 1964-65, asst. corp. controller, 1966-78, dir. fin. systems, 1979-93; ret., 1993. Chmn. fin. com.-exec. com. Winona Meml. Hosp., Indpls., 1979-81, chmn. bd. dirs., 1982-83. Served with U.S. Army, 1951-53. Mem. Beta Alpha Psi, Sigma Iota Epsilon. Republican. Avocations: fishing, swimming. Home: 5427 N Washington Blvd Indianapolis IN 46220-3027

FISHER, GEORGE, gerontological educator; b. May 31, 1915. BS, U. Md., 1956; MBA, Western Mich. U., 1969, SpA, 1977; PhD, U. Mich., 1981. Mech. engr. Keystone Mfg., Boston, 1936-41; commd. C.E., U.S. Army, 1941, advanced through grades to col., ret., 1961; mgmt./computer sys. analyst Def. Logistics Svc., Battle Creek, Mich., 1962-77; prof. gerontology Western Mich. U., Kalamazoo, 1985—. Home: 1129 Par 4 Cir Kalamazoo MI 49008-2917

FISHER, GEORGE A., JR., career officer; b. July 1, 1942. Commd. officer U.S. Army, advanced through grades to lt. gen., 1995—. Office: First United States Army 4705 N Wheeler Dr Forest Park GA 30297

FISHER, GEORGE ALEXANDER, JR., lieutenant general United States Army. BS, U.S. Mil. Acad., 1964; student Armor Officer Advanced Course, U.S. Army Armor Sch., Ft. Knox, Ky., 1968-69; MS in Ops. Rsch. and Analysis, U.S. Naval Post Grad. Sch., Monterey, Calif., 1970-72; student, U.S. Army Command & Staff Coll, Fort Leavenworth, Kans., 1972-73, U.S. Naval War Coll., Newport, R.I., 1983-84. Mortar platoon leader hdqtrs. co., 2d battalion, 508th infantry, 82d airborne divsn. U.S. Army, Fort Bragg, N.C., 1965-66; exec. officer Co. C to comdr. Co. C. 2d battalion, 508th infantry, 82d airborne divsn. U.S. Army, Dominican Republic, 1966-67; instr. U.S. Army Armor Sch., Ft. Knox, Ky., 1969; instr. to asst. prof. dept. math. U.S. Mil. Acad., West Point, N.Y., 1973-76; dep. inspector-gen. Berlin Brigade to battalion exec. officer 3d battalion Berlin Brigade U.S. Army Europe, Germany, 1976-79; ops. rsch./systems analyst Joint Strategic Planning Staff Strategic Air Command, Offutt AFB, Nebr., 1981-83; comdr. 3d battalion, 7th infantry divsn. U.S. Army, Fort Ord, Calif., 1981-83; G-3 (ops.) 7th infantry divsn. to comdr. 3d brigade 7th infantry divsn. U.S. Army, Fort Ord, Calif., 1984-88; chief tech. mgmt. office, Office Chief of Staff, U.S. Army, Washington, 1988-90; asst. comdr. 25th infantry divsn. (light), Schofield Barracks, Hawaii, 1990-91; comdr. joint readiness tng. ctr. U.S. Armed Forces, Little Rock, Ark. then, Ft Polk La, 1991-93; commanding gen. 25th infantry divsn. (light), Schofield Barracks, Hawaii, 1993-95; chief of staff U.S. Army Forces Command, Ft. McPherson, Ga., 1995-97; commanding gen. First U.S. Army, Ft. Gillem, Ga., 1997—. Decorated Defense Disting. Svc. medal, Disting. Svc. medal, Legion of Merit with 2 oak leaf clusters, Bronze Star medal, Defense Meritorious Svc. medal, Meritorious Svc. medal with oak leaf cluster, Air medal, Army Commendation medal with oak leaf cluster, Army Achievement medal. Office: Office of Commanding Gen First US Army Fort Gillem GA 30050

FISHER, GEORGE MYLES CORDELL, photographic imaging company executive, mathematician, engineer; b. Anna, Ill., Nov. 30, 1940; s. Ralph Myles and Catherine (Herbert) F.; m. Patricia Ann Wallace, June 18, 1965; children: Jennifer, Barcy, William. BS in Engring., U. Ill., 1962; MS in Engring., Brown U., 1964, PhD in Applied Maths., 1964-66. Mem. tech. staff Bell Telephone Labs., Murray Hill, N.J., 1965-67; supr. Bell Telephone Labs., Holmdel, N.J., 1967-71; dept. head Bell Telephone Labs., Indpls., 1971-76; dir. mfg. systems Motorola Inc., Schaumberg, Ill., 1976-77; asst. dir. mobile ops. Motorola Inc., Ft. Worth, 1977-78; v.p. portable ops. Motorola Inc., Ft. Lauderdale, Fla., 1978-81, v.p. paging divsn., 1981-84; asst. gen. mgr. comm. sector Motorola Inc., Schaumburg, 1984-86, sr. exec. v.p., 1986-88, pres., CEO, 1988-90, chmn., CEO, 1990-93; chmn., pres., CEO Eastman Kodak Co., Rochester, N.Y., 1993-97, 1997—; bd. dirs. AT&T, GM. Contbr. articles on continuum physics; 3 patents in optical wave guides and digital communications. Chmn. bd. dirs. U. Ill. Found., Nat. Merit Scholarship Bd., Chgo., 1986—; chmn. U.S.-China Bus. Coun. Recipient M. Eugene Merchant Mfg. medal ASME/SME, Am. Soc. Mfg. Engrs., 1994. Mem. IEEE. Office: Eastman Kodak Co 343 State St Rochester NY 14650-0001 Address: PO Box 546 Pittsford NY 14534-0546

FISHER, GERALD PATRICK, criminal justice educator. BA in History, Calif. State U., Northridge, 1979; MS in Criminal Justice, Calif. State U., Sacramento, 1991; postgrad., U. Ala., 1996—. Various positions U.S. Marshals Svc., 1978-95; instr. criminal justice Ala. State U., Montgomery, 1995—. Mem. Ala. Acad. Sci., Omega Phi. Republican. Avocations: camping, woodworking, reading and writing. Office: Dept Sociology and Criminal Justice Ala State U 915 S Jackson St Montgomery AL 36101

FISHER, GLENN DUANE, small business executive; b. Celina, Ohio, Jan. 29, 1947; s. Darrell Donald and Frankie Juanita (Engle) F; m. Linda Kay Brown, June 11, 1971; children: Lisa Marie, Jennifer Lynn, Jeffrey Robert. Student, Ohio State U., 1969; BS in Bus., Wright State U., 1972. Sr. acct. Howard, Beeler and Co. CPA's, Lima, Ohio, 1972-79; treas. Lima Flack Co., Lima, Ohio, 1979-84, owner, 1984—; owner, pres. Lima Flack Co. Celina, 1988—, Lima Scaffolding & Supply, 1988—, G & L Leasing Co., Elida, Ohio, 1989—, Fisher & Assocs., Elida, Ohio, 1992—, McDaniel Equipment, 1998—. bd. dirs., pres. Lima Noon Sertoma, Ohio, 1980-88. Recipient Svc. to Mankind award Wheel Chair Olympics, 1986. Mem. Am. Legion, Elks. Republican. Roman Catholic. Avocations: fishing, woodworking. Office: Lima Flack Co 1420 Elida Rd Lima OH 45805-1598

FISHER, GORDON MCCREA, mathematician; b. St. Paul, Oct. 5, 1925; s. Tully McCrea and Ione Adele (Brown) F.; m. (Helene) Dawn Smith, June 17, 1956; children: Andrea McCrea Rowland, Jennifer Ione Berger. BA in Math. and Philosophy, U. Miami, Coral Gables, Fla., 1951; MS in Computer Sci., U. Va., 1986; PhD in Math., La. State U., 1959. Instr. in math. Princeton (N.J.) U., 1959-62; sr. lectr. in math., history and philosophy of sci. U. Otago, Dunedin, New Zealand, 1962-65; sr. lectr. U. Waikato, Hamilton, New Zealand, 1965-67; prof. math. and computer sci. James Madison U., Harrisonburg, Va., 1967-91, prof. emeritus, 1991—. Contbr. articles to profl. jours. With USN, 1943-45, sgt. U.S. Army, 1947-49. Madison scholar, 1989. Mem. Am. Math. Soc.

FISHER, HANS, nutritional biochemistry educator; b. Breslau, Silesia, Germany, Mar. 4, 1928; s. George and Johanna (Gottheiner) F.; m. Ruth Hirschberg, July 24, 1950; children: Deborah M. Joseph, David E. Fisher, Daniel Z. Fisher. MS, U. Conn., 1952; PhD, U. Ill., 1954. Cert. Am. Bd. Nutrition. Asst. prof. Rutgers U., New Brunswick, N.J., 1954-57, assoc. prof., 1957-62, prof., 1962-72, dept. chair, 1966-88, assoc. provost, 1988-90, disting. prof., 1972—; cons. food and pharm. industries, 1955—. Author: Rutgers Guide to Lowering Your Cholesterol, 1986; contbr. articles to profl. jours. Pres. Highland Park (N.J.) Temple Ctr., 1975-77; v.p. YMHA, Highland Park, 1958-70. Fellow AAAS, Am. Soc. Nutritional Scis., N.Y. Acad. Scis.; mem. Am. Chem. Soc. Jewish. Achievements include research in fiber lowering cholesterol, Tryptophan ameliorates neuroleptic side effects and supresses voluntary alcohol consumption. Discoverer novel treatment for alcohol withdrawal and craving, histamine and carnosine in wound healing and trauma amelioration. E-mail: fisher@aesop.rutgers.edu. Home: 216 N 3rd Ave Highland Park NJ 08904-2412 Office: Rutgers U 96 Lipman Dr New Brunswick NJ 08901-8525

FISHER, HENRY, investment banker; b. Pitts., Feb. 17, 1936; s. Henry Clayton and Dorothea T. (Smith) F.; m. Ann Yeager, Aug. 6, 1960; children: Andrew Clayton, William Bradford. BA, U. Pitts., 1960; attended, Wharton Sch. Investment Bankin, 1967, 68. Gen ptnr. Singer Deane & Scribner, Pitts., 1961-69; exec. v.p. Chaplin McGuiness & Co., Inc., Pitts., 1969-74; mem. N.Y. Stock Exch., 1972-74. Pa. Gov.'s del. Southwestern Pa. Regional Planning Commn., 1995-98, Southwestern Pa. Devel. Coun., 1995-98; commr. Southwestern Pa. Commn., 1999—. Mem., Nat. Securities Traders Assn., Pitts. Mcpl. Analysts Soc., Pa. Boroughs Assn., Pa. League of Cities, Pa Twp. Assn., Pa. Mcpl. Authorities Assn., Pitts. Builders Exch., Sierra Club (co-founder Pitts. chpt.), Am. Youth Hostels, Inc. (past nat. v.p.), Pa. Soc. N.Y., Duquesne Club, Allegheny Club, Rivers Club. Office: 1317 Investment Building Bldg Pittsburgh PA 15222-1712

FISHER, HERBERT CALVIN, retired surgeon; b. Denver, July 7, 1910. MD, Cornell U., 1935. Intern St. Luke's Hosp., Denver, 1935-36; resident in surgery U. Minn.; fellow Mayo Found., Rochester, Minn., 1937-40; pvt. practice, 1946-75, ret., 1975; chief of surg. svc. Children's Hosp.; chief of staff Denver Gen. Hosp., 1971-72; assoc. prof. surgery U. Colo. Sch. Medicine; chief exec. Colo. State Sci. Fair, 1970-75; pres. Internat. Sci. Fair, 1975; chief emergency rom. St Luke's Hosp., 1973-75; chief surg. svc. Brook Gen. Hosp., 1941-45; county judge, Hinsdale County, 1977-80; co-founder Lake City Med. Ctr., 1976. Contbr. numerous articles and editls. to profl. jours. Lt. col. M.C., U.S. Army, 1946. Recipient awards for bronze sculpture, 1950-75, Cert. Svc. Colo. Engring. Coun., 1962, 1st prize for bronze sculpture, N.Y.C., 1972. Fellow ACS (life); mem. AMA (life), Am. Bd. Surgery (diplomate, cert.), Cen. Surg. Assn. (elected, life), Am. Heart Assn. (life), Colo. Surg. Assn., Colo. Med. Assn. (life, 3 Top awards for pub. svc. 1950-75).

FISHER, HERBERT HIRSH, lawyer; b. Rome, N.Y., Mar. 24, 1927; s. Kalman Nathan and Libby (May) F.; m. Ida Curtis; 1 child, Martin. Student, U. Minn., Yale U.; B.A., U. Wis., 1949, LL.B., 1952. Bar: Wis. 1952, Ill. 1953. Practiced in Milw., 1952; mem. firm Landon L. Chapman, Chgo., 1953-56; ptnr. Robinson & Fisher, 1956-60; pvt. practice Chgo., 1960-64, 78—; mem. firm Stradford, Lafontant, Fisher & Malkin, Chgo., 1964-78. Bd. dirs. Nat. Assn. Housing Coops., 1975—, sec., 1980, exec. v.p., 1981-83, pres., 1983-86, chmn. bd. 1986-98; exec. v.p., pres. Chatham Avalon Pk. Cmty. Coun., 1963-66; bd. dirs., officer Chatham Pk. Village Coop., 1962-69. Office: 200 N Dearborn St Ste 1006 Chicago IL 60601-1617

FISHER, JACK, medical educator, plastic surgeon; b. Mar. 10, 1947. BCS, U. Ill., 1969; MD, Emory U., 1973. Assoc. clin. prof. dept. plastic surgery Vanderbilt U., Nashville; assoc. clin. prof. dept. surgery Meharry Med. Coll., Nashville. E-mail: jfishernps@aol.com. Office: 2021 Church St Ste 806 Nashville TN 37203-2077

FISHER, JACK CARRINGTON, environmental engineering educator; b. Cortland, N.Y., Aug. 30, 1932; s. William J. and Jeannette (Carrington) F.; m. Sally Key Retzer, Nov. 15, 1981; children by previous marriage—John C., Margaret Lynn. B.A., Syracuse U., 1956, M.A., 1958, Ph.D. (Ford Found. fellow), 1961. Asst. prof. city and regional planning Cornell U., Ithaca, N.Y., 1962-68; assoc. prof., assoc. dir. urban studies Wayne State U., Detroit, 1969-72; prof. geography and environ. engring. Johns Hopkins U., Balt., 1972—; dir. Center for Met. Planning and Research, 1972-86; spl. asst. to pres. for oversees univ. liaison, dir. spl. projects Johns Hopkins U., 1985-89, coord. internat. internship program Sch. Engring., 1992—. Author: Yugoslavia: A Multinational State; editor: City and Regional Planning in Poland; contbr. articles to profl. jours. Served with U.S. Army, 1952-55. Recipient Golden Placket award U. Ljubljan, Slovenia, 1997. Mem. Am. Assn. Planning Ofcls., Am. Inst. Planning, Am. Assn. Geographers, Regional Sci. Assn. Office: Johns Hopkins U 210 Ames Hall Baltimore MD 21218 Also: 960 Fell St Baltimore MD 21231-3520

FISHER, JAMES A., lawyer; b. Pitts., May 25, 1942; s. David H.W. and Jean K. (Crum) F.; m. Judy Trosper Giefel, aug. 13, 1966; 1 child, Steven Frederick. BA, U. Mich., 1964; JD, Wayne State U., 1968. Bar: Mich. 1968. Pres., atty. Vandervoort, Cooke, McFee, Christ, Carpenter & Fisher, PC, Battle Creek, Mich., 1968—. Past dir. Battle Creek Cmty. Concert Assn.; founder, dir. Silent Observer, Battle Creek, 1970—; past dir. Jr. Achievement, Battle Creek. Paul Harris fellow Rotary Club, 1989. Mem. ABA, Mich. Bar Assn., Calhoun County Bar Assn. (pres. 1971-73), Battle Creek Area C. of C. (chmn. bd. 1981-82), Rotary (pres., dir. 1987-88), Battle Creek Country Club. Avocations: golf, racquetball, biking, reading. E-mail: jfisher@vandervoort-law.com. Home: 53 Minges Rd W Battle Creek MI 49015-7903 Office: Vandervoort Cooke et al 312 Old Kent Bank Bldg Battle Creek MI 49017-7016

FISHER, JAMES AIKEN, industrial marketing executive; b. Pitts., Mar. 15, 1920; s. Chester G. and Margaret R. (Aiken) F.; m. Edith C. Hall, June

12, 1955; children: George S., Chester G. III, James Aiken. BA, Yale, 1942. Engr. Alcoa Niagara Works, 1942-44; with Fisher Sci. Co., Pitts., 1944-85; sales staff Fisher Sci. Co., 1945-50, advt. staff, 1950-60, sr. v.p., dir., 1963-81; asst. to pres., 1981-85; chmn., pres. Kipling Corp., mktg. cons., 1985—; bd. dirs. EFT Corp., Nat. Sci. Programs, Inc., Optical Communications Corp. Trustee Carnegie Inst., Carnegie Mus. Art, Carnegie Sci. Ctr.; mem. Allegheny Conf. Sponsoring Com. Mem. Am. Chem. Soc., Sci. Apparatus Makers Assn. (past pres.), Am. Mktg. Assn., HYP-Pitts. Club (dir.), Duquesne Club, Rolling Rock Club, Pitts. Golf Club. Home: 5414 Kipling Rd Pittsburgh PA 15217-1038 Office: 622 Oliver Bldg Pittsburgh PA 15222-2304

FISHER, JAMES LEE, lawyer; b. Akron, Ohio, Apr. 10, 1944; s. James Lee and Maxine (Sumner) F.; m. Nancy Lorenz, Dec. 20, 1980. BSCE, U. Akron, 1968, JD, 1971. Bar: Ohio 1971. Staff atty. Brunswick Mgmt. Co., Akron, 1972-77; prin. James L. Fisher Co., L.P.A., Akron, 1977-88, Buckingham, Doolittle & Burroughs, Akron, 1988—. City planner City of Akron, 1968-71, community devel. atty., 1971-73; mem. Metro Regional Transit Authority Bd., 1992—; sec.-treas. Summit County Planning Commn., 1978—. Mem. ABA, Ohio Bar Assn., Akron Bar Assn., Home Builders Assn., Am. Planning Assn., Ohio Planning Conf., Copley Lions (pres. 1982). Republican. Mem. United Ch. of Christ. Home: 1135 Forest Pool Rd Akron OH 44333-1509 Office: Buckingham Doolittle & Burroughs PO Box 1500 Akron OH 44309-1500

FISHER, JAMES R., lawyer; b. South Bend, Ind., Apr. 15, 1947; s. Russell Humphries and Virginia Opal (Maple) F.; m. Cynthia Ann Winters, Aug. 14, 1971; children—Gabriel Christopher, Cory Andrew. A.B. in Psychology, Ind. U., 1969, J.D. summa cum laude, 1972. Bar: Ind. 1972, U.S. Dist. Ct. (so. dist.) Ind. 1972. Ptnr. firm Ice, Miller, Donadio & Ryan, Indpls., 1971—. Co-author: Personal Injury Law and Practicesol. 23 of Indiana Practico series; contbr. articles to legal publs. Mem. ABA, Am. Trial Lawyers Assn., Am. Bd. Trial Advs., Ind. Bar Assn., Ind. Trial Lawyers Assn., Indpls. Bar Assn., Order of Coif. Office: Ice Miller Donadio & Ryan 1 Am Sq PO Box 82001 Indianapolis IN 46282

FISHER, JAMES WILLIAM, medical educator, pharmacologist; b. Tucapau (now Startex), S.C., May 22, 1925; s. Ernest Amaziah and Mamie V. (Turner) F.; m. Carol Barbara Brodarick, June 5, 1947; children: Candis Loreen Fisher Smith, Patricia E., Richard W., William E., John C., Elaine Marie Fisher Spurr. B.S., U. S.C., 1947; Ph.D. in Pharmacology (USPHS fellow), U. Louisville, 1958. Devel. chemist Armour Pharm. Rsch. Labs., Chgo., 1950-53; pharmacologist Lloyd Bros. Pharm. Co., Cin., 1954-56; instr. pharmacology U. Tenn., 1958-60, asst. prof., 1960-62, assoc. prof., 1962-66, prof., 1966-68; prof., chmn. dept. pharmacology Med. Sch., Tulane U., 1968-96; Regents prof. pharmacology Tulane U., 1987—, James W. Fisher Disting. Lectureship in Pharmacology, 1991—; vis. prof. U. Zambia, Lusaka, 1987, Keio U., Tokyo, 1987, U. Nairobi, 1993; external examiner U. W.I., Trinidad, 1992; vis. scientist Christie Hosp. and Holt Radium Inst., Manchester, Eng., 1963-64; dir. Tulane-Universidad Nacional del Nordeste, Corrientes, Argentina, Pan Am. Health Orgn. Physiol. Scis. Tng. Program, 1972-77; lectr. in field; mem. Nat. Heart, Lung and Blood Inst. (erythropoietin com. 1971-74), mem. NIH hematology tng. grants com., 1977; mem. Cooley's Anemia Nat. Rsch. Com., 1974; pres. So. Blood Club, 1975-77; mem. Wellcome Professorships Com., 1976, 93, 94, 95; mem. pharmacology com. Nat. Bd. Med. Examiners, 1988-92; mem. ad hoc group med. rsch. funding AAMC, 1990-93. Author: Readings on the History of Pharmacology; editor: Kidney Hormones, Vol. I, 1971, Vol. II, 1977, Vol. III, 1986, Renal Pharmacology, 1971, Handbook of Pharmacology: Blood and Blood Forming Organs, 1992; co-editor: Erythropoiesis, 1975, Erythropoietin and Erythropoiesis, 1981; cons. editor: Erythropoietin, 1968; mem. editl. bd. Proc. Soc. Exptl. Biology and Medicine, 1971-86; contbr. articles to profl. jours. Served to lt. (j.g.) USNR, 1943-46, PTO. Recipient rsch. career devel. award USPHS, 1960-65, Purkinje medal Czechoslovakia Med. Soc., 1975, Golden Sovereign award, 1976, Aspet Exptl. Therapeutics award, 1992; named Disting. faculty AOA Honor Med. Soc., 1993; Ann. Tulane Fisher Lectureship established in his honor, 1992. Mem. AAAS, AAUP, Am. Soc. Pharmacology and Exptl. Therapeutics (Sollman awards com. 1981, exptl. therapeutics award com. 1982, 94, alerting network 1986-90, ednl. affairs com. 1986-89, Krayer awards com. 1990, Exptl. Therapeutics award 1992, nominating com. 1997), Soc. Exptl. Biology and Medicine, Am. Soc. Nephrology, Am. Soc. Hematology (sci. affairs com. 1973-74, chmn. erythropoietin subcom. 1973), Assn. Med. Sch. Pharmacology (exec. com. 1979-82, nominating com. 1975, 86, 94, 96, chmn. essential knowledge base in pharmacology com. 1984-95, pres. 1990-92), N.Y. Acad. Scis., Sigma Xi. Home: 4025 S Pin Oak Ave New Orleans LA 70131-8449 *Creativity and brilliance are very important in science but in order to test one's ideas these qualities must be adequately supplemented by the necessary amount of work at the bench.*

FISHER, JANE ELIZABETH, English educator; b. Morganton, N.C., Jan. 15, 1959; d. Billy Manson and Mary Rusmiselle Fisher; m. Michael Anthony De Freitas, Aug. 15, 1986. BA, Boston U., 1981; MA, Cornell U., 1985, PhD, 1989. Asst. prof. Canisius Coll., Buffalo, 1989-96, assoc. prof. English, 1996—, mem. core curriculum com., 1992-94; non-govtl. del. UN Conf. on Women, Beijing, 1995. Contbr. articles to profl. jours. Grantee N.Y. Pub. Libr., 1991, NEH, 1991. Mem. MLA, N.E. MLA, Internat. Virginia Woolf Soc., Parkside Garden Club (organizer, chair 1998—). Avocations: gardening, films, arts and crafts, architecture. E-mail: jfisher@canisius.edu. Office: Canisius Coll Dept English Buffalo NY 14214

FISHER, JANET WARNER, secondary school educator; b. San Angelo, Tex., July 7, 1929; d. Robert Montell and Louise (Buckley) Warner; m. Jarek Prochazka Fisher, Oct. 17, 1956 (div. May 1974); children: Barbara Zlata Harper, Lev Prochazka, Monte Prochazka. BA, So. Meth. U., 1950, M of Liberal Arts, 1982; student various including, Columbia U., U. Dallas., U. Colo., U. London and others. Cert. English, German and ESL tchr., K-12, Tex., N.Y. Bd. dirs., sec. Masaryk Inst., N.Y.C., 1968-71; with orphan sect. Displaced Persons Commn., Washington, 1950; fgn. editor Current Digest of the Soviet Press, N.Y.C., 1953-55; cable desk clk. Time, Inc., N.Y.C., 1955-56; tchr. of English and reading, langs. Houston Ind. Sch. Dist., 1975-80; tchr. Carmine Ind. Sch. Dist., Round Top, Tex., 1980-82; instr. English Houston Community Coll., 1983-88; adj. prof. English U. Houston, 1983-87; tchr. Royal Ind. Sch. Dist., Brookshire, Tex., 1989-92, Hempstead Ind. Sch. Dist., Waller County, Tex., 1992-94; adj. prof. English, U. Houston, Houston C.C., 1983-87, 1997—; tchr. Amnesty Program, Houston, 1988-90; adj. prof. English Blinn Coll., Brenham, Tex., 1995—, candidate, 1995-96. Candidate sch. bd., South Orangetown, N.Y., 1962, state rep., Houston, 1980; del. Dem. State Conv., 1996, Houston Tchrs. Assn., 1975-80; officer LWV, Nyack, N.Y., 1960-62; trustee Shepherd Drive United Meth. Ch., Houston; del. Tex. ann. conf. United Meth. Ch., 1994, 96, 97, 98, 99; del. Tex. State Dem. Conv., 1996. Recipient award for Svc. to Missions, United Meth. Ch., Houston, 1985. Mem. AAUW, NOW, WILPF, Harris County Women's Polit. Caucus. Avocations: Russian and German lit., real estate devel. Home: PO Box 66067 Houston TX 77266-6067

FISHER, JEFF, professional football coach; b. Culver City, Calif., Feb. 25, 1958; m. Juli; children: Brandon, Trenton, Tara. Student, U. Southern California. Professional football player Chicago Bears, 1981-85; defensive backs coach Philadelphia Eagles, 1986-88, defensive coordinator, 1989-90; defensive coordinator Los Angeles Rams, 1991; defensive backs coach San Francisco 49ers, 1992-93; defensive coordinator Tenn. Titans, 1994; head coach Houston Oilers, 1994—. Fly-fishing, golf, sushi, travel. Office: Tennessee Titans Baptist Sports Park 7640 Highway 70 S Nashville TN 37221-1758*

FISHER, JERID MARTIN, neuropsychologist; b. Houston, July 12, 1953; s. Seymour and Rhoda (Feinberg) F. BS magna cum laude, Duke U., 1975; MS in Psychology, U. Rochester, 1981, PhD in Clin. Psychology, 1981. Diplomate Am. Bd. Profl. Neuropsychology; lic. psychologist, N.Y. Clin. dir. neuropsychiatry lab. U. Rochester, N.Y., 1982-83, asst. dir. neuropsychiatry unit, 1982-83, sr. instr. psychiatry and neurology, 1981-83; dir. Head Injury Ctr. at Highgate, Troy, N.Y., 1984; dir./developer Neurologic Ctr. at Highgate, Cortland, N.Y., 1985; pres., CEO Neurorehab Assocs., Inc., Rochester, 1985-93; pres. Comprehensive Rehab Network, Inc., Rochester, 1987-93, Brain Injury Consultants, Inc., Rochester, 1993—; adj. asst. prof. SUNY, Albany, 1984—; clin. asst. prof. neurology U. Rochester Med. Sch., 1988-95; developer brain injury rehab. program St. Mary's Hosp., Rochester, 1987-91, Our Lady of Victory Hosp., Buffalo, 1986-91. Co-author: The Practice of Forensic Neuropsychology, 1997; contbr. articles to profl. jours. Adv. Compeer, Rochester, 1978--. Mem. APA, Internat. Neuropsychol. Soc., Nat. Acad. Neuropsychology, Am. Bd. of Profl. Disability Cons., Am. Congress Rehab. Medicine, Phi Beta Kappa. Republican. Jewish. Avocations: scuba diving, running, boating. Office: 6780 Pittsford Palmyra Rd Fairport NY 14450-3360

FISHER, (MARY) JEWEL TANNER, retired construction company executive; b. Port Lavaca, Tex., Oct. 31, 1918; d. Thomas M. and Minnie Frances (Dunks) Tanner; m. King Fisher, Aug. 13, 1937; children: Ann Fisher Boyd, Linda Fisher LaQuay. A in Bus., Tex. Luth. Coll., 1937. Sec. treas. King Fisher Marine Svc., Inc., Port Lavaca, 1959-82, dir., cons., 1958-98; artist, poet. Trustee Meml. Med. Ctr., 1976-81, 90-94 Golden Crescent Coun. Govts., 1980-81, Crisis Hotline Calhoun County, 1985-93; pres. bd. trustees, 1992-93; trustee Golden Crescent Coun. Govts., 1980-81, Crisis Hotline Calhoun County, 1985-93. Lic. pvt. pilot. Mem. DAR (regent Guadalupe Victoria chpt. 1986-88), Daus. Republic Tex., 99's, Internat. Orgn. Women Pilots. Home: PO Box 166 Port Lavaca TX 77979-0166

FISHER, JIMMIE LOU, state official; b. Delight, Ark., Dec. 31, 1941. Student, Ark. State U.; grad. John F. Kennedy Sch. Govt., Harvard U., 1985. Treas. Greene County, Ark., 1971-78; auditor State of Ark., Little Rock, 1979, treas., 1981—; sec. Ark. State Bd. Fin. Trustee, ex-offico mem. Ark. Pub. Employees Retirement System, Ark. Tchr. Retirement System; trustee Ark. State Hwy. Retirement System; former vice chair Dem. State Com.; former mem. Dem. Nat. Com.; del. Dem. Nat. Conv., 1988; past pres. Ark. Dem. Women's Club; mem. Ark. Devel. Fin. Authority. Mem. State Bd. Fin. (sec.), State Bd. Election Commrs., Nat. Assn. State Treas. (pres.). Office: Treasury Dept 220 State Capitol Little Rock AR 72201-1059

FISHER, JOEL ANTHONY, sculptor; b. Salem, Ohio, June 6, 1947; s. J. Richard and Marye (Giffin) F.; m. Pamela Robertson-Pearce, Dec. 2, 1977; 1 child, G. Noah. AB magna cum laude, Kenyon Coll., 1969. Educator Shiller Coll., Berlin, 1973-74, Goldsmiths Coll., London (Eng.) U., 1979, Bath Acad. Art, Corsham, 1980-81, 81-82, RISD, Providence, 1985, 90, Vt. Studio Sch., Johnson, 1988—, Sch. Visual Arts, N.Y.C., 1988—, Parsons Sch. Design, N.Y.C., 1990, Boston (Mass.) Mus. Sch., 1990; guest prof. Ecole des Beaux-Arts, Paris, 1991-99; lectr. in field. One-man shows include Diane Brown Gallery, 1992, Farideh Cadot Gallery, Paris, 1991, Gallery Hubert Winter, Wien, Austria, 1991, Galeria Comicos/Luis Serpa, Lisbon, Portugal, 1991, many others; exhibited in group shows at The Bklyn. Mus., Crown Point Press, N.Y.C., 1991, Blum Helman Gallery, N.Y.C., 1988, Albright Knox Gallery, Buffalo, 1987, others; represented in pub. collections Mus. Modern Art, N.Y.C., Tate Gallery, London, Stadfisches Mus. Monchengladback, Germany, Ctr. Georges Pompidou, Paris, Stedlijk Mus., Amsterdam, Kunstmuseum, Bern, Switzerland, many others. Recipient Kress Found. awards in art history, 1967, 68, Thomas J. Watson Traveling fellowship, 1969, 1971-72, Gast der Berliner Kunstlerprogram des DAAD, 1973-74, prize Wroclaw Drawing Triennale, 1978, Nat. Endowment fellowship in sculpture, 1984, George A. and Eliza Gardner Howard Found., 1986-87. Mem. Phi Beta Kappa. Home: PO Box 349 North Troy VT 05859-0349 Office: 99 Commercial St Brooklyn NY 11222-1078

FISHER, JOEL MARSHALL, political scientist, legal consultant, educator; b. Chgo., June 24, 1935; s. Dan and Nell (Kolvin) F.; children: Sara Melinda, Matthew Nicholas. AB, U. So. Calif., 1955; LLB, U. Calif.-Berkeley, MA; PhD in Govt., Claremont Grad. U., 1968. Orgn. dir. Republican Citizens Com. of U.S., Washington, 1964-65; dir. arts and scis. state legis. divs. Rep. Nat. Com., Washington, 1968-69; asst. dep. counsel to pres. U.S. White House, 1969-70; dep. asst. sec. econ. and social affairs U.S. Dept. State, Washington, 1969-71; vis. prof. comparative and internat. law Loyola U. Sch. Law, L.A., 1972-73; dir. World Bus. Inst., L.A., 1974-75; prof. constl. law Southwestern U. Sch. Law, L.A., 1974-76; dir. World Trade Inst. So. Calif., 1976—; prof. internat. law, asst. dean Whitter Coll. Sch. Law, L.A., 1977-80; prin. Ziskind, Greene and Assocs., 1980-83; v.p. Wells Internat., 1983-84; pres. LawSearch Inc., 1984-91; v.p. Clarke Cos., 1991-93; pres. Fisher Group, 1993—; adj. prof. Calif. Internat. U., L.A., 1993—; bd. dirs. Calif. Horse Stalls, spl projects Hollywood Palace, 1998—; ofcl. visitor The European Communities, 1974, 76; mem. U.S. dels. UN confs., 1969-71; chmn. Strategy for Peace Conf. Panel on U.S. and UN, 1972—; coord. Series on the Contemporary Am. Presidency, 1972-73; cons. Robert Taft Inst., 1977-82, World Trade Inst. N.Y., 1977-80. Co-author two books; contbr. articles on polit. sci. and law to profl. publs. Mem. steering com. Calif. Com. for Reelection of Pres., 1972; nat chmn. Community Leaders for Ford, 1976; trustee Rep. Assocs., 1978—, exec. com., 1986—; mem. vestry, sr. warden St. Michael and All Angeles Ch., Studio City, Calif., 1983-86, 89-93, mem. diocesan coun. L.A., 1986-88, chmn. budget com. 1987; bd. dirs. Corp. of the Cathedral, 1988-91; mem. com. on constitution and canons, 1993—. Fellow Nobel Found., 1958; Falk fellow, 1961-62. Mem. Am. Polit. Sci. Assn. (state legis. fellow 1970-73). Home: 4358 Mammoth Ave Apt 26 Sherman Oaks CA 91423-3692 Office: 1735 Vine St Hollywood CA 90028-5248

FISHER, JOHN CROCKER, physicist; b. Ithaca, N.Y., Dec. 19, 1919; m. Jo Ann Johnson; children: Kelly, Mark, Holly. AB, Ohio State Univ., 1941; ScD, Mass. Inst. Tech., 1947. Rsch. engr. Battelle Meml. Inst., 1941-42; asst. & instr. mech. Mass. Inst. Tech., 1942-47; rsch. assoc. Gen. Elec. Co., 1947-51, mgr. phys. metall. sect., 1951-57; physicist, 1957-63; mgr. liaison & transition Rsch. Lab., 1963-64; mgr. physics sci. & info. disciplines Tech. Mil Planning Ops., 1964-68; cons. scientist Re-Entry & Environ. Systems Prod. Divsn., 1969-72; mgr. energy tech. Power Generation Bus. Group, 1972-78; cons. rsch. & devel. Corp. Rsch. & Devel., 1978-81; cons., 1981—, physicist, 1986—; chief scientist USAF, Washington, 1968-69; lectr. Mem. Nat. Acad. Engring., AAAS, Am. Inst. Physicist, Am. Phys. Soc., Am. Soc. Metals. Home: 600 Arbol Verde St Carpinteria CA 93013-2506

FISHER, JOHN HURT, English language educator; b. Lexington, Ky., Oct. 26, 1919; r. Bascom and Franke (Sheddan) F.; m. Jane Elizabeth Law, Feb. 21, 1942 (dec.); children: Janice Carol Fisher Lowe, John Craig, Judith Law; m. Audrey A. Duncan, Aug. 28, 1997. B.A., Maryville Coll., 1940; M.A., U. Pa., 1942, Ph.D., 1945; L.H.D., Loyola U., Chgo., 1970; Litt.D., Middlebury Coll., 1970. Instr., English U. Pa., 1942-45, Yale U., summer 1944; instr. English NYU, 1945-48, asst. prof., 1948-55; lectr. U. So. Calif., summer 1955; instr. English U. Mich., summer 1956; assoc. prof. Duke U., 1955-58, prof., 1958-60; prof. English Ind. U., 1960-62, N.Y. U., 1962-72; John C. Hodges prof. English U. Tenn., 1972-88, chmn., 1976-78; vis. prof. NYU, 1990, U. Tex., San Antonio, 1996. Author: John Gower: Moral Philosopher and Friend of Chaucer, 1964, The Importance of Chaucer, 1991, The Emergence of Standard English, 1995; editor: Tretyse of Loue, 1951, The Medieval Literature of Western Europe: A Review of Research, 1966, The Complete Poetry and Prose of Geoffrey Chaucer, 1977, 2nd edit., 1989; co-editor: The College Teaching of English, 1965, In Forme of Speche is Chaunge: Readings in the History of the English Language, 1973, An Anthology of Chancery English, 1984, The Essential Chaucer: An Annotated Bibliography of Major Modern Studies, 1987; contbr. articles on medieval lit., English linguistics, English edn. to profl. jours. Mem. U.S. Commn. to UNESCO, 1963-69; bd. dirs. Woodrow Wilson Nat. Fellowship Found., 1972-75, Maryville Coll., 1972-74. Nat. Endowment for Humanities sr. fellow, 1975-76. Fellow Medieval Acad. Am. (v.p. 1985-86, pres. 1986), Med. Acad. Soc. Fellows (pres. 1993-96); mem. Modern Lang. Assn. Am. (exec. sec. 1963-71, editor PMLA 1963-71, pres. 1974), New Chaucer Soc. (bd. dirs. 1978-90, exec. sec. 1981-89, pres. 1982-84), Linguistic Soc. Am., Nat. Coun. Tchrs. English, Fedn. Internationale des Langues et Littératures Modernes, UNESCO (Am. v.p. 1972-78), Phi Beta Kappa (senator-a-large 1977-83). Home: 1805 Chicadee Dr Knoxville TN 37919-8956

FISHER, JOHN RICHARD, engineering consultant, former naval officer; b. Columbus, Ohio, Dec. 28, 1924; s. Don Alfred and Katherine Buchanan (Galigher) F.; m. Kitson Overmyer, Oct. 2, 1946; children—Scott Owen, Lani Kitson. BS, U.S. Naval Acad., 1946; BCE, Rensselaer Poly. Inst., Troy, N.Y., 1950, MCE, 1950; grad. Advanced Mgmt. Program, Harvard, 1971. Registered profl. engr., S.C. Commd. ensign U.S. Navy, 1946, advanced through grades to rear adm., 1972; service in North Africa, Cuba, The Philippines, Antarctica, Vietnam, Australia; comdr. 30th Seabee Rgt., Vietnam, 1968-69; dep. comdr. Naval Facilities Engring. Command; also comdr. Chesapeake div. constrn. facilities U.S. Naval Acad. and Omega Nav. System, 1969-73; comdr. Pacific div. Naval Facilities Engring. Command, Constrn. Facilities Diego Garcia, 1973-77; ret., 1977; v.p. Raymond Internat., Inc., 1977-81, sr. group v.p., 1981-83, exec. v.p., 1983-86. Pres. Cmty. Hosp. Assn. Mid-Am., Scottdale, Ariz., 1985-96; past sr. warden St. Anthony Episcopal Ch. Decorated DSM, Legion of Merit with combat V (2). Fellow Am. Soc. Mil. Engrs.; mem. ASCE, Navy League U.S. (nat. pres. 1999—), The Moles, Outrigger Canoe Club (Honolulu), Army-Navy Country Club (Arlington, Va.), Columbia Club (Indpls.), Tau Kappa Epsilon (nat. pres. 1993-95), Tau Beta Pi. Home: 10615 E Arabian Park Dr Scottsdale AZ 85258-6021 Office: PO Box 5585 Scottsdale AZ 85261-5585

FISHER, JOHN WELTON, II, law educator, magistrate judge, university official; b. Fisher, W.Va., Dec. 11, 1942; s. John Welton and Orrie (Shobe) F.; m. Susan Carol Vass, June 6, 1964; children: John Welton III, Jennifer Lynn. BA, W.Va. U., 1964, JD, 1967. Bar: W.Va. 1967, U.S. Dist. Ct. (no. and so. dists.) W.Va. 1967, U.S. Ct. Appeals (4th cir.) 1969. Law clk. to chief judge U.S. Dist. Ct. (no. dist.) W.Va., 1967-68; assoc. Farmer & Farmer, Morgantown, W.Va., 1968-71; mem. faculty W.Va. U. Coll. Law, 1971—, prof. law, 1977—, acting dean, 1981-82, 92-93, 97-98, dean, 1998—, exec. officer univ., 1982-86; magistrate judge U.S. Dist. Ct. No. Dist. W.Va., 1977-98; reporter Speedy Trial Planning Group, No. Dist. W.Va.; mem. W.Va. State Bar Continuing Edn. Com. Reporter: Local Rules of Practice, Northern District of West Virginia, 1980. Mem. ABA, W.Va. State Bar Assn., Fourth Cir. Jud. Conf., Order of Coif. Office: PO Box 6130 Morgantown WV 26506-6130

FISHER, JOHN WESLEY, manufacturing company executive; b. Walland, Tenn., July 15, 1915; s. Arthur Justin and Rachel (Malott) F.; m. Janice Kelsey Ball, Aug. 10, 1940; children: Joan Fisher Woods, Michael J., James A., Jeffrey E., Judith Fisher Oetinger, John Wesley III, Jerrold M. B.S., U. Tenn., 1938; M.B.A., Harvard U., 1942; LL.D. (hon.), Ball State U., 1972, Butler U., 1977, DePauw U., 1981, Ind. U., 1985. Field sec. Delta Tau Delta Frat., Indpls., 1938-40; trainee, various mfg., sales and adminstrv. positions Ball Corp., Muncie, Ind., 1941-70; pres., chief exec. officer Ball Corp., 1970-78, chmn. bd., chief exec. officer, 1978-81, chmn. bd., 1981-86, also dir., chmn. emeritus, 1986—; bd. dirs. Kindel Furniture Co., Grand Rapids, Mich.; ptnr. Blackwood & Nichols Corp., Oklahoma City; chmn. CID Equity Ptnrs., Indpls., Am. Nat. Trust and Investment Mgmt. Co., Muncie; pres. Nature's Catch, Inc., Clarksdale, Miss., Fisher Properties of Ind., Inc. State del. Rep. Party, Ind., 1950-70; mem. Rep. State Fin. Com., 1952-56, del. nat. conv., 1952, 54, 64, 68; chmn. bd. dirs. Ball Meml. Hosp.; pres. Cardinal Health Sys. Mem. NAM (chmn. 1979-80, bd. dirs.), Glass Packaging Inst. (trustee 1962-68, pres. 1965-67), Grocery Mfrs. Assn. (bd. dirs.), Ind. C. of C. (dir. 1959—, pres. 1966-68), Muncie C. of C. (past pres.), Conf. Bd., Ind. Acad., Muncie Club, Delaware Country Club, Indpls. Athletic Club, Columbia Club (Indpls.), Royal Poinciana Country Club, Naples (Fla.) Yacht Club, Rotary, Skyline Club (Indpls.), Naples Nat. Golf Club, Delta Tau Delta. Republican. United Methodist. Home: PO Box 832 Muncie IN 47308-0832 Office: Ball Assocs PO Box 1408 Muncie IN 47308-1408

FISHER, JOHN WILLIAM, civil engineering educator; b. Ancell, Mo., Feb. 15, 1931; s. Nevan August and Nettie (Miller) F.; m. Nelda Rae Adams, Oct. 11, 1952; children: John Timothy, Christopher Lee, Elizabeth Renee, Nevan Andrew. BSCE, Washington U., St. Louis, 1956; MS, Lehigh U., 1958, PhD, 1964; Dr. honoris causa, Swiss Fed. Inst. Tech., Lausanne, Switzerland, 1988. Registered profl. engr., Ill. Asst. bridge research engr. Nat. Acad. Scis., Ottawa, Ill., 1958-61; from research instr. to assoc. prof. Lehigh U., Bethlehem, Pa., 1961-69, prof. civil engring., 1969—, Joseph T. Stuart prof., 1988—, assoc. dir. Fritz Engring. Lab., 1972-84, co-chmn. civil engring., 1984-85, dir. advanced tech. large structural sys. Engring. Rsch. Ctr, 1986—; cons. Washington Metro Area Transit Authority, 1979-93, Minn. Dept. Trans., 1995-96, Conn. Dept. Transp., 1983-96, Triborough Bridge and Tunnel Authority, 1991—; civil col. eminent overseas spkr. Inst. Engrs. Australia, 1983; vis. prof. Swiss Fed. Inst. Tech., Lausanne, Switzerland, 1982; sr. vis. scholar (lectr.) China, 1985; disting. lectr. Transp. Rsch. Bd., 1997, mem. exec. com., 1997—; Portevin lectr. Internat. Inst. Welding, 1997. Author: Structural Steel Design, 1974, Guide to Design Criteria for Bolted Joints, 1974, 2d edit., 1987, Bridge Fatigue Guide, 1977, Fatigue and Fractures in Steel Bridges, 1984, A Fatigue Primer for Structural Engineers, 1998; contbr. over 230 articles to profl. jours. Mem. directory council Southside Ministries, Bethlehem, 1983-98; bd. dirs. New Bethany Ministries, Bethlehem, 1985-90. 2d lt. U.S. Army, 1951-53. Recipient Alumni Achievement award Washington U., 1987, John A. Roebling medal Engrs. Soc. We. Pa., 1995, Frank P. Brown medal Franklin Inst., 1992; named Constrn. Man of Yr. ENR, 1987, Engr. of Yr. in Rsch. Inst. for Bridge Integrity and Safety, 1989. Mem. ASCE (hon. 1989, Huber Rsch. prize 1969, Ernest E. Howard award 1979, R.C. Reese Rsch. prize 1981, Cleve. sect. G. Brooks Earnest award 1997), NAE (chmn. NAE/NRC com. internat. constrn. study 1987-88, mem. Internat. Affairs adv. com. 1988-92, mem. program adv. com. 1992-94), NSPE, Am. Soc. Engring. Educators, Am. Ry. Engring. Assn. (steel structures com.), Am. Welding Soc. (Adams mem.), Internat. Assn. Bridge and Structural Engrs., Am. Inst. Steel Constrn. (specification com. 1976—, T.R. Higgins lectr. 1977), Swiss Acad. Engring. Scis. Republican. United Methodist. Avocations: hiking, canoeing. Office: Lehigh U 117 Atlss St Bethlehem PA 18015-4728

FISHER, JOSEPH ALLEN, retired government official; b. Chgo., Mar. 28, 1924; s. Joseph Marion and Elizabeth Rita (Allen) F.; m. Eleanor May Larsen, Sept. 4, 1948; children: Nancy, JoAnn, Pamela, Joelle, Laurie. BS, Northwestern U., 1948, MS, 1949. Reporter Dubuque (Iowa) Telegraph-Herald, 1949; reporter, polit. editor Rockford (Ill.) Newspapers, 1950-69; press sec. U.S. Senator Ralph T. Smith, Washington, 1969-70; pub. rels. and sec. Postal Rate Commn., Washington, 1971-74; sr. staff, staff dir. Post Office CSC, Washington, 1974-1994; ret., 1994. Served to sgt. USAF, 1942-45, ETO. Decorated 13 air medals and DSC. Avocations: biking, reading, gardening. Home: 8313 Cedardale Dr Alexandria VA 22308-1941*

FISHER, JOSEPH JEFFERSON, federal judge; b. San Augustine County, Tex., 1910; s. Guy B. and Lula (Bl) F.; m. Kathleen Clark; children—Leila (Mrs. Leila F. Thomas), Joseph Jefferson, John Clark, Guy Cade, Anne Fisher Winslow. Student, Stephen F. Austin Coll., 1929; LL.B., U. Tex., 1936. Bar: Tex. 1936. Served as county atty. San Augustine County, 1936-39; dist. atty. 1st Jud. Dist. Tex., 1939-46, dist. judge, 1956-59; partner firm Fisher, Tonahill & Reavley, Jasper, Tex., 1947-56; U.S. dist. judge Eastern Dist. Tex., 1959—, chief judge, 1967—. Mem. ABA (chmn. jud. sect. 1957), 1st Jud. Bar Assn. (pres. 1956), Tex. Bar Assn., State Bar Tex. (legis. and exec. coms. 1957-59), Am. Judicature Soc., Tex. Hist. Assn., Sons of the Republic of Tex., Ex-Student Assn. U. Tex. (life), Stephen F. Austin State U. Ex-Students Assn. (life), Delta Kappa Epsilon. Methodist. Clubs: Mason, Lion (dist. gov., internat. dir., mem. exec. com. 1952-54), Order San Jacinto. Home: 130 Central Caldwood Dr Beaumont TX 77707-1916 Office: PO Box 88 Beaumont TX 77704-0088

FISHER, JOSEPH STEWART, management consultant; b. Athens, Pa., Mar. 3, 1933; s. Samuel Royer and Agnes Corinne (Smith) F.; m. Anita Ann Coyle, May 15, 1954; 1 child, Samuel Royer. BS in Tech. Mgmt., Regis U., 1981; postgrad., U. Colo., 1986-87, Iliff Sch. Theology, 1988-89. With IBM Corp., Kingston, Syracuse & Endicott, N.Y., 1956-60, Boulder, 1960-87; cons., sole propr. Fisher Enterprises, Boulder, 1975—; bd. dirs. Vervcraft Inc., Loveland, Colo. Leadership devel. Boy Scouts Am., 1975—, chmn. long range planning, 1982-86, chaplain, 1991—; bd. dirs. Longs Peak Coun., 1983-87, Colo. Crime Stoppers, 1983-88; exec. dir. Caring About People, Inc., Colo., 1990—; v.p. Helplink, Inc., Boulder, 1991—. With USN, 1952-56, Korea. Recipient Silver Beaver award Boy Scouts Am., Boulder, 1978, God and Svc. award Boy Scouts Am. and United Meth. Ch., 1991, OES Rose award 1994; James E. West fellow Boy Scouts Am., 1997. Mem. Am. Soc. Indsl. Security (cert. CPP, treas. 1985), Colo. Crime Prevention Assn. (cert. CPS), Mason (treas. Columbia lodge #14 1969-85, 90—), Royal Arch Masons, Commandery Knights Templar of York Rite, Scottish Rite (32nd degree), Shriners. Republican. Methodist. Avocations: scouting, church and masonic. Home and Office: 4645 Bedford Ct Boulder CO 80301-4017

FISHER, JOSEPH V., retail executive. Pres., CEO Big V Supermarkets, Florida, N.Y., 1998-99, Penn Traffic Co., Syracuse, N.Y., 1999—. Office: Penn Traffic Co PO Box 4737 Syracuse NY 13221*

FISHER, JULES EDWARD, producer, lighting designer, theatre consultant; b. Norristown, Pa., Nov. 12, 1937; s. Abraham and Ann (Davidson) F. Student, Pa. State U.; BFA, Carnegie Inst. Tech., 1960. Pres. Fisher Dachs Assocs. Inc. Theatre Cons., N.Y.C., 1963—, Fisher Marantz Renfro Stone, Inc., N.Y.C., 1971—, Jules Fisher Enterprises Inc. Lighting Design and Theatrical Prodn., N.Y.C., 1973—. Lighting designer for over 100 Broadway prodns. including Jesus Christ Superstar, Pippin' 1973 (Tony award), Ulysses in Nightown, 1974 (Tony award), Chicago, Beatlemania, Dancin', 1978 (Tony award), La Cage aux Folles, Song & Dance, Grand Hotel, 1990 (Tony award), Will Roger Follies, 1991 (Tony award), Jelly's Last Jam, 1992 (Tony award), Angels in America, 1993, A Christmas Carol, 1994, 95, 96, Victor Victoria, 1995, Bring In Da Noise, Bring In Da Funk, 1996 (Tony award 1996), Ragtime, 1997; producer: Lenny, The Rink, Dancin', Rock n' Roll- The 1st 5,000 Yrs., Elvis-An Am. Musical, Dangerous Games; exec. producer: Big Deal, 1986; prodn. supr., lighting designer: various rock tours including Tommy, Simon & Garfunkel Concert, Central Park, N.Y.C., 1981, Linda Ronstadt's Canciones de mi Padre Tour, 1988, Crosby, Stills & Nash Tour, 1990, The Teenage Mutant Ninja Turtles, 1990, Whitney Houston, 1993; lighting designer film: A Star is Born, 1976, The Birdcage, 1996. Recipient: Antoinette Perry award (Tony), 1973, 74, 78, 90, 91, 92, 96; Theater Hall of Fame, 1994. Mem. United Scenic Artists, Illuminating Engring. Soc., U.S. Inst. Theatre Tech., Internat. Assn. Lighting Designer, Soc. British Lighting Designers, League Am. Theatres and Producers. Office: Jules Fisher/Joshua Dachs Assocs 126 5th Ave New York NY 10011-5606*

FISHER, KENNETH K., councilman; b. Bklyn.; m. Kirsten Fisher; two children. Grad., U. Pacific, Syracuse U. Ptnr. Fisher & Fisher, 1978-91; councilman dist. 33 City of N.Y., 1991—; mem. contracts, econ. devel., parks, recreation, cultural affairs, internat. and intergroup rels. coms., N.Y.C. Coun., chmn. land use subcom. Contbr. articles to profl. jours. Recipient Tenth Annual Goodie award Local 372 DC 37 AFSCME, AFL-CIO, Civilian commendation N.Y.C. Police Dept. Mem. N.Y. State Bar Assn., Bklyn. Bar Assn. E-mail: cyberpol@pipeline.com. Office: 16 Court St Ste 1505 Brooklyn NY 11241-1015*

FISHER, KING, retired marine contracting company executive; b. Port Lavaca, Tex., Jan. 14, 1916; s. Charles Everett and Kittie (Moss) F.; Student pub. schs., Port Lavaca. m. Jewel Tanner, Aug. 13, 1937; children: Ann Fisher Boyd, Linda Fisher LaQuay. Pres. King Fisher Marine Svc., Inc., Port Lavaca, 1941-96, chmn. bd., 1959-98, cons., 1998; marine cons., 1998—; corp. sec. pres. Fisher Channel & Dock Co., Port Lavaca, 1954—; bd. dirs. First Nat. Bank of Port Lavaca, Seaport Bank, Seadrift, Tex. Inducted into Pipeliners Hall of Fame, 1997, Rivers and Harbors Hall of Fame, 1998. Mem. Tex. Mid-Coast Water Devel. Assn., Gulf Coast Intracoastal Canal Assn., Port Lavaca C. of C. Home: Fisher Rd Chocolate Port Lavaca TX 77979 Office: PO Box 166 Port Lavaca TX 77979-0166

FISHER, LAWRENCE EDGAR, market research executive, anthropologist; b. Los Alamos, N.Mex., Jan. 13, 1946; s. Leon H. and Phyllis (Kahn) F.; m. Valerie Joseph, Mar. 25, 1979; children: Lael Sharon, Jonathan Daniel, Matthew Joseph. AB, U. Calif., Berkeley, 1968; MA, Northwestern U., 1969, PhD, 1973; cert. in bus. adminstrn., U. Pa., 1982. Postdoctoral fellow U. Chgo., 1973-74; asst. prof. U. Ill., Chgo., 1974-83; dir. Ethnographic Field Sch. Northwestern U., Evanston, Ill., 1975-78, adj. assoc. prof., 1984-86; vis. scholar Stanford U., 1978; vis. asst. prof. U. Mich., Ann Arbor, 1979-80; account exec., sr. account exec., dir. client svcs. MRCA Info. Svcs., Northbrook, Ill., 1983-88; group mgr. Test Mktg. Group, Control Data Corp., Chgo., 1988-89; dir. client svcs. Info. Resources, Inc., Chgo., 1989-90, v.p. client svcs., 1991-94, sr. v.p., 1994—; mem. external adv. bd. A.C. Nielsen Ctr., Grad. Sch. Bus. U. Wis., Madison, 1991—, bd. chair, 1998—. Author: Colonial Madness, 1985; also numerous articles. Fellow Woodrow Wilson Found., 1972-73, NIH, 1973-74, NEH, 1975. Home: 324 S Euclid Ave Oak Park IL 60302-3508 Office: Info Resources Inc 150 N Clinton St Chicago IL 60661-1402

FISHER, LAWRENCE L., lawyer; b. Mt. Sterling, Ohio, Jan. 4, 1941. BS, Ohio State U., 1964; postgrad., U. Bonn, Germany; JD, Harvard U., 1967. Bar: Ohio 1967. Mem. Vorys, Sater, Seymour & Pease, Columbus, Ohio. Fellow Am. Coll. Trust and Estate Counsel; mem. ABA, Ohio State Bar Assn. (chmn. probate and trust law sect. 1979-80), Columbus Bar Assn. (Community Svc. award 1976-77), Phi Eta Sigma. Office: Vorys Sater Seymour & Pease PO Box 1008 52 E Gay St Columbus OH 43216*

FISHER, LAWRENCE N., lawyer. BA, U. So. Calif., 1965, JD, 1968. Bar: Calif. 1969. Assoc. ptnr. Hahn & Han, 1969-74; tax counsel Fluor Corp., Irvine, Calif., 1974-76; sr. tax counsel Flour Corp., Irvine, Calif., 1976-78; v.p. adminstrn. Fluor Arabia Ltd., 1978-79; v.p., corp. law and asst. sec. Fluor Corp., Irvine, 1984—. Office: Fluor Corp 3333 Michelson Dr Irvine CA 92612-0625*

FISHER, LEONARD EVERETT, artist, writer, educator; b. N.Y.C., June 24, 1924; s. Benjamin M. and Ray Mera (Shapiro) F.; m. Margery Meskin, Dec. 21, 1952; children—Julie Anne, Susan Abby, James Albert. BFA, Yale U., 1949, MFA, 1950. Dean Whitney Art Sch., New Haven, Conn., 1951-53; mem. faculty Paier Art Sch., Hamden, Conn., 1966-78; acad. dean Paier Coll. of Art, Hamden, 1978-82; dean emeritus Paier Coll. of Art, 1982—, vis. prof., 1982-87; vis. prof. Fairfield U., Conn., 1983-85; del. at large White House Conf. on Library and Info. Services, Washington, 1979; lectr. in field, 1957—. Author 80 childrens books; illustrator approximately 260 childrens books; author, illustrator: A Russian Farewell (Nat. Jewish Book award), 1981; designer 10 U.S. postage stamps including 1972 and 1977 U.S. Bicentennial Commemorative issues; paintings and illustrations represented in permanent collections Butler Art Inst., Youngstown, Ohio, Mt. Holyoke Coll., Mass., New Britain Mus. Am. Art, U. Conn., Storrs, U. Minn., Mpls., U. Oreg., Eugene, U. So. Miss., Hattiesburg, Brown U., Providence, Libr. of Congress, Washington, N.Y. Pub. Libr., Mus. Am. Illustration, N.Y.C. Trustee Westport Pub. Library, Conn., 1982-89, v.p., 1985-86, pres. 1986-89; founding mem. Westport-Weston Arts Coun., 1969, pres., bd. dirs., 1973-74, trustee, 1969-76. With U.S. Army, 1942-46, NATOUSA, PTO. Recipient Premio Grafico Internat. Book Fair, Italy, 1968, Medallion, U. So. Miss., 1979, Christopher medal, 1980, Non-Fiction award Childrens Book Guild Washington and the Washington Post, 1989, Regina medal Cath. Libr. Assn., 1991, Kerlan award U. Minn., 1991, Arbuthnot Honor Lectr. citation ALA, 1995, Pulitzer Art scholarship, 1950; Winchester fellow Yale U., 1949. Mem. Soc. Illustrators, Silvermine Guild (trustee 1970-74), Authors Guild N.Y., P.E.N. Home: 7 Twin Bridge Acre Rd Westport CT 06880-1028

FISHER, LESTER EMIL, zoo administrator; b. Chgo., Feb. 24, 1921; s. Louis and Elizabeth (Vodicka) F.; m. Wendy Fisher, Jan. 23, 1981; children: Jane Serrita, Katherine Clark. MDV, Iowa State U., 1943. Supr. animal care program Northwestern U. Med. Sch., 1946-47; attending veterinarian Lincoln Park Zoo, Chgo., 1947-62, zoo dir., 1962-92, dir. emeritus, 1992—; owner, dir. Berwyn (Ill.) Animal Hosp., 1947-68; producer, moderator ednl. closed circuit TV for nat. vet. meetings, 1949-66; asso. prof. dept. biology DePaul U., 1968-98; adj. prof. zoology U. Ill., from 1972. Editor: Brit. Small Animal Jour. and Small Animal Clinician, 1958-72. Mem. citizens com. U. Ill.; chmn. zoo and wildlife div. Morris Animal Found. Served to maj., Vet. Corps AUS, 1943-46. Recipient Alumni Merit award Iowa State U., 1968, Stange award Iowa State U., 1988, Chgo. Superior Pub. Svc. award Chgo. Park Dist., 1973, 92, Laureate Ill. Lincoln Acad., 1993. Mem. Am. Animal Hosp. Assn. (regional dir., outstanding Service award 1969), Am. Vet. Med. Assn., Nat. Recreation and Park Assn., Internat. Union Dirs. Zool. Gardens (v.p. 1980-83, pres. 1983-86), Am. Assn. Zoo Veterinarians (pres. 1966-69), Am. Assn. Zool. Parks and Aquariums (pres. 1972-73, chmn. gorilla species survival plan 1982-92), Chgo. Geographic Soc. (v.p.), Econ. Club Chgo., Theta Xi. Clubs: Adventures (pres. 1971-72), Execs. of Chgo. (bd. dirs. 1968-71), Arts. Assoc., Chgo. Econs. (membership com.) (Chgo.). Home and Office: 3180 N Lake Shore Dr Apt 17H Chicago IL 60657-4868

FISHER, LINDA ALICE, physician; b. Plainfield, N.J., Dec. 27, 1947; d. Alvin Edwin and Bertha Sophie (Steigmann) F. BA, Douglass Coll., New Brunswick, N.J., 1970; M in Med. Sci., Rutgers U., 1972; MD, Harvard U., 1975; MPH, St. Louis U., 1996. Diplomate Am. Bd. Internal Medicine, Am. Bd. Preventive Medicine. Intern, then resident Jewish Hosp. St. Louis, 1975-78; dir. ambulatory care St. Luke's Hosp., St. Louis, 1978-84; chief med. officer St. Louis County Dept. Health, Clayton, 1984-97, dir. rsch., 1997—; project dir. St. Louis STD/HIV Prevention Tng. Ctr., 1995—; chief physician St. Louis Met. Police Dept., 1978-88; clin. instr. medicine Washington U., St. Louis, 1978-94, asst. clin. prof., 1994—; asst. clin. prof. medicine St. Louis U., 1979-95, assoc. clin. prof., 1996—; adj. faculty health svcs. mgmt. U. Mo., Columbia, 1996, St. Louis U. Sch. Pub. Health, 1993—; bd. overseers St. Louis Regional Med. Ctr., 1985-95; cons. Ill. Local Govtl. Law Enforcement Officers Tng. Bd., 1988. Contbr. articles to profl. jours.; author of short stories. Chmn. licensure com. Mo. Bd. Registration for Healing Arts, 1983-86; adv. coun. Greater St. Louis Coun. Girl Scouts U.S., 1986—. Recipient Disting. Alumni award Douglass Coll., 1992, Publ. award Mo. Pub. Health Assn., 1994, St. Louis Woman of Achievement award KMOX Radio and Suburban Jours., 1995. Fellow ACP; mem. AMA, APHA, Am. Med. Women's Assn. (chpt. pres. 1982-85, Cmty. Svc. award 1992), Am. Med. Writers Assn., Nat. Assn. Med. Communicators (Ken Alvord Cmty. Svc. award 1998), St. Louis Met. Med. Soc. (councilor 1982-84, sec. 1986, editor 1989-90), Mo. Women's Forum. Lutheran. Avocation: St. Louis history.

FISHER, LLOYD EDISON, JR., lawyer; b. Medina, Ohio, Oct. 23, 1923; s. Lloyd Edison and Wanda (White) F.; m. Twylla Dawn Peterson, Sept. 11, 1949 (dec. Apr. 1996); children: Karen S., Kirk P. BS, Ohio State U., 1947, JD, 1949. Bar: Ohio 1950. Mem. gen. hearing bd. Ohio Dept. Taxation, 1950-53; trust officer Huntington Nat. Bank, Columbus, 1953-62; ptnr. Porter, Wright, Morris & Arthur and predecessor firm, Columbus, 1962—; adj. prof. law Ohio State U., Columbus, 1967-69, 84-91. Bd. dirs Wesley Glen Retirement Ctr., 1974-80, 88-95; bd. dirs. Grant/Riverside Hospice, 1997—. Served with AUS, 1943-45. Fellow Am. Coll. Trust and Estate Counsel; mem. ABA, Ohio Bar Assn., Columbus Bar Assn., Order of Coif. Home: 6478 Strathaven Ct E Worthington OH 43085-2985 Office: 41 S High St Columbus OH 43215-6101

FISHER, LOUIS MCLANE, JR., management consultant; b. Balt., July 25, 1938; s. Louis McLane and Betty Taylor (Griswold) F.; m. Sue Jane Roderick, Jan. 2, 1977; children: Kathy, Mark, Matthew, Andy; stepchildren: Rolf (dec.), Sonja, Kirsten. B.A. magna cum laude, Hampden-Sydney Coll., 1961; postgrad., U. Va., 1961-62; M.B.A., U. Oreg., 1963. Exec. trainee First Nat. Bank Oreg., Portland, 1963; investment analyst First Nat. Bank Oreg., 1964; owner. Bus. Consulting Svcs., Corvallis, Oreg., 1964-65; administrv. mgr. CH2M HILL, Denver, 1965-70, treas., 1970-75, exec. v.p., 1975-94; pres. Quaere, Littleton, Colo., 1995—; guest lectr. Oreg. State U.; bd. dirs. Open Door Inc., Iotech Inc., OMI Inc., Indsl. Design Corp., Power Interests Holding Corp., Coleman Sperryn-Jones, Mariott Resort, Bahamas, GCSI Tissuscan Tech., Grand Masters of Lacrosse. Contbr. articles to profl. jours. Bd. dirs. Corvallis Arts Ctr. Fellow Profl. Svcs. Mgmt. Assn. (cert. profl. svcs. mgr.; bd. dirs. 1975-78, pres. 1976-77, chmn. coll. fellows 1980—); mem. Am. Mgmt. Assn., Am. Cons. Engrs. Coun., Nat. Assn. Corp. Dirs., Fin. Execs. Inst., Western Regional Coun. (treas. 1987-88), Denver C. of C., Corvallis Area C. of C. (bd. dirs., v.p. 1971), Met. Club, Châine de Rôtisseurs. Republican. Episcopalian. Clubs: Metropolitan. Home: 6093 S Bellaire Way Littleton CO 80121 Office: Quaere 5250 E Arapahoe Rd Ste F7 Littleton CO 80122-2361

FISHER, LUCY J., motion picture company executive; b. N.Y.C., Oct. 2, 1949; d. Arthur Bertram and Naomi (Kislak) F.; m. Douglas Z. Wick, Feb. 16, 1986; children: Sarah, Julia, Tessa. BA, Harvard U., 1971. V.p. prodn. 20th Century Fox, L.A., 1979-80; v.p. worldwide prodns. Zoetrope Studios, Burbank, Calif., 1980-81; v.p., sr. prodn. exec. Warner Bros. Pictures, Burbank, 1981-87, sr. v.p., 1987-89, exec. v.p. prodn., 1989-96; vice chmn. Columbia Tristar Motion Picture Co., Culver City, Calif., 1996—. Office: Columbia Tristar Motion Pic Co Thalberg Bldg Ste 3211 10202 W Washington Blvd Culver City CA 90232-3119*

FISHER, M. JANICE, hospital administrator; b. Phila., Dec. 16, 1937; d. Joseph John and Phyllis R. (Catarro) Ronollo; 1 child, Mary Phillips Talbutt. AS, Delaware County C.C., 1987. Dir. vol. resources Haverford (Pa.) State Hosp., 1971-95; liaison Friends of Haverford State Hosp., 1986-88. Pres. Local 2347 Am. Fedn. State, County, Mcpl. Employees Cheney U., 1976-83, Local 2346, Haverford State Hosp., 1987-88; dir. cmty. health and safety ARC Chester-Wallingford, 1985-86. Mem. Am. Hosp. Assn., Assn. Dirs. Vol. Svcs., Lioness Club Aston Twp., Delt. Valley Assn. Dirs. Vol. Programs, M.L.B. Club (v.p.). Home: 635 E 19th St Chester PA 19013-5610

FISHER, MARGARET ELEANOR, psychologist, lawyer, arbitrator, mediator, educator; b. Newark; d. John T. and Mary (Worden) F.; BS cum laude in Psychology, Seton Hall U., 1958; postgrad. U. Paris, 1958, Carl G. Jung Inst., Switzerland, 1958-59, NYU, 1959-60, U. Md., 1960-63; MA magna cum laude in Ednl. Psychology, San Diego State U., 1966; postgrad. (NDEA grantee), U. Alaska, 1965, MBA, MPA, 1991; PhD cum laude in Psychology, U. Wash., 1970; JD magna cum laude, La Salle U., 1993. Lic. pilot, comml. helicopter, fixed wing. Resident counselor Children's Center, N.Y.C., 1959-60; tchr. Am. Dependents' Schs., Okinawa, Germany, Turkey, France, 1960-64; tchr. English as fgn. lang. Jean Giraudoux Lycée, Chateauroux, France, 1963-64; tchr. English and French, Sweetwater Sch. Dist., Chula Vista, Calif., 1964-66; asst. to editor Rev. of Ednl. Research Jour., Seattle, 1967-68; psychologist vocat. rehab. program Edmonds Sch. Dist., Lynnwood, Wash., 1968-70; cons. psychologist Charles Denny Youth Center, Everett, Wash., 1969-71; instr. psychology Seattle Community Coll., 1971; asst. prof. dept. social scis., humanities and edn. Purdue U., Lafayette, Ind., 1971-72; lang. evaluation specialist Def. Lang. Inst., Monterey, Calif., 1972; research psychologist U. Calif., San Francisco, 1972; asst. prof. psychology U. Calif., Santa Cruz, 1973, Mass. State Colls., 1973-76; pvt. practice psychology, Mass., 1976-78; psychologist N.Y. State Dept. Mental Hygiene, 1978, Alaska div. mental health Harborview Devel. Center, Valdez, 1978-79; psychologist Alaska Psychiat. Inst., Anchorage, 1979-95; psychologist, atty. Alaska Psychol., Arbitration & Mediation Svcs., Inc., 1995—; adj. prof. law & psychology La Salle U.; capt. Civil Air Patrol, Alaska, 1987—; mem. Alaska State Bd. Psychologists and Psychol. Assocs. Examiners, 1984-88; arbitrator, mediator forensic psychologist Am. Arbitration Assn., Soc. Profls. in Dispute Resolution . Amb. to Mauritius, Anchorage organizing com. 1994 Winter Olympics, 1988—. Recipient internat. travel award Purdue U., 1972, scholarly support award Mass. State Coll., 1974, 75, 76; lic. psychologist, Mass., Ind., Alaska. Fellow Am. Coll. Forensic Examiners (diplomate, cert. forensic examiner); mem. APA, DAR, Internat. Council Psychologists (area world chairs coord. 1979-95, pres. 1991-92), Interam. Soc. Psychologists, Mensa. Contbr. articles to psychol. and law jours. Home and Office: PO Box 190925 Anchorage AK 99519-0925

FISHER, MARK JAY, neurologist, neuroscientist, educator; b. Bklyn., Aug. 23, 1949; s. Ralph Aaron and Dorothy Ann (Weissman) F.; m. Janeth Godeau, Aug. 5, 1994. BA in Polit. Sci., UCLA, 1970; MA in Polit. Sci., U. S.D., 1972; MD, U. Cin., 1975; JD, Loyola U., 1997. Diplomate Am. Bd. Psychiatry and Neurology. Intern UCLA Sepulveda VA Hosp., 1975-76; resident UCLA Wadsworth VA Med. Ctr., 1976-79, chief resident, 1979-80; faculty mem., dir. stroke rsch. program U. So. Calif. Sch. of Medicine, L.A., 1980-98, prof. neurology, 1995-98; dir. residency tng. program U. So. Calif. Sch. Medicine, L.A., 1992-96; chmn. dept. neurology U. Calif. at Irvine, Orange, 1998—, prof. neurology and anatomy and neurobiology, 1998—. Editor: Medical Therapy of Acute Stroke, 1989. Recipient Tchr. Investigator award NIH, Bethesda, Md., 1984-89, Program Project grantee, 1994-99. Mem. Am. Acad. Neurology, Am. Neurol. Assn., Am. Heart Assn. (stroke coun.), Nat. Stroke Assn., Internat. Soc. for Thrombosis and Haemostasis, State Bar of Calif. Office: U Calif Irvine Dept Neurology 101 The City Dr S Orange CA 92868-3201

FISHER, MARSHALL LEE, operations management educator; b. Wyandotte, Mich., Feb. 19, 1944; s. Gary Hamilton and Bernice (Druckenbrod) F.; m. Geraldine Ann DeFusco, Nov. 18, 1967; children: Kara, Kimberly, Tobin. BSEE, MIT, 1965, MIT, 1969; PhD, MIT, 1970. Asst. prof. mgmt. sci. Grad. Sch. Bus., U. Chgo., 1970-75; vis. prof. (asst.) dept. ops. rsch. Cornell U., Ithaca, N.Y., 1974-75; assoc. prof. Wharton Sch., U. Pa., Phila., 1975-79, prof. ops. and info. mgmt., 1979-86, co-dir. Fishman-Davidson for Svc. and Ops. Mgmt., 1986—; Thomas Henry Carroll-Ford Found Found. vis. prof. bus. adminstrn. Harvard Bus. Sch., Boston, 1996; cons. Dupont, NASA, Dept. Def., Exxon, FritoLay, Navistar, Air Products & Chems., Inc., USM Corp., Scott Paper, Campbell Soup, Gen. Motors, Spiegel, IBM, Ahold, Allied Signal, others. Editor: Mgmt. Sci, 1979-87, SIAM Jour. Algebraic and Discrete Methodis, 1980-87; contbr. articles to profl. jours. Recipient E. Grosvenor Plowman award Nat. Council Phys. Distbn. Mem. Inst. Mgmt. Sci. (Mgmt. Sci. Practice prize 1983, pres. 1988-89), Math. Programming Soc., Ops. Rsch. Soc. Am. (Lanchester prize 1977), Nat. Acad. Engring. (elected), Sigma Xi. Office: U Pa Wharton Sch Dept Ops and Info Mgmt 3620 Locust Walk Philadelphia PA 19104-6302

FISHER, MARY MAURINE, federal agency official, retired; b. Schenectady, N.Y., July 19, 1929; d. Maurice Lee and Beatrice Mae (Harris) Prescott; m. Eugene T. Fisher, Apr. 16, 1948 (dec. 1982); children: Gene Thomas, William Lee. Cert., Strayer Coll., 1952, U. Va., 1966-89. Credit mgr. Gen. Electric Credit Corp., Washington, 1950-70; with SBA, Washington, 1970-98; ret., 1998; mem. Pres.'s adv. com. on small and minority bus., 1979-85, on Native Am. affairs, 1979-80, on reservation devel., 1978-79, on Native Am. econ. devel., 1977-78. Mem. Fairfax (Va.) Little League, 1956-74, Fairfax Indsl. Devel. Authority, 1985—; v.p. Warren Woods-Joyce Heights Civic Assn., Fairfax, 1958—; active Friends of Fairfax City. Mem. Nat. Contract Mgmt. Assn. Democrat. Methodist. Avocations: reading, sewing, modeling. Home: 4203 Lamarre Dr Fairfax VA 22030-5133

FISHER, MATTHEW P. A., physicist. Rsch. physicist Inst. Theoretical Physics, Santa Barbar, Calif. Recipient Initiatives in Rsch. award NAS, 1997. Office: U California Inst Theoretical Physics 522 University Rd Santa Barbara CA 93106-0002*

FISHER, MICHAEL BRUCE, lawyer; b. Montgomery, Ala., Jan. 2, 1945; s. Philip and Rita (Joss) F.; m. Noreen Rene Zidel, June 25, 1967; children: Anne Elizabeth, Alex Nicholas. BA, U. Minn., 1967; JD, U. Calif.-Berkeley, 1970. Bar: N.Y. 1971, Minn. 1972, U.S. Dist. Ct. Minn. 1972. Assoc. Rosenman, Colin, et al, N.Y.C., 1970-71, Mullin, Swirnoff & Weinberg, P.A., Mpls., 1972-73; staff atty. Fingerhut Corp., Mpls., 1974, assoc. gen. counsel, 1975-80, gen. counsel, 1980-83, v.p., gen. counsel, sec., 1983-90; of counsel Oppenheimer, Wolff & Donnelly, 1990; pres. Warshawsky & Co., Chgo., 1990-91; v.p., gen. counsel Allied Mktg. Group, Inc., Dallas, 1992-93; pvt. practice Mpls., 1993-97; gen. mgr. sys., dir. mktg. Sun Harvest, Ft. Myers, Fla., 1998—; bd. advisors Automated Comms. Inc., 1991-96. Mem. exec. com., dir. Big Sisters Mpls., Inc., 1976-83, Big Bros./Big Sisters Mpls., Inc. 1984-90; v.p., bd. dirs., pres. Herzl Camp Assn., Inc., Mpls., 1971—; vol. Minn. Pub. TV, St. Paul, gen. auction chmn., 1988-89; bd. dirs. Minn. Pub. Lobby, 1989-95. Mem. ABA, Minn. Bar Assn., Am. Corp. Counsel Assn. Minn., Minn. Retail Mchts. Assn. (trustee 1983-89, exec. com. 1988-89), Direct Mktg. Assn. (govt. affairs com. 1980-92), Flying Golf Club, Inc. (v.p. 1998—), 3d Class Mail Assn. (bd. dirs. 1979-89, sec. 1981-86, exec. vice chmn. 1987-88, chmn. bd. dirs. 1988-89), Parcel Shippers Assn. (v.p., bd. dirs. 1980-86, pres. 1987, chmn. bd. dirs. 1988-90). Jewish. Office: 14810 Metro Pkwy Fort Myers FL 33912-4307

FISHER, MICHAEL CHARLES, school administrator; b. N.Y.C., Aug. 10, 1944; s. Samuel and Sadie (Seidenberg) F.; m. Naomi Ruth Morgan, Apr. 8, 1990. BA, CCNY, 1966, MA, 1970. Tchr. social studies N.Y.C. Bd. Edn., 1966-69, edn. adminstr., instrn. specialist, 1979-83; asst. dir. Beta Sch., N.Y.C., 1983-84; chpt. 53 screening adminstr. Comty. Sch. Dist. 4, N.Y.C., 1984-85, attendance improvement coord., 1984-85; dir. Creative Learning Comty., N.Y.C., 1985-98; asst. principal JHS 117 Dist 4; staff developer N.Y.C. Bd. Edn., N.Y.C., 1980-83; mem. curriculum com. Comty. Sch. Dist. 4, N.Y.C., 1993-97; youth leadership coord. Comty. Sch. Dist. 9, N.Y.C., 1972-73. Mem. Seaman North Block Assn., N.Y.C., 1980-90. Mem. ASCD (asst. prin. 1987-98). Avocations: tennis, golf, basketball, coaching basketball. Office: Comty Sch Dist 4 319 E 117th St New York NY 10035-4902

FISHER, MICHAEL ELLIS, mathematical physicist, chemist; b. Trinidad, W.I., Sept. 3, 1931; m. Sorrel Castillejo; children: Caricia J., Daniel S., Martin J., Matthew P.A. B.S. with 1st class honors in Physics, King's Coll., London, 1951, Ph.D., 1957; DSc (hon.), Yale U., 1987, Tel Aviv U., 1992. Lectr. math. RAF, 1952-53; lectr. theoretical physics King's Coll., 1958-62, reader physics, 1962-64; prof. physics U. London, 1965-66; prof. chemistry and math. Cornell U., 1966-73, Horace White prof. chemistry, physics and math., 1973-89, chmn. dept. chemistry, 1975-78; Disting. prof. Inst. for Phys. Sci. and Tech. U. Md., 1987—, Regents prof. Inst. for Phys. Sci. & Tech., 1993—; guest investigator Rockefeller Inst., 1963-64; vis. prof. applied physics Stanford U., 1970-71; Buhl lectr. theoretical physics Carnegie-Mellon U., 1971; Richtmyer Meml. lectr. Am. Assn. Physics Tchrs., 1973; S. H. Klosk lectr. NYU, 1975; 17th F. London Meml. lectr. Duke U., 1975; Walker-Ames prof. U. Wash., Seattle, 1977; Loeb lectr. physics Harvard U., 1979; vis.prof. physics MIT, 1979; Welsh Found. lectr. in physics U. Toronto, Ont., Can., 1979; 21st Alpheus Smith lectr. Ohio State U., 1982; Fairchild scholar Calif. Inst. Tech., 1984; Cherwell-Simon lectr., vis. prof. Oxford U., 1985; Schlapp scholar Edinburgh U., 1987; Marker lectr. Pa. State U., 1988, Nat. Sci. Coun. lectr., Taiwan, 1989; Hamilton Meml. lectr. Princeton U., 1990, 65th J. W. Gibbs lectr. Am. Math. Soc., 1992; E. U. Condon lectr. U. Colo., 1992; M. S. Green Meml. lectr. Temple U., 1992; R&B Sackler Disting. lectr. in solid state physics Tel Aviv U., 1992; 1st Lars Onsager lectr., Norway, 1993; Phi Beta Kappa vis. scholar, 1994; Lennard-Jones lectr. Royal Soc. Chemistry, 1995; Joseph O. Hirschfelder Prize lectr. U. Wis., 1995; Gilbert Newton Lewis Meml. lectr. U. Calif., Berkeley, 1995; George Fisher Bakes lectr. chemistry Cornell U., 1997. Author: (with D. M. MacKay) Analogue Computing at Ultra-High Speed, 1962, The Nature of Critical Points, 1964, The Theory of Equilibrium Critical Phenomena, 1967; assoc. editor: Jour. Math. Physics, 1965-68, 72-75, 86-89; adv. bd.: Jour. Theoretical Biology, 1969-82, Chem. Physics, 1972-84, Discrete Math., 1971-78, Jour. Statis. Physics, 1978-81; mem. editl. bd. Comms. Math. Phys., 1984—, Phys. Rev. A, 1987-92; contbr. numerous articles to profl. jours. Recipient award in phys. and math. scis. N.Y. Acad. Scis., 1978, Guthrie medal and prize Inst. Physics, London, 1980, Wolf prize in physics, 1980, Michelson-Morely award Case Western Res. U., 1982, Boltzmann medal IUPAP, 1983, Hirschfelder prize U. Wis., 1995; Guggenheim fellow, 1970-71, 78-79. Fellow AAAS, Am. Acad. Arts and Scis., Royal Soc. London (Bakerian lectr. 1979, regional editor 1989-93, v.p. 1993—), Phys. Soc. London, Am. Phys. Soc. (Langmuir prize chem. physics 1970, Lars Onsager Meml. prize 1995, Centennial lectr. 1999), Kings Coll. London, Royal Soc. Edinburgh (hon.); mem. NAS (fgn. assoc., James Murray Luck award 1983), Am. Chem. Soc. (Joel H. Hildebrand award 1995), Am. Philos. Soc., Soc. Indsl. and Applied Math., Math. Assn. Am., Brazilian Acad. Scis. (fgn. assoc.), N.Y. Acad. Scis. Office: U Md Inst Phys Sci & Tech College Park MD 20742

FISHER, MILES MARK, IV, education and religion educator, minister; b. Huntington, W.Va., Sept. 25, 1932; s. Miles Mark and Ada Virginia (Foster) F. B.A., Va. Union U., 1954, M.Div., 1959; M.A., N.C. Central U., 1968; D.Min., Howard U., 1978. Ordained to ministry Baptist Ch., 1961; tchr. pub. schs. Durham, N.C., 1959-67; assoc. min. White Rock Bapt. Ch., Durham, N.C., 1959-65; asst. prof. edn., counselor Norfolk (Va.) State U., 1967-69; cons. Model Cities Area of Recreation, Norfolk, 1968-69; exec.-sec., CEO Nat. Assn. Equal Opportunity in Higher Edn., Washington, 1969-78; spl. cons. Inst. for Services to Edn., Washington, 1969-70; vis. asst. prof. Sch. Divinity Howard U., 1978-80; staff dir., com. clk. Com. of Whole, Council of D.C., Washington, 1979-83; spl. asst. to v.p. acad. affairs U. D.C., Washington, 1983-84; dir. policy rev. and analysis Office of the Bd. of Trustees U. D.C., 1985-88, exec. dir. Office of the Bd. of Trustees, 1989-90, interim pres., 1990-91, disting. U. prof., 1991—; chaplain counselor Lincoln Hosp. Sch. Nursing, Durham, N.C., 1962-67; chaplain Fisher Funeral Parlor, Durham, 1963-67; mem. task force employment of minority populations Nat. Recreation and Park Assn., 1970-71; mem. task force on edn. and Vietnam Era vet. VA, 1971-72; mem. steering com. U.S. Office of Edn. Common Core Data for the 70's, 1971-78, Congl. Black Caucus Nat. Policy Conf. on Black Edn., 1972; mem. Nat. task force on Student Financial Aid Problems, 1974-75; bd. trustees Consortium of U. of the Washington Met. Area, 1990-91; bd. dirs. Washington Rsch. Libr. Consortium, 1990-91. Bd. dirs. Cooperative Coll. Registry, 1973-75; mem. adv. bd. Four-Year Servicemen's Opportunity Coll.,

1974-77; mem. adv. com. to bd. dirs. Nat. Student Ednl. Fund, 1974-78; v.p. bd. dirs. Reading is Fundamental Program, 1977-79, Vis. Nurse Assn., 1974-80; bd. dirs. D.C. Citizens for Better Public Edn., 1977, pres., 1981-83; bd. dirs. Voice Informed Community Expression, pres., 1982-84; trustee Va. Union U., 1983-85, Shaw U. Div. Sch., 1982-88. Mem. ACA, Am. Assn. Higher Edn., Am. Acad. Polit. and Social Scis., Am. Acad. Religion, Assn. Multicultural Counseling and Devel., Assn. Spiritual Ethical and Religious Values in Counseling, Am. Soc. Ch. History, Internat. Alumni Assn. Va. Union U. (pres. 1983-85), Am. Tennis Assn. (life), Assn. for Study of Afro-Am. Life and History (life), Assn. for Study of Higher Edn., U.S. Tennis Assn. (life). Home: 4444 Connecticut Ave NW Apt 402 Washington DC 20008-2319 Office: PO Box 2340 Washington DC 20013-2340

FISHER, MORTON POE, JR., lawyer; b. Balt., Aug. 17, 1936; s. Morton Poe Sr. and Adelaide (Block) F.; m. Ann P. Fisher, Aug. 12, 1962; children: Stephen N., Marjorie P. AB, Dartmouth Coll., Hanover, N.H., 1958; LLB, Yale U., 1961. Bar: Md. 1961, D.C. 1961. Law clk. to presiding justice U.S. Dist. Ct. Md., Balt., 1961-62; assoc. Piper & Marbury, 1962-68; asst. gen. counsel Rouse Co., 1968-73; ptnr. Frank, Bernstein, Conaway & Goldman, Balt., 1973-92; mng. ptnr. Balt. office Ballard Spahr Andrews & Ingersoll, Balt., 1992—; faculty mem. U. Md. Law Sch., 1978-87. Mem. Balt. County Econ. Devel. Commn., 1988-90, Mayor's Adv. Commn., Balt. City, Risk Mgmt. Com. Balto City, 1999; bd. dirs. Balt. Downtown Partnership, 1998; dean U. of Shopping ctrs., 1998-99. Mem. ABA (vice chmn. real property divsn 1990-92, chmn. sect. real property, probate and trust law 1993-94), Am. Coll. Real Estate Lawyers (pres. 1988-89), Am. Coll. Constrn. Lawyers, Am. Law Inst., Anglo-Am. Real Property Inst., Internat. Coun. Shopping Ctrs. (co-chmn. law conf. 1995-97, co-dean U. Shopping Ctr. 1998—). Office: Ballard Spahr Andrews & Ingersoll 300 E Lombard St Ste 1900 Baltimore MD 21202-6739

FISHER, NANCY, writer, producer, director; b. Oct. 21, 1941; d. Seymour and Tema Fisher; 1 child, Sarah Olivia. BA, Barbard Coll. Creative group head Benton & Bowles Advt., London, 1970-74, McCann Erickson Advt., N.Y.C., 1974-75; creative dir. Norman, Craig & Kummel Advt., N.Y.C., 1975-78; pres. Nancy Fisher Inc., N.Y.C., 1978—, Creative Programming Inc., N.Y.C., 1981-89. Author: Vital Parts, 1993, Side Effects, 1994, Special Treatment, 1996, Code Red, 1998; creator, writer, prodr. TV series Womanwatch, 1982-89, Celebrity Chefs, 1983-89; numerous home video cassettes, including Look Mom, I'm Fishing (parents Choice award), The Annapolis Book of Seamanship Video Series (Cindy award), The Christmas Carol Video, Video Dog, Video Cat, Video Baby. Recipient 5 broadcast awards Network Documentary Series. Mem. Dirs. Guild Am., Authors Guild. Office: 200 E 84th St New York NY 10028-2906

FISHER, NANCY DEBUTTS, library director; b. Pitts., Apr. 10, 1945; d. Jacob John DeButts and Marie Christine Grills; m. Bruce C. Fisher, May 29, 1971. BS, Cleve. State U., 1968; MSLS, Case We. Res. U., 1973. Reference libr. Cleve. Heights-Univ. Heights Pub. Libr., 1968-79; mgr. Beachwood (Ohio) br. Cuyahoga County Pub. Libr., 1980-90; dir. Wickliffe (Ohio) Pub. Libr., 1990—. Key communicator Wickliffe City Schs., 1992; bd. dirs. Wickliffe Civic Ctr. Inc., 1999—; mem. adv. coun. Wickliffe United Way, 1991-99. Mem. ALA, Ohio Libr. Coun. (mgmt. adminstrn. div. 1992-93), Cleve. Area Met. Libr. Sys. (bd. dirs. 1994-96), Wickliffe C. of C. (v.p. 1998-99, Civic Leader of Yr. 1999), Rotary (pres. 1992-94). E-mail: fisherna@oplin.lib.oh.us. Home: 939 Stuart South Euclid OH 44121 Office: Wickliffe Pub Libr 1713 Lincoln Rd Wickliffe OH 44092

FISHER, NEAL FLOYD, religious organization administrator; b. Washington, Ind., Apr. 4, 1936; s. Floyd Russell and Florence Alice (Williams) F.; m. Ila Alexander, Aug. 18, 1957; children: Edwin Kirk, Julia Bryn. AB, DePauw U., 1957, LHD (hon.), 1982; MDiv, Boston U., 1960, PhD, 1966; STD, MacMurray Coll., Jacksonville, Ill., 1991; DD, Coe Coll., 1994. Ordained to ministry United Meth. Ch., 1958; pastor 1st United Meth. Ch., Revere, Mass., 1960-63, North Andover, Mass., 1963-68; planning assoc. United Meth. Bd. Global Ministries, N.Y.C., 1968-73; dir. planning United Meth. Bd. Global Ministries, 1973-77; assoc. dean, asst. prof. theology and society Boston U. Sch. Theology, 1977-80; pres., prof. theology and society Garrett-Evang. Theol. Sem., Evanston, Ill., 1980—; Mendenhall lectr. DePauw U., Greencastle, Ind., 1982, Willson lectr., Nashville, 1983, Voigt lectr. McKendree Coll., 1984, McKendree Blair lectr. MacMurray Coll., 1986, Henry Martin Loud lectr. U. Mich., Ann Arbor, 1987; Wright lectr. Morningside Coll., 1991; chaplain, preacher, Chautauqua, N.Y., 1984, 88, Lakeside, Ohio, 1996; mem. theol. edn. commn. United Meth. Ch., 1992—, former mem. univ. senate; mem. bd. No. Ill. Conf. United Meth. Ch.; chmn. com. on acad. affairs DePauw U. Bd. Trustees. Author: Parables of Jesus: Glimpses of the New Age, 1979, rev. edit., 1990, Context for Discovery, 1980, Parables of Jesus: Glimpses of God's Reign, 1990; contbg. editor: Truth and Tradition: A Conversation about the Future of United Methodist Theological Education, 1995. Trustee DePauw U., Greencastle, Ind., 1996—. Recipient Disting. Alumnus award Boston U. Sch. Theology, 1985, Disting. Alumni citation DePauw U., 1993; Jacob Sleeper fellow, 1960-61. Mem. Assn. United Meth. Scis., Assn. Chgo. Theol. Schs. (pres. 1985-87, 95-97). E-mail: nfisher@nwu.edu. Home: 3221 Hartzell St Evanston IL 60201-1127 Office: Garrett-Evang Theol Sem 2121 Sheridan Rd Evanston IL 60201-2926

FISHER, PHOEBE GERBER, painter, antique dealer; b. Balt., May 1, 1924; d. Hyman and Blanche (Perel) Gerber; m. Ralph Aaron Fisher, Feb. 10, 1946; children: Harriett, Marsha, Thomas. BA, Md. inst., 1948. Artist, 1944—; interior designer Balt., 1981-91, antique dealer, 1990—. Exhibited in shows at Newport (R.I.) Art Assn., Purdue U., Lafayette, Ind., Soc. fo th Four Arts, West Palm Beach, Fla., Cooperstown (N.Y.) Art Assn., Las Vegas Art League, Miss. Art Assn., Jackson, Lancaster (Pa.) Art Festival, Balt. Mus. Art, Peale Mus., Bowie State Coll., Md. Fedn. Arts, Annapolis, Fairhaven's 5th Biennial Juried Art Exhibit, Ellicott City, Md., 1998, Yorkarts, York, Pa., 1999. Recipient numerous awards for art. Avocations: gardening, reading. Home: 8202 Marcie Dr Baltimore MD 21208-1941

FISHER, PIERRE JAMES, JR., physician; b. Chgo., Oct. 29, 1931; s. Pierre James and Evelyn (Trevithick) F.; m. Carol Ann Walton, Mar. 16, 1951; children—James Walton, David Alan, Steven Edward, Teresa Ann. Student, Taylor U., 1949-51, Ball State U., 1951-52; M.D., Ind. U., 1956. Diplomate Am. Bd. Surgery. Intern U.S. Naval Hosp., San Diego, 1956-57, resident in surgery, 1957-61; pvt. practicee specializing in surgery Surgeons Inc., Marion, Ind., 1965—, pres., 1977—; mem. staff Marion Gen. Hosp., chief staff, 1970. Trustee Meth. Hosp., Indpls., 1972-94. Served with USN, 1956-65. Recipient Physicians Recognition award AMA, 1974, 77, 80, 83, 89; commd. Ky. Col., Gov. Ky., 1997. Fellow ACS; mem. AMA, Grant County Med. Soc. (pres. 1980), Marion Area C. of C. (v.p. 1979-81), N.Am. Med. Golf Assn. (v.p. 1989-90, pres. 1991-93), Rotary (pres. Marion 1983-84, Dist. 656 Disting. Svc. award 1989), Kingsway Country Club (bd. dirs., pres. 1997-99). Methodist. Home: 11250 SW Essex Dr Lake Suzy FL 34266-9162 Office: Surgeons Inc 330 N Wabash Ave Ste 450 Marion IN 46952-2600

FISHER, RAYMOND CORLEY, lawyer; b. Oakland, Calif., July 12, 1939; s. Raymond Henry and Mary Elizabeth (Corley) F.; m. Nancy Leigh Fairchilds, Jan. 22, 1961; children: Jeffrey Scott, Amy Fisher Ahlers. BA, U. Calif., Santa Barbara, 1961; LLB, Stanford U., 1966. Bar: Calif. 1967, U.S. Ct. Appeals (9th cir.) 1967, U.S. Dist. Ct. (no. and cen. dists.) Calif. 1967, U.S. Ct. Claims 1967, U.S. Supreme Ct. 1967. Law clk. to Hon. J. Skelly Wright U.S. Ct. Appeals (D.C. cir.), Washington, 1966-67; law clk. to Hon. William J. Brennan U.S. Supreme Ct., Washington, 1967-68; ptnr. Tuttle & Taylor, L.A., L.A., 1968-88; sr. litigation ptnr. Heller, Ehrman, White & McAuliffe, L.A., 1988-97; assoc. atty. gen. U.S. Dept. of Justice, Washington, 1997—; exec. com. 9th Cir. Jud. Conf., 1989-91; mem. Am. Law Inst., So. Calif. ADR Panel, CPR Inst. for Dispute Resolution. Pres. Stanford Law Rev., 1965-66. Spl. asst. to Gov. of Calif., Sacramento and L.A., 1978—; dir. Constl. Rights Found., L.A., 1978-97, pres., 1983-87; pres. L.A. City Bd. Civil Svc. Commn., 1987-88; dep. gen. counsel Christopher Commn., L.A., 1991-92; pres. L.A. City Bd. Police Commrs., 1996-97. With USAR, 1957. Fellow Am. Coll. Trial Lawyers, Am. Bar Found.; mem. ABA, Fed. Bar Assn. (exec. com. 1990-96), Calif. State Bar, L.A. County Bar Assn., Chancery Club, Order of Coif. Office: U S Dept of Justice 950 Pennsylvania Ave N W Office of Assoc Atty Gen Washington DC 20530*

FISHER, RICHARD B., investment banker; b. Phila., July 21, 1936; s. Ernest W. and Doris Virginia (Rans) F.; m. Emily Hargroves, Sept. 7, 1957; children: R. Britton, Catherine Curtis, Alexander Dylan. A.B., Princeton U., 1957; M.B.A., Harvard U., 1962. Mng. dir. Morgan Stanley & Co., Inc., N.Y.C., 1970—, pres., 1984-91, chmn., 1990-97; chmn. exec. com. Morgan Stanley Dean Witter & Co., N.Y.C., 1997—; mem. N.Y. Stock Exch. Trustee Bar Coll., Urban Inst., Historic Hudson Valley; bd. dirs. Ministers and Missionaries Benefit Bd. of Am. Bapt. Chs., Rockefeller U.; chmn. Bklyn. Acad. of Music Endowment Trust, Princeton U. Investment Co. Mem. Nat. Golf Links, Blin Brook Club, Lyford Cay Club, Mid Ocean Club, Meadow Brook Club. Office: Morgan Stanley Dean Witter & Co 1585 Broadway Fl 40 New York NY 10036-8200*

FISHER, RICHARD FORREST, soils educator; b. Champaign, Ill., May 15, 1941; S. Richard Forrest Fisher and Hannah Elizabeth Ponath; m. Karen Dangerfield, Sept. 4, 1959; children: William Forrest, Marilu, Kevin Royden. BS, U. Ill., 1963; MS, Cornell U., 1967, PhD, 1968. Rsch. scientist Can. Forestry Svc., Sault Sainte Marie, Ont., 1968-69; asst. prof. forestry U. Ill., Urbana, 1969-72; assoc. prof. U. Toronto, Ont., 1972-77; prof. U. Fla., Gainesville, 1977-82; prof., head dept. forest resources Utah State U., Logan, 1982-90; prof., head dept. forest sci. Tex. A&M U., 1990-96, prof., 1996—. Author: (with others) Properties and Management of Forest Soil, 2nd edit.; contbr. articles to profl. jours. Fellow Soc. Am. Foresters, Soil Sci. Soc. Am. (co-editor in chief Forest Ecology and Mgmt.); mem. Ecol. Soc. Am., Internat. Soc. Tropical Foresters, Ecol. Soc. Am., Nat. Assn. Profl. Forestry Schs. and Colls. (pres. 1994-96), Internat. Assn. Round Dance Tchrs. (gen. chmn. 1997-99). Democrat. Avocations: round dance cuer, tchr. E-mail: r-fisher@tamu.edu. Home: 3415 Parkway Ter Bryan TX 77802-3743 Office: Tex A&M U Forest Sci Dept College Station TX 77843

FISHER, RICHARD H., retired orthopaedic surgeon; b. Salem, Va., Nov. 17, 1923; m. Anne Fisher; six children. Student in chemistry, Roanoke Coll., 1942; MD, Med. Coll. Va., 1947. Intern, resident in orthopaedic surgery Med. Coll. of Va., 1947; chief orthopaedic surgery Keesler AFB Hosp., Biloxi, Miss., 1952-54; orthopaedic surgeon Lewis-Gale Clinic and Hosp., 1954-90; pvt. practice, Salem, 1990-94; ret., 1994. Founder Lewis-Gale Med. Found., 1965, past pres.; founder Life Guard, 1980, Salem Edn. Found. and Alumni Assn.; past chmn. Salem Sch. Bd.; active numerous civic activities include Salem Hist. Soc., Civic Ctr., Sports Found., We the People Com., others.

FISHER, RICHARD N., lawyer; b. L.A., Oct. 28, 1943. BA, U. Redlands, 1965; MA, U. Wis., 1966; JD, U. Calif., Berkeley, 1969. Bar: Calif. 1970. Mem. O'Melveny & Myers, L.A. Vice chmn. bd. trustees U. Redlands. Mem. ABA, L.A. County Bar Assn. (labor and employment law sects.). Office: O'Melveny & Myers 400 S Hope St Los Angeles CA 90071-2899

FISHER, ROBERT, gastroenterologist, health facility administrator; b. Bklyn., July 28, 1939; married. BSE, Princeton U., 1960; MD, U. Pa., 1964. Intern Chgo. Wesley Meml. Hosp., 1964-65; resident in internal meedicine Temple U. Hosp., Phila., 1967-70; fellow in gastroenterology Hosp. U. Pa., 1970-72; from asst. prof. to assoc. prof. Temple U. Sch. Medicine, 1972-80, prof. medicine, 1980—; dir. Functional Gastrointestinal Disease Ctr. Temple U. Hosp., Phila., 1984—, chief gastroenterology sect., 1985—. Mem. Am. Coll. Gastroenterology, Am. Gastroent. Assn., Am. Soc. Gastrointestinal Endoscopy, Am. Fedn. Clin. Rsch., Rsch. Soc. Alcoholism. Office: Temple Univ 3400 N Broad St Philadelphia PA 19140-5104

FISHER, ROBERT ABEL, advertising executive; b. Buffalo, Jan. 13, 1951; s. Irving M. and Thelma R. (Abel) F.; m. Roberta L. Leifer, June 30, 1974; children: Michael, Graham. BS in Polit. Sci., SUNY, Buffalo, 1973. Producer Jaguar Prodns. Inc., N.Y.C., 1975-77; exec. producer Bob Giraldi Prodns. Inc., N.Y.C., 1977-80, Michael Ulick Prodns. Inc., N.Y.C., 1981-86; exec. producer, ptnr. UMP and Assocs., Inc., N.Y.C., 1986-90; exec. producer, ptnr. Ptnrs./U.S.A., N.Y.C., 1990-92, exec. producer, gen. mgr. East Coast office, 1992—; exec. prodr., ptnr. Fahrenheit Films, 1992-96; pres. Celcius Films, 1996—. Exec. producer (film) Rocket Gibraltar, 1988. Office: Celsius Films Inc 37 E 18th St New York NY 10003-2001

FISHER, ROBERT ALAN, laser physicist; b. Berkeley, Calif., Apr. 19, 1943; s. Leon Harold and Phyllis (Kahn) F.; children: Andrew Leon, Derek Martin; m. Dixie Sisson, Mar. 8, 1998. AB, U. Calif., Berkeley, 1965, MA, 1967, PhD, 1971. Programmer Stanford (Calif.) linear accelerator Stanford U., Stanford University, 1965; staff mem. Granger Assocs., Palo Alto, Calif., 1966; lectr. U. Calif., Davis, 1972-74; physicist Lawrence Livermore Lab., Calif., 1971-74; laser physicist Los Alamos (N.Mex.) Nat. Lab., 1974-86; cons. to R.A. Fisher Assocs., Santa Fe, N.Mex., 1986—; instr. Engring. Tech., Inc., 1982—; mem. Air Force ABCD Panel, 1982; program com. mem. Internat. Quantum Electronics Conf., 1982, 86; vice chmn. Gordon Conf. on Lasers and Non-linear Optics, 1981; chmn. Soc. Photo-Optical Instrumentation Engrs. conf. on Optical Phase Conjugation/Beam Combining/Diagnostics, 1987—; mem. Air Force Red Team for Space-Based Laser, 1983-86, HEDS II SDI Red Team, 1986; U.S. Ballistic Missile Office Options Team, 1986; mem. secretariat SDI Red/Blue Sensor Teams, 1986, SDI GBL Red/Blue Team Interaction, 1987-88; mem. architecture panel SDI SDS Phase 1, 1990, Air Force Laser 21 Working Group, 1990. Assoc. editor Optics Letters, 1984-86, Applied Optics, 1984-91; editor: Optical Phase Conjugation, 1973; contbr. articles to profl. jours. Vol. coach elem. sch. chess team Pojoaque Elem. Sch. (winner nat. elem. championship 1984), Santa Fe, 1984. Fellow Optical Soc. Am. (guest editor jour. spl. issue on optical phase conjugation), SPIE; mem. IEEE (sr.), Am. Phys. Soc. Avocations: restoring old houses; skiing; music. Home and Office: PO Box 9279 Santa Fe NM 87504-9279

FISHER, ROBERT BRUCE, priest; b. Paragould, Ark., Feb. 6, 1937; s. Lawrence Bruce Fisher and Georgia M. (Paris) Kasper. BA, Divine Word Seminary, Techny, Ill., 1961, MA, 1965; STB, STL, Gregorian Univ., Rome, 1966; STD, Pont. Ateneo di Sant' Anselmo, Rome, 1969. Ordained priest Roman Cath. Ch., 1965. Adminstrv. attache Nunciature of Holy See, Accra, Ghana, 1982-83; pastor Good Shepherd Ch., Tema, Ghana, 1984-86; asst. pastor St. Matthias Ch., New Orleans, 1990-94; pastor St. Martin de Porres Ch., Prairie View, 1996—; asst. prof. Xavier U., New Orleans, 1988-95; dir. studies A. Tolton House of Studies, New Orleans, 1991-96; dist. superior Divine Word Soc. New Orleans, 1990-96; promoter New African Cinema film series; instr. in ethics and critical thinking of Prairie View Tex. A&M U., 1998—; adj. prof. Prairie View A&M U., 1997—. Author: West African Religious Traditions: Focus on the Akan of Ghana, 1998; editor: (liturgical ordo) Ordo for the Phillipines, 1972. Co-chmn. Cath. Returnee Crisis Com., Accra, 1982-83. Mem. Coll. Theology Soc., Am. Acad. Religion, KC (chaplain Met. chpt. 1993-96); African Assn. for Study of Religions. Democrat. E-mail: oburoni@msn.com.

FISHER, ROBERT CHARLES HARU, publishing company executive, editor; b. Burlington, Iowa, Mar. 3, 1930; s. Ray Erwin and Blanche Columbia (Brolin) F. B.A. cum laude, Harvard U., 1955; postgrad., Columbia U. Law Sch., 1955-56, Tokyo U., 1957-59. Analyst, adjutant gen's. office U.S. Army, Kansas City, Mo., 1949-50, Washington, 1950-51; adv. Prime Minister Takeo Miki of Japan, 1957-64; Far Eastern rep. Fodor Travel Guides, Tokyo, 1959-64; exec. editor Fodor Travel Guides, N.Y.C., 1964-66, 75-77; exec. v.p. Fodor Travel Guides, 1975-77, pres., 1977-80; exec. editor Fodor Travel Guides, London, 1966-74; v.p. David McKay Co., N.Y.C., 1976-80; pres. Fisher Travel Guides, 1980-88; gen. editor Crown Insider's Travel Guides, 1988-89; editorial dir. Gault Millau Guides, 1989-90; cons. Simon & Schuster, N.Y.C., 1990-92; editorial dir. Maco Comm., N.Y.C., 1992-94; exec. editor Arthur Frommer, Inc., N.Y.C., 1995—; Founder, dir. Kansas City Open Forum, 1949-50; bd. dirs. Internat. Assn. Med. Assistance to Travelers, 1972—, v.p., 1985—; chmn. Hotel and Restaurant Unsafe Food Labeling Action com., 1995—; pres. Fisher Publs. Inc., 1997—. Author: Picasso, 1967, Klee, 1967, Guide to Japan, 1981, Insider's Guide to Japan, 1986. Served with CIC U.S. Army, 1952-54, Korea. Balt. Scholarship Fund grantee for study in Japan, 1956-59. Mem. Japan Soc. (N.Y.), Internat. House of Japan, Soc. Am. Travel Writers (dir. 1978-80, v.p. 1981-83, pres. 1983-84), N.Y. Travel Writers Assn. (pres. 1979-81); British Guild Travel Writers (chmn. 1970-71), Soc. Am. Travel Writers Found. (pres. 1985-90). Clubs: Harvard of N.Y.C., Am. of Japan.

FISHER, ROBERT DALE, stockbroker, retired naval officer; b. Memphis, July 30, 1924; s. Hollis Welton and Anna Sue (Parrish) F.; m. Joy Lee Chandler, Mar. 30, 1946. B.S., Am. U., 1957. Commd. ensign U.S. Navy, 1944, advanced through grades to comdr., 1963; tng. officer Polaris Missile program, 1955-58; comdr. destroyer, 1959-61, ret., 1963; stockbroker, 1963—; v.p. investments Smith Barney, Washington, 1979—. Mem. Mil. Order of Carabao. Republican. Methodist. Clubs: Kiwanis (pres. Falls Church, Va. 1969, McLean, Va. 1979-80), Nat. Capital Economists, Army-Navy. Lodge: Masons, Shriners, Jesters. Home: 6033 Chesterbrook Rd Mc Lean VA 22101-3213 Office: 1776 I St NW Ste 900 Washington DC 20006-3700

FISHER, ROBERT I., lawyer; b. Bklyn., July 10, 1939; s. Sidney B. and Jeanette (Talisman) F.; m. Debra Kram Fisher, June 30, 1974; children: Daniel I., Elizabeth R. BA, Columbia U., 1960; JD cum laude, Harvard U., 1963; LLM, N.Y.U., 1967. Bar: N.Y. 1964. Assoc. Dewey, Ballantine, Bushby, Palmer & Wood, N.Y.C., 1964-67, Sullivan & Cromwell, N.Y.C., 1967-72; ptnr. Greenbaum, Wolff & Ernst, N.Y.C., 1974-82, Rosenman & Colin, N.Y.C., 1982—; lectr. Practicing Law Inst. Fulbright fellow, Israel, 1963-64. Mem. ABA, N.Y. State Assn., Assn. Bar. City of N.Y.. Home: 150 Factory Pond Rd Locust Valley NY 11560-1416 Office: Rosenman & Colin LLP 575 Madison Ave Fl 26 New York NY 10022-2585

FISHER, ROBERT LLOYD, retired marine geologist and oceanographer; b. Alhambra, Calif., Aug. 19, 1925; s. Howard Bassett and Clara Elizabeth (Michalek) F.; m. Shirley Ann Chapman, Aug. 6, 1948 (div. 1968); 1 child, Carlos Andrew; m. Sarah Coburn Hills, July 18, 1986. BS in Sci., Calif. Inst. Tech., 1949; MS in Marine Geology, UCLA-SIO, La Jolla, 1953; PhD in Oceanography, UCLA, La Jolla, 1957. Geologist U.S. Geol. Survey, St. Lawrence Island, Alaska, 1949; rsch. geologist Scripps Inst. Oceanography, U. Calif.-San Diego, La Jolla, 1950-91, rsch. geologist emeritus, 1991—, assoc. dir., 1974-80, leader deep-sea oceanographic expdns., 1951-84; expert, adviser, mem., chmn. U.S. and fgn. sci. panels and coms. UNESCO, Paris, Monaco, Washington, 1959-99. Contbr. over 100 articles to sci. jours.; editor expdn. reports Jour. Geophys. Rsch., various other jours. With USN, 1944-46, PTO. Rsch. grantee NSF, Office Naval Rsch., 1954-88. Fellow Am. Geophys. Union, Geol. Soc. Am., Explorers Club; mem. Oceanography Soc., Challenger soc. (hon. life), Sigma Xi. Avocations: travel, gardening, history (mainly marine). Office: Scripps Inst Oceanography Geosci Rsch Divsn La Jolla CA 92093-0215

FISHER, ROBERT MORTON, foundation administrator, university administrator; b. St. Paul, Minn., Oct. 15, 1938; s. S.S. and Jean Fisher; m. Elinor C. Schectman, June 19, 1960; children: Laurie, Jonathan. AB magna cum laude, Harvard Coll., 1960; JD, Harvard U., 1963; PhD, London Sch. Econs, Polit. Sci., 1967; LLD, West Coast U., L.A., 1981; DHL, Profl. Sch. Psychology, San Francisco, 1986; DPS, John F. Kennedy U., Orinda, Calif., 1988. Rsch. assoc. Mass. Mental Health Ctr., Cambridge, 1957-62; rsch. asst. Ctr. Study Juvenile Delinquency, Cambridge, 1961-63; spl. asst. to chief psychologist British Prison Dept. Home Office, London, 1963-67; prof. Sch. Criminology U. Calif., Berkeley, 1965-71; profl. race car driver, 1972-77; pres. John F. Kennedy U., Orinda, Calif., 1974-85; exec. dir. 92d St. YMHA, N.Y.C., 1984-85; dir., CEO The San Francisco Found., 1987-97; mayor, councilman Lafayette, Calif., 1968-76; mem. Minn. and Calif. Bar Specialty: charitable gift planning; CEO Fisher Cos., 1997—. Scholar-in-residence Rockefeller Found., Bellagio, 1994; Polit. Sci. vis. fellow London Sch. Econs. and Polit. Sci., 1994; named Outstanding Fundraising Exec. Nat. Soc. Fund Raising Execs. Home and Office: 85 Southwood Dr Orinda CA 94563-3026

FISHER, ROBERT SCOTT, lawyer; b. Detroit, July 16, 1960; s. Alvin Fisher and Beverly (Raider) Levin. BA, U. Mich., 1982; JD, U. Colo., 1985. Bar: Colo. 1985, U.S. Dist. Ct. Colo. 1985, Mich. 1987, U.S. Ct. Appeals (10th cir.) 1989, U.S. Supreme Ct. 1989, U.S. Ct. Appeals (D.C. cir.) 1999. Prin. Law Office of Robert S. Fisher, Colorado Springs, Colo., 1985—. Mem. Colo. Bar Assn., El Paso County Bar Assn., Phi Delta Phi. Avocations: scuba diving, ice hockey, skiing, racquetball. Home: 508 N Sheridan Ave Colorado Springs CO 80909-4518 Office: 502 W Weber Colorado Springs CO 80903

FISHER, ROBERT WARREN, accountant; b. Springfield, Ohio, Sept. 17, 1952; s. Carl Arthur and Frances (Runyan) E.; m. Elizabeth Ann Davies, Dec. 11, 1982; children: Katherine Marie, Anne Margaret, Andrew Robert, David Carl. BA, Wittenberg U., 1974; MBA, U. Toledo, 1975. CPA; registered investment advisor. Mgr., acct. Price Waterhouse, Battle Creek, Mich., 1975-83, Deloitte, Haskins & Sells, Appleton, Wis., 1983-84; ptnr., acct. Wojahn & Fisher, S.C., Appleton, 1984-85; shareholder, v.p. Schumaker, Romenesko & Assocs., Appleton, 1985-97; pres., CEO Trade Winds Pizza, LLC, 1997—; treas., bd. dirs. Wis. Bus. Devel. Fin. Corp., Madison, 1983—; ind. cons. to CPA firms. Mem. fin. com. St. Mary's Ch., 1986—, Appleton Cath. Edn. System, 1986-90; mem. com. St. Paul Home. Mem. AICPA (PCPS peer rev. com. 1991-95), Wis. Soc. CPAs (exec. com., quality rev. com. 1989-95, assn. chmn. 1991, chmn. 1992-94), Nat. Assn. Accts. (v.p. 1982), Appleton C. of C. (small bus. com. 1984—), Riverview Country Club (bd. dirs. 1986-96, treas. 1987-90, v.p. 1990-93, pres. 1993-94), KC, Rotary (membership dir. 1986, treas. 1988-94, Paul Harris fellow 1995). Home: 1027 E Rustic Rd Appleton WI 54911-8547 Office: Trade Winds Pizza LLC 1085 Parkview Rd Green Bay WI 54304-5696

FISHER, ROGER DUMMER, lawyer, educator, negotiation expert; b. Winnetka, Ill., May 28, 1922; s. Walter Taylor and Katharine (Dummer) F.; m. Caroline Speer, Sept. 18, 1948; children: Elliott Speer, Peter Ryerson. AB, Harvard U., 1943, LLB magna cum laude, 1948; LHD, Conn. Coll., 1994; DHL, Bay Path Coll., 1999. Bar: Mass. 1948, D.C. 1950. Asst. to gen. counsel, then asst. to dep. U.S. spl. rep. ECA, Paris, 1948-49; with firm Covington & Burling, Washington, 1950-56; asst. to solicitor gen. U.S., 1956-58; lectr. law Harvard Law Sch., Cambridge, Mass., 1958-60, prof. law, 1960-76, Samuel Williston prof. law, 1976-92; prof. emeritus Harvard Law Sch., 1992—; dir. Harvard negotiation project Harvard Law Sch., Cambridge, Mass., 1980—; vis. prof. internat. rels. dept. London Sch. Econs., 1965-66; cons. pub. affairs editor WGBH-TV, Cambridge, 1969; tech. advisor Found. for Internat. Conciliation, Geneva, 1984-87. Originator, 1st exec. editor: (pub. TV series) The Advocates, 1969-70, moderator, 1970-71; co-originator, exec. editor: (pub. TV series) Arabs and Israelis, 1975; author: International Conflict for Beginners, 1969, Dear Israelis, Dear Arabs, 1972, International Mediation: A Working Guide, 1978, International Crises and the Role of Law: Points of Choice, 1978, Improving Compliance with International Law, 1981; co-author: Getting to Yes: Negotiating Agreement Withoug Giving In, 1981, 2d edit., 1991, Getting Together: Building Relationships as We Negotiate, 1988, Beyond Machiavelli: Tools for Coping with Conflict, 1994, Getting Ready to Negotiate: The Getting to Yes Workbook, 1995, Coping with International Conflict: A Systematic Approach to Influence in International Negotiation, 1997, Getting It Done: How to Lead When You're Not in Charge, 1998; co-author, editor: International Conflict and Behavioral Science--The Craigville Papers, 1964; lectr., contbr. articles on internat. rels., negotiation, internat. law and TV. Bd. dirs. Coun. for Livable World; trustee Hudson Inst., 1962-95. 1st lt. USAF, 1942-46. Recipient Sziland Peace award 1981, Peace Advocate award Lawyers Alliance for Nuclear Arms Control, 1988, Spl. Contbn. award Ctr. Pub. Resources, 1993, Steve Brutsché award Assn. Atty. Mediators, 1994, D'Alemberte-Raven Outstanding Achievements and Contributions to Dispute Resolution award, 1995, Honorato Vasquez Nat. Order Insignia Great Cross Republic Ecuador, 1999, Lifetime Achievement award Am. Coll. Civil Trial Mediators, 1999, Pioneer award New Eng. Soc. Profls. Dispute Reolution, 1999, St. Thomas More award St. Mary's U. Law Sch., 1999; named Guggenheim fellow 1965-66. Fellow Am. Acad. Arts and Scis.; mem. ABA (sect. dispute resolution), Am. Soc. Internat. Law (exec. coun. 1961-64, 66-69, v.p. 1982-84), Mass. Bar Assn., Commn. to Study Orgn. of Peace, Coun. Fgn. Rels., Phi Beta Kappa. Clubs: Metropolitan (Washington); Harvard (N.Y.C.). Office: Harvard U Law Sch Harvard Negotiation Project Pound Hall # 524 Cambridge MA 02138 also: Conflict Mgmt Group 9 Waterhouse St Cambridge MA 02138-3607

FISHER, RONALD C., economics educator; b. Schenectady, Feb. 26, 1950; s. William K. and Agnes M. (McNulty) F.; children: Michael, Charles. BA in Chemistry, Mich. State U., 1972; MA in Econs., Brown U., 1974, PhD in Econs., 1977. Research economist U.S. Adv. Commn. on Interngovtl. Relations, Washington, 1975-76; prof. econs. Mich. State U., East Lansing, 1976—; prof. econs., chmn. dept. econs. Mich. State U., 1988-92, dir. Honors Coll., 1996—; dep. state treas. Mich. Dept. Treasury, Lansing, 1983-85; bd. dirs. Ind. Bus. Rsch. Office of Mich., Detroit, 1988-92; vis. fellow Australian Nat. U., 1992; cons. to the U.S. Adv. Commn. on Intergovtl. Rels., U.S. Dept. HUD, U.S. Dept. Treasury, States of Ariz., Conn., Maine, Mich., Minn., N.J., W.Va., and D.C. Author: State and Local Public Finance, 1989, 96; contbr. articles to profl. jours. Exec. dir. Gov.'s Study Group on Govt. Expenditures, Hartford, 1978-79. NSF grantee, 1980. Mem. AAUP, Am. Econ. Assn., Nat. Tax Assn., Assn. for Pub. Policy Analysis and Mgmt., Midwest Econ. Assn. Office: Mich State U Honors Coll East Lansing MI 48824

FISHER, SALLIE ANN, chemist; b. Green Bay, Wis., Sept. 10, 1923. BS in Chemistry, U. Wis., 1945, MS, 1946, PhD, 1949. Instr. Mt. Holyoke Coll., South Hadley, Mass., 1949-50; asst. prof. U. Minn., Duluth, 1950-51; group leader Rohm & Haas Co., Phila., 1951-60; assoc. dir. rsch. Robinette Rsch. Labs., Berwyn, Pa., 1960-72; v.p. Puricons, Inc., Malvern, Pa., 1972-76; pres. Puricons, Inc., Malvern, 1976—; mem. adv. bd. Internat. Water Conf., Pitts., 1976-91, Reactive Polymers, Netherlands, 1982-88. Contbr. chpts. to books and over 100 articles to profl. jours. Recipient award of merit Engring. Soc. Western Pa., Pitts., 1984. Fellow ASTM (vice-chmn. D-19 1972-78, award of merit 1974, Max Hecht award com. D-19 1975); mem. Soc. Chem. Industry, Am. Chem. Soc., Am. Waterworks Assn., Nat. Assn. Corrosion Engrs. Achievements include patent for regeneration of anion resins; research in process for the concentration and recovery of uranium; devel. of methodology for analysis of resins for nuclear industry. Office: Puricons Inc 101 Quaker Ln Malvern PA 19355-2480

FISHER, SANDRA IRENE, English educator; b. Massillon, Ohio, Aug. 7, 1947; d. Samuel Arnold and Pearl Irene (Wood) Sells; m. John Jay Fisher, July 23, 1978; children: Melissa Pearl, Benjamen Jay. BA in Edn., Harding U., Searcy, Ark., 1969; postgrad., Ohio U., 1980—. Cert. tchr. English grades 7-12, health/phys. edn. K-12, Ohio. Tchr. phys. edn. and health Shenandoah H.S., Sarahsville, Ohio, 1969-72; tchr. English, Belmont Career Ctr., St. Clairsville, Ohio, 1973—. Advisor Lit. Club, St. Clairsville, 1978-97; sec.-treas. Barnesville (Ohio) Track/Cross Country Orgn., 1993, 95-98; sec., charter mem. Mt. Olivet Water Trustees, Barnesville, 1994-96. Martha Jennings scholar, 1979-80. Mem. Belmont County Lang. Arts Coun. (v.p. 1998-2000), Ohio Coun. Tchrs. English Lang. Mem. Ch. of Christ. Avocations: singing, writing, reading, floral designing, traveling. Home: 36815 Morse Ln Barnesville OH 43713-9456 Office: Belmont Career Ctr 110 Fox Shannon Pl Saint Clairsville OH 43950

FISHER, SEYMOUR, psychologist, educator; b. N.Y.C., Nov. 4, 1925; s. George and Fannie (Hesselson) F.; m. Carmen Eldridge, June 20, 1959; children: Mark, Andrew. BA, NYU, 1948; PhD, U. N.C., 1952; postgrad., Washington Sch. Psychiatry, 1954-55. Diplomate Am. Bd. Examiners in Psychol. Hypnosis. Clin. psychologist trainee VA Hosp., Roanoke, 1950, psychology trainee, 1952; intern Psychol. Clinic, U. N.C., Chapel Hill, 1950-51; supervising clin. psychologist Walter Reed Army Inst. Rsch., Washington, 1952-58; rsch. psychologist Psychopharmacology Svc. Ctr., NIMH, Bethesda, Md., 1958-60; chief spl. studies unit Psychopharmacology Rsch Br., NIMH, Bethesda, 1960-63; prof. psychiatry (psychology), dir. rsch. tng., dir. psychopharmacology lab., div. psychiatry Boston U. Sch. Medicine, 1963-78; prof. dept. psychiatry and behavioral scis., U. Tex. Med. Br., Galveston, 1978—, assoc. chmn. for rsch., 1978-80, rsch. advisor to chmn. dept., 1980-91, dir. Ctr. for Medication Monitoring, 1987—; vis. prof. Harvard U., Boston U., May to Nov., 1988; cons. NIMH, Chevy Chase, Md., 1964-66, mem. clin. psychopharmacology rsch. rev. com., 1973-77, mem. treatment devel. and assessment rsch. rev. com., 1979-83; cons. Office Naval Rsch., Washington, 1964-66, Mass. Dept. Mental Health, 1969-78, FDA, 1973-77; pres. Boston Mental Health Found., Inc., 1970-72; mem. Commn. on Cmty. Care of Mentally Ill, chmn. tech. com. Hogg Found., 1987-90, planning com. for 50th anniversary rsch. conf., 1988-89. Mem. editl. bd. Psychopharmacology Svc. Ctr. Bull., 1959-63; assoc. editor Psychol. Record, 1960-66; sr. editor vol. on clin. and biobehavioral aspects of cocaine, Oxford U. Press, 1987; mem. adv. bd. Internat. Jour. Methods Psychiatry, 1998—; contbr. numerous articles to profl. jours., chpts. in books. Recipient Disting. Alumnus award U. N.C., 1981, Donald E. Francke award for best paper Drug Info. Jour., 1987. Fellow APA (mem. exec. coun. divsn. psychopharmacology 1979-82), Am. Coll. Neuropsychopharmacology (life, pres. 1984, asst. sec.-treas. 1974-77, chmn. hon. awards com. 1985-87, mem. other coms. 1973-87, emeritus), Soc. Clin. and Exptl. Hypnosis, Internat. Coll. Psychosomatic Medicine, Collegium Internat. Neuro-Psychopharmacologicum (emeritus); mem. Am. Psychopathol. Assn. (exec. coun. 1970-72), Psi Chi, Sigma Xi, Beta Lambda Sigma. Office: U Tex Med Br Dept Psych Ctr for Med Monitoring Galveston TX 77555-0189 *The difference between intelligence and wisdom: intelligence is knowing that half of what you hear or read is garbage; wisdom is knowing which half.*

FISHER, STEPHEN TODD, naval officer; b. Little Falls, N.Y., Apr. 7, 1941; s. Edwin Morgan and Lillian Wing (Burrell) F.; m. Myra Halcomb, May 15, 1971; children: Arlie, Abby, Ann, Alexandra. BA, Washington & Jefferson, 1963; MBA, Cornell U., 1965; MA, Cath. U., 1985. Commd. ens. USN, 1965, advanced through grades to rear adm.; pers. officer Naval Hosp., Naval Sch. Health Care Adminstrn. USN, Newport, R.I.; dir. mgmt./XO Naval Sch. Health Scis. USN, Bethesda, Md., 1972-82; enlisted cmty. mgr. chief naval ops. USN, Washington, 1982-84; med. adminstrn. officer HQ, Fleet Marine Force Pacific USN, Hawaii, 1984-87; cmdg. officer Naval Med. Clinic USN, Washington, 1987-88; dep. asst. chief pers. mgmt. Bur. Medicine and Surgery, Washington, 1988-92, med. insp. gen., 1992-95, dir. med. svc. corps, 1993-95, asst. chief health care ops., 1993-95, dep. surgeon gen. Navy, 1995—, dep. chief, 1995—. Office: Bur Medicine and Surgery 2300 E St NW Washington DC 20372-5300

FISHER, STEVEN KAY, neurobiology educator; b. Rochester, Ind., July 18, 1942; s. Stewart King and Hazel Madeline (Howell) F.; m. Dinah Dawn Marschall, May 2, 1971; children: Jenni Dawn, Brian Andrew, Steven William. BS, Purdue U., 1964, MS, 1966; postgrad., Johns Hopkins U., 1967-69; PhD, Purdue U., 1969. Postdoctoral fellow Johns Hopkins U., Balt., 1969-71; prof. U. Calif., Santa Barbara, 1971—, dir. Inst. Environ. Stress, 1985-88, dir. Neurosci. Rsch. Inst., 1989—; cons. Ultrastructure Tech., Goleta, Calif., 1984—, Regeneron Pharms., Inc., 1993, 94, Amgen, Inc., 1994, 95. Contbr. numerous articles to profl. jours. Recipient Devel. award NIH, 1980-84, M.E.R.I.T. award NIH, 1989—; NIH grantee, 1971—. Mem. AAAS, Assn. Research in Vision and Ophthalmology (mem. program com. 1979-80), Soc. Neurosci., Am. Soc. Cell Biology, Electron Microscopy Soc. Am., NIH Visual Scis. A2 Study Sect. Avocations: music, gardening, literature, swing dancing, weight lifting. Home: 6890 Sabado Tarde Rd Goleta CA 93117-4305 Office: U Calif Neuroscience Research Institute Santa Barbara CA 93106

FISHER, STEWART WAYNE, lawyer; b. Phila., Mar. 5, 1950; s. Frederick and Evalyn (Wilson) F.; m. Melinda Ruley, Oct. 1, 1994; 1 child, Henry J.; children from previous marriage: Kira H., Amos N., Emily E. BA magna cum laude, Duke U., 1972; MA, Yale U., 1974; JD with honors, U. N.C., 1982. Bar: N.C. 1982, U.S. Dist. Ct. (ea. and mid. dists.) N.C. 1982, U.S. Ct. Appeals (4th cir.) 1993, U.S. Dist. Ct. (west dist.) N.C. 1997, U.S. Supreme Ct. 1997; bd. cert. Civil Trial Advocate Nat. Bd. Trial Advocacy, 1998. Atty. Haywood, Denny & Miller, Durham, N.C., 1982-85; ptnr. Glenn, Mills & Fisher, PA, Durham, 1985—; faculty Nat. Inst. for Trial Advocacy, Durham, 1988—. Coop. atty. ACLU, Raleigh, 1992—. Mem. ABA, ATLA, Nat. Employment Lawyers, N.C. Acad. Trial Lawyers, N.C. Bar Assn., Phi Beta Kappa. Democrat. Avocations: fishing, gardening. Office: Glenn Mills & Fisher PA PO Box 3865 Durham NC 27702-3865

FISHER, THOMAS EDWARD, lawyer; b. Cleve., Sept. 29, 1926; s. McArthur and Ruth Morgan (Dissette) F.; m. Virginia Moore, June 29, 1957; children: Laura, Linda, John. BS in Naval Sci. and Tactics, Purdue U., 1947, BS in Engring. Law, 1950; JD, Ind. U., 1950. Bar: Ohio 1951, U.S. Dist. Ct. (no. dist.) Ohio 1954, U.S. Supreme Ct. 1955, U.S. Ct. Appeals (Fed. cir.) 1973. Asst. to v.p. Lempco Products, Bedford, Ohio, 1950-51; house counsel Willard Storage Battery Co., Cleve., 1951-54; assoc. Schram & Knowles, Cleve., 1954-55; ptnr. Watts, Hoffmann, Fisher & Heinke Co. (predecessor firms), Cleve., 1955—. Councilman Mentor (Ohio) on the Lake, 1955-57; chmn. ARC, Painesville, Ohio, 1956. Lt. USN, 1944. Mem. ABA (divsn. chair), Cleve. Bar Assn. (trustee), Am. Intellectual Property Law Assn. (chair com., bd. dirs.), Cleve. Intellectual Property Law Assn. (pres.), Cleve. World Trade Assn., Nat. Inventors Hall of Fame (pres.), Nat. Coun. Patent Law Assns. (chair). Avocations: woodworking, fishing, travel, gardening. Home: 617 Falls Rd Chagrin Falls OH 44022-2560 Office: Watts Hoffmann Fisher & Heinke Co 1100 Superior Ave Cleveland OH 44114-2518

FISHER, THOMAS GEORGE, lawyer, retired media company executive; b. Debrecen, Hungary, Oct. 2, 1931; came to U.S., 1951; s. Eugene J. and Viola Elizabeth (Rittersporn) F.; m. Rita Knisley, Feb. 14, 1960; children: Thomas G. Jr., Katherine F. Vaaler. B.S., Am. U., 1957, J.D., 1959; postgrad., Harvard U., 1956. Bar: D.C. 1959, Iowa 1977. Atty. FCC, Washington, 1959-61, 65-66; pvt. law practice Washington, 1961-65, 66-69; asst. counsel Meredith Corp., N.Y.C., 1969-72; assoc. gen. counsel Meredith Corp., Des Moines, 1972-76, gen. counsel, 1976-80, v.p. gen. counsel, 1980-94, corp. sec., 1988-94; comml. law liaison ABA Ctr. and East European Law Initiative, Krakow, Poland, 1994-95; atty. Legal Aid Soc. Polk County, 1996—. Contbr. articles to profl. jours. Bd. dirs. Des Moines Met. Opera Co., Indianola, 1980-94, pres., 1990-91; bd. dirs. Civic Music Assn., Des Moines, 1982-92, pres., 1987-88; chmn. legis. com. Greater Des Moines C. of C., 1976-77; bd. dirs. Legal Aid Soc. Polk County, 1986-93, pres., 1993. With U.S. Army, 1952-54. Mem. ABA, Iowa State Bar Assn. (chmn. corp. counsel subcom. 1979-82), Polk County Bar Assn., Embassy Club. Office: Legal Aid Assn Polk County 1111 9th St Ste 380 Des Moines IA 50314-2527

FISHER, THOMAS GEORGE, JR., lawyer; b. Washington, June 1, 1961; s. Thomas George and Rita (Knisley) F.; m. Susan Jane Koenig, June 23, 1990. BA, Iowa State U., 1983; JD with high distinction, U. Iowa, 1986. Bar: Iowa 1986, U.S. Dist. Ct. (so. dist.) Iowa 1987, U.S. Ct. Appeals (8th cir.) 1987, U.S. Dist. Ct. (no. dist.) Iowa 1993. Jud. clk. Iowa Supreme Ct., Davenport, 1986-87; assoc. Duncan, Jones, Riley & Finley, P.C., Des Moines, 1987-91; asst. atty. gen. State of Iowa, Justice Dept., Des Moines, 1991-95; counsel Am. Mut. Life Ins. Co., Des Moines, 1995-96; ptnr. Hogan & Fisher, PLC, Des Moines, 1997—. Precinct chair Polk County Dem. Party, Des Moines, 1988-90, 94-96, 98—; candidate Iowa Ho. of Reps. Dists. 73, 1994; mem. Twenty-First Century Forum, Des Moines Leadership Inst.; bd. dirs., vice chair Anawim Housing. Mem. Blackstone Inn of Ct. Democrat. Roman Catholic. Office: Hogan & Fisher PLC 3101 Ingersoll Ave Des Moines IA 50312-3918

FISHER, THOMAS GRAHAM, judge; b. Flint, Mich., May 15, 1940; s. John Corwin and Bonnie Decou (Graham) F.; m. Barbara Alden Molnar, June 2, 1963; children: Anne Corwin, Thomas Molnar. AB, Earlham Coll., 1962; JD, Ind. U., 1965. Bar: Ind. 1965, U.S. Dist. Ct. (no. dist.) Ind. 1965, U.S. Sup. Ct. 1969. Assoc., John R. Nesbitt, Remington and Rensselaer, Ind., 1965-68; ptnr. Nesbitt & Fisher, Remington and Rensselaer, 1968-73, Nesbitt, Fisher & Daugherty, Rensselaer, Remington, 1973-78, Nesbitt, Fisher, Daugherty & Nesbitt, 1978-82, Nesbitt, Fisher & Nesbitt, 1982-83, Fisher & Nesbitt, 1983-86, judge, Ind. Tax Ct., Indpls., 1986—; pros. atty. Jasper County, Ind., 1967-86; lectr. bus. law St. Joseph's Coll., Rensselaer, 1970-86; trustee Earlham Coll., 1995—. Recipient Eugene Feller award Ind. Pros. Attys. Assn., Indpls., 1986. Mem. ABA, Ind. Bar Assn., Jasper County Bar Assn., Nat. Conf. State Tax Judges, Ind. Soc. Chgo., Columbia Club (bd. dirs. 1991-99, sec. 1992, treas. 1993, pres. 1997), Rotary of Indpls. (v.p. 1998-99, pres.-elect 1999-00), Jaycees (Outstanding Young Man of Am. award 1975). Republican. Mem. Soc. of Friends. Home: 4702 Mallard View Dr Indianapolis IN 46226 Office: Ind Tax Ct 115 W Washington St Ste 1160S Indianapolis IN 46204-3418

FISHER, THOMAS SCOTT, army officer, broadcasting network executive; b. Madison, Wis., June 24, 1963; s. Gale Eugene Fisher and Claudia Jane Clodfelter Killinger; m. Andreina Louisa Zanier Fisher, Aug. 4, 1989; children: Thomas Junior, Maximilian Andreas. BA, U Minn., 1987; MA in Journalism, Marshall U., 1995. Commd. 2d lt. U.S. Army, advanced through grades to maj., 1998; airborne ranger A Co. 2d Bn., 75th Inf., Tacoma, Wash., 1981-83; platoon leader Canadian Army Trophy Team, 7th Corps, Bavaria, 1987-89; exec. officer B Co. 2-64 ARMOR, Schweinfurt, Germany, 1989-90, bn. maintenance officer HQ, 1990; brigade asst. ops. officer 1st Brigade, 3 I.D., Schweinfurt, Germany, 1990-91; co. comdr. A Co. 2-64 ARMOR, Schweinfurt, Germany, 1991-93; ops. officer Am. Forces Network, Frankfurt, Germany, 1996; comdr. AFN-North, Frankfurt, 1997-98, AFN-Balkans, Tuzla, Bosnia, 1998—. Co-author: (book) ...So Are They All, All Honorable Men, 1996, (screenplay) Storm In The Desert, 1995, Reoccurence, 1996. Decorated Army Achievement medal with 4 oak leaf clusters, 1983, Army Good Conduct medal, 1984, Nat. Def. Svc. medal, 1990, Army Commendation medal, 1992, Meritorious Svc. medal, 1993, Armed Forces Svc. medal, 1996, NATO medal, 1997, Joint Svc. Achievement medal, 1998, Def. Superior Svc. medal, 1999. Mem. U.S. Armor Assn., Order of St. George (knight, bronze medallion 1993), World Martial Arts Fedn. (black belt). Baptist. Avocations: golf, skiing, karate.

FISHER, TODD ROGERS, transportation executive; b. Crawfordsville, Ind., July 16, 1949; s. John Rogers and Frances Lois (O'Haver) F. BS Indsl Supv., Engring., Purdue U., 1971. Indsl. engr. United Parcel Service, Altamonte Springs, Fla., 1975-78; terminal mgr. United Parcel Service, Altamonte Springs, 1978-81; branch mgr. Metropolitan Ins., Ormond Beach, Fla., 1981-83; nat. mktg. mgr. Nat. Safe Corp., Clearwater, Fla., 1983-85; dir. ops. Carolina Freight Corp., Cherryville, N.C., 1985-88; sr. engr. Cen. Freight Lines, Inc., Waco, Tex., 1987-89, 90-92; dir. opers. Arnellini Express Lines Inc., Stuart, Fla., 1989-90; dir. ops. devel. Watkins Motor Lines Inc., Lakeland, Fla., 1992-96; dist. mgr. Watkins Motor Lines, Lakeland, FL, 1996-98; dir. ops. planning Overnite Transp., Richmond, Va., 1998—; cons. Meals on Wheels, Dallas, 1987-88, Dallas Greater C. of C., 1987-88, Country Dinner Playhouse, St. Petersburg, Fla., 1982. Capt. USMC, 1971-74. Mem. IIE (community recognition award, 1987), Daytona Beach C. of C., Orange City C. of C., Rotary, Theta Chi (treas. 1970-71, steward, 1969-70), Demolay, Alpha Eta Rho. Republican. Presbyterian. Avocations: scuba diving, boating, golf. Home: 6620 Masada Dr Chesterfield VA 23838-8719 Office: Overnite Transp PO Box 1216 Richmond VA 23218-1216

FISHER, VERNON, artist, educator; b. Ft. Worth. BA, Hardin-Simmons U., 1967; MFA, U. Ill., 1969. Assoc. prof. art Austin Coll., Sherman, Tex., 1969-78; prof. art North Tex. State U., Denton, 1978—. One-man shows Asher-Faure Gallery, L.A., 1986, 91, Barbara Gladstone Gallery, N.Y.C., 1987, Hiram Butler Gallery, Houston, 1987, 90, Lannan Mus., Lake Worth, Fla., 1987, Fred Hoffman Gallery, Buffalo, 1989, Karsten Schubert Ltd., London, 1989, Mus. Fine Arts, Houston, 1990, Rena Bransten Gallery, San Francisco, 1992, also others; exhibited in group shows Bronx (N.Y.) Mus. Arts, 1984, Hirshhorn Mus. and Sculpture Garden, Washington, 1984, New Orleans Mus. Art, 1986, Bklyn. Mus., 1986, Walker Art Ctr., Mpls., 1987, Los Angeles County Mus. Art, 1987, Inst. Contemporary Arts, London, 1987; represented in permanent collections Hirshhorn Mus. and Sculpture Garden, Guggenheim Mus., N.Y.C., Mus. Modern Art, N.Y.C., Albright-Knox Gallery; Author: Navigating by the Stars, 1989, editor, 1992. Grantee SECCA, 1981, 88, Louis Comfort Tiffany Found., 1980-81, 84.

FISHER, WESLEY ANDREW, research administrator, Eurasian studies specialist; b. N.Y.C., Oct. 23, 1944; s. Mitchell Salem and Esther (Oshiver) F.; m. Regine Rayevsky, Sept. 15, 1979; children: Maxim, Katya. BA, Harvard U., 1966; M Phil. in Sociology, Columbia U., 1976, PhD with distinction, 1976, cert. Russian Inst., 1976. Instr. Dept. Sociology, W. Averell Harriman Inst., Columbia U., N.Y.C., 1972-76, asst. prof., 1976-80, adj. assoc. prof., 1981-87; assoc. chmn. Dept. Sociology, Columbia U., N.Y.C., 1980-81; sec. Am. Council Learned Socs. Commns. with USSR Internat. Rsch. & Exch. Bd., N.Y.C. and Princeton, N.J., 1981-89, asst. dir. and dir. Soviet programs, 1989-93; dep. dir. Rsch. Inst., U.S. Holocaust Meml. Mus., Washington, 1993-97, acting dir., 1997-99, spl. asst. to mus. dir., 1997-99; cons. Sakharov Mus., Russia, 1997—; dir. internat. programs U.S. Holocaust Meml. Mus., Washington, 1999—; guest lectr. Foreign Svc. Inst. U.S. Dept. of State, 1976-83; visiting lectr. New Sch. for Social Rsch., 1978-79; rsch. fellow philosophy faculty Moscow (USSR) State Univ., 1970-71, Ctr. for the Study of Population, Moscow State Univ., 1976-86; liaison Soviet Union, Am. Sociological Assn., 1976-86. Author: The Moscow Gourmet: Dining Out in the Capital of the USSR, 1974, The Soviet Marriage Market: Mate Selection in Russia and the USSR, 1980, Social Stratification and Mobility in the USSR, 1973, A Scholar's Guide to the Humanities and Social Sciences in the Baltics and the Soviet Union, 1992; contbr. articles, revs., guidebooks to acad. and profl. jours. Advisor Program for Soviet Emigre Scholars, Nat. Jewish Welfare Bd., Hebrew Immigrant Aid Soc.; bd. dirs. N.Y. Assn. for New Americans. Recipient Herbert H. Lehman fellowship in Pub. and Internat. Affairs,1966, Foreign Area fellowship Ford Found., 1970, two Fulbright-Hays fellowships, 1970-71, 76-77. Mem. Am. Assn. for the Advancement of Slavic Studies, Am. Sociol. Assn., Harvard Club of N.Y.C., Fulbright Assn., Phi Beta Kappa. Jewish. E-mail: wfisher@ushmm.gov. Home: 5920 Edson Ln North Bethesda MD 20852 Office: US Holocaust Meml Museum 100 Raoul Wallenberg Pl SW Washington DC 20024-2126

FISHER, WESTON JOSEPH, economist; b. Glendale, Calif., Aug. 29; s. Edward Weston and Rosalie Eloise (Bailey) F. BS, U. So. Calif., 1962, MA, 1965, MS, 1971, PhD, 1989. Sr. mgr. Naval Undersea Ctr., Pasadena, Calif., 1964-69; chief exec. officer, prin. Ventura County, Ventura, Calif., 1969-73; So. Calif. dir. County Suprs. Assn., L.A., 1974-75; coord. govtl. rels. So. Calif. Assn. Govts., L.A., 1975-78; devel. dir. Walter H. Leimert Co., L.A., 1979-90; bd. dirs. Gray Energy Corp., L.A., Mission Inn Group, Riverside, Calif., Coun. of Leaders and Specialists - UN, Peterson Oil and Gas. Mem. Gov.'s Adv. Coun. for Econ. growth, Channel Islands Conservancy. Mem. Medieval Acad. Am., El Dorado Country Club, Univ. Club, South Coast Yacht Club, Cave Creek Club, Lambda Alpha. Republican. Avocation: medieval and U.S. history. Home: 14373 Tawya Rd Apple Valley CA 92307

FISHER, WILL STRATTON, illumination consultant; b. Nashville, June 27, 1922; s. Will Stratton and Estelle (Carr) R.; m. Patricia A. Fesco, Nov. 10, 1945; children: Patricia Jo, Will Stratton, Robert J. *The earliest Fisher arrived at Philadelphia in the "colonies" about 1730 coming from the small German village of Freinsheim. Frederick Fisher, a second generation native-born son, served in the Revolutionary War in Colonel Campbell's regiment of Washington County, Virginia, and was severely wounded in the Battle of King's Mountain in 1781. For this he received a disability pension of $3.33 per month from the Virginia Assembly. On the distaff side, roots trace back to John Warren who came to America in 1630 aboard the "Arabella".* B.S.E.E., Vanderbilt U., 1947. Registered profl. engr., Ohio. With Lighting Bus. Group, Gen. Elec. Co., Cleve., 1947-87, mgr. advanced application engring., 1971-84, mgr. lighting edn., 1985-87; cons. lighting Moreland Hills, Ohio, 1987—; cons. Lighting Research Inst. Contbr. articles, papers to profl. jours., symposia and internat. profl. meetings. Patentee parabolic wedge louver; developer concepts for utilizing heat from lighting systems to heat bldgs.; designer calorimeter; developer procedure for calculation contbn. of lighting to heating of bldgs. Served to 1st lt. C.E., AUS, 1943-46, Manhattan Project. Fellow Illuminating Engring. Soc. North Am. (pres. 1978-79, Disting. Service award 1980, Louis B. Marks award for exceptional service 1988); mem. Internat. Commn. Illumination (U.S. expert on tech. com., U.S. rep. to div. 3, interior lighting), ASHRAE, IEEE. Methodist. Lodge: Kiwanis (pres. 1990-91). Home and Office: 120 Meadowhill Ln Chagrin Falls OH 44022-1337

FISHER, WILLIAM G.E., nursing home owner and operator, state senator; b. Artesia, Calif., Mar. 24, 1936; m. Darlene F. Fisher; children: William G.E., Darryl E., Rhonda M. BA in Bibl. Langs., Walla Walla Coll., 1965; postgrad., Andrews U., Berrien Springs, Mich., 1966-67, Eastern Wash. State Coll., Cheney, 1968. Owner, operator Rosehaven Nursing Home, Roseburg, Oreg., 1968—; mem. Oreg. Ho. of Reps., 1992-96, Oreg. Senate, 1996—; chmn. Health and Human Svcs. Com., Oreg. Senate, 1997, 99, vice chmn. Agr. and Natural Resources Com., 1997—, mem. Trade and Econ. Devel. Com., Water and Land Use Com., mem. Agr. and Natural Resources Com., 1997—, mem. Ways and Means (Human Resources sub-com.), 1999. Bd. dirs. Riverside Ctr., 1996—, Douglas County Coun. on Alcoholism, 1971-76; mem. Douglas County Pers. Rev. Bd., 1973; bd. dirs. Roseburg Jr. Acad., 1986-89, chmn. bd., 1987-88; mem. Western States Legis. Forestry Task Force, 1993-95; mem. Gov.'s Commn. on Sr. Svcs., 1995-97; mem. Oreg. Health Policy Inst., 1995—; Douglas County Precinct Committeeman, 1990, 92, 94, 96; sec. Douglas County Rep. Exec. com., 1990-93. Served with U.S. Army, 1958-60, also Res. Fellow Am. Coll. Health Care Adminstrs.; mem. Am. Health Care Assn., Oreg. Health Care Assn. (bd. dirs. 1971-73, v.p. 1974-89), Am. Legion, Douglas Timber Operators, Oreg. Farm Bur., Kiwanis Club Roseburg (bd. dirs. 1981—), NRA (life), Oreg. State Shooting Assn. (life), Oreg. Hunters Assn., Roseburg Rod and Gun Club, Am. Assn. Ret. Persons, Sr. Citizens Inc., Aircraft Owners and Pilots Assn., Oreg. Pilots Assn., Exptl. Aircraft Assn., Antique Aircraft Assn., Stearman Restorers Assn., Nat. Biplane Assn., others. Seventh-day Adventist. Office: Oreg State Capitol S-204 Salem OR 97310 also: Profl Bus Ctr 1012 SE Oak Ave Ste 224 Roseburg OR 97470-4946

FISHER, WILLIAM LAWRENCE, geologist, educator; b. Marion, Ill., Sept. 16, 1932; s. Henry Adam and Madge Lenora (Moore) F.; m. Marilee Booth, Dec. 18, 1954; children: Leah, Karl, Peter. BS, So. Ill. U., 1954, DSc, 1986; MS, U. Kans., 1958, PhD (Shell fellow), 1961. Research scientist Tex. Bur. Econ. Geology, Austin, 1960-68; assoc. dir. Tex. Bur. Econ. Geology, 1968-70, dir., 1970-75, 77-94; asst. sec. for energy and minerals Dept. Interior, Washington, 1975-77; prof. dept. geol. scis. U. Tex., Austin, 1969—, Morgan J. Davis prof. petroleum geology, 1984-86, Leonidas T. Barrow chair in mineral resources, 1986—, chmn. dept. geol. scis., 1984-90; dir. Geol. Found. Tex., 1984—; mem. geology assoc. bd. U. Kans., 1972-74, 83—; mem. adv. coun. Gas Rsch. Inst.; mem. Tex. Sci. Adv. Coun.; mem. Gov.'s Energy Coun.; mem. White House Sci. Coun., Nat. Petroleum Coun., Pres.' Coun. of Advisors on Sci. and Tech. Panel on Energy R & D, and Sec. Energy Adv. Bd. Author: Mineral Resources of East Texas, 1964, Depositional Systems in the Wilcox Group, 1969, Delta Systems in the Exploration for Oil and Gas, 1969, Environmental Geologic Atlas of Texas Coastal Zone, 1972, National Energy Policies, Oil and Gas Resources of U.S. Basin Analysis. Served with AUS, 1954-56. Recipient Hedberg medal So. Meth. U. 1995, Sidney Powers Meml. Medal award, Am. Assn. Petroleum Geologists 1995. Fellow Geol. Soc. Am. (councillor); mem. NRC (commn. on geoscis., environ. and resource, chmn. bd. mineral and energy resources, U.S. nat. com. on geology, chmn. bd. on earth scis. and resources, bd. on energy and environ. sys.), Nat. Acad. Engring., Am. Inst. Profl. Geologists (pres. Tex. sect. 1979, pres. 1993, Parker medal pub. svc. award), Assn. Am. State Geologists (hon. pres. 1981-82), Am. Assn. Petroleum Geologists (hon., pres. 1985-86, Powers medal), Am. Geol. Inst. (pres. 1991, Campbell medal, Heroy award), Austin Geol. Soc. (hon., pres. 1973-74), Gulf Coast Assn. Geol. Scis. (hon., pres 1994). Home: 8705 Ridgehill Dr Austin TX 78759-7342 Office: Univ Tex Dept Geological Scis Austin TX 78712

FISHER, WILLIAM P., association executive; b. Ithaca, N.Y., Jan. 15, 1939. BS, Cornell U., 1960, MBA, 1965, PhD, 1968. Past. asst. prof. Sch. acctg., fin. and gen mgmt. courses Hotel Administrn. Cornell U., Ithaca, N.Y.; hospitality industry cons. Gaurnier Assocs., 1965-72; exec. v.p. Nat. Restaurant Assn., 1972-77; exec. v.p. fin. and adminstrn. Service Sys. Corp. (now Marriott Svc. Sys), Buffalo, 1977-84; exec. v.p. to pres. Nat. Restaurant Assn., 1984-96; pres., CEO Am. Hotel & Motel Assn., Washington, 1996—. Author: The Thinker's Guide to Management Action, 1978, Creative Marketing for the Food Service Industry, 1982, Lessons in Leadership, 1993. Served in USAF. Recipient Champion Edn. award Coun. Hotel Restaurant and Instl. Edn., 1996. Office: American Hotel and Motel Assn 1201 New York Ave NW # 600 Washington DC 20005-3917*

FISHER, WILLIAM THOMAS, business administration educator; b. Central Falls, R.I., Mar. 15, 1918; s. William L. and Sarah (Foley) F.; m. Mary Rowena Donnelly, Dec. 26, 1949; 1 son, William Thomas. BS with high honors, Am. Internat. Coll., 1949; MEd, Boston U., 1951; PhD, U. Conn., 1956; postgrad., Clark U., 1954, Columbia U., 1957, St. Thomas Sem., Bloomfield, Conn., 1970-73. Prodn. planner Belding Heminway Corp., Putnam, Conn., 1938-42; prin. Templeton (Mass.) Sch., 1949-50, Tourtellotte High Sch., Thompson, Conn., 1950-57; instr. Becker Jr. Coll., Worcester, Mass., 1955-57; assoc. prof. State U. N.Y. at, Albany, 1957; asst. dean Sch. Ins., U. Conn., 1957-76; asst. dean adminstrn. U. Conn. Sch. Bus. Adminstrn., 1976-77; adminstrv. dir. (Hartford MBA program), 1957-64; vis. prof. Ohio U., summer 1962; dir. (IBM Advanced Ins. Industry Sch.), 1960-70; ednl. cons. IBM Corp., 1960-80; adminstr., asst. dir. Ctr. for Ins. Edn. and Rsch., Hartford, 1976-81; assoc. prof. mgmt. and adminstrv. scis. dept.

Sch. Bus. Adminstrn., U. Conn., Storrs, 1976-81; assoc. prof. mgmt. and orgn. dept. Sch. Bus. Adminstrn., U. Conn., 1981-89, assoc. prof. emeritus, 1989—, adj. prof., 1989-90, 92; ordained permanent deacon Roman Cath. Ch. for Archdiocese of Hartford, 1973; assigned St. Joseph Cathedral, Hartford, part-time 1973-83; rsch. fellow Divinity Sch. Yale U., New Haven, 1989-91, Theol. Opportunities Program Harvard U., Cambridge, Mass., 1994-95; vis. scholar Div. Sch., Duke U., Durham, N.C., 1995, 96, 98, 99, Div. Sch., Vanderbilt U., Nashville, 1996-97, Emory U., Candler Sch. Theology, Atlanta, 1997; real estate broker, 1973-93; mem. Conn. State Ins. Com. and Conn. State Ins. Purchasing Bd., 1963-73, 75-91, chmn. bd., 1971-73; past pres., dir. Conn. Assn. Mcpl. Devel. Commns., 1963-91; mem. Conn. adv. coun. SBA, 1964-70, chmn., 1967; chmn. various coms. Greater Hartford Coun. Econ. Edn., 1958-81; mem. Thompson Bd. Fin., 1963-75; chmn. Thompson Indsl. and Devel. Com., 1964-70, 71-80, 81-91. Editor: Selective Readings in Human Resources Management, 1985, 87, 89; contbr. articles to profl. jours. Pres. Thompson Indsl. Found., 1965-66; mem. Gov.'s Conf. on Human Rights and Opportunities, 1967, Gov.s Conf. on Innovation, 1989; Organizer Conn. small bus. div. Businessmen for V.P. Humphrey, 1968; alumni dir. Am. Internat. Coll., 1961-63, 89-93, trustee, 1963-71, mem. corp., 1972—; chmn. adv. bd. govs. Conn. Library Service Center, Willimantic, 1964-68, mem. exec. com., 1968-70; bd. dirs., sec. Edn. and Research Found. IMA-PIA for States N.Y., N.J. and Conn., Glenmont, N.Y., 1973-83; past trustee, past pres. Thompson Library; corporator Day Kimball Hosp., Putnam, Conn.; mem. region 3 adv. and planning council Conn. Dept. Mental Retardation, 1987-92; trustee Annhurst Coll., Woodstock, Conn., 1977-84; active Conn. Small Bus. Devel. Ctr., summer 1982, 83, 84, 85; bd. dirs. Norwich-Quinebaug unit Am. Cancer Soc. Served with AUS, 1942-45, 39.5 months continuous overseas service. Recipient Yr. award Hartford Assn. Ins. Women, 1969; Presdl. Appreciation cert. Conn. Assn. Mcpl. Devel. Commns., 1968. Mem. NEA (life), Am. Risk and Ins. Assn. (fellowship 1960, 62), Risk and Ins. Mgmt. Soc., Am. Soc. Personnel Adminstrn., Am. Acad. Mgmt., Eastern Acad. Mgmt., Northeastern Indsl. Developers Assn., Conn. Hist. Soc., Nat. Trust Historic Preservation, AAUP, Am. Legion, Phi Delta Kappa, Delta Pi Epsilon. Home: Box 332 Thompson Hill Thompson CT 06277 also: 174 Valleyview Rd Manchester CT 06040

FISHER PRUTZ, MARY LOUISE, coronary care nurse; b. Brownsville, Pa., Sept. 5, 1954; d. Hilden Fredick and Bertha Elizabeth (Radek) Fisher; m. Thomas Prutz; children: Kristie, Farrah, Kelley, Tommy, Timmy. Diploma, Washington Hosp. Sch. Nursing, 1988; BSN, California (Pa.) U., 1995. RN, Pa.; cert. ACLS, BLS. Staff nurse Washington (Pa.) Hosp., 1989—, Monongahela Valley Hosp., Monongahela, Pa., 1991—; co-sponsor Program of Profl. Sharing, Washington, 1991—; sponsor AICD Support Group, Monongahela, 1991—; facilitator Heart to Heart Cardiac Rehab. Support Group. Vol., Am. Cancer Soc., 1985—. Named Nurse of Hope, Am. Cancer Soc., Washington County, 1985-86; recipient Anna Mae Fox pub. edn. award; Dr. Norman Golomb scholarship, 1996. Mem. AACN, AALNC, Nurses Christian Fellowship, Washington Hosp. Sch. Nursing Alumni Assn. (ways and means com. 1990—). Democrat. Lutheran. Avocations: bike riding, sewing, reading, dancing. Home: 307 Madison Heights Rd PO Box 122 Madison PA 15663-0122 Office: Country Club Rd Monongahela PA 15063

FISHKIN, SHELLEY FISHER, English language educator; b. N.Y.C., May 9, 1950; d. Milton and Renee B. Fisher; m. James S. Fishkin; children: Joseph, Robert. BA, Yale Coll., 1971; MA, Yale U., 1974, MPhil, 1974, PhD, 1977. Assoc. Chubb fellow Yale Coll., New Haven, 1974-85, dir. Poynter fellowship in journalism, 1980-85, vis. lectr., 1981-84; sr. lectr. Am. studies U. Tex., Austin, 1985-89, prof. Am. studies, 1993—, prof. English, 1994—. Author: From Fact to Fiction: Journalism and Imaginative Writing in America, 1985 (Frank Luther Mott award Nat. Journalism Scholarship Soc. 1986), Was Huck Black? Mark Twain & African American Voices, 1993 (Outstanding Acad. Book award CHOICE), Lighting Out for the Territory: Reflections on Mark Twain and American Culture, 1997; editor: The Oxford Mark Twain, 1996; co-editor: Listening to Silences: New Essays in Feminist Criticism, People of the Book: Thirty Scholars Reflect on Their Jewish Identity, 1996, (book series) Race and American Culture, 1993, Encyclopedia of Civil Rights in America, 1998. Recipient Disting. Acad. Specialist award U.S. Info. Agy., 1994; Am. Coun. Learned Socs. fellow, 1987-88. Mem. MLA (exec. coun. nonfiction prose divsn 1991-95), Am. Studies Assn. (nominating com. 1990-92, internat. com. 1993-96, program com. 1995), Mark Twain Cir. Am. (pres. 1998—), Charlotte Perkins Gilman Soc. (cofounder, exec. dir. 1990-98). Office: Dept Am Studies U Tex Austin TX 78712

FISHKIND, LAWRENCE, marketing consultant; b. N.Y.C., May 9, 1936; s. Samual and Fanny (Linkoff) F.; m. Lorraine Bernice Diamond, June 19, 1961; 1 child, Paul Leslie. BA in Econs., Bklyn. Coll., 1959. V.p., gen. mgr. Mort N. Marton Corp., Ossining, N.Y., 1964-70; pres. Lawrence Fishkind Assocs., N.Y.C., 1970-77; v.p., gen. mgr. Italglass USA, N.Y.C., 1977-82; v.p. mktg. Crystal Clear Industries, Ridgefield Pk, N.J., 1982-84; pres., chief exec. officer Spl. Mkts., Yorktown Hts., N.Y., 1984—; cons. in mktg. China, S.E. Asia; bd. dirs. Pacific Ave.-Thailand, N.Am. Mktg. Tom's Group U.S.A., Tom's Group Internat. Contbr. articles to profl. jours. With USMCR, 1958-74. Mem. N.Y. Housewares Club, Mensa, Alpha Mu Sigma. Jewish. Avocations: tennis, big game fishing, racquetball, golf, squash. E-mail: infomaster@compuserve.com. Office: 13 Winchester Ave Peekskill NY 10566-6802

FISHMAN, ALFRED PAUL, physician; b. N.Y.C., Sept. 24, 1918; s. Isaac and Anne (Tinter) F.; m. Linda Fishman, Oct. 7, 1984; children: Mark, Jay, Hannah Rae. AB, U. Mich., 1938, MS, 1939; MD, U. Louisville, 1943; MA (hon.), U. Pa., 1971. Diplomate Nat. Bd. Examiners, Am. Bd. Internal Medicine. Intern Jewish Hosp., Bklyn., 1943-44; Dazian Found. fellow pathology Mount Sinai Hosp., N.Y.C., 1946-47; asst. resident, resident medicine Mount Sinai Hosp., 1947-48; Dazian Found. fellow cardiovascular physiology Michael Reese Hosp., Chgo., 1948-49; Am. Heart Assn. research fellow Bellevue Hosp., N.Y.C., 1949-50; established investigator Am. Heart Assn. cardiopulmonary lab. Bellevue Hosp., 1951-55; Am. Heart Assn. research fellow physiology Harvard U., Boston, 1950-51; instr. physiology NYU, 1951-53; assoc. in medicine Columbia Coll. Physicians and Surgeons, N.Y.C., 1953-55; from asst. prof. to assoc. prof. Columbia Coll. Physicians and Surgeons, 1955-66, assoc. prof., 1958-66; prof. medicine U. Chgo., 1966-69; dir. Inst. and Divsn. Cardiovascular Disease Michael Reese Hosp., Chgo., 1966-69; prof. medicine U. Pa., Phila., 1969-72, William Maul Measey prof. medicine, 1972-98, William Maul Measey prof. emeritus, 1998—; assoc. dean Sch. Medicine U. Pa., 1969-75, 90-91, dir. cardiovascular-pulmonary divsn., 1969-90, chmn. dept. rehab. medicine, 1990—; steering com. of dept. chmn. U. Pa. Med. Ctr., 1992; assoc. dean program devel. U. Pa., 1998—; mem. coun. on grad. med. edn. U. Pa. Med. Ctr., 1992-93; dir. Robinette Found., Clin. Cardiovascular Rsch. Center, U. Pa. Med. Ctr., 1969-82; mem. steering com. dept. chmn. U. Pa. Med. Ctr., 1992, coun. on grad. med. edn., 1992-93; dir. Specialized Center of Rsch. (Lung), 1973-81; attending physician Hosp. U. Pa., 1969—; sr. attending physician Phila. Gen. Hosp., 1970-78; physician Mass. Gen. Hosp., 1979; cons. to chancellor U. Mo., Kansas City, 1973-78; vis. prof. Harvard U., 1970, Oxford (Eng.) U., 1972, Washington U., St. Louis, 1973, Johns Hopkins U., 1974, Ben Gurion U., 1975, Emory U., Atlanta, 1976, U. Porto Alegra, Brazilia, Brazil, 1976, U. Zurich, Switzerland, 1978, Duke U., 1986, U. N.C., 1986; vis. scientist for NIH to Peking, China, 1980, to USSR, 1985; cons. Exec. Office Pres., 1961-69, U. Athens, Greece, 1980; mem. WHO Expert Panel, Geneva, 1973-76, Nat. Adv. Heart and Lung Council, NIH, 1968-71, 79-83, Steering Com. of Dept. Chmn U. Pa. Med. Ctrl, 1992, Coun. on Grad. Med. Edn. U. Pa. Med. Ctr., 1992-93; coun. mem. Coll. of Physicians of Phila., 1993—; chmn. Gov.'s Com. for Rsch. on Respiratory Diseases in Coal Miners, 1974-90, Internat. Conf. on Lung, Titisee, Germany, Florence, Italy, 1976, 84, Prague, Czeckoslovakia, 1986, 89, NIH Conf. Proliferative & Obliterative Vascular Disease., steering com. NIH Health Care Financing Adminstrn., Nat. Emphysema Therapy; U.S. chief del. Internat. Union of Physiol. Scis., Helsinki, Finland, 1989; cons. N.Y. State Bd. Health, 1987-91, Cleve. Found., 1984—; vis. com. Case Western Res. Sch. Medicine, Cleve., 1987—, Lankenau Gen. Hosp., Phila., 1985; chmn. Scientific Edn. Partnership, U. Mo-U. Kans.-Merrill Dow, 1989—; chair steering com. NIH Lung Reduction Surgery Ctrs., 1996. Editor: (with D.W. Richards) Circulation of The Blood-Men and Ideas, 1964, (with H.H. Hecht) The Pulmonary Circulation and Interstitial Space, 1969, Handbooks of Respiratory Physiology, Am. Physiol. Soc., 1967-72, 79-87—, Physiology in Medicine, New Eng. Jour. Medicine, 1969-79, Jour. Applied Physiology, 1981-89, cons. editor, 1989—; editor: (with D.W. Richards) Circulation of the Blood Men and Ideas, 1982, Merck Manual, 1972-80, Ann. Rev. Physiology, 1977-81, Heart Failure, 1979; (with E. M. Renkin) Pulmonary Edema, 1979, Pulmonary Diseases and Disorders, 1979, 2d edit., 1988, 3d edit., 1998, Classics in Biology and Medicine, 1989—, The Pulmonary Circulation: Normal and Abnormal, 1990, Pulmonary Rehabilitation, 1994; contbr. articles to profl. jours.; reviewer Health Care Financing Adminstrn., 1995—. Bd. dirs. Polachek Found., Phila. Zool. Soc. Capt. M.C. U.S. Army, 1944-46. Recipient Disting. Alumni award U. Louisville, 1984, Disting. award in nephrology A.N. Richards, 1998. Fellow Am. Coll. Chest Physicians (hon.), Royal Coll. Physicians, ACP; mem. NAS (com. on sci., edn. and pub. policy 1987-90), Inst. Medicine of NAS (chmn. health scis. bd. 1984-90, mem. health scis. bd. 1990—, com. on social and ethical impact of advances in biomedicine 1992—), Am. Physiol. Soc. (chmn. publs. bd. 1974-81, pres. 1983, editor handbook 1986, chmn. centennial celebration com. 1985-87), Am. Soc. Clin. Investigation, AAAS, Am. Acad. Arts and Scis., Royal Soc. Medicine (London), Assn. Am. Physicians, Am. Heart Assn. (bd. dirs. 1988-92, founder, chmn. council on cardiopulmonary disease 1972-74, rsch. coun. 1974-79, Disting. Achievement award 1980, sci. pub. com. 1986-88, chmn. 1988—, Merit award 1989, Gold Heart award 1992, scientific adv. com. 1992—), N.Y. Heart Assn. (pres. 1965-67), Internat. Union Physiol. Scis. (U.S. Nat. Com. 1982-89, chmn. 1986-89), Fedn. Am. Socs. for Exptl. Biology (exec. bd. 1983-85), Am. Coll. Cardiology (hon.), Health Care Financing Adminstrn. (mem. lung transplant ctr. rev. com. 1996—, chair NIH nat. emphysema treatment trial 1997—), Interurban Clin. Club, N.Y. County Med. Soc., Coll. of Physicians of Phila. (coun. 1993—, pres.-elect 1994, pres. 1996-97), Heart Assn. Southeastern Pa. (bd. dirs.), Alpha Omega Alpha. Home: 2401 Pennsylvania Ave Apt 207 Philadelphia PA 19130 Office: Hosp U Pa 3400 Spruce St Philadelphia PA 19104-4204

FISHMAN, ARNIE, marketing executive, consultant, film producer; b. Bklyn., 1965; married; 3 children. BS, CUNY, 1965, postgrad. in Pschology, 1966. Rsch. asst. Liberman Rsch, N.Y.C., 1966, v.p., 1971; founder Lieberman Rsch. Worldwide, L.A., 1973—, also chmn. bd. dirs.; founder, chmn. bd. dirs. Interviewing Svc. Am., 1982—; expert witness Fed. Trade Commn.; spkr. in field; cons. in field. Office: Lieberman Rsch Worldwide 1900 Ave Of Stars #1550 Los Angeles CA 90067-4483

FISHMAN, BARRY STUART, lawyer; b. Chgo., June 14, 1943; s. Jacob M. and Anita (Epstein) F.; B.A., U. Wis., 1965; J.D., DePaul U., 1968; m. Meredith Porte, Mar. 27, 1976; 1 child, Janna. Admitted to Ill. bar, 1968, Fla., Calif. bars, 1969; partner firm Fishman & Fishman, Chgo., 1968-72; counsel real estate fin. dept. Baird & Warner, Inc., Chgo., 1972-75; gen. counsel Biscayne Fed. Savs. & Loan Assn., Miami, Fla., 1976-79; mem. firm, Ea. regional council Logs Nationwide Representation of Lenders; mem. firm Pallot, Poppell, Goodman & Slotnick, Miami, 1977-80; sr. ptnr. Shapiro & Fishman, North Miami Beach, Tampa, Jacksonville, Orlando and Deerfield Beach, Fla., 1984—; dir. investment div. Cushman and Wakefield of Fla., 1978—. Mem. big gifts com. Greater Miami Jewish Fedn., 1977—; dir. Neighborhood Housing Services, Dade County, Fla., 1977—. Mem. Fla., Calif., Ill., Chgo., Dade County bar assns., Nat. Assn. Realtors, Real Estate Securities and Syndication Inst., Mortgage Bankers Assn., Fla. Mortgage Bankers Assn., Comml. Law League. Jewish. Clubs: Turnberry Isle Yacht & Racquet, Turnberry C.C. Home: 1025 NE 203rd Ln Miami FL 33179-2529 Office: 20803 Biscayne Blvd Ste 300 Aventura FL 33180-1400

FISHMAN, BERNARD, mechanical engineer; b. Bklyn., June 26, 1920; s. Max and Mollie (Greenberg) F.; m. Sara Fishman, July 3, 1947; 1 dau., Carol Beth. Student, Bklyn. Coll., 1937-39; B.M.E., CCNY, 1942; M.M.E., Bklyn. Poly. Inst., 1951. Instr. CCNY Sch. Tech., 1942-44; design and mfg. engr. Star Auto Radio, 1944-45; rocket propulsion engr. M.W. Kellogg Co., 1946-53; chief hydro-mech. engr. Simmonds Precision Products, 1953-65; engring. specialist Reaction Motors div. Thiokol Corp., 1965-67; dir. research, dir. ops. exec. office ASME, N.Y.C., 1967-89; freelance consulting engr., 1989—. Contbr. articles to profl. jours. Mem. Bd. Edn., Ft. Lee, N.J., 1968-72. Served with USAF, 1945-46. Fellow ASME; mem. Nat. Soc. Profl. Engrs., Tau Beta Pi, Pi Tau Sigma. Patentee in field.

FISHMAN, BERNARD PHILIP, museum director; b. N.Y.C., July 25, 1950; s. Samuel William and Rosalyn (Schachtel) F.; m. Elizabeth Andersen, Jan. 8, 1983; 1 child, Philip. BA summa cum laude, Columbia U., 1972; MA, U. Pa., 1982. Rsch. fellow Mus. Applied Sci. Ctr. for Archaeology, U. Pa., Phila., 1976-79; Egyptologist Epigraphic Survey Oriental Inst., U. Chgo., Luxor, Chgo., 1979-82; dir. Fenster Mus. Jewish Art, Tulsa, 1982-85, Jewish Mus. Md., Balt., 1985-98, Lehigh County Hist. Soc., Allentown, Pa., 1998—; tchr., lectr. in field. Author, co-author, editor numerous books, exhibit catalogues, jours., articles; art critic World newspaper, Tulsa, 1985. Recipient award NCCJ, 1985; Applied Sci. Ctr. for Archaeology rsch. fellow, 1977-79, William Penn Found. fellow, 1976-77. Mem. Phi Beta Kappa. Home: 717 N 27th St Allentown PA 18104-4223 Office: Lehigh County Hist Soc Hamilton at Fifth PO Box 1548 Allentown PA 18105-1548 *Without the study of history there can be no civilization: without the cultivation of the arts there can be no immortality.*

FISHMAN, BRIAN SCOTT, research assistant; s. Gordon and Dolores Fishman. BS in Packaging, Mich. State U., 1981; MS in Tech. and Human Affairs, Washington U., 1988; PhD in Urban Affairs and Pub. Policy, U. Del., 1997. Cert. packaging profl. Summer student assoc. IBM Corp., Lexington, Ky., 1980; indsl. engr. IBM Corp., Rochester, Minn., 1981-83; staff assoc. Ctr. for Packaging Sci. and Engring., Piscataway, N.J., 1984-86; rsch. assoc. Disaster Rsch. Ctr., Newark, Del., 1990-91, Ctr. for Energy & Environ. Policy, Newark, 1988-96; rsch. assoc. (post-doc) Ctr. for Disabilities Studies, Newark, 1997; rsch. asst. Office Instl. Rsch. Coll. S.I. CUNY, Staten Island, NY, 1998—; program adminstr. coop. ext. U. Del., 1991-92, adminstrv. asst. Coll. Urban Affairs, 1992-96, tchg. asst., 1990-92, rsch. asst., 1992-93; tchg. asst. in field. Author: Emergency Response to Toxic Chemical Releases in the Kanawha Valley of West Virginia, 1988, Tanker Oil Spills in the Delaware Estuary: September 1985 - Apr. 1989, Institutional Response to Oil-Polluting Incidents in the Delaware Estuary: 1967-1990, 1997. Cast mem. and crew Summer Theater, Chatfield, Minn., 1982; cast mem. Rochester (Minn.) Civic Theater, 1981-83; usher Chapel St. Players, Newark, 1990-91. Named Packaging Sr. of Yr., 1981, Mich. State U. Outstanding Sr., 1981; recipient scholarship Packaging Edn., Found., 1980, Nat. Coun. Phys. Distbn. Mgmt., 1984, 85, N.J. Packaging Execs. Club, 1985, Rutgers U. Packaging scholarship, 1985, Washington U. fellowship, 1986, 87, U. Del. Pub. Svc. Assistantship, 1988, 89, 90;. Mem. AAUP, Assn. Instnl. Rsch., Northeast Assn. for Instnl. Rsch., Profl. Staff Congress, Inst. Packaging Profls. Avocations: Internet comm., computers, theatre, ADA advocacy, self empowerment. Home: PO Box 100065 Staten Island NY 10310-0065 Office: Office of Instl Rsch Coll of Staten Island/CUNY 2800 Victory Blvd Staten Island NY 10314

FISHMAN, FRED NORMAN, lawyer; b. N.Y.C., Aug. 21, 1925; s. Arthur Elihu and Frederica (Greenspan) F.; m. Claire S. Powsner, Sept. 19, 1948; children: Robert J., Nancy K. S.B. summa cum laude, Harvard U., 1946, LL.B. magna cum laude, 1948; postgrad., Yale U., 1945-46. Bar: N.Y. State 1950, U.S. Supreme Ct. 1954. Law clk. to Chief Judge Calvert Magruder, U.S. Ct. Appeals, 1st Circuit, Boston, 1948-49; to Asso. Justice Felix Frankfurter, Supreme Ct. U.S., 1949-50; asso. firm Dewey, Ballantine, Bushby, Palmer & Wood (and predecessors), N.Y.C., 1950-57; with Freeport Minerals Co., N.Y.C., 1957-61; asst. sec. Freeport Minerals Co., 1958-59, asst. v.p., 1959-61; partner firm Kaye, Scholer, Fierman, Hays & Handler, N.Y.C., 1962-92, mem. exec. com., 1970-87, chmn. exec. com., 1981-83, spl. counsel, 1993-95. Editor, officer: Harvard Law Rev. chmn. Harvard Law Sch. Fund, 1977-79; mem. bd. overseers' com. to visit Harvard Law Sch., 1975-81, 88-94; chmn. com. Harvard Law Sch. Class of 1948 Twenty-Fifth Anniversary Gift, Forty-Fifth Anniversary Gift; mem. bd. overseers' com. to visit Grad. Sch. Edn., Harvard U., 1971-77, bd. overseers' Com. on Univ. Resources, 1991—, permanent class com. Harvard Coll. Class of 1946; bd. overseers' com. to visit Med. Sch. and Sch. of Dental Medicine Harvard U., 1997—; trustee Public Edn. Assn., N.Y.C., 1956-73, chmn. bd., 1970-71; dir. Harvard Alumni Assn., 1981-83; trustee Hosp. for Joint Diseases and Med. Center, N.Y.C., 1971-73; trustee Lawyers' Com. for Civil Rights under Law, 1979—, bd. dirs., 1983—, co-chmn., 1983-85; mem. steering com. Campaign for Harvard Law Sch., 1991-95. Fellow Am. Bar Found.; mem. ABA, Assn. of Bar of City of N.Y. (chmn. com. fed. legis. 1963-66, exec. com. 1966-70, chmn. com. corp. law 1980-82, treas. 1993-94), N.Y. State Bar Assn., Am. Law Inst. (adviser corp. governance project 1980-92), Legal Aid Soc. (bd. dirs. 1991-94), Harvard Law Sch. Assn. (pres. 1986-88, 1st v.p. 1984-86, coun. 1978-82, exec. com. 1980-82, 88-90, trustee N.Y.C. assn. 1966-69, v.p. N.Y.C. assn. 1974-75, pres. 1988-89), Phi Beta Kappa, Harvard Club N.Y.C. Home: 650 Park Ave Apt 3D New York NY 10021-6115 Office: Kaye Scholer Fierman Hays & Handler LLP 425 Park Ave New York NY 10022-3506

FISHMAN, GLENN I., medical educator. BA in Chemistry cum laude, Cornell U., 1978; MD, Stanford U., 1983. Diplomate Am. Bd. Internal Medicine, Am. Bd. Cardiovascular Diseases. Rschr. Syntex Rsch., Palo Alto, Calif., 1979-81; resident in internal medicine Mass. Gen. Hosp., Boston, 1983-86; clin. fellow in cardiology Columbia-Presbyn. Med. Ctr., N.Y.C., 1986-88, asst. in clin. medicine, 1988-89; postdoctoral rsch. fellow sect. molecular cardiology Albert Einstein Coll. Medicine, Bronx, N.Y., 1988-90, asst. prof. medicine cardiology divsn., 1990-95, asst. prof. molecular genetics, 1991-95, assoc. prof. medicine cardiology divsn., assoc. prof. molecular genetics, acting dir. sect. molecular cardiology, 1995-98; cardiologist, prof. Mount Sinai Sch. Medicine, N.Y.C., 1998—. mem. editl. bd. Circulation Rsch., 1993—; contbr. articles to profl. jours. Recipient Physician Scientist award NIH, 1990, Louis Katz Basic Sci. Rsch. prize Am. Heart Assn., 1990, Established Investigator award, 1995. Fellow Am. Coll. Cardiology; mem. Phi Beta Kappa. *

FISHMAN, JAMES BART, lawyer; s. Ernest Martin and Adele Fishman. AB, Bard Coll., 1976; JD, N.Y. Law Sch., 1979. Bar: N.Y. 1980, U.S. Dist. Ct. (so. dist.) N.Y. 1980, U.S. Dist. Ct. (ea. dist.) N.Y. 1987, U.S. Ct. Appeals (2d cir.) 1993, U.S. Supreme Ct. 1994. Law clk. atty. gen. State of N.Y., N.Y.C., 1979-80, dep. asst. atty. gen., 1980-82, asst. atty. gen., 1982-84; staff atty. The Legal Aid Soc., N.Y.C., 1984-89, sr. staff atty., 1985-89; pvt. practice N.Y.C., 1989-95; ptnr. Fishman & Neil, N.Y.C., 1995—; guest lectr. Touro Law Sch., 1983, N.Y. Law Sch., 1993; arbitrator Small Claims Ct., Civil Ct. of the City of N.Y., 1985-89; judge Moot Ct. Competitions N.Y.U., Cardozo Law Sch., 1982, 83; appeared on CNBC, CBS TV News, WABC, WCBC, WOR, WBAI, WBLS and WNYC Radio. Author: Purchase of New and Used Lemons, 1994, Consumer Law New York Skills Practice, 1996; contbd. articles to profl. jours. Mem. Nat. Assn. Consumer Advocates, Assn. of the Bar of N.Y. Jewish. Office: Fishman & Neil 319 Broadway Ste 400 New York NY 10007-1187

FISHMAN, JOSHUA AARON, sociolinguist, educator; b. Phila., July 18, 1926; s. Aaron S. and Sonia (Horwitz) F.; m. Gella Jeanne Schweid, Dec. 23, 1951; children: M. Manuel, David Elliot, Avrom Avi. B.S., M.S. (Mayor Phila. competitive scholar 1944-48), U. Pa., 1948; Ph.D., Columbia U., 1953; Ped.D. (hon.), Yeshiva U., 1968; LittD (hon.), Free U. Brussels, 1986. Tchr. elem. and secondary Yiddish secular schs., 1945-50; ednl. psychologist, sr. research asso. dept. research and experimentation Jewish Edn. Com. N.Y., 1951-54; from lectr. to vis. prof. psychology CCNY, 1955-58; research assoc. to dir. research Coll. Entrance Exam. Bd., 1955-58; assoc. prof. human relations and psychology U. Pa., 1958-60; prof. psychology and sociology, dean Grad. Sch. Edn. Yeshiva U., 1960-66, disting. univ. research prof. social scis. Ferkauf Grad. Sch. Psychology, 1966-88, emeritus, 1988—, univ. v.p. acad. affairs, 1973-76; vis. rschr., vis. prof. Stanford (Calif.) U., 1990—; Cummings lectr. McGill U., 1979; Linguistics Soc. Am. prof. Linguistics Inst., 1980; disting. vis. prof. Monash U., Melbourne, Australia, 1985; mem. com. on sociolinguistics Social Sci. Rsch. Coun.; adviser, cons. Am. Jewish Congress, Nat. Scholarship Svc. and Fund for Negro Students, Coll. Entrance Exam. Bd., Am. Assn. Jewish Edn., Ministry of Fin., Republic of Ireland; cons. Ctr. for Applied Linguistics, Internat. Rsch. Ctr. on Bilingualism, Secretariat Linguistic Policy Basque Govt., 1986—, Maori Lang. Commn., 1995—; vis. prof. linguistics Stanford U., 1992—, NYU, 1998—, Grad. Ctr. CUNY, 1999—. Author: Studies on Polish Jewry, 1974, Sociology of Bilingual Education, 1976, The Spread of English, 1977, Advances in the Study of Societal Multilingualism, 1978, Never Say Die: A Thousand Years of Yiddish in Jewish Life and Letters, 1981, Bilingual Education for Hispanic Students in the U.S., 1982, The Rise and Fall of the Ethnic Revival, 1985, Readings in the Sociology of Jewish Languages, 1985, Ethnicity in Action, 1985, The Fergusonian Impact (2 vols.), 1986, Ideology, Society and Language, 1987, Language and Ethnicity in Minority Sociolinguistic Perspective, 1988, Yiddish: Turning to Life, 1991, Reversing Language Shift, 1991, The Earliest Stage of Language Planning, 1993, Post-Imperial English, 1996, In Praise of the Beloved Language, 1997, The Multilinges Apple: Languages in New York City, 1997, Handbook of Language and Ethnic Identity, 1999, also numerous profl. publs. including Afn hvel, 1980—, Forverts, 1996—; assoc. editor: Jour. Ednl. Sociology, 1963-65, Yivo Ann., 1970-77, Yidishe Sprakh, 1970—; editor: Yivo Bleter, 1974-77; editor Jour. Social Issues, 1964-69; editor, contbr. Sociology of Lang., 1971—; gen. editor: Internat. Jour. Sociology of Lang., 1973—, Sociology of Jewish Languages, 1985-88. Pres.'s scholar E.C. Morris fellow Columbia Tchrs. Coll., 1952-53, postdoctoral rsch. tng. fellow Social Sci. Rsch. Coun., 1954-55, fellow Ctr. Advanced Study Behavioral Scis., 1963-64, Princeton Inst. Advanced Study fellow, 1975-76, fellow Netherlands Inst. Advanced Study, 1982-83, Israel Inst. Advanced Studies, 1983, Nat. Ctr. Fgn. Langs., 1995-96; NSF European Conf. grantee, 1960, Office of Edn. grantee, 1960-63, 66-68, 72-74, 79-80, Social Sci. Rsch. Coun. European Conf. grantee, 1961, NIMH grantee, Latin Am., 1963, 66, NSF grantee, Europe, 1966, 79-83, Ford Found. grantee, 1969-72, 75-76, Meml. Found. Jewish Culture grantee, 1970-71, 78-79, 82-83, Jewish Culture grantee, 1970-71, 78-79, 82-83, Nat. Inst. Edn. grantee, 1978-79, 79-81; sr. specialist Inst. Advanced Projects, East-West Ctr., 1968-69; sr. assoc. Multicultural-Bilingual divsn. Nat. Inst. Edn., 1976-77. Fellow Am. Psychol. Assn., Am. Sociol. Assn., Am. Anthrop. Assn.; mem. AAAS, Am. Ednl. Rsch. Assn., Linguistic Soc. Am., Yivo Inst. Jewish Rsch., Nat. Assn. Bilingual Edn. (Man of Yr. 1992), TESOL, AAUP. Home: 3340 Bainbridge Ave Bronx NY 10467-2802 Office: Yeshiva U Ferkauf Grad School Rousso Bldg/Einstein Coll 1300 Morris Park Ave Bronx NY 10461-1926 Office: Dept Linguistics Stanford U Stanford CA 94305 *I have had the incredible good fortune to be exposed simultaneously to modern Western as well as both classical and modern Jewish thought, to secular and religious values, beliefs and ideals to theoretical and applied emphases, to the comforts of a language of wider communication (English) and a language of ethnic intimacy (Yiddish), to the infinite world of science, the eternal land of my ancestors and the new world of democracy, opportunity and pluralism to which my parents came as immigrants. I have tried to combine all of these forces within myself and to contribute to them. I consider both the tensions and the creativity resulting from these varied stimuli to be a unique heritage: an American-Jewish heritage to be treasured, cultivated, improved and handed on.*

FISHMAN, LEN, state commissioner. BA in Polit. Sci., Antioch Coll., 1975; JD with honors, U. Md., 1981. Gen. counsel N.J. Assn. Non-profit homes for the Aging, 1991-94; commr. Dept. Health and Sr. Svcs., Trenton, N.J., 1994—; chair N.J. Health Care Financing Authority;. Named Person of Yr. Med. Soc. N.J., 1996. Achievements: created first cabinet-level dept. for srs.; initiated Worlds Aids Day of Learning for Youth, electronic birth cert. in hosps; developed consumer-oriented HMO rules, first report on mortality rates following coronary artery bypass surgery; expanded assisted living and alternate family care for elderly; published HMO report card. Office: Dept Health and Sr Svcs PO Box 360 Trenton NJ 08625-0360

FISHMAN, LEWIS WARREN, lawyer, educator; b. Bklyn., Dec. 19, 1951. BA in Polit. Sci., Syracuse U., 1972; MPA, Maxwell-Syracuse U., 1973; JD, U. Miami, 1976. Bar: Fla. 1976, U.S. Dist. Ct. (so. dist.) Fla. 1977, U.S. Dist. Ct. D.C. 1978, U.S. Ct. Appeals (5th and 11th cirs.) 1981. Assoc. Simons & Fishman P.A. (and predecessor firm), Miami, 1976-80; ptnr., 1980-81; assoc. Wood, Lucksinger & Epstein, Miami, 1982—; adj. prof. law Fla. Internat. U., 1981, 83, 84, 91; mem. bd. legal specialization and edn. Fla. Bar, 1999—. Mem. Fla. Acad. Healthcare Attys. (bd. dirs., sec. 1986-88, pres. 1990-92), Nat. Health Lawyers Assn. (lectr. 1983, 88-89), Fla. Hosp. Assn. (lectr. 1983, 88-89), Fla. Hosp. Assn. (lectr.), Fla.Med. Record Assn. (lectr. 1982, 83, 84), Am. Acad. Hosp. Attys. (lectr. 1989, 90, 91), Nat. Health Lawyers Assn., Cath. Health Assn., Fla. Bar Assn. (mem. exec. coun. health law sect. 1988-97, chmn. health law sect. 1988-97, chmn. health law sect. 1995-96, cert. health law atty., mem. health law cert. com. 1994-99, vice chmn. 1995-96, chmn. 1996-98, bd. legal specialization and edn. 1999—). Jewish. Home: 14140 SW 104th Ave Miami FL 33176-7064 Office: 9130 S Dadeland Blvd Miami FL 33156-7818

FISHMAN, LOUISE, artist; b. Phila., Jan. 14, 1939; d. Edward and Gertrude (Fisher) F.; life partner, Betsy Crowell. Student, Phila. Coll. of Art, 1956-57, Pa. Acad. of Fine Arts, 1958; BFA, BS, Tyler Sch. of Fine Arts, Elkins, Pa., 1963; MFA, U. Ill., Champaign, 1965. lectr. painting Art Inst. Chgo., 1975, Bard Coll., Annandale-on-Hudson, N.Y., 1975-76, Sch. of Visual Arts, N.Y., 1981; asst. prof. painting U. R.I., Kingston, 1976, Sch. of Arts Columbia U., N.Y.C., 1978-84; assoc. prof. painting Dept. Painting and Drawing Pratt Inst., Bklyn., 1982-84; instr. adj. art Cooper Union Sch. Art, N.Y., 1983-86; prof. The Vermont Studio Sch., Johnson, 1987, Harvard U., Cambridge, Mass., 1995-96. One-woman shows include Phila. Art Alliance, 1964, Nancy Hoffman Gallery, N.Y., 1974, 77, 79, U. R.I., 1976, John Doyle Gallery, Chgo., 1976, 55 Mercer St., 1979, Oscarsson-Hood, N.Y. 1980, 82, John Davis Gallery, Akron, 1982, Bakerville and Waston Gallery, N.Y., 1984, 86, Simon Watson Gallery, N.Y., 1989, Lennon, Weinberg, Inc., N.Y., 1989, Lennon, Weinberg, Inc., 1991, Olin Art Gallery, Kenyon Coll., Gambier, Ohio, 1991, The Morris Gallery Pa. Acad. Fine Arts, Phila., 1992, Temple Gallery, Phila., 1992, Tyler Gallery, Phila., 1992, Robert Miller Gallery, N.Y.C., 1992, 93, 94, 95, 96, Cheim & Read Gallery, N.Y.C., 1998; group shows include Paula Cooper Gallery, N.Y., 1972, Whitney Mus. of Am. Art, N.Y., 1973, 87, Nancy Hoffman Gallery, N.Y., 1973, 77, 79, Munson Williams Proctor Mus., Utica, N.Y., 1977, 81, Mary Boone Gallery, N.Y., 1980, Oscarsson-Hood Gallery, N.Y., 1980, 81, Ft. Wayne (Ind.) Mus., 1982, N.C. Mus. of Art, Raleigh, 1985, Baskerville and Watson Gallery, N.Y., 1983, 85, 86, Corcoran Gallery of Art, Washington, 1987, The Jewish Mus., N.Y., 1987, 88, Daniel Weinberg Gallery, L.A., 1979, Lennon, Weinberg, Inc., N.Y., 1989, 91, Margo Leavin Gallery, L.A., 1991, Musee d'Art Moderne et d'Art Contemporain, 1991, Matthew Marks, N.Y.C., 1991, Robert Miller, N.Y.C., 1992, The Carnegie Inst., Pitts., 1996, Rober Miller Gallery, 1998, Cheim & Read Gallery, N.Y.C., 1998. Grantee NEA, 1994; recipient Nat. Endowment for Arts award, 1975, 76, 83, N.Y. Found. for Arts award, 1986, Adolph & Esther Gottlieb Found. award, 1986; Guggenheim fellow, 1979, MacDowell Colony fellow, 1980, CAPS fellow, 1981. Jewish. Office: care Cheim & Read Gallery 521 W 23rd St New York NY 10011-1105

FISHMAN, MARC JUDAH, physician, researcher; b. Washington, June 14, 1960; s. Jacob Robert and Tamar (Hendel) F.; m. Ann Bruner, June 20, 1993; children: Samuel, Hannah. BA, Columbia U., 1983, MD, 1988. Diplomate Am. Bd. Neurology & Psychiatry, Am. Soc. Addiction Medicine. Intern in internal medicine U. Md. Hosp., Balt., 1988-89; resident in psychiatry Johns Hopkins Hosp., Balt., 1989-92, fellow dept. psychiatry, 1992-93, attending physician, 1992—; med. dir. Mt. Manor Treatment Ctr., 1993—; instr. Johns Hopkins U. Sch. Medicine, Balt., 1993-95, asst. prof., 1995—; bd. dirs. Potomac Healthcare Found., Balt., 1993—. Contbr. articles to profl. jours. Bd. dirs. Chesapeake Youth Ctr., 1997—.

FISHMAN, MARK BRIAN, computer scientist, educator; b. Phila., May 17, 1951; s. Morton Louis and Hilda (Kaplan) F.; m. Alice Faber, Feb. 20, 1977 (div. 1986); m. E. Alexandra Baehr, Apr. 13, 1992. AB summa cum laude, Temple U., 1974; postgrad. Northwestern U., 1974-76; MA, U. Tex., 1980. Bilingual tchr. Wilmette Pub. Schs., 1974; rsch. assoc., programmer, asst. instr. U. Tex., Austin, 1976-80; instr. computer and info. scis. U. Fla., Gainesville, 1980-85; asst. prof. computer sci. Eckerd Coll., St. Petersburg, Fla., 1985-90, dept. coord., 1988-90, 91—, assoc. prof. computer sci., 1991—; instrnl. cons. to IBM, 1980—; cons. artificial intelligence, Battelle Corp., 1987-89, USN Naval Tng. Systems Ctr., 1987—, Advanced Techs., Inc., 1988—, LBS Capital Mgmt., 1990—. Series editor: Advances in Artificial Intelligence Rsch., Vol. I, 1989; editor: Proc. of the First Florida Artificial Intelligence Rsch. Symposium, 1988, Proc. of the Second Florida Artificial Intelligence Rsch. Symposium, 1989, Advances in Artificial Intelligence Research, vol. I, 1989, vol. II, 1992, Proc. of the Third Florida Artificial Intelligence Rsch. Symposium, 1990, Proc. of the Fourth Florida Artificial Intelligence Rsch. Symposium, 1991, Proc. of the Fifth Artificial Intelligence Rsch. Symposium, 1992; guest editor: International Journal of Expert Systems, Vol. 5, no. 2; steering com. First Internat. Conf. Human and Machine Cognition; contbr. articles to profl. jours; presenter in field. U. Tex. fellow, 1978-80; F.C. Austin scholar, 1975; Nat. Def. Fgn. Lang. fellow, 1974. Mem. Assn. Computing Machinery (Tchr. of Yr. award U. Fla. 1984), IEEE Computer Soc., Am. Assn. Artificial Intelligence, Assn. Computational Linguistics, Fla. Artificial Intelligence Research Soc. (proc. chair 1988—, sec. 1988-89, v.p. 1989-91, pres. 1991—), Am. Soc. Engring. Edn. (faculty research fellow summer 1986, 91), Internat. Soc. Philosophical Enquiry, Sigma Xi, Phi Beta Kappa, Phi Kappa Phi, Upsilon Pi Epsilon. Home: 20505 Us Highway 19 N # 12175 Clearwater FL 33764-7303 Office: Eckerd Coll Dept Computer Sci Saint Petersburg FL 33733

FISHMAN, MARSHALL H., lawyer; b. Forest Hills, N.Y., Nov. 9, 1955; s. Sanford and Ruth (Lessler) F.; m. Sharon L. Tanzman, Aug. 16, 1980; children: Bradley, Amanda. AB magna cum laude, Syracuse U., 1977; JD, Georgetown U., 1980. Bar: N.Y. 1982, U.S. Ct. Appeals (2d cir.) 1981, U.S. Dist. Ct. (so. and ea. dists.) N.Y. 1981. Shareholder Greenberg Traurig, N.Y.C.; mediator U.S. Dist. Ct. (so. dist.) N.Y., 1995—. Exec. editor: The Tax Lawyer, Georgetown U., 1979. Mem. N.Y.C. Bar Assn. (mem. com. fed. legislature 1992-95), Securities Industries Assn., Futures Industries Assn. (exec. com. lawyers divsn.), Anti Defamation League, Phi Beta Kappa, Phi Kappa Phi. Office: Greenberg Travrig 200 Park Ave New York NY 10166

FISHMAN, MARVIN ALLEN, pediatrician, neurologist, educator; b. Chgo., Feb. 16, 1937; s. Joseph and Mary (Schneider) F.; m. Gloria Brenda Greenberg, Dec. 20, 1959; children: Bradley Steven, Patricia Ann. BS, U. Ill., 1959, MD, 1961. Diplomate Am. Bd. Pediatrics, Am. Psychiatry and Neurology. Intern, then resident in pediatrics Michael Reese Hosp. and Med. Center, Chgo., 1961-64; resident in neurology Mass. Gen. Hosp., Boston, 1966-67; fellow in pediatric neurology St. Louis Children's Hosp., 1967-70, dir. Birth Defects Ctr., 1971-79; prof. pediatrics, neurology and preventive medicine Washington U. Med. Sch., St. Louis, 1970-79; dir. Irene Walter Johnson Inst. Rehab. Washington U. Med. Sch., 1974-79; prof. pediatrics and neurology, dir. pediatric neurology tng. program Baylor Coll. Medicine, Houston, 1979—, vice chmn. dept. pediatrics, 1992—; chief neurology service Tex. Children's Hosp., Houston, 1979—; mem. residency rev. com. for neurology Accreditation Coun. for Grad. Med. Edn., 1991-96, chmn., 1995-96; bd. dirs. Am. Bd. Psychiatry and Neurology, 1991-97, exec. com., 1995-97, v.p., 1996, pres., 1997. Conbr. articles in field, chpts. in books; mem. editorial bd. Jour. Pediatrics, 1980-87, Jour. Child Neurology, Pediatric Neurology, Annals of Neurology; editor textbook. With USAR, 1964-66. Grantee HEW; Grantee Grant Found.; Grantee Ga. Warm Springs Found.; Grantee Nat. Found.-March of Dimes. Mem. Am. Soc. Neurochemistry (councillor 1977-79), Child Neurology Soc. (exec. com., councillor 1980-82, sec.-treas. 1984-86, pres.-elect 1986-87, pres. 1987-89, past pres. 1989-90), Houston Neurol. Soc. (pres.-elect 1989-90, pres. 1990-91), Am. Acad. Pediatrics, Am. Acad. Neurology, Am. Neurol. Assn., Am. Pediatric Soc., Soc. for Pediatric Rsch., Soc. for Neuroscis. Home: 1523-B Potomac Dr Houston TX 77057-1925 Office: Baylor Coll Med 1 Baylor Plz Houston TX 77030-3411

FISHMAN, MITCHELL STEVEN, lawyer; b. N.Y.C., July 27, 1948; s. Abraham and Sylvia (Sher) F.; children: Danielle, Matthew, Jeremy. BA cum laude, Harvard U., 1970, JD cum laude, 1973. Bar: N.Y. 1974, D.C. 1984. Assoc. Breed, Abbott & Morgan, N.Y.C., 1973-74; assoc. Paul, Weiss, Rifkind, Wharton & Garrison, N.Y.C., 1975-81, ptnr., 1981—; exec. dir. Temp. State Commn. on Banking, Ins. and Fin. Svcs., N.Y., 1983-84. Mem. ABA, Assn. of Bar of City of N.Y. (sec. com. on corp. law 1976-79, mem. com. on securities regulation 1998—). Democrat. Home: 200 E 57th St New York NY 10022-2860 Office: Paul Weiss Rifkind Wharton & Garrison Fl 24 1285 Avenue of the Americas New York NY 10019-6064

FISHMAN, PAUL J., lawyer. JD, Harvard U., 1982. Law clk. to Hon. Edward R. Becker U.S. Ct. Appeals 3d Circuit; asst. U.S. atty. Dist. N.J. U.S. Dept. Justice, dep. chief criminal divsn., chief narcotics, 1987-89, chief criminal divsn., 1989-91, 1st asst. U.S. atty., 1991-94, counsel to dep. atty. gen. Jamie S. Gorelick, 1994, assoc. dep. atty. gen., 1995-97; ptnr. Friedman, Kaplan & Seiler, N.Y.C., 1997—. Office: 875 3d Ave New York NY 10022

FISHMAN, RICHARD GLENN, lawyer, accountant; b. Orange, N.J., June 2, 1952; s. Irving and Eleanor (Tanenbaum) F.; m. Jean Goldhammer, Aug. 11, 1974; children: Neil Samuel, Peter Lawrence, Ellen Melissa. BA in Econs. with highest honors and highest distinction, Rutgers U., 1974; JD, Yale U., 1977; LLM in Taxation, NYU, 1980. Bar: N.Y. 1978, N.J. 1978, U.S. Dist. Ct. N.J. 1978, U.S. Ct. Claims 1978, U.S. Tax Ct. 1978, U.S. Dist. Ct. (so. dist.) N.Y. 1979, U.S. Ct. Appeals (3d cir.) 1994. Assoc. Stroock & Stroock & Lavan, N.Y.C., 1977-80, Roberts & Holland, N.Y.C., 1980-85; tax mgr. Spicer & Oppenheim (formerly Oppenheim, Appel, Dixon & Co.), N.Y.C., 1985-87, ptnr., 1987-88; sr. tax. counsel AlliedSignal Inc., Morristown, N.J., 1988-94; dir. internat. taxes and sr. tax counsel AlliedSignal Inc., Morristown, N.J., 1994-96, sector tax dir., engineered materials sector, 1996-97, assoc. gen. tax counsel, 1997—. Contbr. articles to profl. jours. Mem. ABA, AICPA, N.Y. State Bar Assn., N.J. State Bar Assn. Home: 6 Tilden Ct Livingston NJ 07039-2419 Office: Allied Signal PO Box 1057 Morristown NJ 07962-1057

FISHMAN, ROBERT ALLEN, neurologist, educator; b. N.Y.C., May 30, 1924; s. Samuel Benjamin and Miriam (Brinkin) F.; m. Margery Ann Satz, Jan. 29, 1956 (dec. May 29, 1980); children: Mary Beth, Alice Ellen, Elizabeth Ann.; m. Mary Craig Wilson, Jan. 7, 1983. A.B., Columbia U., 1944; M.D., U. Pa., 1947. Mem. faculty Columbia Coll. Physicians and Surgeons, 1954-66, asso. prof. neurology, 1962-66; asst. attending neurologist N.Y. State Psychiat. Inst., 1955-66; asst. attending neurologist Neurol. Inst. Presbyn. Hosp., N.Y.C., 1955-61, asso., 1961-66; co-dir. Neurol. Clin. Research Center, Neurol. Inst., Columbia-Presbyn. Med. Ctr., 1961-66; prof. neurology U. Calif. Med. Ctr., San Francisco, 1966-94, chmn. dept. neurology, 1966-92, prof. emeritus, 1994—; cons. neurologist San Francisco Gen. Hosp., San Francisco VA Hosp., Letterman Gen. Hosp.; dir. Am. Bd. Psychiatry and Neurology, 1981-88, v.p., 1986, pres., 1987. Author: Cerebrospinal Fluid in Diseases of the Nervous System, 1992; chief editor Annals of Neurology, 1993-97; contbr. articles to profl. jours. Nat. Multiple Sclerosis Soc. fellow, 1956-57; John and Mary R. Markle scholar in med. sci., 1960-65; recipient Disting. Alumnus award U. Pa. 1996. Mem. Am. Neurol. Assn. (pres. 1983-84), Am. Fedn. for Clin. Research, Assn. for Research in Nervous and Mental Diseases, Am. Acad. Neurology (v.p. 1971-73, pres. 1975-77), Am. Assn. Physicians, Am. Soc. for Neurochemistry, Soc. for Neurosci., N.Y. Neurol. Soc., Am. Assn. Univ. Profs. Neurology (pres. 1972-73), AAAS, Am. Epilepsy Soc., N.Y. Acad. Scis., AMA (sec. sect. on nervous and mental diseases 1964-67, v.p. 1967-68, pres. 1968-69), Alpha Omega Alpha (hon. faculty mem.). Home: 50 Summit Ave Mill Valley CA 94941-1819 Office: U Calif Med Ctr 794 Herbert C Moffitt Hosp San Francisco CA 94143

FISHMAN, WILLIAM HAROLD, cancer research foundation executive, biochemist; b. Winnipeg, Man., Can., Mar. 2, 1914; s. Abraham and Goldie (Chmelnitsky) F.; m. Lillian Waterman, Aug. 6, 1939; children: Joel, Nina, Daniel. BS, U. Sask., Saskatoon, 1935; PhD, U. Toronto, Ont., Can., 1939; MDhc, U. Umea, Sweden, 1983. Dir. cancer rsch. New Eng. Med. Ctr. Hosp., Boston, 1958-72; rsch. prof. pathology Tufts U. Sch. Medicine, 1961-70, prof. pathology, 1970-77; dir. Tufts Cancer Rsch. Ctr., 1972-76; pres. La Jolla (Calif.) Cancer Rsch. Found., 1976-89, pres. emeritus, 1989—; mem. basic sci. programs merit rev. bd. com. VA, 1971-75; mem. pathobiol. chemistry sect. NIH, Bethesda, Md., 1977-81. Author in field. Rsch. Career award NIH, 1962-77; Royal Soc. Can. rsch. fellow, 1939, 17th Internat. Physiol. Congress-U.K. Fedn. fellow, 1947. Fellow AIC, AAAS, Nat. Acad. Clin. Biochemistry; mem. Am. Assn. Cancer Rsch., Am. Soc. Biol. Chemists, Am. Soc. Cell Biology, Am. Soc. Exptl. Pathology, Histochem. Soc. (pres. 1983-84), Internat. Soc. Clin. Enzymology (hon.), Internat. Soc. Oncodevel. Biology and Medicine (hon., Abbott award 1993), Univ. Club (San Diego). Jewish. Current work: Basic rsch. on expression of placental genes by cancer cells; monoclonal antibodies; oncodevelopmental markers; immunocytochemistry. Home: 715 Muirlands Vista Way La Jolla CA 92037-6202 Office: The Burnham Institute 10901 N Torrey Pines Rd La Jolla CA 92037-1062

FISHWICK, JOHN PALMER, lawyer, retired railroad executive; b. Roanoke, Va., Sept. 29, 1916; s. William and Nellie (Cross) F.; m. Blair Wiley, Jan. 4, 1941 (dec. June 1987); children: Ellen Blair (Mrs. Guyman Martin III), Anne Palmer (Mrs. Wesley Posvar), John Palmer; m. Doreen Allton, Nov. 17, 1989. A.B., Roanoke Coll., 1937; LL.B., Harvard U., 1940. Bar: Va. 1939. Asso. Cravath, Swaine & Moore, N.Y.C., 1940-42; asst. to gen. solicitor N. & W. Ry., Roanoke, Va., 1945-47; asst. gen. solicitor N. & W. Ry., 1947-51, asst. gen. counsel, 1951-54, gen. solicitor, 1954-56, gen. counsel, 1956-58, v.p., gen. counsel, 1958-59, v.p. law, 1959-63, sr. v.p., 1963-70, pres., chief exec. officer, 1970-80, chmn., chief exec. officer, 1980-81, also dir.; ptnr. Windels, Marx, Davies & Ives, N.Y.C., 1981-84; of counsel Fishwick, Jones and Glenn, Roanoke, Va., 1984-95; chmn., chief exec. officer Erie Lackawanna Ry. Co., 1968-70; pres., chief exec. officer Del. and Hudson Ry. Co., 1968-70; pres., dir. Dereco, Inc., 1968-81; chmn. investment com., bd. dirs. Norfolk So. Corp., 1981-89. Trustee Roanoke Coll., 1964-72; trustee Va. Theol. Sem. (former chancellor Diocese S.W. Va.); former bd. dirs. Va. Found. Humanities; former trustee Va. Mus. Fine Arts, Richmond. Served as lt. comdr. USNR, 1942-45. Mem. Met. Club (Washington). Episcopalian. Office: 110 Franklin Rd SE Roanoke VA 24042-0002

FISK, DONALD E., air national guard officer; b. Wichita, Kans., July 4, 1950; s. Floyd Lester and Wilma Ethyl (Unruh) F.; m. Sherry Elaine Megenity, June 19, 1994; chldren: Kris, Bree, Lauren. BA, Wichita State U., 1972; MS, Ark. State U., 1977; JD, Washburn U., 1983. Bar: Kans. 1983. Pres. Omni-Care Health Svc., Topeka, Kans., 1982-84; atty. in pvt. practice, Topeka, 1985-87; with 190th ARW, Kans. Air Nat. Guard, Topeka, 1987—, comdr. maintenance squadron, 1995-96, chief wing plans and programs, 1996—. Capt. USAF, 1972-79. Mem. Custer Battlefield Mus. Hist. Assn., Ft. Phil Kearny/Bozeman Trail, N.G. Assn. U.S., N.G. Assn. Kans. Avocations: history, travel, photography. Home: 4420 Haliday Ln Topeka KS 66618 Office: 190th ARW 5920 SW Coyote Dr Topeka KS 66619-1429

FISK, EDWARD RAY, retired civil engineer, author, educator; b. Oshkosh, Wis., July 19, 1924; s. Ray Edward and Grace O. (Meyer) Barnes; married, Oct. 28, 1950; children: Jacqueline Mary, Edward Ray II, William John, Robert Paul. BCE Marquette U., 1949; student Fresno (Calif.) State Coll., 1954, UCLA, 1957-58; BS, MBA, Calif.-Western U.. Engr., Calif. Div. Hwys., 1952-55; engr. Bechtel Corp., Vernon, Calif., 1955-59; project mgr. Toups Engring Co., Santa Ana, Calif., 1959-61; dept. head Perliter & Soring, Los Angeles, 1961-64; Western rep. Wire Reinforcement Inst., Washington, 1964-65; cons. engr., Anaheim, Calif., 1965; assoc. engr. Met. Water Dist. So. Calif., 1966-68; chief specification engr. Koebig & Koebig, Inc., Los Angeles, 1968-71; mgr. constrn. services VTN Consol., Inc., Irvine, Calif., 1971-78; pres. E.R. Fisk Constrn., Orange, Calif., 1978-81; corp. dir. constrn. mgmt. James M. Montgomery Cons. Engrs., Inc., Pasadena, Calif., 1981-83; v.p. Lawrence, Fisk & McFarland, Inc., Santa Barbara and Orange, 1983—; pres. E.R. Fisk & Assocs., Orange, 1983—, Gleason, Peacock & Fisk, Inc., 1987-92; v.p. constrn. svcs. Wilsey & Ham, Foster City, Calif., 1993-94; adj. prof. engring., constrn. Calif. State U., Long Beach, 1987-90, Orange Coast Coll., Costa Mesa, Calif., 1957-78, Calif. Poly. State U., Pomona, 1974; Instr. U. Calif., Berkeley, Inst. Transportation Studies, 1978—, engring. prof. programs U. Wash., 1994—, internationally for ASCE Continuing Edn.; former mem. Calif. Bd. Registered Constrn. Insps. Served with USN, 1942-43, USAF, 1951-52. Registered profl. engr., Ariz., Calif., Colo., Fla., Idaho, Ky., La., Mont., Nev., Oreg., Utah, Wash., Wyo.; lic. land surveyor, Oreg., Idaho; lic. gen. engring. contractor, Calif.; cert. arbitator Calif. Constrn. Contract Arbitration Com. Fellow ASCE (life fellow, past chmn. exec. com. constrn. div., former chmn. nat. com. inspection 1978—), Nat. Acad. Forensic Engrs. (diplomate); mem. Orange County Engring. Council (former pres.), Calif. Soc. Profl. Engrs. (past pres. Orange County), Structural Engrs. Assn. Calif. (engrs. joint contracts documents com. 1993-95), Am. Arbitration Assn. (nat. panel), U.S. Com. Large Dams, Order Founders and Patriots Am. (past gov. Calif.), Soc. Colonial Wars (dep. gov. gen. Calif. chpt.), S.R. (past dir.), Engring. Edn. Found. (trustee), Tau Beta Pi. Independent. Author: Machine Methods of Survey Computing, 1958, Construction Project Administration, 1978, 82, 88, 92, 97, Construction Engineers Complete Handbook of Forms, 1981, 92, Resident Engineers Field Manual, 1992; co-author: Contractor's Project Guide, 1988, Contracts and Specifications for Public Works Projects, 1992. Home: 1792 N Ridgewood St Orange CA 92865-4454

FISK, IRWIN WESLEY, financial investigator; b. Byers, Kans., Nov. 20, 1938; s. Walter Roleigh Fisk and Mae Pearle Irwin; m. Susie Bea Walters, Sept. 9, 1973; children: Mark Christopher, Paul Steven. Student, L.A. City Coll., 1958-60, Calif. State U., L.A., 1960-64, Pasadena C.C., 1987-88. Lic. pvt. investigator, Calif. Asst. exec. dir. Stores Protective Assn., L.A., 1962-66; sr. spl. investigator Calif. Dept. Corps., L.A., 1966-83, chief investigator, 1983-94; pres. Bus. and Fin. Investigations, Inc., La Crescenta, 1994—; mem. Multi-State Law Enforcement Task Force of Fraudulent Telemarketing, L.A., 1987-94. Contbr. articles to profl. publs. Mem. U.S. Chess Fedn. (life), Am. Radio Relay League (DXCC award 1993), Authors Guild, So. Calif. Fraud Investigators Assn., Masons. Republican. Avocations: chess, ham radio. Home: 343 N 1st St Lindsborg KS 67456-2004 Office: Bus and Fin Investigations Inc PO Box 8246 La Crescenta CA 91224-0246

FISK, LENNARD AYRES, physicist, educator; b. Elizabeth, N.J., July 7, 1943; s. Lennard Ayres and Elinor (Fischer) F.; m. Patricia Elizabeth Leuba, Dec. 28, 1966; children: Ian, Justin, Nathan. AB, Cornell U., 1965; PhD, U. Calif., San Diego, 1969. Postdoctoral fellow NASA/Goddard Space Flight Ctr., Greenbelt, MD., 1969-71, astrophysicist, 1971-77; assoc. prof. U. N.H., Durham, 1977-81, prof., 1981-87, dir. rsch., 1982-83, interim v.p./fin. affairs, 1983-84, v.p. rsch. and fin., 1984-87; assoc. administr. space sci. and applications NASA Hdqrs., Washington, 1987-93; prof. U. Mich., 1993—; advisor NAS, NASA, 1980-87. Contbr. more than 100 articles to profl. jours. Recipient Space Science award Am. Inst. Aeronautics and Astronautics, 1994. Fellow Am. Geophys. Union; mem. Internat. Acad. Astronautics. Office: Univ of Michigan Atmos Oceanic & Space Scis 2455 Hayward St Ann Arbor MI 48109-2143

FISK, MARTIN H., lawyer; b. St. Paul, Apr. 11, 1947. BA, U. Minn., 1969; JD, Harvard U., 1976. Bar: Minn. 1976. Mem. Briggs and Morgan P.A., St. Paul. Mem. ABA, Phi Beta Kappa. Office: Briggs and Morgan PA 2200 1st Nat Bank Bldg Saint Paul MN 55101-3210

FISK, MERLIN EDGAR, judge; b. Great Falls, Mont., Mar. 18, 1921; s. Edgar Anson and Eleanor Sybil (Worden) F.; m. Margery Anne Hall, May 27, 1942; children: Mary Dana, Catherine, Anne, Elizabeth. BSChemE, Mont. State U., 1942. Tech. adminstr. Lago Oil & Transport Co., Ltd. subsidiary Exxon Corp., Aruba, Aruba Netherlands Antilles, 1942-62; v.p., gen. mgr. Antilles Chem. Co. subsidiary Exxon Corp., 1962-64; dir. mfg. Esso Pappas Indsl. Co., Athens, Greece, 1964-67; gen. mgr. Essochem, S.A. subsidiary Exxon Corp., Madrid, 1967-69; mgr. ops. and planning Essochem, S.A. subsidiary Exxon Corp., Brussels, 1969-71, ret., 1971; judge probate div. State of Conn., Newtown, 1979-91; ret., 1991; pres. judge Conn. Probate Assembly, 1990-91. Mem. Commn. on Aging, Newtown, 1987-99; trustee Cyrenius H. Booth Libr., Newtown, 1975-95, 97—; bd. dirs. Newtown Meals on Wheels, Inc., 1974-93, Recording for the Blind, Inc. Conn. chpt., New Haven, 1975-92, Waterbury (Conn.) Ballet Co., 1987-97. Mem. Am. Arbitration Assn. (comml. panel 1991-98), Men's Literary and Social Club of Newtown (pres. 1984-85). Republican. Episcopalian. Avocations: golf, gardening, reading.

FISKE, EDWARD BOGARDUS, editor, journalist, educational consultant; b. Phila., June 4, 1937; s. Edward R., Jr. and Jean (Bogardus) F.; m. Dale Alden Woodruff, July 12, 1963 (div. May 1997); children: Julia F. Hogan, Suzanna F. Wilson; m. Helen F. Ladd, June 29, 1997. B.A., Wesleyan U., Middletown, Conn., 1959; M.A., Princeton Theol. Sem., 1963, Columbia U., 1965; LL.D. (hon.), Occidental Coll., 1991; and others. Religion reporter and editor N.Y. Times, 1964-74, edn. editor, 1974-91; cons. Pew Forum on Edn. Reform, 1991-92, Bus. Roundtable Edn. Initiative, 1991-92, Dana Found., 1992—, UNICEF Edn. Mission to Bangladesh, 1993, Internat. Rescue Com. in Cambodia, 1993-94, Acad. Ednl. Devel., 1993—, World Bank, 1995—, UNESCO, 1996—; edn. analyst Asian Devel. Bank, 1994; fellow Ctr. for Internat. Devel. Rsch., Duke U.; vis. scholar Victoria U. Wellington, New Zealand, 1998. Author: Fiske Guide to Colleges, (annual) Smart Schools, Smart Kids, 1990, Basic Education, 1993, Fiske Guide to Getting into The Right College, 1997, 2d edit., 1999; contbr. articles to nat. periodicals. Trustee Am. Assn. Higher Edn., 1994-98, Am. News Svc., 1995—. Named Wolynsky-Joukowsky fellow Brown U., 1990, Montgomery fellow Dartmouth Coll., 1991. Mem. Phi Beta Kappa. E-mail: efiske@aol.com. Home: 211 Monticello Ave Durham NC 27707

FISKE, ROBERT BISHOP, JR., lawyer; b. N.Y.C., Dec. 28, 1930; s. Robert Bishop and Lenore (Seymour) F.; m. Janet Tinsley, Aug. 21, 1954; children: Linda Goucher, Robert Bishop, Susan Williams. BA, Yale U., 1952; JD, U. Mich., 1955, LLD (hon.), 1997. Bar: Mich. 1955, N.Y. 1956, U.S. Ct. Appeals (2nd cir.) 1957, U.S. Supreme Ct. 1961. Assoc. Davis, Polk, Wardwell, Sunderland & Kiendl, 1955-57; asst. U.S. atty. So. Dist. N.Y., 1957-61; assoc. Davis, Polk & Wardwell, 1961-64, ptnr., 1964-76, 80-99; U.S. atty. So. Dist. N.Y., N.Y.C., 1976-80; ind. counsel for Whitewater, Little Rock, 1994. Fellow Am. Coll. Trial Lawyers (pres. 1991-92); mem. ABA (chmn. standing com. on fed. judiciary 1984-87), Assn. of Bar of City of N.Y., Fed. Bar Coun. (pres. 1982-84), N.Y. State Bar Assn., Noroton Yacht Club, Wee Burn Country Club. Republican. Congregationalist. Home: 19 Juniper Rd Darien CT 06820-5707 Office: 450 Lexington Ave New York NY 10017-3911

FISS, OWEN M., law educator; b. 1938. BA, Dartmouth Coll., 1959; BPhil, Oxford U., 1961; LLB, Harvard U., 1964. Bar: N.Y. 1965. Law clk. to Judge Thurgood Marshall, U.S. Ct. Appeals 2d Cir., 1964-65, to Justice Brennan, U.S. Supreme Ct., 1965; spl. asst. to asst. atty. gen., civil rights div. U.S. Dept. Justice, Washington, 1966-67, acting dir. Office of Planning Coordination, 1968; prof. U. Chgo. Law Sch., 1968-74; prof. Yale U. Law Sch., New Haven, 1974-84, Alexander M. Bickel prof. pub. law, 1984-92, Sterling prof., 1992—; vis. prof. Stanford U., 1973. Mem. Harvard Law Rev.; author: Injunctions, 1972, The Civil Rights Injunction, 1978; (with R.M. Cover) The Structure of Procedure, 1979; (with D. Rendleman) Injunctions, 2d edit., 1984; (with Cover and J. Resnik) Procedure, 1988; (with Cover and Resnik) The Federal Procedural System, 1988, 3d edit., 1991, Holmes Devise History of the Supreme Ct. :Troubled Beginnings of the Modern State, 1888-1910, 1993, Liberalism Divided, 1996, The Irony of Free Speech, 1996, A Community of Equals, 1999; mem. editl. bd. Philosophy and Pub. Affairs and Found. Press, Yale Jour. Criticism, Yale Jour. Law and Humanities, Law, Econs. and Orgns. Office: Yale Law Sch PO Box 401A New Haven CT 06520

FISZEL, GEOFFREY LYNN, investment banker, investment advisor; b. N.Y.C., Aug. 9, 1942; s. John Henry and Rebecca (Wexman) F.; m. Barbara Ann Foohey, Jan. 30, 1970; children: Sharon Lynn, Morgan Bernard, Austin Tyler, Alexander William. BS in Mgmt. and Ops. Rsch., NYU, 1974; M.S. in Acctg. and Tax (Seminar award), U. Hartford, 1976; grad. scholar program econs. of fin. Trinity Coll., 1980; registered securities rep., gen. securities prin., registered investment adviser; m. Barbara Ann Foohey, Jan. 30, 1970; children: Sharon Lynn, Morgan Bernard, Austin Tyler, Alexander William. Cost acct. O'Malley Cos., Phoenix, 1974; regional acct., asst. regional controller Sanitas Service Corp., Hartford, Conn., 1974-75; asst. to corp. controller Bristol (Conn.) Brass Corp., 1975-76; asst. controller Security Ins. Co. of Hartford, 1976-80; controller Chase Enterprises, 1980-81, v.p., controller, 1981, sr. v.p., controller, 1985, sr. v.p. corp. and real estate devel., banking, ins., telecomm., and mergers and acquisitions, 1988-89; CEO, pres., chmn. Equity Investors Holding Co., Glastonbury, Conn., 1989—; v.p. investments Advest, Inc., Hartford, 1993-94, v.p. investments Tucker Anthony, Inc., Hartford, 1994—; tax and fin. cons. U. Conn.; cons. to minority small bus.; cons. to Fortune 100 cos.; lectr. various tax insts. and seminars; mem. Juvenile Diabetes Found. Served with USMC, 1959-63. Mem. Real Estate Bd. of N.Y., Fin. Execs. Inst. (mem. corp. fin. and taxation coms.), The Nature Conservancy. Author: (Book) How to Start Your Own Private Investment Partnership, 1997; pub., author investment adv. newsletter Continuing Walks On The Wild Side. Home: 245 Farmcliff Dr Glastonbury CT 06033-4185 Office: Tucker Anthony Inc One Corporate Ctr Hartford CT 06103

FITCH, COY DEAN, physician, educator; b. Marthaville, La., Oct. 5, 1934; s. Raymond E. and Joey (Youngblood) F.; m. Rachel Farr, Mar. 31, 1956; children: Julia Anne, Jaquelyn Kay. BS, U. Ark., 1956, MS, 1958, MD, 1958. Diplomate Am. Bd. Internal Medicine and Endocrinology. Intern U. Ark. Sch. Medicine, 1958-59, resident, 1959-62, instr. biochemistry, 1959-62, asst. prof. medicine and biochemistry, 1962-66, asso. prof., 1966-67; dir. U. Ark. Sch. Medicine (Honors Med. Student Research Program), 1965-67; asso. prof. internal medicine and biochemistry St. Louis U. Sch. Medicine, 1967-73, prof. internal medicine, 1973—, prof. biochemistry, 1976—, head sect. metabolism, 1969-76, dir. div. endocrinology and metabolism, 1977-85; chief med. service St. Louis U. Hosps., 1976-77, vice-chmn. dept. internal medicine, 1983-85, acting chmn. dept. internal medicine, 1985-88, chmn. dept., 1988—; practice medicine, specializing in internal medicine Little Rock, 1962-67, St. Louis, 1969—; dir. Diabetic Clinic, U. Ark. Med. Ctr., 1962-67, head sect. metabolism and endocrinology, 1966-67; mem. nutrition study sect. div. research grants NIH, 1967-71. Asso. editor: Nutrition Revs., 1964; contbr. articles to profl. jours. Served from capt. to lt. col., M.C. AUS, 1967-69. Recipient Lederle Med. Faculty award, 1966-67; Russell M. Wilder-Nat. Vitamin Found. fellow, 1959-62. Fellow ACP (gov. Mo. chpt. 1995-99); mem. Am. Fedn. Clin. Rsch., Am. Inst. Nutrition, Am., So. Socs. Clin. Investigation, Am. Soc. Biol. Chemists, Ctrl. Soc. Clin. rsch., Phi Beta Kappa, Sigma Xi. Office: 1402 S Grand Blvd Saint Louis MO 63104-1004

FITCH, FRANK WESLEY, pathologist educator, immunologist, educator, administrator; b. Bushnell, Ill., May 30, 1929; s. Harold Wayne and Mary Gladys (Frank) F.; m. Shirley Dobbins, Dec. 23, 1951; children—Mary Margaret, Mark Howard. M.D., U. Chgo., 1953, S.M., 1957, Ph.D., 1960; M.D. (hon.), U. Lausanne, Switzerland, 1990. Postdoctoral research fellow USPHS, 1954-55, 57-58; faculty U. Chgo., 1957—, prof. pathology, 1967—, Albert D. Lasker prof. med. sci., 1976—, emeritus prof., 1996, assoc. dean med. and grad. edn. div. biol. scis., 1976-85, dean acad. affairs, 1985-86, dir. Ben May Inst., 1986-95; vis. prof. Swiss Inst. Exptl. Cancer Research, Lausanne, Switzerland, 1974-75. Editor-in-chief The Jour. of Immunology, 1997—; contbr. chpts. to books, articles to profl. jours. Recipient Borden Undergrad. Research award, 1953, Lederle Med. Faculty award, 1958-61; Markle Found. scholar, 1961-66; Commonwealth Fund fellow U. Lausanne (Switzerland) Institut de Biochimie, 1965-66; Guggenheim fellow, 1974-75. Mem. Fedn. Am. Socs. for Exptl. Biology (pres. 1993-94), Am. Assn. Immunologists (pres. 1992-93), Am. Soc. for Investigative Pathology, Am. Assn. for Cancer Rsch., Chgo. Path. Soc., Transplantation Soc., Sigma Xi, Alpha Omega Alpha. Home: 5449 S Kenwood Ave Chicago IL 60615-5312

FITCH, JAMES MARSTON, architectural preservationist, architectural historian, critic; b. Washington, May 8, 1909; s. James Marston and Ellen (Payne) F.; m. Cleo Rickman (dec. 1995); m. Martica Sawin. Student, U. Ala., 1925-26, Tulane U., 1927-28, Columbia U., 1946-48; LHD (hon.), Columbia U., 1980, N.J. Inst. Tech., 1994; D.A. (hon.), Kans. State U., 1979; LHD (hon.), Tulane U., 1997; PhD (hon.), Parsons Sch. Design, 1997. Housing analyst Fed. Housing Adminstrn., Washington, 1934-35; assoc. editor Archtl. Record, N.Y.C., 1936-42; tech. editor Archtl. Forum, N.Y.C., 1945-49; archtl. editor House Beautiful, N.Y.C., 1949-53; asst. prof. architecture Columbia U., N.Y.C., 1954-60, assoc. prof., 1960-64, prof., 1964-77, prof. emeritus, 1977—; mem. Landmarks Preservation Commn., N.Y.C., 1977-79; dir. hist. preservation Beyer Blinder Belle, Architects & Planners, N.Y.C., 1979—; preservator Central Park, N.Y.C., 1974-76; pres. Ctr. for Bldg. Conservation, N.Y.C., 1980—; vis. prof. U. Ill., Chgo., Ill., 1968, U. Sao Paulo, Brazil, 1978; Centennial vis. prof. Tex. A&M U., 1976; disting. vis. prof. U. Cin., 1979; adj. prof. Grad. Sch. Arts U. Pa., 1979-83. Author: Walter Gropius, 1960, Architecture and Esthetics of Plenty, 1960, 2d edit., 1985, American Building, 2 vols., 2d edit., 1962, Vier Jarhunderte Bauen in U.S.A, 1968, Historic Preservation, 1982, 2d edit., 1990, La Progettanzione Ambiïental, 1985, Walter Gropins Archive, 1991. Bd. dirs. Mcpl. Arts Soc., N.Y.C., 1970-72. Served in USAAF, 1942-45. Recipient Outstanding Achievement award Nat. Trust Hist. Preservation, 1974, Conservation Svc. award U.S. Dept. Interior, 1976, Preservation award Victorian Soc. Am., 1977, recipient cert. of Merit Mcpl. Art Soc. N.Y., 1977, George McEneny medal Am. Hist. Preservation Soc., 1982, Merit award N.Y. Soc. Architects, 1983 , Crowninshield award Nat. Trust Hist. Preservation, 1985, Disting. Prof. award Assn. Collegiate Schs. Architecture, 1986, award of distinction 4th Internat. Passive Low Energy Conf., Venice, 1985, Disting. Svc. medal Nat. Coun. for Preservation Edn., 1990, Lucy B. Moses award for Lifetime Achievements in Architecture, 1992, Lifetime Achievement award Victorian Soc. Am., 1998; Wm. Kenney fellow Greece and Turkey, 1959; Brunner scholar, 1984; Fulbright scholar, Peru, 1975; Guggenheim Found. fellow, 1977-78;, Nat. Endowment Arts fellow, 1980;, Distinctive Designer fellowship Nat. Endowment for Arts, 1988. Fellow Royal British Inst. Architects (hon.); mem. AIA (hon., AIA medal 1976, N.Y. chpt. award of Merit 1979, Presdl. Citation 1990), N.Y. Soc. Architects (award of Merit 1981), Soc. Archtl. Historians (dir. 1973-74), Assn. Preservation Tech. (founding, Harley J. McKee award 1992). Clubs: Century (N.Y.C.); Athenaeum (Phila.). Office: Beyer Blinder Belle Architects 45 E 11th St New York NY 10003-4601

FITCH, LYLE CRAIG, economist, administrator; b. Merriman, Nebr., May 22, 1913; s. Fred B. and Frances (Logsdon) F.; m. Violet Vaughn, Sept. 4, 1937; 1 child, Linda Fitch Andrews. B.S., Chadron (Nebr.) State Coll., 1935; M.A., U. Nebr., 1938; Ph.D., Columbia U., 1946. Econ. depts. Bklyn. Coll., Columbia U., Wesleyan U., 1939-50; assoc. prof. econs. Columbia U., 1953-54; sr. mgmt. econs. Office of Mayor, N.Y.C., 1954-56; 1st dep. city adminstr. Office of Mayor, 1957-60, city adminstr., 1960-61; economist U.S. Treasury Dept., 1942; spl. asst. to Gov. Conn., 1949-50; dir. fiscal research Inst. Pub. Adminstrn., 1956-57, pres., 1961-82, chmn. bd. trustees, 1982-92; cons. govts. in, Africa, S.Am., Europe, Asia, fed., state and local govts., Regents Prof. U. Calif., Los Angeles, 1971, U. Calif., Berkeley, 1984. Author, editor: Planning for Jobs, 1946; author: (with Horace Taylor) Taxing Municipal Bond Income, 1950, (with Robert Haig, Carl Shoup) The Financial Problems of the City of New York, 1952, (with Carl Shoup, others) The Fiscal Systems of Venezuela, 1958, Urban Transportation and Public Policy, 1964, (with Annmarie Hauk Walsh) Agenda for a City, 1970, Financing Transit, 1980, The Rocky Road to Privatization, 1987, Making Democracy Work, 1991, Luther Gulick: Life and Letters, 1996. Mem. Am. Econs. Assn., Nat. Tax Assn., Am. Soc. Pub. Adminstrn., Am. Polit. Sci. Assn., Internat. Pub. Fin. Assn., Nat. Acad. Pub. Adminstrn. Clubs: Century, Cosmos. Home: 41 Meadow Lks Hightstown NJ 08520-3384

FITCH, MARY JANE EARLY, lawyer, computer consultant, writer; b. Phila., Sept. 30, 1955; d. Harold Nathan and Patricia Overton (Owens) F.; m. Franklin Bershir Zimmerman, July 25, 1976; children: Amy Wellington Fitch Zimmerman, Emily Berçir Fitch Zimmerman. Student, Oxford U., Eng., 1968; BA, Temple U., 1969; postgrad. Elec. Engring. studies, U. Pa., 1969-71; JD, Widener U., 1996. Bar: Pa. 1996. Dir. computing lang. and area study rev. U. Pa., Phila., 1969-71, cons. computer ctr., 1971-72, mgr. office of computing activities, 1972-75, asst. dir. ctr. for Phila. studies, 1975-78; sr. assoc., mgr. Ketron Div. Bionetics Corp., Malvern, Pa., 1978-93; CEO Tech. Writers and Translators, Inc., Malvern, 1993-94; database adminstr., tech. cons. The WEFA Group, 1994-97; atty. Fitch & Assocs., Malvern, Pa., 1996—; pvt. practice; cons. intellectual property, Japanese-Am. litigation and record processing, Malvern, 1986—; cons. GMAC Comml. Mortgage. Inventor: AIMILY software sys. for converting mass volumes of Japanese to Eng. litigation database, 1993; contbr. articles to profl. jours.; presenter at numerous confs. in computer sci. and intellectual property. Vol. fundraiser Greenpeace, Phila., 1988—, Save the Ballet, Phila., 1992—. Recipient Acad. scholarship Temple U., Phila., 1966-69, Inst. Internat. Edn. (Oxford), 1968. Mem. ABA (patent, trademark com.), Internat. Machine Translation Assn., Soc. for Tech. Comm. Episcopalian. Avocations: violin, reading, oil painting, gardening. Office: 85 Conestoga Rd Malvern PA 19355-1706

FITCH, MARY KILLEEN, salary design and human resources specialist; b. Carroll, Iowa, July 15, 1949; d. Michael Francis and Mildred (Pauley) Killeen; m. David Paul Fitch, July 3, 1971; 1 child, Emily Grace. BS, Iowa State U., 1971, MS, 1975; postgrad., U. Minn., 1982—. Pers. adminstr. Control Data Corp., Roseville, Minn., 1976-77; sr. compensation analyst/employee rels rep. Honeywell, Inc., Mpls., 1977-80; human resource mgr./compensation and benefits mgr. No. Telecom, Inc., Minnetonka, Minn., 1980-82; compensation cons. Gen. Mills, Wayzata, Minn., 1984-85; mgr. compensation Northwestern Nat. Life Ins., Mpls., 1985-87; prin. compensation specialist Comml. Bldgs. Group, Honeywell, Inc., Mpls., 1987-89; dir. compensation, HRIS, benefits, incentive design Nat. Car Rental System, Inc., Mpls., 1989-99; dir. compensation, HRIS, benefits, and pay system N.Am. Rental Group (combined Alamo and Nat. Car), 1999—; cons. human resources Les Kraus & Assocs., Edina, Minn., 1984; pres. Personnel Mgmt. Services of Twin Cities, St. Paul, 1983—; adj. instr., tchg. asst. Lakewood Cmty. Coll./U. Minn., Mpls., 1982-84. Author: (with Paul) Muchinsky) Organization Behavior and Human Performance, 1975; (with John Fossum) Personnel Psychology, 1985. Former chmn., bd. dirs. Kathadin, United Way Agy., Mpls., 1985—; curriculum com. U. Minn., 1983-84. George Catt Iowa State U. scholar, 1970. Mem. AAUW, Assn. Human Resources Systems Profls., Am. Compensation Assn., Psi Chi, Phi Kappa Pi. Avocations: dressage, karate. Home: 1188 90th St E Inver Grove MN 55077-4206 Office: HR Nat Car Rental Systems Inc 7700 France Ave S Minneapolis MN 55435-5228

FITCH, MORGAN LEWIS, JR., intellectual property lawyer; b. Chgo., Nov. 21, 1922; s. Morgan Lewis and Marian (Ringer) F.; m. Helen Shearer, June 9, 1945; children: Ruth F. White, Mary F. White, Morgan Lewis, Frederick Shearer. B.S. in Chem. Engring., Ill. Inst. Tech., 1943; student, Princeton U., 1943, MIT, 1943-44; J.D., U. Mich., 1948. Bar: Ill. 1948. Since practiced in Chgo.; partner Fitch, Even, Tabin, & Flannery, 1953—; bd. dirs. South Chgo. Bank, Advance Bank; chmn. bd. Advance Bancorp. Pres. Robert Crown Navy Meml. Found., John Crerar Libr. Assocs.; trustee emeritus Tri-State Coll., Angola, Ind.; trustee YMCA, Chgo.; bd. dirs. YMCA Found. Lt. USNR, 1943-46. Recipient Disting. Pub. Service award Sec. Navy, 1960, 65. Mem. ABA, Ill. Bar Assn., Chgo. Bar Assn., Intellectual Property Law Assn. of Chgo., Navy League U.S. (pres. 1965-67), U.S. Naval Sea Cadet Corps (pres. 1963-65), Naval Commandery, Naval Res. Assn., Soc. Mayflower Descs., Union League, Legal Club, Execs. Club. Home: 4640 Clausen Ave Western Springs IL 60558-1640 Office: 135 S La Salle St Chicago IL 60603-4105*

FITCH, NANCY ELIZABETH, historian; b. White Plains, N.Y., June 17, 1947; d. Robert Franklin and Nancy Elizabeth (Harvey) F. BA in Polit. Sci./English Lit., Oakland U., Rochester, Mich., 1969; MA in History, U. Mich., 1971, PhD in History, 1981. Danforth tchg. intern dept. history U. Mich., Ann Arbor, 1970; asst. prof. history and lit. Sangamon State U., Springfield, Ill., 1972-74; sr. social sci. rsch. analyst The Congl. Rsch. Svc. of Libr. of Congress, Washington, 1975-78; asst. to the chmn./historian U.S. EEO Commn., Washington, 1982-89; asst. prof. history Lynchburg Coll. of Va., 1989-91; asst. prof. African Am. studies Temple U., Phila., 1991-92; Jesse Ball Dupont vis. scholar Randolph-Macon Woman's Coll., Lynchburg, Va., 1992-93; assoc. prof. history U. N.C. at Asheville, 1993-95; hist. and assoc. prof. English Coll. New Rochelle, N.Y., 1995—; chmn.'s rep. White House Inst. on Hist. Black Colls. and Univs., U.S. Dept. Edn., 1985-89, EEO com.; pub. rels. vol. S. Africa Exhibit Project, Washington, 1986-88; mem. adv. com. DuPont Vis. Scholars Project, Va. Found. Ind. Colls., 1990-91; adj. prof. in history Shaw U., Asheville, 1994; lectr. Jesse Ball DuPont Found. Coll. Confs. on Diversity, The Aspen Inst., Queenstown, Md., 1995, 96; participating historian, spkr. Schomburg Ctr. for Rsch. in Black Culture, N.Y.C., 1994, Booker T. Washington Jr. Anniversary Commemoration. Anthology Editor: How Sweet the Sound: The Spirit of African American History, 1999; Editl. assoc.: Jour. S. Asian Lit., 1969-79; co-editor: Diversity: A Jour. of Multicultural Issues, 1995-98; mem. editl. adv. bd. Kente Cloth: African Am. Voices in Tex.; book reviewer Jour. S. Asian Lit., Lit. East and West, The Historian, Jour. Asian Studies; author: (series) Essays on Liberty, 1988; contbr. articles to profl. jours. Organizer, producer Ann. Dr. Martin Luther King Jr. Celebration prog., Washington, 1986-88; guest lectr. on history of Am. music Blue Ridge Music Festival, Lynchburg, 1991; participant Radio America African-Am. contbrs. to art and lit., 1990; vol./cons. The Holiday Project, Washington, 1986-88; mem. Widening Horizons Prog. of D.C. Pub. Schs., 1986-88. Recipient Achievement award Mt. Vernon Day Care Ctr., 1983, Spl. Commendation, U.S. EEO Commn., 1985-89, Ft. Drum Sgt. Maj.'s medal for svc. 10th Mountain div. Light Inf., Ft. Drum, N.Y., 1992; fellow Ford Found., 1971-72, Nat. Def. Fgn. Lang., 1970, U. Mich., 1970-71, 78-79, John Hay Whitney Found., 1969-70; Faculty summer seminar fellowship Nat. Endowment for the Humanities, U. Kans., Lawrence, 1996; Alden B. Dow creativity fellow Northwood U., 1998. Mem. Assn. for Study African Am. Life and History, Orgn. Am. Hists., Phi Alpha Theta (faculty advisor 1990-91). Republican. Episcopalian/Buddhist. Avocation: photography. Home: 267 Bedford Ave Mount Vernon NY 10553-1517 Office: Coll New Rochelle 29 Castle Pl New Rochelle NY 10805

FITCH, RACHEL FARR, health policy analyst; b. Deering, Mo.; d. Allen Edward and Rosie Leola (Jones) Farr; R.N., St. Vincent Hosp., 1954; student Little Rock U., 1965-67; B.S., St. Louis U., 1974, M.S., 1976, Ph.D., 1983; m. Coy Dean Fitch, Mar. 31, 1956; children: Julia Anne, Jaquelyn Kay. Psychiat. staff nurse VA Ft. Root Hosp., North Little Rock, Ark., 1954-57; surg.-med. staff nurse St. Vincent Infirmary, Little Rock, 1957-65; acute care nurse Georgetown U. Hosp., Washington, 1968-69; public health nurse to adminstr. South office Vis. Nurse Assn. Greater St. Louis, 1970-73; cons. in edn. St. Louis City Health Dept., 1977-80; rsch. specialist Sen. John C. Danforth, St. Louis, 1980; owner RFF Assocs., 1983-86; project dir. study of infant mortality in city of St. Louis, 1978. Mem. community health edn. com. Am. Heart Assn., 1977-87; bd. dirs. LWV of Mo., 1984—, editor newspaper, 1984-87, dir. health issues, 1987—; chmn. Mo. Consumers Health Care WATCH, 1996—; mem. adv. com. Mo. Medicaid Consumer, 1996-97; mem. Mo. Welfare Coord. Com., 1997—. Mem. Am. Public Health Assn., Acad. Polit. Sci., Grand Jury Assn. St. Louis (bd. dirs.), Woman's Club (St. Louis U. Sch. Medicine, past pres.), Sigma Theta Tau. Address: 23 Lenox Pl Saint Louis MO 63108-1901

FITCH, ROBERT MCLELLAN, business and technology consultant; b. Shanghai, China, Apr. 30, 1928; came to U.S., 1937; s. George A. and Geraldine (Townsend) F.; m. Reta Peck, Aug. 21, 1955; children: David H.A., Douglas G., Christopher M. AB, Dartmouth Coll., 1949; PhD, U. Mich., 1954. Prof. U. Conn., Storrs, 1962-83; v.p. corp. rsch. SC Johnson Wax, Racine, Wis., 1983-85; sr. v.p. R & D SC Johnson Wax, Racine, 1985-89; pvt. practice cons., 1990—. Author: Polymer Colloids, A Comprehensive Introduction, 1997; editor: Polymer Colloids, 1971, Polymer Colloids II, 1980; contbr. numerous articles to profl. jours.; patentee in field. Adv. bd. Nat. Sci. Resources Ctr.; mem. adv. team Nat. Inst. for Sci. Edn.; bd. dirs. Taos Inst. Arts, Taos Talking Pictures, chmn., 1998—. Recipient Disting. Svc. award Am. Chem. Soc., 1987; named to S.E. Wis. Educator's Hall of Fame, 1992. Fellow AAAS. Avocations: bonsai culture, skiing, scuba diving.

FITCH, VAL LOGSDON, physics educator; b. Merriman, Nebr., Mar. 10, 1923; s. Fred B. and Frances Marion (Logsdon) F.; m. Elise Cunningham, June 11, 1949 (dec. 1972); children: John Craig (dec. 1987), Alan Peter; m. Daisy Harper Sharp, Aug. 14, 1976. B. of Engring., McGill U., 1948; Ph.D., Columbia U., 1954. Instr. Columbia, 1953; instr. physics Princeton, 1954-56, asst. prof., 1956-59, assoc. prof., 1959-60, prof., 1960—, Class 1909 prof. physics, 1968-76, Cyrus Fogg Bracket prof. physics, 1976-84, James S. McDonnell Distinguished Univ. prof. physics, 1984—; Mem. Pres.'s Sci. Adv. Com., 1970-73. Trustee Asso. Univ., Inc., 1961-67. Served with AUS, 1943-46. Recipient Research Corp. award, 1967; E.O. Lawrence award, 1968; Wetherill medal Franklin Inst., 1976; Nobel prize in physics, 1980; Grad. Alumnus award Am. Assn. State Colls. and Univs., 1984; Nat. Medal of Sci., 1993; Sloan fellow, 1960. Fellow Am. Phys. Soc. (pres. 1987-88); mem. Am. Acad. Arts and Scis., Nat. Acad. Sci., Am. Philos. Soc. Office: Princeton U Dept Physics PO Box 708 Princeton NJ 08544-0708

FITCH, WALTER M(ONROE), molecular biologist, educator, evolutionist; b. San Diego, May 21, 1929; s. Chloral Harrison Monroe and Evelyn Charlotte (Halliday) F.; m. Eleanor E. McLean, Sept. 1, 1952 (div. Mar. 28, 1988); children: Karen Allyn, Kathleen Leslie, Kenton Monroe; m. Chung-Cha Ziesel, Sept. 9, 1989. AB, U. Calif., Berkeley, 1953, PhD, 1958. USPHS postdoctoral fellow U. Calif. Berkeley, 1958-59, Stanford U., Palo Alto, Calif, 1959-61; lectr. Univ. Coll., London, 1961-62; asst. prof. U. Wis.-Madison, 1962-67, assoc. prof., 1967-72, prof., 1972-86; prof. U. So. Calif., L.A., 1986-89; prof. U. Calif.-Irvine, 1989—, prof., chmn. dept. ecology and evolutionary biology, 1990-95; prof., 1995—; vis. Fulbright lectr. London, 1961-62; NIH vis. prof. Hawaii, 1973-74; Macy Found. vis. prof. U. Calif., L.A., 1981-82; vis. prof. U. So. Calif., L.A., 1985, U. Cambridge, England., 1998-99, Isaac Newton Inst. Math., England, 1998-99. Editor-in-chief Molecular Biology and Evolution, 1983-93; editor Classification Literature, 1975-80; assoc. editor Jour. Molecular Evolution, 1976-80; contbr. articles to profl. jours. Mem. Cupertino Planning Commn., Calif., 1960-61, Madison Planning Commn., 1965-68; mem. Dane County Regional Planning Commn., 1968-73; chmn. Madison Reapportionment, 1979-81. Grantee NIH and NSF, 1962—. Fellow AAAS; mem. NAS, Am. Acad. Arts and Scis., Am. Soc. for Biochemistry and Molecular Biology, Am. Chem. Soc., Am. Soc. Naturalists, Biochem. Soc. (Eng.), Genetics Soc. Am., Soc. Study Evolution, Soc. Systematic Biology, Soc. for Molecular Biology and Evolution (pres. 1992-93), Linnean Soc. (London). Office: U Calif Dept Ecol & Evol Biology Irvine CA 92697-2525

FITCHEN, ALLEN NELSON, publisher; b. Syracuse, Aug. 8, 1936; s. John Frederick and Mary (Nelson) F. III; m. Jane Cady, June 13, 1959 (div. Feb. 1986); children—Anne Wheeler, Christopher Hardy, William Mills; m. Shirley Bergen, May 23, 1991. B.A. in English cum laude, Amherst Coll., 1958; M.A. in English, Cornell, 1960. Coll. traveler Macmillan Co., N.Y.C., 1960-62; editor Macmillan Co., 1962-67; humanities editor U. Chgo. Press, 1968-82, sr. editor, 1971-82; dir. U. Wis. Press, 1982-98, ret., 1998. Mem. Psi Upsilon. Club: University (Madison). Home: 603 Eugenia Ave Madison WI 53705-3404

FITCHEN, DOUGLAS BEACH, physicist, educator; b. N.Y.C., June 8, 1936; s. Paul R. and Eleanor B. Fitchen; m. Janet Mathews (dec. 1995); children: John, Katherine, Sylvia; m. Nancy Mathews, 1996. A.B., Harvard U., 1957; Ph.D., U. Ill., 1962. Asst. prof. physics Cornell U., Ithaca, N.Y., 1962-65; assoc. prof. Cornell U., 1965-71, prof., 1971—, chmn. dept. physics, 1977-82, 86-91, 94-99; vis. prof. Oxford U., 1968, U. Paris, Orsay, 1975. Alfred P. Sloan fellow, 1964-68. Research in optical studies of solids, Raman spectroscopy. Office: Cornell U Clark Hall Ithaca NY 14853*

FITE, GILBERT COURTLAND, historian, educator, retired; b. Santa Fe, Ohio, May 14, 1918; s. Clyde Fite and Mary Jane McCardle; m. Alberta June Goodwin, July 24, 1941; children: James Franklin, Jack Preston. BA, U. S.D., 1941, MA in History, 1941, LittD (hon.), 1975; PhD, U. Mo., 1945, HHD (hon.), 1983; LittD (hon.), Seattle Pacific U., 1962. From asst. prof. to profl. U. Okla., Norman, 1945-68, George Lynn Cross prof. history, 1968-71; pres. Ea. Ill. U., Charleston, 1971-76; Richard B. Russell prof. history U. Ga., Athens, 1976-86, prof. emeritus, 1986—. Author: Peter Norbeck: Prairie Statesman, 1948, Mount Rushmore, 1952, George Peek & The Fight for Farm Parity, 1954, The Farmer's Frontier, 1865-1900, 1966, American Farmers: The New Minority, 1981, Cotton Fields No More, Southern Agriculture, 1865-1980, 1984, Richard B. Russell, Senator from Georgia, 1993, others; contbr. over 50 articles to profl. jours. Trustee Phillips U., Enid, Okla., 1969-76, Lexington (Ky.) Theol. Sem., 1972-76. Fulbright scholar, 1962-63, 69-70; Guggenheim Found. fellow, 1964, Ford Fellow, 1954-55; named to S.D. Hall of Fame, 1990. Mem. Agrl. History Soc. (pres. 1960-61), So. Hist. Assn. (pres. 1974), Western History Assn. (pres. 1985-86), Phi Alpha Theta (pres. 1981-83). Methodist. Avocations: photography, golfing, traveling. Home: 4 Fite Cir Bella Vista AR 72714-5528

FITE, KATHLEEN ELIZABETH, education educator; b. Houston, June 26, 1948; d. Daniel Patrick and Edith Elizabeth (Burnett) F. BS in Edn., S.W. Tex. State U., 1969, MEd, 1970; EdD, N. Tex. State U., 1972. Cert. tchr., Tex. Prof. S.W. Tex. State U., San Marcos, 1973—, dir. Ctr. for Study of Basic Skills, 1980, dir. Race Integration Tng. Inst., 1982-83, dir. elem. edn. dept., 1983-84, assoc. dir. sponsored projects, 1984-86, dir. sponsored projects, 1986-87; cons. U.S. Dept. Edn., numerous pub. cos.; mem. adv. bd. Dushing Pub. Group, Inc. Co-author: A few Favorites of the Total Teacher, The Super Ideas Book, Creative Art Ideas; asst editor SW Tex. U. Faculty Bull., 1977-78, editor, 1978-81; contbr. articles to profl. jours. Mem. sr. citizens adv. com. San Marcos City Coun., Commn. for Women; facilitator, dir. cmty. workshops; pres. Jr. Svc. League; activity chmn. Tex. Spl. Olympics. Named Ky. Col., 1975, named to Hall of Fame, San Marcos Commn. for Women, 1991; grantee U.S. Dept. Edn., L.B. Johnson Inst., 1988-89. Mem. ASCD, Nat. Assn. Edn. Young Children, Tex. Assn. Tchr. Educators, Kindergarten Tchrs. Tex., Tex. Computer Edn. Assn. (bd. dirs. 1984-87, publs. editor, state conf. asst. 1984-88), San Marcos Assn. for Edn. Young Children (treas.), S.W. Tex. State U. Alumni Assn. (Tchg. award of honor, Key of Excellence award, Strutter Hall of Fame), Golden Key, Phi Delta Kappa (pres. 1981, v.p., faculty advisor, ritual team 1986-89), Kappa Delta Pi (hon.). Methodist. Avocations: sewing, needle crafts, painting. Home: 602 Larue Dr San Marcos TX 78666-2410 Office: SW Tex State U Dept Curriculum & Instrn San Marcos TX 78666

FITE, MYRA J. CROPPER, critical care nurse; b. Maysville, Ky., Nov. 29, 1948; d. Wilmar L. and Georgia (Fultz) Cropper; m. Ronald B. Fite, Apr. 20, 1968; children: Jarrett C.,Hayley C., Jeanean C. AAS in Nursing, U. Cin., 1984, BA in Sociology, 1989. RN, Ohio; cert. ACLS, critical care preceptor. Staff-charge nurse cardiac step down unit Christ Hosp., Cin.; clin. nurse mgr. Madeira Health Care Ctr., Cin., 1999—. Home: 1264 Eagle Ridge Dr Milford OH 45150-9613

FITE, PATRICIA PAULETTE, English educator; b. Greensburg, Pa., Oct. 13, 1944; d. George Michael and Anne Lee (Shirley) Lonchar; m. Michael Wayne Fite, June 21, 1969. BA, U. St. Thomas, 1967; MEd, U. Houston, 1972; PhD, Tex. A&M U., 1995. Cert. tchr., Tex. English, history tchr. Marian H.S., Bellaire, Tex., 1967-68; English tchr. M.B. Smiley H.S., Houston, 1968-72, Marian H.S., 1972-75; English, social studies tchr. Gilmary Sch. Girls, Coraoplis, Pa., 1975-76; asst. prin. Marian H.S., 1976-78; adminstrv. asst. Tex. Paralyzed Veterans, Houston, 1978; dir. religious edn. St. Elizabeth Ann Seton Ch., Houston, 1979-80; English tchr., counselor Incarnate Word Acad., Houston, 1980-83; assoc. prof. English U. Incarnate Word, San Antonio, 1983-99, Moody prof. English, 1999—; evaluator Nat. Exam. Svc., Austin, 1997—. Co-author: Union in Christ, 1974. Oversight rev. com. United Way San Antonio, 1996—. Mem. Nat. Coun. Tchrs. English, Internat. Reading Assn., Coll. Coun. Tchrs. English, San Antonio Area Coun. Tchrs. English, Phi Kappa Phi. Roman Catholic. Avocations: gardening, sewing, photography. Office: U Incarnate Word 4301 Broadway St San Antonio TX 78209-6318

FITE, ROBERT CARROLL, retired cosmetics industry executive; b. Atoka, Tenn., May 14, 1934; s. Russel Neal and Mabel H. (Smith) F.; m. Shirley N. Norwood, Nov. 12, 1973; children: Jeff, Camilla. BS, Memphis State U., 1956. Cert. secondary tchr., Tenn. With Coty Cosmetics, 1959-60, Revlon Cosmetics, 1960-72, Gerlain Cosmetics, 1972-89; ret., 1989. With U.S. Army, 1956-58. Republican. Presbyterian.

FITES, DONALD VESTER, tractor company executive; b. Tippecanoe, Ind., Jan. 20, 1934; s. Rex E. and Mary Irene (Sackville) F.; m. Sylvia Dempsey, June 25, 1960; children: Linda Marie. BS in Civil Engring., Valparaiso U., 1956; MS, MIT, 1971. With Caterpillar Overseas S.A., Peoria, Ill., 1956-66; dir. internat. customer div. Caterpillar Overseas S.A., Geneva, 1966-67; asst. mgr. market devel. Caterpillar Tractor Co., Peoria, 1967-70; dir. Caterpillar Mitsubishi Ltd., Tokyo, 1971-75; dir. engine capacity expansion program Caterpillar Tractor Co., Peoria, 1975-76, mgr. products control dept., 1976-79; pres. Caterpillar Brasil S.A., 1979-81; v.p. products Caterpillar Tractor Co., Peoria, 1981-85, exec. v.p., 1985-89; pres., chief opd. officer Caterpillar Inc., Peoria, 1989-90, pres., COO, 1989-90, chmn., CEO, 1990-99, also bd. dirs.; bd. dirs. Caterpillar Inc., Wolverine Worldwide, Mobil Corp., AT&T, Ga.-Pacific Corp.; past chmn. Equip. Mfg. Inst. Trustee Farm Found., 1985—, Meth. Med. Ctr., 1985—, Knox Coll., 1986—; chmn., nat. adv. bd. Salvation Army, 1985—, adminstrv. bd. 1st United Meth. Ch., 1986—; bd. dirs. Valparaiso U., Keep Am. Beautiful; past chmn. U.S.-Japan Bus. Coun. Mem. Agrl. Roundtable (chmn. 1985-87), SAE, ACTPN, Bus. Coun., Bus. Roundtable (past chmn.)., Nat. Assn. Mfrs. and Bus. Coun., Nat. Fgn. Trade Coun., Mt. Hawley Country Club, Creve Coeur Club, Country Club of Peoria. Republican. Office: Caterpillar Inc 100 NE Adams St Peoria IL 61629-0002*

FITILIS, THEODORE NICHOLAS, portfolio manager; b. N.Y.C., July 6, 1937; s. Theris and Katherine (Barbara) F.; children from previous marriage: Jennifer, Hillary. BA in Econs., NYU, 1959, MBA, 1965. Cert. fin. analyst, 1969. Fin. analyst Moody's Investment Service, N.Y.C., 1960-70; fin. analyst Alliance Capital Mgmt., L.P., N.Y.C., 1970-93, sr. v.p., 1986-93; pres., investment portfolio mgr. Fitilis Capital Mgmt. Co., N.Y.C., 1993—; v.p. Printing and Pub. Analyst Group, N.Y.C., 1973-74. Served with U.S. Army, 1960-61. Mem. N.Y. Soc. Security Analysts, Media and Entertainment Analysts Assn. N.Y. Greek Orthodox. Avocations: tennis, travel. Office: Fitilis Capital Mgmt Co 2600 S Ocean Blvd Apt 102N Palm Beach FL 33480-5418

FITTERER, RICHARD CLARENCE, judge; b. Ellensburg, Wash., Jan. 22, 1946; s. L. George and Margeret H. (Lewis) F.; m. Janice M. Ivey, Feb. 14, 1968 (dec.); children: Christian C. (dec.), Zane I., Aaron G. BCS, Seattle U., 1968; JD, U. Puget Sound, 1975. Bar: Wash. 1976, U.S. Dist. Ct. (we. dist.) Wash. 1976, U.S. Dist. Ct. (ea. dist.) Wash. 1977. Assoc. Patrick R. Acres, Moses Lake, Wash., 1977; sole practice Moses Lake, 1977-79, 83-95; ptnr. Milne, Lemargie & Fitterer, Ephrata, Wash., 1979-1983; judge Grant County Dist. Ct., 1995—; instr. Wash. State Jud. Coll. Bd. dirs. Columbia Basin Rodeo Assn. Moses Lake Roundup, 1984-91, United Way, Moses Lake, 1978-81, Moses Lake C. of C., 1979-83, 87-88. Mem. ATLA, ABA, Am. Judges Assn., Wash. State Dist. Judges Assn. (chair rules com.), Grant County Bar Assn. (pres. 1993), Wash. State Trial Lawyers Assn., Moses Lake Golf and Country Club (bd. dirs. 1989-92, pres. 1991-92), Elks (bd. dirs. 1984). Roman Catholic. Avocations: skiing, boating, golfing, photography. Home: 322 N Crestview Dr Moses Lake WA 98837-1412 Office: PO Box 37 Ephrata WA 98823-0037

FITTERON, JOHN JOSEPH, real estate/petroleum products company executive; b. Norwalk, Conn., Sept. 25, 1941; m. Leola Kellogg, Sept. 9, 1967; children: Derek, Deanne. B.S., U. Conn., 1967. C.P.A., Conn. Mgr. Arthur Andersen & Co., N.Y.C. and Stamford, Conn., 1967-75; controller Beker Industries Corp., Greenwich, Conn., 1975-76; v.p., controller Beker Industries Corp., 1976-78, sr. v.p. fin., treas., 1979-86, dir., 1984-86; sr. v.p., treas., CFO Getty Realty Corp. (formerly Getty Petroleum Corp.), Jericho, N.Y., 1986—. Served with USAF, 1959-63. Mem. Am. Inst. C.P.A.s, Conn. Soc. C.P.A.s (Scholastic award 1967), Fin. Execs. Inst. Office: Getty Realty Corp 125 Jericho Tpke Ste 400 Jericho NY 11753-1034

FITTON, HARVEY NELSON, JR., former government official, publishing consultant; b. Washington; s. Harvey Nelson and Ada Hortense (Marshall) F.; m. Bernice Jeanette Sutton, Jan. 8, 1946 (dec. Sept. 1998). Student, Nat. Acad. Theater, 1940; degree in Am. Studies, George Washington U., 1949, MA in Am. Lit. and Cultural History, 1956; postgrad., Am. U., 1963. Editor, rsch. asst. Nat. Acad. Scis., Nat. Rsch. Coun., Washington, 1949-56; med. writer and editor NIH, Bethesda, Md., 1956-58; info. specialist farmer cooperative svc. USDA, Washington, 1958-61, publs. editor office of info., 1961-63, chief editorial br. office of info., 1963-66, head pub. div. office govtl. and pub. affairs, 1966-84, dep. dir. of info., office govt. and pub. affairs, 1984; cons. in writing, editing, publishing and continuing edn. Washington, 1985—; instr. USDA Grad. Sch., Washington, 1962-92, chmn. editl. adv. com., 1976-85, mem. comm. skills adv. com., 1986-97. Editor, rsch. asst. Atlas of Tumor Pathology, 1949-56; editor NIH Record, 1956-58; contbr. articles to profl. jours. Pres. Clermont Woods Community Assn., Fairfax County, Va., 1968, No. Va. Family Svc., Falls Church, 1972-73; elder local Presbyn. Ch. With USN, 1942-45. Recipient Horace Hart award Edn. Coun. of Graphic Arts Industry, 1980; inductee Internat. Poetry Hall of Fame, 1996. Fellow Soc. for Tech. Comm. (pres. Washington chpt. 1972-73, asst. to pres. for recognition programs 1976-77); mem. Acad. Am. Poets, Internat. Soc. Poets, Haiku Soc. Am., Agrl. Communicators in Edn. (pres. Washington chpt. 1968, Spl. Achievement award 1986), Am. Assn. Engring. Schs. (pubs. com.), Nat. Assn. Govt. Communicators (pres. Washington chpt. 1979, nat. pres. 1980, mem. editl. bd. Govt. Comm., 1994—, Communicator of Yr. 1984), St. Andrews Soc., Nat. Assn. Scholars, Assn. Lit. Scholars and Critics, Toastmasters (pres. Alexandria chpt. 1959-60), SAR. Avocations: gardening, tap dancing and singing, book collecting, writing poetry. Home and Office: 5624 Glenwood Dr Alexandria VA 22310-1323

FITTS, C. AUSTIN, investment adviser; b. Phila., Dec. 24, 1950; d. William Thomas Jr. and Barbara Kinsey (Willits) F. AA, Bennett Coll., 1970; student, Chinese U., Hong Kong, 1971; BA, U. Pa., 1974, MBA, 1978; postgrad., MIT. With Dillon, Read & Co., Inc., N.Y.C., 1978-89, sr. v.p., 1984-86, mng. dir., bd. dirs., 1986-89; asst. sec. for housing, urban devel. and fed. housing commr. HUD, Washington, 1989-90; pres., chmn. The Hamilton Securities Group, Inc., Washington, 1990-97; chmn., CEO Solari, Inc., Washington, 1997—; bd. dirs. Student Loan Mktg. Assn. Sallie Mae, 1991-94; adv. bd. Fedn. Nat. Mortgage Assn. Fannie Mae, 1992-93; mem. emerging mkts. adv. com. SEC, 1990-93. Mem. grad. adv. bd. Wharton Sch., U. Pa., Phila., 986-95; mem. adv. bd. Arlington Inst., Hyper Car Inc.; mem. Gertrude Stein Repertory Theatre. Mem. Coun. for Excellence in Govt. (prin. 1991—), Econ. Club N.Y. Office: Solari Inc PO Box 57326 Washington DC 20037

FITTS, DONALD DENNIS, chemist, educator; b. Concord, N.H., Sept. 3, 1932; s. Russell P. and Elisabeth (Reille) F.; m. Beverly Hoffman, July 11, 1964; children: Robert K., William R. A.B., Harvard U., 1954; Ph.D., Yale U., 1957. NSF postdoctoral fellow U. Amsterdam, Netherlands, 1957-58; research fellow Yale U., 1958-59; mem. faculty U. Pa., 1959—, assoc. prof. chemistry, 1964-69, prof. chemistry, 1969—, asst. chmn. dept., 1965-72, assoc. dean grad. studies faculty arts and scis., 1978-82, 83-94, acting dean arts and scis., 1982-83; cons. Am. Cyanamid Co., 1959-63. Author: Nonequilibrium Thermodynamics, 1962, Vector Analysis in Chemistry, 1974, Principles of Quantum Mechanics, 1999; also articles. Mem. Am. Phys. Soc. Achievements include research on theory of optical activity, statis.-mech. theory of transport processes, nonequilibrium thermodynamics, molecular quantum mechanics, theory of liquids, intermolecular forces, surface phenomena. E-mail: dfitts@sas.upenn.edu. Home: 634 Revere Rd Merion Station PA 19066-1008 Office: Dept Chemistry U Pa Philadelphia PA 19104-6323

FITTS, MICHAEL ANDREW, law educator; b. Phila., Mar. 1, 1953; s. William Thomas Jr. and Barbara Kinsey (Willits) F.; m. Renee Judith Sobel, Jan. 2, 1982; children: Alexis, Whitney. AB, Harvard Coll., 1975; JD, Yale U., 1979; MA (hon.), U. Pa., 1991. Law clk. Hon. A. Leon Higginbotham, Jr., U.S. Ct. Appeals (3d cir.), Phila., 1979-81; atty. office legal counsel Dept. of Justice, Washington, 1981-85; asst. prof. law U. Pa., Phila., 1985-90, assoc. prof., 1990-92, prof., 1992—, assoc. dean acad. affairs, 1996-98, Robert G. Fuller Jr. prof. law, 1996—; vis. prof. dept. polit. sci. Swathmore Coll., 1999. Editor Yale Law Jour., 1978-79; contbr. articles to profl. jours. and chpts. to books. Harvard U. scholar, 1971. Mem. Am. Polit. Sci. Assn. (law and polit. process working group), Pa. Bar Assn., Phi Beta Kappa. Mem. Soc. of Friends. Office: U Pa Law Sch 3400 Chestnut St Philadelphia PA 19104-6204

FITZ, BROTHER RAYMOND L., university president; b. Akron, Ohio, Aug. 12, 1941; s. Raymond L. and Mary Lou (Smith) F. B.S. in Elec. Engring., U. Dayton, Ohio, 1964; M.S., Poly. Inst. Bklyn., 1967, Ph.D., 1969. Joined Soc. of Mary, Roman Catholic Ch., 1960; mem. faculty U. Dayton, 1968—, prof. elec. engring. and engring. mgmt., 1975—, exec. dir. Center Christian Renewal, 1974-79, univ. pres., 1979—. Author numerous papers, reports in field. Bd. dirs. various civic organs. Recipient Disting. Alumnus award Poly. Inst. Bklyn., 1980. Office: U Dayton 300 College Park Ave Rm 207 Dayton OH 45469-0001*

FITZALAN-HOWARD, BENNETT-THOMAS HENRY ROBERT, consultant, public administration and policy analyst, political theorist; b. Geneva, Oct. 10, 1955; came to U.S., 1959; s. S. and A. (Argyle-Campbel) FitzA.-H. AA, Jr. Coll. Albany, N.Y., 1973; BA, Union Coll., 1973; MS, Rutgers U., 1980; MA, Russell Sage Coll., 1987; postgrad., NYU, 1989, Yale U., 1989. Cert. fin. analyst, broker; cert. min. Bride in the Light New Testament Ministry. Adminstrv. analyst Todd Logistics, Inc., N.J. and Saudi Arabia, 1980; owner, cons. Fitz Co., Internat., Albany, 1981—; mem. N.Y. Merc. Exch.; insr. Gaton Sch., Yale U., 1987-89, NYU, 1987-89. Author: Expropriation Predictability and Politics, 1979, The Politics of the U.S. Budget, 1987, The Courts in a Democratic System, 1987, White House-Wall Street: The October 87 Crash and the Post Regan Persidency, 1987, The Politics of Deficits, 1988, Enemyless: Can We Survive?, 1989, Responsibility and Accountability: The Forgotten Cornerstones of Democracy, 1990, The Eagle and the UN: Is the US Mature Enough to be the Sole Super-Power?, 1998; contbg. author: Toward a Global Government, 1972, Conservetism: New World Order?, 1990, Tory vs. Labour: Tory: The New English Order, 1992, Hyperinflation, 1992, Eschatology Now, 1992, Eschatology and Current Events, 1992, Bride in the Light: New Testament Church, The Seven Seals of Revelation. Active local ARC, RP Found. Served with U.S. Army, 1973-77, Fed. Republic Germany. Mem. AAAS, ALGA, Acad. Polit. Sci. (life), Am. Philatelic Soc. (life, gideons), Am. Psychol. Assn., Am. Vietnam Vets. Assn., Audubon Soc., Am. Numismatic Assn. (life), Fin. Analysts Fedn. (at large), Fin. Execs. Inst. (at large), Nat. Assn. Securities Dealers (at large), N.Y. Mercantile Exchange, Am. Enterprise Inst., Brookings Inst., Am. Legion, Mensa, Am. Soc. Internat. Law, Am. Bach Found., Am. Soc. Info. Sci., Blind Vets. Assn. (life), Am. Conservative Union, Nat. Press Club, Equestrian Club, Gideons, Barons of Magna Carta. Avocations: oriental antiques and silver, Brit. stamps and coins, photography, reading, piano and cello. E-mail: Norfolk90@aol.com.

FITZGEORGE, HAROLD JAMES, former oil and gas company executive; b. Trenton, N.J., June 15, 1924; s. George T. and Cecilia M. (Jansen) F.; m. Bette M. Weidel, June 23, 1945 (dec. May 1987); children: Barbara Marsh, Virginia Fisher, Patricia Dunning, Elizabeth Brown. A.B., Princeton U., 1948; M.B.M., MIT, 1964. Geologist Magnolia Petroleum Co., Oklahoma City, 1948; numerous positions with petroleum cos., 1948-60; with Mobil U.S. Exploration, N.Y.C., 1960-63; v.p. Mobil Exploration Can., 1964-66; mgr. Mobil Fgn. Exploration, N.Y.C., 1966-68; pres. Mobil de Venezuela, 1968-73; gen. mgr. Western U.S. Exploration & Prodn., Mobil Oil, Denver, 1973-77; cons. in field, 1977-78; pres. Pennzoil Exploration and Prodn., Houston, 1978-84; adv. dir. Pennzoil Exploration and Prodn., 1984—; now ret. Served with USMC, 1943-46, 50-52. Sloan fellow, 1963-64. Mem. Am. Assn. Petroleum Geologists, Assn. Profl. Engrs. and Geologists of Alta., Am. Petroleum Inst. Republican. Roman Catholic. Clubs: Princeton (N.Y.); Moorings; Hawksnest (Vero Beach, Fla.), Vero Beach Yacht Club.

FITZGERALD, BETTY JO, artist, educator, juror, curator; b. Colusa, Calif., Jan. 10, 1942; d. Richard Corwith and Wanda Eloise (Jones) Summerbell; m. James Edward Fitzgerald, Jan. 15, 1966; children: Molly Fitzgerald Keogh, Brant Edward. BS magna cum laude, U. No. Calif., 1963; MS in Botany, U. Wash., 1966. Tchg. asst. U. Wash., Seattle, 1963-66; instr. botany Seattle U., 1967-70; guest lectr. ecology Evergreen State Coll., Olympia, Wash., 1973, guest lectr. art, 1996, 97; artist Olympia, 1980—; juror, workshop tchr. art regional arts workshops, Puget Sound area, Wash., 1990-97; chmn. S.W. Wash. Exhbn., Wash. State Capital Mus., Olympia, 1986-90. Contbr. articles to profl. publs. Fellow Wash. Native Plant Soc. (hon., life, exec. sec., bd. dirs. 1976-86); mem. Nat. Collage Soc. (signature), N.W. Watercolor Soc. (signature, exhbn. chmn. 1995-97, v.p. 1998-99, pres. 1999—), N.W. Collage Soc. (bd. dirs. 1987-99), Women Painters Wash. (elected mem., pres. 1992-93, treas. 1999—). Republican. Avocations: hiking, biking, flying. Studio: 3327 Windolph Ln NW Olympia WA 98502-3836

FITZGERALD, DANIEL LOUIS, securities dealer; b. Salem, Mass., Sept. 27, 1955; s. Richard Wallace and Lucy Marie (Verza) F. BS, Providence Coll., 1977; M in Internat. Mgmt., Am. Grad. Sch. Internat. Mgmt., 1979; postgrad., U. Oxford, Eng., 1979. Ind. polit. cons., 1982-84; account exec. Salomon Smith Barney & Co., Boston, 1984-87; sr. fin. cons. Smith Barney & Co., Boston, 1987-99, 2nd v.p., 1999—. Mem. Marblehead (Mass.) Rep. Town Com., 1984—, fin. chmn., 1985, 91—; del. Mass. State Rep. Conv., Boston, 1990, 98, Worcester, Mass.; field coord. Reagan-Bush 1984 campaign, Peabody, Mass. Recipient AIMR Continuing Edn. awards, 1990-97. Mem. Peabody Hist. Soc., U.S. Naval Inst. Roman Catholic. Office: Salomon Smith Barney & Co 53 State St Boston MA 02109-2804

FITZGERALD, DOROTHY STICKLE, librarian; b. Feb. 23, 1906. BA, Barnard Coll., 1928; MLS, Columbia U., 1937, MA, 1941. Libr. N.Y. Pub. Libr., N.Y.C., 1937, Glen Ridge (N.J.) Pub. Libr., 1937-43, Bloomfield (N.J.) Bd. Edn., 1943-72, Newtown (Pa.) Bd. Trustees, 1972-99. Home: Apt 216 290 E Winchester Ave Langhorne PA 19047

FITZGERALD, EDMUND BACON, electronics industry executive; b. Milw., Feb. 5, 1926; s. Edmund and Elizabeth (Bacon) F.; m. Elisabeth McKee Christensen, Sept. 6, 1947; children: Karen, Kathleen, Edmund Greer, Rogers Christensen. BSEE, U. Mich., 1946. With Cutler-Hammer, Inc., Milw., 1946-78, v.p. in charge engring., 1959-61, adminstrv. v.p., 1961-63, pres., CEO, 1964-69, chmn., chief exec. officer, 1969-78; vice chmn. Eaton Corp., Cleve., 1978-79; mng. dir. Hampshire Assocs., Milw., 1979-80; pres., dir. No. Telecom, Inc., Nashville, 1980-82; pres. No. Telecom Ltd., 1982-84; chmn. bd. dirs. No. Telecom Ltd., Mississauga, Ont., Can., 1985-90, CEO, 1984-89, also bd. dirs.; mng. dir. Woodmont Assocs., Nashville, 1990—; adj. prof. mgmt. Vanderbilt U., Nashville, 1990—; former chmn., bd. dirs. Milw. Brewers Baseball Club, Inc.; former chmn. Com. for Econ. Devel.; mem. President's Nat. Security Telecom. Adv. Com. Capt. USMCR, 1943-46, 51-52. Named Man of Yr., Milw. Jr. C. of C., 1956. Mem. Nat. Elec. Mfrs. Assn. (pres. 1968). Office: Woodmont Assocs 3434 Woodmont Blvd Nashville TN 37215-1422

FITZGERALD, EDWIN ROGER, physicist, educator; b. Oshkosh, Wis., July 14, 1923; s. James C. and Edwina (Brown) F.; m. Carolyn H. Johnson, Aug. 30, 1946; children: Lucia Edwina, Margaret Mary, William Maurice, Alice Ann, Roger Edwin, Douglas Brendan, Thomas Michael, Jane Carolyn. B.S. in Elec. Engring, U. Wis., 1944, M.S. in Physics, 1950, Ph.D. in Physics, 1951. Registered profl. engr., Md. Physicist Phys. Research Lab., B.F. Goodrich Co., 1944-46; Project asso. chemistry U. Wis., 1951-52; mem. faculty Pa. State U., 1953-61, prof. physics, 1959-61; prof. dept. mechanics Johns Hopkins U., 1961—; vis. prof. chemistry U. Wis.-Madison, 1981. Author: Particle Waves and Deformation in Crystalline Solids, 1966; contbr. numerous tech. articles to profl. jours., sects. in books; patentee in field. Fellow Am. Phys. Soc. (exec. com., chmn. high polymer Physics 1958-59); mem. Acoustical Soc. Am., Materials Research Soc., Phi Beta Kappa, Sigma Xi, Eta Kappa Nu, Tau Beta Pi. Achievements include special research on mechanical and dielectric properties solids including dynamic mechanical properties of violin wood in relation to tone qualities of violins and viscoelastic properties of marine mammal tissues. Home: 2445 Traceys Store Rd Parkton MD 21120-9642

FITZGERALD, ERNEST ABNER, retired bishop; b. Crouse, N.C., July 24, 1925; s. James Boyd and Hattie Pearl (Chaffin) F.; m. Sara Frances Perry; children: James Boyd, Patricia Anne Poole. AB, We. Carolina U., 1947; BD, Duke U., 1951; DD, High Point Coll., 1969, Pfeiffer Coll., 1986, Union Coll., 1994; LLD, Greensboro Coll., 1993; DD, Union Coll., 1994. Ordained to ministry United Meth. Ch. as deacon, 1949, as elder, 1950. Pastor Webster Circuit, N.C., 1944-47, Liberty Circuit, 1947-50, Calvary United Meth. Ch., Asheboro, N.C., 1950-55, Abernathy United Meth. Ch., Asheville, N.C., 1955-59, Purcell United Meth Ch., Charlotte, N.C., 1959-64, Grace United Meth. Ch., Greensboro, N.C., 1964-66, Centenary United Meth. Ch., Winston-Salem, N.C., 1966-82, West Market St. United Meth. Ch., Greensboro, 1982-84; bishop United Meth. Ch., Atlanta Area, 1984-92; mem. United Meth. Devel. Fund, Adminstrv. Coun., Southeastern Jurisdiction, Nat. United Meth. Found. for Christian Higher Edn.; bd. trustees Emory U.; bd. visitors Duke U. Author: A Time to Cross the River, 1977, How to be a Successful Failure, 1978, God Writes Straight with Crooked Lines, Diamonds Everywhere, 1983, Keeping Pace: Inspirations in the Air, 1988, others; contbr. AMTRAK mag. Home: 2536 Huntington Woods Dr Winston Salem NC 27103-6634

FITZGERALD, EUGENE FRANCIS, management consultant; b. Jersey City, Mar. 15, 1925; s. Arthur Gregory and Anna (O'Rourke) F.; m. Ellen M. O'Connor, Sept. 1, 1951; children—Timothy, Mary Ellen, Eugene Francis, Maura, John, Ann, Katherine. B.S. in Bus. Adminstrn, Georgetown U., 1949. Spl. agt. FBI, 1951-52; mgr. Prudential Ins. Co. Am., Newark, 1953-65; agy. v.p. K.C., New Haven, 1965-67; v.p. Minn. Mut. Life Ins. Co., St. Paul, 1967-70; pres., dir. North Star Equities Co., St. Paul, 1969-70; exec. v.p. Southland Life Ins. Co., Dallas, 1970-72; also dir. Southland Life Ins. Co.; exec. v.p. Equitable Life Ins. Co., Washington, 1972-73; also trustee Equitable Life Ins. Co.; v.p. Liberty Life Ins. Co., Greenville, S.C., 1974-81; pres. Mountain View Orchard, Inc., 1981-85; mgmt. cons. Phillips Resource Group, Greenville, S.C., 1986—; dir. Nathan Hale Life Ins. Co.; cons. Phillips Resource Group; bd. dirs. Nat. Peach Council, 1984-85. Chmn. bd. United Ministries, Greenville Free Med. Clinic; chmn. Greenville County Human Rels. Commn., 1991—; bd. dirs. Catholic Charities, Diocese of Charleston. Served with USMCR, 1943-45. Decorated Bronze Star. Mem. Nat. Assn. Life Underwriters, Sales and Mktg. Execs. Internat., Newcomen Soc. Roman Catholic. Club: Green Valley Country. Home: 305 Aberdare Ln Greenville SC 29615-2406 Office: Phillips Resource Group PO Box 5664 Greenville SC 29606-5664

FITZGERALD, GARRET ADARE, medical educator; b. May 11, 1950; married; three children. MBBCh with honors, Univ. Coll., Dublin, 1974, MD, 1980; Diploma in Stats., Trinity Coll., Dublin, 1977; MS in Stats., U. London, 1979. FRCP/Ireland, FACP, RCP/U.K. Intern gastroenterology/therapeutics St. Vincent's Hosp., Dublin, 1974, intern, urology, 1975, intern, gen. surgery, 1975, sr. house officer, hematology/oncology, 1975-76; sr. house officer endocrinology/diabetes mellitus Mater Hosp., Dublin, 1976-77, rsch. register, endocrinology/diabetes mellitus, 1977; rsch. fellow Royal Postgrad. Med. Sch., London Clin. Pharmacology, 1977-79; rsch. fellow dept. internal medicine II U. Cologne, 1979-80; rsch. fellow to assoc. dir. Rsch. Ctr. Grant in Pharm. Scis. Vanderbilt U. Sch. Medicine, Nashville, 1980-91, chief. Divsn. Clin. Pharmacology, 1988-91, William Stokes prof. exptl. therapeutics, 1989-91; dir. Ctr. Cardiovascular Sci. U. Coll. Dublin/Mater Hosp., 1991-94; prof. medicine, pharmacology U. Pa., 1994—, chair dept. pharmacology, 1996—, dir. Clin. Res. Ctr., 1994—, Robinette Found. prof., dir. Ctr. Exptl. Therapeutics/Rsch., 1994—; lectr. in field, including vis. prof. Harvard U., U. London, Duke U., Wash. U., numerous others; served numerous coms. and advisory groups in field. Mem. editl. bd. Jour. of Pharmacology and Exptl. Therapeutics, 1987—, Trends in Cardiovascular Medicine, 1990—, Atherosclerosis Thrombosis, and Vascular Biology, 1990-96, Jour. Biol. Chemistry, 1993—, Circulation, 1993—; contbr. numerous articles to profl. jours. and publs. Fellowship Nat. U. Ireland, 1977-80, Wellcome Clin. Rsch. fellow, 1977-79, Alexander von Humboldt Stiftung fellow, Germany, 1979-80; grantee in field. Mem. Assn. Physicians of Gt. Britain and Ireland, Assn. Am. Physicians, Am. Soc. Clin. Investigation, Am. Fedn. Clin. Rsch., Am. Heart Assn. (exec. and long-range planning com. Thrombosis Coun. 1987-91, program dir. 1996, vice chair coun. arterio and vascular biology 1997—), Am. Soc. Pharmacology and Exptl. Therapeutics, Am. Soc. Clin. Pharmacology and Therapeutics, AAAS. Office: 153 Johnson Pavillion 3620 Hamilton Walk Philadelphia PA 19104-6140

FITZGERALD, GERALD FRANCIS, retired banker; b. Chgo., July 6, 1925; s. John J. and Olivia (Trader) F.; m. Marjorie Webb Gosselin, Sept. 10, 1949; children: Gerald Francis Jr., James Gosselin, Thomas Gosselin, Julie Ann Fitzgerald Schauer, Peter Gosselin. BS in Commerce, Northwestern U., 1949. Salesman Premier Printing Co., 1949-53; founder, ptnr. Fitzgerald & Cooke (now Hill and Knowlton, Inc. div. J. Walter Thompson), 1953-60, v.p., 1960-64; chmn. Lake Villa Trust & Savs. Bank, 1961-69, Palatine Nat. Bank, 1961-87, Suburban Nat. Bank of Palatine, Suburban Bank of Hoffman-Schaumburg, Suburban Bank of Cary-Grove, Suburban Bank of Rolling Meadows, Suburban Bank of Barrington, Suburban Bank of Bartlett, 1964-90; pres. Suburban Bancorp, Inc., Palatine, 1982-90, chmn., 1982-94; chmn. So. Colo. Bank Holding Co., 1991—, Citizens Bank of Pagosa Springs, 1991-94; cons. Am. Del. to NATO CCMS, Brussels, 1976; former chmn. Suburban Computer Svcs. Corp., Palatine; lectr. in banking field. Contbr. articles to profl. jours. Bd. dirs., past pres. Inverness Assn.; former mem. Govs. Adv. Coun. of Ill.; past mem. Ill. Racing Bd.; mem. Chgo. Coun. of Fgn. Rels.; cons. Portsmouth, R.I. Abbey Sch., 1978-80; life trustee Newberry Libr.; mem. John Evans Club, Northwestern U. Sgt. U.S. Army, 1944-46, ETO. Mem. Ill. Thoroughbred Owners and Breeders Found., Nat. Assn. of State Racing Commrs., Newcomen Soc., Max McGraw's Wildlife Found., Chgo. Athletic Assn., Inverness Golf Club (bd. govs.), Safari International Club, Caxton Club, Delta Upsilon. Avocations: world travel, opera, rare books, photography, big game hunting and fishing. Home: 19 Creekside Ln Barrington Hills IL 60010-9343 Office: 50 N Brockway St Palatine IL 60067-5076

FITZGERALD, GERALD P., state agency executive; b. N.Y.C.; m. Ellen Roche; 4 children. Student, Fordham U., 1962. With Port Authority of N.Y. and N.J., N.Y.C., gen. mgr. John F. Kennedy Internat. Airport, ast. dir. properties and fin., gen. mgr. mktg., econs. and fin., mgr. John F. Kennedy Airport ops.; asst. mgr. LaGuardia Airport, N.Y.C., supr. John F. Kennedy Airport maintenance, dep. dir., COO aviation dept., acting dir. aviation, 1995, dir. aviation, 1995-96; pres. Parsons Brinckerhoff Aviation Co., N.Y.C., 1996—. Bd. dirs. United Way N.Y.C.; pres. bd. trustees Cath. Charities for Bklyn. and Queens. Mem. Airports Coun. Internat. (chair internat. econs. com., mem. N.Am. econs. com.), Western European Airports Assn., Am. Assn. Airport Execs. (past chmn., mem. bd., exec. com.), Wings Club (mem. fin. com., chmn. membership com.). Office: Parsons Brinkerhoff Aviation Co 1 Penn Plz New York NY 10119-0002*

FITZGERALD, GERALDINE, actress; b. Dublin, Ireland, Nov. 24, 1913; came to U.S. 1938, naturalized, 1954; d. William and Mary (Richards) F.; m. Stuart Scheftel, Sept. 10, 1946; children: Michael Lindsay-Hogg, Susan Scheftel. Student, Queens Coll., London. Appeared in numerous motion pictures, 1936—, including Wuthering Heights (Acad. award nomination), 1939, Dark Victory, 1939, Wilson, 1944, Three Strangers, 1946, 10 North Frederick, 1958, The Pawnbroker, 1964, The Mango Tree, 1977, Diary of the Dead, 1980, Arthur, 1980, Blood Link, 1982, Easy Money, 1983, Pope of Greenwich Village, 1984, Poltergeist II, 1986, Arthur II, 1988; appeared on stage as Mary Tyrone in Long Days Journey into Night (Variety Critics award), 1971, The Lunch Girl; appeared in Broadway prodn. Touch of the Poet, 1980; directed play Mass Appeal, 1980; TV film appearance Do You Remember Love?, 1985, The Best of Everything, Dixie: Changing Habits, 1983, Kennedy, 1983, Street Songs, Circle of Violence, 1986, Night of Courage, 1986, Dick Francis: Twice Shy, 1989, Bump in the Night, 1991; TV guest appearances include Goodyear Television Playhouse, 1951, Alfred Hitchcock Presents, 1955, Naked City, 1958, St. Elsewhere, 1982, The Golden Girls, 1985. Active N.Y. State Council Arts. Recipient Handel medallion N.Y.C., 1974. Mem. AFTRA, Screen Actors Guild, Actors Equity. *

FITZGERALD, JAMES FRANCIS, cable television executive; b. Janesville, Wis., Mar. 27, 1926; s. Michael Henry and Chloris Helen (Beiter) F.; m. Marilyn Field Cullen, Aug. 1, 1950; children: Michael Dennis, Brian Nicholas, Marcia O'Loughlin, James Francis, Carolyn Jane, Ellen Putnam. B.S., Notre Dame U., 1947. With Standard Oil Co. (Ind.), Milw., 1947-48; pres. F.-W. Oil Co., Janesville, 1950—, Total TV, Inc. (cable TV Systems), Wis., 1965-86; bd. dirs. Milw. Ins. Co., Bank One, Janesville N.A.; chmn. bd. Golden State Warriors, Oakland, Calif., 1986-95, Total TV Calif., 1987-96. Bd. govs., chmn. TV com. NBA; chmn. bd., pres. S.P.A.C.E. Inc. subs. Milw. Bucks NBA team, 1976-85; chmn. Greater Milw. Open (PGA Tournament), 1985, Notre Dame Bus. Adv. Coun., 1989—. Served to lt. (j.g.) USNR, 1944-46, 51-53. Mem. Chief Execs. Forum, World Bus. Coun., Wis. Petroleum Assn. (pres. 1961-62), Janesville Country Club, Castles Pines Golf Club, Vintage Club (pres. 1989-91), San Francisco Golf Club, El Dorado Country Club. Roman Catholic. Home and Office: PO Box 348 Janesville WI 53547-0348

FITZGERALD, JAMES MICHAEL, federal judge; b. Portland, Oreg., Oct. 7, 1920; s. Thomas and Florence (Linderman) F.; m. Karin Rose Benton, Jan. 19, 1950; children: Dennis James, Denise Lyn, Debra Jo, Kevin Thomas. BA, Willamette U., 1950, LLB, 1951; postgrad., U. Wash., 1952. Bar: Alaska 1953. Asst. U.S. atty. Ketchikan and Anchorage, Alaska, 1952-56; city atty. City of Anchorage, 1956-59; legal counsel to Gov. Alaska, Anchorage, 1959; commr. pub. safety State of Alaska, 1959; judge Alaska Superior Ct., 3d Jud. Dist., 1959-69, presiding judge, 1969-72; assoc. justice Alaska Supreme Ct., Anchorage, 1972-75; judge U.S. Dist. Ct. for Alaska, Anchorage, from 1975, formerly chief judge, now sr. judge. Mem. advisory bd. Salvation Army, Anchorage, 1962—, chmn., 1965-66; mem. Anchorage Parks and Recreation Bd., 1965-77, chmn., 1966. Served with AUS, 1940-41; Served with USMCR, 1942-46. Office: US Dist Ct 222 W 7th Ave Box 50 Anchorage AK 99513-7564*

FITZGERALD, JAMES PATRICK, lawyer; b. Omaha, Nebr., Nov. 30, 1946; s. James Joseph and Lorraine (Hickey) F.; m. Dianne Fager, Dec. 17, 1968; 1 child, James Timothy. BA, U. Nebr., 1968; JD, Creighton U., 1974. Bar: Nebr. 1974, U.S. Dist. Ct. Nebr. 1974, U.S. Ct. Appeals (8th cir.) 1974. Law clk. U.S. Dist. Ct. Nebr., Omaha, 1974-76; atty. McGrath, North, Mullin & Kratz, P.C., Omaha, 1976—. Sgt. U.S. Army, 1968-71. Mem. ABA, Nebr. Bar Assn., Assn. Trial Lawyers Am., Nebr. Assn. Trial Attys., Def. Rsch. Inst. Home: 16728 Jones Cir Omaha NE 68118-2711 Office: McGrath North Mullin & Kratz 1 Central Park Plz Ste 1400 Omaha NE 68102-1680

FITZGERALD, JAMES T., architect. BA in Philosophy, Josephinum Coll.; BArch, U. Notre Dame. Cert. Nat. Coun. Archtl. Registration Bd.; registered architect 31 states. Chmn., CEO FRCH Design Worldwide (previously Space Design Internat.), 1968—; spkr. in field; tchr. U. Cin. Coll. of Design, Architecture, Art and Planning; bd. advisors Kirk & Blum Co. former chmn. steering com. for downtown retail devel. strategy City of Cin.; v.p., trustee Contemporary Arts Ctr., Cin.; bd. dirs. Archtl. Found., Cin. Fellow AIA (former pres. Cin. chpt., former nat. chmn. interiors com., mem. steering com. AIA internat. com.), Internat. Coun. Shopping Ctrs., Urban Land Inst., Am. Arbitration Assn., Nat. Retail Fedn. Office: FRCH Design Worldwide 311 Elm St # 600 Cincinnati OH 45202-2706

FITZGERALD, JAMES W. (JAY), magazine publisher. BSS, Fordham U., 1961. Advt. dir. Golf Digest, 1972-74; advt. dir. Golf Digest/Tennis, Inc., 1974-76, v.p. advt. and sales, 1976-79, exec. v.p., 1980-84, CEO, 1982-84, pres., CEO, pub., from 1984; exec. v.p., pub. Us Mag., 1979-80; now pres., pub. N.Y. Times Sports/Leisure Mag. Group, Trumbull, Conn., 1980—; former pres., CEO N.Y. Times Co. Mag. Group, chmn., 1998—. Office: NY Times Company Mag Group 5520 Park Ave Trumbull CT 06611-3426*

FITZGERALD, SISTER JANET ANNE, philosophy educator, college president emeritus; b. Woodside, N.Y., Sept. 4, 1935; d. Robert W. and Lillian H. (Shannon) F. BA magna cum laude, St. John's U., 1965, MA, 1967, PhD, 1971, LLD (hon.), 1982. Joined Sisters of St. Dominic of Amityville, Roman Catholic Ch., 1953; NSF postdoctoral fellow Cath. U. Am., summer 1971; prof. philosophy Molloy Coll., Rockville Centre, N.Y., 1969—; pres. Molloy Coll., 1972-96; Trustee L.I. Regional Adv. Coun. on Higher Edn., 1972-96, chmn., 1981-84; trustee Commn. on Ind. Colls. and Univs., 1981-84, 89-92, Fellowship of Cath. Scholars, 1977—, v.p., 1977-80; trustee Cath. Charities, Diocese of Rockville Centre, 1979-82; invited expert peritus Vatican Internat. Conf. on Cath. Higher Edn., Rome, 1989. Author: Alfred North Whitehead's Early Philosophy of Space and Time, 1979. Mem. bd. advisors Sem. of Immaculate Conception, 1975-80; mem. adv. bd. pre-theology program Dunwoodie Sem., Archdiocese of N.Y.; mem. pub. policy com. N.Y. State Cath. Conf., 1992-94; mem. N.Y. State Edn. Dept.-Blue Ribbon Panel on Cath. Schs., 1992-93; 1st woman grand marshal St. Patrick's Day Parade, Glen Cove, 1992. Recipient Disting. Leadership award L.I. Bus. News, 1988, plaque of recognition L.I. Women's Coun. for Equal Edn. Tng. and Employment, 1989, Pathfinder award Town of Hempstead, 1990, Disting. Long Islander in Edn. award Epilepsy Found. L.I., 1991, Educator of Yr. award Assn. Tchrs. N.Y., 1980, Spl. award for arts in edn. L.I. Arts Coun., 1994; honored by L.I. Cath. League for Religious and Civil Rights, 1989; named L.I.'s 100 Influentials, L.I. Bus. News, 1992, 93, 94, 95, 96. Mem. Soc. Cath. Social Scis. (bd. advisors). Office: Molloy College Philosophy Dept 1000 Hempstead Ave Rockville Centre NY 11570-1100

FITZGERALD, JOAN, principal. Prin. Xavier Coll. Prep. Sch. Recipient Blue Ribbon Sch. award 1990-91. Office: Xavier Coll Prep Sch 4710 N 5th St Phoenix AZ 85012-1738*

FITZGERALD, JOHN CHARLES, JR., investment banker; b. Sacramento, May 23, 1941; s. John Charles and Geraldine Edith (McNabb) F.; BS, Calif. State U. at Sacramento, 1964; MBA, Cornell U., 1966; m. Mildred Ann Kilpatrick, June 26, 1965; children—Geraldine Kathrine, Erec John. Dir. corp. planning Bekins Co., L.A., 1966-73; mgr. corp. planning Ridder Publs., Inc., L.A., 1973-75; chief fin. officer City of Inglewood (Calif.), 1975-77; treas./contr. Inglewood Redevel. Agy., 1975-77, Inglewood Housing Authority, 1975-77; v.p. mcpl. fin. White, Weld & Co., Inc., L.A., 1977-78; v.p. pub. fin. Paine Webber Jackson & Curtis, L.A., 1978-79; v.p. and mgr. for Western region, mcpl. fin. dept. Merrill Lynch Capital Markets, L.A., 1979-82, mng. dir. Western region, mcpl. fin. dept., 1982-86; mng. dir. Seidler-Fitzgerald Pub. Fin., L.A., 1986—; sr. v.p. The Seidler Cos., Inc., L.A., 1986—, also bd. dirs., mem. exec. com.; instr. fin./adminstrn. El Camino Coll., Torrance, Calif., 1977-80; bd. dirs., mem. exec. com. The Seidler Cos., Inc. Chmn. bd. dirs., exec. com., treas., chmn. fund raising com. L.A. chpt. Am. Heart Assn., 1977—; bd. dirs. Daniel Freeman Hosps. Inc., Corondelet Health Care Corp.; trustee Mt. St. Mary's Coll., L.A., 1992—; bd. dirs. Tau Kappa Epsilon Ednl. Found., Indpls., 1995—; bd. of dirs., Calif. Soc. for Biomed. Rsch., 1998; alumni coun. mem. Johnson Grad. Sch. of Mgmt. Cornell U., real estate council. Mem. Fin. Execs. Inst., Mcpl. Fin. Officers Assn., Calif. Soc. Mcpl. Fin. Officers, League Calif. Cities, So. Calif. Corp. Planners Assn. (past pres.), L.A. Bond, Beta Gamma Sigma. Republican. Clubs: Jonathan, The Calif., Lake Arrowhead Country. Lodge: Rotary. Address: PO Box 765 27447 Bayshore Dr Lake Arrowhead CA 92352

FITZGERALD, JOHN EDMUND, civil engineering educator; b. Revere, Mass., Sept. 29, 1923; s. John Valentine and Gertrude Margaret (Doyle) F.; m. Elaine Louise Ohlson, Feb. 24, 1945; children: Deborah Lee, Christine Louise, David John, John Paul (dec.). Student, Tufts U., 1941-42, 46; MCE, Harvard U., 1947; MS in Math.-Physics, Nat. U. Ireland, Cork, 1970, DSc, 1972. Registered profl. engr., Utah, N.D.; chartered physicist, U.K. Regional constrn. engr. Liberty Mut. Ins. Co., Dallas, 1947-48; assoc. prof. N.D. State U., Fargo, 1948-51; supr. structures and dynamics Armour Research Found., Chgo., 1951-53; mgr. applied mechanics and med. physics Research div. Am. Machine & Foundry Corp., Chgo., 1953-56; mgr. applied math. and mechanics Borg-Warner Cen. Research Labs., Des Plaines, Ill., 1956-59; dir. devel. br. Lockheed Propulsion Co., Redlands, Calif., 1959-66; prof. civil engring., chmn. dept. U. Utah, Salt Lake City, 1966-74, prof., assoc. dean, 1973-74; prof., dir. Sch. Civil Engring. Ga. Inst. Tech., Atlanta, 1975-89, prof. emeritus, 1991—, assoc. dean, 1989-91; cons. numerous aerospace cos., govt. agys., 1966—; guest lectr. Trinity Coll., Dublin, Ireland, U. Bristol, U.K., U. Marseilles, France, NATO Advanced Study Inst., Italy, others., 1968—; bd. dirs. EFM Corp., Dublin. Author: Engineering Structural Analysis of Solid Propellants, 1971; editor Structural Integrity Handbook, 1972; contbr. over 100 articles to profl. jours.; 27 patents. Served with submarine service USN, 1942-46, ETO. Recipient U.S. Sr. Scientist award for teaching and research Alexander von Humboldt Found., 1973-74. Fellow Inst. Physics U.K., ASCE, AIAA (assoc., Outstanding Achievement in Solid Propulsion award 1987); mem. Soc. Rheology, Am. Acad. Mechanics, Am. Phys. Soc., Irish Sailing Assn. Roman Catholic. Club: Royal Cork Yacht (Crosshaven, Ireland). Avocations: swimming, bicycling, sailing. Home: 4252 Loch Highland Pky Roswell GA 30075-2042 Office: Ga Inst Tech Sch Civil Engring Atlanta GA 30332-0355

FITZGERALD, JOHN EDWARD, III, lawyer; b. Cambridge, Mass., Jan. 12, 1945; s. John Edward Jr. and Kathleen (Sullivan) FitzG. BCE, U.S. Mil. Acad., West Point, N.Y., 1969; JD, M in Pub. Policy Analysis, U. Pa., 1975. Bar: Pa. 1975, N.Y. 1978, Calif. 1983, U.S. Supreme Ct. 1991. Commd. 2d lt. U.S. Army, 1969, advanced through grades to capt., 1971, resigned, 1972; assoc. Saul Ewing Remick & Saul, Phila., 1975-77, Shearman & Sterling, N.Y.C., 1977-78; atty., dir. govt. rels. and pub. affairs Pepsico, Inc., Purchase, N.Y., 1978-82; sr. v.p., dept. head Security Pacific Corp., Los Angeles, 1982-83; ptnr. Schlesinger, FitzGerald & Johnson, Palm Springs, Calif., 1983-87; mng. ptnr. FitzGerald & Assocs., Palm Springs, 1987—; judge pro tem Desert Jud. Dist.; lectr. Calif. Continuing Edn. of the Bar; trustee Nat. Coun. Freedom Found., Valley Forge, Pa.; lectr. Calif. Employment Lawyers Assn. Bd. dirs., chmn.-elect Desert Hosp. Found.; bd. dirs., chmn. Palm Sprngs Boys and Girls Club, Desert Youth Found.; chmn. United Way of the Desert; mem. Com. of 25, Palm Springs; trustee, v.p., Palm Springs Desert Mus. Named Palm Springs Disting. Citizen of Yr., 1999. Mem. ABA, Calif. Bar Assn., Desert Bar Assn. (trustee, chmn. cmty. law sch.), Riverside County Bar Assn., Orange County Bar Assn., Assn. Trial Lawyers Am., Calif. Trial Lawyers Assn. (lectr.), Am. Arbitration Assn. (arbitrator), O'Donnell Golf Club, Desert Bus. Roundtable, World Affairs Coun., Lincoln Club of the Coachella Valley (bd. dirs., jud. nomination com.). Office: Ste 105 3001 Tahquitz Canyon Way Palm Springs CA 92262-6900

FITZGERALD, JOHN THOMAS, JR., religious studies educator; b. Birmingham, Ala., Oct. 2, 1948; s. John Thomas and Annie Myrtle (Walters) F.; m. Karol Bonneaux, May 23, 1970; children: Kirstin Leigh, Kimberly Anne. BA, Abilene Christian U., 1970, MA, 1972; MDiv, Yale U., 1975, PhD, 1984. Instr. Yale Coll., New Haven, Conn., 1979, Yale Divinity Sch., New Haven, Conn., 1980-81; instr. U. Miami, Coral Gables, Fla., 1981-84, asst. prof., 1984-88, assoc. prof., 1988—; vis. assoc. prof. Brown U., Providence, 1992, Yale Divinity Sch., New Haven, 1998-99; dir. honors. program U. Miami, 1987-91, master Hecht Residential Coll., 1987-91, chmn. Rhodes Scholarship com., 1987-91. Author: Tabula of Cebes, 1983, Cracks in an Earthen Vessel, 1988; editor Christian Origins sect. Religious Studies Rev., 1994—, Friendship, Flattery and Frankness of Speech, 1996, Greco-Roman Perspectives on Friendship, 1997; contbr. articles to profl. jours. Judge for Silver Knight awards The Miami (Fla.) Herald, 1988, 90. Recipient Max Orovitz Summer Rsch. award U. Miami, 1985, 87, 94, 95, 98; Rotary Internat. fellow, Tuebingen, Fed. Republic Germany, 1974-76, Two Bros. fellow Yale Div. Sch., 1974-75. Mem. Soc. Bibl. Lit. (chmn. com. 1989-96, editor Texts and Translations Series: Greco-Roman Religion 1993—, rsch. grantee 1997-98), Iron Arrow Honor Soc., Omicron Delta Kappa, Golden Key Nat. Honor Soc. (chmn. scholarship com. 1990-91), Phi Kappa Phi (chpt. pres. 1988-89). Home: 15215 SW 78 Ct Miami FL 33157-2349 Office: U Miami PO Box 248264 Miami FL 33124-8264

FITZGERALD, JOHN WARNER, law educator; b. Grand Ledge, Mich., Nov. 14, 1924; s. Frank Dwight and Queena Maud (Warner) F.; m. Lorabeth Moore, June 6, 1953; children: Frank Moore, Eric Stiles, Adam Warner. B.S., Mich. State U., 1947; J.D., U. Mich., 1954. Bar: Mich. 1954. Practiced in Grand Ledge, 1955-64; chief judge pro tem Mich. Ct. Appeals, 1965-73; justice Mich. Supreme Ct., 1974-83, dep. chief justice, 1975-82, chief justice, 1982; prof. law Thomas M. Cooley Law Sch., Lansing, Mich., 1982—; mem. Mich. Senate from 15th Dist., 1958-64. Served with AUS, 1943-44. Mem. ABA, State Bar Mich. (bd. commrs. 1985-90), Am. Judicature Soc. Office: Thomas M Cooley Law Sch PO Box 13038 Lansing MI 48901-3038

FITZGERALD, JUDITH KLASWICK, federal judge; b. Spangler, Pa., May 10, 1948; d. Julius Francis and Regina Marie (Pregno) Klaswick; m. June 5, 1971 (div. Dec. 1982); 1 child; m. Barry Robert Fitzgerald, Sept. 20, 1986; 1 child. BSBA, U. Pitts., 1970, JD, 1973. Legal rschr. Assocs. Fin., Pitts., 1972-73; law clk. to pres. judge Beaver County (Pa.) Ct. Common Pleas, 1973-74; law clk. to judge Pa. Superior Ct., Pitts., 1974-75; asst. U.S. atty. U.S. Dist. Ct. (we. dist.) Pa., Pitts. and Erie, 1976-87; U.S. bankruptcy judge U.S. Dist. Ct. (we. dist.) Pa., Pitts., Erie and Johnstown, 1987—. Co-author: Bankruptcy and Divorce, Support and Property Division, 1991; editor: Pennsylvania Law of Juvenile Delinquency and Deprivation, 1976; contbr. articles to profl. jours. Mem. Pitts. Camerata, 1978-80, Allegheny County Polit.-Legal Edn. Project, 1980, West Pa. Conservancy, 1990—, Mendelssohn Choir Pitts., 1982—; mem. coun. Program to Aid Citizen Enterprise, 1985-87. Recipient Spl. Achievement awards Dept. Justice, Spl. Recognition award Pittsburgh mag., Operation Exodus Outstanding Performance award Dept. Commerce, 1986. Mem. Allegheny County Bar Assn., Women's Bar Assn. of Western Pa., Nat. Conf. Bankruptcy Judges, Am. Bankruptcy Inst., Nat. Conf. Bankruptcy Clks., Comml. Law League of Am., Fed. Criminal Investigators Assn. (Spl. Svc. award 1988), Zonta. Republican. Lutheran. Avocations: singing, reading, traveling. Office: US Bankruptcy Ct 600 Grant St Ste 5490 Pittsburgh PA 15219-2702

FITZGERALD, LAURINE ELISABETH, university dean, educator; b. New London, Wis., Aug. 24, 1930; d. Thomas F. and Laurine (Branchflower) F. B.S., Northwestern U., 1952, M.A., 1953; Ph.D., Mich. State U., 1959. Instr. English, dir. devel. reading lab., head resident-dir. Wis. State Coll., Whitewater, 1953-55; area dir. residence and counseling Ind. U., 1955-57; teaching grad. asst. guidance and counseling, then instr., counselor Mich. State U., East Lansing, 1957-59; asst. prof. psychology and edn., assoc. dean students U. Denver, 1959-62; asst. prof. counseling psychology, staff counselor for Carnegie Found. project U. Minn., 1962-63; assoc. dean, assoc. prof. Mich. State U., 1963-70, assoc. dean students. prof. adminstrn. and higher edn., dir. div. edn. and rsch., 1970-74; dean Grad. Sch., prof. counselor edn., dir. N.E. Wis. Coop. Regional Grad. Ctr. U. Wis.-Oshkosh, 1974-85; dean/dir. Ohio State U.-Mansfield, 1986-87, prof. edn. policy and leadership, 1985-93, dir. student pers. asst. program, edn. policy and leadership, 1989-92; adj. prof. edn. policy and leadership Ohio State U., 1992-93; vis. lectr. U. Okla., Norman, 1961; vis. prof. Oreg. State U., 1977; cons. in field; vocat. expertwitness, 1962-95. Contbr. numerous articles to profl. jours.; co-author monographs, texts. Adv. bd. Mansfield Gen. Hosp., 1986-94; bd. dirs. Renaissance Theatre, 1986-87, New Beginnings, 1986-94; exec. com. Ohio Consortium on Tng. and Planning, 1985-87; trustee Mt. Carmel Coll. Nursing, chmn. acad. affairs com., 1988-96. Recipient Higher Edn. Rocky Mountain coun. Girl Scouts U.S., 1961, Evelyn Hosmer U. Denver, 1962, Merit award Northwestern Alumni Assn., 1993; named Old Master Purdue U., 1979, Most Disting. Women in Edn., Mich., 1973; Elin Wagner Found. fellow, 1963-64. Mem. AAUW, AAUP (chpt. treas. 1955-56), NEA, Am. Psychol. Assn., Mich. Psychol. Assn., Am. Pers. and Guidance Assn., Am. Coll. Pers. Assn. (sec. 1965-67, exec. bd. 1968-70, chmn. women's task force 1970-71, editor jour. 1976-82, Disting. Scholar award 1985, sr. scholars com. 1985-90, historian 1982-95, chmn. scholars com. 1986-87, sr. scholars diplomate 1990, awards and commendations com. 1988-89, pres.-elect 1989-90, pres. 1990-91, past pres. 1991-92, Esther Lloyd-Jones Disting. Svc. award 1997), Assn. Counselor Edn. and Supervision, Am. Assn. Higher Edn., Nat. Assn. Women Deans, Adminstrs. and Counselors (rsch., ednl. by-laws programs, publs., univ. coms. 1959-72, v.p. 1972-74, KSP Trust Commn. 1979-81, pres. 1980-81, editorial bd. 1991—), Mich. Assn. Women Deans, Adminstrs. and Counselors (pres. 1967-69), Ohio Assn. Women Deans, Adminstrs. and Counselors, Mich. Coll. Pers. Assn., Wis. Coll. Pers. Assn., Midwest Assn. Grad. Schs. (pres. 1980-82), Intercollegiate Assn. Women Students (editorial bd., nat. advisor), Women's Equity Action League (past pres. Mich., nat. sec.-treas. legal and edn. def. fund), Bus. and Profl. Women's Club (chpt. pres. 1980, state officer 1981, Lena Lake Forest fellow 1966-67), Wis. Soc. for Higher Edn. (Achievement award 1985, Pres. award 1982), Altrusa Internat. (mem. bd. dirs. 1986-94), Mortar Bd., Shi-Ai, Beta Beta Beta, Psi Chi, Alpha Lambda Delta, Delta Kappa Gamma, Zonta (pres. Lansing club, chmn. internat. status of women com. 1960-85). Home: 812 Wyman St New London WI 54961-1771

FITZGERALD, LYNNE MARIE LESLIE, family therapist; b. Berea, Ohio, Aug. 21, 1946; d. Glenn Willis and Blanche Marie (Monkosky) Leslie; m. J. Michael Fitzgerald, May 3, 1974; children: Joseph Glenn, Leslie Marie. BA, U. Miami, 1968; MS, St. Thomas U., 1983; PhD, Nova Univ., 1994. Lic. marriage and family therapist, Fla., Va. Sml. group facilitator U. Miami Med. Sch., 1988; family therapist Family Life Ctr. of Fla., Inc., Coral Gables, 1985—; facilitator stress, depression and suicide prevention tng. program Mental Health Assn., Charlottesville, Va., 1995—; facilitator Dade County Pub. Schs./Depression and Suicide Prevention, Miami, 1985-92, Mental Health Assn. Charlottesville/Albemarle/Depression and Suicide Prevention Program for Schs., 1996—; cons. Mediation Ministries, Miami, 1990—, Counseling Ctr., St. Louis Cath. Ch., Miami, 1990-92. Mem. Jr. League, Va., St. Anne's-Belfield Sch. parents aux. bd., 1992-96, Ashlawn-Highland Summer Festival Guild; bd. dirs. The Vizcayans, Miami, 1979-83, Party Parade, Charlottesville, 1995, gen. chmn. 1995-96, pres. 1996-97, bd. dirs., 1998—. Named Woman of Yr., Kappa Kappa Gamma Alumnae Assn., Miami, 1973. Fellow Am. Orthopsychiat. Assn.; mem. Am. Assn. Marriage and Family Therapists (approved supr.), Am. Assn. Christian Counselors, Va. Assn. Marriage and Family Therapists (allied profl. com.), Mental Health Assn Charlottesville (profl. bd. dirs. 1995—), Mothers and Others for a Livable Planet, Kappa Kappa Gamma (U. Va. house bd., 1995—, alumnae exec. bd. 1994—, Woman of Yr. 1973). Roman Catholic. Avocations: horseback riding, needlework, skiing. Home: 888 Tanglewood Rd Charlottesville VA 22901-7817 Office: Family Life Ctr of Fla Inc 1550 Madruga Ave Miami FL 33146-3039

FITZGERALD, MARY JOAN, music educator; b. Chgo., Oct. 2, 1928; d. Arthur Frederick and Mary Naomi (Speidel) F. BA in Music Edn. and Liturgical Music, Alverno Coll. Music, 1965; MA in Ch. Music, DePaul U., 1980; BA in Theology, Loyola U. Chgo., 1982, MPS, 1987. Music edn. tchr. Cath. Sch. System, 1949-59; tchr. primary grades various parochial schs., 1959-67; piano/organ instr. Karnes Music Co., Des Plaines, Ill., 1967-78; pvt. music tchr. Glenview, Evanston, Ill., 1970-88; ch. musician St. Joseph Cath. Ch., Wilmette, Ill., 1973-76, St. Henry Cath. Ch., Chgo., 1981-88; ret., 1994. Author: (liturgical sequences for the ch. yr.) Behold Your Mother: Co-Redemptrix, 1994, Marian Sequences in the 21st Century, 1995, (religious poetry) Salvation in Christ Through Mary, 1995, To Live is Christ, 1996. Roman Catholic. Avocations: reading, sewing. Home: 1615 Hinman Ave # 724 Evanston IL 60201-4509

FITZGERALD, MICHAEL COWAN, art historian; b. Dallas, Sept. 26, 1953; s. James Lawrence and Doris (Cowan) F.; m. May L. Castleberry, June 11, 1976. AB, Stanford U., 1976; MBA, Columbia U., 1986, PhD, 1987. Preceptor Columbia U., N.Y.C., 1981-83; specialist Christie's, N.Y.C., 1986-88; asst. prof. Trinity Coll., Hartford, Conn., 1988-94; assoc. prof. Trinity Coll., Hartford, 1994—, chmn. dept. fine arts, 1996—. Author: (books) Making Modernism, 1995, Bear's Skin, 1992; contbg. author: Picasso and Portraiture, 1996; curator: (exhbn.) Picassoid, 1995; contbr. articles to profl. jours. Fellow NEH, Washington, 1994-95, grantee, 1991; faculty rsch. grantee Trinity Coll., Hartford, Conn., 1989, 93; recipient Rudolf Wittkower fellowship Columbia U., N.Y.C., 1980-81. Office: Trinity Coll Dept Fine Arts Halden Hall Hartford CT 06106

FITZGERALD, MICHAEL LEE, state official; b. Marshalltown, Iowa, Nov. 29, 1951; s. James Martin and Clara Francis (Dankbar) F.; m. Janet Roewe; children: Ryan, Chris, Erin, Bridie. B.B.A., U. Iowa, 1974. Campaign mgr. Fitzgerald for Treas., Colo., Iowa, 1974; market analyst Massey Ferguson, Inc., Des Moines, 1975-83; treas. State of Iowa, Des Moines, 1983—. Democrat. Roman Catholic. Office: Office of State Treas Capitol Bldg Des Moines IA 50319*

FITZGERALD, PETER GOSSELIN, senator, lawyer; b. Elgin, Ill., Oct. 20, 1960; s. Gerald Francis and Marjorie (Gosselin) F.; m. C. Nina Kerstiens, July 25, 1987; 1 child, Jake Buchanan. AB, Dartmouth Coll., 1982; cert. of attendance, Aristotelian U., Salonica, Greece, 1983; JD, U. Mich., 1986. Bar: Ill. 1986, U.S. Dist. Ct. (no. dist.) Ill. 1986. Assoc. Isham, Lincoln & Beale, Chgo., 1986-88; ptnr. Riordan, Larson, Bruckert & Moore, Chgo., 1988-92; mem. Ill. Senate, 1993-98, chmn. state govt. ops. com., 1997-98; U.S. senator from Ill., 1999-; counsel Harris Bankmont, Inc., 1992-96; bd. dirs. Harris Bank Palatine N.A. Translator: Dartmouth Classical Jour., 1982. Pres. Young Rep. Orgn., Palatine, Ill., 1988; bd. dirs. north ctrl. Ill. region Children's Home and Aid Soc. Rotary Found. internat. grad. scholar, 1982-83. Mem. Ill. State Bar Assn., Chgo. Bar Assn., Econ. Club Chgo., Inverness Golf Club, Union League Club, Meadow Club. Roman Catholic. Office: 50 N Brockway St Ste 4-9 Palatine IL 60067-5072

FITZGERALD, ROBERT HANNON, JR., orthopedic surgeon; b. Denver, Aug. 25, 1942; s. Robert Hannon and Alyene (Webber) Fitzgerald Anderson; m. Lynda Lee Lang, Apr. 27, 1968 (div. 1984); children: Robert III, Shannon, Dennis, Katherine, Kelly; m. Jamie Kathleen Dent, Mar. 9, 1985; children: Brian, Steven. BS, U. Notre Dame, 1963; MD, U. Kans., 1967; MS, U. Minn., 1974, Magistri Artivum, U. Pa., 1995. Instr. orthop. surgery Mayo Med. Sch., Rochester, Minn., 1974-77, cons. orthop. surgery, 1974-89, asst. prof., 1977-82, assoc. prof., 1982-86 , prof., 1986-89, chief adult reconstructive surgery, 1987-89, dir. orthop. rsch., 1988-89; prof. chmn. dept. orthop. surgery Wayne State U. Sch. Medicine, 1989-95; chief orthop. surgery Hutzel Hosp., 1989-95, Detroit Receiving Hosp., 1989-95; orthopaedist-in-chief Detroit Med. Ctr., 1989-95, chmn. coun., specialist-in-chief 1993-95; prof., chmn. dept. orthop. surgery U. Pa. Sch. Medicine, Phila., 1995—, P.B. Magnuson prof. bone and joint surgery, 1996—; chief orthop. surgery Hosp. U. Pa., Phila., 1995—, VA Med. Ctr., Phila., Penn. Hosp.; dir. Penn Orthop. Inst., U. Pa. Health Sys., 1997—, cons. Ctr. Disease Control, Atlanta, 1981—, NIH, 1987, chmn. orthop. study sect., 1989-91; bd. dirs. Hutzel Hosp., Detroit, 1989-95. Assoc. editor Jour. Orthop. and Traumatology, 1978—, Jour. Bone Joint Surgery, 1982-86, Clin. Orthop. and Related Rsch., 1988—; trustee Jour. Bone Joint Surgery, 1987-92, sec. 1988-92, Hutzel Hosp., 1989-95. Mem. bd. edn. St. John's Grade Sch./Jr. H.S., Rochester, 1983-87; mem. Bd. Devel. Mayo Clinic, 1984-87; mem. bd. devel. St. John's Ch., 1988-89; trustee Lourdes H.S. Devel. Bd., Rochester, 1982-88. Served to capt. USAF, 1968-70. Decorated Air Commendation medal; recipient Kappa Delta award for musculoskeletal rsch., 1983; . Fellow Am. Acad. Orthop. Surgeons, Phila. Coll. Physicians; mem. Am. Orthopedic Assn., Rsch. Soc., AMA, Assn. Bone and Joint Surgeons, Internat. Soc. Microbiology, Zumbro County Med. Soc., Min-Da-Man Orthop. Soc., Minn. Orthopedic Soc., Am. Soc. Microbiology, N.Y. Acad. Scis., Am. Hip Soc. (Stinchfield award 1985, Charnley award 1986, 95, pres. 1993-94), Internat. Hip Soc., Am. Orthop. Assn. (N. Am. travelling fellow 1974, Am. Brit. Can. traveing fellow, 1981), Surg. Infection Soc. (charter mem.), Clin. Orthop. Soc., Internat. Soc. Orthop. Surgery and Traumatology, Mid-Am. Orthop. Soc. (bd. dirs. 1989-93, 94—, pres. elect 1994, pres. 1996), Detroit Acad. Orthop. Surgery, Mich. Orthop. Soc., Mich. State Med. Soc., Detroit Acad. Medicine, Pa. Orthop. Soc., Phila. Orthop. Soc., Phila. Acad. Medicine, Interurban Club, Sigma Xi, Kappa Delta, Alpha Epsilon Delta. Republican. Roman Catholic. Avocations: cross-country and downhill skiing. Home: 1218 Country Club Rd Gladwyne PA 19035-1418 Office: U Pa Dept Orthopaedic Surgery Sch Medicine II Silverstien Pavilion 3400 Spruce St Philadelphia PA 19104-4204

FITZGERALD, ROBERT MAURICE, financial executive; b. Chgo., Jan. 8, 1942; s. James Patrick and Catherine (McNulty) F.; children: Stephen, Peter, Susan, Martin. BS, Loyola U., Chgo., 1971; postgrad., U. Wis., 1974-76, Northwestern U., 1980. Sr. v.p. Fed. Reserve Bank, Chgo., 1979-85; pres. Chgo. Clearing House Assn., Chgo., 1985—; cons. Currency Bd., Abu Dhabi, United Arab Emirates, 1979; bd. dirs. Nat. Automated Clearing House Assn., Washington; advisor U.S. Coun. on Internat. Banking, N.Y.C. Pres. Coun. on Alcoholism, Ann Arbor, Mich., 1978, Diocesan Bd. Edn., Joliet, Ill., 1981-84; mem. bd. consultors Old St. Patrick's Ch., Chgo.; bd. dirs. Frances Xavier Warde Sch., 1989-91, trustee; vice chmn. Chgo. Crime Commn.; trustee Union Legue Boys and Girls Clubs, sec. Civic and Arts Found.; mem. adv. bd. St. Mary of Nazereth Hosp.; past pres., bd. dirs. v.chmn. exec. com. LaSalle St. Coun. Mem. Nat. Orgn. Clearing Houses (past pres., bd. dirs. Washington chpt.), Execs. Club of Chgo. (bd. dirs., treas.), Econ. Club Chgo., Union League Club (Chgo.) (1st v.p., chair long range plannig com.), Bankers Club Chgo. (sec., treas., exec. com.),. Democrat. Roman Catholic. Office: Chgo Clearing House Assn 230 S La Salle St Ste 700 Chicago IL 60604-1496

FITZGERALD, SCOTT, state legislator; b. Nov. 16, 1963; m. Lisa Fitzgerald; children: Scott William, Brennan, Connor. BS in Journalism, U. Wis., 1985. Senator Wis. State Dist. 13, 1994—; mem. com. on econ. devel., housing and govt. ops., com. on health, human svcs., aging, corrections, vets. and mil. affairs, spl. legis. coun. com. on recodification of fish and game laws, rural econ. devel. com. Wis. State Senate; owner Dodge County Ind. News, 1990—. Chmn. Dodge County (Wis.) Rep. Com.; planning com. City of Juneau, Wis.; former mem. Juneau Planning Commn. Major U.S. Army Res., 1981—. Mem. Juneau Area C. of C., Wis. Newspaper Assn. Address: N4692 Maple Rd Juneau WI 53039-9514*

FITZGERALD, SHARON HOLT, writer, consultant; b. Nashville, July 11, 1956; d. Henry Buford Holt and Sarah Etta Farris; m. John Lendell Fitzgerald, Aug. 26, 1978; 1 child, Kathleen Suzanne. BS in Mass. Comms., U. Tenn., 1978. Corr. Phila. Inquirer, 1980-82; press sec. U.S. Rep. Thomas Carper, Wilmington, 1982-83; chief of info. De. Dept. Natural Resources, Dover, 1983-87; marine info. coord. U. Del., Newark, 1987-89; comms. con. U. Tenn., Nashville, 1990-95; comms. dir. Tenn. Mcpl. League, Nashville, 1995-96; owner Sharon Fitzgerald Comms., Murfreesboro, Tenn., 1996—; adj. prof. Mid. Tenn. State U., Murfreesboro, 1998—; state coord. Project Wild Environ. Curriculum, Dover, 1984-87. Editor mag. Del. Conservationist, 1983-87; assoc. editor mag. Great Smokies, 1979. Recipient Take Pride in Am. award Pres. Ronald Reagan, 1988, Pub. Svc. Achievement award U. Tenn., 1991. Mem. Soc. Profl. Journalists (bd. dirs. Mid. Tenn. chpt. 1992—), Rutherford County C. of C. Democrat. Methodist. Avocation: golf. E-mail: Commfitz@aol.com. Home and Office: 234 Council Bluff Pkwy Murfreesboro TN 37129

FITZGERALD, SUSAN HELENA, elementary educator; b. Ft. Washington, Pa., Sept. 28, 1953; d. John Robert and Helen Etta (Groscost) Payne; m. Richard Michael Fitzgerald, June 8, 1974 (dec. June 1998); children: Kevin Michael, Gregory Thomas, Wendy Elaine. BS in Edn., West Chester (Pa.) U., 1975, M, Reading Specialist, 1992. Cert. reading specialist, elem., spl. edn. tchr. Head start tchr. Chester County IU, Coatesville, Pa., 1987-89; intermediate spl. edn. tchr. Coatesville Sch. Dist., 1989-91, 5th grade tchr., 1991-92, 1st grade tchr., 1992-97, instrl. support tchr., 1997-99, title I reading splst., 1999—; coach Spl. Olympics, Coatesville Sch. Dist., 1989-91, mem. instrn. support team, 1994—; summer sch. tchr. Youth Writing Project, 1995—. Tchr. Penningtonville Presbyn. Ch., Atglen, Pa., 1992-93.

Grantee Coatesville Sch. Dist., 1990, 92. Republican. Presbyterian. Avocations: reading, writing, sewing. Home: 175 Upper Valley Rd Christiana PA 17509-9771 Office: Rainbow Elem Sch 50 Country Club Rd Coatesville PA 19320-1813

FITZGERALD, SUSAN INGE, credit analyst; b. Göppingen, Germany, Oct. 24, 1968; d. John Dean and Heidi Marie (Nicklas) F.; m. Paul Wesley Dickson III, Apr. 22, 1995. AB cum laude, Occidental Coll., L.A., 1990; MA in Internat. Studies, Johns Hopkins U., Washington, 1992. Asst. program officer Internat. Found., Washington, 1992; asst. dir. devel. Johns Hopkins U., Washington, 1992-94; v.p., sr. credit officer Moody's Investors Svc., N.Y.C., 1994—. Mem. Phi Beta Kappa.

FITZGERALD, THOMAS JOE, psychologist; b. Wichita, Kans., July 8, 1941; s. Thomas Michael and Pauline Gladys (Zink) F.; B.A., San Francisco State U., 1965; M.A., U. Utah, 1969, Ph.D., 1971. Dir. behavioral services programs VA Hosp., Topeka, 1971-73; pvt. practice as psychologist, Topeka, 1973-74, Prairie Village, Kans., 1974—; clin. instr. Menninger Sch. Psychiatry, Topeka, 1972-74; v.p. Preferred Mental Health Care Mgmt., Inc., 1986-90, pres., Preferred Mental Health, Inc., 1990—; sec.-treas. Kans. Bd. Psychologist Examiners, 1976-79, 79-80, chmn., 1980—, chmn. psychology examining com.; mem. Behavioral Scis. Regulatory Bd., 1980-82; pres. Psychol. Services Corp., Prairie Village, 1974—. Mem. Gov.'s Commn. on Criminal Adminstrn., 1974-76; vice-chmn. Gov.'s Com. on Med. Assistance, 1978-80; mem. Mid-Am. Health Systems Agy., 1979-82; mem. com. on utilization review orgns. Kansas Ins. Commr. Adv. Com., 1994—. Served with USMC, 1958-61. Mem. Kans. Psychol. Assn. (pres. 1980-81), Kans. Assn. Profl. Psychologists (pres. 1981-82, Outstanding Psychologist award 1979, 80, 81, 82), Greater Kansas City Soc. Clin. Hypnosis (pres. 1978-85). Office: Preferred Mental Health Inc 8220 Robinson St Overland Park KS 66204-3626

FITZGERALD, THOMAS ROLLINS, university administrator; b. Washington, Feb. 23, 1922; s. Thomas Rollins and Bessie (Sheehy) F. BA, Woodstock (Md.) Coll., 1945, MA, 1948; S.T.L., Facultes St. Albert de Louvain, Belgium, 1953; PhD, U. Chgo., 1957. Joined Soc. of Jesus, 1939; ordained priest Roman Cath. Ch., 1952; instr. classics Novitiate St. Isaac Jogues, Wernersville, Pa., 1957-58; dean studies, asst. prof. classics Novitiate St. Isaac Jogues, 1958-64; dean Coll. Arts and Scis., Georgetown U., 1964-66, acad. v.p., 1966-73; pres. Fairfield (Conn.) U., 1973-79, St. Louis U., 1979-87; assoc. prof. fine arts and classics Loyola Coll., Balt., 1987-96, prof. emeritus, 1996—. Pres. Conn. Conf. Ind. Colls., 1975-77; mem. New Eng. Bd. Higher Edn., 1977-79; trustee Gonzaga H.S., Washington, 1969-74, 87-94; chmn. bd. trustees St. Peter's Coll., Jersey City, 1969-75; trustee U. Scranton, Pa., 1974-77, Boston Coll. H.S., 1976-79, Mo. Bot. Garden, 1981-87, U. Detroit, 1982-90, St. Joseph Prep. Sch., Phila., 1988-91; bd. dirs. Nat. Assn. Ind. Colls. and Univs., 1977-79, 82-85. Democrat. Office: 5704 Roland Ave Baltimore MD 21210-1334

FITZGERALD, TIKHON (LEE R. H. FITZGERALD), bishop; b. Detroit, Nov. 14, 1932; s. LeRoy and Dorothy Kaeding (Higgins) F. AB, Wayne State U., 1958. Ordained deacon, 1971, priest, 1978, bishop Eastern Orthodox, 1987. Enlisted U.S. Army, 1954-57; commd. 2 lt. USAF, 1960, advanced through grades to capt., 1971; air staff, 1966-71, released, 1971; protodeacon Holy Virgin Mary Russian Orthodox Cathedral, L.A., 1972-78, rector, archpriest, 1979-87; bishop of San Francisco and the West Orthodox Ch. in Am., L.A., 1987—. Recipient Order of St. Vladimir II Class, Patriarch Aleksy of Moscow, 1993. Democrat. Home: 649 Robinson St Los Angeles CA 90026-3612 Office: Orthodox Ch Am Diocese of the West 650 Micheltorena St Los Angeles CA 90026-3623*

FITZGERALD, TOM, professional soccer coach; b. Saratoga Spring, N.Y., Mar. 14, 1951; m. debi Fitzgerald; children: Shane, Jesse. BA in Phys. Edn., U. South Fla., 1973. Head coach Jesuit H.S., Tampa, 1978-80; asst. coach U. Tampa, 1980-84, head coach, 1987-96; head coach Columbus Crew, 1996—; nat. staff coach U.S. Soccer Fedn., "A" lic. coach; asst. U.S. Men's Nat. "B" team, 1990-94. Office: c/o Columbus Crew 77 E Nationwide Blvd Columbus OH 43215*

FITZGERALD, WILLIAM HENRY G., diplomat, corporation executive; b. Boston, Dec. 23, 1909; s. William Joseph and Mary Ellen (Smith) F.; m. Annelise Petschek, July 2, 1943; children: Desmond, Anne. BS, U.S. Naval Acad., 1931; postgrad., Harvard Law Sch., 1934-35; DSc (hon.), Adelphi U., 1962; LLD (hon.), Cath. U. Am., 1990; D in Pub. Svc. (hon.), Regis U., 1999. With Borden Co., N.Y.C., 1936-41; personal bus. interests Mexico, 1946-47; organized Metall. Research & Devel. Co., Washington, 1947, v.p., treas., 1947-56, pres., 1956-58, 60-82, chmn., 1960-82; chmn. bd. Nat. Metallizing Corp., Trenton, N.J., 1956-58; organizer FitzGerald Corp., 1959, pres., 1980—; chmn. bd. The Cottages, Ltd., Jamaica, 1960-70, Linden Corp., Washington, 1962-70, N.Am. Housing Corp., Washington, 1971-88; chmn. Supramar, Ltd., Lucerne, Switzerland, 1963-69, dir., 1970-75; pres. Nat. Media Analysis, Inc., Washington, 1968-70, chmn., 1970-72; ptnr. Hornblower & Weeks, Hemphill-Noyes, Inc., 1970-72, 1st v.p., 1972-77; vice chmn., dir., exec. com. Fin. Gen. Bankshares, Inc., 1977-82; vice chmn. African Devel. Found., 1990-92; U.S. amb. to Ireland, 1992-93; dir., mem. exec. com. First Am. Bank (N.A.), Washington, 1977-83; dir., mem. exec. com., chmn. investment com. Avemco Corp., Washington, Frederick, Md., 1970-89; Cosmadent, Ltd., Zurich, Switzerland, 1964-75, Chase Fund of Boston, Chase Convertible Fund, Income & Capital Shares Inc., 1970-75, Pyrotector, Inc., Hingham, Mass., 1963-76; cons. to dir. ICA, Washington, 1957; dep. dir. for mgmt. ICA, Dept. State, 1958-60; U.S. conciliator Internat. Center for Investment Disputes, 1975-82; dir. Inst. Inter Am. Affairs, 1958-60; mem. President's Adv. Bd. on Internat. Investments, 1976-78; treas. Presdl. Inaugural Com., 1981; trustee Presdl. Inaugural Trust, 1981-89; mem. nat. adv. com. Internat. Edn., 1982-85. Trustee Fed. City Coun., 1962-90, Wash. Inst. Fgn. Affairs, 1966—; bd. dirs. Atlantic Coun. U.S., 1976—, treas., 1979-92, mem. exec. com., 1980—, vice chmn., 1993—; trustee Fgn. Student Svc. Coun., 1963—, Oblate Coll. (Cath. U.), 1966—; trustee Corcoran Gallery Art, 1977-90, also mem. exec. com., chmn. devel. com.; pres. Soc. for a More Beautiful Nat. Capital, Inc., 1974-77; bd. dirs., mem. exec. com., sr. v.p. Internat. Tennis Hall of Fame, 1964-92, 94—; nat. chmn. Yorktown Internat. Bicentennial Com., 1981; dir., mem. exec. com. Washington Tennis Found., 1987—; U.S. del. Atlantic Treaty Assembly, Reykjavik, Iceland, 1977, Washington, 1979, Rome, 1983, Istanbul, Turkey, 1987, Brussels, 1989, Rome, 1996, sofia, 1997; grand officer Confrérie des Chevaliers du Tastevin, 1979—; grand senechal Sous Commanderie de Washington, 1980-90; trustee White House Preservation Fund, 1979-89, chmn., 1982-89, chmn. emeritus, 1989-90; mem. Nat. Task Force on Prison Industries; trustee, mem. nominating com. U.D.C., 1982-87; mem. nat. com. Vatican Judaica Exhbn., 1987-89; mem. Bretton Woods com., 1992—; mem., dir. Coun. of Am. Ambassadors, 1992—. Ensign USN, 1931-34; from lt. (j.g.) to comdr., 1941-46. Decorated Orden Militar de Ayacucho Peru, knight grand cross Sovereign Mil. Order Malta; knight grand cross Equestrian Order Holy Sepulchre; knight grand cross Sacred Mil. Constantinian Order St. George; elected Mid-Atlantic Tennis Hall of Fame, 1997. Mem. Fed. Assn. in U.S.A. Sovereign Mil. Order of Malta (pres. 1975-79), Assn. for Diplomatic Studies and Tng. (dir. 1993—), Army-Navy Country Club (Washington), Univ. Club (Washington), Harvard Club (Washington), River Club (N.Y.C.), Met. Club (Washington), Essex Country Club (Manchester, Mass.), Portmarnock Golf Club (Dublin, Ireland), FitzWilliam Lawn Tennis Club (Dublin). Roman Catholic. Home: 2305 Bancroft Pl NW Washington DC 20008-4005 Office: Ste 1105 1730 Rhode Island Ave NW Washington DC 20036-3111

FITZGERALD-VERBONITZ, DIANNE ELIZABETH, nursing educator; b. Tampa, Fla., July 11, 1943; d. James Gerald and Bernice Elizabeth (Creel) F.; children: Deborah Elizabeth Guilbault Starr, Fred Anthony Guilbault Jr. AA summa cum laude, Montgomery Coll., 1979; BS in Health Svcs., No. Ariz. U., 1985, MEd, 1987. Nurse in Washington Internship, 1989, Advanced Internship, 1990. Orthopaedic nurse clinician Phoenix, pvt. practice counselor; mem. faculty C.V. Mosby Co., St. Louis; nurse clinician in orthopedics; mgr. orthopedic program Kimberly Quality Care; adminstr. Staff Builders Health Svcs, Phoenix; utilization mgr. CCN, Phoenix, 1998—. Bd. dirs. Valley of Sun Sch. and Rehab. Ctr., Arthritis Found.; mem. Am. Vol. Med. Team; med. vol. Habitat for Humanity. Named one of Top Ten Bus. Women in Managed Health Care, Today's Ariz. Woman, 1998. Mem. Nat. Assn. Orthopedic Nurses (pres. 1989-90), Assn. Rehab. Nurses, Case Mgmt. Soc. Am., Phi Kappa Phi (life). Office: CCN 3636 N Central Ave Ste 950 Phoenix AZ 85012-1971

FITZGIBBON, DANIEL HARVEY, lawyer; b. Columbus, Ind., July 7, 1942; s. Joseph Bales and Margaret Lenore (Harvey) FitzG.; m. Joan Helen Meltzer, Aug. 12, 1973; children: Katherine Lenore, Thomas Bernard. BS in Engring., U.S. Mil. Acad., 1964; JD cum laude, Harvard U., 1972. Bar: Ind. 1972; U.S. Dist. Ct. (so. dist.) Ind. 1972, U.S. Tax Ct. 1977. Commd. 2d lt. U.S. Army, 1964, advanced through grades to capt., 1967; served with inf. U.S. Army, West Berlin, Vietnam; resigned U.S. Army, 1969; assoc. Barnes & Thornburg, Indpls., 1972-79, ptnr., 1979-98, 99—, mem. mgmt. com., 1983-95; speaker various insts. Mem. Sch. Bd. Met. Sch. Dist. Lawrence Twp., 1988-96, pres., 1990-91, 94-95; bd. advs. Eiteljorg Mus. Am. Indian and Western Art. Capt. U.S. Army, 1964-69, Vietnam. Fellow Am. Coll. Tax Counsel, Am. Bar Found.; mem. ABA (tax and bus. law sects.), Am. Law Inst., Ind. State Bar Assn. (tax sect.), Indpls. Bar Assn. (chmn. tax sect. 1982-83, coun. 1982-86), Indpls. Athletic Club, Lawyers Club, Woodstock Club. Home: 6460 Lawrence Dr Indianapolis IN 46226-1035 Office: Barnes & Thornburg 1313 Merchants Bank Bldg Indianapolis IN 46204-3506

FITZGIBBONS, ELEANOR ELIZABETH, retired English educator; b. Sept. 20, 1909. PhD, Cath. U. Am., 1942. Prof. emeritus Marygrove Coll., Detroit, 1973—, poet in residence, 1995—. Home: 8500 Marygrove Dr Detroit MI 48221

FITZGIBBONS, JOHN P., nephrologist; b. Boston, Dec. 3, 1938; s. John Patrick and Helen (Walsh) F.; m. Beverly Elizabeth Adams, June 6, 1964; children: Kathleen, Michael, Stacey, Matthew. BA, Coll. Holy Cross, 1960; MD, SUNY, 1964. Resident Boston City Hosp., 1964-66; rsch. fellow Mayo Clinic, Rochester, Minn., 1966-68; resident U. Calif., San Francisco, 1968-70; fellow in nephrology Tufts New Eng. Med. Ctr., Boston, 1970-73; nephrologist, chief nephrology Baystate Med. Ctr., Springfield, Mass., 1973-88; chair dept. medicine Lehigh Valley Hosp., Allentown, Pa., 1988—. Fellow Am. Coll. Physicians; mem. Internat. Soc. Nephrology, Am. Fedn. Clin. Rsch., Am. Coll. Physician Execs., Assn. Program Dirs. in Internal Medicine, Am. Soc. Nephrology. Office: Lehigh Valley Hosp Cedar Crest I-78 Allentown PA 18105-1556

FITZHUGH, DAVID MICHAEL, lawyer; b. San Francisco, Nov. 24, 1946; s. William DeHart and Betty Jean (Jeffries) F.; m. Jenny Lu Conner, Dec. 22, 1967; children: Ross DeHart, Cameron Hyatt, Michael Jeffries. Student Carleton Coll., 1964-67; B.A., Coll. William and Mary, 1972; J.D., U. Va., 1975. Bar: D.C. 1975, U.S. Dist. Ct. D.C. 1979, U.S. Dist. Ct. Md. 1987, U.S. Ct. Claims 1980, U.S. Ct. Appeals (fed. cir.) 1982, U.S. Ct. Appeals (D.C. cir.) 1987, U.S. Ct. Appeals (4th cir.) 1989, U.S. Supreme Ct. 1982. Assoc. McKenna & Cuneo, Washington, 1975-80, ptnr., 1980-98, chmn. litigation dept., 1984-94; assoc. counsel Office of Counsel, Naval Air Systems Command, 1999—. Mem. editl. bd. Nat. Contract Mgmt. Assn. Jour., 1975—. Contbr. articles to legal publs. Capt. USMC, 1967-71, Vietnam. Mem. ABA (litigation sect., discovery com. pub. contracts sect.). Home: 13261 Clipper Cir Solomons MD 20688-3022 Office: Office of Counsel AIR 7.7 Bldg 2272 Ste 257 47123 Buse Rd Unit IPT Patuxent River MD 20670-1547

FITZ-HUGH, GLASSELL SLAUGHTER, JR., bank executive; b. Charlottesville, Va., May 2, 1939; s. Glassell Slaughter and Dorothea (Meredith) Fitz-H.; m. Susan Harrison, May 11, 1963; children: G.S. III, Meredith H. BA in Sociology, U. Va., 1962; grad., Stonier Grad. Sch. Banking, 1970. Asst. v.p. Va. Nat. Bank, Martinsville, 1964-67, v.p., 1967-73; regional exec. Va. Nat. Bank, Richmond, 1981-84; pres. Va. Nat. Bank of Henry County, Martinsville, 1973-76, Va. Trust Co., Richmond, 1976-81; regional exec. Sovran Bank, Richmond, 1984-89; exec. v.p. Sovran Bank/ Nations Bank, Bethesda, Md., 1989-93; sr. v.p. Nations Bank Mid-Atlantic, Washington, 1993-96; pres. Nations Banks Greater Washington, 1996—. Mem. Martinsville City Coun., 1974-76; mayor City of Martinsville, 1976; pres. Westminster Canterberry, Richmond, 1978-79; chmn. United Way, Richmond, 1988; bd.dirs. Md. C. of C., Greater Washington Bd. Trade, Fed. City Coun. Mem. U. Va. Alumni Assn. (pres. Richmond chpt. 1985), Farmington Country Club, Country Club of Va., Commonwealth Club, Rotary (pres. Martinsville chpt. 1975). Episcopalian. Home: 7608 Arrowood Rd Bethesda MD 20817-2827 Office: Nations Bank 1501 Pennsylvania Ave NW Washington DC 20005-1015

FITZHUGH, WILLIAM WYVILL, JR., printing company executive; b. Bklyn., June 27, 1914; s. William Wyvill and Portia (Starr) F.; m. Florence Hardy, Dec. 13, 1941; children: William, Priscilla, John, Portia. AB, Dartmouth Coll., 1935; BA, Trinity Coll., Cambridge U., 1937, MA, 1938; M in Philosophy, Columbia U., 1977; JD, Pace U. Law Sch., 1980. Fellow Carnegie Endowment for Internat. Peace, 1938-39; sec. rapporteur Internat. Studies Conf., League of Nations, 1938-39; instr. govt. Columbia U., 1939-42; pres. William W. Fitzhugh, Inc., 1945-99, chmn. bd. dirs.; pres. New Haven Bd. & Carton Co., Inc., 1960-64; ptnr. Dalsemer, Fitzhugh & Catzen, N.Y.C., 1964-66; pres. Newspaper Preprint Corp., N.Y.C., 1966-75. Past chmn. Chappaqua Orchestral Assn. Lt. USNR. Mem. Gravure Tech. Assn. (past pres.), Folding Paper Box Assn Am. (past pres. met. N.Y. group), Label Mfrs. Assn. (past dir.), Bklyn. C. of C. (past dir.), Phi Beta Kappa, Sigma Chi. Republican. Episcopalian. Home: 253 Kendal at Hanover 80 Lyme Rd Hanover NH 03755-1225 Office: 148 Main St Montpelier VT 05602 *A long life's enough, there's no need to be famous: just live, while you live: Dum Vivimus Vivamus!.*

FITZMAURICE, CATHERINE THERESA, auditor; b. Cleve., Dec. 11, 1955; d. Thomas Joseph and Margret (Collins) F. BA, Notre Dame Coll., Cleve., 1980; MBA, Cleve. State U., 1990, M in Acctg. and Fin. Info. Syss., 1995. CPA, Ohio; CMA, CIA. Asst. auditor Ohio State Auditors Office, Cleve., 1992—; adj. prof. Ursuline Coll., Cleve., 1995-97. Contbr. articles to profl. jours. John Huntington grantee, 1980; IMA Cleve. East scholar, 1995. Mem. Ohio Soc. CPAs, Inst. Internal Auditors, Inst. Mgmt. Accts., Info. Sys. Auditors Computer Assn., Sigma Beta Gamma. Roman Catholic. Avocation: hiking. Home: 3480 Tuttle Ave Cleveland OH 44111-3027 Office: State Auditor's Office 12th Fl Lausche Bldg 615 Superior NW Cleveland OH 44113

FITZMAURICE, LAURENCE DORSET, bank executive; b. Worcester, Mass., Aug. 7, 1938; s. John Vincent and Alice (Earle) F.; m. Ann McQuaid, Apr. 15, 1961; children: Laura, Peter, Meghan. BS in Mgmt., Babson Coll., 1959; postgrad. in law, Boston Coll., 1961. Prodn. control Sylvania, Needham, Mass., 1959-61; div. controller EG&G, Inc., Bedford, Mass., 1961-69; asst. corp. controller Tyco Labs., Waltham, Mass., 1970; corp. controller Analog Devices, Norwood, Mass., 1971-73; v.p. fin. Balco, Inc., Newton, Mass., 1974-75; comptroller Commonwealth of Mass., Boston, 1976-78, commr. of revenue, 1978; sr. cons. Am. Mgmt. Systems, Arlington, Va., 1979; prin. cons. Boston, 1980-81; sr. v.p. State St. Bank & Trust Co., Boston, 1982—; adj. prof. Northeastern U. Grad. Sch. Polit. Sci., Boston, 1977-78; mem. faculty New Eng. Coll. Fin., 1998—; mem. Bd. Bank Incorp., Boston, 1978. Commr. Mass. State Lottery, Braintree, 1976-78; sec. Mass. Housing Fin. Agy., Boston, 1978; pres. Human Rels. Svc., Wellesley, Mass., 1988-89, trustee, 1986—; bd. dirs. Social Policy Rsch. Group, Boston, 1981-92, Boston Mcpl. Rsch. Bur., 1985—, exec. com. 1999—; mem. allocations com. United Way of Mass. Bay, 1998, multi-yr. audit task force, 1999; bd. overseers USS Constitution Mus., 1999—. Cpl. USMCR, 1957-63. Democrat. Roman Catholic. Club: Union of Boston. Avocations: tennis, golf.

FITZMYER, JOSEPH AUGUSTINE, theology educator, priest; b. Phila., Nov. 4, 1920; s. Joseph Augustine and Anna Catherine (Alexy) F. AB, Loyola U., Chgo., 1943, AM, 1945; Licentiate in Sacred Theology, Facultés St. Albert de Louvain, Belgium, 1952; PhD, Johns Hopkins U., 1956; Licentiate in Sacred Scripture, Pontifical Bibl. Inst., 1957. Joined S.J., 1938, ordained priest Roman Cath. Ch., 1951. Asst. prof. N.T. and Bibl. langs. Woodstock (Md.) Coll., 1958-59, assoc. prof., 1959-64, prof., 1964-69; prof. Aramaic and Hebrew dept. Nr. Ea. langs.-civilizations U. Chgo., 1969-71; prof. N.T. and Bibl. langs. dept. theology Fordham U., Bronx, N.Y., 1971-74, Weston Jesuit Sch. Theology, Cambridge, Mass., 1974-76; prof. dept. Bibl. studies Cath. U. Am., Washington, 1976—; tchr. Gonzaga H.S., Washington, 1945-48; Spkr.'s lectr. Bibl. studies Oxford (Eng.) U., 1974-75. Author: Essays on the Semitic Background of the New Testament, 1971, The Genesis Aprocryphon on Qumran Cave I, 1966, 2d edit., 1971; editor (with R.E. Brown and R.E. Murphy) The New Jerome Biblical Commentary, 1990; The Gospel According to Luke (Anchor Bible), vol. 28, 1981, vol. 28A, 1985, Romans (Anchor Bible), vol. 33, 1993, The Acts of the Apostles, vol. 31, 1998. Mem. Cath. Bibl. Assn. (pres. 1970, editor Quar. 1980-84), Soc. Bibl. Lit. (pres. 1978-79, editor Jour. 1971-76), Studiorum Novi Testamenti Societas (pres. 1992-93). Home: Georgetown U Jesuit Cmty PO Box 571200 Washington DC 20057-1200

FITZPATRICK, CHRISTINE MORRIS, legal administrator, former television executive; b. Steubenville, Ohio, June 10, 1920; d. Roy Elwood and Ruby Lorena (Mason) Morris; student U. Chgo., 1943-44, U. Ga., 1945-46; m. T. Mallary Fitzpatrick, Jr., Dec. 19, 1942; 1 child, Thomas Mallary III. BA, Roosevelt U., 1947; postgrad. Trinity Coll., Hartford, Conn., 1970. Assoc. dir. Joint Human Rels. Project, City of Chgo., 1965-66; tchr. English, Austin Sch. for Girls, Hartford, 1966-70; promotion coord. Conn. Pub. TV, Hartford, 1971-72, dir. community rels., 1972-73, v.p., 1973-77; pub. rels./pub. affairs cons. Commonwealth Edison Co., Chgo., 1977-79; dir. spl. events Chgo. Public TV, 1979-84; v.p. Fitzpatrick Group, Inc., Chgo., 1986-88; adminstrv. dir. Fitzpatrick Law Offices, 1988-94, Fitzpatrick Eilenberg & Zivian, 1994-96; adminstrv. dir. Fitzpatrick Law Offices, Chgo., 1997—; v.p. Pub. Rels. Clinic Chgo., 1980-81. Bd. advisers Greater Hartford Mag., 1975-77; bd. dirs. World Affairs Ctr., Hartford, 1975-77; mem. adv. coun. Am. Revolution Bicentennial Commn. Conn., 1975-77. Mem. Pub. Rels. Soc. Am. (dir. Conn. Valley chpt. 1976-77), Am. Women in Radio and TV (New Eng. chpt. pres. 1976-77), LWV (Chgo. chpt. pres. 1962-64, Hartford chpt. v.p. 1971-73). Home: 5518 S Harper Ave Chicago IL 60637-1830

FITZ-PATRICK, DAVID, endocrinologist, educator; b. Burnley, Lancashire, England, Sept. 1, 1951; came to U.S., 1975; s. Malcolm Milligan and Ada (Maguire) F.; m. Elizabeth Joaquin, Dec. 30, 1972; children: Ian Rodney, Claire Larissa. MB, BS, U. Newcastle-Upon-Tyne, England, 1974. House officer Newcastle (England) Gen. Hosp., 1974-75; resident in internal medicine U. Md. Hosp., Balt., 1975-77; fellow in endocrinology McGill U., Montreal, Que., Can., 1977-81; cons. physician Straub Clinic and Hosp, Honolulu, 1981-91, chief of endocrinology, 1986-91; asst. clin. prof. medicine John Burns Sch. Medicine, Honolulu, 1982-95, assoc. clin. prof., 1995—; med. dir. Diabetes and Hormone Ctr. of Pacific, Honolulu, 1990—, East-West Med. Rsch. Inst., 1999—; mem. house of dels. Hawaii Med. Assn., 1987-90; med. adv. com. Bd. Med. Examiners, Hawaii, 1989—; founding mem., bd. dirs. Juvenile Diabetes Found., Honolulu, 1989-92 (Geraldine Fleming Meml. fellowship 1980-81); dir. East-West Med. Rsch. Inst., 1999—. Contbr. articles to profl. jours.; founder, editor Diabetes & Endocrinology Home Page on Internet. Dir. The Straub Found., Honolulu, 1984-90. Rsch. scholar McGill U., 1977-80. Fellow Am. Coll. Physicians (mem. coun. 1990-93, Gov's prize 1986), Am. Coll. Endocrinology; mem. Am. Diabetes Assn. (pres. 1984-86, 93-94), The Endocrine Soc., Am. Soc. Internal Medicine, Am. Assn. Clin. Endocrinologists (state chair 1992-96, 98—). Avocations: reading, family, tennis, golf. Office: 1329 Lusitana St Ste 304 Honolulu HI 96813-2411

FITZPATRICK, DENNIS MICHAEL, information systems executive; b. Jacksonville, Fla., Jan. 10, 1945; s. John J. Fitzpatrick and Roxanne (Cotsakis) Athanassiades; m. Kathleen Irene McDonough, June 10, 1967; children: Michael, Kara. BS, Manhattan Coll., 1967; MBA, CUNY, 1970. Mgr., system engr. Am. Airlines, N.Y.C., 1967-72; v.p. info. systems Western Airlines, L.A., 1972-87; pres. Info. Resources Assn., L.A., 1987-88; v.p. Pacific Info. Mgmt., Culver City, Calif., 1988-92; pres. Pacific Info. Mgmt., Inc., Canada, 1992-93; exec. dir. Knowledgeware, Inc., Newport Beach, Calif., 1993-94; v.p. Sterling Software, Woodland Hills, Calif., 1994—. Contbg. author: Information Engineering Management Guide, 1989, Information Strategy Planning, 1991, Business Area Analysis, 1990, Information Resource Assessment, 1990. Bd. dirs. Internat. Road Race Assn., 1996—, Internat. Child Abuse Network, 1997—. Named one of Outstanding Young Men Am., 1982. Office: 5900 Canoga Ave Woodland Hills CA 91367-5009

FITZPATRICK, DUROSS, federal judge; b. Macon, Ga., Oct. 19, 1934; s. Mark W. and Jane L. (Duross) F.; m. Beverly O'Connor, Mar. 17, 1963; children: Mark O'Connor, Devon Hart. B.S. in Forestry, U. Ga., 1961, LL.B., 1966. Bar: Ga. 1965. Assoc. Elliott & Davis, Macon, 1966-67; sole practice, Cochran, Ga., 1967-83; ptnr. Fitzpatrick & Mullis, Cochran, 1983-86; judge U.S. Dist. Ct. (mid. dist.) Ga., Macon, 1986-95, chief judge, 1995—; bd. govs. State Bar Ga., 1976-83, mem. exec. com., 1979-84, pres., 1984-85; mem. Ga. Chief Justice's Commn. on Professionalism. Legal counsel Republican del. Gen. Assembly Ga., 1969. Served with USMC, 1954-57. Fellow Am. Bar Found., Ga. Bar Found.; mem. Oconee Bar Assn. (pres. 1970), Am. Inns Ct. (master of the Bench, Joseph Henry Lumpkin chpt.), Macon Bar Assn. Republican. Episcopalian. Home: RR 1 Box 1525 Jeffersonville GA 31044-9768 Office: US Dist Ct PO Box 1014 425 Mulberry St Macon GA 31202*

FITZPATRICK, ELLEN, economist, consultant; b. Newark, June 22, 1957; d. Robert and Joan M. (Tampany) F. BA, Rutgers U., 1979; MS, Poly. U., White Plains, N.Y. Asst. staff mgr. N.Y. Telephone, N.Y.C., 1980-82, staff specialist, 1982-84, staff mgr., 1984-86, assoc. dir., 1986-87; sr. cons. KPMG Peat Marwick, Short Hills, N.J., 1987-89, mgr., 1989-91, sr. mgr., 1991-93; sr. mgr. Arthur Andersen & Co., Chgo., 1993-96; dir. Fin. Mgmt. CP&M Ameritech Network Svcs., 1996—. Mem. Am. Econ. Assn., Nat. Assn. Bus. Economists. Home: 415 W Aldine Ave Apt 15-a Chicago IL 60657-3602 Office: Ameritech Rm 2F08 2000 W Ameritech Center Dr Hoffman Estates IL 60196

FITZPATRICK, HAROLD FRANCIS, lawyer; b. Jersey City, Oct. 16, 1947; s. Harold G. and Anne Marie F.; m. Joanne M. Merry, Sept. 22, 1973; children: Elizabeth, Kevin, Matthew, Christopher. AB, Boston Coll., 1969; MBA, NYU, 1971; JD, Harvard U., 1974. Bar: N.J. 1974, U.S. Dist. Ct. N.J. 1974, U.S. Ct. Internat. Trade, 1986, U.S. Supreme Ct. 1994. Securities analyst Chase Manhattan Bank, N.Y.C., 1970-71, Brown Bros., Harriman & Co., N.Y.C., 1971; staff asst. U.S. Senate, Washington, 1972; law clk. to assoc. justice N.J. Supreme Ct., Trenton, 1974-75; assoc. Cleary, Gottlieb, Steen & Hamilton, N.Y.C., 1975-78; mng. ptnr. Fitzpatrick & Waterman, Secaucus, N.J., 1978—, Bayonne, N.J., 1978—, Hackettstown, N.J., 1996—; gen. counsel Housing Authority City of Bayonne, 1976—, Color Pigments Mfrs. Assn., Alexandria, Va., 1978—, N.J. Assn. Housing and Redevel. Authorities, Brick, N.J., 1979—, Housing Authority Town of Secaucus, N.J., 1980-88, Rahway (N.J.) Geriatrics Ctr. Inc., 1981-92, Housing Authority City of Englewood, N.J., 1985-91, Housing Authority City of Rahway, 1986—, Edgewater Mcpl. Utilities Authority, 1986-93, Housing Authority City of Woodbridge, N.J., 1988-94, Housing Authority City of Asbury Pk., N.J., 1991-94, Bd. Edn. City of Rahway, 1994-97, N.J. Pub. Housing Authority Joint Ins. Fund, 1995—. Mem. ABA, N.J. Bar Assn., Hudson County Bar Assn. (trustee, officer 1984-92, pres. 1993), Beta Gamma Sigma. Office: Fitzpatrick & Waterman 400 Plaza Dr Secaucus NJ 07094-3605

FITZPATRICK, JAMES DAVID, lawyer; b. Syracuse, N.Y., Oct. 21, 1938; s. William Francis and Margaret Mary (Shortt) F. *Mr. Fitzpatrick's twin brothers, Francis and William, have courageously worked to overcome their affliction of cerebral palsy. They have been great examples and inspirations to him to become all that he can be in order to serve God and others and to be a true world citizen.* BS, Holy Cross Coll., Worcester, Mass., 1960; JD, Syracuse U., 1963. Bar: N.Y. 1963, U.S. Dist. Ct. (no. dist.) N.Y. 1965. Assoc. Bond, Schoeneck & King, Syracuse, N.Y., 1963-76, mem., 1976-88, ptnr., 1988—; pres. Hiscock Legal Aid Soc., Syracuse, 1975-76; faculty Nat. Bus. Inst., Eau Claire, Wis., 1990—; del. Russian Conf. on Banking-The Kremlin, Moscow, 1992, 93. Mem. presdl. Roundtable, Washington, 1991-92; founding mem. pres.'s task force Nat. Coalition Against Pornography, Common Cause; chmn. adv. bd. Rep. Nat. Coms., 1994; mem. The Studio Mus. in Harlem, Am. Mus. Nat. History; founding mem. Am. Air Mus.; nat. adv. coun. USN Meml. Found. Recipient Afghanistan Freedom Fighter award Afghan Mercy Fund, 1989, Rep. Senatorial Medal of Freedom, Honored Friend of El Salvador award, 1991. Mem. ABA, NAACP, N.Y. State Bar Assn., Onondaga County Bar Assn. (chmn. real estate com. 1990-96), Internat. Bar Assn., Am. Land Title Assn., UN Assn. of U.S.A.,

Habitat for Humanity Internat., Amnesty Internat. U.S.A., Nat. Audubon Soc., Ctr. for Nat. Independence in Politics, Smithsonian Nat. Assocs., Nat. Trust for Hist. Preservation, Navy League U.S., World Future Soc., Ams. Guild, Internat. Platform Assn. (spkr. Internat. Youth Ctr., New Delhi), Inst. Global Ethics. Republican. Roman Catholic. Avocations: housing education, reading, walking. Home: 201 Croyden Rd Syracuse NY 13224-1917 Office: Bond Schoeneck & King 1 Lincoln Ctr Fl 18 Syracuse NY 13202-1324

FITZPATRICK, JAMES FRANKLIN, lawyer; b. Bluffton, Ind., Jan. 18, 1933; s. Raymond North and Evelyn (Baughman) F.; m. Sandra McNear, July 22, 1961; children: Michael, David, Benjamin. AB, Ind. U., 1955, JD, 1959; postgrad., Cambridge U., 1956. Law clk. to chief judge U.S. Ct. Appeals, Chgo., 1959-61; assoc. Arnold & Porter, Washington, 1961-67, ptnr., 1967—; adj. prof. law Georgetown U., Washington, 1971-75; acad. vis. London Sch. Econs., 1978-79, Trinity Coll., Dublin, Ireland, 1987-88; vice chmn. bd. dirs. Internat. Human Rights Law Group, 1994—; vis. prof. law U. N.Mex., 1997. Author: Law and Roadside Hazards, 1975. Bd. dirs. ACLU, 1983-85, pres. Nat. Capital chpt., Washington, 1982-83; pres. Washington Project for the Arts, 1984-90, Ctr. for Auto Safety, 1984—, The Phillips Collection, 1990—, The Shakespeare Theatre, 1991—, Site Santa Fe, 1997—; Ctr. for Arts and Culture, 1998—; nat. chmn. Young Citizens for Johnson, 1964. Mem. ABA, Phi Beta Kappa. Democrat. Presbyterian. Office: Arnold & Porter 555 12th St NW Washington DC 20004-1206

FITZPATRICK, JOHN HENRY, insurance company executive; b. Chgo., Nov. 1, 1956; s. John Michael; m. Susan Gail Beaman, June 15, 1985; children: Sarah, Kevin, Michael, Brian. BBA, Loyola U., Chgo., 1979. CPA; CFA. Fin. analyst Kemper Corp., Long Grove, Ill., 1978-79, dir. investor rels., 1979-86, v.p. fin., 1986-90, CFO, sr. v.p., dir., 1990-93, exec. v.p., CFO, dir., 1993-96; mng. dir., sr. v.p. Zurich (Switzerland) Ctr. Resource, Ltd., Zurich Ins. Group, 1996-98; sr. pres. Fla. Select Ins. Holdings, Inc. and subs., 1996-98; sr. mng. dir. Securitas Capital, L.L.C., Zurich, 1998; CFO, mem. exec. bd. Swiss Reins. Co., Zurich, 1998—. James S. Kemper Found. scholar, 1974-78. Mem. Investment Analyst Soc. Chgo., Ill. Soc. CPAs and Fin. Execs. Inst. Republican. Roman Catholic. Avocations: sailing, golf. Fax: 41-1-285-6786. E-mail: johnh-fitzpatrick@swissre.com. Office: Swiss Reinsurance Co, Mythenquai 50/60, CH-8022 Zurich Switzerland

FITZPATRICK, JOHN J., bishop; b. Trenton, Ont., Can., Oct. 12, 1918; s. James John and Lorena (Pelkey) F. Ed., Propaganda Fide Coll., Italy, Our Lady of Angels Sem.; B.A., Niagara U., 1941. Ordained priest Roman Catholic Ch., 1942. Titular bishop of Cenae and Aux. of Miami Fla., 1968-71; bishop of Brownsville Tex., 1971-91; bishop emeritus, 1991—. Office: 1904 Barnard Rd Brownsville TX 78520-8247

FITZPATRICK, JOSEPH LLOVERAS, artist, art educator; b. Louisville, Dec. 11, 1925; s. Joseph William and Henriette Lloveras F.; m. Ruth Lerman; children: Josephine, Michael, Tamara. BS, U. Louisville, 1955, MA, 1972. Editor-in-chief Arts in Louisville Mag., 1955-58; instr. Bellarmine Coll., Louisville, 1956-58; art dir. Hi Fi/Stereo Rev. League, N.Y.C., 1959-60; asst. prof. Columbus (Ohio) Coll. Art, 1960-61; chair found. program Ohio State U., Columbus, 1961-69; chair dept. art U. Ky., Lexington, 1974-92; exec. dir., art tchr. Worldscape, Louisville, 1991—. One-man shows include Tri Art Gallery, Louisville, 1998. Sgt. USAF, 1944-46. Residency, Tyrone Guthrie Ctr. Arts, 1999. Democrat. Avocations: gardening, reading, travelling. E-mail: worldscape@ibm.net. Home: 709 S Third St Louisville KY 40202

FITZPATRICK, JOYCE J., nursing educator, former dean. BSN, Georgetown U., LHD (hon.), 1990; MS in Psychiatric-Mental Health Nursing, Ohio State U.; PhD in Nursing, NYU; MBA, Case Western Reserve U., 1992. Dean Frances Payne Bolton Sch. Nursing Case Western Reserve U., Cleve., 1982-97, Elizabeth Brooks Ford prof. nursing, 1998—; dir. WHO Collaborating Ctr. for Nursing Bolton Sch. Editor Applied Nursing Rsch.; co-editor Annual Rev. Nursing Rsch.; contbr. articles to profl. jours. Recipient Am. Jour. Nursing Book of Yr. awards, Midwest Nursing Rsch. Soc. Disting. Contrbn. to Nursing Rsch. award, Pub. Health Svc. Primary Care Policy fellow, 1995; Inst. Medicine/Am. Acad. Nursing/Am. Nurses Found. scholar, 1994-95. Fellow Am. Acad. Nursing; mem. N.Am. Nursing Diagnosis Assn. (chair taxonomy com.). Office: Case Western Res U Frances Payne Bolton Sch Nursing Abington Dr Cleveland OH 44106-4904*

FITZPATRICK, LOIS ANN, library administrator; b. Yonkers, N.Y., Mar. 27, 1952; d. Thomas Joseph and Dorothy Ann (Nealy) Sullivan; m. William George Fitzpatrick, Jr., Dec. 1, 1973; children: Jennifer Ann, Amy Ann. BS in Sociology, Mercy Coll., 1974; MLS, Pratt Inst., 1975. Clk. Yonkers (N.Y.) Pub. Library, 1970-73, librarian trainee, 1973-75, librarian I, 1975-76; reference librarian Carroll Coll. Library, Helena, Mont., 1976-79, acting dir., 1979, asst. prof., 1979-89, dir., 1980—, assoc. prof., 1989—; chmn. arrangements Mont. Gov.'s Pre White House Conf. on Libraries, Helena, 1977-78; mem. steering com. Reference Point coop. program for librs., 1991; mem. adv. com. Helena Coll. of Tech. Libr., 1994—; adv. coun. Mont. Libr. Svcs., 1996—; mem. Networking Task Force, Laws Revision Task Force. Pres. elect Helena Area Health Sci. Libraries Cons., 1979-84, pres., 1984-88; bd. dirs. Mont. FAXNET; co-chmn. interest group OCLC; chmn. local arrangements Mont. Gov.'s Pre White House Conf.; mem. adv. bd. Helena Coll. of Tech.; bd. dirs. Mont. Race for the Cure. Mem. Mont. Library Assn. (task force for White House conf. 1991, chair govt. affairs com. 1996—, mem. EdLINK-MT, 1997—). Democrat. Roman Catholic. Club: Soroptimist Internat. of Helena (2d v.p. 1984-85, pres. 1986-87). Home: 1308 Shirley Rd Helena MT 59602-6635 Office: Carroll Coll.-Jack & Sallie Corette Libr. 1601 N Benton Ave Helena MT 59625-0001

FITZPATRICK, M. LOUISE, nursing educator; b. South River, N.J., May 24, 1942; d. John Francis and Bettina (Galassi) F. Diploma in nursing, Johns Hopkins U., 1963; BSN, Cath. U. Am., 1966; MA, Columbia U., 1968, MEd, 1969, EdD, 1972; cert., Harvard U., 1985. Former assoc. prof., dept. nursing edn. Tchrs. Coll., Columbia U., N.Y.C.; dean, prof. Villanova (Pa.) U. Coll. Nursing, 1978—; cons. Mid. States Assn., Phila.; cons. to numerous univs., also univs. in Morocco, Egypt, Jordan, West Bank, Sultanate of Oman; cons., reviewer USPHS; bd. dirs. Nurses Ednl. Funds, Inc., N.Y.C. Author: The National Organization for Public Nursing, Development of a Practice Field, 1975; editor: Present Realities/Future Imperatives, 1977, Historical Studies in Nursing, 1978, Nursing in Society: A Historical Perspective, 1983; also 21 articles in profl. jours. Recipient Disting. Alumni award Columbia U. Tchrs. Coll., 1966, Cath. Univ. McManus medal, 1992; WHO fellow, Scandinavia and U.K., 1974; Am. Acad. Nursing fellow, 1978. Mem. Am. Nurses Assn. (past chmn. cabinet on nursing edn.), Am. Assn. Colls. Nursing, Nat. League for Nursing (bd. of govs.). Democrat. Roman Catholic. Avocations: music, theater, cooking, international travel. Home: 80 Woodstone Ln Villanova PA 19085-1425 Office: Villanova U Coll Nursing Villanova PA 19085

FITZPATRICK, MARK, professional hockey player; b. Toronto, Ont., Can., Nov. 13, 1968. Goaltender N.Y. Islanders, 1989-93, Quebec Nordiques, 1993, Florida Panthers, 1993-97, Tampa Bay Lightning, 1997-98, Chgo. Blackhawks, 1998—. Recipient Bill Masterton Meml. trophy, 1991-92, Top Goaltender trophy, 1985-86, Meml. Cup All-Star team, 1986-87, 87-88. Office: Chgo Blackhawks United Ctr 1901 W Madison St Chicago IL 60612*

FITZPATRICK, NANCY HECHT, magazine editor; b. Dec. 29, 1942; d. Ira Youngwood and Bettie Jane (Van Cleave) Hecht; m. Alan Rush Fitzpatrick, Dec. 15, 1973 (dec.). Student, Upsala Coll., 1960-62, New Sch. Social Rsch., 1962-64, Johns Hopkins U., summer 1987, Bennington Coll., summer 1988. Asst. copyeditor Am. Home mag., N.Y.C., 1964-68; v.p. Creative Comms. Assocs., Newark, 1968-70; sr. editor Family Circle mag., N.Y.C., 1970-77; corp. sec., v.p. mktg. Alternative Telecom. Corp., N.Y.C., 1977-92; exec. editor Meeting News mag., N.Y.C., 1993-95; prodn. editor The Vineyard Gazette, 1997—. Editor various publs. Mem. NOW, LWV, N.Y. Women in Comms., Empire Women in Telecomm. (pres.), Ea. Bedford Environ. Assn. (treas.).

FITZPATRICK, ROBERT J., transit company executive; b. Newark, Nov. 12, 1964; s. Robert Emmett and Dorothy Marie (Gerrity) F.; m. Catherine M. Hawn, July 8, 1989; 1 child, Kathleen. BA in Polit. Sci., Rutgers Coll., 1989; MA in Politics and Pub. Policy, Rutgers U., 1990. Sheriff's officer Essex County Sheriff's Office, Newark, 1984-87; asst. editor N.J. Reporter Mag., Princeton, 1990; gov.'s fellow State of N.J., Trenton, 1990-91; exec. asst. N.J. Divsn. Codes and Stds., Trenton, 1991-94; sr. planner N.J. Transit Corp., Newark, 1994-96, project mgr. passenger facilities, 1996—; adj. prof. Kean Coll., Union, N.J., 1990-95. Episcopalian. Avocations: books, travel, brewing. Home: 23 3d St Rumson NJ 07760 Office: NJ Transit Corp 1 Penn Plz E Newark NJ 07105-2299

FITZPATRICK, RUTH ANN, education educator; b. Brockton, Mass., July 12, 1941; d. Lenard Burton and Alva D.M. (Goranson) Parent; m. Richard Noll Fitzpatrick, July 9, 1966; 1 child, Elizabeth Ann. BS in Edn., Bridgewater State Coll., 1963, MEd, 1966, cert. advanced grad. study, 1985. Cert. elem. tchr. and prin., reading tchr. and supr., Mass. Tchr. Sharon (Mass.) Pub. Schs., 1963-72, 79-81; assoc. prof. edn., tchr. Bridgewater (Mass.) State Coll., 1982-98; presenter World Congress on Reading, Stockholm, 1990, New Eng. Reading Assn., 1990. Contbr. articles to The Reading Tchr., NALS Jour., The Edn. Digest. Liturgist, chair gifts and memls. com. 1st United Meth. Ch. Stoughton, 1968—, supt. ch. sch., 1968-74, chair pastor/staff/parish com., 1994-97. Mem. Nat. Assn. Lab. Schs. (chmn. N.E. conf. 1990, 95, exec. bd. dirs. 1991—, audit com. 1992-98, nominating com. 1993-94, 97, pres.-elect 1996, pres. 1997, presenter at confs. 1990-98, historian 1998—, Disting. Svc. award 1999), Mass. Reading Assn. (mem. editl. bd. 1990-94, presenter 1990), Delta Kappa Gamma (chpt. corr. sec. 1985-92, treas. 1992—, presenter N.E. conf. Stockholm 1997).

FITZPATRICK, THOMAS BERNARD, dermatologist, educator; b. Madison, Wis., Dec. 19, 1919; s. Joseph J. and Grace (Lawrence) F.; m. Beatrice Devaney, Dec. 27, 1944; children: Thomas B., Beatrice, John, L. Scott, Brian. BA with honors, U. Wis., 1941; MD, Harvard U., 1945; fellow, Mayo Found., 1948-51; PhD, U. Minn., 1952; fellow, Commonwealth Fund, Oxford, 1958-59; DSc (hon.), U. Mass., 1987, U. Rochester Med. Sch., 1996. Intern 4th (Harvard) Med. Service, Boston City Hosp., 1945-46; biochemist Army Med. Ctr., Md., 1946-48; asst. prof. dermatology U. Mich. Med. Sch., 1951-52; prof., head divsn. dermatology U. Oreg. Med. Sch., 1952-58; Edward Wigglesworth prof. dermatology Harvard Med. Sch., 1959-87, prof. emeritus, 1987—, head dept., 1959-87; chief dermatology svc. Mass. Gen. Hosp., Boston, 1959-87; Prosser White orator St. John's Dermatol. Soc., London, 1964; Dohi internat. exch. lectr. dermatology, Japan, 1969; spl. cons. USPHS, NIH; cons. in dermatology Brigham and Women's Hosp., Children's Hosp. Med. Ctr., Boston, 1962—; mem. sci. adv. bd. EPA, 1985; mem. climatic impact com., chmn. health effects NAS; pres. Dermatology Found., 1971, Internat. Pigment Cell Soc., 1978-81, Assn. Profs. Dermatology, 1983. Chief editor: Dermatology in General Medicine, 1971, 4th edit., 1993; mem. editl. bd. New Eng. Jour. Medicine, 1961-69; editor Year Book Dermatology, 1984-97, Fitzpatrick's Dermatology in Gernal Medicine, 5th edit., 1999; columnist Boston Globe, 1984—. Decorated Officer Order of Rising Gold Rays (Japan), 1986; recipient Mayo Found. Alumni Rsch. award, 1951, Outstanding Achievement award U. Minn. Bd. Regents, 1964, Myron Gordon award 6th Internat. Pigment Cell Conf., 1965, Disting. Svc. award Dermatology Found., 1989, U. Wis., 1983, award for discovery of PUVA photochemotherapy for psoriasis Nat. Psoriasis Found., 1993, Nat. Med. Rsch. award Nat. Health Coun., 1994, Am. Skin Assn., 1996, Discovery award Dermatology Found., 1997; Established Thomas B. Fitzpatrick prof. dermatology and endowed chair Harvard U., 1987, Thomas B. Fitzpatrick profl. chair, 1990. Fellow Am. Acad. Dermatology (hon., master, past bd. dirs.); mem. NAS (mem. inst. medicine 1994), Royal Soc. Medicine (hon.), Am. Acad. Arts and Scis., Assn. Am. Physicians, Soc. Investigative Dermatology (hon., pres. 1959-60, Stephen Rothman award, gold medal 1970), Am. Soc. for Clin. Investigation (emeritus 1965), Brit. Assn. Dermatology (hon.), South African Dermatol. Soc. (hon.), Med. Assn. Israel Dermatol. Soc. (hon.), St. John's Hosp. Dermatol. Soc. (London, hon.) Argentina, Danish, Italian, Finnish, German, Polish, Austrian dermatol. socs. (hon.), Pacific Dermatologic Assn. (hon.), French Soc. Dermatology and Syphiligraphy (fgn. corr.), Australasian Coll. Dermatologists, Alpha Omega Alpha. Home: 209 Newton St Weston MA 02493-2338 Office: Mass Gen Hosp Dermatology Svc 55 Fruit St Boston MA 02114-2696

FITZPATRICK, THOMAS MARK, lawyer; b. Anaconda, Mont., June 12, 1951; s. Marcus Leo and Natalie Stephanie (Trbovich) F. BA, U. Mont., 1973; JD, U. Chgo., 1976. Bar: Ill. 1976, Wash. 1978. Asst. to pres.-elect ABA, Chgo., 1976-77, asst. to pres., 1977-78; assoc. Karr, Tuttle, Campbell, Seattle, 1978-85, ptnr., 1985-89; ptnr. Stafford, Frey, Cooper, Seattle, 1989—. Editor: ABA: A Century of Service, 1979. Fellow Am. Bar Found.; mem. ABA (chmn. lawyer and media conf. 1985-88, profl. discipline com. 1988-94, LRIS com. 1994-97, chmn. nat. conf. groups 1982-85, ho. of dels. 1990—, state del. 1993-98, bd. govs. 1998—), Wash. Bar Assn. (pres. young lawyer div. 1986-87), Seattle-King County Bar, U. Chgo. Law Sch. Alumni Assn. (bd. dirs., Seattle regional pres. 1980-86). Roman Catholic. Home: 7345 13th Ave NW Seattle WA 98117-5306 Office: Stafford Frey Cooper 2500 Rainier Tower 1301 5th Ave Ste 2500 Seattle WA 98101-2621

FITZPATRICK, VINCENT DE PAUL, JR., gynecologist; b. Balt., Mar. 24, 1920; s. Vincent de Paul Sr. and Marie Anita (O'Conor) F.; m. Margaret Josephine Schanberger, Oct. 16, 1948 (dec. Apr. 1993); children: Vincent de Paul III, James Lawrence. BA, Loyola Coll., 1942; MD, U. Md., Balt., 1945. Resident Mercy Hosp., Balt., 1948-51; pvt. practice ob-gyn. Balt., 1951-93; head dept. ob-gyn. St. Joseph Hosp., Balt., 1987-98; pres. Mercy Hosp. Med. Staff, Balt., 1975-76; chmn. Cath. Health Care Consortium, Md., 1985-86. Contbr. articles to med. jours. Bd. trustees Loyola H.S., Balt., 1970-76. Capt. Army Med. Corps, 1943-48. Mem. AMA, Am. Coll. Ob-Gyn. (chmn. Md. sect. 1980-83), Balt. City Med. Soc. (bd. dirs.), So. Med. Assn., Knights of Malta (adm. com. 1991). Roman Catholic. Home: 316 Broxton Rd Baltimore MD 21212-3531 Office: 7505 Osler Dr Towson MD 21204-7736

FITZPATRICK, WILLIAM HENRY, retired journalist; b. New Orleans, May 23, 1908; s. Harry William and Clara Mary (Bertel) F.; m. Francis Westfeldt, Aug. 31, 1940; children: William Whitfield, Peter Bryan (dec.), Vaughan Owen, Francis James Gasquet. Student, Tulane U., 1930-32. Reporter New Orleans Item, 1933-35, Times-Picayune, New Orleans, 1935-40; city editor New Orleans States, 1940-41, mng. editor, 1941-45, editor, 1945-52; assoc. editor Wall Street Jour., N.Y.C., 1952-60; editor Ledger Star, Norfolk, Va., 1960-71; exec. editor, bd. dir. Landmark Communications Inc., Norfolk, 1971-75; v.p., bd. dirs. The Times-Picayune Pub. Co., 1948-52. Mem. bd. visitors Tulane U., 1953-64; trustee Woodberry Forest (Va.) Sch., 1975-81. Lt. comdr. USNR, 1942-45, PTO. Awarded 5 battle stars; recipient Pulitzer prize for disting. editl. writing, 1951. Mem. La. Club (New Orleans), Boston Club (New Orleans), Racquet and Tennis Club (N.Y.C.), Biltmore Forest Club (N.C.), Princess Anne Country Club, Norfolk Yacht. Home: 1321 W Princess Anne Rd Norfolk VA 23507-1038

FITZPATRICK, WILLIAM PETER, computer programmer, analyst, state legislator; b. Dublin, Feb. 23, 1961; came to U.S., 1982; s. William Edward and Teresa (Keleghan) F. Grad., Patrician Coll., Dublin, 1979. Computer specialist Revenue Commrs., Dublin, 1979-82, Informatics Gen. Corp., Phoenix, 1982-84, Advanced Tech. Labs., Phoenix, 1984-87, Harvard Cmty. Health Plan of New Eng., Providence, 1987-89, 94-96, Am. Math. Soc., Providence, 1989-94; mem. R.I. State Senate, Providence, 1993-97; cons. Procom Svc., San Francisco, 1997-98; cons., sys. analyst Children's Hosp., Oakland, Calif., 1998—; computer specialist Embarcadero Sys. Corp., 1996-97. Contbr. to profl. jours. Mem. R.I. Campaign to Eliminate Childhood Poverty, 1994. Recipient R.I. Alliance for Mentally Ill, 1993, R.I. Stateside Housing Action Coalition, 1993, 94, Legislator of the Yr. award R.I. Coalition Cmty. Mental Health Ctrs., 1994, award R.I. Coalition for the Homeless, 1994, R.I. Campaign to Eliminate Childhood Poverty, 1994. Democrat. Home: 234 Dore St San Francisco CA 94103-4308

FITZ-PEGADO, LAURI J., telecommunications executive. AB cum laude, Vassar Coll., 1977; MA in Internat. Affairs, Johns Hopkins U., 1986. Asst. cultural affairs officer U.S. Embassy, Santo Domingo, Dominican Republic, 1978-79; fgn. svc. info. officer U.S. Embassy, Mexico City, 1979-81; account exec., sr. v.p. Hill and Knowlton Pub. Affairs Worldwide, 1982-90, mng. dir., sr. v.p. internat. pub. affairs divsn., 1986-93; spl. advisor to Sec. of Commerce U.S. Dept. of Commerce, Washington, 1993-94, asst. sec., dir. gen., 1994-97; v.p. global gateway mgmt. Iridium LLC, 1997—; bd. dirs. Constituency for Africa; mem. Coun. on Fgn. Rels. Mem. The Women's Forum of Washington. Mem. Phi Beta Kappa. Office: Iridium LLC 1575 Eye St NW Washington DC 20005-1105 Home: 1701 Hutchinson Ln Silver Spring MD 20906-5937

FITZROY, NANCY DELOYE, technology executive, engineer; b. Pittsfield, Mass., Oct. 5, 1927; d. Jules Emile and Mabel Winifred (Burr) deLoye; m. Roland Victor Fitzroy, Jr., Mar. 24, 1951. BChemE, Rensselaer Poly. Inst., Troy, 1949; DEng (hon.), Rensselaer Poly. Inst., 1990; DSc (hon.), N.J. Inst. Tech., 1987. Registered profl. engr., N.Y. Heat transfer engr. corp. R & D GE, Schenectady, N.Y., 1950-71, mgr. heat transfer consulting, 1971-74, strategy planner, 1974-76, mgr. program devel. gas turbine divsn., 1976-82; mgr. energy and environ. program Gen. Electric Co., Schenectady, N.Y., 1982-87; dir. West Hill Devel. Corp., Rotterdam, N.Y., 1955-65; mem. adv. com. for rsch. NSF, Washington, 1972-75; mem. transp. rsch. bd. coordinating com. on rsch. and tech. NRC, 1996-99; cons. in field; bd. dirs. ASME Found., 1989-95, 97—, trustee, 1998—. Author, editor: Heat Transfer and Fluid Flow, Data Books, 1955-75; patentee in field. Charter mem. Rensselaer Poly. Inst. Coun., 1972—. Recipient Demers medal Rensselaer Poly. Inst., 1975, Disting. Alumna medal Rensselaer Poly. Inst., 1996, Achievement award Fedn. Profl. Women, 1984; inducted Rensselaer Poly Inst. Hall of Fame, 1999. Fellow ASME (1st woman nat. pres. 1986-87, trustee Gear Rsch. Inst. 1987-89), Instn. Mech. Engrs. London (hon.), Soc. Women Engrs. (Achievement award 1972); mem. AIChE, Nat. Acad. of Engring. (elected), Am. Assn. Engrings. Socs. (gov. 1987-89), Ninety-Nines Club, Whirly-Girls Club, Mohawk Golf Club, Coral Ridge Yacht Club (Ft. Lauderdale, Fla.). Republican. Episcopalian. Home: 2125 Rosendale Rd Niskayuna NY 12309-5418

FITZSIMMONS, (LOWELL) COTTON, professional basketball executive, broadcaster, former coach; b. Hannibal, Mo., Oct. 7, 1931; s. Clancy and Zelda Curry (Gibbs) F.; m. JoAnn D'Andrea, Sept. 2, 1978 (div.); 1 child, Gary. B.S., Midwestern Univ., Wichita Falls, Tex., 1956, M.A., 1957. Head coach, athletic dir. Moberly Jr. Coll, Moberly, Mo., 1958-67; head coach Kans. State U., Manhattan, 1967-70; head coach NBA Phoenix Suns, 1970-72, 1988-94, 96-97, dir. player personnel, 1987-88; head coach NBA Atlanta Hawks, 1972-76; dir. player personnel NBA Golden State Warriors, Oakland, Calif., 1976-77; head coach NBA Buffalo Braves, 1977-78, NBA Kansas City Kings, Mo., 1978-84, NBA San Antonio Spurs, 1984-87; sr. exec. v.p. Phoenix Suns, 1992—, head coach; coach Schick Rookies, 45th ann. All Star Game, America West Arena. Recipient Coach of the Yr. award Nat. Jr. Coll. Athletic Assn., 1966, 67, Coach of the Yr. award Big 8 Conf., 1970, Coach of the Yr. award NBA, 1979, 89, Coach of the Yr. award Sporting News, St. Louis, 1979, 89; inducted into Mo. Sports Hall of Fame, Springfield, Mo., 1981, Nat. Jr. Coll. Basketball Hall of Fame, Hutchinson, 1985. Fellow Nat. Assn. Basketball Coaches. Avocations: golf, fishing. Office: Phoenix Suns 201 E Jefferson St Phoenix AZ 85004-2412

FITZSIMMONS, ELLEN MARIE, lawyer. Sr. gen. counsel CSX Corp., Richmond, asst. gen. counsel, 1995-97, gen. counsel, 1997—. Office: CSX Corp One James Ctr PO Box 85629 901 E Cary St Richmond VA 23285-5629*

FITZSIMMONS, HOLLY B., federal judge, educator; b. 1950. BA, Smith Coll., 1971; MA, JD, U. Va., 1976. Bar: Conn. 1976. Assoc. Robinson, Robinson & Cole, Hartford, Conn., 1976-78; asst. U.S. atty. for dist. Conn., U.S. Dept. Justice, Hartford, 1978-93; magistrate judge for dist. Conn., U.S. Magistrate Ct., Bridgeport, 1993—; instr. Yale Law Sch., New Haven, 1992—. Office: US Magistrate Ct 915 Lafayette Blvd Bridgeport CT 06604-4706

FITZSIMMONS, JOSEPH JOHN, publishing executive; b. Newark, Nov. 10, 1934; s. Joseph A. and Frances E. (Baume) F.; children from previous marriage: Joseph John, Michael, Patricia, Susan, Thomas; m. Beth Berglund Duston, Nov. 30, 1996. B.Chem. Engring., Cornell U., 1957. With Xerox Corp., Rochester, N.Y., 1957-65; v.p., gen. mgr. Xerox Univ. Microfilms, Ann Arbor, Mich., 1974-75; pres. Univ. Microfilms Internat., Ann Arbor, 1976—, pres., chief exec. officer, 1987-94; v.p. Bell and Howell Co., 1987—; chmn. Univ. Microfilms Internat., Ann Arbor, 1994-95, ret., 1995; pres., CEO Nonprofit Enterprise at Work, 1999; bd. dirs. Nat. City Bank Mich./Ill., Bartech Inc., Nematron Corp. Gen. campaign chmn. Wastenaw United Way, 1977-78; mem. devel. com. St. Joseph's Hosp.; pres. Ann Arbor Hands-On-Mus., 1980; mem. adv. bd. for entrepreneurship Ea. Mich. Cen. U., 1986—; adv. bd. U. Pitts. Sch. Libr. and Info. Sci.; bd. dirs. Libr. Mich. Found., 1992, co-chair Capital Campaign, 1995—; trustee Dawn Farm, 1995, Siena Heights U., 1997; Rep. candidate U.S. Congress Mich., 1996. Mem. ALA, Info. Industry Assn. (bd. dirs. 1985, chmn. mktg. com. 1986, chmn. long range planning com. 1987, chmn. bd. elect 1988, chmn. 1989), The White House Conf. on Librs. and Info. Sci. (vice chmn. 1991). Home: 101 N Main St Ste 1005 Ann Arbor MI 48104-1475

FITZSIMMONS, SOPHIE SONIA, interior designer; d. Oleg and Sophie (Ovsianico-Koulikovsky) Yadoff; m. J. Heath Fitzsimmons; children: Gregory James, Raymond Heath, Douglas Paul. AAS with honors, Fashion Inst. Tech., N.Y.C., 1964; student, NYU Wagner Sch., 1994. Design intern Euster Assocs., Inc., Armonk, N.Y., 1964; prin. Sophie Y. Fitzsimmons Interior Design, N.Y., Conn, 1964-77; co-owner Avon (Conn.), Interiors, Inc., 1977-89; prin. Sophie Fitzsimmons Interior Design, N.Y.C., 1989—; pres. Fitz Family Enterprises, 1996; founder, pres. Designers Discovery, 1996; guest exhibitor Fashion Inst. Tech. Symposium, 1984. Author: A Salute, 1996. Chair ann. show Hope Benefit, Hartford, Conn., 1975; mem. Rep. Women's Club Conn., 1978-89; bd. dirs. Friends of Hartford Ballet, 1986-88; vol. N.Y. Commn. UN, Consular Corps and Internat. Bus., 1992—; vol. tchr. East Internat. Community Ctr., 1993—; pres., bd. dirs. Squadron Line PTA, 1976; bd. dirs. Simsbury chpt. Federated Women's Club, 1976. Decorated Medal of Recognition, French Resistance Movement, World War II; recipient Award Edn. Civique Chevalier. Mem. Nat. Soc. Interior Designers (adv. panel 1967), World Affairs Coun., Bamm Hollow Women's Golf Assn. (pres. 1995). Avocations: French and Russian languages, golf, bridge, drawing, travel. Home and Office: 22 Westminster Ln New York NY 10005-1003

FITZSIMONDS, ROGER LEON, bank holding company executive; b. Milw., May 21, 1938; s. Stephen Henry and Wilhelmine Josephine (Rhine) F.; m. Leona I. Schwegler, July 11, 1958; children: Susan Fitzsimonds Hedrick, Stephen. BBA in Fin., U. Wis., Milw., 1960, MBA in Fin., 1971, D in Comml. Sci. (hon.), 1989. From mgmt. trainee to 1st level officer 1st Wis. Nat. Bank, Milw., 1964-69; pres. 1st Wis. Bank Green Bay, 1970-73, 1st Wis. Mortgage Co., Green Bay, 1974-78; exec. v.p. retail banking and real estate fin. 1st Wis. Nat. Bank, Milw., 1978-84, exec. v.p. comml. fin. group, 1984-86; pres. Firstar, Milw., 1986-87; pres. Firstar Corp., 1987-88, vice-chmn., 1990, chmn., CEO, 1991-98, chmn., 1998—; also bd. dirs. Firstar Bank, Milw. Bd. dirs. Milw. Boys and Girls Club, Columbia Health Sys., Milw., Med. Coll. Wis., 1986—; past pres., dir. Competitive Wis., Inc.; past pres. Bankers Round Table, chmn.; chmn., dir. Met. Milw. Assn. Commerce; dir. Wis. Policy Rsch. Inst.; past pres. Greater Milw. Com.; chmn. adv. coun. Sch. Bus. U. Wis. Capt. U.S. Army, 1960-64. Recipient Alumni of Yr. award U. Wis., Milw., 1983. Mem. Wis. Assn. Mfrs. and Commerce (past chmn., bd. dirs. 1988—), Milw. Country Club. Republican. Lutheran. Avocations: tennis, golf, fishing. Home: 7880 N River Rd River Hills WI 53217-3024 Office: Firstar Corp 777 E Wisconsin Ave Milwaukee WI 53202-5300

FITZSIMONS, CORINNE MARIE, medical/surgical nurse; b. Fairfield, Ala., Dec. 7, 1925; d. William Dixon and Marie Rose (Moss) DeBardeleben; m. L. E. FitzSimons, Mar. 18, 1948 (div.); children: Annette, John, Robert. RN, Emory U. Hosp., 1947; BSN, McNeese State U., 1972; MSN, U. Tex. Med. Br., Galveston, 1976. RN, La., Tex. Staff/sch. nurse various hosps./schs., various locations, 1947-77; asst. prof. nursing Tex. Woman's U., Houston, 1977-79, U. South La., Lafayette, 1979-81; coord. nursing edn. St. Patrick Hosp., Lake Charles, La., 1981-82; dir. nursing staff/svc. DeQuincy Nursing Home and Kinder (La.) Nursing Home, 1982-84; charge nurse med./surg. West Calcasieu-Cameron Hosp., Sulphur, La., 1984-86; ind. nurse practitioner Analytical Nurse Mgmt., Lake Charles, La., 1986-88; nurse clinician surgery floor Lake Charles Meml. Hosp., 1988-92, clin. nurse specialist edn. dept., relief nursing supr., 1992—; clin. nurse specialist Sowela Tech. Inst.; relief nursing supr. Grand Cove Nursing Home, 1997—. Mem. ANA, La. Nurses Assn., Cath. Daus. Am., Am. Cancer Soc., Am. Bus. Women's Assn., Sigma Theta Tau.

FITZSIMONS, GEORGE KINZIE, bishop; b. Kansas City, Mo., Sept. 4, 1928. Student, Rockhurst Coll., Immaculate Conception Sem. Ordained priest, Roman Cath. Ch., 1961. Aux. bishop Kansas City-St. Joseph, Kans., 1975-84; bishop Salina, Kans., 1984—. Office: Chancery Office PO Box 980 Salina KS 67402-0980*

FITZWATER, IVAN W., retired superintendant; b. Gaithersburg, Md., May 19, 1931; s. Elmer S. and Cora Dayton (May) F.; m. Elaine F., May 28, 1988; children: Sidney, Elizabeth, Martha. BS, George Washington U., 1955, EdD, 1965. Prin. Montgomery County Elem. and High Schs., Rockville, Md., 1955-66; asst. supt. Elkhart (Ind.) Pub. Schs., 1966-69; dep. supt. Ft. Worth (Tex.) Pub. Schs., 1969-71; supt. San Antonio, 1971-78; prof. Trinity U., San Antonio, 1978-91, prof. emeritus, 1991—. Author 7 books including Time Under Control, You Can Be A Powerful Leader. Recipient Disting. Prof. award. Mem. NASE.

FITZWATER, SIDNEY ALLEN, federal judge; b. Olney, Md., Sept. 22, 1953; s. Ivan Welton and Kathleen Elizabeth (Schroeder) F.; B.A., Baylor U., 1975, J.D., 1976; m. Nancy Jane Ware, Aug. 6, 1976; children—John Welton, Joseph Leon, James Sidney. Bar: Tex. 1977, U.S. Supreme Ct. 1981. Assoc. Vinson & Elkins, Houston, 1976-78, Rain Harrell Emery Young & Doke, Dallas, 1978-82; judge 298th Jud. Dist. Tex., Dallas, 1982-86; judge U.S. Dist Ct. (no. dist.) Tex., 1986—. Bd. dirs. Dallas Services for Visually Impaired Children, 1980-85; mem. exec. com. Dallas County Reps., 1981-82; state del. Tex. Rep. Conv., 1980, 82, 84; mem. exec. com. Tex. Young Reps., 1981-82; bd. dirs. Dallas County Rep. Men's Club, 1984-85. Recipient Baylor U. award of merit, 1983, Ft. Worth Ind. Sch. Dist. Disting. Alumni award, 1986; named Outstanding Young Alumnus, Baylor U., 1985. Fellow Tex. Bar Found.; mem. State Bar Tex., Dallas Bar Assn., Nat. Order of Barristers, Phi Alpha Delta, Omicron Delta Kappa. Office: US Courthouse 1100 Commerce St Ste 15a3A Dallas TX 75242-1016*

FIUMEFREDDO, CHARLES A., investment management company executive; b. Bayonne, N.J., May 12, 1933; s. Charles F. and Alice (Guiliana) F.; m. Joan Kuczynski, June 18, 1955; children—Joanne Fiumefreddo Lewicki, Charles M. B.S., St. Peter's Coll., Jersey City, 1955; postgrad., NYU Sch. Bus. Adminstrn., 1955-57. Asst. v.p. First Jersey Nat. Bank, Jersey City, 1953-65; asst. v.p. investment mgmt. Anchor Corp., Elizabeth, N.J., 1965-69; v.p. Standard & Poor's/InterCapital, N.Y.C., 1969-71, exec. v.p., 1971-74, treas., 1969-77, pres., chief exec. officer, 1974-77; pres. Morgan Stanley Dean Witter Advisors Inc., N.Y.C., 1977-84, treas., 1977-82, chmn., 1982-98, CEO, 1977-98; pres. Morgan Stanley Dean Witter Investment Cos., N.Y.C., 1982—, dir., trustee, 1991—, chmn., 1992—; exec. v.p., bd. dirs. Dean Witter Reynolds Inc., until 1998; trustee, chmn. TCW/DW Investment Cos., N.Y.C., 1992—; chmn. Morgan Stanley Dean Witter Trust FSB, Jersey City, 1989-98; bd. dirs., mem. exec. com. Investment Co. Inst., Washington, 1983—; mem. investment co. com. SIA, N.Y.C., 1984-86. Bd. dirs. Bayonne Hosp., N.J., 1983-89. Lodge: K.C. (Bayonne, N.J.). Avocations: stamps; sport fishing. Office: Morgan Stanley Dean Witter Advisors Inc 2 World Trade Ctr Fl 66 New York NY 10048-0203

FIX, DOUGLAS MARTIN, electrical engineer; b. Lincoln, Nebr., Oct. 20, 1953; s. Raymond Harold and Juliana Marie (Spatz) F. BSEE, BSCS, U. Colo., 1979; MSEE, Southern Meth. U., 1983. Registered profl. engr. Tex. Computer ops. Seismograph Svc. Corp., Denver, 1974-78, seismic analyst, 1978-80; design engr. Tex. Instruments, Dallas, 1980-85, sr. engr., 1985-88, lead engr., 1988—; adj. prof., Eastfield Coll., Mesquite, Tex., 1983—; cons. Computers U2, Allen,Tex., 1990—. Contbr. article to profl. jours.; patent pending for digital video monitor interface arch. Elder, tchr. Zion Luth. Ch., Dallas, 1992—; crime watch coord. Neighborhood Homeowners, Dallas, 1988. Recipient Sundstrand scholarship Sundstrand Corp., 1978. Mem. IEEE, Eta Kappa Nu (sec. 1978), Soc. Info. Display, Mensa, Tau Beta Pi. Republican. Lutheran. Achievements include research in digital pll clocking for TV synch signal processor and preprocessor designs for 4 classified military projects. Avocations: snow skiing, water skiing, foreign travel, classical music, theater. Home: 761 Livingston Dr Allen TX 75002-5229 Office: Texas Instruments 13510 N Central Expy Dallas TX 75243-1108

FIX, JOHN NEILSON, banker; b. Evanston, Ill., Apr. 10, 1937; s. John Leonard and Margaret (Neilson) F.; m. Linda Harris, Dec. 21, 1961; children: John, Christopher, David, Wendy. BS, U. Ill., 1959; grad., Stonier Sch. Banking, Rutgers U., 1971. Asst. cashier, v.p. No. Trust Co., Chgo., 1962-77; v.p., div. head Continental Ill. Nat. Bank & Trust Co., Chgo., 1977-80; sr. v.p., group head Continental Bank N.A., Chgo., 1980-83, sr. v.p., dept. head, 1983-94; sr. v.p, dir. corp. devel. global payment svcs. Bank of Am. N.T.S.A., Chgo., 1994-95, ret., 1995; mng. dir. Fixco, Inc., 1996—; prin. Treasury Strategies, Inc., Chgo., 1997—. Bd. dirs. Kenilworth Dist. 38 Sch. Bd., Ill., 1969-75; trustee, pres. Kenilworth Park Bd., 1981-89; mem. exec. com. Chgo. Area Boy Scouts, 1981-89; pres., treas. Kenilworth Baseball Assn., 1976-85; trustee Kenilworth Union Ch., 1988-93; bd. dirs. Western Golf Assn., 1989—, audit com., 1992—. Lt. U.S. Army, 1959-61. Recipient George Huff award U. Ill., Champaign, 1955; Good Scout award Chgo. Area Boy Scouts Am., 1982. Mem. Bankers Club of Chgo., Ill. State C. of C. (bd. dirs., treas. 1980-82), Exec. Club of Chgo., Econ. Club of Chgo., U. Ill. Alumni Assn. (mem. bd. trustees 1987, exec. com. 1990-93, chmn. investment com. 1992-93), Nat. Corp. Cash Mgmt. Assn. (mem. publs. com. 1987-91, strategic planning com.), Indian Hill Club (bd. govs. 1984-87, 98-02), Old Elm Club (Highland Park, Ill.). Clubs: Chicago; Minneapolis; Indian Hill (bd. govs. 1984-87). Avocations: golf; skiing; paddle tennis.

FIX, MEYER, lawyer; b. Manchester, Eng., July 29, 1906; came to U.S., 1910, naturalized, 1917; s. Morris and Leah (Katz) F.; m. Elizabeth Goldsmith, July 27, 1937; children: Terry E., Brian D. AB, U. Rochester, 1928; JD, Harvard U., 1931. Bar: N.Y. 1932, U.S. Supreme Ct. 1950. Assoc. John Van Voorhis' Sons, Rochester, N.Y., 1936-43; ptnr. Fix & MacCameron, Rochester, 1943-55, Meyer, Fix, Rochester, 1955-61, Fix & Spindelman, Rochester, 1961-74, Fix, Spindelman, Turk & Himelein, Rochester, 1974-77; sr. ptnr. Fix, Spindelman, Turk, Himelein & Schwartz, Rochester, 1977-83, Fix, Spindelman, Turk, Himelein & Shukoff, Rochester, 1983-91, Fix, Spindleman, Brovitz, Turk, Himelein & Shukoff, Rochester, 1991—; lectr. Cornell Law Sch., 1958-68. Contbr. articles to Scribes. Mem. ABA, N.Y. State Bar Assn., Monroe County Bar Assn., Am. Law Inst., Internat. Assn. Ins. Counsel, Fedn. Ins. Counsel, Assn. Ins. Attys., N.Y. State Trial Lawyers Assn. Club: Irondequoit Country. Lodges: Masons, Shriners. Home: 2500 East Ave Apt 30 Rochester NY 14610-3109 Office: Fix Spindelman Brovitz Turk Himelein & Shukoff 500 State St Rochester NY 14608-1645

FIX, R. JOBE, plastic and reconstructive and hand surgeon; b. Sterling, Colo., Dec. 14, 1956; m. Kathleen N. Fix; children: Alexander, Elizabeth, Andrew. MB, U. Nebr., 1978, MD, 1982. Diplomate, Nat. Bd. Med. Examiners, Am. Bd. Surgery, Am. Bd. Plastic Surgery, added qualification in hand surgery. Intern Valley Med. Ctr., Fresno, Calif., 1982-83; resident Valley Med. Ctr., Fresno, 1983-87; resident in plastic surgery U. Ala., Birmingham, 1987-89; burn team instr. Valley Med. Ctr., Fresno, 1986-89; clin. instr. plastic surgery U. Ala., Birmingham, 1989, asst. prof., 1990-97, assoc. prof., 1997—; attending surgeon Children's Hosp., Birmingham, 1990—; chief of plastic surgery VA Med. Ctr., Birmingham, 1990—; domestic vis. prof. Com. Plastic Surgery Ednl. Found., 1991, mem. vis. scholar com., 1995-96; mem. numerous coms. U. Ala. Birmingham. 1992—. Contbr. articles and abstracts to profl. jours., chpts. to books. Mem. Med. Mission to Ecuador Feb., 1996, 97, 98, 99. Recipient Beach-Byer and Drier A&E Honor scholarship U. Nebr., 1976-77, Regent's scholarship, 1975-78. Mem. ACS (Ala. chpt.), Am. Soc. Maxillofacial Surgeons, Am. Soc. Plastic and Reconstructive Surgeons, Assn. Acad. Chmn. of Plastic Surgery, Plastic Surgery Rsch. Coun., So. Med. Assn., Am. Soc. for Surgery of the Hand, Ala. Soc. Plastic and Reconstructive Surgeons, Southeastern Soc. Plastic and Reconstructive Surgery, Alpha Lamba Delta, Phi Eta Sigma. E-mail: Jobe.Fix@CCC.UAB.EDU. Office: U Ala Birmingham 1813 Sixth Ave S MEB 524 Birmingham AL 35294

FIX, WILBUR JAMES, department store executive; b. Velva, N.D., Aug. 14, 1927; s. Jack J. and Beatrice D. (Wasson) F.; m. Beverly A. Corcoran, Sept. 20, 1953; children: Kathleen M., Michael B., Jenifer L. BA, U. Wash., 1950. Credit mgr. Bon Marche, Yakima, Wash., 1951-54; controller, ops. mgr. Bon Marche, Boise, Idaho, 1954-58; sr. v.p. Bon Marche, Seattle, 1970-76; exec. v.p. Bon Marche, 1976-77, pres., chief exec. officer, 1978-87; chmn., chief exec. officer, sr. v.p. Allied Stores Corp., 1987-93; chmn. Fix Mgmt. Group, 1993—; chmn. Wash. Retail Coun., 1983-84; bd. dirs., vice chmn. Wash. Telecomm. Corp.; bd. dirs. BMC West Corp., Vans, Inc., Swirland Apparel Ventures, Inc.; mem. adv. coun. Inst. for Retail Studies, Coll. of the Desert, Palm Desert, Calif., Corp. Coun. of the Arts, Seattle. Mem. pres.'s adv. com. Allied Stores Corp., N.Y., 1968-72; mem. citizens adv. com. Seattle Pub. Schs., 1970-71; v.p. Citizens Council Against Crime; chmn. Seattle King County Conv. & Visitors Bur., 1990. With AUS, 1946-47. Mem. Nat. Retail Mchts. Assn., Controllers Congress, Seattle Retail Controllers Group (past pres.), Fin. Execs. Inst., Western States Regional Controllers Congress (past pres.), Seattle C. of C. (exec. com., bd. dirs.), Assn. Wash. Bus. (fin. adv.), Downtown Seattle Devel. Assn. (exec. com., trustee), Wash. Round Table, Wash. Athletic Club, Mission Hills Country Club (Rancho Mirage, Calif.), Elks, Pi Kappa Alpha, Alpha Kappa Psi, Phi Theta Kappa. Episcopalian. Address: 149 Racquet Club Dr Rancho Mirage CA 92270-1461 Office: The Bon Marché 3rd and Pine St Seattle WA 98181 also: 5403 W Mercer Way Mercer Island WA 98040-4635

FIXEN, RANDALL ROBERT, academic director; b. Marshall, Minn., July 15, 1959; s. Robert LeRoy Sr. and Jeanette Marie Fixen; m. Ahna Lynn Halbakken, July 15, 1989; children: Christopher Aaron, Mariah Lynn. BA, S.W. State U., 1983; MA, U. N.D., 1985, PhD, 1992. Cert. vocat. guidance counselor. Coor. alcohol and drug prevention U. N.D., Grand Forks, 1985-86, dir. internat. student affairs, 1985-90; dir. counseling, housing, student activities, acad. advisement, intramurals U. N.D. Lake Region, Devils Lake, 1992—; v.p. N.D. State Housing Officers, Devils Lake, 1997—; pres. N.D. State Housing Officers, 1998—. Pres. bd. United Way, Devils Lake, N.D., 1994; mem. Devils Lake Sch. Bd., 1997—; problem capt. Odyssey of the Mind, Devils Lake, 1996—; 3rd chair trumpet Devils Lake Elks Band, 1992—. Mem. Am. Counseling Assn., Am. Vocat. Assn., Nat. Assn. Fgn. Student Affairs (chairperson region IV 1990-91, career svcs. grant for internat. students 1988), N.D. Counseling and Personnel Assn., Optimist Club. Avocations: fishing, reading, travel. E-mail: fixenra@stellarnet.com, fixenr@shorelines.und-lr.nodak.edu. Home: 811 4th St Devils Lake ND 58301-2604 Office: UND-Lake Region 1801 College Dr Devils Lake ND 58301-1598

FIXMAN, MARSHALL, chemist, educator; b. St. Louis, Sept. 21, 1930; s. Benjamin and Dorothy (Finkel) F.; m. Marian Ruth Beatman, July 5, 1959 (dec. Sept. 1969); children—Laura Beth, Susan Ilene, Andrew Richard; m. Branka Ladanyi, Dec. 7, 1974. A.B., Washington U., St. Louis, 1950; Ph.D., MIT, 1954. Jewett postdoctoral fellow chemistry Yale U., 1953-54; instr. chemistry Harvard U., 1956-59; sr. fellow Mellon Inst., Pitts., 1959-61; prof. chemistry, dir. Inst. Theoretical Sci., U. Oreg., 1961-64, prof. chemistry, research asso. inst., 1964-65; prof. chemistry Yale U., New Haven, 1965-79; prof. chemistry and physics Colo. State U., Ft. Collins, 1979—. Mem. editorial bd. Jour. Chem. Physics, 1962-64, Jour. Phys. Chemistry, 1970-74, Macromolecules, 1970-74, Accounts Chem. Rsch. 1982-85, Jour. Polymer Sci. B, 1991-93; assoc. editor Jour. Chem. Physics, 1994—. Wwith U.S. Army, 1954-56. Fellow Alfred P. Sloan Found., 1961-63; recipient Governor's award Oreg. Mus. Sci. and Industry, 1964. Mem. NAS, Am. Acad. Arts and Scis., Am. Chem. Soc. (award pure chemistry 1964, award polymer chemistry 1991), Am. Phys. Soc. (high polymer physics award 1980), Fedn. Am. Scientists. Office: Colo State U Dept Chemistry Fort Collins CO 80523

FIZDALE, RICHARD, advertising agency executive; b. 1938. Copywriter BBDO Advt., 1967-68; copywriter Leo Burnett Co., Inc., Chgo., 1969-70, copy supr., 1970-72, assoc. creative dir., 1972-73, creative dir., 1973-74, v.p., 1974-78, exec. creative dir., 1978-79, sr. v.p., exec. creative dir., 1979, sr. v.p., mgr. creative ops., 1979-82, exec. v.p., dep. dir. creative svcs., 1982-85, pres., chief creative officer, bd. dirs., 1985-86, exec. com., 1986-87, pres., chief creative officer, 1987-92, chmn., CEO, chief creative officer, 1992-93, chmn., chief creative officer, 1993-97, chmn., CEO, 1997—. Office: Leo Burnett USA 35 W Wacker Dr Ste 2220 Chicago IL 60601-1614*

FJELL, MICK, principal. Prin. Millard Ctrl. Mid. Sch., 1978—. Recipient Blue Ribbon Sch. award 1990-91. Office: Millard Central Mid Sch 12801 L St Omaha NE 68137-2020*

FLACCO, ELAINE GERMANO, computer programmer; b. Phila., June 20, 1959; d. William Joseph and Rose Angela (Ranelli) Germano; m. Dominick Albert Flacco, Oct. 27, 1984; 1 child, Dominick William. Assoc. in Computer Sci., Peirce Jr. Coll., 1985. Asst. supr. foreclosure Fidelity Bond & Mortgage Co., Phila., 1977-79; adminstrn. asst. multi family U.S. Dept HUD, Phila., 1980-81; computer programmer, analyst Reed & Stambaugh Co., Phila., 1982-86; computer programmer, residential coordinator, prop mgr. Linpro Co./LCOR, Inc., Phila., 1986—. Democrat. Roman Catholic. Avocation: dancing. Home: 28 Briar Creek Rd Sicklerville NJ 08081-1304 Office: Linpro Co/LCOR Inc Five Greentree Ctr Marlton NJ 08053-3409

FLACH, FREDERIC FRANCIS, psychiatrist; b. N.Y.C., Jan. 25, 1927; s. George Raymond and Margaret (Donovan) F.; m. Patricia Anne Kane, June 23, 1951 (div. 1966); children: Frederica, Christopher, Geraldine, Andrew, Winifred; m. Joyce Elizabeth Rasmussen, Sept. 9, 1971. BA summa cum laude, St. Peter's Coll., Jersey City, 1947; MD, Cornell U., 1951. Diplomate Am. Bd. Psychiatry and Neurology. Intern second med. div. Bellevue Hosp., N.Y.C., 1951-52; from resident to chief resident psychiatry Payne Whitney Clinic, N.Y.C., 1953-58; pvt. practice N.Y.C., 1958—; attending psychiatrist N.Y. Presbyn. Hosp., N.Y.C., 1962—, St. Vincent's Hosp., N.Y.C., 1974—; adj. assoc. prof. psychiatry Cornell U. Med. Coll., N.Y.C., 1962—; program dir. Directions in Psychiatry, N.Y.C., 1981—; chmn. The Hatherleigh Co., Ltd., 1990—. Author: The Secret Strength of Depression, 1974, Choices, 1976, Fridericus, 1980, Resilience, 1988, Rickie, 1990, Take Command, 1994, The Secret Strength of Angels, 1998, others. Lt. (j.g.) USNR, 1945-46. Knight Equestrian Order of the Holy Sepulchre of Jerusalem, 1999. Fellow Am. Psychiat. Assn. (life). Roman Catholic. Avocations: travel, swimming, reading. Office: 420 E 51st St New York NY 10022-8058

FLACK, HARLEY E., university president. Provost, exec. v.p. Rowan U., N.J., 1989-94; pres. Wright State U., Dayton, Ohio, 1994—; mem. Miami Rsch. Found., Ohio Aerospace Inst.; chair Area Progress Coun., Ohio Coll. Assn. Composer: (8-pieces for voice and African instruments) The Goree Suite, also numerous works for piano and voice including A Nation: All Families. Bd. dirs. Miami Valley Econ. Devel. Coalition, Nat. City Bank, Dayton Philharm. Orch. Assn., Greene Progress Coun.; hon. adv. bd. A Special Wish Found., Inc.; mem. nat. adv. com. for Acad. Leadership Acad. of Am. Assn. State Colls. and Univs.; bd. trustees Robert K. Greenleaf Servant-Leadership Ctr. Office: Wright State U Office of Pub Rels 3640 Colonel Glenn Hwy Dayton OH 45435-0002

FLACK, JOE FENLEY, county and municipal official, former insurance executive; b. Menard, Tex., Feb. 23, 1921; s. Frank H. and Evelyn (Fenley) F.; m. Ann Tarry, Jan. 21, 1945; children: Kate T., Joan E., Joe Fenley. BBA with honors, U. Tex., 1943. C.P.A., Tex. Acct. Ernst & Ernst (C.P.A.s), Houston, 1946-47; with Am. Gen. Ins. Co., 1947-81, treas., 1951-81, sr. v.p., 1968-81, also dir.; chief fin. officer, auditor Harris County and Port of Houston Authority, 1981—; partner John L. Wortham and Son, Houston, 1947-65; chmn. bd., pres., treas., dir. Knickerbocker Corp.; v.p., dir. Md. Casualty Co., Maine Bonding & Casualty Co., Robert Hampson & Son, Ltd.; v.p., treas., dir. Am. Gen. Fire & Casualty Co., Nat. Standard Ins. Co., Am. Gen. Leasing & Finance Corp., Atlas Realty Co., Am. Gen. Investment Corp., Am. Gen. Realty Co.; v.p. Assurance Co. Am., Marasco Co., Inc., No. Ins. Co. N.Y.; dir. Am. Gen. Capital Corp., Am. Gen. Life, Tex., Am. Gen. Life Del. Exec. bd. Boy Scouts Am.; mayor pro-tem Bunker Hill Village, Tex., 1959-61, mayor, 1961-65; trustee, v.p. sch. bd. Spring Branch Ind. Sch. Dist., 1967-75; bd. dirs. Kappa Sigma Found., U. Tex., Houston chpt. Salvation Army; mem. exec. com. U. Tex. Health Sci. Ctr., Houston. Served to lt. USNR, 1943-45. Mem. U. Tex. Ex-Students Assn. (exec. council, regional v.p.), River Oaks Country Club. Methodist. Office: Dir and Debt Mgmt Harris County PO Box 130450 1001 Preston St Ste 800 Houston TX 77002-1817

FLACK, RONALD DAVID, diplomat, public service educator; b. Cloquet, Minn., Feb. 3, 1934; s. John and Marian Gladys (Steidl) F.; m. Danièle Guigard, Mar. 11, 1961; children: Jean-Marc, Claire-Paule. BA, U. Minn., 1960. Joined Fgn. Svc., Dept of State, Washington, 1962; 3rd sec. Am. Embassy, Athens, Greece, 1963-65; 2nd sec. Am. Embassy, Manila, The Philippines, 1965-69, Abidjan, Ivory Coast, 1969-70; 1st sec. Am. Embassy, Paris, 1970-73, Algiers, Algeria, 1973-75; counselor Am. Embassy, Athens, 1976-80; permanent rep. UN, Geneva, Switzerland, 1983-87; dep. amb. Am. Embassy, Copenhagen, 1987-90; min. counselor U.S. Mission to OECD, Paris, 1990-95; diplomat in residence NYU, N.Y.C., 1995-97; with Tayler Cos., Washington, 1998—. Bd. dirs. Internat. YMCA, N.Y.C., 1997, Jewish Bd. Family and Comty. Svcs., N.Y.C., 1997. Mem. Danish Am. Soc., Scandinavian Am. Soc. Home: 1750 P St NW Washington DC 20036-1340 Office: Taylor Cos 1215 P St NW Washington DC 20005-4406

FLACK, RONALD DUMONT, mechanical engineering educator; b. South Bend, Ind., Dec. 24, 1947; s. Ronald D. and A. Jeanette (Herr) F.; m. Nancy L. Slauson, Aug. 30, 1969; children: Melissa B., Todd A. BSME, Purdue U., 1970, MSME, 1973, PhD, 1975. Analytical design engr. Pratt & Whitney Aircraft, W. Palm Beach, Fla., 1970-71; asst. prof. U. Va., Charlottesville, 1976-81; assoc. prof. U. Va., 1981-87, prof., 1987—, chair dept., 1993—; cons. in field. Contbr. articles to profl. jours. Soccer coach Soccer Orgn. of Charlottesville (Va.)/Albemarle, 1981-86. Fulbright scholar Fulbright Found., Germany, 1988. Fellow ASME, Soc. Tribology and Lubrication Engrs., Am. Soc. Engring. Edn. Office: U Va Thronton Hall Charlottesville VA 22903-2442*

FLADUNG, RICHARD DENIS, lawyer; b. Kansas City, Mo., Aug. 1, 1953; s. Jerome Francis and Rosemary (Voeste) F.; m. Leslie Lynn Cox, June 1, 1985; children: Daniel Edwin, Erica Anne, Derek Richard. BSCE, U. Kans., 1976, postgrad., 1977; JD, Washburn U., 1980. Bar: Kans. 1980, U.S. Dist. Ct. Kans. 1980, Ind. 1981, U.S. Dist. Ct. (so. dist.) Ind. 1981, U.S. Patent and Trademark Office 1982, Mo. 1983, Tex. 1984, U.S. Dist. Ct. (we. dist.) Mo. 1983, U.S. Dist. Ct. (so. dist.) Tex. 1984, U.S. Ct. Appeals (fed. cir.) 1984, U.S. Ct. Appeals (5th cir.) 1987, U.S. Supreme Ct. 1987, U.S. Dist. Ct. (we. dist.) Tex. 1988. Engr. Black and Veatch Cons. Engrs., Kansas City, 1975-80; corp. counsel CTB Inc., Milford, Ind., 1980-82; patent atty. Chase & Yakimo and predecessor firm, Kansas City, 1982-83, Bush, Moseley, Riddle and Jackson and predecessor firm, Houston, 1983-87, Pravel, Hewitt & Kimball, Houston, 1987-98, Akin, Gump, Strauss, Hauer & Feld, Houston, 1999—. Contbr. articles on patent matters and ins. coverage for intellectual property matters to profl. edn. programs. Legal aide to spkr. of Kans. Ho. of Reps., Topeka, 1980. Named One of Outstanding Young Men of Am., 1985. Mem. ABA (vice chmn. patent, trademark sect. young lawyer div. 1988-89), ASCE, Houston Bar Assn. (ex officio bd. dirs. 1987-88, vice chmn. profl. responsibility com. 1991—), Am. Intellectual Property Law Assn., Tex. Young Lawyers Assn. (bd. dirs. 1988), Mo. Bar Assn., Ind. Bar Assn., Houston Young Lawyers Assn. (pres. 1987-88, exec. mem. bd. dirs. 1987-88, Outstanding Com. Chmn. award 1984-86), Kansas City Bar Assn., Houston Intellectual Property Law Assn., Pi Alpha Kappa (treas. 1974-75). Roman Catholic. Avocations: tennis, jogging, biking, golf. Office: Akin Gump Strauss Hauer & Feld 1900 Pennzoil Pl S Tower 711 Louisiana St Houston TX 77002

FLAGG, BARRY DAVID, insurance, corporate benefits, estate planning consultant; b. Summit, N.J., June 11, 1962; s. David Charles and Carole H. (Tresch) F.; m. Kelly M. McCathern, Sept. 12, 1987; children: Kathryn Carole, Samuel Barry II. BS in Fin. with honors, Seton Hall U., 1984. CFP, CLU, ChFC. With Deferred Benefits Corp., Springfield, N.J., 1981-83, Manulife Fin. Corp., Tampa, Fla., 1984-85, Thomas Fin. Group, Tampa, 1985—; adj. mem. faculty Coll. Fin. Planning, Denver, 1987—; lectr. various seminars; speaker radio talk show. Contbr. articles to various jours. Named one of Outstanding Young Men of Am. Mem. Internat. Bd. CFPs, Am. Soc. CLUs & ChFCs, Assn. Advanced Life Underwriters, Fla. West Coast Employee Benefit Coun., Tampa Estate Planning Coun., Million Dollar Round Table (ct. of the table, top of the table, qualifying), Assn. Life Underwriters (Nat. and Tampa chpts.), Beta Gamma Sigma Nat. Hon. Scholastic Soc. Office: Thomas Fin Group 601 Bayshore Blvd Ste 900 Tampa FL 33606-2761

FLAGG, E(LOISE) ALMA WILLIAMS, educational administrator; b. City Point, Va., Sept. 16, 1918; d. Hannibal Greene and Caroline Ethel (Moody) Williams; m. J. Thomas Flagg, Jr., June 24, 1942 (dec. Apr. 1994); children: Thomas L., Lois Luisa. BS, Newark State Coll., 1940, LittD (hon.), 1968; MA, Montclair (N.J.) State Coll., 1943; EdD, Columbia U., 1955. Tchr., Washington, 1941-43; with Newark Pub. Schs., 1943-83, vice-prin., 1963-64, prin., 1964-67, asst. supt., 1967-78, dir., 1978-83; bd. dirs. Krueger-Scott Mansion Cultural Ctr., Share-N.J., v.p., 1996—; cons. edn., 1972—; adj. instr., spkr. in field, poet-in-residence various pub. schs. Author: (poetry) Lines and Colors, 1979, Feelings, Lines, Colors, 1980, Twenty More with Thought and Feeling, 1981, Lines, Colors, and More, 1998; editor: Cardiac Valve Bioprosthesis. Mem. Newark Bicentennial Commn. Recipient various profl. awards; E. Alma Flagg Sch. erected, 1984; E. Alma Flagg Scholarship Fund established, 1984. Mem. NAACP (life), LWV (pres. Newark 1982-84), AAUW, ASCD, N.J. Hist. Soc., Nat. Soc. Study of Edn., Nat. Coun. Tchrs. of English, Nat. Assn. Negro Bus. and Profl. Women's Clubs (Truth award, 1985) Nat. Coun. Tchrs. of Math., Nat. Alliance Black Sch. Educators, Nat. Coun. Negro Women (life), Newark Sr. Citizen's Commn. (editl. cons. 1989—), Alpha Kappa Alpha (life), Kappa Delta Pi. Presbyterian. Home: 67 Vaughan Dr Newark NJ 07103-3470

FLAGG, HELEN CLAWSON, writer; b. Netcong, N.J., May 27, 1921; d. Clyde Leroy and Rose Ann (Wood) Wilgus; m. Raymond E. Clawson, Feb. 7, 1942 (dec. May 1988); children: Lana Hope (Mrs. Dale Hope), Rory Zane; m. Allen Macomber Flagg, Nov. 16, 1991. Student, Rutgers U., 1941-42. CEO, ATS Corp., nat. placement co., Ft. Collins, Colo., 1976-80; pres. Status Unltd., pub. rels., Ft. Collins, 1982-90; fin. planner Waddell & Reed, Ft. Collins, 1984-90; stockbroker Dean Witter, Clearwater, Fla., 1990-91; fin. planner, ins. rep. Walnut Street Securities, Clearwater, 1992-95; former pub. spr. on fin. and religious subjects. Author: Joy in the Morning, 1995; contbr. numerous articles to newspaper and mags., including Fortune mag. Cons., historian Presbyn. Ch., Clearwater, 1995-99; supporter numerous civic orgns; sec. Altrusa, Ft. Collins, 1976-80. Mem. NAFE. Republican. Avocations: writing, poetry, reading history. Home: 2359 Finlandia Ln Apt 49 Clearwater FL 33763-3333

FLAGG, JEANNE BODIN, editor; b. N.Y.C., July 13, 1925; d. G. William and Joan (Lippoth) Bergquist; m. Allen Elias Flagg, Apr. 15, 1955 (div. 1967); children—Jennifer Andrea, Christopher Trevor. B.A., Barnard Coll., 1947; M.A., Columbia U., 1950. Tech. editor Reinhold Pub. Corp., N.Y.C., 1951-57; editor Barnes & Noble, Inc., N.Y.C., 1967-71, Harper & Row Pubs., N.Y.C., 1971-88; sponsoring editor McGraw-Hill Pub. Co., N.Y.C., 1989-95. Home: 1015 Old Post Rd Mamaroneck NY 10543-3901

FLAGG, MICHAEL JAMES, communications and graphics company executive; b. N.Y.C., Aug. 14, 1958; s. Wilbor Thomas and Sylvia (Kobitz) F. BA with highest distinction, U. Va., 1980. Intern, internat. economist U.S. Customs, Washington, 1979; mgmt. assoc. First Nat. Bank Atlanta, 1980-81, cash mgmt. officer, 1981-83, asst. v.p., group mktg. mgr., 1983-84; treasury mgr., asst. to chief exec. officer Contel Corp., Atlanta, 1984-89; v.p. fin. Contel Office Communications, Inc., St. Louis, 1989-91; v.p., treas. Am. Internat., Inc., Chgo., 1991-94; v.p. fin. Alliance Capital, N.Y.C., 1994; sr. v.p. corp. bus. devel. USL Capital, San Francisco, 1995; CFO InterCall, Chgo., 1995, COO, 1996-97; cons. Heidrick & Struggles, Inc., 1997-99, ptnr., 1999—; instr. Am. Inst. Banking, 1982-83; chmn. Contel Profl. Devel. Assn., Atlanta, 1986. Assoc. editor Cash Mgmt. Forum, 1982-84; co-founder, coeditor First Word newsletter, 1983-84. Chmn. fundraising unit United Way, Atlanta, 1985-88, Atlanta unit Am. Cancer Soc., 1985-88, Atlanta Coll. Arts, 1985-88; governing mem. Brookfield Zoo, Chgo., 1992—. Mem. Nat. Corp. Cash Mgmt. Assn. (bd. dirs. 1987-91, exec. com. 1988-91), Fin. Execs.

Inst., Treasury Mgmt. Assn. Chgo., St. Louis Zoo Friends Assn. (bd. dirs. 1990-91). Avocations: sports, arts. Office: 233 S Wacker Dr Chicago IL 60606-6306

FLAGG, NORMAN LEE, retired advertising executive; b. Detroit, Jan. 21, 1932; s. Frank and Harriet (Brown) F.; m. Carolanne Flagg; children: James, Suzanne. BFA, U. Miami, Miami, Fla., 1958. Advt. supr. Smithkline Beckman, Phila., 1970-75, creative dir., 1975-80; owner Illusions Restaurants, Bryn Mawr, Pa., 1979-87, Illusions Restaurant, Tucson, Ariz., 1984-88. Author: Shooting Blanks, 1994. With USMC, 1954-56. Recipient Diana awards Whlse Druggest Assn. 1977, Aesculapius award Modern Medicine 1978. Mem. Acad. Magical Arts.

FLAGG, RONALD SIMON, lawyer; b. Milw., Dec. 3, 1953; s. Arnold and Marian (Levy) F.; m. Patricia Sharin, June 20, 1982; children: Laura Sharon, Emily Rachel, Naomi Erica. AB, U. Chgo., 1975; JD, Harvard U., 1978. Bar: Wis. 1978, U.S. Dist. Ct. (ea. dist.) Wis. 1978, U.S. Ct. Appeals (7th cir.) 1979, D.C. 1980, U.S. Dist. Ct. D.C. 1980, U.S. Ct. Appeals (D.C. cir.) 1980, U.S. Ct. Appeals (3d cir.) 1984, U.S. Supreme Ct. 1986, U.S. Ct. Appeals (5th cir.) 1987, U.S. Ct. Appeals (8th cir.) 1989. Law clk. to presiding judge U.S. Dist. Ct. (ea. dist.) Wis., Milw., 1978-80; atty., adv. office of intelligence policy and rev. U.S. Dept. Justice, Washington, 1980-82; assoc. Sidley & Austin, Washington, 1982-85, ptnr., 1986—. Bd. dirs. Nat. Vets. Legal Svcs. Program. Mem. ABA, D.C. Bar Assn. (pub. svc. activities com). Home: 3909 Garrison St NW Washington DC 20016-4219 Office: Sidley & Austin 1722 I St NW Fl 7 Washington DC 20006-3795

FLAHERTY, BARBARA A., marketing professional, artist; b. Attleboro, Mass., Mar. 14, 1948; d. Charles E. and Marion V. (King) F. BA, U. R.I., 1970; MLS, SUNY, 1974. Libr. dir. FCC, Washington, 1974-79; asst. prof., libr. Law Sch. George Mason U., Arlington, Va., 1979-81; market analyst GTE, Vienna, Va., 1981-84; mgr. strategic planning Northrop-Grumman Corp., Herndon, Va., 1989-94; market cons. INPUT, Inc., Vienna, Va., 1994-96; mgr. strategic planning Lucent Technologies, Washington, 1996-98. Author: Before the Snow Falls, 1997, The Hummingbird at Five O'Clock, 1998. Mem. Bus. and Profl. Womens Orgn., (pres. 1996-98, new membership enrollment 1998-99), Women in Def. (job bank coord., bd. dirs. 1998-99), Psychiat. Rehab. Svcs. (bd. dirs. 1996-97), Tower Club (coun. 1995-97). Avocations: reading, volunteer work, painting, walking on the beach. Office: Fed Data Corp 4800 Hampden Ln Bethesda MD 20814

FLAHERTY, CAROLE L., medical, surgical and mental health nurse; b. Des Moines, Feb. 27, 1938; d. Albert L. and Edythe Evelyn (Kuehl) Hildreth; m. Gary Alan Flaherty, June 2, 1956 (div. Feb. 1967); children: Brian Keith, Kelly Blaine. BS in Sociology-Psychology, Iowa State U., 1970; BSN, U. Iowa, 1972. Lic. counselor drugs and chem.; cert. alcohol and drug abuse counselor. Charge nurse. orthopaedic unit H.E.B. Harris Hosp., Bedford, Tex., 1984-87; relief charge nurse-psychiat., clin. nurse specialist Med. Plaza Hosp., Ft. Worth, 1987-88; charge nurse children's unit Psych. Inst., Ft. Worth, Tex., 1988-90; head nurse psychiat. and behavioral medicine unit N.E. Cmty. Hosp., Bedford, Tex., 1990-91; counselor alcohol and drug abuse and coord. supr. Schick-Shaddel Hosp., Ft. Worth, 1991-94; asst. dir. nursing, med. unit mgr. Park View Ctr., Ft. Worth, 1994-95; supr. weekends Baylor Med. Ctr., Grapevine, Tex., 1995-97; triage and health info. nurse Cigna, Dallas, 1997—; instr. Queens Med. Ctr., Honolulu, 1982. Mem. spl. support group for minorities U., Iowa, 1970; vol. crisis prayer line and Bible study courses 1st Bapt. Ch., Bedford, Tex., 1997—. Recipient Delta Airline award and pin, 1984; Health and Profl. grant U. Iowa, 1970-72. Mem. ANA, Mensa, Am. Assn. Ret. Persons (trip planner). Home: River Forest Estates 2508 Peach Blossom Ct Bedford TX 76021-7235

FLAHERTY, CHARLES FOSTER, JR., psychology educator, researcher; b. Hyannis, Mass., June 25, 1937; s. Charles Foster Sr. and Helen Claire (White) F.; m. Mary Dempsey; children: Brendan Thomas, Jennifer Ellen. BA, Northeastern U., 1964; MA, U. Wis., 1967, PhD, 1968. Prof. psychology Rutgers U., New Brunswick, N.J., 1968—, chmn. psychology dept., 1978-80, 83-86, 91—, assoc. dean arts and scis., 1987-88; reviewer NSF, Animal Learning and Behavior, Am. Jour. of Psychology, Jour. of Comparative Psychology. Author: Learning and Memory, 1977, Animal Learning and Cognition, 1985, Incentive Relativity, 1996; co-editor Current Topics in Animal Learning, 1991. Served with USAF, 1955-59. Grantee NSF, NIMH, Charles and Johanna Busch, 1983—. Mem. AAAS, Soc. for Neurosci., Psychonomic Soc., N.Y. Acad. of Scis., Am. Psychol. Soc. Republican. Office: Rutgers U Psychology Dept New Brunswick NJ 08903

FLAHERTY, DAVID THOMAS, JR., lawyer; b. Boston, June 17, 1953; S. David Thomas Sr. and Nancy Ann (Hamill) F.; m. Margaret Lynn Hoyle, Oct. 2, 1986; children: Alexandra Lynn, David Thomas III. BS in Math., German, U. N.C., 1974, JD, 1978. Bar: Mass. 1979, N.C. 1979, U.S. Dist. Ct. (we. dist.) N.C. 1979, U.S. Dist. Ct. (mid. dist.) N.C. 1981, U.S. Ct. Appeals (4th cir.) 1981, U.S. Tax Ct. 1982, U.S. Supreme Ct., 1987, U.S. Ct. Fed. Claims, 1992. Assoc. Wilson & Palmer, Lenoir, N.C., 1979-80, Ted West P.A., Lenoir, 1980-82; ptnr. Robbins, Flaherty & Lackey, Lenoir, 1982-85, Robbins & Flaherty, Lenoir, 1985-88, Delk, Flaherty, Swanson & Hartshorn, P.A., Lenoir, 1988-89, Delk, Flaherty, Robbins, Swanson & Hartshorn, P.A., Lenoir, 1989-90, Flaherty, Robbins, Swanson & Hartshorn, P.A., 1990-95; dist. atty. 25th prosecutorial dist. Office Dist. Atty., Lenoir, 1995—; mem. N.C. Ho. of Reps., Raleigh, 1988-94, N.C. Cts. Commn., 1989—, N.C. Jud. Adv. Commn., 1997—. Mem. exec. com. Caldwell County Reps., Lenoir, 1985-86, 88—. Mem. N.C. Bar Assn., N.C. Conf. Dist. Attys., 25th Judicial Dist. Bar Assn. (mem. exec. com. 1987-88). Reps. Men's Club, Blue Key. Methodist. Avocations: water and snow skiing, motorcycling. Home: 228 Pennton Ave SW Lenoir NC 28645-4316 Office: Office of Dist Atty Caldwell County Courthouse PO Box 718 Lenoir NC 28645-0718

FLAHERTY, EMALEE GOTTBRATH, pediatrician; b. LaGrange, Ky., May 24, 1944; d. Frank Herman and Katherine Lee (Carothers) Gottbrath; m. Joseph Flaherty, Apr. 28, 1973 (div.); children: Joshua, Megan. BS, Purdue U., W. Lafayette, Ind., 1966; MD, Ind. U., Indpls., 1970. Resident, pediatrics U. Ill. Hosp., 1970-72, Columbus Hosp., 1972-73; med. dir. outpatient dept. Columbus Hosp., Chgo., 1984-96; med. dir. Columbus-Maryville Reception Ctr., Chgo., 1986-95; dir. ambulator pediatrics Columbus Hosp., Chgo., 1979-96, project dir. pediatric primary care tng. grant, 1989-95; med. dir. protective svc. team Children's Meml. Hosp., Chgo., 1996—. Mem. Am. Acad. Pediat. (chpt. treas.), Pediatric Primary Care Rsch. Grp. (steering com.), Pediatric Rsch. Office Setting (dist. coord.), Columbus Hosp. Woman's Bd. (exec. bd. 1988—). Office: Children's Hosp 2300 N Childrens Plz # 16 Chicago IL 60614-3363

FLAHERTY, JOHN JOSEPH, quality assurance company executive; b. Chgo., July 24, 1932; s. Patrick J. and Mary B. F.; BEE, U. Ill., 1959; m. Norrine Grow, Nov. 20, 1954 (dec. Sept. 1995); children: John, Bridgette, George, Eileen, Daniel, Mary, Michael, Amy. Design engr. Admiral Corp., Chgo., 1959-60; project engr. Magnaflux Corp., Chgo., 1960-79, v.p., mgr. research and engring., 1979-84, v.p., mgr. mktg. and sales, 1984-86; v.p., gen. mgr. electronic products, 1986-88; pres. Flare Tech., Chgo., 1988—. Served with AUS, 1951-53. Fellow Am. Soc. Non-Destructive Testing; mem. IEEE, Am. Soc. Metals. Roman Catholic. Numerous patents, publs. on nondestructive testing, including med. ultrasonic; laser scanning. Home: 671 Grosvener Ln Elk Grove Village IL 60007-4203 Office: 2869 Old Higgins Rd Elk Grove Village IL 60007-6416

FLAHERTY, JOHN PAUL, JR., state supreme court chief justice; b. Pitts., Nov. 19, 1931; s. John Paul and Mary G. (McLaughlin) F.; m. Linet Flaherty; 7 children, 2 stepchildren. BA, Duquesne U., 1953; JD, U. Pitts., 1958; LLD (hon.), Widener U., 1993. Bar: Pa. 1958. Pvt. practice Pitts., 1958-73; mem. faculty Carnegie-Mellon U., 1958-73; judge Ct. Common Pleas Allegheny County, 1973-79, pres. judge civil div., 1978-79; justice Supreme Ct. Pa., 1979-96, chief justice, 1996—; USIA speaker in Far East, 1985-86. Mem. Pa. Hist. Soc.; bd. visitors U. Pitts. Sch. Law; chair Pa. County Records Com. Recipient Medallion of Distinction U. Pitts., 1987; named Man of Yr. in law and govt., Greater Pitts. Jaycees, 1978, named to Century Club of Disting. Alumni, Duquesne U., 1994; recipient Judicial award Pa. Bar Assn., 1993. Mem. Pa. Acad. Sci. (chmn. hon. exec. bd. 1978-89, Disting. Alumnus award 1977), Am. Law Inst., Pa. Soc., Mil. History Soc. Ireland, Friendly Sons St. Patrick, Am. Legion. Office: Pa Supreme Ct 6 Gateway Ctr Pittsburgh PA 15222-1318 *The law is the energy of the living world, and although developed and defined by the judiciary in our Anglo-American society, it is applied and is derived by and from the people. It exists only to protect one person from being hurt, physically or economically, by another. Serious problems face our age. In the final analysis, the judiciary must accomodate the various solutions which will be forthcoming. I hope that my brothers have the foresight and the stamina to accomodate what might be quite novel innovations in the law, which is the living energy, to make this world a place in which it's worth living, since that is the function of the law. Every case involves people. There is no such thing as a small case.*

FLAHERTY, LOIS TALBOT, psychiatrist, educator; b. Nashville, Apr. 28, 1942. BA, Wellesley Coll., 1963; MD, Duke U., 1968. Diplomate Nat. Bd. Med. Examiners. Intern D.C. Gen. Hosp., 1968-69; resident in psychiatry Georgetown U. Hosp., 1969-71; resident in child psychiatry Johns Hopkins Hosp., 1971-73; pvt. practice Cross Keys, Md., 1973-81; dir. tng. div. child and adolescent psychiatry U. Md., 1981-89, assoc. prof. med. sch. div. child and adolescent psychiatry, 1982-93, dir. div. child and adolescent psychiatry, 1984-92, adj. assoc. prof., 1994—; clin. assoc. prof. psychiatry U. Pa., 1997—; pvt. practice Blue Bell, Pa., 1994—; instr. depts. psychiatry and pediatrics Johns Hopkins U. Sch. Medicine, 1973-92; attending staff psychiatrist family, child and adolescent div. Sinai Hosp. Balt., 1974-77; staff child psychiatrist Walter P. Carter Ctr., 1977-78, dir. child and adolescent svcs., 1978-92, acting dir. impatient adolescent unit, 1979-80; clin. asst. prof. U. Md., 1977-81; cons. Northwest Drug Alert Sinai Hosp. Balt., 1971-72, St. Vincent's Child Care Ctr., 1973-78, Children's Guild, Inc., 1975-82, SSA, Balt., 1985, many others. Contbr. chpts. to books and articles and book revs. to profl. jours. NIMH grantee, 1983-86. Fellow Am. Psychiat. Assn., Am. Soc. for Adolescent Psychiatry; mem. Am. Acad. Child Psychiatry, Am. Coll. Psychiatrists, Group for Advancement of Psychiatry, Pa. Psychiatr. Soc., Pa. Soc. for Adolescent Psychiatry, Pa. Regional Coun. for Child and Adolescent Psychiatry. Office: Spectrum AQE 6198 Butler Pike Ste 145 Blue Bell PA 19422-2602*

FLAHERTY, MARTIN STEPHEN, law educator; b. Bklyn., Dec. 15, 1958; s. John Edmund and Christine Hovick Flaherty; m. Christine Kelly Loo; 1 child, Aisling Jincui Loo Flaherty. AB, Princeton U., 1981; MA, Yale U., 1982, MPhil, 1987; JD, Columbia U., 1988. Law clk. hon. John J. Gibbons chief judge U.S. Ct. Appeals 3rd Cir., Newark, Phila., 1988-89; law clk. Byron R. White U.S. Supreme Ct., Washington, 1990-91; prof. Fordham Law Sch., N.Y.C., 1989-90, 91—, co-dir. Joseph R. Crowley Program in Internat. Human Rights, 1997—; cons. Lawyers Com. for Human Rights, N.Y.C., 1992—. Ford Found. grantee, Beijing; ITT/Fulbright fellow IIE, Trinity Coll., Dublin, Ireland, 1981-82. Avocations: running, sailing. E-mail: mflaherty@mail.lawnet.fordham.edu. Office: Fordham Law Sch 140 W 62nd St New York NY 10023

FLAHERTY, SISTER MARY JEAN, dean, nursing educator. Dean, prof. Sch. Nursing, Cath. U. Am., Washington. Office: Cath U Am Sch of Nursing Washington DC 20064-0001*

FLAHERTY, PATRICK JOHN, state legislator, economist; b. Hartford, Conn., May 21, 1961; s. Richard James Cromie and Harriette Mildred (Dougherty) Christensen. BA, Harvard U., 1984. Wire operator E.F. Hutton, Hartford, 1984-85; sr. investment acctg. clk. Conn. Nat. Bank, Hartford, 1985-86; asst. economist Shawmut Bank, Hartford, 1986-95; assoc. economist Fleet Fin. Group, 1995—; mem. Conn. Ho. of Reps., Hartford, 1993—, mem. com. on fin., revenue and bonding, 1993—, chmn. select com. on housing, 1995, mem. edn. com., 1999—. Mem. Coventry (Conn.) Town Coun., 1985-87; treas. Booth and Dimock Libr., Coventry, 1987-89; chmn. Coventry Bd. Edn., 1989-92. Democrat. Congregationalist. Home: PO Box 570 Coventry CT 06238-0570 Office: Conn Ho of Reps Legis Office Bldg 4041 Hartford CT 06106

FLAHERTY, ROBERTA D., educational association administrator; b. Sharon, Pa., Aug. 7, 1947; d. Thomas and Esther Dornes Roberts; m. Glassel D. Flaherty, Sept. 4, 1966; 1 child, Erin Leigh. BEd, Washburn U., 1970; MS in Edn., Kans. State U., 1975; postgrad., Harvard U., 1985, Kans. State U., 1985-89. Admissions office staff Kans. State U., Manhattan, 1970-75, acad. advisor divsn. continuing edn., 1975-77, asst. dir. acad. outreach, 1977-78, dir. confs., 1978-88, assoc. dir. divsn. continuing edn., 1986-90; exec. dir. Nat. Acad. Adv. Assn., Manhattan, 1990—; instr. hotel and restaurant mgmt. Kans. State U., Manhattan, 1989—. Bd. dirs. United Way Riley County, Manhattan, 1984-87, campus campaign chmn., 1986; program chmn. Future Manhattan Leadership Program, 1989. Mem. Nat. Univ. Continuing Edn. Assn. (chmn., officer region V 1979-83, nat. chmn. officer confs. and insts. divsn. 1984-90, Leadership award 1988, Stanley C. Robinson Disting. Svc. award 1991), Am. Soc. Assn. Execs. Avocation: antiques. Home: 4427 Tuttle Cove Rd Manhattan KS 66503-8842 Office: Kans State U Coll Edn 2323 Anderson Ave Ste 226 Manhattan KS 66502-2912

FLAHERTY, STEPHEN, composer, orchestrator. Composer songs including: Once On This Island (Tony nomination for best score and best musical, 1995 Olivier award for London's Best Musical), My Favorite Year, Lucky Stiff, Anastasia (Academy Award nominations for best score and best song, 2 Golden Globe nominations); composer incidental music for Neil Simon's play: Proposals; concert pieces include: Suite From Ragtime, Anastasia Swuite. Winner 1998 Tony Award for original musical score "Ragtime", also Drama Desk award, Outer Critics Cir. award. Mem. ASCAP, Dramatists Guild, Drama Dept. Office: c/o Songwriters Guild of Am 1560 Broadway Rm 1306 New York NY 10036*

FLAHERTY, STEPHEN MATTHEW, academic administrator; b. May 27, 1950. MBA, Capital U.; MA, Ohio State U., PhD. Prof. Devry Inst., Columbus, Ohio, 1980-87; dean bus. programs Devry Inst., Columbus, 1987-90; assoc. v.p. Ohio U., Athens, 1990—. E-mail: flaherty@ohiou.edu. Office: 206 Cutler Hall Athens OH 45701

FLAHERTY, TINA SANTI, corporate communications executive; b. Memphis; d. Clement Alexander and Dale (Pendergrast) Santi; m. William Edward Flaherty, Feb. 22, 1975. B.A., Memphis State U., 1961; hon. doctorate, St. John's U., 1979. Commentator host interview program Sta. WMC-TV, Memphis, 1960-61; newscaster, commentator Sta. WHER, Memphis, 1961-62; community rels. specialist Western Electric Co., N.Y.C., 1964-66; v.p. pub. rels. div. Grey Advt., N.Y.C., 1966-72; dep. dir. corp. rels. Colgate-Palmolive Co., N.Y.C., 1972-75; dir. corp. rels. Colgate-Palmolive Co., 1975-76, corp. v.p., v.p. in charge of communications, 1976-84; v.p. pub. affairs GTE Corp., Stamford, Conn., 1984-86; pres., chief exec. officer Image Mktg. Internat., N.Y.C., 1986—. Author: The Savvy Woman's Success Bible, 1997. Former chmn. Bus. Coun. of UN Decade for Women; bd. dirs. Nat. Jr. Achievement, 1978—, Hugh O'Brian Youth Found., 1979-84; mem. The White House Pub. Affairs Advisors, 1981-84; nat. bd. dirs. Animal Med. Ctr.; mem. women's bd. Cen. Park Conservancy, 1992—. Recipient Jr. Achievement Meml. award, 1984; Named One of N.Y.C.'s Outstanding Women of Achievement NCCJ, 1978; One of 100 Top Corp. Women Bus. Week, 1976, One of 73 Women Ready to Run Corp. Am., Working Woman, 1985; named Woman of Distinction Birmingham So. Coll., 1991. Mem. Com. of 200, Internat. Women's Forum. Home and Office: Image Mktg Internat 1040 5th Ave New York NY 10028-0137 *Persistence alone is omnipotent.*

FLAHERTY, WILLIAM E., chemicals and metals company executive; b. 1933. Formerly with GM Overseas Corp., Reynolds Metals Co.; with Gulf & Western, 1974-81, past COO zinc and chems. divsn.; now chmn. bd., CEO Horsehead Industries, N.Y.C.; chmn. bd. Great Lakes Carbon Corp. Office: Horsehead Industries 110 E 59th St New York NY 10022-1304*

FLAKE, FLOYD HAROLD, former congressman; b. L.A., Jan. 30, 1945; m. M. Elaine McCollins; children: Aliya, Nailah, Rasheed, Hasan. BA in Psychology, Wilberforce U., 1967; D in Ministry, United Theol. Sem., Dayton, Ohio, 1995; postgrad., Northeastern U. Social worker, 1968-69; sales rep. Reynolds Tobacco Co., 1969; mktg. analyst Xerox Corp., 1969-70; assoc. dean students, dir. student activities Lincoln U., Pa., 1970-73; dean students, univ. chaplain, dir.Martin Luther King Jr. Afro-Am. Ctr. Boston U., 1973-76; mem. 101st-105th Congresses from 6th N.Y. dist., Washington, 1987-97, mem. banking and fin. svcs. com., mem. domestic & internat. monetary policy subcom., mem. small bus. com.; pastor Allen A.M.E. Ch., Jamaica, N.Y., 1976—; sr. fellow Manhattan Inst., 1998—; bd. dirs. Fannie Mae Found. columnist N.Y. Post, 1999; author: The Way of the Bootstrapper: Nine Action Steps For Achieving Your Dreams. Pastor Allen A.M.E. Ch., Jamaica, N.Y., past chmn. affiliate corps. including Allen Sr. Citizen Complex, Allen Christian Sch. and Multi-Purpose Ctr., Allen Home Care Agy., Allen Housing Corp., So. Jamaica Multi-Svc. Ctr. Alfred Sloan fellow Northeastern U., Danforth fellow Payne Theol. Sem.; Gilbert H. Jones scholar Wilberforce U. Office: Allen AME Ch 11031 Merrick Blvd Jamaica NY 11433-3440

FLAKES, SUSAN, playwright, screenwriter, director; b. San Diego, July 9, 1943; d. Herbert Franklin and Dorothy Jean (Loafman) Barrows; m. Donald Lewis Flakes, Dec. 31, 1964; 1 child, Daniel Keith. BA, U. N.Mex., 1965; MA, San Diego State U., 1969; PhD, U. Minn., 1973. Asst., then assoc. prof. Tisch Sch. Arts NYU, 1973-76, dept. chair Tisch Sch. Arts, 1973-76; founder, artistic dir. Blue Tower Theatre, Stockholm, 1977-80, Strindberg's Intima Teater, Stockholm, 1981-83, Source Prodns., N.Y.C., 1984-90; instr. U.S. Internat. Univ., San Diego, 1972-73; founder, artistic dir. 1st Strindberg Festival, Stockholm, 1977; mem. Women's Project and Prodns., N.Y.C., 1984-90; v.p. Ibsen Soc. Am., N.Y.C., 1986-99; coord. writers unit W. Coast Ensemble Theatre, Hollywood, Calif., 1991-93. Author plays, 1977, 92, 95-97, 98, 99, The Woman Will Play Strindberg's Christina, Silent Star, And Immortality, Portrait of Psyche, My Daddy's Eyes, To Take Arms, Cafe L.A., 4F; (libretto) Take It Higher, Maid of Lorraine, Listening to Angels (with Gabe Green); (screenplays) Angel in the Attic, Hometown, Inc., Cafe L.A., The Rogue; dir. Hughie, 1989, Mother Love, 1994; contbr. articles to profl. jours. and books; creator Exptl. Theatre Wing U.G. Drama Tisch Sch. Arts, NYU, 1975-76. Ensign USN, 1965-67. Fellow Am. Film Inst., 1990; grantee Nat. Endowment for Arts, 1972; travel grantee Am. Scandinavian Found., Norwegian and Swedish Govts., 1985, 86, 89, 94; finalist Susan Smith Blackburn prize, 1996-97. Mem. Dramatists Guild, Phi Beta Kappa. Address: care Barbara Alexander Media Artists Group Lit 8383 Wilshire Blvd Ste 954 Beverly Hills CA 90211-2408

FLAM, JACK DONALD, art historian, educator; b. Paterson, N.J., Apr. 2, 1940; s. Max and Rose Leila (Silverberg) F.; m. Bonnie Suzanne Burnham, Oct. 7, 1972 (div.); 1 child, Laura Rose. BA, Rutgers U., 1961; MA, Columbia U., 1963; PhD, NYU, 1969. Instr. Rutgers U., Newark, N.J., 1962-66; asst. prof. U. Fla., Gainesville, 1966-69, assoc. prof., 1969-72; assoc. prof. Bklyn. Coll., 1975-80, prof. grad. ctr., 1980-90, disting. prof., 1991—. Author: Matisse on Art, 1973, Bread and Butter, 1977, Robert Motherwell, 1983, Matisse, the Man and His Art, 1986, Motherwell, 1991, Richard Diebenkorn: Ocean Park, 1992, Matisse: The Dance, 1993, Western Artists/African Art, 1994, Robert Smithson: The Collected Writings, 1996; art critic Wall St. Jour., N.Y.C., 1984-92. Guggenheim Found. fellow, 1979, NEH, 1986. Mem. Internat. Art Critics Assn., Internat. PEN, Coll. Art Assn. Am. Office: Bklyn Coll Art Dept Bedford Ave # H Brooklyn NY 11210-2889

FLAMINI, JOHN ANTHONY, physician; b. May 31, 1954. BA, U. Pa., 1976; MD, Loyola U., Chgo., 1979. Physician Neurology Assocs. of Erie, Pa., 1983—; trustee St. Vincent Health Sys., Erie, 1996-98. E-mail: jflamini@velocity.net. Office: 3504 State St Erie PA 16508-2834

FLANAGAN, BARBARA, journalist; b. Des Moines; d. John Merrill and Marie (Barnes) F.; m. Earl S. Sanford, 1966. Student, Drake U., 1942-43. With promotion dept. Mpls. Times, 1945-47; reporter Mpls. Tribune, 1947-58; women's editor, spl. writer Mpls. Star and Tribune, 1958-65; columnist Mpls. Star, 1965—. Author: Ovation, Minneapolis. Active Junior League Mpls., Womans Club Mpls.; bd. dirs. Minn. Opera., Friends of Mpls. Pub. Libr. Mem. Mpls. Soc. Fine Arts (life), Mpls. Inst. Arts (founding mem. Minn. Arts Forum), Kappa Alpha Theta, Sigma Delta Chi. Episcopalian. Home: 3200 W Calhoun Pky Apt 301 Minneapolis MN 55416-4650 Office: Mpls Star Tribune 5th and Portland Sts Minneapolis MN 55488

FLANAGAN, CHRISTIE STEPHEN, lawyer; b. Port Arthur, Tex., June 28, 1938; s. Christie John and Rita Catherine (Hancock) F.; m. Gretchen Dowling Neuhoff; children: Mary Eileen, Margaret, Christopher, Michael. BBA, U. Notre Dame, 1960; LLB, U. Tex., Austin, 1962. Bar: Tex. 1962. Assoc. firm Hutcheson & Grundy, Houston, 1962-68; ptnr. Jenkens & Gilchrist, Dallas, 1968-88, mng. ptnr., 1982-87; mem. Jenkens & Gilchrist, P.C., 1988—. Dir. Calif. Preferred Capital Corp., 1997—. Active Dallas Citizens Coun., 1982-92; trustee Hockaday Sch., 1980-86, St. Marks Sch. of Tex., 1986-92, Serra Internat. Found., 1984-88. Mem. ABA, Tex. Bar Assn., Dallas Bar Assn., Salesmanship Club, Serra Club of Dallas, Fishers Island Club, Brook Hollow Golf Club, Coon Creek Club. Office: Jenkens & Gilchrist PC 1445 Ross Ave Ste 3200 Dallas TX 75202-2785*

FLANAGAN, CLYDE HARVEY, JR., psychiatrist, psychoanalyst, educator; b. Louellen, Ky., Aug. 21, 1939; s. Clyde H. Sr. and Ruby Marie (Caldwell) F.; m. Gloria Kay Glymph, June 1,1961 (div. Feb. 1974); children: Clyde H. III, Christpher Shane; m. Carol Anne Ross, Apr. 13, 1974; children: Patrick Ross, Colleen Helen. *Parents, Clyde Sr. and Ruby, of Maryville, Tennessee, celebrate 62 years of marriage October 31, 2000. Mr. Flanagan's oldest child, Clyde III (Jay), his wife Stacy and four children, ages 5 to 11 years, reside near Harrisburg, Pennsylvania, where Jay, an ordained minister, is Director of Second Chance Prison Ministries. His wife, Carol Ross, a registered nurse, was President of the student body during her senior year, in 1970, at Saint Luke's Nursing School, San Francisco. Joining the Army Nurse Corp, she was a top honors graduate of Psychiatric Nursing Training, Walter Reed Army Hospital, Washington, D.C., in 1971, and developed a psychiatric nursing consultation program to medical-surgical wards at Walter Reed in 1971-72.* BS, Maryville Coll., 1962; MD, U. Tenn. Med. Unit, Memphis, 1966. Diplomate Am. Bd. Psychiatry and Neurology, Am. Bd. Child and Adolescent Psychiatry and Neurology, Nat. Bd. Med. Examiners, Am. Bd. Forensic Medicine. Commd. 2d lt. U.S. Army, 1965, advanced through grades to col., 1980; rotating med. intern U.S. Army Tripler Gen. Hosp., Honolulu, 1966-67; gen. psychiatry resident U.S. Army Walter Reed Gen. Hosp, Washington, 1967-69, child psychiatry resident, 1969-71; asst. chief child guidance svc. Walter Reed Army Med. Ctr., Washington, 1971-80; chief cmty. mental health activity Ft. Belvoir, Va., 1980-86; asst. head tri-svc. alcohol rehab. dept. Nat. Navy Hosp., Bethesda, Md., 1986-88, ret., 1988; dir. gen. psychiat. residency program W.S. Hall Psychiat. Inst., Columbia, S.C., 1988-92; prof. dept. of psychiatry/behavioral sci. Sch. Medicine U. S.C., Columbia, 1988—, dir. divsn. psychoanalysis dept. psychiat./behavioral sci., 1992—; candidate in psychoanalysis Washington Psychoanalytic Inst., 1978-88; tng. and supervising analyst U. N.C./Duke PSA Ednl. Program, Chapel Hill, 1991—. Contbr. chpt. to books in field. Recipient Tchr. Yr. award Resident's Gen. Psychiat. Rsch. Program William S. Hall Psychiat. Inst., 1995. Fellow Am. Psychiat. Assn., Am. Acad. Child and Adolescent Psychiatry (Franklin Robinson award 1975); mem. Am. Psychoanalytic Assn. (councilor 1989—, cert. in adult, adolescent, and child psychoanalysis Bd. Profl. Stds. 1991), Am. Coll. Psychiatrists (mem. comm. pub. edn. 1998—), N.C. Psychoanalytic Soc. (councilor 1989-98), S.C. Psychiat. Soc. (membership chmn. 1991—), Am. Coll. Forensic Examiners (diplomate), Am. Group Psychotherapy Assn. (cert. group psychotherapist), Assn. Psychoanalysis Culture and Soc., Internat. Psychoanalytic Assn., Am. Bd. Forensic Medicine. Avocations: fishing, boating, collecting stamps, books, and coins. Office: U SC Sch Medicine Dept Neuropsychiatry 3555 Harden Street Ext Ste 104A Columbia SC 29203-6894

FLANAGAN, DAVID THOMAS, lawyer, attorney general; b. St. Louis, July 25, 1944; s. David Thomas and Mary Jane (Woodley) F.; m. Maureen Anne McGlynn, May 29, 1978; children: Michael, Daniel, Anne Marie. BSCE, U. Mo., Rolla, 1967; JD, U. Wis., 1974. Bar: Wis. 1974, U.S. Dist. Ct. (we. dist.) Wis. 1974, U.S. Ct. Appeals (7th cir.) 1976, U.S. Patent and Trademark Office 1985; registered profl. engr., Wis. Staff atty. Legal Svcs. of N.W. Pa., Erie, 1975; asst. atty. gen. Wis. Dept. Justice, Madison, 1976—. Lt. USNR, 1968-71. Office: Wis Dept of Justice PO Box 7857 Madison WI 53707-7857

FLANAGAN, DEBORAH MARY, lawyer; b. Hackensack, N.J., Sept. 17, 1956; d. Joseph Francis and Mary Agnes (Fitzsimmons) F.; m. Glen H. Koch, Aug. 27, 1983. BA summa cum laude, Fordham U., 1978, JD, 1981; LLM in Taxation, NYU, 1987. Bar: N.Y. 1982 and U.S. Dist. Ct. 1988. V.p., assoc. tax counsel The McGraw-Hill Inc. Cos., N.Y.C., 1981—. Mem. Assn. Bar City N.Y., Fordham U. Law Alumni Assn., NYU Law Alumni Assn. Home: 201 Chestnut Ridge Rd Saddle River NJ 07458-2812 Office: The McGraw-Hill Cos Ste 2401 1221 Avenue of the Americas New York NY 10020-1001

FLANAGAN, DENNIS, journalist; b. N.Y.C., July 22, 1919; s. John Richard and Nan (Apotheker) F.; m. Geraldine A. Lux, Jan. 9, 1948; children: Cara Louise, John Gerard; m. Ellen Raskin; Oct. 17, 1966. A.B., Mich., 1941. Staff writer Life mag., 1941-47; mng. editor Scientific Am., 1947-50, editor, 1950-84; dir. Bull. Atomic Scientists, 1983-93; vis. and supernumerary fellow St. Cross Coll., Oxford, 1974-84; Marsh prof. U. Mich., 1985; Centennial prof. Wash. State U., 1989. Author: Flanagan's Version: A Spectator's Guide to Science on the Eve of the 21st Century, 1988. Trustee Marine Biol. Lab., Woods Hole, Mass., 1975-83, N.Y. Hall of Sci., 1965—; mem. vis. com. for linguistics and philosophy MIT, 1984-86. Recipient Outstanding Achievement award U. Mich., 1961, Kalinga prize UN Ednl., Sci. and Cultural Orgn., 1982, Glenn T. Seaborg award Internat. Platform Assn., 1982 , Olive Br. award Writers' and Pubs. Alliance for Disarmament, 1984; named to Mag. Editors' Hall of Fame, 1999. Fellow Am. Acad. Arts and Scis.; mem. Am. Soc. Mag. Editors (pres. 1977-79), Authors Guild, Century Assn., Sigma Xi. Home: 12 Gay St New York NY 10014-3538

FLANAGAN, DON, coach; m. Wahleah Flanagan; children: Sean, Shane, Brent. BA, Ft. Lewis Coll., 1971. Coach Eldorado H.S., Albuquerque, 1979-95; head coach women's basketball program U. N.Mex., 1995—. Named Albuquerque Jour. Coach of Yr., 1980, 81, 84, 87, 90, 92, Albuquerque Tribune Coach of Yr., 1980, 81, 83, 84, 87, 90, Bank of Am. Coach of Yr., 1993, 94, Albuquerque Sports Hall of Ame Coach of Yr., 1992, Region VIII Coach of Yr., 1985-94. Office: U N Mex South Athletics Complex Athletics Media Rels Dept Albuquerque NM 87131-0041*

FLANAGAN, FIONNULA MANON, actress, writer, producer; b. Dublin, Ireland; came to U.S., 1968; d. Terence Niall and Rosanna (McGuirk) F.; m. Garrett O'Connor, Nov. 26, 1972. C.I.H.E., U. Fribourg, Switzerland, 1962; student, Abbey Theatre Sch., Dublin, 1964-66. pres. The Rejoycing Co., 1978—. Stage appearances include: Ulysses in Nighttown, N.Y.C., 1974, Lovers, 1968, Ghosts, 1989, Happy Days, 1991, Unfinished Stories, 1992, Countess Cathleen, 1992, Summerhouse, 1994; author, actress one-woman shows: James Joyce's Women, 1977 (L.A. Drama Critics award, San Francisco Theatre Critics award, Drama-Logue award); films include: Ulysses, 1967, In the Region of Ice, 1980, Mr. Patman, 1980, James Joyce's Women, 1984, Reflections, 1984, Chain Reaction, 1985, Death Dreams, 1992, Mad at the Moon, 1992, Money for Nothing, 1993, Some Mother's Son, 1996, Wakeing Ned, 1998; TV appearances include: The Picture of Dorian Gray, 1973, The Legend of Lizzie Borden, 1975, Rich Man Poor Man, 1976 (Emmy award for most outstanding support role 1976), How the West Was Won, 1977-79 (Emmy nominee 1978), A Winner Never Quits, 1986, White Mile, 1994, Kings in Grass Castles, 1998, To Have and To Hold, 1998; dir. Freedom of the City, Theatre West L.A., 1988 (Dramalogue award), Faith Healer, 1989, Away Alone, Court Theatre, L.A., 1991, Abbey Theatre, Dublin, 1992. Mem. AFTRA, Actors' Equity, Screen Actors' Guild, Irish Actors Equity. Office: care K&K Entertainment 9034 Sunset Blvd Ste 250 Los Angeles CA 90039

FLANAGAN, FRANCIS DENNIS, retired corporate executive; b. Dunkirk, N.Y., Mar. 6, 1912; s. Mark Francis and Margaret (Ready) F.; m. Margaret L. McNamara, Nov. 23, 1939 (dec. 1986); children: Sheila Flanagan Cones, Mark F., Martha Flanagan Casper, Catherine, Nora Flanagan Nutter, Dennis M., Molly, Patricia; m. Elizabeth Ann Wainwright Bennett, Aug. 8, 1987 (dec. 1995); 1 stepchild, Carole Ann Bennett. Ph.B., Canisius Coll., Buffalo, 1933; LL.B., Georgetown U., 1938. Bar: D.C. bar 1937. Spl. agt. FBI, 1939-44; chief investigator war investigating com. U.S. Senate, 1944-46, asst. chief counsel, then chief counsel permanent subcom. on investigations, 1946-54; asst. v.p. W.R. Grace & Co., 1954-67, v.p., mgr. Washington ops., 1967-86. Mem. Soc. Former Agts. FBI, Friendly Sons St. Patrick, Washington Bar Assn. Clubs: Univ. (Washington); Congressional Country (Bethesda, Md.). Home: 2838 28th St NW Washington DC 20008-4110

FLANAGAN, HARRY PAUL, publishing executive; b. Columbus, Ohio, Dec. 8, 1933; children: Mary Beth, Kevin Hugh, Megan Joan. BS in Mktg., Ohio State U., 1956; Cert. in Mgmt., Capital U., Columbus, 1982, Advanced Mgmt. Cert., 1983. Pers. trainer For Lazarus Co., Columbus, 1960-61; supr. Wesleyan Press Co., Columbus, 1961-65; mgr. Xerox Ednl. Publs., Columbus, 1965-84; mgr. Field Publs., Columbus, 1984-89, ret., 1989; corp. dir. Highlights for Children, Columbus, 1989-94; ret., 1994—; pvt. practice bus. cons., freelance photographer Columbus, 1995—. Chmn. Christ the King Sch. Bd., Columbus, 1975-80, mem. parish coun., 1968-78, 91-94, 96—, pres., 1994-96, chmn. golden jubilee com., 1995-96; bd. dirs. Multiple Sclerosis Soc., Franklin County, Ohio, 1980-83. Recipient citation from Jr. Achievement, Columbus, 1966, Vol. award Ohio Ho. of Reps., 1975. Mem. Am. Mgmt. Assn., Fulfillment Mgrs. Assn., Techs. User Assn., Direct Mail Assn., Customer Svc. Coun. Roman Catholic. Avocations: golf, tennis, photography. Home and Office: 1236 Haddon Rd Columbus OH 43209-2928

FLANAGAN, JAMES HENRY, JR., lawyer; b. San Francisco, Sept. 11, 1934; s. James Henry Sr. and Mary Patricia (Gleason) F.; m. Charlotte Anne Nevins, June 11, 1960; children: Nancy, Christopher, Christina, Alexis, Victoria, Grace. AB in Polit. Sci., Stanford U., 1956, JD, 1961. Bar: Calif. 1962, U.S. Dist. Ct. (no. dist.) Calif. 1962, U.S. Ct. Appeals (9th cir.) 1962, U.S. Dist. Co. (so. dist.) Calif. 1964, U.S. Dist. Ct. (ea. dist.) Calif. 1967, Oreg. 1984. Assoc. Creede, Dawson & McElrath, Fresno, Calif., 1962-64; ptnr. Pettitt, Blumberg & Sherr and successor firms, Fresno, 1964-75; pvt. practice Clovis, Calif., 1975-92, North Fork, Calif., 1992—; instr. Humprey's Coll. Law, Fresno, 1964-69, bus. Calif. State U., Fresno, 1986—, Coll. of Notre Dame MPA prog., Belmont, 1990-91, Nat. U., 1991—, Emerson Inst., 1998—; judge pro tem Fresno County Superior Ct., 1974-77; gen. counsel Kings River Water Assn., 1976-79. Author: California Water District Laws, 1962. Mem. exec. com. parish coun. St. Helen's Ch., 1982-85, chmn. exec. com., 1985; pres. parish coun. St. John's Cathedral, 1974-82; pres. bd. dirs. 3d Fl. Ctrl. Calif.; bd. dirs. Fresno Facts Found., 1969-70, Fresno Dance Repertory Assn., St. Anthony's Retreat Ctr., Three Rivers, Calif.; pres. Inst. for Interactive Edn., Inc. (formerly Dispute Resolution Ctr. Ctrl. Calif.), 1988—; pres. Am. Benefit Devel. Corp., 1995-98; co-founder Am. Benefit Trust; active Clovis Big Dry Creek Hist. Soc. Recipient President award Fresno Jaycees, 1964. Mem. ATLA, Calif. Bar Assn., Fresno County Bar Assn., Calif. Trial Lawyers Assn. (chpt. pres. 1975, 83, mem. state bd. govs. 1990-94), Fresno Trial Lawyers Assn., Am. Arbitration Assn., Stanford Alumni Assn. (life, svc. award), Fresno Region Stanford Club (pres. 1979-80), Celtic Cultural Soc. Ctrl. Calif. (pres. 1977-78), Fresno county and City C. of C. (chmn. natural resources com. 1977-78), Clovis C. of C., North Fork C. of C. (pres. 1993-96, sec. 1998—), Serra Club (pres. Fresno chpt. 1980-81, v.p. 1986-87), Rotary, Elks. Republican. Roman Catholic. Avocations: writing, music, gardening, sailing, fishing. E-mail: jayflanagan@netptc.net. Office: PO Box 1555 North Fork CA 93643-1555

FLANAGAN, JAMES LOTON, electrical engineer, educator. BSEE, Miss. State U., 1948; SMEE, MIT, 1950, ScDEE, 1955; PhD (hon.), U. Madrid, 1992, U. Paris, 1996. Elec. engring. faculty Miss. State U., 1950-52; tech. staff Bell Labs., Murray Hill, N.J., 1957-61; head dept. speech and auditory rsch. Bell Labs., 1961-67, head dept. acoustics rsch., 1967-85, dir. info. prins. rsch. lab., 1985-90; dir. ctr. for computer aids for indsl. productivity Rutgers U., Piscataway, N.J., 1990-93, v.p. for rsch., 1993—. Author: Speech Analysis, Synthesis and Perception, 1972; contbr. numerous articles to profl. jours. Mem. evaluation panel Nat. Bur. Standards/NRC, 1972-77; mem. adv. panel on White House tapes U.S. Dist. Ct. for D.C., 1973-74; bd. govs. Am. Inst. Physics, 1974-77; mem. sci. adv. bd. Callier Center, U. Tex., Dallas, 1974-76; mem. sci. adv. panel on voice communications Nat. Security Agy., 1975-77; mem. sci. adv. bd. div. communications research Inst. Def. Analyses, 1975-77. Recipient Disting. Svc. award in sci. Am. Speech and Hearing Assn., 1977, L.M. Ericsson Internat. prize in telecomms., 1985, Nat. Medal Sci., Nat. Medal Sci. Com., Pres. Clinton, 1996; Marconi Internat. fellow, 1992. Fellow IEEE (fellow selection com. 1979-81, Edison medal 1986), Acoustical Soc. Am. (assoc. editor Speech Comm. 1959-62, exec. coun. 1970-73, v.p. 1976-77, pres. 1978-79, Gold Medal award 1986), Am. Acad. Arts and Sics.; mem. NAE, NAS (chair engring. sect. 1996—), Acoustics, Speech and Signal Processing Soc. (v.p. 1967-68, pres. 1969-70, Achievement award 1970, Soc. award 1976). Achievements include U.S. and foreign patents in field. Office: Rutgers U Ctr Computer Aids for Indsl Productivity Piscataway NJ 08854-8088

FLANAGAN, JOAN WHEAT (MAGGIE FLANAGAN), educational therapist; b. Covina, Calif., Feb. 3, 1941; d. George Stanley Wheat and Elizabeth Virginia (Wilde) von Brecht; m. Connell O'Brien Cowan, Sept. 1959 (div. 1971); children: Sean O'Brien Cowan, Coby Burke Cowan. BA in English, Fontbonne Coll., 1985, teaching cert., 1987. Cert. secondary tchr., Mo. Counselor, instr. DeNovo Ctr., St. Louis, 1982-83; tchr., counselor Logos High Sch., Olivette, Mo., 1987-88; ednl. coord. Care Unit Hosp., St. Louis, 1988-89; treatment coord. Luth. Hosp. New Beginnings, St. Louis, 1989-90; dir. Creative Learning and Counseling Ctr., University City, Mo., 1990—; ednl. cons. University City High Sch., 1992-96; English instr. Logos Sch., 1996-97; instr. Torah Prep, 1997—; cons. University City Bd. Edn., 1992. Pres. Fair in the Square Com., University City, 1991—; bd. dirs. Drug Free Schs. and Communities Adv. Coun., University City, 1992—, Community Partnership for Prevention of Substance Abuse, 1992, CALOP, 1998—; receptionist/sec. U.S. Senate, L.A., 1972-73; vol. various Dem. campaigns, L.A. and St. Louis, 1972-92. Mem. AAUW, Women's Consortium St. Louis, Optimist Internat. (pres. University City club 1992, 96-97, Community Svc. award 1992). Avocations: politics, civic involvement, writing. Home: 8435 Stanford Ave Saint Louis MO 63132-4918 Office: Creative Learning and Counseling Ctr 8515 Delmar Blvd Ste 217 Saint Louis MO 63124-2168

FLANAGAN, JOHN ANTHONY, lawyer, educator; b. Sioux City, Iowa, Nov. 29, 1942; s. J. Maurice and Lorna K. (Fowler) F.; m. Martha Lang, May 8, 1982; children: Sean, Kathryn, Molly. BA, State U. of Iowa, 1964; JD, Georgetown U., 1968. Bar: Iowa 1968, D.C. 1975, Ohio 1977. Law clk. to judge U.S. Tax Ct., Washington, 1968-70; trial atty. U.S. Dept. Justice, Washington, 1970-74; prof. law U. Cin., 1974-78; sr. tax ptnr. Graydon, Head & Ritchey, Cin., 1978—; adj. prof. U. Cin., 1978--. Contbr. articles to profl. jours. Corp. mgr. United Way, Cin., 1988; head lawyers' div. Fine Arts Fund, Cin., 1987-88; mem. Downtown Cin. Inc. Mem. D.C. Bar Assn., Cin. Bar Assn., Order of Coif. Roman Catholic. Avocations: gardening, golf, fly fishing. Home: 5 Walsh Ln Cincinnati OH 45208-3435 Office: Graydon Head & Ritchey 1900 Fifth-Third Ctr PO Box 6464 Cincinnati OH 45202

FLANAGAN, JOHN F., publishing executive; b. Chgo., Feb. 24, 1944. AB, Wabash Univ., 1966; MBA, Univ. Mich., 1968. Pres., CEO Goodheart Willcox Publ., Tinley Park, Ill., 1980—. Office: Goodheart Willcox Publ 18604 W Creek Dr Tinley Park IL 60477-6243*

FLANAGAN, JOHN MICHAEL, editor, publisher; b. Bangor, Maine, Mar. 8, 1946; s. Joseph F. and Dorothy Elizabeth (Albert) F.; m. Mary Katherine Fastenau, June 22, 1990. Student, U. Notre Dame, 1963-65; BJ, U. Mo., 1970. With The News-Jour. papers, Wilmington, Del., 1970-84, mng. editor, 1982-84; editor Marin Ind. Jour., San Rafael, Calif., 1984-87; exec. editor Honolulu Star-Bulletin, 1987-93; editor, pub. Honolulu Star-Bull., 1993—. With U.S. Army, 1965-68. Office: Honolulu Star Bull PO Box 3080 Honolulu HI 96802-3080

FLANAGAN, JOHN T., federal judge; b. 1935. BS, U. Kans., 1958; JD, Washburn U., 1964. Bar: Kans. 1964. Assoc. Payne & Jones, Kansas City, Kans., 1964-83; pvt. practice, Kansas City, 1983-89; judge U.S. Bankruptcy Ct. for Kans., Kansas City, 1989—; adj. prof. Washburn U., Topeka. Fellow ABA, Am. Bar Inst., Assn. Insolvency Accts., Nat. Conf. Bankruptcy Judges, Kans. Bar Assn., Johnson County Bar Assn. Office: US Bankruptcy Ct 125 US Courthouse 500 State Ave Kansas City KS 66101-2403

FLANAGAN, JOSEPH PATRICK, advertising executive; b. Chgo., Jan. 6, 1938; s. Charles Larkin and Helen Mary (Sullivan) F.; children: Charlotte Ahern, Joseph P. Jr., Michael S., Larkin S., Brian A. BA, Mich. State U., 1959; MBA, U. Chgo., 1961. Dist. mgr. sales Time mag., Pitts. and Chgo., 1961-69; gen. mgr. Ctr. Advanced Research in Design, Chgo., 1969-75; v.p., dir. client services BBDO, Chgo., 1975-77; sr. v.p. IMPACT subs. Foote, Cone & Belding Comm. Co., Chgo., 1977-85, pres., 1985—; corp. dir. sales promotion Foote, Cone & Belding Comm. Co., Chgo., 1987-99; pres. Flanagan Mktg., 1999—; pres. Coun. of Sales Promotion Agys., 1986-89, also bd. dirs. Mem. governing bd. Chgo. Symphony Orch., 1974; v.p. Lyric Opera Guild, Chgo., 1974; trustee Loyola Acad.; bd. dirs. Count Theater; dir. arts and letters bd. Nat. Adv. Coun., Mich. State U.; bd. dirs. Total Focus Leo Burnett. Named Sales Promotion Profl. of Yr., Coun. Sales Promotion Agys., 1989; recipient Disting. Alumni award Mich. State U., 1991. Mem. Am. Assn. Advt. Agencies (chmn. sales promotion com.), Exmoor Country Club (Highland Park, Ill.), Assn. of Promotion Mktg. Agys. (Worldwide Hall of Fame award 1998). Roman Catholic. Avocation: classical music, opera. Home: 1520 N State Pky Chicago IL 60610-1634 also: 369 S Lake Dr Palm Beach FL 33480-6509 Office: IMPACT FCB Ctr 101 E Erie St Chicago IL 60611-2812

FLANAGAN, JOSEPH PATRICK, JR., lawyer; b. Wilkes-Barre, Pa., Sept. 18, 1924; s. Joseph P. and Grace B. F.; m. Mary Elizabeth Mayock, Aug. 5, 1950; children: Maureen Elizabeth, Joseph P. III. B.S., U.S. Naval Acad., 1947; J.D., U. Pa., 1952. Bar: Pa. 1953, U.S. Dist. Ct. (ea. dist.) Pa. 1953, U.S. Ct. Appeals (3d cir.) 1953. Assoc. Saul, Ewing, Remick & Saul, Phila., 1952-56; ptnr. Ballard, Spahr, Andrews & Ingersoll, Phila., 1956-94, chmn. pub. fin. dept., 1961-90. Editor: Practicing Law Inst., Health Facilities Financing, 1976; co-author: In Search of Capital-A Trustee's Guide to Hospital Financing; reviewing editor Disclosure Roles of Counsel in State and Local Government Securities Offerings. editor-in-chief: U. Pa. Law Rev., 1951-52; contbr. articles to profl. jours. Bd. dirs. Phila. Com. of 70, 1952-56; former trustee Wyoming Sem., Kingston, Pa.; former mem. bd. visitors U. Pa. Law Sch.; bd. dirs. John Bartram Assn.; adv. coun. of federalism Nat. Govs. Assn., 1988. Served to lt. (j.g.) USN, 1946-49. Fellow Am. Bar Found.; mem. NASD (regulation arbitrator 1998—), ABA (past chmn. urban, state and local govt. sect.), Phila. Bar Assn. (past chmn. bus. law sect., bd. govs., past founding chmn. tax exempt fin. com., past chmn. profl. edn. com., client's security fund com., fee disputes com.), Pa. Bar Assn., Pa. Bar Inst. (pres. 1983, chmn. curriculum and course planning com. 1976-88), Phila. Club, Racquet Club, Phila. Cricket Club, Corinthian Yacht Club, Chesapeake Bay Yacht Club, Army Navy Country Club of Va. Republican. Roman Catholic. Home: 401 E Mill Rd Flourtown PA 19031-1631 Office: Ballard Spahr Andrews & Ingersoll 1735 Market St Fl 49 Philadelphia PA 19103-7501

FLANAGAN, JUDY, marketing specialist, entertainment manager, university official; b. Lubbock, Tex., Apr. 28, 1950; d. James Joseph II and Jean (Breckenridge) F. BS in Edn., Memphis State U., 1972; postgrad., Disney U., 1975-81, Valencia C.C., 1979-81; MS in Comm., U. Tenn., 1998, postgrad., 1999—. Area/parade supr. Entertainment div. Walt Disney World, Orlando, Fla., 1972-81; parade dir. Gatlinburg (Tenn.) C. of C., 1981-85; entertainment prodn. mgr. The 1982 World's Fair, Knoxville, 1982; cons. Judy Flanagan Prodns./Spl. Events, Gatlinburg, 1982—, Miss U.S.A. Pageant, Knoxville, 1983; prodn. coord. Nashville Network, 1983; dir. sales River Terr. Resort, Gatlinburg, 1985-86; account exec. Park Vista Hotel, Gatlinburg, 1986-88; project coord. Universal Studios, Fla., 1988-90; dir. spl. events in univ. rels. U. Tenn., Knoxville, 1990—; dir. Neyland Stadium Expansion Dedication, 1996—; Vt. Bicentennial Events, 1994, 21st Century Campaign Major Events; prodn. mgr. 1984 World's Fair Parades and Spl. Events, New Orleans, Neil Sedaka rock video, Days of Our Lives daytime soap opera. Recipient Gatlinburg Homecoming award, 1986, World Lifetime Achievement award, 1993. Mem. ASPCA, Internat. Spl. Events Soc., Internat. Festivals and Events Assn., Tenn. Festivals and Events Assn. (bd. dirs.), Human Soc. U.S., Tenn. Soc., Defenders of Wildlife, U. Tenn. Pres. Club, Doris Day Animal League. Roman Catholic. Home: 350 Bruce Rd Gatlinburg TN 37738-5612

FLANAGAN, L. MARTIN, lawyer; b. Greenville, S.C., Jan. 22, 1932; s. Leon Smith and Eloise (Martin) F.; m. Mary Georgie deSaussure, Feb. 5, 1955; children: Patrick B.; Michael C., Georgiana M., M. Kathleen. AB, The Citadel, 1953; LLB, U. Va., 1958, JD, 1970. Bar: S.C. 1958, Fla. 1959, U.S. Supreme Ct. 1971, U.S. Dist. Ct. S.C. 1958, U.S. Dist. Ct. (so. dist.) Fla. 1959, U.S. dist. Ct. (mid. dist.) Fla. 1989, U.S. Ct. Appeals (5th cir.) 1965, U.S. Ct. Appeals (11th cir.) 1988; cert. circuit ct. mediator. Clerk Jones, Adams, Paine & Foster, West Palm Beach, Fla., 1958-59, assoc., 1959-64, partner, 1964-75; shareholder Jones, Paine & Foster, P.A., West Palm Beach, 1975-80, Jones & Foster, P.A., West Palm Beach, 1980-89; shareholder Jones, Foster, Johnston & Stubbs P.A., West Palm Beach, 1989-91, of counsel, 1991—; of counsel Flanagan & Maniotis P.A., 1993—. Founder: Trial Advocate Quarterly, 1982, editorial bd. mem., 1982-91. Judge Palm Springs (Fla.) Municipality, 1960-65, Lake Clarke Shores (Fla.) Municipality, 1967; councilman Lake Clarke Shores, 1964-66; committeeman Rep. Exec. Com., Palm Beach County, 1964-74. Capt. U.S. Army, 1953-55. Recipient Execptional Performance citation Def. Rsch. Inst., 1982. Mem. ABA, Am. Bd. Trial Advocates (diplomate 1981-92). Fedn. Ins. and Corp. Counsel, Product Liability Adv. Coun., Fla. Def. Lawyers Assn. (pres. 1982), Fla. Bar, Palm Beach County Bar Assn., The Acad. of Fla. Trial Lawyers, Assn. Trial Lawyer Am. Republican. Presbyterian. Avocations: presidential political buttons, vintage fountain pens, vintage autos. Home: 115 Russlyn Dr West Palm Beach FL 33405-3355 Office: Flanagan & Maniotis 2586 Forest Hill Blvd West Palm Beach FL 33406-5994

FLANAGAN, LOUISE W., federal judge. Bar: N.C. Part-time magistrate judge for ea. dist. N.C. U.S. Magistrate Ct., Greenville, 1995—. Office: 2155 S Evans St Rm 214 Greenville NC 27834-6441

FLANAGAN, MICHAEL PERKINS, lawyer; b. Kinston, N.C., Aug. 2, 1944; s. Roy Chetwynd and Beatrice (Murrey) F.; m. Mary Northup, Nov. 4, 1967 (div. June 1986); m. Louise Wood, June 23, 1990; 1 child, Katherine Gillie. BA, U. N.C., 1968, JD, 1971. Bar: Fla. 1971, N.C. 1972, U.S. Dist. Ct. (ea., mid., we. dists.) N.C., U.S. Ct. Appeals (4th cir.). Assoc. Granville Alley, Atty., Tampa, Fla., 1971, Ward, Tucker, Ward & Smith, New Bern, N.C., 1972-75; dir., shareholder Ward and Smith, P.A., New Bern, N.C., 1975—. Campaign chmn. Crave County Cancer Crusade, New Bern, 1973; active United Way, Greenville, N.C., 1988. Mem. N.C. Bar Assn. (bankruptcy sec., chmn. 1988-89), Ea. Carolina Yacht Club (commodore), New Bern Country Club. Office: Ward & Smith PA PO Box 8088 Greenville NC 27835-8088*

FLANAGAN, PATRICK SEAN LIAM, priest; b. Bethpage, N.Y., Dec. 16, 1964; s. Thomas Joseph Matthew and Claire Mary Agnes (Meiners) F. BS in Biology and Edn., Niagara U., 1987; MDiv in Theology, Sem. of Immaculate Conception, Lloyd Harbor, N.Y., 1992; postgrad., Loyola U. Cert. tchr., N.Y.; ordained priest, Roman Cath. Ch. Parish priest, dir. religious edn. Immaculate Conception Roman Cath. Ch., Phila., 1992-94; sci. tchr. Merion Mercy Acad., Merion Station, Pa., 1993-94; campus min., adj. prof. religious studies Niagara U., N.Y., 1994-98. Mem. Ancient Order of Hibernians (chaplain 1995-98). Republican. Avocations: computers, biking, travel. Office: DePaul Univ Vincentian Res 2233 N Kenmore Ave Chicago IL 60614-3594

FLANAGAN, ROBERT DANIEL, life insurance agent; b. Stamford, Conn., May 2, 1963; s. William H. and Winifred G. (Marston) F.; m. Elaine B. Maloney, May 13, 1989; children: Caitlin, Robert. BA, Trinity Coll., 1985. CLU, ChFC. Advt. asst. Harper Collins Pubs., N.Y.C., 1985-86; sales rep. Addison Wesley Co., Reading, Mass., 1986-88; coll. mktg. coord. W.H. Freeman, N.Y.C., 1988-89; spl. agt. Northwestern Mut. Life, Milw., 1989—; cmty. svc. chmn. Life Underwriters of Westchester County, N.Y., 1995-96, dir., 1994-95. Host: (cable TV show) The United Way of Rye, 1997—. Local bus. chair United Way Rye, N.Y., 1994-95, campaign chair, 1995-96, pres., 1996-97, leadership chair, 1997-98; pres. Rep. Club, Rye, 1996-98, bd. dirs., 1995-98; dist. leader Westchester County Reps., 1995—; bd. dirs. United Way Westchester and Putnam Counties, 1994-95; vol. Jr. Achievement Hudson Valley, 1990—, mem. edn. com., 1994; mem. outreach com. Christ's Ch., Rye, 1997—, co-leader youth group, 1997-99. Recipient Nat. Quality award Nat. Assn. Life Underwriters, 1992, 93, 94, 95, 96, 97, 98, Above and Beyond award Jr. Achievement Hudson Valley, 1994-95, J.A. Hudson Valley Vol. of Month, Jr. Achievement Hudson Valley, 1997. Mem. Million Dollar Round Table. Republican. Episcopalian. Office: Northwestern Mut Life 411 W Putnam Ave Ste 210 Greenwich CT 06830-6233

FLANAGAN, ROBERT JOSEPH, economics educator; b. New Haven, Dec. 16, 1941; s. Russell Joseph and Anne (Macauley) F.; m. Susan Rae Mendelsohn, Aug. 23, 1986. BA, Yale U., 1963; MA, U. Calif., 1966, PhD, 1970. Economist U.S. Dept. Labor, Washington, 1963-64; asst. prof. labor econs. Grad. Sch. Bus. U. Chgo., 1969-75; assoc. prof. labor econs. Grad. Sch. Bus. Stanford (Calif.) U., 1975-86; sr. staff economist Coun. of Econ. Advisors, Washington, 1978-79; sr. fellow The Brookings Instn., Washington, 1983-84; prof. labor econs. Grad. Sch. Bus., Stanford (Calif.) U., 1987-92, Matsushita prof. internat. labor econs. and econ. policy, 1993—, assoc. dean, 1996—; cons. OECD, Paris, 1988, U.S. Civil Rights Commn., Washington, 1982-83, NOAA, Washington, 1981; vis. scholar IMF, 1994. Author: Labor Relations and Litigation Explosion, 1987; (with others) Unionism, Economic Stabilization and Income Policy, 1982, Economics of the Employment Relationship, 1989, numerous others; contbr. articles to profl. jours. Mem. Am. Econs. Assn., Indls. Rels. Rsch. Assn., Inst. for Internat. Econs. (adv. bd.). Office: Stanford U Grad Sch Bus Palo Alto CA 94305

FLANAGAN, SEAN PATRICK, publishing executive; b. Oct. 16, 1963; m. Donna; children: Riley, Owen. BA, Villanova U., 1985. Territory mgr. Playboy, Nat. Geographic Traveler, Am. Bar Assn. Journal, N.Y. mgr.; advertising dir. Men's Health Mag., N.Y.C., 1993-96, assoc. publisher, 1996-97, publisher, 1997—. Mem. AAAA, ACNY, BPAA, CTFA, MPA, NACDS, TFA, Fragrance Found., Beacon Hill Country Club. Avocations: family, Irish music, golf, landscape horticulture. Fax: (212) 949-9455. E-mail: sflanagl@rodalepress.com. Office: Mens Health 733 3rd Ave Fl 15 New York NY 10017-3204*

FLANAGAN, TIMOTHY JAMES, criminal justice educator, university official; b. Pitts., May 16, 1951; s. Norman Patrick and Dorothy Helen (Hoffmann) F.; m. Nancy Ann Rosenbaum, Aug. 4, 1973; children: Erin E., Kevin C. BA, Gannon U., 1973; MA, SUNY, Albany, 1974, PhD, 1980. Asst. prof., then assoc. prof. Sch. Criminal Justice, SUNY Rockefeller Coll. Pub. Affairs and Policy, 1982-91; prof. criminal justice, dean Coll. Criminal Justice Sam Houston State U., Huntsville, Tex., 1991-98; v.p. for acad. affairs SUNY, Brockport, 1998—; presenter numerous papers to profl. meetings, also panel convenor, chmn., discussant; exec. dir. Michael J. Hindelang Criminal Justice Rsch. Ctr., Inc., Albany, 1981-83. Co-editor: Sourcebook of Criminal Justice Statistics - 1978-92; editor: Jour. Criminal Justice Edn., 1989-93; contbr. articles and book revs. to profl. jours., chpts. to books. Recipient Disting. Alumnus award SUNY Rockefeller Coll. Pub. Affairs and Policy, 1992. Fellow Acad. Criminal Justice Scis.; mem. Am. Soc. Criminology , Am. Coun. on Edn. (coun. fellows, leadership devel. fellow 1988-89), Golden Key, Blue Key, Pi Gamma Mu. Roman Catholic. Avocations: photography, bicycling, computers, sports, reading. Office: SUNY Brockport Brockport NY 14420-2914

FLANAGAN, TOMMY (LEE), jazz pianist; b. Detroit, Mar. 16, 1930. Studied clarinet from age 6, piano from age 11. Played with Milt Jackson, Thad Jones, Elvin Jones; pianist, music dir. for Ella Fitzgerald; performed with various groups; albums include: Alone Too Long, The Best of Tommy Flanagan, Beyond the Blue Bird, 1991, It's Magic, 1957, Giant Steps: In Memory of John Coltrane, 1990, Jazz Poet, 1990, The Magnificent Tommy Flanagan, Thelonica, 1982, Something Borrowed, Something Blue, 1978, Tokyo Recital, ALittle Pleasure, 1981, Tommy Flanagan Three: Montreux '77, The Tommy Flanagan Trio, 1960, With the Wilbur Harden Quartet, 1989, Lady be Good...For Ella, 1994, Flanagan's Shenanigans, 1995; albums with Hank Jones include: Our Delights, 1978, More Delights, 1978; album together recorded with Kenny Barron; guest artist Steve

Coleman's Rhythm in Mind, 1992, (with George Marz) Alone Too Long Ballads and Blues, and Eclypso, 1993, Judy Be Good, 1994. Office: Joel Chris & Co 300 Mercer St Ste 3J New York NY 10003-6732 Address: Mesa Bluemoon Rec Inc 9229 W Sunset Blvd Los Angeles CA 90069-3402*

FLANAGAN, VAN KENT, journalist; b. San Antonio, Sept. 20, 1945; s. Marquiss Monroe and Nina Louise (Fowler) F.; m. Janet Dorothy Robinson, Dec. 16, 1972. B.A., Angelo State U., 1968. Reporter, editor San Angelo Standard-Times, Tex., 1966-68; copy editor Fort Lauderdale News, Fla., 1973-74; from news editor to editor Sun. Express-News, San Antonio, 1974-79; from newsman to bur. chief AP, Phila., 1979-80, Columbia, S.C., 1980-82, Bismarck, N.D., 1982-83, Nashville, 1983—. Served with U.S. Army, 1968-72, Vietnam. Mem. Soc. Profl. Journalists (pres. Mid. Tenn. chpt. 1986-87). Presbyterian. Avocations: walking, hiking, reading novels and non-fiction. Home: 613 Riverview Dr Franklin TN 37064-5514 Office: AP 215 Centerview Dr Ste 110 Brentwood TN 37027-5246

FLANAGAN-EGUCHI, BARBARA L., landscape architect, theme park designer; b. Toronto, Ont., Canada, Aug. 4, 1962; m. Miyuki Rei Real Akazawa-Eguchi; children: Jahra Jo Nami Typhina Akazawa-Eguchi, Marlise Satori Alyssa Akazawa-Eguchi. B of Landscape Architecture, U. Toronto, Can., 1985. Landscape architect, designer various landscape architecture and planning firms, 1985-88; design prin. Eguchi Assocs., Landscape Architects, Toronto, Ont., Can., 1988—; sr. theme park planner, designer Forrec Ltd., 1993—; pres. Design with Nature, Inc., Toronto, 1989—; lecturer, Humber Coll., Toronto, Can., 1987; juror, Toronto Real Estate Bd., Annual Garden Competition, 1992-94. Projects include Abu Dhabi Corniche, United Arab Emirates, Kuwait Regional Parks Pre-Devel. Master Plan, Yan Tai Resort Area, China, N. Am. Life Ctr., North York, Ontario, Can. (1st Place Honors award Landscape Ont. Hort. Trades Assn. 1992), WindReach Farm, Ashburn, Ont., Blue Danube Non-Profit Housing, Scarborough, Ont., Can., Lippo Village Supermall, Jakarta, Indonesia, Great World City, Singapore, Cheras Leisureplex, Kuala Lampur, Malaysia., Revolution/Resolution, Toronto, Can., Earth Home, Toronto, Can., Children's Garden -- An Environmental Transformation, Toronto, Can., St. Patrick Catholic Secondary Sch., Toronto, Can., Seniors' Residence and Nursery, Glad Tidings Pentecostal Church, Burlington, Can., many others, and pvt. residences. Recipient B. Harper Bull Conservation Fellowship award Met. Toronto and Region Conservation Found., 1984, Lt. Govern. Silver Medal, U. Toronto, 1985, Prize winner Borough of East York Ann. Garden Competition, 1993, 2nd Place award Nat. Assn. Japanese Cans., 1994, finalist, Mississauga City Centre Park Competition, 1995. Mem. Am. Soc. Landscape Archs. (Honor cert. 1985, 1st Place award 1994), Ont. Assn. Landscape Archs., Can. Soc. Landscape Archs. water color painting, gardening, tennis, parenting, travel. Office: 39 Ferris Rd, Toronto, ON Canada M4B 1G2

FLANAGIN, LUETTA MAE, family and pediatric nurse practitioner; b. Colby, Kans., Aug. 25, 1962; d. Harold Leon and Luella Jane (Kriegh) Duffey; m. Jay Lyndon Flanigan, June 2, 1984; children: Jared Lee, Andrew Tyler, Kaitlyn Rebecca. BSN, Ft. Hays State U., Hays, Kans., 1984; MSN, West Tex. A&M U., Canyon, 1993. RN, Kans.; cert. family nurse practitioner, pediatric nurse practitioner. Nurse Sheridan County Hosp., Hoxie, Kans., 1984-85, Citizens Med. Ctr., Colby, Kans., 1985-92; assoc. dir. nursing Colby C.C., 1987-94; family nurse practitioner Cobly Med. and Surg. Ctr., 1994-97; family nurse practitioner, pediatric nurse practitioner Family Ctr. for Healthcare, Cobly, 1997—; mem. Thomas County Multidisciplinary Team, Cobly, 1995—; mem. nursing adv. bd. Colby C.C., 1994-96, chair, 1996-97. Bd. dirs. for fund drive Am. Heart Assn., Colby, 1998. Mem. ANA, Am. Acad. Nurse Practitioners, Kans. State Nurses Assn., Sigma Theta Tau. Republican. Methodist. Avocations: reading, quilting, cross-stitch, gardening, family activities. Office: Family Ctr for Healthcare 310 E College Dr Colby KS 67701-3716

FLANAGIN, NEIL, lawyer; b. Chgo., Dec. 2, 1930; s. Norris Cornelius and Virginia (Riddell) F.; m. Mary Mead, Nov. 19, 1960; children: John Mead, Margot, Nancy, Jill. B.A., Yale U., 1953; J.D., U. Mich., 1956. Bar: Ill. 1956. Assoc. Leibman, Williams, Bennett, Baird & Minow, Chgo., 1960-66, ptnr., 1966-72; ptnr. Sidley & Austin, Chgo., 1972-95, of counsel, 1996—. Bd. dirs. Dr. Scholl Found., Chgo., 1973—. Served to 1st lt. AUS, 1956-59. Fellow Am. Coll. Investment Counsel (emeritus); mem. Univ. Club, Law Club (Chgo.), Indian Hill Club (Winnetka). Home: 1010 Mt Pleasant Rd Winnetka IL 60093-3615 Office: Sidley & Austin 1 First Natl Plz Chicago IL 60603-2003

FLANARY, DONALD HERBERT, JR., lawyer; b. Texarkana, Ark., July 27, 1949; s. Donald Herbert and Tenney-Margaret (Webb) F.; m. Gina Lynn Rexrod; children: Donald Herbert III, Shannon Gail, Lauren Paige, David Tyerr, John Paul, Noah Toliver. BS with honors, Tex. A&M U., 1971; JD, U. Houston, 1974. Bar: Tex. 1974, U.S. Dist. Ct. (no. dist.) Tex. 1975, U.S. Dist. Ct. (ea. dist.) Tex. 1976, U.S. Dist. Ct. (so. dist.) Tex. 1982, U.S. Tax Ct. 1982, U.S. Ct. Appeals (5th cir.) 1976, U.S. Ct. Appeals (11th cir.) 1984, U.S. Supreme Ct. 1983. Law clk. Hon. Mary Lou Robinson, U.S. Dist. Ct., Amarillo, Tex., 1974-75; asst. dist. atty. Dallas County, Tex., 1975-76; ptnr. Henderson Bryant & Wolfe, Sherman, Tex., 1976-87; ptnr. Vial Hamilton Koch & Knox, Dallas, 1988-99, Arter and Hadden, 1999—; lectr. for bar assns. on tort law, 1981-84. Bd. dirs. Texoma Valley council Boy Scouts Am., Cancer Soc., Sherman. Named one of Outstanding Young Men Am., U.S. Jaycees, 1981; Eagle Scout, Boy Scouts Am., 1963. Fellow Tex. Bar Found. (life); mem. Tex. Assn. Def. Counsel (bd. dirs. 1981-84, 86-88), Grayson County Bar Assn. (pres. 1983-84), Internat. Assn. Ins. Counsel (bd. cert. personal jury trial law), Bd. Legal Specialization (civil trial law), Nat. Bd. Trial Adv., State Bar Assn. Tex. (bd. dirs. 1986-89, pres.-elect 1999), Am. Bd. Profl. Liability Attys. (cert.), Am. Bd. Trial Advocates (cert.). Democrat. Roman Catholic. Office: Vial Hamilton Koch & Knox 1717 Main St Ste 4400 Dallas TX 75201-7388

FLANARY, KATHY VENITA MOORE, librarian; b. Amherst, Tex., Jan. 15, 1946; d. Charles Edward and Jean (Willman) Moore; children: Suzanne Flanary, Charles Flanary. BA, U. Ill., 1972, MLS, 1974. Cert. profl. libr., N.Mex.; cert. tchr., N.Mex. Dir. children's libr. Hayner Pub. Libr., Alton, Ill., 1974-76; dir. Ruidoso (N.Mex.) Pub. Libr., 1978-80; libr. media specialist Horgan Libr., N.Mex. Mil. Inst., Roswell, 1985-93; libr. N.Mex. Sch. Visually Handicapped, Alamogordo, 1993—; workshop presenter Lewis & Clark Regional Libr. Systems, Ill., 1975; outreach programer Hayner Pub. Libr., 1974-76; del. Pre-White Ho. Conf., State of N.Mex., 1991. Contbr. articles to newspapers and profl. jours. Bd. dirs. Alton Symphony, 1975; mem. Altrusa, Ruidoso, 1979-84, Friend of Roswell Pub. Libr.; sec. Ruidoso Summer Festival, 1979; bd. dirs. Supts. Adv. Bd., Roswell, N.Mex., 1987-89; pres. Friends of Libr., Ruidoso, 1980-83, Parent Advocacy for Gifted Edn., 1990-92; v.p. Sunset PTA; bd. dirs. N.Mex. Libr. Found., 1992—. Recipient Svc. award Altrusa, 1979, Sunset PTA, 1989. Mem. N.Mex. Libr. Assn. (libr. devel. com., edn. tech. roundtable vice chair 1991, chair elect 1992, co-chair state conv. local arrangements 1990-91, 2d v.p. 1993-94, 1st v.p. 1994-95, pres. 1995-96), N.Mex. Acad. and Rsch. Librs. (vice chair 1992, pres. 1993), Kiwanis (bd. dirs. 1990-92). Avocations: travel, stained glass, music, hiking. Office: NMex Sch Visually Handicapped 1900 N White Sands Blvd Alamogordo NM 88310-6246

FLANDERS, DONALD HARGIS, manufacturing company executive; b. Memphis, Apr. 26, 1924; s. Henry Jackson and Mae (Hargis) F.; m. Phala Kathryn Davis, Dec. 15, 1946; children: Donald Hargis, Dudley Kennedy, Kathryn Varner. Student, Tex. Christian U., 1943; BBA, Baylor U., 1947. Dir. cost acctg., purchasing agt. McCoy-Couch Furniture Mfg. Co., Benton, Ark., 1947-50, Garrison Furniture Co., Ft. Smith, Ark., 1950-54; pres., founder Flanders Mfg. Co., Ft. Smith, 1954-70, Flanders Industries, Inc., Ft. Smith, 1970—; chmn. bd., CEO Lloyd/Flanders Industries, Inc., Menominee, Mich., bd. dirs. 1st Nat. Bank, Ft. Smith; chmn. Windsor Designs, Ltd., Phoenixville, Pa. Chmn. exec. com. Ft. Smith Freight Bur., 1960-61; chmn. furniture bd. govs. Dallas Mkt. Ctr., 1968; exec. com. Ark. Coun. on Econ. Edn., 1964-67; mem. Ark. Small Bus. Adv. Coun., 1966-68; chmn. Ft. Smith United Fund drive, 1962; dist. chmn. Boy Scouts Am., Ft. Smith, 1960-62, pres. Westark Area coun. 1963-65, regional exec. com., 1964-72, vice chmn. region 5, 1967-69, chmn. region 5, 1969-72, nat. exec. bd., 1969-77; Com. of 100, 1965—; exec. dir. Ark. Indsl. Devel. Commn., 1981-83; trustee, vice chmn. Sparks Regional Med. Ctr., Hendrix Coll., Westark Coll. Found., North Ark. Conf. 1986-95; bd. dirs. Meth. Ch. Served from apprentice seaman to lt. (s.g.) USNR, 1943-46. Recipient Silver Antelope, Silver Beaver, Silver Buffalo, Disting. Eagle Scout awards Boy Scouts Am., Free Enterprise award, 1964; named Industrialist of Yr. Ft. Smith Realtors Bd., 1965. Mem. SW Furniture Mfg. Assn. (pres. 1963), Ft. Smith C. of C. (dir. 1961-63, 73-75), Ark. Wood Products Assn. (dir. 1965-68), Summer Casual Furniture Mfrs. Assn. (pres. 1992-94, chmn. 1994-96), Masons (33 degree), Shriners, KT, Delta Sigma Pi. Methodist. Home: 1925 Jamaica Way Punta Gorda FL 33950-5176 Office: PO Box 1788 1901 Wheeler Ave Fort Smith AR 72902-1788

FLANDERS, GEORGE JAMES, mechanical engineer, engineering development manager; b. Bunker Hill, Ind., June 3, 1960; s. Melvin S. and Edith J. (Mason) F. BSME, Bradley U., 1982, MBA, 1984. Lab. engr. Materials Testing & Rsch. Lab., Peoria, Ill., 1982; rsch. design engr. Caterpillar Tractor Co., Peoria, 1982-85; staff engr. Bristol Myers Co., Englewood, Colo., 1985-86, sr. engr., bus. unit mgr. arthoscopy and reconstructive surgery products, 1986-87; subcontract program mgr. Lockheed Martin, Denver, 1987—; co-founder, CEO WSG Mgmt. and Holding Group, Denver, 1988—; chmn. bd. dirs., sec., chmn., investement com. chmn. Red Rock Fed. Credit Union, 1989-97; ptnr. Advanced Coronary Intervention, 1994—; cons. in field. Area coord. Neighborhood Watch Program, 1988-89; crew leader 10,000 Trees Environ. Project; mem. fin. com. Littleton United Meth. Ch., 1987—; dir. Colo. I Hava Dream Found., 1998—. Mem. NSPE, ASME, Soc. Automotive Engrs., Sigma Phi Delta (grand pres. 1988-90, v.p. 1985-87, trustee chmn. 1988-90), Tau Beta Pi, Pi Tau Sigma, Omicron Delta Kappa. Avocations: Chinese and Russian lang. and writing, fitness, boating, skiing, tae kwon do. Home: 6168 S Lee St Littleton CO 80127-2561 Office: Martin Marietta Astronautics Group PO Box 179 Denver CO 80201-0179

FLANDERS, HENRY JACKSON, JR., religious studies educator; b. Malvern, Ark., Oct. 2, 1921; s. Henry Jackson and Mae (Hargis) F.; m. Tommie Lou Pardew, Apr. 19, 1944; children: Janet Flanders Mitchell, Jack III. BA, Baylor U., 1943; BD, So. Bapt. Theol. Sem., 1948, PhD, 1950. Ordained to ministry Bapt. Ch., 1941. Asst. prof., assoc. prof. Furman U., Greenville, S.C., 1950-55, prof., chaplain, chmn. dept. religion, 1955-62; pastor First Bapt. Ch., Waco, Tex., 1962-69; prof. religion Baylor U., Waco, Tex., 1969-92, chmn. dept., 1980-83; chmn., trustee Golden Gate Bapt. Theol. Sem., Mill Valley, Calif., 1966-76; chaplain Tex. Ranger Commn., 1965—; mem. exec. com. Bapt. Gen. Conv. Tex., Dallas, 1966-68. Author: (with R.W. Crapps and D.A. Smith) People of the Convenant, 1963, 73, 88, 96; (with Bruce Cresson) Introduction to the Bible, 1973; TV spkr. Lessons for Living, WFBC-TV, 1957-62. Trustee Baylor U., Waco, Tex., 1964-68; trustee Hillcrest Bapt. Hosp., 1963-64; chmn. Heart of Tex. Red Cross, 1967-68; narrator Waco Cotton Palace Pageant, 1970-80; chaplain Tex. Aero Commn., 1986—; pastor emeritus First Bapt. Ch., Waco, 1987; mem. grievance oversight com. Tex. Bar, 1979-87. Served to 1st. lt. USAAC, 1943-45, ETO. Named disting. alumnus Baylor U., 1986; grantee Furman U., 1960; grantee Baylor U., 1977, 82. Mem. Assn. Bapt. Profs. Religion (pres. 1958-59), AAUP (chpt. pres. 1973), Soc. Bibl. Lit., Am. Acad. Religion, Inst. Antiquity and Christianity, Waco Bapt. Ministerial Assn. (pres. 1967-68). Lodges: Rotary; Shriners. Home: 3820 Chateau Ave Waco TX 76710-7102 Office: Baylor U Religion Dept Waco TX 76798

FLANDERS, JEFFERSON, publishing executive; b. Montclair, N.J., Feb. 20, 1955; s. Stephen Carver and Carol Marie (Orr) F.; m. Maisie Linette Eng, Jan. 12, 1980; children: Christian, Dana, Clayton. AB in History and Lit., Harvard Coll., 1977; MBA, Columbia U., 1982. Assoc. editor Facts on File, N.Y.C., 1978-80; assoc. to v.p. books, info., edn. The N.Y. Times Co., N.Y.C., 1982-83, sr. analyst planning, 1983-84, project mgr. planning, 1985; dir. mktg. svcs., planning Santa Barbara (Calif.) News-Press, 1986, dir. circulation, 1987, v.p. circulation, 1988; pub., columnist Charlotte/AM. Sarasota Herald-Tribune, Port Charlotte, Fla., 1989-96; v.p. planning Boston Globe, 1997, v.p. promotion, 1997-98, v.p. promotion and mktg., 1999—; seminar leader Am. Press Inst., 1989-93. pres. United Way Charlotte County, Port Charlotte, 1992-93; trustee Mote Marine Lab., Inc., Sarasota, Fla., 1994—. Avocations: tennis, squash racquets, reading, traveling. Office: Boston Globe 135 Morrissey Blvd Boston MA 02125-3338

FLANDERS, RAYMOND ALAN, dentist, governmental health agency administrator; b. Bangor, Maine, Jan. 4, 1929; s. Carroll Benjamin and Mary (Watson) F.; m. Anne-Liss Teisen; children: Molly Olivia and Michael Benjamin (twins). Student, Colgate U., 1948-50; BS, U. Miami, Fla., 1955; DDS, U. Md., 1959; MPH, U. Mich., 1979. Mem. faculty W.Va. U., Morgantown, 1964-65; program dir. Project Hope, Brazil, 1976-78; mem. faculty Coll. Dentistry U. Alagoas, Maceio, Brazil, 1976-78; regional dental dir. Va. State Health Dept., Richmond, 1970-76, 79-85; mem. faculty Med. Coll. Va., Richmond, 1980-85; state dental dir. Ill. Dept. Health, Springfield, 1985-96; mem. faculty Coll. Dental Medicine So. Ill. U., Alton, 1985-96; mem. faculty Coll. Dentistry Sch. Pub. Health U. Ill., Chgo., 1990-96; cons. Project Esperanca, Amazon River, Brazil, 1981, Project HOPE/U.S.A.I.D., Grenda, West Indies, 1984, Project HOPE, Honduras, 1986, Am. Dental Assn., Brazil and Guyana, 1992. Contbr. articles to profl. jours. Served to capt. U.S. Army, 1946-47, 50-51, 60-63. USPHS fellow, 1978-79, Sec's. Excellence in Health Promotion award, 1990. Mem. ADA (Preventive Dentistry award 1983, Cmty. Preventive Dentistry award 1990, 95), Ill. Dental Assn., Am. Pub. Health Assn., Assn. State Territorial Dental Dirs. (exceptional achievement award 1998), Am. Assn. Pub. Health Dentists, Ill. Pub. Health Assn.

FLANIGAN, JAMES J(OSEPH), journalist; b. N.Y.C., June 6, 1936; s. James and Jane (Whyte) F.; m. Patricia Quatrine, Nov. 28, 1997; children: Michael, Siobhan Jane. BA, Manhattan Coll., 1961. Fin. writer N.Y. Herald Tribune, 1957-66; bur. chief, asst. mng. editor Forbes Mag., 1966-86; bus. columnist, sr. econs. editor L.A. Times, 1986—. Office: LA Times Times Mirror Sq Los Angeles CA 90053

FLANIGAN, ROBERT CHARLES, urologist, educator; b. Lima, Ohio, May 2, 1946; children: Nancy, Charles. BA in Chemistry, Coll. of Wooster, 1968; MD, Case Western Res. U., 1972. Resident in surgery and urology Case Western Res. U., 1972-78; vol. asst. prof. urology U. Nebr., 1978-80; asst. prof. surgery U. Ky. Med. Ctr., Lexington, 1980-84, assoc. prof. surgery, 1984-86; prof. urology, chmn. dept. Loyola U. Med. Ctr., Maywood, Ill., 1986—; chief urology Hines VA Hosp., 1986—. Officer M.C., USAF, 1978-80. Recipient Cardinal's Medallion, Archdiocese of Chgo., 1995. Fellow ACS; mem. Am. Urol. Assn., Am. Assn. Genito-Urinary Surgeons, Soc. Pelvic Surgeons, Am. Soc. Transplant Surgeons, Chgo. Urol. Soc. (pres.), Soc. Univ. Urologists (sec.-treas.).

FLANIGEN, EDITH MARIE, materials scientist, consultant. Sr. rsch. fellow materials sci. UOP Tarrytown (N.Y.) Tech. Ctr., ret.; cons. White Plains, N.Y. Recipient Perkin medal Am. Chem. Soc., 1992, Francis P. Garvan-John M. Olin medal Am. Chem. Soc., 1993. Home: 502 Woodland Hills Rd White Plains NY 10603-3136

FLANNAGAN, ROY CATESBY, JR., English literature educator, editor; b. Richmond, Va., Dec. 2, 1938; s. Roy Catesby Flannagan Sr. and Victoria (Iler) Hall; m. Julia Porter, June 8, 1962 (div. 1966); children: Roy Catesby III, Julia Wickham Flannagan; m. Anne Jacqueline Villers, Dec. 30, 1984; 1 child, Elisabeth Welsby Flannagan. BA, Washington & Lee U., 1960; MA, U. Va., 1961, PhD, 1966. Asst. prof. Va. Mil. Inst., Lexington, 1965-66; asst. prof. Ohio U., Athens, 1966-70, assoc. prof., 1970, prof., 1981—; advisor Humanist Electronic Seminar, Brown U., 1990—; advisor Text-Encoding Initiative, 1990—; editorial cons. Shaksper Seminar, U. Toronto, Can., 1990—, Ficino Seminar, 1990—. Editor Milton Quar. Jour., 1966—, John Milton: Paradise Lost, 1993 (Irene Samuel award Milton Soc. of Am. 1994), Oxford Electronic Text Milton, 1992. Folger Shakespeare Libr. fellow, 1967; Fulbright grantee, 1969. Mem. MLA, Renaissance Soc. Am., Renaissance English Text Soc., Milton Soc. Am. (pres. 1989-90), Internat. Milton Symposium (dir. 1987-88), Council Editors of Learned Js. (v.p., 1998-99). Avocations: newspaper writing, book designing, photography, tennis. Home: 216 Longview Heights Rd Athens OH 45701-3359 Office: Ohio U Dept of English Athens OH 45701

FLANNELLY, KEVIN J., psychologist, research analyst; b. Jersey City, Nov. 26, 1949; s. John J. and Mary C. (Walsh) F.; m. Laura T. Adams, Jan. 10, 1981. BA in Psychology, Jersey City State Coll., 1972; MS in Psychology, Rutgers U., 1975; PhD in Psychology, U. Hawaii, 1983. Rsch. asst. dept. psychology U. Ill., Champaign, 1972-73; rsch. intern Alcohol Behavior Rsch. Lab. Rutgers U., New Brunswick, N.J., 1973-75; rsch. scientist Edward R. Johnstone Tng. and Rsch. Ctr., Bordentown, N.J., 1975-78; teaching asst. dept. psychology U. Hawaii, Honolulu, 1980-81, rsch. asst. Pacific Biomed. Rsch. Ctr., 1981-83, asst. prof. Bekesy Lab. Neurobiology, 1983-85; rsch. statistician, statewide transp. planning office Hawaii Dept. Transportation, Honolulu, 1986-89; researcher Office of Lt. Gov., Honolulu, 1989-93; legis. dir., policy analyst energy and environ. protection com. State House of Reps., 1994; with Office of Gov. of State of Hawaii, Honolulu, 1994-97; dir. rsch. Mktg. Rsch. Inst., Honolulu, 1997—; statis cons. U. Hawaii Sch. Nursing, Honolulu, 1986, Hawaii Dept. Health, Honolulu, 1986; mem. State Ridesharing Task Force, 1987; staff mem. gov's. subcabinet on early childhood edn. and childcare, 1989, Hawaii task force on ednl. governance, 1991-92; mem. Gov's. Office State Planning, environ. scanning project, 1992-94; v.p., rsch. dir. Ctr. Psychosocial Rsch., Honolulu, 1987—; instr. dept. social scis. Honolulu Community Coll., 1981; ptnr. Flannelly Cons., 1991—; rsch. dir. Mktg. Rsch. Inst., 1992—; adj. prof. Hawaii Pacific U., 1998. Editor: Biological Perspective on Aggression, 1984, Introduction to Psychology, 1987; reviewer 8 sci. and profl. jours., 1978—; grant reviewer NSF, 1984-92; contbr. numerous articles to profl. jours. Polit. survey cons., Honolulu, 1988—; transp. cons., Honolulu, 1989—; mktg. cons., Honolulu, 1990—; mem. Gov. and Mayor Joint Waikiki Task Force, 1998. Grantee NIH, 1984, Fed. Hwy. Adminstrn., 1987; N.J. State scholar N.J. Dept. Higher Edn., 1968-72. Fellow Internat. Soc. Rsch. on Aggression; mem. AAAS, APA, Am. Psychol. Soc., Am. Statis. Assn., Internat. Soc. Comparative Psychology, N.Y. Acad. Scis., Psychonomic Soc., Sigma Xi. Achievements include research on aggression, educational testing, mental-health services, social and emotional behavior, transportation planning, stochastic models of decision-making. Home: 445 Kaiolu St Apt 1006 Honolulu HI 96815-2239

FLANNELLY, LAURA T., mental health nurse, nursing educator, researcher; b. Bklyn., Nov. 7, 1952; d. George A. Adams and Eleanor (Barragry) Mulhearn; m. Kevin J. Flannelly, Jan. 10, 1981. BS in Nursing, Hunter Coll., 1974; MSN, U. Hawaii, 1984, PhD in Ednl. Psychology, 1996. RN, N.Y., Hawaii. Psychiat. nurse Bellevue Hosp., N.Y.C., 1975, asst. head nurse, 1975-77; psychiat. nurse White Plains (N.Y.) Med. Ctr., 1978-79; community mental health nurse South Beach Psychiat. Ctr., N.Y.C., 1979-81; psychiat. nurse The Queen's Med. Ctr., Honolulu, 1981-83; crisis worker Crisis Response Systems Project, Honolulu, 1983-86; instr. nursing U. Hawaii, Honolulu, 1985-92, asst. prof., 1992—, assoc. grad. faculty, 1998—; adj. instr. nursing Hawaii Loa Coll., Honolulu, 1988, Am. Samoa Community Coll., Honolulu, 1987, 89, 90; mem. adv. bd., planning com. Psychiat. Day Hosp. of The Queen's Med. Ctr., Honolulu, 1981-82; program coord. Premenstrual Tension Syndrome Conf., Honolulu, 1984; dir. Ctr. Psychosocial Rsch., Honolulu, 1987—; program moderator 1st U.S-Japan Health Behavioral Conf., Honolulu, 1988; faculty Ctr. for Asia-Pacific Exch., 1995-99, Internat. Conf. on Transcultural Nursing, Honolulu, 1990; mem. bd. dirs. U. Hawaii Profl. Assembly, 1994-97; mem. Hawaii State Coun. Mental Health, 1997—. Contbr. articles to profl. jours. N.Y. State Bd. Regents scholar, 1970-74; NIH nursing trainee, 1983-84; grantee U. Hawaii, 1986, 91, Hawaii Dept. Health, 1990. Fellow Internat. Soc. Rsch. on Aggression; mem. AAAS, APA, Am. Ednl. Rsch. Assn., Am. Psychol. Soc., Am. Psychiat. Nurses Assn., Am. Statis. Assn., Nat. League for Nursing, N.Y. Acad. Scis., Sigma Theta Tau (rec. sec. chpt. 1995-97). Achievements include research on aggressive behavior, educational testing, learning styles, problem-based learning, cross-cultural differences, statistical modeling. Home: 445 Kaiolu St Apt 1006 Honolulu HI 96815-2239 Office: U Hawaii Sch Nursing Webster Hall Honolulu HI 96822

FLANNERY, ELLEN JOANNE, lawyer; b. Bklyn., Dec. 13, 1951; d. William Rowan and Mary Jane (Hamilla) Flannery. AB cum laude, Mount Holyoke Coll., 1973; JD cum laude, Boston U., 1978. Bar: Mass. 1978, D.C. 1979, U.S. Ct. Appeals (D.C. cir.) 1979, U.S. Ct. Appeals (4th cir.) 1981, U.S. Ct. Appeals (6th cir.) 1983, U.S. Ct. Appeals (3d cir.) 1987, U.S. Dist. Ct. D.C. 1980, U.S. Dist. Ct. Md. 1985, U.S. Supreme Ct. 1983. Spl. asst. to commr. of health Mass. Dept. Pub. Health, Boston, 1973-75; law clk. U.S. Ct. Appeals D.C. cir., Washington, 1978-79; assoc. Covington & Burling, Washington, 1979-86, ptnr., 1986—; lectr. ins. U. Va. Sch. Law, 1984-90, Boston U. Sch. Law, 1993, U. Md. Sch. Law, 1994; mem. Nat. Conf. Lawyers and Scientists, AAAS-ABA, 1989-92. Contbr. to articles to profl. jours. Fellow Am. Bar Found.; mem. ABA (chmn. com. med. practice 1987-88, chmn. life scis div. 1982-84, 88-91, vice chair food and drug law com. 1991-97, chmn. sect. sci. and tech. 1992-93, del. of sci. and tech. sect. to ho. of dels. 1993—, chmn. coordinating group on bioethics and the law 1998—). Office: Covington & Burling PO Box 7566 1201 Pennsylvania Ave NW Washington DC 20044

FLANNERY, HARRY AUDLEY, lawyer; b. New Castle, Pa., June 11, 1947; s. Wilbur Eugene and Ruth (Donaldson) F.; m. Maureen Louise Flaherty, June 28, 1969; children: Preston Wilbur, Courtney Lilyan. BA, Wesleyan U., 1969; JD, Ohio No. U., 1972; LLM in Taxation, Boston U., 1973. Bar: Pa. 1972, U.S. Tax Ct. 1973, U.S. Dist. Ct. (we. dist.) Pa. 1975, U.S. Supreme Ct. 1976, U.S. Ct. Appeals 1984. Sr. gen. svcs. specialist Pitts. Nat. Bank, 1973, asst. trust officer, 1974-75, trust legal officer, 1976; atty. Pa. Power Co., New Castle, 1977-98, FirstEnergy Corp., 1998—; sec. fed. and state polit. coms. Pa. Power Co., New Castle, 1983—; v.p. Euclid Manor Corp.; mem. panel arbitrators Bur. Mediation Dept. Labor and Industry. Assoc. editor Pitts. Legal Jour., 1981—; contbr. numerous articles to legal publs. Bd. dirs. Lawrence County chpt. Pa. Assn. for Blind, 1st v.p., 1994-96, pres. 1996-98; mem. Highland Presbyn. Ch., New Castle, Estate Planning Coun. of Pitts., 1975-77; sec. Lil Maur Found., 1989—; elected mem. sch. bd. dirs. Neshannock Twp. Sch. Bd., Pa., 1993—; mem. Pearson Park Commn., 1993-95; v.p. Neshannock Twp. Sch. Bd., Lawrence County, Pa., 1998—. Mem. ABA (labor and employment law sect. com. on labor arbitration and law of collective bargaining agreements, tax sect. 1973-92, com. excise and employment taxes, subcom. payroll tax issues 1978-80), Pa. Bar Assn. (workmen's compensation sect., adminstrv. law sect., labor and employment law sect., pub. utility law sect., in house counsel com. 1995-98, 99—, dispute resolution com. 1989-91, 99—), Allegheny County Bar Assn. (coun., taxation sect. 1975-77, labor law sect., workmen's compensation sect.), Pitts. Legal Jour. Com., Lawrence County Bar Assn., Allegheny Tax Soc., Pennsylvania Soc. (life), Pa. Assn. Trial Lawyers, Am. Arbitration Assn., The Supreme Ct. Pa. Hist. Soc. (life, trustee 1994—, sec. 1995—, v.p. 1999—), Pa. Sch. Bd. Assn., Duquesne Club, Lawrence Club, New Castle Country Club, Lions (bd. dirs. 1982-91, tailtwister 1983-84, 3rd v.p. 1984-85, 2nd v.p. 1985, 1st v.p. 1986-87, pres. 1987-88), New Castle Lions Charities, Inc. (Lion of Yr. 1988-89), Phi Alpha Delta (life). Republican. Avocations: family, writing, tennis, boating. Home: 116 Valhalla Dr New Castle PA 16105-1037 Office: Pa Power Co 1 E Washington St New Castle PA 16101-3814

FLANNERY, JOHN PHILIP, lawyer; b. N.Y.C., May 15, 1946; s. John Philip and Agnes Geraldine (Applegate) F.; m. Bettina Gregory, Nov. 14, 1981. BS in Physics, Fordham Coll., 1967; BS in Engring., Columbia U., 1969, JD, 1972; student Art Students League, 1972-73. 1 child, Diana Elizabeth. Bar: N.Y. 1973, U.S. Dist. Ct. (so. dist.) N.Y. 1973, U.S. Ct. Appeals (2d cir.) 1973. Mem. staff Ford Found. Project to Restructure Columbia U., 1968; news rep. nat. press relations IBM, 1970; law clk. Adminstrv. Conf. U.S., 1971; law clk. U.S. Ct. Appeals 2d cir., 1972-74; asst. U.S. atty. Narcotics and Ofcl. Corruption units So. Dist. N.Y., 1974-79; sr. assoc. Poletti Freidin Prashker Feldman & Gartner, N.Y.C., 1979-82; spl. counsel U.S. Senate Judiciary Com., 1982; spl. counsel U.S. Senate Labor Com., 1982-83; Dem. candidate for U.S. Congress from Va. 10th Dist., 1983-84; sole practice in civil and criminal litigation, 1984—; spl. counsel Sen. Howard Metzenbaum, 1985-87; asst. dist. atty., Bronx, N.Y., 1986-87; counsel, bd. dirs. Washington Internat. Horse Show Assn., 1989-91; legal expert "Crime in D.C.", Fox-TV, 1993, "Crime Bill", Wis. Pub. Radio, 1994, "People vs. O.J. Simpson", ABC Network Radio, 1994-95, "Va.'s No Parole" Larry King Live CNN, 1994, "Imprisonment" CBS Morning Show, 1994, Habeas Reform Court T.V., 1996, Terrorism, 1996; spl. counsel U.S. House Judiciary Com., 1996-97; project dir., spl. counsel U.S. Edn. and Work Force Com., 1997-98; spl. coun. (impeachment proceedings) U.S. Rep. Zoe Lofgren, 1998—, lectr. in field. Committeeman Dem. Party N.Y. County, 1979-80; mem. legis. commn. Citizen's Union, 1971-72; mem.

Arlington Transp. Commn., 1983-85; chmn. bus. coun. Va. Gov.'s War on Drugs Task Force, 1983-84; committeeman Dem. Party Arlington County, 1983-84; coord. N.Y. State Lawyers Com. for Senator Edward M. Kennedy, 1979-80; dir. Citizens for Senator M. Kennedy, 1980; pres. Franklin Soc., 1979-80; del. Dem. Nat. Conv., 1988, Va. Assembly U. W.Va., 1990; committeeman Loudoun County Dem. Com., 1995—, sec. 1995—, chmn., 1995-97; del. 10th Congress and Dist. Com., 1997—; mem. Ctrl. State (Va.) Com., 1997—. Recipient U.S. Justice Dept. award for Outstanding Contbns. in the Field of Drug Law Enforcement 1977; U.S. Atty. Gen.'s Spl. Commendation for Outstanding Svc., 1979, FLEOA Award, Fed. Law Enforcement Officer's Assn., 1984, NACDL's Marshall Stern Award Outstanding Legis. Achievement, 1997; Mem. ABA, Bar Assn. of City of N.Y., N.Y. County Lawyers Assn., Arlington County Bar Assn., Loudon County Bar Assn., Nat. Assn. Criminal Def. Lawyers (chair briefbank com. 1990-91, legis. co-chair 1991—, dir. 1993—, President's commendation 1991, 92, 95), Acad. Polit. Sci., Va. Coll. Criminal Def. Attys. (bd. dirs. 1993-96). Democrat. Author: Commercial Information Brokers, 1973; Habeas Corpus Bores Hole in Prisoners' Civil Rights Action, 1975; Pro Se Litigation, 1975; Prison Corruption: A Mockery of Justice, 1980; Conspiracy: A Primer, 1988, Is Innocence Relevant to Execution? If Not, Isn't that Murder?, 1994, Equal Justice For All, 1995, Virginia Governor Allen's No-Parole Plan: A Billion Dollar Wasteland of Prisons, 1995. Home: Shamrock Farm 38138 Forest Mills Rd Leesburg VA 20175-9146 Office: Rep Zoe Lofgren 318 Cannon House Off Bldg Washington DC 20515

FLANNERY, JOSEPH EDWARD, retired education association executive; b. Girardville, Pa., Apr. 13, 1930; s. Thomas Edward and Nora Marie (Malloy) F.; m. Joan Marie Whitehorn, June 12, 1954; children: Mystica Rose, Joseph W., Ellen. BS, East Stroudsburg (Pa.) U., 1953; MS, Rowan U., 1976. Tchr., coach Middle Twp. H.S., Cape May Court House, N.J., 1953, Cass Twp. H.S., Minersville, Pa., 1954, Jr. H.S. 3, Trenton, N.J., 1956-58, Burlington (N.J.) H.S., 1958-63; tchr., coach Burlington Twp. H.S., 1963-71, athletic dir., 1971-73; field svc. rep. N.J. Sch. Bds. Assn., Trenton, 1973-80, dir. field svcs., 1980-85, dir. comm., 1985-91; pres., chief cons. CIC (Comm. & Info. Concepts), Beverly, N.J., 1992-95; bd. dirs. Ednl. Press Assn. Am., Glassboro, N.J., 1983-88; v.p. for comm. N.J. Bus.-Industry-Sci. Ednl. Consortium, Hoboken, 1985-91, N.J. Coun. on Econ. Edn., Trenton, 1985-91. Contbr. articles to profl. jours. Mem. Com. on 18, Beverly, 1973-75; chmn. Mcpl. Dem. Com., Beverly, 1974-76; co-chmn. study polit. structure Edgewater Park Municipality, Beverly, 1978. With U.S. Army, 1954-56. Recipient Outstanding Alumnus award pub. rels. dept. Rowan U., 1991; inducted into Interscholastic Athletics Hall of Fame, N.J. Interscholastic Athletic Assn., 1992; grantee Phila. chpt. Am. Chem. Soc., 1970, 73. Mem. VFW, Am. Legion, Moose, Elks. Roman Catholic. Avocations: travel, golf, volunteer activities, walking, writing. Home: 1639 Wood Thrush Dr Murrells Inlet SC 29576-8844

FLANNERY, JOSEPH PATRICK, manufacturing company executive; b. Lowell, Mass., Mar. 20, 1932; s. Joseph Patrick and Mary Agnes Egan F.; m. Margaret Barrows, June 1957; children: Mary Ann, Diane, Joseph, James, David, Elizabeth. BS in Chemistry, Lowell Tech. Inst., 1953; MBA, Harvard U., 1955; PhD, U. Lowell, Mass., 1981. Pres. Uniroyal Chem. Co., Naugatuck, Conn., 1975-77; exec. v.p. Uniroyal, Inc., Middlebury, Conn., 1977, pres., 1977—, chief exec. officer, 1980—; chmn. bd. Uniroyal, Inc., 1982—; chmn., pres., chief exec. officer Uniroyal Holding, Inc., Naugatuck, Conn., 1986—; bd. dirs. Newmont Mining Corp., K Mart Corp., Ingersoll-Rand Co., O.M. Scott & Sons., Newmont Gold Co., Arvin Industries Inc. Mem. Am. Chem. Soc., Country Club of Fla. Roman Catholic. Clubs: Country of Waterbury (Conn.); Vesper Country (Lowell); Oyster Harbors (Osterville, Mass.). Lodge: Knights of Malta. Office: Uniroyal Holding Inc 70 Great Hill Rd Naugatuck CT 06770-2224

FLANNERY, SUSAN MARIE, library administrator; b. Newark, Feb. 18, 1953; d. John Patrick Flannery and Assunta (Lardieri) Ege; m. Stephen A. Coren, Oct. 6, 1984. BA in History of Art, U. Pa., 1974; MLS, Simmons Coll., 1975. Dir. of libr. Newton Country Day, 1975-77, Am. Sch. in Switzerland, Montagnola, 1977-78; young adult libr. Somerville (Mass.) Pub. Libr., 1979-81; reference libr. Cary Meml. Libr., Lexington, Mass., 1981-83; asst. dir. Lucius Beebe Libr., Wakefield, Mass., 1983-87; dir. Reading (Mass.) Pub. Libr., 1987-91; assoc. dir. Cambridge (Mass.) Pub. Libr., 1991-1993, dir., 1993—; steering com. Mass. delegation to White Ho. Conf. on Librs., 1990; corporator East Cambridge Savs. Bank. Reviewer Sch. Libr. Jour.; contbr. articles to profl. jours. Incorporator Cambridge Family YMCA, Cambridge, 1991-93; bd. dirs. Guidance Ctr., Inc., 1994—. Mem. ALA (Mass. councilor 1993-97), ACLU Mass. (adv. bd. 1994-96, bd. dirs. 1996—), Mass. Libr. Assn. (pres. 1985-87, v.p. 1983-85), Rotary (bd. dirs. Cambridge 1993-99, v.p. 1995-96, pres. 1997-98, pres. Reading club). Office: Cambridge Pub Libr 449 Broadway Cambridge MA 02138-4125

FLANNERY, WILBUR EUGENE, health science association administrator, internist; b. New Castle, Pa., June 19, 1907; s. Charles Francis and Mary Catherine (McGrath) F.; m. Ruth Iva Donaldson, June 27, 1929; children: Charles, John, Richard, Harry. Grad., Mercersburg Acad., 1925; BA, Dartmouth Coll., 1929; MA, Oberlin Coll., 1930; MD, Harvard U., 1935. Diplomate Nat. Bd. Medical Examiners. Minister Meth. Ch., New Castle, 1930-31; intern Cleve. City Hosp., 1935-36; resident physician Jameson Meml. Hosp., New Castle, 1936-37; fellowship Cleve. Clinic Found., 1937-40; practice medicine specializing in internal medicine New Castle, 1940—; med. dir. Hospice of St. Francis Hosp., New Castle, 1987—; chmn. bd. Pa. Blue Shield, Harrisburg, Pa., 1975-80. Contbr. numerous articles to med. jours. Pres. Bd. of Edn., New Castle, 1947-53; former trustee Knoville (Tenn.) Coll.; former pres. of chmn. Lawrence County chpt. ARC, Lawrence County chpt. Pa. Assn. for Blind, Lawrence County Mental Health Clinic, New Castle Exec. Club, Greater New Castle C. of C. Recipient Disting. Citizens award Optimists Club, 1974; named Boss of Yr., Am. Bus. Women's Assoc., 1987. Mem. AMA (del. 1953-63), Pa. Med. Soc. (pres. 1963-64), Lawrence County Med. Soc. (sec. 1954-55, pres. 1955-56), Am. Soc. Internal Medicine, Am. Med. Writers Assn., Acad. Hospice Physicians (pres. 1990), Internat. Hospice Inst., Internat. Coll. Hospice/Palliative Care, Internat. Platform Assn., Pa. Soc., New Castle Country Club, Univ. Club (Pitts.), Lawrence Club, Youngstown (Ohio) Club, Elks, Lions (pres. New Castle 1943-44 Disting. Svc. award, Melvin Jones fellow 1995). Republican. Presbyterian. Home: 106 E Hazelcroft Ave New Castle PA 16105-2133 Office: Hospice of St Francis 131 N Columbus Interbelt New Castle PA 16101-7401

FLANSBURG, JAMES MCCAULEY, editor; b. Des Moines, Jan. 21, 1959; s. James Sherman and Carol Ann (McCauley) F. BA, U. Iowa, 1981; MBA, St. Ambrose U., 1991. Reporter Cedar Rapids (Iowa) Gazette, 1981-86; mktg. dir. Gen. Growth Cos., Des Moines, 1986-89; sr. copy editor Quad-City Times, Davenport, Iowa, 1989-91; v.p., mng. editor The Daily Tribune, Ames, Iowa, 1991-95; exec. editor Denton (Tex.) Record-Chronicle, 1995—. Mem. adv. bd. ARC, Denton, 1997—. Mem. Am. Soc. Newspaper Editors. Avocations: house renovations, reading, old movies. Home: 731 Hillcrest St Denton TX 76201-2404 Office: Denton Record Chronicle 314 E Hickory St Denton TX 76201-4272

FLANSBURGH, EARL ROBERT, architect; b. Ithaca, N.Y., Apr. 28, 1931; s. Earl Alvah and Elizabeth (Evans) F.; m. Louise Hospital, Aug. 27, 1955; children: Earl Schuyler, John Conant. BArch, Cornell U., 1954; MArch, MIT, 1957; S.C.M.P., Harvard U. Sch. Bus., 1982. Job capt., designer The Architects Collaborative, Cambridge, Mass., 1958-62; partner Freeman, Flansburgh & Assos., Cambridge, 1961-63; prin. Earl R. Flansburgh & Assos., Cambridge, 1963-69, pres., dir. design, 1969—; bd. dirs. daka, Inc.; exec. v.p. Environment Systems Internat., Inc.; vis. prof. archtl. design Mass. Inst. Tech., 1965-66; instr. art Wellesley Coll., 1962-65, lectr. art, 1965-69; cons. Arthur D. Little, Inc., Cambridge, 1964-70. Archtl. works include Weston (Mass.) High Sch. Addition, 1965-67, Cornell U. Campus Store, 1967-70, Cumnock Hall, Harvard U. Bus. Sch, 1973-75, Acton (Mass.) Elementary schs, 1966-68, 69-71, Wilton (Conn.) High Sch, 1968-71, 14 Story St. Bldg, 1970, Boston Design Ctr., 1985-86, Glenwood Sch., Dallas, 1985-88, New Univ. No. B.C., Prince George, Can., 1991—, Boston Coll. Law Sch., 1992—; exhibited works Light Machine I, IBM Gallery, N.Y.C., 1958, Light Machine II, Carpenter Center, Harvard, 1965, 5 Cambridge Architects, Wellesley Coll., 1969, Work of Earl R. Flansburgh and Assos, Wellesley Coll., 1969, New Architecture in New Eng, DeCordova Mus., 1974-75, Residential Architecture, Mead Art Gallery, Amherst Coll., 1976, works represented in, 50 Ville del Nostro Tempo, 1970, Nuove Ville, New Villas, 1970, Vacation Houses, 1970, Vacation Houses, 2d edit., 1977, Interior Design, 1970, Drawings by American Architects, 1973, Interior Spaces Designed by Architects, 1974, New Architecture in New England, 1974, Great Houses, 1976, Architecture Boston, 1976, Presentation Drawings by American Architects, 1977, Architecture, 1970-1980, A Decade of Change, 1980, Old and New Architecture, A Design Relationship, 1980, 25 Years of Record Houses, 1981, School Ways: The Planning and Design of American Schools, 1992; Author: (with others) Techniques of Successful Practice, 1975. Chmn. architecture com. Boston Arts Festival, 1964, Downtown Boston Design adv. com.; bd. dirs. Cambridge Ctr. Adult Edn.; pres. Downtown North Boston, 1994—; trustee Cornell U., 1972—; chmn. bldgs. and properties com., 1976-87; mem. exec. com. acad. affairs com.; class sec. SCMP VII Harvard Bus. Sch., 1982-89. 1st lt. USAF, 1954-56. Recipient design awards Progressive Architecture, design awards Record Houses, design awards AIA, design awards City of Boston, design awards Mass. Masonry Inst., spl. design citations Am. Assn. Sch. Adminstrs., spl. 1st prize Buffalo-Western N.Y. chpt. AIA Competition., Walter Taylor award Am. Assn. Sch. Adminstrs., 1986, William Candill award Am. Coll. & Univ. Mag., 1993, Award of Honor, Boston Soc. Archs., 1999; Fulbright Rsch. grantee Bldg. Rsch. Sta., Eng., 1957-58. Fellow AIA, Nat. Acad. Design; mem. Royal Inst. Brit. Architects, Boston Soc. Architects (chmn. program com., 1969-71, commr. pub. affairs 1971-73, commr. design 1973-74, dir. 1971-74, pres. 1980-81), Boston Found. Architecture (treas. 1984-89), Cornell U. Coun., Quill and Dagger Soc., St. Botolph Club, Tau Beta Pi. Home: 225 Old County Rd Lincoln MA 01773-4601 Office: 77 N Washington St Boston MA 02114-1908

FLANYAK, CHRISANN MARIE, county court manager; b. Chgo., Mar. 31, 1971; d. John R. and Donelle C. Flanyak. AA, Coll. of DuPage, 1991; BA, No. Ill. U., 1993; MA, U. Ill., Chgo., 1996, postgrad., 1997—. File clk. DuPage County Cir. Clk., Wheaton, Ill., 1994-95; auxiliary police officer Wheaton Police Dept., 1995; adult probation officer Lake County County Cir. Cts., Waukegan, Ill., 1995-98, budget and fin. mgr., 1998—; tchg. asst., rsch. asst. U. Ill., Chgo., 1993-95. Sexual Abuse Intervention Network scholar, 1997. Mem. ASPA, Acad. Criminal Justice Scis., Assn. for Treatment of Sexual Abusers (assoc.), Phi Alpha Alpha. Republican. Roman Catholic. E-mail: cflany1@uic.edu. Office: 19th Jud Cir Ct 18 N County St Waukegan IL 60085

FLASCHEN, DAVID JENKIN STEWARD, marketing executive; b. Summit, N.J., Dec. 10, 1955; s. Steward Samuel and Joyce Davies Flaschen; m. Deborah Nordwall, Apr. 7, 1984; children: Katherine Skylar, David Jenkin Steward Jr. BA, Brown U., 1977; MBA, U. Pa., 1982. Profl. athlete N.Am. Soccer League, Chgo., 1977-79; mgr. product mktg. IBM, Princeton, N.J., 1982-84; materials mgr. Gavilan, Sunnyvale, Calif., 1984; corp. v.p., divsn. gen. mgr. Dataquest, San Jose, Calif., 1985-89; asst. to pres. Dun and Bradstreet Corp., N.Y.C., 1989-91; v.p. software svcs. IMS Internat., London, 1991-93; pres., COO A.C. Nielsen N.Am., Schaumberg, Ill., 1993-95; chmn., CEO Donnelly Mktg. Inc., Naperville, Ill., 1996-97; pres., CEO Thomson Fin. Svcs., Boston, 1997—; bd. dirs. DM Holdings Inc., Chgo. Fund raiser United Way, Chgo., 1993, 94, 95; bd. dirs. Jobs for Mass., 1998—. Recipient Forty Under 40 award Crain's Mag., 1994; mem. All Star Soccer Team, Nat. Collegiate Athletic Assn., 1977. Mem. Direct Mktg. Assn., Kenilworth (Ill.) Club (bd. dirs. 1996-97). Avocations: contemporary art, champagne cap collecting. Home: 180 Clyde St Chestnut Hill MA 02467-2904 Office: Thomson Fin Svcs 22 Thomson Pl Boston MA 02210-1212

FLASCHEN, EVAN DANIEL, lawyer; b. Summit, N.J., July 26, 1957; s. Steward Samuel and Joyce (Davies) F.; m. Cynthia Anne Cromwell, May 24, 1981; children: Reed Cromwell, Joan Steward, Thomas Bevan. BA, Wesleyan U., 1979; JD, U. Conn., 1982. Bar: Conn. 1982. Ptnr. Bingham Dana LLP, Hartford, Conn., 1982—; adj. prof. U. Conn. Sch. Law, 1996—; lectr. in field. Co-editor: International Loan Workouts and Bankruptcies, 1989; contbg. editor: Norton Bankruptcy Law and Practice, 1989—; mem. editorial bd. INSOL Internat. Jour., 1990—, Annual Survey of Bankruptcy Law, 1989—; contbr. articles to profl. jours. Mem. ABA (bus. bankruptcy com. sect. of bus. law 1984—, chmn. secured creditors subcom. 1993-96, vice chmn. 1988-89, vice chmn. Chpt. 11 subcom. 1989-93, internat. bankruptcy subcom. 1986-97), Internat. Bar Assn. (com. creditor's rights and insolvency 1986—), INSOL Internat. (co-chmn. cross-border insolvency project 1989—), Am. Law Inst., Am. Bankruptcy Inst. (chmn. INSOL sect. 1988-92), Am. Coll. Bankruptcy. Home: 43 Riverview Rd Glastonbury CT 06033-3137 Office: Bingham Dana LLP One State St Hartford CT 06103

FLASCHEN, STEWARD SAMUEL, high technology company executive; b. Berwyn, Ill., May 28, 1926; s. Hyman Herman and Ethel (Leviton) F.; m. Joyce Davies, Apr. 21, 1949; children: John, Sheryl, David, Evan. BS in Chemistry, U. Ill., 1947; MA, Miami U., Oxford, Ohio, 1948; PhD in Geochemistry, Pa. State U., 1953. Supr. rsch. dept. Bell Telephone Labs., Murray Hill, N.J., 1952-59; dir. phys. scis., R & D semiconductor products div. Motorola, Inc., Phoenix, 1959-64; sr. v.p., gen. tech. dir., mem. corp. policy bd. ITT Corp., N.Y.C., 1964-86; pres. Flaschen & Davies, New Canaan, Conn., 1986—; chmn. Transwitch Corp., Shelton, Conn., 1988—; chmn. Teco Systems Corp., 1992—, Norwood, Mass.; bd. dirs. Sipex Corp., Billerica, Mass., Merrill Lynch Venture Capital, N.Y.C., Advanced Tech. Venture Ptnrs., Boston, San Jose, Calif., Sipex Corp., Billerica, Mass.; lectr. Pace U. Grad. Sch. Bus. Author: Search and Research, 1965; also articles; patentee in field. Mem. Scottsdale Bd. Edn., 1960-64. Served with USNR, 1944-46. Fellow Am. Inst. Chemists, IEEE, Pa. State U. Alumni; mem. AAAS, Electromech. Soc. Am., Am. Ceramic Soc., Indsl. Research Inst., N.Y. Acad. Scis., Univ. CLub. Avocations: family, exercise. *I was fortunate in my education to have had broad exposure to philosophy, the natural sciences and English. This early training in the basics of problems, concepts, and decisions, and in the skill of communicating effectively, has been of the utmost value to me professionally and personally.*

FLASHBURG, MARSHA LYNNE, community health nurse; b. Bklyn., Apr. 8, 1946; d. Harry and Bertha (Klein) Millendorf; m. Fred Flashburg, Oct. 30, 1965; children: Marlene, Sandra. AAS, N.Y.C. Community Coll., Bklyn., 1965; BSN, Coll. S.I., 1990; MS in Adminstrn., Cen. Mich. U., 1993; DSc, Clayton Sch. Natural Healing, 1994. Cert. community health nurse, hynotherapist; advanced practice Reiki practitioner. Staff nurse Williamsburg Gen. Hosp., Bklyn.; head nurse Coney Island Hosp., Bklyn.; nursing rsch. intern NYC Health & Hosps. Corp., 1994. Contbg. author: Springhouse Review Guides: Nursing Pharmacology. Mem. N.Y. State Nurses Assn., Sigma Theta Tau (Mu Upsilon chpt.).

FLASKAMP, RUTH EHMEN STAACK, retired elementary education educator; b. Moline, Ill., Dec. 11, 1927; d. Henry Frederick and Tjiede Lena (Ehmen) Staack; m. Richard Kresse Flaskamp, June 10, 1950; children: Richard Henry, Thomas Marc. BA, Augustana Coll., 1949; MEd, Bowling Green State U., 1971. Tchr. elem. grades Lanark (Ill.) Consolidated Schs., 1949-50; tchr. elem. grades Sylvania (Ohio) City Schs., 1956-93, ret., 1993; field supr. Coll. Edn., U. Toledo, 1994—; tchr. U. Toledo, 1997-98; part-time faculty dept. of curriculum and instrn. U. Toledo, 1997-99. Contbr. articles to profl. jours., various curriculum guides. Bd. dirs. Sylvania Pub. Libr., 1960-61; mem. ednl. adv. com. Toledo Edison, Toledo Zoo, 1986; active various polit. campaigns. Jennings scholar, 1982-83; recipient award for excellence in edn. NEA/Ladies Home Jour., 1990-91. Mem. NEA, Sylvania Edn. Assn. (sec. 1975-76, 89-90, pres. 1991), Ohio Edn. Assn. (rep.), N.W. Ohio Edn. Assn., Nat. Sci. Tchrs. Assn., Golden Emblem Club. Republican. Lutheran. Avocations: swimming, weaving, music, reading, baking. Home: 6510 Cornwall Ct Sylvania OH 43560-3103 Office: SCI-MA Tech Office U Toledo Bancroft St Toledo OH 43615

FLASTER, RICHARD JOEL, lawyer; b. N.Y.C., Jan. 7, 1943; s. Charles and Sylvia (Moss) F.; m. Esther S. Stomel; children: Kiva Moss, Eben Scott. BS in Econs., U. Pa., 1963; JD, Harvard U., 1966. Bar: N.Y. 1967, U.S. Tax Ct. 1971, N.J. 1972, D.C. 1972. Law clk. to judge U.S. Dist Ct. (ea. dist.), N.Y., 1966-68; Reginald Heber Smith fellow U. Pa., 1968-69; assoc. Stroock & Stroock & Lavan, N.Y.C., 1969-72; pres. Liebman & Flaster, P.C., Cherry Hill, N.J., 1972-86, Flaster, Greenberg et al., Cherry Hill, N.J., 1986—; bd. dirs. Jefferson Bank, N.J.; mem. adv. bd. Living Arts Repertory Theatre; frequent lectr. on various tax subjects ABA, N.J. Inst. Continuing Legal Edn.$d, Harvard U., 1966. Bar: N.Y. 1967, U.S. Tax Ct. 1971, N.J. 1972, D.C. 1972. Law clk. to judge U.S. Dist. Ct. (ea. dist.) N.Y., 1966-68; Reginald Heber Smith fellow U. Pa., 1968-69; assoc. Stroock & Stroock & Lavan, N.Y.C., 1969-72; pres. Liebman & Flaster, P.C., Cherry Hill, N.J., 1972-86; pres. Flaster, Greenberg, Wallenstein, Roderick, Spirgel, Zuckerman, Skinner & Kirchner P.C., Cherry Hill, N.J., 1986—; bd. dirs. Jefferson Bank, N.J.; mem. bd. advisors Living Arts Repertory Theatre; frequent lectr. on various tax subjects ABA, N.J. Inst. Continuing Legal Edn. Mem. N.J. State Bar Assn., N.Y. State Bar Assn., Washington D.C. Bar Assn. Beta Gamma Sigma, Beta Alpha Psi, Pi Gamma Mu. Author: Basic Federal Tax Aspects of Real Estate Transactions, 1976, Tax Aspects of Separation and Divorce, 1982; tax editor N.J. Family Lawyer, 1982-92; editor Tax & Business Report, 1987—. Author: Basic Federal Tax Aspects of Real Estate Transactions, 1976, Tax Aspects of Separation and Divorce, 1982; tax editor N.J. Family Lawyer, 1982-92; editor Tax & Business Report, 1987—. Mem. N.J. State Bar Assn., Washington D.C. Bar Assn., Beta Gamma Sigma, Beta Alpha Psi, Pi Gamma Mu. Office: Flaster Greenberg Et Al 1735 Market St 3 Mellon Bank Ctr Fl 39 Philadelphia PA 19103 also: Three Mellon Bank Ctr 39th Fl 1735 Market St Philadelphia PA 19103

FLATEAU, JOHN, academic administrator; b. Bklyn., Feb. 24, 1950; married. BA, NYU, 1972; MPA, CUNY, 1978, MA in Polit. Sci., 1999. Chief of staff, legis. asst. N.Y. State Assemblyman Albert Vann, 1975-76; exec. dir. N.Y. State Black and Puerto Rican Legis. Caucus, Inc., Albany, 1977-80, 81-82; prin. rsch. analyst N.Y. State Commn. Health Edn. and Illness Prevention, Albany, 1979-80; chmn., CEO Strategic Devel. Svcs. et al, N.Y.C., 1979—; sr. v.p. N.Y. State Urban Devel. Corp., N.Y.C., 1983-90; chief of staff Mayor David Dinkins, N.Y.C., 1991-93; exec. dir. DuBois Bunche Ctr. Pub. Policy Medgar Evers Coll., CUNY, Bklyn., 1994—; adj. lectr. pub. adminstrn. program Medgar Evers Coll., Bklyn., 1994—. Author: The Prison Industrial Complex: Race, Crime and Justice in New York; co-author: Blackout? Media Ownership Concentration and the Future of Black Radio, 1997, Young Lives, American Dreams: An Opinion Survey of African Americans, 1999. Sr. bd. stewards Bridge St. AWME Ch.; mem. Roundtable Instns. People of Color, Vannguard Ind. Dem. Assn.; campaign mgmt./voting rights cons. fed., state, local elections. Pub. Svc. fellow U.S. Office Edn., 1975; Grad. Rsch. fellow N.Y. State Legis. Inst., 1976; Voting Rights fellow So. Regional Coun., 1994; Rsch. fellow Howard Samuels Ctr. State Policy Mgmt., CUNY, 1998. Mem. ASPA, Am. Polit. Sci. Assn., N.Y. Colloquium Am. Polit. Devel., Conf. Minority Pub. Adminstrs. E-mail: jflat@pipeline.com. Office: DuBois Bunche Ctr Pub Policy Medgar Evers Coll CUNY 1650 Bedford Ave Rm 2032C Brooklyn NY 11225

FLATEN, ALFRED N., retired food and consumer products executive; b. 1935. With Nash-Finch Co., Mpls., 1861-98; mgr. Iowa divsn. Nash-Finch Co., 1983-86, v.p. S.E. divsn., 1986-89; v.p. retail ops. Nash-Finch Co., Mpls., 1989-91, past exec. v.p., past pres., CEO, COO, also bd. dirs.

FLATEN, ROBERT ARNOLD, retired ambassador; b. Mpls., May 21, 1934; s. Arnold Wangensten and Evelyn (Solberg) F.; m. Carroll Jean Johnson, Dec. 22, 1956; children: Kristin, Karen, Sonia, Arne. BA, St. Olaf Coll., Northfield, Minn., 1956; MA, George Washington U., 1961. Vice consul Am. Consulate, Strasbourg, France, 1962-63, Peshawar, Pakistan, 1964-66; 2d sec. Am. Embassy, Tel Aviv, 1966-69, dep. chief mission, 1982-86; Fgn. Svc. insp., legis. mgmt. officer, office dir., dep. asst. sec. U.S. Dept. State, Washington, 1970-82, office dir., 1987-90; amb. to Rwanda Am. Embassy, Kigali, 1990-93. Chair exec. com. Peace Prize Forum, 1996, edn. bd. St. John Luteran Ch., Northfield, Minn. 2d lt. USAF, 1956-59. Mem. Am. Fgn. Svc. Assn., Minn. Internat. Ctr., Immortal Chaplains Found., UN Assn./Minn. Home: 5008 90th St E Northfield MN 55057-4349

FLATLEY, LAWRENCE EDWARD, lawyer; b. Erie, Pa., May 24, 1950; s. Willard James and Loretta Grace (Moore) F.; m. Teresa Marie Kadunce, May 17, 1974; children: Daniel Lawrence, Steven James. BA, U. Pitts., 1972; JD, U. Pa., 1975. Bar: Pa. 1975, U.S. Dist. Ct. (we. dist.) Pa. 1975, U.S. Ct. Appeals (3d Cir.) 1975. Assoc. Reed, Smith, Shaw & McClay, Pitts., 1975-83, ptnr., 1983—. Contbg. author Foreign Policy, vol. 2, 1971, Mealey's Ins. Reports, 1990. Mem. Phi Beta Kapp. Democrat. Roman Catholic. Home: 2747 Shamrock Dr Allison Park PA 15101-3146 Office: Reed Smith Shaw & McClay Mellon Sq 435 6th Ave Ste 2 Pittsburgh PA 15219-1886

FLATO, WILLIAM ROEDER, JR., software development company executive; b. Corpus Christi, Tex., Apr. 20, 1945; s. William Roeder and Juanita Flato; m. Beatrice Pesl, Aug. 22, 1974; children: Amanda Leigh, William Roeder III. BBA, U. Houston, 1967. CPA, Tex. Acct. Hughes Tool Co., Houston, 1966-67; acct. Milchem, Inc., Houston, 1967-72, accounting mgr., 1972-73, asst. contr., 1973, corp. contr., 1973-78; v.p. fin., sec., treas. Baker Performance Chems. Inc. (formerly Magna Corp.), Houston, 1978-82, exec. v.p. fin. and planning, sec.-treas., 1982-93; CFO, v.p. fin. CoToCo Techs., Inc., 1993-97; founder, CFO, v.p. fin. Connective Techs., Inc., 1996—. Active Country Village Civic Assn.; state chmn. Young Ams. for Freedom, 1964; precinct chmn. Harris County Rep. Exec. Com., 1966-67. With U.S. Army, 1968-69. Decorated Army Commendation medal. Mem. Am. Inst. CPA's, Tex. Soc. CPA's, Mensa. Presbyterian. Home: 11931 Drexel Hill Dr Houston TX 77077-3009 Office: 7676 Hillmont St Ste 120 Houston TX 77040-6423

FLATT, ADRIAN EDE, surgeon; b. Frinton, Eng., Aug. 26, 1921; came to U.S., 1956, naturalized, 1960; s. Leslie Neeve and Barbara F.; m. Judith Johnson. BA, Cambridge U., 1942, MA, 1945, MBBchir., 1946, MD, 1953, M. chir., 1972. Diplomate: Am. Bd. Orthopedic Surgery. Rotating intern, then resident in gen., plastic and orthopaedic surgery London (Eng.) Hosp., 1946-54, 55-56; mem. faculty U. Iowa Med. Sch., 1956-79; prof. orthopaedic surgery and anatomy, dir. div. hand surgery, chmn. dept. surgery Norwalk (Conn.) Hosp., 1979-82; clin. prof. Yale U. Med. Sch., 1979-82; chief dept. orthopaedics Baylor U. Med. Ctr., Dallas, 1982-92, coord. rsch. Tom Landry Sports Medicine Ctr., 1992-94, dir. edn. dept. orthopaedics, 1995—; Hunterian prof. Royal Coll. Surgeons, 1962; McIlrath guest prof. Royal Prince Alfred Hosp., Sydney, Australia, 1972; Sir R. Watson-Jones lectr. Brit. Orthopaedic Assn., 1986; cons. in hand surgery to surg. gen. U.S. Air Force, 1962—. Editor in chief Jour. Hand Surgery, 1981-91; author textbooks, papers in field. Served as officer RAF, 1948-50. Recipient Kappa Delta award Am. Acad. Orthopaedic Surgeons, 1972. Mem. Am. Soc. Surgery Hand, Brit. Hand Soc., Brit. Assn. Plastic Surgery (hon.), Group Etude de la Main, Am. Orthopaedic Assn., Am. Acad. Orthopaedic Surgeons, Am. Soc. Plastic and Reconstructive Surgery. Patentee artificial wrist and finger joints. Office: Baylor U Med Ctr George Truett James Orthopedic Inst 3500 Gaston Ave Dallas TX 75246-2017

FLATTAU, EDWARD, columnist; b. N.Y.C., May 18, 1937. BA, Brown U., 1958; postgrad., Columbia Law Sch., 1958-60. Polit. corr. UPI, Albany, N.Y., 1962-66; congrl. corr. UPI, Washington, 1967-69; legis. asst. Rep. Benjamin Rosenthal, Washington, 1969-71; asst. dir. of info. European Cmty., Washington, 1971-72; syndicated columnist Global Horizons Syndicate, Washington, 1972—. Author: Tracking the Charlatans, 1998; contbr. articles to mags. Recipient Disting. Journalism citation Scripps Howard Found., 1978, Lorax award Global Tomorrow Coalition, 1985, Global Media award Population Inst., 1986. Avocations: tennis, golf, Civil War buff. Home and Office: 1330 New Hampshire Ave NW Washington DC 20036-6350

FLATTAU, PAMELA EBERT, research psychologist, consultant; b. Chgo., Dec. 24, 1946; d. Raymond Clarence and Sylvia Anne (Jones) E.; m. Edward Samuel Flattau, Feb. 1, 1977; children: Jeremy Paul, Victoria Celeste. BSc with honors, U. Leeds, Eng., 1969; MS, U. Ga., 1972, PhD, 1974. Congrl. sci. fellow AAAS-APA, Washington, 1974-75; staff officer NAS/NRC, Washington, 1975-81, sr. staff officer, 1985-90, unit dir., 1990-95; policy analyst NSF, Washington, 1981-85; pres. Flattau Assocs. LLC, Washington, 1995—; mem. exec. com. Coun. Profl. Assns. for Fed. Stats., Washington, 1986-87. Editor: Research Doctorate Programs in U.S., 1995; author, editor series Biomed and Behavioral Research Personnel 1975-80, 1994; author, contbr.: Science and Engineering Indicators Series, 1981-85. Bd. dirs. Assn. Advancement Psychology, Washington, 1980-82. Mem. AAAS, APA (travel grantee 1992, Young Psychologist 1976), Soc. for Social Studies of Sci.,

Human Resources Planning Soc., Sigma Xi. Office: Flattau Assocs LLC 5335 Wisconsin Ave NW Ste 440 Washington DC 20015-2030

FLATTÉ, STANLEY MARTIN, physicist, educator; b. Los Angeles, Dec. 2, 1940; s. Samuel and Henrietta (Edelstein) F.; m. Renelde Marie Demeure, June 26, 1966; children: Michael, Anne. BS, Calif. Inst. Tech., 1962; student, NYU, 1960-61; PhD, U. Calif.-Berkeley, 1966. Research particle physicist Lawrence Berkeley Lab., Calif., 1966-71; asst. prof. physics U. Calif.-Santa Cruz, 1971-73, assoc. prof., 1973-78, prof., 1978—; dir. Ctr. for Studies of Nonlinear Dynamics La Jolla Inst., 1982-86, dept. chmn., 1986-89; cons. phys. oceanography and underwater sound U.S. Govt.; vis. researcher, Cern, Geneva, 1975, Scripps Inst. Oceanography, 1980, Cambridge U., Eng., 1981. Author: (with others) Sound Transmission Through a Fluctuating Ocean, 1979; contbr. (with others) articles profl. jours. Woodrow Wilson fellow, 1962; NSF fellow, 1962-66; Guggenheim Found. fellow, 1975. Fellow AAAS, Am. Phys. Soc., Acoustical Soc. Am., Optical Soc. Am.; mem. Am. Geophys. Union, Sigma Xi. Discovered cusp phenomenon in particle physics; developed methods for using sound and light waves to probe statis. atmosphere, ocean and earth processes. Office: Univ Calif Physics Dept Santa Cruz CA 95064 *An understanding of science requires two elements: significant, individual research accomplishment, and a knowledge of the historical development of one's discipline. Both are essential. I have tried to balance them in research, and in teaching.*

FLATTERY, THOMAS LONG, lawyer, legal administrator; b. Detroit, Nov. 14, 1922; s. Thomas J. and Rosemary (Long) F.; m. Gloria M. Hughes, June 10, 1947 (dec.); children: Constance Marie, Carol Dianne Lee, Michael Patrick, Thomas Hughes, Dennis Jerome, Betsy Ann Sprecher; m. Barbara J. Balfour, Oct. 4, 1986. BS, U.S. Mil. Acad., 1947; JD, UCLA, 1955; LLM, U. So. Calif., 1965. Bar: Calif. 1955, U.S. Patent and Trademark Office 1957, U.S. Customs Ct. 1968, U.S. Supreme Ct. 1974, Conn. 1983, N.Y. 1984. With Motor Products Corp., Detroit, 1950, Equitable Life Assurance Soc., Detroit, 1951, Bohn Aluminum & Brass Co., Hamtramck, Mich., 1952; mem. legal staff, asst. contract adminstr. Radioplane Co. (divsn. Northrop Corp.), Van Nuys, Calif., 1955-57; successively corp. counsel, gen. counsel, asst. sec. McCulloch Corp., L.A., 1957-64; sec., corp. counsel Technicolor, Inc., Hollywood, Calif., 1964-70; successively corp. counsel, asst. sec., v.p., sec. and gen. counsel Amcord, Inc., Newport Beach, Calif., 1970-72; v.p., sec., gen. counsel Schick Inc., L.A., 1972-75; counsel, asst. sec. C.F. Braun & Co., Alhambra, Calif., 1975-76; sr. v.p., sec., gen. counsel Automation Industries, Inc. (now PCC Tech. Industries Inc. a unit of Penn Cen. Corp.), Greenwich, Conn., 1976-86; v.p., gen. counsel G&H Tech., Inc. (a unit of Penn Cen. Corp.), Santa Monica, Calif., 1986-93; temp. judge Mcpl. Ct. Calif. L.A. Jud. Dist. and Santa Monica Unified Cts., 1987—; settlement officer L.A. Superior and Mcpl. Cts., 1991—; pvt. practice, 1993—; panelist Am. Arbitration Assn., 1991—; jud. arbitrator and mediator Alternative Dispute Resolution Programs L.A. Superior and Mcpl. Cts, 1993—. Contbr. articles to various legal jours. Served to 1st lt. AUS, 1942-50. Mem. ABA, Nat. Assn. Secs. Dealers, Inc (bd. arbitrators 1996, mediators 1997), State Bar Calif. (co-chmn. corp. law dept. com. 1978-79, lectr. continuing legal edn. program), L.A. County Bar Assn. (chmn. corp. law dept. com. 1966-67), Century City Bar Assn. (chmn. corp. law dept. com. 1979-80), Conn. Bar Assn., Santa Monica Bar Assn., N.Y. State Bar Assn., Am. Soc. Corp. Secs. (L.A. regional group pres. 1973-74), L.A. Intellectual Property Law Assn., Am. Ednl. League (trustee 1988—, sec. 1998—), West Point Alumni Assn., Army Athletic Assn., Friendly Sons St. Patrick, Jonathan Club (dir. 1996—), Braemar Country Club, Phi Alpha Delta. Roman Catholic. Home and Office: 439 Via De La Paz Pacific Palisades CA 90272-4633

FLAUM, JOEL MARTIN, federal judge; b. Hudson, N.Y., Nov. 26, 1936; s. Louis and Sally (Berger) F.; m. Delilah Brummet, June 4, 1989; children from previous marriage: Jonathan, Alison. BA, Union Coll., Schenectady, 1958; JD, Northwestern U., 1963, LLM, 1964. Bar: Ill. 1963. Asst. state's atty. Cook County, Ill., 1965-69, 1st asst. atty. gen. Ill., 1969-72; 1st asst. U.S. atty. Chgo., 1972-75; judge U.S. Dist. Ct. (no. dist.) Ill., Chgo., 1975-83, U.S. Ct. Appeals (7th cir.), 1983—; adj. prof. Northwestern U. Sch. Law, 1993—; lectr. DePaul U. Coll. of Law, 1987-88; mem. Ill. Law Enforcement Commn., 1970-72; cons. U.S. Dept. Justice, Law Enforcement Assistance Adminstrn., 1970-71. Mem.: Northwestern U. Law Rev., 1962-63; contbr. articles to legal jours. Mem. vis. com. U. Chgo. Law Sch., 1983-86, Northwestern U. Sch. Law, 1983—; mem. adv. com. USCG Acad., 1990-93. Lt. comdr. JAGC, USNR, 1981-92. Ford Found. fellow, 1963-64. Fellow Am. Bar Found. (life); mem. ABA, Fed. Bar Assn., Ill. Bar Assn., Chgo. Bar Found. (life), 7th Cir. Bar Assn., Chgo. Inn of Ct., Chgo. Bar Assn., Maritime Law Assn., Navy-Marine Corps Ret. Judge Advs. Assn., Am. Judicature Soc., Naval Res. Assn., Legal Club Chgo., Law Club Chgo. Jewish. Office: US Ct Appeals 7th Ct 219 S Dearborn St Chicago IL 60604-1702

FLAUM, MARSHALL ALLEN, television producer, writer, director; b. Bklyn.; s. Mayer and Ethel (Lamkay) P.; m. Gita Faye Miller; children: Erica, Seth Baruch. BA, U. Iowa, 1948; DFA (hon.), So. Ill. U., Edwardsville, 1974. Story editor, writer, assoc. producer TV series for 20th Century, 1957-62; producer, writer, dir. TV spls. for Wolper Prodns., 1962-65; founder Flaum-Grinberg Prodns., 1966; v.p. Metromedia Producers Corp., 1968-76; pres. Marshall Flaum Prodns., Inc., 1976—. Prodr., writer, dir.: TV spls. Day of Infamy, 1963, Hollywood: The Great Stars, 1963, The Yanks Are Coming, 1964, Battle of Britain, 1964, Berlin: Kaiser to Kruschev, 1964, Let My People Go, 1965 (Ohio State award, George Foster Peabody award), Miss Goodall and the Wild Chimpanzees, 1966 (Edinburgh Festival award), Bogart, 1967 (Melbourne Festival award); prodr., writer TV spls. Killy Le Champion, 1969; prodr., writer, dir. TV spls. Hollywood: The Selznick Years, 1969 (Silver Lion award Venice Film Festival), The Time of Man, 1969 (Silver Hugo award Chgo. Internat. Film Festival); exec. prodr., co-writer: (TV series) Undersea World of Jacques Cousteau, 1970-76, Jane Goodall and The World of Animal Behavior, 1972-76, The Wild Dogs of Africa, 1973 (Emmy award best documentary, Chgo. Internat. Festival Gold Hugo award), Baboons of Gombe, 1974, Hyena, 1975, Lions of Serengeti, 1976; prodr. Am. Film Inst. Salute to Bette Davis, 1977; prodr., writer, dir.: (TV spls.) Yabba Dabba Doo! The Happy World of Hanna-Barbera, 1977, Bing Crosby: His Life and Legend, 1978 (Christopher award), Playboy's 25th Anniversary Celebration, 1979, A Bing Crosby Christmas . . . Like the Ones We Used To Know, 1979; prodr., co-writer (with others): TV spls. Ripley's Believe It or Not, 1982, Bob Hope's Who Makes the World Laugh, 1983; prodr., writer, dir.: (TV spls.), Bob Hope's Texaco Star Theatre, Life's Most Embarrassing Moments, 1984, Portrait of Dorothy Stratten, 1985, A Yabba Dabba Doo Celebration, 50 Yrs. of Hanna Barbera, 1989, Arts and Entertainment's Ancient Mysteries, 1996, Celebrate the Century. Recipient Emmy award as best documentary for A Sound of Dolphins, 1972, The Unsinkable Sea Otter, 1972, George Foster Peabody award for TV spls. for Miss Goodall and The Wild Chimpanzees, 1966, Monte Carlo Internat. TV Festival Golden Nymph award for TV spl. The Yanks are Coming, 1964, Silver medal Atlanta Film Festival for Wild Dogs of Africa, 1973, Octopus, Octopus, 1972, Chgo. Internat. Film Festival Silver Hugo award for Tragedy of the Red Salmon, 1971, Oscar nomination for best documentary feature for The Yanks Are Coming, 1964, Let My People Go, 1966, 16 Emmy award nominations. Mem. Writers Guild Am., Dirs. Guild Am., Acad. Motion Picture Arts and Scis., Acad. TV Arts and Scis. Address: 301 S Rodeo Dr Beverly Hills CA 90212-4206

FLAUM, SANDER ALLEN, advertising and marketing executive; b. Apr. 5, 1937; s. Joseph and Rose (Deutsch) F.; children: Pamela, Jonathon; m. Mechele Plotkin, Apr. 25, 1990. BA, Ohio State U., 1958; MBA, Fairleigh Dickinson U., 1970. Product group dir. Lederle Labs. divsn. Am. Cyanamid Co., Wayne, N.J., 1964-84; exec. v.p. Klemtner Advt., N.Y.C., 1984-88; chmn., CEO Robert A. Becker, Inc., N.Y.C., 1988-98, 1998—; vice chmn. Euro RSCG, Healthcare; adj. prof. mktg. Fairleigh Dickinson U. Grad. Sch. Bus., C.W. Post Grad. Sch. Bus., NYU Stern Sch. Bus. Author: The Shortest Road to Success, Focusing Is for Tough Guys, Maximizing Your Convention Spending, There's a Little Consumer in Every M.D., Great Is Better than Good, Hocus Focus, The Agency of the Nineties, Focus on the Future Direction: Outward. Trustee Hollins Coll. Comms. Rsch. Inst.; mem. mktg. com. United Jewish Appeal. With U.S. Army, 1959-61. Mem. Am. Mktg. Assn., Pharm. Advt. Coun. N.Y. (trustee 1981-85). Avocations: tennis, golf. Office: Robert A Becker Inc EURO RSCG 1633 Broadway Fl 27 New York NY 10019-6708

FLAVIN, D. AESCHLIMAN, artist, lecturer, educator; b. June 6, 1931. Student, Washington U., St. Louis, St. Louis C.C., Leon Cooper Art Sch. Lectr. on Georgia O'Keefe and Mary Cassatt. One woman shows include Jr. League St. Louis, 1987; group shows include Christ in Art FEstival Kirkwood United Meth. Ch., 1983, So. Watercolor Soc., 1987, 90, 93, Luth. Women's Missionary League, 1991, Ste. Genevieve Galleria, Mo. Athletic Assn., Springfield (Mo.) Art Assn., Gallery 100-Midwest Minis, Cape Girardeau, Mo., 1993, Ralston Purina, St. Louis, 1993, St. Peter's (Mo.) Cultural Arts Ctr., Monday Club Webster Groves (Mo.); represented in pub. and pvt. permanent collections in U.S., Can., China, France. Art chmn. Mo. 8th dist. Federated Women's Club; artist coord. Mo. Bapt. Hosp., 1987-90. Recipient signature award So. Watercolor Soc., 1987, 90, Grumbacher award for best of show Artworld, 1987; named Artist of Yr., Soc. Ind. Artists, 1982, 85, Woman of Day award. Mem. Nat. League Pen Women (art chmn. St. Louis br.), St. Louis Artist Guild, So. Watercolor Soc. (signature). Address: PO Box 230109 Saint Louis MO 63123

FLAVIN, NANCY ANN, state legislator; b. Northampton, Mass., June 6, 1950; d. James Edward and Margaret (Leveille) F.; div. Student, Northampton Comml. Coll., 1968-69; certificate, Tufts U., 1985; BA, U. Mass., 1987. Sec. sch. nursing U. Mass., Amherst, 1969-87; adminstrv. asst. State Rep. Shannon P. O'Brien, Mass., 1987-92; mem. Mass. Ho. of Reps., 1993—; mem. com. on banks and banking, mem. govt. regulations and taxation com., vice-chair com. on ethics; bd. dir. Riverside Industries; chmn. com. on ins.; mem. com. on long-term debt. Officer Univ. Staff Assn., 1977-86; mem. adv. task force Easthampton Pub. Sch.; bd. dirs. Easthampton Cmty. Ctr., 1991—; mem. Mass. Women's Polit. Caucus, Pascommuck Conservation Trust. Mem. Five Coll. Fed. Credit Union. Office: Mass Ho of Reps State Capitol Rm 254 Boston MA 02133

FLAWN, PETER TYRRELL, businessman, retired university president, educator; b. Miami, Fla., Feb. 17, 1926; s. Stanley Charles and Laura Carolyn (Rotz) F.; m. Priscilla Bernice Pond, June 28, 1946; children: Tyrrell, Laura. BA, Oberlin coll., 1947; MS, Yale U., 1948, PhD, 1951. Jr. geologist mineral deposits br. U.S. Geol. Survey, 1948; rsch. scientist, geologist Bur. Econ. Geology U. Tex., Austin, 1949-60, dir. Bur. Econ. Geology, prof. geology, 1960-70, dir. divsn. natural resources and environment, 1970-72, prof. geol. scis. and pub. affairs, 1970-72, v.p. acad. affairs, 1970-72, exec. v.p., 1972-73; pres. U. Tex., San Antonio, 1973-77; Leonidas T. Barrow prof. mineral resources U. Tex., Austin, 1978-85, pres., 1979-85, pres. emeritus, 1985, pres. ad interim, 1997-98; bd. dirs. Harte-Hanks, Inc., Hester Capital Mgmt., LLP, El Paso Energy Corp.; mem. Tex. Interagy. Coun. on Natural Resources and Environment, 1969-73; mem. various coms. NAS-NCR; mem. Nat. Sci. Bd., 1980-86. Author: Basement Rocks of Texas and Southeast New Mexico, 1956, The Ouachita System, 1962, Mineral Resources, 1966, Environmental Geology in Landuse Planning Resource Management and Conservation, 1970, A Primer for University Presidents, 1990; contbr. articles to profl. jours. Vice chmn. edn. com. Tex. Constl. Revision Commn.; mem. bd. govs., trustee S.W. Found. for Rsch. and Edn., 1973-74, bd. govs., 1974-77; trustee S.W. Rsch. Inst., 1973—, bd. dirs., 1989—, chair bd. dirs., 1997—; trustee Tex. Mil. Inst., 1974-77l St. David's Hosp., 1981-88; bd. dirs. S.W. Ednl. TV. Coun., 1973-74. With USAAF, 1944-45. Recipient Wilbur Cross medal Yale U., 1984, Ben F. Parker medal Am. Inst. Profl. Geologists, 1989; Cooksey fellow, 1948, Binney fellow, 1951. Mem. NAE, Soc. for Mining, Metallurgy and Exploration, Assn. Profl. Geol. Scientists, Am. Assn. Petroleum Geologists (hon.), Assn. Am. State Geologists (hon.; pres. 1969-70), soc. Econ. Geologists (truste 1971-76), Sociedad Geologica Mexicana, Am. Geol. Inst. (dir. 1967-70, pres. 1987-88), Geol. Soc. Am. (councilor 1972-77, v.p. 1977, pres. 1978), Conf. Bd., greater San Antonio C. of C. (dir. 1975-78), Argyle Club (San Antonio), Headliners Club, Tarry House Club (Austin). Home: 3718 Bridle Path Austin TX 78703-2005 Office: U Tex at Austin Geol Scis Rm 526 Austin TX 78712

FLAX, MARTIN HOWARD, pathologist, retired educator; b. N.Y.C., Jan. 19, 1928; s. Abraham and Sadie (Finkel) F.; m. Ann E. Brockway, June 26, 1955; children: Adam, Jonathan, Elizabeth. AB, Cornell U., 1946; AM, Columbia U., 1948, PhD, 1953; MD, U. Chgo., 1955; MS in Health Mgmt., MIT, 1979. Intern Mt. Sinai Hosp., N.Y.C., 1955-56; fellow pathology U. Chgo., 1956-57; chief biophysics br. Armed Forces Inst. Pathology, Washington, 1957-59; clin. fellow Mass. Gen. Hosp., Boston, 1959-61, asst. pathology, 1961-66; fellow pathology Harvard U. Med. Sch., 1959-61, instr. pathology, 1961-63, assoc. pathology, 1961-66, asst. prof., 1966-69; prof., chmn. pathology dept. Tufts U. Sch. Medicine, 1970-97, chmn. vet. sch.; pathologist-in-chief New Eng. Med. Ctr. Hosp., Boston, 1970-97; emeritus prof. Tufts U., 1998—; cons. pathology B study sect. NIH, 1970-74. Capt. M.C., USAF, 1957-59. Recipient Rsch. Career Devel. award NIH, 1966-69; Nat. Cancer Inst. fellow, 1959-61, Med. Found. fellow, 1963-65, Sloan fellow MIT. Mem. Am. Assn. Pathology, Internat. Acad. Pathology, New Eng. Soc. Pathology, Am. Assn. Immunology, Phi Beta Kappa, Sigma Xi. Home: 32 Gate House Rd Chestnut Hill MA 02467-1335

FLAXMAN, HOWARD RICHARD, lawyer; b. Bklyn., Mar. 2, 1948; s. Benjamin Maurice and Thelma (Helfand) F.; m. Lynne Deidre Eysman, July 31, 1969; children: Carrie Yvette, Jill Michelle. BA, SUNY, Binghamton, 1968; JD, U. Pa., 1971. Bar: Pa. 1972, N.J. 1988. Ptnr. Fox, Rothschild, O'Brien & Frankel, Phila., 1971-86, Blank, Rome, Comisky & McCauley, Phila., 1986-96, Fox, Rothschild, O'Brien & Frankel, 1996—. Bd. dirs. Tredyffrn/Easttown Sch. Bd., Berwyn, Pa., 1984-89; twp. supr. Easttown Twp., Berwyn, 1992—; trustee Easttown Twp. Libr., 1978-88. Mem. ABA, Pa. Bar Assn., Phila. Bar Assn. Republican. Jewish.

FLAYHART, MARTIN ALBERT, lawyer; b. Williamsport, Pa., Mar. 1, 1950; s. William Henry and Naomi (Laux) F. BA with hons., U. Va., 1971; JD, U. Pa., 1974. Bar: Pa. 1974, U.S. Dist. Ct. (mid. dist.) Pa. 1976, U.S. Ct. Appeals (3rd cir.) 1985, U.S. Supreme Ct. 1986. Assoc. Smith & Williamson, Lock Haven, Pa., 1974-76; ptnr. Saxton & Flayhart, Lock Haven, 1977-83; dist. atty. Clinton County, Lock Haven, 1979; pvt. practice Jersey Shore, Pa., 1983-84; ptnr. Carpenter, Harris & Flayhart, Jersey Shore, 1984—; lectr. Lock Haven U., 1981-85, 90, Lycoming Coll., Williamsport, Pa., 1993-94, State U. of Chernivtsi Law Sch., Ukraine, 1993. Pres. Jersey Shore Area C. of C., Pa., 1990; com. Lycoming County Dem. Party, 1988-98. Mem. ABA, Fed. Bar Assn., Lycoming County Bar Assn., Pa. Bar Assn., Rotary (pres. Lock Haven club 1991, Rotarian of Yr. 1990), Phi Beta Kappa. Methodist. Avocation: rare book collecting. Office: Carpenter Harris & Flayhart PO Box 505 128 S Main St Jersey Shore PA 17740

FLAYHART, WILLIAM HENRY, history educator; b. Williamsport, Pa., July 12, 1944; s. William Henry II and Naomi (Laux) F.; m. Deborah Ann Smith, June 4, 1977; children: Thomas William, Catherine Ann, Jennifer Nicole. BA with honors, Lycoming Coll., 1966; MA, U. Va., 1968, PhD, 1971. Woodrow Wilson fellow U. Va., Charlottesville, 1966-67, Va. Woodrow Wilson fellow, 1967-68, Danforth Found. Tchg. fellow, 1968-69; Woodrow Wilson Dissertation fellow Inst. of Hist. Rsch. U. London, 1969-70; asst. prof. history Del. State U., Dover, 1970-72, assoc. prof. history, 1972-74, prof. history, 1974-93, chair dept. history, prof., 1993—; vis. prof. U. Leiden, Netherlands, 1994-95. Author: (books) Majesty at Sea, 1981, QE2, 1985, Counterpoint to Trafalgar, 1992, The American Line, 1999. Pres. Friends of Old Dover, 1989-92, v.p. 1993. Recipient Founder's award Phi Alpha Theta, 1996. Fellow London House, USN Inst.; mem. Am. Hist. Assn., Kiwanis Club (pres. Dover club 1977-78), Colonnade Club. Democrat. Presbyterian. Avocations: writing, photography, travel, cruising. Home: 8 Ironwood Cir Dover DE 19904-6522 Office: Dept Hist/Delaware State U 1200 N Dupont Hwy Dover DE 19901-2202

FLECHNER, ROBERTA FAY, graphic designer; b. N.Y.C., June 7, 1949; d. Abraham Julius and Evelyn (Medwin) F. BA, CCNY, 1970; MA, NYU, 1972; cert. Printing Industries Met. N.Y., N.Y.C., 1974, 75, 79. Researcher, asst. editor Arno Press, N.Y.C., 1970-73; free-lance editor Random House, N.Y.C., 1973-74, graphic designer/compositor coll. dept., 1984-88; graphic designer Core Communications in Health, N.Y.C., 1974-76; prodn. mgr. Heights-Inwood News, N.Y.C., 1976-77; art dir., graphic designer Jour. Advt. Research, N.Y.C., 1976-81; prin., graphic designer/compositor Roberta Flechner Graphics, N.Y.C., 1976—; graphic designer/compositor W. W. Norton & Co., Inc., 1977—, McGraw Hill, Inc., 1990-94; mech. artist Fawcett, N.Y.C., 1979-80; graphic designer Avon Internat., N.Y.C., 1982; art dir., compositor, layout artist Source: Notes in the History of Art, N.Y.C., 1982—; graphic designer John Wiley & Sons, Inc., N.Y.C., 1985. Designer stationery, 1979 (Art Direction mag., Creativity-cert. distinction 1979). Art dir. enviroNews, N.Y. State Atty. Gen.'s Environ. Protection Bur., N.Y.C., 1977-78. Mem. Graphic Artists Guild, NOW, Women's Nat. Book Assn. (cons.), Nat. Assn. Female Execs., Women's Caucus for Art, Am. Inst. Graphic Arts, CCNY Alumni, NYU Alumni. Office: 10615 Queens Blvd Flushing NY 11375-4365

FLECK, BELA, country musician. Albums include Deviation, 1985, Bela Fleck and The Flecktones, 1989, Drive, Places, Flight of the Cosmic Hippo, 1991, UFO Tofu, 1992, Three Flew Over the Cuckoo's Nest, 1993, Tabula Rosa, 1994, Tales from the Acoustic Planet, 1995, Live Art, 1996, Left of Cool, 1998. Recipient Best Country Instrumental Performance Grammy award, 1996. Office: Warner Bros Records 20 Music Sq E Nashville TN 37203-4344 Address: PO Box 90125 Nashville TN 37209*

FLECK, GABRIEL ALTON, electrical engineer; b. St. Louis, Oct. 7, 1963; s. Emil Ernst Jr. and Dorothy Marie (Fleck) F.; married. BSEE, Rose Hulman Inst. Tech., 1986. Registered profl. engr., Ill.; cert. plant engr. Maintenance engr. City Water, Light and Power, Springfield, Ill., 1989-91, project engr., 1987-89, 91-98; project mgr. City Water, Light and Power, Springfield, 1999—. Mem. IEEE (mem. at large 1989—), Ill. Soc. Profl. Engrs., Assn. for Facilities Engrs. (cert. plant engr.), Instrument Soc. Am., Order of Engr. Home: 2201 Renwick Dr Springfield IL 62704-6702 Office: City Water Light and Power 3100 Stevenson Dr Springfield IL 62703-4462

FLECK, GEORGE MORRISON, chemistry educator; b. Warren, Ind., May 13, 1934; s. Ford Bloom and Deloris Magdalene (Morrison) F.; m. Margaret Dyer Reynolds, June 27, 1959; children: Margaret Morrison, Louise Elizabeth. BS, Yale U., 1956; PhD, U. Wis., 1961. Asst. prof. Smith Coll., Northampton, Mass., 1961-67, assoc. prof., 1967-76, prof. chemistry, 1976—. Author: Equilibria in Solution, 1966, Chemical Reaction Mechanisms, 1971, Carboxylic Acid Equilibria, 1973, Chemistry: Molecules That Matter, 1974, Patterns of Symmetry, 1977, Shaping Space: A Polyhedral Approach, 1987; contbr.: Nobel Laureates in Chemistry, 1993, Women in Chemistry and Physics, 1993, American National Biography, 1999. Fellow Danforth Found., 1956-61; Dupont fellow, 1960; Danforth assoc., 1982—; grantee NSF, NIH, U.S. Office Edn., Am. Philos. Soc. Mem. Am. Chem. Soc., Mass. Assn. Sci. Tchrs., New Eng. Assn. Chemistry Tchrs., Sigma Xi. Office: Smith Coll Clark Sci Ctr Northampton MA 01063

FLECK, JOHN R., lawyer; b. Huntington, Ind., Oct. 9, 1944; s. Ford Bloom and Deloris (Morrison) F.; m. Susan E., Dec. 31, 1975; children: Todd., Heather Fleck Erekson, Jeremy W. BA, Purdue U., 1966; JD, Ind. U., 1971. Bar: Ind. 1971, U.S. Supreme Ct. 1976, U.S. Dist. Ct. (no. and so. dists.) Ind. 1971. Law clk. Allen Superior Ct., Ft. Wayne, Ind., 1971-72; pvt. practice law Ft. Wayne, 1972—; adj. prof. Ind. U., Ft. Wayne, 1972-75; assoc. city atty. City of Ft. Wayne, 1972-75; atty. Town of Markle, Ind., 1975-80; city atty. City of New Haven, 1998—. Bd. dirs. Canterbury Sch., Ft. Wayne, 1988—; pres., bd. dirs. United Cerebral Palsy, Ft. Wayne, 1972—. Office: 625 Lincoln Tower Fort Wayne IN 46802

FLECK, MARIANN BERNICE, health scientist; b. San Francisco, June 19, 1922; d. Erwin and Grace B. (Fisher) Kahl; m. Jennings McDaniel, June 1946; m. Jack Donald Fleck, Mar. 28, 1980; children: Gary, Eugene. B of Vocat. Edn., Calif. State U., Long Beach, 1965, BA, 1965, MA, 1968; PhD, U. Santa Barbara, 1975. Prof. life sci. div., adminstr. Fullerton (Calif.) Coll., 1960-75; profl. adminstr. Cypress (Calif.) Coll., 1975-80, prof. emeritus, 1980—; dir., owner Profl. Services Assn. Counseling, Santa Ana, Calif., 1977-80, Hypnosis Ctr., La Mirada, Calif., 1975-80; producer Dr. Mariann Health Program, Sta. KJON, Boonville, Ark., 1980-85; dir. Jack Fleck Golf and Health Acad., Magazine, Ark., 1980—; Pres. H.E.P. Internat., 1983-89; cons. and lectr. in field. U. Calif. scholar; recipient Cert. of Appreciation Ronald Reagan Commemorative medal of honor, 1988. Mem. Am. Guild Hypnotherapists (registered 1989), Am. Personnel and Guidance Assn., Calif. Personnel and Guidance Assn., Am. Running and Fitness Assn. (profl. mem.), Hypnotherapists Speakers Platform, Internat. Speakers Platform Assn. Republican. Presbyterian. Home: RR 1 Box 15A Magazine AR 72943-9801 Office: H&P Internat Magazine AR 72943

FLECK, RAYMOND ANTHONY, JR., retired university administrator; b. Bklyn., Mar. 9, 1927; s. Raymond Anthony and Dorothy (Canavan) F.; m. Dorothy Marie Rossow, Aug. 22, 1970; children: Andrew Jerome, Casey Thomas. Student, Manhattan Coll., 1946-48; BS, U. Notre Dame, 1951, PhD, 1954. Brother of Holy Cross, 1949-70. Prof. chemistry St. Edward's U., 1954-69, pres., 1957-69; assoc. research chemist dept. environ. toxicology U. Calif. at Davis, 1969-72; pres. Marygrove Coll., Detroit, 1972-79; acting dir. Food Protection and Toxicology Center, U. Calif., Davis, 1979-83; dir. research Calif. State Poly. U., Pomona, 1983-95; assoc. Anver Biosci. Design, Inc., Sierra Madre, Calif., 1995—; cons. EPA, La. Bd. Regents, U. Wis., Eau Claire, NSF; dir. Monterey Basin Pilot Monitoring Project, 1971-72; rep. Primerica Fin. Svcs., 1996—. Vice pres., bd. dirs. Harmony Village Home Corp. N.W., Detroit, 1977-79. Served with USN, 1945-46. NSF fellow, 1952, 1969; recipient U. Notre Dame Centennial of Sci. medal, 1965; sci. bldg. at St. Edward's U. named Fleck Hall. Home: 4273 Guava St La Verne CA 91750-3010

FLECK, STEPHEN, psychiatrist; b. Frankfort-am-Main, Germany, Sept. 18, 1912; came to U.S., 1935; s. Georg and Anna (Beer) F.; m. Louise Harlan, Oct. 13, 1945 (dec. 1992); children: AnnaLou F.J. Singer, Stephen H., Carra Rockwood. Cand. Medicine, J.W. Goethe U., Frankfort, Fed. Republic of Germany, 1931-33; postgrad., U. Amsterdam, 1933-35; MD, Harvard U., 1940. Diplomate Nat. Bd. Med. Examiners, Am. Bd. Psychiatry and Neurology. Intern Beth Israel Hosp., Boston, 1940-42; clin. trainee Henry Phipps Psychiat. Clinic, Johns Hopkins Hosp., Balt., 1946-48, asst. internal medicine, Commonwealth fellow, 1948-49; asst. prof. psychiatry U. Wash., Seattle, 1949-53; psychiatrist-in-chief Psychiat. Inst., Yale U., New Haven, 1953-83, prof. psychiatry and pub. health Sch. Medicine, 1963-83, prof. emeritus, 1983—; psychiatrist-in-chief Conn. Mental Health Ctr., New Haven, 1969-83; cons. Bridgeport (Conn.) Mental Health Ctr., 1983-95; mem. adv. bd. Whiting Forensic Inst., Middletown, Conn. 1957; mem. Hamden (Conn.) Mental Health Commn., 1970-86. Served to maj. U.S. Army, 1942-46. Fellow Am. Psychiat. Assn. (life), Group for Advancement Psychiatry (life); mem. AMA, Am. Pub. Health Assn., Western New England Psychoanalytic Soc., Conn. Psychiat. Soc. (pres. 1966-67), Conn. Pub. Health Assn. (hon.). Office: Yale U Sch Medicine 25 Park St Rm 608 New Haven CT 06519-1189

FLECK, STEPHEN HARLAN, French language educator; b. Balt., Oct. 16, 1948; s. Stephen and Louise H. (Harlan) F.; m. Maria I. Lajmanovich, Oct. 22, 1989; children: Benjamin H., Nina M. BA in Linguistics, U. Mich., 1971; BA in Music, Sonoma State U., Rohnert Park, Calif., 1986; PhD, U. Calif., Davis, 1993. Assoc. prof. French Calif. State U., Long Beach, 1992—. Author: (book) Music, Dance, and Laughter: Comic Creation in Moliere's Comedy-Ballets. Mem. Pacific Ancient and Modern Lang. Assn., Am. Assn. Tchrs. of French, Soc. des Profs. Francais et Francophones d'Amerique. N. Am. Soc. for Study of Seventeenth Century French Literature.

FLECKENSTEIN, JAMES WILLIAM, elementary school educator; b. Ft. Belvoir, Va., May 14, 1961; m. Martha Richardson, July 22, 1989. BS in Edn., Ga. State U., 1987, MEd, 1994, MA, 1997. Tchr. phys. edn. Wayne County Jr. High Sch., Jesup, Ga., 1988-91, Fayetteville (Ga.) Elem. Sch., 1991—; coach Wayne County High Sch., 1988-91, Sandy Creek High Sch., Tyrone, Ga., 1991-98; mem. tech. com. Ga. Pub. Sch. Excellence, 1993. Mem. AAHPER and Dance, Assn. for Advancement Health Edn., Ga. Athletic Coaches Assn. (Asst. Football Coach of Yr. award region 2AAA 1988), Ga. High Sch. Assn., Nat. Assn. for Sport and Phys. Edn., Profl. Assn. Ga. Educators, Golden Key, Kappa Delta Pi. Home: 41 Strathmore Dr Sharpsburg GA 30277-9221 Office: Fayetteville Elem Sch 440 Hood Ave Fayetteville GA 30214-1119

FLEDER, GARY, film director, producer. T.V. and motion picture dir., prodr. Dir. films Things to Do in Denver When You're Dead, 1995, Kiss the Girls, 1997, Impostor, 1999; T.V. series Tales from the Crypt, 1989,

Homicide: Life on the St., 1993, L.A. Drs., 1998, From Earth to the Moon, 1998; dir. T.V. movie The Companion, 1994; dir., prodr. Air Time, 1992. Office: c/o DGA 7920 Sunset Blvd Los Angeles CA 90046

FLEDER, ROBERT CHARLES, lawyer; b. New London, Conn., Aug. 31, 1948; s. Samuel and Pearl (Perelman) F.; m. Laura Louise Waltuch, Dec. 19, 1971; children: Daniel, Anna, Michael. BA, Columbia U., 1969, MA, 1971, LLB, 1973. Bar: N.J. 1974, N.Y. 1977, D.C. 1991. Law clk. to presiding justice N.J. Supreme Ct., Trenton, 1973-74; assoc. Stryker, Tams & Dill, Newark, 1974-75; assoc. Kramer, Levin, Nessen, et al, N.Y.C., 1976-80, ptnr., 1981-86; ptnr. Paul, Weiss, Rifkind, Wharton & Garrison., N.Y.C., 1986—. Contbr. articles to profl. jours. Mem. ABA, N.Y. State Bar Assn. Office: Paul Weiss Rifkind Wharton & Garrison Rm 202 1285 Avenue Of The Americas Fl 21 New York NY 10019-6028*

FLEEGER, DAVID CLARK, colon and rectal surgeon; b. Neubrucke, Germany, July 11, 1959; s. James Elliott and Madge Ellen (Iseminger) F.; m. Jamie Greenstreet, Aug. 16, 1984; 1 child, Lauren Ann. BS, Baylor U., 1981; MD, Tex. A&M U., 1985. Diplomate Am. Bd. Surgery, Am. Bd. Colon and Rectal Surgeons. Resident in gen. surgery Mayo Clinic, Rochester, Minn., 1985-90; fellow in colon and rectal surgery La. State U., Shreveport, 1990-91; ptnr. Austin (Tex.) Colon and Rectal Clinic, 1991—; chief surgery Columbia St. Davids. S. Hosp., 1996-97; chmn. Cancer Ctr., St. David's Med. Ctr., 1997—. Fellow Am. Coll. Surgeons, Am. Soc. Colon and Rectal Surgeons, Tex. Soc. Colon and Rectal Surgeons (pres-elect 1994, pres. 1994-95); mem. AMA, Am. Soc. Gastrointestinal Endoscopy Surgeons, Am. Soc. Colon and Rectal Surgeons, Soc. Am. Gastrointestinal Endoscopy, Tex. Med. Assn. (chmn. young physician sect., mem. governing coun. 1992—). Avocations: fishing, hunting, photography, kayaking. Office: 4208 Medical Pky Austin TX 78756-3310

FLEEGER, RON, image consultant; b. Miami, Fla., July 5, 1955; s. Donald Raymond and Flora Mae (McDermott) F. BFA cum laude, Fla. State U., 1976. Display mgr. Bloomingdales, N.Y.C., 1981-82; visual dir. Members Only Sportswear, Inc., N.Y.C., 1982-86; owner Fleeger Inc., Comm. Through Design, Imagemakers, N.Y.C., 1986—, designer furniture, home and fashion accessories, N.Y.C., 1986—; custom rugs, fixturing, furniture & lighting, decorative hardware Fleeger Inc./Fleeger Home Products; Products, N.Y.C., 1986—, Fleeger Inc. Virtual Store. Exhibited in group shows at MIT, 1988-89, Design Gallery 91, N.Y.C., 1988, 90, 91, 92; designs included in Ryuko Tsyshsin, 1989, Flatiron, 1990, DNR, 1991, Flooring, 1991, Home Furnishings Daily, 1991, W, 1992, Residential Lighting, 1995, 96, Accessories Merchandising, 1995, Home Accessories, 1996, Decorative Home, 1996, Stores Retail Display and Design, others. Avocations: travel, music. Home and Office: 131 E 23rd St New York NY 10010-4510

FLEENOR, JULIANN EVANS, English language educator, writer; b. Granite City, Ill., Jan. 2, 1942; d. Darwin Everas and Doris Lorraine Evans; m. David L. Fleenor, Oct. 8, 1960; 1 child, David L. Jr. Student, So. Ill. U., 1965-66; BA, Memphis State U., 1971, MA, 1973; PhD, U. Toledo, 1978. Assoc. prof. English, William Rainey Harper Coll., Palatine, Ill., 1992—, pres. faculty senate, 1998—. Editor: The Female Gothic, 1983; contbr. fiction and essays to lit. revs. Co-founder Toledo United Against Rape. Mem. Nat. Coun. Tchrs. English, Mystery Writers Am. Home: 20578 Primrose Ct Deer Park IL 60010 Office: William Rainey Harper Coll English Dept 1200 W Algonquin Rd Palatine IL 60067

FLEETWOOD, MARY ANNIS, education association executive; b. Winfield, Ala., July 31, 1931; d. George A. and Martha Ann (Perry) Sullivan; m. Lewis N. Fleetwood, Aug. 19, 1950; children: Juanita, Dexter Lewis, Melanie Louise. Student, HCC Community Coll., 1973-80. Gen. office staff Able Rose Mercentile Co., Birmingham, Ala., 1949-51; with auditing dept. Bank for Savs. & Trusts, Birmingham, Ala., 1951; account receivables clk. I.W. Phillips, Tampa, Fla., 1972-77; account clk. Sch. Bd. Hill County, Tampa, Fla., 1980, office mgr., 1981-90. V.p. PTA, 1961-62; pres. Woman's Missionary Union, Birmingham, 1963-64. Mem. DAR, Nat. Inst. Govt. Purchasing (cert. profl. buyer). Baptist. Avocations: photography, genealogy, travel.

FLEETWOOD, REX ALLEN, insurance company executive; b. Newton, Kans., Aug. 17, 1951; s. Milburn William and Edna Milton (Hughes) F.; m. Donna Kay Kurr, June 3, 1972. BS, Kans. Wesleyan U., 1973. Programmer First Nat. Bank, Salina, Kans., 1971-73, State of Kans., Topeka, 1973-74; project leader Blue Cross/Blue Shield, Topeka, 1974-77; asst. v.p. data systems Great Central Ins., Peoria, Ill., 1977-81; v.p. data systems Am. Universal Inc., Providence, 1981-84, Pa. Nat. Ins., Harrisburg, 1984-93; v.p. Am. Internat. Group, N.Y.C., 1993-94, Cigna Spl. Risk Facilities, Phila., 1994—. Mem. Diamond Club, United Way, Harrisburg, 1988-92. Named Speaker of Yr., Data Processing Auditors Assn., Harrisburg, 1988. Mem. Pa. Assn. Mut. Ins. Cos. (chmn. data processing com. 1987-90). Republican. Baptist. Home: 276 Ridge Hill Rd Mechanicsburg PA 17055-1748 Office: CIGNA 1600 Chestnut St Philadelphia PA 19103-5113

FLEEZANIS, JORJA KAY, violinist, educator; b. Detroit, Mar. 19, 1952; d. Parios Nicholas and Kaliope (Karageorge) F.; m. Michael Steinberg, July 3, 1983. Student, Cleve. Inst. Music, 1969-72, Cin. Coll.-Conservatory Music, 1972-75. Violinist Chgo. Symphony Orch., 1975-76; concertmaster Cin. Chamber Orch., 1976-80; violinist Trio D'Accordo, Cin., 1976-80; asst. prin. 2d violinist San Francisco Symphony Orch., 1980-81; assoc. concertmaster San Francisco Sympony Orch., 1980-89; acting concertmaster Minn. Orch., Mpls., 1988-89, concertmaster, 1989—; violinist Fleezanis-Ohlsson-Grebanier Piano Trio, San Francisco, 1984—; faculty mem. San Francisco Conservatory of Music, 1983-89, U. Minn., 1989—; founder Chamber Music Sundaes, San Francisco, 1980-89; artist-in-residence U. Calif., Davis, 1995—. Performer World Premiere John Adams Violin Concerto with Minn. Orch., 1994 and Nicholas Maw, Sonata for Solo Violin, commd. by Minn. Pub. Radio, 1997; commd. by Pub. Radio Internat. and Minn. Pub. Radio for world premiere of Nicholas Maw Sonata for Solo Violin, 1998; soloist Am. premier Benjamin Britten Double Concerto, 1998; rec. artist CRI and Koch Classical Records. Democrat. Avocations: photography, cooking. Office: Minn Orch 1111 Nicollet Mall Minneapolis MN 55403-2406

FLEGAL, A(RTHUR) RUSSELL, JR., toxicologist, geochemist, educator; b. Oakland, Calif., Aug. 30, 1946; s. Arthur Russell Sr. and Barbara Flegal; m. Brenda Dolan, Dec. 18, 1970; children: Heather Dolan, John Arthur. BA, U. Calif., Santa Barbara, 1968; MS, Moss Landing (Calif.) Marine Labs., 1976; PhD, Oreg. State U., 1979. Rsch. assoc. Moss Landing Marine Labs., 1981-85; vis. rsch. assoc. Calif. Inst. Tech., Pasadena, 1981-93; assoc. rsch. geochemist U. Calif., Santa Cruz, rsch. geochemist, 1988-92, chair environ. toxicology, 1992—, assoc. dean natural sci. divsn., 1994—; vis. scientist Swiss Fed. Inst. Tech., Zurich, Switzerland, 1988; assoc. dean natural sci. divsn., 1994—; vis. scientist Lawrence Livermore (Calif.) Nat. Labs., 1988-96; mem. com. Nat. Rsch. Coun., Washington, 1989-93, Intergovt. Oceanographic Commn., Paris, 1989—; cons. EPA, Washington, 1989-98. Contbr. chpts. to sci. texts, sects. to ency.; contbr. more than 100 articles to profl. jours. Post doctoral fellow Calif. Inst. Tech., 1980, Rsch. fellow, 1980-81. Office: U Calif Environ Toxicology Santa Cruz CA 95064

FLEGLE, JIM L., lawyer; b. Paducah, Ky., Dec. 3, 1951; s. J.L. and Alice M. (Goodman) F.; m. Ophelia Flegle Camina; children: Lauren Tyler, Brittanie Len, James Brendan, Alexandra Carlisle, James Armand. BA, U. Ky., 1974; JD, U. Va., 1977. Bar: Tex. 1977, U.S. Dist. Ct. (so. dist.) Tex. 1977, U.S. Dist. Ct. (no. dist.) Tex. 1984, U.S. Dist. Ct. (we. dist.) Tex. 1988, U.S. Dist. Ct. (ea. dist.) Tex. 1989, U.S. Ct. Appeals (5th and 11th cirs.) 1981, U.S. Ct. Appeals (9th cir.) 1991, U.S. Ct. Appeals (fed. cir.) 1994, U.S. Supreme Ct. 1993. Assoc. Bracewell & Patterson, Houston, 1977-83, ptnr., 1983-89; ptnr. Bracewell & Patterson, Dallas, 1989—, mng. ptnr., 1992-98, mem. adv. com., 1996-98; mem. Criminal Justice Act Vol. Atty. Panel for the U.S. Dist. Ct. (no. dist.) Tex. Vol. Houston Pro Bono Program; active Tex. Lawyers and Accts. for Arts, Houston, 1982-85, St. Paul's Chamber Music Soc.; mem. corp. campaign com. Dallas Mus. Art, 1994-95, Dallas Hist. Soc., 1991-92. Mem. ABA, Tex. Bar Assn. (grievance com. 1996-99), Houston Bar Assn., Dallas Bar Assn., Houston Bar Found., Tex. Bar Found., Dallas Bar Found., Am. Bd. Trial Advocates (assoc.), Raven Soc., Phi Beta Kappa, Omicron Delta Kappa, Sigma Nu. Methodist. Office: Bracewell & Patterson 500 N Akard St Ste 4000 Dallas TX 75201-3387

FLEHARTY, MARY SUE, secretary; b. Lincoln, Nebr., Aug. 13, 1962; d. Joseph Patrick and Joy Lou (Harnish) Huntley; m. Bradley Daryle Osborne, Mar. 26, 1983 (div. June 1988); m. Terry Lester Fleharty, Aug. 13, 1990. Student, Lincoln Sch. Commerce, 1996-97. Loan processor Am. Charter Fed. Savings and Loan, Lincoln, 1981-84; pub. broadcast exchange operator, sec. Lincoln Clinic, P.C., 1989-91; PBX operator, sec. Woods Park Med. Mgmt. Inc., Lincoln, 1991-93; data reporting asst. Harris Tech. Group, Lincoln, 1993; lease coord. Progressive Lease, Inc., Lincoln, 1993; PBX comms. specialist Branker Buick, Lincoln, 1994-97; sec., receptionist Reel Quick, Inc., Lincoln, 1997-98; case mgmt. sec. Madonna Rehab. Hosp., Lincoln, 1998—. Vol. ARC, Lincoln, 1977—, chmn., 1983-84, pres. Lincoln Fire Dept. Aux., 1993; cert. EMT; notary public Nebr., 1993—. Named Outstanding Vol. ARC, 1985. Mem. NAFE. Republican. Presbyterian. Avocations: church handbell ringing, shuffleboard, playing pool, bowling, gardening. Office: Madonna Rehab Hosp 5401 South St Lincoln NE 68506-2150

FLEISCHAKER, MARC L., lawyer; b. Cin., Feb. 22, 1945; s. Leopold and Betty Jane (Spritz) F.; m. Phyllis S. Schmidt, June 16, 1969; children: Deborah, Julia. BS in Econs., Wharton Sch. U. Pa., 1967; JD, George Washington U., 1971. Bar: D.C. 1971, U.S. Dist. Ct. D.C. 1971, U.S. Supreme Ct. 1974, U.S. Ct. Mil. Appeals, U.S. Ct. Appeals D.C., U.S. Ct. Appeals (3d cir.) 1986, U.S. Ct. Appeals (4th, 5th and 11th cirs.). Assoc. Arent, Fox, Kintner, Plotkin & Kahn, Washington, 1971-78, ptnr., head environ. practice, 1978—, exec. com., 1983—, vice chmn., 1989-96, chmn., 1997—, interim mng. ptnr., 1993; mem. exec. com. Washington Lawyers Com. for Civil Rights and Urban Affairs, 1989—, co-chmn., 1990-91, 99—, chair fin. com. 1992-93; bd. dirs. Nat. Lawyers Com. Civil Rights Under Law, 1995—, co-chmn. 1996-98; chmn. tech. com. legal sect. Am. Soc. Assn. Execs., 1995-96, bd. dirs. tchg., learning and tech. group; gen. counsel to 10 nat. trade assns. Contbr. articles to legal publs. With USNG, 1969-75. Recipient Triangle award Motor and Equipment Mfrs. Assn., 1976. Mem. ABA, Fed. Bar Assn., Univ. Club Washington. Avocations: politics, competitive running, golf, tennis. Home: 6308 Broad Branch Rd Bethesda MD 20815-3342 Office: Arent Fox Kintner Et Al 1050 Connecticut Ave NW Washington DC 20036-5339

FLEISCHAUER, JOHN FREDERICK, retired English language educator; b. Dayton, Ohio, Apr. 29, 1939; s. Paul J. and Ruth (Hedgecock) F.; m. Janet Elaine Patterson, June 17, 1961; children: John Eric, Marc Lawrence, Scott Christopher. BA, Cornell U., 1961; MA, Ohio State U., 1966; PhD, 1970. Tchg. fellow Denison U., 1968-69; asst. prof. English Ohio U., Athens, 1970-74; dir. 100-level English, 1973-74; div. chmn., prof. English, dean Coll. Mt. Union Coll., 1981-87; dean liberal arts Edinboro U., Pa., 1987-88; provost, v.p. acad. affairs, 1989-95, acting pres., 1990-91, provost, v.p. acad. and student affairs, 1995; provost Wright State U., 1995-98; spl. asst. to pres., 1998-99, ret., 1999; cons., lectr. bus. communications, humanities, acad. adminstrn., strategic planning, academic standards, 1975—; moderator Northwest Pa. Health Care Cost Summit, 1993—; co-writer academic grants, 1981—. Author: Writing Skills, 1978; contbr. articles to profl. jours. Served with USN, 1961-65. Rsch. grantee Ohio U., 1973, grantee NEH, 1978. Mem. SOCHE (chair trustees), Am. Assn. State Colls. and Univs. Middle States Assn. (evaluator), Dayton Art Inst. (trustee), Alliance for Edn. (trustee), Ohio Humanities Coun. (scholar), Kiwanis Internat. (dir.). Methodist. Avocations: choral music, canoeing, art.

FLEISCHER, ARTHUR, JR., lawyer; b. Hartford, Conn., Jan. 27, 1933; s. Arthur and Clare Lillian (Katzenstein) F.; m. Susan Abby Levin, July 6, 1958; children: Elizabeth, Katherine. BA, Yale U., 1953, LLB, 1958. Bar: N.Y. 1959. Assoc. Strasser, Spiegelberg, Fried & Frank, N.Y.C., 1958-61; legal asst. SEC, Washington, 1961-62; exec. asst. to chmn. SEC, 1962-64; assoc. Fried, Frank, Harris, Shriver & Jacobson, N.Y.C., 1964-67, ptnr., 1967—, chmn., 1989-97, sr. ptnr., 1997—; vis. lectr. law Columbia U., N.Y.C., 1972-73; adviser to adv. com. Fed. Securities Code Project, Am. Law Inst., 1970-78; adviser to com. to consider new issue proposals Nat. Assn. Securities Dealers, 1973-75, mem. com. corp. financing, 1976-80; bd. dirs. Haleakala, Inc. (The Kitchen), N.Y.; chmn. Ann. Inst. on Securities Regulation, Practising Law Inst., 1969-81; mem. indsl. issuers adv. com. SEC, 1972-73; mem. adv. com. corp. disclosure, 1976-77; bd. govs. Am. Stock Exch., 1977-83; legal adv. com, bd. dirs. N.Y. Stock Exch., 1987-91; mem. adv. bd. J. Ira Harris Ctr. Mich. Bus. Sch. Co-author: Tender Offers, 1978, 5th edit., 1995, Board Games, 1988; co-editor: Annual Institute on Securities Regulation, 1970-81; contbr. articles to profl. jours. Mem. adv. coun. Ctr. for study of fin. instns. U. Pa., 1969—; trustee, mem. photography com. of Whitney Mus.; trustee Ind. Curators, Internat. Recipient Disting. Cmty. Svc. award Brandeis U., 1983, Judge Learned Hand Human Rels. award Am. Jewish Com., 1983, Harold P. Seligson award Practicing Law Inst., 1988, Judge Joseph W. Proskauer award UJA Fedn., 1994. Mem. ABA (mem. com. on fed. regulation of securities regulation 1969—), Assn. Bar City N.Y. (mem. spl. com. on lawyers role in securities transactions 1973-77, chmn. com. securities regulation 1972-74), Century Country Club (N.Y.C.). Home: 1050 Park Ave New York NY 10028-1031 Office: Fried Frank Harris 1 New York Plz Fl 22 New York NY 10004-1980

FLEISCHER, CARL AUGUST, law educator, consultant; b. Oslo, Aug. 26, 1936; s. Carl Johan and Marie (Mathiesen) F.; m. Eva Sylvia Funder, Sept. 15, 1967. Legal exam. laudabilis, U. Oslo, 1960, LLD, 1964. 1st sec. legal divsn. Ministry Fgn. Affairs, 1960-61; spl. cons. internat. law, 1962—; lectr. law U. Oslo Faculty Law, 1961-69, prof., 1969—; adviser in internat. law Ministry Fgn. Affairs, 1986—; lectr., cons., mem. dels. internat. confs.; mem. Internat. Council Environ. Law, Norwegian Petroleum Soc., Norwegian Soc. Int. Law. Author: Jurisdiction on Fisheries, 1963, International Law, 6th edit., 1994, Constitutional Limitations, 1969, The Law on Building and Regulation of Property, 4th edit., 1983, Commentary to the Act of Expropriation and Compensation, 1974, The Economic Zone, 1976, The Law of Expropriation, 1978, Expropriation Procedure, 1980, Application and Interpretation of Judgements, 1981, Petroleum Law, 1983, La pêche (The Fisheries), 1985; co-author: Traitè du Nouveau Droit de la Mer, 1985, Compensation to Fisheries for Offshore Devel. Report, 1986, The New Regime of Maritime Fisheries, 1989, Environment and Resources Management, 1991, 96; co-author: A Handbook on the Law New of the Sea, 1991, Environmental Law, 1992-96, Planning Building Law, 1992, Land-lease Contracts, 1992, Sources of Law, 1995, Private Law Subjects, 1995, Studies in International Law, 1997, Sources of Law and Legal Method, 1998; contbr. articles to profl. jours. Home: 13 Thomas Heftyes, Oslo 2, Norway Office: 7 Juni Pl, Oslo 1, Norway

FLEISCHER, CORNELL HUGH, history educator; b. Berkeley, Calif., Oct. 23, 1950; s. Hugh Warren and Florence Robie Fleischer; m. Kay Marie Fryklund. Student, Brown U., 1968-70; AB, Princeton U., 1972, AM, 1976, PhD, 1982. Instr. Persian and Turkish langs. and lit. Ohio State U., Columbus, 1979-82; asst. prof. Islamic history Washington U., St. Louis, 1982-85, assoc. prof., 1985-89, prof., 1989-93; prof. Ottoman history U. Chgo., 1993-98; prof. Ottoman and Modern Turkish Studies Univ. Chgo., 1998—; dir. Ctr. for Study Islamic Socs. and Civilizations, St. Louis, 1986-91; dir. Ctr. for Mid. Eastern Studies, U. Chgo., 1996—. Author: Bureaucrat and Intellectual in the Ottoman Empire, 1986 (book prize N.W. Assn. Grad. Schs. 1987); assoc. editor Cambridge History of Turkey, 1990—; mem. editorial bd. Internat. Jour. Mid. Ea. Studies, 1994—; contbr. articles to profl. jours. Fulbright-Hays rsch. fellow, 1976-78, MacArthur fellow, 1988-93; rsch. grantee Social Sci. Rsch. Coun., 1984, 86, Fulbright Islamic Civilization grantee, 1986-87; resident Bellagio Ctr., 1991. Mem. Am. Hist. Assn., Mid East Studies Assn., Soc. for Iranian Studies, Turkish Studies Assn. (bd. dirs. 1986-88, pres., 1996—). Office: Ctr Mid Ea Studies U Chgo Chicago IL 60637*

FLEISCHER, DANIEL, minister, religious organization administrator. Pres. Ch. of Luth. Confession, Corpus Christi, Tex.; pastor Resurrection Luth. Ch., Corpus Christi. Office: Resurrection Luth Ch 201 Princess Dr Corpus Christi TX 78410*

FLEISCHER, EVERLY BORAH, academic administrator; b. Salt Lake City, June 5, 1936; s. Arthur and Clare (Katzenstein) F.; m. Harriet Eve Perlysky, June 14, 1959; children: Deborah, Adam Joseph. BS, Yale U., 1958, MS, 1959, PhD, 1961. Asst. prof., then assoc. prof. chemistry U. Chgo., 1961-69; prof. U. Calif., Irvine, 1970-80, dean phys. sci., 1975-80; prof. chemistry, dean Coll. Arts and Scis. U. Colo., Boulder, 1980-88; exec. vice chancellor, prof. chemistry U. Calif., Riverside, 1988-94; program exec. Am. Acad. Arts and Scis., Western Ctr., 1996. Author articles on metalloporphyrins, bioinorganic chemistry. NSF fellow, 1959-61; Alfred P. Sloan fellow, 1962-66; recipient Univ. Svc. award U. Calif., Irvine, 1980. Fellow AAAS; mem. Am. Chem. Soc., Sigma Xi, Alpha Chi Sigma. Home: 8 Tivoli Ct Newport Beach CA 92657-1533 Office: Univ California Dept Chemistry Irvine CA 92697-2025

FLEISCHER, GERALD ALBERT, industrial engineer, educator; b. St. Louis, Jan. 7, 1933; s. Louis Saul and Rita Bashkow F.; m. Ann Ivancic, Dec. 17, 1960 (div. 1992); children: Laural Andrea, Adam Steven; m. Carolyn M. Boyum, Apr. 13, 1993. BS, St. Louis U., 1954; MS, U. Calif., Berkeley, 1959; PhD, Stanford U., Calif., 1962. Ops. analyst Consolidated Freightways, Menlo Park, Calif., 1959-60; instr. Stanford U., Calif., 1961-63; asst. prof. U. Mich., Ann Arbor, 1963-64; assoc. prof. engring. U. So. Calif., Los Angeles, 1964-71, prof. engring., 1971-97, univ. marshal, 1981-87, pres. faculty senate, 1986-87, prof. emeritus, 1998—. Author: Capital Allocation Theory, 1969, Risk and Uncertainty, 1975, Contingency Table Analysis, 1981, Engineering Economy, 1984, Introduction to Engineering Economy, 1994; contbr. to Handbook of Industrial Engineering, 1992, Industrial Engineering Handbook, 1992. Served to lt. (J.G.) USN, 1954-57. Ford Found. fellow, 1960-62, Fulbright sr. lectr. Edcuador, 1974; fellow Inst. Advancement of Engring., 1976. Fellow Inst. Indsl. Engrs. (region v.p. 1984-86); mem. Am. Soc. Engring. Edn., Inst. Mgmt. Scis.

FLEISCHER, JOSEPH LINDEN, architect; b. Bklyn., Oct. 13, 1943; s. Jacob Israel and Jeanne (Lindenbaum) F.; m. Carolyn Stern, Feb. 10, 1968; children: Brian Marc, Eric Robert. BS, CCNY, 1965; BArch, CUNY, 1966. Registered architect, N.Y., N.J., Calif., Colo., Fla., Ga., Ill., La., Mass., Mich., N.C., Pa. Staff architect James Stewart Polshek, Architect, N.Y.C., 1966-70, assoc., 1970-80, ptnr., 1980—; guest lectr. Columbia U. Grad. Sch. Architecture and Planning, Montclair (N.J.) State Coll., Adult Sch. of Montclair; guest critic City Coll. Sch. Architecture, mem. adv. info. com. With USNR, 1965-71. Mem. AIA, Archtl. League, N.Y. Soc. Architects, N.J. Soc. Architects, Am. Arbitration Assn., Am. Assn. Mus., Bldg. Ofcls. and Code Adminstrs., Constrn. Specifications Inst., Architects, Designers and Planners for Social Responsibility. Office: Polshek & Ptnrs Architects 320 W 13th St Fl 8 New York NY 10014-1200*

FLEISCHER, NORMAN SAMUEL, director of endocrinology, medical educator; b. Springfield, Tenn., Jan. 24, 1936; s. Paul and Eva (Cohen) F.; m. Eva Lessy, Apr. 7, 1966; children: Deborah, Arlene. AB, Vanderbilt U., 1958, MD, 1961. Med. resident Albert Einstein Coll. of Medicine, Bronx, 1961-64; fellow in endocrinology Vanderbilt U., Nashville, 1964-66; dir. endocrinology, dir. Diabetes Ctr. Albert Einstein Coll. of Medicine, Bronx, 1976—, prof., 1978—; fellow in endocrinology Sch. of Medicine Vanderbilt U., Nashville, 1964-66; asst. prof. Coll. of Medicine Baylor U., Houston, 1966-71, assoc. prof. Sch. of Medicine, 1971-73; assoc. prof. Albert Einstein Coll. of Medicine, Bronx, 1973-77. Author chpts. in books; contbr. numerous articles to profl. jours. NIH grantee, 1966—. Fellow ACP; mem. Am. Fedn. Clin. Rsch., Am. Soc. Clin. Investigation, Am. Assn. Physicians, Am. Diabetes Assn., Endocrine Soc. Office: Yeshiva U Albert Einstein Coll Medicine 1300 Morris Park Ave Bronx NY 10461-1926

FLEISCHER, ROBERT LOUIS, physics educator; b. Columbus, Ohio, July 8, 1930; s. Leo H. and Rosalie (Kahn) F.; m. Barbara L. Simons, June 10, 1954; children: Cathy Ann, Elizabeth Lee. AB, Harvard U., 1952, AM, 1953, PhD, 1956. Asst. prof. metallurgy MIT, 1956-60; physicist Gen. Elec. Rsch. Lab., Schenectady, 1960-92; rsch. prof. earth and environ. scis. Rensselaer Poly. Inst., Troy, N.Y., 1992—; rsch. prof. geology Union Coll., Schenectady, N.Y., 1997—; sr. rsch. fellow physics Calif. Inst. Tech., 1965-66; adj. prof. physics and astronomy Rensselaer Poly. Inst., 1967-68; adj. prof. geol. sci. SUNY, Albany, 1982-87; cons. U.S. Geol. Survey, 1967-70, GE R&D Ctr., 1992-93; vis. scientist Nat. Ctr. for Atmospheric Rsch., NOAA, 1973-74; adj. prof. applied physics and mech. engring. Yale U., 1984; vis. scientist Materials Rsch. Soc., 1995. Author: Nuclear Tracks in Solids, 1975, Tracks to Innovation, 1998; editor: Intermetallic Compounds: Principles and Practice, 1995; assoc. editor: 1st-4th Lunar Sci. Conf. Procs., 1970-73. Pres. Zoller Sch. PTA, 1968-69; mem. com. on candidates Schenectady Citizens Conv. for Sch. Bd., 1969-72, 82-83, chmn., 1969-70, 71-72, vice chmn. conv., 1977-78, chmn., 1978-79; mem. com. on priorities Schenectady Sch. Bd., 1974-75; Bd. dirs. Schenectady Citizens' League, Freedom Forum, Inc. Recipient awards Indsl. Rsch., 1964, 65, 72, Spl. award Am. Nuclear Soc., 1964, Ernest O. Lawrence award AEC, 1971, Gen. Elec. Silver medallion Inventor's award, 1971, Gold Medallion Inventor's award, 1991, Golden Plate award Am. Acad. Achievement, 1972, Coolidge award Gen. Electric Rsch. and Devel. Ctr., 1972; NASA Exceptional Sci. Achievement award, 1973, spl. recognition, 1979; Disting. Career award Hudson-Mohawk chpt. AIME, 1991. Fellow AAAS, NAE, Am. Acad. Arts and Scis., Am. Phys. Soc., Am. Geophys. Union; mem. Am. Soc. for Metals, Health Physics Soc., Sigma Xi. Achievements include research in charged particle tracks in solids and their use in several fields, including cosmic ray and meteorite sci., geochronology, nuclear physics, radiobiology, environmental radon, personal radon dosimetry, mineral exploration; defects in solids and their effects on mech. properties and superconducting properties, high temperature materials. Home: 1356 Waverly Pl Schenectady NY 12308-2629 Office: Union Coll Dept Geology Schenectady NY 12308

FLEISCHMAN, ALBERT SIDNEY (SID FLEISCHMAN), writer; b. Bklyn., Mar. 16, 1920; s. Reuben and Sadie (Solomon) F.; m. Beth Elaine Taylor, Jan. 25, 1942; children—Jane, Paul, Anne. B.A., San Diego State Coll., 1949. Newspaper reporter San Diego Daily Jour., 1949-50; freelance screenwriter; lectr. fiction writing UCLA. Author: (children's books) Mr. Mysterious & Company, 1962, By the Great Horn Spoon!, 1963, Chancy and the Grand Rascal, 1966, Jingo Django, 1791, Humbug Mountain, 1978, The Hey Hey Man, 1979, McBroom and the Great Race, 1980, McBroom's Almanac, 1984, The Whipping Boy, 1986 (John Newbery medal 1987), The Scarebird, 1988, The Midnight Horse, 1990, Jim Ugly, 1992, The 13th Floor, 1995, The Abracadabra Kid, A Writer's Life, 1996, Bandit's Moon, 1998, (screenplays) Blood Alley, 1955, Goodbye, My Lady, 1956, Lafayette Escadrille, 1958, The Deadly Companions, 1973, Scalawag, 1973, Prince Brat and the Whipping Boy, 1995. Served with USNR, 1941-45. Recipient Spur award Western Writers Am., Commonwealth Club award, Lewis Carrol Shelf award, Mark Twain award. Mem. Writers Guild Am., Authors Guild, Soc. Children's Book Writers. Democrat. Jewish. Office: care Greenwillow Books 1350 Avenue Of The Americas New York NY 10019-4702

FLEISCHMAN, BARBARA GREENBERG, public relations consultant; b. Detroit, Mar. 20, 1924; d. Samuel J. and Theresa (Keil) Greenberg; m. Lawrence A. Fleishman, Dec. 18, 1948; children: Rebecca, Arthur, Martha. BA, U. Mich., 1944. Tchr. Detroit Pub. Schs., 1944-45; psychoanalyst's sec., 1947-49; sec. Greenberg Ins. Agy., 1947-49; customer/pub. rels. cons. Kennedy Galleries, N.Y.C., 1976—. Bd. dirs. Detroit Artists Market, 1958-66, Planned Parenthood, N.Y.C., 1990-96, Am. Craft Coun., 1980-83, Friends of Channel 13, 1968-80, pres., N.Y.C., 1975-79, chmn. auction, 1975, trustee, 1975-84; mem. women's com. Detroit Inst. Arts, 1957-66; pres. Friends of N.Y. Pub. Libr., 1979-84, trustee, 1980—, v.p., bd., 1987—; trustee The Acting Co., 1986-89, pres., 1988-89; mem. gov. bd. Off the Record Luncheons, Fgn. Policy Assn., 1978-85; assoc. prodr. Channel 13 Auction, 1978-80; trustee Mus. TV and Radio, 1988-92, Archives of Am. Art, 1997—; vis. com. Am. Wing, Met. Mus., 1998—; commr. Art Commn. of the City of N.Y., 1995-98; hon. patron Brit. Mus., 1996—, Caryatids com., pres., 1998—, chmn.; v.p. Archives of Am. Art, pres.; mem. trustees com. Libr. Mus. Modern Art, 1998—; mem. Coun. Am. Mus. Nat. History, 1999—; mem. devel. and trust Brit. Mus., 1999—. Mem. Cosmopolitan Club. Office: Kennedy Galleries 730 5th Ave New York NY 10019-4105

FLEISCHMAN, EDWARD HIRSH, lawyer; b. Cambridge, Mass., June 25, 1932; s. Louis Isaac and Jean (Grossman) F.; m. Joan Barbara Walden, Dec. 27, 1953 (dec. 1993), m. Judy Vernon, Sept. 27, 1998. BA, Harvard U.; LLB, Columbia U., 1959. Bar: N.Y. 1959, U.S. Supreme Ct. 1980. Assoc. Beekman & Bogue, N.Y.C., 1959-67, ptnr., 1968-86; commr. SEC, Washington, 1986-92; ptnr. Rosenman & Colin, 1992-94; sr. counsel Linklaters & Paines, N.Y.C., 1994—; adj. prof. NYU Law Sch., 1976—; bd. dirs. Wit Capital Group, Inc. Served with U.S. Army, 1952-55. Mem. ABA (chmn. internat. law com. on internat. securities transactions 1999—, bus. law com. on counsel responsibility 1995-99, com. on devels. in bus. financing 1987-91, subcom. model simplified indenture 1980-83, adminstrv. law com. on securities, commodities and exchs. 1981-84, bus. law subcom. broker-dealer matters 1973-78, subcom. rule 144 1970-72), Am. Law Inst., Am. Coll. Investment Counsel (pres. 1990-91), Am. Soc. Corp. Secs., Internat. Bar Assn., Internat. Law Assn. (chmn. com. on internat. securities regulation 1998—), Security Traders Assn. (bd. govs.). Republican. Jewish. Office: Linklaters 1345 6th Ave New York NY 10105-0302 Home: 897 Franklin Lake Rd Franklin Lakes NJ 07417-2115

FLEISCHMAN, JOSEPH JACOB, lawyer; b. Jersey City, Mar. 10, 1946; s. Benjamin Emanuel and Esther (Robfogel) F.; m. Gloria Damast, May 31, 1975; children: Michael, Richard. BA with highest honors, Rutgers U., 1968; JD, Columbia U., 1972. Bar: N.J. 1972, U.S. Dist. Ct. N.J. 1972, U.S. Ct. Appeals (3d cir.) 1983, U.S. Ct. Appeals (9th cir.) 1986, U.S. Ct. Appeals (2d cir.) 1994, U.S. Supreme Ct. 1983. Assoc. Hannoch Weisman, Roseland, N.J., 1972-77, ptnr., 1977-99; ptnr. Norris, McLaughlin & Marcus, P.A., Somerville, N.J., 1999—. Contbr. articles to legal publs. Mem. ABA, N.J. Bar Assn., Essex County Bar Assn., Phi Beta Kappa. Avocations: reading, golf. Home: 209 Lyncrest Rd Englewood Cliffs NJ 07632-2020 Office: Norris McLaughlin & Marcus PO Box 1018 721 Rt 202-206 Somerville NJ 08876-1018

FLEISCHMAN, KATHRYN AGNES, secondary education educator; b. Buffalo, Jan. 3, 1937; d. Charles Joseph and Catherine (Rydzynski) Baker; m. Jerome Joseph Fleischman, July 16, 1960. Student, Buffalo Sem., 1954; BA in Math., U. Buffalo, 1958; MS in Math., SUNY, Buffalo, 1964. Cert. secondary math. tchr., N.Y. Chmn. math. dept., tchr., enrichment coord. Amherst Cen. Schs., Snyder, N.Y., 1958-92; instr. Niagara C.C., Niagara Falls, N.Y., 1964-65; cons. N.Y. State Edn. Dept., Bur. Math. Edn., 1962-64, 74, 84-86, Addison-Wesley Pubs., 1963-64. Mem. Buffalo Zool. Soc., 1976-98; mem. women's com. Buffalo Philharm. Orch. Soc., 1977-95, mem. edn. com., 1986-90, bd. dirs., 1993-94; mem. World Hospitality Assn., 1976-90, bd. dirs. 1987-88, Encore Soc. Metropolitan Opera, N.Y.C., 1992—, Heritage Soc. Buffalo Seminary, 1992—. Jesse Ketchum scholar, 1950; recipient Citizenship award Am. Legion, 1950, George Washington medal Freedom Found. at Valley Forge, 1988. Mem. Assn. Math. Tchrs. of N.Y. State (pres. 1974-75, exec. com., speaker, coun., county chmn., corr. sec., rec. sec., 2d v.p., 1st v.p), Nat. Coun. Tchrs. of Math. (program com., speaker, nat. del. assembly, jour. referee, rep. to bd. govs. Mu Alpha Theta), Delta Kappa Gamma. Republican. Roman Catholic. Avocations: travel, piano, organ. Home: 15 Oyster Bay Pl Hilton Head Plantation Hilton Head Island SC 29926-2687

FLEISCHMAN, KEITH MARTIN, lawyer; b. Newark, June 13, 1958. BA, U. Vt., 1980; JD, Calif. Western U., 1984. Bar: N.Y. 1985, U.S. Dist. Ct. (so. dist.) N.Y. 1986, U.S. Ct. Appeals (2d cir.) 1989, U.S. Ct. Appeals (11th cir.) 1995. Asst. dist. atty. Bronx (N.Y.) County Dist. Atty., Rackets and Maj. Offense, 1984-88; trial atty. U.S. Dept. Justice, Dallas Bank Fraud Task Force, Washington, 1988-90; asst. U.S. atty. U.S. Atty. Office, Dist. Conn., 1990-92; trial lawyer, ptnr. Milberg Weiss Bershad Hynes & Lerach LLP, N.Y.C., 1992—; inst., lectr. trial practice U.S. Dept. Justice, Washington, 1990-91. Coord. com. mem. New England Bank Fraud Task Force, Dist. Conn., 1990-92. Avocations: skiing, climbing. Office: Milberg Weiss Bershad Hynes & Lerach LLP One Pennsylvania Plaza New York NY 10119

FLEISCHMAN, PAUL, children's author; b. Monterey, Calif., Sept. 5, 1952; s. Albert Sidney and Beth (Taylor) F.; m. Becky Mojica, Dec. 15, 1978; children: Seth, Diana. BA, Univ. of N.Mex., 1977. Author: The Birthday Tree, 1979, The Half-a-Moon Inn, 1980 (Silver medal Commonwealth of Calif. 1980, Golden Kite honor book Soc. Children's Book Writers 1980), Graven Images: Three Stories, 1982 (Newbery honor book 1983), The Animal Hedge, 1983, Finzel the Farsighted, 1983, Path of the Pale Horse, 1983 (Golden Kite honor book Soc. Children's Book Writers 1983, Parents' Choice award Parents' Choice Found. 1983), Phoebe Danger, Detective, in the Case of the Two-Minute Cough, 1983, Coming-and-Going Men: Four Tales, 1985, I Am Phoenix: Poems for Two Voices, 1985, Rear-View Mirrors, 1986, Rondo in C, 1988, Joyful Noise: Poems for Two Voices, 1988 (John Newbery medal 1989), Saturnalia, 1990, Shadow Play, 1990, Time Train, 1991, The Borning Room, 1991, Townsend's Warbler, 1992, Copier Creations, 1993, Bull Run, 1993, Ghosts' Grace: A Poem for Four Voices, 1996, Troy, 1996, Seedfolks, 1997, Whirligig, 1998, A Fate Totally Worse than Death, 1997. Address: 865 17 Mile Dr Pacific Grove CA 93950-4733*

FLEISCHMAN, PAUL ROBERT, psychiatrist, writer; b. Newark, N.J., Aug. 4, 1945; s. Martin L. and Etta G. Fleischman; m. Susan K., June 15, 1974; 1 child, Forrest. BA, U. Chgo., 1967; MD, Albert Einstein Coll. Medicine, N.Y.C., 1971. Diplomate Am. Bd. Psychiatry and Neurology. Seminar leader in psychiatry and religion Yale U., New Haven, 1981-87; pvt. practice psychiatry Amherst, Mass., 1975—; keynote spkr. Highland Hosp., Asheville, N.C., 1992, Albany Med. Coll., Coll. St. Rose, Albany Jewish Family Svcs., 1993, Values in Psychotherapy conf. Nashville Inst. Psychotherapy, 1995; 31st Williamson lectr. in religion and medicine U. Kans., 1995; cons. in psychiatry, Amherst, 1975—; lectr., spkr. U. Mass., Amherst, Hampshire Coll., Smith Coll., Amherst Coll., 1989-98, Med. Group Rounds Albany Med. Coll., 1990, Beth Israel, Boston, 1994; cons. Smith Coll. Chapel, 1995, Smith Sch. for Soc. Work, 1998, Western Mass. Psychiat. Soc., 1994, Jaipur Med. Coll., India, 1994, Bombay Psychiat. Soc., India, 1996, Antioch Coll., Seattle, 1998, U. Wash. Health Svc., 1998, Northwest Rehab. Facility, Seattle, 1998, Mich. Psychoanalytic Found., 1999, Vipassana in Prisons, 1999, Gujarati Sanagi South Mich., 1999, Vipassana, Addictions, Psychotherapy & Mental Health, 1999, U. Mass. Dept. Counseling, 1999, First Ch., Springfield, Mass., Unitarian Meeting, Amherst, Mass., Korf Found., N.Y.C., Johnson Meml. Hosp., Stafford Springs, Conn., 1999, Ctr. for Behavioral Health Holyoke Hosp., 1999, Biennial Jain Conf., Phila., 1999. Author: Therapeutic Action of Vipassana Meditation, 1986, The Experience of Impermanence, 1990, The Healing Spirit, 1990, Spiritual Aspects of Psychiatric Practice, 1993, Cultivating Inner Peace, 1997, Karma & Chaos, Collected and New Essays, 1999; contbr. articles to profl. jours. Recipient Oskar Pfister award for important contbns. to spiritual and humanistic side of psychiatry Am. Psychiat. Assn., 1993. Mem. Phi Beta Kappa, Alpha Omega Alpha. Office: 1394 S East St Amherst MA 01002-3030

FLEISCHMAN, SOL JOSEPH, SR., retired television broadcasting executive; b. Hawkinsville, Ga., Sept. 12, 1910; s. Joseph Simon and Alma (Rockman) F.; Hon. degree U. Tampa (Fla.), 1954; m. Helen Elsberry; children: Sol Joseph Jr., Martin Paul. Profl. musician, Tampa, 1926-32; announcer, control operator WDAE Radio, Tampa, 1928, chief announcer, 1950-57; sports dir., outdoor editor Tampa Daily Times, 1946-57; asst. to gen. mgr. L.S. Mitchell, 1956-57; sports dir., public relations dir. WTVT-TV, Tampa, 1957-81. Mem. Fla. Gov.'s Conservation Com., 1969-72, Tampa Mayor's Bd. Public Recreation, Public Relations and Conv. Centers, 1968—; trustee Land's For You, Inc. Lt. (s.g.) USCG, 1942-46. Named Tampa's Outstanding Citizen, Tampa Sports Club, 1969-70; recipient Disting. Service award U. Tampa, 1975; Merit award Fla. Boxing Assn.; Fightin' Gator award U. Fla., 1975, Achievement Gold medal U. Tampa; named to U. Fla. Sports Hall of Fame, Tampa Sports Hall of Fame; Fla.'s Outstanding Conservationist, Fla. Wildlife Fedn., also other awards; "Salty" Sol Fleischman Boating and Fishing Park named in his honor, Tampa Bay, 1989. Mem. Outdoor Writers Am., Fla. Outdoor Writers Assn. (bd. dirs.), Fla. League Outdoor Writers, Fla. Lunkers Assn., Am. Assn. Ret. Persons, Fla. Sportscasters Assn. (dir. 1970-73), Internat. Fishing Hall of Fame, Greater Tampa C. of C., Manatee C. of C., MacDill AFB Officers Club, Palma Ceia Golf and Country Club, Sword and Shield Club, Tampa Univ. Quarterback Club, Touchdown Club, Santa Rosa Golf Club, Highlands Country Club (N.C.), Sun City North and South Golf Club, Caloosa Golf and Country Club, Masons, Shriners, Rotary, Sigma Delta Chi (Hillsborough County Favorite Son 1998—). Home: 1508 Cloister Dr Sun City Center FL 33573-5048

FLEISCHMAN, STEPHEN, art center director; b. Newton, Mass., July 7, 1954; s. David and Dorothy (Myers) F.; m. Barbara Jane Katz, May 18, 1986; children: Daniel Katz Fleischman, Benjamin Katz Fleischman, Jacob Katz Fleischman. BS in Fine Arts, U. Wis., 1977, MA in Bus. Adminstrn., 1983. Gallery owner, studio potter Seattle, 1977-81; devel. asst. Madison (Wis.) Art Ctr., 1981-83; spl. asst. to dir. Walker Art Ctr., Mpls., 1983-86, dir. program planning, 1986-90; dir. Madison Art Ctr., 1991—. Bd. dirs. So. Theater, Mpls., 1988-90, Minn. Citizens for the Arts, Mpls., 1985-90, Cable Arts Consortium, Mpls., 1986-88, Madison CitiArts, 1991-97; pres. adv. bd. Bolz Ctr. for Arts Adminstrn., U. Wis., 1995-97. Mem. Rotary Internat. Office: Madison Art Ctr 211 State St Madison WI 53703-2214

FLEISCHMANN, ERNEST MARTIN, music administrator; b. Frankfurt, Germany, Dec. 7, 1924; came to U.S., 1969; s. Gustav and Antonia (Koch) F.; children: Stephanie, Martin, Jessica. B of Commerce, U. Cape Town, South Africa, 1950, MusB, 1954; postgrad., South African Coll. Music, 1954-56; MusD (hon.), Cleve. Inst. Music, 1987. Gen mgr. London Symphony Orch., 1959-67; dir. Europe CBS Masterworks, 1967-69; exec. v.p., mng. dir. L.A. Philharm. Assn. and Hollywood Bowl, 1969-88; artistic cons. L.A. Philharm. Assn., 1998—; pres. Fleischmann Arts, Intl. Arts Mgmt. Cons. Svc., 1998—; mem. French Govt. Commn. Reform of Paris Opera, 1967-68; steering com. U.S. nat. commn. UNESCO Conf. Future of Arts, 1975; pres. Fleischmann Arts Internat. Arts Cons., 1998—. Debut as condr. Johannesburg (Republic of South Africa) Symphony Orch., 1942; asst. condr. South African Nat. Opera, 1948-51, Cape Town U. Opera, 1950-54; condr. South African Coll. Music Choir, 1950-52, Labia Grand Opera Co., Cape Town, 1953-55; music organizer Van Riebeeck Festival Cape Town, 1952; dir. music and drama Johannesburg Festival, 1956; contbr. to music publs. Recipient award of Merit, L.A. Jr. C. of C., John Steinway award, Friends of Music award, Disting. Arts Leadership award U. So. Calif., 1989, L.A. Honors award, L.A. Arts Coun., 1989, Live Music award Am. Fedn. Musicians Local 47, 1991, Disting. Authors/Artists award U. Judaism, 1994, Treasures of L.A. award, Ctrl. City Assn. L.A., 1996, Los Amigos de Los Angeles award, L.A. Conv. and Vis. Cur., 1996, Comdrs. Cross of Order of Merit, Germany, 1997, Knight, First Class, of the Order of the White Rose of Finland, Jan., 1999, Officer, Ordre des Arts et Lettres (Legion of Honor), France, 1998, Honored by Mayor and City Coun. as First living Cultural Treasure of Los Angeles, 1998, Gold Baton award Am. Symphony Orch., 1999. Mem. Assn. Calif. Symphony Orchs., Major Orch Mgrs. Conf., Am. Symphony Orch. League, L.A. Philharm. Assn. (bd. dirs. 1984—), L.A. Arts Leaders (exec. com.), Nat. Endowment for Arts. Office: Fleischmann Arts 707 Wilshire Blvd Ste 1850 Los Angeles CA 90017-3507 *Progress in the arts involves taking risks. Safety and blandness go hand in hand and should be banished from the artistic experience: better to stick your neck out and fail than to err on the side of correctness and caution.*

FLEISCHMANN, PAUL, youth minister; b. June 20, 1946; s. Leonard and Viola (Tyler) F.; m. Anntoinette Jordan, June 14, 1973; children: Todd Paul, Tyler Jonathan. BA, Seattle Pacific Coll., 1968; MDiv, Western Bapt. Sem., Portland, Oreg., 1975; postgrad., Internat. Christian Grad. U., San Bernardino, Calif. Ordained to ministry, Conservative Bapt. Assn., 1981. Youth pastor Ballard Bapt. Ch., Seattle, 1965-67; campus staff Seattle Youth for Christ, 1967-68; high sch. ministry staff Campus Crusade for Christ, various locations, 1968-88; exec. dir. Nat. Network of Youth Ministries, San Diego, 1982—; home missionary, 1968—; youth ministry cons., 1974—; officer Bd. Deacons, 1980-82, 88-93, mem. Bd. Christian Edn., 1980-82, ch. planter, 1988-93; adj. prof. Christian edn. Western Bapt. Sem., Portland, Oreg., 1981-83; chmn. Youth Ministry Exec. Coun., 1992—, Atlanta 96 Youth Leaders Conf., 1993-96; chmn. Challenge 2000 Alliance. Author: Where to Turn for Help in Youth Ministry, 1996; exec. editor: Insight for Student Discipleship, 1979-83; contbg. author: Working with Youth, 1982; editor: Discipling the Young Person, 1985; exec. editor Network News, 1983—; contbr. articles to profl. jours.; contbg. author: Magnet Effect, 1995, Reaching a Generation for Christ, 1997. Dir. Continental Singers Choir and Orch., 1977, Nat. Conv. on High Sch. Discipleship, 1979-83; asst. dir. Youth Congress '85, Washington. Recipient Gold Medallion, Evang. Christian Pubrs. Assn., 1986. Office: Nat Network of Youth Min 12335 World Trade Dr Ste 16 San Diego CA 92128-3791

FLEISHER, ERIC WILFRID, retired foreign service officer; b. Washington, Jan. 31, 1926; s. Wilfrid and Greta Agda (Sundberg) F.; m. Elizabeth Fredrikson, Dec. 22, 1948 (div. 1974); children: Emily Susanne, Eric Torsten; m. Thale Gunneng, Aug. 5, 1974; 1 child, Arne Ericsson. Cert., U. Stockholm, 1948; BA, George Washington U., 1950; PhD, U. Lund, Sweden, 1953. Orientation officer U.S. Displaced Persons Commn., French Zone, Germany, 1950-51; program and ops. officer Refugee Relief Dept. State, Washington, 1954-55, intelligence rsch. analyst, 1955-58; polit. officer Am. Embassy, Copenhagen, Denmark, 1959-63; consul Faroe Islands, 1959-63; polit. counselor Helsinki, Finland, 1964-69; dep. country dir., then dir. Nordic countries Washington, 1969-73; press attache Am. Embassy, Stockholm, 1974-76; spl. asst. human rights and refugee affairs Washington, 1977-80, fgn. affairs cons., sr. cons., 1980—. Author: Viking Times to Modern, 1953; translator, editor: Scandinavia in Great Power Politics, 1905-1908, 1958; contbr. articles to various publs. 1st lt. U.S. Army, 1944-47, Tokyo. Mem. Am. Fgn. Svc. Assn., Diplomatic and Consular Officers Ret., Am. Scandinavian Found. Avocations: hiking, hunting, photography. Home: 8300 Thoreau Dr Bethesda MD 20817 Office: Dept State Rm 1434NS Washington DC 20520

FLEISHER, HAROLD, computer scientist; b. Kharkov, Russia, Oct. 12, 1921; came to U.S., 1923, naturalized, 1936; s. Morris and Yetta (Derman) F.; m. Gertrude Lozensky, Dec. 30, 1945; children—Sherry Ann, Leslie Jan, David M. B.A. in Physics, U. Rochester, N.Y., 1942; M.S., 1943; Ph.D. (Ames and AEC fellow 1947-49), Case Inst. Tech., 1951. Mem. staff radiation lab. M.I.T., 1943-45; sr. engr. Rauland Corp., Chgo., 1945-46; instr. physics Case Inst. Tech., 1946-50; with IBM Corp., Poughkeepsie, N.Y., 1950-87; IBM fellow IBM Corp., 1974-87; prof. physics SUNY, New Paltz, 1987—, emeritus prof. physics, 1997—; pres. Hudson Valley Tech. Devel. Ctr., New Paltz, 1987-92; adj. prof. Vassar Coll. Author, editor. Mem. adv. bd. Poughkeepsie Bd. Edn., 1967; mem. Poughkeepsie City Commn. Environ. Quality, 1968-69. Recipient cert. merit OSRD, 1945; Vassar fellow, 1975. Fellow IEEE; mem. Am. Phys. Soc., AAAS, Sigma Xi. Jewish. Patentee in field. Home: 30 Wilmot Ter Poughkeepsie NY 12603-4124 Office: SUNY Coll New Paltz Dept of Physics New Paltz NY 12561*

FLEISHER, JERRILYN, financial planner; b. Phila., May 7, 1952; d. Earl D. and Bette (Romisher) F.; m. Steven M. Bierman, May 28, 1978; 1 child, Emily Larissa. BA, Dickinson Coll., 1973; MBA, Wharton Sch. U. Pa., 1975. Promotion analyst Gillette Co., Boston, 1975-77; product mgr. Chesebrough Ponds Co., Greenwich, Conn., 1977-80, Loreal Co., N.Y.C., 1980-81; account exec. Futterman Orgn., N.Y.C., 1981-83; fin. cons. Shearson Lehman Bros., Greenwich, 1983-92; pres. Fin. Views, Greenwich, 1992—. Mem. Internat. Bd. CFPs, Phi Beta Kappa. Home: 17 Ivanhoe Ln Greenwich CT 06830-3925

FLEISHER, MARK, health care executive. Student, U. N.Mex. Prodr. info. commls. Twin Star Prodns., Scottsdale, Ariz., 1987-93; real estate assoc. Coldwell Banker, Phoenix, 1993-96; pres. Pain Care Clinic, 1996. Chmn. Dem. Party Ariz. State. Mem. Assn. State Dem. Chairs (chmn.). Home: 13635 N 49th St Scottsdale AZ 85254 Office: Ste 105 1337 S Gilbert Mesa AZ 85204

FLEISHER, SEYMOUR, manufacturing company executive; b. Highland Park, N.J., Jan. 21, 1923; s. Benjamin Fleisher and Mary (Grossman) Kivitz; m. Estelle Uram, Aug. 12, 1944; 1 son, Bruce Michael. BS in Mech. Engring., Newark Coll. Engring., 1951. Rsch. engr. Eclipse Pioneer div. Bendix Corp., Teterboro, N.J., 1951-53; asst. gen. mgr. Wayne Engring. Corp., Hackensack, N.J., 1953-56; pres. Pilot Metal Fabricators, Inc., Wayne, 1956-89, chmn. bd., 1989-95; chmn. bd. Pilot Technologies, 1995—. Patentee motorized bicycle with removeable fuel tank. Bd. dirs. YM and YWHa of Wayne, 1985-91, Kenneth L. Jordan Heart Fund, 1985—, Jewish Fedn. North Jersey, 1991—, Wayne Area C. of C., 1991—, United Way, 1990-93; trustee Found. for Handicapped, Wayne, 1986—, St. Joseph's Hosp. and Med. Ctr., Patterson, 1988—, Found. of St. Joseph's Hosp. and Med. Ctr., 1991—, exec. com., 1992—; mem. campaign cabinet United Way Passaic Valley, 1989-91; mem. adv. com. Sch. Indsl. Mgmt., N.J. Inst. Tech., 1990, chmn. athletic adv. bd., 1992-94; exec. bd. Passaic Valley Coun. Boy Scouts Am., 1992—; chmn. Wayne Township Indsl. Commn., 1994; bd. dirs. Am. Friends Tel Aviv U., 1993-94. Capt. U.S. Army, 1942-46, PTO. Decorated Air medal; recipient Edward F. Weston medal for disting. svc. N.J. Inst. Tech., 1985, Benefactors award United Way of Passaic Valley, 1990, Wayne Twp. Corp. Citizen award, 1990; inducted into Athletic Hall of Fame, N.J. Inst. Tech., 1992. Mem. ASME, Precison Metalforming Assn., Soc. Mfg. Engrs., Aircraft Owners and Pilots Assn., Rotary (bd. dirs., past pres.), Masons, Shriners, Preakness Hills Country Club, Frenchman's Creek Yacht, Beach and Country Club, Pi Tau Sigma, Omicron Delta Kappa, Tau Beta Pi. Republican. Jewish. Avocations: flying, fly fishing, golf, jogging, exercise. Home: 3121 Monet Dr Palm Bch Gdns FL 33410 Office: Pilot Technologies 10 Pomeroy Rd Parsippany NJ 07054-3722

FLEISHER, THOMAS ARTHUR, physician; b. Rochester, Minn.; s. Gerard and Gisela Fleisher; m. Mary Fleisher; children: Jeffrey, Jeremy, Matthew. BS, U. Minn., 1969, MD, 1971. Diplomate Am. Bd. Pediatrics, Am. Bd. Allergy and Immunology. Staff physician bone marrow transplant svc. Naval Med. Rsch. Inst., Bethesda, Md., 1975-77; clin. assoc. metabolism br. Nat. Cancer Inst., NIH, Bethesda, 1977-80; asst. chief allergy clin. immunology svc. Walter Reed Army Med. Ctr., Washington, 1980-83; chief immunology svc. Warren G. Magnuson Clin. Ctr., NIH, Bethesda, 1983—, chief clin. pathology dept., 1998—; tng. program dir. clin. lab. immunology NIH, Bethesda, 1992—; bd. dirs. Am. Bd. Allergy and Immunology, Phila., 1991—, chair, 1996. Editor: Clinical Immunology, 1985-89, 93—, Immunology, 1983-86, Clin. Diag. Lab. Immunology, 1993-96; contbr. over 105 articles to sci. jours. Bd. dirs. Bethesda Soccer Club, 1987-95; house capt. Christmas in April, Montgomery County, Md., 1991—; deacon, elder St. Mark Presbyn. Ch., Rockville, Md., 1983-88. With USPHS. Fellow Am. Acad. Allergy, Asthma and Immunology; mem. Am. Assn. Immunologists, Am. Bd. Pediatrics, Am. Fedn. Med. Rsch., Soc. for Pediat. Rsch., Clin. Immunology Soc., Internat. Soc. Analytic Cytology. Avocations: travel, skiing, woodworking. Office: NIH 10/2C306 9000 Rockville Pike Bethesda MD 20892-1508

FLEISHHACKER, DAVID, school administrator; b. San Francisco, May 30, 1937; s. Mortimer and Janet (Choynski) F.; m. Victoria Escamilla, Aug. 1965; children: William, Eleanor, Jeffrey. AB, Princeton U., 1959; MA, U. Calif., 1965. Tchr. Lick-Wilmerding High Sch., San Francisco, 1959-61, Peace Corps, Afghanistan, 1962-64, Marin Country Day Sch., Corte Madera, Calif., 1965, Town Sch., San Francisco, 1965-70; headmaster Katherine Delmar Burke Sch., San Francisco, 1970-95; ret.; interim head Hillbrook Sch., Los Gatos, 1997-98, South Peninsula Hebrew Day Sch., 1998—; pvt. ednl. cons. Contbr. articles to profl. jours. Trustee Internat. House, Berkeley, Calif., 1987-95; pres. Fleishhacker Found., San Francisco, 1990—; bd. dirs. St. Joseph's Hosp./Queen of Angels, L.A., 1976—, San Francisco Youth Orch., 1981—, San Francisco Boys Chorus, 1997—. Mem. Nat. Assn. Prins. Schs. Girls (bd. dirs. 1979-82), Elem. Sch. Heads Assn., Calif. Assn. Ind. Schs. (treas. 1978-81). Home: 3424 Jackson St San Francisco CA 94118-2021

FLEISHMAN, ALAN MICHAEL, marketing consultant; b. Berwick, Pa., June 28, 1939; s. Benjamin Bennet and Ruth (Sadock) F.; m. Ann Arrasmith, Aug. 3, 1963; children: Elizabeth, Gregory, Keith. BA, Dickinson Coll., 1961; postgrad., Xavier U., 1966-67, Calif. State U., Fullerton, 1968-69. Sales and mktg. planning Procter & Gamble, Cin., 1963-67; sr. product mgr. Baxter Internat., Costa Mesa, Calif., 1967-70; dir. mkgt. Allergan, Inc., Irvine, Calif., 1970-76; exec. v.p. Hudson Vitamins, West Caldwell, N.J., 1976-77; v.p. mktg. and sales Cooper Vision, Inc., Mountain View, Calif., 1977-80; pres. Alan M. Fleishman, Mktg. Cons., San Carlos, Calif., 1980—; instr. U. Calif., Berkeley, 1990-96; bd. dirs. Canguard Pharma, Alexon, Purilens. With U.S. Army, 1961-63. Mem. Am. Mktg. Assn., Med. Mktg. Assn. Democrat. Jewish. Home and Office: 3 Bluebell Ln San Carlos CA 94070-1526

FLEISHMAN, EDWIN ALAN, psychologist, author; b. N.Y.C., Mar. 10, 1927; s. Harry E. and Sera (Weinblatt) F.; m. Pauline S. Utman, Feb. 6, 1949; children: Jeffrey B., Alan R. BS, Loyola Coll., Balt., 1945; MA, U. Md., 1949; PhD, Ohio State U., 1951; DSc (hon.), U. Edinburgh, 1982. Dir. Skill Components Rsch. Lab. USAF, San Antonio, 1951-56; prof. indsl. adminstrn. and psychology Yale U., 1956-63; sr. v.p., dir. Washington office Am. Inst. Rsch., 1963-75; pres. Advanced Rsch. Resources Orgn., Washington, 1976-85, Mgmt. Rsch. Inst., Potomac, Md., 1985—; Disting. Univ. prof. George Mason U., Fairfax, Va., 1986—; Guggenheim fellow, vis. prof. Israel Inst. Tech., 1962-63; vis. prof. Grad. Sch. Adminstrn. U. Calif.-Irvine, 1975-76; sr. vis. scholar Japan Soc. for Progress in Sci., 1985, vis. prof., U. Hong Kong; cons. to govt., ednl. instns. and industry., 1957—; mem. adv. panel social sci. Office Sec. Def., 1959-61; mem. adv. panel behavioral scis. Office Surgeon Gen. Army, 1964-68; mem. bd. examiners U.S. State Dept., 1987-97. Author: (with others) Leadership and Supervision in Industry, 1955, (with R. Gagne) Psychology and Human Performance, 1959, Studies in Personnel and Industrial Psychology, 1961, (with A. Bass) Studies in Personnel and Industrial Psychology, 3d edit., 1974, The Structure and Measurement of Physical Fitness, 1964, (with others) Top Management Development and Succession, (with J.G. Hunt) Current Developments in the Study of Leadership, 1973, Human Performance and Productivity, 1982, (with M. Quaintance) Taxonomies of Human Performance, 1984, (with M. Reilly) Handbook of Human Abilities, 1992, Fleischman Job Analysis Survey, 1992; contbr. numerous articles, chpts. to jours., books, encys.; editorial bd., Personnel Psychology, 1961-63, Orgnl. Behavior and Human Performance, 1966-70, Computers in Behavior, 1985—, Human Performance, 1988—, Leadership Quart., 1989—, Contemporary Psychology, 1993-98, Internatl. Jour. of Cognitive Economics, 1997—, Human Resource Mgmt. Review, 1990—, Applied Psychology! An Internatl. Review, 1993—; editor in chief Jour., Erlbaum Series in Applied Psychology, 1989—, Applied Psychology, 1971-76. With USNR, 1945-46. Recipient Franklin Taylor award Soc. Engring. Psychologists, 1974, Disting. Profl. Practice award Soc. Indsl. and Organizational Psychology, 1983; Guggenheim fellow, 1962-63, Awd. for Dist. Contbrs. to the Internatl. Advancememnt of Psych., 1999. Fellow Am. Psychol. Assn. (pres. div. indsl. and organizational psychology 1973-74, pres. div. engring. psychology 1977-78, pres. div. evaluation and measurement 1979-80, Disting. Sci. award for applications psychology 1980); mem. AAAS, Internat. Assn. Applied Psychology (pres. 1974-82), Am. Alliance for Health, Phys. Edn. and Recreation, Psychometric Soc., Am. Ednl. Rsch. Assn., Am. Psychol. Soc. (James McKeen Cattell Fellow award for Dist. Scientific Contbrs., 1993), Fellow, Human Factors and Economics Soc., Cosmos Club (Washington), Sigma Xi. Home: 11304 Spur Wheel Ln Potomac MD 20854-1266 Office: George Mason U Dept Psychology King Hall Fairfax VA 22030-4444

FLEISHMAN, PHIL, radio news executive; b. Saxonburg, Pa., Jan. 8, 1965. Student, U. Pitts., 1984-86. News dir. WPIT, Pitts., 1984-86; prodr., editor Std. News, Washington, 1987-92, sr. editor, newsroom supr., religion editor; bur. chief SRN News, Washington, 1997—. Office: SRN News 1901 N Moore St Ste 201 Arlington VA 22209-1706

FLEISIG, ROSS, aeronautical engineer, engineering manager; b. Montreal, Que., Can., Oct. 12, 1921; came to U.S., 1922, naturalized, 1922; s. Samuel and Ethel (Levy) F.; m. Marjorie M. Hall, June 6, 1943; children—Ann, Dale. B.S. in Aero. Engring., Poly. Inst. Bklyn., 1942, M.S., 1955. Sr. aerodynamicist Chance Vought Aircraft Corp., Stratford, Conn., from 1942, Dallas, to 1950; engring. sect. head Sperry Gyroscope Co., Great Neck, N.Y., 1950-61; project mgr. Grumman Aerospace Corp., Bethpage, N.Y., 1961-84; pres. Therus Dynamics, Inc., 1984—. Editor: Lunar Flight Programs, 1964, Lunar Exploration and Spacecraft Systems, 1962; contbr. articles to tech. jours. Fellow AAAS, BIS, AIAA (assoc., Disting. lectr. 1995-97), Am. Astronautical Soc. (pres. 1957-58, bd. dirs. 1958-68); mem. NSPE, Internat. Acad. Astronautics, Garden City Casino Club, Univ. L.I. Club (bd. dirs. 1979-81), Rotary (dir. local club). Club: Garden City Casino. Home and Office: 58 Kilburn Rd Garden City NY 11530-4135

FLEIT, MARTIN, lawyer; b. Bklyn., Apr. 5, 1926; s. Samuel and Nellie (Greenfield) F.; m. Lois Lenefsky, Dec. 29, 1979; children—Julie, Pam, Douglas, Lauren, David. Student Tufts U., 1944-45; BSChemE, U. N.H., 1948, JD, Georgetown U., 1952. Bar: D.C., 1952, Fla., 1974, N.Y., 1980. Ptnr., Stevens, Davis, Miller & Mosher, Washington, 1948-69, sr. ptnr. Fleit,

Jacobson, Cohn & Price, Washington, 1969-92; of couns. Keck, Mahin & Cate, Washington, 1992-97, Evenson, McKeown, Edwards & Lenahan, 1997—; pres. Martin Fleit P.A., Miami, Fla., 1992—. Mem. adv. bd. Patent, Trademark and Copyright Jour., Bur. Nat. Affairs Inc. With USNR, 1943-46. Mem. ABA, FBA, ATLA, Am. Intellectual Property Law Assn., Patent and Trademark Inst. Can., Internat. Assn. Protection Indsl. Property, Inter-Am. Assn. Indsl. Property, Fedn. Internat. Des Conseils en Propriete Industrielle, Internat. PAT-GOT Assn. (founder). Fax: 305-536-9022. E-mail: martyfleit@aol.com. Home: 520 Brickell Key Dr Miami FL 33131-2660 Office: 1200 G St NW Ste 700 Washington DC 20005-3814

FLEITZ, JOHN, legislative administrator. BA, West Chester (Pa.) U. Dist. dir. to Rep. Curt Weldon U.S. Ho. of Reps., Washington, 1997—. Office: 1554 Garrett Rd Upper Darby PA 19082-4505

FLEMING, ARTHUR WALLACE, physician, surgeon; b. Johnson City, Tenn., Oct. 1, 1935; s. Smith Goerge and Vivian (Richardson) F.; m. Dolores E. Caffey, Apr. 8, 1978; 1 child, Erik. Student, Ill. State U., 1953-54; BA, Wayne State U., 1958-61; MD cum laude, U. Mich., 1961-65. Diplomate Am. Bd. Surgery, Am. Bd. Thoracic Surgery. Intern Walter Reed Gen. Hosp., Washington, 1965-66, resident in gen. surgery, 1966-70, resident in thoracic and cardiovascular surgery, 1970-72; research tng. fellowship Walter Reed Army Inst. of Research, Walter Reed Army Med. Ctr., Washington, 1973-74, mem. staff dept. surgery, 1974-76, chief div. exptl. surgery, 1976-77, dir. dept. surgery, 1977-83; assoc. prof. surgery Uniformed Service U. of Health Scis., Bethesda, Md., 1978-83, clin. assoc. prof. surgery, 1983—; program dir. gen. surgery residency tng. program Martin L. King, Jr./Drew Med. Ctr., Los Angeles, 1983—, dir. trauma ctr., 1983—, chief surgery, 1983—; assoc. prof. surgery UCLA, 1983—; chmn. dept. surgery, assoc. prof. surgery Charles R. Drew Postgrad. Med. Sch., Los Angeles, 1983—. Contbr. numerous articles to profl. jours. Served with USN, 1954-62. Recipient Hoff Medal, 1974, Gold Medal for paper Southeastern Surg. Congress, 1977, Letter of Commendation Commanding Gen. U.S. Army Med. Research and Devel. Command, 1981, Surgeon Gen's. "A" prefix, 1981, Commendation Compton City Council, 1985, Recognition award King-Drew Hosp. Social Service, 1985. Mem. ACS., Nat. Assn. Minority Med. Educators (western region), Golden State Med. Soc., Nat. Med. Assn., Charles R. Drew Med. Soc., Am. Heart Assn., Soc. Surg. Chmn., Assn. Program Dirs. in Surgery, Soc. Thoracic Surgeons, Assn. Acad. Surgery, Am. Assn. Blood Banks, Southeastern Surg. Congress, Am. Fedn. Clin. Research, Assn. Mil. Surgeons. Democrat. Roman Catholic. Avocations: golf, classical music, carpentry crafts. Office: Charles R Drew U 12021 S Wilmington Ave Los Angeles CA 90059-3019*

FLEMING, ARTHUR WILLIAM, ophthalmologist; b. Chgo., Nov. 18, 1938; s. Arthur William and Ann Loretta (Daly) F.; m. Kathleen Anne Gottschalk, June 1965 (div. 1976); m. Margaret Frances Daugherty, July 5, 1980 (dec. 1997); children: Bill, Annemarie, Laura, Margaret, Peter, Will, Jeanne, Timothy, Elisabeth. BA, St. Mary's Coll., Mundelein, Ill., 1960; MD, Loyola U., Chgo., 1965. Intern L.A. County Gen. Hosp. Unit 1, 1965-66; resident in ophthalmology U. Pitts. Eye and Ear Hosp., 1969-72; pvt. practice Pitts. Fellow ACS. Avocations: biking, boating. Office: 2020 Ardmore Blvd Pittsburgh PA 15221-4608

FLEMING, BARBARA JOAN, retired university administrator; b. Chgo., July 23, 1936; d. Otto Albert and Mildred Edith (Coltman) Boehlke; m. Moray Leonard Fleming; children: Patricia Deane, Ian Moray. BS, U. State of N.Y., 1993. Market rsch. asst. Am. Oil Co., Chgo., 1960-64; computer programmer Ins. Co. of N.Am., Phila., 1966-68; libr. reference asst. The Coll. of Wooster, Ohio, 1981-84, dir. rsch. and records, 1984-89; dir. devel. rsch. St. Lawrence U., Canton, N.Y., 1989-93, dir. devel. svcs., 1993-99; ret.; bd. dirs., nat. sec. Am. Prospect Rsch. Assn., 1990-94; dir. habitat for humanity St. Lawrence U. Chpt., 1990-94; trustee APRA Found., 1996-98. Chair Borough Charter Commn., Ringwood, N.J., 1979-80; pres. LWV, Ringwood, 1976-78; mem. Grasse River Players, 1990—, bd. dirs. 1993-98. Recipient Spotlight award for Excellence in Community Theatre Coll.-Community Theatre Com., 1989. Mem. Assn. Profl. Rschrs. for Advancement (founder Upstate N.Y. chpt., bd. trustees Found. 1996-98), Ohio Prospect Rsch. Network (founder). Avocation: community theatre.

FLEMING, BRICE NOEL, retired philosophy educator; b. Hutchinson, Kans., July 29, 1928; s. Augustus Brice and Anna (Noel) F.; m. Barbara Warr, Dec. 20, 1965. B.A., Harvard U., 1950; D.Phil., Oxford (Eng.) U., 1961. Asst. lectr. Manchester (Eng.) U., 1956-57; instr. Yale U., 1957-59, 1960-62; asst. prof. U. Calif. at Santa Barbara, 1962-65, assoc. prof., 1965-69, prof., 1969-91, prof. emeritus, 1991—. Served with AUS, 1951-53. Office: U Calif Dept Philosophy Santa Barbara CA 93106

FLEMING, BRUCE E., English literature educator, writer; b. Salisbury, Md., July 25, 1954; s. Maurice Carl and Jessie K. (Laib) F.; divorced; 1 child, Alexandra. BA, Haverford Coll., 1974; MA, U. Chgo., 1978; PhD, Vanderbilt U., 1982. Lectr. U. Freiburg, Germany, 1983-85; Fulbright prof. Nat. U. Rwanda, Ruhengeri, 1985-87; from asst. prof. to prof. U.S. Naval Acad., Annapolis, Md., 1987—. Author: (novel) Twilley, 1997, (book of dance essays) Sex, Art, and Audience, 1999, (aesthetics) An Essay in Post-Romantic Literary Theory, 1991, (criticism) Caging the Lion, 1992, Modernism and its Discontents, Structure and Chaos in Modernist Works, 1995; author numerous articles and essays. Fellow Free U., Berlin, 1982-83. Mem. MLA, Dance Critics Assn. (pres. 1992-93). Office: US Naval Acad 107 Maryland Ave Annapolis MD 21402

FLEMING, CAROLYN ELIZABETH, religious organization administrator, interior designer; b. Sept. 24, 1946; d. Jerry J. and Mary Josephine (Korten) Maly; m. Roger Earl Fleming, May 26, 1974; children: Karl Joseph, Briana Danika. Student, Texarkana Jr. Coll., 1963-65, Okla. State U., 1965-66; BS in Interior Design, U. Tex., 1970. Asst. to designer Planning/Design Cons., Inc., Tulsa, 1970-72; pvt. cons. Texarkana, Tex., 1972-73; with Anchorage Neuro-Spinal Clinic, 1987-90, 91-96; sec. Nat. Tchg. Com. Bahais of Alaska, Anchorage, 1976-89, mem., 1989-92; mem. Baha'i materials promotion com., Anchorage, 1987-89; active Nat. Spirituality Assembly, Bahais of Alaska, 1992-97, sec. gen., CEO, 1994-96; chmn. Anchorage Bahais Local Spiritual Assembly, 1990-92; mem. Texarkana Bahai Local Spirituality Assembly, 1985, Oceanview (Alaska) Bahai Local Spiritual Assembly, 1986-87; rec. sec. Chena Valley (Alaska) Local Spiritual Assembly Bahais, 1997, mem. internat. goals com., 1997—; coord. Interdenominational Cultural Unity Conf. for Anchorage Area, 1986. Vol. Rural Comty. Action Program, 1986-87, Alaska Coun. on Prevention Alcohol and Drug Abuse, 1987, Spirit Days, 1987-88; trainee Parent and Youth Mediation Program, 1990; mem. Anchorage Local Spiritual Assembly, 1998; asst. aux. bd. for Bahai Oceanview Comty., 1989-92; mem. Arts Coun., Valdez, Alaska, 1974-76, Beyond Beijing Coalition, Anchorage, 1995-96. Mem. Assn. Interior Designers, Beta Sigma Phi. Mem. Baha'i Faith. Office: 1186 Nancy St North Pole AK 99705-5735

FLEMING, CHARLES CLIFFORD, JR., retired airline and jet aircraft sales company executive; b. Gt. Bend, Kans., Dec. 19, 1923; s. Charles Clifford and Nana Gaye (Hanson) F.; m. Barbara Inez Miller, Sept. 15, 1947; children: Charles Clifford III, John Ralph, Robert Mark, Barbara Lisabeth, Roger Andrew. Student, U. Miami, Fla., 1946-48. Ordained deacon Bapt. Ch. With Pan Am. World Airways Inc. (and subs's.), 1942-80; v.p. bus. jets div. Pan Am. World Airways Inc. (and subs's.), N.Y.C., 1970-72; pres., chief exec. officer Falcon Jet Corp., Teterboro, N.J., 1972-80, Bus. Jets Internat., Inc., Cocoa, Fla., 1980-88; pres. Eagle's Nest Homes of Central Fla., 1985-91. Elder Presbyn. Ch.; bd. dirs. United Fund, Brevard County, Fla., 1958. With AC U.S. Army, 1942-46, PTO. Mem. Nat. Bus. Aircraft Assn., Air Force Assn., Nat. Aviation Club. Republican. Club: Wings (N.Y.C.).

FLEMING, DORIS AVEN, mental health nurse; b. Pinehurst, N.C., Sept. 12, 1958; d. Robert Leslie and Margaret Louise (Hunt) F. AS in Nursing, Sandhills C.C., Pinehurst, 1985; BSN, U. N.C., 1995. Cert. biofeedback Biofeedback Cert. Inst. Am. Nurse, biofeedback therapist Moore Regional Hosp., Pinehurst, 1985—. Mem. ANA (cert. psychiat. and mental health nurse), N.C. Biofeedback Assn. Office: Moore Regional Hosp PO Box 3000 Pinehurst NC 28374-3000

FLEMING, DOUGLAS RILEY, journalist, publisher, public affairs consultant; b. Fairmont, W.Va., Jan. 25, 1922; s. Douglas Riley and Sarilda Artemes (Short) F.; m. Irene Stachowicz, Oct. 28, 1944 (dec. 1979), m. Nancy Evelyn Kincaid, May 30, 1992. B.S., Georgetown U., 1953. Commd. ensign U.S. Navy, 1944, advanced through ranks to comdr.; naval aviator; chief protocol NATO, Naples, 1962-67, ret. 1967; with Francis I. DuPont & Co., Investment Banking, Rome, 1968-70; exec. editor, gen. mgr. Daily American, Rome, 1970-75; pres. Stampa Generale, S.R.L., Pubs., Naples, Italy, 1975—; mng. dir. Italo-Am. Assn., Naples; dir. Am. Studies Ctr., Naples, 1975-80; pres. Gen. Press Services, Washington, 1979—; dir. Va. Winery Coop., Inc., Culpeper, 1985-93; proprietor, operator Campicello Vineyards, Madison, Va., 1982-92 . Active Nat. Trust Hist. Preservation, Smithsonian Assocs., Assn. Naval Aviation. Mem. Associazione Della Stampa Estera in Italia, The Cogswell Soc., Georgetown U. Alumni Assn. (pres. Italy 1972-80), Am. C. of C. in Italy, Retired Officers Assn., Navy League of U.S., Nat. Press Club, Vinifera Wine Growers Assn., Jeffersonian Wine Grape Growers Soc., Va. Vineyards Assn. Clubs: Naval and Mil., Steering Wheel, Royal Aero (London); Circolo Canottieri (Naples); N.Y. Athletic; Dist. Yacht (Washington). Address: 400 Madison St Apt 1408 Alexandria VA 22314-1724

FLEMING, EDWARD J., priest, educator; b. Montclair, N.J., Mar. 29, 1924; s. Timothy Joseph and Agnes (Gannon) F. Student, Seton Hall Prep. Sch., South Orange, N.J., 1932-36; A.B., Seton Hall U., 1940, M.A., 1948, LL.D., 1970; student, Immaculate Conception Sem., Ramsey, N.J., 1936-40; S.T.L., Cath. U. Am., 1944; Ph.D., St. John's U., Bklyn., 1955; grad., Inst. Advanced Studies, N.Am. Coll., Rome, 1977; postgrad., Harvard Divinity Sch., 1986. Ordained priest Roman Catholic Ch., 1944, elevated to papal chamberlain, 1963, elevated to prelate to Pope John Paul II, 1983; priest St. Teresa's Ch., Summit, N.J., 1944-49; prof. ednl. psychology and theology Seton Hall U., 1949-51, dean student affairs, 1951-53, dean coll., 1953-59, exec. v.p., 1959-69, pres., 1969-70; pastor Our Lady of Blessed Sacrament Ch., Roseland, N.J., 1970-78; dean Archdiocese of Newark, 1975-77, mem. bd. of consultors; vis. scholar Oxford (Eng.) U., 1987-88; dir. devel. Seton Hall U. Seminary, South Orange, N.J., 1987—; dir. and lectr. Newman studies Univ. Coll., 1987—; dir. devel. Sch. Theology Seton Hall U., South Orange, 1987—; mem. exam. bd. Archdiocesan Clergy and Sem., 1954-64; mem. Archdiocesan Commn. Parish Visitation, 1969—; Episcopal vicar Essex County Archdiocese; coord. dean Essex County, 1975—; pres. Roseland Coun. Chs.; mem. ethics com. N.J. Supreme Ct., 1979—; mem. Senate of Priests, Archdiocese of Newark, 1980—, Archdiocesan Sch. Bd., 1980; vis. scholar Oxford U., Eng., 1964-65; week-end asst. Our Lady Peace, New Providence, N.J., Holy Rosary, Elizabeth, N.J., St. Paul Agostle, Irvington, N.J., St. James, Springfield, N.J., Visitation, Brich, N.J., St. Michael's, Long Branch, N.J., St. Josephs, Rarilian, N.J., St. Peters, Pheasant Beach, N.J. Contbr. articles on higher edn. to ednl. periodicals and jours. Mem. Army Adv. Panel ROTC Affairs, 1961-70; mem. Edn. Commn. U.S.; mem. pres.'s council Caldwell Coll., N.J.; trustee Assumption Coll., Mendham, N.J., Greater Newark Black and White Opera Co., Tri-Hosp. Ecumenical Chaplaincy Council No. N.J., 1979. Recipient Alpha Epsilon Mu award, 1956; Sapientiae Christianae Humanitarian award, 1958; John J. Crecca Found. Humanitarian award, 1967; Irishman of Year award Friends of Brian Boru, Inc., 1967; Zionist Brotherhood award, 1979; named to Athletic Hall of Fame, Seton Hall U., 1986; N.Am. Coll. fellow, Rome, 1971—, fellow Weston Theol. Ctr., Cambridge, Eng., 1986-87. Mem. Eastern Assn. Coll. Deans and Advisers of Men, Nat. Cath. Edn. Assn. (pres. Eastern unit 1965-66), Middle States Accreditation Assn., N.J. Hist. Soc. (com. of 125), Cath. Theol. Soc. Am. Office: Seton Hall Univ Office Dir Devel Sch Theology South Orange NJ 07079 *May I never stop reaching out to others. May I never stop loving. For I should have learned long ago that love is not love 'til I give it away.*

FLEMING, FRANK, sculptor; b. Bear Creek, Ala., June 17, 1940. BS, U. Ala., 1962, MA, 1969, MFA, 1973. One-man shows include Birmingham (Ala.) Mus. Art, 1982, Montgomery (Ala.) Mus. Art, 1983; exhbns. include Mus. Am. Crafts, N.Y., 1986, U. Hawaii Art Gallery, 1991, Contemporary Crafts of the Ams., Ft. Collins, Colo., 1975, Renwich Gallery, 1981, Smithsonian Inst., 1981, Nat. Mus. Art, Washington, 1981; commd. AT&T, Atlanta, 1979, Montgomery Mus. Art, 1989, Birmingham Botanical Gardens, 1990, 92, City of Birmingham, 1991. Recipient Harry Murray award Birmingham Mus. Art, 1990; Ala. State Arts Coun. fellow, 1990, So. Arts Fedn. Sculpture fellow, 1991. Office: 1309 Saulter Rd Birmingham AL 35209-6635*

FLEMING, GRAHAM RICHARD, chemistry educator; b. Barrow-in-Furness, Lancashire, Eng., Dec. 3, 1949; came to U.S., 1979; s. Maurice Norman and Ena (Winter) F.; m. Jean McKenzie, Sept. 16, 1977; 1 child, Matthew. BS with honors, U. Bristol, Eng., 1971; PhD in Phys. Chemistry, U. London, 1974. Rsch. fellow Calif. Inst. Tech., Pasadena, 1974-75; univ. rsch. fellow U. Melbourne, Australia, 1975, Australian Rsch. Grants Commn. rsch. asst., 1976; Leverhulme fellow Royal Instn., London, 1977-79; asst. prof. U. Chgo., 1979-83, assoc. prof., 1983-85, prof., 1985-87, A.H. Compton Disting. Svc. prof., 1987-97, chmn. dept. chemistry, 1988-90; prof. U. Calif., Berkeley, 1997—; dir. phys. bioscis. divsn. Lawrence Berkeley Nat. Lab., 1997—; co-chmn. Ultrafast Phenomena V Meeting, Snowmass, Colo., 1986. Author: Chemical Applications of Ultrafast Spectroscopy, 1986; mem. editl. bd. Chm. Physics Letters, Jour. of Phys. Chemistry, Chem. Physics; contbr. 235 rsch. articles to profl. publs. Recipient Coblentz award Coblentz Soc., 1985; Alfred P. Sloan Found. fellow, 1981, J.S. Guggenheim fellow, 1987; Dreyfus tchr.-scholar, 1982. Fellow Am. Acad. Arts and Scis., Royal Soc. London; mem. Optical Soc. Am., Inter-Am. Photochem. Soc. (award 1996), Royal Soc. Chemistry (Marlow medal 1981, Tilden medal 1991, Centenary medal 1996), Am. Chem. Soc. (Nobel Laureate Signature award for grad. edn. in chemistry 1995, Peter Debye award in phys. chemistry 1998). Avocation: mountaineering. Office: Univ of Calif-Berkeley Dept Chemistry B84 Hildebrand #1460 Berkeley CA 94720-1460

FLEMING, HUBERT LOY, water systems company executive; b. Sutton, W.Va., Aug. 6, 1956; s. Hubert Harrison and Edra Ruth (Crawford) F.; m. Pamela Anne Monteleone, May 6, 1979; children: Jaime, Megan, Benjamin, Amanda. BS, Anderson-Broaddus Coll., 1978; MS, PhD, Cornell U., 1980. Rsch. engr., v.p. Alcoa, Pitts., 1981-88; v.p., gen. mgr. Carbone-USA Corp., Boonton, N.J., 1988-90; v.p. Zenon, Sussex, N.J., 1990-96; pres. Cochrane, Inc., King of Prussia, Pa., 1996—. Co-author: (book) Handbook of Alumina Chemistry and Science, 1986; co-editor: (book) Handbook of Membrane Technology, 1988; patentee in field; contbr. tech. papers to profl. jours. Mem. adv. coun. U. Tex. Edn. Dept., Austin, 1985-88, U. Delaware, Newark, 1983-85; adj. prof. Worcester (Mass.) Poly. Inst., 1984-88; dir. Internat. Bus. Forum, Washington, 1996-97. Mem. AIChE (chmn. separations subgroup 1981—), Am. Chem. Soc., N.Am. Membrane Soc. (past dir. 1988—), N.Y. Acad. Scis., Water Environ. Fedn. Avocation: competitive martial arts. Office: Cochrane Inc 800 3rd Ave King Of Prussia PA 19406

FLEMING, JAMES STUART, JR., pharmaceutical company manager; b. Buffalo, Sept. 1, 1936; s. James Stuart and Pauline (McClurg) F.; m. Marilyn Joyce Bartsch, June 7, 1960; children: Lois Vernette, James Stuart III. BA, Northwestern U., 1958; MS, U. Buffalo, 1962; PhD, Ohio State U., 1965; MBA, Syracuse U., 1983. Rsch. asst. Ohio State U., Columbus, 1962-65; rsch. scientist Bristol-Myers Co., Syracuse, N.Y., 1965-74, sr. rsch. scientist, 1974-82, mgr., 1982-85; assoc. dir. cardiovascular biology Bristol-Myers Co., Syracuse and Wallingford, Conn., 1985-90; assoc. dir. project planning Bristol-Myers Squibb Co., Wallingford, Conn., 1990—. Author: (with others) Platelet Aggregation Inhibitors, 1974-82; editor: Drugs and the Delivery of Oxygen to Tissues, 1989. Cons., tchr. Jr. Achievement, Wallingford, 1988-90. Mem. Am. Soc. Pharmacology and Exptl. Therapeutics, Am. Heart Assn. (coun. on thrombosis), Microcirculatory Soc., Internat. Soc. Oxygen Transport to Tissue, Am. Coll. Clin. Pharmacology, Beta Gamma Sigma. Avocations: golf, tennis, hiking, skiing, gardening. Office: Bristol-Myers Squibb Co 5 Research Pky Wallingford CT 06492-1927

FLEMING, JANE WILLIAMS, retired educator, author; b. Bethlehem, Pa., May 26, 1926; d. James Robert and Marion Pauline (Melloy) Groman; m. George Elliott Williams, July 2, 1955 (div. July 1965); children: Rhett Dorman, Santee Stuart, Timothy Cooper; m. Jérome Thomas Fleming, Sept. 25, 1980. BS, UCLA, 1951; MA, Calif. State U., Long Beach, 1969. Tchr. San Diego Unified Sch Dist., 1951-55, Costa Mesa (Calif.) Sch. Dist., 1955-56, Long Beach (Calif.) Sch. Dist., 1956-58, 62-87, 1990-92; ret. Author: Why Janey Can't Teach, 1999. Mem. Phi Kappa Phi, Ret. Tchrs. Assn., UCLA Alumni Assn., Planetary Soc. (charter), Mus. of Tolerance. Avocations: theater, travel. E-mail: jwilli5687@aol.com. Address: PO Box 13053 Long Beach CA 90803

FLEMING, JOSEPH CLIFTON, JR., dean, law educator; b. Atlanta, July 24, 1942; s. Joseph Clifton Sr. and Claudia Leola (Duncan) F.; m. Linda Wightman, May 27, 1964; children: Allison, Erin, Anne, Matthew Clifton, Stephen Joseph, Michael Grant. BS, Brigham Young U., 1964; JD, George Washington U., 1967. Bar: Wash. 1967, U.S. Dist. Ct. (we. dist.) Wash. 1967, U.S. Tax Ct. 1969, U.S. Ct. Appeals (9th cir.) 1970, Utah 1979. Assoc. Bogle & Gates, Seattle, 1967-73; assoc. prof. Law Sch. U. of Puget Sound, Tacoma, 1973-74; assoc. prof. Law Sch. Brigham Young U., Provo, Utah, 1974-76, prof. Law sch., 1976-98, assoc. dean Law Sch., 1986—; Ernest L. Wilkinson prof. Law Sch. Brigham Young U., Provo, 1998—; Fulbright prof. faculty law U. Nairobi, Kenya, 1977-78; prof. in residence Office of Chief Counsel IRS, Washington, 1985-86; vis. prof. U. Queensland, Brisbane, Australia, 1997. Author: Estate and Gift Tax, 1975, Tax Aspects of Buying and Selling Corporate Businesses, 1984, Tax Aspects of Forming and Operating Closely Held Corporations, 1992, Federal Income Tax: Doctrine, Structure and Policy, 1995, 2nd edit., 1999; notes editor George Washington U. Law Rev., 1966-67; contbr. numerous articles to profl. jours. Bishop Ch. of Jesus Christ of LDS, Orem, Utah, 1981-85. Mem. ABA (subcom. chair tax sect. corp. tax com. 1979-83, chair tax sect. com. on teaching taxation 1992-94), Am. Law Inst. (tax adv. group 1988-94, 98—). Office: Brigham Young U J Reuben Clark Law Sch PO Box 28000 Provo UT 84602-8000

FLEMING, JUANITA W., academic administrator. BS, Hampton Inst., 1957; MA, U. Chgo., 1959; PhD, Cath. U. Am., 1969; D of Pub. Svc., Berea Coll., 1994. Form staff nurse to head nurseMed. Surg. Pediat. Unit Children's Hosp., Washington, 1957-58; pub. health nurse Bur. Pub. Health Nursing, 1959-60; instr. nursing children Sch. Nursing Freedmen's Hosp., Washington, 1962-65; cons. pub. health nursingdept. pediat.Child Devel. Clin. Howard U., 1965-66; from asst. prof. to assoc. prof. Coll. Nursing U. Ky., Lexington, 1969-73, prof. Coll. Nursing, 1973—, spl. asst. to pres. academic affairsctr. administrn., 1991—; mem. grad. faculty Coll. Nursing, U. Ky, 1971—, asst. dean grad. edn., 1975-81, assoc. dean, dir. grad. edn., 1982-86; prof. Coll. Edn. Edpt. Edn. Policy Studies and Evaln., 1979—; assoc. vice-chancellor acad. affairs Med. Ctr., 1984-91; co. project dir. nursing care high risk infants State Maternal and Child Health Divsn., 1972; project dir. advanced nurse tng. grant divsn. nursing Dept. Health Edn. and Welfare, 1977-80, high tech home care chronically ill children Bur. Maternal Child Health, 1989-93; vis. prof. Case We. Res. U., Cleve., 1984, West Chester U., 1997; Martin Luther King/Rosa Parks/Cesar Chavez vis. prof. U. Mich., Ann Arbor, 1989, Elizabeth Carnegie endowed vis. prof. Howard U., 1995; Houston Endowed Minority Health and Rsch. Disting. vis. prof. Prairie View U., 1998; prin. investor Am. Nurses Found., 1970-71. Prin. investor Am. Nurses Found., 1970-71. Recipient Ky. Nurses Assn. award, Marion E. McKenna leadership award, 1988, Disting. Svc. award ANA, 1994. Mem. Am. Acad. Nursing, Nat. Acad. Scis., Inst. Medicine. Office: U Ky 7 Adminstrn Bldg Lexington KY 40536-0032

FLEMING, JULIAN DENVER, JR., lawyer; b. Rome, Ga., Jan. 12, 1934; s. Julian D. and Margaret Madison (Mangham) F.; m. Sidney Howell, June 28, 1960; 1 dau., Julie Adrianne. Student, U. Pa., 1951-53; BChemE, Ga. Inst. Tech., 1955, PhD, 1959; JD, Emory U., 1967. Bar: Ga. 1966, D.C. 1967; registered profl. engr., Ga.; Calif. Rsch. engr., prof. chem. engring. Ga. Inst. Tech., 1955-67; ptnr. Sutherland, Asbill & Brennan, Atlanta, 1967—. Contbr. articles to profl. jours.; patentee in field. Bd. dirs. Mental Health Assn. Ga., 1970-80; bd. dirs. Mental Health Assn. Met. Atlanta, 1970-80, pres., 1974-75; mem. coun. legal advisors Rep. Nat. Com., 1981-85. Fellow Am. Inst. Chemists, Am. Coll. Trial Lawyers, Am. Bar Found.; mem. AAAS, ABA (coun. sect. sci. and tech. 1980-82, vice chmn. 1982-84, chmn. 1985-86, ho. dels. 1990, 94-96, bd. govs. 1994-95, chmn. spl. citation issues com. 1995-96, coord. commn. on legal tech. 1995-97, standing com. on tech. and info. sys. 1997—), AIChE, Nat. Conf. Lawyers and Scientists (chmn. ABA del. 1988-90, ABA liaison 1990-93, standing com. on nat. conf. groups 1990, chmn. 1992-93), Bleckley Inn of Ct. (master of bench). Achievements include patent for data apparatus. Home: 1248 Oxford Rd NE Atlanta GA 30306-2610 Office: Sutherland Asbill & Brennan 999 Peachtree St NE Ste 2300 Atlanta GA 30309-3996

FLEMING, LAURA ELIZABETH, non-profit executive; b. Louisville, Apr. 21, 1969; d. John Marvin and Phyllis Dean (Parker) F. BA, Hanover (Ind.) Coll., 1991; MA, Union Coll., Barbourville, Ky., 1994. Dir. housing Lindsey Wilson Coll., Columbia, Ky., 1991-92; asst. dean student life Union Coll., Barbourville, 1992-95; exec. dir. Cmty. Youth Leadership, Clarksville, Ind., 1995—. Bd. dirs. Hope, Inc., 1995—, Youth as Resources, 1996—, Cynergy: Links to Leadership, 1997—; mem. steering com. Loaves & Fishes Soup Kitchen, Jeffersonville, Ind., 1995—; grad. Leadership So. Ind., 1997; mem., officer Clark & Floyd Youth Coalitions, 1995—, Floyd County Alcohol Task Force, 1995—. Mem. Bus. and Profl. Women (Young Careerist winner 1995). Methodist. Avocations: reading, cooking. Home: 271 Laurie Vallee Louisville KY 40223-3139

FLEMING, LISA L., lawyer; b. Louisville, Nov. 14, 1961; d. Joseph D. Ware. BA cum laude, Hanover (Ind.) Coll., 1982; JD, U. Louisville, 1985. Bar: Ind., Ohio, U.S. Dist. Ct. (so. and no. dists.) Ind.; cert. mediator pursuant to Ind. Trial Rules. Assoc. gen. counsel Midland Enterprises, Inc., Cin.; career cons. Hanover Coll. Mem. Leadership So. Ind., 1990-98, v.p. programming, 1996-97; bd. dirs. Comty. Youth Leadership Collaborative, 1995—. Mem. NAFE, ABA (admiralty and corp. counsel coms.), Ind. State Bar Assn. (articles and by-laws com.), Clark County Bar Assn., Cin. Bar Assn., Am. Corp. Counsel Assn. (bd. dirs., chpt. treas. 1992-95), River City Bus. and Profl. Women, Ky. Women Advs., Focus Louisville, Hanover Coll. Alumni Assn. (bd. dirs. 1990-96, pres. elect 1991-92, pres. bd. dirs. 1992-93, past pres. 1993-94), So. Ind. C. of C. (chair govt. affairs debate subcom. 1991-95, women's bus. coun., 1991-95, chair political skill workshop subcom. 1993-95), Phi Mu (alumnae pres. Louisville chpt. 1985-91, nat. risk mgmt. educator 1996-98, Sigma area collegiate dir. 1996-97, nat. extenstion dir. 1998—). Office: Midland Enterprises 300 Pike St Cincinnati OH 45202-4222

FLEMING, MAC ARTHUR, labor union administrator; b. Walnut Grove, Miss., Sept. 22, 1945; s. Austin J. and Dorothy (Downey) F.; m. Phyllis Jean Tatro, May 18, 1984; children: Vaughn L. Voth, Denise. AA, Jones County Jr. Coll., Laurel, Miss., 1967; student, So. Colo. State Coll., Pueblo, 1967-68; student in trade union program, Harvard U., 1979. System organizer Atchison, Topeka & Santa Fe System Fedn., Pueblo, 1972; asst. gen. chmn. Atchison, Topeka & Santa Fe System Fedn., San Bernardino, Calif., 1972-73; asst. chmn., sec.-treas. Atchison, Topeka & Santa Fe System Fedn., Newton, Kans., 1974-75, vice chmn., 1975-80, gen. chmn., 1980-86; grand lodge sec.-treas. Brotherhood Maintenance Ways Employees, Detroit, 1986-90; pres. Brotherhood Maintenance of Way Employees, Detroit, 1990—; v.p. AFL-CIO, 1995—. Democrat. Avocations: tennis, golf. Home: 21032 Boulder Cir Northville MI 48167-2736 Office: Brotherhood Maintenance Way Employees 26555 Evergreen Rd Ste 200 Southfield MI 48076-4225

FLEMING, MACK GERALD, lawyer; b. Hartwell, Ga., May 3, 1932; s. Mack Judson and Dessie Leola (Vickery) F.; m. Elizabeth McClellan, Mar. 30, 1963; children: Katharine Lee, John McClellan. B.S., Clemson (S.C.) U., 1956; J.D., Am. U., Washington, 1966. Asst. dir. prodn. control Woodside Mills, Simpsonville, S.C., 1959-60; adminstrv. asst. to mem. Congress, 1960-64; dir. Congressional Liaison Office, VA, Washington, 1965-68; spl. asst. to adminstr. Congressional Liaison Office, VA, 1968-69; adminstrv. asst., counsel to mem. congress, 1969-70; pvt. practice law Washington, 1970-74; chief counsel Com. on Vets. Affairs, U.S. Ho. of Reps., 1974-80, staff dir. and chief counsel, 1980-95; pvt. practice Seneca, S.C., 1997—. Served to 1st lt. U.S. Army, 1956-58. Mem. D.C., S.C. bar assns. Democrat. Methodist. Home: 3023 Lake Keowee Ln Seneca SC 29672-6747

FLEMING, MACKLIN, judge, author; b. Chgo., Sept. 6, 1911; s. Ingram Macklin Stainback and Hazel (Caldwell) Fleming; m. Polly Naething, May 17, 1941; children: Penelope, Frances, Ingram. BA, Yale U., 1934, LLB, 1937; LLD, Pepperdine U., 1968. Bar: N.Y. 1938, Calif. 1946. Assoc.

Sullivan & Cromwell, N.Y.C., 1937-39; atty. Bituminous Coal divsn. U.S. Govt., Washington, 1939-41; pvt. practice San Francisco, 1946-49; asst. U.S. atty. U.S. Atty.'s Office, San Francisco, 1949-53; assoc. Mitchell, Silberberg & Knupp, L.A., 1954-59; judge Superior Ct., L.A., 1959-64; justice Calif. Ct. Appeal, L.A., 1964-81; of counsel Troy and Gould, L.A., 1981-91, 98—; assigned judge Superior Ct., L.A., 1992-98. Author: The Price of Perfect Justice, 1974, Of Crimes and Rights, 1978, Lawyers, Money, & Success, 1997. Chmn. Far Eastern Art Coun., L.A. County Mus., 1967-69; v.p. Ctr. Theater Group, L.A., 1970. Capt. U.S. Army, 1941-46. Fellow Am. Bar Found.; mem. ABA, L.A. County Bar Assn., Bar of City of N.Y., Inst. of Jud. Adminstrn., Selden Soc. Democrat. Episcopalian. Avocations: skiing, tennis, gardening. Home: 331 N Carmelina Ave Los Angeles CA 90049-2701 Office: Troy & Gould 1801 Century Park E Ste 1600 Los Angeles CA 90067-2318

FLEMING, MARCELLA, journalist; b. Paoli, Ind., Oct. 14, 1955; d. Kenneth Gale and Neva Louise (Thomas) F.; m. Brian D. Smith. AB in Journalism and English, Ind. U., 1978. Cert. tchr. Reporter Wabash Plain Dealer, 1978-80; reporter Marion Chronicle-Tribune, 1980-83, city editor, 1990-91; city reporter, feature writer, copy editor, Sunday editor Ft. Wayne (Ind.) Jour.-Gazette, 1983-88; editor pubs. Children's Mus. Indpls., 1988-90; freelance writer Indpls. Monthly, 1989-91; nat. editor Indpls. CEO, Columbus (Ohio) CEO mags., 1991-92; writer state desk Indpls. Star & News, 1992—; judge Thomas R. Keating Writing Competition, 1990. Recipient award of Excellence Nat. Down Syndrome Congress, 1988, Best Newsletter, Best Feature Story and Best News Story awards Editor's Forum, 1990, Best Ann. Report award Internat. Assn. Bus. Communicators, 1990. Mem. Ednl. Press Assn. (Breaking News Story Disting. Achievement award 1994). Office: Indianapolis Newspapers Inc PO Box 145 Indianapolis IN 46206-0145

FLEMING, MARJORIE FOSTER, freelance writer, artist; b. Phila., Sept. 12, 1920; d. Major Bronson and Helen Margaret (Vertner) Foster; m. John Joseph Hundermark, Sept. 24, 1949 (div. Sept. 1955); children: John Foster Hundermark, David Laurence Hundermark; m. Paul Stewart Fleming, May 6, 1961. *Marjorie is listed with family in Who's Who in America, Blue Book of America and Who's Who in the Midwest. Her ancestors were early settlers in the Northeast, South, and Midwest, some of which were in the Revolutionary War, Spanish American War and WWI. Her husband, Paul, graduated from the University of Pennsylvania as a chemical engineer. Their son John is an attorney and their son David is an educator. Some of Marjorie's activities include: Red Cross Occupational Therapist, member of the National Library of Poetry, Poetry Guild, International Society of Poetry, International Poetry Hall of Fame Museum, Kappa Chi Delta, Omega Chi, and The Cheltenham Center for the Arts.* BA, Ursinus Coll., 1942; studied with M. Blackburn, R. Goldman, Chgo. Art Inst.; studied with Paul Wieghardt, Cheltenham Twp. Ctr. for Arts. Cert. tchr. Cost acct. Philco Corp., Phila., 1942-43; asst. bank auditor Liberty Title and Trust, Phila., 1943-44; asst. dept. spl. events Phila. Evening Bulletin, 1945-47; asst. stage TV and radio show prodr. Phila., 1947-49; Appeared on Wit's End (live pilot TV show), 1948, guest Poetry Today WRTN Radio, N.Y.C., 1997; adult edn. studies Temple U. Pierce Business Coll, Cheltenham High Sch., Oak Ln. Co. Day Sch., Cheltenham Adult Sch., Arthur Murry Dance Sch.; Painting: Morris Blackburn, Robert Goldman, Paul Wieghardt-Chgo. Art Inst. and Cheltenham Twp. Ctr. for the Arts. Contbr. Northwest Herald, Crystal Lake, Ill., 1996—. Mem. Nat. Libr. Poetry, Internat. Poetry Mus., Cheltenham Ctr. Arts. Republican. Methodist. Avocations: sculpture, photography, creative needlework, pianist, collecting sheet music. Home: 82 Holly Dr Crystal Lake IL 60014-5022

FLEMING, MICHAEL PAUL, lawyer; b. Orlando, Fla., June 25, 1963; s. Joseph Patrick and Therese (Eccles); m. Natalie Jackson, Oct. 15, 1988; children: Shannon Isabel, Nicholas Patrick, Patrick Edward, Michael Paul, Eamon John. BA, U. St. Thomas, 1984; JD, U. Houston, 1987. Bar: Tex. 1987, U.S. Dist. Ct. (so. dist.) Tex. 1988; U.S. Ct. Appeals (5th cir.) 1988, U.S. Supreme Ct. 1991; cert. personal injury. Ptnr. Fleming & Fleming, Houston, 1987-91; asst. county atty. Harris County, Houston, 1991-96; elected Harris county atty. Harris County atty., 1996—. Mem. State Bar of Tex., Houston Bar Assn., Ancient Order of Hibernians, KC, Phi Delta Phi. Roman Catholic. Avocation: genealogy. Home: 6046 Lymbar Dr Houston TX 77096-4713 Office: Harris County Atty 1019 Congress St # 15 Houston TX 77002-1700

FLEMING, NANCY MCADAM, landscape designer; b. Balt., July 24, 1940; d. Robert Martin and Jane Ellen (Weeks) McAdam; m. Samuel Crozier Fleming, Sept. 7, 1963; children: David McAdam, Timothy Crozier. BA, Mt. Holyoke Coll., 1962; cert. in Landscape Design, Radcliffe Coll., 1988. Tchr. The Harley Sch., Rochester, N.Y., 1962-63, Shady Hill Sch., Cambridge, Mass., 1965-67; flower show asst. Mass. Hort. Soc., Boston, 1986-88; pub., owner Country Pl. Books, Weston, Mass., 1995—; landscape designer Nancy Fleming, Inc., Weston, 1989—; mem. landscape vis. com. U. Del., Newark, 1996—; mem. Cornell plantation com. Cornell U., Ithaca, N.Y., 1997—; com. mem. Weston Rds. Trust, 1997—, Weston Land Trust, 1998—; spkr., slide lectr. garden clubs, hort. orgns., Mass., N.H., N.Y., Del., Conn., 1988—. Author: Money, Manure and Maintenance, 1995; (booklet) Weston Town Common, 1988. Chmn. Park and Cemetery Commn., Weston, 1994-96; trustee Walnut Hill Sch., Natick, Mass., 1993—. Mem. Boston Soc. Landscape Architects, Country Club (Brookline, Mass.), Chilton Club (Boston), Weston Garden Club (pres. 1989-91), Lake Sunapee Country Club, Lake Sunapee Yacht Club. Republican. Episcopalian. Avocations: competitive golf and paddle tennis, reading, bridge. Home: 61 Meadowbrook Rd Weston MA 02493-2407 Office: Nancy Fleming Inc 61 Meadowbrook Rd Weston MA 02493-2407

FLEMING, PATRICIA STUBBS, federal official; b. Phila., Mar. 17, 1936; d. Fredrick Douglass Stubbs and Marion Turner Stubbs Thomas; m. Harold S. Fleming, June 1958 (div. Feb. 1971); children: Douglass, Craig, Gordon. BA, Vassar Coll., 1957; postgrad., NYU, 1958-60, U. Pa., 1957-58, Phila. Acad. Fine Arts, 1957-58. Legis. asst. to reps. U.S. Ho. of Reps., Washington, 1971-77; asst. to sec. HEW, Washington, 1977-78, dir. intergovtl. and legis. affairs Office Civil Rights, 1979-80; asst. to sec. U.S. Dept. Edn., Washington, 1979-80, dep. asst. sec. legis., 1980-81; sr. pub. policy assoc. James H. Lowry & Assocs., Washington, 1981-83; chief staff Rep. Ted Weiss U.S. Ho. of Reps., Washington, 1983-86, profl. staff mem. subcom. human resources & intergovtl. rels, 1986-93; spl. asst. to sec. HHS, Washington, 1993-94; dir. Office Nat. AIDS Policy The White House, Washington, 1994-97, cons. on AIDS policy and programs, 1997—. One-person show NYU; exhibited in group shows in N.Y.C. and Washington. Democrat. Episcopalian. Avocations: painting, music, reading. Home and Office: 6009 Massachusetts Ave Bethesda MD 20816-2041

FLEMING, PETER EMMET, JR., lawyer; b. Atlantic Highlands, N.J., Aug. 18, 1929; s. Peter Emmet and Anna (Sullivan) F.; m. Jane Breed, June 2, 1956; children—Peter Emmet III, James M., William B., David W., Jane H. A.B., Princeton U., 1951; LL.B., Yale U., 1958. Bar: N.Y. 1959, U.S. Dist. Ct. (so. and ea. dists.) N.Y. 1960, U.S. Ct. Appeals (2d cir.) 1963, U.S. Ct. Appeals (4th cir.) 1979, U.S. Supreme Ct. 1985. Assoc. Davis, Polk & Wardwell, N.Y.C., 1958-61; asst. U.S. atty. U.S. dist. Ct. (so. dist.) N.Y., N.Y.C., 1961-70; mem. Curtis, Mallet-Prevost Colt & Mosle, N.Y.C., 1970—. Home: 122 Old Church Rd Greenwich CT 06830-4821 Office: Curtis Mallet-Prevost Colt & Mosle 101 Park Ave New York NY 10178

FLEMING, RENÉE L., opera singer; b. Indiana, Pa., Feb. 14, 1959; d. Edwin Davis Fleming and Patricia (Seymour) Alexander; m. Richard Lee Ross, Sept. 23, 1989. BM in Music Edn., Potsdam State U., 1981; MM, Eastman Sch. Music, 1983; student, Juilliard Am. Opera Ctr., N.Y.C., 1983-84, 85-87. Rec. artist Decca Records, London, 1995. Debut engagements include Spoleto Festival, Charleston and Italy, 1986-90, Houston Grand Opera & N.Y.C. Opera, 1988, 89, San Francisco Opera, 1991, Met. Opera, Paris Opera at the Bastille, 1991, Covent Garden, London, 1989, Teatro Colon Buenos Aires, 1991, La Scala, 1993, Lyric Opera of Chgo., 1993, Paris Opera at Palais Garnice, 1996. Winner Met. Opera Nat. Auditions, 1988; recipient George London prize, 1988, Richard Tucker award, 1990, Solti prize Acad. du Disque Lyrique, 1996, Prize Acad. du Disque Lyrique, 1998; Fulbright scholar, Frankfurt, Germany, 1984-85; named Vocalist of Yr. Mus. Am., 1997; nominated 5 Grammy's, 1997-99; recipient Grammy award, 1999. Office: care ML Falcone Pub Rels 155 W 68th St Apt 1114 New York NY 10023-5817

FLEMING, REX JAMES, meteorologist; b. Omaha, Apr. 25, 1940; s. Robert Leonard and Doris Mae (Burrows) F.; m. Kathleen Joyce Ferry, Sept. 3, 1969; children: Thane, Manon, Mark, Noel. B.S., Creighton U., 1963; M.S., U. Mich., 1968, Ph.D., 1970. Commd. lt. U.S. Air Force, 1963, advanced through grades to capt., 1972; research scientist Offutt AFB, Nebr., 1963-67; sci. liaison to Nat. Weather Service for Air Weather Service, Suitland, Md., 1970-72; resigned, 1972; mgr. applications mktg. advanced sci. computer Tex. Instruments, Inc., Austin, 1972-75; dir. U.S. Project Office for Global Weather Expt., NOAA, Rockville, Md., 1975-80, Spl. Research Projects Office, 1980-82, Office of Climate and Atmospheric Research, 1983-84, Internat. Tropical Ocean and Global Atmosphere Project Office and Nat. Storm Program Office, 1984-86; pres. Tycho Tech. Inc., Boulder, Colo., 1986-87, Creative Concepts, Boulder, Colo., 1987-91; sr. mgr., coord. FAA rsch. Nat. Ctr. for Atmospheric Rsch., 1991-92, vis. scientist, 1987-88; NOAA, Boulder, 1993—. *Dr. Fleming has over 30 years experience in managing atmospheric and earth science activities. He has skills in computer programming, numerical analysis, modeling and theoretical understanding of chaos. He managed the U.S. Project Office for the Global Weather Experiment and helped initiate and direct the International Tropical Ocean and Global Atmosphere Program Office. He has presented seminars in computer architecture, atmospheric observing systems, air-sea interaction, and the dynamics of uncertainty. Rex continues to study new technologies that might assist both the business and environmental communities in addressing the environmental challenges of the 21st century.* Contbr. articles to profl. jours. Recipient Gold Medal award Dept. Commerce, 1980. Fellow AAAS; mem. Am. Meteorol. Soc. (chmn. probability and statistics com. 1976-77), The Planetary Soc., Am. Geophys. Union (sec. atmospheric scis. sect. 1984-86). Republican. Home: 7225 Spring Dr Boulder CO 80303-5115 Office: NCAR PO Box 3000 Boulder CO 80307-3000 *One need only be inspired by its spring-morning freshness, stimulated by its magnificent variety of color and form, and humbled by the power of its ever-present energy, to be driven to unveil the secrets of our life-sustaining atmosphere.*

FLEMING, RICHARD, chemical company executive; b. N.Y.C., June 15, 1924; s. James and Caroline (Jung) F.; m. Roberta Marie Seeber, Apr. 8, 1945; children: Richard James, Robert Carleton, Kathleen Teresa Mary. B.Chem. Engring., Pratt Inst., 1944; M.Chem. Engring., N.Y. U., 1949. Devel. engr. Air Reduction Co., Stamford, Conn., 1946-48; design engr. Tex. Co.-N.Y., N.Y.C., 1948-50; devel. engr. Rohm & Haas Co., Bristol, Pa., 1950-52; asst. mgr. corp. devel. Lukens Steel Co., Coatsville, Pa., 1952-54; sect. mgr. research and devel. Sun Oil Co., Marcus Hook, Pa., 1954-59; asst. dir. research and engring. Sun Oil Co., Phila., 1959-62; pres. Avisun Corp., Phila., 1962-69; group v.p., dir., mem. exec. fin. com. Air Products & Chems., Inc., Allentown, Pa., 1969-78; exec. v.p. Air Products & Chems., Inc., 1978-80; pres., chief operating officer, dir. GAF Corp., 1980-81; founder Richard Fleming Assocs., Inc., mgmt. cons., 1981; pres., chief exec. officer Catalytica, Inc., 1985-91, also bd. dirs., 1985—; also bd. dirs. Catalytica Pharms.; bd. dirs., treas. Chem. Industry Inst. Toxicology, 1975-77, chmn. bd., 1977-81, vice chmn., 1986-97; chmn. bd. dirs. Modal Inc.; mgmt. bd. Single Site Catalysts, Inc., 1998—. Bd. dirs. Allentown Hosp., 1976-82; pres., chmn. bd. dirs. Lehigh Valley Hosp. Ctr., 1978-84, bd. dirs., 1984-91; bd. dirs. Lehigh Valley Health Network, 1992-97, emeritus, 1997—; bd. dirs., mem. steering com., exec. com. Am. Indsl. Health Coun., 1978-80; bd. dirs., mem. exec. com. Health East, 1981-92. With USNR, 1942-46. Mem. Am. Inst. Chem. Engrs., Am. Chem. Soc., Am. Mgmt. Assn., Chem. Mfrs. Assn. (vice chmn. chem. regulations adv. com. 1979-80). Home and Office: Windfields 7661 Beryl Rd Zionsville PA 18092-2302 also: Catalytica Inc 430 Ferguson Dr Bldg 1 Mountain View CA 94043-5215*

FLEMING, RICHARD H., finance executive; b. Milw., July 22, 1947; s. David M. and Mildred (Codere) F.; m. Diana Loane, Mar. 21, 1970; children: Douglas Codere, Petria Anne. BA, U. Pacific, 1969; MBA, Dartmouth, 1971. Fin. analyst Graco, Inc., Mpls., 1971-72, mgr. banking and fgn. exchange, 1972-73; fin. analyst Masonite Corp., Chgo., 1973-74, mgr. capital investment, 1974-77, asst. treas., 1977-82, treas., 1982-84, v.p. fin., chief fin. officer, 1985-89; dir. corp. fin. and asst. treas. USG Corp., Chgo., 1989-90, v.p., treas., 1991-94, v.p., CFO, 1994-95, sr. v.p., CFO, 1995-99, exec. v.p., CFO, 1999—; trustee USG Found., 1989—; bd. dirs. Columbus McKinnon Corp. Bd. dirs. Family Care Services Met. Chgo., 1977—, pres. 1983-86; bd. dirs. Child Welfare League Am., Washington, 1987—. Alumni fellow U. Pacific Sch. Bus. Adminstrn. and Pub. Policy, 1990. Home: 311 N Garfield Ave Hinsdale IL 60521-3723 Office: USG Corp PO Box 6721 125 S Franklin St Chicago IL 60680-6721

FLEMING, ROBBEN WRIGHT, retired educator; b. Paw Paw, Ill., Dec. 18, 1916; s. Edmunds Palmer Fleming and Emily Jeannette (Wheeler) Boutwell; children: Nancy Jo, James Edmund, Caroline Elizabeth. BA, Beloit Coll., 1938; LLB, U. Wis., 1941; hon. degree, Mich. State U., 1967, U. Mich., 1968, U. Wis., 1968, U. Ill., 1969, Ohio State U., 1972, Columbia U., 1974, Boston Coll., 1979. Sec., exch. com. lawyer Securities and Exchg. Commn., Washington, 1941-42; mediator Nat. War Labor Bd., Washington, 1942; with Nat. Housing Authority, Washington, 1946-47; asst. prof. U. Wis., Madison, 1947-52; dir. Inst. Lab. & Indsl. Rels., U. Ill., Urbana, 1952-58; prof. law U. Ill. Law Sch., Urbana, 1957-64; chancellor U. Wis., Madison, 1964-67; pres. U. Mich., Ann Arbor, 1967-79; pres. Corp. for Pub. Broadcasting, Washington, 1979-81; chmn. bd. Nat. Inst. for Dispute Resolution, Washington, 1981-88; cons. to fed. judge on desegregation of pub. higher edn., Ala., 1994—. Author: The Labor Arbitration Process, 1965, Tempests Into Rainbows - Managing turbulence, 1996. Capt. U.S. Army, 1943-46. Mem. Rotary (Paul Harris fellow 1997). Avocations: reading, golf. Home: 2108 Vinewood Blvd Ann Arbor MI 48104-2762

FLEMING, RONALD LEE, urban designer, administrator, preservation planner, environmental educator; b. L.A., May 13, 1941; s. Ree Overton and Elizabeth Ann (Ebner) F.; m. Renata von Tscharner, Nov. 9, 1978 (div. Nov. 1998); children: Severine von Tscharner, Siena Antonia von Tscharner, Reynolds Lombard von Tscharner. BA cum laude, Pomona Coll., 1963; M of City Planning, Harvard U., 1967. Urban planner in Boston office of Marshall, Kaplan, Gans and Kahn, San Francisco, 1969-71; townscape designer Cambridge, Mass., 1971-78; pres. Townscape Inst., Cambridge, 1979—; cons., lectr. townscape and planning issues throughout U.S.. Author: Saving Face: How Corporate Franchise Design can Respect Community Identity, 1994, Place Makers, 1981, 2d rev. edit. 1987, On Common Ground, 1982, Facade Stories, 1982; co-author: New Providence: A Changing American Cityscape, 1987; editor: Censored Laughter, 1976; contbr. articles to profl. jours. Founder, chmn. Cambridge Arts Coun., 1975-79; chmn. for Pub. Art, Mass., 1980-87; mem. adv. and standing com. Trustees of Reservations, Beverly, Mass., 1985-97; chmn. Boston chpt. Save Venice, 1993-96; chmn. bd. overseers Strawbery Banke, Portsmouth, N.H., 1980-84; bd. dirs. Victorian Soc. Phila., 1983-89; gov.'s appointee Mass. Hist. Com., 1986-90; co-founder Fleming Fellowships and Lecture Program on the built environment, Claremont Colls., 1985. Capt. Intelligence, U.S. Army, 5th Spec. Forces Group, 1966-68, Vietnam. State Dept. grantee, 1975; fellow Salzburg Seminars Am. Studies, Austria, 1978; recipient 1st prize Architecture and Planning, Columbia U. Urban Film Competition for Newburyport, A Measure of Change, 1975, Merit award Am. Soc. Landscape Architects, 1981, commendation NEA/Dept. Transp., 1981; nominated for Pulitzer prize Mass. Hist. Soc., 1982; winner EDRA/Places award for Urban Design, W. Radnor, Pa. Project, 1998. Fellow Royal Soc. Arts (London); mem. Mass. Hist. Soc., Soc. for Preservation New England Antiquities (past trustee), Mass. Hort. Soc. (past trustee), Inst. for Urban Design, Am. Inst. City Planners, Soc. Archtl. Historians, Scenic America (bd. dirs., sec.). Unitarian. Clubs: Somerset, Union Boat, Harvard (Boston), Club of Odd Volumes, Tavern (Boston); Century Assn., Knickerbocker (N.Y.C.), S.R.B.A. Newport. Home and Office: 8 Lowell St Cambridge MA 02138-4726

FLEMING, SAMUEL CROZIER, JR., health care publishing and consulting firm executive; b. Phila., Sept. 30, 1940; s. Samuel Crozier Sr. and Josephine Coverdale (Plowman) F.; m. Nancy Elizabeth McAdam, Sept. 7, 1963; children: David McAdam, Timothy Crozier. BChemE, Cornell U., 1963; MBA, Harvard U., 1967. Rsch. engr. DuPont Co., 1963; mgmt. cons. Arthur D. Little, Inc., 1967-90, v.p., 1977-83, sr. v.p., 1983-90; pres., CEO ADL Impact Svcs., 1976-79; pres., CEO Arthur D. Little Decision Resources, 1979-83, chmn. bd. dirs., 1983-90; CEO Decision Resources, Inc., Waltham, Mass., 1990—; also bd. dirs., chmn. Decision Resources, Inc., Waltham, 1990—; mem. chem. engring. adv. coun. Cornell U., Ithaca, N.Y., 1989-96, mem. Engring. Coll. coun., 1996—, univ. trustee, 1997—; bd. dirs. Cambridgeport Bank, Cambridge, The Picker Inst., Boston, ImmuLogic Pharm. Corp., Waltham, Charlesbridge Pub., Watertown, Mass.; chmn., bd. dirs. Opinion Rsch. Corp., Princeton, N.J., 1984-88; trustee Standish Ayer & Wood Investment Trust, Boston, 1986—. Vestry Trinity Ch., Boston, 1980-84; chmn. bd. dirs. New Eng. Bapt. Health Care Corp., 1984-90, New Eng. Bapt. Hosp., Boston, 1985-91; bd. dirs. Care Group, Inc., 1996—, Pathway Health Network, Inc., Boston, 1994-96. 1st lt. U.S. Army, 1963-65. Mem. The Country Club (Brookline, Mass.), Harvard Club of Boston, Lake Sunapee Yacht Club, Lake Sunapee Country Club, Cornell Club of N.Y. Episcopalian. Avocation: investments. Home: 61 Meadowbrook Rd Weston MA 02493-2407 Office: Decision Resources Inc 1100 Winter St Bay Colony Waltham MA 02451-1227

FLEMING, SAMUEL M., banker; b. Franklin, Tenn., Apr. 29, 1908; s. Samuel M. and Cynthia Graham (Cannon) F.; m. Josephine Cliffe, Dec. 30, 1930 (dec.); childred: Joanne Cliffe Fleming Hayes, Daniel Milton (dec.); m. Valerie Ellis Johnson, Oct. 17, 1983. Student, Battle Ground Acad., 1919-24; A.B., Vanderbilt U., 1928. Asst. credit mgr. N.Y. (City) Trust Co., 1928-31; with Third Nat. Bank, Nashville, 1931—; dir. Third Nat. Bank, 1947—, pres., 1950-70, chmn. bd., 1970—, chmn. trust bd., 1973-83; cons. in field. Trustee Battle Ground Acad.; past chmn. bd. trustees Vanderbilt U. Served to lt. comdr. USNR, 1942-45. Mem. Am. Bankers Assn. (pres. 1961), SAR, Sigma Alpha Epsilon (past hon. eminent supreme archon). Presbyterian (elder). Clubs: Nat. Golf (Augusta, Ga.), Cumberland, Belle Meade Country, Nashville City Club, Richland Golf (Nashville), Honors Course (Chattanooga), Links, Univ. (N.Y.C. and Nashville), U.S. Seniors Golf, Gulf Stream Golf, Bath and Tennis (Delray Beach, Fla.), Everglades, Seminole Golf, Bath and Tennis, Governors (Palm Beach, Fla.), Garden of the Gods Golf (Colorado Springs, Colo.), Golf of Tenn. (Nashville). Home: 810 Jackson Blvd Nashville TN 37205-4520 also: 365 N County Rd Palm Beach FL 33480-3607 Office: PO Box 305110 Nashville TN 37230-5110

FLEMING, SIDNEY HOWELL, psychiatrist, educator; b. Lubbock, Tex., May 22, 1938; d. McKinley and Wilna Adrian (Simer) Howell; m. J.D. Fleming, Jr., June 28, 1960; 1 child, Julie Adrianne. BA, Agnes Scott Coll., Decatur, Ga., 1959; MD, Emory U., 1964. Diplomate Am. Bd. Psychiatry and Neurology. Intern Emory U./Va. Hosp., Atlanta, 1964-65, resident in psychiatry, 1965-68; mem. faculty Emory U. Med. Sch., 1968—, assoc. prof. psychiatry, 1975—; chmn. Pres.'s Commn. on Status of Women, 1984-85. Grantee NIMH, 1969-71. Mem. Am. Coll. Psychiatry, Am. Psychiat. Assn. (editl. bd. on curriculum on psychol. of women and men 1979-81, com. on women 1985-90), Assn. Acad. Psychiatrists, Ga. Psychiat. Assn., Med. Assn. Ga., Druid Hills Club. Republican. Address: 1248 Oxford Rd NE Atlanta GA 30306-2610

FLEMING, STEVEN ROBERT, minister; b. San Bernardino, Calif., Apr. 30, 1951; s. Robert Ellsworth and Marie Claire (Kitzmiller) F.; m. Brenda Kay Cross, June 9, 1973. BA with honors, U. Md., 1972; D. Ministry, Union Theol. Sem., Richmond, Va., 1976. Ordained to ministry Presbyn. Ch. U.S.A., 1976. Assoc. pastor 1st Presbyn. Ch., Ft. Smith, Ark., 1976-79; pastor Shippensburg (Pa.) Presbyn. Ch., 1979-85; interim assoc. pastor Paxton Presbyn. Ch., Harrisburg, Pa., 1986-87; sr. pastor 1st United Presbyn. Ch., Westminster, Md., 1987-97; regional rep. bd. pensions Presbyn. Ch. USA, 1998—; mem. Carlisle Presbytery; seminar leader; alumni bd. dirs., Union Theol. Sem. in Va., 1995-98. Contbr. articles to profl. jours.; contrbr. Abingdon Preaching Annuals. Bd. dirs. Shippensburg U. Campus Ministry, 1979-85. Recipient Common Ground award Shippensburg U., 1983. Mem. Alban Inst., Am. Acad. Ministry. Republican. E-mail: sfleming@pensions.org. Avocations: photography, gardening, computers, travel, genealogy. Address: 975 Wayne Ave Ste 101 Chambersburg PA 17201-3895

FLEMING, SUSAN, social worker. Social worker United Cerebral Palsy S.W. Ill., dir.; exec. dir. Recreation Coun. Greater St. Louis, 1991—; conf. planner, presenter Assn. Severe Handicaps Mo.; instr. continuing edn. Meramac C.C., 1996; planner, presenter Alliance Inclusion in Edn., 1995-96; asst. fundraiser St. Louis Assn. Retarded Citizens and Therapeutic Horsemanship, 1995; sec. bd. dirs. Tech. Access Bd. Vol. Vincent House, Doorways; block capt. Op. Safe St. Mem. Mo. Park's and Recreation Assn. (Citation of Merit 1994). Office: Recreation Coun Greater St Louis 200 S Hanley Rd Ste 518 Saint Louis MO 63105-3415

FLEMING, SUZANNE MARIE, university official, chemistry educator; b. Detroit, Feb. 4, 1927; d. Albert T. and Rose E. (Smiley) F. BS, Marygrove Coll., 1957; MS, U. Mich., 1960, PhD, 1963. Joined Congregation of Sisters Servants of Immaculate Heart of Mary, Roman Catholic Commn. for Cmty., 1945. Chmn. natural sci. div. Marygrove Coll., Detroit, 1970-75, v.p., dean, 1975-78, acad. v.p., 1978-80; asst. v.p. acad. affairs Eastern Mich. U., Ypsilanti, 1980-82, acting assoc. v.p. acad. affairs, 1982-83; provost, acad. v.p. Western Ill. U., Macomb, 1983-86; vice chancellor U. Wis., Eau Claire, 1986-89; freelance writer, 1989—; vis. scholar U. Mich., 1989—; pres. Mich. Coll. Chemistry Tchrs. Assn., 1975; councilor Mich. Inst. Chemists, 1973-77; bd. dirs. Nat. Ctr. for Rsch. to Improve Postsecondary Teaching and Learning, 1988-90. Contbr. articles to profl. publs. NIH research grantee, 1966-69. Fellow Am. Inst. Chemists; mem. Am. Chem. Soc. (councilor, Detroit 1980-83, Petroleum Research Fund grantee, 1962-88), Am. Assn. Higher Edn., Sigma Xi. Home and Office: 2888 Cascade Dr Ann Arbor MI 48104-6659

FLEMING, SYLVIA SHACKELFORD, secondary school educator, writer; b. Philadelphia, Miss., Feb. 1, 1943; d. John William and Annie Ruth (Fulton) Shackelford. BS, U. So. Miss., 1973; MEd, Miss. State U., 1985, postgrad., 1985-86. Cert. libr. sci. tchr., English edn., educationally handicapped elem. edn., supervision, adminstrn., provisional educator evaluator, Miss. Adj. tch. Am. lit., short story and essay, novel classic Columbia (Miss.) City Schs., 1973-77, chmn. English dept., 1974-76; resource tchr. sr. English, composition and rsch. Leake County Schs., Edinburg, Miss., 1982-83; resource tchr., spl. edn. K-8 Bur. Indian Affairs, Philadelphia, Miss., 1983-85; tchr. spl. edn. English at jr. high sch. Neshoba County Schs., Philadelphia, Miss., 1985-93, tchr. English, accelerated, 12th advanced placement, 1993-97, STAR tchr., 1998, 99; instr. freshman English composition East Ctr. C.C., Decatur, Miss., 1991-92; tchr., cons. Miss. Writing and Thinking Project, Starkville, 1988-97; literacy dir. Winston Bapt. Assn., Louisville, Miss., 1992-93; presenter in field. Tchr. Sunday sch. Bapt. Ch., Philadelphia and Louisville, Miss., 1982-97; tchr. Bible study Ladies Home Bible Study, Philadelphia and Louisville, 1990-97; assoc. interfaith witness Bapt. Conv. Home Mission Bd., Atlanta, 1986-97; dir. interfaith witness Winston County Bapt. Assn., Louisville, 1992-93. Grantee Allies for Edn., 1995, 96, 97, Weyerhaeuser, 1996, BellSouth, 1996, 97. Fellow Miss. Writing and Thinking Inst.; mem. Nat. Coun. Tchrs. English, Miss. Coun. Tchrs. English (presenter). Republican. Avocations: piano, reading.

FLEMING, THOMAS A., academic affairs assistant director, former special education educator. Spl. asst. to the provost Ea. Mich. U., Ypsilanti, Mich. Recipient State Tchr. of Yr. Spl. Edn. award Mich., 1992; named Tchr. of Yr. Mich., 1991, Nat. Tchr. of Yr., 1992. Office: Ea Mich U 106 Welch Hall Ypsilanti MI 48197-2214

FLEMING, THOMAS J., editor, publishing executive; b. Superior, Wis., 1945. BA in Greek, Charleston Coll., 1967; PhD in Classics, U. N.C., 1973. Prof. classics Miami U., Charleston (S.C.) Coll., Shaw U., Raleigh, N.C.; founding editor The Southern Partisan, 1979-83; mng. editor Chronicles, Rockford, Ill., 1984-85, editor, 1985—, pres., 1997—. Author: The Politics of Human Nature, 1987. Office: The Rockford Inst Chronicles 928 N Main St Rockford IL 61103-7061*

FLEMING, THOMAS JAMES, writer; b. Jersey City, July 5, 1927; s. Thomas James and Katherine (Dolan) F.; m. Alice Mulcahey, Jan. 19, 1951; children: Alice, Thomas, David, Richard. A.B., Fordham U., 1950; postgrad., Sch. Social Work, 1950-51. Reporter Yonkers (N.Y.) Herald Statesman, 1951; asst. to Fulton Oursler, 1951-52, lit. executor estate, 1953; asso. editor Cosmopolitan mag., 1954-58, exec. editor, 1959-61; writer, 1961—. Author: Now We Are Enemies, 1960, All Good Men, 1961, The

God of Love, 1963, Beat the Last Drum, 1963, One Small Candle, 1964, King of the Hill, 1966, A Cry of Whiteness, 1967, West Point, The Men and Times of the U.S. Military Academy, 1969, The Man from Monticello, 1969, Romans Countrymen Lovers, 1969, The Sandbox Tree, 1970, The man Who Dared the Lightning, 1971, The Forgotten Victory, 1973, The Good Shepherd, 1974, 1776: Year of Illusions, 1975, Liberty Tavern, 1976, Rulers of the City, 1977, New Jersey, 1977, Promises to Keep, 1978, A Passionate Girl, 1979, The Officers' Wives, 1981, Dreams of Glory, 1983, The Spoils of War, 1985, Time and Tide, 1987, Downright Fighting: The Story of Cowpens, 1988, Over There, 1992, Loyalties: A Novel of World War II, 1994, Remember The Morning, 1997, Liberty! The American Revolution, 1997, The Wages of Fame, 1998, Lights Along the Way, 1998, Hours of Gladnes Duel: Alexander Hamilton, Aaron Bull and the Future of America, 1999; editor Affectionately Yours, George Washington, 1967, Benjamin Franklin, A Biography in His Own Words, 1972, The Living Land of Lincoln, 1980; contbr.: Reader's Companion to American History, 1991, Young Reader's Companion to American History, 1991, Past Imperfect: History According to the Movies, 1995; also various TV scripts, articles, short stories; cons. (movie) The American Revolution The History Channel, 1994; prin. commentator Long Journey Home-The Irish in America, 1998. Chmn. N.Y. Am. Revolution Round Table, 1970-81. Recipient Achievement award in communication arts Fordham U., 1961, Encaenia award, 1965; Mass Media award NCCJ, 1963; Christopher award, 1970; Colonial Dames Am. ann. book award, 1970, 72; award of merit Am. Assn. for State and Local History, 1974; Fiction award Nat. Cath. Press Assn., 1974; Best Book award Am. Revolution Round Table, 1975, 97. Fellow N.J. Hist. Soc., Soc. Am. Historians; mem. Am. PEN (pres. 1971-73), The Century Assn. Home: 315 E 72nd St New York NY 10021-4625

FLEMING, THOMAS MICHAEL, artist, educator; b. Phila, May 12, 1951; s. Thomas Joseph and Eleanor Virginia (Huston) F.; m. Kristin Karen Wigley, Oct. 29, 1977 (dec. Jan. 1980); m. Beverly Jean Folgert, Sept. 25, 1987. AA with honors, Harrisburg (Pa.) Community Coll., 1972; BFA with hons, Pa. State U., 1975; MFA, U. Minn., 1978. Art instr. U. Wis., Wausau, 1978-84, asst. prof., 1985-89, assoc. prof., 1990-97, prof., 1998—; dir., co-founder SoHo Studio Ctr., N.Y.C.; pres. Art Shoot, N.Y.C.; artistic program cons. Anglo-American Workshops, N.Y.C., 1988-89; art. dir. :W/ Co., Wis.; founder Art NYC .com, 1996. Represented in permanent collections Musee Des Arts, Lausanne, Switzerland, Corning (N.Y.) Mus., Internat. Glasmuseum, Ebeltoft, Denmark. One of 100 Art Judges U.S. News and World Report's Best of America, 1990. Grantee U. Wis., 1981, 82, 84, 86, 87, 91, Wis. Arts Bd. Madison, 1985, 91. Mem. Glass Art Soc., Wis. Acad. Scis. Arts and Letters, Internat. Sculpture Assn., Wis. Painters and Sculptors, Artist Space N.Y. Home: 518 S 7th Ave Wausau WI 54401-5362

FLEMING, TOMMY WAYNE, lawyer; b. Canyon, Tex., Nov. 13, 1941; s. Benjamin Dalby and Willie Mildred (Vineyard) F.; m. Sally Ann Moore, Nov. 30, 1968; children: Benjamin Dalby II, Hunter Leah. Student, West Tex. State U., 1960-61; BBA, U. Tex., 1964, JD, 1966. Bar: Tex. 1969, U.S. Dist. Ct. (so. dist.) Tex. 1971, U.S. Supreme Ct. 1978, U.S. Ct. Appeals (5th cir.) 1983. Asst. dist. atty. Office Dist. Atty., Amarillo, Tex., 1969-70; asst. criminal dist. atty. Cameron County Criminal Dist. Atty.'s Office, Brownsville, Tex., 1970-72; ptnr. Wiech, Lewis & Fleming, Brownsville, 1972-74, Wiech, Fleming, Hamilton & Uribe, Brownsville, 1974-82, Wiech & Black, Brownsville, 1982-89, Atlas & Hall, Brownsville, 1989-94, Fleming, Hewitt & Olvera, Brownsville, 1994-98, Fleming & Olvera, Brownsville, 1998—; mem. State Grievance Oversight Com., 1983—. Chmn. Brownsville Cmty. Health Clinci, 1978-79. 1st lt. U.S. Army, 1966-69. Fellow Tex. Bar Found. (life, bd. dirs. 1984-87); mem. Tex. Assn. Bank Counsel, State Bar Tex. (bd. dirs. 1981-84), Cameron County bar Assn. (bd. dirs. 1972-79, pres. 1979-80), Brownsville Hist. Assn. (bd. dirs. 1977-80). Home: 915 Santa Ana Ave Rancho Viejo TX 78575-9749 Office: Fleming & Olvera Ste 102 1650 Paredes Line Rd Brownsville TX 78521

FLEMING, WENDELL HELMS, mathematician, educator; b. Guthrie, Okla., Mar. 7, 1928; s. James Lucian and Helen (Helms) F.; m. Florence Tatum, Apr. 4, 1948; children: Randall, Daniel, William. BS, Purdue U., 1948, MS, 1949, D honoris causa, 1991; PhD, U. Wis., 1951. Mathematician RAND Corp., 1951-55, cons., 1960-65; asst. prof. Purdue U., 1955-58; mem. faculty Brown U., 1958—, prof. math., 1963—, prof. applied math., 1969-95, chmn. dept., 1965-68, 82-85, 1991-94; prof. emeritus, 1995—. Author: Functions of Several Variables, 1965, (with R.W. Rishel) Deterministic and Stochastic Optimal Control, 1975, (with H.M. Soner) Controlled Markov Processes and Viscosity Solutions, 1992; editor SIAM Rev. NSF fellow, 1968-69; Guggenheim fellow, 1976-77. Mem. Am. Math. Soc. (chmn. com. on employment and ednl. policy 1975-77, Steele prize 1987), Soc. Indsl. and Applied Math. (Reid prize 1994), Am. Acad. Arts and Sci. Home: 3 Colley Ct Barrington RI 02806-4005 Office: Brown U Div Applied Math Providence RI 02912

FLEMING, WILLIAM HARE, surgeon; b. Columbus, Ohio, May 1, 1935; s. William Bush and Charlote (Hare) F.; m. Carolyn Etta Swift, June 25, 1959 (div. May 1978); children: Alice Fleming Guzick, William Swift, Edgar Hare. BA, Yale U., 1957; MD, Columbia U., 1961. Diplomate Am. Bd. Surgery, Am. Bd. Thoracic Surgery. Intern in surgery Presbyn. Hosp., N.Y.C., 1961-62, resident in surgery, 1962-66; resident in thoracic surgery Manhattan VA Hosp., N.Y.C., 1967, Harlem Hosp., N.Y.C., 1967, Presbyn. Hosp., N.Y.C., 1968; asst. prof. Emory U., Atlanta, 1971-76; chief thoracic surgery VA Hosp., Atlanta, 1971-76; adj. sr. research scientist Ga. Inst. Tech., Atlanta, 1974-76; assoc. prof. surgery U. Nebr. Med. Ctr., Omaha, 1976-80, prof. surgery, 1980-06, chief thoracic surgery, 1980-92; pres. bd. dirs. Profl. Fees Office Nebr. Clinicians Group, Omaha, 1985-91. Contbr. articles over 70 articles to profl. jours. Served to maj. U.S. Army, 1969-70, Vietnam. Decorated Bronze Star. Fellow ACS, Am. Coll. Cardiology, Am. Acad. Pediatrics; mem. AMA (Physicians Recognition award 1988), Am. Assn. Thoracic Surgery, Soc. Thoracic Surgeons. Republican. Presbyterian. Club: The Omaha. Avocations: tennis, sailing, windsurfing, waterskiing. Home: 2039 S 85th Ave Omaha NE 68124-2127

FLEMING, WILLIAM SLOAN, energy, environmental and technology company executive; b. Long Beach, Calif., Aug. 13, 1937; s. William Sloan and Helen Jean (Disler) F.; m. Jacquline M. Carrio, Mar. 9, 1960; children: Katherine A., Kimberly A. BSME, Calif. Maritime Acad., 1958; MBA, Syracuse U., 1970. Commd. ensign USN, 1958, advanced through grades to lt., 1967, attack pilot, 1958-67, disabled in the line of duty, ret., 1967; mech. engr. Carrier Corp., Syracuse, N.Y., 1967-70; regional sales mgr. Rheem Mfg., Atlanta, 1970-71; market devel. supr. Owens Corning Fiberglas, Toledo, 1971-73; pres. W.S. Fleming & Assocs., Inc., Syracuse, 1975-86; pres. The Fleming Group, Syracuse, 1986-87, CEO, chmn. bd., 1987—; bus. devel. mgr., energy systems group Sci. Applications Internat. Corp./The Fleming Group, Syracuse, 1994-96; bus. devel. mgr. Sci. Applications Internat. Corp./Energy Systems Group, 1996-97; exec. v.p. JacWil Svcs., Cazenovia, N.Y., 1997—; pres. Enterlog Systems, Inc., Syracuse, 1985-94; chmn. bd. Assn. Intelligent System Tech., Inc., Syracuse, 1986-90. Contbr. articles to profl. jours.; author singer energy simulation computer program (SEE), 1975-80. Recipient Energy awards Cen. N.Y., 1981. Fellow ASHRAE (chmn. tech. com. 6.7, solar energy utilization 1984-86, chmn. tech. com. 9.6, sys. energy utilization 1981-83, chmn. ad hoc com. 90, energy stds 1983-84, chmn. nat. program com. 1985-86, mem. edn. coun. 1989-90, rsch. and tech. com. 1991-95, chmn. spl. publs. com. 1998-99); mem. Assn. Energy Engrs. (charter, 1 of 16 in Hall of Fame), DAV, Am. Legion, Ret. Officers Assn. Roman Catholic. Avocations: skiing, boating, homework. Office: JacWil Svcs 4571 E Lake Rd Cazenovia NY 13035-9350

FLEMING, WILLIAM WRIGHT, JR., pharmacology educator; b. Washington, Jan. 30, 1932; s. William Wright and Esme (Reeder) F.; m. Dolores D. Atchison, Sept. 1, 1952; children: Lisa Marie, Jennifer Amelia, David William. AB cum laude, Harvard U., 1954; PhD (Procter fellow), Princeton U., 1957. Mem. faculty W.Va. U. Med. Ctr., Morgantown, 1960—, prof. pharmacology, 1966—, chmn. dept., 1966-86, Mylan Chmn. of Pharmacology and Toxicology, 1986—; vis. prof. U. Melbourne, Australia, 1969, St. George's Hosp. Med. Sch. U. London, 1978, Flinders U., Adelaide, Australia, 1985, 87, U. Adelaide, 1987; cons. Mead Johnson Rsch. Ctr., Evansville, Ind., 1970-77; mem. pharmacology-toxicology rsch. program. Nat. Inst. Gen. Med. Scis., NIH, 1973-77, chmn., 1975-77; mem. drug abuse rsch. rev. com. Nat. Inst. Drug Abuse, 1985-89; mem. pharmacology study sect., div. rsch. grants NIH, 1990-94. Mem. editl. bd. Jour. Pharmacology and Exptl. Therapeutics, 1966-85, Life Scis., 1978-90; contbr. articles to profl. jours. USPHS postdoctoral fellow Harvard U., 1957-60; Fogarty sr. internat. fellow, 1978; recipient P.L. MacLachlan award excellence in teaching W.Va. U. Med. Sch., 1964, 67, 78, 89, 92, 97; named Outstanding Tchr., W.Va. U. Found., 1978. Mem. AAAS, Am. Soc. Pharmacology and Exptl. Therapeutics (councilor 1975-78, pres. 1981-82, chmn. bd publs. trustees 1984-90, Otto Krayer award 1986, Croker Meml. lectr. 1988, Torald Sollman award 1999), Assn. Med. Sch. Pharmacology (councilor 1977-79, treas. 1977-78, pres. 1986-88), Fedn. Am. Socs. for Exptl. Biology (dir. 1980-83), Internat. Union Pharmacology (del. 1980-83, 91-94, mem. internat. adv. com. for Congress of Pharmacology 1987, exec. com. 1994-98, pres. 1998—). Home: 27 Citadel Rd Morgantown WV 26505-3612 Office: WVa U Health Scis Ctr Dept Pharmacology Morgantown WV 26506

FLEMISTER, LAUNCELOT JOHNSON, physiologist, educator; b. Atlanta, Dec. 11, 1913; s. Launcelot Johnson and Willie (Moore) F.; m. Sarah Elizabeth Culbreth, Dec. 25, 1941 (dec. Feb. 1990); m. Mildred Beckham, Feb., 1993. A.B., Duke, 1935, M.A., 1939, Ph.D., 1941. Instr. Med. Sch. George Washington U., 1941-42; research asso. Sharp & Dohme, Phila., 1946-47; asst. prof. Swarthmore Coll., 1947-51, asso. prof., 1951-66, prof. zoology, 1966—; Cons. NSF, 1963-64. Cons. NSF, 1963-64. Lt. USNR, 1942-46. Fulbright fellow Peru, 1959-60. Fellow AAAS; mem. Am. Physiol. Soc., Am. Soc. Zoologists, Sigma Xi, Delta Tau Delta. Office: 36 Deerfield Rd Hilton Head Island SC 29926-1939

FLEMM, EUGENE WILLIAM, concert pianist, educator, conductor, chamber musician; b. Rahway, N.J., Jan. 16, 1944; s. Julius Eugene and Helen Frances (May) F. MusB, Coll.-Conservatory of Music, U. Cin., 1965, MusM, 1972, D in Mus. Arts, 1990. Music dir., condr. Cin. Civic Orch., 1979-83; assoc. prof., chmn. music dept. Mid. Ga. Coll., Cochran, 1983-90; concert pianist, studio tchr. Dunedin, Fla., 1990—; founder, condr. Mid. Ga. Choral Union, 1983-90; chamber musician, founder, dir. The Omega soloists, Dunedin, 1987, Nuveau Ensemble piano quartet, It Takes Three: music dir., condr. Suncoast Symphony Orch., 1996—; ch. musician; bandmaster St. Petersburg Jr. Coll. Symphony Band; guest condr. Clearwater Cmty. Symphony Band; condr. Tampa Oratorio Soc., 1998—; faculty Clearwater Christian Coll. and Fla. Arts Sch. European concert tours include Amsterdam, Baden, Barcelona, Berlin, Brussels, Edinburgh, Geneva, Glasgow, The Hague, Innsbruck, London, Lüneburg, Lucerne, Milan, Monza, Munich, Oslo, Paris, Prague, Püttlingen, Rotterdam, Saarbrücken, Salzburg, Trier, Vienna; solo recitals include Carnegie Recital Hall, Lincoln Ctr., Atlanta-High Mus. Art, Dayton Art Inst., Tampa Bay Performing Arts Ctr., Anderson House, Washington. Mem. Fla. Hist. Soc., Pi Kappa Lambda. Republican. Lutheran. Avocations: cycling, tennis, jogging, training, boating. Home and Office: 1615 Santa Anna Dr Dunedin FL 34698-3722

FLEMMING, ARLENE JOAN DANNENBERG, social worker, psychotherapist; b. N.Y.C., July 21, 1940; d. Melvin and Helen (Ruthberg) Gelb; m. Richard Bruce Dannenberg, Dec. 25, 1962; children: Susan Joy, David Grant. BA, SUNY, White Plains, 1984; MSW, Fordham U., 1988. Lic. social worker, N.Y. Intern in social work, alcoholism counselor The Sharing Community, Yonkers, N.Y., 1985-86, Yorktown Ctr. for Alcoholism and Psychotherapy, Yonkers, 1986-87; alcoholism counselor, psychotherapist Westchester County Med. Ctr., Yonkers, 1986-87; social worker, psychotherapist Middletown (N.Y.) Psychiat. Ctr., 1988-90; clin. social worker, psychotherapist Self Search Labs., Marlboro, N.Y., Newburgh, 1990—; asst. dir. primary care unit Coun. on Alcholism and Chem. Dependency Sullivan County Inc., Monticello, N.Y., 1998—; adj. prof., tutor, SUNY, Empire, State Coll., 1988-94; liaison profl. orgns. Am. Bd. Cert. Managed Care Providers, 1994. Mem. NASW, Mental Health Assn. Ulster County, N.Y. Fedn. Alcoholism and Chem. Dependency Counselors (pres. mid-Hudson region 1990-94, Counselor of Yr. award 1993, regional rep., 1994—, chair managed care com. 1994), Alcoholism and Substance Abuse Coun. Ulster County, Dutchess County Coun. Alcoholism and Chem. Dependency, Sullivan County Coun. on Alcoholism and Chem. Dependency, Alcoholism and Drug Abuse Coun. Orange County, Nat. Coun. Alcoholism and Other Drug Dependencies, Nat. Coun. Alcoholism and Other Drug Addictions Westchester, Rockland County Coun. on Alcoholism and Drug Addictions, N.Y. State Coun. on Alcholism and Other Drug Addictions, N.Y. Fed. Alcoholism and Substance Abuse Counselors, Hudson Valley Addictions Counselor's Assn., Nat. Assn. Alcoholism and Chem. Dependency Counselors (managed care com. 1994), Assn. Diagnostic Excellence and Brief Psychotherapy, N.Y. State Soc. Clin. Social Work Psychotherapists, Inc., Eastern Orange County C. of C. Republican. Avocations: target shooting, hand crafts, sketching, golf. E-mail: Arl108@aol.com. Fax: 1-888-522-4596. Home and Office: Ste 1180 56 N Plank Rd Newburgh NY 12550-2116 Office: Coun on Alcoholism & Chem Dependency Sullivan County Inc 17 Hamilton Ave Monticello NY 12701

FLEMMING, DAVID PAUL, biologist; b. Kittanning, Pa., Oct. 23, 1953; s. Paul Ross and Jeanne Marie (Seaton) F.; m. Diane Frances MacKenzie, Sept. 17, 1983; children: Daniel Robert, Peter David. BS in Biology, Grove City Coll., 1975; MS in Biology, Bowling Green State U., 1977. Child care worker George Jr. Rep., Grove City, Pa., 1978-79; park naturalist State of Pa.-McConnell's Mill State Park, Portersville, 1979; biologist sect. 7 U.S. Fish & Wildlife Svc., Washington, 1979-80, Atlanta, 1980-83; recovery coord. U.S. Fish & Wildlife Svc., Denver, 1983-87; biologist endangered species U.S. Fish & Wildlife Svc., Vero Beach, Fla., 1987-88; chief divsn. endangered species U.S. Fish & Wildlife Svc., Atlanta, 1988-96, chief ecol. svcs., 1997-98, ecol. svcs. supr. Area 2, 1998—. Contbg. author: Conservation and Resource Management, 1993. Asst. coach T-ball and soccer YMCA, Lawrenceville, Ga., 1991-92, premier soccer coach, Snellville, Ga., 1995—, USS Official, 1996—.

FLEMMING, STANLEY LALIT KUMAR, family practice physician, mayor, state legislator; b. Rosebud, S.D., Mar. 30, 1953; s. Homer W. and Evelyn C. (Misra) F.; m. Martha Susan Light, July 2, 1977; children: Emily Drisana, Drew Anil, Claire Elizabeth Misra. AAS, Pierce Coll., 1973; BS in Zoology, U. Wash., 1976; MA in Social Psychology, Pacific Luth. U., 1979; DO, Western U., 1985. Diplomate Am. Coll. Family Practice; cert. ATLS. Intern Pacific Hosp. Long Beach (Calif.), 1985-86; resident in family practice Pacific Hosp. Long Beach, 1986-88; fellow in adolescent medicine Children's Hosp. L.A., 1988-90; clin. preceptor Family Practice Residency Program Calif. Med. Ctr., U. So. Calif., L.A., 1989—; clin. instr. Sch. Medicine U. So. Calif., L.A., 1989-90; clin. instr. Western U. Health Sci., Pomona, Calif., 1989-90; clin. asst. prof. Family Medicine Western U. Health Sci., Pomona, 1987—; exam. commr., expert examiner Calif. Osteo. Med. Bd., 1987-89; med. dir. Cmty. Health Care Delivery System Pierce County, Tacoma, Wash., 1990—; mayor City of University Place, Wash.; clin. instr. U. Wash. Sch. Medicine, 1990—; bd. dirs. Calif. State Bd. Osteo. Physicians Examiners, 1989—, cons., 1989. Mayor, City of University Place, Wash. Col. M.C., U.S. Army, 1976—. Named one of Outstanding Young Men of Am., U.S. Jaycees, 1983, 85, Intern of Yr. Western U. Health Sci. Coll., 1986, Resident of Yr., Greater Long Beach Assn., 1988, Alumnus of Yr., Pierce Coll., 1993, 97; recipient Pumerantz-Weiss award, 1985. Mem. Fedn. State Bds. Licensing, Am. Osteopathic Assn., Am. Acad. Family Practice, Soc. Adolescent Medicine, Assn. Military Surgeons U.S., Assn. U.S. Army (chpt. pres.), Soc. Am. Military Engrs. (chpt. v.p.), Calif. Med. Assn., Wash. Osteopathic Med. Assn. (Physician of Yr. 1993), Calif. Family Practice Soc., Long Beach Med. Assn. (com. mem.), N.Y. Acad. Sci., Calif. Med. Review Inc., Sigma Sigma Phi, Am. Legion. Episcopalian. Home: 7619 Chambers Creek Rd W University Place WA 98467 Office: Family Health Ctr University Place WA 98466

FLESHER, MARGARET COVINGTON, corporate communications consultant; b. San Angelo, Tex., July 29, 1944; d. Charles C. and Helen Irene (Little) F.; m. Alexander Ribaroff, Dec. 11, 1976 (div. June 1988). BA in Polit. Sci., Vassar Coll., 1966. Assoc. editor Harcourt Brace Inc., N.Y.C., 1966-74; prodr. Guidance Assocs. subsidiary of Harcourt Brace, N.Y.C., 1974-76; freelance writer, editor London, 1976-81; sr. editor Franklin Watts, Inc., N.Y.C., 1981-85; pres. The Westport (Conn.) Pub. Group, 1985-89; coord. cmty. rels. Texaco Inc., White Plains, N.Y., 1989-91, sr. coord. media rels., 1991-93; contbg. editor Texaco Inc., White Plains, 1993-97; sr. bus. deve. cons. De.Ditte & Touche, Wilton, Conn., 1998—. Author: Mexico and the United States Today: Issues Between Neighbors, 1985, New Leaves: A Journal for the Suddenly Single, 1987. Mem. The Assn. for Women in Comm. (Westchester chpt. bd. dirs., v.p. profl. devel. 1994-95, Clarion award 1995, Fairfield County chpt. pres. 1986-88), Fairfield County Pub. Rels. Assn. (bd. dirs. 1991-92), Internat. Assn. of Bus. Communicators, Conn. Press Club (v.p. programs 1998-99). Republican. Avocations: hiking, yoga, photography, gardening. Office: 10 Westport Rd Wilton CT 06897

FLETCHER, ANTHONY L., lawyer; b. Washington, Dec. 12, 1935; s. Robert J. and Lyndell (Pickett) F.; m. Juliana Schump, Sept. 3, 1960 (div. 1977); children: Leigh Anne Grinstead, Kristine Marie Giffin, Julie Bowen Cimino; m. Zelda L. Fletcher, Mar. 30, 1986. BA, Princeton U., 1957; JD, Harvard U., 1962. Bar: N.Y. 1963, U.S. Ct. Appeals (2d cir.) 1966, U.S. Ct. Appeals (7th cir.) 1966, U.S. Supreme Ct. 1966, U.S. Ct. Appeals (3d cir.) 1969, U.S. Ct. Appeals (5th cir.) 1973, U.S. Ct. Appeals (1st cir.) 1981, U.S. Ct. Appeals (9th cir.) 1983. Assoc. Simpson, Thacher & Bartlett, N.Y.C., 1962-71; assoc. Conboy, Hewitt, O-Brien & Boardman, N.Y.C., 1971-74, ptnr., 1974-86; ptnr. Hunton & Williams, N.Y.C., 1986-97; prin. Fish & Richardson P.C., N.Y.C., 1997—. Editor-in-chief Trademark Reporter, 1982-84; contbr. articles to profl. jours. With U.S. Army, 1957-59. Mem. Internat. Trademark Assn. (bd. dirs. N.Y.C. 1983-85), Princeton Club. Episcopalian. Office: Fish & Richardson PC 45 Rockefeller Plz Fl 28 New York NY 10111-2889

FLETCHER, BETTY B., federal judge; b. Tacoma, Mar. 29, 1923. B.A., Stanford U., 1943; LL.B., U. Wash., 1956. Bar: Wash. 1956. Mem. firm Preston, Thorgrimson, Ellis, Holman & Fletcher, Seattle, 1956-1979; judge U.S. Ct. Appeals (9th cir.), Seattle, 1979—, sr. judge, 1998-. Mem. ABA (Margaret Brent award 1992), Wash. State Bar Assn., Am. Law Inst., Fed. Judges Assn. (past pres.), Order of Coif, Phi Beta Kappa. Office: US Ct Appeals 9th Cir 1010 5th Ave Ste 1000 Seattle WA 98104-1130

FLETCHER, CARLOS ALFREDO TORRES, video and film production company executive; b. Caracas, Venezuela, Oct. 31, 1959; came to U.S., 1985; s. Carmelo Torres and Miriam Fletcher; m. Patricia Aguilar, Sept. 10, 1988. BS, Cristo Rey, Caracas, 1977; grad., TV and Radio Acad., Caracas, 1981; student, Monterrey Inst. Tech., Mexico City, 1983-85. Editor, cameraman Video Sistema Taurino, Caracas, 1979-82; corr. XHDF TV, Miami, Caracas, 1980—, Venezolana de Television, Miami, Fla., Mex., 1980—; gen. mgr. Estudios Televisivos Internat., Mex., 1982-85; pres. Estudios Televisivos Internat., Miami, 1985—; distbn. agt. Producciones Princess, 1991; tech. dir. Planet Media, Coral Gables, Fla., 1999—; cameraman Colombian TV, 1988; cons., producer Las Americas Horse Race Track, Mexico City, 1983-85. Cameraman, editor (documentary) Latin Tours, 1980; dir.: (documentaries) Cesar Giron, 1981, Un Caminante..Juan Pablo II, 1987; videographer Sports in Mexico City, 1982 (UNESCO award); videographer: Hablando Ingles, 1991; tech. dir. (video mag.) Muscle Flex, 1990-91; dir. (video mag.) Los Toros en el Mundo, 1990; editor (video mag.) Handguns and Home Survival, 1988; video producer XEIPN-TV, Mexico City, 1984; producer (film) Mortal Contact, 1995. Mem. Sindicato Profesional de trabajadores de la industria de la Radio, Cine TV del D.F. y Edo, Miranda. Roman Catholic. Avocation: tennis. E-mail addresses: torrec@idt.net, catfletcher@hotmail.com. Home and Office: Estudios Televisivos Internat 6890 Bamboo St Miami Lakes FL 33014-2942 Other: Planet Media 2100 Coral Way Coral Gables FL 33145

FLETCHER, CATHY ANN, auditor; b. Barnesville, Ga., Aug. 23, 1949; d. John James and Dorothy Lee (Banks) Fletcher; 1 child, Lisa Faye. Student, Ohio State U., 1969-70; AS, Mass. Bay Community Coll., 1982; AS, Northeastern U., Boston, 1984, BS, 1984; MA in HumanResources Mgmt. Emmanuel Coll., Boston, 1993. Mail clk. Fed. Reserve Bank, Boston, 1971-72; office mgr. Breckenridge Sportswear, Boston, 1973-74; asst. dir. Whittier Street Health Ctr., Boston, 1974-81; sec. to dir. Northeastern U., 1981-84; auditor Def. Contract Audit Agy. N.E. Region, Boston, 1984—; sec., bd. dirs. Boston Tenant Policy Coun., 1977-79; mgr. northeastern region Fed. Women's Program, 1989—; mem. adv. bd. DCAA EEO, 1989—; fin. sec. Disciples Baptist Ch., 1999—. Author: Softball Team Book, 1975. V.p., bd. dirs. Bromley Heath Tenant Mgmt. Corp., Jamaica Plain, Mass., 1976-91; mem. fund-raising com. Com. to Elect Jesse Jackson Pres., Boston, 1984; apptd. fed. women program coordinator State of Mass., 1988; mem. women's opportunity com. Boston Fed. Exec. Bd., 1990—, mem. women's coun., 1994—, mem. diversity com., 1997—; bd. dirs. Bromley Health Tenant Mgmt. Corp., Jamaica Plain, Mass., 1997—; past mem. Women's Ednl. Indsl. Union; past mem. NAACP; New Eng. regional mgr. Federally Employed Women, 1997—. Mem. NAFE, Profl. Coun., Nat. Tenants Orgn., Assn. Govt. Accts. (cert. govt. fin. mgr.), Federally Employed Women (treas. Greater Boston chpt. 1992-93, pres. 1994—, New Eng. Regional mgr. 1995—, rep. 1996—), Hawkettes Social (pres., past mem. profl. coun. 1989), Elks, Sigma Epsilon Rho. Avocations: reading, swimming, cooking, walking, travel. Office: Def Contract Audit Agy Boston Br Office 101 Merrimac St Ste 820A Boston MA 02114-4724

FLETCHER, CHARLES RICKEY, public affairs specialist; b. Gadsden, Ala., Nov. 18, 1950. B in Journalism and Mass Comm., N.Mex. State U., 1973. With USDA Forest Svc., Ft. Collins, Colo., 1974—. Editor, author: (newsletter) Rocky Mountain Update, 1970-95; (quarterly mag.) Forestry Research West, 1973— (Blue Pencil award 1981). Office: USDA Forest Svc 240 W Prospect Rd Fort Collins CO 80526-2002

FLETCHER, COLIN, author; b. Cardiff, Wales, Mar. 14, 1922; s. Herbert Reginald and Margaret Elizabeth (Williams) F.; m. Sonia Savage, 1946 (div.); m. Thelma Brad, 1959 (div.). Student, West Buckland Sch., North Devon, Eng. Mfr.'s rep. Nairobi, Kenya, 1947; mgr. hotel Kitale, 1947-48; farmer nr. Nakuru, 1948-52; road builder on estate nr. Inyanga, So. Rhodesia, 1952-53; with mining cos. Can., summers 1954-56; Santa Claus City of Paris Dept. Store, San Francisco, 1956; head janitor Polyclinic Hosp., San Francisco, 1957-58; writer Calif., 1958—. Author: The Thousand-Mile Summer, 1964, The Man Who Walked Through Time, 1968, The Complete Walker, 1968, The Winds of Mara, 1973, The New Complete Walker, 1974, The Man from the Cave, 1981, The Complete Walker III, 1984, The Secret Worlds of Colin Fletcher, 1989; (audio tape) Learn of the Green World, 1991; contbr. articles to Life, Field and Stream, Reader's Digest, Wilderness, other mags. in U.S., Can., Gt. Britain, Africa. Served to capt. Royal Marine Commandos, 1940-47. Office: Brandt & Brandt 1501 Broadway Ste 2310 New York NY 10036-5689*

FLETCHER, DARRIN GLEN, baseball player; b. Elmhurst, Ill., Nov. 3, 1966; s. Tom F. Student, U. Ill. With L.A. Dodgers, 1989-90, Phila. Phillies, 1990-91; catcher Montreal Expos, 1992-97, Toronto Blue Jays, 1997—. Named Nat. League All-Star Team, 1994. Office: Toronto Blue Jays, One Blue Jays Way Ste 3200; Toronto, ON Canada M5V 1J1*

FLETCHER, DOROTHY, community health and primary home care nurse; b. Bklyn., June 10, 1939; d. John and Agnes (Burgio) Duffy; m. Richard Fletcher, May 19, 1962; children: Richard Derek, Leslie. Diploma, St. Anne's Sch. Nursing, Fall River, Mass., 1961; cert., Union Hosp. Sch. Anesthesia, Fall River, 1969. RN, Mass. Staff nurse ICU, Charlton Meml. Hosp., Fall River, nurse anesthetist; primary nurse Olsten Health Care, Braintree, Mass., Profl. Respite, Bridgeport, Mass.; nurse evaluator State of Mass.; nurse cons. Index Corp.; vis. nurse Roger Williams Hosp., Providence, Primary Nurse, Bridgewater, Mass.; case mgr. Primary Health Svcs., Brockton, Mass.; supt. field nurses, ventilator instr., nursing staff, dir. vent program, clin. supr., nursing adminstr., reg. dir. Former instr. CPR, Somerset (Mass.) Fire Dept.; youth leader South Swansea Bapt. Ch. Home: 85 Beach Ave Somerset MA 02726-2832

FLETCHER, EDWARD ABRAHAM, engineering educator; b. Detroit, July 30, 1924; s. Morris and Lillian (Protes) F.; m. Roslyn Silber, June 15, 1948; children—Judith Ellen, Deborah Gail, Carolyn Ruth. B.S., Wayne State U., 1948; Ph.D. (DuPont fellow, AEC fellow), Purdue U., 1952. Head propellant chemistry and flame mechanics sect. NASA, Cleve., 1952-59; assoc. prof. U. Minn., Mpls., 1959-60; prof. U. Minn., 1960—, dir. grad. studies, 1965-86; vis. scientist Byelorussian Acad. Scis., 1964; vis. Fulbright prof. U. Poitiers, 1968; sr. Fulbright lectr. Weizmann Inst., Israel, 1989; vis. scientist, prof. Weizmann inst., 1991-97; cons. U.S. Dept. Commerce Study Waste Heat Mgmt., Minn. Energy Agy., No. States Power Co., Pub. Systems Rsch. Corp.; co-chmn. com. on fire resistant hydraulic fluids NRC-Nat.

Acad. Scis. Nat. Materials Adv. Bd., 1977-78; Participant adv. group for aero. rsch. and devel. NATO Confs. on supersonic combustion, 1960, 61. Editor: Isotopes, 1958-59. Bd. dirs. Minn. Com. for Technion, New Friends of Chamber Music. Served with USNR, 1943-46. Recipient NASA Tech. Devel. award, 1961; Outstanding Ski Patrolman of Western Region award Nat. Ski Patrol, 1969-70. Mem. Combustion Inst. (bd. advisers, sec. Central States sect. 1967-78, vice chmn. 1978-79, chmn. 1979-82), Am. Chem. Soc., AAAS, Internat. Solar Energy Soc., Am. Solar Energy Soc., Sigma Xi, Tau Beta Pi, Pi Tau Sigma, Phi Lambda Upsilon. Home: 3909 Beard Ave S Minneapolis MN 55410-1042

FLETCHER, (ROBERT) ERNIE, congressman; b. Mt. Sterling, Ky., Nov. 12, 1952; m. Glenna Foster; children: Rachael, Benjamin. BS, U. Ky., 1974, MD with distinction, 1984. Physician Lexington, Ky.; CEO St. Joseph Med. Found., Lexington; congressman 6th Dist. Ky., 1999—; mem. Ho. Budget Com., Agr. Com., Com. on Edn. and the Workforce (vice chmn. subcom. on Employer-Employee Rels.); elected freshman liaison to the Ho. Leadership. Elected state rep. for the 78th Dist. Ky.; served on numerous coms. including the Ky. Commn. on Poverty and the Task Force on Higher Edn.; chosen by gov. to play an important leadership role in reforming Ky.'s ailing health care sys.; lay min. Porter Meml. Baptist Ch.; vol. in cmty. With USAF. Office: 1117 Longworth HOB Washington DC 20515*

FLETCHER, GEORGE P., law educator; b. 1939. B.A., U. Calif.-Berkeley, 1960; J.D., U. Chgo., 1964, M.C.L., 1965. Bar: Calif. 1970. Grad. fellow U. Freibur, Fed. Republic Germany, 1964-65; asst. prof. U. Fla. Law Sch., 1965-66, U. Wash., Seattle, 1966-69; acting prof. UCLA Law Sch., 1969-70, prof., after 1971; Charles Keller Beekman prof. law Columbia U., N.Y.C.; Cardozo prof. jurisprudence Columbia U. Sch. Law, N.Y.C.; vis. assoc. prof. Boston Coll., 1968-69; acting prof. UCLA, 1969-71; vis. prof. Hebrew U., Jerusalem, 1972-73, Harvard U., 1973-74, Yale U., 1977, U. Frankfurt, 1980; Guggenheim fellow, 1986-87. Author: Rethinking Criminal Law, 1978, A Crime of Self-Defense: Bernhard Goetz and the Law on Trial, 1988, Loyalty: An Essay on the Morality of Relationships, 1992, With Justice for Some: Victim's Rights in Criminal Trials, 1995. Home: 404 Riverside Dr New York NY 10025-1861 Office: Columbia U Sch Law 435 W 116th St New York NY 10027-7297*

FLETCHER, HARRY GEORGE, III, library director; b. Bklyn., Mar. 25, 1941; s. Harry G. and Helen T. (Dawson) F.; m. Toni A. Owen, 1966 (div. 1987); children: Alexandra, Thomas; m. 2d, Florence Sussman, 1987. A.B., Fordham Coll., 1962, M.A., 1970. Asst. editor, editor, dir. Fordham U. Press, 1966-91; Astor curator of printed books and bindings Pierpont Morgan Libr., N.Y.C., 1991-98; Brooke Russell Astor dir. spl. collections N.Y. Pub. Libr., N.Y.C., 1998—; adj. assoc. prof. NYU, 1996—. Author: Gutenberg and the Genesis of Printing, 1994, New Aldine Studies, 1988, In Praise of Aldus Manutius, 1995; editor: The Heritage of New York, 1970, A Miscellany for Bibliophiles, 1979, The Wormsley Library, 1999; co-editor: Paradosis, 1976; contbr. articles to profl. jours., chpts. to books. Served with AUS, 1963-66. DAAD fellow, 1962-63. Mem. Baker Street Irregulars. Club: Grolier. Office: The NYPL 5th Ave & 42nd St New York NY 10018-2788

FLETCHER, HOMER LEE, librarian; b. Salem, Ind., May 11, 1928; s. Floyd M. and Hazel (Barnett) F.; m. Jacquelyn Ann Blanton, Feb. 7, 1950; children—Deborah Lynn, Randall Brian, David Lee. B.A., Ind. U., 1953; M.S. in L.S. U. Ill., 1954. Librarian Milw. Pub. Library, 1954-56; head librarian Ashland (Ohio) Pub. Library, 1956-59; city librarian Arcadia (Cal.) Pub. Library, 1959-65, Vallejo (Calif.) Pub. Library, 1965-70; city librarian San Jose, Calif., 1970-90, ret., 1990. Contbr. articles to profl. jours. Pres. S. Solano chpt. Calif. Assn. Neurol. Handicapped Children, 1968-69; mem. Presbyn. Ch. Sunnyvale, 1997. Served with USAF, 1946-49. Mem. ALA (intellectual freedom com. 1967-72), Calif. Library Assn. (pres. pub. libraries sect. 1967), Phi Beta Kappa. Democrat. Presbyterian. Home: 7921 Belknap Dr Cupertino CA 95014-4973 *Standing up for what I believe regardless of the consequences. Accepting all human beings as important regardless of their circumstances. Emphasizing honest and forthright behavior in personal and professional life. Retaining a sense of humility and thankfulness.*

FLETCHER, J. S., health educator; b. Hollister, Calif., Aug. 9, 1946. BSN, Calif. State U., Fresno, 1968, MS in Nursing, 1971; EdD, U. San Francisco, 1980. RN, Calif. Instr., chmn. div. Modesto (Calif.) Jr. Coll., 1973-83; staff nurse Scenic Gen. Hosp., Modesto, 1983-90; prof. Calif. State U., Stanislaus, Turlock, 1983—. Co-Author: Essentials in Mental Health Nursing, 4d edit. Pres. Mercer City Sch. Dist. Bd. Edn., 1995-96; pres. Merced County Sch. Bds. Assn., 1995-97. Mem. Calif. Nurses Assn. (pres. region 8 1992-94).

FLETCHER, JAMES ALLEN, video company executive; b. Toledo, Sept. 18, 1947; s. Allen Rae and Ruth Helen (Scharf) F.; m. Kathy Jane Barrett, Jan. 25, 1975. AS, West Coast U., 1977, BSEE, 1979. Electronic technician Hughes Aircraft Co., El Segundo, Calif., 1970-72; engring. technician Altec Corp., Anaheim, Calif., 1972-75, Magna Corp., Santa Fe Springs, Calif., 1975-76; engring. technician Odetics Inc., Anaheim, 1976-79, electronic engr., 1979-86; pres., founder F & B Technologies, Orange, Calif., 1986—. Served as sgt. U.S. Army, 1967-69. Mem. Soc. Motion Picture and TV Engrs., Mensa. Libertarian. Avocations: record collecting, automobile restoration and customization. Office: F & B Technologies 630 N Tustin St Ste 1516 Orange CA 92867-7127

FLETCHER, JAMES WARREN, physician; b. Belleville, Ill., Oct. 6, 1943; m. Mary Bernadette Gatson; children: Michelle Marie, James W., Rebecca Lynn. MD, St. Louis U., 1968. Diplomate Am. Bd. Nuclear Medicine; lic. physician, Mo. Intern in internal medicine St. Louis U. Hosp., 1968-69, asst. resident in internal medicine, 1969-70, resident in nuclear medicine, 1970-71; clin. fellow in radiology Harvard Med. Sch., Boston, 1971-72; sr. resident in nuclear medicine Peter Bent Brigham and Children's Hosp. Med. Ctr., Boston, 1971-72; asst. prof. medicine dept. internal medicine St. Louis U., 1972-75, assoc. prof. medicine dept. internal medicine, 1976-83, assoc. prof. radiology dept. radiology, 1977-84, assoc. dir. divsn. nuclear medicine, 1978-85, prof. medicine dept. internal medicine, 1983—, prof. radiology, 1984—, acting dir. divsn. nuclear medicine, 1985-88, dir. divsn. nuclear medicine, 1988—; staff physician nuclear medicine svc. VA Med. Ctr., St. Louis, 1972-76, med. dir. nuclear medicine network, 1972-79, asst. chief nuclear medicine svc., 1976-79, chief, 1979—, med. dir. AMA nuclear medicine technologist tng. program, 1983—, dir. opers. NMR program project, 1983-88; staff physician St. Louis U. Hosps., 1972—, dir. nuclear medicine dept., 1988—, dir. PET imaging ctr., 1991—; dir., program official nuclear medicine svc., dept. medicine and surgery VA Adminstrn. Ctrl. Office, Washington, 1986-89; dir. diagnostics svc. St. Louis VA Med. Ctr., 1997—; mem. tech. adv. com. to dir. nuclear medicine svc. VA Ctrl. Office, Washington, 1979-86, chmn. spl. interest user groups computer applications in nuclear medicine, 1984-85; spl. soc. liaison rep. Inst. Medicine Com. on Clin. Practice Guidelines, 1990-91; mem. residency rev. com. nuclear medicine Accreditation Coun. Grad. Med. Edn., 1992-97, interagy. NMR task force Office Health Tech. Assessment, 1982, Dept. Vet. Affairs Nat. Task Force on Tech. Assessment, 1992—. Contbr. articles to profl. jours. Second v.p. sch. bd., Mary Queen of Peace Elem. Sch., Webster Groves, Mo., 1981, treas., 1982. Lt. comdr. USNR, 1966-77. Recipient Spl. Commendation award Dept. Vets. Affairs, 1990. Fellow Am. Coll. Nuclear Physicians; mem. AAAS, AMA, Am. Coll. Radiology, Am. Bd. Nuclear Medicine (bd. dirs. 1990-93, vice chmn. 1992-93, chmn. 1994-95), Radiology Soc. N.Am., Soc. Nuclear Medicine (bd. trustees 1988-92, chmn. health care policy com. 1991-92, vice chmn. commn. health care policy 1996-97, chmn. commn. health care policy 1997-98, pres. 1998—), Alpha Omega Alpha. Office: St Louis U Med Ctr PO Box 15250 3635 Vista Ave at Grand Blvd Saint Louis MO 63110-0250

FLETCHER, JEFFREY EDWARD, biochemist, medical writer; b. Toledo, Mar. 11, 1948; s. John Harper and Eleanore (Jackson) F.; m. Marcia Ruth Miller, Mar. 21, 1970 (div. Mar. 1977); m. Jeanne Claire Untied, Aug. 22, 1981; children: Katherine Ann, Lindsay Nicole, Sarah Jeanne. AA, Mohegan C.C., 1974; BA, Conn. Coll., 1976; PhD, U. Conn., 1981. Resident rsch. assoc. NRC, Washington, 1981-83; sr. instr. dept. anesthesia Hahnemann U., Phila., 1983-85, asst. prof., 1985-90, assoc. prof., 1990-95, prof., 1995-96; prof. dept. anesthesia Allegheny U. of Health Scis., 1996-98; v.p. sci. affairs Trinity Comms., Conshohocken, Pa., 1998—. Mem. editl. coun. sci. jour. Toxicon, 1991-98; contbr. articles to profl. jours. With USN, 1967-73, Vietnam. Conn. Coll. scholar, 1974-76. Mem. Am. Soc. Pharmacology and Exptl. Therapeutics, Internat. Soc. Toxinology, Am. Soc. Anesthesiologists, Am. Soc. Biochemistry and Molecular Biology, Soc. Exptl. Biology and Medicine, Soc. for Neurosci., Biophys. Soc., Phi Beta Kappa, Sigma Xi, Rho Chi. Episcopalian. Avocations: photography, tennis, fishing, golf. Office: Trinity Comms Four Tower Bridge 200 Barr Harbor Dr Ste 222 Conshohocken PA 19428-2977

FLETCHER, JOHN CALDWELL, bioethicist, educator; b. Bryan, Tex., Nov. 1, 1931; s. Robert Capers and Estelle Collins (Caldwell) F.; m. Adele Davis Woodall, Sept. 4, 1954; children: John Caldwell, Page Moss, Adele Davis. BA, U. of South, 1953, DCL (hon.), 1993; M.Div. cum laude, Va. Theol. Sem., 1956; MDiv Fulbright scholar, U. Heidelberg, 1957; PhD, Union Theol. Sem., N.Y.C., 1969; DCL (hon.), U. of the South, 1993. Ordained priest Episcopal Ch., 1957-90. Curate St. Lukes Episc. Ch., Mountain Brook, Ala., 1957-60; rector R.E. Lee Meml. Ch., Lexington, Va., 1960-64; chaplain Cornell Med. Sch.-New York Hosp., 1964-66; assoc. prof. Va. Theol. Sem., 1966-71; dir. Interfaith Met. Theol. Edn., Inc., Washington, 1971—; pres. Interfaith Met. Theol. Edn., Inc., 1975-77; chief bioethics program Clin. Center, NIH, 1977-87; Emily Davie and Joseph S. Kornfeld prof. biomed. ethics U. Va., Charlottesville, 1987-97, prof. emeritus, 1997—; vis. fellow Inst. Med. Genetics, U. Oslo, 1984; co-investigator Internat. Survey Med. Geneticists, 1990. Author: (with Celia A. Hahn) Inter-Met: Bold Experiment in Theological Education, 1977, The Futures of Protestant Seminaries, 1983, Coping with Genetic Disorders, 1982; editor: (with Mark I. Evans et al) Fetal Diagnosis and Therapy, Science Ethics and the Law, 1988, (with Albert R. Jonson and Norman L. Quist) Ethics Consultation in Health Care, 1989; editor and author: (with Dorothy Wertz) Ethics and Human Genetics: A Cross-Cultural Perspective, 1989, (with Mary F. Marshall, Franklin G. Miller and Paul A. Lombardo) Introduction to Clinical Ethics, 2d edit., 1997; translator: Creation and Fall, 1959; assoc. editor Ency. of Bioethics, 2d edit., 1995; contbr. articles to profl. jours. Vis. fellow Inst. for Med. Genetics U. Oslo, 1984, Montgomery fellow Dartmouth Coll., 1997. Mem. Soc. Bioethics Consultation (founding, pres., bd. dirs.), Am. Soc. Human Genetics, Am. Soc. Bioethics & Humanities, Soc. for Advancement of Women's Health Rsch., European Soc. for Human Reproduction and Embryology. Home and office: 1454 Bremerton Ln Keswick VA 22947-9145 *My personal philosophy is that responsibility and accountability are the highest goals for human beings. Each situation can be saved from meaninglessness by the courage not to forsake these goals.*

FLETCHER, JOHN GREENWOOD II, state judge; b. Phila., July 27, 1937; s. John Greenwood and Verna Mildred (DeVoe) F.; m. Donna Lynn Gould, Oct. 30, 1965; children: John Greenwood III, Rebecca Lynn. BA, U. Miami, 1959; JD, U. Fla., 1962. Bar: Fla. 1962. Asst. county atty. Pinellas County Fla., Clearwater, Fla., 1963-67, Dade County Fla., Miami, 1967-73; city atty. Sweetwater, Fla., 1975-77, Naples, Fla., 1977-78; gen. counsel Sanibel (Fla.)-Captiva Water Assn., 1978-85; spl. counsel Broward County Expressway Authority, Ft. Lauderdale, Fla., 1985-88, Dade County Sch. Bd., Miami, 1991-96; pvt. practice, South Miami, Fla., 1973-96; dist. judge 3d Dist. Ct. Appeal Fla., Miami, 1996—; asst. adj. prof. U. Miami, Coral Gables, Fla., 1971-73; cons. Dade County Sch. Bd., 1991-96. Contbr. articles to profl. jours., chpt. to book. 1st lt. JAGC, U.S. Army, 1963-68. Mem. Fla. Bar Assn. (grievance com. 1986-88, ethics com. 1989-91), Dade County Bar Assn., Phi Eta Sigma. Avocations: history, films. Home: 11511 Nogales St Coral Gables FL 33156-4231 Office: 3d Dist Ct Appeal Fla Bldg 2001 SW 117th Ave Miami FL 33175-1716

FLETCHER, JOHN LYNN, psychology educator; b. Springdale, Ark., Apr. 18, 1925; s. Lynn Harrington and Elsie Irene (Jones) F.; m. Mary Lou Campbell, Aug. 21, 1949 (div. July 1974); children: Lynn Gray, Jana Lee. BA, U. Ark., 1950, MA, 1951; PhD, U. Ky., 1955. Commd. 2nd lt. U.S. Army, 1953, advanced through ranks to lt. col., 1968; chief audition br. Med. Rsch. Lab. Ft. Knox, Ky., 1953-70; ret. U.S. Army, 1970; prof. psychology Memphis State U., 1970-75; prof., dir. rsch. dept. otolaryngology U. Tenn. Ctr. for Health Sci., Memphis, 1975-81; prof., chair psychology dept. U. Mo., Rolla, 1981-87; lectr. psychology S.W. Tex. State U., San Marcos, 1987—; cons. NASA Space Shuttle, Kennedy Space Ctr., 1972-76; mem. Commn. on Hearing and Bio Acoustics, 1956—. Editor: Effects of Noise on Animals, 1978; contbr. articles to profl. jours. Decorated Bronze Star. Fellow Acoustical Soc. Am., Am Speech, Lang. Hearing Soc.; mem. NAS, NRC, N.Y. Acad. Scis. (life), Human Factors Soc. Republican. Presbyterian. Achievements include patents for Acoustic Reflex Ear Defender. Home: PO Box 309 Martindale TX 78655-0309 Office: SW Tex State Univ Dept Psychology San Marcos TX 78666

FLETCHER, LEROY STEVENSON, mechanical engineer, educator; b. San Antonio, Oct. 10, 1936; s. Robert Holton and Jennie Lee (Adkins) F.; m. Nancy Louise McHenry, Aug. 14, 1966; children: Laura Malee, Daniel Alden. BS, Tex. A&M U., 1958; MS, Stanford U., 1963, Engr., 1964; PhD, Ariz. State U., 1968. Registered profl. engr., Ariz., N.J., Va., Tex., Australia; chartered engr., U.K. Rsch. scientist NASA-Ames Rsch. Ctr., Moffett Field, Calif., 1958-62, dir. aeronautics, 1999—; instr. Ariz. State U., Tempe, 1964-68; prof. aero., engring. Rutgers U., New Brunswick, N.J., 1968-75, assoc. dean, 1974-75; prof., chmn. dept. mech. and aero. engring. U. Va., Charlottesville, 1975-80; dir. Ctr. Energy Analysis, 1979-80; assoc. dean Tex. A&M U., College Station, 1980-88, assoc. dir. Tex. Engring. Expt. Sta., 1985-88, Dietz prof. mech. engring., 1988—, Regents prof., 1998—; vis. prof. Tokyo Inst. Tech., 1993; hon. prof. Ruhr U.-Bochum, Germany, 1988—; disting. vis. prof. Am. U., Cairo, 1998; cons. to various industries, govt. labs. and univs.; mem. exec. com. Internat. Ctr. for Heat and Mass Transfer, Ankara, Turkey, 1994—, fellow, 1998. Author: Introduction to Engineering Including FORTRAN Programming, 1977, Introduction to Engineering Design with Graphics and Design Projects, 1979; editor: Aerodynamic Heating and Thermal Protection, 1978, Heat Transfer and Thermal Control Systems, 1978. Served to capt. USAF, 1958-61. Recipient Disting. Alumni award Ariz. State U., 1985. Fellow ASME (bd. govs. 1983-87, pres. 1985-86, Charles Russ Richards award 1982, Heat Transfer Meml. award 1996, hon.), Accreditation Bd. Engring. and Tech. (dir. 1979-89, 1991-94), Am. Astron. Soc. (bd. dirs. 1993-96), Inst. Engrs. Australia, Inst. Mech. Engrs. U.K., Royal Aeronautical Soc. U.K., Am. Soc. Engring. Edn. (dir. 1974-77, v.p. 1978-80, George Westinghouse award 1982, Ralph Coats Roe award 1983, Donald E. Marlowe award 1986, Leighton W. Collins award 1993), AIAA (dir. 1981-84, 1992-98, v.p. edn. 1992-95, pres. 1996-97, Lee Atwood award 1982, Energy Sys. award 1984, Thermophysics award 1992), Internat. Astro. Fedn. (Frank J. Malina award 1997), Internat. Acad. Astronautics; mem. Sigma Xi, Tau Beta Pi, Pi Tau Sigma, Sigma Gamma Tau, Phi Kappa Phi. Office: Tex A&M Univ Dept Mech Engring College Station TX 77843

FLETCHER, LOUISE, actress; b. Birmingham, Ala., 1936; d. Robert Capers F. BA, U. N.C., 1957; student acting with Jeff Corey; LHD (hon.), Gallaudet U., 1982, Western Md. Coll., 1986. Films include Thieves Like Us, 1973, Russian Roulette, 1974, One Flew Over the Cuckoo's Nest, 1975 (Acad. award as best actress), Exorcist II: The Heretic, 1976, The Cheap Detective, 1977, The Magician, 1978, Natural Enemies, 1979, The Lucky Star, 1979, The Lady in Red, 1979, Strange Behavior, 1980, Brainstorm, 1981, Strange Invaders, 1982, Once Upon a Time in America, 1982, Firestarter, 1983, Overnight Sensation, 1983, Invaders from Mars, 1985, The Boy Who Could Fly, 1985, Nobody's Fool, 1986, Flowers in the Attic, 1987, Two Moon Junction, 1987, Blue Steel, 1988, Best of the Best, 1989, Shadowzone, 1989, Blind Vision, 1990, The Player, 1991, Return to Two Moon Junction, 1993, Tollbooth, 1993, Virtuosity, 1995, Mulholland Falls, 1995, 2 Days in the Valley, 1995, Edie & Pen, 1995, High School High, 1995, Girl Gets Moe, 1996, Heartless, 1996, Love Kills, 1998, A Map of the World, 1999, More Dogs than Bones, 1999, Cruel Inventions, 1999, Time Served, 1999; TV appearances include Maverick, Wagon Train, The Lawman, Playhouse 90, The Millionaire, Alfred Hitchcock, Thou Shalt Not Commit Adultery, 1978, A Summer To Remember, 1984, Island, 1984, Second Serve, 1985, Hoover, 1986, The Karen Carpenter Story, 1988, Nightmare on the 13th Floor, 1988, Twilight Zone, 1988, Final Notice, 1989, The Hitchhiker, 1990, Tales from the Crypt, 1991, In a Child's Name, 1991, Boys of Twilight, 1991, The Fire Next Time, 1992, Civil Wars, 1993, Deep Space Nine, 1994, 95, 96, 97, 98, 99, The Haunting of Cliff House, Dream On, 1994, Someone Else's Child, 1994, VR5, 1994, 95, Picket Fences, 1996, Stepford Husbands, 1996, Twisted Path, 1997, Breastmen, 1997, Married to a Stranger, 1997, Profiler, 1997, The Practice, 1998, Brimstone, 1998, Devil's Arithmetic, 1999. Bd. dirs. Deafness Rsch. Found., 1980—. Mem. Nat. Inst. Deafness and Other Communicable Disorders (adv. bd.). *

FLETCHER, MARJORIE AMOS, librarian; b. Easton, Pa., July 10, 1923; d. Alexander Robert and Margaret Ashton (Arnold) Amos; A.B., Bryn Mawr Coll., 1946; m. Charles Mann Fletcher, May 14, 1949; children: Robert Amos, Elizabeth Ashton, Anne Kennard. Asst. to dir. rsch., then rsch. asst. to pres. Penn Mut. Life Ins. Co., 1946-49; officer A.R. Amos Co., Phila., 1949-66; part-time tchr., 1965-68; librarian Am. Coll., Bryn Mawr, Pa., 1968-77, archivist, 1973—, dir. oral history collection, 1975—, lectr. on archives, 1975—, asst. prof. edn., 1973-87, dir. archives and oral history, 1977—; pres. pub. rels. MAF Enterprises, 1987—. Author articles in field. Recipient awards Phila. Flower Show, 1965—; bd. dirs. Emergency Aid Found.. Mem. Spl. Librs. Assn. (pres. Phila. 1977-78), Soc. Am. Archivists (chairperson oral history sect. 1981-87, award of merit 1987), Oral History Assn., Hist. Soc. Pa., U.S. Pony Club, D.A.R., Nat. Soc. Colonial Dames in Commonwealth of Pa., Emergency Aid Pa. Found., Phila. Skating Club, Davis Creek Yacht Club, Bridlewild Pony Club (sponsor), Bridlewild Trails Club (Gladwyne). Republican. Episcopalian. Home: 1135 Norsam Rd Gladwyne PA 19035-1419 Office: Am Coll Bryn Mawr PA 19010

FLETCHER, MARK ROBERT, political scientist; b. May 4, 1974. BS in Polit. Sci. and Econs., U. Mich., 1996. Legis. dir. Coll. Rep. Nat. Com., Ann Arbor, Mich., 1995-96; first vice-chmn. Coll. Rep. Nat. Com., Ann Arbor, 1997-99; legis. aide Mich. Ho. of Reps., Lansing, 1996—. E-mail: mfletch@hotmail.com. Home: 300 Western Ave A14 Lansing MI 48917

FLETCHER, MARY LEE, business executive; b. Farnborough, Eng.; d. Dugald Angus and Mary Lee (Thurman) F.; B.A., Pembroke Coll., Brown U., 1951. Ops. officer C.I.A., Washington, 1951-53; exec. trainee Gimbels, N.Y.C., 1953-54; head researcher Ed Byron TV Prodns., N.Y.C., 1954; copywriter Benton & Bowles, Inc., N.Y.C., 1955-63; creative dir. Alberto-Culver Co., Melrose Park, Ill., 1964-66; v.p. advt. and publicity Christian Dior Perfumes, N.Y.C., 1967-71; v.p. Christian Dior-N.Y., N.Y.C., 1972-78, exec. v.p., dir., 1978-85. Home: 12 Beekman Pl New York NY 10022-8059

FLETCHER, NORMAN S., state supreme court justice; b. July 10, 1934; s. Frank Pickett and Hattie Sears Fletcher; m. Dorothy Johnson, 1957; children: Mary Kiker, Elizabeth Coan. BA, U. Ga., 1956, LLB, 1958; LLM, U. Va., 1995. Assoc. Matthews, Maddox, Walton and Smith, Rome, Ga., 1958-63; pvt. practice LaFayette, Ga., 1963-90; city atty. City of LaFayette, 1965-89; county atty. County of Walker, 1973-88; spl. asst. atty. gen. State of Ga., Atlanta, 1979-89; justice Supreme Ct. of Ga., Atlanta, 1990—, now presiding justice; mem. State Disciplinary Bd., 1984-87, chair investigative panel, 1986-87. Ruling elder Peachtree Presbyn. Ch., Atlanta; former officer First Presbyn. Ch. of Rome, Ga., LaFayette Presbyn. Ch., Cherokee Presbytery; former commr. Presbyn. Ch. USA Gen. Assembly, 1984, 85; bd. visitors U. Ga. Sch. Law, 1992-95, chmn., 1994-95. Master Joseph Henry Lumpkin Inn of Ct.; fellow Am. Bar Found., Ga. Bar Found.; mem. State Bar Ga. (chair local govt. sect. 1977-78), U. Ga. Law Sch. Alumni Assn. (pres. 1977), Rotary. Office: Supreme Ct Ga 244 Washington St SW Rm 572 Atlanta GA 30334-9007

FLETCHER, OSCAR JASPER, JR., college dean; b. Bennettsville, S.C., Oct. 18, 1938; s. Oscar Jasper and Virginia (Baskin) F.; m. Sybil Morrison, June 3, 1962; children: John, Gregg. BS, Wofford Coll., 1960; DVM, U. Ga., 1964, MS, 1965; PhD, U. Wis., 1968. Asst. prof. U. Ga. Coll. Vet. Medicine, Athens, 1968-74, assoc. prof., 1974-79, prof., 1979-89, assoc. dean, 1975-82, head dept. avian medicine, 1982-89; dean Coll. Vet. Medicine Iowa State U., Ames, 1989-92, N.C. State U., Raleigh, 1992—. Mem. Am. Coll. Vet. Pathologist (cert., pres. 1990). Methodist. Office: NC State U Coll Vet Medicine 4700 Hillsborough St Raleigh NC 27606-1428

FLETCHER, PHILIP B., food products company executive; b. 1933. BA, St. Lawrence U.; MBA, MIT, 1954. With ctrl. foundry divsn. Gen. Motors Corp., 1954-58; various mgmt. positions Campbell Soup Co., 1958-73; gen. mgr. ops. and agriculture H.J. Heinz USA, Inc., 1973-78; v.p. mfg. Heublein Co., 1978-82; pres. Banquet Foods Co., Omaha, 1982-84; corp. pres., COO ConAgra Inc., Omaha, 1982-92, CEO, 1992-97, chmn., 1993—, also dir. Office: ConAgra Inc 1 Conagra Dr Omaha NE 68102-5001

FLETCHER, RAYMOND RUSSWALD, JR., lawyer; b. Schenectady, N.Y., June 7, 1929; s. Raymond Russwald and Elsie Dorothea (Hovemeyer) F.; m. Elsa Ellen Tillema, Dec. 20, 1949 (div. 1973); children—Raymond Russwald III, Nicholas H., Pamela L., William E., Catherine A. B.Ch.E., Rensselaer Poly. Inst., 1949; LL.B., Harvard U., 1956. Bar: N.Y. 1956. Vice-pres., gen. counsel Trans World Airlines, Inc., N.Y.C., 1969-78; ptnr. Chadbourne, Parke, Whiteside & Wolff, N.Y.C., 1978-84; counsel Gilbride, Tusa, Last & Spellane, N.Y.C., 1984—; vice chmn. legal com. Internat. Air Transport Assn., Geneva, Switzerland, 1976-77. Served as lt. (j.g.) USN, 1949-53; Korea. Decorated Air medal. Mem. N.Y. Bar Assn., Harvard Club. Democrat. Presbyterian. Home: 310 E 49th St Apt 7G New York NY 10017-1671 Office: Gilbride Tusa Last Et Al 420 Lexington Ave New York NY 10170

FLETCHER, ROBERT HILLMAN, medical educator; b. Abington, Pa., Mar. 26, 1940; s. Stevenson Whitcomb and Wanda (Moss) F.; m. Suzanne Wright, June 15, 1963; children—John Wright, Grant Selmer. B.A., Wesleyan U., Middletown, Conn., 1962; M.D., Harvard U., 1966; M.Sc., Johns Hopkins U., 1973. Diplomate Am. Bd. Internal Medicine. Asst. prof. Faculty of Medicine McGill U., Montreal, Que., Can., 1973-78; assoc. prof. medicine Sch. Medicine U. N.C., Chapel Hill, 1978-83, prof. medicine, clin. prof. epidemiology, 1983-90, dir. Robert Wood Johnson Clin. Scholars Program, 1983-90, co-dir. Clin. Epidemiology Resource and Tng. Ctr., Internat. Clin. Epidemiology Network, 1986-90; assoc. exec. v.p. ACP, Phila., 1990-92, sr. v.p., 1992-93; prof. Harvard U. Med. Sch., Boston, 1994—; assoc. med. dir. clin. edn. Harvard Pilgrim Health Care, Boston, 1998, dir. teaching ctr., dept. ambulatory care & prevention, 1998—; bd. dirs. IN-CLEN Inc., Boston, chmn., 1993-97. Sr. author: Clinical Epidemiology, The Essentials, 1982, 2d edit., 1988, 3d edit., 1996; co-editor: Jour. Gen. Internal Medicine, 1984-89, Annals of Internal Medicine, 1990-93; primary care editor Up To Date. Served to maj. M.C., U. S. Army, 1968-71. Master ACP (master); mem. Am. Pub. Health Assn., Soc. Gen. Internal Medicine (pres. 1991-92), Phi Beta Kappa, Sigma Xi. Democrat. Quaker. Home: 249 Dudley Rd Newton MA 02459-2831 Office: Dept Ambulatory Care/Prevention 126 Brookline Ave Ste 200 Boston MA 02215-3920

FLETCHER, RONALD DARLING, microbiologist educator; b. Foxboro, Mass., Jan. 18, 1933; s. Howard Wendel and Ada Louise (Darling) F.; m. Barbara Gundersen, Jan. 30, 1954; children: Deborah, Mark Ronald, Christopher Gary. BS, U. Conn., 1954, MS, 1959, PhD, 1963; MA, Harvard U., 1966. Mule skinner U.S. Forest Svc., St. Maries, Idaho, 1952; instr. U. Conn., Storrs, 1959-63; rschr. Am. Cyanamid Co., Pearl River, N.Y., 1964-67; dir. microbiology McKeesport Hosp., Pa., 1971-79; prof., assoc. chairperson dept. microbiology U. Pitts., 1967-86; sr. analyst Armed Forces Med. Intelligence Ctr. Dept. Def., Frederick, Md., 1986-89; prof. microbiology dept. clin. lab. scis. U. Pitts., 1989—; v.p. Affordable Tech., Inc., Pitts., 1990-91; exec. v.p. ATI Bioremediation, Inc., Pitts., 1991-92; mem. biotech. steering com. U.S. Dept. Def., 1987-89; cons. U.S. Army, Frederick, 1978-82, Mellon Inst., Pitts., 1981, Cons.'s Brokerage, Mountain View, Calif., 1981, Battelle Meml. Inst., Columbus, Ohio, 1989-90. Contbr. articles on microbiology to prof. jours. Judge Internat. Sci. and Engring. Fair, Mpls., 1980, judge, Milw., 1981, Dallas, 1982; judge Nat. Jr. Sci. and Humanities Symposium, West Point, N.Y., 1983, 85; dept. state lectr. med. schs. in Ankara and Istanbul, Turkey, 1982. Col. USA & USAR, 1954-85. USPHS fellow U. Zurich, Switzerland, 1963-64; grantee U.S. Army, Am. Cancer Soc., NIH; recipient Postdoctoral fellowship U. Saskatchewan, Can., 1965, cert. of achievement in microbiology Surgeon Gen. U.S. Army, 1973. Fellow AAAS, Am. Acad. Microbiology (registered microbiologist, specialist microbiologists); mem. Internat. Assn. Dental Research (pres. Pitts. 1979-80), AIDA, Assn. Mil. Surgeons, Am. Assn. Microbiologists, N.Y. Acad. Scis., Am. Soc. for Cell Biology, Nat. Mil. Intelligence Assn., Internat. Assn. Chiefs of Police, Am. Legion. Office: U of Pitts 209 Pennsylvania Hall Pittsburgh PA 15261-1802

FLETCHER, SHERRYL ANN, higher education administrator; b. Wyandotte, Mich., July 1, 1956; d. Richard Charles and Pauline L. (Fisher) Seavitt; m. Alan Morris Fletcher, July 26, 1980; children: Christopher Richard, Cameron Morris. BA summa cum laude, Albion Coll., 1978; MA with honors, U. Mich., 1986. Elem. art tchr. East Grand Rapids (Mich.) Schs., 1978-80; asst. dean students, dir. student activities Northwood U., Midland, Mich., 1981-83; admissions counselor Office of Undergrad. Admissions, U. Mich., Ann Arbor, 1983-84, sr. admissions counselor, 1984-88, asst. dir. admissions, 1988-93, assoc. dir. admissions, 1993-95; exec. dir., founder Coll. Access for Rural Am., 1995—; assoc. dir. Office of Undergrad. Admissions Johns Hopkins U., 1996—; guest faculty Annapolis (Md.) Edn. Inst. Inc., 1993-94; adminstrv. univ. liaison Cook Family Found., Mich., 1986—; speaker in field. Chair future planning Jr. League Ann Arbor, 1993-94, chair pub. rels., 1990-93; sustainer Jr. League Annapolis, 1995—; mem. David Hallissey scholarship com. Mem. Nat. Assn. Coll. Admissions Counselors (nat. presdl. com. 1993, 97), Mich. Assn. Coll. Admissions Counselors (state sec. 1992—), Potomac Chesapeake Assn. Coll. Admissions Counselors (chairperson conf. devel. 1997-98, membership chair 1998—), Albion Coll. Shield Club, U. Mich. Alumni Club of Washington, Alumnae Club Annapolis, Alpha Chi Omega. Methodist. Avocations: tennis, golf, swimming, watercolor painting, power walking, interior design, travel. Office: Johns Hopkins U Of Undgrad Adm 3400 N Charles St Baltimore MD 21218-2608

FLETCHER, SUZANNE WRIGHT, physician, educator; b. Jacksonville, Fla., Nov. 14, 1940; d. Robert Dean and Helen (Selmer) Wright; m. Robert H. Fletcher; children: John Wright, Grant Selmer. BA, Swarthmore Coll., 1962; MD, Harvard Med. Sch., 1966; MSc, Johns Hopkins U., 1973. Diplomate Nat. Bd. Med. Examiners, Am. Bd. Internal Medicine. Intern Stanford (Calif.) U. Med. Ctr., 1966-67, resident, 1967-68; physician 22nd med. detachment U.S. Army, New Ulm, Germany, 1969-70; asst. prof. epidemiology and health Mc Gill U., Montreal, Can., 1974-77, assoc. prof., 1977-78, asst. prof. medicine, 1973-78; dir. med. clinic dept. medicine N.C. Meml. Hosp., 1978-82; assoc. prof. medicine U. N.C., 1978-83, co-chief divsn. gen. medicine and clin. epidemiology dept. medicine, 1978-86, rsch. assoc. health svcs. rsch. ctr., 1978-90, vice chmn. clin. svcs., 1981-84, prof. medicine, clin. prof. epidemiology, 1983-90, program dir. faculty devel. gen. medicine and gen. pediatrics, 1985-90, co-dir. internat. clin. epidemiology network program Rockefeller Found., 1986-90; editor Annals of Internal Medicine, Phila., 1990-93; adj. prof. medicine U. Pa., Phila., 1990-93, Jefferson Med. Coll., 1991-93, U. N.C., 1994—; prof. ambulatory care and prevention Harvard Med. Sch., physician internal medicine; chmn. NIH Tech. Assessment Conf., 1992, Nat. Cancer Inst. Internat. Workshop, 1993; active World Bank Seminar on Preventive Strategies in Med. edn., Hangzhou, China, 1986, Ad Hoc NCI Com. on BSE Cancer Detection Rsch. and Applications, 1986. Author: Clinical Epidemiology—The Essentials, 1982, 3rd edit., 1995; contbr. chpts. to books; contbr. articles to profl. jours. Rsch. grantee Conseil de la Recherche en Sante du Quebec, 1975-77; grantee Health and Welfare Can., 1976-78, Robert Wood Johnson Teaching Hosp. Gen. Medicine Group Practice Program, 1980-84, Nat. Ctr. Health Scis. Rsch. and Health Tech., 1985-89, Rockefeller Found. Clin. Epidemiology Resource and Tng. Ctr., 1986-90, NIH, 1987-90, 97—; recipient Can. Nat. Health Rsch. Scholar award Can. Govt., 1975-78. Master ACP (med. knowledge self assessment program 1984-85, clin. practice subcom. 1987, pub. policy subcom. 1988-89); fellow Am. Coll. Epidemiology (chmn. pub. com. 1992-94, bd. dirs. 1990-93), Coll. Physicians Phila.; mem. APHA, Soc. Gen. Internal Medicine (counsellor 1978-81, pres.-elect 1982-83, pres. 1983-84, mem. publs. com. 1990—, chmn. Glaser award com. 1991, co-editor Jour. Gen. Internal Medicine, 1984-89), Inst. Medicine (coun. 1993-96, exec. com. 1993-96), So. Soc. Clin. Investigation, Sydenham Soc., Phila. Epidemiology Soc., Phila. Med. Soc. Democrat. Unitarian. Office: Harvard Med Sch Ambulatory Care/Prevention Dept 126 Brookline Ave Ste 200 Boston MA 02215-3920

FLETCHER, WINONA LEE, theater educator; b. Nov. 25, 1926; m. Joseph Grant; 1 child, Betty. BA, Johnson C. Smith U., 1947; MA, U. Iowa, 1951; PhD, Ind. U., 1968. Prof. speech and theatre Ky. State U., Frankfort, 1951-78; prof. theatre and afro-Am. studies Ind. U., Bloomington, 1978-94, prof. emeritus, 1994; assoc. dean COAS, 1981-84; costumer, dir. summer theatre, U. Mo., Lincoln, 1952-60, 69. Recipient Lifetime Achievement award, 1993; Am. Theatre fellow, 1979. Mem. Am. Theatre for Higher Edn., Black Theatre Network, Nat. Assn. Dramatic and Speech Arts, Nat. Theatre Conf., Alpha Kappa Alpha. Home: 317 Cold Harbor Dr Frankfort KY 40601-3011

FLETCHER ARANCIBIA, PABLO ENRIQUE, internal medicine endocrinology physician, educator; b. Panama, Apr. 15, 1928; s. Paul and Juana (Arancibia) Fletcher; m. Lilia Vasquez, Jan. 19, 1953; children: Juana E., Pablo E., Eduardo E., Lilia E. BS cum laude, Inst. Nat., Panama, 1946; MD cum laude, U. Autonoma de Mexico, Mexico City, 1953. Med. diplomate. Intern Hosp. Santo Tomas, Panama, 1953-54; resident in internal medicine Inst. de la Nutricion, Mexico City, 1954-56; fellow in endocrinology Mass. Gen. Hosp., Boston, 1956-58; chief endocrinology Social Security Hosp., Panama, 1960-89, chief gen. medicine, 1979-85; chief prof. medicine U. Panama, Panama, 1976—, dir. Ctr. of Endocrinology, 1981—; v.p. Panamerican Endocrinology Fedn., 1982-90; med. dir. Social Security Hosp., Panama, 1984-85; adj. prof. medicine U. Miami, Fla., 1989—; nat. health dir. Social Security Panama, 1989-94. Chief editor: Revista Medica-Caja de Seguro Social, Panama, 1982-85; editor: Acta Endocrinological Panamericana, 1969-72; contbr. numerous articles to profl. jours. Treas. Asociacion Medica Nacional de Panama, 1953-54; pres. Asociacion de Medicos, Odontologos y Afines de la Caja de Seguro Social, Panama, 1964-65, Fedn. Internal Medicine Socs. Ctrl. Am., 1969-71, Soc. Bolivariana de Endocrinologia, South Am., Panama, 1971-73. Recipient Best Tchr. award U. Panama, Gold medal U. Panama, 1995. Fellow ACP (gov. 1979-93, Laureate and Masters awards 1995); mem. AAAS, Am. Thyroid Assn., Am. Diabetes Assn., Am. Endocrine Soc., N.Y. Acad. Scis., British Endocrine Soc., Fedn. Panamericana de Endocrinologia (pres. 1982-90), Assn. Panama de Endocrinologia y Metabolismo (pres. 1980-83), Soc. Panamena Medicina Interna (pres. 1971-73), Internat. Soc. Internal Medicine, Latin Am. Soc. Thyroid, Latin Am. Soc. Diabetes, Internat. Diabetes Fedn., Internat. Coun. for Control of Iodine Deficiency Disorders, Internat. Endocrine Soc., N.Y. Acad. Scis. Roman Catholic. Avocations: lecturing, swimming. Home: Calle Septima PO Box 4127, Altos del Golf 12, Panama Panama

FLETTNER, MARIANNE, opera administrator; b. Frankfurt, Germany, Aug. 9, 1933; d. Bernhard J. and Kaethe E. (Halbritter) F. Bus. diploma, Hessel Bus. Coll., 1953. Sec. various cos., 1953-61, Pontiac Motor Div., Burlingame, Calif., 1961-63; sec. Met. Opera, N.Y., 1963-74, asst. co. mgr., 1974-79; artistic adminstr. San Diego Opera, 1979—. Avocations: traveling, hiking, swimming, cooking. Home: 4015 Crown Point Dr San Diego CA 92109-6270 Office: San Diego Opera 18th Fl 1200 Third Ave San Diego CA 92101-4112

FLEURY, PAUL AIMÉ, university dean, physicist; b. Balt., July 20, 1939; m. Carol Anne Moss, Aug. 22, 1964; children: Ellen, Laura, Jennifer. BS in Physics, John Carroll U., 1960; PhD in Physics, MIT, 1965. Mem. tech. staff AT&T Bell Labs., Murray Hill, N.J., 1965-70, head condensed state physics rsch., 1970-79, dir. materials rsch., 1979-84, dir. phys. rsch., 1984-92; v.p. rsch. Sandia Nat. Lab., Albuquerque, 1992-93; dir. materials & process rsch. AT&T Bell Labs., Murray Hill, N.J., 1993-96; dean engring. U. N.Mex., Albuquerque, 1996—. Editor: Coherence and Energy Transfer in Glasses, 1983; contbr. over 120 articles to Phys. Rev., Sci., others. Fellow AAAS, NAE, NAS, Am. Phys. Soc. (Michaelson Morley prize 1985, Frank Isakson prize for optical effects in solids 1992). Achievements include 5 patents for optical devices, lasers, optical fibers; research in laser spectroscopy. Office: U NMex Farris Engring Ctr # 107 Albuquerque NM 87131

FLEURY, THEOREN, hockey player; b. Oxbow, Sask., Can., June 29, 1968; s. Wally and Donna Fleury; m. Veronica Fleury, 1995; children: Josh, Beaux. Hockey player Calgary Flames, 1987-98, Colorado Avalanche, Denver, 1998-99, New York Rangers, N.Y.C., 1999-. Named Juvenile Diabetes Man-of-the-Yr. N.Am., 1997. Office: New York Rangers Madison Sq Garden 2 Penn Plaza New York NY 10121*

FLEXNER, JAMES THOMAS, author; b. N.Y.C., Jan. 13, 1908; s. Simon and Helen (Thomas) F.; m. Beatrice Hudson, 1950; 1 child, Helen Hudson. Grad., Lincoln Sch. of Tchrs. Coll., Columbia U., 1925; BS magna cum laude, Harvard U., 1929; LHD, Ea. Ill. U., 1985. Reporter N.Y. Herald Tribune, 1929-31; exec. sec. Noise Abatement Commn., N.Y.C. Dept. of Health, 1931-32; cons. Colonial Williamsburg, 1956-57, Amon Carter Mus. Western Art, 1974-75; lectr. on founding fathers, history of Am. art and civilization. Author: Doctors on Horseback: Pioneers of American Medicine, 1937, America's Old Masters, 1939, (with Simon Flexner) William Henry Welch and the Heroic Age of American Medicine, 1941, Steamboats Come True, 1944, History of American Painting, Vol. I: First Flowers of Our Wilderness: American Painting, the Colonial Period, 1947 (Life in America prize 1946), John Singleton Copley, 1947, A Short History of American Painting, 1950, The Traitor and the Spy, 1953, History of American Painting, Vol. II: The Light of Distant Skies 1760-1835, 1954, Gilbert Stuart, 1955, Mohawk Baronet: Sir William Johnson of New York, 1959, History of American Painting, Vol. III: That Wilder Image: The Native School from Thomas Cole to Winslow Homer, 1962 (Francis Parkman prize 1963), George Washington, Vol. I: The Forge of Experience 1732-1775, 1965, The World of Winslow Homer 1936-1910, 1966, George Washington, Vol. II: George Washington in the American Revolution 1775-1783, 1968, The Double Adventure of John Singleton Copley, 1969, Nineteenth Century Painting, 1970, George Washington, Vol. III: George Washington and the New Nation 1783-1793, 1970, George Washington, Vol. IV: Anguish and Farewell 1793-1799, 1972 (Nat. Book award for biography 1972), Washington: The Indispensable Man, 1974 (Christopher award 1974, Am. Book award nomination 1980), The Face of Liberty, 1975, The Young Hamilton, 1978, States Dyckman: American Loyalist, 1980, Asher B. Durand: An Engraver's and a Farmer's Art, 1983, An American Saga: The Story of Helen Thomas and Simon Flexner, 1984, Poems of the 1920s, 1991, On Desperate Seas: A Biography of Gilbert Stuart, 1995, Maverick Progress: An Autobiography, 1996, Random Harvest, Shorter Publications Down the Years, 1997; Washington biographies dramatized in CBS miniseries, 1984 (Peaody award 1984); contbr. mags. and newspapers. Trustee emeritus N.Y. Pub. Library. Libr. Congress grantee, 1945; Guggenheim fellow, 1953, 79; recipient Pulitzer Prize spl. citation, 1972, Archives Am. Art award Smithsonian Inst., 1979, Gold medal Am. Acad. Inst. Arts and Letters, 1988. Mem. PEN (pres. 1954-55, hon. v.p. 1963-66), Soc. Am. Historians (pres. 1975-77), Am. Acad. Inst. Arts and Letters (v.p. for lit. 1981-85, Gold medal 1988), Autthors League of Am., Century Assn., Phi Beta Kappa. Club: Century (hon.). Office: 530 E 86th St New York NY 10028-7535 also: Fordham U Press Univ Box L Bronx NY 10458

FLEXNER, JOSEPHINE MONCURE, musician, educator; b. Marion, Va., Oct. 11, 1919; d. Walter Raleigh Daniel and Harriet Ashby (Ogburn) M.; m. Kurt Fisher Flexner, Dec. 20, 1942; children: Thomas Moncure, Peter Wallace. BA, Univ. Richmond, 1941; tchr. cert. in piano, Peabody Conservatory, 1945; MS in piano, Juilliard Sch. Music, 1950. Class piano tchr. Balt. Pub. Sch., 1945-46; mem. piano faculty Peabody Conservatory Prep., Balt., 1945-46, Pius X Sch. Manhatanville Coll. Sacred Heart, N.Y.C., 1946-50, Henry Street Settlement Sch., N.Y.C., 1949-50; piano tchr. Bronxville, N.Y., 1950-54; mem. piano faculty Rhodes Coll., Memphis, Tenn., 1970-82; piano tchr. St. Mary's Episcopal Sch., Memphis, 1982-87; judge for piano auditions, 1980-85, judge in Tenn. Nat. Guild Auditions, 1983-84. Contbr. articles to profl. jours. Den mother Boy Scouts Am., 1963-65, vice chmn., 1964-65; precinct worker, capt. Nat. Elections, Memphis, 1972, 74; mem. Memphis Arts Coun., 1977-79; area chmn. Westchester Soc. Performing Arts, 1964-66, chmn. cultural activities Sch. No. 8, Yonkers, N.Y., 1963-66; vice chmn. music dept. Bronxville Women's Club, 1964-66; pres. chancel choir Dutch Reformed Ch., Bronxville, 1963-66; program chmn. Seoul Internat. Women's Assn., Seoul, Korea, 1967-68, chmn. cultural activities Seoul Am. Schs., 1966-68, chmn. culutral seminars Am. Women's Club, Seoul, 1967-68; treas., pres. Greater Memphis Music Assn., 1975-79; bd. dirs. Young Peoples Piano Concerto Competition, 1979-85, Tenn. Music Tchrs. Assn., 1977-79. Named Tchr. of Yr., Greater Memphis Music, 1983, Tchr. of Yr., Tenn. Music Tchrs. Assn., 1985. Democrat. Presbyterian. Avocations: writing, reading, playing piano. Home: 115 Montgomery St Rhinebeck NY 12572-1108

FLEXNER, KURT FISHER, economist, educator; b. Vienna, Austria, Sept. 26, 1916; came to U.S., 1928; s. Otto Gerard and Wilhelmine (Fisher) F.; m. Josephine Moncure, Dec. 20, 1942; children: Thomas Moncure, Peter Wallace. BS in Econs., Johns Hopkins U., 1946; PhD in Econs., Columbia U., 1954. From asst. prof. to prof. econs. NYU Grad. Sch. Arts and Scis., U. Coll. and Sch. Commerce, 1946-59; chief economist, dep. mgr. The Am. Bankers Assn., 1959-66; adj. prof. banking and fin. NYU, 1965-66, prof., chmn. dept. econs., 1968-78; prof. econs. U. Memphis, 1978-87, prof. emeritus, 1987—; cons. U.S. Savs. and Loan League, 1955-59, N.Y. State Savs. and Loan League, 1955-59; P.K. Seidman Vis. Disting. Prof., Christian Bros. U., Memphis, 1990-94; lectr. intergenerational seminars Bard Coll., Annandale on the Hudson, N.Y., 1987—, Ctr. for Life Studies, Marist Coll., Poughkeepsie, N.Y., 1995—; chief fin. instns. advisor U.S. Agy. for Internat. Devel., Seoul, Korea, 1966-68; spkr. in field; adv. com. to Chancellor Franz Vranitzky, Prime Minister of Austria, 1991-93; guest lectr. Inst. USA and Can. Acad. of Sci., Moscow, 1991-95; advisor to coun. Pres. Mikhail Gorbachev, 1990-91, Pres. Boris Yeltsin, 1991-94. *As director of the National Mortgage Market Committee (N.Y.), Kurt Flexner developed a plan for giving the home mortgage national marketability. This plan became The Government National Mortgage Administration (Ginney Mae), which made home ownership available to many more people. While in Korea, he helped to modernize the Korean financial system, including the creation of the first housing bank in Asia, raising housing starts from three thousand in 1965 to sixty thousand in 1969.* Author: The Enlightened Society: The Economy with a Human Face, 1989; author column Memphis Daily News, 1986-90, Comml. Appeal, 1980-87; contbr. articles to profl. jours. Trustee M.L. Seidman Town Hall Meml. Lecture Series, 1968-87; mem. Gov. Alexander's Action Team, 1980-85. With U.S. Army, 1944-45. Mem. Econ. Club Memphis (exec. dir. 1973-85, pres. 1985-92). Home and Office: 115 Montgomery St Rhinebeck NY 12572-1108

FLIBBERT, JOSEPH THOMAS, English language educator; b. Worcester, Mass., July 24, 1938; s. Hervey John and Marguerite (Gosselin) F.; m. Rosemary Doran Daly, Aug. 10, 1963 (dec. Aug. 1987); children: Michael, Andrew, John; m. Marilyn Jean Sallack, June 24, 1989. AB, Assumption Coll., 1960; MA, Boston Coll., 1963; PhD, U. Ill., 1970. Instr. English Al-Hikma U., Baghdad, Iraq, 1961-62; instr. French Worcester (Mass.) Acad., 1962-63; asst. prof. English Merrimack Coll., North Andover, Mass., 1963-67; prof. English Salem (Mass.) State Coll., 1970—; vis. prof. English U. Du Maine, Lemans, France, 1979; Fulbright vis. lectr., France, 1979. Author: Melville and the Art of Burlesque, 1974, (chpt.) America and the Sea: A Literary History, 1995. Trustee Salem Athenaeum, 1986-92, pres., 1990-92; mem. libr. com. The Essex Inst., Salem, 1981-85. Recipient Disting. Svc. award Salem State Coll., 1981, 84, 88. Mem. Nat. Hawthorne Soc. (pres. 1982-84), Modern Lang. Assn., Melville Soc., Alpha Lambda Delta (hon.), Phi Kappa Phi. Avocations: choral singing, cooking, hiking, reading. Office: Salem State Coll 352 Lafayette St Salem MA 01970-5348

FLICK, CARL, electrical engineer, consultant; b. Vienna, Austria, June 22, 1926; came to U.S., 1939; s. Henry Chaim Ber and Sofie (Dornhelm) F.; m. Frances Ethel Berman, July 4, 1954; children: Lawrence David, Susan Naomi, Jack Bennet. BEE, Poly. U. of N.Y., 1951; MEE, Poly. U., 1953. Registered profl. engr., Fla., Pa. Various engring. positions, adv. engr. Westinghouse Electric Corp., East Pittsburgh, Pa., 1952-84, adv. engr., Orlando, Fla., 1984-89; cons. Techno-Lexic, Orlando, 1989—. Co-author: Handbook of Electric Machines, 1987; contbr. articles to profl. jours.; patentee in field. With U.S. Army, 1945-47, PTO. Fellow IEEE (life; various coms., Centennial medal 1984, Outstanding Engr. award Orlando sect. 1989, Fla. coun. 1989, Region 3 1990, Nikola Tesla award 1994), Power Engring. Soc. (com. Disting. Svc. award); mem. B'nai B'rith. Democrat. Jewish. Avocations: writing, photography, painting.

FLICK, FERDINAND HERMAN, surgeon, prevention medicine physician; b. Bklyn., Feb. 19, 1925; s. Paul Albert and Elizabek Kath (Herz) F.; m. Marie T. Flick, Apr. 7, 1945; children: Paul, Ferdinand, Annette Flick Riddle. BS, Fordham U., MS; MD, Yale U., 1951. Diplomate Am. Bd. Preventive Medicine. Intern SUNY Downstate, 1951-52; resident in ob-gyn Coll. Physicians & Surgeons Columbia U., N.Y.C., 1952; asst. prof. Columbia U. Coll. Physicians & Surgeons, N.Y.C., 1959-62; surgeon 77th Divsn. USAR, N.Y.C., 1962-76; chief plant physician Fort Motor Co., Mahwah, N.J., 1976-80, Edison, N.J., 1980—; asst. prof. U. Calif., Berkeley, 1946-47; trauma lectr. Middlesex C.C., 1984-85. Contbr. articles to profl. jours. including Nature and Am. Jour. Ob-gyn. Mem. smoking intervention team Am. Cancer Soc., New Brunswick, N.J., 1993-95. Col. USAR, 1946-76. Decorated Meritorious Svc. medal. Mem. Am. Coll. Occupl. and Environ. Medicine, Am. Coll. Preventive Medicine, Am. Soc. Abdominal Surgeons, Sigma Xi (Yale chpt.). Avocations: hunting, skiing. Home: 21 Miara St Parlin NJ 08859-1815

FLICK, JAMES DENNIS, journalist, free lance writer; b. Youngstown, Ohio, Dec. 6, 1956; s. James Edmond and Nancy Mae F.; div. July, 1998; 1 child, Michael James. BS in Journalism, Bowling Green State U.; postgrad. studies, Youngstown State U., 1998—. From reporter to columnist, mng. editor Niles (Ohio) Times, 1983-90; mng. editor Ohio Week Mag., Cleve., 1993-94; exec. editor Record Pub. Co., Stow, Ohio, 1994-96.; Mem. Bd. Edn., Niles, Ohio, 1996-99, pres. 1998.; bd. dirs. Niles C. of C., 1991-93. Recipient 2d pl. gen. reporting Ohio Assoc. Press, 1985, Tip of Week, Assoc. Press, Oct., 1985. Mem. Soc. Profl. Journalists. E-mail: J.D. Flick@501. Home: 501 North Rd #2 Niles OH 44446-2000 Office: Youngstown State U 317 De Bartola Hall Youngstown OH 44555

FLICK, JOHN EDMOND, lawyer; b. Franklin, Pa., Mar. 14, 1922; s. Edmond Leroy and Mary M. (Weaver) F.; m. Lois Anna Lange, Apr. 20, 1946; children: Gregory Allan, Scott Edmond, Lynn Ellen, Ann Elizabeth. Student, Northwestern U., 1941-44, U. Pa., 1945; LLB, Northwestern U., 1948. Bar: Ill. 1948, Calif. 1971, U.S. Dist. Ct. (ctrl. dist.) Calif. 1971, U.S. Ct. Appeals (9th cir.) 1971, U.S. Supreme Ct. 1974. Commd. 1st lt. Judge Adv. Gen. Corps U.S. Army, 1950, advanced through grades to lt. col. Res., 1968; ret., 1972; faculty U.S. Mil. Acad., 1954-57, Judge Adv. Gen. Sch., U. Va., 1960-61; counsel Litton Industries, 1963-67; sr. v.p., sec., gen. counsel, dir. Bangor Punta Corp., 1967-69; sr. v.p., gen. counsel Times Mirror Co., Los Angeles, 1970-87, cons., 1987-88. Past chmn. Los Angeles adv. bd. Salvation Army; mem. adv. bd., adult rehab. ctr. corps Santa Barbara, past mem. nat. adv. bd. Salvation Army. Recipient Am. Bar Assn. Acad. award, 1961. Mem. State Bars Calif. and Ill., Wigmore Club (life benefactor, Northwestern U. Law Sch.).

FLICK, THOMAS MICHAEL, mathematics educator, educational administrator; b. Covington, Ky., July 14, 1954; s. Thomas Lawrence and Crystel (Moore) F.; m. Jeanine M. Moran, Nov. 23, 1991. BS, No. Ky. U., 1976, MA, 1981; MEd, Xavier U., 1977; PhD, Southeastern U., 1979; EdD, U. Sarasota, 1989. Cert. secondary tchr., Ohio, Ky. Assoc. vice prin., dean, chmn. math., prin. summer sch. Purcell Marian High Sch., Cin., 1977-89; asst. prof. Xavier U., Cin., 1989-95, assoc. prof., 1995—; lectr. astronomy Wilmington Coll., Ohio, 1977-78, engring. and nat. sci., U. Cin., 1979—. Author: Guidelines for Astronomy Courses, 1976, 78, (with J. Ventre & J. Boothe) Astronomy Teaching Handbook, 1992, Introduction to the Universe, 1991, 93, Eclipses: Presentations for Educators, 1999; contbr. articles to profl. jours. Guest lectr. Cin. Nature Ctr., Milford, 1976—; chmn. edn. Astron. League, Washington; tchr. Super Saturday Program for Gifted and Talented., Cin., 1983; commn. mem. Archdiocese Cin., 1986. Recipient Ohio NSF Presdl. Award for Excellence in Math. Edn., 1986, Greater Cin. Found./GE grantee, 1987. Mem. Ohio Coun. Tchrs. Math. (contest coord. 1983—, Outstanding Math. Tchr. award 1982), Nat. Astron. League (v.p. 1980-82, chmn. edn. 1975—), Nat. Coun. Tchrs. Math., Math. Assn. Am., Ohio Acad. Sci. (Jerry Acker Outstanding Math. Tchr. award 1986-87), Sigma Xi (Outstanding Math. Tchr. award 1985), Pi Mu Epsilon. Roman Catholic. Club: Midwestern Astronomers. Avocations: golf, piano, bicycling, model railroading. Home: 1720 Monticello Dr Fort Wright KY 41011-3765 Office: Xavier U Dept Edn 3800 Victory Pkwy Dept Edn Cincinnati OH 45207-1092

FLICKER, JOHN, foundation executive. With The Nature Conservancy, Great Plains dir., gen. counsel, chief legal officer, exec. v.p., Fla. state dir.; pres. Nat. Audubon Soc., N.Y.C., 1995—. Office: National Audubon Soc 700 Broadway New York NY 10003-9536*

FLICKINGER, CHARLES JOHN, anatomist, educator; b. Bethlehem, Pa., July 13, 1938; s. Wilbur James and Verna (Diehl) F.; m. Agnes Elizabeth Dickel, Feb. 23, 1963; children: Laura Jill, David Paul. AB, Dartmouth Coll., 1960; MD, Harvard U., 1964. Rsch. fellow dept. anatomy U. Colo., Denver, 1964-65, Harvard Med. Sch., Boston, 1965-66; rsch. assoc. Inst. Developmental Biology, U. Colo., Boulder, 1966-67; asst. prof. Inst. Developmental Biology, U. Colo., 1967-70; assoc. prof. dept. anatomy Sch. Medicine, U. Va., Charlottesville, 1971-75; prof. Sch. Medicine, U. Va., 1975—, Harvey E. Jordan prof. anatomy, 1982—, chmn. dept. cell biology (formerly anatomy and cell biology), 1982—; mem. reproductive biology study sect. NIH, 1979-83; mem. anatomy test com. Nat. Bd. Med. Examiners, 1981-84. Author: (with Brown, Kutchai, Ogilvie) Medical Cell Biology, 1979; contbr. articles to profl. jours.; assoc. editor: Jour. Andrology, 1989-92; adv. editor: Internat. Rev. Cytology, 1974-98; mem. editorial bd. Biology of Reprodn., 1986-89, Jour. Andrology, 1986-89, Anatomical Record, 1972-98. NIH research career devel. award grantee, 1968-70. Mem. Am. Soc. Cell Biology, Am. Assn. Anatomists, Soc. Study Reprodn., Am. Soc. Andrology, Phi Beta Kappa, Alpha Omega Alpha. Home: 2009 Meadowbrook Rd Charlottesville VA 22903-1247 Office: University of Virginia Dept of Cell Biology Box 439 Hlth Scis Ctr Charlottesville VA 22902-0439

FLICKINGER, DON JACOB, patent agent; b. Massillon, Ohio, Dec. 31, 1933; s. John Jacob and Elizabeth Ann (Slinger) F.; m. Sonja Loy Jersild (dec. Aug. 1987); 1 child, Packy J. Flickinger. Student, Kent (Ohio) State U., 1951-54, U. Ariz., 1958; BA, Ariz. State U., 1963, MA, 1964. Bar: U.S. Patent and Trademark Office, 1973. Apprentice tool and die maker Spun Steel Corp., Canton, Ohio, 1951-54; staff Ariz. State U., Tempe, 1963-65; law clerk, paralegal Drummond, Cahill & Phillips, Phoenix, 1966-73; reg. patent agent Drummond, Nelson & Ptak, Phoenix, 1973-77, self employed, Phoenix, 1977-94; counsel Parsons & Goltry, Phoenix, 1995—; lectr., instr. Patent Seminars & Courses, Phoenix, 1977—; staff Rio Salado C.C., Phoenix, 1982-84. Patentee Collapsible Dust Pan, Hort. Growing Unit. Comdg. officer Poolee Enrichment Program, Family Marine Force, Poolee Assistance Co., Phoenix; sponsor Thunderbird Little League, Phoenix, 1985, 86, 87; big brother Valley Big Brothers, Phoenix, 1968-70; participant, staff Valley Big Bros./Big Sisters Fish-a-Ree, 1984-87; judge Crown Royal Kinetic Contraption Compeition, 1990. With USMC, 1954-57. Am. Soc. Tool. scholar, Tucson, 1960; recipient Disting. Svc. cert. Valley Big Brothers, Phoenix,1970, Honor award Westside Area Career Project, Glendale, 1981. Mem. BBB, NRA (endowment), Nat. Wildlife Fedn. (leaders club), Am. Legion, Ariz. Heritage Alliance, Phoenix Symphony Guild, Sundome Performing Arts Assn., Wilderness Soc., Nature Conservancy, Sea Shepard Conservation Soc., Legal Defense Fund, Defenders of Wildlife, Am. Legion, Mensa, Kappa Delta Pi. Republican. Buddhist. Avocations: philosophy, reading, woodworking, arts & crafts, fishing. Office: Parsons & Assocs 340 E Palm Ln Ste 260 Phoenix AZ 85004-4530

FLICKINGER, HARRY HARNER, organization and business executive, management consultant; b. Hanover, Pa., July 27, 1936; s. Harry Roosevelt and Goldie Anna (Harner) F.; m. Hsin Yang, May 30, 1961; children: Audrey Mae, Deborah Lynn. B.S. in Psychology, U. Md., 1958. Investigator U.S. Civil Service Commn., Washington, 1962-64; personnel specialist U.S. Naval Ordinance Lab., Silver Spring., Md., 1964-66; from asst. dir. to dir. personnel U.S. OMB, Washington, 1966-73; asst. dir. personnel AEC and Dept. Energy, Washington, 1973-78; dir. personnel U.S. Dept. Justice, Washington, 1978-79, dep. asst. atty. gen. adminstrn., 1979-85, assoc. asst. atty. gen., 1985-87, asst. atty. gen., 1987-92; exec. dir. Am. Consortium for Internat. Pub. Adminstrn., Washington, 1993; pres. Flickinger Enterprises, Gaithersburg, Md., 1994—. Recipient Presdl. Disting. Exec. Rank award, 1988. Office: 8730 Lochaven Dr Gaithersburg MD 20882-4464

FLICKINGER, THOMAS LESLIE, hospital alliance executive; b. Carroll, Iowa, Apr. 22, 1939; s. Leslie Winfred and Evelyn (Hanson) F.; m. Marjorie Ellen Madison, Apr. 19, 1970; children: Benjamin, Samuel. BBA, U. Iowa, 1961, MA, 1963. Adminstrv. asst. Presbyn.-St. Luke's Hosp., Chgo., 1963-64; asst. adminstr. 1 Creighton Meml. St. Joseph Hosp., Omaha, 1964-66, assoc. dir., 1966-68, adminstr., 1968-73; exec. dir. Creighton Omaha Regional Health Care Corp., Omaha, 1973-75; assoc. dir. Vanderbilt U. Hosp., 1975-77; adminstr. Routt Meml. Hosp., Steamboat Springs, Colo., 1977-85; pres. VHA (Vol. Hosps. Am.) Midlands, Omaha, 1986-97; sr. exec. VHA Mid-Am., Omaha, 1998; retired. Mem. Omaha Hosp. Assn. (pres. 1971), Am. Coll. Hosp. Adminstrs., Colo. Hosp. Assn. (chmn. 1982), Phi Kappa Psi. Home: 3421 N 128th Cir Omaha NE 68164-4237 Office: VHA Mid-Am 7912 Davenport St Omaha NE 68114-3631

FLIER, MICHAEL STEPHEN, Slavic languages educator; b. L.A., Apr. 20, 1941; s. Albert and Bonnie F. BA, U. Calif., Berkeley, 1962, MA, 1964, PhD, 1968. Acting vis. asst. prof. Slavic langs. and lits. U. Calif., Berkeley, 1968; asst. prof. Slavic langs. and lits. UCLA, 1968-73, assoc. prof., 1973-79, prof., 1979-91, chmn. dept., 1978-84, 87-89; vis. prof. Slavic langs. Columbia U., fall 1988, Harvard U., fall 1989; Oleksandr Potebnja prof. Ukrainian Philology Harvard U., 1991—, chmn. dept. Linguistics, 1994-99, chmn. dept. Slavic langs. and lits., 1999—. Author: Aspects of Nominal Determination in Old Church Slavic, 1974, Say It In Russian, 1982; editor: Slavic Forum: Essays in Slavic Linguistics and Literature, 1974, Am. Cont. to the Intl. Congress of Slavists, 1983, Ukrainian Philology and Linguistics, 1994; co-editor: Medieval Russian Culture, 1984, Issues in Russian Morphosyntax, 1985, The Scope of Slavic Aspect, 1985, Language, Literature, Linguistics, 1987, Medieval Russian Culture, vol. 2, 1994, For SK: In Celebration of the Life and Career of Simon Karlinsky, 1994, The Language and Verse of Russia: In Honor of Dean S. Worth on His Sixty-fifth Birthday, 1995; mem. editl. bd. Slavic and East European Jour., 1989—, Movoznavstvo, 1991—. Vice chmn. Am. Com. Slavists, 1989-94, chmn., 1994—. Internat. Rsch. and Exchs. Bd. travel grantee Russia, Czechoslovakia, 1966-67, 71, 78, 93, 96; U. Calif. Pres.'s fellow, 1990, John Simon Guggenheim Meml. Found. fellow, 1990-91. Mem. Linguistics Soc. Am., Am. Assn. Tchrs. Slavic and East European Langs., Am. Assn. Advancement Slavic Studies, Western Slavic Assn., Coll. Art Assn., Am. Assn. for Ukrainian Studies (sec.-treas. 1989-93, bd. dirs.). Home: 76 Fresh Pond Ln Cambridge MA 02138-4641 Office: Harvard U Dept Slavic Langs and Lits 301 Boylston Hall Cambridge MA 02138

FLIGG, JAMES EDWARD, retired oil company executive; b. Sydney, N.S.W., Australia, June 1, 1936; came to U.S., 1975; s. Henry Joseph and Florence (Purvis) F.; m. May Dorothea Hunt, Apr. 18, 1959; children: Tracey, Jennifer. B.S., U. N.S.W., 1968; A.M.P., Harvard U., 1980. Mgr. product mgmt., fiber and film intermediates Amoco Chem. Corp., Chgo., 1975-78; mgr. corp. planning Standard Oil Co. (Ind.), Chgo., 1978-80; v.p. mktg. olefins and polymers Amoco Chem. Corp., Chgo., 1980-82, v.p. internat. ops., 1982-85, group v.p. chems. and polymers, 1985-88, group v.p. chem. and specialty products, 1989-91, exec. v.p. internat. ops. and polymer products, 1991, pres., 1991-99; ret., 1999. Bd. mgrs. YMCA Chgo. Mem. Soc. Chem. Industry (exec. com.), Chem. Mfrs. Assn. (bd. dirs.), Nat. Petroleum Refiners Assn. (chair petrochem. com.), Mid-Am. Club, Chgo. Club, Club Internat. Home: Apt 16 B 1120 N Lake Shore Dr Chicago IL 60611-1017*

FLIGSTEN, ANN M., historic foundation director. AB, Goucher Coll., 1968; JD, U. Md., 1975. Pvt. practice law, 1975-92; pres. Hist. Annapolis Found., 1992—; bd. dirs. Hist. Annapolis Found., Preservation Action, AAAC Conf. and Vis. Bur. Mem. Nat. Trust for Hist. Preservation, Md. Heritage Alliance, Friends of Hancock's Resolution, Md. Hist. and Cultural Mus. Assistance Rev. Panel. Office: Hist Annapolis Found 18 Pinkney St Annapolis MD 21401-1718*

FLINK, JANE DUNCAN, publisher; b. Atlanta, Feb. 17, 1929; d. James Archibald and Frances (Watkins) Duncan; m. Richard Albert Flink, Nov. 20, 1954; children: Jennifer, Elizabeth, Caroline, Charles Albert, James Duncan. Student, Carleton Coll., U. Mo. Reporter Tri-Town News, Greendale, Wis., 1958-61; reporter, photographer, feature writer, editor Ctrl. Mo. Rural & Farm Life Mag., Centralia (Mo.) Fireside, 1973-78; editor bus. briefs MFA Oil Co., Columbia, Mo., 1977; editor lifestyles Kingdom Daily News, Fulton, Mo., 1978-82; asst. editor Ctrl. Mo. Rural & Farm Life Mag., Centralia (Mo.) Fireside, 1982-83; assoc. editor Mo. Ruralist, Columbia, 1983-85; dir. external rels. Winston Churchill Meml. & Libr. Westminster Coll., Fulton, 1985-89, dir., 1989-90; owner, pub. Boone County Jour., Ashland, Mo., 1986—. Editor, pub.: Time and the River, 1993. Rep. committeewoman Ward 1 Centralia, 1972, 74, 76; mem. exec. bd. Friends of Winston Churchill Meml. and Libr., Fulton, 1978-97; mem. Boone County Commn. on Child Abuse, 1978-81, Boone County Hist. Soc.; bd. dirs., mem. pub. rels., devel., Maplewood coms., Walters-Boone County Mus. and Visitors Ctr., 1995—, 1st v.p. 1996-98, pres. 1998—; mem. Boone County Gov. Rev. Task Force, 1991-92, chair So. Boone County Sch. Budget Rev. Task Force, 1991-92; pres. Lake Champetra Homewoners Assn., 1993-95, v.p. 1995-96; vice chair Boone County Constn. Writing Commn., 1995-96; mem. ext. coun. U. Mo., 1995-97; co-chmn. Friends So. Boone County Fire Protection Dist., 1995-97. Mem. Nat. Fedn. Press Women (bd. dirs. 1991-93, 21st century com. 1992-93, Nat. Achievement award 1982), So. Boone County C. of C. (chmn. econ. devel. com. 1998—), Mo. Press Women (dist. v.p., v.p., treas. chmn. honors awards, pres. 1991-93. Communicator of Yr. award 1978, 79, 80, 81, 82, 83,85, 86, 95, Woman of Achievement award 1989), Mo. Press Assn., Mo. Soc. Newspaper Editors. Home: 7230 E North Shore Dr Hartsburg MO 65039-9633 Office: Boone County Jour 104 W Broadway Ashland MO 65010-9779

FLINKSTROM, HENRY ALLAN, sales executive; b. Ashby, Mass., Feb. 19, 1933; s. William Elias and Selma Catherine (Aho) F.; m. Marian June Linnus, May 14, 1950; children: Leonard A., Eric A., Carl E. Grad. high sch., Ashby, 1951; diploma in constrn., Fitchburg (Mass.) High, 1953. Ind. carpenter Fitchburg, 1950-54; salesman Webber Lumber, Fitchburg, 1954-64; v.p. Morgan-Price Constrn., Ashburnham, Mass., 1964-66; contractor, sales mgr. Webber Lumber, Fitchburg, 1966-80; sales rep. Sawyer Lumber, Worcester, Mass., 1981-82, Webber Lumber (merger Sawyer Lumber and Webber Lumber), Worcester and Fitchburg, 1982-92, G.V. Moore Lumber, Ayer, Mass., 1993—; home designer HAF Design, Fitchburg; real estate broker Flinkstroms. Charter mem. Rep. Presdl. Task Force, Rep. Nat. Com., 1984—, Mass. Chiefs of Police Assoc., Fitchburg Art Mus. Mem. Am. Plywood Assn., Club of Saima-Fitchburg, U.S. Senatorial Club, Masons. Avocations: classic cars, antiques, music, skiing. Home and Office: HAF Design 19 Ashburnham State Rd Fitchburg MA 01420-6669

FLINN, DAVID LYNNFIELD, financial consultant; b. Atlanta, Aug. 6, 1943; s. William Adams and Caroline Elizabeth (Blackshear) F.; divorced; children: Raymur Elizabeth, Marion Orme. BA, Ga. State U., 1967. With Citizens & So. Nat. Bank, Atlanta and Miami, Fla., 1967-70; asst. to pres. Panelfab Internat. Corp., Miami, 1970-72; v.p. Citibank, Miami, 1972-76; ind. fin. cons. Miami, 1976—; CFO, Aljoma Lumber, Inc., Miami, 1990—; cons. various fgn. corps., 1981—; bd. dirs. Aljoma Lumber, Inc., Medley, Fla., Continental Trust Mortgage Corp., Miami, Hamilton Bank N.A., Miami. Bd. dirs., former pres. La Gorce Island Assn., 1974-89; bd. dirs. Children's Home Soc., Miami, 1980-83. Mem. La Gorce Country Club (Miami Beach, Fla.), Fisher Island Club (Miami), Com. of 100 (Miami). Republican. Episcopalian. Home: 1717 N Bayshore Dr Apt 1231 Miami FL 33132-1150 Office: 10300 NW 121st Way Miami FL 33178-1003

FLINN, MICHAEL JAMES, lawyer; b. Pitts., June 9, 1949; s. George E. and Iris R. (Schartl) F.; m. Eileen McGrady, Aug. 7, 1971; children: Erin, Kevin. BA, U. Notre Dame, 1971; JD, U. Pitts., 1974. Bar: Pa. 1974, U.S. Dist. Ct. (we. dist.) Pa. 1974. Assoc. Moorhead & Knox, Pitts., 1974-81; ptnr. Buchanan Ingersoll, P.C., Pitts., 1981—; dir. Buchanan Ingersoll Ltd., London. Pres. Nat. Aviary, 1992-97; mem. adv. bd. The Salvation Army, Southwestern Pa., 1993—. Home: 728 Harden Dr Pittsburgh PA 15229-1107 Office: Buchanan Ingersoll PC 301 Grant St Ste 21 Pittsburgh PA 15219-1408

FLINN, MICHAEL JOSEPH, marketing executive; b. Balt., May 28, 1958; s. Eugene Aloyuis and Rose Flora (Maranto) F.; m. Toni Lee Staples, June 12, 1982; children: Katy Elizabeth, Sydney Lee, Sarah Michael, Margaret Rose. AB in Religion, Duke U., 1981. Mgr. concessions Durham (N.C.) Bulls, 1979-81; pres. T.E.M.S. Inc., Durham, 1982-85; asst. v.p. Merrill Lynch, Anniston, Ala., 1985-89; v.p., dir. mktg., portfolio mgr. Reiser-Builder/Russell, Atlanta, 1989-91; v.p., prin. Bennington Capital Mgmt., Seattle, 1991-93; v.p., dir. asset allocations svcs. and fin. planning Legg Mason, Balt., 1993-95, v.p., dir. planning and asset allocation, 1995-96; sr. v.p., nat. sales dir. ADAM/PMS Investment Svcs., Atlanta, 1996-98; pres., CEO Timber Ridge Fin. Advisors, Atlanta, 1998—. Fundraiser United Way, Anniston, 1985-89, Atlanta, 1989—. Avocations: tennis, fishing, water sports, hiking. Office: 4797 Old Timber Ridge Rd Marietta GA 30068-1685

FLINN, ROBERTA JEANNE, management and computer applications consultant; b. Twin Falls, Idaho, Dec. 19, 1947; d. Richard H. and Ruth (Johnson) F. Student Colo. State U., 1966-67. Cert. Novell netware engr. Ptnr., Aqua-Star Pools & Spas, Boise, Idaho, 1978—, mng. ptnr., 1981-83; ops. mgr. Polly Pools, Inc., Canby, Oreg., 1983-84, br. mgr. Polly Pools, Inc., A-One Distributing, 1984-85; comptr., Beaverton Printing, Inc., 1986-89; mng. ptnr. Invisible Ink, Canby, Oreg., 1989—. Mem. Nat. Appaloosa Horse Club, Oreg. Dressage Soc., NetWare Users International (Portland chpt.). Home: 24687 S Central Point Rd Canby OR 97013-9743

FLINNER, BEATRICE EILEEN, retired library and media sciences educator; b. Uledi, Pa., Feb. 8, 1924; d. Charles Robert and Esther Marjorie (Sickles) Jeffreys; m. Donald Allayaud, May 18, 1944 (dec.); 1 child, Donald Allayaud; m. Lyle P. Flinner, June 27, 1947; 1 child, Carol Jean Flinner Dorough. AB summa cum laude, So. Nazarene U., 1974; MLS, U. Okla., 1977; MA in Social Studies, So. Nazarene U., 1978, MA in Early Childhood, 1981. Cataloging dept. Asbury Theol. Sem., Wilmore, Ky., 1949-52; aquisitions Geneva Coll., Beaver Falls, Pa., 1959-62, audio visual coord., 1965-68; assoc. prof., head pub. svcs. So. Nazarene U., Bethany, Okla., 1968-96, adj. prof. grad. edn., 1981—; ret., 1996; adv. bd. Bethany Libr., rep. to bd. trustees, 1986-87. Book reviewer The Christian Librarian, 1980-94; indexer Christian Periodical Index, 1988-96; contbr. articles to profl. jours. Mem. AAUW, Okla. Libr. Assn., Assn. Christian Librs. (v.p. 1991-93, program chair internat. conf. 1992), Okla. Assn. Coll. and Rsch. Librs., Univ. Women's Club, U. Okla. Sch. Libr. Info. Sci. Alumni Assn., Assn. Christian Librs. (conf. coord. 1992-95), Rsch. Interest Group (chairperson), Acad. Sr. Profls., Phi Delta Lambda. Republican. Nazarene.

FLINT, GEORGE SQUIRE, lawyer; b. Ft. Wayne, Ind., Oct. 28, 1930; s. A. Verne and Alberta (Minor) F.; m. Emily Gregg McLees, Nov. 23, 1968; 1 son, Alexander C.; children by previous marriage: Julia M., Melissa A., Anthony E. A.B., U. Mich., 1952, J.D., 1955. Bar: N.Y. 1956. Assoc., then sr. assoc. firm Fulton, Walter & Duncombe, N.Y.C., 1955-65; ptnr. Fulton, Duncombe and Rowe, 1983-89; with Tenneco Chems., Inc., 1965-82, v.p., sec., gen. counsel, 1969-82; counsel Jackson & Nash, N.Y.C., 1989—; arbitrator Small Claims Part. Civil Ct., N.Y.C. Served with USNR, 1955-57. Mem. N.Y. State Bar Assn., Assn. Bar City N.Y., Order of Coif. Clubs: Indian Harbor Yacht, Wadawanuck, Stonington. Home: 1185 Park Ave New York NY 10128-1308 Office: 330 Madison Ave New York NY 10017-5001

FLINT, H. HOWARD, II, printing company executive. With Flint Ink Corp., Redford, Milw., 1960—, pres., 1985-92, chmn. bd., ceo, 1992—. Office: Flint Ink Corp 4600 Arrowhead Dr Redford MI 48105*

FLINT, JERRY, writer; b. Detroit, 1931. BA in Journalism, Wayne State U., 1953. Journalist, Chgo./Detroit burs. Wall St. Jour., 1956-57, N.Y. Times, N.Y.C., 1967-73; Washington bur. chief/asst. mng. editor/sr. editor Forbes Inc., N.Y.C., 1973—; auto columnist, N.Y.C., 1996—; columnist Ward's Auto World, Detroit, 1996—; automotive commentator, CNNFN, N.Y., 1996—. Author: The Dream Machine. Office: Forbes Inc 60 5th Ave New York NY 10011-8882

FLINT, JOHN E., historian, educator; b. Montreal, Que., Can., May 17, 1930; s. Alfred Edgar and Sarah (Pickup) F.; m. Nezhat Sepanj, Sept. 19, 1975; children: Helen Sarah, Richard John. B.A., U. Cambridge, 1952, M.A., 1954; Ph.D., U. London, 1957. Asst. lectr., lectr., reader colonial history King's Coll., U. London, 1954-67; vis. prof., Fulbright fellow U. Calif., Santa Barbara, 1960-61; vis. prof., head history dept. U. Nigeria, Nsukka, 1963-64; prof. history Dalhousie U., 1967—, dir. African Studies Centre, 1967-92; prof. emeritus, 1993—; mem. acad. panel Can. Council, 1967-68, Social Scis. and Humanities Research Council Can. Author: Sir George Goldie and the Making of Nigeria, 1960, Nigeria and Ghana, 1966, Cecil Rhodes, 1974; Editor: Cambridge History of Africa, Vol. V, 1790-1870, 1977. Fellow Royal Hist. Soc., Royal Soc. Can.; mem. Canadian Assn. African Studies, Canadian Hist. Assn., Nigerian Hist. Assn., African Studies Assn. U.K.

FLINT, LOU JEAN, retired state education official; b. Ogden, Utah, July 11, 1934; d. Elmer Blood and Ella D. (Adams) F.; children: Dirk Kershaw Brown, Kristie Susan Brown Felix, Flint Kershaw Brown. BS, Weber State Coll., 1968; MEd, U. Utah, 1974, EdS, 1981. Cert. early childhood and elem. edn., Utah Bd. Edn., 1968, edn. adminstrn., 1981. Master tchr. Muir Elem., Davis Sch. Dist., Farmington, Utah, 1968-77; edn. specialist Dist. I Dept. Def., various locations, Eng., Scotland, Norway, 1977-79; ednl. cons. Office Higher Edn. State of Utah Utah Sys. Approach to Individualized Learning, various locations, Tex., S.C., Fla., Utah, 1979-81; acad. affairs officer Commn. Higher Edn. Office, State of Utah, Salt Lake City, 1982-98; mem. Women's Politics Caucus; adv. bd. Women and Bus. Conf.; mem. MHCS Centennial Com., 1995-96; welfare reform demonstration project State of Utah, 1992-96, foster care citizen rev. pilot project. Author: The Comprehensive Community College, 1980, others. Recipient Appreciation award Gov. of Utah, 1983-85, 93, Woman of Achievement award Utah Bus. and Profl. Women, 1985, Pathfinder award C. of C., 1988, Outstanding Educator award YWCA, 1989, Silver Apple award Utah State U., 1992, award for svcs. Utah Mental Health Assn., 1996; named Exemplary Tchr., Utah State Bd. Edn., 1970-77, Outstanding Educator, London Ctrl. H.S., 1979. Mem. AAUW (Edn. Found. award given in her honor 1986, named Woman Who Makes History 1994), Nat. Assn. Women's Work/Women's Worth (Disting. Woman award 1987), Women's Polit. Caucus (Susa Young Gates award 1987), Nat. Assn. Edn. Young Children, Utah Assn. Edn. Young Children (past pres.), Women Concerned About Nuc. War, Utah Jaycee Aux. (past pres. Centerville), Crones Coun., Math. Sci. Network, Mormon.

FLINT-FERGUSON, JANIS DEANE, English language educator; b. Chgo., June 6, 1953; d. Warren Francis Jr. and Dorajean (Buch) F.; m. Robert Rex Ferguson, Sept. 2, 1978. BA, North Ctrl. Coll., 1975; MS, Ill. State U., 1985, DA, 1993. Tchr. lang. arts Paris (Ill.) Union Schs., 1977-79, Gibson City (Ill.) Cmty. Schs., 1979-90; assoc. prof. Gordon Coll., Wenham, Mass., 1990—; dept. chair Gordon Coll., Wenham, 1997—; cons. mid. schs. Co-editor: Readings are Writing, 1995; contbr. articles to profl. jours. Named Coll. Educator of Yr., Mass. Assn. Tchr. Educators, 1997. Mem. Nat. Coun. Tchrs. English, Northeast Alliance Mid. Schs. (chair 1995—), New England League Mid. Schs. (com. chair 1994—). Congregationalist. Avocation: sailing. Office: Gordon Coll 255 Grapevine Rd Wenham MA 01984-1813

FLINTOFF, COREY ALAN, radio newscaster, writer; b. Fairbanks, Alaska, Apr. 8, 1946; s. Alan Dixon and Marjory Doris (Herman) F.; m. Diana Derby, June 24, 1990; 1 child, Claire Parnell. BA, U. Calif., Berkeley, 1970; MA, U. Chgo., 1971. Freelance writer/reporter Chgo., 1971-77; news dir., documentarian KYUK-AM/TV, Bethel, Alaska, 1977-84; host, prodr. Alaska Pub. Radio Network, Anchorage, 1984-89; newscaster NPR, Washington, 1990—; assoc. prof. radio and TV, George Washington U., Washington, 1992—. With USNR, 1966-68. San Diego. Recipient Reporting award Corp. for Pub. Broadcasting, 1989. Mem. AFTRA. Avocations: fiction writing, figure skating. Office: NPR 635 Massachusetts Ave NW Washington DC 20001-3752

FLIPSE, JOHN EDWARD, naval architect, mechanical engineer; b. Montville, N.J., Feb. 4, 1921. SB, MIT, 1942; MME, NYU, 1948. Registered profl. engr., N.Y., Va., Tex. Sr. engr., ship stabilization dept. head, marine div. Sperry Gyroscope Co., Great Neck, N.Y., 1955-57; rsch. engr., dir. rsch., mgr. systems dept., asst. to pres. Newport News (Va.) Shipbuilding and Dry Dock Co., 1957-68; chmn., pres., chief exec. officer Deepsea Ventures, Inc., Gloucester, Va., 1968-77; pres., chief exec. officer Tex. A&M Rsch. Found., College Station, 1983-84; dep. dir. Tex. Engring. Experiment Sta., 1985-88; disting. prof. civil and ocean engring. Tex. A&M U., 1982-92; assoc. dean engring. Tex. A&M U., College Station, 1984-88, assoc. dep. chancellor for engring., 1984-89, Wofford Cain prof. engring., 1988-91, dir. Offshore Tech. Rsch. Ctr., 1988-91; dir. emeritus, 1991—; chmn. Nat. Adv. Com. on Oceans and Atmosphere, 1985-86; mem. marine bd. Nat. Rsch. Coun., 1979-84, chmn., 1982-84; mem. marine facilities panel U.S./Japan Coop. Program in Natural Resources, 1980—; mem. marine petroleum and minerals adv. com. Dept. Commerce, 1974-75; expert mem. U.S. delegation to Law of the Sea Conf., UN, 1975-76; cons., lectr. in field. Contbr. articles to profo. publs., patentee in field. Mem. dean's adv. coun. Sch. Engring. & Applied Sci., U. Va., 1995-98. Fellow Marine Tech. Soc. (pres. 1985-87), Soc. Naval Architects and Marine Engrs. (past chmn. tech. and rsch. steering com.); mem. Nat. Acad. Engring. (membership policy com. 1987-90, membership com. 1987-90, peer rev. com. 1985-86), Va. Inst. Marine Sci. (vice chmn. bd. dirs. 1968-76).

FLISS, RAPHAEL M., bishop; b. Milw., Oct. 25, 1930. Student, St. Francis Sem., Houston, Cath. U., Washington. Ordained priest, Roman Cath. Ch., 1956. Bishop Superior, Wis., 1985—. Office: Chancery Office PO Box 969 1201 Hughitt Ave Superior WI 54880-1631*

FLITCRAFT, RICHARD KIRBY, II, former chemical company executive; b. Woodstown, N.J., Sept. 5, 1920; s. H. Milton and Edna (Crispin) F.; m. Bertha LeSturgeon Hitchner, Nov. 14, 1942; children: Alyce, Anne, Elizabeth, Richard. BS, Rutgers U., 1942; MS, Washington U., 1948. With Monsanto Co., St. Louis, 1942—; dir. inorganic rsch. Monsanto Co., 1960-65, dir. mgmt. info. and systems dept., 1965-67, asst. to pres., 1967-68, group mgr. electronics enterprises, 1968-69, gen. mgr. electronic products div., 1969-71; v.p. Monsanto Rsch. Corp., 1971-75; dir. Mound Lab., 1971-75, v.p. ops., 1975-76; pres. Monsanto Resh. Corp., Dayton, 1976-82, ret., 1982. Past chmn., bd. dirs. United Way, Dayton; bd. dirs. City-Wide Devel. Corp.; former trustee Miami Valley Hosp.; past bd. dirs. Pvt. Industry Coun., Srs., Inc.; chmn. bd. Headstart program Miami Valley Child Devel., Inc. Mem. AAAS, AICE, Am. Chem. Soc., Am. Inst. Chemists, Am. Mgmt. Assn., N.Y. Acad. Scis., Ohio Acad. Scis. (past exec. com.), Dayton C. of C. (past bd. dirs., chmn. small bus. adv. bd., mil. affairs com.), Engrs. Club of Dayton (past bd. dirs.), Engrs. Club Dayton Found. (bd. trustees, chmn.), Moraine Country Club, Dayton Racquet Club. Presbyterian.

FLITTIE, CLIFFORD GILLILAND, retired petroleum company executive; b. Brookings, S.D., Mar. 10, 1924; s. Theodore Ignatius and Grace Eliza (Gilliland) F.; m. Dawn Marie Lee, May 22, 1954. Student, Okla. State U., 1944, Colo. Sch. Mines, 1946; B.S. (Nat. scholar Am. Inst. Mining and Metall. Engrs.), S.D. Sch. Mines and Tech., 1948. Geologist Arabian Am. Oil Co., Dhahran, Saudi Arabia, 1948-57; v.p. exploration Conorada Petroleum Corp., N.Y.C., 1958-63; dir. Conorada Petroleum Corp., 1963-65; v.p., mgr. Amerada Petroleum Corp. of U.K., London, 1964-65, Amerada Petroleum Corp. of Australia, Brisbane, 1966-69; exploration supr. Amerada Hess Corp., N.Y.C., 1970-73; v.p. Shaheen Natural Resources Co., Inc., N.Y.C., 1974-75, Macmillan Oil Co., N.Y.C., 1975-82, Natomas Co., San Francisco, 1982-86; dir. Amerada Exploration Ltd., 1964-65. Served with USNR, 1944-46. Mem. Am. Assn. Petroleum Geologists, Soc. Exploration Geophysicists, Theta Tau, Sigma Tau. Episcopalian. Home: 46 San Jacinto Way San Francisco CA 94127-2033

FLOCH, MARTIN HERBERT, physician; b. N.Y.C., July 24, 1928; s. Samuel and Jean (Scheinman) F.; m. Gladys Wisser, Nov. 24, 1954; children: Jeffrey Aaron, Craig Lawrence, Lisa Suzanne, Neil Robert. B.A., NYU, 1949; M.S., U. N.H., 1950; M.D., N.Y. Med. Coll., 1956. Diplomate: Am. Bd. Internal Medicine, Am. Bd. Gastroenterology Am. Bd. Nutrition. Intern Beth Israel Hosp., N.Y.C., 1956-57; resident in medicine Beth Israel Hosp., 1957-59; fellow in gastroenterology Seton Hall Coll. Medicine, South Orange, N.J., 1959-60; instr. medicine U. P.R., 1960-62; asst. attending physician Montefiore Hosp., N.Y.C., 1962-64; practice medicine specializing in gastroenterology Norwalk, Conn., 1962—; mem. staff Norwalk Hosp., 1964—, chmn. dept. medicine, 1970-94, chief gastroenterology and nutrition, 1970-98; clin. prof. medicine Yale U., New Haven, 1976—; cons. staff Griffin Hosp., Hall-Brooke Hosp., Waveny Care Center; bd. dirs. Norwalk Bank, 1987. Editor Am. Jour. Gastroenterology, 1985-91, The Gastroenterologist, 1992-98; asst. editor Am. Jour. Clin. Nutrition; editor-in-chief Jour. of Clin. Gastroenterology, 1998—; contbr. articles in field to profl. jours. Trustee Aspetuck Valley Health Dist., 1974-76, Norwalk Hosp., 1972-78. Served with M.C. U.S. Army, 1960-62. Conn. Digestive Disease Soc. grantee, 1974-76, NIH grantee, 1975-78, U.S. Army Med. Rsch. grantee, 1964-67, Leslie Found. grantee, 1980, Ednl. Found. Am. grantee, 1989-92. Fellow ACP, Master Am. Coll. Gastroenterology (bd. trustees 1985-90), Am. Soc. Gastroendoscopy, Am. Coll. Nutrition; mem. Am. Soc. Clin. Nutrition, Am. Inst. Nutrition, Am. Gastroenterology Assn. (clin. counselor governing bd. 1997—), Assn. Program Dirs. in Internal Medicine, Am. Soc. Internal Medicine, Am. Fedn. Clin. Rsch., Fairfield County Med. Soc., Conn. Med. Soc. (pres. gastroenterology sect. 1972-74), Assn. Am. Med. Coll., Conn. Digestive Disease Soc. (pres. 1972-74). Home: 32 Woody Ln Westport CT 06880-2259 Office: Norwalk Hosp 30 Stevens St Norwalk CT 06850-3813

FLOCK, JEFFREY CHARLES, news bureau chief; b. Lakewood, N.J., Mar. 16, 1958; s. Byron Harry and Vicki Ruth (Macaulay) F.; m. Elizabeth Brack, Sept. 19, 1998; children: Elizabeth Kathryn, Emily Macaulay. BS in Broadcast Journalism, Boston U., 1980. Writer, producer Cable News Network, Atlanta, 1980-81; corr. Cable News Network, Chgo., 1981-84, bur. chief, 1985—. Methodist. Avocations: running, antiques. Home: 4707 N Magnolia Ave Chicago IL 60640-4903 Office: Cable News Network 435 N Michigan Ave Ste 715 Chicago IL 60611-4076

FLOCK, ROBERT ASHBY, retired entomologist; b. Kellogg, Idaho, July 16, 1914; s. Abraham Lincoln and Florence Louise (Ashby) F.; m. Elsie Marie Ronken, Apr. 8, 1950; children: Karen Marie, Anne Louise Checkai. BS, U. Ariz., 1938, MS, 1941; PhD, U. Calif., Berkeley, 1951. Inspector Ariz. Commn. Agriculture and Horticulture, Phoenix, 1938-41, asst. entomologist, 1941-46; lab. tech. U. Calif., Riverside, 1947-52, asst. entomologist, 1952-63; entomologist Imperial County Dept. Agriculture, El Centro, Calif., 1963-85, part-time entomologist, 1985—. Contbr. articles to profl. jours. Mem. Entomol. Soc. Am., Am. Phytopathol. Soc., Pan-Pacific Entomol. Soc., AAAS, Ctr. for Process Studies, Kiwanis (pres. Imperial Valley chpt. 1984-86, Man of Yr. 1986), Sigma Xi. Republican. Methodist. Avocations: taxonomy and biology of Homoptera, desert ecology, science, religion. Home: 667 Wensley Ave PO Box 995 El Centro CA 92244-0995 Office: Imperial County Dept Agricu 150 S 9th St El Centro CA 92243-2801

FLOCKHART, CALISTA, actress; b. Freeport, Ill., Nov. 11, 1964; d. Ronald and Kay F. BA in acting, Rutgers U. Actress Ally McBeal Twentieth Century Fox, L.A. Appeared in Broadway plays, including The Glass Menagerie, The Three Sisters; television work includes: The Guiding Light, 1978, Darrow, 1991, Ally McBeal, 1997; film work includes: Quiz Show, 1994, Getting In, 1994, Naked in New York, 1994, Pictures of Baby Jane Doe, 1996, The Birdcage, 1996, Milk and Money, 1997, Drunks, 1997, Telling Lies in America, 1997, A Midsummer Night's Dream, 1999, Like a Hole in the Head, 1999, Jane Doe, 1999. Recipient Best Actress award Golden Globes, 1998 for her work on Ally McBeal. Office: Ally McBeal c/o David E. Kelly Productions c/o Twentieth Century Fox 10201 W Pico Blvd Bldg 80 Los Angeles CA 90064-2606*

FLOERSHEIM, SANDRA KELTON, community health nurse; b. Santa Monica, Calif., Jan. 31, 1948; d. Frank B. and Louise C. (Crawford) Kelton; children: Bruce, Todd. Diploma, Rapid City Hosp. Sch. Nursing, 1981; BSN, S.D. State U., 1982. Cert. community health nurse. Staff nurse Rapid City (S.D.) Regional Hosp., 1981-82; charge nurse North County Hosp., Newport, Vt., 1982-84; staff nurse Orleans (Vt.) & No. Essex Home Health Agy., 1984-88, quality assurance coord., 1988, dir. nursing, 1988-96; clin. supr. Ctrl. Vt. Home Health and Hospice, Barre, 1996-99, clin. dir., 1999—. Co-author: Orleans & Northern Essex Home Health Agency Procedure Manual for Nurses and Aides, 1988. Co-chair Lake Region Union High Sch. Grad Night, 1990—, fund raiser, 1989; mem. Drug and Alcohol Abuse Prevention/Edn. adv. coun. Lake Region Union High Sch., 1988—; speaker Vt. Project Graduation, 1987. Recipient Disting. Friend of Edn. award Vt. Headmasters Assn., 1989. Mem. ANA, Vt. Nurses Assn., Sigma Theta Tau. Home: 30 North Ave Orleans VT 05860-1124

FLOHR, DANIEL P., company executive. Pres. C-Phone Inc., Wilmington, N.C., 1986—. Office: C-Phone Inc 6714 Netherlands Dr Wilmington NC 28405-3775*

FLOM, EDWARD LEONARD, retired steel company executive; b. Tampa, Fla., Dec. 10, 1929; s. Samuel Louis and Julia (Mittle) F.; m. Beverly Boyett, Mar. 31, 1956; children—Edward Louis, Mark Robert, Julia Ruth. B.C.E., Cornell U., 1952. With Fla. Steel Corp., Tampa, 1954-93; v.p. sales Fla. Steel Corp., 1957-64, pres., dir., 1964-93, ret., 1993; bd. dirs. Teco Energy Inc., Outback Steakhouse Inc. Bd. dirs., mem. exec. com. Com. of 100, Tampa, United Fund Tampa; mem. adv. com. St. Joseph's Hosp., Tampa; bd. dirs. Family Svc. Assn. Tampa, Jewish Welfare Fedn. Tampa; bd. dirs. temple. With C.E., U.S. Army, 1952-54. Mem. Am. Iron and Steel Inst. (bd. dirs.), Fla. Engring. Soc., Young Pres. Orgn., Univ. Club, Palma Ceia Golf and Country Club, Tampa Yacht Club, Gasparilla Krewe, Rotary (bd. dirs. Tampa). Home: 4936 St Croix Dr Tampa FL 33629-4831

FLOM, GERALD TROSSEN, lawyer; b. Neenah, Wis., Feb. 6, 1930; s. Russell Craig and Lois Eva (Trossen) F.; m. Martha Herrington Benton, Aug. 21, 1954 (div. June 25, 1980); children—Katherine Simmons, Sarah Elizabeth, Russell Craig. BA magna cum laude, Lawrence U., 1952; JD, Yale U., 1957. Bar: Minn. 1957, U.S. Dist. Ct. Minn. 1957. Assoc. Faegre & Benson LLP, Mpls., 1957-64, ptnr., 1964-95; retired, 1995; adj. asst. prof. Law Sch., U. Minn., Mpls., 1966, bd. dirs., Old Republic Natl. Title Holding Co. and Old Republic Natl. Title Ins. Co., 1977-99. Mem. editorial bd. Yale Law Jour. Trustee Mpls. Soc. Fine Arts, 1970-76, Lawrence U., 1974-81, Plymouth Congl. Ch., 1978-81, William Mitchell Coll. Law, St. Paul, 1983-89; bd. dirs. Met. Med. Ctr. Research Found., Mpls., 1975-85. Served with U.S. Army, 1952-54. Mem. ABA, Minn. State Bar Assn., Hennepin County Bar Assn., Assn. Bar City of N.Y., Phi Beta Kappa, Phi Delta Theta, Phi Alpha Delta. Republican. Congregationalist. Clubs: Mace; Minneapolis; Interlachen Country (Edina, Minn.). Home: 3434 Zenith Ave S Minneapolis MN 55416-4663 Office: Faegre & Benson LLP 2200 Norwest Ctr 90 S 7th St Minneapolis MN 55402-3901

FLOM, JOSEPH HAROLD, lawyer; b. Balt., Dec. 20, 1923; s. Isadore and Fannie (Fishman) F.; m. Claire Cohen, Nov. 14, 1958; children: Peter Leslie, Jason Robert. Student, Coll. City N.Y.; LLB cum laude, Harvard U., 1948; LHD (hon.), Queens Coll., 1984; LLD (hon.), Fordham U., 1990. Practice of law N.Y.C., 1949—; bd. dirs. Warnaco, Inc., Am.-Israel Friendship League; spl. counsel subcom. on adminstrn. of internal revenue laws House Ways and Means Com., 1951-52; mem. com. on tender offers SEC, 1983. Editor Harvard Law Rev., 1947-48; co-editor: Disclosure Requirements of Public Corporations and Insiders, 1967, Texas Gulf Sulphur-Insider Disclosure Problems, 1968, Lawyer's Conflicts-The Evolving Case Law, 1991. Mem. N.Y.C. Mayor's Commn. on Status of Women, 1976-77; mem. Mayor's Coun. Econ. Advisors, 1990-93; co-chmn. task force on capital fin. and constrn. N.Y.C. Bd. Edn., 1987-89; co-chmn. N.Y.C. Operation Welcome Home Commn., 1991; chmn. N.Y.C. Commn. on Bicentennial of Constn., 1986-89; trustee Fedn. Jewish Philanthropies N.Y., 1977-86, Barnard Coll., 1983-93, N.Y. Hist. Soc., 1989-94; chair adv. com. Export-Import Bank of U.S., 1995; trustee Mt. Sinai-NYU Health Sys., 1978—; trustee Petrie Stores Liquidating Trust; mem. Archdiocesan Task Force on Crime Prevention and Youth, 1982-87; trustee Skadden Fellowship Found., Constl. Edn. Found., 1989-93, United Way N.Y.C., 1991-97; mayor's rep. Met. Mus. of Art, 1990-93; mem. Mayor's Mgmt. Adv. Task Force, 1991-93; chair Woodrow Wilson Internat. Ctr. for Scholars, 1994-98. Fellow ABA; mem. Assn. Bar City N.Y. Office: Skadden Arps Slate 919 3rd Ave Fl 35 New York NY 10022-3902

FLOM, ROBERT MICHAEL, interior designer; b. Grand Forks, N.D., Oct. 27, 1952; s. John Nicholai and Irene Magdaline (Miller) F.; m. Holly Suzanne Schue, July 20, 1975 (div. June 1986); m. Margaret Elizabeth Moon, Oct. 15, 1988; children: Amy Michelle Moon, Jamie Bryant Moon. Student, Western Tech., 1970-71, U. N.D., 1980-83, LaSalle U., 1994-95, Century U., 1996—. Asst. food and beverage mgr. Holiday Inn/Topeka Inns, Denver, 1970-71; interior designer, fl. mgr. Crossroads Furniture, Grand Forks, 1972-85; store mgr. Greenbaums, Tacoma, 1986-88, interior designer, 1986—; tng. advisor Greenbaums, Bellevue, Wash., 1988—. Mem. Am. Soc. Interior Designers (allied mem.), Autism Soc. Tacoma-Pierce County (treas. 1991—). Avocations: reading, cycling, cross-country skiing, hiking, woodworking. Home: 6816 47th St W Tacoma WA 98466-4912 Office: Greenbaums 929 118th Ave SE Bellevue WA 98005-3889

FLOOD, A. L. (AL FLOOD), retired bank executive; b. Monkton, Ont., Can., 1935; married; 4 children. Grad. program for mgmt. devel., Harvard U. Various mgmt. positions corp. & credit ops. Can. Imperial Bank of Commerce, Toronto, 1951-74; area exec. U.S.A. and Latin Am. Can. Imperial Bank of Commerce, 1974-78, gen. mgr. U.S.A. and Latin Am., 1978-79, v.p. corp. banking, 1979-80, v.p. U.S. ops., 1980-83, sr. v.p. U.S. ops., 1983-84, head internat. ops., 1984, exec. v.p., 1984-86, pres., 1986-92, chmn., CEO, 1992-99, also bd. dirs. Trustee Hosp. for Sick Children; mem. adv. bd. Boys and Girls Club of Can.; mem. dean's adv. coun. Faculty of Mgmt., U. Toronto; dir. Coun. for Can. Unity; chmn. Bus. Coun. on Nat. Issues; bd. govs. Jr. Achievement Can. Office: Can Imperial Bank Commerce, Commerce Court, Toronto, ON Canada M5L 1A2

FLOOD, DIANE LUCY, marketing communications specialist; b. Plainfield, N.J., June 13, 1937; d. William Edward and Lucy (Dycker) Flood. BA, Vassar Coll., 1959; postgrad., Fontainebleau Sch. Fine Arts, France, 1961. Advt. prodn. aide indsl. chem. divsn. Am. Cyanamid Co., Wayne, N.J., 1959-62, prodn. supr., 1962-64, creative coord. organic chems. divsn. advt., 1964-66, design art and copy mgr., 1966-70, advt. rep., 1970-72, advt. rep. paper, process chems. and resins, indsl. chem. divsn., 1972-77, advt. coord. water treating, mining, paper, oil recovery chems., 1977-83, mgr. mktg. comms. indsl. products div., 1983—, mgr. mktg. comms. Venture Chems. divsn., 1986-87, Chem. Products and Indsl. Products divsn., 1987-89, mgr. mktg. comms. Chem. Products Indsl. Products and Interna, 1989-90, mgr. mktg. comms. Chem. Group, 1990-93, mgr. Global Mktg. Comms., 1993-99, retired, 1999; comms. cons. 1999—. Past dir., v.p., past pres. 102 Gedney St. Owners Co-op, 1985-92. Home: 103 Gedney St Apt 3C Nyack NY 10960-2227 Office: 103 Gedney St Lobby Office Nyack NJ 10960

FLOOD, DOROTHY GARNETT, neuroscientist; m. Paul David Coleman, Feb. 26, 1983. BA cum laude, Lawrence U., 1973; student, U. Ill., 1972-73; MS, PhD, U. Rochester, N.Y., 1980. Sr. instr. in anatomy U. Rochester, 1980-83, asst. prof. neurology, neurobiology and anatomy, 1984-90, assoc. prof. neurology, neurobiology and anatomy, 1990-94; sr. sci. Cephalon, Inc., West Chester, Pa., 1994—. Contbr. to book chpts. and articles in field; mem. editl. bd. Neurobiology of Aging, 1989—. Recipient Fenn award U. Rochester, 1980; grantee NSF, NIH, Office of Naval Rsch., 1979-94. Mem. Soc. Neurosci. Office: Cephalon Inc 145 Brandywine Pkwy West Chester PA 19380-4249

FLOOD, (HULDA) GAY, editor, consultant; b. Plainfield, N.J., Aug. 14, 1935; d. William Edward and Lucy (Dycker) F.; BA, Smith Coll., 1957. Picture dept. Sports Illustrated, Time Inc., N.Y.C. 1957-58, letters dept., 1958-59, reporter, 1959-60, writer-reporter, 1960-71, assoc. editor, 1971-85, sr. editor, 1985-90; editor, cons., 1990—. Mem. Alumnae Assn. Smith Coll., Smith Coll. Students Aid Soc., Smith Coll. Club N.Y., Garden Club of Nyack., mem. Greater Consistory 1st Reformed Ch., Nyack, N.Y. Office: 103 Gedney St Apt 3C Nyack NY 10960-2227

FLOOD, JAMES TYRRELL, broadcasting executive, public relations consultant; b. Los Angeles, Oct. 5, 1934; s. James Joseph and Teresa (Rielly) F.; m. Bonnie Carolyn Lutz, Mar. 25, 1966; children: Hilary C., Sean L. BA in Liberal Arts, U. Calif., Santa Barbara, 1956; MA in Communications, Calif. State U., Chico, 1981. Publicist Rogers & Cowan, 1959-60, Jim Mahoney & Assocs., 1960-61, ABC-TV, San Francisco and Hollywood, Calif., 1961-64; cons. pub. relations, Beverly Hills, Calif., 1964-72; pub. relations, advt. dir. Jerry Lewis Films, 1964-72; dir. pub. rels. MTM Prodns., 1970-72; pub. relations cons. Medic Alert Found. Internat., 1976-83; owner, mgr. Sta. KRIJ-FM, Paradise, 1983-88; instr. Calif. State U. Sch. Communications, Chico, 1982-89; gen. mgr. KIXE-TV (PBS), Redding-Chico, Calif., 1991-92; media cons., 1993—. represented numerous artists including Pearl Bailey, Gary Owens, Ruth Buzzi, Allen Ludden, Betty White, Celeste Holm, Jose Feliciano, Tom Kennedy, Shirley Jones, David Cassidy, others. Pub. rels. dir. Warren Miller Prodns., 1967—, Mary Tyler Moore Prodns., 1971. Calif. media cons. Carter/Mondale campaign, 1976; mem. Calif. Dem. Fin. Com., 1982-83. Served with USNR, 1956-58. Mem. Calif. Broadcasters Assn. (bd. dirs. 1986-88).

FLOOD, MARK DAMIEN, finance educator; b. St. Louis, Mo., July 3, 1960; s. Robert E. and Margaret C. F.; m. Rebecca E. Dalton. BS in Fin., Ind. U., 1982, BA in German and Econs., 1983; PhD in Fin., U. N.C., 1990. Fin. adminstrn. trainee Commerzbank AG, N.Y.C., 1984-85; economist Fed. Reserve Bank of St. Louis, 1989-93; asst. prof. fin. Concordia U., Montreal, Quebec, Can., 1993—; economist Office of Thrift Supervision, Washington, 1999—; vis. asst. prof. fin. U. N.C., Charlotte, 1998-99; cons. FDIC, Washington, 1996-97, Fed. Reserve Bank of N.Y., 1996. Author: (book) Financial Markets and the Economy: The Canadian Experience, 1998; (software) Flannery and Flood's Probanker: A financial services simulation, 1998; also articles in profl. jours. Recipient grad. sch. fellowship U. N.C., Chapel Hill, 1985; grantee Social Scis. and Humanities Rsch. Coun., Can., 1994. E-mail address: (O) mdflood@email.uncc.edu. Office: Office Thrift Supervision 4700 G St NW Washington DC 20552

FLOOR, RICHARD EARL, lawyer; b. Lynn, Mass., Aug. 3, 1940; s. Albert C. and Blanche (Goldthwait) F.; m. Elizabeth Wilson, Apr. 19, 1969; children: Amy, Lucy, Rebecca. AB, Fairfield U., 1962; JD, Harvard Law Sch., 1965. Bar: Mass. 1965. Law clk. to Hon. C.P. O'Sullivan U.S. Ct. Appeals (6th cir.), 1965-66; assoc. Goodwin, Procter & Hoar, Boston, 1966-74, ptnr., 1974—, mem. mgmt. com., exec. com., 1987-93; lectr. Harvard Bus. Sch., Cambridge, 1988-92; bd. dirs. Affiliated Mgrs. Group, Inc., New Am. High Income Fund, NYSE, Altamira Mgmt., Ltd. Contbr. articles to profl. jours. Co-chmn. reverse investment com. internat. trade adv. bd. Commonwealth Mass., 1994; organizer Inst. Mgmt. Edn. Thailand; trustee Regis Coll., Wellesley, Mass., 1990-97; vice chmn. Harvard Ctr. Eating Disorders. Mem. ABA, Mass. Bar Assn., Boston Bar Assn. Office: Goodwin Procter & Hoar Exchange Pl Boston MA 02109-2803

FLOR, LOY LORENZ, chemist, corrosion engineer, consultant; b. Luther, Okla., Apr. 25, 1919; s. Alfred Charles and Nellie M. (Wilkinson) F.; BA in Chemistry, San Diego State Coll., 1941; m. Virginia Louise Pace, Oct. 1, 1946; children: Charles R., Scott R., Gerald C., Donna Jeanne, Cynthia Gail. With Helix Water Dist., La Mesa, Calif., 1947-84, chief chemist, 1963—, supr. water quality, 1963—, supr. corrosion control dept., 1956—. 1st. lt. USAAF, 1941-45. Registered profl. engr., Calif. Mem. Am. Chem. Soc. (chmn. San Diego sect. 1965—), Am. Water Works Assn. (chmn. water quality div. Calif. sect. 1965—), Nat. Assn. Corrosion Engrs. (chmn. western region 1970), Masons. Republican. Presbyterian.

FLORA, EDWARD BENJAMIN, research and development company executive, mechanical engineer; b. Phillipsburg, Ohio, June 23, 1929; s. Russell Thomas and Elizabeth Lucille (Hollinger) F.; m. Dolores Genevieve Havrilla, May 3, 1952; children: Christopher Dennis, Stephanie Ann, Christine Marie. BS, Carnegie Mellon U., 1951, MS, 1953. Registered profl. engr., Calif., Ohio. Project engr. Nevis Cyclotron Lab. Columbia U., Irvington, N.Y., 1953-58; sr. engr. Dalmo Victor Co., Belmont, Calif., 1958-63; ptnr. PYRCO Co., San Carlos, Calif., 1960-63; v.p., mgr. Anamet Labs., Inc., San Carlos, 1963-68, v.p., mgr. applied mechanics div., 1968-82; pres., treas. Anamet Labs., Inc., Hayward, Calif., 1982—. Mem. St. Gregory's Cath. Sch. Bd. Edn., San Mateo, Calif., 1971-72. Mem. ASME, AIAA, Soc. Automotive Engrs., Soc. for Exptl. Mechanics (chpt. treas. 1981-84), ASTM, Sequoia Club (Redwood City, Calif.). Avocation: technical analysis of commodity and financial futues markets. Home and Office: 5859 Valle Vista Ct Granite Bay CA 95746-8215

FLORA, GEORGE CLAUDE, retired neurology educator, neurologist; b. Clark, S.D., Apr. 8, 1923; s. Loren and Elma (Lyngbye) F.; m. Kristin Ann Flora; children: George, Elizabeth, John. B.S., U. S.D., 1948; M.D., Temple U., 1950. Diplomate: Am. Bd. Psychiatry and Neurology. Prof. neurology U. Minn., Mpls., 1957-73; prof. neurology U. S.D., Sioux Falls, 1973-92, prof., chairperson; cons. neurology VA Hosp., Sioux Falls, S.D., 1973—. Served to 1st lt. U.S. Army, 1950-54, Korea. Club: Minn. Alumni (Mpls.). Home: 4209 S Lewis Ave Sioux Falls SD 57103-5023*

FLORA, JAIRUS DALE, JR., statistician; b. Northfield, Minn., Mar. 27, 1944; s. Jairus Dale and Betty Ruth (Garvin) F.; m. Sharyl Ann Hughes, Aug. 18, 1967; 1 child, Edward Hughes. BS magna cum laude, Midland Luth. Coll., 1965; postgrad., Tech. U. Karlsruhe, Fed. Republic Germany, 1965-66; MS, Fla. State U., 1968, PhD, 1971. Asst. prof. biostats Sch. Pub. Health U. Mich., Ann Arbor, 1971-73; asst. prof., asst. rsch. scientist Hwy. Safety Rsch. Inst. U. Mich., 1973-76, assoc. rsch. scientist Hwy. Safety Rsch. Inst., 1976-81, assoc. prof. biostats. Sch. Pub. Health, 1976-81, prof. biostats. Sch. Pub. Health, rsch. scientist Transp. Rsch. Inst., 1981-84; prin. statistician Midwest Rsch. Inst, Kansas City, Mo., 1984-90; sr. advisor for stats. Midwest Rsch. Inst., Kansas City, Mo., 1991-99; pres. coun. prin. scientists Midwest Rsch. Inst., 1986; clin. prof. biostats. Sch. Medicine U. Mo., Kansas City, 1984—; prin. statistician Ken Wilcox Assocs., Inc., Grain Valley, Mo., 1999—; cons. statistician Nat. Burn Info. Exchange, 1971-76. Editorial collaborator Annals of Thoracic Surgery, Mathematical Bioscis., Biometrics, Accident Analysis and Prevention, 1979—; contbr. articles to profl. jours.; patentee in field. Mem. adminstrn. bd. Valley View U. Meth. Ch., 1989-92; vol. leader Boy Scouts Am. Recipient CPS Enterprise award, 1985, Dir.'s award, 1987; German Acad. Exch. Svc. fellow, 1965-66; NASA trainee, 1966-69; NIH trainee, 1969-71; Nat Hwy. Traffic Safety Adminstrn. rsch. grantee, 1974-81. Mem. Am. Statis. Assn., Biometric Soc., Inst. Math. Stats., Masons, Blue Key, Sigma Xi (pres. Kansas City chpt. 1990-91, v.p. 1994-96). Republican. Home: 9921 Foster St Shawnee Mission KS 66212-2452 Office: Ken Wilcox Assocs Inc 1125 Valley Ridge Dr Grain Valley MO 64029

FLORA, JOSEPH M(ARTIN), English language educator; b. Toledo, Feb. 9, 1934; s. Raymond D. F. and Frances (Ricica) Neumann; m. Glenda Christine Lape, Jan. 30, 1959; children: Ronald James, Stephen Ray, Peter Joseph, David Benjamin. B.A., U. Mich., 1956, M.A., 1957, Ph.D., 1962. Instr. U. Mich., Ann Arbor, 1961-62; instr. U. N.C., Chapel Hill, 1962-64, asst. prof., 1964-66, assoc. prof., 1966-77, prof. English, 1977—, acting chmn. dept. English, 1980-81, chmn., 1981-91, asst. dean grad. sch., 1967-72, assoc. dean grad. sch., 1977-78. Author: Vardis Fisher, 1965, William Ernest Henley, 1970, Frederick Manfred, 1974, Hemingway's Nick Adams, 1982 (Mayflower Cup award 1982), Ernest Hemingway: A Study of the Short Fiction, 1989; editor: The English Short Story, 1880-1945, 1985; co-editor: Southern Writers, 1979, Fifty Southern Writers Before 1990, 1987, Fifty Southern Writers After 1900, 1987, Contemporary Fiction Writers of the South, 1993, Contemporary Poets, Dramatists, Essayists, Novelists of the South, 1994; editorial bds. Mem. MLA, South Atlantic MLA (v.p. 1997-98, pres. 1998-99), Western Lit. Assn. (bd. dirs 1978-81, 83-86, v.p. 1990, pres. 1992), Soc. for Study So. Lit., Thomas Wolfe Soc. (v.p. 1993-95, pres. 1995-97), Phi Beta Kappa, Phi Eta Sigma. Home: 505 Caswell Rd Chapel Hill NC 27514-2705 Office: UNC Dept of English Chapel Hill NC 27599-3520

FLORA, KENT ALLEN, small business owner; b. Urbana, Ill., Jan. 7, 1944; s. Loyal Lee and Ercel Hannah (Puzey) F.; m. Sharon Jean Bray, Dec. 31, 1974; children: Donald William, William Christopher, Brent Allyn. BS, U. Ill., 1966. Prodn. mgr. Flora Farms, Fairmount, Ill., 1961-70, owner, operator, 1970-89; nat. sales mgr. Marketmatic Ltd., Champaign, Ill., 1990-91; owner AmeriSpec Home Inspection Svc., Champaign, 1994-96; tech. staffing specialist Snelling Search, Champaign, Ill., 1996; tech. staffing specialist dept. agri-bus. quality assurance Grossman & Assocs., Savoy, Ill., 1997—; bd. dirs. Vermilion County Agrl. Extension Adv. Council, 1967-69; nat. pres. Am. Shropshire Registry Assn., 1972-73, nat. bd. dirs., 1965-73; pres. Ill. Shrophire Assn., 1970-72; bd. dirs. Ill. Purebred Sheep Breeder's Assn., 1965-70. Mem. Jamaica Unit Dist. #12 Bd. Edn., Sidell, Ill., 1981-90, v.p. bd. dirs., 1987-90, pres. citizen's adv. council, 1978-82; trustee Vance Twp., Fairmount, 1967-75, mem. Park Bd., 1977-81; mem. exec. com. Vermilion County Rep. Cen. Com., 1986-89; v.p. Vermilion County Merit Commn. for Law Enforcement, 1986-88, pres. 1988-89; pres. Vermilion County Chmn. Unit Am. Cancer Soc., 1972-73; Vermilion County campaign coordinator Mike Houston for Ill. State Treas., 1986; Ill. 19th Congl. Dist. del. Jack Kemp for Pres., 1988. Served to sgt. USAR. Named Outstanding Young Farmer Jaycees, Danville, Ill., 1972, Hon. Chpt. Farmer Jamaica Future Farmers Assn., 1985; recipient Centennial Farm award State of Ill., 1970. Mem. U. Ill. Alumni Assn., Chi Phi, Masons, Shriners. Presbyterian. Avocations: family genealogy, collecting Coca-Cola memorabilia, travel. Home and Office: 3206 B Halifax Dr Champaign IL 61822-5216

FLORANCE, DOUGLAS ALLAN, wholesale distributor; b. Johnson City, N.Y., Feb. 19, 1924; s. Joseph Elmer and Helen (Barton) F.; m. Shirley Rae Gravius, Feb. 10, 1945; 1 child, Deborah. Student, Syracuse U., 1946-49. V.p., asst. mgr. Florance Elec. Supply Co., Inc., Binghamton, N.Y., 1949-52, v.p., mgr., 1952-60, pres., CEO, 1960-84; chief estimator Gersh-Florance Elec. Supply, Binghamton, N.Y., 1984-88; tech. advisor Olsberg-Northeast, Syracuse, N.Y., 1988-93, William H. Posthill Co., Syracuse, N.Y., 1993—; pres. Flo-Root, Inc., Binghamton, 1957—. Patentee in field. Bd. dirs. N.Y. State Industries for Blind Albany, 1981-87, chmn., 1987-88. Staff sgt. U.S. Army, 1942-46. Mem. IEEE (life), Nat. Assn. Elec. Distributors (hon. life), Internat. Assn. Elec. Inspectors, Elec Coun. So. Tier (treas. 1992-98), NRA (life). Office: Flo-Root Inc PO Box 123 Binghamton NY 13903-0123

FLOREA, ROBERT WILLIAM, real estate investment executive; b. N.Y.C., June 6, 1947; s. Stanley Robert and Mildred Barbara (Schneider) F.; m. Barbara Jordan, June 22, 1974; children: Chloe, Dylan. Student, New Sch. for Social Research, 1970-71, Lee Strasberg Inst., 1970-72, L.I. U., 1968-74. v.p., gen. mgr. Pen-Mart, N.Y.C., 1969-71; dir., writer, actor various prodn. cos., Los Angeles, 1971-77; comml. real estate sales agt. Stan Brumer Co., Inc., Los Angeles, 1977-82; sales mgr. investment dept. Schacker Realty, Melville, N.Y., 1982-85; pres., owner Robert Florea Investment Realty, Melville, 1985—; lectr. Real Estate Tng. Ctr. Author: (novel) Manhattan and Me, 1979; assoc. dir. (movie) Jigsaw Puzzle, 1968, Lord of the Dragon, 1974; stage mgr. dir.'s unit Actors Studio, Los Angeles, 1973-74. Campaign rep. Suffolk County (N.Y.) Dems., 1982—. mng. coach Huntington (N.Y.) Little League, 1986—; basketball coach St. Patrick's Girls League, Huntington. Mem. L.I. Advancement Commerce Industry (mem. tennis, golf coms., Bay (Huntington) (co-chair paddle tennis com.), Pine Hollow Club. Avocations: astronomy, art, sailing, tennis, travel. Office: Robert Florea Investment Realty Inc 510 Broadhollow Rd Melville NY 11747-3671

FLOREK, LEONA, nursing educator; b. N.J., Dec. 9, 1945; d. Leo and Viola (Trzaska) F.; children: Maura, Meghan. BS, Georgetown U., 1967; MS, U. Conn., 1990. Pediat. health nurse Pembina County, Cavalier, N.D., 1975-77; nurse coord. pediat. clinic U. Mass. Med. Ctr., Worcester, 1978; asst. prof. nursing Holyoke (Mass.) C.C., 1990—. Mem. Mass. Nurses Assn., Sigma Theta Tau. Home: 24 River Terr Holyoke MA 01040-1821 Office: Holyoke C C 303 Homestead Ave Holyoke MA 01040-1091

FLOREN, DAVID D., advertising executive. BA in Journalism, U. Minn. Copywriter, account svc. rep. GE; with Martin/Williams Advt., Mpls., chmn., CEO, 1998—. Recipient Silver Medal award Am. Advt. Fedn., 1990. Mem. Am. Assn. Advt. Agys. (ctrl. region bd., nat. bd.). Office: Martin Williams Advt Inc 60 S 6th St Ste 2800 Minneapolis MN 55402-4444*

FLORENCE, ERNEST ESTELL, JR., special education educator; b. Grayson, Ky., Feb. 19, 1954; s. Ernest Estell Florence and Margaret Jean (Tittsworth) Ikemire; m. Ginger Lynn Miller, Apr. 19, 1980; children: Ashley Michelle, Charles Todd. BS in Edn., Ea. Ill. U., 1975; MS in Edn., No. Ill. U., 1980. Behavior disorder tchr. Project Advocate Northwestern Ill. Assn., Geneva, 1976-80; behavior disorder tchr. O'Donnell Elem. Sch. Dist. 131, Aurora, Ill., 1980-85, behavior disorder/learning disability tchr. Bardwell Elem., 1985-93; behavior disorder tchr. Prairie Elem. sch. Dist. 203, Naperville, Ill., 1993—. Vol. Spl. Olympics, Aurora, 1990-93; com. mem. Just Say No Com., City of Aurora, 1991-95; com. mem. Aurora 2000 Com., 1993; chmn. scholarship com. Boulder Hill Sch. PTA, Montgomery, Ill., 1992—, reflections chmn., 1995-98; vol. bell ringer Salvation Army, 1995—; vol. Prairie Sch. Market Day, 1995—; mem. Prairie Sch. Bldg. Leadership Team, 1995-98. Named Tchr. of Yr., Bardwell Sch. PTA, 1989, Educator of Yr., Ill. Learning Disabilities Assn., 1989; recipient Chpt. Recognition award Ill. Learning Disabilities Assn., 1992. Mem. NEA (local sch. rep.), Coun. for Exceptional Children, Learning Disabilities Assn. Am. (chmn. Proud Projects 1997-98, state pres. rep. to Nat. Bd. 1998-99), Learning Disabiities Assn. Ill. (regional dir. 1991-94, pres.-elect 1994-96, pres. 1996-98, chmn. scholarship 1992-96, chmn. prin. scholarship programs 1992—, chair nominations com. 1999), Ill. Coun. for Children with Behavior Disorders, Kane Kendall Learning Disabilities Assn. (v.p. 1987—, Kane Kendall Recognition award 1994), Ill. br. Orton Dyslexia Soc., Aurora Moose. Democrat. Avocations: travel, reading, music. Home: 113 Circle Dr W Montgomery IL 60538-2725 Office: Naperville Comty Unit Sch Dist 203 203 W Hillside Rd Naperville IL 60540-6500

FLORENCE, SALLY A., retired school nurse educator, nurse practitioner. BS in Nursing, Alfred U., 1961; cert. school nurse tchr., N.Y. State Edn. Dept., 1967; cert. school nurse practitioner, SUNY, Buffalo, 1978, MS in Nursing, 1979. RN, N.Y.; cert. practitioner in sch. health, N.Y.; cert. pediatric nurse practitioner. Maternal-child health instr. St. James Sch. of Nursing, Hornell, N.Y., 1967-69; sch. nurse tchr. Alfred-Almond Cen. Sch., Almond, N.Y., 1969-70, Canisteo (N.Y.) Cen. Sch., 1970-78; sch. nurse practitioner Steuben-Allegany BOCES, Bath, N.Y., 1978-97, Jasper-Troupsburg Cen. Sch., Jasper, Troupsburg, N.Y.; ret.; pediatric nurse practitioner Office of Arnold Matlin, Geneseo, N.Y., 1979-80; asst. prof., clin. instr. dept. nursing Alfred (N.Y.) State Coll., 1980-85; part-time relief nurse maternity and nursery local hosps., 1961-67, 82-85; part-time nurse practitioner pvt. practice, Office of James McGuire, M.D., Hornell, N.Y., 1989-92. Writer for Update of Guidelines, Bur. of Sch. health Edn. and Svcs., N.Y. State Edn. Dept., Albany, 1987, 90; contbr. articles to profl. jours.; presenter at workshops for profl. orgns.; replicator of phys. assessment skills seminar (PASS) Project, Nat. Assn. Sch. Nurses, N.Y.State, 1987-91. Past vol. worker for local blood bank United Way. Recipient award for Excellence, BOCES. Mem. Nat. Assn. Pediatric Nurse Practitioners and Assocs., N.Y. State Coalition of Nurse Practitioners, Mid So. Tier Nurse Practitioners Assn. (past pres., sec., program and scholarship coms.), N.Y. Assn. Sch. Nurses (charter mem., past rec. sec.), Nurses for Children with Devel Disabilities, Genesee Valley Sports Medicine Coun. Home: 134 Greenwood St Canisteo NY 14823-1234

FLORENCE, VERENA MAGDALENA, business and computer consultant; b. Interlaken, Switzerland, Nov. 4, 1946; came to U.S., 1967; d. Paul Robert and Marie (Raess) Demuth; m. Kenneth James Florence, Dec. 10, 1967. BA, U. Calif., Berkeley, 1974; MS, UCLA, 1979, PhD, 1982. Research scientist Procter & Gamble, Cin., 1983; adminstr. Swerdlow & Florence, Beverly Hills, Calif., 1984-89; pres., chief exec. officer, chmn. of bd. Böl Designs, Inc., L.A., Calif., 1989—. Contbr. articles to profl. jours. Mem. L.A. Computer Soc. (SIG leader). Democrat. Home and Office: 9401 Wilshire Blvd Ste 828 Beverly Hills CA 90212-2921

FLORER, HAYWARD STANLEY, career officer; b. Alexandria, Va., Nov. 2, 1949. Grad., U.S. Mil. Acad., 1972; MA in History, U. Kans., 1984. Commd. 2nd lt. U.S. Army, 1972; advanced through grades to col., 1995; various cmd., staff positions infantry, spl. forces platoon A detachment level, 1978-82; bn. comdr.; two tours of duty Germany; asst. sec. of genl. staff 2nf Inf. Divn., Korea, 1975-76; served in Desert Shield/Storm, Op. Provide Comfort; mem. staff res. component assistnace readiness group Patrick Pretoria, South Africa; fgn. area officer Pretoria, 1984; spec. forces Battalian Exec., 1985-86, Grp. Ops., 1986-88, Readiness Grp. Patrick, 1988-90, Battalian Commdr., 1990-92; dir. tng. and doctrine U.S. Army John F. Kennedy Spl. Warfare Ctr. and Sch., Ft. Bragg, N.C.; comdr. spl. ops. cmd. Atlantic cmd. Decorated Legion of Merit, Expert Infantryman's Badge, Master Parachutist Badge, Spl. Forces Tab, Ranger Tab, Combat Diver Qualification Tab; War Coll. fellow Sch. Advanced Mil. Studies, U.S. Army Cmd. and Gen. Staff Coll. Office: US Army Comdr Spl Ops Cmd US Atlantic Cmd 1283 CV Towway Norfolk VA 23511

FLORES, J. TERRY, accountant; b. Phila., June 19. BS in acctg., Golden Gate Univ., 1972; cert. as expert, Statistical Sampling, Bernard Baruch College. CPA Calif., New Mex., Pa. Auditor Dept. Health, Edn. & Welfare, San Francisco, 1972-73; health care practice ptnr. Morris, Davis & Co., CPA, Oakland, Calif., 1973-84; dir. fin. West Oakland Health Coun., Oakland, Calif., 1984-92; treas., CFO Presby. Medical Svc., Santa Fe, N.Mex., 1992-94; ptnr. Mitchell & Titus LLP, Phila., 1994-98; CFO, sr. v.p. fin. svcs. Davis & Assocs., Washington, 1998—; cons. to Medicare and Medicaid Bureaus of the Healthcare Financing Admin. (HCFA) in Balt., in determining the cost of new fed. regulations. *Terry first became partner with a firm in 1978, and currently serves as the healthcare practice partner for Mitchell & Titus, LLP (M&T), the nations largest minority controlled CPA firm. He also has responsibility for a significant share of the governmental, non-profit audit and financial management engagements in the Philadelphia office of M&T. In addition to his professional career, Terry is also keenly interested in community service for disadvantaged children, and functions on the board of directors for the Maternity Care Coalition (Mommobile Program) and Philadelphia Health Services, Inc.* Author and pub. seperate cost studies by HCFA. With U.S. Army, 1966-69, Vietnam. Mem. PA. Inst. CPAs, Am. Inst. CPAs, Healthcare Fin. Mgmt. Assn., The Health Strategy Network, Acme Healthcare Cons. Coun., Nat. Assn. of Black Acct., Nat. Assn. Health Svcs, Mayor Rendell's annual Gala Finance Com. (Children's Tour Program), Upward Bound adv. bd. for Swarthmore Col., Kappa Alpha Psi. Avocations: chess, basketball, volleyball, card game, billiards. Office: Mitchell & Titus LLP One Logan Sq Ste 2929 Philadelphia PA 19103

FLORES, PATRICK F., archbishop; b. Ganado, TX, July 26, 1929. Grad., St. Mary's Sem., Houston. Ordained priest Roman Catholic Ch., 1956; ordained titular bishop of Italica and aux. bishop San Antonio, 1970; apptd. bishop of El Paso, 1978; archbishop of San Antonio, 1979. Co-founder Mex. Am. Cultural Ctr., San Antonio, 1972; founder Nat. Hispanic Scholarship Fund, 1976. Recipient medal of freedom Ellis Island medal of honor Statue of Liberty 100th Birthday, 1986, Hispanic Heritage award for leadership, 1986, Salute to Edn. award Ford, 1995. Office: Chancery Office PO Box 28410 2718 W Woodlawn Ave San Antonio TX 78228-5124 also: 2600 W Woodlawn Ave San Antonio TX 78228-5122

FLORES, ROBIN ANN, social worker, social services administrator; b. Allentown, Pa., Oct. 6, 1949; d. Norman Henry and Ann May (Huff) Flores. BS in Edn., Kutztown U., 1971; MS in Adminstrn., U. Scranton, 1983. With Lehigh County (Pa.) Area Agy. on Aging, 1973—, info. referral outreach coord., 1975-78, supr. cmty. svcs., 1979-95, exec. dir., 1996—; lectr. cmty. svcs., family care giving and on aging process, 1978—; utilization cmty. resources, Lehigh County. Mem. adv. bd. Cmty. Action Com. of Lehigh Valley, 1979-82, Elder Well, 1987-90; Pa. del. White House Conf. on Aging, Hershey, Pa., 1981; bd. dirs. Vis. Nurse Assn. of Lehigh County, 1982—, Women Inc., 1983-87; adv. bd. Homecare, Inc., 1982—, Geriatric Edn. Modules, Allentown Osteo. Hosp., 1979; mem. profl. adv. com. Lehigh Valley Hospice, 1984—; mem. utilization and rev. bd. Vis. Nurse Assn., 1979—; consumer rep. Pa. Power and Light Co.; co-chmn. Human Svcs. Tng. Coop., 1975-81; bd. assocs. L.V. Hosp. Mem. NAFE, Am. Soc. on Aging, Allentown Art Mus., Quota Internat. Home: 1255 Forest Rd Whitehall PA 18052-6217 Office: Area Agy on Aging Govt Ctr 17 S 7th St Allentown PA 18101-2400

FLORES, ROGER, city official; b. San Antonio; m. Evangelina; children: Roger III, Mariela. City councilman dist. 1 San Antonio, 1997—; restaurant owner, San Antonio, 1975—; mem. world affairs coun. San Antonio, mil affairs coun., coun. com. on ethics, housing task force, mcpl. ct. com., small bus. strategy com., transportation com., water policy com., Alamo Area Coun. Govts., Bexar County Housing Fin. corp., cmty. action bd., firemen's and policemen's pension fund bd. trustees, local govt. approval com. VIA metro. transport sys., urban renewal agy. Adv. com. Conv. & Visitor's Bur., San Antonio. Named small businessman of yr. Hispanic C. of C., 1992, Greater San Antonio C. of C., 1994. Mem. Lions, ARC, Paseo del Rio Assn. Office: City Hall/City Coun PO Box 839966 San Antonio TX 78283-3966*

FLORES, WILLIAM VINCENT, Latin American studies educator; b. San Diego, Jan. 10, 1948; s. William J. and Velia (Aldrete) F.; m. Carole Mary Dische, July 3, 1973 (div. Jan 1986); children: Antonio Ramon, Diana Maria. BA, UCLA, 1970; MA in Polit. Sci., Stanford U., 1971, PhD in Social Theory/Pub. Policy, 1987. Teaching & rsch. fellow Stanford (Calif.) U., 1971-72; lectr. in polit. sci. Calif. State U., Hayward, 1972-75; program coord. Project Intercept, San Jose, Calif., 1976-78; assoc. dir. Gardner Cmty. Health Ctr., San Jose, 1979-84; lectr. U. Santa Clara, Calif., 1985-87; asst. dir. Inter-Univ. Program for Latino Rsch., Stanford, 1987-88; chair dept. Chicano/Latin Am. studies Calif. State U., Fresno, 1988-92, assoc. dean Sch. of Social Scis., 1992-94; dean Coll. Soc. and Behavioral Scis. Calif. State U., Northridge, 1996—; v.p., bd. trustees Arte Americas, 1995-96. Author: Latino Cultural Citizenship, 1997. Mem. CSU Northridge Found. Bd. CSUN pres.'s bus. coun., 1996-98, exec. com. Chicano/Latino Faculty Assn. Calif. State Univ. Sys., 1994-95; chair Com. for Hispanic Ednl. Equity, Fresno, 1990-92; mem. nat. adv. bd. U.S. Students Assn., Washington, 1991-93; v.p. Latino Agenda Coalition Calif., L.A., 1984-86. Chicano Fellows Program fellow Stanford U., 1971-72; Ford Found. fellow Stanford U., 1970-74; Compton-Danforth fellow Stanford U., 1984-85.; Rockefeller Humanities fellow, 1993-94; Am. Coun. on Edn. fellow, 1993-94. Mem. Am. Anthropol. Assn., Am. Studies Assn., Nat. Assn. Chicano Studies (co-chair polit. action com. 1986), Internat. Platform Assn. Democrat. Avocations: poetry, music, racquetball, hiking. Office: Coll Social Behav Scis 18111 Nordhoff St Northridge CA 91330-0001

FLORES, YOLANDA, literature educator; b. Bakersfield, Calif., Mar. 2, 1962; d. Simon and Micaela Flores. BA, U. Calif., Berkeley, 1987; MA, U. Chgo., 1989; PhD, Cornell U., 1995. Lectr. Cornell U., Ithaca, N.Y., 1994-95; prof. Chapman U., Orange, Calif., 1995-99, U. Vt., Burlington, 1999—. Author: The Drama of Gender: Feminist Theater by Women of the Americas, 1998; contbr. articles to profl. publs. Mem. MLA, L.Am. Studies Assn., Am. Soc. for Theater Rsch., Rocky Mountain Modern Lang. Assn., Feministas Unidas. Democrat. Roman Catholic. Avocations: film, music, aerobics, travel. Home: 31 N Willard St Apt 1 Burlington VT 05401-7140 Office: Romane Langs and Lit Dept U Vt 517 Waterman Bldg Burlington VT 05405

FLORESTANO, DANA JOSEPH, architect; b. Indpls., May 2, 1945; s. Herbert Joseph and Myrtle Mae (Futch) F.; m. Peggy Joy Larsen, June 6, 1969. BArch, U. Notre Dame, 1968. Designer, draftsman Kennedy, Brown & Trueblood, architects, Indpls., 1965-69, Evans Woolen Assn., architects, Indpls., 1966; designer, project capt. James Assos., architects and engrs., Indpls., 1969-71; architect, v.p. comml. projects Multi-Planners Inc., architects and engrs., 1972-73; pvt. practice architecture, Indpls., 1973—; pres. Florestano Corp., constrn. mgmt., Indpls., 1973—; co-founder, pres. Solargenics Natural Energy Corp., Indpls., 1975—; pres. Florestano Archery Co., 1985—, Star Archery Corp., Indpls., 1989—; prof. archtl. and constrn. tech. Ind. U.-Purdue U. at Indpls.; instr. in field. Tech. adviser hist. architecture Indpls. Model Cities program, 1969-70; mem. Hist. Landmarks Found. Ind., 1970-72; chmn. Com. to Save Union Sta., 1970-71, founder, pres. Union Sta. Found. Inc., Indpls., 1971—. Dep. commr. and tournament dir. archery Pan-Am. Games, Indpls., 1987. Recipient 2d design award Marble Inst. Am., 1967, 1st design award 19th Ann. Progressive Architecture Design awards, 1972; Design award for excellence in devel. Marriott Inn, Indpls., Met. Devel. Commn.-Office of Mayor, 1977; 1st place award design competition for Visitor's Info. Ctr., Cave Run, Lake, Ky., 1978; 2d design award 1st Ann. Qualified Remodeler, Nat. Competition for Best Rehab. Existing Structures in Am., 1979. Mem. U. Notre Dame Alumni Assn., Notre Dame Club Indpls., AIA (nat. com. historic resources 1974—, commn. on community svcs., Speakers Bur. Indpls. chpt. 1976—), Ind. Soc. Architects (chmn. historic architecture com. 1970—), Ind. Archery Assn. (founder, pres. 1985—, Overall Male State Champion 1987, 90, 94), No. Archery Assn. (bd. dirs., pres. 1987—), Internat. Archery Ctr. (founder, exec. dir. 1992—), Ind. Kyudo Renmei (bd. dirs. 1998—), Constrn. Specifications Inst., Constrn. Mgrs. Assn. Ind. (incorporator, dir. 1976—), World Archery Ctr. Home: PO Box 30089 Indianapolis IN 46230-0089 Office: 6214 Carrollton Ave Indianapolis IN 46220-1925

FLORESTANO, PATRICIA SHERER, university educator; b. Washington, Mar. 15, 1936; d. Wilbur L. and Virginia M. (Moriconi) F.; B.A. in Am. Civilization, U. Md., 1958, M.A. in Govt. and Politics, 1970, Ph.D. in Pub. Adminstrn. and Am. Govt., 1974; m. Thomas Florestano, Nov. 29, 1959; children—Leslie C., Thomas. Research staff State Legis. Commn. on Intergovt. Coop., 1972-75, State Gov.'s Commn. on Functions of Govt., 1973-75; staff asst. to pres. Md. Senate, 1975-78; asst. prof. Inst. Urban Studies, U. Md., College Park, 1974-79, dir. Inst. Govtl. Service, 1979-85, vice-chancellor govtl. relations, 1985-91; prof. govt. Schaefer Ctr. Pub. Policy U. Balt., 1991-95, pub. adminstr., sr. fellow; sec. Md. Higher Edn. Commn., Annapolis, 1995—; cons. ednl. evaluation, mgmt. and survey research. Lector St. Elizabeth Ann Seton Ch., 1970-92; dir. Crofton (Md.) Gymnastics Program, 1972-74; vice chmn. Anne Arundel County (Md.) Commn. on Women, 1975; mem. Transition Exec. Com. for Gov. Elect. State Md., Dec. 1994- Jan. 1995; mem. Anne Arundel County Schs. Adv. Forum, 1975-76, chmn. nominations com., 1976-78; sec. higher edn. Md. Commn. Higher Edn. Recipient Outstanding Teaching award Students Assn. of U. Md., 1979. Mem. Am. Soc. Pub. Adminstrn. (pres. 1983-84, conf. fellow), Am. Polit. Sci. Assn., So. Polit. Sci. Assn., Urban Affairs Assn. (past chmn. governing bd.), So. Consortium Univ. Pub. Service Orgns. (former editor). Democrat. Roman Catholic. Author: (with other) The States and Metropolitan Areas, 1981; Attitudes of Special Interest Groups and the Public on Chesapeake Bay Areas, 1980; also articles. Home: 1 Compromise St Unit D Annapolis MD 21401-1824 Office: Md Higher Edn Commn 16 Francis St Annapolis MD 21401-1714

FLOREY, KLAUS GEORG, chemist, pharmaceutical consultant; b. Dresden, Germany, July 4, 1919; came to U.S., 1947, naturalized, 1952; s. Friedrich Georg and Margarethe Käthe (Pick) F.; m. Anne Major, Nov. 22, 1956; children: Peter, Andrea. Ed., U. Munich, U. Heidelberg, Germany; Ph.D., U. Pa., 1954. Research asst. Bayer, Leverkusen, Germany, 1944-45; research asso. Merck & Co., Rahway, N.J., 1949-50; research chemist Squibb Inst. Med. Research, New Brunswick, N.J., 1954-59; dir. analytical research and devel. Squibb Inst. Med. Research, 1959-84, cons., 1984-90; mem. com. revisions U.S. Pharmacopeia, 1970-95; mem. WHO Expert Adv. Panel Internat. Pharmacopeia, 1976-93. Editor: Analytical Profiles of Drug Substances, 22 vols., 1971—; contbr. articles to profl. jours. Recipient Justin L. Powers award, 1987. Fellow AAAS, Acad. Pharm. Scis. (chmn. pharm. analysis and control sect. 1967-68, pres. 1980-81); mem. Am. Chem. Soc., Soc. Nuclear Medicine, Am. Assn. Pharm. Scientists (Disting. Svc. award 1990), Coun. Sci. Soc. Pres. (chmn. 1983). Patentee in field. Home: 151 Loomis Ct Princeton NJ 08540-3438

FLORI, ANNA MARIE DIBLASI, nurse anesthetist, educational administrator; b. Amsterdam, N.Y., Oct. 29, 1940; d. Tony and Maria (Macario) DiBlasi; children: Tammy, Tina, Toni; m. Gilberto Flori, May 24, 1986. Grad., Albany Med. Ctr. Sch. Nursing, 1962, Fairfax Hosp. Sch. Nurse Anesthetists, Va., 1972; BS in Anesthesia, George Washington U., 1979; M. in Bus. and Pub. Adminstrn., Southeastern U., Washington, 1982; PhD, Columbia Pacific U., 1983. Cert. registered nurse anesthetist. Staff nurse West Seattle Gen. Hosp., 1962-64; office nurse Filmore Buckner, M.D., Seattle, 1964-66; staff nurse anesthetist Fairfax Hosp., 1972-73; staff nurse anesthetist Potomac Hosp., Woodbridge, Va., 1973, chief nurse anesthetist, 1973—; dir. Potomac Hosp. Sch. for Nurse Anesthetists and Sch. for Nurse Anesthesia; faculty mem. Columbia Pacific U., 1973-90; chief nurse anesthetist No. Va. Anesthesia Assn., 1988—; guest lectr. No. Va. Community Coll., Inservice Potomac Hosp., George Washington U.; coord. Free Clinic Prince William County, Woodbridge, Va. Contbr. books on anesthesia. Mem. Am. Assn. Nurse Anesthetists, Va. Nurse Anesthesia Assn., Nat. Italian Am. Found. Home: 12954 Pintail Rd Woodbridge VA 22192-3831

FLORIO, CHRISTOPHER JOHN, multimedia producer; b. Trenton, N.J., Mar. 31, 1961; s. James Joseph and Maryanne (Spaeth) F. BM, Berklee Coll. Music, Boston, 1984. Cert. massage therapist, acupuncture asst., vet. radiologist, Yoga and Oriental med. cert. Pres. IDV Multimedia, Boston, 1993—; dir. Jumpcut Orch., Boston, 1994—; tchr. Wentworth Inst. Interactive Factory, Boston, 1995—, U. Mass., Lowell, 1996, North Ea. U.; med. asst. New Life Health Ctr., Jamaica Plain, Mass., 1985—; multimedia cons. Clark U., Apple Computer, others, 1993—; mem. Desktop Video Group, Cambridge, Mass.; performer 1st Boston CyberArts Festival, 1999. Contbr. articles to profl. jours.; composer: Jungle Afternoon, 1990, others; composer, prodr. recordings including Jingle, Faux Paux, others; contbg. editor: pro-Video Rev., 1999. Vol. instr. IMYA, Jamaica Plain, Mass., 1987—, N.J. Dem. Party, Trenton, 1989—. Avocations: Yoga, film, racquetball, soccer, Oriental medicine. Home and Office: PO Box 2075 Jamaica Plain MA 02130-0018

FLORIO, DAVID PETER, probation and parole counselor; b. Providence, R.I., Feb. 6, 1956; s. John and Simone (Bernard) F.; m. Margaret Mary Boisvert, June 8, 1980; 1 child, Michael David. BA, R.I. Coll., 1977-80, MA in Counseling and Psychology, 1993, postgrad., 1994—. Lic. psychotherapist, Mass.; cert. R.I. probation and parole counselor. Probation counselor R.I. Dept. of Corrections, Wakefield, 1988-89; probation counselor R.I., 1989-91, parole counselor, 1991-92; parole counselor R.I. Home Confinement Program, Cranston, 1992-96; probation, Kent county counselor, superior ct. R.I. Dept. of Corrections, 1996—; psychotherapist, counseling and psych. therapy ctr. The Counseling and Psychotherapy Ctr. of Greater Boston, Needham, Mass., 1996—; chairperson Coventry (R.I.) Juvenile Hearing Bd., 1991—; grievance chairperson R.I. Probation and Parole Assn., Cranston, R.I., 1996-98; mem. R.I. Legis. Commn. Study in Alternative Sentencing, Providence, 1992-98; v.p. emeritus R.I. Arthritis Found., East Providence, 1986-91. Chairperson Coventry Dem. Town Com., 1996—; mem. Dem. City and Town Chairperson Assn., Warwick, 1996—; statewide chair Pres. Clinton's Italian Am. to Elect the Pres. Com., Coventry, 1996—. Recipient Grand Masters award Masons Grand Lodge of R.I., 1990. Mem. Manchester Lodge #12 (master 1989-90, past master 1990), Landmark Chpt. #10 (high priest 1986-87, past high priest 1987), R.I. Grand Lodge (sr. grand deacon 1996-97). Democrat. Roman Catholic. Avocation: soccer coach. Home: 153 Princeton Ave Coventry RI 02816-4234 Office: Kent County Superior Ct Probation 222 Quaker Ln Warwick RI 02886-0100

FLORIO, STEVEN T., magazine executive; b. N.Y.C., Apr. 19, 1949; s. F. Steve and Sophia (Masciale) F.; m. Mariann McNeill, June 1, 1974; children—Steven John, Kelly Anne. A.A., NYU, 1970, B.S., 1972. Rschr. Esquire mag., N.Y.C., 1972-73; New Eng. mgr. Esquire mag., 1974-76, advt. dir., 1976-79, v.p., 1979-80; pub. Gentlemen's Quar., N.Y.C., 1980-85; pres., CEO New Yorker mag., N.Y.C., 1985-94, pub., 1985-88; pres. Condé Nast Publs., Inc., N.Y.C., 1994—; guest speaker lecture series Harvard U., Rice U., NYU, Yale U. Chmn. Namesake Com. USS N.Y.C. USN. Mem. Men's Fashion Assn., Mag. Pubs. Assn. (chmn. conf. 1989). Office: Conde Nast Publ 350 Madison Ave New York NY 10017-3704*

FLORIO, THOMAS, magazine publisher. Formerly advt. dir. Conde Nast Traveler, N.Y.C., pub., 1990-94; pres. The New Yorker, N.Y.C., 1994-99; v.p., pub. Gentleman's Quarterly, N.Y.C., 1999—. Office: Gentlemans Quarterly THE NEW YORKER 350 Madison Ave New York NY 10017*

FLORMAN, SAMUEL CHARLES, civil engineer; b. N.Y.C., Jan. 19, 1925; s. Arthur M. and Hannah (Weingarten) F.; m. Judith Hadas, Aug. 19, 1951; children: David A., Jonathan C. BS, CE, Dartmouth Coll., 1946; MA, Columbia U., 1947; DSc (hon.), Manhattan Coll., 1983, Clarkson U., 1986. Registered profl. engr., N.Y. Field engr. Hegeman Harris Co., Venezuela, 1948; asst. project mgr. Thompson-Starrett Corp., N.Y.C., 1949-54; project mgr. Jos. P. Blitz Inc., N.Y.C., 1954-56; prin. Kreisler Borg Florman Constrn. Co., Scarsdale, N.Y., 1956—. Author: Engineering and the Liberal Arts, 1968, The Existential Pleasures of Engineering, 1976, Blaming Technology, 1981, The Civilized Engineer, 1987, The Introspective Engineer, 1996; contbr. over 200 articles to profl. jours. Bd. overseers Thayer Sch. Engring., Dartmouth Coll., Hanover, N.H., 1971-77; trustee Hosp. for Joint Disease, N.Y.C., 1976—; bd. govs. Ethical Culture Fieldston Schs., N.Y.C., 1983-96; trustee N.Y. Hall of Sci., 1996—. Recipient Stevens award Stevens Inst. Tech., 1976, Ralph Coats Roe medal ASME, 1982, Robert Fletcher award Thayer Sch. Engring., 1983. Fellow AAAS, ASCE; mem. NSPE, Am. Soc. for Engring. Edn., Nat. Acad. Engring., Dartmouth Soc. Engrs. (pres. 1966-67). Home: 55 Central Park W New York NY 10023-6003 Office: 97 Montgomery St Scarsdale NY 10583-5104

FLORSHEIM, RICHARD STEVEN, lawyer; b. Milw., Apr. 2, 1949; s. Ernst Frederick and Ingeborg Miriam (Gotthilf) F.; m. Neena B. Florsheim; children: Ali Brynn, David Ira, Rebecca Lynn. BS, MIT, 1971; JD magna cum laude, Marquette U., 1974. Bar: Wis. 1974, Fla. 1983. Assoc. Foley & Lardner, Milw., 1974-81, ptnr., 1981—, leader intellectual property litigation group, 1987-97, chair intellectual property dept., 1997—. Co-author: Biotechnology Patent Practice, 1994. Pres. North Shore Libr., Milw., 1985-87, Jewish Found. Econ. Opportunity, Milw., 1992-96; bd. dirs. Milw. Jewish Fedn., 1987-93, 96—, NCCJ Wis. region, 1990—. Mem. ABA, Am. Intellectual Property Law Assn. (subcom. chmn. 1992-97), Fed. Cir. Bar Assn., Wis. Bar Assn., Milw. Bar Assn., Marquette Law Alumni Assn. (pres. 1985-86). Office: Foley & Lardner 777 E Wisconsin Ave Ste 3800 Milwaukee WI 53202-5367

FLORY, CURT ALAN, research physicist. BS in Physics with distinction, Stanford U., 1975; MS in Physics, U. Wash., 1977; PhD in Physics, U. Calif., Berkeley, 1981. Prin. dept. scientist, rsch. physicist Hewlett-Packard, Palo Alto, Calif., 1984—; postdoct. SLAC, $D, $D, 1981-84. Recipient Indsl. Physics prize Am. Inst. Physics, 1993-94. Fellow Am. Phys. Soc. Office: Hewlett Packard Co PO Box 10350 3500 Deer Creek Rd # 26M Palo Alto CA 94304-1392

FLORY, MARGARET MARTHA, retired religious organization administrator; b. Wauseon, Ohio, May 13, 1914; d. Arthur Henry and Laura Grace (Gorsuch) F. BA, Ohio U., 1936, MA, 1938; postgrad., Union Theol. Seminary, 1940-43; LLD, Maryville Coll., 1988. Teaching fellow Ohio U., Athens, 1936-38, dir. Westminster Found., 1940-44; tchr. Bainbridge (Ohio) High Sch., 1938-39; mem. drama and speech faculty Ala. State Coll., Montevallo, 1939-40; Eastern area sec. Presbyn. Ch. Nat. Hdqrs., N.Y.C., 1944-51, staff student world rels., 1951-68, staff new dimension in mission, 1969-73; staff ecumenical sharing program dir. Presbyn. Ch. U.S.A., 1973-80; short-term tchr. missions and ecumenical rels. San Francisco Theol. Sem., 1979-80; min. in residence Pacific Sch. Religion, Berkeley, Calif., 1981; mem. Stony Point (N.Y.) ctr. program staff Presbyn. Ch. U.S.A., 1981-87; ret., 1987. Author: Moments in Time, 1995, From Past to Future: Experiments in Global Bridging, 1997, Dear House, 1999; contbr. articles to profl. jours. Active Pres. Kennedy's Women's Com. on Civil Rights, 1963; trustee Maryville (Tenn.) Coll., 1963-78; pres. bd. trustees World Student Christian Fedn., N.Y.C., 1968-90; coun. ch. rels. Warren Wilson Coll., N.C., 1993—. Named Outstanding Alumnae Ohio U.; recipient Human Rights award Korean Christian Scholars, 1985, Woman of Faith award Presbyn. Women, 1987, Cert. of Appreciation Silliman U., 1981; conf. hall named in her honor John Knox Internat. Studies Ctr., Geneva, 1993. Mem. AAUW (exec. bd.), Assn. for Women's Edn. in Asia (pres. 1973-85), Ch. Relationships with Eastern Europe, Ch. Women United, Phi Beta Kappa. Avocations: reading, theater, walking, gardening, floral decoration. Home and Office: 276 College Walk Ln Brevard NC 28712-3155

FLORY, ROBERT MIKESELL, computer systems analyst, personnel management specialist; b. Bridgewater, Va., Feb. 21, 1912; s. John Samuel and Vinnie (Mikesell) F.; m. Thelma Thomas, Sept. 14, 1942; 1 child, Pamela. B.A., Bridgewater Coll., 1932; M.A., U. Va., 1938; postgrad. U. Chgo., 1946-51. Job/methods analyst United Air Lines, Chgo., 1945-47; job analyst Julian Baer, Chgo., 1948; asst. to v.p. Fairbanks, Morse, Chgo., 1949-60; mgmt. cons. Yarger & Assocs., Falls Church, Va., 1961; computer systems analyst, various fed. agys., Washington, 1962-82; tchr. Roosevelt U., Chgo., 1956-61; seminar leader U. Chgo., 1960-61; cons. Va. Gov.'s Commn. for Reorgn. State Govt., 1961. Served to lt. comdr. USN, 1942-45, PTO. Home: 5501 Seminary Rd Apt 1204S Falls Church VA 22041-3907

FLORY, SHELDON, retired clergyman, poet; b. N.Y.C., June 28, 1927; s. Grant Glenwood and Margaret (Atwater) F.; m. Jane Margaret Livsey, June 24, 1950 (div.); children: Christopher Glen, Susan Helen, Sarah Margaret; m. Beth Bishop Odell, July 15, 1978. AB, Middlebury Coll., 1950; MA, Columbia U., 1953; MDiv, Gen. Theol. Sem., N.Y.C., 1958. Ordained deacon and prises Episcopalian Ch., 1958; cert. English, history, secondary edn. tchr., N.Y. Fellow, tutor Gen. Theol. Sem., 1958-60; rector St. Margaret's Ch., Belfast, Maine, 1960-63, Trinity Ch., Geneva, N.Y., 1963-69; chaplain Brown U. and RISD, Providence, 1969-74; tchr. English and Latin, chaplain The Darrow Sch., New Lebanon, N.Y., 1974-76, tchr. English and U.S. history, chaplain, dean faculty, 1978-90; chaplain, tchr. English, Groton (Mass.) Sch., 1976-78; priest-in-charge part-time St. Peter's Ch., Bloomfield, N.Y., 1990-95; chaplain part-time Ontario-Yates Hospice, Geneva, 1993-96; ret., 1996; examining chaplain Dioceses of Maine and Rochester, N.Y., 1960-69; chmn. dept. world mission Diocese of Rochester, 1963-68, mem. racism task force, 1991-93. Author: (poems) A Winter's Journey, 1979; contbr. numerous poems to New Yorker, Poetry, Seneca and Iowa revs., London Sunday Observer, Mangrove, Gulf Coast, Puckerbrush; judge internat. poetry competition Arvon Found., London, 1992. Chmn. ARC, Belfast, 1961-63, Coun. of Chs., Geneva, 1967-69; mem. Geneva Human Rights Commn., 1965-69. Recipient 1st prize Arvon Found., 1990, also various poetry prizes from local arts couns., 1991-95. Mem. Naples Hist. Soc., Naples Arts Network, Friends of Naples Libr. Democrat. Avocations: reading, pastels, birding, canoeing, foreign travel. Home: 6981 Rt 21 Naples NY 14512

FLOSS, FREDERICK GEORGE, economics and finance educator, consultant; b. Buffalo, Feb. 12, 1957; s. Frederick H. and Mary (White) F.; m. Lauren Bodziak, July 26, 1986. BA in Econs. and English, SUNY, Oswego, 1979; MA in Econs., SUNY, Buffalo, 1982, PhD in Econs., 1986. Instr. econs. SUNY, Buffalo, 1980-85, asst. prof., 1986-90, mem. faculty senate, 1986—, assoc. prof., 1990-99, prof., 1999—, co-dir. Ctr. for Econ. Edn., 1997—; rsch. assoc. Ctr. for Applied Rsch. in Urban and Regional Devel., 1983—; dir. Ctr. Econ. Edn. SUNY Coll. Buffalo 1997—; co-dir. Ctr. for Econ. Edn., 1997—; presenter in field. Contbr. articles to profl. jours. Committeeman Erie County Dem. Com., 1979—; mem. cmty. needs assessment com. United Way Western N.Y., 1987-92; mem. adv. coun. Erie-Niagara Planning Bd., 1987-92; chmn. bd. regional dirs. Young Dems. Am., 1988-90; bd. dirs. Literacy Vols. of Buffalo and Erie County, 1992-98; sec. Literacy Vol. of Buffalo and Erie County, 1995-97. Regents scholar, 1975-79; fellow Ctr. for Devel. Human Svcs., 1987-88, 89-98. Roman Catholic. Home: 27 Landers Rd Buffalo NY 14217-2405 Office: SUNY Dept Econs and Fin 1300 Elmwood Ave Dept Econsand Buffalo NY 14222-1004

FLOSS, HEINZ G., chemistry educator, scientist; b. Berlin, Aug. 28, 1934; s. Friedrich and Annemarie F.; m. Inge Sauberlich, July 17, 1956; children: Christine, Peter, Helmut, Hanna. BS in Chemistry, Technische Universitat, Berlin, 1956, MS in Organic Chemistry, 1959; D in Organic Chemistry, Technische Hochschule, Munich, W. Ger., 1961, D in Biochemistry, 1966; DSc (hon.), Purdue U., 1986. Hilfsassistent Technische Universitat, Berlin, 1958-59; hilfsassistent Technische Hochschule, Munich, 1959-61; wissenschaftlicher asst. and dozent Technische Hochschule, 1961-66; on leave of absence at dept. biochemistry and biophysics U. Calif.-Davis, 1964-65; assoc. prof. Purdue U., 1966-69, prof., 1969-77, Lilly Disting. prof., 1977-82, head dept. medicinal chemistry, 1968-69, 74-79; prof. chemistry Ohio State U., Columbus, 1982-87, chmn. dept. chemistry, 1982-86; prof. chemistry U. Wash., Seattle, 1987—, adj. prof. biochemistry medicinal chemistry and microbiology, 1988—; vis. scientist ETH Zurich, 1970; vis. prof. Tech. U. Munich, 1980, 86, 95; mem. bio-organic and natural products study sect. NIH, 1989-93; mem. internat. adv. Natural Product Reports, 1997—. Mem. editorial bd. Lloydia-Jour. Natural Products, 1971—, BBP-Biochemie und Physiologie der Pflanzen, 1971-84, Applied and Environ. Microbiology, 1974-84, Planta Medica, 1978-83, Jour. Medicinal Chemistry, 1979-83, Applied Microbiology and Biotech., 1984-88, Jour. Basic Microbiology, 1989—. Recipient Lederle faculty award, 1967, Mead Johnson Undergrad. Rsch. award, 1968, rsch. career and devel. award USPHS, 1969-74, Volwiler award, 1979, Humboldt sr. scientist, 1980, Newby-McCoy award 1981, award in microbial chemistry Kitasato Inst. and Kitasato U., 1988, White Magnolia Commemoration award and medal, Shanghai, 1995. Fellow Acad. Pharm. Scis. (Research Achievement award in natural products 1976), AAAS; mem. Am. Chem. Soc., Am. Soc. Biol. Chemistry and Molecular Biology, Am. Soc. Microbiology, Am. Soc. Pharmacognosy (Rsch. award 1988), Phytochem. Soc. N.Am., Sigma Xi (Faculty Research award 1976). Office: Univ Wash Box 351700 Seattle WA 98195-1700

FLOURNOY, JOHN CHARLES, SR., training specialist, retired military officer; b. Florala, Ala., Nov. 30, 1936; s. Q. P. and Alice Ruby (Cope) F.; m. Charlene Reneé Lett, June 7, 1957; children: Jamie Lynn, John Charles Jr., Jeffrey Allan. BS, Auburn (Ala.) U., 1959. Commd. 2d lt. USAF, 1959, advanced through grades to col.; asst. dep. chief of staff for ops. 23rd Air

Force; USAF, Scott AFB, 1983-85, dir. ops.; dep. chief of staff for ops. 23d Air Force, Hurlburt Field, Fla., 1985-88; site mgr., tng. mgr. Raytheon Sys., Kirkland AFB, N.Mex., 1988-98, tng. analyst, Air Force Lab., 1998-99; sr. principal engr. Boeing, 1999—. Recipient German Gratitude medal Fed. Republic of Germany, 1962; decorated Leigon of Merit, 1988. Mem. Jolly Green Assn. (1st v.p. 1983-84, pres. 1985-86), Order of Daedalians (former flight capt.), Tanker/Airlift Assn., USAF Helicopter Pilot Assn., Air Commando Assn. Republican. Avocations: fishing, softball, bowling, camping. E-mail: flournoj@jntf.osd.mil. Home: 6817 Medinah Ln NE Albuquerque NM 87111-6419

FLOURNOY, JOHN CRAIG, newspaper reporter; b. Shreveport, La., June 26, 1951; s. Camp Rogers and Carolyn (Clay) F.; m. Nina Planchard, May 21, 1977; children: Kathryn Helene, Louise, Emma. BA in History with honors, U. New Orleans, 1975; MA in History, So. Meth. U., 1986. Freelance writer, landscaper The Courier, New Orleans, 1975; polit. reporter Houma (La.) Daily Courier, 1976; polit. reporter, columnist Shreveport Jour., 1977-78; investigative reporter Dallas Morning News, Dallas, 1978—. Recipient First Place award Investigative Reporting Dallas Press Club, 1981, 82, 83, 85, 93, Pub. Svc. award Assn. Press Managing Editors Assn., N.Y.C., 1986, Silver Gavel award ABA, N.Y.C., 1986, Pulitzer Prize, N.Y.C., 1986, Outstanding Investigative Reporting award Investigative Reporters and Editors, 1989, Worth Bingham prize for investigative reporting, 1993, Edward Meeman award for environ. reporting, 1993. Avocation: gardening. Office: Dallas Morning News Communications Ctr Dallas TX 75265

FLOURNOY, WILLIAM LOUIS, JR., landscape architect; b. Raleigh, N.C., May 6, 1945; s. William Louis and Flossie (Combs) F. Student, Gardner-Webb Jr. Coll., 1964-66; BS in Recreation and Parks Adminstrn., N.C. State U., 1969, M of Landscape Architecture, 1972. Cons. to City of Raleigh N.C. State U. Sch. Design, 1971-72; community planner Wake County Planning Dept., Raleigh, N.C., 1972-80; environ. analysis program mgr. Office Legis. & Intergovtl. N.C. Dept. Environment and Natural Resources, Raleigh, 1980—. Author reports, articles and conf. procs. Bd. dirs. Southeastern U.S. Masters Track and Field, Inc., Raleigh, 1976-82, Triangle Land Conservancy, Rsch. Triangle Pk., N.C., pres. 1991-94, bd. dirs. Triangle Greenways Coun., pres., 1989-91; mem. N.C. bicycle com. N.C. Dept. Transp., 1974-83, chair, 1974-76, 78-79, mem. nat. recreational trails adv. com. U.S. Dept. Transp., 1992-94; mem. steering com. Wake County Cmty. Assessment, 1992-94, mem. organizing com. N.C. Greenways Conf., 1986—, conf. chair, 1992; mem. Triangle Open Space Network, 1997—. Fellow Am. Soc. Landscape Architects (treas. N.C. chpt. 1982-86, v.p. 1978-79, awards 1978, 86, 90, 95), mem. NCSU dept. Landscape and Architecture (alum. adv. bd. 1999—), Nat. Assn. Environ. Profls., N.C. Trails Assn. (bd. dirs. 1977-82, acting pres. 1977), Landscape Architecture Founds., Landscape Architecture Urban Parks Honor Roll, others. Democrat. Methodist. Avocations: trail construction/maintenance, jogging, canoeing, hiking, bicycling. Home: 520 Polk St Raleigh NC 27604-1960 Office: NC ENR Office Legis & Intergovtl Affairs 512 N Salisbury St Raleigh NC 27604-1118

FLOWE, CAROL CONNOR, lawyer; b. Owensboro, Ky., Jan. 3, 1950; d. Marvin C. Connor and Ethel Marie (Thorn) Smith; children: Samantha Kathleen, Andrew Benjamin. BME magna cum laude, Murray State U., 1972; JD summa cum laude, Ind. U., 1976. Bar: Ohio 1977, D.C. 1981, U.S. Dist. Ct. (so. dist.) Ohio 1977, U.S. Dist. Ct. Md. 1983, U.S. Dist. Ct. D.C. 1981, U.S. Supreme Ct. 1987, U.S. Ct. Appeals (2d, 4th, 5th, 7th and D.C. cirs.). Assoc. Baker & Hostetler, Columbus, Ohio, 1976-80, Arent Fox Kintner Plotkin & Kahn, Washington, 1980-87; deputy gen. counsel Pension Benefit Guaranty Corp., Washington, 1987-89, gen. counsel, 1989-95; ptnr. Arent, Fox, Kintner, Plotkin & Kahn, 1995—. Mem. ABA, D.C. Bar Assn., Order of Coif, Alpha Chi, Phi Alpha Delta. Avocations: computers, reading. Home: 8608 Aqueduct Rd Potomac MD 20854-6249 Office: Arent Fox Kintner Plotkin & Kahn 1050 Connecticut Ave NW Ste 500 Washington DC 20036-5339

FLOWER, JEAN FRANCES, art educator; b. Schenectady, N.Y., Apr. 12, 1936; d. Francis Tunis and Marjorie (Colcord) Fort; m. Wesley Allen Flower, Aug. 23, 1958; children: Kimberly Lynn, Kristina Kathleen. BA, Syracuse U., 1958; BFA cum laude, Western Mich. U., 1984, MFA magne cum laude, 1989. Free-lance artist, 1981-86; tech. grad. asst. Western Mich. U., Kalamazoo, 1988, grad. asst. early mgmt., 1989, instr. art, 1989-93; instr. art Kalamazoo Inst. Art, 1993—. One-woman shws include Peoples Ch., Kalamazoo, 1991; exhibited in group shows Kalamazoo Area Art Show, 1992, 94 95, 97, Nat. Art Show, Dallas, 1993, Libr., Parchment, Mich., 1993, EAA Aviation Internat. Art Show, 1992, 95; murals executed Kalamazoo Valley Pub. Mus., 1995, Kalamazoo Aviation History Mus., 1996. Pres., mem. Anna Cir. 1st United Meth. Ch., Kalamazoo, 1980—, mem. communications comm., 1994—; sec.-treas. Airward, Plainwell, Mich., 1986—. Mem. Am. Assn. Aviation Artists, Plainwell Pilots Assn., Kalamazoo Aviatrix Assn. (past v.p.). Avocations: flying, painting, golf, tennis, cross-country skiing. Home and Studio: 8745 Marsh Rd Plainwell MI 49080-8818

FLOWER, WALTER CHEW, III, investment counselor; b. New Orleans, Mar. 3, 1939; s. Walter Chew II and Anne Elisa (Lusk) F.; m. Ella Smith Montgomery, Dec. 21, 1966; children: Anne Stuart, Lindsey Montgomery. BA in Econs., Tulane U., 1960; MBA in Fin., Harvard U., 1964. Cons. AID, State Dept., 1964-65; fin. analyst Delta Capital Corp., New Orleans, 1965-66; v.p., mng. partner Loomis Sayles & Co. Inc., New Orleans, 1967-78; pres. Walter C. Flower & Co., Investment Counsel, New Orleans, 1978—; dir. Starmount Cos.; vice chair Tulane Med. Ctr.; bd. dirs. Longue Vue Found., 1983—; dir GPOA Found., 1985—; vestryman, mem. parish council Trinity Ch., 1978—; dir., fin. adv. Jr. League New Orleans, 1978-82; fin. adv. Hermann Grima Hist. House, 1978—, Beauregard House, 1979—, Metairie Park Country Day Sch., 1991—, New Orleans Mus. Art, 1998—. Lt. USNR, 1960-62. Mem. Boston Club, La. Club., Pickwick Club, New Orleans Lawn Tennis Club, So. Yacht Club (New Orleans), Fishers Island Yacht Club, Stratford Club, Lakeshore Club, Wyvern Club, Confrerie Des Chevaliers Du Tastevin, Phi Beta Kappa. Office: 408 Magazine St New Orleans LA 70130-2435

FLOWERREE, ROBERT EDMUND, retired forest products company executive; b. New Orleans, Jan. 4, 1921; s. Robert E. and Amy (Hewes) F.; m. Elaine Dicks, Sept. 22, 1943; children: Ann D., John H., David R. B.A., Tulane U., 1942. Vice pres. Georgia-Pacific Corp., 1956-63, exec. v.p. pulp, paper and chem. ops., 1963-75, pres., 1974-76, chmn., chief exec. officer, 1976-83, chmn., 1983-84, ret., 1984; chmn. Kilgore Corp.; past bd. dirs. Ga. Gulf Corp. Emeritus adminstr. Tulane U., New Orleans; life trustee Lewis and Clark Coll., Portland, Oreg. Served to lt. USNR, 1942-46. Recipient Disting. Alumnus award Tulane U., 1978. Clubs: Knights of Malta; Arlington (Portland), Waverley Country (Portland); Boston (New Orleans); Links (N.Y.C.). Office: 900 SW 5th Ave Portland OR 97204-1235*

FLOWERS, CREOLE DUANE, publishing executive; b. Vandalia, Ill., Dec. 16, 1942; s. Creole Udell Flowers and Genevieve Eileen Beeson; m. Linda Kay Mollett, Aug. 5, 1966; 1 child, John Curtis. BS in Bus., Greenville Coll., 1965. Quality analyst Allis-Chalmers, Springfield, Ill., 1965-66, quality engr., 1967; jr. ptnr. Bass-Mollett Pubs., Springfield, 1969-72; sales v.p. Bass-Mollett Pubs., Greenville, Ill., 1972-76, pres., 1976—, also bd. dirs.; adv. dir. Mercantile Bank, St. Louis, 1997—; bd. dirs. Masters Engraving Co., Virden, Ill. Trustee bd. Lindenwood U., St. Charles, Mo., 1995—; committeeman Rep. Party, Bond County, 1976-82; trustee 1st Meth. Ch., Greenville, 1974-77; mem. parents adv. com. Rhodes Coll., Memphis, 1993-95. With Ill. Air N.G., 1966-72. Mem. Ill. Funeral Supply Assn. (pres. 1973-76), St. Pats Investment Syndicate (sgt. at arms 1997—), Greenville C. of C., Mo. Athletic Club, Oaks Country Club. Republican. Presbyterian. Avocations: hunting, fishing, golf. Office: Bass-Mollett Pubs 507 Monroe St Greenville IL 62246-2033

FLOWERS, DAMON BRYANT, architect, facility planner; b. Detroit, May 16, 1952; s. Marrell Curtis and Mattie (Rice) F.; m. Adria Faye Burrows, July 28, 1979; children: Lee, Dadria, Damon Bryant II. BS in Architecture, Lawrence Inst. Tech., 1974; BA in Liberal Arts, Cen. Mich. U., 1982; MS in Fin., Ctrl. Mich. U., 1984; JD, Detroit Coll. Law, 1990. Bar: Mich. 1990; registered arch., Mich., Ill., Wis., Ohio, Fla., N.Y. Architect Wayne State U., 1983-85; construction project mgmt. dir. St. Joseph Hosp. and Health Ctrs., 1985-91; v.p. ops. Argus & Assocs., 1991-94; assoc. v.p. facilities devel. and ops. Washtenaw C.C., 1994—. Mem. AIA, APPA, BOCA, Constrn. Spec. Inst., NFPA. Mem. African Methodist Episcopal Ch. Avocation: photography. Home: 22341 Avon Ln Southfield MI 48075-4026 Office: Washtenaw CC Ann Arbor MI 48106

FLOWERS, GLEN DALE, minister; b. Elberfeld, Ind., July 2, 1940; s. Otis Preston and Anna (Hollingsworth) F.; m. Naomi June Bruce, Aug. 13, 1943; children: Theresa Lynne Flowers Carr, Robert Preston. BA, Carson-Newman Coll., Jefferson City, Tenn., 1972; MDiv, So. Bapt. Theol. Sem., Louisville, 1976; real estate diploma, U. Indpls., 1982. Ordained to ministry So. Bapt. Conv., 1969. Driver United Parcel Svc., Evansville, Ind., 1962-69; pastor Mitchell Springs Bapt. Ch., Rutledge, Tenn., 1969-71, Broadway Bapt. Ch., Princeton, Ind., 1972-76, 1st Bapt. Ch., Mooresville, Ind., 1976-85; evangelist, Jefferson City, 1971-72; pastor Oakhill Bapt. Ch., Evansville, 1985—; dir. BSU and ISUE, U. Evansville, 1974-75; mem. nat. steering com. Festival Religion and Rural Life, Home Missions Bd., State Conv. Bapts. in Ind., 1978, mem. exec. bd. and exec. com., 1978-80, 86—, chmn. state exec. bd., 1979-80; mem. various coms. Cen. Ind. Bapt. Assn., Sunday sch. dir., 1978-79, 81-82; tchr. Boyce Bible Ctr., Monrovia, Ind., 1984-85; mem. com. on nominations So. Bapt. Conv., 1988-89; instr., ctr. dir. Extension Ctr. for Okla. Bapt. U., Evansville, 1991-94; numerous others. Contbr. to Ency. So. Bapts., Vol. IV, 1980. Chmn. Vol. Probation Officers for Juvenile Delinquents, Rutledge, 1971; bd. dirs. Mooresville Sr. Ctr., 1983-84, Morgan County Sr. Svcs., Martinsville, Ind., 1983-85; chaplain Morgan County Sheriff's Office and Mooresville Police Dept., 1980-85; vol. chaplaincy program Mooresville High Sch., 1983-84; bd. dirs. Morgan County Weekday Religious Edn., 1983-84; founder Ann. Ladies' Enrichment Day, Mooresville, 1980-85; trustee internat. mission bd. So. Bapt. Conf., 1992-2000; mission trips to Antigua, Zambia, Kenya, Rwanda, Uganda, Malawi, Zimbabwe, South Africa, Switzerland, and Guatemala. With USN, 1958-61. Mem. Southwestern Bapt. Assn. (bd. dirs. 1985—). Republican. Home: 5700 Twickingham Dr Evansville IN 47711-2050 Office: Oakhill Bapt Ch 4615 Oak Hill Rd Evansville IN 47711-2943 *Our generation has a need to be encouraged to express a sincere faith in God while the influences around them are teaching them to be so superficial about their feelings.*

FLOWERS, LANGDON STRONG, foods company executive; b. Thomasville, Ga., Feb. 12, 1922; s. William Howard and Flewellyn Evans (Strong) F.; m. Margaret Clisby Powell, June 3, 1944; children: Margaret Flowers Rich, Langdon Strong, Elizabeth Powell Flowers McKinney, Dorothy Howard Flowers Swinson, John Howard. B.S., MIT, 1944, M.S., 1947; H.H.D., Presbyn. Coll., 1984. Engr., Douglas Aircraft, Los Angeles, 1947; supr. Flowers Baking Co., Thomasville, 1947-50; sales mgr. Flowers Baking Co., 1950-58, v.p. sales, 1958-65; pres., chief operating officer Flowers Industries, Inc., Thomasville, 1965-76; vice chmn. bd., chief exec. officer Flowers Industries, Inc., 1976-80, chmn. bd., 1980-85, ret., 1985. Past pres. Thomasville YMCA, 1958-62; past trustee Presbyn Coll., Clinton, S.C., Archbold Meml. Hosp., Thomasville. Served as lt. (j.g.) USNR, 1943-46. Named Man of Year, Thomas County C. of C., 1974. Mem. Am. Bakers Assn. (exec. com. 1974-75, chmn. 1975-76), So. Bakers Assn. (chmn. bd. 1969-70), NAM (dir., exec. com.), Thomasville C. of C. (pres. 1953-54), Sigma Alpha Epsilon. Presbyterian (chmn. bd. deacons 1952-56, elder 1956—, rep. Gen. Assembly 1966). Club: Rotarian. Home: 207 Fairways Dr Thomasville GA 31792-7626 Office: PO Box 997 Thomasville GA 31799-0997

FLOWERS, MERLE G., legislative staff member; b. Section, Ala.; s. Jack and June Flowers; m. Stacey Reeves. BS in Agrl. Bus. and Econs., Auburn U., 1991; MBA, U. Miss., 1995. Alderman, dir. pks., recreation and beautification City of Section, 1988-92; with Lightfoot, Franklin & White, Birmingham, Ala., Carson-Brooks, Inc., Memphis; dist. mgr. Congressman Roger Wicker, Washington. Pres. bd. dirs. Desoto chpt. Habitat for Humanity; bd. dirs. Kudzu Playhouse. Named Top 40 Under 40 Miss. Bus. Jour. Mem. Mason, Shriner (Clown Unit Rookie of the Yr., 1993). Avocations: marathon, guitar. Fax: 601-342-3883. Office: PO Box 70 8700 Northwest Dr Ste 102 Southaven MS 38671

FLOWERS, ROBERT B., military career officer; b. Pa., July 9, 1947. Grad., Va. Mil. Inst., 1969; MCE, U. Va.; grad., Command & Gen. Staff Coll., Nat. War Coll. Registered profl. engr., Va. Commd. 2nd lt. U.S. Army, 1969, advanced through grades to maj. gen., various positions, 1969-85, comdr. 307th Engr. Battalion, 1985-87; joint staff Nat. Mil. Command Ctr./Counternarcotics Divsn. U.S. Army, Washington, 1987-90; comdr. 20th Engr. Brigade (Combat) (Airborne Corps) U.S. Army, Ft. Bragg, N.C., 1990-92; dep. asst. commandant U.S. Army Engr. Sch., 1992-93; asst. commandant U.S. Army Engr. Sch., Ft. Leonard Wood; dep. commdg. gen. U.S. Army Engring. Ctr., 1993-95; asst. divsn. comdr. 2nd Inf. Divsn. (Mechanized) Eighth U.S. Army; dep. chief staff engring. U.S. Army Europe, 1996; pres. Miss. River Commn. U.S. Army, comdr. Miss. Valley Divsn.; commandant U.S. Army Engr. Sch.; commdg. gen. U.S. Army Engr. Ctr. and Ft. Leonard Wood, 1997—; joint task force engr. Joint Task Force, Somalia. Office: US Army Engr Ctr Fort Leonard Wood MO 65473

FLOWERS, SANDRA JOAN, elementary education educator; b. Newport, R.I., July 17, 1943; d. Joseph A. and Dolores A. (Martino) F. BA, Salve Regina Coll., 1965; MA in Teaching, R.I. Coll., 1968; postgrad., Salve Regina U., 1990—, cert. advanced grad. study, 1994. Cert. elem. tchr., R.I. Tchr. Newport Sch. Dept., 1965-95; ret., 1995; instr., edn. Salve Regina U., Newport, 1979—; mem. adv. bd. Underwood Sch., Newport, 1986, mem. site-based mgmt. team, 1993—; mem. basic ednl. planning team R.I. Dept. Edn., Barrington Pub. Schs., 1986. Mem. Funding and Expenditures Alternatives Strategic Planning, Newport, 1989—; bd. dirs. Aquidneck Collaborative for Edn., 1993—; mem. grad. student coun. Salve Regina U.; religious edn. tchr. St. Joseph's Parish, Newport, 1995—. Moore scholar Salve Regina Coll., 1961-65, R.I. State scholar, 1961-65. Mem. ASCD, AAUW, R.I. Assn. Tchr. Educators. Roman Catholic. Avocations: writing for children, reading, church work, drawing, painting. Home: PO Box # 114 16 Keeher Ave Newport RI 02840-2320

FLOWERS, VIRGINIA ANNE, academic administrator emerita; b. Dothan, Ala., Aug. 29, 1928; d. Kyrie Neal and Annie Laurie (Stewart) F. BA, Fla. State U., 1949; MEd, Auburn U., 1958; EdD, Duke U., 1963. Teaching asst. Duke U., Durham, N.C., 1963; elem. and secondary sch. tchr., adminstr. Dothan and Dalton, Ga., 1949-61; assoc. prof., then prof. edn., head dept. Columbia (S.C.) Coll., 1963-68, assoc. dean, then dean, 1969-72; prof. edn. Va. Commonwealth U., 1968-69; teaching asst. Duke U., 1963; assoc. dean, asst. provost, acting dean, vice provost Trinity Coll. Arts and Scis., Duke U., 1972-74, prof. edn., chmn. dept., asst. provost ednl. program devel., 1974-80; dean Sch. Edn., Ga. So. Coll., Statesboro, 1980-85; asst. vice chancellor acad. affairs Univ. System of Ga., Atlanta, 1985-88, vice chancellor, 1988-90, vice chancellor emerita, 1990—; ind. ednl. cons. Co-author: Law and Pupil Control, 1964, Readings in Survival in Today's Society, 2 vols, 1978; editorial bd.: Jour. Tchr. Edn, 1980-82, Ednl. Gerontology, 1979; ; contbr. articles to profl. jours. Bd. dirs., mem. exec. com. Learning Inst. N.C., 1976-80; mem. bd. visitors Charleston So. U., 1992-93; adv. trustee Queens Coll., Charlotte, N.C., 1976-78; vice chmn. continuing commn. on study of black colls. related to United Meth. Ch., 1973-76. Delta Kappa Gamma scholar Duke U., 1963, State of Fla. scholar Fla. State U., 1949. Mem. NEA, Am. Edn1. Rsch. Assn., So. Assn. Colls. and Schs. (mem. commn. on colls.), Am. Assn. Higher Edn., Am. Assn. Colls. of Tchr. Edn. (pres. 1983-84, bd. dirs., mem. exec. com. 1979-84), Nat. Orgn. Legal Problems in Edn., Kappa Delta Pi, Phi Delta Kappa. Home and Office: PO Box 1603 Marianna FL 32447-5603

FLOWERS, WILLIAM HAROLD, JR., lawyer; b. Chgo., Mar. 22, 1946; s. William Harold and Ruth Lolita (Cave) F.; m. Pamela Mays, Sept. 13, 1980. BA, U. Colo., 1967, JD, 1971. Bar: Colo. 1973, U.S. Dist. Ct. Colo. 1973, U.S. Ct. Appeals (10th cir.) 1978, U.S. Supreme Ct. 1985, U.S. Ct. Appeals (4th cir.) 1994. Atty. Pikes Peak Legal Svcs., Colorado Springs, Colo., 1973; ptnr. Tate, Tate & Flowers, Denver, 1973-76; dep. dist. atty. Office Adams County Dist. Atty., Brighton, Colo., 1977-78; ptnr. Taussig & Flowers, Boulder, 1978-81; pvt. practice Boulder, 1981-89; ptnr. Holland & Hart, LLP, Denver, 1989-97, Hurth Yeager & Sisk, LLP, 1997—; mem. Boulder County Cmty. Corrections Bd., 1985-90. Mem. Boulder Bd. Zoning Adjustment, 1973-78, chmn., 1977-78; mem. Boulder Growth Task Force, 1980-82; mem. exec. bd. Longs Peak coun. Boy Scouts Am., 1983-98; bd. dirs. Sta. KGNU, Boulder County Broadcasting, 1981-84. Mem. ATLA, Nat. Bar Assn. (regional dir. 1983-86, mem. bd. govs. 1983-96, v.p. 1990-91), Colo. Criminal Def. Bar (bd. dirs. 1982-83), Boulder County Bar Assn. (mem. civil litigation com. 1978—, mem. criminal law com. 1979—), Colo. Trial Lawyers Assn. (treas. 1995-96, sec. 1996-97, v.p. 1997-98, pres.-elect 1998-99, pres. 1999—), Cary Bar Assn. (pres. 1987), U. Colo. Boulder Alumni Assn. (bd. dirs. 1987-96, pres. 1994-95), U. Colo. Found. (bd. dirs. 1995—). Democrat. Methodist. Office: Hurth Yeager & Sisk LLP PO Box 17850 4860 Riverbend Rd Boulder CO 80308

FLOWERS, WILLIAM HOWARD, JR., food company executive; b. Thomasville, Ga., Nov. 14, 1913; s. William Howard and Flewellyn Evans (Strong) F.; m. Fontaine Maury Tice, June 22, 1936; children: Fontaine (Mrs. Fontaine Flowers McFadden), Maury (Mrs. Joseph V. Shields Jr.), Daphne (Mrs. C. Martin Wood III), Taliaferro (Mrs. Robert P. Crozer). B.A. in Bus. Adminstrn, Washington and Lee U., 1933. With Flowers Baking Co. div. Flowers Industries, Inc., Thomasville, Ga., 1933-68, pres., chief operating officer, 1937-65, chmn., chief operating officer, 1966-68; chmn., chief exec. officer Flowers Industries, Inc., Thomasville, 1974-76, chmn., 1976-81, chmn. exec. com., 1981-96, chmn. emeritus, 1984-96, retired chmn. bd., 1996—. Chmn. Southeastern Legal Found., Atlanta, 1983-87, emeritus, 1987—; dir. The Prayer Book Soc., 1984-87, Thomas County Bi-Centennial/Sesqui-Centennial Commn.; mem. spl. adv. com. on pub. opinion U.S. Dept. State, 1970-72; mem. Thomas County Sch. Bd., 1953-58, Madeira Sch. Corp., Greenway, Va., 1960-68, Ga. Senate, 1964-68; city commr., Thomasville, 1941; pres. Thomasville YMCA, 1949-52; trustee John D. Archbold Meml. Hosp., 1953-71, Thomasville; pres. William Howard Flowers Jr. Found. Recipient Ga. Freedom award, 1994, Pinnacle award Thomasville-Thomas County, 1994; named Man of Yr., Thomas County C. of C., 1964. Mem. NAM (dir. 1962-66), Young Pres.'s Orgn., Chief Execs. Orgn., Ducks Unltd. (nat. trustee 1967—), University Club (N.Y.C.), Rotary, Lyford Cay (Nassau), Wildcat Cliffs Country (Highlands, N.C.), Ga-Fla Field Trial, Glen Arven Country (Thomasville), Farmington Country (Charlottesville, Va.), Omicron Delta Kappa. Episcopalian. Office: PO Box 1338 2301 Old Monticello Rd Thomasville GA 31799-1338

FLOWERS, WOODIE CLAUDE, mechanical engineering educator and researcher, engineering director. BS, La Polytech U., 1966; MS, MIT, 1968, ME, 1970, PhD, 1972. Rsch. asst. mech. engring. MIT, Cambridge, 1966-68, instr., 1968-72, from asst. to full prof., 1972-88, prof. mech. engring., 1988—, head sys. & design divsn., 1989-91, dir. new prodn. program, 1990—, Pappalardo prof., 1994—; engring. design cons., 1966—; host PBS-TV series, Sci. Am. Frontiers, 1990-93. Recipient Ralph E. Teetor Young Educator award Soc. Automotive Engrs. Mem. AAAS, ASME, NAS, Am. Soc. Engring. Educators. Achievements include research in microcomputer-controlled prostheses for above knee amputees, instrumentation for quantitative assessment of human movement disorders, computer aided design systems. Office: MIT Dept Mech Engring Bldg 3 Rm 439 77 Massachusetts Ave Dept Mech Cambridge MA 02139-4307*

FLOYD, ALTON DAVID, cell biologist, consultant; b. Henderson, Ky., July 17, 1941; s. Frank and Queen Tina (Melton) F.; m. Barbara Wilson, Aug. 18, 1962; children: Fara Alison, Heather Lynn. BS, U. Ky., 1963; PhD, U. Louisville, 1968. From lectr. to asst. prof. U. Mich., Ann Arbor, 1967-72; from asst. to assoc. prof. Sch. of Medicine Ind. U., Bloomington, 1972-83; assoc. prof. Sch. of Medicine Ind. U., Indpls., 1983-84; sect. head cell biology Miles Sci., Inc., Naperville, Ill., 1984-85; sr. staff scientist Miles, Inc., Elkhart, Ind., 1985-89; pvt. practice cons. Edwardsburg, Mich., 1989—; assoc. dir. Ctr. Light Microscope Inaging and Biotech. Carnegie Mellon U., Pitts., 1991; bd. dirs. Endotech Corp., Indpls.; mem. subcom. immunohistochem. stains NCCLS, 1995-96; industry rep. adv. panel hematology and pathology devices FDA, 1996—; trustee Biol. Stain Commn., 1997—. Mem. Am. Assn. Anatomists, Tissue Culture Assn., Soc. Analytical Cytology, Histochem. Soc., Soc. Quantitative Morphology, Soc. Histotech. Avocations: sailing, reading, wood and metal shopwork, computing. Home and Office: 23126 S Shore Dr Edwardsburg MI 49112-8502

FLOYD, BOBBY O., military officer. B in Math., USAF Acad., 1968; M in Bus., Cen. Mich. U., 1977; grad., Armed Forces Staff Coll., 1978, Air War Coll., 1985. Commd. 2d lt. USAF, 1968, advanced through grades to maj. gen., 1996; procurement officer Air Force Contract Mgmt. Divsn., Kirtland AFB, N.Mex., 1975-78; programming officer, dep. chief of staff programs/eval. Hdqs. USAF, Washington, 1978-80, exec. officer to dep. chief of staff programs/eval., 1980-82; comdr. 57th Mil. Airlift Squadron, Altus AFB, Okla., 1982-84; dep. dir., dir. programming and policy, dep. chief staff Hdqs. Mil. Airlift Command, Scott AFB, Ill., 1985-87; dep. chief staff U.S. Transp. Command, Scott AFB, 1987-89; dep. dir. programs and evaluation Hdqs. USAF, Washington, 1991-92; comdr. 23d Wing, Pope AFB, N.C., 1992-94; dir. plans Hdqs. Air Mobility Command, Scott AFB, 1994-95; dir. forces, dep. chief staff Hdqs. USAF, Washington, 1995-96; dir. logistics Hdqs. Air Mobility Command, Scott AFB, 1996—. Decorated Disting. Svc. medal, Def. Superior Svc. medal, Legion of Merit with oak leaf cluster, D.F.C. Office: HQ AMC/LG Unit 2A2 402 Scott Dr Scott Air Force Base IL 62225

FLOYD, BRETT ALDEN, mortgage banker; b. Las Vegas, Nev., Nov. 12, 1963. Branch mgr. Transamerica Fin., West Covina, Calif., 1984-89, Assocs. Fin., San Gabriel, Calif., 1989; area sales mgr. Long Beach Bank, F.S.B., Woodland Hills, Calif., 1989-94; divsn. mgr. Royal Thrift & Loan Co., L.A., 1994-96; v.p. Royal MortgageBanc, Orange, Calif., 1996-97; sr. v.p. retail prodn. mgr. WMC Mortgage Corp., Woodland Hills, Calif., 1997—. Assoc. Ctl. Com., L.A., 1992. Republican. Avocation: snow skiing. Home: 12433 Sebastian Pl Tustin CA 92782-1510 Office: WMC Mortgage Corp 6320 Canoga Ave Ste 720 Woodland Hills CA 91367-2526

FLOYD, CINTHIA ANN, secondary school educator, coach; b. Mobile, Ala., July 26, 1961; d. Joe Merle and V. Marolyn (Whiddon) Crump; children: Cory James, Courtney Marie; m. Martin A. Floyd, Aug. 12, 1994. BS in Phys. Edn., U. South Ala., 1983, MEd, 1984. Cert. phys. edn. tchr., Ala. Grad. tchg. asst. U. South Ala., Mobile, 1984-85; tchr. phys. edn., volleyball coach Palmer Pillans Mid. Sch., Mobile, 1985-98; volleyball and track coach Cranford Burns Mid. Sch., Mobile, 1998—; softball coach B.C. Rain H.S., Mobile, 1989-93; mem. health curriculum adv. bd. Mobile County Pub. Sch. Sys., 1990-91; program dir. Racquetball Club Mobile, 1980-8; track coach Palmer Pillans Mid. Sch., 1994-98. Named Outstanding Tchr. of Yr., Mobile C. of C., 1991, one of Top Three in Nation, Disney's Am. Tchr. awards, 1993. Mem. AAHPERD, NEA, Nat. Assn. Girls and Women in Sports, Ala. Assn. Health Phys. Edn. Recreation and Dance (State Coach of Yr. 1991), Ala. Edn. Assn., Ala. H.S. Athletic Assn., Coaches and Phys. Educators Mobile (v.p. 1989-91), Kappa Kappa Iota (pres. 1991). Baptist. Avocations: volleyball, softball, beach activities, swimming. Home: 607 Montclaire Way Mobile AL 36609-6539 Office: Cranford Burns Mid Sch 6175 Girby Rd Mobile AL 36693

FLOYD, GARY LEON, plant cell biologist; b. Moline, Ill., Dec. 23, 1940; s. Leland L. and Zenta (Henderson) F.; m. Myrna A. Floyd, Aug. 18, 1963. BA, U. No. Iowa, 1962; MS, U. Okla., 1966; PhD, Miami U., Oxford, Ohio, 1971. Sci. tchr. Grinnell (Iowa) Jr. High Sch., 1962-65; instr. Miami U., 1966-68; asst. prof. Rutgers U., New Brunswick, N.J., 1971-75; asst. prof. plant biology Ohio State U., Columbus, 1975-78, assoc. prof., 1978-83, prof., 1983—, assoc. dean biol. scis., 1986-88, dean, 1989-96, prof. and dean emeritus, 1996—; dir. TEM facility plant biology dept. Ohio State U., Columbus, 1978-86. Contbr. articles to profl. jours. NSF scholar, 1965-66; recipient Alumni Teaching award Ohio State U., 1980, Disting. Rsch. award, 1982, Darbaker prize Bot. Soc. Am., 1993; Phycological Soc. Am. nat. lectr., 1983-85. Avocation: golf. Home: 936 Kendale Rd S Columbus OH 43220-4148

FLOYD, JACK WILLIAM, lawyer; b. Columbia, S.C., May 14, 1934; s. Edward Immanuel and Edith Fletcher (Herlong) F.; m. Ruth Parker Matthews, Jan. 10, 1957; children—Connie, Cindy, Jay. BS, U. N.C., 1958, JD with honors, 1961. Bar: N.C. 1961, U.S. Supreme Ct. 1971. Assoc. Smith, Moore, Smith, Schell & Hunter, Greensboro, N.C., 1961-67; ptnr. Smith, Moore, Smith, Schell & Hunter, 1967-87, Floyd, Greeson, Allen & Jacobs, Greensboro, N.C., 1988-90, Floyd, Allen & Jacobs, Greensboro, 1991-97, Floyd & Jacobs, Greensboro, 1998—; lectr. acctg. U. N.C., 1960-

61; lectr. bus. law Guilford Coll., 1962-64; speaker on jury trials Am. Bar Assn., Am. Patent Law Assn.; arbitrator U.S. Dist. Ct. Annexed Arbitration Program. Bd. editors: N.C. Law Rev, 1960-61. Mem. parents' bd. dirs. Meredith Coll., Raleigh, N.C., 1977-79, chmn., 1980-81. Served with USN, 1951-55. Mem. Am. Bar Assn., N.C. Bar Assn. (panelist on family law), Am. Law Inst., N.C. Assn. Trial Lawyers, Order of Coif. Democrat. Baptist. Club: Elks. Home: 1404 Valleymeade Rd Greensboro NC 27410-3938 Office: Floyd & Jacobs 125 S Elm St Greensboro NC 27401-2644

FLOYD, JOHN ALEX, JR., editor, marketing executive, horticulturist; b. Selma, Ala., Feb. 21, 1948; s. John Alex Sr. and Louise (Johnson) F.; m. Pamela Lorene Billups, Aug. 14, 1982; children: Ryan Thomas, James Alex. BS, Auburn (Ala.) U., 1970; MS, Clemson (S.C.) U., 1972, PhD, 1975. Instr. Jefferson State Jr. Coll., Birmingham, Ala., 1975-77; sr. horticulturist So. Living Mag., Birmingham, 1977-84; editorial dir. Classics-So. Accents, Birmingham, 1985-87, Creative Ideas and Cooking Light, Birmingham, 1987-88; dir. mktg. svcs., editor So. Progress Corp, Birmingham, 1988-91; v.p., editor So. Living, 1991—. Author: (with others) Southern Living Trees & Shrubs, 1980, Southern Living Garden Guide, 1982, Southern Living Vegetable & Herbs, 1984. Mem. adv. com. Landscape Architecture Adv. Coun., Auburn U., 1988-93; bd. dirs. U. N.C. Botanical Gardens, Chapel Hill, 1988-90. Grantee NSF, 1977. Mem. Am. Soc. Hort. Sci., Garden Writers Am., Birmingham Bot. Soc. (pres. 1981, trustee 1984—), Am. Hort. Soc. (bd. dirs. 1991-94), The Club, Summit Club, Gamma Sigma Delta, Pi Alpha Xi. Methodist. Home: 369 Palace Dr Trussville AL 35173-1067 Office: So Progress Corp 2100 Lakeshore Dr Birmingham AL 35209-6721

FLOYD, KEVIN R., English educator; b. Mar. 14, 1967. BA, U. North Tex., 1990; PhD, U. Iowa, 1998. Asst. prof. English Kent (Ohio) State U., 1998—. E-mail: kfloyd@kent.edu. Office: Kent State U Dept English Kent OH 44242-0001

FLOYD, RAYMOND LORAN, professional golfer; b. Ft. Bragg, N.C., Sept. 4, 1942; s. Loren B. and Edith (Brown) F.; m. Maria; children: Raymond Loran, Robert Loran, Christina Loran. Student, U. N.C., 1960. Profl. golfer, 1961—; mem. Ryder Cup team, 1969, 75, 77, 81, 83, 85, 89, 91, 93. Winner Doral Ryder Open, 1992, GTE North Classic, 1992, Sr. Tour, 1992, Northville Long Island Classic Senior PGA, 1993, Sr. Tour Championship, 1994; named Rookie of Year Golf Mag., 1963, 77, Player of Yr., 1976. Winner PGA tournament, 1969, 82 St. Petersburg Open, 1963, St. Paul Open, 1965, Jacksonville Open, 1969, Am. Golf Classic, 1969, Kemper Open, 1975, Masters, 1976, World Open, 1976, Byron Nelson Golf Classic, 1977, Pleasant Valley Golf Classic, 1977, Brazilian Open, 1978, Greater Greensboro Open, 1979, Canadian PGA, 1981, Vardon Trophy, 1983, Ryder Cup, 1969, 75, 77, 81, 83, 85, Doral Ea. Open, 1980, 81, Tournament Players Championship, 1981, Westchester Classic, 1981, Meml. Tournament, 1982, Memphis Classic, 1982, PGA Championship, 1982, $1Million Sun City Challenge, 1982, Houston Open, 1985, Chrysler Team Championship, 1985, U.S. Open, 1986, Walt Disney/Oldsmobile Classic, 1986, Skins Game, 1988, RMCC Invitational, 1990, Doral-Ryder Open, 1992, GTE North Classic, 1992, Ralph's Sr. Classic, 1992, Sr. Tour Championship, 1992, Thailand Srs., 1992, Northville L.I. Classic, 1993, The Tradition, 1994, Sr. Skins Game, 1994, 95, 96, 97, 98, Las Vegas Srs. Classis, 1994, Sr. Tour Championship, 1994, PGA Srs. Championship, 1995, Burnet Sr. Classic, 1995, Ford Sr. Players Championship, 1996; capt. Ryder Cup, 1989; inducted in PGA/World Golf Hall of Fame, 1989, winner father-son tourn. w/ son Raymond Jr., 1995, 96, 97. Office: 231 Royal Palm Way Palm Beach FL 33480-4302*

FLOYD, TIM, professional basketball coach, former collegiate basketball coach; b. Hattiesburg, Miss.; m. Beverly Floyd; 1 child, Shannon. BS, La. Tech. Univ., 1977. Coach Univ. El Paso, 1977-86, Idaho Univ., 1986-88, Iowa State Univ., 1994-98. Named Coach of Yr.. Office: Chicago Bulls 1901 W Madison St Chicago IL 60612-2459*

FLOYD, TIMOTHY SHERWOOD, graphic designer; b. Conway, S.C., May 17, 1960; s. Walter Sherwood and Irene Margret (Stevens) F.; m. Carol Ann Lombardi, June 5, 1983; children: Luke Prescott, Felicia Michelle. BA, U. S.C., 1982. Graphic designer U. S.C., Columbia, 1983-85; art dir. Blue Cross & Blue Shield, Columbia, 1985-87, Midlands Tech. Sch., Columbia, 1987-92; graphics mgr. Palmetto Richland Meml. Hosp., Columbia, 1992—. Recipient Addy award Advt. Fedn. Am., 1988, 92, 94, 96, 97, 98, Best of Show, Dist. Gold, 1999, N-Show, Columbia Comm. Acts Soc., 1995-98, Mercury award Pub. Rels. Soc. Am., 1997. 98, Wallie award, 1995, 98; Tim Floyd Appreciation Day named in his honor Palmetto Richland Meml. Hosp., 1999. Republican. Assemblies of God. Avocations: camping, fishing, pranks. Office: Palmetto Richland Meml Hosp 5 Richland Medical Park Dr Columbia SC 29203-6897

FLOYD, WALTER LEO, lawyer; b. St. Louis, May 29, 1933; s. Walter L. Sr. and Estelle E. (Kiess) F.; children: Michael W., Mary Ann, Mark L.; m. Patricia A. Knapko, Sept. 3, 1994. BS, St. Louis U., 1955, LLD, 1959. Bar: Mo. 1959, Ill. 1959, U.S. Dist. (ea. dist.) Mo. 1959. Owner The Floyd Law Firm P.C., St. Louis, 1959—. Contbr. articles to profl. jours. Fellow: Orgn. Nat. Bd. Trial Advocacy; mem. Mo. Assn. Trial Attys. (sec. 1961, v.p. 1962, 85), Am. Trial Lawyers Assn. (lectr.), Mo. Bar Assn., Ill. Assn., Phi Delta Phi. Democrat. Unitarian. Address: Floyd Law Firm 8151 Clayton Rd # 202 Saint Louis MO 63117-1103

FLUCK, J. STEPHEN, disability issues information specialist, writer, educator, poet; b. Quakertown, Pa., Apr. 7, 1944; s. John Jarrett and Florence (Hunsburger) F. *Father J. Jarrett Fluck, Juniata College, member of Board of Directors, Richland Library Company, historical collection with special focus of Pennsylvania history and the Society of Friends, Intellectual Pursuits: Pennsylvania folk artist: Fraktur Schriften, historical researcher on Fraktur-Schriften and Fraktur. Mother, Florence H. Fluck, graduate, Quakertown Community High School,Family member, National Alliance for the Mentally Ill. Legacy, Intellectual and Religious Freedom learned in historical research in Pennsylvania Friends' Meetings, Father's openness, in quiet discussions in little significance but significant love, peace, scholarship, service to man, to God, to history.* AAS, C.C. Phila., 1975. Cert. vocat. rehab. specialist, Pa. Ret. Social Security Disability Ins., 1973; libr. page Lansdale (Pa.) Pub. Libr., 1993-95; cons., fundraiser, creator integrated online sys. for multi-axial med. conditions; mem. planning com. Wellspring Clubhouse, Sellersville, Pa., 1993-94; spkr. Della Landes Found, 1995. *National Writer's Union, UAW Local 1981, AFL-CIO, St. Davids Christian Writer's Association, American Library Association. Association of Specialized and Cooperative Library Agencies: Sections: Independent Librarians Exchange, Interlibrary Cooperation and Networking, State Library Agency, Libraries Serving Special Populations, Independent Libraries Exchange. Forums: Library Service to People with Visual or Physical Disabilities, Library Services to the Deaf, Library Service to the Impaired Elderly, Library Services to Prisoners. Round Tables: Federal Librarians, Government Documents, Library Service to Prisoners, Intellectual Freedom, Social Responsibilities Round Table (ALA Unemployed), Support Staff Interests Round Table. Pennsylvania Library Association. Divisions: College and Research Libraries, Special Librarians, Round Table: Electronic Resources, Library Support Staff. Tables: Staff, Buildings, Equipment and Furnishings, Library Administration and Management. Church and Synagogue Library Association. Friends of the National Library of Medicine: 1999.* Contbr. poetry to various publs. Mem. Com. Support Program Com. Bucks County, Doylestown, Pa., 1992-98; mem. housing task force Bucks County Dept. Mental Health, Doylestown, Pa., 1994-95; spkr. Together We Strive, Bucks County, 1997 Della Landes Found., 1995; participant planning platform State Ind. Living Coun. Conf., Harrisburg, Pa., 1997. Recipient Disting. Character award St. Davids Christian Writers Conf., 1993. Mem. Am. Assn. People with Disabilities, Assn. Macular Diseases, Autism Soc. Am., Nat. Alliance for Mentally Ill, Autism Soc. Am., Acad. Am. Poets (assoc.), Associated Writing Programs, Pa. Coalition Citizens with Disabilities, Pa. Mental Health Consumers Assn., St. Davids Christian Writers Assn., World Affairs Coun. Pa., Pa. Coun. Blind, Heirs, Inc., Sovereign Soc., Mennonite Econ. Devel. Assocs., Highlander Club, Oxford Club, Heirs, Inc. Mennonite. Avocations: surfing the Internet, writing and reading free verse, dining out, shopping, friends. E-mail: stevef@itw.com. Home: 124 S 8th St Quakertown PA 18951-1560 Office: Wellspring Clubhouse 915 Lawn Ave Sellersville PA 18960-1551

FLUELLEN, ABRAHAM P., researcher; b. Columbus, Ga., Sept. 30, 1958; s. King and Elease (Davis) F. BS, Columbus State U., 1981, MS, 1999; postgrad., Alburn U., 1999—. Gen. office asst. Merrill Lynch, Columbus, 1980; intern Mayor of Columbus, 1980-81; gen. office asst. Haley, Bader & Pott Atty., Washington, 1981; statis. analyst U.S. Nuc. Regulatory Commn., Washington, 1981-82; monitor Summer Youth Program, Columbus, 1982. Mem. Nat. Audubon Soc., Sierra Club, Greenpeace. Democrat. Methodist. Avocations: classical music, reading U.S. history, art, traveling, writing. Home: 2116 Garfield Dr Columbus GA 31907-4502

FLUG, JANICE, librarian; b. Mpls., Oct. 19, 1949; d. Albert William and Elberta Edna (Kimball) F.; m. William Raymond LeFevre, Jan. 2, 1982 (dec. June 1986). BA, Hamline U., St. Paul, 1971; MLS, U. Md., 1975; MPA, Am. U., 1980. Acquisitions searcher Am. U. Libr., Washington, 1972-75, asst. to the univ. libr., 1975-91, acquisitions libr., 1991—. Mem. bd. editors The Pub. Mgr., 1996—. Exec. bd. LOMS, 1997—. Mem. ALA (lib. orgn. and mgmt. divsn., mem. LOMS exec. bd. 1997-99), Am. Soc. for Pub. Adminstrn. (mem. nat. coun. 1995-99, pres. Md. chpt. 1994-95, mem. fin. com. fin. vice chair 1999—, chair policy issues com. 1998-99). Democrat. Lutheran. Avocations: swimming, church activities.

FLUHARTY, CHARLES WILLIAM, policy research institute director, consultant, researcher; b. Wheeling, W.Va., Apr. 21, 1947; s. Irwin Adrian and Mary Elizabeth (Foster) F.; m. Marsha Jean Prospal, June 27, 1970; children: Matthew, Joshua, Megan. BA cum laude, U. Steubenville, Ohio, 1969; MDiv with distinctions, Yale U., 1973. Co-dir. Rural Policy Rsch. Inst. U. Mo., Columbia, 1990-92, dir. Rural Policy Rsch. Inst., 1992—, adj. assoc. prof. dept. pub. adminstrn., 1998—, interim dir. Inst. Pub. Affairs, 1998—; human resources cons., 1987—; presenter numerous Congl. hearing/briefing testimonies. Author numerous rural policy rsch. studies, publs., reports, briefings. Recipient Recognition award Nat. Rural Devel. Partnership, 1999, Disting. Svc. award Nat. Assn. Counties, 1998, Recognition award Nat. Orgn. of State Offices of Rural Health, 1998, Columbia Devlin Outstanding Educator award Alpha Chi, 1998. Mem. Baconian Soc. Office: U Mo Rural Policy Rsch Inst Mumford Hall Columbia MO 65211

FLUHR, HOWARD, consulting firm executive; b. Bklyn., Feb. 20, 1943; s. Morton and Evelyn (Cohen) F.; m. Margaret Appel, Sept. 7, 1963; children: Lisa Metaxas, Allison Kaufman. BS in Math. and Philosophy cum laude, NYU, 1964. Various actuarial positions Guardian Life Ins. Co., 1964-66, Eastern Life Ins. Co., 1966-69; various actuarial and mgmt. positions The Segal Co., N.Y.C., 1969-73, v.p., 1973-76, sr. v.p., 1976-87, exec. v.p., 1987-93, pres., CEO, 1994—. Contbr. articles to profl. jours.; speaker in field. Fellow Soc. Actuaries, Conf. Cons. Actuaries (bd. dirs. 1990—, v.p. 1992-94), Can. Inst. Actuaries; mem. Internat. Actuarial Assn., Am. Acad. Actuaries (bd. dirs. 1990-95, v.p. 1993-95), Employee Benefit Rsch. Inst. (trustee 1994—). Office: The Segal Co 1 Park Ave New York NY 10016-5895

FLUKER, JAY EDWARD, middle school art educator; b. Hackensack, N.J., Sept. 26, 1943; s. J. Edward and Betty B. (Berkey) Flucker; m. Eileen Elizabeth Owens, June 22, 1968; children: Colleen Sharon, Maureen Jaye. BA in Art Edn., William Paterson Coll. N.J., 1966, MEd in Art Edn., 1972, MA in Comm. Arts, 1974. Cert. art tchr., elem. tchr. Art tchr. South Plainfield (N.J.) Bd. Edn., 1966-67, Chester (N.J.) Bd. Edn., 1967—; co-developer, workshop instr. West Morris Visual Arts Gifted and Talented Consortium, N.J., 1990-99; spkr. Nat. Conf. Sch. Restructuring, Atlanta, 1991, Phila., 1993, Shore Consortium, Rumson, N.J., 1986; mem. Crayola Art Edn. Coun., 1998. One-man landscape painting exhibit Roxbury, N.J., 1989, 92, Chester, N.J., 1972; creator of weaving, 1966 (pub. in Weaving Without A Loom). With U.S. Army Mil. Police, 1968-71, Vietnam. PTA grantee, 1991-97. Mem. NEA, N.J. Edn. Assn., N.J. Assn. for Mid. Level Edn. (conf. guest spkr. 1991-94, workshop presenter), Art Educators N.J. (presenter 1992, 94-97), Art Assn. in Roxbury (historian 1991-93, exhibitor 1989, 92). Roman Catholic. Avocations: painting, travel, avid sci. fiction Star Trek and Star Wars fan. Office: Black River Mid Sch Rte 513 Chester NJ 07930

FLUNO, JOHN ARTHUR, entomologist, consultant; b. Appleton, Wis., July 21, 1914; s. Arthur Swetland and Elsie (Younger) F.; m. Ruth Margaret Johnson, Aug. 15, 1942; children: Ruth Adaire, Jo Anne. BS, Rollins Coll., 1937; MS, Ohio State U., 1939. Field aide U.S. Dept. Agr., Orlando, Fla., 1937-38; entomologist Orlando, Fla., 1946-56, Beltsville, Md., 1956-72; asst. Ohio Biol. Survey, Columbus, 1938-40; instr. Rollins Coll., Winter Park, Fla., 1941; jr. entomologist USPHS, 1941-46; now cons. Served with AUS, 1943-46. Mem. Entomol. Soc. Washington, Rollins Coll. Alumni Assn. (past pres.), The Lepidopterists Soc., Am. Mosquito Control Assn. Home and Office: 1234 Lakeview Dr Winter Park FL 32789-5038

FLUTH, JOHN ADAM, educational administrator; b. Beeville, Tex., May 19, 1954; s. John and Elouise (Perdue) F.; m. Martye René Glenn, June 22, 1991; children: Craig, Kent, Chad. PhD, Tex. A&M U., 1986; computer technician, Apple Computer, Inc., Culpertino, Calif., 1994. Cert. ednl. adminstr., Tex. Surrogate parent Coastal Bend Youth City, Driscol, Tex., 1977-78; dir. halfway house Coastal Bend Youth City, Corpus Christi, Tex., 1978; tchr. spl. edn. Robstown, Tex., 1978-81; grad. asst. Tex. A&M U., College Station, Tex., 1981-86; coord. assistive tech. Region 5 Edn. Svc. Ctr., Beaumont, Tex., 1986-97; dir. Tex. Acad. Leadership in the Humanities, Beaumont, 1997-98; peer reviewer U.S. Dept. Edn., Washington, 1995—; grant reviewer Entergy, Inc., Beaumont, Tex., 1995-98; fellow Perkins Sch. Theology So. Methodist U., Dallas, 1998—. Pres. Ptnrs. Resource Network, Tex., 1994-96, Cerebral Palsy Rehab. Ctr., 1994-96; mem. exec. bd. Boy Scouts Am., Beaumont, Tex., 1996-98. Olympic Torch Bearer Atlanta Com. for The Olympic Games, 1996; named Cmty. Hero, United Way, Beaumont, Tex., 1996; recipient Perkins-Prothro fellowship, Perkins Sch. of Theology, Dallas, 1998. Mem. Order of Eastern Star (worthy patron), Masons (worshipful master).

FLUTIE, DOUGLAS RICHARD (DOUG FLUTIE), professional football player; b. Manchester, Md., Oct. 23, 1962. Boston Coll. With N.J. Generals, L.A. Rams, 1985; quarterback Chgo. Bears, 1986-87, New Eng. Patriots, 1987-89, B.C. Lions, 1990-91, Calgary Stampeders, 1992-95, Toronto Argonauts, 1996-97, Buffalo Bills, 1998—. Winner Heisman Trophy, 1984; named most valuable player Grey Cup CFL championship game, 1992, 96, Coll. Football Player of Yr. The Sporting News, 1984, quarterback coll. All-Am. first team The Sporting News, 1984; player Grey Cup, 1993. Office: Buffalo Bills 1 Bills Dr Orchard Park NY 14127*

FLYE, M. WAYNE, surgeon, immunologist, educator, writer; b. Tarboro, N.C., June 23, 1942; s. Charlie A. and Martha E. (Bullock) F.; m. Phyllis Webb, June 7, 1964; children: Christopher Warren, Brandon Reid. BS, U. N.C., 1964, MD, 1967; MA in Immunology, Duke U., 1972, PhD in Immunology, 1980; MA (hon.), Yale U., 1985. Diplomate Am. Bd. Surgery, Am. Bd. Thoracic Surgery, Am. Bd. Vascular Surgery. Intern. surg. Case-We. Res. U., Cleve., 1967-68, res. gen. and cardio-thoracic surgery, 1968-75; instr., teaching scholar, vascular and transplantation surgery Duke U. Med. Ctr., Durham, N.C., 1975-76; sr. investigator , chief thoracic surg. svc. NIH, Bethesda, Md., 1977-79; chief vascular surgery U. Tex. Med. Br., Galveston, 1979-82, assoc. prof. surgery and microbiology, 1980-82; dir. div. organ transplantation and immunology, prof. transplantation, dir. sect. gen. surgery Yale U. Sch. Medicine, New Haven, Conn., 1983-85; prof. surgery, molecular microbiology and immunology Washington U. Med. Sch., St. Louis, 1985—; trustee New Eng. Organ Bank, Boston, 1984-85; com. mem. United Network Orgn. Sharing, Richmond, Va., 1986-89; mem. anesthesiology and trauma study sect. NIH Surgery, 1991—; merit rev. com. for surgery VA, 1994—, chmn., 1996—; chief of surgery St. Louis Regional Hosp., 1996; chief thoracic surgery St. Louis VA Hosp., 1996. Editor: Principles of Organ Transplantation, 1989, The Thymus: Regulator of Cellular Immunity, 1993, Atlas of Organ Transplantation, 1994; mem. editl. bd. Clin. Transplantation, 1986—, Prospectives in Gen. Surgery, 1988—, Transplantation, 1989—, Xanthus Intelligence Unit Reports, 1990—, Shock: Molecular, Cellular and Systemic Pathobiology of Injury, 1993—, Transplantation Sci., 1993—, Jour. Surg. Rsch., 1995—, Surgery, 1997—, Graft, Jour. Organ and Cellular Transplantation, 1998—; assoc. editor Jour. Immunology, 1996—. Lt. col. U.S. Army, 1976-78. Recipient James W. McLaughlin medal U. Tex.-Galveston, 1982. Fellow ACP, So. Thoracic Surg. Assn. (Best Sci. Paper award 1980); mem. Am. Assn. Immunologists, Internat. Cardiovascular Soc., N.Y. Acad. Sci., Soc. Thoracic Surgeons, Am. Soc. Transplant Physicians, Am. Soc. Transplant Surgeons (program com. 1984-86, Ethics Com. 1994-95), Brit. Soc. Immunology, Transplantation Soc., Mid-Am. Transplant Assn. (bd. dirs. 1986-89), Am. Fedn. Clin. Rsch., Royal Soc. Medicine, AAAS, Surg. Infection Soc. (edn. and fellowship com. 1998—), Reticuloendothelial Soc., Soc. Univ. Surgeons, Soc. Clin. Vascular Surgery, Brit. Transplantation Soc., So. Assn. Vascular Surgery, Am. Coll. Chest Physicians, Soc. Surg. Oncology, Am. Assn. Thoracic Surgery, Surg. Biology Club I, Am. Assn. Study Liver Diseases, Am. Surg. Assn., So. Surg. Assn., Cen. Surg. Assn., Soc. Internat. de Chirurgie, Midwestern Vascular Surg. Soc., Soc. Vascular Surg., World Ann. Hepato-Pancreato-Bilary Surg., Soc. Surgery of Alimentary Tract, Shock Soc., Gen. Thoracic Surgery Club, Thoracic Surg. Club, Sigma Xi, Alpha Omega Alpha., Chi Psi, Young Republicans N.C. Episcopalian. Avocations: sports, geneology, medical history. Office: Washington U Med Sch 1 Barnes West Dr Ste 5108 Saint Louis MO 63141-6384

FLYNN, BRIDGET MARY, transplant coordinator; b. Pitts., Oct. 25; d. James Michael and Rosemary Karen (Sweeney) F. BSN, U. Pitts., 1982. RN, Pa.; cert. clin. transplant coord., advanced cardiac life support. Staff nurse emergency dept. Presbyn. U. Hosp., Pitts., staff nurse critical care unit, ICU, staff nurse med.-surg./postoperative transplant floor, transplant coord. Author: Annals of Emergency Medicine, 1991, Transplantation, 1997, Transplantation Proceedings, 1997, Transplant Proceedings, 1995. Contbr. articles to profl. jours. Mem. NATCO (North Amer. Transplant Coordinators Orgn.), Amer. Bd. Transplant Coordinators-Clin. Examination Com., Internatl. Transplant Coordinators Soc., Golden Triangle Chap., pres. elect, of Internatl. Transplant Nurses Soc. (ITNS), Soc. of Nursing Profls., bd. dirs., Transplant Recipients Internatl. Orgn. (TRIO), Natl. Transplant Action Com. (NTAC). Home: 65 Sheridan Ave Pittsburgh PA 15202-3617

FLYNN, CATHAL, federal agency amdinistrator; m. Edith Kurtz, 1963; 3 children. BA in Arts and Engring., Trinity Coll., Dublin; MA in Internat. Studies, Am. U. Commd. ensign U.S. Navy, advanced through grades to rear adm., asst. dir. Naval Intelligence for anti-terrorism, comdr. Naval Security and Investigative Command; dep. asst. sec. for spl. ops. Dept. Def.; ret. U.S. Navy, 1990; sr. analyst civil aviation security and mil. spl. ops. Sci. Applications Internat. Corp., 1990-93; assoc. adminstr. for civil aviation security FAA, Washington, 1993—; mem. Air Force studies bd. NRC; mem. task force on techs. for spl. ops. Def. Sci. Bd. Decorated Def. DSM with oak leaf cluster, Def. Superior Svc. medal, Legion of Merit (2), Def. and Navy Meritorious Svc. medals, Navy Commendation medal with combat V. Mem. Phi Kappa Phi. Office: FAA Civil Aviation Security 800 Independence Ave SW Washington DC 20591-0001*

FLYNN, CHERYL DIXON, accountant; b. Hartsville, S.C., Feb. 3, 1952; d. J. Leslie and Peggy E. Dixon; m. Mark A. Thompson, Aug. 17, 1974 (div. 1987); m. Daniel W. Flynn, Apr. 13, 1991; stepchildren: Kimberly, Chris. BS in Acctg., Furman U., 1992. CPA, S.C. Adminstrv. asst. Yeargin Properties, Inc., Greenville, S.C., 1976-89; staff acct. Crisp, Hughes & Assoc., Greenville, 1989-93, Farris, Cooke & Assoc., Charlotte, N.C., 1993-94, Hughes, Boan & Assoc., Columbia, S.C., 1994-95, Ouzts, Ouzts & Varn, PC, Columbia, 1995—. Bd. dirs. Children's Chance. Mem. AAUW, AICPA, S.C. Assn. CPAs, Alpha Sigma Lambda. Presbyterian. Avocations: reading, boating, dancing. Home: 24 Polo Ridge Cir Columbia SC 29223-2819 Office: Ouzts Ouzts & Varn PC 115 Atrium Way Ste 110 Columbia SC 29223-6382

FLYNN, DANIEL FRANCIS, investment company executive; b. Hartford, Conn.; s. Daniel C. and Frances E. (Hurley) F.; m. Barbara L. Quinn, June 12, 1965; children: Daniel F., Garrett S., Laura D. BA, Coll. of the Holy Cross, 1956; JD, U. Conn., 1962. Bar: Conn. 1962. Chmn., CEO John G. Martin Found., Farmington, 1969—; dir., chmn., CEO, pres. JCI Corp., Farmington, Conn., 1968—, Resources Mgmt. Corp., Farmington, 1976—; dir., chmn., CEO Resources Investment Co., Farmington, 1977—, RMC Realty Co., Farmington, 1985—; dir. Security-Conn. Life Ins. Co. Former regent, mem. exec. com. U. Hartford, former chmn. resources com., mem. com. regent mems., mem. investment com.; bd. overseers The Bushnell; bd. vis. Barney Sch.; hon. life mem., bd. mgrs. Silver Hill Found., Inc., past dir., past dir. devel. com.; mem. exec. com., past pres. U. Conn. Law Sch. Found., Inc.; trustee Conn. Policy and Econ. Coun., Inc.; corporator St. Francis Hosp. and Med. Ctr.; founding trustee John G. Martin Scholarship Trust; spl. gifts chmn. United Way Hartford; former trustee Hartford Art Sch.; past pres. Westmont Residents' Assn.; mem. Pres. Coun. Coll. Holy Cross. Mem. Am. Soc. Internat. Law, Am. Judicature Soc., Am. Assn. Individual Investors, Conn. Bar Assn., Newcomen Soc. Am., Twentieth Century Club. Office: Resources Mgmt Corp 2 Batterson Park Rd Farmington CT 06032-2553

FLYNN, DICK, coach; b. Mount Pleasant, Mich., July 17, 1943; m. Mary Flynn; children: Kelly, Katie. BEd, Mich. State U., 1965. Asst. coach, head coach Ea. Lansing (Mich.) H.S., 1965-66, 70-94; coach football Ctrl. Mich. U., Mount Pleasant, 1994—. Office: Ctrl Mich Univ Football SAC 182 Mount Pleasant MI 48859*

FLYNN, ELIZABETH ANNE, advertising and public relations company executive; b. Washington, Aug. 21, 1951; d. John William and Elizabeth Goodwin (Mahoney) F. AA, Montgomery Coll., Rockville, Md., 1972; BS in Journalism, U. Md., 1976; postgrad. San Diego State U., 1976. Writer, researcher, Sea World, Inc., San Diego, 1977-79; sr. writer Lane & Huff Advt., San Diego, 1979-80; account exec. Kaufman, Lansky, Baker Advt., San Diego, 1980-82; mng. dir. Excelsior Enterprises, Beverly Hills, Calif., 1983-84; sr. account exec. Berkhemer & Kline, Inc., L.A., 1985; pres. Flynn Advt. & Pub. Rels., L.A., 1985—; cons. Coca-Cola Bottling Co. L.A., 1982-84; U.S. corr. Aeronovum mag., 1990-98; v.p. mktg. Graffiti Prevention Systems, L.A., 1990-91; dir. new bus. devel. BBDO Hispanica, L.A., 1992-93; pub. rels. dir. Regional Organ Procurement Agy. So. Calif., UCLA Med. Ctr., 1994-97, pub. info. officer/cons. Cmty. Devel. Dept. City of L.A., 1998—. Bd. dirs. Friends of Reconstructive Surgery, Beverly Hills, 1983-89, Nat. Kidney Found., 1994, So. Calif. Coalition on Donation, 1994-97, also mem. steering com., 1995-97; sec. Nat. Coun. Local Coalitions, 1995-97; comms. com. Assn. Organ Procurement Orgns.; cons. Rotary Internat. Give of Yourself program, 1993—; media cons. divsn. transplantation HHS, 1994—. Address: Flynn Advt & Pub Rels 1440 Reeves St Apt 104 Los Angeles CA 90035-2950

FLYNN, GEORGE WILLIAM, chemistry educator, researcher; b. Hartford, Conn., July 11, 1938; s. George William and Rose Margaret (Tummillo) F.; m. Jean Pieri, Oct. 3, 1970; children: David Kenneth, Suzanne MacKay. B.S., Yale U., 1960; A.M., Harvard U., 1962, Ph.D., 1965. Postdoctoral fellow MIT, Cambridge, 1965-67; asst. prof. chemistry Columbia U., N.Y.C., 1967-72, assoc. prof., 1972-76, prof., 1976—, Thomas Alva Edison prof. chemistry, 1986-92, Higgins prof. chemistry, 1994—, dir. lab., 1979—, chmn. dept. chemistry, 1994-96, co-chair dept. chem. engring. and applied chemistry, 1997—; research collaborator Brookhaven Nat. Lab., Upton, N.Y., 1969-78, cons., 1978—. Contbr. articles to profl. jours. Fellow Sloan Found., 1968-70, Guggenheim Found., 1974-75; A. Cressy Morrison award N.Y. Acad. Scis., 1983; recipient Advancement Basic and Applied Sci. award Yale U. Sci. and Engring. Assn., 1994. Fellow Am. Phys. Soc.; mem. Am. Acad. Arts and Scis., Am. Chem. Soc. (chmn. divsn. phys. chemistry, 1996-97), N.Y. Acad. Scis., Sigma Xi. Roman Catholic. Home: 382 Summit Ave Leonia NJ 07605-1337 Office: Columbia U 315 Havemeyer New York NY 10027

FLYNN, HARRY JOSEPH, bishop; b. Schenectady, N.Y., May 2, 1933. Ed., Siena Coll., Loudonville, N.Y., Mt. St. Mary's Coll., Emmitsburg, Md. Ordained priest Roman Cath. Ch., 1960; ordained coadjutor bishop of Lafayette, La., 1986-89. Bishop of Lafayette La., 1989-94; coadjutor archbishop of Diocese of St. Paul and Mpls., 1994-95; archbishop Diocese of St. Paul and Mpls., 1995—. Address: Chancery Office 226 Summit Ave Saint Paul MN 55102-2121*

FLYNN, JOAN MAYHEW, librarian; b. Mpls., Sept. 13, 1927; d. Oscar Koehler and Mabel Victoria (Stein) Mayhew; m. Elliot Colter Dick, Jr., Aug. 19, 1950 (div. May 1966); children: Emily Diane Dick Tuttle, Elliot Mayhew Dick; m. Paul James Flynn, Nov. 4, 1967. BMus, U. Minn., 1950; MLS, U. Hawaii, 1972, cert. in advanced libr. and info. studies, 1986. Circulation clk., 1972-75, reference libr., 1975-85; dir. acad. support svcs., head Sullivan Libr. Chaminade U. of Honolulu, 1986—; mem. Interlibr. Cooperation Coun., 1990, 91; supr. vocal music Forest Lake (Minn.) Pub. Schs. Asst. dir. races Norman Tamanaha Meml., 1982, dir. 1983; bd. dirs. Hawaii Kai Fun Runners. Mem. ALA, Hawaii Libr. Assn., MidPac Road Runners Assn. (bd. dirs.), Hawaii Masters Track Club, Beta Phi Mu, Pi Lambda Theta, Sigma Alpha Iota. Avocations: running, biking, swimming, weight lifting, reading. Home: 130 Opihikao Way Honolulu HI 96825-1125 Office: Chaminade U 3140 Waialae Ave Honolulu HI 96816-1578

FLYNN, JOHN DAVID, writer, educator; b. Jackson, Tenn., Apr. 4, 1948; s. John Aloysius F. and Mary Evelyn Groom; m. Deborah Ann Coleman, Jan. 28, 1978 (div. Dec. 1989); 1 child, Caitlin Rose. BA, B of Journalism, U.Mo., 1971; MA, U. Denver, 1972, Boston U., 1980; PhD, U. Nebr., 1984. Reporter Memphis Press-Scimitar, 1973-74; editor Chapin Pub. Co., Mpls., 1976-77; instr. Tenn. State U., Nashville, 1978-79, asst. prof., 1988-89; asst. prof. U. Hawaii, Honolulu, 1989-91; dir. English Tokai Internat. Coll., Honolulu, 1992-93; assoc. prof. Vol. State C.C., Gallatin, Tenn., 1993—; cons. in field. Author of poems, short stories. Bd. dirs. Hawaii Literary Arts Coun., Honolulu, 1991-92; congrl. intern U.S. Congress, Washington, 1972. Mem. Tenn. Trails Assn., Am. Radio Relay League, Barnard-Seyfort Astron. Soc., Music City Blues Soc. (bd. dirs. 1996—, v.p. 1999—). Avocations: amateur radio, stained glass, astronomy, hiking. Home: 303 Crestmeade Dr Nashville TN 37221 Office: Vol State C C 1480 Nashville Pike Gallatin TN 37066

FLYNN, JOHN FRANCIS, historian, educator; b. Bayshore, N.Y., May 11, 1938; s. John Joseph and Olga (Strutko) F.; m. Jane Louise Frazier, June 3, 1961; children: Rebecca Margaret, Suzanne Monet. BA, Boston Coll., 1959; MA, Columbia U., 1961, PhD, 1971. Instr., asst. prof. St. John's U., N.Y.C., 1961-66; instr., asst. prof., assoc. prof. history U. of South, Sewanee, Tenn., 1966-82; prof. U. of South, Sewanee, 1982—. Contbr. articles to profl. jours. Treas. Sewanee Civic Assn., 1997—. Fellow Churchill Coll., 1994, Wye Fellow Aspen Found., 1988, Mellon Found., 1982, Inst. European Studies, 1983, NEH, summer 1979, 86, Dupont NHC, 1998; Fulbright grantee, 1990. Mem. AAUP (sec. Sewanee chpt.), Am. Hist. Assn., Am. Com. for Study WWII, Soc. Study Am. Fgn. Rels., So. Hist. Assn. (European sect.), Ctrl. European History Group, German Studies Assn., Phi Alpha Theta. Avocations: tennis, travel. Office: U of the South 735 University Ave Sewanee TN 37383-1000

FLYNN, JOHN J., museum curator; b. Wilkes-Barre, Pa., Aug. 10, 1955; s. John J. and Phyllis B. (Allen) F.; m. Alison L. Gold; children: Rachel S., Peter J. BS cum laude, Yale U., 1977; MA, Columbia U., 1979, MPhil, 1980, PhD, 1983. Lectr. dept. geology and geophysics Yale U., New Haven, 1982; asst. prof. geol. scis. Rutgers U., New Brunswick, N.J., 1982-88; assoc. curator dept. geology Field Mus. Natural History, Chgo., 1988-92, curator dept. geology, 1992—, chmn. dept. geology, 1993—, MacArthur curator dept. geology, 1995—; rsch. assoc. Am. Mus. Natural History, N.Y.C., 1984—; co-chair Earth History and Global Change com. Systematics Agenda 2000, 1991-96; lectr. Com. on Evolutionary Biology, U. Chgo., 1990—, assoc. chair, 1995—; adj. prof. dept. biol. scis. U. Ill., Chgo., 1994—. Co-editor: Vertebrate Paleontology in the Neotropics: The Miocene Fauna of La Venta, Colombia, 1997, Mesozoic/Cenozoic Vertebrate Paleontology: Classic Localities, Contemporary Approaches, 1989; assoc. editor Jour. Vertebrate Paleontology, 1988-91; contbr. articles to profl. jours. Grantee in field; recipient William R. Belknap prize, 1977, Best Mus. Curator award Chgo. Mag., 1995. Mem. Soc. Vertebrate Paleontology (chair affiliated soc. liaison 1986-93, mem. devel. com. 1987-89, chair collections computerization com. 1990-93, sec. 1993-96, v.p. 1996-98, pres. 1998—, Alfred Sherwood Romer prize 1982), Geol. Soc. Am., The Paleontological Soc., Soc. Systematic Biologists. Achievements include discovery of oldest S.Am. rodent, oldest well-preserved S.Am. monkey skull, work on geologic time scales. Office: Field Mus Natural History Dept Geology Roosevelt Rd at Lake Shore Dr Chicago IL 60605

FLYNN, KEVIN, healthcare company executive; b. Miami, Fla., July 6, 1964. BS, U. Pa. Owner computer cons. co., Phila., 1989-91; v.p. program devel. Geonex Aero Svc., St. Petersburg, Fla., 1991-96; owner, mgr. Healthcare Advocates, Inc., Phila., 1996—; advisor E-Finity, Wayne, Pa. Bd. dirs. ARC, Phila. Office: Healthcare Advocates Inc 1420 Walnut St Ste 908 Philadelphia PA 19102-4017

FLYNN, KIRTLAND, JR., accountant; b. Orange, N.J., Aug. 27, 1922; s. Kirtland and Jane Elizabeth (Miller) F.; m. Lucy Jane Andrews, June 11, 1948; children: Patricia Carson Flynn Moore, Gail Miller, James Kirtland. BA, Colgate U., 1943. Acctg. staff Celanese Corp., Newark, Houston and Charlotte, N.C., 1947-65; sec.-treas. Little Constrn. Co., Inc., Charlotte, 1965-66; mem. controller's staff J.P. Stevens & Co., Inc., Charlotte, 1966-81, mgr. info. services div., Charlotte and Greer, S.C., 1981-85; pvt. practice acctg., 1985-92; mem. staff Larry R. Swartz, CPA, 1993—. Bd. dirs., treas. Charlotte Exchange Student Program, 1979-83; chmn. Tryon Fire Protection Dist. Bd. Commrs., 1986—; bd. dirs. Tryon Fine Arts Ctr., 1987-89; bd. dirs., treas. Polk County Sheltered Workshop, 1987-91, exec. v.p. 1991-93, pres., 1993-96. 1st lt. USMCR, 1943-46. Decorated D.F.C., Air medals. Mem. Inst. of Mgmt. Accts. (chpt. pres. 1966-67, nat. dir. 1971-73, pres. Carolinas Council 1973-74, nat. v.p. 1978-79), Stuart Cameron McLeod Soc. (bd. govs. 1979-81, treas. 1981-82, sec. 1982-83, v.p. 1983-85, pres. 1985-86), Tryon C. of C. (bd. dirs. 1985-93, treas. 1985-90, v.p. 1990-92). Lodges: Masons, Shriners, K.T. Home: Sourwood Ridge PO Box 1138 Tryon NC 28782-1138 Office: One Tryon Pl Tryon NC 28782-3709

FLYNN, MARTY J., investment company administrator; b. Nov. 15, 1969. BS in Fin., Fordham U., 1991; MBA in Fin., U. Tex., 1998. Assoc. equity rsch. Nomura Securities, N.Y.C., 1992-94, Deutsche Morgan Grendell, N.Y.C., 1994-96; corp. assoc. Invesco, Atlanta, 1998—. E-mail: MFLYNN@ATL.INVESCO.com. Office: Invesco 1315 Peachtree St Ste 500 Atlanta GA 30309

FLYNN, MICHAEL PATRICK, radiologist; b. Rochester, N.Y., Apr. 7, 1946; s. Edwin John and Madeline Lillian (Miller) F.; m. Margaret Ann Spratt; children: Aaron, Nolan. BA, U. Louisville, 1968, MD, 1972. Med. intern L.A. County Hosp./U. So. Calif., 1972-73; resident in radiology U. Louisville, 1973-76; instr. in ultrasound Johns Hopkins U. Med. Ctr., Balt., 1976-77; diagnostic radiologist Sheer-Ahearn & Assocs., Tampa, Fla., 1977—, CEO, 1994—, pres., 1996—; pres. Team Health-Med. Ptnrs., Tampa, 1996—; dir. diagnostic imaging Columbia Regional Med. Ctr., Brandon, Fla., 1987-97, chief of staff, 1992-94; pres. Radiology Ptnrs. Inc., Tampa, 1994—, Fla. Imaging Network, Tampa, 1996—. Mem. Am. Roentgen Ray Soc., Radiol. Soc. N.Am., Am. Inst. Ultrasound in Medicine, Fla. Med. Assn., Fla. West Coast Radiol. Assn., Ctrl. Fla. Ultrasound Soc. (pres. 1987-81, award 1980). Office: Sheer Ahearn 9204 King Palm Dr Tampa FL 33619-1328*

FLYNN, NANCY MARIE, government executive; b. Kalamazoo, Aug. 3, 1947; d. C.L. and Margrete M. (Valentine) Flynn; m. Frank Eugene Camacho, Aug. 22, 1970 (div. Dec. 1980). BA magna cum laude, Western Mich. U., Kalamazoo, 1969; MA, U. Mich., 1970. Investigator Dept. of Labor, Detroit, 1970-76; asst. area dir. Dept. of Labor, Troy, Mich., 1976-79; area dir. Dept. of Labor, Chgo., 1979-82, dep. asst. regional mgr., 1982; from divsn. dir. to dep. dir. human resources Dept. of Labor, Washington, 1983-95; dir. Office of Planning and Analysis, Washington, 1995—; mem. Com. for Purchase from People Who Are Blind or Severely Disabled, Washington, 1988-94. Mem. Exec. Women in Govt., Sr. Execs. Assn. (bd. dirs. 1994—, treas. 1997, vice-chair 1997—), Western Mich. U. Alumni Assn., U. Mich. Alumni Assn., U. Mich. Club of Washington, Delta Zeta Alumni Assn., Presbyterian. Home: 5501 Seminary Rd Apt 2315S Falls Church VA 22041-3912 Office: 200 Constitution Ave NW Washington DC 20210-0001

FLYNN, PAMELA, artist, educator; b. Bellmore, N.Y., Dec. 24, 1948; d. Robert S. and Amalie M. (Debler) Williams; m. Dennis M. Flynn, Aug. 7, 1971; children: Matthew, Amalie. BA, Monmouth U., West Long Branch, N.J., 1971; MA, Kean U., Union, N.J., 1995; MFA, N.J. City U., 1996. Tchr. Freehold (N.J.) Regional Continuing Edn., 1978-95, St. Leo the Great Sch., Lincroft, N.J., 1985—; asst. prof. Holy Family Coll., Phila., 1999—; adj. instr. New Jersey City State U., 1996—, Bergen C.C., 1997—, Brookdale (N.J.) C.C., 1997—, Ocean County (N.J.) C.C., 1997—, asst. prof. art Holy Family Coll., Phila., 1996—. Solo exhbns. include Monmouth U., 1995, Abney Gallery, N.Y.C., 1994, Art Space, New Jersey City State U., 1996; group shows include Nude/Naked Union St. Gallery, Chgo. Women in the Visual Arts, 1998, Erector Gallery, New Haven, ALJIRA Nat. 4, Newark, 1998. Mem. FATE, Coll. Art Assn., Phi Kappa Phi. Home: 13 Dogwood Ln Freehold NJ 07728-1868

FLYNN, PATRICIA MARIE, economics educator; b. Lynn, Mass.. BA in Econs., Emmanuel Coll., 1972; MA in Econs., Boston U., 1973, PhD in Econs., 1980. Rsch. assoc. Inst. for Employment Policy, Boston U., 1975-83; prof. econs. Bentley Coll., Waltham, Mass., 1976—; sr. rsch. fellow New Eng. Bd. Higher Edn., Boston, 1980-82; vis. sch. Fed. Res. Bd., Boston, 1983-84; exec. dir. Inst. for Rsch. & Faculty Devel., Bentley Coll., Waltham, 1986-90; assoc. dean faculty Bentley Coll., Waltham, Mass., 1991-92, dean grad. sch., 1992—; mem. faculty Inst. in Employment and Tng. Adminstrn. Harvard U., Cambridge, Mass., summers, 1979-81; cons. U. Mo., Columbia, 1983-84, First Security Svcs. Corp., Boston, 1985, Devel. Alternatives, Inc., Jakarta, Indonesia, summer, 1987, ABT Assocs., Cambridge, 1987-89; bd. dirs. Fed. Savs. Bank, Waltham, Mass. Author: Technology Life Cycles and Human Resources, 1993; co-author: Turbulence in the American Workplace, 1991; contbr. articles to profl. jours. Adv. panel mem. Office Tech. Assessment, U.S. Congress, Washington, 1989-91; accreditation team mem. New Eng. Assn. Schs. and Colls., 1985—; mem. Newton (Mass.) Econ. Devel. Commn., 1984-87; bd. dirs. Big Sisters Assn., US Trust, 1998—; trustee Mass. Taxpayers Found; active Sloan Found, 1995-98. Grantee Dept. Labor, 1982-84, 88-89, Nat. Inst. Edn., 1982-83, NSF, 1990-93, Sloan Found., 1995—; recipient Gregory H. Adamian award for tchg. excellence Bentley Coll., 1986, Scholar of Yr., 1991, New Eng. Woman's Leadership award, 1998. Mem. Fin. Womens Assn., Am. Econ. Assn., Com. on the Status of Women in Econs. Professions, The Boston Club, The Boston Econ. Club. Office: Bentley Coll 175 Forest St Waltham MA 02452-4705

FLYNN, PATRICK, designer, programmer, consultant; b. Washington, Aug. 11, 1953; s. Walter L. and Virginia B. Flynn. BS in English, East Carolina U., 1977; AAS in Bus. Computer Programming, Coll. of the Albemarle, 1996. Disc jockey Sta. WBXB-FM, Edenton, N.C., 1976; copy coord. BDM Corp., McLean, Va., 1977-80; editor HBH Co., Arlington, Va., 1980-81; audio/visual technician Projection, Inc., Arlington, 1982; carpenter Sandalwood Construction Co., Kitty Hawk, N.C., 1983-86; ind. contractor Patrick Painting, Kitty Hawk, 1986-92; game designer TurnKey Design Group, Kitty Hawk, 1993-96; sr. programmer FC Bus. Systems, Falls Church, Va., 1998—; programmer Airline Tariff Publ. Co., Washington, 1996-97, New Boston Sys., Vienna, Va., 1997-98; sr. programmer FC Bus. Sys., Falls Church, Va., 1998—; media cons., 1973—; pub. SandTraveler, Kitty Hawk, 1992-93. Contbr. articles and editls. to mags. and newspapers; designer Cutthroat Chess, 1993; appeared as extra Matlock series NBC-TV, 1989, (film) Toy Soldiers, 1990. Vol. Transp. Fishnet Ministries, Inc., Front Royal, Va., 1993, Rock Ch. Kitty Hawk, 1983-96. Mem. Alpha Phi Gamma, Phi Theta Kappa. Republican. Avocations: chess, photography. Office: FC Bus Systems 5205 Leesburg Pike Ste 700 Falls Church VA 22041-3887

FLYNN, PATRICK FRANCIS, engineering executive; m. Beverly Collora; children: Bryan, Nicole. BS in Agrl. Engring., U. Minn., 1959, MS in Agrl. Engring., 1965; MBA, Ind. U., 1977; PhD in Mech. Engring., U. Wis., 1971. Design, project engr. Internat. Harvester Co., Chgo., 1961-67; various positions Cummins Engine Co., Inc., Columbus, Ind., 1970-85; v.p. design, technology Cummins Engine Co., Inc., Columbus, 1985-87, v.p. rsch., tech., 1987-89, v.p. rsch., 1985—; draftsman, designer Farmlans Co., Hopkins, Minn., 1957-58; design engr. John Deere Co., East Moline, Ill, 1959; vis. dept. engring., indsl. fellow U. Cambridge, Eng., 1981-82; adv. bd. Combustion Rsch. Facility, U.S. Dept. Energy, Sandia nat. lab., Livermore, Calif., 1988—, sch. engring. U. Wis., 1988-95; exec. adv. bd. Gas Rsch. Inst., Chgo., 1990—; presenter in field. Bd. dirs. Five County Big Brothers, 1973, 79-83, Hoosier H.S. Hockey League, 1991-93; coach Columbus Youth Hockey League, 1982, Columbus Youth Soccer League, 1982-85. NSF fellow, 1960; Minn. Moline Found. scholar, 1956, ALCOA Found. scholar, 1958. Fellow ASME (mem. turbomachinery com. 1977-80), Soc. Automotive Engrs. (advanced power plants com. 1974-76, Arch T. Colwell Merit award 1985); mem. NSPE (exec. com. chpt. 1975-76), Engine Mfrs. Assn. (chmn. com. diesel engine health effects 1979-80, Outstanding Achievement award 1980), Nat. Acad. Engring., Kiwanis, Beta Sigma Gamma, Sigma Iota Epsilon, Sigma Xi, Gamma Sigma Delta, Alpha Epsilon, Alpha Zeta. Achievements include patents for Turbo-machine, Diesel Engine Intake Air Pre-heater Fuel Control. Home: 1743 Franklin St Columbus IN 47201-5116

FLYNN, PAUL BARTHOLOMEW, foundation executive; b. Quincy, Mass., Sept. 17, 1935; s. Bartholomew Joseph and Katherine Marie (Coleman) F.; m. Aline Therese Nicholson, Feb. 11, 1961; children: Bonnie Marie, Laureen P., Elizabeth A., Bernadette J. A.B., Stonehill Coll., 1957; LL.D. (hon.), Allentown Coll., 1985. Sportswriter The Patriot Ledger, Quincy, 1955-63; cmty. rels. dir. The Patriot Ledger, 1963-65; dir. pub. rels. Mass. Tchrs. Assn., Boston, 1965-66; asst. dir. pub. svc. Rochester (N.Y.) Democrat and Chronicle and The Times-Union, 1966-71, dir. pub. svc. and rsch., 1971-72; dir. advt. Huntington (W.Va.) Herald-Dispatch and Advertiser, 1972-74, Binghamton (N.Y.) Press and Sun-Bulletin, 1974-76; dir. mktg. services Gannett Co., Rochester, N.Y., 1976-77; gen. mgr. Jour.-News, Nyack, N.Y., 1977; pres., pub. Fort Myers (Fla.) News-Press, 1977-84; S.E. regional v.p. Gannett Co., 1981-83; exec. v.p. USA Today, Washington, 1983-84; pres. USA Today, 1984; pres., pub. Pensacola News-Jour., Fla., 1984-87; v.p. Gannett South Newspaper Group, 1985-87; exec. v.p. Foster's Daily Democrat, Dover, N.H., 1989-93; dir. mktg. and pub. rels. Strawbery Banke Mus., Portsmouth, N.H., 1993-95; mktg. cons. Jour.-Transcript Newspapers, N.H., Maine, 1995-96; v.p. Susan Bennett Mktg. & Media, Fort Myers, Fla., 1996-97; exec. dir. Southwest Fla. Community Found., Ft. Myers, Fla., 1997—; v.p. Gannett Newspaper Advt. Sales, N.Y.C., 1976-77. Author: You Can Make News, 1996; co-editor: Promoting the Total Newspaper, 1977. Pres. Lend-A-Hand Fund S.W. Fla., S.W. Fla. coun. Boy Scouts Am., 1981, commr. Daniel Webster coun., 1989-96, v.p., 1995-96; bd. dirs. Lee County United Way, 1979-84, campaign chmn., 1981; bd. dirs. Edison C.C. Endowment Fund, 1978-83, Sr. Friendship Ctrs., Inc., 1981-83, United Way Pensacola, Sacred Heart Hosp. Found., Pensacola Jr. Coll. Found.; mem. adv. bd. Stonehill Coll., 1984, trustee, 1987-90. With U.S. Army, 1957-58. Recipient Disting. Service award B'nai B'rith of Cape Coral, Fla., 1979; Gold medal for good citizenship SAR, 1980; disting. alumni award Stonehill Coll., 1984; Patriotism citation Freedom's Found., 1986. Mem. Internat. Newspaper Promotion Assn. (bd. dirs. 1977-78), Greater Dover C. of C. (bd. dirs. 1989-93), Stonehill Coll. Alumni Assn., Rotary (Ft. Myers). Roman Catholic.

FLYNN, PAULINE T., speech pathologist, educator; b. Montclair, N.J., Feb. 22, 1942; d. William J. and Pauline F. Flynn. BA, Paterson State Coll., 1963; MA, Seton Hall U., 1966; PhD, U. Kans., 1970; cert. specialist in aging, U. Mich., 1982. Lic. speech pathologist, Ind.; cert. of clin. competence in speech pathology, Am. Speech Lang. Hearing Assn. Tchr., speech pathologist Bd. Edn., Parsippany-Troy Hills, N.J., 1963-67; prof., chmn. dept. audiology and speech scis. Ind. U. Purdue U., Ft. Wayne, 1970—; ednl. cons. Retirement Ctr., Ft. Wayne, 1982-85. Contbr. articles to nat. and internat. jours. Recipient Outstanding Alumna award William Paterson Coll., 1973, Woman of Achievement award Ft. Wayne YWCA, 1992. Fellow Am. Speech, Lang. and Hearing Assn.; mem. Am. Speech, Lang., Hearing Assn., Ind. Speech, Lang. and Hearing Assn., Phi Kappa Phi. Office: Ind U Purdue U Ft Wayne Dept Audiology & Speech Scis 2101 E Coliseum Blvd Fort Wayne IN 46805-1445

FLYNN, PEGGY LOU, county official; b. Mobridge, S.D., Sept. 27, 1952; d. John and Emeilia (Dikoff) Singer; m. Walter W. Flynn, Oct. 2, 1981; 1 child, John J. AS, Nat. Coll. of Bus., 1971; cert., S.D. Assessor Sch., 1999. Cert. appraiser assessor. Keypuncher Nat. Coll. of Bus., Rapid City, S.D., 1971; credit investigator Household Fin. Corp., Rapid City, 1971-77; loan counselor, processor First Fed. Savs. and Loan, Rapid City, 1977-81; officer mgr., bookkeeper Collins Siding Co., Rapid City, 1981-82; home health aide Dept. of Social Svc., Mobridge, S.D., 1988-90, 90-91; dep. dir. Dewey County, Timber Lake, S.D., 1990-92, dir. equalization, 1992—. Mem. St. Paul's Ladies Aid (sec. 1997—), Am. Legion Aux. (2d v.p.), S.D. Assn. of Assessor Officers, Credit Woman's Internat. (sec. 1981-82). Lutheran. Avocations: designing jewelry, walking, counted cross stitch, golfing, bowling. Home: PO Box 174 706 E Street Timber Lake SD 57656 Office: Dewey County Courthouse PO Box 296 Timber Lake SD 57656-0296

FLYNN, RALPH MELVIN, JR., sales executive, marketing consultant; b. Winchester, Mass., May 2, 1944; s. Ralph Melvin and Mary Agnus (Giuliani) F.; m. Rose Marie Petrock (div. 1988); children: John Patrick, Marc Jeffery; m. Carolyn F. Lee; 1 child, Sean Michael. Engr. Bell Tel. Labs., Holmdel, N.J., 1966-68; tech. coord. Expts. in Art and Tech., N.Y.C., 1968-69; exec. v.p. Bestline Products, San Jose, Calif., 1969-73; pres. Internat. Inst. for Personal Achievement, Palo Alto, Calif., 1975-76, Diamite Corp., Milpitas, Calif., 1977-84; dir. mktg. IMMI, Campbell, Calif., 1973-77; v.p. internat. Neo-Life Co., Fremont, Calif., 1984—; pres. Ultra Promotions, Los Gatos, Calif., 1988-89, Score Publishing, Saratoga, Calif., 1987—; tech. cons. Robert Rauschenberg, N.Y.C., 1968; cons. Std. Oil Co., San Francisco, 1975, I.B.C., Geneva, 1984-88, 1st Interstate Bank, L.A., 1985, Ray Rossi, Design Environs., Los Altos Hills, Calif., 1995; pres. CoffeeSociety.com Your Online Cofffee Store, 1999—; lectr. in field. Author: The Only Variable, 1985, Navigating towards Success, 1986; contbr. articles to profl. pubs. Named adm. State of Nebr., 1987; Joseph Kaplan Trust scholar, 1961. Mem. Direct Selling Assn., Coffee Soc. (founder 1988), Rolls Royce Owners Club. Republican. Avocations: music, sailing, art, interior design, classic automobiles. Office: Coffee Soc 21265 Stevens Creek Blvd Cupertino CA 95014-5715

FLYNN, RAYMOND LEO, ambassador to the Vatican, former mayor; b. Boston, July 22, 1939; m. Catherine Coyne; children: Raymond L. Jr., Edward, Julie, Nancy, Katherine, Maureen. BA, Providence Coll., 1963, PhD (hon.); MEd, Harvard U., 1981; LLD (hon.), Suffolk U., Emmanuel Coll.; PhD (hon.), Northeastern U., 1986, Seton Hall U., St. Anselm's Coll., Stonehill Coll.; D (hon.), Salve Regina U. Mem. Mass. Ho. of Reps., 1971-78, chmn. Boston Harbor Pollution Com.; mem. Boston City Council, 1978-83; mayor City Boston, 1983-93; U.S. ambassador to the Vatican, 1993-97; chmn. U.S. Conf. of Mayors' Task Force on Hunger and Homelessness; pres. U.S. Conf. of Mayors, 1991-92; U.S. amb. to Vatican, 1993-97. Vice chmn. Dem. Nat. Platform Com., 1984, Nat. League of Cities; nat. co-chair Clinton for Pres. Com., 1992. Recipient Outstanding Student Athlete award in U.S., NAACP, 1963, Pub. Svc. award NAACP-Boston, 1985, Silver Ann. award NCAA, 1988, All Am. Silver Ann. award Nat. Assn. Basketball Coaches, 1988, Athletic Alumnus of Yr. award NCAA, 1988, Outstanding Mcpl. Mgr., 1991, Ellis Island medal of Honor, 1994, Michael Joyce Humanitarian award, 1994, St. Martin De Porres Humanitarian award, 1994, John F. Kennedy Nat. award, 1994, Pres. award Assumption Coll., 1994, Silver Anniversary medal Providence Coll., John Boyle O'Reilly Labor Champion award, KC award; fellow Harvard U. Inst. of Politics. Mem. Internat. Longshoremans Assn. Union. Office: 1 Flint Pl South Boston MA 02127-4207

FLYNN, RICHARD MCDONNELL, English educator; b. Evanston, Ill., Jan. 17, 1955; s. Richard James and Joanne Elizabeth (Resseguie) F.; m. Evangline Areti Pappas, Jan. 14, 1979 (div. July 1990); 1 child, Richard Nicholas; m. Patricia Sue Pace, Aug. 7, 1993. BA, George Wash. U., 1977, PhD, 1987; MA, Am. U., 1980. Head libr. Found. FBA, Washington, 1978-88; asst. prof. English Ind. State U., Terre Haute, 1988-90; assoc. prof. English Ga. So. U., Statesboro, 1990—. Author: Randall Jarrell and the Lost World of Childhood, 1990 (Choice Outstanding Acad. Book 1992), The Age of Reason: Poems, 1993; contbr. articles to profl. jours. Grantee NEH, 1989, 95, 98. Mem. MLA, South Atlantic MLA (nominating com. children's lit. discussion cir. 1993—), Children's Lit. Assn. (book award com. 1993-96), Elizabeth Bishop Soc. Democrat. E-mail: rflynn@gsvm2.cc.gasou.edu. Office: Ga So U Dept Lit and Philosophy Box 8023 Statesboro GA 30460-8023

FLYNN, ROBERT JAMES, electronic commerce executive; b. Detroit, Apr. 12, 1941; s. James Vincent and Rita Marie (Cloonan) F.; m. Marilyn Ann Webb, Nov. 21, 1964; 1 child, Sara Louise. BSc, St. John Fischer Coll., Rochester, N.Y., 1964; MSc in Math., U. Windsor, Ont., Can., 1966; postgrad., U. Windsor-U. Mich., 1966-67. Systems engr. IBM, Detroit, 1967-69; applications devel. mgr. IBM/Svc. Bur. Corp., White Plains, N.Y., 1969-76; mktg. dir. Boeing Computer Svcs., McLean, Va., 1976-81; pres., owner Bus. Computer Corp. Am., Reston, Va., 1981-85; ptnr. Office Automation, Vienna, Va., 1985-87; tech. dir. Vanguard Rsch., Inc., Oakton, Va., 1987-93; pres. Ocean Thermal Energy, Inc., Oakton, 1993-95, X-Change Software, Inc., Oakton, 1994-97; exec. v.p., owner Electronic Bus. Svcs., Internat., Vienna, Va., 1997—; tech. cons. World Bank, Washington, 1985-87; software engring. cons. Nat. Test Facility, Colorado Springs, Colo., 1989-93. Inventor in field. Mem. KC (4th degree, grand knight 1993-94, state chmn. 1997-98). Republican. Roman Catholic. Avocations: gardening, piano, chess.

FLYNN, ROBERT LOPEZ, writer; b. Chillicothe, Tex., Apr. 12, 1932; s. James Emmett and Gladys Lopez (Wilkinson) F.; m. Norma Jean Sorrels; children: Deirdre Siobhan Flynn-Bass, Brigid Erin (dec.). BA, Baylor U., 1954, MA, 1956. Prof. Gardner-Webb Coll., Boiling Springs, N.C., 1957-59, Baylor U., Waco, Tex., 1959-63; novelist in residence Trinity U., San Antonio, 1963—. Author: (novels) North to Yesterday, 1967 (Wrangler award), In the House of the Lord, 1969, Sounds of Rescue, Signs of Hope, 1970 (S.W. Booksellers award), Wanderer Springs, 1987 (Spur award), The Last Klick, 1994, (story collections) Season Rain, 1984, Living with the Hyenas, 1996 (Wrangler award), (memoir) Personal War in Vietnam, 1989. With USMC, 1950-52. Mem. PEN, Marine Combat Corrs., Tex. Inst. Letters (pres. 1990-92). Baptist. Home: 101 Cliffside Dr San Antonio TX 78231-1510

FLYNN, THOMAS LEE, lawyer; b. Mitchell, S.D., Feb. 24, 1946; s. Melvin B. and Wilma L. (Jenks) F.; m. Kristine T. Johnson, Dec. 27, 1972; children: Ryan F., Erin M., Rory P. BA, Morningside Coll., 1968; JD, Drake U., 1972. Bar: U.S. Dist. Ct. (no. and so. dists.) Iowa 1972, U.S. Ct. Appeals (8th cir.) 1983. Ptnr. Belin, Lamson, McCormick, Zumbach & Flynn, Des Moines, Iowa, 1989—. Contbr. chpt. Am. Banker's Assn. Jour. Fellow Am. coll. Bankruptcy Law; mem. ABA, Iowa Bar Assn. (comml. and bankruptcy com. 1984-90), Polk County Bar Assn. Democrat. Office: Belin Lamson McCormick Zumbach & Flynn 2000 Financial Ctr Des Moines IA 50309-3909

FLYNN-CONNORS, ELIZABETH KATHRYN, editor; b. Chgo., Aug. 17, 1939; d. Timothy Carver Flynn and Elizabeth Eleanor (Tait) Scanlon; m. Gerald Martin Connors, Dec. 30, 1978; children: Andrew, Kathryn, Elizabeth. Student, Monmouth Coll., 1957-59; BA in Journalism, U. Wis., 1961, postgrad., 1965-66. Cityside reporter Mpls. Tribune, 1961-62; cityside reporter Chgo. Daily News, 1962-66, UN/N.Y. corr., 1966-75, Washington corr., 1968; writer, press officer UN, N.Y.C., 1975-82; sr. writer UN Chronicle, N.Y.C., 1982-85, editor-in-chief, 1985-96; chief editor Yearbook of UN, N.Y.C., 1996—. Troop leader Girl Scouts U.S., Tarrytown, N.Y., 1993-95. Russell Sage fellow U. Wis., 1965-66; recipient Investigative Reporting award Sigma Delta Chi, 1962, 1st Pl. Spot News award AP, 1970. Mem. UN Corrs. Assn. (alumni), Phi Beta Kappa, Kappa Delta. Avocations: reading, watching old movies. Home: 238 Hunter Ave Sleepy Hollow NY 10591-1317 Office: UN Rm DC1-532 New York NY 10017

FLYTHE, STARKEY SHARP, writer; b. Augusta, Ga., Feb. 15, 1935; s. Mary Bradley Bacheller. BA, U. South, Sewanee, Tenn., 1956; MA, U. Ga., 1963; JD, Augusta U., 1969. Editor The Saturday Evening Post, 1971-79; mng. editor Holiday Mag., 1979-80; editor The Country Gentleman, 1980-82; exec. editor Curtis Pub. Co., Indpls., 1978-80. Author short stories. Recipient U. Iowa prize, 1989; lit. fellow NEA, 1987. Episcopalian. Home: 403 Telfair St Augusta GA 30901

FLYZIK, JAMES J., federal official. BA, MBA, U. Md. Dep. asst. sec., chief info. officer Dept. of Treasury; various positions to chief Comms. Divsn. U.S. Secret Svc.; team leader Vice Pres. Gore's Nat. Performance Rev. Info. Tech. Team; chmn. Govt. Info. Tech. Svcs. Working Group; pub. spkr. in field; tchr. U. Md. Recipient numerous awards in field, including Armed Forces Comms. and Electronics Assn. award for Excellence in Info. Tech., 1996, AFFIRM award for Outstanding Svc. to Citizens, 1997, others. Office: Dept of Treasury 1500 Pennsylvania Ave NW Washington DC 20220-0002*

FOARD, DOUGLAS W., educational association administrator; b. Balt., Oct. 23, 1939; s. George Winfield and Anna (Herrmann) F.; m. Janet Hess, Aug. 26, 1961; children: Wendy Lynn, Scott Douglas. BA, Randolph-Macon Coll., 1961; MA, U. Va., 1965; PhD, Washington U., 1972; LHD (hon.), Randolph-Macon Coll., 1992. Asst. to dir. pub. rels. Ferrum (Va.) Coll., asst. prof. history, 1965-70, chair social sci., 1970-79, prof. history, 1972-85, assoc. dean, 1979-81; program officer NEH, Washington, 1985-89; exec. sec. Phi Beta Kappa, Washington, 1989—; adj. prof. history George Mason U., Fairfax, Va., 1986-89; chmn. 7th grade textbook analysis com Va. history Va. Dept. Edn., 1983. Author: The Revolt of the Aesthetes, 1989; contbr. articles to profl. jours.; guest editor Mag. of History, 1991. Bd. dirs. Nat. Humanities Alliance, 1994—, mem. exec. com., 1997—; bd. dirs. Nat. History Day, Washington, 1987—, Health Sys. Agy., Blacksburg, Va., 1978-80, Inst. for the Humanities, Salado, Tex., 1997—; bd. dirs. Va. Found. for Humanities and Pub. Policy, 1990-96, chmn., 1995-96. Grantee Madrid, Am. Coun. Learned Societies, 1985, Ford Found. 1969-70; James Still fellow U. Ky. 1983, Nat. Defense Act fellow Washington U., 1967-70, Philip Dupont fellow U. Va., 1961-62, Ford Found. fellow Asian Studies, 1967, Nat. Meth. scholar Randolph-Macon Coll., 1960-61; NEH summer seminar Vanderbilt U., 1976. Mem. Soc. Spanish & Portuguese Hist. Studies (newsletter editor 1982-83) Va. Soc. History Tchrs. (pres. 1981-83), Phi Beta Kappa, Phi Theta Kappa (hon.). Address: Phi Beta Kappa Society 4th Fl 1785 Massachusetts Ave NW Washington DC 20036-2117

FOARD, SUSAN LEE, editor; b. Asheville, N.C., Aug. 1, 1938; d. Carson Cowan and Anne (Brown) F. AB, Salem Coll., 1960; MA, William and Mary Coll., 1966. Asst. editor Inst. Early Am. Hist. and Culture, Williamsburg, Va., 1961-66; asso. editor Inst. Early Am. Hist. and Culture, 1966; editor U. Press of Va., Charlottesville, 1966—. Office: PO Box 3608 University Sta Charlottesville VA 22903-0608

FOCER-RICHARDS, LINDA JEAN, library director; b. Pitts., Oct. 24, 1935; d. Samuel Walter Focer and Mary Isabelle Murphy; m. Daniel Taddeo, Aug. 6, 1956 (div. Sept. 1984); children: Laurie Lane, Dana Belkot, Christian Focer Taddeo; m. George S. Richards, Feb. 24, 1998. BA in English, Geneva Coll., 1958; M Info. Sci., U. Pitts., 1982. Elem. sch. tchr. Avon (Ohio) Pub. Schs., 1967-70, Sweickley (Pa.) Presch., 1974-78; children's librarian Beaver (Pa.) Meml. Libr., 1978-81; dir. Carnegie Free Libr., Beaver Falls, Pa., 1983—. Mem. adv. bd. Big Bros./Big Sisters, Beaver County, Pa., 1990-92, Adult Literacy Project, Beaver County, 1992-94, Pride, Beaver Falls; mem. Beaver County Tourist Promotion Agy., Monaca, Pa., 1993-95; treas. Beaver Falls Bus. Dist. Authority, 1995—. Recipient cert. of merit CCBC Prevention Project, 1997. Mem. Afro-Am. Folk History Assn. (bd. dirs.), Outlook Club (com. chair 1985—), Merrick Art Gallery. Avocations: little theater work, writing, boating, travel. Office: Carnegie Free Libr 1301 7th Ave Beaver Falls PA 15010

FOCH, NINA, actress, creative consultant, educator, director; b. Leyden, The Netherlands, Apr. 20, 1924; came to U.S. 1927; d. Dirk and Consuelo (Flowerton) F.; m. James Lipton, June 6, 1954; m. Dennis de Brito, Nov. 27, 1959; 1 child, Dirk de Brito; m. Michael Dewell, Oct. 31, 1967 (div.). Grad., Lincoln Sch., 1939; studies with Stella Adler. Adj. prof. drama U. So. Calif., 1966-68, 78-80, adj. prof. film, 1987—; creative cons. to dirs., writers, prodrs. of all media; artist-in-residence U. N.C., 1966, Ohio State U., 1967, Calif. Inst. Tech., 1969-70; mem. sr. faculty Am. Film Inst., 1974-77; founder, tchr. Nina Foch Studio, Hollywood, Calif., 1973—; founder, actress Los Angeles Theatre Group, 1960-65; bd. dirs. Nat. Repertory Theatre, 1967-75. Motion picture appearances include Nine Girls, 1944, Return of the Vampire, 1944, Shadows in the Night, 1944, Cry of the Werewolf, 1944, Escape in the Fog, 1945, A Song to Remember, 1945, My Name Is Julia Ross, 1945, I Love a Mystery, 1945, Johnny O'Clock, 1947, The Guilt of Janet Ames, 1947, The Dark Past, 1948, The Undercover Man, 1949, Johnny Allegro, 1949, An American in Paris, 1951, Scaramouche, 1952, Young Man with Ideas, 1952, Sombrero, 1953, Fast Company, 1953, Executive Suite, 1954 (Oscar award nominee), Four Guns to the Border, 1954, You're Never Too Young, 1955, Illegal, 1955, The Ten Commandments, 1956, Three Brave Men, 1957, Cash McCall, 1959, Spartacus, 1960, Such Good Friends, 1971, Salty, 1973, Mahogany, 1976, Jennifer, 1978, Rich and Famous, 1981, Skin Deep, 1988, Sliver, 1993, Morning Glory, 1993, 'Til There Was You, 1996, Hush, 1998, Shadow of Doubt, 1998; appeared in Broadway plays including John Loves Mary, 1947, Twelfth Night, 1949, A Phoenix Too Frequent, 1950, King Lear, 1950, Second String, 1960; appeared with Am. Shakespeare Festival in Taming of the Shrew, Measure for Measure, 1956, San Francisco Ballet and Opera in The Seven Deadly Sins, 1966; also many regional theater appearances including Seattle Repertory Theatre (All Over, 1972 and The Seagull, 1973); actress on TV, 1947—, including Playhouse 90, Studio One, Pulitzer Playhouse, Playwrights 56, Producers Showcase, Lou Grant (Emmy nominee 1980), Mike Hammer; series star: Shadow Chasers, 1985, War and Remembrance, 1988, LA Law, 1990, Hunter, 1990, Dear John, 1990, 91, Tales of the City, 1993, Dharma and Greg, 1999; many other series, network spls. and TV films; TV panelist and guest on The Dinah Shore Show, Merv Griffin Show, The Today Show, Dick Cavett, The Tonight Show; TV moderator: Let's Take Sides, 1957-59; assoc. dir. (film) The Diary of Anne Frank, 1959; dir. (nat. tour and on-Broadway) Tonight at 8:30, 1966-67, Family Blessings, 1997; assoc. producer re-opening of Ford's Theatre, Washington, 1968. Hon. chmn. Los Angeles chpt. Am. Cancer Soc., 1970. Recipient Film Daily award, 1949, 53. Mem. AAUP, Acad. Motion Picture Arts and Scis. (co-chair exec. com. fgn. film award, membership com., chair foreign lang. award com., 1998-99), Hollywood Acad. TV Arts and Scis. (bd. govs. 1976-77). Avocation: work. Office: PO Box 1884 Beverly Hills CA 90213-1884

FOCHT, JOHN ARNOLD, JR., geotechnical engineer; b. Rockwall, Tex., Aug. 31, 1923; s. John Arnold and Fay (Goss) F.; m. Edith Rials, Aug. 8, 1950; children: John Arnold III, Judith Lynn Schweitzer. BSCE, U. Tex., 1944; MSCE, Harvard U., 1946. Soils engr. U.S. Waterways Expt. Sta., Vicksburg, Miss., 1947-50, 52-53; sr. soils engr. McClelland Engrs., Inc., Houston, 1953-55; v.p. engring. McClelland Engrs., Inc., 1955-72, exec. v.p., 1972-87; v.p. TERA, Inc., 1965-85; chmn. bd. Fugro-McClelland Inc., 1987-90; cons., 1991-99, Focht Consultants, Inc., 1999—. Contbr. articles to tech. jours. Chmn. ofcl. bd. Grace Methodist Ch., 1960-62; bd. dirs. N.W. YMCA, 1957-59; chmn. vis. com. dept. civil engring. U. Tex., Austin, 1974. Served to capt. AUS, 1944-46, 50-52. Recipient Disting. Engring. Alumnus award U. Tex., Austin, 1964. Fellow ASCE (nat. dir. 1980-83, nat. pres. 1989-90, pres. Tex. sect. 1970-71, Thomas A. Middlebrooks award 1957, 76, James Laurie prize 1959, Civil Engring. State of the Art award 1971, 79, Terzaghi lectr. 1993, William H. Wisely Am. Civil Engr. award 1999); mem. NAE, NSPE, Tex. Soc. Profl. Engrs. (Engr. of Yr. award 1987), Am. Cons. Engrs. Coun., Cons. Engrs. Coun. Tex. (dir. 1965-67), Tex. Coun. Engring. Labs. (dir. 1972-75), Houston Engring. and Sci. Soc. (treas., dir. 1973-76), Inst. Profl. Practice (dir. 1996-99). Methodist. Home: 12226 Perthshire Rd Houston TX 77024-4244

FOCHT, MICHAEL HARRISON, health care industry executive; b. Reading, Pa., Sept. 16, 1942; s. Benjamin Harrison and Mary (Hannahoe) F.; m. Sandra Lee Scholwin, May 14, 1964; 1 child, Michael Harrison. Archtl. estimator Caloric Corp., Topton, Pa., 1964-65, cost acct., 1965-66, indsl. engr., 1966-68, mgr. wage rates and standards, 1968-70; indsl. engr. Am. Medicorp. Inc., Fort Lauderdale, Fla., 1970-71; exec. dir. midwest region Am. Medicorp. Inc., Chgo., 1977-78; asst. adminstr. Cypress Community Hosp., Pompano Beach, Fla., 1971-73, adminstr., 1975-77; adminstr. Doctor's Hosp. Hollywood, Fla., 1973-75; v.p. Medfield Corp., St. Petersburg, Fla., 1978-79; v.p. ops. hosp. group Nat. Med. Enterprises, Inc., Los Angeles, 1979-81; regional sr. v.p. hosp. group Nat. Med. Enterprises, Inc., Tampa, Fla., 1981-83; pres., chief exec. officer internat. group Nat. Med. Enterprises, Inc., Los Angeles, 1983-86, pres. chief exec. officer hosp. group, 1986-91; sr. exec. v.p., dir. ops. Nat. Med. Enterprises, Inc., 1991-93, pres., 1993-95; pres., COO Tenet Healthcare Corp., Santa Barbara, 1995—. Mem. Fedn. Am. Hosps. (bd. govs. 1983—), Fla. League Hosps. (bd. dirs. 1982-83). Republican. Roman Catholic. Home: PO Box 703 Santa Ynez CA 93460-0703 Office: Tenet Healthcare Corp 3820 State St Santa Barbara CA 93105-3112*

FOCHT, THEODORE HAROLD, lawyer, educator; b. Reading, Pa., Aug. 20, 1934; s. Harold Edwin and Ruth Naomi (Boyer) F.; m. Joyce Gundy, Aug. 11, 1956; children: David Scott, Eric Steven. AB in Philosophy, Franklin and Marshall Coll., 1956; JD, Coll. of William and Mary, 1959. Bar: Va. 1959. Teaching assoc. Columbia U. Sch. Law, N.Y.C., 1959-60; atty. Office of Gen. Counsel SEC, Washington, 1960-61, legal asst. to Commr., Washington, 1961-63; mem. faculty U. Conn. Sch. Law, Hartford, 1963-71 (leave of absence, 1969-71); spl. counsel on securities legislation Interstate and Fgn. Commerce Com., U.S. Ho. of Reps., Washington, 1969-71; gen. counsel Securities Investor Protection Corp., Washington, 1971-94, pres., 1984-94; adj. prof. law American U. Sch. Law, Washington, 1979-84; mem. Fla. State Comptroller's Task Force on Regulatory DeCoupling, 1995. Mem. Va. State Bar, Phi Beta Kappa. Home: 8436 Pinafore Dr New Port Richey FL 34653-6739

FOCKLER, HERBERT HILL, foundation executive; b. Summersville, W.Va., Feb. 18, 1922; s. William Okey and Annie Lee (Fitzwater) F.; m. Mary Hildegarde Ziegler, May 15, 1950; 1 child, Herbert. BA, W.Va. U., 1947, MA, 1948; cert., Oxford (Eng.) U., 1948, Harvard U., 1949. Adminstr. library Princeton (N.J.) U., 1952-54, Library of Congress, Washington, 1956-58; advisor White House Confs., Washington, 1959-60; exec. NIH, Bethesda, Md., 1961-69; chmn. Sci. and Tech. Coms., Washington, 1969-70; exec. dir. Sci. Founds., Washington, 1971-72; trustee, chmn. Am. Arts Internat. Found., Washington, pres., 1984—, also bd. dirs.; trustee Nat. Mus. of Health and Medicine Found., 1989—; chmn., trustee World Tech. Found., Washington, 1988-89; bd. dirs. Nat. Info. Tech. Ctr., 1992—; advisor NSF, 1975, White House Conf. on Bus., 1975, 78, Montgomery Coll., Rockville, Md., 1978, World Bank, 1986, Winston Churchill Found., 1988, various pub. scos., 1989—, various tech. industries, 1986—, IMF, 1991; mem. adv. coun. Coolfont Found., Berkeley Springs, W.Va., 1980-87; mem. Presdl. Rsch. Group; assoc. Woodrow Wilson Internat. Ctr., 1988—; mem. Bd. on Sci. Edn. Editor: Contemporary South, 1968, also conf. records and newsletters; author sci. research reports and bibliographies. Adv. Stanford U., 1967-69; trustee Threshold Environ. Found., Washington, 1969-75, Nat. Mus. Health and Medicine Found., 1989-90, adv. coun., 1991—; mem. pres.'s coun. Shenandoah Coll., Winchester, Va., 1982-87; mem. Found. Advancement Edn. in Scis., 1980—, Joint Bd. Edn. in Sci. and Engring., 1991—. Served as staff sgt. U.S. Army, 1941-45. Mem. AAAS, Acad. Polit. Sci., Am. Polit. Sci. Assn., Washington Acad. Scis. (bd. dirs. 1992—), U.N. Assn., Smithsonian Assocs., Am. Assn. Mus., Nat. Trust Historic Preservation, Libr. Congress Assocs., Colonial Williamsburg Found., Fgn. Policy Inst., World Affairs Coun., Policy Studies Orgn., Found. for Advancement Edn. in Sci., Internet Soc., Smithsonian Assocs., Am. Film Inst., Am. Assn. Mus., Nat. Trust Hist. Preservation, Harvard Club, Princeton Club, W.Va. Club, W.Va. Acad. Sci., Nat. Press Club. Clubs: Harvard U., Princeton U., W.Va. (Washington). Home and Office: 10710 Lorain Ave Silver Spring MD 20901-1512

FODERARO, ANTHONY HAROLDE, nuclear engineering educator; b. Scranton, Pa., Apr. 3, 1926; s. Edward and Myrtha (Bachman) F.; m. Rita Lacey, May 4, 1953; children—Anthony, John, Diana. B.S. in Physics, U. Scranton, 1950; Ph.D. in Physics, U. Pitts., 1955. Supervisory scientist Westinghouse Atomic Power Div., Pitts., 1954-56; sr. nuclear physicist Gen. Motors Research, Warren, Mich., 1956-60; assoc. prof. nuclear engring. Pa. State U., University Park, 1960-63; prof. Pa. State U., 1963-88; prof. emeritus, 1989—; cons. on radiation protection govt. and industry. Author: The Elements of Neutron Interaction Theory, 1971, The Photon Shielding Manual, 1976; co-author: The Reactor Shielding Design Manual, 1956, The Engineering Compendium on Radiation Shielding, 1968; contbr. articles to publs. in field. Served with U.S. Army, 1944-46. Fellow Am. Nuclear Soc. (chmn. radiation protection and shielding div. 1969-70); mem. Am. Phys. Soc., Am. Assn. Physics Tchrs. Home: 301 S Gill St State College PA 16801-3963

FODIMAN, AARON ROSEN, publishing executive; b. Stamford, Conn., Oct. 10, 1937; s. Yale J. and Thelma F. BS, Tulane U., 1958; LLB, NYU, 1960, MBA, 1961; grad., L'Academie de CuisineCanardier, Washington, 1977. Bar: N.Y. 1960, D.C. 1961, Va. 1965. With FTC, Washington, 1961-65; practiced in Arlington, Va., 1965-78; pres. Fast Food Operators, Inc., N.Y.C., 1978-84, Hampton Healthcare, 1984-91, Kapok Tree Restaurants, Tampa Bay Publs., 1986—. Author: Life is not an Illusion, it Just Looks That Way, 1998; pub., editor: Tampa Bay Mag.; TV host local sports show, Dine Line, Tampa Bay Mag.; Bd. dirs. Tampa Players Inc., Washington Ballet, Manhattan Punch Line Theatre, Kent Jewish Cmty. Ctr.; pres. Dunedin Art Ctr., Bay Ballet Theatre; chmn. Pinellas County Arts Coun., Golda Meir Ctr., Bay Ballet Theatre, A Taste of Pinellas; cmty. advisor Clearwater Dunedin Jr. League; mem. adv. bd. Am. Film Inst.; chmn. Ford Presdl. Campaign, 1976; advisor Fed. Res. Bank Atlanta; participant Leadership Pinellas; participant, founder Leadership Tampa Bay, Nat. Conf. Christians and Jews; Pinellas County amb. to Ringling Mus. Art. Recipient Hyam Soloman Freedom award, 1974, Miniature Palette award Miniature Art Soc. of Fla., 1987, Order of Salvador medal Dali Mus., 1989; honoree award winner Friends of Arts Pinellas County, Svc. to Mankind award Sertoma Club; knighted as Baron Order of St. John of Jerusalem, 1999. Mem. Pinellas County Restaurant Assn. (pres.), Tampa Bay Restaurant Assn. (pres.), Fla. Restaurant Assn. (bd. dirs.), Chaine des Rotisseurs (chpt. officer), Internat. Legal Frat., Phi Delta Phi, Barrister Inn Club (Washington, pres.), B'nai Brith (pres. Washington).

FODOR, GÁBOR BÉLA, chemistry educator, researcher; b. Budapest, Hungary, Dec. 5, 1915; came to U.S., 1969, naturalized, 1976; s. Domokos Victor and Paula Maria (Bayer) F.; m. Ana Maria Ruiz. Cand. Ing., Poly. Tech. Inst., Graz, Austria, 1934; PhD, Szeged U., Hungary, 1937; DSc, Acad. Scis., Budapest, 1952; PhD (hon.), Szeged U., Hungary, 1994. Asst. Szeged U., Hungary, 1935-38, from assoc. prof. to prof., 1945-57; rsch. chemist Chinoin Pharm. Ltd., Budapest, Hungary, 1938-45; head stereochemistry Lab. of Acad., Budapest, Hungary, 1958-65; prof. Laval U., Que., Can., 1965-69; Centennial prof. chemistry W.Va. U., Morgantown, 1969-86, prof. emeritus, 1986—; prof. emeritus József Attila U., Szeged, Hungary, 1990—; project dir. Nat. Found. Cancer Research, Bethesda, Md., 1977-86; vis. prof. U. Munich, 1996, Stevens Tech., Hoboken, 1968, Darmstadt, THD, 1975-76. Author: Organische Chemie I-II, 1966; contbr. articles to prof. jours.; patentee in field. Recipient Kossuth prize Budapest, 1950, 54, Silver medal U. Helsinki, 1958, Golden diploma U. Szeged, 1988, Diamond diploma U. Szeged, 1998, Albert Szent-Györgyi medal, Szeged, Hungary, 1992; fellow Churchill Coll., Cambridge, Eng., 1961—. Mem. Am. Chem. Soc., Can. Inst. Chemistry, Am. Inst. Chemists, Chem. Soc. London, Hungarian Acad. Sci., Sigma Xi. Roman Catholic. Office: WVa U Dept Chemistry Morgantown WV 26506-6045

FODOR, SARAH JOAN, writer, English educator; b. Chgo., July 19, 1956; d. Eugene Dinier Balsley and Joanie Marie (Ruonavaara) Haut; m. David B. Fodor; children: Mark, Timothy. BA, U. Ill., Urbana, 1978, U. Ill., Urbana, 1979; MS, U. Chgo., 1982, PhD, 1994. Tchr. 8th grade Limestone Sch., Kankakee, Ill., 1978-82; English tchr. 9-12 Hamilton (Ill.) H.S., 1982-83; instr. composition Western Ill. U., Macomb, 1983-87; vis. asst. prof. English Wheaton (Ill.) Coll., 1994-98; assoc. dir. found. rels. Northwestern U., 1998—. Avocations: youth advisor, chess.

FODOR, SUSANNA SERENA, lawyer; b. Tg-Mures, Romania, Apr. 24, 1950; came to U.S., 1963; d. Bela Akos and Rachel (Rafira) F.; 1 child, Brooke Alexandra Bodoki-Fodor. BS, U. Wis., Milw., 1969; JD, U. Wis., Madison, 1972. Bar: Wis. 1972, N.Y. 1974. In ho. counsel Wis. Dept. Devel. Natural Resources, Madison, 1972-73, U.S. EPA, N.Y.C., 1973-74, Urban Devel. Corp., N.Y.C., 1975-77; assoc. Schulte, Roth & Zabel, N.Y.C., 1977-79; ptnr. Weil, Gotshal & Manges, N.Y.C., 1979-85, Shea & Gould, N.Y.C., 1985-89, Jones, Day, Reavis & Pogue, N.Y.C., 1989—. Editor chpt. to book; contbr. articles to profl. pubs., chpt. to book. Mem. ABA (real property, probate and trust constrn. form com.), Am. Coll. Real Estate Lawyers, Profl. Women in Constrn., Real Estate Bd. N.Y. (owner labor coordinating com.), Am. Coll. Constrn. Lawyers, Comml. Real Estate Women N.Y., Urban Land Inst., Internat. Assn. Corp. Real Estate Execs., Wis. State Bar Assn., N.Y. State Bar Assn., Hungarian-Am. C. of C. of N.Y./N.J. Avocations: sports, art, languages. Home: 200 E End Ave Apt 14F New York NY 10128-7887 Office: Jones Day Reavis & Pogue 599 Lexington Ave Fl C1A New York NY 10022-6070

FODY, EDWARD PAUL, pathologist; b. Balt., June 11, 1947; s. Edward Paul and Frances Dorothy (Schultz) F.; m. Nancy June Keipe, July 19, 1974. BS, Duke U., 1969; MS, U. Wis., 1971; MD, Vanderbilt U., 1975. Diplomate Am. Bd. Pathology. Resident in pathology Vanderbilt U. Hosp., Nashville, 1975-78; fellow in chemistry U. Tex. Med. Sch., Houston, 1979-80, asst. prof. pathology, 1980-81; chief lab. VA Hosp., Little Rock, 1981-87; assoc. prof. pathology U. Ark. Med. Sch., Little Rock, 1981-87; dir. pathology Bethesda Hosp., Cin., 1987-96; dir. pathology dept. Erlanger Hosp., Chattanooga, 1996—. Editor, author: Clinical Chemistry, 1984, chpt. to book. Fellow Coll. Am. Pathologists, Am. Soc. Clin. Pathologists; mem. AMA, Am. Assn. for Clin. Chemistry, Am. Soc. for Microbiology, Tenn. Med. Assn., Hamilton County Med. Soc. Republican. Lutheran. Avocations: boating, photography. Home: 408 Gentlemens Rdg Signal Mountain TN 37377-3250 Office: Erlanger Hosp Dept Pathology 975 E 3rd St Dept Chattanooga TN 37403-2163

FOEHL, EDWARD ALBERT, chemical company executive; b. Phila., May 30, 1942; s. Edward A. and Geneva (Horner) F.; m. Katherine Broberg, Jan. 13, 1970. BS in Engring., U.S. Mil. Acad., 1965; MBA, George Washington U., 1971. Commd. 2nd lt. U.S. Army, 1965, advanced through grades to capt., 1967, resigned, 1970; fin. product planner Ford Motor Co., Dearborn, Mich., 1971-74; mgr. planning First Nat. Bank Chgo., 1974-76; dir. corp. fin. Mfrs. Hanover Trust Co., N.Y.C., 1977; dir. fin. planning Freightner Corp., Portland, Oreg., 1977-82; pres. Great Western Chem. Co., Portland, 1982-87, 88-92; pres., CEO Systran Fin. Svc. Corp., 1992—; bd. dirs. System Fin. Svcs.; guest lectr. Portland State U., 1979-86. Mem. exec. coun. Boy Scouts Am., Portland, 1986. Decorated Silver Star, Bronze Star, Vietnamese Cross of Gallantry. Mem. Planning Forum (past pres.), Fin. Execs. Isnt., C. of C. (internat. trade com.), West Point Soc. Oreg. (pres.), Multnomah Athletic Club, Pumpkin Ridge Golf Course, Desert Mountain (Phoenix). Home: 360 SE 177th Ave Vancouver WA 98683 Office: Systran Fin Svc Corp 10220 SW Greenburg Rd Ste 551 Portland OR 97223-5577

FOELL, KRISTIE ANN, foreign language educator; b. Seaside, Calif., Oct. 22, 1962; d. Darrell William and Sally Ann (McCampbell) F.; m. Christopher Alan Williams, Aug. 17, 1984. Student, U. Munich, 1982-83; BA cum laude, Yale U., 1984; MA, U. Calif., Berkeley, 1986, PhD, 1992; postgrad., U. Vienna, Austria, 1989-90. Vis. asst. prof. Gustavus Adolphus Coll., St. Peter, Minn., 1991-92, Vassar Coll., Poughkeepsie, N.Y., 1992-95; asst. prof. Bowling Green (Ohio) State U., 1995—. Author: Blind Reflections: Gender in Elias Canetti's Die Blendung, 1994; rev. editor Ars Lyrica, 1994—, H-musTXT (Humanities OnLine), 1996—; contbr. articles and book revs. to profl. jours. Alumni interviewer Yale Alumni Schs. Com., Berkeley and Bowling Green, 1980's, 1996—. Fulbright Rsch. fellow, Vienna, 1989-90, Fulbright Lectr./Rsch. Grantee, Berlin, 1995; grantee in field. Mem. Am. Assn. Tchrs. German, Am. Coun. Tchrs. Fgn. Lang., German Studies Assn. Office: Bowling Green State U GREAL 103 Shatzel Hall Bowling Green OH 43403

FOELSCHE, OTMAR KARL ERNST, German language educator; b. Aug. 26, 1940. BA, Free U. Berlin, 1966; MA, U. Maine, 1970. Tchr. Maine Ctrl. Inst., St. Mark's Sch., Mass., 1966-75; lectr., cons. U. N.H., So. Maine, R.I., 1975-85; lectr. Dartmouth Coll., 1985-87, dir. lang. lab., 1987-91, dir. humanities resources, 1991—; mem. faculty dept. German Dartmouth Coll., Hanover, N.H., dir. humanities resources, 1987—. Mem. MLA (mem., chmn. various coms.), Am. Assn. Tchrs. German, Internat. Assn. Learning Labs. E-mail: otmar@dartmouth.edu. Office: Dartmouth Coll 6192 Bartlett Hall Hanover NH 03755-3530

FOER, SARA, public relations spokesperson, consultant; b. Wilmington, Del., Oct. 6, 1962; d. Norman J. Wohlken and Dian K. (King) Wood; m. Michael N. Foer, May 21, 1989. BA, Barnard Coll., 1984; MSJ, Northwestern U., 1985; MPH, George Washington U., 1994. Assoc. dir. devel. Am. Diabetes Assn., Washington, 1986-88; devel. mgr. St. John's Cmty. Svcs., Washington, 1988-94; asst. dir. comms. Am. Nurses Assn., Washington, 1994—; cons. SEEC, Rockville, Md., 1992—, Nat. Rural Electric, Washington, 1995, Am. Diabetes Assn., 1988-92. Contbr. articles to profl. jours. Vol., donor Am. Diabetes Assn., Washington; promoter of organ donor awareness health fairs, work, speeches, patient advocacy groups, Washington. Recipient Thoth Cert. Pub. Rels. Soc. Am., 1995, 96, 97, Silver Anvil award, 1996. Mem. APHA, Am. Soc. Assn. Execs., Nat. Soc. Fund-Raising Execs., Am. Coll. Healthcare Execs. Avocations: traveling, biking, collecting, writing. Home: 4906 Montgomery Ln Bethesda MD 20814 Office: ANA 600 Maryland Ave SW Ste 100 Washington DC 20024-2520

FOERST, JOHN GEORGE, JR., fundraising executive; b. Queens, N.Y., June 8, 1927; s. John George and Mary Elizabeth (McGinn) F.; m. Marion Theresa Cassidy, June 27, 1953; children: Gerard M. BA, St. Johns U., Queens, 1950. Regional rep. Nat. Found. for Infantile Paralysis, N.Y.C., 1950-52; campaign dir., v.p. Cmty. Counselling Svc., N.Y.C., 1952-59, v.p., asst. to pres., 1965-69, pres., 1969-87, chmn., 1987-96, chmn. emeritus, 1997—; pres. John G. Foerst, Inc., N.Y.C., 1959-65. Contbg. author: complete Guide to Corporate Fund Raising, 1982. Bd. dirs. St. Francis Hosp., Roslyn, N.Y., 1972—, The Ctr. for Devel. Disabilities, Woodbury, N.Y., 1974-87, Nat. Ctr. for Disability Svcs. Inc., Albertson, N.Y., 1988—, Cath. Health Sys. of L.I., 1998—, Help for the Poor Found., 1998—, Mid-Atlantic Hosp. Trust, Bermuda; trustee Pope John Paul II Libr. and Cultural Ctr., Washington, 1998—, Telicare, Uniondale, N.Y.; chmn. Am. Assn. Fund Raising Counsel, N.Y.C., 1982; mem. Cardinal's Com. of Laity, Roman Cath. Archdiocese N.Y., 1984—. Mem. Am. Irish Cultural Inst., Union League, Knights of Malta. Republican. Home: 77 Dover Rd Manhasset NY 11030-3717 Office: Community Counselling Svc Co 350 5th Ave Ste 7210 New York NY 10118-7299

FOERSTER, BERND, architecture educator; b. Danzig, Dec. 5, 1923; came to U.S., 1947, naturalized, 1954; s. Joseph and Martha (Brumm) F.; m. Enell Dowling, May 13, 1950; children: Kent, Mark (dec.). Student, Columbia U., 1948-49; BS in Architecture, U. Cin., 1954; MArch, Rensselaer Poly. Inst., 1957. Various positions Govt. The Netherlands, 1945-47; with various engrs. and architects offices, 1950-59, cons. Ch. bldgs., design cons., 1954—; instr. architecture U. Cin., 1954; instr. architecture Rensselaer Poly. Inst., Troy, N.Y., 1954-56, asst. prof., 1956-62, assoc. prof., 1962-65, prof., 1965-71; dean Kans. State U., Manhattan, 1971-84, prof., 1971-96; adjunct prof. Grad. Program in Hist. Preservation Goucher Coll., 1995—; cons. archtl. and cmty. surveys N.Y. State Coun. Arts, 1962-71; chmn. Gov.'s Adv. Com. Hist. Preservation N.Y. State, 1968-71; cons. Albany Hist. Sites Commn., 1967-71, Independence (Mo.) Heritage Commn., 1975-77; leader U.S. del. Preservation Planning to China, 1982, USSR and Ea. Europe, 1989; leader faculty team Coll. Architecture and Design, Kans. State U. to Poland, The Czech and Slovak Republics, and Hungary, 1990; cons. selection of archs. and design cons. for Fed. projects U.S. GSA, 1994-96. Author: Man and Masonry, 1960, Pattern and Texture, 1961, Architecture Worth Saving in Rensselaer County, N.Y., 1965; (with others) Independence, Missouri, 1978, 2d printing, 1989; (films) Man and Masonry, 1961 (Am. Film Festival selection), What Do You Tear Down Next?, 1964, Earth and Fire, 1964, Assault on the Wynantskill, 1967; editorial adv. bd. Preservation Forum, 1987-93. Bd. dirs. Albany Inst. History and Art, 1967-71, Mohawk-Hudson Council on Edn. TV, 1968-71, v.p., 1970-71; co-chmn. Conf. on Rensselaer County, 1966; pres. Rensselaer County Council for Arts, 1963-64, 66-67; trustee Olana Historic Site, 1969-71; pres. bd. trustees Riley County Hist. Mus., 1977; chmn. Manhattan Downtown Redevel. Adv. Bd., 1979-85, City Fountain Restoration Com., 1983-86; mem. coun. Drayton Hall, Charleston, S.C., 1985-93; mem. Hist. Dist. Rev. Bd. Manhattan, 1997—; mem. planning bd. Riley County, Kans., 1997—; chair Road and Bridge Adv. Com. Riley County, 1997-98; chair steering com. Downtown Tomorrow, Manhattan, 1998—. Named Disting. prof. Assn. Collegiate Schs. Architecture, 1988; recipient Kans. Gov.'s award for historic preservation, 1995. Fellow AIA (com. hist. resources 1977-92, vice chmn. 1986, chmn. 1987, state preservation coordinator 1979-92); mem. AIA Kans. (sec. 1975, exec. com. 1975-80, pres. 1979), Nat. Trust Hist. Preservation (bd. advs. 1979-81, trustee 1981-90, trustee emeritus 1990—), AAUP (chpt. pres. Rensselaer Poly. Inst. 1963-64, Kans. State U. 1987-88, v.p. Kans. conf. 1988-90, pres. 1990-92), The Land Inst. (bd. dirs. 1976-87), Manhattan Arts Coun. (bd. dirs. 1973-78, pres. 1976-77), LWV of Manhattan-Riley County (2d v.p. 1988-91, pres.-elect 91-92, pres. 92-93), Kans. Preservation Alliance (bd. dirs. 1979-85), Nat. Council Preservation Edn. (bd. dirs. 1980-93, vice-chmn. 1981-85), Nature Conservancy, Audubon Soc., Scarab, Tau Sigma Delta, Phi Kappa Phi. Lodge: Rotary (Paul Harris fellow). Home: 920 Ratone St Manhattan KS 66502-5136 *Some places are so important, so fragile, or so beautiful that we must leave them alone.*

FOERSTER, DAVID WENDEL, JR., counselor, consultant, human resources specialist; b. Jacksonville, Fla., Jan. 7, 1953; s. David Wendel Foerster and Estelle Jones Williams. BA cum laude, U. Fla., 1977. Cert. and registered gen. mediator, Ga. Founding dir. Addictive Disease Resouce Ctr., Atlanta, 1979-84; founding exec. dir., crisis mediator Resource Ctr., Atlanta, 1984—; cons. Womble, Carlylse, Sandridge & Rice, Atlanta, Garland Samuel & Loeb, King & Spalding, State Bar Ga., Atlanta Falcons Football Club, Ave. Hosp., Shepard Spinal Hosp., Coca-Cola, Wachovia Corp., Sun Trust Bank, The Kroger Co., Atlanta Humane Soc.; lectr. Ga. State U., Atlanta, 1984—, Atlanta Pub. Schs.; chmn. Lawyers Assistance Com., 1997-98. Contbr. articles to profl. jours.; interviewee, expert CBS, PBS, ABC, CNN, Bus. Week, Atlanta Jour. Cosntn., 1978—. Bd. dirs. Resource Ctr., Atlanta, 1984—; instr. All Saints Episcopal Ch., Atlanta, 1985—. Recipient merit award Mended Hearts, Inc., 1985; grantee HBO, 1987; Will Watt Fellow, 1995. Mem. ACA, Ga. Addiction Counselors Assn., Ga. Employee Assistance Forum, Nat. Assn. Addiction Counselors, Employee Assistance Profl. Assn., Rotary (Paul Harris fellow 1994). Avocations: classical music, reading, photgraphy. Home: 207 Westminster Dr NE Atlanta GA 30309-3312 Office: Resource Ctr 2921 Piedmont Rd NE Ste D Atlanta GA 30305-2785

FOERSTER, SCHUYLER, political science educator, consultant; b. Newport News, Va., Sept. 20, 1949; s. Frederick Henry Jr. and Helen (Yates) F.; m. Janet Louise Johnson, Jan. 29, 1972; children: Allyson, Jennifer. BS, USAF Acad., 1971; MA, Tufts U., 1972; MPA, Am. U., 1976; DPhil, Oxford (Eng.) U., 1983. Comd. 2d lt. USAF, 1971, advanced through grades to col.; intelligence officer Pacific Air Forces USAF, Thailand, 1972-73; intelligence officer Air Force Intelligence Svc. USAF, Washington, 1973-77; tenure assoc. prof., dir. internat. and def. studies USAF Acad., Colorado Springs, 1977-90; polit.-mil. advisor US Mission NATO, Office of the Def. Advisor, Brussels, Belgium, 1986-88; nat. security fellow JFK Sch. Govt. Harvard U., Cambridge, Mass., 1988-89; spl. asst. to amb. U.S. Del. CFE/CSCE, Vienna, Austria, 1990-94; sr. asst. to comdr. in chief U.S. Strategic Command, Offutt AFB, Nebr., 1994-97; ret. USAF, 1997; pres. World Affairs Coun., Pitts., 1997—; adj. prof. U. Pitts., 1998—. Co-editor, author: American Defense Policy, 6th edit., 1990, Defining Stability: Conventional Arms Control in a Changing Europe, 1989; author: (with others) Limited Wars of 1982, 1983; contbr. articles to profl. jours. Mem. Trinity Cathedral, Pitts., 1998—; mem. Leadership Pitts., 1998—; jr. warden Holy Spirit Episcopal Ch., Bellevue, Nebr., 1996-97; sr. warden Anglican Ch., Vienna, Austria, 1991-94. Decorated Legion of Merit, numerous svc. medals. Mem. Internat. Inst. for Strategic Studies, Rotary, Rivers Club, Shannopin Country Club. Episcopalian. Avocations: golf, squash, computers, piano. E-mail: skyfoer@ibm.net. Home: 341 Ritter Rd S Sewickley PA 15143 Office: World Affairs Coun Pitts 400 Oliver Ave Pittsburgh PA 15219

FOFONOFF, NICHOLAS PAUL, oceanographer, educator; b. Queenstown, Alta., Can., Aug. 18, 1929; came to U.S., 1962; s. Paul Alexander and Anna Dimitri (Malakoff) F.; m. Mabel Beryl Hutton Deckard, June 16, 1951; children—Paul Wynn, Stephanie Anne, Timothy Wayne, Nicholas David. B.A., U. B.C., Can.), Vancouver, 1950; M.A., 1951; Ph.D., Brown U., 1955. Postdoctoral fellow Nat. Inst. Oceanography, Eng., 1955-56; scientist Fisheries Research Bd. Can., 1956-62; sr. scientist Woods Hole (Mass.) Oceanographic Instn., 1962-91, chmn. dept. phys. oceanography, 1967-71, 81-85; scientist emeritus Woods Hole (Mass.) Oceanographic Instn., Mass., 1992—; assoc. mem. Ctr. Earth and Planetary Physics, 1971-86, disting. rsch. assoc., 1986-91; prof. practice of phys. oceanography Harvard U., 1968-86; bd. dir. WOCE Internat. Project office, Inst. Oceanographic Scis. Deacon Lab. Eng., 1991-3. Mem. AAAS, Am. Geophys. Union. Research in dynamics of ocean circulation, phys. properties and thermodynamics of seawater, application of satellite data to study ocean currents. Home: 6 Greengate Rd Falmouth MA 02540-2228 Office: Woods Hole Oceanographic Instn Woods Hole MA 02543

FOGARTIE, JAMES EUGENE, retired clergyman; b. Brookhaven, Miss., June 20, 1924; s. Arthur Finley and Eugenia Elizabeth (Vance) F.; m. Ruth Ann Douglass, Aug. 30, 1946 (dec. 1976); children: Ann Douglass, Elizabeth Vance, Arthur Ford, James Eugene, Jr.; m. Vivian M. Reid, Feb. 18, 1978. BA, U. Tex., 1945, MA, 1948; BD, Austin Presbyn. Theol. Sem., 1948; ThM, Union Theol. Sem., Richmond, Va., 1954; DD, Austin Coll., 1969; LHD, Presbyn. Coll., Clinton, S.C., 1989. Ordained to ministry Presbyn. Ch., 1948. Minister First Presbyn. Ch., Marianna, Ark., 1948-52, Ft. Smith, Ark., 1952-55; minister Myers Park Presbyn. Ch., Charlotte, N.C., 1955-74, First Presbyn. Ch., Spartanburg, S.C., 1974-90; pastor emeritus First Presbyn. Ch., Spartanburg, 1991—; supply minister St. Andrews Presbyn. Ch., Wemblen, Eng., 1952; trustee Ctr. of Theol. Inquiry, Princeton, 1986—; mem. instnl. rev. bd. Spartanburg Regional Med. Ctr., 1978—. Author: No Room, 1958, In Search of Christmas, 1959. Recipient Silver Beaver award Mecklenburg Coun. Boy Scouts, 1971, Disting. Alumni award Austin Presbyn. Theol. Seminary, 1990; named one of Outstanding Young Men of Am., 1953. Mem. Spectator Club (pres. Spartanburg chpt. 1990), Rotary. Home: 104 N Carleila Lake Way Spartanburg SC 29037

FOGARTY, CHARLES JOSEPH, state official; b. Providence, Sept. 15, 1955; s. Charles Joseph and Martha Jane (Hague) F. BA, Providence Coll., 1977; MPA, U. R.I., 1980. Policy assoc. Office Gov., Providence, 1978-84; spl. asst. to commr. R.I. Dept. Edn., Providence, 1985; town councilman Glocester, R.I., 1985-91; sr. policy analyst Office Gen. Treas., Providence, 1985-88; dir. policy Office Lt. Gov., Providence, 1989-91; state senator R.I., Providence, 1991-99; majority whip R.I. Senate, 1993-95, pres. pro tem, 1995-99; lt. gov. State of R.I., 1999 . Chmn. Glocester Dem. Town Com., 1979-85, R.I. Longterm Care Coord. Coun., 1996—; del. Dem. Nat. Conv., N.Y.C., 1980, Chgo., 1996; bd. dirs. N.W. Cmty. & Nursing Health Svc., 1994—, R.I. chpt. ARC, 1994—. Mem. Lions (pres. Glocester chpt. 1991—). Roman Catholic. Home: 230 Paris Irons Rd Harmony RI 02829 Office: Rm 116 State House Providence RI 02903

FOGARTY, EDWARD MICHAEL, lawyer; b. Woonsocket, R.I., Feb. 25, 1948; s. Raymond Henry and Mary (Hogan) F.; m. Gail Higgins, Jan. 8, 1977. BA, Providence Coll., 1969; JD, Georgetown U., 1972. Bar: R.I. 1972, D.C. 1973, U.S. Supreme Ct. 1977. Law clk. U.S. Dist. Ct. R.I., Providence, 1972-73; assoc. Wilkinson, Cragun & Barker, Washington, 1973-79, ptnr., 1979-82; ptnr. Baenen, Timme, De Reitzes & Middleton, Washington, 1982-83; counsel Spriggs & Hollingsworth, Washington, 1983-98; legal counsel to speaker R.I. Ho. of Reps., Providence, 1987-93; legal counsel to majority leader R.I. Senate, Providence, 1993—; arbitrator R.I. Superior Ct., 1989—. Trustee Festival Ballet of R.I., pres., 1994-96. Mem. ABA, R.I. Bar Assn. (ho. dels. 1992-94), Am. Arbitration Assn. (nat. panel of arbitrators 1985-96), Univ. Club. Democrat. Roman Catholic. Home: 488 Lloyd Ave Providence RI 02906-4550 Office: 309 State House Providence RI 02903

FOGARTY, JAMES VINCENT, JR., special education administrator, educator; b. N.Y.C., Dec. 12, 1945; s. James Vincent and Dorothy (Hummender) F.; divorced; children: Ann Denise, Brian James. BS in Biology, SUNY, Stony Brook, 1967; MS in Spl. Edn., Adelphi U., 1971; CAS in Adminstrn., Hofstra U., 1974. Tchr. curriculum and mentally handicapped Bd. of Coop. Edn. Svcs.- Rosemary Kennedy Ctr., Nassau County, N.Y., 1967-74; tchr., lead tchr. Town of Oyster Bay, Syosset/Woodbury, N.Y., 1970-74; asst. ctr. adminstr. Bd. of Coop. Edn. Svcs., 2d Supervisory Dist., Patchogue, N.Y., 1974-77, dep. asst. dir., 1977-83, dir. spl. edn., 1983-96, dir. instrnl. programs divsn. spl. edn. & occ./tech. edn., 1996—, exec. dir., 1997—; adj. faculty C. W. Post U., Greenvale, N.Y., 1980—; cons. N.Y.C. Bd. Edn., 1981—; adj. prof. Hofstra U., Hempstead, N.Y., 1986—, Dowling Coll., Oakdale, N.Y., 1988—. Pres. chpts. 72 and 653 Coun. Exceptional Children, 1968—; active Nat. Christina Found., 1985—, Suffolk County Handicapped Adv. Bd., Hauppauge, N.Y., 1985—. Rsch. scholar, grantee NSF, 1967; recipient Svc. award Assn. Children with Down's Syndrome, 1981, Stephen Apter Leadership award N.Y. State Educators Emotionally Disturbed, 1989, Comty. Svc. award St. Charles Hosp., 1997. Mem. Phi Delta Kappa (internat. bd. dirs., internat. v.p. 1991-95, internat. pres.-elect 1995-97, pres. 1997—, Outstanding Kappan award 1971-80, Educator of Yr., Columbia U. 1989). Home: PO Box 1392 Patchogue NY 11772-0796 Office: Eastern Suffolk BOCES James Hines Adminstrn Bldg 201 Sunrise Hwy Patchogue NY 11772

FOGARTY, JOHN PATRICK CODY, lawyer; b. Washington, Sept. 12, 1958; m. Sarah Shiffert, Jan. 20, 1989. BA, George Washington U., 1981; JD cum laude, New Eng. Sch. Law, 1984; postgrad., Georgetown U., 1985-87. Bar: Mass. 1985, D.C. 1985. Sr. atty. NLRG, Inc., Charlottesville, Va., 1984-85; atty., editor Environ. Law Inst., Washington, 1985-87; atty. office of toxic substances EPA, Washington, 1987-89, atty. office of enforcement, 1989-91, sr. atty. office of enforcement, 1991-92, asst. enforcement counsel Superfund, 1992-94; assoc. dir. RCRA Enforcement Divsn., Washington, 1995-98; dep. dir. Office of Planning and Policy Analysis, Washington, 1998—; cons. in field; speaker on environ. issues. Co-author: The Clean Water Desk Book, 1988, Environmental Law and Practice, 1992, 94; editor, co-author: Law of Environment Protection, 1987, 90-91, 95-97; contbr. articles to profl. publs. Bd. trustees Sandy Spring Friends Sch., 1998—. New Eng. scholar, 1982. Mem. D.C. Bar Assn., Environ. Law Inst. (assoc.). Mem. Soc. of Friends. Home: 4408 Fairfield Dr Bethesda MD 20814-4743 Office: EPA 1200 Pennsylvania Ave NW Washington DC 20044

FOGARTY, ROBERT STEPHEN, historian, educator, editor; b. Bklyn., Aug. 30, 1938; s. Michael Joseph and Marguerita (Carmody) F.; m. Geraldine Wolpman, Dec. 30, 1961 (div. Apr. 1984); children: David, Suzanne. B.S., Fordham U., 1960; Ph.D., U. Denver, 1968. Instr. Mich. State U., 1963-67; asst. prof. Antioch Coll., Yellow Springs, Ohio, 1968-73; chmn. humanities area Antioch Coll., 1973-74, 78-79, assoc. prof., 1974-80, prof. history, 1980—; prof. Advanced Internat. Studies, Ctr. for Chinese-Am. Johns Hopkins U., 1986-87; editor Antioch Rev., 1977—; dir. Associated Colls. Midwest/Gt. Lakes Coll. Assn., Program in Humanities, Newberry Library, 1978-79; cons. Nat. Endowment for Arts, 1975-81, U. Waterloo, Ont., Can., 1981; vis. fellow NYU Inst. for Humanities, 1992-93; Darwin lectr. human biology Galton Inst., London, 1994. Author: Dictionary of American Communal and Utopian History, 1980, The Righteous Remnant - The House of David, 1981, All Things New: Communes and Utopian Movements, 1860-1914, 1990, Special Love/Special Sex, 1994; editor Antioch Rev., 1977—. Grantee Am. Philos. Soc., 1976, Am. Coun. Learned Socs.; fellow NEH, 1980, All Souls Coll., Oxford U., 1988, Lloyd Lewis fellow Newberry Libr., 1995, Galton Inst. fellow, 1995; recipient Martha K. Cooper award for editl. achievement, 1981. Mem. Am. Studies Assn. (bibliography com. 1981—), Nat. Hist. Communal Sites Assn. (exec. com. 1975-80), Orgn. Am. Historians. Office: Antioch Rev Inc PO Box 148 Yellow Springs OH 45387-0148

FOGED, LESLIE OWEN, mathematician; b. Cheyenne, Wyo., Sept. 26, 1953; s. Leif Clifford and Darlene Ann (Lutz) F.; m. Robyn Rachel Gilliom, May 30, 1981 (div. 1984); 1 child, Leif Erik. BA in Math., Midland Luth. Coll., 1974; PhD in Math., Washington U., St. Louis, 1979. Asst., assoc. prof. U. Tex., El Paso, Tex., 1979—, chmn. dept. math., 1987-88; dir. U. Tex. H.S. Math. Contest, 1990—. Contbr. articles to Pacific Jour. Math., Proceedings Am. Math. Soc., Topology and Its Applications, Topology Proceedings. Recipient Master Tchr. award Midland Luth. Coll., 1991. Achievements include discovery of an internal characterization of topological spaces which are closed images of metric spaces, constrn. of a consistent example of a quotient space of a separable metric space which is not stratifiable; construction of open-compact image of metric space with no point-countable closed quasibase. Office: U Tex at El Paso Dept Math El Paso TX 79968

FOGEL, HENRY, orchestra administrator; b. N.Y.C., Sept. 23, 1942; s. Julius and Dorothy (Levine) F.; m. Frances Sylvia Polner, June 12, 1945; children—Karl Franz, Holly Dana. Student, Syracuse U., 1960-63. Program dir., v.p. Sta. WONO, Syracuse, N.Y., 1963-78; orch. mgr. N.Y. Philharm., N.Y.C., 1978-81; exec. dir. Nat. Symphony Orch., Washington, 1981-85; pres. Chgo. Symphony Orch., 1985—. Record reviewer Fanfare Mag., 1979—; contbr. to Contemporary Composers. Mem. music panel NEA, 1986-90; past pres. U. Ill. Arts Alliance, 1988-94. Mem. NARAS, Am. Symphony Orch. League (bd. dirs. 1988—), Assn. Recorded Sound Collections (record reviewer jour. 1978). Home: 628 Bonnie Brae Pl River Forest IL 60305-1929 Office: Chgo Symphony Orch 220 S Michigan Ave Chicago IL 60604-2501*

FOGEL, IRVING MARTIN, consulting engineer; b. Gloucester, Mass., Apr. 15, 1929; s. Jacob and Ethel (David) F.; children: Ethan, Ronit. BS, Ind. Inst. Tech., 1954, D of Engring. (hon.), 1982. Registered profl. engr., 22 states, Israel. Civil engr. Ill. Hwy. Dept., Peoria, 1954-55; field engr. Peter Kiewit Sons Co., East Gary, Ind., 1955, field engr., progress engr., cost engr., Ogdensburg, N.Y., 1955-56; supt. grading and paving Merritt, Chapman & Scott, Binghamton, N.Y., 1956; cost engr. Drake-Merritt, Goose Bay, Labrador, 1956-57; constrn. mgmt. engr. Mil. Estimating Corp., Madrid, Spain, also P.I., 1957-58; project mgr. Ministry of Def., State of Israel, 1958-59, Frederic R. Harris (Holland) N.V., The Hague, also Tehran, Iran, 1959-61; project mgr. Solel Boneh & Assocs., Addis Ababa, Ethiopia, 1961-63; asst. to tech. dir. Frederic R. Harris, Madrid, 1963-64; chief engr. McKee-Berger-Mansueto, Inc., N.Y.C., 1964-65, v.p. constrn. mgmt., 1965-69; pres. Fogel & Assocs., Inc., N.Y.C., 1969—; lectr. Fellow ASCE (life); mem. NSPE, Am. Arbitration Assn., Am. Assn. Cost Engrs. Internat. Author guides and handbooks on constrn. bus., latest being Construction Owner's Handbook of Property Development, 1992; contbr. articles to profl. jours. Home: 404 E 79th St New York NY 10021-1466 Office: 1170 Broadway New York NY 10001-7507

FOGEL, J(OAN) CATHY, lawyer; b. Chgo., Mar. 18, 1943; d. Norman Jack and Esther Lois (Grobstein) Friedman; m. Jay Bernard Lichtenberg, June 29, 1968 (dec. Apr. 1981); 1 child, Ian Robert; m. Donald Benjamin Fogel, Sept. 27, 1987; children: Alexis Jill, D. Brandon. BS, U. Wis., 1964; JD, Cath. U., 1977. Bar: U.S. Ct.Appeals (D.C. cir.) 1977, D.C. 1978, U.S. Ct. Appeals (7th cir.) 1979, U.S. Ct. Appeals (2d cir.) 1979, U.S. Supreme Ct. 1981, U.S. Ct. Appeals (3d cir.) 1984. Research librarian Library Congress, Washington, 1964-66; legislative research specialist Am. Pub. Power Assn., Washington, 1966-71; assoc. Duncan, Miller & Pembroke, Washington, 1977-83, ptnr., 1983-88; ptnr. Verner, Liipfert, Bernhard, McPherson and Hand, Washington, 1989—; spl. asst. atty. gen. State of N.D., 1979-86. Contbr. articles to profl. jours. Mem. ABA, Women's Bar Assn., D.C. Bar Assn., Fed. Energy Bar Assn. (chmn. fed. power act parts I & II 1985-86, vice-chmn. power mktg. agys. 1988-89, chmn. power mktg. agys. 1989-90). Democrat. Jewish. Avocations: oenophile, travel. Home: 3804 Woodbine St Chevy Chase MD 20815-4957 Office: Verner Liipfert Bernhard McPherson & Hand 901 15th St NW Ste 700 Washington DC 20005-2327

FOGEL, PAUL DAVID, lawyer; b. Santa Monica, Calif., Sept. 19, 1949; s. Phillip and Betty (Distler) F.; m. Yvette Chalom, Feb. 11, 1981; 1 child, Daniele. AB, U. Calif.-Berkeley, 1971; postgrad., U. Paris II, 1972-73; JD, UCLA, 1976. Bar: Calif. 1976, U.S. Dist. Ct. (ctrl. dist.) Calif. 1977, U.S. Dist. Ct. (no. dist.) Calif. 1987, U.S. Supreme Ct. 1990, U.S. Ct. Appeals (9th cir.) 1981. Grad. fellow Ctr. for Law in Pub. Interest, L.A., 1976-77; dep. state pub. def. State Pub. Defender, L.A., 1977-79; Fulbright fellow U. Paris II Law Sch., 1979-80; dep. state pub. def. State Pub. Def., San Francisco, 1980-82; sr. supervising atty. Calif. Supreme Ct., San Francisco, 1982-87; assoc. Hinton & Alfert, Walnut Creek, Calif., 1987-88; assoc. Crosby, Heafey, Roach & May, San Francisco, Calif., 1988-89, ptnr., 1990—; lectr. Am. law USIA, Washington, 1980; lectr. U. Calif. Berkeley Boalt Hall Sch. Law, 1995, practitioner-advisor, 1991-94, 96—. Mem. Calif. Acad. Appellate Lawyers, Calif. State Bar Assn. (chmn. appellate cts. com. 1990-91), Bar Assn. San Francisco (chair appellate practice sect. 1999—), Amnesty Internat. Office: Crosby Heafey Roach & May 4 Embarcadero Ctr Ste 1900 San Francisco CA 94111-4106

FOGEL, RICHARD, lawyer; b. Bklyn.; m. Sheila Feldman; children: Bruce, Lori Ellen. BA, York Coll., CUNY, 1971; JD, N.Y. Law Sch., 1974. Bar: N.J. 1976, U.S. Dist. Ct. N.J. 1976, N.Y. 1981, U.S. Tax Ct. 1977. Tax law specialist IRS, Newark, 1975-77; sr. pension cons., atty. N.Y. Life, N.Y.C., 1977-81; pvt. practice, Franklin, N.J., 1981-85, Wayne, N.J., 1985-88, McAfee, N.J., 1988—; lectr. Inst. for Continuing Legal Edn., Newark, 1977—; mem. adj. faculty Upsala Coll., East Orange, N.J., 1978-88; presenter 34th ann. meeting. Internat. Soc. for Systems Scis., Portland State U., 1990. Recipient Certs. of Appreciation, IRS, Newark, 1977, Inst. Continuing Legal Edn., Newark, 1981-82, 84, Cert. in Recognition of Accomplishments, Coop. Extension Cook Coll., Rutgers U., 1982, Disting. Grad. award York Coll., 1984, Founder's Day Dist. Alumni award, 1992. Home: 28 Elizabeth Dr Sussex NJ 07461-3402 Office: Vernon Colonial Pla PO Box 737 Rt 94 Mc Afee NJ 07428

FOGEL, ROBERT WILLIAM, economist, educator, historian; b. N.Y.C., July 1, 1926; s. Harry Gregory and Elizabeth (Mitnik) F.; m. Enid Cassandra Morgan, Apr. 2, 1949; children: Michael Paul, Steven Dennis. AB, Cornell U., 1948; AM, Columbia U., 1960; PhD, Johns Hopkins U., 1963; MA, U. Cambridge, Eng., 1975, Harvard U., 1976; DSc, U. Rochester, 1987, U. de Palermo, Argentina, 1994, Brigham Young U., 1995. Instr. Johns Hopkins U., 1958-59; asst. prof. U. Rochester, 1960-64; Ford Found. vis. research prof. U. Chgo., 1963-64, asso. prof., 1964-65, prof. econs., 1965-69, prof. econs. and history, 1970-75; prof. econs. U. Rochester, 1968-71, prof. econs. and history, 1972-75; Taussig research prof. Harvard U., Cambridge, Mass., 1973-74; Harold Hitchings Burbank prof. polit. economy, prof. history Harvard U., 1975-81; Charles R. Walgreen Disting. Svc. prof. Am. instns. U. Chgo., 1981—; Pitt prof. Am. history and insts. U. Cambridge, 1975-76; chmn. com. math. and statis. methods in history Math. Social Sci. Bd., 1965-72; rsch. assoc. Nat. Bur. Econ. Rsch., 1978—, dir. DAE program, 1978-91. Author: The Union Pacific Railroad: A Case in Premature Enterprise, 1960, Railroads and American Economic Growth: Essays in Econometric History, 1964, (with others) The Reinterpretation of American Economic History, 1971, (with others) Dimensions of Quantitative Research in History, 1972, (with S.L. Engerman) Time on the Cross: The Economics of American Negro Slavery, 1974, Ten Lectures on the New Economic History, 1977, (with G.R. Elton) Which Road to the Past? Two Views of History, 1983, Without Consent or Contract: The Rise and Fall of American Slavery, Vol. 1, 1989, (with others) Vols. 2-4, 1992. Gilman fellow, 1957-60, Social Sci. Rsch. Coun. fellow, 1960, Ford Found. Faculty Rsch. fellow, 1970; Faculty Rsch. grantee, 1966, NSF grantee, 1967, 70, 72, 75, 76, 78, 92, 93, 94, 95, 96, Fulbright grantee, 1968, NIH grantee, 1991, 92, 93, 94, 95, 96; recipient Arthur H. Cole prize, 1968; Schumpeter prize, 1971; co-recipient The Bancroft prize, 1975, Gustavus Myers prize, 1990; Nobel Prize in Econ. Sci., Nobel Foundation, 1993. Fellow Econometric Soc., Royal Hist. Soc., AAAS; corr. fellow Brit. Acad.; mem. European Acad. Arts, Scis. and Humanities, Am. Econ. Soc. (pres.-elect 1997), Royal Econ. Soc., Econ. History Assn. (trustee 1972-81, pres. 1977-78), Econ. History Soc., Am. Hist. Assn., Assn. Am. Historians, Social Sci. History Assn. (pres. 1980-81), Agrl. History Soc., Am. Acad. Arts and Scis., Nat. Acad. Scis., Population Assn. Am., Internat. Union for Sci. Study of Population, Phi Beta Kappa. Office: U Chgo Grad Sch Bus 1101 E 58th St Chicago IL 60637-1511*

FOGELBERG, PAUL ALAN, continuing education company executive; b. St. Paul, May 18, 1951; s. Harry William and Dorothy Marie (Dokmo) F.; m. Melissa Rosanne Ormsbee, Oct. 1980; children: Emily Lauren, Julia Christine, Sara Ellen. BS, U. Minn., 1975; JD, Hamline U., 1978. Pub. affairs asst. The Pillsbury Co., Mpls., 1974-75; dir. Nat. Practice Inst., Mpls., 1978-81; CEO The Profl. Edn. Group, Inc., Minnetonka, Minn., 1981—. Mem. Hamline U. Pres. Club, Hamline U. Sch. Law Alumni Assn. (Disting. Svc. 1988, pres. 1985-86). Presbyterian. Office: The Profl Edn Group Inc 12401 Minnetonka Blvd Minnetonka MN 55305-3994

FOGELMAN, ALAN MARCUS, internist; b. Bklyn., 1940. BA in Zoology, UCLA, 1962, MD, 1966. Diplomate Am. Bd. Internal Medicine. Intern UCLA Hosp., 1966-67, resident, 1967-68, 70-71, fellow cardiology, 1971-73, prof. medicine, exec. chair dept. medicine. With USN, 1968-70. Mem. ACP, Am. Coll. Cardiology. Office: UCLA Sch Medicine 10833 Le Conte Ave Los Angeles CA 90095-3075*

FOGELMAN, EVAN MARR, literary agent, entertainment consultant, lawyer; b. Dallas, May 1, 1960; s. M.J. Fogelman and Marilyn (Marr) Klepak; div. BA in English, Tulane U., New Orleans, 1982, JD, 1985. Bar: La. 1986, Tex. 1988, D.C. 1991. Lit. agt., gen. counsel Vicki Eisenberg Lit. Agy., Dallas, 1989-90; pres. Fogelman Pub. Interests, Inc., Dallas, 1990-93, Fogelman Media Mgmt., Dallas, 1993—; book reviewer Dallas Morning News, 1989-95. Author: James Joyce's Chamber Music: Songs of Failure, 1982, How To Think About Literary Agency, 1997. Mem. ABA (forum on entertainment law), Lawyers for the Arts, Assn. Author's Reps., Tex. Bar Assn., La. Bar Assn., D.C. Bar Assn., Romance Writers of Am. (advocacy adv., Industry award 1996), Dallas Bar Assn. (exec. coun. sports and entertainment law sect., 1997—, vice chmn. 1998—). Democrat. Jewish. Office: Fogelman Literary Agy 7515 Greenville Ave Ste 712 Dallas TX 75231-3822 also: 599 Lexington Ave Fl 2300 New York NY 10022-6030

FOGELMAN, HAROLD HUGO, psychiatrist; b. Bronx, N.Y., May 12, 1943; s. Benjamin and Ruth (Nachman) F.; m. Sandra Helene Millman, Mar. 16, 1968; children: Joshua Philip, Benjamin Gabriel. BA, NYU, 1965; MD, Albert Einstein Coll. Medicine, 1969. Diplomate Am. Bd. Psychiatry and Neurology. Med. intern Maimonides Med. Ctr., Bklyn., 1969-70; resident in psychiatry Montefiore Hosp. and Med. Ctr., Bronx, 1972-75; fellow in child psychiatry St. Luke's Hosp. Ctr., N.Y.C., 1975-77; pvt. practice Suffern, N.Y., 1977—; chief psychiatrist Child Devel. Ctr., Pomona, N.Y., 1980—; instr. in psychiatry, Columbia U., N.Y.C., 1977—; clin. supr. and assoc. attending, St. Luke's Roosevelt Hosp. Ctr., N.Y.C., 1977—. Editor: Task Force on Arteriosclerosis, 1972. Pres., trustee Nanuet (N.Y.) Union Free Sch. Dist., 1988—. Lt. comdr. USPHS, 1970-72. Mem. Am. Psychiat. Assn., Am. Acad. Child and Adolescent Psychiatry, N.Y. Coun. on Child Psychiatry, N.Y. Acad. Scis. Jewish. Office: 222 Route 59 Suffern NY 10901-5204

FOGELSON, BRIAN DAVID, educational administrator; b. Newton, N.J., Sept. 25, 1953; s. Edwin Malcolm and Marylyn Jean (Post) F. MusB, Westminster Choir Coll., 1975; EdM, Stetson U., 1989; EdD, Fla. State U., 1992. Cert. music tchr. grades K-12, N.J., tchr. class VIII, N.S., Can.; cert. music tchr., tchrs. K-12, adminstr., ednl. leader, Fla.; cert. elem. and secondary prin., Pa. Tchr. Lunenburg County Dist. Sch. Bd., Bridgewater, N.S., 1975-90; grad. asst., coord. alt. tchr. preparation program Stetson U., Deland, Fla., 1988-89; grad. asst., coord. tutors for at risk students Fla. State U., Tallahassee, 1989-92, rsch. assoc., asst. prof., 1992-93; program adminstr. Fla. Acad. for Excellence in Teaching and the Fla. League Tchrs., Fla. State Univ., Tallahassee, 1992-93; asst. prin. Key West (Fla.) H.S., 1993-95; asst. prin. Catasauqua (Pa.) H.S., 1995-97, prin., 1997—; cons. Fla. Sch. Dists., 1989-95, Fla. Dept. Edn., Tallahassee, 1991-95. Vol. asst. conductor Steton U. Children's Chorus, Deland, 1988-89; mem. sect. leader, soloist Tallahassee (Fla.) Community Chorus, 1989-93; dir. Tallahassee Civic Chorale, 1993. Mem. ASCD, NASSP, PASSP, Nat. Assn. Multicultural Edn., Nat. Coun. of the States, Internat. Soc. for Tchr. Edn., Pa. Elem. and Secondary Sch. Prins. Assn., Kappa Delta Pi, Phi Delta Kappa (newsletter editor 1992-93), Free and Accepted Masons (past master), Order of the Ea. Star (past worthy patron). Avocations: reading, singing, golfing. Office: Catasauqua HS 850 Pine St Catasauqua PA 18032-1013

FOGELSON, ROBERT MICHAEL, history educator, writer, consultant; b. N.Y.C., May 19, 1937; s. Nathan B. and Gussie L. (Richman) F. BA, Columbia U., 1958; MA, Harvard U., 1959, PhD, 1964. Asst. prof. history Columbia U., N.Y.C., 1964-68; assoc. prof. urban studies and history MIT, Cambridge, Mass., 1968-74, prof. urban studies and history, 1974—; cons. Pres.'s Commn. on Law Enforcement and Adminstrn. Justice, Washington, 1966; cons. Nat. Adv. Commn. on Civil Disorders, Washington, 1968-69; cons. O'Melveny & Myers, L.A., 1986-87, Mfrs. Hanover Trust Co., N.Y.C., 1990-91. Author: The Fragmented Metropolis: Los Angeles, 1850-1930, 1967, Violence As Protest: A Study of Riots and Ghettos, 1971, Big-City Police, 1977, America's Armories: Architecture, Society, and Public Order, 1989. Frederick Sheldon traveling fellow, 1961-62, Samuel Stouffer fellow, Harvard-MIT Joint Ctr. Urban Studies, 1962-64, Guggenheim fellow, 1973-74; recipient award Graham Found. Advanced Study in Fine Arts, 1984-85. Home: 41 Linnaean St Cambridge MA 02138-1542 Office: MIT 77 Massachusetts Ave # 3-405 Cambridge MA 02139-4301

FOGERTY, JOHN CAMERON, musician, composer; b. Berkeley, Calif., May 28, 1945. Singer, guitarist Creedence Clearwater Revival, 1968-72; solo performer, 1973—; albums include (with Creedence Clearwater Revival)

Creedence Clearwater Revival, 1968, Bayou Country, 1969, Willy & the Poor Boys, 1969, Green River, 1969, Cosmo's Factory, 1970, Pendulum, 1970, Creedence Gold, 1972, Mardi Gras, 1972, More Creedence Gold, 1973, Live in Europe, 1973, Chronicle, Vol. 1, 1976, Vol. 2, 1986, Down on the Corner, 1976, Hot Stuff, 1977, Greatest Hits, 1979, Concert, 1980, Creedence Country, 1981, Rollin' on the River, 1988, Travelin' Band, 1990; (solo) Blue Ridge Rangers, 1973, John Fogerty, 1975, Hoodoo, 1976, Centerfield, 1985, Knockin' on Your Door, 1986, Eye of the Zombie, 1986, Blue Moon Swamp, 1997. Inducted to Rock and Roll Hall of Fame, 1993. Office: Warner Bros 3300 Warner Blvd Burbank CA 91505-4694*

FOGG, BLAINE VILES, lawyer; b. Boston, Mar. 29, 1940; s. Sanford L. and Dorothy (Viles) F.; m. Diane Abitbol, June 22, 1964; children: William, Matthew, Katherine. AB, Williams Coll., 1962; JD, Harvard U., 1965. Bar: N.Y. 1966. Assoc. Skadden, Arps, Slate, Meagher & Flom, N.Y.C., 1966-71, ptnr., 1971—. Office: Skadden Arps Slate 919 3rd Ave New York NY 10022-3902

FOGG, ERNEST LESLIE, minister, retired; b. Butte, Mont., June 4, 1920; s. Ernest L. Fogg Sr. and Gertrude G. (Waller) Fogg-Parker; m. Margaret E. Fogg, June 17, 1943 (dec. Oct. 1962); children: Judith E., Dennis M. (dec.), Stephen William; m. Carolee Little, Sept. 1, 1965; 1 stepchild, Stephen Babcock. BA, Trinity U., San Antonio, 1943; MDiv, McCormick Theol. Seminary, Chgo., 1946; DD (hon.), Mary Holmes Coll., 1981. Ordained to ministry Presbyn. Ch., 1946. Missionary Bd. of Fgn. Missions/Presbyn. U.S.A., Thailand, 1946-59; field exec. Nat. Coun. of Chs., Indonesia, 1959-65; exec. Commn. on Ecumenical Mission and Rels./Presbyn. U.S.A., N.Y.C., 1965-70, Bd. Nat. Missions/Presbyn. U.S.A., N.Y.C., 1970-72; dir., Fund for Indochina World Coun. Chs., Geneva, 1973-76; sr. minister Cen. Presbyn. Ch., Montclair, N.J., 1977-87; chmn. Am. Leprosy Mission, 1979-86. Contbr. articles to profl. jours. Mem. World Affairs Coun., San Antonio. Mem. Rotary (pres. 1986-87). Democrat. Avocation: woodworking. Home: 10782 Oakland Rd San Antonio TX 78240-2025

FOGG, JOSEPH GRAHAM, III, investment banking executive; b. Cleve., Oct. 22, 1946; s. Joseph G. Fogg; m. Leslie Kirk Solbert, Jan. 23, 1971; children: Nathaniel, Elizabeth Piper, Whitney Solbert. BA, Yale U., 1968; MBA, Harvard Bus. Sch., 1970. Dir. advt. Morgan Stanley & Co., N.Y.C., 1970—; chmn., CEO J.G. Fogg Co., Inc., Westbury, N.Y.; bd. dirs. Silicon Magic Corp., Cooperstown, Calif., GST Telecom., Inc., Vancouver, Wash. Office: JG Fogg & Co Inc 1400 Old Country Rd Westbury NY 11590-5156

FOGG, RICHARD LLOYD, food products company executive; b. Boston, Jan. 22, 1937; s. Lloyd Clark and Mildred Ann (Cass) F.; m. Carolyn Ann Kane, Feb. 12, 1966; children—Amanda C., Jennifer S., Timothy L. AB, Bowdoin Coll., Brunswick, Maine, 1959; MBA, Cornell U., 1961. With brand mgmt. dept. Procter & Gamble Co., Cin., 1961-66; dir. mktg. mgmt. Hunt-Wesson Foods, Fullerton, Calif., 1967-76; sr. v.p. Amfac Food Group, Portland, Oreg., 1977; pres. subs. Fisher Cheese Co., Wapakoneta, Ohio, 1978-83; group v.p., COO Land O'Lakes Dairy Foods, Mpls., 1983-93; pres., CEO Orval Kent Food Co., Wheeling, Ill., 1994-96; pvt. investor, 1997—. Mem. Am. Mktg. Assn. E-mail: sonomafogg@aol.com. Fax #: (707) 939-7859.

FOGGE, LEN, advertising executive; b. N.Y.C.; m. Alison Aldrich; children: Adam, Gina, Vanessa. BA in Philosophy, St. Peter's Coll., 1973. Traffic asst. Charles Schlaifer & Co., N.Y.C., 1973, acct. coord., 1974; acct. coord., acct. exec. Grey Entertainment, N.Y.C., 1974-75, account supr., 1977, v.p. account supr., 1979-84, v.p. mgmt. supr., 1984-86, sr. v.p., gen. mgr., 1986-92, pres., 1992-95; pres. Franklin Spier, Inc., N.Y.C., 1995-96; exec. v.p. creative and mktg. Showtime Networks, Inc., 1996—. Home: 299 W 12th St Apt 11-d New York NY 10014-1824 Office: Showtime Networks Inc 1633 Broadway New York NY 10019-6708

FOGIEL, MAX, publishing executive; b. Magdeburg, Germany, Aug. 29, 1929; came to U.S., 1940; s. Abram and Sara (Pergericht) F. BME, Cooper Union U., N.Y.C., 1952; MME, Poly. Inst., Bklyn., 1954; PhD in Elec. Engring., Tech. U., Munich, Germany, 1965. Bar: U.S. Patent Office, 1958; registered profl. engr., N.Y., N.J. Sr. engr. Ford Instrument, Long Island City, N.Y., 1952-56, Control Instrument, Bklyn., 1956-59; rsch. engr. Loral Electronics, Bronx, N.Y., 1959-61; project engr. RCA, N.Y.C., 1961-64; pres., CEO Rsch. & Edn. Assn., Piscataway, N.J., 1964—, dir. engring. seminars, 1964-66; Instr. in elec. engring. N.J. Inst. Tech., 1965-66. Author: Microelectronics, 1968, 73, Life Insurance, 1972, Beauty Care, 1993, AIDS and HIV, 1995, Handbook of Electrical Engineering, 1996, Handbook of Chemical Engineering, 1998, Handbook of Mechanical Engineering, 1998; editor: Problem Solvers, 1973—; pub. H.S. and coll. study guides and handbooks in sci. and tech.; inventor in field. Avocation: oil painting. Home: 44 Maple Ct Highland Park NJ 08904-1922 Office: Rsch & Edn Assn 61 Ethel Rd W Piscataway NJ 08854-5963

FOGLE, G. LEE, credit union executive, consultant; b. Columbia, S.C., Dec. 16, 1948; s. Gordon Lee, Sr. and Toby Elizabon Sease F.; m. Joanna Elizabeth Sutton, Aug. 23, 1970; 1 child, Elizabeth Lindsay. BS in Social Sci., East Carolina U., 1970. Cert. credit union exec. City exec. State Employees Credit Union, Raleigh, N.C., 1976-82; gen. mgr. EMC Employees Credit Union, Raleigh, N.C., 1982-87; pres., CEO S.C. Telco Fed. Credit Union, Greenville, S.C., 1987-92, SPC Coop. Credit Union, Hartsville, S.C., 1993-97; pres. Fed. Credit Union Duke U., Durham, N.C., 1997—; cons. Lamothe Assocs., Charleston, S.C., 1994; past chmn., bd. dirs., S.C. Credit Union League. Bd. visitors Coker Coll., Hartsville; bd. dirs. 1st Carolina Corp. Credit Union, past vice chmn.; past bd. trustees Byerly Hosp.; past chmn. Darlington County Cities in Schs. Named Profl. Yr., Nat. Assn. Fed. Credit Unions, 1992. Mem. Credit Union Execs. Soc., Credit Union Nat. Assn. (past nat. dir.), Rotary (past pres. Hartsville chpt.). Methodist. Avocations: boating, reading. Office: Duke U Fed Credit Union 1400 Morreene Rd Durham NC 27705-4500

FOGLE, JAMES LEE, lawyer; b. Doniphan, Mo., June 6, 1950; s. Carter Lemuel and Leatha Sue (Logan) F.; m. Pattylynn Raymond, Sept. 18, 1982; children: Kirsten Nicole, Ryan Christopher. BA, Whitman Coll., 1972; JD, Duke U., 1975. Bar: Mo. 1975, Ill. 1976. Assoc. Coburn, Croft & Putzell, St. Louis, 1975-79; ptnr. Coburn & Croft, St. Louis, 1979-96, mng. ptnr., 1980-84, mem. mgmt. com., 1985-89; ptnr. Thompson Coburn, St. Louis, 1996—; bd. dirs. Life Skills Found., 1991—, pres. 1996-98; adj. prof. Fontbonne Coll., St. Louis, 1991—. Alumni admissions rep. Whitman Coll., Walla Walla, Wash., 1980—. Nat. Merit scholar Whitman Coll., 1968. Mem. Estate Planning Coun., Mo. Bar Assn. (tax com.), Mo. Athletic Club, Racquet Club, Masons, Order of Coif, Phi Beta Kappa. Republican. Baptist. Avocations: tennis, snow skiing, golf, collecting polit. memorabilia. Office: Thompson Coburn 1 Mercantile Ctr Ste 3200 Saint Louis MO 63101-1643

FOGLE, MARILYN LOUISE KIPLINGER, hospital administrator; b. Put-in-Bay, Ohio, Jan. 10, 1941; d. Harold Kenton and Elizabeth Louise (Glover) Kiplinger; m. Ronald Willard Fogle, June 15, 1963; children: Jeffrey Alan, Kelly Ann. BSN, U. Cin., 1963; MHA, U. Minn., 1984. Staff nurse Massillon (Ohio) Cmty. Hosp., 1963, mem. faculty Sch. Nursing, 1964-66, asst dir. nursing svc., 1966-68, dir. nursing, 1968-80, v.p. patient svcs., 1980—, v.p. profl. support, 1986—; mem. adv. com. United Bank, Massillon, 1994-96, mem. adv. bd., 1996-98. Co-chmn. United Way Campaign, Massillon, 1992—; bd. dirs. ARC, Massillon, 1980—, Am. Cancer Soc., Canton, Ohio, 1980-93. Fellow Am. Coll. Healthcare Execs.; mem. Massillon Club (bd. dirs. 1987-90). Republican. Presbyterian. Avocation: needlework. Office: Massillon Cmty Hosp 875 8th St NE Massillon OH 44646-8503

FOGLEMAN, GUY CARROLL, physicist, mathematician, educator; b. Lake Charles, La., Dec. 29, 1955; s. Louis Carroll and Peggy Joyce (Trahan) F.; m. Jenny S. Kishiyama, Mar. 14, 1993; children: Elyssa Mayumi, Myles Masaru. BS in Physics, La. State U., 1977; MS in Physics, Ind. U., 1979, MA in Math., 1981, PhD in Physics, 1982. Rsch. assoc. Tri Univ. Meson Facility U. B.C., Vancouver, Can., 1982-84; assoc. prof. San Francisco State U., 1984-87, adj. prof., 1987—; project scientist RCA Govt. Svcs., Moffett Field, Calif., 1987-88; prin. investigator Search for Extraterrestrial Intelligence Inst., Mountain View, Calif., 1988-89; mgr. advanced programs life scis. divsn. NASA Hdqrs., Washington, 1990-93; acting chief environ. sys. and tech. br. Life and Biomed Scis. and Applications divsn. NASA Hdqrs., Washington, 1993-95; program exec. human exploration and devel. of space advanced human support techs. program Life Scis. divsn. NASA, Washington, 1996—; vis. physicist Stanford (Calif.) Linear Accelerator Ctr., 1984-86. Contbr. articles to sci. jours. Travel grantee NSF and NATO, 1980; rsch. grantee NASA, 1988, 89. Mem. AIAA, AAAS, Am. Phys. Soc., Prometheus Soc. (ombudsman), Mega Soc., Sigma Xi (assoc.), Sigma Pi Sigma. Achievements include research in physics of particles in microgravity, theoretical elementary particle physics, technologies for the collection of cosmic dust particles, the origins of life. Office: NASA HQ Code UL Washington DC 20546

FOGLEMAN, JOHN ALBERT, lawyer, retired judge; b. Memphis, Nov. 5, 1911; s. John Franklin and Julia (McAdams) F.; m. Annis Adell Appleby, Oct. 24, 1933; children: John Albert, Annis Adell Fogleman Anderson, Mary Barton Fogleman Williams. Student, U. Ark., 1927-31; LLB, U. Memphis, 1934. Bar: Ark. 1934, U.S. Supreme Ct. 1966. Dep. circuit ct. clk. Crittenden County, 1933-34; pvt. practice law, 1934-44; ptnr. Hale & Fogleman, Marion and West Memphis, Ark., 1944-66; dep. pros. atty. Crittenden County, 1946-57; assoc. justice Ark. Supreme Ct., 1967-79, chief justice, 1980; of counsel firm Gill Skokos Simpson Buford & Owen, Little Rock, 1981-86; of counsel Gill and Elrod, 1986-92, Gill, Wallace, Clayton, Fleming, Elrod and Green, Little Rock, 1992-93, Gill, Fleming & Elrod, Little Rock, 1993, Gill Law Firm, 1994—; mem. State Bd. Law Examiners, 1960-63; chmn. Ark. Judiciary Commn., 1963-65; mem. Ark. Constl. Revision Study Commn., 1967, Fed.-State Jud. Council, Ark., 1971-75, Ark. Criminal Code Revision Com., 1972-74; lectr. Sch. Law, U. Ark., Little Rock, 1981; assoc. justice Delta Theta Phi, 1981-93, chief justice, 1993-95. Active Ark. and Crittenden County Democratic central coms., 1937-44. Served from pvt. to 1st lt. JAGD AUS, 1944-45. Fellow Am. Coll. Trial Lawyers, Am. Bar Found., Ark. Bar Found.; mem. Ark. Bar Assn. (past pres.), NE Ark. Bar Assn. (past pres.), Crittenden County Bar Assn. (past pres.), Pulaski County Bar Assn., Masons, Rotary (charter, past pres. Marion club). Home: PO Box 77 Marion AR 72364-0077 Office: Gill Law Firm 3801 TCBY Bldg Capitol at Broadway Little Rock AR 72201

FOGLEMAN, JULIAN BARTON, lawyer; b. Memphis, Apr. 17, 1920; s. John Franklin and Marie Julia (McAdams) F.; m. Melba Margaret Henderson, Aug. 11, 1950; children: Margaret Elisabeth Heath, Julian Barton, John Nelson, Jennifer Leigh Vaughan, Frances Lorie Irwin. B.S., U. Ark., 1941, LL.B., 1943, J.D., 1969. Bar: Ark. 1943. Practiced in Marion, 1946-54, West Memphis, 1954—, pvt. practice, 1946-52; assoc. Hale & Fogleman, 1952-66, ptnr., 1967-73; ptnr. Hale, Fogleman & Rogers, 1974—; city atty., Marion, 1951-81, dep. pros. atty., 1957-64. Chmn. fin. dir. Crittenden dist. Chickasaw coun. Boy Scouts Am., 1969, mem. exec. bd. coun., 1970-71, 75-80; bd. dirs. Crittenden County Charities, 1994-97, v.p., 1995; bd. dirs. Ark. Good Rds. Transp. Coun., 1976-96; mem. Ark. Cmty. Based Rehab. Commn., 1978-86, Crittenden County Bd. Edn., 1987-92. With inf. AUS, 1943-45, ETO. Fellow Am. Bar Found., Ark. Bar. Found. (bd. dirs. 1989-92)); mem. ABA, Ark. Bar Assn. (ho. of dels. 1972-75, 81-84, exec. council 1972-75, 81-84, outstanding lawyer citizen award 1995-96), N.E. Ark. Bar Assn. (past pres.), Crittenden County Bar Assn. (past pres.), Phi Alpha Delta, Sigma Chi. Methodist. Home: 84 Turner Ave Marion AR 72364-1932 Office: PO Box 1666 108 Dover Rd West Memphis AR 72301-2606

FOGLEMAN, RONALD ROBERT, retired air force officer, consultant; b. Juniata County, Pa., Jan. 27, 1942; s. Harry R. and Sara (Landis) F.; m. M. Jane Lauver, June 22, 1963; children: Harry R., William E. BS, USAF Acad., 1963; MA, Duke U., 1971. Commd. 2d lt. USAF, 1963, advanced through grades to gen., 1992, fighter, mobility and command pilot; chief Tactical Forces Div., The Pentagon, Washington, 1979-81; vice comdr. 388th Tactical Fighter Wing, Hill AFB, Utah, 1981-82; dir. fighter ops. Hdqrs. Tactical Air Command, Langley AFB, Va., 1982-83; comdr. 56th Tactical Tng. Wing, MacDill AFB, Fla., 1983-84, 836th Air Div., Davis-Monthan AFB, Ariz., 1984-86; dep. dir. Programs and Procedure, Hdqrs. USAF, Washington, 1986-88, dir., 1988-90; comdr. 7th Air Force, 1990-92; comdr. in chief U.S. Transp. Command, 1992-94; comdr. Air Mobility Command, 1992-94; chief of staff USAF, Washington, 1994-97, ret. gen., 1997; bd. dirs. Mesa Airgroup, N.Am. Airlines, So. Air Transport, World Airways, Rolls-Royce N.Am. Bd. dirs. Ft. Lewis Coll. Found. Mem. Air Force Assn., USAF Acad. Assn. Grads., Daedalians (flight capt. 1983-84, 89-90), Nat. Aviation Club (bd. dirs. Arlington, Va. chpt. 1986—), Coun. Fgn. Rels. Republican. Methodist. Avocation: rugby. Home: 406 Snow Cap Ln Durango CO 81301-3636*

FOGLE O'KEEFE, MAUREEN ANN, nursing administrator; b. Lawrence, Mass.; d. James Joseph and Dorothy Helen (Hylan) O'Keefe. ADN, North Shore Community Coll., 1974; BS in Health Sci., Northeastern U., Boston, 1976; MEd, U. N.H., 1981; MBA, Pfeiffer U., 1998. Cert. CCRN, CNA, CAGS. Staff nurse Hale Hosp., Havenhill, Mass., 1978; charge nurse Amesbury (Mass.) Hosp., 1979-86; instr. critical care Amesbury Hosp., Mass.; dir. telemetry unit Mercy Hosp., Charlotte, N.C., 1989—. Home: 1062 Woodlake Ln Fort Mill SC 29715-8559

FOGLESONG, ROBERT H., lieutenant general United States Air Force; m. Mary Foglesong; children: David, Mark. BS in Chem. Engring., W. Va. U., 1968, MSc in Chem. Engring., 1969, PhD in Chem. Engring., 1971; student, Nat. War Coll., Ft. Lesley McNair, Washington, 1989; participant, Seminar XXI MIT, on Fgn. and Internat. Rels., 1996. Commd. 2d lt. USAF, 1972, advanced through grades to lt. gen., 1997; instr. pilot 557th Flying Tng. Squadron USAF Acad., Peterson Field, Colo., 1973-76; aide de campe to comdr. Air Forces Korea, 314th Air Divsn., Osau Air Base, S. Korea, 1976-77; instr. pilot, comdr. ops. officer, spl. asst to NORAD region comdr. USAF, Malmstrom AFB, Mont., 1977-80; pilot, squadron scheduler, 9th tactical fighter squadron chief quality 49th figher wing, comdr repair squadron USAF, Holloman AFB, N. Mex., 1980-82; spl. asst. tactical issues, exec. officer dep. chief of rsch , devel. and acquisiton Headqtrs USAF, Washington, 1983-85; spl. asst. to comdr., chief combat analysis divsn. Hdqs. Tactical Air Command, Langley AFB, Va., 1985-87; chief of staff of the air force, chair, prof. joint and combined warfare Nat. War Coll. Ft. Lesley McNair, Washington, 1988-90; pilot F-16, chief of maintenance, 347th Air Tactical Wing USAF, Moody AFB, Ga., 1990-91; comdr. 14 flying tng. wing USAF, Columbus AFB, Miss., 1993; cmdr. 51st fighter wing USAF, Osau Air Base, S. Korea, 1994-95; dep. dir. for politico-mil. affairs Joint Staff, Washington, 1995-97; asst. to chmn. Joint Chiefs of Staff Pentagon, Washington, 1997—. Contbr. 37 articles to mil. and profl. jours. Decorated Defense Superior Svc. medal, Legion of Merit with oak leaf cluster, Meritorious Svc. medal with 3 oak leaf clusters, Aerial Achievement medal with 2 oak leaf clusters, Air Force Commendation medal with 2 oak leaf clusters, Air Force Achievement medal, Korean Nat. Serurity medal (Samil), Korean Nat. Security medal (Cheon-Su). Office: 9999 Joint Staff Pentagon Washington DC 20310-9999

FOGLIETTA, THOMAS MICHAEL, diplomat, former congressman; b. Philadelphia, Pa., Dec. 3, 1928; s. Michael and Rose (Buttari) F. B.A., St. Joseph's Coll.; postgrad., Temple U. Bar: Pa., U.S. Supreme Ct. Pvt. practice law Phila.; mem. 97th-105th Congresses from 1st Pa. dist., Washington, D.C., 1981-97, Phila. City Coun.; U.S. amb. to Italy U.S. Dept. State, Rome, 1997—; mem. subcom. Mil. Constrn. Transp. Appropriations, Congl. Human Rights Caucus, Congl. Arts Caucus, Congl. Narcotics Caucus, Congl. Hispanic Caucus; founder and chmn., Congl. Urban Caucus, Congl. Black Caucus. Mem. Dem. Study group. Democrat. Roman Catholic. Office: US Amb to Italy William J Green Bldg 10402 US State Dept Washington DC 20521-9500*

FOHL, TIMOTHY, consulting and investment company executive; b. Pitts., Apr. 21, 1934; s. Edward Zinn and Dorothy (Umbenhauer) F.; m. Nancy Lee Hattox, Apr. 15, 1961; children: Nicholas, Jeffrey, Peter. AB, Dartmouth Coll., 1956; MS, MIT, 1959, PhD, 1963; postgrad. exec. devel. program, Whittemore Sch. Bus. and Econs., 1977. Rsch. scientist Itek Corp., Lexington, Mass., 1962-63; rsch. scientist Mt. Auburn Rsch. Assocs., Newton, Mass., 1963-68, prin. scientist, dir., 1968-72; with GTE Products Corp., Danvers, Mass., 1972-79, mgr. new product devel. lighting group, 1977-82, mgr. engring. devel., 1982-85, dir. engring. devel., 1985-88; scientist GTE Labs., Inc., Waltham, Mass., 1988-92; pres. Tech. Integration Group, Carlisle, Mass., 1992—; v.p. Light Time in Space, Inc., 1993—. *Dr. Fohl is president and founder of the Technology Integration Group, Inc., a firm which locates, adapts and develops new technology and resources for clients in the fields of lighting and optics. Often these programs are based on unique methods of technology analysis and forecasting which have been recently featured in articles in the Wall Street Journal and Photonics Spectra magazine. An example of TIG's work is a revolutionary laser based lighting system recently announced by Ford Motor Co. TIG programs have resulted in numerous patents and internal awards for clients.* Contbr. articles to profl. jours.; patentee in field. Pres., trustee Carlisle Conservation Found., 1972-79; v.p. Carlisle Trails Assn., 1975—; fin. chmn. Town Republican Com., 1980. Recipient Leslie H. Warner Tech. Achievement award, 1990. Mem. Mass. Bus. Roundtable. Home: 681 South St Carlisle MA 01741-1517

FOHRMAN, BURTON H., lawyer; b. Chgo., July 9, 1939; s. Max and Helen (Naparty) F.; m. Raleigh S. Newman, Dec. 12, 1975. AB cum laude, U. So. Calif., Los Angeles, 1960; JD, UCLA, 1963. Bar: Calif. 1964. Pvt. practice Riverside, Calif., 1964-66; mng. ptnr. Redwine and Sherrill, Riverside, 1966-83; ptnr. Jones, Day, Reavis and Pogue, L.A., 1983-92, former chmn. gen. real estate sect.; ptnr. White & Case, L.A., 1999—. Editor Calif. Real Property Jour., 1978-83. Mem. State Bar Calif. (chmn. real property sect. 1983), Los Angeles County Bar Assn. (chmn. real property fin. com. 1979-80, exec. com. real property sect. 1980-83). Office: White & Case LLP 633 W 5th St Ste 1900 Los Angeles CA 90071-2005*

FOIL, DONALD CARL, accountant; b. Bogalusa, La., Oct. 22, 1946; s. Edward Everett Sr. and Constance Mercedes (Chastant) F. BSBA, U. So. Miss., 1973. Cert. La. sch. bus. offcl., govt. fin. officer, govt. fin. mgr. Sr. auditor Office of the Legis. Auditor, State of La., Baton Rouge, 1974-88; chief acct. St. Tammany Parish Sch. Bd., Covington, La., 1988—; edn. fin. adv. com. State of La., State Dept. of Edn., Baton Rouge, 1990—. Vol. Slidell H.S., 1984—. Sgt. lt. comdr. U.S. Army, 1965-70, USCGR, 1976—. Named La.'s Outstanding Mil. Pers., 1995. Mem. Govt. Fin. Officers Assn. of La. (pres., bd. dirs. 1988—), Southeastern Assn. Sch. Bus. Officers (state dir. 1994-96), Assn. Govt. Accts., Am. Legion, Res. Officers Assn. Republican. Roman Catholic. Avocations: bicycling, cooking, various charitable organizations. Home: 1020 Rue Corton Slidell LA 70458-2202 Office: St Tammany Parish Sch Bd 212 W 17th Ave Covington LA 70433-3162

FOIS, ANDREW, lawyer, educator; b. N.Y.C., June 16, 1958; s. Andrew D. and Lucy (Monaco) F. BA, Georgetown U., 1979; MA, U. Essex, Eng., 1981; JD, Georgetown U., 1983. Bar: Fla. 1983, N.Y. 1984, U.S. Dist. Ct. D.C. 1986, U.S. Ct. Appeals (D.C. cir.) 1985, D.C. 1985. Asst. state's atty. State's Atty.'s Office County of Dade, Miami, Fla., 1983; pres., chief exec. officer Andrew D. Fois and Co., Inc., North Merrick, N.Y., 1983-85; legis. fellow U.S. Senate, Washington, 1985; asst. U.S. atty. U.S. Attys. Office, Washington, 1985-89; counsel crime subcom. Ho. Judiciary Commn., Washington, 1989-92, chief counsel, 1992-95; asst. attorney genl., legis. affairs Dept. of Justice, Washington, 1995; hon. atty. Venable, Baetjer, Howard, Civiletti LLP, Washington, 1998—; adj. instr. in law Am. U. Washington Coll. of Law, 1989-91, Georgetown U. Law Ctr., Washington, 1990—. Co-editor: Federal Grand Jury Practice, 1983, Criminal Practice Institute Trial Manual, 1986, (book rev.) Regulation by Prosecution, 1982. Speaker U.S.A.O., Washington, 1986—; vol. house capt. Christmas in April, Washington, 1985—; mem. Nat. Dems. Club, Washington, 1985—, Dems. for New Direction, Washington, 1989—. Mem. ABA, D.C. Bar Assn., U.S. Atty.'s Assn., Fraternal Order of Police (assoc.), Ho. Legis. Assts. Assn. Roman Catholic. Office: Venable Baetjer Howard Civiletti LLP Ste #1000 1201 New York Ave NW Washington DC 20005-6192*

FOK, THOMAS DSO YUN, civil engineer; b. Canton, China, July 1, 1921; came to U.S., 1947, naturalized, 1956; s D. H. and C. (Tse) F.; m. Maria M.L. Liang, Sept. 18, 1949. B.Eng., Nat. Tung-Chi U., Szechuan, China, 1945; M.S., U. Ill., 1948; M.B.A. Dr. Nadler Money Marketeer scholar, NYU, 1950; Ph.D., Carnegie-Mellon U., 1956. Registered profl. engr., N.Y., Pa., Ohio, Ill., Ky., W.Va., Ind., Md., Fla. Structural designer Lummus Co., N.Y.C., 1951-53; design engr. Richardson, Gordon & Assocs., cons. engrs., Pitts., 1956-58; assoc. prof. engring. Youngstown U., Ohio, 1958-67, dir. computing ctr., 1963-67; ptnr. Cernica, Fok & Assocs., cons. engrs., Youngstown, Ohio, 1958-64; prin. Thomas Fok & Assocs., cons. engrs., Youngstown, Ohio, 1964-65; ptnr. Mosure-Fok & Syrakis Co., Ltd., cons. Engrs., Youngstown, Ohio, 1965-76; cons. engr. to Mahoning County Engr. Ohio, 1960-65; pres. Computing Systems & Tech., Youngstown, Ohio, 1967-72; chmn. Thomas Fok and Assocs., Ltd., cons. engrs., Youngstown, Ohio, 1977—. Contbr. articles to profl. jours. Trustee Pub. Libr. of Youngstown and Mahoning County, 1973—; trustee Youngstown State U., 1975-84, chmn., 1981-83; mem. Ohio State Bd. Registration for Profl. Engrs. and Surveyors, 1992-96. Recipient Walter E. and Caroline H. Watson Found. Disting. Prof.'s award Youngstown U., 1966, Outstanding Person award Mahoning Valley Tech. Socs. Council, 1987. Fellow ASCE; mem. Am. Concrete Inst., Internat. Assn. for Bridge and Structural Engring., Am. Soc. Engring. Edn., Nat. Soc. Profl. Engrs., AAAS, Soc. Am. Mil. Engrs., Ohio Acad. Sci., N.Y. Acad. Sci., Sigma Xi, Beta Gamma Sigma, Sigma Tau, Delta Pi Sigma. Lodge: Rotary. Achievements include development of a design method by computer for a solid-ribbed tied, through arch Ft. Duquesne Bridge; development of Analysis of Continuous Truss by Digital Computer. Home: 325 S Canfield Niles Rd Youngstown OH 44515-4020 Office: 3896 Mahoning Ave Youngstown OH 44515-3022

FOLAND, KENNETH A., geological sciences educator; b. Frederick, Md., May 25, 1945; s. Austin Franklin and P. Lillian (Wachter) F.; m. Ellen Lee Spero, June 18, 1968. BS, Bucknell U., 1967; MSc, Brown U., 1969, PhD, 1972. Postdoctoral fellow U. Pa., Phila., 1972-73, from asst. prof. to assoc. prof., 1973-80; assoc. prof. Ohio State U., Columbus, 1980-87, prof. geological scis., 1987—; cons. divsn. nuclear chemistry Lawrence Livermore Nat. Lab., 1982-86, adv. com. nuclear waste U.S. Nuclear Regulatory Commn., 1990—; mem. indoor radon panel Am. Lung Assn. Ohio, mem. steering and rev. com. Columbus and Franklin County Radon Study, Columbus Health Dept. Assoc. editor Isotope Geosci., 1982-99, Jour. Geophys. Rsch., Solid Earth, 1992-98; reviewer rsch. papers, rsch. proposals; author, co-author numerous rsch. papers, abstracts, revs.; adv. editor: Jour. Geol. Soc. Recipient NSF and NIH grants, 1973—, Deutscher Akademischer Austauschdienst grant Max Planck Inst., Mainz, 1982, Collaborative Rsch. grant NATO, 1986-92. Fellow Geol. Soc. Am.; mem. Am. Geophys. Union, Geochem. Soc., Sigma Xi. Home: 4090 Fenwick Rd Columbus OH 43220-4870 Office: Ohio State U 125 South Oval Mall 379 Mendenhall Lab Columbus OH 43210

FOLBERG, HAROLD JAY, lawyer, mediator, educator, university dean; b. East St. Louis, Ill., July 7, 1941; s. Louis and Matilda (Ross) F.; m. Diana L. Taylor, May 1, 1983; children: Lisa, Rachel, Ross. BA, San Francisco State U., 1963; JD, U. Calif., Berkeley, 1968. Bar: Oreg. 1968. Assoc. Rives & Schwab, Portland, Oreg., 1968-69; dir. Legal Aid Service, Portland, 1970-72; exec. dir. Assn. Family and Conciliation Cts., Portland, 1974-80; prof. law Lewis and Clark Law Sch., Portland, 1972-89; clin. asst. prof. child psychiatry U. Oreg. Med. Sch., 1976-89; judge pro-tem Oreg. Trial Cts., 1974-89; dean, prof. U. San Francisco Sch. Law, 1989—; chair jud. coun. Calif. Task Force on Alternative Dispute Resolution and the Jud. Sys., 1998—; Rockefeller Found. scholar in residence Bellagio, Italy, 1996; vis. prof. U. Wash. Sch. Law, 1985-86; mem. vis. faculty Nat. Jud. Coll., 1975—; mem. Nat. Commn. on Accreditation for Marriage and Family Therapists, 1984-90; cons. Calif. Jud. Coun., U.S. Dist. Ct. (no. dist.) Calif. Author: Joint Custody and Shared Parenting, 1984, 2d edit., 1991; (with Taylor) Mediation-A Comprehensive Guide to Resolving Conflicts without Litigation, 1984; (with Milne) Divorce Mediation-Theory and Practice, 1988; mem. editorial bd. Conciliation Cts. Rev., Jour. of Divorce, Mediation Quar.; contbr. articles to profl. jours. Bd. dirs. Internat. Bioethics Inst., 1989-95, Oreg. Dispute Resolution Adv. Coun., 1988-89. Mem. ABA (chmn. mediation and arbitration com. family law sect. 1980-82), Oreg. State Bar Assn. (chmn. family and juvenile law sect. 1979-80), Am. Bd. Trial Advs., Multnomah Bar Assn. (chmn. bd. dirs. legal aid svc. 1973-76), Am. Arbitration Assn. (mem. panel of arbitrators), Internat. Soc. Family Law, Assn. Family and Conciliation Cts. (pres. 1983-84), Assn. Marriage and Family Therapists (disting. mem.), Am. Assn. Law Schs. (chmn. alternative dispute resolution sect. 1988), Acad. Family Mediators (bd. dirs., pres. 1988), Soc.

Profls. in Dispute Resolution, World Assn. Law Profs. (sec.-gen. 1995—). Office: U San Francisco Sch Law 2130 Fulton St San Francisco CA 94117-1080

FOLDA, JAROSLAV THAYER, III, art historian; b. Balt., July 25, 1940; s. Jaroslav T. Jr. and Rosalie M. (Gilbert) F.; m. Linda E. Whitham, July 25, 1964; children: Natasha K., Lisa K. AB, Princeton U., 1962; PhD, Johns Hopkins U., 1968. Instr. art history U. N.C., Chapel Hill, fall 1968, asst. prof., 1968-72, assoc. prof., 1972-78, prof., 1978-96, N. Ferebee Taylor prof., 1996—, chmn. dept. art, 1983-87. Author: Crusader Manuscript Illumination at St.-Jean d'Acre: 1275-1291, 1976, The Nazareth Capitals and the Crusader Shrine of the Annunciation, 1986, The Art of Crusaders in the Holy Land, 1098-1187, 1995. Rsch. grantee Fulbright Commn., Paris, 1966-67, jr. fellow, Dumbarton Oaks, 1967-68, NEH, 1974-75, 81-82, 98-99, John Simon Guggenheim Meml. Found., 1988-89; vis. scholar J. Paul Getty Mus., Malibu, Calif., 1995; fellow Nat. Humanities Ctr., 1988-89, 98-99. Mem. Am. Soc. Oriental Rsch., Soc. Study of the Crusades (gen. sec. 1983-89), Medieval Acad. Am. (Haskins medal 1999), Coll. Art Assn. Am., Soc. Française Archéologie, U.S. Nat. Com. Byzantine Studies. Office: UNC Dept Art Chapel Hill NC 27599-3405

FOLDEN, NORMAN C. (SKIP FOLDEN), information systems executive, consultant; b. San Francisco, July 28, 1933. BS in Math./English/Engring., U.S. Mil. Acad., 1956. With IBM, various locations, 1966-83; U.S. program mgr. I/S tech. IBM, Sommers, N.Y., 1983-86; owner Folden Mgmt. (Palladin Advocacy), Westchester, N.Y., 1986-91, Folden Mgmt., Las Vegas, 1991—. Author: Drug Criminalization: Organized Crime Cash Cow, Prime Cause of U.S. Victim Crime and Threat to National Sovereignty, 1996, Delegation of Legislative Authority, 1997, Payback to Lippo Group or Grand Coincidence at Grand Staircase, 1997, Kosovo Negotiations Provisions-Five by Five Plan, 1999. Mem. Internat. Platform Assn., Assn. Grads. U.S. Mil. Acad., The Federalist Soc., Little Big Horn Assocs., Calif. Scholarship Fedn. Avocations: ancient history/teachings/exploration, organized crime and drug policy, antiquities, constitutional law. Home and Office: 4329 Silvercrest Ct North Las Vegas NV 89030-0116

FOLDI, ANDREW HARRY, retired singer, educator; b. Budapest, Hungary, July 20, 1926; came to U.S., 1939, naturalized, 1947; s. Alexis and Ann Foldi; children from previous marriage: David John, Nancy Susanne; m. Marta Justus. PhB, U. Chgo., 1945, MA, 1948; pvt. student singing and piano. Pvt. tchr. voice, 1949-61; cantor, mus. dir. Temple Isaiah Israel, Chgo., 1949-61, English-Speaking Jewish Community of Geneva, 1963-71; vis. prof. voice and music Cleve. Inst. Music, 1978-81; chmn. opera dept. Cleve. Inst. Mus., 1981-91; dir. Chgo. Lyric Opera Ctr. for Am. Artists, 1991-95; ret., 1995; mem. faculty U. Chgo., 1947-49, dept. adult edn., 1951-61; instr., dir. opera workshop DePaul U., 1949-57; vis. instr. voice Augustana Coll., 1950-51; mem. faculty apprentice tng. program Santa Fe Opera, 1959, 64, 76, 77; also stage dir.; stage dir. Pa. Opera Festival, 1982, 83, Utah Opera, 1986, 88, 91, Wolf Trap Festival, 1987, Toledo Opera, 1987, 89, Atlanta Opera, 1989, Chgo. Opera Theater, 1990, Chgo. Lyric Opera Ctr., 1992. Author: recorded text An Introduction to Music, 1959; also criticism, program notes; contbr. articles to profl. publs.; Leading bass, Met. Opera, N.Y.C., La Scala, Milan, Vienna Staatsoper, Teatro San Carlo, Naples, Vienna Festival, Grand Théâtre, Geneva, Théâtre Royale de la Monnaie, Brussels, Teatro Regio, Torino, Am. Nat. Opera, Cin. Opera, Stadttheater, Zurich, Teatro Comunale, Genoa, Nederlandsche Opera, Amsterdam, San Francisco Opera Co., Lyric Opera Chgo., Santa Fe Opera, Sociedad Pro Arte Mus., Havana, Cuba; guest soloist, Vienna Festival, Bavarian State Radio, Munich, Concertgebouw Orch., Amsterdam, Orch. de la Suisse Romande, Geneva, Nat. Orch. Monte Carlo, Pitts. Symphony Orch., Clarion Concerts, N.Y., Gulbenkian Found., Lisbon, Concerti sinfonici, Genoa, Atlanta Symphony Orch., Aldeburgh, Lucerne, Lausanne, Ravinia, Glyndebourne, Florence Maggio Musicale festivals, Chgo. Symphony Orch., N.Y. Philharmonic Orch., Boston Symphony, Cleve. Orchestra, San Francisco Symphony, Little Orch. Soc., N.Y., Rochester, Kansas City (Mo.) philharmonic orchs., Radio Sottens, Geneva, Radio Beromunster, Zurich, Grant Park Concerts, Chgo., Indpls. Symphony Orch., Internat. Soc. Contemporary Music, also numerous recitals, radio and TV appearances, recordings for Columbia, Vanguard, Concert Hall, La Voix d'Eglise.

FOLEY, CHARLES BRADFORD, university dean, music educator; b. Indpls., Jan. 30, 1953; s. Charles Lyman and Barbara Ann (Shaw) F.; m. Diane Ellen Berger, June 6, 1976; children: Carolyn Berger, David Bradford. BA with honors, Ball State U., 1975; MusM, U. Mich., 1977, D of Musical Arts, 1983. Grad. tchg. asst. U. Mich., Ann Arbor, 1975-77; instr. Stephen F. Austin State U., Nacogdoches, Tex., 1977-79; instr. East Carolina U., Greenville, N.C., 1979-81, asst. prof., 1981-86, assoc. prof., 1986-92, prof., 1992—, asst. dean Sch. Music, 1984-95, dean Sch. Music, 1995—, mem. adv. bd. Friends of Music, 1984—, mem. adv. bd. Music Alumni Soc., 1985—. Contbr. articles to profl. jours.; performer Brad Foley in Concert, 1984, soloist, chamber music, 1979—. Pres., bd. dirs. Greenville Choral Soc. and New Carolina Sinfonia, 1990-91. Grantee So. Arts Fedn., 1997-99, A.J. Fletcher Found., 1995-99, Presser Found., 1995-99, N.C. Arts Coun., 1997. Mem. N.Am. Saxophone Alliance (regional dir. 1982-88, treas. 1988-93, jour. editor 1989), N.C. Music Tchrs. Assn., Music Tchrs. Nat. Assn. Methodist. Avocations: reading fiction, swimming, travel. E-mail: foleyc@mail.ecu.edu. Fax: 252-328-4780. Home: 1316 Largo Rd Greenville NC 27858-6035 Office: East Carolina U Sch Music Greenville NC 27858

FOLEY, CHERYL M., company executive. V.p., gen. counsel PSI Energy, Inc., Ind., 1989-91; v.p., gen. counsel, corp. sec. PSI Energy, Inc. and PSI Resources Inc., Ind., 1991-94; v.p., sec., gen. counsel Cinergy Corp., Cin., 1994—; pres. Cinergy Global Resources subs. Cinergy Corp., Cin. Office: Cinergy Corp 221 E 4th St # 30 Cincinnati OH 45202-4124*

FOLEY, DANIEL RONALD, business and personnel executive; b. Chgo., Dec. 13, 1941; s. Daniel Edward and Louise Jean (Connolly) F.; m. Mae Geraldine Muscarello, Jan. 30, 1965; children: Louise Ann, Sarah Elizabeth. AB in Psychology, Marquette U., 1965; JD, Depaul U., 1971. Bar: Ill 1971, U.S. Dist. Ct. (no. dist.) Ill. 1971, U.S. Supreme Ct. 1975, Mich. 1989. Pers. recruiter Civil Svc. Commn. City of Chgo., 1965-66; pers. adminstr. Alberto Culver Co., Melrose Park, Ill., 1966-67; pers. dir. Litton Industries, Des Plaines, Ill., 1967-68; equal opportunity coord., mgr. labor rels. Canteen Corp., Chgo., 1968-71; mgr. labor rels. Internat. Telephone and Telegraph World Hdqs., N.Y.C., 1971-79, dir. employee rels., 1979-81, 1981-85; dir. employee rels., environ. health and safety, group v.p. human resources IBP, Dakota City, Nebr., 1985-88; v.p. adminstrn., gen. counsel Domino's Pizza Inc., Ann Arbor, Mich., 1988-93; pres. Exec. Bus. Ptnrs., Inc., 1993-94; v.p. human resources MascoTech, Inc., 1994-96, Masco Corp., 1996—; speaker labor law and bus. seminars, Wharton Sch. U. Pa., St. Mary's Coll., U. Mich., LEGATUS. Mem. Knights of Malta. Roman Catholic (deacon). Avocation: photography. Home: 3399 Robinwood Dr Ann Arbor MI 48103-1748

FOLEY, DAVID, television and film actor; b. Toronto, Jan. 4, 1963. Appeared in films High Stakes, 1986, Three Men and a Baby, 1987, It's Pat, 1994, Hacks, 1997, A Bug's Life (voice), 1998, The Wrong Guy, 1998, Monkey Bone, 1999, Blast from the Past, 1999, Dick, 1999; appeared in TV series Kids in the Hall, 1989, NewsRadio, 1995. Address: care SAG 5757 Wilshire Blvd Los Angeles CA 90036

FOLEY, DAVID E., bishop; b. Worcester, Mass., Feb. 3, 1930. Student, St. Charles Coll., Catonsville, Md., St. Mary's Sem., Balt. ordained priest Roman Cath. Ch., 1952, ordained titular bishop of Octaba and Aux. bishop of Richmond, VA, 1986. Aux. bishop of Richmond Roman Cath. Ch. Va., 1986-94; bishop Diocese of Birmingham, 1994—. Office: Chancery Office PO Box 12047 Birmingham AL 35202-2047*

FOLEY, DAVID W., career officer; b. Toledo, Mar. 28, 1947. Commd. officer U.S. Army, advanced through grades to brig. gen., commdg. gen. Criminal Investigation Command, 1998—. Office: US Army Criminal Investigation Comm 6010 6th St Fort Belvoir VA 22060

FOLEY, EUGENE ARTHUR, pastor; b. San Jose, Calif., May 6, 1953; s. Eugene Frank and Shirley Ann (Merrill) F.; m. Elaine Sayre, July 9, 1995; children: Eugene Welles, Patrick Michael, Brian Ross. BSBA, U. Hartford, 1976; MS in Taxation, Golden Gate U., 1979; MDiv, Princeton Theol. Sem., 1994. CPA, Calif., N.J.; cert. mgmt. acct., info. systems auditor, computer profl., internal auditor. Acct. J.K. Lasser et al, San Jose, 1976-79; internal auditor Carter Hawley Hale, Los Angeles, 1979-81; lectr., asst. prof. Calif. State U., Sacramento, 1979-84; owner, cons. E.A. Foley Accountancy, Sacramento, 1981-84; corp. audit mgr. Emhart Corp., Farmington, Conn., 1984-86; controller Powers Mfg. div. Emhart Corp., Elmira, N.Y., 1986-88; owner, cons. Foley Cos., Elmira, N.Y., 1988-92; asst. prof. Rider U., Lawrenceville, N.J., 1992-94; asst. Christian edn. Cold Spring Presbyn. Ch., 1993-96; pastor Court House Presbyn. Ch., 1996—; bus. mgr. Calif. Polit. Rev., 1987—. Sec.-treas., exec. dir. Elmira YMCA, 1986-87; treas. Supreme Ct. Project, Calif., 1985-86; v.p. fin., 1987, treas., 1988, Sullivan Trail Council Boy Scouts Am., dist. commr. George Washington Coun., 1992-94, So. N.J. Coun., 1994-96, dist. exec., 1996—; treas. Calif. Pub. Policy Found., 1987—; mgr., CFO Lower Township, N.J., 1996-97. Recipient Whitney M. Young Jr. Svc. award Boy Scouts Am. Mem. Am. Inst. CPA's, Calif. Soc. CPA's, Inst. Internal Auditors (cert.), Inst. Mgmt. Accts., EDP Auditors Assn., Mensa, Am. Numismatic Assn., Am. First Day Cover Soc., Am. Topical Assn. (life), Masons, Scottish Rite. Lodges: Masons, Scottish Rite. Avocation: coin collecting. Home: 7 Sheriff Taylor Blvd North Cape May NJ 08204-4476 Office: PO Box 353 Cape May Court House NJ 08210

FOLEY, GARY J., research chemical engineer, computer scientist, federal agency administrator; b. Staten Is.n, N.Y., Mar. 20, 1943; m. Barbar Ickes, 1986; children: William, Karen, Kevin, Ryan, Courtney. BChE, Manhattan Coll., 1964; MS, U. Wis., 1965, PhD in Chem. Engring., 1968. Engr. Am. Oil Co., 1968-73; engr. EPA, 1973-76, 79-86, exec., 1995—; dir. Nat. Exposure Rsch. Lab., 1987-93, acting asst. adminstr. R&D, 1993-94. Mem. AIChE. Achievements include rsch. in air pollution, acid rain, emissions, transport and fate, human and ecosystem exposure and monitoring network design, total quality mgmt. in rsch. orgns. Address: 10705 Spiralwood Ct Raleigh NC 27613-6312

FOLEY, HARRIET ELIZABETH FEALY, retired school librarian; b. Franklin, Ohio, Aug. 11, 1935; d. Milo A. and Nora Lucile (Babb) F. BA in Edn., Coll. of Mt. St. Joseph, Cin., 1957; MS in Libr. Sci., U. Ky., 1961; postgrad., Kent State U., 1965. Cert. tchr. elem. edn., libr. sci., Ohio. Elem. tchr. Carlisle (Ohio) Schs., 1957-61, tchr. secondary French, 1961-63, sch. libr., 1961-82. Editor: (books) Carlisle, the Jersey Settlement in Ohio, 1980-90, Franklin in the Great Miami Valley, 1982, (jour.) Heir Lines, 1986—; co-author: (book) Foleys from County Clare, Ireland, 1994. Trustee, sec. Carlisle Fed. Credit Union, 1962—; mem. Bicentennial Com., Franklin, 1996; mem. various coms. Otterbein-Lebanon Retirement Com., 1990-98. Mem. ALA, DAR (treas. 1988—), New Eng. Geneal. Hist. Soc., Ohio Assn. Sch. Librs. (sec./treas. 1970-75), Ohio Ednl. Libr./Media Assn., Ohio Retired Tchrs. Assn. (life), Franklin Area Hist. Soc. (life, all offices, charter mem., editor newsletter 1986—), Warren County Geneal. Soc. (editor 1982—, treas. 1998—), Ohio Geneal. Soc., Magna Charta Dames, First Families Ohio, First Families Belmont County, First Families Clark County. Republican. Roman Catholic. Avocations: genealogy, local history. Home: PO Box 345 Franklin OH 45005-0345

FOLEY, JACK (JOHN WAYNE HAROLD FOLEY), poet, writer, editor; b. Neptune, N.J., Aug. 9, 1940; s. John Harold and Juana (Terio) F.; m. Adelle Joan Abramowitz, Dec. 21, 1961; 1 child, Sean Ezra. BA, Cornell U., 1963; MA, U. Calif., Berkeley, 1965. Exec. prodr.-in-charge poetry program Sta. KPFA-FM, Berkeley, 1988—; editor-in-chief Poetry USA, Oakland, Calif., 1990-95; resident artist The Djerassi Program, 1994. Author: (poetry and prose) Letters/Lights-Words for Adelle, 1987, (poetry) Gershwin, 1991, Adrift, 1993, (prose) O Her Blackness Sparkles! The Life and Times of the Batman Art Gallery, San Francisco, 1960-65, 1995, Exiles, 1996, (with Ivan Arquelles) New Poetry From California: Dead, Requiem, 1998, Advice to the Lovelorn, 1998; contbr. (film jour.) Bright Lights; contbg. editor: Poetry Flash, 1992—; performances of poetry with wife Adelle, 1985—; author weekly column Foley's Books, in online mag., The Alsop Rev., 1998—. Woodrow Wilson fellow U. Calif., 1963-65; poetry grantee Oakland Arts Coun., 1992-95. Mem. MLA, Poets and Writers, Nat. Poetry Assn. (sec. San Francisco 1989-95), PEN Oakland (program dir. 1990-97). Avocations: playing guitar, tap dancing, writing songs. Home and Office: 2569 Maxwell Ave Oakland CA 94601-5521

FOLEY, JAMES, film director; b. N.Y.C. Dir. films Reckless, 1984, At Close Range, 1986, Who's That Girl, 1987, After Dark, My Sweet, 1990, Glengarry Glen Ross, 1992, Two Bits, 1995, No Fear, 1996, The Chamber, 1996, The Corruptor, 1999. Office: Creative Artists Agy 9830 Wilshire Blvd Beverly Hills CA 90212-1825

FOLEY, JAMES DAVID, computer science educator, consultant; b. Palmerton, Pa., July 20, 1942; s. Marvin Winfield and Stella Elizabeth (Ziegler) F.; m. Mary Louise Herrmann, Aug. 22, 1964; children: Heather, Jennifer. BSEE, Lehigh U., 1964; MSEE, U. Mich., 1965, PhD, 1969. Group mgr. Info. Control Systems, Ann Arbor, Mich., 1969-70; asst. prof. U. N.C., Chapel Hill, 1970-76; sr. systems analyst Bur. of Census, Washington, 1976-77; assoc. prof. George Washington U., Washington, 1977-81, prof., 1981-90, chmn. dept. elec. engring. and computer sci., 1988-90; prof. Ga. Inst. Tech., Atlanta, 1991—; dir. Graphics Visualization and Usability Ctr., Atlanta, 1991-96, Mitsubishi Electric Rsch. Lab. (MERL), Cambridge, Mass., 1996-97; exec. v.p. Mitsubishi Electric Info. Tech. Ctr. Am., Cambridge, 1996-97, chmn., CEO, 1998—; pres. Computer Graphics Cons., Washington, 1979-96; mem. industry program adv. com. NAS, 1997—; bd. dirs. Mitsubishi Am. Author: (with others) Fundamentals of Computer Graphics, 1982, (with others) Computer Graphics: Principles and Practice, 1990, (with others) Introduction to Computer Graphics, 1993; co-author (graphics standard) Core System, 1977. Bd. dirs. Patriot Trails Girl Scout Coun., 1988—. Fellow IEEE, Assn. for Computing Machinery; mem. Human Factors Soc., Spl. Interest Group for Graphics (vice chmn. 1973-75), Nat. Computer Graphics Assn. (bd. dirs. 1982-84), Computing Rsch. Assn. (bd. dirs. 1996—, treas. 1998—). Avocations: skiing, sailing, model railroading. Office: Mitsubishi Elec ITA 201 Broadway Cambridge MA 02139-1955

FOLEY, JAMES EDWARD, scientist, pharmaceutical company executive; b. Newburyport, Mass., Jan. 4, 1950; s. Everett James Foley and Jean Elizbeth (Wade) Doyle; m. Rosemary Ragozzine, June 3, 1972; children: Annarose, Ryan Seamus. BA in Biology, Merrimack Coll., 1972; PhD in Physiology, Dartmouth Med. Sch., 1976. Rsch. assoc. physiology and medicine Dartmouth Med. Sch., Hanover, N.H., 1976-77, postdoctoral fellow, 1977-79; guest scientist Panum Inst., Copenhagen, Denmark, 1979; lectr. physiology U. Århus, Denmark, 1979-80; rsch. asst. prof. medicine U. Tex., Phoenix, 1981; sr. staff fellow NIH/NIADDK, Phoenix, 1981-85; sr. scientist NIH, Phoenix, 1985-86; diabetes group leader Sandoz Rsch. Inst., E. Hanover, N.J., 1986, dir. diabetes, 1986-93, exec. dir. diabetes rsch., 1994-95, exec. dir. metabolic diseases rsch., 1995-96, exec. dir. diabetes pharmacology, 1997; sr. fellow new product mktg. and med. affairs Novartis Pharm. Corp., East Hanover, N.J., 1998—. Contbr. articles to profl. jours. Mem. AAAS, Am. Diabetes Assn., N.Am. Assn. Study of Obesity, Am. Fedn. Clin. Rsch., Am. Jour. Physiology, European Assn. Study Diabetes, N.Y. Acad. Scis. Democrat. Roman Catholic. Avocation: skiing. Home: 73 Seneca Lake Rd Sparta NJ 07871-2825 Office: Novartis Pharmaceutical Corp RR 10 East Hanover NJ 07936

FOLEY, JANE DEBORAH, foundation executive; b. Chgo., May 30, 1952; d. Colin Gray Stevenson and Bette Jane (Cullenbine) Coleman; m. George Edward Foley, Jan. 29, 1972; 1 son, Sy Curtis. BA, Purdue U., 1973, MS, 1977, PhD, 1992. Cert. elem. adminstr., Ind., cert. elem. adminstrn. and supervision. Tchr. phys. edn. and health Lafayette (Ind.) Jefferson H.S., 1973-74; tchr. music and phys. edn. Valparaiso (Ind.) Cmty. Schs., 1974-79, tchr. elem. phys. edn., 1979-90; prin. South Ctrl. Elem. sch., Union Mills, Ind., 1990-93, Flint Lake Elem. Sch., Valparaiso, 1993-98; v.p. Milken Family Found., Santa Monica, Calif., 1998—; mem. panel of experts The Master Tchr., 1996—; key note spkr., presenter state and nat. confs. Contbr. articles to profl. jours. Mem. Valparaiso Sch. Sys. PTA, mem. exec. bd., 1993-98. Recipient Hoosier Sch. award, 1992, Ind. 2000 Designation award 1994, Outstanding Dissertation award Internat. Soc. Ednl. Planning, 1993, Nat. Educator award, Milken Family Found., 1994, Ind. Bell Ringer award Ind. Dept. Edn., 1994, Ind. 4 Star Sch. award, 1995, 96, 97, 98, Internat. Tech. Edn. Assn. award, 1995, Cmty. Improvement award Valparaiso C. of C., 1994, NCREL Pathways to Improvement Pilot Site, 1995, Ind. Sch. Improvement award, Ind. Dept. Edn., 1998, others; Ind. 2000 Planning grantee, 1993, Milken Educator Tech. Project leader, 1997, other grants. Mem. ASCD (assoc.), NAESP, Ind. Assn. Sch. Prins., Valparaiso Tchrs. Assn. (treas. 1989-90), Phi Kappa Phi. Avocations: running, reading, writing, computers. Office: Milken Family Found 1250 4th St Santa Monica CA 90401-1353

FOLEY, JEFF, freelance writer; b. Albany, N.Y., Mar. 16, 1971; m. Tina M. Streett, Jan. 1, 1998. Student, Hudson Valley C.C., 1990-91. mem. Schenectady (N.Y.) Advanced Fiction Writers, 1996—, Impervious to Time Writers' Group, Albany, N.Y., 1997—. Author: (fiction) Rant and Rave, 1995, (nonfiction) Yes, Mother, 1998; singer, songwriter: (music albums) A Little Bit of Soul, 1994, Sonya, 1995. Roman Catholic. Avocation: running. Home: 9 N Church St Apt 202 Schenectady NY 12305-1623

FOLEY, JOHN DONALD, physician; b. Rochester, N.Y., Jan. 2, 1944; s. J. Donald and Mary Margaret (Moran) F.; m. Patricia Susan Scaglione, June 6, 1970; children: Susan Mary, Karen Lynn. BS, U. Notre Dame, 1966; MD, SUNY, Buffalo, 1970. Diplomate Am. Bd. Pediats., Am. Bd. Adolescent Medicine. Intern in pediats. Buffalo (N.Y.) Children's Hosp., 1970-71, resident in pediats., 1971-73; asst. chief pediats. Eisenhower Army Med. Ctr., Augusta, Ga., 1973-82; chief of pediats. Martin Army Cmty. Hosp., Columbus, Ga., 1982-88; fellow in adolescent medicine William Beaumont Army Med. Ctr., El Paso, Tex., 1988-90, chief adolescent medicine, 1990-95; assoc. prof. pediats. Tex. Tech. U. Health Scis. Ctr., El Paso, 1995—; commd. 1st lt. U.S. Army, 1970, advanced through grades to col., 1985. Contbr. articles to profl. jours. Decorated Legion of Merit, Meritorious Svc. medal, Army Commendation medal. Fellow Am. Acad. Pediats., Soc. for Adolescent Medicine (treas. S.W. chpt. 1991-96); mem. El Paso Pediat. Soc., Notre Dame Club of El Paso (treas. 1990—). Avocations: hiking, jogging. Home: 5216 White Oak Dr El Paso TX 79932-2520 Office: Dept Pediats 4800 Alberta Ave El Paso TX 79905-2709

FOLEY, JOHN PATRICK, archbishop; b. Darby, Pa., Nov. 11, 1935; s. John Edward and Regina Beatrice (Vogt) F. BA summa cum laude, St. Josephs Coll., Phila., 1957; BA, St. Charles Borromeo Sem., Phila., 1958; PhL, U. St. Thomas Aquinas, Rome, 1964, PhD cum laude, 1965; MS magna cum laude, Columbia U., 1966; LHD (hon.), St. Joseph's U., Phila., 1985, Allentown (Pa.) Coll., 1990, Cath. U. Am., 1996; DST (hon.), Assumption Coll., Worcester, Mass., 1997; D Journalism, Regis U., 1997; LHD, John Cabot U., 1998. Ordained priest Roman Cath. Ch., 1962, archbishop, 1984. Asst. pastor Sacred Heart Ch., Havertown, Pa., 1962-63; asst. editor Cath. Standard & Times, Phila., 1963, 67-70; Rome corr. Cath. Standard & Times, 1963-65, editor, 1970-84; asst. pastor St. John the Evangelist Ch., Phila., 1966; faculty mem. Cardinal Dougherty High Sch., Phila., 1966-67; assoc. prof. philosophy St. Charles Borromeo Sem., Phila., 1967-84; mem. U.S. Cath. Conf. Communications Com., 1979-82; news sec. gen. meetings Nat. Conf. Cath. Bishops, 1969-84; titular archbishop Neopolis in Proconsulari, 1984—; vice chmn. Pa. State Ethics Commn., 1979-84; apptd. pres. Pontifical Commn. for Social Communications, Vatican City, 1984; pres. Vatican TV Ctr., 1984-89; bd. govs. Internat. Eucharistic Congress. Author: Natural Law, Natural Right and the Warren Court, 1965. Mem. regional bd. dirs. NCCJ, 1969-82. Named hon. prelate Pope Paul VI, 1976; recipient Sourin award Cath. Philopatrian Lit. Inst., Phila., 1990, Knight Comdr. wth Grand Cross, Order of the Holy Sepulchre, 1991, Order of the Northern Star, Kingdom of Sweden, 1991, Pres.'s medal Holy Family Coll., Phila., 1996, Comdr. with Grand Cross Order of Bernardo O'Higgins, Republic of Chile, 1996, Shield of Loyola award St. Joseph's U., Phila., 1997. Mem. Am. Cath. Hist. Soc. (Barry award 1997), Am. Cath. Philos. Assn., Cath. Press Assn. (St. Francis de Sales award 1984). Home: Villa Stritch, Via della Nocetta 63, 00164 Rome Italy Office: Pontifical Coun Social Comm, 00120 Vatican City Vatican City *The most important reality in life is the existence of God, His love for every person exemplified in our redemption by His Son, Jesus Christ, and our eternal destiny to live with Him forever in heaven.*

FOLEY, JOSEPH LAWRENCE, sales executive; b. Albuquerque, June 14, 1953; s. Joseph Bernard and Joan Marie (Johnston) F.; m. Michelle Troglia, Jan., 1992; children: Joseph Louis, Kyle Benjamin. BS in Polit. Sci. and Mktg., Niagara U., 1975. Asst. retail buyer Lord & Taylor, N.Y.C., 1975; asst. retail buyer E.J. Korvette Co., N.Y.C., 1976-78, retail buyer, 1978-80, retail mdse. mgr., 1980; import sales coordinator Block Industries, N.Y.C., 1980-81; v.p. sales Sutton Shirt Co., N.Y.C., 1981-83; exec. v.p. V.I.P. Imports, N.Y.C., 1984-97; prin. Long-Term Care Cons., 1998—. Republican. Roman Catholic. Clubs: Road Runners, Chi Area Racing Assn. Avocations: marathon running; baseball; tennis; skiing; golfing. Home and Office: 3300 N Lake Shore Dr Apt 3A Chicago IL 60657-3938

FOLEY, KATHLEEN M., neurologist, educator, researcher; b. Flushing, N.Y., Jan. 28, 1944; d. Joseph Cyril and Catherine (Cribbin) Maher; m. Charles Thomas Foley, Aug. 10, 1968; children: Fritz, David. BA in Biology magna cum laude, St. John's U., N.Y.C., 1965, DSc (hon.), 1992; MD, Cornell U., 1969. Diplomate Am. Bd. Psychiatry and Neurology (examiner 1980—); lic. physician, N.Y. Intern, then resident in neurology The N.Y. Hosp., N.Y.C., 1969-74; asst. attending neurologist, neurology dept. Meml. Sloan-Kettering Cancer Ctr., N.Y.C., 1974-79, assoc. attending neurologist, 1979-88, chief-pain svc., 1982—, attending neurologist, 1988—; attending neurologist Manhattan (N.Y.) Eye & Ear Hosp., 1974-83; instr. in neurology, Med. Coll. Cornell U., N.Y.C., 1974-75, asst. prof., 1975-79, assoc. prof., 1979-89, assoc. prof. pharmacology, 1979-89, prof. neurology and neuroscience, 1989—, prof. clin. pharmacology, 1990—; rsch. assoc. lab. neurooncology Sloan-Kettering Inst. Cancer Rsch., N.Y.C., 1981-84; vis. asst. physician, cons. in neurology Rockefeller U. Hosp., 1975-79, vis. assoc. physician, 1979—; cons. Calvery Hosp., 1982—; assoc. mem. Meml. Sloan-Kettering Cancer Ctr., 1985-88, mem. 1988—. Editor Clinical Jour. Pain, 1985-87, Jour. Pain and Symptom Mgmt., 1987—, Palliative Medicine Jour., 1993—. Patient Svcs. Adv. Group, Am. Cancer Soc. Genetic Training grant NIH, 1970-71, Program for Pain Rsch. grant Bristol-Myers, 1988-92; Neuro-Oncology spl. fellow Meml. Sloan-Kettering Cancer Ctr., 1975-78; recipient Jr. Faculty award Am. Cancer Soc., 1975-78, Disting. Svc. award, 1992, Nat. Bd. award The Med. Coll. Pa., 1986, Willaim M. Witter award U. Calif. San Francisco, 1987, Annie Blount Storrs award Calvery Hosp., 1988, Balfour M. Mount award Am. Jour. Hospice Care, 1988, Disting. Oncologist award Dayton Oncology Soc., 1990, Tenth Barbara Bohen Pfeifer award Am. Italian Found. for Cancer Rsch., 1993; named Outstanding Women Scientist Women in Sci. Met. N.Y. Chpt., 1987, A. Soriano Jr. Meml. Lectr. The Andres Soriano Cancer Rsch. Found. Inc., 1992. Mem. AAAS, AMA (ad hoc adv. panel mgmt. chronic pain, DATTA reference panel), NAS (Inst. Medicine), Acad. Hospice Physicians, Am. Acad. Neurology (chmn. long range planning com. 1990—, scientific program com. 1990, and other coms.), Am. Fedn. Clin. Rsch., Am. Med. Womens Assn., Am. Neurological Assn. (mem. com. 1984-85, councilor 1984, 94), Am. Pain Soc. (bd. dirs. 1980-82, pres. 1984-85, bylaws com. 1986-87 long range planning task force 1989—), Am. Soc. Clin. Onocology (program com. 1991-92, com. on care at the end of life 1993—, and other coms.), Am. Soc. Clin. Pharmacology and Therapeutics, Assn. Rsch. in Nervous and Mental Diseases, Children's Hospice, Children's Hospice Internat., Cornell U. Med. Coll. Alumni Assn. (bd. dirs., nominating com.), Eastern Pain Assn. (John J. Bonica award 1986), Harvey Soc., Internat. Assn. Study Pain (councilor 1984-90, edn. com. 1986-93, and various coms.), N.Y. Acad. Scis. (USP adv. panel on neurology 1990—), Soc. for Neuscience, Alpha Omega Alpha. Office: Meml Sloan-Kettering Cancer Ctr 1275 York Ave New York NY 10021-6007

FOLEY, L(EWIS) MICHAEL, real estate executive; b. Detroit, Nov. 30, 1938; s. Raymond B. and Mabel (White) F.; m. Pamela Wagner, June 16, 1962; children: Michael D., Kimberly B., Robin E. BS in Sci. Engring., U. Mich., 1960; MBA in Fin. and Mktg., Harvard U., 1964. Lic. real estate broker. Pres. Econ. Devel. Corp., Detroit, 1969-71; v.p. Chrysler Realty Corp., Troy, Mich., 1972-77; exec. v.p. Bell and Howell Video Group, Chgo., 1977-79; v.p. fin., chief fin. officer Bell and Howell Corp., Chgo., 1979-80; sr. v.p. Homart Devel. Co., Chgo., 1981-84, exec. v.p., 1984-93; sr. exec. v.p. Coldwell Banker Real Estate Group Inc., Chgo., 1986-93; chmn., CEO Sears Savs. Bank, Chgo., 1989-93; sr. v.p., CFO Coldwell Banker Corp., 1995-96;

chmn. Borrowers Choice Corp., 1992-93; bd. dirs. BRE Properties, Inc., Western Investment Real Estate Trust. Author: Management of Racial Integration in Business, 1965. Mem. Internat. Council Shopping Ctrs. (v.p., trustee), Sigma Alpha Epsilon. Episcopalian. Club: Mich. Shores (Wilmette, Ill.). Office: 6108 Avenida Cresta La Jolla CA 92037-6508

FOLEY, MARILYN LORNA, artist; b. Arlington, N.J., Aug. 30, 1929; d. Archibald and Mary Ellen (Hall) Lyon; m. William Edward Foley, June 19, 1954; children: Katherine Ann Hastings, William Edward III. BA, Wellesley Coll., 1950; postgrad., Rutgers U., 1950-52. art instr. Wellesley (Mass.) Coll., 1953-54; chair artists com. Art Show: Bedford, 1985-92. One-woman shows include St. Marys Gallery, N.Y.C., 1989, Northridge Art Gallery, Ridgefield, Conn., 1990, 92, Kim Iocovozzi Gallery, Savannah, Ga., 1997, 99; exhibited in group shows at St. Peter's Gallery, Savannah, GA, 1997-99, Salmagundi Club, N.Y.C., 1986, Natl. Arts Club, 1988, Knickerbocker Artists' 40th Annual, 1990, Newington-Cropsey Gallery, Hastings-on-Hudson, N.Y., 1997 (1st prize watercolor), Broome St. Gallery, N.Y.C., 1997 (2d prize watercolor). Juror's Choice Prize, Copley Soc. Mem. Show, 1982; Art Show, Bedford, N.Y., 1983-97, Emille Baker Awd., 1993. Mem. Hudson Valley Art Assn., Landings Art Assn., Catharine Lorillard Wolfe Art Club, Natl. Watercolor Soc. (signature mem.), Hilton Head Art League. Republican. Episcopalian. Avocations: travel, designer of church needlework. Studio: Foley Watercolors 2 Scotch Bonnet Ct Savannah GA 31411-2859

FOLEY, MARK ADAM, congressman; b. Newton, Mass., Sept. 8, 1954. Student, Palm Beach C.C. Owner, mgr. The Lettuce Patch Restaurant, 1975-81; real estate broker, pres. Foley-Smith & Assocs., Inc., 1975-94; commr. City of Lake Worth, 1977-79, commr., vice mayor, 1982-84; state rep. dist. 85 Fla., 1990-92; state senator dist. 35 Fla., 1992-94; mem. 104th-106th Congresses from 16th Fla. dist., 1995—. Republican. Address: 113 Cannon Bldg Washington DC 20515-0916*

FOLEY, MAURICE B., federal judge; b. 1960. BA, Swarthmore Coll., 1982; JD, U. Calif., Berkeley, 1985; LLM in Taxation, Georgetown U., 1988. With Office of Chief Counsel, IRS, Washington, 1985-88; tax counsel, majority staff Com. on Fin., U.S. Senate, Washington, 1988-93; dep. tax legis. counsel U.S. Dept. Treasury, Washington, 1993-95; judge U.S. Tax Ct., Washington, 1995—. Mem. State Bar Calif. Office: US Tax Ct 400 2d St NW Washington DC 20217

FOLEY, MICHAEL FRANCIS, newspaper executive; b. Rockford, Ill., July 6, 1946; s. Richard James and Lucille Nellie (Johnson) F.; children: Shannon Katherine, Corey Lucille. BSJ, U. Fla., 1970; PhD (hon.), Tampa Coll., 1991. Reporter Evening Ind., St. Petersburg, Fla., 1970-74, asst. city editor, 1974-75; city editor St. Petersburg Times, 1975-80, met. editor, 1980-83, asst. mng. editor, 1983-84, mng. editor, 1984-91, exec. editor, 1991-92, v.p. comm. rel., 1992-96, v.p. corp. affairs, 1997—; bd. dirs. Times Pub. Co., St. Petersburg. Named Disting. Alumnus, coll. journalism and comm. U. Fla., 1994. Democrat. Roman Catholic. Avocations: drums, guitar. Office: St Petersburg Times PO Box 1121 Saint Petersburg FL 33731-1121

FOLEY, PATRICIA JEAN, accountant; b. Bridgeport, Conn., Jan. 12, 1956; d. John Edward and Louise (Caselli) F. AA, Housantonic Community Coll., 1978; BS, Cen. Conn. State Coll., 1980; MBA, U. Hartford, 1996. CPA, Conn. Staff acct. Spitz, Sullivan, Wachtel & Falcetta, Hartford, Conn., 1981-82, client acct., 1982-85, sr. acct., 1985-87, supr., mgr., 1987-97; mgr. Falcetta Wachtel & Knochenhauer LLC, Bloomfield, Conn., 1997-98; prin. Patricia J. Foley, CPA, Newington, Conn., 1998—; mem. Acctg. Del. to Russia, Ukraine & Estonia Citizens Amb., 1993. Pres. Woodsedge Condominium Assn., Newington, Conn., 1989-92, treas., 1985-92; dir. Friends of Lucy Robbins Welles Libr. of Newington, 1996—, sec., 1998—. Mem. AICPA (mgmt. adv. svc. com. 1987—, info. tech. divsns., 1992—), Conn. Soc. CPAs, Am. Women Soc. CPAs, Commty. Assn. Inst. (membership chair Conn. chpt. 1991-92), Nat. Assn. Women Bus. Owners. Home: 35 Woodsedge Dr Apt 1B Newington CT 06111-4271 Office: 35-1B Woodsedge Dr Newington CT 06111-4271

FOLEY, PATRICK, air courier company executive. Chmn., CEO DHL Airways, Redwood City, Calif., 1988—. Office: DHL Corp 333 Twin Dolphin Dr Redwood City CA 94065-1496*

FOLEY, PETER MICHAEL, lawyer; b. Detroit, Feb. 10, 1947; s. Paul Emmet and Sophye (Balicki) F.; m. Jane Thurlow Foley, Apr. 25, 1987. BA, Johns Hopkins U., 1969; JD, Georgetown U., 1973. Bar: N.C. 1974, U.S. Supreme Ct., U.S. Ct. Appeals (4th, 5th, & 11th cirs.), U.S. Dist. Ct. (ea., mid. & we. dists.) N.C. Law clk. to Hon. Cornelia Kennedy U.S. Dist. Ct. for Ea. Dist. Mich., Detroit, 1973-75; assoc., ptnr. Moore Ragsdale Liggett Ray & Foley, P.A., Raleigh, N.C., 1975-87; ptnr. LeBoeuf Lamb Leiby & MacRae, Raleigh, 1987-93, Ragsdale, Liggett & Foley, Raleigh, 1994—; adj. prof. Campbell U. Law Sch., Buies Creek, N.C., 1984-87. Mem. Def. Rsch. Inst., N.C. Assn. Def. Lawyers, Am. Bd. Trial Advocates. Office: 2840 Plaza Pl PO Box 31507 Raleigh NC 27622-1507

FOLEY, RICHARD, academic administrator. BA magna cum laude, Miami U., 1969, MA, 1970; PhD, Brown U., 1975. Asst. prof. Ariz. State U., 1975; prof. U. Notre Dame, 1976-90, chair philosophy, 1983-90; prof., chair Rutgers U., New Brunswick, N.J., 1990-92, dean Arts and Scis., 1992-96, exec. dean Arts and Scis., dean Grad. Sch., 1996—; mem. com. on rsch. univs. Coun. of Colls. of Arts and Scis., 1998—. Author: The Theory of Epistemic Rationality, 1987, Working without a Net, 1993; contbr. numerous papers to profl. jours.; mem. editl. bd.: Philos. Issues, 1994—, Philosophy and Phenomenol. Rsch., 1990—, Am. Philos. Quar., 1987-90 (Prize Essay 1979), U. Notre Dame Press, 1985-90; bd. dirs. Jour. of History of Ideas, 1992—; dir. of bd. Thomas A. Edison Papers, 1992—. Nat. Merit scholar, 1965-69; fellow Brown U., 1970-74, NEH fellow, 1989; NEH summer rsch. grantee 1982, 86, Notre Dame rsch. grantee, 1983; recipient Disting. Alumnus award Brown U., 1999. Mem. Am. Philos. Assn. (com. on tchg. 1987-90, adv. com. 1998—, com. on status of future of the profession 1998—), Phi Beta Kappa. E-mail: foley@fas-admin.rutgers.edu. Office: Rutgers U Faculty Arts and Sci 77 Hamilton St New Brunswick NJ 08903

FOLEY, RIDGWAY KNIGHT, JR., lawyer, writer; b. Portland, Oreg., Oct. 7, 1937; s. Ridgway Knight and Eunice Alberta (Ammer) F. BS magna cum laude, Lewis & Clark Coll., 1959; JD, U. Oreg., 1963. Bar: Oreg. Assoc. Mautz, Souther, Spaulding, Kinsey & Williamson, Portland, 1964-71; gen. ptnr. Schwabe, Williamson & Wyatt (and predecessor firms), Portland, 1972-84, sr. ptnr., 1985-92; ptnr., shareholder Foley & Duncan, P.C., Portland, 1993-96; of counsel Greene & Markley PC, Portland, 1997—; com. mem. Multnomah Lawyer Com., 1964-68, 90-93, chair, 1992-93. Contbr. more than 100 articles, essays to profl. jours., 1962—; lectr. profl. orgns., 1970—. Trustee Found. Econ. Edn., Inc., Irvington-on-Hudson, N.Y., 1974-91, 93-96; founding dir. Paulist Fathers Cath. Ctr., Portland, 1978-85. Mem. ABA, Am. Jud. Soc., Oreg. State Bar, Multnomah County Bar (dir. 1993-97), University Club (Portland), Mt. Hood Philos. Soc. (founding trustee, officer 1972-85), Lang Syne Soc., Geneal. Forum of Oreg., Order of Coif. Episcopalian. Avocations: writing, lecturing, genealogy, publishing, history. Office: Greene & Markley PC 1515 SW 5th Ave Ste 600 Portland OR 97201-5449

FOLEY, ROBERT MATTHEW, lawyer; b. N.Y.C., Aug. 28, 1943; s. Nestor Shea and Jacqueline Victoria (Peers) F.; m. Linda-Adèle Swide, Aug. 2, 1969. BA, Lehigh U., 1966; MA, George Washington U., 1968; JD, Am. U., 1972. Bar: D.C. 1973, U.S. Ct. Appeals (Fed. cir.) 1978, U.S. Supreme Ct. 1978, U.S. Ct. Appeals (D.C. cir.) 1982. Sch. psychologist City of Alexandria, Va., 1968-70; staff atty. Broadcast Bur., FCC, Washington, 1972; assoc. firm Shack & Mendenhall, Washington, 1972-78; pvt. practice law Washington, 1978-79; sr. mrm. firm Foley & Chhabra, P.C., 1979-81, Foley & McEvily P.C., 1981-84, Robert M. Foley, P.C., 1984-86, 89—, Landfield, Becker & Green, 1986-89; mem. firm Foley & Saenz, 1991-92, Johnston, Rivlin & Foley, L.L.P., 1995-96, Johnston, Foley & Wasterfield, L.L.P., Washington, 1996-97; of counsel Bogle & Gates PLLC, Seattle, 1997-99, Marks, Holmes, Foley & Morales P.S., Seattle, 1999—. Contbr. articles to legal and bus. jours. Vestryman All Saint's Episcopal Ch., Chevy Chase, Md., 1973-78, 81-87, 93-97, mem. exec. com., 1986-87, 93-97; mem. exec. com. All Saints' All-Day Child Care Ctr., Inc., Chevy Chase, 1973-97, pres., 1979-97. Mem. ABA, D.C. Bar Assn., Va. Bar Assn., Md. Bar Assn., Fed. Comms. Bar Assn., Am. Immigration Lawyers Assn. (sec. D.C. chpt. 1996-97, v.p. 1997), Arab Am. Bar Assn. (pres. 1984-87), Bar Assn. D.C., Chevy Chase Club, West Chop Tennis Club (Martha's Vineyard). Home: 2706 Harvard Ave E Seattle WA 98102-3914 Office: The Washington Harbour 3050 K St NW Ste 170 Washington DC 20007-5123 also: Ste 3130 1001 Fourth Ave Seattle WA 98154-1101

FOLEY, THOMAS STEPHEN, diplomat, former speaker House of Representatives; b. Spokane, Wash., Mar. 6, 1929; s. Ralph E. and Helen Marie (Higgins) F.; m. Heather Strachan, Dec. 1968. B.A., U. Wash., 1951, LL.B., 1957. Bar: Wash. Partner Higgins & Foley, 1957-58; dep. pros. atty. Spokane County, Spokane, 1958-60; asst. atty. gen. State of Wash., Olympia, 1960-61; spl. counsel interior and insular affairs com. U.S. Senate, Washington, 1961-64; mem. 89th-103rd Congresses from 5th Wash. dist., Washington, D.C., 1965-94; House majority whip, 1981-86, House majority leader, 1987-89; speaker U.S. Ho. of Reps., 1989-94; ptnr. Akin, Gump, Strauss, Hauer & Feld, Washington, D.C., 1995-97; U.S. amb. to Japan U.S. Dept. State, Tokyo, 1997—; instr. law Gonzaga U., 1958-60; mem. bd. advisors Ctr. Strategic and Internat. Studies; mem. adv. council Am. Ditchley Found. Bd. overseers Whitman Coll.; bd. advisors Yale U. council; bd. dirs. Council on Fgn. Relations. Mem. Phi Delta Phi. Democrat. Office: Akin Gump Strauss Hauer & Feld Ste 400 1333 New Hampshire Ave NW Washington DC 20036-1564 also: US Amb to Japan US Dept State Washington DC 20521-9800*

FOLEY, WENDY H., library director; b. Cambridge, Mass., Oct. 7, 1948; d. Wilfred G. H. and Elizabeth Joubert; m. James P. Foley, Dec. 24, 1948; 1 child, Anne. BA, Bates Coll., 1966; MS, Simmons Coll., 1974. Br. mgr. Portland Pub. Libr., 1974-88, Clearwater (Fla.) Pub. Libr., 1988-94; libr. dir. Dunedin (Fla.) Pub. Libr., 1994—. Mem. Libr. Adv. Com., Dunedin Friends of Libr. Mem. ALA, Fla. Libr. Assn., Tampa Bay Libr. Cooperative, Dunedin Coun. Orgns., Rotary. Avocations: tennis, camping, reading. E-mail: foleyw@tblc.org. Office: Dunedin Pub Libr 223 Douglas Ave Dunedin FL 34698

FOLK, FRANK ANTON, surgeon, educator; b. Chgo., Dec. 15, 1925; s. Frank A. and Anna (Pilisauer) F.; m. Lorna C. Hill, June 18, 1949; children: Laura, Lawrence, Patricia, Elizabeth, Thomas, James, Mary, Tracy Ann, William. BS, Northwestern U., 1945; postgrad., U. Wis., 1945-46; MD, U. Ill., 1949. Diplomate Am. Bd. Surgery, Nat. Bd. Med. Examiners; lic. Ill., Wis. Rotating intern Cook County Hosp., Chgo., 1949-51; resident in gen. surgery Cook County/Columbus Hosp., Chgo., 1951; resident in gen. surgery Cook County Hosp., Chgo., 1954-57, surgeon, 1958-69, dir. of surgery, 1969-72; mem. faculty Stritch Sch. Medicine Loyola U., Maywood, Ill., 1958—, prof. surgery Stritch Sch. Medicine, 1972-96; prof. emeritus, 1997—; rsch. fellow Hektoen Inst., Chgo., 1959-64; asst. chief surgery VA Hosp., Hines, Ill., 1972-95, chief surg. svc., 1995-96. Mem. editl. bd.: The Am. Surgeon, 1984-92; contbr. articles to med. jours. including Am. Jour. Physiology, Jour. Occupl. Medicine, Annals of Surgery, Archives of Surgery, Jour. Trauma, Surg. Clinics of N.Am. Unit pres., exec. bd. Am. Cancer Soc., Chgo., 1972-89; mem. pres.'s adv. com. Benedictine U., Lisle, Ill., 1965-90. Lt. USN, 1951-53, Korea. Decorated Bronze Star, 1953. Fellow ACS (gov., chmn. gen. surgery Chgo. com. on trauma 1975-83, pres. met. chpt. 1977-78, mem. SESAP com. II and III, instr. ACS advanced trauma life support course 1980-87); mem. Am. Surg. Assn., Am. Assn. for Surgery of Trauma, Assn. Mil. Surgeons of U.S., Assn. for Acad. Surgery, Soc. for Surgery of Alimentary Tract, Assn. VA Surgeons, Collegium Internat. Chirurgiae Digestivae, Cen. Surg. Assn., Midwest Surg. Assn. (pres. 1974-75), Western Surg. Assn., Ill. Surg. Soc. (pres. 1971-72), Chgo. Surg. Soc. (pres. 1989-90), Inst. Medicine of Chgo. Roman Catholic. Avocations: medical history, Civil War history, Central American civilizations. Fax: (708) 202-2180. Office: VA Hosp Surg Svc PO Box 5000 Hines IL 60141-1489

FOLK, JAMES, sales executive; b. Phillipsburg, N.J., Aug. 22, 1948; s. Endress Herwig and June Catherine (Dieda) F.; m. Eileen Maria Berryman, Nov. 29, 1971; children: John Andrew, Elizabeth Anne. BSME, Drexel U., 1971; MBA, Lehigh U., 1974. Reg. profl. engr., Pa. Dir. indsl. engring. Victaulic Co. Am., Easton, Pa., 1971-76; mfg. mgr. Follett Corp., Easton, 1976-82; sr. project mgr. Don Aux Assocs., Inc., Ft. Lee, N.J., 1982-87; sales mgr., v.p. Jacobsen and Co., Elizabeth, N.J., 1986-87; prin. The Folk Group, Doylestown, Pa., 1987—. Mem. Inst. Indsl. Engrs. (pres. 1981-82), Easton-Phillipsburg Indsl. Relations Soc. (chmn. 1983-84). Republican. Presbyterian. Avocations: skiing, field sports, sailing. Home: PO Box 86 Ferndale PA 18921-0086

FOLK, KATHERINE PINKSTON, English language educator, writer, journalist; b. Corsicana, Tex., Feb. 8, 1925; d. Lucian Albert and Katherine (Shell) Pinkston; m. Elmer Ellsworth Folk, Apr. 21, 1946; children: Russell Harter, David Shell, Barbara Kay Folk Nowotny. BA in Journalism, Tex. Tech. U., 1946; postgrad., U. Houston, 1960-71. Reporter Scurry County Times, Snyder, Tex., 1946; dir. advt. Dunlaps Dept. Store, Lubbock, Tex., 1946; instr. English Odessa (Tex.) Coll., 1948-53; dir. communication, editor Viva Mag. Houston Met. Ministries, 1979-80; dir. communication for continuing edn. Houston Community Coll. System, 1989-90, instr. English, 1980—; auditor creative writing Rice U., Houston, 1966; tutor English Spring Br. Ind. Sch. Dist., Houston, 1970-75. Contbr. articles to popular mags. Ann. sponsor Odessa Coll., 1950-53; mem. Harris County Heritage Soc., Houston, 1985-91, Nat. Fedn. Rep. Women, Houston, 1987-99, literacy chair, 1999, Country Playhouse Little Theatre, 1987-96; bd. dirs. Spring Br. YWCA, Houston, 1990-91. Mem. AAUW, Jr. League Houston (patron tea rm.), Nat. Fedn. Press Women, Soc. Children's Book Writers, Romance Writers Am., Delta Delta Delta (chmn. scholarship com. 1972). Episcopalian. Avocations: writing, reading, walking, music, travel. Office: Houston C C Sys 22 Waugh Dr Houston TX 77007-5813

FOLK, ROBERT LOUIS, geologist, educator; b. Cleve., Sept. 30, 1925; s. George Billmyer and Marjorie Marshall (Kinkead) F.; m. Marjorie Thomas, Sept. 7, 1946; children—Robert T., Jennifer Louise, Charles Marshall. B.S., Pa. State Coll., 1946, M.S., 1950, Ph.D., 1952. Research geologist Gulf Oil Co., Houston, 1951-52; mem. faculty U. Tex., Austin, 1952—, prof. geol. scis., 1960—, Dave Carlton prof. geol. scis., 1977-88; vis. lectr. Australian Nat. U., Canberra, 1965, Tong-Ji U., Shanghai, China, 1980; vis. researcher Universita degli Studi, Milan, Italy, 1973. Author: Petrology of Sedimentary Rocks, 1980; contbr. articles to sci. publs. Neil Miner award Nat. Assn. Geology Tchrs., 1989, H.C. Sorby medal Internat. Assn. Sedimentologists, 1990. Fellow Geol. Soc. Am.; mem. Soc. Econ. Paleontologists and Mineralogists (hon., Twenhofel medal 1979). Methodist. Achievements include first discovery of mineralized nannobacteria on earth; the same-appearing organisms were discovered by NASA in Martian meteorite. Home: 1107 Bluebonnet Ln Austin TX 78704-2005 Office: U of Tex Dept Geol Scis Austin TX 78801 *My unique characteristic is that I run my life randomly. At home each day, I put all the things I have/want to do in a list. Then I roll dice to see which thing to do and do that immediately whether it be a painful or pleasurable choice. Since I adopted this method I get immeasurably more work done and much greater pleasure out of daily life. Try it.*

FOLK, THOMAS ROBERT, lawyer; b. Milford, N.J., Jan. 9, 1950; s. Conrad Frank and Isabella Ramsey (Sickels) F.; m. JoAnn Elizabeth Lo Pinto, June 21, 1975; children: Elizabeth Frances, Karina Marie. BS, U.S. Mil. Acad., 1972; JD, U. Va., 1978. Bar: Va. 1978, U.S. Ct. Mil. Appeals 1978, U.S. Ct. Appeals (4th cir.) 1978, U.S. Supreme Ct. 1983, U.S. Ct. Claims 1985, U.S. Ct. Appeals (9th and fed. cirs.) 1985, D.C. 1986., U.S. Dist. Ct. D.C. 1987, U.S. Dist. Ct. Md. 1987. Commd. 2d lt. U.S. Army, 1972, advanced to maj., 1983, resigned, 1986; asst. to gen. counsel U.S. Army, Washington, 1980-82, atty. litigation, 1983-86; assoc. Hazel & Thomas, P.C., Fairfax, Va., 1986-88, owner, 1989—. Contbr. articles to profl. jours. Mem. Com. Armed Svcs. and Vets. Affairs, 1985-88. Col. USAR, 1995. Mem. Va. Bar Assn. (bd. govs. constrn. and pub. contracts), Fairfax Bar Assn. (bd. govs. 1993-97), West Point Soc. D.C. (bd. govs.). Home: 4902 Asquith Ct Fairfax VA 22032-2102

FOLKENBERG, LOIS WAXTER, principal, educator, psychologist; b. Balt., June 17, 1943; d. Frank Shelby and Ruth Virginia (Meyer) Waxter; m. Donald Louis Folkenberg, June 12, 1966; children: Todd Louis, Laura Michelle. BA in Psychology, Columbia Union Coll., 1965; MA in Counseling and Testing, Am. U., 1967. Counselor Montgomery Jr. Coll., Rockville, Md., 1966-67, U. Calif., Riverside, 1967-68; tchr. Maxwell Preparatory Sch., Nairobi, Kenya, 1969; sch. psychologist Spokane (Wash.) Valley Coop., 1979-81; tchr. Ctrl. Valley Sch. Dist., Spokane, 1982-83; prin., tchr. Duluth (Ga.) Jr. Acad., 1986-93, Frederick (Md.) Adventist Sch., 1993-95, Atholton Adventist Sch., Columbia, Md., 1995—; bd. mem. Chesapeake Conf. Ednl. Initiative, Columbia, Chesapeake Conf. Bd. Edn., Columbia, Columbia Union Curriculu Com. Facilitator student projects Global Mission Seventh-Day Adventists, Silver Spring, Md., 1990—. Recipient Zapara Excellence in Tchg. award Office Edn., N.Am. Divsn. Seventh-Day Adventists, Silver Spring, 1991; named Tchr. of the Yr., North Ga. Tchrs.' Assn., Calhoun, 1989-90. Home: 12825 Amberwoods Way Sykesville MD 21784-5525 Office: Atholton Adventist Sch 6520 Martin Rd Columbia MD 21044

FOLKENFLIK, MAX, lawyer; b. Phila., Sept. 9, 1948; s. Bernard Folkenflik and Florence (Rogosin) Field; m. Margaret A. McGerity, Apr., 3, 1971; children: Alexander, Andrew. BS, Cornell U., 1970; JD, Georgetown U., 1975. Bar: N.Y. 1976, U.S. Dist. Ct. (so. dist.) N.Y. 1976, (ea. dist.) N.Y. 1976, U.S. Tax Ct. 1977, U.S. Ct. Appeals (2d cir.) 1994, U.S. Ct. Appeals (3d cir.) 1997. Assoc. Kronish, Lieb, Shainswit, Weiner & Hellman, N.Y.C., 1975-79, Cravath, Swaine & Moore, N.Y.C., 1979-83; ptnr. Morrison, Paul & Beiley, N.Y.C., 1983-84, Morrison, Cohen & Singer, N.Y.C., 1984-85, Wistendahl & Folkenflik, N.Y.C., 1985-88, Folkenflik & McGerity, N.Y.C., 1988—. Mem. staff Georgetown U. Law Review, 1973-74, editor 1974-75. Mem. ABA, Assn. of Bar of City of N.Y. Democrat. Jewish. Avocation: photography. Home: 261 W 90th St New York NY 10024-1119 Office: Folkenflik & McGerity 1370 Ave Of The Americas New York NY 10019-4602

FOLKENS, ALAN THEODORE, clinical and pharmaceutical microbiologist; b. Graceville, Minn., Oct. 26, 1936; s. Martin and Catherine (Laman) F.; m. Pearl June Putnam, July 29, 1961; children: Lee Alan, Kimberly Mae Folkens Anderson, Shannon Lee Folkens Tobin, Eric Martin. BA, Omaha U., 1962; PhD, U. S.D., 1971. Acting dir., dir. allied health professions Ill. State U., Normal, 1971-73; chief clin. microbiologist Peoria (Ill.) Tazewell Pathology Group, 1973-84; lab. dir. Delta Med. Ctr., Greenville, Miss., 1984-85; R&D clin. and pharm. microbiologist Alcon Labs., Inc., Ft. Worth, 1985—, assoc. dir., 1995—; vis. faculty E. Tenn. State U., Johnson City, 1978-86; adj. faculty U. Ill. Peoria Sch. Medicine, 1980-84, Ill. State U., Normal, 1973-84, U. N. Tex., Denton, 1992-94; presenter symposium in field. Contbr. chpt. to book and articles to profl. jours. Bd. edn., past pres. Blessed Sacrament Sch., Morton, Ill., 1978-81; chmn. sickle cell anemia screening Ill. State U., Normal, 1972; chmn. Tootsie Roll drive for retarded children, K.C., Morton, 1975. Trainee NIH, 1967. Mem. Am. Soc. Microbiology, Am. Soc. Clin. Pathology, Am. Acad. Microbiology (diplomate), Assn. Rsch. in Vision and Ophthalmology, Assn. Rsch. to Prevent Blindness, N.Y. Acad. Scis., Phi Sigma, Sigma Xi. Independent. Roman Catholic. Achievements include work in FDA approval of Ciloxan for topical ophthalmic therapy. Home: PO Box 5220 Laguna Park TX 76634-5220 Address: 1822 Union Ave Dow City IA 51528-3118

FOLKER, CATHLEEN ANN, humanities educator; b. West Allis, Wis., May 14, 1956; d. Norman Ralph and Lucille Catherine (Lensing) F. BA in Liberal Arts, Ambassador Coll., 1978; postgrad., U. Wis., Milw., 1986-91; MSBA, Tex. Tech. U., 1995, ABD, 1997. Customer rels. supr. Univ. Acctg. Svc., Milw., 1979-80; mktg. analyst Payco Am. Corp., Brookfield, Wis., 1980; controller West Allis Curtain & Drapery, 1980-92; mgmt. cons., 1992-93; tchg. asst. Tex. Tech U., Lubbock, 1994-97; lectr. U. Wis., Whitewater, 1998-99, U. Nebr., Lincoln, 1999—; freelance writer, Oconomowoc, Wis., 1989-93; tax preparer, 1991-93; grad. tchg. asst. U. Wis., Milw., 1989-90. Avocations: walking, reading, travel, singing, biking.

FOLKMAN, DAVID H., retail, wholesale and consumer products consultant; b. Jackson, Mich., Nov. 6, 1934; s. Jerome D. and Bessie (Schomer) F.; m. Susan Kleppner, June 22, 1958; children: Louis, Sarah, Karen, Jeffrey. A.B., Harvard U., 1957, M.B.A., 1960. Mdse. mgr. Foley's, Houston, 1957-69; v.p. dir. stores Famous-Barr, St. Louis, 1969-74; sr. v.p., gen. mdse. mgr. Macy's Calif., San Francisco, 1974-82; pres., chief exec. officer Emporium Capwell, San Francisco, 1982-87; gen. ptnr. U.S. Venture Ptnrs., Menlo Park, Calif., 1987-90; venture ptnr., 1991-93; pres., chief exec. officer Laurel Burch, Inc., San Francisco, 1990-91; retail investor, cons., 1991-93; CEO Esprit de Corp, San Francisco, 1993-95; prin., Regent Pacific Mgmt. Corp., Cupertino, Calif., 1995—; instr. U. Houston, 1968-69, Wash. U., St. Louis, 1970-73; bd. dirs. Regent Pacific Mgmt. Corp., NeoVista, Natural Wonders, Inc., Shoe Pavilion, Inc. Mem. Harvard Club (N.Y.C.).

FOLKMAN, MOSES JUDAH, surgeon; b. Cleve., Feb. 24, 1933; s. Jerome D. and Bessie Folkman. BA, Ohio State U., 1953; MD, Harvard U., 1957; DSc honoris causa, Mt. Sinai Sch. Medicine, 1996, Northwestern U., 1998; MD honoris causa, Uppsala U., Sweden, 1998; DSc honoris causa, Muhlenberg Coll., 1999, Albany Med. Coll., 1999, U. Mass., Lowell, 1999. Intern, then asst. resident in surgery Mass. Gen. Hosp., Boston, 1957-60, sr. asst. resident in surgery, 1962-64, chief resident, 1964-65; chief resident in pediatric surgery Phila. Children's Hosp., 1969; instr. surgery Harvard U. Med. Sch., 1965-66, assoc. in surgery, 1967, prof. surgery, 1967—, Julia Dyckman Andrus prof. pediatric surgery, 1968—, prof. anatomy and cellular biology, 1989—; asst. surgeon Boston City Hosp., 1965-66; assoc. dir. Sears Surg. Lab., 1966-67; sr. surgeon Children's Hosp. Med. Ctr., Boston, 1968—. With M.C., USN, 1960-62. Recipient Career Devel. award NIH, 1966, Lila Gruber award Am. Acad. Dermatology, 1974, Gairdner Found. Internat. award, Toronto, Can., 1991, Christopher Columbus Commemorative Sci. medal U.S. Congress/NIH, Wolf award Wolf Found., Jerusalem, 1992, Lucian award Royal Coll. Surgeons Can., 1993, Steiner award Josef Steiner Found., Switzerland, 1994, Bristol-Myers Cancer Rsch. award, 1995, Ernst Schering award (Germany), 1996, Gen. Motors Cancer Rsch. award, 1997, Ernst Jung Found. award (Germany), 1997, Med. prize Keio U. (Japan), 1998, Chiron award in medicine, 1999. Fellow ACS (Sheen award 1989); mem. NAS, Am. Coll. Surgeons, Am. Assn. Arts and Scis., Am. Surg. Assn., Assn. Acad. Surgery, Am. Pediatric Surg. Assn., Mass. Med. Soc., Assn. Am. Physicians. Office: 300 Longwood Ave Boston MA 02115-5724

FOLLETT, KENNETH MARTIN, author; b. Cardiff, Wales, June 5, 1949; s. Martin D. and Lavinia C. (Evans) F.; m. Mary Emma Ruth Elson, Jan. 5, 1968 (div. 1985); children: Emanuele, Marie-Claire; m. Barbara Broer, Nov. 8, 1985. BA, U. Coll., London, 1970. Reporter, music columnist South Wales Echo, 1970-73; reporter Evening News, London, 1973-74; editorial dir. Everest Books Ltd., London, 1971-75, 87-96, dep. mng. dir., 1976-77; pres. The Dyslexia Inst.; chair Nat. Year of Reading, 1998-99. Author: The Shakeout, 1975, The Bear Raid, 1976, Secret of Kellerman's Studio, 1976, Eye of the Needle, 1978 (Edgar award Best Novel), Triple, 1979, The Key to Rebecca, 1980, The Man from St. Petersburg, 1982, On Wings of Eagles, 1983, Lie Down with Lions, 1985, The Pillars of Earth, 1989, Night over Water, 1991, A Dangerous Fortune, 1993, Pillars of the Almighty, 1994, A Place Called Freedom, 1995, The Third Twin, 1996, The Hammer of Eden, 1998; (as Martin Martinsen) The Power Twins and the Worm Puzzle, 1976; (as Symon Myles) The Big Needle, 1974, The Big Black, 1974, The Big Hit, 1975; (as Bernard L. Ross) Amok: King of Legend, 1976, Capricorn One, 1978; (as Zachary Stone) The Modigliani Scandal, 1976, Paper Money, 1977; screenwriter: Fringe Banking, 1978, A Football Star, 1979, Lie Down with Lions, 1987. Fellow U. Coll. London. Office: PO Box 708, London SW10 0DH, England

FOLLETT, ROBERT JOHN RICHARD, publisher; b. Oak Park, Ill., July 4, 1928; s. Dwight W. and Mildred (Johnson) F.; m. Nancy L. Crouthamel, Dec. 30, 1950; children: Brian L., Kathryn R., Jean A., Lisa W. AB, Brown U., 1950; postgrad., Columbia U., 1950-51. Editor Follett Pub. Co., Chgo., 1951-55, sales mgr., 1955-58, gen. mgr. ednl. div., developer first multi-racial textbook program, first textbooks for disadvantaged, first beginning-to-read books, 1958-68, pres., 1968-78; chmn., dir. Follett Corp., 1979-94; pres. Alpine Guild, Inc., 1977—; dir. Assn. Am. Pubs., 1972-79; chmn. Rocky Mountain Resource Ctr., Inc., 1997—, Sch. Pubs., 1971-73; dir. Ednl. Systems Corp.; mem. Ill. Gov.'s Commn. on Schs., 1972; pres. Alpine Rsch. Inst., Adv. Coun. on Edn. Stats., 1975-77; chmn. Book Distbn. Task Force of Book Industry, 1978-81; adv. coun. Krannert Sch. of Mgmt., 1988-93; pres. Soda Creek Open Space Assn. Inc., 1994—; dir. Continental Divide Land Trust, 1996—; mem. adv. bd. Ctr. for Living Democracy, 1997—; mem. Consortium on Renewing Edn., 1997—; lectr. Denver U. Pub. Inst., 1997—. Author: Your Wonderful Body, 1961, What to Take Backpacking and Why, 1977, How to Keep Score in Business, 1978, The Financial Side of Book Publishing, 1982, rev. edit., 1988, Financial Feasibility in Book Publishing, 1988, rev. edit., 1996. Bd. dirs. Village Mgr. Assn., 1964-84, Cmty. Found. Oak Park and River Forest, 1959-86, Fund for Justice, 1974-77, For Character, 1983-93, Ctr. Book Rsch., 1985-88; trustee Inst. Ednl. Data Systems, 1965—; elected mem. Rep. State Com. from 7th dist. Ill., 1982-90, vice chmn., 1986-90; chmn. Ill. Reps. Strategic Planning Com., 1986-87; Presdl. Elector, 1988; pres. Keystone Citizens League, 1997—; mem. Keystone Mountain Responsibility Team, 1998—; hon. co-chair Colo. Mountain Coll. Campaign, 1998—. Served in AUS, 1951-53. Mem. Chgo. Pubs. Assn. (pres. 1976-94), Mid.-Am. Pubs. Assn. (mng. dir., 1987-88, dir. 1988-93), Rocky Mountain Book Pubs. Assn., Am. Book Coun. (v.p. 1987-88), Ill. C. of C. (chmn. edn. com. 1977-79), Soc. Midland Authors, Sierra Club, River Forest Tennis Club, Rotary Club Summit County. Office: Alpine Guild Inc PO Box 4848 Dillon CO 80435-4848

FOLLETT, RONALD FRANCIS, soil scientist; b. Laramie, Wyo., June 26, 1939; s. Roy Lawrence and Frances (Hunter) F.; m. Dorothy Mae Spangle, Jan. 1, 1967; children: William, Jennifer, Michael. BS, Colo. State U., 1961, MS, 1963; PhD, Purdue U., 1966. Rsch. soil scientist Agrl. Rsch. Svc., USDA, Mandan, N.D., 1968-75; nat. rsch. program leader Agrl. Rsch. Svc., USDA, Beltsville (Md.) and Ft. Collins (Colo.), 1976-86; rsch. leader soil-plant-nutrient rsch. unit Agrl. Rsch. Svc., USDA, Ft. Collins, 1986—; postdoctoral rsch. U.S. Plant-Soil-Nutrition Lab., Ithaca, N.Y., 1975-76. Co-author: The Potential of U.S. Cropland to Sequester Carbon and Mitigate the Greenhouse Effect, 1998; editor: Soil Fertility and Organic Matter as Critical Components of Production Systems, 1987, Nitrogen Management and Ground Water Protection, 1989, Managing Nitrogen for Ground Water Quality and Farm Profitablity, 1991; guest editor spl. issue Jour. Containmant Hydrol.; contbr. over 100 articles to profl. jours. Officer 1st Presbyn. Ch., Mandan, then Ft. Collins, 1972—; adult leader local Boy Scouts Am., Beltsville, then Ft. Collins, 1975—. Capt. arty., U.S. Army, 1966-68; maj. Res. Recipient Disting. Svc. award USDA, 1984, 92, cert. of merit, 1990, 96. Fellow Soil Sci. Soc. Am. (div. chmn. bd. dirs. 1985-88), Am. Soc. Agronomy, Soil and Water Conservation Soc. Am. Avocations: working with youth, skiing, fishing, gardening. Office: USDA Agrl Rsch Svc Soil-Plant-Nutrient Rsch Unit PO Box E Fort Collins CO 80522-0470

FOLLICK, EDWIN DUANE, law educator, chiropractic physician; b. Glendale, Calif., Feb. 4, 1935; s. Edwin Fulfford and Esther Agnes (Catherwood) F.; m. Marilyn K. Sherk, Mar. 24, 1986. BA, Calif. State U., L.A., 1956, MA, 1961; MA, Pepperdine U., 1957, MPA, 1977; PhD, DTh, St. Andrews Theol. Coll., Sem. of Free Prot. Episc. Ch., London, 1958; MS in Libr. Sci., U. So. Calif., 1963, MEd in Instructional Materials, 1964, AdvMEd in Edn. Adminstrn., 1969; postgrad., Calif. Coll. Law, 1965; LLB, Blackstone Law Sch., 1966, JD, 1967; DC, Cleve. Chiropractic Coll., L.A., 1972; PhD, Academia Theatina, Pescara, 1978; MA in Organizational Mgmt., Antioch U., L.A., 1990. Tchr., libr. adminstr. L.A. City Schs., 1957-68; law librarian Glendale U. Coll. Law, 1968-69; coll. librarian Cleve. Chiropractic Coll., L.A., 1969-74, dir. edn. and admissions, 1974-84, prof. jurisprudence, 1975—, dean student affairs, 1976-92, chaplain, 1985—, dean of edn., 1989—; assoc. prof. Newport U., 1982; extern prof. St. Andrews Theol. Coll., London, 1961; dir. West Valley Chiropractic Health Ctr., 1972—. Contbr. articles to profl. jours. Chaplain's asst. U.S. Army, 1958-60. Decorated cavaliere Internat. Order Legion of Honor of Immaculata (Italy); Knight of Malta, Sovereign Order of St. John of Jerusalem; knight Order of Signum Fidei; comdr. chevalier Byzantine Imperial Order of Constantine the Gt.; comdr. ritter Order St. Gereon; chevalier Mil. and Hospitaller Order of St. Lazarus of Jerusalem (Malta); numerous others. Mem. ALA, NEA, Am. Assn. Sch. Librarians, L.A. Sch. Libr. Assn., Calif. Sch. Libr. Assn., Assn. Coll. and Rsch. Librarians, Am. Assn. Law Librarians, Am. Chiropractic Assn., Internat. Chiropractors Assn., Nat. Geog. Soc., Internat. Platform Assn., Phi Delta Kappa, Sigma Chi Psi, Delta Tau Alpha. Democrat. Episcopalian. Home: 6435 Jumilla Ave Woodland Hills CA 91367-2833 Office: 590 N Vermont Ave Los Angeles CA 90004-2115 also: 7022 Owensmouth Ave Canoga Park CA 91303-2005

FOLLINGSTAD, CAROL C., psychologist, consultant, educator; b. Rantoul, Ill., Jan. 21, 1956; d. James Harvey and Ella May Watson; m. Eugene M. Follingstad; children: Alisha, Angela, Anita, Alayna, Arlyn, Arick. BA, Moorhead State U., 1990, MS, 1992. Lic. sch. psychologist, Minn., clin. psychologist, Minn. Med. sec. Korda Clinic, Pelican Rapids, Minn., 1974-77; news reporter KBRF Radio, Fergus Falls, Minn., 1981-84; rschr. Moorhead State U., 1986-92; sch. psychologist Sheyenne Valley SPED, Valley City, N.D., 1992-93; ind. sch. psychologist Rothsay, Minn., 1993-94, Cass County Spl. Svc., Fargo, N.D., 1994—; dir. After Sch. Program, Moorhead, 1997—; cons. 4-H Vols., Breckenridge, Minn., 1996—. Editor Children's Works mag., 1990-91. Vol. coord. Wilkin County Ext., Breckenridge, 1996—; Blandin Leadership coord. Rothsay Br., Minn., 1996—; adv. bd. Bapt. Ch., Rothsay, 1992—; pres. PTO, Rothsay, 1994; dist. rep. Head Start, Moorhead, 1980-86; Sunday sch. supt. Bapt. Ch., Rothsay, 1988-90. Mem. APA (divsn. 16), Nat. Assn. Sch. Psychologists, N.D. Psychol. Assn., Minn. Sch. Psychol. Assn. Republican. Office: Holiday Office Park 920 28th Ave S Ste 211 Moorhead MN 56560

FOLLMER, JOHN SCOTT, visual effects producer, supervisor; b. Chgo., Apr. 3, 1951; s. Frank Joseph and Lucille Caroline (Fink) F.; m. Carol Jean Lewittes, Feb. 9, 1974; children: Sean Weston, Brian Matthew, Kevin Jeremy. BS with honors, Ill. Inst. Tech., 1973. Animator, designer Crocus Prodns., Evanston, Ill., 1973-75; asst. dir. Phase 5 Prodns., Chgo., 1976; dir., designer Goldsholl Assocs., Northfield, Ill., 1977-84; dir., producer Moore Films, Inc., Hollywood, Calif., 1985; v.p., exec. producer Calico Entertainment, Chatsworth, Calif., 1986-94; v.p., head of prodn., co-exec. producer Metrolight Studios, Hollywood, 1994—. Supervising producer visual effects (films) Batman Forever, Warner Bros., 1995, Mortal Kombat New Line Cinema, 1995, Under Siege II-Dark Territory, Warner Bros., 1995, Virtuosity, Paramount Pictures, 1995, Broken Arrow, 20th Century Fox, 1996, Happy Gilmore, Universal Pictures, 1996, Matilda, Tristar Pictures, 1996, Daylight, Universal Pictures, 1996, Eraser, Warner Bros., 1996, Batman & Robin, Warner Bros., 1997, Kull the Conqueror, Universal Pictures, 1997, Leave it to Beaver, Universal Pictures, 1997, McHale's Navy, Universal Pictures, 1997, Baseketball, Universal Pictures, 1998, From the Earth to the Moon, Imagine Entertainment, 1998, Dragon Heart 2, Universal Pictures, 1998. Mem. Acad. TV Arts and Scis. Office: Metrolight Studios 5724 W 3rd St Ste 400 Los Angeles CA 90036-3078

FOLMSBEE, PATRICIA HURLEY, reading consultant; b. Malden, Mass., Jan. 13, 1939; d. Patrick Francis and Maura Eileen (Earls) Hurley; m. Calvin Coolidge Folmsbee, June 29, 1968; 1 child, John Stephen. AB, Albertus Magnus Coll., 1960; MEd, U. Mass., 1962, postgrad., 1969; cert. in reading and lang. arts, Ctrl. Conn. State U., 1974. Cert. reading and lang. arts cons. Tchr. Chicopee (Mass.) Bd. Edn., 1960-62, 64-69, Air Force Deps. Sch., Toul-Rosieres, France, 1962-64; reading and lang. arts cons. East Windsor (Conn.) Bd. of Edn., 1970-95, English ESL coord., 1990-96, lead tchr. reading & lang. arts, 1995-96; retired. Town meeting mem. Town of So. Hadley Mass., 1961-67; treas. Enfield (Conn.) Cultural Arts Commn., 1989-99; reading edn. del. to China Citizen Amb. Program of People to People Internat., 1993. Mem. NEA, Conn. Edn. Assn., Internat. Reading Assn., Conn. Assn. Reading Rsch. Democrat. Avocations: world traveler, skiing, classical music, theatre, reading. Home: 9 Martin Ter Enfield CT 06082-4528

FOLSOM, DAVID, judge; b. 1947. Student, So. State Coll., 1965-67; BA, U. Ark., 1969, JD, 1974. Assoc. Young & Patton, 1974-76; ptnr. Young, Patton & Folsom, 1974-90; dep. prosecuting atty. Lafayette County, 1978-81; pvt. practice, 1990-95; dist. judge U.S. Dist. Ct. (ea. dist.) Tex., 1995—; tchr. Arks. Sr. H.S., 1969-71. Mem. Ark. Bar Assn., Tex. Bar Assn., Ark. Trial Lawyers Assn., Texarkana Bar Assn., Tex. Trial Lawyers Assn., Northeast Tex. Bar Assn., Assn. of Trial Lawyers of Am., Southwest Ark. Bar Assn., Delta Theta Phi. Office: US Dist Ct 309 US Courthouse 500 Stateline Ave Texarkana TX 75501*

FOLSOM, HYTA PRINE, educational grant writer, consultant; b. Day, Fla., Jan. 6, 1948; d. John Wesley and Estelle Melissa (Weaver) Prine; m. Terrence Franklin Folsom, Aug. 25, 1968 (div. 1995); children: Heather V., Laura E., Teresa A., Tyson F. AA, North Fla. Jr. Coll., Madison, 1967; BS in Elem. Edn., Fla. State U., 1969, cert. in early childhood edn., 1981; MS in Ednl. Leadership, Nova U., 1991. Cert. Fund Raising Executive (CFRE) Nat. Soc. of Fund Raising Execs. (NSFRE), 1996. Tchr. Gladys Morse Elem. Sch., Perry, Fla., 1969-72, 73-74; owner, operator Hyta's Presch. and Nursery, Mayo, Fla., 1979; tchr. Lafayette Elem. Sch., Mayo, 1975-77, 81-93; grants writer Lafayette County Sch. Dist., Mayo, 1989-93; cons. Grant Writers Directory, Jostens Learning Corp., 1991—; dir. alt. resources Coun. of Govts., Odessa, Tex., 1993-97; owner, CEO Devel. Strategies, Inc., 1996—; dir. grants & fed. projects Odessa (Tex.) Coll., Odessa, Tex., 1998—; mem. tchr. edn. coun. Layafette County Sch. Dist., 1983-85, coord. prekindergarten program, 1989-93; rep. Nat. Child Devel. Assocs., 1992; mem. Lafayette Dist. Adv. Coun., 1990-93, Schoolyear 2000 Pub. Schs. Coun., 1991-93; chairperson Lafayette County Early Childhood Coun., 1989-92; dir. grants devel. and fed. projects and Title III coord. Odessa Coll., 1998—. Co-author: Rainbows of Readiness, 1990. Leader Brownie troop Girl Scouts U.S., 1984-85; mem.-at-large Suwannee River Resource Conservation Devel., 1991, sec., 1992-93; nursery coord., tchr. Sunday sch., leader children's ch. Brewer Lake Bapt. Ch., 1984-85. Named Master Tchr., State of Fla., 1986. Mem. Nat. Soc. Fund Raising Execs., Lafayette Edn. Assn. (v.p. 1976-77, 87-89, pres. 1990), Am. Diabetes Assn. (Odessa chpt. v.p. 1997, pres. 1998), Kiwanis (sec. Mayo chpt. 1992), Alpha Delta Kappa. Democrat. Avocation: reading. Home and office: 1513 Custer Ave Odessa TX 79761-3230

FOLSOM, LOWELL EDWIN, English language educator; b. Pitts., Sept. 30, 1947; s. Lowell Edwin and Helen Magdalene (Roeper) F.; m. Patricia Ann Jackson, Aug. 30, 1969; 1 child, Benjamin Bradford. BA, Ohio Wesleyan U., 1969; MA, U. Rochester, 1972, PhD, 1976. Chmn. English dept. Lancaster (Ohio) H.S., 1969-70, 71-72; instr. Eastman Sch. Music, Rochester, N.Y., 1974-75; vis. asst. prof. SUNY, Geneseo, N.Y., 1975-76; asst. prof. U. Iowa, Iowa City, 1976-82, assoc. prof., 1982-87, prof., 1987—, chair English dept., 1991-95, F. Wendell Miller disting. prof., 1997—; cons. Am. Coll. Testing Co., Iowa City, 1980—, Nat. Assessement of Ednl. Progress, Denver, 1980-84; dir. Walt Whitman Centennial Conf., Iowa City, 1992; Fulbright sr. prof. U. Dortmund, Germany, 1996. Author: Walt Whitman's Native Representations, 1994 (Choice Best Acad. Book 1995); editor: Walt Whitman: The Centennial Essays, 1994, Walt Whitman: The Measure of His Song, 1981 (Choice Best Acad. Book 1982), rev. edit., 1998 (Indenpendent Publisher Book Awd., 1999), Walt Whitman and the World, 1995, (CD-ROM) Walt Whitman, 1997 (choice Best Acad. Book, 1998), Walt Whitman Quarterly Rev., 1983—; co-dir. Walt Whitman Hypertext Archive, 1997—; editl. bd. Walt Whitman Encyclopedia, 1994-98. Recipient Rsch. award NEH, Washington, 1991-94; Rochester (N.Y.) Disting. scholar U. Rochester, 1995, Faculty Excellence award Iowa Bd. Regents, 1996. Mem. MLA, Am. Lit. Assn., Am. Studies Assn., Whitman Scholars Assn. (dir. 1992—). Home: 739 Clark St Iowa City IA 52240-5640 Office: Univ Iowa Dept English 308 EPB Iowa City IA 52242

FOLSOM, ROGER LEE, healthcare administrator; b. Hahira, Ga., May 17, 1952; s. Jesse Lee and Virginia (LeGette) F. BS in Biology, Valdosta (Ga.) State U., 1975; postgrad., U. Ga., 1975. From radiol. technologist to adminstrv. asst. Smith Hosp., Inc., Hahira, 1971-78; pharm. rep. The Upjohn Co., Dublin, Ga., 1979-85; cmty. rels. rep. Am. Med. Internat., Dublin, Ga., 1985-86; dir. mktg., pub. rels. Parkside Med. Svcs. Corp., Dublin, 1986-88, corp. mktg. dir. and pub. rels. S.E., 1988-94; owner, CEO Med1st Healthcare, Dublin, 1995—; adv. bd. Ga. Coop. Health Edn. Program, Dublin, 1987, pres., bd. dirs., 1992-95. Mem. Friends of Libr., Dublin, 1983—; coach, mem. adv. bd. Dublin Recreation Dept., 1986—; bd. dirs. Am. Heart Assn., Dublin, pres., 1989-90, chmn. bus. industry com.; bd. dirs. Ga. Assn. Med. Svcs., 1998—; adminstrv. bd., fin. com. Pine Forest United Meth. Ch., Dublin; chmn. planning and devel. com. Laurens 2000. Mem. Acad. Hosp. Mktg., Pub. Rels. and Planning/Am. Mktg. Assn., Dublin-Laurens C. of C. (charter leadership class 1989, mem. alumni com. 1990, bd. dirs. 1990, v.p. 1992, v.p. cmty. devel. 1992-93, pres. 1996—, chmn. bd. 1997-98, chmn. govtl. affairs com. 1999-2000), Ga. C. of C. (mem. govtl. affairs com.), Rotary (fund-raising chmn. Dublin 1986, bd. dirs. 1990-94, pres. Dublin club 1993-94, found. com. dist. 6920 gov.'s group rep., 1996—, lt. gov. 1997—), Dublin Country Club (bd. dirs., v.p. 1995—, pres. 1997). Democrat. Avocations: tennis, nature photography, reading, fly-fishing. Home: 506 Brookwood Dr PO Box 972 Dublin GA 31040-0972 Office: Med1st Healthcare 1016 Claxton Dairy Rd Ste 2-c Dublin GA 31021-7941

FOLTER, ROLAND, rare books company executive; b. Fulda, Fed. Republic of Germany, May 27, 1943; s. Heinz and Annemie (Bennewitz) F.; m. Siegrun Heinecke, Aug. 28, 1967 (dec. 1988); m. Mary Ann Kraus, Apr. 29, 1989; 1 child, Elizabeth. MA, Brown U., 1967, PhD, 1969. Rare books cataloger Yale U., New Haven, Conn., 1966-68; prof. U. Ill., Urbana, 1969-77; dir. H.P. Kraus Rare Books, N.Y.C., 1977—; jury Internat. League Antiquarian Booksellers Prize for Bibliography. Author: Deutsche Dichterbibliotheken, 1975; co-author: Bibliography: Its History, 1984; contbr. to ency. and articles to profl. jours. Violinist Frankfurt (Germany) Youth Symphony Orch., 1960-65. Fellow Brown U., 1968, Faculty fellow U. Ill., 1970-75. Fellow Pierpont Morgan Libr.; mem. Bibliog. Soc. Am. (coun. 1982-90), N.Y. Philharm. Soc., Assn. Internat. de Bibliophilie, Maximilian Gesellschaft, Gesellschaft der Bibliophilen, Antiquarian Booksellers Assn. Am., Old Book Table (pres. 1995-97), Princeton Club. Avocations: violin, chamber music, book collecting, mountaineering. Office: H P Kraus Rare Books 16 E 46th St New York NY 10017-2404

FOLTINY, STEPHEN VINCENT, special education educator; b. Syracuse, N.Y., Feb. 1, 1952; s. Stephen and Ilona T. (Kovacs) F. BA, Rutgers U., 1974; MA, Rider Coll., 1982. Tchr. Princeton (N.J.) Child Devel. Inst., 1986-87; assoc. teaching parent devel. disabilities div. State of N.J. Human Svcs., Trenton, 1988-91; trainer Mercer County (N.J.) Assn. Retarded Citizens, 1991; tchr., job coach EDEN W.E.R.C., Montgomery Twp., N.J., 1991—; behavioral cons. N.J. Ctr. Outreach and Svcs. for Autism Community, Trenton, N.J., 1992—; assoc. teaching parent divsn. Youth and Family Svcs., Autism unit, State of N.J., 1988-89; respite cons. New Horizons in Autism, Cranbury, N.J., 1997. Recipient N.J. State scholarship, 1970-74. Mem. Nat. Teaching Family Assn. (cert.), Coun. Exceptional Children, Coun. Children with Behavioral Disorders, N.J. Assn. for Persons in Supported Employment, United Chess Fedn. (cert. chess coach 1998). Avocations: coaching, sports, reading, stamp and coin collecting.

FOLTZ, ELDON LERCY, neurosurgeon, educator; b. Ft. Collins, Colo., Mar. 28, 1919; s. Leroy Stwart and Emily Louise (Proctor) F.; m. Catherine Churchill Crosby, Oct. 18, 1943; children: Sally J., James. S., Janis A., Suzanne E., Patricia L. BS with highest hons., Mich. State U., 1941; MD, U. Mich, 1943. Diplomate Am. Bd. Neurological Surgery. Intern surgery U. Mich. Hosp., Ann Arbor, 1943-44, asst. resident surgery, 1946-47; neurosurg. resident Dartmouth Coll. Medicine, Hanover, N.H., 1947-49, U. Louisville, Ky., 1949-50; instr. neurosurgery U. Wash., Seattle, 1950-53, asst. prof. neurosurgery, 1953-69; prof., chmn. neurosurg. dept. U. Calif., Irvine, 1969-81, prof. neurosurgery, 1981-89, prof. emeritus, 1989—. contbr. 130 articles to neurosurg. jours., 1950-98. Pres. and other offices Irvine Cove Comty. Assn., 1994—. Lt. MC USN, 1944-46. Named post-doctoral fellow NIMH, U. Wash., Seattle, 1950-51, Markle Med. Sci. scholar, Markle Found., N.Y.C., 1954-59; recipient Outstanding Alumnus award Mich. State U., 1980. Capistrano Bay Yacht Club. Avocation: competitive sailboat racing. E-mail: elfolz@uci.edu. Office: U Calif. Irvine Med Ctr Dept Neurosurgery 101 City Dr Orange CA 92868

FOLTZ, RODGER LOWELL, chemistry educator, mass spectroscopist; b. Milw., Feb. 10, 1934; s. Ross Milton and Ida Louise (Campbell) F.; m. Ruth Lynch Bilbe, June 9, 1956; children—Richard C., Camilla M. BS, MIT, 1956; PhD, U. Wis., 1961. Research chemist Battelle Meml. Inst., Columbus, Ohio, 1961-76; sr. research leader Battelle Meml. Inst., 1976-79; adj. prof. pharmacy Ohio State U., 1972-76, adj. assoc. prof. pharmacology, 1976-79; assoc. dir. Center for Human Toxicology, U. Utah, Salt Lake City, 1979—; rsch. assoc. prof. dept. pharmacology and toxicology U. Utah, Salt Lake City, 1980-85, rsch. prof. pharmacology/toxicology dept., 1985—; pres. CHT, Inc., 1985-87; exec. v.p., lab. dir. N.W. Toxicology Inc., 1987—. Contbr. articles to profl. jours.; editl. adv. bd. Biomed. Mass Spectrometry, 1979-87, 90-95. Pres. N.W. Area Human Relations Council, Columbus, 1968-70; deacon First Congregational Ch., 1971-75; trustee Denison U. Research Found., 1977-79. Mem. Internat. Assn. Forensic Toxicologists, Am. Chem. Soc. (chmn.-elect Columbus chpt. 1978, award Columbus chpt. 1977), Am. Soc. Mass Spectrometry (chmn. nominating com. 1980, 82, bd. dirs. 1988-90), Calif. Assn. Toxicologists (bd. dirs. 1990-91, v.p. 1994, pres. 1995-96), Am. Acad. Forensic Scis., Am. Assn. Pharm. Scientists, Soc. Forensic Toxicologists. Home: 2080 Belaire Dr Salt Lake City UT 84109-1409 Office: U Utah Ctr Human Toxicology 20 S 2030 E Salt Lake City UT 84112-9457 also: NWT Inc 1141 E 3900 S Salt Lake City UT 84124-1215

FOLZ, CAROL ANN, financial analyst; b. Cedar Rapids, Iowa, Dec. 28, 1951; D. Glenn Frederick and Ruth Frances (McIntosh) Rullman; m. Donald Harold McElderry, Oct. 3, 1970 (div. 1981); m. David Charles Folz, Mar. 19, 1983. AA, St. Louis Community Coll., 1973, AS in Library Svcs., 1973; BSBA, U. Mo., St. Louis, 1980. Library asst. Bloomfield (Iowa) Pub. Library, 1968-70, Ferguson (Mo.) Pub. Library, 1972-77; payroll clk. U. Mo., St. Louis, 1977-79, sr. sec., 1979-80, acct., 1980-82, sr. acct., 1982, sr. fiscal analyst, 1982-1989; payroll analyst Blue Cross and Blue Shield of Mo., St. Louis, 1990-91, sr. payroll acct., 1991; acct. Harris-Stowe State Coll., St. Louis, 1996-98, Accoutemps, St. Louis, 1998-99. Methodist. Avocations: genealogy, music, reading, sports, needlework, crafts.

FOLZ, KATHLEEN LOUISE, elementary education educator; b. Chgo.; d. Roman Louis and Dorothy Irene (Krueger) Salik; m. Thomas F. Folz. BS in Edn., Loyola U., Chgo., 1971; MS, St. Xavier U., 1997. Elem. tchr. St. Veronica Sch., Chgo., 1971-73, St. Robert Bellarmine Sch., Chgo., 1973-79; substitute tchr. St. Mary's Sch., Des Plaines, Ill., 1979-80, kindergarten and presch. tchr., 1980-86; kindergarten tchr. South Elem. Sch., Franklin Park, Ill., 1986-92, head tchr., 1989-90; tchr. South Elem. Sch., Franklin Park, 1992-93, 1992-93, tchr. kindergarten, 1993-97; tchr. North Elem. Sch., Franklin Park, 1997—; master tchr. Archdiocese of Chgo., 1982-86. Creator/tchr. kindergarten program, 1975, perceptual-motor program, 1976-86; sold 2 ideas (Spl. Spiders and Little Sprouts to The Mailbox mag., 1995), Plant a Little Flower, 1997, others.

FOMON, SAMUEL JOSEPH, physician, educator; b. Chgo., Mar. 9, 1923; s. Samuel and Isabel (Sherman) F.; m. Betty Lorraine Freeman, Aug. 20, 1948 (div. Apr. 1978); children: Elizabeth Ann Fomon Seiberling, Kathleen Lenore Fomon Anderson, David Bruce, Christopher, Mary Susan Fomon; m. Louise G. Thomson, June 27, 1986. AB cum laude, Harvard U., 1945; MD, U. Pa., 1947; D (hons.), U. Catolica de Cordoba, Argentina, 1974. Diplomate Am. Bd. Pediatrics, Am. Bd. Nutrition. Intern Queen's Gen. Hosp., Jamaica, N.Y., 1947-48; resident Children's Hosp., Phila., 1948-50; research fellow Cin. Children's Hosp. Research Found., 1950-52; asst. prof. pediatrics U. Iowa, Iowa City, 1954-58, assoc. prof., 1958-61, prof., 1961-93, prof. emeritus, 1993—; mem. rev. com. child health and human devel. program project NIH, 1966-69, nutrition study sect., 1978-81; mem. select com. GRAS (generally recognized as safe) substances Life Sci. Research Office, 1974-80. Author: Infant Nutrition, 1st edit., 1967, 2d edit., 1974, Nutrition of Normal Infants, 1993. Recipient Career Devel. award NIH, 1962-67, Rosen von Rosenstein award Swedish Pediatric Soc., 1975, McCollum award Am. Soc. Clin. Nutrition, 1979, F. Cuenca Villoro Found. award, Zaragosa, Spain, 1981, Commr.'s spl. citation FDA, 1984, Nutricia Found. award, Rotterdam, The Netherlands, 1991, Bristol-Myers Squibb/Mead Johnson award, 1992, Harry Schwachman award N.Am. Soc. Pediatric Gastroenterology and Nutrition, 1992. Fellow AAAS; mem. Am. Inst. Nutrition (pres. 1989-90, fellow 1989, Conrad A. Elvehjem award 1990), Am. Acad. Pediatrics (chmn. com. nutrition 1960-63, Borden award 1956), Am. Soc. Clin. Nutrition (pres. 1981-82), Fedn. Am. Socs. Exptl. Biology, Midwest Soc. Pediatric Rsch. (pres. 1963-64, Founder's award 1986), Am. Dietetic Assn. (hon.), El Colegio de Pediatria de Jalisco (hon.).

FONCELLO, MARTIN JOHN, JR., business and intelligence analyst, consultant; b. Bridgeport, Conn., Nov. 22, 1952; s. Martin John Sr. and Geraldine Mary (Parrella) F.; m. Mary Ann Catherine Grandieri, June 23, 1974; 1 child, Martin John III. BS, Boston Coll., 1974, MBA, 1982. Cert. sch. bus. adminstr., Conn. Gen. mgr. Grand Mfg. Corp., Danbury, Conn., 1981-83; EDP auditor Aetna Life & Casualty, Hartford, Conn., 1983-87; EDP audit officer People's Bank, Bridgeport, 1987-90; pres. Candlewood Mktg. & Cons., 1983—; adj. prof. Western Conn. State U., Danbury, 1983—. Pres. Greenridge Tax Dist., Brookfield, Conn., 1986—; sec. Brookfield Econ. Devel. Commn., 1992—; mem. Housatonic Valley Econ. Devel. Partnership, 1997—; rec. sec. Brookfield Rep. Town Com. Capt. U.S. Army, 1974-79, lt. col., battalion comdr. USAR. Mem. Res. Officers Assn. (life), Assn. Former Intelligence Officers, Mil. Intelligence Corps. Assn., First Corps of Cadets, Order Sons of Italy, Brookfield Rotary Club (pres. 1996-97, Paul Harris fellow Rotary Internat.). Republican. Roman Catholic. Avocations: military intelligence, coaching Little League, scouting. Home: 11 Drover Rd Brookfield CT 06804-3508

FONDA, BRIDGET, actress; b. Los Angeles, Jan. 27, 1964; d. Peter and Susan Fonda. Films: Aria, 1987, You Can't Hurry Love, 1988, Shag, 1988, Scandal, 1989, Strapless, 1989, Frankenstein Unbound, 1990, The Godfather, Part III, 1990, Doc Hollywood, 1991, Out of the Rain, (also known as Remains), 1991, Single White Female, 1992, Singles, 1992, Bodies Rest and Motion, 1993, Point of No Return, 1993, Little Buddha, 1994, It Could Happen To You, 1994, Camilla, 1994, The Road to Wellville, 1994, Rough Magic, 1995, Balto (voice), 1995, Grace of My Heart, 1996, City Hall, 1996; TV appearances: (series) 21 Jump Street, 1989, Jacob Have I Loved, WonderWorks episode, 1989, (made for cable movie) Leather Jackets, 1991; TV movie In the Gloaming, 1997; Jackie Brown, 1997, A Simple Plan, 1998, Finding Graceland, 1998, The Break Up, 1998, South of Heaven West of Hell, 1999, South From Hell's Kitchen, 1999, Monkey Bone, 1999, Lake Placid, 1999. *

FONDA, JANE, actress; b. N.Y.C., Dec. 21, 1937; d. Henry and Frances (Seymour) F.; m. Roger Vadim (div.); 1 child, Vanessa; m. Tom Hayden, Jan. 20, 1973 (div.); 1 child, Troy; m. Ted Turner, Dec. 21, 1991. Student, Vassar Coll. Appeared on Broadway stage in There Was a Little Girl, 1960, The Fun Couple, 1962; appeared in Actor's Studio prodn. Strange Interlude, 1963; appeared in films Tall Story, 1960, A Walk on the Wild Side, 1962, Period of Adjustment, 1962, Sunday in New York, 1963, In the Cool of the Day, 1963, The Love Cage, 1963, La Ronde, 1964, Cat Ballou, 1965, The Chase, 1966, Any Wednesday, 1966, The Game Is Over, 1967, Hurry Sundown, 1967, Barefoot in the Park, 1967, Barbarella, 1968, Spirits of the Dead, 1969, They Shoot Horses, Don't They?, 1969, Klute, 1970 (Acad. award best actress), Steelyard Blues, 1973, A Doll's House, 1973, The Blue Bird, 1976, Fun with Dick and Jane, 1976, Julia, 1977, also producer Coming Home, 1978 (Acad. award best actress), California Suite, 1978, Comes a Horseman, 1978, also producer The China Syndrome, 1979, Electric Horseman, 1979, Nine to Five, 1980, On Golden Pond, 1981, Rollover, 1981, The Dollmaker, 1984 (ABC-TV, Emmy award best actress), Agnes of God, 1985, The Morning After, 1986 (Acad. award nomination best actress), Old Gringo, 1988, Stanley and Iris, 1990, producer Lakota Woman, 1994; (TV miniseries) A Century of Women, 1994; author: Jane Fonda's Workout Book, 1981, Women Coming of Age, 1984, Jane Fonda's New Workout & Weight-Loss Program, 1986, Jane Fonda's New Pregnancy Workout & Total Birth Program, 1989, Jane Fonda Workout Video, 12 additional videos. Recipient Golden Apple prize for female star of yr. Hollywood Women's Press Club, 1977, Golden Globe award, 1978; rated no. 1 heroine of young Ams., U.S. News Roper Poll., 1985, 4th most admired woman in Am., Ladies Home Jour. Roper Poll, 1985. Office: CAA care Kim Hodgert 9830 Wilshire Blvd Beverly Hills CA 90212-1804*

FONDA, PETER, actor, director, producer; b. N.Y.C., Feb. 23, 1940; s. Henry and Frances (Seymour) F.; m. Susan Brewer (div. Apr. 1974); 2 children. Student, U. Omaha. Film appearances include Tammy and The Doctor, 1963, The Victors, 1963, Lilith, 1964, The Young Lovers, 1964, The Trip, 1967, The Wild Angels, 1966, The Last Movie, 1971, Two People, 1973, Dirty Mary, Crazy Harry, 1974, Race With The Devil, 1975, 92 in the Shade, 1975, Killer Force, 1975, Fighting Mad, 1976, Futureworld, 1976, Outlaw Blues, 1977, High Ballin', 1978, Wanda Nevada, 1979, Open Season, Smokey and the Bandit II, 1980, Split Image, 1982, Certain Fury, 1985, Dead Fall, 1993, Nadja, 1994, Love and a .45, 1994, Painted Hero, 1996, Grace of My Heart (voice), 1996, Escape From L.A., 1996, Idaho Transfer,

Spasm, Fatal Mission, Reckless; dir., actor in The Hired Hand, 1971, Two People, 1973; writer, co-producer, actor movie Easy Rider, 1969; TV movie appearances include The Hostage Tower, 1980, A Reason To Live, Don't Look Back, 1996, Ulee's Gold(won Golden Globe Award, Best Actor), Me and Will, 1998, South of Heaven West of Hell, 1999, The Passion of Ayn Rand, 1999, The Limey, 1999, Keeping Time, 1999. *

FONDAHL, JOHN WALKER, civil engineering educator; b. Washington, Nov. 4, 1924; s. John Edmund and Mary (DeCourcy) F.; m. Doris Jane Plishker, Mar. 2, 1946; children: Lauren Valerie, Gail Andrea, Meredith Victoria, Dorian Beth. B.S., Thayer Sch. Engring., Dartmouth, 1947, M.S. in Civil Engring, 1948. Instr., then asst. prof. U. Hawaii, 1948-51; constrn. engr. Winston Bros. Co., Mpls., 1951-52; project engr. Nimbus Dam and Powerplant project, Sacramento, 1952-55; mem. faculty Stanford U., 1955—, prof. civil engring., 1966-90, Charles H. Leavell prof. civil engring., 1977-90, prof. emeritus, 1990—. Author reports in field. Served with USMCR, 1943-46. Recipient Golden Beaver award Heavy Constrn. Industry, 1976. Fellow ASCE (Constrn. Mgmt. award 1977, Peurifoy Constrn. Rsch. award 1990), Project Mgmt. Inst. (hon. life, Fellow award 1981); mem. Nat. Acad. Engring., Phi Beta Kappa. Republican. Achievements include patent in field. Home and Office: 12810 Viscaino Rd Los Altos Hills CA 94022-2520

FONDAW, RONALD EDWARD, artist, educator; b. Paducah, Ky., Apr. 25, 1954; s. Lex Alan and Rose Mary (Holley) Kilgore; m. Lynn S. Shepard, Oct. 7, 1987; children: Andrea Rose, Wyler S. BFA, Memphis Coll. Art, 1976; MFA, U. Ill., 1978. Instr. Ohio U., Athens, 1978; assoc. prof. art U. Miami, Coral Gables, Fla., 1978-95, prof., 1997—; prof. art Washington U., St. Louis, 1995—; lectr., presenter workshops Ohio State U., Chgo. Art Inst., Tokyo U. Fine Art, Chautauqua Sch. Art. Exhbns. nat. and internat.; several public art commissions. Ford Found. fellow, 1977, Gla. Arts Coun. fellow, 1981, Guggenheim fellow, 1985, Pollack/Krasner fellow, 1997-98; NEAA grantee, 1988; Kransberg award St. Louis Art Mus., 1998. Home: 7345 Elm Ave Saint Louis MO 63143-3216 Office: Wash U 721 Kingsland Ave Saint Louis MO 63130-3107

FONDILLER, DAVID STEWART, editor, writer; b. N.Y.C., Apr. 20, 1966; s. Harvey V. and Shirley H. (Alperin) F.; m. Jennifer S. Gill, Aug. 16, 1992. BA in History, Columbia U., 1988, M Internat. Affairs, 1992. Mcpl. govt. reporter Gannett Westchester Newspapers, Yonkers and Peekskill, N.Y., 1988-90; deptl. rsch. asst. Columbia U. Sch. Internat. and Pub. Affairs, N.Y.C., 1991-92; press mgr. trainee Treuhandanstalt, Berlin, 1993; reporter Forbes, N.Y.C., 1993-95, staff writer, 1995-97; sr. editor Merrill Lynch, N.Y.C., 1998—; adj. instr. Columbia U. Sch. Internat. & Pub. Affairs, N.Y.C., 1996—. Scholar Scripps Howard Found., 1990-92, Fed. Chancellor scholar Alexander von Humboldt Found., 1992-93; Nat. Press Found. fellow, 1996. Mem. Overseas Press Club Am. (gov.), N.Y. Fin. Writers Assn. Office: Merrill Lynch World Fin Ctr South Tower New York NY 10080-6106

FONDILLER, SHIRLEY HOPE ALPERIN, nursing educator, journalist, historian; b. Holyoke, Mass.; d. Samuel and Rose (Sobiloff) Alperin; m. Harvey V. Fondiller, Dec. 27, 1957 (div. June 1984); 1 child, David Stewart. BS, Columbia U., 1962, MA, 1963, MEd, 1971, EdD, 1980. Dir. ednl. adminstrs., cons. and tchrs. sect. Am. Nurses Assn., N.Y.C., 1964-66, coord. careers program, 1967-70, coord. clin. sessions, 1971-72; editor Am. Nurse, Kansas City, Mo., 1975-78; assoc. prof., asst. to dean for spl. projects Rush-Presbyn.-St. Luke's Med. Ctr., 1979-86; exec. dir. Mid-Atlantic Regional Nursing Assn., N.Y.C., 1986-89; adj. assoc. prof. Columbia U., 1986—; founder, prin. Pub. for Health Dimensions, phd, 1990—. Author of books; contbr. articles to profl. jours. Fellow Am. Acad. Nursing; mem. Kappa Delta Pi, Sigma Theta Tau.

FONDO, EDWIN YOUNG, surgical oncologist; b. Bamenda, Cameroon, West Africa, Mar. 13, 1942; s. Ndom Gwesang and Elizabeth Fondo; m. Pamella Lindo, Oct. 12, 1974; children: Kimberlee, Asher. BA in Chemistry, Hastings Coll., 1966; MD, Howard U., 1970; DLitt (hon.), Christ Theol. Seminary, 1995. Diplomate Am. Bd. Surgery. Intern N.Y. Hosp., N.Y.C., 1970-71; resident in surgery Cornell Med. Ctr., N.Y.C., 1971-73; fellow in surgery Cornell Med. Coll., N.Y.C., 1970-73; resident in surgery Norwalk Hosp./Yale Univ., Norwalk, Conn., 1973-74; fellow in surgical oncology Meml. Hosp., N.Y.C., 1974-75; clin. chemistry rsch. trainee Meml. Sloan-Kettering, N.Y.C., 1975-76; clin. instr. in surgery Mt. Sinai Sch. Medicine, N.Y.C., 1978—; cons. clinician, Breast Exam Ctr. of Harlem, N.Y.C., 1979—; exec. v.p. Akers Labs. Ltd., 1996. Contbr. articles to profl. jours.; host, producer: (cable TV show) The Video Cancer Doctor, 1990—. Bd. dirs. Am. Cancer Soc., N.Y.C., 1978—, mem. profl. edn. and grants com.; dep. chief surgeon N.Y.C. Housing Police, 1979-82, chief surgeon, 1982-90. Named Alumnus of the Yr., Howard U. Alumni Assn. N.Y., 1985, Commandeur, Commanderie de Bordeaux, N.Y.C., 1986, Chevalier, Ordre Mondial, Chaine Des Rotisseur; recipient award of Excellence, Am. Cancer Soc., N.Y. Div., 1980. Republican. Presbyterian. Address: PO Box 324 New York NY 10021-0009

FONER, ERIC, historian, educator; b. N.Y.C., Feb. 7, 1943; s. Jack D. and Liza F.; m. Lynn Garafola, May 1, 1980. BA, Columbia U., 1963, Oxford (Eng.) U., 1965; PhD, Columbia U., 1969. Prof. history City Coll., CUNY, N.Y.C., 1973-82, Columbia U., N.Y.C., 1982—; Pitt prof. Am. history and instns. Cambridge (Eng.) U., 1980-81; Harmsworth prof. Am. history Oxford (Eng.) U., 1993-94. Author: Free Soil, Free Labor, Free Men, 1970, Tom Paine and Revolutionary America, 1976, Politics and Ideology in the Age of the Civil War, 1980, Nothing But Freedom, 1983, Reconstruction: America's Unfinished Revolution, 1988, Readers' Encyclopedia of American History, 1991, Freedom's Lawmakers, 1993, The Story of American Freedom, 1998; editor: The New American History, 1990, The Reader's Companion to American History, 1991, The Story of American Freedom, 1998. Recipient Bancroft prize Columbia U., 1989, L.A. Times Book award, 1989, Parkman prize Soc. Am. Historians, 1989, Owsley prize So. Hist. Assn., 1989, Lit. Lion prize N.Y. Pub. Libr., 1994; named Scholar of Yr., N.Y. Coun. for the Humanities, 1995; fellow ACLS, 1972-73, NEH, 1983-84, Guggenheim fellow, 1974-76. Mem. Am. Hist. Assn. (pres. 2000), Orgn. Am. Historians (Avery O. Craven prize 1989, pres. 1993-94), Am. Antiquarian Soc., Am. Acad. Arts and Scis., British Acad. Home: 606 W 116th St New York NY 10027-7011

FONER, SIMON, research physicist; b. Pitts., Aug. 13, 1925; s. Newton F. Foner. BS, Carnegie-Mellon U., 1947, MS, 1948, DSc, 1952. Research physicist Carnegie-Mellon U., Pitts., 1952-53; staff physicist Lincoln Lab. MIT, Lexington, 1953-61; staff physicist Francis Bitter Nat. Magnet Lab., MIT, Cambridge, 1961-63, project leader, 1963-77, chief scientist, head research div., 1977—; assoc. dir. Francis Bitter Nat. Magnet Lab., MIT, 1988-95; sr. rsch. scientist dept. physics MIT, Cambridge, 1982-95; dir. NATO Advanced Study Insts. in Europe, 1970, 73, 76, 80; chmn. Internat. Cryogenic Materials conf., 1983-85; bd. dirs. Applied Superconductivity Conf., Inc., 1982-88, 92-94, hon. program chmn., 1992-94; bd. dirs. Cryogenic Engring. Conf., 1983-85; mem. Internat. Cryogenics Materials Conf., 1983-92; cons. editor Rev. of Sci. Instruments, 1979—; vis. scientist Francis Bitter Magnet Lab, MIT, 1995—. Editor 4 books in magnetism, superconductivity and applications; contbr. articles to profl. jours.; patentee magnetometers, superconducting materials. Served with USN, 1944-46. Named Disting. lectr. for Magnetic Soc. IEEE, 1982-83. Joseph F. Keithley award. Fellow AAAS, IEEE, Am. Phys. Soc. (exec. com. coun. 1983, chmn. publs. com. 1986-87, mem.-at-large exec. com. condensed matter physics div. 1970-72, chmn. 1978-81, councillor 1982-86, exec. com. magnetics group 1997). Office: Francis Bitter Magnet Lab MIT Albany St Cambridge MA 02139-3529

FONG, HIRAM LEONG, former senator; b. Honolulu, Oct. 15, 1906; s. Lum Fong and Chai Ha Lum; m. Ellyn Lo; children, Hiram, Rodney, Marie-Ellen Fong Gushi, Marvin-Allan (twins). AB with honors, U. Hawaii, 1930, LLD, 1953; JD, Harvard U., 1935; LLD, Tufts U., 1960, Lafayette Coll., 1960, Lynchburg Coll., 1970, Lincoln U., 1971, U. Guam, 1974, St. John's U., 1975, Calif. Western Sch. Law, 1976, Tung Wu (Soochow) U., Taiwan, 1978, China Acad., Taiwan, 1978; LHD, L.I. U., 1968. With supply dept. Pearl Harbor Navy Yard, 1924-27; chief clk. Suburban Water System, 1930-32; dep. atty. City and County of Honolulu, 1935-38; founder, ptnr. law firm Fong, Miho, Choy & Robinson, until 1959; founder, chmn. bd. emeritus Finance Factors, Grand Pacific Life Ins. Co.; founder, chmn bd. Finance Investment Co., Market City, Ltd., Fin. Enterprises Ltd.; pres. Ocean View Cemetery, Ltd.; owner, operator Sen. Fong's Plantation and Gardens, Honolulu; dir. numerous firms, Honolulu; hon. cons. China Airlines. Mem. Hawaii Legislature, 1938-54, speaker, 1948-54; mem. U.S. Senate, 1959-77, Post Office and Civil Service Com., Judiciary Com., Appropriations Com., Spl. Com. on Aging; U.S. del. 150th Anniversary Argentine Independence, Buenos Aires, 1960, 55th Interparliamentary Union (World) Conf., 1966, Ditchley Found. Conf., 1967, U.S.-Can. Inter-Parliamentary Union Conf., 1961, 65, 67, 68, Mex.-U.S. Inter-Parliamentary Conf., 1968, World Interparliamentary Union, Tokyo, 1974; mem. Commn. on Revision Fed. Ct. Appellate System, 1975—; Active in civic and service orgns.; v.p. Territorial Constl. Conv., 1950; del. Rep. Nat. Conv., 1952, 56, 60, 64, 68, 72; founder, chmn. bd. Fin. Factors Found.; founder, pres. Hiram & Ellyn Fong Found.; founder, pres., chmn. bd. Market City Found.; hon. co-chmn. McKinley High Sch. Found., 1989; bd. visitors U.S. Mil. Acad., 1971—, U.S. Naval Acad., 1974—. Served from 1st lt. to maj. USAAF, 1942-44; ret. col. USAF Res. Recipient award NCCJ, 1960, Meritorious Svc. citation Nat. Assn. Ret. Civil Employees, 1963, Horatio Alger award, 1970, citation for outstanding svc. Japanese Am. Citizens League, 1970, award Am. Acad. Achievement, 1971, Outstanding Svc. award Orgn. Chinese Ams., 1973, award Nat. Soc. Daus. Founders and Patriots Am., 1974, cert. Pacific Asian World, 1974, Citizen Among Citizens award Boys & Girls Clubs of Hawaii, 1991, Disting. Alumnus award U. Hawaii Alumni Assn., 1991, Kulia I Ka Nu'u award Pub. Schs. Hawaii Found., 1992, Dedication and Support Svc. award McKinley Found., 1995, ABOTA-Hawai'i Ha'aheo award, 1997; named to Jr. Achievement Hawaii Bus. Hall of Fame, 1995; decorated Order of Brilliant Star with Grand Cordon Republic of China, 1976, Order of Diplomatic Svc. Merit, Gwanghwan Medal Republic of Korea, 1977; Univ. of Hawaii Colls. of Arts and Scis. Hiram L. Fong Endowment in Arts and Scis., 1995; recipient nat. Outstanding Citizen Achievement award Orgn. Chinese Ams., Inc., 1996; named Model Chinese Father of Yr., United Chinese Soc., 1996. Mem. Am. Legion, VFW, Lambda Alpha Internat. (Aloha chpt.), Phi Beta Kappa. Congregationalist. Home: 1102 Alewa Dr Honolulu HI 96817-1507

FONG, JEFFREY TSE-WEI, mechanical engineer; b. Shanghai, China, Nov. 24, 1934; m. Elizabeth Chang, 1956; children: Ivan K., Linda F. BSc in Engring., U. Hong Kong, 1955; MS, Columbia U., 1961; PhD in Applied Mechanics & Math., Stanford U., 1966. Design engr. powerplants Ebasco Svc. Inc., N.Y.C., 1955-63; rsch. assoc. applied mechanics Stanford U., 1964-66; rsch. assoc. applied math. U.S. Nat. Bur. Standards, 1966-68; physicist U.S. Nat. Bur. Standards & Tech., 1968—; sr. policy analyst U.S. Nuclear Regulatory Commn., 1975-76. Recipient Silver medal U.S. Dept. Commerce, 1979. Fellow ASME (disting. lectr. 1988-92, chmn. PVP divsn. 1986-87, pressure vessel & piping medal 1993), Am. Soc. Testing & Mat. (chmn. subcom. E9-01 1978-80); mem. Am. Phys. Soc., Soc. Theology, Soc. Industrial & Applied Math. Am. Statistical Assn. Achievements include research in computational mathematics, applied mechanics and statistical methods for modeling thermo-mechanical behavior of structural materials in both elastic and inelastic states as well as fatigue and fracture to improve quality and reliability. Office: Nat Inst of Standards Tech Rm 388 NIST-North MC8201365 I-270 & quince Orchard Rd Gaithersburg MD 20899*

FONG, MATTHEW KIPLING, state official; b. Oakland, Calif., Nov. 20, 1953; s. Chester and March Fong; m. Paula Fong, May 28, 1978; children: Matthew II, Jade. Grad., U.S. Air Force Acad., 1975; MBA, Pepperdine U., 1982; JD, Southwestern Law. Sch., 1985. Former vice chmn. State Bd. Equalization; treas. State Calif., L.A., -1999; atty. L.A., 1999—. Regent Pepperdine U., Children's Hosp. L.A.; Rep. nominee State Controller, 1990. Lt. col. Air Force Res. Office: Sheppard Mullin Richter & Hampton 333 S Hope St 48th Fl Los Angeles CA 90071*

FONG, WEN CHIH, art historian, educator, author, museum curator; b. Shanghai, People's Republic of China, Dec. 9, 1930; came to U.S., 1948, naturalized, 1961; s. Tse-tsing and Jen-yen (Sha) F.; m. Constance Chih-ming Tang, Aug. 29, 1953; children: Laurence T., Peter C., Serena M. AB, Princeton U., 1951, MFA, 1954, PhD, 1958. Research asst. Cleve. Mus. Art, 1953; instr., then asst. prof. Princeton U., 1955-60; vis. curator Oriental art Yale Art Gallery, 1958-59; mem. faculty Princeton U., 1960—, prof. art and archeology, curator Oriental art, 1967—, chmn. PhD program Chinese and Japanese art and archeology, 1964—, chmn. dept. art and archeology, 1970-73, Sanford Edwards prof. art and archeology, 1971—, chmn. exec. com. Art. Mus., 1970-75; mem. vis com. dept. fine arts Harvard U., 1972-77; cons. chmn. Asian Art Dept., Met. Mus. Art, 1971—; mem. art com. China Inst. Am., 1971—, trustee, 1984; adv. council art dept. Mt. Holyoke Coll.; gallery com. Asia Soc. Art Gallery, N.Y.C. Author: (with Sherman E. Lee) Streams and Mountains Without End, 2d edit., 1966, Lohans and a Bridge to Heaven, 1958, Problems of Forgeries in Chinese Painting, 1963, Sung and Yuan Paintings, 1973, Summer Mountains, The Timeless Landscape, 1975, The Great Bronze Age of China, 1980, (with Murck, Shih, Ch'en and Stuart) Images of the Mind: Selections from the Edward L. Elliott Family and John B. Elliot Collections of Chinese Calligraphy and Painting, 1984, Beyond Representation: Chinese Painting and Calligraphy 8th-14th Century, 1992, Possessing the Past: Treasures from the National Palace Museum, 1996; organizer exhbn. from People's Republic China (The Great Bronze Age in China), Met. Mus. Art, N.Y.C., 1980-81, other exhbns., Princeton Art Mus.; installed permanent Japanese art galleries, Met. Mus. Art, 1987, Weber Galleries of Ancient Chinese Art, Met. Mus. Art, 1988. Hon. fellow Inst. Oriental Studies Hong Kong U., 1961-62, Inst. Advanced Chinese Studies, Republic of China, 1966; Bollingen Found. fellow, 1956-57; Guggenheim fellow, 1961-62; Am. Council Learned Soc., 1965-66, 69-71; McCosh Faculty fellow, Princeton U., 1965-66. Mem. Am. Coll. Art Assn. (bd. dirs. 1971-76), Chinese Art Soc. Am.; mem. Chinese painting delegation to People's Republic of China, 1977 (Comm. Scholarly Communications with PRC), Am. Philos. Soc., Academia Sinica.

FONKEN, GERHARD JOSEPH, retired chemistry educator, academic administrator; b. Krefeld, Germany, Aug. 3, 1928; came to U.S., 1930, naturalized, 1935; s. Henry A. and Wilhelmina Katerina (von Eyser) F.; m. Carolyn Lee Stay, Dec. 20, 1952; children—David, Katherine, Steven, Karen, Eric. BS, U. Calif., Berkeley, 1954, PhD, 1957. Chemist Procter & Gamble Co., 1957-58; chemist Stanford (Calif.) Research Inst., 1958-59; instr. U. Tex., Austin, 1959-61; from asst. to assoc. prof. U. Tex., 1961-72, prof. chemistry, 1972-94, assoc. provost, 1972-75, acting v.p. acad. affairs, 1975-76, exec. asst. to pres., 1976-79, v.p. research, 1979-80, v.p. acad. affairs and research, 1980-85, exec. v.p., provost, 1985-94; retired, 1994. Contbr. articles to chemistry jours. Served with U.S. Army, 1946-49, 50-51, Korea. Decorated Order of the Crown, Kingdom of Belgium; grantee NIH, 1961-64, Robert A. Welch Found., 1962-79. Mem. Am. Chem. Soc. Home: 6612 Lost Horizon Dr Austin TX 78759-6116

FONSECA, JOHN DOS REIS, writer, former law educator; b. New Bedford, Mass., Mar. 13, 1925; s. José dos Reis and Maria (Vicente) F.; m. Joan Fagan, Aug. 27, 1949; children: Kathleen, Patricia, Gwendolyn. AB cum laude, Harvard U., 1949, JD, 1952. Bar: Mass. 1952, N.Y. 1955, U.S. Supreme Ct. 1976. Fin. analyst Dun & Bradstreet, Boston and S.Am., 1952-53; trust administr. Chase Manhattan Bank, N.Y.C., 1953-56; chmn. banking Community Coll., Utica, N.Y., 1956-65; pres. Hamilton Research, Boston, 1965-66; prof. law and banking SUNY, Albany, 1968-85; mem. N.Y. State Consumer Protection Bd., 1972; visiting prof. Wharton Sch. Fin., Phila., 1959-60; cons. State Edn. Dept. on the Regents External Degree Program, 1971-72; developer confs. on estates, trusts, taxes and ins., 1970-72. Author: Law of Business Organizations, vols. I-II, 1971, Law and Society, vols. I-III, 1972, Williston on Sales, 4th edit.Law for the Business Manager, 1977, Law of Modern Commercial Practices, vols. I-II, 1981, Handling Consumer Credit Cases, vols. I-II, 1986, Consumer Credit Compliance Manual, 2nd edit., 1984; editor-in chief Uniform Commercial Code Law Jouranl, 1968-72; editor Banking Law Journal, 1967-72, Encyclopedia of Commercial Laws, 1968-71 and other law jours.; contbr. numerous articles to profl. jours. Served with U.S. Army, 1943-46. Fellow Niagara Mohawk Power Corp., Security Mut. Life Ins. Co., New England Life Ins. Co., Nationwide Ins. Co., Key Banks, Inc. Mem. Saratoga County Bar Assn. Home: Malloy Rd El Rancho Greenfield Center NY 12833

FONSECA, RAYMOND J., dental medicine educator. Prof. oral and maxillofacial surgery Sch. Dentistry U. Mich., until 1989; dean Sch. Dental Medicine, U. Pa., Phila., 1989—. Office: U Pa Sch Dental Medicine 4001 Spruce St 1st Fl Philadelphia PA 19104*

FONSECA, RONALD A., federal judge. Magistrate judge U.S. Dist. Ct. (ea. dist.) La., New Orleans, 1983—. Fax: (504) 589-7190. Office: US Dist Ct (ea dist) La 501 Magazine St Rm B-437 New Orleans LA 70130

FONTAINE, BERNARD LEO, JR., small business owner; b. Holyoke, Mass., Nov. 18, 1956; s. Bernard Leo and Claire Doris (Mathey) F.; m. Susan Eileen Scalia, Apr. 7, 1962. BS, Northeastern U., Boston, 1979; MS, U. Okla., 1983-84. Cert. Am. Bd. Indsl. Hygiene, Bd. Cert. Safety Profls. Indsl. hygiene tech. U.S. Dept. Labor, OSHA, Springfield, Mass., 1976-79; indsl. hygienist U.S. Dept. Labor, OSHA, Hartford, Conn., 1979-83; reg. indsl. hygienist U.S. Dept. Navy, Portsmouth, N.H., 1984-85; health and safety supr. Internat. Tech. Corp., Edison, N.J., 1985-87; corp. indsl. hygienist Atlantic Mut. Cos., Madison, N.J., 1987-90; founder, chief exec. officer The Windsor Group, Inc., Spotswood, N.J., 1990-97, Windsor Consulting Group, Inc., Spotswood, 1997—. Contbr. articles to profl. jours. Mem. Am. Indsl. Hygiene Assn., Am. Soc. Safety Engrs., Am. Conf. Govt. Indsl. Hygienists, Am. Acad. Indsl. Hygiene, Council on Occupational Hearing Conservation. Republican. Roman Catholic. Avocations: golf, tennis, boating. Office: The Windsor Consulting Group Inc 14 Scheinfein St Ste 100 South River NJ 08882-2526

FONTAINE, EUDORE JOSEPH, JR., artist, art historian; b. Springfield, Mass., Aug. 5, 1929; s. Eudore Joseph and Antoinette Marie (Desautels) F.; m. Rose J. Brigada, June 28, 1952; children: Catherine, Christopher, Carolyn, Stephen, Thomas. BA magna cum laude, Tufts U., 1951; LLB, Harvard U., 1958. One-man shows include MIT, 1985, Crane Gallery, 1986, Babson Coll., 1987, Lily Pad Gallery, 1989, The Copley Soc. of Boston, 1989, David Findlay Gallery, N.Y.C., 1990, Mus. Fine Arts, Springfield, Mass., 1991, Elms Coll., 1991; exhibited in numerous galleries in New Eng. Lt. USN, 1951-55. Roman Catholic. Home: 73 Greylock Rd Wellesley MA 02481-1301

FONTAINE, RONALD GERARD, librarian; b. Warwick, R.I., Aug. 15, 1955; s. Theotime A. and Exina Marie-Rose (Caplette) F.; m. Lynn Marie Brown, Apr. 13, 1985; 1 child, Danielle Marguerite. BA in French, U. R.I., 1978, MLS, 1980. Libr. Nat. Marine Fisheries Svc. Lab., Milford, Conn., 1980-83; pub. svcs. libr., adj. faculty Buley Libr., So. Conn. State U., New Haven, 1983-85; pub. svcs. libr. Buley Libbr., So. Conn. State U., New Haven, 1988—; serials libr. Wheaton Coll., Norton, Mass., 1985-86; head reference libr. Sacred Heart U., Fairfield, Conn., 1986-89; evening ref. libr. Sacred Heart U., 1986-88, head ref. libr., 1989; libr. state agy. Office Policy & Mgmt., Hartford, Conn., 1989-92; libr. corrections Cheshire (Conn.) Correctional Instn., 1992-93; reference libr., reference mgr. Hartford (Conn.) Pub. Libr., 1993-95; reference libr. Bridgeport (Conn.) Pub. Libr., 1995—. Mem. ALA, Conn. Libr. Assn. (mem. intellectual freedom com. 1989-90), Elks. Avocation: record collecting. Home: 9 Robert St Milford CT 06460-4052

FONTAINE, SUE (JEANE FONTAINE), public relations professional; b. Rolfe, Iowa; d. Vernette M. and Dorothy (Messinger) Gaskins m. Henry A. Fontaine, Jr., July 1, 1948 (div. 1970); children: Eva Joel, Jeffrey David. BA in Journalism, U. Iowa, 1947; MLS, U. Mo., 1977. Radio and TV dir. Swigart Advt., Inc., New Orleans, 1948-54, 62-65; producer Sta. WDSU-TV, New Orleans, 1948-54; dir. pub. rels. La. State Libr., Baton Rouge, 1960-62, Tulsa City-County Libr., 1965-67, 70-76; spl. projects asst. U. Mo. Sch. Libr., Info. Sci., Columbia, 1976-77; pub. info. officer Wash. State Libr., Olympia, 1977-81; assoc. mgr. pub. rels. N.Y. Pub. Libr., N.Y.C., 1981-85; pub. rels./mktg. dir. Queens Borough Pub. Libr., Jamaica, N.Y., 1985-91; owner SF PR/Mktg., N.Y. and Fla., 1991—; mktg., pub. rels. cons. to various libraries and comml. clients, 1960—. Editor: (with Susan Phelps) Communications for the Humanities, 1975; Public Relations: Tick/Click, 1975; Best of Library Literature, 1981; contbr. articles to profl. jours. Bd. mem. Friends St. Pete Beach Pub. Libr., 1999—. Recipient 5 John Cotton Dana Pub. Rels. awards, 1965-75. Mem. ALA (past sect. chmn., bd. dirs., com. chair 1990—), Pub. Rels. Soc. Am., Women In Comms. (past chpt. pres.), N.Y. Libr. Assn. (chmn. pub. rels. round table, viburnum pub. awareness grant project 1992-95), Iowa-Yucatan Ptnrs., Libr. Pub. Rels. Coun. (mem. exec. bd., past pres.), Alpha Xi Delta. Episcopalian. Summer home: 2612 Lakeside Ave Milford IA 51351-7231

FONTANA, BERNARD LEE, retired anthropologist, writer, consultant; b. Oakland, Calif., Jan. 7, 1931; s. Bernard Campion and Hope Mary (Smith) F.; m. Hazel Ann McFeely, June 27, 1954; children: Geoffrey Earl Francis, Nicholas Anthony, Francesca Ann. BA, U. Calif., Berkeley, 1953; PhD, U. Ariz., 1960. Field historian U. Ariz., Tucson, 1960-62, 78-92; ethnologist Ariz. State Mus., Tucson, 1962-78; writer, cons. Tucson, 1992—; lectr. anthropology dept. U. Ariz., 1962-78; expert witness Papago Tribe of Ariz., Sells, 1962-64; pres. Ariz.-Sonora desert Mus., Tucson, 1983-85; cons. San Xavier Dist. Tohono O'Odham Nation, Tucson, 1992-93, KUAT-TV, Tucson, 1996. Author: Tarahumara: Where Night Is The Day Of The Moon, 1979 (Border Regional Libr. Assn. award 1979), Of Earth and Little Rain: The Papago Indians, 1981 (Border Regional Libr. Assn. award 1981), Entrada: The Legacy of Spain and Mexico in the United States, 1994; editor: Before Rebellion, 1996, A Guide to Contemporary Southwest Indians, 1999. Active western regional adv. com. Nat. Pk. Svc., San Francisco, 1974-76; sheriff Tucson Corral of the Westerners, 1976; sec. Patronato San Xavier, Tucson, 1989—. Calif. Alumni scholar U. Calif. Alumni Assn., Berkeley, 1948; pre-doctoral fellow Wenner Gren Found. for Anthrop. Rsch., 1959; recipient Ben Avery award Ariz. Clean and Beautiful, 1994, Ariz. Gov. Hist. Preservation award Ariz. Heritage Found., 1995. Fellow Ariz. Nev. Acad. Sci.; mem. Soc. For Hist. Arch. (life, pres. 1970, J. C. Harrington medal 1992), Ariz. Arch. and Hist. Soc. (pres. 1960-61, editor 1958-60, Victor R. Stoner award 1990), Am. Soc. for Ethnohistory (pres. 1965, editor 1969-72), S.W. Pks. and Monuments Assn. (life, vice chmn. 1988, Edward Danson award 1989, Emil Haury award 1991). Avocation: philately. Home and Office: 7710 S Mission Rd Tucson AZ 85746-7143

FONTANA, JOHN ARTHUR, employee benefits specialist; b. N.Y.C., Feb. 24, 1955; s. Joseph and Gloria (Rosiello) F.; m. Patricia Ann Cooper, Nov. 10, 1979; children: Adam Vincent, Brian Patrick, Jennifer Ann. BA in Econs., Fordham U., 1977, MBA in Acctg., 1984. Pension analyst George Buck Cons. Actuaries, N.Y.C., 1977-79; retirement plan analyst Sperry Corp., N.Y.C., 1979-80; ops. specialist Bankers Trust Co., N.Y.C., 1980-83; mgr. employee benefits Fidata Corp., N.Y.C., 1983-85; mgr. benefit plan devel. N.Y. Power Authority, White Plains, 1985-90; dir. employee benefits Random House, Inc., N.Y.C., 1990-98; dir. benefits and HRIS Polygram Holding, Inc., N.Y.C., 1998-99; sr. cons. Price-Waterhouse Coopers, N.Y.C., 1999—. Bd. dirs. Monroe (N.Y.) Dem. Com., 1985-87; capt. United Way, N.Y.C., 1992—; musician Ch. of the Sacred Heart, Monroe, 1989—, also mem. fin. com.; team mgr. M-W Little League, 1987-90. Mem. U.S. C. of C. (benefits com. 1987-89), Am. Mgmt. Assn. Democrat. Roman Catholic. Avocations: music, golf, collecting baseball memorabilia. Home: 51 Old Country Rd Monroe NY 10950-4917 Office: Random House Inc 201 E 50th St New York NY 10022-7703

FONTANA, MARIO H., nuclear engineer; b. West Springfield, Mass., Mar. 30, 1933; s. Remo and Sabina F.; m. Sue Janeway, Apr. 12, 1958; children: Richard, Edward. BS, U. Mass., 1955; MS, MIT, 1957; PhD, Purdue U., 1968. Registered engr., Tenn. Mem. rsch. staff Oak Ridge (Tenn.) Nat. Lab., 1957-63, 65-81, asst. dir. nuc. safety rsch., 1968-72, head advanced concepts devel. engring. tech. divsn., 1972-81, asst. to dir. engring. tech. divsn., 1990-92; sr. scientist Avco Rsch. and Advanced Devel., Wilmington, Mass., 1963-64; instr. Purdue U., Oak Ridge, Tenn., 1964-65; dir. industry degraded core program Tech for Energy, Inc., Knoxville, Tenn., 1981-84; v.p. engring. Energex Oak Ridge, 1984-85; dir. nuclear safety tech. IT Corp. and Tenera, L.P., Knoxville, 1985-90; group leader Advanced Concepts, 1993-94; ret., 1994; cons. U.S. AEC, Washington, 1972-73, U.S. NRC, Washington, 1979-81, 91—, U.S. Dept. Energy, Washington, 1986-89; adj. prof. U. Tenn., 1995—; mem. Adv. Com. on Reactor Safeguards, 1995—. Author more than 100 reports and articles. Fellow Am. Nuclear Soc. (chmn. nuclear reactor safety divsn. 1972-73, 94-95); mem. AAAS, ASME, Am.

Mgmt. Assn., Soc. Risk Analysis, Rotary Internat., Sigma Xi, Tau Beta Pi. Achievements include patents for method of arc synthesis of uranium carbide from UF6 and Graphite, others. Office: Oak Ridge Nat Lab PO Box 2009 Oak Ridge TN 37831-2009

FONTANA, MICHAEL, educational foundation administrator, writer, poet. BA in English and Creative Writing, Charter Oak State Coll., 1985; MA in English and Creative Writing, Miami U., Oxford, Ohio, 1989. VISTA worker Ohio Coalition for the Homeless, Columbus, 1986-87; instr. dept. English Miami U., 1987-90; coordinating dir. Greater Cin. Coalition for the Homeless, 1990-94; cons. Caracole, Cin., 1994-95; edn. mgr. Recovery Initiative, Cin., 1995-96; comm. specialist U. Cin. Found., 1996—. Contbr. numerous essays, short stories and poems to jours. in field, anthologies. Trustee Mental Health Assn., Cin., 1991-95, 96—, pres., 1997—, v.p. for advocacy, 1992-95; trustee Found. for Change/Consumer Quality Rev. Team, Cin., 1997-98, pres., 1997—; devel. vol. Recovery Initiative, Cin., 1996—, Jordan Ctr., Cin., 1996—; media liaison Ohio Coalition on Male Survivor Issues, Columbus, 1995-96; mem. cmty. devel. adv. bd. City of Cin., 1991-95; trustee Ohio Coalition for the Homeless/Coalition on Homelessness and Housing in Ohio, Cin., 1991-95, sec., 1994; mem. Ryan White Funding Adv. Com. Greater Cin. AIDS Consortium, 1994-95; mem. housing adv. bd. Hamilton County, Cin., 1992-94; mem. human svcs. adv. bd. St.John Social Svc. Ctr., Cin., 1992-93; mem. organizing com. Coun. Christian Communions, Cin., 1992; co-chair Gen. Assistance Coalition of Greater Cin., 1991-92; mem. steering com. Let Justice Roll! Cin., 1991; state coord. Ohio Housing Now!, Columbus, 1989; trustee Butler County Housing Coalition, Oxford, 1988-90, v.p., 1989-90. Individual Artist fellow in creative writing Ohio Arts Coun., 1995; recipient Helen Isay Smith Meml. award Mental Health Assn. of Cin. Area, 1994, advocacy award Hamilton County Cmty. Mental Health Bd., 1998; named Prominent Cincinnatian, Cin. Enquirer, 1993. Home: 3927 N Clerose Cir Cincinnati OH 45205

FONTANA, ROBERT EDWARD, electrical engineering educator, retired air force officer; b. Bklyn., Nov. 26, 1915; s. Valentino and Secondina (Lesca) F.; m. Victoria E. Mauriello, Dec. 2, 1945; children: Robert Edward, Thomas Paul, Mary Joan. B Elec. Engring, NYU, 1939; MS, U. Ill., 1947, PhD, 1949. Commd. 2d lt. USAAF, 1942; advanced through grades to col. USAF, 1959, ret., 1969; research scientist Sandia Corp., 1949-54; spl. asst. nuclear devel. Hdqrs. USAF, 1954-58; head nuclear applications (Air Research and Devel. Command), 1958-61; dir. (Aerospace Research Labs.), Wright-Patterson AFB, Ohio, 1961-66; chmn. dept. elec. engring. Air Force Inst. Tech., Wright-Patterson AFB, 1966-84, prof. emeritus, 1984—. Pres. Honors Seminars Met. Dayton, 1966-86. Decorated Legion of Merit with oak leaf cluster, Exceptional Civilian service award Dept. Air Force, 1985. Fellow IEEE (chmn. Dayton sect. 1971, editor edn. group newsletter 1970-81, meritorious service award 1983); mem. Am. Soc. Engring. Edn. (editor elec. engring. div. newsletter 1970-81, chmn. energy conversion com. 1978-80), Sigma Xi, Tau Beta Pi, Eta Kappa Nu. Home: 6534 Brook Lake Dr Dallas TX 75248-3915

FONTANA, THOMAS MICHAEL, producer, scriptwriter; b. Buffalo, Sept. 12, 1951; s. Charles Louis and Marie Angelica (Internicola) F. BA in Theater, State U. Coll., Buffalo, 1973; LittD (hon.), SUNY, 1997. Playwright in residence The Writers Theatre, N.Y.C., 1975-93; producer, writer St. Elsewhere NBC-TV, 1982-88; writer The Fourth Wiseman ABC-TV, 1985; exec. producer, writer Tattinger's NBC-TV, 1988-89, Nick and Hillary, 1989, Home Fires NBC-TV, 1991-92, Homicide: Life on the Street NBC-TV, 1993—, Oz HBO-TV, 1997—. Playwright numerous prodns. Recipient Peabody award, 1983, 93, 96, 98, Humanitas prize, 1984, Emmy award for St. Elsewhere, 1985, 87, for Homicide-Life in the street, 1993, Christopher award Nat. Assn. Cath. Broadcasters, 1986, Autism award Nat. Assn. Austistic Children, 1986, Maggie award Planned Parenthood Assn., 1986, Disting. Alumnus award State U. Coll. at Buffalo, 1987, VQT Founder's award, 1995, VQT Best Drama Series award, 1996, Best Drama Series and Program of Yr. award TV Critics Assn., 1996, 97, 98, Nancy Susan Reynolds award, 1996, Marylander of Yr. award Balt. Sun, 1996, Cable Ace award for Oz as best drma series, 1997, Prix Pourla Meillevre Serie, 1997. Mem. Dramatists Guild, Writers Guild Am. (ann. award 1987, 93, 94), Authors League Am., West Side Rowing Club (Buffalo). Democrat. Roman Catholic. Office: Fatima Prodns 448 W 16th St Fl 6 New York NY 10011-7008

FONTANA, VINCENT ROBERT, lawyer; b. Bklyn., Mar. 1, 1939; s. Joseph E. and Sadie (Guastella) F.; m. Joanne F. D'Antonio, Aug. 5, 1967; children: Joseph John, Anne Louise. BS in Acctng., Holy Cross Coll., 1960; JD, Fordham U., 1964. Bar: N.Y. 1965, U.S. Ct. Appeals (2d cir.) 1967, U.S. Supreme Ct. 1974, U.S. Dist. Ct. (ea. so. and we. dists.) N.Y. 1981, U.S. Ct. Appeals (11th cir.) 1985, U.S. Ct. Appeals (9th cir.) 1987, U.S. Ct. Appeals (3d cir.) 1989. Assoc. Wilkie, Farr & Gallagher, N.Y.C., 1965-66; assoc. Mendes & Mount, N.Y.C., 1966-75, ptnr., 1975-77; assoc. Wilson, Elser, Moskowitz, Edelman & Dicker, N.Y.C., 1977-78, ptnr., 1979—. Author: Municipal Liability: Law & Practice Form, 1991-97, Municipal Liability: Law and Practice, 1990-97; contbr. articles to profl. jours. Pres., Bklyn. Assn. Brain Injured Children, 1974-77; pres. N.Y. Assn. Learning Disabled, 1977-79. Recipient Am. Jurisprudence award Fordham Law Review, 1962-64. Mem. ABA, N.Y. State Bar Assn., Internat. Mcpl. Lawyers Assn. Republican. Roman Catholic. Office: Wilson Elser Moskowitz Edelman & Dicker LLP Edelman & Dicker 150 E 42nd St New York NY 10017-5612

FONTANAZZA, FRANKLIN JOSEPH, accountant; b. Balt., Aug. 17, 1953; s. Emanuel Joseph and Mary Jane (Weese) F.; m. Hilda Mae Henry, May 18, 1980 (dec. Feb. 1982); m. Gina Louise De Deo, Sept. 3, 1983; 1 child, Gia. BS in Bus. Adminstrn., Towson (Md.) State U., 1975; MBA, U. Balt., 1988. CPA, Md. Field svcs. mgr. Mid-Atlantic Coun. on Compensation Ins., Towson, 1978-83; tech. svcs. mgr. Md. Casualty Co., Balt., 1983-84; sr. cost acct. Westinghouse Electric Co., Hunt Valley, Md., 1984-91; cost acctg. mgr. Beretta USA Corp., Accokeek, Md., 1991-94; plant contr. GAF Materials Corp., Balt., 1995-99; br. controller divsn. FCI interconnections Framatome Connectors USA Inc., York, Pa., 1999—. Mem. AICPA, Md. Assn. CPAs, Inst. Mgmt. Accts. Roman Catholic. Home: 4107 Sweet Air Rd Baldwin MD 21013-9623 Office: 25 Grumbacher Rd York PA 17402

FONTANIVE, LYNN MARIE, special education educator; b. Detroit, June 29; d. Edward and Violet Fontanive; m. Paul Adasek Jr., Nov. 8, 1985; 1 child, Paul Fontanive. BA, Marygrove Coll., Detroit; MA, Mich. State U.; EdS, Wayne State U., Detroit; EdD, Wayne State U., 1982. Audiologist Plymouth (Mich.) Ctr. for Human Devel.; assoc. dir. Deaf Hearing & Speech Ctr., 1975; ednl. audiologist Oakland Schs., Waterford, Mich., 1976-80; cons. for hearing impaired Oakland Schs., 1980-85, dept. dir. ctr. programs, 1983-99; lectr. in field. Mem. adv. bd. Mich. Sch. for Deaf, Flint, 1986-91; pres. Suprs. for Programs for Hearing Imparied; bd. dirs. Career Leadership and Devel. Bd., 1987-99, State Spl. Edn. Adv. Com., 1994-98. Mem. Am. Speech and Hearing Assn., Mich. Speech, Lang., Hearing Assn. (v.p. 1986-90), Coun. for Exceptional Children Oakland County (membership chmn. 1988-90), Spl. Edn. Adminstrs. of Oakland County, Mich. Supervisors of Pub. Sch. Programs for Hearing Impaired (pres. 1997—). Roman Catholic. Avocations: dance, aerobics, travel, biking, tennis. Office: Oakland Schools 2100 Pontiac Lake Rd Waterford MI 48328-2735

FONTÉ, RICHARD W., university administrator. BS in Internat. Affairs, Georgetown U., 1967; M in Am. Dem. Theory, Ind. U., 1969; PhD in C.C. and Higher Edn. Fin., U. Mich., 1988. Asst. for workforce edn. to Gov. Edgar Ill.; asst. to Gov. Edgar, workforce cons., 1970-77; v.p., interim pres. Triton Coll., Ill.; pres. South Suburban Coll., Ill., 1988, Austin (Tex.) C.C. Co-author: (books) Shaping the Community College Image, Strategic Marketing for Presidents; contbr. articles to profl. jours. Bd. dirs. numerous comty. orgns. including Ill. Philharm. Orch., Austin 2010, Tex. Edn. Agy. Task Force on Adult Edn. Accountability, State Theatre Bd., Capital Area Workforce Devel. Bd., Austin, Capital Area Tng. Found. Mem. Greater Austin C. of C. (bd. dirs.). Address: 5930 Middle Fiskville Rd Austin TX 78752-4390

FONTENOT, ANDREA DEAN, communications executive; b. Drumright, Okla., Mar. 14, 1944; d. Howard G. and Ruby Jewell (Harvison) Harris; m. Lloyd John Culver, Aug. 12, 1962 (widowed Feb. 1966); m. Ronald Ray Fontenot. BS in Speech and Broadcasting, McNeese State U., Lake Charles, 1978, MFA in Creative Writing, 1985; ABD in English, Tex. Tech. U., Lubbock, 1997, PhD in English, 1998. Cert. Distance Educator. Jr. acct. exec. Harris & Weinstein Ad Agy., Atlanta, 1973-75; grad. teaching asst. McNeese State U., Lake Charles, La., 1981-85, adjunct prof., 1985-89; adjunct prof. Davis Monthan Air Force Base, Pima CC Tucson, 1989-90; grad. teaching asst. Tex. Tech. U., Lubbock, Tex., 1990-96; rsch. asst. Distance Edn. College Engring., Lubbock, Tex., 1996; mgr. dir. CLEAR project Southwestern Bell Comms. Found., Lubbock, Tex., 1997—; adv. bd. Teaching Learning and Tech. Ctr., Lubbock, Tex., 1996-98; teaching on internet ind. cons. Lubbock, Tex., 1993—; rsch. asst. Internet Cons. SCATE, Lubbock, Tex., 1996-97. Author: (short story) Minotaur, 1985, Hayden's Ferry Review, 1986; contbr. articles to profl. jours. Rural assistance Initiative Task Force, 1998—; mem. Collaborative Cmty. Network Task Force, 1998—. Recipient Paul Whitfield Horn scholarship, 1995, Outstanding Grad. Tchr., 1993, 95, McNeese Award in Fiction, 1984, 85, Outstanding Classroom Practices award Conf. Coll. Composition and Comm., 1998. Mem. Nat. Coun. Tchrs. English, South Ctrl. Modern Lang. Assn., Soc. for Tech. Comm., Assoc. Writing Program, Grad. English Soc., Tex. Learning Orgn. Home: 5020 Kenosha Ave Apt A Lubbock TX 79413-3948 Office: SBC Found CLEAR Project Southwestern Bell Comm COE Tex Tech University Lubbock TX 79409

FONTENOT, JACKIE DARREL, safety and health consultant; b. Leesville, La., Sept. 22, 1946; s. Oliver Huel and Ida Cora (Abshier) F.; m. Carolyn Luetta Brown, Jan. 2, 1968 (div. Dec., 1968); 1 child, Duane Alan; m. Hilda Marie Lopez, June 7, 1969; 1 child, Kayla Marie. Student, San Houston State U., 1964-66, Lee Coll., 1989-91. Cert. safety profl. (bd. cert. safety profls.); hazard control mgr. (bd. hazard control mgmt.); authorized crane inspector; cert. instr.; approved profl. source Tex. Workers Comp. and Field Safety Rep. Commn. Safety engr. Brown & Root, Monroe City, Tex., 1968-70; field safety rep. Tex. Gulf Sulphur Co., Fannett, Tex., 1970-72; plant safety supr. NL Baroid, Channelview, Tex., 1972-73; prodn. dept. safety coord. NL Baroid, Houston, 1973-76, regional safety mgr., 1976-81; mgr. safety and health NL Baroid Petroleum Svcs., Houston, 1981-86, NL Petroleum Svcs., Houston, 1986-88, Baroid Corp., Houston, 1988-91; safety and health cons. pvt. practice, Anahuac, Tex., 1991—; mem. indsl. com. NFPA, Boston, 1976—; instr. driver safety-fire suppression Tex. Safety Assn., Tex. A&M Extension Svc., 1976—; project dir. Tex. A&M Indsl. Fire Sch., master instr., 1993—; cert. instr. MSHA; speaker in field. Contbr. articles to Safety Coun. Newsletter, 1982-93. Sch. bd. trustee, Anahuac Ind. Sch. Dist., 1981-93; umpire Anahuac Youth Athletic Assn., 1980-82; Anahuac vol. fireman, 1976-86. Recipient Instr. Achievement award Tex. Safety Assn., Austin, 1977. Mem. Am. Soc. Safety Engrs. (nominated for Safety Profl. of Yr. Gulf Coast chpt. Houston 1986), Nat. Safety Coun. (chmn. petroleum sect. 1981—, Masons (past master lodge #995). Avocations: fishing, hunting. Home and Office: PO Box 1207 Anahuac TX 77514-1207

FONTENOTE-JAMERSON, BELINDA, museum director. Pres. Mus. African Am. Art, L.A. Office: Mus African Am Art 4005 S Crenshaw Blvd Fl 3 Los Angeles CA 90008-2534

FONTES, J. MARIO F., JR., lawyer; b. São Paulo, Brazil, Jan. 17, 1964; m. Gladys Fontes, Jan. 7, 1995. BA cum laude in Econs. and Internat. Studies, Am. U., Washington, 1987; JD, Cath. U., Washington, 1992. Bar: Pa. 1993, Fla. 1995, U.S. Ct. Claims 1993, U.S. Ct. Internat. Trade 1993. Assoc. Porter, Wright, Morris & Arthur, Washington, 1992-93, Hughes Hubbard & Reed, Miami, Fla., 1993-96, Baker & McKenzie, Miami, 1996—. Mem. ABA, Inter-Am. Bar Assn., Pa. Bar Assn., Brazilian-Am. Chamber (mem. program com. 1994-95), Phi Kappa Phi. Office: Baker & McKenzie 1200 Brickell Ave Miami FL 33131-3214

FONTES, MANUEL DA COSTA, foreign language educator; b. Altares, Terceira, Portugal, July 2, 1945; came to the U.S., 1961; s. João Silveira and Filomena Augusta (Da Costa) F.; m. Maria João Câmara, June 24, 1974; children: Natacha, Ramiro. BA, Calif. State U. Stanislaus, Turlock, 1969; MA, U. Calif., Berkeley, 1972; PhD, UCLA, 1975. Asst. prof. Kent (Ohio) State U., 1975-79, assoc. prof., 1979-85, prof., 1985—. Author: Portuguese and Brazilian Balladry: A Thematic and Bibliographic Index, 2 vols., 1997; editor: Romanceiro Português do Canadá, 1979, Romanceiro Português dos Estados Unidos, 2 vols., 1980, 83, Romanceiro da Provincia de Trás-os-Montes, 2 vols., 1987, Folklore and Literature: Studies of the Portuguese, Brazilian, Sephardic, and Hispanic Oral Traditions, 1999. Sgt. USMC, 1964-67. Recipient Disting. Scholar award Kent State U., 1997; NEH fellow, Washington, 1978, 80-81, Guggenheim fellow, 1984-85. Mem. MLA, Am. Assn. Tchrs. Spanish and Portuguese, Internat. Assn. Hispanists, Cervantes Soc. Am., Soc. Cantigueiros Santa Maria. Democrat. Roman Catholic. Avocation: jogging. Home: 1294 Gale Dr Kent OH 44240-1614 Office: Modern and Classical Langs Kent State Univ Kent OH 44240

FONTHEIM, CLAUDE G.B., lawyer, advisor; b. Bethlehem, Pa., Aug. 24, 1955; s. Ernest G. and Margot (Hass) F.; m. Orit Frenkel, Dec. 7, 1985. BA in Polit. Sci. & Near East Studies with high distinction and high honors, U. Mich., M in Pub. Policy, 1981, JD, 1981. Bar: D.C. 1981. Assoc. Ginsburg, Feldman & Bress, Washington, 1981-82, Akin, Gump, Strauss, Hauer & Feld, Washington, 1983-87; Crowell & Moring, Washington, 1988-90; mng. dir. IBECS, Inc., Washington, 1990—; CEO Fontheim Internat., Washington, 1990—; lectr. internat. trade and investment; chmn. Dem. Leadership Council Project on Am., the New Global Economy and Trade; gen. counsel Internat. Bus. & Econs. Cons. Svcs., Inc., 1985-88, Export Coun. Renewable Energy, Washington, 1985-87; mem. adv. bd. internat. law study Renewable Energy Inst. Mng. editor Mich. Yearbook Internat. Legal Studies, 1980-81; contbr. articles to legal jours. Policy advisor nat. polit. candidates. Mem. ABA (sec. com. internat. trade 1981-83, steering com. 1983-85, former exec. dir. study internat. trade laws), Phi Beta Kappa. Democrat. Jewish. Office: Fontheim Internat LLC 888 16th St NW Ste 300 Washington DC 20006-4103

FOO, SUN-HOO, physician; b. Malaysia, Mar. 16, 1948; s. Hong Foo and Ah-Noi Long; m. Anastatia Liew, Jan. 14, 1974; children: Farng-Yang, Farng-Yeong, Farng-Yuan, Farng-Yi. Student, Nat. Taiwan U., 1972; MD, St. Vincent's Hosp., 1976; postgrad., NYU Med. Ctr., 1976-79. Attending NYU Med. Ctr., N.Y.C., 1979—; dir. neurology NYU Downtown Hosp., N.Y.C., 1979—; attending VA Med. Ctr., N.Y.C., 1982—, Bellevue Hosp., N.Y.C., 1983—, St. Vincent's Hosp., N.Y.C., 1986—, Hosp. for Joint Disease, N.Y.C., 1990—; pres. med. staff N.Y. Downtown Hosp., 1997-88. Co-founder mag. Medicine Today, 1973, Health World, 1974, (translation) Dream Interpretation, 1974, Man Again Himself, 1974. Trustee NYU Downtown Hosp., 1996-97, 99—, pres. med. bd., 1997-98; exec. dir. Tiananmen Meml. Found., 1989—; co-founder United Chinese Health Found., 1998. Recipient Shell's Merit award, Brunei, 1961-64, Physicians Recognition award AMA, 1980, 85, 90, Courvoisier Leadership award, 1992, Outstanding Asian Am. award N.Y. State, 1993; Trustee of Yr. award, United Hosp. Found., N.Y., 1998. Fellow ACP, Am. Acad. Neurology, Royal Coll. Physicians Can.; mem. Chinese Am. Med. Soc. (pres. 1994-95), Med. Soc. State N.Y. Office: 650 1st Ave New York NY 10016

FOOR, JANE A., school counselor; b. Bristol, Eng., Dec. 26, 1969; came to U.S., 1980; d. John Keith Ord and Janice Ann Derr; m. Jamie Lee Foor, Nov. 5, 1994. BS in Human Devel., Pa. State U., 1992; MEd in Sch. Counseling, U. Pitts., 1994. Nat. cert. counselor. Counselor, social worker Allegany County Girls' Group Home, Cumberland, Md., 1994-95; sch. counselor Washington County Bd. of Edn., Hagerstown, Md., 1995—. Mem. ACA, Am. Sch. Counselor's Assn., Md. Sch. Counselor's Assn., Chi Sigma Iota (treas. 1992-94). Avocations: traveling, watching movies, reading, walking. Office: Bester Elem Sch 30 Memorial Blvd E Hagerstown MD 21740-6220

FOOR-HOGUE, ROBERT L., secondary educator; b. 09161950. BS, U. Md., 1974; MS, Johns Hopkins U., 1976; postgrad., U. Md., 1971-80. Tchr. Dunbar H.S., 1974-80; tchr. South Carroll H.S., 1980-97, dept. chmn., 1990-97; presenter in field. Contbr. articles to profl. jours. Mem. Md. Assn. of Sci. Tchrs., Nat. Assn. of Sci. Tchrs., Nat. Sci. Tech. and Soc. Assn. (nat. adv. bd. 1998). Office: South Carroll High Sch 1300 W Old Liberty Rd Sykesville MD 21784

FOOSE, ROBERT A., higher education administrator; b. East Orange, N.J., Feb. 14, 1942; s. Robert Leinbach and Linda May (Johnson) F.; m. Virginia Lee Clarkson, June 28, 1963; children: Patricia Lynne, Robert Leinbach II. BA, Hamilton Coll., 1963; MBA, Harvard U., 1972. Staff adminstr. Mohawk Airlines, Utica/Buffalo, 1963-68; dir. contract svcs. Northeast Airlines, Boston, 1968-70; dean campus activities Richard Stockton State Coll., Pomona, N.J., 1972-76; asst. to chancellor Fayetteville (N.C.) State U., 1976-79; v.p. fin. Phila. Coll. Art, 1979-82; v.p. adminstrn & fin. Colby Sawyer Coll., New London, N.H., 1982-87; pres. R & G Enterprises, New London, N.H., 1988-93; assoc. dean fin. & adminstrn, sec.-treas. Vermont Law Sch., South Royalton, 1993—. Author: (with Meyerson) Alternative Approaches to Tuition Financing, 1987. Chair New London Budget com., 1991—; trustee Hawthorne Coll., Antrim, N.H., 1989-95; trustee & treas. Woodbury Coll., Montpelier, Vt., 1996—; chmn. bd. trustees New London Hosp., 1989-92. Mem. Ea. Assn. Coll. & Univ. Bus. Officers (dir. 1986-88), ABA. Dem. Avocations: tennis. Home: 3 Twin Lake Villa Rd New London NH 03257-1397 Office: Vermont Law Sch PO Box 96 Chelsea St South Royalton VT 05068

FOOTE, AVON EDWARD, webmaster, communications educator; b. Burnsville, Miss., Sept. 24, 1937; s. Avon Ruble and Lila Frances (Broughton) F.; BS, Florence State U., 1963; MS, U. So. Miss., 1968; PhD, Ohio State U., 1970; m. Dorothy Veronica Gargis, Mar. 15, 1960; children: Anthony E., Kevin A., Michele. *Richard Foote settled in the 1680's in Virginia. The migration was documented in Chotankers: A Family History (Thornwood Publishers, 1982). Further moves included: Cornwall; London; Chotank; Caswell County, North Carolina; Chester County,South Carolina; Lancaster County, South Carolina; Eiles County, Tennessee; Tishomingo County, Mississippi, where Avon Ruble Foote and Lila Frances Broughton Foote reside on January 1, 2000. Chotankers reminds decendants, "To all those who came before; they make this book possible. To all those who will follow; the possibility is all theirs."* Announcer, Sta. WJOI, Florence, Ala., 1958-60; prodn. mgr. Sta. WOWL-TV, Florence, 1960-64; advt. coordinator Plough Inc., Memphis, 1964-66; faculty adviser Sta. WMSU, U. So. Miss., Hattiesburg, 1966-67; producer-dir. telecomm. Ohio State U., Columbus, 1967-69; assoc. prof. broadcasting U. Miss., Oxford, 1971-72; project dir. Ohio Valley TV System, Columbus, 1972-74; mem. faculty, coordinator grad. studies Sch. Journalism and Mass Communication, U. Ga., Athens, 1974-80; prof. broadcasting U. North Ala., Florence, 1980—; prof., London, 1990, 91; awards judge Ohio State Awards, 1968-73; chmn. faculty screening com. Peabody Radio-TV Awards, 1976-79. Bd. dirs. Florence YMCA, 1982-86; founder Worldwide Web Pages including Worldserver, 1995; web cons., 1996—. NDEA fellow, 1967, Nat. Acad. TV Arts and Scis. Meml. fellow, 1970; recipient Cmty. Svc. award Florence Civitan Club, 1990, 1st pl. award Corp. Video Profl. Competition Nat. Broadcasting Soc., 1991; regional 1st pl. award, Nat. 3d pl. award Coll. Emmy award Hollywood Acad. TV Arts and Scis., 1984, Honorable Mention Comedy awards Nat. Broadcasting Soc., 1987, Industry Faculty Seminar fellow Internat. Radio-TV Soc., 1987. Mem. Broadcast Edn. Assn., BBC Networking Club, Alpha Epsilon Rho, Alpha Lamba Delta. Republican. Anglican. Editor: The Challenges of Educational Communications, 1970; CBS and Congress: "The Selling of the Pentagon" Papers, 1972. Author: (with Koenig and others) Broadcasting and Bargaining, 1970; Chotankers, 1982. Editor Nat. Assn. Ednl. Broadcasters Broadcasting Rev., 1969-73. Producer ednl. TV programs. Home: 222 Shirley Dr Florence AL 35633-1434 Office: Comm Bldg Box 5158 Florence AL 35632

FOOTE, CHRISTOPHER SPENCER, chemist, educator; b. Hartford, Conn., June 5, 1935; s. William J. and Dorothy (Bennett) F.; m. Judith L. Smith; children: Jonathan, Thomas. B.S. magna cum laude, Yale U., 1957; Fulbright scholar, U. Goettingen, 1957-58; A.M., Harvard U., 1959, Ph.D., 1961. NSF predoctoral fellow Harvard U., 1958-61; instr. chemistry UCLA, 1961-62, asst. prof., 1962-66, assoc. prof., 1966-69, prof., 1969—, chmn. dept., 1978-81; cons. Chevon, Procter and Gamble; acad. adv. bd. Indsl. Rsch. Inst., 1997—. Sr. editor Accounts of Chem. Rsch., 1995—. Recipient Humboldt sr. scientist award, 1986-87; Sloane fellow, 1965-67; Guggenheim fellow, 1967-68. Fellow AAAS; mem. Am. Chem. Soc. (Baeklund medal, Tolman award 1996, Arthur C. Cope scholar 1994), Chem. Soc. London, Am. Soc. Photobiology (coun. 1978-81, pres. 1988-89), German Chem. Soc., Phi Beta Kappa, Sigma Xi, Phi Lambda Upsilon. Home: 930 Berkeley St Santa Monica CA 90403-2308 Office: U Calif Dept Chemistry & Biochemistry Los Angeles CA 90095-1569

FOOTE, DAVID WARD, JR., insurance agency executive; b. Athens, Ohio, Feb. 26, 1958; s. David W. Sr. and Shirley I. (Harter) F.; m. Sue Ellen Maccombs, Oct. 9, 1983; children: Tessa, Shana, Kyle. Grad. high sch., Madison, Ohio. Dept. mgr. Sears & Roebuck, Mansfield, Ohio, 1977-78; asst. mgr. Sport & Toy City, Mansfield, 1978-79; owner, pres. David Foote Jr. Ins. Agy., Mansfield, 1979-82, Nelsonville, Ohio, 1982-83, Geneva, Ohio, 1983—. Treas. Ashtabula County Young Reps., 1990-93, Ashtabula County Concerts of Prayer, 1991—; bd. dirs. Leadership Ohio, 1992—. Mem. NRA, Ashtabula Life Underwriters (bd. dirs. 1984-85), Ashtabula Farm Bur., Life Underwriters Tng. Coun., Leadership Ashtabula, Civic Devel. Corp., Ducks Unlimited, Geneva C. of C. (v.p. 1987-89, pres. 1989-91), Jaycees (pres. Geneva chpt. 1985-86, named one of Outstanding Young Men of Am. 1982, 83, 90, Jaycee of Yr. 1984-85, Geneva's Citizen of Yr. 1991). Avocations: hunting, fishing, trap and skeet shooting, snow skiing. Home: PO Box 567 Geneva OH 44041-0567 Office: PO Box 567 866 E Main St Geneva OH 44041-1334

FOOTE, EDWARD THADDEUS, II, university president, lawyer; b. Milw., Dec. 15, 1937; s. William Hamilton and Julia Stevenson (Hardin) F.; m. Roberta Waugh Fulbright, Apr. 18, 1964; children: Julia, William, Thaddeus. BA, Yale U., 1959; LLB, Georgetown U., 1966; LLD (hon.), Washington U., St. Louis, 1981, Barry U., 1991; hon. degree, Tokai U., Tokyo, 1984; LLD (hon.), Barry U., 1991. Bar: Mo. 1966. Reporter Washington Star, 1963-64, Washington Daily News, 1964-65; exec. asst. to chmn. Pa. Ave. Commn., Washington, 1965-66; assoc. Bryan, Cave, McPheeters & McRoberts, St. Louis, 1966-70; vice chancellor, gen. counsel, sec. to bd. trustees Washington U., St. Louis, 1970-73, dean Sch. Law, 1973-80, spl. adv. to chancellor and bd. trustees, 1980-81; pres. U. Miami, Coral Gables, Fla., 1981—; mem. exec. com., bd. dirs. Am. Coun. Edn., 1986-88; chmn. citizens com. for sch. desegregation, St. Louis, 1980; chmn. desegregation monitoring and adv. com., St. Louis, 1980-81. Author: An Educational Plan for Voluntary Cooperation Desegregation of School in the St. Louis Met. area, 1981. Mem. Coun. on Fgn. Rels.; founding pres. bd. New City Sch., St. Louis, 1967-73; mem. gov.'s task force on reorganization State of Mo., 1973-74, steering com., chmn. governance com. Mo. Gov.'s Conf. on Edn., UN Assn. Greater St. Louis chpt., 1977-79, adv. com. Naval War Coll., 1979-82, Fla. Coun. of 100, Southern Fla. Metro-Miami Action Plan, exec. com. Miami Citizens Against Crime; founding chmn. Miami Coalition for a Drug Free Community, 1988—. Recipient Order of Sun (Peru). Democrat. Office: U Miami PO Box 248006 Miami FL 33124-8006

FOOTE, EVELYN PATRICIA, retired army officer, consultant; b. Durham, N.C., May 19, 1930; d. Henry Alexander and Evelyn Sevena (Womack) F. BA summa cum laude, Wake Forest U., 1953; student, U.S. Army Command & Gen. Staff Coll., Leavenworth, Kans., 1971-72, U.S. Army War Coll., Carlisle, Pa., 1976-77; MS in Govt. and Pub. Affairs, Shippensburg State U., 1977; student, U. Va. Sch. Bus. Adminstrn., 1980; LLD (hon.), Wake Forest U., 1989. Commd. 1st lt. U.S. Army, 1960, advanced through grades to brig. gen., 1986; platoon officer WAC U.S. Army, Ft. McClellan, Ala., 1960-61; officer selection officer 6th recruiting dist. U.S. Army, Portland, Oreg., 1961-64; comdr. WAC Co. U.S. Army Engr. Brigade, Ft. Belvoir, Va., 1964-66; student Adj. Gen. Officer Advanced Course, Ft. Benjamin Harrison, Ind., 1966; exec. officer, chief adminstrv. div. pub. affairs office U.S. Army, Vietnam, 1967; exec. officer, office personnel ops. WAC, Washington, 1968-71, plans and programs officer OFC, dir., 1972-74; personnel mgmt. officer U.S. Army Forces Command, Ft. McPherson, Ga., 1974-76; comdr. 2d basic tng. bn. U.S. Army Tng. Brigade and Military Police Sch., Ft. McClellan, Ala., 1977-79; faculty mem. U.S. Army War Coll., 1979-82; student Fgn. Service Inst., Dept. of State, Washington, 1982-83; comdr. 42d Mil. Police Group, Mannheim, Fed. Republic of Germany, 1983-85; spl. asst. to comdg. gen. 32d Army Air Def. Command Hdqrs., Darmstadt, Fed. Republic of Germany, 1985-86; dep. insp. gen. for inspections Hdqrs. Dept. of the Army, Washington, 1986-88; dep. comdg. gen. Mil. Dist. Washington, comdr. Ft. Belvoir, Va., 1988-89;

ret. U.S. Army, 1989, recalled to active duty Sr. Rev. Panel, 1996-97, ret., 1997; lectr. various U.S. Army and civilian groups. Contbr. articles to military jours. and books. Bd. visitors Wake Forest U.; mem. Am. Battle Monuments Commn., 1994—, Disting. Fellows Hall of Fame, U.S. Army War Coll., 1996. Decorated D.S.M., Legion of Merit with oak leaf cluster, Bronze star, Meritorious Svc. medal with two oak leaf clusters, German Cross of Svc. 1st class; recipient Dist. Pub. Svc. award Wake Forest U., 1987; inducted into Disting. Fellows Hall of Fame, U.S. Army War Coll., U.S. Army MP Corps. Regimental Hall of Fame, 1998; named Spokesperson of Yr., Dept. of Army, 1997-98. Mem. Zonta. Democrat. Lutheran. Avocations: music, reading, hiking.

FOOTE, FRANCES CATHERINE, association executive, living trust consultant; b. Chgo., Apr. 3, 1935; d. Peter and Ellen Gertrude (Quinn) F. BS in Edn., Cardinal Stritch Coll., 1957; MS in Edn., Ill. State U., 1966. Cert. tchr., Ill. Tchr. Sch. Dist. 123, Oak Lawn, Ill., 1959-84; asst. prin. Sch. Dist. 123, Oak Lawn, 1971-80; instr. geography workshops for tchrs., 1967-70, use of newspaper in classroom workshops, 1973-75; co-chair social Studies Curriculum Revision; living trust cons. Accurate Bus. Assocs., Inc., St. Petersburg; ind. rep. Watkins Products. Officer PTA, Oak Lawn, 1973-76; mem. Rep. Nat. Com., Washington, vol. State of Fla. Guardian ad litem, St. Vincent de Paul Soc.; vol. Day Star, St. Petersburg, Fla. Mem. Am. Fedn. Tchrs. Roman Catholic. Avocations: golf, bridge, cycling. Home: 280 126th Ave E Apt 203 Treasure Island FL 33706-4442

FOOTE, HORTON, playwright, scriptwriter; b. Wharton, Tex., Mar. 14, 1916; s. Albert Horton and Hallie (Brooks) F.; m. Lillian Vallish, June 4, 1945; children—Barbara Hallie, Albert Horton, Walter Vallish, Daisy Brooks. Student, Pasadena Playhouse Sch. Theatre, Calif., 1933-35, Tamara Daykarhanova Sch. Theatre, N.Y.C., 1937-39. Actor N.Y.C., 1939-42; mgr. prodn. co. Productions Inc., Washington, 1942-45; tchr. of playwriting. Author: (novel) The Chase, 1956; (screenplays) Storm Fear, 1956, To Kill a Mockingbird, 1962 (Academy award best screenplay 1962, Writers Guild Am. award 1962), Baby, The Rain Must Fall, 1965, Hurry Sundown, 1966, Tomorrow, 1971, Tender Mercies, 1983 (Academy award best screenplay 1983), 1918, 1984, On Valentine's Day, 1985, The Trip to Bountiful, 1985 (Academy Award nomination best screenplay 1985), Spring Moon, 1987, Convicts, 1991, Of Mice and Men, 1992; (plays) Texas Town, 1942, Out of My House, 1942, Only The Heart, 1944, Celebration, 1948, The Chase, 1952, The Trip to Bountiful, 1953, The Midnight Caller, 1953, A Young Lady of Property, 1954, The Traveling Lady, 1955, The Roads to Home, 1955, Harrison, Texas: Eight Television Plays, 1959, Tomorrow, 1960, Three Plays, 1962, Roots in a Parched Ground, 1962, (musical adaption) Gone with the Wind, 1971, The Road to the Graveyard, 1985, Blind Date, 1986, Selected One Act Plays of Horton Foote, 1988, Habitation of Dragons, 1988, Dividing the Estate, 1989, Talking Pictures, 1990, Horton Foote: Four New Plays, 1994, The Young Man From Atlanta, 1994 (Pulitzer Prize for drama 1995), Night Seasons, 1994, Laura Dennis, 1994, Talking Pictures, 1994, also (play series) "The Orphans' Home Cycle"; (TV movies) Only The Heart, NBC, 1947, Ludie Brooks, CBS, 1951, The Travelers, NBC, 1952, The Old Beginning, NBC, 1953, The Trip to Bountiful, NBC, 1953, Midnight Caller, NBC, 1953, John Turner Davis, NBC, 1953, Young Lady of Property, NBC, 1953, The Oil Well, NBC, 1953, Rocking Chair, NBC, 1953, Expectant Relations, NBC, 1953, Death of the Old Man, NBC, 1953, Tears of My Sister, NBC, 1953, The Shadow of Wilie Greer, NBC, 1954, The Dancers, NBC, 1954, The Roads to Home, ABC, 1955, Flight, NBC, 1956, Drugstore: Sunday Noon, ABC, 1956, Member of the Family, CBS, 1957, Traveling Lady, CBS, 1957, Old Man, CBS, 1959, Tomorrow, CBS, 1960, 71, The Shape of the River, CBS, 1960, The Night of the Storm, CBS, 1961, Gambling Heart, NBC, 1964, The Displaced Person, PBS, 1977, Barn Burning, PBS, 1980, Keeping On, PBS, 1983, The Habitation of Dragons, TNT, 1992; writer (TV film) Mr. and Mrs. Loving, 1996. Recipient Evelyn Burkey award Writer's Guild, 1989. *

FOOTE, JOHN HOLLAND, lawyer; b. Birmingham, Ala., Aug. 4, 1946; s. John Elbert and Wanda Delashaw (Holland) F.; m. Rosamond P. Tompkins, July 26, 1980; children: Nathaniel Lucas, Samuel Tompkins. ABin Govt., La. State U., 1968; JD, U. Va., 1974. Bar: Va. 1974, DC 1976, U.S. Dist. Ct. (ea. dist.) Va. 1977, U.S. Dist. Ct. (we. dist.) Va. 1994, U.S. Ct. Appeals (4th cir.) 1982, U.S. Ct. Appeals (2d cir.) 1977, U.S. Ct. Appeals (11th cir.) 1996, U.S. Supreme Ct. 1979. Policy analyst Office of Policy and Planning U.S. Dept. Justice, Washington, 1974-77; assoc. gen. counsel Pres. Ford's Viet Nam Era Clemency Program, Washington, 1975-76; trial atty. criminal divsn. U.S. Dept. Justice, 1976-77; from dep. county atty. to county atty. Prince William County, Manassas, Va., 1977-89; owner Hazel & Thomas, P.C., Manassas, 1989—, also bd. dirs. Chmn. Prince William-Manassas Regional Jail Bd., 1978-82; bd. dirs. Hist. Manassas, Inc., 1992-96, Project Mend-a-House, 1995-97. Lt. U.S. Army, 1968-71, Vietnam. Mem. Va. State Bar (5th dist. com. disciplinary sys. 1992-95, faculty professionalism 1992-95), Prince William County Bar Assn. (pres. 1987-88), Local Govt. Attys. of Va. (pres. 1987-88). Democrat. Methodist. Avocations: reading, racquetball. Home: 10542 Knollwood Dr Manassas VA 20111-2834 Office: Hazel & Thomas 9324 West St Fl 3 Manassas VA 20110-5198

FOOTE, NATHAN MAXTED, retired physical science educator; b. Woodlawn, Pa., Oct. 8, 1913; s. Myron Tinkham and Ada May (Maxted) F.; m. Laura Belle Gruey, Sept. 5, 1936; children: Jonathan W., L. Nadine, Frances C., Willard G. AB, DePauw U., 1935; MS, Purdue U., 1939. Jr. chemist U.S. FDA, Phila., 1939-40; Rsch. engr. RCA, Camden, N.J., 1940-49; rsch. scientist Colgate Palmolive, Jersey City, N.J., 1950-52; rheologist B.F. Goodrich Chem. Co., Avon Lake, Ohio, 1953-58; acting head, Dept. Physics Baldwin Wallace Coll., Berea, Ohio, 1958-60; vis. asst. prof. Physics Pa. State U., University Park, 1960-61; asst. prof. Physics, Behrend Coll. Pa. State U., Erie, 1964-78, ret., 1979; assoc. prof. Phys. Sci. SUNY, Geneseo, 1961-64. *Professor Foote has suggested that high-flying aircraft have put water vapor where it reacts chemically with single oxygen atoms, forming two hydroxyl radicals, thereby reducing the formation of ozone. Ozone depletion probably altered climates. The magnetically active hydroxyl radical contribute in the oxidation of nitrogen to nitric acid. The deterioration of the atmosphere is being caused by both the increase of energetic light at the ocean surface and by the increases of water in the stratosphere. The process is slow, but nitric acid represents a fully "burned" atmosphere.* Author: Industrial and Engineering Chemistry, 1944, Industrial and Engrineering Chemistry, 1947. Del. Ohio Coun. Am. Bapt. Men, 1955-58. Mem. AAAS, Am. Chem. Soc. (50 Yr. award 1993), Sigma Xi. Avocations: stratospheric chem. change, lawn bowling. Home: 14 E Main St Lot B Mount Dora FL 32757-3470

FOOTE, ROBERT HUTCHINSON, animal physiology educator; b. Gilead, Conn., Aug. 20, 1922; s. Robert E. and Annie (Hutchinson) F.; m. Ruth E. Parcells, Jan. 12, 1946 (dec. Jan. 1992); children: Robert W., Dale H.; m. Barbara J. Johnson, Sept. 25, 1993. BS, U. Conn., 1943; MS, Cornell U., 1947, PhD Animal Physiology/Biochem. Genetics, 1950. Grad. asst. Cornell U., Ithaca, N.Y., 1946-50, asst. prof. animal physiology, 1950-56, assoc. prof., 1956-63, prof., 1963-93, Jacob Gould Schurman chair, 1980-93; emeritus, 1993—; mem. study sect. NIH, 1974-78; cons. Shell Oil, 1985-89, EPA, 1988-96; program mgr. USDA competitive grants, 1986-87. Author: Animal Reproduction, 1954, AI to Cloning, 1998; mem. editl. bds. various jours., 1958-96, Reproductive Physiology, 1992—, Cryobiology, 1991-94; contbr. some 500 articles to profl. jours., chpts. to books. Chmn. trustees Congregation Ch., Ithaca, 1955-60. Served to capt. inf. U.S. Army 1943-46, ETO. Recipient Sci. medal N.Y. Farmers, 1969, SUNY Chancellor award, 1980, Superior Svc. award USDA, 1988, Alumni Merit award U. Conn., 1996; named hon. prof. Beijing Agrl. U., 1995. Fellow AAAS; mem. Soc. Study Reprodn. (bd. dirs. 1976-78, pres. 1985), Nat Assn. Animal Breeders (Physiology award 1970), Am. Soc. Andrology (editorial bd. 1982-88, Outstanding Andrologist 1984, Upjohn physiology award 1985), Am. Soc. Animal Sci. (editorial bd. 1958-60, Nat. physiology and endocrinology award 1970, Casida physiology of reprodn. award 1991, JSPS award 1996), Am. Soc. Theriogenology (editorial bd. 1976-89, Robert H. Foote Symposium in his honor 1992), Sigma Xi, Phi Kappa Phi, Gamma Sigma Delta. Republican. Home: 474 Savage Farm Dr Ithaca NY 14850-6508 Office: Cornell U Dept Animal Sci 204 Morrison Hall Ithaca NY 14853-4801

FOOTE, ROBERT STEPHENS, physician; b. Ft. Worth, July 14, 1944; s. Robert Miller and Elizabeth Carr Foote; m. Nancy Ann Ryan, May 8, 1982; children: Emily Stephens, Hannah Elizabeth, Nora Catherine. BA in English, French, Vanderbilt U., 1966; postgrad., U. Exeter, Devon, Eng., 1969; MD, Vanderbilt U., 1976. Diplomate Am. Bd. Internal Medicine, Nat. Bd. Med. Examiners. Resident Dartmouth Med. Ctr., Hanover, N.H., 1976-79; emergency physician New London (N.H.) Hosp., 1979—, dir. emergency svcs., 1981—; attending physician emergency dept. Dartmouth Hitchcock Med. Ctr., Lebanon, N.H., 1995—; chmn. dept. medicine New London Hosp., 1989-90, sec.-treas. med. staff, 1983-88, 91-94, pres.-elect med. staff, 1995-96; mem. N.H. State Task Force on Pediatric Emergency Care, 1993—; asst. prof. medicine Dartmouth Med. Sch.; pres.-elect med. staff New London Hosp., 1994-95. Author numerous poems. Instr. ACLS, Am. Heart Assn., 1986—; chmn. Hartland, Vt. Sch. Bd., 1989-93, mem. ednl. affairs com., 1993—. Mem. Royal Coll. Surgeons (Eng.). Avocations: gardening, woodworking, hunting and fishing, civil war history, winter sports. Home: PO Box 116 Hartland VT 05048-0116 Office: Dartmouth Hitchcock Med Ctr Lebanon NH 03756

FOOTE, RUTH ANNETTE, business executive, land developer; b. Riverside, Calif., Nov. 2, 1925; d. Edgar Wallace and Murrel (Sibrell) Thomas; m. Harold Dale Borregard, July 15, 1945 (div.); children: Linda Gail, Valerie Louise, Jennifer; m. Robert Earl Foote, June 24, 1951; children: Robin David, James Wayne. Student, pub. schs., San Bernardino, Calif. Comml. closer M.P. Crum Co., Dallas, 1964-67, Trammel Crow Co., Dallas, 1967-69; developer Hidden Valley Airpark, Denton, Tex., 1969-70, exec. sec., 1969-73; escrow officer, mgr. S.W. Land Title, Denton, 1970-75; exec. v.p. Lawyers Title Co., Denton, 1975-80, Attys. Title Co., Dallas, 1984; legal sec. Ray & Gilchrist, Lewisville, Tex., 1984-86; founder, co-owner Am. Title Co., Dallas and Lewisville, 1986—; ins. agt. Alliance for Affordable Health Care, Dallas; assoc. Starcom, Inc.; owner, developer Whitehawk Valley, Denton, 1977—, Rainbow Valley, Denton, 1979—; owner br. office Safeco Land Title Co., North Richland Hills, Tex., 1976-81; exec. v.p. Inpact Mortgage, Inc., 1993—; anti-aging specialist Sterling Health Mktg. Group, Denton, 1995-98. Author: And the Truth Shall Set You Free, 1980. Mem. fund raising com., historian, bd. dirs. Habitat for Humanity, Denton; mem. Women's Forum Dallas. Mormon. Achievements include pioneering efforts (with Robert Foote) in earth sheltered home communities which provide their own electricity, fuel and water. Home and Office: RR 2 Box 1049 Sanger TX 76266-9525

FOOTE, SHELBY, author; b. Greenville, Miss., Nov. 17, 1916; s. Shelby Dade and Lillian (Rosenstock) F.; m. Gwyn Rainer, Sept. 5, 1956; children: Margaret Shelby, Huger Lee. Student, U. N.C., 1935-37; DLitt (hon.), U. of the South, 1981, Southwestern U., 1982, U. S.C., 1991, U. N.C., 1992, Millsaps U., 1993, Notre Dame U., 1994, Coll. of William & Mary, 1999, Loyola U., 1999. Novelist lectr., U. Va., 1963, playwright in residence, Arena Stage, Washington, 1963-64, writer in residence, Hollins Coll., Va., 1968; Author: novels Tournament, 1949, Follow Me Down, 1950, Love in a Dry Season, 1951, Shiloh, 1952, Jordan County, 1954, September September, 1978; history The Civil War, A Narrative: Vol. I, Fort Sumter to Perryville, 1958, Vol. II, Fredericksburg to Meridian, 1963, Vol. III, Red River to Appomattox, 1974; play Jordon County: A Landscape in the Round, 1964, Conversations with Shelby Foote, 1989; editor: Chickamauga and Other Civil War Stories, 1993, Correspondence of Shelby Foote and Walker Percy, 1997. Mem. acad. adv. bd. U.S. Naval Acad., 1988-89. Recipient Disting. Alumnus award U. N.C., 1975, Dos Passos prize for Lit., 1988, Charles Frankel award 1992, St. Louis Literary award 1992, Nevins-Freeman award 1992, Ingersoll-Weaver award, 1997, Richard Wright award, 1997, N.Y. Pub. Libr. Literary Lion, 1994, 98; Guggenheim fellow, 1955-57, Ford Found. fellow, 1963-64. Mem. Am. Acad. Arts and Letters, Fellowship of So. Writers, soc. Am. Historians. Office: 542 E Parkway S Memphis TN 38104-4362

FOOTE, SHERRILL LYNNE, retired manufacturing company technician; b. Marshalltown, Iowa, Apr. 19, 1940; d. Howard Raymond Ellis and Lois Ellen F.; m. Terry D. Downey, July 27, 1958 (div. 1978); children: Patrick L., Holly L. Harrelson; m. Frank H. Foote, Nov. 17, 1979 (div. 1989); stepchildren: Lauri K., Christopher R. Student, Marshalltown C.C., 1981—. Receptionist Drs. Long & Clawson, Marshalltown, 1958-59; clk. Fisher Controls, Marshalltown, 1963-73, cost estimating analyst, 1974-82, sr. cost estimator, 1982-95. Contbr. limericks Des Moines Register (Contest Winner), 1976, Marshalltown Times Rep., 1986. Mem. Mensa (contbr. Bull. Wordplay 1981—, limerick editor M-Pressions Ctrl. Iowa newsletter 1989-91, local sec. 1991-93). Democrat. Methodist. Avocations: games, reading, movies, plays. Home: 702 Ratcliffe Dr Marshalltown IA 50158-3453

FOOTE, WILLIAM CHAPIN, business executive; b. Milw., Mar. 15, 1951; s. Peter Chapin and Mary Jane (Manierre) F.; m. Kari H. Foote, July 27, 1969; children: Tracy, Leslie Suzanne. BA, Williams Coll., 1973; MBA, Harvard U., 1977. Asst. treas. Chase Manhattan Bank, N.Y.C., 1973-75; sr. engagement mgr. McKinsey & Co., Inc., Chgo., 1977-83; v.p. USG Corp., Chgo., 1984—, pres., COO, 1994—; pres. CEO L&W, USG Interiors Inc., 1994, chmn., pres., CEO, 1996—; now chmn. bd., pres., CEO USG Corp., Chgo. Club: Economics Chgo.

FOOTEN, JOHN ANTHONY, video engineer; b. Balt., Jan. 28, 1968; s. John Francis and Susan Jane (Bennett) F. BFA, NYU, 1995. Assoc. prodr. YPL Prodns., Balt., 1983-86; tchg. asst. NYU, N.Y.C., 1986-87, tng. coord., 1987-89, video facilities mgr., 1989-91; prof. New Sch., N.Y.C., 1990-91; tech. dir. Imtech, Internat., N.Y.C., 1991-95; project mgr. Montage Group, N.Y.C., 1995—. Assoc. prodr. (documentary video) Poor Man's Ballet, 1990 (Best Videography 1990). Tchr. Boy Scouts Am., N.Y.C., 1996. Republican. Avocations: racquetball, reading, video games, traveling. E-mail: JFooten@compuserve.com. Home: PO Box 1782 Easton PA 18044 Office: Montage 527 W 34th St New York NY 10001

FOOTMAN, GORDON ELLIOTT, educational administrator; b. L.A., Oct. 10, 1927; s. Arthur Leland and Meta Fay (Neal) F.; m. Virginia Rose Footman, Aug. 7, 1954; children: Virginia, Patricia, John. BA, Occidental Coll., 1951, MA, 1954; EdD, U. So. Calif., 1972. Tchr. Arcadia, Calif., 1952, Glendale, Calif., 1956; psychologist Burbank (Calif.) Schs., 1956-64, supr., 1964-70, dir. pupil pers. svcs., 1970-72; dir. divsn. ednl. support svcs. L.A. County Office Edn., Downey, Calif., 1972-91; cons. ednl. adminstrn., counseling and psychol. svcs., 1991—; pres. Calif. Assn. Adult Devel. and Aging, 1994-95; lectr. ednl. psychology U. So. Calif., 1972-75, asst. prof. ednl. psychology, 1976-85. Pres. Coun. for Exceptional Children, 1969-70; pres. Burbank Coordinating Coun., 1969-70; mem. Burbank Family Svc. Bd., 1972-72. Served with AUS, 1945-47. Mem. ACA (senator 1983-86, gov. coun. 1989-93, exec. com. 1990-93, parliamentarian 1991-92, western region br. assembly publs. editor 1985-87, chair 1988-89, chair bylaws com. 1995-97), Am. Ednl. Rsch. Assn., Am. Assn. Humanistic Edn. and Devel. (bd. dirs., treas. 1996—), Calif. Pers. and Guidance Assn. (pres. 1981-82, exec. coun. 1996—), Nat. Assn. Pupil Pers. Adminstrs., Calif. Assn. Pupil Pers. Adminstrs. (monograph editor 1977-80), Calif. Assn. Counselor Educators and Suprs. (trustee), Calif. Soc. Ednl. Program Auditors and Evaluators (sec. 1975-76, v.p. 1976-77, pres.), Calif. Assn. Measurement and Evaluation in Counseling and Devel. (sec. 1976, pres. 1979-80, 96-97, pres. 1997-98, cons. ednl. and pupil svcs. adminstrn. 1991—), Calif. Inst. Tech. Assocs., Assn. Humanistic Edn. and Devel. (bd. dirs. 1996—, treas. 1996—, pres.-elect 1999—), Huntington Libr. Soc. Fellows, Coun. Exceptional Children (pres. Foothill chpt. 1969-70), Phi Beta Kappa, Phi Alpha Theta, Psi Chi. Republican. Presbyterian. Home and Office: 1259 Sherwood Rd San Marino CA 91108-1816

FORAN, KEVIN RICHARD, television station executive; b. Tucson, Apr. 6, 1972; s. Richard Charles and Mary Ann (Corella) F. BA in Media Arts, U. Ariz., 1995. Prodn. operator Sta. KUAT-TV, PBS, Tucson, 1994-95, Sta. KOLD-TV, CBS, Tucson, 1995; assoc. dir. Sta. KGUN-TV, ABC, Tucson, 1995—. asst. prodr. TV program Beat the Pro, 1996; prodr. TV program 1996 U. Ariz. Wildcat Football Preview, 1996, 97, 98 (AP award for editing 1998). Avocations: musician, soccer, golf. Office: Sta KGUN-TV 7280 E Rosewood St Tucson AZ 85710-1643

FORASTE, ROLAND, psychiatrist; b. N.Y.C., Mar. 1, 1938; s. Paul Foraste and Anita Schonbachler. AB honors cum laude, Coll. Holy Cross, 1960; cert. neurology, U. London, 1965; MD, SUNY, Downstate, 1965. Med. intern Jefferson Hosp., Phila., 1965-66; resident in psychiatry N.Y. Hosp., 1966-69, resident in child psychiatry, 1968-71, chief resident in adolescent psychiatry, 1970-71, asst. attending psychiatrist, 1973-86; med. dir. psychiatry U.S. Healthcare and Total Health, N.Y.C., 1986-90, cons., 1990—; clin. instr. psychiatry Cornell Med. Coll., 1967-73, clin. asst. prof. psychiatry, 1973-86; attending physician Gracie Sq. Hosp., N.Y.C., 1969—, Rye (N.Y.) Hosp. Ctr.; mem. adv. bd. Med. Rsch. Industries, Inc., 1997—. Co-author: (audiotext) The Drug Syndrome and the Teacher, 1971; co-editor, contbr. Biology Jour. of Coll. of Holy Cross, 1957-58. Benefit chmn. Hosp. Audiences, Inc., N.Y.C., 1984; benefit com. Cultural Coun. Found., N.Y.C., 1984-86, Big Apple Circus, 1984-86, Five Men Named Moe, 1992; bd. dirs. Cmty. Ctrs., Inc., Greenwich, Conn., 1990-97, mem. adv. bd., 1997—; mem. Met. Mus. Art, Mus. Modern Art, Bruce Mus., Greenwich, Friends of Greenwich Libr. Recipient Physicians Recognition award AMA. Fellow Am. Soc. Adolescent Psychiatry (asst. continuing med. edn. officer 1989-90, continuing med. edn. officer 1990-96; mem. Am. Acad. Child and Adolescent Psychiatry, N.Y. Coun. Child and Adolescent Psychiatry, N.Y. Soc. for Adolescent Psychiatry (bd. dirs. 1987-88, sec. 1988-90, pres. 1991-93, ex-officio 1993—), Am. Psychiat. Assn. (N.Y. dist. br.), Flying Physicians Assn. (instrument rated), N.Y. Hosp.-Cornell Med. Ctr. Alumni Assn., Aircraft Owners and Pilots Assn., Greenwich Boat and Yacht Club, Greenwich Polo Club, Westchester Flying Club, Porsche Club Am., Westchester Country Club (mem. nominating com. 1987-88, membership com. 1987-88, 90-91, entertainment com. 1987-88, 90-93), U.S. Ski Assn., Wintergreen Club (dir.-trustee 1990-93, chmn. entertainment com. 1990-96), KC. Republican. Roman Catholic. Avocations: flying, riding, sailing, sking, windsurfing. Home: 623 Steamboat Rd Greenwich CT 06830-7140 also: 420 E 51st St New York NY 10022-8014 Office: 60 Sutton Pl S Ste C New York NY 10022-4168 also: 2 Greenwich Plz Ste 100 Greenwich CT 06830-6353

FORAUER, ROBERT RICHARD, elementary education educator; b. New Britain, Conn., May 14, 1946; s. Joseph Philip and Marion Margaret (Zotter) F.; children: Jason Alan, Melissa Lynn. BS, Cen. Conn. State Coll., 1968; MA, Castleton State Coll., 1975. Tchr. Meriden Sch. Dist., Meriden, Conn., 1968-72; tchr. Wallingford Sch. Dist., Wallingford, Vt., 1972-98, ret., 1998; machinist Bryant Grinder Corp., Springfield, Vt., 1980-81. Mem. NEA, Vt. Edn. Assn., Vt. State Tech. Coun., Wallingford Tchrs. Assn. (pres. 1981-92), Vt. Fish and Game (instr. hunter safety 1976-96). Avocations: guitar, photography. Home: 197 Aube Ridge Rd Hinesburg VT 05461

FORBES, ALFRED DEAN, religious studies researcher, biomedical consultant; b. Pomona, Calif., Mar. 2, 1941; s. Paul Edward and Lela Irene (Randall) F.; m. Ellen Moss, May 8, 1971. BA in Physics, Harvard Coll., 1962; MDiv, Pacific Sch. Religion, 1969. With U.S. Peace Corps, Nigeria, 1962-64; prin. med. dept. scientist Hewlett-Packard Labs., Palo Alto, Calif., 1971-98; vis. scholar U. Calif., San Diego, 1999—; vis. scholar religious studies Stanford (Calif.) U., 1986-89; adj. prof. Jewish studies Pa. State U., 1998—. Author: (with F.I. Andersen) Spelling in the Hebrew Bible, 1986, The Vocabulary of the Old Testament, 1989; (with F.I. Andersen and D.N. Freedman) Studies in Hebrew and Aramaic Orthography, 1992, others; algorithms editor Jour. Clin. Monitoring and Computing; contbr. articles to profl. jours. Trustee, v.p. Whitney Edn. Found., Los Altos, Calif., 1981-88. Mem. Soc. Bibl. Lit., IEEE (sr. mem.). Avocations: travel, magic. E-mail: adforbes@ix.netcom.com. Home: 820 Loma Verde Ave Palo Alto CA 94303-4112

FORBES, ARTHUR LEE, III, lawyer; b. Houston, Sept. 3, 1928; s. Arthur Lee Jr. and Corinne (Mayfield) F.; m. Nita R. Harrison, Mar. 25, 1957; children—Tricia, Kim, Arthur Lee. B.S.C.E., U. Tex.-Austin, 1952; J.D., S. Tex. Coll. Law, 1959. Bar: Tex. 1959, U.S. Ct. Appeals (5th cir.) 1960, U.S. Supreme Ct. 1967. Ptnr. firm Lee & Forbes, Houston, 1960-73, Shapiro, Forbes & Cox, Houston, 1974-88; gen. counsel Bay Houston Towing Co., 1989—. Served to lt. USMC, 1952-54. Mem. ABA, Tex. Bar Assn., Houston Bar Assn., Assn. Trial Lawyers Am., Houston Trial Lawyers Assn., Sigma Chi, Phi Delta Phi, Unitarian. Club: Houston Racquet. Home: 5 Leisure Ln Houston TX 77024-5123 Office: Three Riverway Ste 450 Houston TX 77056

FORBES, CHRISTOPHER (KIP FORBES), publisher; b. Morristown, N.J., Dec. 5, 1950; s. Malcolm Stevenson and Roberta Remsen (Laidlaw) F.; m. Baroness Astrid Cornelia Mathilde Von Heyl Zu Herrnsheim, Sept. 7, 1974; 1 child, Charlotte Adelaide Mathilde. BA in Art History magna cum laude, Princeton U., 1972; LHD (hon.), N.H. Coll., Manchester, 1986. Curator Forbes Mag. Collection, N.Y.C., 1970-80; ad salesman Forbes Mag., N.Y.C., 1972-76, assoc. pub., v.p., 1978-89, sec., 1981-92, vice-chmn., corp. sec. 1989—; also dir.; pub. Nineteenth Century, Phila., 1976-78. Author books and catalogues, including: Victorians in Togas, Paintings by Sir Lawrence Alma-tadema from the Collection of Allen Funt, 1973; the Royal Academy (1836-1901) Revisited, 1975; (with Margaret Kelly) War a la Mode: Meisonier Detaille, de Neuville, and Berne-Bellecour, 1975; (with Hermione Waterfield) Faberge: Imperial Eggs and Other Fantasies, 1978; (with Dr. Armand Hammer) Faberge Eggs, 1980, (with Susan Casveras) Victorian Childhood, 1986; editor: Masterpieces from the House of Faberge, 1984. Mem. Cultural and Hist. Commn. Somerset County, N.J., 1984-96; bd. dirs. Newark Mus., Victorian Soc. Am., Friends of N.J. State Mus.; bd. advisers Princeton U. Art Mus., N.J., Bklyn. Mus. of Art; nat. trustee Balt. Mus. Art; mem. adv. com. dept. European decorative arts Mus. Fine Arts, Boston. Decorated assoc. knight Venerable Order St. John Jerusalem. Mem. Grolier Club, Nat. Arts Club, Salmagundi Club, Century Club. Republican. Episcopalian. Office: Forbes Inc 60 5th Ave New York NY 10011-8882

FORBES, COLIN AMES, graphic design consultant; b. London, Mar. 6, 1928; came to U.S., 1978; s. John Cumming and Kathleen Ethel (Ames) F.; m. Elizabeth Hopkins, Jan. 31, 1950 (div. 1978); 1 child, Christine Coppe; m. Wendy Maria Schneider, June 6, 1961; children: Aaron, Jessica Forbes Russo. BFA, Ctrl. Sch. Arts & Crafts, London, 1952. Graphic design asst. Herbert Spencer Studio, London, 1952-53; freelance graphic designer, lectr. Ctrl. Sch., London, 1953-57; art dir. Stuart Advt., London, 1957-58; head graphic design dept. Ctrl. Sch. Arts & Crafts, London, 1958-60; freelance graphic designer London, 1960-62; ptnr. Fletcher, Forbes, Gill, London, 1962-65, Crosby, Fletcher, Forbes, London, 1965-72, Pentagram Design Ltd., London, 1972-78, Pentagram Design Inc., N.Y.C., 1978-93; sr. critic graphic design Yale Sch. Art, New Haven, 1989; cons. ptnr. Pentagram Design AG, Zug, Switzerland, London, N.Y.C., San Francisco, 1993—; chmn. Stanford Design Forum, Stanford U., Palo Alto, Calif., 1988. Co-author: Graphic Design: Visual Comparisons, 1963, A Sign Systems Manual, 1970, New Alphabets A-Z, 1973, Living By Design, 1978, Pentagram: The Compendium, 1993. Staff sgt. Brit. Army, 1946-49. Recipient Silver medal Biennale Internat. Art Book Prize, Israel, 1975, Pres. award Designers and Art Dirs. Assn., London, 1977. Mem. Am. Inst. Graphic Arts (pres. 1983-84, medal 1992), Royal Soc. Arts, Alliance Graphique Internat. (pres. 1976-79), Am. Ctr. for Design (hon.). Home: Forbes Farm 2879 Horseshoe Rd Westfield NC 27053 Office: Pentagram Design Inc 204 5th Ave New York NY 10010-2101

FORBES, CYNTHIA ANN, small business owner, marketing educator; b. Richmond, Calif., Dec. 27, 1951; d. James Martin and Mary Jane (Clafferty) Forbes; m. Larry Charles Osofsky, Mar. 20, 1970 (div. 1980); 1 child, Anna; m. William Charles Ham, Aug. 30, 1986. BA, U. Calif., 1977; MS, Golden Gate U., 1981. Rsch. asst. U. Calif., Berkeley, 1975-77, Chevron Rsch., Richmond, 1977-79; specialist dealer affairs Chevron USA, San Francisco, 1979-80, sales rep., San Fafael, Calif., 1981-84, adminstrv. supr., San Ramon, Calif.; 1984-85, advt. mgr. Chevron Chem. Co., San Francisco, 1986-88; assoc. prof. Golden Gate U., San Francisco, 1981-92. Vol., lectr. child abuse prevention; pres. Sierra County Arts Coun. Democrat. Avocations: mountaineering, bicycling. Home: PO Box 427 Downieville CA 95936-0427

FORBES, DAVID CRAIG, musician; b. Seattle, Feb. 12, 1938; s. Douglas James and Ruby A. (Niles) F.; m. Sylvia Sterling, Aug. 29, 1965 (div. Apr. 1973); 1 child, Angela Rose. Grad., USN Sch. Music, 1957; student, Western Wash. U., 1960-64. Prin. horn La Jolla (Calif.) Civic Orch., 1958-60, Seattle Worlds Fair Band, 1962, Seattle Opera Co., 1964—, Pacific Northwest Ballet, Seattle, 1964—; asst. prin. horn Seattle Symphony Orch., 1964—; prin. horn Pacific Northwest Wagner Fest., Seattle, 1975—; instr. horn Western Wash. State U., 1969-81, Cornish Inst., Seattle, 1964-78. Served with USN, 1956-60. Mem. NARAS, Internat. Horn Soc. Avocations: piano, golf, fishing. Home: 9050 15th Ave NW # 2 Seattle WA 98117-3429

FORBES, FRANKLIN SIM, lawyer, educator; b. Kingsport, Tenn., Sept. 21, 1936; s. Harvey Sim and Virginia Smith (Pooler) F.; m. Suzanne Marie Willard, June 30, 1962; children—Franklin Sim, Anne Marie. BA, U. Hawaii, 1959; JD, U. Iowa, 1963. Bar: Hawaii 1963, Nebr. 1964. Law clk. Hawaii Supreme Ct., 1963; mem. faculty U. Nebr. Coll. Bus. Adminstrn., Omaha, 1965—, prof. law, 1965—, chmn. dept. law and society, 1970-97, acting chmn. dept. profl. acctg., 1986-87, Peter Keweit disting. prof. law, 1987-93; pvt. practice, Omaha, 1964—. Author: Going Into Business in Nebraska: The Legal Aspects, 1983, Instructor's Resource Guide-Business Law, 1983-88, Starting and Operating a Business in Nebraska, 1995, Debtors and Creditors Rights, 1988, Legal Environment of Telemarketing, 1991; contbr. articles to legal publs. Mem. integration com. Omaha Sch. Bd., 1974; mem. St. James Bd. Edn., Omaha, 1974; pres. parish coun. St. James Roman Cath. Ch., 1975, St. Elizabeth Ann Ch., 1983-84, 90-91. Recipient Real Dean award U. Hawaii, 1959, Gt. Tchr. award U. Nebr., 1978, 81, Chancellor's medal U. Nebr., 1977, Outstanding Achievement award U. Nebr. Coll. Bus. Adminstrn., 1983, 84, 85, 87, 88; Rotary Found. grantee Australia, 1972. Mem. ABA, Am. Arbitration Assn., Am. Judicature Soc., Midwest Bus. Adminstrs. Assn., Midwest Bus. Law Assn. (pres. 1975), Nebr. Bar Assn., Omaha Bar Assn. (del. conf. Future Law 1979), Hawaii Bar Assn., Nat. Golden Key Soc., Alpha Phi Omega, Phi Alpha Delta, Beta Gamma Sigma, Phi Theta Chi. Democrat. Club: Rotary. Office: Univ Nebr Coll Bus Adminstrn Omaha NE 68182

FORBES, GILBERT BURNETT, physician, educator; b. Rochester, N.Y., Nov. 9, 1915; s. Gilbert DeLeverance and Lillian Augusta (Burnett) F.; m. Grace Moehlman, July 8, 1939; children: Constance Ann (Mrs. Joseph F. Citro), Susan Young (Mrs. William A. Martin). B.A., U. Rochester, 1936, M.D., 1940. Intern Strong Meml. Hosp., Rochester, 1940-41; resident St. Louis Children's Hosp., 1941-43; practice medicine, specializing in pediatrics Los Alamos, 1946-47; instr. pediatrics Sch. Medicine, Washington U., St. Louis, 1943-46; asst. prof. Sch. Medicine, Washington U., 1947-50; prof. pediatrics, chmn. dept. Southwestern Med. Sch., Dallas, 1950-53; assoc. prof. pediatrics Sch. Medicine, U. Rochester, 1953-57, prof., 1957-68, prof. pediatrics, prof. radiation biology, 1968—, Alumni Disting. Service prof. pediatrics, 1978—, chmn. faculty council, 1969-70, acting co-chmn. dept. pediatrics, 1974-76; cons. Nat. Inst. Child Health and Human Devel.; mem. sci. adv. com. Nutrition Found., 1963-66; mem. Nat. Council on Radiation Protection; mem. com. infant nutrition, com. dietary allowances NRC, 1960-63; vis. research fellow U. Oxford, Eng., 1970-71. Author: Human Body Composition, 1987; assoc. editor: Am. Jour. Diseases Childhood, 1964-72; chief editor, 1973-82; assoc. editor: Nutrition Revs, 1961-71; editor Pediatric Nutrition Handbook, 1985; contbr. numerous articles to profl. jours. Recipient Research Career award USPHS, NIH, 1962—, Borden award Am. Acad. Pediatrics, 1964, Alumni award to faculty U. Rochester, 1975; Albert David Kaiser award, Rochester Acad. Medicine, 1979, Arthur Kornberg Rsch. award, 1997. Mem. AAAS, AMA, Am. Pediatric Soc. (coun., v.p. 1975-76, John Howland award 1992), Soc. Pediatric Research (past pres.), Am. Acad. Pediatrics (com. on nutrition 1974-80), U. Rochester Med. Alumni Assn. (past pres., Gold medal 1982), Rotary, Sigma Xi, Alpha Omega Alpha, Theta Chi. Home: 1570 East Ave Apt 119 Rochester NY 14610-1635 Office: Univ of Rochester Dept of Pediatrics 601 Elmwood Ave Rochester NY 14642-0001

FORBES, GORDON MAXWELL, sports journalist, commentator; b. Bellport, N.Y., Feb. 6, 1930; s. Harlow Campbell and Grace Bain (DeVall) F.; m. June Lolita Cassidy, July 16, 1960 (dec. Jan. 1994); children—James Douglas, Christopher Bryan. B.A. in English, Duke U., 1955. Sports writer Fla. Times Union, Jacksonville, 1957-62; pro-football writer Phila. Inquirer, 1962-82; pro-football editor USA Today, Rosslyn, Va., 1982—; sports commentator Home Box Office Cable TV, 1988, Sta. WIP Radio, Phila., 1992-95; corr. Sports Illustrated, N.Y.C., 1963-89; selector Pro Football Hall of Fame, Canton, Ohio, 1975-87. Author: How to Win at the Trotters, 1966; contbr. numerous articles to jours. and mags. Served to cpl. U.S. Army, 1952-54. Recipient Dick McCann award for outstanding pro football coverage, 1988. Mem. Duke U. Alumni Assn., Pro Football Writers of Am. Republican. Episcopalian. Avocations: jogging, tennis, weightlifting. Home and Office: USA Today 13 Carriage Ln Marlton NJ 08053-1109

FORBES, J. RANDY, state senator; b. Cheaspeake, Va., Feb. 17, 1952. BA, U. Va., JD. Mem. Va. State Senate, 1998—, mem. cts. of justice, mem. local govt. com., mem. privileges & elections com., mem. 1998 bills & resolutions com. Chmn. Rep. Party Va. Republican. Baptist. Office: Gen Assembly Bldg 910 Capitol St Rm 320 Richmond VA 23219-3400 also: 524 Johnstown Rd Chesapeake VA 23322-5617

FORBES, JAMES WENDELL, publishing consultant; b. Evansburg, Alta., Can., Oct. 8, 1923; s. Prescott and Annie Alvira (MacLean) F.; m. Carolyn J. Irvine, May 14, 1965; children: James Wendell Jr., Elizabeth MacLean. B in Commerce, U. B.C., 1948. Various positions, circulation dept. Time Inc., 1948-70; dir. circulation Life mag., 1962-64, adminstr. book pub. div., 1964-68; asst. planning dir. Time-Life Books, 1969; asst. to mng. dir. Time-Life Records, 1970; pub. cons. Ridgefield, Conn., 1970—; cons. dep. pub. Guideposts mag., 1975-91; mgr. direct response advt. Young & Rubicam Internat., Inc., 1973-74; founder Sch. Mag. Mktg., 1979; chmn. bd. Direct Mktg. Assn., 1964-65. Author newsletter On Publishing; contbr. articles to profl. jours. Bd. dirs. Peale Ctr. Christian Living, 1985-95, Insts. Religion and Health, 1986-91; incorporator Ridgefield Boys' Club, 1986—; chmn. bd. missions Conglist. Ch., 1976, deacon, 1977, chmn. bd. deacons, 1978-79, chmn. parish rels. com., 1985-86. With RCAF, 1943-45. Recipient Mag. Circulation Hall of Fame award Direct Mktg. Assn., 1987, Silver Apple award Direct Mail Club N.Y., 1989, Lee C. Williams award Fulfillment Mgmt. Assn./X.Y.Z./The Circulation Mktg. Com. Mag. Pubs. Assn., 1990; elected to Direct Mktg. Assn. Hall of Fame, 1995. Mem. Literary and Sci. Exec. Assn. U. B.C. (hon.). Address: 87 Peaceable Hill Rd Ridgefield CT 06877-3618

FORBES, JOHN DOUGLAS, architectural and economic historian; b. San Francisco, Apr. 9, 1910; s. John Franklin and Portia (Ackerman) F.; m. Margaret Funkhouser, Feb. 4, 1937 (dec.); children: Pamela, Peter; m. Mary Elizabeth Lewis, July 26, 1980 (div.); 1 child, Michael. A.B., U. Calif.-Berkeley, 1931; M.A., Stanford U., 1932; A.M., Harvard U., 1936, Ph.D., 1937. Accountant J.F. Forbes & Co. (C.P.A.'s), San Francisco, 1937-38, 42-43; asst. to dir. fine arts, curator paintings San Francisco World's Fair, 1938-40; chmn. dept. fine arts U. Kansas City, Mo., 1940-42; faculty history Bennington Coll., 1943-46; assoc. editor Am. Enterprise Assn., 1944-46; assoc. prof. history and fine arts Wabash Coll., 1946-50; prof. U. Va., 1950-54; prof. bus. history Darden Sch. U. Va., 1954-80; prof. emeritus U. Va., 1980, lectr. art history Div. Continuing Edn., 1982—; adv. bd. Historic Am. Bldgs. Survey, 1974-78. Author: Israel Thorndike, 1953, Victorian Architect, 1953, Murder in Full View, 1968, Death Warmed Over, 1971, Stettinius, Sr., Portrait of a Morgan Partner, 1974, J.P. Morgan, Jr. (1867-1943), 1981, Death Among the Artists, 1993; editor: Jour. Soc. Archtl. Historians, 1953-58; asst. editor industry Ency. Britannica, 1956-58. 2d lt. AUS, 1942. Decorated officier Ordre des Palmes Académiques (France); cavaliere Ordine al Merito (Italy); named Hon. Alumnus Class of 1950, Assn. of Wabash Men, 1993. Mem. Am. Hist. Assn. (life), Coll. Art Assn. (life), Mystery Writers Am., Soc. Archtl. Historians (pres. 1962-64, life), Colonial Soc. Mass. (life), AAUP, AIA (hon.), Audubon Soc., Nat. Trust Historic Preservation, Wilderness Soc. (life), Sierra Club (life), Nature Conservancy (life), Mechanics Inst. (life), Victorian Soc. (life), Victorian Soc. in Am., Calif. Hist. Soc., Soc. Calif. Pioneers (life), Friends of Sea Otter (life), Tamalpais Conservation Club (life), Am. Kitefliers Assn. (life), Am. Soc. Dowsers (life), Save-the Redwoods League (life), Phi Beta Kappa. Clubs: Colonnade (Charlottesville) (life), Pacific-Union (San Francisco); Farmington Country (Charlottesville); Cambridge (Mass.) Boat. Home: PO Box 3607 Charlottesville VA 22903-0607 also: 1250 Jones St San Francisco CA 94109-4261

FORBES, JOHN EDWARD, financial consultant; b. Chgo., Sept. 18, 1925; s. Harry Charles and Jeanette Anne (Field) F.; m. Dorsey Connors, Aug. 10, 1961. Student, Rensselaer Poly. Inst., 1943-44, Franklin and Marshall Coll., Lancaster, Pa., 1943; BA, Monmouth coll., 1949; postgrad., Northwestern U., 1949-50. Account exec. and commodity mgr. Merrill Lynch, Pierce, Fenner and Smith, Inc., Chgo., 1949-61; pres. San Jose Cigarette Co., Calif., 1958-68; account exec. Hornblower & Weeks, Hemphill, Noyes, Inc., Chgo., 1961-71, assoc. resident mgr., 1971-75, v.p., resident mgr., 1975-78; corp. v.p. Loeb, Rhoades, Hornblower & Co., Chgo., 1981—, Shearson Lehman Bros., Chgo., 1961—; v.p. fin. cons. Smith Barney, Chgo., 1995—; pres. 227 E. Delaware Corp, Chgo., 1980-86; bd. dirs. Trend Industries, Chgo. Lt. USN, 1943-46, PTO. Clubs: Econ., Chgo. Bond, Hundred Club of Cook County, Tavern (pres. 1981-82), Saddle and Cycle (bd. dirs. 1983-86). Lodge: Soc. St. Andrew. Home: 227 E Delaware Pl Chicago IL 60611-7758 Office: Smith Barney Inc 10 S Wacker Dr Ste 2800 Chicago IL 60606-7407

FORBES, JOHN FRANCIS, government official; b. Ossining, N.Y., Aug. 19, 1946; s. Frank Joseph and Sara A. (Howell) F. BA, Marist Coll., 1968; MBPA, Southeastern U., Washington, 1981; MA, Boston U., 1986. Spl. agt. U.S. Customs Svc., Rouses Point, N.Y., 1972-73; spl. agt. enforcement U.S. Customs Svc., Buffalo, 1974-78; sr. spl. agt. U.S. Customs Svc., Reston, Va., 1978-82; customs rep. U.S. Customs Svc., Bonn, Fed. Republic Germany, 1982-87; program mgr. U.S. Customs Svc., Washington, 1987-88, chief gen. smuggling sect., 1988, chief gen. smuggling br. fin. investigations divsn., 1988-91, investigator senate permanant subcom. on investigations, fin. investigation div., 1992-94, with customs congl. affairs, 1994; with group IV-El Dorado task force U.S. Customs Svc., N.Y.C., 1994-99; mem. banking subcom. on oversight and investigation U.S. Ho. of Reps., 1999—; spl. agt. Drug Enforcement Agy., Rouses Point, 1973-74; investigator Senate Permanent Subcom. on Investigations, 1992-94. Contbr. articles to profl. mag. Mem. Nat. Trust for Hist. Preservation, Washington, Friends of Kennedy Ctr., Washington. 1st lt. U.S. Army, 1968-71, Vietnam. Mem. VFW, Internat. Police Assn., Assn. Cert. Fraud Examiners, Fraternal Order of Police, World Affairs Coun. Washington, Fed. Law Enforcement Officers Assn., Wilson Ctr. Assocs., Lincoln Soc., Cousteau Soc., World Future Soc., The Acad. of Polit. Sci., ASPA, Fed. Planning Network, Nat. Capitol Hist. Soc. Roman Catholic. Avocations: running, reading, scuba diving, cross country skiing. Office: US Customs Svc 6 World Trade Ctr Rm 508 New York NY 10048-0206

FORBES, JOHN RIPLEY, museum executive, educator, naturalist; b. Chelsea, Mass., Aug. 25, 1913; s. Kenneth Ripley and Ellen Elizabeth (Barker) F.; m. Margaret Sanders, Dec. 10, 1951; children: Ripley, Anne. Spl. student, U. Iowa, 1933-34, Bowdoin Coll., 1934-35; LHD (hon.), Bowdoin Coll., 1987. Founder, dir. Stamford (Conn.) Mus., 1935-37; ornithologist, taxidermist Lee Mus. Biology, Bowdoin Coll., MacMillan-Arctic Expdn., Labrador and Baffin Island, 1937; founder, dir. William T. Hornaday Meml. Found., N.Y., 1938-50; organizer, dir. Kansas City (Mo.) Mus., 1939-41; founder Nashville Children's Mus., 1944, acting dir., 1945-46, trustee for life, 1975; exec. dir. Jacksonville (Fla.) Children's Mus., 1945; founder Fernbank Children's Nature Mus., Atlanta, 1946; organizer, dir. Oreg. Mus. Sci. and Industry, Portland, 1947-49; founder Nat. Found. for Jr. Mus., N.Y., dir., 1951-60; founder Sacramento Jr. Mus., dir., 1951-53; co-founder, dir. ops. Nature Centers for Young Am., 1959-60; founder, pres., chmn. bd. Natural Sci. for Youth Found., Conn., 1961—; founder Big Cypress Nature Center, Naples, Fla., 1959; organizer Ft. Worth's Children's Mus., 1945. Founder, pres. William T. Hornaday Meml. Trust, Conn., 1961-77; founder Mid-Fairfield County Youth Mus., Westport, Conn., 1958, pres., 1963-66, trustee for life, 1966; founder Am. Assn. Youth Mus., 1964, hon. life mem., 1976; co-founder, v.p. Aspetuck Land Trust, Fairfield County; pres. St. John's on the Lake Assn., 1963-64; pres. emeritus, trustee John and Anna Newton Porter Found., 1974-89; founder Outdoor Activity Ctr., Atlanta, chmn., 1977-80; founder Chattahoochee Nature Ctr., Roswell, Ga., pres., 1977-78; founder Reynolds Arboretum and Nature Preserve Morrow, Ga., 1976; founder, pres. Lakes Region Conservation Trust, Meredith, N.H., 1977; founder Forbes Nature Ctr., Beckett Preserve and Ragged Island Lake Winnipesaukee, N.H., 1979; trustee Hilla Von Rebay Found., 1968; trustee Milford (Pa.) Reservation 1977, pres. 1977-82 1983; founder, pres. Natural Sci. Solar Ctr., Milford, 1983; founder, trustee Cochran Mill Nature Ctr. and Arboretum, Atlanta, Ga., 1987; founder Autrey Mill Nature Ctr., Alpharetta, Ga., 1988; founder, pres. Big Trees Forest Preserve and Edn. Ctr., Sandy Springs, Ga., 1989; founder Lake Careco Nature Ctr., Austell, 1992; naturalist, lectr. on Bahia Paraiso, Argentine polar transport ship sunk near U.S. Palmer Base at Arthur Harbor, Antarctic Peninsula, 1989; bd. mem. Environ. Adv. Commn. State of Ga., 1992-94. With M.C., USAAF, 1942-. Recipient conservation award Am. Motors, 1971, William T. Hornaday gold medal, 1977, Founder's award Natural Sci. for Youth Found., 1979, Conservationist of Yr. award Ga. Wildlife Fedn., 1991, Nature Educator of Yr. award Roger Tory Peterson Inst., 1995. Mem. Am. Assn. Mus. (chmn. children's mus. sec. 1965), Nat. Audubon Soc. (life), Am. Nature Study Soc., Nature Conservancy, Wilderness Soc., Am. Ornithologist Union (life), N.Y. Zool. Soc., Am. Birding Assn. (life), Nat. Wildlife Fedn., Conn. Conservation Assn. (pres. 1969-70), Sierra Club, Audubon Soc. N.H. (pres. 1975). Clubs: Explorers (N.Y.C.); Mazamas (Portland, Oreg.). Home: 11 Wildwood Vly Atlanta GA 30350-4461 Office: Natural Scis for Youth Found 130 Azalea Dr Roswell GA 30075-4804

FORBES, JUDIE, program manager; b. Fullerton, Calif., Sept. 27, 1942; d. James Franklin and Lois Virginia (Couse) F.; m. Ralph M. Hawk, Nov. 10, 1990; children: Laurel Alice Schader, James Joseph Resha, Edward John Resha III. BA in Physics, Calif. State U., Fullerton, 1974; MS in Engring., Calif. State U., 1979; MBA, U. So. Calif., 1983; postgrad., Claremont Grad. Sch. Engr. electromech. div. Northrop, Anaheim, Calif., 1975-80; project engr., mgr. electronic div. Northrop, Hawthorne, Calif., 1981-87; tech. staff TRW, San Bernadino, Calif., 1981; project mgr. Gen. Rsch. Corp., El Segundo, Calif., 1987-89; v.p. D.C. Caldwell & Co., Inc., Buena Park, Calif., 1987—; European program mgr. TRW Technar, Irwindale, Calif., 1989—. Active Town Hall Calif., Los Angeles, 1983—. Calif. State U. Found. grantee, 1974; named Disting. Alumni Calif. State U., 1986; recipient Engring. Merit award Orange County Engring. Council, 1985. Fellow Inst. for Advancement Engring., AIAA (assoc., pres. Orange County 1986-87), Soc. Women Engrs. (pres. Los Angeles chpt. 1981-82, nat. v.p. 1983-84). Democrat. Home: 14742 Beach Blvd # 611 La Mirada CA 90638-4259 Office: TRW Technar 6010 N Irwindale Ave Azusa CA 91702-3207

FORBES, KENNETH ALBERT FAUCHER, urological surgeon; b. Waterford, N.Y., Apr. 28, 1922; s. Joseph Frederick (dec.) and Adelle Frances (Robitaille) Faucher; adopted s. James Peter Forbes; m. Jeanne Ann Bonacci, June 18, 1947 (dec.); 1 child: Michael; m. Eileen Ruth Gibbons, Aug. 4, 1956; children: Diane, Kenneth E., Thomas, Maureen, Daniel. BS cum laude, U. Notre Dame, 1944; MD, St. Louis U., 1947. Diplomate Am. Bd. Urology. Intern St. Louis U. Hosp., 1947-48; resident in urol. surgery Barnes Hosp., VA Hosp., Washington U., St. Louis. U. schs. medicine, St. Louis, 1948-52; asst. chief urology Letterman Army Hosp., San Francisco, 1952-54; fellow West Roxbury (Harvard) VA Hosp., Boston, 1955; asst. chief urology VA Hosp., East Orange, N.J., 1955-58; practice medicine specializing in urology Green Bay, Wis., 1958-78, Long Beach, Calif., 1978-85; mem. cons. staff Fairview State Hosp. U. Calif. Med. Ctr., Irvine, VA Hosp., Long Beach; chmn. Legal Def. Com., State Med. Soc. Wisc., 1976-77; pres. Wisc. Urological Soc., 1977-78; asst. clin. prof. surgery U. Calif., Irvine, 1978-85; cons. Vols. in Tech. Assistance, 1986—. *American medical care flourished during the 20th Century because the Constitution/Bill of Rights guarantees all citizens freedom of choice in all basic rights. Federal laws have infringed upon these rights, resulting in unjustifiable over-regulation and loss of freedom of choice for patients and physicians. Politically, we have the Right (Republicans) and the Left (Democrats). Erik von Kuehnelt-Leddihn in Leftism Revisited (Regnery Gateway 1990, ISBN 0-89526-537-0, p.29) states: "To identify-the Right with freedom, personalism and variety, and the Left with slavery, collectivism and uniformity is to make sense of semantics." Thus, Right is right and Left is Wrong!.* Contbr. articles to profl. jours. Served with USNR, 1944-46, ensign 1947-51; capt. U.S. Army, 1952-54. Named Outstanding Faculty Mem. by students, 1981. Fellow ACS, Royal Soc. Medicine, Internat. Coll. Surgeons; mem. AMA, AAAS, Calif. Med. Assn., Am. Urol. Assn. (exec. com. North Ctrl. sect. 1972-75, Western sect. 1980—), N.Y. Acad. Scis., Surg. Alumni Assn. U. Calif.-Irvine, Justin J. Cordonnier Soc. Washington U., Urologists Corr. Club, Notre Dame Club (Man of Yr. award 1965), Union League Club of Chgo., Miles City Club (Mont.), Phi Beta Pi. Republican. Roman Catholic. Home and Office: 14425 W Via Tercero Sun City West AZ 85375-2741

FORBES, MARJORIE WEBSTER, counselor; b. Providence, July 25, 1930; d. George Wickliffe and Kathryn Craig (Annable) Webster; m. Richard Daniel Forbes, Aug. 4, 1951; 1 child, Richard Bruce. BA in Psychology, U. R.I., 1988; MA in Counseling, R.I. Coll., 1992. Vol. pres. Get Out and Live Successfully, Warwick, R.I., 1984—. Vocal tape Panic Disorder, 1987. Chairperson adv. coun. John A. Ferris Health Ctr., 1988—; vol. Samaritans, Providence, 1988. Recipient Jefferson award Am. Inst. for Pub. Svc., 1989, Community Svc. award U. R.I., 1989. Mem. Phobia Soc. R.I. (treas. 1987-91). Avocations: reading, musicals, visiting friends, travel..

FORBES, MICHAEL P., congressman; b. Riverhead, N.Y., July 16, 1952; m. Barbara; children: Abby, Ted. BA, SUNY Albany. Coord. various local, state, fed. Rep. campaign, 1980-89, exec. asst. to U.S. Senator Alfonse D'Amato, 1981-84, adm. asst. to U.S. Rep. Connie Mack, 1985-87; owner small bus., 1985-89; regional adminstr. U.S. Small Bus. Adminstrn., 1989-92; legis. dir., regional mgr. U.S. C. of C., 1993-94; mem. 104th-106th Congress from 1st N.Y. dist., 1995—. Office: US House Reps 125 Cannon HOB Washington DC 20515-3201*

FORBES, MICHELLE, television and film actress; b. Austin, Tex., Feb. 17, 1967. Appeared in films Love Bites, 1993, Kalifornia, 1993, Swimming with Sharks, 1994, The Road Killers, 1994, Black Day Blue Night, 1995, Escape from L.A., 1996, Bullfighter, 1999; appeared on TV in The Guiding LIght, 1952, Star Trek: The Next Generation, 1987, Homicide: Life on the Street, 1996-98, The Prosecutors, 1996.

FORBES, MORTON GERALD, lawyer; b. Atlanta, July 12, 1938; s. Arthur Mark and Mary Dean (Power) F.; m. Eunice Lee Haynsworth, Jan. 25, 1963; children: John, Ashley, Sarah. AB, Wofford Coll., 1962; JD, U. Ga., 1965. Bar: Ga. 1965, U.S. Dist. Ct. (mid. dist.) Ga. 1965, U.S. Dist. Ct. (so. dist.) Ga. 1968, U.S. Dist. Ct. (no. dist.) Ga. 1993, U.S. Ct. Appeals (5th cir.) 1974, U.S. Ct. Appeals (4th cir.) 1972, U.S. Ct. Appeals (11th cir.) 1981. Assoc. Pierce, Ranitz, Lee, Berry & Mahoney, 1967-70; ptnr. Pierce, Ranitz, Berry, Mahoney & Forbes, 1970-76, Pierce, Ranitz, Mahoney, Forbes & Coolidge, 1976-81; ptnr., sec. Ranitz, Mahoney, Forbes & Coolidge, P.C., 1981-91, Forbes & Bowman, 1991—; gen. counsel Ga. Fen. Young Rep. Clubs, 1971-72; guest lectr. dept. dental hygiene Armstrong State Coll., 1970-72. Mem. Savannah Port Authority, 1973—, chmn., 1979-81; mem. Chatham County Devel. Authority, 1973-80; mem. nat. com. Nat. Fedn. Young Reps., 1973; mem. econ. adv. coun. Coastal Area Planning and Devel. Authority, 1980—; bd. dirs. Savannah Symphony Soc., 1971-75; Ga. del. to Japan/Southeast Trade Mission, Kyoto, Japan, 1983, S.E. U.S.A./Japan Assn. meeting, Birmingham, Ala., 1984. Served with USN, 1965-67. Recipient Outstanding Service award Savannah Port Authority, 1981. Mem. ABA, State Bar Ga., Am. Judicature Soc., Nat. Assn. Bond Counsel, Ga. Def. Lawyers Assn. (v.p. 1987—, mem. exec. com. 1988, bd. dirs., exec. v.p. 1990-91, pres. 1991-92), Savannah Bar Assn. (exec. com. 1989-94, pres. 1992-93), Libel Def. Resource Ctr., Def. Rsch. Inst. (state chmn. 1992—), Savannah Econ. Devel. Action Council (founding), Savannah Area Wofford Coll. Alumni Club (past pres.), Soc. of the Cincinnati (Va.), St. Andrews Soc., Soc. Colonial Wars, Sons of Revolution (sec. 1988-92). Republican. Presbyterian. Clubs: Chatham, Savannah Yacht, 1st City, The Landings Club. Office: Forbes & Bowman PO Box 13929 Savannah GA 31416-0929

FORBES, PETER, architect; b. Berkeley, Calif., May 22, 1942; s. John Douglas and Margaret (Funkhouser) F.; m. Patricia Ann Marsh, Aug. 27, 1966 (div. 1982); children: Alexander John, Anne deMarken; m. Erica Longfellow deBerry, July 21, 1990; 1 child, Allegra Longfellow. BArch, U. Mich., 1966; MArch, Yale U., 1967; Dr. Engring. Tech. (hon.), Wentworth Inst. Tech., 1991. Registered architect, Mass., Va., Calif., Maine, R.I., N.Y., Mich., Conn., D.C.; cert. Nat. Council Archtl. Registration Bds. Project designer Skidmore, Owings & Merrill, Chgo., 1965-66; assoc. ptnr. PARD Team, Inc., Boston, 1967-71; pres. Forbes Hailey Jeas Erneman, Inc., Boston, 1972-80, Peter Forbes and Assoc., Inc., Boston, 1980—; mem. Commonwealth of Mass. Designer Selection Bd., 1986-89; mem. Spl. Comm. Concerning State and County Bldgs., 1978-81; bd. dirs. continuing edn. Boston Archtl. Ctr.; vis. critic U. Mich., 1980-82, Cath. U. Am., Rome, 1982; vis. lectr. Cath. U., Washington, 1997; lectr., vis. critic Va. Poly. Inst. and State U., 1989-92, 96, Columbia U., 1984; vis. critic N.C. State U., 1997; Thomas S. Monaghan Disting. vis. prof. U. Mich., 1987; vis. prof. Harvard U., 1989, 91, 94, G. Truman Ward vis. lectr. Va. Poly. Inst. and State U., 1996; vis. lectr. Lawrence Tech. U., 1996, Evergreen State Coll., 1996, U. B.C., 1996; guest lectr. Boston Mus. Fine Arts, 1997, Guido A. Binda vis. lectr. U. Mich., 1997. Author: Ten Houses: Peter Forbes and Associates, 1995; exhbns. include Cath. U. Am., 1982, 97, U. Mich., 1982, 87, 97, Va. Poly. Inst. and State U., 1983, Boston Athenaeum, 1986, Harvard U., 1986, Lawrence Tech. U., 1996; contbr. articles to profl. jours. Recipient Record House award, 1983, 86, 87, 89, New Eng. Design awrd, 1986, 87, 89, 91, 94, 96, 97, 98, Archtl. Excellence award Am. Inst. Steel Constrn., 1987, Tucker award Bldg. Stone Inst., 1987, 90, Best and Brightest award, 1995, Honor award Am. Wood Inst., 1989, Nat. Housing Design award, 1990, Silver award Indsl. Designers Soc. Am., 1993, 94. Fellow AIA (nat. jud. coun. 1987—, Nat. honor award 1986, 92, New Eng. regional coun./design award 1986, 87, 89, 91, 94, 96, 97, 98, Washington D.C. merit award 1994; Excellence in Arch. award Maine chpt. 1995), Boston Soc. Archs. (bd. dirs., commr. pub. affairs, chmn. ethics com., v.p., pres. 1988-89, Excellence in Arch. award 1988-89, 91-94, 98, Honor award 1995, 97, 98, Excellence in Housing design award 1996, 98), Soc. Archtl. Historians (life), Century Club, Newport Reading Rm., Racquet and Tennis Club, Nat. Tennis Club, Yale Club, Boston Athenaeum. Home: Greenings Is Southwest Harbor ME 04679 Office: Peter Forbes and Assocs 70 Long Wharf Boston MA 02110-3602

FORBES, RICHARD MATHER, biochemistry educator; b. Wooster, Ohio, Jan. 8, 1916; s. Ernest Browning and Lydia Maria (Mather) F.; m. Mary Medlicott, Feb. 26, 1944; children—Sally Allen, Anne Mather, Stephen Harding. B.S., Pa. State Coll., 1938, M.S., 1939; Ph.D., Cornell U., 1942. Instr. biochemistry Wayne State U., 1942; research fellow Cornell U., Ithaca, N.Y., 1942-43; asst. prof. U. Ky., Lexington, 1946-49; assoc. prof. U. Ill., Champaign-Urbana, 1949-55; prof. nutritional biochemistry U. Ill., 1955-85, emeritus prof., 1985—. Contbr. articles to profl. jours. Served to capt. U.S. Army, 1943-46. Recipient H. H. Mitchell award U. Ill., 1981. Fellow AAAS, Am. Inst. Nutrition (Borden award 1984); mem. Am. Soc. Animal Sci. (Gustav Bohstedt award 1968), Sigma Xi. Republican. Mem. United Ch. of Christ. Clubs: Nat. Exchange, Izaak Walton League. Home: 101 W Windsor Rd Apt 2105 Urbana IL 61802-6663

FORBES, STEVE (MALCOLM STEVENSON FORBES, JR.), publishing executive; b. Morristown, N.J., July 18, 1947; s. Malcolm and Roberta (Laidlaw) F.; m. Sabina Beekman, June 19, 1971; 5 children. BA, Princeton U., 1970; LHD, Lycoming Coll., Jacksonville U., Kean Coll.; LLD (hon.), Lock Haven U., Westminster Coll., Sacred Heart U., Centenary Coll., Iona Coll., Pepperdine U., LeHigh U., 1997, New Hampshire U.; LittD, Heidelberg Coll.; ScD (hon.), N.Y. Inst. Tech., Lynn U.; SScD, U. Francisco Marroquin; D.P.S. (hon.), U. Rio Grande; PhD (hon.), Hillsdale Coll. With Forbes Inc., N.Y.C., 1970—, pres., COO, 1980-90, dep. editor-in-chief, 1982-90, editor-in-chief, pres., CEO, 1990—. Author: (filmscript) Some Call It Greed, 1977; editor: Fact and Comment, 1974. Pres. Somerset County Park Commn., N.J., 1981-91; mem. Bd. for Internat. Broadcasting, 1983-93, chmn., 1985-93; trustee Brooks Sch., North Andover, Mass., 1978-97; pres. bd. trustees Princeton U., 1987-96; trustee Found. Student Comm., 1970—, Ronald Reagan Presdl. Found., 1990—, Am. Enterprise Inst., 1990—, Princeton U., 1992—, Freedom House, 1993—; bd. overseers Meml. Sloan-Kettering Cancer Ctr., 1989—; chmn. bd. dirs., Empower America, 1993-96, Americas Soc., 1992-97, Nat. Endowment for Democracy, 1994—; Rep. presdl. primary campaign candidate, 1995-96, 99—; bd. dirs. Nat. Taxpayers Union, 1997—, Jackie Robinson Found., 1996—; mem. Coun. for Nat. Policy, 1998—. Republican. Office: Forbes Inc 60 5th Ave New York NY 10011-8882

FORBES, THEODORE MCCOY, JR., arbitrator, mediator, retired lawyer; b. Atlanta, Oct. 28, 1929; s. Theodore M. and Mary Beatrice (Christie) F.; m. Margaret Paty, Dec. 12, 1953; children: Theodore McCoy, Margaret Paty. BS in Chemistry, Ga. Inst. Tech., 1950; LLB, U. Va., 1953. Bar: Ga., 1952, D.C. 1973, U.S. Ct. Appeals (5th cir.) 1976, U.S. Ct. Appeals (11th cir.) 1981. Instr. Culver (Ind.) Summer Naval Sch., 1950; assoc. Smith, Gambrell & Russell, and predecessor firms, Atlanta, 1953-58, ptnr., 1958-91; solo practice, 1992-95. Bd. dirs. Travelers Aid Soc., Atlanta, 1974-90, pres., 1975-76, 86-89; bd. dirs., corp. sec. Shepherd Spinal Ctr., Atlanta, 1975-95; bd. dirs. Ga. Fund for Edn., 1986-89. Lt. (j.g.) USNR, 1950-62. Fellow Ga. Bar Found.; mem. ABA, Atlanta Bar Assn., State Bar Ga., Ga. C. of C. (bd.

dirs. 1986-95), Capital City Club (life). Avocations: golf, American history, fishing. Home: 1760 Marlborough Dr Atlanta GA 30350-4507

FORBES, TIMOTHY CARTER, publisher; b. Morristown, N.J., Oct. 5, 1953; s. Malcolm Stevenson and Roberta (Laidlaw) F.; m. Anne Shepard Harrison, Mar. 4, 1983. AB with honors, Brown U., 1976, LHD (hon.), 1996. Prodr. Seven Seas Cinema, N.Y.C., 1977-81; prodr., screenwriter N.Y.C., 1981-85; v.p. Forbes Inc., N.Y.C., 1986—, COO, 1996, also bd. dirs.; pres. Am. Heritage Mag., N.Y.C., 1986—. Dir., producer: (films) Some Call It Greed, 1977, Lost to the Revolution, 1979, Golden Age of Toy Boats, 1981, Whatever Happened to Childhood?, 1987, Margaret Thatcher Found., 1993—, Hist. House Trust N.Y.C., 1990—. Trustee St. Vincent's Hosp., N.Y.C., 1986—; trustee Brown U., 1987-94, 95—, Tougaloo Coll., 1992—; bd. dirs. United Hosp. Fund, 1992—, Margaret Thatcher Found., 1993—, Hist. House Trust N.Y.C., 1990—. Mem. Am. Antiquarian Soc. Office: Forbes Inc 60 5th Ave New York NY 10011-8882

FORBES-RICHARDSON, HELEN HILDA, state agency administrator; b. Detroit, July 26, 1950; d. Henry and Trunetta (Adams) Forbes; m. Leon Richardson (div.); 1 child, Leon Ronald Jr. BA in Edn. and Human Svcs., U. Detroit, 1972; MPA, Harvard U., 1989. Cert. tchr. Mich. Substitute tchr. Detroit Bd. Edn., 1972-75; assistance payment worker State Dept. Social Svcs., Detroit, 1975-79, supr. assistance payment, 1979-85, section mgr., 1985—; adminstrv. asst. to chief dep. dir. Wayne County Dept. Social Svcs., Detroit, 1989-90; mem. case rev. com. Mich. Dept. Social Svcs. Gen. Assistance, 1985, 87, labor rels. subcom., quality initiative task force tng. com., 1985; co-chairperson quality initiative error reduction com. and conf. planning com.; mem. tng. com. quality initiative task force Mich. Dept. Social Svcs., 1984, client svc. subcom., 1989—, coord. employee recognition program, 1989-90, chmn. procedure com., Grand River Warren local office, 1990—, coord. state employee recognition program, Wayne County, 1980-90; chair security plan com. client info. system County of Wayne, 1989, mem. UAW Secondary Contract Negotiations Team, 1988; mem. conf. planning com. Mich. County Social Svcs. Assn., 1988; chairperson Grand River/Warren Procedures Com., 1990, employee recognition awards program level 1 Grand River/Warren Dept. Social Svcs., 1990; pres. Forbes-Richardson Ltd., 1990—, mgmt. cons., 1990; owner, editor Adams-Forbes Pub. Co., Detroit. Pub.: (poetry) I Am, 1997. Coordinator Social Svc. United Found. Dr., Lafayette local office 1985, Social Svc. Black United Fund Dr. 1987, speaker Nat. Polit. Congress Black Women, 1986; student project coord. Wayne County Community Coll., Wayne County Dept. Social Svcs., 1989; coord. scholarship project Mary Holmes Coll. Spirit of Detroit Leadership award, 1985. Mem. Am. Pub. Welfare Assn. (planning com. 1986), Am. Legion Aux. Avocations: reading, sewing, billiards. Office: Mich Dept Social Svcs 1200 6th St Detroit MI 48226-2424

FORBIS, BRYAN LESTER, state agency administrator; b. Jefferson City, Mo., Aug. 14, 1957; s. Lewis Wagner and Thelma Rose (Thompson) F.; m. Mary Beth Dobbs, Nov. 1987. BA in Polit. Sci. with honors, U. Mo., 1979, MA in Polit. Sci., 1981. Rsch. asst. Mo. Office of Lt. Gov., Jefferson City, 1980; teaching asst. U. Mo., Columbia, 1980-81; mgmt. analysis specialist I, Mo. Div. Family Svcs., Jefferson City, 1981-83; mgmt. analysis specialist II, Mo. Div. Med. Svcs., Jefferson City, 1983-85; asst. to dir. Mo. Div. of Aging, Jefferson City, 1985-89, dir., 1992-93, special asst. to dir., 1996—; asst. dir. Mo. Dept. of Natural Resources, 1989, dir. program coordination, 1989-90, dir. policy devel., 1991-92; dep. dir. Mo. Div. Child Support Enforcement, 1993-95; spl. asst. Mo. Divsn. Aging, 1995—. Mem. Capital City Coun. on Arts, Jefferson City, 1985-89, Mo. Mansion Preservation Inc., Jefferson City, 1985-89; steering com. March of Dimes, Jefferson City, 1986; mem. Conservation Fedn. of Mo., 1992—; sec. U. Mo. Arts & Scis. Leaders, 1996—, Fund Distbn. Com., United Way, 1995—. Named One of Outstanding Young Men of Am., 1985, 86; curator scholar U. Mo., 1975, 77, 78, William Bradshaw scholar U. Mo., 1979. Mem. ASPA, Acad. Polit. Sci., Capital Area Mo. U. Alumni Assn. (exec. asst., pres. bd. dirs., dist. bd. dirs. 1992—), Phi Beta Kappa, Pi Sigma Alpha, Omicron Delta Kappa. Republican. Lutheran. Club: Pachyderms (Jefferson City). Avocations: chess, collecting polit. campaign buttons, football. Home: 935 Fairmount Blvd Jefferson City MO 65101-3544 Office: Mo Divsn Aging 615 Howerton Ct Jefferson City MO 65109-6806

FORBIS, RICHARD GEORGE, archaeologist; b. Missoula, Mont., July 30, 1924; s. Clarence Jenks and Josephine Marie (Hunt) F.; m. Marjorie Helen Wilkinson, Nov. 12, 1960; children: Michael, David, Amanda. B.A., U. Mont., 1949, M.A., 1950; Ph.D., Columbia U., 1955. Sr. archeologist Pacific N.W. Pipeline Corp., Western U.S., 1955-56; archeologist Glenbow Found., Calgary, Alta., Can., 1957-63; mem. faculty U. Calgary, 1963—, prof. archaeology, 1968-88, prof. emeritus, 1988—, interim chmn. dept., Killam Meml. fellow, 1977; chmn. Alta. Public Adv. Com. Hist. and Archeol. Resources, 1971-74; mem. Alta. Historic Sites Bd., 1974-78; vis. scientist Can. Nat. Museum Man, 1970. Author: Cluny: An Ancient Fortified Village in Alberta, 1977; co-author: An Introduction to the Archaeology of Alberta, Canada, 1965. Served with AUS, 1943-46. Mem. AAAS, Soc. Am. Archaeology, Can. Archaeol. Assn. (Smith-Wintemberg award 1984), Am. Anthrop. Assn., Plains Anthrop. Conf., Champlain Soc., Sigma Chi. Office: U Calgary Dept Archeology, 2500 University Dr NW, Calgary, AB Canada T2N 1N4*

FORCE, ELIZABETH ELMA, retired pharmaceutical executive, consultant; b. Phila., Sept. 6, 1930; d. Harry Elgin and Loretta G. (Werner) F. BA, Temple U., 1952; postgrad., U. Pa., 1965-67; MPh, George Washington U., 1972, PhD, 1973. Cons. sr. scientist Booz-Allen Hamilton, Bethesda, Md., 1967-68; rsch. cons. scientist GEOMET, Inc., Rockville, Md., 1968-70; profl. assoc. div. med. scis. NAS-NRC, Washington, 1970-74; mgr. clin. adminstrn. dept. clin. rsch. and devel. Wyeth Labs., Radnor, Pa., 1974-77; exec. dir. regulatory affairs Merck Sharp and Dohme Rsch. Labs., West Point, Pa., 1977-88; cons. Clin. Regulatory Systems, Sarasota, Fla., 1988-91; asst. professorial lectr. epidemiology and environ. health Sch. Medicine George Washington U., Washington, 1972-74; vis. assoc. prof. cmty. health and preventive medicine Med. Coll. Jefferson U., Phila., 1981-83. Editor Clin. Rsch. Practice and Drug Regulatory Affairs, 1983-85, Drug Info. Jour., 1984-88; contbr. 60 articles to profl. jours. Pres. Sterling Lakes Owners Assn., Boynton Beach, 1996-98, pres. Women's Resource Ctr., Sarasota, 1992-94; pres., bd. dirs. Siesta Tower Condominium Assn., Sarasota, 1990-92; vice chmn. Com. for Minority Contracts, Sarasota County, 1991; chmn. adv. coun. bd. trustees Ringling Mus. of Art, 1991-95, Coun. on Violence, Sarasota County, 1994. Ruhland Pub. Health fellow George Washington U. Sch. Medicine, 1971-73. Mem. Drug Info. Assn. (pres. 1986-87, Outstanding Dir. award 1985), Heritage Soc. of George Washington U., Harid Conservatory (advancement coun.), Boynton Women's Club, Pres.' Club, Fla. Atlantic U. Avocations: collecting Oriental art, sailing. Office: 7555 Northport Dr Boynton Beach FL 33437-5066

FORCE, ROBERT, law educator; b. Phila., Aug. 11, 1934; s. Charles and Dora (Woloshin) F.; m. Ruth Morris, Aug. 18, 1962; children: Joshua Simon, Seth Daniel. B.S., Temple U., 1955, LL.B., 1958; postgrad., U. Adelaide, 1958-59; LL.M., NYU, 1960. Bar: Pa. 1961. Law clk. to presiding justice Pa. Ct. Common Pleas., Phila., 1960-61, U.S. Dist. Ct., Phila., 1961-62; instr. Temple U., Phila., 1960-61; assoc. Kleinbard, Bell & Brecker, Phila., 1963-64; asst. prof. Ind. U. Law Sch., Indpls., 1964-67, assoc. prof., 1968; prof. Tulane U., New Orleans, 1969—, Thomas Pickles prof. law, 1979-89, Niels F. Johnsen prof. maritime law, 1989—, acting dean, 1977-78; dir. Tulane Maritme Law Ctr. Co-author: Hall's Criminal Law, 1993, Admiralty and Maritime Law: Cases, Notes and Text, vols. 1 and 2, 1997, Marine Pollution: Conventions, Statutes, Cases and Text, 1998. Fulbright fellow, 1958-59. Mem. ABA, Beta Gamma Sigma, Omicron Delta Kappa. Home: 1038 Eleonore St New Orleans LA 70115-4311 Office: 6329 Freret St Ste 255 New Orleans LA 70118-6231

FORCE, RONALD WAYNE, librarian; b. Sioux City, Iowa, Sept. 7, 1941; s. Robert N. and Madeline (Heine) F.; m. Jo Ellen Hitch, May 31, 1964; children: Emily, Alicia. BS, Iowa State U., 1963; MA, U. Minn., 1968; MS, Ohio State U., 1975. Asst. to head dept. librs. Ohio State U., Columbus, 1968-70, head engring. librs., 1970-72, head edn./psychology libr., 1972-79; asst. dir. pub. svcs. Wash. State U. Librs., Pullman, 1979-82; asst. sci. libr. U. Idaho Libr., Moscow, 1982-84, pub. svcs. libr., 1984-85, humanities libr., 1985-88, assoc. dean libr. svcs., 1988-91, dean libr. svcs., 1991—; mem. adv. coun. Libr. Svcs. and Constrn. Act. Author: Guide to Literature on Biomedical Engineering, 1972; contbr. articles to profl. jours. Mem. Sacajawea Coun. Campfire Bd., 1980-85, mem. Pullman Dist. Campfire Com., fin. com., 1980-82, chair, 1983-84, treas., 1985, Sacajawea County Self-Study Com., 1986; mem. adv. bd. N.W. Net Info. Resources, 1994-95; mem. Idaho Network Adv. Com., 1993-95; mem. LSCA Adv. Coun., 1989-95. Mem. ALA, Idaho Libr. Assn. (2d v.p. 1997-98, 1st v.p. 1998-99, pres. 1999—). Home: 545 N Blaine St Moscow ID 83843-3626 Office: U Idaho Libr Moscow ID 83844-2371

FORCHESKIE, CARL S., former apparel company executive; b. Shamokin, Pa., Feb. 3, 1927; s. John A. and Helen F.; m. Barbara Ann Pierz; children from previous marriage: Carl, Gail, Caroline Karen. B.A., Pa. State U., 1951. Mgr. Coopers & Lybrand, 1951-62; cons. U.S. Dept. Treasury, 1962-63; chief fin. officer Loral Corp., 1963-69; exec. v.p. Salant Corp., N.Y.C., 1969-81; pres., chief exec. officer Salant Corp., 1981-85. Mem. Planning Bd. Hastings-on-Hudson, N.Y. Served with AUS, 1945-46. Mem. AICPA, N.Y. State Soc. CPAs, Fin. Execs. Inst., Am. Apparel Mfrs. Assn., St. Andrews Golf Club, Union League, Paupack Hills Golf and Country Club. Roman Catholic. Home: 192 Eagle Crest Greentown PA 18426-9052

FORCIER, LAWRENCE KENNETH, natural resource educator; b. Gardner, Mass., Aug. 17, 1943; married, 1995; 3 children. BA, Dartmouth Coll., 1966; M in Forest Sci., Yale U., 1968, MPhil, 1970, PhD in Forest Ecology, 1973. From asst. to assoc. prof. forest ecology U. Mont., Missoula, 1970-76, acting dean forestry, 1977; assoc. prof. ecology-silviculture U. Wis., Stevens Point, 1975-76; from asst. to assoc. dir. U. Vt., Burlington, 1977-83, acting dir., 1983-84, dean natural resources, 1984-99, dean agr. and life scis., dir. extension, 1991—, sr. advisor to pres., 1999—. Mem. Soc. Am. Foresters. Achievements include research in forest tree population dynamics and the response of forest ecosystems to disturbance. Office: U Vt Divsn Agrl Natural Resources & Extension 601 Main St Burlington VT 05401-3439*

FORCIER, RICHARD CHARLES, information technology educator, computer applications consultant; b. Chicopee, Mass., Feb. 17, 1941; s. Rudolph Joseph and Rachel Lena (Chagnon) F.; m. Peggy Jean Prosser, July 30, 1983; children: Laura, Andrea, Richard J. BSE, Westfield (Mass.) State Coll., 1962; MEd, U. Mass., 1964; postgrad., U. Colo, 1966; PhD, Mich. State U., 1969. Media cons. Mich. State U., East Lansing, 1967-69; prin. Lincoln County Sch. Dist., Newport, Oreg., 1969-70; instructional cons. U. Wis., Madison, 1970-72; prof. info. tech. Western Oreg. U., Monmouth, 1972-97, asst. dean Sch. Edn.; computer tech. cons. numerous cos., schs. and chs. Co-author: Computer: Tool for the Teacher, 1985; author: The Computer as a Productivity Tool in Education, 1996, The Computer as an Educational Tool: Productivity and Problem Solving, 1999; producer film Systems Analysis, 1971; contbr. numerous articles to profl. jours. Mem. Assn. Ednl. Comms. and Tech., Oreg. Ednl. Media Assn. Avocations: fishing, bowhunting. Home: 25335 SW Neill Rd Sherwood OR 97140-7301 Office: Western Oreg U Sch Edn 345 Monmouth St Monmouth OR 97361

FORCIER, TERESA ELAINE, state legislator; b. Oct. 6, 1953; d. Waid Stanley and Elaine Agusta (Swift) Fosburg; children: Christopher, Delaine. Student, Alliance Coll., Edinboro U. Legis. aide 6th Legis. Dist., Meadville, Pa., 1979-86, 5th Legis. Dist., Meadville, 1987; per diem employee Crawford County, Meadville, 1988-89, asst. dir. tax claim bur., 1989-90; mem. Pa. Ho. of Reps., Titusville, 1991—; mem. appropriations com., transp. com.; sec. Legis. Office for Rsch. Liaison; co-chmn. Emergency Svcs. Outreach Group; active Fire Fighters Caucus, Task Force on Jobs and Bus. Expansion, Task Force on Environ., Task Force on Welfare Reform, Antigambling Caucus. Former editor Crawford County GOP Newsletter. Former asst. coord. Cambridge Springs (Pa.) Little League and Little Griddlers; former mem. Miss Crawford County Pageant Scholarship Exec. Bd., Cambridge Springs Presbyn. Food Pantry; mem. adv. bd. U. Pitts., Titusville; past dist. leader GOP Cambridge Dist.; active Cambridge Springs Presbyn. Ch., also former mem. bd. deacons; active Meadville Med. Ctr. Aux., Pa. Ag Reps., Craford County GOP Exec. Bd., Northwest Coun. Rep. Women, Capitol Area Coun. Rep. Women in Govt. Mem. NRA, Bus. and Profl. Women, Meadville Sportsmen Club, Pa Ruffled Grouse Soc., Kiwanis Club of Cambridge Springs. Home: 629 State St Meadville PA 16335-2262 Office: 401 S OFC PO Box 202020 Harrisburg PA 17120-2020*

FORCINIO, HALLIE EUNICE, editor; b. Cleve., Aug. 25, 1952; d. Quentin L. and Bertha W. (Bolman) Schirch; m. Robert K. Forcinio, Jan. 24, 1981. BA cum laude, Baldwin-Wallace Coll., Berea, Ohio, 1974. Traffic mgr. Jaeger Advt., Berea, 1975; editorial asst. Arthur G. McKee & Co., Cleve., 1975-78; comm. asst. Work Wear Corp., Cleve., 1978-82; assoc. editor HBJ Publs. (name now Advanstar Comm.), Cleve., 1982-84, mng. editor, 1984-91, editor in chief, 1991-93; freelance writer, editor Cleve., 1993—. Mem. Friends Cleve. Pub. Libr. Mem. Internat. Assn. Bus. Communicators (sec., facilitator, membership chair, dir. Cleve. chpt.), Am. Soc. Bus. Press Editors, Inst. Packaging Profls. (sec., v.p., pres. Cleve. chpt.), Internat. Packaging Press Orgn., Cleve. Zool. Soc., Kappa Phi (editor 1976-83, pres. 1983-87, 89-91). Republican. Lutheran. Avocations: stamps, reading, Chinese cooking.

FORD, ANDREW THOMAS, academic administrator; b. Cambridge, Mass., May 22, 1944; s. Francis Lawler and Eleanor (Vahey) F.; m. Anne M. Monahan, July 2, 1966; 1 dau., Lauren Elizabeth. B.A., Seton Hall U., 1966; M.A., U. WIs., 1968; Ph.D., U. Wis., 1971. Asst. prof. history Stockton State Coll., Pomona, N.J., 1971-72, asst. to v.p. for acad. affairs, 1972-74; acting dir. Nat. Materials Devel. Ctr. for French and Portuquese, Bedford, N.H., 1976-77; acad. programs coordinator N.H. Coll. and Univ. Council, Manchester, 1975-78; v.p. acad. affairs R.I. Sch. Design, Providence, 1978-81; dean Allegheny Coll., Meadville, Pa., 1981-93; provost Allegheny Coll., Meadville, 1983-93; pres. Wabash Coll., Crawfordsville, Ind., 1993—; mem. adv. bd. Marine Bank, 1987-93; founding mem. Commonwealth Partnership. Author: (with R. Chait) Beyond Traditional Tenure, 1982. Bd. dirs. Vis. Nurse Assn., Providence, 1979-81, Allegheny Summer Music Festival, Meadville, 1981-89, Meadville Med. Ctr., 1985-87; bd. incorporators Spencer Hosp., 1981-85; mem. Nat. Com. on U.S.-China Rels., 1986—. Democrat. Home: 400 E Pike St Crawfordsville IN 47933-2520 Office: Wabash Coll Office of Pres Crawfordsville IN 47933

FORD, ANNA MARIE, language professional; b. Starachowice, Poland, Aug. 17, 1940; came to U.S., 1954; d. Antoni Niedzwiedzki and Wanda Gluszkiewicz; married; 1 child, Alexandra Joanna Paszkowski. BA, Wayne State U., 1963, MA, 1972. Cert. secondary edn. tchr., Mich., S.C. Tchr. French and Spanish Ford Mid. Sch., Highland Park, Mich., 1965-66; tchr. fgn. lang. dept. Highland Park Cmty. H.S., 1966-97, head fgn. lang. dept., 1968-70, 73-78, lang. arts facilitator, 1991-94; owner, founder Horizons-Internat., Grosse Pointe Park, Mich., 1993-97; dist.-wide lang. cons./coord. Highland Park Pub. Schs., 1994-97; Spanish, French and English lang. tchr. Georgetown (S.C.) County Sch. Dist., 1997—; ind. contractor, cons. Langs. and Svcs. Agy., 1993—; assessor, field study, tchr. performance lang. arts Nat. Bd. Profl. Tchg. Stds., Mich., 1994; scorer writing proficiency assessments Mich. Dept. Edn., 1994-97, trainer of tchrs., 1995, trainer of trainers, 1995-97; mem. Elem. and Secondary Content Literacy Com. of Mich. Dept. of Edn., 1995—, instrnl./profl. devel. task force Mid. Cities Assn., Lansing, Mich., 1995-97; mem. North Ctrl Accreditation Evaluations Teams, 1970-97; cons. Coastal Area Writing Project, S.C., 1998—. Advisor: (h.s. yearbook) Polar Bear, 1985-86 (Big E award Josten's Printing Divsn. 1986); editor: (newsletter) Happenings, 1977-79, Mich. Writing Assessment News, 1994-97. Bd. dirs. French Inst. Mich., Southfield, 1985-97, Friends of Polish Art, Mich., 1995-97. Recipient cert. appreciation for participation in Classrooms of Tomorrow program, Mich. Gov., 1990. Mem. AAUW, Alliance Française: Detroit/Grosse Pointe/Charleston. Roman Catholic. Avocations: travel, sailing, skiing, literature, music. Home: 38 Wexford Ln River Club Pawleys Island SC 29585-7614 Office: Horizons Internat 38 Wexford Ln Pawleys Island SC 29585-7614

FORD, ASHLEY LLOYD, lawyer, retired consumer products company executive; b. Cin., Mar. 10, 1939; s. Starr MacLeod and Mary Lloyd (Mills) F.; m. Barbara Hill, Apr. 23, 1965; children: Christopher Ashley, Elizabeth Hill. AB, Princeton U., 1960; JD, Yale U., 1963. Bar: Ohio 1963. Assoc. Dinsmore & Shohl, Cin., 1965-69; counsel Procter & Gamble Co., Cin., 1969-71, divsn. counsel, 1971-89, sec., 1979-94; ret., 1994. Shareholder Cin. Mus. Assn.; dir. Hist. S.W. Ohio; mem. Cin. History Mus. Adv. Bd. Lt. USNR, 1966-72. Mem. Cin. Country Club, Queen City Club, Univ. Club, Sailfish Pt. Country Club, Order of Coif, Phi Beta Kappa. Episcopalian.

FORD, BETTY BLOOMER (ELIZABETH FORD), health facility executive, wife of former President of United States; b. Chgo., Apr. 8, 1918; d. William Stephenson and Hortence (Neahr) Bloomer; m. Gerald R. Ford (38th Pres. U.S.), Oct. 15, 1948; children: Michael Gerald, John Gardner, Steven Meigs, Susan Elizabeth. Student, Sch. Dance Bennington Coll., 1936, 37; LL.D. (hon.), U. Mich., 1976. Dancer Martha Graham Concert Group, N.Y.C., 1939-41; fashion dir. Herpolscheimer's Dept. Store, Grand Rapids, Mich., 1943-48; dance instr. Grand Rapids, 1932-48; chmn. bd. dirs. The Betty Ford Ctr., Rancho Mirage, Calif. Author: autobiography The Times of My Life, 1979, Betty: A Glad Awakening, 1987. Bd. dirs. Nat. Arthritis Found. (hon.); trustee Martha Graham Dance Ctr., Eisenhower Med. Ctr., Rancho Mirage; hon. chmn. Palm Springs Desert Mus.; nat. trustee Nat. Symphony Orch.; bd. dirs. The Lambs, Libertyville, Ill. Episcopalian. Home: PO Box 927 Rancho Mirage CA 92270-0927

FORD, BYRON MILTON, computer consultant; b. Hayden, Colo., Feb. 24, 1939; s. William Howard and Myrtle Oretta (Chistian) F.; BS, U. Colo., 1964; MS in Mgmt. Sci., Johns Hopkins U., 1971; m. Shirley Ann Edwards, Sept. 4, 1958; children: Gregory Scott, Barry Matthew. Sr. mathematician Applied Physics Lab., Johns Hopkins U., Laurel, Md., 1964-79; computer cons., Laurel, 1979-95, Longmont, 1996—. Mem. Ops. Rsch. Soc. Am., Nat. Assn. Self-Employed. Address: 13545 Weld County Road 13 Longmont CO 80504-9660

FORD, CHARLES NATHANIEL, otolaryngologist, educator; b. N.Y.C., June 25, 1940; s. Charles Nathaniel and Marie (Casa) F.; children: C. David, Brian C.; m. Sharon L. James, Feb. 3, 1990; stepchildren: Scott James, Julie James. BA, SUNY, Binghamton, 1961; MD, U. Louisville, 1965. Intern and resident Henry Ford Hosp., Detroit, 1965-70, staff, 1970-71; with Gundersen Clinic, LaCrosse, Wis., 1973-81; chief otolaryngology Middleton VA Hosp., Madison, Wis., 1982-94; prof. otolaryngol. div. dept. surgery U. Wis., Madison, 1981-93, chmn. otolaryngol. div. dept. surgery, 1993—; mem.-at-large med. bd. U. Wis. Ctr. for Health Scis., 1989-91, sec., 1992-93, v.p., 1994-95, pres. med. staff, chair med. bd. 1996-98; DeWeese lectr. U. Oreg., 1994; Manion Meml. lectr. Ind. U., 1995; Hough lectr. U. Okla., 1996; Sartian lectr. U. Tex., 1998. Author, editor: Phonosurgery: Assessment and Surgical Management of Voice Disorders, 1991; mem. editl. bd.: Jour. Voice, Laryngoscope, Microsurgery; author editor numerous sci. papers, chpts. and abstracts. Maj. USAF, 1971-73. Avalon Found. scholar, 1962-63; named to Best Drs. in Am., Woodward/White, Inc., 1991—. Fellow ACS, Am. Laryngol. Rhinol. and Otolog. Soc., Am. Bronchoesophical Assn., Am. Laryngol. Assn. (sec.), Am. Soc. for Head and Neck Surgery, Am. Acad. Otolaryngology, Head and Neck Surgery (honor award 1992), Am. Acad. Facial Plastic and Reconstructive Surgery; mem. AMA, Soc. Univ. Otolaryngologists-Head and Neck Surgeons (coun. mem.), Internat. Assn. Phonosurgeons, Am. Speech-Lang.-Hearing Assn., Collegium Theatrical and Internat. Arts, Medicine Assn. Democrat. Unitarian Universalist. Avocations: tennis, golf, theater, art, music. Office: U Wis Ctr Health Sci 600 Highland Ave Madison WI 53792-0001

FORD, CHARLES REED, state senator; b. Tulsa, Aug. 2, 1931; s. Juell Reed and Marzee (Lane) F.; m. Patricia Ann Ojers, 1951; children: Christopher Reed, Roger Howard, Karin Rebecca, Robyn Ann. Attended Okla. State U., 1949-51. Engr., aide, U.S. Corps. Engrs., 1951-53; designer SunrayDX, 1953-55, asst. mktg. engr. Tidewater Oil Co., 1955-58, real estate investor Charles Ford Co., 1958—; pres. Gothic Investments, Inc., 1963; mem. Okla. Ho. of Reps., 1967-81, minority floor leader, 1970-76, asst. minority leader, 1981; mem. Okla. Senate, 1981—, caucus chmn., 1982-83, caucus whip, 1984-86, asst. minority leader, 1987-88, minority leader, 1991-92; mem. Southwest region adv. com. Nat. Park Service, 1982-88. Trustee Tulsa Expn. and Fair Corp., 1955-67; vice chmn. Tulsa Met. Area Planning Commn., 1960-65; former officer Tulsa County Young Republicans; del. Rep. Nat. Conv., 1972, 84, 88; bd. govs. Spartan Sch. Aeronautics, 1993—. Served with USNR, 1948-53. Named Legislator of Yr. Rep. Legis. Assoc., 1988, Outstanding Legis. Leader Nat. Conf. State Legislators, 1992. Mem. Jaycees (Okla. pres. 1959-60, U.S. v.p. 1960-61, internat. v.p. 1963, chmn. trustees War Meml. Fund 1963—), Nat. Petroleum Coun., Alpha Sigma Eta. Republican. Office: Okla Senate Rm 527A Oklahoma City OK 73105

FORD, CHARLES WILLARD, university administrator, educator; b. Bloomsburg, Pa., Oct. 28, 1938; s. John Willard and Pauline Teresa (Rakocy) F.; m. Barbara Marie Hanawalt, June 6, 1959; children: Lane, Lori, Lanae, Lanette. BA, Taylor U., 1960; BS, Pa. State U., 1961, MEd, 1962; PhD, SUNY, Buffalo, 1970; postgrad., U. Mich., 1976-77. High sch. instr., 1961-64; faculty Erie Community Coll., 1965-70; fgn. svc. officer Peace Corps, Ghana, 1970-72; various positions Sch. Health Related Professions SUNY, Buffalo, 1972-75, 77-79; assoc. dean Sch. Health Related Professions SUNY, 1978-79; with Grand Rapids (Mich.) Med. Edn. Ctr., 1975-77; dean U. Health Scis./Chgo. Med. Sch., 1979-81; dean undergrad. colls. U. New Eng., Biddeford, Maine, 1982-84; pres. U. New Eng., Biddeford, 1984-91, prof. health sci., 1983—; cons. in accreditation and curriculum program in 35 states; vis. prof. Israel Coll., 1999. Author: (with M.K. Morgan) Teaching in the Health Professions, Clinical Education for the Allied Health Professions; contbr. articles to profl. jours. Pres. Maine Higher Edn. Coun., 1987-88, Maine Ind. Coll. Assn., 1988-89; bd. govs. Am. Assn. Coll. Osteo. Medicine, 1984-91. Rotary Internat. Study Exch., Germany and Turkey, 1995. Mem. NEA (life), Am. Assn. Higher Edn. (charter life), Assn. of Schs. of Allied Health Profls. (life). Home: 21 Magnolia Dr Kennebunkport ME 04046-6102 Office: U New Eng Hills Beach Rd Biddeford ME 04005

FORD, CHRIS, professional basketball coach; b. Atlantic City, NJ, Jan. 11, 1949; m. Kathy Ford; children: Chris, Katie, Anthony, Michael. Ed., Villanova Univ. Player Detroit Pistons, NBA, 1973-78; player Boston Celtics, NBA, 1978-82, broadcaster, 1982-83, asst. coach, 1983-90, head coach, 1990-95; head coach Milw. Bucks, NBA, 1996-98, L.A. Clippers, NBA, 99-. Mem. NBA Championship teams, as player, 1981, as coach, 1984, 86. Office: Los Angeles Clippers 3939 S Figueroa St Los Angeles CA 90037-1200*

FORD, CLARENCE QUENTIN, mechanical engineer, educator; b. Glenwood, N.Mex., Aug. 6, 1923; s. Clarence Noel and Elsie May (Jones) F.; m. Ruth Madge McKinney, June 11, 1950; children—Glenn Mac, Dabney Ann. B.S., U.S. Mcht. Marine Acad., 1944; B.S. in Mech. Engring., N.Mex. State U., 1949; M.S. in Mech. Engring., U. Mo., 1950; Ph.D., Mich. State U., 1959. Registered profl. engr. Inst. U. Mo., 1949-50; instr. Wash. State U., 1950-53, asst. prof., 1953-56; instr. Mich. State U., 1956-59; prof. N.Mex. State U., Las Cruces, 1959-88, head dept. mech. engring., 1960-70, assoc. dean engring., 1974-80, 81-88, dean engring., 1980-81, prof. and assoc. dean emeritus, 1988—; prin. Ford & Assocs., 1964—; mem. N.Mex. Bd. Registration Profl. Engrs. and Land Surveyors, 1978-88, chmn., 1980-81, 86-87, mem. emeritus, 1989—; mem. N.Mex. State Hwy. Commn., 1989-95, sec., 1991-95. Editor: Space Technology and Earth Problems, Vol. 23 Sci. and Tech. Series, 1969. Served to lt. USNR, 1942-46. Fellow AAAS; mem. ASME, Am. Soc. Engring. Edn., Nat. Coun. Examiners for Engring. and Surveying (v.p. 1986-88, Disting. Svc. award 1989, Disting. Svc. award with spl. commendation 1990), N.Mex. Soc. Profl. Engrs. (Outstanding Engr. 1964), Masons, York Rite, Kiwanis, Sigma Xi, Phi Kappa Phi, Pi Tau Sigma, Tau Beta Pi, Pi Mu Epsilon. Presbyterian. Home: 1985 Crescent Dr Las Cruces NM 88005-3300

FORD, DANIEL (FRANCIS), writer; b. Nov. 2, 1931; s. Patrick Joseph and Anne Theresa Ford; m. Sarah Lansing Paine; 1 child, Katharine Serena. BA, U. N.H., 1954; postgrad., U. Manchester, Eng., 1954-55. Reporter Overseas Weekly, Frankfurt, Germany, 1958; asst. editor N.H. Profiles mag., Portsmouth, 1959-60; publs. editor U. N.H., 1961-68; freelance writer Durham, N.H., 1969—; corr. The Nation, South Vietnam, 1964; contbg. editor Air & Space/Smithsonian Mag., 1994—. Author: Now Comes Theodora, 1965, Incident at Muc Wa (transl. in Dutch, filmed as Go Tell the Spartans), 1967, The High Country Illuminator, 1971, The Country Northward, 1976, Flying Tigers: Claire Chennault and the American Volunteer Group, 1991, Glen Edwards: The Diary of a Bomber Pilot, 1998. With U.S. Army, 1956-57. Recipient award of excellence Aviation-Space Writers, 1992; Fulbright fellow U. Manchester, 1954-55, Verville fellow Nat.

Air & Space Mus., 1989-90; Stern Found. Mag. Writers grantee, 1964; resident scholar U. N.H., 1996—. Mem. Met. Opera Guild, Phi Beta Kappa, Phi Kappa Phi. Office: 433 Bay Rd Durham NH 03824-3439

FORD, DAVID CLAYTON, lawyer, senator; b. Hartford City, Ind., Mar. 3, 1949; s. Clayton I. and Barbara J. (McVicker) F.; m. Joyce Ann Bonjour, Aug. 22, 1970; children: Jeff, Matthew, Kelly, Andrew. BA in Polit. Sci., Ind. U., 1973; JD, Ind. U., 1976, MBA Internat. Trade, Ball State U., 1988. Bar: Ind. 1975, U.S. Dist. Ct. (so. dist.) Ind. 1976, U.S. Dist. Ct. (no. dist.) Ind. 1977, U.S. Tax Ct. 1988, U.S. Supreme Ct. 1983. City atty. City of Montpelier, Ind., 1977-79; town atty. Town of Shamrock Lakes, Ind., 1977—; gen. counsel, internat. trade dir. Ind. Farm Bur. Inc., 1988—; chief dep. prosecutor, Blackford County, 1979; pros. atty. 71st Jud. Cir., Blackford County, Hartford City, Ind., 1983-86; mem. com. on character and fitness State Bd. of Law Examiners. Rep. nominee for 19th Dist. Ind. State Sen., 1986, elected 1994, Ind. Agrl. Leadership Program, 1990-91; bd. dir. Blackford County Young Reps., 1977-82, pres., 1977-78; chmn. Town of Shamrock Lakes Rep. Com., 1983, Ind. Lawyers for Bush and Quayle, 1988; vice chmn. Blackford County Rep. Cen. Com., 1978-82, chmn. 1993—; precinct committeeman Blackford County, Licking 7, 1980-93; mem. Ind. 10th Congl. Dist. Rep. Caucus, 1978-82, U.S. Edn. Appeals Bd., U.S. Dept. Edn., 1982-90, Nat. Def. Execs. Res. 1983—; former mem. bus. adv. com. to Congressman Dan Burton; chmn. bus., industries and devel. com. Ptnrs. of Ams., Ind. chpt., 1983-84; mem. Blackford County Bd. Aviation Commrs., 1977-83, pres., 1979-83; bd. dirs. Dollars for Scholars, Blackford County, 1977-95, v.p., 1977-95; mem. St. John's-Riedman Meml. Sch. Bd., 1978-82, pres., 1978-82; mem. Blackford County Sheriff's Merit Bd., 1981-82. Named Man of Yr. Hartford City C. of C., 1978, Sagamore of the Wabash, Gov. Otis Bowen, 1978; Hon. Sec. of State Edwin J. Simcox, 1981; participant Rotary group study exch. to São Paulo, Brazil, 1981; named Outstanding Young Man of Am. U.S. Jaycees, 1982. Mem. ABA, Assn. Trial Lawyers' Am., Ind. State Bar Assn., Blackford County Bar Assn., World Trade Club Ind., Mensa, Sigma Iota Epsilon. Home: 1023 N Walnut St Hartford City IN 47348-1553 Office: 210 W Main St Hartford City IN 47348-2209

FORD, DAVIS L., sanitary & environmental engineer; b. May 18, 1937. BCE, Tex. A&M U.; M in Engring., U. Tex., Austin; PhD in Environ. Engring., U. Tex. Cons. environ. engring. Davis L. Ford & Assocs., 1985—; adj. prof. U. Tex., Austin, 1968—; bd. mem. Sci. Adv. Bd. Nat. Rsch. Coun.; chair Program Com., Water Pollution Control Fedn. Contbr. over 100 tech. papers to profl. publs. Mem. Nat. Acad. Engring. Office: Davis L Ford & Assocs 701 Brazos St Ste 550 Austin TX 78701-3232*

FORD, DEXTER, retired insurance company executive; b. Utica, N.Y., Nov. 18, 1917; s. David E. and Anna Mae (Dexter) F.; m. Jean Brand McGowan, Nov. 1, 1944; children: David K., Dexter T., Nancy E. B.S., St. Lawrence U., 1939. With Aetna Life & Casualty Co., Hartford, Conn., 1946—; v.p. mktg. Aetna Life & Casualty Co., 1968-76, v.p. personal ins. dept., 1976-80. Chmn. bd. mgmt. YMCA, 1978-80. Served to lt. (s.g.) USNR, 1941-45. Recipient St. Lawrence U. Alumni citation, 1978. Mem. St. Lawrence U. Alumni Assn. (pres. 1974-75). Republican. Congregationalist (chmn. bd. trustees 1970). Clubs: Lake Pleasant Golf (N.Y.); Codgers (Simsbury, Conn.). Home: 39 Wickham's Fancy Collinsville CT 06022

FORD, DONALD HAINLINE, lawyer; b. Chgo., Dec. 5, 1906; s. Matthew Henry and Ethel (Griffith) F.; m. Siri Ann Enegren, Aug. 22, 1934; children—Carol Ann (Mrs. Raymond D. McMullin), Barbara Jean (Mrs. Robert A. Harrington), Richard Donald. B.S., Oreg. State U., 1929; J.D., U. Mich., 1932. Bar: Calif. bar 1933. Park ranger Lassen Volcanic Nat. Park, 1931-32; assoc. firm Overton, Lyman & Prince, Los Angeles, 1933-41; partner Overton, Lyman & Prince, 1941—; chmn. bd. Stocks Mill & Supply Co.; dir. W.W. Henry Co., Macpherson Oil Co. Served with USAAF, 1941-46; col. USAF; Ret. Decorated Bronze Star; Cloud and Banner spl. class (China). Mem. ABA, Calif. Bar, Los Angeles County Bar Assn. Presbyterian. Lodge: Rotary. Office: 520 S Grand Ave Fl 7 Los Angeles CA 90071-2600

FORD, DONALD HERBERT, psychologist, educator; b. Sioux City, Iowa, Aug. 15, 1926; s. Herbert Owen and Esther (Sanow) F.; m. Carol Clark, May 30, 1948; children—Russell, Martin, Douglas, Cameron. B.S., Kans. State U., 1948; M.S., 1951; Ph.D., Pa. State U., 1955. Counselor Kans. State U., 1948-52; asst. prof. psychology Pa. State U., University Park, 1955-64, assoc. prof., 1964-67, assoc. prof. human devel., 1967-72, prof. human. devel., 1972—, prof. biobehavioral health, 1992—; asst. dir. div. counseling, 1956-59, dir., 1959-67; dean Coll. Human Devel., 1967-77, head dept. Communications Disorders, 1988-89, head biobehavioral health, 1992. Author: Systems of Psychotherapy; A Comparative Study, 1963, Humans as Self-Constructing Living Systems, 1987, 2d edit., 1992, Developmental Systems Theory, 1992, Contemporary Models of Psychotherapy, 1998. Served with USAAF, 1944-45. Mem. AAAS, Am. Psychol. Assn., Am. Psychol. Soc., Ea. Psychol. Assn. Home: 130 Slab Cabin Rd State College PA 16801-6971 Office: Penn State U Coll Health & Human Devel University Park PA 16802 *My basic values are rooted in the "teaching by example" of my parents, serving the objectives of being of service to others as well as to self, utilizing a strong, caring family unit as the best cornerstone of psychological, social, and economic health. My basic professional goal is to help harness the fruits of technological advances, resulting from the intensive application of the principle of specialization, to the evolution of humanistic societies designed to serve people as open, living systems. This requires a new scientific model of Man as a coherent unit, enabling us to synthesize the fruits of analytical science and to put "Humpty Dumpty" back together again as a person with purposes and values as well as productive potential.*

FORD, DOROTHY MARY, principal; b. June 29, 1948. BS, Marian Coll., 1971; MS, U. Wis., 1991. Tchr. Sch. Dist. Waupaca (Wis.), 1971-78; tchr., prin. St. Patrick Sch., Ripon, Wis., 1978-88; prin. Sacred Hearts Sch., Sun Prairie, Wis., 1988—. Office: 221 Columbus St Sun Prairie WI 53590-2202

FORD, EDWARD CHARLES (WHITEY FORD), retired baseball player; b. N.Y.C., Oct. 21, 1928. Baseball player N.Y. Yankees, 1950-67. Named to Baseball Hall of Fame, 1974; mem. World Series Champions, 1950-54, 56, 58, 61-62. Home and Office: 3750 Galt Ocean Dr Fort Lauderdale FL 33308*

FORD, EILEEN OTTE (MRS. GERARD W. FORD), modeling agency executive; b. N.Y.C., Mar. 25, 1922; d. Nathaniel and Loretta Marie (Laine) Otte; m. Gerard William Ford, Nov. 20, 1944; children: Margaret (Mrs. Robert Craft), Gerard William, M. Katie (Mrs. Andre Balazs), A. Lacey (Mrs. John Williams). B.S., Barnard Coll., 1943. Stylist Elliot Clarke Studio, N.Y.C., 1943-44, William Becker Studio, 1945; copywriter Arnold Constable, N.Y.C., 1945-46; reporter Tobe Coburn, 1946; co-founder Ford Model Agy., N.Y.C., 1946—, now chmn. bd. Author: Eileen Ford's Model Beauty, Secrets of the Model's World, A More Beautiful You in 21 Days, Beauty Now and Forever, 1977. Bd. dirs. London Philharmonic, 1948—. Recipient Harpers Bazaar award for promotion internat. understanding., Woman of Yr. in Advt. award, 1983. Office: Ford Modeling Agy 142 Greene St New York NY 10012-3236

FORD, EMORY A., chemist, researcher; b. South New Berlin, N.Y., Oct. 17, 1940; s. Merritt L. and Verda M. (Manwaring) F.; m. Susan Dorothy Rogers, Sept. 14, 1963; children: Kelly Diane, Kendra Lee. BA, Hartwick Coll., 1962; PhD, Syracuse U., 1966. Sr. rsch. chemist Monsanto Co., Springfield, Mass., 1966-72, rsch. group leader, 1972-76, sr. rsch. group leader, 1976-78; tech. mgr. Monsanto Co., Pensacola, Fla., 1978-81; rsch. mgr. No. Petrochem. Co., Morris, Ill., 1981-84; dir. basic rsch. Enron Chem. Co., Rolling Meadows, Ill., 1984-86, Quantum Chem. Co., Cin., 1987-97; chief scientist Equistar, Cin., 1997—. Mem. AAAS, Am. Chem. Soc., N.Y. Acad. Sci., Chemists Club of Chgo., Internat. Union Pure and Applied Chemistry, Sigma Xi. Unitarian. Avocations: reading, running, traveling. Office: Equistar 11530 Northlake Dr Cincinnati OH 45249-1642

FORD, FAITH, actress; b. Alexandria, La., Sept. 14, 1964; d. Charles and Pat F., m. Robert Nottingham, 1989. Actress: (TV) One Life to Live, thirtysomething, Hardcastle & McCormick, Popcorn Kid, Almost Home; regular on TV series Murphy Brown, CBS, 88-97, Emmy nominations, Supporting Actress - Comedy Series, 1989, 90, 91, 94); (TV film) Poisoned by Love: The Kern County Murders, 1993, A Weekend in the Country, 1996, Night Visitors, 1996, Her Desperate Choice, 1996, (film) You Talkin' to Me, North, 1994; Sometimes They Come Back...For More, 1998,(TV Series) Maggie Winters, 1998. *

FORD, FORD BARNEY, retired government official; b. Norton, Va., Nov. 19, 1922; s. William Zachary and Annis Louvinia (Ford) Godbey; m. Norma Isabel Lentz, Jan. 16, 1945; children: Robert Barney, Jack T. (dec.). Student, Va. Mil. Inst., Lexington, 1942-43; BS, U. Calif., Berkeley, 1948, LLD (hon.) Huston Tillotson Coll., 1985. Registered indsl. and safety engr. Acting postmaster, Bishop, Calif., 1951-54; adminstrv. analyst Calif. Joint Legis. Budget Com., Sacramento, 1955-59; exec. dir. Calif. Senate Fact-Finding Com. on Natural Resources, Sacramento, 1959-67; dep. sec. Calif. Resources Agy., Sacramento, 1967-73; chmn. and mem. Calif. Occupational Safety and Health Appeals Bd., Sacramento, 1973-78; v.p. Calif. Inst. Indsl. and Govtl. Relations, Sacramento, 1978-81; asst. sec. labor for mine safety and health Dept. Labor, Arlington, Va., 1981-83, undersec. Dept. Labor, Washington, 1983-85, acting sec. 1984-85; chmn. Mine Safety and Health Rev. Commn., 1985-92; retired, 1992. Served with U.S. Army, 1943-46, ETO. Decorated Combat Infantryman badge. Mem. DAV., SAR, VFW (comdr. Bishop, Calif. 1948-50). Methodist. Lodges: Elks, Masons, Shriners. Research publs. on fire prevention, geothermal devel. East Wilmington oil field.

FORD, FRANKLIN LEWIS, history educator, historian; b. Waukegan, Ill., Dec. 26, 1920; s. Frank Leland and Dorothy Elsey (Lewis) F.; m. Eleanor Rose Hamm, Jan. 8, 1944; children: Stephen Joseph, John Franklin. A.B., U. Minn., 1942; M.A., Harvard U., Ph.D., 1950. Mem. faculty Bennington Coll., 1949-52; mem. faculty Harvard U., 1953-91, prof. history, 1959-91, McLean prof. ancient and modern history, 1968-91; emeritus, 1991—; dean faculty arts and scis. Harvard U., 1962-70, acting dean, 1973; chmn. bd. dirs. Harvard Univ. Press, 1986-91; mem. Inst. for Advanced Study (Princeton), 1974. Author: Robe and Sword, 1953, Strasbourg in Transition, 1958, Europe, 1780-1830, 1970, rev. edit., 1989, Political Murder, 1985, French and German transl., 1990; co-editor: Traditions of Western Civilization, 1966. Served with U.S. Army and O.S.S., 1943-46. Fulbright research fellow France, 1952-53; Guggenheim fellow Germany, 1955-56; fellow Ctr. Advanced Study Behavioral Scis., 1961-62; fellow Nat. Humanities Ctr., 1983-84, 88, 89. Mem. Am. Philos. Soc., Phi Beta Kappa. Home: 1010 Waltham St # C-557 Lexington MA 02421-8044 Office: Harvard Univ Widener Libr P Cambridge MA 02138

FORD, FREDERICK JAY, clergyman; b. Franklin, Ind., Aug. 11, 1960; s. William Frederick and Janice Marie (Houston) F.; m. Wendi Carol Platt, Feb. 19, 1983; children: Tonya Dawn, Clint Boone. BS in Ministry and Bible Studies, Platte Valley Bible Coll., 1988; diploma in fin. counseling, Christian Fin. Concepts, 1989; diploma in behavior analysis, Inst. for Christian Living, 1989. Ordained to ministry Christian Ch., 1987. Automotive Svc. Excellence cert. mechanic. Min. Glenrock (Wyo.) Christian Ch., 1987-88; youth min. Cen. Christian Ch., Claremore, Okla., 1988-95; dir. Ctrl. Youth Mission Programs, 1990—; owner Ford Imaging - Slides for Praise and Worship; assoc., youth min. First Christian Ch., Sierra Vista, Ariz., 1996—; organizer T.L.C. Autocare Ministry, 1990; dean, asst. dean H.S. Wilderness Challenge, 1989-95; dean So. Ariz. H.S. Wilderness Challenge, 1997—; dean Camp Christian Echoes Christian Svc. Camp, 1997—, bd. sec., 1996—; trustee and mem. exec. bd. Agape Christian Youth Ctr., Sierra Vista, Ariz., 1998—. Town councilman City Coun., Hartman, Colo., 1987. With U.S. Army, 1979-83. Republican. Office: First Christian Ch 55 Kings Way Sierra Vista AZ 85635-3619

FORD, GEORGE BURT, lawyer; b. South Bend, Ind., Oct. 1, 1923; s. George W. and Florence (Burt) F.; m. Charlotte Ann Kupferer, June 12, 1948; children: John, Victoria, George, Charlotte. BS in Engring. Law, Purdue U., 1946; LLB, Ind. U., 1949. Bar: Ind. 1949, U.S. Dist. Ct. (no. dist.) Ind. 1949. Assoc. Jones, Obenchain & Butler, South Bend, Ind., 1949-52; ptnr. Jones, Obenchain, Ford, Pankow & Lewis, South Bend, 1953-93, of counsel, 1994—. Co-author: Forms for Indiana Corporations, 1967, 2nd edit. 1977. With U.S. Army, 1943-45, ETO. Fellow Am. Coll. of Trust and Estate Counsel; mem. ABA, Ind. Bar Assn., St. Joseph County Bar Assn. (pres. 1976-77), Phi Gamma Delta, Phi Delta Phi. Presbyterian (trustee 1966-68, elder 1967-70). Office: Jones Obenchain LLP 1800 City Center PO Box 4577 South Bend IN 46634-4577

FORD, GERALD RUDOLPH, JR., former President of United States; b. Omaha, July 14, 1913; s. Gerald R. and Dorothy (Gardner) F.; m. Elizabeth Bloomer, Oct. 15, 1948; children: Michael, John, Steven, Susan. A.B., U. Mich., 1935; LL.B., Yale U., 1941; LL.D., Mich. State U., Albion Coll., Aquinas Coll., Spring Arbor Coll. Bar: Mich. 1941. Practiced law at Grand Rapids, 1941-49; mem. law firm Buchen and Ford; mem. 81st-93d Congresses from 5th Mich. Dist., 1949-74, elected minority leader, 1965; v.p. U.S., 1973-74, pres., 1974-77; del. Interparliamentary Union, Warsaw, Poland, 1959, Belgium, 1961, Bilderberg Group Conf., 1962; dir. The Travelers, Inc.; adv. dir. Tex. Commerce Bancshares, Inc., Am. Express Co.; mem. internat. adv. coun. Inst. Internat. Studies. Served as lt. comdr. USNR, 1942-46. Recipient Grand Rapids Jr. C. of C. Distinguished Service award, 1948; Distinguished Service Award as one of ten outstanding young men in U.S. by U.S. Jr. C. of C., 1950; Silver Anniversary All-Am. Sports Illustrated, 1959; Distinguished Congressional Service award Am. Polit. Sci. Assn., 1961. Mem. Am., Mich. State, Grand Rapids bar assns., Delta Kappa Epsilon, Phi Delta Phi. Republican. Episcopalian. Clubs: University (Kent County), Peninsular (Kent County). Lodge: Masons. Home: PO Box 927 Rancho Mirage CA 92270-0927

FORD, GORDON BUELL, JR., English language, linguistics, and medieval studies educator, author, retired hospital industry accounting financial management executive; b. Louisville, Sept. 22, 1937; s. Gordon Buell Sr. and Rubye (Allen) F. AB summa cum laude in Classics, Medieval Latin, and Sanskrit, Princeton U., 1959; AM in Classical Philology and Linguistics, Harvard U., 1962, PhD in Linguistics, Slavic and Baltic Langs. and Lits., 1965; postgrad., U. Oslo, 1962-64, U. Sofia, Bulgaria, 1963, U. Uppsala, Sweden, 1963-64, U. Stockholm, 1963-64, U. Madrid, 1963. CPA. Yeager, Ford, and Warren Found. Disting. prof. Indo-European, Classical, Slavic, and Baltic linguistics, Sanskrit, and Medieval Latin Northwestern U., Evanston, Ill., 1965—; Lybrand, Ross Bros., and Montgomery Found. Disting. prof. English and linguistics U. No. Iowa, Cedar Falls, 1972—; sr. exec. v.p. for real estate accounting fin. mgmt. Gorgay, Inc., The Real Estate Co., Louisville, 1976-77, also bd. dirs.; sr. exec. v.p. for reimbursement and rates acctg. fin. mgmt. hosp. acctg. divsn. Humana, Inc., The Hosp. Co., Louisville, 1978-93; ret., 1993; dir. Southeastern Investment Trust, Inc., Louisville, 1976—, ret., 1993; rsch. prof. The Southeastern Investment Trust, Inc. Rsch. Found., Louisville, 1976—; vis. prof. Medieval Latin, U. Chgo., 1966—; vis. prof. linguistics U. Chgo., Downtown Ctr., 1966—; prof. English evening divs. Northwestern U., Chgo., 1968-69, prof. anthropology, 1971-72. Author: The Ruodlieb: The First Medieval Epic of Chivalry from Eleventh-Century Germany, 1965, The Ruodlieb: Linguistic Introduction, Latin Text with a Critical Apparatus, and Glossary, 1966, The Ruodlieb: Facsimile Edition, 1965, 3d edit. 1968, Old Lithuanian Texts of the Sixteenth and Seventeenth Centuries with a Glossary, 1969, The Old Lithuanian Catechism of Baltramiejus Vilentas (1579): A Phonological, Morphological, and Syntactical Investigation, 1969, Isidore of Seville's History of the Goths, Vandals, and Suevi, 1966, 2d edit. 1970, The Letters of Saint Isidore of Seville, 1966, 2d edit. 1970, The Old Lithuanian Catechism of Martynas Mazvydas (1547), 1971, others; translator: A Concise Elementary Grammar of the Sanskrit Language with Exercises, Reading Selections, and a Glossary (Jan Gonda), 1966, The Comparative Method in Historical Linguistics (Antoine Meillet), 1967, A Sanskrit Grammar (Manfred Mayrhofer), 1972; contbr. numerous articles to many scholarly jours. Appointed to Hon. Order Ky. Cols. (life). Mem. Linguistic Soc. Am. (life, Sapir life patron), Internat. Linguistic Assn. (life), Societas Linguistica Europaea (charter, life), Am. Philol. Assn. (life), Classical Assn. of the Atlantic States (life), Classical Assn. of the Middle West and South (life), Classical Assn. of N.Eng. (life), Medieval Acad. of Am. (life), Renaissance Soc. of Am. (life), MLA (life), Am. Assn. Tchrs. Slavic and East European Langs. (life), Am. Assn. Advancement Slavic Studies (life), Am. Coun. Tchrs. Russian (life), Assn. for Advancement Baltic Studies (life), Inst. Lithuanian Studies (life), Tchrs. of English to Speakers of Other Langs. (charter, life), SAR (life), Princeton Club (N.Y.C., Chgo.), Princeton Alumni Assn. (Louisville), Harvard Club (N.Y.C., Chgo., Louisville, Lexington, Ky.), Pres.'s Soc. Bellarmine Coll. (life), Louisville Country Club, KC (life), Phi Beta Kappa (life). Baptist. Home: 3619 Brownsboro Rd Louisville KY 40207-1863 also: PO Box 2693 Clarksville Br Jeffersonville IN 47131-2693

FORD, HAROLD EUGENE, congressman; b. Memphis, Tenn., May 20, 1945; s. Newton J. and Vera (Davis) F.; m. Dorothy Bowles, Feb. 10, 1969; children: Harold, Newton Jake, Sir Isaac. BS, Tenn. State U., 1967; AA, John Gupton Coll., 1969; MBA, Howard U. Mem. Tenn. Ho. of Reps., 1970-74; mem. 94th-106th Congresses from 9th Tenn. dist., 1975—, mem. edn. and workforce com., mem. govt. reform and oversight com.; mem. ways and means com., subcom. on oversight, mem. subcom. human resources, Dem. whip representing Tenn., La., Miss. during 99th Congress. Bd. dirs. Met. Memphis YMCA affiliated with Alpha Phi Alpha frat.; mem. nat. adv. bd. St. Jude Children's Research Hosp. Named Outstanding Young Man of Year Memphis Jaycees, 1976, Outstanding Young Man of Year Tenn. Jaycees, 1977, Child Advocate of Yr. Child Welfare League Am., 1987. Office: US House Reps 325 Cannon HOB Washington DC 20515-4209*

FORD, HARRIET-LYNN, English educator; b. Wichita Falls, Tex., May 27, 1952; d. Wesley Craig and Alice Ann Stallcup; 1 child, Michael Adam Brown; m. John Ceburn Ford Jr., Aug. 20, 1983. BA in English Edn., Okla. Ctrl. State U., 1977, MA in English, 1979. Adj. instr. Pellissippi State Tech. C.C., Knoxville, Tenn., 1989-90, instr. to assoc. prof. English, 1990-99, interim dept. head acad. devel. divsn., 1994-95; program coord. for remedial and devel. English Pallissippi State Tech. C.C., Knoxville, Tenn., 1995—. Co-editor, co-author: (textbook) Preparing for College Writing, 1996; editor, co-author: Preparing for College Writing, 1997, 2d edit., 1999. Docent Knoxville Zoo, 1990-97. Mem. AAUP (chpt. pres.), AAUW, Nat. Coun. Tchrs. English. Avocations: reading, Celtic music, golf. Office: Pellissippi State Tech CC Hardin Valley Rd Knoxville TN 37933

FORD, HARRISON, actor; b. Chicago, Ill., July 13, 1942; m. Mary Ford; children: Willard, Benjamin; m. Melissa Mathison; children: Malcolm, Georgia. Ed., Ripon Coll. Appeared in motion pictures including: Dead Heat on a Merry-Go-Round, 1966, Luv, 1967, The Long Ride Home, 1967, Getting Straight, 1970, Zabriskie Point, 1970, The Conversation, 1974, American Graffiti, 1974, Star Wars, 1977, Heroes, 1977, Force 10 From Navarone, 1978, Hanover Street, 1979, Frisco Kid, 1979, Apocalypse Now, 1979, The Empire Strikes Back, 1980, Raiders of the Lost Ark, 1981, Blade Runner, 1982, Return of the Jedi, 1983, Indiana Jones and the Temple of Doom, 1984, Witness, 1985, Mosquito Coast, 1986, Frantic, 1988, Working Girl, 1988, Indiana Jones and the Last Crusade, 1989, Presumed Innocent, 1990, Patriot Games, 1992, The Fugitive, 1993, Clear and Present Danger, 1994, Sabrina, 1995, A Hundred and One Nights, 1995, Devil's Own, 1996, Air Force One, 1997, Six Days Seven Nights, 1998, Random Hearts, 1999; appeared in TV movie James A. Michener's Dynasty, 1976; numerous TV appearances including Judgement: The Court-Martial of Lt. William Calley, 1975, The F.B.I., Gunsmoke, The Virginian, The Possessed, Young Indiana Jones Chronicles. *

FORD, JAMES CARLTON, human resources executive; b. Portland, Mar. 10, 1937; s. John Bernard and Margaret (Reynolds) F.; m. Carolyn Tadina, Aug. 22, 1959; children: Scott, Michele, Mark, Brigitte, Deidre, John. BA in History, U. Portland, 1960; MS in Edn., Troy State U., 1969; MPA, U. Puget Sound, 1976. Cert. sen. profl. in human resources. Commd. 2d lt. USAF, 1960, advanced through grades to lt. col., 1976, adminstr., tng. officer, 1960-70, personnel mgmt. officer, 1971-76; dep. inspector gen. U.S. Air Force Acad., Colorado Springs, Colo., 1977-80; ret. U.S. Air Force Acad., 1980; employment mgr. Western Fed. Savs. (name changed to Bank Western), Denver, 1980-82, v.p. human resources, 1982-88, sr. v.p. mgmt. svcs., 1988-92; dir. career mgmt. AIM Exec., Inc., Cons. Svcs., 1992-95; owner Orgn./Individual Strategies, Inc., Cons., 1995—; bd. dirs. Rocky Mountain chpt. Am. Inst. Banking, Denver, 1988-92; adj. prof. U. Colo., Colorado Springs, 1978-79, USAF Acad., Colorado Springs, 1978-80; adv. bd. U. Colo. Contemporary Mgmt. Program, Regis Coll. Career Svcs.; mem. faculty U. Phoenix, Colo., 1995—; mediator Pikes Peak Better Bus. Bur., 1995—. Mediator Neighborhood Justice Ctr., Colorado Springs, 1980; vol. allocations com. Pikes Peak United Way, Colorado Springs, 1978-79; vol. campaign exec. Mile Hi United Way, Denver, 1986-89; vol. mgmt. cons. Tech. Assistance Svc., Denver, 1991. Mem. Assn. for Mgmt. of Orgn. Design, Soc. for Human Resource Mgmt. (state dir. certification 1996-97). Republican. Roman Catholic. Office: Orgn/Individual Strategies, Inc 975 Tari Dr Colorado Springs CO 80921-2256

FORD, JEREMIAH, III, architect; b. Phila., Apr. 22, 1932; s. Jeremiah II and Mary Sterling (Hewitt) F.; m. Judith Oakes Seidler, June 17, 1954 (div. 1973); children: Amanda Hewitt, Katerine Brewster; m. Elizabeth Dana Stewardson, Mar. 1, 1975; children: Elizabeth Connolly, Caroline Thornewill, Dana H. Stewardson. AB, Princeton U., 1954, MFA, 1959. Registered architect, N.J., Mass., Pa., Fla., Del. Designer Harrison and Abramovitz Architects, N.Y.C., 1960-61, Port of N.Y. Authority World Trade Ctr., N.Y.C., 1961-62; archtl. apprentice Kenneth Kassler Architect, Princeton, 1962-64; ptnr. Walker Sander Ford and Kerr Architects, Princeton, 1965-74, Short and Ford Architects, Princeton, 1974-93, Ford Farewell Mills and Gatsch Architects, Princeton, 1993—. Prin. works include Marriott Hotel and Conf. Ctr., Trenton, N.J. State House, Trenton, Princeton (N.J) Coalition, Summit(N.J.) City Hall, Mary Jacob's Libr., Rocky Hill, N.J., 1973, Morristown (N.J.) Libr., 1985, Princeton Cmty. Housing, 1982, Cranbury (N.J.) Sr. Housing, 1990, pvt. residences. Capt. USMC, 1954-57, Korea, Japan. Episcopalian. Avocations: painting, gardening. Home: 820 Pretty Brook Rd Princeton NJ 08540-7532 Office: Ford Farewell Mills Gatsch 864 Mapleton Rd Princeton NJ 08540-9538

FORD, JERRY LEE, service company executive; b. Muncie, Ind., July 11, 1940; s. Robert Thomas and Thelma Adrien (Stricker) F.; m. Margaret Annette Bailey, Sept. 10, 1966; children: Duane A., Diana K., Brenda D. BS in Acctg., Ind. U., 1962. CPA, Ind. Sr. auditor KPMG Peat Marwick, Indpls., 1964-67; contr. Georgia Kraft Co., Rome, Ga., 1967-71; asst. dir. acctg. Gen. Mills, Inc., Mpls., 1971-75, sys. contr. foods group; v.p. fin., contr. Ship N Shore subs. Gen. Mills, Inc., Phila., 1979-80; v.p. fin., treas. Poppin Fresh Pies divsn. Pillsbury Co., Mpls., 1980-81; v.p. fin. foods group Pillsbury Co., Mpls., 1981-84, v.p. adminstrn. svcs., 1984-87; COO, exec. dir. Lindquist & Vennum, Mpls., 1988-93; chief operating officer Comdisco Network Svcs., Minnetonka, Minn., 1994-98; chief devel. officer and gen. mgr. western U.S. Jetways, Inc., 1998—; instr. Def. Contract Audit Agy. Exec. Program, Memphis 1987; dir. Nash Finch Co. Co-author: Controllers Handbook, 1984, 92. Bd. dirs. Min. Acctg. Aid Soc., 1986-88, 90-94, Mpls. YMCA, 1974-78. Mem. Fin. Execs. Inst. (chpt. pres., nat. bd. dirs.), Inst. Mgmt. Accts. (nat. v.p. 1984-85), Inst. Cert. Mgmt. Accts. (cert., chmn. bd. dirs. 1982-84), Ind. U. Alumni Assn. (bd. dirs. 1989-93). Republican. Methodist. Avocations: golf, racquetball.

FORD, JOE THOMAS, telephone company executive, former state senator; b. Conway, Ark., June 24, 1937; s. Arch W. and Ruby (Watson) F.; m. Jo Ellen Wilbourn, Aug. 9, 1959; children: Alison, Scott. BS, U. Ark., 1959. With Allied Telephone Co., Little Rock, 1959-83, v.p.-treas., 1963-77, pres., 1977-83; pres. ALLTEL Corp., 1983-87, pres., chief exec. officer, 1987-91, chmn., pres., chief exec. officer, 1991-93, chmn., CEO, 1993—; now chmn. Alltel Corp., Little Rock, A.R.; mem. Ark. Senate, 1967-82; dir. Comml. Nat. Bank, 1970-85, Little Rock, Security Bank, Conway. Recipient Disting. Alumni cert. U. Ark., 1987. Baptist. Home: 2100 Country Club Ln Little Rock AR 72207-2040 Office: Alltel Corp PO Box 2177 1 Allied Dr Little Rock AR 72202-2099*

FORD, JOHN GILMORE, interior designer; s. John Gilmore and Marian Brunner (Mainhart) F.; m. Berthe Diana Hanover, Aug. 19, 1972. B.F.A., Md. Inst. Coll. Art. Founder, 1962; since pres. John Ford Assocs., Inc., Balt.; tchr. seminars Md. Inst. Coll. Art; lectr. Indo-Asian art Johns Hopkins U., Towson State Coll. Served with USCGR. Recipient citation of merit Md. Inst. Coll. Art, 1960. Fellow Am. Soc. Interior Designers (past nat. v.p., pres. Md. chpt.; Presdl. citation); mem. Internat. Chinese Snuff Bottle Soc. (pres., co-editor jour.), Asia Soc., Am. Soc. Appraisers (sr.

mem.). Club: Masons (32 deg.). Office: 2601 N Charles St Baltimore MD 21218-4514

FORD, JOHN STEPHEN, treasurer; b. Clinton, Mass., Apr. 27, 1957; s. James Joseph and Rita (Hart) F.; m. Mary Andrejczyk, Apr. 15, 1978; children: Michelle, Amanda, William. BS, Lowell U., 1979. CPA, Mass.; notary pub., Mass. Staff acct. Main, Hurdman, Cranston, CPA's, Worcester, Mass., 1979; sr. acct. William S. Reagan & Co. CPA's, Fitchburg, Mass., 1979-82; treas. Peterborough Oil Co., Inc., Leominster, Mass., 1982—; cons. in field. Active Lancaster (Mass.) Dem. Town Com.; former treas. Lancaster Soccer; former mem. Lancaster Recreation Com.; coach Pop Warner football; treas. Lancaster Baseball Assn.; bd. dirs. Worker's Credit Union, Fitchburg, Mass. Fellow Mass. Soc. CPA; mem. AICPA (tax divsn.), Am. Turners, Lancaster Recreation Com., Elks. Roman Catholic. Avocations: sports, local politics, home improvements. Office: Peterborough Oil Co PO Box 787 665 N Main St Leominster MA 01453-1894

FORD, JOHN T., JR., art, film and video educator; b. Rotan, Tex., Feb. 17, 1953; s. John T. and Lala Fern (Shipley) F.; m. Betty Jean Crawford; children: Casey, Craig, Kirk. BA, U. Redlands, 1975. Cert. tchr., Calif. Tchr. art, film, video Yucaipa (Calif.) Joint Unified Sch. Dist., 1976-88; tchr. art and crafts Vacaville (Calif.) Unified Sch. Dist., 1990-92, tchr. video prodn., 1992—, sr. prodn. video, 1994—; cons. Dist. Fine Arts Insvc., Yucaipa, 1987; co-sponsor Art Club, Will C. Wood High Sch., Vacaville, sponsor Video Club. Creator, coord. (conceptual art) Whole School Environments, Caves, Tubes and Streamers, Forest Edge, 1980-84; creator (comml. art prints) Toy Horse Series, 1982-83; prodr. ann. sr. video, 1994—. Mem. Yeoman Svc. Orgn., U. Redlands, 1972, Vacaville Sch. Dist. Tech. Com., Dist. Fine Arts Task Force, Yucaipa, 1984-87, Dist. Task Force for Vocat. Edn., 1992; interim dir. Hosanna House, Redlands, Calif., 1975; liaison Sch. Cmty. Svc./San Bernardino County (Calif.) Fire Dept., 1980-81. Recipient Golden Bell award Calif. Sch. Bd. Rsch. Found., 1987, Ednl. Svc. award Mason's, 1987-88; named one of Outstanding Young Men of Am., 1987, Tchr. of Yr. Calif. Continuation Edn. Assn., 1987-88; grantee Calif. Tchrs. Instructional Improvement Program, 1985; scholar U. Redlands, 1975. Mem. Am. Film Inst. Avocations: art, media fabrication, writing, collecting books, backpacking. Office: Will C Wood High Sch 998 Marshall Rd Vacaville CA 95687-5735

FORD, JUDITH ANN TUDOR, retired natural gas distribution company executive; b. Martinsville, Ind., May 11, 1935; d. Glenn Leyburn and Dorotha Mae (Parks) Tudor; m. Walter L. Ford, July 25, 1954 (dec. 1962); children: John Corbin, Christi Sue. Student, Wichita State U., 1953-55; student, U. Nev.-Las Vegas. Legal sec. S.W. Gas Corp., Las Vegas, 1963-69, asst. corp. sec., 1969-72, corp. sec., 1972-82, v.p., 1977-82, sr. v.p., 1982-88, also bd. dirs., dir. 7 subs. Bd. dirs. NBA Svcs., Nev., residence for handicapped, 1989-97, treas., 1990-91, chmn., 1994-97; trustee Nev. Sch. Arts, Las Vegas, 1979-90, chmn. bd. dirs., 1985-86; trustee Disciples Sem. Found., Claremont Sch. Theology and Pacific Sch. Religion, San Francisco, 1985-91, 92-98, 99—, vice chmn., 1993-94, chmn., 1994-98; mem . Ariz. Acad., Ariz. Town Halls, 19 86-92. Mem. Am. Soc. Corp. Secs., Greater Las Vegas C. of C. (bd. dirs. 1979-85), Pacific Coast Gas Assn. (bd. dirs. 1984-88), Ariz. Bus. Women Owners (exec. com. 1985-88). Democrat. Mem. Christian Ch. (Disciples of Christ).

FORD, KENNETH WILLIAM, physicist; b. West Palm Beach, Fla., May 1, 1926; s. Paul Hammond and Edith (Timblin) F.; m. Karin Stehnike, Aug. 27, 1953 (div. 1961); m. Joanne Baumunk, June 9, 1962; children: Paul T., Sarah E., Caroline A., Adam B., Jason L., Ian L.; 1 stepdau., Nina Tannenwald. Student, John Carroll U., 1945, U. Mich., 1945-46; AB, Harvard Coll., 1948; PhD, Princeton U., 1953. Rsch. asst. Los Alamos Sci. Lab., 1950-51; rsch. assoc. Princeton U., 1951-52; rsch. assoc. Ind. U., 1953-54, asst. prof. physics, 1954-57, assoc. prof., 1957-58; assoc. prof. Brandeis U., 1958-1961, prof., 1961-64; prof. U. Calif., Irvine, 1964-70, chmn. dept. physics, 1964-68; prof. physics U. Mass., Boston, 1970-75; pres. N.Mex. Inst. Mining and Tech., Socorro, 1975-82; exec. v.p. U. Md., Adelphi, 1982-83; pres. Molecular Biophysics Tech. Inc., 1983-85; edn. officer Am. Phys. Soc., 1986-87; exec. dir. Am. Inst. Physics, 1987-93; tchr. Germantown Acad., 1995-98; sci. program dir. David and Lucile Packard Found., 1998-99; mem. Commn. Coll. Physics, 1968-71. Author: The World of Elementary Particles, 1963, Basic Physics, 1968, Classical and Modern Physics, 3 vols., 1972-74, (with John Wheeler) Geons, Black Holes, and Quantum Foam: A Life in Physics, 1998; mem. bd. editors Phys. Rev., 1960-62; contbr. articles on nuclear physics and field theory to tech. publs. With USNR, 1944-46. Fulbright fellow Max Planck Inst., Germany, 1955-56, NSF sr. postdoctoral fellow Imperial Coll. London, 1961-62, MIT, 1962. Fellow AAAS (coun. del. physics electorate 1983-86), Am. Phys. Soc. (chmn. forum on physics and soc. 1981, councilor 1984-87); mem. Am. Assn. Physics Tchrs. (pres. 1972, Disting. Svc. citation 1976), Fedn. Am. Scientists.

FORD, KIMBALL SUDDERTH, middle school educator; b. Weisbaden, Germany, Nov. 17, 1948; naturalized citizen, 1966; d. Ralph Manning and Emily Spindler Sudderth; m. Mabry Eugene Ford, Sept. 29, 1973. BA, Hendrix Coll., 1970; MEd, U. Ark., 1976; postgrad., U. Memphis, 1986-88. Cert. tchr. English, libr. sci., Tenn. English tchr. Little Rock Pub. Schs., 1970-78; rsch. asst. U. Tenn. Ctr. for Health Scis., Memphis, 1978-84; English tchr., libr. Cypress Jr. High, Memphis, 1984—; textbook evaluator Tenn. State Textbook Commn., 1991, 93; cons. Libr. of Congress, Washington, 1995; fellow Tenn. Collaborative Leadership Acad., 1995; reviewer English Jour., 1995—; presenter in field. Editor: (newsletter) TCTE Newsletter, 1996-97. Bd. dirs. Theatre Memphis, 1984-97; theatre judge Memphis Arts Coun., 1996—. Named Outstanding Tchr. of Humanities, Tenn. Humanities Coun., 1989, Thanks to Tchr.'s award Apple Computer, Memphis, 1990, Rotary award for Tchr. Excellence, Memphis City Schs., 1995. Mem. Shelby Memphis Coun. Tchrs. English (bd. dirs. 1988—), Tenn. Coun. Tchrs. English (bd. dirs. 1992—, pres. 1994-95, Award of Excellence 1993), Nat. Coun. Tchrs. English (adv. bd. for Promising Young Writers award 1996—), Tenn. Assn. Mid. Schs., Tenn. Assn. Sch. Librs. Episcopalian. Avocations: NASCAR Winston Cup Auto Racing. Home: 162 Adney Gap Dr Memphis TN 38134-6320 Office: Cypress Jr High Sch 2109 Howell Ave Memphis TN 38108-2264

FORD, KISHA, basketball player; b. Apr. 4, 1975. Degree in mgmt., Ga. Tech. U., 1997. Basketball player N.Y. Liberty Women's NBA, 1997-98, guard Orlando Miracle's, 1998—. All-time leading scorer Ga. Tech. U. basketball. Avocations: reading, bike riding, the park. Office: Orlando Miracle Ea Conf Two Magic Pl 8701 Maitland Summit Blvd Orlando FL 32810*

FORD, LUCILLE GARBER, economist, educator; b. Ashland, Ohio, Dec. 31, 1921; d. Ora Myers and Edna Lucille (Armstrong) Garber; m. Laurence Wesley Ford, Sept. 1, 1946; children: Karen Elizabeth, JoAnn Christine. AA, Stephens Coll., 1942; BS in Commerce, Northwestern U., 1944, MBA, 1945; PhD in Econs., Case Western Res. U., 1967; PhD (hon.), Tarkio Coll., 1991, Ashland U., 1995. Cert. fin. planner. Instr. Allegheny Coll., Meadville, Pa., 1945-46, U. Ala., Tuscaloosa, 1946-47; personnel dir., asst. sec. A.L. Garber Co., Ashland, Ohio, 1947-67; prof. econs. Ashland U., 1967-95, chmn. dept. econs., 1970-75; dir. Gill Ctr. for Econ. Edn. Ashland Coll., 1975-86, v.p., dean Sch. Bus., Adminstrn. and Econs., 1980-86, v.p. acad. affairs, 1986-90, provost, 1990-92; exec. asst. to pres., 1993-95; pres. Ashland Comm. Found., 1995—; bd. dirs. Western Res. Econ. Devel. Coun., Morgan Freeport Corp., Ohio Coun. Econ. Edn.; lectr. in field; mem. govs. adv. com. on econ. devel. Author: University Economics-Guide for Education Majors, 1979, Economics: Learning and Instruction, 1981, 91; contbr. articles to profl. jours. Mem. Ohio Gov.'s Commn. on Ednl. Choice, 1992; candidate for lt. gov. of Ohio, 1978; trustee Stephens Coll., 1977-80; elder Presbyn. Ch.; bd. dirs. Presbyn. Found., 1982-88; chair, trustee Synod-Presbyn. Ch., 1994—; active ARC. Recipient Outstanding Alumni award Stephens Coll., 1977, Outstanding Prof. award Ashland U., 1971, 75, Roman F. Warmke award, 1981, Women of Achievement award, 1998. Mem. Am. Econs. Assn., Nat. Indsl. Research Soc., Am. Arbitration Assn. (profl. arbitrator), Assn. Pvt. Enterprise Edn. (pres. 1983-84), North Ctrl. Assn. Colls. & Schs. (commr.), Omicron Delta Epsilon, Alpha Delta Kappa. Republican. Office: Ashland Comm Found PO Box 733 Ashland OH 44805-0733

FORD, MAUREEN MORRISSEY, civic worker; b. St. Joseph, Mo., July 1, 1936; d. Albert Joseph and Rosemary Kathryne (FitzSimons) Morrissey; m. James Henry Lee Ford Jr., Feb. 12, 1954; children: Kathryne Elizabeth, Maryellen, James Henry Lee III, William Charles, Maureen Lee. Student, U. N.Mex., 1953-54, U. Bridgeport, Conn., 1966-68; BS, Fairfield U., 1986, postgrad. in applied ethics, 1986—. Charity and sch. vol., 1959—, fundraiser for cmty. causes, mus., agys., 1964—, active presdl. campaign Barry Goldwater, 1963-64, congl. campaign Senator Lowell Weiker, 1968; pre-sch. tchr. Nature Ctr. Environ. Activities, 1966-68, trustee, v.p. bd. dirs., 1968-75; assoc. program in applied ethics Fairfield U., 1986—. Author: (with Lisa H. Newton) Taking Sides: Controversial Issues in Business Ethics, 1990, 5th edit., 1998. V.p. Women's League, 1966-70; mem. exec. com. Rep. Women's Club, Westport, 1967-68; leader, trainer Troops on Fgn. Soil br. Girl Scouts US, Caracas, Venezuela, 1971-72; founding trustee, treas. Kara Mus., Norwalk, Conn.; mem. adv. coun. Fairfield County (Conn.) for spl. edn. Staples H.S.; bd. dirs. CLASP; mem. exec. com. Group Home Search; pres. Ind. Assocs. Cons. Firm, 1991—; cons., facilitator life planning workshops Merideth Assocs., Westport; v.p., bd. dirs. Isaiah 61:1, Inc., 1989—; active grants com. Bridgeport Pub. Edn. Fund and Devel. Commn., 1984—; mem. 1st selectmen's com. on recycling, 1974-75; bd. dirs. PTA, 1976-79; mem. YWCA of Bridgeport Com. of 100 and Task Force; v.p. bd. dirs. YWCA, 1980-87, pres., 1984-85; v.p. Conf. Women's Orgns., Bridgeport; founding mem. Concerned Women Colleagues of Bridgeport; pres. Jr. League Ea. Fairfield County, Inc., 1977-78; v.p., sec. J.H.L.F. Inc., Westport; mem. grants com. Conn. Cares Hartford Fund, 1995-97. Mem. Assn. Jr. League Am., Westport Tennis Assn. Roman Catholic. Home: 204 Stillson Rd Fairfield CT 06432-3227

FORD, NANCY LOUISE, composer, scriptwriter; b. Kalamazoo, Oct. 1, 1935; d. Henry Ford III and Mildred Wotring; m. Robert D. Currie, June 7, 1957 (div. 1962); m. Keith W. Charles, May 23, 1964. BA, DePauw U., 1957; D of Arts (hon.), Eastern Mich. U., 1986. Composer: off-Broadway musicals (in collaboration with Gretchen Cryer) Now is the Time for All Good Men, 1967, The Last Sweet Days of Isaac, 1970, I'm Getting My Act Together and Taking It On the Road, 1978, The American Girls Revue, 1998, (Broadway musical) Shelter, 1972; performer stage and cabaret., scriptwriter: (TV daytime serials) Love of Life, 1971-74, Ryan's Hope, 1975, Search for Tomorrow, 1981-82, Guiding Light, 1977-78, As the World Turns, 1978-80, 87-95. Trustee DePauw U., 1988-97. Recipient Emmy awards, 1983, 84. Mem. Dramatists Guild, Writers Guild Am. East, AFTRA, Actors Equity, Am. Fedn. Musicians, League Profl. Theatre Women N.Y.

FORD, ORAL IVAN (VAN FORD), retired engineer; b. Ind., Mar. 21, 1925; s. Arnold Saris and Zetta May F.; m. Betty Joyce Taulman, Feb. 5, 1947; children: Joellen, Deanne, Charalyn. BSME, Purdue U., 1949; MS in Engring., Calif. Coast U., 1977, PhD, 1978. Aircraft engine design and devel. engr. Allison Divsn. GMC, Marquardt Corp., Pratt and Whitney, GE, Sacramento, Calif., 1951-60; engring. mgr. Aerojet Gen. Corp., Sacramento, 1961-72; rsch. dir. Norris Industries, L.A., 1972-74; engring. mgr. Communications Tech., L.A., 1974-75; cons. O.I. Ford Engring., Canoga Park, Calif., 1975-77; rschr., troubleshooter GE Co., San Jose, Calif., 1977-89. Author: Low Emission G.T. Combuster, 1972, Rubbing Contact Wear in Water Handling Equipment, 1976; inventor in field. With USNR, 1943-45. Decorated Air medal with 2 stars, DFC.

FORD, PATRICK KILDEA, Celtic studies educator; b. Lansing, Mich., July 31, 1935; s. Oliver Patrick and Ina Mildred (Spence) F.; m. Carol Mae Larsen, June 20, 1959 (div. 1978); children: Anne Kristina, Paul Kildea, James Oliver; m. Chadine Pearl Bailie, Nov. 17, 1979. B.A., Mich. State U., 1959; M.A., Harvard U., 1966, Ph.D., 1969. Asst. prof. English Stanford U., 1968-70; asst. prof. Indo-European studies UCLA, 1970-71, asst. prof. English, 1971-74, assoc. prof., 1974-79, prof. English and Celtic studies, 1979-91, dir. Folklore and Mythology Ctr., 1979-84, chmn. Indo-European Studies program, 1972-73, 74-75, 79-82, dir. writing programs, 1989-91; Margaret Brooks Robinson prof. Celtic Harvard U., Cambridge, Mass., 1991—; Wallace E. and Grace Connolly prof. Celtic Stanford U., 1986; founder, pres. Ford & Bailie Pubs./Book Distbrs. Author: The Poetry of Llywarch Hen, 1974, The Mabinogi and Other Medieval Welsh Tales, 1977, Ystoria Taliesin, 1992, The Celtic Poets: Songs and Tales from Early Ireland and Wales, 1999, Math uab Mathonwy, 1999, Manawydan uab Llyr, 1999; editor, contbr.: Celtic Folklore and Christianity: Essays in Memory of William W. Heist, 1983; co-author: Sources and Analogues of Old English Poetry: Celtic and Germanic, 1984, The Irish Literary Tradition, 1992. Served with AUS, 1956-57. NEH fellow, 1972; UCLA fellow, 1973; Fulbright fellow, 1973-74; Skaggs Found. grantee, 1981-83; Am. Council Learned Socs. grantee, 1985; NEH grantee, 1986; hon. fellow Ctr. for Advanced Welsh and Celtic Studies/U. Wales. Mem. MLA, Internat. Arthurian Soc. (pres. N.Am. br. 1981-83), Medieval Acad. Am., Celtic Studies Assn. N.Am. (v.p. 1984-86, pres. 1987-89). Office: Harvard U Dept Celtic Lang and Lit Barker Ctr 12 Quincy St Cambridge MA 02138-2030

FORD, PETER C., chemistry educator; b. Salinas, Calif., July 10, 1941; s. Clifford and Thelma (Martin) F.; children: Vincent, Jonathan. BS with honors, Calif. Inst. Tech., 1962; MS, Yale U., 1963, PhD, 1966. Postdoctoral fellow Stanford U., 1966-67; asst. prof. chemistry U. Calif., Santa Barbara, 1967-72, assoc. prof. chemistry, 1972-77, prof. chemistry, 1977—; grad. advisor dept. chemistry U. Calif., 1980-81, co-grad. advisor, 1985-92, chmn., 1994-96; vis. fellow Australian Nat. U., 1974; guest prof. H.C. Oersted Inst., Denmark, 1981; lectr. U. Berne, Switzerland, 1989, MITI-ASTI, Japan, 1990; guest investigator radiation biology br. Nat. Cancer Inst., 1994. Contbr. to profl. jours. Fellow NIH, 1963-66, NSF, 1966-67, Sterling fellow Yale U., 1963, sr. fellow Fulbright Found., 1974; Dreyfus Found. Tchr. scholar, 1971-76; recipient Alexander von Humboldt-Stiftung U.S. Sr. Scientist Rsch. award, 1992, Richard C. Tolman medal Am. Chem. Soc., 1993. Fellow AAAS. Achievements include research in the photochemical, photocatalytic and photophysical mechanisms of transition metal complexes and with homogeneous catalysis mechanisms as probed by modern kinetics techniques; the bioinorganic chemistry of metal nitrosyl complexes. Office: Univ of California Dept of Chemistry 552 University Rd Dept Of Santa Barbara CA 93106-0001

FORD, RICHARD EDMOND, lawyer; b. Ronceverte, W.Va., May 3, 1927; s. Grady Williams and Hazel Loraine (Fry) F.; m. Sally Frances Alexander, June 14, 1952; children: Richard Edmond Jr., Sally Anne, Melinda J. Student, U. N.C., 1950; B.S. in Bus. Adminstrn., W.Va. U., 1951, LL.B., 1954. Bar: W.Va. 1954. Assoc. Holt & Haynes, Lewisburg, W.Va., 1954-55; ptnr. Haynes & Ford, Lewisburg, 1955-74, Haynes, Ford & Rowe, Lewisburg, 1975-96, The Ford Law Firm, Lewisburg, 1997-98, Ford & Richardson Law Firm, Lewisburg, 1998—; dir. W.Va. Power Co., First Nat. Bank Ronceverte, Greenbrier Cable Corp. Mem. W.Va. Legislature, 1961-64; bd. dirs. W.Va. U. Found., Daywood Found. (v.p. 1986—), Faculty Merit Found. W.Va., W.Va. Legal Services Plan, 1973-79; trustee Greenbrier Coll. for Women, 1960-73; mem. exec. bd. Buckskin council Boy Scouts Am.; mem. adv. bd. Greenbrier Community Coll. Center; mem. vis. com. Coll. Law, W.Va. U., 1972-74. Served as ensign U.S. Maritime Service, 1945-47. Recipient Outstanding Alumnus award W.Va. U. Law Sch., 1980, W.Va. U., 88. Fellow Am. Bar Found., Am. Judicature Soc.; mem. ABA (ho. of dels. 1977-80), W.Va. Bar Assn. (v.p. 1965-66, 75-76, pres. 1978-79), Greenbrier County Bar Assn. (pres. 1964-66, 81-82), W.Va. Law Sch. Assn. (pres. 1966-67), Nat. Conf. Commrs. Uniform State Laws, Am. Coll. Real Estate Lawyers, W.Va. U. Alumni Assn. (pres. 1971), Phi Beta Kappa, Sigma Chi, Phi Delta Phi, Order of Vandalia. Democrat. Methodist. Clubs: Masons, KT, Shriners, Lewisburg Elks. Home: Buckingham Acr Lewisburg WV 24901 Office: Ford & Richardson Law Firm 203 W Randolph St Lewisburg WV 24901-1023

FORD, ROBERT DALE (DALE FORD), umpire; b. Jonesboro, Tenn., July 6, 1942; married; 3 children. Former umpire Fla. State League, Carolina League, So. League, Am. Assn.; umpire maj. league baseball Am. League, N.Y.C., 1975—; with Umpires Union, Phila.; spkr. in field. Active St. Jude Children's Hosp., Heart Fund. With U.S. Army. Avocations: golf, racquetball. Office: Am League 350 Park Ave New York NY 10022 also: Umpires Union 1735 Market St Philadelphia PA 19103

FORD, ROBERT MACDONALD, III, architect, educator; b. Seattle, Apr. 4, 1934; s. Robert MacDonald Jr. and Nancy Elizabeth (McFate) F.; m. Ruth Evelyn Keene, 1957 (div. 1980); children: Karen, Judith, Robert IV; m. Martha Evelyn Cooper, Mar. 11, 1983. BArch, U. Wash., Seattle, 1962; MArch, U. Ill., 1963. Registered architect, Miss. Asst. prof. architecture U. Ill., Urbana, 1963-66; asst. prof. architecture Wash. State U., Pullman, 1966-69, assoc. prof. architecture, 1969-74, prof. architecture, 1974-75; prof. architecture Miss. State U., Starkville, 1975-96, prof. emeritus architecture, 1996—; vis. prof. Oreg. Sch. Design, Portland, fall 1982, U. P.R., San Juan, spring 1990; pres. Ford & Assocs., Architects, Miss., 1975-92; pres. Architecture/South, Miss., Tenn., 1992-97, Ford Properties, 1997—. Councilman City of Pullman, 1969-74. With U.S. Army, 1953-56. Fellow AIA (bd. dirs. Miss. 1987, 90, 98, sec.-treas. 1988, v.p. 1989, pres.-elect 1991, pres. 1992, state design awards 1981, 82, 83, 88, regional design awards 1981, 84, 85, 91, 92), Archtl. Found., Tau Sigma Delta. Democrat. Avocations: sailing, travel. Home and Office: 308 Mangrove Palm St Starkville MS 39759-2746

FORD, S. THEODORE, JR., academic administrator; b. Nov. 27, 1954. BA, Ohio State U., 1977, MA, 1978. Exec. asst. Office of Gov., Columbus, Ohio, 1988-91; pres. Environ. Devel. Cons., Columbus, 1991-93; devel. dir. Edison Welding Inst., Columbus, 1993-97; sr. v.p. No. Ariz. U., Flagstaff, 1997-98. E-mail: TED.FORD@NAU.EDU.

FORD, SCOTT T., telecommunications company executive. Pres., chief oper. officer Alltel Corp., Little Rock. Ofice: Alltel Corp One Allied Dr Little Rock AR 72202*

FORD, STEVEN MILTON, insurance agent; b. Owensboro, Ky., Mar. 20, 1954; s. Wendell Hampton and Ruby Jean (Neel) F.; Sarah Whitley Ratliff, Aug. 28, 1976; children: Wendell Clay Hampton, Steven Neel, Morgan Ratliff. BBA, U. Ky., 1976. Agt., ptnr., mgr. E.M. Ford & Co., Owensboro, 1976-97; dir., organizer First Security Bank of Owensboro, 1997—. Bd. dirs. Owensboro-Daviess County Family-Y, 1977-85, Audubon Coun. Econ. Edn., Owensboro, 1986-92, Owensboro Symphony Orch., 1985-92, pres. 1991. Mem. Ind. Ins. Agts. Ky. (vice chmn. nat. young agts. 1987-88, chmn. 1988-89, treas. county bd. 1981-82, pres. 1983—, bd. dirs., state v.p. 1997-98, pres.-elect 1998-99, Outstanding Young Agt. award 1986), Owensboro C. of C. (bd. dirs., mem. leadership class 1984). Democrat. Baptist. Avocations: golf, fishing, hunting. Office: EM Ford & Co PO Box 22880 2100 Frederica St Owensboro KY 42304-2880

FORD, TERRY LYNN, fire department executive; b. Highland, Ill., June 4, 1953; s. Robert Elmer and Beverly June (Pashea) F.; divorced, Nov. 1996; children: Carolyn M., Jacquelyn S., Laura L., Kaitlyn E. AAS, Lewis and Clark Coll., 1987. From firefighter to capt. Godfrey (Ill.) Fire Dept., 1976-87, fire chief, 1987—; chmn. bd. dirs. Madison County Emergency Telephone Sys., Edwardsville, Ill., 1990—; exec. fire officer Nat. Fire Acad., Emmitsburg, Md., 1993-97; mem. Ill. fire adv. bd. U. Ill., Springfield, 1996—. Mem. Medal of Honor com. State of Ill., Springfield, 1992—. Mem. Internat. Assn. Fire Chiefs, Internat. Assn. Fire Fighters, Ill. Firefighters Assn. (v.p. 1992-96, pres. 1996—), Madison County Firefighters (pres. 1997-99), Ill. Fire Svcs. Assn. (lobbyist 1990—). Roman Catholic. Avocations: coin collecting, golf, Cardinal baseball fan. Home: 1214 Douglas St Alton IL 62002-2221 Office: Godfrey Fire Dept PO Box F Godfrey IL 62035-0615

FORD, THOMAS PATRICK, lawyer; b. Wausau, Wis., Dec. 29, 1918; s. John Patrick and Matild (Flatley) F.; m. Jean Ann Smith, Feb. 6, 1943 (dec. 1969); children: Thomas Patrick, Howard Michael, John Timothy, James J.; m. Mary Louise McGovern, Oct. 2, 1970; children: Mary Dolph Adkins, Louise D. Madsen, William McGovern Ford. Ph.B., U. Notre Dame, 1940; LL.B., Harvard U., 1947. Bar: N.Y. 1948, Fla. 1975. Assoc. Shearman & Sterling, N.Y.C., 1947-55, ptnr., 1955-88, ret., 1988—. Bd. dirs. W.M. Keck Found., Calif., Cord Found., Nev. Lt. comdr. USNR, 1942-46. Mem. Bath and Tennis Club (Palm Beach, Fla.), Everglades Club (Palm Beach, Fla.), Madison (Conn.) Beach Club. Home: 315 Tangier Ave Palm Beach FL 33480-3518

FORD, VICTORIA, author, educator; b. South Bend, Ind., Dec. 29, 1952; d. G. Burt and Charlotte Ann (Kupferer) F. .BA, Ohio Wesleyan U., 1975; MA, Ind. U., 1978. Design team mem. Morningside Acad., Seattle, 1995—; adj. faculty Seattle Ctrl. C.C., 1990—, Antioch U., Seattle, 1995—. Author: Following the Swan, 1988, Rain Psalm, 1996.

FORD, WENDELL HAMPTON, former senator; b. Owensboro, Ky., Sept. 8, 1924; s. Ernest M. and Irene (Schenk) F.; m. Jean Neel, Sept. 18, 1943; children: Shirley Jean (Mrs. Dexter), Steven. Student, U. Ky., 1942-43. Past ptnr. Gen. Ins. Agy., Owensboro; chief asst. to gov. Ky., 1959-61; mem. Ky. Senate, 1966-67; lt. gov. Ky., 1967-71, gov. Ky., 1971-74, U.S. senator from Ky., 1974-99, former Dem. whip, 1991—; past chmn. Dem. Senatorial Campaign Com., Nat. Dem. Gov.'s Caucus; chmn. Dem. Nat. Campaign Com., 1976; ranking minority mem. Commerce, Sci. and Transp. Subcom. on Aviation, Rules and Adminstrn. Com.; mem. Energy and Natural Resources Com., Joint Com. on Printing, Senate Dem. Policy Com., Senate Dem. Steering and Coordination Com., Senate Dem. Tech. and Comm. Com. Served with AUS, 1944-46, Ky. N.G., 1949-62. Disting. fellow Martin Sch. Pub. Policy and Adminstr. U. Ky., 1999—. Baptist. Club: Elk, Jaycees. *

FORD, WHITEY See **FORD, EDWARD CHARLES**

FORD, WILLIAM CLAY, automotive company executive; b. Detroit, Mar. 14, 1925; s. Edsel Bryant and Eleanor (Clay) F.; m. Martha Firestone, June 21, 1947; children: Martha, Sheila, William Clay, Elizabeth. BS, Yale U., 1949. Sales and advt. staff Ford Motor Co., 1949; indsl. relations, labor negotiations with UAW, 1949; quality control mgr. gas turbine engines Lincoln-Mercury Div., Dearborn, Mich., 1951, mgr. spl. product ops., 1952, v.p., 1953, gen. mgr. Continental Div., 1954, group v.p. Lincoln and Continental Divs, 1955, v.p. product design, 1956-80; dir., 1948—, vice chmn. bd., 1980-89; mem. fin. com. Ford Motor Co., 1987—; pres., owner Detroit Lions Profl. Football Club. Chmn. emeritus Edison Inst.; hon. life trustee Eisenhower Med. Ctr. Mem. Soc. Automotive Engrs. (asso.), Automobile Old Timers, Econ. Club Detroit, Masons, K.T., Phelps Assn., Psi Upsilon. Office: Ford Motor Co Design Ctr PO Box 6012 Dearborn MI 48121-6012 also: Detroit Lions 1200 Featherstone Rd Pontiac MI 48342-1938*

FORD, WILLIAM D., English educator; b. July 15, 1939. BA, Occidental Coll., 1965; PhD, U. Iowa, 1972. Assoc. prof. English Lycoming Coll., Williamsport, Pa., 1972-83; instr. Coe Coll., Cedar Rapids, Iowa, 1990-94, Kirkwood C.C., Cedar Rapids, 1994—.

FORD, WILLIAM F., banker; b. Huntington, N.Y., Aug. 14, 1936; s. William and Margaret (Mueller) Freithaler; m. Diane McDonald, June 11, 1960; children: Eric W., Kristin E. BA in Econs. summa cum laude, U. Tex., 1961; MA, U. Mich., 1962, PhD, 1966; DSc (hon.), Fla. Inst. Tech., 1981; grad. sr. exec. program, Stanford U., 1983. Part-time teaching asst. U. Mich., 1962-63, instr., 1965-66; economist Rand Corp., 1966, cons., 1967-68, 70-71; asst. prof. econs. U. Va., 1967-69; assoc. prof. Tex. Tech. U., Lubbock, 1969-70; prof. econs., dean Transylvania Coll., Lexington, Ky., 1970-71; exec. dir., chief economist rsch. and planning group Am. Bankers Assn., 1971-75; sr. v.p., chief economist Wells Fargo Bank, San Francisco, 1975-80; pres., chief exec. officer Fed. Res. Bank Atlanta, 1980-83; pres., chief operating officer First Nationwide Savs., 1983-85; pres., chief exec. officer Broadview Savs. Bank, Cleve., 1986-89; dean coll. bus. U. Denver, 1990-91; prof. and chair fin. Mid. Tenn. State U., Murfreesboro, 1992—; mem. faculty Stonier Grad. Sch. Banking, 1976-80; mem. fed. open market com. Fed. Res. System, 1982-83; sr. econ. advisor TeleCheck Svcs. Inc., 1992—; bd. dirs. Beech St. Inc.; spkr. in field. Author: Mexico's Foreign Trade and Economic Development, 1968; also articles, revs., TV script. Bd. vis. Berry Coll., 1984-89. With USN, 1954-57. Woodrow Wilson fellow, 1961; NDEA fellow, 1961-63; Ford Found. fgn. area fellow, Mex., 1964-65; Rotary fellow, Chile, 1970; co-winner Fred M. Taylor Prize U. Mich. Mem. Stanford Grad. Sch. Bus. Adminstrn. Alumni Assn. (bd. dirs. 1985-86), Am. Econ. Assn., Nat. Assn. Bus. Economists, U.S. C. of C. (bd. dirs. 1989-91, chmn. econ. policy com. 1990-93), Phi Beta Kappa. Methodist. Office: Mid Tenn State U Coll Bus PO Box 27 Murfreesboro TN 37133-0027

FORD, WILLIAM FRANCIS, retired bank holding company executive; b. Albany, N.Y., Mar. 11, 1925; s. Patrick J. and Ellen M. F.; m. Marcia J. Whalen, Jan. 7, 1956; children: William Francis, Michael P., Timothy K., Daniel J., Cathleen A. B.A. in Acctg. with honors, St. Michaels Coll., 1950. V.p. Equitable Credit Corp., Albany, 1950-60, Am. Fin. Systems Inc., Silver Spring, Md., 1960-65, Gen. Electric Credit Corp., Stamford, Conn., 1965-74; chmn., chief exec. officer Security Pacific Fin. Corp., San Diego, 1974-81; exec. v.p., adminstr. specialized fin. services group Security Pacific Corp., Los Angeles, 1981-84; vice chmn. Security Pacific Corp., 1984-91; bd. dirs., vice chmn. Ford Fin. Svcs., 1991—. Served with USN, 1943-46. Mem. Am. Fin. Svcs. Assn. (chmn., dir. emeritus exec. com.). Club: Stone Ridge Country.

FORD, WILLIAM R., federal agency administrator; b. Highland Park, Mich.. BS in Physical Sci., Mich. State U., 1957, MA in Adminstrv. and Ednl. Svcs., 1959; MA in Internat. Pub. Policy, Johns Hopkins U., 1983. Tchr. math. and sci. Mich. Dept. Social Welfare; rsch. cons. Mich. Dept. Pub. Instrn., 1963-65; dir. Lansing (Mich.) Job Tng. Ctr. Mich. Cath. Conf., 1965-66, exec. dir. job tng. projects, 1966-67; dir. Mich. Economic Opporunity Office, 1967-69, Mich. Employment Security Commn., 1969-71; dir. Mission to Nigeria USAID, 1971-76; CEO Delta Oil, Ltd., Nigeria, 1976-79; dir. D.C. Dept. Labor, 1979-81; office dir. for Indonesia USAID, 1981-89, desk officer office coastal and ctrl. West Africa, 1989-90; dep. dir. office internat. tng. USAID, Washington, 1990--92; dep. dir. mission to South Africa USAID, Pretoria, South Africa, 1992-95; pres. African Devel. Found., Washington, 1995—. Office: African Development Found Office of Chmn 1400 I St NW Fl 10 Washington DC 20005-2208

FORD-CATRON, MARY ELAINE, nurse; b. New Castle, Ind., Sept. 6, 1950; d. John Ward and Greedle Elizabeth (Jones) F.; m. James H. Catron, Sept. 1, 1967; children: James A., Jonathon Lee. RN, BSN, Ind. U., 1995. Bookkeeper McGrady Furniture, New Castle, Ind., 1968-87; nurse, mgr. Jacwil Casket Co., Inc., Knightstown, Ind., 1987-93; LPN New Castle health Care, 1993-96; nurse, pvt. duty, 1996—. Active Mother's March, March of Dimes, New Castle, 1995—; area chmn. Leukemia Soc., New Castle, 1997. Mem. Women of the Moose. Avocation: cross-stitch. Home: 710 New York Ave New Castle IN 47362-4967

FORDEMWALT, JAMES NEWTON, microelectronics engineering educator, consultant; b. Parsons, Kans., Oct. 18, 1932; s. Fred and Zenia (Chambers) F.; m. Suzan Lynn Hopkins, Aug. 26, 1958 (div. June 1961); m. Elizabeth Anna Hoare, Dec. 29, 1963; children: John William, James Frederick. BS, U. Ariz., 1955, MS, 1956; PhD, U. Iowa, 1960. Sr. engr. GE Co., Evandale, Ohio, 1959-60, U.S. Semcor, Inc., Phoenix, 1960-61; sect. mgr. Motorola Semiconductor Products Div., Phoenix, 1961-66; dept. mgr. Philco-Ford Microelectronics Div., Santa Clara, Calif., 1966-68; assoc. dir. R & D Am. Microsystems Inc., Santa Clara, 1968-71; assoc. rsch. prof. U. Utah, Salt Lake City, 1972-76; dir. microelectronics lab. U. Ariz., Tucson, 1976-87; assoc. prof., lab. mgr. Ariz. State U., Tempe, 1987—, assoc. chair microelectronics, 1992—, asst. chair dept. electronic and computer tech., 1993—; cons. Integrated Cirs. Engring., Scottsdale, Ariz., 1976—, Western Design Ctr., Mesa, Ariz., 1980—; mem. semiconductor com. United Techs. Corp., Hartford, Conn., 1978-87. Author: Silicon Wafer Processing Technology, 1979; editor: Integrated Circuits, 1965; contbr.: MOS Integrated Circuits, 1972. Mem. IEEE, Internat. Soc. for Hybrid Microelectronics (chpt. pres. 1982-83), Electrochem. Soc. Avocations: pilot, photographer. Home: 613 W Summit Pl Chandler AZ 85224-1556

FORDEN, DIANE CLAIRE, magazine editor; b. N.Y.C., Apr. 6, 1951; d. Joseph Anthony and Helen (Nash) F. BA in English Edn. summa cum laude, Montclair (N.J.) State U., 1973. Fashion editor Seventeen Mag., N.Y.C., 1975-81; fashion and beauty dir. YM Mag., N.Y.C., 1981-85; fashion dir. Avon Fashions, N.Y.C., 1985-87, Prima Mag., N.Y.C., 1987-88; freelancer fashion and beauty dept. Family Circle Mag., N.Y.C., 1989; fashion and beauty editor Bridal Guide Mag., N.Y.C., 1989-95, fashion editor, 1992-95, editor in chief, 1995—. Mem. Am. Soc. Mag. Editors, Fashion Group Internat. Avocations: piano, biking, skiing, photography. Home: 10 River Rd Apt F Nutley NJ 07110-3459 Office: Bridal Guide Mag 3 E 54th St New York NY 10022-3108

FORDHAM, CHRISTOPHER COLUMBUS, III, university dean and chancellor, medical educator; b. Greensboro, N.C., Nov. 28, 1926; s. Christopher Columbus and Frances Long (Clendenin) F.; m. Barbara Byrd, Aug. 16, 1947; children: Pamela Fordham Richey, Susan Fordham Crowell, Betsy Fordham Templeton. Cert. in medicine, U. N.C., 1949; MD, Harvard U., 1951. Diplomate Am. Bd. Internal Medicine. Intern Georgetown U. Hosp., 1951-52; asst. resident Boston City Hosp., 1952-53; prof. medicine emeritus U. N.C. Sch. Medicine, 1993—; sr. asst. resident N.C. Meml. Hosp., Chapel Hill, 1953-54; fellow in medicine U. N.C. Sch. Medicine, 1954-55, instr. medicine, 1958-60, asst. prof., 1960-64, assoc. prof., asst. dean, Sch. Medicine, 1964-68, prof., assoc. dean, 1968-69; acting asst. sec. for health Dept. HEW, Washington, 1977; dean Sch. Medicine U. N.C., 1971-79; prof. medicine U. N.C. Sch. Medicine, 1971—, vice chancellor for health affairs, 1977-80, chancellor, 1980-88, chancellor emeritus and prof. medicine, 1988-93, chancellor emeritus, dean emeritus, prof. medicine emeritus, 1993—; prof. medicine, v.p. for medicine, dean Sch. Medicine, Med. Coll. Ga., Augusta, 1969-71; practice medicine, specializing in internal medicine Greensboro, N.C., 1957-58; chair Gov.'s Com. on N.C. Awards, 1993—. Bd. dirs. Royal Soc. Med. Found., N.Y.C., 1990-95; chmn. N.C. Awards Com., 1993—. Officer USAF, 1955-57. Master ACP; fellow AAAS; mem. AAUP, AMA (spl. award 1990), Nat. Assn. State Univs. & Land Grant Colls. (chair coun. univ. governance 1990-91), N.C. Med. Soc., So. Soc. Clin. Investigation, Am. Soc. Nephrology, Am. Fedn. Clin. Rsch., Soc. Health and Human Values, Am. Assn. Med. Colls. (exec. coun. 1975-78, rep. liaison com. med. edn. 1977-79), Am. Assn. Med. Coll. So. Regional Deans (chmn. 1972-73, 75-76, chmn. nat. coun. deans 1977), N.Y. Acad. Scis., Inst. Medicine of Nat. Acad. Sci. (council 1985-90), Elisha Mitchell Sci. Soc., Order Golden Fleece, Sigma Xi, Alpha Omega Alpha. Office: Univ NC Sch Medicine Campus Box 7000 Rm 5023 Clin Wing Chapel Hill NC 27514

FORDICE, KIRK (DANIEL KIRKWOOD FORDICE, JR.), governor, construction company executive, engineer; b. Memphis, TN, Feb. 10, 1934; s. Daniel Kirkwood and Clara Aileen (Augustine) F.; m. Patricia Louise Owens, Aug. 13, 1955; children: Angela Leigh Fordice Roselle, Daniel K. III, Hunter L., James Owens. BSCE, Purdue U., 1956, MS in Indsl. Mgmt., 1957. Registered profl. engr., Miss., La. Engr. Exxon, Baton Rouge, 1956-62; ptnr. Fordice Constrn. Co., Vicksburg, Miss., 1962-76, pres., chief exec. officer, from 1976; gov. State of Miss., 1992—; bd. dirs. Mchts. Nat. Bank, Vicksburg, Miss.; vice-chmn. So. Gov.'s Assn., 1992—, chmn., 1994—. Sec. Miss. Rep. Party, Jackson, 1981-88; vice-chmn. Vicksburg-Tallulah Dist. Airport Bd.; chmn. Econ. Devel. Found., Vicksburg, 1984. Served to col. C.E., USAR. Recipient Teddy Roosevelt award Cons. Engrs. Coun. Miss., 1992, Captain of Industry award Miss. Cystic Fibrosis Found., 1992; named one of Outstanding Young Men of Am., U.S. Jaycees, 1969, Vol. Laureate in Indsl. Devel., Gov. of Miss., 1985; achievement recognition Engineering News Record mag., 1982, 91, A Grade for Fiscal Policy award Cato Inst., 1994. Fellow ASCE (pres. Vicksburg br. 1982, Outstanding Civil Engr. of Yr. Miss. sect. 1992); mem. NSPE, NRA, Associated Gen. Contractors of Miss., (Outstanding Mem. of Yr. award 1992), Am. Inst. Constructors, Cons. Constructors Coun. Am., Soc. Am. Mil. Engrs., Assoc. Gen. Contractors Am. (nat. pres. 1990, nat. life dir., pres. Miss. Valley flood control br. 1970, Man of Yr. award 1992), Am. Constrn. Industry Forum (pres. 1991), Confederation Internat. Contractor's Assns. (v.p. 1990—), So. Govs. Assn. (chmn.), Aircraft Owners and Pilots Assn., Nat. Aero. Assn., Reserve Officers Assn., Quiet Birdmen, Am. Quarter Horse Assn., Safari Club Internat., Game Conservation Internat., Rivertown Club (Vicksburg), The Moles, Nature Conservancy, Sigma Chi (Significant Sig award 1993), Tau Beta Pi, Chi Epsilon. Republican. Methodist. Office: Office of the Governor PO Box 139 Jackson MS 39205-0139*

FORD-ROEGNER, PATRICIA A., health services professional; b. May 25, 1947. AD, Gwynedd Mercy Coll., 1967; BA, West Chester State U., 1969; MSW, U. Pa., 1973. Pres. pub. affairs PFR, Washington, 1992-94; regional dir. Dept. Health and Human Svcs., Atlanta, 1994—; vice-chair White House Task Force Health Care Reform, 1993. E-mail: pford-roegner@osophs.dhhs.gov. Office: Sam Nunn AFC 61 Forsyth St Ste 5B95 Atlanta GA 30303-8909

FORDYCE, JAMES GEORGE, physician; b. Detroit, Jan. 9, 1945; s. James Alexander and Stella Marie (Pakron) F.; m. Kathleen Marie Ray, June 17, 1967; children: James A., Jonathan A., Jared A. BS, Mich. State U., 1966, DVM, 1968; MD, Wayne State U., 1974. Diplomate Am. Bd. Pediats., Am. Bd. Allergy and Immunology. Intern, resident Children's Hosp. Mich., Detroit, 1973-76; fellow allergy and clin. immunology Henry Ford Hosp., Detroit, 1976-78; physician Dearborn (Mich.) Allergy and Asthma Clinic, PC, 1978—; cons. Metro Med. Group, Detroit, 1979-95. Author: Asthma in Clinical Pulmonary Medicine, 1992. Bd. trustees Oakwood Healthcare, Inc. Fellow Am. Acad. Pediats., Am. Acad. Allergy, Asthma and Clin. Immunology; mem. Am. Bd. Quality Assurance and Utilization Rev. Physicians, Inc. (diplomate), Mich. Allergy and Asthma Soc. (pres. 1991-92). Avocations: fishing, sailing. Office: Dearborn Allergy & Asthma Clinic PC 20200 Outer Dr Dearborn MI 48124-2634

FORDYCE, JAMES STUART, non-profit organization executive; b. London, Dec. 10, 1931; came to U.S., 1947; s. James Wilfred and Doris Vera (Macrae) F.; m. Beverly Ann Arnold, June 12, 1954; children: Cameron James, Jean Margaret. AB, Dartmouth Coll., 1953; PhD in Phys. Chemistry, MIT, 1959. Rsch. scientist Parma (Ohio) rsch. lab. Union Carbide Corp., 1959-66; rsch. scientist Lewis rsch. ctr. NASA, Cleve., 1966-68, head electrochemical fundamentals, 1968-73, mgr. environ. monitoring office, 1973-76, chief electrochemistry br., 1976-80, dep. chief space power tech. divsn., 1980-81, chief, 1981-84, dep. dir. aerospace tech., 1984-85, dir., 1985-91, dep. ctr. dir., 1991-94; v.p., chief scientist Ohio Aerospace Inst., Cleve., 1995—; spl. lectr. Internat. Space U.; disting. space tech. lectr. Columbia U., 1988; bd. trustees Edison Polymer Innovation Corp., Akron, Ohio, 1991—. Author: (with others) Solar Power Satellites, 1993; contbr. articles to profl. jours. Mem. spl. com. Mus. Natural History, Cleve., 1991-96; active Leadership Cleve., 1992—. Fellow AIAA (assoc.); mem. AAAS, Am. Chem. Soc., Fedn. Am. Scientists, Electrochem. Soc. (lectr. 106th mtg. 1985), Sigma Xi. Democrat. Unitarian. Home: 21295 Cromwell Ave Fairview Park OH 44126-2714 Office: Ohio Aerospace Inst PO Box 3531 Akron OH 44309-3531

FORE, ANN, counselor, educator, country dance instructor; b. Artesia, N.Mex., July 16, 1948; d. Stanley William and Jackie (Hightower) Blocker; divorced; 1 child Richard Todd. BS, Eastern N.Mex. U., Portales, 1971, MA, 1976. Instr. sociology Eastern N.Mex. U., Clovis, 1974; counselor, instr. So. Plains Jr. Coll., Plainview, Tex., 1975-76; drug and alcohol counselor U.S. Dept. Army, Ft. Hood, Tex., 1976-77; group leader Forest Svc., USDA, Estacada, Oreg., 1980-81; owner Women's Issues Counseling Svcs., Salem, 1985—; tchr. country western ptnr. dancing and line dancing various ednl. settings, Salem, Oreg., Portland C.C., Salem Keizer Schs. Author: founder, adminstr. award-winning, nationally televised country dance team Koda Kountry Drifters. U. N.Mex. rsch. dept. grantee, 1972; recipient Star award United Country/Western Dance Coun., 1998. Mem. APGA, Willamette Writers Assn., Nat. Tchrs. Assn. for Country/Western Dance Instrs., Internat. Platform Assn. Republican. Christian. Avocations: reading, camping, photography, public speaking. Home and Office: PO Box 13851 Salem OR 97309-1851

FOREE, EDWARD GOLDEN, environmental engineer, consultant; b. Sulphur, Ky., Feb. 24, 1941; s. Edward Cecil and Sarah Coleman (Golden) F.; m. Jo Ellen Chilton, Sept. 9, 1962; children: Molly Chilton, Macy Samuel. BSCE, U. Ky., 1964; MSCE, Stanford U., 1965, PhD in CE, 1968. Registered profl. engr., Ind., Ky., Va., W.Va., Ohio, Pa., S.C. Asst. prof. civil engring. U. Ky., Lexington, 1968-74, assoc. prof., 1974-80; pres. Commonwealth Tech., Inc., Lexington, 1980—. Mem. ASCE, Water Pollution Control Fedn. (nat. dir. 1985-88), NSPE, Am. Water Works Assn., Am. Acad. Environ. Engrs. Office: Commonwealth Tech Inc 2520 Regency Rd Lexington KY 40503-2921*

FORELL, DAVID CHARLES, financial executive; b. Sheboygan, Wis., Dec. 13, 1947; s. Gerald Franklin and Eleanor (Wahlstrom) F.; m. Luann Coleman, July 29, 1972; children: Leslie Ann, Geoffrey Scott. B.S.B.A., Northwestern U., 1970, M.B.A., 1971. C.P.A., Ill. Mgr., Arthur Andersen & Co., Chgo., 1971-81; asst. contr. Marshall Field & Co., Chgo., 1981-82; dir. acctg. Batus, Louisville, 1982-83; v.p. fin. Hutzlers, Balt., 1983-87; exec. v.p., chief fin. officer Catherine's, Stores Corp., Memphis, 1988—. Mem. bd. dirs. St. Mary's Episcopal Sch., 1994—, Jr. Achievement, Memphis, 1995—. Contbr. articles to profl. jours. Barker fellow Northwestern U., 1971; Austin scholar Northwestern U., 1966-70. Mem. AICPA, Fin. Execs. Inst. (pres. Memphis chpt. 1994-95). Republican. Home: 8592 Edenfield Cv Memphis TN 38138-7319 Office: Catherine's Stores Corp 3742 Lamar Ave Memphis TN 38118-3743

FORELL, GEORGE WOLFGANG, religion educator; b. Breslau, Germany, Sept. 19, 1919; came to U.S., 1939, naturalized, 1945; s. Frederick J. and Madeleine (Kretschmar) F.; m. Elizabeth Jean Rossing, June 14, 1945; children: Madeleine Helene (Mrs. Gary Marshall), Mary Elizabeth (Mrs. Christopher Davis). Student, U. Vienna, 1937-38; BD, Luth. Theol. Sem., Phila., 1941; Th.M., Princeton Theol. Sem., 1943; ThD, Union Theol. Sem., N.Y.C., 1949; DD (hon.), Wartburg Theol. Sem., 1967; LHD, Gustavus Adolphus Coll., 1974; LLD, Luther Coll., 1983; LittD, Upsala Coll., 1983. Ordained to ministry Luth. Ch., 1941. Pastor Luth. Chs., N.J. and N.Y., 1941-47; asst. prof., then assoc. prof. philosophy Gustavus Adolphus Coll., St. Peter, Minn., 1947-54; asst. prof., then assoc. prof. theology U. Iowa, 1954-58, prof. religion, 1961-73, Carver prof., 1973-89, Carver Disting. prof. emeritus, 1989—, dir. Sch. Religion, 1965-71; prof. systematic theology Luth. Sch. Theology, Chgo., 1958-61; vis. prof. U. Hamburg, Germany, 1957-58, All Africa Theol. Seminar, Marangu, Tanzania, 1960, Japan Luth. Coll., Tokyo, 1968, Gurukul Theol. Rsch. Inst., Madras, India, 1978, Luth. Coll., Hong Kong, 1980; Eli Lilly vis. prof. Berea Coll., Ky., 1979, 86, Pacific Luth. U., Tacoma, Wash., 1987, Luth. Theol. Sem., Phila., 1988-91, Luth. Sch. Theology, Chgo., 1991-92, China Evang. Sem., Taipei, Taiwan, 1993, Pacific Luth. Theol. Sem., Berkeley, Calif., 1995, Concordia U., Irvine, Calif., 1996-98; cons. dept. studies Luth. World Fedn., Geneva, 1981-84. Author: Faith Active in Love, 1954, Ethics of Decision, 1955, The Protestant Faith, 1960, The Christian Year, 1964-65, Understanding the Nicene Creed, 1965, Christian Social Teachings, 1966, The Augsburg Confession, A Contemporary Commentary, 1968, Zinzendorf: Nine Public Lectures, 1973, The Proclamation of the Gospel in a Pluralistic World, 1973, The Christian Lifestyle, 1975, The Revolution at the Frontier: Reports from Moravian Missionaries Among the American Indians, 1976, History of Christian Ethics, Vol. I, 1979, The Luther Legacy, 1983, Martin Luther: Theologian of The Church, 1994. Mem. Ch. Coun. Evang. Luth. Ch. Am., 1987-91. Mem. Am. Philos. Assn., Am. Soc. Ch. History, Am. Soc. Reformation Research (pres. 1959), Omicron Delta Kappa. Democrat. Home: PO Box 2300 Iowa City IA 52244-2300

FOREMAN, ALFRED G., theologian, philosopher; b. Sulfur, La., Mar. 19, 1960; s. Grover Foreman and Stella Kibodeaux. BA, U. Southwestern La., 1987; MA, Liberty U., 1991. Founder S. La. Weather Sta., Crowley, 1986—; pastor Ch. of God, Crowley, 1986—; dir. La. Philos. Inst., Crowley, 1989—; lectr. Islamic Ctr., Lafayette, La., 1983-84, La. Philos. Inst. Humanities, Crowley, 1993—. Dir. S. La. Weather Jour., 1986—. Mem. Internat. Palm Soc. (La. and Calif. chpts.). Home: 130 Palms Rd Crowley LA 70526-1907

FOREMAN, CAROL LEE TUCKER, consumer advocate; b. Little Rock, May 3, 1938; d. James Guy and Willie Maude (White) Tucker; A.A., William Woods Coll., Fulton, Mo., 1958; A.B., Washington U., St. Louis, 1960; postgrad. Am. U.; LL.D. (hon.), William Woods Coll., Fulton, Mo., 1976; m. Jay Howell Foreman, June 13, 1964; children: Guy Tucker, Rachel Marian. Rsch. asst. Com. on Govt. Ops., U.S. Senate, 1961; assoc. Fed. Counsel Assocs., 1961-63; instr. Am. govt. William Woods Coll., Fulton, 1963-64; exec. asst. to Rep. James Roosevelt, 1964; dir. rsch. and publs. Dem. Nat. Com., 1965-66; Congressional liaison aide HUD, 1967-69; chief info. liaison Ctr.for Family Planning Program Devel., Planned Parenthood-World Population, 1969-71; dir. policy coordination Commn. on Population and Am. Future, 1971-72; exec. dir. Citizens Com. on Population and Am. Future, 1972-73, Paul Douglas Consumer Rsch. Ctr., 1973-77, Consumer Fedn. Am., 1973-77; asst. sec. food and consumer svcs. Dept. Agr., Washington, 1977-81; dir. U.S. Commodity Credit Corp., 1977-81; dir. U.S. Consumer Cooperative Bank, 1979-81; pres. Foreman & Co., 1981-86, ptnr. Foreman & Heidepriem, 1986-94; pres. Foreman & Heidepriem, Inc., 1994-97; pres. Foreman Heidepriem & Mager, Inc., 1997-99, dir., disting. fellow, Foord Policy Inst., Consumer Fedn. Am.; coord. Safe Food Coalition, 1987—; mem. Pres.' Commn. on White House Fellows, 1996—; mem. Nat. Adv. Com. Meat & Poultry Inspection, 1997—. Editor: Regulating for the Future, 1991. Exec. dir. Ctr. for Women Policy Studies, 1983-84; mem. Interdeptl. Task Force on Women; mem. D.C. Commn. on Status Women, 1973-74; bd. dirs. Consumer's Union, 1982-83, chmn., 1993—; bd. dirs. Food Rsch. and Action Ctr., 1983—, Christianity and Crisis, 1990-92; vice-chmn. Ctr. Nat. Policy, 1982-84, bd. dirs., 1981—; trustee Washington U., St. Louis, 1987-95. Recipient Disting. Alumni award Washington U., 1979. Mem. Women's Equity Action League (past pres. local chpt.), Nat. Policy Assn. (dir. 1985—), Pi Beta Phi. Presbyterian. Home: 5408 Trent St Chevy Chase MD 20815-5514 Office: Consumer Fedn Am 1424 16th St NW Ste 604 Washington DC 20036

FOREMAN, DALE MELVIN, lawyer, state official; b. Los Angeles, May 1, 1948; s. C. Melvin and Sylvia (Ahnlund) F.; m. Gail Burgener, June 24, 1972; children: Mari Elizabeth, Ann Marie, James Sterling. AB cum laude, Harvard U., 1970, JD, 1975. Bar: Wash. 1976, U.S. Dist. Ct. (we. dist.) Wash. 1977, U.S. Ct. Claims 1977, U.S. Dist. Ct. (ea. dist.) Wash. 1981, U.S. Ct. Appeals (9th cir.) 1981, Calif. 1986, U.S. Ct. Appeals (3rd cir.) 1987. Ptnr. Jeffers, Danielson & Foreman, Wenatchee, Wash., 1975-81, Jardine, Foreman & Arch, Wenatchee, 1981-88; sr. ptnr. Foreman, Arch, Dodge, Volyn & Zimmerman, Wenatchee, 1988—; mem. 12th legis. dist. Wash. Ho. of Reps., 1993-96, majority leader, 1995-97; mem. Spl. Adv. Commn. on Pub. Opinion, U.S. Dept. of State, 1970-72. Author: Washington Trial Handbook, 1988, Dental Law, 1989, How to Become an Expert Witness, 1989, Crucify Him! A Lawyer Looks at the Trial of Jesus, 1989. Chmn. Chelan County Rep. Cen. Com., Wenatchee, 1977-79, 82-84; bd. dirs. Am. and Fgn. Christian Union, N.Y.C., 1985—, Greater Wenatchee Community Found., 1987—. Mem. ABA, Assn. Trial Lawyers Am., Wash. State Bar Assn., State Bar Calif., Wash. State Trial Lawyers Assn. (bd. govs. 1990—), Harvard Club, Rotary. Presbyterian. Avocation: horticulture. Home: 323 Chatham Hill Rd Wenatchee WA 98801-5931 Office: Foreman Arch Dodge & Volyn 124 N Wenatchee Ave # A Wenatchee WA 98801-2239*

FOREMAN, EDWARD RAWSON, lawyer; b. Atlanta, May 15, 1939; s. Robert Langdon and Mary (Shedden) F.; m. Margaret Reeves, Oct. 19, 1968; children: Margaret Langdon, Mary Rawson. BA, Washington & Lee U., 1962; JD, Emory U., 1965. Bar: Ga. 1965. Assoc. Jones, Bird & Howell, Atlanta, 1965-70, ptnr., 1970-82; ptnr. Alston & Bird, Atlanta, 1982—; chmn. McAliley Endowment Trust, 1978—; lectr. Inst. for Continuing Legal Edn. in Ga., 1989; panelist, moderator Bus. Atlanta's Office Leasing and Tenant Opportunities in 1990s. Bd. editors Comml. Leasing Law and Strategy, 1996—. Bd. dirs. Ansley Park Beautification Found., Atlanta, 1984—; bd. dirs. Midtown Alliance, Atlanta, 1988-96, sec., chmn. fundraising com., 1989-91, v.p., 1991, pres., 1992; trustee Paidela Sch. Endowment Fund, Atlanta, 1980—, Woodruff Arts Ctr., Atlanta, 1985-90; chmn. Emory U. Law Fund, Atlanta, 1981; chmn. legal divsn. United Way Met. Atlanta, 1984; chmn. strategic planning com. High Mus. Art, 1986-95, chmn., bd. dirs. 1998—, chmn. nominating com., 1993-95; vestryman, sr. warden St. Luke's Episc. Ch., 1975, 94, mem. com., 1975—; pres. Atlanta Legal Aid Soc., 1975-76, Atlanta Preservation Ctr., 1986-91; trustee Miss Hall's Sch., Pittsfield, Mass., 1990—. Recipient Cmty. Svc. award Martin Luther King Jr. Ctr. Nonviolent Social Change, 1980, Outstanding Svc. award Atlanta Preservation Ctr., Inc., 1983. Mem. ABA (mem. comml. leasing com. 1987—), State Bar Ga. (chmn., panelist, moderator comml. leasing seminars 1979-86), Atlanta Bar Assn. (chmn., panelist, moderator leasing seminars 1979-86, chmn. hdqrs. search com. 1988-96), Lawyers Club Atlanta (chmn. long-range planning com. 1989-90), Atlanta Bar Found. (bd. dirs.), Old War Horse Lawyers Club, Nine O'Clocks Club (mem. centennial com. 1983), Highlands Country Club N.C. Democrat. Episcopalian. Home: 238 15th St NE House 16 Atlanta GA 30309-3594 Office: Alston & Bird 4200 One Atlantic Ctr 1201 W Peachtree St NW Ste 4200 Atlanta GA 30309-3424

FOREMAN, EDWIN FRANCIS, economist, real estate broker; b. Syracuse, N.Y., July 24, 1931; s. Herve Joseph and Ruth Margaret F.; m. Colleen Frances Tapp, July 7, 1962; children: Lisa C., Eric E. BAE in Econs. and Fgn. Trade, U. Fla., 1957; postgrad. in real estate Fla. Internat. U., 1974-75. Owner, prin. Edwin F. Foreman, Mortgage Broker, Hollywood, Fla., 1974—; with Consol. Energy Corp., Hollywood, 1977—, pres., chmn. bd., 1977—; v.p. Ea. State Securities, Inc., 1977—; owner, prin. Edwin F. Foreman, Real Estate Broker, 1978—; pres., chmn. One-Fore-Devel., Inc., 1985, Three-Fore-Devel., Inc., 1985, L&E Comm. Inc., 1985; chmn., CEO Universal Traction, Hollywood, 1988—; gen. ptnr. Four-Fore Devel. Ltd., Five-Fore-Devel. Ltd., Six-Fore Devel., Ltd., 1987—, CCS Ventures, 1990—; mem. Funds Coordinating Group Internat., L.L.C., 1998—. Econ. cons. Michael I. Warde de Colombia Ltd.; guest lectr. econs. Xavier U., Bogota, Colombia. Served with USAF, 1950-53. R.J. Reynolds fellow U. N.C., 1961. Fellow NSF; mem. Hollywood C. of C. (econ. devel. com.), Ft. Lauderdale World Trade Council. Democrat. Unitarian. Clubs: Jockey, Grove Isle (Miami), Fisher Island. Avocations: camping, fishing, music, photography, travel. Office: PO Box 7570 Hollywood FL 33081

FOREMAN, GEORGE, boxer, minister, boxing broadcaster; b. Marshall, Tex.; s. J. D. and Nancy Foreman; children from previous marriages: Michi, Freeda, Natalie, George Jr., George 3d, George 4th. Profl. boxer, 1969-77, 87—, minister, 1977—; founder, minister Ch. Lord Jesus Christ, Houston, 1984—; heavyweight champion 1968 Olympics; world heavyweight champion, 1973-74; WBA & IBF heavyweight champion, 1994, abandoned titles, 1994. Author: By George, 1995; boxing analyst HBO; numerous TV commercials and endorsements. Founder George Foreman Cmty. Ctr., Houston. Oldest Heavyweight Champion in boxing history-45 yrs. Office: 2202 Lone Oak Rd Houston TX 77093-3336*

FOREMAN, JAMES LOUIS, retired judge; b. Metropolis, Ill., May 12, 1927; s. James C. and Anna Elizabeth (Henne) F.; m. Mabel Inez Dunn, June 16, 1948; children: Beth Foreman Banks, Rhonda Foreman Riepe, Nanette Foreman Love. BS in Commerce and Law, U. Ill., 1950, JD, 1952. Bar: Ill. Ind. practice law Metropolis, Ill.; ptnr. Chase and Foreman, Metropolis, until 1972; state's atty. State of Ill., Massac County; asst. atty. gen. State of Ill.; chief judge U.S. Dist. Ct. (so. dist.) Ill., Benton, 1979-92, sr. status, 1992—. Pres. Bd. of Edn., Metropolis. With USN, 1945-46. Mem. Ill. State Bar Assn., Metropolic C. of C. (past pres.). Republican. Home: 38 Hilanoa-East Dr Metropolis IL 62960-2533 Office: US Dist Ct 301 W Main St Benton IL 62812-1362

FOREMAN, JOHN DANIEL, financial executive; b. Wheeling, W.Va., Aug. 24, 1940; s. William Carroll and Mary Katheryn (Leese) F.; m. Helen Virginia Donato, Sept. 2, 1967; children: Sean, Christopher. BA, Wheeling (W.Va.) Coll., 1962; MA, W.Va. U., 1965. Banking officer Wheeling Dollar Bank, 1964-67; prof., dept. chair Seton Hill Coll., Greensburg, Pa., 1967-81; mem. faculty, adminstr. Westmoreland County Community Coll., Youngwood, Pa., 1971-81; dir. continuing edn. St. Vincent Coll., Latrobe, Pa., 1981-84, dean enrollment and planning, 1984-87; chief fin. officer The Eye and Ear Inst., Pitts., 1987-93; pres. Aquillian Corp., Greensburg, Pa., 1981—. Contbr. articles to profl. jours. Treas. bd. dirs. Westmoreland Symphony Orch., Greensburg, 1989—; bd. dirs. SUC Small Bus. Devel. Ctr., Latrobe, 1983-90, Westmoreland Trust, 1992—. Mem. Pitts. Athletic Assn., Pitts. Club. Office: 419 College Ave Greensburg PA 15601-3030

FOREMAN, JOHN WILLIAM, pediatrician, educator; b. Washington, June 23, 1947; s. William Roy and Elizabeth Roberts (McLean) F.; m. Linda Poffenberger, May 27 1973; children: Matthew John, Jennifer Lynne. BS, Duke U., 1969; MD, U. Md., 1973. Diplomate Nat. Bd. Med. Examiners, Pa., Va., N.C., Am. Bd. Pediatrics, subbd. pediatric nephrology. Intern, resident Montreal (Que., Can.) Children's Hosp., 1973-75; asst. chief resident pediatrics Children's Hosp. Phila., 1975-76, fellow pediatric nephrology, 1976-79, staff physician, 1979-86; instr. pediatrics U. Pa. Sch. Medicine, Phila., 1976-79, clin. asst. prof., 1979-85, assoc. prof., 1985-86; assoc. prof. pediatrics Med. Coll. Va., Va. Commonwealth U., Richmond, 1986-90, prof., 1990-93; prof., chief divsn. pediatric nephrology Duke U. Med. Ctr., Durham, N.C., 1993—; cons. WHO, 1984; chmn. med. adv. bd. Nat. Kidney Found. Va., 1989-92, mem. exec. com. pediatric urology and nephrology coun.; mem. pediatric delegation to Chinese Med. Assn. of People's Republic of China. Contbr. articles to profl. jours., chpts. to books. Bd. dirs. Transplant Found., Richmond, 1991. Daland fellow Am. Philos. Soc., Phila., 1980-81; grantee Am. Heart Assn., 1984-88, NIH, 1988-91. Fellow Am. Acad. Pediatrics; mem. Soc. Pediatric Rsch., Am. Pediatric Soc., So. Soc. Pediatric Rsch. (councillor 1989-91), Internat. Pediatric Nephrology Soc. (councillor 1993-98), Am. Soc. Pediatric Nephrology (mem. manpower subcom. 1991-93), Am. Soc. Nephrology. Avocations: reading, bicycling. Home: 9 Streamley Ct Durham NC 27705-5396 Office: Duke U Med Ctr PO Box 3959 Durham NC 27710

FOREMAN, JULIE LYNN, volunteer coordinator; b. Omaha, Mar. 4, 1974; d. Larry Lee and Joan Terese Foreman. BS in Edn., U. Nebr., 1996; postgrad., U. Nebr., Omaha, 1998—. Mem. vol./aux. support staff Immanuel Med. Ctr., Omaha, 1996-97; vol. coord. Henry Doorly Zoo, Omaha, 1997—. Mem. Am. Soc. Pub. Adminstrn., Nebr. Pub. Health Assn. Democrat. Roman Catholic. Avocations: travel, biking. E-mail: educate@omahazoo.com. Home: 5304 Emiline St Bellevue NE 68157 Office: Henry Doorly Zoo 3701 S 10th St Omaha NE 68107

FOREMAN, LAURA, dancer, choreographer, conceptual artist, writer, educator; b. L.A.; d. Michael and Gladys (Charnas) F.; m. John Everett Watts. Dir. dance, physical fitness and recreation depts. and movement specialist cert. program, Foreman Dance Theatre artist-in-residence. New Sch. Social Rsch., N.Y.C., 1971—; founder, dir. Choreographers Theatre, N.Y.C.; artist-in-residence Channel 13 TV Lab., 1978, Holographic Film Found., N.Y.C., 1983; dance dir., bd. dirs. Composers and Choreographers Theatre, Inc.; cons. Nat. Endowment Humanities; mem. Artists Talk on Art, The Performance Project, N.Y. Theater Bridge, Writers Rm., N.Y.C.; mem. dance panel N.Y. State Coun. on Arts; visual arts panel Ill. Arts Coun., Seattle Arts Commn.; documentary and arts panel Nat. TV Emmy Awards; bd. dirs. Ear Inc., N.Y.C.; tchr. master classes New Sch., Parsons Sch. of Design, Art Student League, Met. Mus. Art, Chapin Sch. Choreography and performanc art includes Memorials, Study, A Time, Perimeters, Epicycles, SkyDance for skywriters and helicopters, Margins, Signals, Laura's Dance, Spaces (Collage I-IV), Locrian, Performance, a deux, Postludes, Monopoly, Program, Heirlooms, Entries, others.; video includes TimeCoded Woman I, II, III (2 silver, 1 gold award Houston Internat. Film Festival 1979, 80, 81, Bronze medal Internat. Film and TV Festival of N.Y., 1981); conceptual work (with John Watts) includes WallWork, crowd-created art work, 1981, Coney Island Cray-Pas, 1981, Concourse Cray-Pas, The Philadelphia Story, 1981; installations include Roomwork, 1981, WindoWork, 1982, 91; one-woman shows Portico Gallery, Phila., Limbo, N.Y.C., Souyun Yi Gallery, N.Y.C., Kleinert Arts Ctr., Woodstock, N.Y.; two-person shows Souyun Yi Gallery, Webb & Parsons Gallery, Vt.; over 50 group shows including Bronx, N.Y., Wustum., Wis., Hudson Highlands, N.Y., Chgo. Peace, Ill., and Pasadena, Calif., museums; permanent collections include Antwerp Mus.; off-Broadway shows City Junket, 1980 (Best Short Story in English); published in The Act, Downtown, Letters, Pinehurst Jour., Confrontation, ACM, Santa Clara Review, Up Front Muse Internat., Lamia, Ink mags., Sundown Books, (short story collection) Pig Iron Anthology. Grantee CAPS, 1970, 73, N.Y. State Coun. Arts, 1970-74, Nat. Endowment Arts, 1971, 73, 77, 78, Vogelstein Found., 1985, Pub. Arts Commn., JBR Found., 1989; fellow Blue Mountain, 1985, 90, Dorset Colony, 1985, 88, MacDowell Colony, 1986, Djerassi Found., 1987, Vt. Studio Sch. and Colony, 1988, Act II Colony, 1988, Ragdale Found., 1990, Watershed Ctr. for Ceramic Arts, Edward Albee Found., Byrdcliffe Arts Colony, 1991, Cummington Cmty. for the Arts, 1992, Lookout Sculpture Park, 1994, Pallenville Found., 1994, Mary Anderson Ctr., 1994, Hambidge Ctr., Ga., 1995, Pouch Cove Studio Cst. John's NK, 1996, Contemporary Artists Ctr., Mass., 1996, Saltonstall Found., N.Y., 1998, Yaddo Artists Colony, 1999, Vt. Studio Ctr., 1999; recipient 1st prize 8th Abiko Quar. Internat. Fiction Contest, 1997. Mem. Artists and Scis. in Collaboration (founder), Artists Talk on Art. Home: 94 Chambers St New York NY 10007-1800

FOREMAN, RICHARD, theater director, playwright; b. N.Y.C., June 10, 1937; s. Albert and Claire (Levine) F. BA, Brown U., 1959, ArtsD (hon.), 1993; MFA, Yale U., 1962. Artistic dir. Ontological-Hysteric Theater, N.Y.C., 1968—; dir.-in-residence N.Y. Shakespeare Festival, N.Y.C., 1975-76; artistic dir. Theatre O.H., Paris, 1973-85. Dir. Broadway and off-Broadway plays including 3-Penny Opera, 1976; author, dir. Dr. Selavy's Magic Theater, 1972, Rhoda in Potatoland, 1976 (Obie award Village Voice 1976), Film Is Evil: Radio is Good, 1987 (Obie award Village Voice, 1987), Pearls for Pigs, 1997 (Obie award Village Voice, 1997), Benita Canova, 1998 (Obie award Village Voice, 1998); over 40 others; author: Unbalancing Acts, 1992 and others. Mem. panel theatre div. Nat. Endowment for Arts, Washington, 1976-79. Guggenheim fellow, 1972, Rockefeller fellow, 1974, Creative Artist's Pub. Svc. fellow, 1974, Creative Artist's Pub. Svc. fellow N.Y. State Arts Coun., 1971, MacArthur fellow, 1995—; recipient Lifetime Achievement award NEA, 1990, Am. Acad. Arts and Letters prize in lit., 1992. Mem. Dramatist's Guild, Soc. Stage Dirs., PEN. Jewish. Avocations: philosophy, psychoanalysis. Home and Office: 152 Wooster St New York NY 10012-5330

FOREMAN, SPENCER, pulmonary specialist, hospital executive; b. Phila., Nov. 10, 1935; s. Samuel and Freda F.; m. Sandra Lee Finkelstein, June 10, 1961; children: Corinne, Todd, Cheryl, Andrea. BS, Ursinus Coll., 1957; MD, U. Pa., 1961. Diplomate Am. Bd. Internal Medicine (subspecialty bd. pulmonary disease). Intern Henry Ford Hosp., Detroit, 1961-62; med. officer USPHS, San Pedro, Calif., 1962-63; resident in internal medicine USPHS Hosp., New Orleans, 1963-65; fellow in pulmonary diseases Tulane U., 1965-67; asst. chief dept. internal medicine USPHS Hosp., Balt., 1967-68; chief dept. internal medicine USPHS Hosp., 1968-73, hosp. dir., 1971-73; CEO Sinai Hosp., Balt., 1973-86; pres. Montefiore Med. Ctr., Bronx, N.Y., 1986—; prof. medicine, prof. social medicine and epidemiology Albert Einstein Coll. Medicine, Bronx; mem. Accreditation Coun. on Med. Edn., 1981-87, ProPAC (Prospective Payment Assessment Commn.) 1996. Contbr. articles to med. jours. Commr. Md. Health Resources Commn., 1982-86, Liaison Com. for Med. Edn., 1989-91; bd. dirs. Am. Jewish Joint Distribution Com., Inc., Ursinus Coll., Collegeville, Pa. Capt. USPHS, 1962-73. Fellow ACP, N.Y. Acad. Medicine; mem. Inst. Medicine Nat. Acad. Scis., Assn. Am. Med. Colls. (rep. assembly, chmn. 1986, adminstrv. bd. Coun. Tchg. Hosps., chmn.-elect assembly 1991-92, chmn. 1992-93), Am. Hosp. Assn. (bd. dirs. 1995-98), Health Forum (bd. dirs.), Greater N.Y. Hosp. Assn. (bd. dirs., vice chmn., chmn.), League Vol. Hosps. (bd. dirs., sec.-treas., chmn.). Office: Montefiore Med Ctr 111 E 210th St Bronx NY 10467-2401

FOREMAN, THOMAS ALEXANDER, dentist; b. Tionesta, Pa., Oct. 24, 1930; s. James Aura and May (Lanson) F.; student Grove City Coll., 1948-50; BS, Allegheny Coll., 1952; DDS cum laude, U. Pitts., 1957, DMD, 1970; m. Dorothy Jean Wolf, June 12, 1953; children: Bonnie Jean, Julie Marie, Mary Aleta, Lloyd George. Gen. practice dentistry, Clarion, Pa., 1961—. Mem. Clarion Hosp. Assn., 1965—; mem. exec. bd. Colonel Drake Council Boy Scouts Am., 1969-72, mem.-at-large French Creek council, 1972-73, vice chmn. Indian Trails dist., 1971-73; mem. governing coun. Alpha Christian Acad. Sch., 1977-81. Served with Dental Corps, USAF, 1957-61. Fellow Pierre Fauchard Acad. Fellow Acad. Dentistry Internat., Am. Coll. Dentists, Internat. Coll. Dentists, Royal Soc. Health; mem. Am. Dental Assn., Pa. Dental Assn. (dir. 8th dist. 1964-87, 91—, pres. 1974-76, trustee 1987-91), Acad. Gen. Dentistry (mem. 1977, fellow 1984, master 1988), AMA (affiliate), Clarion County Dental Soc. (pres. 1983-87), S.A.R., (pres. Capt. Samuel Brady chpt. 1970-71, 77-80), Soc. Mayflower Descs., Pilgrim Edward Doty Soc., Fedn. Dentaire Internationale, Pa. Soc., Western Pa. Conservancy, Cook Forest Ctr. for Arts, Clarion County Hist. Soc., Phi Beta Phi, Omicron Kappa Upsilon, Delta Sigma Delta, Theta Chi. Presbyn. (pres. bd. trustees 1966-67, supt. Sunday sch. 1966-67, chmn. endowment trust fund dirs. 1980-84). Mason (Shriner). Home: 147 S 7th Ave Clarion PA 16214-2006 Office: 832 E Main St Clarion PA 16214-1168

FOREMAN, THOMAS ELTON, drama critic; b. Forsythe, Mont., May 13, 1918; s. Thomas Benjamin and Dora Mabel (Regester) F.; m. June Elizabeth McNeil, Apr. 2, 1949; children: Steven Thomas (dec.), Rebecca June, Kimberly Annette. AB, Fresno State U., 1946; MA, Calif. State U., Fresno, 1957. Tchr., dir. pub. rels. Coll. Sequoias, Visalia, Calif., 1953-57; staff writer, drama critic, columnist Press-Enterprise, Riverside, Calif., 1957—, drama critic. With U.S. Army, 1941-45. Mem. Am. Theater Critics, L.A. Drama Critics Circle. Democrat. Avocations: acting, distance running, writing childrens' books. Home: 4773 Newbury Ct Riverside CA 92507-5817 Office: Press-Enterprise PO Box 792 Riverside CA 92502-0792

FORER, ARTHUR H., biology educator, researcher, editor; b. Trenton, N.J., Dec. 17, 1935; immigrated to Can., 1972; s. Bernard and Rose Ethel Forer; m. Alexandra Engberg Westengaard, Dec. 18, 1964; children—Michael, David. B.Sc., MIT, Cambridge, 1957; postgrad., U. Rochester, 1957-59, U. Wash.-Friday Harbor, summer 1959; Ph.D. in Molecular Biology, Dartmouth Med. Sch., 1964. Postdoctoral fellow Am. Cancer Soc. Carlsberg Labs., Copenhagen, Denmark, 1964-66; research asst. Cambridge U., Eng., 1966-67, Helen Hay Whitney Found. fellow, 1967-69; Helen Hay Whitney Found. fellow Duke U., Durham, N.C., 1969-70; lektor Odense U., Denmark, 1970-72; assoc. prof. biology York U., Toronto, Ont., Can., 1972-75, prof. biology, 1975—; mem. grant selection panel Natural Scis. and Engring. Research Council, 1976-78. Editor: Mitosis/Cytokinesis, 1981; mem. editorial bd. Jour. Cell Sci., 1972-84, Can. Jour. Biochemistry and Cell Biology, 1982-93, Cell Biology Internat. Reports, 1984—; contbr. articles to profl. jours. Active Amnesty Internat., Ottawa, Ont., 1980—, Cmty. Theatre Orchs., Toronto, A Pack-O-Lips Now Saxophone Quartet, Toronto. Fellow Royal Soc. Can., Acad. Scis.; mem. AAAS, Am. Soc. Cell Biology, Microscopical Soc. Can., Stankel Ben Soc. (charter mem. 1960—), Tarragon Theatre, Shaw Festival (supporting). Avocations: music; gardening; cycling; hiking. Home: 17 Michigan Dr, Willowdale, ON Canada M2M 3H9 Office: York U Biology Dept, 4700 Keele St, Downsview, ON Canada M3J 1P3

FOREST, BOB, author, poet; b. Hawkesbury, Ont., Can., Apr. 11, 1943; s. Joseph Gerard and Anita (Babin) F.; . Chongchit Vacharothayangkura, Sept. 12, 1969; children: Paul Richard, John David. Student, Corning Cmty. Coll. Presdl. asst. Internat. Stock Food Corp., Waverly, N.Y., 1970-84; author, poet Waverly, 1990—. With USN, 1962-65. Mem. Am. Acad. of Poetry. Avocations: scriptural studies, ancient history buff, chess, literature. Home: 35 Lincoln St Waverly NY 14892-1118

FOREST, EVA BROWN, songwriter, producer; b. Ontario, Va., July 7, 1941; d. William Butler and Ruth Pauline (Simpson) Brown; m. Willie J. Forest Jr., Sept. 16, 1961; children: Geraid, Darryl, Angela. AA, Bismarck (N.D.) State Coll., 1981; BSN, U. Mary, Bismarck, 1984. RN, Colo. Charge nurse St. Alexius Med. Ctr., Bismarck, 1984-85, Cedars Health Care Ctr., Lakewood, Colo., 1989-90; staff devel. coord. Park Avenue Bapt. Home, Denver, 1990-91; supr., charge nurse Cedars Health Care Ctr., Lakewood, Colo., 1991—; charge nurse Villa Manor Health Ctr., Lakewood, Colo., 1991-93; charge nurse Stovall Care Ctr., Denver, 1995-96, supr., 1997-98. Songwriter, prodr., 1999; recorded (CD) God Has Begun a Good Work in Me, 1999. Vol. for cultural exch. lang., culture and fashions YWCA, Kano, Nigeria; vocalist gospel music workshop, N.D.; pianist adult and children's choir, N.D.; mem. MADD, Habitat for Humanity Internat., HALT, Vols. of Am. Mem. Nat. Multiple Sclerosis Soc., Internat. Platform Assn., DAV Commdrs. Club.

FOREST, HERMAN SILVA, biology educator; b. Chattanooga, Feb. 18, 1921; s. William Hirsh and Frances (Schutzer) Silva; m. Grace Marie Wyman, Apr. 5, 1963; children: Samuel, Benjamin. B.A., U. Tenn., 1942; M.S., Mich. State U., 1948, Ph.D. with honors, 1951. Instr. biology Coll. William and Mary, Williamsburg, Va., 1953-54; instr. botany U. Tenn., Knoxville, 1954-55; asst. prof. U. Okla., Norman, 1955-58; research assoc. U. Tenn. Research Ctr., Knoxville, 1958-60; research asst. U. Okla. Med. Ctr., Oklahoma City, 1960-61; research assoc. U. Rochester, N.Y., 1961-65; mem. faculty SUNY, Geneseo, 1965-92, prof. biology, 1965-92; SUNY exchange prof. U. Moscow, 1979; vis. scholar SUNY, 1974-92; sr. scientist PAI Environ. Cons., 1995—; prin. scientist Environ. Resource Ctr., Geneseo, 1968-80, dir., 1986; advisor N.Y. State Depts. Health and Environ. Conservation, 1965-74, Fedn. N.Y. Lake Assns., 1983-89, Monroe County Parks, 1984-86, Rochester City Water Supply Lakes, 1985-87; nat. lectr. Am. Inst. for Biol. Scis., 1970; mem. Monroe County Environ. Mgmt. Coun., 1971-74; assoc. herbarium Tenn. Tech. U., 1996—; cons. in field. Author: Handbook of Algae, 1954, The Limnology of Conesus Lake, in Lakes of New York State, 1978; chief editor Studies of Pollution Control in a Lake Front Community, 1982; co-author: Natural Survival and Reproduction of American Chestnut Trees, 1988; co-editor: Geology of the Genesee Valley Region since H.L. Fairchild, 1983, American Chestnut, a bibliography, 1990; editor, contbr. Prehistory of Lake Baikal Limnological Inst., Siberia, 1991; production editor: Translation of Fish Culture in Rice Fields (V.A. Meien), Bibl. Rice Field Ecology and Fish Culture C.H. Fernando, 1993, Aquatic Angiosperms of the Genesee Valley Region, Western N.Y., 1996; contbr. to Ency. Brit. Yearbook, 1986, articles to profl. jours. With U.S. Army, 1944-46, 51-53. Fellow Scientists Inst. for Pub. Info. (Nat. lectr.), 1974; fellow Rochester Acad. Sci., 1981; Nat. Acad. Scis. Exchange scholar, 1964, 80. Mem. Am. Inst. Biol. Scis., Internat. Congress Ecology, Internat. Great Lakes Research Assn. (conf. chmn. 1979), Ecol. Soc. Am., Bot. Soc. Am., Phycol. Soc. Am., Am. Soc. Plant Taxonomists, So. Appalachian Bot. Soc., Lucy Braun Forest Soc. (dir. 1998—), Sierra Club (Tenn. state dir. 1997-99). Jewish. Email: hforest@usit.net. Home: 215 Cherry Ave Cookeville TN 38501-2500

FOREST, JAMES JARED-FRANZEN, educator, reseacher; b. Pocatello, Idaho; s. John J. Franzen and Jeri Lynn Mallard. BS, Georgetown U., 1993; MA, Stanford U., 1994; PhD, Boston Coll., 1998. Computer lab. mgr. Stanford (Calif.) U., 1993-94; rsch. assoc. B.C. Ctr. for Internat. Higher Edn., Boston, 1994-97; policy analyst Mass. Bd. Higher Edn., Boston, 1994-97; rsch. and tech. coord. Nat. Ctr. for Urban Partnerships, N.Y.C., 1996—; dir. strategic analysis Franklin Pierce Coll., Rindge, N.H., 1999—; cons. GEAR UP initiative, Dept. Edn., Washington, Ctr. for Rsch. and Pub. Policy, New Haven, Conn. Editor: University Teaching: International Perspectives, 1998; contbr. articles to profl. jours. Recipient Grad. Student award Boston Coll., 1996, Kinane Higher Edn. Excellence award, 1996, A. Robert DeHart Pres.'s award De Anza Coll., 1991. Mem. Am. Ednl. Rsch. Assn. (tech. facilitator 1997—), Assn. for the Study Higher Edn. (chair internat. com. 1998-99), Boston Coll. Grad. Edn. Assn. (pres. 1995-96). Avocations: music, website development. E-mail: JF@Higher-ed.org. Office: Franklin Pierce Coll Box 60 College Road Rindge NH 03461

FOREST, PHILIP EARLE, housing finance consultant; b. San Mateo, Calif., Dec. 4, 1931; s. Percy Egbert and Charlotte Elizabeth (Copeland) F.; m. Sally Annette Cauble, Apr. 30, 1988. BS, U. Md., 1972. Enlisted U.S. Army, 1950, advanced through grades to maj., 1964; various pos. FHA, HUD, Washington, 1966-77; spl. asst. to asst. sec. for housing HUD, Washington, 1977-78, spl. asst. to dep. asst. sec. for single family housing, 1978-83, spl. asst. to undersec., 1979, acting dep. asst. sec. for single family housing, 1980-81; housing and housing finance cons. Arlington, Va., 1983—. Author: Building the Single Family Loan Package, 1988, Collection Department Responsibilities and Operations, 1986, Processing the Loan, 1986, FHA/VA Servicing Handbook, 1990, Mortgage Loan Servicing, 1994. Pres. Columbia (Md.) Commuter Bus Corp., 1975-83. Mem. Mortgage Bankers Assn. Am. (assoc. single family and loan adminstrn. coms. 1983—), Nat. Assn. Rev. Appraisers and Mortgage Underwriters (sr., registered mortgage underwriter 1983-93), Appraisal Inst. (affiliate), Suburban Md. Bldg. Industry Assn. (fin. com. 1984—), Nat. Assn. Home Builders (standing com. housing fin. 1989-91, 93—, single family govtl. subcom., vice-chmn. 1990, chmn. 1991, single family subcom., vice-chmn. 1995, chmn. 1996, task force on crisis in fin. housing prodn., chmn. HUD subcom. 1990, task force on internat. bus. devel. 1991, internat. housing com. 1998—), Am. Alliance for Loan Mgmt. (incorporator, dir., exec. v.p. 1989—).

FORESTER, JOHN GORDON, JR., lawyer; b. Wilkesboro, N.C., Jan. 14, 1933; s. John Gordon and Mary Hope (Hendren) F.; m. Georgina Ramirez, June 26, 1957; children: John Gordon III, Robert Raoul, Georgina Yasué, Richard Alexander. B.S.; in Indsl. Relations, U. N.C., 1955; LL.B., George Washington U., 1962. Bar: D.C. 1962, Md. 1993. Internat. economist Dept. Commerce, 1958-62; confidential asst. to dep. asst. sec. commerce, 1962-63; law clk. to U.S. Dist. Judge L.P. Walsh, 1963-64; pvt. practice Washington, 1964-80; ptnr. Pohoryles & Greenstein, P.C., Washington, 1980-89, Greenstein Delorme & Luchs, P.C., Washington, 1989-95; pvt. practice, 1995—; mem. Jud. Conf. D.C. Cir., 1981, 82, 92, adv. com. Civil Justice Reform Act, U.S. Dist. Ct., 1991-93; pres. Lawyers Mut. Ins. Co. of D.C., 1990-92. Contbr. articles to profl. jour. Pres. Friendly Citizens Assn., 1963, Gonzaga Fathers Club, 1974-76; chmn. bd. dirs. Henson Valley Montessori Sch.; bd. dirs. Sursum Corda Neighborhood Center, 1975-77. Lt. comdr. USNR, 1955-58. Mem. ABA, D.C. Bar Assn. (sec. 1999), Md. bar Assn., Coun. for Ct. Excellence (chmn. ct. improvement com.), George Washington U. Law Alumni Assn. (pres. D.C. chpt. 1988-89), Counsellors (pres. 1984-85), Barrister Inn (pres. 1976-77), Order Golden Fleece, Kappa Alpha Order, Phi Delta Phi. Roman Catholic. Home: 10701 Laurel Leaf Pl Potomac MD 20854-1770 Office: 1742 N St NW Washington DC 20036-2907

FORESTER, KARL S., federal judge; b. 1940. BA, U. Ky., 1962, JD, 1966. With Eugene Goss Esp., 1966-68; mem. firm Goss & Forester, 1968-75, Forester, Forester, Buttermore & Turner, P.S.C., 1975-88; judge U.S. Dist. Ct. (ea. dist.) Ky., Lexington, 1988—. Mem. Ky. Bar Assn., Harlan County Bar Assn., Fayette County Bar Assn. Office: US Dist Ct PO Box 2165 Lexington KY 40595*

FORESTER, RUSSELL, artist; b. Salmon, Idaho, May 21, 1920; s. Alvin R. and Mary (Isley) F.; m. Marie-Christine Meynet, Feb. 2, 1968; 1 dau., Lynn; 1 stepson, William C. Attinger. Student, Inst. Design Chgo., 1950. Prin. Russell Forester Architect, Inc., 1948-76. One-man exhbn. La Jolla Mus. Contemporary Art and Everson Mus. Art, Syracuse, N.Y., Willard Gallery, N.Y., Galerie Maurer, Zurich, Switzerland, Track 16, L.A., 1997; group shows include, La Jolla Mus. Contemporary Art, Guggenheim Mus., N.Y.C., San Francisco Mus. Modern Art; represented in permanent collections, Guggenhmem Mus., Cedars-Sinai Med. Center, Los Angeles, McCrory Corp., N.Y.C., 1st Nat. Bank of Chgo. Fellow AIA (emeritus). *

FORESTI, ROY, JR., chemical engineer; b. Balt., Mar. 25, 1925; s. Roy Sr. and Katherine (Kirk) F.; m. Barbara Mills, June 27, 1953; children: Lois, Carl. BS in Chem. Engring., Johns Hopkins U., 1947; MS, Carnegie-Mellon U., 1948; PhD, Pa. State U., 1951. Registered profl. engr., Md. Research engr. U.S. Bur. Mines, Pitts., 1951-54; group leader Monsanto Chem. Co., Dayton, Ohio, 1954-59; sr. engr. U. Dayton Research Inst., 1959-61; assoc. prof. U. Conn., Storrs, 1961-63; head chem. engring. dept. Cath. U. of Am., Washington, 1963-80; staff engr. Vitro Corp., Silver Spring, Md., 1980-89; engring. cons. Silver Spring, 1989-99; adj. prof. Howard U., 1989, 93. Bd. dirs. Jr. Engring. Tech. Soc., 1971-75; chmn. Joint Bd. Sci. Edn., Washington, 1966-71. Served with U.S. Army, 1944-46. Fellow Am. Inst. Chem. Engrs.; mem. Am. Chem. Soc., Am. Soc. Heating Refrigeration Air Conditioning Engrs., Nat. Assn. Corrosion Engrs., Tau Beta Pi, Phi Lambda Upsilon, Sigma Xi. Avocations: gardening, hiking, wood and metalworking. Home: 301 Willington Dr Silver Spring MD 20904-2856

FORET, MICKEY PHILLIP, air transportation company executive; b. McComb, Miss., Oct. 23, 1945; s. Fadias Phillip and Christine (Brown) F.; m. Mary Ann Tramonte, Aug. 12, 1966; 1 child, Keri. BS in Fin., La. State U., 1971, MBA in Fin., 1971. Dir. credit/interim dir. internal audit Tex. (Houston) Internat. Airlines, 1975-77, dir. cash mgmt., 1977-78, asst. treas., 1978-81, v.p. fin. svcs., 1981-82; v.p., treas. Continental Airlines, L.A., 1982-84, v.p., chief fin. officer, 1984-86, also bd. dirs.; sr. v.p. fin. and internat. Eastern Airlines, Miami, Fla., 1987-88, v.p., chief fin. officer, 1986—, also bd. dirs.; sr. v.p. Tex. (Houston) Air Corp., 1988—; exec. v.p. fin. and planning Continental Airlines, Houston, 1988-89, pres., 1989-90; exec. v.p., CFO Northwest Airlines, 1992-96; pres. Atlas Air, Inc., 1996-1997; spec. projects offcr. Northwest Airlines, 1998—, CFO, exec. v.p., 1998—; chmn. bd. dirs., chief exec. officer Chelsea Catering Co., Houston. Pres. Clear Wood Improvement Assn., Houston, 1975-78; coach Friendswood (Tex.) Girls Softball Team, 1981. Served with USAF, 1966-69, Vietnam. Mem. Phi Kappa Phi, Beta Gamma Sigma. Republican. Baptist. Avocations: boating, water skiing, biking. Home: 7001 Valley View Rd Edina MN 55439-1652

FORÊT, RANDY BLAISE, insurance executive; b. New Orleans, June 29, 1954; s. John Morris and Della Antoinnette Forêt; m. Tanya Lynn Mason, May 28, 1977; children: Tabitha, Blaise, Marshall, Joshua. BS, Liberty Coll., 1977; A in Claims, Ins. Inst. Am., 1991. English instr., football coach Liberty High Sch., Pensacola, Fla., 1979-84; editor Wise Publs., Denton, Tex., 1984-85; field claims rep. State Farm Ins. Co., Dallas, 1985-89; claims supt. State Farm Ins. Co., Abilene, Tex., 1989-96; mgr. claims ctrl. ops. State Farm Ins. Co., Dallas, 1997-99; mgr. property & casualty ops. Cornerstone Tng. Devel. Svcs., Dallas, 1999—; lic./ordained cons. Liberty Fellowship, Pensacola, 1977-85. Pres. Denton TTA, 1984; precinct chmn. Rep. Party, Ft. Worth, 1984, mem. exec. com., 1994-96, chmn. permanent orgn. com., 1996, chmn. leadership com., 1995-96; instr. Jr. Achievement; bd. dirs., dir. fgn. missions, pub. rels. Liberty Inst. of Biblical Studies. Mem. Abilene Claims Assn, Abilene C. of C. (leadership com.). Avocations: tennis, golf, hunting, reading, fishing. Office: Cornerstone Tng and Devel. Svcs Ste #203 16980 Dallas Parkway Dallas TX 75248

FORGAN, DAVID WALLER, retired career officer; b. Chgo., Sept. 28, 1933; s. Harold Nye and Ruth Ada (Waller) F.; m. Shirley Dobbins, Oct. 18, 1958; children—Bruce Dobbins, Todd Macmillan. B.S. in Mktg., U. Colo., 1955; M.S. in Mgmt., George Washington U., 1966. Commd. 2d lt. U.S. Air Force, 1956, advanced through grades to maj. gen., 1985, various positions worldwide, 1956-77; dir. programs hdgrs. tactical air command U.S. Air Force, Langley AFB, Va., 1977-79; dir. force devel. U.S. Air Force, Washington, 1979-80; dep. comdr. spl. ops. command U.S. Air Force, Fort Bragg, N.C., 1980-82; asst. chief staff ops. Allied Forces Central Europe, Brunssum, The Netherlands, 1982-85; dep. chief staff ops. U.S. Air Force Europe, Ramstein Air Base, Fed. Republic Germany, 1985-87; comdr. Sheppard Tech. Tng. Ctr. Sheppard AFB, Tex., 1987-89; ret., 1989. Decorated Silver Star, D.F.C. (3), Legion of Merit, Air medal, Def. Disting. Svc. medal, Def. Superior Svc. medal; Aero Cross of Merit (Spain). Mem. Delta Tau Delta. Republican. Avocations: military history, skiing, golf. Home: 4935 Newstead Pl Colorado Springs CO 80906-5978

FORGANG, DAVID M., museum curator; b. N.Y.C., Mar. 26, 1947; s. Joseph Hyman and Clarice (Ishbia) F.; m. Joyce Enid Blumenthal, June 15, 1968 (div. May 1979); children: Adam, Bradley. B in Anthropology, U. Ariz., 1968, M in Anthropology, 1971. Mus. curator So. Ariz. Group Nat. Pk. Svc., Phoenix, 1971-77; regional curator we. region Nat. Pk. Svc., San Francisco, 1977-82; curator Yosemite (Calif.) Mus. Nat. Pk. Svc., 1982—; pres. Yosemite Renaissance Art Competition, 1983-94; dir. Yosemite Artist in Residence Program, 1985—. Mariposa County advisor El Portal (Calif.) Town Planning Adv. Bd., 1984-94. Recipient Unit Award citation US Dept. Interior, 1974. Democrat. Jewish. Avocations: fishing, canoeing, hunting, gardening. Office: Nat Pk Svc PO Box 577 Yosemite National Park CA 95389*

FORGER, ROBERT DURKIN, retired professional association administrator; b. Norwalk, Conn., May 24, 1928; s. Alois John and Elsie Marie (Durkin) F.; m. Eleanor Marie Goddard, May 14, 1951; children: Gary Robert, Jeffrey Alois. B.S., Norwich U., Northfield, Vt., 1949; grad., U.S. Army Command and Gen. Staff Coll., 1970. Research and devel. engr., mgr. tech. publicity Dorr-Oliver Inc., Stamford, Conn., 1949-59; conf. mgr., pub., exec. dir. Soc. Plastics Engrs., Brookfield, Conn., 1959-93; ret., 1993. Chmn. Westport (Conn.) Pub. Housing Authority, 1959-64; treas. Plastics Edn. Found., 1971-75; bd. dirs. Norwich U. Alumni Assn., 1981-86, pres., 1984-86; trustee Norwich U., 1987-92, Nat. Plastics Mus., 1983-93; mem. plastics engring. curriculum adv. com. U. Mass., Lowell, 1974-93. Lt. col. USAR. Named Conn. Assn. Exec. of Yr., 1983, elected to Plastics Hall of Fame, 1996. Mem. AIChE, Soc. Plastics Engrs. (disting. mem. 1984, pres.'s cup, 1992), Am. Soc. Assn. Execs. (life), Coun. Engring. and Sci. Soc. Execs. (bd. dirs. 1983-85, sec. 1985-86, v.p. 1986-87, pres. 1987-88), Plastics Pioneers Assn. Home: 42 DeForest Rd Wilton CT 06897-1909

FORGEY, BENJAMIN FRANKLIN, architecture and art critic; b. Ashland, Ky., July 31, 1938; s. Chauncey Eaton F. and Joyce Evangeline (Shafer) Heinzen; m. Julie A. Savage, Sept. 1963 (div. 1967); 1 son, Benjamin Eric; m. 2d Gabriella A. von Joeden, Aug. 14, 1967; children: Elisa Gabriella, Martina Jane. B.A., Princeton U., 1960. Reporter, editor, art critic Washington Star, 1964-81; architecture critic Washington Post, 1981—. Served with USAR, 1961-67. Fulbright fellow, Japan, 1985-86. Home: 2856 28th St NW Washington DC 20008-4110 Office: Washington Post 1150 15th St NW Washington DC 20071-0002

FORGUE, KERRY JO, artist, educator; b. McMinnville, Oreg., Sept. 10, 1963; d. Tyrone Yoshikazu and Sandra Joan (Gilbert) Kuhns; m. David Mumm Forgue, Dec. 31, 1987; 1 child, Shawnie Jo. Student, Linfield Coll., McMinnville, 1981-82, Chemeketa C.C., Salem, Oreg., 1982-83; BS in Art, Western Oreg. State Coll., Monmouth, 1995. Artist/painter Phoenix, 1985-92, Salem, Oreg., 1993-94; artist, instr. Bush Barn Art Ctr., Salem, 1994-96; pvt. art instr. Salem, 1994—; floor mgr. Art Media, Salem, 1998—; co-owner Forgue's Painting, Phoenix, 1985-92, Salem, 1993—; art demonstrator/instr. Salem Art Assn. Art Fair and Festival, 1994-96. One person shows include Presidents Gallery, Western Oreg. State Coll., Monmouth, 1994, Concourse Gallery, Werner Coll. Ctr., Western Oreg. State Coll., 1994, 95, Majestic Theater, Corvallis, Oreg., 1996, Timberhill Athletic Club, Corvallis, 1996, Illahe Hills Country Club, Salem, Oreg., 1996-97, Corinne Woodman Gallery, Corvallis Art Ctr., 1998; exhibited in group shows at Bush Barn Art Ctr., Salem, 1997, Oreg. Soc. Artist Gallery, Portland, 1997, Celebration of the Arts, Portland, 1995, 97, New Orleans XVIII Nat. Exhbn. at the World Trade Ctr., Elsinore Ctr.for the Arts Gallery, Salem, 1997, 7th Ann. Colored Pencil Soc. Am. Exhbn., Portland, 1998, 8th Ann. Colored Pencil Soc. Am. Exhbn., Portland, 1999. Recipient numerous awards for art, including New Orleans World Trade Ctr. and Art Experience '96 award for excellence in drawing; named Artist of Month Mid-Valley Arts Coun., 1997. Mem. Nat. Colored Pencil Soc. Am., Colored Pencil Soc. Am. (dist. chpt. 210), Salem Art Assn., Corvallis Fine Arts Guild, Arts in Oreg. Coun., Mid-Valley Arts Coun., Oreg. Coast Coun. for the Arts. Baptist. Avocations: art and art events, photography, working with children, music, psychology. Home: 1113 Martin Ct S Salem OR 97306 Office: Art Media Commercial SE Salem OR 97306

FORGUE, STANLEY VINCENT, physics educator; b. Cleve., Oct. 6, 1916; s. John Napoleon and Mary Elizabeth (Smith) F.; m. Dorothy Jeanne Huber, Feb. 14, 1942; children, Mary Jeanne Forgue Metz, Stanley T., Wesley V. BS in Physics, Ohio State U., 1939, BEE, 1940, MS in Physics and Elec. Engring., 1940. Registered profl. engr., Ohio. Grad. asst. in physics Ohio State U., Columbus, 1939-40; asst. engr. Ohio Experiment Sta., Columbus, 1940-41; rsch. fellow Ohio State U., 1941-42; rsch. engr., sr. mem. tech. staff RCA Labs., Princeton, N.J., 1942-52, rsch. group head, 1952-72, ret.; engring. cons. Gen. Electrodynamics, others, Tex., 1972-76; assoc. prof., prof. physics Cen. Fla. Coll., Ocala, 1976—. Contbr. articles to jours. and author gov. reports; patentee in electronics field. Recipient Disting. Alumnus award Ohio State U., 1970, 5 rsch. awards RCA. Fellow IEEE; mem. Am. Phys. Soc., N.Y. Acad. Sci. (life), Sigma Xi., Tau. Beta Pi. Eta Kappa Nu (Disting. mem. Ariz. 1970), Pi Mu Epsilon, Sigma Pi Sigma (past pres. Ohio state chpt.). Avocations: teaching astronomy, travel, boating, camping. Home: Apt FF 304 431 Maple Tree Dr Altoona FL 32702-9047 Office: Cen Fla Coll PO Box 1388 Ocala FL 34478-1388

FORKER, OLAN DEAN, agricultural economics educator; b. Kendallville, Ind., Aug. 18, 1928; s. Fred Forrest and Mary May (Butler) F.; m. Kathleen Rose Buuck, Apr. 21, 1951; children: Michael, Brent, Susan. BS, Purdue U., 1950; MS, Mich. State U., 1958; PhD, U. Calif., Berkeley, 1962. Fieldman Halderman Farm Mgmt. Service, Wabash, Ind., 1954-58; extension economist U. Calif. at Berkeley, 1961-65; assoc. prof. Cornell U., Ithaca, N.Y., 1965-70; prof. Cornell U., 1971-95, prof. emeritus, 1995—; chmn. dept. agrl. econs., 1976-85; fellow U. Manchester, 1981-82; dir. Universal Foods Corp., Inc., Milw., 1974-96; cons. AID, Turkey, 1970-71, Ford Found., 1978, Nat. Dairy Promotion and Rsch. Bd., 1984-88; Naumes Family vis. prof. Santa Clara U., 1985-86; adj. prof. U. Fla., 1988-89; dir. Tompkins Co. Nutrition for Elderly, Inc. Author: (with Ron Ward) Commodity Advertising: The Economics and Measurement of Generic Programs, 1993; contbr. articles to profl. jours. Officer, council mem. Trinity Luth. Ch., Ithaca, 1967-69, 72—; trustee Cornell U., 1984-88. Lt. col., ret., U.S. Army. Recipient award for profl. excellence for quality of discovery in pub. research Am. Agrl. Econs. Assn., 1975. Mem. Am. Agrl. Econs. Assn., Am. Agrl. Econs. Found. (pres. 1988-89), N.E. Agrl. and Resource Econs. Assn. (life, pres. 1991-92, Jour. award 1991, Disting. Mem. award 1994). Home: 13 Stormy View Rd Ithaca NY 14850-9774 Office: Cornell U 312 Warren Hall Ithaca NY 14853-7801

FORLEY, BRYAN G., plastic surgeon; b. N.Y.C., Apr. 15, 1957; s. Erwin and Ruth Forley. AB, Brown U., 1979; MD, Mt. Sinai Sch. Medicine, 1984. Diplomate Am. Bd. Plastic Surgery. Pvt. practice N.Y.C., 1994—. Contbr. chpts. to books and articles to profl. jours. Recipient Investigator Category First Prize award Plastic Surgery Ednl. Found., 1988; Biomed. Rsch. Support grantee NIH, 1987; N.Y. State Regents scholar, 1975, Nat. Merit scholar, 1975. Fellow ACS (assoc.), Am. Soc. for Laser Medicine and Surgery, Royal Soc. Medicine; mem. Am. Soc. Plastic and Reconstructive Surgeons, Alpha Omega Alpha. Avocations: travel, art and antique collecting, tennis, skiing. E-mail: bgf57@asprsdial.org. Office: 5 E 82nd St New York NY 10028

FORLINI, FRANK JOHN, JR., cardiologist; b. Newark, Mar. 30, 1941; s. Frank Sr. and Rose Theresa (Parussini) F.; m. Joanne Marie Horch, July 19, 1969; children: Anne Marie, Victoria, Frank III, Anthony. BS in Biology, Villanova (Pa.) U., 1963; MD, George Washington U., 1967. Diplomate Am. Bd. Internal Medicine, Am. Bd. Cardiovascular Disease. V.p., bus. agt. Cooks, Countermen and Cafeteria Workers Union Local 399 AFL, 1960-61; intern Bklyn.-Cumberland Med. Ctr., N.Y., 1967-68, resident in internal medicine, 1968-70; fellow in cardiology Inst. Med. Sci. Pacific Med. Ctr., San Francisco, 1970-72; practice medicine specializing in cardiology Rock Island, Ill., 1974—; sr. ptnr. Forlini Med. Speciality Clinic, Rock Island, 1974—; owner Forlini Farm and Forlini Devel. Enterprises; assoc. prof. pharmacy L.I. U., Bklyn., 1969-70; pres., CEO U.S. Oil & Transp. Co., Inc., 1966-89; pres. Profl. and Execs. Ins. Assocs., 1973-89, Profls. Assocs., 1973-89; med. and exec. dir. Cardiovasc. Inst. Northwestern Ill., 1984—; exec. dir., owner Franksoft Pub., 1988—; Shelter for Abused Women and Children, Rock Island, 1992-94, pres., chmn., 1994, chmn. capital campaign com., 1994; bd. dirs. Rescue Missions and Christian Family Care Ctr., 1992-94, pres., 1994. Contbr. articles to profl jours. Chmn. D.C. Coll. Young Reps., 1965-66; mem. exec. com. Rep. Cen. Com., Washington, 1965-66; mem. nat. com. Coll. Young Reps., 1965-66; mem. exec. com. Young Rep. State Cen. Com., Washington, 1965-66; mem. Physicians for Reagan-Bush, 1980, 84; vice chmn. Rock Island Reps., 1985-90, precinct committeeman, 1985-90, 92-93; dep. registrar County of Rock Island, 1985—; trustee South Rock Island Twp., Rock Island County, 1987-97; truste Twp. Intergovtl. Agy., 1993-97, Friends of Twp. Govt. of Rock Island County, chmn., 1995—; alderman City of Rock Island, Rock Island County, 1997—; mem. Rock Island Comml. Indsl. Revolving Loan Fund, 1998—; mem. exec. com. Rock Island County Rep. Cen. Com., 1992-94; del. Ill. State Rep. Conv., 1992; pres. parish coun. Roman Cath. Ch. Maj. USAF, 1972-74. Nat. Inst. Heart Disease NIH-USPHS grantee, 1964-66, 70-72; Fellowship of Cath. Scholars, 1994—. Fellow Am. Coll. Cardiology, N.Am. Soc. Pacing and Electrophysiology; mem. AMA, Ill. State Med. Soc., Rock Island County Med. Soc. (chmn. com. on ins. 1990—), Western Ill. Ind. Physicians Assn. (bd. dirs. 1995—, mem. exec. com. 1996—, sec. 1996-97, treas. 1997—), Rock Island County Twp. Assn. (v.p. 1994, pres. 1994-95, mem. exec. com. 1994-97), Soc. Cath. Social Scientists, Univ. Faculty for Life, KC (3d deg. 1994—). Office: 2508 25th St Ste B Rock Island IL 61201-5419

FORLITI, AMY MARIE, reporter; b. St. Paul, Feb. 2, 1973; d. Richard M. and Kathleen M. (Lethert) F. BA summa cum laude, U. St. Thomas, St. Paul, 1995. Pub. rels. intern Evans Larson Comm., Mpls., 1994-96; news prodr. Sta. WEAU-TV, Eau Claire, Wis., 1996-97; reporter Chippewa Herald, Chippewa Falls, Wis., 1997-98, ABC newspapers, Anoka, Minn., 1998; copy editor Star Tribune, Mpls., 1998; reporter AP, Indpls., 1999—; freelance writer, 1998—. Mem. Soc. Profl. Journalists. Avocations: running, reading. Office: AP 251 N Illinois St Ste 1600 Indianapolis IN 46204-1943

FORMAN, BETH ROSALYNE, specialty food trade executive; b. N.Y.C., Oct. 15, 1949; d. Philip and Dorothy Lea (Vilensky) F. BA in English with honors, NYU, 1971; MA with honors, Columbia U., 1972; MBA in Fin., Rutgers U., 1980. Asst. to contr. Colin Hochstin Co., N.Y.C., 1971-78; instr. Columbia U., N.Y.C., 1974-76; adj. faculty Bergen Community Coll., Paramus, N.J., 1985-87; communications cons. B.R. Forman & Co., Paramus, 1981-87; proposal mgr. Ogden Svcs.Corp., N.Y.C., 1988-89; dir. tech. svcs. Ogden Entertainment Svcs., Rosemont, Ill., 1990-92; dir. mktg. comms. Ogden Entertainment Svcs., N.Y.C., 1993-96; dir. mktg. Euro-Am. Brands, LLC, Paramus, N.J., 1999—. Bd. dirs. new leadership div. United Jewish Community Bergen County, River Edge, N.J., 1981-87, chmn. fundraiser, 1983, chmn. edn. com., 1983-86, treas., 1984-86; mem. steering com. Viewpoints div. Am. Jewish Com., 1991-93. Pres.'s fellow Columbia U., 1973; recipient Masters award Ogden Svcs. Corp., 1994. Mem. NAFE, Women in Comm. (v.p. spl. programs 1992-93 Chgo. chpt., mem. career devel. com. 1994-95, mem. pub. rels. com. and Matrix awards fundraising com. 1995-96), Columbia U. Club of N.Y., Mensa. Democrat. Avocation: acting. Home: 421 Yuhas Dr Paramus NJ 07652-4125 Office: Euro-Am Brands LLC 15 Prospect St Paramus NJ 07652

FORMAN, CHARLES WILLIAM, religious studies educator; b. Gwalior, India, Dec. 2, 1916; s. Henry and Sallie (Taylor) F.; m. Helen Janice Mitchell, Mar. 12, 1944; children—David, Sarah, Harriet. B.A., M.A., Ohio State U., 1938; Ph.D., U. Wis., 1941; B.D., Union Theol. Sem., N.Y.C., 1944, S.T.M., 1947. Ordained to ministry Presbyn. Ch., 1944. Prof. North India United Theol. Coll., Saharanpur, 1945-50; sec. program emphasis Nat. Council Chs., 1951-53; mem. faculty Div. Sch., Yale U., New Haven, 1953—, D. Willis James prof. missions, 1961-87, D. Willis James prof. missions emeritus, 1987—; chmn. theol. edn. fund World Coun. chs., 1965-70, mem., 1970-77; mem. commn. ecumenical mission United Presbyn. Ch., 1962-71, chmn., 1965-71; chmn. Found. for Theol. Edn. in SE Asia, 1970-89, mem. 1966-69, 90—. Author: A Faith for the Nations, 1958, The Nation and the Kingdom, 1964, Christianity in the Non-Western World, 1967, The Island Churches of the South Pacific, 1982, The Voice of Many Waters, 1986. Mem. bd. edn., Bethany, Conn., 1957-66; bd. dirs. Community Action Agy., New Haven, 1978-81, Overseas Ministries Study Center, New Haven, 1979—. Home: 200 Leeder Hill Dr Hamden CT 06517-2758

FORMAN, DONALD T., biochemist; b. N.Y.C., Feb. 27, 1932; s. Jack and Fannie (Jaffee) F.; m. Florence Sporn, Aug. 22, 1953; children: Joan Diane, Steven Lawrence, Debra Helene. B.S., Bklyn. Coll., 1953; M.S., Wayne State U., 1957, Ph.D., 1959. Clin. biochemist Mercy Hosp. Med. Center, Chgo., 1959-63; dir. clin. biochemistry, asso. prof. biochemistry and pathology Evanston Hosp./Northwestern U. Med. Sch., Chgo., 1963-78; research prof. U. Stockholm and Royal Postgrad. Med. Sch., London, 1975; prof. pathology and biochemistry U. N.C., Chapel Hill, 1978—; dir. clin. chemistry U. N.C., 1978—; cons. clin. chemist, industry and govt., 1965—. Editor: Clinical Chemistry, 1976. Served with AUS, 1953-55. Recipient Chgo. Clin. Chemists award, 1974, Sunderman award as clin. scientist for 1986; Mich. Heart Assn. fellow, 1957-59. Mem. AAAS, AAUP, Assn. Clin. Scientists (pres. 1973-74), Am. Assn. Clin. Chemistry (dir., award for outstanding contbn. to animal clin. chemistry 1995), Sigma Xi, Phi Lambda Upsilon. Jewish. Achievements include research on enzymology, inborn errors of metabolism, tumor-associated markers, atherosclerosis, human alcohol metabolism, and clinical biochemistry. Home: 2559 Owens Ct Chapel Hill NC 27514-1737 Office: U NC Med Sch Dept Pathology Chapel Hill NC 27514

FORMAN, HARRIET, nursing publication executive; b. Bklyn., Dec. 13, 1936; d. Herman Schulman. Diploma, The Mount Sinai Hosp. Sch., of Nursing; BS in Nursing cum laude, Adelphi U.; M of Health Care Adminstrn., L.I. U.; EdD, Tchr.'s Coll. Columbia U. RN, N.Y., Fla. Adminstrv. nursing supr. to asst. dir. nursing The Jewish Inst. for Geriatric Care, 1971-73, assoc. dir. nursing, 1973-76; dir. nursing svcs. Kingsbrook Jewish Med. Ctr., 1976-78, asst. adminstr., 1977-78; dir. of nursing to exec. dir. nursing Hempstead Gen. Hosp. Med. Ctr., 1978-81, assoc. adminstr., 1981-88; adminstr. Met. Jewish Geriatric Ctr., 1988-89; exec. dir. Greater N.Y./N.J. met. edit. The Nursing Spectrum, 1989-92, corp. editorial dir., 1992-93; exec. editor, start-up mng. editor HT-The Mag. for Health Care Travel Profls., 1993—; exec. dir. Fla. divsn. Nursing Spectrum, Ft. Lauderdale, 1994—; cons. in mgmt. and edn.; adv. com. nursing edn., nursing edn. and nursing adminstrn. com.; expert witness in managerial comm. and nursing adminstrn. Editor Courier, Nursing Edn. Alumni Assn. newsletter, Columbia U.; contbr. articles to profl. jours. Mem. ANA, Fla. State Nurses Assn., Am. Orgn. Nurse Execs., South Fla. and Tampa Orgn. Nurse Execs., South Fla. Sigma Theta Tau. Home: 520 N Ocean Blvd Apt 20 Pompano Beach FL 33062-4621

FORMAN, HOWARD IRVING, lawyer, former government official; b. Phila., Jan. 12, 1917; s. Jacob and Dora (Moses) F.; m. Ada Pressman, Aug. 2, 1938; children: Kenneth J., Harvey R. *Sons Kenneth and Harvey are internists and cardiololgists. Son, Kenneth, BA (1964) University of Pennsylvania, MD (1969) George Washington University, married Barbara J. Rifkind, BS (1964) University of Pennsylvania, PhD (1969) Georgetown University, who is a physical organic chemist and president of Art Goes to School of Delaware Valley. Their daughter, Stacy J., BA (1998) Temple University. Son, Harvey, BS (1968) Ursinus College, MD (1973) Temple University, married Arlene I. Pekter, BS (1972) Temple University who taught elementary education in Lower Moreland, Pa. schools. Their son, David J., attends West Chester University, and daughter, Julie M., is a middle school student at Lower Moreland, Pa.* BS in Chemistry, St. Joseph's Coll., 1937; LLB, Temple U., 1944; MA, U. Pa., 1949, PhD, 1955. Bar: D.C. 1945, Pa. 1973. Research chemist Frankford Arsenal, Dept. Army, Phila., 1940-44; patent atty. Frankford Arsenal, Dept. Army, 1944-46, chief patents br., 1946-56; asst. dir. Pitman-Dunn Rsch. Labs., 1955-56; lectr. polit. sci. Temple U., 1956-63; from patent atty. to trademark and internat. corp. counsel Rohm and Haas Co., Phila., 1956-76; dep. asst. sec. U.S. Dept. Commerce, Washington, 1976-81; also dir. Office of Product Standards Policy; chmn. interagy. com. on standards policy Weiser, Stapler & Spivak, Phila., 1974-76; head. U.S. dels. to UN internat. confs., Geneva, 1976-81; sec., dir. Rohm & Haas Asia, Inc., 1973-76; v.p., gen. counsel, dir. Brilliant Internat., Inc., Bala-Cynwyd, Pa., 1974-83; sec., dir. Far East Chem. Services, Inc., Wilmington, Del., 1973-76; Rohm and Haas Far East Chem. Services, Inc., GmbH, Zug, Switzerland, 1975-76; dir. U.S. Pharm. Corp., 1975-83; pvt. practice Phila., 1981—; advisor to asst. sec. for econ. affairs relative to internat. intellectual property matters Dept. State, 1968-72; orginator Internat. Lab. Accreditation world-wide biennial confs. (ILAC), 1977—; chmn. accredited stds. com., Z21, on performance and installation gas burning appliances and accessories, 1981-97. Author: Inventions, Patents and Related Matters, 1957, Patents-Their Ownership and Administration by the U.S. Government, 1957; Editor: Patents, Research and Management, 1961, The Law of Chemical, Metallurgical and Pharmaceutical Patents, 1967; author plays: The Birth of the American Patent System, 1976, The Birth of the American Patent and Copyright Systems , 1990.; contbr. to publs. in field. Bd. dirs. Lower Moreland Twp. Sch. Bd., Montgomery County, Pa., 1969-75; bd. dirs. Eastern Montgomery County Vocat.-Tech. Sch., 1969-75, sec., 1970-75; bd. dirs. Warminster (Pa.) Gen. Hosp., 1983-91; emeritus dir. Allegheny United Hosps., Inc., 1991-94; life trustee Med. Coll. Pa. and Hahnemann U. Hosps., 1994—. Recipient Robert J. Painter Meml. award Stds. Engring. Soc.-ASTM, 1978, Leo B. Moore award Stds. Engring. Soc., 1981. Fellow Am. Inst. Chemists; mem. ABA, FBA, AAAS, ASTM (hon. life, bd. dirs. 1985-87), Internat. Assn. Protection Indsl. Property, Am. Nat. Stds. Inst. (bd. dirs. 1977-80, Finegan Stds. medal 1996, chmn. Z 21 Accredited Standards com. performance installation of gas burning appliances and related accessories, 1981-97), Nat. Coun. Patent Law Assn. (chmn. 1967-68), Am. Chem. Soc., Sci. Rsch. Soc. Am., Am. Assn. Lab. Accreditation (dir. 1983-91), Am. Patent Law Assn. (bd. mgrs. 1970-73), Am. Coll. Legal Medicine, Phila. Bar Assn. (sec. 1973-74, com. on jurimetrics, tech. and patents, v.p. 1975), Phila. Patent Law Assn. (pres. 1964-66), Licensing Execs. Soc., Stds. Engring. Soc. (Robert J. Painter Meml. award 1978, Leo B. Moore award 1981), Franklin Inst. (vice chmn. Futures Ctr. campaign), Nat. Lawyers Club, Gas Appliance Mfrs. Assn. (meritorious svc. award 1996), Am. Soc. Gas Engrs. (hon.), Sigma Xi. Principal draftsman, prime mover in devel. original OMB Circular A-119 which established nat. policy calling for primary dependence of Fed. Gov. on private sector standards orgns. for devel. of standards required for procurement and regulatory purposes by govt. agencies. Fax: (215) 947-5036. Home: 1033 Corn Crib Dr Huntingdon Valley PA 19006-3335 Office: Albidale-Windmill Circle PO Box 66 Huntingdon Valley PA 19006-0066 *My life has been a slow-but-sure progression in which patience, diligence and determination, mixed with a readiness to adapt myself to each new circumstance, have enabled me to overcome numerous obstacles and forge a useful career and a happy life as a husband, father and grandfather that have been personally gratifying and rewarding. My creed consists of truth, simplicity, candor, tolerance, genuine humility and faith in God and my fellow men and women.*

FORMAN, J(OSEPH) CHARLES, chemical engineer, consultant, writer; b. Chgo., Dec. 22, 1931; s. Joseph O. and Marie (Smith) F.; m. Ursula Diane Weston, July 22, 1953; children: Stephen Charles, Diane Brigitte, Mary Erika. S.B., M.I.T., 1953; M.S., Northwestern U., 1957, Ph.D., 1960. Registered profl. engr., Ill. Trainee chem. engring. Dow Chem. Co., Midland, Mich., 1953-54; from sr. chem. engr. to dir. mfg. ops. agrl. vet. div. Abbott Labs., North Chicago, Ill., 1956-77; assoc. exec. dir. Am. Inst. Chem. Engrs., N.Y.C., 1977-78; exec. dir., sec., pub. Am. Inst. Chem. Engrs. Jour., Internat. Chem. Engring., Biotech Progress, Plant/Ops. Progress, Energy Progress, Environ. Progress, 1978-87; pres. and prin. Forman Assocs. Cons. and Tech. Svcs., 1987—; cons. in field, accreditation insp. chem. engring. curricula; mem. ednl. council MIT, 1961-74, 78-95; mem. chem. engring. consultor coun. Manhattan Coll., N.Y.C., 1985—. Mem. ednl. coun. MIT, 1961-74, 78-95; mem. Lake Bluff (Ill.) Bd. Edn., 1967-73, pres., 1971-73; pres. Lake County (Ill.) Sch. Bd. Assn., 1969-71; mem. Lake Bluff Plan Commn., 1973-77, chmn., 1976-77; mem. Darien (Conn.) Pers. Adv. Commn., 1986-92, Darien Park and Recreation Commn., 1999—; dist. chmn. Boy Scouts Am., 1994-97. With USAF, 1954-56. Fellow Am. Inst. Chem. Engrs., AAAS; mem. Soc. Plastics Industry (profl. mem.), Am. Chem. Soc., Am. Soc. Assn. Execs., Coun. Engring. and Sci. Soc. Execs. (dir. 1980-83, sec. 1983-84, v.p. 1984-85, pres. 1985-86), Nat. Eagle Scout Assn., Sigma Xi, Tau Beta Pi, Phi Lambda Upsilon, Alpha Tau Omega. Patentee in field. Home and Office: 77 Stanton Rd Darien CT 06820-5128

FORMAN, LEONARD P., media company executive; b. N.Y.C., June 7, 1945; s. William and Jean (Feldman) F.; m. Barbara Rubin, June 2, 1968; children: Daniel, Matthew. BA, CUNY, 1967; PhD, NYU, 1975. Asst. prof. econs. Fordham U., N.Y.C., 1971-72; economist Fed. Res. Bank, N.Y.C., 1972-73; dir. planning N.Y. Times Corp., N.Y.C., 1974-86; sr. v.p. ops. Telemundo Group, Inc., N.Y.C., 1987-96; sr. vp. corp. devel. N.Y. Times Corp., N.Y.C., 1996-98; pres. and CEO N.Y. Times Mag. Group, 1998—; adj. asst. prof. Queens Coll. CUNY, 1972-75; assoc. prof. Pace U., 1975-77; lectr. Fordham U., 1977-80; adj. prof. Yale U., 1981; prin. researcher CEAR, N.Y.C., 1982—; chmn. telecommunications com. Am. Newspaper Pubs. Assn.; cons. Social Systems Inc., Chapel Hill, N.C., 1977-82. Editor Managerial and Decision Econs. jour., 1981-84; contbg. editor Managerial Planning jour.; contbr. articles to profl. jours. Named teaching fellow U. Mass., 1969-70; recipient research assistantship N.Y.U., 1972-73. Mem. Am. Econ. Assn., Managerial Econ. Assn., Econometric Soc., Nat. Assn. Bus. Economists, N.Am. Soc. Corp. Planning, Planning Execs. Inst., Ops. Research Soc., Inst. Mgmt. Sci., Omicron Delta Epsilon. Avocations: race car driving, reading, tennis. Home: Ridge Rd Glen Cove NY 11542 Office: NY Times Co 229 W 43rd St New York NY 10036-3959*

FORMAN, PAULA, advertising agency executive. Market rsch. trainee BBDO; sr. v.p., mgmt. supr. Wells, Rich, Greene; now exec. v.p., exec. mgmt. dir. Saatchi & Saatchi Advt. Worldwide, N.Y.C.

FORMAN, PETER, sheriff, former state legislator; b. Plymouth, Mass., Apr. 28, 1958; m. Dawn M. David; children: David, Chandler, Sarah. BA, Colby Coll., 1980. Mem. Mass. Ho. of Reps., Boston, 1981-94, asst. house whip, 1989-90, ho. Rep. leader, 1991-94; sheriff Plymouth County, Mass., 1995—. Home: 51 Warren Ave Plymouth MA 02360-2437 Office: Sheriff's Office Obery St Plymouth MA 02360

FORMAN, RICHARD T. T., ecology educator; b. Richmond, Va., Nov. 10, 1935; s. Henry Chandlee and Caroline (Lippincott) F.; m. Barbara J. Lee, 1963; children: Sabrina, Adrian, Brent. BS, Haverford Coll., 1957; postgrad., Duke U., 1959-60; PhD, U. Pa., 1961; MA (hon.), Harvard U., 1985; LHD (hon.), Miami U., 1987. Vol. Am. Friends Svc. Com., Guatemala and Honduras, 1961-63; asst. prof. U. Wis., 1963-66; mem. faculty Rutgers U., New Brunswick, N.J., 1966-84, prof. botany, 1976-84; dir. grad. program Rutgers U., 1979-83; prof. landscape ecology Harvard U., Cambridge, Mass., 1984—; dir. Hutcheson Meml. Forest Ctr., N.J., 1972-84; instr. Orgn. Tropical Studies, Costa Rica, 1970, W.I. Lab., St. Croix, 1973, Ft. Burgwin Research Ctr., N.Mex., 1976; fellow Clare Hall, U. Cambridge, Eng., 1985—; hon. prof. acad. Sinica, Shenyang, China, 1995. Author: Landscape Ecology, 1986, Land Mosaics, 1995, Landscape Ecology Principles for Landscape Architecture and Land-use Planning, 1996; editor: Pine Barrens: Ecosystem and Landscape, 1979, 2nd edit., 1998, Changing Landscapes: An Ecological Perspective, 1990; mem. editl. bd. Ecology and Ecol. Monographs, 1973-77, Biosci., 1978-84, Landscape Ecology, 1987—; contbr. articles to profl. jours. Recipient award for excellence in tchg. Lindback Found., 1984, medal U. Florence, Italy, 1997, Charles U., Prague, Czech Republic, 1998; Fulbright scholar, Bogota, Colombia, 1970-71; chercheur CNRS, Montpellier, France, 1977-78; Mieguny̆ah fellow U. Melbourne, 1999. Fellow AAAS; mem. Ecol. Soc. Am. (v.p. 1982-83), Torrey Bot. Club (pres. 1980-81, editorial bd. Bull. 1967-70), Nature Conservancy, Internat. Assn. Landscape Ecology (v.p. 1982-88, Disting. Landscape Ecologist award U.S. Sect., 1992). Office: Harvard U Grad Sch Design Cambridge MA 02138

FORMAN, ROBERT, painter; b. Jersey City; s. Edward and Deborah (Amel) F.; married. BFA, Cooper Union, 1975. Lectr. Newark Mus., 1995, William Paterson Coll., Wayne, N.J., 1996, R.I. Sch. Design, Providence, 1996, Bklyn. Mus., 1996, Radford (Va.) U., 1997, others. Exhibited in solo shows at Elaine Benson Gallery, Bridgehampton, N.Y., 1980, Stevens Inst., Hoboken, N.J., 1983, Bologna/Landi Gallery, East Hampton, N.Y., 1985, Anne Reid Gallery, Princeton, N.J., 1988, AMB Gallery, Hoboken, N.J., 1989, Schenectady Mus., 1995, Bergen Mus. Art, Paramus, N.J., 1997; exhibited in group shows at Walter Moos Gallery, Toronto, NAD, N.Y.C., Gallery Henock, N.Y.C., Noyes Mus., Oceanville, N.J., Zenith Gallery, Washington, Newark Mus., N.J. State Mus., Allan Stone Gallery, N.Y.C., 1980, 84, 87, The Renwick Gallery, Washington, 1998, others; represented in collections at Walter Moos Gallery, Broad Nat. Bank, Perth Amboy, N.J., Renwick Gallery/Nat. Mus. Am. Art, Washington. Nat. Endowment for Arts fellow, 1979, N.J./Hudson County Artist fellow, 1985, Fulbright fellow, 1992, Ludwig Vogelstein Found. fellow, 1994, N.J. Coun. Arts Artist fellow, 1998; Adolf and Esther Gottlieb Found. grantee, 1997. Mem. Fulbright Found. Alumni, Cooper Union Alumni Assn. Home: 412 Grand St Hoboken NJ 07030-2791

FORMAN-BELLO, JUDITH, clinical social worker; b. Boston, July 27, 1951; d. George William and Florence (Saberlinsky) Forman; m. Martin Glen Bello, Sept. 11, 1982. BA, Boston U., 1970; MSW, Boston Coll., 1972. Lic. ins. clin. social worker, Mass.; diplomate Am. Bd. Examiners in Clin. Social Work. Clin. social worker Cath. Charitable Bur., Boston, 1972-74; clin. social worker Boston City Hosp., 1974-94, tchr. sociology high sch. program, 1985-86, clin. social work supr., 1994—; pvt. practice, Boston, 1984—. Coord. Mass. Tenants' Union, 1988-89. Mem. NASW, Acad. Cert. Social Workers, Mass. Acad. Clin. Social Workers, Nat. Coun. Jewish Women, Jewish Women's College Club. Avocations: ballet, aerobics. Home: 89 Pleasant St Brookline MA 02446-3421 Office: Boston Med Ctr 732 Harrison Ave Boston MA 02118

FORMAN-MASON, MONICA N., speech and language pathologist; b. Boise, Idaho, Sept. 15, 1951; d. M. Neal and Eugenia T. (Mis) F. BS in Speech Pathology, Idaho State U., 1974, MS in Speech Pathology, 1976; student, Boise State Coll., 1969-72. lic. speech pathologist, Wash.; cert. clin. competence in speech pathology. Speech pathologist St. Boniface Hosp., Winnipeg, Man., Can., 1976-77, Soc. for Crippled Children and Adults, Winnipeg, 1977-78, Trade Winds Rehab. Ctr., Gary, Ind., 1978-79, West Cen. Ohio Hearing and Speech Ctr., Springfield, Ohio, 1979-80, St. Anthony Community Hosp., Pocatello, Idaho, 1980-82, Gresham (Oreg.) Community Hosp., 1982-83, Irwin Lehrhoff & Assocs., Seattle and Portland, Oreg., 1983-85, Good Shepherd Luth. Home, Cornelius, Oreg., 1988-91; medicare and rehab. specialist Gresham, 1991-92; medicare and rehab. specialist Puget Sound Therapy Svcs., Seattle and Tacoma, 1992-95, 96—, speech/lang. pathologist, 1996—; speech/lang. pathologist Speech & Rehab. Svcs., Edmonds, Wash., 1995-96; pvt. practice, Portland, 1990. Leader Oreg. Cath. Charismatic Renewal. Mem. Assn. Christian Therapists. Avocation: bowling.

FORMELLER, DANIEL RICHARD, lawyer; b. Chgo., Aug. 15, 1949; s. Vernon Richard and Shirley Mae (Gruber) F.; m. Ann M. Paa, Aug. 17, 1974; children: Matthew Daniel, Kathryn Ann, Christina Marie. BA with honors, U. Ill., 1970; JD cum laude, DePaul U., 1976. Bar: Ill. 1976, U.S. Dist. Ct. (no. and cen. dists.) Ill. 1976, U.S. Ct. Appeals (7th cir.) 1976, U.S. Ct. Appeals (D.C. cir.) 1995. Assoc. McKenna, Storer, Rowe, White & Farrug, Chgo., 1976-82, ptnr., 1982-86; ptnr. Tressler, Soderstrom, Maloney & Priess, Chgo., 1986—. Exec. editor DePaul U. Law Rev., 1975-76. With USN, 1970-72, Vietnam. Mem. ABA, Ill. Bar Assn., Ill. Assn. Def. Trial Counsel (pres. 1994-95), Chgo. Bar Assn., Assn. Def. Trial Attys. Office: Tressler Soderstrom et al 233 S Wacker Dr Chicago IL 60606-6306

FORMENTO, DANIEL, radio company executive, writer; b. Pitts., Aug. 11, 1954; s. Stephen P. and Betty Jean (McCorkle) F.; m. Alison Ashley, Oct. 7, 1995; children: Alexander Daniel, Natalie Annette. Grad. high sch., Mt. Lebanon, Pa. Program mgr. The Source/NBC Radio Network, N.Y.C., 1979-82; prin. Dan Formento Prodns., N.Y.C., 1982-84; pres. Radio Today Entertainment, N.Y.C., 1984—, West Hill Studios, N.J., 1993—; v.p., creative dir. ABC Radio Network, 1998. Author: Rock Chronicle, 1982; producer radio programs including Flashback, 1984 , Rock Stars, 1985—, Walter Cronkite's 20th Century, 1988, Pop Quiz, 1992—; radio comml. Grog Shop, 1976 (Aftra award 1976); announcer radio feature Today in Rock History, 1979—; TV comml. Short Cuts, 1989—; producer radio feature One Minute With, 1976 (Golden Quill award 1976), Pop Quiz, 1992— (Internat. Radio Festival of N.Y. grand award 1992). Democrat. Avocations: swimming, tennis, audio enthusiast. Office: Radio Today Entertainment 1776 Broadway New York NY 10019-2002

FORMO, BRENDA TERRELL, travel company executive; b. Greensboro, N.C., May 18, 1946; d. Walter C. Terrell and Eunice W. Kirkman; m. Robert A. Formo, Oct. 14, 1978; 1 child, Eric Victor. BSBA, East Carolina U., 1968; MA in Bus. Adminstrn., Webster U., 1977; postgrad., 1970, 72, 77, 84, 87; grad., Army War Coll., 1990. Commd. 2d lt. U.S. Army, 1969, advanced through grades to col., 1991, ret., 1993; acctg. instr. U.S. Army Fin. Sch., Ft. Harrison, Ind., 1969-71; women's officer recruiter U.S. Army Kansas City Recruiting Main Sta., 1971-73; recruiting ops. officer U.S. Army SW Recruiting Command, San Antonio, 1973-75; area comdr. U.S. Army San Antonio Dist. Recruiting Command, 1975-77; chief pay and examination divsn. U.S. Army Fin. and Acctg. Office, Yongsan, Korea, 1977-78; asst. chief acctg. U.S. Army Mil. Dist. Washington Fin. and Acctg. Office, 1978-80; banking officer U.S. Army Europe Office of the Dep. Chief of Staff for Resource Mgmt., 1980-84; fin. and acctg. officer Def. Nuclear Agy., 1984-87; investigator Office of Dept. of the Army Inspector Gen., 1987-91; chief programs and analysis divsn. Dept. Army Office of Dep. Chief of Staff for Logistics, 1991-93; fin. mgmt. cons., 1993-96; co-founder, pres. BRE Travel, 1996—. Pres. Browne Acad. PTA, Alexandria, Va., 1987; active Guilford Coll. United Meth. Ch., Greensboro. Decorated Legion of Merit with oak leaf cluster (2 awards), Meritorious Svc. medal with 3 oak leaf clusters (4 awards), Army Commendation medal with 4 oak leaf clusters (5 awards). Mem. Am. Soc. Travel Agts., Assn. of the U.S. Army, Terrell Soc. Am., Cardinal Golf and Country Club (Greensboro). Address: 4116 Obriant Pl Greensboro NC 27410-8372

FORMO, JEROME LIONEL, chemist; b. Mpls., Aug. 24, 1915; s. John Martin and Jennie Marie (Imsdahl) F.; m. Martha Winifred Helland, Aug. 12, 1939; children: David (dec.), Philip, Katherine Whitaker. BA in Chemistry, Math. and Music, Augsburg Coll., Mpls., 1937; postgrad., U. Minn., Mpls. Tchr. high sch. sci. Verndale, Minn., 1937-41; chemist Honeywell, Inc., Mpls., 1941-43, dir. plastics rsch., 1943-61; v.p. Plastics Corp. Am., 1961-62; cons. plastics, 1962-63; v.p. rsch. and devel. and engring. Plastics Inc., St. Paul, 1963-78; cons. in plastics Formo & Assocs., Roseville, Minn., 1978-93; mem. U.S. Dept. Commerce Trade Mission Team to Poland representing U.S. Plastics Industry, 1959; mem. Internat. Exec. Svc. Corps, Guatemala, 1988, 92, El Salvador, 1989. Regional corr. Plastic Trends, 1985-88; contbr. articles to profl. jours. Fellow Am. Inst. Chemists; mem. Am. Chem. Soc. (emeritus), Soc. Plastics Engrs. (disting., pres. Upper Midwest sect., nat. pres. 1956), Soc. Plastics Industry (chmn. tech. confs. 1973, 79). Lutheran. Achievements include over 10 patents in field.

FORN, RICK, talent agent. Ptnr. Artists Mgmt. Group, Beverly Hills, Calif. Office: Artists Management Group 9465 Wilshire Blvd #519 Beverly Hills CA 90212*

FORNADEL, WILLIAM MARK, university dean; b. Elizabeth, N.J., June 19, 1951; s. Paul and Margaret Beatrice F.; m. Sarah Gudaitis, July 3, 1982; children: Laura Elizabeth, Erin Katherine. BA in Psychology, Trenton State Coll., 1973; MS in Edn. Student Pers., So. Ill. U., 1975; PhD in Higher Edn./Mgmt., U. Va., 1993. Dir. conf. and insts., student union dir. SUNY, Stony Brook, 1980-85, divsn. dir. student life, 1985-90; asst. intern Office of Sr. and CFO U. Va., Charlottesville, 1992-93, ADA assoc. coord., 1991-93; assoc. dean Inst. Textile Tech., Charlottesville, 1993, dean, v.p. acad. affairs, 1994—; lectr. in field. Contbr. articles to profl. jours. Mem. task force Planning & Cmty. Devel., County of Albemarle, 1995—. Recipient dissertation of the Yr. award Ctr. for Study of Higher Edn., 1984, Anette Gibbs Rsch. award, 1993, William M. Fornadel Ann. Student Life award SUNY, Stony Brook, 1990. Mem. Nat. Coun. Textile edn. (treas. 1996—), Faculty Student Assn. (bd. dirs. 1988-90), Charlottesville C. of C., Soc. for Coll. and Univ. Planning, Assn. Instl. Rsch., Assn. Psychol. Type, Raven Soc., , AIR, SCUP, NACUBO, Phi Delta Kappa. Office: Inst Textile Tech 2551 Ivy Rd Charlottesville VA 22903-4614

FORNARA, CHARLES WILLIAM, historian, classicist, educator; b. N.Y.C., Nov. 19, 1935; s. Charles and Dorothy Mae (Stind) F.; 1 son, Charles William III. B.A., Columbia U., 1956; M.A., U. Chgo., 1958; Ph.D., UCLA, 1961. Instr. Ohio State U., Columbus, 1961-63; from asst. prof. to prof. classics and history Brown U., Providence, 1963—, David Benedict prof. classics, 1989—; vis. prof. U. Tex., Austin, 1976; prof. Greek history Inst. Ancient History, Ann Arbor, Mich., summer 1977; vis. fellow Humanities Rsch. Ctr. Australian Nat. U., Canberra, spring 1983; lectr. Australian univs., 1983, English univs., 1987, U. Amsterdam, 1995. Author: Herodotus, An Interpretative Essay, 1971, The Athenian Board of Generals, 1971, Archaic Times to the End of the Peloponnesian War, 1977, 2d edit., 1983, The Nature of History in Ancient Greece and Rome, 1983, (with Loren Samons II) From Cleisthenes to Pericles, 1991 (commentary) Continuation of Felix Jacoby, Die Fragmente der griechischen Historiker III c, 1994; contbr. articles and revs. in field to profl. jours. John Simon Guggenheim fellow, 1988-89. Mem. Am. Philol. Assn., Soc. for Promotion Hellenic Studies. Club: Providence Art. Home: 527 Mooresfield Rd Saunderstown RI 02874-1208 Office: Brown Univ Dept Classics Providence RI 02912

FORNATTO, ELIO JOSEPH, otolaryngologist, educator; b. Turin, Italy, July 2, 1928; came to U.S., 1953; s. Mario G. and Julia (Stabio) F.; m. Mary Elizabeth Pearson, Dec. 17, 1960; children: Susan, Robert, Daniel. MD, U. Turin, Italy, 1952. Diplomate Am. Bd. Otolaryngology. Intern Edgewater Hosp., Chgo., 1956-57; resident U. Ill., Chgo., 1953-56; chief otolaryngologist Elmhurst (Ill.) Clinic, 1958—; sr. otolaryngologist Elmhurst (Ill.) Meml. Hosp., 1964—; med. dir. Chgo. Eye Ear Nose Throat Hosp., 1966-69; clin. asst. prof. Loyola U., Chgo., 1967-87; bd. dirs. DuPage County unit Am. Cancer Soc., 1977-94; chmn. Elmhurst Clinic, 1980-89. Founder Centurion Club, Deafness Research Found., N.Y.C., 1960—. Recipient Disting. Svc. award Elmhurst Meml. Hosp., 1994. Mem. AMA, Ill. Med. Soc., Am. Acad. Facial Plastic and Reconstructive Surgery, Am. Acad. Otolaryngologic Allergy, Am. Acad. Otolaryngology and Head and Neck Surgery. Roman Catholic. Avocations: music, bicycling. Home: 200 W Jackson St Elmhurst IL 60126-4807 Office: Elmhurst Clinic 172 Schiller St Elmhurst IL 60126-2885

FORNEK, SCOTT PATRICK, journalist; b. Chgo., Apr. 16, 1959; s. Edward John and Patricia Lavergne (Skalecki) F.; m. Angela C. Rodriquez, Jan. 27, 1987; 1 step son, Joseph Rodriquez. BA summa cum laude, Loyola U., Chgo., 1991. Reporter Chgo. Sun-Times, 1991-95, polit. writer, 1995—. Panelist: (TV show) Chgo. Tonight Sta. WTTW-TV, 1997, Chgo. Week in Review WTTW, 1997—; guest: (TV show) Inside Politics CNN, 1995, Washington Journal C-SPAN, 1996. Recipient Woelfl Polit. Sci. award Loyola U. Chgo., 1991; named Co-Winner for Best Team Report, Nat. Assn. Real Estate Editors, 1993, Co-winner for Salute to Excellence, Nat. Assn. Black Journalist, 1993, Co-winner of Newsmakers, Chgo. Assn. Black Journalists, 1995. Mem. Chgo. Newspaper Guild, Gold Key, Pi Sigma Alpha, Alpha Sigma Nu. Office: Chgo Sun-Times 401 N Wabash Ave Chicago IL 60611-5642

FORNELL, CLAES, management consultant, marketing educator. Fil.Kand., U. Lund, Sweden, 1971, MBA, 1971, D Econs., 1976; postgrad., U. Calif., Berkeley, 1972-75. Vis. asst. prof. Duke U., 1977-78; asst. prof. mktg. Northwestern U., Evanston, Ill., 1978-80; assoc. prof. mktg. U. Mich., Ann Arbor, 1980-84, prof. mktg., 1984—, Donald C. Cook prof. bus. adminstrn., 1987—; chmn., founder CFI Group, Ann Arbor; vis. prof. Stockholm Sch. Econs., 1987, INSEAD, France, 1987; dir. Nat. Quality Rsch. Ctr., 1993—; mem. editl. bd. Mktg. Sci., 1988-94, Mktg. Letters, 1989—, Jour. Mktg. Rsch., 1983-91, Jour. Mktg., 1990-94, Jour. Internat. Consumer Mktg., 1988—, Jour. Consumer Rsch., 1986-89, Internat. Jour. Rsch. in Mktg., 1992—. Author: Konsumentkontakt-Ett medel for Battre Marknadsanpassning, 1976, Consumer Input for Marketing Decisions—A Study of Corporate Departments for Consumer Affairs, 1976; editor: A Second Generation of Multivariate Analysis, Vol. 1: Methods, 1982, vol. 2, Measurement and Evaluation, 1982; contbr. articles to profl. jours., chpts. to books. Office: CFI Group Inc 625 Avis Dr Ann Arbor MI 48108

FORNESS, STEVEN ROBERT, educational psychologist; b. Denver, May 13, 1939; s. Robert E. and Rejeana C. (Houck) F. BA in English, U. No. Colo., 1963, MA in Ednl. Psychology, 1964; EdD in Spl. Edn., UCLA, 1968. Tchr. Santa Maria High Sch., Calif., 1964-66; counselor Sch. Edn. UCLA, 1966-68; spl. educator Neuropsychiat. Inst., 1968—, chief ednl. psychology child outpatient dept., 1970—, mem. mental retardation research ctr., 1970—, prof. dept. psychiatry, 1972—, prin. inpatient sch., 1976—, dir. mental retardation and developmental disabilities tng. program, 1985-92; grant rev. panelist U.S. Dept. Edn., 1974—; cons. Nat. Assn. Exceptional Children, Venezuela, 1974—; commn. ednl. psychology Calif. State Bd. Behavioral Scis. Examiners, 1977-99. Specialist in classroom observation tech. early identification of children with learning and behavior disorders; author publs. including (with Frank Hewett) Education of Exceptional Learners, 3d edit., 1984, (with K. Kavale) Science of Learning Disabilities, 1985, (with Kavale and Bender) Handbook of Learning Disabilities, vols. I, II and III, 1987, 88; (with K. Kavale) Nature of Learning Disabilities, 1995, Efficacy of Special Education, 1999; cons. editor various jours. Sr. scholar Shaklee Inst. on Spl. Edn., 1996—. Fulbright scholar Ministry of Edn., Portugal, 1976. Fellow Internat. Acad. Rsch. in Learning Disabilties, Am. Assn. Mental Retardation; mem. Tchr. Educators of Children with Behavior Disorders (pres. 1985-86), Coun. Children with Behavior Disorders (pres. 1987-88, Leadership award 1995), Am. Assn. Univ. Affiliated Programs in Developmental Disabilities (interdisciplinary coun. 1972-89), Internat. Coun. for Exceptional Children (del. Assembly 1988-91, Wallin award 1992, Excellence in Tchr. Edn. award 1995), Acad. on Mental Retardation (exec. com. 1989-91), Nat. Mental Health and Spl. Edn. Coalition (co-chair of Definition Task Force 1987—), Am. Psychiat. Assn. (DSM IV subcom. on learning disorders 1988-94), Profl. Group for Attention and Related Disorders (com. profl. advisors 1990-91), Midwest Symposium on Behavioral Disorders (Leadership award 1993), Am. Acad. Child and Adolescent Psychiatry (cochmn. practice parameters on learning disabilities 1996-98), Knights of Malta (Order of St. John 1994). Home: 11901 W Sunset Blvd Los Angeles CA 90049-4240 Office: UCLA Dept Psychiatry 760 Westwood Plz Los Angeles CA 90095-8353

FORNEY, G(EORGE) DAVID, JR., retired electronics company executive; b. N.Y.C., Mar. 6, 1940; s. George David Forney and Priscilla (Brush) Forney McDonnell; m. Harriet A. Bascom, June 9, 1962 (div. 1989); children: Mark Hamilton, Priscilla Jean, William McDonnell. BS in Engring., Princeton U., 1961; MSc, MIT, 1963, ScD, 1965. Mem. tech. staff Codex Corp., Watertown, Mass., 1965-70; v.p. rsch. Codex Corp., Newton, Mass., 1970-75; v.p. R & D Codex Corp., 1975-78; v.p. rsch. Codex Corp., Mansfield, Mass., 1978-82, v.p., 1986-89; v.p., dir. tech. and planning Motorola Info. Sys. Group, Mansfield, 1982-86; v.p. tech. staff Motorola, Inc., Mansfield, 1980-99; vis. scientist Stanford (Calif.) U., 1971-72, vis. prof., 1990, mem. adv. coun., 1990-94; adj. prof. MIT, Cambridge, 1980-82, Bernard M. Gordon adj. prof., 1996— ; mem. adv. coun. dept. elec. engring., Princeton (N.J.) U., 1977—, Columbia ., N.Y.C., 1986-93, Harvard U., Cambridge, 1995—. Author: Concatenated Codes, 1966; contbr. articles to profl. jours.; patentee in field. Bd. dirs. Am. Field Svc., N.Y.C., 1971-74; trustee Lehrman Inst., N.Y.C., 1973-80, Mt. Auburn Hosp., Cambridge, 1986—; overseer Shady Hill Sch., Cambridge, 1980-86. Recipient Christopher Columbus award in Internat. Comm., 1996; Marconi Internat. fellow, 1997. Fellow AAAS, Am. Acad. Arts and Scis., IEEE (editor jour. 1970-73, Info. Theory Group award 1970, Browder J. Thompson prize paper award 1972, Centennial medal 1984, Donald G. Fink prize paper award 1990, Edison medal 1992, Shannon award 1995); mem. NAE, IEEE Info. Theory Soc. (pres. 1992), Popov Soc. (Russia, hon.). Home and Office: 1010 Memorial Dr Apt 3G Cambridge MA 02138-4853

FORNEY, ROBERT CLYDE, retired chemical industry executive; b. Chgo., Mar. 13, 1927; s. Peter Clyde and Hildur (Hoglund) F.; m. Marilyn Glenn, Apr. 3, 1948; children: Gerald Glenn, Barbara Dale, Robert C. BSChemE, Purdue U., 1947, MS, 1948, PhD, 1950. With E.I. DuPont de Nemours, Wilmington, Del., 1950—, asst. gen. mgr. textile fibers dept., 1970-75, v.p., gen. mgr., 1975-77, v.p. plastic products and resins, 1977-78, sr. v.p., 1979-81, exec. v.p., 1981-89, also bd. dirs.; ret. E.I. DuPont de Nemours, Wilmington, 1989; bd. dirs. Wilmington Trust Corp. Mem. AIChE, NAE, AAAS, Am. Chem. Soc., Sigma Xi. Republican. Lutheran. Home: PO Box 549 Unionville PA 19375-0549

FORNEY, RONALD DEAN, elementary school educator, consultant, educational therapist; b. Kearney, Nebr., June 28, 1954; s. Carl Roger and Florence Alyce (Gordon) F. Student, Community Coll. Denver, 1972-73; BA in Liberal Arts, Loretto Heights Coll., Denver, 1975; AS in Devel. Psychology, Arapahoe Community Coll., Denver, 1977; MBA, Calif. State Coll., San Bernardino, 1992; MS in Ednl. Adminstrn., Nat. U., 1993. Cert. tchr., English tchr., Calif.; cert. ednl. therapist. Tchr. Lake Elsinore (Calif.) Sch. Dist., 1985-87; tchr. Banning (Calif.) Unified Sch. Dist., 1987—, master tchr., classroom mgmt.-assertive discipline cons., 1990—, asst. prin. Ctrl. Elem. Sch., 1996-98; cons. visual and performing arts, motivation and self-esteem bldg; ednl. therapist in pvt. practice, 1998—. Recipient cert. in affective domain Lake Elsinore Sch. Dist., 1986, Outstanding Tchr. award Hemmerling Sch., Banning, 1989. Avocations: theatre, reading, writing and reading Haiku poetry.

FORNEY, VIRGINIA SUE, educational counselor; b. Little Rock, Sept. 15, 1925; d. Robert Millard and Susan Amanda (Ward) Tate; m. J.D. Mullen, Jr., Oct. 13, 1945 (div. 1966); children: Michael Dunn, Patricia Sue; m. Bill E. Forney, Apr. 29, 1967. Student Tex. State Coll. for Women, 1943-46; BFA, U. Okla., 1948; postgrad. Benedictine Heights Coll., Tulsa, 1957-58; M.Teaching Arts, Tulsa U., 1969; postgrad. Okla. State U., intermittently, 1969—. Cert. secondary tchr., sch. counselor, vis. sch. counselor, Okla. With Sta. WNAD, U. Okla., 1947-49; tchr. lang. arts Tulsa Bd. Edn., 1959-73; women's counselor Tulsa YWCA, 1980; vis. sch. counselor Tulsa County Supt. of Schs. Office, 1980-86; dir. spl. project Tulsa County Supt. Schs. Office, 1986-91; owner, dir. Svc. to Families in Bus. and Industry, 1991—. Mem. budget com. United Way Greater Tulsa, 1980-86, edn. com. Planned Parenthood Greater Tulsa, 1980-86; mem. Tulsa County adv. coun. Okla. State U., 1983-85; chairperson Tulsa Coalition for Parenting Edn., 1983-84; chairperson problems of youth study Tulsa Met. C. of C., 1984-85; mem. gen. bd. March of Dimes Greater Tulsa, 1985; pres. evening alliance All Souls Unitarian Ch., 1993-94. Mem. Am. Assn. for Counseling and Devel., Internat. Assn. Pupil Personnel Workers (state bd. dirs. 1982-86), Okla. Assn. Family Resource Programs (regional v.p. 1982-86, state pres. 1986-87), Program Internat. Ednl. Exchange (community coordinator for Tulsa 1986-90), LWV Okla. (chairperson juvenile justice study 1976-77), LWV Met. Tulsa (mem. exec. bd. 1993-95), Tulsa Parents As Tchrs. Inc. (founding pres. 1991-92, exec. bd. 1992-96). Democrat. Unitarian. Avocation: piano.

FORNI, PATRICIA ROSE, nursing educator, university dean; b. St. Louis, Feb. 14, 1932; d. Harold and Glenda M. (Keay) Brown. B.S.N., Washington U., St. Louis, 1955, M.S. (USPHS trainee), 1957; Ph.D. (USPHS fellow), St. Louis U., 1965; postgrad. (USPHS scholar), U. Minn., summers 1968, 70. Staff nurse McMillan EENT Hosp., St. Louis, summer 1955, Renard Psychiat. Hosp., St. Louis, part-time 1955-57; rsch. asst. Washington U. Sch. Nursing, St. Louis, 1957-59, rsch. assoc., 1959-61, asst. prof., 1964-66, assoc. dean in charge grad. edn., assoc. prof. gen. nursing sci., 1966-68; assoc. prof. pub. health nursing Wayne State U., Detroit, 1968-69; asst. dir. for manpower and edn. Ill. Regional Med. Program, Chgo., 1969-71; project dir. Midwest Continuing Profl. Edn. for Nurses, St. Louis U., 1971-75; dean, prof. nursing So. Ill. U., Edwardsville, 1975-88; dean, prof. Coll. Nursing U. Okla., Oklahoma City, 1988—; grant proposal reviewer Divsn. Nursing, USPHS, 1972-79, 88, 91, NSF, 1978, U.S. Dept. Edn., 1980; mem. Ill. Implementation Commn. on Nursing, 1975-77, Okla. State Health Plan Adv. Com., 1994—. Mem. peer rev. panel Nursing Outlook, 1987-91; mem. editl. bd. Health Care for Women Internat., 1984—, Jour. Profl. Nursing, 1988-90. Chairwoman articulation of nursing programs task force Okla. State Regents for Higher Edn., 1990-91; bd. dirs. Greater St. Louis Health Sys. Agy., 1976-81, Adult Edn. Coun. Greater St. Louis, 1973-76, Edwardsville unit Am. Cancer Soc., 1981-88. Fellow WHO, Sweden, Finland, 1985. Mem. Nat. League for Nursing (accreditation site visitor 1979—, nominating com. Coun. Baccalaureate and Higher Degree Programs 1979-82, pub. policy and legis. com. 1981-85, bd. dirs. 1991-93, treas. 1991-93, mem. fin. com. 1991-95), Nat. League for Health Care (trustee 1991-93), Nat. League for Nursing Accrediting Commn. (peer review panel, baccalaureate and higher degree programs 1997—), Am. Nurses Assn. (chmn. continuing edn. publs. com. 1975-76), Mo. Nurses Assn. (chmn. edn. com. 1973-77), Greater St. Louis Soc. Health Manpower Edn. and Tng. (chmn. legis. com. 1974-75), Midwest Alliance in Nursing (1st governing bd. 1979-80, 93-96, chmn. nominations com. 1980, 81, mem. fin. com. 1993-94, chair fin. com. 1994-96, treas. 1994-96, pres. 1998-2000), Am. Assn. Colls. Nursing (program com. 1978-82, mem.-at-large, bd. dirs. 1990-92, chair rsch. com. 1990-92), Ill. Coun. Deans/Dirs. Baccalaureate and Higher Degree Programs in Nursing (chmn. 1979-81), Am. Acad. Nursing (treas., chairwoman fin. com., mem. gov. coun. 1989-93, editor Newsletter 1982-87), Ill. Nurses Assn. (commn. on adminstrn. 1983-87, commn. on edn. 1987-89), Okla. Nurses Found. (pres. bd. trustees 1990-93), Sigma Theta Tau Internat. (charter mem. Epsilon Eta chpt. 1980). Office: U Okla Coll Nursing PO Box 26901 Oklahoma City OK 73190

FORNOFF, ANN LYNETTE, secondary school educator; b. McCook, Nebr., June 17, 1962; d. Dale Arthur and Eva Marie (Sughroue) Hofman; m. Kevin Ray Fornoff, June 15, 1985; children: Kyle Ryan, Amanda Lynette. BA in English Lang. Arts and Bus., Kearney State Coll., 1984. Tchr. English Palco (Kans.) H.S., 1985; tchr. English, journalism Hayes Center (Nebr.) Schs., 1985—; journalism advisor, Hayes Ctr. Schs., 1987—, sophomore class advisor, 1985—, sr. class advisor, 1996. Treas. Sacred Heart Ch. Altar Soc., Hayes Center, 1997—, catechism class coord., 1995—. Mem. NEA, NCTE, Nebr. Edn. Assn., Hayes Center Tchrs. Assn. (past pres., v.p., sec. and scholarship chmn.). Avocations: gardening, reading. Home: HCR 62 Box 19 Hayes Center NE 69032

FORNOFF, FRANK J(UNIOR), retired chemistry educator, consultant; b. Mt. Carmel, Ill., Mar. 29, 1914; s. Frank and Ada (Arnold) F. A.B., U. Ill., 1936; M.S., Ohio State U., 1937, Ph.D., 1939. Asst. prof. Lehigh U., Bethlehem, Pa., 1942-44; chem. engr. Western Electric Co., N.Y.C., 1944-45; asst. prof. chemistry Lehigh U., 1945-47, assoc. prof., 1947-53; assoc. prof. Kans. State U., Manhattan, 1953-56; lectr. Rutgers U., New Brunswick, N.J., 1956-84; sr. examiner Ednl. Testing Svc., Princeton, N.J., 1956-93, group head, 1956-83. Editor AP Chemistry newsletter, 1976-90; contbr. articles to profl. jours. Active Boy Scouts Am., Princeton, 1957-93. NRC fellow U. Calif., Berkeley, 1939-40; Procter and Gamble fellow Ohio State U., 1938-39. Mem. AAAS, Am. Chem. Soc. (chmn. local sect. assn. publs. 1960-70), Am. Soc. Engring. Edn., Nat. Sci. Tchrs. Assn., Nat. Council Measurements in Edn., N.J. Acad. Sci., N.Y. Acad. Sci. Methodist. Home: 110 E 7th St Mount Carmel IL 62863-2033

FORNOS, PETER SECUNDINO, pulmonary medicine physician; b. Havana, Cuba, May 18, 1952; s. Pedro G. and Caridad (Lopez) F.; married 1987; 2 children. BS, S.W. Tex. State U., San Marcos, 1978; MD, U. Autonoma, De Nuevo Monterrey, Mexico, 1984. Bd. cert. pulmonary and critical care. Intern Mt. Sinai, Elmhurst, N.Y., 1984-85, resident, 1985-87; pulmonary and critical care fellow Audie Murphy VA Hosp., 1987-90; chief staff Bapt. Hosp. Systems, San Antonio, 1995, chmn. medicine, 1996-97. Mem. Am. Coll. Chest Physicians, So. Med. Assn. Republican. Episcopalian. Office: P Fornos MD & Assocs 311 Camden St Ste 201 San Antonio TX 78215-2011*

FORNSHELL, DAVE LEE, educational broadcasting executive; b. Bluffton, Ind., July 9, 1937; s. Harold Christman and Mary Ann Elizabeth (Fox) F.; 1 child, John David; m. Delphia Crum, May 18, 1991. BA, Ohio State U., 1959. Continuity dir. Sta. WTVN-TV, Columbus, Ohio, 1959-61; traffic dir., asst. program mgr. Sta. WOSU-TV, Columbus, 1961-69; ops. mgr. Md. Center for Pub. Broadcasting, Balt., 1969-70; exec. dir. Ohio Ednl. TV Network Commn., Columbus, 1970—; pres. Ohio Radio Reading Services; dir., mem. exec. com. Central Ednl. Network, 1972—, chmn. bd. dirs., 1986—; mem. exec. com., chmn. Postsecondary Edn. Council of Central Ednl. Network; chmn. Higher Edn. Telecomm. Coun. of Ohio; mem. adv. com. Ohio State Awards. Pres. Landings Residents Assn., 1973; active March of Dimes, 4-H. Served with USAF, 1961-62. Recipient award Dayton Fedn. Women's Clubs, 1974, Civil Air Patrol, 1994. Mem. N.G. Assn., Ohio State U. Alumni Assn., Nat. Acad. TV Arts and Scis. (bd. govs. Columbus chpt. 1970—), Nat. Assn. Ednl. Broadcasters (chmn. state adminstrs. council), Broadcast Pioneers, Ohio State Awards Adv. Com., Health Scis. Communications Assn., Nat. Assn. TV Program Execs., Nat. Press Club, Am. Assn. Higher Edn., Alpha Epsilon Rho, Alpha Delta Sigma, Sigma Delta Chi. Clubs: University, Athletic (Columbus), Symposiarchs, Rotary. Home: 3388 Scioto Run Blvd Hilliard OH 43026-3002 Office: Ohio Ednl Broadcasting 2470 N Star Rd Columbus OH 43221-3405*

FORONDA, ELENA ISABEL, secondary school educator; b. N.Y.C., Jan. 15, 1947; d. Severino Deliso and LaVerne (Ibanez) F. BS in Music, Hunter Coll., CUNY, 1969, MA in Music Edn., 1971. Tchr. vocal music N.Y.C. Pub. Sch. System, 1970—; asst. dir. tchr. placement Hunter Coll., City U. N.Y., summers 1971-72; examination asst. N.Y.C. Pub. Sch. System Bd. Examiners, 1987-89. Sponsor children in World Vision Internat., 1973-97; del. Asian Am. Women's Caucus, 1977; mem. Hunter Coll. choirs, 1968-69, 71; pianist, minister of music Ch. of The Holy Spirit, Bklyn., 1988-90; lay reader, lay eucharistic minister L.I. Diocese Episcopal Ch., 1993. Dist. winner Nat. Piano Playing Auditions, 1965; recipient N.Y. State permanent cert. Dept. Edn., 1971. Mem. Music Educators Nat. Conf., Music Educators Assn. N.Y.C., N.Y. State Sch. Music Assn., Amateur Chamber Music Players (N.Y.C.). Democrat.

FORREST, ALLEN WRIGHT, tax and financial services firm executive, accountant, financial planner; b. Quincy, Mass., Nov. 8, 1941; s. Edwin Wright and Sylvia (Locke) F.; m. Helen Frances Kolb, Nov. 10, 1962; children: Deborah, Teresa, Sandra, William. BBA, U. N. Fla., 1980, MS in Acctg., 1981. Enrolled agt., IRS. Enlisted USN, 1958, advanced through grades to sr. chief petty officer, 1972, resigned, 1977; treas., contr. Fla. Bonded Pools, Inc., Jacksonville, 1977-89; pvt. practice Jacksonville Beach, Fla., 1982-89; pres. Profl. Computer Support Inc., Jacksonville Beach, 1988-90, Forrest & Co., Inc., Jacksonville, Fla., 1989—. Treas. Beaches United Citizens, Jacksonville Beach, 1982. Recipient Carl Burger Meml. Manuscript Nat. Assn. Accts., 1982-83. Mem. Inst. Cert. Fin. Planners, Fleet Res. Assn., Beaches Bus. Assn., Phi Kappa Phi, Beta Gamma Sigma. Avocations: jogging, weightlifting, microcomputers. Home: 259 Coral Way Jaxville Bch FL 32250-2911 Office: Forrest & Co Inc 1500 Roberts Dr Jacksonville Beach FL 32250-3222

FORREST, DAVID VICKERS, psychiatrist, educator; b. N.Y.C., July 8, 1938; s. Melbourne Arthur and Cleo Florence (Garello); m. Lynne Putnam Stetson; children: Daniel Stetson, Susannah Nissly. AB summa cum laude, Princeton U., 1960; MD, Columbia U., 1964, cert. in psychoanalysis, 1974. Cert. in psychiatry Am. Bd. Psychiatry and Neurology. Intern in medicine St. Luke's Hosp., N.Y.C., 1964-65; resident psychiatry N.Y. State Psychiat. Inst., Columbia Presbyn. Med. Ctr., N.Y.C., 1965-68; chief psychiatric clinic 935th Med. Det. (KO) 93d Evacuation Hosp., Long Binh, Vietnam, 1968-69; chief psychiatric consultation Letterman Army Med. Ctr., San Francisco, 1969-70; pvt. practice psychiatry N.Y.C., 1970—; mem. psychiatry faculty Columbia U., N.Y.C., 1970—; dir. edn. ednl. rsch. dept. N.Y. State Psychiat.

Inst., 1970-77; assoc. prof. clin. psychiatry Columbia U., Coll. Physicians and Surgeons, N.Y.C., 1984—; faculty psychoanalytic ctr. Columbia U., Coll. Physicians and Surgeons, 1974—, liaison psychiatrist neurology, 1977—; lectr. psychiatry U. Saigon Med. Sch., Vietnam, 1968-69; lectr. abnormal psychology Far East div. U. Md., Long Binh, Vietnam, 1969. *Dr. Forrest's contributions in pscyhoanalytic anthropology related mythology andpersonality development in Asian societies, particularly Vietnam. Based on his research in 1968-69, when he was chief of the largest psychiatric clinic at the peak of that war. Writing on language in psychopathology, he explored how literary analysis can comprehend the purposes of expression in psychiatric disorders, including poiesis, neologism, and the rhetoric of character styles. Analogously, he explicated the psychotherapy of patients with neuropsychiatric disorders, and wrote a "Mind, Brain, Machine" series describing how principles of neurocomputing can elucidate studies of mind-brain relationships.* Author: Selected American Expressions, 1974, 76, 82; co-author: Treating Schizophrenic Patients, 1983, (video cassette series) Electronic Textbook of Psychiatry, 1972-77; co-author, pub: The Ballet Company Game, 1973; founding editor, pub. Spring: The Jour. of the E. E. Cummings Soc., N.Y.C., 1980—; editor: Neural Net News, N.Y. State Psychiat. Inst., 1989-91; technical cons. Star Trek TV series, 1997—; contbr. articles to profl. jours., textbooks. Psychiat. cons. N.Y.C. Ballet Co., 1973; first aid instr. Boy Scouts Am., 1983—. Capt. USAF, 1968-70, Vietnam. Decorated Bronze Star; Gen. Motors nat. scholar. Fellow Am. Psychiat. Assn., Am. Coll. Psychiatrists, Am. Acad. Psychoanalysis (program chair), Am. Coll. Psychoanalysts (program chair 1987-89, bd. regents 1989-92, v.p. 1993, pres.-elect 1994, pres. 1995), Explorers Club; mem. Am. Acad. Neurology (assoc.), N.Y. Clin. Soc. (v.p. 1995, pres. 1996). Episcopalian. Avocations: invention, discovery, magic. Office: 133 E 73rd St Ste 211 New York NY 10021-3556 also: 155 W 68th St Apt 1219 New York NY 10023-5818

FORREST, DOUGLAS WILLIAM, banker; b. Hackensack, N.J., Feb. 16, 1945; s. Harvey Sinclair and Marjorie Elizabeth (Stagg) F.; m. Marie M. Rakowsky, Oct. 1, 1967 (div. Oct. 1984); children: Chad Douglas, Kimberly Marie; m. Janet Valerie Dearborn, May 27, 1989. BS, Ithaca Coll., 1967. Capt. Eastern Airlines Inc., Boston, 1972-91; mgmt. Fleet Bank, Nashua, N.H., 1991-94; v.p. Cmty. Bank & Trust Co., Exeter, N.H., 1994—. Coach, hockey, baseball Recreation Dept., Exeter, N.H., 1978-83; mem. Sounding Bd., Exeter, 1979; mem. Congl. Ch., 1973—, diaconate chmn., 1982. Capt. USAF, 1967-72. Mem. Airline Pilots Assn. (Hat in the Ring 1986), Ea. Pilots Assn., Rotary (Exeter treas. 1995-98, Paul Harris fellow 1998), Exeter C. of C. (bd. dirs. 1995—, chmn. 1998—). Republican. Avocations: golf, tennis, skiing, boating. Home: 9 Little Pine Ln Exeter NH 03833-3109 Office: Cmty Bank & Trust Co 80 Main St Exeter NH 03833-2428

FORREST, HERBERT EMERSON, lawyer; b. N.Y.C., Sept. 20, 1923; s. Jacob K. and Rose (Fried) F.; m. Marilyn Lefsky, Jan. 12, 1952; children: Glenn Clifford, Andrew Matthew. Student, CCNY, 1941, Ohio U., 1943-44; BA with distinction, George Washington U., 1948, JD with highest honors, 1952. Bar: Va. 1952, D.C. 1952, U.S. Supreme Ct. 1956, Md. 1959, U.S. Ct. Appeals (D.C. cir.) 1953, (1st cir.) 1992, (2d cir.) 1971, (3d cir.) 1957, (4th cir.) 1956, (5th cir.) 1981, (7th cir.) 1996, (8th cir.) 1991, (9th cir.) 1994, (11th cir.) 1981. Plate printer Bur. Engraving and Printing, Washington, 1942-43, 1946-52; law clk. to chief judge Bolitha J. Laws U.S. Dist. Ct., Washington, 1952-55; pvt. practice Washington, 1952-87; with Welch & Morgan, 1955-65; with Steptoe & Johnson, 1965-85, of counsel, 1986-87; trial atty. fed. programs br. civil divsn. U.S. Dept. Justice, Washington, 1987—; chmn. adv. bd. D.C. Criminal Justice Act, 1971-74; sec. com. admissions and grievances U.S. Ct. Appeals, D.C., 1973-79; title-1 audit hearing bd. U.S. Office Edn. HEW, 1976-79; edn. appeals bd. U.S. Dept. Edn., 1979-82; mem. Lawyer's Support Com. for Visitors Service Center, 1975-87. Contbr. articles to legal jours.; advisory bd.: Duke Law Jour, 1969-75. Pres. Whittier Woods PTA, 1970-71. Served with F.A., Signal Corps U.S. Army, 1943-46. Recipient Walsh award in Irish history, 1952, Goddard award in commerce, 1952. Fellow Am. Bar Found. (life); mem. George Washington Law Assn., Am. Judicature Soc., ABA (council 1972-75, 1981-84, budget officer 1985-88, vice chmn. task force on sect. devel. 1987-89, chmn. com. on agy. rule making 1968-72, 1976-81, chmn. membership com. 1984-85, editor ann. reports 1973-88, adminstrv. law sect., mem. comm. com. public utilities law sect., vice chmn. industry regulation com. 1985-86, chmn. comm. subcom. 1983-85, antitrust law sect., internat. law sect., sec. judicial adminstrn., sect. sci. and tech., comm. forum), Va. State Bar Assn., Fed. Bar Assn. (chmn. jud. rev. com. 1981-85, vice chmn. adminstrv. law sect. 1985-87), Fed. Comm. Bar Assn. (del. to ABA Ho. Dels. 1979-81, exec. com. 1967-71, 76-84, v.p. 1981-82, pres. 1982-83, chmn. telecomm. com. 1983-87), D.C. Bar Assn. (past sec., exec. com.), NAM, Nat. Conf. Bar Pres., Washington Council Lawyers, Legal Aid and Pub. Defender Assn., Am. Arbitration Assn. (comml. panel 1976-87), D.C. Unified Bar (bd. govs. 1976-79, chmn. com. on employment discrimination complaint service 1973-79, chmn. task force on services to public 1974-78, chmn. com. on appointment counsel in criminal cases 1978-88, co-chmn. com. on participation govt. employees in pro bono activities 1977-79), Broadcast Pioneers, Order of Coif, Phi Beta Kappa, Pi Gamma Mu., Artus, Phi Eta Sigma, Phi Delta Phi. Democrat. Lodge: B'nai Brith. Home: 8706 Bellwood Rd Bethesda MD 20817-3033 Office: US Dept Justice 901 E St NW Rm 1050 Fed Washington DC 20004-2037

FORREST, KAY V., educator, editor, writer; b. Newport News, Va., Oct. 5, 1948; d. John James, Jr. and June (Hek) Verser; m. Henry Stephen Forrest, III, Dec. 22, 1966; children: Kelly Ann, Cleveland James. BA in English, Christopher Newport U., 1973; MA in Profl. Writing, Old Dominion U., 1995. Lic. postgrad. profl. English, journalism, speech comm., Va. Reporter pub. info. office U.S. Armed Forces, Ft. Eustis, 1966; sec. bursar's office U. Va., Charlottesville, 1968, sec., clerk periodicals Alderman Libr., 1968-69; homebound tchr. Hampton (Va.) Pub. Schs., 1973-74; tchr. Poquoson (Va.) Pub. Schs., 1974, Hampton Pub. Schs., 1975-81; substitute tchr. York (Va.) County Pub. Schs., 1981-82, tchr., 1982—. Freelance editor and writer, 1995—. Mem. Colonial Uniserv Coun., 1996—, chair, 1999—. Mem. NEA, Internat. Reading Assn., Nat. Coun. Tchr. English, York Edn. Assn. (bldg. rep. 1977-81, 86-92, bd. dirs. 1992-93, treas. 1996, 99—, pres. 1996-99), Va. Edn. Assn., Journalism Edn. Assn., Va. Reading Assn., Va. Journalism Edn. Assn., Columbia Scholastic Press Assn., Christopher Newport U. Alumni Assn., Delta Kappa Gamma (Gamma Phi chpt.). Democrat. Presbyterian. Avocations: pool, needlework, hiking, reading, traveling. Office: Tabb High Sch 4431 Big Bethel Rd Yorktown VA 23693-3124

FORREST, KENTON HARVEY, science educator, historian; b. Fort Lauderdale, Fla., Oct. 3, 1944; s. Harvey William and Marjorie A. (Boxrud) F. BA, Colo. State Coll., 1968; MA, U. No. Colo., 1981. Science tchr. Dunstan Middle Sch., Jefferson County Pub. Schs., Lakewood, Colo., 1968-98, dept. chmn., 1994-98; pres. Tramway Press, Inc., 1983-98. Author: Denver's Railroads, 1981; (with William C. Jones) Denver-A Pictorial History, 1973; (with others) The Moffat Tunnel, 1978; Rio Grande Ski Train, 1984, History of the Public Schools of Denver, 1989, Route 3 Englewood, 1990, The Railroads of Coors Field, 1995. Trustee Colo. Railroad Hist. Found., Golden, 1975-98, trustee emeritus, 1998—, pres. 1994-95; archivist Richardson Railroad Libr., 1998—; mem., 1st pres. Lakewood Hist. Soc. (Colo.), 1976; office Jeffco Credit Union. Mem. NEA (life) Colo. Assn. Sci. Tchrs., Nat. Railway Hist. Soc. (Intermountain chpt. pres. 1980-83, chmn. hist. plaque commn.), Mobile Post Office Soc. Home: PO Box 15607 Lakewood CO 80215-0007

FORREST, SIDNEY, clarinetist, music educator; b. N.Y.C., Aug. 21, 1918; s. Paul and Esther (Tannenhaus) F.; m. Faith Levine, Nov. 16, 1941; 1 child, Paula Forrest Helmuth. Student, Juilliard Sch. Music, 1935-37; BA, U. Miami, Fla., 1939; MA, Columbia U., 1941; studied with Simeon Bellison, Otto Conrad, Alexander Williams. Prof. Peabody Conservatory of Music, Johns Hopkins U., Balt., 1946-85, prof. emeritus, 1985; dir. placement and career counseling Peabody, Balt., 1969-85; clarinet soloist U.S. Marine Band and Symphony Orch., Washington, 1941-45; prin. clarinet Nat. Symphony, 1946-50; adj. prof. faculty Cath. U., 1954—; faculty Interlochen Ctr. for the Arts, Mich., 1959—, Am. U., 1961—, Levine Sch. Music, Washington, 1980—; adjudicator Nat. Fulbright Commn., 1980-84, Que. Can. Nat. Conservatoire, 1969-84; mem. faculty major conservatories and univs. Editor and arranger clarinet solos including Nocturne No. 20: Chopin, Pastorale: Baermann, Twelve Fantasies for Solo Clarinet: Telemann, Variations on a Theme of Corelli: By Tartini, Four Hebraic Pictures (arranged by S. Bellison), Twelve Fantasies for Solo Saxophone: Telemann, Twelve Fantasies for Solo Oboe: Telemann, others; major full clarinet recitals include Carnegie Recital Hall, Bklyn. Mus., Nat. Art Gallery, Phillips Collection, Libr. Cong., others; solo clarinet recordings and recitals; contbr. articles to profl. jours.; former students in major Am. and overseas opera and symphony orchs. Mem. Music Tchrs. Nat. Assn. Avocations: photography, gardening, stamps, travel. Home: 9611 Kingston Rd Kensington MD 20895-3521 Office: Cath U Rome Sch Music Harewood Rd NW Washington DC 20064-0001

FORRESTAL, ROBERT PATRICK, banker, lawyer; b. N.Y.C., Oct. 31, 1931; s. Patrick A. and Lillian D. (Moran) F.; m. Wilma Anderson, Sept. 29, 1956; 1 child, Renee Marie. BA, St. John's U., 1953; JD, Georgetown U., 1961. Bar: D.C. 1961, U.S. Supreme Ct. 1964. Atty. Spencer & Whalen, Washington, 1961-64; atty. Fed. Res. Bd., Washington, 1964-68, asst. sec., 1968-70; v.p., gen. counsel Fed. Res. Bd., Atlanta, 1970-74; sr. v.p., gen. counsel Fed. Res. Bank of Atlanta, 1974-79, 1st v.p., 1979-83, pres., 1983-95; ptnr. Smith, Gambrell and Russell, Atlanta, 1996—; bd. dirs. ING Corp., Genuine Parts Co., Equifax Corp., ING Ins. Co. Bd. dirs. Leadership Atlanta, 1971-73, Child Svcs. and Family Counseling Ctr., Atlanta, 1974-81, Ga. Worlds Congress Inst., 1979-83, United Way of Met. Atlanta, 1984-90, So. Ctr. for Internat. Studies, 1986-94; bd. sponsors Atlanta Symphony Orch., 1973-75; divsn. chmn. United Way, Atlanta, 1980-81; bd. dirs., exec. com. Ga. State U., Atlanta, 1972-83, chmn. recognition fund, 1975, chmn. trustees, 1976-78, mem. bd. advisors Coll. Bus. Adminstrn.; bd. dirs. Ctrl. Atlanta Progress, Piedmont Hosp. Found.; trustee Atlanta Arts Alliance, Oglethorpe U.; mem. adv. bd. Atlanta Humanities Program; bd. visitors Emory U., 1986-89, Berry Coll., 1987-89, Ga. State U. Sch. Law; mem. bd. councilors Carter Ctr.; active Friends of Piedmont Hosp., Piedmont Med. Care Found. Lt. USN, 1953. Fulbright scholar, 1953. Mem. Atlanta C. of C. (bd. dirs. 1984-87, 93-94), Rotary (bd. dirs. 1985-88, 93—), Commerce Club (bd. dirs.), World Trade Club of Atlanta, Buckhead Club. Home: 3949 Vermont Rd NE Atlanta GA 30319-1212 Office: Smith Gambrell & Russell 1230 Peachtree St NE Ste 3100 Atlanta GA 30309-3592

FORRESTER, ALAN MCKAY, capital company executive; b. Cleve., Oct. 13, 1940; s. John Carens and Mary Ann (Bryan) F.; m. Donna Dee Forrester, June 1964 (div. 1976); children: Sheri Lynn, Stephan Alan; m. Nancy V. Sullivan (div. 1990). Bachelor in Civil Engring, Ohio State U., 1963, Masters in Bus. Adminstrn. 1963. Registered Profl. engr., CPA. Indsl. engr. E.I. DuPont de Nemours and Co., Virginia, 1964-66; mgr. program mgmt. support Tex. Instruments, Dallas, 1966-69; ptnr. Cons. Assocs. Inc., Dallas, 1969; v.p. fin. Medicus Systems Corp., Chgo., 1969-73, Acts Computing, Southfield, Mich., 1973-74; pres. Van Arnem Co., Mich., 1974-80, First Nat. Capital, Birmingham, 1980—, McDonnell Douglas Capital Corp., Troy, Mich., 1987-89; bd. dirs. First Nat. Capital Corp., Troy, First Nat. Capital Leasing Corp., Meresco Corp., Bloomfield Hills, Mich., First Nat. Energy Corp.; pres. Classic Investment Cars Corp., 1990—, The Forrester Group, 1992—, Worldwide Software Solutions, 1998—; ptnr. The Lewis Group, 1995—; internat. exec. Interior Design Nutritionals, Bloomfield Hills, 1992—. Contbr. articles to profl. jour. Chmn. bd. trustees St. Joseph Mercy Hosp., Pontiac, 1988-89, vice chmn. bd. trustees, 1987, chmn. fin. com., 1985; trustee Sta. WTVS-TV, Detroit, 1982-88. Mem. AICPA, Internat. Assn. Fin. Planners, Am. Assn. Equipment Lessors, Computer Dealers and Lessors Assn., Oakland U. Pres. Club, Beta Theta Pi (v.p. 1962-64). Republican. Avocations: cross country, downhill skiing, golf, classic cars, woodworking. Office: First Nat Capital Corp Classic Investment Cars Worldwide Software Solutions Inc 6596 E Washington Ave Clarkston MI 48346-2172

FORRESTER, ANN, nurse. AD in Nursing, Craven Community Coll., New Bern, N.C., 1977; LPN, Durham Tech. Inst., 1972. RN, N.C.; cert. by N.C. Eye and Tissue Bank for enucleation of donor eyes. Staff nurse ob-gyn., labor and delivery and nursery Carteret Gen. Hosp., Morehead City, N.C., 1977-78, head nurse, 1978-80; asst. dir. nursing, then dir. nursing Harborview Nursing Home, Morehead City, 1980-81; nursing supr. Calhoun County Med. Care Facility, Battle Creek, Mich., 1982-83; staff nurse, relief charge nurse med.-surg. unit Craven Regional Med. Ctr., New Bern, N.C., 1983-85, relief nursing supr., 1984-85, asst. dir. nursing, 1985-87; nursing supr. Britthaven Nursing Home, New Bern, N.C., 1987—; staff nurse in orthopedics Craven Regional Med. Ctr., 1987-88, asst. nurse mgr. orthopedics, 1988-94; nursing supr. Britthaven Nursing Home, New Bern, N.C., 1994-95, dir. nursing, 1995-97, 97-98; asst. dir. nursing Guardian Care of New Bern, N.C., 1998-99; dir. nursing New Bern Health Care Ctr. (formerly Guardian Health Care of New Bern), New Bern, N.C., 1999—; asst. dir. nursing Twin Rivers Nursing Ctr., New Bern, N.C. Mem. Internat. Platform Assn. Address: PO Box 12975 New Bern NC 28561-2975

FORRESTER, J. OWEN, federal judge; b. 1939. B.S., Ga. Inst. Tech., 1961; LL.B., Emory U., 1966. Bar: Ga. 1966. Staff atty. Ga. gubernatorial candidate, 1966-67; assoc. Fisher & Phillips, Atlanta, 1967-69; magistrate U.S. Dist. Ct. (no. dist.) Ga., Atlanta, 1976-81, judge, 1981—. Office: US Dist Ct 1921 US Courthouse 75 Spring St SW Atlanta GA 30303

FORRESTER, JAY WRIGHT, management specialist, educator; b. Anselmo, Nebr., July 14, 1918; s. Marmaduke M. and Ethel Pearl (Wright) F.; m. Susan Swett, July 27, 1946; children: Judith, Nathan Blair, Ned Cromwell. B.Sc., U. Nebr., 1939, D.Eng. (hon.), 1954; M.Sc., MIT, 1945; D.Sc. (hon.), Boston U., 1969, Union Coll., 1973; D.Eng. (hon.), Newark Coll. Engring., 1971, U. Notre Dame, 1974; D.Polit. Sci. (hon.), U. Mannheim, 1979; LHD (hon.), SUNY, 1988. Tchr., X-ray equipment research MIT, 1939-40, co-founder servomechanisms lab., 1940, devel. electric and hydraulic servomechanisms for gun mounts and radar, 1940-44, asso. dir. servomechanisms lab., also supr. Whirlwind I digital computer devel., 1944-51, founder Digital Computer Lab., dir., 1951-56, div. head Lincoln Lab. for Air Def., 1951-56, prof. mgmt. Sloan Sch. Mgmt., 1956-72, Germeshausen prof., 1972-89, prof. emeritus, sr. lectr., 1989—; owner Forrester Cattle Ranch, Dunning, Nebr.; head System Dynamics Group, Sloan Sch., 1960-89. Lectures and tech. papers on digital computers and indsl. mgmt.; also dynamics indsl. and econ. behavior.; author: Industrial Dynamics, 1961, Principles of Systems, 1968, Urban Dynamics, 1969, World Dynamics, 1971, Collected Papers, 1975; patentee servomechanisms, digital info. storage, indsl. control. Recipient Inventor of Yr. award George Washington U., 1968, Valdemar Poulsen Gold medal Danish Acad. Tech. Scis., 1969, Outstanding Accomplishment award Systems, Man and Cybernetics Soc. of IEEE, 1972, Computer Pioneer award IEEE Computer Soc., 1982, Benjamin Franklin fellow Royal Soc. Arts, London, 1972, New Eng. award Engring. Socs. New Eng., 1973, Potts medal Franklin Inst., 1974; Harry Goode Meml. award Am. Fedn. Info. Processing Socs., 1977, Common Wealth award of Disting. Service, 1979, James R. Killain Jr. Faculty Achievement award MIT, 1987, Agricultura 2000 award, Italy, 1987, Info. Storage award IEEE Magnetics Soc., 1988, Lord Found. Leadership award, 1988, U.S. Nat. Medal of Tech., 1989, Pioneer award IEEE Aerospace & Electronic Systems Soc., 1990; named to Nat. Inventors Hall of Fame, 1979; Jay W. Forrester chair named in his honor, MIT. Fellow IEEE (medal of Honor 1972, Pioneer award 1990), Am. Acad. Arts and Scis., Acad. Mgmt.; mem. Nat. Acad. Engring., Inst. Mgmt. Scis., Soc. Mfg. Engrs. (hon.), Am. Phys. Soc., Assn. Computing Machinery, Eta Kappa Nu, Sigma Xi, Sigma Tau. Office: MIT Bldg E60-389 Cambridge MA 02139*

FORRESTER, PATRICIA TOBACCO, artist; b. Northampton, Mass., 1940. Student, Yale Summer Sch. Music and Art, 1961; BA, Smith Coll., 1962; BFA, Yale U., 1963, MFA, 1965. resident Yaddo Found., 1979, The MacDowell Colony Residency, 1980, Hand Hollow Found., 1981. One woman shows include Trutton Gallery, San Francisco, 1968, Capper's Gallery, San Francisco, 1970, William Sawyer Gallery, San Francisco, 1974, 81, 83, Smith Coll. Fine Arts Bldg., Northampton, 1975, M. H. de Young Meml. Mus., San Francisco, 1977, Kornblee Gallery, N.Y.C., 1978, 79, 81, 82, 83, Fendrick Gallery, Washington, 1978, 79, 81, 88, 90, Sebastian Moore Gallery, Denver, 1981, Contemporary Art Ctr., Honolulu, 1984, Frick Gallery, U. Pitts., 1984, U. Conn., 1984, New Orleans Acad. Fine Arts, 1984, 91, Mattingly-Baker Gallery, Dallas, 1985, Fischbach Gallery, N.Y.C., 1987, 89, 90, 92, Reynolds/Minor Gallery, Richmond, Va., 1987, Braunstein/Quay Gallery, San Francisco, 1987, 89, 91, 94, Gail Severn Gallery, Sun Valley, Idaho, 1988, Sierra Nevada Mus., Reno, 1988, N.Y. Stock Exch. Bldg., N.Y.C., 1989, Luria Gallery, Bay Harbor Island, Fla., 1990, Kalamazoo Inst. Arts, 1991, Stephen Scott Gallery, N.Y.C., 1992, Addison/Ripley Gallery, Washington, 1993, Gerald Peters Gallery, Santa Fe, 1994; exhibited in group shows Mattingly-Baker Gallery, Dallas, 1982, Springfield (Mo.) Art Mus., 1983, Pa. Acad. Fine Arts, Phila., 1983, Art Inst. Chgo., 1983, Corcoran Gallery, Washington, 1984, Bklyn. Mus., N.Y.C., 1985, William Sawyer Gallery, San Francisco, 1985, 88, Coll. of Mainland, Texas City, Tex., 1985, William's Coll. Art Ctr., Williamstown, Mass., 1985-86, Akron (Ohio) Art Mus., 1985-86, Madison (Wis.) Art Ctr., 1985-86, San Francisco Mus. Art, 1985-86, DeCordova and Dana Mus. Art, Lincoln, Mass., 1985-86, Archer M. Huntington Art Gallery U. Evanston, Ill., 1985-86, William's Coll. Art Ctr., Williamstown, Mass., 1985-86, Akron (Ohio) Art Mus., 1985-86, Madison (Wis.) Art Ctr., 1985-86, Metro. Mus., Miami, 1986, Springfield (Mo.) Art Mus., 1986, Art Mus. Santa Cruz County, 1987, The Sierra Nevada Mus. Art, Reno, Nev., 1988, William Sawyer Gallery, San Francisco, 1988, Kohler Arts Ctr., Sheboygan, Wis., 1988, Grand Ctrl. Art Galleries, N.Y.C., 1989, Fendrick Gallery, Washington, 1989, Gallery K., Washington, 1989, The Palmer Mus. Art, Pa., 1990, Steven Scott Gallery, Balt., 1990, Am. Acad. and Inst. Arts and Letters, N.Y.C., 1991, The Gallery at Bristol-Myers Squibb, Princeton, N.J., 1991, The Noyes Mus., N.J., 1991, Ctr. Contemporary Arts, Miami, 1991, Nat. Mus. Women in the Arts, 1991-92, The Miyagi Mus. Art, Sendai, Japan, 1991-92, Sogo Mus. Art, Yokohama, Japan, 1991-92, Tokushima (Japan) Mod. Art Mus., 1991-92, Mus. Modern Art, Shiga, Japan, 1991-92, Kochi (Japan) Prefectural Mus. Folk Art, 1991-92; Kavesh Gallery, Ketchum, Idaho, 1993, Nat. Acad. Design, N.Y.C., 1993, Sewall Art Gallery Rice U., Houston, 1993, Gerlad Peters Gallery, Santa Fe, N. Mex., 1993; represented in numerous pub. and pvt. permanent collections including The Achenbach Found., Art Inst. Chgo., Hawaii Arts Ctr., Indpls. Mus. Art., Meml. Art Gallery, Oakland Mus., N.Y. Pub. Lib., San Antonio Mus. Art, San Francisco Art Commn., Springfield Mus., The British Mus., The Brooklyn Mus., University Art Mus., others. Guggenheim fellow in printmaking, 1967. Mem. Nat. Acad. Design, Phi Beta Kappa. Address: Addison Ripley Fine Art 9 Hillyer Ct NW Washington DC 20008-1930 also: 2220 20th St NW Washington DC 20009-5074

FORROW, BRIAN DEREK, lawyer, corporation executive; b. N.Y.C., Feb. 6, 1927; s. Frederick George and Doris (Williams) F.; m. Eleanor Reid, Mar. 8, 1952; children: Lisa Coggins, Brian Lachlan, Catherine Frances, Derek Skylstead. AB, Princeton U., 1947; JD, Harvard U., 1950. Bar: N.Y. 1950, Conn. 1967. From assoc. to ptnr. Cahill, Gordon, Sonnett, Reindel & Ohl (and predecessors), 1950-68; v.p., gen. counsel Allied Chem. Corp., 1968-85, dir., 1969-85; sr. v.p., gen. counsel Allied-Signal Inc., 1985-92; pvt. practice, Greenwich, Conn., 1992—; of counsel Whitman Breed Abbott & Morgan, 1992-94; bd. dirs. Union Tex. Petroleum, 1985-92. Contbr. articles to profl. publs. Mem. Greenwich Represenative Town Meeting, 1993—; vestryman, former sr. warden, former diocesan rep., Episcopal Ch. Served to 1st lt. USAF, 1951-53. Mem. ABA, Am. Law Inst., Conn. Bar Assn., N.Y. State Bar Assn., Assn. Bar City of N.Y. (past chmn. com. corp. law depts.), Assn. Gen. Counsel, Am. Arbitration Assn. (bd. dirs. 1987-97), Corp. Bar Assn. Westchester-Fairfield (past pres., bd. dirs. 1986-91), Am. Corp. Counsel Assn. (bd. dirs. 1987-89), Assn. Corp. Counsel N.J. (past pres.), Indian Harbor Yacht Club, Harvard Club N.Y. Republican. Home and Office: 704 Lake Ave Greenwich CT 06830-3361

FORRY, JOHN EMERSON, retired aerospace company executive; b. Coweta, Okla., Feb. 13, 1920; s. Fred and Elizabeth (Ingram) E.; m. Marion Carlotta MacArthur, May 24, 1941; children: John Ingram, Anne Elizabeth. BSME, Okla. State U., 1939; LLB, George Washington U., 1953. Bar: D.C. 1953, Mo. 1960; registered profl. engr., D.C. Asst. chief engr. Piper Aircraft Corp., 1939-41; project engr. CAA, Kansas City, Mo., 1942; head aircraft design rsch. br. Bur. Aeros., USN, 1946-54; asst. dir. Office Aircraft and Marinecraft Dept. Def., 1954-57; with McDonnell Douglas Corp., St. Louis, 1957—, v.p., contr., 1968-77; exec. v.p. fin. Douglas Aircraft Co., Long Beach, 1977-79; ret.; bus. cons., 1979—. Various offices P.E. Diocese Mo.; trustee Maryville Coll.; vol. in healthcare and politics. Lt. USNR, 1943-46. Mem. Sigma Tau, Phi Delta Phi. Home and Office: 450 E Lockwood Ave Apt 209 Webster Grvs MO 63119-3160

FORSBERG, CAROLINE BERNICE, academic administrator; b. Pueblo, Colo., Sept. 6, 1944; s. Gustaf Adolf and Donna Lucy F. BA, William Smith Coll., 1967; MEd, SUNY, Albany, 1977, EdD, 1984. Tchr. Northeastern Assn. Blind, Albany, 1970-78, Computing & Disability, Albany, 1987-96; coord. disability SUNY Ctrl. Adminstrn., Albany, 1986-93; dir. disability, coord. ADA SUNY System Adminstrn., Albany, 1993—; cons. in field. Bd. dirs. Northeastern Assn. Blinc, 1980-85; mem. AHEAD Nat., Columbus, Ohio, 1986—; mem. steering com. Taskforce (Disabled), Albany, 1998—. Avocations: writing, dog training, software testing, philosophy. Office: SUNY 353 Broadway Albany NY 12246

FORSBERG, CHARLES ALTON, computer, information systems engineer; b. Wilmette, Ill., May 6, 1944; s. Delbert Alton and Margery (McCleary) F. Student, Rensselaer Poly. Inst.; BSEE, U. Wis., 1966, MSEE, 1968; postgrad., various univs. and colls. From design engr. to project leader Tektronix, Portland, Oreg., 1968-74; mgr. R&D Sidereal, Portland, 1974-80; chief engr. Computer Devel. Inc., Portland, 1980-84; pres. Omen Tech. Inc., Portland, 1984—. Developer YMODEM and ZMODEM Protocols for worldwide data transfer. Recognized for outstanding contbn. to field IBM-PC Users Group, Madison, Wis., 1988, Alamo PC Orgn., San Antonio, 1988. Home and Office: 10255 NW Old Cornelius Pass Rd Portland OR 97231-2515

FORSBERG, PETER, professional hockey player; b. Ornskoldsvik, Sweden, July 20, 1973. Profl. hockey player MODO Hockey Swedish League, 1990-94, Swedish Olympic Team, 1994, Quebec Nordiques, Colo. Avalanche, 1994—. Named to Swedish League All-Star team, 1991-92; named Swedish League Player of Yr., 1993-94, NHL Rookie of Yr., Sporting News, 1994-95; recipient Calder Meml. award 1994-95; mem. Gold Medal winning Swedish Olympic Team, 1994. Office: c/o Colorado Avalanche 1635 Clay St Denver CO 80204-1743*

FORSDALE, (CHALMERS) LOUIS, education and communication educator; b. Greeley, Colo., Mar. 8, 1922; s. John Aaron and Wilhelmina (Thorkildsen) F.; m. Elinor Wulfekuhler, Aug. 22, 1947 (dec. 1963); children: Lynn, John; m. Joan Ida Rosengren, May 28, 1964 (div. 1966). B.A., Colo. State Coll., 1942; M.A., Columbia U. Tchrs. Coll., 1947; Ed.D., Columbia U., 1951. Instr. English Tchrs. Coll., Columbia U., N.Y.C., 1947-51; asst. prof. Tchrs. Coll., Columbia U., 1951-55, assoc. prof., 1955-58, prof. communication and edn., 1958-87, prof. emeritus, 1987; vis. assoc. prof. edn. U. So. Calif., Los Angeles, 1957; cons. in communication various businesses, industries and schs., 1965—; vis. scholar Iran Communication and Devel. Inst., Tehran, 1977. Author: Nonverbal Communication, 1974, Perspectives on Communication, 1981; Editor: (with others) Communication in General Education, 1961, 8MM Sound Film and Education, 1962. Served to 1st lt. USAAF, 1943-45. Recipient Tchrs. Coll. Disting. Alumni award Merit, 1989. Democrat. Home: 330 Otero St Santa Fe NM 87501-1906

FORSEE, JOE BROWN, library director; b. Fulton, Ky., Oct. 25, 1949; divorced; children: Amy, Matthew. BS in Libr. Sci., Murray State U., 1971, MS in Libr. Sci., 1972. Assoc. regional libr. Barren River Regional Libr., Russellville, Ky., 1972-73; dir. interlibr. cooperation Ky. Dept. Libr. and Archives, Frankfort, 1973-76; libr. cons. Miss. Libr. Commn., Jackson, 1976, asst. dir. adminstrn., 1976-78, dir., 1978-80; dir. pub. libr. svcs. Ga. Dept. Edn., Atlanta, 1980-95; dir. N.W. Ga. Regional Libr., Dalton, 1995—; co-chmn. Gov.'s Conf. on Libr. and Info. Svcs.; past vice-chmn. White House Conf. Libr. and Info. Svcs. Task Force.; del. 1st and 2d White House Confs. Libr. and Info. Scis.; libr. bldg. cons., mgmt. cons. Contbr. articles to profl. jours., fed. and state docs.; guest spkr. in field. Mem. ALA, S.E. Libr. Assn. (past pres.), Ga. Libr. Assn. Home: 515 College St Calhoun GA 30701-1915 Office: NW Ga Regional Libr 310 Cappes St Dalton GA 30720-4123

FORSEN, HAROLD KAY, retired engineering executive; b. Sept. 19, 1932; s. Allen Kay and Mabel Evelyn (Buehler) F.; m. Betty Ann Webb, May 25, 1952; children: John Allen, Ronald Karl, Sandra Kay. AA, Compton Jr. Coll., 1956; BS, Calif. Inst. Tech., 1958, MS, 1959; PhD, U. Calif., Berkeley, 1965. Rsch. assoc. Gen. Atomic, San Diego, 1959-62; rsch. assoc., elec. engr. U. Calif., Berkeley, 1962-65; assoc. prof. nuclear engring. U. Wis., Madison,

1965-69, prof., 1969-73, dir. Phys. Sci. Lab., 1970-72; v.p. Exxon Nuc. Co., Bellevue, Wash., 1973-75, v.p., bd. dirs., 1975-80, exec. in charge of laser enrichment, 1981; exec. v.p. Jersey-Avco Isotopes, Inc., 1975-80, pres., 1981, dir., 1975-81; mgr. engring. and materials Bechtel Group, Inc., San Francisco, 1981-83, dep. mgr. rsch. and engring., 1983-84, mgr. advanced sys., 1984-85, mgr. R & D, 1986-91; sr. v.p. Bechtel Corp., San Francisco, 1986-95; mgr. Bechtel Tech. Group, 1992-93; v.p., dir. Bechtel Hanford Inc., 1994-95, ret., 1995; mem. fusion power reactor sr. rev. com. U.S. Dept. Energy, 1977, mem. magnetic fusion adv. com., 1982-86, mem. fusion policy adv. com., 1990, mem. fusion energy adv. com., 1994-96; mem. tech. adv. com. Internat. Thermonuc. Exptl. Reactor, 1996-98; mem. Fusion Indsl. Coun., U.S., 1994-96; chmn. U.S. del. to former Soviet Union on ion sources AEC, 1972; mem. vis. com. dept. nuc. energy Brookhaven Nat. Lab., 1992-96; mem. external rev. com. accelerator ops. and tech. divsn. Los Alamos Nat. Lab., 1993-96, mem. indsl. adv. bd. Lawrence Livermore Nat. Lab., 1994-98, univ. rsch. assn. overseer-at-large Fermilab Bd., 1995—, Univ. Chgo. rev. com. tech. devel. divsn., Argonne Nat. Lab., 1996—; mem. German-Am. Acad. Coun., 1996—, mem. exec. com., 1997—. Trustee, v.p. Pacific Sci. Ctr. Found., 1977, pres., 1978-80, chmn., 1981; mem. dean's vis. com. Coll. Engring., U. Wash., 1981—, dept. nuclear engring. and engring. physics indsl. rels. coun. U. Wis., 1987-92; mem. com. magnetic fusion in energy policy Nat. Rsch. Coun., 1987; pres. bd. dirs. Bay Area Sci. Fair, Inc., 1988-89; bd. dirs. Plasma and Materials Tech., Inc., 1988-91, Pepco, 1998-99; West Coast adv. bd. Inst. Internat. Edn., 1991-94; mem. bd. overseers Superconducting Super Collider, 1991-92; mem.-at-large bd. on assessment Nat. Inst. Standards and Tech., 1991-95; mem. adv. bd. to coll. engring. U. Calif., Berkeley, 1993-96; bd. visitors Coll. of Scis., Wash. State U., 1994-96. Served with USAF, 1951-55. Named San Francisco Bay Area Eminent Engr., 1990. Fellow Am. Phys. Soc., Am. Nuclear Soc. (Arthur H. Compton award 1972, chmn. tech. group controlled nuclear fusion 1973); mem. NAE (councillor 1993-95, fgn. sec. 1995—), Tau Beta Pi, Sigma Xi. Address: 386 Skidder Trl Truckee CA 96161-3929

FORSETH, PAUL, member of parliament; b. Dec. 14, 1946; m. Maureen Forseth; 2 children. B in Edn., U. B.C.; cert. pub. adminstrn., U. Victoria. M.P. for New Westminster-Burnaby House of Commons, 1993-97, M.P. for New Westminster-Coquitlam-Burnaby, 1997—, reform party dep. justice critic, 1997-98, vice chmn. standing com. on justice and legal affairs, 1997-98, reform party environment critic, 1995-97, mem. standing com. on environment and sustainable devel., mem. subcom. on econ. disincentives for environ., 1995, reform party justice critic, 1993-95, reform party dep. revenue critic, 1998—. Probation officer, family ct. counsellor B.C. Atty. Gen. Ministry, 1972-93. Office: House of Commons, 248 Wellington Bldg, Ottawa, ON Canada K1A 0A6*

FORSGREN, JOHN H., JR., financial executive; b. Cleve., Aug. 31, 1946; s. John H. and Jeanne Marie (Sullivan) F. B.A., Georgetown U., 1967; M.B.A., Columbia U., 1969; M.S., U. Geneva, Switzerland, 1972. With Alcan, 1969-75; dir. internat. fin. Sperry Corp., N.Y.C., 1977-80, staff v.p., 1980-83, treas., 1983-86; v.p., treas. The Walt Disney Co., Burbank, 1986-90, sr. v.p., chief fin. officer Euro Disney, 1990-91, exec. v.p., CFO, 1996—. Trustee Georgetown U. Library, Washington, 1983. Republican. Roman Catholic. Clubs: N.Y. Athletic; Essex Yacht (Conn.); Cercle de l'Union Internalliee (Paris); Metropolitan (N.Y.C.). *

FORSHAY, STEVEN R., marketing professional, consultant; b. Knoxville, Tenn., Nov. 17, 1942; s. Raymond Leroy and Majorie Zoe Forshay; m. Judith Ann West, Sept. 7, 1963; children: Steven William, Ann Marie, Sarah Lewis. BS, U. Tenn., 1964; MBA, U. Tenn., Chattanooga, 1972. Mfg. engr. Am. Lava Corp., Chattanooga, 1967-75; indsl. ceramic sales staff 3M-Tech. Ceramics, Sunnyvale, Calif., 1976-78; mktg. mgr. 3M-Tech. Ceramics, St. Paul, 1979-89; bus. mgr. 3M-Tech. Ceramics, Dusseldorf, Germany, 1990-94; mktg. ops. staff 3M-New Products Dept., St. Paul, 1995—; mktg. cons. in field. Chmn. staff parish Centennial United Meth., Roseville, Minn., 1988, chmn. long range planning, 1996. Capt. U.S. Army, 1964-66. Mem. Am. Ceramic Soc., Am. Soc. Metals, Am. Inst. Indsl. Engrs., Internat. Soc. Hybrid Microelectronics (com. chair 1976-78), Kiwanis Club Signal Mountain (pres. 1975-76). Avocation: international travel. Home: 19 Spring Farm Ln North Oaks MN 55127-2142 Office: 3M Bldg 220-9E-10 Saint Paul MN 55144

FORSLEFF, LOUISE STEWART, psychologist; b. Portland, Maine, Oct. 7, 1933; d. Roland and Gertrude (More) Peterson; m. Elmer Andrew Forsleff Dec. 24, 1965 (dec. June 4, 1993); children: Mary Anne, John Clark. AB, Lake Erie Coll., 1959; MA, Western Mich. U., 1962; PhD, Mich. State U., 1967. Lic. psychologist, Mich.; diplomate Am. Bd. Sexology. Testing, rsch. Kalamazoo Pub. Schs., 1962; counselor Western Mich. U., U. Counseling Ctr., Kalamazoo, 1962-68, dir., 1968-85; assoc. v.p. student svcs. Western Mich. U., Kalamazoo, 1985-90, prof. Sch. Cmty. Health Svcs., 1990-98, prof. emeritus, 1998—; coord. Profl. Exchg. Clearing House, 1977-79. Contbr. editor: An Outline of Sexology, 1993. Loaned exec. United Way, 1988; bd. dirs. Homestead, Inc., 1990-97, West Main Hill Neighorhood Assn., 1993-97. Recipient Faculty Rsch. grant Western Mich. U., 1992. Mem. Internat. Assn. Counseling Svcs. (bd. dirs. 1976-79, pres.-elect 1983-84, pres. 1984-85), Soc. Human Ecology, Inst. Noetic Scis. (del. Threads to the Future Conf. 1996). Mem. Soc. of Friends. Avocations: gardening, traveling, sailing. Office: Western Mich U Coll Health & Human Svcs Kalamazoo MI 49008

FORSLING, PETER J., defense analyst; b. Casper, Wyo.; m. Suzanne Forsling. BS in Physics, U. Wyo., 1984; MS in Physics, U. Iowa, 1988; diploma, U.S. Naval War Coll., 1996. Def. analyst NSWCDD, Dahlgren, Va., 1990-98. Republican. Roman Catholic. E-mail: pforsli@uwyo.edu. Office: Coll Engring Univ Wyo Laramie WY 82070

FORSMAN, CATHERINE ANNE, poet, webmaster; b. Denver, June 2, 1965; d. John Franklin Forsman and Marjorie Hildegard Jochum. BS, Columbia U., 1999. Editor Columbia U., N.Y.C., 1996-97, webmaster, 1998—. Mem. Assn. Computing Machinery, Siggraph.

FORSMAN, DAN BRUCE, professional golfer; b. Phinelander, Wis., July 15, 1958; m. Trudy Forsman; children: Ricky, Thomas. Grad., Ariz. State U., 1976. Winner matches including Shearson Lehman Hutton Open, 1990, Buick Open, 1992. Ranked 8th on PGA tour, 1992. Home: Riverside CC 2701 N University Ave Provo UT 84604-3817 Office: PGA Tour 112 Tpc Blvd Ponte Vedra Beach FL 32082-3077 also: PGA Am PO Box 109601 100 Ave of the Americas West Palm Beach FL 33410*

FORSON, NORMAN RAY, controller; b. Port Arthur, Tex., July 12, 1929; s. Hollis G. and Annie (Butler) F.; m. Nancy McAnelly, Dec. 6, 1952; children: James Hollis, Diana Nancy. BA, Baylor U., 1952; MBA, U. Houston, 1961. CPA, N.Y. Sales engr. Macgobar, New Orleans and Houston, 1956-57; buyer Transcontinental Gas Pipe Line, Houston, 1957-61; supr. Ernst & Young, Houston, 1961-65; sr. v.p., treas. Gulf & Western Inc., N.Y.C., 1965-83; sr. v.p., chief fin. officer Hi-Shear Industries, Inc., North Hills, N.Y., 1984-85, Jonathan Logan Inc., Teaneck, N.J., 1985-97; sr. v.p., comptroller United Mchts. & Mfgrs., Inc., Teaneck, 1987-97; cons., 1997—. Served to 1st lt. USAF, 1952-56. Home: 7315 Marigold Dr Irving TX 75063-5501

FORST, EDMUND CHARLES, JR., communications educator, consultant; b. Chgo., June 25, 1961; s. Edmund Sr. and Patricia Ann (Dopek) F.; m. Kelly Lee Globke; children: Morgan Mae, Shannon Rose. BA, Ea. Ill. U., 1983, MA, 1984; EdD, W. Va. U., 1994. Leader, mem. staff Neighborhood Boys Club, Chgo., summer 1975-84; instr. in communication DePaul U., Chgo., 1988-93; instr. Waubonsee C.C., Sugar Grove, Ill., 1993-94, assoc. dean comms. and humanities, 1994-98; dean arts & scis. Triton Coll., River Grove, Ill., 1998—; cons. communication for Leon Spinks, 1990. Contbr. articles to profl. jours. Eucharist minister Our Lady of Mercy, Chgo., 1989-90; bd. dirs. Neighborhood Boys Club, Chgo., 1988-92. Mem. Aurora-Naperville Rotary. Republican. Roman Catholic. Avocations: sports, reading, movie collecting, model railroads. Home: 101 Wesley Ave Oak Park IL 60302-2907

FORST, JUDITH DORIS, mezzo-soprano; b. New Westminster, B.C., Can., Nov. 7, 1943; d. Gordon Stanley and Euna Jessie (Thompson) Lumb; m. Graham Nicol Forst, May 30, 1964; children: Noel Graham, Paula Judith. MusB, U. B.C., Vancouver, 1965, LittD (hon.), 1991; LLD (hon.), U. B.C., 1992, D Music (hon.). featured lectr. U. B.C., U. Mont. Debut with Seattle Opera Co., 1967; debut with Met. Opera, 1968-74, guest artist, 1977, 89—; guest artist appearances throughout U.S. including San Francisco, New Orleans, Ft. Worth, Dallas, Santa Fe and Seattle opera cos., N.Y.C. Opera, Opera Soc. Washington, Can. Opera Co., Toronto, Ont., Miami Opera Co., Vancouver Opera Assn., Edmonton Opera Assn., Winnipeg Opera Assn., Calgary Opera Assn., Montreal Symphony, Vancouver Symphony., Balt. Opera Co., Nat. Arts Ctr., Ottawa, Ont., Can., appeared in performance for Queen Elizabeth, Vancouver, 1983; European debut Orchestre de la Radio-Diffusion Française, Paris, 1985, Bayersiche Staatsoper, Munich, 1987, State Orch. of Spain, Barcelona, English Nat. Opera, 1994. Decorated Order of Can.; named Can. Woman of Yr., 1978, Walter and Ida Olsen Young Am. Artist of Yr., Miami Opera Assn., 1980; recipient Disting. Alumnus award U. B.C., 1986. Mem. Actors Equity, Am. Guild Musical Artists, Assn. Canadian TV Radio Artists, Vancouver Symphony Soc. (bd. dirs.), Order Can. (officer 1992). Winner N.W. regional finals Met. Opera auditions, 1968; Canadian Broadcasting Co. Cross-Can. Talent Contest, 1968. Office: care Columbia Artists Mgmt 165 W 57th St New York NY 10019-2201

FORST, MARION FRANCIS, bishop; b. St. Louis, Sept. 3, 1910; s. Frank A.J. and Bertha T. (Gulath) F. Grad., Kenrick Sem., Webster Groves, Mo., 1934. Ordained priest Roman Catholic Ch., 1934; pastor St. Mary's Cathedral, Cape Girardeau, Mo., 1949-60; vicar gen. Diocese of Springfield-Cape Girardeau, 1956-60; bishop Dodge City, Kans., 1960-76; aux. bishop Archdiocese of Kansas City, Kans., 1976-86; ret., 1986; Kan. chaplain K.C., 1964—. Served with Chaplains Corps USNR, World War II. Office: 12615 Parallel Ave Kansas City KS 66109-3718*

FORSTADT, JOSEPH LAWRENCE, lawyer; b. Bklyn., Feb. 21, 1940; BA, CCNY, 1961; LLB, NYU, 1964. Bar: N.Y. 1965, U.S. Supreme Ct. 1968. spl. legal counsel to bd. justices Supreme Ct. N.Y. County, 1965-67; dep. commr. N.Y.C. Dept. Licenses, 1967-68, acting commr., 1968-69; acting commr. N.Y.C. Dept. Consumer Affairs, 1969; asst. adminstr. Econ. Devel. Adminstrn., 1969; assoc. Stroock & Stroock & Lavan, N.Y.C., 1969-75, ptnr., 1976—; lectr. in trial practice N.Y. County Lawyers Assn., Practising Law Inst., 1993; mem. N.Y.C. Rent Guidelines Bd., 1984-97; arbitrator U.S. Dist. Ct. (ea. dist.) N.Y.; spl. counsel Appellate div. First Dept., Disciplinary Com. Author: (monograph) Prosecuting and Defending Title Insurance Claims, 1993, 94. Dist. campaign mgr. John V. Lindsay for Mayor of N.Y.C., 1965; campaign mgr. Congressman Theodore Kupferman, 1966; chmn. N.Y.C Young People for Nixon, 1968; pres. N.Y. Young Rep. Club, 1969-71; chmn. N.Y. State Assn. Young Rep. Clubs, 1970-72; vice chmn. N.Y. Com. to Re-elect Pres. Nixon, 1972. Recipient Brotherhood award NCCJ, 1987; Judge Jacob Markowitz scholar NYU, N.Y.C., 1964. Mem. Fed. Bar Council, Am. Judicature Soc., Phi Alpha Delta. Office: Stroock Stroock & Lavan 180 Maiden Ln New York NY 10038-4925

FORSTER, ARNOLD, lawyer, author; b. N.Y.C., June 25, 1912; s. Hyman Lawrence and Dorothy (Turits) Fastenberg; m. May Kasner, Sept. 29, 1940; children: Stuart William (dec.), Janie Forster Berman. LLB, St. John's U., 1935. Bar: N.Y. 1935, U.S. Supreme Ct. 1949. Gen. practice law, 1935-40; dir. law dept. Anti-Defamation League of B'nai Brith, 1940-46; asso. dir. Anti-Defamation League of B'nai B'rith, 1946-78, gen. counsel, 1946—; of counsel Shea & Gould, N.Y.C., 1979-94, Baer Marks and Upham, N.Y.C., 1994—; police justice N.Y. State, 1954-57. Author: Anti-Semitism in the United States, 1947, A Measure of Freedom, 1950, The Troublemakers, 1952, Cross-Currents, 1956, Some of My Best Friends, 1962, Danger on the Right, 1964, (with B.R. Epstein) Report on the Ku Klux Klan, 1965, Report on the John Birch Society, 1966, Radical Right: Report on the John Birch Society and Its Allies, 1967, Report From Israel, 1969, The New Anti-Semitism, 1974, Square One, 1988, Stubs-A Letter to His Children, 1994; author (TV/radio) Dateline Israel, 1967-83. Mem. bd. edn., New Rochelle, N.Y., 1962-66. Recipient Emmy award for film Avenue of the Just, 1980, Emmy award for film Zubin and the I.P.O., 1983. Home: 79 Wykagyl Ter New Rochelle NY 10804-3207 Office: Baer Marks and Upham 805 Third Ave New York NY 10022-7513 *In one's vintage years, it becomes unarguably clear that the only true satisfaction is in understanding that one's achievements, however small or large, made others happy and this earth a better place for living.*

FORSTER, BRUCE ALEXANDER, dean; b. Toronto, Ont., Can., Sept. 23, 1948; m. Margaret Jane Mackay, Dec. 28, 1968 (div. Dec. 1979); 1 child, Kelli Elissa; m. Valerie Dale Pendock, Dec. 8, 1979; children: Jeremy Bruce, Jessica Dale. BA in Math., Econs., U. Guelph, Ont., 1970; PhD in Econs., Australian Nat. U., Canberra, 1974. From asst. prof. to assoc. prof. U. Guelph, 1973-83; prof. econs. U. B.C., Vancouver, 1979; vis. assoc. fellow U. Wyo., 1979-80, vis. prof., 1983-84, 87, prof. econs., 1987—, dean Coll. Bus., 1991—; vis. prof. Profl. Tng. Ctr., Ministry of Econ. Affairs, Taiwan, 1990-97; acad. assoc. The Atlantic Coun. of the U.S., cons. in field; Jayes-Qantas vis. scholar U. Newcastle, Australia, 1983. Author: The Acid Rain Debate: Science and Special Interest in Policy Formation, 1993; co-author: Economics in Canadian Society, 1986; assoc. editor: Jour. Applied Bus. Rsch., 1987, mem. editl. adv. bd., 1987—; editl. coun.: Jour. Environ. Econs. and Mgmt., 1989, assoc. editor, 1989-91; contbr. articles to profl. jours. Trustee Wyo. Retirement Sys., 1995—, Laramie Sr. Housing, Inc., 1995-96. Mem. Internat. Assn. Mgmt. Edn. (bus. accreditation com. 1995-98), Am. Econ. Assn., Assn. Environ. and Resource Economists, Mid-West Assn. Bus. Deans and Divsn. Heads (pres. 1995-96), Faculty Club U. Guelph (treas. 1981-82, v.p. 1982-83, 85-86, pres. 1986-87). Avocations: weight lifting, swimming, skiing, scuba diving. Home: 3001 Sage Dr Laramie WY 82070-5751 Office: U Wyo Coll Bus Laramie WY 82071

FORSTER, FRANCIS MICHAEL, physician, educator; b. Cin., Feb. 14, 1912; s. Michael Joseph and Louise Barbara (Schmid) F.; m. Helen Dorothy Kiley, June 15, 1937; children—Denis, Susan, Kathleen, Mark, Gabrielle. Student, Xavier U., Cin., 1930-32, LL.D., 1955; B.S., U. Cin., 1935, B.M., 1936, M.D., 1937; D.Sc. hon., Georgetown U., 1982. Diplomate: Am. Bd. Psychiatry and Neurology (dir.). Rotating intern Good Samaritan Hosp., Cin., 1936-37; house officer neurology and neurosurgery Boston City Hosp., 1937-38, resident neurology, 1939-40; fellow psychiatry Pa. Hosp., Phila., 1938-39; asst. neurology Harvard Med. Sch., 1939-40; Rockefeller Found. research fellow physiology Yale Sch. Medicine, 1940-41; instr. neurology Boston U. Sch. Medicine, 1941-43; asst. prof. neurology Jefferson Med. Sch., 1943-47, asso. prof. neurology, 1947-50; prof. neurology, dir. dept. Georgetown U. Sch. Medicine, 1950-58, dean Sch. Medicine, 1953-58; prof., chmn. dept. neurology U. Wis. Sch. Medicine, 1958-78; emeritus, 1978—; dir. Epilepsy Center, VA Hosp., Madison, Wis., 1977-82; cons. neurology. Author: Synopsis of Neurology, 1962, 66, 73, 78, Reflex Epilepsy, Behavioral Therapy and Conditional Reflexes, 1977; editor: Modern Therapy in Neurology, 1957, Evaluation of Drug Therapy, 1961. Mem. AMA (chmn. nervous and mental diseases sect. 1952-53), AAAS, D.C. Med. Soc. (chmn. sect. neurology and psychiatry 1955-56, pres. 1958), Am. Acad. Neurology (chmn. survey com. 1948-51, pres. 1957-59), Am. Neurol. Assn. (chmn. com. internat. collaboration 1954-55), Am. Epilepsy League (pres. 1951-52), Assn. Rsch. Nervous and Mental Diseases, Am. Physiol. Soc., Am. Assn. Electroencephalographers, Med. Soc. Wis., Cosmos Club (Washington), Sigma Xi, Alpha Omega. Club: Cosmos (Washington). Home: 21 Fallen Br Cincinnati OH 45241-3242 Office: U Wis Med Sch 600 Dept Neurology Madison WI 53792

FORSTER, FREDERICK HARWOOD, air force officer; b. Huntsville, Ala., Sept. 22, 1946; s. Melancthon Graham and Harriet (Canterberry) F.; m. Carolyn DeLozier, July 10, 1981; children: Joy Elizabeth, Katherine Anne, Rebecca Lynne. BA in English Lit., U. of the South, 1968; MS in Founds. of Edn., Troy State U., 1972. Commd. 2d lt. USAF, 1968, advanced through grades to brig. gen., 1998, pilot/staff officer, 1968-76; group plans officer 134th Arg, Tenn. Air N.G., Knoxville, 1976-77, aircraft maintenance officer, 1977-87, wing comdr., 1987—; regional bd. dirs. Bank of East Tenn., Maryville, 1989-93, First Tenn. Bank, Maryville, 1996—; mem. sr. seminar U.S. Dept. State, Washington, 1993-94; chancellor's assocs. U. Tenn., Knoxville, 1996—. Chmn. Blount County C. of C., Maryville, 1992, United Way of Blount County, 1997; mem. Leadership Knoxville, 1990, Leadership Blount County, 1996. Decorated Bronze star, Legion of Merit; recipient Citizen of Yr. award Boy Scouts Am., 1992. Mem. N.G. Assn. Tenn., N.G. Assn. U.S., Kiwanis (pres. elect 1990-92). Home: 1046 Nina Delozier Rd Maryville TN 37804-2329 Office: 201 S Washington St Maryville TN 37804-5728

FORSTER, JOHN, JR., federal judge; b. 1942. BA, North Tex. State U., 1965; JD, U. Ark., 1969. Pvt. law practice North Little Rock, Ark., 1969-72, 78-86; dep. pros. atty. Sixth Jud. dist., 1972; asst. U.S. atty. ea. dist. Ark. Dept. Justice, 1972-76; spl. commr. Ark. Workers Compensation Commn., 1979; adj. faculty U. Ark., Little Rock, 1973; mem. faculty Memphis State U., 1987. Office: 600 W Capitol Ave Ste 399 Little Rock AR 72201-3323

FORSTER, JULIAN, physicist, consultant; b. N.Y.C., Aug. 31, 1918; s. Meyer Kivetz and Rose (Sommer) F.; m. Frieda Bain, July 2, 1941; children: Jeffrey M., Laura Gherman. BS in Physics, CCNY, 1940. Registered nuclear engr., Calif. Sr. physicist US Naval 4th Dist., Phila., 1941-56; sr. nuclear engr. GE, San Jose, Calif., 1956-70, sr. project mgr. nuclear energy dept., 1970-80; sr. mgmt. tech. Quadrex Corp., Campbell, Calif., 1980-85, cons., 1985-96; cons. GE-NE, 1996—. Contbr. articles to profl. jours. Commr. Fine Arts, San Jose, 1987-95. Fellow IEEE (life, emeritus; standards bd. 1970—, computer soc. 1985—, nuclear scis. soc. 1963—, power engring. soc. 1975—, coord. pace divsn. IV 1993—, chmn. awards and recognition com. 1986-95, Divsnl. Profl. Achievment award 1994, Standards Bd. Spl. Achievement award 1995); mem. Internat. Electro Tech. Com. (nuclear power com. SC45A 1969—, R.F. Shea Svc. award 1992). Democrat. Jewish. Avocations: music, wine, fine arts, golf. Fax: (408) 925-5312. Fax: 408-925-5312. E-mail: jay.forster@gene.ge.com. Home: 6962 Castlerock Dr San Jose CA 95120-4704 Office: GE NE MC/801 175 Curtner Ave San Jose CA 95125-1014

FORSTER, LANCE ALLEN, technical researcher animal science; b. Phila., Oct. 8, 1963; s. Lance Allen and Arlene Marie (Janisheck) F.; m. Kristina Krim, Sept. 26, 1992. BS in Animal Husbandry, Delaware Valley Coll. Sci., 1985, BS in Dairy Husbandry, 1985; student dairy herdsmanship, Delware Valley Coll. Sci., 1981-84; MS in Animal Sci., Va. Poly. Inst., 1988; PhD, U. Ark., 1993. Mechanics asst. Delaware Valley Coll., Doylestown, Pa., 1984; grad. rsch. asst. Va. Poly. Inst. & State U., 1985-87; tech. rschr. Dept. Animal Sci. U. Ark., Fayetteville, 1988-93; nutritionist oilseed processing divsn. Archer Daiels Midland Co., Memphis, 1993-98. Contbr. articles to profl. jours. Mem. Am. Soc. Animal Sci., Am. Forage & Grassland Coun., Tristates Oil Mill Supts., Internat. Oil Mill Supt. Assn., Sigma Xi, Delta Tau Alpha. Avocations: hunting, fishing, reading, philately, gardening. Office: Archer Daniels Midland Co PO Box 1470 Decatur IL 62525-1820

FORSTER, MERLIN HENRY, foreign languages educator, author, researcher; b. Delta, Utah, Feb. 24, 1928; s. Henry and Ila Almeda (Rawlinson) F.; m. Vilda Mae Naegle, Apr. 25, 1952; children: Celia Marlene, David Merlin, Angela, Daniel Conrad, Elena Marie. BA, Brigham Young U., 1956; MA, U. Ill., 1957, PhD, 1960. Instr. in Spanish U. Tex., Austin, 1960-61, asst. prof., 1961-62; asst. prof. Spanish and Portuguese U. Ill., Urbana, 1962-65, assoc. prof., 1965-69, prof., 1969-78, dir. Latin Am. studies, 1972-78; prof., chmn. dept. Spanish and Portuguese, U. Tex., Austin, 1978-87; disting. prof. Latin Am. lit. Brigham Young U., Provo, Utah, 1987-98, chmn. dept. Spanish and Portuguese, 1989-93; prof. emeritus Brigham Young U., Provo, 1998—; dir. summer seminars NEH, 1978, 89, 90, 93, 96, 98. Author: Los Contemporáneos, 1964, Fire and Ice, 1976, Historia de la Poesia Hispanoamericana, 1981; editor: Index to Mexican Journals, 1966, Tradition and Renewal, 1975, De la Crónica a la Nueva Narrativa, 1986, Vanguardism in Latin American Literature: An Annotated Bibliographical Guide, 1990. Rsch. grantee Social Sci. Rsch. Coun., Mexico City, 1965, Fulbright-Hays, Buenos Aires, 1971, NEH, Austin, 1986-87, Am. Coun. Learned Socs. and German Acad. Exch. Svc., 1993-94; fellow Ctr. for Advanced Study, Urbana, 1976-77. Mem. MLA, Latin Am. Studies Assn., Am. Assn. Tchrs. Spanish and Portuguese, Internat. Inst. Iberoam. Lit. (pres. 1981-83, 94-96). Mem. LDS Ch. Avocations: classical music, quartet singing, gardening, woodworking. Office: Brigham Young Univ Dept Spanish and Portuguese Provo UT 84602

FORSTER, ROBERT, history educator; b. N.Y.C., June 7, 1926; s. Theodore and Elise (Strobel) F.; m. Elborg Hamacher, July 8, 1955; children: Marc Richard, Thomas Theodore. B.A., Swarthmore Coll., 1949; M.A. in Modern European History, Harvard U., 1951; Ph.D., Johns Hopkins U., 1956; D. honoris causa, U. Toulouse, France, 1985. Instr. modern European history Johns Hopkins U., 1956-57; Bissing fellow U. Toulouse, France, 1957-58; asst. prof. U. Nebr., 1958-62; assoc. prof. Dartmouth, 1962-65; prof. history Johns Hopkins, 1966-96, prof. emeritus, 1996—; fellow Inst. for Advanced Study, Princeton, N.J., 1975-76, Center for Advanced Study in Behavioral Scis., Stanford U., 1979-80; U.S. rep. Internat. Congress Hist. Scis., 1975-80. Author: The Nobility of Toulouse in the 18th Century, 1960, The House of Saulx-Tavanes: Versailles and Burgundy, 1700-1830, 1971, Seeds of Change: Peasants, Nobles, and Rural Revolution in 18th Century France, 1975; author: Merchants, Landlords, Magistrates: The Depont Family in 18th Century France, 1980; Author also articles.; Editor: (with Elborg Forster) European Society in the 18th Century, 1969, (with Jack P. Greene) Preconditions of Revolution in Early Modern Europe, 1970, (with Elborg Forster) European Diet from Pre-Industrial to Modern Times, 1975, (with Orest Ranum) Biology of Man in History, 1975, Family and Society, 1976, (with E. Carter and J. Moody) Enterprise and Entrepreneurs in 19th and 20th Century France, 1976, (with Orest Ranum) Rural Society in France, 1977, Deviants and the Abandoned, 1978, Food and Drink in History, 1979, Medicine and Society in France, 1980, Ritual, Religion, and the Sacred, 1981, (with Elborg Forster) Sugar and Slavery, Family and Race, 1996, European and Non-European Societies, 1450-1800, 2 vols., 1997. Served with AUS, 1944-46. French Govt. fellow, 1953-55; Social Scr. Rsch. Coun. fellow France, 1962, 64; Guggenheim fellow Paris, 1969-70; NEH fellow, 1983-84; recipient Prix Gaussail Acad. Toulouse, 1954, Chevalier de l'Ordre des Palmes Academiques award French Govt., 1994; named Hon. Citizen Vieillevigne, France, 1977; Doctor Honoris Causa, Toulouse, 1985. Mem. Internat. Commn. for Study of French Revolution, Soc. French Hist. Studies (pres. 1974), French Colonial Hist. Soc., Soc. Caribbean History, Am. Hist. Assn. (coun. 1985-88), Phi Beta Kappa. Home: 208 Oakdale Rd Baltimore MD 21210-2520

FORSTER, ROBERT, actor, speaker; b. Rochester, N.Y., July 13, 1941; s. Robert Wallace and Grace (Montanarella) F.; m. June Carol Provenzano (div.); children: Robert, Elizabeth, Kathrine, Maeghen; m. Tsvia Mizrahi (div.). BA in History and Psychology, U. Rochester, 1964; student, Heidelberg Coll., Tiffin, Ohio, 1959-60, Alfred (N.Y.) U., 1960-62. Actor, 1966—; motivational speaker Interacting, L.A.; instr. actor workshops. Appeared in Broadway plays Mrs. Dally Has a Lover, 1965, Streetcar Named Desire; Off-Broadway plays include Glass Menagerie, Twelve Angry Men, The Sea Horse, others; films include Reflections in a Golden Eye, 1966, Medium Cool, 1968, The Don is Dead, Stunts, Avalanche, Jackie Brown, 1997 (Acad. award nominee), American Perfekt, Psycho, 1998, others; T.V. appearances in Banyon, 1972, Nakia, 1974, Death Squad, Standing Tall, Police Story, Once a Hero, others, TV movie Rear Window, 1998; prodr., dir. Hollywood Harry, 1985. *

FORSTER, WILLIAM HULL, aerospace executive; b. Shelby, Miss., June 24, 1939; s. William Oskar Hermann and Amy B. (Hull) F.; children: William Hull Jr., Robert Brown. BS in Chemistry and Physics, U. Ala., 1960; PhD in Nuclear Chemistry, U. Calif., 1965; grad. Air Force War Coll., Navy Test Pilot Sch. Entered U.S. Army, 1965, advanced through grades to lt. gen.; comdr. Battery C, 6/56th Arty., Vietnam, 1965-66, 173d Assault Helicopter Co., Vietnam, 1971-72, 10th Combat Aviation Bn., Ft. Lewis, Wash., 1976-78; chief aviation systems div. hdqrs. U.S. Army, Washington, 1981-82; project mgr. Army Helicopter Improvement Program, 1982-85; dep. comdg. gen. Army Aviation Systems Command, 1985-86; program mgr. Apache Advanced Attack Helicopter, 1986-87; program exec. officer Combat Aviation, 1987-88; dir. requirements hdqrs. U.S. Army, Washington, 1988-91; comdr. Army Operational Test and Evaluation Command, Alexandria, Va., 1991-92; dep. asst. sec. rsch., devel., and acquisition U.S. Army, Washington, 1992-95; ret., 1995; now v.p. land combat systems Northrop G. Corp. Chmn. Nat. Rsch. Coun. Bd. Army Sci. and Tech. Decorated D.F.C., D.S.M. with oak leaf cluster, Bronze Star with oak leaf cluster, Legion of Merit with oak leaf cluster, Air medal (15 awards). Fellow Am.

Helicopter Soc.; mem. Am. Phys. Soc., Russian Acad. Natural Sci., Army Aviation Assn. (v.p.), Nat. Aeronautic Assn. Presbyterian. Avocations: boating, automobile repair. Home: 5224 Lighthorne Rd Burke VA 22015-1726

FORSTOT, STEPHAN LANCE, ophthalmologist; b. N.Y.C., Aug. 19, 1943; s. Shepard and Edith Forstot; m. Lynne Rochelle Bitton, June 15, 1945; children: Michele, Jordan. AB, Princeton U., 1965; MD, Johns Hopkins U., 1969. Diplomate Am. Bd. Ophthalmology. Ophthalmologist Corneal Cons. of Colo., Denver, 1982—; ophthalmologist U. Colo. Sch. of Medicine, Denver, 1976-82, clin. prof., 1982—. Contbr. articles to profl. jours. Recipient Honor award Am. Acad. Ophthalmology. Mem. Contact Lens Assn. of Ophthalmology (bd. dirs. 1985-87), Internat. Soc. Refractive Surgery (bd. dirs. 1995-96). Avocation: tennis. Office: Corneal Cons of Colo 8381 Southpark Ln Littleton CO 80120-4508

FORSYTH, BARBARA JEAN, elementary reading specialist, writer, poet; b. Detroit, Nov. 20, 1946; d. Henry Gurney and Alice Elaine Shreve; m. Sid H. Forsyth, May 28, 1966.; children: Janelle Forsyth Bauer, Linette Forsyth Donovan. BS in Edn., Taylor U., 1966; M in Edn., Calif. State U., L.A., 1980; adminstrv. credential, Calif. State U., Fullerton, 1997. Cert. tchr., reading specialist, Calif. Tchr. Rivera Elem. Sch., El Rancho Unified Sch. Dist., Pico Rivera, Calif., 1967-72; tchr. 3d and 4th grade LEP Class Hacienda La Puenta Unified Sch. Dist., Hacienda Hghts., Calif., 1979-80; reading specialist Monrovia Unified Sch. Dist., Monrovia, Calif., 1981-86, Alicia Cortez Elem. Sch., Chino, Calif., 1986—; cons. Houghton-Mifflin, San Jose, Calif., 1997—; mentor Tchrs. of English Conf., San Diego, Calif., Calf. Reading Conf., Long Beach and Anaheim, Internat. Reading Assn., Albuquerque, N. Mex. Author: poetry, childrens' books; presenter How to Teach Reading using Readers' Theatre, 1996. Vol. Rep. campaign for state senate Chino, Calif., 1998. Recipient Editor's Choice award Nat. Libr. Poetry, Washington, 1997, 98. Fellow Internat. Soc. Poets; mem. ASCD, PTA, Internat. Reading Assn., Calif. Reading Assn., Foothill Reading Coun. Republican. Avocations: reading, writing plays, poetry, planning curriculum materials and weddings. Home: 1341 Mallard Ct #A Chino CA 91709 Office: Cortez Sch 12756 Carissa Chino CA 91710

FORSYTH, BEN RALPH, academic administrator, medical educator; b. N.Y.C., Mar. 8, 1934; s. Martin and Eva (Lazansky) F.; m. Elizabeth Held, Aug. 19, 1962; children: Jennifer, Beverly, Jonathan. Attended, Cornell U., 1950-53; MD, NYU, 1957. Diplomate Am. Bd. Internal Medicine. Intern, then resident Yale Hosp., New Haven, 1957-60; postdoctoral fellow Harvard U. Med. Sch., Boston, 1960-61; rsch. assoc. NIH, Bethesda, Md., 1963-66; assoc. prof. med. microbiology, prof. med. coll. U. Vt., Burlington, 1966-90, assoc. dean div. health scis., 1971-85, assoc. v.p. acad. affairs, 1977-78, v.p. adminstrn., 1978-85, sr. v.p., 1985-90; sr. exec. asst. to pres. Ariz. State U., Tempe, 1990—, prof. health adminstrn. and policy, 1991—, interim v.p. adminstrv. svcs., 1991-93; interim provost Ariz. State U. West, Phoenix, 1992-93, Ariz. State U. East, Mesa, 1994-96; provost, v.p. Ariz. State U. West, Phoenix, 1993-96; sr. cons. Univ. Health Ctr., Burlington, 1986-90. Contbr. articles to profl. jours. V.p., chmn. United Way Planning Com., Burlington, 1974-75, Ops. Com., 1975-76, bd. dirs., officer, 1977-89; bd. trustees U. Vt., Burlington, 1996—; mem. New England Bd. Higher Edn. Com., Burlington, 1985-89; chmn. U. Vt. China Project Adv. Bd., Burlington, 1989-90. Lt. comdr. USN, 1962-63. Sinsheimer Found. faculty fellow, 1966-71. Fellow ACP, Infectious Diseases Soc. Am.; mem. Phi Beta Kappa, Alpha Omega Alpha. Avocations: hiking, gardening, travel. Office: Arizona State Univ PO Box 872203 Tempe AZ 85287-2203

FORSYTH, ILENE HAERING, art historian; b. Detroit, Aug. 21, 1928; d. Austin Frederick and Eleanor Marie (Middleton) H.; m. George H. Forsyth, Jr., June 4, 1960. A.B., U. Mich., 1950; A.M. (univ. fellow), Columbia U., 1955, Ph.D. (Fulbright, AAUW, Fels Found. fellow), 1960. Lectr. Barnard Coll., 1955-58; instr. Columbia U., 1959-61; mem. faculty U. Mich., Ann Arbor, 1961—; prof. history of art U. Mich., 1974-97, prof. emerita, 1998—, Arthur F. Thurnau prof., 1984—; vis. prof. Harvard U., 1980; Mellon vis. prof. U. Pitts., 1981; vis. prof. U. Calif., Berkeley, 1996; mem. Nat. Com. History Art, 1975-97; bd. dirs. Internat. Ctr. Medieval Art, 1970-95, v.p., 1981-85; mem. supervisory com. Woodrow Wilson Found., 1985-88; Rome prize juror Am. Acad. in Rome, 1986-88; bd. advisors Ctr. Advanced Study in the Visual Arts, Nat. Gallery Art, 1985-88; mem. vis. com. medieval dept. Met. Mus. Art, N.Y.C., 1990-95; Samuel H. Kress prof. Ctr. Advanced Study in the Visual Arts, Nat. Gallery Art, 1998—. Author: The Throne of Wisdom, 1972 (Charles Rufus Morey Book award 1974), The Uses of Art: Medieval Metaphor in The Michigan Law Quadrangle, 1993 (Annie award for non-fiction 1994); co-editor: Current Studies on Cluny, 1988; contbr. articles to profl. jours. Rackham research grantee and fellow, 1965-66, 75-76; grantee Am. Council Learned Socs., 1972-73; mem. Inst. Advanced Study Princeton, 1977. Mem. Coll. Art Assn. (dir. 1980-84), Archaeol. Inst. Am., Medieval Acad. Am. (bd. advs. 1985-86, editorial bd. 1986-90), Medieval Club N.Y., Soc. francaise d'archéologie, Soc. Archtl. Historians, Acad. Arts, Scis. et Belles Lettres Dijon (France), Centre de recherches et d'études préromanes et romanes. Home: 5 Graddes Hts Ann Arbor MI 48104 Office: U Mich Dept Art History Ann Arbor MI 48109

FORSYTH, JOSEPH, privacy and information management consultant; b. County Durham, Eng., Aug. 15, 1942; emigrated to Can., 1966; s. James Frederick and Maisie (Appleby) F.; m. Kay Frances Appleby, Oct. 3, 1964; children: Julian Alastair, Andrew Stuart. Asso. of Library Assn., Newcastle (Eng.) Sch. Librarianship, 1963; MA in Library Sci., U. London, 1976, Fellow of Library Assn., 1971. Library asst. Durham County Library, 1960-62; coll. librarian Easington (Eng.) Tech. Coll., 1962-63; regional librarian North Riding County (Eng.) Library, 1964-66; reference librarian Calgary (Alta., Can.) Public Library, 1966-70; library devel. officer Govt. Alta., Edmonton, 1970-77; dir. library services Alta. Dept. Culture, Edmonton, 1977-86; regional supt. air navigation programming and adminstrn. Transport Can., 1986-87; spl. intergovtl. advisor Alta. Fed. and Intergovtl. Affairs Dept., 1988, asst. dep. min. cultural devel., 1990-93; dir. libr. svcs. Alta. Culture and Multiculturalism, Edmonton, 1988-91; asst. dep. min. Individual Rights and Citizenship Svc., Alta., Edmonton, 1993-95; dir. Freedom of Info. and Protection of Privacy and Records Mgmt./Alta Comm. Devel., 1995-97; prin. foippassociates, 1997—. Author: Government Publications Relating to Alberta, 1972. Anglican. Office: 4552-99 St, Edmonton, AB Canada T6E 5H5

FORSYTH, RAYMOND ARTHUR, civil engineer; b. Reno, Mar. 13, 1928; s. Harold Raymond and Fay Exona (Highfill) F.; BS, Calif. State U., San Jose, 1952; M.C.E., Auburn U., 1958; m. Mary Ellen Wagner, July 9, 1950; children: Lynne, Gail, Alison, Ellen. Jr. engr., asst. engr. Calif. Div. Hwys., San Francisco, 1952-54; assoc. engr., sr. supervising, prin. engr. Calif. Dept. Transp., Sacramento, 1961-83, chief geotech. br., 1972-79, chief soil mechanics and pavement br., 1979-83, chief Transp. Lab., 1983-89; cons., lectr. in field. Served with USAF, 1954-56. Fellow ASCE (pres. Sacramento sect., chmn. Calif. council 1980-81); mem. Transp. Research Bd. (chmn. embankments and earth slopes com. 1976-82, chmn. soil mechanics sect. 1982-88, chmn. group 2 council 1988-91), ASTM. Contbr. articles to profl. publs. Home: 5017 Pasadena Ave Sacramento CA 95841-4149

FORSYTHE, HENDERSON, actor; b. Macon, Mo., Sept. 11, 1917; s. Cecil Proctor and Mary Catherine (Henderson) F.; m. Dorothea Maria Carlson, May 26, 1942; children: Eric, Jason. Student, Culver-Stockton Coll., 1935-37; B.A., State U. Iowa, 1939, M.F.A., 1940. mem. faculty, dir. U. Iowa, summers 1953-55. Numerous appearances Broadway and off-Broadway plays, TV and film prodns., 1955—; sheriff in U.S. and London prodns. Best Little Whorehouse in Texas (Tony award); prin. role in TV series Eisenhower and Lutz, CBS, 1987-88, Nearly Departed, 1989; appeared in running role in daytime TV drama As the World Turns, 1960-91; prin. role in 110 in the Shade, N.Y.C. Opera, 1992; lead in Quarrel of Sparrows, 1993; TV comml./Col. Sanders for Kentucky Fried Chicken, 1994. Served with U.S. Army, 1941-46. Mem. Actors Equity Assn., AFTRA, Screen Actors Guild, ANTA. Presbyterian.

FORSYTHE, JANET W., lawyer; b. L.A., May 12, 1957; d. John Winston and Madeleine S. (Henry) F. BA, George Washington U., 1979; JD, Georgetown U., 1982. Bar: Calif. 1983. Head atty. City and County of San Francisco, 1983-97; criminal law specialist, 1988-98. Bd. dirs. No. Calif. Svc. League, San Francisco, 1985-87, Black Coalition in AIDS, v.p., 1996—; founding mem. Women Across Generations - The Vol. Resource, 1997—. Coro Found. City Focus fellow, 1989-90. Mem. Bar Assn. San Francisco (chmn. community law week 1988, jud. evaluation com. 1989-91, bd. dirs. Barristers Club 1987-88, Barrister of Yr. 1988, bd. dirs., 1992-93, criminal justice adv. com., 1992-96), Calif. Women Lawyers, Lawyers Club San Francisco. Democrat. Judeo-Christian. Avocations: biking, weight training, embroidery, crocheting. Office: PO Box 320115 San Francisco CA 94132

FORSYTHE, PATRICIA HAYS, development professional; b. Curtis, Ark.; d. John Chambers and Flora Jane (Eby) Hays; m. Kurt G. Pahl, Dec. 15, 1962 (div. Dec. 1980); children: Thomas Walter, Susan Clara; m. Robert E. Forsythe, June 20, 1981; 1 child, Nathaniel Ryan. BA, Calif. State U., Los Angeles, 1974; MSLS, U. So. Calif., 1976. Asst. to dir. devel. office The Assocs., Calif. Inst. Tech., Pasadena, 1978-81; exec. dir. Iowa City Pub. Library Found., 1982-89; dir. devel. Hoover Presdl. Libr. Assn., West Branch, Iowa, 1989-94, exec. dir., 1994—. Contbr. articles to profl. jours. Recipient Outstanding Fund Raising Exec. award Ea. Iowa, 1990, honorary Paul Harris fellow, 1994. Mem. ALA, LWV (editor 1985-87), Nat. Soc. Fund Raising Execs. (bd. dirs. 1987-89, chmn. Ea. Iowa Philanthropy Day 1990-91, bd. dirs. Ea. Iowa chpt. 1986-91), Iowa City C. of C., West Branch C. of C. (bd. dirs.), Iowa Life Shares Assn. (bd. dirs., pres. 1995-96), Libr. Adminstrn. and Mgmt. Assn., Johnson County Area Women's Network, Hancher Guild (audience devel. 1981-85, pres. 1985-86), Univ. Athletic Club, Rotary (program chair 1992-98). Congregationalist. Avocations: travel, writing, cooking, drama. Home: 1806 E Court St Iowa City IA 52245-4643 Office: Hoover Presdl Libr Assn PO Box 696 West Branch IA 52358-0696

FORSYTHE, RANDALL NEWMAN, paralegal, educator; b. Hammond, Ind., Mar. 24, 1959; s. Perry Newman and Elwanda (Cox) F.; children: Kenneth Newman, Keith Randall. AA in Law Enforcement, Calumet Coll., Whiting, Ind., 1979, BA in Criminal Justice magna cum laude, 1982, BS in Mgmt. magna cum laude, 1982; Lawyer's Asst. Cert., Roosevelt U., Chgo., 1986. Labor leader/painter Inland Steel Co., East Chicago, Ind., 1978-86; ins. and securities rep. Primerica, Portage, Ind., 1984-91; paralegal Katz, Brenman & Angel, Merrillville, Ind., 1987-91, Komyatte & Freeland, P.C., Highland, Ind., 1991—; coord. paralegal divsn. Sawyer Coll., Merrillville, 1989-92, paralegal instr., 1989—; ct. apptd. spl. advocate Juvenile divsn. Lake County Superior Ct., Gary, Ind., 1987—. Manuscript/book reviewer West Pub. Co., St. Paul, 1991—. Parliamentarian Orchard Dr. Bapt. Ch., Hammond, Ind., 1981-91. Mem. Assn. Trial Lawyers Am., Nat. Assn. Legal Assts., Ind. Legal Assts. (Ind. Legal Asst. of Yr. 1990, liaison to nat. orgn. 1989-92, 97). Avocations: coaching children's Little League baseball, basketball, football teams, adult softball, hunting, fishing, camping. Office: Komyatte & Freeland PC 9650 Gordon Dr Highland IN 46322-2909

FORSYTHE, ROBERT ELLIOTT, economics educator; b. Pitts., Oct. 25, 1949; s. Robert Elliott and Dolores Jean (Davis) F.; m. Lynn Maureen Zollweg, June 17, 1970 (div. July 1978); m. Patricia Ann Hays, June 20, 1981; 1 child, Nathaniel Ryan. BS, Pa. State U., 1970; MS, Carnegie-Mellon U., Pitts., 1972, Carnegie-Mellon U., Pitts., 1974; PhD, Carnegie-Mellon U., Pitts., 1975. Ops. rsch. analyst PPG Industries Inc., Pitts., 1970-72; instr. Carnegie-Mellon U., Pitts., 1974-75; asst. prof. Calif. Inst. Tech., Pasadena, 1975-81; assoc. prof. U. Iowa, Iowa City, 1981-86, prof. econs., 1986-90, chmn. dept. econs., 1990-94, sr. assoc. dean Coll. Bus., 1994—; founder Iowa Polit. Stock Market; pres. Iowa Market Systems, Inc., 1993—. Author: Forecasting Presidential Elections: Polls, Markets, Models; assoc. editor Jour. Econ. Behavior and Orgn., Jour. Exptl. Econs., 1997—. Univ. faculty scholar U. Iowa, 1985-88. Mem. Econometric Soc., Am. Econ. Assn., Econ. Sci. Assn. (sect. head 1989-92, pres.-elect 1992-93, pres. 1993-95). Congregationalist. Home: 1806 E Court St Iowa City IA 52245-4643 Office: U Iowa Tippie Coll Bus 108 Pappajohn Bus Bldg Iowa City IA 52242-1000

FORT, ARTHUR TOMLINSON, III, physician, educator; b. Lumpkin, Ga., Sept. 24, 1931; s. Thomas Morton and Gladys (Davis) F.; m. Jane Wilmer McClelland, June 15, 1957; children: Abby Lucinda, Arthur Tomlinson IV, Juliana Melody, Ernest Arlington, II. BBA, U. Ga., 1952; MD, U. Tenn., 1962. Diplomate: Am. Bd. Ob-Gyn, Am. Bd. Family Practice. Intern, then resident in ob-gyn U. Tenn.-City of Memphis Hosp., 1962-66; asst. prof. U. Tenn. Med. Sch., 1966-70; prof. ob-gyn, head dept. Sch. Medicine La. State U., Shreveport, 1970-73; prof. maternal-child health and family planning, head program family health Sch. Pub. Health Tulane U., 1973-74; practice medicine specializing in rural family medicine Vacharie, La., 1974-79; prof. ob-gyn and family medicine, head dept. family medicine and comprehensive care Sch. Medicine La. State U., Shreveport, 1980—. Author articles in field. Adv. bd. mem. State of La. Dept. Health and Human Resources, 1986-88. With USAF, 1952-57. Recipient Golden Apple Teaching award Student AMA, 1969, Golden Apple Teaching award Western Interstate Commn. on Higher Edn., 1973. Fellow Am. Coll. Ob-Gyn, Am. Acad. Family Practice; mem. AMA. Office: PO Box 33932 Shreveport LA 71130-3932

FORT, JAMES TOMLINSON, lawyer; b. Albany, N.Y., Apr. 12, 1928; s. Tomlinson and Beatrice (Lawson) F.; m. Judith Anne Davis, May 9, 1959; children: Edward Tomlinson, Madeline Annabelle. A.B., Allegheny Coll.; LL.B., Yale U. Bar: Supreme Ct. Assoc. Reed Smith Shaw & McClay, Pitts., 1954-62, ptnr., 1962—. Trustee Allegheny Coll., Meadville, Pa., 1975—; dir. Pitts. Dance Council, 1977-83, Pitts. Ballet Theatre Inc. With USMC, 1953-54. Mem. ABA, Pa. Bar Assn., Pitts. Acad. Trial Lawyers, Bar Supreme Ct. U.S., Am. Coll. Trial Lawyers. Republican. Presbyterian. Clubs: Duquesne (Pitts.), Rivers; Rolling Rock (Ligonier, Pa.). Home: 204 Woodcock Dr Pittsburgh PA 15215-1546 Office: Reed Smith Shaw & McClay Mellon Sq 435 6th Ave Ste 2 Pittsburgh PA 15219-1886

FORT, JEFFREY C., lawyer; b. Burlington, Iowa, Oct. 10, 1950; s. Lyman R. and Lucille (Gibb) F.; m. Diane Locandro; children: Christopher Glen, Elizabeth Anne. BA, Monmouth, 1972; JD, Northwestern U., 1975. Bar: Ill. 1975, U.S. Dist. Ct. (no. dist.) Ill. 1976, U.S. Ct. Appeals (7th cir.) 1977, U.S. Ct. Appeals (D.C. cir.) 1985, U.S. Supreme Ct. 1980. Law clk. to John M. Karns, Jr. Appellate Ct., Belleville, Ill., 1975-76; assoc. Martin Craig Chester, et al, Chgo., 1976-83, ptnr., 1983-88; ptnr. Gardner Carton & Douglas, Chgo., 1988-90, Sonnenschein Nath & Rosenthal, Chgo., 1990—; adj. prof. Northwestern U. Sch. Law, Chgo., 1990-92; presenter in field. Author: Establishing an Effective Environmental Law Compliance Program, 1993—; editl. bd. Environmental Law for the Transactional Lawyer, 1991, rev. edit., 194, Illinois Environmental Law, 1993; contbr. articles to profl. jours. Chair Lake Mich. States sect. Air & Waste Mgmt. Assn., Chgo., 1988-89; elder 1st Presbyn. Ch. Wilmette, Ill., 1990-93. Mem. ABA, Chgo. Bar Assn. (chair environ. law com. 1987-88), Met. Club, Mich. Shores Club. Office: Sonnenschein Nath & Rosenthal 8000 Sears Tower Chicago IL 60606

FORT, RANDALL MARTIN, investment banking executive; b. Richmond, Ind., July 4, 1956. Student, U. Cin., 1974-76; BA in Pub. Affairs with distinction, George Washington U., 1978. Various positions with rep. Willis D. Gradison Jr., Cin. and Washington, 1976-80; rsch. asst. office of hon. Roo Watanabe M.P., Tokyo, 1980-81; asst. dir., dep. exec. dir. Pres's. Fgn. Intelligence Adv. Bd., Washington, 1982-87; spl. asst. to sec. nat. security U.S. Dept. Treasury, Washington, 1987-89; dep. asst. sec. for functional analysis and rsch. U.S. Dept. State, Washington, 1989-93; dir. spl. projects TRW, Inc., Washington, 1993-96; v.p. Goldman Sachs, 1996—. Luce scholar Henry Luce Found., 1980. Mem. The Asia Soc. (del.), Phi Beta Kappa. Republican. Methodist. Office: Goldman Sachs 85 Broad St Fl 22 New York NY 10004-2456

FORT, ROBERT BRADLEY, minister; b. Portsmouth, Va., Dec. 27, 1948; s. Richard Gould and Hazel Naomi (McBride) F.; m. Esther Faith Hardin, June 10, 1967; children: Yvonne René, Nathan Michael. Ordained to ministry United Evang. Ch., 1973. Evangelist United Evang. Chs., Monrovia, Calif., 1966, nat. youth dir., 1968-70, asst. to the pres., 1970-73, Calif. dist. supt., 1973-75; evangelist Assemblies of God, Springfield, Mo., 1976-78; sr. pastor Lynden (Wash.) Assembly of God, 1978-81, County Christian Ctr., Bellingham, Wash., 1981-87, First Assembly of God, Salinas, Calif., 1988—; exec. dir. Life Mgmt. Sems., Salinas, 1989—; pres. Fort Ministries, Salinas, 1967—; exec. v.p., chmn. bd. United Evang. Chs., Hollister, Calif., 1996—; plenary spkr. World Congress Evang. Chs., Nairobi, Kenya, Africa, 1993. Composer Love was the Color, 1980 (Grand prize 1981); singer, musician 15 records. Republican. Office: Fort Ministries PO Box 1000 San Juan Bautista CA 95045-1000

FORT, TOMLINSON, chemist, chemical engineering educator; b. Sumter, S.C., Apr. 16, 1932; s. Tomlinson and Madeline A. Kean (Scott) F.; m. Martha Kirby, Oct. 13, 1956; children: Tomlinson, III, Frances Clare; m. Nancy H. Blackwelder, Dec. 19, 1998. B.S. in Chemistry, U. Ga., 1952; M.S., U. Tenn., 1957, Ph.D. in Phys. Chemistry, 1957; A.E. and F.A.Q. Stephens postdoctoral fellow, U. Sydney, Australia, 1957-58; cert., Inst. Ednl. Mgmt., Harvard U., 1978. Instr. surface chemistry U. Sydney, 1957-58; rsch. chemist, then sr. rsch. chemist and project leader duPont Co., 1958-65; mem. faculty Case Western Res. U., 1965-73, prof. chem. engring., dir. surfaces research lab., 1971-73; prof. chem. engring. and chemistry, head dept. chem. engring. Carnegie-Mellon U., 1973-80, adj. prof., 1980-83; prof. chemistry and chem. engring., provost U. Mo., Rolla, 1980-82; v.p. acad. affairs Calif. Poly. State U., San Luis Obispo, 1982-83, provost, 1983-86, prof. chemistry and materials sci., 1986-89; Centennial prof. chem. engring. Vanderbilt U., Nashville, 1989—, prof. materials sci., 1990—, chair dept. chem. engring., 1989-96; summer vis. prof. Nat. U. Mex., 1973, U. Copenhagen, 1978, 80; pres. Frances Fort Brown Realty Co., Chattanooga, 1970-94. Author papers on surface and colloid sci. Mem. AAAS, Am. Chem. Soc., Am. Inst. Chem. Engrs., Internat. Assn. of Colloid and Interface Scientists, Sigma Xi, Phi Beta Delta, Gamma Sigma Epsilon, Alpha Chi Sigma, Sigma Chi. Home: 1015 Carlisle Ln Franklin TN 37064 Office: Vanderbilt U Dept Chem Engring PO Box 1604 Nashville TN 37235

FORTADO, MICHAEL GEORGE, lawyer; b. Wichita Falls, Tex., Oct. 29, 1943; s. Antonio and Flossie Juanita (Bowers) F.; m. Avis Ann Smith, Mar. 12, 1964; children: Michael Scott, Angela Avis, Shannon Michelle. BBA, Midwestern U., Wichita Falls, 1965; LLB, U. Tex., Austin, 1968. Bar: Tex. 1968. Assoc. atty. firm McClure & Sharpe, Houston, 1968-69; atty. Enserch Corp. (and predecessor), Dallas, 1969-71, corp. sec., asst. gen. counsel, 1971-88, v.p., corp. sec., asst. gen. counsel, 1988-96; sr. v.p., gen. counsel, corp. sec. Enserch Exploration, Inc., Dallas, 1996-97; v.p., gen. counsel, corp. sec. Trinity Industries, Inc., Dallas, 1997—. Mem. ABA, Am. Soc. Corp. Secs. (bd. dirs. 1980-83), State Bar Tex., Dallas Bar Assn., DAC Country Club, Kappa Alpha Order, Delta Sigma Pi, Phi Alpha Delta. Office: Trinity Industries Inc 2525 N Stemmons Fwy Ste 1000 Dallas TX 75207-2400

FORTADO, ROBERT JOSEPH, librarian, educator; b. Jacksonville, Ill., Apr. 22, 1933; s. Joseph G. and Nellie Louise (Hawk) F.; m. Shirley Ann Scoggins, Aug. 8, 1975 (dec. Mar. 1988); m. Marjorie Francis Neuhaus Dreith, Sept. 10, 1992; children: Mark Edward, Theodore John, Laura Marie, Kimberly, David Dreith. *Fortado, a variation of more numerous Furtado, is of Portuguese origin, some by way of Madeira and some France. The family name means "the Hidden one," the 1st, son of Urraca, Queen of Leon and Castile who ruled from 1109-1126. Today, the name and coat of arms are on the ceiling of Palacio Nacional de Sintra. They represent Portuguese XVI century noblemen. For many years the family was closely associated with a 2nd family and the name on the ceiling is Mendonca Furtados. Grandfather Matthew immigrated to Illinois in 1904. Grandmother Maria Baptist was a descendant of the governor of Madeira and his daughter the 1st wife of Christopher Columbus.* BA, Ill. Coll., 1960; MS in LS, U. Ill., 1967. Agt., telegrapher Chgo., Burlington & Quincy R.R., Beardstown and Galesburg, Ill., 1951-61; libr., tchr. Triad H.S., St. Jacob, Ill., 1961-64; U.S. documents libr. So. Ill. U., Edwardsville, 1964—, assoc. prof., 1981-96, assoc. prof. emeritus, 1996—; advisor, mem. documents coordinating coun. Ill. State Libr., Springfield, 1992-94. Mem. bd. editors Microform Rev.; contbr. articles to profl. jours. With USN, 1952-56, Korea. Mem. Ill. Libr. Assn., Govt. Documents Roundtable, VFW. Avocations: fishing, travel to France and Portugal, walking. Home: 3713 Western Ave Alton IL 62002-3159

FORTALEZA, JUDITH ANN, school system administrator; b. Dayton, Ohio, Sept. 10, 1936; d. Jesse Beldon and Vivian (Bussert) Moore; m. Alfred Little, Aug. 28, 1954 (div. Oct. 1974); m. Leslie Comdey, July 8, 1988; children: Allen Dale, Jeffrey, Stuart. BS, Wright State U., 1971, MA, 1976; EdD, U. Sarasota, Fla., 1981. Tchr. Bellbrook (Ohio) City Schs., 1969-73, Greene Vocat. Sch., Xenia, Ohio, 1973-74, London (Ohio) City Schs., 1974-75; cons. C.O.S.E.R.R.C., Columbus, Ohio, 1975-78; coord. Hopewell Special Edn. Regional Resource Ctr., Hillsboro, Ohio, 1978-81, Ctrl. Ohio Special Edn. Regional Resource Ctr., Columbus; supr. Westerville (Ohio) City Schs., 1986-90; dir. Newark (Ohio) City Schs., 1990—; lectr. U. Dayton, 1976, Capital U., Columbus, 1983, Ohio U., Athens, 1986-89. Co-author: Identification of SBH Students, 1975, Intervention Assistant Teams, 1983. Mem. Coun. of Exceptional Children (exec. com. 1989-90), Coun. of Adminstrs. of Spl. Edn. (nat. bd. dirs. 1989-90, pres. 1990). Home: 2840 Hollow Cove Ct Columbus OH 43231-1698 Office: Newark City Schs 85 E Main St Newark OH 43055-5605

FORT-BRESCIA, BERNARDO, architect; b. Peru, Nov. 19, 1951. BA in Architecture and Urban Planning magna cum laude, Princeton U., 1973; MArch, Harvard U., 1975. Registered arch., Calif., Colo., Conn., Del., Fla., Ga., La., Md., Mass., Mich., Minn., N.H., N.J., Nev., N.Y., N.C., Pa., Tex., Va.; cert. Nat. Coun. Archtl. Reigstration. Founding prin. Arquitectonica, Miami, Fla., 1977—; lectr. in field. Key projects include Disney's All Star Resorts, Orlando, E-Walk at Times Sq., N.Y.C., Miami Internat. D-E-F Wrap, Atlanta Arena and CNN Ctr., Am. Airlines Arena, Miami, Miami Fed. Courthouse, Festival Walk Retail and Office Complex, Hong Kong, Orchard Scotts, Singapore, Performing Arts Ctr., Dijon, France, U.S. Embassy, Lima, Peru, Four Seasons Hotel, Caracas, Hyatt Regency Hotel, Lima, Bank of Luxembourg Hdqrs., Shanghai Info. Ctr. Fellow AIA. Office: Arquitectonica 550 Brickell Ave Ste 200 Miami FL 33131-2517*

FORTE, STEPHEN FORREST, interior designer; b. Shreveport, La., Oct. 18, 1947; s. Forrest Lee and Alva (Clary) F. BA, Centenary Coll., Shreveport, 1971; postgrad., La. Tech U., 1971, Parsons Sch. Design, Paris, 1981. Lic. interior designer, La., Fla. Interior designer Interiors, Inc., Shreveport, 1974-75, Yarbrough Interior Designers, Shreveport, 1975-85; pres. Stephen Forte Interior Design, Shreveport, 1985—. Prin. works include: Strand Theatre Restoration, Shreveport, 1981-85, One Tex. Ctr., Shreveport, 1986, Southdown Retirement Ctr., Baton Rouge, 1988, Goodrich Oil Co., 1990, Caddo Parish Commn. Offices, 1993, Champion Lake Complex, Shreveport, La., 1995-96; featured in The Designer, Designers West and So. Living mag. articles. Mem. Internat. Interior Design Assn. Democrat. Roman Catholic. Office: # 5 6104 Line Ave # 5 Shreveport LA 71105-3117

FORTENBAUGH, SAMUEL BYROD, III, lawyer; b. Phila., Nov. 6, 1933; s. Samuel Byrod Jr. and Katherine Francisca (Wall) F.; children: Samuel Byrod IV, Cristina Fortenbaugh Alemany, Katherine Dooley, Francesca Cowden. BA, Williams Coll., 1955; LLB, Harvard U., 1960. Bar: N.Y. 1961, U.S. Dist. Ct. (so. dist.) N.Y. 1961. Assoc. Kelley Drye & Warren, N.Y.C., 1960-69, ptnr., 1970-79; ptnr. Morgan, Lewis & Bockius, N.Y.C., 1980—; bd. dirs. Baldwin Tech. Co., Inc., Norwalk, Conn., Goodman Equipment Corp., Chgo.; bd. dirs., sec. Furgueson Capital Mgmt. Inc., N.Y.C.; chmn. bd. dirs., sec. Wall Industries, Inc., Kannapolis, N.C.; chmn. bd. dirs. Knight Textile Corp, Saluda, S.C.; trustee Patroni Scholastici, New Brunswick, N.J., 1978—, sec. 1985—; lectr. profl. seminars. Contbr. articles to profl. jours. Mem. ABA, Assn. of Bar of City of N.Y. (mem. Young Lawyers com. 1962-65, corp. law com. 1976-79, com. on securities regulation 1982-85, chmn. com. on issue distbn. of securities 1984-85), Racquet and Tennis Club, Univ. Club. (N.Y.C.), Bay Head (N.J.) Yacht Club, Indian Harbor Yacht Club (Greenwich, Conn.), Phi Beta Kappa. Office: Morgan Lewis & Bockius LLP 101 Park Ave Fl 45 New York NY 10178-0060

FORTENBERRY, CAROL LOMAX, real estate appraiser; b. Charlotte, N.C., Apr. 23, 1959; d. Henry Clyde and Anne Tristram (Holt) Lomax; m. Mark Kevin Fortenberry, July 14, 1984; children: Liza Holt, Joseph Tristram. BA in radio, TV, motion pictures, U. N.C., Chapel Hill, 1981; MBA, Queens Coll., Charlotte, 1988. Lic. real estate salesman, N.C.; cert. gen. real estate appraiser, N.C.; MAI. Various positions Jefferson Pilot Communications Co., Charlotte, 1981-85; asst. show mgr. So. Shows, Inc., Charlotte, 1985-87; bus. mgr. Mark Fortenberry Photography, Charlotte, 1987-88; comml. real estate appraiser Stout-Beck & Assocs., Charlotte, 1988-94, Fitzhugh L. Stout & Assoc., Charlotte, 1994-97; mng. ptnr. Fortenberry & Assocs., Charlotte, 1997—. Mem. zoning bd. adjustment City of Charlotte.

Mem. Appraisal Inst. (chmn. Metrolina subchpt., bd. dirs. N.C. chpt.), Comml. Real Estate Women, U. N.C. Alumni Assn., Nat. Bone Marrow Registry, Cool Hand Investing and Conversing Soc. Avocations: salt water fishing, gardening, hiking, outdoor activities. Home: 4106 Tottenham Rd Charlotte NC 28226-6600 Office: Fortenberry and Assocs 2123 E 7th St Charlotte NC 28204-3337

FORTGANG, CHARLES, wholesale distribution executive; b. 1932. Grad., Syracuse U., 1953. With M. Fabrikant & Sons Inc., 1955—, CEO, now chmn. Address: Lazard Freres & Co 30 Rockefeller Plz Fl 59 New York NY 10112-5999*

FORTH, KEVIN BERNARD, beverage distributing industry consultant; b. Adams, Mass., Dec. 4, 1949; s. Michael Charles and Catherine Cecilia (McAndrews) F.; m. Deborah Newport; children: Melissa, Brian. AB, Holy Cross Coll., 1971; MBA with distinction, NYU, 1973. Divsn. rep. Anheuser-Busch, Inc., Boston, 1973-74; dist. sales mgr. Anheuser-Busch, Inc., L.A., 1974-76; asst. to v.p. mktg. staff Anheuser-Busch, Inc., St. Louis, 1976-77; v.p. Straub Distbg. Co., Ltd., Orange, Calif., 1977-81; pres. Straub Distbg. Co., Ltd., Orange, 1981-93, chmn., CEO, 1986-93, also bd. dirs. Commr. Orange County Sheriff's Adv. Coun., 1988—; mem. adv. bd. Rancho Santiago C.C. Coll. Dist., 1978-80; bd. dirs. Children's Hosp. of Orange County Padrinos Found., 1983-85, St. Joseph's Hosp. Found., Orange County Sports Hall of Fame, 1980-89; exec. com., bd. dirs. Nat. Coun. on Alcoholism, 1980-83; mem. pres. coun. Holy Cross Coll., 1987-91; bd. dirs., pres. Calif. State Fullerton Titan Athletic Found., 1983-85, 89-90; mem. Calif. Beer Wholesalers Assn., dir., 1978-89, v.p., 1984, chmn., 1985; bd. dirs. Freedom Bowl, 1984-93, v.p., 1984-85, pres., 1986, chmn., 1986-87, Anaheim Vis. and Conv. Bur., 1989-93; bd. dirs. Orangewood Children's Found., 1988-93; mem. Calif. Rep. State Ctrl. Com., 1988-93, Orange County Probation Dept. Cmty. Involvement Bd., 1992-93. Recipient Founders award Freedom Bowl, 1993; Benjamin Levy fellow NYU, 1971-73. Mem. Industry Environ. Coun., Holy Cross Alumni Assn., NYU Alumni Assn., Nat. Assn. Stock Car Auto Racing, Sports Car Club Am. (Ariz. state champion 1982), Holy Cross Club (So. Calif.), Nat. Beer Wholesalers Assn. (bd. dirs. 1986-93, asst. sec. 1989-90, sec. 1989-91, vice-chmn. 1992, chmn. 1993), Beta Gamma Sigma. Roman Catholic. Home: 27750 Tamara Dr Yorba Linda CA 92887-5840

FORTH, STUART, librarian; b. Manistee, Mich., Aug. 13, 1923; s. Wade Stuart and Nan (Rumans) F.; m. Pearl Elizabeth Brown, Dec. 24, 1951. BA, U. Mich., 1949, MLS, 1950; PhD in History, U. Wash., 1961. Catalog librarian Oreg. State U., Corvallis, 1950-52, adminstrv. asst. to dir. libraries, 1952-54; reference librarian Seattle Pub. Library, 1954-59; undergrad. librarian U. Kans., Lawrence, 1959-61, assoc. dir. libraries, 1961-65; dir. libraries U. Ky., Lexington, 1965-73, prof. library sci., 1966-73, v.p. for student affairs, 1968-70; dean, univ. libraries Pa. State U., University Park, 1973-88, dean emeritus, 1988—; teaching fellow history U. Wash., 1954-55, 57-58; instr. dept. Western Civilization U. Kans., 1960-65; Pres. Reagan appointee to adv. com. White House Conf. on Libr. and Info. Svcs., 1989—. Staff sgt. USAAF, 1942-45, PTO. Mem. ALA (past chmn./mem. various coms.) AAUP (pres. U. Kans. chpt. 1965), Assn. Coll. and Rsch. Librs., Assn. Rsch. Librs. (mem. or chair various coms.), Rsch. Librs. Group, Inc. (bd. govs. 1974-82, 84-86), Am. Hist. Assn., Orgn. Am. Historians, Manuscript Soc., Bibliog. Soc. Am., Pacific N.W. Libr. Assn. (sec. 1953-54), Kans. Libr. Assn. (chmn. coll. and univ. libr. sect. 1963-64), Pa. Libr. Assn. (pres. 1979-81). Anglican. Avocations: archtl. history, reading, music. Home: PO Box 713 State College PA 16804-0713

FORTI, CORINNE ANN, corporate communications executive; b. N.Y.C., July 26, 1941; d. Wilbur Walter and Sylvia Joan (Charap) Bastian; B.A., CUNY, 1963; m. Joseph Donald Forti, Aug. 18, 1962 (dec.); 1 child, Raina. Adminstrv. asst. Ednl. Broadcasting Corp., 1963-65; adminstrv. asst. W.R. Grace & Co., N.Y.C., 1965-67, pub. relations rep., 1967-70, mgr. info. services, 1970-79, dir. info. services, 1980-86, dir. info. and advt., 1986-87; pres. Bastian-Forti Communications, 1988-89, Forti Communications Inc., 1989—; lectr. photography and graphics Am. Mgmt. Assn. Bd. dirs. YM/YWCA Day Care, Inc. Named to Acad. Women Achievers, YWCA, 1979; recipient citation award in communications Nat. Council of Women, 1979. Mem. Am. Women in Radio and TV, Chem. Mfrs. Assn., Am. Mgmt. Assn., Women Execs. in Pub. Relations. Republican. Roman Catholic. Home and Office: 1246 Calle Yucca Thousand Oaks CA 91360-2239

FORTI, LENORE STEIMLE, business consultant; b. Houghton, Mich., Sept. 9, 1924; d. Russell Nicholas and Agnes (McCloskey) Steimle; m. Frank Forti, May 29, 1950 (dec.). BBA summa cum laude, Northwood U., 1973, Dr.Laws, 1969. Asst. corp. sec., purchasing agt. Fed. Life & Casualty Co., Detroit, 1942-53; supr. sectl. J.L. Hudson Co., Detroit, 1953-57, adminstrv. asst. to exec. v.p., 1957-86; instr. Wayne State U. and U. Mich. Adult Edn., Detroit, 1958-71; creator, dir. Seminars for Profl. People, 1971—. Co-author: The Professional Secretary; contbr. articles to profl. jours. Asst. br. dir. planning City of Detroit for Civil Def.; chmn. bd. trustees PSI Rsch. and Ednl. Found.; trustee PSI Retirement Home Complex, Albuquerque; elected dir. Property Owners and Residents Assn., Sun City West Mcpl. Govt., 1994-97; past pres. Women's Bd. Northwood U., Midland, Mich.; pres. parish coun. Our Lady of Lourdes Ch., Sun City West, Ariz., 1988, pres. ladies guild, 1990, pres. singles club, 1995; 1st v.p. Vol. Bur. of Sun Cities, 1989; bd. dirs. Sun City West Cmty. Fund, 1998—; dir., corp. sec., Sun City West Found., 1998—, Sch. Found. Elected One of Detroit's Top Ten Working Women, 1969; elected to Exec. and Profl. Hall of Fame. Mem. Internat. Assn. Adminstrv. Profls. (internat. pres. 1967-69), Future Secs. Assn. (nat. coord.), Lioness Club (pres. 1991-92), Sun City West Singles Club (pres. 1988, pres. Singles Club Ch. 1995). Republican. Roman Catholic. Avocations: golf, bridge, Mah Jongg, line dancing. Home and Office: 12613 W Seneca Dr Sun City West AZ 85375-4635

FORTIER, JEAN-MARIE, retired archbishop; b. Que., Can., July 1, 1920; s. Joseph and Alberta (Jobin) F. Student, Grand Sem. Que., 1940-45; L.Th., Laval U., Que., 1945; postgrad., U. Louvain, Belgium, 1946-48; Licentiate in Ch. History, Gregorian U., Rome, 1950. Ordained priest Roman Catholic Ch., 1944; sec. to bishop of Hearst, Ont., Can., 1945-46; tchr. ch. history Grand Sem. Que., 1950-60; consecrated bishop Ste. Anne de la Pocatiere, Que., 1961-65, Gaspe, Que., 1965-68; archbishop Sherbrooke, Que., 1968-96, archbishop emeritus, 1996—; mem. Congregation for Sacraments and Divine Cult, 1975-84; v.p. Can. Cath. Conf., 1971-73, pres., 1973-75; pres. Comité Episcopal des Communications Sociales, 1976-84; v.p. l'Assemblee des Evêques du Quebec, 1981-85, pres., 1985-89. Mem. Knights Holy Sepulchre of Jerusalem, Assn. Eveques de Que. (pres. 1985-89), Assn. des Chevaliers de Colomb de Que., Filles d'Isabelle. Address: 2 rue Port Dauphin CP 459, Quebec, PQ Canada G1R 4R6

FORTIER, L. YVES, barrister; b. Quebec City, Que., Can., Sept. 11, 1935; s. Francois and Louise (Turgeon) F.; m. C. Carol Eaton, Sept. 26, 1959; children: Michel, Suzanne, Margot. BA summa cum laude, U. Montreal, 1955; BCL, McGill U., 1958; BLitt, Oxford U., 1960, LLD (hon.), 1989, 92, 93. Created Queen's counsel, 1976. Sr. ptnr., chmn. Ogilvy, Renault Advs., Barristers and Solicitors, Montreal, 1960—, on leave; Can. amb. to UN N.Y.C., 1988-92; counsel for Can. in Can.-USA, Gulf Maine Case in World Ct., 1984, Royal Commns., Commn. Inquiry War Criminals, Commn. Inquiry Lang. Air Traffic Control, Commn. Inquiry R.C.M.P.; mem. Permanent Ct. Arbitration The Hague, 1984-89; pres. London Ct. Internat. Arbitration, 1998—; chief negotiator Can.-France fishing dispute, 1987-89, Can.-U.S. Pacific Salmon Treaty dispute, 1993-98; Can.'s chief del. to 43d, 44th, 45th, 46th sessions of UN Gen. Assembly, Can. rep. UN Security Coun., 1989-90; v.p. UN 45th Gen. Assembly; gov. Hudson's Bay Co.; bd. dirs. Royal Bank Can., Nantel Networks Corp., Nova Corp., duPont Can. Inc., Southam Inc. Bd. dirs. Can. Inst. Advanced Legal Studies, Internat. Peace Acad., UN Internat. Sch., Montreal Gen. Hosp. C.D. Howe Inst., Clin. Rsch. Inst., Can. Found. for AIDS Rsch. Decorated officer and companion Order of Can.; Rhodes scholar, 1960. Mem. ABA (hon.), Can. Bar Assn. (pres. 1982-83, founding dir. Law for Future Fund), Internat. Commn. Jurists (Can. sect.), Internat. Law Assn. (Can. br.), Am. Coll. Trial Lawyers (regent 1991-95), Internat. Assn. Permanent Reps. to UN (exec. bd.), Mount Royal Club, Univ. Club, Montreal Indoor Tennis Club, Hermitage Country Club, The Brook Club (N.Y.). Roman Catholic. Avocations: tennis, squash, skiing, golf. Home: 19 Rosemount Ave, Westmount, PQ Canada

FORTIER, MARDELLE LADONNA, English educator; b. Brookings, S.D., Sept. 15, 1947; d. Leon Doneval and Edna Pearl (Rosenstock) Eide; m. Robert Frederic Fortier, July 27, 1974. BA, U. Minn., 1970; MA, U. Ill., 1971, PhD, 1978. Instr. Berlitz, Hinsdale, Ill., 1983-84, North Ctrl. Coll., Naperville, Ill., 1985; sr. lectr. Loyola U., Chgo., 1984-95; instr. Coll. DuPage, Glen Ellyn, Ill., 1985—; English instr. Benedictine U., Lisle, Ill., 1985, 95—; cons. in field. Author: The Utopian Thought of St. Thomas More, 1994; author numerous poems. Mem. Ill. State Poetry Soc., Poets and Patrons, Inc. (1st prize 1992, 2d prize 1995), Poets Club Chgo. Roman Catholic. Avocations: music, travel. Home: 5515 E Lake Dr Apt A Lisle IL 60532-2664

FORTIN, JUDY, cable news anchor. BA in Govt. and French, Bowdoin Coll. Gen. assignment reporter various stas.; nat. corr. CNN Newsource, Atlanta, 1990; anchor CNN Airport Network, Atlanta; weekend anchor CNN Headline News, Atlanta. Recipient AP awards. Office: c/o CNN 1 CNN Ctr PO Box 105366 Atlanta GA 30348-5366*

FORTIN, RAYMOND D., lawyer. BA, U. Fla., 1974, JD, 1977. Bar: Ga. 1977. Pvt. practice, 1977-81; staff counsel The Citizens & So. Corp., 1981-89; mng. atty. SunTrust Banks, Inc., Atlanta, 1989-91, sr. v.p., 1991—. Office: SunTrust Banks Inc 30th Fl 303 Peachtree St NE Atlanta GA 30308-2900*

FORTMAN, MARVIN, law educator, consultant; b. Bklyn., Oct. 20, 1930; s. Herman and Bess (Smith) F.; m. Sorale Esther Elpern, Aug. 3, 1958; children: Brian E., Anita J., Deborah J. BS in Acctg., U. Ariz., 1957, JD magna cum laude, 1960; LLM, NYU, 1961. Bar: Ariz. 1960, N.Y. 1961, U.S. Tax Ct. 1962, U.S. Ct. Appeals 1962, U.S. Supreme Ct. 1962. Assoc. Aranow, Brodsky, Bolinger, Einhorn & Dann, N.Y.C., 1961-63, O'Connor, Cavanaugh, Anderson, Westover & Beshears, Phoenix, Ariz., 1963-65; prof. bus. law, bus. and pub. adminstrn. U. Ariz., Tucson, 1965—; legal cons. various corps., 1963—. Author: Legal Aspects of Doing Business in Arizona, 1970; contbr. articles to profl. jours. Mem. legal com. Ariz. Coun. on Econ. Edn., Tucson, 1975—, Sabbar Shrine Temple, Tucson, 1978—, legal advisor, chmn. wills and gifts, 1981-84, 1990—. With U.S. Army, 1951-53; ETO. Kenneson fellow NYU, 1960-61. Mem. N.Y. State Bar Assn., Ariz. Bar Assn. (wills, trusts, estates sect.), Phi Kappa Phi, Beta Gamma Sigma (v.p., treas. 1972—), Beta Alpha Psi, Alpha Kappa Psi. Home: 5844 E 15th St Tucson AZ 85711-4508 Office: U Ariz Coll of Bus and Pub Adminstrn Tucson AZ 85721

FORTMANN, THOMAS EDWARD, research and development company executive; b. Evanston, Ill.; s. Daniel John and Mary Annette (Van Halteren) F.; m. Carla Ann Vaccariello, June 18, 1966; children: Daniel, Stephen, Andrew. BS in Physics, Stanford U., 1965, MSEE, 1966; PhDEE, MIT, 1969. Sr. lectr. U. Newcastle, NSW, Australia, 1969-73; sr. v.p. BBN Systems & Techs., Cambridge, Mass., 1974-97; vol. tchr. Boston Pub. Schs., 1997—. Author: An Introduction to Linear Control Systems, 1977, Tracking and Data Association, 1988; also articles. Mem. Lexington (Mass.) Town Meeting, 1982-87. Fellow IEEE; mem. Assn. for Computing Machinery, Phi Beta Kappa. Avocations: bicycling, skiing, sailing, windsurfing. Home: 5 Harrington Rd Lexington MA 02421-4805

FORTNER, BILLIE JEAN, small business owner; b. Tarrytown, Ga.; d. Willard and Sara (Beckworth) Burch; m. Randall Carroll; m. David Jones (div.); m. Robert F. Fortner, Jr., Sept. 20, 1981; children: Gina Sumner, Simone Dixon, Natalie Garner. AA summa cum laude, Brewton Parker Coll., 1970; BS, Ga. So. Coll., 1972, MEd, 1975, EdS, 1977. Math & sci. tchr. Toombs County Schs., Lyons, Ga., 1971-76, gifted tchr., 1976-81; gifted tchr. Montgomery County Schs., Mt. Vernon, Ga., 1985-88; ptnr. Rabbit's Quik Stop, Vidalia, Ga., 1985—, Rabbit's Cargo Inc., Vidalia, 1987—, Fortner Rentals, Vidalia, 1988—, Rabbit On the Strip, Vidalia, 1988—, Fortner Farms, Vidalia, 1989—; artist-in-residence, ptnr. F.C.F. Investments, Vidalia, 1992—; ptnr. Kipling B. Collins; artist-in-residence, Vidalia, Ga. Troup leader Girl Scouts, Vidalia, 1972-76; block coord. Ga. Heart Assn., Vidalia, 1976. Mem. Phi Beta Kappa. Baptist. Home: 404 Slayton St Vidalia GA 30474-4436 Office: Rabbit's Quik Stop Hwy 292 W Vidalia GA 30474

FORTNER, JOSEPH GERALD, surgeon, educator; b. Bedford, Ind., May 30, 1921; s. Everett Rex and Lula Alice (Robbins) F.; m. Roberta Olson, Nov. 4, 1948; children: Kathleen Alice Fortner Lewis, Joseph Jr. BS, U. Ill., 1944, MD, 1945; MSc in Immunology, Birmingham (Eng.) U., 1965. Diplomate: Am. Bd. Surgery. Intern St. Luke's Hosp., Chgo., 1945-46; resident in pathology Tulane U., New Orleans, 1948-49; surg. resident Bellevue Hosp., N.Y.C., 1949-51, Meml. Hosp., N.Y.C., 1952-54; clin. asst. surgeon, asst. to clin. dir. Meml. Hosp., 1955-59, asst. attending surgeon, 1958-66, assoc. attending surgeon, 1966-69, attending surgeon, 1969-94, chief gastric and mixed tumor service, 1970-78, chief surg. research service, 1978-91, assoc. chmn. for lab. affairs dept. surgery, 1978-84, chief div. surg. research, 1968-77; chief Gen. Motors Surg. Rsch. Lab., 1977-92; instr. surgery Sloan-Kettering Inst., N.Y.C., 1954-58; asst. prof. clin. surgery Sloan-Kettering Inst., 1958-64; clin. asst. prof. surgery Cornell U. Med. Coll., N.Y.C., 1964-70; assoc. prof. surgery Cornell U. Med. Coll., 1970-72, prof., 1972—. Contbr. articles to profl. jours.; editor Accomplishments in Cancer Research. Pres. Gen. Motors Cancer Research Found., 1978-96, pres. emeritus, 1996—, also mem., trustee; mem. WHO Collaborating Center for Evaluation of Methods of Diagnosis and Treatment of Melanoma. Served with U.S. Army, 1946-48. Recipient Alfred P. Sloan award Sloan-Kettering Inst. Cancer Research, 1963. Fellow ACS, N.Y. Acad. Scis., Royal Coll. Surgeons Edinburgh (hon.); mem. AMA, AAAS, Am. Assn. Cancer Research, Am. Gastroent. Assn., Am. Radium Soc., Am. Soc. Clin. Oncology, European Soc. Exptl. Surgery, Harvey Soc., Soc. Surg. Oncology, N.Y. County, N.Y. State med. socs., Am. Surg. Assn., N.Y. Surg. Soc., Soc. Univ. Surgeons, Hellenic Surg. Soc. (hon.), Chgo. Surg. Soc., Korean Surg. Soc., Am. Soc. Transplant Surgeons, Transplantation Soc., N.Y. Cancer Soc., Econ. Club of N.Y., Explorer Club N.Y., Met. Club N.Y., Madison Beach Club, Sigma Xi, Alpha Omega Alpha. Republican. Home: 131 E 66th St New York NY 10021-6129

FORTSON, EDWARD NORVAL, physics educator; b. Atlanta, June 16, 1936; s. Charles Wellborn and Virginia (Norval) F.; m. Alix Madge Hawkins, Apr. 3, 1960; children—Edward Norval, Lucy Frear, Amy Lewis. B.S., Duke U., 1957; Ph.D., Harvard U., 1963. Research fellow U. Bonn., Federal Rep. Germany, 1965-66; research asst. prof. physics U. Wash., Seattle, 1963-65, asst. prof., 1966-69, assoc. prof., 1969-74, prof., 1974—. Fulbright travel grantee, 1965-66; Nat. Research Council fellow Oxford, Eng., 1977; Guggenheim fellow, 1980-81. Fellow AAAS, Am. Phys. Soc.; mem. NAS. Office: U Wash Dept Physics PO Box 351560 Seattle WA 98195-1560

FORTSON-RIVERS, TINA E. (THOMASENA ELIZABETH FORTSON-RIVERS), information technology specialist; b. Anderson, S.C.; d. Thomas Henry and Mary (Oliver) Fortson; m. Michael M. Rivers, Sept. 12, 1962 (div. 1973); children: Michael II (dec.), George Thomas, Kashiya Elaine. BA, Spelman Coll., 1962; MEd, Bowie State U., 1979; MS, Johns Hopkin U., 1982. Cert. adminstrn., supervision, Md. Tchr. Tulip Grove Elem. Sch., Bowie, Md., 1973-79, Kenmoor Elem. Sch., Landover, Md., 1979-82; computer coord. Benjamin Stoddert Mid. Sch., Temple Hills, Md., 1982-86; info. tech. specialist Prince Georges County Pub. Schs., Upper Marlboro, Md., 1986—; ednl. cons. Wicat, Provo, Utah, 1985-91; design cons. Computer Lady, Capitol Heights, Md., 1990-92; del. U.S.-Russia Conf. on Edn., 1994; del. Initiative for Edn., Sci. and Tech. to Republic of South Africa, 1995. Author: Education Software Correlation to PGCPS Social Studies Curriculum, 1992. Mem. Com. of 100, Prince Georges County Schs., Upper Marlboro, 1985; bd. trustees Gethsemane United Meth. Ch. Mem. Mid. States Coun. for Social Studies (bd. dirs. 1979—, conf. program chair 1989, 97, regional conf. coord. 1992-93, pres. 1994-96, awards chair 1996-99, sec. 1999—), Md. Coun. for Social Studies (treas. 1982-83), Prince Georges County Coun. for Social Studies (pres. 1981-82), Nat. Coun. for Social Studies (membership com. chmn. 1994, task force on governance, 1999), Alpha Delta Kappa (sec. MD Eta 1992-94, membership chair 1994-96, pres.-elect 1996-98, pres. 1998—, Md. dist. chair 1994-96, Md. state rec. sec. 1998—, corr. sec. 1996-98). Avocations: watercolor painting, sewing. Office: Prince Georges County Pub Schs 8437 Landover Rd Landover MD 20785-3502

FORTUIN, FLOYD D., neurologist; b. Providence, Dec. 28, 1937; s. Astrid Fortuin; m. Phyllis Fortuin, Dec. 12, 1964; children: David, Brian, Kathy. BA cum laude, Amherst Coll., 1959; MD with honors, Cornell U., 1963. Diplomate Am. Bd. Psychiatry and Neurology. Resident in medicine and neurology U. Wash., 1964-67; chief resident neurology U. Wash. Hosp., VA, Children's Hosp, King County Hosp., Wash., 1965-67; electroencephalographist U. Wash. Laboratory, 1966; neuropathologist U. Wash., 1967; chief neurology USAF Hosp., Elmendorf AFB, Anchorage, 1967-69, St. Luke's Hosp., San Francisco, 1970-83; asst. chief neuroscis. Mt. Zion VC Med. Ctr. Hosp., San Francisco, 1984-98; pvt. practice San Francisco, 1969—. Contbr. articles to profl. jours. Neurologist Peniel Mission, Oakland, Calif., 1997—. Mem. Nat. Bd. Med. Examiners, Am. Acad. Neurology, Calif. Med. Assn., San Francisco Med. Soc. (co-chmn. med. review and adv. com. 1978-85), San Francsico Neurol. Soc. Republican. Avocations: flying, fishing, motorcycle riding, roller blading, mountain biking. Home: 1871 Piedras Cir Alamo CA 94507

FORTUNA, ANTHONY FRANK, retired educator, consultant; b. Thomas, W.Va., Apr. 8, 1914; s. Anton and Rose (Secna) F.; m. Ann Marie Barthel, Sept. 27, 1938; children: Richard, Eugene. Student, L.A. Trade Tech. Coll., Pierce Coll., Valley Coll.; grad. Warren Sch. Astronautics, L.A. Coll.; student, U.S. Aviation Cadets. Registered profl. engr., Calif. Leadman Vultee Aircraft, Downy, Calif., 1939-40; gen. supr. Hindustan Aircraft, Bangalore, India, 1942-44; supr., inspector U.S. Air Corp., Long Beach, Calif., 1945-46; tng. supr. Douglas Aircraft Co., El Segundo, Calif., 1946-55; mgr. Northrop Ventura Div., Newberry Park, Calif., 1955-79; devel. engr. Hughes Space, El Segundo, 1981-86; dir. Talley Corp., Newberry, 1980-81; tchr., instr. Pierce Coll., Woodland Hills, Calif., 1962-98; source engr. BQS, Inc., 1982-98; cons. in field. Mem. Am. Inst. Astronautic/Aeronautic. Republican. Mormon. Avocations: teaching, reading. Home and Office: 3415 Loadstone Dr Sherman Oaks CA 91403-4513

FORTUNA, WILLIAM FRANK, architectural engineer, architect; b. Paris, Ill., Apr. 3, 1948; s. William F. Sr. and Mary O. (Komatz) F. BArch, U. Ill., 1972, MS in Archtl. Engring., 1973. Lic. arch., Ill., Wis., Iowa, lic. structural engr., Ill., lic. profl. engr., Wis., lic. archtl. engr. specializing in crisis mgmt., Nat. Coun. Examiners for Engring. and Surveying, Nat. Coun. Archtl. Registration Bds. Designer Unteed Assocs. Ltd., Champaign, Ill., 1973-76; structural engr. Consoer Townsend, Chgo., 1976-79, Schmidt, Garden & Erikson, Chgo., 1979-83; sr. project structural engr. Skidmore Owings & Merrill, Chgo., 1983-87; pres. W.F. Fortuna Ltd., Archtl. Engring., Lake Bluff, Ill., 1987—; project engr. World Trade Ctr., Cairo; structural engr. exhbn. ctr. McCormick Place Annex, Chgo., United Airlines terminal O'Hare Airport, Bishop's Gate, London; contract adminstr. One and Two Prudential Plaza, Chgo. (SEAOI Best Structure award and tallest concrete bldg. in the world). Active mem. Illinois Emergency Mgmt. Agency. Mem. AIA, NCARB, Structural Engrs. Assn. Ill., Nat. Coun. Examiners for Engring. and Surveying, Am. Concrete Inst., Am. Inst. Steel Constrn., Chgo. Hist. Soc., Nat. Trust His. Preservation. Home: WF Fortuna Ltd Archtl Engr 1420 Ridge Rd Highland Park IL 60035 Office: WF Fortuna Ltd Archtl Engr 28A E Center Ave Ste 2 Lake Bluff IL 60044-2545

FORTUNATO, NANCY, artist; b. Highland Park, Ill., Nov. 29; d. Charles Fortunato and Virginia (Ashel) Niemuth; m. Donald William Anstedt. Student, Zhejiang Acad. Fine Art, Hangzhou, China. bd. dirs. Nat. Arts Found., Ill. Author: So You Want to be An Artist, 1980, Watercolor Tips, 1982, reprinted 1999; exhibited in group shows Nat. Zool. Park, 1995, Midwest Watercolor Soc., Green Bay, Wis., 1997, Mystic Maritime Gallery, Conn., 1995, Frye Art Mus., Seattle, 1996, Maritime and Yachting Mus., Stuart, Fla., 1997, Amsterdam (The Netherlands) Open Harbour Mus., 1998, others. Fellow Am. Art Profl. League (award 1995); mem. Midwest Watercolor Soc. (v.p., 1995-97, pres. 1997—), Tex. Watercolor Soc. (Excellence award 1999), Purple Sage Honor Soc., Ariz. Watercolor Soc., Coatimundi Honor Soc., Acad. Artists Am. Avocations: photography, computers, visiting lighthouses, birdwatching, travel. Fax: 847-359-5543. Studio: 249 N Marion St Palatine IL 60067-5470

FORTUNATO, PAT DEAKIN, fine artist; b. Buffalo, Apr. 30, 1934; d. Edmund J. Deakin and Jane Wilson (Danahy) Ray; m. Thomas A. Fortunato, Apr. 7, 1956; children: Kathleen Yoder, Mark, Susan, Karen Voight, Steven, Thomas J. BS in Edn., State U., Buffalo, 1955. Elem. tchr. Buffalo Sch. System, 1955-57; substitute tchr. Williamsville (N.Y.) Schs., 1974-76; part-time workshop instr. Niagara C.C., Sanborn, N.Y., 1991-93; workshop instr. 1990—, pvt. instr., Orchard Park, N.Y., 1992—. Exhibited at Albright-Knox Mems. Gallery, Buffalo, 1993; paintings included in several books. Liason Williamsville Sch. System, 1972-79. Recipient Award of Merit Nat. League of Am. Pen Women, 1988, Holbein award Batavia Internat. Exhibit, 1997. Mem. Midwest Watercolor Soc. (Award of Excellence 1987), Am. Watercolor Soc. (assoc.), Allied Artists of Am. (assoc.), Niagara Frontier Watercolor Soc. (editor 1983-87, chmn. 1988-94, Grumbacher Gold medal 1990), Buffalo Soc. of Artists (bd. dirs. 1994-95). Roman Catholic. Avocation: photography. Home and Office: 70 Southwick Dr Orchard Park NY 14127-1650

FORTUNE, JAMES MICHAEL, network analyst; b. Providence, Sept. 6, 1947; s. Thomas Henry and Olive Elizabeth (Duby) F.; m. G. Suzanne Hein, July 14, 1973. Student, Pikes Peak Community Coll., Colorado Springs, Colo., 1981-83; BSBA, BS in Computer Info. Systems, Regis Coll., 1991. Owner Fortune Fin. Svcs., Colorado Springs, Colo., 1975-79; ptnr. Robert James and Assocs., Colorado Springs, 1979-81; pres. Fortune & Co., Colorado Springs, 1981-88; sr. v.p. mktg. and editorial Phoenix Communications Group, Ltd., Colorado Springs, 1985-95, also bd. dirs.; sr. network analyst Coastal States Mgmt. Corp., 1995—; bd. dirs. Interstate Gas Credit Union, Inc., N.Am. Internet, LLC; talk show host Sta. KRCC, fin. commentator Wall Street Report, Sta. KKHT, 1983-84. Editor Fortune newsletter, 1981-85, The Can. Market News, 1981-83; editor, pub. Penny Fortune newsletter, 1981-95, The Low Priced Investment newsletter, 1986-87, Women's Investment Newsletter, 1987-95; pub. Internal Revenue Strategies, 1990, Tax and Investment Planning Strategies for Medical Professionals, 1991; contbr. articles to profl. jours. Cons. Jr. Achievement bus. project, Colorado Springs, 1985, 97-98. Sgt. U.S. Army, 1968-70, Vietnam. Mem. Direct Mktg. Assn., Elks. Avocations: fly fishing, skiing, hiking, backpacking. Office: PO Box 1087 2 North Nevada Ave Colorado Springs CO 80944

FORTUNE, LOWELL, lawyer; b. Colorado Springs, Colo., Dec 12, 1941; s. Benjamin Acres and Wilma E. (Henry) F.; m. Beverly Jane Sanborn, June 30, 1963; children: Sabrina Fortune Allen, Christina. BA, U. Denver, 1963, JD, 1966. Bar: U.S. Dist. Ct. Colo. 1966, U.S. Ct. Appeals (10th cir.) 1966, U.S. Supreme Ct. 1976. Assoc. White & Steele, Denver, 1966-71, ptnr., 1971-75; pres. Lowell Fortune, P.C., Denver, 1975-79, Fortune & Lawritson, P.C., Denver, 1979-95; pvt. practice Fortune Law Firm, P.C., Denver, 1995-99; spl. counsel Montgomery, Kolodny, Amatuzio, Dusbabek and Parker, L.L.P., Denver, 1999—. Author: The Year 2000 Problem and the Economic Loss Rule, 1999. Mem. ABA, Am. Bd. Trial Advocates, Denver Bar Assn., Colo. Bar Assn. Republican. Episcopalian. Home: 5237 Bear Mountain Dr Evergreen CO 80439-5605 Office: 475 17th St Ste 1600 Denver CO 80202

FORTUNE, MICHAEL JOSEPH, religion educator; b. N.Y.C., Aug. 28, 1922; s. John and May (Vaughan) F.; m. Genevieve Hintz, May 27, 1945 (div. Apr. 1977); children: Michael, Patrick, Richard, Ronald, Susan, Sandra, Sharon, Laura. BS, U. Wis., Stevens Point, 1949; PhD, U. Wis., Madison, 1965; MA, U. Minn., 1952. Prof. lit. U. Wis., Stevens Point, 1956-67, chmn. comp. lit., fgn. lang., 1972-74; prof. religious lit. Mundelein Coll., Chgo., 1968-72, 74-87; sr. prof. Loyola U./Mundelein Coll., Chgo., 1987—, dir. grad. liberal studies, prof. emeritus, 1992—. Author: (play) Metamorphosis, 1991; contbr. articles to jours. in field. Named Tchr. of Yr., Johnson Found., Racine, Wis., 1965. Mem. Sigma Tau Delta, Alpha Mu Gamma. Home: 5555 N Sheridan Rd Apt 1702 Chicago IL 60640-1629 Office: Loyola U Mundelein Coll Dept Religious Studies 6363 N Sheridan Rd Chicago IL 60660-1727

FORTUNE, PHILIP ROBERT, retired metal manufacturing company executive; b. Gouverneur, N.Y., Feb. 14, 1913; s. Robert J. and Mary (Cain)

F.; m. Margaret E. Burns, Apr. 15, 1944 (div. Aug. 15, 1980); children: Joanne, Terence, David, Christopher, Stephen; m. Kathryn T. Crawford, Oct. 4, 1980 (dec. July 1986); m. Naomi K. Buryan. B.A., St. Joseph's Coll., 1933; M.A., Niagara U., 1939. Instr. Niagara U., 1938-40; with N.Y. Air Brake Co. (merged with Gen. Signal Corp. 1967), Watertown, 1940—; gen. mgr. N.Y. Air Brake Co. (merged with Gen. Signal Corp. 1967), 1955-63, v.p., 1959-65, group exec., 1961-65, pres., 1965-67, chmn. exec. com., 1967-77, cons., 1977—, also dir.; ret.; dir. Hamworthy Hydraulics Ltd., 1963-82, chmn. bd., 1971-82; trustee Watertown Savs. Bank. Served to lt. col. AUS, World War II, ETO. Home: 9 Church Ln S Scarsdale NY 10583-5603*

FORTUNE, ROBERT RUSSELL, financial consultant; b. Collingswood, N.J., Nov. 22, 1916; s. Colin C. and Minnie M. (Brown) F.; m. Christine E. Dent, Nov. 10, 1956. B.S. in Econs., U. Pa., 1940. C.P.A., Pa. With Haskins & Sells (C.P.A.s), 1940-42, 46-48; with Pa. Power & Light Co., Allentown, 1948-84; v.p. fin. Pa. Power & Light Co., 1966-75, exec. v.p. fin., dir., 1975-84; chmn., CEO Assoc. Electric and Gas Ins. Svcs. Ltd., 1984-93; bd. dirs. Ind. Sq. Income Securities, Inc., chmn. pres., 1994—; bd. dirs. Chestnut St. Exch. Fund, chmn. pres., 1994—. Tech. adv. com. on fin. FPC, 1974-75. Treas. Allentown Sch. Dist. Authority, 1963-85, Lehigh-Northampton Airport Authority, 1985-94. With USN, 1942-46. Mem. Fin. Execs. Inst., Am., Pa. insts. C.P.A.s. Republican. Club: Lehigh Country. Home: 2920 Ritter Ln Allentown PA 18104-2823

FORWARD, DOROTHY ELIZABETH, legal assistant; b. Medford, Mass., Oct. 12, 1919; d. Roy Clifford and Julia (Lane) Hurd; m. Winston W. Forward, Sept. 29, 1942. Student, UCLA, 1964. Sec. nat. dir. fund raising ARC, Washington, 1943-46; legal sec. William W. Waters, Esq., L.A., 1953-56; office mgr. Winston W. Forward, Ins. Adjuster, Arcadia, Calif., 1956-64; legal asst. John M. Podlech, Esq., Pasadena, 1964-79; dir. Calif. Probate Insts., Arcadia, 1970—; ind. probate legal asst., 1979—; condr. workshops in probate procedures, 1967-92; vol. lectr. to sr. citizens in estate planning; vol. sec. All-Ch. Coun. United Meth. Ch., Arcadia, 1998, 99; pres. Philathea (women's club), Arcadia, 1999, 2nd v.p., Arcadia Travelers, 2000, Arcadia, Calif. Recipient ARC Meritorious Svc. award, 1945. Office: PO Box 660311 Arcadia CA 91066-0311

FORWARD, GORDON E., manufacturing executive; m. Heather Forward; children: Mark, Paul. BS, U. B.C., Vancouver; MS, U. B.C.; PhD in Metallurgy, MIT; LLD (hon.), Queen's U., 1993. Sr. rsch. engr. Steel Co. of Can.; gen. supt. Lake Ontario Steel Co.; v.p. prodn. Chaparral Steel, Midlothian, Tex., 1975-82; pres., CEO Chaparral Steel, Midlothian, 1982-98; pres., CEO Cement/Concrete divsn. Tex. Industries, 1988-91, vice chmn., 1998—; bd. dirs. Tex. Industries, Noranda Forest Inc. of Can. Mem. adv. coun. Queen's U., So. Meth. U., Stanford U. Grad. Sch. Bus., U. B.C., MIT Materials Sci. Sch.; past chmn. Gifted Students Inst. of Tex., Nat. Super Collider Edn. Consortium. Recipient John Chipman medal Am. Inst. Metall. Engrs., 1972, named Howe Meml. Lectr., 1985, Benjamin Fairless award 1988; recipient Corporate Leadership award MIT, 1987; named CEO of Yr., Fortune mag., 1987; named U.S. Steelmaker of Yr., Iron Age mag., 1992. Mem. Steel Mfg. Assn. (bd. dirs.), Nat. Acad. Engring., Bus. Coun. for Sustainable Devel. Home: 1341 W Mockingbird Ln Dallas TX 76247*

FORWARD, ROBERT L(ULL), physicist, businessman, consultant, writer; b. Geneva, N.Y., Aug. 15, 1932; s. Robert Torrey and Mildred (Lull) F.; m. Martha Neil Dodson, Aug. 29, 1954; children—Robert Dodson, Mary Lois, Julie Elizabeth, Eve Laurel. BS in Physics, U. Md., 1954, PhD, 1965; MS in Applied Physics, UCLA, 1958. With Hughes Aircraft Co., 1956-87, assoc. mgr. theoretical studies dept., 1966-67, mgr. exploratory studies dept., 1967-74; sr. scientist Hughes Research Labs., Malibu, Calif., 1974-87; owner, chief scientist Forward Unltd., Clinton, Wash., 1987—; ptnr., chief scientist Tethers Unlimited, 1994-97; v.p., chmn. bd. dirs., sec., treas., chief scientist Tethers Unltd., Inc., 1997—; popular sci. writer and lectr. Author: (sci. fiction) Dragon's Egg, 1981, The Flight of the Dragonfly, 1983, Starquake, 1985, Rocheworld, 1986, Martian Rainbow, 1991, Timemaster, 1992, Camelot 30K, 1993, (with Julie Forward Fuller) Return to Rocheworld, 1993, Rescued from Paradise, 1995, (with Martha Dodson Forward) Marooned on Eden, 1993, Ocean under the Ice, 1994, Saturn Rukh, 1997, (nonfiction) (with Joel Davis) Mirror Matter: Pioneering Antimatter Physics, 1988, Future Magic, 1988, Indistinguishable from Magic, 1995; contbr. numerous articles to sci. jours. Capt. USAF, 1954-56. Hughes fellow, 1956-62. Fellow AIAA (assoc.), Brit. Interplanetary Soc.; mem. Am. Phys. Soc., Author's Guild, Sci.-Fiction and Fantasy Writers' Am., Sigma Xi, Sigma Pi Sigma. Home and Office: 8114 S Pebble Ct Clinton WA 98236-9240

FORYST, CAROLE, computer electronics executive; b. Chgo., Apr. 8; d. James M. and Marie V. Foryst; m. Anthony H. Cordesman, Feb. 14, 1976; children: Justin G., Alexander Scott. Student, Rosary Coll., 1958-61, Cite Universite de Grenoble, France, 1961, Hunter Coll., 1964-67, Roosevelt U., 1970-71. Fin. reporter Chgo. Sun-Times, 1969-72, L.A. Times, 1972; staff asst. to sec. U.S. Dept. Treasury, Washington, 1973-76; dep. dir. pub. affairs U.S. Dept. Interior, Washington, 1976; asst. v.p. Assn. Am. R.R.'s, Washington, 1977-78; v.p. AMTRAK, Washington, 1979-81; assoc. adminstr. budget and policy Urban Mass Transp. Adminstrn., Washington, 1981-84; comml. real estate broker Barnes, Morris & Pardoe, Washington, 1984-88, Larry Hogan & Assocs., Inc., Landover, Md., 1988-93; mortgage broker Mortgage Investment Corp., Vienna, Va., 1993-94, Windsor Mortgage Co, McLean, Va., 1994—; v.p. ops. Floating Images Inc., Westbury, N.Y., 1997-98; v.p. ops. DynaFirm, Inc., Los Alamos, N.Mex., 1998-99, CEO, 1999—; mem. fin. svc. com. Treas. Dept., Fed. Credit Union, 1991-93, Pub. Internat. Bus. Insights, 1991-93, Hotels and Comm. Real Estate Co., 1993-96. Republican. Home: RR 5 Box 417A Espanola NM 87532-8917 Office: DynaFirm Inc 127 Eastgate Dr Los Alamos NM 87544-3300

FOSCARINIS, MARIA, lawyer; b. N.Y.C., Aug. 8, 1956; d. Nicolas and Rosa F. BA, Barnard Coll., 1977; MA, Columbia U., 1978, JD, 1981. Bar: N.Y. 1982, U.S. Dist. Ct. (so. and ea. dists.) N.Y. 1983, D.C. 1986, U.S. Dist. Ct. D.C., U.S. Ct. Appeals (D.C. cir.). Law clk. to judge U.S. Ct. Appeals (2d cir.), N.Y.C., 1981-82; assoc. Sullivan & Cromwell, N.Y.C., 1982-85; counsel Nat. Coalition for Homeless, Washington, 1985-89; founder and dir. Nat. Law Ctr. on Homelessness and Poverty, Washington, 1989—. Notes editor Columbia U. Law Rev., 1980-81. Harlan Fiske Stone scholar, 1978-79; John Dewey fellow. Mem. ABA (commr. homelessness and poverty, 1989-95). Home: 4515 Willard Ave Apt 1207S Chevy Chase MD 20815-3656 Office: Nat Law Ctr Homelessness and Poverty 918 F St NW Ste 412 Washington DC 20004-1406

FOSCARINIS, ROSA, pediatrician, allergist; b. Burlington, Vt., Apr. 7, 1916; d. Gerassimos and Maria (Focarinis) Moshopoulos; m. Nicolas Foscarinis, July 22, 1946; 1 child, Maria. MD, Nat. U. Athens, 1940. Diplomate Am. Bd. Pediat. Rotating intern Fordham Hosp., N.Y.C., 1948-49; pediat. resident Gouverneur Hosp., N.Y.C., 1949-50, attending pediat. allergy, 1977-97; pediat. resident Postgrad. Hosp., N.Y.C., 1950-51; allergy tng. Mount Sinai Hosp., N.Y.C., 1955-72; pvt. practice N.Y.C., 1951-86; attending pediat. Med. Ctr. NYU, N.Y.C., 1951-93, clin. assoc. prof., 1971—; attending pediat. Bellevue Hosp. Ctr., N.Y.C., 1963-91; cons. pediatrician Manhattan State Hosp., N.Y.C., 1965-75; attending pediatrician Astoria Gen. Hosp., N.Y.C., 1973-87; cons. allergy T. Cardinal Cooke, N.Y.C., 1982-97. Recipient award City of N.Y. Dept. Hosps., 1964, citation Med. Soc. State N.Y., 1990. Fellow Am. Acad. Pediat.; mem. Am. Coll. Allergy and Immunology (com. food allergy 1984-86), N.Y. State Med. Soc., N.Y. County Med. Soc., N.Y. Allergy Soc. Home: 64 E 94th St New York NY 10128-0773*

FOSCHIO, LESLIE GEORGE, lawyer; b. Oct. 29, 1940; s. Frank George and Sonia (Kaczynski) F.; m. Virginia Rose Kostur, June 27, 1964; children: John, Michael, Amy, Robert, Christa. BA cum laude, U. Buffalo, 1962; LLB cum laude, SUNY, Buffalo, 1965. Bar: N.Y. 1966, U.S. Dist. Ct. (we. dist.) N.Y. 1975, U.S. Tax Ct. 1980, U.S. Ct. Appeals (7th cir.) 1973, U.S. Ct. Appeals (2d cir.) 1977, U.S. Ct. Appeals (D.C. cir.) 1977, U.S. Supreme Ct. 1975. Law clk. to Hon. William B. Lawless, Jr. N.Y. State Supreme Ct., 1965; atty. Counsel's Office, SUNY, 1965-66; asst. dist. atty. Erie County, Buffalo, 1966-69; assoc. prof., asst. dean U. Notre Dame Law Sch., Ind., 1969-74; corp. counsel City of Buffalo, 1975-77; ptnr. Cohen Swados Wright Hanifin Bradford & Brett, Buffalo, 1978-80; commr. Dept. Motor Vehicles, State of N.Y., Albany, 1981-83; gen. counsel, sec., v.p. Barrister Info. Sys. Corp., Buffalo, 1983-91; U.S. magistrate judge U.S. Dist. Ct. (we. dist.) N.Y., 1991—; lectr. law SUNY, Buffalo, 1966-68, 78-80. Comment editor Buffalo Law Rev., 1944-65; contbr. articles to profl. jours. Dem. candidate for N.Y. State Assembly from Erie County, 1968; Dem. primary candidate for mayor, Buffalo, 1977; pres. Theodore Roosevelt Inaugural Nat. Hist. Site Found., Buffalo, 1978-87, trustee, 1978—; trustee Theodore Roosevelt Assn., 1981—; dist. chmn. Greater Niagara Frontier coun. Boy Scouts Am., Buffalo, 1980-82. Recipient T. R. McConnell Leadership, Scholarship and Character award U. Buffalo, 1962, Disting. Pub. Svc. award N.Y. Jaycees, Buffalo, 1976, Outstanding Svc. to Hwy. Safety award N.Y. State Assn. Traffic Safety, 1982, Alumnus of Yr. award H. C. Tech. H.S., 1997. Fellow N.Y. State Bar Found. (life), Am. Bar Found. (life); mem. Fed. Magistrate Judges Assn., N.Y. State Bar Assn. (Action Unit 5 1980-83), Bar Assn. Erie County (dir. 1988-91), U. Buffalo Alumni Assn. (dir. 1995-99, v.p. membership 1988-99, pres. 1981-82, Disting. Alumnus award 1983), Phi Alpha Delta (hon.). Roman Catholic. Home: 46 Woodley Rd Buffalo NY 14215-1321 Office: 424 US Courthouse 68 Court St Buffalo NY 14202-3405

FOSDICK, CORA PRIFOLD (CORA PRIFOLD BEEBE), government official; b. San Francisco, Nov. 3, 1937; d. George and Beatrice (Ehni) Prifold; m. Ronald Beebe, Jan., 1959 (div.); m. Donald James Fosdick, Oct. 12, 1997. Student, Hollins Coll., Va., 1955-57, Am. U., 1957-58; BA, U. Mich., 1959, MA, 1961; LHD (hon.), Southeastern U., 1993. Adminstrv. asst. Am. Polit. Sci. Assn., 1962-64; research assoc. Inst. Comparative Studies of Polit. Systems, Washington, 1963-65; program planning and evaluation specialist U.S. Office Edn., Washington, 1965-68, planning coordinator, 1968-73, dir. planning and budget div., 1973-80; prin. dep. asst. sec. for elem. and sec. edn. Dept. Edn., Washington, 1980-81; asst. sec. adminstrn. U.S. Treasury Dept., Washington, 1981-84; dir. office of policy, budget and program mgmt. OSWER, EPA, Washington, 1984-86; dir. office of planning, budget and evaluation Dept. Commerce, Washington, 1986-87; commerce & justice br. chief Office of Mgmt. and Budget, 1987-94, advisor to assoc. dir. gen. govt. and fin., 1994; exec. dir. adminstrn., chief fin. officer Office of Thrift Supervision, Washington, 1994—. Mem. women's com. Washington Performing Arts Soc., 1983—. Recipient HEW Superior Svc. award, Presdl. Rank award, 1989; Inst. World Affairs fellow, 1956, Am. Edn. Abroad former fellow, 1960. Fellow Nat. Acad. Pub. Adminstrn.; mem. Exec. Women in Govt. Program and Budget Analysis, Nat. Press Club. Home: 550 N St SW Apt S702 Washington DC 20024-4643 Office: Office Thrift Supervision 1700 G St NW Washington DC 20552-0003

FOSGATE HEGGLI, JULIE DENISE, producer; b. El Paso, Tex., Feb. 17, 1954; d. Orville Edward and Patricia (Ward) Fosgate; m. Bjarne Heggli, June 20, 1980; children: Elise Mai, Kristin April. BA in Broadcasting, U. So. Calif., 1976, MA in Journalism, 1978. On-board editor Royal Viking Line, San Francisco, 1978-80; editor Stentor, Trondheim, Norway, 1981; staff Grunion Gazette, Long Beach, Calif., 1981; news editor Nine Network Australia, Los Angeles, 1981-82; editor South Coast Metro News, Costa Mesa, Calif., 1981-82; v.p. The Newport Group, Newport Beach, Calif., 1982-85; exec. editor Orange County This Month, Newport Beach, 1985; exec. dir. mktg. Gen. Group Cos.,, Harbor City, Calif., 1985-87; sr. v.p. mktg. Automax Corp., L.A., 1987-88, Gen. Group Internat., Harbor City, Calif., 1988-90; assoc. producer Zoo Life Tv Spls., L.A., 1991; asoc. producer NBC News, Burbank, Calif., 1992-94; v.p. mktg. Western Nat., Scottsdale, Ariz., 1994—. Mem. Phi Beta Kappa. Avocations: collecting, reading, art. Home: 9640 E Davenport Dr Scottsdale AZ 85260-1426 Office: Western Nat 4150 Civic Center Blvd Scottsdale AZ 85251-3921

FOSLER, R. SCOTT, academic administrator. Student, Johns Hopkins U., Italy, U. Oslo, Norway, 1965-66; BA, Dickinson Coll., 1967; MPA, Princeton U., 1969. Pres. Nat. Acad. Pub. Adminstrn., Washington, 1992—. Author of numerous book chpts.; contbr. articles to profl. jours.; co-author (with Alonso, Meyer, Kern) Demographic Change and the American Future, 1990. Office: Nat Acad Pub Adminstrn Office of the President 1120 G St NW Ste 850 Washington DC 20005-3801*

FOSS, CHARLES R., transportation operations specialist; b. Chgo., Nov. 1, 1945; s. Raymond C. and Marilyn (Halas) F. Assoc. in Transp., Davenport Coll., 1973, B in Mktg., 1985, BS in Mgmt., 1994. Cert. purchasing mgr., Nat. Assn. Purchasing Mgmt.; cert. profl. mgr., Inst. Cert. Profl. Mgrs.; cert. transp. and logistics profl., Am. Soc. Transp. Logistics. Yardmaster Chesapeake and Ohio Ry., Benton Harbor, Mich., 1963-66; ticket agt. Chesapeake and Ohio Ry., Holland, Mich., 1969-71; freight agt., train dispatcher Penn Cen. Ry., Ft. Wayne, Ind., 1971-76; crew dispatcher Consol. Rail Corp., Grand Rapids, Mich., 1976-78; trainmaster Mich. No. Ry., 1978-85; customer service rep. Superior Brand Produce, Hudsonville, Mich., 1985; purchasing buyer U.S. Dept. Def., Dayton, Ohio, 1986-89; contract adminstr. U.S. Dept. Def., Grand Rapids, Mich., 1989-94; transp. specialist, ops. CSX Transp. Inc., Grand Rapids, 1994—; part-time sales rep. Foss Police Equipment and Communications, Battle Creek, Mich., 1978-85. Author: Evening Before The Diesel, 1980. Coord. Susquicentennial Commemorative Winchester Carbine, Byron Twp., Byron Ctr., Mich., 1985; hon. life mem. RR History Mus., Durand, Mich. With U.S. Army, 1966-69, Vietnam. Mem. NRA (life), Nat. Assn. Purchasing Mgmt. (cert. purchasing mgr.), Nat. Contract Mgmt. Assn., Am. Soc. Transp. and Logistics (cert. in transp. and logistics mgmt.), Chgo. and North Western Hist. Soc. (contbr.), So. Mich. R.R. Soc. (contbr.), Am. Truck Hist. Soc. (life). Republican. Avocations: firearms collection, antique cars and trucks, transp. art works collector.

FOSS, CLIVE FRANK WILSON, history educator; b. London, Aug. 30, 1939; came to U.S., 1945, naturalized, 1980; s. Victor Albert and Jeanne Francoise (Beurton) W. A.B. magna cum laude, Harvard U., 1961, M.A., 1965, Ph.D., 1973. Instr., U. Mass., Boston, 1967-69, lectr., 1969-73, asst. prof., 1973-76, asso. prof., 1976-80, prof. history, 1980—; faculty Boston Coll., 1968-69; vis. prof. U. Lyon, France, 1977-79, U. South Africa, 1981, U. Calif., 1985, Harvard U., 1990-91; mem. Sardis Expdn., 1969-75, 79-83; dir. Medieval Castles Survey of Anatolia, 1982-85; assoc. Ephesus Excavations, 1973-74. Author: Byzantine and Turkish Sardis, 1976, Rome and Byzantium, 1977, Ephesus After Antiquity, 1979, Medieval Castles Survey I: Kutahya, 1985, II, Nicomedia, 1996, Byzantine Fortifications, 1986, History and Archaeology of Byzantine Asia Minor, 1990, Roman Historical Coins, 1991, Nicea, 1996, Cities, Fortresses and Villages of Byzantine Asia Minor, 1996, Juan and Eva Peron, 1999; contbr. articles to profl. jours. Norton fellow Am. Sch. Classical Studies, Athens, 1961-62; Am. Coun. Learned Socs. grantee, 1974, 80; Indo-U.S. fellow (CIES), 1983; CNRS rsch. assoc., Paris, 1983; NEH fellow, 1975-76; Guggenheim fellow, 1983-84; vis. fellow Dumbarton Oaks, 1973-74, All Souls Coll., Oxford U., 1983-84, Trinity Coll., Oxford U., 1997; fellow Inst. Advanced Studies, Hebrew U., Jerusalem, 1993. Fellow Soc. Antiquaries, Royal Numismatic Soc.; mem. Am. Philol. Assn., Am. Numismatic Soc., Brit. Inst. Archaeology of Ankara, Numismatic Soc. India, Harvard Club (N.Y.C.), Tavern Club (Boston), Phi Beta Kappa. Republican. Episcopalian. Home: 5 Birch St Cambridge MA 02138-1205 Office: U Mass Dept History Boston MA 02125

FOSS, DONALD JOHN, university dean, research psychologist; b. Mpls., Mar. 28, 1940; s. Bernard J. and Elizabeth (Cody) F.; m. Patricia R. Diamond, Sept. 18, 1965; children—Melissa, Lara. BA, U. Minn., 1962, PhD, 1966. Postdoctoral fellow Harvard U., Cambridge, Mass., 1966-67; asst. prof. psychology U. Tex., Austin, 1967-71, assoc. prof., 1971-75, prof., 1975-95, chmn. dept., 1983-95; dean Coll. Arts and Scis., Fla. State U., Tallahassee, 1995—. Author: (with others) Psycholinguistics, 1978, Mental Health Research in Texas, 1990; editor Contemporary Psychology, 1980-85; assoc. editor Am. Psychologist, 1987-92, Ann. Rev. of Psychology, 1994-98; contbr. articles to profl. jours. Mem. adv. coun. Hogg Found., 1988-91, USAF Cognition Group, 1989-93, Mellon Found. Literacy Coun., 1989-93, U. Corp. Atmospheric Rsch. 1995—, Fla. State U. Rsch. Found, 1995—, bd. dirs., 1993—; co-chair Nat. Rsch. Agenda Steering Com., Univ. Corp. Atmospheric Rsch., 1995—;. Grantee NSF, 1969-72, NIMH, 1976-81, Army Rsch. Inst., 1982-85, Tex. Advanced Rsch., 1988-92; recipient Outstanding Grad. Tchg. award U. Tex., 1986, Outstanding Achievement award U. Minn., 1993. Fellow AAAS, APA (mem. publs. and comm. bd. 1985-94, chmn. 1991-93), Am. Psychol. Soc.; mem. Psychonomics Soc., Soc. Engring. Psychologists, Chancellors Coun. U. Tex., Pres.'s Club U. Minn. E-mail: dfoss@mailer.fsu.edu. Home: 3933 Bobbin Brook Cir Tallahassee FL 32312-1239 Office: Fla State U Coll Arts and Scis Tallahassee FL 32312

FOSS, JOHN FRANK, mechanical engineering educator; b. Washington, Pa., Mar. 24, 1938; s. Maurice Felker and C. Catharine (Reynard) F.; m. Jacqueline Kay Voss, July 24, 1960; children: Judith Kathleen, Janette Diane. Student, Wilmington Coll., 1956-58; B.S., Purdue U., 1961, M.S., 1962, Ph.D., 1965. Mem. faculty Mich. State U., East Lansing, 1964—; asso. prof. mech. engring. Mich. State U., 1968-75, prof., 1975—; dir. fluid dynamics & hydraulics program NSF, 1998—; cons. McDonnel Douglas Helicopter Co., Ford Motor Co., Bd. Water and Light, Lansing, Tranter Corp., United Techs. Rsch. Ctr., East Hartford, Conn. Author: (with M.C. Potter) Fluid Mechanics, 1975. Mem. Oaks Recreation Program staff, 1976-78; moderator Edgewood United Ch., 1975-77. Sloan fellow John Hopkins U., Balt., 1970-71; Alexander von Humboldt fellow U. Karlsruhe, Fed. Republic Germany, 1978-79, U. Erlangen, Fed. Republic Germany, 1985-86, rsch. fellow U. Melbourne, Australia, 1995. Fellow ASME; mem. AIAA, AAAS, AAUP, Am. Soc. Engring. Edn., Am. Phys. Soc., Soc. Scholars Johns Hopkins U., Sigma Xi, Tau Beta Pi, Pi Tau Sigma. Mem. United Ch. of Christ. Home: 4731 Nakoma Dr Okemos MI 48864-2024 Office: Mich State U Dept Mech Engring East Lansing MI 48824

FOSS, KARL ROBERT, auditor; b. Aug. 26, 1938; s. Robert Henry and Ethel Caroline (Huston) F. Student, U. Wis., 1956-59, 62; BS, Madison Bus. Coll., 1961. Auditor Wis. Dept. Revenue, Madison, 1962-95; owner, mgr. LIST, Middleton, Wis., 1968-76; Bd. dirs. Middleton Hist. Soc., 1976-93, v.p., 1980; legis. adv. Old Car Hobby, 1971—. Co-recipient Spl. Interest Autos Appreciation award, 1971. Mem. Wis. Automobile Clubs in Assn. Inc. (co-founder 1971, bd. dirs. 1971—, pres. 1972-74, 77-78, 80, 86-87, v.p. 1975-76, 79, 85, 95-99), Oldsmobile Club Am. (nat. dir. 1973-85, treas. 1981-85), Contemporary Hist. Vehicle Assn., Studebaker Drivers Club, Nash Car Club Am., Crosley Car Club, Antique Automobile Club Am., Vintage Chevrolet Club of Am., The Marmon Club, Model T Ford Club Am. Pub.: Suppliers List, 1968, Suppliers List Directory, 1969. Home: 1619 Middleton St Middleton WI 53562-3723

FOSS, LUKAS, composer, conductor, pianist; b. Berlin, Germany, Aug. 15, 1922; came to U.S. from Paris, 1937, naturalized, 1942; s. Martin and Hilde (Schindler) F.; m. Cornelia Brendel, Sept. 1951; 2 children. Student, Paris Lycée Pasteur, 1932-37; grad., Curtis Inst. Music, 1940; spl. study, Yale U., 1940-41; pupil of, Paul Hindemith, Julius Herford, Serge Koussevitzky, Fritz Reiner, Isabelle Vengerova; hon. doctorate, Yale U., 1991; 14 other hon. doctorates. Former prof. UCLA (in charge orch. and advanced composition); faculty Harvard U., 1970-71; prof. of composition Boston U., 1992—; founder Ctr. Creative and Performing Arts, Buffalo U.; vis. prof. Carnegie Mellon U., Pitts., 1987-90; composer in residence Tanglewood, 1989, 90; Mellon lectr. Nat. Gallery, Washington, 1987. Former condr., music dir., Buffalo Philharmonic; music dir., condr., Bklyn. Philharmonic, 1971-90, condr. laureate, 1990—; music dir., condr. Milw. Symphony Orch., 1981-86, condr. laureate, 1986—; orchestral compositions performed by many major orchs.; best known works include (opera) Griffelkin, Baroque Variations (orch.), Echoi (4 instruments), Time Cycle (songs with orch.), Renaissance concerto (flute and orch.); orch., chamber music, ballets, works commd. by, League of Composers, Nat. Endowment for Arts, N.Y. Arts Coun., NBC opera on TV, Am. Choral Condrs. Assn., Ind. U., 1979 Olympics, Boston Symphony, Chgo. Symphony; (recipient N.Y. Critic Circle citation for Prairie 1944, Soc. for Pub. Am. Music award for String Quartet in G 1948, Rome prize 1950, Horblit award for Piano concerto #2 1951, Naumburg Rec. award for Song of Songs 1957, Creative Music grant Inst. Arts and Letters 1957, N.Y. Music Critics Circle award for Time-Cycle orch. songs 1961, for Echoi 1963, Ditson award for condr. who has done the most for Am. music 1973, N.Y.C. award for spl. contbn. to arts 1976, ASCAP award for adventurous programming 1979, CRI rec. award for Thirteen Ways of Looking at a Blackbird 1979). Guggenheim fellow, 1945; Creative arts award Brandeis U., 1983; Laurel leaf award Am. Composers Alliance, 1983. Mem. Am. Acad. of Arts and Letters.

FOSS, RICHARD JOHN, bishop; b. Wauwatosa, Wis., Dec. 27, 1944; s. Harlan Funston and Beatrice Naomi (Lindaas) F.; m. Nancy Elizabeth Martin, June 21, 1969; children: Susan, John, Naomi Foss Welsh, Elizabeth, Peter, Andrew. BA, St. Olaf Coll., 1966; MDiv, Luther Theol. Seminary, 1971; ThM, Luther N.W. Theol. Seminary, 1984. Ordained to ministry Luth. Ch., 1971. Pastor St. Andrews Ch. and Ch. of Christ the Redeemer, Mpls., 1971-77; assoc. pastor First Luth., Fargo, N.D., 1977-79; sr. pastor Prince of Peace Luth., Seattle, 1979-86, Trinity Luth., Moorhead, Minn., 1986-92; bishop Ea. N.D. Synod, Fargo, ND, 1992—. Soloist F-M Opera Co., Fargo, 1979; coach St. James Girls' Basketball Team, Settle, 1982-84; vol. Wash. State Patrol Crisis Chaplaincy, Seattle, 1983-86; bd. dirs. Discovery, Inc., Mpls., 1972-77, Highline Boys' and Girls' Club, Burien, Wash., 1980-81, Luth. Compass Ctr., Seattle, 1983-86, v.p., 1985-86; mem. Master Chorale, 1987—; bd. regents Concordia Coll., 1993—; bd. dirs. Daily Bread, 1991—, Luth. Social Svcs. of N.D., 1992—, Oak Grove Luth. H.S., 1990—, Luth. Resources Network, 1994-97, Healthy Congregations Adv. Bd., 1997—. Avocations: racquetball, golf, reading, travel, vocal performance. Home: 1510 2nd St S Moorhead MN 56560-4014 Office: Ea ND Synod 1703 32nd Ave S Fargo ND 58103-5936

FOSSEEN, NEAL RANDOLPH, business executive, former banker, former mayor; b. Yakima, Wash., Nov. 27, 1908; s. Arthur Benjamin and Florence (Neal) F.; m. Helen Witherspoon, Sept. 26, 1936; children: Neal Randolph Jr., William Roger. BA, U. Wash., 1930; LD (hon.), Whitworth Coll., 1967. With Wash. Brick, Lime & Sewer Pipe Co., 1923-32, v.p., 1932-38; pres. Wash. Brick & Lime Co., 1938-58; dir. Securities Intermountain Co., 1954-71; v.p., dir. Old Nat. Bank Wash., 1958-68; v.p., dir. Wash. Bancshares, 1968-71, vice chmn., 1971-72, chmn. bd., pres., 1972-73; dir. Utah-Idaho Sugar Co., 1968-79, 1st Nat. Bank Spokane, 1972-79; dir. Spokane Indsl. Park, 1959-72, treas., 1959-66; dir. North Coast Life Ins. Co., 1965-76, Quarry Tile Co., 1965-68, Day Mines, Inc., 1968-81; chmn. emeritus, dir. Old Nat. Bancorp., 1973-77; pres. 420 Investment Co., 1982-84; hon. dir. Met. Mortgage Co., 1995—. Mem. exec. com. Expo '74; mem. adv. bd. Mus. Native Am. Culture, 1957-81; mayor City of Spokane, 1960-67, mayor emeritus, 1967—; mem. adv. bd. emeritus Spokane Intercollegiate Rsch. and Tech. Inst., 1993-96; past chmn. adv. bd. Wash. State Inst. Tech.; bd. dirs., past pres. coun. Boy Scouts Am.; bd. dirs. Wash. Rsch. Coun., sec., 1968-74; bd. dirs. YMCA, 1969-80, Pacific Sci. Found., 1970-73, Mountain States Legal Found., 1979-85; mem. adv. bd. Grad. Sch. Bus., U. Wash., 1974-81, emeritus, 1981—, mem. adv. bd. dept. history, 1981—; chmn. Regent Gonzaga U., 1948-61, emeritus, 1961—, benefactor, (hon.) LD, 1999; mem. adv. bd. Coll. Engring., Wash. State U., 1949-79; hon. trustee Found. N.W.; trustee Rockwood Cmty. Found., 1993-97, Gonzaga Dussault Found., Fosseen-Kusaka Disting. Professorship, Jackson Found. Scholarship, U. Wash., 1998; mem. adv. bd. Advanced Tech. Ctr., 1989-94, Mukogawa Fort Wright Inst., Whitworth Coll. Internat. Mgmt., City Innovation; founding. dir. Athetic Round Table. Col. USMCR, ret. Recipient Shrine award El Katif Temple, 1974, Non Sibi, Sed Patriae award Marine Corps. Res. Officers Assn., Outstanding Svc. award Fairchild AFB, Spokan Mcpl. League, Forward Spokane award Spokane County Hotel and Restaurant Coun., Liberty Bell award Spokane County Bar Assn., Book of Golden Deeds, Exchange Club, Sister City Outstanding Svc. award Town Affiliation Assn., Disting. Citizen award Ea. Wash. U., 1982, Founders Day award, 1994, Disting. Citizen award Air Force Air Mobility Command, 1995, Citizen League Lifetime Svc. award, 1997; named hon. citizen Nishinomiya, Japan. Mem. VFW, Ret. Officers Assn., Assn. Wash. Bus. (past pres.), Spokane C. of C. (v.0. 1946-51), Spokane-Nishinoniya Sister City Soc. (pres.), Srs. N.W. Golf Assn. (gov.), Mil. Order World Wars (Perpetual), Order of the Rising Sun (Japan), Balboa de Mazatlan Club (Mex.), Spokane Club (life), Spokane Country Club (life), Prosperity Club, Travellers Century Club, Spokane Ski Club, Rotary (Paul Harris fellow, benefactor), Beta Theta Pi, Alpha Kappa Psi. Home: Rockwood Manor 701 2903 E 25th Ave Spokane WA 99223 Office: 1420 US Bank Bldg Spokane WA 99201

FOSSELLA, VITO JOHN, congressman; b. Staten Island, N.Y., Mar. 9, 1965; s. Vito John and Elizabeth Lucey Fossella; m. Mary Patricia Rowan, 1990. BS, U. Pa., 1987; JD, Fordham U., 1993. Mem. Cmty. Bd. 3 Staten Island, 1989-90; city councilman N.Y.C., 1994-97; U.S. Congressman 13th Dist. Staten Island, 1997—; mem. commerce com., subcoms. on fin., energy and telecomms. U.S. Ho. of Reps. Mem. Phi Sigma Epsilon. Republican. Roman Catholic. Address: 4434 Amboy Rd 2nd Fl Staten Island NY 10312 Office: US House of Representatives 451 Cannon HOB Washington DC 20515

FOSSIER, MIKE WALTER, consultant, retired electronics company executive; b. New Orleans, Mar. 30, 1928; s. Louis Joseph and Thelma (Titus) F.; m. Donna Scott, Apr. 16, 1953 (dec.), m. Linda Furman, Nov. 11, 1990; children: Michael, Michele, Scott. BS, La. State U., 1945; MS, Calif. Inst. Tech., 1946, Profl. Degree, 1947. Aerodynamicist Douglas Aircraft, El Segundo, Calif., 1947-50; guidance engr. Raytheon Co., Oxnard, Calif., 1950-54; project engr. Raytheon Co., Bedford, Mass., 1954-59, chief engr. Missile System div., 1959-65, v.p., asst. gen. mgr. tech., 1965-90; pvt. cons. Winchester, Mass., 1990—. Contbr. articles to profl. jours.; inventor yaw damper, 1950, radome, 1953, missile guidance, 1977, radar system, 1983. Fellow AIAA; mem. IEEE.

FOSSLAND, JOEANN JONES, professional speaker, personal coach; b. Balt., Mar. 21, 1948; d. Milton Francis and Clementine (Bowen) Jones; m. Richard E. Yellott III, 1966 (div. 1970); children: Richard E. IV, Dawn Joeann; m. Robert Gerard Fossland Jr., Nov. 25, 1982. Student, Johns Hopkins U., 1966-67; cert., Hogan's Sch. Real Estate, 1982. Cert. values coach, behaviors coach, 1998, GRI; master cert. coach. Owner Kobble Shop, Indiatlantic, Fla., 1968-70, Downstairs, Atlanta, 1971; seamstress Aspen (Colo.) Leather, 1972-75; owner Backporch Feather & Leather, Aspen and Tucson, 1975-81; area mgr. Welcome Wagon, Tucson, 1982; realtor assoc. Tucson Realty & Trust, 1983-85; mgr. Home Illustrated mag., Tucson, 1985-87; asst. pub., gen. mgr. Phoenix, Scottsdale, Albuquerque, Tricities Tucson Homes Illustrated, 1990-93; pres. Advantage Solutions Group, Cortaro, Ariz., 1993—; power leader Darryl Davis Seminars Power Program, 1995—; personal and profl. coach. Designer leather goods (Tucson Mus. Art award 1978, Crested Butte Art Fair Best of Show award 1980); author: Personal and Professional Coaching: Coach University, Certified Training Program, 1996. Voter registrar Recorder's Office City of Tucson, 1985-91; bd. dirs. Hearth Found., Tucson, 1987-96, pres., 1994; bd. dirs. Ariz. Integrated Residential & Ednl. Svcs., Inc., 1989-95, pres. 1994-95). Mem. NAFE, Internat. Fedn. Coaches (master cert. coach), Women's Coun. Realtors (leadership tng. grad. designation, pres. Tucson chpt. 1995, Ariz. state gov. 1997-98, Tucson Affiliate of Yr. award 1991), Tucson Assn. Realtors (Affiliate of Yr. award 1988). Democrat. Presbyterian. Avocations: tennis, gardening, reading, traveling, public speaking. Office: Advantage Solutions Group PO Box 133 Cortaro AZ 85652-0133

FOSSUM, JERRY GEORGE, electrical engineering educator; b. Phoenix, July 18, 1943; s. George Clayton and Lillian Edith (McNeilis) F.; m. Mary Ellen Turner; children: Kerry Ray, Kelly Lynn. AA, Phoenix Coll., 1963; BSEE, U. Ariz., 1966, MS, 1969, PhD, 1971. Mem. tech. staff Sandia Labs., Albuquerque, 1971-78; assoc. prof. elec. engring. U. Fla., Gainesville, 1978-80, prof., 1980—; cons. Burr-Brown Rsch. Corp., Tucson, 1970-71, Jet Propulsion Lab., Pasadena, Calif., 1979, Harris Corp., Melbourne, Fla., 1984, Tex. Instruments, Inc., Dallas, 1988-89, 94-96, Ibis Tech. Corp., Danvers, Mass., 1995, Meta-Software, Campbell, Calif., 1995-96, Dynamics Rsch. Corp., San Diego, 1996—; mem. adv. com. Semiconductor Rsch. Corp., 1991-95; mem. exec. com. IEEE SOI Conf., 1994-97. Contbr. articles to profl. jours.; assoc. editor: Solid-State Electronics, 1979—, IEEE Trans. Computer-Aided Design, 1988-91; patentee in field. Recipient Outstanding Rsch. award Am. Soc. Engring. Edn., 1979. Fellow IEEE (Best Paper award SOI Conf. 1992). Office: U Fla Dept Elec and Computer Engr Gainesville FL 32611-6130

FOSSUM, JUDY KAYE, radio news reporter; b. Bowman, N.D., Feb. 25, 1975; d. Albert Leroy and Joyce Adelina (Jalbert) F. BS in Mass Comms., Moorhead (Minn.) State U., 1997. On-air announcer 1340 KPOK Radio, Bowman, 1989-93; news reporter 790 KFGO AM Radio, Fargo, N.D., 1997—. Mem. Soc. Profl. Journalists (sec. 1995-96), Sons of Norway, Am. Legion Aux. Avocations: piano, accordion, walking, reading.

FOSSUM, ROBERT H(EYERDAHL), retired English literature educator; b. Beloit, Wis., Mar. 19, 1923; s. Hans Martinius and Talma Irene (Heyerdahl) F.; m. Terry O'Brien Barker, Sept. 12, 1945 (div. Feb. 1951); m. Virginia Adelaide Hammond, June 7, 1952; children: Kristin, Robert Paul, Elizabeth. BA, Beloit Coll., 1948; MA, U. So. Calif., 1950; PhD, Claremont Grad. Sch., 1963. Tchg. asst., lectr. dept. English, U. So. Calif., L.A., 1948-50; instr., asst. prof., then assoc. prof. Beloit Coll., 1950-62; assoc. prof., prof. Calif. State U., L.A., 1962-63; assoc. prof., then prof. Claremont (Calif.) McKenna Coll., 1963-87, Josephine Olp Weeks prof. lit., 1972-87, prof. emeritus, 1987—; Fulbright prof. Am. lit. U. Vienna and U. Graz, Austria, 1969-70, 76-77. Author: William Styron, 1968, Hawthorne's Inviolable Circle, 1972; co-author: Facing Mirrors, 1980, The American Dream, 1981; co-editor: American Ground, 1988. With inf. U.S. Army, 1943. Fellow Lilly Found., 1959-60, Shell Found., 1960-61. Mem. MLA, Phi Beta Kappa. Avocations: reading, spectator sports, theater, film. Home: 403 University Cir Claremont CA 91711-4251

FOSSUM, ROBERT MERLE, mathematician, educator; b. Northfield, Minn., May 1, 1938; s. Inge Martin and Tina Otelia (Gaudland) F.; m. Cynthia Carol Foss, Jan. 30, 1960 (div. 1979); children: Karen Jean, Kristin Ann; m. Barbara Joel Mason, Aug. 4, 1979 (div. 1993); children: Jonathan Robert, Erik Anton; m. Robin Karyl Goodman, Aug. 10, 1997. BA, St. Olaf Coll., 1959; AM, U.Mich., 1961, PhD, 1965. Instr. U. Ill., Urbana, 1964-66; asst. prof. U. Ill., 1966-68, assoc. prof., 1968-72, prof. math., 1972—; lectr. Aarhus U., Denmark, 1971-73, Copenhagen U., Denmark, 1976-77; vis. prof. Université de Paris VI, 1978-79, Oslos U., 1968-69. Contbr. numerous articles to profl. jours. Fulbright grantee Oslos U., 1967-68. Mem. AAAS, Nat. Assn. Mathematicians, Math. Assn. Am., Am. Math. Soc. (assoc. sec. ctrl. sect. 1983-87, sec.-designate 1988, sec. 1989-99), Dansk Matematisk Forening, Inst. Algebraic Meditation (sec.), Swedish Math. Soc., Det Kongelig Norske Videnskabers Selskab (elected natural scis. sect.). Democrat. Lutheran. Club: Heimskringla (Urbana). E-mail: r-fossum@uiuc.edu. Office: U Ill Dept Math 1409 W Green St Urbana IL 61801-2943

FOSTER, ALAN HERBERT, financial consultant, educator; b. Somerville, Mass., Nov. 7, 1925; s. Herbert and Margaret J. (Griffin) F.; m. Cynthia Ann Brooks, June 26, 1954; children—Mark Brooks, Andrew Herbert. B.S., B.A., Boston Coll., 1951; M.B.A., Harvard U., 1953. With Sylvania Electric Products, Inc., 1953-63; with Am. Motors Corp., 1963-77, corp. dir. financial planning and analysis, 1963-67, treas., 1967-68, v.p., treas., 1968-77; pres. A.H. Foster & Co. (Cons. in Corp. Fin.), Ann Arbor, Mich., 1977—, Fin. Risk Mgmt. Inc., Ann Arbor, 1983—; adj. prof. ethics corp. strategy Grad. Sch. Bus., U. Mich. Author: Practical Business Management, 1962, Treasurer's Handbook; also articles. Served with USNR, 1945-46. Mem. Commanderie de Bordeaux, Fin. Execs. Inst. (pres. Detroit chpt. 1972-73), Baker Street Irregulars, Speckled Band Boston, Inst. Mgmt. Scis. (past nat. chmn. coll. planning), U. Mexico Club, Samuel Pepys Club, Harvard Club N.Y.C. Home: 810 Earhart Rd Ann Arbor MI 48105-2711

FOSTER, AMY NICOLE, television station sales administrator. BS, Appalachian State U., 1971. Sale promotions, creative svcs. dir., kids club coord. WSFX-TV, Wilmington, N.C., 1997—. E-mail: afoster@wsfx.com. Office: Apt 140 6211 Wrightsville Ave Wilmington NC 28403

FOSTER, ARTHUR KEY, JR., lawyer; b. Birmingham, Ala., Nov. 22, 1933; s. Arthur Key and Vonceil (Oden) F.; m. Jean Lyles Foster, Jan. 7, 1967; children: Arthur Key III, Brooke Oden. B.S.E., Princeton U., 1955; JD, U. Va., 1960. Bar: Ala. 1960. Ptnr. Balch & Bingham, Birmingham, 1965—. Trustee Episcopal Found. Jefferson County; bd. dirs. Met. YMCA, Downtown Club, Highlands Day Sch., Altamont Sch. Served to lt., USN, 1955-60. Mem. ABA, Ala. Bar Assn., B'ham Bar Assn., Estate Planning Council of Birmingham, Nat. Assn. Bond Lawyers, Newcomen Soc. of U.S. Republican. Episcopalian. Club: Kiwanis (bd. dirs.). Office: Balch & Bingham PO Box 306 Birmingham AL 35201-0306

FOSTER, ARTHUR ROWE, mechanical engineering educator; b. Peabody, Mass., Apr. 22, 1924; s. Francis Joel and Helen Almira (Rowe) F.; m. Nettie Claire Pease, July 12, 1947 (dec. Mar. 1997); children: Jackson Judd, Cynthia Grace. B.S. in Mech. Engring, Tufts U., 1945; M.Engring. in Mech. Engring, Yale, 1949. Registered profl. engr., Mass. Engr. material devel. lab. Pratt & Whitney aircraft div. United Aircraft Corp., 1947-48; mem. faculty Northeastern U., 1949—, prof. mech. engring., 1961-89, prof. emeritus, 1989—, chmn. dept., 1961-75; Latin Am. teaching fellow Escuela Politecnica Nacional, Quito, Ecuador, 1975-76; Fulbright lectr. solar engring. Colombia, summer 1979; vis. prof. Escuela Politecnica Nacional, Quito, Ecuador, 1984. Author: (with R. L. Wright, Jr.) Basic Nuclear Engineering, 1968, 4th edit., 1983, (with Melvin Mark) Thermodynamics: Principles and Applications, 1979. Served to ensign USNR, 1945-46. Fellow ASME (life, Centennial medal 1980); mem. Am. Soc. Engring. Edn. (life), Delta Tau Delta, Pi Tau Sigma, Tau Beta Pi. Home: 10 Longwood Dr #121 Westwood MA 02090

FOSTER, BENJAMIN, JR., educational administrator; b. Raleigh, N.C., Mar. 30, 1946; s. Benjamin and Miriam Foster; 1 child, Benjamin Bayete; m. Walton L. Brown, Dec. 28, 1994. BA, Trinity Coll., Hartford, Conn., 1971; MA in Teaching with honors, Wesleyan U., Middletown, Conn., 1973; EdD, U. Mass., 1989, cert. advanced grad. study, 1984. Cert. social studies tchr., Mass., N.Y.; cert. intermediate adminstrn., Conn. Prin. planning analyst for human svcs. Conn. Office Policy and Mgmt., Hartford; rsch. fellow Ctr. for Study Pub. Policy, Cambridge, Mass.; staff rsch. asst. U. Mass., Amherst; asst. chief staff devel. Conn. Dept. Social Svcs., Hartford; asst. dir. A.I. Prince Regional Vocat. Sch., Hartford; prin. Bloomfield (Conn.) H.S.; dir. H.C. Wilcox Tech. Sch., Meriden, Conn., 1989—; vis. practitioner Harvard Grad. Sch. Edn., 1994—. Author: Looking for Payoff: A New Schooling for Inner-City Youth, 1990; contbr. numerous articles to profl. jours. Trustee Trinity Coll., Hartford. With U.S. Army, 1965-67. Nat. urban fellow, 1982-83. Mem. Inst. Ednl. Leadership (v.p. fellowship edn. policy program 1978-79), Nat. Dropout Prevention Network, Omega Psi Phi. Home: 6 Croydon Dr Bloomfield CT 06002

FOSTER, BILL See FOSTER, WILLIAM EDWIN

FOSTER, BRUCE DUDLEY, retired clergyman; b. Gage, Okla., May 1, 1935; s. Ernest Edward and Ruth Anna (Berry) F.; m. Barbara Anne Walker; children: Teresa Lynn, Robyn Kathleen, Karen Leigh, Connie Ruth. BS in Biology, Pittsburg (Kans.) State U., 1958, MS in Edn., 1959; DD (hon.), Hyles-Anderson Coll., 1980. Cert. tchr., Kans., Colo., La.; ordained minister Bapt. Ch. Tchr. Thayer (Kans.) High Sch., 1958-59, New Castle (Colo.) High Sch., 1959-62, Mid-City Bapt. High Sch., New Orleans, 1962-63; athletic dir. Tenn. Temple U., Chattanooga, 1963-75; exec. v.p. Okla. Bapt. Coll., Oklahoma City, 1979-86; adminstr. College Heights Bapt. Acad., Farmington, N.Mex., 1986-92; pastor College Heights Bapt. Ch., Farmington, 1986-92, 2d Bapt. Ch., Festus, Mo., 1992—; evangelist, conf. spkr., Christian author, speaker in field. Author: Creation Considered From a Biblical and a Scientific Viewpoint, 1970, The Home, 1976, The Doubt Problem, 1975; writer weekly column Teen Talks, 1976-79. Pres. Twin City Christian Acad., Festus, 1992-98, Living Springs Camp, Festus, 1992-98. With U.S. Army, 1954-55. Mem. Phi Delta Kappa. Republican. Avocations: hunting, fishing. Home: PO Box 987 South Fork CO 81154 Office: 488 Wolf Creek Rd South Fork CO 81154

FOSTER, CATHERINE RIERSON, manufacturing company executive; b. Balt., Mar. 14, 1935; d. William Harman and Ella Fredericka (Magsamen) Rierson; m. Morgan Lawrence Foster, Nov. 17, 1957 (dec. Jan. 1990); children: Diana Kay, Susan Ann, Morgan Lawrence, Heather Lynne. Student, Balt. City Coll., 1955, Johns Hopkins U., 1956-57, Glendale Coll., 1962-63. Sec. Martin Co., Balt., 1956-57, adminstrv. sec., 1957-58; v.p., corp. sec. Fostermation, Inc., Meadville, Pa., 1971-90, pres., chmn. bd., 1990-97; ret., also bd. dirs.; pvt. practice cons., 1997—; mem. adv. com. Vocat./Tech. Sch., Meadville, 1982-86, export coun. We. Pa. Dist., 1995—, Meadville Area Indsl. Commn., 1996—, Meadville Med. Ctr. Bd. Corporators, 1996—; mem. Western Pa. Dist. Export Coun., 1995-98. Pres. La Crescents, La Crescenta, Calif., 1962; active City Hosp. Aux., Meadville, 1969-86, Rep. Women's Workshop, Glendale, Calif., 1966-68, Com. to Elect Ronald Reagan, Glendale, 1967; bd. dirs. YWCA, Meadville, 1988-89, 98—, also chmn. fin. com., 1988-89; bd. dirs. Jr. Achievement, Crawford County, Meadville, 1992-94. Recipient Tribute to Women award YWCA, 1998. Mem. DAR (chpt. regent 1989-92), NAFE, Svc. Corps Ret. Execs., Rotary (pres. 1996-97). Lutheran. Avocations: genealogy, history, bridge. Home: 1121 Lakemont Dr Meadville PA 16335-2826 Office: Fostermation Inc 200 Valleyview Dr Meadville PA 16335-7916

FOSTER, C(HARLES) ALLEN, lawyer; b. Monroe, La., Aug. 26, 1941; s. Charles Shearer and Bessie Lea (Long) F.; m. Susan Coomes; children: Charles Shearer Sanders II, Susan Elizabeth Coomes, Charles Henry Edward. BA summa cum laude, Princeton U., 1963; postgrad., BA in Jurisprudence with 1st class honors, Oxford (Eng.) U., 1965, MA in Jurisprudence, 1971; JD magna cum laude, Harvard U., 1967. Bar: N.C. 1967, U.S. Dist. Ct. (mid. dist.) 1968, U.S. Dist. Ct. (we. dist.) 1968, U.S. Dist. Ct. (ea. dist.) 1968, U.S. Tax Ct. 1970, U.S. Ct. Appeals (4th cir.), U.S. Ct. Appeals (5th cir.) 1970, U.S. Ct. Appeals (11th cir.) 1991, U.S. Ct. Appeals (10th cir.) 1993, U.S. Ct. Appeals (fed. cir.), 1995, U.S. Supreme Ct. 1971, D.C. 1984, U.S. Dist. Ct. D.C. 1985, U.S. Dist. Ct. (no. dist.) Tex. 1990, U.S. Dist. Ct. (so. dist.) Tex. 1991, U.S. Ct. Fed. Claims 1994. Assoc., McLendon, Brim, Brooks, Pierce & Daniels, Greensboro, N.C., 1967-72, ptnr., 1972-73; sec., dir., gen. counsel Spanco Industries, Inc., Greensboro and Sanford, N.C. and Conestee, S.C., 1973-75; ptnr. Turner, Enochs, Foster, Sparrow & Burnley, Greensboro, 1975-81, Foster, Conner & Robson, 1983-88, Patton, Boggs LLP, 1988-98, Greenberg, Traurig, Hoffman & Rosen, 1999—; sr. lectr. law Duke U., 1981-88; arbitrator Am. Arbitration Assn., mem. nat. panels of labor, constrn. and internat. comml. arbitrators; mem. Nat. Acad. Arbitrators; pub. mem. N.C. Tax Rev. Bd., 1972-76; mem. N.C. Judicial Selection Study Commn., 1987-88; U.S. rep. Internat. Energy Agy. Dispute Resolution Centre, Paris, 1984—; permanent panel arbitrator Martin Marietta and Atomic Trades and Labor Coun.; hearing officer Guilford Tech. Inst., Greensboro, others. Co-founder, sec., bd. dirs. Greensboro Day Sch.; dir. Greensboro Opera Co.; alumni council; exec. com. Princeton U. Alumni Assn.; exec. com. Harvard Law Sch. Assn. N.C., 1970; group chmn. United Fund Dr., 1969-70; precinct chmn. Guilford County Rep. Exec. Com., 1974-76, 84-92, chmn. fin. com., 1975-76; Rep. candidate for atty.-gen. N.C., 1984. Mem. ABA, Am. Law Inst., N.C. Bar Assn. (council sect. constitutional law), Greensboro Bar Assn., 18th Jud. Dist. Bar Assn., Phi Beta Kappa, Cap and Gown Club. Author: Construction and Design Law, 1984—; Construction and Design Law Digest, 1981—; Law and Practice of Commercial Arbitration in North Carolina, 1984; contbr. articles to profl. jours. Active N.C. Tax Rev. Bd., 1975-79; spl. counsel Rep. Nat. Com., 1989—; spl. litigation counsel N.C. Rep. Cen. Com., 1987—; co-founder, sec., bd. dirs. Greensboro Day Sch., bd. dirs. Greensboro Opera Co., 1980-83, Young Women's Christian Assn., 1968-84, atty.; group chmn. United Fund Drive, 1979. Mem. ABA (litigation sect., labor and employment discrimination law sect., forum com. on constrn. industry), N.C. Bar Assn. (labor and employment law sect., constrn. law sect.), Am. Arbitration Assn. (bd. dirs. 1980-83, nat. panels labor, constrn., internat. comml. arbitrators 1975—, chmn. N.C. regional adv. coun. 1979-83), Am. Coll. Constrn. Arbitrators (pres. 1983-84), Princeton U. Alumni Assn. (pres. alumni coun., exec. com. 1978-79, pres. middle N.C. chpt. 1968-80), and others. Home: 3060 Q St NW Washington DC 20007

FOSTER, CHARLES F., communications executive. Group pres SBC Comm., San Antonio. Office: SBC Comm 175 E Houston St Rm 1309 San Antonio TX 78205-2233*

FOSTER, CHARLES HENRY WHEELWRIGHT, former foundation officer, consultant,author; b. Boston, Mar. 18, 1927; s. Reginald Candler and Frances Helen (Hoar) F.; m. Barbara Ann Duchaine, Sept 19, 1953; children: Frances H., Jonathan R., Susan Foster Swensen. BA, Harvard U., 1951; BSF, U. Mich., 1953, MS, 1956; PhD, Johns Hopkins U., 1969; DPA (hon.), Suffolk U., 1971; MA (hon.), Yale U., 1977. Exec. sec. Wildlife Conservation Inc., Boston, 1953-55; cons. Mass. Water Resources Commn., Boston, 1956-59; commr. Mass. Dept. Natural Resources, Boston, 1959-66; pres. Nature Conservancy, Washington, 1966-67; sr. staff mem. Conservation Found., Washington, 1967-68; chmn. bd. N.E. Natural Resources Ctr., Boston, 1969-70; sec. Mass. Exec. Office Environ. Affairs, Boston, 1971-75; sr. staff mem. A. D. Little, Inc., Cambridge, Mass., 1975-76; prof. environ. policy U. Mass., Amherst, 1975-76; dean Sch. Forestry and Environ. Studies Yale U., 1976-81; vis. scholar Stanford U., 1981-82; rsch. assoc. U. Calif., Santa Cruz, 1982; scholar in residence U. Va., 1983; pres. W. Alton Jones Found., Charlottesville, Va., 1983; adj. prof. environ. studies Tufts U., 1984-85; vis. rsch. prof. Clark U., 1985-86; adj. rsch. fellow and lectr. Harvard U., 1986—; vis. prof. environ. studies Brown U., 1987; cons., lectr. in field. Trustee of numerous natural resources and ednl. orgns. With U.S. Army, 1945-47. Bullard fellow Harvard U., 1969-70. Fellow AAAS; mem. Soc. Am. Foresters, Am. Water Resources Assn., Harvard Club (Boston).

FOSTER, COLLEEN, library director. BA in English Lit., Coll. Notre Dame, Belmont, Calif., 1967; MLS, U. Denver, 1968. Br. reference libr. San Francisco Pub. Libr., 1968-69; reference libr. Stockton-San Joaquin County Pub. Libr., Calif., 1969-77, audiovisual libr., 1977-78, br. supr., 1978-81, libr. divsn. mgr. for adult svcs., 1990-92, dep. dir. libr. svcs., 1992-94, dir. libr. svcs., 1994—. Five gallon blood donor, Delta Blood Bank; mem. League of Women Voters of San Joaquin County, 1981—, sec., 1983-84, mem. speakers bureau, pros and cons presenter, 1985—, voter editor (newsletter), 1984-88, voter distbn. coord., 1991-97, participant candidates' forum, 1984-92, bd. dirs., 1983-84, 88-90, mem. League Study Com.; mem. Leadership Stockton, Class of 1995; reading tutor vol. Marshall Middle Sch. HOSTS (Help One Student to Suceed), 1996—. Mem. ALA, ACLU, NOW, MADD, Calif. Libr. Assn. (coun. mem. 1984-91, chair Coun. Rules Com. 1986, 88-89, bd. dirs. Calif. Soc. Librs. 1987-89, chair Bylaws Reorganization Com. 1990, mem. future of the profession task force, 1995, sec., treas. Calif. County Librs. Assn. 1995, mem. assembly 1995-98, mem. Conf. Planning Com. 1996, Fin. Com. 1996-98, Exec. Com. 1997-98, Mgmt. Svcs. Divsn. Excellence in Libr. Mgmt. award 1997), Habitat for Humanity, So. Poverty Law Ctr., Amnesty Internat., Greenpeace, Nature Conservancy, World Wildlife Found., Sierra Club, Rotary (Stockton chpt., vol. Asparague Festival 1994—, Rotary Read-in 1994—, Su Salud Health Fair 1995). Fax: 209-937-8683. Office: Stockton-San Joaquin County Pub Libr 605 N El Dorado St Stockton CA 95202-1907*

FOSTER, DALE WARREN, political scientist, educator, management consultant, real estate broker, accountant; b. Bryan, Tex., Mar. 7, 1950; s. William Henry and Maysie Blanche (Hembree) F. BBA, Tex. A&M U., 1972, MA, 1979, Cert. in Profl. Teaching, 1987; BS, U. Houston, 1981, MEd, 1983; AAS, Houston C.C. Sys., 1982. Cert. in property mgmt. Dept. mgr. J.C. Penney Co., Bryan, 1973-74; shopper advt. mgr. Harte-Hanks Newspapers/Daily Eagle, Bryan, 1975-76; bus. mgr., contr. S.M. Hardee Enterprises, College Station, Tex., 1976-78; ops. mgr. Western Food Svcs., Inc., Pasadena, Tex., 1978-80; internal auditor Hermann Hosp., Houston, 1980-82; high sch. tchr. Cypress-Fairbanks Independent Sch. Dist., Houston, 1983-84; alternative sch. tchr. Alief Independent Sch. Dist., Houston, 1984-88; gov. prof. Houston C.C. System, 1980—, chmn. govt. dept. co-op program, 1992—; lead instr. Houston C.C. Sys., 1993—; supr. student tchr. U. Houston, 1989-90; adj. instr. North Harris County Coll., Houston, 1983-96; fin. cons. Pro-Trac Econ. Planning Adv. Bd., Denver, 1985-86; Presdl. Scholars lectr. Minority Students Honors Program, Houston, 1986-89; coord. legis. practicum Harris County Congl. Internship Program, 1988—; exch. tchr., The Netherlands, 1992. Co-editor textbook supplement, curriculum guide, departmental political reader; author classroom instructional project. Mem. adv. com. Hermann Affiliated Fed. Credit Union, Houston, 1980-82; mem. fin. coun. Harris County Dem. Com., 1991-93; mem. dean's coun. U. Houston, 1992-96; trustee, treas. Wilmington-Barnard Found., 1992—. Named Tchr. of Yr., Cy.-Fair H.S., 1984, Alief Individualized Study Ctr., 1987, Master Tchr. Nat. Leadership Inst. U. Tex., Austin, 1991, host tchr. Washington Week Intern Program, 1995; recipient Adj. Teaching and Comty. Svc. award North Harris County Coll. Dist., 1990, Teaching Excellence medal Nat. Inst. Staff and Orgn. Devel., 1991, 98; Fulbright scholar, 1992, 98; Acad. Polit. Sci. inductee, 1994; Robert A. Taft fellow L.B.J. Sch. Pub. Affairs, 1995, Fulbright-Hays fellowship U.S. Dept. Edn., 1998. Fellow Am. Bd. Master Educators; mem. ASCD, Tex. Jr. Coll. Tchrs. Assn., Tex. Coun. Social Studies, Inst. Mgmt. Accts., Internaat. Platform Assn., Am. Fin. Assn., Fulbright Assn., Houston C.C. Sys. Faculty Assn. (treas. 1997—, Outstanding Tchr. award 1991, Tchr. of Yr. 1997), Phi Theta Kappa, Alpha Phi Omega, Kappa Delta Pi. Democrat. Baptist. Avocations: travel, reading, bowling, water sports, outdoor activities. Office: Houston C C NW 5514 Clara Rd Houston TX 77041-7204

FOSTER, DANIEL W., medical educator; b. Marlin, Tex., Mar. 4, 1930; married, 1955; 3 children. BA, Tex. Western Coll., 1951; MD, U. Tex., 1955. Intern internal medicine Parkland Meml. Hosp., 1955-56, asst. resident, 1956-58, chief resident, 1958-59; fellow biochemistry U. Tex. Southwestern Med. Sch., 1959-60; investigator Nat. Inst. Arthritis and Metabolic Disease, 1960-62; from asst. prof. to assoc. prof. U. Tex. Southwestern Med. Sch., 1962-69; prof. U. Tex. Southwestern Med. Sch., Dallas, 1969-86, Jan and Henri Bromberg prof., 1986-89, chmn. dept. internal medicine, 1988—, Donald W. Seldin Disting. chair, 1989—; mem. metabolism study sect. NIH, 1968-70, chmn. sect., 1970-72, mem. NIDDK adv. coun., 1987-90, bd. sci. counselors Clin. Ctr., 1991-95, 98—; chief internal medicine Parkland Meml. Hosp. and Univ. Med. Ctr., Tex.; mem. Nat. Diabetes Adv. Bd., 1981-84; chair sci. adv. bd. Hartford Found.; cons. VA Hosp., Dallas, Presbyn. Hosp., Baylor U. Med. Ctr.; mem. sci. adv. bd. Merck, Inc., 1991-94; mem. sci. adv. coun. Abbott Labs., 1998—. Assoc. editor: Jour. Clin. Investigation, 1972-77; editor: Diabetes, 1978-83. Fellow AAAS; master ACP; mem. Am. Acad. of Arts and Scis., Assn. of Profs. of Medicine (pres. 1997-98), Inst. Medicine-NAS, Am. Soc. Clin. Investigation, Am. Diabetes Assn. (Banting medal 1984, Joslin medal 1984, Upjohn award 1988), Am. Fedn. Clin. Rsch., Am. Soc. Biol. Chemists, Assn. Am. Physicians. Office: U Tex Health Sci Ctr Dept Internal Medicine Dallas TX 75235-9030

FOSTER, DAVID BEN, creative writing educator, freelance writer; b. Cleve., June 1, 1945; s. Harold Paul and Pearl Lorraine (Baldwin) F.; m. Cathering Marie Somerville, Mar. 24, 1989; children: Emily R., David B. II, Timothy A., Byron K., Thomas J. BA, Mt. Vernon Nazarene Coll., 1979; MA, Ashland (Ohio) U., 1972; postgrad., Cleve. State U., 1997—. Tchr. h.s. Rapides Parish Schs., Alexandria, La., 1982-86; tchr. h.s. Medina County Schs., Medina, Ohio, 1987-96, tchr. creative writing, tchr. gifted students, 1995-97; tchr. creative writing, poet Lorain (Ohio) C.C., 1997—. Author: A View of Ourselves, 1995, Anthology In Blue, 1998, Love Listens, 1998; contbr. essays and poetry to jours., newspapers and mags. Mem. Medina County Arts Coun., 1997—; mem. Medina County Con. Rep. Party, 1989-90. Served with U.S. Army, 1979-80. Named Poet Laureate of Medina County, 1996. Mem. Nat. Coun. Tchrs. English, Ohio Coun. Tchrs. English Lang., Cleve. Poetry Consortium, DAV (life). Congregationalist. Avocations: reading, attending plays (musicals, comedy, drama), swimming. Office: PO Box 1793 Medina OH 44258-1793

FOSTER, DAVID JOHN, journalist; b. Phila., Aug. 24, 1961; s. John. G. and Constance (Walter) F. BS in Secondary Edn. and Social Studies, West Chester (Pa.) U., 1983. Journalist News Gleaner Publs., Phila., 1983—; editor, staff writer West Coast Video/Nat. Video Corp., Phila., 1986-90. Co-author: Take a Trip Through Time, 1996. Recipient 1st pl. editl. comment award Phila. Press Assn., 1994, hon. mention feature writing, 1995, 3d pl. editl. comment, 1996, hon. mention editl. comment, 1996, hon. mention feature writing, 1996, 1st pl. news writing, 1997, 1st pl. bus. writing, 1997, hon. mention editl., 1997; 1st pl. feature story Pa. Newspaper Pubs. Assn. Keystone Press awards, 1993, , 2d pl. news story, 1994, 2d pl. health story, 1994, 1st pl. feature story, 1995, 2d pl. news series, 1995, 1st pl. feature beat reporting, 1996, 2d pl. series, 1996, 2d pl. editl. comment, 1996, hon. mention feature story, 1996, 1st pl. news beat reporting, 1997, 1st pl. editl. comment, 1997, 2d pl. series, 1997; Golden Dozen award Internat. Soc. Weekly Newspaper Editors, 1997. Mem. Soc. Profl. Journalists (Keystone chpt., Phila. chpt., 1st pl. environ. story 1995, 2d pl. non-deadline news story 1995, hon. mention feature story 1995, 1st pl. health story 1996, 2d pl. non-deadline news story 1996, 3d pl. editl. comment 1996, 1st pl. editl. 1997, 2d pl. health story 1997), Phi Alpha Theta. Home: 8624 Hickory Dr Philadelphia PA 19136-2018 Office: News Gleaner Publs 1612 Margaret St Philadelphia PA 19124-2712

FOSTER, DAVID LEE, lawyer; b. Des Moines, Dec. 13, 1933; s. Carl Dewitt and Dorothy Jo (Bell) F.; m. Marilyn Lee Bokemeier, Aug. 12, 1957 (div. June 1978); children: Gwendolyn Foster Reed, Cynthia Foster Curry, David Lee Jr.; m. Kathleen Carol Walsh, Mar. 24, 1979; 1 child, John Wickersham. Student, Simpson Coll., 1951-52; BA, U. Iowa, 1954, JD, 1957. Bar: Iowa 1957, N.Y. 1958, Ohio 1964, U.S. Supreme Ct. 1975. Assoc. Cravath, Swaine & Moore, N.Y.C., 1957-63; from assoc. to ptnr. Jones, Day, Cockley & Reavis, Cleve., 1963-72; ptnr. Willkie Farr & Gallagher, N.Y.C., 1972—; lectr. So. Meth. U., 1979-84, U. Pitts., 1984, Practicing Law Inst., N.Y.C., 1984-85; mem. adv. bd. Civil RICO Report LRP Publs., 1988—; bd. govs. N.Y. Ins. Exch., 1987-96. Contbr. chpts. to book, articles to legal jours. Mem., bd. trustees Cardigan Mountain Sch., 1995—. Served with USNR, 1952-60. Fellow Am. Coll. Trial Lawyers, Internat. Acad. Trial Lawyers (bd. dirs. 1987-92); mem. Am. Counsel Assn. (pres. 1994-95, bd. dirs. 1992—), River Club, Order of Coif, Phi Beta Kappa. Avocations: flying; fishing. Office: Willkie Farr & Gallagher 787 7th Ave New York NY 10019-6099

FOSTER, DAVID MARK, retired bishop; b. Fancher, Ill., Feb. 11, 1932; s. Homer Foster; m. Joy Lee Clark, Oct. 4, 1952; children: Kathleen Litton, LaDon Birk, Coleen Jeffery, David A. BA, Greenville (Ill.) Coll., 1956; MA, Azusa Pacific U., 1972; PhD, Calif. Grad. Sch. Theology, Los Angeles, 1974. Ordained to ministry Free Meth. Ch., 1955. Pastor Free Meth. Ch., 1952-79; conf. supt. Pacific Northwest Conf. Free Meth. Ch., Seattle, 1979-85; bishop Free Meth. Ch., Indpls., 1985-97. Pres. Free Meth. World Fellowship, 1995—. Address: 1617 S Kline Ct Lakewood CO 80232-6336*

FOSTER, DAVID RAMSEY, soap company executive; b. London, May 24, 1920; (parents Am. citizens); s. Robert Bagley and Josephine (Ramsey) F.; m. Anne Firth, Aug. 2, 1957 (dec. June 1994); children: Sarah, Victoria; m. Alexandra Chang, May 24, 1996. Student in econs., Gonville and Caius Coll., Cambridge (Eng.) U., 1938. With Colgate-Palmolive Co. and affiliates, 1946-79; v.p., gen. mgr. Europe Colgate-Palmolive Internat., 1961-65; v.p., gen. mgr. household products divsn. parent co. Colgate-Palmolive Internat., N.Y.C., 1965-68, exec. v.p., 1968-70, pres., 1970-75, CEO, 1971-79, chmn., 1975-79. Author: Wings Over the Sea, 1990. Trustee Woman's Sport Found. Served to lt. comdr. Royal Naval Vol. Res., 1940-46. Decorated Disting. Svc. Order, D.S.C. with bar, Mentioned in Despatches (2); recipient Victor award City of Hope, 1974, Herbert Hoover Meml. award, 1976, Adam award, 1977, Harriman award Boys Club N.Y., 1977, Charter award St. Francis Coll., 1978, Walter Hagen award, 1978, Patty Berg award, 1986, Commr.'s award LPGA, 1995. Mem. Soc. Mayflower Descs., Hawks Club (Cambridge U.), Royal Ancient Golf Club (St. Andrews, Scotland), Royal Cinque Ports Golf Club (life), Sunningdale Golf Club, Swinley Forest Golf Club (U.K.), Sankaty Head Golf Club, Racquet and Tennis Club (N.Y.C.), Mission Hills Country Club, Bally Bunion Golf Club (life). Home: 540 Desert West Dr Rancho Mirage CA 92270-1310

FOSTER, DAVID SCOTT, lawyer; b. White Plains, N.Y., July 13, 1938; s. William James and Ruth Elizabeth (Seltzer) F.; m. Eleanore Stalker, Dec. 21, 1959; children: David Scott, Robert McEachron. BA, Amherst Coll., 1960; LLB, Harvard U., 1963. Bar: N.Y. 1963, D.C. 1977, Calif. 1978. Jud. law clk. U.S. Dist. Ct. (so. dist.) N.Y., 1963-64; assoc. Debevoise & Plimpton, N.Y.C., 1964-72; internat. tax counsel U.S. Treasury Dept., Washington, 1972-77; ptnr. Brobeck, Phleger & Harrison, San Francisco, 1978-90, Coudert Bros., San Francisco, 1990-91, Thelen, Reid & Priest LLP, San Francisco, 1991—. Mem. ABA, San Francisco Bar Assn., Internat. Fiscal Assn., Western Pension and Benefits Confs., St. Francis Yacht Club (San Francisco). Presbyterian. Office: Thelen Reid & Priest LLP 2 Embarcadero Ctr San Francisco CA 94111-3823

FOSTER, DUDLEY EDWARDS, JR., musician, educator; b. Orange, N.J., Oct. 5, 1935; s. Dudley Edwards and Margaret (DePoy) F. Student Occidental Coll., 1953-56; AB, UCLA, 1957, MA, 1958; postgrad. U. So. Calif., 1961-73. Lectr. music Immaculate Heart Coll., L.A., 1960-63; dir. music Holy Faith Episcopal Ch., Inglewood, Calif., 1964-67; lectr. music Calif. State U., L.A., 1968-71; assoc. prof. music L.A. Mission Coll., 1975-83, prof., 1983—, also chmn. dept. music, 1977—; mem. dist. acad. senate L.A. Community Colls., 1991-92; mem. acad. senate L.A. Mission Coll., 1993-97; dir. music 1st Luth. Ch., L.A., 1968-72. Organist, pianist, harpsichordist; numerous recitals; composer O Sacrum Convivium for Trumpet and Organ, 1973, Passacaglia for Brass Instruments, 1969, Introduction, Arioso & Fugue for Cello and Piano, 1974. Fellow Trinity Coll. Music, London, 1960. Recipient Associated Students Faculty award, 1988. Mem. Am. Guild Organists, Am. Musicol. Soc., Nat. Assn. of Scholars, Acad. Senate, Town Hall Calif., L.A. Coll. Tchrs. Assn. (pres. Mission Coll. chpt. 1976-77, v.p., exec. com. 1982-84), Mediaeval Acad. Am. Republican. Anglican. Office: LA Mission Coll Dept Music 13356 Eldridge Ave Sylmar CA 91342-3200

FOSTER, EDWARD PAUL (TED FOSTER), process industries executive; b. Pawtucket, R.I., Aug. 23, 1945; s. Edward Francis and Vivian Adrienne (Davagne) F.; m. Barbara Philomena Cook, Dec. 17, 1965 (div. Apr. 1978); children: Edward Robert, Gwendolyn Lucy; m. Johanna Helena Klaassen, June, 1985 (div. 1988). BSChemE with distinction, U. R.I., 1967; MSChemE, Worcester Poly. Inst., 1970; MBA, Lehigh U., 1981. Mfg. melting engr. Corning Glass Works, Central Falls, R.I., 1966-67; group leader rsch. and devel. The Babcock & Wilcox Co., Alliance, Ohio, 1968-71; mgr. tampella process The Babcock & Wilcox Co., Barberton, Ohio, 1972-74; from comml. devel. engr. to dir. bus. devel. in gases, metallurgy, coal, energy, chems. and polymers, and environ. areas Air Products and Chem., Inc., Allentown, Pa., 1974—; cons. U.S. Army Natick (Mass.) Lab., 1966-67. Contbr. articles to profl. jours.; patentee in field. Chmn. fin. Unitarian Ch., Bethleham, Pa., 1985, chmn. social, 1983-84. NDEA fellow HEW, 1967-69; ROTC scholar U.S. Army, 1965, Nat. Merit scholar, 1963. Mem. AIChE, Comml. Devel. Assn. (vice chmn. fall meeting 1996, nat. program chmn. 1997-98, bd. dirs. 1998—), Am. Chem. Soc., Phi Kappa Phi, Tau Beta Pi, Theta Chi. Avocations: tennis, downhill skiing, sailing, biking. Home: 6023 Fairway Ln Allentown PA 18106-9610 Office: Air Products and Chems 7201 Hamilton Blvd Allentown PA 18195-1526

FOSTER, ERIC HAROLD, JR., retail executive; b. Nov. 8, 1943; s. Eric H. Sr. and Dorothy (Schwarz) F.; married; children: Dawn, Eric III, Kimberly, Meredith. BS in Mgmt., Rutger's U., 1969; student grad. sch. acctg. and taxation, Farleigh Dickinson U., 1973-74. Computer and peripheral equipment operator N.J. Bell Tel. Co., 1965-66; mem. prodn. planning and scheduling 3M Co., St. Paul, 1966-68, data analyst, 1968-69; supr. customer and geog. info. ctr. McGraw-Hill Book Co., Hightstown, N.J., 1969-71, staff asst. to gen. mgr. distbn. ctr., 1971-75, 78, mgr. retail accounts receivable credit and collection dept., 1975-78, 79, responsible McGraw-Hill club and retail customer svc. depts., 1979, mgr., 1979-80, mgr. spl. svcs. and returns, 1980-82, gen. mgr. profl. pub. svcs., 1982-88. Councilman Borough of Freehold, pres., chmn. water and sewer dept., mem. planning bd., fin. and econ. devel. com.; bd. dirs. Freehold Presbyn. Nursery Sch.; chmn. bd. The Rugby Sch.; vice chmn. Freehold Borough Zoning Bd.; mem. vestry, bus. and pers. com., maintenance and repair com. St. Peter Episc. Ch., chmn. fin. com.; advisor Youth Group; charter mem., 1st pres., mem. founding group East Freehold Fire Co.; coord. troop 151 Boy Scouts Am. Recipient Bronze Palm award Eagle Scouts Am., 1960. Mem. Direct Mktg. Assn., Direct Mktg. and Credit Assn. (bd. dirs.), Internat. Consumer Credit Assn. (bd. dirs. region II N.Y./N.J. chpts.), N.J. Assn. Schs. and Agys. for the Handicapped, Internat. Credit Assn. (cert. consumer credit exec.). Episcopalian. Home: 35 Broadway Freehold NJ 07728-1864

FOSTER, FRANCES BARRETT, advanced nurse practitioner; b. Boston, Jan. 26, 1966; d. Martin Leo and Marian (Dow) Barrett; m. Charles Stephen Foster, Jan. 4, 1997. BS in Nursing, Boston Coll., 1988, MS in Nursing, 1994, postgrad., 1995—. Primary nurse Mass. Gen., Boston, 1988-91; intern in clin. nurse specialist Deaconness Hosp., Boston, 1993-94; intern in advanced practitioner Boston Med. Ctr, Home Care, 1993-94, Lasell Coll., Newton, Mass., 1993-94; advanced practitioner Carney Hosp., Boston, 1994-99; advanced nurse practitioner Mass. Eye and Ear Infirmary, Boston, 1999—, Mass. Gen. Hosp., Boston; stress mgmt. facilitator Newton-Wellesley Hosp., 1994—; rschr., cons. Functional Health Pattern Assessment Screening Tool, Boston Coll., 1992—;. Patentee in field; contbr. articles to profl. jours. Co-leader, developer Uveitis Support Group Mass. Eye and Ear, Boston, 1997—. Mem. ANA, Am. Heart Assn. (CPR instr. 1987—), Mass. Nurses Assn., Ea. Nursing Rsch. Soc., N.Am. Nursing Diagnosis Assn., Mass. Coalition Nurse Practitioners. Avocations: water skiing, down hillskiing, watercolors, gardening. Home: 348 Glen Rd Weston MA 02493-1403 Office: Mass Gen Hosp Bulfrench Med Group Feiders 3 Fruit St Boston MA 02114

FOSTER, GEORGE MCCLELLAND, JR., anthropologist; b. Sioux Falls, S.D., Oct. 9, 1913; s. George McClelland and Mary (Slutz) F.; m. Mary Fraser LeCron, Jan. 6, 1938; children: Jeremy, Melissa Bowerman. BS, Northwestern U., 1935; PhD, U. Calif. at Berkeley, 1941; DHL (hon.), So. Meth. U., 1990. Instr. Syracuse U., 1941-42; lectr. UCLA, 1942-43; vis. prof. U. Calif.-Berkeley, 1953-55, prof. anthropology, 1955-79, prof. emeritus, 1979—, chmn. dept., 1958-61; acting dir. Mus. Anthropology, 1955-57; lectr. pub. health, 1955-64; anthropologist Inst. Social Anthropology, Smithsonian Instn., 1943-52, dir., 1946-1952; field rsch. Calif. Indians, 1937, Spain, 1949-50, Mexico, 1940—; adviser AID, India-Pakistan, 1955, Afghanistan, 1957, Zambia, 1961, 62, Nepal, 1965, Indonesia, 1973-74, WHO, Sri Lanka, 1975, Malaysia, 1978, India, 1979, 80, 81, Manila, 1983; adviser UNICEF, Geneva, 1976. Author: Traditional Cultures and the Impact of Technological Change, 1962, Tzintzuntzan: Mexican Peasants in a Changing World, 1967, Applied Anthropology, 1969, (with B. Anderson) Medical Anthropology, 1978, Hippocrates' Latin American Legacy, 1993, others, also monographs and articles. Recipient Berkeley citation, 1979; Guggenheim fellow, 1949; fellow Center for Advanced Study in Behavioral Scis., 1969-70. Fellow Am. Anthrop. Assn. (pres. 1970, Disting. Service award 1980); mem. Southwestern Anthrop. Assn. (Disting. Research award 1981), Nat. Acad. Scis., Am. Acad. Arts and Scis., Soc. Applied Anthropology (Malinowski award 1982). Club: Cosmos (Washington). Home: 790 San Luis Rd Berkeley CA 94707-2030

FOSTER, GLENN KEVIN, former christian relief agency executive, social service agency executive; b. Grand Rapids, Mich., Mar. 3, 1957; s. Glenn Ellsworth and Dorothy Mae (Burgess) F.; m. Kimberly Corinne Andrews, June 30, 1984; children: Kevin Andrew, Abigail Michelle, Joy Corrine, Katharine Ann. BS in Indsl. Engring., Mich. State U., 1981; MBA, Claremont (Calif.) Grad. Sch., 1988. Cert. quality auditor. Dist. sales mgr. The Southwestern Co., Nashville, 1981-82; regional sales mgr. Universal Scheduling Co., Chgo., 1983-84; from mgr. quality & reliability to project mgr. Rockwell Internat., Anaheim, Calif., 1985-93; quality mgr. Haworth, Inc., Holland, Mich., 1994-99, mgr. global product introduction, 1997—; trustee Mich. Quality Coun., Lansing, 1994—; cons. Ctrl. Wesleyan Ch., Holland, 1994-95, Holland City Mission, 1995-96, Lakeland Cmty. Ch., Zeeland, 1997-98, Reformed Bapt. Ch., Holland, 1999—, Pine Creek Ch., Holland, 1996-97, Calvary Presbyn. Ch., Glendale, Calif., 1989-94, bd. examiners Malcolm Baldridge Nat. Quality award, 1998—, sr. examiner Mich. Quality Leadership award, 1995—. Mem. Am. Soc. Quality, Product Devel. Mgmt. Assn. Republican. Presbyn. Office: Holland Rescue Mission 166 S River Ave Holland MI 49423

FOSTER, HENRY WENDELL, medical educator; b. Pine Bluff, Ark., Sept. 8, 1933; s. Henry Wendell and Ivie (Hill Watson) F.; m. St. Clair Anderson, Feb. 6, 1960; children: Myrna Faye, Henry Wendell. B.S., Morehouse Coll., 1954; M.D., U. Ark., 1958. Am. Bd. Ob-Gyn. Chief ob-gyn. John Andrew Hosp., Tuskegee, Ala., 1965-73; prof., chmn. dept. ob-gyn. Meharry Med. Coll., Nashville, 1973—, prof. emeritus; dir. maternal and infant care project Tuskegee Inst., Ala., 1970-73; sr. program cons. Robert Wood Johnson Found., Princeton, N.J., 1981-86; chmn. ob-gyn exec. com. Nat. Med. Assn., 1977-79. Mem. editorial bd.: Jour. Med. Edn., 1974-77. Bd. dirs. Planned Parenthood Assn. Am., 1975-81; bd. dirs. Alan Guttmacher Inst., N.Y.C., 1975-81. Served to capt. USAF, 1959-61. Fellow Am. Coll. Obstetricians and Gynecologists; mem. Alpha Omega Alpha. Democrat. Am. Baptist. Home: 4140 W Hamilton Rd Nashville TN 37218-1829 Office: Meharry Med Coll 1005 D B Todd Blvd Nashville TN 37208*

FOSTER, J. DON, lawyer. IM, Ga. Inst. Tech., 1968; postgrad., U. Ala., 1968, JD, 1971. Assoc. Gallalee, Denniston & Edington, Mobile, Ala., 1971-76, Foley and Fairhope, 1976-95; U.S. atty. So. Dist. Ala., Mobile, 1995—; mcpl. judge City Foley, Ala., 1977-78; bar commr. 28th Jud. Cir., Baldwin County, Ala., 1980-86; apptd. Jud. Inquiry Comm., 1986-95; mem. Com. New Jud. Bldg., 1992. 2d lt. U.S. Army, 1971; capt. U.S. Army Res., 1971-75. Mem. Ala. Bar Assn. (chmn. state bar disciplinary panel 1983-86), Baldwin County Bar Assn. Office: US Atty's Office 63 S Royal St Ste 600 Mobile AL 36602*

FOSTER, JAMES CALDWELL, academic dean, historian; b. Madison, Wis., Apr. 10, 1943; s. Mark A. and Ruth C. (Caldwell) F.; m. Diane L. Mohn, Sept. 3, 1966; children: Jeffrey, Justin, Joshua. BS, U. Wis., 1967; PhD, Cornell U., 1972. Assoc. dir. Wis. Humanities Commn., NEH, Madison, 1977-78; asst. prof. U. Alaska, College, 1971-74; dir. labor studies Ariz. State U., Tempe, 1974-81, Sch. for Workers, U. Wis., Madison, 1981-84; assoc. dean of campus Ohio State U., Newark, 1984-87; dean Coll. Arts, Scis. and Lit. U. Mich., Dearborn, 1987-92; dir. acad. affairs Pa. State U.-Fayette, Uniontown, 1993-95; dean of the coll. Walsh U., Canton, Ohio, 1995—, acad. v.p., 1996—. Author: The Union Politic, 1975, American Labor in the Southwest, 1982; newspaper columnist, Kenosha (Wis.) Labor, 1981— (1st, 2d and 3d best story awards for column Lest We Forget, AFL-CIO 1984); commentator Wis. Pub. Radio, Madison, 1981-84. Exxon Edn. grantee, Tempe, 1976, Rockefeller Found. grantee, Tempe, 1977, German Marshall Fund grantee, Madison, 1981. Mem. Indsl. Rels. Rsch. Assn., Am. Arbitration Assn. Office: Walsh U Office Acad Affairs 2020 Easton St NW North Canton OH 44720-3336

FOSTER, JAMES HENRY, advertising and public relations executive; b. Kansas City, Mo., May 14, 1933; s. Wendell F. and Lillian M. (East) F. BA, Drake U., 1955, postgrad., 1957. Reporter, editor Des Moines (Iowa) Register, 1951-61; pub. rels. and advt. exec. J. Walter Thompson Co., N.Y.C., 1961-73, 79-99, v.p., 1970-73; sr. v.p., gen. mgr. Brouillard Communications div., N.Y.C., 1979-81, exec. v.p., gen. mgr., 1981-84, pres., CEO, 1984-94; chmn., CEO Brouillard Communications, 1994-97, chmn., 1997-99, chmn. emeritus, 1999—; v.p. pub. affairs Western Union Corp., Uppper Saddle River, 1973-79; pres. Reputation Mgmt. Strategies, Durango, Colo., 1999—. Bd. dirs. J. Walter Thompson, 1987-99; Music in the Mountains, Durango, Colo., 1998—. Presbyterian. Clubs: Union League (N.Y.C.), Petroleum Club (Durango). Office: Reputation Mgmt Strategies 1472 E Third Ave Durango CO 81301-5244

FOSTER, JAMES REUBEN, investment company executive; b. Chgo., May 28, 1930; s. Reuben Aaron and Marion (Philipson) F.; m. Claire Lynn Block, Aug. 16, 1953; children: Kim Petracca, Craig James, Kyle Foster Weinstein. BA, Trinity Coll., 1952; JD, Yale U., 1955. Bar: Ill. 1955, U.S. Ct. Claims 1955, U.S. Ct. Mil. Appeals 1956, U.S. Ct. Customs and Patent Appeals, 1956. Trial atty. U.S. Dept. of Justice, Washington, 1955-57; v.p. L.B. Foster Co., Pitts., 1957-82; pres. Fosco Fabricators, Chgo., 1961-64; v.p., sec. Foster Industries, Inc., Pitts., 1977-97; gen. ptnr. Real Estate Partnerships, 1975-93; v.p., sec. Fostin Securities, Inc., 1978—; pres., 1994—; chmn. bd., chief exec. officer Travel Profls. Inc., 1984—; v.p. Fostin Mgmt. Co., Chgo., 1998—, also bd. dirs.; sec. United Comms. Sys. Inc., Chgo.; bd. dirs. Foster Industries, Inc., Pitts., Fostin Capital Co., Pitts., Travel Profls., Inc., Chgo., Pelouze Scale, Evanston, Ill., 1990-94, United Comm. Sys., Inc., Chgo., Fostin Securities, Inc., Fostin Mgmt. Inc. Pres. Temple Jeremiah, Northfield, Ill., 1980-83; chmn. com. Chgo. Assn. Commerce and Industry, 1971-73; trustee, chmn. com. Lakeland Health Svcs./Highland Park Hosp., 1978-84, life trustee, 1985—; vice chmn., committeeman Lake County Reps. Ctrl. Com., Ill., 1964-74; bd. dirs., sec., treas. Groveland Health Svcs., Highland Park, 1982-90; v.p. Am. Jewish Com., 1990-96, nat. coun., 1996—, exec. bd. Chgo. chpt. 1981—; exec. bd. dirs., chmn. Great Lakes region Am. Assocs. Ben Gurion U. of the Negev, 1991-95; treas. collectors forum Mus. of Contemporary Art, Chgo., 1994—. Mem. ABA, Am. Inst. Mgmt., Std. Club (bd. dirs. 1985-92), Northmoor Country Club. Republican. Jewish. Avocations: art collector, travel, golf. Office: Travel Profls Inc 401 N Michigan Ave Ste 206 Chicago IL 60611-4282

FOSTER, JODIE (ALICIA CHRISTIAN FOSTER), actress; b. L.A., Nov. 19, 1962; d. Lucius and Evelyn (Almond) F.; 1 child, Charles. BA in Lit. cum laude, Yale U., 1985. Acting debut in TV show Mayberry, R.F.D, 1969; numerous other TV appearances including My Three Sons, The Courtship of Eddie's Father, Gunsmoke, Bonanza, Paper Moon, 1974-75; TV spl. The Secret Life of T.K. Dearing, 1975, A Salute to Martin Scorsege, 1997; TV movies Rookie of the Year, Smile, Jenny, You're Dead; motion picture appearances Napoleon and Samantha, 1972, Menace on the Mountain, One Little Indian, 1973, Tom Sawyer, 1973, Kansas City Bomber, 1972, Bob & Carol & Ted & Alice, 1973, Alice Doesn't Live Here Anymore, 1974, Taxi Driver, 1976 (Acad. award nominee for Best Supporting Actress), Echoes of a Summer, 1976, Bugsy Malone, 1976, Freaky Friday, 1976, Moi, Fleur Bleue, 1977, Casotto, 1977, The Little Girl Who Lives Down the Lane, 1977, Candleshoe, 1977, Foxes, 1980, Carny, 1980, O'Hara's Wife, 1982, Svengali, 1983, Hotel New Hampshire, 1984, The Blood of Others, 1984, Mesmerized, 1986, Siesta, 1986, Five Corners, 1986, Siesta, 1987, Stealing Home, 1988, Five Corners, 1988, The Accused, 1988 (Acad. award for Best Actress, 1989), Backtrack, 1989, The Silence of the Lambs, 1991 (Golden Globe award for Best Actress in Drama, 1992, Acad. award for Best Actress, 1992), Shadows and Fog, 1992, Sommersby, 1993, Maverick, 1994, Contact, 1997; dir., actress: Little Man Tate, 1991; prodr., actress: Nell, 1994 (Acad. award nominee for Best Actress 1995); dir., prodr. Home For the Holidays, 1995; prodr. Contact, 1996; exec. prodr. (Showtime) Babydance, Waking the Dead, Anna, 1999. Recipient Golden Globe award, 1989. Office: EGG Pictures Production Co Jerry Lewis Annex 5555 Melrose Ave Los Angeles CA 90038

FOSTER, JOE B., oil company executive; b. Arp, Tex., July 25, 1934; s. William R. and Ruth D. (Knox) F.; m. Harriet; children: Warren, Ken, Jennifer. BS in Petroleum Engring., Tex. A&M U., 1957, BBA, 1957. Jr. petroleum engr. Tenneco Oil Co., Oklahoma City, 1957-59; petroleum engr. Tenneco Oil Co., Lafayette, La., 1959-62; dist. engr. Tenneco Oil Co., 1962-66; adminstrv. asst. to exec. com. Tenneco Oil Co., Houston, 1966-68, chief econ. planning and analysis, 1968-70, mgr. exploration, 1970-72, v.p., 1972-74, sr. v.p., 1974-76, exec. v.p., 1976-78, pres. Tenneco Oil Exploration and Prodn., 1978-81; exec. v.p. Tenneco, Inc., Houston, 1981-89; chmn. Newfield Exploration Co., Houston, 1989—; bd. dirs. Baker Hughes, Houston, N.J. Resources, Meml. Hermann Hosp. Sys., 1998—. Bd. dirs. Houston Mus. Natural Sci., Houston Hospice, YMCA of Greater Houston; chmn. Nat. Petroleum Coun. 2d lt. U.S. Army, 1958. Mem. AIME, Soc. Petroleum Engrs. Ind. Petroleum Assn. Am., Nat. Assn. Ocean Industries, All-Am. Wildcatters Com., Met. Racquet Club. Methodist. Office: Newfield Exploration Co Ste 2020 363 N Sam Houston Pkwy E Houston TX 77060-2421

FOSTER, JOE C., JR., lawyer; b. Lansing, Mich., Feb. 5, 1925; s. Joe C. and Grace E. (McComb) F.; m. Janet C. Shanks, July 6, 1946; children—Cathy Foster Young, Susan Foster Ambrose, Thomas, John, Amy. Student, Wabash Coll., Ind., 1943-44; JD, U. Mich., 1949. Bar: Mich. 1949, Fla. 1986. Assoc. Fraser, Trebilcock, Davis & Foster, and predecessors, Lansing, Mich., 1949-53; ptnr. Fraser, Trebilcock, Davis & Foster, and predecessors, 1954—. Co-author: Independent Probate Administration, 1980, 3d edit., 1995. Trustee, sec. Renaud Found., Lansing, 1960-87; bd. dirs., sec. Abrams Found., Lansing, 1960—; bd. dirs., officer ACTEC Found., L.A., 1983-87, 98—; trustee Jr. League Endowment Found., Lansing, 1984-90; trustee, chmn. Sparrow Hosp., Lansing, 1970-84; trustee, pres. Okemos Bd. Edn., Mich., 1962-66; bd. dirs., pres. county unit Am. Cancer Soc., 1950-60; bd. dirs., pres. Community Nursing Bur., Lansing, 1956-57. Lt. USNR, 1943-46, PTO. Fellow Am. Coll. Trust and Estate Counsel (pres. 1985-86), Am. Coll. Tax Counsel, Am. Bar Found., Mich. Bar Found.; mem. ABA, Fla. Bar Assn., Mich. Bar Assn. (chmn. probate and estate planning sect. 1977-78), Internat. Acad. Estate and Trust Law (exec. coun. 1990-94, joint editl. bd. for Uniform Probate Code 1991—), Rotary (bd. dirs. Lansing 1968-70), Phi Beta Kappa, Phi Gamma Delta. Avocations: sailing; running; tennis. Home: 1965 Yuma Trl Okemos MI 48864-2746 Office: Fraser Trebilcock Et Al 1000 Michigan Nat Tower Lansing MI 48933 *Honesty and kindness are two of our best precepts. They also are good business.*

FOSTER, JOHN HORACE, consulting environmental engineer; b. Quincy, Mass., June 2, 1927; s. Horace Herbert and Alice Gertrude (Hatch) F.; m. Claire Alice Sabean, Aug. 31, 1952; children—Janet, Mark, David. B.S., Tufts U., 1952; M.S., Harvard U., 1953. Engr. Malcolm Pirnie Engrs., White Plains, N.Y., 1953-63; partner Malcolm Pirnie, Inc., 1963-70, pres., 1970-88, chmn. bd. dirs., 1988-95; chmn. emeritus, 1997—. Contbr. articles to profl. jours. Served with USN, 1945-47. Recipient Distinguished Service award Dept. Civil Engring. Tufts U., 1977. Mem. ASCE, Am. Acad. Environ. Engrs., Water Environment Fedn., Am. Water Works Assn., Am. Cons. Engrs. Coun. (v.p. 1989-91, pres. 1992-93), N.Y. Assn. Cons. Engrs. (v.p. 1987-92, Engr. of Yr. 1995). Club: Cedar Point Yacht. Home: 53 Farrell Rd Weston CT 06883-2306 Office: Malcolm Pirnie Inc PO Box 751 104 Corporate Park Dr White Plains NY 10604-3335

FOSTER, JOHN MCNEELY, accounting standards executive; b. Denver, Mar. 7, 1949; s. Wallin G. and Marilyn Hope (Coxhead) F.; m. Bonnie McCune, Aug. 23, 1970 (div. 1978); m. Sharon Kay Sheffield, May 8, 1982 (div. 1991); children: Katherine McNeely, Matthew Thomas. BA in Econs., Colo. Coll., 1971. CPA, Tex. Treas. Meis and Co., Inc., Colorado Springs, Colo., 1971-73; sr. audit mgr. Price Waterhouse Co., Houston, 1973-81; v.p. fin. Krusen Energy Co., Houston, 1981-83; v.p., treas. Compaq Computer Corp., Houston, 1983-92; bd. dirs. Fin. Acctg. Standards Bd., Norwalk, Conn., 1993—. Mem. AICPA, Phi Beta Kappa. Republican. Episcopalian. Avocations: golf, fishing. Office: Fin Acctg Standards Bd 401 Merritt 7 Norwalk CT 06851-1000

FOSTER, JOHN ROBERT, lawyer; b. Long Beach, Calif., Feb. 13, 1940; s. Orlon c. and Catherine Rose (Rhind) F.; m. Nancy Crandall, June 17, 1962; children: John Crandall, Christopher Peter, Blayney Robert, Courtland William. BA in History, San Jose State U., 1961; LLB, U. Calif., Berkeley, 1964. Bar: Calif. 1965, U.S. Dist. Ct. (no. dist.) Calif. 1965, U.S. Ct. Appeals (9th cir.) 1965; cert. specialist in probate, estate planning, and trust law. Dep. legis. counsel State of Calif., Sacramento, 1964-65; pres. Rusconi, Foster, Thomas & Wilson, APC, Morgan Hill, Calif., 1965—; asst. dist. atty. San Benito County, Hollister, Calif., 1967. Mem. Morgan Hill Unified Sch. Dist. Bd. Edn., 1967-74, 79-83, chmn. bd., 1969-71; councilman City of Morgan Hill, 1984-88, 97-98, mayor, 1984. Named Citizen of Yr., City of Morgan Hill. Mem. Calif. State Bar (past state bar exec. com. on estate planning, probate and trusts), Santa Clara County Bar Assn., Gilroy-Morgan Hill Bar Assn. (past pres.), Morgan Hill C. of C. (past pres.), Masons, Rotary (past pres. Morgan Hill). Republican. Methodist. Avocations: skiing, fly fishing, backpacking, camping. E-mail: bob@rftw.com. Home: 17630 Black Oak Ct Morgan Hill CA 95037-9442 Office: Rusconi Foster Thomas & Wilson 30 Keystone Ave Morgan Hill CA 95037-4325

FOSTER, JOHN STANTON, nuclear engineer; b. Halifax, N.S., Can., June 14, 1921; s. Stanton Ray and Mabel Rose (Davies) F.; m. Margaret Charlotte Lane, Oct. 9, 1948; 1 dau., Margaret Anne. *Dr. Foster is a descendant of one Thomas Foster who settled near Boston in 1634 and of Edward Foster who left Massachusetts to settle as a planter in Port Medway, Nova Scotia in 1760, when the British, after the victories at Louisburg (1758) and Quebec (1759), were populating the colony. His wife, Margaret, is a descendant of a branch of the Locke family with a similar history.* Diploma in Engring., Dalhousie U., 1941; B in Engring., N.S. Tech. Coll., 1943, Dr. in Engring., 1967; Dr. in Engring., Carleton U., 1967. With Montreal Engring. Co., Ltd., 1946-54, asst. chief mech. engr., 1952-54; head nuclear design Can. Gen. Electric Co., 1955-58; gen. mgr. power projects Atomic Energy of Can. Ltd., 1958-66, v.p., 1966-74, pres., 1974-77; v.p. Monenco Ont. Ltd., Toronto, 1978-83; mem. Tech. Adv. Panel on Nuclear Safety, Ontario Hydro, 1991-98. *Dr. Foster was a member of the Nuclear Power Group - half a dozen engineers fromthe power industry - who, in 1954, went to Atomic Energy of Canada Limited's Chalk River Laboratory and working with members of AECL, investigated the feasibility of employing a heavy water reactor for power production. He headed the early stages of design of the nuclear part of Canada's first nuclear powerstation, and later led the engineering and project management for 11 nuclear units in Canada and 3 abroad a heavy water production plant and a 1000 MW 555 mile long HVDC transmission system in Manitoba.* Served to lt. Royal Can. Navy, 1943-45. Decorated Can.'s Centennial medal, 1967, Queen Elizabeth II Silver Jubilee medal, 1977; named Pioneer of Nuclear Era Am. Nuclear Soc., European Nuclear Soc., 1992. Fellow Royal Soc. Can., Can. Acad. Engring., Engring. Inst. Can. (Julian C. Smith medal 1987); mem. Profl. Engrs. Ont. (mem. coun. 1970-73, Gold medal1986), World Energy Coun. (chmn. programme com. 1980-86, chmn. internat. exec. coun. 1986-89, pres. 1989-92, hon. chmn., pres. 1992—), Can. Nat. Com. World Energy Coun. (hon. chmn.), Can. Nuclear Assn. (past chmn.), Univ. Toronto Faculty Club., Blvd. Club. Home: 10 Thornbury Crescent, Toronto, ON Canada M9A 2M2

FOSTER, JOHN STUART, JR., physicist, former defense industry executive; b. New Haven, Sept. 18, 1922; s. John Stuart and Flora (Curtis) F.; m.

Frances Schnell, Dec. 28, 1978; children: Susan, Cathy, Bruce, Scott, John. BS, McGill U., 1948; PhD in Physics, U. Calif., Berkeley, 1952; DSc (hon.), U. Mon., 1979. Dir. Lawrence Livermore (Calif.) Lab., 1952-65; dir. def. rsch. and engring. Dept. Def., Washington, 1965-73; v.p. TRW Energy Systems Group, Redondo Beach, Calif., 1973-79; v.p. sci. and tech. TRW Inc., Cleve., 1979-88, also bd. dirs.; mem. nat. adv. bd. Am. Security Coun.; chmn. Def. Sci. Bd., 1989-93; chmn. Pilkington Aerospace; chmn. Tech. Strategies & Alliances. Decorated knight Comdr.'s Cross, Badge and Star of Order of Merit (Federal Republic of Germany); comdr. Legion of Honor (France); recipient Ernst Orlando Lawrence Meml. award AEC, 1960, Disting. Pub. Svc. medal Dept. Def., 1969, 73, 93, Cromwell medal, 1972, Enrico Fermi Award, U.S. Dept. of Energy, 1992, Eugene Fubini award, U.S. Dept. Def., 1998. Mem. NAE (Founders award 1989), AIAA, Am. Def. Preparedness Assn., Nat. Security Indsl. Assn. Office: TRW Inc 1 Space Park Blvd Bldg E1-5010 Redondo Beach CA 90278-1071

FOSTER, JOY VIA, library media specialist; b. Besoco, W.Va., Aug. 11, 1935; d. George Edward and Burgia Stafford (Earls) Via; m. Paul Harris Foster, Jr., Dec. 8, 1956 (dec. Dec. 20, 1962); children: Elizabeth Lee, Michael Paul. BS, Radford Coll., 1971; MS, Radford U., 1979. Cert. pub. sch. libr., Va. Clk. Va. Tech. and State U., Blacksburg, 1955-57; clk. Christiansburg (Va.) Primary Sch., 1971-72, libr., 1972-85; libr. Auburn Mid. and High Sch., Riner, Va., 1985—. Meml. chmn. Am. Cancer Soc., Christiansburg, 1965-66; area chmn. Am. Heart Fund, Christiansburg, 1990-93, block worker, 1985-91. Mem. NEA, ALA, Am. Assn. Sch. Librs., Montgomery County Edn. Assn. (v.p. 1988-89, sec. 1989-91, bldg. rep. 1991, sec. 1995-96), Va. Ednl. Media Assn., Va. Ednl. Assn. Presbyterian. Avocations: reading, bowling, sailing, flea marketing, antique collecting. Office: Auburn Mid and H S 4163 Riner Rd Riner VA 24149-2513

FOSTER, JULIAN FRANCIS SHERWOOD, political science educator; b. London, July 27, 1926; came to U.S., 1953; s. George Sherwood and Norah Patrickson (Langford) F.; m. Beatrice Ingrid Joerer Lindner, Feb. 22, 1957; children—Hugh, Fiona, Jennifer. B.A. with first class honours, New Coll., Oxford, 1951, M.A. (English Speaking Union fellow, Fulbright scholar), 1955; Ph.D., UCLA, 1963. Asst. prof. polit. sci. U. Santa Clara, Calif., 1957-61; asst. prof. polit. sci. Calif. State U., Fullerton, 1963-65, assoc. prof., 1965-70, prof., 1970-93, chmn. faculty council, 1966-67, acad. senator, 1971-78, dept. chmn., 1978-84, chmn. acad. senate, 1986-88; vis. prof. politics U. Durham, U.K., 1984-85; intern univ. adminstrn. Am. Council on Edn., 1967-68. Author: None Dare Call it Reason, 1964; editor, frequent contbr.: Reason: A Review of Politics, 1965-66; editor, contbr.: Protest: Student Activism in America, 1970, Politics in the United States and California, 1995. Served with Royal Navy, 1945-47. Home: 12593 Vista Panorama Santa Ana CA 92705-1390

FOSTER, KATHRYN WARNER, newspaper editor; b. Charleston, S.C., Sept. 16, 1950; d. Jack Huntington Warner and Theodora (Warner) Miller; m. William Chapman Foster, Sept. 11, 1971; children: William Huntington, Jonathan Chapman. BA in English, Newberry Coll., 1972. Obituary writer, TV editor Greenville (S.C.) Piedmont, 1971-72; asst. lifestyle editor Greenville (S.C.) News-Piedmont, 1972-73, feature editor, 1973-78; Living Today copy editor Miami (Fla.) Herald, 1978-83, asst. weekend editor, 1984-86, asst. travel editor, 1986-91, 96-98, editor Getaways midweek travel page, 1993-94, editor Youth Only (YO), 1994, assoc. editor Health Beat, 1995-96; editor Tropical Life, 1999—; editor Miami Herald Dining Guide, 1988-91; speaker S.W. Fla. Writer's Conf., Ft. Myers, 1992; mem. bi-racial/tri-ethnic adv. com., Dade County Pub. Schs., 1997—; contbr. travel writing to Fodor's, newspapers. Sec. Palmetto Elem. PTA, Miami, 1990-91. Recipient Penney-Mo. 1st pl. award for feature sects. U. Mo. Sch. Journalism, Columbia, 1978. Lutheran. Avocations: bicycling, swimming, canoeing, reading, camping. Office: Miami Herald Travel Dept 1 Herald Plz Miami FL 33132-1693

FOSTER, KENNARD P., federal judge; b. 1944. Student, Purdue U., 1962-64; BS, Ball State U., 1966; JD, Ind. U., 1970. Bar: Ind. Spl. agt. FBI, 1970-71; atty. Jones, Foster & Loveall, 1971-76; asst. U.S. Atty., 1976-86; magistrate judge U.S. Dist. Ct. (so. dist.) Ind., Indpls., 1986—. Mem. Fed. Bar Assn., Johnson County Bar Assn., Fed. Magistrate Judges Assn. Office: US Courthouse Rm 277 46 E Ohio St Indianapolis IN 46204-1903

FOSTER, KIM, art dealer, gallery owner; b. Washington, Nov. 22, 1956; d. James R. and Clair Lynn (Block) Foster; m. Antonio Petracca, Oct. 30, 1994. BA, Sarah Lawrence Coll.; MA, Johns Hopkins U. Lic. stockbroker, N.Y. Asst. treas. Bankers Trust Co., N.Y.C., 1980-83; asst. v.p. Marine Midland, N.Y.C., 1984-85; commodities credit mgr. Shearson Lehman, N.Y.C., 1985-86; v.p. Bayerische Vereinsbank, N.Y.C., 1988-94; pres. Kim Foster Gallery, N.Y.C., 1993—; bd. dirs. Foster Holdings, Inc., Pitts., Fostin Securities, Inc., Wilmington, Del. Speech writer Gov. James R. Thompson, Chgo., 1975. Mem. Mus. Modern Art., Whitney Mus. Am. Art. Republican. Jewish. Avocations: swimming, travel. Office: Kim Foster Gallery 529 W 20th St New York NY 10011

FOSTER, LAWRENCE, concert and opera conductor; b. Los Angeles, 1941. Student, Bayreuth Festival Masterclasses; studied with, Fritz Zweig. Debut as condr., Young Musicians' Found., Debut Orch., 1960; condr., mus. dir., 1960-64, condr., San Francisco Ballet, 1961-65, asst. condr., Los Angeles Philharmonic Orch., 1965-68, chief guest condr., Royal Philharmonic Orch., Eng., 1969-75, guest condr., Houston Symphony, 1970-71, condr. in chief, 1971-72, music dir., 1972-78, Orch. Philharmonique of Monte Carlo, 1979, gen. music dir., Duisburg & Dusseldorf Opera (Ger.), 1982-86, former music dir. Lausanne Chamber Orch., 1991-96, music dir. Aspen (Colo.) Music Festival and Sch.; currently music dir. Orquestra Ciutat de Barcelona; artistic dir. Bucharest Festival and Competition; guest condr. orchs. in, U.S., Europe, Australia and Japan; recorded, condr. world premiere Paul McCartney's Standing Stone, 1997; (Recipient Koussevitsky Meml. Conducting prize 1966, Eleanor R. Crane Meml. prize Berkshire Festival, Tanglewood, Mass. 1966); condr. Jerusalem Symphony Orch., 1990. Address: ICM Artists Ltd c/o Jenny Vogel 8942 Wilshire Blvd Beverly Hills CA 90211-1934

FOSTER, LESTER ANDERSON, JR., retired steel company executive; b. Apr. 4, 1929; s. Lester Anderson and Annie Lee (Swink) F.; m. Patricia White, July 9, 1955; children: Leslie Ann, Caroline Suzann, Lester Anderson, Samuel Timothy. Student, Elon Coll., 1947-50; BS, N.C. State U., 1952. With Bethlehem Steel Corp., Sparrows Point, Md., 1952-94, engr., 1956-57, med. foreman, 1957-59, asst. gen. foreman, 1959-61, asst. master mechanic, 1961-67, master mechanic, 1967-92, cons., 1992—; v.p. L&M Cons. Steel Plant Facilities, Inc. Pres. PTA, Sparrows Point, 1963-65; mem. exec. bd. nominating com. Balt. County Sch. Bd., 1964-65; dist. field svc. chmn. Boy Scouts Am., Balt., 1972-78, bicentennial show program chmn., 1976, dist. commr., 1979-83, dist. chmn., 1983—; pres. 7th dist. Rep. Club, 1969-72; mem. Md. Rep. State Cen. Com., 1980-90. With U.S. Army, 1952-54. Recipient Silver Beaver award Boy Scouts Am., 1975, award of Merit, 1984. Mem. SAR (pres. Md. Soc. 1993, v.p. gen. Mid-Atlantic, Silver Good Citizenship medal, Meritorious medal, Patriot meda, Minuteman medal 1999), Am. Inst. Iron and Steel Engrs., Soc. Mfg. Engrs., Am. Mgmt. Assn., Soc. Advancement Mgmt., Nat. Football Found. and Hall of Fame, Sparrows Point Country Club, Sparrows Point Engrs. Clubs, Masons, Shriners, K.T. (Grand Comdr.). Lutheran. Home: 3006 Dunmore Rd Baltimore MD 21222-5131

FOSTER, LINDA NEMEC, poet, educator; b. Garfield Heights, Ohio, May 29, 1950; d. John Joseph and Helen Agnes (Kumor) Nemec; m. Anthony Jesse Foster, Oct. 26, 1974; children: Brian Jesse, Ellen Kathleen. BA, Aquinas Coll., 1972; MFA, Goddard Coll., 1979. Social demographer Ctr. Environ. Study, Grand Rapids, Mich., 1971-74; clk. Jones & Laughlin Steel Corp., Detroit, 1974-77; lectr. art Ferris State U., Big Rapids, Mich., 1982-84; tchr. poetry and writing Mich. Coun. for Arts, Detroit, 1980—; prof. English, poetry workshops Aquinas Coll., 1999—; bd. dirs. Mecosta County Coun. for the Humanities, Big Rapids, 1982-85; bd. dirs. Urban Inst. for Contemporary Arts, Grand Rapids, 1989-95, dir. lit. programming, 1989-96. Author: (poetry) A History of the Body, 1987, A Modern Fairy Tale: Baba Yaga Poems, 1992, Trying to Balance the Heart, 1993, Living in the Fire Nest, 1996. Corr. sec. Lakeside Sch. Parents Assn., East Grand Rapids, 1992-93; vol. East Grand Rapids H.S., 1994-98, Degage Homeless Shelter, Grand Rapids, 1995-97. Poetry fellow Arts Found. Mich., 1996; grantee Mich. Coun. for Arts & Cultural Affairs, Detroit, 1984, 90. Mem. Detroit Women Writers, Urban Inst. for Contemporary Arts, Creative-Writers-In-Schs., Acad. Am. Poets, Poetry Soc. Am., Nat. Writers Voice Project. Roman Cath. Avocations: hiking, camping, boating, travelling. Home: 2024 Wilshire Dr SE Grand Rapids MI 49506-4014

FOSTER, LLOYD ARTHUR, principal; b. Stamford, Conn., June 11, 1933; s. Lloyd Allister and Ruth Celeste (Olmstead) F.; m. Virginia Grace Wood, June 5, 1959; children: Heidi, Leigh, Lance, Jonathan, Barry, Daniel, Victoria, Rikio. BA, Gordon Coll., Beverly, Mass., 1960; MA, U. Hartford, 1964; EdD, Nova U., 1987. Cert. elem. and secondary edn. adminstr. Sales rep. Conn. Blue Cross Ins. Co., 1960-63; tchr. Ellington (Conn.) Bd. Edn., 1963-66, prin., 1966-68; prin. Hartford (Conn.) Bd. Edn., 1968-94, Annie Fisher Sch., 1971-94; founder First Acad., 1994-96; dir. Essential Learning Ctr. of New Eng., 1995—; prin. Union Elem. Sch., 1997—; co-founder program to reduce racial isolation Across the Lines, program to assist mainstream tchrs. to meet the needs of students with spl. learning needs, Target; co-founder program to prepare high risk students for world of work Annie Fisher Work Readiness; with portfolio assessment program to monitor and motivate at-risk students Annie Fisher Portfolio Assessment Program. With USAF, 1951-55. Mem. Assn. Supvs. and Curriculum Devel., Hartford Prins. and Suprs. Assn. (v.p. 1980-94), Phi Delta Kappa. Republican. Baptist. Home and Office: 133 Dunn Rd Coventry CT 06238-1113

FOSTER, LUCILLE CASTER, school system administrator, retired; b. Vallejo, Calif., Sept. 28, 1921; d. Lewis Caster and Mabel Estelle (Witt) Beidleman; m. Donald Foster, Nov. 21, 1942 (deceased). AB in History, U. Calif., Berkeley, 1943; MA in Elem. Edn., San Francisco State U., 1953; EdD, Stanford U., 1959. Cert. sch. adminstr., Calif. Elem. tchr. Alameda (Calif.) Unified Sch. Dist., 1948-55; curriculum cons. Laguna Salada Elem. Sch. Dist., Pacifica, Calif., 1955-60, asst. supt., 1960-81; ret., 1981; bd. dirs. Fir br. Children's Med. Ctr. No. Calif. co-author (handbook) Grant Writing for Non-Profits, 2d edit., 1994; contbr. articles to Calif. Jour. Elem. Edn., 1957, 61. Mem. Santa Rosa Cultural Heritage Bd. Mem. AAUW, Internat. Fedn. U. Women, Calif. Sch. Adminstrs. Assn. (life), Calif. Tchrs. Assn. (life), Calif. Sch. Personnel Commrs. Assn. (life), Nat. Assistance League, Assistance League Sonoma County, No. Calif. Coun. Alumnae Panhellenics (v.p. 1997-99), Pi Lambda Theta. Avocations: community volunteer, bridge, traveling. Fax: 707-538-3507. Home: 245 Mockingbird Cir Santa Rosa CA 95409-6245

FOSTER, M. J., JR. (MIKE FOSTER), governor; b. Shreveport, La.; married. BSCE, La. State U. Sugar cane farmer La.; founder Bayou Sale, La.; pres. Sterling Sugars, Inc.; senator St. Mary/Assumption Parish Dist. La. State Senate, 1987, chmn. commerce com., 1991; gov. State of La. Jr. warden St. Mary's Episcopal Ch.; pres. St. Mary Parish Farm Bur. With USAF, Korea. Mem. Am. Legion. Avocations: hunting, fishing, tennis. Office: Office of the Governor PO Box 94004 Baton Rouge LA 70804-9004*

FOSTER, M. JOAN, lawyer; b. Cin.; d. William and Marguerite (DeHaven) Moeller; children: Peter Graf, James DeHaven. BA, Duke U., 1961; JD cum laude, Seton Hall U., 1976. Bar: N.J. 1976, U.S. Dist. Ct. N.J. 1976, U.S. Ct. Appeals (3d cir.) 1980, U.S. Dist. Ct (no. dist.) Calif. 1982. Assoc. Lowenstein, Sandler, Kohl, Fisher & Boylan, Roseland, N.J., 1976-79; assoc. Grotta, Glassman & Hoffman, PA, Roseland, 1980-85, prin., 1986—; adj. prof. Seton Hall Law Sch., Newark, 1978-80. Trustee N.J. Symphony Orch., Newark, 1989—, vice chair, 1997—. Mem. ABA (labor and employment law sect. 1980—, internat. law sect. 1988—), N.J. State Bar Assn. (exec. com. labor and employment sect. 1982—, editor-in-chief 1984-88, sec. 1991-92, vice chair 1992-93, chair 1993-94, health and hosp. law sect. 1988—), N.J. Pub. Employer Labor Rels. Assn. (trustee 1993—), N.J. Network of Bus. and Profl. Women (trustee 1980—, pres. bd. trustees 1991-93), U.S. Dist. Ct. Hist. Soc. (trustee, exec. com. N.J. dist. 1989-92). Office: Grotta Glassman & Hoffman PA 75 Livingston Ave Ste 13 Roseland NJ 07068-3701*

FOSTER, MARK EDWARD, lawyer, consultant, international lobbyist; b. Detroit, May 12, 1948; s. Herbert Edward and Joyce Mary (Campbell) F.; m. Miyoko Katabami, Apr. 20, 1974; children: Lorissa Chieko. *Wife Miyoko Katabami is one of the leading English-Japanese translators in the world, having worked for various U.S. and Japanese government agencies and multinational companies. Daughter Lorissa Chieko will graduate Dartmouth College in 2000 and studies engineering, pre-med and studio art. She was a Westinghouse Competition Award recipient in 1996 for her paper "Optimal Methods for Quantifying Mitral Regurgitant in Prolapsed Mitral Valves".* BA, Alma Coll., 1970; MA, U. Calif.-Berkeley, 1972; JD, U. Calif.-Hastings, 1981; postgrad., Stanford Ctr., Tokyo, 1983. Japanese lang. cert., 1982; bar: Calif. 1981, Oreg. 1989. Law clk. U.S. Dist. Ct., San Francisco, 1980-81; atty. Hetland & Hansen, Berkeley, Calif., 1981-82, Braun Moriya Hoashi, Tokyo, 1982-84; spl. counsel U.S. Embassy, Tokyo, 1984-85; Japan counsel U.S. Electronic Industries Assn., 1985-86; mng. ptnr. Law Offices Mark E. Foster, Portland, Tokyo, 1988—; lectr., cons. on internat. law and tech. stds., tech. transfer, product compliance, engring. Internat. Stds. Orgn., Geneva, Ministry of Internat. Trade and Industry of Japan, U.S. Dept. Commerce, U. So. Calif., World Trade Inst.; mem. tech. stds. com. for Optoelectronics, Japanese Ministry of Posts and Telecom., 1984-86, tech. stds. com. for Intelligent Office Systems, Japanese Patent Office, Japanese Ministry of Internat. Trade and Industry, 1984-86. *Mark Foster is referred to by the Wall Street Journal as "a full time lobbyist for American interests in Japan". He was Special Counsel to the U.S. Embassy, Tokyo, part of the team assembled by Malcolm Baldridge, President Reagan's Secretary of Commerce. Foster's efforts as negotiator are credited with opening Japan's telecom business, and it's previously closed system of product technical standards to U.S. suppliers. Foster was the first full time lobbyist in Japan for a U.S. industry association, and served on several Japanese Government councils. His firm has successfully negotiated approvals by various Japanese Ministries of over two dozen U.S. manufacturers, enabling export to Japan of U.S. products from rice to industrial machinery to telecom equipment, valued over $2 billion.* Author articles, books in internat. law and tech. Grantee Rockefeller Found. Presbyn. Ch., Geneva and Tokyo, 1972-74; sr. fellow Conf. of World Regions. Mem. ABA, Am. Soc. Quality Control, Internat. Bar Assn., Calif. Bar Assn., Oreg. Bar Assn., Am. C. of C. in Japan, Portland World Trade (bd. advisors), World Affairs Coun. Presbyterian. Office: 9615 SW Allen Blvd Ste 103 Portland OR 97005-4814

FOSTER, MARK STEPHEN, lawyer; b. Edgerton, Mo., Feb. 6, 1948; s. George Elliott and Annabel Lee (Bradshaw) F.; m. Camille Pepper, June 27, 1970; children: Natalie Ashley, Stephanie Ann. BS, U. Mo., 1970; JD, Duke U., 1973. Bar: Mo. 1973, U.S. Ct. Mil. Appeals 1974, Hawaii 1975, U.S. Dist. Ct. Hawaii 1975, U.S. Dist. Ct. (we. dist.) Mo. 1977, U.S. Ct. Appeals (8th cir.) 1986, U.S. Supreme Ct. 1994. Assoc. Stinson, Mag & Fizzell, Kansas City, 1977-80, ptnr., 1980—, mng. ptnr., 1987-90, bd. dirs., 1991—, chmn. bd. dirs., 1998—; arbitration panelist Nat. Assn. Securities Dealers, N.Y.C., 1985—, Pvt. Adjudication Found., Durham, N.C., 1988—. Active Citizens Assn., Kansas City, 1982-92; pres. Spelman Med. Found., Smithville, Mo., 1984-88; bd. dirs. Alzheimers Assn. Metro. Kansas City, 1997—, 1st v.p., 1998—. Lt. comdr. USNR, ret. Mem. ABA, Hawaii Bar Assn., Mo. Bar Assn., Kansas City Met. Bar Assn., Am. Arbitration Assn. (panelist 1990—, large complex case adv. com. 1993—), Carriage Club, Masons. Home: 1035 W 65th St Kansas City MO 64113-1813 Office: Stinson Mag & Fizzell PC PO Box 419251 1201 Walnut St Ste 2800 Kansas City MO 64106-2117

FOSTER, MARTHA TYAHLA, educational administrator; b. Coaldale, Pa., Apr. 22, 1955; d. Stephen and Frances (Solomon) Tyahla; m. David Marion Foster, Jan. 3, 1981. BA with distinction, U. Va., 1977, MEd, 1981, EdS, 1981. Legis. asst. U.S. Ho. of Reps., Washington, 1977-79; asst. dean summer session U. Va., Charlottesville, 1981; program cons. campus activities U. Houston, 1981; coordinator student affairs Capitol Inst. Tech., Kensington, Md., 1982-83, asst. dean students, Laurel, Md., 1983-84, assoc. dean students, 1984-86, dean students, 1986-87; bd. dirs. Curry Sch. Edn. Found. U. Va., 1987-90. Mem. Arlington County Commn. on Status of Women, 1985-88; chmn. Christian edn. Christ Meth. Ch., 1994-97; dir. Resurrection Luth. Presch., 1997—; coun. mem.- at-large Arlington United Way, 1995—; pres. PTA Arlington Traditional Sch., 1997-98, treas. 1994-96. Named Woman of Yr. Bus. and Profl. Women's Club, Vienna, Va., 1986. Methodist. Lodge: Order of Eastern Star (worthy matron 1988-89, trustee 1993-96).

FOSTER, MARY CHRISTINE, motion picture and television executive; b. L.A., Mar. 19, 1943; d. Ernest Albert and Mary Ada (Quilici) F.; m. Paul Hunter, July 24, 1982. BA, Immaculate Heart Coll., Los Angeles, 1967; M of Journalism in TV News Documentary, UCLA, 1968. Dir. research and devel. Metromedia Producers Corp., Los Angeles, 1968-71; dir. devel. and prodn. services Wolper Prodns., Los Angeles, 1971-76; mgr. film programs NBC-TV, Burbank, Calif., 1976-77; v.p. movies and mini series Columbia Pictures TV, Burbank, 1977-81, v.p. series programs, 1981; v.p. program devel. Group W. Prodns., L.A., 1981-87; agt. The Agency, Los Angeles, 1988-90, Shapiro-Lichtman Agy., Los Angeles, 1990—; lectr. in field, 1970—. Creator: (TV series) Sullivan, 1985, Auntie Mom, 1986. Bd. dirs. Immaculate Heart High Sch., L.A., 1980—; mem. exec. com. Humanitas Awards, Human Family Inst., 1985—, L.A. Roman Cath. Archdiosesan Comm. Commn., L.A., 1986-90, Catholics in Media Exec. Com., 1992—. Mem. Women in Film (bd. dirs. 1974-78), Nat. Acad. TV Arts and Scis. Democrat. Office: 8827 Beverly Blvd Los Angeles CA 90048-2405 *Fidelity to God's will yields life's greatest satisfaction. Love of family and community gives life fulfillment.*

FOSTER, MARY FRANCES, accounting firm executive, accountant; b. Yonkers, N.Y., Sept. 16, 1952; d. John Andrew Bordash and Dolores Becker; m. Donald J. Foster, Dec. 30, 1978; children: Scott I., Kelly Belle. BBA, Pace U., 1975, MBA, 1976. CPA, N.Y. Staff acct. Haskins & Sells, N.Y.C., 1975-78; from assoc. to mgr. Deloitte, Haskins & Sells, N.Y.C., 1978-87, ptnr., 1987-90; ptnr. Deloitte & Touche, N.Y.C., 1990-99. Co-author: GAAP for Not-for-Profit Organizations, Plus Tax and Regulatory Reporting; contbr. articles to profl. jours. V.p., bd. dirs. Mental Health Assn. Westchester County, mem. strategic planning com., fin. com., personnel com.; treas., bd. dirs. Multiple Sclerosis Soc. So. N.Y.; mem. fin. com. United Way Am.; chairperson, trustee Search for Change; chair exec. com., adv. com. Pace U., Lubin Sch. Bus. Acctg. Dept.; mem. Lubin Sch. Bus. Alumni Fedn. Mem. AICPA (chair com. nonprofit orgns. 1989-92), N.Y. State Soc. CPAs (mem. com. nonprofit orgns. 1982-84, 85-87, com. computer usage and EDP auditing 1985, com. pub. sch. accounting 1988, mem. com. ops. 1993-97). Democrat. Roman Catholic. Office: Deloitte & Touche 2 World Fin Ctr New York NY 10281-1414

FOSTER, MICHAEL PAUL, sales and marketing representative; b. Lubbock, Tex., Dec. 21, 1947; s. William Paul and Helen Warren (Chapman) F.; m. Sheryl Leigh Steffens, Feb. 16, 1974. BA, Baylor U., 1970; MBA, U. South Fla., 1986. Tech. specialist Sci. Product div. Am. Hosp. Supply Corp., Dallas, 1974-79; instrument salesman diagnostics div. Boehringer Mannheim Gmbh, Tampa, Fla., 1979-84; area sales mgr. Cooper/Technicon, Tampa, 1985-89; sales mgr. southeastern region Chemistry div. Coulter Electronics, Inc., Tampa, 1989—; nat. sales mgr. Serono Diagnostics, 1993—; pres., CEO Sierra Resource Internat. Inc.; med. mktg. cons. Ferraz and Foster, Tampa, 1986—; pres., CEO Sierra Resources Internat. Inc., 1997. Mem. Radiology Soc. Am., Am. Assn. Clin. Chemistry. Republican. Methodist. Home: 2103 Isle Of Palms Dr Valrico FL 33594-7256

FOSTER, MICHELE, educator; b. May 5, 1947. PhD, Harvard U., 1987. Asst. prof. U. Pa., Phila., 1987-91; assoc. prof. U. Calif., Davis, 1991-94; prof. Claremont (Calif.) Graduate U., 1994—. E-mail: michelfg@idt.net.

FOSTER, NANCY MARIE, environmental analyst, government official; b. Electra, Tex., Jan. 23, 1941; d. evelyn Ann (Spurrier) F. BS, Tex. Women's U., 1963; MS, TEx. Christian U., 1965; PhD, George Washington U., 1969. Chmn. biology dept. Dunbarton Coll. for Women, Washington, 1969-73; environ. analyst U.S. Fish & Wildlife Svc., Washington, 1973-74; sr. environ. analyst Dept. Interior, Washington, 1974-78; dir. U.S. Nat. Marine and Estuarine Sanctuary Programs NOAA, Washington, 1978-87, dir. protected resources, 1987—; speaker to profl. and cultural groups on govt. involvement in hist. preservation of nationally significant maritime cultural resources, 1981—. Contbr. articles to profl. jours. Mem. AAAS, Women's Aquatic Network (founding trustee), Caribbean Is. Directorate (UNESCO), Biosphere Res. Directorate (UNESCO). Avocations: ceramics, aerobics, English history. Office: Nat. Ocean Service SSMC, Bldg 4 1305 E West Hwy Silver Spring MD 20910-3278*

FOSTER, NORMAN HOLLAND, geologist; b. Iowa City, Oct. 2, 1934; s. Holland and Dora Lucinda (Ransom) F.; m. Janet Lee Grecian, Mar. 25, 1956; children: Kimberly Ann, Stephen Norman. BA, U. Iowa, 1957, MS, 1960; PhD, U. Kans., 1963. Instr. geology U. Iowa, 1958-60; sr. geologist, geol. specialist, exploration team supr. Sinclair Oil Corp. and Atlantic Richfield Co., Casper, Wyo., also Denver, 1962-69; dist. geologist Trend Exploration Ltd., 1969-72, v.p., 1972-79; ind. geologist Denver, 1979—; instr. geology U. Kans., 1960-62; chmn., pres., CEO Voyager Exploration, Inc., Denver, 1995—; guest lectr. geology Colo. Sch. Mines, 1972—, U. Colo., 1972—, U. Iowa, 1975—, U. Kans., 1975—; adv. bd. U. Kans., 1982—, U. Iowa, 1988—, U. Colo., 1990—; chmn. fin. com. 28th Internat. Geol. Congress, 1987-89, ofcl. U.S. rep., Washington, 1989; dir. MarkWest Hydrocarbon, Inc., Denver, 1996—. Assoc. editor Guidebook to Geology and Energy Resources of Piceance Basin, Colorado, 1974, Mountain Geologist, 1967-68, 71-85, editor, 1968-70; co-editor, compiler Treatise of Petroleum Geology, 1984—; contbr. papers on geology to profl. publs. Served to capt. inf. AUS, 1957. Recipient Haworth Disting. Alumni award dept. geology U. Kans., 1977, Disting. Alumni award dept. geology U. Iowa, 1992. Fellow Geol. Soc. Am.; mem. Am. Assn. Petroleum Geologists (del. 1972-75, 79-82, disting. lectr. 1976-77, pres. Rocky Mountain sect. 1979-80, treas. 1982-84, adv. coun. 1985-88, chmn. astrogeology com. 1984-88, nat. pres. 1988-89, found. trustee 1979—, hon. mem. 1993—, Levorsen award 1980, Disting. Svc. award 1985, founder astrogeology com. 1984, mem. 1984—, mem. resource evaluation com. 1992—), Rocky Mountain Assn. Geologists (sec. 1970, 1st v.p. 1974, pres. 1977, best paper award 1975, Explorer of Yr. award 1980, Disting. Svc. award 1981, hon. mem. 1983—), Soc. Econ. Paleontologists and Mineralogists, Am. Inst. Profl. Geologists, Soc. Ind. Profl. Earth Scientists, Soc. Exploration Geophysicists, Soc. Petroleum Engrs., Nat. Acad. Scis. (bd. earth scis. and resources, U.S. nat. com. geology, com. earth resources, com. adv. to U.S. Geol. Survey 1989-92), Colo. Sci. Soc., Sigma Xi, Sigma Gamma Epsilon. Republican. Mem. Christian Ch. Office: 1625 Broadway Ste 370 Denver CO 80202-4725*

FOSTER, SIR NORMAN ROBERT, architect; b. Reddish, Eng., June 1, 1935; s. Robert and Lilian (Smith) F. Dip.Arch., Manchester U.; M.Arch., Yale U.; LittD (hon.), East Anglia, 1980; DSc (hon.) Bath, 1986, Valencia, 1992, Humberside, 1992, Manchester, 1992, Royal Coll. Art, 1990, Kent Inst. Design, 1994, Eindhoven, 1996, Oxford, 1996, London, 1996. Cons. architect Imperial Coll. London and U. East Anglia, 1978-87; prin. Foster and Ptnrs. (formerly Foster Assocs.), London, 1967—; collaborator with Buckminster Fuller, from 1968-83; former external examiner Royal Inst. Brit. Architects; former mem. Archtl. Assn. Council, v.p., 1974; former tchr. U. Pa., Archtl. Assn., London, London Poly., Bath Acad. Arts; mem. council R.C.A., 1981. Archtl. works include: Pilot Head Office, IBM, Hampshire, 1970; Sainsbury Centre for Visual Arts, Norwich, 1978 (R.S. Reynolds Internat. Meml. award 1979); Head Office, Willis, Faber and Dumas, Ipswich (R.S. Reynolds Internat. Meml. award 1976), 1979; devel. project Whitney Gallery, N.Y.C., 1979; Centre for Renault Car Co. U.K., 1983; Hong Kong and Shanghai Banking Corp. Hdqrs., 1986 (R.S. Reynolds Internat. Meml. award 1986); Stockley Park B3, 1989; Carré d'Art Arts Centre, Nimes, 1993; Century Tower, Tokyo, 1991; Barcelona Telecom. Tower, 1991; King's Cross Master Plan, London, 1991; Third London Airport Terminal Zone at Stansted, 1991, Sackler Galleries, Royal Acad. of Arts, London, 1991, Libr. Cranfield U., 1993, Joslyn Art Mus. addition, Omaha, 1994, Reichstag new German Parliament (winner competition Berlin 1993), Micro-Electronic Centre, Duisburg, 1993, Lycée Sch., Fréjus, France, 1993, Marine Simulator Ctr., Rotterdam, The Netherlands, 1994, Bilbao Metro Sys., 1995; U. Cambridge Law Faculty, 1995; exhbns.: Mus. Modern Art, N.Y.C., 1979; also in Barcelona, London, Parma, Copenhagen, Paris, Nimes, Madrid, Florence, Venice, Milan, Berlin, Tokyo, Zurich, Bordeaux, Bilbao, Hong Kong, Antwerp, Munich, Valencia; represented in permanent collection: Mus. Modern Art, N.Y.C.; contbr. articles to archtl. and tech. publs. Recipient of over 130 awards for design excellence including Fin. Times Indsl. Architecture award, 1967, 74, 84, 93, R.S.A. Bus. and Industry awards, Internat. Design awards, Finniston award, Structural Steel award, 1972, 78, 84, 86, 92, Ambrose Congreve award, Royal Gold Medal for Architecture, 1983, Berlin art grand prize, 1989, Knighthood, 1990. Trustees medal Royal Inst. Brit. Architects, Mies Van Der Rohe Pavilion award, 1990, Royal Inst. Brit. Archs. awards, Chgo. Arts award, 1990, Gold medal French Acad. Arch., 1991, Arnold W. Brunner Meml. prize, 1992, Premio Alcantara award, 1992, Concrete Soc. awards, Benedictus award, 1993, Interiors USA award, 1988, 92, 93, Queens Export achievement award, 1995, Order of N. Rhine Westphalia; named Man of the Yr. MIPIM, 1996; IBM fellow Aspen Design Conf., 1980. Fellow AIA (hon., Gold Medal 1994), Officer of the Order of Arts and Letters Ministry of Culture, France, Royal Acad. Engring. (hon.); mem. AAAS (fgn. hon.), C.S.D., Royal Acad. (assoc.), Royal Designers for Industry, Chartered Soc. Designers, Assn. Academie Royale de Belgique, Royal Acad. Fine Arts Sweden (fgn.), European Acad. Scis. and Arts. Office: Foster and Ptnrs, Foster & Ptnrs, Riverside 3 22 Hester Rd, London SW11 4AN, England*

FOSTER, PAUL, zoo director; b. Opp, Ala., Mar. 1, 1939. Zoo keeper Montgomery Zoo, 1970-80, gen. curator, 1980-90, mgr. animal care, 1990-97, acting dir., then dir., 1997—. Mem. Am. Zool. Assn. Office: Montgomery Zoo PO Box Zebra Montgomery AL 36109-0313*

FOSTER, PAUL, playwright; b. Penn's Grove, N.J., Oct. 15, 1931; s. Elderidge M. and Mary (Manning) F. BA, Rutgers U., 1954; LLB, St. John's U., 1958. Pres. La Mama Theater Club, N.Y.C., 1962—; tchr. drama dept. NYU and U. Calif.-San Diego, 1983. Author: The Birthday Party Stories, 1962, Hurrah for the Bridge, 1963, The Recluse, 1964, Balls, 1964, Madonna In the Orchard, 1965, The Hessian Corporal, 1966, Tom Paine, 1967, Heimskringla, 1969, Satyricon, 1970, Elizabeth I, 1971, Silver Queen Saloon, 1972, Marcus Brutus, 1973-74, Murderers' Row, 1976, A Kiss is Just a Kiss, 1983, (stage trilogy) The Dark and Mr. Stone, 1985-87, (TV) The Tragedy of the Commons, 1979, The Vampyre and Dr. Frankenstein, 1980, Silver Saloon, 1992, (film) Andrew Mellon and the National Gallery of Art, 1980, Cop and the Anthem, 1982, Smile, 1983, Cinderella Story, 1984, (stage play based on Dickens) A Tale of Two Cities, 1988, Kisses, Bites and Scratches, 1990, Elizabeth Eins, 1992, Make Believe Musical Book and Lyrics, 1993, Murder in the Hollyhocks, 1995; translator: (Horvath) Back & Forth, Faith, Hope, Charity, 1983, Fritz Lang's M for stage, 1997; donated collection of theatrical lit. to Rutgers U. Libr. Served to lt. (j.g.) USNR, 1955-57. Recipient Play award Irish Univs., 1967, 71, N.Y. Drama Critics award, 1968, Tony award nomination, 1973; Rockefeller Found. fellow, 1967-68; Creative Artists Pub. Service grantee, 1972; Nat. Endowment Creative Writing fellow, 1973; Guggenheim fellow, 1974. Mem. Eugene O'Neill Meml. Theater Found., New Dramatists, Dramatists Guild, Player's Club, Societe des Auteurs. Home: PO Box 867 Avondale PA 19311-0867

FOSTER, REBECCA ANNE HODGES, secondary school educator; b. Waurika, Okla., Mar. 29, 1941; d. Robert Lee and Ouida (Gregory) Hodges; m. Jim Foster, Sept. 27, 1963; children: Krista Michelle, Lisa Rene. BS, Abilene Christian U., 1963; MEd, Middle Tenn. State U., 1989; student, SW Mo. State U., North Tex. State U. Cert. vocat. home econs., English, libr. Tchr. English and home econs. Dallas Christian Sch., 1963-70; tchr. vocat. home econs. Garland (Tex.) High Sch., 1971-73; tchr. English, home econs. Alternative Edn. Ctr., Corpus Christi, Tex., 1974-77; tchr. English, Mid. Tenn. Christian Sch., Murfreesboro, 1984-90; tchr. English, Coyle Mid. Sch., Garland Ind. Sch. Dist., 1990-92, libr. Meml. Prep. Sch., 1992—. Mem. ASCD, NEA, Tex. State Tchrs. Assn., Garland Edn. Assn., Nat. Coun. Tchrs. English, Tex. Libr. Assn., Phi Kappa Phi. Home: PO Box 473063 Garland TX 75047-3063 Office: 2825 S 1st St Garland TX 75041-3429

FOSTER, RICHARD, journalist; b. Chgo., Oct. 16, 1938; s. James Edward and Mary (Sebat) F.; m. Susanne Elisabeth Hill, Sept. 28, 1996; 1 child, Katherine Elisabeth. B.A., Lawrence Coll., 1963. Reporter City News Bur., Chgo., 1963-64; reporter Chgo. Sun-Times, 1964-72, editorial writer, mem. editorial bd., 1972-78; editorial writer Des Moines Register & Tribune, 1978-82, Milw. Journal Sentinel, 1983—; journalist-in-residence Colo. State U., spring 1982. Served with AUS, 1958-61. Recipient 1st place award UPI, 1984, Inter-Am. Press Assn. award, 1988; NEH profl. journalism fellow Stanford U., 1976-77. Mem. Nat. Conf. Editorial Writers, Nat. Press Club. Home: 4645 N Murray Ave Whitefish Bay WI 53211-1259 Office: 333 W State St Milwaukee WI 53203-1305

FOSTER, ROBERT CARMICHAEL, banker; b. Toledo, Ohio, Apr. 1, 1941; s. Robert Albert and Kate (Thompson) F.; m. Phyllis Lorainne Schmidt, Nov. 25, 1974; children: Brian Clinton, Suzanne Pamela, Robert Carmichael Jr. AB, Colo. Coll., 1963; MBA, U. Chgo., 1965; AMP, Harvard U., 1982. Analyst, programmer McDonnell-Douglas Corp., St.Louis, 1965-67; systems cons. Bristol-Myers Co., N.Y.C., 1967-70; comptroller Toledo Trust Co., 1970-73, sr. v.p., 1973-77, exec. v.p., 1977-87, also bd. dirs.; v.p. Trustcorp, Inc., 1975-86, exec. v.p., 1986-87; pres., dir. Sea-Gate Aviation Corp., Toledo, 1983—; pres., chief exec. officer, bd. dirs. West Mich. Nat. Bank, Frankfort, Mich., 1987—; bd. dirs. Traverse Bay Econ. Devel. Corp., 1988—. Bd. dirs. Riverside Hosp., Toledo, 1978-85, Northcoast Health Sys., Inc., 1983-88, Lucas County Children Svcs., Toledo, 1981-85, Munson Healthcare Inc., 1990—, Traverse City, Mich.; trustee YMCA, Toledo, 1974-87; assoc. trustee Boys Club of Toledo, 1984-86, trustee, 1986-87; chmn. Lucas County U.s. Savs. Bond Program, Toledo, 1972-87; mem. planning commn. Crystal Lake Twp., 1988-97; sec.-treas. Paul Oliver Meml. Hosp., 1989-90, pres., 1990—; pres. Frankfort Indsl. Pk. Devel. Corp., 1989—; mem. Traverse Bay Cmty. Found., 1995—; chmn. Frankfort City-County Airport Authority, 1995—. Mem. Am. Inst. Banking, Bank Adminstrn. Inst., Toledo Area Govtl. Rsch. Assn. (pres., bd. dirs. 1974-79), Toledo C. of C. (aviation com.), Ottawa Skeet Club (treas.), Crystal Downs Country Club, Rotary. Presbyterian. Avocations: airline transport-rated pilot; water and snow skiing; hunting; tennis. Home: 70 Thomas Rd Frankfort MI 49635-9538

FOSTER, ROBERT FRANCIS, communications executive; b. Chgo., June 4, 1926; s. William John and Anna Alice (O'Farrell) F.; m. Mary D. Palella, May 4, 1963; children: Sean Terence, Nancy Marie, Patrick Daniel. Student, Cath. schs., Chgo. and Evanston, Ill. News and sports writer Sta. WGN, Chgo., 1943-55; with Chgo. Pub. Rels. Counselors, 1955-60, WGN Continental Broadcasting Co., Chgo., 1960-82; news bur. chief WGN Continental Broadcasting Co., Springfield, Ill., 1961-63; Washington news bureau chief WGN Continental Broadcasting Co., Washington, 1964-82; press sec. to Ill. Congressman Philip M. Crane, 1982-96; reporter and analyst at 10 nat. polit. convs. WGN-TV and WGN-Radio; Chgo. Stadium announcer Chgo. Blackhawks, 1955-64. Goalie 78th Div. ice hockey team, 1946. With AUS, 1944-46. Decorated Combat Inf. badge, Bronze Star. Recipient award best pub. service news Am. Coll. Radio Arts, Crafts and Scis., 1961. Mem. Radio-TV Corr. Assn. Washington (pres. 1976), Broadcast Pioneers, Am. Legion. Roman Catholic. Home: 5718 Marble Arch Way Alexandria VA 22315-4037

FOSTER, ROBERT LAWSON, retired judge, deacon; b. Putnam, Okla., Nov. 17, 1925; s. Mark M. and Jessie Marie (Gregory) F.; m. Mary Jo Hull, July 1, 1949 (dec.); children: Candace Ann (Mrs. Dan Sebert), Martha Denise (Mrs. Gerald Speed), Karen Sue Greenfield, Robert L., John Michael (dec.), Cynthia Kay. B.A., U. Okla., 1949, LL.B., 1950, J.D., 1970. Bar: Okla. 1950; ordained deacon Roman Cath. Ch., 1979. Pvt. practice Chandler, 1950-51; county judge Lincoln County, Okla., 1951-69; assoc. dist. judge 23d Jud. Dist., Chandler, Okla., 1969-86; ret., 1986. Chmn. dist. council Boy Scouts Am., 1968-69; chmn., an organizer Chandler Combined Appeal, 1954—; sec., pres. Lincoln County Jr. League Baseball, 1960-68; county dir. Civil Def., 1953-70; mem. bd. Permanent Deacon Candidates for Okla., mem. deacon perceiver team, 1985-97; adv. to registrants Selective Svc., 1953—. Served with USAF, 1944-45. Mem. Lincoln County Bar Assn. (pres. 1965, sec. 1960-64, 67-69, 70-73), C. of C. (sec. 1964-68), Okla. Assn. County Judges (sec.-treas. 1964-67), Okla. Jud. Conf. Club: Chandler Parents. Lodge: Lion (dir. 1964-65, pres. 1967, treas. 1968-70, zone chmn. 1973-74, dep. dist. gov. 1974—, ret. 1990).

FOSTER, ROBERT W., state legislator; b. Springfield, Mass., Mar. 6, 1920; m. Mary Ann (dec.); two children. Student, Northeastern U., 1946-48, U. Mass. Former mktg. mgr. Mobil Oil Corp.; past town trustee; state rep. N.H. Dist. 10; chmn. emeritus health, human svcs. and elderly affairs com.; mem. rules com. chmn. N.H. Hosp. Assoc. Trustee Forum, Huggins Hosp.; mem. Moultonborough Acad. Scholar Trust; chmn. Amherst Sch. Bd., 1966-68. Mem. Bald Peak Colony Club (bd. dirs.), Mason. Address: PO Box 602 Holland St Moultonborough NH 03254

FOSTER, ROGER SHERMAN, JR., surgeon, educator, health facility administrator; b. Washington, Jan. 8, 1936; s. Roger Sherman and Genevieve Wakeman (Bartlett) F.; m. Joan Crile, June 25, 1960; children: Roger Sherman III, Charles Bartlett, Elizabeth Crile, Halle Crile Foster Moore. AB, Haverford Coll., 1957; MD, Case Western Res. U., 1961. Diplomate Am. Bd. Surgy, Nat. Bd. Med. Examiners; lic. Vt., Ga. Intern then resident in surgery Univ. Hosps., Cleve., 1961-66; research fellow Roswell Park Meml. Inst., Buffalo, 1966-68; asst. prof. surgery U. Vt., Burlington, 1970-73, assoc. prof. surgery, 1973-80, prof. surgery, 1980-92, dir. comprehensive cancer ctr., 1984-92; attending surgeon Med. Ctr. Hosp. of Vt., 1970-92; Wadley Glenn prof. surgery Emory U., Atlanta, 1992—; chief surgical svcs. Crawford Long Hosp. of Emory U., 1992—; mem. cancer clin. investigation rev. com. NIH, 1987-92, chmn., 1991-92, chmn. various coms.; cons. Am. Internat. Health Alliance for Tblisi, Georgia Hosp., 1992-96. Assoc. editor: Clinical Surgery, 1987; co-editor: Essentials of Clinical Surgery, 1991; editor-in-chief: Breast Surgery: Index and Reviews, 1993-95; assoc. editor: Surgery: Problem-Solving Approach, 2d edit., 1995; co-editor: Q & A Review for Surgery, 1995; manuscript reviewer: Jour. AMA, Jour. Trauma, others; contbr. more than 100 articles to profl. jours. Trustee Univ. Health Ctr., Burlington, 1986-89. Served to maj. U.S. Army, 1968-69. Grantee NIH, 1971-92; summer rsch. fellow Josiah Macy Jr, Found., 1958-59. Fellow Am. Surg. Assn., ACS (bd. regents 1991—, bd. govs. 1981-87, adv. coun. for gen. surgery 1989-92, 95—, sec./treas. Vt. chpt. 1979-80, v.p. 1980-81, pres. 1981-82, mem. orgn. com. 1992-93, mem. comms. com. 1992-93, chmn. comms. com. 1993, mem. com. on ethics 1992-97, chmn. com. on ethics 1994-97, mem. exec. com. 1992, 93, 96—, mem. fin. com. 1994-96, mem. fellowship com. 1996, chmn. fellowship com. 1998—, mem. exec. com. commn. on cancer 1993—); mem. AMA, AAAS, New Eng. Surg. Soc. (treas. 1986-89, exec. com. 1981-92), Soc. Univ. Surgeons, So. Surg. Assn., Southeastern Surg. Congress, Soc. Surg. Oncology, Ea. Surg. Soc. (pres. 1994), Am. Endocrine Surg. Soc. (coun. 1992-95), Am. Soc. Clin. Oncology (pub. rels. 1989-91 and pub. issues coms. 1989-94), Transplantation Soc., New Eng. Cancer Soc. (treas. 1983-87, v.p. 1988-89, pres. 1989-90), Assn. Acad. Surgery, Newfoundland Club Am. (bd. dirs. 1976-78, 1st v.p. 1979), Nat. Surg. Adjuvant Breast Project, 1971-92 (exec. com. 1978-81). Avocations: white water canoeing, breeding Newfoundland dogs, wilderness travel, chamber music. Home: 1750 Winterthur Close NW Atlanta GA 30328-4626 Office: Crawford Long Hosp Emory U 550 Peachtree St NE Atlanta GA 30365-3900

FOSTER, RUTH MARY, dental association administrator; b. Little Rock, Jan. 11, 1927; d. William Crosby and Frances Louise (Doering) Shaw; m. Luther A. Foster, Sept. 8, 1946 (dec. Dec. 1980); children: William Lee, Robert Lynn. Grad. high sch., Long Beach, Calif. Sr. hostess Mon's Food Host of Coast, Long Beach, 1945-46; dental asst., office mgr. Dr. Wilfred H. Allen, Opportunity, Wash., 1946-47; dental asst., bus. asst. Dr. H. Erdahl, Long Beach, 1948-50; office mgr. Dr. B.B. Blough, Spokane, Wash., 1950-52; bus. mgr. Henry G. Kolsrud, D.D.S., P.S., Spokane, 1958—, Garland Dental Bldg., Spokane, 1958—. Sustaining mem. Spokane Symphony Orch. Mem. NAFE, Nat. Assn. Dental Assts., DAV Aux., DAV Comdrs. Club, Wash. State Fedn. Bus. and Profl. Women (dir. dist. 6), Spokane's Lilac City Bus. and Profl. Women (past pres.), Nat. Alliance Mentally Ill, Wash. Alliance Mentally Ill, Internat. Platform Assn., Spokane Club, Credit Women's Breakfast Club, Dir.'s Club, Inland N.W. Zool. Soc., Pioneer Circle of Women Helping Women. Democrat. Mem. First Christian Ch. Avocations: gardening, reading, continuing education studies. Office: Henry G Kolsrud DDS PS 3718 N Monroe St Spokane WA 99205-2850 *Keep the joy of accomplishment in your chosen profession with fresh ideas and zeal! Always remember to lend a helping hand to people in need that will let them work towards this joy. Vision and focus!.*

FOSTER, SCARLETT LEE, public relations executive; b. Charleston, W.Va., Dec. 14, 1956; d. William Christoph Foster, Jr. and Anne (Howes) Conway. B in Comm., Bethany Coll., 1979. Dir. pub. rels. Allergy Rehab. Found., Charleston, 1979-80; dir. pubs. Contractors Assn. W.Va., Charleston, 1980-82; comm. rep. Monsanto Co., Nitro, W.Va., 1982-84, 1984-87; mgr. environ. and community rels. Monsanto Co., St. Louis, 1987-89, mgr. pub. rels., 1989-91, mgr. fin. pub. rels., 1991-93, dir. pub. rels., 1993-94, dir. pub. affairs, 1994—. Bd. dirs. Sta. KWMU Pub. Radio, St. Louis, 1992—; trustee Bethany (W.Va.) Coll., 1994—. Named Outstanding Alumni of Achievement Bethany Coll., 1990. Mem. Internat. Assn. Bus. Communicators (3 Gold Quill awards of Merit). Episcopalian. Avocations: sculling, biking, reading, cooking, gardening. Office: Monsanto Co A2SP 800 N Lindbergh Blvd # A2sp Saint Louis MO 63167-0001

FOSTER, SERRIN MARIE, non-profit organization executive; b. Washington, Sept. 17; d. William A. and Donna R. (Hayden) F. BA in Pub. Rels., Old Dominion U., 1977. Freelance pub. rels. specialist Springfield, Va., 1978-82; program mgr., regional rep. St. Jude Children's Rsch. Hosp., Arlington, Va., 1982-89; dir. devel. Nat. Alliance for Mentally Ill., Washington, 1989-94; exec. dir. Feminists for Life of Am., Washington, 1994—; mem. adv. bd. Ivy League Coalition for Life, Harvard U., 1997, Am. Collegians for Life, Washington, 1998. Editor-in-chief, contbr. The Am. Feminist mag., 1994—; contbr. to Boston Globe. Susan B. Anthony List, Alexandria, 1997. Mem. Alpha Phi Women's Found. Avocations: gardening, travel, oil painting. Office: Feminists for Life of Am 733 15th St NW Ste 1100 Washington DC 20005-2112

FOSTER, STEPHEN KENT, banker; b. St. Louis, Dec. 14, 1936; s. John William and Josephine Fladune (Bushman) F.; m. Rosanne Pleier, Sept. 13, 1958; children: John Andrew, Stephanie Mary. B.B.A., U. Wis., 1959, M.B.A. (H.B. Earhart fellow), 1964. Asst. export mgr. Cargill, Inc., Portland, Oreg., 1959-61; with 1st Interstate Bank Oreg. (formerly 1st Nat. Bank Oreg.), Portland, 1964-81, sr. v.p. loan adminstrn., 1973-75, sr. v.p. br. and loan adminstrn., 1975-76, exec. v.p., 1976-81; exec. v.p. First State Bank Oreg. (later Pacific Western Bank), Milwaukie, 1981-82; pres., chief operating officer, dir. Pacific Western Bank, Milwaukie, 1983-86; sr. v.p. Pacwest Bancorp, 1981-83, pres., 1983-86; pres., chief adminstrv. officer Key Bank of Oreg., 1986-89, also bd. dirs., mem. exec. com.; pvt. investor, 1990—; bd. dirs., treas. Lake Oswego Corp.; gov.'s appointment to Oreg. State Banking Bd., 1985, chmn., 1986, mem., 1987-89. Bd. dirs. United Cerebral Palsy of N.W. Oreg., 1967-80; bd. dirs. Oreg. Council on Econ. Edn., 1970-80, Portland Opera Assn., 1970-74, United Way of Columbia-Willamette, 1973-75, Oreg. Ind. Coll. Found., 1983-91, vice chmn., 1985-91, mem. exec. com., 1985-91; bd. regents U. Portland, 1976-88, mem. fin. com., 1976-78, mem. exec. com., 1979-88, chmn. acad. affairs com., 1980-88, chmn. presdl. rev. com., 1981; mem. adv. coun. chair Entrepreneurship, 1998—; trustee St. Vincent's Hosp. Med. Found., 1986-90. Served with U.S. Army, 1958, 61-62. Recipient Service to Legal Edn. award Oreg. Bar Assn., 1971, Ednl. and Service award Bank Adminstrn. Inst., 1971. Mem. Portland C. of C., Oreg. Assn. Credit Mgmt. (Leadership Svc. award 1973), Am. Bankers Assn., Robert Morris Assocs., Am. Fin. Assn., Nat. Assn. Accts. (Ednl. and Svc. award 1971), Arlington Club (bd. dirs. 1986-89, treas. 1987-88, 2d v.p. 1988-90), Univ. Club Portland (bd. dirs. 1986-95, chmn. libr. and reciprocal mems., sec. 1990-91, chmn. membership com. 1991-92, treas. 1992-93, v.p. 1993-94, pres. 1994-95), Waverley Country Club (long-range planning com. 1990-94), Astoria Golf and Country Club, Phi Beta Kappa, Phi Kappa Phi, Phi Eta Sigma, Beta Gamma Sigma, Sigma Chi.

FOSTER, TEREE E., law educator, dean. BA in English Lit., U. Ill., Chgo., 1968; JD, Loyola U., Chgo., 1976. Bar: Ill. 1976, U.S. Dist. Ct. (no. dist.) Ill. 1976, U.S. Dist. Ct. (we. dist.) Okla. 1976, U.S. Ct. Appeals 7th and 10th cirs.) 1983, Okla. 1984. Admissions officer U. Ill., Chgo., 1968-69; co-dir. Dept. Def., Hanau, Germany, 1969-72; intern Office of State Appellate Defender, Springfield, Ill., 1974; law clk. Philip H. Corboy and Assocs., Chgo., 1974-76; instr., teaching asst. Loyola U., Chgo., 1975-77; jud. law clk. U.S Ct. Appeals, Chgo., 1976-77; of counsel Hastie & Kirschner, Oklahoma City, 1984-90; from asst. prof. to assoc. prof. U. Okla., Norman, 1980-83, prof., 1983-93, assoc. dean, 1990-92; dean, prof. law U. W.Va., Morgantown, 1993-97, mem. bd. advisors, 1994-96, facilitator social justice common ground forum, 1994-97; dean, prof. law DePaul U., Chgo., 1997—; vis. prof. U. Denver, 1992-93, U. Fla., 1988-89, Ohio State U., 1987-88; mem. Chgo. com. Chgo. Coun. on Fgn. Rels., 1997—; mem. Chgo. Lawyers Com. for Civil Rights under Law, 1997—. Contbr. articles to profl. jours. Host Perspectives, 1986-87, The Law in Your Life, 1995-97, Legal Lines, 1996-97; co-host Encounter, 1983-85; gov. bd. W.Va. Rape and Domestic Violence Info. Ctr., 1993-97, W.Va. Women's Alliance, 1993-97, Okla. Com. Prevention Child Abuse, 1990-93; instr. Rite Christian Initiation Adults St. Thomas More U., 1983-87; exec. com. Southwest Ctr. Human Rels. Studies, 1983-86, directorship search com., 1984-85; task force Quality of Okla. Life, 1983-84; mem. Chgo. com. Chgo. Coun. on Fgn. Rels., 1997—; mem. Chgo. Com. for Civil Rights Under Law, 1997—. Mem. ABA, Ill. Bar Assn., Soc. Am. Law Tchrs., Assn. Am. Law Schs., Am. Judicature Soc. Home: 851 W Roscoe St Chicago IL 60657-2303 Office: DePaul U Office of Dean College of Law 25 E Jackson Blvd Chicago IL 60604-2289*

FOSTER, VICTOR LYNN, translator; b. Oklahoma City, Jan. 17, 1959; s. William James and Barbara Jean (Langston) F. BA in French Studies, U. Ctrl. Okla., 1995; MA in French Lit., Okla. U., 1999. Mgr. Hardees Food Sys., Oklahoma City, 1987-89; asst. Conseil Regional Auvergne, Clermont-Ferrand, France, 1996-97; translator Jean-Paul Pavlus, Clermont-Ferrand, 1996-97; French tutor, asst. French dept. U. Okla., 1998—. Mem. Kappa Alpha Psi, Kappa Gamma Epsilon (pres. 1998-99, ways and means com. 1998-99). Democrat. Baptist. Avocations: reading, writing, sports. Home: PO Box 11842 Oklahoma City OK 73136-0842

FOSTER, VIRGINIA, retired botany educator; b. Joseph, Oreg., Feb. 4, 1914; d. Perry Alexander and Genevieve (Shain) F. BS, U. Wash., 1949, MS, 1950; PhD, Ohio State U., 1954. Prof. Judson Coll., Marion, Ala., 1956-58; prof. Miss. State Coll. for Women, Columbus, 1958-59, LaVerne (Calif.) Coll., 1959-60, Calif. Western U., San Diego, 1960-61, Pensacola (Fla.) Jr. Coll., 1962-84. Author: (lab. manual) The Botany Laboratory, 1976, rev. edit., 1985, 3d edit., 1991. Avocations: gardening, travel, photography. Home: 9270 Scenic Hwy Pensacola FL 32514-8054

FOSTER, WALTER HERBERT, JR., real estate company executive; b. Belmont, Mass., Nov. 2, 1919; s. Walter Herbert and Gertrude (Sullivan) F.; m. Hazel Campbell, Aug. 7, 1942 (div. July 1979); children: Katherine D., Walter H. III, Stephen C., Banton T.; m. Nedra Ann Thompson, July 3, 1981; 1 child, Timothy John. Student, Harvard U., 1937-38; BS, U. Maine, 1947; grad. in real estate, Tri-State Inst., 1968-70. Cert. gen. appraiser, Maine. Owner, mgr. Foster Bros., Lyndeborough, N.H., 1947-56; ter. sales mgr. Beacon Milling Co., Oakland, Maine, 1956-64; v.p. Sherwood & Foster, Inc., Old Town, Maine, 1964-67; sales rep. Bangor (Maine) Real Estate, 1967-73; chief appraiser James W. Sewall Co., Old Town, 1970-73; mgr. J.F. Singleton Co., Bangor, 1973-80; pres. Coldwell Banker Am. Heritage, Bangor, 1980—; dean Tri-State Inst., 1981; mem. Maine Real Estate Commn., 1987-93, chmn. 1991. Mem. Rep. Nat. Com., Washington, 1980; mem. assessment bd. appeals Old Town, Maine, Holden Assessment Bd. of Appeals; bd. dirs. Penobscot Theatre, 1987-92, treas., 1989, mem. Maine State Bd. Property Rev., 1998. Capt. USAF, 1941-46, USAFR ret., 1966. Mem. Nat. Assn. Realtors (bd. dirs. 1980-81), Maine Assn. Realtors (life, bd. dirs. 1976-80, pres. 1980, Realtor of Yr. 1984), Bangor Bd. Realtors (bd. dirs. 1973-74, pres. 1976, Realtor of Yr. 1976, 84), Maine Real Estate Commn. (chmn. 1991-92), Maine State Bd. Property Tax Review, Commn. to Study Real Estate Appraiser Cert. and Licensing, Nat. Assn. Rev. Appraisers, Am. Assn. Cert. Appraisers, Res. Officers Assn., Appraisal Inst. (assoc.), Nat. Assn. Ind. Fee Appraisers (sr.), Harvard Club of Ea. Maine (treas.), Rotary (bd. dirs. local club), Am. Legion., Ret. Officers Assn. Episcopalian. Avocations: woodworking, gardening. Home: Mistover Dole Hill Rd RR 2 Box 692 East Holden ME 04429-9802 Office: Coldwell Banker Am Heritage 510 Broadway Bangor ME 04401-3468

FOSTER, WALTER HERBERT, III, mechanical and manufacturing engineer, executive; b. Old Town, Maine, Apr. 15, 1945; s. Walter Herbert Jr. and Hazel Gertrude (Campbell) F.; m. Grace Irene Damon Jordon, Jan. 22, 1965 (div. Feb. 1980); 1 child, Walter Herbert IV; m. JoAnn Mary Doherty, Feb. 21, 1996. BSME, U. Maine, 1977; MSME, Worcester Poly. Inst., 1987. Registered profl. engr. Various positions Gen. Electric, Fitchburg, Mass., 1977-80; mgr. engring. support Gen. Electric, Bangor, Maine, 1980-84; sr. engr. turbine devel. Gen. Electric, Fitchburg, 1984-85, sr. engr. Navy programs, 1985; mgr. product assurance Gen. Electric, Bangor, 1986-89; mgr. indsl. product svc. Gen. Electric, Fitchburg, 1989-91, mgr. comml. customer svc., 1991-92; product line mgr. Gen. Electric, Schenectady, 1992-93; sales mgr. Gen. Electric/Power Generation, Schenectady, 1993-95; pres., CEO Foster Steam Turbine Cons. Ltd., Jaffrey, N.H., 1995—, Foster Steam Holding Ltd., Jaffrey, N.H., 1995—, Foster Power Generation Equipment Reapplication, Ltd., Jaffrey, N.H., 1999—. Served with U.S. Army, 1965-69, Korea. Decorated Army Commendation medal. Mem. ASME. Achievements include patent for steam turbine rotor weld repair. Avocations: building, solar energy, masonry, automobiles, computers. Home and Office: 551 Thorndike Pond Rd Jaffrey NH 03452-5150

FOSTER, WENDELL, councilman; b. Elba, Alaska, Feb. 14, 1929; s. Harrison and Annie (Yelberton) Foster; m. Helen Somersall, 1956; children: Rebekah Ann Joy, Helen Diane. Student, Daniel Payne Coll., Armed Forces Edn. Inst., U. Hawaii, Columbia U., Union Theol. Sem. City councilman 16th dist. N.Y.C. Coun., 1978—; chmn. parks, recreation, cultural affairs, internat. intergroup rels., fin., edn., rules and privileges, and election coms. N.Y.C. Coun. Pastor Mount Zion AME Ch., St. John's Ch., Niagara Falls, N.Y., Bethel Ch., Springfield, Mass., Vernon Temple and St. Paul's Ch., Bermuda, British West Indies; sr. mem. United Ch. Christ, Bronx; founder United Black Ch. Appeal & Shepherds Restoration Corp. Ensign USN, 1943-45. Recipient Citizen of Yr. award, Springfield, Mass., 1962. Mem. NAACP, Urban League. Home: 1225 Woodycrest Ave Bronx NY 10452-3743 Office: 1377 Jerome Ave Bronx NY 10452-3325*

FOSTER, WILLIAM ANTHONY, management consultant, educator; b. Washington, Nov. 26, 1929; s. Willard Hill and Evelyn Marie (Serrin) F.; m. Donna Roy Hayden, Feb. 5, 1955 (div. July 1985); children: Serrin M., Donna L., Shickel, Laura A. Valentine; m. Frances Christian Meacham, Dec. 6, 1995. BS in Bus. and Pub. Adminstrn., U. Md., 1956; MSPA, Nova Southeastern U., 1975, DPA, 1977. Registered profl. engr., Calif. Dir. indsl. engring. Washington region U.S. Postal Svc., 1969-71, mgr. indsl. engring. and plant maintenance Ea. Region, 1971-72; mgr. indsl. engring. U.S. Postal Svc., Washington, 1972-80, nat. coord., 1980-83, program mgr. tng., 1983-86; pres., educator, trainer, cons. William A. Foster Assoc., Washington, 1986—; educator, trainer, cons. U.S. Postal Svc., Washington, 1983-86, Embry-Riddle U., Daytona Beach, Fla., 1993, U. D.C., Washington, 1977-83, Southeastern U., 1980; dir., mgr. ops. U.S. Postal Svc., Washington, 1962-83. Author exec. tng. books; moderator TV show (Inaugural award 1991). Charter mem. Charleston Assn., Springfield, Va., 1968-84. Mem. ASTD (com. mem. 1986—), Am. Inst. Indsl. Engrs. (govt. liaison 1976-80, Nat. award for excellence 1969), Am. Soc Pub. Adminstrn. (cons. 1980-84), D.C. Coun. Engring. and Archtl. Socs. (chmn., PBS chair 1979-81, Outstanding Svc. award 1981, Bicentennial Engring. and Archtl. award 1976). Republican. Roman Catholic. Avocations: public speaking, American history, family, travel. Home: 1441 Northgate Sq Apt 12B Reston VA 20190-3754

FOSTER, WILLIAM EDWIN (BILL FOSTER), nonprofessional basketball coach; b. Ridley Park, Pa., Aug. 19, 1930; s. Howard M. and Viola Jane (Beaston) F.; m. Shirley Ann Junkin, June 17, 1957; children: Vicki R., Debra Jo, Julia Ann, Mary K. BS, Elizabethtown Coll., 1954; MEd, Temple U., 1957. Coach, tchr. Chichester (Pa.) High Sch., 1954-57, Abington (Pa.) High Sch., 1957-60; coach, instr. Bloomsburg (Pa.) State Coll., 1960-63; head basketball coach Rutgers U., New Brunswick, N.J., 1963-71, U. Utah, Salt Lake City, 1971-74; head basketball coach, asst. athletic dir. Duke U., Durham, N.C., 1974-80, U. S.C., Columbia, 1980-86; head basketball coach, interim athletic dir. Northwestern U., Evanston, Ill., 1986-93, athletic dir., 1993; assoc. commr. S.W. Conf., Dallas, 1993-96; pres. BF Sports Ltd., Carrollton, Tex., 1996-98; cons. Com. of Big 12 Conf. for basketball, 1996—; chmn. of the bd. Naismith Meml. Basketball Hall of Fame; pres. Nat. Sports Video Seminars; cons. to commr. of Big 12 for Basketball. Served with USAF, 1951-52. Named Nat. Coach of Yr., Sporting News Playboy Mag.,

1978, S.C. Coach of Yr., 1981; named to Elizabethtown Coll. Sports Hall of Fame, Pa., Pa. Sports Hall of Fame, Rutgers Basketball Hall of Fame, Delaware County (Pa.) Hall of Fame. Mem. Nat. Assn. Basketball Coaches (past pres., co-coach of yr. 1978), Nat. Speakers Assn. Fax: 972-323-6341. Office: BF Sports Ltd 1080 E Sandy Lake Rd S # 74 Coppell TX 75019

FOSTER, WILLIAM SILAS, JR., minister; b. Kansas City, Mo., Nov. 5, 1939; s. William Silas and Edna LaResta (Scott) F.; m. Susan Jean Mannle, June 5, 1983; children Robert Light, Beth Light, Stacey Light; children from previous marriage, Beth Ann, Amy Lynne. BA, Mo. Valley Coll., 1962; MDiv, McCormick Sem., 1966. Ordained to ministry Presbyn. Ch. (USA), 1966. Asst. min. 1st Presbyn. Ch., Edwardsville, Ill., 1966-68; min. St. Paul's Presbyn. Ch., St. Louis, 1968-71, Moro (Ill.) Presbyn. Ch., 1971-83; min. 1st Presbyn. Ch., North Kansas City, Mo., 1983-84, Worland, Wyo., 1985—; commr. to Gen. Assembly Presbyn. Ch. (U.S.A), Omaha, Balt., Albuquerque, 1973, 91, 95; stated clk. Presbytery Wyo., Casper, 1990—, Com. of the Office of Gen. Assembly; instr. calligraphy Synod Sch., 1982-83; pres. Presbyn. Alcohol Info. Network, 1982-83, Ill. Impact Bd., 1983. Resource person 1980 Youth Triennium, Bloomington, Ind., 1980; bd. dirs. Edwardsville Sch. Bd., 1976-83, Mental Bd. Washakie County, 1989—. Recipient M. Keith Upson award U.S. Jaycees, 1974; named Outstanding New Mem., Ill. Jaycees, 1972, Outstanding Mem., 1973. Mem. Lions (2d v.p. 1989-91). Home: 1515 Yellowstone Ave Worland WY 82401-2206 Office: 1st Presbyn Ch PO Box 53 Worland WY 82401-0053 *In the 21st Century, we are called as Abraham to live on a wilderness frontier of life. This radically unique environment demands creative risks and personal ethical choices. Listening to one another's wilderness journeys, learning from each other and supporting others are the keys for genuine faith, hope and love in the future.*

FOTA, FRANK GEORGE, artist; b. Northampton, Pa., Feb. 20, 1921; s. Frank Michael and Elizabeth Rose (Simko)F.; m. Christine June Ringwald, Oct. 18, 1947. Student, Chgo. Acad. of Fine Art, 1951-53. Artist Studio Maintained in Residence, S. Holland, Ill.; comml. artist, designer Triangle Outdoor Advt. Co., Chgo., 1956-61, Gen. Outdoor Advt. Co., Chgo., 1961-63; art dir. Triangle Outdoor Advt. Co., Chgo., 1963-83. Artist: (paintings) The Juniper Tree, 1971, Moab, Utah, 1974, Give Us This Day, Crete, Ill., 1972; exhibits include Wally Findlay Gallery, Chgo., 1953, 54, 55, Richard H. Love Gallery, Steger, Ill., Olympia Fields, Ill., Chgo., 1973, 74, 75, others. Mem., photographer Dolton (Ill.) Civic Assn., 1983-85. Roman Catholic. Clubs: Veteran of Foreign Wars, Dolton, Ill. (Trustee), Am. Legion, Riverdale, Ill. (Photog.). Avocations: photography, music. Home: 16748 Clyde Ave South Holland IL 60473-2611

FOTH, BOB, Olympic athlete, riflery. Olympic shooter Barcelona, Spain, 1992, Seoul, Korea, 1988, Atlanta, 1996. Recipient Shooting Silver medal Olympics, Barcelona, 1992. Office: USA Shooting One Olympic Plaza Colorado Springs CO 80909*

FOTI, MARGARET ANN, association executive, publisher, editor; b. Phila., Dec. 15, 1944; d. Samuel A. and Margaret M. (DiBiase) F. B.A., Temple U., 1975, M.A. in Communications, 1985, PhD in Comm., 1995. Tech. editor U. Pa., Phila., 1962-64, asst. to bus adminstr., 1964-65; sr. editorial asst. Cancer Rsch. Jour., Phila., 1965-69, mng. editor, 1969—; CEO, Am. Assn. Cancer Rsch., Phila., 1982—, pub., 1999—; adminstrn., pub. edn., devel., editorial and pub. cons., lectr. in field. Contbr. articles to profl. jours. Pres. Nat. Coalition for Cancer Rsch., 1994-96. Recipient cert. of appreciation Am. Assn. Cancer Rsch., 1975, 85, 90. Mem. AAAS, Am. Soc. Assn. Execs., Am. Assn. Cancer Rsch., European Assn. Cancer Rsch., European Assn. Sci. Editors, Internat. Fedn. Sci. Editors, Soc. Sch. Publs., Soc. for Scholarly Publs. (pres. 1996-97), Coun. Biology Editors (pres. 1980-81), Coun. Engrs. and Sci. Soc. Execs. Democrat. Roman Catholic. Home: 220 Locust St Apt 24A Philadelphia PA 19106-3932 Office: Am Assn Cancer Rsch Ste 826 150 S Independence Mall W Philadelphia PA 19106-3483

FOTOPOULOS, DANIELLE, soccer player; b. Camp Hill, Pa., Mar. 24, 1976. Student, U. Fla. mem. U.S. Nat. Women's Soccer Team, 1996—. Recipient Southeastern Conf. Player of Yr. award 1996; appeared twice in Faces in the Crowd, Sports Illustrated. Office: US Soccer Fedn 1801-1811 S Prairie Ave Chicago IL 60616*

FOTOPOULOS, SOPHIA STATHOPOULOS, medical scientist, administrator; b. Kansas City, Mo., Nov. 6, 1936; d. Marinos G. and Stavroula (Fotopoulos) Stathopoulos; m. Chris K. Fotopoulos, Aug. 27, 1963 (div.). BA, U. Kans., 1958, MA, 1964, PhD, 1970. Diplomate Behavioral Scis. Regulatory Bd. State of Kans., Council for Nat. Register of Health Svc. Providers. Rsch. asst. U. Kans. Med. Ctr., Kansas City, 1958-61; rsch. assoc. Inst. Cmty. Studies, Kansas City, Mo., 1965-66; lectr. U. Kans., Lawrence, 1969-70; dir. Psychophysiology-pharmacology Lab. Greater Kansas City (Mo.) Mental Health Found., 1970-73; staff assoc. neuropsychophysiology, 1973, Midwest Rsch. Inst., Kansas City, Mo., 1974-75, sr. scientist, head Psychophysiology Lab., 1975-77, assoc. dir. chem. scis. div., 1977-79, dir. life scis. div., 1979-84; dean, dir. rsch. Am. U., Washington, 1984-87; exec. v.p., CEO Immucomp, Inc., 1987-92; pres., CEO Bioactive Tech., 1992—. rsch. prof. dept. medicine Kansas U. Med. Ctr., 1987—; spl. rev. com. Nat. Cancer Inst., 1978—; mem. adv. com. Am. Cancer Soc., 1982-96; lectr. U. Mo.-Kansas City Sch. Medicine, 1970-84. NIH research fellow, 1962-64, HHS research fellow, 1965-69; recipient Creative Scientist award Am. Inst. Research, 1971. Mem. AAAS, Claude Bernard Soc., Internat. Soc. for Antiviral Rsch., N.Y. Acad. Scis., Biofeedback Soc. Am., Mo. Biofeedback Soc. (pres. 1979-80), Sigma Xi. Greek Orthodox. Clubs: Zonta Internat. (pres. KCII 1983-85). Contbr. articles to profl. jours. and books. Office: Bioactive Tech 8433 Quivira Rd Lenexa KS 66215-2802

FOTSCH, DAN ROBERT, elementary education educator; b. St. Louis, May 17, 1947; s. Robert Jarrel and Margaret Louise (Zimmermann) F.; m. Jacquelyn Sue Rotter, June 12, 1971; children: Kyla Michelle, Jeffrey Scott, Michael David. BS in Edn. cum laude, U. Mo., 1970; MS in Edn., Colo. State U., 1973. Cert. K-12 phys. edn. and health tchr. Mo., Colo. Tchr. phys. edn., coach North Callaway Schs., Auxvasse, Mo., 1970-71; grad. teaching asst., asst. track coach Colo. State U., Ft. Collins, 1971-73; tchr. elem. phys. edn., coach Poudre R-1 Sch. Dist., Ft. Collins, 1973—; tchr. on spl. assignment Elem. Phys. Edn. Resource, 1990; adminstrv. asst. Moore Sch., Ft. Collins, 1990—, acting prin., 1997; tchr. on spl. assignment dist. phys. edn. coord. Moore Sch., 1998, k-12 coord. dist. phys. edn., 1998—; co-dir. Colo. State U. Handicapped Clinic, Ft. Collins, 1973-93; dir. Moore Elem. Lab. Sch., Ft. Collins, 1979—; dir. Colo. State U. Super Day Camp, 1979—; presenter for conf. in field. Contbr. articles to profl. jours. State dir. Jump Rope for Heart Project, Denver, 1981. Recipient Scott Key Acad. award, Sigma Phi Epsilon, 1969, Honor Alumni award, Coll. of Profl. Studies of Colo. State U., 1983; grantee Colo. Heart Assn., 1985; recipient Coaching Excellence award Ft. Collins Soccer Club, 1991-92. Mem. NEA, AAHPERD (exec. bd. mem. coun. on phys. edn. for children 1983-86, reviewer Jour. Phys. Edn., Recreation and Dance 1984—, fitness chairperson, conv. planner 1986), ASCD, Poudre Edn. Assn., Colo. Edn. Assn., Colo. Assn. Health, Phys. Edn., Recreation and Dance (pres. 1979-82, Tchr. award 1977, Honor award 1985), Internat. Platform Assn., Ctrl. Dist. Alliance for Health, Phys. Edn., Recreation and Dance (elem. divsn. chairperson for phys. edn. 1989—), Phi Delta Kappa (found. rep. 1985), Phi Epsilon Kappa (v.p. 1969, pres. 1970). Republican. Avocations: marathons, triathlons, racketball, volleyball, swimming (Colo. State Swimming Championship Village Green Team, 1987, 89). Home: 2807 Blackstone Dr Fort Collins CO 80525-6190 Office: Moore Elem Sch 1905 Orchard Pl Fort Collins CO 80521-3210

FOUCHARD, JOSEPH JAMES, retired government agency administrator; b. Chgo., June 6, 1928; s. Joseph Narcisse and Nell Gladys (Rowe) F.; m. Martha Jean Swiney, Aug. 20, 1950; children: James M., Melissa A., Lisa E. BS in Journalism, U. Ill., 1950. Asst. news editor Champaign-Urbana Courier, Urbana, Ill., 1953-56; chief copy editor Globe-Democrat, St. Louis, 1957-60; info. officer U.S. AEC, Washington, 1960-65, asst. dir. pub. info., 1966-74; asst. dir. U.S. NRC, Washington, 1975-78, dir. pub. affairs, 1978-94, pub. affairs counsel, 1994—; pub. affairs advisor Pres.' Task Force on Chernobyl Reactor Accident, Washington, 1986, U.S. Del. to Conf. on Chernobyl Accident, Vienna, Austria, 1986, Internat. Conf. on Nuclear Info., Paris, 1993; dir. NRC info. activities Three Mile Island Reactor Accident, 1979. 1st lt. U.S. Army, 1950-53. Recipient Presdl. Meritorious Sr. Exec. award Pres. Reagan, 1988, Presdl. Disting. Sr. Exec. award Pres. Bush, 1992. Presbyterian. Home: 4840 Flower Valley Dr Rockville MD 20853-1627

FOUCHEUX, RICHARD, actor, artist; b. Houma, La., Aug. 18, 1954; s. O.J. and Yvonne (Domangue) F.; m. Mary Jeanne Jacobsen, Nov. 19, 1977; children: Joanna Clay, Nina Marie. BA, Nicholls State U., 1976. Announcer KHOM-FM, Houma, 1971-76; TV host/prodr. KALB-TV, Alexandria, La., 1976, WOWK-TV, Huntington, W.Va., 1977-78, KTVK-TV, Phoenix, 1979-82; TV host WJLA-TV, Washington, 1982-83; actor/artist Washington, 1983—; v.p. A. Salon, Washington, 1992-93; prodr. U.S. Info. Agy., Washington, 1998—. Appeared in theatrical prodns. including An Ideal Husband, Romeo and Juliet, Much Ado About Nothing, The Cherry Orchard, The Death of Humpty Dumpty, 1992 (Mary Goldwater award 1992); exhbited in group shows, 1990—. Mem. Screen Actors Guild, Am. Fedn. TV and Radio Artists, Actors Equity Assn. FAX: 301-589-5974. Home: 2912 Woodstock Ave Silver Spring MD 20910 Office: 2912 Woodstock Ave Silver Spring MD 20910

FOUDREE, BRUCE WILLIAM, lawyer; b. Des Moines, Mar. 27, 1947; s. Shie Wilbur and Dorothy Mable (Lynde) F.; m. Suzanne Joan Floss Reade, May 31, 1986; children: Andrew A., Grant R. BA, Drake U., 1969; student, U. Geneva, Switzerland, 1968, U. Vienna, Austria, 1968; JD, Drake U., 1972; LLM, U. Pa., 1975. Bar: Iowa 1972, U.S. Ct. Appeals (8th cir.) 1976, U.S. Supreme Ct. 1977, Ill. 1986. Asst. atty. gen. Iowa Dept. Justice, Des Moines, 1976-80; ins. commnr. Iowa Ins. Dept., Des Moines, 1980-86; of counsel Mitchell, Williams, Selig and Tucker, Little Rock, 1986-88; shareholder Keck, Mahin & Cate, Chgo., 1988-96; ptnr. Lord, Bissell & Brook, Chgo., 1996—; commr., chmn. Iowa Ins. Dept., 1980-86; commr. Iowa Health Data Commn., 1983-86, chmn. 1985. *Business insurance lawyer providing advice and representation on a wide variety of corporate and regulatory matters. Experience includes counseling in complex litigation involving insurance issues and advising clients on multi-state and alternative-market insurance programs.* Assoc. editor Drake Law Rev., 1971-72; dir. Jour. Ins. Regulation, 1982-89. Mem. ABA (TIPS scope and correlation com. 1991-94, chmn. fin. svcs. com. 1990-91, professionalism com. 1994-96), Nat. Assn. Ins. Commrs. (chmn. 1984, pres. 1985), Ins. Regulatory Examiners Soc. Found. (bd. dirs. 1991—, chmn), Iowa State Bar Assn., Union League Club of Chgo. (chmn. ins. group 1989-92), The Chicago Lighthouse (bd. dirs. 1995—, sec.). Avocations: travel, history, literature, music. Office: Lord Bissell & Brook 115 S La Salle St Ste 3600 Chicago IL 60603-3972

FOUDREE, CHARLES M., financial executive. BS in Acctg., Truman State U., 1966. CPA, Kans., Mo. Mem. audit staff Peat Marwick Mitchell & Co., Kansas City; CFO, Harmon Industries, Inc., Blue Springs, Mo., 1972—; bd. dirs. Harmon Industries, Inc., Blue Springs; bd. dirs. OTR Express, Inc., Olathe, Kans. Past chmn. bd. assocs. St. Mary's Hosp., Blue Springs; bd. dirs. Harry S. Truman Libr. Inst., treas., Truman State U. Found.; trustee St. paul Sch. Theology, Kansas City, Mo. Mem. AICPA, Mo. Soc. CPAs, Fin. Execs. Inst. (bd. dirs., past pres. Kansas City chpt., nat. bd. dirs. 1995-98), Inst. Mgmt. Accts., Independence C. of C. (past dir., treas.), Rotary, Blue Key, Sigma Tau Gamma. Home: 4124 NE Pembroke Ln Lees Summit MO 64064-1622 Office: Harmon Industries Inc 1600 NE Coronado Dr Blue Springs MO 64014

FOUDY, JULIA MAURINE, soccer player; b. San Diego, Jan. 23, 1971; m. Ian Sawyers, July 1995. BSW in Biology, Stanford U., 1993. Mem. U.S. Women's Nat. Soccer Team; color commentator Men's World Cup, ESPN, 1998. Mem. Tyresco Football Club, Sweden,m 1994. Appeared on cover Women's Soccer World mag., 1997; recipient Gold medal Centennial Olympic Games, 1996; mem. championship team World Championships, Sweden, 1995, CONCACAF, Montreal, 1994. Office: c/o US Soccer Fedn 1801 S Prairie Ave # 1811 Chicago IL 60616-1357

FOULADVAND, HENGAMEH, artist; b. Tehran, Iran; naturalized U.S. citizen, 1974; d. Mansour and Mahin F.; m. Masoud B. Mansouri, Feb. 20, 1981; 1 child, Tia. BA, San Jose State U., 1976; master's degree, Calif. State U., 1979. Exec. dir. Ctr. Iranian Modern Arts, 1998-99; art cons. T.H.E. Graphics & Design, 1990-96; graphic & prodn. cons. Metro Lables, 1994-96; exec. dir. Ctr. for Iranian Moderan Arts, 1998-99. Exhibited in solo and group shows including Columbia U., N.Y.C., 1989, L.I. U., 1989, 91, Strathmore Arts Ctr., Md., 1991, Port Washington Pub. Libr., 1991, Huntington Arts Coun., Hecksher Mus., 1993, 95, McArthur Airport Terminal Bldg., L.I., 1996-97, Columbia U., Hamilton Bldg., N.Y.C., 1997, Lindberg Gallery, N.Y.C., 1999, GORA Gallery, Montreal, 1999; represented in permanent collections Ency. Iranica Found., N.Y., Line & Tone Typographics, N.Y., numerous pvt. collections. Mem. N.Y. State Coun. Arts, N.Y. Found. Arts, Huntington Art League and Coun. Long Island. E-mail: the3dimas@aol.com. Home: 301 E 19th St Huntington Station NY 11746-3311

FOULKE, EDWIN GERHART, JR., lawyer; b. Perkasie, Pa., Oct. 30, 1952; s. Edwin G. and Mary Claire (Keller) F. BA, N.C. State U., 1974; JD, Loyola U., New Orleans, 1978; LLM, Georgetown U., 1993. Bar: S.C. 1979, U.S. Dist. Ct. S.C. 1979, U.S. Ct. Appeals (4th cir.) 1979, Ga. 1986, U.S. Ct. Appeals (11th cir.) 1986, D.C. 1989, U.S. Ct. Appeals (D.C. cir.) 1989, U.S. Supreme Ct. 1990, N.C. 1997. Assoc. Thompson, Mann & Hutson, Greenville, S.C., 1978-83, Rainey, Britton, Gibbes & Clarkson, Greenville, 1983-85; ptnr. Constangy, Brooks & Smith, Columbia, S.C., 1985-90; chmn. Occupational Safety and Health Rev. Commn., Washington, 1990-95; ptnr. Jackson Lewis, Greenville, S.C., 1995—; instr. St. Mary's Dominican Coll., New Orleans, 1977-78. Field rep. Reagan/Bush Campaign, Columbia, 1980, S.C. state coord., 1984; sec., treas. Employment Labor Law Sect., Columbia, 1981-82. Mem. ABA, S.C. Bar Assn., Ga. Bar Assn., Greenville County Bar Assn. (chmn. pub. rels. com. 1984-85), SAR, Rotary. Roman Catholic. Avocations: swimming, tennis, skiing, golf. Office: Jackson Lewis & Krupman 301 N Main St Ste 2100 Greenville SC 29601-2122

FOULKE, ROBERT DANA, English educator, travel writer; b. Mpls., Apr. 25, 1930; s. Robert William and Bertha Almeda (Peterson) F.; m. Patricia Ann Nelson, Dec. 29, 1953; children: David William, Carolyn Denise, Deborah Ann. AB, Princeton U., 1952; MA, U. Minn., 1957, PhD, 1961. Instr. English U. Minn., Mpls., 1956-61; asst. prof. English Trinity Coll., Hartford, Conn., 1961-66, assoc. prof. English, 1966-70; prof. English Skidmore Coll., Saratoga Springs, N.Y., 1970-92, chmn. dept. English, 1970-80, dir. NEH grant, 1981-83; scholar, writer, 1992—; vis. prof. Sea Edn. Assn., Woods Hole, Mass., 1980, 83, mem. corp., 1990—; vis. prof. Williams-Mystic (Conn.) Program, 1982, Regents Coll., London, 1989; vis. assoc., life mem. Clare Hall, Cambridge (Eng.) U., 1976-77, 90-91; vis. fellow dept. English Princeton U., 1988. Author, co-editor: An Anatomy of Literature, 1972; author: Europe Inder Canvas, 1980, Fielding's Motoring and Camping Europe, 1986, Daytrips, Getaway Weekends and Vacations in New England, 1983, 88, 91, 94, 97, 99, Daytrips, Getaway Weekends and Vacations in the Mid-Atlantic States, 1986, 89, 93, 96, 99, Exploring Europe by Car, 1991, Fielding's The Great Sights of Europe, 1992, Fielding Worldwide, 1994, A Guife to Colonial America, 1995, The Sea Voyage Narrative, 1997, Romantic Weekends: New England, 1998; co-author: (with Patricia Foulke) Colonial America, 1995, also 7 other travel guides on Europe and Am., 1980-99; script writer, host (TV series) Sailing with Confidence, 1989; co-editor: The Writer's Mind, 1983. Dir. The Lake George Club, Diamond Point, N.Y., 1977-82, commodore, 1981-82; elder First Presbyn. Ch., Glens Falls, N.Y., 1982—; trustee Glens Falls Hist. Assn., 1988-93; exec. com. Black Watch Coun., N.Y.C., 1993-96. Fulbright fellow U. London, 1959-60, Alexander O. Vietor fellow John Carter Brown Libr., Brown U., 1993. Mem. MLA, Am. Soc. Journalists and Authors, N.Am. Soc. Oceanic History (exec. coun. 1995—), N.Am. Snowsports Journalists Assn., Soc. Am. Travel Writers, N.Am. Snowsports Journalists Assn., Travel Journalists Guild, Coll. English Assn. (dir. 1981-84), Travel Journalists Guild, Lake George Rotary Club (dir. 1984-86, 98—). Presbyterian. Avocations: sailing, skiing, canoeing, heritage travel, cruises. Home and Office: 25 Dark Bay Ln Lake George NY 12845

FOULKE, WILLIAM GREEN, retired banker; b. Whitemarsh, Pa., Nov. 20, 1912; s. Walter Longfellow and Helen (Pardee) F.; m. Louisa Lawrence Wood, Nov. 2, 1934; children: Louisa Lawrence Foulke Newlin, Walter Longfellow, William Green. A.B., Princeton U., 1934. Asst. treas. Provident Trust Co., Phila., 1940-41; trust officer Provident Trust Co., 1945-50, v.p., 1950-57; sr. v.p. charge trust div. Provident Tradesmens Bank and Trust Co., Phila., 1957-60; exec. v.p. Provident Tradesmens Bank and Trust Co., 1960-62, pres., 1962-64; pres. Provident Nat. Bank, Phila., 1964-69; chmn. chief exec. officer Provident Nat. Bank, 1969-74; chmn., chief exec. officer Provident Nat. Corp., 1969-73, chmn., 1973-74; ret. Gen. chmn. United Campaign, 1975. Served to lt. comdr. USNR, 1941-45. Mem. Pa. Bankers Assn. (pres. 1970-71). Episcopalian. Clubs: Racquet; Ivy (Princeton). Home: 321 Evergreen Ave Philadelphia PA 19118

FOULKES, JULIA LAWRENCE, historian; b. Rochester, N.Y., Dec. 18, 1964; d. Thomas Schuyler and Anne Schley (Fitch) F. BA, Williams Coll., 1986; MA, Loyola U., Chgo., 1991; PhD, U. Mass., 1997. Pres. The Museum Group, Chgo., 1988-91; instr. John Jay Coll., N.Y.C., 1995; postdoctoral fellow Ctr. for Black Music Rsch., Chgo., 1997-98; instr. Bennington Coll., 1997-99; core faculty BA program New Sch. U., N.Y.C. Contbr. articles to Am. Jewish History, Dance Rsch. Jour., Am. Hist. Rev., others. Grantee Houghton Libr./Harvard U., 1997, Newberry Libr., Chgo., 1997, Rockefeller Archive Ctr., Tarrytown, N.Y., 1997; Am. Jewish Archives fellow, 1995. Mem. Am. Studies Assn. (Annete K. Baxter travel award 1995), Soc. Dance History Scholars (Selma Jeanne Cohen award 1994-95), Congress on Rsch. in Dance.

FOUNTAIN, ANDRE FERCHAUD, academic program director; b. Oklahoma City, Nov. 12, 1951; s. J. E. and Neaumatta Abilene (Edwards) F.; m. Linda K. Young. BS in Nursing, U. Okla., 1978. RN, Okla; cert. master hyrdotherapist, Kniepp Inst., Germany, massage therapist. Exec. dir. New Life Programs, Oklahoma City, 1981-87; dir. Praxis Coll. Health, Arts and Scis., Oklahoma City, 1988—; speaker in field. Author: A Psychoprophylactic Workbook, 1981; co-author: Psychological Reports, 1977. Found. Caucus for Men in Nursing, Norman, 1976. Recipient 1st Pl. award Internat. Sci. Fair Balt., 1970; honored for Oklahoma City bombing vol. work, U.S. Dept. Justice. Mem. Internat. Childbirth Edn. Assn. (state coord. 1982-84), Am. Soc. Psychoprophylaxis in Obstetrics, Body Workers and Wellness Therapies Assn., Okla. Sports Massage Assn., Masons.

FOUNTAIN, EDWIN BYRD, minister, educator, librarian, poet; b. Manassas, Ga., Mar. 11, 1930; s. David Theodore and Laura Bertha (Phillips) F. BFA, U. Ga., 1951; BRE, ThB, Lexington Bapt. Coll., 1980, MRE, 1981, DD (hon.), 1990; MLS, U. Ky., 1984; PhD in Edn., Am. Bible Coll. and Seminary, 1998. Ordained to ministry Bapt. Ch., 1982. Pastor Riverview Bapt. Ch., Lexington, Ky., 1982-87; libr. asst. Lexington Bapt. Coll., 1980-81, tchr., libr., 1981-90; divisional chmn. libr. svcs. Tenn. Temple U., Chattanooga, 1990-91; librarian Statesboro (Ga.) Regional Libr., 1991-93. Author: The Sovereignty and Rightousness of God, 1997; compiler indexes for religious books: (by B.H. Carroll) An Interpretation of the English Bible, (by T.P. Simmons) A Systematick Study of Bible Doctrine, (with Jim Jeffries) A Student's Writers Guide; contbr. articles to profl. publs., poetry to anthologies. U. Ky. fellow, 1990. Mem. ALA, SAG, SAR (local sec.), S.R., SCV, Christians Librs. Assn., Actors Equity Assn., Bulloch County Hist. Soc., Darlington County Hist. Soc., Lexington Bapt. Coll. Alumni Assn. (pres. 1982-87, 89-90), Armstrong State Coll. Alumni Assn., Beta Phi Mu. Home: 2365 Womack Rd E Garfield GA 30425-4208

FOUNTAIN, ELIZABETH BEAN, home economist, musician, philanthropist; b. Washington, Apr. 16, 1932; d. Louis Hyman and Dorothy May (Wile) Bean; m. Robert Roy Fountain, June 4, 1955; children: Robert, Dorothy, Sally, Edwin. BA in English, U. Rochester, 1954; BS in Music Performance, Old Dominion U., 1976. Sec. Speedwriting Sch., Washington, 1954-55; counselor, advisor YWCA, San Diego, 1955-56; sec. Humphrey, Inc., San Diego, 1956-57; tchr. B.F. Williams Elem. Sch., Norfolk County, Va., 1957-58; pvt. piano tchr. Va., Conn., Guam, 1970-81; sec. State Dept. Adv. Panel on Security, Washington, 1984-86. Vice pres. Rappahannock (Va.) Cmty. Concert Assn., 1994—; mem. Rappahannock Music Study Group, 1995—. Mem. Naval Officers Wives Club (pres. 1983-84), Friday Morning Music Club. (sec. 1994-96), Sigma Alpha Iota (People-to-People project dir., 1993—, pres. D.C. alumni chpt. 1991-93). Avocations: music, gardening, reading. Home: 4750 Zacata Rd Montross VA 22520-3510

FOUNTAIN, JANE ELLEN, public policy educator; b. Medford, Mass., Feb. 8, 1955; d. Anthony Aloysius and Matilda Viola (D'Alessandro) F.; m. Michael Anthony Serio, July 5, 1981; children: Elena Fountain Serio, Emily Fountain Serio. BMus cum laude, Boston Conservatory Music, 1977; EdM, Harvard U., 1982; MA, Yale U., 1986, MPhil, 1988, PhD, 1990. Instr. Kennedy Sch. govt. Harvard U., Cambridge, Mass., 1989-91, asst. prof., 1991-96, assoc. prof., 1996—. Co-editor: Proposition 2 1/2: Its Impact on Massachusetts, 1983; contbg. author: Customer Service Excellence, 1992, Investing in Innovation, 1997; mem. editl. adv. bd. Informatization and the Pub. Sector, 1992-95. Mem. Am. Polit. Sci. Assn. (mem.-at-large exec. com. sect. 12 1997—), Assn. Pub. Policy and Mgmt., Acad. Mgmt. Democrat. Office: Harvard U Kennedy Sch Govt 79 Jfk St Cambridge MA 02138-5801*

FOUNTAIN, KAREN SCHUELER, physician; b. Aberdeen, S.D., Oct. 14, 1947. BA, No. State Coll., Aberdeen, S.D., 1968; MD, U. Md., Balt., 1972. Diplomate Nat. Bd. Med. Examiners, Am. Bd. Radiology in Therapeutic Radiology. Intern Md. Gen. Hosp., Balt., 1972-73, resident in radiation oncology, 1973-74; fellow in radiation oncology Mayo Clinic, Rochester, Minn., 1974-76, cons. in oncology, 1976-81; clin. asst. prof. Columbia U., N.Y.C., 1981-83, residency program dir. dept. radiation oncology, 1981-93, clin. assoc. prof., 1983—; mem. med. bd. Presbyn. Hosp., N.Y.C., 1983-86; faculty coun. mem. Columbia U., 1982-89; del. N.Y. State Radiological Soc., N.Y.C., 1987—. Fellow Am. Coll. Radiology (councilor 1999—), N.Y. Acad. Medicine; mem. Am. Soc. Therapeutic Radiology and Oncology, Radiol. Soc. N.Am., Am. Radium Soc., Am. Soc. Clin. Oncology, Am. Assn. for Women Radiologists (bd. dirs. 1995-96), N.Y. Roentgen Soc. (sect. chmn. 1989-90), N.Y. State Radiol. Soc. (bd. dirs. 1996—). Office: Columbia-Presbyn Med Ctr Rad Onc 622 W 168th St New York NY 10032-3720

FOUNTAIN, LINDA KATHLEEN, health science association executive; b. Fowler, Kans., Apr. 30, 1954; d. Ralph Edward and Ruth Evelyn (Cornelson) Young; m. Andre Fountain. BS in Nursing, Cen. State U., Edmond, Okla., 1976. RN, Okla. Staff nurse med./surg. and coronary care unit Presbyn. Hosp., Oklahoma City, 1976-79; mgr. nursing Hillcrest Osteo. Hosp., Oklahoma City, 1979-80; staff nurse, mgr. Oklahoma U. Teaching Hosp., Oklahoma City, 1981-82; pres. New Life Programs, Oklahoma City, 1981-88, Nursing Entrepreneurs, Ltd., Oklahoma City, 1988—; mgr. Internat. Health Supply, Oklahoma City, 1988—; coord. lactation cons. program State of Okla., 1981-98, new life car seat rental program at various hosps., 1983-92, also speaker Success Co., Oklahoma City, 1984—; owner Rainbows Overhead Graphic Media, Oklahoma City, 1984-91; speaker in field. Founder Praxis Coll., Oklahoma City, 1988. Named Mentor of Yr., Okla. Metroplex Childbirth Network, Oklahoma City, 1984; honored for vol. work with families and rescue after Oklahoma City bombing, U.S. Dept. Justice, 1995. Mem. Am. Nurses Assn., Internat. Lactation Cons. Assn., Internat. Platform Assn., Bodyworkers and Wellness Therapies Assn. Avocations: gemology, travel.

FOUNTAIN, ROBERT ALLEN, organizational management executive; b. Toledo, Nov. 19, 1947; s. Ellis Allen Fountain and Florence Delores (Hay) Stump; m. Mary Ann Buckmaster, Mar. 7, 1975 (div.); children: Donna, Meredith; m. Clare Bradshaw, Dec. 5, 1993. AS, State Tech. Inst., 1987; BS summa cum laude, Tusculum Coll., 1989. Quality controller Burroughs Corp. (UNISYS), Holland, Ohio, 1969-73, field service rep., 1973-78, internat. traffic analyst and specialist, 1978-81; gen. traffic mgr. Buckman Labs., Inc., Memphis, 1981-85, mgr. transp. and credit adminstrn., 1985-90, spl. projects mgr., 1990—; Past master of Tipton # 226 Free & Accepted Masons (F&AM); owner De'Novo Decorating and Design. Author computer programs. With USN, 1967-69. Recipient Cert. honor Internat. Trade Mart, 1983, Acad. Excellence award State Tech. Inst.; named Hon. Harbor Master of Port of New Orleans Bd. Commrs. of Port of New Orleans, 1983. Mem. State Tech. Inst. Alumni Assn. (v.p. 1988-89), Tenn. Grand Lodge of F&AM, Phi Theta Kappa (v.p. 1986-87). Republican. Avocations: painting, carpentry. Home: 301 Yarbrough Rd Covington TN 38019 Office: Buckman Labs Inc 1256 N Mclean Blvd Memphis TN 38108-1241

FOUNTAIN, ROBERT ROY, JR., farmer, industrial executive, naval officer; b. Norfolk, Va., Jan. 25, 1932; s. Robert Roy and Hilda (Burton) F.; m. Elizabeth Whitmarsh Bean, June 4, 1955; children: Robert, Dorothy, Sally, Edwin. Student, U. Rochester, 1950-51; B.S. Engring. with distinction, U.S. Naval Acad., 1955. Commd. ensign U.S. Navy, 1955, advanced through grades to rear adm., 1980; nuclear engr. serving in destroyers, cruisers, and nuclear submarines; comdg. officer U.S.S. Sea Devil, 1970-74; comdr. Submarine Devel. Squadron 12, New London, Conn., 1976-78; comdr. U.S. Naval Forces Marianas, comdr. U.S. Naval Base Guam comdr. in chief Pacific rep. Guam and Trust Ter. Pacific Islands, 1979-81; dep. chief Naval Sea Systems Command, ASW and Undersea Warfare Systems, Navy Dept., Washington, 1981-85; ret., 1985; dir. Offshore Systems Marine Systems div. Honeywell, Seattle, 1986-88; v.p. Honeywell Advanced Marine Systems Operation, Mpls., 1988, San Diego, 1989, Arlington, Va., 1990-91; dir. tech. plans & resources Alliant Techsystems Inc., Arlington, Va., 1991-92; chmn. Indsl. Devel. Authority, Westmoreland County, Va. Mem. Va. River Country Econ. Devel. Exec. Bd.; mem. bd. Rappahannock C.C.; presdl. elector, 1996; mem. Virginia Rep. State Ctrl. Com. Decorated Legion of Merit (3), Def. Superior Service medal, Meritorious Service medal (2), Navy Commendation medal. Mem. SAR, Nat. Def. Indsl. Assn. (undersea warfare adv. com.), Va. Small Grains Assn., Naval Submarine League, Ret. Officers Assn. (v.p. Va. Coun.), Naval Acad. Alumni Assn., Va. and No. Neck Hist. Socs. Home: Stillwater 4750 Zacata Rd Montross VA 22520-3510

FOUNTAIN, RONALD GLENN, management consultant, finance/marketing executive; b. Mason City, Wash., Feb. 12, 1939; s. Aldine Shirah and Ella Maude (Fordham) F.; m. Ethel Joan Hightower, Aug. 22, 1968; children: John Hightower, Dana Leigh. AS, Ga. Southwestern Coll., 1959; BS, Valdosta State Coll., 1965; MBA, Case Western Res. U., 1983, ExecDrMgmt, 1999. V.p. nat. accounts Ctrl. Bancshares, Birmingham, Ala., 1973-74; cash control mgr. White Consol., Cleve., 1974-76, asst. treas., 1976-79, treas., dir. investor rels., 1979-82, v.p., treas., 1982-83, v.p. fin., treas., 1983-86; pres. Dix & Eaton, 1986-88; v.p. fin., CFO M.A. Hanna Co., Cleve., 1988-93; mng. prin. The Commonwealth Group, Cleve., 1993-04; sr. exec. v.p. Roulston & Co., Cleve., 1994-96; adv. dir. InfoSource, Harris Co., 1995-98; ptnr. The Parkland Group, 1996—; pres., CEO United Truck Fin. & Mktg., 1998—; bd. dirs., asst. sec. Inst for Rsch., Epilogue Coun. Issues Mgmt.; adj. faculty Weatherhead Sch. Mgmt.; trustee NCC Funds, Inc., 1984-92. Trustee Notre Dame Coll., Cleve., 1984-90, Laurel Sch., 1986-90, Pub. Radio Sta. WCPN, 1990-93, MetroHealth Sys., Ctr. Families and Children; chmn. N.E. Hospice Study Com., 1989-93; bd. dirs. Jr. Achievement Cleve., 1982, Nat. Adoption Exch., Phila., 1983, Cleve. Edn. Fund, 1983-87. Mem. Alumni Assn. Weatherhead Sch. Mgmt. (pres. 1985-88), Fin. Execs. Inst. (membership chmn. 1983-84), Assn. Corp. Growth, Nat. Investor Rels. Inst. (pres. 1978-79), Planning Forum (pres. 1992-94), Union Club, Country Club. Home: 2908 Paxton Rd Cleveland OH 44120-1824

FOURAKER, LAWRENCE EDWARD, retired business administration educator; b. Bryan, Tex., Oct. 28, 1923; s. Leroy L. and Laura (Broach) F.; m. Patricia Orr, June 14, 1949; children: Senter Fouraker Jones, Lawrence Anderson. BA, Tex. A.&M. Coll., 1947, MS, 1948; PhD, U. Colo., 1951; MA (hon.), Harvard U., 1963; PhD (hon.), U. Pan Americana, Mex., 1987, St. Norbert Coll., West De Pere, Wis., 1974. Instr. U. Wyo., 1948-49; from asst. prof. to prof. Pa. State U., 1951-61; mem. faculty Bus. Sch. Harvard U., Cambridge, Mass., 1961-83, prof. bus. adminstrn., 1962-82, Edsel Bryant Ford Prof., 1968-70, 80-83, dir. divsn. rsch., 1968-70, George Fisher Baker prof. bus. adminstrn., 1970-80, dean Bus. Sch., 1970-80, prof. emeritus. Author: (with S. Siegel) Bargaining and Group Decision Making, 1960, Bargaining Behavior, (with H. Bierman and R. Jaedicke) Quantitative Analysis for Business Decisions, 1961. Trustee Dana Farber Med. Inst., Mass. Gen. Hosp., 1974-80, Pine Manor Coll., Mus. Fine Arts, Boston, 1971—, pres., 1980-84; mem. Resources for the Future; mem. vis. com. Harvard U. Meml. Ch., 1980—. With AUS, 1943-46. Home: 80 Fernwood Rd Chestnut Hill MA 02467-2907

FOURER, ROBERT HAROLD, industrial engineering educator, consultant; b. Phila., Sept. 2, 1950; s. Herbert S. and Priscilla (Silver) F. BS in Math., MIT, 1972; MS in Ops. Rsch., Stanford U., 1979, MS in Stats., 1979, PhD in Ops. Rsch., 1980. Rsch. analyst Nat. Bur. Econ. Rsch., Cambridge, Mass., 1974-77; asst. prof. dept. indsl. engring. and mgmt. scis. Northwestern U., Evanston, Ill., 1979-85, assoc. prof., 1985-93, dept. chair, 1989-95, prof., 1993—; vis. mem. tech. staff AT&T Bell Labs., Murray Hill, N.J., 1985-86, 95-96; cons. AT&T, Exxon, Goldman Sachs & Co., Keebler Co., Kraft Foods, Sears Roebuck & Co. Co-author: AMPL: A Modeling Language for Mathematical Programming, 1993; assoc. editor Mgmt. Sci., 1983—, Ops. Rsch., 1986—; contbr. articles to profl. jours. Grantee NSF; recipient Computer Sci. Tech. Sect. prize, Ops. Rsch. Soc. Am., 1993. Mem. Inst. Indsl. Engrs., Soc. Indsl. and Applied Math, Inst. Ops. Rsch. and Mgmt. Scis. (chair Computer Sci. Tech. sect., 1996-97), Math. Programming Soc. (mem.-at-large, coun. 1994-97). Achievements include AMPL modeling lang. Office: Northwestern Univ Dept Ind Eng and Mgmt Scis 2145 Sheridan Rd Evanston IL 60208-0834

FOURKAS, JOHN T., chemistry educator. Prof. dept. chemistry Boston Coll., Chestnut Hill, Mass. Chemistry grantee Camille and Henry Dreyfus Found., 1994; Cottrell scholar, 1997, Camille Dreyfus tchr.-scholar, 1999; Sloan Rsch. fellow, 1998; named Beckman Young Investigator, 1997. Office: Boston College Dept Chemistry Chestnut Hill MA 02467

FOURNELLE, RAYMOND ALBERT, engineering educator; b. St. Louis, Dec. 9, 1941; s. August Carl and Adella Emma (Fleer) F. BS in Metall. Engring., U. Mo., 1964, MS in Metall. Engring., 1968, PhD in Metall. Engring., 1971. Registered profl. engr., Wis. Rsch. engr. Shell Oil Co., Wood River, Ill., 1964-66; rsch. assoc. Northwestern U., Evanston, Ill., 1971-72; asst. prof. Marquette U., Milw., 1972-78, assoc. prof., 1978-86, prof., 1986—; interim chairperson Dept. of Mech. and Indsl. Engring., 1998—. Contbr. articles to profl. jours. 1st lt. U.S. Army, 1964-66, Fed. Republic Germany. Rsch. grantee NSF, 1975, 79, 86; Fulbright fellow U. Stuttgart (Germany), 1983-84, 90-91, Alexander von Humboldt fellow, 1985-88, Mac-Planck-Forschungspreis, 1994, ASM Internat. fellow, 1996. Mem. ASME, ASTM, AAUP, ASM Internat. (bd. rev. 1981—), Minerals, Metals and Materials Soc. (com. mem.), Am. Ceramic Soc., Am. Soc. Engring. Edn. Achievements include development of theories and models for various solid state reactions in metals and alloys, including discontinuous precipitation, coarsening, and dissolution, diffusion induced grain boundary and liquid film migration. Home: 1129 N Jackson St Apt 1207 Milwaukee WI 53202-3290 Office: Marquette U Dept Mech/Indsl Engring PO Box 1881 Milwaukee WI 53201-1881

FOURNIER, DONALD JOSEPH, JR., mechanical engineer, consultant, educator; b. Norwich, Conn., July 27, 1962; s. Donald Joseph Sr. and Juanita L. (Malone) F.; children: Catherine, Jacqueline, Evan. BSME, U. Fla., 1986, MSME, 1988. Registered profl. engr., Fla. Rsch. engr. Combustion Lab. U. Fla., Gainesville, 1985-88; mech. engr. Envireco, Gainesville, 1987-88; project engr. Acurex Environ., Jefferson, Ark., 1988-94; rsch. engr. and cons. Gould, Lewis & Proctor, Gainesville, 1992-98; project engr. Combustion Tec, Orlando, Fla., 1995-96; v.p., pres. Spectrum Design and Cons., Orlando and Hattiesburg, 1996—; asst. prof. U. So. Miss., Hattiesburg, 1998—; bd. dirs. Internat. Process Tech. Alliance. Contbr. articles on topics related to combustion, incineration, accident reconstruction, training, education, safety and engring. edn. to profl. jours. U. Fla. grad. scholar's fund fellow, 1986. Mem. ASTM, ASME, ASSE, Soc. of Automotive Engrs., Am. Soc. Engring. Edn., Air and Waste Mgmt. Assn., Internat. Process Tech. Alliance (bd. dirs.), Tau Beta Pi, Pi Tau Sigma. Achievements include identification of metal behavior in hazardous waste incineration. Office: Sch of Engring Tech U So Miss PO Box 5137 Hattiesburg MS 39406-5137

FOUSE, ANNA BETH, education educator; b. Austin, Tex., Jan. 11, 1947; d. Wilfred Davis and Doris Faye (Thomas) Chrisner; m. William Douglas Fouse; children: Douglas Lee, Alan Dale, Michael Wade, Robert Lynn. BS, U. Tex., Austin, 1967; MEd, Tex. Woman's U., 1973, PhD, 1976; various postgrad., Tex., 1980-81, 85-89. Cert. elem. tchr., spl. edn. tchr., Tex. 1st grade tchr. Austin Ind. Sch. Dist., 1967-68, Pasadena Ind. Sch. Dist., 1968-69; 3rd grade tchr. Harlingen (Tex.) Ind. Sch. Dist., 1969-70; homebound tchr. Irving (Tex.) Ind. Sch. Dist., 1970-71, tchr. emotionally disturbed, 1971-73; spl. edn. dir. Paris (Tex.) Ind. Sch. Dist., 1975-85, Region VII ESC, Kilgore, Tex., 1985-91; instr. U. Tex., Tyler, 1990-91; asst. prof. U. Tex., 1991-96, assoc. prof., 1996-98; ret., 1999; consulting editor bd. Acad. Therapy Jour., Austin, 1988-89. Author: Creating a Win-Win/EP for Students with Autism, 1996; co-author: (tech. asst. manual) Assessment Manual for Appraisal Personnel, 1987, Guidelines for Speech Pathologists, 1987, Accreditation for Special Educators, 1988, A Primer About Attention Deficit Disorder, 1993, A Treasure Chest of Behavioral Strategies for Individuals with Autism, 1997. Chairperson Paris Regional Habilitation Ctr. Adv. Bd., 1980-85, High Priority Infant Transitional Svcs. Adv. Bd., Longview, Tex., 1989-90; chair mental retardation/DD adv. bd. Sabine Valley Ctr., 1997-99; profl. adv. bd. so. region Attention Deficit Disorders Assn., 1990—; mem. adv. bd. Lamar County Alcohol and Drug Ctr., Paris, 1984-86. Mem. Autism Soc. of Ams., Tex. Coun. for Exceptional Children (v.p., pres., pres.-elect, bd. dirs.), Tex. Coun. of Adminstrs. in Spl. Edn., Assn. for Children with Learning Disabilities, Tex. Ednl. Diagnosticians Assn., Internat. Coun. for Exceptional Children, Phi Delta Kappa (pres. chpt. 1324 1991-93). Avocations: ceramics, crocheting, reading. Home and Office: 517 E Fairmont St Longview TX 75601-3804

FOUSE, SARAH VIRGINIA, geriatrics nurse; b. Florence, Ala., Apr. 24, 1948; d. John E. and Violet (Chandler) Perkins; m. Alvin Fouse Jr., Feb. 9, 1967; children: Anthony, Alicia, Alvin III. LPN, Gateway Tech. Coll., 1975, ADN, 1984; BSN, Alverno Coll., 1987; MSN, U. Wis., Milw., 1992. Cert. psychiat.-mental health nurse; cert. gerontology nurse. Staff nurse VA Med. Ctr., North Chicago, Ill., LPN, nursing asst., head nurse, adminstrv. clin. nurse specialist, mental health clin. coord., 1995—. Mem. ANA, Kans. Nurses Assn., Wis. Nurses Assn., Kenosha-Racine Nurses Assn., Milw. Assn. Black Nurses, Sigma Theta Tau. Home: 1900 21st St Racine WI 53403-2425

FOUST, DONNA ELAINE MARSHALL, women's health nurse; b. Sacramento, May 11, 1959; d. Donald H. and Diana Janet (O'Day) Marshall; m. Jennings Franklin Foust, Mar. 29, 1980; children: Andrew Donald, Sheri Diane. LPN, Harriman Vocat. Sch., 1979; ADN, Walter State C.C., 1983. RN, Tenn.; cert. RN first asst., CNOR. Staff nurse labor and delivery Meth. Med. Ctr., Oak Ridge, Tenn., 1979-83, staff nurse oper. rm., 1983-90; 1st asst. ob/gyn office Women's Health Assocs., Oak Ridge, 1988—. Mem. Assn. Oper. Rm. Nurse, RN First Asst. Specialty Assembly. Democrat. Avocations: breeding and showing malamutes. Home: 2512 Clinton Hwy Powell TN 37849-7613 Office: Westmall Med Park 200 New York Ave Ste 150 Oak Ridge TN 37830-5227 also: 9330 Park West Blvd Ste 300 Knoxville TN 37923-4311

FOUST, ROBERT SCHMERTZ, legislative director; b. New Holland, Pa., Jan. 20, 1941. BA in Polit. Sci., Upsala Coll., 1964; MA in Internat. Rels., Lehigh U., 1971. Asst. dir. admissions Upsala Coll., East Orange, N.J., 1965-69; legis. asst. Office of Senator Claiborne Pell, Washington, 1970-89; cons. Indochinese Cmty. Ctr., Washington, 1990-91; legis. dir. Office of Senator Kent Conrad, Washington, 1991—; panelist Nat. Edn. Assn. Safety Summit, L.A., 1995. Bd. mem. Indochinese Cmty. Ctr.; active Meridian Internat. Ctr. Named Outstanding Young Men of Am., Jaycees, 1973. Office: 530 Hart Senate Office Bldg Washington DC 20510-3403

FOUSTE, DONNA H., association executive; b. N.Y.C., Feb. 26, 1944; d. Donald Lynn and Edna (Parker) Ham; m. James Edward Fouste, Nov. 2, 1980. AA in Mgmt. and Supervision, Coastline Community Coll., Fountain Valley, Calif., 1980; BS in Organizational Behavior, U. San Francisco, 1985, MS in Orgnl. Devel., 1988. Officer mgr., bus. mgr. Fulwider, Patton, Rieber, Lee & Utecht, L.A., 1971-79, 89-91; patent adminstrn. specialist Discovision Assocs., Costa Mesa, Calif., 1979-82; law office mgr. City of Anaheim, Calif., 1982-89; exec. dir. Orange County Bar Assn., Santa Ana, Calif., 1992—; instr. Rancho Santiago Coll., Santa Ana, with legal asst. program, 1987—; instr. U. Calif., Irvine, 1997; mem. adv. bd. Pub. Svc. Inst., Santa Ana, 1986-88. Patron Friends of South Coase Repertory, Costa Mesa, Calif., 1985; mem. applause chpt. Performing Arts Ctr., Costa Mesa, 1986-87. Recipient Silver medal in Chess Corp. Challenge, 1988, Tribute to Women award YWCA, 1997, Spirit of Volunteerism award Vol. Ctr. of Greater Orange County, 1996. Mem. Assn. Legal Adminstrs., Nat. Assn. Bar Execs. (membership chair 1999), State Bar Calif. (minimum continuing legal edn. com.), Am. Soc. Assn. Execs., So. Calif. Soc. Assn. Execs., Execs. of Calif. Law Assns. Avocations: gourmet cooking, skiing, gardening. Office: Orange County Bar Assn PO Box 17777 Irvine CA 92623-7777

FOUTCH, MICHAEL JAMES, actor, dancer, lighting designer, producer; b. Dallas, Dec. 18, 1951; s. G.E. and Mary Muriel (Stanphill) F. BFA in Theatre, So. Meth. U., 1973. Cert. tchr. theatre and speech. Tech. dir. Eastfield Theatre, Dallas, 1973-77; dancer San Antonio Ballet, 1982, Dallas Concert Ballet, 1982-83; gen. ptnr. Stanphill Energy Partnership, Dallas, 1990-91; exec. dir. The Dallas Gilbert and Sullivan Soc., 1991-92; lighting designer Dallas Repertory Theatre, 1975; dancer TV Project, Shreveport, La., 1981; tchr. various ballet cos., Tex., La., 1983—; hist. dance study Early Dance Inst., Balt., 1988. Appeared in play The Mousetrap, 1976, ballets Giselle, 1980, Les Sylphides, 1982, The Nutcracker, 1983, 84, 92, 93, 94, 97, Cinderella, 1983, Swan Lake, 1983, Romeo and Juliet, 1984, dancer in operas Orfeo, 1986, Andrea Chenier, 1987, Iolanthe, 1989. Mem. S.W. Theatre Assn., Mensa. Avocations: tennis, music, movies. Office: PO Box 170711 Dallas TX 75217-0711

FOWLER, ALAN BICKSLER, retired physicist; b. Denver, Oct. 15, 1928; s. Alan Bruce and Minnie Edna (Bicksler) F.; m. Kathleen Teresa Devlin, Sept. 4, 1950; children: Stephen B., Susan Fowler-Finn, Andrew A., Sarah A. BS, Rensselaer Poly. Inst., 1951, MS, 1952; PhD, Harvard U., 1958. Rsch. staff mem. Raytheon Mfg. Co., Rsch. Div., Waltham, Mass., 1953-56, IBM Rsch. Div., Yorktown Heights, N.Y., 1958-83; IBM fellow Yorktown Heights, N.Y., 1983-93, IBM fellow emeritus, 1993—. With U.S. Army, 1946-48, 1st lt. Signal Corps, 1952-53. Recipient John Price Wetherill medal Franklin Inst., 1981, Alexander von Humboldt Preistraeger, 1982, David Sarnoff medal IEEE, 1987, Buckley prize Am. Phys. Soc., 1988. Mem. IEEE, NAS, NAE, Am. Phys. Soc., Am. Acad. Arts and Scis. Office: IBM T J Watson Rsch Ctr PO Box 218 Yorktown Heights NY 10598-0218

FOWLER, ANDREA, teachers academy administrator. Dir. Delta Tchrs. Acad., Atlanta; dir. Delta Tchrs. Acad., sr. program exec. Nat Faculty, Atlanta, v.p. programs, to 1998; cons. for edn. and non-profits Atlanta, 1998—. Office: Nat Faculty 83 Dartmouth Ave Avondale Estates GA 30002

FOWLER, BARBARA HUGHES, classics educator; b. Lake Forest, Ill., Aug. 23, 1926; d. Fay Orville and Clara (Reber) Hughes; m. Alexander Murray Fowler, July 14, 1956; children: Jane Alexandra, Emily Hughes. BA, U. Wis., 1949; MA, Bryn Mawr Coll., 1950, PhD, 1955. Instr. classics Middlebury (Vt.) Coll., 1954-56; asst. prof. Latin Edgewood Coll., Madison, Wis., 1961-63; mem. faculty U. Wis., Madison, 1963—; prof. classics U. Wis., 1976—, John Bascom prof., 1980—, prof. emeritus, 1991—. Author: The Hellenistic Aesthetic, 1989, The Seeds Inside a Green Pepper, 1989, Hellenistic Poetry, 1990, Archaic Greek Poetry, 1992, Love Lyrics of Ancient Egypt, 1994, Songs of a Friend, 1996, Vergil's Eclogues, 1997; also articles. Fulbright scholar Greece, 1951-52; Fanny Bullock Workman travelling fellow, 1951-52. Mem. Am. Philol. Assn., Archaeol. Inst. Am. Home: 1102 Sherman Ave Madison WI 53703-1620 Office: U Wis 910 Van Hise Hall Madison WI 53706

FOWLER, BRUCE ANDREW, toxicologist; b. Seattle, Dec. 28, 1945; s. Andrew and Dolores Yvonne F.; children by a previous marriage: Glenn Andrew, Randall Bruce. BS in Fisheries, U. Wash., 1968; PhD in Pathology, U. Oreg., 1972. Staff fellow Nat. Inst. Environ. Health Scis., Research Triangle Park, N.C., 1972-74, sr. staff fellow, 1974-77, rsch. biologist, 1977-87, sr. scientist, 1978-86, head Metal Toxicology, 1986-87; dir. U. Md. Toxicology program, 1987—; prof. pathology U. Md. Med. Sch., 1987—; dir. office collaborative studies on adaptive responses estuarine species U. Md., 1988; Meyer Bodansky lectr. Dept. of Pathology, U. Tex med. br., Galveston; adj. assoc. prof. pathology and toxicology curriculum U. N.C.; temporary adv. WHO; mem. work group Internat. Agy. Research Against Cancer; mem. Internat. Commn. on Occupl. Health, Sci. Com. on Toxicology of Metals (chmn.); mem. Md. Gov.'s Coun. on Toxic Substances, 1988-93, chmn., 1990-93; chmn. Dahlem Workshop on Mechanisms of Cell Injury: Implications for Human Health, Berlin, 1985; mem. toxicology info. program com., com. on toxicology, chmn. com. on measuring lead in critical populations, com. on women in sci. and engring., com. on biologic markers in urologic toxicology NAS/NRC, 1989-93, com. on evaluation of viability of augmenting potable water supplies with reclaimed water NAS/NRC, 1996-97; Subcom. on arsenic in drinking water of the com. on toxicology NAS/NRC, 1997; co-chmn. N.Y. Acad. of Scis. Conf. on Mechanisms of Chem.-Induced Porphyrinopathies, Rye, N.Y.; Swedish Med. Rsch. Coun. vis. prof. Karolinska Inst., 1994-95; Colgate-Polmolive vis. prof. U. Washington, 1998. Editor: Biological and Environmental Effects of Arsenic, 1983; Mechanisms of Cell Injury: Implications for Human Health; (with E.K. Silbergeld) Mechanisms of Chemical Induced Porphyrinopathies; mem. editorial bd. Chemico-Biol. Interactions, 1980-85, Environ. Health Perspectives, 1981-97, Toxicology and Applied Pharmacology, 1985-96, Jour. Toxicology and Environ. Health, 1986-97, Internat. Archives Environ. Health, 1986—, Renal Failure, 1988—, Internat. Jour. Occupl. and Environ. Health, 1994-96; contbr. articles to profl. jours. and chpts. to books. Rsch. fellow Japanese Soc. for Promotion of Sci., 1990; Fulbright scholar Karolinska Inst., 1994. Mem. AAAS, APHA, Am. Soc. Pharmacology and Exptl. Therapeutics, Am. Assn. Pathologists, Soc. Toxicology (councilor mechanisms of toxicity sect., pres. metals specialty sect. 1996, councilor nat. capital area regional chpt. 1994-95), Am. Coll. Toxicology (councilor 1995-98), Soc. for Occupational and Environ. Health (councilor 1988, v.p. 1993), N.Y. Acad. Sci., Internat. Commn. on Occupl. Health (chmn. scientific com. on the toxicology of metals 1996—), Profl. Assn. Diving Instructors, Sigma Xi. Office: U Md Tech Ctr Program in Toxicology Ctr 1450 S Rolling Rd Baltimore MD 21227-3831

FOWLER, CHARLES ALBERT, electronics engineer; b. Centralia, Ill., Dec. 17, 1920; s. Clarence J. and Bess (Maxwell) F.; m. Kathryn Elizabeth Grimes, Oct. 23, 1943; children: Patricia Ann Paul, Mary Catherine Leathem. B.S. in Engring. Physics, U. Ill., 1942. Mem. staff radiation lab. MIT, 1942-45; head radar systems dept. Airborne Instruments Lab., Deer Park, N.Y., 1946-66; dep. dir. (tactical warfare) def. research and engring. Dept. Def., 1966-70; v.p., mgr. equipment devel. labs. Raytheon Co., Sudbury, Mass., 1970-76; sr. v.p., gen. mgr. Bedford (Mass.) ops. Mitre Corp., 1976-85; pres C.A. Fowler Assocs., 1986—; mem. sci. adv. com. Def. Intelligence Agy., 1971—, chmn. sci. adv. com., 1976-82; mem. Air Force Sci. Adv. Bd., 1971-77, Def. Sci. Bd., 1972-98, chmn., 1984-88, vice chmn., 1988-90. Contbr. articles in field. Mem. East Norwich Sch. Bd., 1955-61, East Norwich Library Bd., 1956-62. Fellow IEEE, AAAS, AIAA; mem. Nat. Acad. Engring. Office: 15 Woodberry Rd Sudbury MA 01776-2227

FOWLER, CHARLES ALLISON EUGENE, architect, engineer; b. Halifax, N.S., Can., Jan. 24, 1921; s. Charles Allison and Mildred (Crosby) F.; m. Dorothy Christine Graham, Aug. 30, 1947; children: Graham Allison, Beverly Anne. BSc, Dalhousie U., 1942; B in Engring., McGill U., 1944; BArch., U. Man., 1948; DEng (hon.), Tech. U. of Nova Scotia, 1975. With C.A. Fowler, Bauld & Mitchell, Ltd. (and predecessor firms), Halifax, 1946-80; sr. ptnr. C.A. Fowler, Bauld & Mitchell, Ltd. (and predecessor firms), 1950-70, pres., 1970-80, chmn., 1980-81; pres. C.A. Fowler & Co., 1981—; assoc. Vaughan Engring. Assocs. Ltd., Halifax, 1992-94. Prin. works include Miners Mus., Glace Bay, N.S., Dalhousie U. Fine Arts Ctr., 1970, univ. ctr. Acadia U., Acad. Ctr. at Mt. St. Vincent U., Halifax Law Cts., Canadian Martyrs Ch., Can. Permanent Bldg. Hfx., Halifax Metro Ctr., Stadacona Hosp., Victoria Gen. Hosp., Centre 200, Sydney, N.S. Past chmn. bd. dirs. N.S. Coll. Art and Design. With Can. Army, 1943-46. Fellow AIA (hon.), Royal Archtl. Inst. Can. (pres. 1965), Can. Soc. for Civil Engring.; mem. Engring. Inst. Can. (life). Mem. United Ch. Home and Office: 2 Hall's Rd, Halifax, NS Canada B3P 1P3

FOWLER, CONRAD MURPHREE, retired manufacturing company executive; b. Montevallo, Ala., Sept. 17, 1918; s. Luther J. and Elsie (Murphree) F.; m. Virginia Evelyn Mott, June 15, 1945; children: Conrad, Randolph. BS, U. Ala., 1941, JD, 1948. Bar: Ala. 1948. Practiced in Columbiana, 1948-53; mem. firm Ellis and Fowler, 1948-53; dist. atty. 18th Jud. Circuit Ala., 1953-59; probate judge, chmn. Shelby County Commn. Shelby County Ct., Columbiana, 1959-77; v.p. pub. affairs West Point-Pepperell, Inc., 1977-89, ret., 1989; Mem. Presdl. Adv. Commn. on Intergovtl. Relations, 1970-77. Mem. Ala. Dem. Exec. Com., 1966-77; chmn. Ala. Constl. Commn., 1970-76; bd. dirs. Associated Industries Ala., 1979-87, Pub. Affairs Coun., 1979-89; v.p. Am. Lung Assn., 1980-82, pres., 1982-83; mem. coun. Nat. Mcpl. League, 1976-82; vice chmn. Pub. Affairs Coun., 1987-89; bd. dirs. Ga. Bus. Coun., 1987-89. Col. USMCR, 1941-78. Decorated Silver Star with gold star, Purple Heart (2); named to Ala. Acad. Honor, 1981; recipient William Crawford Gorgas award Ala. Med. Assn., 1985, Paul Harris fellow, 1997. Mem. Nat. Assn. Counties (pres. 1969-70), Assn. County Commrs. Ala. (pres. 1970-71), U. Ala. Nat. Alumni Assn. (pres. 1969, Alumnus of Yr. 1992), Probate Judges Assn. Ala. (pres. 1968-69), Murphree Geneal. Assn. (pres. 1990-91), Tuscaloosa Exch. Club. Home: 1605 Bellingrath Dr Tuscaloosa AL 35406-2020

FOWLER, DAVID LUCAS, corporate lawyer; b. Heidelberg, Germany, Sept. 26, 1952; s. James Daniel and Nannie Romay (Lucas) F.; m. Cynthia Lou Smith, Aug. 19, 1989. BS, U.S. Mil. Acad., 1974; JD, Georgetown U., 1981. Bar: N.J. 1982, Calif. 1990, U.S. Ct. Fed. Claims 1990, U.S. Dist. Ct. (cen. dist.) Calif. 1990. 2d lt. U.S. Army, 1974, advanced through grades to maj.; infantry platoon leader U.S. Army, Berlin, 1975-76, asst. protocol officer, 1976-77, aide-de-campe U.S. Commander, 1977-78; minority augmentation recruit officer U.S. Mil. Acad., 1978; chief adminstrv. law sect. U.S. Army Tng. Ctr., Ft. Dix, N.J., 1983-86; command judge advocate U.S. Army Field Sta., Sinop, Turkey, 1985-86; trial atty. U.S. Army Legal Svcs. Agy., Falls Church, Va., 1986-89; resigned U.S. Army, 1989; corp. staff counsel Hughes Aircraft Co., L.A., 1989-94; sr. staff counsel Electro-Optical Sys. Hughes Aircraft Co., El Segundo, Calif., 1994-95; asst. gen. counsel Hughes Aircraft Co., Arlington, Va., 1996-97; v.p., dep. gen. counsel Raytheon Sys. Co., Arlington, Va., 1998—; asst. sec. Hughes Electronics and Hughes Aircraft Co., 1996—. Bd. dirs. West Point Soc. L.A., 1993. Mem. ABA (public contract law sect.), Armed Svcs. Bds. of Contract Appeals Assn., Army Sci. Bd. Avocations: reading, weightlifting, golf. Office: Raytheon Sys Co 1100 Wilson Blvd Ste 2000 Arlington VA 22209-2297

FOWLER, DAVID WAYNE, architectural engineering educator; b. Sabinal, Tex., Apr. 25, 1937; s. Otis Lindley and Sadie Gertrude (Cox) F.; m. Maxine Yvonne Thomson, Mar. 31, 1961; children: Teresa, Leah. BS in Archtl. Engring., U. Tex., 1960; MS, U. Tex., Austin, 1962; PhD in Civil Engring., U. Colo., 1965. Design engr. W.C. Cotten (Cons. Engr.), Austin, Tex., 1961-62; asst. prof. archtl. engring. U. Tex., Austin, 1964-69, assoc. prof., 1969-75, prof., 1975—, Taylor prof., 1981—, dir. Ctr. Aggregates Rsch., 1992—, Joe J. King chair; vis. prof. Nihon U., Japan, 1981; bd. dirs. Univ. Fed. Credit Union, 1976-84; pres. Internat. Congress on Polymers in Concrete, 1981-87, bd. dirs.; chmn. Concrete Rsch. Coun., 1996—. Editor procs. 2d Internat. Congress on Polymers in Concrete, 1978; contbr. articles to profl. jours. Recipient Teaching award Gen. Dynamics, 1975, Teaching award Amoco Found., 1978, Disting. Engring. Alumnus award U. Colo., 1993, Owen Nutt award ICPIC, 1995; cited by Engring.-News Record, 1975, Concrete Repair, 1995; Ford Found. faculty devel. grantee, 1962-64. Fellow ASCE (pres. Austin br. 1976-77), Am. Concrete Inst. (Delmar L. Bloem award 1985, bd. dirs. 1993-96); mem. NAE, Concrete Rsch. Coun./Concrete Rsch. Found. (chmn. 1996—), Am. Soc. Engring. Edn. (chmn. archtl. engring. div. 1971-72), Tex. Soc. Profl. Engrs. (bd. dirs. Travis chpt. 1968), Russian Acad. Engring. (hon.), Tau Beta Pi, Chi Epsilon. Mem. Ch. of Christ. Home: 612 Brookhaven Trl Austin TX 78746-5455 Office: Univ Tex ECJ 5208 Archtl Engring Group Austin TX 78712

FOWLER, EMIL EUGENE, nuclear technology consultant; b. Morgantown, W.Va., Sept. 15, 1923; s. Jesse Lash and Lillian May (Everly) F.; m. Jo Ann Vigor, July 9, 1949; children: Joycelyn Elizabeth Fowler Sharp, Christopher Lash, David Vigor. BS, W.Va. U., 1945, MS, 1947. Chief licensing then dep. dir. isotopes div. AEC, Oak Ridge, Tenn., 1950-56; dept asst., dir. div. civilian applications AEC, Washington, 1957-60, dep. dir isotopes devel. div., 1961-65, dir. isotopes div., 1966-74; head chemistry and indsl. applications IAEA, Vienna, Austria, 1975-79, coord. regional coop. Asia-Pacific area, 1980-82; dir. and chief tech. adviser Office Indsl. Tech. Transfer UN, Tokyo, 1982-85; sr. adviser Mitsubishi Kasei, Tokyo, 1986—; sr. sci. tech. adviser Asian Rare Earth Co., Ipoh, Malaysia, 1986-90; founder and chief exec. officer Kakihana & Fowler Assocs., various countries, from 1987; now ret., 1995—; offical U.S. rep. UN Internat. Confs. 2d-4th on Uses of Atomic Energy, Geneva; offical U.S. rep. 5th-13th Japan Conf. on Radioisotopes. Contbr. articles to profl. jours. Oak Ridge (Tenn.) Nat. Lab. fellow, 1950, 51. Fellow Am. Inst. Chemists; mem. APHA, AAAS, Royal Soc. Health, Am. Nuclear Soc., Washington Acad. Sci., N.Y. Acad. Sci., Am. Chem. Soc. Nuclear Medicine, Am. Heart Assn., Kenwood Golf and Country Club. Republican. Episcopalian. Home: 5124 Westpath Way Bethesda MD 20816-2318

FOWLER, FLORA DAUN, lawyer; b. Washington, Aug. 11, 1923; d. Herman Hartwell and Flora Elizabeth (Adams) Sanford; m. Kenneth Leo Fowler, Aug. 22, 1941; children: Kenneth Jr., Michael, Kathleen, Daun, Jonathan, Colin, Kevin, James, Shawn, Maureen, Wendelyn, Liam, Tobias, Melanie. Student, Wilson Tchrs. Coll., 1940-41; AA, U. Md., 1973; JD, U. Balt., 1976. Bar: Fla. 1977, U.S. Dist. Ct. (mid. dist.) Fla. 1979, U.S. Ct. Appeals (5th and 11th cirs.) 1981. Staff atty. Cen. Fla. Legal Services Inc., Daytona Beach, 1978-80, mng. atty., 1980-81; pvt. practice, Daytona Beach, 1981-93; ret., 1993. Past editor Seabrook Acres Citizens' League Newsletter; columnist Bowie Express & Community Times; contbr. poems to New Voices in American Poetry, 1974. V.p. Seabrook (Md.) Acres Citizens League, 1970; past v.p. Prince Georges County Civic Fedn., Md.; past unit chmn. League of Women Voters, Prince Georges County; past pres., v.p., publicity chmn. Lanham-Bowie Dem. Club, Seabrook. Recipient Evening Star Trophy award Prince Georges County Civic Fedn., 1969. Mem. Fla. S. Ct. Hist. Soc. Democrat. Roman Catholic. Avocations: swimming, creative writing, Cursillo.

FOWLER, GEORGE SELTON, JR., architect; b. Chgo., Jan. 20, 1920; s. George Selton and Mabel Helena (Overton) F.; m. Yvonne Fern Grammer, Nov. 25, 1945; 1 child, Kim Ellyn. Cert. in European geo-politics andadvanced language study, Hamilton Coll. (ASTP), 1944; BS in Architecture, Ill. Inst. Tech., 1949, postgrad. City and Regional Planning, 1968. Cert. Elec. Assn. Ill., 1976; reg. arch., Ill., Ohio. Co-founder, pres. The Modern Arts Press, Chgo., 1946; instr. archtl. and related engrng. subjects Am. Sch. Tech. Soc., Chgo., 1948-65; urban planner Chgo. Land Clearance Commn., 1949-50; liaison architect Chgo. Housing Authority, 1950-68, chief design-tech. divsn., 1968-80, dir. dept. engrng., 1980-84; prin. George S. Fowler Architect, Chgo., 1984-90; treas., bd. dirs. Chgo. Housing Authority Credit Union, 1963-65; architect, cmty. planner and cons. Interconco., 1965-66. Author: (textbook study guide) Reinforced Concrete Design, 1959. Patentee Subcom. chmn., founder Mayor's Adv. Commn. to Revise the Bldg. Code, 1986-91; founder, pres., EFCO, Chgo., 1988—. Served with Corp. of Engrs., U.S. Army, 1942-46, group sgt. maj., 1944-46. Recipient citation for residential devel. Mayor Richard J. Daley, Chgo., 1960, Black Achievers of Industry Recognition award YMCA, Chgo., 1977; Kappa Alpha Psi grantee, 1936. Mem. Nat. Assn. Archs., Assn. Archs. in Industry, Nat. Assn. Housing and Redevel. Officials, Internat. Platform Assn. Home and Office: 8209 S Rhodes Ave Chicago IL 60619-5005

FOWLER, HENRY HAMILL, investment banker; b. Roanoke, Va., Sept. 5, 1908; s. Mack Johnson and Bertha (Browning) F.; m. Trudye Pamela Hathcote, Oct. 19, 1938; children: Mary Anne Fowler Smith, Susan Fowler-Gallagher, Henry Hamill (dec.). AB, Roanoke Coll., 1929, LLD, 1962; LLB, Yale U., 1932, JSD, 1933; LLD, William and Mary U., 1966, Wesleyan U., 1966. Bar: Va. 1933, D.C. 1946. Counsel TVA, 1934-38, asst. gen. counsel, 1939; spl. asst. to atty. gen. as chief counsel subcom. Senate Com. Edn. and Labor, 1939-40; spl. counsel Fed. Power Commn., 1941; asst. gen. counsel Office Prodn. Mgmt., 1941, War Prodn. Bd., 1942-44; econ. advisor U.S. Mission Econ. Affairs, London, 1944; spl. asst. to adminstr. Fgn. Econ. Adminstrn., 1945; dep. adminstr. N.P.A., 1951, adminstr., 1952; adminstr. Def. Prodn. Adminstrn., 1952-53; dir. Office Def. Moblzn., mem. NSC, 1952-53; sr. mem. firm Fowler, Leva Hawes & Symington, Washington, 1954-61, 1963-61, 64-65, undersec. Treasury, 1961-64, sec. Treasury, 1965-68; gen. partner Goldman, Sachs & Co., N.Y.C., 1969-81; ltd. ptnr., 1981—; chmn. Goldman, Sachs Internat. Corp., N.Y.C., 1969-84; dir. Corning Glass Works, U.S. and Fgn. Securities Corp., U.S. Industries Inc., Norfolk and Western Co., Trans-World Airlines. Trustee Franklin D. Roosevelt Four Freedoms Found., 1982-87, Lyndon B. Johnson Found., 1973—, Roanoke Coll., 1954—, Christ Ch., Alexandria, Va., Atlantic Coun. U.S., vice chmn., 1978—; co-chmn. Citizens Network for Fgn. Affairs, 1987—, Com. on the Present Danger, 1976-88, Bretton Woods Commn., 1985-89; chmn. bd. trustees Roanoke Coll., 1974-81; chmn. Atlantic Coun. U.S., 1973-78; chmn. bd. trustees Inst. Internat. Edn., 1972-77; mem. coun. Miller Ctr. for Pub. Affairs, U. Va., 1980-91; bd. dirs. Alfred E. Sloan Found., 1971-81, Carnegie Found. for Peace, 1974-80, Japan Soc., 1974-78. Mem. Councilor Conf. Bd. Yale Law Sch. Assn. Washington (pres. 1955), Links Club (N.Y.C.), River Club (N.Y.C.) Met. Club (Washington), Bohemian Club (San Francisco), Pi Kappa Phi, Phi Delta Phi. Democrat. Episcopalian. Home: 209 S Fairfax St Alexandria VA 22314-3303 Office: Goldman Sachs 85 Broad St New York NY 10004-2456 also: 200 E 66th St New York NY 10021-6728

FOWLER, H(ORATIO) SEYMOUR, retired science educator; b. Detroit, Mar. 1, 1919; s. Horatio Seymour and Bessie Liona (Ladd) F.; m. Kathleen M. Marshall, Nov. 21, 1945 (dec.); 1 dau., Kathleen Marie Fowler Barto. B.S., Cornell U., 1941, M.S., 1946, Ph.D., 1951. Tchr. sci. McLean (N.Y.) Central Sch., 1946-47, Dryden (N.Y.) Freeville Central Sch., 1947-49; asst. prof. sci. edn. So. Oreg. Coll., Ashland, 1951-52; asst. prof. biology U. No. Iowa, Cedar Falls; also dir. Iowa Tchrs. Conservation Camp, 1952-57; prof. edn., dir. Pa. Conservation Lab. for Tchrs., Pa. State U., University Park, 1957-83, chmn. sci. edn. faculty, 1969-83, coordinator div. acad. curriculum and instrn., 1974-76, prof. nature and sci. edn. emeritus, 1983—; dir. Pa. Gov.'s Sch. for Scis., 1978-79; sci. advisor Nat. Jr. Sci. and Humanities Symposium, Program U.S. Army Research Office, Acad. Applied Sci., 1979—. Author: Secondary School Science Teaching Practices, 1964, Las Ciencias en la Esquelas Secundarias, 1968, Fieldbook of Natural History, 1974; contbr. articles to profl. jours. Served with 9th inf. div. AUS, 1942-45, ETO. Fulbright lectr. Korea, 1968-69; recipient citation Pa. Dept. Edn., 1970, 83, Centre County (Pa.) Conservation award, 1973, Faculty Service award Nat. Univ. Continuing Edn. Assn., 1983, citation Pa. Ho. of Reps., 1983, Service award U.S. Army Office of Research, 1983; Paul Harris fellow Rotary Club, 1983. Fellow AAAS, Iowa Acad. Sci., Explorers Club; mem. Am. Nature Study Soc. (pres. 1967), Nat. Assn. Biology Tchrs. (v.p. 1956, dir. region II 1971-74, hon. mem. 1974), Nat. Assn. Rsch. in Sci. Teaching, Nat. Sci. Tchrs. Assn. (Disting. Svc. citation 1976), Pa. Sci. Tchrs. Assn. (dir. 1971—, v.p. 1975, pres. 1976, meritorious svc. to sci. teaching citation 1975), Korean Sci. Tchrs. Assn., Royal Asiatic Soc., Masons, Shriners, Rotary (1st v.p. 1981, pres. 1982, gov. dist. 735 1988-89), Elks, Sigma Xi, Phi Kappa Phi, Phi Delta Kappa (chpt. v.p. 1973, pres. 1974-75, Leadership award 1983), Beta Beta Beta. Clubs: Masons, Shriners, Rotary (1st v.p. 1981, pres. 1982, gov. dist. 735 1988-89), Elks. Home: 1342 W Park Hills Ave State College PA 16803-3273 Office: Pa State U Sci Edn Dept University Park PA 16802

FOWLER, J. EDWARD, lawyer. AB, Princeton U., 1953; LLB, Yale U., 1959. Bar: N.Y. 1960. Atty. Debevoise, Plimpton, Lyons & Gates, 1959-68; gen. counsel internat. divsn. Mobil Oil Corp., 1974-77, asst. gen. counsel, 1977-78, assoc. gen. counsel, 1979-83, gen. counsel mktg. and refining divsn., 1983-86; gen. counsel Mobil Corp., Fairfax, Va., 1986-95; sr. ptnr. Holland & Knight, Washington, D.C., 1995-98. Bd. editors Yale Law Jour., 1958-59. Bd. dirs. Nat. Symphony Orch. Assn., 1991—, pres., 1995-98; trustee Shakespeare Theatre, 1993—. Fax: 202-797-9546. Office: 10 Kalorama Cir NW Washington DC 20008-1616

FOWLER, JAMES D., JR., marketing and human resources consulant; b. Washington, Apr. 24, 1944; s. James D. and Romay (Lucas) F.; m. Linda Marie Raiford, May 25, 1968; children—Scott, Kimberly. Student, Howard U., Washington, 1962-63; B.S., U.S. Mil. Acad., West Point, N.Y., 1967; M.B.A., Rochester Inst. Tech., 1975. With Xerox Corp., Rochester, N.Y., 1971-75; sr. cons. D.P. Parker & Assocs., Inc., Wellesley, Mass., 1975-76; mgr. staffing ITT World Hdqrs., N.Y.C., 1976-78; v.p. dir. of adminstrn. ITT Aetna, Denver, 1978; sr. v.p., dir. adminstrn. ITT Consumer Fin. Corp., Mpls., 1978-84, sr. v.p., dir. adminstrn. and mktg., 1984-87, exec. v.p., dir. adminstrn. and mktg., 1987-90, exec. v.p., dir. product mgmt., mktg. and adminstrn., 1990-92; exec. v.p., dir. of adminstrn., 1992-93; dir. govt. rels. ITT Washington Office, 1993-96; pres. Fowler & Assocs., 1996—; exec. dir. Exec. Leadership Coun., 1997—. Trustee U.S. Mil. Acad., West Point, N.Y., 1977-86, 87—; bd. dirs., chmn. legal and pub. affairs com. ITT Ednl. Svcs., Inc.; bd. dirs. Duke Ellington Sch. Arts, Suburban Hosp., Bethesda, Md., Folger Shakespeare Libr., Washington; charter mem., bd. dirs. Exec. Leadership Coun., 1992-97. Capt. U.S. Army, 1967-71, Vietnam. Decorated Bronze Star with oak leaf cluster. Mem. Sigma Pi Phi. Office: 1010 Wisconsin Ave NW Ste 520 Washington DC 20007-3678*

FOWLER, JAMES RAYMOND, surgeon; b. Feb. 4, 1937. MD, Emory U., 1964. rear admiral USNR, 1991-97, surgeon gen., 1993-97. Office: 1220 E 3900 S Ste 2H Salt Lake City UT 84124-1327

FOWLER, JENNEFER RAE, sculptor; b. Bay City, Tex., Feb. 14, 1973; d. Bobby Owens and Ygerne Roxanne Michalec Hubbell; 1 child, Lexis DeVoe Beauford. Student, Richland Jr. Coll., 1991, 92; BFA with honors, U. Ctrl. Ark., 1998. Intern, apprentice Richard Hunt Studios, Chgo., 1997; mem. com. Kramer Artist Coop., Little Rock, 1997; v.p. Kramer Sch. Artist Coop. Sculptor, Moon Meditation, 1997. Mem. Art History Assn. (v.p. 1997). Democrat. Avocations: painting with oil, watercolors, acrylic; camping, canoeing, swimming, figure drawing. Home: 715 Sherman St Apt 7 Little Rock AR 72202-2685

FOWLER, JOSEPH CLYDE, JR., protective services official; b. Knoxville, Tenn., Jan. 22, 1927; s. Joseph Clyde and Elizabeth (Baker) F.; m. Wanda Sue Carroll, Aug. 4, 1956; 2 children. Student, U. Tenn., 1946, 47, Bob James Jr. Coll., 1947, FBI Nat. Acad., 1967. Various positions Knoxville Police Dept., 1959-65, detective, sgt., lt. juvenile bur., 1965-70, asst. chief police, 1970-78, chief of police, 1979-82; pres. Ctrl. Comm. & Elecs., 1982-90; sheriff Knox County (Tenn.) Sheriff's Dept., 1990-94; warden Tenn. Dept. Corrections, Knoxville, 1994—; U.S. Marshall Ea. Tenn., 1994—. With USN, 1945-46, res., 1959-63. Mem. Kiwanis, Vestal Boys Club, Knoxville Lodge 769, Scottish Rite, Kerbala, Mystic Shriners, Am. Legion, FOP, Phi Gamma Delta. Methodist. Avocations: boating, horseback riding, swimming. Office: US Courthouse 800 Market St Ste 320 Knoxville TN 37902

FOWLER, LINDA MCKEEVER, hospital administrator, management educator; b. Greensburg, Pa., Aug. 7, 1948; d. Clay and Florence Elizabeth (Smith) McKeever; m. Timothy L. Fowler, Sept. 13, 1969 (div. July 1985). Nursing diploma, Presbyn. U. Hosp., Pitts., 1969; BSN, U. Pitts., 1976, M in Nursing Adminstrn., 1980; D in Pub. Adminstrn., Nova U., 1985. Supr., head nurse Presbyn. Univ. Hosp., Pitts., 1969-76; mem. faculty Western Pa. Hosp. Sch. Nursing, Pitts., 1976-79; acute care coord. Mercy Hosp., Miami, 1980-81; asst. adminstr. nursing North Shore Med. Ctr., Miami, 1981-84, v.p. patient care, 1984-88; v.p. patient care Golden Glades Regional Med. Ctr., Miami, 1988-89, Humana Hosp.-South Broward, Hollywood, Fla., 1989-91; assoc. exec. dir. nursing Humana Hosp.-South Broward, Hollywood; v.p./CNO Columbia Regional Med. Ctr., Bayonet Point, 1991-96; COO/CNO Greenbrier Valley Med. Ctr., 1996-97; quality mgmt. coord. Greenbrier Valley Hospice, 1997-98; pvt. practice healthcare cons., 1998—; mem. adj. faculty Barry U., Miami, 1984-97, Broward C.C., Ft. Lauderdale, 1984—, Nova U., 1986—; cons. Strategic Health Devel. Inc., Miami Shores, Fla., 1986—, So. Coll., Cleveland, Tenn., 1995-96. Dept. HEW trainee, 1976, 79-80; bd. dirs. Pasco County Am. Cancer Soc., 1992-95. Mem. Am. Orgn. Nurse Execs. (legis. com. 1988-90), Fla. Orgn. Nurse Execs. (bd. dirs. 1986-88), South Fla. Nurse Adminstrs. Assn. (sec. 1983-84, bd. dirs. 1984-86), U. Pitts. Alumni Assn., Presbyn. U. Alumni Assn., Portuguese Water Dog Club Am. (bd. dirs. 1988-89), Ft. Lauderdale Dog Club (bd. dirs. 1981-82, 83-85, v.p. 1982-83), Am. Kennel Club (dog judge), Sigma Theta Tau. Lutheran. Home and Office: 27 Potomac Crossway Lewisburg WV 24901-8917

FOWLER, MARK STAPLETON, lawyer, corporation counsel; b. Toronto, Ont., Can., Oct. 6, 1941. B.A., U. Fla., 1966, J.D., 1969. Bar: Fla. 1970, D.C. 1970. Assoc. firm Smith & Pepper, Washington, 1970-75; ptnr. Fowler & Meyers, Washington, 1975-81; chmn. FCC, 1981-87; vice chmn. Adminstrv. Council U.S., Washington, 1981-1987; bd. dirs. Telecommunications Tng. Inst., 1983-87; sr. comm. counsel Latham & Watkins, Washington, 1987—; pres., CEO Powerfone, Inc., 1992-94, Bell Atlantic Personal Comm., Inc., 1992-94; chmn. Uni Site, Inc., 1994—, AssureSat, Inc., 1998—; mem. bd. dirs. The St. Paul Cos., 1987-94. Named Virginian of Yr. Va. Assn. Broadcasters, 1981; recipient Thomas Jefferson award U. Tex., 1982, Clarence Darrow award Broadcast Pioneers, 1985, Sol Taishoff award, 1985, 1st Amendment award Radio TV News Dirs. Assn., 1986. Mem. D.C. Bar, D.C. Bar Assn., Fla. Bar Assn., Delta Theta Phi. Office: 324 N Interlachen Ave Winter Park FL 32789-3808

FOWLER, MARTI, secondary education educator; b. St. Louis, Mar. 25, 1952; d. Chester Felix and Emily (Kohout) Czarcinski; m. Robert Lee Fowler, Mar. 26, 1988. BA, So. Ill. U., 1973, MA, 1981. Cert. tchr. English, speech and theatre, Mo. Tchr. asst. Hazelwood Sch. Dist., St. Louis, 1974-76; instr. Jefferson Coll., 1991-92, St. Louis C.C. at Meramec, St. Louis, 1990—; tchr. Hazelwood East H.S., St. Louis, 1976-97; dept. chair fine arts Hazelwood East H.S. and Kirby Jr. H.S., 1997—; cons. Hazelwood Sch. Dist., 1999—. Co-playwright/lyricist: (musical theatre) Difficult Choices, 1988; dir. and choreographer numerous prodns., 1973—. Mem. Am. Alliance for Theatre in Edn. (Mo. state chmn. 1993-97, Dina Reese Evans award 1998), Theatre Edn. Assn. (Mo. State chmn. 1993-97, coord. Mo. State Thespian Conf. 1996, Dina Rees Evans award for theatre in our schs. advocacy), Mo. State Thespian Bd. Dirs., Speech Theatre Assn. of Mo., Speech Comm. Assn., Internat. Thespian Soc., Zeta Phi Eta (pres. 1972-73). Avocations: attending theatre, reading. Home: 15685 Silver Lake Ct Chesterfield MO 63017-5128 Office: Hazelwood E High Sch 11300 Dunn Rd Saint Louis MO 63138-1047

FOWLER, NOBLE OWEN, physician, university administrator; b. Vicksburg, Miss., July 14, 1919; s. Noble Owen and Annie Lou (Robertson) F.; m. Charlotte Ruth Walters, June 13, 1942; children: Joann, Michael, Anne Stewart. Student, Memphis State U., 1936-38; M.D., U. Tenn., 1941. Diplomate Am. Bd. Internal Medicine (examining bd. 1970-72, cardiovascular subspecialty examining bd. 1966-72, chmn. cardiovascular subspecialty bd. 1970-72). Intern Cin. Gen. Hosp., 1942-43, resident in internal medicine, 1945, 47-48, fellow in cardiology, 1948-52; resident in internal medicine Peter Bent Brigham Hosp., Boston, 1946; instr. U. Cin., 1950-51, asst. prof. medicine, 1951-52, assoc. prof., 1957-64, prof., 1964—, prof. pharmacology and cell biophysics, 1980-84, prof. emeritus, 1984—, assoc. dir. dept. medicine, 1970-79, dir. div. cardiology, 1970-86; asst. prof. SUNY, 1952-54; chmn. cardiovascular research Emory U., 1954-57; mem. adv. com. on cardiovascular and renal drugs FDA, 1970-78, chmn., 1974-78; mem. sci. adv. com. Nat. Inst. Aging, NIH, Balt., 1983-86. Author: Cardiac Diagnosis and Treatment, 3d edit., 1980, Myocardial Diseases, 1973, Cardiac Arrhythmias; Diagnosis and Treatment, 1977, Pericardium in Health and Disease, 1985, Diagnosis of Heart Disease, 1991, Diagnosis in Color: Physical Signs in Cardiology, 1998. Served with M.C., AUS, 1943-44. Recipient award for contbns. to cardiology Georgetown U., 1978; Nat. Heart and Lung Inst. grantee, 1961-73. Fellow ACP, Am. Coll. Cardiology (Master Tchr. award 1974), Am. Heart Assn. Coun. on Clin. Cardiology; mem. Am. Clin. and Climatol. Assn., Am. Physiol. Soc., Cttrl. Soc. Clin. Rsch., Am. Fedn. Clin. Rsch., Assn. Univ. Cardiologists (founding mem., pres. 1976), Am. Heart Assn. (local chpt. trustee, exec. com., pres. 1979—, Samuel Kaplan Rsch. award 1994, Spl. Recognition award Laennec Soc. 1994), U. Tenn. Coll. Medicine (Disting. Alumnus award 1992), Sigma Xi, Alpha Omega Alpha, Phi Chi. Presbyterian. Home: 3533 Deepwoods Ln Cincinnati OH 45208-2530 Office: U Cin Coll Medicine 231 Bethesda Ave Cincinnati OH 45229-2827 *Dig deeply. Know more about one area than anyone else. Do things for other people. At the end of your career these will be more important than your research.*

FOWLER, PAUL RAYMOND, physician, lawyer; b. Washington, Apr. 30, 1958; s. Charles Raymond and Dora E. (Burger) F.; m. Mary Jane Weber, Oct. 4, 1986; children: Christina D., Laura M., Joshua P. BS, U. Md., 1980, postgrad., 1980-81; DO, U. Osteopathic Medicine, Des Moines, Iowa, 1985; JD with honors, Drake U., 1994. Diplomate Am. Bd. Family Practice, Am. Bd. Forensic Examiners, Am. Osteo. Bd. Family Practice, Am. Osteo. Bd. Preventive Medicine; bar: Fla. 1995, Ill. 1996, D.C. 1996, Ky. 1998. Intern Des Moines Gen. Hosp., 1985-86; resident Ea. Va. Grad. Sch. Medicine, Norfolk, 1986-88; pvt. practice medicine Norfolk, 1988-90; staff Iowa Meth. Med. Ctr., Des Moines, 1990-95, Mercy Med. Ctr., Des Moines, 1992-94; med. dir. Occupational Health Svcs., Des Moines, 1990-95; chief physician Ford Motor Co., Hapeville, Ga., 1995-97; med. dir. Mary Black Health Sys., Spartanburg, S.C., 1997—; assoc. clin. prof. U. Osteo. Medicine, 1990—; clin. prof. Pikevill Coll. Osteo. Medicine, 1997—; judge Nat. Mock Trial Coll. Comp., 1992; mem. mock trial team Drake U. Law Sch., 1992, Med. Malpractice Rev. Bd., Commonwealth of Va., 1988-90; pvt. practice law, 1994—. Reviewer Am. Forensic Examiner, 1997—; contbr. articles to profl. jours. Active Silver Spring Vol. Fire Dept., 1978-81; mem. bioethics com. Iowa Meth. Med. Ctr., Des Moines, 1992-95. Recipient Good Citizen award Clifton Park Citizens Assn. Fellow Am. Acad. Family Physicians, Am. Coll. Legal Medicine; mem. Fla. Bar Assn., Ky. Bar Assn., Ill. Bar Assn., D.C. Bar Assn., Am. Bd. Med. Specialties, S.C. Acad. Family Physicians, Am. Osteo. Assn. (tech. task force), Phi Sigma (pres. 1984-85). Avocations: tennis, running, stamp collecting. Home: 225 Mosspoint Cir Apt 7 Spartanburg SC 29303-1430 Office: 2995 Reidville Rd Ste 160 Spartanburg SC 29301-5668

FOWLER, RAYMOND DALTON, professional association executive, psychologist; b. Jasper, Ala., Dec. 22, 1950; s. Raymond Dalton and Willie (Sanders) F.; m. Nancy Allebach, Aug. 13, 1955 (dec.); children: Karen Sydney, Derek Tyson, Michael Allan; m. Sandra Mumford, May 5, 1984. Student, Vanderbilt U., 1948-50; BA, U. Ala., 1952, MA, 1953; PhD, Pa. State U., 1957; D in Psychology (hon.), Forest Inst. Profl. Psychology, 1996. Diplomate in clin. psychology Am. Bd. Profl. Psychology; lic. psychologist, Ala. Rsch. asst. Psychoacoustics Lab., Pa. State U., University Park, 1953-54; fellow USPHS, 1954-56; asst. prof. psychology, asst. dir. Psychol. Clinic, U. Ala., Tuscaloosa, 1956-59; assoc. prof., dir. Psychol. Clinic U. Ala., Birmingham, 1959-65, prof., chmn. dept., 1965-83, prof. (on leave), 1983-86, prof. emeritus, 1986—; sr. cons. Psych. Sys. and Nat. Computer Sys., Balt. and Washington, 1983-86; prof. psychology, head dept. U. Tenn., Knoxville, 1986-89; exec. v.p., CEO APA, Washington, 1989—; participant White House Conf. on Health, 1965, Nat. Conf. on Criminal Justice Stds. and Goals, 1973; mem. nat. adv. com. on alcoholism HEW, 1970-72, chmn. com. on rsch., 1970; mem. task panel on manpower and pers. President's Commn. on Mental Health, 1977-78; mem. Ala. Gov.'s Adv. Com. on Alcoholism and Drug Abuse, 1973-82; vice chmn. program com. N.Am. Congress on Alcohol and Drug Addiction, 1974; mem. sci. adv. com. Nat. Coun. on Alcoholism, 1974-78; mem. rsch. tng. rev. com. Nat. Inst. Alcohol Abuse and Clcoholism, 1975-78; dir. Ala. Prison Classification Project, 1976-77; chmn. So. Sch. Alcohol Studies, 1960-62; cons. Ala. Commn. on Alcoholism, 1958-70, VA, 1959-65, Estate of Howard R. Hughes, 1976-84; prin. cons. Roche Psychiat. Svc. Inst., Nutley, N.J., 1966-77, Med. Computer Svc., Basel, Switzerland, 1968-76, Med. Computer Svc., Hans Huber Verlag, Berne, Switzerland, 1976-89; cons. to adminstr. Law Enforcement Assistance Adminstrn., U.S. Dept. Justice, Washington, 1971-73; program cons. div. alcoholism Ala. Dept. Mental Health, 1973-75; sr. cons. Nat. Computer Sys., Mpls., 1983-89. Contbg. author: Assessment for Decision, 1987, Handbook of Psychological Assessment, 1990; editor Am. Psychologist, 1989-95; contbr. articles and revs. to profl. jours. Vice pres. Ala. Coun. on Human Rels., 1965-68, Rehab. Rsch. Found., 1965-80; alumni fellow Pa. State U., 1988—; bd. dirs. Rosalynn Carter Inst. for Human Devel., 1988. Named Disting. Practitioner, Nat. Acad. Practice, 1986; recipient significant Minn. Multiphasic Personality Inventory contbn. award U. Minn., 1988; grantee Ala. Commn. on Alcoholism, 1962-63, 64-68, NIMH, 1963-64, Roche Psychiat. Svc. Inst., 1967-76, Ala. Dept. Mental Health, 1969-70, U.S. Dept. Justice, 1971-82, Ala. Bd. Corrections, 1972-73, Ala. Law Enforcement Planning Agy., 1972-74, Nat. Inst. Alcohol Abuse and Alcoholism, 1973-83. Fellow APA (pres. div. 13, 1978-79, coun. reps. 1965-68, 70-73, 75-78, bd. dirs. 1979—, treas. 1983-87, pres.-elect 1987-88, pres. 1988-89, presdl. citation 1990), Soc. for Personalaity Assessment; mem. AAUP (pres. U. Ala. chpt. 1969-70), Southeastern Psychol. Assn. (pres. 1971-72, dir. continuing edn. 1973-89, dist. speaker 1982, 87), Ala. Psychol. Assn. (pres. 1962, award for outstanding contbns. 1979), Alcohol and Drug Problems Assn. N.Am. (program chmn. 1974-76, bd. dirs. 1975-77), Internat. Coun. Psychologists, Sigma Xi (life), Psi Chi (nat. v.p. 1980-84, disting. speaker 1977, 88), Omicron Delta Kappa, Phi Kappa Phi. Democrat. Avocations: running, gardening, cooking. Home: 4020 Linnean Ave NW Washington DC 20008-3805 Office: Am Psychological Assoc 750 1st St NE Washington DC 20002-4241

FOWLER, ROBERT ARCHIBALD, infosystems company executive; b. Lewistown, Pa., May 29, 1931; s. Harry K. Fowler and Margaret (Elder) Mann; m. Gail Brewer; children: R. Wendell, Ann, Allen. BS in Econs., Franklin and Marshall Coll., 1953; MBA, Cornell U., 1958. Auditor Gen. Motors Corp., Rochester, N.Y., 1953-54; exec. trainee Mfr.'s Hanover Bank, N.Y.C., 1958-60; credit rep. Cen. Trust Corp., Rochester, 1960-61; mktg. exec. Voplex Corp., Rochester, 1961-70; chmn. 5 W Info. Services, Rochester, 1970—; treas. Clover Investment Group, Rochester, 1960—. Author: Careerism, 1970, Buyerism, 1971, Creative Winemaking, 1973; contbr. articles to profl. jours. Served with U.S. Army, 1954-56. Mem. Am. Legion, Midtown Tennis Club, Counterpointe Golf Club, Rockledge Country Club. Republican. Presbyterian. Avocation: tennis. Office: 5W Info Svcs Inc Ste 107B 2509 Browncroft Blvd Rochester NY 14625-1522

FOWLER, ROBERT ASA, diplomat, consultant, business director; b. Sewickley, Pa., Aug. 5, 1928; s. William Henry and Violet Lee (Baker) F.; m. Monica Hedén; children: William Henry, Thomas Grasselli, Robert Saxton, Mary Antonia. B.A., Princeton U., 1950; M.B.A., Harvard U., 1955. With Conoco, Inc., 1955-85; comml. mgr. Conch Methane Services Ltd., U.K., 1960-65; gen. mgr. adminstrv. and ops. Conoco Ltd. (U.K.), London, 1965-68; mktg. devel. mgr. Conoco Inc. (U.S.A.), Houston, 1968-73; area mgr. Conoco Inc. (U.S.A.), N.W. Europe, 1973-78; chmn., mng. dir. Conoco Ltd., U.K., 1978-81; v.p. internat. mktg. Conoco Inc. (U.S.A.), Houston, 1981-85; owner, prin. cons. Fowler Internat., 1986—; counsul gen. Sweden, 1989—. Served to lt. USNR, 1950-53, Korea. Mem. Am. Petroleum Inst. Republican. Episcopalian. Clubs: Knickerbocker (N.Y.C.), River (N.Y.C.); Allegheny Country (Sewickley, Pa.); Chagrin Valley Hunt (Gates Mills, Ohio); Hurlingham (London). Office: 4422 First City Tower 1001 Fannin St Houston TX 77002-6706

FOWLER, ROBERT EDWARD, JR., agricultural products company executive; b. Camden, Tenn., Oct. 7, 1935; s. Robert Edward and Rebecca (Watson) F.; m. Margaret Caroline Armstrong, Dec. 28, 1957; children: Robert, William, Margaret. B.Engring., Vanderbilt U., 1957. With GE, Louisville, 1957-78, v.p., 1978-81; pres., COO, Rubbermaid, Inc., Wooster, Ohio, 1981-87, bd. dirs., 1981-87; chmn., CEO, pres. Josephson Office Products, Chgo., 1987-90; pres., CEO, BCC Indsl. Svcs., 1991-93; pres., COO, The Vigaro Corp., 1993-94, pres., CEO,, 1994-96; pres., COO, IMC Global (merged with The Vigoro Corp. 1996), Northbrook, Ill., 1996-97; CEO, pres. IMC Global, Northbrook, 1997—, chmn., chief exec. officer; bd. dirs. Alltrista Corp., Anixter Internat. Mem. Chgo. Christian Indsl. League (bd. dirs.). Office: IMC Global 2100 Sanders Rd Ste 200 Northbrook IL 60062-6146*

FOWLER, ROBERT F., JR., chemicals executive. BSChemE, Vanderbilt U., 1957. From mgmt. trainee to corp. v.p. GE, 1957-78; pres., COO Rubbermaid, Inc., Wooster, Ohio, 1981-87; chmn., COO, pres. Josephson Office Products, Chgo., 1987-90; pres., COO BCC Indsl. Svcs., Inc., 1991-93; pres., COO, dir. Vigoro Corp., Chgo., 1993-94; pres., COO IMC Global, Northbrook, Ill., 1996—, also CEO, 1997—, also chmn. bd. dirs., 1998—; dir. Anixter Internat., Chgo. Christian Indsl. League, Nat. Mining Assn. Office: IMC Global 2100 Sanders Rd Ste 200 Northbrook IL 60062-6146

FOWLER, ROBERT RAMSAY, Canadian government official; b. Ottawa, Ont., Can., Aug. 18, 1944; s. Robert MacLaren and Sheila Gordon (Ramsay) F.; m. Mary Stoker, June 13, 1981; children: Linton, Ruth, Antonia, Justine. BA, Queen's U., Kingston, Ont., 1968. Joined Fed. Pub. Svc. Can. Internat. Develop. Agy., Ottawa, 1968-69, dept. external affairs, 1969-71; 2nd sec. Can. Embassy, Paris, 1971-74; with comml. policy divsn. external affairs, 1974-76; 1st sec., counsellor Can. Permanent Mission to UN, N.Y.C., 1976-78; exec. asst. to under-sec. state, external affairs Can. Ottawa, 1978-80; asst.ssec. to cabinet, fgn. and def. policy Privy Coun. Office, Ottawa, 1980-86; asst. dep. min. (policy) Dept. Nat. Def., Ottawa, 1986-89, dep. min., 1989-95; amb. and permanent rep. UN Permanent Mission of Can. to UN,

N.Y.C., 1995—. Avocation: photography. Office: Perm Mission of Canada to UN 885 2nd Ave Fl 14 New York NY 10017-2201*

FOWLER, SUSAN MICHELE, real estate broker, entrepreneur; b. East Liverpool, Ohio, Jan. 6, 1952; d. George Robert and Mary Helen (Gilliland) F.; m. Paul Joseph Cusumano, Nov. 5, 1988. BA, West Liberty Coll., 1973; MEd, Kent State U., 1995. Lic. real estate broker, Ohio. Sales rep. Tropic-Cal, L.A., 1974-76; project mgr. R&B Enterprises, L.A., 1977-80; regional leasing mgr. First Union Mgmt., Inc., Cleve., 1981-82; comml. real estate broker Adler, Galvin, Rogers, Inc., Cleve., 1983-86, Coldwell Banker Comml. Real Estate, Cleve., 1986-90; pres. Comml. Real Estate Co., Cleve., 1990—; owner Susan M. Fowler Comml. Real Estate Co., Chagrin Falls, Ohio, 1990—, Empower Yourself Seminars, Chagrin Falls, 1992—; v.p., dir. offices First Union Real Estate Investment Trust, Cleve.; pres. Christopher Real Estate Investment, Cleve., 1989—, Christopher Mgmt. Co., Cleve., 1989—; founder, speaker Empower Yourself Seminars, 1992. Trustee, pres. West Side Community Mental Health Ctr., Cleve., 1985—; trsutee, v.p. Child Conservation Coun., Cleve., 1988—; trustee Big Bros. and Big Sisters Greater Cleve., 1989, Visions for Youth, 1991; mem. Cleve. Mus. Art, Geauga County Humane Soc., Fairmount Arts Centre. Mem. Comml. Real Estate Women, Cleve. Area Bd. Realtors (speakers bur.), Nat. Assn. Realtors, Ohio Assn. Realtors, Cleve. Mus. Art, Pine Lake Trout Club. Home: 1014 Oakland Dr Barrington IL 60010

FOWLER, SUSAN ROBINSON, theatre executive; b. Chattanooga, July 17, 1946; d. Samuel Francis and Ruth Elizabeth (Cates) Robinson; m. Herbert Oliver Fowler, Aug. 26, 1978; 1 child, Kathryn Elizabeth. BA, Carnegie-Mellon U., 1968. Activities dir. Hotel Hershey, Pa., 1969-71; svcs. rep. L.A. Conv. Ctr., 1971; banquet coord. Alexandria Hotel, L.A., 1972-73; dir. Hershey Edn. and Cultural Ctr., 1974-76; exec. dir. Hershey Theatre, 1976—. Named Miss Pa., 1968. Mem. Rotary (pres. Hershey 1997-98). Avocations: sewing, baking, gardening. Office: Hershey Theatre E Caracas Ave Hershey PA 17033

FOWLER, THOMAS KENNETH, physicist; b. Thomaston, Ga., Mar. 27, 1931; s. Albert Grady and Susie (Glynn) F.; m. Carol Ellen Winter, Aug. 18, 1956; children—Kenneth, John, Ellen. B.S. in Engring, Vanderbilt U., 1953, M.S. in Physics, 1955; Ph.D. in Physics, U. Wis., 1957. Staff physicist Oak Ridge Nat. Lab., 1957-65, group leader plasma theory, 1961-65; staff physicist Gen. Atomic Co., San Diego, 1965-67, head plasma physics div., 1967; group leader plasma theory Lawrence Livermore Lab., Livermore, Calif., 1967-69, div. leader, 1969-70, assoc. dir. magnetic fusion, 1970-87; prof., chmn. dept. nuclear engring. U. Calif., Berkeley, 1988-94, prof. emeritus, 1995—. Calif. Coun. Sci. Tech. fellow, 1997—. Fellow Am. Phys. Soc. (chmn. plasma physics div. 1970); mem. Nat. Acad. Scis., Sigma Xi, Sigma Nu. Home: 221 Grover Ln Walnut Creek CA 94596-6310 Office: U Calif 4167 Etcheverry Hall Berkeley CA 94720-1731

FOWLER, TILLIE KIDD, congresswoman; b. Milledgeville, Ga., Dec. 23, 1942; d. Culver and Katherine Kidd; m. L. Buck Fowler, 1968; children: Tillie, Elizabeth. BA in Polit. Sci., Emory U., 1964, JD, 1967. Legis. asst. Rep. Robert G. Stephens, 1967-70; counsel White House Office of Consumer Affairs, 1970-71; mem. 103d-106th Congresses from 4th Fla. dist., 1993—, mem. nat. sec. com., transp. and infrastructure com.; majority dep. whip 103d-105th Congresses from 4th Fla. dist. Pres. Jr. League Jacksonville, Fla., 1982-83; chmn. Fla. Humanities Coun., 1989-91; pres. Jacksonville City Coun., 1989-90, mem., 1985-91; mem. bd. visitors U.S. Naval Acad., 1995—; chmn. ho. page bd., 1996—. Republican. Office: US Ho of Reps 106 Cannon Bldg Ofc Bldg Washington DC 20515-0904*

FOWLER, VINCENT R., dermatologist; b. South Bend, Ind., Dec. 15, 1944; s. Vincent R. and Miriam Frances (Alward) F.; m. Madeline M. Morales, Apr. 26, 1975; children: Debra, Michael, Peter. BA in Pscyhology, Calif. State U., L.A., 1969; MD, U. Autonoma Guadalajara, Mex., 1973. Diplomate Am. Bd. Dermatology; lic. Calif. Intern Long Beach (Calif.) Med. Ctr., 1974-75; resident in internal medicine SUNY Med. Ctr., Stonybrook, N.Y., 1975-78; resident in dermatology Letterman Army Med. Ctr., Presido San Francisco, Calif., 1978-80; chief medicine/dermatology Reynolds Army Hosp., Fort Sill, Okla., 1980-82; chief dermatology W. L.A. Kaiser Med. Ctr., 1982—; asst. clin. prof. UCLA Sch. Medicine, 1984—. Major Army Med. Corps., 1978-82. Fellow Am. Acad. Dermatology; mem. L.A. Met. Dermatol. Soc. Avocations: surfing, skiing, tennis. Office: Kaiser W LA Med Ctr 5971 Venice Blvd Los Angeles CA 90034-1713

FOWLER, VIVIAN DELORES, insurance company executive; b. Knoxville, Tenn., Sept. 26, 1946; d. Rance James Pierce and Margaret Willadene (Crowe) Compton; m. James Hubert Fowler, May 12, 1979. Student, U. Tenn., Knoxville. CPCU. Clk. The Travelers Ins. Co., Knoxville, 1967-84, adminstv. staff, 1984, comml. mktg. asst., 1984-86; comml. account analyst The Travelers Ins. Co., Nashville, 1986-89, sr. account analyst, 1989-90, account mgr., 1990-93; regional asst. mgr. small bus. unit comml. lines The Travelers Ins. Co., Atlanta, 1993—; regional underwriting mgr. select accounts mktg. Travelers/Aetna Ins. Co. (name changed to Travelers Property and Casulty Co.), Atlanta, 1996. Lay witness speaker, United Meth. Ch., Knoxville 1979-82; charter mem. St. Thomas Hosp. Found. Soc., 1990; mem. Arthritis Found., 1991. Mem. NAFE, Soc. CPCU, Soc. Cert. Ins. Counselors (cert. 1987), Nat. Assn. of Ins. Women (cert. Profl. Ins. Woman 1975), Internat. Platform Assn., Ins. Professionals of Atlanta, 1998. Republican. United Methodist. Home: 604 Ashley Forest Dr Alpharetta GA 30022-6133 Office: Travelers Property and Casulty Co 4400 Northpoint Pkwy Alpharetta GA 30022-2411

FOWLER, WALTON BERRY, franchise developer, educator; b. Tulsa, Dec. 4, 1946; s. Walton Rector Fowler and Martha Jean (Berry) Oliver; m. Deborah Martz, Oct. 1, 1972 (div. Feb. 1985); 1 child, Cullen Brian; m. Anne Sadler, Sept. 23, 1985; children: Nicole Anne, William Dean, Catherine Elizabeth. BA, Chapman Coll., 1972; teaching cert., Calif. State U., Fullerton, 1973. Mgr. Al Mayton Prodns., Universal City, Calif., 1968-72; dept. chmn., tchr. Anaheim (Calif.) High Sch. Dist., 1973-78; founder, chmn. Sylvan Learning Corp., Montgomery, Ala., 1979-88; v.p., treas. Vincent, Hanna, Fowler Investments, Bellevue, Wash., 1987-92; chmn. The Little Gym Internat. Inc., Kirkland, Wash., 1992-94; founder, pres. Krypton Inst., Spokane, Wash., 1995-97; pres. W. Berry Fowler & Assocs., 1997—; dept. chmn., tchr. Anaheim (Calif.) High Sch. Dist., 1968-72; bd. dirs. The Wilcox Group, Mercer Island; lectr. Nat. Honor Soc. Mem. Com. for Tchr. Tng. Chapman Coll., Orange, Calif., 1973, planning com. Boy Scouts Am., Mercer Island; founder, chmn. A Thousand Points of Knowledge Learning Ctrs. Mem. NEA, Internat. Franchise Assn., Venture Founders Assn. Republican. Avocations: boating, traveling, reading, art. Office: W. Berry Fowler & Associates Third Fl 421 W Riverside Ave Fl 3 Spokane WA 99201-0405

FOWLER, WAYNE LEWIS, SR., internist; b. Topeka, Kans., Jan. 5, 1923; s. Morrill George and Grace Anna (Carlson) F.; m. Violet June Ransom, Sept. 4, 1948; children: Wayne Jr., Deborah. BS, Washburn U., 1945; MD, U. Ind., 1947. Diplomate Am. Bd. Internal Medicine. Intern Kansas City (Mo.) Gen. Hosp., 1947-48, resident internal medicine, 1948-51; internist Galvin-Haughey Clinic, Concordia, Kans., 1953-95, NCK Med. Clinic, Concordia, Kans., 1995—; past pres. med. staff St. Joseph Hosp., Concordia Kans. Capt. US Air Force, 1951-53,. Fellow Am. Coll. Physicians (Laureate award Kans. chpt. 1994), Am. Coll. Chest Physicians; mem. AMA, Cl. County Med. Soc., Kans. Med. Soc., Am. Soc. Internal Medicine, Concordia Elks, Concordia Moose, Topeka Masonic Lodge # 17, Scottish Rite Bodies Topeka, ISIS Shrine alina. Republican. Episcopalian. Avocation: amateur radio. Home: 332 W 8th St Concordia KS 66901-3406 Office: NCK Med Inc 1010 3rd Ave Concordia KS 66901-4003

FOWLER, WESLEY CASWELL, JR., obstetrician, gynecologist; b. Dunn, N.C., Feb. 18, 1940. MD, U. N.C., 1966. Diplomate Am. Bd. Ob.-Gyn. Intern N.C. Meml. Hosp., Chapel Hill, 1967; resident N.C. Meml. Hosp, Chapel Hill, 1967-71; obstetrician-gynecologist U. N.C. Hosps., Chapel Hill, 1972—; prof., vice chmn. dept. ob.-gyn. U. N.C. Sch. of Medicine, Chapel Hill, 1972—. Mem. ACS, ACOG, AMA, Soc. Gynecologists and Obstetricians. Office: Univ NC Dept Ob-gyn CB # 7570 MacNider Chapel Hill NC 27599-7570

FOWLER, WILLIAM E., JR., government official; m. Norma June Roxborough; children: Claude, John. Grad., U. Akron, 1949, Fordham U., 1952; JD, Akron U., 1954. City prosecutor Akron, Ohio, 1957-58; 1st asst. law dir. City of Akron, 1958-59; asst. atty. gen. State of Ohio, 1959; chief hwy. divsn. Ohio Atty. Gen.'s Office, 1959-61; spl. asst. to atty. gen. U.S. Dept. Justice, 1961-65; hearing examiner U.S. Dept. Labor, 1965; mem. appeals counsel Social Security Adminstrn., 1965-66; mem. Bd. Appeals and Rev. U.S. Civil Svc. Commn., 1966-68, exec. vice chmn. interagy. adv. group, 1968-69; hearing examiner Nat. Transp. Safety Bd., Washington, 1969-77, chief judge, 1977—. Past pres. D.C. Mental Health Assn. Mem. Fed. Adminstrv. Law Judges Conf. (past pres.). Office: Nat Transp Safety Bd 490 Lenfant Plz SW Washington DC 20024-2104*

FOWLER, WILLIAM MAYO, JR., rehabilitation medicine physician; b. Bklyn., June 16, 1926. BS, Springfield Coll., 1948, MEd, 1949; MD, U. So. Calif., L.A., 1957. Diplomate Am. Bd. Phys. Medicine and Rehab. Intern UCLA, 1958, resident in pediatrics, 1959, resident in phys. medicine, rehab., 1963; chmn. dept. phys. medicine, rehab. U. Calif., Davis, 1968-82, mem. faculty dept. phys. medicine, rehab., 1972-91, prof. emeritus, 1991—. Fellow Am. Acad. Phys. Medicine and Rehab. (pres. 1981, Krusen award 1994), Am. Coll. Sports Medicine; mem. Assn. Acad. Physiatrists. Office: U Calif Davis Dept Phys Med Rehab One Shields Ave Davis CA 95616*

FOWLER, WYCHE, JR., ambassador; b. Atlanta, GA, Oct. 6, 1940; s. William Wyche and Emelyn (Barbre) F.; 1 dau., Katherine Wyche. BA, Davidson Coll., 1962; JD, Emory U., 1969. Bar: Ga. 1970. Chief asst. to Congressman Charles Weltner, 1965; mem. Atlanta Bd. Aldermen, 1969-73; pres. Atlanta City Council, 1973-77; mem. 95th-99th Congresses from 5th Ga. Dist., 1977-87; U.S. Senator from Ga., 1987-92; with Powell, Goldstein, Frazer & Murphy, Washington & Atlanta, 1993-95; pvt. practice law, 1996; U.S. amb. Saudi Arabia, 1996—. Served in U.S. Army. Recipient Myrtle Wreath award, 1972, Congl. sunbelt coun. ann. award, 1981, Ga. Citizens Coalition on Hunger award, 1982; named Outstanding Young Man Atlanta Jaycees, 1972, Outstanding Young Man Ga. Jaycees, 1973. Mem. ABA, State Bar Ga., Phi Delta Theta. Democrat. Office: US Embassy Unit 61307 APO AE 09803-1307

FOWLER-DIXON, DEBORAH LEA, family physician; b. Chicago Heights, Ill., July 24, 1967; d. Roger Haslewood and Esther Gladys (Aboab) F. AB with honors, Washington U., St. Louis, 1988; MD, So. Ill. U., 1993. Diplomate Am. Bd. Family Practice. Resident family practice So. Ill. U., Belleville, 1993-96; physician Southside Family Practice, St. Louis, 1996-97; asst. prof. dept. cmty. and family medicine Belleville Family Practice Residency Program, 1997-98; pvt. practice, 1998—. Named Young Careerist Collinsville Bus. and Profl. Women, 1995. Mem. Am. Acad. Family Practice, Ill. Acad. Family Practice, Am. Med. Women's Assn., Soc. Tchrs. Family Medicine, Phi Beta Kappa. Office: Family Health Assocs LLC 60 Regency Pl Millstadt IL 62260-2210

FOWLES, GEORGE RICHARD, physicist, educator; b. Glenwood Springs, Colo., Apr. 2, 1928; s. Howard Payne and Phyllis Kathleen (Gibson) F.; m. Dorothy Ellen Evans, Oct. 8, 1954 (dec. Dec. 1987); children: John Reed Maxon, Louise, Kathleen, Jefferson; m. Colleen Elizabeth Murphy, Sept. 17, 1988; stepchildren: Karla Sanger, Joseph Sanger, Kristina Sanger. BS, Stanford U., 1952, MS, 1954, PhD, 1962. Geophysicist Phelps Dodge Corp., Douglas, Ariz., 1954-55; physicist SRI Internat., Menlo Park, Calif., 1955-62, group leader, 1962-66; assoc. prof. Wash. State U., Pullman, 1966-73, prof. physics, 1973-95, prof. emeritus physics, 1995—, chmn. dept., 1984-90; cons. Nat. Materials Adv. Bd., Washington, 1970, 77-78; cons. numerous govt. labs., Washington, 1968—; vis. prof. Australian Nat. U., Canberra, 1983. Contbr. 50 sci. articles to physics jours. Served with USN, 1946-48. Fulbright research fellow Nat. Edn. Found., U. Auckland, New Zealand, 1975. Fellow Am. Phys. Soc., Am. Assn. Physics Tchrs. Avocation: guitar making. Home: PO Box 327 Eastsound WA 98245-0327

FOWLES, JOHN, author; b. Essex, Eng., Mar. 31, 1926; s. Robert and Gladys (Richards) F.; m. Elizabeth Whitton, Apr. 2, 1954 (dec. 1990); m. Sarah Smith, Sept. 3, 1998. Honours degree in French, Oxford U., 1950; D.Litt., Exeter U., 1983; LittD, U. East Anglia, 1997. Author: The Collector, 1963, The Aristos, 1964, The Magus, 1966, The French Lieutenant's Woman, 1969, Poems, 1973, The Ebony Tower, 1974, Shipwreck, 1977, Daniel Martin, 1977, Islands, 1978, The Tree, 1979, Mantissa, 1982, A Maggot, 1985, Wormholes, 1998. Hon. fellow New Coll., Oxford, 1997. Office: Jonathan Cape Ltd, 20 Vauxhall Bridge RD, London SW1V 2SA, England

FOWLKES, NANCY LANETTA PINKARD, social worker; b. Athens, Ga.; d. Amos Malone and Nettie (Barnett) Pinkard; m. Vester Guy Fowlkes, June 4, 1955 (dec. 1965); 1 child, Wendy Denise. BA, Bennett Coll., 1946; MA, Syracuse U., 1952; MSW, Smith Coll., 1963; MPA, Pace U., 1982. Dir. publicity Bennett Coll., Greensboro, N.C., 1946-47, 49-50; asst. editor Va. Edn. Bull. ofcl. organ Va. State Tchrs. Assn., Richmond, 1950-52; asst. office mgr. Cmty. Svc. Soc., N.Y.C., 1952-55; social caseworker, asst. supr. Dept. Social Svcs., Westchester County, White Plains, N.Y., 1959-67, supr. adoption services, 1967-77, supr. adoption and foster care, 1977-89; mem. adv. bd. White Plains Adult Edn. Sch. First v.p. Eastview Jr. High Sch., 1970-71; area chmn. White Plains Community Chest, 1964; sec. Mt. Vernon Concert Group, 1952-54; fund raising co-chmn. Urban League Guild of Westchester, 1967; pres. White Plains Interfaith Council, 1972-74; pres. northeastern jurisdiction United Meth. Ch., 1988-92; chmn. adminstrv. bd. Meth. Ch., 1970-72, 82-83, vice chmn., 1978-80, vice chmn. trustees, 1973-77, treas., 1978-83; lay speaker, v.p. Met. dist. United Meth. Women, 1977-79, exec. bd. N.Y. conf., N.Y. conf. rep. Upper Atlantic Regional Sch., 1981-83, mem. nominating com., 1982-83, trustee N.Y. conf., 1982-88, pres. N.Y. conf., 1983-87, conf. United Meth. Women, bd. dirs. Global Ministries United Meth. Ch., 1988-96, women's divsn., 1988-96, v.p., chair sect. finance women's divsn., 1992-96, supt., 1997—, chair program divsn. N.Y. Conf., 1989-93; v.p. superintendency commn. Met. North Dist., 1997—; chair Episcopal residence N.Y. Conf. Episcopancy Commn., 1997—; bd. dirs. Family Service of Westchester, Bethel Meth. Home, Ossining, N.Y.; bd dirs White Plains YWCA, 1985-93, Scarritt Bennett Ctr., Nashville, Tenn., 1990—, Gum Moon Women's Residence, San Francisco, 1992-96, White Plains-Greenburg NAACP, 1993—. Mem. Nat. Assn. Social Workers, Acad. Cert. Social Workers, Jack and Jill of Am. Inc. (chpt. pres. 1954-56, regional sec.-treas 1967-71), Nat. Bus. and Profl. Women's Club (chpt. sec. 1954-56), Internat. Platform Assn., Theta Sigma Phi (Sec.-Treas.), Zeta Nu Omega, Alpha Kappa Alpha (pres. 1960-64, treas. 1975-78). Club: Regency Bridge (pres. 1963-65). Home: 107 Valley Rd White Plains NY 10604-2316

FOX, ALAN HUGO, musical instrument manufacturing company executive; b. Chgo., Apr. 1, 1934; s. Hugo Eugene and Mary Margaret F.; m. Pamela Ann Michne, June 13, 1964; 1 child, Karen. BS in Chem. Engring., Purdue U., 1955. Engr. Procon Inc., Des Plaines, Ill., 1957-60; v.p. gen. mgr. Fox Products Inc., S. Whitley, Ind., 1960-70, pres., 1970—. Designer Fox double reed symphonic instruments. Recipient Outstanding Chem. Engring. award Purdue U., 1992. Mem. Internat. Double Reed Soc. (co-founder 1972—), Wawasee Yacht Club (commodore 1982—). Office: Fox Products Corp 6110 South State Rd 5 South Whitley IN 46787

FOX, ANNE C., state agency administrator; 1 child. BS in Edn., Bucknell U., 1967; MS in Reading, Syracuse U., 1973, PhD in Tchr. Edn., 1975. Cert. elem. tchr., adminstr., Idaho. Postdoctroal work in edn. adminstrn. U. Idaho; tchr. elem.; prin., supt. pub. schs., 1978-84; assoc. prof. edn. adminstrn. Gonzaga U., 1987-94; supt. pub. instrn. State of Idaho, 1995—; mem. State Bd. Edn., State Land Bd., State Libr. Bd., State Endowment Fund, Investment Bd.; founder Children's Village for Abused Children; grant writer. *

FOX, ARTHUR CHARLES, physician, educator; b. Newark, Sept. 16, 1926; s. Jacob and Mae (Bonda) F. Student, Harvard U., 1943-44; M.D., N.Y. U., 1948. Intern, asst. resident and chief resident in medicine Bellevue Hosp., N.Y.C., 1948-52; from asst. to prof. N.Y. U. Sch. Medicine, N.Y.C., 1954—; chief cardiology sect. N.Y. U. Sch. Medicine, 1969—; cons. Manhattan VA Hosp. Contbr. articles to profl. jours. Served with M.C. USAF, 1952-54. NIH fellow, 1954-56; grantee, 1956-80. Master ACP (gov. region 1981-86); fellow Am. Coll. Cardiology; mem. Am. Fedn. Clin. Research, N.Y. Heart Assn. (pres. 1987-89), N.Y. Cardiologic Soc. (pres. 1992-93), Alpha Omega Alpha, AAAS, Sigma Xi. Home: 330 E 33rd St New York NY 10016-9466 Office: 550 1st Ave New York NY 10016-6481

FOX, ARTHUR JOSEPH, JR., editor; b. Bklyn., Sept. 19, 1923; s. Arthur Joseph and Mary Loretta (Foley) F.; m. Ann Marie McElroy, Sept. 7, 1946; children: Jane Ann, John Arthur; m. Lorraine Cecelia Hodge, Sept. 10, 1993. BS in Civil Engring, Manhattan Coll., 1947, DSc (hon.), 1982. Structural designer Sanderson & Porter, N.Y.C., 1947-48; asst. editor Engring. News-Record, McGraw-Hill Publs., N.Y.C., 1948-54; asso. editor Engring. News-Record, McGraw-Hill Publs., 1954-58, sr. editor, 1956-57, sr. staff editor, 1957-60, mng. editor, 1960-64, editor-in-chief, 1964-88; mng. dir. Constrn. Industry Presidents Forum, Potomac, Md., 1989-97; exec. dir. Constrn. Industry Round Table, 1998. Mem. N.Y.C. Environ. Control Bd., 1974-77. Served with AUS, 1943-45. Decorated Bronze Star; recipient award of merit Am. Cons. Engrs. Council, 1975, medal of profl. excellence, 1985; recipient Met. Civil Engr. of Year award, 1975, We Dig America award Nat. Utility Contractors Assn., 1987, Golden Beaver svc. award, 1988; recipient Silver Shovel award Am. Subcontractors Assn., 1975, hon. mem. 1987; named hon. mem. AIA, 1986. Fellow ASCE (pres. 1975-76); mem. Am. Acad. Environ. Engrs. (past trustee), Engrs. Council for Profl. Devel. (dir. 1969-75), Nat. Constrn. Industry Council (exec. com. 1976-77, Saul Horowitz Career Achievement award 1987), N.Y. Bldg. Congress (bd. govs. 1969-73, 78-86), Engrs. Joint Council (dir. 1976-77, v.p. 1978-80), The Moles, Manhattan Coll. Alumni Soc. (past pres.), Chi Epsilon, Tau Beta Pi. Club: Congrl. Country. Home and Office: 10108 Garden Way Potomac MD 20854-3966

FOX, ARTURO ANGEL, Spanish language educator; b. Hoguín, Cuba, Aug. 2, 1935; came to U.S., 1962, naturalized, 1972; s. Arturo Roberto and Dulce Maria (Macle) F.; m. Rosa del Carmen Portilla, Jan 17, 1959; children: Franz, Alexandra. B. Letters and Scis., Friends Sch., Holguin, Cuba, 1952; LL.D., U. Havana, 1960; M.A. in Spanish, U. Minn., 1968, Ph.D., 1971. Bar: Cuba 1960. Pvt. practice law Holguin, 1960-62; instr. Spanish Luther Coll., Decorah, Iowa, 1963-66; asst. prof. Spanish Dickinson Coll., Carlisle, Pa., 1966-72, assoc. prof., 1972-79, prof., 1979-98, chmn. dept. modern langs., 1972-74, chmn. depts. Spanish and Italian, 1978-79, chmn. dept. Spanish, 1981-84, 90-93; coord. Latin Am. Studies program, 1968-77; dir. Colombia Semester program Ctrl. Pa. Consortium, 1977-78, Dickinson in Spain, Malaga, 1985-86, 88-90, 93-95; apptd. William W. Edel prof. humanities; endowed chair, 1992. Author: three Spanish textbooks, (novel) Anecdotario del Comandante, 1976; contbr. articles in field to profl. publs. Ford grantee, 1969-70; Lilly and Mellon faculty devel. grantee, 1978, 79; recipient Christain R. and F. Lindback Found. Disting. Teaching award, 1981. Mem. Am. Assn. Tchrs. Spanish and Portuguese. Office: Dickinson Coll Dept Spanish Carlisle PA 17013

FOX, BERNARD HAYMAN, cancer epidemiologist, educator; b. N.Y.C., Dec. 26, 1917. BS, U. Mass., 1940; MS, Tufts U., 1947; PhD, U. Rochester, 1949. Teaching fellow U. Mass., 1941; asst. prof. George Washington U., Washington, 1949-56; chief exptl. rsch. Div. Accident Prevention, HEW, Washington, 1957-60, 62-67, assoc. chief rsch., neurol. and sensory disease control program, 1967-70; dir. lab. of exptl. psychology Cleve. Psychiat. Inst., 1960-62; asst. to chief perinatal rsch. program Nat. Inst. Neurol. Diseases and Blindness, NIH, Bethesda, Md., 1970-73, mgr. social sci., biometry br. Nat. Cancer Inst., 1973-82; prof. psychiatry Boston U. Sch. Medicine, 1983—; mem. sci. adv. coun. Inst. for Advancement of Health, 1982-90. Served to 1st lt. USAAC, 1942-46. Fellow APA; mem. Internat. Psycho-Oncology Soc. (bd. dirs. 1986—). Co-editor: Alcohol and Traffic Safety, 1963; Minimal Brain Dysfunction, 1971; Cancer: The Behavioral Dimensions, 1976; Perspectives on Behavioral Medicine, 1981; Impact of Psychoendocrine Systems in Cancer and Immunity, 1984. Office: 99 Florence St Apt 320 Malden MA 02148-3955

FOX, BETH WHEELER, library director; b. Oklahoma City, May 4, 1945; d. Robert R. and Marjorie (Woodberry) Wheeler; m. Dennis Dean Fox, July 15, 1963; children: Rebecca, Julia, Bryce. BS in Libr. Sci./History cum laude, U. North Tex., 1967. Cataloger George Williams Coll., Downers Grove, Ill., 1967-68; br. libr. Libr., Ft. Benning, Ga., 1968-69; ref. libr. Palos Verdes (Calif.) Pub. Libr., 1969-72; libr. vol. Am. Luth. Sch. Libr., Burbank, Calif., 1979-81, Stevenson Elem. Sch. Libr., Burbank, 1981-82; libr. dir. Westbank Community Libr., Austin, Tex., 1983—; presenter in field. Author: The Dynamic Community Library: Practical, Creative and Inexpensive Ideas of the Library Director, 1988, Behind the Scenes at the Dynamic Library: Simplifying Essential Operations, 1990. Bd. dirs. Westbank Community Bds. Recipient Hon. Svc. award Burbank Coun. PTA, 1981, Vol. of Yr. award, 1982. Mem. ALA (John Cotton Dana award 1986, 90), Tex. Libr. Assn. (co-founder small cmty. libr. round table 1986, program chmn. dist. III 1986, rep. state fin. rev. 1991, structure/orgn. coun. 1994, rsch. grant recipient 1987, pub. rels. com. 1995-98, scholarship com. 1995-98, Access Tex. com. 1996—Cmty. Libr. of Yr. 1988), Ctrl. Tex. Libr. Sys. (automatiion com. 1986), Network for Smaller Librs. (founder 1985), Tex. Mcpl. Libr. Dirs. Assn., Vol. League of Austin, Rotary (scholarship com. 1996, 98), Rotary (tchr. excellence com. 1997, program com. 1997-98), Phi Alpha Theta. Avocations: genealogy, gardening, home repair, stained glass, sailing. Home: 1606 Bay Hill Dr Austin TX 78746-6248

FOX, BRUCE I., federal judge; b. 1949. BS, SUNY, Stony Brook, 1971; JD, Harvard U., 1975. Bar: Pa. Bankruptcy judge for ea. dist. Pa., U.S. Bankruptcy Ct., Phila., 1986—. Office: US Bankruptcy Ct 900 Market St Rm 400 Philadelphia PA 19107-4299

FOX, BYRON NEAL, lawyer; b. St. Louis, May 15, 1948; s. Meyer and Thelma (Werber) F.; m. Cynthia Penner, Aug. 25, 1984. BS, Tulane U., 1970; MBA, Boston U., 1974; JD, Kans. U., 1973. Bar: Mo. Pres. Fox & Partee, Kansas City, Mo., 1988-93. Chmn. Kans. City Bd. of Zoning Adjustment, 1993-98. Stockbroker Dain Rauscher, Inc., 1998—. Homestead Commn., 1993—. 1st lt. U.S. Army, 1973. Mem. ABA, Mo. Bar Assn., Kansas City Bar Assn. Jewish, Nat. Assn. Criminal Defense Lawyers, Am. Royal Assn. (bd. govs.), Kans. City Club. Office: Fox & Partee 410 Archibald St Fl 2 Kansas City MO 64111-3001

FOX, CARL ALAN, research executive; b. Waukesha, Wis., Nov. 24, 1950; s. Frank Edwin and Margaret Alvilda (Rasmussen) F.; m. Susan Jane Smith, June 18, 1977; children: Thomas Gordon, James David, Joseph Carl. BS, U. Wis., River Falls, 1973; MS, U. Minn., 1975; PhD, Ariz. State U., 1980; postgrad., Stanford U., 1993. Lab. asst. dept. biology U. Wis., River Falls, 1971-73; rsch. asst. dept. agronomy and plant genetics U. Minn., St. Paul, 1973-75; tchr. high sch. Le Center (Minn.) Pub. Schs., 1975-76; rsch. fellow dept. botany Ariz. State U., Tempe, 1976-79; rsch. asst. Lab. Tree-Ring Rsch. U. Ariz., Tucson, 1978-79; rsch. scientist, then sr. rsch. scientist So. Calif. Edison Co., Rosemead, 1979-87; rsch. assoc. agrl. experiment sta. U. Calif., Riverside, 1986-87; exec. dir. Desert Rsch. Inst., Reno, 1987-96, assoc. v.p. rsch., 1994-95; dir. Office of Rsch. and Program Devel. U. N.D., Grand Forks, 1996—, rsch. prof. dept. tchg. and learning and biology; rsch. adviser Electric Power Rsch. Inst., Palo Alto, Calif., 1983-87; liaison Utility Air Regulatory Group, Washington, 1983-87, cons., 1989-91; mem. peer rev. panel EPA, 1986, 97, 98, 99; invited reviewer air quality rsch. div. Nat. Park Svc., Denver, 1989; peer rev. panel Minn. Legis. Commn. on Resources, 1998. Contbr. numerous papers to profl. publs. Asst. troop leader Newport Beach (Calif.) area Boy Scouts Am., 1981-82, cub scout leader Reno area, 1990-91; bd. dirs. World Rainforest Found., Reno, 1989-92, Internat. Visitors Coun. No. Nev., Reno, 1991-96; coach YMCA, Reno, 1989-95, Grand Forks, N.D., 1996—; deacon Covenant Presbyn. Ch., 1989-92; judge State of Nev. Odyssey of the Mind. NSF fellow, 1976-79; grantee EPA, 1978-79, 83-85, 89-95, NSF, 1987-95, 98—, Dept. of Def. and Energy, 1987. Mem. AAAS, Air Pollution Control Assn., Ecol. Soc. Am., Am. Soc. Agronomy, Greentree Gators Swim Team (pres. 1986-87), N.D. Acad. of Scis., Nat. Coun. of Univ. Rsch. Adminstrs., Soc. of Rsch. Adminstrn., Sigma Xi, Beta Beta Beta. Republican. Presbyterian. Avocations: camping, canoeing, tennis, gardening, basketball. Office: U ND Office Rsch/Program Devel PO Box 7134 Grand Forks ND 58202-7134

FOX, CLAUDE EARL, federal health official; b. Charleston, Miss., Nov. 8, 1946; s. Claude Earl Jr. and Shirley (Houston) F.; m. Carolyn Tedford, May 15, 1971; children: Stephanie Ryan, Victoria Crossley. BS with distinction,

Miss. Coll., 1968; MD, U. Miss., 1972; MPH, U. N.C., 1975. Diplomate Am. Bd. Preventive Medicine, Am. Bd. Pub. Health; qualified Am. Bd. Pediatrics. Pediatric intern U. Miss. Med. Ctr., Jackson, 1972-73, pediatric resident, 1979-80; pediatric resident Johns Hopkins Hosp., Balt., 1978-79; with Miss. State Dept. Health, 1973-86; local health officer Charleston, 1973-74; dist. health officer Tupelo, Miss., 1975-78; chief Bur. Family Health Service Jackson, 1980-81, chief Bur. Personal Health Service, 1980-86; state health officer Ala. Dept. Pub. Health, Montgomery, from 1986; now administr. health resources and svcs. administrn. Dept. HHS, Rockville, Md.; med. cons. N.C. Dept. Health, Chapel Hill, 1974-75, Rockwell Internat., Tupelo, 1976-78, Mo. Dept. Health, 1984; vis. tchr. maternal and child health U. Miss. Med. Ctr., 1980-86, mem. adv. council; vis. teaching staff Sch. Pub. Health and Sch. Medicine, U. Ala.; adv. group on prevention Sen. Com. Labor and Human Resources, Washington; mem. Ala. Statewide Health Coordinating Council; mem. Ala. State Child Abuse and Negelect Prevention Bd., Ala. Commn. on Aging, Ala. Youth Services Bd., Planning and Adv. Council for Devel. Disabilities, Pesticides Adv. Com., Ala. Bd. Examiners Nursing Home Adminstrs.; chmn. Ala. Task Force Prevention and Perinatal Health, Ala. Radiation Adv. Bd. Health; adv. com. Emergency Med. Services; past mem. work group to revise 1988 U.S. standard birth certificate Nat. Ctr. Health Stats., primary care work group Miss. Gov.'s Office; past chmn. infant mortality task force, adolescent pregnancy task force Gov.'s Council on Children and Youth; adj. assoc. prof. George Washington U. Mem. Ala. Resource Devel. Com.; bd. dirs. Montogmery chpt., bd. .dirs. Ala. div., med. adv. com. ARC.; mem. external adv. com. Sch. Pub. Health U. Ala. Birmingham; mem. Ala. State Bldg. Commn. Recipient Sidney Chipman award for Outstanding Achievement in Maternal and Child Health U. N.C., 1982; named Pub. Citizen of Yr. Nat. Assn. Social Workers, Montgomery unit, 1987, Ala. chpt. 1987, Disting. Alumnus award sch. pub. health U. N.C., 1999, Leadership award Washington Bus. Group on Health and Nat. Assn. Cmty. Health Ctrs., 1999. Mem. Nat. Assn. Maternal and Child Health and Crippled Children's Dirs. (past steering com., legis. com., data com., pres-elect), Med. Assn. State Ala , Montgomery County Med. Soc., Am. Pub. Health Assn. (past Miss. del. Governing Council, Young Profl. Yr. award Maternal and Child Health sect. 1984), Ala. Pub. Health Assn., Assn. State and Terr. Health Officials (past forms revision com.), Am. Coll. Ob-gyn (past com. revision natality terminology). Baptist. Avocations: antique cars, antique clocks, photography, music. Office: Dept HHS Health Resources and Svcs Adminstrn 5600 Fishers Ln Rockville MD 20852-1750

FOX, DANIEL MICHAEL, foundation administrator, author; b. N.Y.C., Aug. 20, 1938; s. Alexender E. and Rose (Leitner) F.; m. Carol Anne Kemps, Sept. 8, 1963 (div. 1985); children: Aaron, Miriam, Joshua, Benjamin; m. Louise O. Vasvari, Dec. 26, 1988. AB, Harvard U., 1959, AM, 1961, PhD, 1964. Instr. Harvard U., Cambridge, Mass., 1964-65, asst. prof., 1967-72; dir. field ops. Applachian Vols., Berea, Ky., 1965-67; prof., v.p. SUNY, Stony Brook, 1972-89; assoc. dir. Nat. Ctr. for Health Svcs. Rsch., Rockville, Md., 1975-78; pres. Milbank Meml. Fund, N.Y.C., 1990—; cons. in field. Author: Engines of Culture, 1963, rev. edit., 1994, The Discovery of Abundance, 1967, Economists and Health Care, 1979, Health Policies, Health Politics, 1986, Photographing Medicine, 1988, AIDS: The Burdens of History, 1989, AIDS: The Making of a Chronic Disease, 1992, Power and Illness: The Failure and Future of American Health Policy, 1993, 95. Bd. mem. Village Care of N.Y., Inc., vice chmn. 1996—; bd. dirs. Employee Benefits Rsch. Inst. Shaw travel fellow Harvard U., 1959-60, Sheldon travel fellow, 1962; also numerous grants. Mem. NAS, Inst. Medicine, Am. Hist. Assn. (Beveridge prize 1965), Am. Assn. for the History of Medicine, N.Y. Acad. Medicine, Harvard Club of N.Y. Jewish. Office: Milbank Meml Fund 645 Madison Ave Fl 15 New York NY 10022-1010

FOX, DAVID ALAN, rheumatologist, immunologist; b. Montreal, July 5, 1953; s. Lester L. and Zelda L. (Rothbart) F.; m. Paula L. Bockenstedt, July 10, 1977; children: Sharon Elizabeth, Michelle Caroline, Jonathan William. BS, MIT, 1974; MD, Harvard U., 1978. Diplomate Am. Bd. Internal Medicine, Am. Bd. Rheumatology. Intern, then resident Brigham and Women's Hosp., Boston, 1978-81; fellow in rheumatology and immunology Harvard U. Med. Sch., Boston, 1981-85; asst. prof. U. Mich., Ann Arbor, 1985-90, assoc. prof., 1990-95, prof., 1995—, acting chief divsn. rheumatology, 1990-91, chief divsn., 1991—; dir. U. Mich. Multipurpose Arthritis Ctr., Ann Arbor, 1990—; trustee Arthritis Found., 1992-98. Assoc. editor Jour. Clin. Investigation, 1997—; contbr. chpts. to books, articles to profl. jours. Mem. Am. Coll. Rheumatology, Am. Assn. Immunologists, Am. Soc. Clin. Investigation. Achievements include discovery of T lymphocyte surface molecules and development of various monoclonal antibodies. Office: U MichMed Ctr Rackham Arthritis Rsch Unit 3918 Taubman Ctr Ann Arbor MI 48109

FOX, DAWNE MARIE, safety scientist; b. West Lafayette, Ind., Aug. 3, 1948; d. Gerhard P. and Betty M. (Norris) F.; m. Gerald C. Newmeyer, Oct. 4, 1969 (div. 1981); children: Mimie, Jerry. Grad. magna cum laude, Lord Fairfax, Middletown, Va., 1979; grad., Casper (Wyo.) Coll., 1985; cert. in indsl. safety and health, Ga. Inst. Tech., 1998. Cert. environ. trainer Nat. Environ. Tng. Assn.; EPA cert. instr. in asbestos abatement, supr., insp. and mgmt. planner, project designer tng. courses; approved instr. occupl. safety and health adminstrn., U.S. Dept. Labor, Nat. Tng. Inst.; cert. in disl. safety and health. Regional safety coord. Milchem Inc., Casper, 1979-83; safety dir. Energy Insulation Inc., Casper, 1983-85; safety mgr. Western States Constrn., Loveland, Colo., 1985-86; safety officer Govt. of D.C., 1987-89; dir. safety, health svcs. Denver and Rio Grande R.R., Denver, 1989-90; safety mgr. Browning-Ferris Inc., Hyattsville, 1990-91; sr. safety scientist Gen. Physics Corp., Columbia, Md., 1991—; cons., Casper, 1983-85. Instr. ARC, Casper, 1981-85, Am. Heart Assn., Casper, 1982-85; spl. aide to Spl. Olympics, Casper, 1983-85. Mem. Nat. Safety Coun., Am. Soc. Safety Engrs. (v.p. 1982-83, pres. 1983-84, Safety Profl. award 1982), Assn. Am. Railroads Safety Coun. (past del.). Republican. Roman Catholic. Avocations: skiing, bowling. Home: 9119 Bryant Ave Laurel MD 20723-1700

FOX, DONALD LEE, mental health counselor, consultant; b. Seymour, Ind., Sept. 9, 1948; s. John L. and Thelma P. (Engel) F.; m. Patricia L. Sain, Aug. 26, 1978; children: Ashley M., Aimee E. BA, Ind. U., Indpls., 1978; MS, Ind. State U., 1979. Lic. clin. social worker, social worker, marriage and family therapist. Coord. mental health Cath. Social Svcs., Indpls., 1979-85; coord. psychiat. assessment Valley Vista Hosp., Greenwood, Ind., 1985-86; clin. dir. Pathways, Speedway, Ind., 1986—; lectr., cons. Butler U., Indpls., 1988-89; adj. prof. U. Indpls., 1990—; cons. Wayne Twp. Vol. Fire Dept., Indpls., 1984—, La Porte (Ind.) Child Welfare Dept., 1988—. Pres., CEO Five Stop of Ind.: A Program for Youth, Inc., 1987-92. Mem. APA (assoc.), ACA, Am. Mental Health Counselors Assn. (nat. conf. com. 1990), Ind. Assn. Counseling and Devel. (conf. chmn. 1989), Ind. Mental Health Counselors Assn. (pres.-elect 1989-91, pres. 1991-92, Outstanding Svc. award 1989), Soc. Personality and Social Psychology (assoc.). Roman Catholic. Avocations: gardening, woodworking, fin. planning, money mgmt. Home: 730 Greenlee Dr Indianapolis IN 46234-2237

FOX, DONALD THOMAS, lawyer; b. Council Bluffs, Iowa, June 12, 1929; s. Donald and Genevieve (Tinley) F.; m. Ana Clemencia Tercero-Graham; children: Mark, Matthew, Genevieve, Melissa. AB magna cum laude, Harvard U., 1951; LLB, N.Y. U., 1956; Brevet de Traduction et de Terminologie Juridiques, U. Paris, 1957, Diplôme de Droit Comparé, 1960. Bar: N.Y. 1957, U.S. Ct. Claims 1960, U.S. Dist. Ct. (so. and ea. dists.) N.Y. 1960, U.S. Ct. Appeals (2nd cir.) 1960, D.C. 1968, U.S. Tax Ct. 1973. Instr. Inst. Comparative Law, NYU, 1957-59; assoc. Davis, Polk, Wardwell, Sunderland & Kiendl, N.Y.C., 1958-67; ptnr. Fox Horan & Camerini, LLP and predecessor firms, N.Y.C., 1968—; bd. dirs. Washington Sq. Legal Svcs., Inc., N.Y.C., 1974-85, Uniroyal Goodrich Tire Co., 1990-96, Michelin Licensing Svcs. Inc., Globalstar do Brazil, 1995-99; mem. adv. com. on history and theory Harvard U. Grad. Sch. Design, 1990—. Author: Conciliation of International Economic Disputes, 1964, Human Rights in Guatemala, 1979, Report on Contra Activity in Nicaragua, 1985, Violence in Colombia, 1989, Hungarian Constitutional Reform and the Rule of Law, 1993, Elections in Ethiopia, 1995, Elections in Nicaragua, 1996, Elections in Mexico, 1997; editor: The Cambodian Incursion: Legal Issues, 1971; mem. panel advisors Jour. Internat. Law and Politics, 1968—; contbr. articles to legal jours. Trustee Law Ctr. Found., N.Y.U., 1975-86, chmn. campaign fund, , 1980; mem. Am. Soc., 1975—; Coun. on Fgn. Rels., 1973—. 1st lt. USAF, 1951-53. Named to Com. of Honor, Giulio Romano Exhbn., Mantova, Italy, 1989; Albert Gallatin fellow, 1978. Fellow Am. Bar Found. (life); mem. Am. Law Inst., Am. Assn. Internat. Commn. Jurists (exec. com., bd. dirs. 1970—, chmn. 1991—), Am. Arbitration Assn. (panel arbitrators 1970—), Assn. of Bar of City of N.Y. (chmn. com. lawyers role in search for peace 1969-71, chmn. com. audit 1978-80, treas. 1982-84, chmn. com. profl. responsibility 1971-74, chmn. fin. com. 1982-84), NYU Law Alumni Assn. (pres. 1971-73), NYU Alumni Fedn. (pres. 1983-85), Humanitarian Found. for Nicaragua (exec. com. bd. dirs. 1991-96), The Century Assn. (chmn. wine com.), The DownTown Assn., Harvard Club of N.Y.C. Office: Fox Horan & Camerini LLP One Broadway New York NY 10004

FOX, DOUGLAS ALLAN, retired religion educator; b. Mullumbimby, Australia, Mar. 20, 1927; came to U.S., 1960; s. Cecil Edwin Madison and Lilly Louise (Tucker) F.; m. Margaret Eileen Porter, Sept. 10, 1958; children: Elizabeth Rachel, Michael Glenn. BA, U. Sydney, Australia, 1954; MA, U. Chgo., 1957; STM, Pacific Sch. Religion, Berkeley, Calif., 1958, ThD, 1962. Minister Congl. Union of New South Wales, Wollongong, Australia, 1955-56; minister Congl. Union of New South Wales, Sydney, Australia, 1958-61; prof. religion Colo. Coll., Colorado Springs, 1963-98, David and Lucille Packard prof., 1982-86. Author: Buddhism, Xianity and the Future, 1972, The Vagrant Lotus, 1973, Mystery and Meaning, 1975, Meditation and Reality, 1986, The Heart of Buddhist Wisdom, 1986, Dispelling Illusion, 1993, Direct Awareness of the Self, 1995. Trustee Penrose Meml. Hosp., Colorado Springs, 1980-82. World Ch. fellow World Council of Churches, Chgo., 1956-57; research fellow Soc. Religion in Higher Edn., 1966; named carnegie Found. Colo. Prof., 1995. Mem. Am. acad. Religion, Highlands Inst. for Am. Religious Thought. Mem. United Ch. of Christ. Avocations: fishing; hiking. Home: 1413 Querida Dr Colorado Springs CO 80909-3212

FOX, EDWARD A., business executive; b. N.Y.C., July 17, 1936; s. Herman and Ruth F.; divorced; children: Brian, Laura, Jacqueline; m. Arletta Ashe. AB, Cornell U., 1958; MBA, NYU, 1975. Pres., CEO, Student Loan Mktg. Assn., Washington, 1973-90; dean Amos Tuck Sch. Dartmouth Coll., Hanover, N.H., 1990-94; chmn. SLM Holding Corp., 1997—; bd. dirs. Delphi Fin. Group, Inc., Greenwich Capital Holdings, Inc., New Eng. Life Ins. Co.; chmn. bd. dirs. Eldorado Bancshares. Office: SLM Holding Corp 11600 Sallie Mae Dr Reston VA 20190-4796

FOX, EDWARD INMAN, education administrator and Spanish educator; b. Nashville, Aug. 22, 1933; s. Herbert Franklin and Ladye (Inman) F. BA, Vanderbilt U., 1954, MA, 1958; student, U. Montpellier, France, 1956-57; AM, Princeton U., 1959, PhD, 1961; LHD, Knox Coll., 1982, Monmouth Coll., 1982. Tchg. asst. Vanderbilt U., 1957-58; preceptor European lit. Princeton U., 1959; asst. prof. Romance langs. Vanderbilt U., 1960-64, acting dir. admissions, 1960-61, assoc. prof. Spanish, 1964-66; assoc. prof. Romance langs. U. Mass., 1966-67; prof. chmn. dept. Hispanic studies Vassar Coll., 1967-74, John Guy Vassar prof. modern langs., 1972-74, acting dean faculty, 1971-72, dir. long range ednl. planning, 1972-73; pres. Knox Coll., Galesburg, Ill., 1974-82; prof., chmn. dept. Hispanic studies Northwestern U., Evanston, Ill., 1982-98; retired; cons. on univ. reform in Uruguay, Brazil, Colombia, Chile, Ecuador, Jordan, Syria, 1988—; sr. cons. on higher edn. Kittleman Assocs., 1989-91; cons. Libr. of Congress on Spanish Newspapers, NEH; exec. com. Fedn. Ill. Ind. Colls. and Univs.; chmn. bd. Asso. Colls. Midwest; chmn. Ill. Rhodes Scholarship Com., 1974-77, Gt. Lakes Rhodes Com., 1979-83; bd. advisors Patterson Sch. Diplomacy and Internat. Commerce; chmn. selection com. Fulbright awards to Spain, 1989-92. Author: Azorin as a Literary Critic, 1962, La Crisis Intelectual del 98, 1976, Liberalismo y Socialismo, 1984, Ideologia y Politica en las Letras de Fin de Siglo, 1989, Azorin: Guia de la Obra Completa, 1992, La invención de España, 1996; also articles, translations poetry; editor: La voluntad, 1969, 5th edit., 1985, Antonio Azorin, 1970, 2d edit., 1992, Articulos desconocidos de R. de Maeztu, 1977, Meditaciiones de Ortega y Gasset, 1987, Castilla, 1991; co-editor: Spanish Thought and Letters in the Twentieth Century, 1966. Served to lt. (j.g.) USNR, 1954-56; capt. Res. Decorated Order of Queen Esabella the Cath. (Spain), 1985; Am. Philos. Soc. grantee, 1963, 68; Woodrow Wilson fellow, 1956-57, Herbert Montgomery Bergen fellow, 1958-59, Guggenheim fellow, 1970-71, NEH fellow, 1983, 94-95, Rockefeller Found. fellow, 1995; Fulbright scholar France, 1955-57, Fulbright Rsch. scholar Spain, 1965-66, 94-95; recipient Spain's Gold medal of Merit in Arts and Letters., 1993. Fellow Spanish Soc. for Intellectual History (hon.); mem. MLA (mem. exec. and nominating com. Spanish 4 1965-68, chmn. Spanish 5 1968, mem. exec. com. Spanish 5 1980-84), Real Acad. de Alfonso X el Sabio, Vanderbilt U. Alumni Assn. (bd. dirs.), Assn. Princeton Grad. Alumni (mem. bd. govs.), Internat. Assn. Hispanists, Phi Beta Kappa, Omicron Delta Kappa, Sigma Alpha Epsilon. Home: 4113 Dorman Dr Nashville TN 37215-2404

FOX, ELAINE SAPHIER, lawyer; b. Chgo., Nov. 18, 1934; d. Nathan Abraham and Rhoda M. (Schneidman) Saphier; m. Alan A. Fox, Apr. 25, 1954; children: Susan Fox Lorge, Wendy Fox Schneider, Mimi. BS, Northwestern U., 1955; JD, Ill. Inst. Tech., 1975. Bar: Ill., 1975, U.S. Dist. Ct. (no. dist.) Ill., 1975, U.S. Ct. Appeals (7th cir.) 1975, U.S. Ct. Appeals (fed. cir.) 1985. Trial atty. NLRB, Chgo., 1975-80; assoc. Hirsh & Schwartzman, Chgo., 1980-81; assoc. Gottlieb & Schwartz, Chgo., 1981-84, ptnr., 1984-90; ptnr. D'Ancona & Pflaum, Chgo., 1990—. Contbr. articles to profl. jours. and mags. Bd. dirs., exec. com. Am. Cancer Soc., Chgo., 1993—; mem. nat. and local governing coun. Am. Jewish Congress, Chgo., 1991—; bd. dirs. Jewish Vocat. Svc. Mem. ABA (subcom. nat. labor rels. bd. practice and procedures, employment and labor rels. law, labor and employment law com., Women Rainmakers, midwest regional mgmt. chair Nat. Labor Rels. Bd. practice and procedure com.), Women's Bar Assn., Chgo. Bar Assn. (labor and employment rels. vice chmn. 1989-90, chmn. 1990-91, co-chmn. Alliance for Women 1994-95, co-chair bd. mgrs. 1996—), Decalogue Assn. Avocations: swimming, walking, reading, theater, art. Office: Dancona and Pflaum 11 E Wacker Dr Ste 2800 Chicago IL 60601*

FOX, ELEANOR MAE COHEN, lawyer, professor, author; b. Trenton, N.J., Jan. 18, 1936; d. Herman and Elizabeth (Stein) Cohen; children: Douglas Anthony, Margot Alison, Randall Matthew. BA, Vassar Coll., 1956; LLB, NYU, 1961. Bar: N.Y. 1961, U.S. Dist. Ct. N.Y. 1964, U.S. Supreme Ct. 1965. Editor high sch. textbooks Cambridge Book Co., N.Y.C., 1956-57; editor labor service publ. Bur. Nat. Affairs, Washington, 1957-58; assoc. Simpson Thacher & Bartlett, 1962-70, partner, 1970-76, of counsel, 1976—; assoc. prof. law NYU, 1976-78, prof., 1978—, dir. Root-Tilden program, 1979-81, assoc. dean Law Sch., 1987-90, Walter Derenberg prof. trade regulation, 1994—; lectr. on antitrust and competition policy, domestic, internat. and comparative; mem. Pres. Carter's Nat. Commn. Rev. Antitrust Laws and Procedures, 1978-79; mem. adv. bd. Bur. Nat. Affairs Antitrust and Trade Regulation Reporter, 1977—, coun. fgn. rels., 1993—; trustee NYU Law Ctr. Found., 1974-92; trustee Lawyers' Com. Civil Rights Under Law, 1988—; mem. Coun. Fgn. Rels., 1993—; mem. internat. competition policy adv. com. to advise the U.S. Atty. Gen., 1998—. Author: (with Byron E. Fox) Corporate Acquisitions and Mergers, Vol. 1, 1968, Vol. 2, 1970, Vol. 3, 1973, Vol. 4, 1981, rev. edit., 1998; (novel) W.L., Esquire, 1977, (with G. Bermann, R. Goebel, W. Davey) European Community Law, Cases and Materials, 1993, supplement, 1998; (with Lawrence A. Sullivan) Antitrust—Cases and Materials, 1989, supplement, 1995; (with J. Fingleton, D. Neven, P. Seabright) Competition Policy and the Transformation of Central Europe, 1996; bd. editors N.Y. Law Jour., 1976-99, Antitrust Bull., 1986—; mem. adv. bd. Antitrust Law and Econs. Rev., 1988—, Rev. Indsl. Orgn., 1990—, EEC Merger Control Reporter, 1992—, Gaceta Juridica de la CE y de la Competencia, 1992—; contbr. articles to legal jours. Fellow Am. Bar Found., N.Y. Bar Found.; mem. ABA (chmn. merger com. antitrust sect. 1974-77, chmn. publs. com. 1977-78, chmn. Sherman Act com. 1978-79, mem. council antitrust sect. 1979-83, 90-94, vice chmn. antitrust sect. 1992-94, chair NAFTA Task Force, 1993—), N.Y. State Bar Assn. (chmn. antitrust sect. 1978-79, mem. exec. com. antitrust sect. 1979-83), Fed. Bar Council (trustee 1974-76, v.p. 1976-78), Assn. of Bar of City of N.Y. (v.p. 1989-90, exec. com. 1977-81, chmn. trade regulation com. 1973-76, lawyer advt. com. 1976-77, chmn. com. on U.S. in a global economy, 1991-94), Am. Law Inst., Assn. Am. Law Schs. (chmn. sect. antitrust and econ. regulation 1981-83), NYU Law Alumni Assn. (bd. dirs. 1974-79, 87-91), Am. Fgn. Law Assn. (v.p. 1979-82).

FOX, ELIZABETH TALBERT, writer, artist; b. Iowa City, Iowa, Dec. 19, 1950; d. Samuel Stubbs and Frances Selzer Talbert; m. Peter John Fox, Jan. 23, 1971 (div.); children: Seth Talbert, Caleb John. BA in Liberal Arts, U. Miss., 1975, postgrad., 1995-96; postgrad., Millsaps Coll., 1982, Hinds C.C., 1989. Pre-admissions sec. U. Miss., University, 1968-70, grad. asst., 1995-96; adminstrv. asst. Downtown YMCA, Jackson, Miss., 1986-89. Contbr. articles to profl. jours., newspapers, and mags. Usher New Stage Theater, Jackson, 1989; cub scout leader Boy Scouts Am., 1980, 87; sec. PTA, Alternative Elem. Sch., Jackson, 1985; mem. sch. bd. St. Therese Sch., Jackson, 1988; docent Miss. Mus. Art, Jackson, 1989. Hinds C.C. Pres.' scholar, 1989. Mem. Soc. Profl. Journalists, U. Miss. Alumni Assn., Yoknapatowpha Arts Coun. Home: PO Box 2002 Oxford MS 38655

FOX, ELLEN, academic administrator; b. N.Y.C., Apr. 5, 1946; d. Edward and Faith-Hope (Green) Kahn; divorced; 1 child, Jenny Fox. BA in English magna cum laude, L.I. U., 1967, MA in English, 1969. With student affairs office grad. sch. arts and scis. Harvard U., Cambridge, Mass., 1980—, dir. student svcs., 1994—. Author: (poem) A Break in the Clouds, 1993. Co-founder, pres. Nat. Lymphatic and Venous Found Inc., Cambridge, 1978-81. Mem. Nat. Assn. Student Personnel Adminstrs., Assn. Coll. and Univ. Housing Officers Internat. Avocations: writing poetry, lyrics and articles; movies, music. Address: PO Box 400748 Cambridge MA 02140-0008

FOX, FRANCIS HANEY, lawyer; b. Attleboro, Mass., May 28, 1933; s. Francis Joseph and Mary Frances (Brady) F.; m. Cynthia Ann Blundell, Dec. 27, 1959; children: Cynthia, Martin, Matthew, Kalarn. BS in Econs., Coll. Holy Cross, 1955; LLB, Harvard U., 1963. Bar: Mass. 1963, U.S. Ct. Appeals (1st cir.) 1963, U.S. Supreme Ct. 1977. Assoc. Bingham, Dana & Gould, Boston, 1963-70, ptnr., 1970—; mem. adv. com. on civil rules Jud. Conf. of U.S., 1992—. Capt. USNR, 1955-78. Fellow Am. Coll. Trial Lawyers. Home: 77 Cottage St Sharon MA 02067-2132 Office: Bingham Dana LLP 150 Federal St Boston MA 02110-1713

FOX, FRANCIS HENRY, veterinarian; b. Clifton Springs, N.Y., Mar. 11, 1923; s. Henry Sylvester and Alma (Lindner) F.; m. Mildred Genevieve Cullen, Aug. 6, 1946; children—Rosanna, Laurinda, Teresa, Henry. D.V.M., N.Y. State Veterinary Coll., 1945. Diplomate: Charter diplomate Am. Coll. Veterinary Internal Medicine. Research asst. N.Y. State Veterinary Coll.-Cornell U., 1945-46, mem. faculty, 1947—, prof. veterinary medicine and obstetrics, 1953—, chmn. dept. large animal medicine, obstetrics and surgery, 1972-77; instr. surgery Veterinary Coll., Ohio State U., 1946-47. Author articles in field. Mem. Nat. Acad. Practice, Am. Vet. Med. Assn. (exec. bd. dist. I 1966-81, chmn. 1973-74, 77-78), So. Tier (sec.-treas. 1957-62), N.Y. State veterinary med. assns., N.Y.State Assn. Professions, Am. Assn. Bovine Practitioners (pres. 1971-72), Sigma Xi, Alpha Psi, Phi Zeta, Phi Kappa Phi., Omega Tau Sigma. Home: 11 Muriel St Ithaca NY 14850-1835

FOX, GARY DEVENOW, lawyer; b. Detroit, Sept. 8, 1951; s. Edward J. Fox. BA in Polit. Sci. and Drama, Drury Coll., 1973; JD, U. Fla., 1976. Bar: Fla. 1976, U.S. Dist. Ct. (so. and mid. dists.) Fla. 1977, U.S. Ct. Appeals (5th and 11th cirs.) 1977, U.S. Supreme Ct. 1981. From assoc. to ptnr. Frates, Floyd, Pearson, Stewart, Richman & Greer, Miami, 1976-84; ptnr. Stewart, Tilghman, Fox & Bianchi, PA, Miami, 1984—. Exec. editor U. Fla. Law Rev.; contbr. articles to profl. jours. Mem. ABA, Fla. Bar (cert. civil trial advocacy 1983, chmn. code and rules of evidence com. 1997—, civil procedure rules com.), Fla. Bd. Bar Examiners, Dade County Bar Assn., Assn. Trial Lawyers Am. (substaining, lectr.), Acad. Fla. Trial Lawyers (diplomate, lectr.), Dade County Trial Lawyers Assn. (bd. dirs. 1986-89), Am. Bd. Trial Advocates (pres. Miami chpt. and Fla. fedn.), Bankers Club. Avocations: tennis, skiing. Office: 1 SE 3rd Ave Ste 3000 Miami FL 33131-1715

FOX, GEOFFREY E., educational administrator; b. Chgo., Apr. 3, 1941; s. Oswald Irvin and Dorothy Mae Knickerbocker F.; m. Sylvia Herrera, 1966 (div. 1975); m. Susana Amelia Torre, 1980; children: Alex, Jaoqumn. AB, Harvard U., 1963; PhD, Northwestern U., 1975. Cmty. developer ACCION en Venezuela, Caracas, 1963-64; rsch. supr. U. P.R., San Juan, 1966-67; instr. U. Ill., Chgo., 1970-75; asst. prof. varius schools, Ill., Wis., Ohio, Minn., 1975-79; UN rep. World Fedn. Trade Unions, N.Y.C., Prague, Czech Republic, 1979-80; freelance writer, translator N.Y.C., 1980-94; dir. comm. N.Y.C. Commn. Human Rights, 1994-95; coord. sch./coll. articulation Bronx Ednl. Alliance, 1998—; cons. in field. Author: Wellcome to my Contri, 1988, Hispanic Nation: Culture, Politics and the Constructing of Identity, 1996, The Land and People of Argentina, 1990, The Land and People of Venezuela, 1991. NEH fellow, 1977, 81, rsch. fellow NYU, 1983-84. Mem. Nat. Writers Union (steering com. 1991-94), Authors Guild. Avocations: guitar, sailing. Home: 14 E 4th St #812 New York NY 10012 Office: Bronx Ednl Alliance Lehman Coll 250 Bedford Pk Blvd W Bronx NY 10468

FOX, GRADY HARRISON, library director; b. Stephens County, Tex.; d. Henry Grady Harrison and Annie Eudora Fade; m. William Whitley Fox, Aug. 12, 1944 (div. June 1971); dec.); children: Charles Harrison Fox (dec.), William Bruce Fox (dec.). AD, Tarleton Coll., 1943; BS summa cum laude, Tex. Wesleyan Coll., 1946; MLS, North Tex. State U., 1975. Tchr. Lovington (N.Mex.) Pub. Schs., 1959-65; tchr. Artesia (N.Mex.) Pub. Schs., 1965-74, libr., 1974-76; libr. h.s. Breckenridge (Tex.) Ind. Sch. Dist., 1976-90, supr. elem. librs., 1986-90; libr. dir. Breckenridge Pub. Libr., 1985—. Charter mem. Beautify Breckenridge, 1986—; mem. Historic Breckenridge Assn., 1998—, U.S. Congressman's Com. Edn., Tex., 1984, Breckenridge Cmty. Tech. Team, 1997. Mem. Tex. Libr. Assn., Delta Kappa Gamma (scholar 1975), Phi Beta Mu. Democrat. Presbyterian. Avocations: travel, reading, needlework. Office: Breckenridge Pub Libr 207 N Breckenridge Ave Breckenridge TX 76424

FOX, GRETCHEN HOVEMEYER, staff assistant, freelance editor, genealogical consultant; b. Erie, Pa., Jan. 2, 1940; d. Ernst Henry and Marjory Etta (Hollister) Hovemeyer; m. Kenneth Roland Fox, Apr. 23, 1989. AB, Radcliffe Coll., 1961. Manuscript sec. Internat. Tax Program Harvard U. Law Sch., Cambridge, Mass., 1961-63; copy editor Internat. Tax Program Harvard U. Law Sch., Cambridge, 1963-65, editorial asst., 1965-66, publs. asst., 1966-76, editorial and pub. dir., 1976-89; freelance editor, cons. pub. and genealogy Cambridge, 1989—; database/rsch. asst. innovations program John F. Kennedy Sch. of Govt., Harvard U., Cambridge, Mass., 1991-93, staff asst. innovations program, 1993—. Co-compiler: Bibliography on Taxation of Foreign Operations and Foreigners: 1968-75, 1976, Bibliography on Taxation of Foreign Operations and Foreigners: 1976-82, 1983; contbr. articles on geneal. to prof. jours.; designer computer software. Mem. New Eng. Hist. Geneal. Soc., Orange County Geneal. Soc. (pub. cons. 1983-91), Sullivan County (N.Y.) Hist. Soc., DAR (chpt. registrar, chpt. historian 1978-83). Office: Innovations Program John F Kennedy Sch Govt 79 Jfk St Cambridge MA 02138-5801

FOX, GWEN, artist, educator; b. Jefferson City, Tenn., Jan. 25, 1943; d. Arthur Crowell and Margaret Fox; children: Mary, John. Student, Carson Newman Coll., Jefferson City, 1962-63. Tchr. art Belstead House, Ipswich, Eng., 1978-80, Barton Mills (Eng.) Edn., 1979-80, Bemis Art Ctr., Colorado Springs, Colo., 1992-94; tchr. art adult edn., Panama City, Fla., 1981-82; tchr. art Cheyenne Mountain Heritage Ctr., Colorado Springs, 1995—; tchr. Cottonwood Art Acad. One-woman shows, Honolulu, 1971, Mildenhall, Eng., 1977, Panama City, Fla., 1982, Monument, Colo., 1986, 87, Colorado Springs, Colo., 1995, 97; exhibited in group shows Poudre Valley Art League, 1993, N.W. Watercolor Soc., 1993, Fine Arts Ctr. and Taylor Mus., Colorado Springs, 1995 (MCI award 1995), Tex. Watercolor Soc., 1995, Colo. Watercolor Soc., 1995, U. Colo., 1997; represented in numerous pub. collections including Ctr. for Creative Leadership, also numerous pvt. collections; represented in Flowers in Watercolor, 1996; included in Best of Watercolor Painting Color. Recipient Best of Show award Colorado Springs Nat., 1994, Golden award Rocky Mountain Nat., 1994, award Catherine Lorillard Wolfe, 1996. Mem. NOW, Colo. Watercolor Soc. (signature), Ala. Watercolor Soc., Pikes Peak Watercolor Soc. (pres. 1991-93). Avocations: gardening, reading, hiking. Home: 2017 Brookwood Dr Colorado Springs CO 80918-1135

FOX, HAROLD EDWARD, obstetrician, gynecologist, educator, researcher; b. East Orange, N.J., Feb. 19, 1945; s. Willis Edward and Elizabeth (Strathearn) F.; m. Rhea Keller, June 18, 1966; children: Harold Hamilton, Andrhea Alicia. BA, U. Rochester, 1967, MS, MD with honors, 1972.

Diplomate Am. Bd. Ob-Gyn., Am. Bd. Maternal-Fetal Medicine. Intern, resident Strong Meml. Hosp., Rochester, N.Y., 1972-75; dir. Regional Perinatal Program, Rochester, N.Y., 1975-79; dir. obstetrics and maternal fetal medicine U. Rochester, 1977-79; dir. maternal fetal medicine Columbia U., N.Y.C., 1979-95, dir. obstetrics, 1985-88, vice-chmn. ob-gyn., 1988-91, chmn. protem dept. ob-gyn., 1991-95; Oscar I. and Mildred S. Dodek prof., chmn. ob-gyn. George Washington U., Washington, 1995-96, exec. dir. Ctr. Excellence for Women's Health, 1995-96; ob-gyn. in-chief Johns Hopkins Medicine, Balt., 1996—, Dr. Dorothy Edwards prof. ob-gyn., 1996—, chair women's health ctr. oversight com., 1997—; trustee Johns Hopkins Med. Svc. Corp., Johns Hopkins Home Care Group; mem. med. bd. Johns Hopkins Hosp.; mem. adv. bd. Johns Hopkins Medicine, mem. agenda com. adv. bd.; dir. ob-gyn Johns Hopkins Medicine, 1996—; chmn. women and infant transmission study NIH, 1988-93; mem. pediatric com. AIDS clin. trials group, 1988-91; organizing mem. women's com.; mem. obstet. adv. com. N.Y.C. Dept. Health; bd. midwifery N.Y. State Edn. Dept., 1994-95; chmn. N.Y. Acad. Medicine Ob-gyn. sect., 1993-94. Editor Pediatric AIDS, 1991—; contbr. articles to profl. jours. Grantee NIH, 1988-95, USPHS, 1991-95, March of Dimes. Fellow Soc. Gynecologic Investigation, ACOG; mem. Internat. AIDS Soc., Am. Gynecol. and Obstet. Soc., Am. Inst. Ultrasound in Medicine, Perinatal Rsch. Soc., Washington Acad. Medicine, Washington Gynecol. Soc., Alpha Omega Alpha, Phi Beta Delta. Avocations: boating, art, fitness. Home: PO Box 142 Gibson Island MD 21056-0142 Office: Johns Hopkins Medicine Dept Gyn-Ob 600 N Wolfe St Rm 264 Baltimore MD 21287-0005

FOX, HAZEL MARY, barrister, editor; b. Maymyo, Burma, Oct. 22, 1928; d. John Matthew Stuart and Joan Daria (Elliott-Taylor) Denning; m. Michael John Fox, June 6, 1954; children: Matthew, Patrick, Jane, Charles. MA in Jurisprudence, Oxford U., 1949. Bar: London, 1950. Barrister in practice Fountain Court Temple, London, 1950-54, London, 1994—; lectr. Jurisprudence Oxford (Eng.) U., 1951-58, lectr. in law, 1992-95; lectr. Coun. Legal Edn. Inn Sch. Law, London, 1962-76; dir. Brit. Inst. Internat. and Comparative Law, London, 1982-89; gen. editor Internat. and Comparative Law Quar., London, 1987-98, editor, 1999—; gov. Summerfields, Oxford, 1969-98; mem. dept. com. jury svc, Home Office, London, 1963-65; chmn. Juvenile Magistrates Ct., Tower Hamlets, London, 1968-76. Author: (with J.L. Simpson) International Arbitration, 1959; editor International Economic Law and Developing States, Vol. I, 1988, Vol. II, 1992, Joint Development of Offshore Oil and Gas, Vol. I, 1989, Vol. II, 1990, (with Michael A. Meyer) Effecting Compliance, 1993. Active Inner London Borough Juvenile Panel, London, 1959-77; chmn. London Rent Assessment Panel, 1977-98, Leashold Valuation Tribunal, London, 1981-98. Hon. fellow Somerville Coll., Oxford U., 1988; named Queens Counsel Lord Chancellor, 1993. Mem. Internat. Law Assn., Lincolns Inn (additional bencher). Anglican. Avocation: gardening. Office: 4/5 Grays Inn Sq, London WC1R 5AY, England

FOX, HOWARD ALAN, physician, medical educator; b. N.Y.C., Apr. 14, 1933; s. Julius and Cynthia Ruth (Vogel) F.; m. Barbara Ellen Samo, Mar. 7, 1965; children: Marjorie Laura, Sarah Diana. BS, Union Coll., 1954; MD, Columbia U., 1962. Diplomate Nat. Bd. Med. Examiners, Am. Bd. Pediats., Am. Bd. Perinatal/Neonatal Medicine. Intern N.C. Meml. Hosp., Chapel Hill, 1962-63; resident in pediat. Babies Hosp., Columbia Presbyn. Med. Ctr., N.Y.C., 1963-65; fellow in neonatology Yale U. Sch. Medicine, New Haven, Conn., 1967-68, clin. rsch. trainee in neonatology, devel. biochemistry, ins, 1967-68; asst. prof. pediat., asst. attending pediatrician, dir. newb Mt. Sinai Sch. Medicine, N.Y.C., 1968-73, assoc. prof. pediat., attending pediatrician, dir. newborn s, 1973-74; assoc. prof. pediat. U. Kans. Med. Ctr., Kansas City, 1974-80, dir. divsn. newborn medicine, 1974-81, prof. pediat., 1980-85; chmn. dept. pediat., dir. residency tng. program Monmouth Med. Ctr., Long Branch, N.J., 1985—; prof. clin. pediat. M.C.P., Hahnemann Sch. Medicine, Phila., 1985—; spl. com. on infant mortality N.Y. County Med. Soc., 1969-72; chmn. sub-com. for establishment of stds. for infant transport N.Y.C. Dept. Health, 1970-74, sub-com. for establishment of stds. for neonatal intensive care ctrs., 1970-74; adv. com. N.Y.C. Hosp. Corp., High Risk Infant Transport Svc., 1970-74; dir. statewide program Regionalization of Perinatal Care in Kans., 1974-76, mem. perinatal med. coun., 1976-85; consulting neonatalogist Bur. Maternal and Child Health, Kans. Dept. Health and Environ., 1974-85; med. dir. neonatology MidAm. Regional Coun. Emergency Rescue, Kansas City, Mo., 1977-80; cons. maternal and child health Bur. Cmty. Health Svcs., U.S. HEW; chmn. Kans. Bur. Emergency Svcs. Com. on Neonate, 1978-80; profl. adv. bd. Parents of Prematures, Inc., 1983-85; mem. coun. of acad. socs. Assn. Am. Med. Colls., 1991-94; mem. curriculum com. Med. Coll. Pa.-Hahnemann U., 1992—, Robert Wood Johnson Found. generalist initiative grant, coordinating coun., 1992—. Contbr. articles to profl. jours. Bd. dirs. Kaw Valley chpt. Nat. Found. March of Dimes, 1979-85; mem. exec. com. Monmouth Ocean Regional Perinatal Ctr., 1986-92, chmn., 1986-87; bd. trustees, exec. com. Monmouth Kids, Inc., Ronald McDonald House, Long Branch, N.J., 1986—; med. adv. com. United Cerebral Palsy Ctr., Long Branch, 1987—; exec. dir. Ctr. for Infant/Toddler Devel., Early Intervention Program, Long Branch, 1988—. Served as sr. surgeon USPHS, 1965-67. Recipient For the Love of Children award Nat. Found. March of Dimes, 1980, Outstanding Svc. citation Kans. State Dept. Health and Environ., 1985. Fellow Am. Acad. Pediat. (perinatal/neonatal pediat. sect., fetus and newborn com. dist. III 1970-74, 3d party reimbursement com. Kans. chpt. 1979-85, resident edn. com. 1986—); mem. AMA, APHA (breast feeding sub-com. maternal and child health sect. 1984-86), Am. Acad. Pediat., Am. Assn. for History of Medicine, Assn. Pediat. Program Dirs. (mem. coun., exec. com. 1991-94), Nat. Perinatal Assn. (steering com., founding mem. 1974-76), Perinatal Assn. N.J., Sigma Xi. Office: Monmouth Med Ctr 300 2nd Ave Long Branch NJ 07740-6300

FOX, JACK, financial service executive; b. Bklyn., Mar. 8, 1940; s. Benjamin and Rebecca (Shure) F.; m. Carole Olafson, July 8, 1987; children: Neal, Stuart. BBA, CCNY, 1961; MBA, CUNY, 1969. Sales specialist Am. Can Corp., N.Y.C., 1962-63; talent agt. Gen. Artists Corp., N.Y.C., 1963-66; bus. specialist N.Y. Times, 1966-70; pres. Ednl. Learning Systems, Inc., Washington, 1971-78; budget dir. Nat. Alliance of Bus., Washington, 1979-80; pres. Computerized Fin. Services, Rockville, Md., 1980-87; regional v.p. Govt. Funding Corp., L.A., 1987-90; owner, mgr. Jack Fox Assocs., Ventura, Calif., 1986; founder Acctg. Resources Group, Ventura, 1993—; adj. prof. Am. U., Washington, 1983-85; tchr. fin. Montgomery Coll., Rockville, 1978-86. Author: How to Obtain Your Own SBA Loan, 1983, Starting and Building Your Own Accounting Business, 1984, 2d rev. edit. 1991, Accounting and Record Keeping Made Easy for the Self Employed, 1994, God's Business Game Book, 1999. Mem. Internat. Platform Assn. Democrat. Jewish. Avocation: stand-up comedy. Office: Atlanta GA 30309-1148

FOX, JACK JAY, chemist, educator; b. N.Y.C., Dec. 21, 1916; s. Samuel and Celia (Stern) F.; m. Ruth C. Inabu, June 13, 1939; children: Dolores M. Emspak, John Reed. A.B., U. Colo., 1939, Ph.D., 1950. With Sloan-Kettering Inst. for Cancer Research, N.Y.C., 1952-88, mem. emeritus, 1988—; head Lab. Organic Chemistry, prof. biochemistry Cornell U. Grad. Sch. Med. Scis., N.Y.C., 1958—. Recipient Alfred P. Sloan award cancer rsch., 1956, C.S. Hudson award in carbohydrate chemistry Am. Chem. Soc., 1977, Pap award for sci. achievement, 1983, Norlin award U. Colo. Alumni Assn., 1984; NRC fellow, 1950-52; postdoctoral fellow Free U. Brussels, 1950-52; Damon Runyon Meml. Fund fellow, 1952-54. Mem. Am. Chem. Soc., Westchester Chem. Soc., Am. Soc. Biol. Chemists, Am. Assn. Cancer Rsch., Am. Soc. Antiviral Rsch., Sigma Xi. Research, numerous publs. on design, synthesis and structural elucidation of anticancer and antiviral agts., specific syntheses of compounds related to nucleic acid components, carbohydrate and heterocyclic chemistry. Fax: 914-946-1352. Home: 424 S Lexington Ave White Plains NY 10606-2501 Office: Meml Sloan-Kettering Cancer Ctr 1275 York Ave New York NY 10021-6007

FOX, JAMES CARROLL, federal judge; b. Atchison, Kans., Nov. 6, 1928; s. Jared Copeland and Ethel (Carroll) F.; m. Katharine deRosset Rhett, Dec. 30, 1950; children: James Carroll, Jr., Jane Fox Brown, Ruth Fox Jordan. BSBA, U. N.C., 1950, JD with honors, 1957. Bar: N.C. 1957. Law clk. U.S. Dist. Ct. (ea. dist.) N.C., Wilmington, 1957-58; assoc. Carter & Murchison, Wilmington, N.C., 1958-59; ptnr. Murchison, Fox & Newton, Wilmington, N.C., 1960-82; judge U.S. Dist. Ct. (ea. dist.) N.C., Wilmington, 1982—; lectr. in field. Contbr. articles to profl. jours. Vestryman, St. James Episcopal Ch., 1973-75, 79-82. Mem. Hew Hanover County Bar Assn. (pres. 1967-68), Fifth Jud. Dist. Bar Assn. (sec. 1960-62), N.C. Bar Assn. Office: US Dist Ct Alton Lennon Fed Bldg PO Box 2143 Wilmington NC 28402-2143

FOX, JAMES MICHAEL, orthopedic surgeon; b. Milw., July 20, 1942; m. Ellen Fox. BS, U. Wis., 1964, MD, 1968. Diplomate Nat. Bd. Med. Examiners, Am. Bd. Orthop. Surgery. Intern Bronx (N.Y.) Mcpl. Hosp./Albert Einstein Coll. Medicine, 1968-69, surg. resident, 1969-70, orthop. surgery resident, 1970-72, chief resident orthop. surgery, 1972-73; asst. instr. orthop. surgery Albert Einstein Coll. Medicine, 1972-73; sports medicine fellow Nat. Athletic Health Inst., Inglewood, Calif., 1973-74, mem. med. adv. bd., 1974—; pvt. practice Sherman Oaks, Calif., 1976-81, So. Calif. Orthop. Inst., Van Nuys, Calif., 1981—; mem. staff Centinela Valley Cmty. Hosp., Inglewood, 1973-74, Daniel Freeman Hosp., Inglewood, 1973-74, View Park Hosp., L.A., 1973-74, Keesler Med. Ctr., Keesler AFB, Miss., 1974-76, Encino (Calif.) Hosp., 1976-81, Sherman Oaks Cmty. Hosp., 1976-83, Valley Presbyn. Hosp., 1981—; med. cons. sports medicine video cassettes VCI-Nat. Athletic Health Inst., 1974-76; cons. cmty. outreach program on emergency treatment of athletic injuries Sherman Oaks Cmty. Hosp., 1978-80; cons., presenter in field; cons. Youth Soccer Mag.; med. dir. Ctr. for Disorders of Knee, Van Nuys; mem. Ctr. for Sports Medicine, Calif. State U., Northridge, 1990; med. examiner State of Calif. Dept. Indsl. Rels., 1993-95. Author: Save Your Knees; co-editor: Patello-Ferral Joint; mem. editl. bd. Jour. of Arthroscopy, 1989-93, video supplement, 1989, The Knee, 1994. Mem. Summer Olympics, 1984. Maj. Med. Corps USAF, 1974-76. Fellow ACS; mem. Am. Athletic Trainers Adv. Assn. and Cert. Bd. Inc. (mem. com.), Arthroscopy Assn. N.Am. (mem. rsch. com. 1986-89, bd. dirs. 1989-91, chmn. pub. rels. com. 1989, program chmn. 1993, sec. 1994-97), Calif. Med. Assn. Office: So Calif Orthop Inst 6815 Noble Ave Van Nuys CA 91405-3796

FOX, JAMES WALTON, artist; b. Summit, N.J., Jan. 17, 1969; s. John William and Susan Elizabeth (McCotter) F. BA, Hobart Coll., 1991. Creator cycle of paintings Forty Seasons, 1997. Office: 51 MacDougal St Ste 106 New York NY 10012

FOX, JEAN, piano educator; b. Madison, Wis., Mar. 1, 1941; d. Robert Lewis and Virginia Leonie (Burnier) Meriwether; m. Virgil Grant Fox, Mar. 3, 1962; children: Linda, Frederick, Steven, Barbara. BA, Kans. State U., 1965. Pvt. piano tchr. Manhattan, Kans., 1963-66, Denver, 1966-74, Allentown, Pa., 1974—; founder Cmty. Music Sch., Allentown, 1981, mem. faculty, 1981-88; spkr. del. Music Tchrs. Conv., Wichita, Kans., 1989; lectr. workshop clinician on pvt. music tchg., Del., Md., Kans., Fla., N.Y., Pa., N.J., Oreg., Calgary, B.C.; sec. Advanced Speechmasters, 1992-93. Author: Performance with Pleasure, 1987 Piano Guild Notes; contbr. articles to profl. jours. Music del. People to People Program, S.E. Asia, 1989; v.p., bd. dirs. Pa. Sinfonia Orch., 1991-94. Named to Hall of Fame Am. Coll. Musicians, Austin, Tex., 1986. Mem. AAUW, Nat. Guild Piano Tchrs. (adjudicator 1980—), Nat. Music Tchrs. Assn. (chair ind. music tchr. com. Ea. divsn. 1985-90), Pa. Music Tchrs. Assn. (sec. 1987-89, 1st v.p. 1989-91, pres. 1991-93), Lehigh Valley Music Tchrs. Assn. (pres. 1987-89, treas. 1998—), Ind. Music Tchrs. (chair 1985-90), Music Tchrs. Nat. Assn. (pres. Ea. divsn. 1994-96, v.p 1989-91, bd. dirs. 1996-98), Rotary. Avocations: gourmet cooking, reading. Home: 4102 Kilmer Ave Allentown PA 18104-3310

FOX, JEANNE MARIE, lawyer; b. Phila., May 30, 1952; d. Samuel Cooper and Palmira Caroline (Ungerbuehler) F.; m. Stephan DeMicco, Sept. 29, 1979. BA, Douglass Coll., Rutgers U., New Brunswick, 1975; JD, Rutgers Sch. of Law, Camden, 1979; completed Program for State and Local Govt. Execs., Harvard U., 1990. Lawyer. Letter carrier U.S. Post Office, Wildwood, 1971, Delran, 1973, Willingboro, 1976; intern U.S. Dept. of Environ. Protection, Edison, Phila., 1974, 77; law clerk Bd. of Pub. Utilities, Newark, N.J., 1978, N.J. Supr. Court, Camden, N.J., 1978, 79; policy dir. N.J. Democrat. State Com., Trenton, N.J., 1979-80; atty. N.J. Office of the Sec. of State, 1980-81; regulatory officer N.J. Bd. Pub. Utilities, Newark, 1981-85, dep. dir., 1985-87; dir. N.J. Bd. of Pub. Utilities, Newark, 1987-90, sr. advisor for policy and mgmt., 1990-91; chief of staff N.J. Dept. of Environ. Protection and Energy, Trenton, 1991-92; dep. commr. N.J. Dept. Environ. Protection and Energy, Trenton, 1992-93, commr., 1993-94, commr. Delaware River Basin Commn., 1991-94; regional adminstr. Region II, EPA, N.Y.C., 1994—. Contbr. articles to profl. jours. Mem. Com. on Status of Women, Middlesex, 1985-94, chmn., 1985-89; pres. Middlesex County Women's Polit. Caucus, 1984-86, Women's Polit. Caucus N.J., 1988-91; v.p. Nat. Women's Polit. Caucus, 1991-94, mem. steering and adminstrn. coms., 1989-94; bd. dirs. Douglass Coll. Assoc. Alumnae, 1986—; trustee Rutgers U., 1989—; mem. N.J. Commn. on Sex Discrimination in Statutes, 1989-94; del. Dem. Nat. Conf., 1992; chmn. Dem. Task Force Women's Polit. Caucus, N.J., 1991-94. Named Outstanding Young Woman N.J., N.J. Woman of Achievement, N.J. Women's Clubs and Douglass Coll., 1986, Jerseyan of Week, Star Ledger, 1986, Bus. and Profl. Woman of Yr., Bus. and Profl. Women, 1993; recipient Alumni Meritorious Svc. award Rutgers U. Alumni Fedn., 1991, award Douglass Soc., 1994; honored in Rutger U.'s Hall of Disting. Alumni, 1997. Mem. Nat. Women's Polit. Caucus, N.J. State Bar Assn., Rutgers Sch. of Law Alumni Assn., Rutgers Club. Democrat. Home: 227 New York Ave New Brunswick NJ 08901-1715 Office: EPA Region II 290 Broadway Lowr 26 New York NY 10007-1823

FOX, JOHN BAYLEY, JR., university dean; b. Cambridge, Mass., Nov. 6, 1936; s. John Bayley and Eunice (Jameson) F.; m. Julia Garrett, July 22, 1967; children—Sarah Cleveland, Thomas Bayley. A.B., Harvard U., 1959; B.A., Oxford U., Eng., 1961, M.A., 1962. Assoc. div. internat. fellowships Commonwealth Fund of N.Y., N.Y.C., 1963-67; dir. Office Career Services Harvard U., Cambridge, 1967-71, spl. asst., asst. dean of faculty, 1971-76, dean Harvard Coll., 1976-85, adminstrv. dean Grad. Sch. Arts and Scis., 1985-94; sec. faculty arts and scis., sec. faculty coun., 1992—. Unitarian. Home: 125 Prince St West Newton MA 02465-2603 Office: Harvard U Faculty Arts and Scis University Hall 1 Cambridge MA 02138-5722

FOX, JOHN DAVID, educator, physicist; b. Huntington, W.Va., Dec. 8, 1929; s. David and Eleanor (Griffin) F.; children: Heidi Roberts Fox, Lise, Peter, Paul, Michelle Fox Lundy; m. Georgiana Fry Vines, Oct. 23, 1993. SB, MIT, 1951; Fulbright fellow, Rijksuniversiteit, Groningen, Netherlands, 1951-52; MS, U. Ill., 1954, PhD, 1960. Asst. physicist Brookhaven Nat. Lab., Upton, N.Y., 1956-59; asst. prof. physics Fla. State U., Tallahassee, 1959-63, asso. prof., 1963-65, prof., 1965-94, prof. emeritus, 1994—; adj. prof. U. Tex., El Paso, 1996; guest scientist Max-Planck Inst. für Kernphysik, Heidelberg, Germany, 1968-69, Inst. für Kernphysik U. Köln, 1975; cons. physics divsn. Argonne Nat. Lab., 1982—; guest scientist Oak Ridge Nat. Lab., 1994—, program dir. nuclear physics NSF, 1990-92, 95-97; dir. Branchland Pipe & Supply Co., Huntington, W.Va., 1965-81; mem. MIT Ednl. Coun., 1981-90. Co-editor: Isobaric Spin in Nuclear Physics, 1966, Nuclear Analogue States, 1976; Contbr. articles to sci. jours. Mem. Leon County Dem. Com., 1970-74; Bd. dirs. LeMoyne Art Found., Tallahassee, 1971-73. NSF Grad. fellow, 1955-56; Sr. postdoctoral fellow, 1968-69; sr. U.S. scientist award Alexander von Humboldt-Stiftung, 1975. Fellow Am. Phys. Soc.; mem. AAAS, ACLU, Sigma Xi.

FOX, JON D., congressman; b. Abington, Pa., Apr. 22, 1947; s. William L. and Elainne (Brickman) F.; m. Judithann Wilbert, June 27, 1992. B in Pub. Svc., Pa. State U., 1969; JD, Widener U., 1975. Asst. dist. atty. County of Montgomery, Pa., 1976-80, bd. commrs., 1991-94; bd. commrs. Twp. of Abington, Pa., 1980-84; mem. Pa. Ho. of Reps., 1984-91, 104th-105th Congress from Pa. 13th dist., 1995-98; mem. banking and fin. svcs., internat. rels., vets. affairs com. Co-founder Montgomery County AIDS Task Force; active Montgomery County Legal Aid, Ea. Montgomery County Red Cross, Jewish Cmty. Rels. Coun., Aldersgate Youth Svc. Bur., Montgomery County Spinal Cord Assn., Am. Cancer Soc., Manor Jr. Coll., Willow Grove Sr. Citizens Ctr., Citizens' Com. for Environ. Control, Friends of Abington Free Libr., Montgomery County Office on Aging and Adult Svcs. Sgt. USAF, 1969-75. Mem. VFW, Am. Legion, Optimist Club of Ea. Montgomery County, Elks, Masons, Kiwanis, B'nai B'rith. Republican. Jewish. Office: US Ho of Reps 435 Cannon HOB Washington DC 20515-3813

FOX, KARL AUGUST, economist, eco-behavioral scientist; b. Salt Lake City, July 14, 1917; s. Feramorz Young and Anna Teresa (Wilcken) F.; m. Sylvia Olive Cate, July 29, 1940; children: Karl Richard, Karen Frances Anne. BA, U. Utah, 1937, MA, 1938; PhD, U. Calif., 1954. Economist USDA, 1942-54; head div. statis. and hist. rsch. Bur. Agrl. Econs., 1951-54; economist Coun. Econ. Advisers, Washington, 1954-55; head dept. econs. and sociology Iowa State U., Ames, 1955-66; head dept. econs. Iowa State U., 1966-72, disting. prof. scis. and humanities, 1968-87, prof. emeritus, 1987—; vis. prof. Harvard, 1960-61, U. Calif., Santa Barbara, 1971-72, 78, vis. scholar, Berkeley, 1972-73; William Evans vis. prof. U. Otago, N.Z., 1981; Bd. dirs. Social Sci. Rsch. Coun., 1963-67, mem. com. econ. stability, 1963-66, chmn. com. areas for social and econ. statistics, 1964-67; mem. Com. Reg. Accounts, 1963-68. Author: Econometric Analysis for Public Policy, 1958, (with M. Ezekiel) Methods of Correlation and Regression Analysis, 1959, (with others) The Theory of Quantitative Economic Policy, 1966, rev. edit., 1973, Intermediate Economic Statistics, 1968, rev. edit, (with T.K. Kaul), 1980, (with J. K. Sengupta) Economic Analysis and Operations Research, 1969, (with W.C. Merrill) Introduction to Economic Statistics, 1970, Social Indicators and Social Theory, 1974, Social System Accounts, 1985, The Eco-Behavioral Approach To Surveys and Social Accounts for Rural Communities, 1990, repub., 1994, Demand Analysis, Econometrics and Policy Models, 1992, Urban-Regional Economics, Social System Accounts and Eco-Behavioral Science, 1994; author-editor: Economic Analysis for Educational Planning, 1972; co-editor: Readings in the Economics of Agriculture, 1969, Economic Models, Estimation and Risk Programming (essays in honor of Gerhard Tintner), 1969, Systems Economics, 1987; contbr. articles to profl. jours. Recipient superior service medal USDA, 1948, award for outstanding pub. research Am. Agrl. Econs. Assn., 1952, 54, 57, for outstanding doctoral dissertation, 1953. Fellow Econometric Soc., Am. Statis. Assn. (Census Research fellow 1980-81), Am. Agrl. Econs. Assn. (v.p. 1955-56, award for publ. of enduring quality 1977), AAAS; mem. Am. Econs. Assn. (research and publs. com. 1963-67), Regional Sci. Assn., Ops. Research Soc. Am., Am. Ednl. Research Assn., Phi Beta Kappa, Phi Kappa Phi. Home: 1801 20th St Apt J-31 Ames IA 50010-5166 Office: Iowa State U Econs Dept Ames IA 50011

FOX, KELLY DIANE, financial advisor; b. Brockton, Mass., Sept. 9, 1959; d. James H. and Betty Jane (Calloway) F.; m. Alan David Goldberg, July 6, 1985; 1 child, Andrew Jason. BA, Allegheny Coll., 1980; postgrad. in Bus. Adminstrn., Suffolk U., 1983-84; student, Temple U., London, 1978, Syracuse U., London, 1949. Asst. mgr. Casual Male, Braintree, Mass., 1980, Hit or Miss, Braintree, 1981-82; merchandiser Foxmoor, West Bridgewater, Mass., 1982; distbr. Hill's Dept. Stores, Canton, Mass., 1982-85; asst. buyer BJ's Wholesale Club, Natick, Mass., 1985-92; advanced advisor team, personal fin. advisor Am. Express Fin. Advisors, 1993—; Am. Express Fin. Advisors Boston steering com., diversity chair 1995-96; mem. spkrs. bur. Women's Ednl. and Indsl. Union, 1997—; contbr. ADVICE program State Atty. Gen's. Office for Elder Affairs. Cheerleading coach Avon H.S., Mass., 1982-83; co-chair enrichment program Falls Elem. Sch., 1994-95, 97-98; mem. John Woodcock Sch. Coun., 1993-94; treas., bd. mem. Attleboro Area Coun. for Children, 1993—; bd. dirs. Attleboro Area Parents Anonymous, 1996, New Hope, 1996-98; vol. Foxborough Regional Charter Sch. Methodist. Avocations: dance, exercise, cooking, art galleries.

FOX, LINDA CHODOSH, Spanish educator; b. Charlottesville, Va., May 20, 1943; d. Maurice Allen Chodosh and Miriam Yuter; m. William R. Fox, Aug. 20, 1967; children: Daniel Eric, Jeremy Seth. BA with honors, Douglass Coll., 1965; MA, Ind. U., 1967; PhD, U. Wis., 1974. Cert. secondary tchr., N.J. Lectr. Ind. U., Fort Wayne, 1971-74, asst. prof., 1974-96, assoc. prof., 1996—. Sunday sch. tchr. The Temple, Fort Wayne, Ind.; mem. Ft. Wayne Women's Bur. Named Tchr. of Yr. Ind.-Purdue Ft. Wayne Friends, 1996. Mem. MLA, Am. Assn. of Tchrs. of Spanish and Portuguese, Ft. Wayne Women's Bur., Am. Coun. for Tchg. of Fgn. Langs., Nat. Women's Studies Assn., Feministas Unidas (newsletter editor 1980-95), Phi Beta Kappa. Avocations: piano, reading. E-mail: fox@ipfw.edu. Office: Ind U-Purdue U Fort Wayne 2101 E Coliseum Blvd Fort Wayne IN 46805

FOX, LLOYD ALLAN, insurance company executive; b. Bklyn., Sept. 20, 1945; s. Samuel Morris and Adele (Sheingold) F.; m. Lenore Judith Weinstock, Aug. 10, 1968; children: Jennifer Lynn, Elizabeth Susan. BS in Pharmacy, Long Island U., 1968; JD, U. Mich., 1974. Bar: Ga. 1974, D.C. 1979; lic. ins. agent, Ga. Mng. ptnr. Stokes, Shapiro, Fussell, Fox & Wedge, Atlanta, 1974-87; exec. v.p., gen. counsel Splty. Systems, Inc., Indpls., 1987-90; chmn., CEO Environ. Mgmt. Group Inc., Atlanta, 1987-90; pres. Synergy Ins. Svcs. Inc., Atlanta, 1990—, Am. Safety Casualty Ins. Co., 1993—, Am. Safety Ins. Group, Ltd., 1997—; bd. dirs. Performance Contracting Group, Inc., Charlotte, N.C., Am. Safety Casualty Ins. Co., 1993—, Am. Safety Ins. Group, Ltd., 1996—. Author: Employer's Guide to Employee Retirement Income Security Act, 1974, Businessman's Guide to Mergers and Acquisitions, 1977, Business Planning for the Closely-Held Company, 1980, Asbestos Management and Removal-Legal Considerations and Planning, 1985, Legal Considerations of Asbestos Management Plans, 1987. Pres. Chastain Park Civic Assn., Atlanta, 1976; bd. dirs., v.p. Nat. Kidney Found., Atlanta, 1977-88, bd. dirs. emeritus, 1988—; bd. dirs. Asbestos Abatement Coun. Assn. Wall and Ceiling Industries Internat., Washington, 1987-90, pres., 1989-90. Lt. USPHS, 1968-71. Recipient Pres.'s award Nat. Kidney Found. Ga., 1984. Mem. State Bar Ga., D.C. Bar, Environ. Info. Assn., Alpha Zeta Omega. Jewish. Office: 1845 The Exchange Ste 200 Atlanta GA 30339-2019

FOX, LORRAINE SUSAN, marketing professional; b. L.A., Feb. 8, 1956; d. Robert Lazar and Valerie Joan (Barker) Fox; m. Clark Byron Siegel, July 19, 1981 (div. Nov. 1989). AB with distinction, Stanford U., 1979; MBA, U. Chgo., 1983. Sr. fin. analyst MacIntosh div., Apple Computer, Cupertino, Calif., 1983-84; sr. fin. analyst Sun Microsystems Inc., Mountain View, Calif., 1984-85, mgr. fin. planning and analysis, 1985-86, project mgr., 1986-88, mgr. project mgmt., 1988-90, sr. product mktg. mgr., 1990-93, mgr. mktg. strategy, 1993-95; dir. multimedia product mktg. new media divsn. Oracle Corp., Redwood Shores, Calif., 1995, sr. dir. product mktg. Sun Products divsn., 1995-96; v.p. mktg. Centerview Software, Inc., San Francisco, 1996; sr. dir., bus. strategy Apple Computer, Inc., Cupertino, Calif., 1997; gen. ptnr. Crescendo Ventures, Inc., Palo Alto, Calif., 1997—. Vol. fundraiser Stanford (Calif.) U., 1983-88; vol. Sun Microsystems Cmty. Vols., Mountain View, 1989—; alumni rep. undergrad. commn. on edn. Stanford U. Mem. Commonwealth Club, Stanford Profl. Women's Club, Churchill Club. Avocations: reading, running, cycling, ballet, music. Home: 2017 Columbia St Palo Alto CA 94306 Office: Crescendo Ventures Inc 505 Hamilton Ave Ste 315 Palo Alto CA 94301-2013

FOX, LYNN SMITH, federal government official; b. Spartanburg, S.C., Apr. 19, 1955; d. James Leonard and Dorothy Harriet (Wilson) Smith; m. William Lloyd Fox, Aug. 1, 1981; 1 child, Harriet Buffington. Student, Wofford Coll., 1974; BA cum laude, Smith Coll., 1977; MBA, George Washington U., 1982. Legis. asst. Rep. John J. LaFalce, Washington, 1982-83; profl. staff mem. Subcom. on Econ. Stabilization, Ho. Banking Com., Washington, 1983-85; congl. liaison asst. Fed. Res. Bd., Washington, 1986-88, spl. asst. to bd., 1992-94, dep. congl. liaison, 1994-98, asst. to bd. for pub. liaison, 1998—; dir. corporate rels. Harvey Mudd Coll., Claremont, Calif., 1990-92. Vice chair Inland Hospice, Claremont, 1992; class pres. Smith Coll. Alumnae, Northampton, Mass., 1997—. Univ. fellow George Washington U., 1981-82. Mem. Women in Housing and Fin. Found. (bd. dirs. 1997—), Washington Literacy Coun. (bd. dirs. 1996-98). Home: 3526 Woodbine St Chevy Chase MD 20815-4039 Office: Fed Res Bd 20th & Constitution Ave NW Washington DC 20551*

FOX, MARGARET LOUISE, retired secondary education educator; b. Newport News, Va., Nov. 27, 1919; d. Preson Curtis and Lydia Enos (Diggs) Watson; m. Jesse Emerson Todd, Sr., Apr. 5, 1947 (dec. 1992); children: Frances Diggs, Jesse Emerson Jr.; m. Russell E. Fox, Aug. 3, 1996. AB, Coll. William and Mary, 1943; MA, Hampton U., 1978. Elem. tchr. Newport News (Va.) Sch. System, 1943-45; newspaper reporter Times-Herald, 1945-46; tchr. English Goerge Wythe Jr. High, 1946-47; tchr. English Bethel High Sch., Hampton, 1970-82, ret., 1982; speaker in field and tchr. workshops. Author: (with others) Hampton From the Sea to the Stars, 1985; author: (biograph) C. Alton Lindsay: Educator and Community Leader, 1994; contbr. articles to profl. jours. Cert. lay speaker United Meth. Ch., Peninsula, 1970s-95; judge Va Forensics Debate, 1970s-82; debate coach Bethe H.S., Hampton, 1971-82. Mem. AAUW (life), Va. Ret. Tchrs. Assn.

(trustee Va. conf. UM Hist. Soc.), Nat. Assn. Parliamentarians, Great Books Group, Planned Parenthood (pres. 1967-68), Hampton Hist. Found., Nat. Blackstone Coll. Alumnae Assn. (pres. 1995—). Avocations: reading, visiting historical sites, teaching, travel. Home: 3 Carrington Ct Hampton VA 23666-6030

FOX, MARK D., judge; b. N.Y.C., Aug. 4, 1943; s. Morris J. and Susan (Sciaky) F.; m. Jean Amatucci, Nov. 22, 1975; 1 child, Michael Louis. BA, SUNY, Buffalo, 1964; LLB (JD), Bklyn. Law Sch., 1967. Investigator criminal investigation divsn. U.S. Army, 1968-70; asst. dist. atty. rackets bur. Bronx County, 1970-71; asst. dist. atty. Orange County, 1971-72; sr. staff atty. Orange County Legal Aid Soc., 1973-75, chief atty., 1975-77; ptnr. Bavoso, Fox & Coffill, Port Jervis, N.Y., 1977-91; part time U.S. magistrate judge, 1988-91; U.S. magistrate judge U.S. Dist. Ct. (so. dist.) N.Y., White Plains, 1991—; past mem. adv. bd. divsn. criminal justice svcs., Bur. of Prosecution & Defense Svcs. N.Y. State; former mem. adv. com. appellate divsn. 2d dept. Law Guardian Adv. Com.; former mem. grievance com. 9th Judicial Dist., 1983-91; lectr. in field; mem. com. on security and facilities Jud. Conf. of U.S. Mem. editl. bd. Fed. Bar Coun. Newsletter, 1997—. Mem. N.Y. State Bar Assn. (former mem. exec. com. criminal justice sect.), N.Y. State Defenders Assn. (past dir.), Orange County Bar Assn. (past chmn. criminal law com.). Office: US Court House 300 Quarropas St White Plains NY 10601-4140

FOX, MARY ANN WILLIAMS, librarian; b. Savannah, Ga., Jan. 16, 1939; d. Alton F. and Arthur (Colquitt) Williams; m. William Francis Fox, Dec. 26, 1960 (div. 1984); children: Katherine Frances, William Francis Jr. BA, U. Ga., 1960; MLS, Rutgers U., 1984. Libr. Metuchen (N.J.) Pub. Libr., 1983-85, Mable Smith Douglas Libr. Rutgers U., New Brunswick, N.J., 1984, Firestone Libr. Princeton (N.J.) U., 1985, The Hun Sch. of Princeton, 1985—; bd. dirs. Ctrl. Jersey Regional Libr. Coop., 1997—, Region 5 Libr. Coop., N.J., 1985-92. Trustee East Brunswick (N.J.) Pub. Libr., 1979-92; bd. dirs. Ctrl. Jersey YWCA, New Brunswick, 1985-88, Ctrl. Atlantic Conf. United Ch. of Christ, 1985-88, Ctrl. Jersey Regional Libr. Coop., 1997—. Mem. ALA, N.J. Libr. Assn., N.J. Ind. Sch. Assn. (chair libr. sect. 1988—), Edn. Media Assn. N.J. (bd. dirs. 1987—), Librs. of Middlesex (pres.). Democrat. Mem. United Ch. of Christ. Home: 10 Redcoat Dr East Brunswick NJ 08816-2759 Office: Hun Sch Princeton Edgerstone Rd Princeton NJ 08540

FOX, MARY MASELLI, psychologist; b. Chgo.. BA, Carleton Coll., 1964; PhD, Duke U., 1970. Cert. clin. psychologist, N.Y. With Marin County Mental Health Services, San Rafael, Calif., 1970-71; dir. Adult Mental Health Services of Gaston County, Gastonia, N.C., 1971-72; co-founder Family Therapy Services, Gastonia, 1972-73; asst. prof. psychiatry U. Rochester (N.Y.) Sch. Medicine, 1979-84, dir. psychotherapy and group relations program, 1979-84, clin. asst. prof. psychiatry, 1984-87, clin. assoc. prof. psychiatry, 1987-90; assoc. prof. psychology Coll. Arts and Scis. U. Rochester, 1990—. Contbr. articles to profl. jours. Office: 988 Park Ave Rochester NY 14610-1734

FOX, MARYE ANNE, university chancellor, chemistry educator; b. Canton, Ohio, Dec. 9, 1947. BS, Notre Dame Coll. of Ohio, 1969; MS, Cleve. State U., 1970; PhD, Dartmouth Coll., 1974; postgrad., U. Md., 1974-76. Prof. chemistry U. Tex., Austin, 1976-91, Rowland Pettit Centennial prof., 1986-92, M. June and J. Virgil Waggoner regents chair chemistry, 1992-98, v.p. rsch., 1994-98; chancellor N.C. State U., Raleigh, 1998—; mem. Nat. Sci. Bd., 1991-96, vice-chair, 1994-96. Assoc. editor Jour. Am. Chem. Soc., 1986-94; mem. adv. bd. Jour. Organic Chemistry, Chem. Engring. News, Chem. Review; contbr. numerous articles to profl. jours. Recipient Agnes Faye Morgan Rsch. award Iota Sigma Pi, 1984, Arthur C. Cope scholar award Am. Chem. Soc., 1988; Garvan medal Am. Chem. Soc., 1988, Havinga medal Leiden U., 1991, Monie A. Ferst award, 1996; named to Hall of Excellence, Ohio Found. Ind. Colls., 1987, The Best of the New Generation, Esquire Mag., 1984; Alfred P. Sloan Rsch. fellow, 1980-82, Camille and Henry Dreyfus tchr. scholar, 1981-85. Fellow AAAS; mem. NAS, Am. Acad. Arts and Sci., Am. Philos. Soc. Office: NC State U Chancellor's Office Box 7001 Raleigh NC 27695

FOX, MATTHEW IGNATIUS, publishing company executive; b. N.Y.C., Apr. 10, 1934; s. Matthew I. and Lucille V. (Reilly) F.; children: Cathleen, Matthew, Patricia. A.B., Rutgers U., 1956. Field rep. Prentice-Hall, Inc., N.Y.C., 1958-60; editor engring. Prentice-Hall, Inc., 1960-67, exec. editor, asst. v.p., 1967-71, exec. editor, 1981-83, editor-in-chief, 1983-85, pub., 1985—; pres. Reston Pub. Co., Va., 1971-81; cons. in pub., 1987—; bd. dirs. Fairmont Press, Atlanta. Dep. mayor, mayor, Rivervale (N.J.), 1964-67, commr., Bergen County (N.J.), 1966-70; del. Fairfax County Democratic Com., Va., 1976-81. Mem. Assn. Am. Pubs., Rutgers U. Alumni Assn., Washington, N.Y. pubs. groups. Democrat. Roman Catholic. Club: Cape May Cottagers and Beach. Home: 1103 Illinois Ave Cape May NJ 08204-2608

FOX, MAURICE SANFORD, molecular biologist, educator; b. N.Y.C., Oct. 11, 1924; s. Albert and Ray F.; m. Sally Cherniavsky, Apr. 1, 1955; children: Jonathan, Gregory, Michael. BS in Meteorology, U. Chgo., 1944, MS in Chemistry, 1951, PhD, 1951; Docteur Honoris causa, Université Paul Sabatier, Toulouse, France, 1994. Instr. U. Chgo., 1951-53; asst. Rockefeller Inst., 1953-55, asst. prof., 1955-58, assoc. prof., 1958-62; assoc. prof. MIT, Cambridge, 1962-66, prof., 1966-79, Lester Wolfe prof. molecular biology, 1979-96, head dept. biology, 1985-89; mem. Radiation Effects Rsch. Found., Hiroshima; mem. internat. bioethics com. UNESCO. Served with USAAF, 1943-46. USPHS fellow, 1952-53; Nuffield Research fellow, 1957; Fogarty scholar, 1991. Fellow AAAS; mem. NAS, Am. Acad. Arts and Scis., Inst. Medicine. Office: MIT Dept Biology 77 Massachusetts Ave Cambridge MA 02139-4307

FOX, MICHAEL DAVID, art educator, visual imagist artist; b. Cortland, N.Y., Dec. 29, 1937; s. Donald F. Fox and Ethel (Allen) Sullivan; m. Carol Ann Hampston, Nov. 5, 1967; 1 child, Kathryn Gabrielle. BS, SUNY, Buffalo, 1962, MS, 1969; cert. in sculpture Bklyn. Mus. Sch., 1964. Tchr. art City Schs., Rochester, N.Y., 1962-63, 64-65; prof. art. Morehead State Univ., Ky., 1965-67, SUNY, Oswego, 1967—; speaker in field; vis. artist univs. and art ctrs., U.S.A., Can.; dir. Popular Image Gallery, Oswego, 1967—; vis. artist various Us. and art ctrs.; speaker art shows; adjudicate local, regional, state and nat. exhbns., 1965—. Work featured on CBS-TV, 1976, 78, 80, also featured in N.Y. Times, Look, Evergreen Review, Nat. Lampoon, Scanlon's Monthly, Cavalier, Sch. Arts, others, 1970—; featured in textbook Sculpture: Techniques, Form and Content, 1988; represented in pvt. and pub. collections U.S.A., Can., Japan, Africa, Asia, Europe, S.Am.; reviewer textbooks. Recipient Outstanding Teaching award Morehead State Univ., 1967; Chancellors award for Excellence in Teaching, SUNY, 1981; numerous awards for drawing, painting, and sculpture, 1962—. Mem. United Univ. Profs. (v.p., del.). Home: 38 W End Ave Oswego NY 13126-1758 Office: SUNY Tyler Hall Oswego NY 13126-1737

FOX, MICHAEL J., museum director. Pres., CEO Mus. of No. Ariz., Flagstaff. Office: Mus of No Ariz 3101 N Fort Valley Rd Flagstaff AZ 86001-8348

FOX, MICHAEL J., actor; b. Vancouver, B.C., Can., June 9, 1961; s. Bill and Phyllis Fox; m. Tracy Pollan, July 16, 1988; 1 son, Sam Michael. TV series include Leo and Me (CBC), 1976, Palmerstown USA, 1980, Family Ties, 1982-89 (Emmy Award, 1987, 88), Spin City, 1996; TV films include Letters From Frank, 1979, Poison Ivy, 1985, High School USA, 1985, I Am Your Child, 1997, Tales From the Crypt: The Trap (guest, dir.), HBO, Don't Drink the Water, 1994; film appearances include Midnight Madness, 1980, Class of '84, 1981, Back to the Future, 1985, Teen Wolf, 1985, Light of Day, 1986, The Secret of My Success, 1987, Bright Lights, Big City, 1988, Casualties of War, 1989, Back to the Future, Part II, 1989, Back to the Future, Part III, 1990, The Hard Way, 1991, Doc Hollywood, 1991, (voice over) Homeward Bound: The Incredible Journey, 1993, Life with Mikey, 1993, For Love or Money, 1993, Where the Rivers Flow North, 1993, Greedy, 1994, Cold Blooded, 1995, Blue in the Face, 1995, The American President, 1995, Mars Attacks!, 1996, Homeward Bound II: Lost in San Francisco, 1996, The Frighteners, 1996. Office: CAA care Kevin Huvane 9830 Wilshire Blvd Beverly Hills CA 90212-1804*

FOX, MICHAEL VASS, Hebrew educator, rabbi; b. Detroit, Dec. 9, 1940; s. Leonard W. and Mildred (Vass) F.; m. Jane Schulzinger, Sept. 4, 1961; children: Joshua, Ariel. BA, U. Mich., 1962, MA, 1963; PhD, Hebrew U., Jerusalem, 1972. Ordained rabbi, 1968. Lectr. Haifa U., Israel, 1971-74, Hebrew U., Jerusalem, 1975-77; prof. Hebrew U. Wis., Madison, 1977—, chmn. dept., 1982-88, 92—, Weinstein-Bascom prof. in Jewish studies, 1990—, Halls-Bascom prof., 1999—. Author: The Song of Songs and the Ancient Egyptian Love Songs, 1985, Shirey Dodim Mimitzrayim Ha'atiqa, 1985, Qohelet and his Contradictions, 1988, The Redaction of the Books of Esther, 1991, Character and Ideology in the Book of Esther, 1991; editor SBL Dissertation series, 1994—, A Time to Tear Down and a Time to Build Up: A Rereading of Ecclesiasted, 1999; contbr. articles to profl. jours. Recipient Wahrburg prize Hebrew U., 1971-72; Leverhulme fellow U. Liverpool, Eng., 1974-75; Brit. Friends of Hebrew U. fellow, Liverpool, 1974-75; NEH fellow, 1992; Vilas assoc., 1988-90. Mem. Soc. for Bibl. Lit. (editor SBL Dissertation Series 1994—, editl. bd. Jour. Bibl. Lit. 1991-95), Nat. Assn. Profs. Hebrew (editor Hebrew Studies 1985-93). Home: 2815 Chamberlain Ave Madison WI 53705-3607 Office: U Wis Dept Hebrew 1220 Linden Dr Rm 1338 Madison WI 53706-1525

FOX, MICHAEL W., lawyer; b. Sulphur Springs, Tex., June 11, 1950; s. Clovis Dean and Doris Louise (Watson) F.; m. Christine Simpson, June 12, 1971 (div. 1985); 1 child, Dru Anne; m. Suzan O'Connor, Aug. 9, 1986 (div. 1996). BA with honors, Stephen F. Austin State U., 1972; JD with high honors, U. Tex., 1975. Bar: Tex. 1975, U.S. Dist. Ct. (so. dist.) 1976, U.S. Dist. Ct. (we. dist.) 1978, U.S. Dist. Ct. (ea. dist.) 1981, U.S. Dist. Ct. (no. dist.) 1991, U.S. Ct. Appeals (5th cir.) 1976, U.S. Ct. Appeals (11th dist.) 1979, U.S. Supreme Ct. 1998. Assoc. Butler & Binion, Houston, 1975-78; assoc., then sharcholder Soules & McCamish, San Antonio, 1978-82; assoc., then partner McGown & McClanahan, San Antonio, 1982-87; ptnr. Haynes and Boone L.L.P., San Antonio, 1987—. Pres., bd. dirs. San Antonio Food Bank, 1984-90; bd. dirs. Blue Bonnet Region Epilepsy Found., San Antonio, 1982-85, Bexar County Detention Ministry, San Antonio, 1985-86. Episcopal. Office: Haynes and Boone LLP 112 E Pecan St Ste 1600 San Antonio TX 78205-1517

FOX, MICHAEL WILSON, veterinarian, animal behaviorist; b. Bolton, Eng., Aug. 13, 1937; came to U.S., 1962; s. Geoffrey and Elizabeth (Wilson) F.; m. Deanna L. Krantz, May 1989; children by previous marriage: Michael Wilson, Camilla, Mara. B. in Vet. Medicine, Royal Vet. Coll., London, 1962; Ph.D., U. London, 1967, D.Sc., 1975. Postdoctoral fellow Jackson Lab., Bar Harbor, Maine, 1962-64; med. research assoc. State Research Hosp., Galesburg, Ill., 1964-67; assoc. prof. psychology Washington U., St. Louis, 1967-76; v.p. Humane Soc. U.S., Washington, 1986-98, sr. scholar bioethics, 1998—. Author: syndicated newspaper column Ask Your Animal Doctor; author: Canine Behavior, 1965, Canine Pediatrics, 1966, Integrative Development of Brain and Behavior in the Dog, 1971, Behavior of Wolves, Dogs and Related Canids, 1971, Understanding Your Dog, 1972, Understanding Your Cat, 1974, Concepts in Ethology: Animal and Human Behavior, 1974, Between Animal and Man: The Key to The Kingdom, 1976, The Dog, Domestication and Behavior, 1977, Wild Dogs Three, 1977, What is Your Cat Saying?, 1978; (juveniles), The Wolf, 1973 (Christopher award), Vixie, The Story of a Fox, 1973, Sundance Coyote, 1974, Ramu and Chennai, 1975 (Sci. Tchrs.' award); co-author: What Is Your Dog Saying?, 1977, Dr. Fox's Fables, 1980, The Touchlings, 1981, Understanding Your Pet, 1978, The Soul of the Wolf, 1980, One Earth One Mind, 1980, Returning to Eden: Animal Rights and Human Responsibility, 1980, How to be Your Pet's Best Friend, 1981, The Healing Touch, 1982, Love is a Happy Cat, 1982, Farm Animal Husbandry, Behavior and Veterinary Practice, 1983, The Whistling Hunters: Field Studies of the Asiatic Wild Dog (Cuon alpinus), 1984; The Animal Doctor's Answer Book, 1984; Laboratory Animal Care, Welfare and Experimental Variables, 1986, Agricide-The Hidden Crisis That Affects Us All, 1986, The New Animal Doctor's Answer Book, 1989, The New Eden, 1989, Superdog, 1990, Inhumane Society, The American Way of Animal Exploitation, 1990, Animals Have Rights Too, 1991, You Can Save The Animals 50 Things To Do Right Now, 1991, Supercat, 1991, Superpigs and Wondercorn: How the Brave New World of Biotechnology Will Affect Us All, 1992, The Boundless Circle: Caring for Creatures and Creation, 1996, Eating With Conscience: The Bioethics of Food, 1997, Beyond Evolution: The Genetically Altered Future of Plants, Animals, The Earth...and Humans; editor: Abnormal Behavior in Animals, 1968, Readings in Ethology and Comparative Psychology, 1973, The Wild Canids, 1975, On the Fifth Day: Animal Rights and Human Ethics, 1978, Internat. Jour. for Study of Animal Problems, Advances in Animal Welfare Sci. Mem. AVMA, AAAS, Brit. Vet. Assn., Animal Behavior Soc. *My life was shaped in childhood by close contact with animals and nature. Empathy and concern for the well-being of non-human beings led to a veterinary degree and curiousity about their behavior and inner awareness to several years research. Most influential teacher: the wolf. My philosophy: reverence for all life; humankind as steward living in co-creative communion with nature and all.*

FOX, MIRIAM ANNETTE, state legislative fiscal analyst; b. Cuba, N.Y., May 27, 1959; m. Frederick S. Fox, Jan., 1991. BA in Polit. Sci., Idaho State U., 1984; MS in Pub. Mgmt. & Policy, Carnegie-Mellon, 1986. Semiconductor line technician Gould/AMI, Pocatello, Idaho, 1978-84; legal rsch. analyst Manning, Holmes And Winmill Law Firm, Pocatello, 1983-84; market rsch. intern Internat. Trade Adminstrn., Pitts., 1985; rsch. intern Health & Welfare Planning Assn., Pitts., 1985-86; acctg. clk. Carnegie Mellon U., Pitts., 1986; tax revenue analyst Pa. House Appropriations Com., Harrisburg, 1987-91, sr. tax revenue analyst, 1991-93, sr. fiscal analyst, 1993—; designee to Pa. Sch. Employees Retirement Sys. Bd., 1993—. Mem. Capitol Hill Dem. Women's Club, Phi Kappa Phi. Avocations: downhill skiing, swimming, piano. Office: Pa House Reps Appropriations Com 512 E9 Main Capitol Bldg Harrisburg PA 17108-0054

FOX, MITCHELL, magazine publisher. Pub. Vanity Fair mag., N.Y.C., 1994—, v.p., 1998—. Office: Vanity Fair Conde Nast Publs 350 Madison Ave New York NY 10017-3704*

FOX, MURIEL, public relations executive; b. Newark, Feb. 3, 1928; d. M. Morris and Anne L. (Rubenstein) F.; m. Shepard G. Aronson, July 1, 1955; children: Eric R., Lisa S. Student, Rollins Coll., 1944-46; BA summa cum laude, Barnard Coll., 1948. Art critic, bridal editor Miami (Fla.) News, 1946; reporter U.P.I., 1946-48; polit. speechwriter, publicist, 1949-50; from TV-radio writer to exec. v.p. Carl Byoir & Assos., N.Y.C., 1950-85; pres. subs. MediaCom Comm. Tng., 1975-85, By/Media Inc., 1981-85; sr. cons. Hill & Knowlton, Inc., 1986-90; dir. Harleysville Ins. Co., Rorer Group Inc.; Co-chmn. Vice Presdl. Task Force on Women, 1968; mem. steering com. Women's Forum, 1974-79, pres., 1976-78; mem. Women's Econ. Adv. Com., N.Y.C., 1974-78; mem. nat. adv. com. Nat. Women's Polit. Caucus; nat. adv. bd. Women Today, Ethnic Woman. Bd. dirs. N.Y. Diabetes Assn., 1956-66, Holy Land Conservation Fund, United Way of Tri-State, Internat. Rescue Com., 1977-84; v.p. Rockland Ctr. for the Arts, 1985—; pres. Hickory Hill Coop., Inc., 1995—. Named one of 100 Top Corp. Women Bus. Week mag., 1976; recipient Matrix award Women in Communications, 1977, Bus. Leader of Year award ADA, 1979; Disting. Alumna award Barnard Coll., 1985, Eleanor Roosevelt Leadership award, 1985. Mem. NOW (founder, v.p. 1967-70, chmn. bd. 1971-73, chair nat. adv. com. 1973-74, bd. dirs. legal defense and edn. fund 1974—, v.p. fund 1977-78, pres. 1978-81, chair bd. 1981-92, hon. chair bd. 1993—, Muriel Fox Comm. Leadership award 1991, Our Hero award 1995, Caroline Lexow Babcock award 1997), Am. Women in Radio and TV (bd. dirs. 1950-51, chair nat. publicity com. 1955-57, chair nat. pub. rels. com. 1957-59, Achievement award 1983), Am. Arbitration Assn. (bd. dirs. 1983-87). Home and Office: 66 Hickory Hill Rd Tappan NY 10983-1804 *As a business executive, a founder and leader of the modern women's movement, and a fulfilled wife and mother, I hope I have helped to prove that women can enjoy success at many levels-professionally, politically and personally-without being forced to sacrifice one aspect of life for another. I also hope I've helped make such multifaceted success more attainable for other women in the present and future.*

FOX, NED, professional sports team owner. BS in Accounting, U. So. Calif., 1969, MBA, 1971. With real estate Arthur Andersen & Co., 1971-78; sr. ptnr. Maguire Thomas Ptnrs., 1978-93; Founder, co-mng. dir. CommonWealth Ptnrs., L.A., 1993—; adv. com. U. So. Calif. Grad. Sch. Bus.; adv. coun. U. So. Calif. Sch. Arts & Architecture. Exec. com., bd. dirs. L.A. Convention & Vis. Bur., 1993—; chmn. real estate/constrn. com. L.A. County Music Ctr Unified Fund Campaign, 1992-93; urban devel./mixed-use coun. Urban Land Inst.; vol. Boy Scouts Am. Mem. Am. Inst. Cert. CPAs. Office: Sacramento Kings One Sports Pkwy Sacramento CA 95834 also: Commonwealth Ptnrs 633 W 5th St Ste 5610 Los Angeles CA 90071-3502*

FOX, PAUL T., lawyer; b. N.Y.C., Jan. 17, 1953. BA, Northwestern U., 1975, JD cum laude, 1978. Bar: Ill. 1978, U.S. Dist. Ct. (no. dist. trial bar) Ill. 1979, U.S. Ct. Appeals (7th cir.) 1979, U.S. Supreme Ct. 1986, U.S. Ct. Appeals (fed. cir.) 1987, Wis. 1989. Mng. shareholder Greenberg Traurig, Chgo.; faculty mem. Nat. Inst. for Trial Advocacy. Mem. ABA (mem. litigation sect.), State Bar Wis., Chgo. Bar Assn., Order of Coif. Office: Greenberg Traurig 227 W Monroe St Ste 3500 Chicago IL 60606

FOX, PAULA (MRS. MARTIN GREENBERG), author; b. N.Y.C., Apr. 22, 1923; d. Paul Hervey and Elsie (de Sola) F.; m. Richard Sigerson (div. 1954); children: Adam, Linda, Gabriel; m. Martin Greenberg, June 9, 1962. Student, Columbia U. Condr. writing Seminars U. Pa. Author: 22 children's books and 6 novels, including How Many Miles to Babylon, 1966, Portrait of Ivan, 1968, Blowfish Live in the Sea, 1970; (novels) Poor George, 1967, Desperate Characters, 1970, The Western Coast, 1972, The Slave Dancer, 1974 (John Newbery medal), The Widow's Children, 1976, The Little Swineherd and Other Tales, 1978, A Place Apart, 1983 (Am. Book award), A Servant's Tale, 1984, One-Eyed Cat, 1985 (Newbery honor book 1985), Maurice's Room, 1985, The Moonlight Man, 1986, The Stone-Faced Boy, 1987, The Village by the Sea, 1988, Lily and the Lost Boy, 1989, The God of Nightmares, 1990, Monkey Island, 1991, Amzat and His Brothers, 1993, Western Wind, 1993, The Eagle Kite, 1995, Radiance Descending, 1997. Recipient Arts and Letters award Nat. Inst. Arts and Letters, 1972, Hans Christian Andersen medal, 1978, fiction citation Brandeis U., 1984, Empire State award for children's lit., 1994; Guggenheim fellow, 1972. Mem. Authors League. Office: care Robert Lescher 47 E 19th St New York NY 10003-1323*

FOX, RAYMOND GRAHAM, educational technologist; b. Portland, Oreg., May 31, 1923; s. George Raymond and Georgia Dorothy (Beckman) F.; B.S., Rensselaer Poly. Inst., 1943; m. Harriet Carolyn Minchin, Apr. 17, 1948; children—Susan, Christine, Ellen, Laura, John. Salesman IBM Corp., N.Y.C., 1946-48, br. mgr., 1949-56, systems mgr., 1957-65, edn. systems devel. mgr., 1965-76; chmn. bd. Learning Tech. Inst., Warrenton, 1975—. Mem. Va. Council for Deaf, 1978-84; chmn., 1980-83; mem. Sec. of Navy Adv. Bd. on Edn. and Tng., 1972-77; cons. for tech. Va. Legis. Adv. Com. on Handicapped, 1970; mem. Nat. Def. Exec. Reserve, 1970-83; mem. emeritus, 1983—. Served with USNR, 1943-46. Mem. Soc. Applied Learning Tech. (pres. 1972—), Nat. Security Indsl. Assn. (chmn. tng. group 1974-76). Anglican. Clubs: Army & Navy (Washington); Fauquier (Warrenton, pres. 1993-94); Columbia Country (Chevy Chase, Md.); Moorings (Vero Beach, Fla.). Patentee interactive multimedia instruction delivery sys. Home: PO Box 376 Warrenton VA 20188-0376 Office: 50 Culpeper St Warrenton VA 20186-3207

FOX, RENÉE CLAIRE, sociology educator; b. N.Y.C., Feb. 15, 1928; d. Paul Fred and Henrietta (Gold) F. AB summa cum laude, Smith Coll., 1949, LHD, 1975; PhD, Harvard U., 1954; MA (hon.), U. Pa., 1971, U. Oxford, 1996; ScD (hon.), Med. Coll. Pa., 1974, St. Joseph's Coll., Phila., 1978; D honoris causa, Katholieke U., Belgium, 1978; LHD (hon.), La Salle U., Phila., 1988; DSc (hon.), Hahnemann U., 1991. Rsch. asst. Bur. Applied Social Rsch., Columbia U., 1953-55, rsch. assoc., 1955-58; lectr. dept. sociology Barnard Coll., 1955-58, asst. prof., 1958-64, assoc. prof., 1964-66; lectr. sociology Harvard U., 1967-69; rsch. fellow Center Internat. Affairs, 1967-68, research assoc. program tech. and soc., 1968-71; prof. sociology, psychiatry and medicine U. Pa., Phila., 1969-98, Annenberg prof. social scis., 1978-98, chmn. dept. sociology, 1972-78, Annenberg prof. social scis. emerita, 1998—, faculty assoc. Ctr. for Bioethics, 1999—; faculty assoc. Ctr. for Bioethics, U. Penn., 1999—; sci. adviser Centre de Recherches Sociologiques, Kinshasa, Zaïre, 1963-67; vis. prof. sociology U. Officielle du Congo, Lubumbashi, 1965; vis. prof. Sir George Williams U., Montreal, Que., Can., summer 1968; Phi Beta Kappa vis. scholar, 1973-75; dir. humanities seminar med. practitioners NEH, 1975-76; maître de cours U. Liège, Belgium, 1976-77; vis. prof. Katholieke U., Leuven, Belgium, 1976-77; Wm. Allen Neilson prof. Smith Coll., Mass., 1980; dir. d'Etudes Associé, Ecole des Hautes Etudes en Sciences Sociales, Paris, summer 1989; George Eastman vis. prof. Oxford U., 1996-97; mem. bd. clin. scholars program Robert Wood Johnson Found., 1974-80; mem. Pres.'s Commn. on Study of Ethical Problems in Medicine, Biomed. and Behavioral Rsch., 1979-81; dir. human qualities of medicine program James Picker Found., 1980-83; Fae Golden Kass lectr. Harvard U. Sch. Medicine and Radcliffe Coll., 1983, Kate Hurd Mead lectr. Med. Coll. Pa./Coll. Physicians Phila., 1990, Lori Ann Roscetti Meml. lectr. Rush-Presbyn.-St. Luke's Med. Ctr., Chgo., 1990; vis. scholar Women's Ctr., U. Mo., Kansas City, 1990, vis. scholar Case Western Reserve Sch. of Med., 1992; opening address 13th Internat. Conf. on Social Scis. and Medicine, Hungary, 1994, vis. prof. U. Calif., San Francisco Sch. of Med., 1994; lectr. founds. of medicine Faculty of Medicine McGill U., Montreal, Can., 1995; Supernumerary fellow Balliol Coll. Oxford U., 1996-97; WHR Rivers disting. lectr. Dept. of Social Medicine, Harvard Med. Sch., 1998; assembly series lectr. Washington U., St. Louis, 1998; William J. Rashkind Meml. lectr, Am. Heart Assn., 1998. Author: Experiment Perilous, 1959, (with Willy DeCraemer) The Emerging Physician, 1968, (with Judith P. Swazey) The Courage to Fall, 1974, rev. edit. 1978, Essays in Medical Sociology, 1979, 2d edit., 1988, L'Incertitude Medicale, 1988, The Sociology of Medicine: A Participant Observer's View, 1989, (with Judith P. Swazey) Spare Parts: Organ Replacement in American Society, 1992, In the Belgian Château: The Spirit and Culture of European Society in an Age of Change, 1994, French language edit., 1997, Organ Transplantation: Meanings and Realities (edited with Stuart Youngner and Laurence O'Connell), 1996; assoc. editor: Am. Sociol. Rev. 1963-66, Social Sci. and Medicine; mem. editorial com.: Ann. Rev. Sociology, 1975-79; assoc. editor Jour. Health and Social Behavior, 1985-87, Perspectives in Biology and Medicine, 1996—; mem. editorial adv. bd. Tech. in Soc., Sci., 1982-83; mem. editorial bd. Bibliography of Bioethics, 1979—, Culture, Medicine and Psychiatry, 1980-86, Jour. of AMA, 1981-94, Am. Scholar, 1994—, Current Revs. in Publs., 1994—; vice chair adv. bd. Am. Jour. Ethics and Medicine; contbr. articles to profl. jours. Bd. dirs. Medicine in Pub. Interest, 1979-94; mem. tech. bd. Milbank Meml. Fund, 1979-85; mem. overseers com. to visit univ. health svcs. Harvard Coll., 1979-86; trustee Russell Sage Found., 1981-87; vice chmn. bd. dirs. Acadia Inst., 1990-97; mem. adv. com. Sch. Nursing LaSalle U., 1998—; mem. advancement com. King Baudouin Found. U.S. Inc., 1998—. Recipient E. Harris Harbison Gifted Teaching award Danforth Found., 1970, Radcliffe Grad. Soc. medal, 1977, Lindback Found. award for teaching U. Pa., 1989, Centennial medal Grad. Sch. Arts and Scis. Harvard U., 1993, Chevalier de l'Ordre de Leopold II (Belgium), 1995; Wilson Ctr., Smithsonian Instn. fellow, 1987-88, Guggenheim fellow, 1962; Fulbright Short-Term Sr. scholar to Australia, 1994; 1st W.H.R. Rivers Disting. lectr. Harvard Med. Sch., 1998. Fellow African Studies Assn., AAAS (dir. 1977-80, chmn. sect. K 1986-87), Am. Sociol. Assn. (council 1970-73, 79-81, v.p. 1980-81), Am. Acad. Arts and Scis. (co-chair Class III section I membership com., 1994-96), Inst. Medicine (Nat. Acad. Scis., council 1979-82), Inst. Soc., Ethics and Life Scis. (founder, gov.); mem. AAUP, AAUW, Assn. Am. Med. Colls., Social Sci. Research Council (v.p., dir.), Eastern Sociol. Soc. (pres. 1976-77, Merit award 1993), N.Y. Acad. Scis., Soc. Sci. Study Religion, Inst. Intercultural Studies, 1969-93, (asst. sec. 1969-78, sec. 1978-81, 89-92, v.p. 1987-89), Am. Bd. Med. Specialists, Coll. of Physicians of Phila. (coun. 1993-98), Phi Beta Kappa (senate 1982-87, Ralph Waldo Emerson book award com. 1998—). Home: The Wellington 135 S 19th St Philadelphia PA 19103-4912

FOX, RICHARD GABRIEL, anthropologist, educator; b. N.Y.C., Mar. 3, 1939; s. Joseph Fox and Elizabeth(Cetron) Swig; m. Judith Lynn Huff, Dec. 18, 1974; 1 child, Sarah. BA, Columbia U., 1960; MA, U. Mich., 1961, PhD, 1965. Asst. prof. Brandeis U., Waltham, Mass., 1965-68; assoc. prof. Duke U., Durham, N.C., 1968-74, prof. anthropology, 1974-93; prof. Washington U., St. Louis, 1993—; pres.-elect, Wenner-Gren Found. for Anthropological Rsch., 1999—; vis. scholar Sch. Am. Rsch., Santa Fe, 1987-88; mem. Inst. Advanced Study, Princeton, N.J., 1972-73. Author: Kin, Clan, Raja and Rule, 1972, Urban Anthropology, 1977, Lions of the Punjab, 1985, Gandhian Utopia, 1989. John Simon Guggenheim Found. fellow, N.Y.C.,

1987-88; grantee NSF, NEH, NIH. Fellow Am. Anthropol. Assn. Office: Washington U Dept Anthropology Saint Louis MO 63130

FOX, ROBERT AUGUST, food company executive; b. Norristown, Pa., Apr. 24, 1937; s. August Emil and Elizabeth Martha (Deimling) F.; m. Linda Lee Carnesale, Sept. 19, 1964; children: Lee Elizabeth, Christina Carolyn. B.A. with high honors, Colgate U., 1959; M.B.A. cum laude, Harvard U., 1964. Unit sales mgr. Procter & Gamble Co., 1959-62; gen. sales mgr. T.J. Lipton Co., 1964-69; v.p. mktg. Can. Dry Corp., 1969-72; pres., chief exec. officer, dir. Can. Dry Internat., 1972-75; exec. v.p., dir. Hunt-Wesson Foods, Inc., 1975-78; pres., chief exec. officer, dir. R.J. Reynolds Tobacco Internat. S.A., 1978-80; chmn., chief exec. officer, dir. Del Monte Corp., San Francisco, 1980-85; vice chmn. Nabisco Brands, Inc., East Hanover, N.J., 1986-87; pres., chief oper. officer Continental Can Co., Norwalk, Conn., 1988-90; chmn., chief exec. officer Clarke Hooper Am., Irvine, Calif., 1990-92, also bd. dirs.; pres. Revlon Internat., N.Y.C., 1992; pres., CEO Foster Farms, Livingston, Calif., 1993—; bd. dirs. New Perspective Fund, Growth Fund Am., Income Fund Am., Am. Balanced Fund, Clarke Hooper, plc, Crompton & Knowles Corp.; trustee Euro-Pacific Growth Fund. Trustee Colgate U. Mem. San Francisco C. of C. (bd. dir., pres. 1984), Pacific Union Club, The Olympic Club. Office: Foster Farms PO Box 457 Livingston CA 95334-0457*

FOX, ROBERT KRIEGBAUM, manufacturing company executive; b. Covington, Ohio, Apr. 1, 1907; s. Ammon L. and Josephine (Kriegbaum) F.; m. Dorothy Carroll Bush, Aug. 28, 1934; children: Susan, Hannah, Robert L. A.B., Ohio State U., 1929, M.A., 1930, Ph.D., 1932. Chemistry instr. Bethany Coll., W.Va., 1932-36; mem. faculty Hiram Coll., Ohio, 1936-41; partner Fox Chem. Co., Coshocton, Ohio, 1941-45; pres. Lancaster Glass Corp., 1945-76, chmn. bd., 1976-91; chmn. bd. Indiana Glass Co., 1956-74; v.p., treas. Lancaster Colony Corp., 1962-82; dir. Hocking Valley Nat. Bank, 1948-77, Lancaster Colony Corp., 1962-91. Mem. Sigma Xi, Phi Lambda Upsilon. Clubs: Mason, Shriner, Rotarian. Home: 1445 Cin-zanesville Rd SW Lancaster OH 43130 Office: 220 W Main St Lancaster OH 43130-3720

FOX, ROBERT WILLIAM, mechanical engineering educator; b. Montreal, Que., Can., July 1, 1934; s. Kenneth and Jessie (Glass) F.; m. Beryl Williams, Dec. 15, 1962; children—David, Lisa. B.S. in Mech. Engring, Rensselaer Poly. Inst., 1955; M.S., U. Colo., 1957; Ph.D., Stanford U., 1961. Instr. mech. engring. U. Colo., Boulder, 1955-57; research asst. Stanford (Calif.) U., 1957-60; mem. faculty Purdue U., Lafayette, Ind., 1960-99; assoc. prof. Purdue U., 1963-66, prof., 1966-99, asst. head mech. engring., 1971-72, asst. dean engring. for instrn., 1972-76; acting head Purdue U. (Sch. Mech. Engring.), 1975-76, asso. head, 1976-98, chmn. univ. senate, 1971-72, prof. emeritus, 1999; cons. Owens-Corning Fiberglass Co., Edn. Services Inc., Nelson Mfg. Co., Peoria, Ill., B. Offen Co., Chgo., Agard Co., Johns-Marsville Co., Richmond, Ind., Babcox & Wilcox, Alliance, Ohio. Named Standard Oil Outstanding Tchr. Purdue U., 1967; recipient Harry L. Solberg Outstanding Tchr. award, 1978, 83, Donald E. Marlowe awd., Am. Soc. for Engineering Education, 1992. Fellow ASME, Am. Soc. for Engring. Edn.; mem. Sigma Xi, Pi Tau Sigma, Tau beta Pi, Delta Tau Delta. Home: 3627 Chancellor Way Lafayette IN 47906-8809 Office: Purdue U Sch Mech Engring Lafayette IN 47907

FOX, RONALD ERNEST, psychologist; b. Conover, N.C., May 11, 1936; s. Fred Yount and Carolyn Victoria (Weeks) F.; m. Margaret Elizabeth Smith, Dec. 27, 1956; children: Kelley Victoria, Brett Anthony, Jonathan Eric. A.B., U. N.C., 1958, M.A., 1961, Ph.D., 1962. Diplomate: Am. Bd. Profl. Psychology. Asst. prof. dept. psychiatry and psychology U. N.C., 1963-68; asso. prof. dept. psychiatry and psychology Ohio State U., 1968-74, prof., 1974-77, coord. edn. and tng. dept. psychiatry, 1968-77, dir. Family Therapy Clinic, Med. Sch., 1970-77; dean Sch. Profl. Psychology, Wright State U., 1977-92; CEO Piedmont Care, Chapel Hill, N.C., 1992-95; sr. ptnr. Norton, Fox and Assocs., Inc., Chapel Hill and Cin., N.C., 1993-97; exec. dir. The Cons. Group divsn. HRC, 1997—. Author: (with others) Patients View Their Psychotherapy, 1968, Abnormal Psychology, 1972, (with Norton) The Change Equation: Capitalizing on Diversity for Effective Organizational Change, 1997; contbr. articles to sci. jours. Fellow APA (pres. 1994); mem. Ohio Psychol. Assn., N.C. Psychol. Assn., Nat. Acads. Practice. Home: 309 Brookside Dr Chapel Hill NC 27516-2905 Office: 104 S Estes Dr Ste 301 Chapel Hill NC 27514-2866

FOX, RONALD FORREST, physics educator; b. Berkeley, Calif., Oct. 1, 1943; s. Sidney Walter and Raia (Joffe) F.; children: Daniel, Lara. BA, Reed Coll., 1964; PhD, Rockefeller U., 1969. Postdoctoral fellow Miller Inst., U. Calif., Berkeley, 1969-71; asst. prof. Ga. Inst. Tech., Atlanta, 1971-74, assoc. prof., 1974-79, prof., 1979—, Regents prof. physics, 1991—, asst. dir. Sch. Physics, 1982-84, assoc. dir. Sch. Physics, 1986-89, 97—. Author: Biological Energy Transduction, 1982, Energy and the Evolution of Life, 1988; contbr. over 100 articles to sci. jours., over 20 chpts. to books. Recipient W. Roane Beard Outstanding Tchr. award Ga. Inst. Tech., 1992, Sigma Xi Sustained Rsch. award Ga. Inst. Tech., 1997; fellow Alfred P. Sloan Found., 1974-78, Guggenheim fellow, 1985; grantee NSF, 1973—. Fellow Am. Phys. Soc.; mem. N.Y. Acad. Scis. Avocations: racquetball, jazz piano. Office: Ga Inst Tech Dept Physics Atlanta GA 30332-0430

FOX, SANDRA GAIL, insurance marketing executive; b. N.Y.C., Aug. 12, 1960; d. Joseph A. and Rhoda (Levine) Fried; m. David A. Fox, Sept. 21, 1986; children: Alexander, Peter. BA, Ind. U., 1982. Examiner nat. compliance Dean Witter, N.Y.C., 1983-84, from sales supr. active assets acct. to mktg. assoc., 1984-86; pvt. practice Hackensack, N.J., 1986-87; dir. alt. distbn. mktg. Mut. of N.Y., Teaneck, N.J., 1987-89, dir. spl. markets and annuities, 1989-94, asst. v.p. annuities mktg., 1994-97; product developer Prudential, Newark, 1997—, v.p. annuity product devel., 1998, 1998—; mem. work life force com. Mut. N.Y., Teaneck, 1991-97. Vol. presch. activities YW-YMHA, Wayne, N.J., 1993-94; vol. Wayne PTA (fundraisers), 1996—; fundraiser United Jewish Fedn., Bergen and Passaic, N.J., 1992-96, Kidney Found., 1994; mem. annuity exam. rev. panel LOMA, 1998-99, annuity programs steering com., 1999, expert reviewer for Annuity Principles and Products book. Griswald acad. scholar Ind. U., 1980, 81. Mem. Nat. Assn. Variable Annuities (edn. com. 1996—, publ. chmn. 1996), Phi Beta Kappa. Avocations: tennis, running, theater. Office: Prudential 3 Gateway Ctr 8th Fl 100 Mulberry St Newark NJ 07102

FOX, SARAH, lawyer; b. Buffalo, Dec. 12, 1951; d. Austin McCracken and Jean McLean (Coatsworth) F. BA, Yale U., 1973; JD, Harvard U., 1982. Bar: N.Y. 1982, D.C. 1983. Reporter Buffalo Courier-Express, 1973-79; staff counsel Internat. Union of Bricklayers & Allied Craftsmen, Washington, 1982-90; chief labor counsel Senate Labor and Human Resources Com., Washington, 1990-94, minority chief labor counsel, 1995-96; bd. mem. NLRB, Washington, 1996—. Office: NLRB 1099 14th St NW Ste 11300 Washington DC 20045-2001*

FOX, SAUL LOURIE, physician, researcher; b. Boston, July 5, 1906; s. Isadore H. and Bessie (Cohen) F.; m. Matilda R. Aronson Fox, Jan. 26, 1933 (widowed March 1975); children: Myra D., John O. AB cum laude, Harvard U., 1927, MD, 1931. Intern Sinai Hosp., Balt., 1931-32; asst. res., 1932-33; vol. fellow Johns Hopkins Hosp., Balt., 1933-34; intern Charles V. Chapin Hosp., Providence, 1934-35; physician in Internal Medicine Beverly Hills, Calif., 1935-77; attending physician Cedars Sinai Hosp., L.A., 1935-77; Harbor Gen. Hosp., Torrence, Calif., 1961-70; asst. clin. prof. UCLA Med. Sch., L.A., 1961-70. Contbr.: Textbook on Diseases of the Breast, 1950; contbr. articles to profl. jours. Capt. U.S. Med. Corps., 1944-46. Named Pres., 1968, Gov., 1969-71, Beverly Hills Med. Soc. Fellow ACP; mem. AMA, Am. Internal Medicine, Med. Bd. Med. Examiners, Nat. Bd. Med. Examiners, L.A. County Med. Assn., Phi Delta Epsilon Club. Home: 1324 Sunset Plaza Dr Los Angeles CA 90069-1235

FOX, SHELDON, retired radiologist, medical educator; b. N.Y.C., May 11, 1919; s. Max and Sara (Lefcowitz) Fuchs; m. Anitta Ruth Boyko, 1948; children: Serena, Daniel, Judith. BA, Johns Hopkins U., 1938, MD, 1942. Diplomate Am. Bd. Radiology, Am. Bd. Nuclear Medicine. Intern in Pediatrics Yale U., 1942; pediatric fellow Vanderbilt U., 1945-46; fellow med. mycology Duke U.; resident in diagnostic radiology N.Y.U.- Bellevue Med. Ctr., 1947; radiology postgrad. fellow Columbia Presbyn. Hosp.; NCI fellow in radiation Therapy Bellevue; attending radiologist Meml. Hosp.-Sloan Kettering Inst., 1951-54; radiologist Elizabeth (N.J.) Gen. Hosp. and Wuester Cancer Clinic; pvt. practice Elizabeth, N.J., 1956-70; dir. radiology dept. Alexian Brothers Hosp., 1960-83, attending radiologist, 1983-90, ret., 1990; asst. clin. vis. prof. radiology N.Y.U.-Bellevue. avocations: tennis, music, reading, swimming, skiing. Home: 936 Westminster Ave Hillside NJ 07205-2923

FOX, STUART IRA, physiologist; b. Bklyn., June 21, 1945; s. Sam and Bess F.; m. Ellen Diane Berley; 1 child, Laura Elizabeth. BA, UCLA, 1967; MA, Calif. State U., L.A., 1967; postgrad., U. Calif., Santa Barbara, 1969; PhD, U. So. Calif., 1978. Rsch. assoc. Children's Hosp., L.A., 1972; prof. physiology L.A. City Coll., 1972-85, Calif. State U., Northridge, 1979-84, Pierce Coll., 1986—; cons. William C. Brown Co. Pubs., 1976—. Author: Computer-Assisted Instruction in Human Physiology, 1979, Laboratory Guide to Human Physiology, 2d edit., 1980, 8th edit., 1999 Textbook of Human Physiology, 1986, 6th edit., 1999, Human Anatomy and Physiology, 1986, 5th edit., 1999, Perspectives on Human Biology, 1991, Laboratory Manual for Anatomy and Physiology, 1986, 5th edit., 1999; contbg. author: Biology, 5th edit., 1999, Synopsis of Anatomy and Physiology, 1997. Mem. AAAS, Am. Physiol. Soc., Sigma Xi. Home: 5556 Forest Cove Ln Agoura Hills CA 91301-4047 Office: Pierce Coll 6201 Winnetka Ave Woodland Hills CA 91371-0001

FOX, SUSAN E., legal assistant; b. Uniontown, Pa., June 17, 1955; d. James Ira Sr. and Elizabeth Ann (Kirk) F. BS in Journ., W.Va. U., 1977; Cert. Completion, Nat. Ctr. for Paralegal Tng., Atlanta, 1977. Legal asst. Jackson, Kelly, Holt & O'Farrell, Charleston, W.Va., 1978-79, Dennis, Corry, Webb & Carlock, Atlanta, 1979-84, Dennis, Corry, Porter & Thornton, Atlanta, 1984-89, Ga.-Pacific Corp., Atlanta, 1989-98, Radcliffe, DeHaas & Monaghan, Uniontown, Pa., 1998—. Bd. dirs. Met. Atlanta Coun. on Alcohol and Drugs, 1991-92, treas., 1992-93, pres., 1993-94; bd. dirs. DeKalb Rape Crisis Ctr., 1994-96; bd. dirs. Ga.-Pacific Svc. Force, 1995-96; chmn., mem. devel. Jr. League of DeKalb County, Decatur, Ga., 1989-90, cmty. rsch. chmn., 1990-91, corr. sec., 1991-92, pres.-elect, 1994-95, pres., 1995-96; mem. Leadership DeKalb, 1995; Olympic vol., Equestrian Venue Comm. Ctr., 1996. Republican. Presbyterian. Avocations: needlework, reading, collecting foxes and seashells. Home: 26 Belmont Cir #2 Uniontown PA 15401-1611 Office: Radcliffe DeHaas & Monaghan 99 E Main St Uniontown PA 15401

FOX, SYLVAN, journalist; b. Bklyn., June 2, 1928; s. Louis and Sophie (Shapiro) F.; m. Gloria R. Endleman, Sept. 8, 1948; 1 child, Erica. BA, Bklyn. Coll., 1951; MA, U. Calif., Berkeley, 1952. Reporter Little Falls (N.Y.) Evening Times, 1954, Schenectady (N.Y.) Union Star, 1954-55, Buffalo Evening News, 1955-59; successively rewriteman, asst. city editor, city editor N.Y. World Telegram and Sun, 1959-66; dep. police commr. for press relations City of N.Y., 1966-67; successively rewriteman, reporter, dep. met. editor, Saigon bur. chief N.Y. Times, N.Y.C., 1967-73; Nassau editor Newsday, L.I., N.Y., 1973-77, nat. editor, then asst. mng. editor nat. and fgn. news, 1977-79, editor editorial pages, 1979-88; travel columnist, 1994-95; tchr. journalism NYU, 1965, L.I.U., 1967, Baylor U., Waco, 1985, 88; asst. prof. journalism NYU, 1989-90. Author: The Unanswered Questions About President Kennedy's Assassination, rev. edit., 1975. Recipient Pulitzer prize local reporting, 1963. Mem. Soc. of Silurians. Home: 401 E 65th St New York NY 10021-6943

FOX, TERRY LYNN, art psychotherapist; b. Bryn Mawr, Pa., June 10, 1967; d. Charles Henry and Mary E. Fox; m. Willis W. Moore IV, Feb. 1, 1991. BFA, U. of the Arts, 1989; MA, Hahnemann U., 1993. Registered art therapist; cert. addictions counselor, Pa. Graphic designer STG Graphics, Phila., 1989-91; art therapist Cmty. Coun., Phila., 1992-94; art psychotherapist Belmont/Einstein, Phila., 1994—; student supr. Hahnemann U., Phila., 1993—. Mem. Am. Art Therapy Assn., Delaware Valley Art Therapy Assn., South Jersey Bead Soc. (co-founder, sec. 1997—). Avocations: beading, old movies, drawing, computers, knitting.

FOX, THOMAS GEORGE, health science educator; b. N.Y.C., Sept. 15, 1942; s. Thomas Peter and Alice Cecilia (Ehler) F.; m. Mary Patricia Palmer, Aug. 29, 1980; children: Christopher Adam, Thomas Andrew, Stephen Baron. BA, Coll. N.J., 1964; MEd, U. Vt., 1966; PhD, U. Mich., 1972. Asst. to dean U. Mass., Amherst, 1966; dir. counseling and student svcs. U. Mich., Ann Arbor, 1966-68, sr. adminstrv. asst. Med. Ctr., 1968-69, adminstrv. assoc., 1969-71; asst. dean Robert Wood Johnson Med. Sch., Piscataway, N.J., 1972-77, assoc. dean, 1977-83; sr. v.p. Robert Wood Johnson U. Hosp., New Brunswick, N.J., 1983-86; exec. v.p. U. Health System of N.J., New Brunswick, 1986-90; prof., v.p. devel. and univ. rels. Oreg. Health Scis. U., Portland, 1990-94; CEO Univ. Found., 1990-94; pres., CEO, Liberty Sci. Ctr., Jersey City, 1994-96; CEO, Operation Smile, Norfolk, Va., 1996—; asst. prof. U. Medicine and Dentistry N.J., 1973-79, assoc. prof., 1979-83, clin. assoc. prof., 1983-90. Contbr. articles to profl. jours. Trustee Francis E. Parker Meml. Home, 1981-90, 96—. Fellow Acad. Medicine N.J.; mem. Am. Coll. Healthcare Execs.(diplomate), Am. Soc. Assns. Execs. (Key Philanthropic Orgns. Com.). Home: 1217 Masters Row Chesapeake VA 23320-9455 Office: Operation Smile 6435 Tidewater Dr Norfolk VA 23509-1600

FOX, WARREN HALSEY, academic administrator, consultant; b. Loma Linda, Calif., Apr. 20, 1945; s. Gaylord Hollis and Helen Elizabeth (Halsey) F.; Candace A. Evart, June 7, 1970. BA, U. Calif., Berkeley, 1967; PhD, U. So. Calif., 1973. Program mgr. U. Calif., Berkeley, 1970-72; vis. prof. U. Tex., Austin, 1973-74; prof. polit. sci. U. Nev., Reno, 1974-79, assoc. dean; 1979-82; vice chancellor U. Nev. System, Reno, 1982—; acting dir. computer system ctr. U. Nev. System, 1987-88; Chmn. Burroughs' Project "Reducing the Risk", U. Consortium, Detroit, 1984-85. Contbr. articles to jours. Commr. Gov.'s Com. Future of Nev., 1980; mem. Gov.'s Task Force on MX Missile, 1981, Gov.'s Com. Econ. Devel., 1984; vice chmn. Truckee Meadows Adv. Bd., 1984; chmn. exec. com. Nat. Forum for System Chief Acad. Officers, 1985-86. Named Faculty Speaker of Yr., U. Nev., 1975; Econ. Devel. grantee Nev. Commn., 1984; Am. Council Edn. fellow, 1981, NASA fellow, 1968-71. Mem. Am. Soc. Pub. Adminstrn. (pres. Reno chpt. 1978), Internat. Indsl. Relation Assn., Acad. Polit. Sci., Western Govt. Research Assn. Democrat. Presbyterian.

FOX, WILLIAM RICHARD, retired physician; b. Bozeman, Mont., Oct. 12, 1915; s. William Edward Fox and Anah Grace Bump; m. Esther Viola Jorgenson, Aug. 15, 1948 (dec. 1985); 1 child, Susan Jane Fox. MD, U. Manitoba, Can., 1941. Intern St. Joseph Hosp., St. Paul, 1940-41; staff Good Samaritan Hosp. Johnson Clinic, 1941-85; pub. health officer Pierce County, 1948-85; surgeon Gt. No. Ry., 1950-70. Past pres. Rugby Econ. Devel. Assn. Recipient N.D. Physicians Community and Profl. Svc. award, 1984. Mem. Union Hills County Club (Sun City Ariz.), Mason (past master), Shriners, Elks. Avocations: golf, bowling, crafts.

FOXEN, RICHARD WILLIAM, manufacturing company executive; b. N.Y.C., Nov. 12, 1927; s. William Aloysius and Mae Dorothea (Scully) F.; m. Hilda Duran-Ballen, Feb. 11, 1956; children: Richard, Theresa, Thomas, Patricia, Anthony. B.M.E., Bklyn. Poly. Inst., 1950. V.p. corp. staffs Westinghouse Air Brake Co., Pitts., 1961-69; pres. European indsl. group Am. Standard, Brussels, 1969-73; v.p. Europe bus. div. GE, Brussels, 1973-78, sr. v.p. Rockwell Internat., 1978-88; adj. prof. bus. adminstrn. Carnegie Mellon U., U. Pitts. Chmn. Western Pa. Family Ctr., Pitts.; chmn. Pitts. Mercy Health Systems Inc., Pitts.; bd. trustees N.Y. Poly. U.; bd. dirs. Cordis Corp., Mannesmann U.S. Adv., Conflict Resolution Ctr. Internat.; chmn. Mendelssohn Choir of Pitts., Pressley-Ridge Schs. With U.S. Army, 1946-48. Mem. Pitts. Athletic Assn., Tau Beta Pi, Pi Tau Sigma. Roman Catholic. Clubs: Duquesne, Pitts. Athletic, Seabrook Island. Home: 5529 Dunmoyle St Pittsburgh PA 15217-1014

FOX-FREUND, BARBARA SUSAN, real estate executive; b. Rocky Mount, N.C., Jan. 17, 1949; d. Albert Richard and Anita (Levinson) Fox; m. James Coleman Freund, Jan. 12, 1985. Student, Centenary Coll., 1968, Boston U., 1970. Real estate broker Whitbread-Nolan, Inc., N.Y.C., 1972-80; v.p. Stribling and Assocs., Ltd., N.Y.C., 1980-82; exec. v.p. Cross and Brown Residentials, Inc., N.Y.C., 1982-88; pres. Fox Residential Group, Inc., N.Y.C., 1988—. Bd. dirs. Riverside Symphony, N.Y.C., 1989; bd. dirs., pres. 55 W. 73d St. Corp., N.Y.C., 1986—. Mem. Real Estate Bd. N.Y. (chmn. residential com. 1986-89, ethics com. 1989-92, bd. dirs. brokerage com. 1988-92, tchr. 1986—, chmn. inter-firm rels. com. 1991-93, bd. dirs. residential divsn. 1994-99, bd. govs. 1994-99, chmn. interfirm forum 1995—, residential ethics com. 1995—). Republican. Jewish. Avocations: sculpture, tennis, skiing. Home: 55 W 73rd St New York NY 10023-3136 Office: Fox Residential Group Inc 1015 Madison Ave New York NY 10021-0261

FOX-GENOVESE, ELIZABETH ANN TERESA, humanities educator; b. Boston, May 28, 1941; d. Edward Whiting and Elizabeth Mary (Simon) Fox; m. Eugene Dominick Genovese, 1969. BA, Bryn Mawr Coll., 1963; MA, Harvard U., 1966, PhD, 1974; LittD (hon.), Millsaps Coll., 1992. Teaching fellow Harvard U., Cambridge, Mass., 1965-66, 1967-69; asst. prof. U. Rochester, N.Y., 1973-76, assoc. prof., 1976-80; prof. SUNY, Binghamton, 1980-86; prof. Emory U., Atlanta, 1986—, Eleonore Raoul prof. of humanities, 1988—; adj. prof. Auburn (Ala.) U., 1987; Eudora Welty prof. Millsaps Coll., 1990. Author: Origins of Physiocracy, 1976, (with others) Fruits of Merchant Capital, 1983, Within the Plantation Household, 1988, Feminism Without Illusions, 1991, Feminism Is Not the Story of My Life: How the Elite Women's Movement Has Lost Touch with the Real Concerns of Women, 1996; mem. editl. adv. bd. First Things; mem. editl. bd. Books and Culture; The Jour. of the Historical Soc. (editor), contbr. numerous articles to profl. jours.; editor: The Jour. Hist. Soc. Mem. acad. adv. bd. Inst. for Am. Values, 1994—; adv. bd. Campaign for the Am. Family, 1995—, Ind. Women's Forum, 1993—. Mem. LWV, MLA, Soc. Am. Historians, The Hist. Soc. (mem. exec. com.), So. Hist. Assn. (life), So. Assn. for Women Historians (life), Am. Comparative Lit. Assn. (adv. bd. 1991-95), Orgn. Am. Historians (life, proglram com. 1991), Am. Studies Assn. (program com. 1987), Soc. for Study So. Lit. (exec. coun. 1990-93), South Atlantic MLA (chair women's studies network 1989-90), Social Sci. Hist. Assn. (exec. coun. 1986-88), Am. Hist. Assn., Am. Polit. Sci. Assn., Assn. of Lit. Scholars and Critics, Am. Acad. Liberal Edn. (bd. dirs.), Nat. Coun. on Hist. Standards (steering commn.), Hist. Soc. (mem. exec. com.), Atlanta Hist. Assn. (acad. adv. com.), Am. Antiquarian Soc., Nat. Alumni Forum (adv. bd.), Cosmos Club, Harvard Club of Boston. Roman Catholic. Avocations: family, films, fashion, reading, needle point, major league baseball. Home: 1487 Sheridan Walk NE Atlanta GA 30324-3253 Office: Emory U Dept History Atlanta GA 30322

FOXHOVEN, JERRY RAY, lawyer; b. Yankton, S.D., July 24, 1952; s. Elmer William and Ida Elizabeth (Lubbers) F.; m. Julie Ann Greco, Apr. 6, 1985; children: Anthony Michael, Peter Joseph. BS summa cum laude, Morningside Coll., 1974; JD, Drake U., 1977. Bar: Iowa 1977, U.S. Dist. Ct. (so. and no. dists.) Iowa 1977, U.S. Ct. Appeals (8th cir.) 1977, U.S. Supreme Ct. 1981, Nebr. 1985, U.S. Dist. Ct. Nebr. 1985, Wis. 1986. Assoc. Critelli & Pille, Des Moines, 1977-79; ptnr. Critelli & Foxhoven, Des Moines, 1979-82, Foxhoven & McCann, Des Moines, 1982-88; ptnr. Peddicord, Wharton, Thune, Foxhoven & Spencer, P.C., 1988-91, pvt. practice, 1991—; instr. criminal justice dept. Des Moines Area Community Coll., Ankeny, Iowa, 1978-81, Am. Inst. Banking, 1982-85. Mem. steering com. Culver for U.S. Senate, Des Moines, 1980; chmn. Iowa State Foster Care Rev. Bd.; bd. dirs., nat. pres. Nat. Assn. Foster Care Reviewers; mem. parish council Sacred Heart Roman Cath. Ch., West Des Moines, 1982. Democrat. Lodge: Masons (master 1990). Home: 1155 Prairie View Dr West Des Moines IA 50309-2317 Office: 505 5th Ave Des Moines IA 50309-2317

FOXLEY, CECELIA HARRISON, commissioner. BA in English, Utah State U., 1964; MA in English, U. Utah, 1965, PhD in Ednl. Psychology, 1968. English tchr. Olympus H.S., Salt Lake City, 1965-66; asst. prof. edn., assoc. dir. student activities U. Minn., Mpls., 1968-71; from asst. prof. to assoc. prof., asst. dean Coll. Edn. U. Iowa, Iowa City, 1971-81; prof. psychology Utah State U., Logan, 1981-85, from asst. v.p. student svcs. to assoc. v.p. for student svcs. and acad. affairs, 1981-85; assoc. commr. for acad. affairs Utah State Bd. Regents, Salt Lake City, 1985-93, commr., 1993—; Utah rep. Am. Coun. on Edn. Office Women in Higher Edn., 1982-92; mem. nat. adv. coun. on nurse tng. U.S. Dept. Health and Human Svcs., 1987-91; mem. nat. adv. bd. S.W. Regional Ctr. for Drug Free Schs., 1988-93; mem. edn. bd. Utah Alliance for Edn. and Humanities, 1989-93; mem. prevention subcom. Utah Substance Abuse Coordinating Coun., 1991-93; mem. exec. bd. U.S. West Comm., 1995—; mem. adv. bd. Salt Lake Buzz, 1995—; active Consortium for Women in Higher Edn. Bd., 1981-85, Utah State Libr. Bd., 1990-93, Compact for Faculty Diversity, 1994—; presenter in field; cons. in field. Author: Recruiting Women and Minority Faculty, 1972, Locating, Recruiting, and Employing Women, 1976, Non-Sexist Counseling: Helping Women and Men Redefine Their Roles, 1979; co-author: The Human Relations Experience, 1982; editor: Applying Management Techniques, 1980; co-editor: Multicultural Nonsexist Education, 1979; author chpts. to books; contbr. articles to profl. jours. Grantee Utah State Dept. Social Svcs., 1984-85, 85-86; recipient Pres. Leadership award Assn. Utah Women Edn. Adminstrs., 1990, Disting. Alumni award Utah State U., 1991. Mem. APA, Am. Assn. Counseling and Devel., Am. Coll. Pers. Assn., Nat. Forum Sys. Chief Acad. Officers, State Higher Edn. Exec. Officers (mem. exec. com. 1994—), Western Interstate Cooperative Higher Edn. (mem. exec. com. 1994—). Office: Utah State Bd Regents 3 Triad Ctr Ste 350 355 W North Temple Salt Lake City UT 84180-1205*

FOXMAN, ABRAHAM H., advocacy organization administrator; came to U.S., 1950; s. Helen and Joseph F. BA in Polit. Sci., CCNY; JD, NYU; postgrad., Jewish Theol. Sem., New Sch. Social Rsch.; LLD (hon.), Fla. Internat. U., 1992. Asst. dir. law dept. Anti-Defamation League of B'nai B'rith, N.Y.C., 1965-68, dir. Mid. Ea. affairs, 1968-73, assoc. nat. dir., 1973-87, nat. dir., 1987—. Mem. Pres.'s U.S. Holocaust Meml. Coun., N.Y.C. Holocaust Meml. Commn. (adv. coun.), Am. Gathering, Jewish Holocaust Survivors. Office: Anti-Defamation League 823 United Nations Plz New York NY 10017-3518*

FOXMAN, BRUCE MAYER, chemist, educator; b. Youngstown, Ohio, Mar. 12, 1942; s. Jerome Jay and Phyllis E. (Altshuler) F.; B.S. with distinction, Iowa State U., 1964; Ph.D. in Inorganic Chemistry, M.I.T., 1968; m. Carole J. Wittkopf, Sept. 14, 1968; children—Gregory Michael, Andrew Craig. Research fellow Australian Nat. U., Canberra, 1968-72; asst. prof. Brandeis U., Waltham, Mass., 1972-78, assoc. prof., 1978-85, prof., 1985—; vis. prof. Thomas J. Watson Rsch. Ctr., IBM, Yorktown Heights, N.Y., 1975, Max-Plank-Inst. fur Polymerforschung, Mainz, Germany, 1995-96; cons. Polaroid Corp. Mem. Am. Chem. Soc., Am. Crystallographic Assn., Materials Rsch. Soc., Royal Soc Chemistry, Coll. Bd. Advanced Placement Exam. Com. (chair, Chemistry 1993-96), Sigma Xi, Phi Kappa Phi, Phi Lambda Upsilon. Home: 74 N Hill Ave Needham MA 02492-1223 Office: Brandeis Univ Dept Chemistry Waltham MA 02454-9110

FOXWELL, ELIZABETH MARIE, editor, writer; b. Somerville, N.J., Aug. 30, 1963; d. James Adolph and Rita Ann (Drohan) F. BS in Journalism, U. Md., 1985; MA in Liberal Studies with distinction, Georgetown U., 1990. Coord. publs. internat. student exch. program Georgetown U., Washington, 1987-91; editor Am. Assn. Colls. for Tchr. Edn., Washington, 1992-97, dir. publs. and mktg., 1994-97; publs. mgr. Soc. for Am. Archaeology, 1998—; bd. dirs. Malice Domestic, Bethesda, Md., publicity liaison, 1988-94, vice chair, 1993-95, chair, 1995-97; presenter Vera Brittain Centenary Conf., 1993, Popular Culture Assn. Conf., 1995, 96. Editor The Usual Suspects, 1992-95; co-editor (anthologies) Malice Domestic 5, Malice Domestic 6; editor Malice Domestic 7, 1995-97, Malice Domestic 8, 1998, Malice Domestic 9, 1999; co-editor Murder, They Wrote I, 1997, Murder, They Wrote II, 1998, More Murder, They Wrote, 1999; editor-in-chief The Armchair Detective, 1997-98; contbr. short stories to Crime Through Time II, 1998, Cat Crimes Through Time, 1999; contbr. articles to profl. jours. Recipient 2d prize in play contest N.J. Ctr. for the Performing Arts, 1981, honorable mention in writing contest Interlochen Arts Acad., 1981. Home: 1568 Mt Eagle Pl Alexandria VA 22302-2120

FOXWORTH, JO, advertising agency executive; b. Tylertown, Miss., G-rad. in Journalism, U. Mo. Exec. McCann-Erickson, Interpub. Group of Cos.; owner Jo Foxworth Inc., N.Y.C., 1968—; co-owner Foxworth-Gold, Inc. Author: Boss Lady, 1979, Wising Up, 1981, Boss Lady's Arrival and Survival Plan, 1986, The Bordello Cookbook, 1996. Named to AAF Hall of Fame, 1997. Office: 740 Broadway New York NY 10003-9518

FOXWORTHY, JEFF, comedian, actor, writer; b. Hapeville, Ga., Sept. 6, 1958; m. Pamela Gregg Grethe, 1985; children: Jordan, Juliane. Grad., Ga. Inst. Tech., 1979. Computer engr. IBM, 1979-84; performing and rec. artist, comdedian, writer, 1984—. Star TV show The Jeff Foxworthy Show, ABC-TV, 1995-96, NBC-TV, 1996—; author: You Might Be a Redneck If..., 1989, Hick Is Chic: A Guide to Etiquette for the Grossly Unsophisticated, 1990, Red Ain't Dead: 150 More Ways To Tell If You're a Redneck, 1991, Check your Neck: More of "You Might Be a Redneck If...," 1992, You're Not a Kid Anymore, 1993, (with Vic Henley) Games Rednecks Play, 1994, Redneck Classic: The Best of Jeff Foxworthy, 1995; albums include You Might Be a Redneck If..., 1994 (platinum cert.), Games Rednecks Play, 1995 (platinum cert.). Office: care Warner/Reprise 1815 Division St Nashville TN 37203-2732*

FOY, CHARLES DALEY, retired soil scientist; b. Buena Vista, Ky., Aug. 19, 1923; s. Charles Clinton and Zylphia Gertrude (Binkley) F.; m. Doris Blanche Hornbaker, June 4, 1950; 1 child, David Alden. BS in Agriculture, U. Tenn., 1949; MS in Soil Sci., Purdue U., 1953, PhD in Soil Fertility, 1955. Tchr. Vets. Inst. on Farm Tng. Program, Connersville, Ind., 1949-51; rsch. fellow Purdue U., West Lafayette, Ind., 1951-55; asst. prof. agronomy Purdue U., West Lafayette, 1955-57; rsch. soil scientist, dept. agronomy USDA U. Ark., Fayetteville, 1957-61; rsch. soil scientist, climate stress lab. USDA Agrl. Rsch. Sta., Beltsville, Md., 1961-95; collaborator, 1995—; cons. and lectr. in U.S. and abroad. Contbr. articles to profl. jours. With U.S. Army, 1943-46, PTO. Recipient Environ. Quality award Am. Soc. Hort. Sci., 1974, Cert. of Recognition for outstanding contbn. Orgn. Com. of IV Internat. Symposium on Plant-Soil Interactions at Low pH and Nat. Maize and Sorghum Rsch. Ctr., Belo Horizonte, Brazil, 1996; Purdue U. grad. rsch. fellow, 1953-55. Fellow Am. Soc. Agronomy, Soil Sci. Soc. Am., Crop Sci. Soc. Am.

FOY, EDWARD DONALD, financial planner; b. Omaha, June 2, 1952; s. Donald Edward and Eloise Annette (Knudson) F.; m. Kathleen Joyce Sykora, Oct. 1, 1971; children: Becky Jo, Stacy Ann, Cindy Lee. BS cum laude, Dana Coll., Blair, Nebr., 1974. Pharm. sales rep. Schering-Plough, Inc., Lincoln, Nebr., 1974-80; account exec. Dain Bosworth, Inc., Lincoln, 1980-84, E.F. Hutton & Co., Inc., Lincoln, 1984-87; prin. Investment Advisors, Lincoln, 1987-95; mgr. SELECTOR Money Mgmt., Lincoln, 1993—; pres. Foy Fin. Svcs., Lincoln, 1994—; gen. securities prin. FFP Securities, Inc., Chesterfield, Mo., 1989—, registered agt. FFP Adv. Svcs., Inc., Chesterfield, 1990—; regional v.p. 1st Fin. Planners, Inc., Chesterfield, 1991—, mem. adv. bd., 1990—. Vocalist A Song with Class, Lincoln, 1987-91; soloist St. John's Ch., Lincoln, 1986—, chmn. fin. com., 1989-91, sponsor godparent program, 1988-92; pres. Meadowlane Area Residents Assn., Lincoln, 1990. Republican. Roman Catholic. Avocations: fishing, cycling. Office: Foy Fin Svcs 12501 Holdrege St Lincoln NE 68527-9430

FOY, THOMAS PAUL, lawyer, retired state legislator, retired banker; b. Silver City, N.Mex., Oct. 19, 1914; s. Thomas J. and Mary V. Foy; m. Joan Carney, Nov. 17, 1948 (dec. June 1994); children: Celia, Thomas Paul Jr. (dec.), Muffet (Mary Ann), J. Carney, James B.. BS in Commerce, Notre Dame U., 1938, JD, 1939. Bar: N.Mex. 1946. Dist. atty. N.Mex. 6th Jud. Dist., Silver City, 1949-57; atty. Village of Bayard, N.Mex., 1954-68, Village of Ctrl., N.Mex., 1960-70; v.p., counsel, bd. dirs. Sunwest Bank, Silver City, 1946-84, chmn. bd. dirs., 1969-84, chmn. emeritus, 1984-97; state rep. Dist. 39 State of N.Mex., Grant-Hidalgo, 1971-98; chmn. jud. com. N.Mex. State Legis., Santa Fe, 1984-98; pres. Foy & Vesely and Foy, Foy & Castillo, Silver City, 1946—. 1st lt. U.S. Army, 1941-46; prisoner of war, PTO, 1942-45. Decorated Bronze Star, Purple Heart, Asiatic-Pacific Ribbon with 3 oak leaf clusters; recipient Citizen of Yr. award Silver City-Grant County C. of C., 1965, Dedication to Advancement award Trial Lawyers Assn., 1993, N.Mex. Disting. Svc. medal, 1994. Mem. ABA, N.Mex. Bar Assn. (bar commr. 1967-85, v.p. N.Mex. bar commn. 1978-79, Disting. Svc. of Laws award 1987), Am. Judicature Soc., Bataan Vets. Orgn. (state comdr. 1965-66, 98-99), KC (Grand Knight 1936-37), VFW (state comdr. 1959-60), Lions (dist. gov. 1956-57), Elks. Democrat. Roman Catholic. Avocations: football, baseball, travel, conventions. Office: Foy Foy & Castillo PC 210 W Broadway St Silver City NM 88061-5353

FOYE, LAURANCE VINCENT, physician, hospital administrator; b. Seattle, Nov. 26, 1925; s. Laurance Vincent and Sara Pauline (Given) F.; m. Laura Marian Love, June 22, 1951; children: Patricia Marian, Michael Laurance. A.B., U. Calif., Berkeley, 1949; M.D., U. Calif., San Francisco, 1952. Diplomate: Am. Bd. Internal Medicine. Intern San Francisco Gen. Hosp., 1952-53; resident in medicine VA Hosp., San Francisco, 1953-55, 56-57, Stanford U. Hosp., San Francisco, 1955-56; asst. chief med. service VA Hosp., San Francisco, 1958-66; chief clin. investigations br. Nat. Cancer Inst., Bethesda, Md., 1966-70; dir. edn. service VA, Washington, 1970-74; dep. chief med. dir., 1974-78; dir. VA Med. Center, San Francisco, 1978-86; assoc. clin. prof. medicine U. Calif. Sch. Medicine, San Francisco, 1979-86; mem. adv. council Nat. Heart and Lung Inst., 1971-73. Contbr. articles on cancer research to profl. jours. Mem. governing bd. West Bay Health Systems Agy., 1978-82; mem. Fed. Exec. Bd., San Francisco, 1978-86. Served with U.S. Army, 1944-46. Recipient Exceptional Service award VA, 1978, Disting. Career award, VA, 1986. Fellow ACP; mem. Phi Beta Kappa, Sigma Xi, Alpha Omega Alpha. Address: 125 Cambon Dr Apt 10-h San Francisco CA 94132-2512

FOYE, THOMAS HAROLD, lawyer; b. Rapid City, S.D., Nov. 23, 1930; s. Harold Herbert and Jean Winifred (McCormick) F.; m. Laurene Fowler, Aug. 7, 1972; children: David Snyder, Stewart Snyder. BS in Commerce, Creighton U., 1952; LLB, Georgetown U., 1955. Bar: S.D. 1955, D.C. 1955, U.S. Supreme Ct. 1968. Trial atty. tax div. U.S. Dept. Justice, Washington, 1955-58; assoc. Bangs, McCullen, Butler, Foye & Simmons, predecessor firms, Rapid City, 1958-60, ptnr., 1960—; lectr. in field. Fellow Am. Coll. Trust and Estate Counsel, Am. Bar Found.; mem. ABA, State Bar S.D. (pres. 1982-83), Pennington County Bar Assn. (pres. 1962), Am. Coll. Real Estate Lawyers, Internat. Acad. Estate and Trust Law., Am. Coll. Tax Counsel. Democrat. Roman Catholic. Club: Arrowhead Country (Rapid City). Avocations: snow skiing, water skiing, hiking. Office: Bangs McCullen Butler Foye & Simmons PO Box 2670 Rapid City SD 57709-2670

FOYT, A(NTHONY) J(OSEPH), JR., auto racing crew chief, former professional auto racer; b. Houston, Jan. 16, 1935; m. Lucy Zarr, 1955; children: A.J. 3d, Jerry, Terry Lynn. Ed. pub. schs. Auto racer, 1953-82; owner Conseco/A.J. Foyt Enterprise Corp.; profl. horse breeder and trainer, Houston; bd. dirs. Riverway Bank, Houston, SCI Corp., Houston. Named Racing Driver of Yr., Auto Racing Frat. Greater N.Y., 1963, Outstanding Am. Driver of Yr., 1967. Winner Indpls. 500, 1961, 64, 67, 77; winner U.S. Auto Club championship, 1960, 61, 63, 64, 67, 75, 79; winner Twenty Four Hours of Le Mans (France), 1967, Schaefer 500, 1973, Pocono 500, 1975, 79, Daytona 500, 1972, nat. championship stock car div. U.S. Auto Club, 1968, 78, 79, Twenty Four Hours of Daytona, 1983, 85, Twelve Hours of Sebring, 1985. Address: AJ Foyt Enterprises 6415 Toledo St Houston TX 77008-6207*

FOYT, ARTHUR GEORGE, electronics research administrator; b. Austin, Tex., June 17, 1937; s. Arthur George and Virginia (Watkins) F.; m. Michelle Swanzy, May 28, 1978; children—Claire, John. B.S.E.E., M.S.E.E., MIT, 1960, Sc.D. in Elec. Engring., 1965. Staff mem. Bell Telephone Labs., Murray Hill, N.J., 1960-62; group leader MIT Lincoln Labs, Lexington, 1962-82; mgr. electronics research United Tech. Research Ctr., East Hartford, Conn., 1982—. Fellow IEEE; mem. Sigma Xi, Eta Kappa Nu. Office: United Tech Rsch Ctr MS 129-15 411 Silver Ln East Hartford CT 06118-1127*

FOZZATI, ALDO, automobile manufacturing company executive; b. Italy, Mar. 10, 1950; came to U.S., 1978; s. Danilo and Piera (Bretto) F.; m. Ana Maria Ruiz, June 7, 1977; children: Giacomo, Hugo, Daniel. PhD in Aero. Engring., Poly. U. of Turin, Italy, 1975. Registered profl. engr., Europe, U.S. and Can. Project mgr. Fiat Aerospace, Turin, 1975-78; U.S. rep. Fiat Corp., N.Y.C. and Detroit, 1978-82; ind. internat. bus. cons. Los Angeles, Paris and N.Y.C., 1982-84; program dir. GM, Detroit, 1984-87; dir. new bus. devel. GM Europe, Zurich, Switzerland, 1987-91; purchasing exec. dir. GM Europe, Rüsselsheim, Germany, 1991-92; v.p., gen. mgr. Kelsey-Hayes Europe, Wiesbaden, Germany, 1992-94, Delco Remy Internat. Europe, Frankfurt, Germany, 1995-98; mem. adv. bd. Citicorp Venture Capital, N.Y.C., 1998—; bd. dirs. Erido European Investment Agy., Brussels, Frankfurt (Germany) Internat. Sch.; mem. global adv. coun. Thunderbird Am. Mgmt. Sch., Phoenix; sr. advisor Mitchell Madison Group N.Y.; mem. adv. bd. Artoc Group, Cairo. Mem. Soc. Automotive Engrs., Am. Security Council. Republican. Roman Catholic. Avocations: skiing, tennis, golf. Home: 250 Marlborough Dr Bloomfield Hills MI 48302-0644 Office: Delco Remy Internat Germany, Frankfurter St 92, Eschborn Germany

FRACKMAN, NOEL, art critic; b. N.Y.C., May 27, 1930; d. Walter David and Celeste (Barman) Stern; m. Richard Benoit Frackman, July 2, 1950; 1 child, Noel Dru Pyne. Student Mt. Holyoke Coll., 1948-50; BA, Sarah Lawrence Coll., 1952, MA, 1953; postgrad. Columbia U., 1964-67; MA, Inst. Fine Arts, NYU, 1976, PhD, 1987. Art critic Scarsdale Inquirer (N.Y.), 1962-67, Patent Trader, Mt. Kisco, N.Y., 1962-71; assoc. Arts Mag., N.Y.C., 1968-92; lectr. Aldrich Mus. Contemporary Art, Ridgefield, Conn., 1967-75, Gallery Passport Ltd., N.Y.C., 1968-96; contractual lectr. Met. Mus. Art, N.Y.C., 1994-95; curator of edn. Storm King Art Ctr., Mountainville, N.Y., 1973-75; instr. continuing edn. div. SUNY, Purchase, 1988—; adj. assoc. prof. humanities, 1997—; bd. dirs. Friends of the Neuberger Mus. Art, Purchase (N.Y.) Coll., SUNY, 1994—. Author (catalogue) John Storrs, Whitney Mus. of Am. Art, 1986; contbr. articles and/or revs. to various mags. including: Arts Mag., Harper's Bazaar, Feminist Art Jour., Art Voices. Sarah Williston scholar, 1948-50; recipient 1st prize, coll. publs. contest Mademoiselle mag., 1961. Mem. Internat. Assn. Art Critics, Art Table Inc., Coll. Art Assn. Home: 3 Hadden Rd Scarsdale NY 10583-3327

FRACKMAN, RICHARD BENOIT, investment banker; b. N.Y.C., Apr. 14, 1923; s. H. David and Ruth (Warren) F.; m. Noel Stern, July 2, 1950; 1 dau., Noel Dru Frackman Pyne. Grad., Pratt Sch. Bus., 1941; student, U. Pa., 1941-42, NYU, 1946-48, N.Y. Inst. Fin., 1962-63. Mdse. mgr. R.H. Miller Stores, Inc., N.Y.C., 1946-49; v.p., mdse. mgr. Darling Stores Corp., N.Y.C., 1949-61; stockbroker, sr. security analyst, ltd. partner Burnham & Co., N.Y.C., 1962; v.p., corp. Burnham & Co. Inc., 1972; sr. v.p. Drexel Burnham Lambert, Inc., 1972-89; mem. hearing bd. N.Y. Stock Exchange, 1978—; ltd. ptnr. Cowen & Co., N.Y.C., 1989-98; mng. dir., 1992—; mem. exec. com. Securities Industry Assn., N.Y.C., 1980—; arbitrator NYSE, N.Y.C., 1992—; mng. dir. S.G. Cowen Securities Corp., 1998—. Pres. Greenville Community Coun., 1967-70; vice chmn. Town of Greenburgh (N.Y.) Planning Bd., 1970-77; bd. dirs. N.Y. State Planning Fedn., 1975-78; mem. Westchester County Regional Plan Assn., 1970-92; trustee Sarah Lawrence Coll., Bronxville, N.Y., 1979-87; mem. Coun. of N.Y. State U. at Purchase, 1996—, chmn. 1998—, , Purehouse Coll. Found., 1997—; mem. N.Y. State Rep. Com., 1976-82, 97—. Capt. USAAC, 1942-46. Recipient Silver Box award Greenville Community Council, 1970. Mem. N.Y. Soc. Security Analysts (sr. mem.), Fin. Analysts Fedn. Clubs: Metropolis Country (White Plains, N.Y.) (gov. 1974—, v.p. 1977-78, treas. 1979-80, pres. 1981-83); Harmonie (N.Y.C.). Home: 3 Hadden Rd Scarsdale NY 10583-3327 Office: SG Cowen Securities Corp Financial Sq New York NY 10005

FRACKMAN, RUSSELL JAY, lawyer; b. N.Y.C., July 3, 1946; s. Sam and Doris (Wasserberg) F.; m. Myrna D. Morganstern, Aug. 3, 1980; children: Steven Howard, Abigail Zoe. BA in History, Northwestern U., 1967; JD cum laude, Columbia U., 1970. Bar: Calif. 1971, U.S. Dist. Ct. (ctrl., ea. and no. dists.) Calif., U.S. Ct. Appeals (2d and 9th cirs.), U.S. Supreme Ct. Assoc. Mitchell, Silberberg & Knupp, L.A., 1970-76, ptnr., 1976—, chmn. litigation dept., 1994-96; lectr. on intellectual property and entertainment law various instns. including Practising Law Inst., L.A. Copyright Soc., Beverly Hills Bar Assn., U. So. Calif. Sch. Law, Am. Film Mktg. Assn., Calif. Copyright Conf. Bd. editors Columbia Law Rev., 1969-70; contbr. articles and revs. to legal jours. Co-chmn. internat. leadership devel. forum CARE, 1990; bd. trustees CARE Found., 1991—, Twitty, Milsap, Sterban Found., 1988-92. Mem. ABA (chmn. copyright subcom. litigation sect. 1990-93, lectr. various confs.), Am. Film Mktg. Assn. (mem. arbitration tribunal). Democrat. Jewish. Office: Mitchell Silberberg & Knupp 11377 W Olympic Blvd Los Angeles CA 90064-1625

FRADE, PETER DANIEL, chemist, educator; b. Highland Park, Mich., Sept. 3, 1946; s. Peter Nunes and Dorathea Grace (Gehrke) F.; m. Karen L. Kovich, Mar. 14, 1992. B.S. in Chemistry, Wayne State U., 1968, M.S., 1971, Ph.D., 1978. Chemist Henry Ford Hosp., Detroit, 1968-75, analytical chemist, toxicologist dept. pathology, div. pharmacology and toxicology, 1975-86, sr. clin. lab. scientist dept. pathology div. clin. chemistry and pharmacology, 1987-96; assoc. prof. Coll. of Pharmacy and Allied Health Professions Wayne State U., Detroit, 1996—; research assoc. in chemistry Wayne State U., Detroit, 1978-79; vis. scholar U. Mich., Ann Arbor, 1980-90; vis. scientist dept. Hypertension Research, Henry Ford Hosp., Detroit, 1986-88; adj. prof. Coll. Pharmacy and Allied Health Professions Wayne State U., 1991-96. Contbr. sci. articles to profl. jours.; peer reviewer for profl. jours., 1988—. Mem. Rep. Presdl. Task Force, 1984-88; organist St. John's Episcopal Ch., Royal Oak, Mich., 1995-97. Recipient David F. Boltz Meml. award Wayne State U., 1977. Fellow Am. Inst. Chemists, Nat. Acad. Clin. Biochemistry, Assn. Clin. Scientists; mem. Am. Coll. Forensic Examiners, Am. Chem. Soc., Am. Assn. Clin. Chemistry, Am. Guild Organists, European Acad. Arts, Scis. and Humanities, Assn. Analytical Chemists, Mich. Inst. Chemists (treas. 1994—), N.Y. Acad. Scis., Am. Coll. Toxicology, Royal Soc. Chemistry (London), Titanic Hist. Soc., Virgil Fox Sox., Sigma Xi, Phi Lambda Upsilon, Alpha Chi Sigma. Episcopalian. Home: 20200 Orleans St Detroit MI 48203-1356 Office: Wayne State U 627 W Alexandrine Detroit MI 48201-1633

FRADIS, ANATOLY ADOLF, film producer; b. Odessa, USSR, Sept. 26, 1948; came to U.S., 1980; s. Adolf Fradis; m. Marlene Gerdts, Dec. 17, 1983 (div. Dec. 1993); 1 child, Olga. Film dir. Mosfilm Studios, Moscow, 1973-80; pres. Afra-Film Enterprises, L.A., 1980—; film commr. Russian Film Commn., L.A., 1991—. Prodr. films: Haunted Symphony, 1993, Beyond Forgiveness, 1994, Burial of the Rats, 1995, Marquis DeSade, 1996, Business for Pleasure, 1996, Termination Man, 1996, Red Shoe Diaries, 1998, others. Mem. Union of Russian Filmmakers (hon.). Republican. Jewish. Avocation: boxing. Office: Afra-Film Enterprises Inc 137 S Robertson Blvd # 254 Beverly Hills CA 90211-2832

FRADKIN, DAVID MILTON, physicist, educator; b. Los Angeles, Apr. 20, 1931; s. Aaron and Annie (Gordon) F.; m. Dorothea Edna Fairweather, Nov. 25, 1959; children: Lee, Mark, Steven. BS, U. Calif., Berkeley, 1954; PhD, Iowa State U., 1963. Exploitation engr. Shell Oil Co., Los Angeles, 1954-56; research assoc. Iowa State U. and Ames Lab., Ames, Iowa, 1963-64; NATO postdoctoral fellow U. Rome, 1964-65; asst. prof. physics Wayne State U., Detroit, 1965-69, assoc. prof., 1969-75, prof., 1975-94, chmn. dept. physics, 1981-91; prof. emeritus, 1994—; del. Argonne (Ill.) Univs. Assn., 1981-83; vis. fellow U. Durham, Eng., 1991-92. Contbr. articles to profl. jours. Vice chmn. adv. bd. Detroit pub. schs., 1972-73; trustee Detroit Sci. Ctr., 1986-94. Recipient award Probus Club, 1973; sr. postdoctoral fellow U. Edinburgh, Scotland, 1977-78. Mem. Am. Phys. Soc., Sigma Xi. Avocations: tennis, fishing, golf, sailing.

FRADLEY, FREDERICK MACDONELL, architect; b. Bronxville, N.Y., July 31, 1924; s. Justis Frederick and Helen Josephine (Macdonell) F.; m. Dorothy Davis Richard, Aug. 7, 1948; children: Stephen Davis, Wendy Fradley Monroe. B.S., Brown U., 1948; M.F.A. (Lowell M. Palmer fellow), Princeton, 1954. Office engr. Turner Constrn. Co., Phila., 1948-51; project architect Vincent G. Kling, Phila., 1954-61; partner Bower & Fradley Architects, Phila., 1961-78. Important works with Bower in Phila. area include 1500 Walnut St. Office Bldg., Internat. House Student Ctr., Wharton Grad. Ctr. (Vance Hall), Gallery at Market East, 1234 Market St. Office Bldg., Yarway Corp. Hdqs., SKF Industries Hdqrs., in Balt. the W.R. Grace Bldg. Served with USAAF, 1942-46, PTO. Mem. Phi Delta Theta. Home: PO Box 8314 Cruz Bay VI 00831-0373 also (summer): 20 McFarland Shore Rd New Harbor ME 04554-4827

FRAEDRICH, ROYAL LOUIS, magazine editor, publisher; b. Weyauwega, Wis., Apr. 23, 1931; s. Clarence Otto and Libbie Clara (Trojan) F.; m. Phyllis Bohren, June 26, 1955; children—Lynn, Craig, Ann, Sarah, Paul. B.S., U. Wis., 1955. With Doane Agrl. Service, St. Louis, 1955-57; info. specialist Mich. State U., East Lansing, 1957-59; mng. editor Agrl. Pubs., Inc., Milw., 1959-64; editor Big Farmer mag., Milw., 1964-69, Frankfort, Ill., 1969-73; editor Farm Futures mag., Milw., 1973-81; pub. Farm Futures mag., 1981-85; exec. v.p. Top Farmers Am. Assn., Milw., 1973-81; pub. print services AgriData Resources, Inc., 1981-85, v.p. editorial and adminstrn., 1986-89, v.p., sr. editorial dir., 1990-92; sr. editorial dir. ARI Network Svcs. Inc., 1992-94; sr. editor AgEd Network Stewart-Peterson Group, West Bend, Wis., 1994-96, cons. editor, 1996—; v.p., dir. Big Farmer Inc., 1969-73; v.p. Market Communications Inc., Milw., 1973-78. Vice pres. Grace Lutheran Ch., Menomonee Falls, Wis., 1963, mem. stewardship com., 1965-67, sec. bd. elders, 1974-77, mem. bd. elders, 1987-89. Mem. Am. Agrl. Editors Assn. Home: N95w16529 Richmond Dr Menomonee Falls WI 53051-1452 Office: 137 S Main St West Bend WI 53095-3321

FRAENKEL, GEORGE KESSLER, chemistry educator; b. Deal, N.J., July 27, 1921; s. Osmond Kessler and Helene (Esberg) F.; m. Johanna-Maria Herzog, June 30, 1951 (div. Aug. 1965); m. Elizabeth R. Rosen, Nov. 11, 1967 (div. Jan. 1990); m. Eva S. Cantwell, Feb. 3, 1990. BA, Harvard U., 1942; PhD, Cornell U., 1949. Research group leader National Def. Research Com., 1943-46; instr. chemistry Columbia U., N.Y.C., 1949-53; asst. prof. Columbia U., 1953-57, assoc. prof., 1957-61, prof., 1961-91, Eugene Higgins prof. Grad. Sch. Arts and Scis., 1986-91, prof. emeritus, 1992—, chmn. dept. chemistry, 1966-68, dean grad. sch. arts and scis., 1968-83, dean emeritus, 1983—, v.p. spl. projects, 1983-86; mem. postdoctoral fellowship com. Nat. Acad. Sci.-NSF, 1964-65; chmn. Gordon Research Conf. Magnetic Resonance, 1967; mem. Arts Coll. adv. council Cornell U., 1964-74; mem., bd. dirs. Atran Found., N.Y.C., 1968—, com. on budget and fin., 1986—; treas. Atran Found., 1988—. Assoc. editor: Jour. Chem. Physics, 1962-64; Mem. adv. editorial bd.: Chemical Physics Letters, 1966-71; editorial bd.: Jour. Magnetic Resonance, 1969-70. Trustee Columbia U. Press, 1968-71, Walden Sch., N.Y.C., 1964-66. Recipient Army-Navy certificate of appreciation, 1948; Harold C. Urey award Phi Lambda Upsilon, 1972; decorated officer Ordre des Palmes Académiques. Fellow AAAS, Am. Phys. Soc., Am. Chem. Soc., Internat. Electron Spin Resonance Soc.; mem. Assn. Grad. Schs. (exec. com. 1976-80, v.p. 1977-78, pres. 1978-79, chmn. com. policies on grad. edn. 1969-71), Phi Beta Kappa, Sigma Xi, Phi Kappa Phi. Achievements include research in field of electron spin resonance with particular emphasis on the electron spin resonance of organic free radicals. Home: 520 W 114th St Apt 82 New York NY 10025-7852

FRAENKEL, STEPHEN JOSEPH, engineering and research executive; b. Berlin, Germany, Nov. 28, 1917; came to U.S., 1938, naturalized, 1943; s. Max S. and Martha (Plessner) F.; m. Josephine Rubnitz, June 28, 1941; children: Richard Mark, Charles Matthew, Martha Ann. B.S. in Civil Engring. with distinction, U. Nebr., 1940, M.S. in Civil Engring, 1941; Ph.D., Ill. Inst. Tech., 1951. Registered profl. engr., Ill., registered structural engr., Ill. Engr. Pitts.-Des Moines Steel Co., 1941-44, Link Belt Co., 1944-46; with Ill. Inst. Tech. Research Inst., successively research engr., supr., dept. mgr., head dept. propulsion and structural research, 1946-55; dir. research and devel. Stanray Corp., Chgo., 1955-62; dir. research engring. Continental Can Co., 1962-64; gen. mgr. research and devel. Container Corp. Am., Chgo., 1964-75; dir. research and devel. Container Corp. Am., 1975-82; pres., dir. Tech. Services, Inc., Chgo., 1982—; dir. Tech. Commercialization Ctr., Ill. Inst. Tech., 1986-89; arbitrator Am. Arbitration Assn., 1983—; adviser effects nuclear weapons Dept. Def., 1950—; cons. space flight programs ABC. Mem. bd. editors Research Mgmt., 1976-82; contbr. articles to profl. jours. Ency. Chem. Tech. Recipient certificate of achievement for atomic test Greenhouse, U.S. Joint Task Force Three. Mem. TAPPI (chmn. Chgo. sect. 1968-69, dir. 1969—, chmn. acad. adv. group 1971-73, chmn. acad. rels. div. 1973-76), AIAA (pres. Chgo. sect. 1958-59, dir. 1959—), Soc. Exptl. Stress Analysis, Navy League, Sigma Xi, Sigma Tau, Tau Beta Pi, Chi Epsilon. Home: 1252 Spruce St Winnetka IL 60093-2148 Office: 1252 Spruce St Winnetka IL 60093-2148

FRAENKEL-CONRAT, HEINZ LUDWIG, cell biology educator; b. Breslau, Germany, July 29, 1910. MD, Breslau U., 1933; PhD in Biochemistry, U. Edinburgh, 1936. Asst. Rockefeller Inst., 1936-37; rsch. assoc. Butanan Inst., Sao Paulo, 1937-38, Inst. Exp. Biol., U. Calif., 1938-42; from assoc. chemist to chemist We. Regional Rsch. Lab., USDA, 1942-50; Rockefeller fellow England & Denmark, 1951; rsch. biochemist, virus lab. of molecular cell biology U. Calif., Berkeley, 1952-58; Guggenheim fellow, 1963, 67; faculty rsch. lectr. U. Calif., 1968; vis. prof. Postgrad. Med. Coll. U. London, 1986—. Recipient Lasker award APHA, Humbolt Sr. US Scientist award. Mem. Nat. Acad. Sci., Internat. Soc. Toxinology, AAAS, ACS, Am. Soc. Biol. Chemistry. Office: U. Calif. Stanley Hall Berkeley CA 94720

FRAGA, FELIX, councilman. City councilman City of Houston, 1994—. Office: Houston City Coun PO Box 1562 Houston TX 77251-1562*

FRAGER, ALBERT S., retired retail food company executive; b. Boston, Dec. 29, 1922; s. Oscar and Anna (Polterak) F.; m. Marion Nathan, June 15, 1950; children: Owen R., Bonnie L. Frager Franks, Laurie J. Burton, Sherri Frager Goodstein. Student, Amos Tuck Sch. Bus., Dartmouth Coll., 1943; B.S. in Bus. Adminstrn, Northeastern U., 1944. Internal revenue agt. IRS, 1945-56; v.p., controller Stop & Shop, Inc., Boston, 1956-67; treas. Stop & Shop, Inc., 1967-86, fin. v.p., 1969-79, sr. v.p., 1979-86. Past trustee South Palm Beach County Jewish Fedn.; bd. dirs. Donna Klein Jewish Acad.; mem. corp., past bd. overseers Northeastern U.; past pres. Jewish temple. With USNR, 1943-44. Mem. AICPA, Mass. Soc. CPAs. Home: 4740 S Ocean Blvd Apt 911 Highland Beach FL 33487

FRAGNER, MATTHEW CHARLES, lawyer; b. N.Y.C., Jan. 12, 1954; s. Berwyn N. and Marcia R. (Salkind) F.; m. Mariann Donahue, June 19, 1983; children: Rachel Jade, Jaron Roark, Bailyn Natalie, Talia Colby. BA, Yale U., 1975; JD, U. Calif., Berkeley, 1978. Bar: Calif. 1978, U.S. Tax Ct. 1979, U.S. Ct. Appeals (9th crct.) 1979. Atty. Thomas Shafran & Wasser, L.A., 1978-83; ptnr. Shafran & Fragner, L.A., 1984-87, Lane & Edson, L.A., 1987-88, Mayer Brown & Platt, L.A., 1989-92, Sonnenschein Nath & Rosenthal, L.A., 1992—; pres. Somnolence, Inc., L.A., 1989—; lectr. U. So. Calif., 1994—. Active Berkeley (Calif.) Law Found., 1978-83. Mem. Los Angeles County Bar Assn. (co-chair comml. devel. and landing subsect.). Office: Sonnenschein Nath Rosenthal 601 S Figueroa St Ste 1500 Los Angeles CA 90017-5720

FRAGOLA, JOSEPH RALPH, executive; s. Caesar F. and Phyllis C. F.; children: Christopher, Kimberly, Meredith. BS in Physics, Polytech Inst. Bklyn., 1968, MS in Physics, 1971, postgrad., 1971-78. Prin. investigator NASA Space Sta. Reliability Data Analysis Project, 1993; prin. investigator Space Shuttle Risk Assessment NASA, 1994-95; program mgr. Probabilistic Risk Assessment, Dodewaard Plant, The Netherlands, 1990-91; task leader Asco Probabilistic Safety Assessment, Spain, 1990-92, Garona PSA, Spain; prin. investigator NRC Programmatic Performance Indicator, 1988-89; v.p. Sci. Applications Internat. Co., N.Y.C., 1980—; tech. and managerial guidance Operational Safety and Reliability Rev.; cons. in field. Prin. author Nat. Reliability Evaluation Program Procedures Guide; co-author: Human Reliability Analysis. Recipient R.K. McElroy award Reliability and Maintainability Symposium, 1994, award SAIC, 1995. Fellow IEEE (regional award). Office: Sci Applications Internat Co 7 W 36th St Fl 10 New York NY 10018-7911

FRAGUELA, JAMES, publishing executive; b. Bklyn.; s. G. and Sophie (Vidal) F.; m. Susan Baron, Aug. 15, 1988; 1 child, Kate. BA in Bus. Adminstrn., Curry Coll. Sales rep. Seventeen Mag., 1970-72; advt. sales dir. Seventeen's Make-It, 1972-73; sales rep. Woman's Day Mag., 1973-75; account mgr. Family Cir. Inc., 1975-81, assoc. Eastern mgr., 1981-82, Eastern advt. mgr., 1982-84, v.p., advt. dir., 1984-87; pub. Lear Pub., Inc., 1988-91; v.p., mktg. dir. Electronic Mktg. and Retail Comm., 1992-95; sr. v.p., pub. Globe Comm. Corp., N.Y.C., 1995—. Avocations: motorcycling, jogging, tennis. Home: 300 E 74th St New York NY 10021-3712 Office: Globe Comm Corp 3 E 54th St New York NY 10022-3108

FRAHM, SHEILA, association executive, former government official, academic administrator; b. Colby, Kans., Mar. 22, 1945; m. Kenneth Frahm; children: Amy, Pam, Chrissie. BS, Ft. Hays State U., 1967. Mem. bd. edn. State of Kans., 1985-88; mem. Kans. Senate, Topeka, 1988-94, senate majority leader, 1993-94; lt. gov. State of Kans., 1995-96; mem. from Kans., U.S. Senate, Washington, 1996; exec. dir. Kans. Assn. C.C. Trustees, Topeka, 1996—. Mem. AAUW (Outstanding Br. Mem. 1985), Thomas County Day Care Assn., Shakespeare Fedn. Women's Clubs, Farm Bur., Kans. Corn Growers, Kans. Livestock Assn., Rotary (Paul Harris fellow 1988). Republican. Home: 6005 SW 39th St Topeka KS 66610-1380 Office: 700 SW Jackson St Ste 401 Topeka KS 66603-3757

FRAHM, VERYL HARVEY, JR., laboratory manager; b. Lewellen, Nebr., Sept. 11, 1948; s. Veryl Harvey and Elaine Eloise Frahm; m. Vicki Anne, May 29, 1971; children: Errin Wilson, Megan Joy, Branden Corey. BA in Chemistry, U. Colo., 1971; MBA, U. Phoenix, 1989. Rsch. asst. Nat. Ctr. for Atmospheric Rsch., Boulder, Colo., 1968-72; support scientist Nat. Ctr. for Atmospheric Rsch., Boulder, 1976-79; rsch. metallurgist Cato Rsch. Corp., Wheatridge, Colo., 1972-75, 79-86; chemist scientist U.S. Geol. Survey, Denver, 1975-76; sr. radiochemist Pub. Svc. Co. of Colo., Denver, 1986-89; radiochemistry supr. Omaha Pub. Power Dist., 1989-92; lab. mgr. Scientech Inc. Environ. Labs., Gaithersburg, Md., 1992-94; labs. mgr., quality assurance mgr., vitreous state lab. The Cath. U. Am., Washington, 1994—. Treas. Alpha Chi Sigma Chemistry Frat., Boulder, 1967-71; guild mem. Nebr. Choral Arts Soc., Omaha, 1990-91; chmn. property com. Evang. Reformed Ch., Frederick, Md.; mem.-at-large Frederick County Md. Solid Waste Mgmt. Adv. Com. Mem. Am. Nuclear Soc., Mensa, Intertel. Office: Cath U Am Vitreous State Lab Hannan Hall Rm 307 Cardinal Station Washington DC 20064

FRAIDIN, STEPHEN, lawyer; b. Boston, July 29, 1939; s. Morris and Freda (Rozeff) F.; m. Susan Greene, July 4, 1963; children: Matthew, Sam, Sarah. AB, Tufts U., 1961; JD, Yale U., 1964. Bar: N.Y. 1965. Ptnr. Fried, Frank, Harris, Shriver & Jacobson, N.Y.C., 1964—; vis. lectr. Yale U. Law Sch., 1988—, mem. exec. com.; mem. editl. adv. bd. Prentice Hall Law and Bus.; bd. dirs. Selfhelp Cmty. Svcs. Inc. Contbr. numerous articles to profl. jours. Mem. bd. overseers Tufts U. Arts and Scis.; bd. dirs. UJA-Fedn. N.Y. Mem. ABA, Assn. of Bar of City of N.Y. Office: Fried Frank Harris Shriver & Jacobson 1 New York Plz Fl 22 New York NY 10004-1980

FRAILEY, STEPHEN A., photographer; m. Mary Ehni, Oct. 9, 1988. Attended, San Francisco Art Inst.; BA, Bennington Coll., 1979. prof. photography Sch. Visual Arts, N.Y.C., 1995—, chmn. photography dept., 1998—; instr. Internat. Ctr. Photography, N.Y.C., 1994—; mem. faculty Milton Avery Grad. Sch. Arts Bard Coll., 1996—; vis. artist Bennington (Vt.) Coll., 1998—. One man exhbns. include New Mus. Contemporary Art, N.Y.C., 1984, Real Art Ways, Hartford, Conn., 1986, U. Ariz., 1986, 303 Gallery, N.Y.C., 1986, Lieberman and Saul Gallery, N.Y.C., 1989, 1990, Vassar Coll., 1990, others; group exhbns. inlcude Murray (Ky.) State U., 1981, Ohio State U., 1981, Pensacola (Fla.) Coll, 1981, Foto Gallery, N.Y.C., 1981, Sarah Spurgeon Gallery, Wash., 1982, Waco (Tex.) Art Ctr., 1982, Contemporary Art Mus., Houston, 1982, Artists Space, 1983, Jack Tilton Gallery, N.Y.C., 1983, Amarillo Art Ctr., 1984, Bennington Coll, 1984, Nature Morte Gallery, N.Y.C., 1984, Galerie Vivian Esders, Paris, 1984, L.A. Ctr. Photographic Studies, 1985, Camerawork, San Francisco, 1985, Daniel Wolf Gallery, N.Y.C., 1985, Light Gallery, N.Y.C, 1986, Whitney Mus./Fairfield, Stamford, Conn., 1986, Internat. Ctr. Photography, N.Y.C, 1986, 90, White Columns, N.Y.C., 1986, Josh Baer Gallery, N.Y.C., 1986, L.A. County Mus. Art, 1987, U. Ill., Chgo., 1987, Visual Arts Gallery, N.Y.C., 1988, Catskill Ctr. Photography, Woodstock, N.Y., 1988, Nat. Mus. Am. Art, Smithsonian Inst., 1989, Friends of Photography, San Francisco, 1989, Janet Borden Gallery, N.Y.C., 1989, Tampa Mus. Art, 1989, Calif. Coll. Arts and Crafts, San Francisco, 1990, Hokkaido Mus. Modern Art, Sapporo, Japan, 1990, Inst. Contemporary Art, Boston, 1990, Dept. Cultural Affairs, N.Y.C., 1991, Maier Mus. Art, Lynchburg, Tenn., 1991, Cleveland Ctr. for Contemporary Art, 1991, Jayne Baum Gallery, N.Y.C., 1992, High Mus. Art, Atlanta, 1992,The Burden Gallery/Aperture Found., N.Y.C., 1992 others; represented in pub. collections Allen Meml. Art Mus., Oberlin, Ohio, Fogg Art Mus. Harvard U., Cambridge, Mass., Chase Manhattan Bank, N.Y.C., Polaroid Collection, Frankfurt, W. Germany, Internat. Ctr. Photography, N.Y.C., Vassar Coll., Poughkeepsie, N.Y., Mus. Fine Art, Houston, Princeton (N.J.) U. Art Mus.; contbr. articles to profl. jours. MacDowell Colony fellow, 1988, 95, NEA grantee photography, 1988, Aaron Siskind Found. grantee, 1992. Avocation: bee keeping.

FRAISTAT, NEIL RICHARD, English language educator; b. Bronx, N.Y., Apr. 19, 1952; s. Louis and Shirley (Putterman) F.; m. Rose Ann Cleveland, July 28, 1979; children: Shawn Cleveland, Ann Cleveland. BA, U. Conn., 1974; MA, U. Pa., 1976, PhD, 1979. From asst. prof. to assoc. prof. English U. Md., College Park, 1979-91, prof. English, 1991—. Author: The Poem and the Book, 1985; editor: Poems in Their Place, 1986, The "Prometheus Unbound" Notebooks, 1991, The Complete Poetry of Percy Bysshe Shelley, 1999; (Website) Romantic Circles; mem. editl. bd.: Keats-Shelley Jour., 1996—, Studies in Romanticism, 1995—, Romanticism, 1993—, Romanticism on the Net, 1996—. Recipient Fredson Bowers Meml. prize for best essay on textual scholarship Soc. for Textual Scholarship, 1994; fellow for univ. tchrs. NEH, 1990, Am. Coun. Learned Socs. fellow, 1982, Huntington Libr. fellow, 1981. Home: 4202 Woodberry St Hyattsville MD 20782-1171 Office: U Md Dept English College Park MD 20742

FRAKES, JAMES TERRY, physician, gastroenterologist, educator; b. Burlington, Iowa, Feb. 22, 1946; s. Harold Decatur amd Marjorie Marie (Kinnison) F.; m. Nancy Jean French, June 15, 1968; children: Sarah Jean Frakes Wallin, David Harold Frakes. BS, U. Ill., Urbana, 1968, MS, 1972; MD, U. Ill., Chgo., 1976. Diplomate Am. Bd. Internal Medicine and Gastroenterology, Nat. Bd. Med. Examiners; lic. Ill. Staff engr. Westinghouse Astronuc. Lab., Pitts., 1968-69; staff scientist Los Alamos (NMex.) Sci. Lab., 1970-71; intern, resident in internal medicine U. Mo. Med. Ctr., Columbia, 1976-78; fellow in gastroenterology U. N. Carolina Sch. Medicine, Chapel Hill, 1978-80; physician, gastroenterologist Rockford (Ill.) GE Assoc., Ltd., 1980—; clin. prof. medicine U. Ill. Coll. Medicine, Rockford, 1981—; dir. digestive disease unit Saint Anthony Med. Ctr., Rockford, 1983—; course dir. AGA/ASGE, 1991—; med. lectr., 1987—. Bd. dirs. U. Ill. Alumni Assn., 1991-96; mem. U. Ill. Found., Urbana, 1991—, mem. pres.'s coun., 1994—. Fellow ACP, Am. Coll. Gastroenterology; mem. AMA, Am. Digestive Health Found. (numerous coms., bd. dirs. 1998—), Am. Gastroenterol. Assn. (numerous coms.) Am. Soc. Gastrointestinal Endoscopy (treas. 1995-98, pres.-elect 1998-99, pres. 1999-00). Republican. Avocations: gardening, wine collecting, college sports. Office: Rockford Gastroenterology Assocs Ltd 401 Roxbury Rd Rockford IL 61107-5078

FRAKES, ROD VANCE, plant geneticist, educator; b. Ontario, Oreg., July 20, 1930; s. Wylie and Pearl (Richardson) F.; m. Ruby L. Morey, Nov. 27, 1952; children: Laura Ann, Cody Joe. BS, Oreg. State U., 1956, MS, 1957; PhD, Purdue U., 1960. Instr. dept. agronomy Purdue U., West Lafayette, Ind., 1959-60; asst. prof. dept. crop sci. Oreg. State U., Corvallis, 1960-64, assoc. prof., 1964-69, prof., 1969—, assoc. dean research, 1981-88, emeritus dean of rsch., prof. emeritus crop sci., 1989—. Author numerous papers and abstracts; contbr. to books in field. Served with USCG, 1950-53. Named Man of Yr., Pacific Seedsmen's Assn., 1972; recipient Elizabeth P. Ritchie Disting. Prof. award Oreg. State U., 1980. Fellow Am. Soc. Agronomy, Crop Sci. Soc. Am.; mem. AAAS, Soc. Research Adminstrs., Nat. Council Univ. Research Adminstrs., Western Soc. Crop Sci. (pres. 1978), Model A Ford Club of Am., Model T Ford Club of Am., Rotary. Avocations: antique autos, Am. history, amateur radio. Home: 2625 NW Linnan Cir Corvallis OR 97330-1221 Office: Oreg State U Rsch Office Corvallis OR 97331

FRAKES, RONALD LAVERNE, JR., systems analyst; b. Manassus, Va., May 29, 1960; s. Ronald LaVerne and Stella Francis (Zefo) F.; m. Nov. 7, 1987 (dec.); children: Justin Shawn, Aaron Trevor. BA in Math., Knox Coll., 1980; postgrad., Wash. State U., 1992-93. Clk. Giant Foods, Galesburg, Ill., 1975-85; sr. sys. analyst Merdan Group Inc., San Diego, 1993-94; sr. security engr., task leader Merdan Group Inc., Vienna, Va., 1994—. Sunday Sch. tchr. Evang. Free Ch. Am., Manassas, 1995—. Capt. USAF, 1985-92. Mem. AFCEA. Avocations: photography, fitness, reading, video games, electronic repair. Home: 9629 Branchview Ct Manassas VA 20110-6009 Office: Merdan Group Inc 1953 Gallows Rd Vienna VA 22182-3934

FRALEY, DEBRA LEE, critical care nurse; b. San Antonio, June 19, 1961; d. Billy C. and Martha Sue (Schooler) F. BSN, U. Tex., San Antonio, 1983. CCRN; cert. ACLS, ACLS instr. Nursing care coord. Univ. Hosp.; asst. head nurse Med. Ctr. Hosp., San Antonio; surg. ICU insvc. coord. Med. Ctr. Hosp., chmn. ICU flow sheet com., SICU rep. for transplant liaison com., product evaluation com., expert rater for patient acuity; mem. nurse practice com., mem. critical care amb. team to South Africa-People to People Internat.; chair nurse practice com. Recipient George W. Brackenridge Nursing scholarship. Mem. AACN, Sigma Theta Tau. Address: 227 Twilight Terrace St San Antonio TX 78233-6557

FRAME, JOHN FAYETTE, sculptor; b. Colton, Calif., Nov. 27, 1950; s. Rudolph Randolph and Mildred Louise (Jones) F.; m. Laura Lynn Dierker, Sept. 3, 1977; children: Katherine, Ashley, Lilian. BA in English, San Diego State U., 1975; MFA in Art, Claremont Grad. Sch., 1980. One person shows include Francine Seders Gallery, Seattle, 1981, Jan Turner Gallery, L.A., 1982, 84, 87, 90, 93, 96, Mattingly Baker Gallery, Dallas, 1982, Installation Gallery, San Diego, 1983, L.A. County Mus. Art, 1992; exhibited in group shows L.A. Mcpl. Art Gallery, 1981, 86, 87, The Fountain Gallery, Portland, Oreg., 1982, Triton Mus., Santa Clara, Calif., 1984, Montgomery Art Gallery, Claremont, 1984, Galerie Hartje, Berlin, 1985, San Diego State U., 1987, Artspace Gallery, L.A., 1988, Nakazawa Gallery, Tokyo, 1989, U. Hawaii, Honolulu, 1990, Sezon Mus. Art, Tokyo, 1991, Susan Cummins Gallery, Mill Valley, Calif., 1992, 93, Koplin Gallery, L.A., 1993, Dorothy Goldeen Gallery, Santa Monica, 1993, Lew Allen Gallery, Santa Fe, 1993, Tawain Mus. Art, Taichung, 1994, Louis Newman Gallery, Beverly Hills, Calif., 1994, Armory Ctr. for Arts, Pasadena, Calif., 1994, Laband Art Gallery, Loyola Marymount U., L.A., 1994, Garth Clark Gallery, L.A., 1994, Palm Springs Desert Mus., 1995, Cheney Cowles Mus., Spokane, Wash., 1995, Las Vegas Inst. Contemporary Art, 1995; works included in publs. including Artweek, L.A. Weekly, L.A. Times, Images and Issues, World Art Trends 1983-84, L.A. Herald Examiner, Daily News, Reader, Sculpture, Visions, Connections, Angeles Mag., San Francisco Chronicle. Recipient Young Talent award L.A. County Mus., 1985; individual artist fellow Nat. Endowment for Arts, 1984, 86, J. Paul Getty Mus., 1995. Home: 2421 S Santa Fe Ave Ste 21 Los Angeles CA 90058-1147*

FRAME, LAWRENCE MILVEN, JR., inventor; b. Adrian, Mich., Apr. 13, 1951; s. Lawrence M. Sr. and Margret L. Frame. Student, Art Instrns. Sch., Cin., North Light Sch., Cin. Gen. laborer USAF. Patentee; songwriter; author: 100% Service Connected and Social Security Disability, Golden Book of Short Stories, Part VI; art exhibited in show at Scioto Paint Valley Mental Health Ctr., 1993. With USAF, 1971-75. Recipient several art and writing awards. Mem. Am. Legion, Disabled Am. Vets. Avocations: art, writing, electrophysics. Home: 117 Cherry St Apt A Georgetown OH 45121-1207

FRAME, NANCY DAVIS, lawyer; b. Brookings, S.D., Dec. 13, 1944; m. J. Davidson Frame, Mar. 28, 1970 (div. Oct. 1994); 1 child, Katherine Adele. BS, S.D. State U., 1966; MA, Georgetown U., 1968, JD, 1976. Bar: D.C. 1976. Atty., advisor AID, Washington, 1976-81, asst. gen. counsel, 1981-86; dep. dir. Trade and Devel. Agy., Washington, 1986—. Recipient Superior Honor award AID, 1984, Presdl. Meritorious Rank award, 1993, Disting. Alumnus award S.D. State U., 1998, Presdl. Disting. Rank award, 1998; Fulbright fellow , 1966, NDEA fellow, 1967. Mem. ABA, Fed. Bar Assn. Home: 5819 Magic Mountain Dr Rockville MD 20852-3231 Office: Trade and Devel Agy 1621 N Kent St Arlington VA 22209-2131

FRAME, PAUL SUTHERLAND, medical educator, physician; m. Gay Krause; children: Patrick Sutherland, Ryan Paul. BA in Chemistry with honors, Oberlin Coll., 1967; MD, U. Pa., 1971. Diplomate Am. Bd. Family Practice. Resident in family practice Hunterdon (N.J.) Med. Ctr., 1971-74; mem. Nat. Health Svc. Corps. Tri-County Family Medicine, Dansville, N.Y., 1974-76, mem. med. staff, 1976—; clin. instr. in family medicine U. Rochester Sch. Medicine, N.Y., 1976-84; pres. med. staff Noyes Meml. Hosp., Dansville, N.Y., 1981-83; clin. asst. prof. family medicine U. Rochester Sch. Medicine, N.Y., 1985-89, clin. assoc. prof. family medicine, 1989—; mem. attending staff Noyes Meml. Hosp., Dansville, N.Y., 1976—; med. dir. Tri-County Family Medicine; participant in Surgeon Gen.'s Conf. on Breast Feeding and Human Lactation, Rochester. 1984; sr. advisor to U.S. Preventive Svcs. Task Force, HHS, 1985-88; participant Internat. Symposium on Preventive Svcs. in Primary Care: Issues and strategies, Montreal, 1987; cons. to Dartmouth-COOP grant "Improving Cancer Control by Primary-Care Physicians", 1987-89; mem. U.S. Prevention Svcs. Task Force, 1990-95. Contbr. numerous articles to Jour. Family Practice and other med. publs. Recipient Lillie M. Erk prize U. Pa. Sch. Medicine, 1971, Max Cheplove award Erie County Med. Soc., Buffalo, 1987. Mem. Inst. Medicine NAS, N.Y. State Acad. Family Physicians, Am. Acad. Family Physicians, Soc. Tchrs. Family Medicine, Sigma Xi. Home: 8922 Reeds Corners Rd Dansville NY 14437-9782 Office: Tri-County Family Medicine PO Box 112 Cohocton NY 14826-0112*

FRAME, TED RONALD, lawyer; b. Milw., June 27, 1929; s. Morris and Jean (Lee) F.; student UCLA, 1946-49; AB, Stanford U., 1950, LLB, 1952; m. Lois Elaine Pilgrim, Aug. 15, 1954; children: Kent, Lori, Nancy, Owen. Bar: Calif. 1953. Gen. agri-bus. practice, Coalinga, Calif., 1953—; sr. ptnr. Frame & Matsumoto, 1965—. Trustee, Baker Mus.; dir. West Hills Coll. Found. Mem. ABA, Calif. Bar Assn., Fresno County Bar Assn., Am. Agrl. Law Assn., Coalinga C. of C. (past pres.), Masons, Shriners, Elks. Avocations: bicycling, hiking. Home: 1222 Nevada St Coalinga CA 93210 Office: 201 Washington St Coalinga CA 93210-1645

FRAMPTON, GEORGE THOMAS, SR., legal educator; b. N.Y.C., Mar. 24, 1917; s. Harry Vinton and Mary Louise (Fottrell) F.; m. Margaret Anne Raup, May 2, 1941; children: George Thomas Jr., Mary Louise. A.B., Duke U., 1938, J.D., 1941. Bar: N.Y. 1942, Ill. 1956, U.S. Supreme Ct. 1956. Assoc. firm Cravath, deGersdorff, Swaine & Wood, N.Y.C., 1941-42; atty. OPA, Washington, 1942-43; assoc. Fulton, Walter & Halley, N.Y.C., 1945-53; teaching fellow Harvard Law Sch., 1953-54; mem. faculty U. Ill. Coll. Law at Urbana-Champaign, 1954—, prof., 1957-87, prof. emeritus, 1987—; vice chancellor Urbana-Champaign, 1970-72; vis. summer prof. N.Y. U., 1954, Stanford U., 1957, Salzburg (Austria) Seminar Am. Studies, 1965; vis. prof. U. Calif. at Berkeley, 1959-60, N.Y. U., 1967-68; cons. Joint Congressional Com. Atomic Energy, 1963, Nat. Council Radiation Protection, 1964, project corp. debt financing ABA, 1963-65, AEC, 1974, ERDA, 1975, U.S. Dept. Energy, 1979-80; arbitration-mediator panelist Am. Arbitration Assn., N.Y. Stock Exch., Nat. Assn. Securities Dealers, Nat. Futures Assn., Pvt. Adjudication Ctr., Inc.; arbitration tribunal Internat. Ct. Arbitration, Paris, 1995-98. Author: (with E.R. Latty) Basic Business Associations, 1963. Mem. Democratic County Com., Westchester County, N.Y., 1946-53, Champaign County, Ill., 1960-70. Served with AUS, 1943-45, ETO. Mem. ABA, ABA Fellows, FBA, Am. Soc. Internat. Law, Ill. State Bar Assn., Ill. Coun. Mediators, Assn. Bar of City of N.Y., Champaign County Bar Assn., Soc. Profls. in Dispute Resolution. Home: 803 W Delaware Ave Urbana IL 61801-4808 Office: U Ill Coll Law 504 E Pennsylvania Ave Champaign IL 61820-6909

FRAMPTON, JAMES SCOTT, career officer; b. Norman, Okla., Jan. 18, 1967; s. Richard Kelly Frampton and Glenna Ann McNeil; m. Elizabeth Pauline Frampton, Jan. 18, 1967; children: Nick, James. BS in Polit. Sci., Tex. A&M, 1990; MS in Bus., Boston U., 1994; postgrad., Naval Postgrad. Sch. Capt. USMC, 1988—; co. comdr. USMC, Camp Lejeune, N.C., 1994, Camp Butler, Japan, 1997. Asst. scoutmaster Boy Scouts Am., 1991-95. Mem. Am. Polit. Sci. Soc., Mason (sec. 1992). Democrat. Episcopalian. Avocations: scuba, investing, reading. E-mail: jsframpt@nps.navy.mil. Home: 372-B Bergin Dr Monterey CA 93940

FRAMPTON, PAUL HOWARD, physics researcher, educator; b. Kidderminster, Eng., Oct. 31, 1943; came to U.S., 1968; naturalized citizen, 1989; s. Harold Albert and Grace Elizabeth (Howard) F.; m. Anne-Marie Curran, 1993. BA, U. Oxford, Eng., 1965, MA, 1968, DPhil, 1968, DSc, 1984. Rsch. assoc. U. Chgo., 1968-70; fellow CERN, Geneva, 1970-72; vis. prof. Bielefeld (Germany) U., 1972, 99, Syracuse U., 1972-75; vis. assoc. prof. UCLA, 1975-77, Harvard U., Cambridge, Mass., 1978-81; from asst. prof. physics to prof. U. N.C., Chapel Hill, 1981-96; disting. prof. physics The Louis D. Rubin Jr., 1996—; vis. prof. U. Tex., fall 1983, Boston U., 1986-87, U. d'Aix-Marseille, 1993, CERN, 1996, 98; chmn. steering com. Workshops on Grand Unification, 1980-89. Author: Dual Resonance Models, 1974, Dual Resonance Models and Superstrings, 1986, Gauge Field Theories, 1986; editor books in field; contbr. over 250 articles to profl. jours. Gov.'s project dir. for supercollider in N.C., 1987. Fellow AAAS, Am. Phys. Soc., Brit. Inst. Physics. Home: 101 Cedar Ridge Way Durham NC 27705-1980 Office: U NC Dept Physics and Astromomy Chapel Hill NC 27599-3255

FRANANO, SUSAN MARGARET KETTEMAN, orchestra administrator, soprano; b. Kansas City, Mo., Sept. 30, 1946; d. Charley Gilbert and Mary Elizabeth (Bredehoeft) Ketteman; m. Frank Salvatore Franano, Dec. 20, 1969; 1 child, Domenico Frank. AA, Stephens Coll., Columbia, Mo., 1966, BFA, 1967; postgrad., U. Mo., Kansas City, 1967-68; MusM, So. Ill. U., Edwardsville, 1969. Gen. mgr. Kansas City (Mo.) Symphony Orch.; mgr. Lyric Opera Group, Kansas City, 1976-82; tour coordinator Lyric Opera Kansas City, 1978-85; dir. outreach Kansas City Symphony, 1982-84, asst. mgr., 1984-85, ops. mgr., 1985-86, gen. mgr., 1986-95; Daniel Hart exec. dir. Columbus (Ohio) Symphony Orch., 1998—; exec. dir. Ohio Citizens for the Arts, Columbus, 1998—. Regional liaison Mo. Citizens for Arts, Kansas City, 1984-86; regional rep. Am. Guild Mus. Artists, Kansas City, 1977-81; regional ammenities task force mem. Mid-Am. Regional Coun., 1989—; panelist Nat. Endowment for the Arts, 1991. Mem. Am. Symphony Orch. League, Mo. Citizens for Arts, Symphony Women's Assn., Jr. Women's Symphony Alliance, Friends of Symphony, Kansas City Consensus, Cen. Exchange Club (Kansas City), Woodside Racquet Club (Shawnee Mission). Democrat. Roman Catholic. Avocations: tennis, cooking, travel. Office: Ohio Citizens for the Arts 77 S High St Columbus OH 43215*

FRANCA, CELIA, ballet director, choreographer, dancer, narrator; b. London, Eng., June 25, 1921; m. James Morton, Dec. 7, 1960. Student, Guildhall Sch. Music, Royal Acad. Dancing; LLD (hon.), Assumption U. of Windsor, 1959, Mt. Allison U., 1966, U. Toronto, 1974, Dalhousie U., 1976, York U., 1976, Trent U., Peterborough, Ont., Can., 1977, McGill U., 1986; DCL (hon.), Bishop's U., 1967; DLitt (hon.), Guelph U., 1976; DFA, Carleton U., Ottawa, 1995. Founder, artistic dir. Nat. Ballet Can., Toronto, 1951-74; co-founder Nat. Ballet Sch., Toronto, 1959; Mem. jury 5th Internat. Ballet Competition, Varna, Bulgaria, 1970, 2d Internat. Ballet Competition, Moscow, 1973. Debut: corps de ballet Mars, The Planets (Tudor), Mercury Theatre, London, 1936; soloist, Ballet Rambert, London, 1936-38, leading dramatic dancer, Ballet Rambert, 1938-39, guest artist, Ballet Rambert, 1950, dancer, Ballet des Trois Arts, London, 1939, Arts Theatre Ballet, London, 1940, Internat. Ballet, London, 1941, leading dramatic dancer, Sadler's Wells Ballet, 1941-46, guest artist, choreographer, Sadler's Wells Theatre Ballet, London, 1946-47, dancer, tchr., Ballets Jooss, Eng., 1947, ballet mistress, leading dancer, Met. Ballet, London, 1947-49, dancer, Ballet Workshop, London, 1949-51, prin. dancer, Nat. Ballet Can., 1951-59; prin. roles include Black Queen in Swan Lake; title roles in Lady from the Sea; choreographer: ballets, including Midas, London, 1939, Cancion, London, 1942, Khadra, London, 1946, Dance of Salome, BBC-TV, 1949, The Eve of St. Agnes, BBC-TV, 1950, Afternoon of a Faun, Toronto, 1952, Le Pommier, Toronto, 1952, Casse-Noisette, 1955, Princess Aurora, 1960, The Nutcracker, 1964, Cinderella, 1968, numerous others for CBC, Can. Opera Co.; author: The National Ballet of Canada: A Celebration, 1978. Hon. patron Osteoporosis Soc. Can. Decorated Order of Can.; recipient Key to City of Washington, 1955, Woman of Yr. award B'nai B'rith, 1958, award for outstanding contbn. to arts Toronto Telegram, 1965, Centennial medal, 1967, Hadassah award of merit, 1967, Molson award, 1974, award Internat. Soc. Performing Arts Adminstrs., 1979, Can. Dance award, 1984, Gold Card IATSE local 58, 1984, diplôme d'honneur Can. Conf. Arts, 1986, Woman Yr. award St. George's Soc. Toronto, 1987, Order of Ont., 1987, Gov. Gen. award, 1994, Children's Charity award Variety Club of Ont., 1995; twice visited China at invitation of Chinese govt. to teach; in Beijing mounted full-length Coppelia, 1980; honored as one of founders of Can.'s maj. ballet cos. at Alta. Ballet Co.'s 15th anniversary, 1981. Home: 203 350 Queen Elizabeth Dr, Ottawa, ON Canada K1S 3N1 also: Nat Ballet Canada, 470 Queens Quay West, Toronto, ON Canada M5V 3K4*

FRANCAVILLA, DONNA T., news reporter; b. Camden, N.J., Dec. 4, 1960; d. Lelio and Aurora (DeVuono) Ciccotelli; m. Thomas Louis Francavilla, May 29, 1957; children: Michael, Lisa, Jessica, Gregory. BS, Emerson Coll., Boston, 1985. Talk show prodr. WWDB-FM Talkradio, Phila., 1980-81; desk asst., prodn. asst. KYW Newsradio 1060 AM, Phila., 1981-82; talk show prodr. WRKO-AM, Boston, 1982-85; news anchor radio network Internat. Media News, Washington, 1986-88; program dir., news dir. Westinghouse WPGC AM & FM, Washington, DC, 1988-90; traffic reporter Metro Traffic Control, Phila., 1990-92; news anchor, all news radio WINZ-AM, Miami, 1993-94; news reporter NBC, WVTM-TV, Birmingham, Ala., 1996—; radio corr. UPI, 1996—; founder Donna Francavilla Public Relations. V.p. Greystone Ladies Club, Birmingham, 1995. Mem. Jefferson County Med. Alliance; public rels. dir., Jefferson County Med. Alliance. Roman Catholic. Avocations: exercising, dancing, skiing, cooking, writing. Home: 5079 Greystone Way Birmingham AL 35242-6456 Office: WVTM-TV Birmingham AL 35209 also: Ala Radio Network Birmingham AL 35000

FRANCE, BELINDA TAKACH, lawyer, business owner; b. Jacksonville, Fla., June 10, 1964; d. Bruce Albert and Bertha Loretta (Hawkins) Takach; m. Alden Whitney France, July 27, 1985. BS, U. Tampa, Fla., 1985; JD, Stetson U., 1987; LLM in Taxation, U. Fla., 1989. Bar: Fla. 1989, U.S. Dist. Ct. (mid. dist.) Fla. 1989, U.S. Ct. Claims 1989, U.S. Tax Ct. 1989, U.S. Ct. Appeals (11th cir.) 1989, U.S. Ct. Appeals (Fed. cir.) 1990. Tax preparer H&R Block, Tampa, 1983-84; acct. Robert Osborne & Assocs., Tampa, 1984-85; assoc. Thomas C. Little, P.A., Clearwater, Fla., 1987-88; co-counsel Bruce R. Young, P.A., Clearwater, 1988; prin. Belinda Takach France, P.A., Tallahassee, Fla., 1988—; prof. Ft. Lauderdale Coll., Tallahassee, 1989; adj. instr. Tallahassee C.C., 1991—; vice chmn. bd. dirs. Someplace Else, Tallahassee; owner Catalyst Seminars; expert witness in taxation and pension matters. Mem. Tallahassee Rep. Women, 1989-90. Mem. ABA (com. domestic rels. tax problems, com. attys. in small law firms), Fla. Bar Assn., Tallahassee Bar Assn., Tallahassee Women Lawyers Assn., Tallahassee C. of C. Office: 703 E Tennessee St Tallahassee FL 32308-4984

FRANCE, JOSEPH DAVID, securities analyst; b. Smithville, Mo., July 24, 1953; s. Raymond Hughes and Bonnie Lee (Cavin) F; m. Tina Rachel Sidney; 1 child, Lucille Terrell. BS in Pharmacy, U. Kans., 1977, MBA, 1980. Registered pharmacist; chartered fin. analyst. Staff pharmacist U. Kans. Med. Ctr., Kansas City, 1977-80; securities analyst First Nat. Bank Chgo., 1980-82; securities analyst Smith Barney, Harris Upham & Co., Inc., N.Y.C., 1982-86, mng. dir., 1986-93; 1st v.p. Merrill Lynch, N.Y.C., 1993-95; sr. v.p. Dillon, Read & Co., 1995-96; dir. CS First Boston, N.Y.C., 1996—. Mem. Am. Soc. Health-Syss. Pharmacists, N.Y. Soc. Securities Analysts, Assn. for Investment Mgmt. and Rsch., Am. Math. Soc., Am. Fin. Assn. Democrat. Jewish. Avocations: reading, computers. Office: 11 Madison Ave Fl 6 New York NY 10010-3629

FRANCE, NEWELL EDWIN, former hospital administrator, consultant; b. Massillon, Ohio, Sept. 30, 1927; s. Lawrence Joel and Marcella Ruth (Nelson) F.; m. Eve Elisabeth Voluter, 1953; children: Philip J., Corinne E., Anne-Claire I., Stephen C., Louise A. B.S., Northwestern U., 1953, M.S. in Hosp. Adminstrn, 1955. Adminstrv. resident Herrick Meml. Hosp., Berkeley, Calif., 1954-55; evening supt. Chgo. Wesley Meml. Hosp., 1955-56; asst. adminstr. St. Lukes Episcopal and Tex. Children's hosps., Houston, 1956-58, assoc. adminstr., 1958-64, adminstr., 1964-73, exec. dir., 1973-83; pres. emeritus Tampa Gen. Hosp., Fla., 1983-91, 91—; pres. Patrick Philbin & Assocs., Austin, 1993—; cons. Hok Architecture, 1995—; asso. adminstr. Tex. Heart Inst., Houston, 1958-64, adminstr., 1964-73, exec. dir., 1973-83; cons. adv. council HEW and NIH; staff cons. AID, 1969—; cons. program projects rev. com. Nat. Inst. Neurol. and Communicative Disorders and Stroke; acad. planning bd. health care scis. Walden U., Naples, Fla.; mem. com. pediatrics NRC-Nat. Acad. Scis., 1975—; chmn. Greater Houston Hosp. Council, Children's Hosps. Execs. Council, 1972-73; dir. Child Care Center, Tex. Med. Center, 1967—; adj. asso. prof. Sch. Architecture, Rice U.; prof. health scis. Tex. Women's U. Bd. dirs. Met. Houston chpt. Nat. Found. March of Dimes, First City Bank Med. Center; trustee Pin Oaks Charity Horse Show Assn., Houston Bot. Soc.; mem. exec. bd. South Main Center Assn., Inc.; active Houston/Baku Sister City Assn. Served with USNR, 1946-48, 51-52. Fellow Am. Coll. Hosp. Adminstrs.; mem. Am. Hosp. Assn., Tex. Hosp. Assn. (chmn. coun. hosp. auxs. 1969-73, trustee

1972—, adviser, chmn. coun. on profl. svc. 1976—), Houston Area Hosp. Assn. (pres. 1968-69), Nat. Assn. Childrens Hosps. and Related Instns. (pres. 1969-70, conf. chmn. 1969, trustee 1971—, chmn. coun. past pres.'s 1973-74), Am. Assn. Hosp. Planning, Statutory Teaching Hosps. Coun. (Fla.) (chmn. 1988-91). Methodist. Clubs: Rotary Internat; Doctors (Houston). Home: 6609 Coolglen Dr Dallas TX 75248-2902

FRANCE, RICHARD WILLIAM, finance executive; b. Evanston, Ill., Oct. 24, 1947; s. Norman Marshall and Carolyn (Andersen) F.; m. Dianne M. Vlasak, May 5, 1979; children: Jennifer Sara, Hilary Ann, Justine Elizabeth. AA, Kendall Coll., 1968; BS in Bus. Adminstrn., Am. U., 1970. Auditor Pick Hotels Corp., Chgo., 1970-72; comptroller K St. Hotel Corp., Washington, 1972-74; controller Registry Hotel Corp., Dallas, 1974-83, Fairmont Hotel Co., Dallas, 1983-86; corp. controller Signet Hotel Corp., Dallas, 1986-87, v.p. fin., 1987-92, chief fin. officer, 1992-98. Mem. Internat. Assn. Hospitality Accts. (v.p., pres., and chmn. Minn. Chpt. 1975-82), Hospitality Fin. & Technology Profls. Assn. Republican. Roman Catholic. Avocation: swimming.

FRANCE-DEAL, JUDITH JEAN, English as a Second Language educator; b. Falls City, Nebr., June 27, 1941; d. Paris and Georgia Elizabeth (Reiger) France; m. Gary Arthur Deal, Dec. 30, 1960; children: Kevin, Timothy. Student, Bapt. Inst. Christian Workers, Bryn Mawr, Pa., 1959; grad., Liberty Bible Inst., 1994, Barbizon Sch. Modelling, 1998. Cert. and lic. chaplain. Vol. worker with many orgns., 1957—; receptionist Central Ins. Co., Omaha, Nebr., 1960-62; vol. PTA, Cub Scouts, etc., Wis., 1966-76; tchr. spl. edn. First Bapt. Ch., Dallas, 1985-88, vol. tutor ESL, 1985—; inspirational spkr.; tchr. English and Bible studies 1st Bapt. Ch., Richardson, Tex., 1989—; pres., founder God's Internat. ABCs, Inc.; model for numerous advts. and commls. Author: Center of Our Lives, 1994. Chaplain-min. to cancer patients Tulsa Cancer Treatment Ctr.; vol. chaplain Plano Specialty Hosp. Recipient numerous writing awards. Mem. Internat. Platform Assn. Republican. Avocations: sewing, reading, writing poetry, helping others, songs. Office: Gods Internat ABC 1000 14th St Ste 122 Plano TX 75074-6220

FRANCESCHI, ERNEST JOSEPH, JR., lawyer; b. L.A., Feb. 1, 1957; s. Ernest Joseph and Doris Cecilia (Beluche) F. BS, U. So. Calif., 1978; JD, Southwestern U., L.A., 1980. Bar: Calif. 1984, U.S. Dist. Ct. (cen. dist.) Calif. 1984, U.S. Dist. Ct. (ea. dist.) Calif. 1986, U.S. Dist. Ct. (no. and so. dists.) Calif. 1987, U.S. Ct. Appeals (9th cir.) 1984, U.S. Supreme Ct. 1989. Pvt. practice law L.A., 1984—. Mem. Assn. Trial Lawyers Am., Calif. Trial Lawyers Assn., L.A. Trial Lawyers Assn., Trial Lawyers for Pub. Justice, Fed. Bar Assn. Office: 445 S Figueroa St Ste 2600 Los Angeles CA 90071-1630

FRANCESCONE, JOHN BERNARD, accountant; b. Camden, N.J., Jan. 7, 1968; s. Isidore Anthony and Mary Joan (Meiler) F. BS, Villanova U., 1990. CPA, N.J., Pa. From staff mem. to mgr. Arthur Andersen, Phila., 1990—. Zoning bd. Mt. Laurel Twp., N.J., 1996—, chmn. zoning bd., 1999, parks and recreation adv. com., 1995—; mem. Camden County (N.J.) Rep. Com., 1988-94, Burlington County (N.J.) Rep. Com., 1998—; mem. World Affairs Coun. Phila., 1990—. Fellow N.J. Soc. CPAs; mem. AICPAs, Pa. Inst. CPAs, Healthcare Fin. Mgmt. Assn. Roman Catholic. Avocations: public service, golf, tennis. Home: 301B Cypress Point Cir Mount Laurel NJ 08054-2740 Office: Arthur Andersen 1601 Market St Philadelphia PA 19103-2301

FRANCESE, JOSEPH, Italian language and literature educator; b. Westerly, R.I., Sept. 5, 1955; s. Frank J. and Anna M. (Pellegrino) F.; m. Gina Crocco, Apr. 22, 1979; children: Anna, Luciana. BA, U. R.I., 1977; postgrad., U. Rome, 1981; PhD, U. Conn., 1990. Tchg. asst., lectr. U. Conn., Storrs, 1986-90; asst. prof. Italian, Mich. State U., East Lansing, 1990-95, assoc. prof., 1995-99, prof., 1999—. Author: Il realismo impopolare di Pier Paolo Pasolini, 1991, Narrating Postmodern Time and Space, 1997, Cultura e Politica Negli Anni Cinquanta: Salinari Pasolini Calvino; editor: The Craft and the Fury. Essays in Honor of Glauco Cambon; contbr. articles to profl. jours., chpts. to books. Grantee Midwest Univs. Consortium for Internat. Activities, 1995, 97. Avocations: gardening, woodworking. Office: Mich State U Dept Romance Langs Old Horticulture Bldg East Lansing MI 48824

FRANCH, RICHARD THOMAS, lawyer; b. Melrose Park, Ill., Sept. 23, 1942; s. Robert and Julia (Martino) F.; m. Patricia Staufenberg, Apr. 18, 1971 (dec. Apr. 1994); children: Richard T. Jr., Katherine J.; m. Susan L. Rice, Sept. 1, 1995. B.A. cum laude, U. Notre Dame, 1964; J.D., U. Chgo., 1967. Bar: Ill. 1967, U.S. Dist. Ct. (no. dist.) Ill. 1967, U.S. Supreme Ct. 1980, U.S. Ct. Appeals (2d cir.) 1984, U.S. Ct. Appeals (3d cir.) 1981, U.S. Ct. Appeals (6th cir.) 1991, U.S. Ct. Appeals (7th cir.) 1971, U.S. Ct. Appeals (8th cir.) 1981, U.S. Ct. Appeals (9th cir.) 1997, U.S. Dist. Ct. (no. dist.) Wis. 1989, U.S. Tax Ct. 1994. Assoc. Jenner & Block, Chgo., 1967-68, 70-74, ptnr., 1975—; former mem. Ill. Supreme Ct. Rules Com. Served to capt. U.S. Army, 1968-70. Decorated Bronze star, Army Commendation medal. Fellow Am. Coll. Trial Lawyers; mem. Am. Law Inst. Office: Jenner & Block Ste 4700 One IBM Plz Chicago IL 60611

FRANCHINI, GENE EDWARD, state supreme court justice; b. Albuquerque, May 19, 1935; s. Mario and Lena (Vaio) F.; m. Glynn Hatchell, Mar. 22, 1969; children: Pamela, Lori (dec.), Gina, Joseph James, Nancy. BBA, Loyola U., 1955; degree in adminstrn., U. N.Mex., 1957; JD, Georgetown U., 1960; LLM, U. Va., 1995. Bar: N.Mex. 1960, U.S. Dist. Ct. N.Mex. 1961, U.S. Ct. Appeals (10th cir.) 1970, U.S. Supreme Ct. 1973. Ptnr. Matteucci, Gutierrez & Franchini, Albuquerque, 1960-70, Matteucci, Franchini & Calkins, Albuquerque, 1970-75; judge State of N.Mex. 2d Jud. Dist., Albuquerque, 1975-81; atty.-at-large Franchini, Wagner, Oliver, Franchini & Curtis, Albuquerque, 1982-90; chief justice N.Mex. Supreme Ct., Santa Fe, 1990-99, justice, 1999—; v.p. bd. dirs. Conf. Chief Justices, 1997-98. Chmn. Albuquerque Pers. Bd., 1972, Albuquerque Labor Rels. Bd., 1972, Albuquerque Interim Bd. Ethics, 1972. Capt. USAF, 1960-66. Recipient Highest award Albuquerque Human Rights Bd., 1999. Mem. Am. Bd. Trial Advocates, N.Mex. Trial Lawyers (pres. 1967-68), N.Mex. Bar Assn. (bd. dirs. 1976-78), Albuquerque Bar Assn. (bd. dirs. 1976-78, Outstanding Judge award 1997). Democrat. Roman Catholic. Avocations: fishing, hunting, golf, mushroom hunting. Home: 4901 Laurene Ct NW Albuquerque NM 87120-1026 Office: NMex Supreme Ct PO Box 848 Santa Fe NM 87504-0848

FRANCHINI, ROXANNE, banker; b. N.Y.C., Mar. 20, 1951; d. Tullio and Jean (Brady) F. Student, Emerson Coll., Ricker Coll., New Sch. Social Rsch. With Princess Marcella Borghese div. Revlon, N.Y.C., 1972-73; stewardess TWA Airlines, 1973-74; asst. to pres. N.Y. Shipping Assn., N.Y.C., 1974-79; benefits mgr. Kidde, Inc., N.Y.C., 1979-83; 2d v.p. pension trust fin. svcs. Chase Manhattan Bank, N.A., N.Y.C., 1983-85, v.p. mgr. global securities, 1985-89; v.p., sales dir. global custody worldwide securities svcs. Citibank, N.Y.C., 1989-91; v.p. Mellon Bank, Pitts., 1991—. Chair fin. local fund raising campaigns. Mem. AAUW, Internat. Ops. Assn., Nat. Investment Co. Svc. Assn., Nat. Assn. Colls. and Univ. Bus. Offices, Ea. Assn. Coll. and Univ. Bus. Offices.

FRANCIOSA, ANTHONY (ANTHONY PAPALEO), actor; b. N.Y.C., Oct. 28, 1928; s. Anthony and Jean (Franciosa) Papaleo; m. Rita Thiel; children: Christopher, Marco, Nina. Ed. high sch., N.Y.C.; studied drama with Joseph Geiger; scholarship Dramatic Workshop, New Sch. Social Rsch.; studied Actor's Studio. Worked with drama groups including Off Broadway, Inc., N.Y. Repertory Theatre; internat. tour Grand Hotel, 1990-91, Love Letters, 1992, 93, 94, 95; appeared in Broadway prodns. End as a Man, 1953, Wedding Breakfast, 1954-55, A Hatful of Rain, 1955 (Tony award nomination 1956, Acad. award nomination 1957); motion pictures include A Face in the Crowd, 1957, This Could Be the Night, 1957, Long Hot Summer, 1958, Naked Maja, 1959, Career, 1960 (Golden Globe award for best motion picture actor), Story on Page One, 1960, Go Naked in the World, 1960, Senilita, 1961, Period of Adjustment, 1962, Assault on a Queen, 1966, A Man Could Get Killed, 1966, The Swinger, 1966, Fathom, 1967, A Man Called Gannon, 1968, The Sweet Ride, 1968, In Enemy Country, 1968, Across 110th Street, 1972, Ghost in the Noonday Sun, 1973, The Drowning Pool, 1975, Firepower, 1979, The World is Full of Married Men, 1979, Death Wish II, 1982, Soot gli occhi dell'Assassino, 1982, Tenebrae, 1983, Avitami ai Sognare, 1984, La Cicala, 1985, Death House, 1988, La Morte e di Mona, 1990, Backstreet Dreams, 1990, Double Threat, 1992, City Hall, 1995; TV mini-series: Aspen, 1974, Wheels, 1975; movies for TV: Fame Is the Name of the Game, 1970, Earth II, 1971, The Deadly Hunt, 1974, Hide and Go Seek, 1975, The Catcher, 1976, This Is the Week That Was, 1977, Sideshow, 1979, The Black Widow, 1980, Matt Helm, 1982, Till Death Do Us Part, 1983, Stagecoach, 1987, Ghost Writer, 1990; star TV series Valentine's Day, 1964-65, The Name of the Game, 1968-72, Search, 1972-73, Matt Helm, 1975-76, Finder of Lost Loves, 1984-85; narrator for A Lincoln Portrait with St. Louis Symphony Orch., 1971. Recipient Count Volpe Di Misurata cup Venice Film Festival, Daniel Blum's Theatre World award, Critics Outer Circle award.

FRANCIOSA, JOSEPH ANTHONY, health care consultant; b. Easton, Pa., Apr. 24, 1936; s. Joseph and Letitia Beatrice (Cascioli) F.; m. Antonietta Battistoni, Feb. 8, 1964 (div. 1972); m. Barbara Ann Neilan, Aug. 3, 1973 (div. 1989); 1 child, Christopher David; m. Robin J. McGarry, Oct. 4, 1999. BA, U. Pa., 1958; MD, U. Rome, 1963. Diplomate Am. Bd. Internal Medicine; lic. in Pa., Md., Ark. Intern USPHS Hosp., S.I., N.Y., 1964-65; resident Washington Hosp. Ctr., 1967-69; cardiology fellow VA Hosp.-Georgetown U., Washington, 1969-71; chief ICU Va. Hosp., Washington, 1971-73; asst. prof. medicine Georgetown U. Med. Sch., 1971-73, assoc. dir. cardiovascular tng. program, 1974-75; dir. CCU Va. Hosp., Mpls., 1974-76; asst. prof. medicine U. Minn., Mpls., 1977-79; chief cardiology VA Hosp., Phila., 1979-82; assoc. prof. U. Pa., Phila., 1979-82; adj. prof. 1987—; adj. prof. medicine Mt. Sinai Med. Sch., N.Y.C., 1989—; dir. cardiology div. U. Ark., Little Rock, 1982-86; prof., 1982-86; dir. cardio-renal drugs ICI Americas Inc., Wilmington, Del., 1986-88; v.p. R&D Zambon Corp., East Rutherford, N.J., 1988-90; exec. dir. med. affairs Ciba-Geigy Pharm., Summit, N.J., 1990-91; exec. dir. med. svcs. Ciba-Geigy, 1992-95; health care/pharm. cons., N.Y.C., 1995—. Contbr. numerous articles to med. jours. Mem. med. rsch. com. Am. Heart Assn., Mpls., 1976-79, Phila., 1981-82. Lt. comdr. USPHS, 1965-67. VA grantee, 1974-84, U. Ark. grantee, 1982-83. Fellow ACP, Am. Coll. Cardiology, Am. Coll. Chest Physicians (chmn. hypertension com. 1981-83, gov. Ark. 1984-86), Am. Heart Assn. (circulation coun. 1978—, coun. high blood pressure rsch. 1982—, clin. cardiology coun. 1984, bd. dirs. N.J. affiliate 1994-98); mem. Am. Soc. Clin. Pharmacology and Therapeutics (vice chmn. cardiopulmonary com. 1981-89), Assn. Univ. Cardiologists, Am. Acad. of Pharm. Physicians (charter mem.). Avocations: computers, gardening, physical fitness.

FRANCIOSI, BARBARA LEE, designer, fiber artist; b. Batavia, N.Y., Oct. 25, 1931; d. Henry Curtis and Ferne Marie (Jewitt) Parcells; m. Raymond Louis Cates, June 23, 1950 (div. 1960); children: Gwynne Cates Eldridge Edward Paul Cates; m. Pat. Grad., Ctrl. City Bus. Coll., Syracuse, N.Y., 1949. Med. sec., asst. Harold Courtney, MD, Syracuse, N.Y., 1949-51; dir., owner Barbara Schs. of Dance, Preble, N.Y., and Groton, Conn., 1951-63; legal asst. Melvin Scott, Atty., New London, Conn., 1961-75; designer, owner Fiber Artistry by Barbara Lee, Groton, 1978—. Sec. Dem. City Com., Groton, Conn., 1972-76; candidate dist. judge of probate State of Conn., 1974; vice chmn. Dem. Town Com., Groton, 1976-80; elected Groton Town Coun., 1971, Rep. Town Meeting, Groton, 1969-71, 77-79; mem. Lyman Allyn Art Mus. Mem. Am. Craft Coun., Coun. Am. Embroiderers, Mystic Art Assn., Soc. Conn. Crafts. (bd. dirs., corr. sec. 1983-86). Avocations: early Am. primitive antiques collecting, interior design, travel, ballroom dancing, swimming. Office: Fiber Artistry by Barbara Lee 30 W Elderkin Ave Groton CT 06340-4933

FRANCIS, CAROLYN RAE, music educator, musician, author, publisher; b. Seattle, July 25, 1940; d. James Douglas and Bessie Caroline (Smith) F; m. Barclay Underwood Stuart, July 5, 1971. BA in Edn., U. Wash., 1962. Cert. tchr., Wash. Tchr. Highline Pub. Schs., Seattle, 1962-64; musician Olympic Hotel, Seattle, 1962-72; 1st violin Cascade Symphony Orch., 1965-78; tchr. Bellevue (Wash.) Pub. Schs., 1965-92; founder Innovative Learning Designs, Mercer Island, Wash., 1984-96; profl. violinist for TV, recs., mus. shows, 1962-85; violist Eastside Chamber Orch., 1984-86; pvt. tchr. string instruments, 1959-96; spkr. in-svc. workshops, convs., music educators numerous cities, 1984-96; adjudicator music festivals; instr. MIDI applications for educators, 1992-96. Author-pub. Music Reading and Theory Skills (curriculum series), Levels 1, 2, 1986, Level 3, 4, 1984; contbr. articles to profl. jours., 1984—. Mem. Snohomish Indian Tribe. Bellevue Schs. Found. grantee, 1985-86, 86-87, 89-90. Mem. NEA, Am. String Tchrs. Assn. (regional mem. chmn. 1992-94), Music Educators Nat. Conf., Music Industry Coun. Avocations: hiking, traveling, reading, sewing, sketching. Office: Innovative Learning Designs 7811 SE 27th St Ste 104 Mercer Island WA 98040-2961

FRANCIS, CHARLES K., medical educator; b. Newark, May 24, 1939. BA, Dartmouth Coll., 1961; MD, Jefferson Med. Coll., 1965. Med. intern Phila. Gen. Hosp., 1965-66; med. resident Boston City Hosp., Tufts U., 1969-70; clin. fellow cardiology Tufts Circulation Lab., 1970-71; clin. and rsch. fellow cardiology Mass. Gen. Hosp., 1971-72, sr. med. resident, 1972-73; chief cardiac catheterization lab. divsn. cardiology Martin Luther King Jr. Gen. Hosp., L.A., 1973-74, chief cardiology divsn., 1974-77; dir. cardiology divsn. Mt. Sinai Hosp., Hartford, Conn., 1977-80; assoc. dir. hypertension svc., assoc. prof. medicine, dir. cardiac catheterization lab. Yale Med. Sch., Hartford, Conn., 1980-87; dir. dept. medicine Harlem Hosp. Ctr., N.Y.C., 1987—; prof. clin. medicine Columbia U. Coll. Physicians and Surgeons, 1987—; clin. instr. medicine Sch. Medicine, Tufts U., 1970-71; tchg. fellow Harvard Med. Sch., 1971-72, clin. fellow, 1972-73; asst. prof. medicine Charles R. Drew Postgrad. Med. Sch. & Sch. Medicine, U. So. Calif., 1973-77; asst. prof. medicine, dir. Burgdorf Hypertension Clin., Med. Sch., U. Conn., 1977-80; mem. cardiac adv. comty. Nat. Heart, Lung & Blood Inst., NIH, 1977-79; asst. prof. medicine Sch. Medicine, Yale U., 1980-81, assoc. prof., 1981-87. Fellow ACP, Am. Coll. Cardiology; mem. Inst. Medicine-NAS, Am. Fedn. Clin. Rsch., Am. Heart Assn., Assn. Black Cardiologists (chmn. bd. 1994—). Office: Harlem Hosp Ctr 506 Lenox Ave Rm 14101 New York NY 10037-1802*

FRANCIS, CHARLES MACKENZIE, wildlife biologist; b. Pretoria, South Africa, Dec. 1, 1958. BSc in Fisheries and Wildlife Biology with honors and distinction, U. Guelph, 1980; MSc in Biology, Queen's Univ., Kingston, 1987, PhD in Biology, 1990. Computer programmer, sys. mgr. U. Wollongong, Australia, 1981; CUSO vol. ornithologist wildlife sect. Sabah Forest Dept., Malaysia, 1981-84; computer programmer Can. Wildlife Svc., 1986; Natural Scis. & Engring. Rsch. Coun. postdoctoral fellow Duke U., Durham, N.C., 1990-92; wildlife biologist Can. Wildlife Svc. and U.S. Nat. Biol. Surveys, 1993-95; sr. sci. Bird Studies Can./Long Point Bird Obs., Port Rowan, Ont., Can., 1995—; adj. prof. biol. dept. Queen's U., 1995—; adj. prof. geography dept. U. Western Ont., 1996—; rsch. assoc. Wildlife Conservation Soc., 1991—, zool. dept. U. Malaya, 1991-96, Royal Ont. Mus., 1997—; tchg. asst. Queen's U., 1985, 88, 89, 90, Guelph U., 1978, 79. Author: A Pocket Guide to the Birds of Borneo, 1985, A Pocket Checklist of the Birds of Sabah, 1986; co-author: A Field Guide to the Mammals of Borneo, 1986; contbr. articles to profl. jours. Urlla Carmichael scholar, 1989, Alma Mater scholar, 1979, Audubon Wildlife scholar, 1980, Can. Nat. Sportsman's Fund scholar, 1979, Natural Scis. & Engring. Rsch. Coun. scholar, 1985-88; grantee Wildlife Conservation Soc., 1991—, AOU Travel award, 1994, AOU Marcie Brady Tucker Travel award, 1990; Can. Wildlife Svc. Rsch. grantee, 1989, Am. Mus. Nat. History Chapman Fund grantee, 1986, 87, 89, Queen's Sch. Grad. Studies and Rsch. Travel grantee, 1985, 87, 88, 89. Mem. Wildlife Soc., Am. Ornithologists' Union, Brit. Ornithologists' Union, Assn. Tropical Biologists, Royal Australian Ornithologists' Union, Cooper Ornithol. Soc., Assn. Field Ornithologists, Oriental Bird Club, Can. Soc. Ornithologists, Am. Soc. Mammalogists. Office: Bird Studies Canada, PO Box 160, Port Rowan, ON Canada N0E 1M0

FRANCIS, CONNIE L., retired secondary education educator; b. Bellevue, Ohio, July 19, 1940; d. Edward and Viola (Kreh) Dick; divorced; children: Cynthia, Kelli, Scott. BS in Edn., Bowling Green State U., 1961; MS in Edn., Kearney State Coll., 1969, MA in Edn., 1989. Tchr. Tiffin (Ohio) Pub. Schs., 1961-64, Old Fort (Ohio) Pub. Schs., 1964-65, Kearney Pub. Schs., 1965-97; lectr. U. Nebr., Kearney, 1985—; judge speech & drama Nebr. Sch. Activities Assn., 1965—. Avocations: reading, writing. Home: 215 Heavenly Dr Omaha NE 68154-2135

FRANCIS, D. MAX, healthcare management executive; b. Miltonvale, Kans., May 29, 1938; s. Emery James and Neva Orene (Geist) F.; m. Joyce Marie Behrle, Aug. 27, 1971; children: Kimberly Kay, Jeffery Scott, Heather Lyn. AB in Bus. Adminstrn., Kans. Wesleyan U., 1962; M Health Adminstrn., Wash. U., St. Louis, 1966. Adminstr. Clay County Hosp., Clay Center, Kans., 1966-68, Spelman Meml. Hosp., Smithville, Mo., 1968-71; pres. United Hosp. Ctr., Clarksburg, W.Va., 1971-87, Clarkson Regional Health Sys., Omaha, 1987-94, Hosp. Health Plan Mgmt. Corp., White Bear Lake, Minn., 1994-96, Sage Health, Stillwater, Minn., 1996—. Chmn. W.Va., C. of C, Charleston, 1985-86; treas. W.Va. Bus. Roundtable, Charleston, 1984-87; bd. dirs. Nebr. C. of C., Lincoln, 1992-94. Named Lifetime Bd. dirs. W.Va. C. of C., 1986. Mem. White Bear Lake C. of C., Minn. C. of C. Republican. Methodist. Avocations: tennis, biking, wine collecting, travel. Home: 4736 Mcdonald Drive Pl Stillwater MN 55082-2152

FRANCIS, DICK (RICHARD STANLEY FRANCIS), novelist; b. Tenby, Wales, U.K., Oct. 31, 1920; s. George Vincent and Catherine Mary (Thomas) F.; m. Mary Margaret Brenchley, June 21, 1947; children: Merrick, Felix. LHD (hon.), Tufts U., 1991. Steeplechase jockey, 1946-57; journalist London Sunday Express, 1957-73. Author: (autobiography) The Sport of Queens, 1957, Dead Cert, 1962, Nerve, 1964, For Kicks, 1965 (Silver Dagger award 1965), Odds Against, 1965, Flying Finish, 1966, Blood Sport, 1967, Forfeit, 1968 (Edgar Allen Poe award 1969), Enquiry, 1969, Rat Race, 1970, Bonecrack, 1971, Smokescreen, 1972, Slay-Ride, 1973, Knock Down, 1974, Risk, 1977, Trial Run, 1978, Whip Hand, 1979 (Gold Dagger award 1980, Edgar Allen Poe award 1980), Reflex, 1980, Twice Shy, 1981, Banker, 1982, The Danger, 1983, Proof, 1984, Break In, 1985, Lester (biography of Lester Piggott), 1986, Bolt, 1986, Hot Money, 1987, The Edge, 1988, Straight, 1989, Longshot, 1990, Comeback, 1991, Driving Force, 1992, Decider, 1993, Wild Horses, 1994, Come to Grief, 1995, 2 Edgar Allen Poe award for Best Novel and Grand Master, 1996.RD To The Hilt, 1996, 10 lb. Penalty, 1997, Field of Thirteen, 1998, Second Wind, 1999; co-editor: (with John Welcome) The Racing Man's Bedside Book, 1969, Best Racing and Chasing Stories, 1966, part II, 1969, The Dick Francis Treasury of Great Racing Stories, 1991; contbr. anthologies Winter's Crimes, 1973, Stories of Crime and Detection, 1974, Ellery Queen's Crime Wave, 1976, Ellery Queen's Searches and Seizures, 1977; contbr. articles to periodicals. Officer RAF, 1940-46. Decorated Order Brit. Empire, Nibbies award 1998; champion steeplechase jockey The Jockey Club, London, 1954. Mem. Mystery Writers Am., Crime Writers Assn., Detection Club, Racecourse Assn. Avocations: traveling, racing. Home: care of John Johnson Ltd, 45-47 Clerkenwell Green, London ECIR OHT, England Office: Putnam Pub Group 200 Madison Ave New York NY 10016-3903

FRANCIS, EDWARD D., architect; b. Cleve., Aug. 15, 1934; s. Michael and Anna (Buchinsky) F.; m. Betty-Lee Ellen Seydler, Aug. 25, 1956 (div. 1982); children—Tameron, Theron; m. Lynne Marie Merrill, Sept. 6, 1984. B.Arch, Miami U., 1957. Draftsman, designer David Maxfield, Oxford, Ohio, 1953-59; draftsman Austin Co., Cleve., summers 1954, 56; designer Meathe, Kessler & Assoc., Grosse Pointe, Mich., 1959-68; prin. William Kessler & Assoc., Detroit, 1968-94, pres., 1985—; pres. Kessler Assoc. Inc., 1995—. Chmn. Franklin Village Hist. Commn., Mich., 1971-79; pres. Friends of Capitol, Lansing, 1984-85; dir. Mich. State Hist. Preservation Rev., 1984-94. Fellow AIA (Gold medal Detroit chpt.); Mich. AIA (Detroit chpt.), mem. Nat. Trust for Hist. Preservation (bd. dirs.), Gabriel Richard Hist. Soc., Engring. Soc. Detroit. Office: Kessler Assocs Inc 409 E Jefferson Ave Detroit MI 48226-4322

FRANCIS, JAMES CLARK, IV, judge; b. Tulsa, Okla., Oct. 3, 1952; s. James C. and F. Ruth Francis; m. Elizabeth Bradford, Aug. 19, 1978; children: Nathaniel, Jeremy. BA, Yale Coll., 1974, JD, 1978; M of Pub. Policy, Harvard U., 1978. Bar: N.Y. 1979, U.S. Dist. Ct. (so. dist.) N.Y. 1979, U.S. Dist. Ct. (ea. dist.) N.Y. 1980, U.S. Ct. Appeals (2nd cir.) 1980. Law clk. Hon. Robert L. Carter, N.Y.C., 1978-79; staff atty. Legal Aid Soc., N.Y.C., 1979-85; U.S. Magistrate judge U.S. Dist. Ct. (so. dist.) N.Y., N.Y.C., 1985-98, chief U.S. Magistrate judge, 1998—. Author: (chpts.) Moore's Federal Practice, 1997; curator (exhibit) Discreet Persons Learned in Law, 1995. Mem. profl. adv. bd. Epilepsy Inst., N.Y.C.; bd. dirs. Port Washington (N.Y.) Soccer Club. Mem. N.Y. State Bar Assn. (jud. com. 1989—), Assn. Bar of City of N.Y. (fed. cts. com. 1995-98). Democrat. Avocations: travel, sports, coaching soccer. Office: US Court 500 Pearl St New York NY 10007-1316

FRANCIS, JAMES DELBERT, oil company executive; b. Orange, N.J., Jan. 8, 1947; s. Delbert Matthew and Margaret Janet (Thornley) F.; m. Shirley Ann Waters; children: Elizabeth M., John A., David S., Virginia a., Grace A., J. Thornley. B.S. in Commerce, U. Va., 1970; J.D., U. Fla., 1973. Bar: Fla. 1973. Ptnr. Smith and Hulsey, Jacksonville, Fla., 1973-82; exec. v.p. Charter Oil Co., Fla., 1982-83, pres., 1983-86; chmn., chief exec. officer Ray Distbg. Co., 1987—; bd. dirs. Petro Distbg., Inc. Bd. dirs., chmn. Children's Home Soc., Jacksonville, 1976-94; elder St. Johns Presbyn. Ch., 1985—. Mem. ABA, Fla. Bar, Jacksonville Bar Assn. Republican. Clubs: Fla. Yacht; River (Jacksonville). Home: 4284 Mcgirts Blvd Jacksonville FL 32210-4368 Office: Ray Distbg Co PO Box 43250 Jacksonville FL 32203-3250

FRANCIS, JOHN WAYNE, educator; b. May Pen, Jamaica, June 9, 1963; came to U.S., 1986; s. Keith George and Ella Elizabeth Francis; m. Ouida Binnie, Sept. 28, 1988 (div. July 1993); children: Richard, John; m. Sheryl R. Goldson, Mar. 11, 1994. BSc, U. W.I., Jamaica, 1986; PhD, Loyola U., Chgo., 1991; postgrad., Franklin U., 1998—. Asst. prof. Felician Coll., Lodi, N.J., 1993-95, safety officer, 1993-95; sci. safety officer Bloomfield (N.J.) Coll., 1993-97; pres. JWF & Assocs., Fairlawn, N.J., 1993-97; asst. prof. chemistry U. Bridgeport, Conn., 1995-97; instr. chemistry Columbus (Ohio) State C.C., 1997—. Contbr. articles to profl. jours. Soccer coach Ctrl. Cmty. House, Columbus; neighborhood revitalization coord. U. Bridgeport, 1995-97. Mem. Am. Chem. Soc., N.Am. Catalysis Soc., Organic Reaction Catalysis Soc. Anglican. Avocations: photography, computing, classic cars, reading. E-mail: jfrancis@cscc.edu. Office: Columbus State CC 550 E Spring St Columbus OH 43215-1722

FRANCIS, KAREN See **RUGALA, KAREN FRANCIS**

FRANCIS, LORNA JEAN, nutritionist; b. Mt. Carmel, Ill., July 2, 1955; d. Adolph William and Edna Louise (Kleinschmidt) Kirsch; m. Lionel Jackie Bush, Oct. 2, 1976 (div. Mar. 1988); children: Leah Joann, Lucas Jeffrey; m. Terry Glen Francis, Dec. 30, 1989; 1 child, Ashley Michelle. BS in Dietetics, So. Ill. U., 1976, MS in Cmty. Nutrition, 1984. Cert. nutrition support dietitian Am. Soc. Parenteral and Enteral Nutrition. Tchr.'s asst. So. Ill. U., Carbondale, 1982-84; cons. dietitian, Ill., Ind., 1984-86, Hillhaven Corp., Columbus, Ohio, 1986-89; clin. dietitian Deaconess Hosp., Evansville, Ind., 1989-91; mgr. clin. nutrition Marriott-Welborn Bapt. Hosp., Evansville, 1991-96; dept. dir. Sodexho-Marriott, Evansville, 1996-98; food svc. dir. U. Evansville, 1998—; mem. adj. faculty U. Evansville, 1989—; mem. adv. bd. Riverfront Home and Health Agy., Vincennes, Ind., 1993—; mem. med. adv. bd. YMCA, 1998—; exam. writer Nat. League for Nursing, N.Y.C., 1991, 97. Contbr. articles to profl. jours. Co-chmn. Parent Tchr. League, Evansville Luth. Sch., 1993-95, chmn. health com., 1997; bd. dirs. Meals on Wheels, Evansville, 1994—; vol. Center City Corp., Evansville, 1996—. Mem. Am. Dietetic Assn. (registered), Ind. Cons. Dietitians (chmn. 1987-88), Ind. Nutrition Edn. Network, S.W. Ind. Dietetics Assn. (edn. chmn. 1992—, pub. rels. com. 1983-84, co-chmn. 1984-85, chmn. 1985-86). Avocations: choir, golf, gardening, reading. Home: 513 Red Bud Ln Evansville IN 47710-4977 Office: U Evansville 1800 Lincoln Ave Evansville IN 47722

FRANCIS, MARION DAVID, consulting chemist; b. Campbell River, B.C., Can., May 9, 1923; came to U.S., 1949; s. George Henry and Marian (Flanagan) F.; m. Emily Liane Williams, Aug. 27, 1949 (dec. 1995); children: William Randall, Patricia Ann; m. Jacqueline S. Lohman, June 14, 1997. BA, U. B.C., Vancouver, 1946, MA, 1949; PhD, U. Iowa, 1953. Instr. U. B.C., Vancouver, Can., 1946-49; chemist Can. Fishing Co., Vancouver, Can., 1946; research asst. U. Iowa, Iowa City, 1949-51; research chemist Procter & Gamble Co., Cin., 1952-76, sr. scientist, 1976-85; sr. scientist Norwich Eaton Pharms., Inc., Norwich, N.Y., 1985-89; rsch. fellow Victor Mills Soc., Cin., 1990-93; cons. Cin., 1993—; chmn. Gordon Rsch.

Conf., N.H., 1968, 79, session chmn., 1985; invited speaker, panel discussion mem. 1st Internat. Conf. on Crystal Deposition and Dissolution in Tissues, Evion, France, 1985; invited speaker Internat. Workshop on Flouride in Bone, 1988, Bisphosphonates: Current Status and Future Prospects, London, 1990; invited speaker for Tng. for Pharm. Industry, London, 1992, 24th Internat. Sun Valley Workshop on Hard Tissue Biology, 1993, Internat. Bone Disease Symposium, Chantilly, Va., 1996; session chmn. workshop, Sienna, Italy, 1992; invited symposium speaker Japanese Bone & Mineral Soc., Yokahoma, 1993; invited speaker, co-chmn. "Bisphosphonate Therapies for Osteoporosis: Today and Tomorrow" Symposium, Davos, Switzerland, 1996, spkr./chmn. XIV Internat. Conf. on Phosphorus Chemistry, Cin., 1998, others; lectr. numerous univs., U.S., Can., Europe and China, 1965-90; spkr. in field. Contbr. articles to sci. jours.; patentee in field. Dist. chmn. Cin. United Appeal, 1956-60. Recipient Profl. Accomplishment award Tech. and Sci. Socs. Cin., 1979, Tech. Innovation award Victor Mills Soc., 1990, Perkin medal U.S. Soc. Chem. Industry, 1996; U.S. Pub. Health predoctoral fellow, 1951-52. Fellow AAAS, Am. Inst. Chemists; mem. Soc. Nuclear Medicine, Am. Assn. Dental Rsch., Internat. Assn. Dental Rsch., Am. Pharm. Assn., Am. Soc. Bone and Mineral Rsch., Am. Chem. Soc. (program chmn. cen. regional meeting 1983, invited symposium spkr. nat. meeting 1987, 92, invited awards symposium spkr. 1994, Cin. Chemist of Yr. award 1977, Nat. Indsl. Chemist award 1994, Morley medal 1996), Am. Assn. Pharm. Scientists, Am. Coll. Rheumatologists, N.Y. Acad. Scis., Ohio Acad. Sci., Dance Club (pres. 1972-73), Wyo. (Ohio) Sunday Supper Club (pres. 1998-99). Republican. Roman Catholic. Home and Office: 23 Diplomat Dr Cincinnati OH 45215-2074

FRANCIS, MARK OWEN, landscape architecture educator; b. Des Moines, Oct. 19, 1950; s. James E. Francis and Elizabeth Wright; m. Kirsten Lovik, Dec. 4, 1976; children: Linn Lovik, Bjørn. BA in Landscape Arch. with honors, U. Calif., Berkeley, 1972; M Landscape Arch. in Urban Design, Harvard U., 1975. Lic. landscape architect, Calif., Mass., N.Y. Asst. prof. environ. psychology CUNY, N.Y.C., 1977-80; prof. landscape arch. U. Calif., Davis, 1980—, chair dept. environ. design, landscape arch. program, 1984, 95-97; prin. Codesign Inc., Landscape Archs., Davis, 1984—; sr. design cons. Moore, Iacofano, Goltsman, Berkeley, 1999—; mem. nat. urban and cmty. forestry adv. coun. USDA, Washington, 1995-98. Author: Community Open Spaces, 1984, Public Space, 1992 (USLA Book award 1995), The California for a Landscape Garden, 1999; editor: The Meaning of Gardens, 1990 (USLA Honor award 1993); contbr. over 60 articles to profl. jours. Chair Downtown Parking and Pedestrian Task Force, Davis, 1981-83; mem. Pub. Arts Selection Com., Davis, 1995-96; mem. adv. bd. Nearby Nature, 1992—. Fellow Royal Norwegian Coun. for Sci. and Indsl. Rsch., 1984-85; recipient awards for planning, rsch. and comm. Am. Soc. Landscape Architects, 1985, 87, 90, 93, 95. Mem. San Francisco League of Urban Gardeners (adv. bd. 1990—), Trust for Pub. Land (adv. bd. 1994—), Sacramento Harvard Club. Avocations: cross country skiing, travel, hiking, photography. E-mail: mofrancis@ucdavis.edu. Home: 720 Robin Pl Davis CA 95616 Office: U Calif Dept Environ Design Davis CA 95616

FRANCIS, MARY FRANCES VAN DYKE, real estate executive, editor; b. Sedalia, Mo., Nov. 17, 1925; d. Frank B. and Mary Irene (Sims) Van Dyke; student Central Mo. State Coll.; m. Harold E. Francis, Apr. 23, 1944 (div. 1980); children—David Eugene, Lois Irene Valero, Roland Wayne, Eric Brian. Tchr. grade sch. Pettis County, Mo., 1943-44; timekeeper Montgomery Ward & Co., Kansas City, Mo., 1944-45; instr. new operators Southwestern Bell Telephone Co., Independence, Mo., 1945-47; real estate salesman Russell Realtors, Independence, 1958-66; owner Mary Francis, Realtor, Independence, 1967—; exec. sec., editor Eastern Jackson County Bd. Realtors, 1962-68; exec. asst., pub. relations dir., editor Kansas City Realtor, 1968-71; marketing asst. South Central region Chgo. Title Ins. Co., Kansas City, 1971-75; pres. Maranco, Inc., real estate, 1975—; v.p. Raintree Lake Realty, 1980-83 . Cub Scout den mother council Boy Scouts Am. Recipient Outstanding Service award Eastern Jackson County Bd. Realtors, 1964, Salesmanship award, 1965, CPW Real Estate Exchange award, Expo, 1983. Mem. Nat. Assn. Real Estate Bds. (charter pres. Greater Kansas City chpt., gov., pres. Mo. Women's Council), Mo. Real Estate Assn. (mem. Speakers Bur.). Club: Soroptomist (past pres., Independence). Contbr. articles to realty publs. Address: PO Box 1158 Independence MO 64051-0658

FRANCIS, MERRILL RICHARD, lawyer; b. Iowa City, Jan. 28, 1932; m. Mardi Munson, Dec. 22, 1991; children from previous marriage: Kerry L., David M., Robin A. B.A. magna cum laude, Pomona Coll., 1954; J.D., Stanford U., 1959. Bar: Calif. 1960, Supreme Ct. 1970. Ptnr. Sheppard, Mullin, Richter & Hampton, Los Angeles, 1959—. Mem. Fellows of Contemporary Art, 1980—. Served to lt. (j.g.) U.S. Navy, 1954-56. Fellow Am. Bar Found., Am. Coll. Bankruptcy (chmn. 9th cir. admissions com. 1992-95, bd. dirs. 1995—, chair bd. regents 1995—); mem. ABA Bus. Law Sect. (chmn. secured creditors com. 1981-85, chmn. bus. bankruptcy com. 1986-89, chmn. Task Force on Fed. Ct. Structure 1990-93, mem. Coun. Bus. Law sect. 1991-95, chmn. ad hoc com. on brown bag programs 1994-97), State Bar of Calif. (mem. debtor/creditor and bankruptcy com. of bus. law sect. 1978-79), L.A. County Bar Assn. (mem. real property sect., exec. com. 1970-80, mem. comml. law and bankruptcy sect., sect. chmn. 1976-77), Fin. Lawyers Conf. (bd. govs. 1970—, pres. 1972-73), La Canada-Flintridge C. of C. and Cmty. Assn. (pres. 1971-72), Order of the Coif, Jonathan Club, Phi Beta Kappa. Office: Sheppard Mullin Richter & Hampton 333 S Hope St Fl 48 Los Angeles CA 90071-1406

FRANCIS, MICHAEL G., political party official; b. Jena, La.; m. Diana Istre; children: Mackey, Bryan. Pres., owner Francis Drilling Fluids, Ltd., 1977—; state fin. chmn. La. Rep. Party, 1993-94, state chmn., 1995—. Mem. St. Michael the Archangel Roman Cath. Ch.; mem. exec. bd. United Way Acadiana, Welcome House of Acadia Parish, Acadia Parish Boy Scouts Am. Recipient Silver Beaver award Boy Scous Am. Mem. Soc. Petroleum Engrs. Avocations: work, politics, hunting, fishing. Office: 7916 Wrenwood Blvd Ste E Baton Rouge LA 70809-1782

FRANCIS, MILES N., JR., muncipal official; b. Roanoke, Va., Mar. 14, 1941. BS, U. Fla., 1969. Aviation rsch. and devel. Pratt Whitney Aircraft, West Palm Beach, Fla.; mgr. mass transit ops. Jacksonville (Fla.) Transp. Authority, 1982-87, exec. dir., 1987—. Mem. Am. Pub. Transit Assn., Nat. Transit Rsch. Bd., Fla. Transit Assn., Fla. Assn. Transp. and Expressway Authorities. Office: Jacksonville Transp Authority PO Drawer O 100 N Myrtle Av Jacksonville FL 32203*

FRANCIS, NORM, computer software executive, accountant. BSc in computer science, U. B.C. CPA. Co-owner Basic Software Group (acquired by Computer Assocs. Internat., 1979; pres, CEO Pivotal Software Inc., North Vancouver, B.C., Can.; lectr. in field. Office: Pivotal Software Inc. 300-224 W Esplanade, N Vancouver Can V7M3MG

FRANCIS, PETER T., gas and oil industry executive; b. 1952. Grad., Middlebury Coll.; MBA, Stanford U., 1987. Bd. dirs. JM Huber Corp., Edison, N.J., 1985-87, 1990-93, chmn. bd., 1993, now pres., CEO; pres. AMS Subsidiary Corp., Seattle, Wash., 1988—; chmn., CEO, pres. Cascade Cabinet Corp., Woodinville, Wash., 1990—. Office: J M Huber Corporation 333 Thornall St Edison NJ 08837-2220*

FRANCIS, PHILIP HAMILTON, management consultant; b. San Diego, Apr. 13, 1938; s. William Samuel and Ruth Kathryn (Allison) F.; m. Regina Elizabeth Kirk, June 10, 1961 (div. May 1971); m. Diana Maria Villarreal, July 15, 1972; children: Philip Scott, Edward Philip, Mary Allison, Kenneth Joseph. BSME, Calif. Poly. State U., 1959; MSME, U. Iowa, 1960, PhD in Engring. Mechanics, 1965; MBA in Mgmt., St. Mary's U., San Antonio, 1972. Registered profl. engr., Tex. With Douglas Aircraft Co., Santa Monica, Calif., 1960-62, S.W. Rsch. Inst., San Antonio, 1965-79; prof., chmn. dept. mech. and aerospace engring. Ill. Inst. Tech., Chgo., 1979-84; with Indsl. Tech. Inst., Ann Arbor, Mich., 1984-86; dir. advanced mfg. tech. Motorola Inc., Schaumburg, Ill., 1986-88; corp. v.p. Square D Co. (Schneider-N.Am.), Palatine, Ill., 1988-94; client ptnr. AT&T Solutions, AT&T, Chgo., 1995-96; mng. ptnr. Mascon Info. Tech., Ltd., Schaumburg, Ill., 1996—. Mem. various indsl. and acad. adv. bds. Recipient Gustas Larson award ASME and Pi Tau Sigma, 1978. Fellow ASME; mem. Ill. Math. and Sci. Acad. (fund bd. dirs.), Soc. Mfg. Engrs., Sigma Xi, Tau Beta Pi, Pi Tau Sigma. Roman Catholic. Avocation: writing. Home: 52 Ridge Rd Barrington IL 60010-2602

FRANCIS, RICHARD HAUDIOMONT, government administrator; b. Boston, Mar. 8, 1925; s. Dalton Edward and Dusolina Mary (Arratto) F.; m. Della May Bailey, June 18, 1949 (dec. Feb. 1986); children: Mark, Clare Siegel, Daniel; m. Sarah Marie Splaine Leonard, Sept. 6, 1986. BS, U.S. Naval Acad., 1949; MA, Yale U., 1958; PhD, U. Md., 1977. Commd. USMC, 1949, advanced through grades to lt. col., ret., 1969; served in Korean War, battalion in Okinawa; project officer for research and devel.; asst. naval attache Madrid; mem. Office Joint Chiefs of Staff; v.p. Washington Coll., Chestertown, Md., 1970-71; exec. dir. Md. Ind. Coll. Univ. Assn., Annapolis, 1971-74; asst. dir. fed. relations Assn. Am. Colls., Washington, 1974-76; dir. govt. relations Nat. Assn. Ind. Colls. and Univs., Washington, 1976-78; exec. v.p. Nat. MultiHousing Council, Washington, 1978-81; sr. policy advisor HUD, Washington, 1981-82, pres. solar bank, 1982-87; v.p. Profl. Lobbying and Cons. Ctr., 1987-88; exec. dir. Marine Exec. Assn., 1988-98; former asst. prof. Yale U.; pres. Am. Embassy Personnel Assn., 1965. Contbr. articles to profl. jours. Active various polit. campaigns, Va., various Cath. groups and PTAs. Recipient Letter of Commendation Republic of Korea, Cross of Naval Merit, Spain. Republican. Clubs: Fairfax (Va.) Country, Woodlawn Country (v.p. 1974-76) (Fairfax). Avocations: golf, badminton. Home: 10540 Anita Dr Lorton VA 22079-3527

FRANCIS, RON, professional hockey player; b. Sault Ste Marie, Ont., Can., Mar. 1, 1963. Center Pitts. Penguins, 1991-98, Carolina Hurricanes, 1998—. Office: c/o Carolina Hurricanes KTR Hockey Ltd Partnership 5000 Aerial Ctr Ste 100 Morrisville NC 27560*

FRANCIS, SAMUEL TODD, columnist; b. Chattanooga, Apr. 29, 1947; s. Todd Ware and Julia (Ford) F. BA, Johns Hopkins U., 1969; MA, U. N.C., 1971, PhD, 1979. Policy analyst Heritage found., Washington, 1977-81; legis. asst. U.S. Senator John P. East, Washington, 1981-86; editorial writer Washington Times, 1986-87, dep. editorial page editor, 1987-91, acting editorial page editor, 1991, columnist, 1991-95; pres. Ctr. for Nat. Rsch., Alexandria, Va., 1995—. Author: Soviet Strategy of Terror, 1981, Power and History: The Political Thought of James Burnham, 1984, Beautiful Losers: Essays on the Failure of American Conservatism, 1994, Revolution from the Middle, 1997; contbg. editor Chronicles: A Mag. of Am. Culture, Rockford, Ill., 1987—; editor: The Samuel Francis Letter; mem. bd. editl. advisors Modern Age, College Park, Md., 1987—. Nat. bd. dirs. Coun. of Conservative Citizens, 1995—. Recipient Disting. Editorial Writing award Am. Soc. Newspaper Editors, 1988, 89. Mem. The Phila. Soc. (bd. dirs. 1989-93), The John Randolph Club (bd. dirs.), Phi Kappa Psi. Office: PO Box 19627 Alexandria VA 22320-0627

FRANCIS, TIMOTHY DUANE, chiropractor; b. Chgo., Mar. 1, 1956; s. Joseph Duane and Barbara Jane (Sigwalt) F. Student, U. Nev., 1974-80, We. Nev. C.C., 1978; BS, L.A. Coll. Chiropractic, 1982, Dr. of Chiropractic magna cum laude, 1984; postgrad., Clark County C.C., 1986—; MS in Bio/Nutrition, U. Bridgeport, 1990. Diplomate Internat. Coll. Applied Kinesiology, Am. Acad. Pain Mgmt., Am. Naturopathic Med. Bd.; cert. kinesiologist, applied kinesiology tchr.; lic. chiropractor, Calif., Nev. Instr. dept. recreation and phys. edn. U. Nev., Reno, 1976-80; from tchng. asst. to lead instr. dept. principles & practice L.A. Coll. Chiropractic, 1983-85; pvt. practice Las Vegas, 1985—; asst. instr. Internat. Coll. Applied Kinesiology, 1990, chmn. exam review com., 1993, chmn. syllabus review com., 1994; adj. faculty The Union Inst. Coll. of Undergrad. Studies, 1993; joint study participant Nat. Olympic Tng. Ctr., Beijing, China, 1990. Mem. editl. rev. bd. Alternative Medicine Rev., 1996; contbr. articles to profl. jours. including Internat. Coll. Applied Kinesiology. Charles F. Cutts scholar, 1980. Fellow Internat. Acad. Clin. Acupuncture, British Inst. Homeopathy (homeopathy diploma 1993); mem. Am. Chiropractic Assn. (couns. on sports injuries, mutrition, roentgenology, technic, and mental health), Nev. State Chiropractic Assn., Nat. Strength and Conditioning Assn., Gonsted Clin. Studies Soc., Found. for Chiropractic Edn. and Rsch., Internat. Chiropractors Assn., Internat. Coll. Applied Kinesiology, Internat. Fedn. Practitioners Natural Therapeutics, Nat. Inst. Chiropractic Rsch., Nat. Strength and Conditioning Assn., Am. Naturopathic Med. Assn., Nat. Acad. Rsch. Biochemists, Phi Beta Kappa, Phi Kappa Phi (v.p. 1979-80, Scholar of the Yr. award, 1980), Delta Sigma. Republican. Roman Catholic. Avocations: karate, weightlifting. Home: 3750 S Jones Blvd Las Vegas NV 89103-2283

FRANCIS-BRUCE, RICHARD, film editor. Editor: (films) Goodbye Paradise, 1982, Careful, He Might Hear You, 1983, Mad Max Beyond Thunderdome, 1985, Short Changed, 1985, The Mosquito Coast, 1986, Bullseye, 1986, (with Hubert de la Bouillerie) The Witches of Eastwick, 1987, Dead Calm, 1989, The Blood of Heroes, 1990, Cadillac Man, 1990, (with Marcus D'Arcy and Lee Smith) Lorenzo's Oil, 1992, Sliver, 1993, The Shawshank Redemption, 1994 (Acad. award nomination best film editing 1994), Speechless, 1994, Seven, 1995 (Acad. award nomination best film editing 1995), The Rock, 1996, Air Force One, 1997 (Acad. award nomination best film editing 1997), Instinct, 1999; (TV movies) The Dismissal, 1984, The Cowra Breakout, 1985, The Nightman, 1992. Office: Mirisch Agency #700 10100 Santa Monica Blvd Los Angeles CA 90067

FRANCISCO, IRVING, landmark administrator; b. Ft. Defiance, Ariz., July 6, 1952. Student, Yavapai Coll., Coconino Coll., No. Ariz. U. Pk. ranger U.S. Pks. Svc., 1972-93; chief ranger Navajo Nat. Monument, Tonalea, Ariz., 1993—. Office: Navajo National Monument HC 71 Box 3 Tonalea AZ 86044-9708*

FRANCISCO, ROMA MERCEDES, educator; b. Santiago, Dominican Republic, Sept. 5, 1964; s. Jose Miguel and Lucrecia (Balbuena) F.; children: Carlos Felix, Diego Felix, Sade Ortiz. AA, Hostos C.C., Bronx, N.Y., 1996; BS, CCNY, 1998. Cert. tchr., N.Y. Mentor CCNY, 1997; rsch. asst. Dominican Studies Inst., N.Y.C., 1996—. Mem. ASCD, Nat. Assn. for Edn. of Young Children, Phi Theta Kappa. Roman Catholic. Avocations: classical music, arts and crafts, photography. Home: 575 E 140th St Bronx NY 10454 Office: CUNY Dominican Studies Inst 138th St at Convent Ave New York NY 10031

FRANCISCO, WAYNE H., criminalist, educator; b. Owosso, Mich., July 24, 1926; s. Leon D. and Louella E. Francisco; m. Donna J. Francisco; children: Judith Lynn, Carolyn Sue. BS, Ea. Mich. U., 1950, MA, 1967; M in Criminal Justice, Mich. State U., 1971; PhD in Criminalistics/Law, Columbia Pacific U., 1987. Chief investigator, owner Peninsula Security and Investigations, Atlanta, Mich., 1958—; dep. sherriff Oakland County, Mich., 1952-56; patrolman in Pontiac area Mich., 1969-73; spl. investigator Prosecutors Office, Montmorency County, 1974-79; dep. sheriff, evidence technician, criminalist Montmorency County, 1969-88; dep. sheriff, criminalist Chippewa County, 1973-88; capt., tng. officer Onaway Police Dept., 1989-91, Albee-Maple Grove Met. Police Dept., 1991-92; dir. Regional Law Enforcement Ctr., Atlanta, Mich., 1991—; recreational safety instr. DNR, Lansing, Mich., 1991—; criminalist cons., spkr. in field, U.S., Can., 1983—; sci./law enforcement instr. Walled Lake Schs., Mich., 1969-73; law enforcement instr. Schoolcraft Coll., 1969-73; prof. criminal justice/pub. safety/resident criminalist Lake Superior State U., 1973-83; dir., prof. criminal justice, cons. Mich. Christian Coll., Rochester Hills, 1992-97; prof. emeritus Lake Superior State U., pres. criminal justice adv. coun., 1983—. Recipient Conspicuous Heroism in the Performance of Duty Am. Police Hall of Fame, 1980, John Edger Hoover Gold medal for Disting. Svc., 1985, Knighted Am. Police Conf., 1989. Mem. Internat. Narcotic Enforcement Officers Assn., Nat. Assn. of Fed. Investigators, NEA (life), Mich. Edn. Assn. (life), DAV/NOTR, VFW (life). Avocations: fishing, hunting, music, hiking, bowling. Home: 23001 Storm Lake Trail Atlanta MI 49709-9501

FRANCISKOVICH, JOLENE ANN, library administrator; b. Morris, Ill., Aug. 22, 1958; d. Donald Eugene and Marcia Kay Togliatto; m. Michael John Franciskovich, June 19, 1976; children: Alison, Megan. Circulation clk. Coal City (Ill.) Pub. Libr., 1988-91, asst. dir., 1991—. Mem. ALA, Carbon Hill Women's Club. Roman Catholic. Avocations: reading, swimming, bicycling, gardening. E-mail: jfranciskovich@starbase.1.lib.il.us. Office: Coal City Pub Libr Dist 85 N Garfield Coal City IL 60416

FRANCK, FREDERICK SIGFRED, artist, author, dental surgeon; b. Maastricht, The Netherlands, Apr. 12, 1909; came to U.S., 1939, naturalized, 1945; s. Daniel and Helen (Foyer) F.; m. Claske Berndes Franck, July 15, 1960; 1 son, Lukas van Witsen Franck. Student, U. Amsterdam, 1926-31; Chirurgien Dentiste, Antwerp Dental Sch., 1935; LDS, Royal Coll. Surgeons, Edinburgh, Scotland, 1937; DMD, U. Pitts., 1942, DFA (hon.), 1963; ArtsD (hon.), Mt. St. Mary Coll., 1994. Practice dentistry London, 1937-39; resident oral surgery U. Pitts., 1942-44; anaesthetist Elizabeth Steel Magee Hosp.; staff Children's Hosp., Pitts., 1942-44; service cons. Netherlands East Indies govt., 1944-46; dentist N.Y.C., 1946-66; vis. staff Albert Schweitzer Hosp., 1958-60; chief mission Med. Internat. Coop., 1958; research fellow Nanzan U., Nagoya, 1981. Author: Open Wide, Please, 1957, Au Pays de Soleil, 1958, Days with Albert Schweitzer, A Lambarene Landscape, 1959, reissued 1992, (juvenile) My Friend in Africa, 1960, reissued 1995, African Sketchbook, 1961, My Eye is in Love, 1963 (Art Am. 50th Anniversary spl. citation 1963), Au Fil de L'Eau, 1964, Outsider in the Vatican, 1965, Met Het Oog Op Het Vatikaan, 1965, Au Pays Du Soleil, 1965, I Love Life, 1967, Exploding Church, 1968, Open Boek, 1967, Au Fil De L'Eau, 1968, Croquis Parisiens, 1969, Tutte le Strade portano a Roma, 1969, Le Paris de Simenon, 1969, Simenon's Paris, 1970, Tussen Broek en Brooklyn, 1971, The Zen of Seeing, 1973, Pilgrimage to Now/Here, 1973, (play) Inquest on a Crucifixion, 1975, An Encounter with Oomoto, 1975, The Book of Angelus Silesius, 1976, Zen and Zen Classics, 1977, EveryOne, The Timeless Myth of Everyman Reborn, 1978, The Awakened Eye, 1979, Art as a Way, A Return to the Spiritual Roots, 1981, The Buddha Eye, An Anthology of the Kyoto School, 1982, The Supreme Koan, Confessions of a Journey Inward, 1982, Messenger of the Heart, The Book of Angelus Silesius, 1982, De Zen van het Zien, 1983, 92, Echoes from the Bottomless Well, 1985, De Droomzolder--Oog in Oog met Venetie, 1985, Life Drawing Life, 1989, Little Compendium on that Which Matters, 1989, reissued 1993, To Be Human Against All Odds, 1991, reissued 1996, Zen Seeing, Zen Drawing: Meditation in Action, 1993, Fingers Pointing at the Sacred, 1996, The Tao of the Cross, 1998; co-author What Does It Mean to be Human?, Beyond Hiroshima, 1999; contbg. editor Parabola Quar.; rsch. editor Nanzan Monograph Series; contbr. articles, drawings to various mags. and periodicals; one-man shows include Contemporary Arts Gallery, Lilienfield Galleries, Passedoit Gallery, Albert Landry Gallery, (all N.Y.C.), 1959-60, Saginaw (Mich.) Mus., Doll & Richards Gallery, Boston, Ringling Mus. Art, M.H. De Young Mus., San Francisco, Waddell Gallery, Far Gallery, both N.Y.C., Foster-White Gallery, Seattle, 1976, U. Puget Sound Gallery, Seattle, 1977, Thorpe Intermedia Gallery, N.Y.C., 1977, others; shows in Paris, Amsterdam, Geneva, London, Rotterdam, Brussels, Rome, Tokyo, Kyoto, 1971, U. Maine, 1970-72, Melbourne, Australia, 1972, Interchurch Ctr. Gallery, 1972, Greater Middletown Arts Coun., 1973, Far Gallery, 1973, Singer Meml. Mus., The Netherlands, 1986, Pa. State U., 1989, Cathedral of St. John the Divine, N.Y.C., 1993, Albert Schweitzer Ctr., Great Barrington, Mass., 1993, Quinnipiac Coll., Hamden, Conn., 1994, Amber Gallery, Leiden, The Netherlands, 1994, Van Rijn Gallery, Maastricht, The Netherlands, 1994, Oude Kerk, Amsterdam, The Netherlands, 1994, Paul Mellon Arts Ctr. Choate Rosemary Hall, Wallingford, Conn., 1996; touring exhbn. Drawings of Lambarene, Albert Schweitzer's Hospital in Action, 1995, 96, 97, 98, Cathedral of St. John the Divine, N.Y.C., Newark, 1996, Weimar Gallery, Germany, 1999; group shows include Met. Mus., Whitney Mus., Corcoran Biennale, Indpls. Mus., Mpls. Mus., Nanzan U. Mus., Nagoya, Japan, 1981; represented in permanent collections including M.H. De Young Mus., Fogg Art Mus., San Francisco Mus. U. Ill., Mus. Modern Art, The Vatican, Witherspoon Gallery, Raleigh, N.C., Tokyo Nat. Mus., Nat. Collection Fine Arts, Washington, Santa Barbara, Amsterdam, Eindhoven, Maastricht, N.Y. Pub. Libr., Seattle Mus., Dartmouth Coll., Cornell U., Aschenbach Found., Ga. Mus., Whitney Mus., N.Y.U., State Capitol Mus., Wash., Fordham U. Lowenstein Gallery, Roanoke Mus. Fine Arts, Cathedral of St. John the Divine, N.Y.C., U. Nymegen, The Netherlands, U. Pa., Kans. State U., New Harmony, Ind., Cath. Ctr., others; traveling exhbn. to 12 univs. and colls., 1970-72, to The Netherlands and Belgium, 1991, 92; drawing exhbn. Amber Gallery, Leiden, Holland, 1999; built Pacem in Terris Trans-religious Sanctuary, Warwick, N.Y., 1966; steel sculptures comml. Genesis Farm, N.J., 1990, Omega Inst., N.Y., 1991, Pa. State U., 1991, Ch. of Saviour, Washington, 1991, Wainright House, Rye, N.Y., 1991, Fondacion Elpis, Buenos Aires, 1991, Cath. St. John the Divine, N.Y.C., Bucknell U., Peace Garden, Harrisburg, Pa., The Netherlands, 1993, Sarajevo, 1994, Belgium, 1995, New Cmty. Corp., Newark, 1995, Choate Rosemary Hall, Wallingford, Conn., 1995, Santa Cruz, Calif., 1995, Ittoen Found., Kyoto, Japan, 1997. Bd. dirs. Temple of Understanding, St. Francis Assisi, Italy, 1999. Recipient Chapman U. and Albert Schweitzer Inst. award of Excellence, 1995, purchase prize U. Ill., Am. Inst. Arts Letters, Living Arts Found., 1st prize Garnegie Inst., prize Musées Nationaux Francais, medal for drawings Pope John XXIII, 1963. Fellow Internat. Inst. Arts and Letters, Soc. for Arts, Religion and Contemporary Culture (dir.), Knighthood Order of Orange Nassau; mem. Artists Equity Assn. (hon. dir. N.Y.), P.E.N. Home: Pacem in Terris 96 Covered Bridge Rd Warwick NY 10990-2854 *I discovered that to defy the general trend towards specialization as a writer, painter, draughtsman, playwright, sculptor, does not mean "to spread oneself thin", is only seemingly a multiple commitment, and is in my case a single-minded obedience to what my very nature bids me to express in any medium I can handle.*

FRANCK, THOMAS MARTIN, law educator; b. Berlin, July 14, 1931; naturalized, 1977; s. Hugo and Ilse (Rosenthal) F. BA, U. B.C., 1952, LLB, 1953, LLD (hon.), 1995; LLM, Harvard U., 1954, SJD, 1956. Asst. prof. law U. Nebr., 1954-56; from assoc. prof. to prof. law NYU, 1960—, dir. Ctr. Internat. Studies, 1965—; acting dir. internat. law Carnegie Endowment Internat. Peace, 1973-75, dir., 1975-79; vis. prof. Stanford U., 1963, U. East Africa, 1964, 65, York U. Osgoode Hall Law Sch., 1972-73, 74-76; dir. rsch. UN Inst. Tng. and Rsch., 1980-82; cons. U.S. AID Dept. State, 1970-72, 85; constl. adviser govts. Tanganyika, 1963, Zanzibar, 1963, 64, Mauritius, 1965; mem. Sierra Leone Govt. Commn. Legal Edn., 1964, Nat. Liberal Adv. Coun. Can., 1952-53; lectr. Woodrow Wilson Sch., Princeton U., 1979, Hague Acad. Internat. Law, 1993; vis. fellow Trinity Coll., Cambridge, Eng., 1996-97. Author: Race and Nationalism, 1960, The United Nations in the Congo, 1963, East African Unity Through Law, 1965, Comparative Constitutional Process, 1968, The Structure of Impartiality, 1968, Why Federations Fail, 1968, A Free Trade Association, 1968, Word Politics, 1971, Secrecy and Foreign Policy, 1973, Resignation in Protest, 1975, Control of Sea Resources by Semi-Autonomous States, 1978, Foreign Policy by Congress, 1979, The Tethered Presidency, 1981, Human Rights in Third World Perspective, 1982, Nation Against Nation: What Happened to the U.N. Dream and What the U.S. Can Do About It, 1985, Judging the World Court, 1986, Foreign Relations and National Security Law, 1987, The Power of Legitimacy Among Nations, 1990, Political Questions/Judicial Answers, 1992, Fairness in the International Legal and Institutional System, 1993, Fairness In International Law and Institutuions, 1995; co-author: U.S. Foreign Relations Law, vols. I-III, 1980-81, vols. IV & V, 1984, Foreign Relations and National Security Law, 2d edit., 1993; editor-in-chief Am. Jour. Internat. Law, 1984-93; co-editor: Internat. Law Decisions in Nat. Cts., 1996. Lt. Can. Army, 1953. Guggenheim fellow, 1973-74, 82-83. Mem. Inst. de Droit Internat., State Dept. Adv. Com. on Internat. Law, Can. Coun. Internat. Law, African Law Assn., Assn. Am. Law Schs., Am. Soc. Internat. Law (pres.), Internat. Law Assn. (v.p. U.S. br.), Coun. on Fgn. Rels. Home: 15 Charlton St New York NY 10014-4910

FRANCK, WALTER ALFRED, rheumatologist, medical administrator, educator; b. Shanghai, China, Sept. 2, 1941; s. August Albert and Hilda Sylvia (Vandamme) F.; m. Linda Ashley Callanen, June 6, 1964; children: Christopher, Patrick, Kevin, Natalee. BA, Yale U., 1960; MD, Columbia U., 1964. Intern U. Mich., Ann Arbor, 1964-65, resident in medicine, 1965-68; fellow in rheumatology Harvard U./Mass. Gen. Hosp., Boston, 1971-73; attending physician in medicine and rheumatology Mary Imogene Bassett Hosp., Cooperstown, N.Y., 1973—, chief of medicine, 1980—; prof. clin. medicine Columbia U., N.Y.C., 1981—, assoc. dean Bassett Healthcare-Coll. Physicians and Surgeons, 1998—; adj. prof. clin. medicine Rochester (N.Y.) Sch. Medicine, Albany (N.Y.) Sch. Medicine, Dartmouth Sch. Medicine, Hanover, N.Y. Contbr. numerous articles to profl. pubs. Trustee, mem. fin. com. St. Mary's Ch., Cooperstown, 1991—. Maj. U.S. Army, 1968-71. Fellow ACP, Am. Coll. Rheumatology. Roman Catholic. Avocations: philately, gardening, fishing, hiking. Home: 6 Lakeview Dr S Cooperstown NY 13326-3003 Office: Bassett Hosp 1 Atwell Rd Cooperstown NY 13326-1394

FRANCKE, GLORIA NIEMEYER, pharmacist, editor, publisher; b. Dillsboro, Ind., Apr. 28, 1922; d. Albert B. and Fannie K. (Libbert) Niemeyer; m. Donald Eugene Francke, Apr. 15, 1956. BS in Pharmacy, Purdue U., 1942; PharmD, U. Cin., 1971; postgrad. U. Mich., 1945; PharmD (hon.) Purdue U., 1988—. Pharmacist, Dillsboro Drug Store, 1943-44; instr. Sch. Pharmacy, Purdue U., Lafayette, Ind., 1943; asst. to chief pharmacist U. Mich. Hosp., Ann Arbor, 1944-46; assoc. editor Am. Jour. Hosp. Pharmacy, Washington, 1944-64; asst. dir. Div. Hosp. Pharmacy of Am. Pharm. Assn., Washington, 1946-56; exec. sec. Am. Soc. Hosp. Pharmacists, Ann Arbor, 1949-60; acting dir. dept. comms., Washington, 1963-64; drug lit. specialist Nat. Library Medicine, Bethesda, Md., 1965-67; clin. pharmacy teaching coord. VA Hosp., Cin., 1967-71; asst. clin. prof. clin. pharmacy Coll. Pharmacy, U. Cin., 1967-71; chief program evaluation br. Alcohol and Drug Dependence Svc., VA, Ctrl. Office, Washington, 1971-75; dir. Pharmacy Intelligence Ctr., Am. Pharm. Assn., Washington, 1975-85; mem. Roche Hosp. Pharmacy Adv. Bd., 1971-74; judge for ann. Lunsford Richardson Pharmacy awards, 1963, 64; mem. com. standards for drug abuse treatment and rehab. programs Joint Commn. Accreditation of Hosps., 1974-75. Author: (with D. E. Francke, C. J. Latiolais and N.F. H. Ho) Mirror to Hospital Pharmacy, 1964. Contbr. articles on hosp. pharmacy and clin. pharmacy to profl. jours. Recipient Harvey A.K. Whitney award Mich. Soc. Hosp. Pharmacists, 1953, Disting. Alumnus award Purdue U. Sch. of Pharmacy, 1985, Remington Honor medal, 1987, Career Achievement award Profl. Frat. Assn., 1991, Fedn. Internat. Pharm. Lifetime Achievement in the Practice of Pharmacy award, 1996; also various commendations. Mem. Internat. Pharm. Fedn., Am. Inst. History of Pharmacy (exec. sec. 1968-78), Tex. Soc. Hosp. Pharmacists (hon.), Am. Pharm. Assn. (hon. chmn. 1986, named the Gloria Niemeyer Francke Leadership Mentor award in her honor 1995), Am. Soc. Hosp. Pharmacists (Donald E. Francke medal 1995), Drug Info. Assn., Kappa Epsilon, Rho Chi. Presbyterian. Home and Office: Apt 208A 3900 Cathedral Ave NW Washington DC 20016-5291

FRANCKE, LINDA BIRD, journalist; b. N.Y.C., Mar. 14, 1939; d. Samuel Curtis and Janet (King) Bird; m. G.D. Mackenzie, Jan. 12, 1961; 1 son, Andrew Mackenzie; m. Albert Francke III, Oct. 7, 1967; 2 daughters: Caitlin, Tapp. Student, Bradford Jr. Coll., 1958. Copywriter Young & Rubicam, Inc., N.Y.C., 1960-63, Ogilvy & Mather, Inc., N.Y.C., 1965-67; contbg. editor N.Y. Mag., N.Y.C., 1968-72, 80—; gen. editor Newsweek Mag., N.Y.C., 1972-77; columnist N.Y. Times, 1977—; TV news commentator Spl. Edit., 1978-79; dir. New Directions; juror Am. Book Awards, 1981; Co-chmn. Writer's Resource Center, Southampton, N.Y. Works in numerous anthologies, including, The New York Spy, 1967, The Power Game, 1970, Running Against the Machine, 1969, Women: A Book for Men, 1979, Hers: Through Women's Eyes, 1985, America Firsthand, Vol. II: From Reconstruction to the Present, 1994; author: The Ambivalence of Abortion, 1978, Growing Up Divorced, 1983, Ground Zero: The Gender Wars in the Military, 1997; collaborator: First Lady from Plains, 1984, Ferraro: My Story, 1985, A Woman of Egypt, 1987, Daughter of Destiny, 1989, Signature Life, 1998. Mem. Women's Commn. for Refugee Women and Children, Internat. Rescue Com. Inc.; chmn. East End Choice; candidate N.Y. State Assembly, 2d Dist., 1990; del. to Dem. Nat. Conv., 1992; bd. dirs. Bridgehampton Child Care & Recreational Ctr., Inc., The Retreat. Recipient award Cannes Film Festival, 1969, Nat. Clarion award, 1994. Mem. Authors Guild, Women's Media Group N.Y.C., Eastville Hist. Soc., Women Mil. Aviations, Inc.

FRANCKE, UTA, medical geneticist, genetics researcher, educator; b. Wiesbaden, Germany, Sept. 9, 1942; came to U.S., 1969; d. Kurt and Gertrud Müller; m. Bertold Richard Francke, May 27, 1967 (div. 1982); m. Heinz Furthmayr, July 27, 1986. MD, U. Munich, Fed. Republic Germany, 1967; MS, Yale U., 1985. Diplomate Am. Bd. Pediatrics, Am. Bd. Med. Genetics (bd. dirs. 1981-84). Asst. prof. U. Calif., San Diego, 1973-78; assoc. prof. Yale U., New Haven, 1978-85, prof., 1985-88; prof. genetics Stanford (Calif.) U., 1989—; investigator Howard Hughes Med. Inst., Stanford, 1989—, mem. sci. rev. bd., Bethesda, Md., 1986-88; mem. mammalian genetics study sect. NIH, Bethesda, 1990-94; bd. dirs. Am. Soc. Human Genetics, Rockville, Md., 1981-84. Profl. advisor March of Dimes Birth Defects Found., White Plains, N.Y., 1990, Marfan Assn., Port Washington, N.Y., 1991. Mem. Inst. Medicine of NAS (fgn. assoc.), Human Genome Orgn., Soc. for Pediatric Rsch., Soc. for Inherited Metabolic Disorders, Am. Soc. Human Genetics (pres. 1999). Avocation: piloting. Office: Stanford U Med Sch Howard Hughes Med Inst Beckman Ctr Stanford CA 94305-5323

FRANCO, ANTHONY M., public relations executive; b. Detroit, July 7, 1933; s. John Richard and Evelyn Louise F.; m. Melissa R. Rohde, Aug. 27, 1983; children: Catherine, Suzanne, Anne, Anthony, Patricia, Michael, David, Meredith, Christopher. Student, U.S. Naval Acad., 1955-57; BS, Wayne State U., 1958. Dir. pul. rels. Dawson-Murray Advt., Detroit, 1958-60, Fred M. Randall Co., Detroit, 1960-62, Denman & Baker Advt., Detroit, 1962-64; founder, chmn. Anthony M. Franco, Inc., Detroit, 1964-95; editl. dir. WJBK-TV (Fox), 1994-97; bd. dirs. Ziebart Internat.; adj. prof. Walsh Coll., Mich.; cons. Broad, Vogt and Conant; cons. Stone, August, Medrich Co. Past trustee Marygrove Coll., Detroit; trustee U. Detroit; corp. bd. dirs. Boys Clubs Met. Detroit, 1972-87; emcee Celebrity Night fundraising dinner, St. Joseph Mercy-Oakland Hosp.; pres. Met. Detroit coun. Boy Scouts Am., 1985; chmn. Channel 56, 1988-90; bd. dirs. Mich. Libr. Found., 1988-95, Mich. Hist. Found.; bd. dirs. Alma (Mich.) Coll. Comms. Ctr. at St. Joseph Mercy-Oakland Hosp. named in his honor; named one of 100 superstars in pub. rels. Pub. Rels. Quarterly, 1990. Mem. Internat. Pub. Rels. Group of Cos. (v.p., dir.), Pub. Rels. Soc. Am. (pres. 1986, dir. Detroit chpt., pres. 1974, chmn. east ctrl. dist.), Mich. C. of C., Greater Detroit C. of C. (vice-chmn. exec. com., chmn. 1990-91), U.S. Naval Acad. Alumni Assn., Bloomfield Open Hunt Club (pres. bd. dirs.), Royal Poinciana Golf Club, Bloomfield Hills Country Club, McAuley Club. Presbyterian. Home: 6621 George Washington Way Naples FL 34108-8222

FRANCO, CAROLE ANN, international consultant; b. Hartford, Conn., Dec. 21, 1948; d. Nicholas Lawrence and Mary Elizabeth (LaRosa) F. BA in Spanish, Duke U., 1970; grad. cert. in edn., Trinity Coll., Hartford, 1971; postgrad. in French, Sorbonne, Paris, 1980; M Internat. Rels., Cambridge (Eng.) U., 1981. Tchr. West Hartford (Conn.) Pub. Schs., 1970-76; researcher on biography of Sumner Welles Washington, 1976-77; adminstr. Ctr. for Strategic and Internat. Studies, Washington, 1978-79; broker, mgr. Parks Capital Mgmt., N.Y.C., 1981-83; assoc., cons. Burgess Mgmt. Assocs., N.Y.C., 1984-88; producer, owner Kingdom Prodns., New Paltz, N.Y., 1988-93; internat. cons. Strategic Ptnrs. Internat., New Paltz, 1993-96, Lady Mayoress of City of Westminster, London, 1996-97. Mem. Duke U. Alumni Assn. N.Y., Cambridge U. Alumni Assn. N.Y. (founder, bd. dirs. 1987—), United Oxford-Cambridge U. Club (London), Pilgrims. Republican. Roman Catholic. Home: 79 Two Stone Dr Wethersfield CT 06109

FRANCO, RALPH ABRAHAM, lawyer; b. Montgomery, Ala., Dec. 27, 1921; s. Abraham and Matilda (Habib) F.; m. Lila Keene, June 9, 1974; 1 stepchild, Charles Walton deCelle. BS, U. Ala., 1943; JD, U. Ala., 1948. Bar: Ala. 1948. Assoc. Hill, Hill, Carter, Franco, Cole & Black P.C. and predecessor firms, Montgomery, 1948-53, ptnr., 1953-88, stockholder, 1988—; mem. adv. bd. dirs. internal medicine residency program med. sch. U. Ala., Montgomery. Past pres. Jewish Fedn., Montgomery; bd. dirs., past pres. St. Margaret's Hosp. Found., St. Margaret's Found.; bd. dirs. Cath. Social Svc., Montgomery, pres., 1984-86, dir. emeritus; bd. dirs., pres. U. Ala. Law Sch. A Found.; bd. dirs., past pres. Etz Ahayem Synagogue. Capt. inf. U.S. Army, 1943-52, PTO, JACG, 1952-74, ret. col. Fellow Am. Bar Found.; mem. ABA, Ala. Bar Assn. (past pres. young lawyers, chmn. real property and probate sect. 1985-86), Montgomery County Bar Assn. (bd. dirs.), llth Jud. Cir. Hist. Soc. (bd. dirs. 1985—), Ala. Law Inst., Ret. Officers Assn., Blue and Gray Assn. (bd. dirs.), U. Ala. Law Sch. Alumni Assn. (past pres., bd. dirs.), Chancellors Soc. (Auburn U. Montgomery), Lions (bd. dirs. Montgomery, past pres.), Standard Country Club (bd. dirs. 1970-76). Home: 3609 Thomas Ave Montgomery AL 36111-2013 Office: Hill Hill Carter et al 425 S Perry St Montgomery AL 36104-4235

FRANCO, RAMON S., plastic surgeon; b. Atlanta, Ga., Dec. 10, 1942. MD, Emory U., 1966. Diplomate Am. Bd. Facial, Plastic, and Reconstructive Surgery. Resident Emory U., 1966-68, L.A.V.A. and UCLA, 1970-73; pvt. practice Atlanta, 1973—. Capt. USAF, 1968-72. Fellow ACS, Am. Coll. Facial, Plastic, and Reconstructive Surgery. Office: 980 Johnson Ferry Rd NE Atlanta GA 30342-1626

FRANCO, ROBERT, economist; b. Cairo, Aug. 11, 1941; came to U.S., 1960; s. Edgard and Speranza Franco; m. Martine Pastor, June 9, 1978; children: Erik, Arnaud. BA, U. Calif., 1963, PhD, 1970; MA, San Diego State U., 1965. Economist Transp. Inst., Washington, 1970-72; mgr. CACI, Arlington, Va., 1972-74; asst. divsn. chief IMF, Washington, 1974-94; resident rep. IMF, Senegal, 1984-87; sr. country economist World Bank, Washington, 1994-96; resident rep. IMF, Harare, Zimbabwe, 1996—; cons. OECD, Paris, 1970-74; prof. U. Md., College Park, 1970-80. Mem. Am. Econ. Assn., AAUP, Omicron Delta Epsilon. Avocations: tennis, music, fishing, boating. Home: PO Box 2960 IMF, Harare Zimbabwe Office: IMF C-200 700 19th St NW # C-200 Washington DC 20431-0001

FRANCO, VICTOR, theoretical physics educator; b. N.Y.C., Dec. 15, 1937; s. Isaac and Regina (Ferezy) F.; m. Jieying Zong, Sept. 12, 1983; children: Zachary M., Anna L., Eugene R. BS, NYU, 1958; MA, Harvard U., 1959, PhD, 1964. Research assoc. MIT, Cambridge, 1963-65, Los Alamos Sci. Lab., 1965-67, Lawrence Radiation Lab., Berkeley, Calif., 1967-69; assoc. prof. Bklyn. Coll., 1969-72, prof., 1973—; guest sci. Internat. Centre for Theoretical Physics, Trieste, 1970, 75; vis. staff mem. Los Alamos Nat. Lab., 1969-75; vis. physicist Lawrence Berkeley Lab., 1974; fgn. collaborator Centre d'Etudes Nucleaires, Saclay, France, 1975-76, 86; vis. sci. U. Trondheim, Norway, 1980, U. Alta., Can., 1982, U. Karlsruhe, Germany, 1985; vis. scholar U. Wash., Seattle, 1980; sr. rsch. assoc. Harvard U. Cambridge, 1983-84; NAS exch. scholar Inst. High Energy Physics, Beijing, China, 1984; guest prof. New Sch. Social Rsch., N.Y.C., 1988, 89; cons. in the field 1973—. Contbr. numerous articles to sci. jours. Recipient various fellowships and research grants. Fellow Am. Phys. Soc.; mem. Sigma Xi. Office: Brooklyn College Physics Dept Brooklyn NY 11210

FRANCOIS, FRANCIS BERNARD, association executive, lawyer; b. Barnum, Iowa, Jan. 21, 1934; s. Rudolph John and Irene Frances (McDonough) F.; m. Eileen M. Schmelzer, Feb. 6, 1960; children: Joseph, Marie, Michael, Monica, Susan. B.S., Iowa State U.; LL.B., George Washington U. Bar: Md. 1960, U.S. Patent and Trademark Office. Chief judge Orphan's Ct. Prince George's County, Upper Marlboro, Md., 1962-66; commr. Prince George's County, Upper Marlboro, Md., 1966-71, councilman, 1971-80; exec. dir. Am. Assn. State Hwy. and Transp. Ofcls., Washington, 1980-99; retired; adv. com. Ctr. Transp. Studies, MIT, 1983—; mem. adv. panel White House Intergovtl. Sci. and Engring. Tech., 1976-80; mem. Washington Suburban Transit Commn., 1978-80, chmn., 1979; dir. Washington Met. Area Transit Authority, 1978-80; exec. com. Transp. Rsch. Bd., 1980—, Strategic Hwy. Rsch. Program, 1986—; mem. permanent internat. commn. Permanent Internat. Assn. Rd. Congresses, 1990—; bd. dirs. Internat. Rd. Fedn., 1991—, Nat. Ctr. for Asphalt Tech., 1991—, Intelligent Transp. Soc. Am., 1991—, chmn., 1992-93; lectr. in field. Contbr. articles to profl. jours. Mem. adv. council Nat. Community Energy Mgmt. Ctr., 1981-82; mem. local govt. energy policy adv. com. Dept. of Energy, 1979-80; vice chmn. Md. Potomac Water Authority, 1970-80; air quality control adv. council State of Md., 1975-80; chmn. Water Resources Planning Bd., 1975-77; mem. Gov.'s Interstate Water Quality Planning Com., 1973-74; v.p. Md. Com. for Fair Representation, 1962; counselor Washington Career Inst., 1963; bd. dirs. Bowie Jaycees, Bowie Fine Arts Soc., Bowie YMCA; trustee Md. Easter Seal Soc., Prince George's United Way, Md. Soc. Crippled Children and Adults. Recipient Community Service award Nat. Capital chpt. ASCE, 1980, Community Service award Bowie Jaycees, 1980, Community Service award Cedar Heights Civic Assn., 1978, Profl. Achievement on Engring. award Iowa State U., 1984, W.N. Carey Jr. Disting. Svc. award Transp. Rsch. Bd., 1990, Theodore M. Matson Meml. award, 1993; named Washingtonian of Yr. Washingtonian Mag., 1973; Theodore M. Matson Meml. award, Am. Assn. State Hwy. and Transp. Officials, Am. Rd. and Transp. Builders Assn., Fed. Hwy. Adminstrn., Am. Hwy. Users Alliance, Inst. Transp. Engrs., Matson Meml. Assocs., and Transp. Rsch. Bd., 1993; Pioneer award Conf. Minority Transp. Officials, 1995, Chi Epsilon, Nat. Civil Engring Honor Soc., 1995. Mem. Nat. Assn. Counties (pres. 1979-80), Nat. Assn. Regional Coun. (pres. 1972-73), Washington Met. Coun. Govts. (dir. 1966-80, pres. 1971), Cmty. Assns. Inst. (dir. 1975-80, pres. 1979-80), Chi Epsilon. Democrat. Roman Catholic. Lodge: K.C. Home: 12421 Seabury Ln Bowie MD 20715-3113 Office: Am Assn State Hwy and Transp Ofcls 444 N Capitol St NW Ste 249 Washington DC 20001-1512*

FRANCOIS, WILLIAM ARMAND, packaging company executive, lawyer; b. Chgo., May 31, 1942; s. George Albert and Evelyn Marie (Smith) F.; m. Barbara Ann Sala, Aug. 21, 1965; children—Nicole Suzanne, Robert William. B.A., DePaul U., 1964, J.D., 1967. Bar: Ill. 1967. Pvt. practice Lyons, Ill., 1967-68; with Am. Nat. Can Co., Chgo., 1970—, sec., 1974—, v.p., 1978—, assoc. gen. counsel, 1987, v.p., dep. gen. counsel, sec., 1988—; dep. gen. counsel N.Am. Pechiney Group, 1996—. Served to capt. U.S. Army, 1968-70. Mem. ABA, Ill. Bar Assn., Chgo. Bar Assn., Am. Soc. Corp. Secs., Am. Corp. Counsel Assn. Home: 530 Oak Knoll Dr Lake Forest IL 60045-2630 Office: Am Nat Can Co 8770 W Bryn Mawr Ave Chicago IL 60631-3515

FRANCONA, TERRY JON, manager professional athletics; b. Aberdeen, S.D., Apr. 22, 1959; s. Tito F.; m. Jacque Lang, Jan. 9, 1982; children: Nick, Alyssa, Leah, Jamie. Student, U. Ariz. First baseman/outfielder maj. league baseball Montreal Expos, 1980, Chgo. Cubs, Cin. Reds, Cleve. Indians, Milw. Brewers; hitting instr. Sarasota, Gulf Coast Rookie League Chgo. White Sox orgn., 1991; mgr. S. Bend, 1992; coach Grand Canyon, Ariz. Fall League, 1992; mgr. Birmingham AA, 1993-95, Dominican Winter League, 1995-96, Phillies, Phila., 1996—. Recipient So. League Title, 1993, Minor League Mgr. of Yr., So. League, 1993, Minor League Mgr. of Yr., Baseball Am., 1993; named Top Managerial Prospect among minor league mgrs. Baseball Am., 1994. Avocation: golf. Fax: (215) 389-3050. Office: The Phillies PO Box 7575 Philadelphia PA 19101

FRANDEN, BLANCHE M., nursing educator; b. June 9, 1923; d. Samuel and Rebekah (Stern) Randall; m. Robert Jacob Franden, Aug. 20, 1950; children: Richard Jules, Peter Herb, Daniel Ethan. Grad., Mass. Meml. Hosp. Sch. Nursing, 1945; B Vocat. Edn., Calif. State U., L.A., 1980. RN, Calif. Dir. student health Mass. Meml. Hosp., Boston, 1947-49; staff nurse various hosps. N.Y. and Calif., 1949-91; instr., coord. hosp. related occupations East San Gabriel Valley Regional Occupl. Program, 1973-90, instr., coord. EMT 1, 1986—; program dir., instr., EMT 1 La Puente Valley Regional Occupl. Program, 1985-93; CPR instr.-trainer; mem. CPR com., local governing bd. Am. Heart Assn; mem. L.A. County Com. to Revise Curriculum for EMT1 recertification, 1992-95. Author student manual. Bd. dirs. Pathways to Hope chpt. City of Hope. Mem. VFW Women's Aux., Calif. Assn. Regional Occupl. Ctrs./Programs, Am. Vocat. Assn., Calif. Assn. Health Career Educators, So. Calif. Assn. EMT Instrs. and Coords. Democrat. Jewish. Office: E San Gabriel Valley Regional Occupl Program 1501 Del Norte St West Covina CA 91790-2105

FRANGIPANE, AMY CHRISTINA, media planner; b. Phila., May 1, 1976; d. Leo George Frangipane Jr. and Joyce Ann Miller. Student, U. Seville, Spain, 1996; BS in Journalism, Northwestern U., 1998. Reporter Reading (Pa.) Eagle/Times, 1995, 96, N.W. Herald, Crystal Lake, Ill., 1997; publicist Planned TV Arts, Chgo., 1997; radio prodr. Real Estate USA, Chgo., 1998; asst. media planner Euro RSCG Tatham, Chgo., 1998—. Tutor Ptnrs. in Edn., Chgo., 1998—. Mem. Soc. Profl. Journalists, Delta Delt Delta (pres. 1997-98). Democrat. Roman Catholic. Avocations: reading, art, movies, theater, athletics. E-mail: amy.frangipane@tatham.com. Address: 3343 N Sheffield Ave # 2 Chicago IL 60657-2212

FRANGIPANE, FRANCIS A., minister, religious organization executive, writer; b. Lodi, N.J., Nov. 26, 1946; s. Frank and Ann (Mac) F.; m. Denise Frangipane; 5 children. Ed. high sch., Lodi, 1964. Ordained to ministry, 1971. Pastor Ch. at Hilo, Hawaii, 1972-73, Berach Chapel, Flat Rock, Mich., 1973-80, Victory Christian Ctr., Marion, Iowa, 1983-89, River of Life Ministries, Cedar Rapids, Iowa, 1989—; pres. Advancing Ch. Ministries, Cedar Rapids, 1990—; bd. dirs. Morning Star Publs., Charlotte, N.C. Author: Holiness, Truth and the Presence of God, 1986, The Three Battlegrounds, 1989, The House of the Lord, 1991, The River of Life, 1993, The Place of Immunity, 1994, The Divine Antidote, 1994, The Days of His Presence, 1995. With USAF, 1965-69. Office: River of Life Ministries 3801 Blairs Ferry Rd NE Cedar Rapids IA 52402-1763 *As I have been serving the Lord these past years, He has led me to seek for two things, and two things only: to know the heart of God in Christ, and to know my own heart in Christ's light.*

FRANGOPOULOS, ZISSIMOS A., banker; b. Athens, Greece, Dec. 16, 1944; s. John and Thalia (Landi) F.; m. Ruth Snowdon Hoopes, Nov. 21, 1981. BA, Yale U., 1967; MBA, Columbia U., 1969. Lending officer Chem. Bank, N.Y.C., 1969-74; v.p. energy group Chem. Bank, London, 1974-79; sr. v.p. merchant banking Chem. Bank, N.Y.C., London, 1979-84; mng. dir., chief exec. officer Chem. Bank Internat. Ltd., London, 1981-84; sr. v.p., dir. for corp. fin. Chem. Banking Corp., N.Y.C., 1984-90, treas., 1990-92; sr. v.p., treas. Chem. Bank, N.Y.C., 1992-94; mng. dir. Chase Securities, Inc., N.Y.C., 1994—. Home: 17 E 96th St New York NY 10128-0783 Office: Chase Securities Inc 270 Park Ave Fl 12 New York NY 10017-2036

FRANK, ALAN I W, manufacturing company executive; b. Pitts., Mar. 6, 1932; s. Robert and Cecelia F.; children: Darcy Mackay, Kimberly Frank Shaw. AB cum laude, Harvard U., 1954; LLB, Columbia U., 1960. Bar: N.Y., 1961, Pa., 1982. Pres. Nat. Petroleum Corp., 1954-69; pres., chmn. bd. AIWF Corp., 1962—; pres. & bd. dirs. numerous corps. Patentee in field. Gen. chmn. $200 million campaign Pitts. area, Columbia U., N.Y.C., 1968-70, mem. nat. devel. bd., 1974—; mem. Rensselaer coun. Rensselaer Poly. Inst., 1974-83; mem., chmn. various coms. Harvard Coll., 1961—; trustee Pitts. History and Landmarks Found., 1996—. Served with Counter Intelligence Corps, Spl. Agt. U.S. Army, 1955-57. Mem. N.Y. Bar, Pa. Bar., Mid Ocean Club (Bermuda). Address: 96 E Woodland Rd Pittsburgh PA 15232-2861

FRANK, ALAN W., television station executive. V.p., gen. mgr. WDIV, Detroit, 1988—. Office: WDIV 550 W Lafayette Blvd Detroit MI 48226-3140*

FRANK, ANN-MARIE, sales administration executive; b. Omaha, July 27, 1957; d. Joseph Anthony and Louise Virginia (DiMauro) Malingagio; m. Jon Lindsay Frank, July 13, 1985; 1 child, Jon L. BA in Fine and Communication Arts, Loyola Marymount U., L.A., 1980, MBA, 1988. Region adminstrv. mgr. Data Gen. Corp., Manhattan Beach, Calif., 1986-90; contracts/sales adminstrn. mgr. Candle Corp., Santa Monica, Calif., 1991-96; dir. records and royalties Herbalife Internat., Inglewood, Calif., 1996-98; dir. customer svc. and internat. ops. G.B. Data Sys., Marina del Rey, Calif., 1998—. Dir., editor: (creative drama) Patchwork, 1982 (Rochester, N.Y. trophy). Republican. Roman Catholic. Avocations: travel, Victorian architecture, music, antiques. Home: 3311 Raintree Ave Torrance CA 90505-6618 Office: GB Data Sys 330 Washington Blvd Marina Del Rey CA 90292

FRANK, ANTHONY MELCHIOR, federal official, former financial executive; b. Berlin, Germany, May 21, 1931; came to U.S., 1937, naturalized, 1943; s. Lothar and Elisabeth (Roth) F.; m. Gay Palmer, Oct. 16, 1954; children: Tracy, Randall. BA, Dartmouth Coll., 1953, MBA, 1954; postgrad. in fin., U. Vienna, 1956. Asst. to pres., bond portfolio mgr. Glendale (Calif.) Fed. Savs. Assn., 1958-61; v.p., treas. Far West Fin. Corp., Los Angeles, 1962; adminstrv. v.p., v.p. savs. First Charter Fin. Corp., Beverly Hills, Calif., 1962-66; pres. State Mut. Savs. and Loan Assn., Los Angeles, 1966-68, Titan Group, Inc., N.Y.C. and Los Angeles, 1968-70, INA Properties, Inc., 1970-71; pres. Citizens Savs. & Loan, San Francisco, 1971-73, vice chmn., chief exec. officer, 1973-74; chmn. bd., pres., chief exec. officer FN Fin. Corp., 1974-88; postmaster gen. U.S. Postal Svc., 1988-92; chmn. Belvedere Capital Ptnrs., San Francisco; also pres., vice chmn., industry dir. Fed. Home Loan Bank San Francisco, 1972-77; trustee, treas. Blue Shield of Calif., from 1976-88; bd. dirs. Gen. Am. Investors, Trans Am. Home First, Temple Inland, Schwab, Bedford Property Investors Inc., Irvine Apts. Cmtys., Crescent Real Estate Equities. Chmn., bd. dirs. Calif. Housing Fin. Agy., Sacramento, 1978-86; trustee Am. Conservatory Theater; chmn. bd. visitors Sch. Architecture and Planning UCLA, 1971-86; bd. overseers Tuck Sch.; del. Calif. Dem. Conv., 1968. Served with AUS, 1954-56. Mem. SAG, Chief Execs. Orgn., World Bus. Forum, Dartmouth Club No. Calif., Bohemian Club. Office: Belvedere Capital Ptnrs One Maritime Plz Ste 825 San Francisco CA 94111-6114

FRANK, ARTHUR J., lawyer; b. Chgo., Mar. 18, 1946; s. Maurice A. and Elizabeth H. (Hoffmann) F.; m. Fredrica Frank, Oct. 22, 1969 (div. 1976); m. Mary Kay Dawson, Oct. 16, 1983; 1 child, Rebecca Anne. BSBA, Babson Coll., 1967; JD, U. Ill., 1971. Bar: Ill. 1971, U.S. Dist. Ct. (no. dist.) Ill. 1971, U.S. Dist. Ct. Md. 1989, U.S. Supreme Ct. 1989, D.C. 1989, U.S. Dist. Ct. D.C. 1990, Md. 1990. Mng. ptnr. Frank Assocs., Ltd., Chgo., 1971-86; regional ptnr. Hyatt Legal Svcs., Washington, 1986-90; sr. ptnr. Frank & Breads, Washington, 1990—. Pres. Lawyers for the Creative Arts, Chgo., 1974-75; bd. dirs. Neighborhood Justice of Chgo., 1979-81, Legal Assistance Found., Chgo., 1981-82; chmn. Second City Ballet, Chgo., 1986; mem. Dem. Nat. Com., 1994—, Dem. Congl. Campaign Com., 1994—. Mem. ATLA, ABA, Chgo. Bar Assn. (bd. mgrs., chmn. creative arts com. young lawyers sect. 1974-75, chmn. commn. on profl. responsibility young lawyers sect. 1975-76, bd. dirs. young lawyers sect. 1976-77, chmn.-elect young lawyers sect. 1977-78, chmn. legis. task force 1977, chmn. planning com. young lawyers sect. 1977-79, chmn. young lawyers sect. 1978-79, spl. com. on appointive selection of judges 1979, mem. spl. commn. code profl. responsibility of Supreme Ct. Ill. 1979), Md. Bar Assn. (mem. sect. estates and trusts), D.C. Bar Assn. (chmn. law firm mgmt. com. 1990-91, working group on reform of D.C. courts 1997-98, family law action group 1998—), Montgomery County Bar Assn., Prince George's County Bar Assn. Home: One Tripoli Ter North Potomac MD 20878-2853 Office: Frank & Assocs 1700 K St NW Ste 700 Washington DC 20006-3813

FRANK, BARNEY, congressman; b. Bayonne, N.J., Mar. 31, 1940; s. Samuel and Elsie (Golush) F. AB, Harvard U., 1962, JD, 1977. Exec. asst. to mayor City of Boston, 1968-71; adminstrv. asst. to U.S. congressman, 1971-72; mem. Mass. Ho. of Reps., 1972-80, 97th-105th Congresses from 4th Dist. Mass., 1981—; mem. banking and fin. svcs. com., mem. judiciary com.; teaching fellow govt. Harvard U., 1963-67, asst. to dir. Inst. Politics John F. Kennedy Sch. Govt., 1966-67, fellow Inst. Politics, 1971. Democrat. Office: US Ho of Reps 2210 Rayburn HOB Washington DC 20515

FRANK, BARRY H., lawyer; b. Nov. 19, 1938; s. David and Rose (Pearl) F.; divorced; children: Toby L., S. Kenneth, Gary A. BS, Pa. State U., 1960; LLB, Temple U., 1963. Bar: Pa. 1964. Staff atty. IRS, Phila., 1963-66; tax mgr. Ernst & Whinney, Phila., 1966-74; exec. v.p., gen. counsel Nat. Freight, Inc., Vineland, N.J., 1974-75; ptnr. Pechner, Dorman, Wolffe, Rounick & Cabot, Phila., 1975-87, Mesirov, Gelman, Jaffe, Cramer & Jamieson, LLP, Phila., 1987—; instr. Temple U. Tax Inst., Phila., 1976—. Co-author: Alimony, Child Support and Counsel Fees; mem. editl. bd. The Practical Acct.; contbr. numerous articles to profl. jours. Mem. exec. com. Mayor's Small Bus. Adv. Coun., Phila., 1981-83. Mem. ABA, AICPA, Phila. Bar Assn., Pa. Inst. CPAs, Phila. C. of C. (chmn. small bus. coun. 1977-78, chmn. emeritus 1981-83, bd. dirs. 1977-78, 80-81). Republican. Jewish. Office: Mesirov Gelman Jaffe Cramer & Jamieson 1735 Market St Ste 3901 Philadelphia PA 19103-7503

FRANK, BERNARD, lawyer; b. Wilkes-Barre, Pa., June 11, 1913; s. Abraham and Fanny F.; m. Muriel I. Levy, June 19, 1938; children: Roberta R. Penn, Allan R. PhB, Muhlenberg Coll., Allentown, Pa., 1935, LHD, 1987; JD, U. Pa., 1938; postgrad., NYU, 1940-42. Bar: Pa. 1939. Since practiced in Allentown; asst. U.S. atty. Eastern Dist. Pa., 1950-51; asst. city solicitor Allentown, 1956-60. Author articles on ombudsmen in profl. jours. Vice chmn. B'nai B'rith Nat. Commn. Adult Jewish Edn., 1959-61, chmn., 1961-63; bd. dirs. Muhlenberg Coll., 1987-93. With AUS, 1943-46. Decorated comdr. Order of North Star Sweden; recipient Disting. Service award Internat. Ombudsman Inst., 1980. Mem. ABA (chmn. com. ombudsman 1970-76, vice chmn. com. on pub. advs. and pub. representation adminstrv. law sect. 1984-92), Internat. Bar Assn. (chmn. com. ombudsman 1973-80), Fed. Bar Assn. (chmn. com. ombudsman 1973-80), Pa. Bar Assn., Lehigh Bar Assn., Inter-Am. Bar Assn., World Assn. Lawyers, U.S. Assn. Ombudsmen (hon.), Internat. Ombudsman Inst. (hon. life mem., bd. dirs. 1978-89, pres. 1984-88), Jewish Pub. Soc. Am. (bd. dirs. 1982—, v.p. 1986-

89, 94-98), 94th Inf. Div. (pres. 1953-54). Home: 3203 W Cedar St Allentown PA 18104-3407 Office: 640 Hamilton Mall Allentown PA 18101-2110

FRANK, CHARLES RAPHAEL, JR., financial executive; b. Pitts., May 15, 1937; s. Charles Raphael and Lucille (Briscoe) M.; m. Susan Patricia Backman, Mar. 9, 1963 (div. June 1976); children: Elizabeth Grace, Stephen Raphael; m. Eleanor Sebastian, July 19, 1976; children: Paul Sebastian, Philip Sebastian; stepchildren: Joyce Oxman, Alan Oxman. BS in Math., Rensselaer Poly. Inst., 1959; MA in Econs., Princeton U., 1961, PhD in Econs., 1963. Sr. rsch. fellow East African Inst. Social Rsch. Makerere U. Coll., Kampala, Uganda, 1963-65; asst. prof. econs. Yale U., New Haven, 1965-67; assoc. prof. econs. and internat. affairs Princeton (N.J.) U., 1967-70, prof., 1970-74; assoc. dir. rsch. program econ. devel. Woodrow Wilson Sch., 1967-70, dir., 1970-74; sr. fellow Brookings Inst., 1972-74; mem. policy planning staff U.S. Dept. State, 1974-77, dep. asst. sec. state for econ. and social affairs, 1977-78; v.p. Salomon Bros. Inc., 1978-87; pres. Frank & Co. Inc., 1987-88; v.p. project fin. GE Capital Corp., Stamford, Conn., 1988-97; 1st v.p. European Bank for Reconstrn. and Devel., London, 1997—; ops. rsch. analyst U.S. Steel, summers 1960, 61; cons. Govt. Uganda, 1964, UN Econ. Commn. for Asia and Far East, 1969, IBRD, 1969-72, Korea Devel. Inst., 1973-74, Mathematica, 1967-68, Nat. Conf. Bd., 1969-70, Nat. Bur. Econ. Rsch., 1970-75, Brookings Instn., 1969; mem. rsch. adv. com. AID, 1971-75, cons., Washington, 1966-68, Korea, 1971-73. Author: Production Theory and Indivisible Commodities, 1969, The Sugar Industry in East Africa, 1965, (with Brian Van Arkadie) Economic Accounting and Development Planning, 2d edit., 1969, Debt and the Terms of Aid, 1970, Statistics and Econometrics, 1971, American Jobs and Trade with the Developing Countries, 1973, Foreign Exchange Regimes and Economic Development, The Case of South Korea, 1975, Foreign Trade and Domestic Adjustment, 1976, Income Distribution and Economic Growth in the Less Developed Countries, 1977. Mem. Council Fgn. Relations. Home: 70-72 Cadogan Sq Flat 5 London SW1X 0EA, England Office: European Bank Recon & Devel, One Exchange Sq, London ED2A 2EH, England

FRANK, DAVID ANTHONY, educator; b. Topeka, Kans., Mar. 23, 1955; s. Arthur Martin and Rosemary Boles Frank; m. Marjorie Machie Enseki, July 3, 1988; children: Michael, Justin. BA, Western Wash. U., 1978, MA, 1979; PhD, U. Oreg., 1983. Grad. tchg. fellow Western Wash. U., Bellingham, 1978-79; grad. tchg. fellow U. Oreg., Eugene, 1979-81, instr., 1981-82, asst. prof., 1982-88, assoc. prof., 1988—; cons. U.S. Forest Svc., Eugene, 1993—; expert witness in field, 1994; speech cons. Oreg. Sec. of State, Salem, 1998—. Author: Debating Values, 1993, Creative Speaking, 1994, Lincoln Douglas Debate, 1995; contbr. articles to profl. jours. Co-chair Savage com. on peace U. oreg., 1995—; chmn. bd. dirs. Koinia Ctr., Eugene, 1991-94. Recipient Prof. of Month award Mortar Bd., 1988, 90, Disting. Svc. award N.W. Forensics Conf., 1998. Democrat. Congregationalist. Office: U Oreg Honors Coll Eugene OR 97403

FRANK, DAVID STANLEY, medical diagnostics company executive; b. Bklyn., Dec. 3, 1944; s. Joseph Allen and Jeanne (Holdowsky) F.; m. Mina Freidstern; children: Jeffrey, Marcy. BS, U. Pa., 1966; MS, Cornell U., 1968, PhD, 1971. Rsch. assoc. Eastman Kodak Co., Rochester, N.Y., 1972-81, regional bus. gen. mgr. Asia, Africa, Australia, 1981-90, group product mgr. dispersed testing, 1990-94; dir. bus. devel. Johnson & Johnson, Rochester, N.Y., 1994-97, Ortho-Clin. Diagnostics, Raritan, N.J., 1997—. Inventor in field of in vitro diagnostics. Pres. Hillel Found., Rochester, 1995-96, Congregation Beth Hakneses, Rochester, 1975-79; fin. dir. Hillel Sch., Rochester, 1983-85. Mem. AAAS, Am. Chem. Soc. (bd. dirs. 1979-81, Outstanding Student 1966), Am. Assn. Clin. Chemistry, Licensing Execs. Soc. Democrat. Jewish. Avocation: tennis. Office: Ortho-Clinical Diagnostics 1001 Us Highway 202 Raritan NJ 08869-1424

FRANK, DIETER, technical consultant, retired chemical company executive; b. Erfurt, Thuringia, Germany, May 21, 1930; came to U.S., 1975; s. Karl Hermann and Luise (Metz) F.; m. Edith Anna Laufer, July 19, 1957; children: Martin, Susanne, Beate. DEng, Tech. U., Berlin, 1963. Rsch. chemist Glanzstoff A.G., Obernburg, Federal Republic of Germany, 1965-69, sect. head, 1969-71; assoc. dir. AKZO Corp. Rsch., Obernburg, Federal Republic of Germany, 1971-75; dir. rsch. ARMAK (AKZO), Chgo., 1975-76; v.p. rsch. AKZO Chems., Chgo., 1976-90, ret., 1990; tech. cons., 1991—; mem. indsl. adv. bd. U. Fla., Gainsville, 1987-90. Contbr. to Ullman Ency., 1985, 90, also articles on organic chemistry; patentee chemicals. County vice chmn. Social Dem. Party of Germany, Obernburg, 1968; pres. Soccer Club, Elsenfeld, Federal Republic of Germany, 1974, 75. Mem. AAAS, Sugar Industry Technologists (G.E. Meade award 1986), Indsl. Rsch. Inst. (rep. 1979-90, bd. editors 1981-83). Avocations: woodworking, jazz player. Home and Office: An der Hauptstr 93, 98553 Schleusingen-Gethles Germany

FRANK, EDGAR GERALD, retired financial executive; b. Cin., May 15, 1931; s. Carl F. and Marcella M. F.; m. Joy Hueber, Oct. 30, 1954; children: Thomas, Phillip, Angela, Walter. B.B.A., U. Cin., 1955. Acct. Wm. S. Merrell Co., Cin., 1960-61; asst. sec. Emery Industries, Cin., 1961-66; fin. v.p. Samuel Moore & Co., Aurora, Ohio, 1966-79; v.p. fin. Telex Corp., Tulsa, 1979-88, ret., 1988. Served with USN, 1955-58. Mem. AICPA, Fin. Execs. Inst.

FRANK, ELIZABETH AHLS, art educator, artist; b. Cin., Sept. 27, 1942; d. Edward Henry and Constance Patricia (Barnett) Ahls; m. James Russell Frank, Aug. 10, 1963; children: Richard Scott, Robert Edward. Student, Hiram (Ohio) Coll., 1960-63; BA, U. Denver, 1964; MA, U. South Fla., 1988. Cert. profl. educator, Fla. Remedial reading tchr. Willoughby-Eastlake (Ohio) Schs., 1971-72; elem. tchr., grade level chmn. Lee County Pub. Schs., Ft. Myers, Fla., 1972-79, tchr. art, 1979—, mem. arts coun., long range and model schs. planning coms., 1997-98. Contbg. author Davis Art Edn. Publs., Worcester, Mass. Vol. Mann Performing Arts Hall, Fort Myers, 1986-98, Harborside Convention Ctr., 1991-95; sec. Colonial Acres Homeowners Assn., North Fort Myers, Fla., 1994-99. Mem. NEA, Fla. Art Edn. Assn. (workshop presenter), S.W. Fla. Audubon Soc. (Educator of Yr. 1998), Southwest Fla. Rose Soc., Calusa Nature Ctr., Lee Art Edn. Assn. (founder, pres. 1991-92, Art Educator of Yr. 1991-92), Fla. Tchg. Profession, Tchrs. Assn. Lee County (rep. bd. 1972-99, mem. exec. bd. 1990-91, M.M. Bethune Humanities award 1992), Edison African Violet Soc. (1st v.p. 1997—), Phi Kappa Phi, Phi Delta Kappa, Delta Kappa Gamma (scholar 1988, v.p. 1986-88, pres. 1988-90, sec. 1996-98, state chmn. arts and crafts com. 1997-99). Democrat. Avocations: gardening, camping, boating, arts and crafts, rock collecting. Home: 8236 W Jamestown Cir Fort Myers FL 33917-3602 Office: Suncoast Elem 1858 Suncoast Ln Fort Myers FL 33917-1898

FRANK, ERICA, preventive medicine physician; b. Trenton, N.J., June 17, 1962; m. Randall White, 1990; 1 child, Ridge. MD, Mercer U., 1988. Intern Cleve. Clin., 1988-89; resident in preventive medicine Yale U., New Haven, Conn., 1989-90; fellow in mass media Stanford U., 1990-92; asst. prof. Sch. Medicine Emory U., Atlanta, 1993-99, assoc. prof., 1999—; Co-editor-in-chief Preventive Medicine. Recipient Clinician-Scientist award Am. Heart Assn., 1995-96. Office: Emory U 69 Butler St SE Atlanta GA 30303-3033*

FRANK, EUGENE MAXWELL, bishop; b. Cherryvale, Kans., Dec. 11, 1907; s. Ade W. and Emma W. (Maxwell) F.; m. Wilma A. Sedoris, June 20, 1930; children: Wilmagene Frank Noonan, Gretchen Frank Beal, Susan Frank Parsons, Thomas E. BS, Kans. State Tchrs. Coll., 1930, Garrett Bibl. Inst., 1932; DD, Baker U., 1947; LLD, Central Coll., 1957; DD, Depauw U., 1959, St. Paul Sch. Theology, Methodist, 1962. Ordained to ministry Meth. Ch., 1932; pastor Tonganoxie, Kans., 1932, Americus, Kans., 1933-36, Olathe, Kans., 1936-42, Kansas City, Kans., 1942-48, Topeka, 1948-56; consecrated bishop, 1956; bishop of Mo. St. Louis, 1956-72, Ark. Area, Little Rock, 1972-76; vis. prof. ch. ministry Candler Sch. Theology, Emory U., 1976-79; bishop-in-residence Central United Meth. Ch., Kansas City, Mo., 1979—; pres. Council of Bishops of Meth. Ch., 1968—; mem. bd. global missions, bd. ch. and soc. Mem. Kappa Delta Pi, Pi Kappa Delta, Phi Mu Alpha, Tau Kappa Epsilon. Address: 10000 Wornall Rd Apt 4111 Kansas City MO 64114-4369

FRANK, FRANCINE HARRIET, language educator, linguist; b. Bklyn., Apr. 18, 1931; d. William Myron and Irma (Turteltaub) W.; m. Peter J. Frank, June 13, 1954 (div. 1959). BA magna cum laude, NYU, 1952; MA in Linguistics, Cornell U., 1953; PhD in Spanish Linguistics, U. Ill., 1955. Instr. U. Ill., Urbana, 1955-57; lang. tng. officer Intergovtl. Com. for European Migration, Geneva, 1957-66; from asst. to assoc. prof. Spanish and linguistics SUNY, Albany, 1966-97; prof.; asst. dean coll. arts and sci. SUNY, Albany, 1972-73, dir. linguistics program, 1973-85, assoc. dean coll. humanities and fine arts, 1985-86, acting dean coll. humanities and fine arts, 1986-87, dean coll. humanities and fine arts, 1987-93, prof. women's studies, 1990-97, prof. emerita, 1997—; cons. in field. Co-author: Language and the Sexes, 1984, Language, Gender and professional Writing, 1989; contbr. articles to profl. jours. Pres. Millay Colony for the Arts, Austerlitz, N.Y., 1986—; bd. dirs. Neighborhood Resource Ctr., Albany, 1986—; adv. bd. Capitol Chamber Artists; bd. dirs. Capital Repertary Co., 1989-98. Named Fulbright-Hays prof. Rome, 1971-72, Buenos Aires, 1980. Mem. MLA, Linguistic Soc. Am., Nat. Women's Studies Assn., Fulbright Alumni Assn., Zonta (bd. dirs. 1983-385, 87-89), Phi Beta Kappa. Avocations: travel, art, music. Home: 489 State St Albany NY 12203-1004

FRANK, FREDERICK, investment banker; b. Salt Lake City, May 31, 1932; s. Simon and Suzanne (Seller) F.; m. Mary Ann Nahum (div. 1979); children: Jenny Ann, Laura Kim, Frederick S.; m. Mary Catherine Tanner. BA, Yale U., 1954; MBA, Stanford U., 1958. Chartered fin. analyst. Mng. dir. Smith Barney & Co., N.Y.C., 1958-69; mng. dir. Lehman Bros., N.Y.C., 1969-85, sr. mng. dir., 1985-95, vice chmn., 1995—; bd. dirs. Pharm. Product Devel., Wilmington, N.C., Physicians Computer Network, AXS, Verkeley, Calif., Automated Call Processing, San Francisco, Diagnostic Products, L.A. Chmn. Nat. Genetics Found., N.Y.C., 1985—; trustee Hotchkiss Sch., Lakeville, Conn.; adv. dir. Yale U. Sch. Mgmt.; bd. dirs. Salk Inst., La Jolla, Calif. With U.S. Army, 1954-56. Mem. Chartered Fin. Analysts, N.Y. Soc. Security Analysts. Avocations: skiing, tennis, running. Home: 109 E 91st St New York NY 10128-1601 Office: Lehman Bros Am Express Tower World Fin Ctr New York NY 10285

FRANK, GERALD WENDEL, civic leader, journalist; b. Portland, Oreg., Sept. 21, 1923; s. Aaron Meier and Ruth (Rosenfeld) F. Student, Stanford U., 1941-43, Loyola U., L.A., 1946-47; BA with honors, Cambridge U., 1948, MA, 1953; D Bus. Adminstrn. (hon.), Greenville (Ill.) Coll., 1971; LLD (hon.), Pacific U., 1983. Mgr. Meier & Frank Co., Salem, Oreg., 1955-65; v.p. Meier & Frank Co., Ltd., 1948-65; also bd. dirs.; pres. Gerry's Frankly Speaking, Salem, Oreg., 1996—; co-owner Gerry Frank's Konditorei, Inc., Salem, Oreg., 1982—; bd. dirs. Oreg. Baking Co., World Masters Games 1998, Inc. Author: Where to Find It, Buy It, Eat It in New York, 10 edits., 1980—, Joan and Gerry's Little Black Book of Shopping Secrets, 1991, Friday Surprise, 1995; sr. corres. Northwest Reports, 1992-96; commentator/reporter Morning news shows KPTV, Portland, 1993—. Trustee Lorene Sails Higgins Charitable Trust, 1993—; chief of staff to Sen. Mark O. Hatfield, 1973-92; gen. chmn. Mark Hatfield for U.S. Sen., 1966, 72, 78, 84, 90; mem. Culver Commn. on Reorganization of U.S. Senate, 1975-76; mem. mgmt. com. U.S. Senate, 1978; active Nat. Found. Infantile Paralysis, Arthritis and Rheumatism Found., Portland C. of C., Salem Area C. of C., Sunshine Divsn., Portland Police Res., Portland Area Coun., Cascade Area Coun., Cascade Pacific Coun., Nat. Coun., Boys Scouts Am., Portland Rose Festival Assn., Jr. Achievement, Travelers Aid Soc. Portland, Nat. Mcpl. League, Salem Pub. Libr. Found., Portland United Fund, Marion-Polk Counties United Good Neighbors, Salem Gen. Hosp., Nat. Retail Merchants Assn., Citizens' Conf. for Govtl. Coop., Gov.'s Econ. Devel. Commn., Oreg. Retail Distributors' Inst., Am. Heart Soc., Oreg. Rsch. Assn., Salem 4-H Club, Willamette River Days, Salem YWCA, Willamette U. bd. trustees, League Women Voters, Oreg. Grad. Inst. Sci. & Tech., Portland Met. Futures Unltd., Inc., Marion-Salem Bldg. Study Com., Oreg. Symphony Soc., Am. Legion, Oreg. Coast Aquarium, 1990—, exec. com., U.S. Com. for UNICEF, 1990—, Oreg. High Desert Mus., Salvation Army, Salem Art Assn., Parry Ctr. for Children, St. Vincent Hosp. & Med. Ctr., Oreg. Health Scis. U., OMSI, chair, dir., 1996-97, Oreg. Tourism Coun., chair, 1996—, Oreg. Ind. Colls. Found., AAA of Oreg., Oreg. Garden Found., Oreg. State Bar Ho. Dels., Miss Oreg. Scholarship Program. Recipient numerous awards including Silver Beaver Boy Scouts Am., 1963, Reginald H. Vincent trophy United Good Neighbor of Yr., 1980, Brotherhood Nat. Conf. Christians and Jews, Portland, 1984, Glenn Jackson leadership Willamette U., 1984, Tom Lawson McCall fellowship Pacific U., 1987. Mem. Am. Legion, Elks, Rotary (Paul Harris fellow 1986). Avocations: travel, gourmet dining. Home: 3250 Crestview Dr S Salem OR 97302-5959 Office: Gerry's Frankly Speaking Inc Ste 130 475 Cottage St NE Salem OR 97301-3825 also: PO Box 2225 Salem OR 97308-2225

FRANK, HARVEY, lawyer, author; b. N.Y.C., Aug. 24, 1930; s. Leon and Hannah (Lehr) F.; m. Judith Ellen Lewis, Nov. 29, 1959; 1 child, David L. AB, NYU, 1951, LLM, 1961; JD, Harvard U., 1954. Bar: N.Y. 1954, Md. 1981, Ohio 1982. Ptnr. Hays Feuer Porter & Spanier, N.Y.C., 1963-69, Burns, Summit, Rovins & Feldesman, N.Y.C., 1970-74; prof. law Coll. William and Mary, Williamsburg, Va., 1974-80; adj. prof. Johns Hopkins U., Balt., 1981; ptnr. Benesch Friedlander, Coplan & Aronoff, Cleve., 1982-93, Law Offices of Harvey Frank, Phila., 1993—; sec. Banner Aerospace, 1990-93. Author: The ERC Closely Held Corporation Guide, 1981, 2d edit., 1984; contbr. articles to legal jours. Mem. ABA, Am. Law Inst. Home and Office: Law Offices of Harvey Frank 1215A Waverly Walk Philadelphia PA 19147

FRANK, HOWARD, college dean. BEEE, U. Miamai, 1962; MS, Northwestern U., 1964, PhD, 1965. Prin., owner Contel Information Sys.; dir. info. tech. office Dept. Defense, Washington, 1993-97; dean Robert H. Smith Sch. U. Md., College Park, 1998—; assoc. prof. U. Calif., Berkeley, 1965-70; adj. prof. Wharton Sch. U. Pa., Phila., 1991-93; bd. dirs. Intek Global Corp.; speaker in field. Mem. 6 editl. bds.; contbr. over 190 articles to profl. jours. Recipient Distinguished Svc. medal Sec. Defense. Fellow IEEE (Eric Sumner award). Office: Robert H Smith School Bus Univ Md Van Munching Hall College Park MD 20742

FRANK, ISAIAH, economist, educator; b. N.Y.C., Nov. 7, 1917; s. Henry and Rose (Isserles) F.; m. Ruth Hershfield, Mar. 23, 1941; children: Robert E., Kenneth D. B in Social Sci., CCNY, 1936; MA in Econs., Columbia U., 1938, PhD in Econs., 1960. Rsch. assoc. in econs. Columbia U. Council for Research in Social Scis., 1936-39; tchg. fellow, instr. econs. Amherst Coll., 1939-41; Carnegie fellow Nat. Bur. Econ. Rsch., 1941-42; cons. WPB, 1942; sr. economist OSS, 1942-44; various positions U.S. Dept. State, 1945-63; dir. Office Internat. Trade, 1957-59; dir. Office Internat. Financial and Devel. Affairs, 1961-62, dep. asst. sec. for econ. affairs, 1962-63; William L. Clayton prof. internat. econs. Sch. Advanced Internat. Studies, Johns Hopkins U., 1963—; Mem. Industry-Govt. Iron and Steel Mission to Europe, 1947; adviser U.S. del. Econ. Commn. for Europe, 1948; dep. dir. fgn. resources div. Pres.'s Materials Policy Commn., 1951-52; head U.S. del. Conf. on Dollar Liberalization, OEEC, Paris, 1955-56; chmn. U.S. del. GATT, Geneva, 1958; alt. U.S. rep. Fourth Meeting Devel. Assistance Group, London, 1961; chmn. U.S. del. to prep. com. UN Conf. Trade and Devel., Geneva, 1963—; U.S. rep. Spl. Trade Conf. OAS, Alta Gracia, Argentina, 1964; exec. dir. Pres.'s Commn. on Internat. Trade and Investment Policy, 1970-71; adv. com. UN Trade and Devel. Bd.; dir. internat. econ. studies Com. Econ. Devel.; mem. adv. council Inst. for Latin Am. Integration; mem. adv. com. Inst. Internat. Econs.; cons. World Bank; chmn. adv. com. on internat. investment State Dept.; mem. svcs. policy adv. com. U.S. Trade Rep.; mem. adv. com. on internat. econ. policy U.S. Dept. State. Author: The European Common Market: An Analysis of Commercial Policy, 1960, Foreign Enterprise in Developing Countries, 1980, Finance and Third-World Economic Growth, 1988, Breaking New Ground in U.S. Trade Policy, 1991, U.S. Trade Policy Beyond the Uruguay Round, 1994, U.S. Economic Policy Toward the Asia-Pacific Region, 1997; co-author, editor: The Japanese Economy in International Perspective, 1975; contbr. articles to profl. publs. 1st lt. AUS, 1944-45. Recipient Rockefeller Pub. Svc. award, 1959-60. Mem. Coun. Fgn. Rels., Am. Econ. Assn., Cosmos Club, Phi Beta Kappa. Home: 3102 Hawthorne St NW Washington DC 20008-3539 Office: Johns Hopkins U 1740 Massachusetts Ave NW Washington DC 20036-1903

FRANK, JACOB, lawyer; b. Albany, Apr. 4, 1936; s. Isidore and Sara F.; m. Yoelith Frank, Aug. 26, 1936; children: Eytan, Michael, Adam, Orly. BEE, Rensselaer Poly. Inst., 1957; LLB, Am. U., 1963; postgrad., George Washington U. Coll. Law, 1964-67, NYU Law Sch., 1969-73. Bar: D.C. 1963, Mass. 1979, U.S. Patent Office. V.p., gen. counsel Data Gen. Corp., Westboro, Mass.; chmn. pension com.; adj. prof. of law Suffolk Law Sch., Boston. Home: 16 Cakebread Dr Sudbury MA 01776-1206 Office: Data Gen Corp 4400 Computer Dr Westborough MA 01580-0001*

FRANK, JAMES AARON, magazine editor, author; b. Englewood, N.J., Apr. 13, 1954; s. Reuven and Bernice (Kaplow) F.; m. Belle Gross, Aug. 14, 1977; children: William Moses, Rebecca Ann. BA, Kenyon Coll., 1976. From editorial asst. to assoc. editor Diversion Mag., N.Y.C., 1976-79; sr. editor US Air Mag., N.Y.C., 1979-82; editor Amtrak Express Mag., N.Y.C., 1982-84; exec. editor Golf Mag., N.Y.C., 1984—, now editor; v.p. Golf Mag. Properties. Author: The Golfer's Companion, 1993, Golf Secrets, 1994, Precision Putting, 1998; editor: Golf Magazine's Private Lessons, 1990; co-author, co-editor: Golf in America: The First 100 Years, 1988; co-author: PGA Championship 1916-84, 1984, The Golf Magazine Complete Book of Golf Instruction, 1997, Dave Pelz's Short Game Bible, 1999. Avocation: golf. Office: Golf Magazine Times Mirror Mags 2 Park Ave New York NY 10016-5675

FRANK, JAMES S., automotive executive; b. 1942. BS, Dartmouth Coll.; Masters, Stanford U. With ZF, Inc., 1965, Wheels, Inc., Des Plaines, Ill., 1965; pres. Four Wheels, Inc., Des Plaines, 1965; pres., CEO Frank Consol Enterprises, Des Plaines. Office: Frank Consol Enterprises 666 Garland Pl Des Plaines IL 60016-4725*

FRANK, JOHN, editor; b. Aug. 31, 1912; s. John Ernest and Elizabeth L. (Baughman) F.; m. Ann Canon, July 10, 1945; 1 child, Ralpha Ernest (Skip). AB, Centre Coll., 1935; postgrad., U. Ky., 1940-47, U. Tex., 1948. Radio operator Sta. WDOB, Chattanooga, 1935-38, Sta. WLAP, Lexington, Ky., 1938-40; tchr. Danville (Ky.) H.S., 1940-42, Lincoln Meml., Harrogate, Tenn., 1947-48; ins. agy. Frank Ins. Agy., Danville, 1950-72; owner, editor Danville Examiner, 1979—. Avocations: church work, genealogical studies. Office: Danville Examiner 226 N 2d St Danville KY 40422-1604

FRANK, JOHN LEROY, lawyer, government executive, educator; b. Eau Claire, Wis., Mar. 13, 1952; s. George LeRoy and Frances Elaine (Torgerson) F. BS summa cum laude, U. Wis., Eau Claire, 1974; JD cum laude, U. Wis., Madison, 1977. Bar: Wis. 1977, U.S. Dist. Ct. (we. dist.) Wis. 1977, U.S. Supreme Ct. 1982. Instr. law U. Wis., Madison, 1976-77; assoc. Garvey, Anderson, Kelly & Ryberg, S.C., Eau Claire, 1977-81; legis dir., counsel Congressman Steve Gunderson, Washington, 1981-85, chief of staff, counsel, 1985-89; staff coord. 92 Group, Washington, 1987-89; paralegal instr., program dir. Chippewa Valley Tech. Coll., 1989-93, 97—; pvt. practice Eau Claire, Wis., 1990-93, 97—; counsel, minority cons. House Subcommittee on Livestock, Washington, 1993-95; counsel Congressman Steve Gunderson, Washington, 1993-97; dep. minority counsel House Com. on Agr., Washington, 1993-95, dep. chief counsel, 1995-97; commr. W. Ctrl. Wis. Regional Planning Commn., Eau Claire, 1998—. Named One of Outstanding Young Men in Am., U.S. Jaycees, 1977. Mem. ABA, Fed. Bar Assn., Wis. Bar Assn., U. Wis. Alumni Assn. (outstanding sr. arts & scis. 1974), Phi Delta Phi, Phi Gamma Delta (Durrance award 1978). Republican. Lutheran. Address: 2113 Meadow Ln Eau Claire WI 54701-7965

FRANK, JOHN PAUL, lawyer, author; b. Appleton, Wis., Nov. 10, 1917; s. Julius Paul and Beatrice (Ullman) F.; m. Lorraine Weiss, May 11, 1944; children: John Peter, Gretchen, Karen, Andrew, Nancy. B.A., U. Wis., 1938, M.A., LL.B., 1940; J.S.D., Yale U., 1946; LL.D., Lawrence U., 1981; HHD, Ariz. State U., 1997. Bar: Wis. 1940, D.C. 1966, Ariz. 1954, U.S. Supreme Ct. 1954. Law clk. U.S. Supreme Ct. Justice Hugo L. Black, 1942; asst. to sec. interior, 1943, to atty. gen., 1944-45; asst. prof. law Ind. U., 1946-49; asso. prof. law Yale, 1949-54; vis. lectr. law U. Wash., 1966, U. Ariz., 1967, Ariz. State U., 1969, 72; with firm Covington & Burling, Washington, 1947, Arnold & Porter, Washington, 1948, 53; mem. firm Lewis & Roca, Phoenix, 1954—; Mem. adv. com. civil procedure Jud. Conf. U.S., 1960-70; chmn. U.S. Circuit Judge Nominating Commn.-9th Circuit Panel, South, 1977; mem. exec. com. Adv. Com. on Appellate Justice; mem. Ariz. Commn. Appellate Ct. Appointments, 1974-85; chmn. sr. adv. bd. 9th Cir. Ct. Appeals. Author: Mr. Justice Black, 1949, Cases on Constitutional Law, 1950, Cases on the Constitution, 1951, My Son's Story, 1952, Marble Palace, 1958, Lincoln as a Lawyer, 1961, Justice Daniel Dissenting, 1964, The Warren Court, 1964, American Law: The Case for Radical Reform, 1969, Clement Haynsworth, The Senate and the Supreme Court, 1991; also articles. Dem. precinct committeeman, 1956-86; counsel Ariz. Dem. Com., 1962-67, 79-99. Recipient Lewis F. Powell, Jr. award, Am. Inns of Ct. Found., 1997. Fellow Am. Bar Found.; mem. ABA, Maricopa County Bar Assn., Am. Law Inst. (coun.), Ariz. Club. Home: 5829 E Arcadia Ln Phoenix AZ 85018-3220 Office: Lewis and Roca 40 N Central Ave Ste 1900 Phoenix AZ 85004-4429

FRANK, JOHN V., foundation executive; b. Cleve., Oct. 14, 1936; s. Paul A. and Frances (Halbert) F. Student Babson Coll., 1956-57; BBA, U. Miami-Fla., 1960. Mgmt. trainee Nat. City Bank, Cleve., 1960-62; investment analyst officer First Nat. Bank, Akron, 1962-70, asst. trust officer, 1970-73, trust officer, 1973-80, v.p., trust officer, 1980-81; pres. Summit Capital Mgmt. Co., Akron, 1982—. Treas., Fairlawn Heights Assn., Inc., Akron, 1971—; pres. Ohio Ballet, 1973-74; trustee Howland Meml. Fund, Akron, 1974—; pres., trustee Burton D. Morgan Found., Akron, 1976—; councilman City of Akron, 1978-98; trustee Akron Art Mus., 1976-83, pres., 1979-81; trustee Akron City Hosp. Found., 1980-83, 1992, Summa Health Systems Found., 1992—, The Rectory Sch., 1999—; mem. Coun. on Founds. Com. on Legis. and Regulations, 1990-94; nat. steering com. Coll. Wooster, 1992-96; mem. Akron Charter Rev. Commn., 1980, vice chmn., 1990; mem. fin. & fiscal policy investment subcom. U. Akron, 1996—; mem. 50th anniversary com. UN, Grace Cathedral Ch., San Francisco, 1993-95, St. Paul's Episc. Ch.; bd. overseers Blossom Music Ctr., 1996—; trustee Akron Rural Cemetery, 1994—, The Rectory Sch., Pomfret, Conn., 1999—; pres., trustee Akron Civil War Meml. Soc., 1996—; mem. Akron Emergency Med. Adv. Bd., 1986—. 1st lt. USAR, 1963-69. Mem. Cleve. Soc. Security Analysts, Portage Country Club, Hillsboro Club (Hillsboro Beach, Fla.). Republican. Episcopalian. Avocation: art collecting. Office: Burton D Morgan Found PO Box 1500 Akron OH 44309-1500

FRANK, JOSEPH NATHANIEL, comparative literature educator; b. N.Y.C., Oct. 6, 1918; s. William and Jennie (Garlick) F.; m. Marguerite J. Straus, May 11, 1953; children: Claudine, Isabelle. Student, NYU, 1937-38, U. Wis.-Madison, 1941-42, U. Paris, 1950-51; Ph.D., U. Chgo., 1960. Editor Bur. Nat. Affairs, Washington, 1942-50; spl. researcher Am. Embassy, Paris, 1951-52; lectr. dept. English Princeton U., 1955-56, prof. dept. comparative lit., 1966-83, dir. Christian Gauss Seminars in Criticism, 1966-83, prof. emeritus comparative lit., 1983-85; asst. prof. U. Minn., Mpls., 1958-61; assoc. prof. Rutgers U., 1961-66; vis. mem. Inst. Advanced Study, 1984-87; prof. comparative lit. and Slavic languages and lits. Stanford U., Palo Alto, Calif., 1986; vis. prof. Harvard U., 1965. Author: The Widening Gyre, Crisis and Mastery in Modern Literature, 1963, F.M. Dostoevsky: Seeds of Revolt (1821-1849), 1976, F.M. Dostoevsky: The Years of Ordeal (1850-1859), 1983, Dostoevsky: the Stir of Liberation (1860-1965), 1986, Dostoevsky, The Miraculous Years (1865-1871), 1995, Through the Russian Prism, 1990, The Idea of Spatial Form, 1991; editor: A Primer of Ignorance, 1967; co-editor: Selected Letters of Fyodor Dostoevsky, 1987, Dostoevsky: The Miraculous Years, 1865-1871, 1995; contbr. of numerous articles and reviews to profl. jours. Grantee Am. Council Learned Socs., 1961-62, 64-65, 67-68, 70-71; grantee Rockefeller Found., 1979-80, 83-84; recipient Phi Beta Kappa award, 1977, 96; recipient Nat. Book Critics Circle award, 1984. Elected fellow Am. Acad. Arts Scis.; mem. MLA (James Russell Lowell prize 1977, 87), Am. Assn. Advancement of Slavic Studies, Nat. Acad. Arts and Scis. Address: 78 Pearce Mitchell Pl Stanford CA 94305-8534

FRANK, JUDITH ANN (JANN FRANK), retired entrepreneur, small business owner; b. Fresno, Calif., Feb. 10, 1938; d. Walter R. Frank and Ethel Joan (Klomburg) Brinkerhoff; m. David Rogers, Oct. 1956 (div. June 1973). BA, Calif. State U., Fullerton, 1989, postgrad., 1990-91; postgrad., Chapman U., 1991-93. Vault teller, new accounts, comml. Bank of Am., Fresno, 1956-64; new accounts and note teller Security First Nat. Bank, Fresno, 1965-68; br. bookkeeper, supr. Wells Fargo Bank, Santa Clara and San Jose, Calif., 1968-78; student asst. Fullerton Coll. Career Planning and

Placement Ctr., 1982-83; founder, pres. Distant Drums Native Arts, 1994-97, Jann Frank Enterprises, Placentia, Calif., 1996-98; ret., 1997. Phys. and occupl. intern transitional tng. program for brain injured adults and impaired sr. citizens Rehab. Inst. So. Calif., Orange, 1978-80, vol., 1993; vol. Sr. Citizens Transp., Lunch and Counseling Program, Fullerton, 1981-82; vol. City Wide Disaster Drill, Whittier, Calif., 1987; vol. grad. Evolution of Psychotherapy Conf., Anaheim, Calif., 1990; bd. dirs. Native Am. Inst.; former amb. Placentia (Calif.) C. of C. Recipient Commendation for Vol. Svc. Orange County Coun. Women in C. of C., 1980, Woman of Distinction in Social Scis. award, 1984, Disting. Svc. award Rehab. Inst. So. Calif., Orange, 1993, Key award, 1997; tuition scholarship grantee Chapman U., Orange, 1991. Bd. dirs. Native Am. Inst., mem. Smithsonian Instn., Mus. Am. Indian, Am. Biog. Inst. Rsch. Assn. (lifetime dep. gov.), Order of Internat. Fellowship, Golden Key, Alpha Gamma Sigma, Libr. of Congress (Disting. Leadership award 1996, Internat. Cultural diploma of honor 1996, Twentieth Century Achievement award 1996, Woman of Yr. 1996, Millennium Hall of Fame 1997-98, Internat. Woman of Yr. 1997-98). Avocations: American Indian and other cultural events, reading, travel, music, walking.

FRANK, JUHAN, astrophysicist; b. Dec. 16, 1944. MS, U. Buenos Aires, 1970; PhD, Cambridge U., 1978. Post-doctoral rsch. asst. Astronomy Centre, U. Sussex, Eng., 1977-79; post-doctoral rsch. asst. dept. astronomy U. Leicester, Eng., 1979-82; staff scientist Max-Planck-Institut for Astrophysics, Munich, 1982-89; prof. dept. physics and astronomy La. State U., Baton Rouge, 1990—. E-mail: frank@rouge.phys.lsu.edu. Office: La State Univ 212B Nicholson Hall Baton Rouge LA 70803-4001

FRANK, LAURA JEAN, computer scientist; b. New Rochelle, N.Y., May 21, 1945; d. James Florian and Erma (Guttag) F. BA, U. Vt., 1967; MBA, Iona Coll., New Rochelle, 1971; postgrad. China Inst., N.Y.C., Polytechnic Inst., White Plains, N.Y. With Equitable Life Assurance Soc., N.Y.C., 1967-79, project leader, 1978-79; sr. planning specialist PHH Relocation, Wilton, Conn., 1979-80, project mgr., 1980-83, system mgr., 1983-88, mgr. office tech., 1988-91, founding prof. Homequity U., 1985-91; system's cons., LJF Assocs., 1991-95; sys. mgr. Fiberlux, 1994-98, pjt mgr. New Sub Svcs., 1998—. Editor Stamford First Nighter, bd. dirs. Tri-State Trainers; contbr. articles and featured in profl. jours. Mem. Stamford Hist. Soc., Women in Mgmt., Friends of Stamford Symphony. Home: 20250 Soundview Ave Stamford CT 06902-7123

FRANK, LAWRENCE J., library administrator; b. Detroit, Oct. 9, 1943; s. George A. and Marjorie J. (McConkey) F.; m. Bonnie L. Bonsky, Aug. 4, 1973; children: Alyssa Ann, Nathan D. BA with honors, Western Mich. U., 1976, MA magna cum laude, 1977; AMLS, U. Mich., 1979; cert. pub. adm. advanced mgmt. program, Miami U., Oxford, Ohio, 1983; cert. edn., U. Wis., 1996. Pub. Librs. Profl. cert., N.Y., Librs. Permanent Profl. cert., Mich., Profl. cert., Ky. Libr. intern Ann Arbor (Mich.) Pub. Libr., 1979; reference libr. Toledo-Lucas County Pub. Libr., 1979-81; exec. dir. Amos Meml. Pub. Libr., Sidney, Ohio, 1981-85; dir. Troy (Mich.) Pub. Libr., 1985-86, Boyd County Pub. Libr., Ashland, Ky., 1986-95, St. Clair County Libr., Port Huron, Mich., 1995-99, Onondaga County Pub. Libr., Syracuse, N.Y., 1999—; tchr., missionary The Lang. Inst., Japan Luth. Ch., Tokyo and Niigata, Japan, 1968-71; cons. in libr. design and orgn., Port Huron, 1996-98. Contbr. articles to jours.; author of poems. Bd. dirs. Ky. Coun. on Econ Edn., Ashland, 1986-95; mem. steering com. U. Cin. Children's Hosp., Ashland, 1987-90; active Main St. Port Huron, 1996-98. Named Boss of the Yr., Jaycees, Ashland; Tuition scholar U. Mich., Ann Arbor, 1978-79. Mem. APHA, ALA, Libr. Adminstrn. and Mgmt. Assn., Pub. Libr. Adminstrn., N.Y. Libr. Assn., The Libr. Network (steering com. 1996-98, strategic planning com.). Avocations: wine and art collecting, writing, drawing, hiking, environmental design. Office: Onondaga County Pub Libr The Galleries Syracuse 447 S Salina St Syracuse NY 13202-2494

FRANK, LEONA VEDA, artist; b. Kew Gardens, N.Y., Nov. 23, 1946; d. Edward Elliot and Sylvia Lois (Moskowitz) Kliegman; m. Richard P. Frank, June 15, 1968; children: Hillary Dena, Joshua Eric. BA in Art cum laude, Queens Coll., 1968. Calligrapher, 1970—, fine art painter, 1989—; mem. visual arts com. Westport (Conn.) Arts Ctr., 1992-95. One-person shows include Slater Meml. Mus., Norwich, Conn., 1992, Ctr. for Fin. Studies, Fairfield U., 1993, Design Ctr., Boston, 1994, Westport Arts Ctr., 1994, Picture This Gallery, Westport, 1996; exhibited in group shows Castle Gallery, Coll. New Rochelle, N.Y., 1993, Nan Miller Gallery, Rochester, N.Y., 1994, Met Life Windows Exhbn., N.Y.C., 1994; represented in pub. and corp. collections Hale & Dorr, Boston, Linsco Pvt. Ledger, Boston, Westport schs.; works featured in publs. including Woman's Day Mag., Conn. Artists' Calendar, The William & Mary Rev., Conn. Mag. Recipient Best in Show awards Ridgefield Guild of Artists, 1990, Conn. Artists' Exhbn.-Slater Meml. Mus., 1991. Mem. Conn. Women Artists.

FRANK, LEONARD ARNOLD, physician; b. Phila., Nov. 28, 1935; s. Charles and Rose F.; m. Barbara Balis, Aug. 17, 1958; children: Michael, Brad. BS, Franklin & Marshall Coll., 1957; MD, Hahnemann U., 1961. Intern Phila. Gen. Hosp., 1961-62; resident Bryn Mawr (Pa.) Hosp., 1964-65, Jefferson Med. Coll., Phila., 1965-68; co-chmn. urology Sacred Heart Hosp., Norristown, Pa., 1980-85, Montgomery Hosp., Norristown, Pa., 1980-85; chmn. urology Sacred Heart Hosp., 1985-93; clin. prof. urology Jefferson Med. Coll., 1996—; pres. med. staff Sacred Heart Hosp., 1982-84. Lt. USN, 1962-64. Rsch. grantee Hahnemann Med. Coll., 1960. Mem. AMA, Am. Urologic Assn., Pa. Med. Soc., Urologic Assn. Pa. (pres. 1988-89), Montgomery County Med. Soc., Phila. Urologic Soc. (pres. 1980-81). Avocations: gardening, hiking, skiing, sculpture. Office: Jefferson Med Coll 1025 Walnut St Philadelphia PA 19107

FRANK, LLOYD, lawyer, retired chemical company executive; b. N.Y.C., Aug. 9, 1925; s. Herman and Selma (Lowenstein) F.; m. Beatrice Silverstein, Dec. 26, 1954; children: Margaret Lois, Frederick. B.A., Oberlin Coll., 1947; J.D., Cornell U., 1950. Bar: N.Y. 1950, U.S. Supreme Ct. 1973. Practiced law N.Y.C., 1950—; sr. ptnr, exec. com., chmn. corp. dept. Parker Chapin Flattau & Klimpl LLP; sec., dir. Grow Group, Inc., N.Y.C., 1964-95; bd. dirs. Madison Industries, Inc., N.Y.C., Metro-Tel Corp., Miami, Fla., Pub. Art Fund, Inc., N.Y.C., Park Electrochem. Corp., Lake Success, N.Y., Internat. Longevity Ctr. U.S.A. Ltd.; sec. Esquire Radio & Electronics, Inc., Bklyn.; lectr. Am. Mgmt. Assn., 1967-77, Probe Internat., Inc., 1975-77, Corp. Seminars, Inc., 1968-71. Mem. ABA (com. negotiated acquisitions), Assn. Bar City of N.Y. (com. on internat. environ. law com. on product liability, com. on lawyers in transition, com. on securities law), N.Y. County Lawyers Assn. (com. on corp. law depts.). Home: 25 Central Park W Apt 17Q New York NY 10023-7211 Office: Parker Chapin Flattau & Klimpl LLP Ste 1700 1211 Avenue Of The Americas New York NY 10036-8735

FRANK, MARTIN, physiology educator, health scientist, association executive; b. Chgo., Oct. 22, 1947; s. Edward D. and Ann (Horwitz) F.; m. Cheryl Lynn Motel, Aug. 19, 1970; children: Beth Susan, Eric Lawrence. AB (Evans scholar), U. Ill., 1969, MS, 1971, PhD, 1973. USPHS predoctoral research trainee U. Ill., 1971-73; research assoc. Mich. Cancer Found., Detroit, 1973-74; dept. pharmacology Mich. State U., 1974-75; assoc. prof. physiology George Washington U., 1980—; exec. sec. physiology study sect. div. research grants NIH, Bethesda, Md., 1978-85; exec. dir. Am. Physiol. Soc., Bethesda, 1985—; pres., treas., bd. dirs. Commn. on Profls. in Sci. and Tech., 1986—; mem. internat. adv. panel Galileo found., 1990—, life scis. subcom. NASA Space Sci. and Applications Adv. Com., 1991-94. Editor Physiologist, 1985—; contbr. articles to profl. jours. Vice pres., bd. dirs. Bennington Community Assn., Gaithersburg, Md., 1976-78, 80-81, mem. Gaithersburg City Planning Commn., 1982-85. Nations' Capitol Affiliate Am. Heart Assn. grantee-in-aid, 1975-78. Mem. AAAS, Am. Physiol. Soc., Soc. Gen. Physiologists, Am. Soc. Assn. Execs., Coalition Engring Scientific Soc. Execs., Sigma Xi. Office: Am Physiol Soc 9650 Rockville Pike Bethesda MD 20814-3998

FRANK, MICHAEL SANFORD, dermatologist; b. New Castle, Pa., Nov. 11, 1949; s. Hyman Harry and Cecelia (Grossman) F.; m. Sara Beverly Newman, May 21, 1972; children: Daniel Philip, Amy Carolyn. BS, U. Mich., 1971, MD, 1975. Pres. Georgetown Dermatologists, P.C., Sterling Heights, Mich., 1979—; clin. instr. Wayne State U., Detroit, 1980—. Mem. Am. Acad. Dermatology, Skin Cancer Found., Am. Soc. Dermatological Surgery, AMA, Mich. State Med. Soc., Oakland County Med. Soc., Mich. Dermatology Soc. Office: Georgetown Dermatologists 37300 Dequindre Rd Ste 200 Sterling Heights MI 48310-3597*

FRANK, MICHAEL VICTOR, risk assessment engineer; b. N.Y.C., Sept. 22, 1947; s. David and Bernice (Abrams) F.; m. Jane Griminger, Dec. 21, 1969; children: Jeffrey, Heidi, Heather. BS, UCLA, 1969; MS, Carnegie-Mellon U., 1972; PhD, UCLA, 1978. Registered profl. engr., Calif.; cert. profl. cons. to mgmt., cert. hazard and operability study leader. Engr. Westinghouse Electric Corp., Pitts., 1970-72, Southern Calif. Edison, Los Angeles, 1972-74; lectr. U. Calif., Santa Barbara, 1976-77; task leader General Atomics, San Diego, 1977-81; sr. exec. engr. NUS Corp., San Diego, 1981-85; with Mgmt. Analysis Co., San Diego, 1985-86; sr. cons. PLG, Newport Beach, Calif., 1986-89; pres. Safety Factor Assocs., Inc., Encinitas, Calif., 1989—; tech. dir. risk and reliability studies of NASA facilties, space and launch vehicles, space nuclear power systems and terrestrial nuclear facilities worldwide; risk assessment cons., mem. U.S. Interagy. Nuclear Safety Rev. Panel, NASA hdqrs., NASA Ames Rsch. Ctr.; lectr. on risk assessment at NASA ctrs.; probabilistic risk assessment cons. to U.S. nuclear regulatory commn., ctr. for nuclear waste regulatory analysis and utility co., qualified forensic cons. in product defects and hazards, fires and explosions, safety and reliability; engring. risk mgmt. cons. European Space Agy.; mem. tech. program com. probabilistic safety assessment and mgmt. confs.; risk mgmt. cons. European Space Agy. Contbr. over 60 articles to Reliability Engring. and System Safety, Nuclear Engring. and Design, ASME, others. Mem. ASME, IEEE, Soc. for Risk Analysis, Cons. Round Table, Forensic Cons. Assn. (past pres.), Nat. Bur. Cert. Cons. Avocations: family activities, running, skiing. Office: Ste 16 1410 Vanessa Cir Encinitas CA 92024-2440

FRANK, MIKEL R., art museum manager, artist; b. June 23, 1954. BFA, Md. Inst., 1977; MFA, Pratt Inst., 1983. Stage mgr. dept. concerts and lectrs. Met. Mus. Art, N.Y.C., 1986—. One-person shows include Dean's Gallery, Balt., 1977, Carnegie Recital Lobby, N.Y.C., The Pargot Gallery, Edison, N.J.; group shows include San Francisco Art Inst., 1978, Vered Gallery, East Hampton, N.Y., Robin Hutchins Gallery, Maplewood, N.J., 1986, Burghdorff Cultural Ctr., Maplewood, 1996, Gallery of South Orange, N.J., 1996, RC Fine Arts, Maplewood, 1999. Recipient Hon. Mention, Summit (N.J.) Art Ctr., 1980; Ford Found. grantee Pratt Inst., 1982; grantee Pratt Inst., 1983. E-mail: mikesbrain@msn.com.

FRANK, MYRA LINDEN, consultant; b. Richmond, Va., Oct. 26, 1950; d. J. C. and Myra Teresa (Lanzarone) Frank; m. Timothy Franklin Long (div. Jan. 1981); m. Robert Andrew Hudson (div. 1994). BA, Erskine Coll., 1972; student, Inst. Fin. Edn., 1982-88. Chief activities therapist S.C. Dept. Corrections, Columbia, 1973-75, acting prin., 1975-77, coll. coord., 1977-78; owner, operator Carolina Coast Seafood, Aiken and Beaufort, S.C., 1978-80; from teller to savs. counselor Security Fed. Savs. & Loan, Aiken, 1981-83; customer svc. rep. Bankers 1st Savs. & Loans, Augusta, Ga., 1983-84, mgr. br. adminstrn., 1984-85; coord. automated teller machines, banking officer 1st Fed. Savs. Bank, Brunswick, Ga., 1985-88; ptnr., cons. electronic banking/software devel. RAH Systems, Brunswick, 1988-93; ptnr. specific application computer programming, software tng. Details & More, Greenville, S.C., 1989-90, ptnr. event planning, various mfg. positions and mktg./sales, 1989-91; cons. office and computer svcs. Mauldin, S.C., 1992-93; lectr. S.C. Edn. Tchrs. Assn., Columbia, 1974, S.C. Assn. Social Workers, Columbia, 1975, Bus. and Profl. Women's Club, Columbia, 1978; small bus. owner, distbr. Nuskin product line, 1987-90; ind. mktg. rep. Network 2000/U.S. Spring, 1988-92; computer specialist Top Food Svcs. Carolina, Inc., Duncan, S.C., 1989-90; adminstrv./sales mgr. Custom Catering, Duncan, 1990; cons. Contract Office/Computer Svcs., Greenville, 1992—; Shaklee ind. distbr., 1998—. Book rev. writer A Class Act, Greenville, 1996—; appeared with Aiken Cmty. Theatre, 1981. Bd. dirs. Quest Soc., Greenville, 1992-95; mem. hospice com. Am. Cancer Soc., Augusta, 1981; lectr. St. John's United Meth. Ch., 1981-82, A Class Act, 1998; registrar, treas. Sugar Creek Soccer Club, Greenville, 1996-97. Mem. A Creative Gathering Writers Group, Writer's Roundtable. Democrat. Avocations: writing, reading, travel, study/research exploring the internet. Home and Office: PO Box 333 Mauldin SC 29662-0333

FRANK, PAULA ELIZABETH, nursing educator; b. East Cleveland, Ohio, Oct. 31, 1946; d. Harry and Sarah (Snyder) Dennis; m. Richard T. Frank, Mar. 8, 1969; children: Rebecca J., Laurel A. BS in Nursing, Ohio State U., 1968; MN in Nursing, U. Wash., 1970; PhD, U. Utah, 1982. Dir., instr. N.Mex. State U., Alamogordo, 1975-77; asst. to dean liberal edn. U. Utah, Salt Lake City, 1981-82; asst. prof. Wright State U., Miami Valley Sch. Nursing, Dayton, Ohio, 1983-87; lectr. Coll. Nursing U. N.Mex., Albuquerque, 1990-91; assoc. prof. Ind. State U. Sch. Nursing, Terre Haute, 1994-98, prof., 1998—, prof., chmn. Baccalaureate and Higher Degree Nursing Dept., 1999—; vis. asst. prof. Coll. Nursing U. N.Mex., 1991-94; cons. in continuing edn. Torrejon AB Hosp., 1987-90. Contbr. articles to profl. jours. Vol. ARC programs. Mem. ANA, Nat. League Nurses, Assn. Women's Health Obs. and Neonatal Nursing, Phi Delta Kappa (rsch. rep. 1989-90), Sigma Theta Tau (faculty counselor Gamma Sigma chpt. 1992-94, faculty counselor Lambda Sigma chpt. 1994-96, 1999—, internat. eligibility com. 1996-99, treas. CGEAN 1996-99). Home: 1250 N Pointer St Terre Haute IN 47803-9573

FRANK, RICHARD ASHER, lawyer, health products executive; b. Omaha, Nov. 4, 1936; s. Alexander David and Sarah R. (Katz) F.; m. Susan Marie Kling; children: Brian, Hilary, Alexander, Nicholas. AB, Harvard U., 1958, JD, 1962. Bar: D.C. 1962, U.S. Supreme Ct. Asst. legal advisor U.S. State Dept., Washington, 1962-69; dir. Ctr. Law and Social Policy, Washington, 1970-77; adminstr. NOAA, Washington, 1977-81; ptnr. Wald, Harkrader, Ross, Washington, 1981-87; pres. Population Svcs. Internat., Washington, 1987—; adj. prof. Georgetown Law Sch., 1988—. Editor: The Constitution and the Conduct of Foreign Policy, 1976; contbr. articles to profl. jours. 1st lt. U.S. Army, 1959-66. Mem. Coun. Fgn. Rels., Am. Soc. Internat. Law. Avocations: sailing, tennis. Home: 3405 Lowell St NW Washington DC 20016-5024 Office: Population Svcs Internat 1120 19th St NW Washington DC 20036-3605

FRANK, RICHARD CALHOUN, architect; b. Louisville, May 17, 1930; s. William George and Helen (Calhoun) F.; m. Janet Nickerson, Feb. 12, 1966; children—Richard, Scott, Elizabeth, William, Jennifer, Philip. BArch, U. Mich., 1953. Assoc. archtl. firms Lansing, Mich., 1953-61; pres. Frank & Stein Assocs., Inc., Lansing, 1961-70; prin. Johnson, Johnson & Roy, Ann Arbor, 1971-75; pres. Preservation/Urban Design/Inc., Ann Arbor and Washington, 1975-84; pvt. practice Saline and Gregory, Mich., 1985—; hist. preservation counsel Smith Group/Archs. Four, Ann Arbor, 1997—. Life trustee Hist. Soc. Mich. Fellow AIA (gold medal Mich. 1992); mem. Nat. Trust for Historic Preservation (trustee emeritus), Victorian Soc. Am. (v.p.). Home and Office: 7172 Glencoe Dr Gregory MI 48137-9657

FRANK, RICHARD SANFORD, retired magazine editor; b. Paterson, N.J., July 28, 1931; s. David and Shirley (Dwoskin) F.; m. Margaret Schwartz, June 30, 1957; children: Daniel, Peter. B.A., Syracuse U., 1953; M.A., U. Chgo., 1956. Reporter Balt. Evening Sun, 1957-64, Phila. Bull., 1965-71; asst. to mayor City of Balt., 1964-65; reporter Nat. Jour., Washington, 1971-72, editor, 1972-76, editor-in-chief, 1976-97. Served with U.S. Army, 1953-55. Mem. Am. Soc. Mag. Editors. Home: 5111 Wessling Ln Bethesda MD 20814-1232

FRANK, ROBERT ALLEN, advertising executive; b. Albany, N.Y., Sept. 26, 1932; s. Edward and Marian (Kostelanetz) F.; m. Cynthia Tull, Aug., 1984; children: David, Chelsea, Alison. B.A., Colby Coll., 1954; MBA, Amos Tuck Sch. Bus. Adminstrn., Dartmouth Coll., 1958. Cost control adminstr. ABC-TV, N.Y.C., 1958-59; corp. auditor CBS, Inc., N.Y.C., 1959-60, TV sales svc. account exec., 1961, account exec. radio network sales, 1962-69; exec. v.p., co-founder SFM Media Corp., N.Y.C., 1969—, pres. Media Svc. div., 1981; pres., CEO SFM Media LLC, N.Y.C., 1998—. Radio-TV cons. Nat. Kidney Fund., 1974; active radio TV for various polit. campaigns including Robert Kennedy for Senator, 1964, Richard Nixon for Pres., 1972, Ford for Pres., 1976, Bush for Pres., 1980, Reagan for Pres., 1980, Du Pont for Pres., 1988; mem. Leadership Coun. Nat Rep. Congl. Com., Rep. Nat. Com., Pres.' Club, 1984-88, Rep. Nat. Senatorial Com. Inner Circle, 1985-88, Citizens for Rep. Pres. Com., 1984-88; trustee Nat. Child Labor Com., 1984-96, vice chmn., 1994-96; trustee Myasthenia Gravis Found., 1984-93. Served to capt. USAF, 1954-56. Mem. Internat. Radio-TV Soc., Amos Tuck Alumni Assn. N.Y. (pres. 1976-77, dir. 1979), Dartmouth Club (N.Y.C.), Pi Gamma Mu. Home: 35 Lounsbury Rd Ridgefield CT 06877-4710 Office: SFM Media Corp 1180 Ave Of The Americas New York NY 10036-8401

FRANK, ROBERT DONALD, flight nurse; b. Elyria, Ohio, Nov. 7, 1959; s. Donald Edward and Janet Ann (Clement) F.; m. Donna Jean Dyer, July 22, 1995; 1 child, Robert Donald II. BS in Biology, U. Akron, 1983, BSN, 1986. RN, Ohio, CCRN, CEN, CFRN, ENPC-I, TNCC-I. Staff nurse burn ICU MetroHealth Med. Ctr., Cleve., 1986-88, staff nurse emergency dept., 1988-93, flight nurse MetroLife Flight, 1993—. Com. mem. Citizens of North Ridgeville (Ohio) for Paramedics, 1993, 94. Mem. AACN, Am. Burn Assn., Nat. Flight Nurses Assn., Emergency Nurses Assn. (state coun. mem., pres. Greater Cleve. chpt. 1993, treas. Ohio chpt. 1994-95). Office: MetroHealth Med Ctr MetroLife Flight 2500 Metrohealth Dr Cleveland OH 44109-1900

FRANK, ROBERT E., artist; b. Oct. 29, 1931. BA, U. Cin., 1956. Comml. artist Ohio, 1951-90; landscape painter Fla., 1990—. E-mail: rainbow-send@webtv.net. Address: 4004 Acoma Dr Ormond Beach FL 32174-9327

FRANK, ROBERT LOUIS, lawyer; b. Balt., Mar. 26, 1958; s. Louis Jr. and Beryl (Oppenheimer) F.; m. Carolyn Moses; children: Robert Louis Jr., Michael David, Cameron Alexander, Victoria Rochelle. BSEE, Duke U., 1980; JD, U. Md., 1983. Bar: Md. 1983. Assoc. Belsky & Akman, Towson, Md., 1984-85; pvt. practice Reisterstown, Md., 1985; ptnr. Blitz Frank & Blitz, Owings Mills, Md., 1986-92, Needle, Montague & Frank, P.C., 1992-94; mem. Md. Ho. Dels., Annapolis, 1994-98; pvt. practice, 1994—; vice-chair sci. and tech. subcom. Pres. Pikesville (Md.) Recreation Parks Bd., 1988, Pikesville Baseball, 1984-86; bd. dirs. Soldier's Delight Conservation, Inc. Mem. ABA, Md. State Bar Assn. (bd. govs. 1987-88, chmn. gen. practice sect. 1987-88), Balt. County Bar Assn., Balt. City Bar Assn., Psi Upsilon (scholarship 1978). Democrat. Home: 15 Sunnyking Dr Reisterstown MD 21136-6143

FRANK, ROBERT WORTH, JR., English language educator; b. Logansport, Ind., Apr. 8, 1914; s. Robert Worth and Grace Alice (Haun) F.; m. Gladys Martine Loeb, May 11, 1940 (dec. Mar. 1994); children: Thaisa, Elizabeth Ann. A.B., Wabash (Ind.) Coll., 1934; M.A., Columbia U., 1939; Ph.D., Yale U., 1948; DLitt in Humanities (hon.), Wabash Coll., 1997. Instr. English Lafayette Coll., Easton, Pa., 1937-39, U. Rochester (N.Y.), 1940-42, Princeton U., 1942-44, Northwestern U., 1944-48; asst. prof., then assoc. prof. Ill. Inst. Tech., 1948-58; prof. English Pa. State U., 1958-79, head dept., 1975-79, emeritus, 1979—; O'Connor prof. lit. Colgate U., 1980, 85; Charles Rahter Meml. lectr., Susquehanna U., 1977, 91. Author: Piers Plowman and the Scheme of Salvation, 2d edit, 1969, The Responsible Man: The Insights of the Humanities, rev. edit, 1965, The Critical Question, 1964, Chaucer and the Legend of Good Women, 1973; editor The Chaucer Rev., 1966—; mem. editorial bd. Revised Chaucer Analogues, 1988—. Fellow Am. Coun. Learned Socs., 1951-52, 60-61, Fund Advancement Edn., 1955-56, Guggenheim Found., 1970-71, assoc. fellow Clare Hall, Cambridge (Eng.) U., 1971, 76, vis. fellow, 1972-73. Mem. Mediaeval Acad. Am., MLA, New Chaucer Soc. (trustee 1980-84, pres. 1986-88). Democrat. Club: Lit. (State College, Pa.). Home: 749 W Hamilton Ave State College PA 16801-4110 Office: 116 Burrowes Pa State Univ University Park PA 16802 also: Chaucer Rev Pa State U Press Barbara Bldg 820 N University Dr Ste C University Park PA 16802-1012

FRANK, ROBERTA, English language educator; b. N.Y.C., Nov. 9, 1941; d. Norman Berton and Doris (Birnbaum) F.; m. Walter André Goffart, Dec. 31, 1978. BA, NYU, 1962; MA, Harvard U., 1964, PhD, 1968. Asst. prof. U. Toronto, Ont., Can., 1968-73, assoc. prof., 1973-78, prof. English, 1978—, univ. prof., 1995—, dir. grad. studies dept. English, 1980-85, dir. Ctr. for Medieval Studies, 1994—; mem. bus. bd. U. Toronto Press. Author: Old Norse Court Poetry, 1978; also articles; co-editor: Computers and Old English Concordances, 1970, A Plan for the Dictionary of Old English, 1973; gen. editor: Toronto Old English Series, 1976—; publs. of Dictionary of Old English, 1984—. Recipient Guggenheim award, 1985; Bowdoin prize humanities Harvard U., 1968. Fellow Medieval Acad. Am. (councillor 1981-84, Elliott prize 1972), Royal Soc. Can.; mem. Internat. Soc. Anglo-Saxonists (pres. 1985-87), MLA (mem. Old English exec. com. 1974-78, 95—). Home: 171 Lowther Ave, Toronto, ON Canada M5R 1E6 Office: U Toronto Ctr Medieval Studies, 39 Queens Park Crescent E, Toronto, ON Canada M5S 2C3

FRANK, RONALD EDWARD, marketing educator; b. Chgo., Sept. 15, 1933; s. Raymond and Ethel (Lundquist) F.; m. Iris Donner, June 18, 1958; children: Linda, Lauren, Kimberly. BSBA, Northwestern U., 1955, MBA, 1957; PhD, U. Chgo., 1960. Instr. bus. statistics Northwestern U., Evanston, Ill., 1956-57; asst. prof. bus. adminstrn. Harvard U., Boston, 1960-63, Stanford U., 1963-65; assoc. prof. mktg. Wharton Sch., U. Pa., 1965-68, prof., 1968-84, chmn. dept. mktg., 1971-74, vice dean, dir. rsch. and PhD programs, 1974-76, assoc. dean, 1981-83; dean, prof. mktg. Krannert Grad. Sch. Mgmt., Purdue U., 1984-89; dean, Asa Griggs Candler prof. mktg. Goizueta Bus. Sch. Emory U., Atlanta, 1989-98, dean, Asa Griggs Candler prof. mktg. emeritus, 1999—; bd. dirs. Lafayette (Ind.) Life Ins. Co., The MAC Group, Home Hosp., Lafayette; cornerstone rsch. cons. to industry; mem. strategic issues com. Am. Assembly Collegiate Schs. of Bus., 1988-92, bd. dirs., 1992-96, chmn. audit com., 1993-94, mem. strategic planning and ops. com., 1994-95; chmn. Orgn. for the Future Task Force, 1996-97. Author: (with Massy and Kuehn) Quantitative Techniques in Marketing Analysis, 1962, (with Matthews, Buzzell and Levitt) Marketing: an Introductory Analysis, 1964, (with William Massy) Computer Programs for the Analysis of Consumer Panel Data, 1964, An Econometric Approach to a Marketing Decision Model, 1971, (with Paul Green) Manager's Guide to Marketing Research, 1967, Quantative Methods in Marketing, 1967, (with Massy and Lodahl) Purchasing Behavior and Personal Attributes, 1968, (with Massy and Wind) Market Segmentation, 1972, (with Marshall Greenberg) Audience Segmentation Analysis for Public Television Program Development, Evaluation and Promotion, 1976, The Public's Use of Television, 1980, Audiences for Public Television, 1982. Bd. dirs., fin. com. Home Hosp. of Lafayette, 1985-89; bd. dirs. The Washington Campus, 1984-89, 95-98. Recipient pub. TV rsch. grants John and Mary R. Markle Found., 1975-82. Mem. Am. Mktg. Assn. (dir. 1968-70, v.p. mktg. edn. 1972-73), Inst. Mgmt. Sci., Assn. Consumer Rsch. Home and Office: Westfield Sq 6 Downing Ln Decatur GA 30033-1403

FRANK, RONALD RAY, elementary school educator; b. Vernonia, Oreg., Sept. 24, 1948; s. E.R. and Frances (John) F.; m. Debra Holland, June 11, 1977; children: Jennifer Nicole, Jeffrey Scott. BA, N.W. Nazarene Coll., 1971; MEd, Seattle Pacific U., 1982, postgrad., 1984. Cert. continuing elem./secondary educator, ednl. staff assoc. reading resource, elem. prin., Wash. 6th grade tchr. Warrenton (Oreg.) Grade Sch., 1975-77; 4th grade tchr. Seattle Christian Sch., 1977-78, 6th grade tchr., 1978-84; 4th grade tchr. Kent (Wash.) Sch. Dist. 415, 1984-85, 6th grade tchr., 1985—; lectr. Seattle Pacific U. summer writing camp, Whidby Island, Wash., 1981-83, Seattle Pacific U. Young Authors conf., Seattle, 1982-84; adj. prof. City U., Mercer Island, Wash., 1990—, Seattle Pacific U., 1990—. Day camp dir. Kentview Christian Sch., Kent, 1985-86; bd. dirs. Church of the Nazarene, Kent, 1985, Sunday sch. tchr. With USAF, 1971-75. Co-recipient Outstanding Contbn. award, Internat. Reading Assn., 1986. Mem. Nat. Coun. Tchrs. English. Republican. Avocations: camping, sports activist, fishing, gardening. Home: 18633 110th Pl SE Renton WA 98055-7140

FRANK, RONALD WILLIAM, lawyer, financier; b. Greensburg, Pa., Mar. 11, 1947; s. William John and Louise (Mautino) F.; m. Marsha Ann Kolesar, Aug. 30, 1969. BSChemE, Carnegie-Mellon U., 1969; JD, Duke U., 1972. Bar: Pa. 1972. Ptnr. Buchanan Ingersoll P.C., Pitts., 1972-93, Babst, Calland, Clements & Zomnir, P.C., Pitts., 1993—; mng. dir. Morgan Franklin & Co., 1994—; bd. dirs. Analytical Network Design, Inc., Morgan Franklin & Co. Contbr. articles to profl. jours. Chmn. Nat. Fund Raising Com., Carnegie-Mellon U., Pitts., 1983-88; mem. exec. com. Andrew Carnegie Soc., Pitts., 1983-92; mem. bd. visitors sch. law Duke U., Durham, N.C. Mem. ABA, Pa. Bar Assn. (coun., corp. sec. 1982-85, chmn. Internat. and Comparative law sect. 1992—), Allegheny County Bar Assn., Internat. Bar Assn.,

Duquesne Club, Shannopin Country Club. Avocations: golf, skiing, computers, amateur radio. Home: 1675 Gloucester Ct Sewickley PA 15143-8518 Office: Babst Calland Clements & Zomnir PC 2 Gateway Ctr Pittsburgh PA 15222-1402

FRANK, RUBY MERINDA, employment agency executive; b. McClusky, N.D., June 28, 1920; d. John J. and Olise (Stromme) Hanson; m. Robert G. Frank, Jan. 14, 1944 (dec. 1973); children: Gary Frank, Craig. student Coll. Mankato, Minn., Aurora (Ill.) U. Home: 415 Dunham Place Commons Saint Charles IL 60174-1421 Office: Arcada Theater Bldg 12 S 1st Ave Saint Charles IL 60174-1947

FRANK, STANLEY DONALD, publishing company executive; b. N.Y.C., June 30, 1932; s. Arthur and Jessie (Schwartz) F.; m. Sheila Rose, Dec. 25, 1958; children: Bradley Scott, Tracy Lynne. BS, CCNY, 1953, MS, 1956; EdD, Columbia U., 1961. Counselor N.Y.C. Pub. Schs., 1955-61; dir. pupil pers. svcs. San Diego County Dept. Edn., 1959-61; dir. mktg. Sci. Rsch. Assocs. subs. IBM, Chgo., 1961-68, v.p. mktg. and ops., 1968-73; pres. Holt, Rinehart & Winston, Inc. subs. CBS, N.Y.C., 1974-77, CBS Ednl. Pub. Div., 1975-78; exec. v.p., chief oper. officer CBS Pub. Group, 1978-80, pres., 1980-84; pres. Britannica Learning Corp., Chgo., 1985-90; exec. v.p. Ency. Britannica, Inc., 1985-93; pres. Comptons Multi Media Pub. Group, Inc., Chgo., 1991—; chmn. bd. dirs. Am. Learning Corp., 1985—; pres., CEO Ctr. for the Assessment of Human Potenial Inc., Boca Raton, Fla., 1994—; mng. ptnr. New Media Ventures, Boca Raton, 1995; bd. dirs. Childcraft Ednl. Corp., Designware, Inc. Mem. Bd. Edn. Dist. 67, Niles, Ill., 1972-73; mem. council Rockefeller U. Served with AUS, 1953-55. Andrew Wellington Cordier fellow Columbia U. Sch. Internat. Affairs. Mem. Am. Psychol. Assn., Phi Delta Kappa. Office: Ctr Assessment Human Potential Inc 5047 Suffolk Dr Boca Raton FL 33496-1654

FRANK, STEPHEN IRA, political science educator; b. Seattle, Oct. 14, 1942; s. Nancy Ann (Schwartz) Frank; m. Barbara Ann Covey; 1 child, Thomas Aaron. BS in Edn., History and Polit. Sci., Cen. Mich. U., 1966, MA in Polit. Sci., 1969; PhD in Polit. Sci., Wash. State U., Pullman, 1976. Tchr. social sci. Clarkston (Mich.) High Sch., 1967-69; instr. in polit. sci. Gogebec Community Coll., Ironwood, Mich., 1967-69, Lamar U., Beaumont, Tex., 1975-76; prof. polit. sci. N.E. La. U., Monroe, La., 1976-78, St. Cloud (Minn.) State U., 1978—; co-dir., founder St. Cloud State U. Survey. Contbr. articles to profl. jours. Mem. Am. Polit. Sci. Assn., Am. Assn. Pub. Opinion, Nat. Assn. Prelaw Advisors, Midwest Prelaw Advisors Assn. (bd. dirs.), St. Cloud State U. Faculty Assn. (pres. 1993-94), Phi Kappa Delta. Avocations: gardening, walking, reading. Office: St Cloud State U Dept Polit Sci 319 Brown Hall Saint Cloud MN 56301-4444

FRANK, STEVEN NEIL, chemist; b. Red Oak, Iowa, Feb. 15, 1947; s. Robert Joseph and Joyce (Erickson) F.; m. Carol Bert Femmer, Jan. 4, 1975. BS, Colo. State U., 1969; PhD, Calif. Inst. Tech., 1974. Sr. mem. tech. staff, solar energy project Tex. Instruments, Dallas, mgr. fuel cell devel., 1980-83, mgr. charge coupled imagers, 1983-86, mgr. wafer fabrication, focal plane array, 1986-88, mfg. mgr., focal plane array, 1988-90, mgr. focal plane array assembly and testing, 1990-91, mgr. uncooled IR imaging, 1990—. Author: (with others) Laboratory Techniques in Electro-Analytical Chem, 1996; referee Jour. Applied Physics, 1977—, Jour. Phys. Chemistry, 1977—; contbr. articles to profl. jours. Robert A. Welch fellow U. Tex., 1974-77. Fellow Am. Inst. Chemists; mem. AAAS, Am. Chem. Soc., Electrochem. Soc. Achievements include 19 patents and numerous papers and presentations. Home: 471 Hackberry Dr Mc Kinney TX 75069-1569 Office: Raytheon Co MS 37 PO Box 660246 Dallas TX 75266-0246

FRANK, STUART, cardiologist; b. N.Y.C., Dec. 25, 1934; s. Henry and Kitty (Sternberg) F.; m. Nanchen O'Brien, Aug. 1976 (div. Feb. 1980); children: Rachel Arthur, Sebastian Noah; m. Amber Barnhart, June 22, 1982; children: Amelia Elizabeth, Abigail Kitty, Jessica Cole. BS in Chemistry, MIT, 1956; MD, NYU, 1960. Diplomate Am. Bd. Internal Medicine, Am. Bd. Cardiovascular Disease. Intern and resident in internal medicine Yale U. New Haven Hosp., 1960-64; postdoctoral fellow Inst. Cardiology, London, 1964-65, Nat. Heart Inst., Bethesda, Md., 1965-67; chief cardiology Kaiser Permanente Med. Ctr., San Francisco, 1967-77; assoc. prof. dept. medicine So. Ill. U., Springfield, 1977-86, chief div. cardiology, 1977-90, asst. chmn. dept. medicine, 1981-88, prof. dept. medicine, 1986—, dean of students, 1990-95. Author: The People's Handbook of Medical Care, 1972; contbr. numerous articles to profl. jours. Recipient Nellie Westerman prize Am. Fedn. Clin. Research, 1986. Fellow ACP, Am. Coll. Cardiology, Am. Coll. Chest Physicians, Am. Heart Assn. (council clin. cardiology), Laennec Soc. Office: So Ill Univ Medicine Dept Cardiology PO Box 19230 Springfield IL 62794-9230

FRANK, THEODORE DAVID, lawyer; b. Bklyn., Apr. 1, 1941; s. Paul and Bessie (Frank) F.; m. Louise Quinby Gorrell, Oct. 19, 1969; chilren: Carolyln Quinby, Rachel Jackson. BS in Math., Rensselaer Polytech. Inst., 1963; LLB, U. Tex., 1966; LLM, Harvard U., 1969. Bar: Tex. 1966, D.C. 1969, U.S. Ct. Appeals (1st cir. and 2d cir.) 1977, U.S. Ct. Appeals (5th and 9th cir.) 1980, U.S. Ct. Appeals (3rd cir. and 11th cir.) 1981, U.S. Ct. Appeals (D.C. cir.) 1970. Law clk. to Hon. Walter P. Gewin U.S. Cir. Ct., 5th cir., Tuscaloosa, Ala., 1966-67; faculty asst. for Ames Competition Harvard Law Sch., Cambridge, Mass., 1967-69; assoc. Arent, Fox, Kintner, Plotkin & Kahn, Washington, 1969-75, ptnr., 1976-97; ptnr. Arent & Porter, Washington, 1997—; mem. hearing com. bd. profl. responsibility D.C. Bar, 1997—. Chair zoning and tax Springfield Civic Assn., Bethesda, Md., 1989-97. Mem. ABA, Fed. Comm. Bar Assn. (exec. com. 1996-98). Jewish. Avocations: woodworking, bike riding. Office: Arent & Porter 555 12th St NW Washington DC 20004-1200

FRANK, VICTOR ROBERT, electrical engineer; b. Grand Rapids, Mich., Dec. 21, 1937; s. Victor Lambert Leo and Lillian Lorraine (Krueger) F.; m. Katsuko Miyazato, May, 1963; children: Mary, Arthur. AS, Weber Jr. Coll., Ogden, Utah, 1957; student, Stanford Univ., 1960-63; BSEE, Utah State Univ., 1959, MSEE, 1960. Electronic technician Douglas Aircraft, Santa Monica, Calif., 1957, Hughes Aircraft, Culver City, Calif., 1958; physicist Nat. Bur. Standards, Boulder, 1959-60; rsch. assoc. Stanford (Calif.) Univ., 1960-70; sr. rsch. engr. SRI Internat., Menlo Park, Calif., 1970—. With Calif. Army Res. Nat. Guard, 1968. Republican. Lutheran. Avocations: amateur radio. Home: 12450 Skyline Blvd Woodside CA 94062-4554

FRANK, WILLIAM EDWARD, JR., executive recruitment company executive; b. Pitts., Aug. 28, 1943; s. William Edward and Grace (Hankey) F.; m. Lesley Ann Austin, July 22, 1992; children: William John, Jorell. BS in English, Slippery Rock U., 1965. Corp. employment mgr. Wometco Enterprises, Inc., Miami, Fla., 1967-71; v.p. human resources ITT Community Devel. Corp., Miami, 1971-79; ptnr. TASA, Inc., Coral Gables, Fla., 1979-80; pres., ceo The Curtiss Group, Inc., Boca Raton, Fla., 1980—. Bd. dirs. IIC Ptnrs.; mem. pres.'s adv. coun. Slippery Rock U. Mem. Boca Grove Country Club, Boca Raton Premier Club. Avocations: golf, boating, baseball. Home: 7859 Mandarin Dr Boca Raton FL 33433-7427 Office: The Curtiss Group No Trust Plz 301 Yamato Rd Ste 2112 Boca Raton FL 33431-4929

FRANK, WILLIAM FIELDING, computer systems design executive, consultant; b. N.Y.C., Oct. 27, 1944; s. Karl Frederick and Margaret Ruth (Denisson) F.; m. Linda Carol Hainfield, Dec. 20, 1965 (div. 1972); children: Aaron, Tobin. BA, Middlebury Coll., 1966; MA, U. Chgo., 1969; PhD, U. Pa., 1976. Assoc. prof. Oreg. State U., Corvallis, 1969-79; mem. tech. staff Bell Labs., Whippany, N.J., 1979-81; pres. Enterprise Engring. Assts. Inc., Warren, Vt., 1982—; vis. scholar MIT, Cambridge, 1981-85; cons. Citibank, 1982—, AT&T, 1984, N.Y. Times, 1985, Bank of Am., 1985, State of Calif., 1986—, Digital Equipment Corp., 1987-89, Soviet Ministry of Trade, 1990, Bankers Trust, 1991, Fidelity Investments, 1993—, Reuters, 1996, Ameritech, 1996, NEC, 1998—. *EEA, the firm Dr. Frank founded in 1982, is a systems engineering firm devoted to business process engineering and technology planning, serving international banks, institutional investors, investment banks, electronic commerce participants, and their technology vendors. Dr. Frank's purpose is to increase the effectiveness of his client's technology through improved quality, reliability, flexibility, integration, and reuse. EEA's commitment to excellence results in long-term relationships some as long as 15 years, and an almost 100% success rate for EEA directed client projects.* Contbr. articles to profl. jours. Rsch. grantee NSF, 1971, 77, NEH, 1976, 81. Mem. Assn. for Computing Machinery, Computer Soc. IEEE. Republican. Congregationalist. Achievements include pioneering of object-oriented enterprise modelling and research in business rule driven software design. Office: EEA 53-102 E Shearwater Ct Jersey City NJ 07305

FRANKE, LINDA FREDERICK, lawyer; b. Mankato, Minn., Aug. 28, 1947; d. Cletus and Valeria (Haefner) Frederick; m. Willis L. Franke, Dec. 17, 1966; children: Paul W., Gregory J. BA, U. Mo., 1981, JD, 1984. Bar: Mo. 1985, U.S. Dist. Ct. (we. dist.) Mo. 1985. Rsch. assoc. Koenigsdorf, Kusnetzky and Wyrsch, Kansas City, Mo., 1984-85; asst. gen. counsel dept. revenue State of Mo., Independence, 1985-86; claims rep. workers' compensation Cigna Ins. Co., Overland Park, Kans., 1986-87; sr. claims rep. workers' compensation Gulf Ins. Co., Kansas City, Mo., 1987-88; worker's compensation atty. Fireman's Fund Ins. Co., Kansas City, 1988—; mem. Mo. Worker's Compensation Com. U. Mo. scholar, 1980, 81. Mem. Platte County Bar Assn., Kansas City Met. Bar Assn. (adv. bd. workers' compensation com.). Home: 8117 NW Eastside Dr Weatherby Lake MO 64152 Office: Bren Przybeck & Stotler 1100 Walnut Kansas City MO 64105

FRANKE, RICHARD JAMES, retired investment banker; b. Springfield, Ill., June 23, 1931; s. William George and Frances Marie (Brennan) F. BA, Yale U., 1953; MBA, Harvard U., 1957. With John Nuveen & Co., Chgo., 1957-96, v.p., 1965-69, exec. v.p., 1969-74, chief adminstrv. officer, 1970-74, pres., 1974-89, CEO, 1974-96, chmn., 1988-96, also dir., chmn., CEO emeritus, 1996—; vice chmn. Yale Corp., 1987-94, chmn., 1994—. Chmn. investment com. Yale U.; mem. Pres.'s Com. on the Arts and Humanities; trustee Chgo. Symphony Orch.; trustee U. Chgo.; bd. dirs. Lyric Opera, Newberry Libr. 1st lt. U.S. Army, 1953-55. Office: # 300 400 N Michigan Ave Ste 300 Chicago IL 60611-4130*

FRANKE, THOMAS, investment company executive. Pres. Raymond James & Assocs., St. Petersburg, Fla. Office: Raymond James & Assocs 880 Carillon Pkwy Saint Petersburg FL 33716*

FRANKE, WAYNE THOMAS, retired government affairs director, consultant; b. San Angelo, Tex., June 23, 1950; s. Bernard Raymond and Henrietta Elizabeth (Kozelsky) F.; 1 child, Mauri Jane. BBA in Gen. Bus., Angelo State U., 1972. Adminstrv. clk. Gen. Telephone Co. of the S.W., San Angelo, 1968-72; comm. cons. Gen. Telephone Co. of the S.W., Irving, Tex., 1972-75; asst. govt. affairs mgr. Gen. Telephone Co. of the S.W., San Angelo, 1975-78; govt. affairs mgr. Gen. Telephone Co. of the S.W., Austin, Tex., 1976-86; govt. affairs dir. Gen. Telephone Co. of the S.W., Austin, 1986-98; owner MJWT Cons., Austin, 1998—; legis. affairs com. Tex. Indsl. Devel. Council, College Station, 1977-84, chmn., Austin, 1981-83; mem. energy and awards coms., 1978-79; mem. U.S. Speaker Jim Wright's Diplomatic Mission to Moscow, 1987. Fundraiser Boy Scouts Am., Austin, 1987-88; loaned exec. Tarrant County United Way, 1973-74; issues mgmt. adv. coun. North Tex. Commn., Dallas, 1985-87; program chmn. John Ben Shepperd Leadership Forum, Odessa, Tex., 1986, chmn., Austin, 1987, John Ben Shepperd Alumni Forum, 1988; mem. John Ben Shepperd Governing Bd., 1990-91, chmn. fin., 1990-91, fin. com. 1990-92, adv. bd., 1991-93, vice-chmn. John Ben Shepperd Found., 1997-98, chmn., 1998—; corp. co-chmn. drive United Cerebral Palsy Assn., Austin area, 1990-96; mem. Hys a Country Oaks Archtl. Control & Protection Com., 1993-96; steering com., fundraising Travis County Assn. Retarded Citizens; trustee West Tex. Boy's Ranch Found., 1995—; chmn. Tex. Statehood Sesquicentennial Program, 1996; bd. dirs. Angelo State U. Ex-Students Assn. Recipient External Team Excellence award GTE, 1992-93, Strive for Excellence award, 1992; named Lobbyist of the Year for GTE Corp., 1987, 91, 1989 Disting. Alumnus, Angelo State U.; Wayne Franke Day proclaimed by San Angelo, Tex. City Council Oct. 14, 1989, one of ten Rising Stars of Tex., Tex. Bus. mag., 1988. Mem. Tex. Assn. Bus. and C. of C. (statewide state affairs com., chmn. state affairs com. 1977-79, bd. dirs. Austin chpt. 1985-88, vice chmn. 1987), Tex. Taxpayers and Rsch. Assn. (state affairs com. 1985—), Tex. Self-Ins. Assn. (co-chair legis. com. 1993), Homeowners Assn., West Tex. C. of C. (state affairs com., legis. adv. coun.), Bus. Ins. Consumers Assn. (exec. com. 1990-95), Lewisville/San Angelo C. of C. (amb. 1974-77, Amb. of the Yr. 1975, 76). Roman Catholic. Lodge: Optimists (sec. Irving chpt. 1973-74, v.p. youth work, 1974-75, pres., 1975, bd. dirs. San Angelo chpt. 1977, lt. gov. North Tex. dist., 1978-79). Avocations: golf, rock work, fishing, tree trimming, camping.

FRANKE, WILLIAM AUGUSTUS, corporate executive; b. Bryan, Tex., Apr. 15, 1937; s. Louis John and Frances (Hanna) F.; m. Carolyn Diane Franke; children: Catherine Anne, Paige Estelle, Brian Hanna, David Parker. BA, Stanford U., 1959, LLB, 1961. Bar: Wash. 1961. With MacGillivray, Jones, Clark & Schiffner, Spokane, 1962-69; ptnr. S.W. Forest Industries, Phoenix, 1970-86; CEO, S.W. Forest Industries (merged with Stone Container Corp.), Phoenix, 1978, chmn. bd. dirs., 1986—; pres., owner Franke & Co., Inc., Phoenix, 1987—; chmn., CEO, Am. West Holdings Corp., Phoenix, 1995—; chmn. bd. Am. West Airlines, Tempe, 1992-93, chmn. bd., CEO, 1993-97; mng. ptnr. Newbridge Latin Am. LLP; bd. dirs. Phelps Dodge Corp., Ctrl. Newspapers, Inc., Air Transport Assn., Aerfi Grp. plc., Beringer Wine Estates. Mem. dean's council Ariz. State U. Sch. Bus. Served to capt. U.S. Army, 1961-62. Mem. ABA, Wash. Bar Assn., Chief Execs. Orgn. Episcopalian. Clubs: Paradise Valley Country, Phoenix Country, Arizona Club, Desert Mountain Country. Home: 7701 N Saguaro Dr Paradise Valley AZ 85253-3043 Office: 2525 E Camelback Rd Ste 800 Phoenix AZ 85016-4230

FRANKEL, ANDREW JOEL, management consultant; b. N.Y.C., Oct. 7, 1945; s. Lazar Hirsch and Estelle Rose (Fuchs) F.; m. Marilyn Judith Marcus, Dec. 24, 1967; children: Jennifer Lauren, Jonathan Matthew. B-SChemE, N.J. Inst. Tech., 1968; M in Nuclear Engring., NYU, 1970; postgrad. in fin., U. Hartford, 1971-72. Cert. paralegal mediator Am. Arbitration Assn. Physicist ABB Combustion Engring., Windsor, Conn., 1970-76, lead engr., 1976-77; dir. non-proliferation programs Oak Ridge (Tenn.) Nat. Lab., 1977-78; mgr. mkt. intelligence dept. NAC Internat., Inc., Atlanta, 1978-80; gen. mgr., dir. energy info. products divsn. NAC Internat., Inc., 1980-86; mgr. mktg. info. systems Martin Marietta Energy Systems, Inc., Oak Ridge, 1986-89, mgr. info. resources, 1989-91, mgr. bus. analysis and decision support, 1991-92; cons. bus. devel. Martin Marietta Corp., Bethesda, Md., 1992-93; mgr. fin. and strategic planning Martin Marietta Utility Svcs., Inc., Oak Ridge, 1993-94; mgr. cost reduction programs Lockheed Martin Utility Svcs., Inc., Bethesda, Piketon, Ohio, Paducah, Ky., 1994-96; ops. cons. Lockheed Martin Corp., Bethesda, 1996-97; sr. mgr. info. tech., bus. proc. re-engring Universal Scheduling Co., Bala Cynwyd, Pa., 1997—. Contbr. articles to profl. jours. U.S. del. Internat. Nuclear Fuel Cycle Evaluation, Washington, 1977-78; nuclear safety advisor Conn. Gov.'s Office, Hartford, 1975-77. NSF fellow, 1968-70. Mem. Am. Nuclear Soc. (sec. Conn. chpt. 1976-77), Tau Beta Pi (v.p. N.Y.C. Met. chpt. 1969, pres. 1970), Omega Chi Epsilon. Republican. Methodist. Achievements include research in nuclear power, nuclear safety, nuclear arms control and nuclear non-proliferation; privatization of U.S. government uranium enrichment program; business process re-engineering, ERP packaged software solutions. Home: 200 Jalusian Trl Paducah KY 42001-8856 Office: Universal Scheduling Co One Bala Cynwyd Plaza Bala Cynwyd PA 19004

FRANKEL, BENJAMIN HARRISON, lawyer; b. Trenton, N.J., Nov. 13, 1930; s. Abraham and Fannie (Lavine) F.; m. Phyllis Sanders, Mar. 29, 1959; children—Faith, Rachel, Eleanor. B.A., U. Calif.-Berkeley, 1951; LL.B., Harvard U., 1954. Bar: N.Y. 1954. Assoc. Kelley Drye & Warren, N.Y.C., 1954-62, ptnr., 1962—. Author: (with Prof. Rohan) Real Estate Syndications; editor Harvard Law Rev., 1953-54; contbr. articles on three dimensional real property law, partnership tax allocations and real property gains tax to profl. jours. Chairperson 25th Anniversary Class Gift to Harvard Law Sch.; treas. Scenic Hudson Land Trust Inc.; bd. dirs. Am. Soc. Protection Nature in Israel; pres. P.E.F. Israel Endowment Funds, Inc. Robert Gordon Sproul assoc. U. Calif. Mem. ABA, N.Y. State Bar Assn., Assn. Bar City of N.Y., Phi Beta Kappa, Phi Beta Kappa Assocs., Harvard Club (N.Y.C.), Century Assn. Club. Democrat. Jewish. Home: 50 Euclid Ave Hastings Hdsn NY 10706-1110 Office: Kelley Drye & Warren LLP 101 Park Ave New York NY 10178-0002*

FRANKEL, BERNARD, advertising executive; b. 1929. B in Mktg., U. Buffalo, 1951. Sales rep. Rugby Knitting Mi, Chgo., 1951-54; midwest rep. E.O. Hirsch & Assocs., Chgo., 1954-57; dir. sales promotion Kling Studios, Chgo., 1957-59; account exec., account supr., v.p. Knipschild-Robinson, Inc. (now William A. Robinson and Co.), 1959-62; CEO Frankel & Co., Chgo., 1962—, also chmn. bd. dirs.; media rep., advt. sales mgr., advertising and promotion mgr. Concrete Pub. Co., Chgo., 1955-57. Office: Frankel & Co 111 E Wacker Dr Chicago IL 60601-3713*

FRANKEL, CHARLES JAMES, III, banker; b. Charlottesville, Va., Feb. 14, 1944; s. Charles James II and Gladys (Birmingham) F.; m. Dawn Marie Hornung, Oct. 23, 1964; 1 child, Kimberly Mavourneen. Student, U. Va., 1961-65; BS, Fla. Atlantic U., 1966, MEd, 1967. Asst. v.p. Wachovia Bank & Trust Co., Winston-Salem, N.C., 1967-74; exec. v.p. Sun Bank/So. Fla., Nat. Assn., Ft. Lauderdale, 1974-85; pres. Pan Am. Bank of Broward, Ft. Lauderdale, 1985-86; sr. v.p. and dir. private banking, ea. U.S. and internat. Nations Bank, Ft. Lauderdale, 1989-91; with Fla. pvt. banking, 1986-88, 92-93; mng. dir. U.S. Trust Co. Fla., Boca Raton, Fla., 1993—; private lending com. Robert Morris Assocs., Phila., 1990-93; speaker various profl. confs. Pres. Greater Ft. Lauderdale Touchdown Club, 1981; chmn. Blockbuster Bowl, Ft. Lauderdale, 1992; bd. dirs. City of Ft. Lauderdale Bch. Redevel. Bd., 1991, Greater Ft. Lauderdale C. of C. Found., 1992, City of Ft. Lauderdale Pks. and Recreation Bd., 1992-96, bd. dirs. Fla. Atlantic Univ. Found., 1997—; mem. Va. Student Aid Found., U. of Va. Nat. Campaign Com., nat. leadership gifts coun. 1996—; lay Eucharistic minister All Saints Episcopal Ch., 1994-98, St. Paul's Episcopal Ch., 1998—; mem. corp. advocates com. Boca Raton Cmty. Hosp., 1998—. Recipient Disting. Am. award Nat. Football Found., Brian Piccolo chpt., 1991. Mem. Am. Bankers Assn. (pvt. banking exec. com. 1991-92), Jr. Achievement (bd. advisors 1988-91), Lauderdale Yacht Club (bd. govs. 1984-88), Tower Club (bd. dirs. 1985-93), Boca Raton C. of C. (bd. dirs. 1997—), Lago Mar Beach Club, Boca Raton Hist. Soc. (bd. dirs. 1995—), Boca Raton Chamber Senate, Scuttlebutt Club, Museum of Sci. and Discovery Planned Giving Coun., New River Club, Sunshine Football Classic (bd. trustees, exec. com., 1992—), Gulf Stream Bath and Tennis Club, The Hundred Club of Palm Beach County. Episcopalian. Avocations: tennis, arts, sporting events, volunteerism.

FRANKEL, DONALD LEON, retired oil service company executive; b. San Francisco, May 23, 1931; s. Donald A. and Sallie A. F.; m. Donna J. Frankel; children: Michael, Pamela, Karen, Mark, Steven. B.B.A., U. Okla., 1956. Vice pres. fin., treas., then v.p. internat. Gardner Denver Co., Dallas, 1956-78; also dir.; sr. v.p. fin., treas. Galveston Houston Co., 1979-80; sr. v.p. fin. Geosource, Inc., Houston, 1980-84; pres., chief exec. officer, dir. Delta Drilling Corp., Tyler, Tex., 1985-95, ret., 1995; dir. Protection Mut. Ins. Co., EMSCO; cons. oil svc. industry. Served with USAF, 1951-53. Mem. Petroleum Club, Hollytree Country Club. Republican. Home: 5918 Foxcroft Rd Tyler TX 75703-4519*

FRANKEL, ERNST GABRIEL, shipping and aviation business executive, educator; b. Beuthen, Germany, Oct. 17, 1923; came to U.S., 1959, naturalized, 1964.; s. Siegfried Samuel and Martha (Blumenthal) F.; m. Inna Kordonsky, Sept. 9, 1990; 1 child, Michael. BS, London U., 1948; MS in Marine-Mech. Engring., MIT, 1960; MBA, Boston U., 1979, D of Bus. Adminstrn., 1986; PhD in Econs., U. Wales, 1985. Chief engr. ZimNav Co., Haifa, Israel, 1950-59; asst. prof. MIT, Cambridge, Mass., 1960-64; assoc. prof. MIT, Cambridge, 1964-65, mem. faculty, 1970—, prof. marine systems, 1970—, prof. mgmt. Sloan Sch., 1993—; chief divsn. operation analysis maritime adminstrn. Dept. of Commerce, 1965-66; tech. dir. Litton Industries, Beverly Hills, Calif., 1966-70; pres. E.G. Frankel, Inc., Boston, 1969—; port, shipping and aviation advisor World Bank, 1983-86; sr. advisor on ports to sec. gen. Internat. Maritime Orgn., 1987—; chmn. Am. Pres. Lines, Inc., 1997—; dir. Am. Eagle Tankers, 1997—; dir. Neptune Orient Lines Inc., 1988—. Author: Ocean Transportation, 1973, Regulation and Policies of American Shipping, 1982, Management and Operations of American Shipping, 1982, Systems Reliability and Risk Analysis, 1984, Port Planning and Development, 1986, The World Shipping Industry-Economics Transition, 1987, Project Management, 1989, Management of Technological Change, 1989, In Pursuit of Technological Excellence, 1993, Ocean Environmental Management, 1994, America's Institutional Dilemma, 1998. Served with Royal Navy, 1942-45. Recipient Gold medal Brit. Govt., 1956. Mem. Am. Soc. Civil Engrs., Soc. Naval Architects and Marine Engrs., Ops. Rsch. Am., The Inst. of Man Scis., Soc. Internat. Devel., Royal Inst. Naval Architects, Inst. Marine Engrs. Home: 283 Buckminster Rd Brookline MA 02445-5841

FRANKEL, FRANCINE RUTH, political science educator; b. N.Y.C., Aug. 31, 1935; d. William and Dora (Tuchschneider) Goldberg; m. Douglas Vernon Verney, Nov. 28, 1975; stepchildren: Andrew, Jonathan. BA, CCNY, 1956; MA, Johns Hopkins U., 1958; PhD, U. Chgo., 1965. Asst. prof. U. Pa., Phila., 1965-70, assoc. prof., 1970-79, prof., 1979—, prof. South Asian studies, 1978—, chmn. grad. program polit. sci., 1980-83; dir. Ctr. Advanced Study of India, 1992—; vis. fellow Ctr. of Internat. Studies, Princeton (N.J.) U., 1969-73; resident scholar Bellagio Study and Conf. Ctr., 1975; vis. mem. Inst. Advanced Study, 1976; mem.-at-large Commn. Internat. Rels., Nat. Acad. Scis., 1973-79; mem. del. South Asian specialists to China, 1986; mem. task force on non-proliferation and South Asian security Carnegie Endowment for Internat. Peace, 1986-88; founding mem., mem. Gov. Coun. U. Pa. Inst. for Advanced Study of India, New Delhi, 1995—. Author: India's Political Economy, 1947-77, The Gradual Revolution, 1978, Chinese edit., 1990, India's Green Revolution, 1971; editor, contbr. Dominance and State Power in Modern India, Decline of a Social Order, 2 vols., 1989-90, Bridging the Non-Proliferation Gap: India and the United States, 1995; contbr. articles on India's polit. economy to profl. jours. Grantee Am. Inst. Studies, 1979-80, Smithsonian Instn., 1983-86, Social Sci. Rsch. Coun., 1989-91; Woodrow Wilson fellow, 1997—. Mem. Am. Polit. Sci. Assn., Assn. Asian Studies, Coun. Fgn. Rels. (ind. task force on new U.S. policy toward India 1996, ind. task force on U.S. policy toward India and Pakistan in the Wake of the Tests 1998). Club: Univ. (Toronto). Home: 104 Pine St Philadelphia PA 19106-4312 Office: U Pa Dept Polit Sci Stiteler Hall Philadelphia PA 19104

FRANKEL, GENE, theater director, author, producer, educator; b. N.Y.C., Dec. 23, 1923; s. Barnet and Anna (Talerman) F.; m. Pat Ruth Carter, May 1, 1963; children: Laura Ann, Ethan-Eugene. BA, NYU, 1943. Artistic dir. Gen. Frankel Theatre, N.Y.C., 1963—, exec. dir., 1973—; founding dir. Berkshire Theatre Festival, Stockbridge, Mass., 1965-66; vis. Arena Stage, Washington, 1969-71; cultural exchange dir. U.S. Dept. State, Belgrade, Yugoslavia, 1968-69; dir. Hartman Theatres, Stamford, Conn., 1976-79; vis. prof. Boston U., 1967-69, Queens Coll., N.Y.C., 1969-71, Columbia U., N.Y.C., 1972-73; cons. dir. Nat. Shakespeare Co., N.Y.C., 1966—; dir. various regional theaters, 1969-80. Dir.: Broadway, 1969 (Burns Mantle 1969, Best Play award), Emperor Jones, European tour, 1970, Oh Dad, Poor Dad, Belgrade, Yugoslavia, 1969, Lost in the Stars, Broadway, 1971, The Night That Made American Famous, 1975, Cry of Players, 1967, The Blacks, Off-Broadway, 1961 (Obie award 1963), also European tour, Brecht on Brecht, Off-Broadway, 1965, To Be Young Gifted and Black, Off-Broadway, 1970, Enemy of the People, Off-Broadway, 1969, Indians, On Broadway, 1979, Pueblo, 1981, 27 Wagons Full of Cotton, 1985, Talk To Me Like the Rain, 1985, War Play, 1986, The Marriage, 1986, Private Wars, 1987, Sister Aimee, 1987, The Dutchman, 1988, Carreno, 1989—; author, dir. The Actor Then Ma, 1979; co-author, dir.: (play/concert) Carreno, 1990, See Moscow and Die, 1991, (play) Hallowed Ground The Private Thoughts of Abraham Lincoln, 1997; author: So This is the Wicked Stage, 1993; taught and directed numerous actors and actresses including Anne Bancroft, Maya Angelou, Morgan Freeman, Vincent Gardenia, Frank Langella, Fred Gwynne, Louis Gosset, Jr., Walter Matthau, Rod Steiger, Beau Bridges, James Earl Jones, Loretta Swit, Judd Hirsh, Stacy Keach, Lee Marvin, Raul Julia, others. With U.S. Army Air Force, World War II. Recipient Lola D'Annunzio award, 1958; recipient Obie award for Volpone, Village Voice, 1958, Obie award for Machinal Village Voice, 1963, Vernon Rice award for Machinal, Drama Desk-N.Y. Post, 1963; Ford Found. fellow, 1969-71. Mem. SAG, Soc. Choreographers and Dirs., Actors Equity Assn. Office: 4 Washington Square Vlg New York NY 10012-1936 also: Gene Frankel Theatre 24 Bond St New York NY 10012-2424 *"To acquire knowledge and insight, one must learn from others. In so doing, it can happen that a pygmy standing on the shoulders of a giant may see further than the giant. So learn-learn-learn-then teach so that you can learn some more".*

FRANKEL, GLENN, journalist; b. N.Y.C., Oct. 2, 1949; s. Herbert A. and Betty Beck; m. Betsyellen Yeager; children: Abra, Margo, Paul. BA, Columbia U., 1971. Staff reporter Richmond Mercury, 1973-75; staff writer The Record, Hackensack, N.J., 1975-79; Richmond bur. chief The Washington Post, 1979-82, So. Africa bur. chief, 1983-86, Jerusalem bur. chief, 1986-89, London bur. chief, 1989-92, staff writer, editor-in-chief, 1993—. Author: Beyond the Promised Land: Jews and Arabs on the Hard Road to a New Israel, 1994. Recipient Pulitzer Prize for internat. reporting, 1989; Stanford U. fellow, 1982-83. E-mail: frankelg@aol.com. *

FRANKEL, JEFFREY, neurologist; b. Washington, N.J., Sept. 1, 1941; s. Leon and Libby (Kor) F.; m. Trina Gail Newstein, June 21, 1964; children: Laura Frankel Harper, Katherine Frankel Azaro. Student, U. Pa., 1959-62; MD, U. Chgo., 1966. Diplomate Am. Bd. Psychiatry and Neurology. Intern Mt. Sinai Hosp., N.Y.C., 1966-67; resident in neurology Alfert Einstein Coll. Medicine Affiliated Hosps., N.Y.C., 1967-70; pvt. practice, Livingston, N.J., 1972—; chmn. profl. adv. com., trustee No. N.J. chpt. Nat. Multiple Sclerosis Soc., 1982-94, mem. profl. adv. com., 1996—; mem. profl. adv. com. Epilepsy Found. N.J. Asst. surgeon USPHS, 1970-72. Fellow Am. Acad. Neurology; mem. Am. Assn. for Study Headache, Am. Soc. Neuroimaging, Acad. Medicine N.J. (chmn. neurology sect. 1984-94). Jewish. Avocation: ballroom dancing. Office: Essex Neurol Assocs 340 E Northfield Rd Livingston NJ 07039

FRANKEL, JEFFREY ALEXANDER, economist; b. San Francisco, Nov. 5, 1952; s. Jack Earle and Donna (Lyons) F.; m. Jessica Eve Stern, June 10, 1990. BA, Swarthmore Coll., 1974; PhD, MIT, 1978. Asst. prof. U. Mich., Ann Arbor, 1978-79; asst. prof. econs. U. Calif., Berkeley, 1979-84, assoc. prof., 1984-87, prof., 1987—, dir. Ctr. for Internat. and Devel. Econ. Rsch., 1991-96; chief economist Pres.'s Coun. Econ. Advisors, Washington, 1996-97; mem. Pres.'s Coun. Econ. Advisers, White House, Washington, 1997-99; vis. scholar Fed. Res. Bd., Washington, 1977, 79, 81, 86, IMF, Washington, 1985, 86, 89, 92, 93; vis. asst. prof. Yale U., New Haven, 1980; sr. staff economist Coun. Econ. Advisors, Washington, 1983-84; sr. fellow Inst. Internat. Econs., Washington, 1984, 90, 91, 94-95; vis. prof. Harvard U., Cambridge, Mass., 1988-89; rsch. assoc. Nat. Bur. Econ. Rsch., dir. internat. fin. and macroecons., 1993—, co-chmn. Internat. Seminar on Macroecons., 1994—; mem. Bus. Cycle Dating Com., 1994—; mem. panel on fgn. trade stats. NAS, 1992-94. Co-author: World Trade and Payments, 8th edit., 1999; also articles and books. New century chair Brookings Instn., Washington, 1999; Harpel chair Kennedy Sch. Harvard U., 1999—. Recipient 1st prize for essay Am. Express Bank Rev., London, 1991, 10th ann. Ohira Meml. Prize, 1994; NSF fellow, grantee, 1974-86; rsch. fellow Alfred P. Sloan Found., 1986-88; Japan-U.S. Friendship Commn. grantee, 1990-96. Mem. Ctr. for Pacific Basin Monetary and Econ. Studies (vis. scholar 1990-96). Office: Kennedy Sch Harvard U 79 JFK St Cambridge MA 02138

FRANKEL, JUDITH JENNIFER MARIASHA, clinical psychologist, consultant; b. Bklyn., May 25, 1947; m. Anthony R. D'Augelli, Sept. 1, 1968 (div. 1985); children: Jennifer Hadley Frankel, Rebekah Lindsey Frankel. BA, New Coll. at Hofstra U., 1968; MA, U. Conn., 1971, PhD, 1972. Lic. psychologist, Pa. Rsch. psychologist Family Consultation Ctr., Roslyn, N.Y., 1968, Conn. State Dept. Mental Health, Hartford, 1969-71; staff intern VA Hosp., West Haven, Conn., 1971-72; asst./assoc. prof., dir. program devel. and evaluation Pa. State U., University Park, 1972-81; spl. admissions asst. Schreyer Honors Coll. Pa. State U., State Coll., 1998; pvt. practice psychology and clin. health psychology State College, 1976—; pvt. practice psychology Larry Clayton and Counseling Assocs., 1998—; psychol. cons. PYRAMID Orgn., Walnut Creek, Calif., 1975-78, N.Y. Dept. Mental Health, 1976, Nat. Inst. Alcohol Abuse Prevention, Nat. Inst. Drug Abuse Prevention, Nat. Youth Alternatives Program, 1975-79, Meadows Psychiatric Ctr. Women's Program, 1993-95; v.p. Mental Health Profls., State College, 1978-80, pres., 1980-82; exec. bd. Ctrl. Pa. Psychol. Assn., 1989-90. Author: Decisions Are Possible, 1975, Communication and Parenting Skills, 1976, Helping Others, 1980; contbr. articles to profl. jours. Campaign cosn. Stein for Rep., 1982, Wachob for Congress, 1984; chair cmty. action Congregation Brit Shalom, State College, 1985-87, coord. ednl. liaison, 1985-87; v.p. Jewish Cmty. Coun. Women, 1988-90, pres., 1990-93, bd. dirs. Congregation Brit. Shalom, 1985-87, 90-93; v.p. Hadassah, 1995—. USPHS fellow, U. Conn., 1969-71. Mem. APA (clin. psychology, psychology of women, ind. practice, & health psychology divsns.), Pa. Psychol. Assn., Ea. Psychol. Assn., Ctrl. Pa. Psychol. Assn. (exec. bd. 1989-90), Jewish Cmty. Coun. women (bd. dirs. 1990-94), Hadassah (v.p. programming 1995-98, v.p. fundraising, 1998—), Phi Beta Kappa, Phi Kappa Phi. Democrat. Jewish. Avocations: art, music, film, literature, gardening.

FRANKEL, KENNETH MARK, thoracic surgeon; b. Bklyn., July 29, 1940; s. Clarence Bernard and Ruth (Rutes) F.; m. Felice Cala Oringel, Dec. 10, 1967; children: Matthew David, Michael Jacob. B.A., Cornell U., 1961; M.D., SUNY, Bklyn., 1965. Diplomate Am. Bd. Surgery, Am. Bd. Thoracic Surgery. Intern in surgery Yale New Haven Hosp., 1965-66; resident in surgery Kings County-SUNY Med. Ctr., Bklyn., 1966-67, 69-71, chief resident in gen. surgery, 1971-72, resident in thoracic surgery, 1972-73, chief resident thoracic and cardiovascular surgery, 1973-74; attending thoracic surgeon Mercy Hosp., Springfield, Mass., 1974—, Holyoke (Mass.) Hosp., 1974—; pvt. practice medicine specializing in thoracic surgery Springfield, 1974—; chief thoracic surgery Baystate Med. Ctr., Springfield, 1977—; clin. prof. cardiothoracic surgery Tufts U. Sch. Medicine, 1978—; cons. in throacic surgery Noble Hops., Westfield, Mass., 1976—; cons. Shriners Hosp. for Children, Mary Lane Hosp., Ware, Mass., 1997—; bd. dirs. Pioneer Health Care Inc., 1997—, sec. of bd., 1998—. Contbr. articles to profl. jours. Corporator Springfield (Mass.) Symphony Orch., Stage West, Springfield; rep. to Blue Cross/Blue Shield Regional Health Care Improvement Coun., 1995-98. Capt. U.S. Army, 1967-69. Decorated Bronze Star, Gallantry Cross (Republic of Vietnam). Fellow ACS, Am. Coll. Chest Physicians; mem. AMA, ACLU, Soc. Thoracic Surgeons, Am. Thoracic Soc., New Eng. Cancer Soc., Springfield Acad. Medicine (past pres.), Mass. Med. Soc. (councilor 1981-83), Hampden Dist. Med. Soc. (exec. com. 1990-96), Physicians for Social Responsibility, Maimonides Med. Club (past pres.), AMnesty Internat., Internat. Physicians for Prevention Nuc. War, Union Concerned Scientists, Cornell Club Wester Mass., Porsche Club Am. Democrat. Jewish. Home: 202 Ellington Rd Longmeadow MA 01106-1510 Office: Baystate Med Ctr Office Bldg 2 Medical Center Dr Ste 304 Springfield MA 01107-1271

FRANKEL, MARTIN RICHARD, statistician, educator, consultant; b. Washington, June 16, 1943; s. Lester R. and Vera B. Frankel; m. Jean L. Kaiser, Mar. 24, 1970; children: Jennifer, Margaux. AB, U. N.C., 1965; MA, U. Mich., 1967, PhD, 1971. Asst. prof. stats. U. Chgo., 1971-73, assoc. prof., 1974-76; prof. stats. and computer info. systems Baruch Coll., CUNY, 1977—, assoc. chair, 1995—; tech. dir. Nat. Opinion Research Ctr., U. Chgo., 1972-96; sr. statis. scientist Abt Assocs., Cambridge, Mass., 1996—; chmn. Quality Research Council, Advtg. Research Found., 1988—; cons. statis. methods and quality control, 1965—; mem. panel on occupational and health stats., com. on nat. stats. Nat. Rsch. Coun., NAS, 1985-87; pres. Market Rsch. Coun., 1995—. Author: Inference from Survey Samples: An Empirical Investigation, 1971; (co-author) SEPP: Sampling Error Program Package, 1972, Total Survey Error: Applications to Improve Health Surveys, 1979; also articles; mem. editorial bd. Pub. Opinion Quar., Ency. Statis. Scis., Sociol. Research and Methods. Fellow Am. Statis. Assn. (chmn. census adv. com. 1981, chmn. sect. survey research methods 1975-76, editorial bd. jour.), Royal Statis. Soc., Internat. Statis. Inst.; mem. Am. Assn. Pub. Opinion Research (chmn. standards com.), Market Rsch. Coun. (pres. 1995-96). Home: 14 Patricia Ln Cos Cob CT 06807-1734 Office: Baruch Coll 17 Lexington Ave New York NY 10010-5518

FRANKEL, MARVIN E., lawyer; b. N.Y.C., July 26, 1920; s. Charles and Anne (Brody) F.; m. Betty Streich, June 20, 1945 (div. 1965); 1 child, Eleanor; m. Alice Kross, Aug. 22, 1965; 1 dau., Mara; stepchildren: David K. Schorr, Ellen Schorr. A.B., Queens Coll., 1943; LL.B., Columbia U., 1948. Bar: N.Y. 1949, U.S. Supreme Ct 1952. Asst. to U.S. solicitor gen., 1952-56; ptnr. Proskauer Rose Goetz & Mendelsohn, 1956-62, 78-83, Kramer, Levin, Naftalis & Frankel, N.Y.C., 1983—; prof. law Columbia U., 1962-65; U.S. dist. judge So. Dist. N.Y., 1965-78. Author: Criminal Sentences, 1973, (with Gary P. Naftalis) The Grand Jury--An Institution on Trial, 1977, Partisan Justice, 1980, (with Ellen Saideman) Out of the Shadows of Night, 1989, Faith and Freedom--Religious Liberty in America, 1994; editor-in-chief Columbia Law Rev., 1948. Chmn. Lawyers Com. for Human Rights, 1980-95, chmn. emeritus, 1996—. With AUS, 1942-46. Mem. ABA, N.Y. State Bar Assn., Assn. of Bar of City of N.Y. Office: Kramer Levin Naftalis & Frankel 919 3rd Ave New York NY 10022-3902*

FRANKEL, MAX, journalist; b. Gera, Germany, Apr. 3, 1930; came to U.S., 1940, naturalized, 1948; s. Jacob A. and Mary (Katz) F.; m. Tobia Brown, June 19, 1956 (dec. Mar. 1987); children: David M., Margot S., Jonathan M.; m. Joyce Purnick, Dec. 11, 1988. A.B., Columbia, 1952, M.A. in Polit. Sci, 1953. Mem. staff N.Y. Times, 1952-94, chief Washington corr., 1968-73, Sunday editor, 1973-76, editorial pages editor, 1977-86, exec. editor, 1986-94, 94—; columnist N.Y. Times mag. Served with AUS, 1953-55. Recipient Pulitzer prize for internat. reporting, 1973. Office: NY Times Co 229 W 43rd St New York NY 10036-3959

FRANKEL, PAUL WARREN, insurance executive, physician; s. Clarence Bernard and Ruth (Rutes) F. AB magna cum laude, Harvard U., 1970; MA, Princeton U., 1972, PhD, 1973; MD with honors, Dartmouth Med. Sch., 1975. Intern in internal medicine Peter Bent Brigham Hosp., Harvard Med. Sch., Boston, 1975-76, resident in internal medicine, 1976-77, fellow in gastroenterology, 1977-79; Physician Williamstown Med. Assoc., P.C., Williamstown, Mass., 1979-88; asst. in medicine Williams Coll., Williamstown, 1979-88; group med. dir. MultiGroup Health Plan, Williamstown, 1984-88, Harvard Community Health Plan, Williamstown, 1984-88; med. dir. Corp. Health Strategies, Westport, Conn., 1988; regional med. dir. Corp. Health Strategies, Westport, 1988-89; v.p. and nat. med. dir. Met. Life Ins. Co., Westport, 1989—. Office: Met Life Ins Co 276 Post Rd W Westport CT 06880-4703

FRANKEL, STANLEY ARTHUR, columnist, educator, business executive; b. Dayton, Ohio, Dec. 8, 1918; s. Mandel and Olive (Margolis) F.; m. Irene Baskin, Feb. 20, 1946; children—Stephen, Thomas, Nancy. BS with high honors, Northwestern U., 1940; student, Columbia U., 1940, U. Chgo., 1946-49. Reporter Chgo. News Bur., 1940; publicist CBS, 1941; asst. to pres. Esquire and Coronet mags., N.Y.C., 1946-56; pres. Esquire Club, 1956-58; with McCall Corp., N.Y.C., 1958-61; asst. to pres. and pub. McCall Corp., 1958-61, v.p., 1959-61; v.p., dir. corporate devel. Ogden Corp., 1961-88, cons., 1988—; cons. Manning, Selvage & Lee Pub. Relations Corp., N.Y.C., 1987—; weekly columnist This Week mag., 1990—; dir. Michaelis Prodns., Inc., Rockwood Corp., Careful Office Service Inc., Western Calif. Canners Corp., Internat. Terminal Operating Co., Inc., Ogden Am. Corp.; adj. prof. Baruch Coll., CUNY, 1974—, Pace U., 1983—; bd. dirs. Baruch Coll. Ctr. of Mgmt., 1986—; bd. visitors PhD Program Baruch Coll., 1986—, bd. mgmt. dept. Baruch Coll., CUNY; guest lectr. NYU, 1974; mem. Pres.'s Adv. Council on Pece Corps, 1965, Pres.'s Adv. Council on Youth Opportunity.; Mem. chancellor's panel SUNY, 1970-72 ; mem. N.Y. State Task Force on Higher Edn., 1974-76; bd. mem., exec. com. Nat. Council Crime and Delinquency; bd. mem., vice chmn. Nat. Businessmen's Council; bd. dirs., officer Scarsdale Adult Sch.; adv. bd. Channel 14 Cable TV Sta. Author: History of 37th Division, 1947, Frankel-y Speaking About WWII In the South Pacific, 1992; columnist The Week mag., 1989—; regular guest cable TV series Frankel-y Speaking, Westchester County, N.Y., 1944—; contbr. articles to popular mags. Exec. bd. Writers for Stevenson, 1952, 56, for Kennedy, 1960, McGovern for Pres., 1972; pub. rels. dir. Stevenson-for-Pres., 1956; chmn. Writers for Senator Humphrey Vice-Presidl. campaign, 1964; exec. bd. Businessmen for Humphrey-Muskie, 1968; mem. nat. exec. com. McGovern for Pres., 1972; vice chmn. N.Y. State McGovern for Pres. Com., 1972; bd. overseers Rutgers U., 1977-80; chancellor's external rels. com. CUNY, 1977-80; bd. dirs., v.p., mem. exec. com. YMCA of Greater N.Y.; founder Pub. Rels. Bd., Inc., N.Y.C. and Chgo., Bedford Stuyvesant Project (T.R.Y.); mem. V.P.'s Task Force on Youth Unemployment, 1979-80; mem. Cable TV Adv. Coun., Scarsdale, N.Y., 1996—. Maj. AUS, 1940-46. Decorated 2 Presdl. Citations, 3 Bronze Stars; recipient Peabody award for TV Series Adlai Stevenson Reports, 1961-63; Northwestern U. Alumni Merit award, 1964. Mem. Town Club (bd. govs.), Sunningdale Country Club, Dutch Treat Club, Northwestern U. Club N.Y. (pres. 1964), Overseas Press Club, Scarsdale Town Club, Phi Beta Kappa, Phi Beta Kappa Assocs. (pres. 1983-90, trustee, disting. lectr. 1988), Phi Beta Kappa Assn. Westchester County (pres 1980—85). Home and Office: 109 Brewster Rd Scarsdale NY 10583-2001 *Peace of heart and of mind ... among races and among nations ... in families and in neighborhoods ... at schools and at churches ... in cities and in space ... on streets and on highways ... between you and me and between them and us.*

FRANKEN, AL, humorist, actor, writer; b. Mpls., 1952; s. Joe and Phoebe Franken; m. Franni Bryson, 1975; 1 child, Thomasin. Grad., Harvard U., 1973. Stand-up comic, Mpls.; writer, performer Saturday Night Live, NBC-TV, 1973—; network commendator for presdl. campaigns Comedy Ctrl., 1992. Author: I'm Good Enough, I'm Smart Enough, and Doggone It, People Like Me, 1992, Rush Limbaugh Is a Big Fat Idiot and Other Observations, 1996, (screenplay) Stuart Saves His Family, 1995; co-author: (screenplay) When a Man Loves a Woman, 1994; creator character Stuart Smalley. Recipient Emmy award for Saturday Night Live. Democrat.

FRANKEN, DARRELL, counselor, writer, publisher; b. Oskaloosa, Iowa, Oct. 28, 1930; s. Henry E. and Harriet J. (Dykshorn) F.; m. Marilyn (Tanis); children: Kent, Julie, Todd. BA, Ctrl. U. Iowa, 1952; MDiv, Western Theol. Sem., Holland, Mich., 1955; MA, U. Chgo., 1963; PhD, La Salle U., 1995. Pastor Everglades Reformed Ch., Grand Rapids, Mich.; missionary Bahrain Arabian Gulf; counselor Christian Counseling Svc., Holland, Mich. Author: Health Through Stress Reduction, 1985, Psychological First Aid Kit, 1992, Psychology II Optimum Psycho-Social Lifestyles, 1996, 13 Core Values, 1995, Optimum Christian Lifeskills, founder of Lifeskills Trng. Ctrs. Inc.; creator various computer software programs. Fellow Am. Assn. Pastoral Counselors, Mich. Lic. Marriage and Family Counselors. Avocation: photography. E-mail: darrell@lifeskillstraining.org. Home: PO Box 2397 930 S Shore Dr Holland MI 49423-4539

FRANKEN, LYNN, English educator; b. Columbus, Ohio, Mar. 23, 1944; d. Robert Franken and Georganna Mae Boyd; children: Robert, Charles, Erik. PhD, U. Tex., 1983. Prof. English Butler U., Indpls., assoc. dean Coll. Liberal Arts and Scis., 1991-93, head dept. English, 1994—. Contbr. articles to profl. jours. Office: Butler U 4600 Sunset Ave Indianapolis IN 46208

FRANKEN, MARTIN, public relations company executive; b. 1950. BA, Rutgers U., 1974, MBA, 1975. Sr. audit mgr. Peat Marwick KPMG, N.Y.C., 1975-86; CFO Yankelovich Clancy Shulman, Inc., N.Y.C., 1986-87; sr. exec. v.p., CFO Rowland Worldwide, Inc., N.Y.C., 1988—, now COO, pres.; now COO, pres. Saatchi & Saatchi/Rowland, Sofia, Bulgaria; with Saatchi & Saatchi, N.Y.C. Fax: 212 463-2204. E-mail: STEAM@internet.BG.BG. Office: Saatchi & Saatchi, 5 Kaliakar St, 1421 Sofia Bulgaria*

FRANKENBERGER, BERTRAM, JR., investor, consultant; b. New Haven, Jan. 24, 1933; s. Bertram and Thelma (Wisan) F.; m. Marjorie Green, Dec. 20, 1953 (dec. June 1997); children: Linda Frankenberger Reason, Wendy Frankenberger Goldstein; m. Harriet Feldman Newman, July 26, 1998. B.S. cum laude, U. Conn., 1954. CPA, Conn. Auditor Haskins & Sells, New Haven, 1956-61; ptnr. Weinstein & Timm CPAs, New Haven, 1961-70, Deloitte Haskins & Sells, New Haven, 1970-76; U.S. ptnr in charge mergers and acquisitions exec. office N.Y.C., 1976-85; dir. Sheffield Mgmt. Co., N.Y.C., 1985—, Sheffield Investments, Inc., N.Y.C., 1985-96, Lafayette Am. Bank & Trust, Hamden, 1985-96; treas. Human Rels. Area Files, New Haven, 1963-70, 86—, assoc. sec., 1985—; cons., New Haven, 1985-94, Boynton Beach, Fla., 1994—; chmn. bd. Chargar Corp., Hamden, Conn., Graham-Worldtek Travel, New Haven; lectr. in field. Contbr. articles to profl. pubs., chpt. to book. Pres., dir. Camp Laurelwood, Madison, Conn., 1970-72; pres., trustee Congregation Mishkan Israel, Hamden, Conn., 1974-76; bd. trustees Union Am. Hebrew Congregations, N.Y.C., 1976-84; treas. Religion in Am. Life, N.Y.C., 1983-89, dir., 1983-94. Capt. USAF, 1954-56. Recipient Pres.'s award New Haven Jaycees, 1960; Pres.'s award Camp Laurelwood, 1969. Mem. AICPA, Conn. Soc. CPAs, Assn. Corp. Growth, Woodbridge Country Club (pres. 1994-95), Hunters Run Golf and Racquet Club (Boynton Beach). Avocations: skiing, golf, tennis, stamp collecting.

FRANKENHEIM, SAMUEL, lawyer; b. N.Y.C., Dec. 20, 1932; s. Samuel and Mary Emma (Ward) F.; m. Nina Barbara Mennerich, Sept. 2, 1960; children: Robert Mennerich, John Frederick. BA, Cornell U., 1954, LLB, 1959. Bar: N.Y. 1959, Mass. 1976. Law clk. N.Y. Ct. Appeals, 1959-61; assoc. Shearman & Sterling, attys., N.Y.C., 1961-68, ptnr., 1968-69; sr. v.p., dir. Damon Corp., Needham Heights, Mass., 1969-78; sr. v.p., gen. counsel mem. Office of Chmn. Gen. Cinema Corp., Chestnut Hill, Mass., 1979-92; counsel Ropes & Gray, Boston, 1992—; mem. corp. Ptnrs. Healthcare Sys., Inc., 1999—; trustee Ea. Enterprises. Overseer Newton-Wellesley Hosp., Newton, Mass., 1973-85, pres., 1980-82; bd. givs. Newell Health Care Sys., 1983-93; overseer Wang Ctr. for Performing Arts, Boston, 1985-87, trustee, 1987-97; trustee Huntington Theatre Co., Boston, 1993—; assoc. First Night, Inc., 1988, chmn. bd., 1991-93; chmn. bd. Internat. Alliance of First Night Celebrations, 1994-99, treas., 1999—. 1st lt. USAF, 1955-57. Mem. ABA. Home: 115 Shornecliffe Rd Newton MA 02458-2420 Office: Ropes & Gray 1 International Pl Boston MA 02110-2602

FRANKENHEIMER, JOHN MICHAEL, film and stage director; b. Malba, N.Y., Feb. 19, 1930; s. Walter Martin and Helen Mary (Sheedy) F.; m. Carolyn Diane Miller, Sept. 22, 1954 (div. 1961); children: Elise, Kristi; m. Evans Evans, 1964. Grad., LaSalle Mil. Acad., 1947; B.A., Williams Coll., 1951. Actor, 1950-51; dir.: CBS-TV programs You Are There, Danger, Climax (Emmy award 1956), Studio One, Playhouse 90, 1954-59 (Emmy awards 1957, 58, 59); programs directed include For Whom the Bell Tolls, The Comedian (Brotherhood award 1959, Acapulco Film Festival award 1962), The Days of Wine and Roses, Old Man, The Browning Version, The Turn of the Screw, The Rainmaker, Against the Wall (Emmy award, Best Direction of a Miniseries or Special, 1994), The Burning Season, 1994 (Emmy award, 1995); motion pictures include The Young Stranger, 1956, The Young Savages, 1961, Birdman of Alcatraz, 1962, All Fall Down, 1962, Manchurian Candidate, 1962, Seven Days in May, 1963, The Train, 1964, Seconds, 1965, Grand Priz, 1966, The Fixer, 1968, Gypsy Moths, 1969, I Walk the Line, 1970, The Horsemen, 1971, Impossible Object, 1972, The Iceman Cometh, 1973, 99 and 44/100% Dead, 1974, French Connection II, 1975, Black Sunday, 1977, Prophecy, 1979, Challenge, 1982, The Holcroft Covenant, 1984, 52-Pick-up, 1986, Dead Bang, 1989, The Fourth War, 1990, Year of the Gun, 1991, The Island of Dr. Moreau, 1996, Ronin, 1998; (TV movie) The Burning Season, 1994; films have been nominated for 38 Oscars. Recipient of the Christopher award, 1954; grand prize for best film dir. Lacarno Film Festival, 1955; Critics award for best direction of year, 1956-59. *

FRANKENTHALER, HELEN, artist; b. N.Y.C., Dec. 12, 1928; d. Alfred and Martha (Lowenstein) F.; m. Robert Motherwell, Apr. 5, 1958 (div.); m. Stephen DuBrul, Jr., July 1994. BA, Bennington Coll., 1949; LHD (hon.), Skidmore Coll., 1969, Hofstra U., 1991; DFA (hon.), Smith Coll., 1973, Moore Coll. Art, 1974, Bard Coll., 1976, NYU, 1979; DFA, Phila. Coll. Art, 1980, Williams Coll., 1980; DFA (hon.), Marymount Manhattan Coll., 1989, Adelphi U., 1989, Washington U., St. Louis, 1989; DArt, Radcliffe Coll., 1978, Amherst Coll., 1979; DArt (hon.), Harvard U., 1980; DFA (hon.), Yale U., 1981, Brandeis U., 1982, U. Hartford, 1983, Syracuse U., 1985, Dartmouth Coll., 1994, Parsons Sch. Design, 1996, U. Pa., 1996, R.I. Sch. Design, 1996. tchr., lectr. Yale U., 1966, 67, 70, Hunter Coll., 1970, Princeton U., 1971, Cooper Union, N.Y.C., 1972, Washington U. Sch. Fine Arts, 1972, Skidmore Coll., 1973, Swathmore Coll., 1974, Drew U., 1975, Harvard, 1976, Radcliffe Coll., 1976, Bard Coll., 1977, Detroit Inst. Arts, 1977, NYU, U. Pa., Sch. Visual Arts, Goucher Coll., Wash. U., Yale Grad. Sch., U. Ariz., 1978, Graphic Arts Council N.Y., 1979, Harvard U., 1980, Phila. Coll., 1980, Williams Coll., 1980, Yale U., 1981, Brandeis U., 1982, U. of Hartford, 1983, Syracuse U., 1985, Sante Fe Inst. Fine Arts, 1986, 90, 91; U.S. rep. Venice Biennale, 1966, lectr. in field. One-woman shows include, Tibor de Nagy Gallery, N.Y.C., 1951-58, Andre Emmerich Gallery, N.Y.C., 1959-73, 75, 77, 78, 79, 81, 82, 83, 84, 86, 87, 89, 90, 91, 92, 93, Jewish Mus., N.Y., 1960, Everett Ellin Gallery, Los Angeles, 1961, Galerie Lawrence, Paris, 1961, 63, Bennington Coll., 1962, 78, Galleria dell'Ariete, Milan, 1962, Kasmin Gallery, London, 1964, David Mirvish Gallery, Toronto, 1965, 71, 73, 75, Gertrude Kasle Gallery, Detroit, 1967, Nicholas Wilder Gallery, Los Angeles, 1967, Andre Emmerich Gallery, Zurich, 1974, 80, Swarthmore (Pa.) Coll., 1974, Solomon R. Guggenheim Mus., N.Y.C., 1975, Corcoran Gallery Art, Washington, 1975, Seattle Art Mus., 1975, Mus. Fine Arts, Houston, 1975, 85, 86, Ace Gallery, Vancouver, B.C., Can., 1975, Rosa Esman Gallery, N.Y.C., 1975, 83, 89, 3d Internat. Contemporary Art Fair, Paris, 1976, 81, retrospective Whitney Mus. Am. Art, 1969, Whitechapel Gallery, London, Eng., 1969, Kongress-Halle, Berlin, Kunstverein, Hannover, 1969, Heath Gallery, Atlanta, 1971, Galerie Godard Lefort, Montreal, 1971, Fendrick Gallery, Washington, 1972, 79, John Berggruen Gallery, San Francisco, 1972, 79, 82, Portland (Oreg.) Art Mus., 1972, Waddington Galleries II, London, 1973, 74, Janie C. Lee Gallery, Dallas, 1973, Houston, 1975, 76, 78, 80, 82, Met. Mus. Art, N.Y.C., 1973, Gallery Diane Gilson, Seattle, 1976, Greenberg Gallery, St. Louis, 1977, Galerie Wentzel, Hamburg, Germany, 1977, Jacksonville (Fla.) Art Mus., 1977-78, Knoedler Gallery, London, 1978, 81, 83, USIA exhbn., 1978-79, Atkins Mus. Fine Art, William Rockhill Nelson Gallery Art, Kansas City, Mo., 1978, 80, Saginaw Art Mus., Mich., 1980, Gimpel and Hanover and Andre Emerich Galleries, Zurich, 1980, Gallery Ulysses, Vienna, 1980, Knoedler Gallery, London, 1981, 83, Buschlen/Mowalt Fine Arts, Vancouver, 1989, Mus. Modern Art, N.Y.C., 1989, Douglas Drake Gallery, N.Y.C., 1989, Mizografia Gallery, L.A., 1989, Gerald Peters Gallery, Santa Fe, 1990, Kukje Gallery, Seoul, Korea, 1991, Assn. Am. Artists, N.Y.C., 1992, Knoedler & Co., N.Y.C., 1992, 94, 95, 96, 97, Nat. Gallery Art, Washington, 1993, San Diego Mus. Art, 1993, Mus. Fine Arts, Boston, 1994, Contemporary Arts Ctr., Cin., 1994, Meredith Long and Co., Houston, 1994, 95, 96, 97, Dennos Mus. Ctr. Northwestern Mich. Coll., Travers City, 1995, Tyler Graphics Ltd., Mt. Kisco, N.Y., 1995, Bobbie Greenfield Gallery, Santa Monica, Calif., 1995, Meyerovich Gallery, San Francisco, 1995, Greg Kucera Gallery, Seattle, 1995, Gallery One, Toronto, Canada, 1995, 97, Ace Contemporary Exhbns., L.A., 1996, Tasenda Gallery, L.A., 1997, Remba Gallery, West Hollywood, Calif., 1997, Thomas Segal Gallery, Balt., 1997, numerous others; exhibited in group shows including, Whitney Mus., 1958, 71, 75-79, 82, 89, Carnegie Internat., Pitts., 1955, 58, 61, 64, Columbus Gallery Fine Arts, 1960, Guggenheim Mus., 1961, 76, 80, 82, Seattle World's Fair, 1962, Art Inst. Chgo., 1963, 69, 72, 76, 77, 82, 83, San Francisco Mus. Art, 1963, 68, Krannert Mus., U. Ill., 1959, 63, 65, 67, 80, Washington Gallery Modern Art, 1963, Pa. Acad. Fine Arts, 1963, 68, 76, N.Y. World's Fair, 1964, Am. Fedn. Arts Circulating Exhbn., 1964, U. Austin Art Mus., 1964, Rose Art Mus. Circulating Exhbn., 1964, Detroit Inst. Arts, 1965, 67, 73, 77, U. Mich. Mus. Art, 1965, Md. Inst., 1966, Norfolk Mus. Arts and Scis., 1966, Venice Biennale, 1966, Smithsonian Instn., 1966, Expo '67, Montreal, 1967, Washington Gallery Modern Art, 1967, Ga. Mus. Art, Athens, 1967, U. Okla. Mus. Art, Norman, 1968, Philbrook Art Center, Tulsa, 1968, Cin. Mus., 1968, U. Calif. at San Diego, 1968, Mus. Modern Art, N.Y.C., 1969, 75, 76, 80, 82, Met. Mus., N.Y.C., 1969-70, 76, 79, 81, Va. Mus., Richmond, 1970, 74, 87, Balt. Mus. Art, 1970, 76, 89, Boston U., 1970, Boston Mus. Fine Arts, 1972, 82, 90, Des Moines Art Center, 1973, Mus. Fine Arts, Houston, 1974, 82, Smith Coll. Mus. Art, Northampton, Mass., 1974, El Instituto de Cultura Puertorriquena, San Juan, 1974, Basil (Switzerland) Art Fair, 1974, 76, Finch Coll. Mus. Art, N.Y.C., 1974, S.I. Mus., 1975, Denver Art Mus., 1975, Visual Arts Mus., N.Y.C., 1975, 76, Mus. Modern Art, Belgrade Yugoslavia, 1976, Chrysler Mus., Norfolk, Va., 1976, Everson Mus., Syaracuse, N.Y., Galleria d'Arts Moderna, Rome, 1976, Grey Art Gallery, N.Y.C., 1976-78, 81, Bklyn Mus., 1976-77, 82, Edmonton Art Gallery, Alta., Can., 1977, 78, Albright-Knox Mus., Buffalo, 1978, Fogg Art Mus., Harvard U., 1978, 83, Art Gallery Ont., 1979, Hirshorn Mus. and Sculpture Garden, Washington, 1980, Phoenix Art Mus., 1980, Nat. Gallery Art, Washington, 1981, Tate Gallery, London, 1981, Walker Art Ctr., Mpls., 1981, Milw. Art Mus., 1982, Mus. Fine Arts, Boston, 1982, Whitney Mus. Am. Art , N.Y., 1982, St. Louis Art Mus., 1982, High Mus. Art, Atlanta, 1989, Nelson-Atkins Mus. Art, Kansas City, Nat. Gallery Can., 1990, Williams Coll. Mus. Art, Williamstown, Mass., 1991, Aldrich Mus. Contemporary Art, Ridgefield, Conn., 1992, Mus. Modern Art, Mexico City, 1992, Yokohama Mus. Art, Japan, 1992, Marugame Inokuma-Genichiro Mus. Contemp. Art, 1992, Mus. Modern Art, Wakayama, 1992, Tokushima Modern Art Mus., Japan, 1992, Hokkaido Obihiro Mus. Art, 1993, Whitney Mus. Am. Art, Stamford, Conn., 1993, Gallery One, Toronto, Can., 1994; represented in permanent collections, Bklyn. Mus., Met. Mus. Art N.Y., , Solomon R. Guggenheim Mus., NYU, Mus. Modern Art, Albright-Knox Art Gallery, Buffalo, Whitney Mus., N.Y.C., U. Mich., High Mus., Atlanta, Milw. Art Inst., Wadsworth Atheneum, Hartford, Newark Mus., Yale U.

Art Gallery, U. Nebr. Art Gallery, Carnegie Inst., Pitts., Detroit Inst. Art, Balt. Mus. Art, Univ. Mus., Berkeley, Calif., Bennington (Vt.) Coll., Art Inst. Chgo., Cin. Art Mus., Cleve. Mus. Art, Columbus Gallery Fine Arts, Honolulu Acad. Arts, Contemporary Arts Assn., Houston, Pasadena Art Mus., William Rockhill Nelson Gallery Art, Kans. City, Kans., Kans. City Art Inst., Atkins Mus. Fine Arts, Kans. City, Kans., City Art Mus., St. Louis, Mus. Art, R.I. Sch. Design, Providence, San Francisco Mus. Art, Everson Mus., Syracuse, N.Y., Smithsonian Instn., Walker Art Inst., Mpls., Washington Gallery Modern Art, Wichita Art Mus., Brown Gallery Art, Nat. Gallery Victoria, Melbourne, Australia, Australian Nat. Gallery, Canberra, Victoria and Albert Mus., London, Eng., Tokyo Mus., Ulster Mus., Belfast, No. Ireland, Elvehjem Art Center, U. Wis., Israel Mus.-Instituto Nacional de Bellas Artes, Phila. Mus. Art, Phoenix Art Mus., Corcoran Gallery Art, Boston Mus. Fine Arts, Springfield (Mass.) Mus. Fine Arts, Witte Mus., San Antonio, Abbott Hall Art Gallery, Kendal, Eng., Mus. Contemporary Art, Nagaoka, Japan, Guggenheim Mus., N.Y.C., 1984, others; was subject of film Frankenthaler: Toward a New Climate, 1978. Trustee Bennington Coll., 1967—. Fellow Calhoun Coll., Yale U., 1968—; recipient 1st prize for painting Paris Biennale, 1959, Gold medal Pa. Acad. Fine Arts, 1968, Great Ladies award Fordham U., Thomas Moore Coll., 1969, Spirit of Achievement award Albert Einstein Coll. Medicine, 1970, Gold medal Commune of Catania, III Biennale della Grafica d'Arte, Florence, Italy, 1972, Garrett award 70th Am. Exhbn., Art Inst. Chgo., 1972, Creative Arts award Nat. Women's div. Am. Jewish Congress, 1974, Art and Humanities award Yale Women's Forum, 1976, Extraordinary Woman of Achievement award NCCJ, 1978, Alumni award Bennington Coll., 1979, N.Y.C. Mayor's award , 1986, Lifetiem Achievement award Coll. Art Assn., 1994. Mem. NEA, Am. Acad. (vice-chancelor 1991), Am. Acad. Arts and Scis., Nat. Coun. Arts, Nat. Inst. Arts and Letters. Office: M Knoedler & Co Inc 19 E 70th St New York NY 10021-4907*

FRANKER, STEPHEN GRANT, investment executive; b. Spencer, Iowa, July 29, 1949; s. Oscar Grant and Betty Jean (Greenwaldt) F.; m. Dianne Alice Russell, Aug. 23, 1970; children: Derek, Leah. BA, U. No. Iowa, 1971. CPA, Iowa. Staff acct. McGladrey, Hansen, Dunn & Co., CPA's, Mason City, Iowa, 1971-75; audit supr. Clinton, Iowa, 1975-76; contr. 1st Fed. Savs. & Loan Assn., Spirit Lake, Iowa, 1976-82, pres., 1982-83; v.p. NW Fed. Savs. Bank, Spencer, 1983-90; investment exec. Piper Jaffray, Inc., Spencer, 1990—. Republican. Lutheran. Avocations: reading, running, bicycling. Home: 503 9th St Spirit Lake IA 51360-1701 Office: Piper Jaffray Inc 4 E 4th St Spencer IA 51301-4009

FRANKFORTER, WELDON DELOSS, retired museum administrator; b. Tobias, Nebr., May 1, 1920; s. Archie and Mary Ann (Schroder) F.; m. Laura Glea Nicholas, Sept. 12, 1943; children—Mary Glea, Nicholas Dean, Gary Don, Matthew Jason, Lori Ann. BSc, U. Nebr., 1944, MSc, 1949. Student asst., assoc. curator U. Nebr. State Mus., Lincoln, 1941-50; dir. Sanford Mus. and Planetarium, Cherokee, Iowa, 1951-62; asst. dir. Grand Rapids Pub. Mus., Mich., 1962-64; dir. Grand Rapids Pub. Mus., 1965-88; mem. faculty Williamsburg Seminar, Va., 1971-73; mem. adv. council Nat. Mus. Act, Washington, 1971-76, Mich. Hist. Preservation Act, 1971-78; advisor for Mich. Nat. Trust Hist. Preservation, 1972-78, regional v.p., 1975-76; mem. Kent County Council for Historic Preservation, 1972—, pres., 1973-74; mem. extension inst. Mich. State U., East Lansing, 1973-75. Contbr. articles to profl. jours. Active Family Svc. Assn., Grand Rapids, 1967-73, West Mich. Environ. Action Coun., Grand Rapids, 1967—, Mich. Sesquicentennial Found., 1983-87; mem. Western Mich. World Affairs Coun., 1973—, pres., 1980-83; city liaison Grand Rapids Hist. Commn., 1974-88; bd. dirs. Hispanic Ctr. Western Mich., 1988-91; bd. govs. Aquinas Emeritus Coll., 1991-97, chmn., 1993-95; bd. dirs. West Mich. Interactive Sci. Ctr., 1990—. Fellow Geol. Soc. Am.; mem. Am. Assn. Mus. (exec. bd. 1973-75, v.p. 1977-80, mem. mus. accreditation com. 1970), Midwest Mus. Conf. (pres. 1966-67), Mich. Archaeol. Soc. (pres. 1968-69), Nebr. State Hist. Soc., Hist. Soc. Mich., Soc. Vertebrate Paleontology, Nebr. Acad. Scis., Mich. Acad. Scis., Arts and Letters, Iowa Acad. Scis., Iowa Archaeol. Soc., Mich. Mus. Assn., Nebr. State Genealogical Soc., Grand Rapids Hist. Soc. (v.p. 1993-94), Grand Forum (bd. dirs. 1995—), Edelweiss Club Grand Rapids (v.p. 1991-93), Torch Club (v.p. 1993-94, pres. 1994-95), Collectors Club Grand Rapids, Rotary, Sigma Xi. Episcopalian. Avocations: travel; photography; landscape gardening; building log cabins; art. Home: 4856 Fuller Ave SE Grand Rapids MI 49508-4738

FRANKFURTER, DAVID THOMAS MUNRO, religious studies educator; b. N.Y.C., Feb. 24, 1961; s. Alfred Moritz Frankfurter and Eleanor (Munro) Kahn; m. Anath Chana Golomb, Aug. 28, 1988; children: Raphael, Sariel. BA, Wesleyan U., 1983; MTS, Harvard U., 1986; MA, Princeton U., 1988, PhD, 1990. Asst. prof. religious studies The Coll. of Charleston, S.C., 1990-95; asst. prof. history and religious studies U. N.H., Durham, 1995-98, assoc. prof., 1998—. Author: Elijah in Upper Egypt, 1993, Religion in Roman Egypt, 1998. Bd. dirs. Planned Parenthood of Mid-Mich., Ann Arbor, 1989-90. Fairchild fellow Inst. for Advanced Study, 1993-95; grantee Nat. Endowment for Humanities, 1992. Mem. Am. Acad. Religion, Soc. Bibl. Lit., Internat. Assn. for Coptic Studies, Egyptian Exploration Soc., N.Am. Patristics Soc. Office: U NH U NH Dept History Durham NH 03824-3586

FRANKHOUSER, HOMER SHELDON, JR., engineering and construction company executive; b. Reading, Pa., Sept. 6, 1927; s. Homer Sheldon Sr. and Helen May (Geisewite) F.; m. Betty Carpenter, Sept. 2, 1972; children: Karl, Lorelei, Kurt, Michelle, Brandt. BCE, Lehigh U., 1952. Engr., then supt. Dravo Corp., Pitts., 1954-69; v.p. Dravo Ocean Structures, New Orleans, 1969-72; sr. project mgr. Brown & Root Inc., Houston, 1972-74, v.p., 1977-85; v.p. Brown & Root (U.K.) Ltd., London, 1974-77, dep. chmn., COO, 1980-89; sr. v.p. Brown & Root Inc., Houston, 1985-92; pres. Frankhouser & Assocs. Inc., Houston, 1992—, Internat. Indsl. Devel. Corp., 1997—, PetroAm. Corp., 1997—; chmn. Pulse Radar, Inc., 1997—; chmn. bd. Brown & Root Norge A.S., Oslo. 1st lt. U.S. Army, 1952-54, Korea. Mem. ASCE (life), Oil Industries Club (London), Inst. Dirs. (London), Masons. Republican. Avocation: oil painting. Home: 9095 Briar Forest Dr Houston TX 77024-7221 Office: Frankhouser & Assocs Inc 3535 Briarpark Dr Ste 207 Houston TX 77042-5234

FRANKL, DANIEL RICHARD, physicist, educator; b. N.Y.C., Sept. 6, 1922; s. William and Frances (Lerner) F.; m. Estelle Marder, Aug. 26, 1951; children—Joseph Frederick, Phyllis Gail. BSChemE, Cooper Union, 1943; Ph.D., Columbia, 1953. With U.S. Rubber Co., Detroit, 1943-50; with Gen. Telephone & Electronics Labs., Inc., Bayside, N.Y., 1953-63; vis. prof. phys. metallurgy U. Ill., Urbana; (on leave Gen. Telephone & Electronics Labs.), 1962-63; prof. physics Pa. State U., University Park, 1963-88, emeritus, 1988—; Vis. sr. research assoc. U. Sussex, 1969-70; vis. research physicist U. Calif., San Diego, 1978-79; vis. fellow Fitzwilliam Coll. U. Cambridge, 1986. Author: Electrical Properties of Semiconductor Surfaces, 1967; Electromagnetic Theory, 1986. Fellow Am. Phys. Soc. Research, publs. on internal friction, electroluminescence, surface properties of solids, thermal conduction, atomic beam scattering. Home: 438 Sierra Ln State College PA 16803-1409 Office: Pa State Univ Dept Physics University Park PA 16801

FRANKL, SPENCER NELSON, dentist, university dean; b. Phila., Nov. 19, 1933; s. Louis and Vera F.; m. Rhoda Lee, June 12, 1955; children—Elizabeth Ann, Catherine Susan. D.D.S., Temple U., 1958; postgrad., Children's Hosp. D.C., 1958-59; M.S., Tufts U., 1961. Asst. prof. dentistry Tufts U., 1961-64; asso. prof. Boston U., 1964-67, prof., 1967—, chmn. dept. dentistry, 1964-67, asst. dean, 1970-73, asso. dean, 1973—; dean Boston Univ. Sch. of Dental Medicine, 1977—; dep. dir. Boston U. Med. Ctr., 1980—; chief pedodontics Boston U. Med. Center U. Hosp., 1964; head pediatric dentistry Beth Israel Hosp., 1964; chief dental service Joseph P. Kennedy Jr. Meml. Hosp., Brighton, Mass., 1968—. Contbr. articles to profl. jours. Fellow Am. Coll. Dentists, Internat. Coll. Dentists, Am. Acad. Pediatric Dentistry; mem. APHA, ADA, Am. Soc. Dentistry for Children, Mass. Soc. Dentistry for Children (past pres.), Internat. Assn. for Dental Rsch., Am. Bd. Pedodontics (examiner). Office: 100 E Newton St Boston MA 02118-2308

FRANKL, WILLIAM STEWART, cardiologist, educator; b. Phila., July 15, 1928; s. Louis and Vera (Simkin) F.; m. Razelle Sherr, June 17, 1951; children: Victor S. (dec.), Brian A. BA in Biology, Temple U., 1951, MD, 1955, MS in Medicine, 1961. Diplomate Am. Bd. Internal Medicine, Am. Bd. Cardiovasc. Disease. Intern Buffalo Gen. Hosp., 1955-56; resident in medicine Temple U., Phila., 1956-57, 59-61; faculty Temple U. Sch. Medicine, 1962-68, dir. EKG sect. dept. cardiology, 1966-68, dir. cardiac care unit, 1967-68; prof. medicine, dir. divsn. cardiology Med. Coll. Pa., Phila., 1970-79; prof. medicine, assoc. dir. cardiology divsn. Thomas Jefferson U., Phila., 1979-84; physician-in-chief Springfield (Mass.) Hosp., 1968-70; pvt. practice Phila., 1962-68, 70—; prof. medicine, co-dir. William Likoff Cardiovascular Inst. Hahnemann U., Phila., 1984-86, dir. William Likoff Cardiovascular Inst., dir. div. cardiology, 1986-92, Thomas J. Vischer Prof. medicine, chmn. dept. medicine, 1987-92; prof. medicine, dir. cardiovascular regional programs Allegheny U. of the Health Scis., 1992-98; dir. cardiovascular regional programs Allegheny U. Hosps., 1992-98; v.p. cardiovascular program devel. Allegheny U. Hosps. System, 1995-98; prof. medicine cardiology divsn. dept. medicine Temple U. Sch. Medicine, 1998—; cons. cardiology Phila. Va Hosp., 1970-79; Fogarty Sr. Internat. fellow Cardiothoracic Inst., U. London, 1978-79; pres. Pa. affiliate Am. Heart Assn., 1985-86. Contbr. articles to profl. jours. Capt. (M.C.), U.S. Army, 1957-59. Cardiovascular Rsch. fellow U. Pa., Phila., 1961-62; recipient Golden Apple award Temple U. Sch. Medicine, 1967; award Med. Coll. Pa., 1972; Lindback award for distinguished teaching, 1975. Fellow ACP, Am. Coll. Cardiology (gov. Ea. Pa. 1986-89), Phila. Coll. Physicians, Am. Coll. Clin. Pharmacology (regent 1980-85, 93-98), Coun. Clin. Cardiology of Am. Heart Assn. (coun. on arteriosclerosis); mem. AAUP, AAAS, N.Y. Acad. Scis., Am. Fedn. Clin. Rsch., Assn. Am. Med. Colls., Am. Heart Assn. (bd. govs. S.E. Pa. chpt. 1972-84, pres. 1976, Pa. affiliate pres. 1984-85), Am. Soc. Clin. Pharmacology and Exptl. Therapeutics, Phila. County Med. Soc. (pres. 1993-94, 1st dist. trustee to Pa. Med. Soc. bd. trustees 1998—). Home: 536 Moreno Rd Wynnewood PA 19096-1121 Office: Temple U Hosp 3401 N Broad St Philadelphia PA 19140 *The essence of humanity and being human is caring. When one cares, life takes on a new dimension and provides one the ability to transcend the thin veneer which separates human and animal.*

FRANKLE, EDWARD ALAN, lawyer; b. N.Y.C., Dec. 14, 1946; m. Myrna Elaine Friedman, Feb. 22, 1986. BSE, Cath. U. Am., 1968, MSE, 1971; JD, Georgetown U., 1974. Bar: Md. 1974, D.C. 1980, U.S. Ct. Claims, 1976, U.S. Supreme Ct. 1978. Aerospace engr. Naval Ordnance Sta., Indian Head, Md., 1968-71; trial atty. Navy Gen. Counsel, Washington, 1974-78, asst. to gen. counsel, 1978-79, assoc. chief trial atty., 1979-80; assoc. dir. for policy SSS, Washington, 1980-82; chief counsel Goddard Space Flight Ctr., NASA, Greenbelt, Md., 1982-85; dep. gen. counsel NASA, Washington, 1985-88, gen. counsel, 1988—. Recipient Presdl. Rank, Meritorious Exec., 1988, Disting. Exec., 1992, NASA Disting. Svc. medal, 1993. Mem. ABA, AIAA (legal aspects com.), Internat. Inst. Space Law. Office: NASA Gen Counsel 300 E St SW Washington DC 20546-0005

FRANKLIN, AL, artistic director; b. Oceanside, Calif., Mar. 3, 1951; m. Elizabeth Amey Sanchez, June 22, 1985; children: Jacob Sanchez, Caleb Alexander. Freelance stage mgr., tour mgr., line prodr. various locations, 1979-86; prodn. mgr. Walnut St. Theatre, Phila., 1987-91; producing artistic dir. Gretna Theatre, Mt. Gretna, Pa., 1991-94; exec. dir. Theatre Assn. of Pa., 1995-96; artistic dir. Fort Wayne Civic Theatre, Ind., 1996—; founder, chmn. C-PATH, Lancaster, 1992-96. Prodr., dir. large and small musicals, new plays, Shakespeare and other classic plays, contemporary dramas and comedies, children's plays, workshops, play readings, spl. projects and fundraising events. Bd. dirs. Fort Wayne Civic Theatre, 1996—, Leadership Lebanon (Pa.) Valley, 1993-95, Friends of Colonial, Lebanon, 1992-94. With USAF, 1969-73, The Netherlands. Avocations: writing, martial arts, painting, clay sculpting. Home: 4811 Old Mill Rd Fort Wayne IN 46807-2927 Office: Ft Wayne Civic Theatre 303 E Main St Fort Wayne IN 46802-1907

FRANKLIN, ARETHA, singer; b. Memphis, 1942; d. Clarence L. and Barbara (Siggers) F.; m. Ted White (div.); m. Glynn Turman, Apr. 11, 1978. First record at age 12; rec. artist with Columbia Records, N.Y.C., 1961, then with Atlantic records, now with Arista Records; albums include Aretha, 1961, Electrifying, 1962, Tender Moving and Swinging, 1962, Laughing on the Outside, 1963, Unforgettable, 1964, Songs of Faith, 1964, Running Out of Fools, 1964, Yeah, 1965, Soul Sister, 1966, Queen of Soul, Take it Like You Give It, 1967, Lee Cross, Greatest Hits, 1967, I Never Loved a Man, 1967, Once in a Lifetime, Aretha Arrives, 1967, Lady Soul, 1968, Greatest Hits, Vol. 2, 1968, Best of Aretha Franklin, Live at Paris Olympia, 1968, Aretha Now, 1968, Soul 69, 1969, Today I Sing the Blues, 1969, Soft and Beautiful, Aretha Gold's, 1969, Satisfaction, I Say a Little Prayer, 1969, This Girl's in Love With You, 1970, Spirit in the Dark, 1970, Don't Play that Song, 1970, Live at the Fillmore West, 1971, Young Gifted and Black, 1971, Aretha's Greatest Hits, 1971, Amazing Grace, 1972, Hey Hey Now, 1973, Star Collection, 1978, First 12 Sides, 1973, Let Me Into Your Life, 1974, With Every Thing I Feel in Me, 1975, You, 1975, Sparkle, 1976, Ten Years of Gold, 1976, Sweet Passion, 1977, Almighty Fire, 1978, La Diva, 1979, Aretha, 1980, Who's Zoomin' Who, 1985, One Lord, One Faith, One Baptism, 1987, Aretha Sings the Blues, 1965, 85, Lady Soul, 1988, Through the Storm, 1989, What You See Is What You Sweat, 1991, Jazz to Soul, 1992, Aretha After Hours, Chain of Fools, 1993, Unforgettable: A Tribute to Dinah Washington, 1995, Love Songs, 1997; appeared in film: Blues Brothers, 1980; performer: (Showtime prodn.) Aretha, 1986; concert tours in U.S. and Europe. Named Top Female Vocalist, 1967; named Number One Female Singer 16th Internat. Jazz Critics Poll, 1968; recipient Grammy award for best female rhythm and blues vocal, 1967-74, 81, 85, 87, 88 for best rhythm and blues rec., 1967, for best soul gospel performance, 1972, for best rhythm and blues duo vocal (with George Michael, 1987); Am. Music award, 1984; Kennedy Center Honor, 1994; inducted into Rock and Roll Hall of Fame, 1987. Address: 8450 Linwood St Detroit MI 48206-2379 Office: care Arista Records c/o Gwen Quinn 6 W 57th St New York NY 10019*

FRANKLIN, BARBARA HACKMAN, business executive, former government official; b. Lancaster, Pa., Mar. 19, 1940; d. Arthur A. and Mayme M. (Haller) Hackman; m. Wallace Barnes, Nov. 29, 1986. BA with distinction, Pa. State U., 1962; MBA, Harvard U., 1964; D of Bus. Adminstrn. (hon.), Bryant Coll., 1973; D of Commerce (hon.), Drexel U., 1990; D of Comml. Sci. (hon.), U. Hartford, 1994; JD (hon.) Briarwood Coll., 1996. Mgr. environ. analysis Singer Co., N.Y.C., 1966-68; asst. v.p. Citibank, N.Y.C., 1969-71; asst. on White House staff for recruiting of women to positions in govt., Washington, 1971-73; commr., vice chmn. U.S. Consumer Product Safety Commn., Washington, 1973-79; sr. fellow, dir. govt. and bus. program Wharton Sch., U. Pa., Phila., 1979-88; pres., CEO Franklin Assocs., Washington, 1984-92; alt. rep. pub. del. 44th session UN Gen. Assembly, 1989-90; sec. commerce Dept. Commerce, Washington, 1992-93; pres. and CEO Barbara Franklin Enterprises, Washington, 1995—; adviser to comptroller gen. U.S., 1984-92, 94—; bd. dirs. Aetna, Inc., 1979-92, chair audit com., 93—; bd. dirs. Cinn. Milacron Inc., 1996—, Dow Chem. Co., 1980-92, chair audit com., 1985-92, 93—; bd. dirs. AMP, Inc., 1993—, J.A. Jones, Inc., 1995-98, MedImmune, Inc., 1995—, NASDAQ Stock Market, 1996-98, Guest Svc., Inc., 1995—; Automatic Data Processing, Inc., 1984-92, Armstrong World Ind., 1989-92, Black & Decker Corp., 1985-92, Westinghouse Electric Corp., 1980-92, Nordstrom, 1988-92; pub. mem. Auditing Standards Bd. Planning Com., 1989; pub. mem., bd. dirs., chair audit com. Am. Inst. CPA's, 1979-86. Apptd. by Pres. Reagan then Bush to Pres.'s Adv. Com. Trade Policy and Negotiations, 1982-86, 89-92, chair task force on tax reform, 1985-86; co-chmn. Nat. Fin. Com. George Bush for Pres., 1987-88; Conn. reps. fin. chair, 1993-94; bd. visitors Def. Systems Mgmt. Coll., Dept. Def., 1986-89; svcs. policy adv. Com. of U.S. Trade Representatives; apptd. by Gov. Thornburgh to State Bd. Edn., Commonwealth Pa., 1980-81; bd. regents U. Hartford, 1986-88. Commentator Nightly Bus. Report, 1997—. Trustee Pa. State U., 1976-82; bd. dirs. Harvard Bus. Sch., 1998—. Recipient Disting. Alumni award Pa. State U., 1972, Disting. Woman award Northwood Inst., 1972, Mother Gerard Phelan medal Marymount Coll., 1972, Catalyst award for Corp. Leadership, 1981, Excellence in Mgmt. award Simmons Coll., 1981, Am. Assn. Poison Control Ctrs. award, 1979, cert. appreciation, Am. Acad. Pediatrics, 1979, Dirs. Choice award Nat. Women's Econ. Alliance, 1987, Corp. Social Responsibility award CUNY, 1988, John J. McCloy Auditing award, 1992, Womens Nat. Rep. Club award, 1993; Kappa Alpha Theta Graduate fellow, 1962, Edith Gratia Stedman, Harvard U., fellow, 1962; named one of 50 Most Influential Corp. Dirs. Am. Mgmt. Assn., 1990. Fellow Nat. Assn. Corp. Dirs.; mem. NACD (Blue Ribbon commn. bd. and CEO evaluation 1994), Women's Forum Washington, Nat. Women's Econ. Alliance Found. (bd. govs. 1984-92, 94-96, Nixon Ctr. for Peace and Freedom (adv. coun.), Dir.'s Choice award 1987), U.S. China Bus. Coun., Nat. Com. U.S.-China Rels. (dir.), Atlantic Coun. (bd. dirs.), Internat. Women's Forum (founding mem.), Asia Soc., Coun. Fgn. Rels., Exec. Women in Govt. (founding mem., vice chmn. 1973—), Heritage Found. (chair internat. trade adv. coun.), Bretton Woods Com., Alumni Coun. Pa. State U., 1925 F Street Club, Washington, Women's Nat. Rep. Club (bd. govs. 1969-71), Econ. Club N.Y. (trustee 1998—), Econ. Club D.C, Union League Club N.Y. Congregational. Avocations: exercise, hiking, reading. Office: 2600 Virginia Ave NW Ste 506 Washington DC 20037-1905 also: 1875 Perkins St Bristol CT 06010-8910*

FRANKLIN, BILLY JOE, international higher education specialist; b. Honey Grove, Tex., Jan. 30, 1940; s. John Asia and Annie Mae (Castle) F.; m. Sonya Kay Erwin, June 1, 1958; children: Terry Daylon, Shari Dea. BA, U. Tex., 1965, MA, 1967, PhD, 1969. Asst. prof. sociology U. Iowa, Iowa City, 1969-71; chmn. Western Carolina U., Cullowhee, N.C., 1971-72, Wright State U., Dayton, Ohio, 1973-75; dean S.W. Tex. State U., San Marcos, 1975-77; v.p. acad. affairs Stephen F. Austin State U., Nacogdoches, Tex., 1977-81; pres. Tex. A&I U., Kingsville, 1981-85, Lamar U., Beaumont, Tex., 1985-91; exec. v.p. Tex. Internat. Edn. Consortium, Austin, 1991-96, pres., 1996—; mem. nat. agrl. rsch. com. USDA, 1982-85; policies and purposes com. Am. Assn. State Colls. and Univs., 1985-91, nominating com., 1986-88, mem. exec. com. bd. dirs., 1990-91; pres. Assn. Tex. Colls. and Univs., 1985-86, Tex. Acad. Sci., 1986-87; commr. commn. on colls. So. Assn. Colls. and Schs., 1985-90, chmn., 1987-90, pres.-elect, 1990-91; chmn. Coun. Pub. Univ. Pres. and Chancellors, 1988-91; bd. dirs. Tex. Ptnrs. of Am. Co-editor: Research Methods: Issues and Insights, 1971, Social Psychology and Everyday Life, 1973; contbr. articles to profl. jours. Mem. sr. adv. bd. Tex. Lyceum, Inc., 1982-88; bd. dirs. United Way of Coastal Bend, 1981-84, United Way of Beaumont, Tex., Tex. Ptnrs. of the Ams., 1994—; chmn. Austin-Oita (Japan) Sister Citis, 1995-96; ; bd. dirs. Energy Mus., 1987, pres., 1987-90; mem. exec. com. Muscular Dystrophy Assn., 1985-91. Presbyterian. Fellow Tex. Acad. Sci.; mem. Am. Sociol. Assn., Kingsville C. of C. (bd. dirs. 1981-83, pres. 1984), Beaumont C. of C. (bd. dirs. 1986-91, chmn. 1988-89), East Tex. C. of C. (bd. dirs. 1985-87), East Tex. Venture Capital Group (bd. dirs. 1985-87), Sigma Xi. Presbyterian. Office: PO Box 7667 Austin TX 78713-7667

FRANKLIN, BLAKE TIMOTHY, lawyer; b. San Mateo, Calif., Sept. 28, 1942; s. Harvey James and Marie Agnes (Leane) F. AB, Dartmouth Coll., 1963; JD, Harvard U., 1966. Bar: Calif. 1966, D.C. 1969, U.S. Supreme Ct. 1970, N.Y. 1976. AID contractor Peace Corps; vis. prof. comml. law U. Costa Rica, San Jose, 1966-68; assoc. Coudert Bros., Washington, 1969-74; ptnr. Coudert Bros., N.Y.C., 1975-83, Gibson Dunn & Crutcher, N.Y.C., 1983—; bd. dirs. Minera, S.A., Union Theol. Sem., N.Y., Nat. Law Ctr. for Inter-Am. Free Trade, Tucson. Chancellor of vestry St. Michael's Ch., N.Y.C., 1987-93; trustee Aids Svc. Found. of Orange County, Calif., 1994-97; St. Hilda's and St. Hugh's Sch., N.Y.C., 1988-92; mem. bd. gov.'s USO, 1987-90. Mem. ABA, Inter-Am. Bar Assn., Am. Soc. Internat. Law, Assn. of Bar of City of N.Y. Episcopalian. Office: Gibson Dunn & Crutcher 200 Park Ave Fl 47 New York NY 10166-0193

FRANKLIN, BONNIE GAIL, actress; b. Santa Monica, Calif., Jan. 6, 1944; d. Samuel Benjamin and Claire (Hersch) F. B.A., UCLA, 1966. Mem. regional theatres in, N.Y., Mass., Ohio, Maine, N.H., Conn., Pa., 1972-99. Stage appearances include Your Own Thing, San Francisco, L.A., N.Y.C., 1968, Dames At Sea, 1969, Applause, N.Y.C., 1970-72 (Aegis Theatre Club award 1970, Theatre Club award 1970, Outer Critics Circle award 1960-70, Tony nomination), Happy Birthday and Other Humiliations, N.Y., 1987, Frankie & Johnny in the Clair de Lune, 1988, Grace & Glorie, 1996; tv appearances include One Day At A Time, 1975-84. Mem. AFTRA, SAG, Actors Equity Assn., Dirs. Guild Am. Democrat. Jewish. Address: 15745 Royal Oak Rd Encino CA 91436-3907 *To avoid criticism: say nothing, do nothing, be nothing.*

FRANKLIN, BONNIE SELINSKY, federal agency administrator; b. Oakland, Calif., Mar. 17, 1944; d. Harold Joseph and Madge (Warden) Selinsky; m. Alfred Carl Franklin, Jan. 24, 1981; 1 child, Amy Beth. AB in Am. Studies, George Washington U., 1966, MBA in Acctg., 1977. Tax auditor IRS, Baileys Crossroads, Va., 1966-71; from program analyst to tax law specialist IRS, Washington, 1971-77, from program analyst appeals to chief procedures sect., 1979-82, tech. asst. to nat. dir. appeals, 1985—; regional analyst conf. IRS, Atlanta, 1977-79. Chair Arlingtonians for a Better County, Arlington, Va., 1994-97, archivist, 1999; active Friends of the Libr., Arlington, 1996—. Mem. LWV (treas. Arlington Va. chpt. 1998—), Womens Nat. Dem. Club. Democrat. Lutheran. Avocations: reading, travel.

FRANKLIN, BRUCE WALTER, lawyer; b. Ellendale, N.D., Feb. 26, 1936; s. Wallace Henry and Frances (Webb) F.; m. Kristy Ann Jones, Feb. 7, 1944; children: Kevin, Monica, Taylor. Student, U. Mich., 1954-56; LLB, Detroit Coll. Law, 1962. Bar: Mich. 1963. Sole practice Troy, Mich., from 1962; mng. ptnr. Franklin, Bigler, Berry & Johnston, P.C., Troy, 1991-98; now mng. ptnr. Bruce Franklin P.C., Troy; pres., CEO Lanward III Devel. Corp. (Arbor Springs Plantation). *Highly successful trial attorney for 35 years. Currently president and CEO of Landward III (Arbor Springs Plantation), a major 2000 acre golf residential development in Metro Atlanta. Also president of Arbor Springs Realty and Alta Vista Properties, a commercial developer. Chairman of the board of the United Methodist Retirement Communities form 1994-1997. UMRC is a multiple CCRC facility with emphasis on dementia care in southeastern Michigan. Accomplishments during his tenure included the implementation of a 15 million dollar state of the art dementia center and the creation of a foundation board for an innovative and highly successful fund raising program.* Past chmn. Mich. Young Reps., United Meth. Retirement Cmtys. Served with U.S. Army. Office: Landward III 250 Arbor Springs Plantation Dr Newnan GA 30265

FRANKLIN, CABE GERARD, information systems specialist; b. East Patchogue, N.Y., June 8, 1973; s. Stephen Anthony Franklin and Janet Marie (Gough) Bedol. BA, Amherst Coll., 1995. Rsch. asst. Obilvy, Adams & Rinehart, Washington, 1995, acct. coord., 1995-96, rsch. assoc., 1996, asst. acct. exec., 1996-97, acct. exec., 1997-98, assoc., 1998, dir. interactive svcs., 1998—; co-host Technology Today, WTEM Radio, WBIG Radio, Washington, 1998—. Author: Just Between Friends, 1992. Mem. Friends of Amherst Coll. Libr., 1990—. Recipient Featured Website award ASAE, 1995, Best Ann. Report award ARC awards, 1997. Mem. Hexagon, Amherst Alumni Assn. of Washington (sec. 1994-98), Chi Psi. Avocations: creative writing, mathematics, singing. Office: Ogilvy Adams & Rinehart 1901 L St NW Ste 300 Washington DC 20036-3515

FRANKLIN, CARL, director; b. Richmond, Calif., Apr. 11, 1949. Student, U. Calif., Berkeley. *Attended the American Film Institute.* Dir. (films) One False Move, 1992, Devil in a Blue Dress, 1995, One True Thing, 1998, (TV) Laurel Avenue, 1993, Punk, 1993, Partners, 1999; appeared in TV series Caribe, 1975, The Fantastic Journey, 1977, McClain's Law, 1981-82, also TV episodes; writer Devil in a Blue Dress, 1995, Punk, 1993. Avocation: poetry. Office: Internat Creative Mgmt 8942 Wilshire Blvd Beverly Hills CA 90211-1934

FRANKLIN, CHARLES SCOTHERN, lawyer; b. Knoxville, Tenn., Dec. 12, 1937; s. Samuel Leroy and Mildred (Gibson) F.; m. Lynn Kerr; children: Jill Parvin, Melissa Ann, Samuel Arthur. B.S., U. Tenn., 1958, MS, 1960; LL.B., Vanderbilt U., 1966. Bar: Calif. 1967, Nev. 1971. Instr. econs. U. Tenn., Knoxville, 1960-61; Ford Found. fellow in econs. U. Calif., Berkeley, 1962; assoc. firm Kent Brookes & Anderson, San Francisco, 1966-70; gen. counsel, sec. Harrah's, Reno, 1970-79; pvt. practice Reno, 1980-85, Sacramento, 1985-94. Mem. Nev. State Bar, Calif. State Bar. Home: 2814 Greenrock Trl Atlanta GA 30340-5014

FRANKLIN, CHERYL JEAN, engineer, author; b. Pasadena, Calif., Sept. 11, 1955; d. Peter Gordon and B. Joyce (Jette) F. BS in Math., U. Redlands, 1975; postgrad studies engring., U. Calif., Irvine, 1975-76, Calif. State U., Fullerton, 1980-81. Tech. staff mem. Boeing, Anaheim, Calif., 1976—; mem. Creative Writing adv. bd. Calif. State U., Fullerton, 1996. Author: (books) Fire Get, 1987, Fire Lord, 1989, Fire Crossing, 1991, Inquisitor (et al), 1992. Mem. Authors Guild, Sci. Fiction and Fantasy Writers of Am. Episcopalian. Avocations: conchology, painting, musical theater. Home: 19502 Old Ranch Rd Yorba Linda CA 92886-4307 Office: Boeing DF07 3370 Miraloma Ave Anaheim CA 92803

FRANKLIN, CORY MICHAEL, medical administrator, educator; b. Chgo., June 30, 1954; s. Murray and Charlotte (Ringel) F.; m. Suzanne Drabant, Aug. 15, 1982; children: Shana, Celia, Samuel, Charlotte-Frances. BS, Northwestern U., 1973, MD, 1977. Cert. internal medicine and critical care medicine. Dir. med. intensive care U. Ill., Chgo., 1981-82, Cook County Hosp., Chgo., 1982—; prof. medicine/med. ethics Finch U., North Chicago, Ill., 1991—; sci. advisor Critical Care Investigation Network, Chgo., 1995—. Author: (med. book) Yearbook of Critical Care, 1995—; tech. advisor: (film) The Fugitive, 1993; contbr. articles to med. jours. Mem. Free Clinic of Cleve., 1980-81. Mem. N.Y. Acad. Scis., Inst. Medicine of Chgo. (bd. dirs. 1993—). Office: Cook County Hosp 1900 W Polk St Chicago IL 60612-3736

FRANKLIN, EDWARD WARD, international investment consultant, lawyer, actor; b. N.Y.C., Sept. 23, 1926; s. Albert Ward and Edith (Meyers) F.; m. Joan Rice, Aug. 25, 1956; children—Caroline, Melissa, Edward Ward. AB magna cum laude, Harvard U., 1947, LLB, 1950. Bar: N.Y. 1951. Assoc. Cadwalader, Wickersham & Taft, N.Y.C., 1950-56; gen. counsel N.Y. Air Brake Co., 1956-67, v.p. internat. and legal, 1962-67; v.p., gen. counsel Gen. Signal Corp., N.Y.C., 1967-80; sec. Gen. Signal Corp., 1969-80, sr. v.p., 1980-83, vice chmn., 1983-85, also dir., mem. exec. com.; chmn. bd. Hamworthy Hydraulics, Ltd., Poole, Eng.; dir. Holborn Internat. Portfolio Mgrs., Ptnrs. Fund, Inc., Pacus Ventures Ltd., Chase NBW Bank. Life gov., trustee N.Y. Presbyn. Hosp.; bd. dirs. York Theatre Co.; trustee Trinity Episcopal Schs. Corp. Mem. AEA, SAG, AFTRA, Assn. Bar City of N.Y., The Players, Knickerbocker Club, Harvard Club (N.Y.C.), Misquamicut Club (Watch Hill, R.I.), Phi Beta Kappa. Home and Office: 1185 Park Ave New York NY 10128-1308

FRANKLIN, GENE FARTHING, engineering educator, consultant; b. Banner Elk, N.C., July 25, 1927; s. Burnie D. and Delia (Farthing) F.; m. Gertrude Stritch, Jan. 1952; children: David M., Carole Lea. BSEE, Ga. Inst. Tech., 1950; MSEE, MIT, 1952; DEngSc, Columbia U., 1955. Asst. prof. Columbia U., N.Y.C., 1955-57; prof. elec. engring. Stanford (Calif.) U., 1957-95, prof. emeritus, 1995—; cons. IBM, Rochester, Minn., 1982-94. Author: Sampled-Data Control, 1958, Digital Control, 1980, 3d edit., 1997, Feedback Control, 1986, 2d edit., 1991, 3d edit., 1994. With USN, 1945-47. Recipient Edn. award Am. Automatic Control Coun., 1985. Fellow IEEE (life), Control Soc. of IEEE (Bode lectr. 1994). Democrat. Office: Stanford U Dept Elec Engring Stanford CA 94305

FRANKLIN, G(EORGE) CHARLES, academic administrator; b. Normangee, Tex., Dec. 27, 1935; married; 3 children. BBA, Sam Houston State U., 1958, postgrad., 1958—. Chief acct., instr. acct. Sam Houston State U., Huntsville, Tex., 1959-62; asst. to dir. Commn. on Coord. Higher Edn. Fin. State of Ark., 1962-64; contr. Ark. State U., Jonesboro, 1964-65; v.p. for bus. affairs Midwestern U., Wichita Falls, Tex., 1965-69; bus. mgr. U. Tex., Austin, 1969-71; v.p. for fiscal affairs U. Tex., San Antonio, 1971-72; v.p. for adminstrn. and fin., Health Sci. Ctr. U. Tex., Houston, 1972-79; v.p. adminstrv. svcs. U. Tex., Austin, 1979-80, v.p. for bus. affairs, 1980—. 2d lt. U.S. Army, 1958-59. Mem. Nat. Assn. Coll. and Univ. Bus. Officers, So. Assn. Coll. and Univ. Bus. Officers, Tex. Assn. State Sr. Coll. and Univ. Bus. Officers (pres. 1988). Home: 6603 Cypress Pt N Austin TX 78746-7104 Office: U Tex Austin VP Bus Affairs PO Box 8179 Austin TX 78713-8179

FRANKLIN, GODFREY, adult education educator; b. Ghana, West Africa; came to U.S., 1976; s. Mercy Lydia Kyeiwa-Franklin; m. Kay Tidmarsh, Dec. 29, 1973; children: Jared J., Trina T. Diploma in theology, Melbourne Coll. Div., Australia, 1973; BD, Ref. Theol. Coll., Geelong, Australia, 1975; MA, U. Ala., 1978, PhD, 1983. Ordained Reformed Presbyn. pastor, 1976. Pastor Ref. Presbyn. Ch., Selma, Ala., 1976-81; counseling psychologist U. West Fla., Pensacola, 1983-91, asst. prof. edn., 1991-95, assoc. prof., 1996—, dir. Multicultural Ctr., 1998—; founding pastor Multiracial Ref. Presbyn. Ch., Pensacola, 1989—; cons. USAF S.O.S., Hurlburt Field, Fla., 1985—. Contbr. articles to profl. jours. Recipient Golden Apple award Escambia County Sch. Sys., Pensacola, 1993, 99, Disting. Tchr. award U. West Fla., 1993, 99, Outstanding Undergrad. Tchg. and Advising award, 1994. Mem. ASCD, ACA, Am. Assn. Christian Counselors, Phi Kappa Phi. Avocations: travel, soccer, racquetball, jogging, golf. Home: 5625 Saint Adamnan Ave Pensacola FL 32503-7916 Office: Univ of West Florida 11000 University Pkwy Pensacola FL 32514-5732

FRANKLIN, H. BRUCE, language educator, writer; b. Bklyn., Feb. 28, 1934; s. Robert and Florence (Cohen) F.; m. Jane Morgan, Feb. 11, 1956; children: Karen, Gretchen, Robert Morgan. BA, Amherst Coll., 1955; PhD, Stanford U., 1961. Tugboat deckhand, mate Pa. R.R., Jersey City, 1955-56; asst. prof. English, assoc. prof. Stanford (Calif.) U., 1961-64, 65-72; asst. prof. English Johns Hopkins U., Balt., 1964-65; vis. prof. English Wesleyan U., Middletown, Conn., 1974-75; prof. English Rutgers U., Newark, N.J., 1975-87; John Cotton Dana prof. English Rutgers U., Newark, 1987—; cons. Stanford Rsch. Inst., 1962-64, Sugarloaf Films, 1993; adv. bd. mem. Vietnam Generation, 1994—. Author: The Wake of the Gods: Melville's Mythology, 1963, rev. edit., 1983, Future Perfect: American Science Fiction of the 19th Century, 1966, 4th edit., 1995, Herman Melville's Mardi: And a Voyage Thither, 1964, The Scarlet Letter, Together With Main Street, Ethan Brand, and Hawthorne's Published Critical Writings, 1967, Herman Melville's the Confidence-Man: His Masquerade, 1967, Who Should Run the Universities, 1969, From the Movement: Toward Revolution, 1971, The Essential Stalin: Major Theoretical Writings, 1905-52, 1972, Back Where You Came From, 1975, The Victim as Criminal and Artist: Literature From the American Prison, 1978, Robert A. Heinlein: America as Science Fiction, 1980, American Prisoners and Ex-Prisoners: An Annotated Bibliography of Their Writings, 1798-1981, 1982, Countdown to Midnight, 1984, Vietnam and America: A Documented History, 1985, rev. edit., 1995, War Stars: The Superweapon and the American Imagination, 1988, M.I.A. or Mythmaking in America, 1992, the Vietnam War in American Stories, Songs, and Poems, 1996, Prison Writing in 20th Century America, 1998; edit. bd. cons. Sci.-Fiction Studies, 1973—; contbr. articles to profl. jours. 1st lt. USAF, 1956-59. Fellow Am. Coun. Learned Societies, 1968-69, grantee, 1967; Stanford Wilson fellow, 1960-61, Rockefeller Found. Humanities fellow, 1975-76; grantee Nat. Endowment Humanities, 1982, William Joiner Ctr., 1987; recipient Alexander Cappon prize, 1978, Eaton award, 1981, Pilgrim award, 1983, Disting. Scholar award Internat. Assn. Fantastic in Arts, 1990, Pioneer award, 1991. Office: English Dept Rutgers Univ Newark NJ 07102

FRANKLIN, HARDY R., retired library director; b. Rome, Ga., May 9, 1929; B.A. in Sociology, Morehouse Coll., 1950; M.L.S., Atlanta U., 1956; Ph.D. (Higher Edn. Act fellow), Rutgers U., 1971; m. Barbara Washington; children: Petey, Regan Hayes. Tchr., librarian Rockdale County Bd. Edn., Conyers, Ga., 1950-53; various positions Bklyn. Pub. Library, 1956-64, sr. community coordinator, 1964-68; asst. prof. library sci. dept. Queens Coll. City U. N.Y., Flushing, 1971-74; dir. D.C. Pub. Library, Washington, 1974-97, ret., 1997; cons., guest lectr. in field. Pres., Middle Schs. PTA, Hempstead, N.Y., 1973-74; mem. advisory council to supt. schs., Hempstead, 1973-74; mem. advisory bd. D.C. Citizens for Better Edn., 1975—; mem. advisory bd. Streets for People, 1975—; co-chmn. One Fund campaign, 1975, 76. Served with U.S. Army, 1953-55. Recipient Bklyn. Friends of Library award, 1963, Community Leader award Freedom Nat. Bank, 1968, Disting. Svc. award Rutgers U., 1992; Council on Library Resources grantee, 1970-71; Nat. Endowment for the Humanities grantee, 1970-71; named Washingtonian of Yr., 1987. Mem. ALA (pres. 1993-94, Allie Beth Martin award 1983), D.C. Libr. Assn. (v.p., pres. elect. 1991-92, bd. trustees Disting. Svc. award 1990), Am. Film Inst., Assn. Study of Afro-Am. Life and History, Urban League, NAACP, Sigma Pi Phi, Alpha Phi Alpha. Contbr. articles to profl. jours. Home: 4417 46th St NW Washington DC 20016-2031

FRANKLIN, HAROLD LEROY, graphic artist, filmmaker; b. Mobile, Ala., Mar. 14, 1934; s. Harold Leroy and Julia (Nicholson) F.; m. Frances Sanders, Aug. 24, 1996; 1 child, Lavarr K. Zuber. Diploma, Phila. Coll. Art, 1958. Art dir. City of Phila., 1961-97; film prodr., dir. EKO Prodns., Phila., 1969—; freelance artist Phila. Inquirer Sunday Mag., 1970, N.Y. Times Sunday Mag., Bus. Week Mag., 1971. Author: Which Way to Go, 1969, A Garden on Cement, 1971, Once Around the Track, 1974, A Trip Back to Elmwood, 1991; film prodr. The Classroom Channel, Lakewood, Colo., 1987-90, WHYY-TV, Channel 12, Phila., 1986, 92, The Black Filmmaker Found., 1987-88. Mem. Black Peoples' Unity Movement, Phila., 1968-71. With U.s. Army, 1958-60. Recipient Spl. Jury's prize Phila. Internat. Film Festival, 1986; Pa. Coun. Arts film fellow, 1992. Mem. Phila. Ind. Film/Video Assn. Democrat. Baptist. Avocations: writing, historical research, movies, plays, flea markets. Home: 1315 S 53rd St Philadelphia PA 19143-4901 Office: EKO Prodns PO Box 5492 Philadelphia PA 19143-0492

FRANKLIN, JOEL NICHOLAS, mathematician, educator; b. Chgo., Apr. 4, 1930; m. Patricia Anne; 1 dau., Sarah Jane. B.S., Stanford, 1950, Ph.D., 1953. Research asso. N.Y. U., 1953-55; asst. prof. math. U. Wash, 1955; mem. faculty Calif. Inst. Tech., 1957—, prof. applied sci., 1966-69, prof. applied math., 1969—. Author: Matrix Theory, 1968, Methods of Mathematical Economics, 1980, also articles. Mem. Am. Math. Soc., Soc. Indsl. and Applied Math., Phi Beta Kappa. Home: 1763 Alta Crest Dr Altadena CA 91001-2130 Office: Calif Inst Tech 217-50 Pasadena CA 91125

FRANKLIN, JOHN HOPE, historian, educator, author; b. Rentiesville, Okla., Jan. 2, 1915; s. Buck Colbert and Mollie (Parker) F.; m. Aurelia E. Whittington, June 11, 1940; 1 son, John Whittington. AB, Fisk U., 1935; AM, Harvard, 1936, PhD, 1941; hon. degrees, Morgan State Coll., Va. State Coll., Lincoln (Pa.) U., Cambridge (Eng.) U., Drake U., Mich. State U., U. Ill. at Chgo., Carnegie-Mellon U., Columbia U., Columbia Coll., Chgo., Loyola U., Chgo., Bklyn. Coll., Bard Coll., Boston Coll., Brown U., Tuskegee Inst., Grand Valley Coll., Marquette U., Lincoln Coll., Ill., Princeton, Hamline U., Fisk U., R.I. Coll., Dickinson Coll., Howard U., U. Md., U. Notre Dame, Tulsa U., Morehouse Coll., Miami U., Johnson C. Smith U., Lake Forest Coll., Tougaloo Coll., Union Coll., Northwestern U., Whittier Coll., U. Mass., U. Mich., Seattle U., U. Toledo, Yale U., L.I. U., Catholic U. Am., Tulane U., Temple U., Kalamazoo Coll., Washington U., St. Louis, Trinity Coll. (Conn.), Ariz. State U., SUNY, Albany, No. Mich. U., U. Utah, Coll. New Rochelle, George Washington U., Governors State U., Harvard U., U. Pa., Ripon Coll., Atlanta U., Wayne State U., U. N.C.-Chapel Hill, Dillard U., Manhattan Coll., Roosevelt U., N.C. Central U., Ind. State U., St. Olaf Coll., Emory U., U. Miami, U. Conn., U. N.C.-Charlotte, Brandeis U., Wake Forest U., Wilkes Coll., Queen's Coll., N.Y., Wilmington Coll., Hope Coll., Bryant Coll., SUNY-Binghamton, Indiana U., N.C. Weslyan U., N.C. State U., So. Meth. U., Berea Coll., Grad Ctr. CUNY, Suffolk U., Washington Coll., Eckerd Coll., Rutgers U., U. N.C., Greensboro, St. Augustine Coll., U. Okla., Oreg. State U., Winston-Salem State U., Queens Coll., Charlotte, N.C., Ill. State U., Bates Coll., Williams Coll., U. of the South, U. N.C.-Wilmington, Am. U.; hon. degree, Furman U., Georgetown U., Tufts U., Elizabeth City State U., Shaw U., San Francisco U., Washington and Lee U., Columbia U., Chgo., Lincoln Meml. U., Elmira Coll., Lane Coll., Bethune-Cookman Coll., Amherst Coll., U. Cin., Dartmouth Coll., U. Ky., Duke U., San Francisco State U., York Coll., Northeastern U., Occidental Coll. Instr. history Fisk U., 1936-37; prof. history St. Augustine's Coll., 1939-43, N.C. Coll. at Durham, 1943-47, Howard U., 1947-56; chmn. dept. history Bklyn. Coll., 1956-64; prof. Am. history U. Chgo., 1964-82, chmn. dept. history, 1967-70, John Matthews Manly Distinguished Service prof., 1969-82; James B. Duke prof. history Duke U., 1982-85; prof. legal history Duke U. Law Sch., 1985-92; Elizabeth City State U., Shaw U., U. San Francisco, Washington and Lee U.; Pitt prof. Am. history and instns. Cambridge U., 1962-63; vis. prof. Harvard U., U. Wis., Cornell U., Salzburg Seminar, U. Hawaii, U. Calif., Cambridge U.; chmn. Bd. Fgn. Scholarships, 1966-69, Nat. Coun. on Humanities, 1976-79; trustee Nat. Humanities Ctr., 1980-91, chmn. adv. bd. to pres.'s initiative on race, 1997—; Fulbright prof., Australia, 1960; Jefferson lectr. in humanities, 1976; Fulbright disting. lectr., Zimbabwe, 1986; chmn. Adv. Bd. to the Pres.'s Initiative on Race, 1997—. Author: Free Negro in North Carolina, 1943, From Slavery to Freedom: A History of African Americans, 7th edit, 1994, Militant South, 1956, Reconstruction After the Civil War, 1961, The Emancipation Proclamation, 1963, A Southern Odyssey, 1976, Racial Equality in America, 1976, George Washington Williams, A Biography, 1985, Race and HIstory, 1990; (with others) Land of the Free, 1966, Illustrated History of Black Americans, 1970, The Color Line: Legacy for the 21st Century, 1993; editor: Civil War Diary of James T. Ayers, 1947, A Fool's Errand by Albion Tourgee, 1961, Army Life in a Black Regiment by Thomas Higginson, 1962, Color and Race, 1968, Reminiscences of an Active Life by John R. Lynch, 1970; editor: (with August Meier) Black Leaders in the Twentieth Century, 1982 (with Abraham Eisenstadt) Harlan Davidson's American History Series; mem. editorial bd.: Am. Scholar, 1972-76, 94—, My Life and An Era (with John W. Franklin). Bd. dirs. Salzburg Seminar, Mus. Sci. and Industry, 1968-80, DuSable Mus., 1970—; trustee Chgo. Symphony, 1976-80, Fisk U., 1947-80. Recipient Cleanth Brooks medal Fellowship So. Writers, 1989, Gold medal Ency. Brit., 1990, Caldwell medal N.C. Coun. on Humanities, N.C. medal, 1992, 93, Charles Frankel medal, 1993, NAACP Spingarn medal, 1995, others; Bruce Catton award Soc. Am. Historians, 1994, Cosmos Club award, 1994, Sidney Hook award Phi Beta Kappa Soc., 1994, Pres. Medal of Freedom, 1995, Peggy V. Helmerich Disting. Author award, 1997, Smithson Bicentennial medal, 1997; named to Okla. Hall of Fame, 1978, Okla. Historians Hall of Fame, 1996; Edward Austin fellow, 1937-39, Guggenheim fellow, 1950-51, 73-74, Pres.'s fellow Brown U., 1952-53, Ctr. for Advanced Study in Behavioral Scis. fellow, 1973-74, sr. Mellon fellow. Fellow Am. Acad. Arts and Scis.; mem. Am. Hist. Assn. (pres. 1978-79), So. Hist. Assn. (pres. 1970-71), Orgn. Am. Historians (pres. 1974-75), Assn. for Study Negro Life and History, Am. Studies Assn. (past pres.), Am. Philos. Soc. (Jefferson medal 1993), AAUP, Phi Beta Kappa (senate 1966-82, pres. 1973-76), Phi Alpha Theta. Home: 208 Pineview Rd Durham NC 27707-2846

FRANKLIN, JOHN THOMAS IKEDA, English educator; b. Knoxville, Tenn., July 12, 1956; s. John Wesley and Yoshiko (Ikeda) F. BA in English and Econs., Rice U., 1978; MA in English, Miami U., Oxford, Ohio, 1986; PhD in English, U. Fla., 1994. Cert. educator, Tex. Tchr. English Jesse Jones H.S., Houston, 1978-84; TV prodr. Fredonia Hill TVM, Nacogdoches, Tex., 1991-94; prof. English Pitts. (Kans.) State U., 1995—, dir. writing ctr., 1997—; chair grad. student forum South Atlantic MLA, Tampa, Fla., 1990; advisor Sigma Tau Delta, Pittsburg, 1995-99. Producer: (TV program) 21st Century Composition, 1991-94. Vol. Women's Shelter, Nacogdoches, 1992-93, St. John's Hospice, Joplin, Mo., 1996—. Recipient scholarship English Speaking Union, Houston, 1981, Herbert fellowship U. Fla., Gainesville, 1986. Mem. Midwest Writing Ctrs. Assn., Nat. Coun. Tchrs. English, Kans. Assn. Tchrs. English (exec. bd. mem. 1997—, editor Kans. English, 1999—), Acad. Am. Poets. Avocations: travel, video prodn., cigars, correspondence, baseball. Office: Pittsburg State U 1701 S Broadway St Pittsburg KS 66762-7500

FRANKLIN, JON DANIEL, writer, journalist, educator; b. Enid, Okla., Jan. 12, 1942; s. Benjamin Max and Wilma Irene (Winburn) F.; m. Nancy Sue Creevan, Dec. 12, 1959 (div. 1976, dec. 1987); children: Teresa June, Catherine Cay; m. Lynn Irene Scheidhauer, May 20, 1988. B.S. with high honors, U. Md., 1970; LHD (hon.), U. Md., Balt. County, 1981, Coll. Notre Dame, Balt., 1982. With USN, 1959-67; reporter/editor Prince Georges (Md.) Post, 1967-70; sci. and feature writer Balt. Evening Sun, 1970-85; assoc. prof. U. Md. Coll. Journalism, 1985-88, prof., 1988-89; prof., chmn. dept. journalism Oreg. State U., Corvallis, 1989-91; prof. creative writing, dir. U. Oreg., Eugene, 1991-98; sci. writer, spl. assignments editor Raleigh News and Observer, Raleigh, N.C., 1998—. Author: Shocktrauma, 1980, Not Quite a Miracle, 1983, Guinea Pig Doctors, 1984, Writing for Story, 1986, The Molecules of the Mind, 1987. pub.: *Bylines*, WriterL. Recipient James T. Grady medal Am. Chem. Soc., 1975, Pulitzer prize for feature writing, 1979, Pulitzer prize for explanatory journalism, 1985, Carringer award Nat. Mental Health Assn., 1984, Penney-Mo. Spl. award for health reporting, 1985; named to Newspaper Hall of Fame, Md.-Del.-D.C. Press Assn. Mem. Nat. Assn. Sci. Writers (bd. dirs.), Soc Profl. Journalists, The Writers Guild.

FRANKLIN, JUDE ERIC, electronics executive; b. St. Marys, Pa., Aug. 3, 1943; s. William Nelson and Elizabeth (Kronenwetter) F.; m. Mary Frances Bizot, Sept. 17, 1966; children: Pamela Mary, Erik Jude. BEE, Cath. U., 1965, MEE, 1968, PhDEE, 1980. Program mgr. Chesapeake Instrument Corp. (now divsn. of GE), Shadyside, Md., 1966-75; v.p. MAR, Inc., Rockville, Md., 1975-81; mgr. Navy Artificial Intelligence Ctr. Naval Rsch. Lab., Washington, 1981-85; sr. v.p. tech. div. Planning Rsch. Corp., McLean, Va., 1985-87, sr. v.p., 1987-92, chief tech. officer and v.p., 1991—; bd. dirs. Am. Univ., Washington Juvenile Diabetes Found. Contbr. to Artifical Intelligence Ency., 1987; also articles to profl. jours. V.p. Prince Mont Swim League; vol. U.S. Swimming Referee and Starter; PRC team leader Juvenile Diabetes Found., 1995. Recipient Meritorious Svc. award Armed Forces Communications and Electronics Assn., 1988, Fed. "100" award Fed. Computer News, 1992, Best Paper of Yr. award Signal Mag., 1995. Fellow Washington Acad. Sci.; mem. IEEE (sr., guest editor Expert Mag., 1989), Kettering Civic Fedn. (pres. 1971-72), Sigma Xi. Democrat. Roman Catholic. Home: 7616 Carteret Rd Bethesda MD 20817-2021 Office: Planning Rsch Corp 1500 Planning Rsch Corp Dr Mc Lean VA 22102-5001

FRANKLIN, JULIAN HAROLD, political science educator; b. N.Y.C., Mar. 26, 1925; s. Jerome A. and Molly (Seidenstein) F.; m. Paula Angle, Feb. 23, 1928. BA summa cum laude, Queens Coll., 1946; MA, Columbia U., 1950, PhD, 1960. Instr. Columbia U., N.Y.C., 1951-59, assoc. prof., 1962-68, prof., 1968-96, prof. emeritus, 1997—; vis. asst. prof. New Sch. for Social Research, N.Y.C., 1959-60; asst. prof. Princeton (N.J.) U., 1960-62; acting chmn. summer session Columbia U., 1962—, dir. grad. studies polit. theory, 1968—, dept. rep., 1971-72, 86—, dept. del. com. on instruction faculty polit. sci., 1971-73, 81-82, chmn., 1973-74, co-founder, adj. chmn. sem. on polit. and social thought; mem. adv. council dept. politcs. Princeton U., 1973-76. Author: Jean Bodin and the Sixteenth Century Revolution in the Methodology of Law and History, 1963, Constitutionalism and Resistance in the Sixteenth Century, 1969, Jean Bodin and the Rise of Absolutist Theory, 1973, rev. edit. (in French), 1993, John Locke and the Theory of Sovereignty, 1978; editor and translator: Jean Bodin on Sovereignty, 1992; editl. cons. in polit. theory Polity, 1977-79; mem. editl. bd. Polit. Theory; contbr. articles to profl. jours. Served with USAF, 1943-46. Queens Coll. scholar, 1946, Social Sci. Research Council fellow, 1950-51, William Bayard Cutting travelling fellow, 1950-51, NEH fellow, 1975-76, 89-90, Phi Beta Kappa fellow, 1990. Mem. Conf. for Study Polit. and Social Thought. Jewish. Office: Columbia U Dept Polit Sci 116th St And Broadway New York NY 10027

FRANKLIN, KENNETH RONALD, franchise company executive, consultant; b. N.Y.C., June 6, 1932; s. Lawrence and Gladys (Siegel) Franklin; m. Harriet Faye Lewis, Dec. 27, 1960; children: Gregg E., Erica G. BS, Syracuse U., 1953, MBA, 1954. Cert. mgmt. cons. Instr. Harpur Coll. Syracuse U., Vestal, N.Y., 1956-57; sales rep. IBM, Pitts., 1957-64; br. mgr. ABS, Pitts., 1964-66; v.p. franchising Arby's Inc., Youngstown, Ohio, 1966-70; pres. Franchise Devel. Inc., Pitts., 1970—. With Spl. Svcs., 1954-56, ETO. Mem. Inst. Mgmt. Cons., Pitts. Athletic Assn., Concorcia Club, Westmoreland C.C. Avocations: tennis, reading, traveling. Office: Franchise Devel Inc Hampshire Hall 4730 Centre Ave Pittsburgh PA 15213-1759

FRANKLIN, LARRY BROCK, publishing executive; b. Greenville, S.C., June 28, 1951; s. Billy Center and Elizabeth (Brock) F.; m. Janice Ann Roberts, Jan. 8, 1972; children: Stacie Lyn, Kevin Brock. BA in Journalism, U. S.C., 1974. Mgr. advt. Clinton (S.C.) Chronicle, 1974-78, mng. editor, 1978-86, gen. mgr., 1986-89, pub., 1989—. Recipient News Photograph award S.C. Press Assn., 1979-81, Best Column award, 1985, 87, 90, 93, Best Editorial award, 1987, Reporting In Depth award, 1990, Best Investigative Series award Nat. Newspaper Assn., 1991, 2nd place George Andrew Buchanan award for excellence in health care news writing; winner 20 bus. and editl. awards from Smith Newspapers Inc. Baptist. Avocations: reading, sports. Office: Clinton Chronicle PO Box 180 Clinton SC 29325-0180

FRANKLIN, LARRY DANIEL, communications company executive; b. Commerce, Tex., July 16, 1942; s. John Asia and Annie Mae (Castle) F.; m. Charlotte Anne Walker, Aug. 18, 1962; children: Kelly Leigh, Kristi Lynn. BBA, East Tex. State U., 1965; MBA, Tex. Tech. U., 1966. Mem. audit staff Arthur Andersen Co., Dallas, 1966-67; controller, treas. Paris Milling Co., Tex., 1967-69; mem. audit staff Price Waterhouse Co., Dallas, 1969-71; asst. copr. dir. acctg. Harte-Hanks Communications Inc., San Antonio, 1971, corp. dir. fin. services, 1971-72, chief fin. officer, treas., 1972-74, v.p. fin., treas., 1974-75, v.p. fin., sec.-treas., 1975-78, sr. v.p., pres. newspaper ops., 1978-80, pres., chief oper. officer, 1980—, exec. v.p., 1980-84, COO, 1984-91; pres., CEO Harte-Hanks, Inc., San Antonio, 1991—, chmn., CEO; bd. dirs. Interfirst Bank, San Antonio; bd. dirs. Mailers Coun., 1992—; chmn. audit com. AP; mem. adv. coun. Incarnate Word Coll. Sch. Bus.; past mem. graphic arts adv. com. Rochester Inst. Tech.; mem. mass comm. adv. com. Tex. Tech U., Lubbock; mem. Coll. Comm. Found. adv. coun. U. Tex., Austin, 1989—. Mem. mass comm. adv. com. St. Thomas Episcopal Ch., San Antonio; past mem. program ops. com. United Way, bd. dirs., 1993—; bd. dirs. East Tex. State U. Found., Commerce; bd. dirs. Tex. Rsch. League, 1992—, mem. exec. com., 1994—, mem. chmn.'s leadership coun.; bd. dirs. San Antonio Area Found., 1993—, mem. devel., comm. and mktg. com.; bd. dirs. San Antonio Econ. Devel. Found., 1992—, mem. exec. com., 1993—; trustee S.W. Rsch. Inst., 1993—; mem. devel. bd. U. Tex., San Antonio, 1992—. Recipient Disting. Alumnus award East Tex. State U., 1982, Disting. Acctg. Alumnus award Tex. Tech U., 1984. Mem. AICPA, Fin. Execs. Inst. (founding bd. dirs., past pres. South Tex. chpt.), Am. Newspaper Pubs. Assn. (newsprint com.), So. Newspaper Pubs. Assn. (bd. dirs. 1988—), Newspaper Assn. Am. (bd. dirs. 1991—, chmn. audit com., vice chmn. pub. policy subcom. on state rels.), Am. Press Inst. (bd. dirs.), Tex. Daily Newspaper Assn. (recycling task force), Beta Alpha Psi (Disting. Alumnus award 1984). Office: Harte-Hanks Inc 200 Concord Plaza Dr Ste 800 San Antonio TX 78216-6942*

FRANKLIN, LEONARD G., engineer; b. Peoria, Ariz., Aug. 20, 1934; s. William Geruous and Francis (Maldonado) F.; m. Janet E. Gilbert, Mar. 5, 1953 (div. 1959); 1 child, Gwendolyn Jean Norton; m. Gayle Irene Minor, Feb. 1, 1963; children: Keith, Robin, Peter, Leonard Jr., Suzanne, Mary, Steven. BS in Psychology, Clayton U., 1982; M in Mgmt., Nat. Louis U., 1995; PhD summa cum laude, So. Calif. U., 1999. Instrument engr. Ariz. Pub. Svc. Co., Phoenix, 1960-66; computer engr. GE Co., Phoenix, 1966-75; computer engr., regional tng. coord. Honeyell, St. Louis, 1975-82; sr. digital inpector, engr. Shell Oil Co., Roxana, Ill., 1983—; mem. diversity coun. Shell Oil Co., Roxana, 1997—. Author: (book) Eight Guiding Principles for Top-Level Leaders, 1999. Bishop, first counselor Bethalto Ward Ch., Ill., 1987-97. With USAF, 1956-60, Korea. Mem. Toastmasters Club (pres. 1986). Republican. Mem. LDS Ch. Avocations: writing, walking, grandchildren. E-mail: lgfranklin@juno.com. Home and Office: 421 Morning Sun Drive Nampa ID 83686

FRANKLIN, LYNNE, business communications consultant, writer; b. St. Paul, Minn., Aug. 24, 1957; d. Lyle John Franklin and Lois Ann (Cain) Kindseth; stepdau. Thomas John Kindseth; m. Lawrence Anton Pecorella, Sept. 2, 1989; 1 stepchild, Lauren. BA in Psychology and English, Coll. St. Catherine, 1979; MA, Hamline U., 1989. Residential treatment counselor St. Joseph's Home, Mpls., 1979-80; staff writer Comml. West Mag., Mpls., 1980-81; acct. exec. Edwin Neuger & Assocs., Mpls., 1981-83, Hill and Knowlton, Mpls., 1983-84; mgr. pub. rels. Gelco Corp., Eden Prarie, Minn., 1984-86; dir. financial rels. Dunstan & Assocs., Mpls., 1986; cons. MC Assocs., Chgo., 1986-87; v.p. Fin. Rels. Bd., Chgo., 1987—; prin. Wordsmith, Glenview, Ill., 1993—; trustee Lawrence Hall Youth Svcs.; judge achievement awards Internat. Assn. of Bus. Communicators, Mpls., 1986, presenter fin. rels., 1990; judge achievement awards Publicity Club of Chgo., 1992-94; presenter annual report seminar Nat. Investor Rels. Inst., Chgo., 1992. Author: (novel) Second Sight, 1989. tchr. Great Books Program, St. Paul, 1976-79, Minn. Literacy Coun., 1985-87. Recipient Ann. Report Excellence award Fin. World Mag., 1991-97, MerComm-ARC Competition, 1992-98, Nat. Assn. Investors Corp., 1994-98. Office: Wordsmith 2019 Glenview Rd Glenview IL 60025-2849

FRANKLIN, MARC ADAM, law educator; b. Bklyn., Mar. 9, 1932; s. Louis A. and Rose (Rosenthal) F.; m. Ruth E. Korzenik, June 29, 1958; children—Jonathan, Alison. AB, Cornell U., 1953, LLB, 1956. Bar: N.Y. 1956. Assoc. Proskauer Rose Goetz & Mendelsohn, N.Y.C., 1956-57; law clk to Hon. Carroll C. Hincks, New Haven, 1957-58, to Earl Warren, U.S. Supreme Ct., Washington, 1958-59; prof. law Columbia U., 1959-62, Stanford U., Calif., 1962-76; Frederick I. Richman prof. law Stanford U., 1976—. Author: Biography of a Legal Dispute, 1968, Dynamics of American Law, 1968, Cases and Materials on Tort Law and Alternatives, 1971, (with R.L. Rabin) 6th edit., 1996, Mass Media Law, 1977, (with D.A. Anderson) 5th edit., 1995, The First Amendment and the Fourth Estate, 1977, (with T.B. Carter and J.B. Wright) 7th edit., 1997, The First Amendment and the Fifth Estate, 1986, (with T.B. Carter and J.B. Wright) 4th edit., 1996. Fellow Ctr. for Advanced Study in Behavioral Scis., 1968-69; Fulbright rsch. scholar Victoria U., Wellington, N.Z., 1973. Home: 2870 Pacific Ave San Francisco CA 94115-1107 Office: Stanford U Law Sch Nathan Abbott Way Stanford CA 94305

FRANKLIN, MARGERY BODANSKY, psychology educator, researcher; b. N.Y.C., Mar. 18, 1933; d. Oscar and Barbara (Biber) Bodansky; m. Raymond S. Franklin, Aug. 22, 1962; children—Kenneth, David. A.B., Swarthmore Coll., 1954; M.A., Clark U., 1956, Ph.D., 1961. Instr. psychology Vassar Coll., Poughkeepsie, N.Y., 1960-62, asst. prof., 1962-64; research assoc. Bank St. Coll. Edn., N.Y.C., 1967-72; prof. Sarah Lawrence Coll., Bronxville, N.Y., 1965—. Co-editor: Developmental Processes: Heinz Werner's Selected Writings, 1978, Symbolic Functioning in Childhood, 1979, Child Language: A Reader, 1988, Development and the Arts: Critical Perspectives, 1994; contbr. articles to profl. jours., chpts. to books. Fellow Am. Psychol. Assn. (pres. psychology and arts divsn. 1990-91); mem. Soc. for Rsch. in Child Devel. Avocation: photography. Office: Sarah Lawrence Coll Psychology Dept Bronxville NY 10708*

FRANKLIN, MICHAEL HAROLD, arbitrator, lawyer, consultant; b. Los Angeles, Dec. 25, 1923; m. Betty Chernow, 1989; children from previous marriage: Barbara, John, James, Robert. A.B., UCLA, 1948; LL.B., U. So. Calif., 1951. Bar: Calif. 1951. Practiced in Los Angeles, 1951-52; pvt. practice, 1951-52; atty. CBS, 1952-54, Paramount Pictures Corp., 1954-58; exec. dir. Writers Guild Am. West, Inc., 1958-78; nat. exec. dir. Dirs. Guild Am., Inc., 1978-88; Mem. Fed. Cable Adv. Commn. Served with C.E. AUS, 1942-46. Mem. Order of Coif.

FRANKLIN, MORTON JEROME, emergency physician; b. Boston, Dec. 25, 1927; s. Jacob and Rose Ann (Borax) F. BA, Harvard U., 1949, MD, 1954. Diplomate Am. Bd. Emergency Medicine. Many positions as emergency physician various cities and states, 1955-97. Lt. cmmdr. USN, 1955-57. Home: 20 Hammond Pond Pkwy Apt 11 Chestnut Hill MA 02467-2129 Address: 320 Hammond Pond Pkwy Apt 304 Chestnut Hill MA 02467-2661

FRANKLIN, MURRAY JOSEPH, retired steel foundry executive; b. Orange, N.J., Apr. 1, 1922; s. Joseph Charles and Edna S. F.; m. Jane Modlin, Oct. 25, 1946; children: Gail Lee, Martha Ann. BA, Ohio Wesleyan U., 1943; MA (univ. fellow 1946-49), U. Mich., 1947, PhD, 1963. Assoc. prof. bus. U. Mich., 1963-65; with Hayes-Albion Corp., Jackson, Mich., 1968-70; v.p., gen. mgr. Westinghouse Airbrake div. Am. Standard Corp., Pitts., 1970-77; pres. transp. equipment div. Dresser Industries, Inc., DePew, N.Y., 1977-84; adj. assoc. prof. SUNY, Buffalo, 1990-95; pres. Coll. Counseling Assocs., Orchard Park, N.Y., 1990-98. Bd. dirs. Better Bus. Bur. Chgo., 1966-67. With USMCR, 1943-46. Mem. Ry. Progress Inst. (exec. com., bd. govs.). Home: 20 Lancaster Ln Orchard Park NY 14127-2852

FRANKLIN, PATRICIA LYNN, special education educator; b. East St. Louis, Ill., Nov. 28, 1953; d. William and Alice Alfreda (Sowers) Powell; m. Stephen Reed Franklin, July 27, 1974; 1 child, Ashley Lynn. BS in Edn., So. Ill. U., 1976, M in Elem. Edn., 1992. Cert. elem. edn., early childhood edn., learning disabilities, behavior disorder, and educable mentally handicapped tchr., Ill. Primary spl. edn. tchr. Highland (Ill.) Community Sch. Unit #5, 1976—; insvc. presenter Madison County Region II Svc. Ctr., Edwardsville, Ill., 1976, 89, 91, 92, coach, supr. Spl. Olympics, 1977-90; supervising tchr. So. Ill. U., Edwardsville, 1976, 91, 93, 96—, Greenville (Ill.) Coll., 1976-84; chmn. exec. orgnl. com. Very Spl. Arts Festival, Madison County Supr. Schs., Edwardsville, 1983; chmn. com. Very Spl. Arts Festival, Ill. Arts for Handicapped, 1983-855; participating tchr. Title IV-C learning disabilities program St. Clair County Supr. Schs., 1979-81; spl. edn. summer program tchr. Madison County Region II Svc. Ctr., 1998—. Vol. Angel choir St. Paul United Meth. Ch., Rosewood Heights, Ill., 1990-92; Sunday sch. tchr. St. John's United Meth. Ch., Edwardsville, brownie leader Girl Scouts U.S., 1991—. Mem. Ill. Reading Assn., Tchrs. Applying Whole Lang., Zoo Tchrs., Coun. for Exceptional Children, Highland Profl. Educators, Lewis & Clark Reading Coun., Ill. Whole Lang., Early Childhood Spl. Interest Coun. Avocations: needlework, crafts, camping, fishing, travel. Office: Highland Community Unit 5 1800 Lindenthal St Highland IL 62249

FRANKLIN, PETER CHARLES, brigadier general; b. Tokyo, Oct. 26, 1949; came to U.S., 1950; s. Charles Francis and Beverly Jean (Keyse) F.; m. Diane Jean Wallace Franklin, June 12, 1971; children: Jeffrey, Jonathan, Jillian. BS in Aerospace Engring., Va. Polytechnic Inst., 1971; MS in Guided Weapons Systems Engring., Royal Military Coll. Sci., Eng., 1979. Project officer Strategic Def. Initiative Orgn., 1985-87; commdr. 2nd Battalion 62nd Air Def. Artillery Brigade, Fort Ord, Calif., 1987-89, 35th Air Def. Artillery Brigade, Fort Lewis, Wash., 1990-92; exec. officer U.S.A. Space and Strategic Def. Command, Washington, 1993-94; asst. deputy for systems mgmt. Office Asst. Sec. of Army for Rsch. Devel. and Acquisition, Washington, 1994—. Brigadier General U.S. Army, 1971—. Recipient Legions of Merit U.S. Army, Def. Meritorious Svc. medal, Meritorious Svc. medal. Mem. Assn. of U.S. Army. Office: Asst Secretary of Army Pentagon Washington DC 20310

FRANKLIN, PHYLLIS, professional association administrator; b. N.Y.C., Apr. 21, 1932; d. Matthew Pine and Helen Lutsky; m. Irwin Franklin, Apr. 21, 1958 (div. 1971); children: James, Jody. AB, Vassar Coll., 1954; MA, U. Miami, 1965, PhD, 1969; LHD (hon.), George Washington U., 1986. From asst. to assoc. prof. U. Miami, Coral Gables, 1969-80; spl. asst. to dean Coll. Arts & Scis. Duke U., Durham, N.C., 1980-81; dir. English programs MLA, N.Y.C., 1981-85, exec. dir., 1985—; adj. prof. English programs NYU, 1987-88. Editor ADE Bull., 1981-85, Profession, 1985—. Fellowship, Danforth Found., 1966-68, Am. Council on Edn., 1980-81; stipend NEH, 1971. Mem. USSR Acad. Scis., Am. Coun. Learned Socs. (bd. dirs. 1987-89, commn. on humanities and social scis. 1987-88, chair conf. secs. 1987-90), Nat. Humanities Alliance (bd. dirs. 1986-88, v.p. 1990-91, pres. 1991-96), Nat. Fedn. Abstracting and Info. Svcs. (bd. dirs. 1994-96). Democrat. Jewish. Office: Modern Language Assn 10 Astor Pl Fl 4 New York NY 10003-6981

FRANKLIN, RAYMOND A., medical facility administrator. MPA, U. Kans., 1995. Adminstr. U. Kans. Med. Ctr., Kansas City, 1979—; bd. dirs. Kans. U. Credit Union, 1992-95, 97—; mem. site coun. Piper Mid. Sch., Kansas City, Kans., 1997—. Telethon vol. Children's Miracle Network, Fairway, Kans., 1997, 98. Mem. Am. Soc. for Pub. Adminstrn. Avocations: bowling, skating, golf, church activities, family activities.

FRANKLIN, RICHARD MARK, lawyer; b. Chgo., Dec. 13, 1947; s. Henry W. and Gertrude (Gross) F.; m. Marguerite June Wesle, Sept. 2, 1973; children: Justin Wesley, Elizabeth Cecilia, Catherine Helena, Caroline Lucinda. BA, U. Wis., 1970; postgrad., U. Freiburg, Fed. Republic Germany, 1968-69; JD, Columbia U., 1973. Bar: Ill. 1973, U.S. Dist. Ct. (no. dist.) Ill. 1973, U.S. Ct. Appeals (7th cir.) 1973. Assoc. Baker & McKenzie, Chgo., 1973-79, Frankfurt, Fed. Republic Germany, 1979-80; ptnr. Baker & McKenzie, Chgo., 1980—. Mem. ABA, Ill. Bar Assn., Chgo. Bar Assn. Mem. United Ch. Christ. Avocations: music, lit., theatre, outdoor activities. Home: 1161 Oakley Ave Winnetka IL 60093-1437 Office: Baker & McKenzie 1 Prudential Plz 130 E Randolph St Ste 3700 Chicago IL 60601-6342

FRANKLIN, ROBERT ALLEN, broadcast executive, radio producer; b. Jackson, Miss., Aug. 22, 1958; s. Ellen Myers Franklin. BS, Jackson State U., 1981, MA, 1983. Gen. mgr. WRCR, Rust Coll., Holly Springs, Miss., 1983-84, WMUW-FM, Miss. U. Women, Columbus, 1984-86, WIUM-WIUS-FM, Western Ill. U., Macomb, 1986-87; media coord. Dept. Energy and Transp., Jackson, 1988-89; gen. mgr. WESM-FM, U. Md. Ea. Shore, Princess Anne, 1989—. Exec. prodr.: (radio talk show) Like It Is, 1990— (Gavel awards Md. State Bar Assn. 1990, 92, 84, Media award Md. Press Club 1994); prodr.: (radio series) Still Going On, 1994-95, The Blues Project, 1993-94. Congl. fellow with Congresswoman Eddie Bernice Johnson, Dallas, 1995-96. Avocations: basketball, jogging, television, radio producing and directing. Home: 407 Brookridge Dr Apt 1 Salisbury MD 21804-3966 Office: Univ Md Ea Shore Backbone Rd Princess Anne MD 21853

FRANKLIN, ROBERT BREWER, journalist; b. Phila., Mar. 31, 1937; s. John Jay and Sarah Louise (Redman) F.; m. Norma Jean Belke, June 18, 1966; children: James Robert, Mary Jean. B.A. in Journalism, Pa. State U., 1959; postgrad., U. Minn. News editor Hatboro (Pa.) Public Spirit, 1959-60; reporter No. Va. Sun, Arlington, 1960-62; journalist AP, Phila., 1962, Mpls., 1962-67; reporter, then asst. city editor Mpls. Tribune, 1967-74, city editor, 1975-82; city editor Mpls. Star and Tribune, 1982-83, state editor, 1983-86, reporter, 1986—; adj. faculty U. St. Thomas, St. Paul, 1985—. Mem. Medina (Minn.) City Council, 1971-76, chief police, 1971-73, commnr. public safety, 1974-76. Served with U.S. Army, 1960-62. Mem. Soc. Profl. Journalists (pres. Minn. profl. chpt. 1986-87). Lutheran. Home: 2819 Lakeshore Ave Maple Plain MN 55359-9665 Office: 425 Portland Ave Minneapolis MN 55488-1511

FRANKLIN, ROBERT DRURY, oil company executive; b. Mead, Okla., June 6, 1935; s. Sam Wesley and Frankie Marjorie (Gooding) F.; m. Barbara Jean Bellis, May 30, 1958 (div. 1973); children: Philip Foster, Elizabeth Jean. BS in Petroleum Engring., U. Okla., 1957; JD, So. Methodist U., 1964. Registered profl. engr., Tex. Petroleum engr. Mobil Oil Corp., Denver City, Tex., 1957-59; prodn. mgr. Bayview Oil Corp., Dallas, 1959-65; sec., dir. Siboney Corp., Dallas, 1965-70; pres., dir. Northland Oils Ltd., Dallas, 1970-89, Costa Resources, Inc., Dallas, 1972—; v.p., dir. Internat. Oil & Gas Corp., Dallas, 1979-84. Mem. Rep. Eagles, Washington. Mem. State Bar Tex., Ind. Petroleum Assn. Am., Soc. Petroleum Engrs., Am. Petroleum Inst., Energy Club of Dallas, Mensa. Presbyterian. Clubs: Willow Bend Polo, Midland Country, Beverly Hills. Avocations: polo, tennis, skiing. Home: 3700 Binkley Ave Dallas TX 75205-2138 Office: Costa Resources Inc 3103 W Golf Course Rd Midland TX 79701-2914

FRANKLIN, ROBERT MCFARLAND, book publisher; b. Memphis, Mar. 13, 1943; s. Robert Dumont and Mary McFarland (Wilson) F.; m. Cheryl Jane Roberts, Jan. 18, 1975; children: Charles McRee, Nicholas Roberts, William Holliday. AB, Yale U., 1965. Cataloger Columbia U. Libr., N.Y.C., 1965-66; editor to exec. editor Scarecrow Press, Metuchen, N.J., 1969-79; pres., founder McFarland & Co., Inc., Publishers, Jefferson, N.C., 1979—. pub. Jour. Info. Ethics, 1992—; contbr. articles to profl. jours. Dir., actor Ashe County Little Theatre, Jefferson, 1980—; libr. adv. bd. Appalachian State U. With U.S. Army, 1966-68. Recipient Gov.'s Bus. award in arts and humanities, State of N.C., 1984, 87, 97, N.C. State Arts Coun. Outstanding Vol. award 1991. Mem. ALA (pub. com. 1984-88, coun. governing body 1988—, pay equity com. 1991-93, intellectual freedom com. 1994-96), Am. Soc. for Psychical Rsch. (dir. 1984-88). Avocations: chess, French language and culture, fine art commissioning and collecting, acting, piano. Home: 338 Cut Laurel Gap Rd Creston NC 28615-9049 Office: care McFarland & Co Inc Pubs PO Box 611 Jefferson NC 28640-0611

FRANKLIN, ROBERT RICHARD, retired federal agency administrator, farmer; b. Middletown, Conn., Mar. 11, 1943; s. John Henry and Helen (Morris) F.; m. Anne Marie Henderson, Aug. 20, 1971; children: Charles Michael, Amy Louise. BS in Acctg., U. Conn., 1965; cert., Naval Postgrad. Sch., 1981. Cert. acquisition profl. Dept. Def.; cert. internal auditor Inst. Internal Auditors. Auditor Def. Supply Agy., Alameda, Calif., 1965-67; supervisory auditor Def. Supply Agy., Boston, 1967-75; dep. comptr. Def. Logistics Agy., Boston, 1975-88; dep. comdr. Def. Logistics Agy., Hartford, Conn., 1988-98; ret., 1998; farmer Aroostook County, Maine, 1998—. Recipient Outstanding Young Man Am. award U.S. Jaycees, 1976. Mem. Def. Acquisition Corps, Conn. Fed. Exec. Assn. (chmn. 1992-93, sec.-treas. 1996-98), KC (3d deg.). Democrat. Avocations: fishing, gardening, genealogy, travel, birding. Home: 181 Pokorny Rd Higganum CT 06441-4418 Office: Def Contract Mgmt Command 130 Darlin St East Hartford CT 06108-3234

FRANKLIN, RONALD, neuropsychologist; b. Pinehurst, N.C., Jan. 1, 1946; s. Carl D. and Cletus I. F.; divorced; children: Leslie, Alyssa. BA in Psychology, East Carolina U., 1977, MA in Psychology, 1979; PhD in Psychology, N.C. State U., 1986. Mgr. mental health program N.C. Dept. Corrections, Raleigh, 1986-90; sr. psychologist South Fla. State Hosp., Pembroke Pines, 1991-95; mgr. behavioral medicine St. Mary's Hosp. Child Devel., West Palm Beach, Fla., 1995—; pres. Ctr. Forensic Neuropsychology, Boca Raton, Fla., 1998—. Editor: Design & Analysis of Single Case Research, 1997. Tax commr. Town of Candor, N.C., 1979-81, chmn. united fund, 1982. Pediatrics fellow Johns Hopkins Sch. Medicine, 1990-91. Fellow Am. Bd. Pediatric Neuropsychology; mem. APA, Nat. Acad. Neuropsychology, Internat. Neuropsychology Soc., Phi Kappa Phi. Office: 21301 Powerline Rd Ste 201 Boca Raton FL 33433

FRANKLIN, ROOSEVELT, minister; b. Chattanooga, Aug. 30, 1933; s. James R. and Cora Ann (Ponds) F.; m. Darnell Pinkston, Sept. 30, 1972; children: Sophia, Siemoran Dellazar. BS, Northeastern U., 1958; MA (hon.), Savannah State Coll., 1962; M. of Cybernetics, Grad. Sch. Wicca, St. Charles, Mo. Lic. metaphysician. Pastor Free For All Bapt. Ch., Greenwood, S.C., 1959-61; radio min. Spiritual Ch., Aiken, S.C., 1961-63; nat. lectr. United Coun. Spiritual Ch., Raleigh, N.C., 1963-66; min. Holy Trinity House of God, Macon, Ga., 1966—; youth dir. Holy Trinity Ch., Macon, 1966-72, talent coord., 1966-73; dir. Spiritual Singers, 1966—; lectr. in field; world renown authority on witchcraft and transcendental meditation; expert in clairvoyance, spiritual meditation. Organizer voters registration, Macon, 1977; pub. relations vol. Nat. Dem. Party, Atlanta, 1984; bd. dirs. Retired Persons Assn., 1980—. Capt. U.S. Army, 1951-54, Korea. Named extrovert promoter Music Workshop, 1979; recipient Afro Am. Heritage award Afro Am. Heritage Mus., 1987, Golden Eagle award Macon Courier, 1988, Nat. Achievers award Nat. Black Secs. Assn., 1990, Ednl. award Ptnrs. Youth Club, 1991, Golden Eagle award 500 Black Men of Am. Club, 1992, Black Achievement award Nat. Negro Achievers Assn., 1993, Nat. Rschrs. Occult award United Spiritual Coun. Chs., 1994, Mahogny Triump award Am. Black Affluent Assn. Am., 1995, Concerned Citizens award People in Action Club, 1996, Good Samaritan award United Youth Fellowship Club, 1997, Registered Spiritual award, Registered Psychic award and Mystic award United Spiritual Coun. Assn., 1998, Dr. of Metaphysics award, Dr. of Biblical Counseling award and Dr. of Religion award, 1999. Mem. NAACP (life), SCLC (life), Inner Circle Congl. Aids, C. of C., Minister's Alliance (v.p. 1966—, Citizens award 1979), Ga. Black Am. Pageant (coord. 1980—, Leadership award 1982), Direct Sellers League, Smooth Ashlar (dist. dep. 1970—), Rolls-Royce Club, Woodsmen of Am., Pioneer Club, Shriners (nat. amb.), Masons (33 deg., sovereign grand gen. inspector), Optimist, Kiwanis, Civitan, Elks, Nat. Lodge (treas. 1987—), Potentate of the Rosicrucisns, Sertoma, Lions. Democrat. Avocations: martial arts, billiards. Office: Holy Trinity House of God 280 Straight St Macon GA 31204-6100

FRANKLIN, ROSEMARY F., English educator; b. Birmingham, Dec. 15, 1941; d. James Hardy and Mary Elizabeth F.; m. Thomas J. Crowley, Mar. 19, 1935. AB, Birmingham So. Coll., 1963; MA, Wake Forest U., 1964; PhD, Emory U., 1968. Asst. prof. English Ga. State U., Atlanta, 1967-69; asst. then assoc. prof. English U. Ga., Athens, 1969—; Sandy Beaver prof. English, U. Ga., 1988-91. Contbr. articles to profl. jours. Founder Five Points Neighborhood Assn., Athens, 1977; mem. Oconee Citizens Responsible Growth, Watkinsville, Ga. Mem. MLA, Am. Lit. Assn. (chair various panels), S. Atlantic MLA (chair various panels), Soc. Study So. Lit., Nathaniel Hawthorne Soc., Melville Soc., Phi Beta Kappa. Office: U Ga Dept English Athens GA 30602

FRANKLIN, SHIRLEY MARIE, marketing consultant; b. Kansas City, Mo., Apr. 13, 1930; d. Eric E. and Marie M. (Kilpatrick) Snodgrass; div. 1967; 1 child, Scot Wesley. BA, State U. Iowa, 1952; MS, Simmons Coll., 1954; MA, Kans. U., 1974. Cert. tchr., Kans., Mass., N.J., Ariz., Calif. Tchr., adminstr. various schs., 1952-76; gifted student program designer Leavenworth County (Kans.) Pub. Schs., 1976-77; sales cons., mgr. Sealight Co., Inc., Kansas City, Mo., 1978-82; dir. chain sales Haagen Dazs Ice Cream Co., Teaneck, N.J., 1982-87; program dir. case space mgmt. Ice Cream Industry, 1986-88; prin. Shirley Franklin Consulting, Basehor, Kans., 1987—; U.S. brands dir. Mövenpick Co., Zurich, Switzerland, 1990—; mktg. cons. Franklin & Assocs., 1994—; speaker at dairy industry meetings, seminars. Contbr. articles to profl. jours. and mags. Foster parent World Vision, Pasadena, Calif., 1986—; mem. nat. com. steering com. U.S. Congress Arts Caucus, Washington, 1988, 89; vol. ct. appointed spl. advocate for children in trouble, Kans., 1994; apptd. City Planning Commn., 1996—. Recipient Excellence in Sales Promotions award Dairy and Food Industries Supply Assn. Mem. Internat. Ice Cream Assn. (mktg. coun. 1979—), Internat. Platform Spkrs. Assn., Alpha Delta Kappa, Delta Delta Delta. Republican. Episcopalian. Avocations: writing, walking, reading, travel, bridge. Home and Office: PO Box 233 Basehor KS 66007-0233

FRANKLIN, STANLEY PHILLIP, computer scientist, cognitive scientist, mathematician, educator; b. Memphis, Aug. 14, 1931; s. Sam and Lily (Rosenblum) F.; m. Jeannie Stonebrook, Apr. 1, 1979; children—Lynn Ann, Michele Suzanne, Phillip Byron, Bruce Eric, Halli Eileen, Elena Simone, Sunny Patrice, Sam Elliot. B.S., U. Memphis, 1959; M.A., UCLA, 1962, Ph.D., 1963; NSF postdoctoral fellow, U. Wash., Seattle, 1963-64. Asst. prof. math. U. Fla., 1964-65; assoc. prof., then prof. Carnegie-Mellon U., 1965-72; prof. math., chmn. dept. math. scis. U. Memphis, 1972-84, prof. computer sci., 1984—, co-dir. Inst. for Intelligent Systems, 1987—; vis. prof. Indian Inst. Tech., Kanpur, Technion, Haifa, Israel; vis. mem. Mathematische Centrum, Amsterdam, Netherlands; condr. workshops, cons. in field. Author research papers and books in field. Served with USMCR, 1951-53. Recipient Bd. Visitors Eminent Faculty award, 1997. Mem. Assn. for Computing Machinery, Am. Assn. for Artificial Intelligence, Cognitive Sci. Soc., Internat. Neural Network Soc., Sigma Xi, Pi Mu Epsilon. Home: 5736 Rich Rd Memphis TN 38120-2086 Office: U Memphis Dept Math Sci Memphis TN 38152

FRANKLIN, WILLIAM EDWIN, bishop; b. Parnell, Iowa, May 3, 1930. Attended, Loras Coll., Mt. St. Bernard Sem., Dubuque, Iowa. Ordained priest Roman Cath. Ch., 1956. Priest Roman Cath. Ch., Dubuque, titular bishop Surista aux. bishop, 1987-93; bishop Davenport, Iowa, 1994—. Office: Diocese of Davenport St Vincent Ctr 2706 N Gaines St Davenport IA 52804-1914*

FRANKLIN, WILLIAM EMERY, international business educator; b. Sedalia, Mo., Apr. 6, 1933; s. Russell George and Edith Mae (Van Dyke) Franklin; m. Beverly Jean Feig, Mar. 25, 1933 (div. 1963); children: Stephen, Julia, Angela. BS in Bus., U. Mo., 1954; postgrad., Harvard U., 1982. With forestry ops. Weyerhaeuser Co., Longview, Wash., 1954; pres. Weyerhaeuser Far East Ltd., Hong Kong, 1980-96, Franklin Internat., Ltd., Seattle, 1996—; chmn. Weyerhaeuser China Ltd.; pres. Weyerhaeuser Korea; mem. U.S.-Japan Bus. Coun., Pacific Basin Econ. Coun.; bd. dirs. NCR Japan Ltd.; mem. Eisenhower Fellowship Com., adv. com. on investment and devel. U.S. Dept. State; past chmn. forestry working group industry coop. program of UN-FAO, com. on internat. trade U.S. Dept. Commerce; adj. prof. U. Puget Sound, Am. Grad. Sch. Internat. Mgmt.; guest lectr. U. Internat. Bus. Econs., Beijing, Columbia U., Internat. U. of Japan, Seattle U. Trustee Pacific N.W. Ballet; chmn. Far East Coun. Friends of Scouting. Mem. Am. C. of C. in Japan (pres.), Yomiuri Internat. Econ. Soc. (bd. dirs.), Coun. Fgn. Rels., World Affairs Coun., U.S.-Asian Bus. Coun., Fgn. Corrs. Club, Tokyo Lawn Tennis Club, Tokyo Club. Avocations: tennis, music, sailing.

FRANKO, BERNARD VINCENT, pharmacologist; b. West Brownsville, Pa., June 9, 1922; m. Marie Burke, June 25, 1946; 9 children. BS in Pharmacy, W.Va. U., 1954, MS in Pharmacology, 1955; PhD in Pharmacology, Med. Coll. Va., 1958. With A.H. Robins Co., Richmond, Va., 1958—, assoc. dir. pharmacology, 1968-71, 73-77, dir. pharmacologic research, 1971-73, monitor, dir. good lab. practices dept., 1978-81, mgr. research coordination and tng. sect., 1981-90, ret., 1990; asst. prof., adj. asst. prof. pharmacology Med. Coll., Va. Commonwealth U., Richmond, 1961—. Contbr. numerous articles to profl. jours. Fellow AAAS; mem. Am. Soc. Pharmacology and Exptl. Therapeutics, Soc. Exptl. Biology and Medicine, Internat. Soc. Biochem. Pharmacology, Va. Acad. Scis. Home: 4012 Patterson Ave Richmond VA 23221-1913

FRANKS, CHARLES LESLIE, investments executive; b. Columbus, Miss., Jan. 21, 1934; s. Leslie J. and Almeda (Morris) F.; m. Cecile Alice Cronovich, Feb. 7, 1959; children—Carolyn Anne, Charles Christopher. B.S. summa cum laude, Miss. State U., 1956. Cert. internal auditor; C.P.A.; chartered bank auditor. Acct. Arthur Andersen & Co., Houston, 1959-61; mgr. internal audit dept. Bank of S.W., Houston, 1961-71; gen. auditor Southwest Bancshares, Inc., 1972-79; v.p., auditor Merc. Nat. Bank, Dallas, 1979-82, sr. v.p., auditor, 1982-86; sr. v.p., dir., internal auditor Bright Banc, Dallas, 1986-89, sr. v.p., chief fin. officer, 1989-90; pvt. practice investments, 1991—; instr., speaker various Bank Adminstrn. Inst. seminars, meetings and convs. Served to capt. USAF, 1956-59. Mem. Tex. Soc. C.P.A.s (sec. Houston chpt. 1971-72), Bank Adminstrn. Inst. (v.p. Gulf Coast chpt. 1971-72, pres. 1973-74, dir. 1974-75, state dir. 1975-77, dir. Dallas chpt. 1980-84), Am. Inst. Banking, Inst. Internal Auditors (gov. 1973-78, pres. Houston chpt. 1974-75), Houston C. of C., Arnold Air Soc., Phi Eta Sigma, Chi Lambda Rho, Phi Kappa Phi, Alpha Kappa Psi. Roman Catholic. Home: 206 Brocket Pl Stafford TX 77477-4708

FRANKS, DAVID A., computer engineer; b. Washington, June 24, 1929; s. David Ransom and Lela Becton (Duncan) F.; m. Erta Mae Williford, June 20, 1953; children: David Bryan, Kathleen Elva. BS in Math., Howard U., 1951, MS in Math., 1952; postgrad., U. Ill., 1953-54. 1st lt. U.S. Army, 1953-57; various engring. positions Westinghouse Electric Corp., Balt., 1957-92, mgr. applications software, 1968-91; cons. Dafer Enterprises, Columbia, Md., 1992—. Mem. Assn. for Computing Machinery, Data Processing Mgmt. Assn., Balt. Computer Users Group, Capital Computer Users Group. Home: 8505 Moon Glass Ct Columbia MD 21045-5630

FRANKS, DAVID BRYAN, internist, emergency physician; b. Washington, D.C., Nov. 18, 1956; s. David Ardell and Erta Mae (Williford) F.; m. Deborah Ann Hayek, Jan. 31, 1987; children: Ariel Ann, David Henry, Theodore Gabriel. BS, U. Md., 1978, MD, 1980. Diplomate Am. Bd. Internal Medicine, Am. Bd. Emergency Medicine. Resident Thomas Jefferson U. Hosp., Phila., 1980-83; physician Temple U. Hosp., Phila., 1983-85, St. Joseph Health Ctr., St. Charles, Mo., 1985-87, Belleville (Ill.) Meml. Hosp., 1987—. Fellow Am. Coll. Emergency Physicians. Office: 4500 Memorial Dr Belleville IL 62226-5360

FRANKS, GARY ALVIN, former congressman, real estate professional; b. Waterbury, Conn., Feb. 9, 1953; s. Richard Dobbs and Jenary Minnie (Petteway) F.; m. Donna Williams, Mar. 10, 1990; children: Jessica Lynn, Gary Alvin; 1 stepchild, Azia Forrest. BA, Yale U., 1975. Indsl./labor rels. profl. Continental Can, Conn., 1976-78, Chesebrough-Ponds, Conn., 1978-82, Cadbury Schweppes, Conn., 1982-86; pres., founder GAF Realty, Waterbury, Conn., 1986-90; mem. 102nd-103rd Congresses from 5th Conn. Dist, 1990-96; pres. Franks & Genoa Assocs. LLC, 1996—; candidate for senate; mem. policy com., commerce comn. vice chmn. energy and power subcom., heal and the environment subcom.. Alderman City of Waterbury, 1986-90, pres. pro tempore, 1986-87; vice chmn. Waterbury Zoning Com., 1986-87; mem. Environ. Control Commn., Waterbury, 1988-90; dir. ARC, Naugatuck, Conn., 1984-87, Waterbury C. of C., 1987-90; mem. Waterbury Found., 1989-90; mem. Waterbury Fire Bd., 1986-87, Waterbury Housing Assistance Program Commn., 1986-90; bd. dirs. Waterbury Opportunities Industrialization Ctr., 1985-90, Waterbury Boys Club, 1984-89, YMCA, 1988-90. Named Outstanding Young Man Waterbury Boys Club, 1971, Man of Yr. Negro Profl. Women's Club. Mem. Congl. Black Caucus, Conservative Opportunities Soc. Republican. Baptist.*

FRANKS, HERBERT HOOVER, lawyer; b. Joliet, Ill., Jan. 25, 1934; s. Carol and Lottie (Dermer) F.; m. Eileen Pepper, June 22, 1957; children: David, Jack, Eli. BS, Roosevelt U., 1954; postgrad., Am. U., 1960. Bar: Ill. 1961, U.S. Dist. Ct. (no. dist.) Ill. 1961, U.S. Supreme Ct. 1967. Ptnr. Franks, Gerkin & McKenna, 1985—; chmn. Wonder Lake State Bank, Ill., 1979—, First Nat. Bank, Marengo, Ill., 1976-84, mem. exec. com., 1976—; vice-chmn. hotel mgmt. orgn. Bricton Group, Park Ridge, Ill., 1992-98. Bus. editor Am. U. Law Rev., 1959, 60. State pres. Young Dems. of Ill., 1970-72; trustee Hebrew Theol. Coll., Skokie, Ill., 1974—; trustee, sec. Forest Inst. Profl. Psychology, Springfield, Mo., 1979-91; chmn. Forest Hosp., Des Plaines, 1980-88. With U.S. Army, 1956-58. Fellow Ill. State Bar (bd. govs. 1994-97, treas. 1996-97, 3d v.p. 1997-98, 2d v.p. 1998-99, pres.-elect 1999—);

mem. Ill. Trial Lawyers (mng. bd. 1975-92, treas. 1985-87), Masons, Shriners, Sigma Nu Phi (pres. 1980-82). Home: 19324 E Grant Hwy Marengo IL 60152-9438 Office: Franks Gerkin & McKenna 19333 E Grant Hwy Marengo IL 60152-8234

FRANKS, HERSCHEL PICKENS, judge; b. Savannah, Tenn., May 28, 1930; s. Herschel R. and Vada (Pickens) F.; m. Judy Black; 1 child, Ramona. Student U. Tenn.-Martin, U. Md.; JD, U. Tenn.-Knoxville; grad. Nat. Jud. Coll. of U. Nev. Bar: Tenn. 1959, U.S. Supreme Ct. 1968. Claims atty. U.S. Fidelity & Guaranty Co., Knoxville, 1958; ptnr. Harris, Moon, Meacham & Franks, Chattanooga, 1959-70; chancellor 3d Chancery div. of Hamilton County, 1970-78; judge Tenn. Ct. Appeals, Chattanooga, 1978—; spl. justice Tenn. Supreme Ct., 1979, 86, 87; presiding judge Hamilton County Trial Cts., 1977-78; spl. judge Tenn. Ct. of Criminal Appeals, 1990-92; mem. commn. to study appellate cts., 1990-92. Served with USNG, 1949-50, USAF, 1950-54. Mem. ABA (award of merit), Tenn. Bar Assn. (award of merit 1968-69), Tenn. Bar Found., Chattanooga Bar Found., Chattanooga Bar Assn. (pres. 1968-69, Founds. of Freedom award 1986), Am. Judicature Soc., Inst. Jud. Adminstrn., Optimists (pres. 1965-66), Community Service award 1971), Mountain City Club, City Farmers Club, Phi Alpha Delta. Mem. United Ch. of Christ. Address: 540 Mccallie Ave Ste 562 Chattanooga TN 37402-2039

FRANKS, HOLLIS B., retired investment executive; b. Sugar Tree, Tenn., Jan. 18, 1916; s. Louis Berry and Mary Maggie (Oxford) F.; m. Anne Moody, June 22, 1940 (dec. Jan 1993); children: Robert Berry, June Anne Franks Johnson. BS in Agr., U. Tenn., 1937; MEd, U. Mo., 1940. Cert. tchr. Tchr. Tenn. Dept. Edn., various locations, 1922-39; tchr. vocat. agriculture Sardis, Tenn., 1937-38; tchr. vocat. agr. and vocat. edn. U. Mo., Columbia and Richland, 1939-42; mgr. The Large Mo. Turkey Show, Richland, 1940-41; regional mgr. Ralston Purina Co., 1942-60; stock and commodity broker Bache & Co., Greensboro, N.C., 1960-70; 2d v.p. investments Shearson Lehman & Hutton, Memphis, 1970-81; fin. advisor to sr. citizens, 1982—; gen. sales mgr. adv. bd. Ralston Purina Co., 1947-57. Mem. Henderson County Ret. Tchrs. (v.p. 1986—), Lexington Rotary Club (bd. dirs. 1989-90), Phi Kappa Phi, Phi Delta Kappa. Republican. Baptist. Avocations: landscaping, travel, lawn care, fishing, playing bridge. Home: Decatur County Manor Nursing Ctr 726 Kentucky Ave Parsons TN 38383

FRANKS, JOHN JULIAN, anesthesiology educator, medical investigator; b. Pueblo, Colo., Apr. 9, 1929; s. Frank Alec and Lila Ethelda (Ownbey) F.; m. Kathryne Jean Sammon, Dec. 27, 1951; children: John Alec, William Thomas, Margaret Lila, Elizabeth Ellen. BA, U. Colo., 1951, MD, 1954. Assoc. dir., dir. clin. rsch. ctr. U. Colo., Denver, 1969-81; assoc. chief of staff rsch. Denver VA Hosp., 1969-82, chief hematology div., 1983; resident in anesthesiology Vanderbilt U. Hosp., Nashville, 1984-86; prof., dir. rsch. div. Vanderbilt U., Nashville, 1987-98, dir. div. organ transplant anesthesia, 1989-98, interim chmn. dept. anesthesiology, 1993-94; prof. emeritus Vanderbilt U., 1999—. Author chpts. in books; contbr. articles to Jour. of Gen. Physiology, Jour. of Clin. Investigation, New Eng. Jour. of Medicine, Anesthesiology and N.Y. Acad. Sci.; contbr. numerous articles to profl. jours. Col. USAF, 1955-63, 68-69. NIH grantee U. Colo., 1963-69, 64-82, Vanderbilt U., 1992-96, U.S. VA grantee Denver VA Hosp., 1969-83. Mem. Am. Soc. Anesthesiologists, Am. Physiol. Soc., Cen. Soc. Clin. Rsch., Internat. Soc. Thrombosis Haemostosis, Soc. Gen. Physiologists. Home: 216 Vaughns Gap Rd Nashville TN 37205-3532 Office: Vanderbilt U Med Ctr Nashville TN 37232-2125

FRANKS, LEWIS E., electrical and computer engineering educator, researcher; b. San Mateo, Calif., Nov. 8, 1931; s. Lloyd C. and Leora (Embree) F.; m. Mary B. Harris, June 21, 1954; children: Janet K., Jill M., Daniel J. BSEE, Oreg. State U., 1952; MSEE, Stanford U., 1953, PhD, 1957. Mem. tech. staff Bell Telephone Labs., Murray Hill, N.J., 1958-62; supr. Bell Telephone Labs., North Andover, Mass., 1962-69; assoc. prof. U. Mass., Amherst, 1969-71, prof., 1971-96, chmn. dept elec. and computer engring., 1975-78, acting head dept. elec. and computer engring., 1991-93, prof. emeritus, 1996—. Author: Signal Theory, 1969; editor: Data Communication, 1974; contbr. over 60 articles to profl. jours. Hewlett-Packard fellow, Stanford U., 1952. Fellow IEEE; mem. NSF (program dir. networking and communications rsch., 1988-90). Office: Univ of Mass Dept of Elec & Computer Engring Amherst MA 01003

FRANKS, LUCINDA LAURA, journalist; b. Chgo., July 16, 1946; d. Thomas Edward and Lorraine Lois (Leavitt) F.; m. Robert M. Morgenthau, Nov. 1977; children: Joshua Franks Morgenthau, Amy Elinor Morgenthau. B.A., Vassar Coll., 1968. Journalist specializing youth affairs, civil strife in No. Ireland UPI, London, 1968-73, N.Y. Times, N.Y.C., 1974-77; freelance writer N.Y. Times Mag., N.Y. Times Book Rev., The Atlantic, The New Yorker, N.Y. mag., The Nation; Vis. prof. Vassar Coll., 1977-82; Ferris prof. journalism Princeton U., 1983. Author: Waiting Out A War: The Exile of Private John Picciano, 1974, Wild Apples, 1991. Recipient Pulitzer prize for nat. reporting, 1971, N.Y. Newspaper Writers Assn. award, 1971; Nat. Headliners award, Soc. Silurians journalism award, 1976. Mem. Am. PEN Club (membership bd.), Author's League, Coun. on Fgn. Rels., Writers Rm. Inc. (past pres.). Address: 64 E 86th St New York NY 10028-1016*

FRANKS, ROBERT D. (BOB FRANKS), congressman; b. Hackensack, N.J., Sept. 21, 1951; s. Norman A. and June Evans F. BA, Depauw U., 1973; JD, So. Methodist U., 1976. Exec. dir. People for Bateman, 1977; cons. Jim Courter for Congress Com., 1978; v.p. Med Data Inc., 1978-80; co-owner County News, 1980-83; cons. Tom Kean for Gov. Com., 1981; mem. N.J. State Assembly from 22nd Dist., Trenton, 1979-93, 103d-106th Congresses from 7th N.J. Dist., 1993—; mem. budget com., mem. transp. and infrastructure com.; Bd. dirs. Intrenet.; mgmt. cons. in field; founder CREO; mem. Econ. Steering Com., 1980, Com. on Energy and Nat. Resources, 1981-83, Com. on State Govt., Civil Svc., Elections, Pensions and Vet. Affairs, 1981-85, N.J. State Pension Study Commn., 1982, Com. Revenue, Finance and Appropriations, 1984-93, State and Local Expenditure and Revenue Policy Commn., 1985-93, Waste Mgmt. Planning and Recycling Com., 1990-91; chmn. Task Force to Reform Congress Redistricting Process, 1982, N.J. Coalition for Regulatory Efficiency, 1985-93, Republican Policy Com., 1990-91, N.J. State Rep. Party, 1988-93; campaign mgr. Congressman Jim Courter, 1982, Congressman Dean Gallo, 1984; assembly liaison Rep. Majority. 1985. Bd. mgrs. Children's Specialized Hosp., Mountainside, N.J., 1980; mem. long range planning com. Overlook Hosp., Summit, N.J., 1982; mem. domestic task force Hands Across Am., 1986; mem. N.J. Jaycees. Named Legislator of Yr. Nat. Rep. Legislators Assn., 1986. Office: 2333 Morris Ave Ste B17 Union NJ 07083-5714 Office: US Ho of Reps 225 Cannon HOB Washington DC 20515-3007*

FRANKS, RONALD DWYER, university dean, psychiatrist, educator; b. Balt., Jan. 15, 1946; s. Wylie and H. Jeanette (Dwyer) F.; m. Vicky Ruth Vicklund; children: Aaron Matthew, Alexis Linda. Student, Albion Coll., 1964-67; MD with distinction, U. Mich., 1971. Intern Virginia Mason Hosp., Seattle, 1971-72; resident in psychiatry U. Colo. Med. Ctr., Denver, 1972-76; instr. psychiatry U. Colo. Sch. Medicine, Denver, 1976-77, asst. prof. psychiatry, 1977-83, assoc. prof., 1983-88, asst. dean student affairs, 1982-84, asst. dean student and curricular affairs, dir. inpatient svcs. dept. psychiatry, 1986-88; dean, prof. psychiatry U. Minn. Sch. Medicine, Duluth, 1988-97; dean, prof. psychiatry and behavioral scis. East Tenn. State U. Coll. Medicine, Johnson City, 1997—. Contbr. numerous articles to profl. jours. Mem. AMA, Lake Superior Med. Soc., Am. Psychiat. Assn., Alpha Omega Alpha. Home: 3007 Moss Creek Dr Johnson City TN 37604-2203 Office: East Tenn State U James H Quillen Coll Med PO Box 70694 Johnson City TN 37614-1212*

FRANKS, SUZAN L. R., state legislator; b. Everett, Mass., Sept. 18, 1949; m. Richard A.; three children. State rep. N.H., 1991—. Office: NH Ho of Reps State Capitol Concord NH 03301*

FRANKS, TOMMY RAY, army officer; b. Wynnewood, Okla., June 17, 1945; m. Cathryn Carley, Mar. 22, 1969; 1 child, Jacqueline Franks Matlock. BSBA, U. Tex., Arlington, 1971; MS in Pub. Adminstrn., Shippensburg U. Pa., 1985; grad., Armed Forces Staff Coll., U.S. Army War Coll. Commd. 2d lt. U.S. Army, 1967, advanced through grades to lt. gen., 1997; comdr. 2d bn. 78th F.A. 1st Armored Divsn., Germany, 1981-84; dep. asst. chief staff G3 III Corps, Ft. Hood, Tex., 1985-86; comdr. div. arty. 1st Cav. Div., 1987-88, chief staff, 1988-89; asst. divsn. comdr. Operation Desert Shield-Storm, 1st Cav. Div., Saudi Arabia, Iraq, 1990-91; asst. comdt. U.S. Army F.A. Sch., Ft. Sill, Okla., 1991-92; dir. La. Maneuvers Task Force, Office Chief of Staff U.S. Army, Ft. Monroe, Va., until 1994; asst. chief staff C3/J3/G3 UN and combined forces command U.S. Forces Korea, 8th U.S. Army, 1994; commdr. second infantry divsn. Korea, 1995-97; comdr. 3d United States Army Ft. McPherson, Ga., 1997—. Decorated Def. Disting. Svc. Medal, Disting. Svc. Medal, Legion of Merit with 3 oak leaf clusters, Bronze Star medal with V device and 4 oak leaf clusters, Purple Heart with 2 oak leaf clusters. Home: 1299 Staff Row SW Atlanta GA 30310-5124 Office: 1777 Hardee Ave SW Atlanta GA 30330-1062

FRANKSON-KENDRICK, SARAH JANE, publisher; b. Bradford, Pa., Sept. 24, 1949; d. Sophronus Ahimus and Elizabeth Jane (Sears) McCutcheon; m. James Michael Kendrick, Jr., May 22, 1982. Customer svc. rep. Laros Printing/Osceola Graphics, Bethlehem, Pa., 1972-73; assoc. editor Babcox Publs., Akron, Ohio, 1973-74, Bill Comms., Akron, Ohio, 1974-75; sr. editor Bill Comms., Akron, 1975-77, editor-in-chief, 1977-81; assoc. pub. Chilton Co./ABC Pub., Chgo., 1981-83, pub., 1983-89; group pub. Chilton Co./ABC Pub., Radnor, Pa., 1989-93; group v.p. Cahners Bus. Info. (formerly Chilton Co.), Radnor, Pa., 1993-98; divsn. v.p. Primedia Intertec, Chgo., 1999—; exec. MBA prof. Northwood U., mem. adv. coun. Recipient Automotive Replacement Edn. award Northwood Inst., 1983, award for young leadership and excellence Automotive Hall of Fame, 1984; bd. dirs. Automotive Hall of Fame. Mem. Automotive Found. for Aftermarket (trustee), Automotive Parts and Accessories Assn. (bd. dirs., exec. com., sec., treas., strategic planning com., edn. com., Disting Svc. award 1993), Automotive Svc. Industry Assn. (bd. dirs. automotive divsn. com.), Automotive Svc. Assn. Mgmt. Inst. (trustee, exec. com.), Knollwood Country Club (Lake Forest, Ill.). Republican. Office: Primedia Intertec 29 N Wacker Dr Chicago IL 60606

FRANO, ANDREW JOSEPH, lawyer, civil engineer; b. Chgo., July 14, 1953; s. Joseph Neil Frano and Lorraine Rose (Jeczalik) Patchett; children: Alaina Marie, Jacqueline Elyse. BSCE, Bradley U., 1975, MSCE, 1976; JD, Ill. Inst. Tech., 1982. Bar: Ill. 1982, Nebr. 1986, U.S. Dist. Ct. (no. dist.) Ill. 1982, U.S. Dist. Ct. Nebr. 1992, Ariz. 1993, Tex. 1997; registered profl. engr., Ill., Ind., Nebr.; lic. gen. engring. constrn. contractor Fla., Utah. Soils lab. instr. and residence hall dir. Bradley U., Peoria, Ill., 1975-76; civil engr. Harza Engring. Co., Chgo., 1976-85; pvt. practice Chgo., 1982-85; pres. GEC Engring. Co. Inc., Chgo., 1985-86; corp. constrn. atty. Peter Kiewit Sons Inc., Omaha, Nebr., 1986-92; asst. gen. counsel Harza Engring. Co., Chgo., 1992-95; owner The Law and Engring. Office of Andrew J. Frano, 1996—; adj. asst. prof. dept. civil and architectural engring., Ill. Inst. Tech., Chgo., 1993—; corp. atty., civil engr. T.J. Lambrecht Constrn., Inc., Joliet, Ill., 1996-98; prin. engr. Mirza-RSV Engring., Inc., Chgo., 1998—. Chmn. San. Improvement Dist. 111, Sarpy County, Nebr., 1987-92; vol. atty. Chgo. Vol. Legal Svcs., 1983-85; bd. dirs., treas. Trails Assn. Inc., Roselle, Ill., 1983-86. Mem. ASCE, Tau Beta Pi, Chi Epsilon. Republican. Roman Catholic. Avocations: basketball, tennis. Home: 2 N Dee Rd #107 Park Ridge IL 60068-2871 Office: Mirza-RSV Engring Inc 7221 W Touhy Ave Chicago IL 60631

FRANO, RONALD A., non-profit executive; b. East Paterson, N.J.; s. Michael and Ida Frano; children: Ron Jr., Lisa, Lynn, Cheryl. BS in Bus. Adminstrn., Rutgers U., Newark, 1968; MBA in Gen. Mgmt., Fordham U., 1972. City mgr. Twp. of Ocean, N.J., 1970-74; area dir. state and local affairs Nat. Fedn. Ind. Bus., 1974-81; exec. dir. Plastic Pipe Inst. Soc. of the Plastics Industry, NY.C., 1981-84; fin./tax cons. Ronald A. Frano and Assocs., Ocean, 1984-90; exec. dir. Am. Small Bus. Assn., Grapevine, Tex., 1990-94; CFO U. Tex., Southwestern Med. Ctr., Dallas, 1994—. Mem. MGMA, ASOA, AUPO, Healthcare Fin. Mgmt. Assn. E-mail: ronald.franocerail.swmed.edu. Office: U Southwestern Med Ctr Bldg E 7 142A 5323 Harry Hines Blvd Dallas TX 75235-9057

FRANTZ, ANDREW GIBSON, physician, educator; b. N.Y.C., May 22, 1930; s. Angus Macdonald and Virginia (Kneeland) F. A.B. magna cum laude, Harvard U., 1951; M.D., Columbia U., 1955. Intern Presbyn. Hosp., N.Y.C., 1955-56; resident in medicine Presbyn. Hosp., 1956-58; fellow in endocrinology Columbia U., N.Y.C., 1958-60; asst. prof. medicine Columbia U., 1966-68, assoc. prof., 1968-73, prof., 1973—, chief div. endocrinology, 1971-87; chmn. admissions com., assoc. dean for admissions Columbia U. (Coll. Physicians and Surgeons), 1981—; assoc. in medicine Harvard U., 1962-66; asst. in medicine Mass. Gen. Hosp., Boston, 1962-66; mem. staff Presbyn. Hosp., N.Y.C.; mem. med. adv. bd. Nat. Pituitary Agy., 1970-73; established investigator Am. Heart Assn., 1968-73. Contbr. articles on prolactin and other pituitary hormones and functions to med. and sci. jours.; mem. editorial bd.: Jour. Clin. Endocrinology and Metabolism, 1971-76; assoc. editor: Metabolism, 1969—. Served to lt. comdr. USNR, 1960-62. Recipient Silver Medal Coll. Physicians and Surgeons, Columbia U., 1981, Alumni Fedn. medal Columbia U., 1984, Disting. Tchr. award, Coll. Physicians and Surgeons, Columbia U., 1989. Mem. AAAS, Endocrine Soc., Assn. Am. Physicians, Am. Soc. Clin. Investigation, Internat. Soc. for Neuroendocrinology, Harvey Soc., Practitioners Soc. (pres. 1993—), Peripatetic Club, Charaka Club, Am. Fedn. Clin. Rsch., N.Y. Acad. Scis., N.Y. Acad. Medicine, Union Club, Century Assn. (N.Y.C.), P and S Alumni Assn. (pres. 1991-93), Alpha Omega Alpha. Episcopalian. Home: 1185 Park Ave New York NY 10128-1308 Office: 630 W 168th St New York NY 10032-3702

FRANTZ, CECILIA ARANDA, psychologist; b. Nogales, Ariz., Aug. 6, 1941; d. Tomas Návarro and Maria Guadalupe (Covarrubias) A.; m. Roger Allen Frantz, May 27, 1972; 1 child, Kimberly Marie Whelan. BA, U. Ariz., 1966; MA, Ariz. State U., 1972, PhD, 1975. Lic. clin. psychologist, Ariz., sch. psychologist, Va. Tchr. Wilson Sch. Dist., Phoenix, 1966-70; psychologist Child Evaluation Ctr., Phoenix, 1973-75; sch. psychologist Wilson Sch. Dist., Phoenix, 1975-78, spl. edn. dir., 1977-78, schs. supt., 1978-81; acting dir. Nat. Inst. Handicap Rsch. U.S. Dept. Edn., Washington, 1981-82, dep. asst. sec. dept. elm. and secondary edn., 1982-87; asst. dir. Bush's Nat. Steering Com. Campaign Hdqrs., Washington, 1987-88; pvt. practice Washington, 1988—; sch. psychologist Cath. Diocese of Arlington, Va., 1990-92; Arlington County Schs., Arlington, Va., 1992—; cons. U.S. Dept. Edn., Washington, 1987—. Mem. APA, Am. Assn Sch. Adminstrs., Ariz. State Psychol. Assn., Ariz. State Sch. Psychologists Assn., Maricopa Soc. Clin. Psychologists (sec. 1976-77). Republican. Roman Catholic. Home: 4501 Arlington Blvd Apt 609 Arlington VA 22203-2740

FRANTZ, IVAN D., III, pediatrician; b. Boston, Feb. 26, 1945. BA in Chemistry, U. Minn., 1967, BS, 1971, MD, 1971. Diplomate Am. Bd. Pediatrics. Intern in pediatrics U. Minn. Hosps., 1971-72, resident in pediatrics, 1972-73; fellow in newborn medicine Montreal Children's Hosp., Quebec, Canada, 1973-74; clin. fellow in neonatology Children's Hosp. Med. Ctr., Boston, 1974-75; rsch. fellow in pediatrics Harvard Med. Sch., Boston, 1974-75; instr. in pediatrics Harvard Med. Sch., 1975-77, asst. prof. pediatrics, 1977-84, assoc. prof. pediatrics, 1984-85; assoc. prof. pediatrics Tufts U. Sch. Med., Boston, 1985-87; prof. pediatrics Tufts U. Sch. Med., 1987—; lectr. pediatrics Harvard Med. Sch., 1985—, Boston U. Sch. Med., 1985—; dir. Tufts affiliated program in newborn medicine, 1985—; asst. in newborn medicine, Children's Hosp. Med. Ctr., Boston, 1975-77, assoc. in medicine, 1977-80, assoc. chief divsn. newborn medicine, 1977-85, sr. assoc. in medicine, 1981-86; pediatrician Boston Hsop. for Women, 1975-78; sr. pediatrician Brigham & Women's Hosp., Boston, 1978-85; assoc. in pediatrics Beth Israel Hosp., Boston, 1975—; assoc. dir. Joint Program in Neonatology, Boston, 1979-85; assoc. neonatologist Brigham and Women's Hosp., Boston, 1985—; pediatrician New England Med. Ctr., Boston, 1985—, dir. Neonatal ICU, 1985—, dir. Boston Perinatal Ctr., 1985—, chief divsn. newborn medicine dept. pediatrics, 1987—; pediatrician St. Margaret's Hosp. for Women, Boston, 1985-92; assoc. vis. physician Boston City Hosp., 1985—; cons. Children's Hosp. Med. Ctr., Boston, 1986—; mem. courtesy staff South Shore Hosp., South Weymouth, Mass., 1991—, Beverly (Mass.) Hosp., 1991—, Salem (Mass.) Hosp., 1991—; mem. assoc. staff Lowell (Mass.) Gen. Hosp., 1994—; mem. gen. hosp. and personal use device classification panel dept. health edn. and welfare FBA, 1976-81; mem. numerous coms. Mem. Am. Pediatric Soc., Soc. Pediatric Rsch., Am. Physiol. Soc., Am. Thoracic Soc. (rsch. rev. com. 1986—), Am. Acad. Pediatrics, Perinatal Rsch. Soc. (coun. mem. pediatrics 1989—), New England Perinatology Soc. (pres. 1982, program com. chmn. 1984-87), European Soc. Pediatric Rsch., Eastern Soc. Pediatric Rsch., Mass. Thoracic Soc. (rsch. allocations com. 1986—). Office: Tufts U New England Med Ctr Box 44 750 Washington St Boston MA 02111-1526*

FRANTZ, JACK THOMAS, advertising executive; b. Indpls., Dec. 27, 1939; s. John Richard and Edna Louise (Bennett) F.; m. Georgene Mary Meyers, Aug. 18, 1962; 1 child, John Bennett. B.S. in Mktg. Ind. U., 1961. Media buyer Ted Bates & Co., N.Y.C., 1962-65; account exec. Papert, Koenig, Lois Inc., N.Y.C., 1965-69; account exec. Grey Advt. Inc., N.Y.C., 1969, account supr., 1969-72; v.p. mgmt. supr. Grey Advt. Inc., 1972-79; sr. v.p. account mgmt. Grey Advt., Inc., 1979-83, exec. v.p., 1983-93, exec. v.p., group dir., 1993-96, cons., 1996—. Served with USAR, 1962. Recipient numerous advt. awards. Office: Grey Advt Inc 777 3rd Ave New York NY 10017-1401

FRANTZ, PHARES ALBERT, architect; b. New Orleans, Nov. 1, 1923; s. Roy Florestan and Marie Lucile (O'Kelley) F.; m. Elinor Mae McCloskey, Feb. 20, 1954; children—Ninette Marie, Colleen Marie, Melinda Marie. B.Arch., Tulane U., 1950. Registered architect, La., Miss., Tenn. Draftsman, Richard Koch Architect, New Orleans, 1950-52, architect, 1952-55; assoc. Richard Koch & Samuel Wilson Jr. Architects, New Orleans, 1955-72; ptnr. Koch and Wilson Architects, New Orleans, 1972-86; pres. Koch & Wilson, Architects, P.C., 1986—. Mem. Citizens Adv. com. Studying Revisions to City Zoning Ordinance, 1969; bd. dirs. Incarnate Word Parish Sch. Bd., 1971-80, pres., 1977-80; bd. dirs. France Amerique, 1981; pres. La. Polit. Com. Design Profls., 1984. Decorated Order of St. Louis Archdiocese of New Orleans. Mem. La. Inst. Bldg. Scis. (dir. 1980), AIA (mem. hist. resources com. 1975-83, mem. New Orleans chpt. 1950—, pres. 1969, dir. 1970-71, state preservation coordinator 1982), La. Architects Assn. (pres. 1980), Construction Specifications Inst. (pres. New Orleans chpt. 1960), Friends of Cabildo, La. Landmarks Soc., Sons of the Revolution, Nat. Trust, Mag. St., Delta Tau Delta. Republican. Roman Catholic. Club: Round Table Club (v.p. 1992-93, pres. 1994-95). Home: 7525 Pearl St New Orleans LA 70118-3835 Office: Koch and Wilson 1100 Jackson Ave New Orleans LA 70130-5652

FRANTZ, RAY WILLIAM, JR., retired librarian; b. Princeton, Ky., Aug. 17, 1923; s. Ray William and Marjorie (Kevil) F.; m. Doris Methvin, Aug. 26, 1951; children: Katherine Kevil, Paul William. AB, U. Nebr., 1948; MLS, U. Ill., 1949, MA, 1951, PhD in English, 1955. Dir. libr. U. Richmond, Va., 1955-60; asst. dir. Ohio State U. Libr., Columbus, 1960-62; dir. libraries U. Wyo. Libr., 1962-67; libr. U. Va. Libr., Charlottesville, 1967-93; chmn. bd. dirs. Southeastern Libr. Network, 1975-76; vice chmn., bd. dirs. 18th Century Short-Title Catalogue, N.Am., 1985—. With inf. AUS, 1943-46. Mem. ALA, Assn. Rsch. Librs. (pres. 1977-78), Assn. Southeastern Rsch. Librs. (chmn. 1975—), Bibliog. Soc. Am., Bibliog. Soc. U. Va. (sec.-treas. 1967—). Home: 540 Worthington Dr Charlottesville VA 22903-4651

FRANTZ, ROBERT WESLEY, lawyer; b. Long Branch, N.J., Dec. 31, 1950. BS, Rutgers U., New Brunswick, N.J., 1973; JD, Rutgers U., Newark, 1977. Bar: N.J. 1977, U.S. Dist. Ct. N.J. 1977, U.S. Ct. Appeals (4th and 10th cirs.) 1978, U.S. Ct. Appeals (6th, 7th and 8th cirs.) 1979, D.C. 1980, U.S. Ct. Appeals (9th cir.) 1980, U.S. Dist. Ct. D.C. 1981. Trial atty. U.S. Dept. Justice, Washington, 1977-80; assoc. Hamel and Park, Washington, 1980-82; asst. gen. counsel Chem. Mfrs. Assn., Washington, 1982-85; counsel, environ. protection GE, Fairfield, Conn., 1985-88, Pittsfield, Mass., 1988-89; mgr. and counsel Environ. Remediation Program, Fairfield, Conn., 1989-95; mgr., sr. counsel Environ. Ops. Program, Fairfield, 1995-98; gen. mgr., counsel GE Engines Svcs., Cin., 1998—; mem. sci. adv. bd. subcom. on risk reduction options U.S. EPA, 1996—. Contbr. articles to profl. publs.; editorial bd. Rutgers Law Rev., 1976. Mem. Newtown (Conn.) Charter Revision Commn., 1986-87. Mem. ABA (exec. editor Natural Resources and Environment 1986-93, coun. mem. sect. natural resources 1993-96). Avocations: sailing, golf, skiing, bicycling, woodworking. Office: GE Engine Svcs 1 Neumann Way # Md-t164 Cincinnati OH 45215-1915

FRANTZEN, HENRY ARTHUR, investment company executive; b. Orange, N.J., Nov. 28, 1942; s. Henry and Natalie (Johnson) F.; m. Julie Louise Haverty, Aug. 14, 1965; children—John Blair, Jill Marie, Eric Patrick. Student, Hamline U., 1960-62; B.S.B.A., U. N.D., 1964. Sr. securities analyst Chem. Bank, 1968-71; adminstrv. asst. Coll. Retirement Equities Fund, 1971, asst. investment officer, 1972, investment officer, 1973, asst. v.p., 1974-76, 2d v.p., 1976, v.p., investment mgr., mem. investment com., 1976; sr. v.p., investment mgr. Tchrs. Ins. and Annuity of Am., N.Y.C., 1980-87, Coll. Retirement Equities Fund, N.Y.C., 1980-87; dir. SBC Portfolio Mgmt. Internat. Inc., Amsterdam, 1987-89; chmn., chief investment officer Yamaichi Capital Mgmt. Corp., 1987-89; pres. Yamaichi Funds Inc., 1987-89, chmn., 1988-89; exec. v.p., dir. equities Oppenheimer Mgmt. Corp., N.Y.C., 1989-91; CEO, exec. v.p. Federated Global Investors, N.Y.C., 1995—; mgr. Brown Bros Harriman & Co., 1992-95, Brown Bros. Harriman & Co. Investment Mgmt. Ltd., London, 1992-95; exec. v.p. Federated Global Rsch. Corp., 1995—; exec. v.p. Federated Rsch. Corp., 1995—; v.p. Federated Investors, 1995; chief investment officer Global Equities and Fixed Income. Served to lt. USNR, 1964-68. Fellow Fin. Analysts Fedn.; mem. N.Y. Soc. Security Analysts, Econs. Club (N.Y.C.), Sigma Nu, Alpha Kappa Psi. Republican. Episcopalian. Avocations: sailing; golfing; tennis; body surfing. Home: 2 Fireside Dr Colts Neck NJ 07722-1354 Office: Federated Global Investors 175 Water St New York NY 10038-4918*

FRANZ, DANIEL THOMAS, financial planner; b. Dayton, Ohio, Jan. 30, 1949; s. Albin Benedict and Monica Elizabeth (Moeller) F.; m. Sally Ann Stickley, Oct. 11, 1968; children: Amanda Marie, Stephanie Ann. BS, Charleston So. U., 1971, postgrad., 1975; postgrad., S.C. State U., 1974. Cert. fin. aid adminstr., fin. planner. Coach, admissions officer Bapt. Coll., Charleston (S.C.) So. U., 1971-72; dir. fin. aid Bapt. Coll., Charleston, S.C., 1972-76; pvt. practice fin. planning Greenville, Ohio, 1977—; cons. S.C. Bapt. Conv., Columbia, 1974-76, U.S. Office Edn., Atlanta, 1974-76, Corning Glass Works, Greenville, 1984—, Franklin-Monroe High Sch., Pitsburg, Ohio, 1985—, United Telephone Co., Bellefontaine, Ohio, 1986—. Bd. dirs. Darke County Supts. Roundtable, Greenville, 1983—, Darke County Widows Assn., 1984-86; mem., chmn. bd. dirs. S.C. Com. Higher Edn., Columbia, 1974-76, Darke County Mental Health Clinic, 1984-90; bd. dirs. Coun. on Rural Svcs. Programs, 1991—; chmn. bd. dirs. Ch. of the Transfiguration Cath. Ch., West Milton, Ohio, 1978-82. Mem. Inst. Cert. Fin. Planners, Internat. Assn. Fin. Planners, Nat. Assn. Life Underwriters, Miami Valley Assn. Life Underwriters, S.C. Assn. Student Fin. Aid Adminstrs. (bd. dirs. 1971—), Darke County C. of C. (bd. dirs. 1993—), Lions. Republican. Avocation: sports. Office: Fin Achievement Svcs PO Box 657 5116 Childrens Hm Bradford Rd Greenville OH 45331-9327

FRANZ, DENNIS, actor; b. Maywood, IL, Oct. 28, 1944. stage appearances include: Bleacher Bums, 1978, Borhters, 1983; films include: The Fury, 1978, Remember My Name, 1978, Stony Island, 1978, A Wedding, 1978, A Perfect Couple, 1979, Dressed to Kill, 1980, Popeye, 1980, Blow Out, 1981, Psycho II, 1983, Body Double, 1984, A Fine Mess, 1986, The Package, 1989, Die-Hard 2, 1990, The Player, 1992, American Buffalo, 1996, City of Angels, 1998; TV appearances include: (series) Chicago Story, 1982, Hill Street Blues, (as "Bad Sal" Benedetto) 1982-83 (as Lieutenant Norman Buntz) 1987-88, Bay City Blues, 1983, Beverly Hills Buntz, 1987-88, Nasty Boys, 1990, NYPD Blue, 1993— (Emmy award 1994) (movies) Deadly Messages, 1985, Kiss Shot, 1989, Moment of Truth: Caught in the Crossfire, 1994, Texas Justice, 1995. Office: Paradigm Talent Agency 10100 Santa Monica Blvd Fl 25 Los Angeles CA 90067-4003*

FRANZ, ELIZABETH, actress. Actress with Broadway credits in: Death of a Salesman, The Cripple of Inishmaan, Brighton Beach Memoirs (Tony and Drama Desk nominations), Broadway Bound, Uncle Vanya, Getting Married, The Cemetery Club, The Octette Bridge Club, The Cherry Orchard; off-Broadway credits include: Sister Mary Ignatius (Obie award, Drama Desk nomination), Minutes from the Blue Route, The Comedy of Errors; regional credits include: Eleanor of Aquataine in The Lion in Winter (Cleve.), Amanda in The Glass Menagerie, Dividing the Estate (Great

Lakes), A View From the Bridge, Woman in Mind (Berkshire Theatre Festival), Dolly in The Matchmaker, Agnes of God, Hamlet, Buried Child, The Wicket Witch in The Wizard of Oz, Miss Haversham in Great Expectations; appeared in numerous TV series and movies including: Roseanne, Sister, A Town's Revenge (Emmy nomination), Notes for My Daughter, Nothing Personal, Shameful Secrets, Face of a Stranger, Dottie, The Rise and Rise of Daniel Rocket, Love and Other Sorrows; film credits include: Sabrina, The Substance of Fire, The Pallbearer, Thinner, Twisted, Jacknife, Secret of My Success, School Ties. Winner 1999 Tony award for featured actress in Death of a Salesman, also Drama Desk award, Outer Critics Circle award. Office: c/o Michael Slessinger Assocs 8730 Sunset Blvd #220 Los Angeles CA 90069*

FRANZ, FRANK ANDREW, university president, physics educator; b. Phila., Sept. 16, 1937; s. Russell Ernest and Edna (Keller) F.; m. Judy Rosenbaum, July 11, 1959; 1 child, Eric Douglas. BS in Physics, Lafayette Coll., 1959; MS in Physics, U. Ill., 1961, PhD in Physics, 1964. Research assoc. U. Ill., Urbana, 1964-65; asst. prof. physics Ind. U., Bloomington, 1967-70, assoc. prof., 1970-74, prof., 1974-85, assoc. dean Coll. Arts and Scis., 1974-77, dean faculties, 1977-82; prof. physics, provost, v.p. academic affairs and research W.Va. U., Morgantown, 1985-91; prof. physics, pres. U. Ala., Huntsville, 1991—; guest scientist Swiss Fed. Inst. Tech., Zurich, 1965-67, U. Munich, 1978. Contbr. articles to profl. jours. NSF fellow, 1965-67, Alfred P. Sloan fellow, 1968-70. Fellow Am. Phys. Soc.; mem. AAAS, AAUP (pres. Bloomington, Ind. chpt. 1972-73), Am. Assn. Physics Tchrs., Sigma Xi. Avocation: tennis. Office: Office of President Univ Alabama in Huntsville Huntsville AL 35899

FRANZ, JENNIFER DANTON, public opinion and marketing researcher; b. Oakland, Calif., Oct. 31, 1949; d. Joseph Periam and Lois (King) Danton; m. William Edwin Behnk, July 30, 1978. BA, Antioch Coll. West, 1973; MA, Stanford U., 1974; PhD, U. Calif., Berkeley, 1991. Cert. Community Coll. Student Personnel Worker, Calif., Community Coll. Supr., Calif. Cons. Alum Rock Union Elem. Sch. Dist., San Jose, Calif., 1973-75; rsch. asst. Far West Lab. for Ednl. Rsch. and Devel., San Francisco, 1974-75; project dir. Hartnell Coll., Salinas, Calif., 1975-77; project dir. Chancellor's Office Calif. Community Colls., Sacramento, 1978-80; pres., owner J.D. Franz Rsch., Sacramento, 1981—; topic expert Nat. Mktg. Summit, 1995; adj. asst. prof. Golden Gate U., 1982—; instr. mktg. cert. program U. Calif. at Davis Extension, 1990—; lectr. Calif. State U., Sacramento, 1995—; instr. U. Calif.-Berkeley Ext., 1997—. Contbr. numerous articles to profl. jours. Mem. small bus. adv. com. Calif. Senate, Sacramento, 1986-92; bd. dirs. Jr. Achievement Sacramento, 1989-91, Episcopal Cmty. Svcs. Sacramento, 1991-92. Recipient various rsch., svc. awards. Mem. Am. Mktg. Assn., Am. Assn. Pub. Opinion Rsch., Am. Ednl. Rsch. Assn. (editor 1984-86, mem. div. H evaluation steering com. 1984-85, polit. edn. spl. interest group, survey rsch. spl. interest group, judge div. H awards competition 1984, program reviewer 1982—), Mktg. Rsch. Assn., Sacramento Met. C. of C. (bd. dirs. 1990-93, state govt. affairs, local govt. affairs, pub. rels. coms. 1985—), Sacramento Valley Mktg. Assn. (bd. dirs. 1987-94, pres. 1993-94). Democrat. Episcopalian. Avocations: playing piano, swimming, reading. Address: JD Franz Rsch 1804 Tribute Rd Ste K Sacramento CA 95815-4313

FRANZ, JOHN E., bio-organic chemist, researcher; b. Springfield, Ill., Dec. 21, 1929; m. Elinor Theilken, Aug. 7, 1951; children: Judith, Mary, John, Gary. BS, U. Ill., 1951; PhD, U. Minn., 1955. Sr. research chemist Monsanto Agrl. Co., St. Louis, 1955-60, research group leader, 1960-63, fellow, 1963-75, sr. fellow, 1975-80, disting. fellow, 1980-90; ret., 1991. Co-author: Glyphosate: A Unique Global Herbicide, 1997; Inventor roundup herbicide; holder 840 U.S. and fgn. patents; contbr. 42 articles to sci. publs. Recipient Indsl. Rsch. Mag. award, 1977, Indsl. Rsch. Inst. Achievement award, Washington, 1985, J.F. Queeny award Monsanto Co., 1981, Inventor of Yr. award St. Louis Bar Assn., 1986, The Nat. Medal of Tech., Washington, 1987, Outstanding Achievement award, U. Minn., 1988, The Mo. award, Gov. of Mo., 1988. Mem. Am. Chem. Soc. (Carother's award Del. sect. 1989, Perkin medal. Am. sect., 1990).

FRANZ, JUDY R., physics educator. BA in Physics, Cornell U., 1959; MS in Physics, U. Ill., 1961, PhD in Physics, 1965. Rsch. physicist IBM Rsch. Lab., Zurich, Switzerland, 1965-67; asst. prof. dept. physics Ind. U., 1968-74, assoc. prof., 1974-79, prof., 1979-87; prof. dept. physics W.Va. U., 1987-91, U. Ala. Huntsville, 1991—; exec. officer Am. Phys. Soc., 1994—; vis. prof. Tech. U. Munich, 1978-79, Cornell U., 1985-86, 88, 90; assoc. dean coll. arts and scis. Ind. U., 1980-82; mem. coun. on materials sci. Dept. of Energy; mem. rev. com. for materials sci and tech. divsn. Los Alamos Nat. Lab. Mem. editorial bd. Am. Jour. Physics, 1985-88; contbr. numerous articles to profl. jours. Mem. divsn. materials rsch. adv. com. NSF, 1986-89, mem. divsn. undergrad. edn. adv. com., 1991-93. Humboldt rsch. fellow Munich, 1978-79; recipient Distinguished Service Citation awd., Am. Assn. of Physics Teachers, 1993, Disting. Alumni award Coll. Eng., U. Ill., Urbana-Champaign, 1997. Fellow AAAS (coun. 1995-98), Am. Phys. Soc. (various coms. and offices, chair exec. com. divsn. condensed matter physics 1993-94); mem. Am. Assn. Physics Tchrs. (pres. 1990-91), Assn. Women in Sci., Am. Inst. Physics (various coms., gov. bd. 1994—, exec. com. 1996—), Coun. Sci. Soc. Pres. (exec. bd. 1990), Phi Beta Kappa, Sigma Xi (pres. local chpt. 1981-82). Avocations: tennis, reading. Office: Am Phys Soc One Physics Ellipse College Park MD 20740

FRANZ, MARIAN C., association administrator; b. Newton, Kans., Oct. 12, 1930; d. Ernest G. and Justine (Wiebe) Claassen; m. Delton W. Franz, Dec. 12, 1932; children: Gregory, Gayle, Coretta. BA, Bethel Coll., Newton, 1954; M Religious Edn., Mennonite Bibl. Sem., Chgo., 1957. Elem. sch. tchr. Whitewater, Kans., 1951-52, Hillsboro, Kans., 1954-55; ch. sch. supr. Ch. Fedn. Greater Chgo., 1957-63; dir. Dunamis, Washington, 1970-80. Author: Questions That Refuse to Go Away, 1991; contbr. chpts. to books, 1990—. Mennonite. Avocations: swimming, walking. Home: 6151 31st St NW Washington DC 20015-1515 Office: Nat Campaign for Peace Tax Fund 2121 Decatur Pl NW Washington DC 20008-1923

FRANZ, WANDA, association administrator. BA in Anthropology, U. Washington, 1965; MS in Family Resources, W. Va. U., 1970, PhD in Developmental Psychology, 1974. Pres. Nat. Right to Life Com., D.C.; prof. divsn. of family resources W.Va. U., Morgantown, 1974—. Office: Nat Right to Life Com 419 7th St NW Ste 500 Washington DC 20004-2293*

FRANZBLAU, CARL, biochemist, consultant, researcher; b. Bklyn., Sept. 26, 1934; s. William and Fannie (Gerber) F.; m. Myrna Tucker, Aug. 24, 1958; children: William, Rachel. BS, U. Mich., 1956; PhD, Yeshiva U., 1962; DSc (hon.), Roger Williams Coll., 1988. Prof., chmn. dept. biochemistry Sch. Medicine, Boston U., 1978—, assoc. dean for grad. studies, 1989—; mem. coun. Nat. Heart, Lung and Blood Inst., Bethesda, Md., 1985-88; cons. study sects. NIH. Contbr. numerous articles to profl. jours.; patentee in field. Fellow Am. Heart Assn., Am. Thoracic Soc.; mem. Am. Assn. Biochemistry and Molecular Biology, Fedn. Am. Socs. of Exptl. Biology. Office: Boston U Sch Medicine 80 E Concord St Roxbury MA 02118-2307*

FRANZE, ANTHONY JAMES, pharmacist, lawyer; b. Albany, N.Y., Sept. 22, 1941; s. Vincent J. and Susie (Special) F.; m. Kaoru Marie Nakamura, July 15, 1940; children: Vincent, Francis. BS in Pharmacy, St. John's Coll., 1963, JD, 1966. Bar: N.Y. 1996, U.S. Ct. Appeals (D.C. cir.) 1971, U.S. Patent Ct 1971; lic. pharmacist. Patent counsel Norwich (N.Y.) Eaton Pharms., 1970-84; assoc. city ct. judge City of Norwich, 1981-84; assoc. trademark and copyright coun. Bristol-Myers Squibb Co., N.Y.C., 1984—; mem. Emergency Svcs. Commn., Norwich, 1982-84; arbitrator N.Y.C. Small Claims Ct., N.Y.C., 1991—. Pres. PTO, Norwich, 1980-82; com. mem. Boy Scouts Troop 43, Princeton, N.Y., 1986-92. Col. U.S. Army, 1966-93 (active duty 1966-70). Mem. ABA, Am. Pharm. Assn., Am. Intellectual Property Assn., N.Y. State Bar Assn., Internat. Trademark Assn. Home: 387 Gallup Rd Princeton NJ 08540-7315 Office: Bristol-Myers Squibb Co 345 Park Ave New York NY 10022-6000

FRANZEL, BRENT STEVEN, lawyer; b. St. Louis, June 29, 1961; s. Richard and Lorraine Franzel; m. Ellen B. Brown. BJ, U. Mo., 1983; JD, Duke U., 1986. Bar: D.C. 1988, Mo. 1988. Legis. counsel Office of Senator Kit Bond, Washington, 1986-94; staff dir. Senate Banking Subcom. on Internat. Fin., Washington, 1995-96; ptnr. Tighe, Patton, Tabackman & Babbin, Washington, 1996—; sr. advisor US-Asean Bus. Coun., Washington, 1996—. Office: Tighe Patton Tabackman & Babbin # 300 1747 Pennsylvania Ave NW Washington DC 20006

FRANZEN, BYRON T. (JOHN FRANZEN), media specialist; b. Britton, S.D., Apr. 16, 1946; s. Harold G. and Marian E. (Swenson) F. BA in English and Philosophy, Concordia Coll., 1968; MA in English, McGill U., Montreal, Que., Can., 1970. Press sec. McGovern for Pres. Campaign, N.H., Ill. Oreg., N.Y., 1971-72; pub. rels. and press. sec. various orgns., Washington, Ala., N.Y., 1973-74; lesig. aide Hon. Michael Harrington U.S. Ho. Reps., Washington, 1975-76; mgr. Panetta for Congress Campaign, Calif., 1976; chief staff Hon. Leon Panetta U.S. Ho. Reps., Washington, 1977-78; pres., prin. Franzen & Co., Washington, 1979—; lectr. U.S. Info. Agy., various countries, 1988—. Designer Harriman Comm. Ctr., Nat. Dem. Hdqs., Washington, 1982-85; works represented in permanent collection Smithsonian Mus. Am. History. Recipient Excellence award Internat. TV Assn., 1985, Silver award Houston Internat. Film Festival, 1987, Gold award, 1988, Nat. Telly award, 1987, 93, 98, 99, Nat. Silver Microphone award, 1987, 94, 97, Addy award, 1987, Vision award, 1992, 95. Mem. Am. Assn. Polit. Cons. (bd. dirs. 1991—, Pollie award 1986, 88, 94). Avocations: reading, architectural design, carpentry, art, antiques. Office: Franzen & Co 610 C St NE Washington DC 20002-6002

FRANZEN, JANICE MARGUERITE GOSNELL, magazine editor; b. LaCrosse, Wis., Sept. 24, 1921; d. Wray Towson and Anna Heldena (Renstrom) Gosnell; m. Ralph Oscar Franzen, Feb. 15, 1964. BS cum laude, Wis. State U., LaCrosse, 1943; MRE, No. Bapt. Theol. Sem., 1947. Tchr. history and social sci. Galesville (Wis.) High Sch., 1943-45; registrar Christian Writers Inst., Chgo., 1947-49; dir. Christian Writers Inst., 1950-63, dir. studies, 1964-86; fiction editor Christian Life Mag., Wheaton, Ill., 1950-63, woman's editor, 1964-72, exec. editor, 1972-86; mem. editorial bd. Creation House, Wheaton, 1972-86; with Christian Life Missions, Lake Mary, Fla., 1971-95; speaker writers confs. Author: Christian Writers Handbook, 1960, 61, The Adventure of Interviewing, 1989; editor: Christian Author, 1949-54, Christian Writer and Editor, 1955-63; compiler, contbr.: The Successful Writers and Editors Guidebook, 1977; contbr. articles to various mags. Sec. Christian Life Missions, 1971-95. Home: 3N455 Mulberry Dr West Chicago IL 60185-1185

FRANZEN, LARRY WILLIAM, aerospace electronics engineer; b. Joliet, Ill., Sept. 6, 1945; s. Elmer William and Evelyn M. (Leonard) F.; m. Pennie Ann Gardner, Aug. 10, 1968 (div. Aug. 1975). A in Applied Tech., DeVry Tech. Inst., 1966; BSEE, Marquette U., 1969. Assoc. engr. McDonnell Douglas Aerospace, St. Louis, 1969-70, engr., 1970-76; sr. engr. McDonnell Douglas Aerospace, Langley AFB, Va., 1977-78; lead engr. McDonnell Douglas Aerospace, Eglin AFB, Fla., 1978-93, sr. project engr., 1994—. Mem. Choctaw Multihull Assn., Ft. Walton Yacht Club, Emerald Coast Cyclist. Avocations: sailing, cycling, skiing. Home: 358 Marie Cir NW Fort Walton Beach FL 32548-4632 Office: McDonnell Douglas Aerospace PO Box 1867 Eglin AFB FL 32542-0867*

FRANZEN, LAVERN GERHARD, bishop; b. Leigh, Nebr., May 18, 1926; s. Frank L. and Addie (Korfhage) F.; m. Mary Ann Karen Langeuin, Aug. 20, 1948; children: Kathryn, Frank, Sheryl, Deborah. BS in Edn., Concordia Coll., Seward, Nebr., 1948; MA in Religion, Concordia Sem., St. Louis, 1963; D of Ministry, Columbia Sem., Decatur, Ga., 1985; DD (hon.), Newberry Coll., 1988. Ordained to ministry Evang. Luth. Ch. in Am., 1963. Tchr. St. Paul Luth. Sch., Omaha, 1948-49, Luth. High Sch., Detroit, 1949-64; pastor Messiah Luth. Ch., Saginaw, Mich., 1964-68, Our Redeemer Luth. Ch., Temple Terrace, Fla., 1969-87; bishop Fla. synod Evang. Luth. Ch. in Am., Tampa, 1988-95, bishop emeritus, 1995—; lectr. on Ecumenism, 1995—. Author: Smile, God Loves You, 1971, Smile, Jesus Is Lord, 1973, The Good News from Luke, 1975, The Good News from Matthew, 1977. Bd. dirs. Trinity Sem., Columbus, Ohio, 1988-95, Newberry (S.C.) Coll., 1988-93. Mem. Kiwanis (editor, pres. local chpt.). Democrat. Home: 512 Hibiscus Dr Tampa FL 33617-3706*

FRANZEN, ULRICH J., architect; b. Rhineland, Germany, Jan. 15, 1921; s. Erik and Elizabeth (Hellersberg) F.; m. Joan Cummings, May, 1942 (div. 1962); children—Peter, David, April; m. Josephine Laura Hughes, Sept. 2, 1980. BFA, Williams Coll., 1942, LHD (hon.), 1972; MArch, Harvard U., 1949. Designer I.M. Pei & Ptnrs., N.Y.C., 1950-55; head Ulrich Franzen & Assocs., N.Y.C., 1955—; vis. critic, prof. Washington U., St. Louis, 1960-61, Yale U., New Haven, 1962-69, 79, 80, 81, Harvard U., Cambridge, Mass., 1961, Columbia U., N.Y.C., 1983, 84; chmn. Archtl. Bd. Rev., Rye, N.Y., 1960-62; mem. Cin. Archtl. Bd. Rev., 1964-66. Prin. works include Alley Theatre, 1968 (AIA honor 1970), Agronomy Bldg., 1970 (AIA honor 1971), Christensen Hall, 1970 (AIA honor 1972), Harlem Sch. of Arts, 1982, Hunter Coll. N.Y.C., 1983, Philip Morris World Hdqrs., 1984, Whitney Mus. Br., 1984, Champion Internat. World Hdqrs. with Whitney Mus. Br., 1985. With U.S. Army, 1943-45. Decorated Bronze Star, Croix de Guerre Avec Palme, Belgium; recipient Bruner prize Inst. Arts and Letters, N.Y.C. Fellow AIA (Thomas Jefferson award); mem. AIA (gold medal N.Y. chpt.), Archtl. League N.Y. (pres. 1968-70, bd. dirs. 1962—), N.Y.C. Landmarks Preservation Commn. (commr. 1992-96), Century Assn. Home: 168 E 74th St New York NY 10021-3561 Office: Ulrich Franzen Architect 168 E 74th St New York NY 10021-3561

FRANZETTA, BENEDICT C., bishop; b. Liverpool, Ohio, Aug. 1, 1921. Attended, St. Charles Coll., Calonsville, Md., St. Mary Sem., Cleve. Ordained priest Roman Cath. Ch., 1950. Priest Roman Cath. Ch., Youngstown, Ohio; titular bishop Oderzo and aux. bishop Roman Cath. Ch., Youngstown, from 1980. Office: 144 W Wood St Youngstown OH 44503-1030*

FRANZINI-ARMSTRONG, CLARA, biologist; b. Florence, Italy, Oct. 3, 1938. Grad., U. Pisa, Larea, 1960. Asst. prof. to assoc. prof. physiology U. Rochester, 1970-81; prof. U. Pa. Sch. Med., 1981—. Mem. NAS, Am. Soc. Cell Biology, Biophysics Soc. (K.C. Cole award), Soc. Gen. Physiologists. Office: Dept Cell and Devel Biology Anaton Chemistry Bldg B1 Philadelphia PA 19104*

FRANZKE, RICHARD ALBERT, lawyer; b. Lewistown, Mont., Mar. 7, 1935; s. Arthur A. and Senta (Clark) F.; divorced; children: Mark, Jean, Robert. BA in Polit. Sci., Willamette U., 1958, JD with honors, 1960. Bar: Oreg. 1960, U.S. Dist. Ct. Oreg., 1960, U.S. Supreme Ct., 1961. Ptnr. Stoel, Rives, Portland, 1960—; bd. dirs., chmn. various coms. Assn. Gen. Contractors Am., Portland, 1972-79; mem. com. on legis. affairs Assn. Builders & Contractors, Portland, 1983—. Author: A Study of the Construct by Contract Issue, 1979. Mem. Gov.'s Task Force on Reform of Worker's Compensation, Salem, Oreg., 1980-81; atty. gen.'s com. on Pub. Contracting. Recipient SIR award Assn. Gen. Contractors, 1979, Nat. Winner Outstanding Oral Argument award U.S. Moot Ct., 1959. Mem. ABA (sect. pub. contract law), Oreg. Bar (law sch. liaison, com. on practice and procedure specialization), Multnomah County Bar Assn. Republican. Avocations: antique autos, antique furniture, boating, water skiing. Home: 14980 SW 133rd Ave Tigard OR 97224-1646 Office: Stoel Rives 900 SW 5th Ave Ste 2300 Portland OR 97204-1235

FRANZMANN, ALBERT WILHELM, wildlife veterinarian, consultant; b. Hamilton, Ohio, July 19, 1930; s. Wilhelm Heinreich and Louise Marie (Schlichter) F.; m. Donna Marie Grueser, Dec. 13, 1953; children: Karl Wilhelm, Louise Ann. DVM, Ohio State U., 1954; PhD, U. Idaho, 1971. Diplomate Am. Coll. Zool. Medicine (hon.). Veterinarian Tiffin (Ohio) Animal Hosp., 1956-59; gen. practice vet. medicine Hamilton, 1959-68; NDEA rsch. fellow U. Idaho, Moscow, 1968-71; wildlife cons. F-2 Wildlife Cons., Moscow, 1971-72; dir. Kenai Moose Rsch. Ctr. Alaska Dept. Fish and Game, Soldotna, 1972-87; cons. AWF Profl. Svcs.; affil. assoc. prof., U. Alaska, Fairbanks, 1972-87; bd. dirs. Internat. Wildlife Vet. Svc. Inc., Laramie, Wyo., Hamilton Tool co., Bd. of Game State of Alaska, Alaska Outdoor Coun. Contbr. more than 100 articles to profl. jours., 15 chpts. to books. Served to capt. USAF, 1954-56. Named Disting. Moose Biologist, N.Am. Moose Conf., Prince George, B.C., Can.,1983; recipient Disting. Alumnus award Ohio State U. Coll. Vet. Medicine. Mem. AVMA, Am. Assn. Wildlife Veterinarians (pres. 1979-81), Wildlife Disease Assn. (council 1980-81, Emeritus award 1996), Am. Assn. Zoo Veterinarians, Am. Coll. Zool. Medicine (hon. diplomate), The Wildlife Soc. (cert. wildlife biologist, Einarsen award N.W. sect.), Phi Zeta, Xi Sigma Pi. Republican. Lodge: Elks. Avocations: photography, hunting, fishing, travel, exploration. Home and Office: PO Box 666 Soldotna AK 99669-0666 *The anxioms that were important in my life were: prepare myself, follow my instincts, and don't fear failure.*

FRANZMEIER, DONALD PAUL, agronomy educator, soil scientist; b. Greenwood, Wis., May 13, 1935; s. Paul Herman and Esther Rose (Humke) F.; m. Karen Elizabeth Hanson, June 18, 1960; children: Sonya, Gail, Julie. BS, U. Minn., 1957, MS, 1958; PhD, Mich. State U., 1962. Rsch. soil scientist USDA, Beltsville, Md., 1962-67; prof. Purdue U., West Lafayette, Ind., 1967—. Fellow Soil Sci. Soc. of Am., Ind. Acad. Sci.; mem. Internat. Soil and Sci. Soc., Am. Soc. Agronomy, Coun. Agr. Sci. and Tech. Home: 162 Reba Dr West Lafayette IN 47906-1616 Office: Purdue U Dept Agronomy West Lafayette IN 47907

FRAPPIA, LINDA ANN, management executive; b. St. Paul, May 14, 1946; d. Orville Keith Ferguson and Marilyn Ardis (Morris) Bidwell; 1 child, Jennifer Frappia Barrett. Grad. high sch., Seattle. Cert. claims adminstr. Claims rep. Fireman's Fund Ins., L.A., 1965-68; adminstrv. asst. to v.p. Employee Benefits Ins., Santa Ana, Calif., 1969-72; claims specialist Indsl. Indemnity Ins., Orange, Calif., 1972-83; claims supr. CNA Ins., Brea, Calif., 1983-85; claims mgr. EBI Ins. Svcs., Tustin, Calif., 1985; v.p. United Med. Specialists, Santa Ana, Calif., 1985-91; chief exec. officer United Ind. Specialists, Santa Ana, 1990—; chief executive officer United Chiropractic Specialists, Santa Ana, 1987—; instr. Ins. Edn. Assn., Brea, 1988—; speaker Western Ins. Info. Svc., Orange, 1976-83. Mem. Calif. Mfrs. Assn., Pub. Agencies Risk Mgmt. Assn., Calif. Self-Insured Assn., Toastmasters Internat. (v.p. Orange chpt. 1978). Republican. Avocations: sailing, reading, traveling.

FRAPPIER, CARA MUNSHAW, school social worker; b. Grand Rapids, Mich., Feb. 13, 1942; d. Carroll Lambert and Ruth (Switzer) Munshaw; m. Calvin Leslie Frappier, July 30, 1966; 1 child, Arielle. BA, Mich. State U., 1963, MA, 1966, MSW, 1973. Lic. social worker, marriage and family counselor, Mich.; diplomate in clin. social work. Elem. tchr. Lansing (Mich.) Pub. Schs., 1963-65; sch. social worker Ingham Intermediate Sch. Dist., Mason, Mich., 1965—; bd. dirs. profl. staff assn. Ingham Intermediate Pub. Schs., 1981-85; founding mem. Family Therapy and Consultation Program for Sch. Social Workers. Contbr. articles to profl. jours. and books. Mem. Nat. Assn. Social Workers, Am. Assn. Marriage and Family Counselors, Am. Orthopsychiat. Assn., Mich. Sch. Social Workers Assn. Democrat. Avocations: downhill skiing, sailing. Home: 5706 Bearcreek Dr Lansing MI 48917-1400 Office: Ingham Intermediate Sch Dist 2630 W Howell Rd Mason MI 48854-9329

FRARY, JOHN NEWTON, history educator; b. Farmington, Maine, Dec. 2, 1940; s. George Hubert and Margaret (Palmer) F. BA, U. Maine, 1965; MA, Rutgers U., 1971. Lathe operator Frary Wood Turning Co., Wilton, Maine, 1957-65; asst. dean Middlesex County Coll., Edison, N.J., 1972-82; prof. history Middlesex County Coll., Edison, 1982—; assoc. editor The Internat. Mil. Ency., Gulf Breeze, Fla., 1989—; editor LU/English Newsletter, New Brunswick, N.J., 1983—; asst. editor Continuity: A Jour. of History, Bryn Mawr, Pa., 1981-84. Contbr. articles to profl. jours. and publs. Freeholder candidate Middlesex County Rep. Orgn., Metuchen, N.J., 1981; com. New Brunswick Rep. Orgn., 1981-85. Fellow Princeton U., N.J., 1983. Mem. Nat. Assn. Scholars, U.S. Naval Inst. Republican. Congregational. Home: 11 Llewelyn Pl New Brunswick NJ 08901-3026 Office: Middlesex County Coll Mill Rd Edison NJ 08818

FRASCA, ROBERT JOHN, architect; b. Niagara Falls, N.Y., May 10, 1933; s. John and Jean Marie (Delgross) F.; m. Marilyn Margaret Buys, Sept. 23, 1937; children: Jason Robert, Andrea Melina. BArch, U. Mich., 1957; M in City Planning, MIT, 1959. Registered architect, Oreg., Wash., Calif., N.Y., Ariz., Utah. Ptnr. in charge of design Zimmer Gunsul Frasca Partnership, Portland, Oreg., 1966—, chief exec. officer, 1979—; design commn. U. Wash.; vis. prof. architecture U. Mich., U. Calif., Berkeley; design juror numerous nat., state and chpt. AIA awards programs. Prin. works include Justice Ctr., 1983, KOIN Ctr., 1985, Vollum Inst. for Advanced Biomed. Rsch., 1986, Oreg. Conv. Ctr., 1990, Oreg. Mus. of Sci. and Industry, 1992, Fred Hutchinson Cancer Rsch. Ctr., 1993; contbr. articles to profl. jours. and mags. Charter adv. bd. mem. Portland State U., 1987—; trustee Nat. Bldg. Mus., Washington; bd. dirs. Assn. for Portland Progress. Fellow AIA; mem. Arlington Club (Portland), Multnomah Athletic Club, Century Club (N.Y.). Clubs: Arlington (Portland), Multnomah Athletic. Office: Zimmer Gunsul Frasca 320 SW Oak St Ste 500 Portland OR 97204-2737*

FRASCELLA, DANIEL WILLIAM, JR., scientist; b. New Brunswick, N.J., July 6, 1934; s. Daniel William Sr. and Jenny (Revere) F.; m. Mary Patricia Fitzpatrick, Sept. 2, 1956; children: Daniel III, Nancy, Thomas. BS in Pharmacy magna cum laude, Rutgers U., 1960, MS in Physiology, 1962, PhD in Physiology and Biochem., 1968. Jr. pharmacologist Carter-Wallace Pharm., Cranbury, N.J., 1960-61; rsch. assoc. U. Pa., Phila., 1962-63; rsch. fellow Rutgers U., New Brunswick, 1963-65, asst. prof., 1965-68; rsch. fellow Merck Inst. Med. Rsch., Rahway, N.J., 1968-69; asst.prof. St. John's U., Jamaica, N.Y., 1970-74; assoc. dir. Hoechst-Roussel Pharm., Somerville, N.J., 1974—; vis. assoc. prof. City U. S.I., N.Y., 1972-74; diabetes cons. Hoechst-Roussel, 1974-96, CE program devel., 1974-82; ind. med. mktg. cons. on diabetes; pres. Diabetologics, 1996—. Author: (with others) Secondary Diabetes, 1980. With USN, 1952-55. Recipient H.A.B. Dunning award Am. Pharm. Assn., 1986, Edn. award Calif. Pharm. Assn., 1985. Fellow Royal Soc. of Medicine; mem. AAAS, Am. Diabetes Assn. (profl.), Am. Coll. Clin. Pharmacology, N.Y. Acad. Sci., Sigma Xi. Republican. Roman Catholic. Avocations: early American antiques, books and paper Americana, collecting stamps. Home: 1006 Stanton Lebanon Rd Lebanon NJ 08833-3109 Office: Diabetologics PO Box 197 Stanton NJ 08885-0197

FRASCH, BRIAN BERNARD, lawyer; b. San Francisco, Apr. 13, 1956; s. Norman Albert Frasch and Elizabeth Louise (Michelfelder) Milsten. BA magna cum laude, U. Calif., Santa Barbara, 1978; JD, U. Calif., Berkeley, 1982. Bar: Calif. 1982, U.S. Dist. Ct. (no. dist.) Calif. 1982, U.S. Dist. Ct. (so. dist.) Calif. 1983. Law clk. to chief judge U.S. Dist. Ct. (so. dist.) Calif., 1983-84; assoc. Graham & James, San Francisco, 1984-86, Lillick & McHose, San Diego, 1986-90; ptnr. Stephenson Prairie & Frasch, San Diego, 1990-96, Hillyer & Irwin, San Diego, 1996—. Assoc. editor: California Law Rev., 1981-82. Mem. ABA (litigation sect.), Calif. Bar Assn. (litigation sect.), San Diego County Bar Assn., San Diego Bldg. Owners and Mgrs. Assn. (bd. dirs. 1990-98, gen. counsel 1995-98), Westside Athletic Club. Office: Hillyer & Irwin 550 W C St Ste 1600 San Diego CA 92101-3568

FRASER, BRAD, playwright, theatrical director, screenwriter; b. Edmonton, Alta., Can., June 28, 1959. Works include: (plays) Two Pariahs At A Bus Stop In A Large City Late At Night, Mutants, Wolfboy, 1981, Rude Noises (For A Blank Generation), 1982, Chainsaw Love, 1985, Return Of The Bride, 1985, Unidentified Human Remains and the True Nature of Love, 1989 (Floyd S. Chalmers award for best new Can. play), Blood Buddies, Prom Night of the Living Dead, The Ugly Man, 1992, Poor Super Man, 1994 (Floyd S. Chalmers award for best new Can. play); (screenplay) Love and Human Remains, 1993. Office: Int'l Arts Entertainment 8899 Beverly Blvd Ste 800 Los Angeles CA 90048-2428*

FRASER, BRENDAN, actor; b. Indianapolis, Dec. 3, 1968. Movies include: Dogfight, 1991, Encino Man, 1992, School Ties, 1992, Twenty Bucks, 1993, Son in Law, 1993, Younger and Younger, 1993, With Honors, 1994, In the Army Now, 1994, Airheads, 1994, The Scout, 1994, The Passion of Darkly Noon, 1995, Balto (voice), 1995, Now and Then, 1995, Kids in the Hall: Brain Candy, 1996, Mrs. Winterbourne, 1996, Glory Daze, 1996, George of the Jungle, 1997, Still Breathing, 1998, Gods and Monsters, 1998, Sinbad: Beyond the Veil of Mists (voice), 1999, Ringside, 1999, Monkey Bone, 1999, Blast from the Past, 1999, The Mummy, 1999, Dudley Do-Right, 1999. Office: William Morris Agy 151 S El Camino Dr Beverly Hills CA 90212-2775*

FRASER, CAMPBELL, business consultant; b. Dunblane, Scotland, May 2, 1923. B Comm., Dundee Sch. Econs., 1950; LLD (hon.), Strathclyde U., 1977; D of Univ. (hon.), Stirling U., 1977; DCL (hon.), Bishop's U., 1990. Chmn. Dunlop Holdings plc, 1978-83, Dunlop Tire & Rubber Corp., U.S., 1978-83, Green Park Health Care, London, 1975-88, Scottish TV plc, 1975-91, Pauline Hyde and Assocs. Corp., 1988-93, Barkers Scotland, 1994; bd. dirs. Brit. Petroleum, 1978-91, Brit. Am. Co. plc, 1980-93; chmn. adv. bd. Wells Fargo, 1980-95; chmn. Tandem Ltd.; mem. adv. bd., Tandem Inc., 1985-97; chmn. Riversoft Tech. Ltd. Pres. Confedn. Brit. Industry, London, 1982-84; trustee The Economist, 1978—. Awarded Knighthood, 1978.

FRASER, CATHERINE ANNE, Canadian chief justice; b. Campbellton, N.B., Can., Aug. 4, 1947; d. Antoine Albert and Anne (Slevinski) Elias; m. Richard C. Fraser, Aug. 17, 1968; children: Andrea Claire, Jonathan James. BA, U. Alta., Can., 1969, LLB, 1970; ML, U. London, 1972. Assoc., ptnr. Lucas, Bishop & Fraser, Edmonton, Alta., 1972-89; justice Ct. Queen's Bench Alta., Edmonton, 1989-91; justice Ct. Appeal Alta., Edmonton, 1991-92, chief justice Alta. and NW Ter., 1992—; dir. Can. Inst. Adminstrn. Justice, 1991-95. Recipient Tribute to Women award YWCA, 1987. Mem. Can. Bar Assn., Edmonton Bar Assn., Law Soc. Alta. Office: Ct Appeal Alta, Law Courts Bldg, Edmonton, AB Canada T5J 0R2

FRASER, DAVID CHARLES, investment banker; b. Phila., Aug. 2, 1942; s. Charles Walter and Althea Mary (Mathis) F.; m. Carole Ann Geren, June 16, 1962 (div. 1989); children: Mark Samuel, Steven David, Tanya, Adam Scott, Luke Wesley; m. Mary Kay Naumann, Nov. 18, 1993. BA, Taylor U., 1965. Pres. Am. Intertel Corp., Mt. Holly, N.J., 1969-74, Figure World, Inc., Moorestown, N.J., 1978-80; corp. fin. Herzog, Heine, Geduld, Inc., N.Y.C., 1982-84; v.p. Goldman Sacks & Co., 1983-84; sr. v.p. Lord Securities Corp., N.Y.C., 1984—, dir. 28 fin. cos. managed by Lord Securities; pres., CEO Lord Capital Corp., 1989—; vice chmn. Tex. State Optical, 1990-94; chmn., CEO Providence Energy Co. Ltd., Houston, 1992-95, Covenent Capital Corp., Colorado Springs, Colo., 1993-95; chmn., CEO Internat. Vehicle Care, Inc., Kansas City, 1997—; gen. ptnr. Ammex Captial Ptnrs., Ltd., Houston; chmn. Way Refining and Mktg., Inc., Houston, 1990-92; bd. dirs. Rio Grande Mining Co., Plainsboro, N.J., BelCor, Inc., Plainsboro, Silver Assets, Inc., Plainsboro, N.J. Mem. Taylor U. Alumni Assn. (pres. 1972-74). Republican. Avocations: tennis, golf, music. Home and Office: PO Box 3298 Olathe KS 66063-3298

FRASER, DAVID WILLIAM, epidemiologist; b. Abington, Pa., May 10, 1944; s. Grant Clippinger and Ella Finlaw (Ayars) F.; m. Barbara Josephine Gaines, June 25, 1966; children: Evan Grant, Leigh Robertson. B.A., Haverford (Pa.) Coll., 1965, D.Sc. (hon.), 1991; M.D., Harvard U., 1969; Sc.D. (hon.), Moravian Coll., 1987. Diplomate Am. Bd. Internal Medicine. Intern in internal medicine U. Pa. Hosp., Phila., 1969-70, resident, 1970-71, chief resident in internal medicine, 1973-74, fellow in infectious diseases, 1974-75; commd. officer USPHS, 1971-73, 75-82; chief spl. pathogens br., bacterial diseases div. Bur. Epidemiology, Center Disease Control, USPHS, Atlanta, 1975-80; med. epidemiologist, asst. dir. bacterial diseases div. Bur. Epidemiology, Center Disease Control, USPHS, 1981-82; pres. Swarthmore (Pa.) Coll., 1982-91; head dept. social welfare Secretariat of His Highness Aga Khan, Gouvieux, France, 1991-95; cons. in internat. health and edn., 1996; exec. dir. INCLEN, Inc., 1996—; adj. prof. medicine U. Pa. Sch. Medicine, 1983-91, adj. prof. epidemiology, 1997—. Author: A Guide to Weft Twining and Related Structures with Interacting Wefts, 1989; editl. bd. Annals of Internal Medicine, 1991-94; contbr. articles to profl. med. and textile jours. Bd. mgrs. Haverford Coll., 1980-83; bd. advisors Educators for Social Responsibility, 1986-91; chmn. bd. Consortium on Financing Higher Edn., 1986-87; trustee The Textile Mus., Washington, 1986—, v.p., 1990-91, 96, pres., 1997—; bd. dirs. Albert G. Oliver Found., 1985-91; sci. adv. bd. Ctr. for Infectious Diseases, 1989-91; mem. immunization practices adv. com. Ctrs. for Disease Control, 1988-92; mem. com. to visit med. sch. and sch. dental medicine Harvard U., 1988-94; costume and textile com. Phila. Mus. Art, 1988-91. Recipient Meritorious Svc. medal USPHS, 1978, John Scott award, 1986; Clementine Cope fellow Haverford Coll., 1965, Daland fellow Am. Philos. Soc., 1974. Fellow ACP (Richard and Hinda Rosenthal Found. award 1979), Infectious Diseases Soc. Am., Am. Coll. Epidemiology; mem. Am. Epidemiol. Soc., Aesculapian Club, Founders Club (Haverford Coll.). Home: 907 N Pennsylvania Ave Yardley PA 19067-2023 Office: INCLEN Inc 3600 Market St Ste 380 Philadelphia PA 19104-2645

FRASER, DONALD ALEXANDER STUART, mathematics educator; b. Toronto, Ont., Can., Apr. 29, 1925; s. Maxwell John and Ailie (Stuart) F.; children: Julie, Danae, Maia, Andrea, Ailana, Cristin, Donelle. B.A., U. Toronto, 1947, M.A. in Math, 1947; M.A. in Math., Princeton U., 1948, Ph.D., 1949, DMath (hon.), 1992. Mem. faculty dept. math. U. Toronto, 1949—, assoc. prof., 1953-58, prof., 1958—, prof. dept. statistics, 1977—; vis. prof. Princeton U., 1955, Stanford U., 1961-62, U. Wis., Madison, 1965, U. Copenhagen, 1964, U. Hawaii, 1969-70, U. Geneva, 1978-79, Stanford U., 1982-83; adj. prof. math. York U., 1984-86, prof. math, 1986—; adj. prof. stats. U. Waterloo, 1984—, U. Western Ontario, 1991—. Author: Nonparametric Methods in Statistics, 1957, Statistics, An Introduction, 1958, The Structure of Inference, 1968, Probability and Statistics, Theory and Applications, 1976, Inference and Linear Models, 1979. Fellow Inst. Math. Stats., Am. Statis. Assn., Royal Statis. Soc., Royal Soc. Can., AAAS. Office: Dept Statistics, U Toronto, Toronto, ON Canada M5S 3G3

FRASER, DONALD C., engineering executive, educator; b. N.Y.C., Apr. 20, 1941; s. Donald Fraser and Anna Thurston; children: Lynn, Eric. S.B., MIT, Cambridge, 1962, M.S., 1963, Sc.D., 1967. Tech. staff MIT Instrumentation Lab., Cambridge, Mass., 1967-69; div. leader C.S. Draper Lab., Inc., Cambridge, 1969-81, v.p. tech. ops., 1981-88, exec. v.p., 1988-90; dep. dir. operational test and evaluation Office Sec. Def., Washington, 1990-91; prin. deputy under sec. def. for acquisition Office Sec. of Def., Washington, 1991-93; vis. prof. Stanford U., Calif., 1970-71; lectr. MIT Aero/Astro Dept., Cambridge, 1972-91; founder, dir. Ctr. Photonics prof. engring. and physics Boston U., 1993—; active Air Force Studies Bd. Com. Advanced Avionics, 1979-83; chmn. Air Force Studies Bd. Com. Fault Isolation, 1982-85; active USAF Aero Systems Divsn. Adv. Group, 1984-90; mem. NASA Adv. Coun. Space Systems and Tech. Adv. Com., 1982-91, U.S. Army Sci. Bd., 1987-90, NRC Aeronautics and Space Engring. Bd., 1995—. Assoc. editor AIAA Jour. Spacecraft and Rockets, 1970-72, editor-in-chief, 1974-78; founder, editor-in-chief AIAA Jour. Guidance, Control and Dynamics, 1977-91. Recipient Def. Disting. Svc. medal. Fellow AAAS, AIAA (bd. dirs. New Eng. sect. 1973-75, publs. com. 1973-74); mem. NAE, Tau Beta Pi, Sigma Xi, Sigma Gamma Tau. Avocations: pilot; hiking; skiing; bicycling.

FRASER, DONALD MACKAY, former mayor, former congressman, educator; b. Mpls., Feb. 20, 1924; s. Everett and Lois (MacKay) F.; m. Arvonne Skelton, June 30, 1950; children: Thomas Skelton, Mary MacKay, John DuFrene, Lois MacKay (dec.), Anne T. (dec.), Jean Skelton. BA cum laude, U. Minn., 1944, LLB, 1948. Bar: Minn. 1948. Ptnr. Lindquist, Fraser & Magnuson (and predecessors), 1948-62; Minn. State senator, 1954-62; sec. Senate Liberal Caucus, 1955-62; mem. 88th-95th Congresses from 5th Dist. Minn., mem. fgn. affairs com., chmn. subcom. on internat. orgn., mem. budget com.; mayor City of Mpls., 1980-93; mem. study and rev. com. Dem. Caucus; mem. Commn. on Role and Future Presdl. Primaries, 1976; adj. prof. law and pub. affairs U. Minn., Mpls.; Vice chmn., dir. Mpls. Citizens Com. on Pub. Edn., 1950-54; Sec. Minn. del. Democratic Nat. Conv., 1960; chmn. Minn. Citizens for Kennedy, 1960; mem. platform com. Dem. Nat. Conv., 1964, mem. rules com., 1972, 76; vice chmn. Com. Dem. Selection Presdl. Nominees, 1968; chmn. Democratic Study Group Congress, 1969-71, chmn. Commn. on Party Structure and Del. Selection Dem. Party, 1971-72; 1st Am. co-chmn. Anglo-Am. Parliamentary Conf. on Africa, 1964; mem. U.S. del. 7th spl. session and 30th session UN Gen. Assembly, 1975; Congl. adviser to U.S. del. to UN Conf. on Disarmament, 1967-73, to U.S. del. to 3d Law of Sea Conf., 1972, to UN Commn. on Human Rights, 1974. Chair health com. U.S. Conf. Mayors; bd. dirs. Mpls. United Way, 1986-93; co-chair Ctr. for Internat. Policy, 1976—; co-founder, pres. Dem. Farmer-Labor Edn. Found.; initiated numerous youth programs such as Transitional Work Internship Program, Youth Work Internship Program, Neighborhood Early Learning Ctrs., Youth Coordinating Bd., Youth Trust. Lt. (J.G.) USNR, 1944-46. Recipient 1st Minn. Internat. Human Rights award, 1985, Disting. Svc. award Mpls. United Way, 1992. Mem. Mpls. Fgn. Policy Assn. (pres. 1952-53), Citizens League Greater Mpls. (sec. 1951-54), Minn. Bar Assn., Hennepin County Bar Assn., Ams. for Dem. Action (nat. chmn. 1973-76), Dem. Conf. (nat. chmn. 1976-78), U. Minn. Law Alumni Assn. (dir. 1958-61), Univ. Dist. Improvement Assn. (pres. 1950-52), Nat. League of Cities (2d v.p. 1991, 1st v.p. 1992, pres. 1993), Minn. Advocates for Human Rights (co-founder, bd. dirs. 1983-92), League of Minn. Cities (bd. dirs. 1991-93).—.

FRASER, ELEANOR RUTH, radiologist, administrator; b. Woodlake, Calif., May 31, 1927; d. Morton William and Dorothy Jean (Harding) F. BA magna cum laude, Pomona Coll., 1949; MD, Stanford U., 1954. Diplomate Am. Bd. Radiology. Resident in radiology Los Angeles County Hosp., L.A., 1957; radiologist St. Joseph Hosp., Orange, Calif., 1957-61; pvt. practice Anaheim, Calif., 1961-78; radiologist Radiology Nuclear Med. Group, Bakersfield, Calif., 1978-85; dir. radiology Kern Valley Hosp., Lake Isabella, Calif., 1985—, chief of staff, 1992—. Mem. AMA, Calif. Med. Assn., Kern County Med. Assn., Soc. Nuclear Medicine, Kern Valley Exchange Club (sec. 1992-94), Phi Beta Kappa. Methodist. Avocations: music, percussion, writing. Home & Office: PO Box 1657 Lake Isabella CA 93240-1657

FRASER, HENRY S., lawyer; b. Oswego, N.Y., July 11, 1900; s. Hector A. and Minnie (Salmon) F.; m. Myrtle Gosse, June 15, 1937; children: Bruce, Rosene, Roger. A.B., Haverford Coll., 1922; J.D., Cornell U., 1926. Bar: N.Y. State bar 1927, U.S. Supreme Ct. bar 1930. Tech. adviser League of Nations Com. Experts for Progressive Codification of Internat. Law, 1927; chief research staff N.Y. State Constl. Conv., 1938; chmn. N.Y. State Uniform Law Commn., 1948-70; chief counsel U.S. Senate, Spl. Com. Investigating Petroleum Resources and to recommend a nat. and internat. petroleum policy, 1945-47; pvt. practice Syracuse, N.Y., 1927-88; mem. Harvard Research in Internat. Law, 1927-54. Author various legal publs. and U.S. Senate Documents. Mem. Am. Law Inst. (life), ABA, N.Y. State Bar Assn. (Fifty-Yr. Lawyer award 1986), Onondaga County Bar Assn. (Disting. Lawyer award 1980), N.Y. City Bar Assn., Phi Beta Kappa, Chi Phi. Club: Century. Lodge: Rotary. Home: Jefferson Tower Presidential Plz Syracuse NY 13202 Office: 220 S Warren St Ste 700 Syracuse NY 13202-1663

FRASER, JOHN FOSTER, management company executive; b. Saskatoon, Sask., Sept. 19, 1930; s. John Black and Florence May (Foster) F.; m. Valerie Georgina Ryder, June 21, 1952; children: John Foster Jr., Lisa Ann. B of Commerce, U. Sask., 1952; LLD (hon.), U. Winnipeg, 1993. Pres. Empire Freightways Ltd., Saskatoon, Sask., 1953-60, Empire Oil Ltd., Saskatoon, 1960-62, Hanford Drewitt Ltd., Winnipeg, 1962-68, Norcom Homes Ltd., Mississauga, Ont., 1969-78; pres., chief exec. officer Fed. Industries Ltd., Winnipeg, 1978-91, chmn., chief exec. officer, 1991-92, chmn. bd., 1992-95; vice chmn. Russel Metals, Winnipeg, 1995-97; chmn. bd. Air Canada, 1996—; bd. dirs. Internat. Comfort Products Corp., Bank of Montreal, Air Can., Investors Group, Inc., Can. Devel. Investment Corp., Shell Can. Ltd., The Thomson Corp., Ford Motor Co. Can. Ltd., Man. Telecom Svcs. Inc., Centra Gas Man. Inc., Coca-Cola Beverages Ltd., Inter-City Products Corp., Continental Airlines, Inc., Am. West Airlines; past chmn. Coun. for Bus. and Arts in Can. Bd. dirs., founding chmn. Assocs. Faculty of Mgmt. Studies U. Man.; past pres. Man. Theatre Centre; past bd. govs. St. John's Ravenscourt Sch., Winnipeg; mem. cultural rev. policy com. Province of Man., 1979; past pres. Royal Winnipeg Ballet, 1992-93. Decorated officer Order of Can., 1990; recipient Peter D. Curry award U. Man., 1984, Outstanding Bus. Achievement award as Citizen of Yr. Man. C. of C., 1984; named Transp. Person of Yr. Nat. Transp. Week, 1990. Mem. Am. Mgmt. Assn. (pres.'s assn.), Royal Lake of the Woods Yacht Club, Toronto Club. Progressive Conservative. Presbyterian. Avocations: boating, reading. Office: 201 Portage Ave Ste 3100, Winnipeg, MB Canada R3B 3L7*

FRASER, JOHN WAYNE, insurance executive, consultant, underwriter; b. Ashland, Ala., Jan. 19, 1944; s. Elliott Nathaniel and Maurice Jennette (Glenn) F.; m. Diana Louise Renn, Jan. 20, 1963; children: Christine Celeste, Sean Elliott. AA in Bus. Adminstrn., St. Petersburg Jr. Coll., 1969; BA with honors, U. South Fla., 1974. Dir. mfg. svcs. Milton Roy Co., St. Petersburg, Fla., 1965-74; sales rep. Fla. Forms Co., Tampa, 1975-76, Graphic Bus. Systems, St. Petersburg, 1976-79; dist. mgr. Blue Cross/Blue Shield Fla., St. Petersburg, 1979-86; sr. v.p. Wittner Cos., 1986-98; pres. Advocate Cons., Inc., Clearwater, Fla., 1998—. Mem. editl. bd., monthly contbr. COBRA Advisory, 1997—. Former mem. Internat. Found. Employee Benefit Welfare Plans; pres. Benefit One of Am., Inc., 1997-98. With U.S. Army, 1962. Mem. Bay Area Benefits Assn. (pres. 1989-90), Fla. West Coast Employee Benefit Coun. (bd. dirs. 1994—), Nat. Assn. Health Underwriters (trustee West Coast chpt. 1988—, pres. 1992-93), Fla. Assn. Health Underwriters (bd. dirs. 1992-93, 1st v.p. 1993-94, pres. 1994-95), Cen. Pinellas Jaycees (treas. 1975, v.p. 1976), U. South Fla. Alumni Assn. Unitarian-Universalist. Avocations: photography, golf. Office: Ste 460 13555 Automobile Blvd Clearwater FL 33762

FRASER, KATHLEEN JOY, poet, creative writing educator; b. Tulsa, Mar. 22, 1935; d. James Ian and Marjorie Joy (Axtell) F.; m. Jack Marshall, July 10, 1960 (div. 1970); 1 child, David Ian; m. Arthur Kalmer Bierman, June 30, 1984. BA in English Lit., Occidental Coll., 1958; doctoral equivalency, San Francisco State U., 1976. Vis. prof. writing, lectr. in poetry The Writer's Workshop, U. Iowa, Iowa City, 1969-71; writer in residence Reed Coll., Portland, Oreg., 1971-72; dir. Poetry Center San Francisco State U., 1972-75, prof. creative writing, 1972-92; founder-dir. Am. Poetry Archives, San Francisco, 1973-75; founder-editor How(ever), Jour. for poets/scholars interested in modernism and women's innovative writing, 1983-91. Author: (children's book) Stilts, Somersaults and Headstands, 1967; (poetry) What I Want (New and Selected Poems), 1974, New Shoes, 1978, Something (even human voices in the foreground) A Lake, 1984, Notes Preceding Trust, 1988, When New Time Folds Up, 1993, Il Cuore: The Heart, Selected Poems 1970-95, 1997. Recipient Frank O'Hara Poetry prize, 1964; Nat. Endowment for Arts fellow, 1978, Guggenheim fellow, 1981. *

FRASER, MAC ROBERT (ROB FRASER), livestock auction owner, auctioneer; b. Mont., Mar. 3, 1958; s. William Sidney III and Catherine Lee (Arneson) F.; m. Cynthia Jo Leland, Nov. 4, 1989; 1 child, Kelsey. BS in Agrl. Bus., Mont. State U., 1981. Ptnr. Valley Ranch and Feedlot Supply, Billings, Mont., 1984-89; auctioneer Billings Livestock Commn., 1988-94; ptnr. Mont. Video Contract Auction, 1991—; owner Miles City (Mont.) Livestock Commn. Co., 1991—. Active Miles City Club, 1995—. Mem. Nat. Cattlemen's Beef Assn. (mem. internat. mktg. com. 1997), Mont. Stockgrowers (mem. mktg. com. 1997), Mont. Assn. Livestock Auction Markets, Miles City C. of C. Avocations: snow skiing, travel, hunting, horsemanship. Office: Miles City Livestock Commn Co W Main St Miles City MT 59301

FRASER, MARGOT, consumer products company executive; b. Bremen, Germany. Pres., founder Birkenstock Footprint Sandals, Inc. Inductee Footwear News Hall of Fame. Office: Birkenstock Footprint Sandals PO Box 6140 Novato CA 94948

FRASER, MARILYN ANNE, state legislator; b. Concord, N.H., Apr. 24, 1936; d. Louis Nicholas and Clarissa Blanchard N.; m. Maurice Henri Dupuis, 1990; 1 child, John E. Jr. BEd, U. N.H., MEd. Tchr. Concord, 1991-95; co-chmn. Concord Area Transp., 1992—, cons., 1993—, chmn. airport adv. com., 1993—; mem. Concord City Coun., 1991-95, N.H. Ho. of Reps., 1994—; chmn. state and city rels. N.H. Ho. of Reps., 1995—. Democrat. Address: 84 Branch Tpke #54 Concord NH 03301-5715*

FRASER, PAMELA, artist; b. Smyrna, Tenn., 1965. BFA, Sch. Visual Arts, N.Y.C., 1988; MFA, UCLA, 1992. One-woman shows include Casey Kaplan, N.Y.C., 1996, 98; group shows at Lotus Motel, Inglewood, Calif., 1995, White Columns, N.Y.C., 1996, Exit Art, N.Y.C., 1999, Elga Wimmer Gallery, N.Y.C., 1999, others. Recipient Louis Comfort Tiffany award, 1997; fellow Skowheghan Sch. Painting and Sculpture, 1988. Fax: 212-226-6294. Office: care Casey Kaplan Gallery 48 Greene St New York NY 10013

FRASER, ROBERT BURCHMORE, lawyer; b. Newton, Mass., Aug. 13, 1928; s. Alfred Alexander and Helen Louise (Comiskey) F.; m. Mary-Ann Jackson, Sept. 7, 1963; children: Melanie, Jennifer Amy, Matthew John. AB, Harvard U., 1949, LLB, 1952, LLM, 1955. Bar: Mass. Assoc. Goodwin, Procter & Hoar, Boston, 1955-63, ptnr., 1964-97, chmn., 1984-97; spl. advisor to Mayor of Boston and Boston Police Commr., 1997—; bd. dirs. Investors Fin. Svcs. and Investors Bank and Trust Co. Mem. Mass. Gov.'s Jud. Nominating Commn., 1979-82; mem. adv. com. Mass. Commr. Revenue, 1979-82; chmn. adv. com. Mass. Housing Fin. Agy, 1979-83; chmn. Boston Pub. Health Commn., 1996-97, Vol. Lawyers for Arts of Mass., 1990-97; bd. dirs. Greater Boston YMCA, 1981-87, Greater Boston Arts Fund, 1987—, Boston Pvt. Industry Coun., 1988—, Citywide Ednl. Coalition, 1988—, Boston Against Drugs, 1988-93, chmn. 1990;-93, Boston Ptnrs. in Edn., 1989—, Am. Student Assistance Corp., 1989-97, Greater Boston C. of C., 1993—, Jobs for Mass., 1993-98, Boston Pub. Libr. Found., 1992—, Boston Mgmt. Consortium, 1994—, NCCJ, 1994—, chmn. 1997—, Mass. Bus. Alliance Edn., 1995—, Ctr. for Collaborative Edn., 1998—, The Med. Found., 1995—, MassInc., 1996—; trustee New Eng. Conservatory Music, 1982—, Boston Plan for Excellence in Pub. Schs., 1987—, chmn., 1992-95, Boston Adult Literacy Fund, 1989-96; pres. Lesley Coll., 1994-96; overseer Boston Lyric Opera, 1994—. With AUS, 1952-54. Mem. ABA, Mass. Bar Assn., Boston Bar Assn., Harvard Mus. Assn. Harvard Club (Boston.). Home: 90 Allandale St Jamaica Plain MA 02130-3442 Office: Goodwin Procter & Hoar Exchange Pl Boston MA 02109-2803

FRASER, ROBERT CARSON, business consultant; b. Port Washington, N.Y., Apr. 11, 1925; s. Irving Thomas and Elizabeth Armstrong (Kennedy) F.; m. Constance Anne Morell, May 25, 1957; 1 child, Robert Carson Jr. BA in Econs., William and Mary Coll., 1951. Pub. relations mgr. Martin Marietta Corp., Washington, 1966-69; mkt. mgr. RCA, Washington, 1969-73, Lockheed Aircraft Co., Washington, 1973-75; exec. asst. to treas. U.S. Treasury Dept., Washington, 1975-79; sr. mgr. NASA Hdqrs., Washington, 1979-88; pvt. practice cons., 1988—. Mem. Nat. Space Club (v.p.), Capitol Hill Exch. Club (pres. Washington chpt. 1986-87). Episcopalian. Avocation: boating. Home: 543 Lakeview Cir Severna Park MD 21146-2312

FRASER, ROBERT GORDON, diagnostic radiologist; b. Winnipeg, Man., Can., June 30, 1921; s. William Gordon and Amy Dena (Rumball) F.; m. Joanne Elsa Williams, June 15, 1974; children by previous marriage: Richard S., Merrill A., John R., Nancy L. DS (hon. causa), McGill U., Can., 1994. Resident in radiology Royal Victoria Hosp., McGill U., 1948-51; radiologist-in-chief Royal Victoria Hosp., Montreal, Que., 1964-76; prof. diagnostic radiology McGill U. Med. Sch., Montreal, 1964-76; chmn. dept. McGill U. Med. Sch., 1971-76; prof. diagnostic radiology U. Ala. Med. Sch., Birmingham, 1976-89, prof. emeritus, 1989—; vis. prof. U.S. and fgn. univs. Sr. author: Diagnosis of Diseases of the Chest, 3rd edit., 4 vols., 1988-90; co-author: Synopsis of Diseases of the Chest, 2nd edit., 1993. Served with Can. Navy, 1945-46. Fellow Royal Coll. Physicians Can., Royal Coll. Radiologists (hon.), Am. Coll. Radiologists, Am. Coll. Chest Physicians (Ann. Gold medal 1972); mem. Fleischner Soc., Radiol. Soc. N.Am. (Gold medal 1990), Am. Roentgen Ray Soc. (Gold medal 1989), Can. Med. Assn. Office: 619 S 19th St Dept Diagnostic Radiology Birmingham AL 35233

FRASER, RUSSELL ALFRED, author, educator; b. Elizabeth, N.J., May 31, 1927; s. Roger John and Mary Louise (Narden) F.; m. Eleanor Jane Phillips, May 31, 1947 (div. 1979); children—Karen Mildred, Alexander Varennes; m. Mary Nelva Zwiep, July 5, 1980. A.B., Dartmouth Coll., 1947; M.A., Harvard U., 1949, Ph.D., 1950. Instr. English UCLA, 1950; postgrad. study, Eng., 1951-52; instr., then asst. prof. English Duke U., 1952-56; asst. prof., then assoc. prof. English Princeton U., 1956-65, assoc. dean Grad. Sch., 1962-65; prof., chmn. English Vanderbilt U., Nashville, 1965-68; prof. English U. Mich., Ann Arbor, 1968—; chmn. dept. U. Mich., 1968-73, Austin Warren prof., 1983-95, prof. emeritus, 1995—; resident Inst. for Advanced Study, Princeton U., 1976. Author: Shakespeare's Poetics, 1962, The War Against Poetry, 1970, An Essential Shakespeare, 1972, The Dark Ages and the Age of Gold, 1973, The Language of Adam, 1977, A Mingled Yarn: The Life of R.P. Blackmur, 1982, The Three Romes, 1985, Young Shakespeare, 1988, Shakespeare, The Later Years, 1992; editor: The Court of Venus, 1955, The Court of Virtue, 1961, King Lear, 1963, Oscar Wilde, 1969, (with others) Drama of the English Renaissance, 2 vols, 1976; All's Well That Ends Well, 1985. Served with USNR, 1944-46. Grantee Am. Council Learned Socs., 1951-52, 60, 68; Grantee Am. Philos. Soc., 1951-52, 60, 68; Grantee Dartmouth, 1951-52; jr. fellow Council Humanities, Princeton, 1960; NSF grantee, 1964-67; Guggenheim fellow Rome, 1973-74; Rockefeller resident scholar Bellagio, 1975; sr. Fulbright-Hays scholar, 1975; Nat. Endowment Humanities fellow, 1978-79. Mem. Renaissance Soc. Am., Shakespeare Assn. Am., Caledonian Soc. of Hawaii, Harvard Club of Mich. Office: U Mich Dept English Ann Arbor MI 48109

FRASER, WILLIAM NEIL, government official, retired; b. Vancouver, B.C., Can., May 25, 1932; s. James Herbert and Katherine Baikie (Grieve) F.; m. Marie Helm, Dec. 19, 1986; children by previous marriage: Gordon, Alan, Katherine, Ian. Student, Banff Sch. Advanced Mgmt., 1967. Product mgr. Masonry, Deeks-McBride Ltd., Vancouver, 1952-68; gen. mgr. Masonry Contractors Assn. B.C., Vancouver, 1968-71; exec. dir. Can. Masonry Contractors Assn., Toronto, 1971-87; mem. Ont. Labour Rels. Bd., 1988-98, ret., 1999; mem. Bd. Trade Met. Toronto. With Can. Navy Res., 1953-57. Mem. Inst. Assn. Execs. (past pres. Toronto chpt.), Royal Can. Mil. Inst., Clan Fraser Soc. Can. (chmn.), Vancouver Golf Club, Clans and Scottish Socs. of Can. (sec.-treas., past pres.), St. Andrew's Soc. of Toronto, Scottish Studies Found. (patron, gov.), Heraldry Soc. Can., Grant of Arms Can. Heraldic Authority, Capt. Olde 78th Fraser Highlanders. E-mail: CDNEXPLORER@msn.com. Home: 71 Charles St E, Apt 1101, Toronto, ON Canada M4Y 2T3

FRASIER, RALPH KENNEDY, lawyer, banker; b. Winston-Salem, N.C., Sept. 16, 1938; s. LeRoy Benjamin and Kathryn O. (Kennedy) F.; m. Jeannine Quick, Aug. 1981; children: Karen D. Frasier Alston, Gail S. Frasier Cox, Ralph Kennedy Jr., Keith Lowery, Marie Kennedy, Rochelle Doar. BS, N.C. Cen. U., Durham, 1963, JD, 1965. Bar: N.C. 1965, Ohio 1976. With Wachovia Bank and Trust Co., N.A., Winston-Salem, N.C., 1965-70; v.p., counsel Wachovia Bank and Trust Co., N.A., 1969-70; asst. counsel, v.p. parent co. Wachovia Corp., 1970-75; v.p., gen. counsel Huntington Nat. Bank, Columbus, Ohio, 1975-76; sr. v.p. Huntington Nat. Bank, 1976-83, sec., 1981-98, exec. v.p., 1983-98, cashier, 1983-98; v.p. Huntington Bancshares Inc., 1976-86, gen. counsel, 1976-98, sec., 1981-98; sec., dir. Huntington Mortgage Co., Huntington State Bank, Huntington Leasing Co., Huntington Bancshares Fin. Corp., Huntington Investment Mgmt. Co., Huntington Nat. Life Ins. Co., Huntington Co., 1976-88; v.p., asst. sec. Huntington Bank N.E. Ohio, 1982-84; asst. sec. Huntington Bancshares Ky., 1985-97; sec. Huntington Trust Co., N.A., 1987-97, Huntington Bancshares Ind., Inc., 1986-97, Huntington Fin. Services Co., 1987-98; dir. The Huntington Nat. Bank, Columbus, Ohio, 1998—; of counsel Porter Wright Morris & Arthur LLP, Columbus, 1998—; trustee Online Computer Libr. Ctr., Inc., Columbus, 1999—. Bd. dirs. Family Svcs. Winston-Salem, 1966-74, sec., 1966-71, 74, v.p., 1974; chmn. Winston-Salem Transit Authority, 1974-75; bd. dirs. Rsch. for Advancement of Personalities, 1968-71, Winston-Salem Citizens for Fair Housing, 1970-74, N.C. United Community Svcs., 1970-74; treas. Forsyth County (N.C.) Citizens Com. Adequate Justice Bldg., 1968; trustee Appalachian State U., Boone, N.C., 1973-83, endowment fund, 1973-83, Columbus Drug Edn. and Prevention Fund, Inc., 1989-92; trustee, vice chmn. employment and Edn. Commn. Franklin County, 1982-85; mem. Winston-Salem Forsyth County Sch. Bd. Adv. Coun., 1973-74, Atty. Gen's Ohio Task Force Minorities in Bus., 1977-78; bd. dirs. Inorads Columbus, Inc., 1986-95, Greater Columbus Arts Coun., 1986-94, Columbus Urban League Inc., 1987-94, vice chmn., 1990-94; trustee Riverside Meth. Hosp. Found., 1989-90, Grant Med. Ctr., 1990-95, Grant/Riverside Meth. Hosps., 1995-97; trustee Ohio Health Corp., 1997—; dir. Cmty. Mutual Ins. Co., 1989-92, mem. audit com., 1989-92; trustee N.C. Ctrl. U., Durham, 1993—, vice-chmn., 1993-94, chmn. 1995, chair ednl. planning and acad. affairs com., 1995—, mem. audit devel. coms., 1998—; mem. Ohio Bd. Regents, 1987-96, vice-chmn., 1993-95, chmn., 1995-96; trustee Nat. Jud. Coll., Reno, Nevada, 1996—, fin. and audit com., 1997—, treas. 1998—, Columbus Bar Found., 1998— (fellows com. 1998—, grants com., 1998—); AEFC Pension Adminstrn. Com. defined benefit plan of the ABA, Am. Bar Endowment, Am. Bar Found., and Nat. Jud. Coll., Chgo, Ill., 1998—. With AUS, 1958-60. Mem. ABA, Nat. Bar Assn., Ohio Bar Assn., Columbus Bar Assn. Office: Porter Wright Morris & Arthur LLP 41 S High St Ste 3100 Columbus OH 43215-6194

FRASIER, S. DOUGLAS, medical educator; b. L.A., Nov. 29, 1932; m. Robin D'Arvin; children: Karen Lynn, Eric Marc, Sara Leslie. BA, U. Calif., L.A., 1953; MD with highest honors, U. Calif., 1958. Diplomate Am. Bd. Pediatrics (chair sub-bd. endocrinology, 1997-98). Intern in pediat. Strong Meml. Rochester (N.Y.) Mcpl. Hosps., 1958-59; asst. resident pediat. U. Calif. Hosps., L.A., 1959-61; postdoc. trainee U. Calif., L.A., 1963-65; from asst. prof. to prof. pediat. U. So. Calif. Sch. Medicine, L.A., 1965-86; prof. pediat. UCLA Sch. Medicine, L.A., 1986—; attending physician Children's Mercy Hosp., Kansas City, Mo., 1962-63, L.A. county-Harbor Gen. Hosp., Torrance, Calif., 1965-67; endocrine cons. Pacific State Hosp., Pomona, Calif., 1965-69, tng. cons., 1965-70; med. adv. Human Growth Found. L.A. Chpt., 1967-74, chmn. adv. com., 1967-72, co-chmn. rsch. com., 1972-75; med. adv. bd. Nat. Pituitary Agy., 1971-74; chief divsn. pediat. endocrinology, L.A. County-U. So. Calif. Med. Ctr., 1967-86, physician, 1967-86, dir. pediat. endocrine and diabetic clinics., 1967-72; exec. asst. Calif. Student Health Project, L.A., 1967-68, faculty dir., 1968-69; coord. curriculum U. So. Calif. Sch. Medicine, L.A., 1969-76, assoc. dean student affairs, 1970-76, vice-chair dept. pediat., 1986—; assoc. attending physician divsn. endocrinology/metabolism children's Hosp. L.A., 1976-79, cons., 1979-82; cons. Calbiochem Corp., 1969-78, Hoechst-Roussel Pharmaceutical Corp., 1978-79, maternal and child health br. genetics disease sect. Calif. Dept. Health Scis., 1978—, Soreno Labs., Inc., 1979-94, growth hormone program Can. Med. Rsch. Coun., 1981, program on drugs AMA, 1985; endocrine cons. Lanterman State Hosp., Pomona, 1980-82; chief pediat. Olive View-UCLA Med. Ctr., Sylmar, Calif., 1986—; mem. med. staff UCLA Med. Ctr., L.A., 1986—; vis. lectr. Milwaukee Children's Hosp., 1977; vis. prof. U. Ariz. Sch. Medicine, 1978, Kapiolani/Children's Med. Ctr., Honolulu, 1983, U. Montreal/Hosp. Sainte-Justine, 1988, Australasian Pediat. Endocrine Group, 1990, Tripler Army Hosp., Honolulu, 1993; mem., chmn. various other hosp. coms. Mem. editl. bd. Jour. Pediat. Endocrinology; rev. Pediats., Jour. Pediats., Jour. Clin. Endocrinology and Metabolism, Am. Jour. Diseases Children, Pediat. Rsch., Med. Letter, Metabolism, Endocrine Revs. Capt. U.S. Army Med. Corps, 1961-63. Fellow U. Calif. Sch. Medicine, L.A., 1955-56, Cecil E. Vesy scholar, 1956-58; recipient Sheard-Sanford prize Am. Soc. Clin. Pathologists, 1958. Mem. L.A. Pediat. Soc., Am. Acad. Pediat., Western Soc. Pediat. Rsch. (chmn. nominating com. 1975-76), Endocrine Soc., Lawson Wilkins Pediat. Endocrine Soc. (membership com. 1971-74, chmn. membership com. 1973-74, dir. 1978-82, ad hoc com. uses human growth hormone 1981-87, 88-90, pres.-elect 1988-89, chmn. awards com. 1988—, pres. 1989-90, past pres. 1990-91, chmn. drug and therapeutic com., 1990-94), Soc. Pediat. Rsch., Am. Pediat. Soc. Home: 10428 Lorenzo Pl Los Angeles CA 90064-4449 Office: UCLA-Ssch of Med Dept Pediatrics/Endocrin 10833 Le Conte Ave Los Angeles CA 90095-3075*

FRASK, ROBIN ANN KOSTANESKY, secondary school educator; b. Hazleton, Pa., Apr. 27, 1971; d. John F. and Karen A. (Brandmier) Kostanesky; m. Randy Michael Frask, July 2, 1999. BS in Edn., Mansfield U., 1993; MEd, Wilkes U., 1999. Substitute tchr. Weatherly (Pa.) Area Sch. Dist., 1994-96; substitute tchr. Hazelton (Pa.) Area Sch. Dist., 1994-96, tchr. sci., 1996—. Mem. NEA, Pa. State Edn. Assn. E-mail: rmf@ccomm.com. Home: 345 Shingle Mill Dr Drums PA 18222

FRASSINELLI, GUIDO JOSEPH, retired aerospace engineer; b. Summit Hill, Pa., Dec. 4, 1927; s. Joseph and Maria (Grosso) F.; m. Antoinette Pauline Clemente, Sept. 26, 1953; children: Lisa, Erica, Laura, Joanne, Mark. BS, MS, MIT, 1949; MBA, Harvard U., 1956. Treas. AviDyne Rsch., Inc., Burlington, Mass., 1958-64; asst. gen. mgr. Kaman AviDyne divsn. Kaman Scis., Burlington, 1964-66; asst. dir. strategic planning N. Am. ACFT OPNS, Rockwell Internat., L.A., 1966-69; from mgr. program planning to project mgr. advanced programs Rockwell Space Sys. Divsn., Downey, Calif., 1970-94; ret. Rockwell Space Systems Div., Downey, 1994. Mem. Town Hall of Calif., L.A., 1970—; treas. Ecology Devel. and Implementation Commitment Team Found., Huntington Beach, Calif., 1971-75; founding com. mem. St. John Fisher Parish Coun., Rancho Palos Verdes, Calif., 1978-85. Recipient Tech. Utilization award, NASA, 1971, Astronaut Personal Achievement award, 1985. Fellow AIAA (assoc.; tech. com. on econs. 1983-87, exec. com. L.A. sect. 1987-91, 94-98), Inst. for Advancement of Engrng.; mem. Sigma Xi, Tau Beta Pi. Roman Catholic. Achievements include determination of aircraft damage limits and atomic-weapon-delivery capabilities of aircraft; development of cost models to account for advances in engineering state of art, of cost prioritization techniques for space shuttle improvements, of software to produce business plans. Home: 29521 Quailwood Dr Palos Verdes Peninsula CA 90275-4930

FRASURE, CARL MAYNARD, political science educator; b. Morgantown, W.Va., Aug. 21, 1938; s. Carl Maynard and Louise (Durham) F.; m. Beverly Brown, Sept. 1, 1962 (div. Aug. 1980); 1 child, Stephanie Frasure Goff. BS, W.Va. U., 1962, MA, 1965, MS, 1966, PhD, 1980; postgrad., Ohio U., 1985. Cert. secondary tchr., W.Va. Extension prof. W.Va. U., Morgantown, 1966-82; dir. student svcs. Bluefield (W.Va.) State U., 1982-83; prof. Salem (W.Va.)-Teikyo U., 1983—, chmn. polit. sci. dept., 1983—, asst. to acad. dean, 1984-86; cons. W.Va. Dept. Edn., Charleston, 1990; chairperson social scis. divsn., 1994—. Author, editor: W.Va. U. Non-credit Programs Catalog, 1980. Treas. Polit. Action Com. for Better Edn., Clarksburg, 1990; mem. Bridgeport (W.Va.) Police Civil Svc. Commn., 1993—; mem. Clarksburg Police Civil Svc. Commn, 1994—. Sgt. U.S. Army, 1957-63. U.S. Dept. Edn. grantee, 1966-70, 82-87, Options grantee Brown U., 1991. Mem. Am. Polit. Sci. Assn., W.Va. Polit. Sci. Assn., Phi Delta Kappa (treas. W.Va. U. chpt. 1984), Lions (treas. Bridgeport chpt. 1987-93, pres. 1993—), Elks (essay judge Clarksburg chpt. 1983—). Democrat. Episcopalian. Avocations: reading, politics, travel. Home: 1088 Taylor St Clarksburg WV 26301-4227 Office: Salem-Teikyo U Political Sci Dept Penn Ave Salem WV 26426

FRATANTONI, JOSEPH CHARLES, medical researcher, hematologist, medical and regulatory consultant; b. Bklyn., May 14, 1938; s. Joseph Edward and Providence Adeline (Bellante) F.; m. Pauline F. Jones, Jan. 30, 1965; children: David, Michael, Joan. BS in Chemistry egregia cum laude, Fordham Coll., 1959; MA in Chemistry, Harvard U., 1961; MD, Cornell U., 1965. Diplomate Am. Bd. Internal Medicine. Rsch. assoc. Sloan-Kettering Inst., N.Y.C., 1960-61; fellow dept. pharmacology Cornell U., 1961-64; intern, resident in medicine Cornell-N.Y. Hosp., 1965-67; staff assoc. Nat. Inst. Arthritis and Metabolic Diseases NIH, 1967-69; resident in medicine Cornell-N.Y. Hosp., 1969-70, fellow in hematology dept. medicine, 1970-71; instr. in medicine Cornell U., 1970-71; asst. prof. medicine, dir. Coagulation Lab. Georgetown U., 1971-72, from clin. asst. to assoc. prof. medicine and pharmacology, 1972-85; sr. staff physician hematology svc. Clin. Ctr. NIH, 1972-74; thrombosis program dir. Nat. Heart, Lung and Blood Inst., 1974-75, chief blood diseases br., 1975-77, chief blood resources br., 1977-78; chief lab. of cellular hematology Ctr. for Biologics Evaluation and Rsch., FDA, 1978-92; from assoc. prof. to clin. prof. medicine Uniformed Svcs. U., 1976-96; dir. divsn. hematology FDA, 1992-96; v.p. biologics C.L. McIntosh and Assocs., Rockville, Md., 1996—; cons., lectr. Nat. Naval Med. Ctr., 1975; presenter in field. Patentee in non-invasive optical assessment of platelet viability, measurement of platelet aggregation using a microplate reader; contbr. over 100 articles to profl. jours. Served to capt. USPHS, 1967-96, ret. Recipient Spl. Citation, FDA Commr., 1988, Citation, USPHS, 1989, Meritorious Svc. medal USPHS, 1991. Fellow ACP; mem. Am. Fedn. for Clin. Rsch., Am. Soc. Hematology, Am. Assn. Blood Banks (Disting. Svc. award 1998), Sigma Xi, Alpha Omega Alpha. Achievements include rsch. in hemostasis, platelet function and blood substitutes. Home: 9412 Overlea Dr Rockville MD 20850-3735 Office: C L McIntosh & Assocs 12300 Twinbrook Pkwy Ste 625 Rockville MD 20852-1606

FRATESCHI, LAWRENCE JAN, economist, statistician, educator; b. Chgo., Oct. 7, 1952; s. Lawrence and Olga (Los) F. BS in Math. and Psychology, U. Ill., Chgo., 1975, MA in Econs., 1979, MS Pub. Health in Biostats. and Epidemiology, 1990, PhD in Econs., 1992. Teaching asst. math, lectr. dept. info. and decision scis. U. Ill., Chgo., 1978-80, rsch. assoc. epidemiology and biostatistics Sch. Pub. Health, 1989-90; statistician Argonne (Ill.) Nat. Labs., 1980-81; asst. prof. econs. and stats. Coll. of DuPage, Glen Ellyn, Ill., 1981-86, assoc. prof., 1986-90, prof. econs., stats., 1990—; rsch. prof. epidemiology and biostats. Sch. Pub. Health U. Ill., Chgo., Ill., 1993—. Contbr. articles to profl. publs. Mem. Am. Econ. Assn., Am. Statis. Assn., Am. Pub. Health Assn., Soc. Epidemiologic Rsch., Midwest Econs. Assn., Ill. Econs. Assn., Ill. Pub. Health Assn., Phi Eta Sigma, Phi Kappa Phi, Delta Omega. Office: Coll of DuPage 422 22nd St Glen Ellyn IL 60137-6700

FRATIANNE, DAVID MICHAEL, architect; b. Columbus, Ohio, Dec. 17, 1960; s. Douglas G. and Carol J. (Sidman) F. BArch, Ohio State U., 1983, MArch, 1987; student, Oxford U., Eng., 1983. Architect Bly Ryder, N.Y.C., 1989-97. Mem. AIA (N.Y.C. chpt.). Fax: 212-929-8807. Studio: # 4-G 720 Greenwich St Apt 4G New York NY 10014-2547

FRATKIN, LESLIE, photographer; b. Schenectady, N.Y., 1960. BA in Comm., SUNY, Albany, 1983. curator, coord., mgr. touring internat. photog. exhbn., film series, web site and book project Sarajevo Self-Portrait: The View From Inside, 1995—. Works exhibited at Barney's, N.Y.C., 1995, Foster Goldstrom Gallery, N.Y.C., 1995, Children in Crisis Benefit, Germany, 1997, Riverside Studios, London, 1998, Florence, Italy, 1999; contbg. photographer various publs., 1983—. Grantee The Trust for Mutual Understanding, 1997; Individual Project fellow and grantee Soros Found./Open Soc. Inst., 1997. E-mail: leslief@interport.net. *

FRATT, DOROTHY, artist; b. Washington, Aug. 10, 1923; d. Hugh and Martha (Holt) Miller; m. Nicholas Diller Fratt, Sept. 4, 1943 (div. 1965); children: Nicholas, Hugh, Gregory, Peter; m. Curtis Calvin Cooper, Nov. 3, 1972. Studied with Nicolai Cikovsky, 1940; student, Mt. Vernon Coll., 1940-42, Am. U., 1942-43, Phillips Collection Art Sch., 1942-43; studied with Karl Knaths, 1943. mem. commissioning panel for NEA grant, Scottsdale, Ariz., 1971; mem. adv. bd. U. Art Mus. Ariz. State U., Tempe, 1989-95. Exhibited at UN Club Gallery, 1948, Desert Art Gallery, Scottsdale, Ariz., 1959, Tucson Art Ctr., 1964, Phoenix Art Mus., 1964, 75, Riva Yares Gallery, Scottsdale, 1965, 82, 89, 94, 95, Calif. Legion Honor, San Francisco, 1965, Mickelson Gallery, Washington, 1967, State-Wide Touring Exhibit, 1974, Scottsdale Ctr. for Arts, 1980, Carson-Sapiro Gallery, Denver, 1981, Thomas Beabor Gallery, La Jolla, Calif., 1985, U. Ariz. Gallery, Tucson, 1986; represented in pub. collections at Phoenix Art Mus., Tucson Mus., Ariz. State Mus., Tempe, Mus. Fine Arts, Santa Fe, Mus. No. Ariz., Flagstaff; represented in various corp. collections; contbr. to Archives of Am. Art, 1996. Mem. Fine Arts Commn., Phoenix, 1965-71; mem. Sotheby Symposium Quality in Art, N.Y.C., 1990. Home: 6010 E Cholla Ln Scottsdale AZ 85253-6902

FRATTI, MARIO, playwright, educator; b. L'Aquila, Italy, July 5, 1927; came to U.S., 1963, naturalized, 1974; s. Leone and Palmira (Silvi) F.; children: Mirko, Barbara, Valentina. Ph.D., Ca Foscari U., 1951. Tchr., 1964-65; mem. faculty Columbia U., 1965-66; mem. Adelphi Coll., 1964-65; mem. faculty Hofstra U., 1973-74; prof. lit. New Sch. Hunter Coll., N.Y.C., 1967—; drama critic. Drama critic: Paese, 1963—, Progresso, 1963—, Ridotto, 1963—, Ora Zero, 1963—; playwright: Cage-Suicide, 1964, Academy-Return, 1967, Mafia, 1971, Races, 1972, Bridge, 1971, Eleven Plays in Spanish, 1977, Refrigerators, 1977; author: Eleonora Duse-Victim, 1981, Nine, 1982 (Tony), Biography of Fratti, 1982, A.I.D.S., 1987, V.C.R., 1988, (mus.) Encounter, 1989, Family, 1990, Friends, 1991, Lovers, 1992, Leningrad Euthanasia, 1993, Holy Father, 1994, Sister, 1995, Sacrifices, 1996, Jurors, 1997, also 8 plays in Russian, 1997, 4 plays in Japanese, 1997, 7 minidramas in Spanish, 1998. Served to lt. Italian Army, 1951-53. Recipient awards for plays and musicals. Mem. Drama Desk, Am. Theatre Critics, Outer Critics Circle (v.p.). Democrat. Home: 145 W 55th St Apt 15D New York NY 10019-5355 Office: Hunter Coll 695 Park Ave New York NY 10021-5024

FRAUENFELDER, HANS, physicist, educator; b. Neuhausen, Switzerland, July 28, 1922; came to U.S., 1952, naturalized, 1958; s. Otto and Emma (Ziegler) F.; m. Verena Anna Hassler, May 16, 1950; children: Ulrich Hans, Kätterli Anne, Anne Verena. Diploma, Swiss Fed. Inst. Tech., 1947, Ph.D. in Physics, 1950. Asst. Swiss Fed. Inst. Tech., 1946-52; asst. prof. physics U. Ill. at Urbana, 1952-56, assoc. prof., 1956-58, prof., 1958-92, prof. emeritus, 1992—; mem. staff Los Alamos (N.Mex.) Nat. Labs., 1992—; Guggenheim fellow, 1958-59, 73; vis. scientist CERN, Geneva, Switzerland, 1958-59, 63, 73. Author: The Mossbauer Effect, 1962, (with E.M. Henley) Subatomic Physics, 1974, 2d edit., 1991, Nuclear and Particle Physics, 1975; contbr. articles to profl. jours. Recipient Humboldt award, 1987-88. Fellow AAAS, Am. Phys. Soc. (Biol. Physics prize 1992), N.Y. Acad. Sci.; mem. Royal Swedish Acad. Scis., NAS, Am. Inst. Physics (chmn. governing bd. 1986-93), Am. Acad. Arts and Sci., Am. Philos. Soc., Acad. Leopoldina.

FRAUMANN, WILLARD GEORGE, lawyer; b. San Francisco, July 21, 1948; m. Anne C. Derleth, Dec. 18, 1971; children: Ellen, Robert, Sarah. AB, U. Mich., 1970; JD, Harvard U., 1973. Bar: Ill., U.S. Dist. Ct. (no. dist.) Ill. Ptnr. Kirkland & Ellis, Chgo., 1977—. Served to lt. USNR, 1973-77. Office: Kirkland & Ellis 200 E Randolph St Fl 54 Chicago IL 60601-6636*

FRAUMENI, JOSEPH FRANCIS, JR., scientific researcher, medical educator, physician, military officer; b. Boston, Apr. 1, 1933; s. Joseph Francis and Pauline (Malta) F.; m. Patricia Welch D'Arcy, Apr. 23, 1977. AB, Harvard U., 1954; MD, Duke, 1958; ScM, Harvard U., 1965. Diplomate Am. Bd. Internal Medicine. Commd. lt. USPHS, 1962, advanced through grades to rear admiral (asst. surgeon gen.), 1997; med. intern, resident Johns Hopkins Hosp., Balt., 1958-60; med. resident, chief resident Meml. Sloan-Kettering Cancer Ctr., N.Y.C., 1960-62; staff assoc. Nat. Cancer Inst., Bethesda, Md., 1962-65, assoc. chief, 1966-75, chief environ. epidemiology br., 1975-82, dir. epidemiology & biostats. program, 1979-95, dir. epidemiology & genetics divsn., 1995—; attending physician Clin. Ctr. NIH, Bethesda, 1966—; prof. epidemiology uniformed svcs. U. Health Scis., Bethesda, 1985—; adj. prof. harvard U. Sch. Pub. Health, Boston, 1993—, George Washington U. Med. Ctr., 1997—. Editl. bds. Jour. Nat. Cancer Inst., 1966-69, Teratology, 1974-78, Med. and Pediat. Oncology, 1974-78, Cancer Rsch., 1974—, Am. Jour. Indsl. Medicine, 1979—, Oncology, 1980—, Cancer Investigation, 1980-98, Preventive Medicine, 1982-98, Genetic Epidemiology, 1984-97, Cancer Causes and Control, 1989-97, Cancer Epidemiology, Biomarkers and Prevention, 1990—, Cancer, 1991—, Internat. Jour. Oncology, 1992—; contbr. more than 700 articles to profl. jours. Recipient Disting. Svc. medal USPHS, 1983, Gorgas medal Assn. Mil. Surgeons U.S., 1989, W.W. Sutow award U. Tex. M.D. Anderson Cancer Ctr., 1992, Disting. Alumnus award Duke U. Med. Ctr., 1992, Alumni Award of Merit, Harvard Sch. Pub. Health, 1993, Wick Williams Meml. award Fox Chase Cancer Ctr., 1993, Dir.'s award NIH, 1994, Charles Mott prize GM Cancer Rsch. Found., 1995, John Snow award APHA, 1995, Selikoff award Ramazinni Inst., 1996, Robert S. Gordon award NIH, 1996; vis. prof. GM Cancer Rsch. Found. Internat. Agy. Rsch. Cancer, 1990. Fellow AAAS, ACP (James D. Bruce Meml. award 1997), Am. Coll. Epidemiology (Lilienfeld award 1993, hon. fellow 1998, bd. dirs. 1985-89), Am. Coll. Preventive Medicine; mem. Inst. Medicine NAS, Am Soc. Preventive Oncology (Disting. Achievement award 1993, pres. 1981-83), Am. Assn. Cancer Rsch. (bd. dirs. 1983-87, Am. Cancer Soc. award rsch. excellence epidemiology, prevention 1993), Assn. Am. Physicians. Achievements include research in environmental and genetic determinants of cancer. Office: Nat Cancer Inst EPS/8070 Div Cancer Epidemiology & Genetics Executive Plz N Rm 543 Bethesda MD 20892

FRAUNFELDER, FREDERICK THEODORE, ophthalmologist, educator; b. Pasadena, Calif., Aug. 16, 1934; s. Reinhart and Freida Fraunfelder; m. Yvonne Marie Halliday, June 21, 1959; children—Yvette Marie, Helene, Nina, Frederick, Nicholas. BS, U. Oreg., 1956, MD, 1960, postgrad. (NIH postdoctoral fellow), 1962. Diplomate Am. Bd. Ophthalmology (bd. dirs. 1982-90). Intern U. Chgo., 1961; resident U. Oreg. Med. Sch., 1964-66; NIH postdoctoral fellow Wilmer Eye Inst., Johns Hopkins U., 1967; prof., chmn. dept. ophthalmology U. Ark. Health Scis. Ctr., 1968-78, 78-98, Oreg. Health Scis. U., 1998—; dir. Casey Eye Inst., 1992-98, Nat. Registry Drug-Induced Ocular Side Effects, 1976—; vis. prof. ophthalmology Moorfields Eye Hosp., London, 1974. Author: Drug-Induced Ocular Side Effects and Drug Interactions, 1976, 4th edit., 1966, Current Ocular Therapy, 1995, 5th edit., 1999, Recent Advances in Ophthalmology, 8th edit., 1985; assoc. editor: Jour. Toxicology: Cutaneous and Ocular, 1984—; mem. editl. bd. Am. Jour. Ophthalmology, 1982-92, Ophthalmic Forum, 1983-90, Ophthalmology, 1984-89; contbr. numerous articles lens and eye toxicity rsch. to profl. jours. Served with U.S. Army, 1962-64. FDA grantee, 1976-86; Nat. Eye Inst. grantee, 1970-87. Mem. AMA, ACS, Am. Acad. Ophthaolmology, Assn. Univ. Profs. in Ophthalmology (pres. 1976), Am. Ophthalmol. Soc., Am. Coll. Cryosurgery (pres. 1977), Assn. Research in Ophthalmology. Lutheran. Clubs: Lions, Elks. Home: 13 Cellini Ct Lake Oswego OR 97035-1307 Office: Casey Eye Inst 3375 SW Terwilliger Blvd Portland OR 97201-4197

FRAUTSCHI, STEVEN CLARK, physicist, educator; b. Madison, Wis., Dec. 6, 1933; s. Lowell Emil and Grace (Clark) F.; m. Mie Okamura, Feb. 16, 1967; children—Laura, Jennifer. B.A., Harvard U., 1954; Ph.D., Stanford U., 1958. Research fellow Kyoto U., Japan, 1958-59, U. Calif.-Berkeley, 1959-61; mem. faculty Cornell U., 1961-62, Calif. Inst. Tech., Pasadena, 1962—; prof. theoretical physics Calif. Inst. Tech., 1966—, exec. officer physics, 1988-97, master student houses, 1997—; vis. prof. U. Paris, Orsay, 1977-78. Author: Regge Poles and S-Matrix Theory, 1963, The Mechanical Universe, 1986. Guggenheim fellow, 1971-72. Mem. Am. Phys. Soc. Research, publs. on Regge poles, bootstrap theory, cosmology. Home: 1561 Crest Dr Altadena CA 91001-1838 Office: 1201 E California Blvd Pasadena CA 91125-0001

FRAUTSCHI, TIMOTHY CLARK, lawyer; b. Madison, Wis., Apr. 8, 1937; s. Lowell E. and Grace C. (Clark) F.; m. Pamela H. Hendricks, June 23, 1964; children—Schuyler, Jason, Jacob; m. Susan B. Brumm, June 13, 1981. B.A., U. Wis., 1959; LL.B., London Sch. Econs., U. Wis., 1963. Bar: Wis. 1963, U.S. Ct. Claims 1976, U.S. Tax Ct., 1976. Assoc. firm Foley & Lardner, Milw., 1963-70, ptnr., 1970—. Editor Wis. Law Rev. Co-founder Milw. Forum; pres. Lakeside Community Council; bd. dirs. Am. Players Theater, Milw., Repertory Theater, Northcott Neighborhood House, United Performing Arts Fund, Inc., Milw., Children's Svc. Soc., Wis., Theatre Tesseract, Next Act theatre, Frank Lloyd Wright Wis. Conservancy; pres. Present Music, Inc., 1991-98, Skylight Comic Opera Ltd., 1980-85; pres. Watertower Landmark Trust, 1986-89. Mem. Milw. Jr. Bar Assn. (pres. 1969-70), Milw. Bar Assn. (dir. 1971-74), Order of Coif, Phi Beta Kappa (pres. Milw. chpt. 1968-70), Phi Kappa Phi, Phi Eta Sigma. Office: Foley & Lardner First Wis Ctr 777 E Wisconsin Ave Ste 3800 Milwaukee WI 53202-5367

FRAVEL, ELIZABETH WHITMORE, accountant; b. Hagerstown, Md., Oct. 17, 1951; d. John W. and Dorothy E. (McCullough) Whitmore; children: Christine E., John W. BBA, Bridgewater Coll., 1973. CPA. Jr. staff acct. Rockingham Meml. Hosp., Harrisonburg, Va., 1973-75; mgr. customer service Pentamation Enterprises Inc., Sparks, Md., 1975-83; sr. acct. Good Samaritan Hosp., Balt., 1983-84; pvt. practice acctg. Balt., 1984-86, Annapolis, Md., 1986—; staff acct. Hammond & Heim Chartered Accts., Annapolis, Md., 1987-89; contr. Smith Bros., Inc., Galesville, Md., 1989-94; v.p. fin. Md. Spl. Olympics, Columbia, Md., 1995—. Treas. Belmont Condominium Assn., Balt., 1983-85. Mem. AICPAs, Md. Assn. CPAs, Md. Soc. Accts. Avocations: jewelry, music, gardening, computers.

FRAWLEY, THOMAS FRANCIS, retired physician; b. Rochester, N.Y., June 27, 1919; s. Thomas J. and Mary (Leddy) F.; m. Marigrace Cecelia Gould, Feb. 23, 1946; children—Thomas Joseph II, Colleen, Brian (dec.). A.B., U. Rochester, 1941; M.D., U. Buffalo, 1944. Diplomate Am. Bd. Internal Medicine, Am. Bd. Endocrinology and Metabolism. Intern St. Mary's Hosp., Rochester, 1944-45; resident Buffalo Gen. Hosp., 1945-48; research fellow Harvard Med. Sch., 1948-52; resident Peter Bent Brigham Hosp., Boston, 1948-52; chief endocrinology and metabolism Albany (N.Y.) Med. Sch., 1952-58, assoc. prof. medicine, 1952-58, prof. medicine, 1960-63; research assoc. NIH, 1958-60; prof. medicine St. Louis U. Sch. Medicine, 1963-97, chmn. dept. internal medicine, 1963-73, chmn. emeritus, 1977—; chmn. Office of Grad. Med. Edn., St. John's Mercy Med. Center, St. Louis, 1981-95; physician-in-chief St. Louis U. Hosp., 1963-73; mem. durg effecacy study panel Nat. Acad. Scis., 1966-69; med. adv. com. Cath. Hosp. Assn., 1966-69; mem. sci. rev. com. NIH, 1970—; commr. Joint Commn. Accreditation of Hosps., 1976—, mem. resident rev. com. Int. Medicine, 1980-82, 89-93. Author books in field; contbr. articles to profl. jours. Served to capt., M.C. AUS, 1946-47; surgeon USPHS, 1958-60. Recipient Disting. Alumni award U. Buffalo Sch. Medicine, 1989. Fellow ACP (gov. Mo. 1971-75, regent 1976—, pres. 1981, master 1982, Laureate award 1986, Stengel award 1993), Royal Coll. Physicians Ireland, Royal Soc. Medicine London; mem. Assn. Am. Physicians, Am. Fedn. Clin. Rsch., Endocrine Soc., Ctrl. Soc. Clin. Rsch., So. Soc. Clin. Investigation, Am. Thyroid Assn., Am. Diabetes Assn. (profl. edn. com. 1983), Am. Clin. and Climatol. Assn., St. Louis Med. Soc. (Schlueter award 1994), Sigma Xi, Alpha Omega Alpha. Home: 14003 Baywood Villages Dr Chesterfield MO 63017-3450

FRAWLEY BAGLEY, ELIZABETH, government advisor, ambassador; b. Elmira, N.Y., July 13, 1952; m. Smith Bagley; 2 children. BA in French and Spanish cum laude, Regis Coll., 1974; JD in Internat. Law, Georgetown U., 1987. Staff Office Congl. Rels. Dept. State, spl. asst. to Amb. Sol Linowitz, congl. liaison Conf. on Security and Cooperation in Europe; amb. to Portugal Dept. State, Washington, 1993—; adj. prof. law Georgetown U. Washington. Home: 1539 29th St NW Washington DC 20007-3061

FRAWLEY-O'DEA, MARY GAIL, clinical psychologist, psychoanalyst, educator; b. Lowell, Mass.; d. John Edward and Mary Gail (Quinn) Frawley; m. Dennis Michael O'Dea, Jan. 1, 1996; 1 stepson, Daniel Patrick, 1 adopted son, Igor Ibradzic. BA, St. Mary's Coll., Notre Dame, Ind., 1972; MBA, So. Meth. U., 1975; PhD, Adelphi U., 1988, postdoctoral diploma in psychoanalysis, 1996. Psychologist II Pomona (N.Y.) Mental Health Clinic, 1987-91; asst. clin. prof. Adelphi U., Derner Inst., Garden City, N.Y., 1989—; pvt. practice clin. psychologist/psychoanalyst Nyack, N.Y., 1990—; faculty supr. Minn. Inst. Contemporary Psychoanalysis, Mpls.-St. Paul, 1996—, continuing edn. faculty, N.Y. Psychol. Assn. for Psychoanalysis, 1998—. Co-author: treating the Adult Survivor of Childhood Sexual Abuse, 1994; contbr. chpts. to books, articles to profl. jours. Mem. APA, Adelphi Soc. Psychoanalysis and Psychotherapy. Avocations: hiking, cooking, theater, symphony, reading. Home and Office: 75 N Broadway Nyack NY 10960-2624

FRAY, LIONEL LOUIS, management consultant; b. Paris, Jan. 17, 1935; came to U.S., 1942; s. Maurice and Esther Fray; m. Joanne Caroline Liberman, June 30, 1963; children: Sharon June, Elizabeth Ann. BS, MIT, 1957, MS, 1958; MBA, Harvard U., 1962. Co-founder U.S. Sonics, Inc., Cambridge, Mass., 1957-58; with Mitre Corp., Bedford, Mass., 1958-60, Mgmt. Systems Corp., 1962-64; v.p. Harbridge House, Boston, 1964-73, TBS Capital Corp., Lexington, Mass., 1973-86, Temple, Barker & Sloane, Lexington, Mass., 1973-86; pres. Lionel L. Fray Assocs., Inc., Lexington, Mass., 1986—; bd. dirs. Am. Technion Soc., AOA Geophysics, Inc. Author: Handbook of Strategic Management, 1985, How to Develop the Strategic Plan, 1987; contbr. articles to profl. jours. Mem. Strategic Leadership Forum, Inst. Mgmt. Cons. Club: Harvard. Avocations: tennis, skiing, jazz violin, flying. Home: 2361A Massachusetts Ave Lexington MA 02421-6733 Office: Lionel L. Fray Assoc Inc 1620 Massachusetts Ave Lexington MA 02420-3826

FRAYSSINET, DANIEL FERNAND, software company executive; b. Rodez, Aveyron, France, June 25, 1956; came to U.S., 1979; s. Leon Privat and Fernande Marie (Foulquier) F.; m. Chantal Luce Hebrard, June 30, 1979 (div. 1988); m. Corinne Yollande Guillaud, Mar. 4, 1989; children: Jennifer, Malorie. BA in Math., Lycee Chaptal, Mende, France, 1974; diploma in Math., Institut Nat. des Scis. Appliquees, Villeurbanne, France, 1976, MSME, 1979. Registered mech. engr. Rsch. asst. Onser, Bron, France, 1977-78; devel. engr. Centech, Glenview, Ill., 1979-82; pres., dir. JMS Inc., Camarillo, Calif., 1985—; CEO, pres., dir. D.P. Tech. Corp., Camarillo, 1982—; dir. Acaso Bus. Ctr., Oxnard, Calif. Author: Adverse Effect of Inertia and Rigidity of Truck Colliding with Lighter Vehicle, 1979; co-author: (software) Arcade, 1979, Esprit, 1984. Mem. Soc. Mfg. Engrs., Acad. Magical Arts, Inc. Avocations: flying, windsurfing, scuba diving, magic, hypnosis. Office: D P Tech Corp 1150 Avenida Acaso Camarillo CA 93012-8719

FRAZER, DAVID HUGH, JR., allergist; b. Montgomery, Ala., Mar. 31, 1937; s. David H. and Sue Ray (Durrett) F.; m. Johnnie Bowie Swetenburg, July 5, 1941; children: David Hugh III, Bowie Swetenburg Frazer Campbell, Wills Findley. BS, Tulane U., 1958, MD, 1961. Private practice Atlanta, 1966-67, Montgomery, 1967—. Bd. dirs. S. Ala. State Fair, Montgomery,

Brantwood Children's Home, Montgomery Metro YMCA Bd. With USAF, 1962-64. Fellow Am. Coll. Allergy and Immunology; mem. Am. Acad. Allergy and Immunology. Republican. Presbyterian. Office: 1420 Narrow Lane Pky Montgomery AL 36111-2654

FRAZER, JOHN HOWARD, tennis association executive, retired manufacturing company executive; b. Cin., June 3, 1924; s. H. Howard and Amelia (Spieth) F.; m. Joann Elizabeth McEvoy, Nov. 3, 1956; children: John Howard Jr., Victoria F. Fuller. BA, U. Cin., 1948, JD, 1950. Bar: Ohio 1950. V.p. H. Howard Frazer Co., Cin., 1950-62; pres. H. Howard Frazer Co., 1962-76; treas., dir. Cin. Transit Co., 1957-73; dir. Am. Controlled Industries, Cin., 1973-86; pres. Am. Controlled Industries, 1974-75, exec. v.p., 1975-86; dir. Vulcan Corp., Cin., 1960-91; pres. Vulcan Corp., 1975-88; sec., dir. Valley Industries, 1973-86, Colorpac, Inc., 1973-86; chmn. U.S. Open Tennis Championships, 1993-94. Chmn. men's com. Cin. Symphony Orch., 1971-73; pres. Cincinnatus Assn., 1969-70; chmn. Western Tennis Championships, Cin., 1970-73; bd. dirs. Internat. Tennis Hall of Fame, 1979—, exec. com. 1985—, chmn. internat. coun. 1996—. Served with USAAF, 1942-45. Recipient Highest Effort award SAE Fraternity, 1995. Mem. USTA (mem. exec. com. 1975—, chmn. sanction and schedule com. 1973-86, bd. dirs. 1986-96, v.p. 1986-88, sec. 1988-90, 1st v.p. 1990-92, pres. 1993-94, chmn. nat. men's ranking com. 1971-73, long-range planning com. 1981-87), Internat. Tennis Fedn. (del. 1991-96, mem. com. mgmt. 1993-97, v.p. 1995-97, hon. life counsellor 1997—, mem. vets. com. 1996—, chmn. vets. com. 1996-97, mem. constl. com. 1997—, Svc. to the Game award 1998), Am. Footwear Industries Assn. (dir.), Rubber Mfrs. Assn. (dir.), Shoe Last Mfrs. Assn. (pres. 1978-79), Univ. Club, Cin. C.C., Cin. Tennis Club, Pelican Bay Club (Naples, Fla.), Quail Creek C.C., (Naples), Bay Colony Club (Naples), River Club (N.Y.C.), All-Eng. Lawn Tennis Club (Wimbledon). Home: 8171 Bay Colony Dr Apt 1701 Naples FL 34108-7566

FRAZER, JOHN PAUL, surgeon; b. Rochester, N.Y., Sept. 14, 1914; s. Edward and Annie Margaret (Burdick) F.; m. Doris V. Larsen, Sept. 23, 1950; children: Karin Ann, Gail Sherry. MD, U. Rochester, 1939. Intern in pathology Cornell U. Med. Center - N.Y. Hosp., 1939-40; intern in surgery L.I. Coll. Hosp., 1940-41; resident ENT in ear, nose and throat Yale-New Haven Hosp., 1941-44, instr., 1945-48; practice medicine specializing in ear, nose and throat Honolulu, 1948-63; prof. surgery, chmn. dept. ENT surgery U. Rochester Sch. Medicine and Dentistry, 1963-81, prof., 1981-93, prof. emeritus, 1993—; cons. to surgeon gen. Tripler Hosp., 1950-63, Tb and leprosy Sanitoria, Hawaii, 1949-63. Mem. ACS, Am. Laryngol. Assn., Am. Bronchoesophagological Assn., Am. Laryngol-Rhinol-Otol. Soc., N.Y. State Soc. Medicine. Address: 329 Orchard Park Blvd Rochester NY 14609-3314

FRAZER, LANCE WILLIAM, writer; b. Ann Arbor, Mich., Aug. 19, 1954; s. William James and Helen Marie (Kennedy) F.; m. Celia Marie Burki, July 24, 1976; 1 child, Logan Donovan. BA, U. Santa Clara, 1976; student, Sonoma State Coll., 1982, Santa Rosa Jr. Coll., 1987. Corr. Space World Mag., 1988-89; staff writer The Inter-City Express, 1988-91; corr. Ad Astra Mag., 1989-92. contbr. articles to Trials Digest Mag., Napa-Solano Bus. Jour., Santa Rosa Bus. Jour., Environ. Health Perspectives Mag., USAIR Mag., Air & Space, New Physician. Recipient First award for Excellence in Mag. Journalism Soc. Nat. Assn. Publs., 1989. Mem. Am. Soc. Journalists and Authors (Outstanding Article award 1993), Nat. Writers Assn. (profl. divsn.), Nat. Assn. Sci. Writers. Avocations: sailing, travel, astronomy, outdoor activities. Home and Office: 3521 Santos Cir Cameron Park CA 95682-8247

FRAZER, NIMROD THOMPSON, financial services company executive; b. Montgomery, Ala., Dec. 10, 1929. BA, Huntingdon Coll., 1954; MBA, Harvard U., 1956. Securities salesman Sterne Agee & Leach, Montgomery, 1956-57; adminstr. State of Ala., Montgomery, 1957-60; from salesman to exec. v.p. Thornton, Farish & Gauntt, Montgomery, 1961-75; chmn. The Frazer Lanier Co., Montgomery, 1976-96; chmmn, pres., CEO The Enstar Group, Montgomery, 1990—. Mem. bd. visitors USAF Air U.; trustee Atlanta Internat. Sch. 1st lt. U.S. Army, 1950-53. Decorated Silver Star. Mem. Montgomery C. of C. (vice-chmn.; mem. exec. com.). Home: 663 Cloverdale Rd Montgomery AL 36106-1805 Office: Enstar Group Inc 176 Commerce Ct Montgomery AL 36104-2586*

FRAZER, RICARDO AMANDO, program director; b. Kingston, Jamaica, May 11, 1953; came to U.S., 1959; s. Neman Wesley and Vera Olive (Reid) F.; m. Katana L. Hall, May 15, 1987 (div. Mar. 10, 1995). BS, BA, U. Conn., 1977; EdM, Harvard U., 1979; PhD, Bowling Green State U., 1993. Dir. Dittmar Gallery, Evanston, Ill., 1992—; art svcs. mgr. Northwestern U., 1992—. Editor: (univ. publ.) Cultural Crossroads, 1994, (jour.) Crucial Roots, 1987, Assn. Coll. Unions Internat., 1996. Trustee Bowling Green State U., 1989-90. Recipient Jacob Lawrence award Bowling Green State U., 1990. Mem. APA, Artists United (pres. 1997), Ritual Artists Group (founder 1996). Avocations: poetry, photography, conga drumming, oil painting. Home: 1347 W Estes Ave Chicago IL 60626-5441 Office: Northwestern U Norris Ctr 1999 S Campus Dr Evanston IL 60208-0001

FRAZER, ROBERT LEE, landscape architect. BS in Landscape Architecture, Tex. A&M U., 1948; MS in Agriculture, East Tex. State U., 1951. Registered landscape architect, Tex. Landscape architect, instr. vocat. horticulture San Antonio Sch. Dist., 1948-49; landscape architect, instr., head campus maintenance East Tex. State U., Commerce, 1949-54; dir. parks and recreation City of San Antonio, 1955-73; univ. landscape architect, prof. landscape architecture Tex. Tech. U., Lubbock, 1973-74; v.p., prin., dir. landscape architecture Groves Fernandez Frazer & Assocs., Inc., San Antonio, 1974-83; v.p., prin., dir. landscape architecture Fernandez Frazer White & Assocs., Inc., San Antonio, 1984-92, v.p. emeritus, 1992—; adj. prof. U. Tex., Arlington, 1993. Contbr. articles to profl. jours. Recipient Robert H. Hugman award for devel. San Antonio River Walk, 1987, Disting. Svc. award San Antonio Conservation Soc., 1973. Fellow Am. Soc. Landscape Architects (Terry Hershey award for Excellence in Field of Recreation Parks or Tourism), Am. Inst. Park Execs., Am. Acad. for Park and Recreation Adminstrn., Tex. Recreation and Park Soc.; mem. S.W. Park and Recreation Tng. Inst. (past pres., co-organizer), Tex. Mcpl. Park and Recreation Assn. (past pres., organizer), Tex. Turfgrass Assn. (past pres., co-organizer), Nat. River Parks and Waterfront Assn. (past bd. dirs.), Nat. Recreation Assn. (past mem. nat. adv. com.). Office: Fernandez Frazer White & Assoc 11824 Radium St San Antonio TX 78216-2711

FRAZER, STUART HARRISON, III, cotton merchant; b. Montgomery, Ala., Feb. 13, 1948; s. Stuart Harrison Jr. and Myrta Frances (Garrett) F.; m. Linda Gail Patterson, Nov. 21, 1971 (div. 1983); 1 child, Heather Allison; m. Mary Prue Coleman, Oct. 28, 1983; children: Laura Goldman, Meredith Jane. Student, Huntingdon Coll., Montgomery, 1966-68, Auburn (Ala.) U., 1970-73. V.p. Weil Bros. Cotton Inc., Montgomery, 1970-88; sr. v.p. Rollins Cotton Co., Montgomery, 1988-92, pres., 1992-94; pres. Prodn. Mktg., Montgomery, 1994—; mem. USDA adv. com. con Cotton Clasing, Washington, 1988—; bd. dirs. N.Y. Cotton Exch., Cotton Coun. Internat., Nat. Cotton Coun.; mem. agrl. adv. com. to Commodity Futures Trading Commn., Washington. Mem. YMCA Boys Work Com., pres. 1986-87. With U.S. Army, 1968-69. Mem. Am. Cotton Shippers Assn. (dir., 1st v.p. 1992, 2nd v.p. 1991, pres. 1993), Nat. Cotton Coun., Atlantic Cotton Assn. (pres. 1981-82), Montgomery Cotton Exch. (pres. 1976—), Montgomery Country Club. Episcopalian. Home: 2517 Darrington Rd Montgomery AL 36111-1527 Office: Prodn Mktg PO Box 210309 Montgomery AL 36121-0309

FRAZIER, AMY, professional tennis player; b. St. Louis, Mo., Sept. 19, 1972. 4th ranked woman USTA, now ranked 25th, 1998; winner Japan Open, 1995; now ranked 66th USTA, 1999. World Team Tennis MVP, 1994. Office: USTA 70 W Red Oak Ln White Plains NY 10604-3602*

FRAZIER, ANN LYNETTE, medical/surgical nurse; b. Oxford, N.C., Jan. 18, 1960; d. James Edward and Gerald Rene (Hite) F. BSN, Atlantic Christian Coll., Wilson, N.C., 1982. RN, N.C.; cert. med.-surg. nurse ANCC. Staff nurse med.-surg. unit, asst. head nurse Duke U. Med. Ctr., Durham, N.C., 1988-92, advanced staff nurse, 1992—. Recipient Spl. Achievement-Excellence in Nursing Practice award Duke U. Med. Ctr. Friends of Nursing, 1989. Mem. ANA. Home: 3476 Sandy Creek Dr Durham NC 27705-6033 Office: Duke U Med Ctr PO Box 3714 Durham NC 27710

FRAZIER, CHET JUNE, advertising agency executive; b. Waldron, Ark., May 17, 1924; s. R.C. and Alice (Terry) F.; m. Lucille Whetzel, Nov. 17, 1942; children: John, Lynette, Terry, Luanna. B.S., Okla. State U., 1949, M.S., 1950. Editor Okla. News Service, Stillwater, 1949-50; product sales mgr. Ralston Purina Co., St. Louis, 1951-58; advt. mgr. Ralston Purina Co., 1958-63; v.p. Bozell & Jacobs Internat., Inc., N.Y.C., 1964-68; sr. v.p. Bozell & Jacobs Internat., Inc., 1968-71, exec. v.p., 1971-76, pres., 1976-89; pres. Bozell & Jacobs Internat., Inc. (Agrl. Div.), 1978-89, also dir., 1972-89; ret., 1989, pvt. practice agrl. mktg. cons., 1989—; chmn. bd. Henke Machine, Inc., 1972—; bd. dirs. Fed. Land Bank Adminstrn. of Midlands, 1989. Contbr. articles on agrl. advt. to profl. jours. Served with U.S. Army, 1943-46, PTO. Named Advt. Man of Year Advt. Fedn. Am., 1968. Mem. Nat. Agrl. Advt. and Mktg. Assn. (pres. 1967-68, dir. 1967-70), U.S. Feed Grains Council (bd. dirs., chmn. pub. relations com.), Am. Feed Mfg. Assn., Agrl. Council Am. (bd. dirs.), Farm Equipment Mfg. Assn., Agrl. Pubs. Assn. Methodist. Club: Kiwanis. Home: 9770 Westchester Dr Omaha NE 68114-3875 *My business philosophy has always been one of honesty, integrity, hard work and respect for the rights of those with whom I work.*

FRAZIER, DOUGLAS ALMEDA MCREE, former energy facility analyst; b. Soddy, Tenn., Feb. 6, 1923; d. Clarence Douglas and Nannie (Eldridge) McRee; m. Earl Lee Frazier, Aug. 25, 1963. BA, U. Chattanooga, 1944, B of Music, 1949, MEd, 1958. Various positions TVA, Chattanooga, power supply analyst, 1945-87. Vol. for TVA retirees, Chattanooga Visitors Ctr., Chattanooga Health Coun.; mem. Adult Edn. Coun., Chattanooga Employees Recreation Assn., Sr. Neighbors Orch., Chattanooga, 1990—, v.p. Ret. Sr. Vol. Program; organist, pianist Soddy United Meth. Ch.; past sec. Soddy-Daisy H.S. Alumni Assn.; life mem. First Presbyn. Ch.resbyn. Ch. Grand Organist, O.E.S., Tennessee, 1999—; Listed in 1st Families Tenn., 1996. Mem. AAUW (life; past pres., Names Gift award 1965), AARP (past pres., Cmty. Citizen award), DAR, East Tenn. Hist. Soc., Chattanooga Engrs. Club (past. sec., v.p., pres., People-to-People award 1989), U. Chattanooga Alumni Coun., Soddy C. of C., Soddy Lioness Club, Order of Eastern Star (past matron, grand rep. 1965-67, grand rep. Tenn. 1996, 97, grand organist 1999), Soddy High Alumni Assn. (past sec., past pres.), Pilot Club of Chattanooga. Life-long mem. of the First Presbyterian Church of Soddy, Tennessee. Home: 11313 Hixson Pike Soddy Daisy TN 37379-6371 Mailing: PO Box 223 Soddy Daisy TN 37384-0223

FRAZIER, DOUGLAS BYRON, health care consultant; b. Danville, Va., Jan. 18, 1957; s. Calvin Luther and Frances Ann (Benbow) F.; m. Linda Camille Kane, Apr. 25, 1981; 1 child, John Byron. BS in Fin. with honors, U. Fla., 1979. Ops. analyst Whittaker Gen. Med., Miami, Fla., 1980, div. mgr., 1980-85; health care cons. Abbott Labs., Abbott Park, Ill., 1985-86, sr. health care cons., 1986-92; dir. cons. svcs. Abbott Labs, Abbott Park, Ill., 1992-93, dir. cons. and supply channel svcs., 1993—. Mem. Chgo. Coun. Fgn. Rels., Citizens Against Govt. Waste, Abbott Labs. Better Govt. Fund. Republican. Avocations: golf, tennis. Office: Abbott Labs Bldg Apt 6B Abbott Park IL 60064

FRAZIER, ELAINE C., public health nurse; b. Beverly Farms, Mass., Dec. 27, 1942; d. George Ranceford and Eleanor Cashman (McKeigue) Frazier; children: Julia, Stuart. BS, Boston Coll., 1964; MS, U. Md., 1991. RN, Md. Pub. health nurse Washtenaw County Health Dept., Ann Arbor, Mich., 1964-65, 67-69; vol. nurse Afghan Mission Hosp., Peshawar, Pakistan, 1966-67; rsch. asst. Johns Hopkins, CMRT, Calcutta, India, 1970-72; vol. nurse with Mother Theresa Calcutta, India, 1971-72; mgr., nurse Balt., 1983-84; staff nurse Md. Gen. Hosp., Balt., 1986-88, nursing practice specialist, 1989-91; case mgr. Johns Hopkins Home Care, Balt., 1991-97; mem. planning com. U. Md. Community Health Conf., Balt., 1989—; guest lectr. grad. sch. nursing U. Md., Balt., 1990; witness U.S. Subcom. on Health, Washington, 1989; mem. Am. Community Svcs., Riyadh, Saudi Arabia, 1987-88. Mem. ANA, Md. Nurses Assn., Sigma Theta Tau. Roman Catholic. Avocations: international travel, volunteering professional services to Third World countries, swimming, tennis. Home: 904 Kingston Rd Baltimore MD 21212-1910 Office: Network Health Svcs Baltimore MD 21244

FRAZIER, HENRY BOWEN, III, retired judge, government official, lawyer; b. Bluefield, W.Va., Aug. 9, 1934; s. Henry Bowen and Margaret Beale (West) F.; m. Joan McIntosh, Dec. 30, 1959. BA with honors, U. Va., 1956; JD with honors, George Washington U., 1967; LLM in Labor Law, Georgetown U., 1969, MLT, 1985. Bar: Va. 1967, D.C. 1980, U.S. Supreme Ct. Personnel adminstr. Army Dept. Washington, 1959-63, spl. projects officer, 1963-67; dep. for civilian personnel policy and civil rights Office Sec. Army, 1967-70; chief program div. Fed. Labor Relations Council, Exec. Office Pres., 1970-71, dep. exec. dir., 1971-72, exec. dir., 1973-78; mem. Fed. Labor Relations Authority, Washington, 1979-87, acting chmn., 1984-85; adminstrv. law judge EPA, Washington, 1987-89, chief adminstrv. law judge, 1990-94; chmn. Employee Relations Commn., U.S. Fgn. Service, 1979-81; acting chmn. Fgn. Service Labor Relations Bd., 1984-85. With USAF, 1961-62. Mem. SAR, Fed. Adminstrv. Law Judges Conf., Jefferson Soc., U. Va. Alumni Assn. (nat. v.p. 1984-85, nat. pres. 1985-86, bd. mgrs. 1980-87), Va. Student Aid Found. (trustee 1990-97, v.p. 1995, pres. 1996), U. Va. Athletic Adv. Coun., Raven Soc., Order of Coif, Colonnade Club (bd. govs. 1997—), Glenmore Country Club, Duck Woods Country Club, Phi Beta Kappa, Omicron Delta Kappa, Phi Kappa Psi.

FRAZIER, HOWARD STANLEY, physician; b. Oak Park, Ill., Jan. 16, 1926; s. Cecil Austin and Harriet DeGolyer (Greenleaf) F.; m. Lenore Callahan, June 10, 1950; children—Mark C., Reid J., Anne K., Peter B. Ph.B., U. Chgo., 1949; M.D., Harvard U., 1953. Intern, then resident in medicine Mass. Gen. Hosp., Boston, 1953-55; postdoctoral fellow Harvard U. Med. Sch., 1955-56, Cambridge U., 1956-57, Case Western Res. U. Med. Sch., 1957-58; mem. faculty Harvard U. Med. Sch., 1958—, prof. medicine, 1978-96, prof. emeritus, 1996—; cons. NIH, Nat. Center Health Care Tech., Congl. Office Tech. Assessment. Author papers in field. Served with USNR, 1943-46. Mem. Am. Soc. Clin. Investigation, Am. Physiol. Soc., Am. Soc. Nephrology, Inst. Medicine. Office: 677 Huntington Ave Boston MA 02115-6028*

FRAZIER, JAMES MARTELL, JR., retired insurance company official; b. Van Buren, Mo., Mar. 23, 1940; s. James Martell and Grace Rosella (Holt) F.; m. Donna Lee Gossett, Feb. 19, 1968 (dec. Sept. 1981); 1 child, Troy A. m. Joyce Ann Barnes Wallace, Mar. 9, 1989; 3 stepchildren. CLU; ChFC. Collector Van Buren City Clk.'s Office, 1970-74, city clk., 1971-72; owner, operator variety store, Van Buren; ins. agt. Mo. Farm Bur. Ins. Co., Van Buren, 1972-75; agy. mgr. Mo. Farm Bur. Ins. Co., Van Buren, Jefferson City, 1972-85; regional sales mgr. Mo. Farm Bur. Ins. Co., Jefferson City, 1985-95, ret., 1995. Author: Fraziers in Carter County, 1997, The Holts of Missouri and the Pacific Northwest, 1998. Mem. Carter County R-1 Sch. Dist. Bd., Van Buren, 1977-85, teas., 1977-78, pres., 1979-80. With U.S. Army, 1962-64. Democrat. Avocations: recreational vehicling, travel, family research. Home: 617 W Main St Fordland MO 65652-9406

FRAZIER, J(OHN) PHILLIP, manufacturing company executive; b. Beech Grove, Ind., Mar. 2, 1939; s. Stanley C. and Dorothy E. Frazier; m. Carole Gilbert, Aug. 15, 1964; children: Gregory and Bradley (twins), Natalie. BS, Butler U., 1965; MBA, Harvard U., 1969. Acct. Wolf & Co., Indpls., 1962-65; fin. acct. Cummins Engine Co., Inc., Columbus, Ind., 1965-73, contr., 1970-73; dir. fin. planning Hyster, 1973-74, v.p. fin., 1974-82, sr. v.p. fin. and adminstrn., 1982-83; sr. v.p., mng. dir. Hyster Europe, 1983-85; pres., chief operating officer Hyster Co., 1985-88; pres., CEO, 1988-89; chmn., chief exec. officer Hyster-Yale Materials Handling, Inc., 1989-92; cons., 1993-94; operating ptnr. Stonebridge Ptnrs., 1995-96; pres., CEO Niagara Mohawk Energy sub. Niagara Mohawk Power Corp., 1996—; bd. dirs. Guy F. Atkinson Co. Calif. Bd. dirs. Oreg. Pub. Broadcasting. With USN, 1957-61. Mem. Harvard Univ. Bus. Sch. Assn. (past pres., chmn. Oreg. chpt.), Portland Golf Club, Arlington Club, Multnomah Athletic Club. Republican. Presbyterian. Avocations: golf, skiing, fly fishing. Home: Mission Landing 429 N Franklin St Apt 101 Syracuse NY 13204-1455

FRAZIER, JOHN W., physiologist, researcher; b. Wilmington, Ohio. With Wright-Patterson AFB, 1956—, rsch. physiologist. Recipient Eric Liljencrantz award, 1996. Fellow Aerospace Med. Assn.; mem. SAFE (Sr. Scientist award, Pres. award), Aerospace Physiology Soc. (space medicine br., Paul Bert award), Aerospace Human Factors Assn. (life scis. & biomed. engrng. br.). Office: AFRL/HESA 2245 Monahan Way Bldg 33 Wright Patterson AFB OH 45433-7008

FRAZIER, LEROY See DYYON, FRAZIER MARIO

FRAZIER, MARIE DUNN, speech educator, public relations and human resources specialist; b. Milton, Mass., Oct. 26, 1932; d. Lawrence Daniel and Margaret Ethel (Henry) D.; m. M. Timothy Sullivan, Apr. 17, 1960 (div. 1974); 1 child, M. Timothy Dunn Sullivan; m. John Robinson Frazier, Aug. 28, 1975. BA, Emerson Coll., 1954, MA, 1958. Cert. tchr., Mass. Mng. theater dir. Peabody Playhouse, Boston, 1955-60; dir. alumni rels. Emerson Coll., Boston, 1971-73; dir. activities, personal devel. faculty Katharine Gibbs, Boston, 1974-78; dir. rsch. and devel. Aquinas Coll., Milton, Mass., 1981-82; dir. cmty. rels. Bryman Sch., Brookline, Mass., 1981-84; resource developer Quincy (Mass.) Cmty. Action, 1987-89; adjunct faculty, lead program Eastern Nazarene Coll., Quincy, Mass., 1993—; adv. bd. Ctr. Lifelong Learning, Curry Coll., Milton, 1977; tng. in speech comm. for Digital Corp., Am. Sci. and Engring. Co., Gen. Time and Security Corp., Children's Hosp., Milton Savs. Bank; mem. speech comm. faculty Garland Jr. Coll., Boston, 1967-70, Aquinas Coll., Newton, Mass., 1991. Developed (seminar) Reflections on Tea, 1993. Bd. dirs. ACCLAIM Arts Group, Milton, 1989, D.W. Dunn Co., Jamaica Plain, Mass., 1962-65, Milton Hist. Soc., 1990-92, Coastline Coun. for Children, 1987; mem. bd. Mayor's Commn. for Women, Quincy, 1989—; ambassador South Shore C. of C., Quincy, 1990-91. Mem. AAUP, Zeta Phi Eta. Home: 25 Whitelawn Ave Milton MA 02186-3514

FRAZIER, PHILLIP M., federal judge. Magistrate judge U.S. Dist. Ct. (so. dist.), Benton, 1987—. Office: US Courthouse 301 Main St Benton IL 62812

FRAZIER, ROSA MAE, medical/surgical and hemodialysis nurse; b. Jacksonville, Fla., Feb. 16, 1925; d. John Oliver and Zeller M. (Chavious) Laster; m. Timothy Frazier, June 4, 1944; 1 child, Timothy Russell. Lic. practical nurse diploma, Phila. Pub. Schs., 1952; cert. in hemodialysis, U. South Fla.-VA Hosp., Tampa, 1975. Lic. practical nurse, Pa., Fla. Nurse orhopedic unit Pa. Coll. Medicine Osteo. Hosp., Phila.; operating room technician Episcopal Hosp., Phila., Hahnemann Med. Coll., Phila.; practical nurse, attending nurse for Alzheimer's patients Meth. Hosp., Jacksonville, Fla. Vol. emergency dept. U. Med. Ctr., Jacksonville. Fellow Salvation Army. Mem. Nat. Nurses Assn. Home: 3176 Ray Rd Jacksonville FL 32209-1840

FRAZIER, THOMAS C., protective services official; married; 3 children. BA in Social Scis., San Jose State U., MS in Adminstrn. of Criminal Justice. Mem. San Jose (Calif.) Police Dept., 1967-94, dep. chief bur. field ops.; commr. Balt. Police Dept., 1994—. Trustee Milton S. Eisenhower Found.; v.p. exploring Balt. Area coun. Boy Scouts Am.; mem. Empower Balt. Mgmt. Corp.; co-chair Gov.'s Coun. on Criminal and Juvenile Crime; active Md. Spl. Olympics, Project RAISE, Hist. East Balt. Cmty. Action Coalition, Inc., Downtown Partnership Pub. Safety Coalition; mem. Mayor's Adv. Commn. on Tourism, Entertainment and Culture. Decorated Bronze Star, Air medal. Mem. Internat. Assn. Chiefs of Police, Police Exec. Rsch. Forum, Major Cities Chiefs, Md. Chiefs of Police Assn., Fraternal Order of Police. Office: Balt Police Dept 601 E Fayette St Baltimore MD 21202-4014*

FRAZIER, TODD MEARL, retired health science adminstrator, epidemiologist; b. Lima, Ohio, Nov. 9, 1925; s. Todd M. and Gertrude (Blanks) F.; m. Barbara Welday, Sept. 28, 1946; children—Michael, Sarah, Nancy, David. A.B., Kenyon Coll., 1949; Sc.M., Johns Hopkins U., 1957. Dir. biostats. Balt. City Health, 1953-63; assoc. dir. planning and research D.C. Dept. Pub. Health, Washington, 1963-68; asst. dir. Harvard Ctr. Community Health and Med. Care, Harvard U., Boston, 1968-78; chief surveillance br. Nat. Inst. Occupational Safety and Health, Cin., 1978-92; assoc. prof. Harvard Sch. Pub. Health, Boston, 1968-78; cons. WHO, Geneva, 1971-78. Served with USN, 1943-46, U.S. Army, 1950-51. Fellow Am. Pub. Health Assn.; mem. Johns Hopkins U. Sch. Hygiene and Pub. Health Alulmni Soc. (alumnus award 1997), Sigma Xi, Delta Omega. Home: 2164 Cablecar Ct Cincinnati OH 45244-4101

FRAZIER, WALTER RONALD, real estate investment company executive; b. Dallas, Mar. 3, 1939; s. Walter and Gracie Neydene (Bowers) F.; m. Bertina Jan Simpson, May 10, 1963; children: Ronald Blake, Stephen Bertram. BS in Civil Engring., Tex. A&M U., 1962, BS in Archtl. Constrn., 1962. Tech. dir. Marble Inst., Washington, 1965-68; dir. mktg. Yeonas Co., Vienna, Va., 1969-72; pres. McCarthy Co., Anaheim, Calif., 1972-76, The Frazier Group, Annandale, Va., 1977-79; chmn. Equity Programs Investment Corp., Falls Church, Va., 1980-85; pres., dir. Community Constrn. Co., Falls Church, 1982-85; pres. Palestrina Corp., Falls Church, 1986—; pres. bd. dirs. Annandale Jaycees, 1967-69, Annandale Nat. Little League, 1983-85. Served to 1st lt. U.S. Army, 1963-65. Named to Outstanding Young Men Am., U.S. Jaycees, 1973. Mem. Nat. Assn. Home Builders (bd. dirs. 1991-95), No. Va. Bldg. Industry Assn., (1st v.p., bd. dirs. 1991-95, pres. 1994), Prince William County C. of C. (pres. bd. dirs. 1989-92). Republican. Methodist. Avocations: golf, boating. Home: 4203 Elizabeth Ln Annandale VA 22003-3668 Office: Palestrina Corp 5119A Leesburg Pike Ste 249 Falls Church VA 22041-3207

FRAZIN, RHONA SONDRA, non-profit executive; b. Chgo., Feb. 4, 1949; d. Herman C. and Harriet (Pozner) Berkowitz; m. Julian J. Frazin, Oct. 6, 1990. BS in Comm., U. Ill., 1970; postgrad., DePaul U., Chgo., 1971-72. Pub. info. coord. Ill. Arts Coun., Chgo., 1970-71; pub. rels. dir. Goodman Theatre, Chgo., 1971-76; asst. dir. The Nature Conservancy, Chgo., 1976-80; prin. Rhona Schultz & Assocs., Chgo., 1977-80; dir. devel./alumni The John Marshall Law Sch., Chgo., 1980-86; exec. v.p. Met. Family Svcs., Chgo., 1986—; comm. cons. Rhona Schultz & Assocs., 1977-80; devel. cons. Internat. Theater Festival of Chgo., 1986. Contbr. articles to profl. jours.; collaborator gridiron rev. Chgo. Bar Assn. Christmas Spirits, 1989-98. Mem. com. justice for youth Chgo. Bar Assn., 1989-93; mem. Chgo. coun. of Planned Giving; mem. frieds com., pub. chair Jesse Owens Found., 1993-97; founding dir. A Sporting Chance Found., mem. exec. com., 1995-99. Recipient Bronze Tablet award U. Ill., 1970. Mem. Nat. Soc. Fundraising Execs., U. Ill. Chgo. Scholarship Assn. Avocations: writing satire, tennis, hiking. Home: 1560 N Sandburg Ter Chicago IL 60610-1351 Office: Metropolitan Family Svcs 14 E Jackson Blvd Ste 1400 Chicago IL 60604-2217

FRAZZA, GEORGE S., lawyer, business executive; b. Paterson, N.J., Jan. 21, 1934; s. Paul T. and Myrtle Mary (Van Riper) F.; m. Marie Pollara, Sept. 17, 1955; children: Caren, Janine, Leslie, Lauren. A.B., Marietta Coll., 1955; LL.B., Columbia U., 1958. Bar: N.Y. 1959. Atty. Rogers & Wells, N.Y.C., 1958-66; atty. Johnson & Johnson, New Brunswick, N.J., 1966, assoc. gen. counsel, 1973, corp. sec., 1975, v.p., gen. counsel, 1978-97; of counsel Patterson, Belknap, Webb & Tyler, N.Y.C., 1997—. Bd. dirs. N.J. Ballet, Morristown, 1983-97. Mem. Assn. Gen. Counsel (pres.), ABA (chair elect bus. sect.), N.Y. State Bar Assn., Assn. of Bar of City of N.Y., Am. Corp. Counsel Assn., Am. Arbitration Assn. (bd. dirs.). Club: Roxiticus. Office: Patterson Belknap Webb & Tyler 1133 Avenue of Americas New York NY 10036-6710*

FRAZZETTA, THOMAS HENRY, evolutionary biologist, functional morphologist, educator; b. Rochester, N.Y., May 13, 1934; s. Joseph H. and Louise V. (Cross) F. B.S., Cornell U., 1957; Ph.D., U. Wash., 1964. Instr. in zoology U. Wash., Seattle, 1963-64; assoc. in herpetology Harvard U., Cambridge, Mass., 1964-65; asst. prof. U. Ill., Urbana, 1965-71, assoc. prof., 1971-76, prof. dept. ecology, ethology, evolution, 1976—. Author: Complex Adaptations in Evolving Populations, 1975; contbr. articles to jours. Active ACLU, World Wildlife Fedn., Planned Parenthood Fedn. Am., Zero Population Growth, Amnesty Internat. NIH postdoctoral fellow, 1964; NSF research grantee, 1969, 77, 86. Mem. AAAS, Am. Soc. Naturalists, Soc. Study of Evolution, Am. Soc. Ichthyologists and Herpetologists, Am. Elasmobranch Soc., Soc. for Integrative and Comparative Biology. Democrat.

E-mail: tomfrazz@uiuc.edu. Office: Univ Ill Dept Ecology Ethology and Evolution 515 Morrill Hall Urbana IL 61801

FREARS, STEPHEN, film director; b. Leicester, Eng., June 20, 1941; m. Anne Rothenstein; 4 children. BA in Law, Cambridge (Eng.) U. Lectr. in film Nat. Film Sch., Beaconsfield, U.K., 1987. Dir.: (stage) Waiting for Godot, 1964, Inadmissable Evidence, (TV) A Day Out, 1971, Match of the Day, 1972, Sunset Across the Bay, 1973, Playthings, 1975, Early Struggles, 1975, Last Summer, 1976, Cold Harbor, 1977, Three Men in a Boat, 1978, Long Distance in Formation, 1979, Going Gently, 1980, Bloody Kids, 1980, December Flower, 1984, Loving Walter, 1987, (films) The Burning, 1967, Gumshoe, 1972, Bloody Kids, 1979, Saigon-Year of the Cat, 1983, The Hit, 1984, My Beautiful Laundrette, 1985, Prick Up Your Ears, 1987, Sammy and Rosie Get Laid, 1987, Mr. Jolly Lives Next Door, 1987, Dangerous Liaisons, 1988, The Grifters, 1990, Hero, 1992, The Snapper, 1993, Mary Reilly, 1995, The Van, 1996, High Fidelity, 1999. Office: William Morris Agency 151 S El Camino Dr Beverly Hills CA 90212-2775*

FREAS, GEORGE WILSON, II, computer consultant; b. Franklin, Ky., Oct. 27, 1955; s. George Wilson and Audrey Carolyn Freas; m. Cynthia Anne Fleming, Feb. 19, 1984 (div. Oct. 1990); 1 child, Alexander Morange. BS in Computer Sci., Western Ky. U., 1979; MS in Computer Sci., U. Ala., Huntsville, 1994. Software cons. Bell South Telecom., Birmingham, Ala., 1995-98; pres. Synergistic Cons., Inc., Huntsville, 1991—; software cons. Internat. Space Station MSFC, AL Boeing, Ala., 1999—; adj. prof. Am. Inst. for Computer Sci., Birmingham, Ala., 1997—. Author: Canny Canon, 1990; author: (software) GEN7 Desktop, 1993, LALL-LL(1), 1992. Home: PO Box 2885 Huntsville AL 35804-2885 Office: Synergistic Consultants Inc PO Box 18888 Huntsville AL 35804-8888

FRÉCHET, JEAN MARIE JOSEPH, chemistry educator; b. Chalon, France, Aug. 18, 1944; came to U.S., 1967; s. Victor H. and Renée F.; m. Janet R. Manning, Nov. 25, 1967; children: Jacques Christopher, Marc Alexander. MSc, SUNY, Syracuse, 1969, PhD, 1971; PhD, Syracuse U., 1971. Asst. prof. chemistry U. of Ottawa, Can., 1973-78, assoc. prof. chemistry, 1978-82, prof. chemistry, 1982-87; IBM prof. chemistry Cornell U., Ithaca, N.Y., 1987-95, P.J. Debye chair chemistry, 1996—; prof. chemistry U. Calif., Berkeley, 1996—; vis. scientist IBM Rsch. Lab., San Jose, Calif., 1979, 83; vice dean grad. studies and rsch. U. Ottawa, 1983-87; cons. Xerox Corp., 1979-88, Allied Signal Corp., Morristown, 1986-93, Exxon Corp., Linden, N.J., 1988—, E.I. duPont de Nemours, Wilmington, 1990-93, Loctite, 1993—, Pharmacia, 1993-95, Miles, 1994, Bayer, 1996—, Symyx, 1996—, Rhone Poulenc, 1994—, Pharmacopeia, 1995—, Kodak, 1997—, Unilever, 1997; bd. dirs. Ont. Ctr. for Materials Rsch., Toronto. Contbr. numerous articles to profl. jours.; patentee in field. Recipient Award Internat. Union Pure and Applied Chemistry, 1983, Polymer Soc. of Japan, 1986, A.K. Doolittle award, 1986, Coop. Rsch. award Am. Chem. Soc., 1994, Applied Polymer Chem. award Am. Chem. Soc., 1996; numerous grants for rsch. Avocation: oenophile. Office: U Calif 718 Latimer Hall Berkeley CA 94720-1460

FRECHETTE, BONNIE L., secondary education educator; b. Green Bay, Wis., Oct. 23, 1946; d. Frank martin and Grace Emilia (Yindra) Jirovetz; m. David H. Frechette, June 23, 1973. BS, U. Wis., Oshkosh, 1969; MA, Viterbo Coll., LaCrosse, Wis., 1992. English tchr. West DePere H.S., DePere, Wis., 1969—. Recipient Golden Apple Tchr. of Distinction award Ptnrs. in Edn., 1996; named Dist. Tchr. of Yr., Wis. State Dept. Instrn., 1986-87; Kohl Found. scholar, 1997. Mem. Nat. Coun. Tchrs. English, Wis. Coun. Tchrs. English (dist. dir. 1987—). Avocations: reading, theater and film. walking. Office: West DePere HS 665 Grant St De Pere WI 54115-1367

FRÉCHETTE, LOUISE, Canadian diplomat. With dept. external affairs Govt. of Can., from early 1970s, amb. to Argentina and Uruguay, 1985; asst. dep. min. for L.Am. and Caribbean Ministry of Fgn. Affairs, 1988, asst. dep. min. for internat. econ. and trade policy, 1991-92; amb. to UN, 1992-94; assoc. dep. min. Can. Dept. Fin., 1994-95, Can. Dept. of Fin., 1995; dep. minister def. Govt. of Can., 1995-98; dep. sec. gen. UN, 1998—.

FRECHETTE, PETER LOREN, dental products executive; b. Janesville, Wis., Aug. 15, 1937; s. Francis Michael and Gladys Jean F.; m. Patricia Jean O'Brien, June 24, 1961; children: Kathleen and Kristen (twins). B.S. in Econs., U. Wis., 1960; M.B.A., Northwestern U. 1980. Pres. Sci. Products, McGaw Park, Ill., 1975-82; pres., CEO Patterson Dental Co., Mpls., 1982—. Served with U.S. Army, 1961-63. Mem. Am. Dental Trade Assn. Office: Patterson Dental Co 1031 Mendota Heights Rd Mendota Heights MN 55120

FRED, ROGERS MURRAY, III, veterinary oncologist; b. Leesburg, Va., July 22, 1955; s. Rogers Murray Jr. and Barbara Ann (Stewart) F.; m. Kimberly Edna Shepherd, Oct. 15, 1989; 1 child, Asa Hugh Shepherd. BS, Washington and Lee U., 1977; postgrad., U. Ga., 1979-81; DVM, Va. Poly. Inst., 1985. Staff veterinarian Abbey Animal Hosp., Balt., 1986-89; resident in vet. oncology U. Pa., Phila., 1989-91; clin. oncologist Red Bank (N.J.) Vet. Hosp. & Referral Svc., 1991—; lectr. in field. Co-author: Connective Tissues in Health & Disease, 1980. Bd. dirs. Ebenezer Chs. and Cemetery Co., Bloomfield, Va., 1986—, Monmouth Hills (N.J.), Inc. Mem. SCV (camp comdr. 1988-90), Am. Vet. Med. Assn., Vet. Cancer Soc., N.J. Vet. Med. Assn., Assn. for Preservation of Civil War Sites, Phi Kappa Phi, Phi Zeta. Republican. Episcopalian. Avocations: reading, walking, battlefield touring, ornithology. Home: 15 Monmouth Hills Highlands NJ 07732 Office: Red Bank Vet Hosp 210 Newman Springs Rd Red Bank NJ 07701-1465

FREDEN, SHARON ELSIE CHRISTMAN, state education assistant commissioner; b. Watertown, S.D., Jan. 11, 1941; d. Harlon Arthur and Mildred Lillian (Jensen) Christman; m. Noble Everett Freden, July 3, 1973; 1 child, Anne Victoria. B.S., No. State Coll., Aberdeen, S.D., 1962; M.A., U. Iowa, 1966; Ed.D., U. Colo., 1973. Tchr. Manitowoc Pub. Schs., Wis., 1962-64, Boulder Valley Pub. Schs., Colo., 1966-70, K-12 lang. arts cons., 1970-72; cons. Colo. Dept. Edn., Denver, 1973-76, 77-80; ITV inservice coordinator Sta. KCPT Channel 19, Kansas City, Mo., 1980-81; dir. Kans. State Dept. Edn., Topeka, 1981-84, asst. commr., 1984—. Editor: Basic Skills: Promising Practices in Colorado, 1979; (with others) Pupil Progress in Colorado, 1978. Contbr. to books. Precinct com. chmn. Democratic Party, Broomfield, Colo., 1978. Hildegard Sweet Meml. scholar, 1972, YWCA Leadership award, 1990. Mem. Assn. Supervision and Curriculum Devel., Kans. Assn. Supervision and Curriculum Devel., United Sch. Adminstrs., Phi Delta Kappa. Home: 3711 SW 31st St Topeka KS 66614-2809 Office: Kans State Dept Edn 120 E 10th Topeka KS 66612

FREDERES, MARSHALL, stockbroker; b. June 28, 1948. BA, Univ. Fla., Gainesville, FL, 1970. Fin. cons. Shearson Lehmax Hutton, San Francisco, CA, 1985-90; assoc. vice pres. Raymond James & Assoc., Greenville, SC, 1990—. Home: 5 Cannon Lane Taylors SC 29687

FREDERICH, KATHY W., social worker; b. Ashland, Ky., Apr. 19, 1953; d. James Greeley and Jo Ann (Sparks) Walker; divorced; m. Harry Donald Frederich, Sept. 5, 1987; stepchild, David Scott. BA with distinction, U. Ky., 1978; MS with honors, Ea. Ky. U., 1994. Tng. supr. Blue Grass Assn. for Retarded Citizens, Lexington, Ky., 1971-75, Bur. Vocational Rehab., Lexington, 1976-77; social worker Ky. Dept. for Social Svcs., Lexington, 1978-79, field office supr., 1979-85; social work/domestic violence prog. specialist, conf. coord. Ky. Dept. for Social Svcs., Frankfort, 1985-97, tng. instr., 1987—; assoc. dir. families and children tng. project Ea. Ky. U., Richmond, 1997—; instr. Ky. Sheriff's Acad., 1986-92; cert. instr. domestic violence Ky. State Police, 1995—; cert. instr. Levington Fayette div. police, 1981-87, 90-91; cons., trainer for social svcs., 1983—; mem. adv. bd. Assn. for Older Kentuckians, 1983-89; mem. Ky. Law Enforcement Tng. Project, 1989-91; mem. Atty. Gen.'s Task Force on Domestic Violence Crime, 1991-93, Legis. Task Force on Domestic Violence, 1994-95; coord. 1st Nat. Teleconf. on Domestic Violence and Family Preservation Svcs., 1994; mem. Gov.'s Coun. Domestic Violence, 1996-97; staff facilitator Nat. Coll. Dist. Attys. domestic violence conf., 1995; mem. Domestic Violence Jud. Edn. Planning Com., 1995-96; asst. course dir., presenter Nat. Coll. Dist. Attys., 1997, 98; cons. in field. Contbr. articles to profl. jours. Ad hoc grant com. Violence Against Women Act, 1995. Recipient Outstanding Svc. award Lexington Fayette div. of Police, 1984, Ky. Sheriff's Acad. Hon. Grad., 1989, tributes, 1986-88, Outstanding Kentuckian award Gov. Martha Layne Collins, 1987, Outstanding Young Am. Women award, 1987, Outstanding Victim Adv. award Lexington Urban County Govt., 1990, Outstanding Victim Advocacy award Ky. Victims' Coalition, 1993, Outstanding Svcs. Recognition Senate Ky. Gen. Assembly, 1995, Ky. Commn. Women, 1996, Exemplary Svc. award Ky. Dept. for Social Svcs., 1997; named Ky. Col., 1985, 96, Outstanding Alumni, Ea. Ky. U. Coll. Law Enforcement, 1996. Mem. Ky. Domestic Violence Assn. (homicide-suicide task force 1990-94), Ky. Law Enforcement Coun. (cert.). Democrat. Avocations: camping, hiking, reading, music, boating.

FREDERICI, C. CARLETON, lawyer; b. Sioux City, Iowa, Jan. 17, 1938; s. Cecil Carleton and Lois Alida (Selzer) F.; m. Virginia A. Gregori, Oct. 14, 1961 (div.); m. Susan A. Low, Oct. 1, 1983; children: Gloria M., Carleton J., Charles W., Seth L. Student Iowa State U., 1956. BA, U. Iowa, 1960, JD with high distinction, 1965. Bar: Iowa 1965, N.Y. 1966, U.S. Dist. Ct. (no. dist.) Iowa 1968, U.S. Dist. Ct. (so. dist.) Iowa 1969, U.S. Supreme Ct. 1970, U.S. Ct. Appeals (8th cir.) 1970, U.S. Ct. Appeals (3d cir.) 1973. Assoc. firm Willkie, Farr & Gallagher, N.Y.C., 1965-68, firm Shull, Marshall & Marks, Sioux City, Iowa, 1968-69; assoc. firm Davis, Brown, Koehn, Shors & Roberts, P.C., Des Moines, 1969-71, jr. ptnr., 1971-73, sr. ptnr., 1973-90, shareholder, 1990-95, counsel, 1996—; speaker Supreme Ct. Day, Law Sch. Drake U., 1973. Contbr. articles to legal publs. Vestryman St. Luke's Ch., bd. dirs. 1976-78, 1982-85; mem. Polk County Rep. Cen. Com., 1969-71. Served to 1st lt. U.S. Army, 1961-62. Mem. ABA (chmn. 8th cir. commn. on class actions and derivative suits), Iowa Bar Assn. (chmn. prison reform com., adv. mem. fed. practice commn., litigation sect. bench and bar com.), Polk County Bar Assn. (bench and bar com.), Assn. Bar City N.Y., Am. Judicature Soc. (bd. dirs. Iowa 1990-96), Order of Coif, Wakonda Club (Des Moines). Episcopalian. Office: Davis Brown Koehn Shors & Roberts PC 666 Walnut St Ste 2500 Des Moines IA 50309-3904

FREDERICK, CRAIG MATTHEW, sculptor; b. New Britain, Conn., Feb. 27, 1963; s. Theodore John and Joyce Chase Frederick; m. Laura Jean Wixon, Oct. 4, 1997. BA in Geology and Biology, Skidmore Coll., 1985; MFA in Sculpture, U. Pa., 1992. Tchr. St. Mary's Hall, San Antonio, 1986-89, U. Pa., Phila., 1991, Galveston (Tex.) Coll., 1992-94; sculptor The Bob Wilson Art Foundry, Houston, 1993-94; sculptor, owner Sculpture by Craig, New Britain, 1994—; tchr. The Black Brick Studio and Gallery, Plainville, Conn., 1994—; devel. bd. mem. N.B. Landmark Com., City Hall, New Britain, 1994-95, Summer Learning Arts Mentorship, 1997; lectr. in field. One-man shows include The Colonade, Phila., 1991, The Stanley Works World Hdqrs., Farmington, Conn., 1992, The Loomis Chaffee Sch., Windsor, Conn., 1992, Two Houston Ctr., 1993, The Geary Gallery, Darien, Conn., 1996, The Black Brick Studio and Gallery, Plainville, 1997, 98; exhibited at group shows at Inst. Contemporary Art, Phila., 1990, Meyerson Gallery, U. Pa., 1991, 92, Gutman Ctr., New Hope, Pa., 1992, Galveston (Tex.) Art Ctr., 1992, Machorro Gallery, Houston, 1993, Jack Meier Gallery, Houston, 1993, Black Brick Studio and Gallery, Plainville, 1994, 96, 98, New Britain Mus. Am. Art, 1995, New Britain Art League, 1995, Pump House Gallery, Hartford, Conn., 1997, Hartford Fine Art and Framing, 1998, Pfizer, Inc., Groton, Conn., 1998, 99, Charter Oak Cultural Ctr., Hartford, 1998; represented in permanent collections New Britain Pub. Libr., Petrolios Mexicanos, Mexico City, Art Foundry Carpino, Houston, Yarde Metals, Inc., Bristol, Conn. Cons., mem. Vision New Britain, 1994-97; mem. long range planning com. New Britain Mus. Am. Art, 1995-97; mem., activist New Britain Archtl. Preservation Trust, 1996-97; original mem. initial concepts The New Arch Com., New Britain, 1997-98. Holt/Dupont grantee Holt/Dupont Orgns., San Antonio, 1988. Mem. Internat. Sculpture Ctr., Greater New Britain Arts Alliance (co-founder, pres. 1996-97), Guild.Com (represented artist). E-mail: SculptByC@aol.com.

FREDERICK, DOLLIVER H., investment banker; b. Edmonton, Alta., Can., Apr. 2, 1944; s. Henry and Gladys (Gaede) F.; student Alta Coll., U. Alta., grad. bus. adminstrn. No. Alta. Inst. Tech., 1965; m. Joan B. Dickau, Aug. 28, 1965; children: Blayne Jeffrey, Tamara Lea. With Imperial Oil Ltd., Edmonton, 1965-72, sr. analyst mktg., Toronto, Ont., 1972-73; corp. devel. mgr. Hees Internat. (formerly Bovis Corp. Ltd.), 1973-75, corp. v.p., 1975-79; pres., chief operating officer Gen. Supply Co. Can. (1973) Ltd., 1975-79, Equipment Fed. Que. Ltd., 1975-79; pres., chief exec. officer, dir. CanWest Investment Corp., Toronto, Ont., 1979-81; chmn. exec. com., dir. Na-Churs Plant Food Co., Marion, Ohio, 1979-81, Macleod-Stedman, Inc., Winnipeg and Toronto, 1980-81; chmn., pres., chief exec. officer, dir. Cochrane-Dunlop Ltd., 1982-87, Frederick Capital Corp. (Can.) Inc., 1981—, pres., chief exec. officer, dir. Comterm Inc., 1989-90; Electrohome Limited, 1985-87, Can. Coun. of Christians and Jews, Engineers Club of Toronto; adv. bd. mem. Noram Capital Mgmt. Mem. Assn. Corp. Growth, World Pres.'s Orgn. Republican. Clubs: Nat., Cambridge, Can. Club N.Y., Pacific Club. Office: Frederick Capital Corp Ste 3000 5000 Birch St Newport Beach CA 92660-2127

FREDERICK, EDWARD CHARLES, university official; b. Mankato, Minn., Nov. 17, 1930; s. William H. and Wanda (MacNamara) F.; m. Shirley Lunkenheimer, Aug. 16, 1951; children: Bonita Frederick Treangen, Diane Frederick Fox, Donald, Kenneth, Karen Frederick Swenson. B.S. in Agrl. Edn, U. Minn., 1954, M.S. in Dairy Husbandry, 1955, Ph.D. in Anatomy and Physiology, 1957. Animal scientist, instr. N.W. Sch. and Expt. Sta. U. Minn., Crookston, 1958-64; supt. So. Sch. and Expt. Sta. U. Minn., Waseca, 1964-69, provost Tech. Coll., 1969-85, chancellor Tech. Coll., 1985-90; sr. fellow Hubert H. Humphrey Inst. Pub. Affairs, 1990-91, U. Minn. Coll. of Agriculture, 1991—; Mem. Tech. Agrl. Edn. Study Team to Morocco, 1977. Contbr. articles on dairy physiology, mgmt., agrl. edn. and adminstrn. to tech. jours. and popular publs. Bd. dirs. Bob Hodgson Student Loan Fund, 1971-90, Minn. Agrl. Interpretive Ctr., 1978—, chair, 1994—; bd. dirs. Minn. Agri-Growth Coun., 1980—, pres. 1992—; bd. dirs. Southeastern Minn. Initiative Fund, 1986-92, v.p., 1991-92; bd. dirs. Waseca area United Way, 1988-94, pres., 1992; bd. dirs. Minn. Agriculture in the Classroom, 1993—, pres., 1995-96. Recipient Alumni award 4-H, 1972, Good Neighbor award, WCCO, 1990, Ed Frederick Day award State of Minn., 1990, Award of Merit Gamma Sigma Delta, 1994. Mem. Am. Dairy Assn., Am. Soc. Animal Prodn., AAAS, Nat. Assn. Colls. and Tchrs. Agr. (pres. 1976-77), Am. Assn. Community and Jr. Colls. (pres. Council of Two Yr. Colls. of Four Yr. Instns. 1988-90), Minn. FFA Alumni Assn. (pres. 1998—), South Central Edn. Assn. (Disting. Service award 1971), Waseca Area C. of C. (dir. 1979), Phi Kappa Phi. Roman Catholic. Club: Foresters. Lodges: Rotary (gov. dist. 596 1982-83); K.C. Home: 39031 State Highway 13 Waseca MN 56093-4212 Office: U Minn Coll Agrl Food and Env Sci Waseca MN 56093

FREDERICK, GEORGE FRANCIS, manufacturing executive; b. Cleve., Jan. 24, 1937; s. George Henry and Margaret Mary (Gibson) F.; m. Mary Jane Masielli, Oct. 20, 1956; children: Denise Marie, George Charles, Donna Marie, Karl Stephen. Assoc. in Machine Design, Cleve. Engring. Inst., 1957; BS, SUNY, Albany, 1977. Cert. mfg. engr. Supr. mfg. engring. Sq. D Co., Cleve., 1956-66; supr. stds. engring. TRW, Cleve., 1966-69; mgr. engring. Rossgear divsn. TRW, Ind. and Tenn., 1969-80; ops. mgr. Control Concepts divsn. TRW, Newton, Pa., 1980-82; gen. mgr. Falcon Products, Greeneville, Tenn., 1982-84; sr. v.p. ops. Lockley Mfg. Group divsn. of Entwistle Co., Hudson, Mass., 1984-92, pres., 1992-95; exec. v.p., gen. mgr., dir. Advanced Tech. and Rsch. Corp., Burtonsville, Md., 1996—; bd. dirs. Jameson Health Care System, Lawrence County Econ. Devel. Corp. Co-chmn. New Castle Area Labor Mgmt. Com., 1987-95; dist. chmn. Boy Scouts Am., Greeneville, 1982-83, 1987-88; bd. dirs. United Way, 1981. Mem. KC, Inst. Indsl. Engrs. (sr. mem. exec. bd. 1972-74), The Mfrs. Assn., Lions. Republican. Roman Catholic. Avocations: golf, reading, computers. Home: 255 Par Ln Greeneville TN 37743 Office: Advanced Tech and Rsch Corp 15210 Dino Dr Burtonsville MD 20866-1172

FREDERICK, LIZETTA MARY, educator, counselor; b. Franklin, La., May 15, 1954; d. Joseph and Juanita Mary (Goulas) F. BA in English, U. New Orleans, 1977, MA in English Tchg., 1988; postgrad., Nicholls State. Cert. secondary education educator, La. Writer, reporter St. Mary Jour. Newspaper, Morgan City, La., 1980-81; instr. English JTPA Program Delgado Coll., New Orleans, 1988-89; instr. writing ctr. Xavier U. of La., New Orleans, 1989-91; coord. vols. Meals on Wheels, San Francisco, 1991-92; devel. assoc. Lighthouse for the Blind, San Francisco, 1992-93; instr. English Nicholls State U., Thibodaux, La., 1994-97; acad. skills specialist, 1997—; tchr. English Franklin (La.) Sr. H.S., 1995-96, Ctrl. Cath. H.S., Morgan City, 1996-97; faculty rep. Ctrl. Cath. Devel. Com., Morgan City, 1996-97. Sponsor Beta Club, Franklin Sr. H.S., 1995-96, SADD, Ctrl. Cath. H.S., 1996-97. Mem. Nat. Coun. Tchrs. English, La. Acad. Advising Assn., U. New Orleans Alumni Assn., Delta Zeta (del. to nat. conv. 1975, 83, 89, editor alumnae newsletter New Orleans chpt. 1977-78, pres. house corp. Theta Kappa chpt. 1979, province alumnae dir. 1980-82, dir. coll. chpt. 1988-90, Collegiate award 1976). Democrat. Roman Catholic. Avocations: reading, travel.

FREDERICK, LLOYD RANDALL, soil microbiologist; b. Shannon, Ill., Aug. 5, 1921; s. Elmer Lewis and Ina Hattie (Hendricks) F.; m. Shirley Althea Miller, Oct. 20, 1943; children: June Ann, Mary Lou, David Randall. BS, U. Nebr., 1943; PhD, Rutgers U., 1950. Asst. prof. soil microbiology Purdue U., West Lafayette, Ind., 1949-55; prof. soil microbiology Iowa State U., Ames, 1955-78; sr. soil microbiologist U.S. Agy. Internat. Devel., Washington, 1978-89; cons. Ames, Iowa, 1989—; cons. W.R. Grace & Co., Princeton, Ill., 1966-70, Rsch. Seeds, St. Joseph, Mo., 1970-74; cons., Cambridge, Iowa, 1989-98, Ames, Iowa, 1998—. Author (with others): Methods of Soil Analysis, 1985; contbr. articles to profl. jours. Pres. Collegiate Meth. Credit Union, Ames, 1962-71; lay speaker United Meth. Ch., Iowa, 1960-75. Soil Sci. Soc. Am. fellow, 1961; Fulbright scholar, 1962. Mem. Am. Soc. Agronomy (fellow 1961). Republican. Achievements include research on temperature relationship of conversion of ammonium to nitrate in soil, importance of very high number of rhizobia for good nodulation and nitrogen fixation by legumes, retention of ammonia by soils, delayed conversion to nitrate in application zone of ammonia in soils. Home and Office: 2344 Hilton Ct Ames IA 50014-8264

FREDERICK, NORMAN L., JR., electrical engineer; b. Hopkinsville, Ky., Feb. 7, 1965; s. Norman L. and Nancy A. (Bass) F. ASES, Hudson Valley C.C., 1985; BSEE, Union Coll., Schenectady, 1987; MSEE, Syracuse U., 1990. Comm. engr. GE, Schenectady, 1986; systems engr. Rome Air Force devel. ctr. MITRE, Griffiss AFB, Rome, N.Y., 1987-89; researcher, teaching asst. Syracuse (N.Y.) U., 1989-90; R&D elec. engr. HP EESOF divsn. Hewlett Packard, Westlake Village, Calif., 1991-98; sr. RF engr. Qualcomm, Inc., San Diego, 1998—. Mem. IEEE, Tau Beta Pi, Eta Kappa Nu, Sigma Xi. Achievements include research on one to three phase converter circuits, near fields for phased array antennas; development of T-Matrix method for relation of current distribution to near field, communication systems and RF-microwave circuit simulators, RX,TX design for cellular phones. Office: Qualcomm Inc 6455 Lusk Blvd San Diego CA 92121

FREDERICK, RAYMOND JOSEPH, sales engineering executive; b. Chgo., Oct. 27, 1948; s. Clarence W. and Lorraine T. (Frey) F.; m. Doreen Lynne Thompson, Nov. 7, 1970; children: Victoria Lynne, Steven, Joseph. Student, U. Ill., Chgo., 1966-68, Tri-State Coll., Angola, Ind., 1968-69; BSEE, Chgo. Tech. Coll., 1974. Technician, jr. engr. Rauland-Borg Corp., Chgo., 1970-74, assoc. engr., 1974-75, design engr., 1975-78, application engr., 1978-79, sales engr., 1979-81, product mgr., 1981-83; sales engr. Nichimen Am. Inc., Chgo., 1983-87; mgr. sales engring. Nichimen Am. Inc., Farmington Hills, Mich., 1987—. Pres. Westgate Civic Assn., Farmington Hills, 1989—. Eagle Scout. Mem. Soc. Automotive Engrs., Intelligent Vehicle Hwy. System Am., Nat. Assn. Broadcasters. Roman Catholic. Avocations: golf, fishing, boating, home repairs, computers. Home: 30180 Richmond Hl Farmington Hills MI 48334 Office: Nichimen Am Inc 32000 Northwestern Hwy Ste 155 Farmington Hills MI 48334

FREDERICK, ROBERT ALLEN, history educator; b. Mishawaka, Ind., Feb. 3, 1928; s. Ralph Leon and Garnet Laree (Bowles) F.; m. Mary Billington Swartz, Nov. 23, 1950 (div. Sept. 1967); children: Carol Heren Frederick Asi, John Billington, Peter Carey; m. Saradell Carolyn Ard, Sept. 9, 1969 (div. April 1983). BA, Hanover Coll., 1950; MS in Edn., Ind. U., 1951, PhD in History, 1960. Assoc. dean students Tex. Technol. Coll., Lubbock, 1951-53; instr. history U.S. Naval Acad. Prep Sch., 1953-56; grad. asst. history Ind. U., Bloomington, 1956-58, fellow dept. history, 1958-60; assoc. prof. history Alaska Meth. U., Anchorage, 1960-66, prof. history, chmn. dept., 1966-73; exec. dir. Alaska Hist. Commn., Anchorage, 1973-80; ind. rschr./writer Alaska Hist. Soc., Anchorage, 1980-85; editor Ind. German Heritage Soc., Indpls., 1986-88; Richard Lieber rschr. Brown County Hist. Soc., Nashville, Ind., 1988-93; dir. Alaska humanities task force NEH, 1972-73. Editor/contbr. Frontier alaska: Historical Opportunity, 1968, writing Alaskas History: A Guide to Research, 1974, Anchorage: Star of the North, 1982; author: Alaska's quest for Statehood: 1867-1959, 1985; editor newsletter Ind. German Heritage Soc., 1986-89. Pres. Cook Inlet Hist. Soc., Anchorage, bd. dirs., 1963—; pres. Alaska Hist. Soc., 1968-69, bd. dirs., 1967-74; mem. nat. archives adv. bd. Nat. Archives and Records Svcs., Regions IX and X, 1974-77; chmn. Nat. Trust for Hist. Preservation, 1975-77, bd. advisors, 1969-78; dir. A Pioneer Family in Alaska (film) U. Alaska Found., Homer, 1982. Lt. USNR, 1953-56. Ind. Heritage Rsch. grantee Ind. Humanities Coun., 1987-91. Mem. Historic Landmarks Found. Ind., Sigma Chi (life). Democrat. Avocations: hiking in wilderness, visiting natural and historical sites. Home: 352 Wilmington Ct Bloomington IN 47401-4246

FREDERICK, ROBERT MELVIN, farm organization executive; b. Wadsworth, Ohio, Feb. 1, 1923; s. Llewellyn Rorthrock and Golda May (Joycox) F.; m. Rosemary Rothgary, Feb. 14, 1955; children: Pamela Sue, Mark Llewllyn. BA, Ohio State U., 1948. Horticulturist family farm, Wadsworth, 1948-56; ext. horticulturist Purdue U., Vincennes, Ind., 1957-59; exec. sec. Am. Vegetable Growers Assn., Washington, 1959-61; gen. mgr. Fla. Flower Assn., Ft. Myers, 1961-63, Fla. Growers Coop., Ft. Myers, 1963-66; pres. Ruke Transport, Ft. Myers, 1966-67; sales mgr. Green Thumb Products, Toledo, 1967-68; legis. dir. Nat. Grange, Washington, 1968-96, dir. adminstrn., 1996—; mem. agr. policies adv. com. USDA/U.S. Trade Rep., Washington, 1970-80, mem. fruit and vegetable com., 1981-84; mem. agr. census adv. com. Dept. Commerce, Washington, 1971-85. Mem. Medina County (Ohio) Rep. Com., 1956. Sgt. USMCR, 1942-45, PTO. Recipient Alumni Disting. Svc. award Ohio State U., 1995, Agr. Frat. Centennial hon. Alpha Zeta, 1997. Mem. Nat. Planning Assn. (food and agr. com.), Nat. Grange (7th degree, past master, ec., exec. com. Potomac chpt.). Avocation: gardening. Office: Nat Grange 1616 H St NW Washington DC 20006-4999

FREDERICK, SHERMAN, publishing executive. Pub. Las Vegas (Nev.) Rev.-Jour. Office: Las Vegas Rev-Journal 1111 W Bonanza Rd Las Vegas NV 89106-3545

FREDERICK, VIRGINIA FIESTER, state legislator; b. Rock Island, Ill., Dec. 24, 1916; d. John Henry and Myrtle (Montgomery) Heise; B.A., U. Iowa, 1938; postgrad. Lake Forest Coll., 1942-43, LLD, 1994; m. C. Donnan Fiester (dec. 1975); children—Sheryl Fiester Ross, Alan R., James D.; m. Kenneth Jacob Frederick, 1978. Free-lance fashion designer, Lake Forest, Ill., 1952-78; pres. Mid Am. China Exchange, Kenilworth, Ill., 1978-81; mem. Ill. Ho. of Reps., Springfield, 1979-95, asst minority leader, 1990-95. Alderman, first ward Lake Forest, 1974-78; del. World Food Conf., Rome, 1974; mem. Ill. Commn. on Status of Women subcom. pensions and employment, 1976-79; co-chmn. Conf. Women Legislators, 1982-85; bd. trustees Lake Forest Coll., 1995—; city supr. City of Lake Forest, Ill., 1995-98; bd. dirs. Lake Forest Symphony Guild, 1998—. Named Chgo. Area Woman of Achievement, Internat. Orgn. Women Execs., 1978. Recipient Lottie Holman O'Neal award, 1980, Jane Addams award, 1982, Outstanding Legislator award Ill. Hosp. Assn., 1986, VFW Svc. award, 1988, Joyce Fitzgerald Meml. award, 1988, Susan B. Anthony Legislator of the Yr. award, 1989, award Delta Kappa Gamma, 1991, Outstanding Legislator award, 1995, Svcs. for Srs. award, Ill. Dept. Aging, 1991, Ethics in Pols. award, Rep. Women's Club, 1992, Woman of Achievement award YWCA North Eastern Ill., 1994, Ill. Women in Govt. award, 1994. Mem. LWV (local pres. 1958-60, state dir. 1969-75, mem. nat. com. 1975-76), AAUW (local pres. 1968-70, state pres. 1975-77, state dir. 1963-69, mem. nat. com. 1967-69, Legislator of Yr. award 1993), UN Assn. (dir.), Chgo. Assn. Commerce and Industry (dir.). Methodist. Home: 1290 N Western Ave Lake Forest IL 60045-1237

FREDERICK-MAIRS, T(HYRA) JULIE, administrative health services official; b. Islip, N.Y., Jan. 4, 1941; d. Manuel and Thyra C. (thorsen)

Cajiao. BA, Adelphi U., 1961; MSW, U. So. Calif., 1972, MPA, 1991. Social worker L.A. County Dept. Social Svcs., 1966-67, social work supr., 1967-70, planning cons., 1972-76; dep. to supr. 4th dist. L.A. County, 1976-80; asst. dir. L.A. County Office Alcohol Programs, 1980-90; assoc. adminstr. ELACO Health Ctrs., 1990-97; CEO East Country Health Ctrs., 1997—; fellow U. So. Calif., 1988-90. Author: (with others) Youth Program Planning, 1975. Trustee LEARNS, 1992; active L.A. Child Sexual Abuse Project, Commn. for Sexual Equality, L.A. Unified Sch. Dist., Harbor Policy Cmty. Adv. Coun., L.A.; mem. Perinatal Substance Abuse Coun. L.A.; mem. ops. com. Interagy. Coun. Child Abuse and Neglect; adv. com. UCLA Alcohol Rsch. Ctr. c. Mem. Los Amigos de la Humanidad, DHS Latino Mgrs., Alpha Epsilon Delta, Beta Beta Beta, Bus. and Profl. Women's Club, Soroptimists (pres. L.A. County chpt. 1986-88, dir. Found. of L.A. 1986-88).

FREDERICKS, ALAN, editor-in-chief; b. N.Y.C., Sept. 11, 1934; s. Arthur Joseph and Sylvia Ernestine (Herzberg) Israel; m. Natalie Levinson, Nov. 6, 1955 (div. 1977); children: Lon Scott, Todd Steven. BA, NYU, 1955; MA, New Sch. Social Rsch., 1986. Radio announcer WBRE, Wilkes Barre, Pa., 1954, WABJ, Adrian, Mich., 1955-56, WGBB, Freeport, N.Y., 1956-58, WHOM, N.Y.C., 1958-59, WADO, N.Y.C., 1960-66; assoc. editor Travel Weekly, N.Y.C., 1966-67, mng. editor, 1967-72, editor, 1972-87; editor-in-chief Travel Weekly, Secaucus, N.J., 1987—, v.p., editl. dir. Fellow Inst. Cert. Travel Agts. Office: Reed Travel Group 500 Plaza Dr Secaucus NJ 07094-3685*

FREDERICKS, BARRY IRWIN, lawyer; b. Bklyn., Oct. 3, 1936; m. Beverly Sharon Cohen, June 21, 1987; children from a previous marriage: Elizabeth, Jessica, Amanda, Alexander. AB, Ohio State U., 1958; JD, U. Mich., 1961. Bar: D.C. 1961, N.Y. 1965, N.J. 1972, Colo. 1992, U.S. Dist. Ct. D.C. 1961, U.S. Dist. Ct. (ea. and so. dists.) N.Y. 1965, U.S. Dist. Ct. N.J. 1972, U.S. Dist. Ct. (no. dist.) N.Y. 1985, U.S. Dist. Ct. (we. dist.) N.Y. 1991, U.S. Dist. Ct. (ea. dist.) Wis. 1985, U.S. Dist. Ct. Ariz. 1992, U.S. Dist. Ct. (we. dist.) Wis. 1996, U.S. Ct. Internat. Trade 1985, U.S. Tax Ct. 1974, U.S. Ct. Mil. Appeals, 1961, U.S. Ct. Appeals (D.C. cir.) 1961, U.S. Ct. Appeals (2nd cir.) 1965, U.S. Ct. Appeals (3rd cir.) 1978, U.S. Ct. Appeals (1st cir.) 1994, U.S. Ct. Appeals (7th cir.) 1996, U.S. Supreme Ct. 1965. Asst. chief counsel divsn. corp. fin. SEC, Washington, 1961; trial attyl divsn. civil rights U.S. Dept. Justice, Washington, 1962, asst. U.S. atty., 1962-65, U.S. commr. for D.C., 1965-66; assoc. Robinson, Silverman, Pearce, et al, N.Y.C., 1967-71; ptnr. Harris, Fredericks, et al, N.Y.C., L.A., 1971-77, Goldschmidt, Fredericks & Oshatz, N.Y.C., 1977-85; sr. ptnr. Law Office Barry I. Fredericks, N.Y.C., Englewood Cliffs, N.J., 1987—; counsel Gilberg & Kurent, Englewood Cliffs, N.J., 1996; govs. adv. com. N.J. Criminal Justice Standards and Goals, 1975-77; mem. bd. govs. N.J. State Law Enforcement Agy., 1977-79; pres., chief operating officer Operation Raleigh USA, 1983-87; lectr. on trial advocacy Practicing Law Inst., 1984—, Victorian Bar Coun., Melbourne, Australia, 1990; faculty Univ. Va. Sch. Law Trial Advocacy Inst., 1986—, Univ. Mich. Sch. Law Inst. Continuing Legal Edn., 1988-96, Nat. Inst. for Trial Advocacy, 1992—; sec. Cardoza U. Law Sch. Trial Advocacy Inst., 1993; mediator U.S. Dist. Ct. (so. dist.) N.Y., 1993. Councilman, Ridgewood, N.J., 1980-84; mem. planning bd., Ridgewood, 1980-81. Recipient William S. Brennan Jr. award U. Va. Law Sch., 1994. Mem. ABA, Assn. Trial Lawyers Am., N.Y. County Lawyer's Assn., N.Y. State Trial Lawyers Assn., Fed. Bar Assn. N.Y., N.J. Fed. Bar (v.p. 1981-90), N.J. State Bar Assn., D.C. Bar Assn. Office: 560 Sylvan Ave Englewood Cliffs NJ 07632

FREDERICKS, DALE EDWARD, lawyer; b. Springfield, Ill., Mar. 12, 1943; m. Jean Schmidt, June 8, 1968; children: Michael J., Amy C. BS with honors, Bradley U., 1965; JD, U. Ill., 1968. Bar: D.C. 1969, Calif. 1971, U.S. Supreme Ct. 1978. Gen. counsel Summit Fidelity and Surety Co., Minneapolis, 1988-93, Hampton Ct. Holdings, Inc., San Francisco, 1989-93; ptnr. Sheppard, Mullin, Richter & Hampton, 1991-96, mng. ptnr. San Francisco office, 1993-95; pres. Sangamon Properties Co., Incline Village, Nev., Sangamon Devel. Co., Sangamon Energy Co., Lafayette, Calif. Capt. USMCR, 1968-72. Mem. ABA (antitrust law and litigation sects.), Calif. Bar Assn., San Francisco Bar Assn., Internat. Bar Assn., World Trace Club. Republican. Avocation: golf, real estate development. Office: 3 Embarcadero Ctr Ste 1060 San Francisco CA 94111-4056

FREDERICKS, MICHAEL EDWIN, criminal investigator; b. Merced, Calif., Sept. 16, 1946; s. Edwin W. and Rachel A.; m. Barbara June Alley, July 9, 1966 (div. 1972); children: Traci Ann Mapps, Michael Rae Mendoza; m. Virginia Veleva Taneva; children: Tor Michael, Kay C. Pederson. AS in Law Enforcement, Spokane C.C., 1977. Security officer U.S. Customs Agy. Svc., Portland, Oreg., 1971; spl. agent Customs Office of Invest, Portland, Oreg., 1971-73; spl. agent Drug Enforcement Adminstrn., Portland, Oreg., 1973-74, Spokane, Wash., 1974-80; spl. agent El Paso Intelligence Ctr., El Paso, Tex., 1981-83, US Embassy-DEA, Bogota, Columbia, 1983-85, DEA, Lahore, Pakistan, 1985-88; supervising spl. agt. U.S. Drug Enforcement Adminstrn., San Juan, P.R., 1988-91; country attaché Am. Embassy U.S. Drug Enforcement Adminstrn., New Delhi, 1991-98; chief chem. ops. U.S. Drug Enforcement Adminstrn., Arlington, Va., 1999—. Mem. Internat. Narcotic Enforcement Officer's Assn. (Commendation 1991), Fed. Law Enforcement Officer's Assn., Internat. Police Assn. Avocations: scuba, golf, tennis, writing. E-mail: chemops1@hotmail.com. Office: 600 Army Navy Dr Arlington VA 22202

FREDERICKS, PATRICIA ANN, real estate executive; b. Durand, Mich., June 5, 1941; d. Willis Edward and Dorothy (Plowman) Sexton; m. Ward Arthur Fredericks, June 12, 1960; children: Corrine Ellen, Lorraine Lee, Ward Arthur II. BA, Mich. State U., 1962. Cert. Grad. Real Estate Inst., residential broker, residential salesperson; cert. real estate broker. Assoc. Stand Brough, Des Moines, 1976-80; broker Denton, Tuscon, 1980-83; broker-trainer Coldwell Banker, Westlake Village, Calif., 1984-90; broker, br. mgr. Brown, Newbury Park, Calif., 1990-94; dir. tng. Brown Real Estate, Westlake Village, Calif., 1994—; gen. mgr., dir. mktg. Coldwell Banker Town & Country Real Estate, Newbury Park, Calif., 1994—; dir. mktg. Coldwell Banker Town and Country, 1995—; bd. sec. Mixtec Corp., Thousand Oaks, 1984—. Contbr. articles to profl. jours. Pres. Inner Wheel, Thousand Oaks, 1991, 96-97; bd. dirs. Community Leaders Club, Thousand Oaks, 1991, Conejo Future Found., Thousand Oaks, 1989-92, Wellness Community Ventura Valley, 1994—. Mem. Calif. Assn. Realtors (dir. 1988-95 regional chairperson 1995, vice chairperson expn. 1997, chair Calif. Expo 1998), Conejo Valley Assn. Realtors (sec., v.p., pres.-elect 1989-92, pres. 1993, Realtor of Yr. 1991), Pres.'s Club Mich. State U., Com. 100, Cmty. Concerts Assn., Alliance for the Arts, Conejo Valley Symphony Guild, Wellness Cmty., Indian Wells Country Club, North Ranch Country Club, Sherwood Country Club. Office: 2235 Michael Dr Newbury Park CA 91320-3340

FREDERICKS, WARD ARTHUR, venture capitalist, food industry consultant; b. Tarrytown, N.Y., Dec. 24, 1939; s. Arthur George and Evelyn (Smith) F.; BS cum laude, Mich. State U., 1962, MBA, 1963, PhD. m. Patricia A. Sexton, June 12, 1960; children: Corrine E., Lorrine L., Ward A. Assoc. dir. Technics Group, Grand Rapids, Mich., 1964-68; gen. mgr. logistics systems Massey-Ferguson Inc., Toronto, 1968-69, v.p. mgmt. svcs., comptr., 1969-73, sr. v.p. fin., dir. fin. Americas, 1975—; comptr. Massey-Ferguson Ltd., Toronto, Ont., Can., 1973-75; prin. W.B. Saunders & Co., Washington, 1962—; sr. v.p. mktg. Massey/Ferguson, Inc., 1975-78, also pres., gen. mgr. Tractor div., 1978-80; gen. mgr. Rockwell Graphic Sys., 1980-82; pres. Goss Co.; v.p. ops., Rockwell Internat., Pitts., 1980-84; v.p. Fed. MOG., 1983-84; chmn. MIXTEC Group LLC, 1998—, also dir., chmn.; principal Venture Assocs., 1993—. dir. Polyfet RF, Inc., Venture Assocs., Badger Northland Inc., MST, Inc., Calif., Tech-Mark Group Inc., Spectra Tech., Inc., Mixtec Group-Venture Capital, Inc., Unicorn Corp., Mixtec Food Group Calif., Mixtec Signal Tech., Harry Ferguson Inc., M.F. Credit Corp., M.F. Credit Co. Can. Ltd. Bd. dirs., mem. exec. com. Des Moines Symphony, 1975-79; exec. com. Conejo Symphony, pres. 1988-90, pres. Westlake Village Cultural Found., 1991; mem. exec. com. Alliance for Arts.; pres. Conejo Valley Indsl. Assn., 1990, 93; mem. Constn. Bicentennial Com., 1987-88, Ventura County Airport Commn., 1995—, LaQuinta Arts Found.; bd. dirs. Ventura County Bus. Incubator, 1996—; v.p. Com. Leaders Club, 1988, pres., 1989-90, pres. Westlake Cultural Found, 1991; vice chair Alliance for the Arts; regent Calif. Lutheran U., 1990—, exec. com. 1993—, chmn. acad. affairs 1993—, exec. com. 1992—, chmn. acad. affairs, 1992—, vice chmn., 1997—; v.p. Aviation C.C. of Calif. Fellow Am. Transp. Assn., 1992-63, Ramlose, 1962-63; mem. AAAS, IEEE, SAR, Am. Mktg. Assn., Nat. Council Phys. Distbn. Mgmt. (exec. com. 1974), Produce Mktg. Assn., United Fresh Fruit and Vegetable Assn., Internat. Fresh-cut Produce Assn., Soc. Automotive Engrs., U.S. Strategic Inst., Tech. Execs. Forum (Tech. Corridor 100 award, 1989), Internat. Food Mfg. Assn., Produce Mktg. Assn., Toronto Bd. Trade, Westlake Village C. of C. (chmn. 1990), Cochella Valley Community Concerts Assn. (bd. dirs. 1992-95), Old Crows, Assn. for Advanced Tech. Edn., Air Force Assn., Aerospace Soc., Experimental Aircraft Assn., Mil. Order World Wars, Conf. Air Force (col.), Westlake Village C. of C. (chmn. bd. 1990-91), Republican Ctrl. Com., State of Calif., 1993-98, Community Leaders Club, Pres.'s Club Mich. State U., North Ranch Country Club, Indian Wells Country Club, Sherwood Country Club, St. Georges Club (U.K.), Aviation Country Club of Calif. (v.p. 1999), Rotary, Flying Rotarians, Beta Gamma Sigma. Author: (with Edward W. Smykay) Physical Distribution Management, 1974; author: Management Vision, 1988, Competitive Advantage in Technology Organizations, 1996, Competitive Advantage in Technology Organizations, 1996; contbr. articles to profl. jours. Lutheran. Home: 1640 Aspenwall Rd Westlake Village CA 91361 also: 48143 Vista Cielo La Quinta CA 92253-2256 Office: 31255 Cedar Valley Dr Westlake Village CA 91362-4014

FREDERICKS, WENDY ANN, graphic designer; b. Queens, N.Y., Oct. 27, 1955; d. Robert John and Margaret Ellen (Wright) Politica; children: Dawn, Kurt. BFA in Graphic Design cum laude, SUNY, Buffalo, 1978. Freelance book designer and promoter, 1980-86; book promotions and cover designer Thieme Med. Pubs., N.Y.C., 1986-88; sr. designer Caliber Design, Long Island City, N.Y., 1988-91; sr. designer HarperCollins Pubs., N.Y.C., 1992-93, design mgr., 1993-96; design mgr. Addison Wesley Longman, N.Y.C., 1996—. Brownie and jr. scout leader Girl Scouts U.S., Valley Stream, N.Y., 1990-93. Regents scholar, 1973; recipient 1st Place series design Bookbinders Guild, 1998. Mem. Unity Ch. of Christianity. Home: 7 Hunter Ave Valley Stream NY 11580-3027 Office: Addison Wesley Longman 1185 Avenue Of The Americas New York NY 10036-2601

FREDERICKS, WESLEY CHARLES, JR., lawyer; b. N.Y.C., Mar. 31, 1948; s. Wesley Charles and Dionysia W. (Bitsanis) F.; m. Jeanne Maria Judson, May 19, 1973; children: Carolyn Anne, Wesley C. III. BA Johns Hopkins U., 1970; JD, Columbia U., 1973. Bar: N.Y. 1974, Conn. 1976, U.S. Supreme Ct. 1979. Assoc. Shearman & Sterling, N.Y.C., 1973-83, Cummings & Lockwood, Stamford, Conn., 1976; chmn. bd. Lotus Performance Cars, L.P., Norwood, N.J., 1983-87; group exec. cons. Group Lotus PLC, 1987; automotive industry cons., 1988-90; pres, CEO Mfrs. Products Co., 1990-94; counsel Gersten, Savage, Kaplowitz & Fredericks, LLP, N.Y.C., 1994, ptnr., 1995-98, Dorsey & Whitney LLP, N.Y.C., 1998—. Mem. Johns Hopkins U. Alumni Schs. Com. With USMC, 1968-69. Mem. ABA (co-chmn. bus. law sect. subcom. multinat. mergers and acquisitions 1996—, mem. com. on negotiated acquisitions 1997—), Mashomack Fish and Game Preserve, Campfire Am. Club (N.Y.), Weston Gun Club (Conn.), Sigma Phi Epsilon. Republican. Congregationalist. Home: 221 Benedict Hill Rd New Canaan CT 06840-2913 Office: Dorsey & Whitney LLP 250 Park Ave New York NY 10177

FREDERICKS, WILLIAM JOHN, chemistry educator; b. San Diego, Sept. 18, 1924; s. William and Jenney (Cunnion) F.; m. Lola M. Schneider, Sept. 20, 1942. BS, San Diego State Coll., 1951; PhD, Oreg. State U., 1955. Technician, planner USN, San Diego, 1942-46; electronics technician Waldorf Appliance Co., San Diego, 1946-47; jr. civil engr. Calif. Div. Architecture, San Diego, 1947-51; phys. chemist, solid state mgr. Stanford Research Inst., Menlo Park, Calif., 1956-62; prof. chemistry Oreg. State U., Corvallis, 1962-87, prof. chemistry emeritus, 1988—; rsch. prof. chemistry and materials sci. U. Ala., Huntsville, 1988-94, ret.; vis. acad. Atomic Research Establishment, Harwell, Eng., 1973-74; sr. vis. fellow U. Western Ont. Ctr. Chem. Physics, 1982; cons. in field; faculty advisor Oreg. State U. Flying Club. Contbr. articles to profl. jours. Chmn. Corvallis Airport Commn., 1979-83. Fulbright fellow 1955-56. Mem. AAAS. Am. Assn. Crystal Growth (mem. exec. bd. West Sect. 1976-86), Am. Chem. Soc. (sect. chmn.), Am. Phys. Soc., Materials Research Soc. Democrat. Avocations: flying, fishing, bonzai, golfing. Office: 11443 SW 82nd Court Rd Ocala FL 34481-3566

FREDERICKSEN, WALTER MAILAND, behavioral and ocean sciences educator emeritus; b. Kansas City, Mo., Dec. 30, 1934; s. Walter Mailand Sr. and Aurelia Helene (Christensen) F.; m. Demaris Lou Nebgen, Aug. 11, 1957; children: Erik Mailand, Kirsten Demaris. BA, U. Kans., 1960; MA, U. Copenhagen, 1961; postgrad., U. Oreg., 1961-63. Master USCG; lic. archaeologist, Hawaii. Teaching fellow U. Oreg., Eugene, 1961-63; head counselor Lahainaluna H.S., Lahaina, Maui, Hawaii, 1965-66; prof. U. Hawaii Maui, Kahului, 1967-95; prof. emeritus U. Hawaii, 1995—; scientist, co-dir. Xamanek Rschs., Pukalani, Maui, Hawaii, 1964—; Tsunami surveyor JIMAR, U. Hawaii, Honolulu, 1975—; capt. rsch. vessel Glass Slipper II, Lahaina, 1964—; speaker in field. Author: An Introduction to Sailing, Cruising, Navigation, 1977; author more than 100 reports Sci. Archives, State of Hawaii, 1965—. Mem., chair Marine Adv. Coun., Lahainam 1975—. Sgt. USMC, 1953-56, Korea. Mem. numerous profl. orgns. Avocations: martial arts, ocean diving, ocean vessel cruising, poetry, music. E-mail: xamanek@juno.com. Home: PO Box 131 Pukalani HI 96788-0131 Office: Xamanek Rschs PO Box 880131 Pukalani HI 96788-0131

FREDERICKSON, ARMAN FREDERICK, minerals company executive; b. Glenbore, Man., Can., May 5, 1918; came to U.S., 1923, naturalized, 1940; s. Albert F. and Ethel M. (Wilton) F.; m. Mary Maxine Stubblefield, Sept. 23, 1943; children—Mary Christene, Clover Diane, Penny Kathlene, Kimberly Mei, Sigrid, Janice. B.S. in Mining Engring, U. Wash., 1940; M.S. in Metall. Engring, Mont. Sch. Mines, 1942; Sc.D. in Geology, Mass. Inst. Tech., 1947. Registered profl. engr., Tex., Colo., Nev., Mo.; cert. petroleum geologist. Mining engr., chief geologist Cornucopia Gold Mines, Oreg., 1939-40; instr. mineral dressing Mont. Sch. Mines, 1941-42; research asst. Mass. Inst. Tech., 1942-43; prof. geology and geol. engring. Washington U., St. Louis, 1947-56; organizer, supr. geol. research Standard (Amoco) Oil and Gas Co., Tulsa, 1955-60; prof. geology, chmn. dept. earth and planetary sci., dir. oceanography U. Pitts., 1960-65; sr. v.p., dir. research, mgr. petroleum prospecting and mineral programs in U.S., Middle East, Africa, Latin Am., 1965-71; pres., chief engr. Sorbotec, Inc., Houston, 1971-74; pres. Global Survey, 1972—; v.p. Samoco (Panama) Challenger Desert Oil Corp., 1977-81; cons. in mining and petroleum exploration, 1971—; v.p. SAMOCO, Del., 1977-81; v.p. ops. CHADOIL, 1978-81, Crown Gems, Inc., Thailand; pres. Global-Thai Exploration Corp., Thailand; organizer, past chmn. clay minerals com. Nat. Acad. Sci.-NRC; organizer, econ. analyst land and real estate projects, Calif.; negotiator oil, gemstone and mining programs, U.S., Africa, Thailand, Middle and Far East, Latin Am., exploration specialist. Author tech. papers in field, hist. novels; patentee fertilizer, oil and water pollution processes and products. Served with USNR, 1943-45. Fulbright prof. Norway, 1955. Fellow Geol. Soc. Am., Mineral Soc. Am.; mem. Am. Inst. Mining, Metall. and Petroleum Engrs., Am. Assn. Petroleum Geologists, Soc. Econ. Geologists, Geochem. Soc. Am., Underwater Soc. Am. Republican. Lutheran. numerous clubs. Home: 1525 Eastman Ln Petaluma CA 94952-3649

FREDERICKSON, CHRISTOPHER JOHN, neuroscientist; b. Norman, Okla., Aug. 1, 1945; s. John Henry and Joan Munson Frederickson; m. Cathleen Jean McCartney, Apr. 30, 1995; 1 child, Isabel. AB magna cum laude, Harvard Coll., 1968; PhD, U. Chgo., 1972. Asst. prof. neurosci. Carnegie Mellon, Pitts., 1972-75; asst. prof. neurosci. U. Tex. Dallas, Richardson, 1975-78, assoc. prof. neurosci., 1978-85, full prof. neurosci., 1985-99; CEO NeuroBio Tex, Little Elm, Tex., 1999—; dir. biotechnology MicroFab Tech., Inc., Plano, Tex., 1996—; mem. adv. bd. Tex. A&M Biomed. Engring., College Station, 1998-99; spkr. in field. Editor: Zinc Neurobiology, 1985; contbr. articles to profl. jours.; patentee in field. Bd. mem. YMCA, Richardson, 1995. Small Bus. Innovation and Rsch. grantee NIH, Washington, 1998. Mem. Soc. for Neurosci., Soc. Photo-Optical Instrumentation Engrs., Am. Chemosensory Soc. Avocation: sailing. E-mail: cjfrederickson@hotmail.com. Office: NeuroBio Tex 921 Sealy-Smith Bldg 200 University Blvd Galveston TX 77550

FREDERICKSON, DENNIS RUSSEL, senator, farmer; b. Morgan, Minn., July 27, 1939; s. Louis Bernard and Mary (Kragh) F.; m. Marjorie Davidson, July 15, 1961; children: Kari, Karl, Disa. BS, U. Minn., 1961. Farmer Morgan, 1967—; commr. Redwood County, Minn., 1973-80; mem. Minn. Senate, St. Paul, 1981—; past bd. dirs. Redwood Electric Coop. Author: (with others) The Fairy Tale Grim of Prince Perp, 1986. Served to lt. comdr. USN, 1962-67. Mem. S.W. Farm Mgmt. Assn. Republican. Lutheran. Avocation: running. Home: 4 Sunrise Dr New Ulm MN 56073-3615 Office: Minn Senate State Office Bldg Rm 143 Saint Paul MN 55155-1201

FREDERICKSON, HORACE GEORGE, former college president, public administration educator; b. Twin Falls, Idaho, July 17, 1937; s. John C. and Zelpha (Richins) F.; m. Mary Williams, Mar. 14, 1958; children—Thomas, Christian, Lynne, David. B.A., Brigham Young U., 1959; M.P.A., UCLA, 1961; Ph.D., U. So. Calif., 1967; LL.D. (hon.), Dongguk U., Korea. Intern Los Angeles County, 1960; research asst. Bur. Govtl. Research, U. Calif., Los Angeles, 1960-61; lectr. pub. adminstrn. U. So. Calif., 1962-64; lectr. govt. and politics U. Md., 1964-66; asst. prof. polit. sci. Maxwell Sch., Syracuse U., 1967-71; assoc. dir. Met. Studies Program, 1970-72, assoc. prof. polit. sci., 1971-72; fellow in higher edn. fin. adminstrn. U. N.C. System, 1972; chmn. Grad. Program, Sch. Pub. and Environ. Affairs, Ind. U., 1972-74, assoc. dean for policy and adminstrv. studies, 1973-74; dean Coll. Pub. and Community Services, prof. regional and community affairs U. Mo., Columbia, 1974-76; pres. Eastern Wash. U., Cheney, 1976-87; Edwin O. Stene Disting. prof. pub. adminstrn. U. Kans., Lawrence, 1987—. Author: New Public Administration, 1980, The Spirit of Public Administration, 1997; editor: Ethics and Public Administration, 1993, Public Policy and the Two States of Kansas, 1994, Ideal and Practice in Council-Manager Government, 2nd edit., 1994; editor in chief Jour. Pub. Adminstrn. Rsch. and Theory, 1991—. Haynes Found. fellow U. So. Calif., 1963-64. Mem. Am. Soc. Pub. Adminstrn. (pres.), Nat. Acad. Pub. Adminstrn. Home: 3420 Doral Ct Lawrence KS 66047-2131 Office: U Kans 318 Blake Hall Lawrence KS 66044-7508

FREDMAN, HOWARD S, lawyer; b. St. Louis, Feb. 1, 1944; s. Manuel and Sydine Fredman; children: Jocelyn Bly, Amber Alexandra, Cameron Penn. BA, Princeton U., 1966; JD, Columbia U., 1969. Bar: Calif. 1970, U.S. Dist. Ct. (no. dist.) Calif. 1970, U.S. Ct. Appeals (9th cir.) 1970, U.S. Dist. Ct. (so. dist.) Calif. 1974, U.S. Dist. Ct. (ctrl. dist.) Calif. 1975, U.S. Dist. Ct. (ea. dist.) Calif. 1997. Law clk. to Hon. Milton Pollack U.S. Dist. Ct. (so. dist.) N.Y., N.Y.C., 1969-70; assoc. McCutchen, Doyle, Brown & Enersen, San Francisco, 1970-75; counsel, sr. atty., atty. legal divsn. Atlantic Richfield Co., L.A., 1975-87; assoc. Frandzel & Share, L.A., 1987-90; ptnr. Frandzel Share Robins & Bloom, L.A., 1991—. Mem. L.A. County Bar Assn. (chmn. antitrust sect. 1986-87, exec. com. antitrust sect. 1982—, nominating com. 1986-87). Democrat. Jewish. Office: Frandzel Share Robins & Bloom 6500 Wilshire Blvd Fl 17 Los Angeles CA 90048-4920

FREDMANN, MARTIN, ballet artistic director, educator, choreographer; b. Balt., Feb. 3, 1943; s. Martin Joseph and Hilda Adele (Miller) F.; m. Kaleriya Fedicheva, Jan. 2, 1973 (div.); m. Patricia Renzetti, June 12, 1980. Student, Nat. Ballet Sch., Washington, 1962-64, Vaganova Sch., Leningrad, 1972. Prin. dancer The Md. Ballet, Balt., 1961-64; dancer The Pa. Ballet, Phila., 1964-65, Ballet of the Met. Opera Co., N.Y.C., 1965-66; prin. dancer Dortmund (Fed. Republic Germany) Ballet, 1973-75, Scapino Ballet, Amsterdam, Holland, 1975-76; tchr. German Opera Ballet, West Berlin, Fed. Republic Germany, 1979, Netherlands Dance Theater, 1979, Royal Swedish Ballet, 1980, San Francisco Ballet, 1981; tchr., coach Australian Ballet, 1982; tchr. Tokyo City Ballet, Hong Kong Ballet, 1985, 86, 87, London Festival Ballet, 1981-83; dir. ballet Teatro Comunale, Florence, Italy, 1984-85; artistic dir. Tampa (Fla.) Ballet, 1984-90; artistic dir. in alliance with The Tampa Ballet Colo. Ballet, Denver, 1987-90; artistic dir. Colo. Ballet, 1987—; tchr. German Opera Ballet, 1982, Ballet Rambert, London, Bat Dor summer course, Israel, 1983, Cullberg Ballet, Sweden, 1983, Hong Kong Acad. For Performing Arts, 1985, 86, 87, 89, 91, Tokyo City Ballet, 1985, 86, 87, 89, 90, Ballet West, 1990, Nat. Ballet Korea, 1991, Dance Divsn. Tsoying High Sch., Kaohsiung, Taiwan, R.O.C., 1992; guest lectr., tchr. Cen. Ballet China, Beijing Dancing Acad., P.L.A. Arts Coll., Beijing, 1990; tchr. Legat Sch., 1978, examiner, 1980; tchr. Eglevsky Sch., N.Y.C., 1980; asst. dir., ballet master Niavaron Cultural ctr., Tehran, Iran, 1978; tchr. Ballet Arts Sch. Carnegie Hall, N.Y.C., 1979-81, choreographer Estonia Nat. Theatre, USSR, 1991; dir. Marin Ballet, Calif., 1981. Choreographer Romeo and Juliet, 1983, Sachertorte, 1984, A Little Love, 1984, Ricordanza, 1986, Cinderella, 1986, Coppelia, 1987, The Nutcracker, 1987, Beauty and the Beast, 1988, Masquerade Suite, 1989, Silent Woods, 1989, The Last Songs, 1991, Centenial Suite, 1994. Recipient Mayor's award Denver, 1996, Dance Mag. award, 1999. Mem. Am. Guild Mus. Artists, Fla. State Dance Assn., Nat. Assn. Regional Ballet. Avocations: cooking, cook book collecting, travel, opera. Home: 836 E 17th Ave Apt 3A Denver CO 80218-1449 Office: Colo Ballet 1278 Lincoln St Denver CO 80203-2114

FREDO, BART, educator; b. Norwalk, Conn., Nov. 12, 1938. AB, Duke U., 1964; MS in Journalism, Northwestern U., 1995. News reporter Sta. KHVH TV and Radio, Honolulu, 1966-70, Sta. KGMB TV and Radio, Honolulu, 1970-84; documentary maker Hawaii Pub. TV, Honolulu, 1984-90; tchr. New Canaan (Conn.) Country Sch., 1990-96, 97—; lectr. Calif. Poly. State U., San Luis Obispo, 1996-97. Lance cpl. USMC, 1958-60. Recipient Documentary Gold award Houston Internat. Film Festival, 1989, Documentary Blue and Red ribbons Am. Film and Video Assn., 1990. Mem. Kappa Tau Alpha. Home: 29 Arthur Pl Stamford CT 06906-1802

FREDO, PETER W., public relations executive. V.p. customer comm. and pub. rels. United Parcel Svc., Atlanta. Office: United Parcel Svc 55 Glenlake Pkwy NE Atlanta GA 30328-3498*

FREDRICK, DAVID WALTER, university administrator; b. Oelwein, Iowa, May 12, 1944; s. Walter Junior and Jean Louise (Carran) F.; m. Merry Lou Bunger, Mar. 18, 1967; children: Erika Fredrick Stein, Adrian, Andre. BA, Wartburg Coll., 1965; MA, Clark U., 1970. Mktg. svcs. mgr. Koehring Comp., Waverly, Iowa, 1966-69; U.S. diplomatic svc. U.S. Agy. for Internat. Devel., Washington, 1969-96; internat. admissions Wartburg Coll., Waverly, 1996—. Contbr. articles to profl. jours. Councilman at large City of Waverly, 1967-69; bd. dirs. Self Help Found., Waverly, 1996—. Recipient Disting. Svc. award U.S. Agy. for Internat. Devel., 1996, Meritorious Svc. award, 1993. Mem. Nat. Assn. Fgn. Students, Am. Fgn. Svc. Assn., Rotary. Lutheran. Avocations: fishing, hiking, travel. Home: 1105 Gateway Blvd Waverly IA 50677-1462

FREDRICK, LAURENCE WILLIAM, astronomer, educator; b. Stroudsburg, Pa., Aug. 27, 1927; s. Ishmeal T. and Grace (Slider) F.; m. Frances I. Schwenk, Feb. 5, 1949; children—Laura Grace, Theodore David, Rebecca Lyn. B.A., Swarthmore Coll., 1952, M.A., 1954; Ph.D., U. Pa., 1959. Research asst. Sproul Obs., Swarthmore, Pa., 1952-56; research assoc. Flower and Cook Obs., Malvern, Pa., 1957-59; astronomer Lowell Obs., Flagstaff, Ariz., 1959-63; mem. faculty U. Va., Charlottesville, 1963-95, prof. astronomy, 1965-95, rsch. prof., 1995—; prof. U. Vienna, Austria, 1972-73; cons. in field; Fulbright-Hays exch. lectr., Austria, 1972-73; assoc. astronomer European So. Obs., Munich, Fed. Republic Germany, 1982-83; vis. fellow Australian Nat. U., Canberra, 1991-92. Co-author: Astronomy, 10th edit., 1976, Descriptive Astronomy, 1978, An Introduction to Astronomy, 9th edit., 1980. Served with USN, 1945-48. Named Alumnus of Yr., Milton Hershey Sch., 1961. Mem. Am. Astron. Soc. (sec. 1969-80), Internat. Astron. Union (sec. U.S. nat. com. 1970-80), Am. Inst. Physics (bd. govs. 1969-79), Univs. for Space Research Assn. (trustee), Royal Astron. Soc., Sci. Exploration (sec. 1981—), Sigma Xi. Home: 2602 Bennington Rd Charlottesville VA 22901-2211

FREDRICKSON, DONALD SHARP, physician, scientist; b. Canon City, Colo., Aug. 8, 1924; s. Charles Arthur and Blanche (Sharp) F.; m. Henriette Priscilla Dorothea Eekhof, Sept. 5, 1950; children: Eric Henderikus, Rurik Charles. Student, U. Colo., 1942-43; BS, U. Mich., 1946, MD, 1949; MD (hon.), Karolinska Inst., Stockholm, 1977; DSc (hon.), U. Mich., 1977, Mt. Sinai Sch. Medicine, 1978, U. N.C., 1979, Georgetown U., 1981, Yeshiva U., 1981, N.J. U. Medicine and Dentistry, 1982, Med. U. S.C., 1985, George Washington U., 1985, U. Rochester, 1986. Intern Peter Bent Brigham

Hosp., Boston, 1949-50; house staff mem., fellow Peter Bent Brigham and Mass. Gen. hosps., 1950-53; mem. sr. research staff lab. cellular physiology and metabolism Nat. Heart and Lung Inst., Bethesda, Md., 1953-61, clin. dir. inst., 1961-66, dir. inst., 1966-68, chief molecular disease br. div. intramural research, 1966, dir. div. intramural research, 1968-74; pres. Inst. Medicine, NAS, 1974-75; dir. NIH, 1975-81; scholar-in-residence NAS, 1981-83; v.p. Howard Hughes Med. Inst., Bethesda, 1983, pres., chief exec. officer, trustee, 1984-87; scholar Nat. Libr. Medicine, 1987—; professorial lectr. medicine George Washington U. Sch. Medicine, 1956-84; lectr. preventive medicine Georgetown U. Sch. Medicine, 1963-84; pres. DS Fredrickson Assocs., 1987—; researcher Nat. Heart, Lung and Blood Inst., 1987-90. Editor: (with others) The Metabolic Basis of Inherited Disease, 1st-6th edit, 1989; Contbr. articles to profl. jours. Served with AUS, 1943-45. Recipient Internat. award James F. Mitchell Found. for Med. Edn. and Rsch., 1968, Disting. Achievement award Modern Medicine, Superior Svc. award HEW, 1970, Disting. Svc. award, 1971, Jimenez Das award, 1971, McCollum award Am. Soc. Clin. Nutrition/Am. Inst. Nutrition, 1971, Modanina prize, 1975, Irving Cutter medal, 1978, Gairdner Found. ann. award, 1978, Purkinje medal Czechoslovakian Med. Soc., 1980, Fondazione Lorenzini medal, 1980, Disting. Pub. Svc. award HHS, 1981, Disting. Svc. award Miami Winter Symposium, 1985, Svc. to Sci. award Arthur M. Sackler Found., 1986, Sandoz Lifetime Achievement award, 1993. Fellow AAAS, ACP, Royal Coll. Physicians (London), Am. Coll. Cardiology (gold medal 1967, Disting. Svc. award 1983); mem. NAS, Am. Acad. Arts and Scis., Am. Philos. Soc., Am. Soc. Clin. Investigation, Assn. Am. Physicians, Harvey Soc. (hon.), Acad. Kingdom of Morocco, Med. Soc. Sweden, Phi Beta Kappa, Alpha Omega Alpha, Phi Kappa Phi.

FREDRICKSON, GEORGE MARSH, history educator; b. Bristol, Conn., July 16, 1934; s. George Fredrickson and Gertrude (Marsh) F.; m. Helene Osouf, Oct. 16, 1956; children: Anne, Laurel, Thomas, Caroline. A.B., Harvard U., 1956, Ph.D., 1964. Instr. history Harvard U., Cambridge, Mass., 1963-66; assoc. prof. history Northwestern U., Evanston, Ill., 1966-71; prof. Northwestern U., Evanston, 1971-84, William Smith Mason prof. Am. history, 1979-84; Edgar E. Robinson prof. U.S. history Stanford U., Calif., 1984—; Fulbright prof. Moscow U., 1983, Harmsworth prof. Am. history Oxford U., 1988-89. Author: The Inner Civil War, 1965, 2d edit., 1993, The Black Image in the White Mind, 1971, 2d edit., 1987 (Anisfield-Wolf award 1972), White Supremacy, 1981 (Ralph Walso Emerson award 1981, Merle Curti award, 1982, Pulitzer prize finalist 1982), The Arrogance of Race, 1988, Black Liberation, 1995, The Comparative Imagination, 1997; co-author: America: Past and Present, 5th edit., 1998; editor: A Nation Divided, 1975. Served to lt. USN, 1957-60. Guggenheim fellow, 1967-68; NEH fellow, 1973-74; Ctr. for Advanced Studies in Behavioral Scis. fellow, 1977-78; NEH fellow, 1985-86; Ford sr. fellow DuBois Inst., Harvard U., 1993. Fellow Soc. Am. Historians, Am. Antiquarian Soc., Am. Acad. Arts and Scis.; mem. Am. Hist. Assn., Orgn. Am. Historians (pres. 1997-98), So. Hist. Assn. Home: 741 Esplanada Way Palo Alto CA 94305-1013 Office: Stanford Univ Dept History Stanford CA 94305

FREDRICKSON, GLENN HAROLD, chemical engineering and materials educator; b. Washington, May 8, 1959. BS in Chem. Engrng. with honors, U. Fla., 1980; MS in Chem. Engrng., Stanford U., 1981, PhD in Chem. Engrng., 1984. Mem. tech. staff AT&T Bell Labs., Murray Hill, N.J., 1984-89, disting. mem. tech. staff, 1989-90; assoc. prof. dept. chem. engrng. and engrng. materials dept. U. Calif., Santa Barbara, 1990-91, dir. Macromolecular Sci. and Engrng. Ctr., prof. dept. chem. engrng. and engrng. materials dept., 1991—, vice-chair chem. engrng., 1996-98, chair chem. engrng., 1998—; Allan P. Colburn lectr. U. Del., 1991; George T. Piercy disting prof. chem. engrng. and materials sci. U. Minn., Mpls., 1992; vis. rsch. prof. Miller Inst. U. Calif., Berkeley, 1993; lectr. in field. Mem. editorial bd. Jour. Polymer Sci. physics edit., 1992—, Macromolecules, 1994-96; mem. internat. editorial adv. bd. Acta Polymerica, 1992—. Exxon Teaching fellow Stanford U., 1982-84, Alfred P. Sloan Rsch. fellow, 1992; recipient Presdl. Young Investigator award NSF, 1990, Camille and Henry Dreyfus Tchr.-Scholar award, 1991. Fellow Am. Phys. Soc. (publs. com. 1992-94, John H. Dillon medal Divsn. High Polymer Physics 1992); mem. Phi Kappa Phi. Office: U Calif Chem Engrng Eng II Rm 3329 Santa Barbara CA 93106-5080

FREDRICKSON, L(AWRENCE) THOMAS, composer; b. Kane, Pa., Sept. 5, 1928; s. Eric Lawrence Fredrickson and Esther Linnea (Skoog) Bussell; m. Betty Jean Blessing, July 30, 1950; children: Lawrence Alan, Linda Kay, Gail Diane. MusB, Ohio Wesleyan U., 1950; MusM, U. Ill., Urbana, 1952, MusD, 1960. Jazz musician Ill., 1952—; composer, arranger Urbana, Ill., 1952—; instr. music U. Ill., Urbana/Champaign, 1952-60, asst. prof., 1960-63, assoc. prof., 1963-67, prof., 1967-93, prof. emeritus, 1993, dir. Sch. of Music, 1970-74. Composer: Brass Quintet, Impressions, Deja Vu, Music for the Double Bass Alone; commns. include works for orch., band, chamber music, solo works; performer double bass in chamber music and jazz groups, symphony orchs. Mem. ASCAP, Am. Fedn. of Musicians. Home: 1814 Robert Dr Champaign IL 61821-6031

FREDRICKSON, SCOTT ALFRED, instructional technology educator, consultant; b. San Mateo, Calif., Nov. 4, 1950; s. Raymond Anton William and Lois Elaine (Austin) F.; m. Lynn Ann Traylor, June 17, 1973; children: Lance Raymond, Jeffrey Ryan. BS in Criminal Justice, U. Nebr., Omaha, 1976; MED, Tex. Tech U., 1983, EdD, 1989. With identification divsn. FBI, Washington, 1970; aircraft mechanic USAF, 1970-74; dep. sheriff Lubbock (Tex.) Sheriff's Dept., 1979-82; tchr. Lubbock Ind. Sch. Dist., 1981-89; asst. prof. U. Alaska SE, Sitka, 1989-92; assoc. prof. U. Nebr., Kearney, 1992—; presenter in field. Author: Teaching Incarcerated Youths Using MicroComputer Distance Education Technology, 1989, Alaskan High Schools Graduates: A Study of the 1986-1989 Graduates, 1990, Contemporary Issues in Education, 1993, Going The Distance in Central Nebraska: A Distance Education Needs Assessment, 1994, Distance Education: Technologies and Teaching Strategies for University Faculty, 1995; contbr. articles to profl. jours. Lt. U.S. Army, 1976-79. Mem. Phi Delta Kappa (v.p. Sitka chpt. 1989-92). Republican. Lutheran. Avocations: scuba diving, chess, reading. Office: U Nebr Kearney Coll Edn Kearney NE 68849-1260

FREDRICKSON, SHARON WONG, accountant; b. Cleve., Nov. 24, 1956; d. Jack Don and Fung Suey (Chow) Wong; m. Brant M. Fredrickson, Mar. 19, 1988; children: Eric Brant, Saul Wong. BS in Acctg. summa cum laude, Case Western Res. U., 1978, MBA, 1987. CPA, Ohio. Acct. Price Waterhouse, Cleve., 1978-81, sr. acct., 1981-84; acctg. rsch. and planning analyst BP Am., Inc. (formerly Standard Oil Co.), Cleve., 1984-85, sr. fin. analyst rsch. and devel. acctg., 1985-88, bus. analyst, regional ctr. fin. reporting, 1989-93; fin. reporting analyst BP Oil Co., 1994-96; project mgr. control svcs. Key Svcs. Corp. subs. Key Corp., Cleve., 1996-97; acct. Glazer & Co., Pepper Pike, Ohio, 1997—. Bus. advisor Inroads Cleve., Inc., 1982-84. Mem. AICPA, Am. Woman's Soc. CPAs (Northeastern Ohio affiliate pres. 1985-86, v.p. 1984-85, sec. 1983-84), Ohio Soc. CPAs (state bd. dirs. 1985-86, 88-89, sec. Cleve. chpt. 1987-88, chpt. bd. dirs. 1986-87), Young Profls. Cleve. (trustee 1984-85). Avocations: travel, exercise, reading. Office: Glazer & Co 29225 Chagrin Blvd Ste 100 Pepper Pike OH 44122-4629

FREDRICKSON, WILLIAM ROBERT, scientist, company executive; b. Chgo., Sept. 2, 1960; s. Robert Arnold and Mary Eileen (Cleary) F. Student, Wabash Coll., Crawfordsville, Ind., 1979, Purdue U., West Lafayette, Ind., 1980-82, 90, Ind. U./Purdue U., Indpls., 1984, 87. Rschr. in amino acids Ind. U./Purdue U., Indpls., 1984-85; rsch. in HIV antivirals Fredrickson & Strecker Trading Co., Indpls., 1987-98; CEO, vice chmn. of bd., head of R&D F and S Biogenesis Group Inc., Indpls., 1998—; cons. in fields of mktg. and mgmt. Author: The Tree of Life, 1994, Genesis, 1994; composer: (anthology of music) Believe, 1995; 1 patent pending. Republican. Avocations: guitar, chess, mathematics, physics, philosophy. Home and Office: F & S Biogenesis Group Inc 5461 N Illinois St Indianapolis IN 46208-2639

FREDRIK, BURRY, theatrical producer, director; b. N.Y.C., Aug. 9, 1925; d. Fredric Kreuger and Erna Anita (Burry) Gerber; m. Gerard E. Meunier, Dec. 27, 1945 (div. 1949). Grad., Sarah Lawrence Coll., 1947. Ind. theatrical dir., producer U.S. and abroad, 1955—; lit. mgr., dir. Boston Post Road Stage Co., 1988-92; artistic dir. Fairfield County Stage Co. (formerly Boston Post Road Stage), 1992-93. Producer: (Broadway plays) Too Good To Be True, 1964-65 (nominated Tony award 1965), Travesties, 1975-76 (Tony award 1976), An Almost Perfect Person, 1977, The Night of the Tribades, 1978, To Grandmother's House We Go, 1981, The Royal Family, 1975-76, (off-Broadway plays) Thieves Carnival, 1955 (Spl. Tony award 1955), Exiles, 1956 (OBIE award 1956), Buried Child (Pulitzer prize 1980); dir.: (nat. tours) Misalliance, 1953, Milk and Honey, 1963, Dark at the Top of the Stairs, 1958, Dear Love, 1971, To Grandmother's House We Go, 1982, (off-Broadway prodns.) The Decameron, 1961, Catholic School Girls, 1981, (Broadway prodn.) Wild and Wonderful, 1972. Chmn. Weston Commn. for Arts, 1997-99; mem. fin. commn. Long Wharf Theatre, New Haven, 1998-99. Home: 51 Hillside Rd N Weston CT 06883-1513

FREDRIKSEN, MARYELLEN, physician assistant; b. New Brunswick, N.J., Oct. 21, 1963; d. Joseph Saverio and Naomi Yolanda (Alvarado) Iacovacci; m. Olaf Rune Fredriksen, May 13, 1990 (div. 1996). BA in Chemistry, Boston U., 1986; BS in Health Science, CUNY/Columbia U., 1996; postgrad., U. Nebr. Reg. physician assistant, N.Y.; cert. in basic life support, advanced cardiac life support, neonatal advanced life support, pediatric advanced life support, advanced trauma life support; cert. HIV/AIDS counselor. Biochem. rsch. tech. Boston U., 1984-86; biochem. rsch. tech. Sch. Medicine Harvard U., Boston, 1986-87; rsch. tech. Cold Spring Harbor (N.Y.) Lab., 1987-90, buyer, 1990-94; physician asst., house staff officer dept. surgery and medicine Samaritan Med. Ctr., Watertown, N.Y., 1997—. With Students Teaching AIDS to Students, 1995-96; vol. physician asst. student N.Y.C. Marathon, 1995, 96; participant Teddy Bear Clin., 1997. N.Y. State Soc. Physician Assts. scholar, 1996. Fellow Am. Acad. Physician Assts. (treas. Student Soc. Student Acad. 1994-96); mem. N.Y. State Soc. Physician Assts. (cert., student treas. local chpt. 1994-96, rep. Project Access program 1995-96). Democrat. Avocations: archery, skiing. Home: 261 Ten Eyck St Apt 4 Watertown NY 13601-3902 Office: Samaritan Med Ctr 830 Washington St Watertown NY 13601-4034

FREE, E. LEBRON, lawyer; b. Cleveland, Tenn., Jan. 27, 1940; s. James D. and Mary Kathleen (Hunt) F.; children: Jason LeBron, Ryan Edward. BA, Berea Coll., 1963; ThM, So. Meth. U., 1966; JD, Okla. City U., 1974. Bar: Ga. 1974, Fla. 1975, U.S. Dist. Ct. (mid. dist.) Fla. 1975, U.S. Supreme Ct. 1975. Litigation atty. Jim Walter Corp., Tampa, Fla., 1975-79; prin. E. Lebron Free, P.A., Clearwater, Fla., 1980—. Editor Res. IPSA Loquitur, 1996—. Bd. dirs. Ye Mystice Krewe of Neptune, Pinellas County, Fla., 1980-90, capt., 1984; bd. dirs. Hospice of the Fla. Suncoast, 1981-91; chmn., 1984; mem. Met. Planning Orgn., Pinellas County, 1984, Zoning Bd., Clearwater, 1984; bd. dirs. Family Svc. Ctrs., 1993—. Mem. ABA, ATLA, Canakaris Inns of Ct. (bd. dirs. 1997—), Fla. Bar Assn. (family law sect., chmn. fee arbitration com. 1991), Fla. Acad. Trial Lawyers, Clearwater Bar Assn., Rotary (Paul Harris fellow 1992), Masons. Avocation: sailing. Office: 2725 Park Dr Ste 3 Clearwater FL 33763-1023

FREE, HELEN MAE, chemist, consultant; b. Pitts., Feb. 20, 1923; d. James Summerville and Daisy (Piper) Murray; m. Alfred H. Free, Oct. 18, 1947; children: Eric, Penny, Kurt, Jake, Bonnie, Nina. BA in Chemistry, Coll. of Wooster, Ohio, 1944, DSc (hon.), 1992; MA in Clin. Lab. Mgmt., Ctrl. Mich. U., 1978, DSc (hon.), 1993. Cert. clin. chemist Nat. Registry Clin. Chemistry. Chemist Miles Labs., Elkhart, Ind., 1944-78, dir. mktg. svcs. rsch. products div., 1978-82, chemist, mgr., cons. diagnostics divsn. Bayer Corp., 1982—; mem. adj. faculty Ind. U., South Bend, 1975—. Author: (with others) Urodynamics and Urinalysis in Clinical Laboratory Practice, 1972, 76. Contbr. articles to profl. jours. Patentee in field. Women's chmn. Centennial of Elkhart, 1958. Recipient Disting. Alumni award Coll. of Wooster, 1980, award Medi Econ. Press, 1986, Lab. Pub. Svc. Nat. Leadership award, 1994; named to Hall of Excellence, Ohio Found. Ind. Colls., 1992; named Woman of Yr. YWCA, 1993; Kilby Found. laureate, Engring and Scis. Hall of Fame, 1996. Fellow AAAS, Am. Inst. Chemists (co-recipient Chicago award 1967), Royal Soc. Chemistry; mem. Am. Chem. Soc. (pres. 1993, bd. dirs., chmn. Chemistry Week task force, bd. com. pub. affairs and pub. rels., chmn. women chemists com. internat. activities com., grants and awards com., profl. and member relations com., nominating com., council policy pub. affairs and budget, Service award local chpt. 1981, councilor; Garvan medal 1980, co-recipient Mosher award, 1983, (first recipient) Helen M. Free Pub. Outreach award, 1995, Helen M. Free award named in honor 1995), Am. Assn. for Clin. Chemistry (council, bd. dirs., nominating com. and pub. relations com., nat. membership chmn., profl. affairs coordinator, pres.), Assn. Clin. Scientists (diploma of honor 1992), Am. Soc. Clin. Lab. Sci. (chmn. assembly, Achievement award 1976), Nat. Com. Clin. Lab. Standards (bd. dirs.), Fellow, Royal Soc. Chem. (London), Am. Assn. Adv. Scis., Am. Inst. Chemistry, Soc. Chem. Industry (hon.), Iota Sigma Pi (hon.), Sigma Delta Epsilon (hon.). Presbyterian. Lodge: Altrusa (pres. 1982-83, bd. dirs.). Home: 3752 E Jackson Blvd Elkhart IN 46516-5205 Office: Bayer Corp Diagnostics Divsn 1884 Miles Ave Elkhart IN 46514-2291

FREE, MARY MOORE, biological and medical anthropologist; b. Paris, Tex., Mar. 6, 1933; d. Dudley Crawford and Margie Lou (Moore) Hubbard; m. Dwight Allen Free Jr., June 26, 1954 (dec.); children: Hardy (dec.), Dudley (dec.), Margery, Caroline. Student, Ward-Belmont Coll., 1951; BS, So. Meth. U., 1954, MLA, 1981, MA, 1987, PhD, 1989. Instr. So. Meth. U., Dallas, 1982-89, prof. continuing edn., 1989-90; prof. So. Meth. U., Dedman Coll., Dallas, 1990—; adj. asst. prof. dept. anthropology So. Meth. U., Dallas, 1990—; prof. Richland C.C., Dallas, 1986; house anthropologist Baylor U. Med. Ctr.; cardiothoracic transplantation team Baylor U. Med. Ctr., S.W. transplantation team Baylor U. Med. Ctr./U. Tex. Southwestern Med. Sch., 1990— (cardiothoracic transplantation award for excellence in svc., 1998); adv. bd. geriatrics Vis. Nurse Assn., Dallas, 1984-91; presenter in field anthropology, medicine, women's issues; bd. Dedman Coll. SMU Excellence in Sci. Lecture Series.; contbr. AMA/JAMA protocol on authorship; spokesperson, adv. bd. Lisa Landry Childress Found. for Organ Donation Awareness. Author: The Private World of the Hermitage: Lifestyles of the Rich and Old in an Elite Retirement Home, 1995; contbr. chpts. in sci. books, ednl. TV, and articles to Anthropology Newsletter, Am. Anthropologist, Am. Jour. Cardiology, Cahiers de Sociologie Economique et Culturelle-Ethnopsycholie, Jour. Heart Failure, Jour. Internat. Soc. Dermatology; mem. editl. bd. Baylor U. Med. Ctr. Procs.; contbr. articles to profl. jours. Bd. dirs. New Hearts and Lungs, Baylor Med. Ctr., 1994—, Lisa Landry Children's Found. for Organ Donor Awareness, Victims Outreach, 1997—, Isis Soc. and internat. issues com. Baylor U. Med. Ctr.; active various svc. and social orgns. Named one of Notable Women of Tex., 1984; recipient Outstanding Svc. Cardiothoracic Transplantation award Baylor U. Med. Ctr., 1998; provide Dr. Mary Moore Free Endowment for grad. study fieldwork in anthropology So. Meth. U. Fellow Am. Anthrop. Assn., Inst. for Study of Earth and Man; mem. AAAS, Internat. Soc. Heart Failure (sci. adv. bd.), Internat. Acad. Cardiology Inc. (internat. sci. adv. bd.), Internat. Congress Heart Disease (internat. sci. adv. bd.), Internat. Soc. Heart Disease (sci. adv. bd.), Soc. Heart Edn. (sci. adv. bd.), Dallas Women's Club, Dallas Petroleum Club, Brook Hollow Golf Club, Pi Beta Phi. Methodist. Achievements include development of position of house anthropologist in non-academic medical center, community medicine program; cross-cultural research on old age, women and cardiology. Home: 4356 Edmondson Ave Dallas TX 75205-2602 Office: Baylor U Med Ctr 3500 Gaston Ave Dallas TX 75246-2017

FREEARK, ROBERT JAMES, surgeon, educator; b. Chgo., May 14, 1927; s. Ray H. and Lizette (Stauffer) F.; m. Ruth Nelson, June 24, 1950; children: Kris, Kim. BS, Northwestern U., 1949, MD magna cum laude, 1952; grad., Oak Ridge Inst. Nuclear Studies, 1953. Diplomate Am. Bd. Surgery (dir. 1980-86), Nat. Bd. Med. Examiners. Rotating intern, then resident in gen. surgery Cook County Hosp., 1952-58; dir. surgery Cook County Hosp., 1958-68, attending physician, 1960-70, hosp. dir., 1968-70; research fellow Jerome D. Solomon Found. Chgo., 1953-54; mem. faculty Northwestern U. Med. Sch., 1960-70, prof. surgery, 1968-70; prof. surgery, chmn. dept. Loyola U.-Stritch Sch. Medicine, Maywood, Ill., 1970-95; surgeon-in-chief Loyola U.-Foster G. McGaw Hosp., 1970-95, prof. emeritus, 1995—; asst. to pres. Loyola U. Health Sys., 1995—; asst. to pres.. Loyola U. Med. Ctr., 1995—. Served with USMCR, 1945-46. Recipient Outstanding Clin. Prof. award Stritch Sch. Medicine, 1973, Alumni medal Northwestern U., 1980, Stritch medal Loyola U., 1981; named to Navy Pier Hall of Fame, Alumni Assn./U. Ill., Chgo, 1991. Fellow ACS (Surgeons award Nat. Safety Council 1987); mem. Am. Assn. Surgery Trauma (pres. 1982), Am. Surg. Assn. (v.p. 1995), AMA, Am. Trauma Soc. (pres. 1982), Central Surg. Assn. (pres. 1980-81), Soc. Internat. de Chirurgie, Soc. Surgery Alimentary Tract, Soc. Surg. Chmn., Soc. U. Surgeons, Western Surg. Assn., Ill. Surg. Soc. (pres. 1983-84), Ill. Med. Soc., Midwest Surg. Soc. (pres. 1970), Chgo. Med. Soc., Inst. Medicine Chgo., Chgo. Surg. Soc. (pres. 1984), Alpha Omega Alpha, Omega Beta Pi. Congregationalist. Office: 2160 S 1st Ave Maywood IL 60153-3304

FREEBURG, RICHARD GORMAN, financial derivatives company executive; b. Princeton, Ill., July 2, 1938; s. Eugene Victor and Mary Catherine (Albrecht) F.; m. Cheryl Rue, Mar. 16, 1957; children: Wesley Eugene, Michael James, Margaret Denise. BS in Fin., Ariz. State U., 1961. Account exec. Merrill Lynch & Co., San Diego, 1962-67; trade devel. mgr. Merrill Lynch & Co., N.Y.C., 1967-72, nat. mktg. mgr. futures divsn., 1972-76, regional office mgr., 1976-81; pres. Merrill Lynch Futures, N.Y.C., 1981-85; ind. cons. N.Y.C., 1985-88; mng. dir. Chase Futures Mgmt., Inc., N.Y.C., 1988-95; pres., CEO Derivatives Cons. Group, Inc., 1995—; bd. govs. N.Y. Coffee & Sugar Exch., 1973-79, Chgo. Mercantile Exch., 1984-85. Founder Bowling Green Improvement Assn., 1982-85; chmn. Vt. State Rep. Fin. Com., 1997—, bd. dirs. Ethan Allen Inst., 1997—. Recipient Fin. award Wall St. Jour., 1961; Ariz. Bankers Fin. scholar Ariz. Bankers Assn., 1960. Mem. Futures Industry Assn., Internat. Winston Churchill Soc. Episcopalian. Avocations: Winston Churchill book collector, gardening, birdwatching. Home: PO Box 105 Perkinsville VT 05151-0105 Office: Upper Falls Rd Perkinsville VT 05151

FREEBURG, RICHARD L., elementary education educator. Elem. tchr. Nicollet Jr. High Sch. Recipient Tchr. Excellence award Internat. Tech. Edn. Assn., 1992. Office: Nicollet Jr High Sch 400 E 134th St Burnsville MN 55337-4010*

FREED, CHARLES, engineering consultant, researcher; b. Budapest, Hungary, Mar. 21, 1926; came to U.S., 1949; s. Erno and Ernestine (Duschnitz) F.; m. Florence Joan Wallach, Apr. 16, 1956; children: Lisa Ernestine, Josie Anne. BEE, NYU, 1952; SM, MIT, 1954, EE, 1958. Registered profl. engr., Mass. Rsch. asst. MIT, Cambridge, Mass., 1952-55, mem. staff, 1955-58; sr. engr., dept. head Raytheon, Waltham, Mass., 1958-62; mem. staff Lincoln Lab., Lexington, Mass., 1962-78, sr. staff mem., 1978-94; lectr. dept. elec. engrng. and computer sci. MIT, Cambridge, 1969-99. Contbr. over 60 articles to profl. jours. Fellow IEEE; mem. Tau Beta Pi, Eta Kappa Nu, Sigma Xi. Achievements include patent in field. Home: 16 Browning Ln Lincoln MA 01773-3911 Office: MIT Lincoln Lab 244 Wood St Lexington MA 02421-6426

FREED, DANIEL JOSEF, law educator; b. New York, May 12, 1927; s. Julius Leon and Sara (Lobel) F.; m. Judith Darrow, June 30, 1967; children: Peter Jacob, Emily Sara; children from previous marriage: Jonathan Michael, Amy. BS, Yale U., 1948, LLB, 1951; LLD (hon.), New England Coll., 1994. Bar: N.Y. 1952, D.C. 1953, U.S. Supreme Ct. 1955. Atty.-investigator, preparedness subcom., com. on armed svcs., U.S. Senate, Washington, 1951-52; assoc. Ford, Bergson, Adams & Borkland, Washington, 1952-59; sr. trial atty. antitrust divsn. U.S. Dept. Justice, Washington, 1959-64, assoc. dir. office of criminal justice, 1964-66, acting dir., 1966-68, dir., 1968-69; prof. law and its adminstrn. Yale U., New Haven, 1969-75, clin. prof., 1975-94, clin. prof. emeritus, profl. lectr. in law, 1994—; dir. clin. program law Yale U., 1969-72, dir. Daniel and Florence Guggenheim program in criminal justice, 1972-87, dir. criminal sentencing program, 1988-96. Co-author: (with Wald) Bail in the United States: 1964, publ.1964; editor (periodical) Fed. Sentencing Reporter, 1988—; contbr. articles to profl. jours. Trustee Vera Inst. Justice, N.Y., 1970—; pres. Yale Law Sch. Assn. Washington, 1986. With USN, 1945-46. Recipient Glenn R. Winters award Am. Judges Assn., 1992. Democrat. Jewish. Avocations: metal sculpture, swimming. Home: 226 Lawrence St New Haven CT 06511-2419 Office: Yale Law Sch 127 Wall St PO Box 208215 New Haven CT 06520-8215

FREED, DAVID CLARK, artist; b. Toledo, May 23, 1936; s. J. Clark and Thelma F.; m. Mary Lichtenwald, Sept. 3, 1962; children—Aaron, Michael. BFA, Miami U., Oxford, Ohio, 1958; MFA, U. Iowa, 1962; postgrad., Royal Coll. Art, 1963-64. instr. art Toledo Mus., 1964-66; prof. printmaking Va. Commonwealth U., Richmond, 1966—; instr. Central Sch. Art, London, 1969. One-man shows include Franz Bader Gallery, Washington, 1967, 70-71, 73, 76, 79, 82, Va. Mus. Fine Arts, 1977, Am. Cultural Ctr., Belgrade, 1982, Il Bisonte, Florence, Italy, 1989; exhibited in group shows at World Print Show, San Francisco Mus. Modern Art, 35 Artists of the S.E., High Mus., Atlanta Art of Poetry, Nat. Coll. Fine Arts; represented in permannet collections Corcoran Gallery Washington, Mus. Modern Art, N.Y.C., Nat. Mus. Am. Art, Washington, Chgo. Art Inst., Victoria and Albert Mus., London; artist books include (with Steven Lautermilch) What Light Guides This Hand—Poems by Izumi Shikibu; (with Charles Wright) 6 Poems, 1964, Yard Journal, 1985; (with Larry Levis) Elegy with a Thimbleful of Water, 1995; (with Philip Levine) An Ordinary Morning, 1995. Fulbright grant, 1963-64; Va. Mus. fellow, 1983-84, Nattie Marie Jones fellow creative work, 1983. Home: 1825 W Grace St Richmond VA 23220-2104 Studio: 308 S Laurel St Richmond VA 23220-6231

FREED, DEBOW, college president; b. Hendersonville, Tenn., Aug. 26, 1925; s. John Walter and Ella Lee (DeBow) F.; m. Catherine Carol Moore, Sept. 10, 1949; 1 child, Debow II. B.S., U.S. Mil. Acad., 1946; grad., U.S. Inf. Sch., 1953, U.S. Army Command and Gen. Staff Coll., 1959; M.S., U. Kans., 1961; Ph.D., U. N.Mex., 1966; grad., U.S. Air War Coll., 1966; LL.D. (hon.), Monmouth (Ill.) Coll., 1987. Comdg. officer U.S. Army, 1946; comdr. 35th Inf. Japan, 1947-48; asst. to cmdr. 17th Airborne Div., 1948-49; comdr. 26th Inf., Federal Republic of Germany, 1949-51; asst. to chief U.S. Mission, Iran, and chief Middle Ea. Affairs, 1951-53; instr. The Inf. Sch., 1953-56; comdr. 32d Inf., Korea, 1956-57; instr. Command and Gen. Staff Coll., 1957-58; chief nuclear br. U.S. Atomic Energy Agy., 1961-65; chief Plans Div. Vietnam, 1966-67; prof. physics dept. U.S. Mil. Acad., 1967-69, ret., 1969; dean Mt. Union Coll., 1969-74; pres. Monmouth Coll., 1974-79, Ohio No. U., Ada, 1979—; chmn. Assoc. Colls. of Midwest, 1977-79, also officer other consortia of colls. and univs. Author: Using Nuclear Capabilities, 1959, Pulsed Neutron Techniques, 1965; contbr. articles, revs. to profl. publs.; editor: Atomic Development Report, 1962-64. Bd. dirs. Presbyn. Coll. Union, 1974-79; trustee Ctr. Sci. and Industry, 1982—, Toledo Symphony; v.p., dir. Buckeye coun. Boy Scouts Am., 1972-74, dir. Prairie coun., 1974-78. Decorated Bronze Star, (2) Legion of Merit, Legion of Honor Iran, Army Commendation medal, Air medal, Joint Svcs. Commendation medal, others; recipient various civic awards; Associated Western Univs. fellow, 1963-65; AEC fellow, 1963-65; Fgn. Policy Research Inst. fellow, 1966. Mem. Assn. Meth. Colls. and Univs. (bd. dirs. 1979—), Ohio Coll. Assn. (bd. dirs. 1980-84, 85-88, pres. 89-90), Ohio Found. Independent Colls. (bd. dirs. 1979—), Ohio Athletic Conf. (chmn., pres. coun. 1989-90), Sigma Xim Phi Kappa Phi, Phi Eta Sigma, Delta Theta Phi, Omicron Delta Kappa, Mortar Bd. Home: 115 W Lima Ave Ada OH 45810-1633 Office: Ohio No U Office of Pres Ada OH 45810

FREED, DONALD CALLEN, vocal and choral musician, educator; b. Holdrege, Nebr., Aug. 19, 1952; s. Donald William and Mary Louise (Callen) F. BM, Nebr. Wesleyan U., 1974; MM, U. Nebr., 1978, PhD, 1991. Instr. music Peru (Nebr.) State Coll., 1983-87; vis. prof. music U. Nebr., Lincoln, 1992-93, Hastings (Nebr.) Coll., 1993—. Composer/arranger choral music, including What a Friend We Have in Jesus, A Place for You, Away in a Manger; contbr. articles to profl. jours. Adjudicator music contests Nebr. Sch. Activities Assn., 1984—; program writer Nebr. Chamber Orch., 1987-88; instr. Malone Cmty. Ctr., Lincoln, 1987-90. Peru State Coll. travel grantee, 1986; musical pieces commd. Mem. ASCAP, Nat. Assn. Tchrs. Singing (bd. dirs., auditions chmn. West Ctrl. region 1996—), Am. Choral Dirs. Assn., Am. Guild of Organists, Coll. Music Soc., Kappa Delta Pi. Avocations: writing, bicycling, train travel, theatre. Home: 2660 Ryons St Lincoln NE 68502-4028 Office: Hastings Coll 46 Fuhr Hall 800 Turner Blvd Hastings NE 68902

FREED, JACK HERSCHEL, chemist, educator; b. N.Y.C., Apr. 19, 1938; s. Nathan and Pauline (Wolodarsky) F.; m. Renée Strauch, Mar. 25, 1961; children: Denise Elaine, Nadine Debra. BE, Yale U., 1958; MS, Columbia U., 1959, PhD, 1962. NSF fellow Cambridge U., 1962-63; asst. prof. chemistry Cornell U., 1963-67, asso. prof., 1967-73, prof., 1973—; vis.

prof. Tokyo U., 1969, Weizmann Inst. Sci., 1970, Aarhus U., 1974, U. Geneva, 1977, Delft U. of Tech., 1978, École Normale Supérieure, Paris, 1984-85, Hebrew U., Jerusalem, 1990, U. Padua, Italy, 1991, Yamagata U., 1998; fellow Inst. for Advanced Study, Hebrew U. Mem. edit. bd. Jour. Chem. Physics, 1976-78, Jour. Phys. Chemistry, 1979-83, Chem. Phys. Letters, 1988-90, Applied Magnetic Resonance, 1990—, Magnetic Resonance Rev., 1993—; contbr. numerous articles to profl. jours. Recipient Buck-Whitney award Ea. N.Y. sect. Am. Chem. Soc., 1981, Gold medal award Internat. Electron Spin Resonance Soc., 1994, Irving Langmuir prize in chem. physics Am. Phys. Soc., 1997, Internat. Zavoisky award Zavoisky Inst. of Russian Acad. Scis., 1998; named Ramsay Meml. fellow, 1962-63, A.P. Sloan Found. fellow, 1966-68, sr. Weizmann fellow, 1970, Guggenheim fellow, 1984-85, Bruker lectr. Chem. Soc. U.K., 1990, MacDowell lectr. in chemical physics, U.B.C., 1997. Fellow Am. Phys. Soc., Am. Acad. Arts and Scis. Jewish. Home: 108 Homestead Cir Ithaca NY 14850-6214 Office: Cornell U Dept Chemistry Baker Lab Ithaca NY 14853-1301

FREED, KARL FREDERICK, chemistry educator; b. Bklyn., Sept. 25, 1942; s. Nathan and Pauline Freed; m. Gina P. Goldstein, June 14, 1964; children: Nicole Yvette, Michele Suzanne. B.S., Columbia U., 1963; A.M., Harvard U., 1965, Ph.D., 1967. NATO postdoctoral fellow U. Manchester (Eng.), 1967-68; asst. prof. U. Chgo., 1968-73, assoc. prof., 1973-76, prof. chemistry, 1976—, dir. James Frank Inst., 1983-86. Author: Renormalization Group Theory of Macromolecules, 1987; editl. bd. Jour. Statis. Physics, 1976-78, Advances in Chem. Physics, 1985—, Computational Theoretical Polymer Sci., 1996—; adv. editor Chem. Physics, 1979-92, Chem. Revs., 1981-83, Internat. Jour. Quantum Chemistry, 1995—; assoc. editor Jour. Chem. Physics, 1982-84; contbr. articles to profl. jours. Recipient Marlow medal Faraday div. Chem. Soc. London, 1973; recipient Pure Chemistry award Am. Chem. Soc., 1976; fellow Sloan Found., 1969-71; Guggenheim fellow, 1972-73; fellow Dreyfus Found., 1972-77. Fellow Am. Phys. Soc.; mem. Royal Soc. Chemistry (London), Am. Chem. Soc. Office: U Chgo 5640 S Ellis Ave Chicago IL 60637-1433

FREED, KATHRYN E., councilwoman, lawyer. BA, Temple U., 1970; LLD, N.Y. Law Sch., 1977, JD, 1979. News editor Washington Market Rev., 1978-80; atty., 1980—. Chmn. County Exec. Com. on Housing, 1981-85; dem. dist. leader 61st AD, 1981—; city councilwoman Dist. 1, N.Y.C., 1992—, chairwoman contracts com., 1995—, mem. consumer affairs, contracts, environ. protection and transp. coms.; mem. City Coun., 1992—. Democrat. Office: 51 Chambers St Rm 429 New York NY 10007-1209*

FREED, KENNETH ALAN, lawyer; b. Buffalo, Apr. 28, 1957; s. Sherwood E. and Renee (Liebesman) F.; m. Odette Ashley Freed; children: David Benjamin, Daniel Lawrence. BA in Econs. magna cum laude, Boston U., 1979; JD, U. Chgo., 1982. Bar: Calif. 1982, U.S. Dist. Ct. (no. dist.) Calif., 1982. Prin., shareholder Feldman, Waldman & Kline, San Francisco, 1982-95; sr. v.p., gen. counsel Sydran Svcs., Inc., San Ramon, Calif., 1995—. Mem. ABA, Calif. Bar Assn. Home: 3291 Blackhawk Meadow Dr Danville CA 94506-5805 Office: 3000 Executive Pkwy Ste 515 San Ramon CA 94583

FREED, LISA ERNESTINE, research scientist; b. Boston, Jan. 2, 1961; d. Charles and Florence (Wallach) F.; m. Theodore Sussman, June 12, 1993; children: Sara, Rachel. SB in Biology, MIT, 1982, SM in Nutritional Biochemistry and Metabolism, 1982, PhD in Biotech., 1988; MD, Harvard Med. Sch., 1988. Lectr. Harvard-MIT divsn. of Health Scis. and Tech., Cambridge, Mass., 1990-92, prin. rsch. scientist, prin. investigator, 1993—; instr. Dept. of Anatomy and Cell Biology Harvard Med. Sch., Boston, 1991-93, prin. rsch. scientist, 1998—; mem. NASA-NIH Adv. com. on biomed. and behavioral rsch., 1995-97. Contbr. articles to profl. jours. Am. Heart Assn. fellowship Harvard Med. Sch., 1985-86, Whitaker Health Scis. and Tech. fellowship MIT, 1986-88, Fulbright scholarship Inst. of Internat. Edn., 1988-89, Rsch. Svc. fellowship NIH, 1991-93. Jewish. Avocations: classical music, violinist, athletics, travel. Home: 34 Palfrey Rd Belmont MA 02478-2259 Office: MIT E25-342 45 Carleton St Cambridge MA 02142-1323

FREED, MAYER GOODMAN, law educator; b. Phila., Oct. 26, 1945; s. Abraham H. and Fannie (Rothenberg) F.; m. Paulette Kleinhaus, Aug. 23, 1970; children: Daniel, Joshua. A.B. cum laude, Columbia Coll., 1967, JD, 1970. Bar: N.Y. 1971, Ill. 1975, U.S. Dist. Ct. (so. and ea. dists.) N.Y. 1972, U.S. Ct. Appeals (2d cir.) 1972, U.S. Supreme Ct. 1974. Assoc. Proskauer Rose Goetz & Mendelsohn, N.Y.C., 1970-71; staff atty. Nat. Employment Law Project, N.Y.C., 1971-73, sr. staff atty., 1973-74; asst. prof. law Northwestern U., 1974-77, assoc. prof., 1977-79, prof., 1979—, assoc. dean acad. affairs, 1986-95. Contbr. articles to legal publs.; bd. editors Columbia Law Rev., 1969-70. Bd. dirs. Legal Assistance Found. Chgo., 1980-82. Stone scholar, 1968-69. Mem. ABA. Office: Northwestern U Sch Law 357 E Chicago Ave Chicago IL 60611-3059*

FREED, MELVYN NORRIS, writer, retired higher education educator; b. Kansas City, Mo., Apr. 30, 1937; s. Carl and Betty (Wachtel) F.; m. Janet Lea Triplitt, Dec. 26, 1971; children: David A., Edward L. BA in Econs. with distinction, U. Mo., Kansas City, 1959; MS in Edn., So. Ill. U., Carbondale, 1962, PhD in Higher Edn., 1965. Dir. instl. rsch. Ark. State U., Jonesboro, 1965-72, v.p. for adminstrn., 1972-76; v.p. for adminstrn. Govs. State U., University Pk., Ill., 1977-82; univ. prof., rsch. assoc. Govs. State U., University Pk., 1982-87; writer, 1987—; co-founder, past dir. measurement and rsch. So. Ctrl. Region Edn. Lab., Little Rock; past evaluator rsch. grants U.S. Office of Edn., Washington; founder U.S. River Acad. (chartered by Congress) in the late 1960s. Author: The Educator's Desk Reference, 1989 (1 of 30 Best Reference Books 1989), Business Information Desk Reference, 1991, Patient's Desk Reference, 1994, others; contbr. articles to profl. jours.; editor: Handbook of Statistical Procedures and Their Computer Applications, 1991; tool inventor. Village trustee Hazel Crest, Ill., 1997—, plan commr., 1988-97; adminstrv. asst. Congressman William Alexander, Washington, 1969; v.p., bd. dirs. Calumet Coun. Boy Scouts Am., Munster, Ind., 1978-95. Recipient U.S. Congl. citation, Washington, 1971, Silver Beaver award Boy Scouts Am., 1976, Disting. Svcs. award Ark. State U., 1975. Mem. Masons, Scottish Rite of Freemasonry (named Knight Comdr. of the Ct. of Hon. 1979), Alpha Epsilon Pi (life), Phi Kappa Phi, Omicron Delta Kappa.

FREED, RITA EVELYN, curator, Egyptologist, educator; b. Newark, June 29, 1952; d. Samuel David and Gertrude (Houseman) F. BA in Classical and Nr. Ea. Archaeology, Bibl. Studies, Wellesley Coll.; cert. in museology, NYU, MA, PhD. Exhbn. asst. Egypt's minor arts Mus. Fine Arts, Boston, 1978-82, curator dept. Ancient Egyptian, Nubian and Near Ea. Art, 1989—; curator Egyptian exhbn. univ. gallery U. Memphis, 1983, curator Egyptian antiquities, founding dir., 1984-89, assoc. prof. dept. art, 1983-89; adj. prof. Wellesley Coll., 1991—; part-time rsch. asst. dept. Egyptian and classical art Bklyn. Mus., 1976-78; rschr. Egyptian dept. Met. Mus. Art, 1977-78, lectr. dept. pub. edn., 1978; lectr. art Adelphi U., 1978-79; mem. archaeol. survey team Idalion Excavations, Dhali, Cyprus, 1973; site supr. excavation of Philistine temple, Tel Qasile, Tel Aviv, 1973; field archaeologist expdn. photographer Mendes Excavations, Ea. Delta, Egypt, 1977; small finds registrar Memphis Excavations, Mitrahineh, Egypt, 1988; epigrapher Giza Mastabas Project, Egypt, 1989; co-project dir. Boston-Penn Expdn., Bersheh, Egypt, 1990, Saqqara, Egypt, 1992—. Contbr. articles and revs. to profl. jours. and books; author exhbn. catalogues. U.S. trustee Schiff-Giorgini Found. Ford Found. fellow, Slater Fgn. Study fellow; Trustee fellow and Durant scholar of Wellesley Coll.; NSF rsch. grantee. Mem. Am. Rsch. Ctr. in Egypt (past bd. govs.), Soc. for Study Egyptian Antiquities, Egypt Exploration Soc., Egyptological Seminar, Internat. Assn. Egyptologists (N.Am. rep.), Internat. Coun. Mus. (Am. rep.), Am. Assn. Mus., Com. Internat. Egyptology (chmn.), Phi Beta Kappa. Jewish. Office: Mus Fine Arts 465 Huntington Ave Boston MA 02115-5597

FREED, STANLEY ARTHUR, museum curator; b. Springfield, Ohio, Apr. 18, 1927; s. Aaron Arthur and Belle (Kilstein) F.; m. Ruth Shelley, Sept. 12, 1955. Ph.B., U. Chgo., 1949; B.A., U. Calif. at Berkeley, 1951, Ph.D., 1957. Vis. asst. prof. anthropology U. N.C., 1959-60; mem. staff Am. Mus. Natural History, N.Y.C., 1960—; curator, chmn. dept. anthropology Am. Mus. Natural History, 1969-76, curator, 1976—; adj. prof. Columbia U., 1992—; research fellow Am. Inst. Indian Studies, 1977-78. Served with AUS, 1945-46. Postdoctoral fellow Social Sci. Research Council, 1957; Postdoctoral fellow NSF, 1958. Mem. N.Y. Acad. Scis. (chmn. anthropology sect. 1974-75). Home: 344 W 72nd St New York NY 10023-2625 Office: Am Mus Natural History Central Park W & 79th St New York NY 10024

FREEDBERG, A. STONE, physician; b. Salem, Mass., May 30, 1908; s. Hyman and Rachel Leah (Freedberg) F.; m. Beatrice Gordon, Aug. 29, 1935; children: Richard Gordon, Leonard Earl. A.B., Harvard U., 1929; M.D., U. Chgo. (Rush), 1935. Diplomate: Am. Bd. Internal Medicine (cardiology). Intern Mt. Sinai Hosp., Chgo., 1934-35, Mass. Meml. Hosp., Boston, summer 1935; resident Cook County Hosp., Chgo., 1935-36; house officer pathology R.I. Hosp., 1936-37; practice medicine, specializing in internal medicine Boston, 1946—; asst. in medicine Beth Israel Hosp., 1938-40, jr. vis. physician, 1940-46, assoc. in med. research, 1940-50, assoc. vis. physician, 1946-48, vis. physician, 1949-63, assoc. dir. med. research, 1950-63, sr. Ziskind fellow, 1956, physician, 1964-84, acting physician-in-chief dept. medicine, 1973, dir. cardiology unit, 1964-69, bd. consultation, 1984-87, hon. bd. consultation, 1988—; research fellow medicine Med. Sch., Harvard U., 1941-42, asst. in medicine, 1942-46, instr. medicine, 1946-47, assoc. in medicine, 1947-50, asst. prof., 1950-57, assoc. prof., 1958-69, prof., 1969-74, prof. emeritus, 1974—, adminstrv. bd. faculty medicine, 1958-62; physician Harvard U. Health Svcs., 1974—; cons., com. mem. med. div. Oak Ridge Inst. Nuclear Studies, 1955-56; spl. cons. metabolism study sect. USPHS, 1956-60; mem. sr. cons. staff Nuclear Medicine Inst., 1966-67. Mem. editorial bd.: Circulation, 1956-60, 62-67; contbr. articles profl. jours. Guggenheim fellow Oxford U., 1967-68. Fellow Am. Heart Assn. (bd. dirs.; mem. council clin. cardiology); mem. Mass. Heart Assn. (dir., past pres., com. chmn.), Am. Thyroid Assn. (v.p.), Mass., Charles River Dist. med. socs., Am. Soc. Clin. Investigation, Am. Physiol. Soc., Assn. Am. Physicians, New Eng. Cardiovascular Soc. (pres. 1971-72), Assn. Profs. Medicine. Home: 111 Perkins St Boston MA 02130-4313 Office: 275 Longwood Ave Boston MA 02115-5704

FREEDBERG, DAVID ADRIAN, art educator, historian; b. Capetown, South Africa, June 1, 1948; s. William and Eleonore (Kupfer) F.; children: Hannah, William. BA, Yale U., 1969; DPhil, Oxford U., 1973. Lectr. art Westfield Coll., U. London, 1973-76, Courtauld Inst. Art, U. London, 1976-84; prof. Barnard Coll., Columbia U., N.Y.C., 1984-86, Columbia U., 1986—; Slade prof. fine art U. Oxford, 1983-84; dir. Print Quar., London, 1983—; Andrew W. Mellon prof. Nat. Gallery Art, 1996-98. Author: Dutch Landscape Prints of the Seventeenth Century, 1980, Rubens: The Life of Christ After the Passion, 1984, Iconoclasts and Their Motives, 1985, Iconoclasm and Painting in the Revolt of the Netherlands, 1566-1609, 1988, The Prints of Pieter Bruegel the Elder, 1989, The Power of Images Studies in the History and Theory of Response, 1989, Joseph Kosuth the Play of the Unmentionable, 1992, Peter Paul Rubens: Paintings and Oil Sketches, 1995, (with E. Baldini) The Paper Museum of Cassiano dal Pozzo: Citrus Fruit, 1997. Mem. Am. Acad. Arts and Scis., Am. Philos. Soc. Office: Columbia University Schermerhorn Hall New York NY 10027

FREEDBERG, IRWIN MARK, dermatologist; b. Boston, July 4, 1931; s. Arthur Harris and Sayde Ruth (Bixby) F.; m. Irene Sybil Lisman, July 4, 1954; children—Marjorie, Kenneth, Deborah. Student, Dartmouth Coll., 1949-52; M.D., Harvard U., 1956. Intern Beth Israel Hosp., Boston, 1956-57; resident in internal medicine Beth Israel Hosp., 1957-59; resident in dermatology Mass. Gen. Hosp., Boston, 1959-62; instr. to prof. dermatology Harvard U. Med. Sch., Boston, 1962-77; prof., chmn. dept. dermatology Johns Hopkins Sch. Medicine, Balt., 1977-81; George Miller McKee prof. and chmn. dept. dermatology NYU Sch. Medicine, N.Y.C., 1981—; adv. council Nat. Inst. Arthritis, Diabetes and Digestive and Kidney Diseases, 1984-86, musculoskeletal and skin diseases, 1986-87. Contbr. articles in field to profl. jours.; editor: Jour. Investigative Dermatology, 1972-77. Guggenheim fellow, 1969-70; NIH grantee, 1962—; Am Cancer Soc., Am. Contract Bridge League faculty research asso., 1965-70. Fellow AAAS; mem. Inst. Medicine of Nat., Acad. Sci.; mem. Coun. Biologic Editors, Am. Soc. Biol. Chemistry, Am. Soc. Clin. Investigation, Soc. Investigative Dermatology (pres. 1981-82), Harvey Soc., Am. Fedn. Clin. Rsch., Assn. Am. Physicians, Assn. Profs. Dermatology (pres. 1986-88), Am. Dermatologic Assn. (treas. 1987-92, dir. 1992-97, pres. 1997-98), Am. Soc. Cell Biology, Am. Bd. Dermatology (dir. 1984-94, v.p. 1992, pres. 1993), Am. Med. Assn. (Ho. of Dels. 1990—), N.Y. Acad. Medicine (sect. on dermatology 1986-87, chmn. 1987-88), Am. Acad. Dermatology (dir. 1991-96), French Dermatology Soc. (hon.), Korean Dermatology Soc. (hon.). Home: 333 E 68th St New York NY 10021-5693 Office: 562 1st Ave New York NY 10016-6402

FREEDLAND, RICHARD ALLAN, retired biologist, educator; b. Pitts., May 9, 1931; s. Milton and Gertrude (Davis) F.; m. Beverly Jane Pachefsky, June 22, 1958; children: Howard M., Judith L., Stephen J. BS, U. Pitts., 1953; MS, U. Ill., 1955; PhD, U. Wis., 1958. Research assoc. U. Wis., Madison, 1958-60; lectr. U. Calif., Davis, 1960-61, asst. prof., 1961-65, assoc. prof., 1965-69, prof. physiol. chemistry, 1969-74, prof., chmn. physiol. scis., 1974-93; Wellcome vis. prof. U. Ga., Athens, 1990-91. Author: A Biochemical Approach to Nutrition, 1977, Biochemistry: A Short Course, 1997; mem. editorial bd. Archives Biochemistry and Biophysics, 1978—, Jour. Biol. Chemistry, 1985-91, Fedn. Am. Socs. for Exptl. Biology Jour., 1991-94; assoc. editor Jour. of Nutrition, 1984-88, editor, 1988-89. Fulbright scholar, Australia, 1987-88. Fellow AAAS, Am. Soc. Nutrition Sci.; mem. Am. Soc. Biol. Chemists. Office: U Calif Dept Molecular BioSci Davis CA 95616

FREEDLENDER, SUSAN See HOMESTEAD, SUSAN

FREEDMAN, AARON DAVID, medical educator, former university dean; b. Albany, N.Y., Jan. 4, 1922; s. Jacob Abraham and Pauline Rebecca (Hoffman) F.; m. Alice Maurer, Sept. 10, 1948; children: Abigail, Jonathan, Jeremy. AB, Cornell U., 1942; MD, Albany Med. Coll., 1945; PhD, Columbia U., 1958; MA, U. Pa., 1972. Diplomate Am. Bd. Internal Medicine. Asst. prof. medicine and biochemistry Columbia U., N.Y.C., 1958-65; clin. prof. U. Kans., Kansas City, 1965-69, chmn. dept. medicine Menorah Med. Ctr., 1965-69; prof., assoc. dean U. Pa., Phila., 1969-75, exec. dir. Grad. Hosp., 1972-75; prof. medicine Med. Sch. CUNY, 1975—, acting dean, 1978-79, dep. dean acad. affairs, 1990-92; examiner N.Y. State Bd. Med. Examiners, Albany, 1962-65; cons. Touro Coll., N.Y.C., 1980; career investigator N.Y. Pub. Health Rsch. Coun., 1963-65; dir. Danciger Med. Inst., Kansas City, Mo., 1966-69. Mem. Ardsley (N.Y.) Bd. of Edn., 1962-65. Libman Fund fellow, 1951-54, USPHS fellow, 1958-60. Mem. Am. Soc. for Cell Biology, Am. Soc. Biochemistry and Molecular Biology. Jewish. Office: CUNY Med Sch 135th St & Convent Ave New York NY 10031

FREEDMAN, ALBERT ZURO, publishing company executive; b. Taunton, Mass.; s. Frank and Bessie (Kanaber) F.; m. Esther Hilda Katz, Sept. 23, 1954 (dec.); children: Mara, Lisa, Tani, Derek; m. Nancy Lee Dworman, Aug. 17, 1984. Student, Boston U., 1945-46; BA, U. So. Calif., 1948; postgrad., Inst. Hautes Etudes Cinématagraphiques, Paris, 1949-50; PhD, Inst. for Advanced Study Human Sexuality, San Francisco, 1981. Radio writer Los Angeles, N.Y.C., 1950-52; TV writer, producer WOR-TV, N.Y.C., 1952, NBC, CBS, 1952-58; playwright Mex., 1959-60; with KTLA, ABC-TV, L.A., 1961-64; free lance writer London, 1964-66; editor Forum, Jour. Human Rels., London, 1967-75; co-pub. Forum, Jour. Human Rels., N.Y.C., 1975—; mng. dir. Penthouse Publs., London, 1970-75; v.p. Penthouse Internat., 1982—. Mem. Am. Bd. Sexology (diplomate), Soc. Sci. Study of Sex. Home: 11 Laderman Ln Greenbrae CA 94904-2482 Office: Gen Media Inc 11 Penn Plz New York NY 10001

FREEDMAN, ANNE BELLER, public speaking and marketing consultant; b. Gardner, Mass., June 22, 1949; d. Gabriel Philip Freedman and Natalie Engler (Beller) Lyons; m. Edward A. Fischer, May 20, 1979; 1 child, Lynne Heather. BSJ, U. Fla., 1971. Writer Coral Gable Times, Miami, Fla., 1972-73; reporter Miami News, 1973-74; assoc. editor Miami Phoenix, 1974-75; freelance writer Miami, 1975-80; corr. Advt. Age, Miami, 1977-81; pres. Exec. S.O.S., Inc., Miami, 1980-9-, Speak Out, Inc., Coral Gables, Fla., 1990—; ptnr. Speak Out/ Lewison-Singer, Inc., Coral Gables, 1991-94; instr. Fla. Internat. U. Author: Unforgettalbe Speeches and Sales Presentations in 8 Easy Steps, 1991, rev. edit. 1998; mem. editl. bd. Enterprising Women Mag., 1996-97; host Focus South cable TV show; prodr. cable TV show Not for Women Only, 1992, pub. rels., 1990-92. Bd. dirs. Miami/ Bogota-Calé Sister Cities Program, 1983-85; mem. steering com. Fla. Internat. U. Coun. of 100, 1995—; co-pres. South Miami Middle Sch. Band Parent Assn., 1997-98, 98—. Mem. Nat. Assn. Women Bus. Owners (chair pub. rels. 1981, dir. tng. and devel. 1987—, chmn. corp. ptnrs., v.p. 1989-91, co-chmn. Recognition awards, 1992, pub. rels. chair 1990-93, dir. tng. and devel. 1993-94, exec. chair 1994—, established bus. chair 1995-96, comm. coun. 1998—, bd. dirs., recognition honoree, 1999), South Miami/Kendall C. of C. (editor monthly newsletter 1980-83, dir., 1982-85, chmn. bus. com. 1985-89, editor ann. directory and buyer's guide 1986-87, 89—, Presdl. award 1983, 89), Euro-Am. Women's Coun. (del. spkr., dir. 1998—), Coral Gables C. of C. (chmn. dir. 1993-94, mem. editl. bd. 1995-96), Toastmasters (pres. 1984). Home: 6721 SW 113th Pl Miami FL 33173-1954 Office: 1541 Sunset Dr Ste 201 Coral Gables FL 33143-5777

FREEDMAN, BART JOSEPH, lawyer; b. New Haven, Sept. 27, 1955; s. Lawrence Zelic and Dorothy (Robinson) F.; m. Esme Detweiler, Sept. 28, 1985; children: Luke Edward, Samuel Meade, Benjamin Zelic. BA, Carleton Coll., 1977; JD, U. Pa., 1982. Bar: Wash. 1984, U.S. Dist. Ct. (we. dist.) Wash. 1984, U.S. Ct. Appeals (9th cir.) 1985, U.S. Dist. Ct. (ea. dist.) Wash. 1988. Law clk. to chief justice Samuel Roberts Supreme Ct. Pa., Erie, 1982-83; asst. city solicitor City of Phila., 1984; assoc. Perkins Coie, Seattle, 1984-90; ptnr. Preston Gates & Ellis, Seattle, 1990—. Editor: Natural Resource Damages, 1993. Bd. dirs. Seattle Metrocenter YMCA, 1988-97, chmn. 1993-97; bd. dirs. Leadership Tomorrow, 1996-97; chair Sierra Club Inner City Outings Program, Seattle, 1986-90; chmn. bd. advisors Earth Svc. Corps/ YMCA, Seattle, 1990-97. Mem. ABA (com. on corp. counsel 1985—), Wash. State Bar Assn., Seattle-King County Bar Assn. (participant neighborhood legal clinics 1985-94). Office: Preston Gates & Ellis 701 5th Ave Ste 5000 Seattle WA 98104-7078

FREEDMAN, CHARLES, bank executive; b. Toronto, Ont., Can., Sept. 1, 1941; s. Nathan and Freda (Glicksman) F.; m. Aviva Kravetz, Aug. 21, 1966; children: Barry, Daniel. BComm., U. Toronto, 1963; BA (hon.), Oxford (Eng.) U., 1965; PhD, MIT, 1970. Asst. prof. U. Minn., Mpls., 1969-74; rsch. advisor Bank of Can., Ottawa, 1974-78, dep. chief, 1978-79, chief, 1979-84, advisor to gov., 1984-88, dep. gov., 1988—. Author: Foreign Currency Business of Canadian Banks, 1974; contbr. 55 articles to profl. jours. Gov.'s Gen. medal U. Toronto, 1963; Can. Coun. fellow, 1968. Mem. Am. Econs. Assn., Can. Econs. Assn. Jewish. Avocations: reading, traveling, cross-country skiing. E-mail: cfreedman@bank-banque-canada.ca. Fax #: (613) 782-7003. Home: 1757 Dunkirk Crescent, Ottawa, ON Canada K1H 5T3 Office: Bank of Can, 234 Wellington St, Ottawa, ON Canada K1A 0G9

FREEDMAN, DAVID AMIEL, statistics educator, consultant; b. Montreal, Que., Can., Mar. 5, 1938; came to U.S., 1958; s. Abraham and Goldie (Yelin) F.; children: Deborah, Joshua. B.Sc., McGill U., Montreal, 1958; M.A., Princeton U., 1959, Ph.D., 1960. Prof. stats. U. Calif.-Berkeley, 1961—; Miller prof., 1991, chmn. dept. stats., 1981-86; cons. Bank of Can., Ottawa, 1971-72, WHO, 1973, Carnegie Commn., 1976, Dept. Energy, 1978—, Bur. Census, 1983, Dept. Justice, 1984, 89-92, Brobeck, Phleger & Harrison, 1985—, Skadden Arps, 1986, County of Los Angeles, 1989. Author: Markov Chains, 1971, Brownian Motion and Diffusion, 1971, Approximating Countable Markov Chains, 1972, Mathematical Methods in Statistics, 1977, Statistics, 1978, 3d edit., 1997; contbr. numerous articles to profl. pubs. Fellow Can. Council, 1960, Sloan Found., 1964. Mem. Am. Acad Scis. Home: 901 Alvarado Rd Berkeley CA 94705-1551 Office: U Calif-Berkeley Dept Stats Berkeley CA 94720*

FREEDMAN, DAVID NOEL, religion educator; b. N.Y.C., May 12, 1922; s. David and Beatrice (Goodman) F.; m. Cornelia Anne Pryor, May 16, 1944; children: Meredith Anne, Nadezhda, David Micaiah, Jonathan Pryor. Student, CCNY, 1935-38; AB, UCLA, 1939; BTh, Princeton Theol. Sem., 1944; PhD, Johns Hopkins U., 1948; LittD, U. Pacific, 1973; ScD, Davis and Elkins Coll., 1974. Ordained to ministry Presbyn. Ch., 1944; supply pastor in Acme and Deming, Wash., 1944-45; tchg. fellow, then asst. instr. Johns Hopkins U., 1946-48; asst. prof., then prof. Hebrew and Old Testament lit. Western Theol. Sem., Pitts., 1948-60; prof. Pitts. Theol. Sem., 1960-61, James A. Kelso prof., 1961-64; prof. Old Testament San Francisco Theol. Sem., 1964-70, Gray prof. Hebrew exegesis, 1970-71, dean of faculty, 1966-70, acting dean of sem., 1970-71; prof. Old Testament Grad. Theol. Union, Berkeley, Calif., 1964-71; prof. dept. Nr. Ea. studies U. Mich., Ann Arbor, 1971-92, Thurnau prof. Bibl. studies, 1984-92, dir. program on studies in religion, 1971-91; prof., endowed chair in Hebrew Bibl. studies U. Calif., San Diego, 1987—; dir. religious studies program U. Calif., 1989-97; Danforth vis. prof. Internat. Christian U., Tokyo, 1967; vis. prof. Hebrew U., Jerusalem, 1977, Macquarie U., N.S.W., Australia, 1980, U. Queensland (Australia), 1982, 84, U. Calif., San Diego, 1985-87; Green vis. prof. Tex. Christian U., Ft. Worth, 1981; dir. Albright Inst. Archeol. Rsch., 1969-70, dir., 1976-77; centennial lectr. Johns Hopkins U., 1976; Dahood lectr. Loyola U., 1983; Soc. Bibl. Lit. meml. lectr., 1983, Smithsonian lectr., 1984; prin. bibl. cons. Reader's Digest, 1984, 88, 89, 90, 94; disting. faculty lectr. Univ. Mich., 1988; Stone lectr. Princeton Theol. Sem., 1989; Mowinckel lectr., Oslo U., 1991; lectr. Uppsala U., Sweden, 1991; vis. lectr. Brigham Young Ctr. Near Eastern Studies, Jerusalem, 1993. Author: Divine Commitment and Human Obligation, 1997; co-author: (with J.D. Smart) God Has Spoken, 1949, (with F.M. Cross, Jr.) Early Hebrew Orthography, 1952, (with John M. Allegro) The People of the Dead Sea Scrolls, 1958, (with R.M. Grant) The Secret Sayings of Jesus, 1960, (with F.M. Cross, Jr.) Ancient Yahwistic Poetry, 1964, rev. edit., 1975, 97, (with M. Dothan) Ashdod I, 1967, The Published Works of W.F. Albright, 1975, (with L.G. Running) William F. Albright: Twentieth Century Genius, 1975, 2d edit., 1991, (with B. Mazar, G. Cornfeld) The Mountain of the Lord, 1975, (with W. Phillips) An Explorer's Life of Jesus, 1975, (with G. Cornfeld) Archaeology of the Bible: Book by Book, 1976, Pottery, Poetry and Prophecy, 1980, (with K.A. Mathews) The Paleo-Hebrew Leviticus Scroll, 1985, The Unity of the Hebrew Bible, 1991, (with D. Forbes and F. Andersen) Studies in Hebrew and Aramaic Orthography, 1992,(with Sara Mandell) The Relationship between Herodotus' History and Primary History, 1993; co-author, editor: (with F. Andersen) Anchor Bible Series Hosea, 1980, Anchor Bible Series Amos, 1989; editor: (with G.E. Wright) The Biblical Archaeologist, Reader I, 1961, (with E.F. Campbell, Jr.) The Biblical Archaeologist, Reader 2, 1964, Reader 3, 1970, Reader 4, 1983, (with W.F. Albright) The Anchor Bible, 1964—, including, Genesis, 1964, James, Peter and Jude, 1964, Jeremiah, 1965, Job, 1965, 2d edit., 1973, Proverbs and Ecclesiastes, 1965, I Chronicles, II Chronicles, Ezra-Nehemiah, 1965, Psalms I, 1966, John I, 1966, Acts of the Apostles, 1967, II Isaiah, 1968, Psalms II, 1968, John II, 1970, Psalms III, 1970, Esther, 1971, Matthew, 1971, Lamentations, 1972, 2d edit., 1992, To the Hebrews, 1972, Ephesians 1-3, 4-6, 1974, I and II Esdras, 1974, Judges, 1975, Revelation, 1975, Ruth, 1975, I Maccabees, 1976, I Corinthians, 1976, Additions, 1977, Song of Songs, 1977, Daniel, 1978, Wisdom of Solomon, 1979, I Samuel, 1980, Hosea, 1980, Luke I, 1981, Joshua, 1982, Epistles of John, 1983, II Maccabees, 1983, II Samuel, 1984, II Corinthians, 1984, Luke II, 1985, Judith, 1985, Mark, 1986, Haggai-Zechariah 1-8, 1987, Ecclesiasticus, 1987, 2 Kings, 1988, Amos, 1989, Titus, 1990, Jonah, 1990, Leviticus I, 1991, Deuteronomy I, 1991, Numbers 1-20, 1993, Romans, 1993, Jude and 2 Peter, 1993, Zechariah 9-14, 1993, Zephaniah, 1994, Colossians, 1995, Joel, 1995, James, 1995, Obadiah, 1996, Tobit, 1996, Ecclesiastes, 1997, Ezekiel 21-37, 1997, Galatians, 1997, Malachi, 1998, Acts of the Apostles, 1998; editor Anchor Bible Ref. Libr., Jesus Within Judaism, 1988, Archeology of the Land of the Bible, 1990, The Tree of Life, 1990, A Marginal Jew Vol. 1, 1991, The Pentateuch, 1991, The Rise of Jewish Nationalism, 1992, History and Prophecy, 1993, Jesus and the Dead Sea Scrolls, 1993, The Birth of the Messiah, 1993, The Death of the Messiah, 2 vols., 1994, Introduction to Rabbinical Literature, 1994, A Marginal Jew, vol. 2, 1994, The Scepter and the Star, 1995, An Introduction to the New Testament, 1997, Education in Ancient Israel, 1998, Warrior, Dancer, Seductress, Queen, 1998, (with J. Greenfield) New Directions in Biblical Archaeology, 1969, (with J.A. Baird) The Computer Bible, 1971, A Critical Concordance to the Synoptic Gospels, 1971, An Analytic Linguistic Concordance to the Book of Isaiah, 1971, I, II, III John: Forward and Reverse Concordance and Index, 1971, A Critical Concordance to Hosea, Amos, Micah, 1972, A Critical Concordance of Haggai, Zechariah, Malachi, 1973, A Critical Concordance to the Gospel of John, 1974, A Synoptic Concordance of Aramaic Inscriptions, 1975, A Linguistic Concordance of Ruth and Jonah, 1976, A Linguistic Concordance of Jeremiah, 1978, Syntactical and Critical Concordance of Jeremiah, 1978, Synoptic Abstract, 1978, I and II Corinthians, 1979, Zechariah, 1979, Galatians, 1980, Ephesians, 1981, Philippians, 1982, Colossians, 1983, Pastoral Epistles, 1984, 1 & 2 Thessalaians, 1985, Density Plots in Ezekiel, 1986, Exodus, 1987, Hebrews, 1988, Ruth, 1989, James, 1991, 1 & 2 Peter, 1991, 1, 2 & 3 John and Jude, 1991, Psalms, Job and Proverbs, 1992, Apocalypse, 1993, The Pentateuch, 1995, Aramaic Inscriptions, 1975, (with T. Kachel) Religion and the Academic Scene, 1975, Am. Schs. Oriental Research publs; co-editor: Scrolls from Qumran Cave I, 1972, Jesus: The Four Gospels, 1973, Pomegranates and Golden Bells, 1995; Reader's Digest editor: Atlas of the Bible, 1981, Family Guide to the Bible, 1984, Mysteries of the Bible, 1988, Who's Who in the Bible, 1994, The Bible Through the Ages, 1996, Complete Guide to the Bible, 1998; gen. editor: (facsimile edit.) Complete Guide to the Bible, 1998; The Leningrad Codex, 1998; assoc. editor Jour. Bible Lit., 1952-54, editor, 1955-59; cons. editor Interpreter's Dictionary of the Bible, 1957-60, Theologisches Wörterbuch des Alten Testaments, 1970-92, English Translation Theological Word-Book of the Old Testament, 1975—; editor in chief The Anchor Bible Dictionary, 6 vols., 1992; co-editor (with W.H. Propp and Baruch Halpern) The Hebrew Bible and Its Interpreters, 1990; contbr. numerous articles to profl. jours. Recipient prize in New Testament exegesis Princeton Theol. Sem., 1943, Carey-Thomas award for Anchor Bible, 1965, Layman's Nat. Bible Com. award, 1978, 3 awards for Anchor Bible Bibl. Archaeol. Soc., 1993; William H. Green fellow in Old Testament, 1944, William S. Rayner fellow Johns Hopkins U., 1946, 47, Guggenheim fellow, 1959, Am. Assn. Theol. Schs. fellow, 1963; Am. Coun. Learned Socs. grantee-in-aid, 1967, 76. Fellow U. Mich. Soc. Fellows (sr., chmn. 1980-82); mem. Soc. Bibl. Lit. (pres. 1975-76), Am. Oriental Soc., Am. Schs. Oriental Rsch. (v.p. 1970-82, editor bull. 1974-78, editor Bibl. Archeologist 1976-82, dir. publs. 1974-82), Archaeol. Inst. Am., Am. Acad. Religion, Bibl. Colloquium (sec.-treas. 1960-90). Office: U Calif San Diego Dept History 0104 9500 Gilman Dr La Jolla CA 92093-0104

FREEDMAN, ERIC, journalist, educator, writer; b. Brookline, Mass., Nov. 6, 1949; s. Morris and Charlotte (Nadler) F.; m. Mary Ann Sipher, May 24, 1974; children: Ian Sipher, Cara Sipher. BA, Cornell U., 1971; JD, NYU, 1975. Bar: N.Y. 1976, Mich. 1985. Congl. aide U.S. Rep. Charles Rangel, Washington and N.Y.C., 1971-76; reporter Knickerbocker News, Albany, N.Y., 1976-84, Detroit News, Lansing, Mich., 1984-95; asst. prof. journalism Mich. State U., 1995—. Author: Pioneering Michigan, 1992, On the Water, Michigan, 1992, Michigan Free, 1993, Great Lakes, Great National Forests, 1995; co-author: What to Study, 1997; contbr. numerous articles to profl. jours. Recipient Merit citation Am. Judicature Soc., Journalism awards AP, Pulitzer prize for beat reporting, 1994. Mem. Am. Soc. Writers on Legal Subjects, Investigative Reporters and Editors, State Bar Mich. (journalism award), N.Y. State Bar Assn. (journalism awards), Ingham Country Bar Assn., Lansing Area Folksong Soc. (bd. dirs.). Avocations: bicycling, travel, writing. Home and Office: 2698 Linden Dr East Lansing MI 48823-3814

FREEDMAN, FRANK HARLAN, federal judge; b. Springfield, Mass., Dec. 15, 1924; s. Alvin Samuel and Ida Hilda (Rosenberg) F.; m. Eleanor Labinger, July 26, 1953; children: Joan Robin Goodman, Wendy Beth Greedman Mackler, Barry Alan. LL.B., Boston U., 1949, LL.M., 1950; Ph.D. (hon.), Western New Eng. Coll., Springfield, 1970. Pvt. practice law, 1950-68; mayor City of Springfield, 1968-72; judge U.S. Dist. Ct. Mass., Springfield, 1972-86, chief judge, 1986-92; now sr. judge, 1992—. Chmn. fund raising drs. Muscular Dystrophy, Leukemia Soc.; mem. Susan Auchter Kidney Fund Raising Com.; mem. Springfield City Council, 1960-67, pres., 1962; del. Republican Nat. Conv., 1964, 68; mem. Springfield Rep. Com., 1959-72. Served with USNR, 1943-46. Greenaway Drive Elem. Sch. rededicated as Frank H. Freedman Sch., 1974; recipient Silver Shingle award for disting. service Boston U., 1984. Mem. Hampden County (Mass.) Bar Assn., Lewis Marshall Club on Jurisprudence (pres.). Jewish. Office: US Dist Ct 1550 Main St Rm 525 Springfield MA 01103-1428*

FREEDMAN, GERALD M., lawyer; b. Hampton, Va., July 26, 1943; s. Henry and Arlene L.; m. Kristin King. BA, Columbia U., 1964, JD, 1967. Bar: N.Y. 1968, U.S. Dist. Ct. (so. and ea. dists.) N.Y. 1970, U.S. Ct. Appeals (2d cir.) 1976. Adminstr. Columbia U., N.Y.C., 1967-69; assoc. Kelley, Drye & Warren, N.Y.C., 1969-71; assoc. Trubin Sillcocks Edelman & Knapp, N.Y.C., 1971-76, ptnr., 1976-84; ptnr. Morgan, Lewis & Bockius, N.Y.C., 1984—. Contbr. articles to profl. jours. Mem. ABA, Assn. of Bar of City of N.Y., Am. Bankruptcy Inst., Univ. Club. Office: Morgan Lewis & Bockius 101 Park Ave Fl 44 New York NY 10178-0060*

FREEDMAN, GERALD STANLEY, radiologist, healthcare administrator, educator; b. Bklyn., May 28, 1936; s. Martin and Adele (Goodman) F.; m. Karen Johnson, May. 13, 1972; children: David, Julia, Sarah. BME, Cornell U., 1959; MD, Columbia U., 1964; MPH, Yale U., 1999. Resident in gen. radiology Columbia-Presbyn. Hosp., N.Y.C., 1965-68; mem. faculty Sch. Medicine Yale U., New Haven, 1968-98, assoc. clin. prof. radiology, 1978—; dir. radiology Temple Med. Ctr., New Haven, 1978-95, Yale Health Svcs., 1992; pres. Radiol. Cons. P.C., 1977-87; dir. radiology Yale Health Svcs., New Haven, 1991; with Yale-New Haven Ambulatory Svcs., 1994-98; pres. Freedman Nuc. Medicine, 1978-97; adj. prof. radiology Vanderbilt U., 1978—; mem. Conn. Computerized Tomography Task Force, 1978; indsl. cons.; mem. med. adv. bd. Blue Cross/Blue Shield, 1978-85. Editor: Tomographic Imaging in Nuclear Medicine, 1973, Management Concepts in Nuclear Medicine, 1977; contbr. numerous articles to profl. jours., chpts. to books; patentee in field. Fellow Timothy Dwight Coll. Yale U. Fellow Am. Coll. Radiology; mem. Radiol. Soc. N.Am., Am. Coll. Nuc. Physicians, Soc. Nuc. Medicine (trustee, chairperson fin. 1980, co-chairperson sci. program). E-mail: Gerald.Freedman@yale.edu. Home: 104 Riverview Ave Branford CT 06405-4719 Office: 60 Temple St New Haven CT 06510-2716

FREEDMAN, GREGG, real estate appraisal company executive; b. Burbank, Calif., Feb. 1, 1957; s. Morton Ira and Charlotte (Chernick) F.; m. Laura Jean Anderson, May 20, 1989; 1 child, Hillary Anne. Student, U. So. Calif., Calif. State U., L.A. Cert. gen. real estate appraiser Calif.; cert. rev. appraiser, sr. cert. prof. appraiser, cert. comml. property appraiser, cert. real estate owned appraiser, cert. appraiser; independent fee appraiser-senior Am. Soc. Appraisers. Appraiser, mgr. Freedman and Freedman Cons., Monrovia, Calif., 1984-88; pres. Gregg Freedman and Assocs., Inc., Arcadia, Calif., 1988—; Tchr. real estate appraisal classes Monrovia H.S. Adult Edn.; chmn., bd. dirs. Pacific Commerce Credit Union. Prodr. Music Theater of So. Calif. Former commr. City of Duarte Econ. Devel. Coun.; bd. dirs. Meth. Hosp. Arcadia Found. Fellow Coll. Real Estate Appraisers; mem. Appraisal Inst. (assoc.), U. So. Calif. Alumni Assn. Avocations: gourmet food and wines, international travel, community service. E-mail: gifreedman@gfassociates.com. Home: 195 S Canon Ave Sierra Madre CA 91024-2601 Office: G Freedman & Assocs 124 N 1st Ave Arcadia CA 91006

FREEDMAN, HARRY, composer; b. Lodz, Poland, Apr. 5, 1922; came to Can., 1925; s. Max and Rose (Nelken) F.; m. Mary Louise Morrison, Sept. 15, 1951; children: Karen Liese, Cynthia Jane, Lori Ann. Student, Winnipeg Sch. Art, 1936-40, Royal Conservatory Music, 1945-50. Musician Toronto Symphony, 1946-70; dir. Canadian Music Centre. Composer: Tableau, 1952, Images, 1958, Tokaido: chorus and wind quintet, 1964; Tangents (orch.), 1967; ballet Rose Latulippe, 1966; Toccata, 1968; Debussy orchestration Piano Preludes, 1971; children's choir Keewaydin, 1971; orch. Tapestry, 1973; Romeo and Juliet Ballet, 1973; violin and piano Encounter, 1974; clarinet Lines, 1974; orch. Nocturne 2, 1975; narrator and chamber ensemble The Explainer, 1976; Celebration (saxophone concerto for Gerry Mulligan), 1977; choir Green...Blue...White, 1978; 1-act jazz opera Abracadabra, 1979; chorus and orch. Nocturne 3, 1980; brass quintet and orch. Royal Flush, 1980; string quartet Blue, 1980; clarinet and string quartet Chalumeau, 1981; Concerto for Orch., 1982; Third Symphony, 1983; ballet Oiseaux Exotiques, 1984; Passacaglia for jazz band and orch., 1984; narrator and orch. A Garland for Terry, 1985; string orch. Contrasts, The Web and the Wind, 1986; children's choir Rhymes from the Nursery, 1986; music theater Fragments of Alice, 1987; orch. A Dance on the Earth, 1988; wind ensemble Sonata for Symphonic Winds, 1988; Touchings, concerto for percussion ensemble and orch., 1989, marimba solo Bones, 1989, orch. Town, 1991; soprano and string quartet Spirit Song, 1993; 22 solo strings, Indigo, 1994; Touchpoints for flute, viola and harp, 1994; soprano and lute Bright Angels, 1995; saxophone quartet, Saxtet, 1995, flute, clarinet, violin, cello, piano Blue Light, 1995; Higher, bass clarinet, and cello, 1996; Marigold, viola, synthesizer, percussion, 1996; orchestra and 4 choirs, Borealis, 1997, harp solo Dances, 1997, choir Voices, 1999; also many scores for Stratford Shakespeare Festival, films, stage, TV; host Music on a Sunday Afternoon, 1987. Served with RCAF, 1942-45. Officer Order of Can., 1984; Can. Coun. sr. arts grantee, 1960, 63, 73-74, 81; recipient Can. film awards, 1970, Composer of Yr. award Can. Music Coun., 1979, Lynch-Staunton award, 1998; Tanglewood scholar, 1949, Royal Conservatory scholar, 1950. Mem. Canadian League Composers (founding mem., pres. 1975-78). Address: 35 St Andrews Gardens, Toronto, ON Canada M4W 2C9

FREEDMAN, HELEN EDELSTEIN, justice; b. New York, N.Y., Dec. 15, 1942; d. David Simeon and Frances (Fisher) Edelstein; m. Henry A. Freedman, June 7, 1964; children: Katherine Eleanor, Elizabeth Sarah. BA, Smith Coll., 1963; JD, NYU, 1967. Bar: N.Y. 1970, U.S. Dist. Ct. (so. and ea. dists.), U.S. Supreme Ct. 1979. Staff atty. office of gen. counsel Am. Arbitration Assn., N.Y.C., 1967-69; assoc. Hubbel, Cohen & Stiefel, N.Y.C., 1970-71, Shaw, Bernstein, Scheuer, Boyden & Sarnoff, N.Y.C., 1971-74; law sec. Civil Ct., N.Y.C., 1974-76; sr. atty. housing litigation bur. N.Y.C. Dept. Housing Preservation and Devel., 1976; supervising atty. Dist. Coun. 37 Legal Svcs. Plan, N.Y.C., 1976-78; judge Civil Ct., N.Y.C., 1979-88; acting justice Supreme Ct., N.Y.C., 1984-88, justice, 1989-95; apptd. to appellate term 1st dept. NY Supreme Ct., N.Y.C., 1995—; co-chair State Judges Mass Tort Litigation Com.; mem. pattern jury instrns. com., Supreme Ct. Justices; adj. prof. N.Y. Law Sch., 1999; lectr. in field. Author: New York Objections, 1999; contbr. articles to profl. jours. Fellow Am. Bar Found.; mem. ABA (chair small claims ct. com. 1986-89, bioethics com. nat. conf. spl. ct. judges, N.Y. State Ct. del. to ann. meetings, nat. conf. spl. ct. judges, 1987, 88, Spl. Cts. Conf. award 1987, 88, 93, Jud. Excellence award 1998), Nat. Assn. Women Judges, N.Y. State Bar Assn., N.Y. Women's Bar Assn., N.Y. State Assn. Women Judges (pres. 1995-97), Assn. of Bar of City of N.Y. (mem. various coms., chair com. med. malpractice, v.p. 1994-95). Home: 150 W 96th St New York NY 10025-6469 Office: NY Supreme Ct 60 Centre St New York NY 10007-1402

FREEDMAN, HOWARD MARTIN, financial planner; b. Bronx, N.Y., Mar. 5, 1953; s. Ralph and Jean (Hoffman) F.; m. Ann Beth Roberts, Aug. 20, 1978; children: Richard, Andrew, Tania. BA, Bradley U., Peoria, Ill., 1974; MBA in Fin. Mgmt., Pace U., 1977; postgrad., NYU, 1978. Registered investment advisor. Fin. planner personal fin. planning div. E.F. Hutton Group, N.Y.C., 1978-83; account supr. E.F. Hutton Group, Providence, 1983-86; sr. fin. advisor E.F. Hutton Group-Shearson Lehman Hutton, Stamford, Conn., 1987-89; prin. Freedman Planning & Mgmt., Norwalk, Conn., 1989—; advisor planned giving com. Pace U., N.Y.C., 1983-86. Advisor gifting program, fin. com., budget com. Temple Shalom, Norwalk. Republican. Avocations: photography, travel. Office: 360 Connecticut Ave Ste 365 Norwalk CT 06854-1824

FREEDMAN, JAMES OLIVER, university president, lawyer; b. Manchester, N.H., Sept. 21, 1935; s. Louis A. and Sophie (Gottesman) F. AB, Harvard U., 1957; LLB, Yale U., 1962; LLD (hon.), Cornell Coll., 1982, So. Meth. U., 1988, Mt. Holyoke Coll., 1988, Vt. Law Sch., 1992, U. N.H., 1992; LHD (hon.), St. Ambrose U., 1984, Hebrew Union Coll., 1998, Dartmouth Coll., 1998. Bar: N.H. 1962, Pa. 1971, Iowa 1982. Prof. law U. Pa., 1964-82, assoc. provost, 1978, dean, 1979-82, also univ. ombudsman, 1973-76; pres., disting. prof. law and polit. sci. U. Iowa, 1982-87; pres. Dartmouth Coll., Hanover, 1987-98; 8th ann. Roy R. Ray lectr. So. Meth. U. Sch. Law, 1985; Tyrell Williams lectr. Washington U. Sch. Law, 1994; Francis Greenwood Peabody lectr. Harvard U., 1998, Margaret MacVicker lectr. MIT, 1999; bd. dirs. Houghton Mifflin Co. Author: Crisis and Legitimacy: The Administrative Process and American Government, 1978, Idealism and Liberal Education, 1996; mem. editl. bd. U. Pa. Press, 1974-81, chmn., 1979-82; contbr. aritcles to profl. jours. Mem. Phila. Bd. Ethics, 1981-82; chmn. Pa. Legis. Reapportionment Commn., 1981; chmn. Iowa Gov.'s Task Force on Fgn. Lang. Studies and Internat. Edn., 1982-83; trustee Jewish Pub. Soc., 1979—; bd. dirs. Salzburg Seminar Am. Studies, 1988-92, 94-97, 99—, Am. Coun. on Edn., 1986-89; bd. Jacob K. Javits fellows program U.S. Dept. Edn., 1993-97. Recipient scholarship award Pa. chpt. Order of Coif, 1981, Am. Book award, 1990, William O. Douglas First Amendment Freedom award Anti-Defamation League, 1991, Gilda Radner award Wellness Cmty. Greater Boston, Frederic W. Ness award Assn. Am. Coll. and Univ., 1997; fellow NEH, 1976-77; Phi Beta Kappa vis. scholar, 1999-2000. Mem. Am. Law Inst., Am. Acad. Arts & Scis., Clare Hall Cambridge U. (life). Office: Dartmouth Coll 236 Baker Libr Hanover NH 03755-3529

FREEDMAN, JAY WEIL, lawyer; b. Washington, May 19, 1942; s. Walter and Maxine (Weil) F.; m. Linda Newman, Aug. 7, 1966; children—Courteney, Spencer. B.A., Williams Coll., 1964; J.D., Yale U., 1967. Bar: D.C. 1968, U.S. Supreme Ct. 1973. Atty. office of gen. counsel FCC, 1967-68; assoc. Freedman, Levy, Kroll & Simonds, Washington, 1968-72, ptnr., 1972—. Pres. Washington Hebrew Congregation, 1982-84, Am. Jewish Com., Washington, 1987-89. Mem. ABA, D.C. Bar, Woodmont Country Club (pres. 1997—), Econ. Club Washington, Phi Delta Phi. Office: Freedman Levy Kroll & Simonds 1050 Connecticut Ave NW Ste 825 Washington DC 20036-5366

FREEDMAN, JONATHAN BORWICK, journalist, author, lecturer; b. Rochester, N.Y., Apr. 11, 1950; s. Marshall Arthur and Betty (Borwick) F.; m. Maggie Locke, May 4, 1979; children: Madigan, Nicholas. AB in Lit. cum laude, Columbia Coll., N.Y.C., 1972. Reporter AP of Brazil, Sao Paulo and Rio de Janeiro, 1974-75; editorial writer The Tribune, San Diego, 1981-90; syndicated columnist Copley News Service, San Diego, 1987-89; freelance opinion writer L.A. Times, 1990—; free-lance editorial writer N.Y. Times, 1990-91; dir. Hope Lit. Project, 1998—; dist. vis. lectr. and adj. faculty San Diego State U., 1990—; mem. U.S.-Japan Journalists Exch. Program, Internat. Press Inst., 1985. Author, illustrator: The Man Who'd Bounce the World, 1979; author: The Editorials and Essays of Jonathan Freedman, 1988; contbg. author: Best Newspaper Writing, From Contemporary Culture, 1991, (nonfiction) From Cradle to Grave: The Human Face of Poverty in America, 1993; freelance columnist, 1979-81; dir. (TV documentary) Pedaling Hope, 1998; contbr. articles to N.Y. Times, Chgo. Tribune, San Francisco Examiner, Oakland Tribune, others. Moderator PBS, San Diego, 1988; bd. dirs. Schs. of the Future Commn., San Diego, 1987. Recipient Copley Ring of Truth award, 1983, Sigma Delta Chi award, 1983, San Diego Press Club award, 1984, Spl. citation Columbia Grad. Sch. Journalism, 1985, Disting. Writing award Am. Soc. Newspaper Editors, 1986, Pulitzer prize in Disting. Editorial Writing, 1987; Cornell Woolrich Writing fellow Columbia U., 1972, Eugene C. Pullian Editorial Writing fellow Sigma Delta Chi Found., 1986, Media fellow Hoover Instn., Stanford, Calif., 1991, Kaiser Media fellow, 1995, Peacemaker awarad San Diego Mediation Ctr., 1999, one of 45 Am. Heroes, Esquire mag., 1998. Mem. Soc. Profl. Journalists (Disting. Svc. award 1985, Casey medal for meritorious journalism 1994), Nat. Conf. Editl. Writers, Authors Guild, Phi Beta Kappa. Jewish. Avocations: skiing, tai chi. Office: 4506 Adair St San Diego CA 92107-3804

FREEDMAN, JOSEPH, sanitary and public health engineering consultant; b. Brighton, Mass., Oct. 16, 1923; s. Edwin Akiva and Fanny (Wine) F.; m. Emily Ann Feltman, Nov. 4, 1959; children: Susan Alexandra. BS in Pub. Health Engring., Ga. Tech., 1943; MS in Sanitary Engring., U. N.C., 1945; SM in Sanitary Engring., Harvard U., 1955; cert. in groundwater devel., U. Minn., 1959. Registered profl. engr., Mass. Sanitary engr. Holmes & Narver, Architect Engrs., Okinawa, Japan, 1946-48; chief sanitary engr. R & U div. Mariannas Bonins Command, Dept. of the Army, Guam, 1948-50; engr. Charles T. Main, Consulting Engrs., Boston, 1951-54; sanitary engr. Pan Am. Health Orgn., Honduras, 1955-61; advisor Govt. of Honduras, Tegucigalpa, 1955-61; chief sanitary engr., advisor to govts. U.S AID, La Paz, Bolivia and Asuncion, Paraguay, 1961-63; chief sanitary engr. Inter-Am. Devel. Bank, Washington, 1963-73; sr. sanitary engr. Latin Am. Caribbean region World Bank, Washington, 1973-79; water/waste advisor Ctrl. Office World Bank, Washington, 1979-86; cons. various water supply, sewage and pollution control and tourist projects World Bank, OAS, VITA, 1989—; cons. on devel. North Coast and Bay Islands, Honduras Govt./OAS, 1986-87; cons. Arthur Young Assocs., Reorgn. and Decentralization Nat. Water and Sewer Authority, Honduras, 1987; World Bank rep. on bd. dirs. Internat. Ref. Ctr. for Cmty. Water Supply and Sanitation, The Hague, Netherlands, 1983-85. Author: Plan for the Development of the Hydraulic Resources of Honduras, 1953; asst. contbr. report Unified Devel. of the Hydraulic Resources of the Jordan River Valley, 1951-52; co-author: National Health Plan and Training Center for Government of Honduras, 1956-57, Development of National and Local Institutions for Planning, Building, Maintaining and Financing Urban and Rural Water and Sewer Programs. Buenos Aires Convention fellow, 1953. Fellow ASCE; mem. Inter-Am. Soc. Sanitary Engrs. (charter mem.), World Bank 1818 Soc., Sigma Xi, Phi Eta Sigma, Phi Kappa Phi. Avocation: genealogy. Home: 6504 Elgin Ln Bethesda MD 20817-5442

FREEDMAN, JOSEPH MARK, optometrist; b. Bklyn., Jan. 28, 1951; s. Milton and Bernice (Lobele) F.; m. Lynn M. Gewant, Oct. 22, 1978; children: Rachel, Margot. BS summa cum laude, Bklyn. Coll., 1973; OD, SUNY, 1977. Lic. optometrist, N.Y., N.J. Dir. contact lens svc. Bronx, N.Y., 1977-83; pvt. practice North Shore Contact Lens Assocs. (name changed to North Shore Contact Lens & Vision Cons., P.C.), Roslyn, N.Y., 1983—; v.p. Vision Rsch. Tech., Inc., Great Neck, N.Y., 1985—; v.p., rsch. & devel. Natural Ceuticals, Inc., Deer Park, N.Y., 1992—. Contbr. articles to profl. jours. Office: N Shore Contact Lens Assoc 1025 Northern Blvd Roslyn NY 11576-1506

FREEDMAN, LOUIS MARTIN, dentist; b. Newark, Mar. 19, 1947; s. Morris and Sylvia (Swimmer) F.; m. Elizabeth Norine Palmer, June 17, 1978; children: Steven, Julie, Brian. Student, Emory U., 1963-66, DDS, 1970. Gen. dentist Freedman, Freedman & Weitman DDS, P.C., Atlanta, 1970—; clin. instr. Emory U. Dental Sch., Atlanta, 1970-77; team dentist Atlanta Hawks Basketball Team, 1971—, Atlanta Flames Hockey Team, 1979-80, Atlanta Knights Hockey Team, 1992-96, Atlanta Fire Ants Roller Hockey Team, 1994-96. Mem. Exch. Club, Atlanta, 1970-73; mgr. Sandy Springs Youth Sports Little League Baseball, 1979-96; head coach Sandy Springs United Meth. Ch. basketball program, 1991-96. Mem. Acad. Osseointegration, Alpha Epsilon Delta, Omicron Kappa Upsilon. Jewish. Avocations: softball, little league managing, gardening, snow skiing, water skiing, swimming. Office: Freedman Freedman & Weitman 3111 Piedmont Rd NE Atlanta GA 30305-2507

FREEDMAN, MARC ALLAN, investment company executive; b. Buffalo, Sept. 8, 1958; s. Gerald Kenneth and Marlene (Celniker) Freedman; m. Sheryl Renee Lechtner, May 23, 1982; children: Hallie Michelle, Max Aaron. Student, Rochester Inst. Tech., 1976-78, George Washington U., 1978-80. Cert. investment mgmt. analyst; cert. investment mgmt. cons. Account exec. Clayton Brokerage of St. Louis, Inc., McLean, Va., 1982-83, Smith Barney Harris Upham & Co., Rockville, Md., 1983, E.F. Hutton & Co., Inc., Alexandria, Va., 1983-86; v.p. investments Gruntal & Co., Inc., Washington, 1986-91, Prudential Securities, Inc., Washington, 1991-93; mng. ptnr. TriCapital Investment Mgmt., North Bethesda, Md., 1993—. pres. Washingtonian Towns Homeowners Assn., Gaithersburg, Md., 1984-91; treas. Congregation B'nai Tzedekh, Potomac, Md., 1989-91, v.p. fin., 1991-93, pres. Brotherhood, 1995-97. Republican. Jewish. Avocations: golf, skiing, reading, landscape design, racquetball. Office: TriCapital Investment Mgmt Inc 11140 Rockville Pike Ste 600 Rockville MD 20852-3117

FREEDMAN, MARK, marketing executive. BA in Sociology, Clark U. Licensing exec. Long Ranger, Buck Rogers Leisure Concepts, 1980-82; mgr. licensing Flintstones, Scooby-Doo Taft Merchandising Group, 1983-85; mgr. Alvin & the Chipmunks Mode Prodns., 1985; pres., founder, licensor Teenage Mutant Ninja Turtles Surge Licensing, 1986—; mgr. Street Sharks Surge Entertainment, Inc., 1994—. Office: Surge Licensing Inc 100 Jericho Quadrangle Ste 233 Jericho NY 11753-2710

FREEDMAN, MARYANN SACCOMANDO, lawyer; b. Buffalo, N.Y., Sept. 12, 1934; d. James Vincent and Rosaria (Rizzo) Saccomando; m. Robert Paul Freedman, Apr. 9, 1961; children: Brenda Marie, Donald Vincent. JD, U. Buffalo, 1958. Bar: N.Y. 1959, U.S. Dist. Ct. (we. dist.) N.Y. 1959, U.S. Supreme Ct. 1963. Law clk. Saperston McNaughton & Saperston, Buffalo, 1957-59, assoc., 1959-61; ptnr. Freedman & Freedman, Buffalo, 1961-75; confidential legal rsch. asst. Buffalo City Ct., 1972-75; asst. atty. gen. N.Y. State Dept. Law, Buffalo, 1977-90; spl. counsel Lavin & Kleiman, Buffalo, 1991-95; of counsel Cohen & Lombardo, P.C., Buffalo, 1995—, 1995—; asst. prof. Erie C.C., Buffalo, 1975-76; lectr. Erie County Emergency Med. Technician Program, Buffalo, 1975-83, Buffalo and Erie County Police Acad., 1975-86; referee N.Y. State. Jud. Conduct Commn., 1998—. Bd. editors N.Y. State Bar Jour., 1983-97. Founder, panel mem. Alliance for Dispute Resolution, 1997—; trustee YMCA, Buffalo, 1982-87; chmn. United Way Task Force on Legal Svcs., Buffalo, 1983; chair Buffalo Philharm. Orch. Stabilization Com., 1991-94; mem. dean's adv. coun. sch. law State U. Buffalo, 1991-93; bd. dirs. Downtown Nursing Home, Buffalo, 1982-91, Better Bus. Bur., Buffalo, 1983-92; mem. Gov.'s Departmental and Statewide Jud. Screening coms., 1997—, Jud. Compensation Commn., 1997—; co-host Ask Women radio, 1996-98. Recipient Buffalo Bison award City of Buffalo, 1976, Legal Svcs. for Elderly and Handicapped award, 1986, SUNY Buffalo Disting. Alumni award, 1986, Hilbert Coll. Pres.'s medal, 1987, Wise Woman award Nat. Orgn. Italian-Am. Women, 1987, Barrister award Nat. Columbus Day Com., 1987, Westchester Legal Svcs. award, 1987; named Outstanding Woman in Law, U. Buffalo Cmty. Adv. Coun., 1984, Outstanding Citizen Buffalo News, 1986, Disting. Alumnus, U. Buffalo Law Alumni, 1988, Woman of Yr. Buffalo Philharm. Orch., 1993. Mem. ABA (ho. dels. 1986—), N.Y. State Bar Assn. (pres-elect, chair ho. of dels. 1986-87, pres. 1987-88, Ruth G. Schapiro award 1994), N.Y. State Bar Found. (bd. dirs., v.p. 1994-97, pres. 1997—), Erie County Bar Assn. (pres. 1981-82, Spl. Svc. award 1984, Lawyer of Yr. 1987), Cattaraugus County Bar Assn. (Law Day award 1986), Assn. of Italian-Am. Women of West N.Y. (Lifetime Achievement award 1999), Aid to Indigent Prisoners Soc. (pres. 1981-82), Women Lawyers Assn. Western N.Y. (pres. 1962-64), Buffalo Geol. Soc. (treas. 1999). Clubs: Zonta (pres. 1978-79, area dir. dist. IV 1979-80, 82-83). Office: 343 Elmwood Ave Buffalo NY 14222-2203

FREEDMAN, MERVIN BURTON, psychologist, educator; b. N.Y.C., Mar. 6, 1920; s. Eli and Rose (Weithorn) F.; m. Marjorie Ellingson, Feb. 16, 1952; children: Eric, Kristin, Rolf, Anne Marie. B.S., Coll. City N.Y., 1940; Ph.D., U. Calif. at Berkeley, 1950. Lectr. dept. psychology U. Calif. at Berkeley, 1950-53; research asso. Mellon Found. for Advancement Edn., Vassar Coll., 1953-58; dir. Mellon Found., 1958-60; research assoc. Inst. for Study Human Problems Stanford U., 1962-63, asst. dean undergrad. edn. Stanford U., 1963-65; chmn. dept. psychology San Francisco State U., 1965-68, prof. psychology, 1968—; dean grad. sch. Wright Inst., Berkeley, 1969-79; sr. Fulbright research scholar U. Oslo, 1961-62; fellow Center for Advanced Study Behavioral Sci., 1960-61. Author: The College Experience, 1967; (with others) Search for Relevance, 1969, Academic Culture and Faculty Development, 1978, Human Development in Social Settings, 1983, Personality and Social Change, 1986, Americans and the Irrational, 1988, A Traveller in Inner Landscapes, 1999, Closing Time, 1999; assoc. editor: Polit. Psychology. Vice pres. San Francisco Am.-Scandinavian Found. Served with AUS, 1941-45. Decorated Bronze Star. Fellow Am. Psychol. Assn., Am. Psychol. Soc.; mem. Western Psychol. Assn., Internat. Soc. Polit. Psychology. Home: 866 Spruce St Berkeley CA 94707-2043

FREEDMAN, MICHAEL HARTLEY, mathematician, educator; b. Los Angeles, Apr. 21, 1951; s. Benedict and Nancy (Mars) F.; 1 child by previous marriage, Benedict C.; m. Leslie Blair Howland, Sept. 18, 1983; children: Hartley, Whitney, Jake. Ph.D., Princeton U., 1973. Lectr. U. Calif., 1973-75; mem. Inst. Advanced Study, Princeton, N.J., 1975-76; prof. U. Calif., San Diego, 1976—; Charles Lee Powell chair math. U. Calif., 1985—. Author: Classification of Four Dimensional Spaces, 1982; assoc. editor Jour. Differential Geometry, Math. Rsch. Letters and Topology, 1982—, Annals of Math., 1984-91, Jour. Am. Math. Soc., 1987—. MacArthur Found. fellow, 1984-89; named Calif. Scientist of Yr., Calif. Mus. Assn., 1984; recipient Veblen prize Am. Math. Soc., 1986, Fields medal Internat. Congress of Mathematicians, 1986, Nat. Medal of Sci., 1987, Humboldt award, 1988; Guggenheim fellow, 1989, 94. Mem. Nat. Acad. Scis., Am. Assn. Arts and Scis., N.Y. Acad. Scis., Guggenheim Fellowship award, 1994. Avocation: technical rock climber (soloed Northeast ridge Mt. Williamson 1970, Great Western boulder climbing champion 1979). Office: U Calif San Diego Dept Math 0112 9500 Gilman Dr La Jolla CA 92093-0112*

FREEDMAN, MICHAEL LEONARD, geriatrician, educator; b. Newark, Dec. 12, 1937; s. David Hyman and Alice Ella (Zwain) F.; m. Cora Ruth Singer, June 24, 1962; children: Lawrence Andrew, Deborah Lynn. AB with honors, Colgate U., 1959; MD cum laude, Tufts U., 1963. Diplomate Am. Bd. Internal Medicine, Am. Bd. Hematology, Am. Bd. Geriatric Medicine. Intern, then resident NYU/Bellevue Med. Ctrs., 1963-65, 68-69; rsch. assoc. lab physiology to staff investigator Nat. Cancer Inst., NIH, Bethesda, Md., 1965-68; asst. prof. NYU Med. Ctr., 1969-74, assoc. prof., 1974-77, prof., 1977—, firm chief, dir. geriatrics, 1979—; Diane and Arthur Belfer prof. geriatric medicine NYU, 1987—; cons. CBS, Inc., Bristol Meyers Corp., Kimberly-Clark Corp., Pfizer Corp., Nutrasweet Corp., Citicorp. Editor: Hematology in the Elderly, 1985; contbr. over 175 articles to profl. jours. Lt. comdr. USPHS, 1965-68. NIH rsch. grantee, 1969—; recipient Wholeness of Life award Hosp. Chaplaincy, 1988; named one of the Heroes of Bellevue, 1987. Fellow ACP, Am. Geriatrics Soc. (com. chmn. 1985—), Am. Soc. Hematology, Gerontol. Soc. Am. (com. chmn. 1984—); mem. Am. Soc. Clin. Investigation, Am. Soc. Hematology, AAAS, Am. Fed. Aging Rsch. (founder, mem. nat. adv. coun.), Alpha Omega Alpha. Democrat. Jewish. Avocations: photography, travel, tennis. Office: NYU Med Ctr 550 1st Ave New York NY 10016-6481

FREEDMAN, MONROE HENRY, lawyer, educator, columnist; b. Mt. Vernon, N.Y., Apr. 10, 1928; s. Chauncey and Dorothea (Kornblum) F.; m. Audrey Willock, Sept. 24, 1950 (dec. 1998); children: Alice Freedman Korngold, Sarah Freedman Izquierdo, Caleb (dec. 1992), Judah. AB cum laude, Harvard U., 1951, LLB, 1954, LLM, 1956. Bar: Mass. 1954, Pa. 1957, D.C. 1960, U.S. Dist. Ct. (ea. dist. N.Y.), U.S. Ct. Appeals (D.C. cir.) 1960, U.S. Supreme Ct. 1960, U.S. Ct. Appeals (2d cir.) 1968, N.Y. 1978, U.S. Ct. Appeals (9th cir.) 1982, U.S. Ct. Appeals (11th cir.) 1986, U.S. Ct. Appeals (Fed. cir.) 1987. Assoc. Wolf, Block, Schorr & Solis-Cohen, Phila., 1956-58; ptnr. Freedman & Temple, Washington, 1969-73; dir. Stern Community Law Firm, Washington, 1970-71; prof. law George Washington U., 1958-73; dean Hofstra Law Sch., Hempstead, N.Y., 1973-77, prof. law, 1973—, Howard Lichtenstein Disting. prof. legal ethics, 1989—; Drinko-Baker & Hostetler chair in law Cleve. State U., 1992; assoc. dir. Inst. for the Study of Legal Ethics, 1995—; faculty asst. Harvard U. Law Sch., 1954-56, instr. trial advocacy, 1978—; lectr. on lawyers' ethics; exec. dir. U.S. Holocaust Meml. Coun., 1980-82, gen. counsel, 1982-83, sr. adviser to chmn., 1982-87; cons. U.S. Commn. on Civil Rights, 1960-64, Neighborhood Legal Services Program, 1970; legis. cons. to Senator John L. McClellan, 1959; spl. com. on courtroom conduct N.Y.C. Bar Assn., 1972; exec. dir. Criminal Trial Inst., 1965-66; expert witness on legal ethics state and fed. ct. proceedings, U.S. Senate and House Coms., U.S. Dept. Justice, FDIC; spl. investigator Rochester Inst. Tech., 1991; reporter Am. Lawyer's Code of Conduct, 1979-81; mem. Arbitration panel U.S. Dist. Ct. (ea. dist.) N.Y., 1986—; Inaugural Wickwire lectr. Dalhousie Law Sch., N.S., 1992; lectr. S.C. Bar Found., 1993, numerous profl. confs; adv. subgroup on ethics U.S. Dist. Ct. (ea. dist.) N.Y., 1994-96. Author: Contracts, 1973, Lawyers' Ethics in an Adversary System, 1975 (ABA gavel award, cert. of merit 1976), Teacher's Manual Contracts, 1978, American Lawyer's Code of Conduct, 1981, Understanding Lawyers' Ethics, 1990, Group Defamation and Freedom of Speech—The Relationship Between Language and Violence, 1995; co-editor; columnist Cases and Controversies, Am. Lawyer Media, 1990—, (with Supreme Ct. Justice Ruth Bader Ginsburg) Freedom, Life, & Death: Materials on Comparative Constitutional Law, 1997; television appearances include Donohue, CNN Money Line, CBS 60 Minutes, CNN Late Edition, Court TV, and others; contbr. articles to profl. jours. Recipient Martin Luther King Jr. Humanitarian award, 1987, The Lehman-LaGuardia Award for Civic Achievement, 1996. Fellow Am. Bar Found. (life); mem. ABA (ethics adv. to chair criminal justice sect. 1993—, Michael Franck award 1998), ACLU (nat. bd. dirs. 1970-80, nat. adv. coun. 1980—, spl. litigation counsel 1971-73), Am. Law Inst. (consultative group on the law governing lawyers, 1990-99, consultative group on Uniform Comml. Code art. 2 1990—), Soc. Am. Law Tchrs. (mem. governing bd. 1974-79, exec. com. 1976-79, chmn. com. on profl. responsibility 1974-79, 87-90), ABA (vice chmn. ethical considerations com. criminal justice sect. 1989-90, ethics advisor to chmn. criminal justice sect., 1993-96), N.Y. State Bar Assn. (com. on legal edn. and admission to bar 1988-92, criminal justice sect. com. on profl. responsibility, 1990-92, award for Dedication to Scholarship and pub. svc. 1997), Assn. Bar City N.Y. (com. on profl. responsibility 1987-90, com. on profl. and jud. ethics 1991-92), Fed. Bar Assn. (chmn. com. on profl. disciplinary standards and procedures 1970-71), Am. Jewish Congress (nat. governing coun. 1984-86), Am. Arbitration Assn. (arbitrator, nat. panel arbitrators 1964—, cert. svc. award 1986), Nat. Network on Right to Counsel (exec. bd., exec. com. 1986-90), Nat. Prison Project (steering com. 1970-90), Nat. Assn. Criminal Def. Lawyers (vice chmn. ethics adv. com. 1991-93, co-chmn., 1994), Inst. Study Legal Ethics (assoc. dir. 1995—). Democrat. Jewish.

FREEDMAN, PHILIP, physician, educator; b. London, June 25, 1926; came to U.S., 1963, naturalized, 1970; s. Myer and Mildred (Frankel) F.; m. Jean Kennis Cunningham, Dec. 21, 1954; children: Simon John, Marion Rose, Mark Alexander, Paul Daniel, Adam James. MB, BS with honors, Univ. Coll. Hosp. Med. Sch., London, 1948, MD, 1951. House surgeon Univ. Coll. Hosp., 1948, med. registrar, 1953-56, rsch. asst. professorial med. unit, 1956-57, Bilton Pollard fellow, 1957-59; sr. house physician Chase Farm Hosp., 1949; 1st asst. physician St. George's Hosp., London, 1959-60; cons. Woolwich Hosp. Group, London, Redhill Hosp. Group, Surrey, Eng., 1960-63; chief Chgo. Med. Sch. Div., Dept. Medicine Cook County Hosp., 1963-66; prof., chmn. dept. medicine Chgo. Med. Sch., 1967-74; dir. renal unit Cook County Hosp., Chgo., 1963-66; chmn. dept. medicine Mt. Sinai Hosp. Med. Ctr., Chgo., 1966-79; professor and sr. attending physician Rush Med. Coll., Rush-Presbyn.-St. Luke's Med. Ctr., Chgo., 1975-96. Contbr. articles to profl. jours. With M.C. Brit. Army, 1951-53. Fellow ACP, Royal Coll. Physicians; mem. Ctrl. Soc. Clin. Investigation, Med. Rsch. Soc. London, Alpha Omega Alpha (faculty mem.). Home: 2304 Sand Point Champaign IL 61822-9297

FREEDMAN, ROBERT LOUIS, lawyer; b. Phila., Apr. 8, 1940; s. Abraham L. and Jane G. (Sunstein) F.; m. Diane Stoller, July 25, 1965; children: Elizabeth, Paul, Jonathan. AB, Harvard U., 1962; MA in Econs., Columbia U., 1963, LLB, 1966. Bar: Pa. 1967. Law clk., 1966-68; assoc. Dechert Price & Rhoads, Phila., 1968-75, ptnr., 1975—; lectr. in law Temple U. Law Sch., 1969-74; adj. prof. U. Pa. Law Sch., 1997—. Mem. adv. com. on decedents' estates Pa. Joint State Govt. Commn. Mem. Am. Law Inst., Am. Coll. Trust and Estate Counsel, Phila. Bar Assn. (chmn. sect. on probate and trust law 1983). Jewish. Club: Germantown Cricket. Office: Dechert Price & Rhoads 4000 Bell Atlantic Tower 1717 Arch St Philadelphia PA 19103-2793

FREEDMAN, RONALD, sociology educator; b. Winnipeg, Man., Can., Aug. 8, 1917; came to U.S., 1924, naturalized, 1930.; s. Isador and Ada (Greenstone) F.; m. Deborah Gail Selin, May 4, 1941; children: Joseph Selin, Jane Ilene. BA, U. Mich., 1939, MA, 1940; PhD, U. Chgo., 1947. Mem. faculty U. Mich., Ann Arbor, 1946—; prof. sociology U. Mich., 1954—, Roderick D. McKenzie prof. sociology, 1979-87, now Roderick D. McKenzie prof. emeritus; rsch. assoc. Survey Rsch. Ctr., 1954-70; dir. Population Studies Ctr., 1962-71; co-dir. Taiwan Population Studies Ctr., 1962-64; cons. to Taiwan govt., 1962-88; mem. tech. adv. com. 1970 Census of Population, 1965, Pres.'s Adv. Com. on Population and Family Planning. Author: The Sociology of Human Fertility, 1960, (with others) Family Planning, Sterility and Population Growth, 1959, Principles of Sociology, 1952, Family Planning in Taiwan, 1969; also articles and monographs. With USAAF, 1942-45. Recipient award excellence on teaching U. Mich. Class of, 1952, Disting. Faculty Svc. award U. Mich., 1970, Taeuber award, 1981; Guggenheim fellow, 1957-58; Fulbright fellow, 1957-58; fellow Center for Advanced Study in Behavioral Scis., 1970; Lady Davis fellow and Einstein fellow Hebrew U., 1987. Fellow Am. Acad. Arts and Scis., U.S. Nat. Acad. Sci., Am. Statis. Assn.; mem. NAS, Population Assn. Am. (pres. 1964-65), Internat. Union Study Population (v.p. 1966-67), Am. Sociol. Assn., Sociol. Rsch. Assn., Phi Beta Kappa. Home: 2125 Nature Cv Apt 206 Ann Arbor MI 48104-4989

FREEDMAN, RUSSELL BRUCE, author; b. San Francisco, Oct. 11, 1929; s. Louis Nathan and Irene (Gordon) F. BA, U. Calif., Berkeley, 1951. Newsman AP, San Francisco, 1953-56; with dept. TV publicity J. Walter Thompson Co., N.Y.C., 1956-60; faculty New Sch. for Social Rsch., N.Y.C., 1969-86. Author: Teenagers Who Made History, 1961, Jules Verne: Portrait of a Prophet, 1963, 2000 Years of Space Travel, 1965, Thomas Alva Edison, 1966, Scouting with Baden-Powell, 1967, Animal Architects, 1971, The First Days of Life, 1974, Growing Up Wild, 1975, Animal Fathers, 1976, Animal Games, 1976, Hanging On: How Animals Carry Their Young, 1978, Getting Born, 1978, Tooth and Claw, 1980, They Lived with the Dinosaurs, 1980, Immigrant Kids, 1980, When Winter Comes, 1981, Farm Babies, 1981, Animal Superstars, 1982, Killer Fish, 1982, Killer Snakes, 1982, Can Bears Predict Earthquakes? Unsolved Mysteries of Animal Behavior, 1982, Dinosaurs and Their Young, 1983, Children of the Wild West, 1983 (Western Heritage Wrangler award, Outstanding Western Juvenile Book award 1984), Rattlesnakes, 1984, Cowboys of the Wild West, 1985, Sharks, 1985, Holiday House: The First Fifty Years, 1985, Indian Chiefs, 1987, Abraham Lincoln: A Photobiography, 1987 (John Newbery medal 1988, Jefferson Cup award 1988), Buffalo Hunt, 1988, Franklin Delano Roosevelt, 1990 (Orbis Pictus award 1991, Jefferson Cup award 1991), The Wright Brothers: How They Invented the Airplane, 1991 (Newbery Honor Book 1992, Jefferson cup award 1992, Golden Kite award 1991), An Indian Winter, 1992 (Western Heritage Wrangler award 1993), Eleanor Roosevelt: A Life of Discovery, 1993 (Newbery Honor Book 1994, Golden Kite award 1993, Boston Globe Horn Book award 1993), Kids at Work, 1994 (Golden Kite award 1994, Jane Addams Book award 1995), The Life and Death of Crazy Horse, 1996 (Spur award Best Western Juvenile Non-fiction 1996), Out of Darkness: The Story of Louis Braille, 1997, Martha Graham: A Dancer's Life, 1998, Babe Didrikson Zaharias: The Making of a Champion, 1999; co-author: (with James E. Morris) How Animals Learn, 1969, Animal Instincts, 1970, The Brains of Animals and Man, 1972. With M.I., U.S. Army, 1951-53; Korea. Mem. PEN, Author's Guild.

FREEDMAN, SAMUEL ORKIN, university official; b. Montreal, Que., Can., May 8, 1928; s. Abraham Orkin and Elvira (Gottheil) F.; m. Norah Lee Maizel, Aug. 28, 1955; children—David Orkin, Daniel Ari, Abraham Edward, Elizabeth Vera. B.Sc., McGill U., Montreal, 1949, M.D., C.M., 1953, D.Sc. (hon.), 1992. Intern Jewish Gen. Hosp., Montreal, 1953-54; resident in internal medicine and allergy Montreal Gen. Hosp., also Roosevelt Hosp., N.Y.C., 1954-59; mem. faculty McGill U. Med. Faculty, 1959—, prof. medicine, 1968—, dean, 1977-81, vice-prin. (acad.), 1981-91; dir. rsch. Sir Mortimer B. Davis Jewish Gen. Hosp., 1991—; vis. prof. U. London, Eng., 1973-74; dir. div. clin. immunology and allergy Montreal Gen. Hosp., 1967-77; bd. dirs. Nat. Cancer Inst. Can., 1979—; chmn. com. immunology and transplanatation Med. Research Council Can., 1968-73, mem. program grants com., 1975-78. Editor: Clinical Immunology, 2d edit, 1976. Decorated Order of Can.; recipient Queen's Silver Jubliee medal, 1977; Gairdner Internat. award for outstanding med. rsch., 1978, Commemorative medal for the 125th Anniversary of the Confedn. of Can., 1992, prix Armand Frappier, 1998, prix de Que., 1998. Fellow Royal Soc. Can., Royal Coll. Physicians and Surgeons Can., ACP, Am. Acad. Allergy; Mem. Internat. Assn. Allergology and Clin. Immunology (v.p. 1982-88); mem. Am. Soc. Clin. Investigation, Am. Assn. Immunology, Am. Thoracic Soc., Canadian Soc. Clin. Investigation. Jewish. Club: Univ. (Montreal). Co-discoverer CEA test for cancer, 1969. Home: 658 Murray Hill Ave, Montreal, PQ Canada H3Y 2W6 Office: McGill U/Lady Davis Inst Med Rsch, 3755 Cote Ste Catherine Rd, Montreal, PQ Canada H3T 1E2

FREEDMAN, SANDRA WARSHAW, former mayor; b. Newark, Sept. 21, 1943; m. Michael J. Freedman; 3 children. BA in Govt., U. Miami, 1965. Mem. Tampa (Fla.) City Coun., 1974—, chmn., 1983-86; mayor City of Tampa, 1986-95. Bd. dirs. Jewish Cmty. Ctr., Boys and Girls Clubs Greater Tampa, Hillsborough Coalition for Health, Tampa Cmty. Concert Assn., Hillsborough Edn. Found., Judeo Christian Clinic, NCCJ, Human Rights Task Force; mem. sports adv. bd. Hillsborough Community Coll., 1975-76; sec. Downtown Devel. Authority, 1977-78; bd. dirs., v.p. Fla. Gulf Coast Symphony, 1979-80; vice chmn. Met. Planning Orgn., 1981-82; corp. mem. Neighborhood Housing Service; bd. fellows U. Tampa; mem. steering com. Hillsborough County Council of Govt.'s Constituency for Children; mem. exec. bd. Tampa/Hillsborough Young Adult Forum; chmn. bd. trustees Berkeley Prep. Sch.; trustee Tampa Bay Performing Arts Ctr., Inc., Tampa Mus.; mem. ethics com. Meml. Hosp.; mem. Tampa Preservation, Inc., Tampa/Hillsborough County Youth Council, Davis Islands Civic Assn., Tampa Hist. Soc., Met. Ministries Adv. Bd., Rodeph Sholom Synagogue, Sword of Hope Guild of Am. Cancer Soc., Friends of Arts. Recipient Spessar L. Holland Meml. award Tampa Bay Com. for Good Govt., 1975-76, Human Rights award City of Tampa, 1980, award Soroptimist Internat. Tampa, 1981, Status of Women award Zonta of Tampa II, 1986, Woman of Achievement award Bus. & Profl. Women, Jewish Nat. Fund Tree of Life award, Disting. Citizen award U. South Fla., 1995, Nat. Conf. of Christian and Jews Humanitarian award, 1995; named to Fla. Home Builders Hall of Fame. Mem. Hillsborough County Bar Aux., Greater Tampa C. of C., C. of C. Com. of 100 (exec. com.), Fla. League of Cities (bd. dirs.), Tampa Urban League, Nat. Council Jewish Women, U. Miami Alumni Assn., Athena Soc., Hadassah. Office: 3435 Bayshore Blvd Apt 700 Tampa FL 33629-8800

FREEDMAN, SARAH WARSHAUER, education educator; b. Wilmington, N.C., Feb. 23, 1946; d. Samuel Edward and Miriam (Miller) Warshauer; m. S. Robert Freedman, Aug. 20, 1967; 1 child, Rachel Karen. BA in English, U. Pa., 1967; MA in English, U. Chgo., 1970; MA in Linguistics, Stanford U., 1976, PhD in Edn., 1977. Tchr. English Phila. Sch. Dist., 1967-68, Lower Merion H.S., 1968-69; instr. English U. N.C., Wilmington, 1970-71; instr. English and linguistics Stanford U., 1972-76; asst. and assoc. prof. English San Francisco State U., 1977-81; asst. prof. edn. U. Calif., Berkeley, 1981-83, assoc. prof. edn., 1983-89; dir. Nat. Ctr. for the Study of Writing and Literacy, 1985-96; prof. edn. U. Calif., 1989—; resident Bellagio Conf. and Study Ctr., Rockefeller Found., 1997; mem. nat. task force Nat. Writing Project, 1998—. Author: Response to Student Writing, 1987, Exchanging Writing, Exchanging Cultures, Lessons in School Reform from the United States and Great Britain, 1994, (with E.R. Simons, J.S. Kalnin) Inside City Schools, Investigating Literacy in Multi-cultural Classrooms, 1999; editor: The Acquisition of Written Language: Response and Revision, 1985; contbr. chpts. to books and articles to profl. jours. Recipient Richard Meade award for Pub. Rsch. in Tchr. Edn. Nat. Coun. Tchrs. English, 1989, 94, Ed Fry book award, 1996; fellow Nat. Conf. on Rsch. in English, 1986; Rockefeller Found. grantee Bryn Mawr Coll., 1992, Nat. Ctr. for Study of Writing and Literacy grantee Office Ednl. Rsch. and Improvement, 1985-95, Minority Undergrad. Rsch. Program grantee U. Calif., 1988, 89, 92, 93, numerous other grants. Mem. Nat. Coun. Tchrs. English (mem. standing com. on rsch. 1981-87, ex-officio 1987—, chair bd. trustees rsch. found. 1990-93), Am. Ednl. Rsch. Assn. (chair spl. interest group on rsch. in writing 1983-85, numerous other coms.), Linguistic Soc. Am., Am. Assn. Applied Linguistics, Internat. Reading Assn. Office: U Calif Dept Edn Berkeley CA 94720

FREEDMAN, STANLEY MARVIN, manufacturing company executive; b. Frederick, Md., Aug. 26, 1923; s. Jacob Menaham and Ethel (Freiman) F.; m. Lynn Maureen Katchen, Apr. 24, 1957 (dec.); children: Rita, Lynn, Michael, Richard, Jon, Jack; m. Lottie Carnell, Dec. 31, 1994 (div.). Student, Georgetown U., 1944; AB in English, High Point Coll., 1946. Owner, operator retail bus. Bound Brook, N.J., 1949-63; dir. mktg. Franklin State Bank, Somerset, N.J., 1963-65; program dir. mktg. div. Am. Mgmt. Assn. N.Y.C., 1965-67; exec. dir. Internat. Bus. Forms Industries, Washington, 1967-69; dir. communications, dir. office machines group Bus. Equipment Mfrs. Assn., Washington, 1969-72; div. pres. Litton Industries, Hampton, Va., 1972-74; group v.p., paper, printing and forms group Litton Industries, Virginia Beach, Va., 1974-86; cons. bus. planning and devel; univ. lectr., 1986-91; dir. Somerset County Savs. & Loan; exec. in residence U. Wis. Grad. Sch. Bus., 1973; entrepreneur in residence U. of the Pacific, Stockton, Calif., 1996. Mem. Bound Brook Bd. Edn., 1955-63; trustee Raritan Valley Hosp., Somerset, N.J., 1960-62; chmn. Urban Devel., Bound Brook, N.J., 1963; mem. def. conversion team AID, Warsaw, Poland, 1995-96. Served with U.S. Army, 1943-46, PTO. Mem. Am. Transfer Print Assn. (conf. bd.), Am. Mgmt. Assn. Home and Office: 33322 N 71st St Scottsdale AZ 85262-7194

FREEDMAN, THEODORE JARRELL, healthcare executive; b. St. Boniface, Man., Can., Nov. 13, 1943; s. Lou and Nydia (Omansky) F.; m. A. Judith Hyman, June 16, 1969; children: Lisa Gaye, Randal Asher. BSc in Pharmacy, U. Man., 1965; DHA, U. Toronto, 1970. Cert. health care exec. Can. Coll. Health Care Execs. Hospital pharmacist Winnipeg (Man.) Health Sci. Ctr., Can., 1965-68; adminstrv. asst. new bldg. coord. Mt. Sinai Hosp., Toronto, Ont., Can., 1970-72, asst. adminstr., 1972-74, asst. exec. dir., 1974-77, assoc. exec. dir., 1977-82, 1977-82, sr. assoc. exec. dir., 1982-84, sr. v.p., 1984-86, exec. v.p., 1986-89, exec. v.p., COO, 1989-93, pres., CEO, 1993—, also bd. dirs., bd. govs.; assoc. prof. dept. health adminstrn. faculty of medicine U. Toronto, 1993—, preceptor, 1988-94; vis. prof. Nanjing (China) Med. U., 1996—; vice chair Toronto Acad. Health Sci. Coun., 1994-96, chair, 1996-98; vice chair Ont. Coun. Tchg. Hosp., 1997-98, chair, 1998-99; mem. regional coun. exec. com. Ont. Hosp. Assn., 1994-98, bd. dirs. Change Found., 1997—; bd. govs. Baycrest Ctr. for Geriatric Care, Toronto, 1993—; bd. mem. Home Care Program for Met. Toronto, 1995-97; bd. mem. Toronto Dist. Health Coun., 1995-98; mem. Health Sci. Consortium of Toronto, 1992-93; preceptor faculty of adminstrn. U. Ottawa, Ont., 1985-94. Contbr. articles to profl. jours. Recipient Robert Wood Johnson award dept. health adminstrn. U. Toronto, 1971, Eugenie M. Stuart award, 1993, Regent's award Am. Coll. Health Care Execs., 1998. Fellow Am. Coll. Health Care Execs.; mem. Can. Coll. Health Svc. Execs., Mandarin Club, Univ. Club. Avocations: golf, travel. Office: Mount Sinai Hosp, 600 University Ave, Toronto, ON Canada M5G 1X5

FREEDMAN, WALTER, lawyer; b. St. Louis, Oct. 30, 1914; s. Sam and Sophie (Gordon) F.; m. Maxine Weil, June 23, 1940; children—Jay W., Sandra Freedman Sabel. A.B., Washington U., 1937, J.D., 1937; LL.M., Harvard, 1938. Bar: Mo. bar, Ill. bar, D.C. bar. Atty. SEC, Washington, 1938-40, U.S. Dept. Interior, Washington, 1940-42; chief counsel Office Export Control, Foreign Econ. Adminstrn., 1942-44, dir., 1944-45; partner Freedman, Levy, Kroll & Simonds (and predecessor firm), Washington, 1946—; Fairchild fellow Harvard U. Law Sch., 1937-38. Editor-in-chief: Washington U. Law Quarterly, 1936-37; Contbr. articles to profl. jours. Decorated chevalier de l'Order de la Couronne (Belgium), 1950; recipient Disting. Alumni award Washington U. Sch. Law, 1995. Mem. Washington Bd. Trade, Am. Law Inst., ABA, Fed. Bar Assn., D.C. Bar Assn., Woodmont country Club (bd. mgrs.), Cosmos Club, Phi Beta Kappa, Omicron Delta Kappa, Phi Sigma Alpha. Jewish (trustee temple). Home: 4545 W St NW Washington DC 20007-5366 Office: 1050 Connecticut Ave NW Washington DC 20036-5366

FREEDMAN, WALTER G., corporate services executive; b. Sherman, Tex., Sept. 10, 1938; s. Samuel B. and Marian (Kirschner) F.; children: Debora Freedman Clower, Amy Freedman Jurkowitz, Michael, Douglas; m. Karen G. Harrison, Aug. 25, 1984. BA, Dartmouth Coll., 1960, MBA, 1961. Data processing salesman IBM, Boston, 1961-64; dir. systems Kitchens of Sara Lee div. Sara Lee Corp., Chgo., 1964-67; pres. Oz Food Corp., Chgo., 1967-70; v.p. corp. devel. Sara Lee Corp., Chgo., 1970-74; pres. Fuller Brush Co. div. Sara Lee Corp., Chgo., 1974-75, Yoplait, USA, Chgo., 1975-77; exec. v.p. Wheels, Inc., Des Plaines, Ill., 1978-86; pres. IVI Bus. Travel Internat., Northbrook, Ill., 1986-95; chmn. VIEWnet, Inc., Madison, Wis., 1995—; bd. dirs. VIEWnet, Inc., Madison, Wis., Cloverleaf Investments, Inc., Northbrook, Ill. Bd. dirs. Chgo. Lung Assn., 1984—, Chgo. Conv. & Visitors Bur., 1988—; benefactor Chgo. Children's Mus., 1987—. Named one of 25 Most Influential Travel Industry Execs. Bus. Travel News, 1987, 89, 90. Mem. Assn. Corp. Travel Execs. (bd. dirs. 1989—). Office: VIEWnet Inc 1 N Franklin St Ste 960 Chicago IL 60606-3421

FREEDMAN, WILLIAM MARK, lawyer; b. Washington, Dec. 8, 1946; s. Henry E. and Dorothy (Markowitz) F.; m. Harriet Arnold, Mar. 9, 1980; children: Alex, Emily. BA, Carleton Coll., 1968; JD, Harvard U., 1973. Bar: Ohio 1973, U.S. Dist. Ct. (so. dist.) Ohio 1973, U.S. Tax Ct. 1974. Assoc. Dinsmore & Shohl, Cin., 1973-80, ptnr., 1980—. Contbr. articles to profl. jours. Trustee Jewish Fedn. Cin., 1983-94, Yavneh Day Sch., Cin., 1988—, Norther Hills Synagogue, 1988—, Cin. Symphony Orch., 1990-94; v.p. No. Hills Synagogue, Cin., 1992-94, pres., 1994-96; chair Jewish Fedn. Cin. Endoment Fund Profl. Advisers Roundtable. With U.S. Army, 1968-70. Mem. ABA, Ohio State Bar Assn., Cin. Bar Assn., Am. Health Lawyers Assn., Soc. Ohio Hosp. Attys. E-mail: freedman@dinslaw.com. Fax: 513-977-8141. Home: 10405 Stablehand Dr Cincinnati OH 45242-4652 Office: Dinsmore & Shohl 1900 Chemed Ctr 255 E 5th St Cincinnati OH 45202-4700

FREEH, LOUIS JOSEPH, federal agency administrator; b. Jan. 6, 1950. AB, Rutgers U., 1971, JD, 1974; LLM in Criminal Law, NYU, 1984. Pvt. practice, 1974-75; spl. agt. FBI, 1975-80, spl. agt. supr., 1980-81; dir. FBI, Washington, 1993—; dep., assoc. U.S. Atty. Office, 1987-91; asst. U.S. atty. U.S. Dist. Ct. (so. dist.) N.Y., 1981-91; judge U.S. Dist. Ct. (so. dist.) N.Y., N.Y.C., 1991-93; adj. assoc. prof. Fordham Law Sch., 1988-92. 1st lt. JAGC USAR, 1985-91. Recipient Fed. Law Enforcement Officers award, 1989, Presdl. award, Disting. Svc. award Atty. Gen., 1987, 91. Mem. N.Y. County Lawyers Assn., Res. Officers Assn. U.S., Phi Beta Kappa. Office: US Dept. of Justice FBI J Edgar Hoover Building 935 Pennsylvania Ave NW Washington DC 20535-0001

FREEHILL, MAURICE F., retired educational psychology educator; b. Chgo., Nov. 29, 1915; s. Pat and Anna (Dillon) F.; m. Kay M. Cronan, Nov. 3, 1924; 1 child, Bernard J. B.Ed., U. Alta., Can., 1945; M.A., Stanford U., 1947, Ed.D., 1948. Cert. tchr., Alta. Tchr., then prin. Alta., 1937-45; prof. ednl. psychology Western Wash. U., Bellingham, 1948-62; prof. ednl. psychology U. Wash., Seattle, 1962-86, prof. emeritus, 1986—. Author: Gifted Children, Their Psychology and Education, 1961, repub., 1982; editor: Disturbed and Troubled Children, 1973; contbr. numerous articles to profl. jours., chpts. to books. Ellwyn Morey fellow, Australia. Fellow APA (diplomate). Home: 5600 S Tara Dr Freeland WA 98249-9472

FREEHLING, ALLEN ISAAC, rabbi; b. Chgo., Jan. 8, 1932; s. Jerome Edward and Marion Ruth (Wilson) F.; m. Lori Golden; children: Shira Susman, David Matthew, Jonathan Andrew. Student, U. Ala., 1949-51; AB, U. Miami, Fla., 1953; B of Hebrew Letters, Hebrew Union Coll., 1965, MA, 1967; PhD, Kensington U., 1977; DD (hon.), Hebrew Union Coll., 1992. Ordained rabbi, 1967. Asst. to pres. Stylaneze, Inc., 1953-54, Univ. Miami, 1954-56; exec. dir. Temple Israel, Miami, 1956-57; asst. to pres. Stevens Markets, Inc., 1957-59; acct. exec. Hank Meyer Assocs., 1959-60; exec. dir. Temple Emanu-El, Miami Beach, Fla., 1960-62; assoc. rabbi The Temple, Toledo, Ohio, 1967-72; sr. rabbi Univ. Synagogue, L.A., 1972—; adj. prof. Loyola-Marymount U., St. Mary's Coll.; v.p. Westside Ecumenical Coun., 1979-81; v.p. Bd. Rabbis of So. Calif., 1981-85, pres., 1985-87; mem. com. on rabbinic growth Cen. Conf. Am. Rabbis; chair Regional Synagogue Coun., 1984-86; bd. dirs., mem. several coms. and commns. Jewish Fedn. Coun.; cons. social actions Union of Am. Hebrew Congregations, mem. nat. and Pacific-S.W. region coms. on AIDS; mem. Rabbinic Cabinet, United Jewish Appeal; bd. dirs. Israel Bonds Orgn., Nat. Jewish Fund; bd. govs. Synagogue Coun. Am.; bd. dirs., newsletter editor Am. Jewish Com. Guest columnist L.A. Hearld Examiner (Silver Angel award Religion in Media, 1987, 88); guest religion progs. Sta. KCBS, KABC; radio/TV host Nat. Conf. Christians and Jews. Chaplain L.A. Police Dept., 1974-86; bd. dirs., mem. exec. com., chair com. on pub. policy, chair govt. affairs com. AIDS Project L.A.; founding chair, exec. com. chairperson AIDS Interfaith Coun. So. Calif.; mem. adv. bd. L.A. AIDS Hospice Com.; apptd. mem., founding chair L.A. County Commn. on AIDS, 1987-89, chair svcs. com., 1989-91, L.A. County Commn. on Mental Health, 1992-95; mem. AIDS-related grants proposal rev. com. Robert Wood Johnson Found., AIDS Task Force of United Way; mem. com. on ethics, medicine and humanity Santa Monica Hosp., L.A. County Commn. on Pub. Social Svcs., 1984-86, Gate Ways Hosp. bd dirs., 1992-95, Jewish Big Bros., 1994—; City of L.A. Task Force on Diversity of Families, Commn. to Draft Ethics Code for L.A. City Govt.; mem. L.A. County Commn. on Juvenile Delinquency and Adult Crime, 1991—; bd. dirs. Jewish Homes for Aging of Greater L.A., NCCJ, 1989, Health of the Bay ; adv. bd. Westside Children's Mus., Interreligious Info. Ctr.; chmn. com. on fed. legislation commn. on law and legislation L.A. Jewish Cmty. Rels. Com., trustee; chair CCAR/UAHC com. on HIV AIDS, Progressive Religious Alliance, City of L.A. 1998 Vol. Festival Adv. Com., First Internat. Conf. on Allocation of Health Resources, Washington, 1997; mem. exec. com., bd. dirs. Heal the Bay; mem. adv. com. Disability Rights Advocates; hon. bd. mem. Jewish Fedn. Western Region Bd. Recipient Bishop Daniel Corrigan commendation Episcopal Diocese, 1987, Humanitarian award NCCJ, 1988, Social Responsibility award L.A. Urban League, 1988, Nat. Friendship award Parents and Friends of Lesbians and Gays, 1989, AIDS Hospice Found. Gene La Pietra Leadership award, 1989, Cath. Archdiocese's Serra Tribute award, 1989, Univ. Synagogue's Avodah award for Cmty. Svc., 1990, Am. Jewish Congress Tzedek award for Cmty.

Leadership and Svc., 1990, Crystal Achievement award AIDS Project L.A., 1996, Planned Parenthood Disting. Svc. award, 1996, Cmty. Leadership award Beeth Chayim Chadashim Congregation. Mem. Am. Jewish Congress (pres. 1977-80, 82-84), Physicians Assn. for AIDS Care (nat. adv. bd.), AIDS Nat. Interfaith Network (bd. dirs.), Jr. C. of C. (chair internat. rels. com.), Sigma Alpha Mu, Omnicron Delta Kappa, Phi Mu Alpha. Office: Univ Synagogue 11960 W Sunset Blvd Los Angeles CA 90049-4200

FREEHLING, DANIEL JOSEPH, law educator, law library director; b. Montgomery, Ala., Nov. 13, 1950; s. Saul Irving and Grace (Lieberman) L. BS, Huntingdon Coll., 1972; JD, U. Ala., 1975, MLS, 1977. Ref. libr., asst. to assoc. dean U. Ala. Sch. Law, Tuscaloosa, 1975-77; assoc. law libr. U. Md., Balt., 1977-79, Cornell U., Ithaca, N.Y., 1979-82; law libr. dir., assoc. prof. U. Maine, Portland, 1982-86; law libr. dir., assoc. prof. law Boston U., 1986-92, prof., 1992—, assoc. dean for adminstrn., 1993-97; mem. steering com., law program com. Rsch. Librs. Group, 1989-91; treas. New Eng. Law Libr. Consortium, 1989-91; vice chair, chair-elect sect. on law librs. Assn. Am. Law Schs., 1990-91, chair, 1992. Mem. ABA (accreditation com. 1995—), Am. Assn. Law Librs. (chair acad. law librs. spl. interest sect. 1981-82, edn. com. 1982-83, membership com. 1983-84, program chair 1987-88, local arrangements co-chair 1992-93, chair mentoring and retention com. 1995-96). Home: 6 Priscilla Ln Winchester MA 01890-4021 Office: Boston U Law Sch Pappas Law Libr 765 Commonwealth Ave Boston MA 02215-1401

FREEHLING, HAROLD GEORGE, JR., respiratory therapist, consultant; b. Benton Harbor, Mich., Nov. 20, 1947; s. Harold George and Wilma Louise (Backus) F.; m. Janet Louise Peppel, June 10, 1971; children: Wendy Brooke, Joel Zachary, Bret Jeromy, Melissa Bethann. AS, Lake Mich. Coll., 1972; Diploma in Respiratory Therapy, U. Chgo., 1977; B in Liberal Studies, Bowling Green State U., 1978; MA in Health Care Adminstrn., Cen. Mich. U., 1987. Dir. respiratory care Providence Hosp., Sandusky, Ohio, 1974-84; v.p. support svcs. O.E. Meyer Co., Sandusky, 1984—; bd. dirs., 1989-93; clin. evaluator Calif. Coll. of Helath Sci., Nature City, 1981—; chmn. Firelands Coll. Respiratory Care Adv., Huron, Ohio, 1984—; cons. Ohio Bd. Regents, Columbus, 1986. Pres. Erie County Cancer Svcs., 1990, 94. With USN, 1967-70, Vietnam. Recipient Ed Ruff Community Svc. award, Am. Lung Assn., South Shore, Milan, Ohio, 1987, Disting. Alumnus/Alumna award Bowling Green State U. Firelands Coll., 1993. Mem. Am. Assn. Respiratory Care (cert. tech., registered respiratory therapist), Ohio Soc. Respiratory Care (sec. 1986), Ohio Thoracic Soc., Ohio Assn. Med. Equipment Svcs. (sec. 1991-92, treas. 1992-93, v.p. 1994-96, pres. 1996-99), Erie County Health Planning Assn. Avocation: golf. Home: 154 Fairway Cir Norwalk OH 44857-1970 Office: O E Meyer Co PO Box 479 Sandusky OH 44871-0479

FREEHLING, STANLEY MAXWELL, investment banker; b. Chgo., July 2, 1924; s. Julius and Juliette (Stricker) F.; m. Joan Steif, Jan. 26, 1947; children: Elizabeth, Robert Stanley, Margaret J. Student, U. Chgo., 1942-43, Ind. U., 1943-44, U. Stockholm, Sweden, 1946-47. With 1st Nat. Bank Chgo., 1947-52; ptnr. Freehling Bros., Chgo., 1948—, Freehling & Co., Chgo., 1960-87; spl. ltd. ptnr. Cowen & Co., 1987—; bd. dirs. Chgo. Sun Times Cos. Mem. Ill. Pub. Employees Pension Laws Commn., 1962-66; chmn. Ravinia Festival Assn., 1967-71; pres. men's coun. Art Inst. Chgo., 1962-65, trustee, 1970—, now life trustee; trustee Glenwood (Ill.) Sch. for Boys, 1967-80, Lake Forest Coll., 1972-83, Found. for Excellence in Tchg., Shedd Aquarium, U. Chgo., 1983—, Cradle Soc.; hon. mem. The Court Theatre; chmn. bd. Ill. Arts Coun., 1971-72; hon. chmn. Chgo. Theatre Group; bd. dirs. Northwestern Meml. Hosp., Chgo., Chgo. Pub. Libr. Found.; hon. chmn. bd. Goodman Theatre; chmn. Pub. Arts Adv. Com., 1978-90; mem. Pres.'s Com. on Arts and Humanities, Washington, 1984-88; bd. govs. Smart Mus. Art. Mem. Northwestern U. Assocs., Arts Club, Bond Club, Commercial Club (Chgo.), Lake Shore Country Club (Glencoe, Ill.), Old Elm Country Club (Highland Park, Ill.), Mid-Day. Clubs: Arts, Bond, Commercial (Chgo.); Lake Shore Country (Glencoe, Ill.); Mid-Day. Home: 121 Belle Ave Highland Park IL 60035-2503 Office: 190 S La Salle St Chicago IL 60603-3410

FREEL, EDWARD J., state official; b. Elizabeth, N.J., June 18, 1947; m. Maureen Freel. BA, Gannon Coll.; MA, U. Del., MEd. Dep. dir. Office Econ. Opportunity; spl. asst. to asst. dir. Fed. Cmty. Svc. Adminstr.; dir. Fed. Low Income Energy Asst. Program; asst. to Congressman Thomas R. Carper; posit. dir. Carper for Gov. Campaign; chief of staff to Gov.; sec. of state State of Del., 1994—. Bd. mem., treas. Bayard House. Home: 4633 Talley Hill Ln Wilmington DE 19803-4815 Office: 401 Federal St Ste 3 Dover DE 19901-3639*

FREELAND, ALAN EDWARD, orthopedic surgery educator, physician; b. Youngstown, Ohio, July 30, 1939; s. Harold Edward and Esther Amelia (Hanley) F.; m. Janis Ann Foerschl, Oct. 11, 1969; children: Matthew, Jennifer, Rebecca, Michael. BA, Johns Hopkins U., 1961; MD, George Washington U., 1965. Cert. hand surgery Am. Bd. Orthopedic Surgery. Intern Church Home and Hosp., Balt., 1965-66; resident Johns Hopkins Hosp., Balt., 1967-70, Letterman Army Med. Ctr., San Francisco, 1973-75; prof. dept. orthopaedic surgery U. Miss. Med. Ctr., Jackson, 1978—, chief of staff, 1986-87, also bd. dirs. Rowland Med. Libr., 1996-98; chief surgery Miss. Meth. Rehab. Ctr., Jackson, 1991-93, pres. elect med. staff, 1994, pres. med. staff, bd. dirs., 1995-97. Author: Stable Internal Fixation of the Hand and Wrist, 1986, The First Twenty-Five Years: History of the American Association for Hand Surgery, 1996; mem. editl. bd. Orthopedics, Slack, Inc., 1986—, Jour. Orthopaedic Trauma, Raven Press, 1993—, Year Book of Hand Surgery, 1997—; sect. editor, sr. editor hand surgery Jour. Orthopedic Trauma, 1997—; sect. editor Hand Surgery, 1997—. Mem. Fire Protection Dist., Brandon, Miss., 1990-93. Lt. col. U.S. Army, 1971-78. Fellow Am. Acad. Orthopaedic Surgeons, Am. Orthopaedic Assn.; mem. Am. Soc. Surgery of Hand (governing coun. 1989-92), Am. Assn. Hand Surgeons (parliamentarian 1994, historian 1995, mem. exec. com., bd. dirs. 1994—, treas. 1996-98, Nat. Clinician/Tchr. of Yr. 1997), Internat. Fedn. Socs. for Surgery of Hand (chmn. bone and joint com. 1992—), Miss. State Orthopaedic Assn. (pres. 1986, pres. Jackson chpt. 1985), S.E. Hand Club (sec.-treas. 1998—). Home: 303 Swallow Dr Brandon MS 39047-6454 Office: 2500 N State St Jackson MS 39216-4500

FREELAND, HERBERT THOMAS, minister; b. Rahway, N.J., Feb. 2, 1953; s. Donald Grant and Elva Margaret (Smeal) F.; m. Lynn Elizabeth McLaughlin, June 5, 1976; children: Thomas Paul, Jodie Lynn. AA, Valley Forge Mil. Coll., 1973; BA, Ramapo Coll., 1975; MDiv, Drew Theol. Sch., 1978. Ordained to United Meth. Ch. as deacon, 1978, as elder, 1980. Min. Wesley United Meth. Ch., Belleville, N.J., 1978-80, St. John's United Meth. Ch., Hope, N.J., 1980-83, Oxford and Summerfield United Meth. Chs., Belvidere, N.J., 1983-87; assoc. min. First United Meth. Ch., Westfield, N.J., 1987-89, United Meth. Ch., Pearl River, N.Y., 1989-91; min. St. Paul's United Meth. Ch., Nyack, N.Y., 1991-98, Cmty. United Methodist Ch., Roselle Park, N.J., 1998—; mem. Rockland Youth Adv. Coun., New City, N.Y., 1990-92; founder, pres. No. N.J. Truckstop Ministries, Columbia, 1982-87; trustee Domestic Abuse & Rape Crisis Ctr., Belvidere, 1985-87, Interfaith Coun. for the Homeless, Summit, N.J., 1987-89; coord. Orangetown Interfaith CROP Walk, 1990—. Contbr. article on clocks to profl. jour. Named one of Outstanding Young Men of Am., Jaycees, 1984. Mem. Nat. Assn. Watch & Clock Collectors (life), No. N.J. Ann. Conf. (chairperson parish and cmty. devel. 1988-92), Nyack Rotary Club. Democrat. Home: 309 Chestnut St Roselle Park NJ 07204 Office: Cmty United Meth Ch 301 Chestnut St Roselle Park NJ 07204 *It is a curious fact of life that the heart which is never broken can never truly be made whole. It would certainly seem that God most greatly uses those who have been deeply hurt.*

FREELAND, JAMES M. JACKSON, lawyer, educator; b. Miami, Fla., Feb. 17, 1927; s. Byron Brazil and Mary Helen (Jackson) F.; m. Valerie; children: Carole Leigh, Thomas Byron, James Jackson Jr. AB, Duke U., 1950; JD, U. Fla., Gainesville, 1954; postgrad. fellow, Yale U. Law Sch., 1960-61. Bar: Fla. 1954. Assoc. firm Dowling & Culverhouse, Jacksonville, 1954-57; mem. faculty Law Sch. U. Fla., Gainesville, 1957-60, 61-62, 65—, prof. law, 1970-95; dir. grad. tax law program U. Fla., 1977-82, disting. svc. prof. law, emeritus, 1995—, prof. emeritus, 1995—; of counsel August & Kulunas, P.A., West Palm Beach, Fla., 1995—; prof. law NYU Law Sch., 1963-65; vis. prof. U. Ariz. Law Sch., Tucson, 1969-70; mem. tax faculty Practicing Law Inst., 1969-76; vis. tax prof. Leiden U., The Netherlands, 1983. Co-author: Federal Income Taxation of Estates, Trusts and Beneficiaries, 1970, 3d edit., 1998, The Florida Will and Trust Manual, 1983, The Tennessee Will and Trust Manual, 1984, Fundamentals of Federal Income Taxation, 1972, 10th edit., 1998; adv. editor Jour. Corp. Taxation, 1977—, S Corp. Tax Jour., 1989—. Served with USNR, 1944-46. Named Outstanding prof. U. Fla., 1968, Outstanding Law Prof., 1970-73, 75; Designated Disting. Service Prof. Law, 1982. Mem. ABA, Am. Law Inst., Am. Coll. Tax Counsel, The Fla. Bar Tax Sect., (Outstanding Tax Lawyer State of Fla. 1982), Am. Judicature Soc., Order of Coif, Fla. Blue Key, Phi Kappa Phi. Republican. Methodist. Home: 7700 NW 41st Ave Gainesville FL 32606-4114 *Always be aware of others, but compete only with yourself.*

FREELAND, MARCIA STEPHAN, nursing educator; b. Buffalo, Nov. 5, 1946; d. William Mathias and Marguerite Loretta (Sontag) Stephan; m. Gary C. Freeland, Sept. 9, 1978; children: Joshua, Ashley. Diploma in nursing, St. Joseph's Hosp., Syracuse, N.Y., 1967; BSN magna cum laude, Boston Coll., Chestnut Hill, Mass., 1970, MS in Nursing, 1975. RN, Ill. Various nursing positions, 1967-70; asst. instr. med.-surg. nursing Northeastern U., Boston, 1970; staff nurse surg. ICU, U. Rochester (N.Y.) Med. Ctr., 1971; staff-charge nurse med.-surg. unit, Peter Bent Brigham Hosp., Boston, 1972-74, staff nurse in ICU; instr. staff edn. and devel. Beth Israel Hosp., Boston, 1974-75; staff-charge nurse CCU, Boston U. Med. Ctr. Hosp., 1975-76; instr. staff devel. New England Deaconess, 1976-78; staff nurse infant spl. care unit Evanston (Ill.) U., 1978-79, instr. Sch. Nursing, 1979, coord. nursing arts lab., 1981-82; staff nurse mother-baby unit Lake Forest (Ill.) Hosp., 1987—; instr. neonatal resuscitation Lake Forest Hosp.; instr. obstetric nursing Oakton C.C., DesPlaines, Ill, 1992. Nursing scholar N.Y. State Regents. Mem. Sigma Theta Tau. Home: 6319 Rfd Long Grove IL 60047-7679

FREELAND, ROBERT FREDERICK, retired librarian; b. Flint, Mich., Dec. 20, 1919; s. Ralph V. and Susan Barbara (Goetz) F.; m. June Voshel, June 18, 1948; children: Susan Beth Visser, Kent Richard. BS, Eastern Mich. U., 1942; postgrad., Washington & Lee U., 1945; MS, U. So. Calif., 1948, postgrad., 1949; postgrad., U. Mich., 1950-52, Calif. State U., 1956-58, UCLA, 1960; LittD (hon.), Linda Vista Bible Coll., 1973. Music supr. Consol. Schs. Warren, Mich., 1946-47; music dir. Carson City (Mich.) Pub. Schs., 1948-49; librarian, audio-visual coord. Ford Found., Edison Inst., Greenfield Village, Dearborn, Mich., 1950-52, Helix High Sch. Library, 1952-77; librarian, prof. library sci. Linda Vista Bible Coll., 1976—; reference libr. San Diego Pub. Libr. System, 1967-97; cons. edn., libr. and multimedia. Editor book and audio-visual aids review, Sch. Musician, Dir. and Teacher, 1950-75. Former deacon and elder Christian Reform Ch., libr., 1969-72, Classis archivist, 1991—; pub. affairs officer, sr. program officer, moral leadership officer Sq. 57 GP III, Calif. wing CAP. With USAAF, 1942-46. Named Scholar Freedoms Found., Valley Forge, Pa., 1976-80. Mem. NEA (life), ALA, Nat. Music Camp, Calif. Tchrs. Assn., Music Libr. Assn. So. Calif. (adviser exec. bd.), Calif. Libr. Assn. (pres. Palomar chpt. 1972-73), Sch. Libr. Assn. Calif. (treas. 1956-73), Calif. Media and Libr. Educators (charter mem.), Am. Legion (Americanism chmn. 22d dist. San Diego County, chmn. oratorical contest com. La Mesa post), Ret. Officers Assn., San Diego Aero Space Mus., San Diego Mus. Art, Alumnia Assn. Ea. Mich. U. Home: 4800 Williamsburg Ln Apt 223 La Mesa CA 91941-4651

FREEMAN, ALBERT E., agricultural science educator; b. Lewisburg, W.Va., Mar. 16, 1931; s. James A. and Grace Vivian (Neal) F.; m. Christine Ellen Lewis, Dec. 23, 1950; children: Patricia Ellen, Lynn Elizabeth, Ann Marie. BS, W.Va. U., Morgantown, 1952, MS, 1954; PhD, Cornell U., 1957. Grad. asst. W.Va. U., Morgantown, 1952-54; grad. asst. Cornell U., Ithaca, N.Y., 1955-57; asst. prof animal sci Iowa State U., Ames, 1957-61, assoc. prof. animal sci., 1961-65, prof. animal sci., 1965-78, Charles F. Curtiss Disting. prof. agriculture, 1978—. Contbr. numerous articles to profl. jours. Active Collegiate Presbyterian Ch., Ames. Recipient 1975, Sr. Fulbright-Hays award, 1975, First Miss. Corp. award, 1979, award of appreciation for contbns. to Dairy Cattle Breeding 21st Century Genetics, 1984, Disting. Alumni award W.Va. U., 1985, faculty citation Iowa State U., 1987; named Charles F. Curtiss Disting. Prof. Agr., 1978. Fellow Am. Soc. Animal Sci. (Rockefeller Prentice Meml. award 1979, award of Honor 1987), Am. Dairy Sci. Assn. (bd. dirs. 1981-83, Nat. Assn. Animal Breeders Research award 1975, Borden award, 1982, J.L. Lush award 1984, Disting. Svc. award); mem. Biometrics Soc., First Acad. Disting. Alumni W.Va. U., Gamma Sigma Delta (award of Merit). Office: Iowa State Univ 239 Kildee Hall Ames IA 50010

FREEMAN, ANTONIO MICHAEL, professional football player; b. Balt., May 27, 1972. Student, Va. Poly. U. Wide receiver Green Bay (Wis.) Packers, 1995—; mem. Superbowl 31 championship team, 1996, lost Superbowl 32 to New Eng. Patriots, 1997. Holder Super Bowl record for longest pass reception, 1997; shares NFL postseason record for most touchdowns by punt return. Office: c/o Green Bay Packers PO Box 10628 Green Bay WI 54307-0628*

FREEMAN, ARTHUR, veterinarian, retired association administrator; b. Youngstown, Ohio, Jan. 12, 1925. Student, Stanford U., 1949-50; D.V.M., Ohio State U., 1955. Pvt. practice Bellingham (Wa.) Vet. Hosp., 1955-56; dir. profl. rels. Jensen Salsbery Labs., Kansas City, Mo., 1956-59; editor Am. Vet. Med. Assn., Chgo., 1959-72; asst. exec. v.p. Am. Vet. Med. Assn., Schaumburg, Ill., 1977-84, editor-in-chief, 1972-84, exec. v.p., 1985-89; dir. Coun. of Biology Editors, Chgo., 1982-85, pres., 1985-86; adj. asst. prof. vet. med. Purdue U., 1997. Contbr. articles to profl. publs. Mem. Indpls. Mus. Art, Indpls. Symphony Orch. 1st lt. USAF, 1942-60. Recipient Disting. Alumnus award Ohio State U., 1976, Ind. Vet. of the Yr. award, 1995. Mem. AVMA, Ohio Vet. Med. Assn. (Meritorious Svc. award 1989), Ind. State Vet. Med. Assn. (hon.), Ill. Vet. Med. Assn. (hon.), Mich. Vet. Med. Assn. (hon.), Indpls. Exec. Svc. Corps (Frederic M. Hadley Svc. award 1995), Ind. Hist. Soc., Indpls. Aero. Club.

FREEMAN, ARTHUR J., physics educator; b. Lublin, Poland, Feb. 6, 1930; s. Louis and Pearl (Mandelbaum) F.; m. Rhea B. Landin, June 21, 1952 (div. 1990); children: Jonathan (dec.), Seth, Claudia, Sarah; m. Doris Caro, Mar. 1991. B.S. in Physics, Mass. Inst. Tech., 1952, Ph.D., 1956. Instr. Brandeis U., 1955-56; solid state physicist Army Materials Research Agy., Watertown, Mass., 1956-62; instr. Northeastern U., 1957-59; assoc. lab. dir., leader theory group Francis Bitter Nat. Magnet Lab., Mass. Inst. Tech., 1962-67; prof. physics Northwestern U., Evanston, Ill., 1967-83; Morrison prof. physics Northwestern U., 1983—, chmn. dept. physics, 1967-71; cons. Argonne Nat. Lab., Los Alamos Nat. Lab. Editor: Hyperfine Interactions, 1967, The Actinides: Electronic and Related Properties, Handbook on the Physics and Chemistry of the Actinides, Internat. Jour. Magnetism, 1970-75, Jour. Magnetism and Magnetic Materials, 1975—; mem. editl. adv. bd. Computational Materials Sci., 1992, Jour. Computer-Aided Materials Design, 1993; contbr. numerous articles to tech. lit. Guggenheim fellow, 1970-71; Fulbright-Hays fellow, 1970-71; Alexander von Humboldt Stiftung fellow 1977-78; 1st recipient medal Materials Rsch. Soc., 1990, award in magnetism Internat. Union Pure and Applied Physics, 1991. Fellow Am. Phys. Soc.; fgn. mem. Acad. Natural Scis. Russia, Russian Acad. Scis., Polish Acad. Scis. Home: 2739 Ridge Ave Evanston IL 60201-1719 Office: Northwestern Univ Dept Of Physics Evanston IL 60208-3112*

FREEMAN, ARTHUR L., state commissioner; m. Laura Freeman; 1 child, Will. Computer programmer; v.p. Mercer County Nat. Bank, Harrodsburg, Ky.; exec. v.p., CEO Mercer Fed. Savs. and Loan Assn., Harrodsburg; regional v.p. Cumberland Fed. Savs. Bank, Lexington, Ky.; v.p. Lexington Fed. Savs. Bank; v.p. Ky. League Savs. Instns., pres., exec. dir.; v.p., dir. thrift membership Ky. Bankers Assn.; commr. Ky. Dept. Fin. Instns., Frankfort. Office: Fin Instns Dept 1025 Capital Ctr Ste 200 Frankfort KY 40601-3868

FREEMAN, ARTHUR MERRIMON, III, psychiatry educator, dean; b. Birmingham, Ala., Oct. 10, 1942; s. Arthur Merrimon Freeman II; m. Linda Poynter; children: Arthur M. IV, Katherin Leigh, Edward Todd. AB in Philosophy, Harvard U., 1963; MD, Vanderbilt U., 1967. Diplomate Am. Bd. Psychiatry and Neurology; lic. psychiatrist, Ala., N.C., La. Asst. prof. dept. psychiatry and behavioral scis. Stanford (Calif.) U., 1974-77; prof., vice chmn. dept. psychiatry U. Ala., Birmingham, 1977-90; med. dir. Appalachian Hall Hosp., Asheville, N.C., 1990-91; prof., chmn. dept. psychiatry La. State U. Med. Ctr., Shreveport, 1991—, dean, 1993-96; regional med. dir. divsn. mental health La. Dept. Health and Hosps., 1992-94. Author: Psychiatry for the Primary Care Physician, 1979. Bd. dirs. Vols. of Am., Shreveport, 1993-96, Shreveport Symphony, C. of C., 1993-96. Lt. comdr. M.C., USN, 1972-74. Nat. Merit scholar Harvard U., 1959-63; Biochemistry fellow Karolinska Inst., Stockholm, 1965, fellow in hepatic disease Royal Free Hosp., London, 1966. Fellow APA, Am. Coll. Psychiatrists (Laughlin fellow 1971), Acad. Psychosomatic Medicine, So. Psychiat. Assn.; mem. Am. Assn. Chmn. of Depts. of Psychiatry, Biomed. Rsch. Found. N.W. La. (bd. dirs. 1993-96). Home: 5929 E Ridge Dr Shreveport LA 71106-2423 Office: La State U Med Ctr Dept of Psychiatry 1501 Kings Hwy Shreveport LA 71103-4228

FREEMAN, BOB A., retired microbiology educator, retired dean; b. Eastland, Tex., May 7, 1926; s. Oswald Ledbetter and Osielee (Wilcox) F.; m. Rosemary David, June 4, 1960; children: Susan A., Robert D., Katherine E., Andrew W. BA, U. Tex., 1949, MA, 1950, PhD, 1954. Instr. biology Tex. A & M U., College Station, 1950-51; rsch. scientist I U. Tex., Austin, 1951-54; instr., asst. prof. U. Chgo., 1954-64; assoc. prof. U. Tenn., Memphis, 1964-66, prof., 1966-88, chmn. microbiology dept., 1970-83, vice chancellor, 1982-88, Disting. Svc. prof., 1988-96, interim dean Coll. Grad. Health Scis., 1993-96, dean, prof. emeritus, 1997—; cons. WHO, Calcutta, India, 1968. Author: Burrows Textbook of Microbiology, 21st edit., 1979, 22d edit., 1984; mem. edit. bd. Jour. Dental Edn., 1980-83, U. Tenn. Press., 1983—; contbr. articles to microbiology jours. Bd. dirs. Memphis Heart Gala, 1984-90. With USN, 1944-46, PTO. Grantee U.S. Army Rsch. and Devel. Command, USPHS, U.S. Dept. Agr. Mem. AAAS, Am. Soc. for Microbiology (br. councillor 1969-71), Imhotep Soc. (Memphis), Sigma Xi (chpt. pres. 1974-75). Republican. Methodist. Avocations: woodworking, outdoor activities. Home: 1319 E Crestwood Dr Memphis TN 38119-5000

FREEMAN, CAROLYN RUTH, radiation oncologist; b. Kettering, Eng., Jan. 2, 1950; emigrated to Can., 1974, naturalized, 78; d. Ivor Thomas and Winifred Mary (Scotney) F.; m. J.C. Negrete, July 25, 1981. Student, King's Coll. London U., 1967-69; MB, BS, Westminster Med. Sch. London U., 1972. Prof., chmn. dept. radiation oncology, faculty medicine McGill U., Montreal, 1979—; radiation oncologist-in-chief McGill U. Hosps., Montreal, 1979—. Contbr. articles to med. publs. Fellow Royal Coll. Physicians (Can.); mem. Can. Assn. Radiol. Oncologists (pres. 1991-93), Am. Soc. Therapeutic Radiology and Oncology. Home: 4270 deMaisonneuve W, Montreal, PQ Canada H3Z 1K6 Office: 1650 Cedar Ave, Montreal, PQ Canada H3G 1A4

FREEMAN, CHARLES E., state supreme court justice; b. Richmond, Va., Dec. 12, 1933; m. Marylee Voelker; 1 child, Kevin. BA in Liberal Arts, Va. Union U., 1954; JD, John Marshall Law Sch., 1962, LLD (hon.), 1992. Bar: Ill. 1962. Pvt. practice, 1962-76; pvt. practice, Cook County, Chgo., Ill., 1962-76; asst. state's atty. Cook County, 1964; asst. atty. gen., then asst. state's atty. Cook County, Chgo., 1964; asst. atty. Bd. Election Commrs., Chgo., 1964-65; mem. Ill. Indsl. Commn., Chgo., 1965-73, Ill. Commerce Commn., Chgo., 1973-76; judge law and chancery divsns. Cook County Circuit Ct., Chgo., 1976-86; judge Appellate Ct. Ill., 1986-90; chief justice Ill. Supreme Ct., 1990—. First African-Am. to swear in a Mayor city Chgo., to serve on Ill. Supreme Ct., 1990; leader in case disposition by published opinion, 1988, 89; recipient cert. Achievement, Internat. Christian Fellowship Missions, Earl B. Dickerson award Chgo. Bar Assn., Merit award Habilative Systems, award Statesmanship, Monarch Awards Found. of Alpha Kappa Alpha. Mem. ABA (cert. Recognition, task force opportunities minorities in jud. adminstrn. divsn. and coms. opportunities minorities in profession), Am. Judges' Assn., Am. Judicature Soc., Ill. State Bar Assn., Ill. Jud. Coun. (Kenneth Wilson Meml. award, Meritorious Svc. award), Ill. Judges' Assn., Cook County Bar Assn. (Kenneth E. Wilson award, Cert. Merit, Ida Platt award, Presdl. award, Jud. award), Du Page County Bar Assn. Office: Supreme Ct Ill 160 N La Salle St Fl 20 Chicago IL 60601-3103*

FREEMAN, CHAS. W., JR., government official, ambassador, author; b. Washington, Mar. 2, 1943; divorced; 3 children; m. Margaret Van Wagenen Carpenter, 1993. BA, Yale U.; JD, Harvard U. Joined Fgn. Svc., 1965, assigned to India and Taiwan; Am. interpreter for Pres. Nixon, People's Republic China, 1972; vis. fellow East Asian Legal Rsch. Ctr., Harvard U., 1974-75; dep. dir. for Taiwan affairs, dir. pub. programs, dir. plans and mgmt. U.S. Dept. State, Washington, 1975-78; dir. program coord. and devel. USIA, Washington, 1978, acting U.S. coord. for refugee affairs; dir. China affairs U.S. Dept. State, 1979; dep. chief of mission Am. Embassy, Beijing, 1981, Bangkok, 1984; prin. dep. asst. sec. state for African affairs U.S. Dept. State, Washington, 1986; amb. to Saudi Arabia, Riyadh, 1989-92; asst. sec. def. The Pentagon, Washington, 1993-94; dist. fellow U.S. Inst. of Peace, Washington, 1994-95; chmn. bd. Projects Internat. Inc., Washington, 1995—; mem. internat. adv. bd. Fleishman-Hillard, 1995; co-chmn. U.S. China Policy Fou nd., 1996; vice-chmn. Atlantic Coun., 1997, pres. Middle East Policy Coun.; bd. dirs. Inst. for Def. Analyses; bd. dirs. World Affairs Coun. Washington, 1998; mem. bd. visitors Dept. Def. Regional Ctrs., 1998—; mem. U.S. Nat. Security Study Group, 1998—. Author: The Diplomat's Dictionary, 1994, revised edit., 1997; Arts of Power, 1997. Recipient Sec. Def. Meritorious Civilian Svc. award, 1991, Disting. Pub. Svc. awards, 1993-94, Sec. State Disting. Honor, 1991, Dir. Ctrl. Intelligence Shield Medallion award, 1991, First Class Order of Abd Al-Aziz award Saudi Arabian Govt., 1992. Mem. Am. Acad. Diplomacy, Metropolitan Club. Home: 2805 31st St NW Washington DC 20008-3524 Office: Project Internat Inc 1800 K St NW Ste 1018 Washington DC 20006-2202

FREEMAN, CHESTER WILLIE, small business owner; b. Cullman, Ala., June 3, 1922; s. Willis Jessie and Sarah Ethel (Ponder) F.; m. Hilda Wood, Mar. 10, 1946; children: Carolyn, Phillip. Student, West Ga. Coll., 1974. Pres. Chester W. Freeman Enterprises, Cullman. Bd. advisors Wallace State Coll., Hanceville, Ala., 1962-93; pres. Cullman Lions Club, 1959-60; vice chmn. Cullman Reg. Med. Ctr., 1979—; chmn. Cullman Parks and Recreation, 1970-97; pres. City of Cullman Parks Found., 1988-97. With U.S. Army, 1942-45. Mem. Nat. Recreation and Park Assn. (life trustee, pres.), N.Am. Fedn. Fairs (pres. 1987), Cullman Area C. of C. (pres. 1991), Ala. Sight Assn. (pres.), Cullman County Fair Assn. (pres. 1962), Assn. Ala. Fairs (pres. 1975). Methodist. Avocations: travel, music, reading, hiking. Home: 1827 Edgewood Dr NW Cullman AL 35055-5721 Office: PO Box 543 Cullman AL 35056-0543

FREEMAN, CLARENCE CALVIN, financial executive; b. Lancaster, Pa., July 2, 1923; s. Clarence Calvin and Margaret (Hollinger) F.; m. B. Virginia Miller, Aug. 26, 1944; children—Margaret Ann, Elizabeth Ann, Martha Suzanne. A.B. cum laude, Franklin and Marshall Coll., 1951. Asst. bookkeeper Battery & Brake Service Co., Lancaster, 1941-42; supr. inventory records and receiving Armstrong Cork Co., Lancaster, 1946-48; accountant Internat. Latex Corp., Dover, Del., 1951-52, Ebasco Services, Inc., Holtwood, Pa., 1952-53; office mgr., accountant A.O. Smith Corp., Leola, Pa., 1953-54; office mgr., plant accountant Sybron-Permutit div. Lancaster, 1954-57; div. controller BCA div. Fed. Mogul Corp., Lancaster, 1957-64; controller Fed. Mogul Corp., Southfield, Mich., 1964-74; v.p., controller Addressograph-Multigraph Corp., Cleve., 1974-78; adminstrv. v.p., controller Irvin Industries, Stamford, Conn., 1978-79; v.p. fin. Technical Tape Inc., New Rochelle, N.Y., 1979-80; v.p. fin., treas., dir. K-D Mfg. Co., Lancaster, 1980-83; chief fin. officer C-F Manbeck, Inc., 1984-86; exec. v.p. Sensenich Corp., Lancaster, 1986-90, also bd. dirs.; sr. v.p. fin., chief fin. officer Sensenich Propeller Co., Lancaster, 1991-94; ret.; owner acctg. svc., 1953-64, Dairy Queen, 1956-60; lectr. Franklin and Marshall Coll., 1957-58, adj. faculty, 1983-89; lectr. Wayne State Grad. Sch., 1966-67; guest speaker Nat. Assn. Accts. Mem. Oakland County Planning Commn., 1967-68; adviser Jr. Achievement, 1957-58. Served with AUS, 1943-46, PTO. Mem. Nat. Assn. Accountants, Fin. Execs. Inst., Phi Beta Kappa (v.p. Detroit), Pi Gamma Mu. Republican. Presbyterian (elder, deacon). Club: Conestoga Country. Lodges: Masons, Kiwanis, Elks. Home: 1411 Newton Rd Lancaster PA 17603-2462 *To succeed in life, it is important to have faith and confidence in one's own capability but to rely on this alone is disastrous; a faith and belief in a supreme being (God) more powerful than any human being is necessary not only to sustain us in times of our own failure, but each and every day as we face life's challenges.*

FREEMAN, CLIFFORD LEE, advertising agency executive; b. Vicksburg, Miss., Feb. 14, 1941; s. James Evans and Lillian (Pennebaker) F.; m. Susan Jane Kelner, Sept. 3, 1976; 1 child, Clifford Scott. BS, Fla. State U., 1963. Copywriter Sears & Roebuck, Atlanta, 1964-65, Liller Neal Battle & Lindsey, Atlanta, 1965-68, McCann-Grickson, Atlanta, 1968-70; copywriter Dancer Fitzgerald & Sample, N.Y.C., 1970-75, group head, 1976-80, assoc. creative dir., 1981-83, creative dir., 1984-85, exec. creative dir., 1986-87; exec. creative dir., chmn. Cliff Freeman and Ptnrs., N.Y.C., 1987—. With Ga. N.G., 1964-70. Winner 44 Clio awards including Best Campaign of Yr. for Philips Lighting, 1988, Child World, 1992, Little Ceasars, 1994, 96, Best of Show 1997 Fox Network; winner 23 One Show Pencils inclyding Best Campaign of Yr. awards for Little Ceasars, 1984, 88, 90, 92, 94, 97, Philips Lighting, 1987, Comedy Channel, 1991; winner 19 Cannes Lion awards; named Creative Agy. of Yr., Am. Assn. Advt. Agys., 1992, 94, 97, Adweek's Copywriter of Yr. for Where's the Beef for Wendy's, MVP in Advt. for Little Ceasars Pizza! Pizza! campaign. Mem. Sigma Chi (Significant Sig 1994). Office: Cliff Freeman and Ptnrs 375 Hudson St 8th Fl New York NY 10014-3658*

FREEMAN, CORINNE, financial services, former mayor; b. N.Y.C., Nov. 9, 1926; d. Bernard J. Hirschfeld and Sidonie (Daxe) Lichtenstein; m. Michael S. Freeman, Mar. 14, 1948; children: Michael L., Stephan J. Adelphi Coll. Sch. Nursing, 1944-47. RN, N.Y., Mass. Nurse numerous hosps. in N.Y. and Mass., 1948-64; mayor St. Petersburg, Fla., 1977-85; mem. Pinellas County Sch. Bd., St. Petersburg, Fla., 1989—, chmn., 1996-98; fin. advisor Prudential Securities; bd. dirs. Creativity in Child Care. Chmn. Social Svc. Allocations Com., St. Petersburg, 1972-76, City Budget Rev. Com., 1973-76, Youth Svc. System, Pinellas County, 1975-76, West Coast Regional Water Supply Authority; past mem. community redevel. com. U.S. Conf. of Mayors; past pres. Fla. League Cities; past mem. Pinellas County Mayors Coun.; past mem. Nat. League of Cities Revenue and Fin. Task Force; pres. LWV, St. Petersburg, 1970-72, 75-76; trustee Fire Pension Bd., St. Petersburg, 1989-92, Bayfront Med. Ctr., Palms of Pasadena Hosp., 1999—; adv. com. Jr. League St. Petersburg, 1990-92. Recipient Disting. Alumni award Adelphi U. Mem. Fla. Nursing Assn. Republican. Home: 2101 Pelham Rd N Saint Petersburg FL 33710-3659 Office: 5858 Central Ave Saint Petersburg FL 33707-1728

FREEMAN, CORWIN STUART, JR., investment adviser; b. Elmhurst, Ill., July 31, 1947. AA in Edn., Waubonsee C.C., Sugar Grove, Ill., 1971. CLU; cert. estate counselor; registered investment advisor; cert. sr. advisor. Pres. Valley Estate Planners Ltd., Elgin, Ill., 1980—; chmn. Leaders Coun. Can. Life Assurance Co., 1988; mem. agts. coun. Delta Life and Annuity Co., 1993-95. With USMC, 1965-68, Vietnam. Named to Million Dollar Round Table, 1982-99, life and qualifying mem., 1997, Ct. of Table Status, 1988. Fellow Life Underwriter Tng. Coun.; mem. Nat. Tax Sheltered Annuity Assn. (charter mem. 1991-93), Elgin Area Life Underwriters (past pres. 1987-88), Ill. Life Underwriters Assn. (bd. dirs. 1991-93, region III v.p.). Home and Office: Valley Estate Planners Ltd 14n555 Tyrrell Rd Elgin IL 60123-7846 also: 150 Terrane Rdg Peachtree City GA 30269

FREEMAN, DAVID FORGAN, retired foundation executive; b. Chgo., June 25, 1918; s. Halstead Gurnee and Marion Kerr (Forgan) F.; m. Hazel Sims Farr, Sept. 5, 1947; children: David Forgan, Sims, Marion, John, Francis. AB, Princeton U., 1940; LLB, Yale U., 1947. Bar: N.Y. 1948. Atty. Debevoise, Plimpton & McLean, N.Y.C., 1947-50; exec. assoc. Ford Found., 1950-52; sec. Fund for the Republic, N.Y.C., 1952-54; v.p. Fund for the Republic, 1954-57; assoc. Rockefeller Bros. Fund, N.Y.C., 1957-67; pres. Council on Founds., N.Y.C., 1968-78; exec. dir., treas. Scherman Found., N.Y.C., 1979-93; pres. So. Edn. Found., Atlanta, 1965-79; bd. dirs. Fund for N.J., 1980-87; exec. sec. major awards program Gulf & Western Found., 1981-86. Author: The Handbook on Private Foundations, 1981, rev. edit., 1991. Mem. Rumson Bd. Edn., N.J., 1952-55; mem. Monmouth County Mental Health Bd., N.J., 1985-90; mem. com. on religion and race Presbyn. Ch., 1958-61. With USNR, 1940-45. Decorated Legion of Merit. Mem. Seabright Tennis Club. Home: 6 Clay Ct Rumson NJ 07760-2307

FREEMAN, DAVID JOHN, lawyer; b. N.Y.C., Aug. 9, 1948; s. John L. and Josephine F. (Wilding) F.; m. Ellen Gogolick, Dec. 29, 1974; children: Matthew, Julie. B.A., Harvard U., 1970; J.D., 1975. Bar: Mass. 1975, D.C. 1977, N.Y. 1982, U.S. Dist. Ct. D.C. 1981, N.Y. 1982, U.S. Dist. Ct. D.C. 1981, U.S. Dist. Ct. (so. and ea. dists.) N.Y. 1982, U.S. Ct. Appeals (D.C. cir.) 1979, U.S. Ct. Appeals (2nd cir.) 1982, U.S. Cupreme Ct. 1988. Spl. asst. to U.S. Senator Frank E. Moss, 1970-72; trial atty. FTC, Washington, 1975-77; assoc. Ginsburg, Feldman & Bress, Washington, 1977-81, Holtzmann, Wise & Shepard, N.Y.C., 1981-84; ptnr., 1984-94; ptnr., chmn. environ. dept. Battle Fowler, 1994—; spl. legal counsel N.Am. Environ. Affairs, UN Environ. Programme; co-chair emeritus ISO 14000 Legal Issues Forum, U.S. Tech. Com. to TC-207, Internat. Com. Standardization. Editor-in-chief: Jour. Environ Law Practice (West). Mem. ABA (natural resources sect.), Assn. Bar City of N.Y., Harvard Law Sch. Assn., N.Y. STate Bar Assn. (environ. law sect., co-chair hazardous waste com.). Office: Battle Fowler LLP 75 E 55th St New York NY 10022-3205

FREEMAN, DONALD CHESTER, JR., health care company executive; b. Haverhill, Mass., May 15, 1930; s. Donald C. and Isabelle (Brown) F.; m. Wilhelmina Lind, June 23, 1978; children: Robert M., Christopher B., Dorian M. BS, Brown U., 1951; PhD, U. Md., 1955; postgrad., Duke U., 1960-61. Dir. tech. materials system div. Union Carbide Corp., Indpls., 1968-69; gen. mgr. instrument dept. Union Carbide Corp., White Plains, N.Y., 1969-71, dir. new bus. devel., 1971-78; pres. Davol, Inc., Providence, 1978-80; group v.p. C.R. Bard, Inc., Murray Hill, N.J., 1980-83; pres., CEO Xenotech Labs., Inc., 1984-87; pres. Intra-Sonix, Inc., 1988-93; ptnr. Grayson & Assocs., Denver, 1993-96; pres., CEO HydroCision, Inc., 1996—; bd. dirs. In-X Corp., RadioMed Corp., Integrated Chem. Sensors Corp. Contbr. articles to sci. jours.; patentee in field. Mem. Am. Phys. Soc., N.Y. Acad. Scis., Greater Providence C. of C. (dir. 1982), Sigma Xi, Alpha Tau Omega. Unitarian. Home: 23 Arborwood Dr Burlington MA 01803-3816 Office: 220 Ballardvale St Wilmington MA 01887-1050

FREEMAN, ERNEST ROBERT, engineering executive; b. Bklyn., Oct. 3, 1933; s. Nathan and Rose (Beginsky) F.; m. June Gladys Moser, June 6, 1954; children—Jesse David, Miriam Lisa, Sarah Ellen, Beth Bayla. B.S.E.E., U. Miami, Coral Gables, Fla., 1955; M.E.A., George Washington U., 1966; Sc.D. (hon.), London Inst., 1977. Registered profl. engr., Md., N.J. Mem. tech. staff Bell Telephone Labs., Whippany, N.J., 1959-61; mgr. engring. dept. IIT Research Inst., Annapolis, Md., 1961-68; dir. engring. dept. Vertex Corp., Kensington, Md., 1968-69; pres., chief exec. officer SFA Inc., Landover, Md., 1969-91, exec. advisor, 1991-98; pres., chmn., CEO SFA Inc., Largo, Md., 1998—; lectr. Am. U., Ctr. for Tech. and Adminstrn.; dir. Data Range Ltd., High Wycombe, U.K. Author: (with others) Electromagnetic Compatibility Design Guide, 1981; Interference Suppression Techniques for Antennas and Transmitters, 1982; contbg. editor Attorney's Guide to Engring., 1986; editor-in-chief IEEE NCAC Scanner, 1997-98. Served with USAF, 1956-59. Recipient Bausch & Lomb award, 1951, Electro '76 Best Session award. Fellow IEEE, Washington Acad. Sci.; mem. Assn. Fed. Comm. Cons. Engrs. (life mem.), Spectrum Planning Adv. Coun. (dept. commerce), Dept. Justice (peer rev. panel), Mensa. Avocations: scuba, flying, sailing. Home: 5357 Strathmore Ave Kensington MD 20895-1160 Office: SFA Inc 1401 Mccormick Dr Largo MD 20774-5396

FREEMAN, GEORGE STANLEY, city manager, city and regional planner; b. Atlantic, Iowa, Feb. 10, 1948; s. Stanley Leroy and Emma (Forbes) F.; m. Roberta Ann Rapp, Mar. 11, 1974; 1 child, Sharon. BS in Physics, U. Wyo., 1970, BS in Sociology, 1973; MPA, U. S.C., 1988. Planner City-County Planning Bd., Billings, Mont., 1974-76, dir. planning, 1976-85; asst. prof. U. S.C., Columbia, 1985-89; maintenance officer 84th divsn., Milw., 1989-93; exec. officer 139th Ordnance Bn., Irvine, Calif., 1993-94; dep. comdr. 304th Materiel Mgmt. Ctr., L.A., 1994-98; city mgr. City of Reed City, Mich., 1998—. Lt. col. U.S. Army, 1985-99. Mem. Am. Planning Assn., Res. Officer Assn., Am. Soc. for Pub. Adminstrn., Internat. City/County Mgmt. Assn., Rotary. Democrat. Avocation: history. Office: City of Reed City 227 E Lincoln Ave Reed City MI 49677

FREEMAN, GERALD RUSSELL, lawyer; b. Mpls., Feb. 14, 1928; s. Samuel W. Freeman and Mildred Lorraine (Linton) Wofford; m. Ann Leslie Alton; 1 child, Brady Michael; children by previous marriage: Gerald Russell, Jon L., Craig V., Pamela A., Kelley M. BA, U. Minn., 1952; BS in Law, William Mitchell Coll. Law, Mpls., 1958, JD, 1960. Bar: Minn. 1960. Sole practice Mpls., 1960-67; ptnr. Collins, Freeman & Flakne, Mpls., 1967-73, Freeman, Gill, Keating & Ebersold, Mpls., 1973-86, Freeman, Alton, Dodd & Greer, Mpls., 1986-91, Freeman & Alton, Ltd., Mpls., 1991—; lectr. Golden Valley Med. Ctr., Mpls., 1976-81; adj. prof. Hamline Law Sch., St. Paul, 1981; legal counsel, bd. dirs. Vinland Nature Ctr., Mpls., 1984-85. Mem. chm. dependency adv. com. United Hosp., St. Paul, 1988-94. With U.S. Army, 1946-48. Mem. ABA (com. on alcohol and drug abuse), Minn. Bar Assn., Hennepin County Bar Assn., Am. Trial Lawyers Assn., Minn. Trial Lawyers Assn., Am. Judicature Soc., Am. Arbitration Assn. (nat. panel arbitrators), Minn. Bd. Profl. Responsibility, Minn. Hist. Soc., Douglas K. Amdahl Inn of Ct., Minn. Lawyers Concerned for Lawyers (bd. dirs. 1996—). Fax: 612-475-1214. Home: 2105 Xanthus Ln N Minneapolis MN 55447-2055 Office: 12450 Wayzata Blvd Ste 224 Minnetonka MN 55305-1927

FREEMAN, GILL SHERRYL, judge; b. N.Y.C., June 24, 1949; d. Norman and Arlene (Vigdor) Jacovitz. BS in Edn. cum laude, Temple U., 1970; student, U. Wis., 1966-68; MEd, U. Miami, Miami, Fla., 1973; JD cum laude, U. Miami, 1977. Bar: Fla. 1977, U.S. Dist. Ct. (so. dist.) 1977, U.S. Dist. Ct. (mid. dist.) Fla. 1984, U.S. Ct. Appeals (5th cir.) 1977. Tchr. Dade County Pub. Schs., Miami, 1970-76; assoc. Walton, Lantaff, Schroeder & Carson, Miami, 1977-82; assoc. Ruden, McClosky, Smith, Schuster & Russell, Miami, 1982-97, ptnr., 1983-97; apptd. cir. ct. judge Dade County Fla., 1997—; vice chair Fla. Supreme Ct. Gender Bias Commn., 1987-90; chair Fla. Supreme Ct. Gender Bias Study Implementation Commn. Elected Fellow of the ABA, 1993; Master, Family Law Inns. of Ct., 1992. Mem. Fla. Bar Assn. (pres. 1984-85), Fla. Assn. Women Lawyers, Supreme Ct. Commn. on Fairness. Avocations: alpine skiing, travel, tennis. Office: Courthouse Ctr 175 WW 1st Ave Miami FL 33128

FREEMAN, HARRY LOUIS, investment executive; b. Omaha, Mar. 1, 1932; s. Joseph H. and Celia (Rivonne) F.; m. Lucile Carpenter, Dec. 26, 1965; children: Bennett, Lansing, Rachel, Alexandra. AB, U. Mich., 1953; JD, Harvard U., 1956. Bar: Nebr. 1956, Calif. 1957, U.S. Supreme Ct. 1967, D.C. 1968. Clk. U.S. Ct. Appeals, 9th Circuit, 1956-57; mem. Janin, Morgan, Brenner & Freeman, San Francisco, 1957-66; dir. Ins. div. AID, Dept. State, Washington, 1966-69; v.p. corp. planning OPIC, Washington, 1969-71; v.p. fin. OPIC, 1974-75; mgr. comml. projects, mgr. project fin. group Bechtel Corp., San Francisco, 1972-74; v.p. Am. Express Co., Washington, 1975-77; sr. v.p. Am. Express Co., N.Y.C., 1977-79; sr. v.p., office of chmn. Am. Express Co., 1979-83, exec. v.p., 1984-89; pres. The Freeman Co., Washington, 1989—; adj. prof. internat. law U. Calif., Berkeley, 1974, Georgetown U., 1975-76; prin. Ctr. for Excellence in Govt.; trustee U.S. Council for Internat. Bus. Contbr. articles to profl. jours. Trustee World Affairs Council No. Calif., 1960-66, Overseas Devel. Coun., Ctr. Excellence in Govt.; bd. dirs. Calif. Clinic for Psychotherapy, San Francisco, 1964-66, Fund for Multinat. Edn., 1984—; trustee Com. Econ. Devel., 1983—. Recipient Disting. Service award AID, 1969, Disting. Service award OPIC, 1971. Mem. ABA, Calif. Bar Assn., Nebr. Bar Assn., Washington Bar Assn., Coun. on Fgn. Rels., Harvard Club (N.Y.C.). Democrat. Jewish. Home: 4708 Dorset Ave Chevy Chase MD 20815-5446

FREEMAN, HARRY LYNWOOD, accountant; b. L.A., May 5, 1920; s. Edward Church and Mildred Eaton (Noyes) F.; m. Ruth Turner, Feb. 14, 1941; children: Tracy Ruth (Mrs. Richard W. Flatow), Martin Harry. BS, UCLA, 1942. CPA, Calif. With Price Waterhouse & Co., CPAs, 1942-56; ptnr. Price Waterhouse & Co., CPAs, Mexico City, 1956-73; ptnr.-in-charge Middle Americas firm Price Waterhouse & Co., CPAs, 1973-80. Chmn. auditing com. Am. Brit. Cowdray Hosp., 1962-68; bd. dirs., treas. YMCA of Mexico, 1967-73; bd. dirs. Inst. Mexicano-Norteamericano de Relaciones Culturales, 1961-69; trustee, v.p. Fallbrook Hosp. Found., 1987-90, pres., 1990-92; bd. dirs. Fallbrook Hosp. Dist., 1994-98, v.p., 1996-98. With AUS, 1944-46. Mem. AICPA, Calif. Soc. CPAs, Am. C. of C. Mex. (past pres.), Assn. Am. C. of C. in Latin Am. (past pres.), Aero Club of So. Calif., Book Club Calif. Home: 1002 Ridge Heights Dr Fallbrook CA 92028-3671

FREEMAN, HENRY MCCALL, newspaper publisher; b. Savannah, Ga., Jan. 9, 1947; s. Henry McCall and Helen (Powell) F.; m. Rae Jean Harris, Sept. 20, 1968 (div. 1976); Margaret Crabtree, Sept. 11, 1977; 1 child, Helen McCall. Student, U. Ga., 1965-69. Reporter Athens (Ga.) Daily News, 1968-69; sports editor The Anderson (S.C.) News Leader, 1969; asst. sports editor The Greenville (S.C.) News, 1969-76; asst. sports editor The News Jour., Wilmington, Del., 1976-79, editor, 1989-93; sports editor The Oakland (Calif.) Tribune, 1979-80, asst. mng. editor, 1980-82; planning editor USA Today, Washington, 1982, mng. editor sports, 1982-89; pres., pub. The Courier News, Bridgewater, N.J., 1993—; mem. Newspaprer Assn. Am., bd. dirs. N.J. Press Assn. Staff sgt. USMCR, 1969-76. Mem. Am. Soc. Newspaper Editors, Assn. Press Sports Editors (v.p. 1984-87, pres. 87-88). Office: The Courier News 1201 Us Highway 22 Bridgewater NJ 08807-2977*

FREEMAN, HERBERT, computer engineering educator; b. Frankfurt, Germany, Dec. 13, 1925; came to U.S., 1938; s. Leo and Johanna (Friedmann) F.; m. Joan Sleppin, Nov. 25, 1955; children: Nancy, Susan, Robert. BSEE, Union Coll., 1946; MSEE, Columbia U., 1948, DEngSc, 1956. Registered profl. engr., N.Y. Project engr. Sperry Gyroscope Co., Great Neck, N.Y., 1948-53, section head, 1953-57, dept. head, 1957-60; assoc. prof. computer engring. NYU, 1960-64, prof., chmn., 1965-75; prof. Rensselaer Poly. Inst., Troy, N.Y., 1975-85; dir. Ctr. for Computer Aids for Indsl. Productivity Rutgers U., New Brunswick, N.J., 1985-90; dir. Nat. Ctr. Geographic Info. and Analysis, 1988-93. Author: Discrete-Time Systems, 1965; co-editor: Map Data Processing, 1980, Software Engineering, 1981; editor: Introduction to Computer Graphics, 1981, Machine Vision for Three-Dimensional Scenes, 1990. NSF postdoctoral fellow, 1966, Guggenheim fellow, 1972; recipient Medaglia Teresiana award U. Pavia, Italy, 1996. Fellow IEEE (Computer Pioneer award 1999), Internat. Assn. for Pattern Recognition (treas. 1982-88, pres. 1978-80, K.S. Fu award 1994); mem. Computer Soc. of IEEE (chmn. Pattern Analysis and Machine Intelligence sect. 1976-78), Internat. Fedn. Info. Processing (program chmn. 1974, Silver Core award 1974), Assn. Computing Machinery, Pattera Recognition Soc. Avocations: stamp collecting, skiing, swimming. Office: Rutgers U Elec & Computer Engring PO Box 909 Piscataway NJ 08855-0909

FREEMAN, J. P. LADYHAWK, underwater exploration, security and transportation executive, educator, fashion model; b. Berkley, Calif., Feb. 21, 1951; d. Gilbert Richard Freeman (dec.) and P. M. (Ann) Raistrick; m. B.M. McGlynn, Feb. 9, 1974; children: Jennifer Patricia (dec.), Schne F. (dec.). BA in English, Davis & Elkins Coll., W.Va., 1973; grad., USAF Air Weapons Controller Sch., Tyndall AFB, Fla., 1973, USAF Air Command and Staff Coll., 1982, U.S. Marine Corps Command and Staff Coll., 1982, Dept. Def. Computer Inst., 1984; M in Aviation Mgmt., Embry-Riddle Aeronautical U., Daytona Beach, Fla., 1986, postgrad., 1986; grad., USAF Air War Coll., Montgomery, Ala., 1988. Cert. EMT. Mem. 56th spl. ops. rescue for Southeast Asia NKP Royal Thai Air Force Base, 1974, 75; chief wing radar standardization/evaluation RAF Alconbury, England, 1980-83; commdr. joint U.S. forces Operation Raleigh, 1986; support chief of staff Hdqs. NORAD, Colorado Springs, Colo., 1987-89; dep. base commdr. NATO Hdqs. Allied Forces No. Europe, Norway, 1989-91; chief airport mgmt. divsn. Whiteman AFB, Knob Noster, Mo., 1991-93; dir. spl. projects USAF Acad. Regional Hosp., Colorado Springs, 1993-94; systems performance specialist Colo. Sport & Spine Rehab., Colorado Springs, 1994-95; dir. FLEET Internat. Explorations and Svcs. Co., Colorado Springs, 1995-97; fashion model, 1996—; spl. adv. for anti and counter terrorist security design for 1994 Internat. Olympic Games, Oslo, Norway, 1989-91; designer Automated Provider Credentialing System USAF Acad. Regional Hosp., USAF Acad., Colo., 1993-94; spl. adv. coms. NATO German High Commd., 1977-80; experience in 37 countries. Poet, poems included in numerous anthologies. Mem. bd. dirs. Johnson County (Mo.) United Way, 1991-93; surgery life support specialist ARC, USAF Acad. Regional Hosp., 1993-95; mem. nat. scholarship com. Red River Valley Fighter Pilots Assn., 1993—; hosp. vol., med. technician, provider credentialing system designer, oral surgery life support system specialist. Recipient 53 awards and decorations including Defense Meritorious svc. medal with 1 oak leaf cluster, Meritorious Svc. medal with 2 oak leaf clusters, Joint Svc. Commendation medal with 1 oak leaf cluster, air force commendation medal, Armed Forces Expeditionary medal with 2 bronze stars, 2 Humanitarian Svc. medals, 2 Kuwait Liberation medals, 2 Southwest Asia medals; named Adminstrn. Officer of Yr. USAF, 1986; named one of the six top Support Officers USAF, 1986-87; 1st woman named dir. Fleet Internat. Mem. VFW, DAV, Am. Legion, Air Force Assn., Soc. of Profl. Journalists, Assn. of Old Crows, Lambda Lambda, Alpha Phi Omega, Iota Beta Sigma. Mem. Anglican Ch. Avocations: writing, skiing, horseback riding, oil painting, music. Home: 4861 Chaparral Rd Colorado Springs CO 80917-1413 Office: FLEET Internat Explorations & Svcs Co PO Box 14192 Colorado Springs CO 80914-0192

FREEMAN, JAMES ATTICUS, III, lawyer, insurance and business consultant; b. Gadsden, Ala., Jan. 27, 1947; s. James Atticus and Dorothy Mae (Watson) F.; m. Judith Gail Davis, June 19, 1970; children: Gwendolyn Gail, James Atticus IV, Laura Marie. BS, Vanderbilt U., 1969, JD, 1972. Bar: Tenn. 1972. Broadcaster, newsman GE Broadcasting, Nashville, 1965-72; atty. The Murray Ohio Mfg. Co., Nashville, 1972-73, legal officer, 1973-81; asst. v.p., legal officer, asst. sec. The Murray Ohio Mfg. Co., Brentwood, Tenn., 1981-86, asst. v.p., legal officer, dir. risk mgmt., 1986-90, sec., 1988-90; of counsel Blackburn, Little, Smith & Slobey, Nashville, 1990-92; atty. Blackburn & Slobey, 1992-94; shareholder Blackburn Slobey Freeman & Happell PC, 1995—; pres. Litigation Mgmt. Specialists, Inc., 1989—; founder Nat. Alternative Dispute Resolution Svcs. Tenn., Inc.; bd. dirs. Puhl Leasing, Inc., Some Assembly Required, Inc., Phoenix Property Mgmt. Svcs., Inc., Product Assembly, Inc.; lectr. corp. law, mem. bd. advisers Southeastern Inst. Paralegal Edn., Nashville, 1982-98); guest lectr. U. Wis. Sch. Engring., Madison, 1983; resource cons. Med Marc Ins., 1992—. Mem. ABA, Tenn. Bar Assn., Nashville Bar Assn. (chmn. membership com. 1984, program chmn. corp. sect. 1985-86), Def. Rsch. Inst., Soc. Metals (mem. adj. faculty Cleve. chpt. 1984-88), Outdoor Power Equipment Inst. (chmn. corp. counsel com. 1976-84), Bicycle Mfrs. Assn. (chmn. legal affairs com. 1978-81), Vanderbilt Alumni Assn., Risk and Ins. Mgmt. Soc. (v.p. Cumberland chpt. 1988, 89, Phi Alpha Delta. Episcopalian. Office: Litigation Mgmt Specialists One Nat Bank Plaza 414 Union St Ste 2051 Nashville TN 37219-1790 also: Blackburn Slobey Freeman& Happell One Nat Bank Plaza 414 Union St Ste 2050 Nashville TN 37219-1789

FREEMAN, JAMES BEAUMONT, philosophy educator; b. Paterson, N.J., Mar. 27, 1947; s. Theodore Roosevelt and Marion Elizabeth (Evans) F. BA, Drew U., 1968; AM, Ind. U., 1971, PhD, 1973. Lectr. Ind. U., Bloomington, 1973-74, Butler U., Indpls., 1974, Bloomfield (N.J.) Coll., 1974-75; rsch. assoc. U. Victoria, B.C., Can., 1975-78; asst. prof. philosophy Hunter Coll., CUNY, 1978-84, assoc. prof., 1985-92, prof., 1993—, chmn. dept., 1992-98. Author: Thinking Logically: Basic Concepts for Reasoning, 1988, 93, Dialectics and the Macrostructure of Arguments: A Theory of Argument Structure, 1991; contbr. articles to jours. in field; mem. editl. bd. Argumentation. Mem. Am. Philos. Assn., Soc. Christian Philosophers, Assn. for Informal Logic/Critical Thinking. Republican. Anglican. Avocation: physical fitness. Home: 478 Park Ave Paterson NJ 07504-1806 Office: Hunter Coll CUNY 695 Park Ave New York NY 10021-5024

FREEMAN, JEFFREY VAUGHN (JEFF FREEMAN), art educator, artist; b. Bismarck, N.D., Oct. 19, 1946; s. Dorrance Samuel Evan and Ethel Beatrice (Peterson) F. BS, Moorhead State U., 1970; MA, U. N.D., 1972; MFA, U. Wis., 1980. Grad. teaching asst. U. N.D., Grand Forks, 1970-72, U. Wis., Madison, 1978-80; prof. art U. S.D., Vermillion, 1980—; subst. tchr. Moorhead (Minn.) Pub. Schs., 1973; mem. faculty adult edn. Ctrl. Cass Pub. Schs., 1973-74; adj. prof. Moorhead State U., 1973-75; coord. S.D. Coll. Art Assn. Painting Conf., U. S.D., Vermillion, 1981; cons., W.H. Over Mus., Vermillion, 1985; lectr. in field. One man shows include Jamestown (N.D.) Coll., 1973, Bison Gallery, Fargo, N.D., 1975, Plains Art Mus., Moorhead, 1979, U. Wis., Madison, 1980, Ritz Gallery, S.D. State U, Brookings, 1982, No. State Coll, Lincoln Hall Gallery, Aberdeen, S.D., 1984, Buena Vista Coll., Storm Lake, Iowa, 1985, S.D. Meml. Art Ctr., Brookings, 1985, Gallery 306, Sioux Falls, S.D., 1987, Gallery 72, Omaha, 1988, Ruddell Gallery, Black Hills State Coll., Spearfish, S.D., 1988, LeMars (Iowa) Civic Fine Arts Ctr., 1989, Nobles County Art Ctr., Worthington, Minn., 1990, U. S.D. Art Galleries, Vermillion, 1990, Olivet Nazarene U., Bourbonnais, Ill., 1990, Mount Vernon (Ohio) Nazarene Coll., 1990, Coffee Shop Gallery, Vermillion, 1991, U. Ark., 1992, DuPont Gallery, Lexington, Va., 1992, Nordstrand Gallery, Wayne, Nebr., 1993, The New Gallery, Rapid City, S.D., 1993, Bede Art Gallery, Yankton, S.D., 1993, Gus Lucky Gallery, Minn., 1998, others; exhibited in group shows at Minn. Mus. Art, St. Paul, 1975, Moorhead State U., 1975, 76, U. Minn., Morris, 1975, Thief River Falls C.C., Minn., 1976, 1st Nat. Bank, Moorhead, 1976, U. Wis., 1978, Plains Art Mus., Moorhead, 1978, 79, 93, U. S.D., 1981, 82, 83, 84, 85, 87, 88, 90, 92, 94, 96, Rourke Art Gallery, Moorhead, Minn., 1982, 83, 84, 85, 86, 89, 90, 97, 98, No. State Coll., Student Union Gallery, 1981, Sioux City Art Ctr., 1983, 88, 90, 92, N.D. State U. Art Gallery, Fargo, 1984, N.D. Mus. Art, Grand Forks, 1984, Sioux Falls (S.D.) Civic Fine Arts Ctr., 1987, Gallery 72, Omaha, 1988, 90, Dahl Fine Arts Ctr., Rapid City, S.D., 1988, Joslyn Art Mus., Omaha, 1990, S.D. Art Mus., Brookings, 1991, 93, 95, 97, Sheldon Meml. Art Gallery, Lincoln, Nebr., 1991, The New Gallery, Rapid City, 1992, 94, 96, Thimmesh Gallery, Mpls., 1992, 93, 94, Chgo. Art Expo, 1993, Jamestown (N.D.) Art Ctr., 1993, Mus. Der Stadt Ratingen, Germany, 1997, others; represented in permanent collections Joslyn Art Mus., Donaghey Found., Little Rock, U. Ark., Little Rock, Sheldon Meml. Art Gallery, Lincoln, Nebr., Legrand and Co., Sioux City, Sioux City Art Ctr., Sioux Falls Civic Fine Arts Ctr., Klinger Corp., Sioux City, S.D. Art Mus., Brookings, Plains Art Mus., Moorhead, N.D. Mus. of Art, Grand Forks, Madison Art Ctr., Comstock Meml. Union, Moorhead State U., U. S.D., Vermillion, Norwest Bank, Moorhead, Grafton, N.D. and various pvt. collections in N.D., S.D., Minn., Nebr., Iowa, Ohio, Ill., Alaska, Wis., La., Mass, Calif., N.Y., Ariz., N.C., Tex., Wash., Oreg. and N.J. Rsch. grantee S.D. Rsch. Inst., U. S.D., 1982, 86, Bush Found. grantee, 1988; Visual Artist grantee S.D. Arts Coun., 1988-89; Painting fellow Arts Midwest/Nat. Endowment for the Arts, 1990-91, Nat. Endowment for the Arts, 1991-92; recipient 1st Place and Purchase award Plains Art Mus., Moorhead, 1978, Jury Purchase award Madison Art Ctr., 1978, Best Painting award Sioux City Fall Biennial, 1983, Merit award ARTQUEST, 1985. Home: 900 W Main St Vermillion SD 57069-2915 Office: U SD Art Dept 414 E Clark St Vermillion SD 57069-2307

FREEMAN, JOEL ARTHUR, behavioral consultant; b. Lewiston, Maine, July 24, 1954; s. Arthur Fickett and Katherine Ann (Schroeder) F.; m. Shirley Lee Burkhardt, Jan. 6, 1996; children: David Joel, Jesse Andrew, Jacob Edward, Shari Adelaide. MS in Pastoral Counseling, Loyola Coll., Balt., 1986; PhD in Pastoral Counseling, Evang. Theol. Sem., Dixon, Mo., 1991. Ordained to ministry Calvary Chapel Outreach Fellowship, 1975. Pastor Glorious Gospel Ch., Friendship, Maine, 1975-77, Balt., 1977-80, Columbia, Md., 1980-88; pastor Stillmeadow Christian Fellowship, Balt., 1988-93; pres. Freeman Inst., Severn, Md., 1993—; chaplain NBA Washington Wizards Basketball Team, 1979—; host radio talk show Sta. WABS, 1977-88; TV host Howard Cable Co., Ellicott City, Md., 1980-86; interviewer CBN Satellite Radio Network, 1988—; mentor, corp. chaplain The Shepherd's Guide, 1980—; chaplain Sports World Ministries, 1998—. Author: The Doctrine of Fools, 1984, God Is Not Fair, 1987, Living with Your Conscience without Going Crazy, 1989, Kingdom Zoology, 1991, Return to Glory: The Powerful Stirring of the Black Man, 1997; co-prodr., co-writer (film) Return to Glory, 1998. Instr. chaplain's office Johns Hopkins U., Balt., 1977-79; mem. steering com. Word Renewal Pastor's Fellowship, Balt., 1977-83, County Exec. Prayer Breakfast, Howard County, 1983-86; area coord. Washington for Jesus, 1980. Mem. Inst. in Basic Life Principles (coord. 1979-86). Republican. Home: 1103 Burkhardt Ln Severn MD 21144 Office: Freeman Inst 1103 Burkhardt Ln Severn MD 21144 *I choose to keep the eternal perspective in clear view. I want to invest my life in that which will be important one thousand years from now. Jesus Christ is the same yesterday, today and forever.*

FREEMAN, JOHN CLINTON, meteorologist, oceanographer; b. Houston, Aug. 7, 1920; s. John Clinton and Ann (Dotson) F.; m. Marjorie Schaefer, June 14, 1947; children: John C. III, Walter H., Jill F. Hasling, Cathryn F. Disch, Helen, Paul D. BA, Rice U., 1941; MS, Calif. Inst. Tech., 1942; postgrad., Brown U., 1946-48; PhD, U. Chgo., 1952. Commd. 2d lt. USAF, 1941, advanced through grades to lt. col., 1970; weather officer U.S. Army, 1941-46; math. rschr. grad. divsn. applied math. Brown U., Providence, R.I.,

1946-48; rschr. in meteorology U.S. Weather Bur., Washington, 1948-49, Inst. Advanced Study, Princeton, N.J., 1949-50, U. Chgo., 1950-52; rschr. in meteorology and oceanography, prof. Tex. A&M, College Station, Tex., 1952-55; meteorology and oceanography rschr. Gulf Cons.-NESCO, Houston, 1955-66; prof., chmn. and dir. rsch. Inst. Storm Rsch.-U. St. Thomas, Houston, 1957-88; dir. rsch., pres. Weather Rsch. Ctr., Houston, 1988—; convenor, chmn. Internat. Conf. Coastal Engring., Houston, 1984; presenter in field. Contbr. chpts. to books. Fellow Am. Meteorology Soc. (chmn. com. applied meteorology 1975-76, Meisinger award 1950, spl. award Tex. tornado radar network 1961); mem. Am. Geophys. Union, Marine Tech. Soc. (local chmn. 1970). Democrat. Church of Christ. Avocation: dog training. Office: Weather Rsch Ctr 3227 Audley St Houston TX 77098-1901

FREEMAN, JOHN MARK, pediatric neurologist; b. Bklyn., Jan. 11, 1933; s. Leon Lucas and Florence (Kann) F.; m. Elaine Kaplan, Aug. 26, 1956; children: Andrew David, Jennifer Beth, Joshua Leon. B.A., Amherst Coll., 1954; M.D., Johns Hopkins U., 1958. Intern Harriet Lane Home, Johns Hopkins U., Balt., 1958-59; resident in pediatrics Harriet Lane Home, Johns Hopkins U., 1959-61; fellow in neurology Columbia Presbyn. Hosp., N.Y.C., 1961-64; asst. prof. pediatrics and neurology Stanford (Calif.) U., 1966-69; asso. prof. neurology and pediatrics Johns Hopkins U., Balt., 1969-82, prof., 1982—, Lederer prof. pediatric epilepsy, 1991—; dir. pediatric neurology Johns Hopkins, Balt., 1969-90; dir. pediatric epilepsy ctr. Johns Hopkins U., Balt., 1973—, dir. birth defects treatment center, 1969-90; Pres. Epilepsy Assn. Md., 1977-82; mem. profl. adv. bd. Epilepsy Found. Am., 1975-82, sec., 1977, v.p., 1982—, hon. life dir., 1991—. Contbr. articles to profl. jours. Served with AUS, 1964-66. Named Physician of Yr. Gov.'s Com. on Employment Handicapped, 1979, Health Care Profl. of Yr. Gov.'s Com. on Employment of Persons with Disabilities, 1990; recipient Community Leadership award Epilepsy Assn. Md., 1991, Lennox award Am. Epilepsy Assn., 1993. Fellow Am. Acad. Neurology, Am. Acad. Pediatrics (chmn. neurology sect. 1978-80); mem. Profs. of Child Neurology (pres. 1980-82), Child Neurology Soc. (exec. com. 1979-81), Am. Acad. Pediatrics, Am. Pediatric Soc., Am. Fedn. Clin. Research, Am. Epilepsy Soc. (Lennox award 1993), Am. Neurol. Assn. Home: 1026 Rolandvue Ave Baltimore MD 21204-6815 Office: John Hopkins Med Inst 600 N Wolfe St 2-147 Meyer Baltimore MD 21287-0005

FREEMAN, JUDI H., curator, art historian; b. New Hyde Park, N.Y., Nov. 4, 1957; m. Kenneth Slade, Aug. 20, 1978; children: Jessica and Rebecca Freeman-Slade. AB in Art, Vassar Coll., 1978; MA in Art History, Johns Hopkins U., 1979; MPhil in Art History, Yale U., 1982, postgrad., 1994—; MAT in History, Tufts U., 1999. Curatorial intern Hirshhorn Mus. and Sculpture Garden, 1978; lectr. dept. edn. Nat. Gallery Art, Washington, 1980; vis. rsch. scholar Courtauld Inst. Art, London, 1983-84; assoc. curator 20th century art L.A. County Mus. Art, 1985-93; Joan Whitney Payson curator Portland (Maine) Mus. Art, 1993-94; fellow Harvard U., 1994-95; ind. curator, educator; vis. fellow Harvard U., 1994-95. Author: The Spiritual in Art: Abstract Painting 1890-1985, 1986, The Dada and Surrealist Word-Image, 1989, The Fauve Landscape, 1990, Mark Tansey, 1993, Picasso and the Weeping Women, 1994, The Fauves, 1995, The Fridart Foundation, 1999. Recipient Rsch. award Inst. français de Washington, 1982; fellow Smithsonian Inst., 1979, Yale U., 1980-82, Danforth Found., 1978-83, Vassar Coll. Alumni, 1984-85, U.S.-France Mus. Profls. Exhange/Nat. Endowment Arts, 1988, Andrew W. Mellon, 1992; Chester Dale fellow Met. Mus. Art, N.Y.C., 1984-85; grantee Kress Found., 1978, Coun. We. European Studies, 1981, Swedish Inst. Rsch., 1982-83, Fulbright-Hays, 1982-83, Coll. Art Assn., 1983, Assn. Française d'Action Artistique/French Min. Culture, 1993; named Chevalier dans l'Ordre des Arts et Lettres French Govt., 1991. Address: 19 Cushing Rd Wellesley MA 02481-2903

FREEMAN, LEE ALLEN, JR., lawyer; b. Chgo., July 31, 1940; s. Lee Allen and Brena (Dietz) F.; m. Glynna Gene Weger, June 8, 1968; children: Crispin McDougal, Clark Dietz, Cassidy Bree. A.B. magna cum laude, Harvard U., 1962, J.D. magna cum laude, 1965. Bar: Ill. 1966, D.C. 1966, Mont. 1986, U.S. Supreme Ct. 1969. Practiced in Washington, 1965-68, Chgo., 1968—; law clk. to Justice Tom C. Clark, Washington, 1965-66; asst. U.S. atty., 1966-68; v.p. Freeman, Freeman & Salzman, P.C., 1970—; spl. asst. atty. gen. Ill., W.Va., 1969-82, Mich., Wis., Minn., Colo., Ky., N.D., 1973-79; spl. dep. atty. gen. Pa., 1971-82; spl. asst. corp. counsel Chgo., 1971-76. Pres. Chgo. Lyric Opera Guild; pres. Fine Arts Music Found.; dir. Chgo. Lyric Opera, 1995—. Named Outstanding Young Citizen Chgo. Jaycees, 1976. Fellow ABA Found.; mem. ABA (coun. mem. antitrust sect. 1985-87), Am. Coll. Trial Lawyers, Std. Club, Chgo. Inn of Ct., Am. Law Inst. Home: 232 E Walton St Chicago IL 60611-1507 also: PO Box 1295 Livingston MT 59047-1295 Office: 401 N Michigan Ave Chicago IL 60611-4255

FREEMAN, LEONARD MURRAY, radiologist, nuclear medicine physician, educator; b. N.Y.C., Apr. 20, 1937; s. Joseph and Tillie (Krutman) F.; m. Marlene Carolyn Held, Apr. 28, 1967; children: Eric Lawrence, David Robert, Joy Esther. B.A., N.Y. U., 1957; M.D., Chgo. Med. Sch., 1961. Diplomate: Am. Bd. Radiology, Am. Bd. Nuclear Medicine. Intern Beth Israel Hosp. and Med. Center, N.Y.C., 1961-62; resident in radiology Bronx Municipal Hosp. Center, 1962-65; mem. staff Albert Einstein Coll. Medicine, N.Y.C., 1965—; co-dir. div. nuclear medicine Jacobi Med. Ctr., N.Y.C., 1965-83; dir. nuclear medicine Montefiore Med. Center, N.Y.C., 1976—, attending radiologist, 1977—; cons. nuclear medicine USPHS Hosp., S.I., N.Y., 1967-82, St. Barnabas Hosp., Bronx, 1967—, Beth Israel Hosp. and Med. Center, 1974—, Maimonides Hosp. and Med. Center, 1974—, Bklyn. VA Hosp., 1984—; asst. instr. radiology Albert Einstein Coll. Medicine, Bronx, 1964-65, instr., 1965-67, asst. prof., 1967-72, assoc. prof., 1972-77, prof., 1977—, prof. nuclear medicine, 1983—, vice chmn. dept. nuclear medicine, 1987—; mem. adv. com. nuclear medicine program Brookhaven Nat. Labs., Upton, N.Y., 1972-82; examiner nuclear medicine Am. Bd. Radiology. Author: Clinical Scintillation Scanning, 1969, Clinical Scintillation Imaging, 1975, Freeman and Johnson's Clinical Radionuclide Imaging, 1984; co-editor Seminars in Nuclear Medicine, 1970—, Physicians Desk Reference for Radiology and Nuclear Medicine, 1971-80; reviewer Jour. Nuclear Medicine, 1972—; editor Nuclear Medicine Ann., 1980—, Current Concepts in Diagnostic Nuclear Medicine, 1983-87, Advances in Functional Neuroimaging, 1988-90; mem. editl. bd. European Jour. Nuclear Medicine, 1979—, Jour. Nuclear Medicine and Allied Scis., 1982-96, Nuclear Medicine Communications, 1986—, Quar. Jour. Nuclear Medicine, 1996—; contbr. numerous articles to jours., also book chpts. Fellow Am. Coll. Radiology, Am. Coll. Nuclear Physicians, N.Y. Acad. Medicine; mem. AMA, Soc. Nuclear Medicine (gov. local chpt. 1973—, nat. trustee 1973-77, nat. v.p. 1977-78, nat. pres. 1979-80, chmn. pub. rels. com. 1981-91, chmn. correlative imaging coun. 1982-84, chmn. awards com. 1983-86, Disting. Edn. award 1993, Berson-Yallow award Greater N.Y. chpt. 1997), Am. Roentgen Ray Soc., Radiol. Soc. N.Am., N.Y., Roentgen Soc., L.I. Radiol. Soc., Soc. Gastrointestinal Radiologists, N.Y. State Med. Soc., Nassau County Med. Soc., Pan Am. Med. Assn. (hon. life), European Assn. Nuclear Medicine, Gissellschaft für Nuklearmedizin (hon. corr.), L.I. Soc. Nuclear Med. Technologists (hon. life), Alpha Omega Alpha (hon.). Home: 50 Sutton Pl S New York NY 10022 Office: 111 E 210th St Bronx NY 10467-2401

FREEMAN, LESLIE GORDON, anthropologist, educator; b. Warsaw, N.Y., Sept. 9, 1935; s. Leslie Gordon and Theresa Rosalie (Stanbro) F.; m. Susan Tax, Mar. 20, 1964; 1 child, Sarah Elisabeth. AB, U. Chgo., 1954, AM, 1961, PhD, 1964. Asst. prof. anthropology Tulane U., 1964-65; asst. prof. U. Chgo., 1965-70, assoc. prof., 1970-76, prof., 1976—; pres. Inst. Prehistoric Investigations, Chgo., 1983—. Author: (with J. Gonzalez) Cueva Morin, 2 vols., 1971, 73, Vida y Muerte en Cueva Morin, 1978, Le Paleolithique Inferieur et Moyen en Espagne, 1998; editor: Views of the Past, 1978, (with Sol Tax) Horizons of Anthropology, 1976, (with others) Altamira Revisited, 1987, Beato de Liebana, 1995. Corporator Internat. Inst. Spain. With U.S. Army, 1957-59. Recipient Silver Plaque Provincial Deputation of Santander, Spain, 1973. Fellow AAAS, Am. Anthropol. Assn., Royal Anthropol. Inst.; mem. Reial Academia Catalana de Belles Arts de Sant Jordi Barcelona (corr.), Reial Academia Catalana de Bones Lettres Barcelona (corr.), Chgo. Acad. Scis. (trustee, 2d v.p. 1981-83). Home: 5537 S Woodlawn Ave Chicago IL 60637-1620 Office: U Chgo Dept Anthropology Haskell Hall M-135 Chicago IL 60637 also: Inst for Prehistoric Investigations 5537 S Woodlawn Ave Chicago IL 60637

FREEMAN, LESLIE JEAN, neuropsychologist, researcher; b. San Diego, Feb. 17, 1965; d. Richard Joseph and Jean Doris (Weber) Currier; m. Drue Scott Freeman, Sept. 6, 1986. BA, U. Calif., Irvine, 1989; MA in Clin. Psychology, Antioch U., L.A., 1992; postgrad., Calif. Sch. Profl. Psychology, Fresno, 1993-98. Marriage, family and child counselor intern So. Calif. Counseling Ctr., L.A., 1990-93; marriage, family, child counselor intern/psychology intern Bakersfield (Calif.) Med. Hosp., 1993-94; intern, resident in neuropsychology pvt. practice and Drs. Hosp., Modesto, Calif., 1994-97; resident in neuropsychology VA Med. Ctr., Cleve., 1997-98; resident, fellow in neuropsychology U. Rochester (N.Y.) Med. Ctr., 1998—; guest lectr. in field. Contbr. articles to profl. jours. Mem. APA, Nat. Acad. Neuropsychology, Internat. Neuropsychol. Soc., Am. Neuropsychiat. Assn., Calif. Assn. Marriage and Family Therapy, Calif. Assn. Psychology Providers. Avocations: collecting first edition mystery novels, collecting original animation art and Disneyana, cooking, skiing, photography. Home: 20 Tobey Ct Pittsford NY 14534 Office: U Rochester Strong Meml Hosp U Rochester Rochester NY 14642

FREEMAN, LILLIE BROOKS, communications company administrator; b. Newark, Aug. 16, 1944; d. John Louis and Lillie (Hill) Brooks; m. Andrew L. Freeman, May 23, 1970; 1 child, Kyle E. BS, Howard U., Atlantic Community Coll., Mays Landing, N.J. Long distance telephone operator, supr. N.J. Bell Telephone Co., Pleasantville, staff clk., 1980-92; sr. admstrv. asst. RMS Techs., Inc., Pleasantville, 1992-96, facilities adminstr., 1996-99; facilities adminstr. Intellesource Info. Sys., 1999—. Recipient Lay Speaker award, others. Mem. Toastmistress Club, Zonta Internat., Nat. Black Coalition of Fed. Aviation Employees, Nat. Bawling Assn. Address: 22 N 2nd St Pleasantville NJ 08232-2610

FREEMAN, LINTON CLARKE, sociology educator; b. Chgo., July 4, 1927; s. Willis and Kathryn Clarke (Kieffer) F.; m. Sue Carole Feinberg, Aug. 2, 1958; children: Stacey Elizabeth Vanhanswyk, Michael Andrew. B.A., Roosevelt U., Chgo., 1952; M.A., U. Hawaii, 1953; Ph.D., Northwestern U., 1956. Asst. prof., then assoc. prof. sociology Syracuse (N.Y.) U., 1956-67; prof. sociology and computer sci. U. Pitts., 1967-69; prof. sociology and info. sci. U. Hawaii, 1969-72; Lucy G. Moses distinguished prof. sociology Lehigh U., Bethlehem, Pa., 1973-79; prof. Sch. Social Scis., U. Calif., Irvine, 1979—, dean, 1979-82; Killam sr. lectr. sociology and anthropology Dalhousie U., Halifax, N.S., Can., 1972; directeur d'Etudes Associé Maison des Sciences de l'Homme, Paris, 1991; Ward supr. Onondaga County (N.Y.) Bd. Suprs., 1966-68. Author: Elementary Applied Statistics, 1965, Patterns of Local Community Leadership, 1968; co-author: Residential Segregation Patterns, 1970; editor: Social Networks; contbr. to profl. jours. Served with USNR, 1944-46. Home: 2705 Temple Hills Dr Laguna Beach CA 92651-2037 Office: U Calif Sch Social Scis Irvine CA 92697-5100

FREEMAN, LOUIS S., lawyer; b. Cin., Apr. 21, 1940; s. Emanuel and Sadye (Harris) F.; m. Diane Ruth Edson, Jan. 27, 1967; children: Matthew E., James H., Jill E. BBA, U. Cin., 1963; JD, Harvard U., 1966; LLM in Taxation, NYU, 1972. Bar: Ohio 1966, N.Y. 1968, Ill. 1975. CPA. Mem. staff Coopers & Lybrand, N.Y.C., 1966-68; assoc. Mudge, Rose, Guthrie & Alexander, N.Y.C., 1968-74; assoc. Sonnenschein Nath & Rosenthal, Chgo., 1974-76, ptnr., 1976-97; ptnr. Skadden, Arps, Slate, Meagher & Flom, Chgo., 1997—; adj. prof. of taxation Ill. Inst. Tech., Chgo.-Kent Coll. of Law Grads. Program in Taxation, 1985-89. Mem. bds. of contbg. editors Jour. Corp. Taxation, Jour. Real Estate Taxation, Jour. Taxation of Investments; bd. advisors the M&A Tax Report, Jour. Corp. Taxation; also author articles. Fellow Am. Coll. Tax Counsel; mem. ABA (tax sect. com. on corp. tax), Chgo. Bar Assn., (chmn. exec. com. of fed. tax com. 1986-87), N.Y. Sate Bar Assn. (tax sect. exec. com. 1990-92), Am. Law Inst. (tax adv. group subchpt. C. Fed. Income Tax Project), Met. Club of Chgo. Home: 333 W Wacker Dr Chicago IL 60606

FREEMAN, MARGARET H., English educator; b. Leicester, England, U.K., Jan. 1, 1940; came to U.S., 1962; d. William Ernest and Helen Milton Chalmers Shepherd Hay Rawson; m. Donald C. Freeman, Dec. 19, 1970. BA in English and Philosophy with honors, U. Manchester, England, 1962; MA in English, U. Mass., Amherst, Mass., 1970, PhD in English, 1978. Assoc. prof. SUNY/Coll. at Old Westbury, Old Westbury, N.Y., 1975-87; assoc. prof. dept. English U. So. Calif., L.A., 1987-89; prof. of English L.A. Valley Coll., Van Nuys, Calif., 1989—. Contbr. chpts. to books, articles to profl. jours. N.E.H. fellow Princeton, 1989; N.E.H. grantee, 1995. Mem. Emily Dickinson Internat. Soc. (pres. 1988-92), Poetics and Linguistics Assn, Modern Lang. Assn., Cognitive Linguistics Assn., European Soc. for Study of English, Internat. Assn. Empirical Aesthetics. Office: L A Valley Coll 5800 Fulton Ave Van Nuys CA 91401-4096

FREEMAN, MARJORIE SCHAEFER, mathematics educator; b. Chevy Chase, Md., Sept. 23, 1924; d. Herbert Stanley and Helen (Hummer) Schaefer; m. John C. Freeman, June 14, 1947; children: John C. III, Walter H., Jill F. Hasling, Cathryn F. Disch, Helen Freeman, Paul D. AB, Randolph-Macon Womans Coll., 1946; MS, Brown U, 1949; postgrad., U. Houston, 1973-75. Computer asst. Inst. for Advanced Study, Princeton, N.J., 1949-50; rsch. asst. Tex. A&M Rsch. Found., College Station, 1954-55; instr. Tex. A&M U., College Station, 1955; cons. Gulf Cons., Houston, 1955-56; instr. South Tex. Jr. Coll., Houston, 1961-74; asst. prof. U. Houston-Downtown, 1974-90, asst. prof. emeritus, 1990—; systems analyst, programmer TERA, Inc., Houston, 1985; cons. Inst. for Storm Rsch., Houston, 1979-86; adv. bd. Weather Rsch. Ctr., Houston, 1987—. Mem. Math. Assn. Am., South Tex. Obedience Club, S.W. Tracking Assn., Am. Chesapeake Club. Avocations: dog training, camping, crafts. Home: 4404 Mount Vernon St Houston TX 77006-5814

FREEMAN, MARK, artist; b. Zaleszczyki, Austria, Sept. 27, 1908; came to U.S., 1923, naturalized, 1929; s. David and Henrietta (Schlaf) F.; m. Pauline Allen, Sept. 15, 1935; children: David, Stephen. A.B., Columbia Coll., 1930; M.Arch., Columbia U. Sch. Architecture, 1932, postgrad. in fine arts, 1932-34; postgrad. (Carnegie fellow), Sorbonne, Paris, summer 1930, NAD, 1927-30. One-man shows include Parrish Art Mus., Southampton, N.Y., 1964, Ringwood Manor Mus., N.Y., 1966, Sylvan Cole Gallery, N.Y., 1987, Elliott Mus., Stuart, Fla., 1991, Sragow Gallery, 1992, Hirschl-Adler Gallery, 1993, Avery Hall Sch. of Architecture, 1993, Vienna (Austria) Mus., 1994, Passau, Germany, 1994; group shows include, Nat. Soc. Painters in Casein and Acrylic, 1962—, Am. Watercolor Soc., Audubon Artists, N.Y., 1968—, Internat. Biennial Color Lithography, Cin. Mus., 1951-53, Washington Water Color Assn., 1955-65, Soc. Am. Graphic Artists, N.Y., 1958, N.Y.C. Center Gallery, 1960-62, Knickerbocker Artists, N.Y., 1959-68, Boston Printmakers, 1950-60, Parrish Mus., N.Y., 1954-65, Portland (Oreg.) Mus., 1955-62, Wichita Art Assn., 1954-62, Print Club., Phila., 1960-64, Pa. Acad. Fine Arts, Art in U.S.A., N.Y., 1959, NAD, 1960, 64, 82, 97, Nat. Inst. Arts and Letters, N.Y., 1968, 69, Butler Art Inst., 1970, Wichita Watercolor Centennial, Columbia U., 1995; represented in permanent collections Mus. Modern Art, N.Y.C., Whitney Mus., N.Y., British Mus., Met. Mus. Art, Boston Library, Wichita Art Mus., Johnson Mus. (Ithaca, N.Y.), Ft. Wayne (Ind.) Mus. Art, East Hampton Guild Hall, Mitchell Wolfson Miami Collection, Norfolk Art Mus., Phila. Mus. Art, Library of Congress, Parrish Art Mus., Butler Art Inst., Holyoke Art Mus., St. Vincent Coll., Hengelose Kunstzaal, Holland, Slater Art Mus., Springfield Art Mus., Mus. of City of N.Y., Bklyn. Mus., Nat. Mus. Am. History Smithsonian Instn., Queens Mus., Corcoran Art Gallery, Washington, Cleve. Mus., Worcester Mus., Mass., New Britain Mus. Am. Art, Mus. Modern Art, Passau, Germany, Bawag Found., Vienna, Austria, pvt. colls.; author Reaching for the Sky, 1992 (drawings N.Y. 1929-32). Artists' fellowship, 1992; recipient Clinedinst Merit medal, 1994. Artists fellow, 1994, Columbia U. 65th Retrospective, 1995; named to Nat. Acad., 1992. Mem. NAD1992, Audubon Artists (pres. 1977-79, hon. life pres.), Nat. Soc. Painters in Casein and Acrylic (pres. 1972-88), Am. Soc. Contemporary Artists (pres. 1975-77), League Present Day Artists (pres. 1975), N.Y. Artists Equity (v.p. 1976-79, 81-83, editor-in-chief newsletter 1977-80, 81-84, cons.), Lotos Club (art chmn. 1977-92, medal of merit 1992). Home: 117 E 35th St New York NY 10016-3805 Studio: 32 Union Sq W New York NY 10003-3202

FREEMAN, MARSHALL, publishing executive. BA in Econs., Stanford U., 1955. Advt. sales McGraw-Hill, N.Y.C., Boston, L.A., 1957-63; from salesman to chmn., CEO Miller Freeman Publs., San Francisco, 1963-98. Office: Miller Freeman Inc 600 Harrison St Ste 400 San Francisco CA 94107-1391*

FREEMAN, MARY ANNA, librarian; b. Sentinal, Okla., July 24, 1943; d. Wylie Lee and Thelma Anna (Elam) Johnson; m. Charles Edward Freeman, Jr., Aug. 26, 1963; children: Charles Edward III, Juliana Elizabeth, Mark Adrian, Lee Agustin. BS, Abilene Christian U., 1963; MLS, Tex. Woman's U., 1981. Tchr. 4th grade Las Cruces Pub. Sch. (N.Mex.), 1963-64; tchr. 2d grade, 1964-67; head audiovisual dept. El Paso (Tex.) Pub. Library, 1972; head librarian Guillen Jr. H.S., El Paso, 1974-95; asst. librarian Andress H.S., El Paso, 1995-96, head libr., 1996—. Treas., Guillen PTA, El Paso, 1983-85, 86-89; mem. partnership in edn. liaison, 1986-90; Westside police area rep. El Paso Police Dept., 1997—. Mem. ALA, Tex. Library Assn. Office: Andress HS 5400 Sun Valley Dr El Paso TX 79924-3418

FREEMAN, MEREDITH NORWIN, former college president, education educator; b. Elvins, Mo., June 1, 1920; s. William J. and Zelpha (McGuire) F.; m. Helen Lorene Larkin, Aug. 3, 1941 (dec. Nov. 1970); children: James Michael, Judith Ann; m. Joyce Mary Liebsch, Oct. 23, 1971; stepchildren: Mary Ann, Dawn Joy. BS, Southeast Mo. State Coll., Cape Girardeau, 1949; MEd, U. Mo., 1951, EdD, 1955. Rural sch. tchr. St. Francis County, Mo., 1940-41; elementary tchr., also prin. New Haven, Mo., 1941-42, 46-50; high sch. sci. tchr., prin., 1947-50; supt. schs. Wright City, Mo., 1951-52, New Haven, Mo., 1952-54; tchr. chemistry and physics Hickman High Sch., Columbia, Mo., 1954-55; assoc. prof. edn. Fort Hays State Coll., Kans., 1955-57; dir. spl. services, prof. edn. Mankato (Minn.) State U., 1957-64, asst. acad. dean, 1964-66, academic dean, 1966-67; pres. Black Hills State U., Spearfish, S.D., 1967-76, Concord Coll., Athens, W.Va., 1976-85; regents prof. edn. W.Va. Coll. Grad. Studies, Institute, 1985-90, ret., 1990; mem. exec. com. Minn. Assn. Colls., 1964-67; sec. S.D. Council Coll. and Univ. Pres.'s, 1967-68, chmn., 1969-70, 74-75; mem. S.D. Indian Scholarships Com., 1967-76; pres. emeritus BlCK Hills State Coll., 1976, Concord Coll., 1985. Mem. exec. com. Black Hills Area Council Boy Scouts Am., 1968-76; mem. S.D. Gov.'s Scholarship Com., 1970-76; mem. exec. com. W.Va. Assn. Coll. Pres.'s; mem. W.Va. Adv. Council on Profl. Personnel, 1976-82; bd. dirs. Appalachia Regional Lab., 1981-85, Princeton Community Hosp. Served to sgt. U.S. Army, 1942-46, ETO. Mem. NEA, Am. Assn. Sch. Adminstrs., Am. Assn. State Colls. and Univs. (S.D. rep. 1971-75, W.Va. rep. 1981-83), Princeton C. of C. (dir.), Phi Delta Kappa (past faculty sponsor Epsilon Iota chpt.), Sigma Tau Gamma. Republican. Methodist. Lodges: Masons, Rotary. Avocations: painting, wood sculpture, hunting, fishing, traveling.

FREEMAN, MICHAEL J., inventor, professor, author, corporate executive; b. Bronx, N.Y., July 26, 1946; s. Harry and Anne Freeman; m. Lois L. Sheffield; children: Joan, Zachary, Casey, Matthew, Amy. BBA, City Coll., N.Y., 1969; MBA, Baruch Coll., 1970; PhD, City U., N.Y., 1977. Honors prof. City U., 1969-77; adj. prof. Cornell U., N.Y., 1970-72; found. Comtec, Inc., N.Y., 1981, ACTV, Inc., N.Y., 1983; adj. prof. Hofstra U., N.Y., 1983-85. Author: Writing Resumes & Locating Jobs, 1983-92; inventor 2-XL Robot (Toy of Yr., 1978, 1992), Activity Fun Alpha, Talk N Play; inventor, patentee toys, telecom., and TV industries; holds 20 US commercialized and numerous internat. Patents. Office: ACTV Inc Ste 2401 1270 Avenue Of The Americas New York NY 10020-1801

FREEMAN, MICHAEL LEE, veterinarian; b. Dallas, Sept. 4, 1947; s. Harold Hix and Maxine Evelyn Meyers Freeman; m. Lana Joan Currey, Dec. 30, 1965; children: Chris, Todd, Susie. BS in Vet. Sci., Tex. A&M U., 1970, DVM, 1972. Veterinarian Dallas, 1972—; cons. Synbiotics, San Diego, 1998-99. Bd. dirs. Angel Flight, 1995-97. Mem. Am. Vet. Medicine Assn., Soc. Theriogeniology, White Rock Rotary (bd. dirs. 1995-98). Avocations: flying, outdoors. E-mail: petcare@htcomp.net. Home and Office: Rt 1 Box 273M Hamilton TX 76531

FREEMAN, MILTON MALCOLM ROLAND, anthropology educator; b. London, Apr. 23, 1934; came to Can., 1958; s. Louis and Fay (Bomberg) F.; m. Mini Christina Aodla; children: Graham, Elaine, Malcolm. BS, Reading U., Eng., 1958; postgrad., U. Coll., London, 1962-64; PhD, McGill U., 1965. Research scientist No. Affairs Dept., Ottawa, Ont., Can., 1965-67; asst. prof. Meml. U., St. John's, Nfld., Can., 1967-71, assoc. prof., 1971-72; dir. Inuit Land Use Study, Hamilton, Ont., 1973-75; prof. anthropology McMaster U., Hamilton, 1976-81; Henry Marshall Tory prof. U. Alta., Edmonton, Can., 1982—; adj. prof. East Asian studies U. Alta., Edmonton, Can., 1993—; adj. prof. environ. studies U. Waterloo, Ont., 1977-81; sr. sci. advisor Indian and No. Affairs, Ottawa, 1979-81; chmn. No. Sci. Network, UNESCO-MAB, 1983-87; sr. rsch. scholar Can. Circumpolar Inst., U. Alta., 1990—; McLean prof. Trent U., Peterborough, Can., 1995. Author: People Pollution, 1974, Cultural Anthropology of Whaling, 1989, Recovering Rights, 1992, Inuit, Whaling, and Sustainability, 1998; editor: Inuit Land Use and Occupancy Report, 1976, Procs. Internat. Symposium on Renewable Resources and the Economy of the North, 1981, Japanese Small-type Coastal Whaling, 1988; co-editor: Elephants and Whales: Resources for Whom?, 1994. Bd. dirs. Sci. Inst. N.W.T., 1985-87; chmn. adv. bd. Circumpolar Inst., 1990-96; chmn. Man-Environ. Commn., Internat. Union Anthrop. and Ethnol. Scis., 1977-82. Fellow Am. Anthropol. Assn., Arctic Inst. N.Am., Soc. Advancement Socio-Economics, Soc. Applied Anthropology; mem. Soc. Applied Anthropology Can. (pres. 1984-85), Can. Anthropology Soc., Japan Social Studies Assn. Can., Internat. Assn. Study of Common Property. Home: 305 10710 80th Ave, Edmonton, AB Canada T6E 1V8 Office: U Alta, Dept Anthropology, Edmonton, AB Canada T6G 2H4

FREEMAN, MILTON VICTOR, lawyer; b. N.Y.C., Nov. 16, 1911; s. Samuel and Celia (Gelfand) F.; m. Phyllis Young, Dec. 19, 1937; children: Nancy Lois (Mrs. Gans), Daniel Martin, Andrew Samuel, Amy Martha (Mrs. Malone). AB, CCNY, 1931; LLB, Columbia U., 1934. Bar: N.Y. 1934, D.C. 1946, U.S. Supreme Ct. 1943. With gen. counsel's office SEC, 1934-42, asst. solicitor, 1942-46; staff securities div. FTC, 1934; with Arnold & Porter (and predecessor firms), Washington, 1946—; adj. prof. Yale U., 1947, Georgetown U. Law Sch., 1952; vis. scholar various univs., 1978-79; mem. adv. bd. Bur. Nat. Affairs, Securities Regulation and Law Report, Washington, Internat. Fin. Law Rev., London. Contbr. articles to profl. jours.; bd. editors Columbia Law Rev., 1933-34 (Ordronaux prize 1934). Mem. adv. bd. Securities Regulation Inst., U. Calif., San Diego. Mem. ABA (chmn. subcom. SEC practice and enforcement 1972-83, exec. com. fed. regulation of securities com. 1983—, ad hoc com. on ALI corp. governance project, ad hoc com. on insider trading), Am. Law Inst. (advisor, corp. governance project), Fed. Bar Assn., D.C. Bar Assn., Internat. Law Inst. (hon. chmn. 1977-81, trustee 1955-86), Anxiety Disorders Assn. Am. (bd. dirs.). Home: 3405 Woolsey Dr Chevy Chase MD 20815 Office: 555 12th St NW Washington DC 20004-1200

FREEMAN, MORGAN, actor; b. Memphis, 1937; s. Grafton Curtis and Mayme Edna (Revere) F.; m. Jeanette Adair Bradshaw, Oct. 22, 1967 (div. 1979); m. Myrna Colley-Lee, June 16, 1984; children: Alphonse, Saifoulaye, Deena, Morgana. Student, L.A. City Coll. Actor: (stage prodns.) Niggerlover (debut), 1967, Hello Dolly (Broadway), 1967, Jungle of Cities, 1969, The Recruiting Officer, 1969, Scuba-Duba, 1969, Purlie (ANTA Theatre, N.Y.C.), 1970, Black Visions, 1972, Sisyphus and the Blue-Eyed Cyclops, 1975, Cockfight, 1977, Mighty Gents, 1978 (Clarence Derwent award, Drama Desk award, Tony award nomination), White Pelicans, 1978, Coriolanus, also Julius (N.Y. Shakespeare Festival), 1979, Mother Courage and Her Children, 1980, Othello, also All's Well That Ends Well (both Dallas Shakespeare Festival), 1982, Buck, 1983, Medea and the Doll, 1984, The Gospel at Colonus (Obie awards), Driving Miss Daisy, 1987, (feature films) Who Says I Can't Ride a Rainbow, 1971, Brubaker, 1980, Eyewitness, 1980, Harry and Son, 1983, Teachers, 1984, Street Smart, 1987 (Acad. award nomination), Clean and Sober, 1988, Lean On Me, 1989, Johnny Handsome, 1989, Driving Miss Daisy (Golden Globe award, Acad. award nomination), 1989, Glory, 1989, The Bonfire of the Vanities, 1990, Robin Hood, 1991, Unforgiven, 1992, The Shawshank Redemption, 1994, Outbreak, 1995, Seven, 1995, Chain Reaction, 1996, Moll Flanders, 1996, Deep Impact 1997, The Flood, 1997, Kiss The Girls, 1997, The Long Way Home, 1996, Hard Rain, 1998, Water Damage, 1999, Under Suspicion, 1999, Mutiny, 1999, others; dir.: Bopha!, 1993; regular cast (TV show) The Electric Company; TV films include: Hollow Image, 1979, Attica, 1980, The Marva Collins

Story, 1981, The Atlanta Child Murders, 1985, Resting Place, 1986, Flight for Life, 1987, Clinton and Nadine (Showtime TV), 1988. With USAF, 1955-59. Office: William Morris Agency 151 S El Camino Dr Beverly Hills CA 90212-2775 also: 2472 Broadway # 227 New York NY 10025-7449*

FREEMAN, MORTON S., former bar association executive, retired lawyer; b. Phila., Dec. 12, 1912; s. Samuel S. and Serena G. (Singer) F.; m. Mildred Hurwitz, May 31, 1942; children: Janet Freeman Gallo, Roberta Freeman Cooperman. A.B. with first honors, Pa. State U., 1934; J.D., U. Pa., 1937. Bar: Pa. bar 1937. Practiced law Phila., 1937-42, 1966-70; spl. agt. FBI, 1942-51; partner Reynolds Shoes (retail chain), Phila., 1951-60; pres. Admiral Fin. Corp., Phila., 1959-66; dir. office publs. Am. Law Inst.-Am. Bar Assn., Phila., 1970-83. Author: The Grammatical Lawyer, 1979, Pennsylvania Equity Digest, a biennial supplement, 1954—, A Treasury for Word Lovers, 1983, The Story Behind the Word, 1985, Japanese edit., 1995, A Handbook of Problem Words and Phrases, 1987, A Professional Guide to Effective Communication, 1989, A Wordwatcher's Guide to Good Writing & Grammar, 1990, Words to the Wise, 1991, The One-Minute Grammarian, 1992, Japanese edit., 1994, Hue and Cry and Humble Pie (the stories behind the words), 1993, Even Steven & Fair and Square (more stories behind the words), 1993, Japanese edit., 1997, A New Dictionary of Eponyms; columnist The Grammatical Lawyer in The Practical Lawyer, 1976-83, Word Watcher, St. Louis Post-Dispatch, Phila. Inquirer, Buffalo News, San Diego Herald Tribune, other newspapers. Trustee Big Bros. Assn., Phila. Recipient Book of Yr. award Am. Soc. Legal Writers; named to Cultural Hall of Fame, South Phila. High Sch. Alumni. Mem. Phila. Bar Assn., Am. Law Inst. Home: Green Hill Condo W-508 1001 City Ave Wynnewood PA 19096-3902 also: 2001 N Ocean Blvd Boca Raton FL 33431-7848

FREEMAN, MYRNA FAYE, county schools official; b. Danville, Ill., Oct. 30, 1939; d. Thomas Gene and Dorothy Olive (Chodera) F.; m. Lonnie Lee Choate, Aug. 16, 1959 (div. 1987); children: Leslie Rene, Gregory Lonn. BA in Pub. Adminstrn., San Diego State U., 1977, MA in Edn. Adminstrn., 1987. Employee benefits mgr. City of San Diego, 1974-84; asst. risk mgr. San Diego County Office Edn., San Diego, 1984—; instr. Sch. Bus. Mgrs. Acad., Assn. Calif. Sch. Adminstrs., 1985—, Ins. Edn. Assn., Cert. Employee Benefits Specialist courses, 1991—. Author: Adm. Impact of Implement Leg. 1987; Author: Article Risk Mgmt.-Emp. Benefits 1985, Risk Mgmt.-Workers' Comp. 1986, Risk Mgmt.-Loss Control 1986. Mem. Kaiser Consumer Coun., 1977-84, pres., 1979-80; bd. dirs. S.D. County Affirmative Action Adv. Bd., 1985; mem. adv. com. Vista Health Plan Pub. Policy, 1994—; adv. coun. Kaiser On-the-Job, 1994—. Recipient Appreciation award COMBO-Cultural Arts of San Diego 1977. Mem. Risk Ins. Mgmt. Soc. (pres. San Diego chpt. 1988), Calif. Assn. Sch. Bus. Ofcls. (chmn. risk mgmt. R&D comm. 1987-88), San Diego Group Ins. Claims Coun. (pres. 1987), S.D. Employers Health Cost Coalition (vice-chmn. 1987), Calif. Women in Govt. (bd. dirs. 1983-84), Calif. Assn. of Joint Powers Authority, Pub. Agys. Risk Mgmt. Assn., Pub. Risk Ins. Mgmt. Assn., Internat. Found. Employee Benefits Plans, San Diego Workers' Compensation Forum, Sigma Kappa, Phi Kappa Phi, Internat. Platform Assn. Republican. Methodist. Fax: 619-279-6236. E-mail: ffreeman@sdcoe.k12.ca.us. Home: 4345 Cartulina Rd San Diego CA 92124-2102 Office: San Diego County Office Edn 6401 Linda Vista Rd Rm 505 San Diego CA 92111-7319

FREEMAN, NEAL BLACKWELL, communications corporation executive; b. N.Y.C., July 5, 1940; s. Malcolm T. and Virginia (Neal) F.; m. Jane Louise Metze, Mar. 19, 1966; children: Malcolm Trowbridge II, James Bragdon, Kathryn R. BA magna cum laude, Yale U., 1962. Asst. to pres. Washington Star Syndicate, 1965-66; assoc. producer TV show Firing Line, 1966-67; exec. editor King Features Syndicate, N.Y.C., 1968-73; v.p., editor King Features div. Hearst Corp., 1973-76; pres. Jefferson Communications, Inc., 1976-86; chmn. bd., chief exec. officer Blackwell Corp., 1982—; exec. prodr. Pub. TV; bd. dirs. Comsat Corp., Nat. Rev. Forum Network, Inc., Denver Nuggets Profl. Basketball Club, Colo. Avalanche Profl. Hockey Club; chmn. Inst. on Polit. Journalism, Georgetown U.; mem. Pres.'s Commn. on White House Fellows, 1974-77; chmn. of agts. Yale Alumni Fund; bd. dirs. Ctr. for Pub. Broadcasting, 1972-75; bd. dirs., vice-chmn. Ethics and Pub. Policy Ctr. Bd. dirs. Wolf Trap Found., 1984-90. Mem. Colony Found., Cosmos Club (Washington), Yale Club (N.Y.C.), York Country Club (Maine), Nat. Press Club, Sigma Delta Chi. Office: The Blackwell Corp USA Today Bldg 1000 Wilson Blvd Ste 2707 Arlington VA 22209-3906

FREEMAN, NEIL, accounting and computer consulting firm executive; b. Reading, Pa., Dec. 27, 1948; s. Leroy Harold and Audrey Todd (Dornhecker) F.; m. Janice Lum, Nov. 20, 1981. BS, Albright Coll., 1979; MS, Kennedy-Western U., 1987, PhD, 1988. Cert. systems profl., data processing specialist, info. system security profl. Acct. Jack W. Long & Co., Mt. Penn, Pa., 1977-78; comptroller G.P.C., Inc., Bowmansville, Pa., 1978-79; owner Neil Freeman Cons., Bowmansville, 1980-81; program mgr., systems cons. Application Systems, Honolulu, 1981-82; instr. Chaminade U., Honolulu, 1983-96; owner Neil Freeman Cons., Kaneohe, Hawaii, 1982-96, Grand Junction, Colo., 1996—; instr. Mesa State Coll., Grand Junction, 1997—. Author: (computer software) NFC Property Management, 1984, NFC Mailing List, 1984; (book) Learning Dibol, 1984. Served with USN, 1966-68, Vietnam. Mem. Nat. Assn. Accts., Am. Inst. Cert. Computer Profls., Assn. Systems Mgmt. Office: PO Box 60070 Grand Junction CO 81506-8758

FREEMAN, ORVILLE LOTHROP, lawyer, former governor of Minnesota, think tank executive; b. Mpls., May 9, 1918; s. Orville E. and Frances (Schroeder) F.; m. Jane C. Shields, May 2, 1942; children: Constance Jane, Michael Orville. B.A. magna cum laude, U. Minn., 1940; LL.B., 1946; LL.B. (hon.), U. Seoul, (Korea); hon. degree, Am. U., Fairleigh Dickinson U., St. Joseph's Coll. Bar: Minn. 1947. Mem. Larson, Loevinger, Lindquist and Freeman, Mpls., 1947-55; gov. Minn., 1955-61; sec. U.S. Dept. Agr., 1961-69; pres. E.D.P. Tech. Internat. Inc., 1969-70; pres., chief exec. officer Bus. Internat. Corp., N.Y.C., 1970-81; chmn. bd. Bus. Internat. Corp., 1981-84; sr. ptnr. internat. law Popham, Haik, Schnobrich, Kaufman & Doty, Ltd., Washington, 1985-95; dir. Natomas Corp., Multinat. Agribus. Sys., Inc., Franklin Mint, Grumman Corp., Slater, Michael Foods, Mycogen Corp., San Diego; mem. faculty Salzburg (Austria) Seminar, 1974, 77; vis. scholar Hubert Humphrey Inst., U. Minn., Mpls., 1995—. Asst. charge vets. affairs to mayor Mpls., 1945-49; chmn. Mpls. Civil Svc. Commn., 1946-49; sec. Minn. Dem. Farmer Labor Party, 1946-48, chmn., 1948-50; mem. exec. com. Japan-U.S. Bus. Adv. Coun.; chmn. India-U.S. Bus. Adv. Coun., CARESBAC, 1986-96, chmn. emeritus; mem. adv. com. Hubert Humphrey Inst.; chmn. U.S.-Nigerian Agrl. Consultative Com.; chmn. bd. dirs. World Watch Inst., 1970-96, chmn. emeritus, 1997—; pres. Agr. Coun. Am., 1985-90; chmn. bd. govs. UN Assn. U.S.A.; mem. Presdl. Commn. on World Hunger; past trustee Luth. Ch. in Am. Lt. col. USMCR, 1941-45. Mem. Exec. Alumni Assn., Phi Beta Kappa, Delta Sigma Rho. Home: Walker Pl #802 3701 Bryant Ave S Minneapolis MN 55409-1051

FREEMAN, PATRICIA ELIZABETH, library and education specialist; b. El Dorado, Ark., Nov. 30, 1924; d. Herbert A. and M. Elizabeth (Pryor) Harper; m. Jack Freeman, June 15, 1949; 3 children. BA, Centenary Coll., 1943; postgrad., Fine Arts Ctr., 1942-46, Art Students League, 1944-45; BSLS, La. State U., 1946; postgrad., Calif. State U., 1959-61, U. N.Mex., 1964-74; EdS, Peabody Coll., Vanderbilt U., 1975. Libr. U. Calif., Berkeley, 1946-47; libr. Albuquerque Pub. Schs., 1964-67, ind. sch. libr. media ctr. cons., 1967—. Painter lithographer; one-person show La. State Exhibit Bldg., 1948; author: Pathfinder: An Operational Guide for the School Librarian, 1975, Southeast Heights Neighborhoods of Albuquerque, 1993; compiler, editor: Elizabeth Pryor Harper's Twenty-One Southern Families, 1985; editor: SEHNA Gazette, 1988-93. Mem. task force Goals for Dallas-Environ., 1977-82; pres. Friends of Sch. Librs., Dallas, 1979-83; v.p., editor Southeast Heights Neighborhood Assn., 1988-93. With USAF, 1948-49. Honoree AAUW Ednl. Found., 1979, 96; vol. award for outstanding service Dallas Ind. Sch. Dist., 1978; AAUW Pub. Service grantee 1980. Mem. ALA, AAUW (dir. Dallas 1976-82, Albuquerque 1983-85), LWV (sec. Dallas 1982-83, editor Albuquerque 1984-88), Nat. Trust Historic Preservation, Friends of Pub. Libr., N.Mex. Symphony Guild, Alpha Xi Delta. Home: 3016 Santa Clara Ave SE Albuquerque NM 87106-2350

FREEMAN, PAUL DOUGLAS, symphony conductor; b. Richmond, Va., Jan. 2, 1946; s. Louis H. and Louise (Willis) F.; m. Cornelia Perry; 1 son, Douglas Cornel. MusB, Eastman Sch. Music, 1956, MusM, 1957; PhD, 1963; PhD Fulbright scholar, Hochschule für Musik, Berlin, Germany, 1957-59. Dir. Hochstein Music Sch., Rochester, N.Y., 1960-66; music dir., condr. Chgo. Sinfonietta, 1987—; first v.p. Nat. Guild Community Music Schs., 1964-66; bd. dirs. N.Y. State Opera League, 1963-66, Detroit Community Music Sch.; music adv. com. San Francisco chpt. Young Audiences, 1966—; mem. Calif. Framework Com. for Arts and Humanities, 1967-68; music dir.-chief condr. Czech Nat. Symphony Orch., Prague. Founder, conductor Faculty-Community Orch.; music dir. Opera Theatre, Rochester, 1961-66, San Francisco Little Symphony, 1967-68, Victoria (B.C.,Can.) Symphony, 1979, Saginaw Symphony, 1979-88, music dir. emeritus, 1988—; dir., San Francisco Community Music Ctr., 1966-68, condr. San Francisco Conservatory Orch., 1966-67; assoc. condr. Dallas Symphony, 1968-69, 69-70; condr.-in-residence, Detroit Symphony Orch., 1970-79; artistic dir. Delta Fstival Music and Art, 1977-79, Can. Music Educator's Artist Rec. Svcs., Mozart Rec. Project Philarmonic of London; numerous guest appearances with maj. orchs. in U.S. and Europe; rec. artist Columbia Records, Vox Records, Orion Records; music dir., conductor Chgo. Sinfonetta, 1987—. Recipient prize Dimitri Mitropolous Internat. Conductor's competition, 1967—; Spoleto award Festival of Two Worlds, 1968. Office: Chgo Sinfonietta 105 W Adams St Ste 3330 Chicago IL 60603-6210*

FREEMAN, PETER A., computer science educator, dean. PhD in Computer Sci., Carnegie-Mellon U., 1970. Asst. prof. to prof. info. and computer sci. U. Calif., Irvine, 1971-90; divsn. dir. Computer and Computation Rsch. NSF, 1987-89; vis. disting. prof. info. tech. George Mason U., Fairfax, Va., 1989-90; dean, Coll. Computing Ga. Inst. Tech., Atlanta, 1990—; former Chief Info. Officer, Ga. Inst. Tech.; bd. dirs. Computing Rsch. Assn., 1988—; mem. rev. coms. IRS and FAA Air-traffic Control Modernization efforts; chair Vis. Com. Schlumberger Austin Rsch.; active cons. to industry and govt. Author: Software Perspectives: The System is the Message, 1987, Software System Principles, 1975; editor, co-editor 4 books, including Software Design Techniques, and Software Reusability; founding editor McGraw-Hill Series in Software Engineering and Technology; contbr. numerous papers to scientific and profl. jours. Fellow IEEE (past chair IEEE/CS Tech. Com. on Software Engring.), AAAS. *

FREEMAN, RALPH CARTER, management consultant; b. La Grange, Ga.; s. Ralph Carter and Alice (Cordell) F.; m. Carole Stephens, July 31, 1957 (div. 1977); children: Carter III, Allyson, Stephens, LeAnna; m. Nancy Lynn Brown, Apr. 8, 1977. BBA, Emory U., 1959. CPA, Mont. From mem. staff to ptnr. Pannell Kerr Forster, Atlanta, Honolulu, 1959-72; mgmt. cons. Touche Ross & Co., Honolulu, Am. Samoa, Asia, South Pacific, 1972-75; pres. FP Industries, Inc., Hawaii, Mont., Ga., 1975-85, Janas Consulting, Huntsville, Ala., 1986-90; prin. Janas Consulting, San Francisco and L.A., 1990—; Calif. real estate broker. Contbr. articles to profl. jours. and nat. trade mags. Mem. Inst. Mgmt. Cons. (cert.), All Cities Resource Group, Bus. Opportunities Coun., Turnaround Mgmt. Assn., L.A. Ventura Assn., Sigma Alpha Epsilon. Avocations: fishing, tennis, camping.

FREEMAN, RICHARD CAMERON, federal judge; b. Atlanta, Dec. 14, 1926. A.B., Emory U., 1950, LL.B., 1952. Bar: Ga. 1953. Since practiced in Atlanta; mem. firm Haas, Holland & Blackshear, 1955-58; ptnr. Haas, Holland, Freeman, Levison & Gibert, 1958-71; judge U.S. Dist. Ct. (no. dist.) Ga., Atlanta, 1971—, sr. judge; alderman City of Atlanta, 1962-71; pres. Atlanta Humane Soc., 1981. Mem. Ga. Bar Assn., Atlanta Bar Assn., Chi Phi, Phi Delta Phi. Office: US Dist Ct 2121 US Courthouse 75 Spring St SW Atlanta GA 30303-3309*

FREEMAN, RICHARD DEAN, new business start-up service company executive; b. Rushville, Ind., Nov. 27, 1928; s. Verne Crawford and Mary Phyllis (Dean) F.; m. Mary Jane Barkman, Aug. 21, 1950; children: Debra Dean, Phyllis Lynn, Richard Paul, Tom Crawford. BS in Aero. Engring., Purdue U., 1950, BS in Naval Sci. and Tactics, 1950, MS in Indsl. Mgmt., 1954. Supr. indsl. engring. Gen. Motors Corp., Warren, Ohio, 1954-58; prodn. mgr. Ramo Wooldridge div. TRW Corp., Denver, 1958-62; mgr. missile programs Hughes Aircraft Co., Los Angeles, 1962-68; v.p. E-Systems Inc., Dallas, 1968-72, Rockwell Internat. Co., Los Angeles, 1972-74; pres. Internat. Pacific Co., Newport Beach, Calif., 1974—; sr. lectr. West Coast U., L.A., 1974-78; sec. proteus Corp., Newport Beach, 1978-80; chmn. Tech. Assocs. Corp., Newport Beach, 1984-85; chief exec. officer Equicenters, Inc., Irvine, 1988—. Author: Economation Approaches, 1958, Equator, 1984 (also film); prod. documentary film Zeros of the Pacific, 1979. Cubmaster, scoutmaster, dist. chmn. Boy Scouts Am., various locations, 1966-76; mem. librs. devel. adv. com. Purdue U., 1992; mem. restoration adv. bd. Marine Corps Air Sta., Tustin, 1994; pres. bd. trustees, elder Presbyn. Ch. Capt. USMC, 1946-58, Korea. Named Man of Yr., Sigma Alpha Tau, West Lafayette, Ind., 1971; recipient Disting. Engring. Alumnus award Purdue U., 1973, Outstanding Aerospace Engr. award Purdue U. Sch. Aeronautics and Astronautics, 1999. Mem. Am. Inst. Indsl. Engrs., Purdue U. Alumni Assn., Nat. Eagle Scout Assn. (pres. 1998), Exch. Club of Newport Harbor (pres. 1998—), Kappa Sigma (inducted into Hall of Fame 1997). Republican. Lodge: Masons (consistory 32 degree v.p.). Avocation: exploration for Amelia Earhart's missing aircraft. Home: 3910 Topside Ln Corona Del Mar CA 92625-1628

FREEMAN, RICHARD FRANCIS, banker; b. Mt. Kisco, N.Y., Apr. 19, 1934; s. Richard Francis and Nora Frances (O'Connell) F.; m. Barbara Jean Calhoun, Nov. 30, 1957; children: Kathleen, Kevin, Kelley, Keith. B.S. in Finance and Banking, Miami U., Oxford, Ohio, 1956; grad., Stonier Grad. Sch. Banking, Rutgers U., 1973. With Central Nat. Bank, Cleve., 1956-60, No. Westchester Nat. Bank, Chappaqua, N.Y., 1960-67; with State Nat. Bank Conn., Bridgeport, 1967-78, exec. v.p., dir., 1974-78; pres., chief exec. officer The Bank Mart (formerly City Savs. Bank Conn.), Bridgeport, 1978-91; pres., CEO Bridgeport Area Found., to 1999, dir., 1999—; bd. dirs. Conn. Energy Corp., So. Conn. Gas Co., Physicians Health Svcs., Inc. Former chmn. bd. trustees Park City Hosp., Bridgeport; bd. dirs. Bridgeport Econ. Devel. Corp., Ctr. for Fin. Studies, Inc.; mem. bus. adv. coun. Miami U. Sch. Bus. Adminstrn. Office: Bridgeport Area Found 940 Broad St Bridgeport CT 06604-4809*

FREEMAN, RICHARD MERRELL, lawyer, corporate director; b. Crawfordsville, Ind., July 2, 1921; s. F. Rider and Ruth (Merrell) F.; m. Joanne Spears, Nov. 26, 1943; children: Randy, Mark, Candy, Marcia. AB, Wabash (Ind.) Coll., 1943; LLB, Columbia U., 1948. Bar: Tenn. 1948, Ill. 1957. Atty. TVA, Knoxville, 1948-57, dir., 1978-86; partner firm Belnap, Spencer, Hardy & Freeman, Chgo., 1957-67; v.p. law Chgo. & Northwestern Transp. Co., Chgo., 1967-78, also dir., voting trustee. Exec. com. Fla. West Coast Symphony. With USNR, 1943-46. Mem. Phi Beta Kappa. Democrat. Mem. Community Ch. Home: 775 Longboat Club Rd Longboat Key FL 34228-3843

FREEMAN, ROBERT SCHOFIELD, musicologist, educator, pianist; b. Rochester, N.Y., Aug. 26, 1935; s. Henry Schofield and Florence Margaret (Knope) F.; m. Carol Jean Morgan, Dec. 10, 1976; children: John Frederick, Elizabeth Katharine, Scott Alan Henry. AB summa cum laude, Harvard U., 1957; MFA, Princeton U., 1960, PhD, 1967; MusD (hon.), Hamilton Coll., 1988. Instr., asst. prof. Princeton U., 1963-68; asst. prof., assoc. prof. MIT, 1968-73; dir., prof. musicology Eastman Sch. Music, U. Rochester, 1972-96; pres. New England Conservatory, Boston, 1996—; chmn. nat. adv. bd. Ctr. for Black Music Research, Chgo., 1985-90; cons. for various Am. U.; vis. assoc. prof. Harvard U., 1972. Author: Opera Without Drama, 1981; contbr. articles to profl. jours. Trustee Rochester YMCA, Greenwood Music Camp; bd. dirs. Rochester Downtown Devel. Corp. Harvard Sheldon fellow, 1958, Woodrow Wilson Found. fellow, 1959, Martha Baird Rockefeller Fund fellow, 1963, Fulbright fellow, 1960-62; recipient Civic medal Rochester C. of C., 1982. Mem. Am. Musicol. Soc. (chair New Eng. chpt. 1970-72, coun. mem. 1973-76), Coll. Music Soc. (coun. mem. 1973-76), Neue Bach Gesellschaft (chmn. 1977-82), Nat. Assn. Schs. Music (grad. commn. 1981-85), Harvard Music Assn., St. Botolph Club of Boston, Princeton Club of N.Y., Harvard Club of Boston. Avocations: baseball, reading, animal welfare. Office: New England Conservatory 290 Huntington Ave Boston MA 02115-5018

FREEMAN, ROBERT TURNER, JR., insurance executive; b. N.Y.C., Apr. 25, 1918; s. Robert Turner and Eva (Boyd) F.; m. Mary Frances Jones, Nov. 28, 1942; children: Veronica (Mrs. Wisdom F. Coleman, Jr.), Robert Turner III. BA, Lincoln (Pa.) U., 1941, LLD (hon.), 1987; student, N.Y.U. Grad. Sch., 1941-42. Econ. statistician WPB, 1942-45; v.p., actuary United Mut. Life Ins. Co., N.Y.C., 1945-55; founder, mng. dir. Ghana Ins. Co. Ltd., Accra, 1955-62, Ghana Gen. Ins. Co., Ltd., Accra, 1959-62; cons. actuary Providence Ins. Co., Monrovia, Liberia, 1958-59, Nigerian Broadcasting Corp., Lagos, 1964-65; founder, dir. Great Nigeria Ins. Co. Ltd., Lagos, 1960-63; mng. dir. Ghana State Ins. Corp., Accra, 1962-65; asso. dir. for mgmt. Peace Corps, 1965-66; cons. minority affairs USIA, 1966-68; pres. Freeman, Cole and Assos., Inc., Washington, 1966-68; dir. office capital devel. and finance Bur. Africa AID, 1968-71; ins. adviser to Govt. Ethiopia, 1971-73; pres. Consumers United Ins. Co., 1973-83, Freeman Internat. Ins. Co., 1984-86; dir. Ghana Nat. Investment Bank, 1962-65, First Ghana Bldg. Soc., 1958-63, Lafayette Fed. Credit Union, Washington, 1966—, Riggs Nat. Bank, Washington; exec. dir. Washington Life & Health Ins. Guaranty Assn., 1992-95; mem. Washington Bd. Trade; bd. govs. Internat. Ins. Seminars Hall of Fame, 1977—; guest lectr. Howard U. Sch. Ins., 1983—. Dir. Commn. Ednl. Exchange between U.S. and Ghana, 1964-65; mem. Fulbright Scholarship Com., Accra, 1960-61, Bus. Community Scholarship Com., 1958-61; co-chmn. United Negro Coll. Fund, Bklyn., 1952; cons. Korry com. on Africa, ept. State, 1966, NAACP Task Force on Africa, 1977, World Bank, 1978; Trustee, chmn. Phelps-Stokes Fund; trustee Solebury Sch., New Hope, Pa., Lincoln U., 1977—; bd. dirs., 1st v.p. Nation's Capital council Girl Scouts U.S.A., 1978—, African Am. Scholars Council, 1978—, Friends of Senghor Found., 1977—; bd. dirs., mem. corp. bd. Children's Hosp., Washington, 1978—; mem. Washington Mayor's Commn. Fire Safety, 1984-85, mem. Internat. Adv. Council, 1984—; mem. Nat. Conf. Black Mayors' Econ. Devel. Task Force, 1982—; bd. dirs. Davis Meml. Goodwill Industries, 1985. Bob Freeman Clinic dedicated in his honor, Accra, Ghana, 1987. Mem. Lincoln U. Alumni Assn. (pres. N.Y.C. 1952-55), Alpha Phi Alpha. Club: Rotarian (pres. Ghana 1963-65). Home: 3001 Veazey Ter NW Apt 801 Washington DC 20008-5403

FREEMAN, RUSSELL ADAMS, lawyer; b. Albany, N.Y., July 22, 1932; s. Russell Marvin and Edith (Adams) F.; m. Elizabeth Frances McHale, June 30, 1956; children: Lynn, James. BA, Amherst Coll., 1954; JD, Albany (N.Y.) Law Sch., 1957; LLM, U. So. Calif., 1966. Bar: N.Y. 1957, Calif. 1960. Practiced in Albany, 1957-59; with Security Pacific Nat. Bank, L.A., 1959-92, v.p., 1968-72, counsel, 1968-74, head legal dept., 1968-74; sr. v.p. Security Pacific Corp., L.A., 1972-81, exec. v.p., 1981-92, gen. counsel, 1972-92; sr. counsel O'Melveny & Myers, L.A., 1992-94; bd. govs. Fin. Lawyers Conf., 1972-74; faculty Pacific Coast Banking Sch., 1980-81; lectr. in field, 1965-94. Contbr. articles to profl. publns. Trustee Flintridge Prep. Sch., La Canada, Calif., 1978-80. Mem. ABA (mem. banking com.), Am. Bankers Assn. (mem. govt. rels. com. 1981-84, del. to Leadership Conf. 1984-86, 90-92), Assn. Banking Holding Cos., Calif. Bankers Assn. (dir., chmn. govt. rels. group 1979-81, 86-88, dir. and chmn. fed. govt. rels. 1985-86, Almon B. McCallum award for disting. and meritorious legal svc. 1986), Calif. Bankers Clearing House Assn. (chmn. pub. policy adv. com. 1980-81, 88-89), Calif. State Bar, L.A. County Bar Assn. past chmn. comml. law and bankruptcy sect., Outstanding Corp. Counsel award 1989, corp. law dept. sect., Constl. Rights Found. (bd. dirs. 1986-94).

FREEMAN, SUSAN TAX, anthropologist, educator, culinary historian; b. Chgo., May 24, 1938; d. Sol and Gertrude Tax.; m. Leslie G. Freeman, Jr., Mar. 20, 1964; 1 dau., Sarah Elisabeth. BA, U. Chgo., 1958; MA, Harvard U., 1959, PhD, 1965. Asst. prof. anthropology U. Ill., Chgo., 1965-70; assoc. prof. U. Ill., 1970-78, prof., 1978—, chmn., 1979-82; panelist NEH, Council for Internat. Exchange of Scholars; mem. anthropology screening com. Fulbright-Hays Research Awards, 1975-78; mem. ad hoc com. on research in Spain Spain-U.S.A. Friendship Agreement, various yrs., 1977-84; field researcher Mex., 1959, Spain, 1962—, Japan, 1983; instr. Radcliffe Coll. Seminars on Food in History and Culture, 1998. Author: Neighbors: The Social Contract in a Castilian Hamlet, 1970, The Pasiegos-Spaniards in No Man's Land, 1979; assoc. editor: Am. Anthropologist, 1971-73, Am. Ethnologist, 1974-76. Named to Inst. for the Humanities, U. Ill. Chgo., 1987-88; Wenner-Gren Found. for Anthrop. Research grantee, 1966, 83; NIMH grantee, 1967, 68-71; NEH fellowships, 1978-79, 89-90. Fellow Am. Anthrop. Assn. (nominating com. 1981-82), Royal Anthrop. Inst. Gt. Britain and Ireland; mem. Soc. for Anthropology of Europe (exec. com. 1987-88), Soc. Spanish and Portuguese Hist. Studies (exec. com. 1990-92), Coun. European Studies (steering com. 1980-83), Internat. Inst. Spain (corporator, bd. dirs. 1982-87), Centro Estudios Sorianos (hon.), Assn. Anthropologia Castilla y Leon (hon.). Home: 5537 S Woodlawn Ave Chicago IL 60637-1620 Office: U Ill Dept Anthro M/C 027 1007 W Harrison St Chicago IL 60607-7135

FREEMAN, THEODORE MONROE, physician; b. Orlando, Fla., Jan. 3, 1955; s. Fred Monroe and Mary Ann (Ridgeway) F.; m. Karen Bonaccorso, Aug. 11, 1978; children: Kathryn Maria, Michelle Terese, Jeannine Nicole, Jason Monroe. BS in Chemistry, Duke U., 1977; MD, U. So. Fla., 1980. Diplomate Am. Bd. Internal Medicine, Am. Bd. Allergy and Immunology. Intern Jacksonville (Fla.) U. Hosp., 1980-81; commd. capt. USAF, 1981, advanced through grades to col.; resident internal medicine Keesler AFB USAF, Biloxi, Miss., 1981-83; staff physician Dyess AFB USAF, Abilene, Tex., 1983-84; fellow allergy and immunology Wilford Hall Med. Ctr. Lakeland AFB USAF, San Antonio, 1984-86; fellow diagnostic lab. immunology Mass. Gen. Hosp. USAF, Boston, 1986-87; staff allergist and immunology Wilford Hall Med. Ctr. USAF, 1987-89, chmn. dept. allergy and immunology, program dir., 1989—; med. dir. transplants Wilford Hall Med. Ctr., 1989—. Contbr. articles to profl. jours. Fellow Am. Coll. Physicians, Am. Coll. Allergy and Immunology, Am. Acad. Allergy and Immunology; mem. AMA, Soc. Air Force Physicians. Roman Catholic. Office: MMIA Wilford Hall Med Ctr 2200 Bergquist Dr Ste 1 San Antonio TX 78236-5302

FREEMAN, TODD IRA, lawyer; b. Mpls., Nov. 24, 1953; s. Earl Stanley and Gretta Lois (Rudick) F.; m. Judy Lynn Sigel, June 15, 1975; children: Jennifer, Katie, Zachary. BS in Mktg., U. Colo., 1974; JD, U. Minn., 1978. Bar: Minn. 1978, U.S. Dist. Ct. Minn. 1978, U.S. Tax Ct. 1980; CPA, Minn. Acct. Coopers & Lybrand, Mpls., 1978-80; shareholder Larkin, Hoffman, Daly & Lindgren, Mpls., 1980—, treas., 1990—, also bd. dirs., 1990-93. Bd. dirs. Temple of Aaron, St. Paul, 1983—, Sholom Home, Inc., St. Paul, 1983-89. Mem. ABA (tax sect., past chmn. personal svc. orgns.), AICPA, Minn. Soc. CPAs (tax conf. com. 1987—), Minn. State Bar Assn., Hennepin County Bar Assn. Avocations: tennis, racquetball, football. Office: Larkin Hoffman Daly & Lindgren 7900 Xerxes Ave S Ste 1500 Minneapolis MN 55431-1128

FREEMAN, TOM M., lawyer; b. Wauwatosa, Wis., Oct. 5, 1952; s. Max and Betty J. (Zimmerman) F.; m. Judith Casper, June 23, 1974; children: Sarah Carolyn, Benjamin Robert. BA with honors, U. Wis., 1974; JD cum laude, Harvard U., 1977. Bar: Wis. 1977, Ill. 1978, Calif. 1980, U.S. Dist. Ct. (we. dist.) Wis. 1977, U.S. Ct. Appeals (7th cir.) 1978, U.S. Dist. Ct. (no. dist.) Calif. 1980, U.S. Ct. Appeals (9th cir.) 1982. Law clk. Wis. Supreme Ct., Madison, 1977-78; staff atty. U.S. Ct. Appeals (7th cir.), Chgo., 1978-80; assoc. Brobeck, Phleger, Harrison, LLP, San Francisco, 1980-85. Democrat. Jewish. Office: Brobeck Phleger & Harrison LLP Spear St Tower 1 Market San Francisco CA 94105*

FREEMAN, TYLER IRA, physician; b. N.Y.C., Feb. 1, 1934; s. Jules and Mildred (Cohen) F.; m. Alice Fruchter, Dec. 22, 1957; children: Julie, Nancy. BA, Johns Hopkins U., 1955; MD, Chgo. Med. Sch., 1959. Intern L.I. (N.Y.) Coll. Hosp., 1959-60, resident in internal medicine, 1960-62; chief med. resident North Shore U. Hosp., Manhasset, N.Y., 1962-63; pvt. practice internal medicine, dir. Employee Health Svc., Mt. Sinai-Elmhurst Hosp., N.Y.C., 1965-75; asst. med. dir. Hoechst/Celanese, N.Y.C., 1975-78; med. dir. adminstrv. svcs. Consolidated Edison Corp., N.Y.C., 1978-82; corp. med. dir. Fielderest/Cannon Inc., Eden, N.C., 1981-88; med. dir. A.T. & T. Network Systems, Columbus, Ohio, 1988-90; pvt. cons. Bus. Health Mgmt., Cleve., 1990-94; dir. occupational and environ. medicine Charlotte/Mecklenburg Hosp. Assn., N.C., 1994-96; pres. Med. Evaluations Unltd., Charlotte, N.C., 1996—; MD cons. Health Ins. Plan-Greater N.Y., N.Y.C., Combustion Toxicity Task Group, Am. Textile Mfg. Assn.; pres. occupational med. com. Am. Indsl. Hygiene Assn., N.C. and S.C.; pres. Component

Soc. Am. Coll. Del. steering com. Wellness Coun., Greensboro, N.C.; advisor Hospice Task Force, Rockingham, N.C.; bd. dirs. ARC, Eden. Capt. USAF, 1963-65. Fellow Am. Coll. Preventive Medicine, Am. Coll. Occupational Medicine; mem. AMA, N.Y. Acad. Sci., Am. Diabetes Assn., Am. Soc. Internal Medicine, Am. Pub. Health Assn. Jewish. Avocations: classical music, classical automobiles, literature, golf. Home: 12033 Delmahoy Dr Charlotte NC 28277-9635 Office: 1005 S Kings Dr Charlotte NC 28207-1603

FREEMAN, VAL LEROY, geologist; b. Long Beach, Calif., June 25, 1926; s. Cecil LeRoy and Marjorie (Austin) F.; BS, U. Calif., Berkeley, 1949, MS, 1952; m. June Ione Ashlock, Sept. 26, 1959 (div. June 1962); 1 child, Jill Annette Freeman Michener; m. Elizabeth Joann Sabia, Sept. 4, 1964 (div. Oct. 1972); 1 child, Rebecca Sue Freeman Shepard; 1 stepchild, Frank J. Sabia; m. Betty M. Avey, Oct. 9, 1993. Geologist, U.S. Geol. Survey, 1949-85, Fairbanks, Alaska, 1955-57, Denver, 1957-70, 74-85, Flagstaff, Ariz., 1970-74, dep. chief coal resources br., until 1985. With USNR, 1943-45. Fellow Geol. Soc. Am. Contbr. articles to profl. jours. Home: 26 S Indiana Pl Golden CO 80401-5082

FREEMARK, MICHAEL SCOTT, pediatric endocrinologist and educator; b. Phila., Dec. 10, 1950; s. Morton and Molly (Blumberg) F.; m. Anne R. Slifkin, May 8, 1979; children: Samara, Yonah. BA magna cum laude, Brandeis U., 1972; postgrad., Temple U., 1972-74; MD, Duke U., 1976. Diplomate Am. Bd. Pediatrics, subspecialty bds. pediatric endocrinology, Nat. Bd. Med. Examiners; lic. physician, N.C. Resident pediatrics Duke U. Med. Ctr., Durham, N.C., 1976-79, fellow in pediatrics, 1980-84, asst. prof. pediatrics, 1984-90, asst. prof. cell biology, 1989—, assoc. prof. pediatrics, 1991—; chief pediatric endocrine divsn. Duke U. Med. Ctr., Durham, 1991—; med. dir. Pediatric Clinics, Harnett and Hoke Counties, N.C., 1979-80; ad hoc reviewer human embryology and devel. study sect. NIH, 1989, 90; dir. weekly endocrine and pediatric fellows rsch. seminars; lectr. in field. Contbr. numerous articles, abstracts to profl. jours., chpts. to books; editorial bd. Jour. Clin. Endocrinology and Metabolism, 1990-93, Endocrinology, 1998—. Bd. dirs. Durham Nursery Sch. Assn., 1983-88; chmn. People's Alliance Subcom. on Pub. Edn.; mem. Durham County Commn. Merger Issues Task Force, 1988-89; tchr. Triangle Children's Shule, Chapel Hill, N.C., Durham Co. Comm. Child Protection Team, 1994-96. Recipient NIH-Nat. Rsch. Svc. award, 1982-85, NIH Clin. Investigator award, 1985-88, Rsch. award March of Dimes, 1988-92, NIH Rsch. Career Devel. award, 1990—; March of Dimes-Basil O'Connor Starter grantee, 1985-87, Trent Found. grantee, 1984-85, NIH grantee, 1988—; USEPA fellow, 1972, USPHS fellow, 1974, 75, Fogarty fellow, Paris, 1993. Mem. Am. Fedn. Clin. Rsch., N.C. Med. Assn., Am. Acad. Pediatrics, Endocrine Soc., Lawson-Wilkins Pediatric Endocrine Soc. (chair program com. 1991-94, chair drug and therapeutics com. 1999—), Soc. for Pediatric Rsch. (coun. endocrinology, metabolism and nephrology 1991-94). Home: 1309 Oakland Ave Durham NC 27705-3243 Office: Duke Univ Med Ctr PO Box 3080 Durham NC 27710*

FREENY, PATRICK CLINTON, radiology educator, consultant; b. Kansas City, Mo., July 16, 1942; s. Joseph Bernard and Grace Elizabeth (Hardin) F.; m. Marsha Nye, 15 June, 1968; children: Kristen E., Kevin P. BA, Davidson Coll., 1964; MD, U. Okla., 1968. Intern UCLA, 1968-69; resident U. Oreg., Portland, 1972-75; clin. fellow Am. Cancer Soc., Portland, 1974-75; chief angiography-intreventional radiology Virginia Mason Clinic, Seattle, 1974-91; prof. radiology U. Wash. Sch. Medicine, Seattle, 1991—; vis. prof. Royal Soc. Medicine, London, 1987. Author: Radiology of the Pancreas, 1983, 2d edit., 1989, Alimentary Tract Radiology, 5th edit., 1994; assoc. editor Radiology; mem. editorial bd. Internat. Jour. Pancreatology; contbr. papers, book chpts. to profl. publs. Mem. World Affairs Coun., Seattle, 1985—. Lt. comdr. USPHS, 1969-72. Fellow Am. Coll. Radiology, Soc. Cardiovascular Interventional Radiology; mem. Soc. Gastrointestinal Radiologists (pres. 1995), Soc. Computed Body Tomography (pres. 1994), Pacific N.W. Radiol. Soc. (pres. 1985), West Angio-Interventional Soc. (pres. 1992), Am. Alpine Club (N.Y.C.). Republican. Avocations: mountain climbing, skiing, photography, kayaking. E-mail: freeny@u.washington.edu. Home: 3 Columbia Key Bellevue WA 98006-1007 Office: U Wash Sch Medicine Dept Radiology PO Box 357115 Seattle WA 98195-7115

FREER, COBURN, English language educator; b. New Orleans, Nov. 5, 1939; s. Wilbert Coburn and Lillian Jackson (Hicks) F.; m. Ramona Jean Salminen; children: Meagan, Elinor. BA, Lewis and Clark Coll., 1960; PhD, U. Washington, 1967. Instr. U. Ariz., Tucson, 1965-67; asst. prof to prof. U. Mont., Missoula, 1967-80; head dept. U. Ga., Athens, 1980-92, prof., 1980—. Author: Music for a King, 1972, The Poetics of Jacobean Drama, 1981; contbr. articles to profl. jours. Recipient Sr. Fulbright-Hays lectureship U. Oulu, Finland, 1971-72, NEH fellowship, London, 1974-75. Mem. MLA, Internat. Assn. Univ. Profs. English, Milton Soc., South Atlantic MLA, Southeast Renaissance Conf. Home: 400 Saint George Dr Athens GA 30606-3940 Office: Univ Ga Dept English Athens GA 30602

FREER, ROBERT ELLIOTT, JR., lawyer; b. Washington, Jan. 19, 1941; s. Robert E. and Alice (Barry) F.; m. Roberta Stapleton Renchard, Dec. 31, 1972; children: Kimberly Dunlap, R. Elliott III, Ashleigh Hamilton, Daniel Renchard. AB, Princeton U., 1963; JD, U. Va., 1966. Bar: Va. 1966, D.C. 1968, U.S. Supreme Ct. 1973. Trial atty. FTC, 1966-69, atty. advisor to chmn., asst. to gen. counsel, 1970-71; exec. asst. to gen. counsel U.S. Dept. Transp., Washington, 1971-74; Washington counsel Kimberly Clark Corp., 1974-83; staff v.p., 1975-80, corp. v.p., 1980-84; gen. counsel Roswell, Ga., 1983-84; pvt. practice Washington, 1984—; mem. President's Commn. on White House Fellowships, 1985-93; pub. mem. Adminstrv. Conf. U.S., 1981-86; capt. land team President's Pvt. Sector Survey on Cost Control in Fedn. Govt., 1982-83; sec., gen. counsel U.S.-Cuba Bus. Coun., 1994—; bd. dirs. Natural Solutions Corp., 1998—. Contbg. author, editor: Finding Our Roots/Facing Our Future: America in the 21st Century, 1997; contbr. articles to profl. jours. Founder, chmn. bd. trustees Washington Episc. Sch., 1986-94, chmn. emeritus, 1994; chmn. bd. visitors Regent U. Sch. Law, 1995—; trustee Corcoran Gallery Art, 1986-93, asst. sec., chmn. bylaws com., 1990, sec., 1991; chmn. Lawyers for the Republic, 1988—; asst. gen. counsel Rep. Nat. Conv., 1988, 92, 96. Mem. Rep. Nat. Lawyers Assn. (bd. govs. 1985—, gen. counsel 1985-89, vice chmn. 1988-89), Washington Met. Area Corp. Counsel Assn. (founder, pres. 1980-81, bd. dirs. 1980-84), Am. Arbitration Assn. Home: 1 W Melrose St Chevy Chase MD 20815-4243 Office: Baise Miller & Freer PC 1020 19th St NW Washington DC 20036-6101

FREESE, ANDREW, neurosurgeon, educator, scientist; b. Boston, July 4, 1959; s. Ernst and Elisabeth (Bautz) F.; m. Marcia Geary, June 14, 1986; children: John Alexander, Elisabeth Marguerite, Ernst Timothy, Matthew Andrew. BA, Harvard U., 1981; MD, Harvard U., Boston, 1990; PhD, MIT, 1990. Lic. physican, Pa.; trauma cert. Rsch. assoc. NIH, Bethesda, Md., 1982-83; surg. intern U. Pa., Phila., 1990-91, neurosurgery resident, 1991-97, dir. Lab. Molecular Neurosurgery Grad. Hosp., 1994-97, mem. Inst. Human Gene Therapy, 1994—; assoc. prof. neurosurgery, dir. neurosurgery rsch. Thomas Jefferson U., Phila., 1997—, assoc. dir CNS Gene Therapy Ctr., 1998—; vis. scientist Wistar Inst., Phila., 1994-95; pres. Neurel, Inc., Boston, 1987-88, sci. dir., 1988-90; cons. Polykinetix, Inc., N.Y.C., 1993; exec. dir. Parkinson's Disease Gene Therapy Consortium. Editor: Biotechnology Processing, 1988, Neurological Disorders: Novel Experimental and Therapeutic Approaches, 1992; editor spl. issue Exptl. Neurology, 1997; contbr. articles to profl. jours. Fellow Sigma Xi; mem. AMA, Internat. Brain Rsch. Orgn., Soc. Neurosci., Congress Neurol. Surgeons, Controlled Release Soc. Achievements include patents for controlling the release of drugs using drug delivery system for neurological disorders; one of the first viral vector systems to deliver genes into neurons; the demonstration of the precursor effect on brain kynurenines; gene therapy for Parkinson's disease, epilepsy, pituitary adenomas, neurogenetic disorders, and stroke. Home: 101 Buck Ln Haverford PA 19041-1104 Office: Thomas Jefferson U Dept Neurosurgery 1015 Chestnut St Ste 1400 Philadelphia PA 19107-5211 also: Thomas Jefferson U Neurosurgery Rsch Labs Ste #511 1025 Walnut St Philadelphia PA 19107-5001

FREESE, BARBARA T., nursing educator; b. Kansas City, Mo., Oct. 1, 1944; d. Ernest M. and Marjorie (McIntosh) Tapp; m. Hal Freese, Feb. 3, 1968; 1 child, Tiffany Jo. BSN, U. Mo., 1967; MSN, Clemson U., 1980; EdD, U. Ga., 1989. Nursing faculty Lander U., Greenwood, 1975—, dean sch. nursing, 1989—. Contbr. articles to profl. jours. Trustee Neuman Sys. Model Group. Fellow Royal Coll. Nursing, Australia; mem. ANA, Nat. League for Nursing, Mensa, Sigma Theta Tau., Kappa Delta Pi.

FREESE, KATHERINE, physicist, educator; b. Freiburg, Germany, Feb. 8, 1957; came to U.S., 1957; d. Ernst and Elisabeth Gertrude Maria (Bautz) F.; 1 child, Douglas Quincy Adams. BA, Princeton U., 1977; MA, Columbia U., 1981; PhD, U. Chgo., 1984. Postdoctoral fellow Harvard/Smithsonian Ctr. for Astrophysics, Cambridge, Mass., 1984-85, Inst. for Theoretical Physics, Santa Barbara, Calif., 1985-87, U. Calif., Berkeley, 1987-88; asst. prof. physics MIT, Cambridge, 1988-91; assoc. prof. physics U. Mich., Ann Arbor, 1991—; gen. mem. Aspen Ctr. for Physics, 1991—. Contbr. articles to profl. jours. William Rainey Harper fellow U. Chgo, 1982; Sloan Found. fellow, 1989; Presdl. Young Investigator NSF, 1990, rsch. grantee, 1991, 94; Presdl. fellow U. Calif., 1987. Mem. Am. Phys. Soc., Assn. for Women in Sci. Democrat. Avocations: water polo, swimming, skiing, tennis. Office: U Mich Dept Physics Ann Arbor MI 48109

FREESE, MELANIE LOUISE, librarian, professor; b. Mineola, N.Y., May 12, 1945; d. Walter Christian and Agnes Elizabeth (Jensen) F. BS in Elem. Edn., Hofstra U., 1967, MA in Elem. Edn., 1969; MLS, L.I. U., 1977. Cert. tchr., N.Y. Bibliographic searcher acquisitions dept. Adelphi U. Swirbul Libr., Garden City, N.Y., 1973-79, res. desk libr., 1979-83; catalog libr., assoc. prof. Hofstra U. Axinn Libr., Hempstead, N.Y., 1984—; ch. librarian St. Peters Evang. Luth. Ch., Baldwin, N.Y., 1977—. Founder libr. Salvation Army Wayside Home and Sch. for Girls, Valley Stream, N.Y., 1993. Mem. ALA, Nassau County Libr. Assn. (corr. sec. acad. and spl. librs. divsn. 1986-88, v.p., pres.-elect 1989-90, pres. 1991), Bus. and Profl. Women's Club (pres. Nassau County chpt. 1990-92, 95-97, Woman of Yr. 1994). Republican. Avocations: needlework, knitting, crocheting. Office: Hofstra U Axinn Library 1000 Fulton Ave Hempstead NY 11550-1030

FREESE, RAYMOND WILLIAM, mathematics educator; b. Foristell, Mo., Dec. 17, 1934; s. Herman E. and Lydia D. (Giessmann) F.; m. Celia Ann Staubach, Aug. 10, 1957; children: Carl, William, Timothy. BS in Agrl., U. Mo., 1956, BS in Edn., 1958, MA in Math., 1958, PhD in Math., 1961. Asst. prof. math. St. Louis U., 1961-64, assoc. prof. math., 1964-67, prof. math., 1967-83, prof. math., chmn. dept., 1971-83, prof. math. and computer sci., chmn. dept., 1983-86, prof. math. and computer sci., 1983—, prof. edn., 1989—. Contbr. articles to profl. jours. Mem. Francis Howell Sch. Dist. Bd. Edn., St. Charles, Mo., 1967-69. Mem. Mo. Sch. Bd. Assn. (exec. com. 1968-70), Math. Assn. Am. (Mo. sect. chmn. 1964-65, Mo. sect. gov. 1973-76), Am. Math. Soc., Math. Educators of Greater St. Louis, Nat. Coun. Tchrs. of Math., Sigma Xi. Mem. United Ch. of Christ. Avocations: ham radio, sci. fiction. Office: St Louis U Dept Math/Computer Sci 221 N Grand Blvd Saint Louis MO 63103-2006

FREESE, UWE ERNEST, physician, educator; b. Bordesholm, Germany, May 11, 1925; s. Heinrich and Frida (Lessau) F.; m. Gabriela Friederici, Oct. 11, 1961; children: Axel, Pamela. M.D., U. Kiel, W.Ger., 1951. Diplomate: Am. Bd. Obstetrics and Gynecology. Resident U. Kiel, 1954-56; resident U. Chgo. Lying-in Hosp., 1956-59, prof. ob-gyn., 1971-75; prof., chmn. dept. Chgo. Med. Sch., 1975-95; prof. emeritus, 1995; chmn. dept. ob-gyn. Cook County Hosp., 1976-95, chmn. emeritus, 1995—; prof., chair emeritus ob/gyn The Chgo. Med. Sch., 1995—. Patentee cervical cap. Mem. Soc. Gynecol. Investigation, Perinatal Research Soc. (founding mem.), Central Assn. Obstetrics and Gynecology (cert. of merit 1967), Perinatal Soc. Ill. East (chmn.), N.Y. Acad. Scis., Sigma Xi. Lutheran. Home: 238 Forest Ave Oak Park IL 60302-1908 Office: U Health Scis Chicago Med Sch 3333 Green Bay Rd North Chicago IL 60064-3037

FREESTONE, JEANNETTE WARREN, nurse practitioner; b. Danville, Va., May 19, 1945; d. Robert Lee and Alma Irene (Howerton) Gourley; m. Daniel Lee Freestone, Aug. 15, 1970; 1 child, Elizabeth Helen. Student, U. Wash., 1965-67; AS, Ind. U., 1971; cert. ob-gyn. nurse practitioner, Ohio State U., 1979; BS, Ind. Wesleyan U., 1995, MS in Primary Health, Family Nursing, 1997. RN, Ind.; cert. family nurse practitioner ANCC. Staff nurse Cmty. Hosp., Anderson, Ind., 1971-76; educator childbirth Pvt. Lamaze Classes, Anderson, Ind., 1975-79; staff nurse ob-gyn. Ball Meml. Hosp., Muncie, Ind., 1977-78; nurse practitioner Planned Parenthood, Muncie, Ind., 1978-81; chair practical nursing sch. Ind. Vocat. Tech. Coll., Richmond, Ind., 1981-83; staff devel. coord. Henry City Meml. Hosp., New Castle, Ind., 1983-93; nurse practitioner Family Planning/Madison County, Anderson, 1982-94, Dr. Mark Jennings, Internal Medicine, Anderson, 1992-94, St. John's Health System, Anderson, 1994-97, Open Door Health Clinic, Muncie, Ind., 1997—; adj. faculty continuing edn.-women's health practitioner program, Ind. U., 1994-95; chair health occupations adv. com. Area Vocat. Sch., New Castle, 1983-93; owner Advanced Practice Edn. Inst., Inc., Indpls., 1998—; instr. trainer CPR, ARC, Anderson, 1984-92; owner, operator Practical Nursing Rev. Course, Anderson, 1985-88; owner, instr. Pvt. Lamaze Instrn., Anderson, 1985-88; instr. nurse practitioner program Ball State U., 1997—. Chair Task Force on Teen Pregnancy, New Castle, 1987. Mem. ANA, Am. Coll. Nurse Practitioners, Ind. State Nurses Assn., Advanced Practice Nurses, East Central Ind. (edn. chair coalition advanced practice nurses in Ind.), Sigma Theta Tau. Avocation: travel. Home: 824 Hemlock Ct Anderson IN 46012-1813 Office: Open Door Health Clinic 905 S Walnut St Muncie IN 47302-2333

FREEZE, JAMES DONALD, administrator, clergyman; b. Balt., Sept. 15, 1932; s. Frank Leo and Helen Angela (Sweeney) F. A.B., Boston Coll., 1956, M.A., 1957; S.T.L., U. Innsbruck, Austria, 1964. Joined S.J., Roman Catholic Ch., 1950, ordained priest, 1963; mem. faculty dept. philosophy Wheeling (W.Va.) Coll., 1965-70, chmn. dept., 1967-70; asst. dean Coll. Arts and Scis., Georgetown U., Washington, 1971-74; asst. v.p. for acad. affairs Coll. Arts and Scis., Georgetown U., 1974-79, exec. v.p., provost, 1979-91; dir. Loyola Retreat House, Faulkner, Md., 1992-97; v.p., treas. Corp. Roman Cath. Clergyman, Balt., 1997—. Trustee Georgetown Prep. Sch., Rockville, Md., 1975-79, chmn. bd., 1978-79; trustee Loyola Coll., Balt., 1982-88, U. Detroit, 1983-90, Fairfield U., 1990-96, Manresa Retreat House, Staten Island, N.Y., 1997-98. Home and Office: 5704 Roland Ave Baltimore MD 21210-1334

FREGOSI, JAMES LOUIS, professional baseball team manager; b. San Francisco, Apr. 4, 1942; m. Joni Fregosi; children: Jim Jr., Jennifer, Nicole, Robbie. Student, Menlo Coll. Profl. baseball player Angels, Calif., 1961-71, N.Y. Mets, 1972-73, Tex. Rangers, 1973-77, Pitts. Pirates, 1977-78; mgr. Calif. Angels, 1978-81, Louisville Redbirds, 1983-86, Chgo. White Sox, 1986-88; spl. assignment scout, coach Phila. Phillies, 1989-90, minor league pitching instr., spl. assignment scout, 1990, mgr., 1991-97; spl. asst. to gen. mgr. San Francisco Giants, 1997-98; mgr. Toronto (Ont.) Blue Jays, 1999—. Named to All-Star team, 1964, 66-70; recipient Gold Glove award, 1967. Office: Toronto Blue Jays, 1 Blue Jays Way Ste 3200, Toronto, ON Canada M5V 1J1*

FREI, BRENT R., computer software executive. BS in Engrg., Dartmouth Coll., Hanover, N.H., 1989; MS, Dartmouth Coll. Mech. engr. Motorola Corp., 1989-90; progammer analyst Microsoft Info. Tech. Group, 1991-94; dir. ONYX, 1994—, pres., sec., treas., 1995-98, pres., CEO, Chmn., 1998—. Office: ONYX Software Corp 310 120th Ave NE Ste 101 Bellevue WA 98005-3013

FREI, EMIL, III, physician, medical researcher, educator; b. St. Louis, 1924; m. Elizabeth Smith (dec. Apr. 1986); children: Mary, Emil, Alice, Nancy, Judy; m. Adoria Smetana Brock, May 1987; stepchildren: Stephen, Francis, Peter, Vincent, John. MD, Yale U., 1948. Diplomate Am. Bd. Internal Medicine, Am. Bd. Med. Oncology. Intern St. Louis U. Hosp., 1948-49; resident in pathology Barnes Hosp., St. Louis, 1952-53; resident in internal medicine St. Louis U., 1953-54, VA Hosp., St. Louis, 1954-55; chief gen. medicine br. Nat. Cancer Inst., Bethesda, Md., 1955-65; head devel. therapeutics, assoc. dir. M.D. Anderson Hosp. and Tumor Inst., Houston, 1965-72; dir., physician-in-chief Children's Cancer Research Found. (now Dana-Farber Cancer Inst.), Boston, 1972-91; physician-in-chief emeritus Dana-Farber Cancer Inst., 1991—; prof. medicine Med. Sch. Harvard U., Boston, 1972—, Richard and Susan Smith prof. medicine, 1985, Richard and Susan Smith disting. prof. medicine, 1994—; nat. cons. in internal medicine-oncology USAF, 1968-72; mem. Eleanor Roosevelt internat. cancer fellowships com. Internat. Union Against Cancer, 1968-72; NAS, 1968-72; nat. cons. in internal medicine-oncology USAF; mem. Eleanor Roosevelt internat. cancer fellowships com. Internat. Union Against Cancer; chmn. anti-neoplastic disease drug panel, drug efficacy study NAS; mem. bd. sci. counselors Nat. Cancer Inst., 1986-90, mem. Presdl. Commn. for New Drugs for Cancer and AIDS, 1988-90; chmn. antitumor drug panel Nat. Acad. Scis., 1996. Lt. M.C. USNR, 1950-52. Recipient Lasker award 1972, Kettering prize GM, 1983, Hamao Umezawa award 1985, Armand Hammer Cancer Rsch. award 1989, Disting. Alumnus award NIH, 1990, Emil Frei III Professorship in Medicine, 1992, Morse award, 1996, Sidney Farber medal for contbns. to cancer rsch., 1998. Fellow ACP, Am. Acad. Arts and Scis.; mem. AMA, Am. Assn. for Cancer Rsch. (past pres.), Am. Soc. Clin. Oncology (pres. 1968-69, Disting. Scientist award 1992), Am. Cancer Soc. (ann. Nat. award 1981), Am. Soc. Hematology, Am. Soc. Clin. Investigation, Assn. Am. Physicians, Inst. of Medicine, Nat. Acad. Medicine. Office: Dana Farber Cancer Inst 44 Binney St # 1240 Boston MA 02115-6084*

FREIBERG, LOWELL CARL, financial executive; b. N.Y.C., May 15, 1939; s. Joseph and Esther (Merns) F.; m. Cathy Taub, May 7, 1994; children: Jill, Edward, Oliver, Julian. BA, NYU, 1961; MBA, Columbia U., 1962. Second v.p. Chase Manhattan Bank, N.Y.C., 1964-69; asst. treas. Reliance Group Holdings, N.Y.C., 1969, treas., 1969—, v.p., 1972-74, sr. v.p., 1974—, chief fin. officer, 1985-98, exec. v.p., 1998—, also bd. dirs.; bd. dirs. Symbol Technologies, Inc., Bohemia, N.Y., LandAmerica, Richmond, Va. With U.S. Army, 1962-64. Recipient Human Relations award Am. Jewish Com., 1978. Office: Reliance Group Holdings Inc 55 E 52nd St New York NY 10055

FREIBERG, ROBERT JERRY, laser physicist, engineer, technology administrator, consultant; b. Chgo., Mar. 26, 1939; s. Jerry and Mildred (Lukes) F.; m. Deanna Corrine Qualls, July 8, 1968; children: Joseph, Sean, Jamison. BS in Physics, Rensselear Poly. Inst., 1961; MS in Physics, U. Ill., 1963, PhD, 1966. Postgrad. rsch. assoc. U. Ill., Urbana, 1966-67; rsch. scientist Hughes Rsch. Labs., Malibu, Calif., 1967-69; group mgr. United Tech. Rsch. Labs., East Hartford, Conn., 1969-75; gen. mgr. United Tech. Optical Sys., West Palm Beach, Fla., 1975-79; bus. mgr. optics TRW, Redondo Beach, Calif., 1979-83; program dir. Baxter Healthcare, Inc., Irvine, Calif., 1983-86; dir. engrng. and mfg. ops. Pfizer Laser Sys., Irvine, 1986-92; dir. engrng. Lumonics, Inc., Camarillo, Calif., 1992-94; sr. v.p. engrng. and program mgmt. View Engrng., Inc., Simi Valley, Calif., 1994-97; v.p. engrng. Indsl. Electronic Engrs. Inc., Van Nuys, Calif., 1997—; gen. ptnr., sr. tech. cons. Internat. Mktg. and Cons. Assocs., Thousand Oaks, Calif., 1991—; chmn. tech. adv. bd. Premier Laser Sys., Irvine, 1992—; numerous presentations in field. Contbr. numerous articles to Procs. IEEE, Laser Focus, Applied Optics, IEEE Jour. Quantum Electronics, Jour. Applied Physics, Phys. Rev., Applied Physics Letters, Bull. Am. Phys. Soc. Asst. scoutmaster Boy Scouts Am., Mission Viejo, Calif., 1989-92, varsity scoutmaster, Newbury Park, Calif., 1994-96. Fellow NSF, 1962-66. Fellow Internat. Soc. for Optical Engring. (mem. membership com. 1994-99, chmn. 1994-96); mem. IEEE, Am. Electronics Assn., Optical Soc. Am., Am. Soc. for Laser Surgery and Medicine, Nat. Ctr. Mfg. Scis. (Strategic Initiative Group com. 1995-97), Soc. Info. Displays, Sigma Xi. Achievements include numerous patents for surgical lasers, endoscopic instrumentation, medical catheters, novel optical resonators, laser devices, and diagnostic instruments. Avocations: water and snow skiing, volleyball, fishing, tennis. Home: 325 Fox Ridge Dr Thousand Oaks CA 91361-1328 Office: Indsl Electronic Engrs Inc 7740 Lemona Ave Van Nuys CA 91405-1136

FREIBERGER, KATHERINE GUION, composer, retired piano educator; b. Mineral Wells, Tex., May 2, 1927; d. Waldo Burton and Kate Francis (Guion) Lasater; m. John Jacob Freiberger, July 22, 1950; children: John J., Kate Fentress Huxel, Erich D. AA, HocKaday Jr. Coll., Dallas, 1946; BA, U. Tex., 1949; MusB, So. Meth. U., 1966. Sec., translator Murray Cotton Gin Co., Dallas, 1949; tchr. Dallas Ind. Schs., 1949-50; pvt. practice piano tchr. Dallas, 1961-85. Composer piano solos and duets, chamber, choral and incidental music. Mem. Dallas Civic Chorus, 1962-69, 72-76, chorus Dallas Civic Opera, 1959; alto soloist Preston Hollow Presbyn. Ch., Dallas, 1956-63; alto soloist, dir. youth choir Churhill Way Presbyn. Ch., Dallas, 1963-70; sole trustee David W. Guion Edn. and Religious Trusts I and II, Dallas, 1978-91; bd. dirs. Dallas Music Tchrs. Assn., 1979-91, Voices of Change, Dallas, 1980s, Dallas Civic Music, 1970s-80s, Durango/Purgatory Music in the Mts., Colo., 1990—, The Dallas Opera, 1989-97. Mem. Musical Arts Club, Mu Phi Epsilon Alumni (First prize for composition 1989). Avocations: creative writing, tennis, snow skiing, horseback riding. Home: 7407 Stonecrest Dr Dallas TX 75240-2746

FREIBERGER, WALTER FREDERICK, mathematics educator, actuarial science consultant, educator; b. Vienna, Austria, Feb. 20, 1924; came to U.S., 1955, naturalized, 1962; s. Felix and Irene (Tagany) F.; m. Christine Mildred Holmberg, Oct. 6, 1956; children: Christopher Allan, Andrew James, Nils H. BA, U. Melbourne, 1947, MA, 1949; PhD, U. Cambridge, Eng., 1953. Rsch. officer Aero. Rsch. Lab. Australian Dept. Supply, 1947-49, sr. sci. rsch. officer, 1953-55; tutor U. Melbourne, 1947-49, 53-55; asst. prof. div. applied math. Brown U., 1956-58, assoc. prof., 1958-64, prof., 1964—, prof. applied math., prof. cmty. health, 1994—, dir. Computing Center, 1963-69, dir. Ctr. for Computer and Info. Scis., 1969-76, chmn. div. applied math., 1976-82, chmn. grad. com., 1985-88, assoc. chmn. div. applied math., 1988-91, chmn. univ. ctr. for statis. sci., 1991—; joint appointment Brown U. Med. Sch., 1994—; lectr., cons. program in applied actuarial sci. Bryant Coll., 1986—; joint appointment as prof. cmty. health Sch. Medicine Brown U., 1994—; mem. fellowship selection panel NSF, Fulbright fellowship selection panel. Author: (with U. Grenander) A Short Course in Computational Probability and Statistics, 1971; editor: The International Dictionary of Applied Mathematics, 1960, (with others) Applications of Digital Computers, 1963, Advances in Computers, Volume 10, 1970, Statistical Computer Performance Evaluation, 1972; mng. editor: Quarterly of Applied Mathematics, 1965—; Contbr. numerous articles to profl. jours. Served with Australian Army, 1943-45. Fulbright fellow, 1955-56; Guggenheim fellow, 1962-63; grantee NSF Office Naval Rsch. NIH. Mem. Am. Math. Soc. (assoc. editor Math. Reviews 1957-62), Soc. for Indsl. and Applied Math., Am. Statis. Assn., Inst. Math. Stats., Assn. Computing Machinery, Edgewood Yacht Club. Republican. Episcopalian. Home: 24 Alumni Ave Providence RI 02906-2310 Office: Brown U 182 George St Providence RI 02912-9056

FREIBOTT, GEORGE AUGUST, physician, chemist, priest; b. Bridgeport, Conn., Oct. 6, 1954; s. George August and Barbara Mary (Schreiber) F.; m. Jennifer Noble, July 12, 1980 (div.); children: Jessica, Heather, George; m. Arlene Ann Steiner, Aug. 1, 1982, Bethany, Bethiah, Solomon, Joel, Rachel. BD, Am. Bible Coll., Pineland, Fla., 1977; BS, Nat. Coll. NHA, International Falls, Minn., 1978; ThM, Clarksville (Tenn.) Sch. Theology, 1979; MD, Western U., Phoenix, 1982; ND, Am. Coll., 1979; MsT, Fla. Sch. Massage, 1977. Diplomate Nat. Bd. Naturopathic Examiners; ordained priest Ea. Orthodox Ch., 1983. Chief mfg. cons. in oxidative chemistry Am. Soc. Med. Missionaries, Priest River, Idaho, 1976-88; mfg. cons. Oxidation Products Internat. div. ASMM, Priest River, 1974—; chemist/oxidative chemistry Internat. Assn. Oxygen Therapy, Priest River, 1985—; oxidative chemist, scientist, priest A.S. Med. Missionaries, Priest River, 1982—; CEO Internat. Oxydative Products Techs., Ltd., Las Vegas, Nev., 1996—; massage therapist Fla. Dept. Profl. Registration, Tallahassee, 1977-91; cons. Benedict Lust Sch. Naturopathy; cons. mem. World Natural Health Orgn., Washington, Internat. Colon Hydrotherapy Found., London; lectr. in field. Author: Nicola Tesla and the Implementation of His Discoveries in Modern Science, 1984, Warburg, Blass and Koch: Men With a Message, 1990, Free Radicals and Their Relationship to Complex Oxidative Compounds, 1991, Complex Oxidative Molecules: Their Implication in the Rejuvenation of the Human Cell, 1994, History of Naturopathy or Pseudomedicalism: Naturopathy's Demise?, 1990, 95; contbr. articles to profl. jours. Recipient Tesla medal of Scientific Merit, Benedict Lust Sch. Natural Scis., 1992. Mem. Am. Chem. Soc., Tesla Meml. Soc., Tesla Coil Builder's Assn., Internat. Bio-Oxidative Med. Found. (Disting. Spkr. award 1994), Brit. Guild Drugless Practitioners, Internat. Assn. for Colon Therapy, Am. Massage Therapy Assn., Am. Naturopathic Med. Assn., Am. Soc. Med. Missionaries, Am. Coll. Clinic Adminstrs., Nat. Assn. Naturopathic Physicians, Am. Psychotherapy Assn., Am. Soc. Metals, Am. Naturopathic Assn. (trustee, pres.), Internat. Traders. Achievements include research conducted in organic and inorganic oxidative chemistry, thermoelectric/thermionic materials in relation to oxygen, oxygen as related to superconductivity and molecular makeup, energy studies, material science, archaeology, ancient Biblical and medical studies; developer and co-designer advanced oxidative equipment and testing apparatus of oxidation and oxidative studies. Home: PO Box 1360 Priest River ID 83856-1360 Office: Am Sch Naturopathy 200 N Tamiami Trail Ste E Venice FL 34285

FREIDHEIM, CYRUS F., JR., management consultant; b. Chgo., June 14, 1935; s. Cyrus F. and Eleanor Freidheim; m. Marguerite VandenBosch; children: Marguerite Lynn, Stephen Cyrus, Scott. BSChE, U. Notre Dame, 1957; MS in Indsl. Adminstrn., Carnegie Mellon U., 1963. Plant mgr. Union Carbide Corp., Whiting, Ind., 1961; cons. Price Waterhouse, Chgo., 1962; fin. analyst Ford Motor Co., Dearborn, Mich., 1963-66; vice chmn. Booz, Allen & Hamilton, Chgo., 1966—; dir. Household Internat. Inc., 1989—, Security Capital Group, 1991—, Microage, 1988—, Dir. Chef, 1999—. Author: The Trillion Dollar Enterprise, 1998. Chmn. bd. trustees Thunderbird, The Am. Grad. Sch. Internat. Mgmt.; dir. Chgo Coun. Fgn. Rels.; trustee Rush-Presbyn.-St. Luke's Med. Ctr., 1981—; assoc. Northwestern U., 1981—; trustee Chgo. Symphony Orch.; vice chmn. bd. overseers Rush U., bd. dirs.; trustee Brookings Instn., 1994—. With USN, 1957-61. Mem. Coun. Fgn. Rels., U.S. Japan Bus. Coun., Am.-China Soc. (bd. dirs.), Chgo. Club, Mid Day Club, Econ. Club, Comml. Club (Chgo.), Stanwich Club (Greenwich, Conn.), Old Elm club, Lost Tree Club (North Palm Beach). Home: 1320 N State Pkwy Chicago IL 60610-2118 Office: 225 W Wacker Dr Chicago IL 60606-1224

FREIDHEIM, LADONNA, dance company director; b. Chgo., Nov. 15, 1967; d. J. Thomas and Janet Rae (Garr) F. BS, U. Ill., 1991. Corp. asst. dir. Advanced Quality Custom Graphics, Champaign, Ill., 1990-91; adminstrv. coord. Classical Symphony Orch., Chgo., 1991-92; adminstrv. asst. Chgo. Sinfonietta, 1992-93; bus. mgr. Organic Theater, Chgo., 1993-94, mng. dir., 1994-96; mng. dir. Hedwig Dances, Chgo., 1997—; lighting designer, 1992-95; founding mem. Lucid Theatre Co. Bd. dirs. Ministry to the Disadvantaged, Champaign; vol. phys. assistance Rehab. Inst., Chgo., 1993-96; vol. dance instr. Pace Program, Evanston, 1993; vol. Children's Meml. Hosp., Chgo., 1996-99. Roman Catholic. Avocations: lighting design, exercise, cycling. Office: Hedwig Dances Chgo Cultural Ctr 78 E Washington Chicago IL 60606

FREIDIN, JACK, architect; b. N.Y.C., Jan. 16, 1930; m. Marta Neufeld Freidin, Feb. 3, 1966. BArch, Pratt Inst., 1951; M of Planning, Columbia U., 1954; Postgrad. in Computer-Aided Design, Harvard U. Registered architect N.Y., N.J., Conn. Former designer Marcel Breuer; design critic Pratt Inst., 1959-70; sr. ptnr. Freidin Bolcek Assocs., N.Y.C., 1956—; lectr. numerous profl. seminars. Contbr. articles to profl. jours., newspapers. Recipient numerous awards in field, including design honors from Nat. Assn. Home Builders, The Queens County C. of C., Ponderosa Pine Wood Co., Mus. of Modern Art. Mem. AIA, Nat. Coun. Archtl. Registration Bds., Am. Arbitration Assn. Office: Freidin Bolcek Assocs Ltd 331 E 18th St New York NY 10003-2845

FREIHEIT, CLAYTON FREDRIC, zoo director; b. Buffalo, Jan. 29, 1938; s. Clayton John and Ruth (Miller) F. Student, U. Buffalo, 1960; DHL (hon.), U. Denver, 1996. Caretaker Living Mus., Buffalo Mus. Sci., 1955-60; curator Buffalo Zool. Gardens, 1960-70; dir. Denver Zool. Gardens, 1970—. Contbr. articles to profl. jours. Named Outstanding Citizen, Buffalo Evening News, 1967. Mem. Internat. Union Dirs. Zool. Gardens, Am. Assn. Zool. Pks. and Aquariums (pres. 1967-68 Outstanding Svc. award). Home: 3855 S Monaco Pky Denver CO 80237-1271 Office: Denver Zool Gardens City Park Denver CO 80205

FREIJE, PHILIP CHARLES, lawyer; b. Princeton, N.J., July 27, 1944; s. Brahim K. and Evelyn M. (Haddad) F.; m. Karen Mae Janovic, Oct. 18, 1969; children: Michael P., James C., Christine L. BA, U. Conn., 1966, JD, 1969; LLM, George Washington U., 1972. Bar: Conn. 1970, D.C. 1970, U.S. Supreme Ct. 1973. Assoc. Conway, Londregan, Leuba & McNamara, New London, Conn., 1969; atty.-advisor Office of Fgn. Direct Investment, U.S. Dept. Commerce, Washington, 1970-73, asst. dir. litigation, 1974; legal advisor Social & Econ. Statistics Adminstrn., U.S. Dept. Commerce, Washington, 1974-75; dep. asst. gen. counsel adminstrn./econ. affairs Office of Gen. Counsel, U.S. Dept. Commerce, Washington, 1975-81, dep. asst. gen. counsel econ. affairs/regulation, 1981-85, dep. chief counsel for econ. affairs, 1985-92, chief counsel for econ. affairs, 1992-98; bureau coun. U.S. Census Bureau U.S. Dept. Commerce, 1998—. Dir. Lake Barcroft Community Assn., Falls Church, Va., 1980-82. Mem. ABA, Fed. Bar Assn., Conn. Bar Assn., D.C. Bar Assn., Am. Judicature Soc. Home: 6212 Beachway Dr Falls Church VA 22041-1423 Office: US Dept Commerce 14th & Constitution Ave NW Washington DC 20230-0002

FREIJOSO, RICARDO, microbiologist; b. Puerto Padre, Cuba, Sept. 24, 1949; came to U.S., 1980; s. Ricardo Freijoso and Elsie M. Santiesteban; m. Gloria Pelaez, Nov. 24, 1979 (div. 1980). BS in Microbiology, Havana (Cuba) U., 1979; postgrad., St. John U., 1982; MS, Iona Coll., 1992. Phlebotomist, microbiologist Kings County Hosp. Ctr., Bklyn., 1983-89, coord. mgr. A phlebotomy, 1989-92, coord. mgr. B AIDS, 1992-93, assoc. lab. microbiologist, 1993, prin. microbiologist, 1993—; instr. Kings County Hosp. Ctr., Bklyn., SUNY, King Jewish Hosp. Ctr., 1993—. Mem. Am. Soc. Clin. Pathologists, Am. Soc. Microbiologists, Am. Soc. Phlebotomy Technicians. Republican. Roman Catholic. Avocations: traveling, photography, antiques, gardening. Home: 85-43 121st St Kew Gardens NY 11415 Office: Kings County Hosp Ctr 451 Clarkson Ave # P20 Brooklyn NY 11203-2057

FREILICH, IRVIN M., lawyer; b. Ulm, Germany, Mar. 3, 1949; came to U.S., 1949; s. Charles J. and Sylvia (Schaengold) F.; m. Judith Ellen Pines, June 20, 1971; children: Jared P., Emily R. BA, U. Cin., 1971; JD, Georgetown U., 1974. Bar: N.Y. 1975, N.J. 1977, U.S. Dist. Ct. (so. and ea. dist.) N.Y. 1975, U.S. Dist. Ct. (no. dist.) N.Y. 1985, U.S. Dist. Ct. N.J. 1975, U.S. Ct. Appeals (3d cir.) 1983, U.S. Ct. Appeals (2d cir.) 1975, U.S. Ct. Appeals (D.C. cir.) 1996, U.S. Supreme Ct. 1987. Assoc. Kaye, Scholer, Fierman, Hayes & Handler, N.Y.C., 1974-77; from assoc. to ptnr. Hannoch Weisman, Roseland, N.J., 1977-90, 94-99; ptnr. Edwards & Angell, Newark, 1990-94, Robertson, Freilich, Bruno & Cohen, Morristown, N.J., 1999—. Office: Robertson Freilich Bruno & Cohen North Tower 14th Fl 89 Headquarters Plz Morristown NJ 07960*

FREILICH, JEFF, television producer, writer, director; b. N.Y.C., June 29, 1948; s. Seymour David and Natalie Freilich; m. Marguerite Hester Copp, Nov. 17, 1979; children: Nicholas Brandon, Molly Alyssa. BA, Antioch Coll., 1969; postgrad., U. So. Calif., Los Angeles, 1969-71. Freelance writer New World Pictures, Am. Internat. Pictures, Los Angeles, 1972-75; pres. Magnum TV, 1992—; creative cons. Baretta, Universal Studios, Universal City, Calif., 1976; exec. story cons. Quincy, 1979. Freelance writer New World Pictures, Am. Internat. Pictures, L.A., 1972-75; prodr., writer The Incredible Hulk, 1980, Galactica, 1980, A Nightmare on Elm Street: The Series, 1988—; exec. story editor Flamingo Road, 1980-82; supr. prodr. Boone, 1983, Picture Windows, 1994-95; exec. prodr., creator Better Days, 1986; exec. prodr., writer, dir. Falcon Crest, 1986—, Dark Justice, 1990—, Naked City, 1997-98; exec. prodr. Against the Grain, 1993, Frogmen, 1994; prodr. Rescuers: Stories of Courage, 1996-97, Execution of Justice, 1999, Meanstreak, 1999. Mem. Writers Guild Am. West, Dirs. Guild Am., Screen Actors Guild. Avocations: playing blues saxophone, golf, video games. Office: Magnum TV Inc Paramount Pictures Hollywood CA 91311-5107 also: Warner Bros Television Burbank CA

FREILICH, JOAN SHERMAN, utilities executive; b. Albany, N.Y., Nov. 3, 1941; d. Julius and Bess (Bergner) Sherman; m. Sanford J. Freilich, Jan. 24, 1965. AB in French magna cum laude, Barnard Coll., 1963; MA in French, Columbia U., 1964, PhD in French, 1971, MBA in Fin., 1980. Instr. CCNY, Columbia U., N.Y.C., 1965-75; tchr. Walden Sch., N.Y.C., 1970-74; asst. to dean Coll. of New Rochelle, N.Y., 1974-75, dir. admissions, 1975-78; sr. acct. Consol. Edison Co. N.Y., N.Y.C., 1978-81, mgr. acctg. rsch., 1981-82, contr. power generation, 1982-86, gen. mgr. power generation, 1986-89, exec. asst. to pres., 1989, asst. v.p. corp. planning, 1989-90, v.p. corp. planning, 1990-92, v.p., contr., chief acctg. officer, 1992-96, sr. v.p., CFO, 1996-98, exec. v.p., CFO, 1998—; also bd. dirs. Consol. Edison, Inc. and Consol. Edison of N.Y., Inc., N.Y.C.; bd. dirs. Con Edison Solutions, Inc. Author: Paul Claudel's "Le Soulier de satin": A Stylistic, Structuralist and Psychoanalytic Interpretation, 1973; assoc. editor Claudel Studies, 1973-78; contbr. articles to profl. jours. Trustee Citizen's Budget Commn. Publ. grantee Humanities Rsch. Coun. Can., 1972; Pres.'s fellow Columbia U., 1964, Henry Todd fellow, 1967; recipient scholarship N.Y. State Bd. Regents, 1959, Nat. Merit Found., 1959, Columbia U., 1965. Mem. Fin. Execs. Inst., N.Y. State Women in Comms. and Energy (pres.), YWCA Acad. of Women Achievers, Phi Beta Kappa, Beta Gamma Sigma. Office: Consolidated Edison Co NY 4 Irving Pl New York NY 10003-3598

FREILICHER, JANE, artist; b. N.Y.C., Nov. 29, 1924; d. Martin and Bertha (Niederhoffer); m. Joseph Hazan, Feb. 17, 1957; 1 dau., Elizabeth. AB, Bklyn. Coll., 1947; postgrad., Hans Hoffman Sch. Fine Arts, 1947; MA, Columbia U., 1948. vis. lectr., critic art schs., colls. One-woman shows include Tibor de Nagy, 1952-68, 98, John Bernard Myers Gallery, 1971, Fischbach Gallery, 1975, 77, 79-80, 83, 85, 88, 90, 92, 95, Utah Mus. Fine Arts, 1979, Lafayette Coll., 1981, Kansas City Art Inst., 1983, David Heath Gallery, Atlanta, 1990, Reynolds Gallery, Richmond, Va., 1993; group exhbns. include Met. Mus. Art, 1979-80, Denver Art Mus., 1979, Pa. Acad., 1981, Am. Acad. and Inst. of Arts and Letters, 1981, 84-85, Bklyn. Mus. 1984, Yale U., 1986, Tibor de Nagy Gallery, 1992, Whitney Mus., Stanford, Conn., 1995, 99; represented in permanent collections Met. Mus. Art, Hirschorn Mus., Bklyn. Mus., NYU, Rose Art Mus., Whitney Mus., Cleve. Mus. Art, San Francisco Mus. Art, others; travelling retrospective in Currier Gallery Art, Parrish Mus., Contemporary Arts Mus., McNay Mus., 1986-87; illustrator Turandot and Other Poems, 1953, Paris Review, 1965, Descriptions of a Masque, 1998. Recipient Eloise Spaeth award Guild Hall Mus., East Hampton, N.Y., 1991, Lifetime Achievement award Guild Hall Mus., 1996; AAUW fellow, 1974; Nat. Endowment Arts grantee, 1976; Benjamin West Clinedinst Meml. medal Artists' Fellowship, 1997. Mem. NAD (academician) (Saltus Gold medal 1987, Benjamin Altman landscape prize 1995), Am. Acad. Arts and Letters.

FREILICHER, MORTON, lawyer; b. N.Y.C., June 23, 1931; s. Morris and Gertrude D. (Pedowitz) F.; m. Yseult A. Snepvangers, Dec. 3, 1972. BA, Columbia Coll., N.Y.C., 1953, JD, 1956. Bar: N.Y. 1957. Assoc. Hartman & Craven, N.Y.C., 1956-60; assoc. Phillips, Nizer, Benjamin, Krim & Ballon, N.Y.C., 1960-67, ptnr., 1967-94; counsel Phillips, Nizer, Benjamin, Krim & Ballon LLP, N.Y.C., 1995—; adj. prof. Law Sch. Fordham U., N.Y.C., 1982-92. Author: Estate Planning Handbook, 1970; editor-in-chief Jour. of Estate and Tax Planning for the Elderly and Disabled, 1986-91. Chmn. trusts and estates lawyers divsn. UJA Fedn., 1985. Harlan Fiske Stone scholar Columbia Law Sch., 1956. Fellow Am. Coll. Trusts and Estates Counsel; mem. ABA, N.Y. State Bar Assn., N.Y.C. Bar Assn. Democrat. Jewish. Avocations: hiking, exercise, reading. Home: 45 W 54th St New York NY 10019-5404 Office: Phillips Nizer et al 666 5th Ave New York NY 10103-0001

FREILINGER, JAMES EDWARD, insurance and investments company executive; b. Ft. Thomas, Ky., Mar. 11, 1939; s. Otto Peter and Martha Jane (Hancock) F.; m. Mary Catherine Danoski, Aug. 15, 1969; children: Sarah Anne, Peter Joseph. BA in Philosophy, Ill. Benedictine Coll., 1962; BA in Theology, Cath. U. Am., 1966; MS in Fin. Svcs., Am. Coll., Bryn Mawr, Pa., 1989. CLU, ChFC. Owner, pres. James E. Freilinger & Co., Portland, Maine, 1969—. Bd. mem. Bd. Zoning Appeals, Cape Elizabeth, Maine, 1982-88; bd. dirs. Portland (Maine) Symphony Orch., 1988; bd. dirs., pres. Diocesan Bd. of Religious Edn., Portland, 1972-78; bd. dirs., officer The Waynflete Sch., Portland, 1981-90; mem. fin. com. Maine Coun. of Chs., 1993-97, mem. endowment com. 1993-96; pres. Maine Assn. Life Underwriters, 1983; mem. planned giving com. Maine Med. Ctr., 1996—. Recipient J. Putnam Stevens award Maine Assn. Life Underwriters, 1988. Fellow Life Underwriters Tng. Coun.; mem. Nat. Assn. Life Underwriters (chmn. nat. com. on edn. 1989-92), Am. Soc. CLU's and ChFC's, Maine Estate Planning Coun. (bd. dirs. 1990-98, pres. 1993-94), New Eng. CLU Conf. (bd. dirs. 1992—, pres. 1996-97), So. Maine Assn. Life Underwriters (bd. dirs. 1992-93, pres. 1973), Million Dollar Round Table, Order Ky. Cols. Roman Catholic. Avocations: golf, reading, private piloting. Office: 482 Congress St Ste 400 Portland ME 04101-3420

FREIMAN, DAVID GALLAND, pathologist, educator; b. N.Y.C., July 1, 1911; s. Leopold and Dorothy (Galland) F.; m. Ruth Schein, Sept. 2, 1949; children: Nancy, Leonard. AB, CCNY, 1930; MD, L.I. Coll. Medicine (now Downstate Med. Center SUNY), 1935; AM (hon), Harvard U., 1962. Intern, house physician Jewish Hosp. of Bklyn., 1935-36; intern Kingston Ave. Hosp. (for Contagious Disease), Bklyn., 1938; intern, resident pathology Montefiore Hosp., 1938-43; asst. pathologist Mass. Gen. Hosp., 1944-50; attending pathologist Cin. Gen. Hosp., Drake Meml. Hosp., 1952-56; pathologist-in-chief, dir. labs. Beth Israel Hosp., Boston, 1956-79, emeritus, 1979—, spl. asst. to pres., 1979—; cons. pathologist VA, Hosps., Cin., Ft. Thomas, Ky., 1954-56, Boston, 1962-85; instr. pathology Med. Sch. Tufts U., 1947-48; instr. pathology Harvard U. Med. Sch., 1949-50, clin. prof. pathology, 1956-62, prof., 1962-84, Mallinckrodt prof. pathology, 1969-79, emeritus, 1984—; prof. anatomy, interim chmn. dept. anatomy U. Mass. Coll. Medicine, 1985-87; asst. prof. pathology Coll. Medicine, U. Cin., 1950-52; assoc. prof. U. Cin. Coll. Medicine, 1952-56; lectr. pathology Simmons, 1962-78; cons. pathology Cambridge Hosp., 1968-85, Uniformed Services U. Health Scis., 1974-75, Children's Hosp. Med. Center, Boston, 1977-90; mem. joint faculty Harvard-MIT, 1975-79. Mem. editorial bd. Am. Jour. Pathology, 1961-82, Circulation, 1962-67, Human Pathology, 1969-93, assoc. editor, 1979-91; mem. editorial adv. com. Atlas of Tumor Pathology, 1966-87; contbr. articles to profl. jours. Recipient Stratford prize CCNY, 1931, Alumni prize L.I. Coll. Medicine, 1935; Kirstein fellow in med. edn. Harvard U., 1971-72. Mem. Am. Assn. Pathologists, Internat. Acad. Pathology, Histochem. Soc., Am. Soc. Clin. Pathologists, AAAS, Mass. Med. Soc., New Eng. Soc. Pathologists, Internat. Soc. for Haemostasis and Thrombosis, Phi Beta Kappa, Sigma Xi, Alpha Omega Alpha. Home: 182 Homer St Newton MA 02459-1518 Office: Beth Israel Deaconess Med Ctr 330 Brookline Ave Boston MA 02215-5400

FREIMARK, JEFFREY PHILIP, retail supermarket executive; b. Bklyn., Mar. 11, 1955; s. Benjamin and Fay (Lefton) F.; m. Hollis Joan Hauser, Aug. 27, 1978; children: Samara, Brandon. BS, U. So. Fla., 1976; MBA, NYU, 1980; JD, N.Y. Law Sch., 1984. Bar: N.J. 1985; CPA, N.J., Fla. Sr. staff acct. Abraham and Straus, Bklyn., 1976-78; internal audit dir. Stern's Dept. Store, Paramus, N.J., 1978-79; dir. acctg. Kings Super Markets, West Caldwell, N.J., 1979-82, controller, 1982-83, controller, sec., 1983-84, v.p. fin., 1985-86; sr. v.p. fin. and adminstrn., chief fin. officer, treas., dir. PXC & M Holdings Inc./Pueblo Xtra Internat. (formerly Pueblo Internat. Inc.), Pompano Beach, Fla., 1986-91, exec. v.p., chief fin. officer, sec., 1992-97; exec. v.p., CFO, sec. dir. Pueblo Xtra Internat., Inc., Pompano Beach, Fla., 1993-97, PXC&M, Inc., Pompano Beach, 1993-97; exec. v.p., CFO The Grand Union Co., 1997—. Vol. dir. NYU Grad. Sch. Bus. Mgmt. Decision Lab., 1980-81. Mem. ABA, N.J. Bar Assn., Am. Inst. CPA's, Fla. Soc. CPA's, N.J. Soc. CPA's, Assn. MBA Execs., Fin. Execs. Inst. Republican. Jewish. Avocations: reading, tennis, golf. Home: 26 E Greenbrook Rd N Caldwell NJ 07006-4320 Office: Grand Union Co 201 Willowbrook Blvd Fl 1 Wayne NJ 07470-7010

FREIMARK, ROBERT (BOB FREIMARK), artist; b. Doster, Mich., Jan. 27, 1922; s. Alvin O. and Nora (Shinaver) F.; m. Mary Carvin (dec.); 1 son, Matisse Jon; m. Lillian Tihlarik; 1 child, Christine Gay. B.E., U. Toledo, 1950; M.F.A., Cranbrook Acad. Art, 1951. Prof. art emeritus San Jose State U., 1964-86; W.I.C.H.E. prof. Soledad State Prison, 1967; established artist in residence program Yosemite Nat. Park,1984-85, Fire Clay and Tile, Aromas, Calif., 1998. Guest artist Harvard U., 1972-73; first Am. to make tapestries in Art Protis technique at Atelier Vlnena, Brno, Czechoslovakia.; contbr. to profl. publs.; Numerous solo shows including, Minn. Inst. Arts, Toledo Mus. Art, Salpeter Gallery, Morris Gallery, N.Y.C., Des Moines Art Center, Santa Barbara Mus., Moravska Mus., Czechoslovakia, Brunel U., London, Amerika Haus, Munich, Stuttgart, Regensburg, Joslyn Ctr. for Arts, Torrance, Calif, Stanford U., San Jose (Calif.) Mus. Art, Triton Mus., Santa Clara, Calif., Guatemalteco, Guatemala City, Dum Umeni Brno, CSFR, Strahov Closter, Prague, 1990, Walter Bischoff Gallery, Stuttgart, 1990, Kunstler aus den USA, Kunsthaus Ostbayern and Amerika Haus, Stuttgart, 1991, Max Planck Inst., Munich, The Gag Theatre, Prague, 1992, Haus Wiegand, Munich, 1993, San Jose State U., 1994, Viva!, Tokyo, 1994, Gallery Q, Sacramento, 1997, Parish Gallery, Wash. D.C., 1997, Barton Gallery, Sacramento, Calif., 1997; Galeria Galiano Havana, 1998, Galerie Weber, Viechtach, Germany, 1998, Point Gall., Brno, Czech Rep., 1998, Galerie Divadlo, Uherske Hradiste, C.R., 1998, exhibited in group shows, Art Inst. Chgo., 1952, Pa. Acad. Fine Arts, 1953 (Lambert Fund prize), Detroit Inst. Arts, 1956, Mich. State U., 1956, N.A.D., 1956, Boston Print Symposium, 1997, Internat. Print Exhibition Portland (Oreg.) Art Mus., 1997, Honolulu Acad. Art, 1998, Internat. Graphic Triennial, Krakow, Poland, 1998, Internat. Small Engraving Salon, Romania, 1999, Florean Mus. 1999, Internat. Woodprint Assn., Kyoto, Japan, 1999, Bklyn. Mus., Mus. Modern Art, Michael Stone Collection, D.C., Contempo Collection, Tokyo, others, L.A., Boston, San Francisco, Omaha, Oklahoma City, Des Moines, Dallas, Phoenix, San Jose, Havana, Tokyo, Manila, Rio de Janeiro, Mexico City, Sao Paulo, Brasilia, Buenos Aires, Prague, exhbn. 50 States toured, European Mus., 1970-71, represented in collections, Pa. Acad. Fine Art, Boston Mus. Fine Arts, Fogg Mus., Butler Inst. Am. Art, Ford Motor Co., South Bend Art Assn., Joslyn Art Mus., Seattle Art Mus., Ga. Mus., Huntington Gallery, Des Moines Art Center, Smithsonian Instn., Libr. Congress, L.A. County Art Inst., Brit. Mus., Nat. Gallery, Prague, Birmingham (Eng.) Mus., Moravske Mus., Brno, Czechoslovakia, Bibliotheque Nationale, Paris, Harn Mus., Gainsville, Fla., Portland Mus. Art (complete prints), Nat. Mus., Washington, Natl. Mus. of Cuba, La Habana, others; numerous tapestries in pub. and pvt. collections, created tapestry representing U.S. for Olympic Games, Moscow, 1980; produced film El Dia Tarasco, 1982; prodr. video documentary: Arte Cubano (Contemporary Art and Culture in Cuba, 1999; guest artist, Joslyn Meml. Mus., 1961, instr. painting and drawing, Ohio U., 1955-59, artist in residence, Des Moines Art Center, 1959-63, dir., Crystal Lake Art Center, Frankfort, Mich., (1955-57), guest lectr., one man show, Columbia U., 1963, cultural exchange exhibit, Northamerican Cultural Inst., Mexico City, 1963; guest artist, Riverside Art Center, 1964, Agora Vienna, Austria, 1994; curated exhibit Stuttgart, 1993; founder Bob & Lil Freimark Collection Portland Art Mus.; contbr. to craft and fibre publs. Served with USNR, 1939-46. Recipient 2d award for oil Northwest Territorial exhibit, 1954, Roulet medal Toledo Mus. Art, 1957, 1st award Print Exhbn., 1958, purchase award Midwest Biennial and Northwest Printmakers, Jurors award Berkeley Art Ctr, 1996; Calif. State Coll. Sys. spl. creative leave edit. serigraphs; elected to New Talent in U.S.A., 1957; Ohio U. rsch. grantee, 1958-59, Ford Found. grantee, 1965; Western Interstate Commn. for Higher Edn. grantee, 1967, San Jose State Coll. Found. grantee, 1966, 67, 68, 69, 70, 71, 85; designated ofcl. U.S. Bicentennial Exhbn. Amerika Hausen, Fed. Republic Germany, 1976; donated Bob & Lil Freimark Collection, Mexican Arts & Crafts, Gavilan Coll., Gilroy, Calif., 1996; represented by Parish Gallery, Washington, Triad Gallery, Seal Rock, Oreg., Yukiko Lunday Gallery, Houston, Haus Wiegand, Munich, Konfese, Brno, Czech Republic. Subject of TV interview, 1993. Home: 539A Dougherty Ave Morgan Hill CA 95037-9241 Office: Grass Valley Studios Morgan Hill CA 95037

FREIMAUER, JACQUELINE LINDA, secondary educator; b. N.Y.C., Sept. 13, 1946; d. Daniel and Rose (Oresky) Miller; m. Richard M. Freimauer, Dec. 13, 1969; children: Stacey M., Scott M. BA in English, Am. Internat. Coll., Springfield, Mass., 1968; MEd, Seton Hall U., South Orange, N.J., 1996. Cert. English tchr., N.J.; cert. supr., N.J. Tchr. English Rockland (Mass.) H.S., 1968-69; tchr. English and social studies Savannah (Ga.) Pub. Schs., 1969-71; tchr. English Rockaway Twp. (N.J.) Pub. Schs., 1971-72; tchr. English Roxbury Twp. Pub. Schs., Roxbury H.S., Succasunna, N.J., 1979—, tennis coach, 1987-90, newspaper advisor, 1991—. Author: Following Directions, 1980, Sequence Writing, 1980. Mem. ASCD, NEA, Nat. Coun. Tchrs. English. Avocations: tennis, net surfing, reading, golf. Home: 5 Copeland Rd Denville NJ 07834-9603 Office: Roxbury HS 1 Bryant Dr Succasunna NJ 07876-1632

FREIRE, ERNESTO, biophysicist, educator; b. Peru, July 28, 1949. BS, U. Herida, 1972, MS, 1973; PhD, U. Va., 1977. Postdoctoral rsch. assoc. U. Va., Charlottesville, 1977-78; asst. prof. biology and biophysics The Johns Hopkins U., Balt., 1986-87, assoc. prof. biology and biophysics, 1987-89, prof. biology and biophysics, 1989—; dir. Biocalorimetry Ctr. Johns Hopkins U., Balt., 1988—; lectr., speaker at nat. and internat. sci. symposiums, seminars, workshops and meetings, 1982—. Contbr. over 117 articles to profl. jours. including Biophys. Chemistry, Biochemistry, J. Mol. Biol., Proteins and Proceedings of U.S. Nat. Acad. Scis. Mem. AAAS, Am. Chemical Soc., Biophysical Soc., Protein Soc. Achievements include biomedical research on structure based molecular design using thermodynamic principles. Office: Johns Hopkins U Biocalroimetry Ctr Dept Bio 3400 N Charles St Baltimore MD 21218-2680

FREIRE, GLORIA MEDONIS, social worker; b. Pitts., Apr. 19, 1929; d. Vincent X. and Anastasia T. (Puida) Medonis; m. Luis Francis Freire, Aug. 30, 1958; children: Michael, Charles. BA in Polit. Sci. & Econs., Carlow Coll., 1950; MSSA, Case-Western Res. U., 1955; MPA, Cleve. State U., 1986; PhD, Union Inst., 1995. Teen-age dir. Merrick House, Cleve., 1955-62; group psychotherapist Cleve. Psychiat. Inst., 1966-73; lectr. sch. applied social scis. Case-Western Res. U., Cleve., 1973-75; cluster dir. Golden Age Ctrs., Cleve., 1975-76; specialist Cmty. Guidance & Human Svcs., Cleve., 1976, staff tng. & devel. coord., 1977, dir. consultation & edn., 1978-84; coord. psychiat. emergency svcs. systems Lake County Mental Health Bd., Ohio, 1984-86; adminstr. Hispanic office Cath. Social Svcs., Cleve., 1986-97; asst. prof. social work Cleve. State U., 1997—. Editor SASS mag., Case Western Res. U. Alumni, 1973-79. Chmn. steering com. East Cmty. Task Force on Desegregation; chmn. subcoun. of Ohio Cmty. Mental Health Ctrs. Consultations & Edn.; chmn. consultation & Edn. Coun. Cleve.; coord. Christian Formation cmty. of St. Malachi, 1975-77, coord. liturgy commn., 1978-80, coord. social concerns com., 1982-84; mem. Diocesan Commn. on Cath. Cmty. Action, 1982-88, vice chmn., 1986-87; mem. Urban League Edn. Adv. and Task Force on Minium Competency, 1978-80. Recipient Disting. Leadership award Alumnae Assn. Carlow Coll., 1982. Mem. AAUW, NASW (task force on desegregation 1974-83, co-chmn. 1981-83, coord. polit. action com. 1977, dir. Cleve. chpt., 1975-77, sec.-treas. Ohio coun. chpts., 1975-76, steering com. Clevel chpt. 1987-89), Acad. Cert. Social workers, Am. Soc. Pub. Adminstrn. (trustee Cleve. chpt. 1987-92, 98—), Am. soc. Profl. & Exec. Women, Nat. and Cuyahoga County Women's Polit. Caucus (exec. bd.), Am. Group Psychotherapy Assn., Am. Planning Assn., Coun. Social Work Edn., Union Inst. Learner Coun. ADvocacy and Adv. Task Force (alt. chmn. 1991-92), Tri-State Group Psychotherapy Soc., Nat. Image Hispanic Profls. (trustee 1991-92, pres. N.E. Ohio chpt. 1992-94), Julia Burgos Ctr. (bd. dirs. 1998—), Japan Soc. Cleve. (bd. dirs. 1996-98, exec. com. 1997-98), Japanese Am. Citizens League, Esperanza/Hispanic Edn. (mem. adv. bd. 1998-99, exec. bd. 1999—). Democrat. Roman Catholic. Home: 5001 Tuxedo Ave Cleveland OH 44134-1007 Office: Dept Social Work Cleve State U Euclid Ave at E 24th St Cleveland OH 44115

FREIREICH, EMIL J, hematologist, educator; b. Chgo., Mar. 16, 1927; s. David and Mary (Klein) F.; m. Haroldine Lee Cunningham, Mar. 13, 1953; children: Debra Ann, David Alan, Lindsay Gail, Thomas Jon. B.S., U. Ill., 1947, M.D. with honors, 1949, D.Sc. (hon.), 1982. Diplomate Am. Bd. Internal Medicine. Intern Cook County (Ill.) Hosp., Chgo., 1949-50; resident in internal medicine Presbyn. Hosp., Chgo., 1950-53; research asso. in hematology Mass. Meml. Hosp., Boston, 1953-55; sr. investigator, head Leukemia Service USPHS, Nat. Cancer Inst., Bethesda, Md., 1955-65; prof. medicine U. Tex. System Cancer Ctr., Houston, 1965—; chief research in hematology U. Tex. System Cancer Ctr., 1965-85, head dept. devel. therapeutics, 1972-83, chmn. dept. hematology, 1983-85, dir. Adult Leukemia Rsch. Program, 1985—; prof. medicine U. Tex. Health Sci. Ctr. (Sch. Medicine), 1973—, chief div. oncology, 1973-81; mem. faculty Grad. Sch. Med., Health Scis. Ctr., 1965—; mem. rev. com. drug. devel. div. cancer treatment NIH, 1975-80, Ruth Harriet Ainsworth chair in devel. therapeutics, 1980—. Assoc. editor Cancer, 1976—, Cancer Research, 1977-86; mem. editorial bd. Oncology News, 1975-90, Cancer Treatment Reports, 1976-80, Leukemia Research, 1976-87, Med. and Pediatric Oncology, 1974—, Leukemia 1987—; contbr. numerous articles on research in hematology and oncology to profl. jours. Recipient Albert Lasker Med. rsch. award, 1972, Charles F. Kettering prize Gen. Motors Cancer Rsch. Found., 1983, Outstanding Investigator award Nat. Cancer Inst., NIH, 1985-92, Alumnus award NIH, 1990; named Alumnus of Yr., U. Ill. Alumni Assn., 1974. Fellow ACP, AAAS; mem. Internat. Soc. Hematology, Am.

Soc. Hematology, Am. Fedn. Clin. Research, Am. Soc. Clin. Pharmacology and Therapeutics, Am. Soc. Clin. Oncology (David A. Karnofsky award 1976, pres. 1980-81), Am. Soc. Clin. Investigators, Am. Assn. Cancer Research, Leukemia Soc. Am. (pres. Gulf Coast chpt. 1968-70, trustee 1968-70, Robert Roesler DeVilliers award 1979, grant rev. subcom. 1986-89), Tex. Med. Assn., AMA (editorial bd. jour. 1973-83), Assn. Am. Physicians, Alpha Omega Alpha. Research in therapy of human acute leukemia and leukocyte physiology. Home: 810 Monte Cello St Houston TX 77024-4515 Office: M D Anderson Cancer Ctr 1515 Holcombe Blvd Houston TX 77030-4009 *The search for eternal physical and mental health has been at the forefront of man's striving to understand and to control his destiny. The opportunity to investigate, to discover and to apply new remedies for major human illness is a rare privilege, one of man's highest callings.*

FREISE, EARL JEROME, univeristy administrator, materials engineering educator; b. Chgo., Dec. 30, 1935; s. Otto H. and Mary A. (Hoffman) F.; m. Lenore A. Serpico, Dec. 27, 1958; children: Christopher E., Timothy P., Nora A., Lawrence M. BSMetE, Ill. Inst. Tech., 1958; MS in Materials Sci., Northwestern U., 1959; PhD in Metallurgy, U. Cambridge, Eng., 1962. From asst. to assoc. prof. Northwestern U., Evanston, Ill., 1962-77; dir. rsch. office, prof. mech. engring. U. N.D., Grand Forks, 1977-82; asst. vice chancellor rsch., prof. mech. engring. U. Nebr., Lincoln, 1982-87; dir. rsch. office Inst. Material Sci., Calif. Inst. Tech., Pasadena, 1987-96, asst. v.p. adminstrv. process engring., 1996—. Contbr. articles to profl. jours. Recipient award for Excellence in Engring. Edn., Western Elec. Co., 1971; Fulbright fellow, 1959-61. Mem. AIME, Am. Soc. Metals (v.p., pres. Chgo. chpt. 1971-72), Am. Soc. Engring. Edn. (sec.-treas. Ill.-Ind. sect. 1963-64, 73-74), Assn. Univ. Tech. Mgrs., Nat. Coun. Univ. Rsch. Adminstrs. (pres. 1984-85). Office: Calif Inst Tech MC1-10 1200 E California Blvd Pasadena CA 91106

FREITAG, CAROL WILMA, state official; b. Ada, Okla., July 21, 1939; d. Lowell William and Lois Marie (Robertson) Petersen; m. Henry Wesley Freitag, Dec. 20, 1961 (dec. Nov. 1985); children: Bonita Louise, Henry Lowell. Diploma in Dental Hygiene, Northwestern U., 1959; BA, Purdue U., Hammond, Ind., 1988. Registered dental hygienist, Ill. Pvt. practice dental hygiene Henry W. Freitag, D.D.S., Homewood, Ill., 1959-85; faculty, interim dir. dental hygiene Prairie State Coll., Chicago Heights, Ill., 1971-72; pvt. practice James J. Kreuz, D.D.S., Homewood, 1985-90; contbr. articles to profl. jours. Chair U.S. Constn. Bicentennial Commn., Village of Matteson, Ill., 1986-89; pres. Matteson Hist. Soc., 1987-89; panel spkr. South Suburban Heritage Assn., Homewood, 1990. Calumet rep. Bicentennial Com. Purdue U., 1998; vis. com. Northwestern Dental Sch., 1997-98. Recipient Key to City, Village of Matteson, 1990, Svc. award Northwestern U., 1980, Good Neighbor award Village of Matteson, 1989. Mem. Am. Dental Hygienists' Assn. (chairperson Ann. Session Program 1975), Ill. Dental Hygienists Assn. (pres. 1968-69, bd. dirs., Merit award 1979), G.V. Black Soc. (leader, pres. 1997—), Evelyn E. Maas Soc. (pres. 1989-90, bd. dirs., Merit award 1993), Northwestern Dental Sch. Alumni Assn. (bd. dirs., pres. 1977-78, v.p. 1976-77, 90-93), Sigma Phi Alpha (mem. dental hygiene soc.), Alpha Chi (scholarship soc.). Avocation: travel. Home: 7926 Belle Rive Ct Tinley Park IL 60477-4583

FREITAG, DONNA, head women's basketball coach. BA, U. Iowa, 1983. Player/coach Team Trivoli, Dublin; asst. coach U. Wis., Platteville; recruiting coord. Bradley U., Peoria, Ill., asst. coach women's basketball, head coach women's basketball, 1996—. Office: Bradley Univ Women's Athletics Dept 1501 W Bradley Ave Peoria IL 61625-0002*

FREITAG, FREDERICK GERALD, osteopathic physician; b. Milw., Feb. 12, 1952; s. Frederick August and Shirley June (Siewert) F.; m. Lynn Nadene Stegner, Sept. 10, 1977; children: Crescentia Adella, Abigail Amadea, Genevieve Angelica. BS in Biochemistry, U. Wis., 1974; DO, Chgo. Coll. Osteo. Medicine, 1979. Intern Brentwood Hosp., Warrensville Heights, Ohio, 1979-80, resident in family practice, 1980-81; dir., physician Twinsburg (Ohio) Family Clinic, 1981-83; assoc. prof. family medicine Coll. Osteo. Medicine, Ohio U., Warrensville Heights, 1982-83; staff Diamond Headache Clinic, Chgo., 1983-86, assoc. dir., 1986—; attending staff mem. Louis A. Weiss Meml. Hosp., Chgo., 1983-93; attending staff Columbus Hosp., 1993—; mem. Janssen Rsch. Coun.; sec. Diamond Headache Rsch. and Edn. Found.; vis. lectr. dept. family medicine Chgo. Coll. Osteo. Medicine, 1985—; clin. assoc. dept. medicine Pritzker Sch. Medicine U. Chgo., 1989-93; mem. editl. bd. Headache Quar., 1991—; chmn. instnl. rev. bd. Louis A. Weiss Meml. Hosp., 1991-93; mem. Evidence Based Headache Outcomes Rsch. Group; mem. migraine adv. coun. Abbott, 1995—, mem. primary care adv. coun., 1997—; mem. adv. group Glaxo Wellcome, 1996—; mem. migraine adv. coun. Zeneca, 1996—; Am. Osteo. Assn. rep. to Nat. Consortium on Stds. of Care of Migraine, 1998—; mem. Nat. Consortium for Stds. of Care for Migraine, 1998—. Coord. editor Headache Quar.; contbr. articles to profl. jours., chpts. to books. Bd. dirs. Nat. Headache Found., liaison standards of care com. to Am. Acad. Neurology. Fellow Am. Assn. for Study of Headache; mem. AMA, Am. Coll. Gen. Practioners in Osteo. Medicine, Am. Osteo. Assn., Am. Soc. Clin. Pharmacology and Therapeutics (vice chmn. headache sect. 1995-96), Ill. Assn. Osteo. Physicians and Surgeons, Ill. Med. Soc., Internat. Assn. Study Pain, Am. Pain Soc., Nat. Headache Found., Chgo. Med. Soc. (speakers bur.), German Wine Soc. (past pres. Chgo. chpt.), U. Wis. Alumni Assn. Lutheran. Avocations: German oenophile, gardening, model railroading, home carpentry. Home: 931 Clinton Pl River Forest IL 60305-1503 Office: The Diamond Headache Clinic 467 W Deming Pl Ste 500 Chicago IL 60614-1726

FREITAG, HARLOW, retired computer scientist and corporate executive; b. Bklyn., Apr. 17, 1936; s. Abraham and Eva (Levine) F.; 1 son, Adam. B.S. with honors, NYU, 1955; M.S., Yale U., 1958, Ph.D., 1959. Research staff mem. IBM, Yorktown Heights, N.Y., 1961-70, asst. dir. computer sci., 1970-77; asst. dir. computer sci. IBM, White Plains, N.Y., 1977-80; staff v.p., group exec. IBM, White Plains, NY, 1980-82; editor Jour. Rsch. and Devel. IBM, White Plains, N.Y., 1982-83; dep. dir. Supercomputing Rsch. Ctr., Bowie, Md., 1986-91; tech. staff Inst. for Def. Analysis, Alexandria, Va., 1991-94; ret., 1994. Recipient Outstanding Innovation award IBM, 1966; recipient Francis Mills Turner award Electrochem. Soc., 1959. Fellow IEEE (editor procs. of IEEE 1979-82, Centennial medal 1984), Yale Sci. and Engring. Assn. (exec. v.p. 1981-83, pres. 1983-85).

FREITAG, WOLFGANG MARTIN, librarian, educator; b. Berlin, Germany, Oct. 27, 1924; came to U.S., 1955, naturalized, 1961; s. Georg and Anne Marie (Friess) F.; m. Doris Christiane Pfeil, Oct. 25, 1952; children—Thomas Martin, Tilman George. Dr. Phil., U. Freiburg, W. Ger., 1950; postgrad., Harvard U., 1951-52; M.S. in Library Sci., Simmons Coll., Boston, 1956. Reference libr., program dir. U.S. Info. Ctr., Frankfurt, Germany, 1950-53; editor Droemer-Knaur Publ., Munich, 1953-55; cataloger Harvard Coll. Library, Cambridge, Mass., 1955-60; head librarian Gordon McKay Library, Harvard U., 1960-62; chief undergrad. library planning Stanford U., Calif., 1962-64; librarian Fine Arts Library Fogg Art Mus., Harvard U., 1964-91, lectr. bibliography and art historiography, 1967-75, sr. lectr., 1975-91; lectr. libr. sci. Simmons Coll., Boston, Mass., 1991-92; libr. cons. J.P. Getty Trust, L.A., 1982-83, U. Pitts, 1983, The Frick Collection, N.Y. 1984, Inst. Fine Arts, NYU, 1987; mem. vis. com. Met. Mus. Art, 1972-92; bd. vis. Sch. Info. Studies, Syracuse U., 1981-85, SUNY, Stony Brook, 1986, NYU Inst. Fine Arts, 1987. Editor: Artist Resource Manuals, Art Books: Monographs on Artists, 1985, 2d edit., 1997; cons. to pubs.; contbr. articles to profl. jours. Fulbright fellow, 1951, 68, Council Library Resources fellow, 1975. Mem. Art Libraries Soc. N.Am. (pres. 1980), Coll. Art Assn., Internat. Fedn. Library Assns. (exec. com. art librs. sect. 1985-93), Goethe Soc. New Eng. Avocation: autograph collecting. Home: 43 Fair Oaks Dr Lexington MA 02421-6931

FREITAS, ANTOINETTE JUNI, insurance company executive; b. Kansas City, Mo., Feb. 14, 1944; d. Anthony P. and Mariam L. Freitas; BA, Calif. State U.-Long Beach, 1966; MA, U. So. Calif., 1974; m. Stephen R. Krajcar, July 4, 1980. Chartered life underwriter, chartered fin. cons. Counselor, U. So. Calif., 1967-70, assoc. dir. fin. aid, 1970-75; sales agt. Equitable Life Assurance Co., 1975-79, dist. mgr., San Francisco, 1979-84; pres. Group Mktg. Services, Inc., field dir. Northwestern Mut. Life, San Francisco, 1984-86; pres. Peninsula Fin. Group, Inc., 1986—; mktg. mgr. Home Life, H.L. Fin. Group, San Jose, Calif., 1986—; registered rep. Carrilon, Investments, Securities, 1987-91; pres. Peninsula Fin. Group, Inc., 1991. Bd. dirs. San Francisco 300, 1996—. Recipient various sales and mgmt. awards; mem. Million Dollar Round Table. Mem. Nat. Assn. Life Underwriters, AAUW, U. So. Calif. Alumni Assn., Women Life Underwriters Conf. Republican. Episcopalian. Author: A Study in Changing Youth Values, 1974. Office: Peninsula Fin Group Inc 2995 Woodside Rd Ste 400 Woodside CA 94062-2446

FREITAS, DAVID PRINCE, lawyer; b. San Francisco, Oct. 21, 1940; s. Walter Francis and Marno Catherine (Prince) F.; m. Alice Urrutia, June 24, 1961 (div. 1972); children: Diane Phillips, Nancy Freitas, Megan Neale; m. Patricia Garbarino, June 20, 1996. BS, U. San Franciso, 1964; JD, San Francisco Law Sch., 1968. Bar: Calif. 1969. Atty. Freitas Law Firm, San Rafael, Calif., 1969-96, Ragghianti, Freitas, Montobbio & Wallace LLP, San Rafael, 1996—; bd. dirs. St. Vincent's Sch.; lectr. in field; judge pro tempore San Francisco and Marin Counties; spl. master Superior Cts. of Marin and Sonoma. Contbr. articles to profl. jours. Bd. dirs. Guide Dogs for the Blind, San Rafal, 1994-95, Marin Agrl. Land Trust, 1991-92, Marin County Humane Soc., 1967-71. Fellow Am. Coll. Trial Lawyers, Internat. Acad. Trial Lawyers, Internat. Soc. Barristers; mem. Internat. Assn. Def. Counsel, Am. Bd. Trial Adv. (San Francisco chpt., pres. 1993, nat. bd. dirs. 1992—, exec. com. 1990—), Nat. Bd. Trial Adv. (diplomate), Assn. Def. Counsel N.C. (pres. 1985, bd. dirs. 1977-86), Calif. State Bar Assn. (adminstrn. justice com. 1982, jury instrns. com. 1977), Calif. Def. Counsel (bd. dirs. 1984), Marin County Bar Assn. (secr. 1987, treas. 1984), Def. Rsch. Inst. (Nat. Execptional Performance award 1985), Cal-ABOTA (bd. chair 1995), Edward J. McFetridge Am. Inn Ct. (pres. 1993, exec. com. 1990—), San Rafal C. of C. (bd. dirs. 1995—). Home: 90 Convent Ct San Rafael CA 94901-1334 Office: Ragghianti Freitas Montobbio Wallace LLP 874 4th St San Rafael CA 94901-3246

FREITAS, ELIZABETH FRANCES, lawyer; b. N.Y.C., Aug. 19, 1963; d. Joao A. and Alva Marie (Alvarez) F. BA cum laude, Cath. U. Am., 1985; BBA cum laude, CUNY-Baruch Coll., 1994; JD, Bklyn. Law Sch., 1993. Bar: N.J. 1993, N.Y. 1994, D.C. 1995. Intern U.S. Internat. Trade Com., Washington, 1985-86; archivist asst. Nat. Leadership Coun./GOPAC, Washington, 1985; telephone mgr. Citizen Action, Washington, 1986-87; telemarketer Decision Ctr., N.Y.C., 1988; intern Lawyers Com. for Human Rights, N.Y.C., 1992-93; pvt. practice Advocacy Inc., N.Y.C., 1994—; part-time atty. Americana Agy., N.Y.C., 1995-96; chair film com. L.I. U., 1981-82. Editor: (lit. mag.) New Leaf, 1980. Mem. Get Out the Vote com. Citizen Action, Washington, 1986-87. Recipient Bausch and Lomb Sci. award, 1981; Phillips fellow L.I. U., 1981-82. Mem. ABA, ACLU, N.Y. Bar Assn., Amnesty Internat., Pi Gamma Mu, Beta Gamma Sigma, Golden Key Nat. Honor Soc. Democrat. Catholic. Home and Office: 969A Argyll Cir Lakewood NJ 08701-6806

FREIWALD, DAVID ALLEN, physicist, mechanical engineer; b. Cleve., June 4, 1941; s. Harry Herman and Arline Mildred (Woehrman) F.; m. Karen Lee Eaton, Aug., 1960 (div. 1976); children: Wesley, Todd, Christopher; m. Joyce Darlyne Gross, Apr. 3, 1976. BSME, Northwestern U., 1963, PhD, 1968. Rsch. scientist Sandia Nat. Labs., Albuquerque, 1967-72; scientist, staff dir.'s office Los Alamos (N.Mex.) Nat. Lab., 1972-81; program mgr. SEA, Inc., McLean, Va., 1981-82, MRJ, Inc., Oakton, Va., 1982-85; dir., gen. mgr. Gen. Dynamics, San Diego, 1985-90; v.p.. F2 Assocs., San Diego, 1991-92, Albuquerque, 1992—; adv. bd. USAF, Washington, 1985; team leader 20-Yr. Look Ahead Study Gen. Dynamics, St. Louis, 1986-87; SMES adv. bd. Bechtel, Inc., San Francisco, 1986-87. Active N.Mex. Gov.'s Land Use Legislation Com., Santa Fe, 1971, Energy Task Force, 1973-74; pres. Whispering Ridge Homeowners Assn., 1988. Mem. Am. Def. Preparedness Assn., Marine Corps Assn., N.Mex. Acad. Sci. (pres. 1981), Tau Beta Pi, Pi Tau Sigma, Sigma Xi. Republican. Methodist. Achievements include patents pending for magnetically protected laser fusion cavity, burst laser communication mode for satellite-submarines, explosive driven shock tubes for top-atmosphere weapon effects simulation, numerous patent applications for robotic laser-based industrial decoating systems. Home: 1708 Soplo Rd SE Albuquerque NM 87123-4485 Office: 14800 Central Ave SE Albuquerque NM 87123-3905

FREIZER, LOUIS A., radio news producer; b. N.Y.C., Oct. 10, 1931; s. Morris and Celia (Lassersohn) F.; m. Michèle Suzanne Orban, July 6, 1968; children: Sabine, Eric. BS, U. Wis., 1953; postgrad., U. Heidelberg, Germany, 1956; MA, Columbia U., 1964, postgrad., 1966—. Corr. UPI, Madison, Wis., 1953-54; desk asst. CBS News, N.Y.C., 1956-59, newswriter, 1959-60; newswriter Sta. WCBS, N.Y.C., 1960-62, news editor, 1963-68, sr. news prodr., 1968-73, sr. exec. news prodr., 1973—; adj. prof. comm. Fordham U.; lectr., cons. journalism and internat. rels. Prodr.: (pub. affairs series) Let's Find Out, 1966, International Briefing series, 1968-72. Served to 1st lt. U.S. Army, 1954-56; capt. USAR. Recipient Am. Legion medal; Radio Journalism award AMA, Radio Journalism award Nat. Headliners Club, Radio Journalism Nat. award for Outstanding Newscast UPI, 1st place award for Best Regularly Scheduled Local News Program N.Y. State AP Broadcasters Assn., spl. mention for Best One Day News Effort N.Y. State AP Broadcasters Assn., Bene Merenti medal Fordham U.; winner German Study Program for U.S. Journalists sponsored by KIAS Berlin Commn. and the Radio and TV News Dirs. Found.; fellow CBS News Found. Mem. Am. Polit. Sci. Assn., Acad. Polit. Sci., Am. Acad. Polit. and Social Scis., Radio-TV News Dirs. Assn., Broadcast Pioneers, Sigma Delta Chi. Home: 1619 3rd Ave New York NY 10128-3459 Office: Sta WCBS 51 W 52nd St New York NY 10019-6119

FRELICK, ROBERT WESTCOTT, physician; b. Potsdam, N.Y., Feb. 27, 1920; s. H. Victor and Ruth (Scott) F.; m. Jane Hayden, Jan. 22, 1944; children: Susan, Alcy, Sally, William, Scott. AB, Union Coll., 1941; MD, Yale, 1944. Diplomate Am. Bd. Internal Medicine, Am. Bd. Medical Onocology, Am. Bd. Nuclear Medicine. Intern New Haven Hosp., 1944-45; resident Meml. Hosp., Wilmington, Del., 1947-49, Meml. Hosp. Ctr., N.Y.C., 1949-50; pvt. practice Wilmington, Del., 1950-82; program dir. Nat. Cancer Inst., Bethesda, Md., 1982-87; cons. Del. Divsn. Pub. Health, Wilmington, 1987-96; med. dir. South Jersey Cancer Ctr., 1995-97, cons., 1998—; chief medicine Wilmington Med. Ctr., Del., 1965-72. Contbr. to profl. jours. Bd. overseers, CARE, N.Y.C. then Atlanta, 1980-97; pres. Assn. Cmty. Cancer Ctrs., Rockville, Md., 1979-80. Capt. (Med. Svc. Corps.) U.S. Army, 1944-47. Recipient Disting. Svc. award Del. Med. Soc., 1977, Outstanding Svc. to Cmty. award Assn. Cmty. Cancer Ctrs., 1987, St. George's medal Am. Cancer Soc., 1990. Fellow ACP (laureate, gov.); mem. AMA, ACS (surveyor hosp. cancer programs 1988-97), Med. Soc. Del. (chair com. ethics, pres. 1980-81), Soc. Surg. Oncology, Am. Soc. Internal Medicine, Am. Soc. Clin. Oncology, Am. Pub. Health Assn., Am. Sch. Health Assns. Home: 1018 Overbrook Rd Wilmington DE 19807-2236

FRELINGHUYSEN, RODNEY P., congressman; b. Apr. 29, 1946; m. Virginia Frelinghuysen; children: Louisine, Sarah. State and fed. aid coord., adminstrv. asst. Morris County, 1972; mem. Morris County Bd. of Chosen Freeholders, 1974-83, dir., 1980, mem. welfare and mental health bds., human svcs. and pvt. industry couns., mem. freeholder fin. com.; mem. N.J. Gen. Assembly, 1983-94, chmn. assembly appropriations com., 1988-89, 92-94; mem. 104th-106th Congresses from 11th N.J. Dist., 1995—. With 93d Engr. Bn. U.S. Army, 1969-71, Vietnam. Named Legis. of Yr. N.J. Assn. of Mental Health Agencies, Legis. of Yr. N.J. Assn. of Retarded Citizens. Mem. Am. Legion, VFW (Legis. of Yr.). Office: US House Reps 228 Cannon Bldg Ofc Bldg Washington DC 20515-3011*

FREMON, DAVID KENT, writer, consultant; b. Chgo., Feb. 17, 1949; s. William Joe and Irene (McGoldrick) F.; m. Sonja Yap Pacana, June 24, 1988; 1 child, Kent Joseph; children from previous marriage: Palomila, Karl, Tommy. BA, Lawrence U., 1970. Ind. writer, 1986—; cons. Chgo. Bd. Edn., 1991-92. Author: Chicago Politics Ward by Ward, 1988, The Trail of Tears, 1994, The Negro Baseball Leagues, 1994, Running Away, 1996, Japanese-American Internment in American History, 1996, The Great Depression in American History, 1997, The Watergate Scandal in American History, 1998, The Holocaust Heroes, 1998, The Salem Witchcraft Trials in American History, 1999; author media sect.: Restoration '89, 1991. Recipient Hispanic Journalism award Cermak Rd. C. of C., 1990, Investigative Journalism award Chgo. Electric Options Campaign, 1991, Spur award Western Writers Am., 1995, N.Y. Pub. Libr. Books for the Teenager award, 1977, Voya, Best Young Adult Books award, 1997; named best local polit. columnist New City Poll, 1993. Mem. St. Louis Browns Fan Club, Merrie Gangsters Lit. Soc. Mem. United Ch. of Christ. Home: 4451 N Rockwell St Chicago IL 60625-3018

FREMON, RICHARD C., retired infosystems specialist; b. St. Louis, May 28, 1918; s. Richard Horatio and Hazel Pauline (Rhea) F.; m. Virginia Isabelle Moore, Sept. 7, 1940; children: Carolyn E. Fremon Maycher, Richard L., James N., Nancy I. Brown. AB, Columbia U., 1939; BEE, 1940, MEE, 1944. With personnel Bell Telephones, N.Y.C., 1941-54, dir. salary adminstrn., Murray Hill, N.J., 1954-73, dir. adminstrv. systems, 1973-81; dir. computer ctr. Centenary Coll., Hackettstown, N.J., 1981-89. Contbr. chpt. to book. Trustee Sea Cliff Sch. Bd., N.Y., 1950-52; past chmn. Engring. Manpower Commn., N.Y.C., 1965. Mem. Inst. Indsl. Engrs. (sr.), Panther Valley Club. Democrat. Presbyterian. Home: 32 Barn Owl Dr Hackettstown NJ 07840-3205

FREMONT-SMITH, MARION R., lawyer; b. Boston, Oct. 29, 1926; d. Max and Frances (Davis) Ritvo; m. Joseph Miller, Sept. 12, 1948 (div.); m. 2d, Paul Fremont-Smith, July 6, 1961; children by previous marriage: Beth Miller Johnsey, Keith Lane Miller, E. Bradley Miller. BA with high honors, Wellesley (Mass.) Coll., 1948; LLB cum laude, Boston U., 1951. Bar: Mass. 1951, U.S. Supreme Ct. 1979. Instr. dept. polit. sci. Wellesley Coll., 1958-59; asst. atty. gen. Commonwealth Mass., Boston, 1961-62; project dir. Russell Sage Found., Boston, 1963-65; assoc. Choate, Hall & Stewart, Boston, 1964-71, ptnr., 1971-96, sr. counsel 1997—; sr. rsch. fellow Hauses Ctr. for Nonprofit Orgns., Harvard U., 1998—; dir. Fed. Tax Inst. New Eng., Mount Auburn Cemetery, Aid to Artisans; former dir. Ind. Sector, Washington. Hon. trustee Carnegie Endowment for Internat. Peace, Washington; trustee Mass. Environ. Trust. Fellow Am. Acad. Arts and Scis., Am. Bar Found., Am. Coll. Trust and Estate Counsel, Am. Coll. Tax Counsel, Internat. Acad. Estate and Trust Law; mem. ABA (former chmn. com. on exempt orgns. tax sect.), Am. Law Inst. Author: Foundations and Government: State and Federal Law and Supervision, 1965, Philanthropy and the Business Corporation, 1972; contbr. articles to profl. jours. Office: Exchange Pl 53 State St Boston MA 02109-2804*

FREMONT-SMITH, THAYER, judge; b. Boston, June 17, 1931; s. Mary (Dixon) Thayer; m. Anne Jeffery, 1960; children: Matthew, James, Thomas, Phillip. AB, Harvard U., 1953, JD, 1960. Bar: N.H. 1960, U.S. Dist. Ct. N.H. 1961, Mass. 1963, U.S. Dist. Ct. Mass. 1964,U.S. Supreme Ct. 1965. Assoc. Goodnow, Arwe & Ayer, Keene, N.H., 1960-63; city solicitor , Keene, N.H., 1961-63; assoc. Choate, Hall & Stewart, Boston, 1963-69, ptnr., 1969-93; assoc. justice Superior Ct. Mass., 1993—. Mem. Melrose (Mass.) Planning Bd., 1985-89; bd. dirs. Melrose YMCA, 1985-89. With U.S. Army, 1953-55. Republican. Roman Catholic.

FREMOUW, EDWARD JOSEPH, physicist; b. Northfield, Minn., Feb. 23, 1934; s. Fred J. and Marion Elizabeth (Drozda) F.; m. Rita Lorraine Johnson, June 26, 1960; children: Thane Edrik, Sean Fredrik; 2nd marriage: Marilyn Call Allred, Feb. 15, 1998. BSEE, Stanford U., 1957; MS in Physics, U. Alaska, 1963, PhD in Geophysics, 1966. Asst. prof. geophysics U. Alaska, Fairbanks, 1966-67; physicist Stanford Research Inst., Menlo Park, Calif., 1967-70, sr. physicist, 1970-75; program mgr. SRI Internat., Menlo Park, 1975-77; v.p. Phys. Dynamics, Inc., Bellevue, Wash., 1977-86; pres. Northwest Research Assocs., Inc., Bellevue, Wash., 1986—, also bd. dirs.; cons. Geophys. Inst., College, 1967-68; assoc. La Jolla (Calif.) Inst., 1981-89. Contbr. articles to profl. jours. Trustee East Shore Unitarian Ch., 1984-86; co-chair adv. com. on econ. diversification Wash. State, 1991-96; bd. dirs., pres. Banchero Friends Svc., Inc., 1994-95. Geographic feature Fremouw Peak named in his honor, 1968. Mem. IEEE, Am. Geophys. Union (Excellence in Refereeing award 1984, 89), Union Radio Sci. Internat., Stanford Club of Western Wash. (trustee 1984-86). Democrat. Unitarian Universalist. Avocations: hiking, skiing. Home: 2873 W Lk Sammamish Pkwy NE Redmond WA 98052-5913 Office: Northwest Rsch Assocs Inc PO Box 3027 Bellevue WA 98009-3027*

FREMUND, ZDENEK ANTHONY, manufacturing company executive; b. Prague, Czechoslovakia, Oct. 6, 1946; came to U.S., 1969; s. Karl and Francis (Davidek) F.; div.; children: Brian David, Michelle Jean. Elec. Engring. degree, Czech Inst. Tech., 1969; BSME, Newark Coll. Engring., 1976. Profl. engr., N.J. Design engr. Computer Tech. Corp., Prague, 1965-68; machinist R.G. Laurence Co., Inc., Tenafly, N.Y., 1969-71, designer, 1971-74, prodn. mgr., 1974-79, v.p. mfg., chief engr., 1979-81; v.p. ops. Kleiner Metal Specialties, Inc., South Plainfield, N.J., 1981-86, pres., 1986-89; pres. & CEO Sava Industries, Inc., Riverdale, N.J., 1989—; ptnr. Jordan Mfg. LLC, Lafayette, N.J., 1995—, DécorCable Innovations, LLC, Chgo., 1996—. Mem. ASME, Wire Assn. Internat. Republican. Roman Catholic. Avocation: racquetball. Home: 24 Shadow Ridge Rd Wayne NJ 07470-4967 Office: Sava Industries Inc PO Box 30 4 N Corporate Dr Riverdale NJ 07457

FRENCH, ANTHONY PHILIP, physicist, educator; b. Brighton, Eng., Nov. 19, 1920; came to U.S., 1955; s. Sydney James and Elizabeth Margaret (Hart) F.; m. Naomi Mary Livesay, Oct. 6, 1945; children: Martin Charles, Gillian Ruth. BA with honors, Cambridge (Eng.) U., 1942, MA, 1946, PhD, 1948; ScD (hon.), Allegheny Coll., 1989. Mem. atomic bomb projects Tube Alloys and Manhattan Project, 1942-46; demonstrator, lectr. physics Cambridge U., 1948-55; fellow Pembroke Coll., 1950-55; prof. physics U. S.C., 1955-63, chmn. dept., 1956-62; vis. prof. MIT, 1962-64, prof., 1964-91, prof. emeritus, 1991—; vis. fellow Pembroke Coll., Cambridge, 1975; chmn. Internat. Commn. on Physics Edn., 1975-81. Author: Principles of Modern Physics, 1958, Special Relativity, 1968, Newtonian Mechanics, 1971, Vibrations and Waves, 1971, (with Edwin F. Taylor) Introduction to Quantum Physics, 1978, (with M.G. Ebison) Introduction to Classical Mechanics, 1986; editor: Einstein: A Centenary Volume, 1979, Physics in a Technological World, 1988; co-editor: Niels Bohr: A Centenary Volume, 1985, Physics History from AAPT Jours. II, 1995; contbr. articles to profl. jours. Recipient Univ. medal Charles U., Prague, 1980, Bragg medal Inst. Physics, U.K., 1988, Oersted medal Am. Assn. Physics Tchrs., 1989. Fellow Am. Phys. Soc.; mem. Am. Assn. Physics Tchrs. (pres. 1985-86, Oersted medal 1989, Melba Newell Phillips award 1993), Sigma Xi, Sigma Pi Sigma. Office: Mass Inst Tech Rm 6-101 Cambridge MA 02139

FRENCH, CLARENCE LEVI, JR., retired shipbuilding company executive; b. New Haven, Oct. 13, 1925; s. Clarence L. Sr. and Eleanor (Curry) F.; m. Jean Sprague, June 29, 1946; children: Craig Thomas, Brian Keith, Alan Scott. BS in Naval Sci., Tufts U., 1945, BSME, 1947; ScD (hon.), Webb Inst., 1992. Registered profl. engr., Calif. Foundry engr. Bethlehem Steel Corp., 1947-56; staff engr., asst. supt. Kaiser Steel Corp., 1956-64; supervisory engr. Bechtel Corp., 1964-67; with Nat. Steel & Shipbldg. Co., San Diego, 1967-86; exec. v.p., gen. mgr. Nat. Steel & Shipbldg. Co., to 1977, pres., chief operating officer, 1977-84, chmn., chief exec. officer, 1984-86, outside dir., 1989-98; past mem. maritime transp. rsch. bd. NRC. Bd. dirs. United Way, San Diego, YMCA, San Diego; past chmn., bd. dirs. Pres. Roundtable; chmn. emeritus bd. trustees Webb Inst. Lt. USN, 1943-53. Fellow Soc. Naval Architects and Marine Engrs. (hon., past pres.), Shipbuilders Council Am. (past chmn. exec. com.), ASTM, Am. Bur. Shipping; mem. Am. Soc. Naval Engrs., U.S. Naval Inst., Navy League U.S., Propeller Club U.S.

FRENCH, DANA LEWIS, computer consultant; b. Stillwater, Okla., Nov. 17, 1958; s. Hilton Victor O'Daniel and Fern Ethel (Dennis) F. BS in Zoology, U. Okla., 1983, postgrad., 1983-84. Chem. engring. technician Applied Tech. Inc., Norman, Okla., 1979; sr. systems analyst Energ Analysts, Inc., Norman, 1981-89; owner French Consulting Svcs., Norman, 1989-93; sr. tech. cons. Applied Intelligence Group, Edmond, Okla., 1993—. Developer various computer programs, including Shell Curses, French Menus, KshEvents, KshSchedule, others. Mem. Open View Forum. Avocations: hang gliding, sky diving, scuba diving, snow skiing, water skiing. Office: Applied Intelligence Group 13800 Benson Rd Edmond OK 73013-6417

FRENCH, EDWARD RONALD, plant pathologist; b. Buenos Aires, Apr. 28, 1937; s. Daniel Argentino and Federica Romana (Tonizzo) F.; m. Delia G. Monar-Peralta, Mar. 9, 1968; children: Vivian Marie, Ronald David, Sandra Janice. BS, U. R.I., 1960; MSc, U. Minn., 1963; PhD, N.C. State U.,

1965. Plant pathologist agrl. mission to Peru N.C. State U., Raleigh, 1965-71, asst. prof. dept. plant pathology, 1971-72; head pathology dept. Internat. Potato Ctr., Lima, Peru, 1972-91, leader disease mgmt. program, 1992-95, assoc. dir. rsch., 1996-97, scientist emeritus, 1998—; vis. prof. U. Agraria La Molina, Lima, 1967—; vis. plant pathologist Cen. Agrl. Rsch. Inst., Gannoruwa, Sri Lanka, 1980-81; vis. scientist Sta. de Pathologie Vegetale, Rennes, France, 1990; mem. Jakob Eriksson Prize Com., Stockholm, 1980—; v.p. French Realty Co., Inc., North Kingston, R.I., 1981—. Author, editor: Prospects For The Potato in the Developing World, 1972; author: (with T.T. Hebert) Metodos de Investigacion Fitopatologica, 1980; editor: (with G. Galvez) Plant Pathologists in Latin America, 1990. Pres. Tuqui Urco Housing Devel., Monterrico, Lima, 1977-78, 84-85, 93-94; pres. bd. dirs. F.D. Roosevelt Am. Sch. Lima, Camacho, 1987-89; assoc. bd. dirs. F.D. Roosevelt Ednl. Inst., Lima, 1986—; pres. Am. Sch. Lima Found., Wilmington, Del., 1990—. Named Hon. Citizen City of Huanuco, Peru, 1985; E.R. French Bd. Rm. named in his honor FDR Am. Sch. Lima, Camacho, 1989. Fellow Am. Phytopathol. Soc.; mem. Internat. Soc. Plant Pathology (v.p. 1983-88, coun. 1973—), Peruvian Phytopathol. Soc. (hon.), Assn. Latin Am. Fitopatologia (hon., pres. 1970-74, 85-87, exec. sec. 1974-80, 92—), Rinconada Country Club, Club Tenis Terrazas Miraflores, R.I. Club Sports Honor Soc., Sigma Chi (magister 1958-59, Freshman award 1957, Found. award 1960), Alpha Zeta (Centennial Honor Roll 1997), Gamma Alpha, Sigma Xi (hon.), Phi Sigma (hon.), Phi Kappa Phi (hon.). Roman Catholic. Avocations: tennis, swimming. E-mail: e.french@cgiar.org. Office: Internat Potato Ctr, Apartado 1558, Lima 33, Peru

FRENCH, HAROLD STANLEY, food company executive; b. Bklyn., Oct. 2, 1921; s. Morris and Fay (Kaufman) F.; m. Claire E. Weingart, Oct. 3, 1943 (dec. Mar. 1983); children: Madelaine Diane, Janet Gail. BA, L.I. U., 1942; postgrad., NYU, 1950, Columbia U., 1960; PhD in Philosophy, Am. Coll., 1998. Asst. buyer R.H. Macy Co., N.Y.C., 1949-52; group mgr. Abraham & Straus Co., Hempstead, N.Y., 1952-54; mdse. mgr. Popular Club Plan, Passaic, N.J., 1954-60, Nat. Silver Co., N.Y.C., 1964-69; mktg. dir. Waverly Products Co., Phila., 1970-74; pres. Pet Food Industries, Inc., N.Y.C., 1974—, Harold French & Co., Inc., N.Y.C., 1974—, African Fruit Co. Inc., 1993—, Harold French Engring. Corp., 1993—; pres. King Agro-Indsl. Corp., 1986, Globe King Agro-Indsl. Co. Ltd., Nigeria, 1988—; trade agt. to Nigerian Govt., 1992—, also builder workers' housing, supplier of housing materials; founder, pres. The People Speak mag., 1995; founder, pres., pub. New Century Pub. Co. Inc., 1998. Dating and Mating for Women Over Fifty, 1998. Chmn., pres. The Nigeria Fund, Inc., 1989—; contbg. patron N.Y. Met. Opera, N.Y.C. Ballet; home builder for Nigerian Govt. Workers. With M.I., U.S. Army, 1943-45. Decorated Bronze Star. Home: 60 E 8th St New York NY 10003-6514

FRENCH, JEFFREY STUART, architect; b. Arlington, Va., Sept. 18, 1954; s. Orville Sidney and Doris G. French; m. Anne Harvey Hollibaugh, Sept. 26, 1981; children: Courtney Allen, Kyle Stuart, Allison Calvert. BA, Princeton U., 1976; MArch, U. Va., 1978. Registered architect, Pa., N.J., Mich., S.C., Ga., Del., Va., Mo., Ind., N.C., Ky., Tenn. V. p., dir. R&D facilities, COO The Ballinger Co., Architects/Engrs., Phila., 1978—; instr. U. Wis., Madison, 1986; lectr. in rsch. facility design; grant rev. panel NSF, 1990. Co-author NSF guidebook on planning acad. rsch. facilities. Mem. AIA (cert., coll. of fellows), Nat. Coun. of Archtl. Registration Bds., Soc. Coll. and Univ. Planning, N.Y. Acad. Scis., Internat. Soc. Pharm. and Med. Device Profls. Avocations: semi-professional baseball, golf, watercolor painting, violin. Office: Ballinger One Commerce Sq 2005 Market St Ste 1500 Philadelphia PA 19103-7088

FRENCH, JERE STUART, landscape architect; b. St. Louis, Jan. 18, 1929; s. Charles Lewis and Elizabeth Park (Smith) F.; m. Joan Marion Edwards, Jan. 16, 1953; children: Daniel, Susan, Cecily, Andrew. BA, Washington U., St. Louis, 1951; BS in Landscape Arch., Mich. State U., 1956; MA, Calif. State U., Fullerton, 1970. Registered landscape architect, Calif., 1958. Intelligence officer CIA, Washington, 1951-52; landscape architect F.B. Stresau, Ft. Lauderdale, Fla., 1956-57; prof. landscape arch. Calif. State Poly. U., Pomona, 1965, dean Coll. Environ. Design, 1979-83; prin. Boltz, French & Moore, Pomona, 1958-60, Environ. Planning Assocs., Pomona, 1960-63; pvt. practice landscape arch. Claremont, Calif., 1963-94; Author: The Public Park Movement in the Age of Industry, 1971, Urban Green, 1973, Urban Space, 1978, Urban Space Revised, 1983, City Landscape, 1983, The California Garden, 1993, End of Fall, 1996. Mem. trees and parkways commn. City of Claremont, 1966-68, park commn., 1968-71, arch. commn., 1975-79. With USNR, 1952-53. Recipient Ann. Heritage prize W. Fla. Literary Fedn., 1999. Fellow Am. Soc. Landscape Architects (Bradford Williams medal 1970); mem. Audubon Soc. (editor The Skimmer 1998—), Phi Kappa Phi, Phi Alpha Theta, Sigma Delta Pi, Sigma Lambda Alpha (Disting. mem. 1982—). Democrat. Unitarian. Avocations: environmental causes, birding. Home and Office: 2738 Sunrunner Ln Gulf Breeze FL 32561-5509

FRENCH, JOHN, III, lawyer; b. Boston, July 12, 1932; s. John and Rhoda (Walker) F.; m. Leslie Ten Eyck, Jan. 11, 1957 (div. 1961); children: John B., Lawrence C.; m. Anne Hubbell, Jan. 9, 1965 (div. 1983); children: Daniel J., Susanna H.; m. Marina Kellen, Nov. 21, 1987. BA, Dartmouth Coll., 1955; JD, Harvard U., 1958. Bar: N.Y. 1959, D.C. 1988. Assoc. Milbank, Tweed, Hadley & McCloy, N.Y.C., 1961-68, Satterlee & Stephens, N.Y.C., 1968-73; asst. gen. counsel Continental Group, Inc., Stamford, Conn., 1973-81; v.p., gen. counsel, sec. Peabody Internat. Corp., Stamford, Conn., 1981-82; ptnr. Appleton, Rice & Perrin, N.Y.C., 1982-84; ptnr. Beveridge and Diamond, N.Y.C., 1985-93, counsel, 1993-99; counsel Tudor Assocs., LLC, N.Y.C., 1999—; lectr. Practising Law Inst., 1979-83, Am. Law Inst., 1978; bd. dirs. Resorts Mgmt., Inc., Tudor Assocs., LLC, N.Y.C. Contbr. articles to profl. jours. Trustee Hudson River Found., YMCA-YWCA Camping Svcs. of Greater N.Y., Inc.; bd. dirs. Third St. Music Sch. Settlement House, Inc., N.Y.C., Internat. House, Inc., N.Y.C., Young Concert Artists, Inc., 33 E. 70th St. Corp., Teatro alla Scala Found.; mem. Westchester County Planning Bd., 1974-85; mem. N.Y. State Environ. Bd., 1976-88. Capt. JAGC, USAF, 1958-61. Mem. ABA, N.Y. State Bar Assn. (lectr.), Assn. of Bar of City of N.Y. (lectr.), Environ. Law Inst., Am. Soc. Corp. Secs., Met. Opera, Soc. Mayflower Descs., river Club, Harvard Club, Knickerbocker Club, The Pilgrims, Century Assn. Republican. Home: 33 E 70th St New York NY 10021-4941 Office: Tudor Assocs LLC 33 E 70th St New York NY 10021

FRENCH, JOHN DWYER, lawyer; b. Berkeley, Calif., June 26, 1933; s. Horton Irving and Gertrude Margery (Ritzen) F.; m. Annette Richard, 1955; m. Berna Jo Mahling, 1986. BA summa cum laude, U. Minn., 1955; postgrad, Oxford U., Eng., 1955-56; LLB magna cum laude, Harvard U., 1960. Bar: D.C. 1960, Minn. 1963. Law clk. Justice Felix Frankfurter, U.S. Supreme Ct., 1960-61; legal asst. to commr. FTC, 1961-62; assoc. Ropes & Gray, Boston, 1962-63; assoc. Faegre & Benson, Mpls., 1963-66, ptnr., 1967-75, mng. ptnr., 1975-94, chmn. mgmt. com., 1989-94; mem. adj. faculty Law Sch. U. Minn., 1965-70, mem. search com. for dean of Coll. of Liberal Arts, 1996; mem. exec. com. Lawyers Com. for Civil Rights Under Law, 1978—; co-chmn. U.S. Dist. Judge Nominating Commn., 1979; vice chmn. adv. com., mem. dir. search com., chmn. devel. office search com. Hubert Humphrey Inst., 1979-87. Contbr. numerous articles and revs. to legal jours. Chmn. or co-chmn. Minn. State Dem. Farm Labor Party Conv., 1970-90, 94, chmn. Mondale Vol. Com., 1972, treas., 1974; assoc. chmn. Minn. Dem.-Farmer-Labor Party, 1985-86; mem. Dem. Nat. Com., 1985-86; mem. Dem. Nat. Conv., 1976, 78, 80, 84, 88; trustee Twin Cities Public TV, Inc., 1980-86, mem. overseers com. to visit Harvard U. Law Sch., 1970-75, 77-82; chmn. Minn. steering com. Dukakis for Pres., 1987-88; mem. Sec. of State's Commn. on Electoral Reform, Minn., 1994; mem. Mayor's Commn. on Regulatory Reform, Mpls., 1995. With U.S. Army, 1955-56. Rotary Found. fellow, 1955-56. Mem. ABA (editorial bd. jour. 1976-79, commn. to study fed. trade 1969—), Minn. Bar Assn., Hennepin County Bar Assn., Jud. Coun. Minn., Lawyers Alliance for Nuclear Arms Control (nat. bd. dirs. 1982-84), U. Minn. Alumni Assn. (exec. com. 1985-87, v.p. 1989-91, pres. 1991-92, Vol. of Yr. award 1988), Phi Beta Kappa. Episcopalian. Office: Faegre & Benson 2200 Norwest Ctr 90 S 7th St Ste 2200 Minneapolis MN 55402-3901

FRENCH, JOSEPH JORDAN, JR., lawyer; b. Shreveport, La., Jan. 3, 1931; s. Joseph Jordan and Minnie Graham (Tomlinson) F.; m. Carol Jean Wesner, Dec. 22, 1954; children: Mary French Breckeen, Joseph Jordan III, Elizabeth French Pospick, Charles Robert. BS, Washington & Lee U., 1950; LLB, U. Tex., 1956. Bar: Tex. 1956, U.S. Dist. Ct. (no. dist.) Tex. 1956, U.S. Ct. Appeals (5th cir.), U.S. Tax Ct. Staff acct. W.O. Ligon & Co., Dallas, 1950-51; assoc. Thompson & Knight, Dallas, 1956-59; ptnr., shareholder Locke Purnell Rain Harrell, Dallas, 1959-93; prin. Joe French & Assocs., P.C., Dallas, 1993—; sec. Trinity Industries, Inc., Dallas, 1969-97, Halter Marine Group Inc., 1996-97. 2nd lt. USAF, 1951-53. Home: 4440 Fairfax Ave Dallas TX 75205-3028 Office: Joe French & Assocs PC 8300 Douglas Ave Ste 800 Dallas TX 75225-5813

FRENCH, JUDSON CULL, government official; b. Washington, Sept. 30, 1922; s. Morrison Brady and Ethel Haviland (Cull) F.; m. Julia A. McAllister, Aug. 1, 1951; 1 child, Judson Cull. BS cum laude, Am. U., 1943; MS, Harvard U., 1949, postgrad. at bus. sch., 1968; postgrad., Johns Hopkins U., 1943-44, George Washington U., 1944-45, MIT, 1951. Instr. physics Johns Hopkins U., Balt., 1943-44, George Washington U., Washington, 1944-47; sec., dir. Home Title Ins. Co., Washington, 1956-71; with Nat. Bur. Standards (now Nat. Inst. Standards and Tech.), Commerce Dept., Washington, 1948—; asst. chief electron devices sect. Nat. Bur. Standards (now Nat. Inst. Standards and Tech.), Commerce Dept., 1964-68, chief electron devices sect., 1968-73, chief electronic tech. div., 1973-78, dir. Ctr. for Electronics and Elec. Engring., 1978-91; dir. Electronics and Elec. Engring. Lab., Nat. Inst. Standards and Tech., Gaithersburg, Md., 1991-99, dir. emeritus Electronics and Elec. Engring. Lab., 1999—; mem. policy bd. Optoelectronic Computing Sys. Ctr. U. Colo., 1992—; bd. dirs. Nat. Electronics Mfg. Intitiative, Inc., 1998—; co-chmn. jt. mgmt. com., U.S.-Japan Jt. Optoelectronics Project, 1992—. Contbr. articles to profl. jours. Recipient Silver medal for meritorious svc. Commerce Dept., 1964, Gold medal for exceptional svc., 1978, Edward Bennett Rosa award Nat. Bur. Standards, 1971, presdl. rank of Meritorious Exec., Sr. Exec. Svc., 1980, Disting. Exec., 1984, 93. Fellow IEEE; mem. ASTM, Am. Phys. Soc., Nat. Acad. Engring., Sigma Pi Sigma, Pi Delta Epsilon, Alpha Kappa Pi. Office: Nat Inst Standards and Tech Metrology Bldg Rm B352 Electronics Electrical Engr Lab Gaithersburg MD 20899

FRENCH, KATHLEEN PATRICIA, educational administrator; b. Elizabeth, N.J., July 31, 1951; d. Raymond Patrick and Dorothy Ann (Gerber) F. BA, Kean U. N.J., 1974; MS in Edn., Fordham U., 1978; MS in Edn. Admin., Kean U., 1998. Cert. learning disabilities tchr.-cons., prin., supr., spl. edn. tchr., elem. sch. tchr., N.J. Tchr. spl. edn. Elizabeth Sch. Dist., 1974-87; with pub. affairs dept. Merck and Co., Inc., Rahway, N.J., 1987-89; tchr. spl. edn. Woodbridge (N.J.) Twp. Sch. Dist., 1989-92; intervention strategist Phillipsburg (N.J.) Sch. Dist., 1992-93; adj. prof. Kean U. N.J., Union, 1992-94; learning cons. on child study team Union Twp. Sch. Dist., N.J., 1993-99; supr. spl. edn. Piscataway Twp. Schs., Piscataway, N.J., 1999—; alumni vol. to undergrad. admissions office Fordham U., N.Y.C., 1990-97; adviser Union County Narcotics Bd., Elizabeth, 1992-97. Mem. Assn. Learning Cons., Coun. for Exceptional Children, Kappa Delta Pi. Avocation: travel. Home: 183 Gibson Blvd Apt 8 Clark NJ 07066-1455 Office: Piscataway Twp Schs Adminstrn Bldg PO Box 1332 1515 Stelton Rd Piscataway NJ 08855-1332

FRENCH, KENNETH RONALD, finance educator; b. Franklin, N.H., Mar. 10, 1954; s. Vernon Cecil and Barbara Jean (Craig) F.; m. Vickie Anne Welch, Sept. 18, 1976; children: Robert Timothy, Laura Nancy, Elizabeth Anne. BSME, Lehigh U., 1975; MBA, U. Rochester, 1978, MS in Fin., 1981, PhD in Fin., 1983. Machine design engr. Eastman Kodak, Rochester, N.Y., 1975-77; rsch. fellow Found. for Rsch. in Econs. and Edn., UCLA, 1982-83; asst. prof. Grad. Sch. Bus., U. Chgo., 1983-85, assoc. prof., 1985-87, prof., 1987-89, Chgo. Mercantile Exch. prof., 1989-91, Leo Melamed prof., 1991-94; Edwin J. Beinecke prof. Yale Sch. Mgmt., New Haven, 1994-98, mng. dir. Intenat. Ctr. Fin., 1994-98; NTU prof. fin. Sloan Sch. Mgmt., MIT, Cambridge, Mass., 1998—; rsch. assoc. Nat. Bur. Econ. Rsch., Cambridge, Mass., 1989—; dir. Ctr. for Rsch. in Security Prices, Chgo., 1990-94. Contbr. numerous articles to profl. jours. Batterymarch Investment fellow, 1986; Sloan Found. grantee, 1989. Home: 85 Trescott Rd Etna NH 03750-4505 Office: MIT Sloan Sch Mgmt 50 Memorial Dr Cambridge MA 02139

FRENCH, KENNETH WAYNE, radio station executive, consultant; b. Damascus, Va., May 18, 1952; s. Kenneth Park and Adelphia (Sluder) F.; m. Patsy Baker, Sept. 1, 1979. BA in Broadcast Journalism, U. S.C., 1974. Cert. radio mktg. cons. Sports announcer Sta. WSSC, Sumter, S.C., 1974-76; gen. sales mgr. Sta. WWDM-FM, WFIG, Sumter, S.C., 1976-80; gen. mgr. Sta. KIXY-FM, KQSA, San Angelo, Tex., 1981-83; v.p., gen. mgr. Sta. KELS-FM, Ardmore, Okla., 1983-84; gen. sales mgr. Sta. KKCS-FM KKHT, Colorado Springs, Colo., 1984-85; local sales mgr. KEYN-FM/KQAM, Wichita, Kans.; gen. mgr. Sta. KBUY-FM, KDJW, Amarillo, Tex., 1986-87; operating ptnr., gen. mgr. Sta. KMVR-FM KOBE, Las Cruces, N.Mex., 1987-88; gen. mgr. Sta. WYBB-FM/WNST-FM, Charleston, S.C., 1989—; exec. v.p. The French Group, Charleston, S.C., 1990—. Actor in films Rich In Love, 1993, Die Hard III, 1995, Stranger Than Fiction, 1996, O, 1999, TV movies Queen, 1993, Class of '61, 1993, Scarlet, 1994, Bionic Everafter, 1994, Twisted Desire, 1996, Liar, 1997, Carriers, 1997, The Tempest, 1998, TV series Sweet Justice, 1995. Bd. dirs. YMCA, San Angelo, 1981-82, Conv. and Visitors Bur., Las Cruces, 1987-88, Aggie Sports Assn., Las Cruces, 1987-88; dir.-elect Las Cruces C. of C., 1988-89, Dona Ana Arts Coun., 1988-90; bd. dirs. Happy Days, Spl. Times, Charleston, 1993—, v.p., pres.-elect, 1994—, v. chmn., 1996-98. Recipient Key Man award Jaycees, 1980, N.Mex. Gov. award of appreciation, 1989, S.C. Gov.'s Vol. award, 1996. Mem. SAG, Charleston Area Broadcasters (pres. 1993-94), Internat. Platform Assn., (founding, charter mem., exec. bd. 1998—, chmn. exec.com. 1999) Carolina Film Alliance. Baptist. Avocations: helping children, all sports, 4 wheel drive off-road, snow and water skiing, reading. E-mail: Frenchgrp@aol.com. Office: Sta WYBB-FM/WNST-FM 59 Windermere Blvd Charleston SC 29407-7411

FRENCH, KIRBY ALLAN, transportation engineer, computer programmer; b. San Angelo, Tex., Oct. 12, 1948; s. Leland Wayne French and Helen Lois (Stennett) French-Vance; m. Verda Jane Amyl Schaffer, Oct. 11, 1970; children: Tammy Lyrae, Adrian Allyn. Diploma in Computer Programming, Mkt. Tng. Inst., 1968. Transp. engr. Calif. Dept. Transp., San Bernardino, 1969-98; ret., 1998. Author: Speed Math, 1991, Trigonometric Formulas, 1991, Speed Reading, 1994, Microsoft Word 6 Macros for Spec Writers, 1996, Power Macintosh Apple Script Programs, 1996. Avocations: computer programming, writing, painting, Star Trek conventions. Home: 1257 Poplar St San Bernardino CA 92410-2522

FRENCH, LAURENCE ARMAND, social science educator, psychology educator; b. Manchester, N.H., Mar. 24, 1941; s. Gerald Everett and Juliette Teresa (Boucher) F.; m. Nancy Picthall, Feb. 13, 1971. BA cum laude, U. N.H., 1968, MA, 1970, PhD, 1975; postdoctorate, SUNY, Albany, 1978; PhD, U. Nebr., 1981; MA, Western N.M. U., 1994. Diplomate Am. Bd. Forensic Medicine, Am. Bd. Forensic Examiners, Am. Bd. Psychol. Specialties in Forensic Psychology & Neuropsychology; lic. psychologist, Ariz. Instr. U. So. Maine, Portland and Gorham, 1971-72; asst. prof. Western Carolina U., Cullowhee, N.C., 1972-77, U. Nebr., Lincoln, 1977-80; psychologist I N.H. Hosp., Concord, 1980-81; psychologist II Laconia (N.H.) State Sch., 1981-88; sr. psychologist N.H. Divsn. for Children & Youth Svcs., Concord, 1988-89; prof., chair dept. social scis. Western N.Mex. U., Silver City, 1989—; Psi Chi Nat. Honor Soc. in psychology Western N.Mex. faculty adviser; adj. assoc. prof. U. So. Maine, 1980-84; cons. N.C. Dept. Mental Health, 1972-77, Nebr. Indian Commn., Lincoln, 1977-80, Cherokee (N.C.) Indian Mental Health Program, 1974-77; cons. alcohol program Lincoln Indian Ctr., 1977-80; profl. adv. bd. Internat. Coll. Prescribing Psychologists. Author: The Selective Process of Criminal Justice, 1976, (with Richard Crowe) Wee Wish Tree: Special Qualla Cherokee Issue, 1976, (with Hornbuckle) Cherokee Perspective, 1981, (with Letman et al) Contemporary Issues in Corrections, 1981, Indians and Criminal Justice, 1982, Psychocultural Change and the American Indian, 1987, The Winds of Injustice, 1994, Counseling American Indians, 1997, The Qualla Cherokee Surviving in Two Worlds, 1998; spl. issue editor Quar. Jour. Ideology, Vol. II, 1987; contbr. articles to profl. jours. Commr. Pilsbury Lake Village Dist., Webster, N.H., 1985-90. With USMC, 1959-63, Badge of Honor, Republic of China, 1998. Recipient Hon. medal Rep. China, 1998, Nat. Int. Drug Abuse 1st Leadership award Conducting Rsch., 1999; U. N.H. fellow, 1971-72, Nebr. U. System fellow, 1978. Fellow APA, Prescribing Psychologists Register (diplomate), Soc. Psychol. Study Social Issues; mem. NASP, VFW (life), Am. Soc. Criminology (life), Internat. Coll. Prescribing Psychologists Inc. (profl. adv. bd.), Nat. Assn. Alcohol and Drug Abuse Counselors (nat. chmn., clin. issue com. 1996-98), N.Mex. Alcohol and Drug Abuse Counselors Assn. (educator of the yr. award 1997), Phi Delta Kappa (treas. 1990-91, pres. 1991-92). Office: Western NMex U Dept Social Scis Silver City NM 88062

FRENCH, MARILYN, author, critic; b. N.Y.C., Nov. 21, 1929; d. E. Charles and Isabel (Hazz) Edwards; m. Robert M. French, Jr., June 4, 1950 (div. 1967); children: Jamie, Robert. BA, Hofstra Coll., 1951, MA, 1964; PhD, Harvard U., 1972. Secretarial, clerical worker, 1946-53; lectr. Hofstra Coll., 1964-68; asst. prof. Holy Cross Coll., Worcester, Mass., 1972-76; Mellon fellow Harvard U., 1976-77; writer, lectr., 1967—. Author: (criticism) The Book as World: James Joyce's Ulysses, 1976, Shakespeare's Division of Experience, 1981; (novels) The Women's Room, 1977, The Bleeding Heart, 1980, Her Mother's Daughter, 1987, Our Father: A Novel, 1994, My Summer with George, 1996; (non-fiction) Beyond Power: On Women, Men and Morals, 1986, The War Against Women, 1992, A Season in Hell, 1998; introductions to Edith Wharton's Summer and The House of Mirth, 1981. Mem. Virginia Woolf Soc., Phi Beta Kappa. *

FRENCH, MARK, women's basketball coach university level; b. Bakersfield, Calif.. BS in Polit. Sci., U. Calif., Santa Barbara, 1973; MA, Pacific Union Coll., Anowin, Calif., 1983. Head coach women's basketball Pacific Union Coll., Angwin, Calif., 1979-83, U. Idaho, Moscow, 1983-87, U. Calif., Santa Barbara, 1987—. Named Coach of Yr., Big West Athletic Conf., 1991-2, 95-96, 96-97. Mem. Women's Basketball Assn. Office: Women's Athletic Dept U Calif Santa Barbara Santa Barbara CA 93106-7211*

FRENCH, MARY B., English educator; b. Dallas, July 21, 1942; d. Harry Blake and Mary Virginia (Jones) F.; m. Richard Edelin Crouch, Feb. 6, 1965; children: John, Virginia. BA, Coll. William and Mary, 1965; MA, U. Va., 1966. Columnist, reporter Va. Gazette, Williamsburg, 1961-65; mng. editor William and Mary Rev., Williamsburg, 1963-64; asst. editor Microfilm Publs., U. Va., Charlottesville, 1966-67; lectr. Am. lit. and women in lit. U. Va., Falls Church, 1968—; instr. English, No. Va. C.C., Annandale, 1968-69; instr. English composition George Washington U., Washington, 1970; cons. in lit. humanities project Arlington County Libr., 1976. Author: The State Slate: A Guide to Legislative Procedures and Lawmakers, 1977; compiler: Women in Literature: A Bibliography, 1973; editor (with J.L. Anderson) Microfilm Edition of the Papers of R.M.T. Hunter, 1817-1887, 1966; editor Spokeswoman Mag., 1979-82, Washington Women's Rep. Newsletter, 1979-82; mng. editor Women's News Svc., 1979-82; assoc. editor Career Opportunities News, 1983—; mng. editor Army Mag., 1984-93, editor, 1993—; contbr. poetry to several anthologies. Active Com. on Status of Women, Arlington, Va., 1976, steering com. Coalition on Optimum Growth, 1970-73. Mem. MLA, AAUW (rsch. women's studies, dir. Arlington br. 1974-76, assoc. editor Grad. Women mag. 1982, mng. editor publs. 1983), ACLU, AAUP, Women's Caucus of Modern Langs., Washington Women's Network, Nat. Women's Polit. Caucus, English-Speaking Union, Edgar Allan Poe Found., Thoreau Soc., Jane Austen Soc., U.S. Congress Periodical Press Corrs.'s Assn., Nat. Trust Hist. Preservation, Preservation Soc. Loudoun County, Old House Group Loudoun County, Soc. Profl. Journalists, Am. Soc. Mag. Editors, Women in Comm. Inc., Soc. Nat. Assn. Publs., Am. Folk Art Mus. Democrat. Episcopalian. Office: 2425 Wilson Blvd Arlington VA 22201-3326

FRENCH, MICHAEL BRUCE, beverage company executive; b. Arlington, Va., Sept. 18, 1954; s. Orville Sidney and Doris (Goldberg) F.; m. Robin Ann Abenstein, Oct. 15, 1978; children: Brian Michael, Matthew Jeffrey, Sean Thornton. BA, Princeton (N.J.) U., 1976; M in Mgmt., Northwestern U., Evanston, Ill., 1978. Brand asst., asst. brand mgr. Procter & Gamble Co., Cin., 1978-80, brand mgr., 1981-84; mktg. dir. Coca-Cola Bottling Mideast Inc. subs. P&G, Lexington, Ky., 1984-85; v.p. mktg. Coca-Cola Botting Mideast, Inc., Lexington, 1985-87; brand mgr. Coca-Cola USA, Atlanta, 1987-89; mktg. mgr. chain accounts Coca-Cola Fountain, Atlanta, 1989, dir. channel mktg., 1989-93, dir. product definition and devel., 1993, asst. v.p. mktg. ops., 1993-94, v.p. mktg., 1994-95; dir. edn. mktg. Coca-Cola USA, Atlanta, 1995-97, dir. consumer occasions mktg., non-retail, 1997-99; dir. Coca-Cola Connection, 1999—. Mem. Rep. Party of Ga., Atlanta, 1988—; mem. baseball steering com. U. Ky., Lexington, 1986-87; fundraising chmn. Jr. Achievement of the Bluegrass, Lexington, 1986-87; chmn. pub. awareness subcom. Gov.'s Anti-Substance Abuse Commn., Frankfort, Ky., 1986-87; divsn. coord. Coca-Cola United Way Campaign, 1996. Named to Hon. Order of Ky. Cols., 1986. Mem. Princeton Club of Ga. Avocations: golf, youth baseball and basketball, reading, family. E-mail: sheba2@earthlink.net, MFRENCH@NA.KO.com. Home: 4352 Highborne Dr Marietta GA 30066-2429 Office: Coca-Cola USA Coca-Cola Plz Atlanta GA 30313

FRENCH, MICHAEL FRANCIS, non-profit education agency administrator; b. La Crosse, Wis., July 25, 1948; s. Albert Frank Jr. and Kathryn Patricia (MacKoske) F.; m. Janet Alan Street Head, Nov. 26, 1991. BS in Edn., U. Wis., 1972. Cert. emergency med. technician. Tng. coord. emergency med. svcs. Wis. Dept. Health and Social Svcs., Madison, 1975-80, tng. dir. emergency med. svcs., 1980-84, chief emergency med. svcs., 1984-90; co-dir. Mo. Area Health Edn. Ctrs. Kirksville (Mo.) Coll. Osteo. Medicine, 1990—, adj. instr. cmty. health, 1990—; emergency med. svcs. cons., Kirksville, 1984—; founding mem. Continuing Edn. Coordinating Bd. for Emergency Med. Svcs., Inc., Kirksville, 1992. Author: (tng. curriculum) EMS Instructor Training Course-U.S. Dept. Transportation, 1985; editor newsletter, editor-in-chief publs. Nat. Assn. Emergency Med. Technicians, 1983-91; author book chpts. V.p., pres. bd. dirs. Adair County Ret. Sr. Vol. Program, Kirksville, 1992-95. Recipient Lunda Trauma award Am. Trauma Soc., 1982, Svc. awards Nat. Coun. State EMS Tng. Coords., 1982, 83, A. Roger Fox Founders award Nat. Assn. Emergency Med. Technicians, 1989, others. Mem. ASTM, ASCD, ASTD, APHA, Nat. Rural Health Assn. (rural health policy bd. 1998—), Mo. Rural Health Assn. (bd. dirs. 1995-96, pres.-elect 1996-97, pres. 1997-99), Mo. PEW Health Professions Partnership (chair exec. com. 1994-95), Mo. Pub. Health Assn. (awards chair 1996), Wis. Emergency Med. Tech. Assn., Internat. Soc. Fire Svc. Instrs., Am. Coll. Healthcare Execs. (assoc.), Nat. Orgn. Area Health Edn. Ctr. Program Dirs. (nominations com. 1996), Mensa. Avocations: bicycling, reading, computer games. Office: Mo AHEC Program 800 W Jefferson St Kirksville MO 63501-1443

FRENCH, RICHARD FREDERIC, retired music educator; b. Randolph, Mass., June 23, 1915; s. Herbert F. and Edith (MacGregor) F. BS, Harvard U., 1937, MA, 1939; MusD, Concordia U., 1998. Asst. prof. music Harvard U., 1947-51; dir. publs., v.p. Asso. Music Pubs., 1951-60; pres. N.Y. Pro Musica, 1959-70, dir., 1959—; Robert S. Tangeman prof. sacred music Union Theol. Sem., N.Y.C., 1961-73; adj. prof. sacred music Union Theol. Sem., 1973-77; prof. music Inst. Sacred Music, Yale U., 1973-85, prof. emeritus; grad. faculty, dir. doctoral studies Julliard Sch., N.Y.C., 1985-99; vis. prof. music Yale Sch. of Music, 1994, 96, 99. Contbr. articles to books, mags. Trustee Schola Musicae Liturgicae, Bklyn. Music Sch. Served with USAAF, 1942-45. Decorated Bronze Star. Mem. Am. Musicol. Soc., Internat. Soc. Contemporary Music (treas. U.S. sect.). Clubs: Harvard (N.Y.C.), Yale (N.Y.C.), Century Assn. (N.Y.C.). Home: 88 Notch Hill Rd # 323 North Branford CT 06471-1820 Office: PO Box 208246 New Haven CT 06520-8246

FRENCH, RICHARD VAUGHN, federal agency administrator; b. Beckley, W.Va., Feb. 8, 1966; s. Zina Harold and Betty Jo (Hutchison) F.; m. Jamie Lyn Hart, Oct. 12, 1996. BA in Polit. Sci., W.Va. U., 1988, MPA, 1989. Staff asst. Rep. Nick J. Rahall II, Washington, 1990; labor rels. specialist U.S. Dept. Labor, Washington, 1990-95, program mgmt. specialist, 1995-97, program analyst, 1997-98, spl. asst. to asst. sec., 1998—; spl. asst. Corp. Nat. Svc., Washington, Phila., 1997. Mem. Am. Soc. Pub. Adminstn., W.Va. Soc. Washington (1st v.p. 1997—). Office: US Dept Labor Rm S-2203 200 Constitution Ave NW Washington DC 20210

FRENCH, STANLEY GEORGE, university dean, philosophy educator; b. Hamilton, Ont., Can., Sept. 24, 1933; s. Reginald George and Marie (Larson) F.; children: Shona, Sean, Lina, Ewan. BA, Carleton U., 1955; MA, U.

Rochester, 1957; PhD, U. Va., 1959; spl. student, Oxford U., 1961, U. Nice, France, 1975-76, Royal Victoria Hosp., McGill U., Montreal, 1987-88. Assoc. prof. philosophy U. Western Ont., London, 1965-68; prof. philosophy Sir George Williams U., Montreal, Que., 1968; chmn. dept. philosophy Sir George Williams U., 1969-71; prof. philosophy, dean grad. studies Concordia U., Montreal, 1971-86, dir. humanities interdisciplinary doctoral program, 1992—; mem. joint com. on programs Council of Univs., 1972-75; chmn. Westmount Sch. Commn., 1972; pres. London Council for Adult Edn., 1965-66; chmn. Bd. Edn. City of London, 1968; bd. govs. Sir George Williams U., 1969-71; internat. vis. scholar The Hastings Ctr., 1992. Author: The North West Staging Route, 1957, Philosophers Look at Canadian Confederation, 1979, Interpersonal Violence, Health and Gender Politics, 1993, Violence Against Women: Philosophical Perspectives, 1998, also monographs; cons. editor: Humanities Research Coun. Can., 1970—; editorial adv.: Gnosis, 1977—; contbr. articles to profl. jours., chpts. to books. Served as officer RCAF, 1951-56. Can. Council grantee, 1962; Internat. vis. scholar The Hastings Ctr., 1992. Mem. Soc. for Philosophy and Pub. Affairs (exec. bd. dirs.), Montreal Conf. Polit. and Social Thought, Sociète de Philosophie du Montreal, Sociète de Philosophie du Quebec, Can. Philos. Assn., Am. Philos. Assn., Am. Soc. Polit. and Legal Philosophy, Mind Assn., Can. Assn. Grad. Schs. (sec.-treas. 1980-81), Can. Bioethics Soc. Home: Le Mas, 585 Newaygo Rd, Montfort, PQ Canada J0T 1YO Office: Concordia U, Dept Philosophy, Montreal, PQ Canada H3G 1M8

FRENCH, STEPHANIE TAYLOR, arts administrator; b. Newark; d. William Taylor and Connie V. French; B.A., Wellesley Coll., 1972; M.B.A., Harvard U., 1978; children: Christina French Houghton, Amory Taylor Houghton. Free-lance on-air performer, producer San Francisco and Oakland cable TV stas., 1973-76; dir. European Gallery, San Francisco, 1974-75; acct. exec. Young & Rubican, N.Y.C., 1978-79; acct. supr. Rives Smith Baldwin & Carlberg, Houston, 1980-81; mgr. cultural affairs and spl. programs Philip Morris Cos. Inc., N.Y.C., 1981-86, dir. cultural and contbns. programs, 1986-90, v.p. corp. contbn. ans cultural programs bds., 1990—. Bd. dirs. The Joffrey Ballet of Chgo., Am. Fedn. of Arts, Ams. for Arts, Dance Com. Julliard Sch., Am. Craft Mus., Parsons Dance Co., Nat. AIDS Fund, the Thomas S. Kenan Inst. for the Arts, Harkness Ctr. for Dance Injuries, Bus. Com. of the Met. Mus. Art, The Contbns. Coun. of the Conf., Arts and Edn. Adv. Coun. for Harvard Grad. Sch. Edn., Bd. Adv. Com. of Bill T. Jones/ Arnie Zane Co., Dance Theatre Workshop. Apptd. mem. Gov. of N.Y. to Empire State Arts Commn., Mayor of N.Y.C. to the N.Y.C. Econ. Devel. Corp. Clubs: Harvard Bus. Sch. Network of Women Alums, Harvard Bus. Sch., Wellesley. Home: 320 E 72nd St Apt 8C New York NY 10021-4769 Office: Philip Morris Cos Inc 120 Park Ave New York NY 10017-5592

FRENCH, TALMADGE L., clergyman, educator; b. Flint, Mich., Nov. 7, 1955; s. Alvin French and Christine Butler Grant; m. Rebecca Lynn French, Aug. 25, 1978; children: Ryan A., Jonathan A., Nathan A. Ed., Apostolic Bible Inst., St. Paul, 1976; grad., Wheaton Coll., 1985; student, Wheaton Grad. Sch., 1998. Ordained to ministry Pentecostal Ch., 1978. Asst. min. First United Pentecostal Ch., West Memphis, Ark., 1978-80; sr. min. First Pentecostal Ch., Wheaton, Ill., 1983—; prof. N.T. Ind. Bible Coll., Indpls., 1994—. Named to Outstanding Young Men of Am., 1985. Mem. Soc. for Pentecostal Studies. Republican. Home: 626 S Beverly St Wheaton IL 60187-4518 Office: First Pentecostal Ch 112 S Dorchester Ave Wheaton IL 60187-4710

FRENCH, THOMAS, journalist; 2 children. BJ, Ind. U., 1980. Feature writer St. Petersburg Times, 1980—, now writer serial narratives; nat. TV appearances include Oprah Winfrey Show, Good Morning America, Sally Jesse Raphael, numerous local TV shows. Author: A Cry in the Night, South of Heaven, Babyland, Angels & Demons (serial narratives); author: (books) Unanswered Cries, 1991, South of Heaven, 1993. Winner 1998 Pulitzer for feature writing for Angels and Demons series, Soc. of Profl. Journalists' nat. award for best feature reporting, 1998, Livingston Award Am. Soc. Newspaper Editors, 1998. Office fax: (727) 893-8675; email: french@sptimes.com. Office: St Petersburg Times PO Box 1121 Saint Petersburg FL 33731-1121*

FRENCH, WILLIAM HAROLD, retired newspaper editor; b. London, Ont., Can., Mar. 21, 1926; s. Harold Edward and Isabel (Brash) F.; m. Margaret Jean Rollo, June 23, 1951; children—Jane, Mark, Paul, Susan. B.A., U. Western Ont., 1948; Nieman fellow, Harvard, 1954-55; DLitt (hon.), U. Western Ont., 1991. With The Globe and Mail, Toronto, Ont., Can., 1948-90; lit. editor The Globe and Mail, 1960-90; instr. journalism Ryerson Poly. Inst., 1955-88; asso. fellow York U., 1969-77; broadcaster Canadian Broadcasting Corp., 1964-90, ret., 1990; cons. Can. Council, 1969—. Author: A Most Unlikely Village, 1960. Recipient President's medal U. Western Ont., 1966; Nat. Newspaper award for critical writing, 1978, 79. Home: 78 N Hills Terr, Don Mills, ON Canada M3C 1M6

FRENI, MIRELLA, soprano; b. Modena, Italy, Feb. 27, 1935; d. Ennio and Gianna F.; m. Leone Magiera, 1955; 1 dau., Micaela; m. Nicolai Ghiaurov. Debut as Micaela in Carmen, Modena, 1955, since has appeared in maj. opera houses throughout world including Covent Garden, 1961, La Scala, 1962, Royal Opera House, Met. Opera, 1965, Vienna State Opera, Paris Opera, Salzburg Festival, Glyndebourne Festival; appeared in film Madame Butterfly and U.S. pub. TV broadcast of The Marriage of Figaro; maj. roles include: Zerlina in Don Giovanni, Nanette in Falstaff, Mimi in La Boheme, Violetta in La Traviata, Desdemona in Otello, title role in Adriana Lecouvrer, 1994; numerous operatic recs., including Carmen (Grammy award for best opera rec. 1964). Address: care John Coast Opera Mgmt, 31 Sinclair Rd, London W14 ONS, England Office: c/o J F Mastroianni Assoc Inc 80 Central Park W Apt 5E New York NY 10023-5247*

FRENKEL, EDWARD VLADIMIR, mathematician, educator; b. Kolomna, Russia, May 2, 1968; came to U.S., 1989; s. Vladimir Iosifovich and Lidia Vladimirovna Frenkel; m. Zvezdelina Stankova. BA, Gubkin Inst., Moscow, 1989; PhD, Harvard U., 1991. Jr. fellow Soc. Fellows, Harvard U., Cambridge, Mass., 1991-94, assoc. prof. math., 1994-97; prof. U. of Calif., Berkeley, 1997—; vis. prof. Kyoto (Japan) U., 1992, 93, 95, U. Paris VII, 1992, U. Paris VI, 1996, Ecole Normale Superieure, Paris, 1998, Weizmann Inst., Israel, 1992; invited spkr. Internat. Congress Mathematicians, Zurich, Switzerland, 1994, Internat. Congress Math. Physics, Paris, 1994; mem. Inst. for Advanced Study, Princeton, 1997. Editl. bd. Inventiones Mathematical, Internat. Math. Rsch. Notices, Inventiones Mathematical; contbr. articles to profl. jours. Harvard prize fellow, 1989, Packard Found. fellow, 1995; grantee NSF, 1992, 95, Sloan Found., 1995. Mem. Am. Math. Soc. Office: U Calif at Berkeley Evans Hall Berkeley CA 94720

FRENKEL, EUGENE PHILLIP, physician; b. Detroit, Aug. 27, 1929; s. David Eugene and Eva (Antin) F.; m. Rhoda Beth Smilay, Dec. 21, 1958; children: Lisa Michelle, Peter Alan. BS, Wayne State U., 1949; MD, U. Mich., 1953. Diplomate Am. Bd. Internal Medicine (hematology, med. oncology; bd. govs. 1980-87, chmn. subspecialty com. hematology 1980-85). Intern Wayne County Gen. Hosp., Eloise, Mich., 1953-54; resident in internal medicine Boston City Hosp., 1954-55; resident in internal medicine, then instr. U. Mich. Med. Center, 1957-62; mem. faculty U. Tex. Southwestern Med. Ctr., Dallas, 1962—, prof. internal medicine and radiology, 1969—, chief divsn. hematology-oncology, 1962-91, Patsy R. and Raymond D. Nasher Disting. chair in cancer rsch., 1990—, A. Kenneth Pye prof. in cancer rsch., 1994—; chief nuclear medicine, cons. hematology-oncology VA Med. Center, Dallas, 1962-80; Sydney and J.L. Huffines, Jr. disting. chair U. Tex. Southwestern Med. Ctr., 1998—; cons. com. on evaluation rsch. hematology; nutrition Nat. Inst. Arthritis and Metabolic Diseases, 1979-82; active Am. Joint Commn. on Cancer, 1986-95; interim dir. divsn. hematology-oncology VA Med. Ctr., Dallas, 1995-97. Author numerous research papers in field. Served as officer M.C. USAF, 1955-57. Fellow ACP (coun. of subspecialty socs. 1992—), Internat. Soc. Hematology; mem. Am. Soc. Hematology (treas. 1976-84), Am. Soc. Clin. Oncology (chmn. membership com. 1982-85), Am. Cancer Soc. (pres. Dallas unit 1970-71, dir. Tex. divsn. 1978—, sci. adv. com. on clin. investigations II-chemotherapy and hematology 1978-82, Emma Freeman prof., 1981-91, nat. clin. fellowship com. 1978-87, internat. rsch. grants com. 1988-90, sci. adv. coun. 1991-97), Assn. Am. Physicians, Am. Assn. Cancer Rsch., Am. Assn. Cancer Edn., Am. Soc. Biol. Chemists, Am. Soc. Clin. Investigation, So. Soc. Clin. Investigation, Soc. Nuclear Medicine, Am. Fedn. Clin. Rsch., Internat. Soc. Hematology (elected councillor 1992-97), Internat. Assn. Study Lung Cancer, Alpha Omega Alpha. Office: U Tex Southwestern Med Ctr Dallas TX 75235-8852

FRENKIEL, RICHARD HENRY, systems engineer, consultant; b. N.Y.C., Mar. 4, 1943; s. Lucjan and Stefani (Komorowska) F.; m. Annamae Mary Rollason, Dec. 28, 1963; children: Scott Thomas, Kathleen Ann. BSME, Tufts U., 1963; MS in Engring. Mechanics, Rutgers U., 1965. Mem. tech. staff Bell Labs., Holmdel, N.J., 1963-71, supr., 1973-77, dept. head, 1977-88, dir. R & D, 1988-93, ret., 1993; vis. prof. Rutgers U., sr. cons. to WINLAB at Rutgers, 1994—. Patentee in field. Mem. twp. com., Manalapan Twp., N.J., 1995—, dep. mayor, 1996, mayor, 1999—. Recipient N.J. Inventor of Yr. award 1995, Achievement award Indsl. Rsch. Inst., 1992, Alexander Graham Bell medal IEEE, 1987, Nat. medal of Tech. U.S. Dept. of Commerce, 1994; Bell Labs fellow, 1990. Fellow IEEE (spkr. Outstanding Lecture Tour 1975-76); mem. NAE, Electronics Industry Assn. (mem. cellular stds. com., 1980). Republican. Achievements include contributions to design and deployment of first cellular telephone systems in U.S.; leadership in design of cordless telephone products; invention of the Metroliner Radiotelephone System; inventor of a cell splitting method. Office: Rutgers WINLAB PO Box 909 Piscataway NJ 08855-0909

FRENSLEY, JOE THOMAS, elementary education educator; b. Camden, Tenn., July 7, 1950; s. Charles Thomas and Sylvia Athalie (Herrin) F. BS in Edn., S.E. Mo., 1973; MA in Edn., Murray State U., 1979. Tchr. Hollow Rock (Tenn.)-Bruceton Sch. Dist., 1974-75; substitute tchr. Henry County Sch. Sys., Paris, Tenn., 1975-77; homebound tchr. Henry County Sch. Sys., Paris, 1977-78; resource tchr. Grove Jr. High, Paris, 1978-80, Puryear (Tenn.) Sch., 1980-84; assessment specialist Henry County Bd. Edn., Paris, 1984-87; resource tchr. Henry (Tenn.) Sch., 1987-91; learning disabled, gifted resource Grove Middle Sch., Paris, 1991-94; facilitator success for all Lakewood Sch., Buchanan, Tenn., 1994—; com. study inclusion State Dept. Edn., 1994-96. Bd. dirs. Paris-Henry County Arts Coun., 1996—. Recipient Spirit award Effective Adv. Citizens with Handicaps, 1985. Mem. NEA (del. rep. 1984-99), Henry County Edn. Assn. (bd. dirs. 1984—), Tenn. Edn. Assn. (bd. dirs. 1991-94), Internat. Reading Assn. Democrat. Home: 1317 McFadden St Paris TN 38242-3209 Office: Lakewood Sch 6745 Highway 79 N Buchanan TN 38222-5100

FRENZ, DOROTHY ANN, cell and developmental biologist; b. New Rochelle, N.Y., Jan. 17, 1954; d. Anthony Joseph and Angelina Marie (Guida) Chiodo; m. Michael Richard Frenz, Sept. 15, 1974; children: Christopher, Elizabeth. BA summa cum laude, Iona Coll., 1978; MS, N.Y. Med. Coll., 1986, PhD, 1988. Postdoctoral fellow Albert Einstein Coll. Medicine, Bronx, N.Y., 1988-91; asst. prof. dept. otolaryngology Albert Einstein Coll. Medicine, Bronx, 1991-97, asst. dir. rsch., 1993—, anatomy instr., 1991-92, asst. prof. anatomy and structural biology, 1993—, assoc. prof., 1997—; chairperson resident rsch. com. Albert Einstein Coll. Medicine, 1991—, senator faculty senate, 1991—, mem. faculty bone biology group. Contbr. chpts. in books and articles to profl. jours. Bd. dirs. New Rochelle YMCA, 1991-97, Songcatchers, Inc.; pres. Isaac E. Young Mid. Sch. PTA, 1992-93, mem. adv. coun., 1993-94; tchr., lectr. Blessed Sacrament Ch., New Rochelle, 1986—, parish bull. editor, 1988-96, parish coun. rec. sec., 1990—, parish trustee. Recipient Martha Pate award N.Y. Med. Coll., 1988, New Rochelle Interreligions Coun. award, 1995. Mem. Soc. for Cell Biology, N.Y. Acad. Sci., Assn. for Rsch. in Otolaryngology. Roman Catholic. Office: A Einstein Coll Medicine 1300 Morris Park Ave Bronx NY 10461-1926

FRERET, RENÉ JOSEPH, minister; b. Pass Christian, Miss., Jan. 3, 1944; s. James Carroll and Pearl (Gordy) F.; m. Freda Rester; children: Katherine, Grace, Stephen, Rachel. AA, Perkinston Jr. Coll., 1964; BA, Bapt. Christian Coll., 1973; MA, Bapt. Christian U., 1978, PhD, 1984. Ordained to ministry Ind. Bapt. Ch., 1967. Pastor New Hope Bapt. Ch., McNeil, Miss., 1966-68, Cen. Bapt. Ch., Gulfport, Miss., 1968-70, Forest Hills Bapt. Ch., Benton, Ark., 1970-72; assoc. pastor Bapt. Tabernacle, Shreveport, La., 1972-73; pastor Temple Bapt. Ch., Gulfport, Miss., 1973-97; adminstr. Temple Christian Acad., Gulfport, Miss., 1974-97; pres. Temple Bapt. Inst., 1981—; instr. Maranatha Inst. Missions, Natchez, Miss., 1983—; dir. Maranatha Mens Retreat, Natchez, 1990—; pres. Bible Edn. and Missionary Svc., 1996. Author: Patriotism, 1990. Chmn. Harrison County (Miss.) Fire Commn., 1990; chmn., mayor Gulfport City Councilmen Task Force, 1994-97; chaplain Orange Grove Vol. Fire Dept., Gulfport, 1989, Harrison County Bd. Suprs., 1992-95; trustee Meml. Hosp. Gulfport, 1996-97. Mem. Miss. State Assn. Christian Schs. (exec. dir. student state competition 1984-93, v.p. 1988-93, pres. 1993-95, exec. dir. 1995-96), Am. Assn. Christian Schs. (bd. dirs. 1996-97). Home: 13092 Quail Ridge Rd Gulfport MS 39503-4835 Office: Bible Edn and Missionary Svc 14190 Dedeaux Rd Gulfport MS 39503-3358 *If you will stand by the Word of the God, the God of the Word will stand by you.*

FRERICHS, ERNEST SUNLEY, religious studies educator; b. S.I., N.Y., Apr. 30, 1925; s. Ernest V. and Eva (Sunley) F.; m. Sarah Hazel Cutts, Aug. 20, 1949; children: John Allen (dec.), David Sunley, Elizabeth Ann. AB, Brown U., 1948; AM, Harvard U., 1949; STB, Boston U., 1952, PhD, 1957; DHL, Hebrew Union Coll., 1992. Mem. faculty Brown U., Providence, 1953—, prof. religious studies, 1966-95, chmn. dept., 1964-70, asst. dean. coll., 1958-59, dean grad. sch., 1976-82, dir. program in Judaic studies, 1982-95, prof. religious and Judaic studies emeritus, 1995—; exec. dir. Dorot Found., 1995—; mem. Grad. and Profl. Schs. Fin. Aid Coun., 1978-82; mem. Grad. Record Exam. Bd., 1980-82; mem. com. on testing Coun. Grad. Schs., 1980-82; mem. N.Am. com. Mellon Fellowship Program, 1982-92; chmn. Coun. Grad. Studies in Religion, 1989-93. Mem. region I and II selection com. Woodrow Wilson Found., 1959-69; trustee Am. Schs. Oriental Rsch., 1976-82, 93—, v.p., 1993-96; trustee Hiatt Inst., Brandeis U., 1979-82, Roger Williams Hosp., Providence, 1981-97; trustee Albright Inst. Archeol. Rsch., Jerusalem, 1974—, pres., 1976-82; bd. dirs. Assn. of Jewish Studies, 1990-98. With inf. AUS, 1943-46. Recipient Disting. Alumnus award Boston U., 1994; Beebe fellow Boston U., 1952-53, Lilly postdoctoral fellow Heidelberg U., 1962-63. Mem. Soc. Bibl. Lit. (exec. com. New Eng. coun. 1977-82), Am. Acad. Religion (pres. New Eng. 1970-71), Phi Beta Kappa (sec. Brown U. chpt. 1964-68, pres. 1975-77). Home: 32 Vassar Ave Providence RI 02906-3420 Office: Dorot Found 439 Benefit St Providence RI 02903-2934

FRERICHS, JOY ROBERTA, elementary education educator; b. Sweetwater, Tenn., July 21, 1946; d. Elton F. and Lenis Abby (Edwards) F. AA, Hiwassee Jr. Coll., Madisonville, Tenn., 1966; BS, East Tenn. State U., 1968; MEd, West Ga. Coll., 1977. Tchr. Dug Gap, Dalton, Ga., 1966-75; lead lang. arts tchr. Valley Point Mid. Sch., Dalton, Ga., 1975—; mem. Ga. state textbook adv. com., 1979-80. Author (tchg. ideas) English Counselor, 1986, Mailbox, 1993-98; reviewer children's jours., contbr. articles to profl. jours. Pres. Friends of the Libr., Dalton, 1994—. Named Reading Tchr. of Yr., Cherokee Coun., Northwest Ga., 1986-87; NEH scholar, Ark., 1993, Tex., 1998. Mem. NEA (com. mem.), Nat. Coun. Tchrs. English (coord. Young Writers Program 1986), Internat. Reading Assn. (S.E. team leader Young Adult Choices), Pilot Club (various offices including pres. 1986—, Ga. state parliamentarian 1988-89, lt. gov. 1991-93, team leader young adult choices 1998), Alpha Delta Kappa. Democrat. Methodist. Avocations: reading, serving community. Home: 4156-29A Hwy 225 N Chatsworth GA 30705 Office: Valley Point Mid Sch 3976 S Dixie Rd Dalton GA 30721-5111

FRESE, ALAN D.R., publishing executive; b. N.Y.C., Oct. 6, 1932. BA, Middlebury Coll., 1955. Editor Hasting House Pubs., N.Y.C., 1971-86; pres., sr. edit. Arctl. Book Pub. Co. Inc., Stamford, Conn., 1986—. Recipient Reginald Townsend award New Eng. Soc., N.Y.C. Mem. Dutch Treat Club. Office: Archtl Book Pub Co Inc 268 Dogwood Ln Stamford CT 06903-4518*

FRESHWATER, MICHAEL FELIX, surgeon, educator; b. N.Y.C., Feb. 4, 1948; s. Jack and Rhonda F. BS magna cum laude, Bklyn. Coll., 1968; MD, Yale U., 1972. Diplomate Nat. Bd. Med. Examiners, Am. Bd. Plastic Surgery. Asst. resident in surgery Yale New Haven Hosp., 1972-74; fellow in plastic surgery Med. Sch. Johns Hopkins U., Balt., 1974-77; resident, then chief resident in plastic surgery Jackson Meml. Hosp., 1977-78; Kleinert fellow hand and microsurgery U. Louisville, 1979; pvt. practice medicine specializing in hand surgery Miami, 1979—; pres., dir. Miami (Fla.) Inst. Hand and Microsurgery, 1980—; dir. hand and microsurgery Cedars Med. Ctr., 1985—, chief surgery, 1988-90, bd. dirs., 1990-92; mem. vol. faculty U. Miami Sch. Medicine, 1979—, Barry U. Sch. Podiatric Medicine and Surgery, 1989—; vis. prof. Javeriana U., Bogota, 1983-85, Centro Medico de los Andes, 1983-86; cons. Fla. Children's Med. Svc., Tallahassee, 1979—, Fla. Elks Crippled Children Svc., Orlando, 1983—, Fla. Dept. Profl. Regulation, Tallahassee, 1984-95, Fla. Agy. for Health Care Adminstrn., Tallahassee, 1995—, League Against Cancer, 1983—, Scientists Inst. for Pub. Info., 1985—, USCG, Miami Beach, 1992—. Contbr. chpts. to books and articles to profl. jours.; mem. bd. reviewers Plastic and Reconstructive Surgery, 1976—. Trustee Yale U. Med. Libr., New Haven, 1972-77, D.R. Millard Found., 1987—; bd. dirs. V and A Gildred Found., Miami, 1980-86; bd. dirs. Yale Sch. Medicine Fund, 1991-97; active nat. campaign com. Yale Sch. Medicine, 1993-97. Recipient Letter Commendation Gov. Bob Graham, 1984; Weinberger fellow NIH, 1974-76; Jonas Salk scholar CUNY, 1968-72. Fellow Internat. Coll. Surgeons; mem. AMA (Physicians Recognition award 1976, 79, 82, 85, 88, 90, 93, 96, 99), Am. Assn. Hand Surgery, Am. Burn Assn., Am. Soc. Reconstructive Microsurgery, Internat. Soc. Reconstructive Microsurgery, Royal Soc. Medicine, Greater Miami Soc. Plastic and Reconstructive Surgeons (sec.-treas. 1987-88, pres.-elect 1988-89, pres. 1989-90), Am. Soc. Peripheral Nerve, Miami Assn. for Surgery of Hand (dir. 1991—), Assn. Yale Alumni in Medicine (bd. dirs. 1998—), Yale Club (Miami, N.Y.), Grove Isle Club (Miami), Phi Beta Kappa. Avocation: skiing. Office: 1 Datran Ctr Ste 502 Miami FL 33156-7814

FRESHWATER, PAUL ROSS, consumer goods company executive; b. Columbus, Ohio, Aug. 16, 1941; s. Fayne F. and Lillian (Ross) F.; m. Robertine Ann Nekervis, June 14, 1964; 1 child, Ross Foley. BArch, Ohio State U., 1964; SM in Mgmt., MIT, 1968. Brand asst., mgr. Procter & Gamble, Cin., 1968-74, asst. to v.p., 1974-80, mgr. spl. projects, 1980-83, mgr. issues analysis, 1983-89, regional pub. affairs mgr., 1989—; treas., dir. The Film House, Inc., Cin., 1986—; treas. Ohio Alliance for Environ., Columbus, 1986-89; founding mem. Ohio Issues Scanning Network, Akron, 1988-89; founding bd. dirs., vice chair So. States Waste Mgmt. Coalition, Atlanta, 1992—; chair So. States Energy Bd. Assocs., Atlanta, 1994—. Editor Kennedy Heights Community News, 1973-75; editor-in-chief The Ohio State Engr., 1961-62. V.p., dir. Charter Com. of Greater Cin., 1979—; pres., mem. Kennedy Hts. Cmty. Coun., Cin., 1973— (Citizen of Yr. 1977); founding mem. Neighborhood Support Program Rev. Bd., Cin., 1980-82; high adventure exploring chmn. Dan Beard coun. Boy Scouts Am., Cin., 1983—. Lt. Civil Engring. Corp, USNR, 1964-66. Recipient Silver Beaver award Boy Scouts Am., 1992. Mem. Calumet Theater Soc., Keweenaw County Hist. Soc., Buick Club Am., Miscowaubik Club Calumet, Lit. Club Cin., Ohio Soc. Colonial Wars, Sigma Phi Epsilon (pres. Ohio Gamma Alumni Corp. 1970-71). Avocations: Sea Scouts, piano, summer home. Office: The Procter & Gamble Co 1 Procter And Gamble Plz Cincinnati OH 45202-3393

FRESTEDT, JOY LOUISE, scientist; b. Oak Park, Ill., Jan. 31, 1959; d. James Albert Machnicki and Wanda Louise (McConnaughhay) Katzman; m. Robert LeVance Frestedt, Aug. 8, 1987; 1 child, Megan Marie. BA in Biology, Knox Coll., 1980; PhD in Pathobiology, U. Minn., 1996. Rsch. asst. Knox Coll., 1978-80; cytogeneticist Ill. Masonic Med. Ctr., Chgo., 1980-81; med. tech., asst. scientist, rsch. scientist, lab. dir. U. Minn., Mpls., 1981-89, 91-96; cancer rsch. scientist III, lab. dir. Roswell Park Cancer Inst., Buffalo, 1989-90; rsch. scientist, lab. dir. Mpls. Children's Med. Ctr., 1990-91; grad. fellow Sci. Mus. Minn., St. Paul, 1993—; rsch. scientist St. Jude Med. Inc., St. Paul, 1996-97; grants reviewer U. Minn., 1994; mem. Grad. Women in Sci., Inc., 1984—, pres., 1996—, bd. dirs.; exec. bd. Minn. Acad. Sci., St. Paul, 1994-96, 97—; adj. faculty Mpls. Cmty. Tech. Coll., 1996—, North Hennepin C.C., 1997-98, Anoka Ramsey C.C., 1997-98, Rasmussen Bus. Coll., 1998-99, Medtronic/Mpls. Cmty. Tech. Coll., 1998. Co-author: Writing About Science, 1997, Researching the Right Way: Doing Research Like the Pros, 1997; referee, reviewer Jour. Women and Minorities in Sci. and Engring; contbr. articles to profl. jours. and books. Adv. bd. Operation Smart, YWCA, St. Paul, 1994-97. Mem. AAAS, Nat. Assn. Biology Tchrs., Coalition of Women Grad. Students, Preparing Future Faculty, Am. Assn. Cancer Rsch., Assn. Molecular Pathology, Am. Soc. Investigative Pathology, Am. Soc. Leukocyte Biology, Assn. Women in Sci., Am. Soc. Human Genetics, Sci. by Mail, Sigma Xi. Avocations: softball, mentoring activities, camping, corresponding scientist. E-mail: frest001@maroon.tc.umn.edu. Home: 5727 W 42nd St Saint Louis Park MN 55416-3101 Office: Biology Dept Mpls Cmty and Tech Coll 1501 Hennepin Ave Minneapolis MN 55403-1710

FRESTON, THOMAS E., cable television programming executive; b. N.Y.C., Nov. 22, 1945; s. Thomas E. and Winifred (Geng) F.; m. Margaret Badali, Oct. 18, 1980; 1 child, Andrew. BA, St. Michaels Coll., 1967; MBA, NYU, 1969. Dir. mktg.- MTV MTV Networks, N.Y.C., 1980-81, dir. mktg.- The Movie Channel, 1982-83; v.p. mktg.-MTV MTV Networks Inc., N.Y.C., 1983-84, v.p. mktg., 1984-85, sr. v.p./gen. mgr. affiliate sales, mktg., 1985, sr. v.p./gen. mgr. MTV, VH-1, 1985-86, pres. entertainment, 1986-87, pres., CEO, 1987-89; chmn., CEO MTV Networks, N.Y.C., 1989—; bd. dirs. Cable Advt. Bur., N.Y.C., 1987—, MTV Europe, London, 1986—, Rock 'n Roll Hall of Fame, N.Y.C., 1986—. Mem. Smithsonian com. Music in Am., 1987—. Mem. Cable TV Adminstrn. & Mktg. Assn., Nat. Acad. Cable Programming. Avocations: photography, travel, antique rugs. *

FRETER, MARK ALLEN, marketing and public relations executive, consultant; b. Chgo., Oct. 31, 1947; s. John Maher and Christopher Patricia (Allen) F. BA, U. Calif., Santa Barbara, 1969; MBA, U. Calif., Berkeley, 1971. Regional dir. HBO Svcs., Inc., L.A. and Denver, 1979-84; v.p. affiliate rels. X-Press Info. Svcs., Denver, 1984-85; v.p. mktg. Telecrafter Corp., Denver, 1985-86; mktg. dir. Computer Svcs. Corp., Boulder, Colo., 1986-87; prin., v.p. pub. rels. svcs. MultiMedia, Inc., Denver, 1987-88; dir. documentation and corp. comm., product specialist, op. cons. Data Select Systems Inc., Woodland Hills, Calif., 1988-91; pres., CEO The Aspen Group Ltd., Valencia, Calif., 1988—; mgr. mktg. comm. WorldCom, San Antonio, 1991-96; sr. mgr. product devel. GCI, Inc., Anchorage, 1996-97; sr. product mgr. LCI Internat., San Antonio, 1997-98; sr. product mgr. mgmt. Earthlink Network, Inc., Pasadena, Calif., 1998—; lectr. Internat. Coun. Shopping Ctrs., N.Y.C., 1977; conf. planner ICSC-West, San Francisco, 1978-79; tng. program devel. HBO, N.Y.C., 1982. Youth coach South Suburban YMCA, Littleton, Colo., 1984-86. Recipient First Pl. cert. for Retail Ad Campaign San Diego Advt. Assn., 1980. Mem. Calif. Cable TV Assn., No. Calif. Promotion Mgrs. Assn. (v.p. 1977-78), So. Calif. Promotion Mgrs. Assn. (sec., treas. 1976-77). Democrat. Mem. Soc. Friends. Avocations: skiing, ice hockey, reading, coaching youth sports.

FRETWELL, ELBERT KIRTLEY, JR., retired university chancellor, consultant; b. N.Y.C., Oct. 29, 1923; s. Elbert Kirtley and Jean (Hosford) F.; m. Dorris Shearer, Aug. 25, 1951; children: Barbara Alice (Mrs. Peter Cooke), Margaret Jean (Mrs. John C. Cross), James Leonard, Katharine Louise (Mrs. Robert Saul). A.B. with distinction, Wesleyan U., Middletown, Conn., 1944; M.A. in Tchg., Harvard U., 1948; Ph.D., Columbia U., 1953; hon. doctorate, Tech. U. Wroclaw, Poland, 1976; LL.D. (hon.), Wesleyan U., 1981; D in Pub. Svc. (hon.), U. N.C., Charlotte, 1998. Stringer AP, 1942-44; staff writer ARC, 1944-45; vice consul Am. embassy, Prague, Czech Republic, 1945-47; tchr. Brookline (Mass.) Pub. Schs., 1948, Evanston (Ill.) Twp. High Sch. and Community Coll., 1948-50; adminstrv. sec. John Hay Fellowships, John Hay Whitney Found., 1951-53; asst. prof., asst. to dean Tchrs. Coll., Columbia U., 1953-56, assoc. prof., 1956; asst. commr. for higher edn. N.Y. State Dept. Edn., 1956-64; summer faculty U. Calif. at Berkeley, 1964; dean acad. devel. CUNY, 1964-67; pres. SUNY, Buffalo, 1967-78; chancellor U. N.C., Charlotte, 1979-89, chancellor emeritus, 1989—; sr. assoc. MDC Inc., 1989-91; interim pres. U. Mass. System, 1991-92; chair N.C. edn. Stds. and Accountability Commn., 1993-97, N.C. Transit 2001 Commn., 1995-97; interim pres. U. North Fla., 1998; mem. commn. higher instns. Mid. States Assn. of Schs. and Colls., 1965-71, pres., chmn., 1973-74; trustee Carnegie Found. for Advancement Tchg., chmn., 1975-77; mem. Carnegie Coun. on Policy Studies in Higher Edn., 1973-79; bd. dirs. Microelectronics Ctr., N.C., 1981-89, N.C. Transp. History Found., 1996—; trustee Wesleyan U., 1967-70, Nichols Sch., Buffalo, 1969-78, Canisius Coll., 1969-76, Peace Coll., 1997—; bd. dirs. Found. of U. N.C., Charlotte, 1981-89; exec. dir. com. on edn. N.Y. State Constl. Conv., 1967; mem. N.C. State Goals and Policy Bd., 1983-91; cons. U.S. Info. Svc., Austria, 1989, Spain and Hungary, 1990. Author: Founding Public Junior Colleges, 1954, The

Interim Presidency: Guidelines for University and College Governing Boards, 1995, (with David W. Leslie) Wise Moves in Hard Times: Creating & Managing Resilient Colleges & Universities, 1996, also articles, chpts. in profl. yearbooks. Vice chmn. N.Y. State Am. Revolution Bicentennial Commn., 1969-76; pres. Mecklenburg coun. Boy Scouts Am., 1985-87. Carnegie Corp. grantee, 1964, 74; decorated Order of Cultural Merit Poland; recipient ann award N.Y. State Assn. Jr. Colls., 1962, Disting. Alumnus award Wesleyan U., 1974, Tchrs. Coll., Columbia U., 1983, Boy Scouts Am. Silver Beaver award. Mem. Am. Assn. State Colls. and Univs. (pres. 1978-79), Am. Assn. for Higher Edn. (pres. 1964-65), Am. Coun. Edn. (chmn. 1980-81), N.C. Assn. Colls. and Univs. (pres. 1985-86), Nat. Rlwy. Hist. Soc., Adirondack Mountain Club, Rotary (pres. Charlotte chpt. 1994-95). Home: 124 Amrita Ct Charlotte NC 28211-4019 Office: U NC-Charlotte 9201 Univ City Blvd Charlotte NC 28223-0001

FRETZ, MARK JONATHAN HOCHSTETLER, editor, religion educator; b. Lansdale, Pa., Dec. 4, 1958; s. Merrill Emerson and Nancy Carol (Reichley) F.; m. Angela Kathryn Hochstetler, Dec. 21, 1979; 1 child, Elyse Audrey Hochstetler. BA in Bible and Psychology, Ea. Mennonite Coll., 1979; MDiv in Bibl. Studies, Mennonite Bibl. Sem., 1984; PhD in Bibl. Studies and Hebrew, U. Mich., 1993. Hebrew lang. asst. Mennonite Bibl. Sem., Elkhart, Ind., 1982; tchg. fellow Goshen (Ind.) Coll., 1983-84; instr. bible and religion Freeman (S.D.) Jr. Coll., 1984-86; grad. tchg. asst. U. Mich., Ann Arbor, 1986-89; editl. asst., writer Anchor Bible Dictionary Project, Ann Arbor, Mich., 1987-90; asst. prof. religion Bluffton (Ohio) Coll., 1990-91; asst. prof. bible Ea. Mennonite Coll., Harrisonburg, Va., 1991-93; sr. editor religious pub. Doubleday, N.Y.C., 1994—. Contbr. articles to books. Arthur F. Thurnau fellow and Radcliffe Ramsdell fellow U. Mich., 1987-88. Mem. Am. Acad. Religion, Am. Schs. Oriental Rsch., Soc. Bibl. Lit. Avocations: computer, reading, gardening, swimming, genealogies. Office: Doubleday Religion Dept 1540 Broadway New York NY 10036-4039

FRETZ, THOMAS A., agricultural studies educator; b. Buffalo, Oct. 9, 1942; m. Susan Fretz; children: Peter, Christian. BS in Hort., U. Md., 1964; MS in Hort. and Plant Sci., U. Del., 1966, PhD in Hort. and Plant Sci., 1970. Mem. faculty U. Ga.-Ga. Experiment Sta., 1969-72, Ohio State U., Columbus, 1972-79; chair dept. hort. Kans. State U., 1979-81, Va. Poly. Inst. and State U., Blacksburg, 1981-89; assoc. dean Coll. Agr. Iowa State U., College Park, 1989-94; assoc. dir. Iowa Agr. and Home Econs. Experiment Sta. Iowa State U., 1989-94; dean Coll. Agr. and Natural Resources U. Md., College Park, 1994—; dir. Md. Agrl. Experiment Sta., 1994—, Md. Coop. Extension Svc., 1994—; mem. USDA adv. bd. U.S. Nat. Arboretum 1981-87, 92-94; rschr. on weed control in field and container grown nursery crops. Contbr. numerous articles and reports to profl. publs. Fellow Am. Soc. Hort. Sci. (mem. numerous coms. and bds., chmn. bd. dirs. 1992-93, pres. 1991-92, v.p. edn. divsn. 1988-89, publs. com. 1978-81, fin. com. 1984-90, co-chair program com. 1979, gen. chair ann. meeting 1985, assoc. editor jour. 1976-82, co-recipient Kenneth Post award 1979); mem. Am. Hort. Soc. (bd. dirs. 1982-84). Avocation: outdoor activities. Office: U Md Coll Agr 1104 Symons Hall College Park MD 20742-5500*

FREUD, NICHOLAS S., lawyer; b. N.Y.C., Feb. 6, 1942; s. Frederick and Fredericka (von Rothenburg) F.; m. Elsa Doskow, July 23, 1966; 1 child, Christopher. AB, Yale U., 1963, JD, 1966. Bar: N.Y. 1968, Calif. 1970, U.S. Tax Ct. 1973. Ptnr. Chickering & Gregory, San Francisco, 1978-85, Russin & Vecchi, San Francisco, 1986-93, Jeffer, Mangels, Butler & Marmaro, LLP, San Francisco, 1993—; mem. joint adv. bd. Calif. Continuing Edn. of Bar, chair taxation subcom. 1987-87; mem. fgn. income adv. bd. Tax Management Internat. Jour., mem. bd. advs. The Jour. of Internat. Taxation; mem. adv. bd. NYU Inst. on Fed. Taxation. Author: (with Charles G. Stephenson and K. Bruce Friedman) International Estate Planning, rev. edit., 1997; contbr. articles to profl. jours. Fellow Am. Coll. of Tax Counsel (cert. specialist in taxation law) mem. ABA (tax sect. coun. dir. 1995-97, chair com. on U.S. activities of foreigners and tax treaties 1989-91, vice chair 1987-89, chair subcom. on tax treaties 1981-87), Calif. State Bar Assn. (taxation sect. exec. com. 1981-85, vice chair 1982-83, chair 1983-84, vice chair income tax com. 1981-82, chair 1982-83, vice chair personal income tax subcom. 1979-80, chair 1980-81, co-chair fgn. tax subcom. 1978-79), N.Y. State Bar Assn. (taxation sect., mem. com. on U.S. activities of fgn. taxpayers and fgn. activities of U.S. taxpayers), Bar Assn. of San Francisco, Bar Assn. of City of N.Y., San Francisco Tax Club (pres. 1988), San Francisco Internat. Tax Group. Office: Jeffer Mangels Butler & Marmaro LLP 1 Sansome St Fl 12 San Francisco CA 94104-4430

FREUDENBERGER, HERMAN, retired economics educator; b. Eberbach, Germany, Apr. 14, 1922; came to U.S., 1934; s. Alfred and Frieda (Gruenebaum) F.; m. Paulette Ethel Gross, June 17, 1951; children—Joseph, Alfred Carl. B.S., Columbia U., 1950, M.A., 1951, Ph.D., 1957. Instr. Bklyn. Coll., 1956-58, 59-60; lectr. Rutgers U., New Brunswick, N.J., 1958-59; asst. prof. U. Mont., Missoula, 1960-62; assoc. prof. Tulane U., New Orleans, 1962-66, prof. econs., 1966-92, prof. emeritus, 1992—. Author: The Industrialization of a Central European City, 1977, (with others) Von der Provinzstadt zur Industrieregion, 1975, A Redemptorist Missionary in Ireland 1851-1854, 1998; contbr. articles to profl. jours. Served with U.S. Army, 1942-46, ETO. Home: 709 Ashlawn Dr New Orleans LA 70123-3809

FREUDENBURG, WILLIAM R., sociology educator; b. Norfolk, Nebr., Nov. 2, 1951; s. Eldon G. and Betty D. Freudenburg. BA, U. Nebr., 1974; MA, Yale U., 1976, MPhil, 1977, PdD, 1979. Research assoc. Yale U., New Haven, 1975-77; asst. prof. sociology and rural sociology Wash. State U., Pullman, 1978-83; assoc. prof. rural sociology Wash. State U., 1983-86, U. Wis., Madison, 1986-91; prof. rural sociology and environ. studies U. Wis., 1991—; mem. sci. com. U.S. Dept. Interior, minerals mgmt. svc., 1982-91, chair socioecon. sub-com., 1986-91; researcher, cons. in field. Author: Public Reactions to Nuclear Power: Are There Critical Masses?, 1984, Paradoxes of Western Energy Development, 1984, Oil in Troubled Waters: Perceptions, Politics and the Battle Over Offshore Drilling, 1994; contbr. articles to profl. jours. Recipient award for disting. contbns. Soc. Environment and Tech., 1996; Hawksworth scholar, 1970-72, Nat. Merit scholar, 1970-74; NSF grad. fellow, 1975-79. Fellow Soc. for Applied Anthropology; mem. Am. Sociol. Assn. (coun., sect. on environ. sociology 1980-83, chair-elect 1987-89, chair sect. on environ. and tech. 1989-91, congl. fellow 1983-84, award Disting. Contbns. to Sociology of Environment & Tech. 1996), Internat. Assn. for Impact Assessment, NAS (panelist, adv. com. on future nuclear power 1984, com. Alaska outer continental shelf oil and gas program 1992-94, com. N.Y. low level radioactive waste program 1993-96), Rural Sociol. Soc. (v.p. 1993-94, chmn. natural resources rsch. group 1982-83, program chmn. 1983-84, mem. various coms., local arrangements chmn. 1986-87, award of merit, natural resources rsch. group 1991), AAAS (life, Rural Sociol. Soc. rep. 1979-86, sec., sect. on social, econ. and polit. scis. 1986-94, chair-elect, sect. on social econ. and polit. scis. 1994-95, chair sect. on social, econ. and polit. scis. 1995-96, retiring chair sect. on social, econ. and polit. scis. 1996-97), Soc. for Risk Analysis, Coun. for Agrl. Sci. and Tech., Wis. Sociol. Assn., Law and Soc. Assn. (life), Midwest Sociol. Assn., Phi Beta Kappa, Phi Eta Sigma. Office: Univ Wis Dept Rural Sociology 350 Agriculture Hall 1450 Linden Dr Madison WI 53706-1522

FREUDENHEIM, MILTON B., journalist; b. New Rochelle, N.Y., Mar. 4, 1927; s. Milton Benjamin and Lenore Patricia (Kroh) F.; m. Elizabeth Ege, Mar. 7, 1952 (dec. Dec. 30, 1996); children: Jo Louise, Susan Patricia, John Milton Otto, Tom Henry. A.B., U. Mich., 1948. Reporter Louisville (Ky.) Courier-Jour., 1948-49; reporter Akron (Ohio) Beacon Jour., 1949-52, Washington corr., 1953-56; UN corr. Chgo. Daily News, 1956-66, nat. and fgn. editor, 1966-69, Paris corr., 1969-77; dir. public affairs for Region V HEW, Chgo., 1978-79; copy editor, writer N.Y. Times Week in Rev., 1979-87, bus. and health reporter, 1987—; adv. U.S. del. UNESCO Gen. Conf., 1978; Pres. UN Corrs. Assn., 1966, Anglo-Am. Press Assn., Paris, 1975. Mem. Phi Beta Kappa, Sigma Delta Chi. Home: 123 W 74th St New York NY 10023-2209 Office: NY Times 229 W 43rd St New York NY 10036-3959

FREUDENHEIM, TOM LIPPMANN, museum administrator; b. Stuttgart, Germany, July 3, 1937; came to U.S., 1938, naturalized, 1943; s. Ernest Simon and Margot Ruth (Freund) F.; m. Leslie Ann Mandelson, Nov. 15, 1964; children: Alexander Darius, Adam Jeremy. AB, Harvard U., 1959; postgrad., Hebrew Union Coll., 1959-61; MA, NYU, 1966; DFA (hon.), U. Md., 1982. Asst. curator Jewish Mus., N.Y.C., 1962-65; asst. dir. Univ. Art Mus., U. Calif. at Berkeley, 1966-71; dir. Balt. Mus. of Art, 1971-78; dir. museum programs Nat. Endowment for Arts, Washington, 1979-82; dir. Worcester Art Mus., Mass., 1982-85; asst. sec. for museums Smithsonian Instn., Washington, 1986-92, asst. sec. for arts and humanities, 1992-95; guest scholar Woodrow Wilson Ctr., 1996; exec. dir. Yivo Inst. for Jewish Rsch., N.Y.C., 1996-98; dep. dir. Jewish Mus. Berlin, 1998—. Contbr. articles on decorative and modern art to profl. publs. Trustee Harvard Pierian Found., Am. Fedn. Arts; chmn. Nat. Found. Jewish Culture. USIA grantee Romania, Czechoslovakia, 1969, State Dept. grantee Japan, 1971, Romania, 1974. Mem. Coll. Art Assn., Am. Assn. Mus., Century Assn., St. Botolph Club. Office: Yivo Inst for Jewish Rsch, Lindenstrasse 9-14, 10969 Berlin Germany Address: 425 Riverside Dr Apt 9K New York NY 10025-7729

FREUDENRICH, DAVID ROBERT, civil engineer, traffic engineer; b. Pitts., Dec. 22, 1961; s. Robert David and Frances M. (Feduska) F.; m. Tara Ann Howey; 1 child, Mackenzie Lee. BS in Bioloy, Pa. State U., 1984; BS in Civil Engring. Tech., Point Park Coll., 1994. Engr. in tng. Design engr. Boswell Engring., South Hackensack, N.J., 1984-87, Travers Assocs., Clifton, N.J., 1987-89; engr. Mackin Engring. Co., Inc., Pitts., 1989; sr. planner Wilbur Smith Assocs., Pitts., 1989-94; sr. traffic engr. Maguire Group Inc., Pitts., 1994—. Chmn. computer practices group ASCE, 1991-93; info. tech. chmn. focus group Maguire Group Inc., 1998—; jr. bd. dirs. Rehab. Inst. Pitts., 1991-93; indsl. adv. bd. Point Park Coll., 1994—; co-chmn. reservations Burger King Cancer Caring Ctr.-Steeler Fashion Show Fundraiser, 1994—; mem. corp. stds. com. Maguire Group Inc., 1998—. Mem. ASCE (bd. dirs. Pitts. sect., exec. sec. Pitts. sect.), ASME, Am. Soc. Hwy. Engrs. (sr.), Inst. Transp. Engrs. (assoc.), Acoustical Soc. Am., Pitts. Squash Racquets Assoc., Corp. Computer Stds. (chair corp. info. tech.), Pitts. Regional Intelligent Transp. System (steering com.). Republican. Roman Catholic. Avocations: squash, tennis, computers, photography, gardening. Home: 106 Timberlane Dr Pittsburgh PA 15229-1059 Office: Maguire Group Inc 564 Forbes Ave Ste 1212 Pittsburgh PA 15219-2903

FREUDENTHAL, DAVID D., prosecutor. U.S. atty. for Wyo. U.S. Dept. Justice, Cheyenne, 1994—. Office: US Atty Dist Wyo 2120 Capitol Ave Rm 4002 Cheyenne WY 82001-3633*

FREUDENTHAL, ERNEST GUENTER, technology and business educator; b. Mannheim, Germany, July 22, 1920; came to the U.S., 1937; s. Leopold and Selma (Rosenthal) F.; m. Stephanie Karlsruher, Dec. 26, 1948; children: Pamela Hausman, Joan Fraifeld. BA in Econs., Vanderbilt U., 1948, MA in Econs., 1971. Employee Werthan Industries, Nashville, 1942-44, 46-48, middle mgmt. staff, 1948-69, v.p. mfg., 1969-71, sr. v.p., 1971-90; adj. assoc. prof. bus., tech., pub. policy, indsl. mktg. Vanderbilt U., Nashville, 1971—. Mem. Bus. Res. Adv. Coun. to the Bur. Labor Statis., Washington, 1981—; chmn. Metro Social Svcs. Commn., Nashville, 1989—, Com. on Employment Projections of the Bus. Rsch. Adv. Coun., Washington, 1997—; commr. Tenn. Holocaust Commn., Inc., 1998—; pres. Jewish Cmty. Ctr., Nashville, 1965-67. Staff sgt. U.S. Army, 1944-46, PTO. Recipient Sage award Coun. on Aging, Nashville, 1995. Mem. Jewish Fedn. Nashville (pres. 1974-76), The Temple (pres. 1986-88), Vanderbilt Inst. Pub. Policy Studies, Univ. Club, Phi Beta Kappa. Avocation: hiking. Home: 4406 Sunnybrook Dr Nashville TN 37205-3860 Office: Vanderbilt Univ Box 6188 Nashville TN 37235

FREUDENTHAL, RALPH IRA, toxicology consultant; b. N.Y.C., Aug. 27, 1940; m. Susan E. Loy; children: Judith, Jennifer, Ralph D. BS, NYU, 1963; PhD, SUNY, Buffalo, 1969. Biochem. pharmacologist Rsch. Triangle Inst., Research Triangle Park, N.C., 1969-73; assoc. mgr. Battelle Meml. Inst., Columbus, Ohio, 1973-77; dir. toxicology Stauffer Chem. Co., Farmington, Conn., 1977-84; dir. health, safety and regulatory affairs Stauffer Chem. Co., Westport, Conn., 1984-88; cons. Toxicology Consultancy, West Palm Beach, Fla., 1988—; steering com. Rene Dubos Ctr. for Environ., N.Y.C., 1982-89. Co-author: Polycyclic Aromatic Hydrocarbons, Chemistry, Metabolism and Carcinogenesis, 1976, What You Need to Know to Live With Chemicals, 1989, Food Facts and Fictions, 1991, Material Safety Data Sheets, The Writer's Desk Reference, 1992, 1995 Directory of Toxicology Laboratories Offering Contract Services, 1995; contbr. articles to profl. jours. Mem. Soc. of Toxicology, Am. Soc. Pharmacology and Exptl. Therapeutics, Am. Assn. for Cancer Rsch., Soc. for Environ. Toxicology and Chemistry. Home and Office: 8737 Estate Dr West Palm Beach FL 33411-6594

FREUDENTHAL, STEVEN FRANKLIN, lawyer; b. Thermopolis, Wyo., June 8, 1949; s. Lewis Franklin and Lucille Iola (Love) F.; m. Janet Mae Mansfield, Aug. 30, 1969 (div. Sept. 1996); children: Lynn Marie, Kristen Lee; m. Barbara A. Crofts, Jan. 1, 1998; stepchildren: Shane C., Jeanne N. B.A., Trinity Coll., Hartford, Conn., 1971; J.D., Vanderbilt U., 1975. Bar: Wyo. 1975, U.S. Supreme Ct. 1981. Tax acct. Conn. Gen. Life Ins. Co., Hartford, Conn., 1971-72; asst. atty. gen. Wyo. Cheyenne, 1975-77, atty. gen. Wyo., 1981-82; state planning coordinator Office Gov. Wyo., Cheyenne, 1977-78; dep. under sec. Dept. Interior, Washington, 1978-79, exec. asst. to sec., 1979-80; ptnr Sherman & Howard, Cheyenne, Wyo., 1980-81; ptnr. Herschler, Freudenthal, Salzburg & Bonds, Cheyenne, 1982—; mem. Wyo. Ho. Reps., 1987-91. Trustee United Med. Ctr., 1990—, pres., 1993-96; bd. dirs. Cheyenne LEADS, 1990-93, 97; chmn. Wyo. Dem. Party, 1999—. Office: 314 E 21st St PO Box 387 Cheyenne WY 82003-0387

FREUKES, PATRICIA E., pediatrics nurse, nursing supervisor; b. St. Louis, Oct. 13, 1954; d. Lawrence D. Sr. and Helen L. (Wooliver) F. Student, Jefferson Coll., 1973-74; RN, Luth. Med. Ctr. Sch. Nursing, 1977; student, Maryville Coll., 1977-78; BSN, St. Louis U., 1987. Staff nurse in orthopedics Luth. Hosp., St. Louis, 1977-79; staff nurse neurology/neurosurgery St. Louis Children's Hosp., 1979-88, adminstrv. supr., 1988—. Home: 3270 Bayshore Pky Arnold MO 63010-4034

FREUND, CYNTHIA M., dean, nursing educator. BSN, Marquette U., 1963; MSN, U. N.C., 1973, FNP, 1974; PhD in Bus. and Health Adminstrn., U. Ala., 1981. Staff nurse McHenry (Ill.) Hosp., 1963, 64-65, VA Hosp., Wood, Wis., 1963-64; instr. Milw. County Instns., Wauwatosa, Wis., 1965-68, supr. Milw. County Rehab. and Chronic Disease Hosp., 1968-70; instr. Sch. Nursing U. Wis., Milw., 1972-73; dir. FNP program Area L Health Edn. Ctr., Tarboro, N.C., 1973-74; asst. prof., assoc. dir. FNP program U. N.C., Chapel Hill, 1974-78, assoc. prof., chair social and adminstrv. sys. dept., 1984-92, dean, prof. nursing, 1992—; asst. prof. U. Pa., Phila., 1981-84, sr. rsch. assoc. Leonard Davis Inst. Health Econs., 1981-84, dir. MSN nursing adminstrn. program, PhD in nursing/MBA joint degree, 1981-84; mem. Gov. Advocacy Com. for Children and Youth State of Wis., 1973; bd. dirs. N.C. Ctr. for Child and Family Health, 1996, N.C. Inst. Medicine, 1996—; mem. N.C. Med. Data Base Commn., N.C. Gen. Assembly, 1985-89; mem. nursing adv. panel P.E.W. Health Professions Commn., 1991-92; mem. nat. adv. com. for project future requirements for nurse practitioners and nurse midwives Dept. Health and Human Svcs., 1993-94, mem. joint adv. com. to project future requirements for primary care physicians, and others, Bur. Health Professions, 1994-95; cons., presenter in field. Author: (with D. del Bueno) Power and Politics in Nursing Administration, 1986 (Am. Jour Nursing Book of Yr. 1986), Nursing: A Kaleidoscopic View, 1991 (Am. Jour. Nursing Book of Yr. 1991); author chpts. to books; mem. editl. bd. Nursing Econs., 1982-84, manuscript reviewer, 1982—; manuscript reviewer Jour. Profl. Nursing, 1984—, Health Svc. Rsch., 1984—, Planning for Higher Edn., 1986; contbr. articles to profl. jours. Bd. dirs. N.C. Ctr. Child and Family Health, 1996, N.C. Inst. Medicine, 1996—. Pub. Health Svc. Doctoral fellow Nat. Ctr. for Health Svcs. Rsch., 1980-81, Rsch. fellow Nat. Health Care Mgmt. Ctr., 1980-81; recipient Profl. Svc. Alumni award Marquette U., 1992. Fellow Am. Acad. Nursing; mem. ANA (vice-chair coun. FNP and clinicians 1977-78, cert. adult nurse practitioner 1977, Jessie M. Scott award 1990), Nat. League Nursing, Acad. Mgmt., Am. Orgn. Nurse Execs., Am. Hosp. Assn. Office: U NC Sch Nursing CB # 7460 Carrington Hall Chapel Hill NC 27599-7460*

FREUND, DEBORAH MIRIAM, transportation engineer; b. Bklyn., Apr. 9, 1957; d. Harry and Bertha (Fried) F.; m. Garey Douglas White, Feb. 22, 1981. BSCE, Washington U., 1979, MSc, 1982. Registered profl. engr., Tex. Grad. rsch. asst. Washington U., St. Louis, 1979-81; transp. planning engr. Mid-Am. Regional Coun., Kansas City, Mo., 1981-83; civil engr. Fed. Hwy. Adminstrn., Washington, 1983-85, rsch. hwy. engr., 1985-90, transp. specialist, 1990-92, sr. transp. specialist, 1992—; mem. Com. Operator and Vehicle Performance and Simulation Transp. Rsch. Bd., Washington, 1993-96, Com. on Vehicle User Characteristics, 1997—; presenter in field. Fellow Coun. for Excellence in Govt., Washington, 1995-96; recipient U.S Dept. Transp. award for meritorious achievement, 1996. Mem. ASCE (sec. hwy. divsn. rsch. com. 1988-90), Soc. Automative Engrs. (co-chair total vehicle com. 1997—), Inst. Transp. Engrs., Sigma Xi (assoc.). Achievements include leadership in research on commercial motor vehicle driver safety; innovation in pavement infrastructure information systems. Avocations: photography, bicycling. E-mail: deborah.freund@fhwa.dot.gov. Office: Fed Hwy Adminstrn 400 7th St SW Rm 3107 Washington DC 20590-0001

FREUND, ECKHARD, electrical engineering educator; b. Düsseldorf, Germany, Feb. 28, 1940; s. Karl and Margret (Meya) F.; m. Brigitte Keudel; children: Viviane, Ariane. Diploma in engring., Tech. Sch. Darmstadt, Fed. Republic Germany, 1965; D Engring., Tech. U. Berlin, 1968. Scientist U. Raumfahrt, Oberpfaffenhofen, Fed. Republic Germany, 1965-70; guest prof. aero. engring. U. So. Calif., L.A., 1972-76, 83; guest scientist European Space Ops. Ctr., Darmstadt, Fed. Republic Germany, 1970-71; sci. coord. Fraunhofer Inst., Karlsruhe, Fed. Republic Germany, 1976-78; prof. dept. elec. engring. Fernuniversität, Hagen, Fed. Republic Germany, 1978-84; prof. dept. elec. engring., dir. Inst. Robotics Rsch. U. Dortmund, Fed. Republic Germany, 1985—; sci. adviser Jet Propulsion Lab., NASA, Pasadena, Calif., 1983. Author: Zeitvariable Mehrgrössensysteme, 1971, Regelungssysteme in Zustandsraum, I/II, 1986, 87; contbr. some 250 articles on robotics and automation to tech. publs. Office: Inst Robotics Rsch Dortmund, Otto Hahn Strasse 8, D 44221 Dortmund Germany

FREUND, EMMA FRANCES, medical technologist; b. 1922; d. Walter R. and Mabel W. (Loveland) Ervin; m. Frederic Reinert Freund, March 4, 1953; children: Frances, Daphne, Fern, Frederic. BS, Wilson Tchrs. Coll., Washington, 1944; MS in Biology, Cath. U., Washington, 1953; MEd in Adult Edn., Va. Commonwealth U., 1988. Tchr. math and sci. D.C. Sch. Sys., Washington, 1944-45; technician in parasitology lab. U.S. Dept. Agr., Beltsville, Md., 1945-48; histologic technician dept. pathology Georgetown U. Med. Sch., Washington, 1948-49; clin. lab. technician Kent and Queen Anne's County Gen. Hosp., Chestertown, Md., 1949-51; histotechnologist Med. Coll. Va. Hosp., Richmond, Va., 1951—; cons. profl. meetings and workshops; mem. exam. coun. Nat. Cert. Agy. Med. Lab. Pers. Co-author: (mini-course) Instrumentation in Cytology and Histology, 1985; editor Histo-Scope Newsletter. Asst. Cub Scout den leader Robert E. Lee coun. Boy Scouts Am., 1967-68, den leader, 1968-70. Fellow Internat. Biographical Assn.; mem. AAAS, NAFE, AAUW, APA, Am. Mgmt. Assn., Am. Soc. Clin. Lab. Sci. (rep. to sci. assenbly histology sect. 1977-78, chmn. 1983-85, 89-96), Am. Psychol. Soc., Va. Soc. Med. Tech. (Richmond chpt. corr. sec. 1977-78, bd. dirs. 1981-82, pres. 1984-85), Va. State Soc. Histotech. (pres. 1994-96), Nat. Certification Agy. (clin. lab. specialist in histotech., clin. lab. supr. clin. lab. dir.), N.Y. Acad. Scis., Am. Assn. Clin. Chemistry (assoc.), Am. Soc. Clin. Pathologists (cert. histology technician), Nat. Geog. Soc., Va. Govtl. Employees Assn., Nat. Soc. Histotech. (by-laws com. 1981—, C.E.U. com. 1981—, program com. regional meeting 1984, 85, 97, chmn. regional meeting 1987, program chmn. regional meeting 1987, 92, Conv. scholarship award 1997, program chmn. state meeting 1998, 99), Am. Mus. Natural History, Smithsonian Inst., Am. Mgmt. Assn., Clin. Lab. Mgmt. Assn., Van Slyke Soc., Nat. Soc. Historic Preservation, Sigma Xi, Phi Beta Rho, Kappa Delta Pi, Phi Lambda Theta. Home: 1315 Asbury Rd Richmond VA 23229-5305

FREUND, FRED A., retired lawyer; b. N.Y.C., June 18, 1928; s. Sidney J. and Cora (Strasser) F.; m. Rosalie Sampo, Nov. 18, 1975 (div. Apr. 1983); m. Patricia A. Gardner, Mar. 13, 1957 (div. Jan. 1967); children: Gregory G., K. Bailey. A.B., Columbia U., 1948, J.D., 1949. Bar: N.Y. 1949, U.S. Supreme Ct. 1968. Law clk. to chief judge U.S. Dist. Ct. So. Dist. N.Y., N.Y.C., 1949-51; assoc. Kaye, Scholer, Fierman, Hays & Handler, N.Y.C., 1953-58, ptnr., 1959-93, ret., 1993. Served to 1st lt. USAF, 1951-53. Mem. ABA, Assn. Bar City N.Y., Phi Beta Kappa. Home: 1085 Park Ave Apt 4C New York NY 10128-1179 *Balancing the quest for excellence with humility and humor.*

FREUND, FREDRIC S., real estate broker, property manager; b. Denver, Sept. 23, 1930. AB, Brown U., 1952. Sr. v.p. Hanford, Freund & Co., San Francisco, 1956—; past adv. dir. Western Investment Real Estate Trust; bd. dirs. Berkeley Antibody Co.; instr. real estate mgmt. U. Calif. Ext.; guest lectr. Stanford U. Sch. Bus. Adminstrn. Commr. Calif. Senate Adv. Commn. on Cost Control in State Govt. Mem. Am. Soc. Real Estate Counselors (CRE, pres. no. Calif. 1987-88), San Francisco Assn. Realtors (pres. 1974-75, Realtor of Yr. 1975), Bldg. Owners & Mgrs. Assn. San Francisco, Realtors Nat. Mktg. Inst. (CCIM), Inst. Real Estate Mgmt. (CPM). E-mail: ffreund@hanfordfreund.com. FAX: 415-296-0725. Office: Hanford Freund & Co 47 Kearny St Ste 300 San Francisco CA 94108-5582

FREUND, JOHN RICHARD, former English educator; b. Chgo., Nov. 16, 1926; s. Charles Anton and Helen Mary Freund; m. Barbara Ann Krohn, Sept. 11, 1948; children: David Eric, Alaric James. BA, Miami U., Oxford, Ohio, 1949, MA, 1950; PhD, Ind. U., 1955. Asst. prof. English Western Mich. U., Kalamazoo, 1954-64; assoc. prof. English Grand Valley State Coll., Allendale, Mich., 1964-68; prof. English King's Coll., Wilkes-Barre, Pa., 1968-71; prof. English Ind. U. of Pa., Indiana, Pa., 1971-90, English prof. emeritus, 1990—; supr. English Program for Disadvantaged Pre-Coll. Youth, Ind. Colls. Tng. Program, Kalamazoo, 1968; specialist, Adult Basic Edn. Tchr. Tng. Inst., Wilkes-Barre, 1971; cons. Consultant Cadre, Right to Read, State of Pa., 1977-78. Author: Broken Symmetries: A Study of Agency in Shakespeare's Plays, 1991; (with Arnold Nelson) Where Minds Meet ednl. radio series, 1963; author/performer: The Nature of Perception closed-circuit TV program, 1964 (Ohio State Award); editor: Studies in the Humanities Jour., 1972-81. With USN, 1944-46, PTO. Mem. MLA, Assoc. Lit. Scholars and Critics. Democrat. Avocations: raising dogs and cats. E-mail: jrfreund@wideopen.net. Home: 8 Deborah Trail Fairfield PA 17320

FREUND, LAMBERT BEN, engineering educator, researcher, consultant; b. McHenry, Ill., Nov. 23, 1942; s. Bernard and Anita (Schaeffer) F.; m. Colleen Jean Hehl, Aug. 21, 1965; children: Jonathan Ben, Jeffrey Alan, Stephen Neil. B.S., U. Ill., 1964, M.S., 1965; Ph.D., Northwestern U., 1967. Postdoctoral fellow Brown U., Providence, 1967-69; asst. prof. Brown U., 1969-73, assoc. prof., 1973-75, prof. engring., 1975—, Henry Ledyard Goddard prof., 1988—, chmn. div., 1979-83; vis. prof. Stanford (Calif.) U., 1974-75, 95; cons. Aberdeen Proving Ground, U.S. Steel Corp.; vis. scholar Harvard U., 1983-84; mem.-at-large U.S. Nat. Com. for Theoretical and Applied Mechanics, NRC, 1985-97; mem. IUTAM Gen. Assembly, 1987—, treas., 1996—; Russell Severance Springer prof. U. Calif., Berkeley, 1995; cons. Advanced Rsch. Projects Agy. Def. Scis. Rsch. Coun.; disting. vis. scientist Jet Propulsion Lab NASA, 1994—. Author: Dynamic Fracture Mechanics, 1990; editor in chief: ASME Jour. Applied Mechanics, 1983-88, editor Cambridge monographs on Mechanics and Applied Mathematics, 1989—, Jour. Mechanics and Physics of Solids, 1992—; mem. editorial adv. bd. Acta Mechanica Sinica, 1990—; contbr. articles to tech. jours. NSF trainee, 1964-67; grantee NSF, Office Naval Rsch., Army Rsch. Office, Nat. Bur. Stads., Air Force Office Sci. Rsch., Dept. Energy; recipient Alumni Honor award Coll. Engring., U. Ill., 1996. Fellow ASME (Henry Hess award 1974, mem. applied mechanics divsn. exec. com. 1989-94), Am. Acad. Mechanics, Am. Acad. Arts and Scis.; mem. NAS, NAE, ASTM (George R. Irwin medal 1987), Am. Geophys. Union. Home: 4 Connor Ln Barrington RI 02806-2750 Office: Brown U Dept Engngring Box D Providence RI 02912

FREUND, RICHARD L., communications company executive, consultant, lawyer; b. N.Y.C., Jan. 30, 1921; s. Sidney J. and Cora (Strasser) F.; m. Esta Neiman, Apr. 16, 1950; children: Alice, Robert, Charles. BA, NYU, 1941; LLB, Columbia U., 1944. Bar: N.Y. 1944, U.S. Dist. Ct. (so. dist.) N.Y. 1944. Assoc. Lauterstein, Spiller, Bergerman & Dannett, N.Y.C., 1943-46; labor adminstr. Publix Shirt Corp., N.Y.C., 1946-47; atty. R.H. Macy & Co. Inc., N.Y.C., 1947-54; labor atty. NBC, N.Y.C., 1954-57; dir. labor relations ABC-Paramount Theatres Inc., N.Y.C., 1957-60; v.p. labor relations ABC, N.Y.C., 1960-72, corp. v.p. labor relations, 1972-86; corp. v.p. labor relations

Capital Cities/ABC Inc., N.Y.C., 1986-87, cons., 1987-91; co-chmn. bd. trustee Am. Fedn. Musicians Pension Fund, N.Y.C., 1967-87; trustee AFTRA Health and Retirement Fund, N.Y.C., 1964-87, Nat. Assn. Broadcast Employees and Technicians Pension Fund, N.Y.C., 1964-87. Contbg. author: Susbidiary Rights and Residuals, 1968. Mem. Phi Beta Kappa. Jewish. Avocations: collecting antique silver and pewter, numismatics, golf. Home and Office: 90 Gerard Ave W Malverne NY 11565-1232

FREUND, ROLAND PAUL, farm management extension agent; b. Finschhafen, Papua New Guinea, June 16, 1939; came to U.S., 1976; s. August Paul Harold and Dorothea Martha (Ey) F.; m. Josephine Lenola Bailey, July 7, 1971; 1 child, Ernest Andreas. Diploma of agrl., Roseworthy Agrl. Coll., 1959; student, U. New England, 1964; MS, Mich. State U., 1971. Mission agriculturalist New Guinea Luth. Mission, Wabag, Papua New Guinea, 1959-71; rural devel. officer Dept. Primary Industries, Wabag, 1972-73; lectr. agrl. econs. Vudal Agrl. Coll., Mt. Hagen, Papua New Guinea, 1974-76; county agrl. agy. Penn State Extension, Carlisle, 1976-80; regional farm mgmt. agt. Penn State Extension, York, 1980-82, 84—; agrl. econ. Penn State/USAID, Swaziland, Africa, 1982-84. Feature article writer Pa. Farmer Mag., 1980—; farm mgmt. columnist Lancaster Farming, 1985—; contbr. articles to profl. jours. Mem. Nat. Assn. County Agrl. Agts. (North-east regional winner farm fin. mgmt. 1991, Disting. Svc. award 1992), Pa. Assn. County Agrl. Agts. (regional dir. 1992-95, Search for Excellence Farm Income State winner 1982), Pa. Joint Coun. Ext. Profls. (chmn. 1997-98), Epsilon Sigma Phi (pres. Pa. chpt. 1996). Lutheran. Avocations: auto mechanics, music, photography, travel. Home: 382 Petersburg Rd Carlisle PA 17013-9219 Office: Penn State Extension 1100 Claremont Rd Carlisle PA 17013-8893

FREUND, RONALD S., management consultant, marketing company executive; b. Hanford, Calif., Mar. 13, 1934; s. Wayne S. and Bluebell (McConihe) F.; m. Jane Mary Thaler, Dec. 10., 1964; children: Nancy Anne, Timothy Wayne. BA, Stanford U., 1956, MBA, 1959. Ind. economist Stanford Research Inst., Menlo Park, Calif., 1956-63; dir. bus. planning J.C. Penney Co. Inc., N.Y.C., 1963-72; pres. Corwin Co., Kansas City, Mo., 1972-85, Midpoint Nat. Inc., Kansas City, 1988—, Summit Assocs., Kansas City, 1985—; cons. Menninger Clinic, Topeka, Kans., 1991; v.p., 1991-93; chmn. exec. com. Midpoint Trade Books, N.Y.C., 1995—; cons. Nat. Renewable Energy Lab., Golden, Colo., 1987—; cons., trustee Midwest Research Inst., Kansas City, 1974—. Mem. Kansas City Club. Office: Midpoint Nat Inc 1263 Southwest Blvd Kansas City KS 66103-1901

FREUND, WILLIAM CURT, economist; b. Nuremberg, Ger., Sept. 4, 1926; came to U.S., 1937, naturalized, 1942; s. Hugo and Paula (Gruenstein) F.; m. Judith Irmgard Steinberger, Aug. 14, 1951; children: Hugo, Nancy, Sandra. BBA, CCNY, 1949; MS, Columbia U., 1950, PhD, 1954. Economist Prudential Ins. Co. Am., 1950-59; assoc. prof. fin. N.Y. U. Grad. Sch. Bus. Adminstrn., 1959-62; exec. dir., chief economist Prudential Ins. Co. Am., 1963-67; sr. v.p., chief economist N.Y. Stock Exchange, 1968-85; prof. econs. Grad. Sch. Bus. Pace U., 1972—, N.Y. Stock Exchange prof. econs., dir. Ctr. Study Equity Mkts., 1992—; mem. econ. policy coun. to Gov. of N.J., 1969-90. Author: Investment Fundamentals, 5th edit, 1981, (with E. Epstein) People and Productivity, 1984; also articles. Named Disting. Alumnus Coll. City N.Y., 1974. Mem. Am. Econ. Assn., Am. Finance Assn., Nat. Assn. Bus. Economists. Office: Pace U Pace Plaza One Pace Plz New York NY 10038

FREVERT, DONALD KENT, hydraulic engineer; b. Des Moines, Mar. 23, 1950; s. Richard Keller and Corine (Twetley) F.; m. Maria Carmen Tarazon, Mar. 16, 1973; children: Richard Paul, Erica Lynn. BS in Hydrology, U. Ariz., 1972; MS in Hydrology and Water Resources, Colo. State U., 1974, PhD in Irrigation and Drainage, 1983. Registered profl. engr., Colo. Engring. aid USDA Agrl. Rsch. Svc., Tucson, 1970-72; grad. rsch. asst. Colo. State U., Fort Collins, 1972-74; hydrologist, water rights engr. Woodward-Clyde Cons., Denver, 1975-76; grad. rsch. asst. Colo. State U., Fort Collins, Colo., 1977-80; hydraulic engr. U.S. Bur. Reclamation, Lakewood, Colo., 1980—; faculty affiliate civil engring. dept. Colo. State U., Ft. Collins, 1986—; trustee Rocky Mountain Hydrologic Rsch. Ctr., 1992—, treas., 1996—; tech. co-chair Fed. Interagy. Hydraulic Modeling Conf., 1998. Co-author: (manuals) Comparison of Equations Used for Estimating Agricultural Crop Evapotranspiration with Field Research, 1983, Applied Stochastic Techniques Users Manual, 1990; contbr. articles to profl. jours. Age group coord. Lakewood Swim Club, 1988-97, treas. 1995-96. Paul Elliott Ullman scholar U. Ariz., Tucson, 1969, Pima Mining Co. scholar, U. Ariz., 1970. Mem. ASCE (chmn. surface water com. 1988-90, chmn. exec. com. water resources engring. divsn. 1994-95, exec. com. irrigation and drainage divsn. 1991-94, chmn. water resources engring. awards com. 1995-96, sec. watershed mgmt. com. 1997—), Phi Kappa Phi, Alpha Epsilon. Home: 2034 S Xenon Ct Lakewood CO 80228-4355 Office: US Bur Reclamation D-8510 PO Box 25007 Denver CO 80225-0007

FREVERT, JAMES WILMOT, financial planner, investment advisor; b. Richland Twp., Iowa, Dec. 19, 1922; s. Wesley Clarence and Grace Lotta (Maw) F.; m. Jean Emily Sunderlin, Feb. 12, 1949; children: Douglas James, Thomas Jeffrey, Kimberly Ann. BS in Gen. Engring., MIT, 1948. Prodn. mgr. Air Reduction Chem. Co., Calvert City, Ky., 1955-61; plant mgr. Air Products & Chems., West Palm Beach, Fla., 1961-62; pres. Young World HWD, Ft. Lauderdale, Fla., 1962-66; v.p. Shareholders Mgmt. Co., L.A., 1966-73, Thomson McKinnon Secs., North Palm Beach, Fla., 1973-89, Raymond James & Assoc., West Palm Beach, Fla., 1989-91. Founder, past pres. MIT Club Palm Beach County, dir., 1976—; ednl. council mem. 1977-81. Served to 1st lt. USAF, 1943-46. Mem. Palm Beach Pundits. Republican. Presbyterian. Home: 883 Country Club Dr No Palm Beach FL 33408-3742

FREY, ANDREW LEWIS, lawyer; b. N.Y.C., Aug. 11, 1938; s. Daniel B. and Ruth J. Frey; children: Matthew S., Alexandra S. BA with high honors, Swarthmore Coll., 1959; LLB, Columbia U., 1962. Bar: N.Y. 1962, D.C. 1966, U.S. Supreme Ct. 1972. Law clk. to judge U.S. Ct. Appeals (D.C. cir.), 1962-63; spl. counsel to Gov. U.S. V.I., 1963-65; assoc. Koteen & Burt, Washington, 1965-70; ptnr. Dutton, Gwirtzman, Zumas, Wise & Frey, Washington, 1970-72; dep. solicitor gen. Office U.S. Solicitor Gen., Washington, 1972-86; ptnr. Mayer Brown & Platt, Washington, N.Y.C., 1986—. Recipient John Marshall award Dept. Justice, 1975, Disting. Service award Atty. Gen., 1980, Presdl. award for Meritorious Service, 1985. Mem. Am. Law Inst., Am. Acad. Appellate Lawyers, D.C. Bar Assn., Phi Beta Kappa. Notes editor Columbia Law Rev., 1961-62. Office: Mayer Brown & Platt 1675 Broadway Fl 19 New York NY 10019-5889

FREY, CHARLES FREDERICK, surgeon, educator; b. N.Y.C., Nov. 15, 1929; s. Charles N. and Julia (Leary) F.; m. Jane Louise Tower, July 20, 1957; children: Jane Elizabeth, Susan Ann, Charles Frederick, Robert Tower, Nancy Louise. BA, Amherst Coll., 1951; MD, Cornell U., 1955. Diplomate Am. Bd. Surgery. Intern Cornell Med. Ctr., N.Y.C., 1955-56, asst. resident, 1956-57, 59-61, 1st asst. resident, 1962, chief resident, 1963; instr. surgery U. Mich., Ann Arbor, 1964-65, asst. prof. surgery, 1965-68, assoc. prof., 1968-72, prof., 1972-76; prof. U. Calif., Davis, 1976—, vice. chmn. dept. surgery, 1976-81, exec. vice-chmn. dept., 1981-95, emeritus prof. surgery, vice chmn. dept. surgery, 1998—; mem. staff VA Hosp., Martinez, Calif., chief surg. service, 1976-80; attending surgeon Sutter Hosps., Sacramento; surg. cons. U. Mich., 1966-76, VA, 1971—, Highway Safety Research Inst., 1973-76. Assoc. editor, mem. editorial bd. The Pancreas, Internat. Jour. of Pancreatology; mem. editorial bd. Western Jour. Medicine, Jour. Gastrointestinal Surgery; contbr. numerous articles to profl. jours. Served to capt. USAF, 1957-59. Fellow ACS (chief regional com. on trauma 1976-89, disaster preparedness com. 1978—, med. motion picutres com. 1981-91, allied health com. 1981-82, program com. No. Calif. chpt., 1981—, credentials com. No. Calif. chpt. 1982—, mem. bd. govs. 1989-94, gov. 1988-94, adv. com. on ambulatory surgery, chmn. ambulatory surg. care com. 1990-94, pres. No. Calif. chpt. 1995-96), Am. Assn. Surgery Trauma; mem. AMA, Calif. Med. Assn., El Dorado-Scarmento Med. Soc., Am. Fedn. Clin. Rsch., Am. Assn. Automotive Medicine (bd. dirs. 1970-74), Internat. Assn. Accident and Traffic Medicine, Am. Trauma Soc. (founding, standards devel. com. 1978—, v.p. Calif. divsn. 1979—, bd. dirs. 1980—), Calif. Trauma Soc. (trustee 1977—), Nat. Trauma Com. of ACS (chmn. membership com. 1980-84, exec. com. 1981-85), Assn. Acad. Surgery, Am. Surg. Assn., Brazilian Surg. Soc., Western Surg. Assn., Ctrl. Surg. Assn. (membership com. 1971-73), Pacific Coast Surg. Assn., Sacramento Surg. Soc. (pres. 1994), Assn. VA Surgeons (publs., program coms. 1981—), Soc. Univ. Surgeons, Soc. Surgery Alimentary Tract (constn. and by-laws com. 1969—, chmn. 1972-76, v.p. 1995-96), Internat. Assn. Pancreatology (mem. editl. bd. 1986, steering com.), Internat. Biliary Assn., Am. Gastroenterology Assn., Pancreas Club (chmn. 1975-96). Home: 11450 Grinding Rock Pl Gold River CA 95670-7703 Office: U Calif Med Ctr Dept Surgery 4301 X St Sacramento CA 95817-2214

FREY, DALE FRANKLIN, financial investment company executive, manufacturing company executive; b. Lancaster, Pa., Aug. 14, 1932; s. Franklin W. and Mary A. (Strickler) F.; m. Betty Ann Heistand, Aug. 22, 1953; children—Scott, Philip, Kyle, Susan. BS in Econs., Franklin and Marshall Coll., 1954; MBA, NYU, 1957. With Gen. Elec. Co., Fairfield, Conn., 1957-97, mgr. group fin. ops., 1975-77, internat. and Can. group staff exec., internat. sector, 1977-80, v.p., treas., 1980-84, 86-93; chmn. bd., pres. Gen. Elec. Investment Corp., Stamford, Conn., 1984-97; bd. dirs. Praxair Inc., Danbury, Promus Hotel Corp., Memphis, Damon Runyon-Walter Winchell Cancer Rsch. Fund, Roadway Express, Akron, After Market Tech., Aurora Capital Ptnrs., Cmty. Health Sys. Trustee Franklin and Marshall Coll. Capt. USAF, 1955-57. Mem. Fin. Execs. Inst. (chmn. com. corp. fin. 1983-85), Aspetuck Valley Country Club (Weston, Conn.). Clubs: Aspetuck Valley Country (Weston, Conn.). Office: c/o Michael Allen Co One Gorham Island Westport CT 06880

FREY, DONALD NELSON, industrial engineer, educator, manufacturing company executive; b. St. Louis, Mar. 13, 1923; s. Muir Luken and Margaret Bryden (Nelson) F.; m. Bonnie A. Gore, May 28, 1989; children by previous marriage: Donald Nelson, Judith Kingsley, Margaret Bente, Catherine, Christopher, Elizabeth. Student, Mich. State Coll., 1940-42; BS, U. Mich., 1947, MS, 1949, PhD, 1950, DSc (hon.), 1965; DSc, U. Mo., Rolla, 1966. Instr. metall. engring. U. Mich., 1949-50, asst. prof. chem. and metall. engring., 1950-51; rsch. engr. Babcock & Wilcox Tube Co., Beaver Falls, Pa., 1951; various rsch. positions Ford Motor Co. (Ford div.), 1951-57, various engring. positions, 1958-61, product planning mgr., 1961-62, asst. gen. mgr., 1962-65, gen. mgr., 1965-68, co. v.p. for product devel., 1965-67; pres. Gen. Cable Corp., N.Y.C., 1968-71; pres. Bell & Howell Co., Chgo., 1973-81, chmn., chief exec. officer, 1971-88, also bd. dirs.; prof. of indsl. engring. and mgmt. sci. Northwestern U., Evanston, Ill., 1988—. Co-chmn. Gov.'s Commn. of Sci. and Industry, Ill., 1988—. With AUS, 1942-46. Named Young Engr. of the Yr., Engring. Soc. Detroit, 1953, Outstanding Alumni, U. Mich. Coll. Engring., 1957, Outstanding Young Man of the Yr., Detroit Jr. Bd. of Commerce, 1958, Man of the Yr., Weissmann Inst., 1988; recipient Nat. medal for tech., 1990. Fellow AAAS; mem. Am. Inst. Mining Metall. and Petroleum Engrs. (chmn. Detroit chpt. 1954, chmn., editor Nat Symposium on Sheet Steels 1956), Am. Soc. Metals, Nat. Acad. Engring. (mem. coun. 1972), ASME, Soc. Automotive Engrs. (vice chmn. Detroit 1958, Russell Springer award 1956), Detroit Engring. Soc. (pres., bd. dirs. 1962-65), Coun. on Fgn. Rels., Chgo. Club, Saddle and Cycle Club, Sigma Xi, Phi Kappa Phi, Tau Beta Pi, Phi Delta Theta. Home: 2758 Sheridan Rd Evanston IL 60201-1728 Office: Northwestern U 2225 Sheridan Rd Rm M237 Evanston IL 60208-0834

FREY, DONALD RAY, medical association administrator; b. Leavenworth, Kans., Jan. 7, 1952; s. Raymond Donald and Emma Margaret (Beach) F.; m. Leticia Darlene Schneider, June 6, 1975; children: Zachary, Dustin. BA, William Jewell Coll., 1974; MD, U. Mo., 1978. Am. Bd. Family Practice with cert. added qualification in Geriat. Physician Savannah (Ga.) Med. Ctr., 1981-84; family practice residency dir. United Hosp. Ctr., Clarksburg, W.Va., 1984-89; residency devel. dir. Clarkson Hosp., Omaha, 1989-90; v.p. med. affairs United Hosp. Ctr., 1990-93; family practice residency dir. Creighton U. Sch. Medicine, Omaha, 1993-95, family practice dept. chmn., 1995—; mem. Nebr. Rural Health Commn., 1998—. Maternal Mortality Rev. Panel W. Va. Dept. of Health, Charleston, 1989, med. adv. comm., Child Health, 1991-93; mem. rural health adv. commn. Nebr. Dept. Health, 1998—. Named Ronald L. Kleeberger Endowed Chair Creighton Univ, Omaha, 1996—; recipient Creighton U. Disting. Continuing Edn. award, 1997. Fellow Am. Acad. Family Physicians; mem. Am. Bd. Family Practice, Nebr. Med. Assn., Soc. Tchrs. Family Medicine. Fax: 402-280-5165. Office: Creighton Univ., Dept. Family Practice 601 N 30th St Ste 6720 Omaha NE 68131-2137

FREY, FREDERICK AUGUST, geochemistry researcher, educator; b. Milw., Apr. 1, 1938; s. Frederick August and Evelyn Dorothy (Lange) F.; m. Julie Ann Golden; 1 child, Oren. BSCE, U. Wis., 1960, PhD in Chemistry, 1967. Prof. dept. earth, atmospheric and planetary scis. MIT, Cambridge, 1966—; Francqui Found. prof. MIT, Belgium, 1996-97. Assoc. editor: Geochimica et Cosmochimica Acta; contbr. over 160 articles to profl. jours. Fellow Am. Geophys. Union (pres.-elect VGP sect. 1998—, VGP Bowen award 1986); mem. Geochem. Soc., Geol. Soc. Am. Office: MIT Dept Earth Atmos & Plan Sci 54 # 1226 Cambridge MA 02139

FREY, GERARD LOUIS, retired bishop; b. New Orleans, May 10, 1914; s. Andrew and Marie Therese (DeRose) F. DD, St. Joseph's Sem. Coll., St. Benedict, La., 1933; student, Notre Dame Sem., New Orleans. Ordained priest Roman Cath. Ch., 1938; asst. pastor Taft, La., 1938-46; asst. dir. (Confraternity Christian Doctrine, Archdiocese New Orleans); also asst. (St. James Ch.), New Orleans, 1946; dir. (Confraternity Christian Doctrine), Archdiocese New Orleans, 1946-67; also in residence Archdiocese New Orleans (St. Leo the Great Parish), 1946-54; founding pastor (St. Frances Cabrini Ch.), New Orleans, 1952-63; pastor (St. Frances de Sales Parish), Houma, La., 1963-67; clergy rep. 2d Vatican Council, 1964; dir. Diocesan Friendship Corps, New Orleans, 1966; bishop of Savannah Ga., 1967-72; bishop of Lafayette La., 1972-89; retired, 1989—; episcopal moderator Therseians Am., 1968—. Recipient Bishop Tracy Vocation award St. Joseph's Sem. Alumni Assn., 1959. Fax: 228-466-6477. Office: PO Box 2458 Bay St Louis MS 39521-2458*

FREY, GLENN, songwriter, vocalist, guitarist; b. Detroit, Nov. 6, 1948. Performed with Bo Diddly and Linda Ronstadt; founding mem. mus. group Longbranch Penny Whistle, mus. group Eagles; songs include Take it Easy; albums with Eagles include Desperado, 1973, On the Border, 1974, One of These Nights, 1975, Hotel California (Grammy award for album of yr. 1977), The Long Run, Hell Freezes Over; albums as a solo artist include No Fun Aloud, 1982, The Allnighter, 1984, Soul Searchin', 1988, Strange Weather, 1992, Glen Frey Live, 1993, Solo Collection, 1995; co-recipient Grammy award for Lyin' Eyes 1975, for New Kid in Town 1977; composer theme song for TV shows Miami Vice, Body by Jake, 1988; TV appearance Wiseguy, 1988; actor: (TV series) South of Sunset, 1993, (movie) Jerry Maguire, 1996. Named (with Eagles) to Rock and Roll Hall of Fame, 1998. *

FREY, HARLEY HARRISON, JR., anesthesiologist; b. Toledo, Feb. 22, 1920; s. Harley Harrison and Mina Rosina (Wiedemann) F.; m. Jane Luceia Murray, Aug. 28, 1944 (dec. 1964); children: Richard E., Martha J., Thomas C.; m. Emma Jean Hamilton, Apr. 15, 1966; 1 stepchild, Rick A. Gregory. BS, U. Toledo, 1942; MD, U. Cin., 1945. Diplomate Am. Bd. Anesthesiology. Intern Akron City Hosp., Ohio, 1946-49; fellow anesthesia U. Minn., Mpls., 1950; hon. mem. staff St. Elizabeth Hosp. Med. Ctr., Lafayette, Ind., 1950—, Lafayette Home Hosp., 1950—. Bd. dirs. Lafayette Symphony Orch., 1952-54; counselor, committeeman Lafayette coun. Boy Scouts Am., 1955-63; ruling elder Presbyn. Ch., 1964-67, active deacon, 1991-94; bd. dirs. Lafayette Citizens Band, 1997—. Fellow Am. Coll. Anesthesiology; mem. Am. Soc. Anesthesiology (bd. dirs. 1965-74), Ind. Soc. Anesthesiology (pres., bd. dirs. 1961-74, Disting Svc. award 1992), Ind. State Med. Soc. (Cert. Distinction 1995), Tippecanoe County Med. soc. (pres. 1961), Rotary (bd. dirs. 1992-95) Lafayette Country Club (bd. dirs. 1963-65). Avocations: music, painting. Home and Office: 3513 Creek Ridge Lafayette IN 47905-5619 Office: 2323 Ferry St Ste 209 Lafayette IN 47904-3049 *Personal philosophy: My philosophy of life is simple, whatever talent or wisdom I may have has been given to me by God as a gift. In any task I undertake, this gift should be used to the best of my ability, be fair, build goodwill, better friendships, exhibit truth and benefit all concerned.*

FREY, HERMAN S., publishing company executive; b. Murfreesboro, Tenn., Apr. 19, 1920; s. Saleem McCool and Minnie May (Felts) F.; m. Daisy Rook Corlew, Apr. 3, 1946; 1 child, Pamela Anne. Student electronic Navigation MIT, 1943, Fgn. Svc. Sch., Washington, 1958; cert. in Commerce, U. Va., 1958; cert. internat. law, internat. ct. justice, The Netherlands, 1959; Course in naval intelligence U.S. Naval War Coll., 1948; grad. student in Am. History, U. Md., 1955, 66; BA, Am. U., 1964; MBA, George Washington U., 1965; postgrad., Oxford U., 1974; cert. constl. history, Oxford U., 1974, cert. fgn. and imperial policy, 1975. Commd. ensign USN, 1942; advanced through grades to lt. comdr., 1955; with navigation dept. USS Quincy, 1937-41, navigator USS Sagamore, 1941-42, asst. navigator USS Iowa, 1942-44, with Naval Schs., Norfolk, Va., N.Y.C., Miami, 1944-45, navigation and gunnery officer USS Zuni, 1945-46, exec. officer USS Chickasaw, 1946-47, comdg. officer, 1947-48; instr. Naval Sch., Boston, 1948-51; comdg. officer USS Sisken, 1951-52; conducted Cts. Inquiry for comdr. Mine Force Atlantic Fleet, 1953; comdr. mine divsn., task unit, 1952-54; exec. officer USS McClellan, 1954-55; officer detailer Bur. Naval Pers., Washington, 1955-58; advisor, liaison Am. Embassy, The Netherlands, 1958-61; stock broker Auchincloss, Parker & Redpath, Arlington, Va., 1966-67; asst. prof. Georgetown U., Washington, 1967, U. Va., Charlottesville, 1967-69; freelance journalist Europe, U.S., 1972-76; pres. Frey Enterprises, 1976—; faculty U. Md., College Park, 1978; condr. cts. inquiry Comdr. Mine Force Atlantic Fleet, 1953-54; mem. bd. govs. Am. Sch. of Hague, Netherlands, 1959-61; cons. State of Tenn., 1969-70; mem. World Affairs Coun., Washington, 1994—. Author: Jefferson Davis, 1977. Ran for U.S. Senate, Tenn., 1970, 72; mem. adv. com. Nat. Naval Meml. Found., Washington, nat. adv. coun. A Tribute to the United States Navy, 1941-45; bd. govs. Meth. Ch., Arlington, 1962-64; mem. U.S. Hist. Soc., Nat. Trust for Hist. Preservation, Battle of Normandy Found., 50th ann. Coun. Battle of Normandy; honorary citizen Colonial Williamsburg, Va. Mem. AAUP, VFW (life), Am. Bus. Men's Assn., The Hague, 1958-61, Naval Order of U.S. (life), World Inst. Achievement, Soc. Advancement Mgmt. (pres. 1964), Internat. Platform Assn., U.S. Naval Inst. (life), U.S. Capitol Hist. Soc., Tenn. Hist. Soc., Tenn. Sheriff's Assn., Ret. Officers Assn. (life), Nat. Assn. Uniformed Services (life), World Affairs Coun. (Washington), Am. Legion (life), Navy League of U.S., U.S. Navy Mine Warfare Assn., Vets. Assn. of USS Iowa, U.S.S. Chickasaw Vets. Assn., Mil. Dist. Officer's Club (Washington), Phi Alpha Theta. Democrat. Avocations: history, literature, collecting rare books, travel, amateur cooking. Participant in the atom bomb tests at Bikini Atoll, 1946. Office: Frey Enterprises Ste 115-12 1007 Murfreesboro Pike Nashville TN 37217-1509

FREY, JAMES MCKNIGHT, government official; b. Mattoon, Ill., Dec. 7, 1932; s. Raymond Matthew and Virginia Laurel (McKnight) F.; m. Jean Meyer, June 18, 1954 (div. 1977); children—Katherine Marie Frey Glenn, Nancy Elizabeth Frey Longo; m. Nancy E. Hitt, Apr. 28, 1978. A.B., Harvard U., 1954, M.B.A., 1956. With Bur. of Budget, 1954-62, 65-70, mgmt. analyst internat. programs, 1960-62, dir. internat. programs div., 1970-75; asst. to spl. asst. to Pres. U.S.; also staff mem. Nat. Security Council, 1962-64; spl. asst. for policy coordination to asst. sec. state inter-Am. affairs, also policy planning officer Bur. Inter-Am. Affairs, State Dept., 1964-65, chief internat. programs div., 1970-75; asst. dir. for legis. reference U.S. Office Mgmt. and Budget, Washington, 1975-88; mem. Pres.'s Task Force Govt. Reorgn., 1964; ret., 1988; participant Internat. Symposium on Pub. Adminstrn. Reform in China, Beijing, 1989. Mem. Harvard Club (Washington), Cosmos Club. Home: 8106 Inverness Ridge Rd Potomac MD 20854-4013

FREY, JEFFERY PAUL, internist, geriatrician; b. Ossining, N.Y., Mar. 23, 1948; s. John Joseph and Barbara (Gerlach) F.; m. Linnea Raye Hollis; children: Jeffery W., Charles, Benjamin B. BA, Cornell U., 1970; MD, SUNY, Syracuse, 1974. Diplomate Am. Bd. Internal Medicine, Am. Bd. Geriatrics with added qualifications. Intern Syracuse Med. Ctr., 1974-75, asst. med. resident, 1975-76, resident, 1976-77; clin. assoc. prof. Tulane U. Sch. Medicine, New Orleans, 1979-91; clin. asst. prof. La. State U. Med. Ctr., New Orleans, 1981-91; clin. asst. prof. medicine U. Mo., Columbia, 1991—; staff physician Ochsner Clin., New Orleans, 1981-91; pvt. practice Columbia, 1991—; staff Columbia Regional Hosp., 1991—, Boone Hosp. Ctr., Columbia, 1991—. Contbr. articles to profl. jours.; presenter in field. Lt. commdr. USPHS, 1977-81. Mem. ACP, So. Med. Assn., Mo. State Med. Soc., Boone County Med. Sco. Episcopalian. Avocations: sailing, skiing, vegetable gardening. Office: 201 W Broadway Columbia MO 65203-3842

FREY, JOHN WARD, landscape architect; s. Philip Rockel and Sarah Helen (Dempwolf) F.; m. Wilma Emma Weggel, Feb. 11, 1961; children: Holly Frances, Allison Margaret, Frederika Elizabeth, Marietta Isabel. BA in Math., Coll. of Wooster, 1952; MLA, Harvard U., 1955. Urban designer The Architects Collaborative, 1955; assoc., designer Sasaki (Walker) Assocs., Inc., 1957-62; ptnr. Mason and Frey, Landscape Architects, 1963—; Registered landscape architect N.Y., Conn., Mass. Prin. works include Arlington (Mass.) Bicentennial Park, 1975, S.W. Corridor Park, Sect. III, Jamaica Plain, Boston, 1988, State U. Agricultural and Tech. Coll., Farmingdale, N.Y., 1963-71, State U. Coll., Geneseo, N.Y., 1963-73, Fulton Montgomery C.C., Johnstown, N.Y., 1967-70, Burlington (Mass.) High Sch., 1968-74, Wellesley Coll. Sci. Ctr., 1973, Lexington Ctr. Mall, 1967, Murray Hill, Manchester, 1973, Polaroid Corp., Waltham, Mass., 1970, Sandoz Pharm., East Hanover, N.J., 1964, 73, others incl. indsl., comml. office bldgs., land devel. and pvt. res. Adv. com. to planning bd. Lexington Design, 1973-76; mem. Revere Beach Design Rev. Bd., 1976-78, Lexington Tree Com., 1990—, Lexington Minuteman Commuter Bikeway Com., 1993-95, Mass. Recreational Trails Adv. Com., 1993—; chmn. Design Adv. Com., Lexington, 1988—. Recipient Boston Soc. of Architects award 1973, "A" Citation, Mass. Audubon Soc., 1968, Indsl. Plant Beautification award Govs. Conf. on Natural Beauty, 1967, NEA Presdl. Design award Fed. Design Achievement award, 1988. Fellow Am. Soc. of Landscape Architects (Merit award 1973, trustee Boston chpt. 1980-83); mem. BSLA (treas. 1966-67, program com. 1966-67, com. landscape architectural registration in Mass. 1966-67, pub. svc. com. 1963-71, examining bd. 1971-75, others) Charles River Watershed Assn., Appalachian Mountain Club, Appalachian Trail Conf., The Nature Conservancy, Mass. Audubon Soc., Rails to Trails Conservancy. Avocations: gardening, bicycling, hiking, canoeing, jogging. Home: 1133 Massachusetts Ave Lexington MA 02420-3818 Office: Mason & Frey Landscape Architects 1133 Massachusetts Ave Lexington MA 02420-3818

FREY, JUDITH LYNN, elementary education educator; b. Ashland, Ohio, Sept. 10, 1956; d. Lloyd Baeder and Norma Claire (Hostettler) Wygant; m. Daniel K. Frey, Nov. 21, 1981; children: Jennifer Lynn, Lynnette Danielle. BS in Edn., Otterbein Coll., 1978. Elem. remedial reading tchr. Norwalk (Ohio) City Schs., 1978-79; elem. remedial reading tchr. Bucyrus (Ohio) City Schs., 1979-81, 87-98, kindergarten tchr., 1981-87, 7th grade English tchr., 1998—. Co-dir. Holy Trinity Cath. Ch. Pre-Sch. Religion, Bucyrus, 1987-92. Mem. DAR, Internat. Reading Assn. (Crawford County chpt., bldg. rep. 1991-94), Eden Homemakers Club (sec./treas. 1995—), Bucyrus Acad. Boosters. Avocations: reading, bike riding, walking, crafts. Home: 9940 County Highway 134 Nevada OH 44849-9763 Office: Bucyrus Middle Sch 245 Woodlawn Ave Bucyrus OH 44820-2460

FREY, JULIA BLOCH, French language educator; b. Louisville, July 25, 1943; d. Oscar Edgeworth and Jean Goldthwaite (Russell) Bloch; m. Roger G. Frey, Dec. 27, 1968 (div. Mar. 1976); m. Ronald Sukenick, Mar. 9, 1992. BA, Antioch Coll., 1966; MA, U. Tex., 1968; MPhil, Yale U., 1970, PhD, 1977. Instr. Brown U., Providence, 1972-73; chargée de cours U. Paris, 1974-75; lectr. Yale U., New Haven, 1975-76; prof. Inst. Internat. Comparative Law, U. San Diego, Paris, 1979-89, adminstrv. dir., 1989; assoc. prof. French, U. Colo., Boulder, 1976—, dir. undergrad. studies, 1985-95, assoc. chmn. for grad. studies, 1996-97, 98-99, chmn., 1999—; guest prof. Sarah Lawrence Coll., Bronxville, N.Y., 1983. Author: Toulouse-Lautrec, a life, 1994, Toulouse-Lautrec l'homme qui aimait les femmes, 1996; editor: Gustave Flaubert's La Lutte du Sacerdoce et de L'Empire (1837), 1981; contbr. articles and monographs to profl. publs., chpts. to books; translator: René. Recipient Conn. Grad. Study award, 1970-73; grantee NDEA, 1967, Brown U. Research and Travel, 1973, Boulder Arts Com., 1979, 80, Ctr. for Applied Humanities, 1985, S.W. Inst. for Research on Women, 1985-86, NEH, 1986; fellow NDEA, 1966-68, Yale U., 1968-72, Gilbert Chinard, Inst. Français de Washington, 1977; Pen Ctr. USA West Lit. award for non-fiction, 1995; Finalist Nat. Book Critics Cir. award for Biography, 1994. Mem. MLA, PEN U.S.A., CAA, Yale Club. Unitarian. E-mail:

freyj@spot.colorado.edu. Home: 1505 Bluebell Ave Boulder CO 80302-8041 Office: U Colo Dept French and Italian PO Box 238 Boulder CO 80309-0238

FREY, KATIE MANCIET, educational administrator; b. Tucson, Ariz., Dec. 31, 1952; d. Hector Encinas and Lilian Eloisa (Hanna) Manciet; m. Richard Patrick Frey, Jul. 20, 1974; 1 child, Stacy Ann. BS, U. Ariz., 1974, MEd, 1982, PhD, 1987. Tchr. physical edn. Amphitheater Pub. Schs., Tucson, 1974-81, rsch. specialist, 1982-85, dir. rsch. & devel., 1985-88, asst. supt., 1988-89, assoc. supt., 1989—; gymnastics coach Amphitheater Pub. Schs., Tucson, 1974-81, rsch chair Ad Hoc Adv. Coun. on Sch. Dropouts, Ariz., 1987, mem. Gov. Edn. Conf., Ariz., 1989, mem. State Supr. Task Force on Sch. Violence, Ariz., 1993-94, Mayor's Sch. Dist. Action Task Force, Tucson. 1993—; mem. NCAA recertification equity subcom. U. Ariz., 1997-98. Mem. APEX, Tucson, 1987—, Traveler's Aid Soc. of Tucson, 1993-98, Citizen's Adv. Coun. U. Ariz., 1994—; mem. tech. adv. bd. Town of Oro Valley, 1995-96; mem. exec. steering com. K-16 Edn. Coun. So. Ariz.; bd. dirs. YWCA, 1999—. Recipient APEX Apple award U. Ariz., 1994. Mem. Assn. for Supervision and Curriculum Devel., Nat. Organ. for Women, Am. Assn. of U. Women, U. Ariz. Hispanic Alumni Assn., Coll. Assn. for the Devel. and Renewal of Edn., U. Ariz. Letterwinners Club. Avocations: reading, traveling, family, Tai Chi.

FREY, LAURA MARIE, special education administrator; b. Waterloo, Iowa, Dec. 21, 1958; d. Eugene Richard and Mary Ellen (Beckman) F. BS in Secondary Spl. Edn., U. Iowa, 1981; MSE in Behavior Disorders with honors, U. Kans., 1988, PhD in Spl. Edn., 1996. Cert. in learning disabilities, Kans. Spl. edn. tchr. Decorah (Iowa) High Sch., 1981-83, Tipton (Iowa) High Sch., 1983-87; behavior disorders tchr. J.C. Harmon High Sch., Kansas City, Kans., 1988-90, Wyandotte High Sch., Kansas City, 1990-93; tchr. Bridges Program, Kansas City, 1993-97; coord. therapeutic learning ctr. Wentzville (Mo.) R-IV Sch. Dist., 1997—; adj. prof. Lindenwood U., St. Charles, Mo.; presenter in field. Mem. NOW (bd. dirs. Kansas City Urban chpt., bd. pres. St. Louis chpt.), Assn. for Retarded Citizens, Overland Park, Kans., 1983—, Woman Source, Kansas City, Mo., 1987—, Women's Equality Coalition. Recipient Fenichel Dissertation Rsch. award Coun. for Children with Behavior Disorders, 1996. Mem. NAFE, AAUW, ASCD (network co-facilitator Network for Affective Factors in Learning), NEA, Coun. for Exceptional Children (divsn. learning disabilities, divsn. behavior disorders, dir. tchr. edn., divsn. tchr. edn., divsn. R & D), Coun. Learning Disorders, Phi Delta Kappa. Avocations: aerobics, sewing, reading, writing, movies. Home: 1573 Bittersweet Ct Saint Charles MO 63303-3805

FREY, MARY ELIZABETH, artist; b. Yonkers, N.Y., Nov. 25, 1948; d. Harold and Matilda F.; m. William M. Bennett, Jan. 31, 1976; children: Jacob F. and Nicholas F. BA in Fine Arts, Coll. New Rochelle, 1970; postgrad., Pratt Inst., 1970-71; MFA in Photography, Yale U., 1979. Instr. photography Project Art Ctr., Cambridge, Mass., 1975-77, dir. photography, 1976-77; assoc. prof. photography Hartford Art Sch., West Hartford, Conn., 1989—; NEA, Washington, 1994; vis. artist Harvard U., Cambridge, 1984, Cooper Union, N.Y.C., 1985, Yale U., New Haven, 1986, NYU, N.Y.C., 1987, Cornell U., Ithaca, N.Y., 1988, Northfield Mt. Hermon, Northfield, Mass., 1989, Mills Coll., Oakland, Calif., 1989, Hampshire Coll., 1992; Harnish vis. artist Smith Coll., Northampton, Mass., 1994-95; guest lectr. Hudson River Mus., Yonkers, N.Y., 1984, Hartford Art Sch., 1988, Smith Coll. Mus. Art, Northampton, 1994. One-woman shows include Panopticon Gallery, Boston, 1974, Hollins College (Va.) Art Gallery, 1977, Project Art Ctr., Cambridge, Mass., 1979, Hudson River Mus., Yonkers, N.Y., 1984, Blue Sky Gallery, Portland, 1985, ZONE Art Ctr., Springfield, Mass., 1988, Ledel Gallery, N.Y.C., 1989, Arno Maris Gallery, Westfield, Mass., 1991, Springfield (Mass.) Mus. of Fine Arts, 1993, Laelia Mitchell Gallery, Boston, 1995, Marlboro (Vt.) Coll., 1998; group shows include Commonwealth Armory, Boston, 1974, Project Art Ctr., Cambridge, 1975, Boston City Hall, 1976, Yale U., New Haven, 1977, Webb & Parsons Gallery, New Bedford, Mass., 1978, Pleasant St. Gallery, Amherst, Mass., 1979, Hampshire Coll., Amherst, 1980, Light Gallery, N.Y.C., 1981, Memphis Acad. Art, 1982, Carpenter Ctr. for Visual Arts, Cambridge, 1984, Blue Sky Gallery, Portland, 1985, Mus. Modern Art, N.Y.C., 1986, Aperture Gallery, N.Y.C., 1986, 87, Real Art Ways, Hartford, Conn., 1988, MS Gallery, Hartford, 1990, Smith Coll. Mus. Art, Northampton, 1992, 100 Pearl St. Gallery, Hartford, 1993, Artspace, New Haven, 1994, ICP-Midtown Eye of the Beholder, 1997, others; represented in permanent collections at Art Inst. Chgo., Mus. Fine Arts, Houston, Smith Coll. Mus. Art, Northampton, Internat. Polaroid Collection, Cambridge, Mus. Modern Art, N.Y.C., Coca-Cola Corp., Atlanta, Bank of Boston, Springfield Tech. C.C., Avon Corp., others. Home: 70 Firglade Ave Springfield MA 01108-2531

FREY, PAUL HOWARD, chemical engineer, engineering consultants company executive; b. Gilman, Ill., Feb. 12, 1922; s. Carl Fredrick and Doretta Mary (Koritz) F.; m. Patricia Anne Leonard, Oct. 6, 1942; children: Paul H. Jr, Elizabeth Ann. BSChE, U. Ill., 1943. Registered profl. engr., Ill. Tech. advisor Manhatten Dist. (Atom Bomb Project) Union Carbide Corp., Tonawanda, N.Y., 1943-46, rsch. and devel. engr., 1946-49; project engr. Union Carbide Corp, Chgo., 1960-80, engrng. mgr., 1980-86; plant engr. U.S. Reduction Co., East Chicago, Ind., 1949-54; project and sales engr. Sunbeam Corp., Chgo., 1954-58; plant mgr. Detinning Corp., Chgo., 1958-60; owner Freytone Co. Cons. Engrs., Spooner, Wis., 1986—. Inventor/patentee in field. Leader Citizens for Improved Edn., LaGrange, Ill., 1967-69; mem. vestry St. Alban's Episc. Ch., 1993—. Mem. AIChE, Lions (Lion Tamer officer Spooner chpt., 1992—), Jaycees (Key award Hammond, Ind. 1951), Waukegan Yacht Club (bd. dirs. to commodore 1976-82), No. Ill. Venture Assn. (various officers to commodore 1974-78). Avocations: sailboat racing, long-distance sailing. Home and Office: N5683 Tanglewood Dr Spooner WI 54801-8480

FREY, STUART MACKLIN, automobile manufacturing company executive; b. Peoria, Ill., Feb. 13, 1925; s. Muir Luken and Margaret Bryden (Nelson) F.; m. Lillian Maxine Paxton, 1951; children: Mellissa June, Muir Paxton. BS in Mech. Engrng, U. Mich., 1949; SM in Indsl. Mgmt, MIT, 1961. With Budd Co., 1949-53; with Ford Motor Co., 1953—; chief car research engr. Ford Motor Co., Dearborn, Mich., 1974-75; chief vehicle engr. Ford Motor Co., 1975-80, v.p. car engring., 1980-83, v.p. car product devel., 1983-87, v.p. engrng. and mfg. staff, 1987-88, v.p. tech. affairs, 1988-90; with TRW, 1990—; v.p. auto tech. affairs, 1990-94. Contbr. articles to profl. jours. Served as officer AUS, 1943-46, 51-52. Sloan fellow, 1960-61. Fellow Soc. Automotive Engrs., Engring. Soc. Detroit; mem. Am. Soc. Body Engrs., Tau Beta Pi, Pi Tau Sigma. Home: 3790 Darlington Rd N Bloomfield Hills MI 48301-2000 *The key ingredient that has contributed most importantly to my success has been the understanding and employment of the principles of employee involvement and participative management.*

FREY, VIOLA, sculptor, educator; b. Lodi, Calif., Aug. 15, 1933. AA, Delta Coll.; BFA, Calif. Coll. Arts and Crafts; MFA, Tulane U. Assoc. prof. ceramics Calif. Coll. Arts and Crafts, 1965—; chmn. dept. ceramics Noni Eccles Treadwell Ceramic Arts Ctr. Exhibited sculpture in numerous shows including Overglaze Imagery Calif. State U., Fullerton, 1977, Soap Box Derby San Francisco Mus. Modern Art, 1978, A Century of Ceramics in the U.S. Everson Mus. Art, Syracuse, N.Y., 1979, Renwick Mus., Washington, 1979, Cooper-Hewitt Mus., N.Y., 1979. Grantee Nat. Endowment Arts, 1978. Office: Calif Col Arts & Crafts Dept Ceramics 5212 Broadway Oakland CA 94618-1426 Office: c/o Rena Bransten Gallery 77 Geary St San Francisco CA 94108-5723*

FREY, WILLIAM RAYBURN, healthcare educator, consultant; b. Springfield, Tenn., July 20, 1948; s. Rayburn and Elma Faye (Nunley) F.; m. Carol Jackson, Jan. 2, 1971. BS in Occupational Therapy, U. Ill., Chgo., 1971; MEd, Ga. State U., 1973; MHA, Washington U., St. Louis, 1976; PhD, Ohio State U., 1987. Registered occupational therapist. Asst. prof. U. Ill., Chgo., 1974; hosp. adminstr. The Toledo Hosp., 1975-81; instr. Ohio State U., Columbus, 1981-85; hosp. adminstr. Nat. Med. Enterprises, York, Pa., 1985-87; assoc. prof. Slippery Rock (Pa.) U., 1987-88; prof. Coll. St. Francis, Joliet, Ill., 1988-92, St. Mary's Coll., Moraga, Calif., 1992—; cons. Commn. on Accreditation of Rehab. Facilities, Samuel Merritt Coll., Nat. Med. Enterprises. Author: Cross National Perspective on Health Care Reform, 1995; (jours.) Health Care Mgmt. Rev., Archives of Phys. Medicine and Rehab., Jour. of Head Trauma Rehab., Jour. of Allied Health. Juror Acad. Med. Films; bd. dirs. Easter Seals Rehab., Quincy Found. for Med. Rsch., 1997—; pres. Child Abuse Prevention, hon. adv. bd., 1982. Capt. U.S. Army, 1971-73. Fellow Am. Coll. Healthcare Execs.; mem. Am. Hosp. Assn., Am. Occupational Therapy Assn., Assn. Univ. Programs Health Adminstrn. Avocations: acting, musical comedy. Office: St Marys College PO Box 4700 Moraga CA 94575-4700*

FREYD, PETER JOHN, mathematician, computer scientist, educator; b. Evanston, Ill., Feb. 5, 1936; s. Paul Robert and Pauline Margaret (Pattinson) F.; m. Pamela Parker, Jan. 1, 1957; children: Jennifer Joy, Gwendolyn Ann. AB magna cum laude, Brown U., 1958; MA (Woodrow Wilson fellow), Princeton U., 1959, PhD, 1960. J.F. Ritt instr. math. Columbia U., N.Y.C., 1960-62; faculty U. Pa., Phila., 1962—; prof. math. U. Pa., 1968—, chmn. grad. group math., 1982-87, prof. computer info. sci., 1987—; dir. Lab. for Logic and Computation, 1993—; Adviser Pahlavi U., Shiraz, Iran, 1968; lectr. Canadian Nat. Rsch. Seminar, 1974; vis. rschr. Swiss Fed. Inst. Tech., Zurich, 1969; vis. researcher U. Mex., 1975, U. Sydney, 1985, U. Milan, 1986, U. Parma, 1990; vis. prof. U. Chgo., 1980, U. Louvain, Belgium, 1981; vis. prof. in computer sci. Carnegie Mellon U., 1988-89. Author: Abelian Categories, 1964; (with Andre Scedrov) Categories, Allegories, 1990; founder Jour. Pure and Applied Algebra, 1970; editor Theoretical Computer Sci., 1988—, Math. Structures in Computer Sci., 1989—, Internat. Jour. Algebra and Computation, 1990—, Jour. Knot Theory and its Ramifications, 1991—. Fulbright scholar Australia, 1971; fellow St. John's Coll., Cambridge U., Eng., 1980-81. Mem. Isaac Newton Inst. 1995, Phi Beta Kappa, Sigma Xi. Home: 2020 1/2 Addison St Philadelphia PA 19146-1307 Office: U Pa Dept Maths 33 E Walnut Ln Philadelphia PA 19144-2002

FREYD, WILLIAM PATTINSON, fund raising executive, consultant; b. Chgo., Apr. 1, 1933; s. Paul Robert Freyd and Pauline Margaret (Pattinson) Gardiner; m. Diane Marie Carlson, May 19, 1984. BS in Fgn. Svc., Georgetown U., 1960. Field rep. Georgetown U., Washington, 1965-67; campaign dir. Tamblyn and Brown, N.Y.C., 1967-70; dir. devel. St. George's Ch., N.Y.C., 1971; assoc. Browning Assocs., Newark, 1972-73; regional v.p. C.W. Shaver Co., N.Y.C., 1973-74; founder IDC, Henderson, Nev., 1974—. Inventor PHONE/MAIL program. Bd. dirs. Nev. Symphony Orch., 1994—, N.J. Symphony Orch., 1991-94; apptd. Nev. Charitable Solicitation Task Force, 1994. Mem. Nat. Soc. Fund Raising Execs. (nat. treas. 1980-81, pres. N.Y. chpt. 1974-76, cert. 1982), Am. Assn. Fund Raising Counsel (sec. 1984-86), World Fund Raising Coun. (bd. dirs. 1995—, treas. 1998—), Georgetown U. Regional Club Coun., N.Y. Yacht Club, Union League Club N.Y., Masons, Nassau Club, Circumnavigators Club (regional club coun. 1996—). Achievements include the invention of the Phone Mail Program. Office: The IDC Ctr 2920 N Green Valley Pkwy Henderson NV 89014

FREYER, VICTORIA C., fashion and interior design executive; b. Asbury Park, N.J.; d. Spiros Steven and Hope (Pappas) Pappaylion; m. Cyril Steven Arvanitis, Dec. 26, 1950 (div. 1975); children: Samuel James, Hope Alexandra. BA, Georgian Court Coll., 1950; student, N.Y. Sch. Interior Design, 1971-72. Mgr. Homestead Restaurant, Ocean Grove, N.J., 1946-58; art supr. Lakewood (N.J.) Pub. Schs., 1950-51; interior designer London, 1975-76, F. Korasic Assocs., Oakhurst, N.J., 1977-78; owner, operator Virginia Interiors, McLean, Va., 1974-90; interior designer Anita Perlut Interiors, McLean, 1986; owner, operator Victoria Freyer Interiors, McLean, 1986—; fashion cons. Nordstrom Splty. Store, McLean, 1988-92; fashion seminar coord. Nordstrom Splty. Store, Tysons Corner, Va., 1992—; lectr. Girl Scouts U.S., Rep. Women of Capitol Hill, Washington Hosp. Ctr., Women's Am. ORT, Nat. Assn. Cath. Women, Bethesda Naval Hosp., NIH, others. Pres. Monmouth County Med. Aux., 1964; originator 1st lecture series Monmouth Coll., Long Branch, N.J., 1965; guest moderator Alexandria (Va.) Hosp. Series, 1988; mem. Women's Symphony Com., Washington, 1988—; guest speaker Girl Scouts U.S. Coun. Nation's Capitol, 1988-90, Nuclear Energy Coun., 1989, pers. dept. CIA, 1989-90, Internat. Women's Group Washington, 1989-90. Recipient Recognition awards Girl Scout Coun. Nation's Capitol, 1991, No. Region Beta Pi, 1991, Beta Sigma Pi, 1991. Mem. AAUW (program chmn. 1968, guest speaker many orgns.). Greek Orthodox. Avocations: Greek and Roman archeology and antiquities, painting, gourmet cooking, traveling. Home and Office: Apt # 203 7630 Provincial Dr Mc Lean VA 22102-7631

FREYERMUTH, CLIFFORD L., structural engineering consultant. BS in Civil Engrng., State U. Iowa, 1956, MS in Structural Engrng., 1958. Registered structural engr., Ariz. Consulting engr. structural design Ned L. Ashton, 1955-57; grad. teaching asst. structural mechanics State U. Iowa, 1957-58; with bridge divsn. Ariz. State Hwy. Dept., 1958-64; with Portland Cement Assn., Chgo., Skokie, Ill., 1964-71; dir. post-tensioning divsn. Prestessed Concrete Inst., 1971-76; mgr. Post-Tensioning Inst., 1976-88; pres. Clifford L. Freyermuth, Inc., 1988—; mem. cable-stayed bridges com. Post-Tensioning Inst, editor various publs.; prin. investigator Nat. Coop. Hwy Rsch. Project, Washington, 1988. Contbr. articles to profl. jours. Recipient Martin P. Korn award Prestressed Concrete Inst., 1969. Fellow Am. Concrete Inst. (prestressed concrete com., standard bldg. code com., bd. dirs. 1991—, Henry C. Turner medal 1992); mem. ASCE (prestressed concrete com.), Internat. Assn. Bridge and Structural Engrs., Structural Engrs. Assn. Ariz., Chi Epsilon. Office: Clifford L Freyermuth Inc 9201 N 25th Ave Ste 150B Phoenix AZ 85021-2721

FREYERMUTH, GUNDOLF S., writer; b. Hannover, Germany, Jan. 3, 1955; s. Georg and Ursula (Toennies) Schneider-Freyermuth; m. Elke M.M. Waldvogel, Dec. 23, 1983; children: Leon Sebastian, George Samuel. MA in Comparative Lit., Free U., Berlin, 1979. Sr. editor TransAtlantik, Munich, 1981-82; sr. editor, writer Stern Mag., Hamburg, Germany, 1983-90; advisor to editor-in-chief Elle Mag., Munich, 1990-92; head reporter Tempo Mag., Hamburg, 1992-94; lectr. Free U., Berlin, 1985-90. Author: The Way Out, 1989, Bogart's Brother (writing as John Cassar), 1991, A Travel Into a Past Lost, 1990, Endgamer, 1993, Spy Among the Stars, 1994, Cyberland, 1996, That's It. Last Words with Charles Bukowski, 1996, (writing as Peter Johannes) Pearls Before Swine, 1999. Home and Office: PO Box 1001 Canyon Creek Ranch Snowflake AZ 85937

FREYERMUTH, VIRGINIA KAREN, secondary art educator. BFA cum laude, Boston U., 1973, MFA, 1975; edn. cert., Suffolk U., 1975. Cert. art tchr., Mass. Grad. asst. Boston U., 1973-75; art tchr. Quincy (Mass.) Pub. Schs., 1975-76, Plymouth (Mass.) Pub. Schs., 1976-78, 83-85; painting tchr. Brockton (Mass.) Fuller Mus. Art, 1978-79; art coord. grades K-12 Duxbury (Mass.) Pub. Schs., 1985-99; vis. lectr. art edn. U. Mass., Dartmouth, 1999—; art reviewer Patriot Ledger, Quincy, 1975-85; dir. Freyermuth Fine Arts Ctr., Plymouth, 1990-94; mem. adv. coun. Mass. Field Ctr. Tchg. & Learning, 1993-96; tchr. in electronic residence MCET, Cambridge; instr. art Massasoit C.C., Brockton, 1991-92; dir. Helen Bumpus Gallery, Inc., Duxbury, 1992-94; forum tchr. Goals 2000 U.S. Dept. of Edn., 1994—, internat. space camp, 1994. Columnist Learning for Life, 1994. Mem. commn. on common core of learning Mass. Dept. Edn.; bd. dirs. Mass. Alliance for Arts Edn., 1994-95. Named Mass. Tchr. of Yr., Mass. Dept. Edn., 1994, Nat. Outstanding Visual Art Tchr., Walt Disney and McDonald's, 1995, 1995-96 Profiled in Disney Channel. Mem. Mass. Art Edn. Assn., Nat. Art Edn. Assn., Mus. Fine Arts Boston, Nat. State Tchrs. of the Yr., Tchr. Leadership Acad. Mass. (bd. dirs.), Lucretia Crocker Acad. of Tchg. Fellows (bd. dirs.). Office: PO Box 6132 Plymouth MA 02362-6132

FREYSS, DAVID, producer, director; b. Morristown, N.J., Jan. 20, 1933; s. Jean-Paul and Beatrice (Strobel) F.; m. Eva-Kersti Ström, May 30, 1964; children: Eva-Katerine, Anika. AB, Hamilton Coll., 1954; MBA, Columbia U., 1959. Supr. programs McCann-Erickson, N.Y.C., 1959-61; mgr. TV bus. McCann-Marschalk, N.Y.C., 1961-63; prodr. Fuller & Smith & Ross, N.Y.C., 1963-65; sr. prodr. Benton & Bowles, N.Y.C., 1965-68; sr. prodr., art dir. J. Walter Thompson, N.Y.C., 1968-78; prodr. Sesame Street, Children's TV Workshop, N.Y.C., 1978-81; exec. prodr. and dir. CBN Cable Prodns., Virginia Beach, Va., 1981-90; owner, prodr., dir. David Freyss Prodns., Virginia Beach, 1990—; cons. U.S. AID, Washington, 1979. With U.S. Army, 1954-57. Mem. NATAS (Emmy award 1980), Broadcast Advt. Prodrs. Soc. Am. (pres. 1975-77). Home and Office: David Freyss Prodns 1034 Red Oak Rd Virginia Beach VA 23452-6006

FREYTAG, DONALD ASHE, management consultant; b. Chgo., Apr. 17, 1937; s. Elmer Walter and Mary Louise (Mayo) F.; m. Elizabeth Ritchie Robertson, Dec. 19, 1964; children: Donald C., Gavin K., Alexander M. BA, Yale U., 1959; MBA, Harvard U., 1963. Pres. Mgmts. West, LaJolla, Calif., 1963-65; mktg. asst. Norton Simon, Inc., Fullerton, Calif., 1965-67; product mgr. Warner-Lambert, Inc., Morristown, N.J., 1967-70; group mgr. mktg.-planning dir. advt. Pepsi-Cola Co., Purchase, N.Y., 1970-72; from v.p. mktg. to exec. v.p. Beverage Mgmt., Inc., Columbus, Ohio, 1972-76, pres., 1976-79, vice-chmn., 1979-80; pres. Freytag Mgmt. Co., Columbus, 1980-82, 84—, G.D. Ritzy's, Inc., Columbus, 1982-84; bd. dirs. Antolino & Assoc., Atlas-Butler, Barney Corp., Century Resources, Contract Sweepers, Contrax Corp., Inc., Columbus Showcase Co., Columbus Paper and Copy Supply Co., Custom Concepts, Inc., Eastway Supplies, Inc., People Serve, Inc., Profitworks Ltd., Paul Werth & Assoc., Shared Resources, Inc., Saturday's Family Hair Care, Horizons Real Estate Group, all in Columbus, Coughlin Automotive Group, Newark, Ohio, Hugo Bosca Co., Springfield, Ohio; ctrl. region dir. Ohio Com. for Employer Support of the Guard and Res., 1992-95. Pres. Cen. Ohio Ctr. for Econ. Edn., 1978-80, 81-87; bd. dirs. Columbus Acad., 1982-84. Capt. U.S. Army, 1959-61. Recipient Roman F. Warmke award, Ohio Coun. on Econ. Edn., 1991. Mem. Nat. Assn. Corp. Dirs., HBS Club Columbus, Yale Club. Avocations: jogging, bicycling, scuba diving, golf, reading. Office: 7955 Riverside Dr Dublin OH 43016-8234

FREYTAG, RICHARD ARTHUR, banker; b. Chgo., Oct. 26, 1933; s. Elmer Walter and Mary Louise (Mayo) F.; m. Pamela Burge, Feb. 11, 1989; children: Richard Christopher Hughes Freytag, Bliss Louise Mayo Freytag. AB, Trinity Coll., Hartford, Conn., 1955; MBA, Harvard U., 1961; MS, MIT, 1971. Map salesman Rand McNally & Co., Chgo., 1955-56; internat. salesman Diversey Corp., Chgo., 1959-60; with Citibank, Japan, Taiwan, Korea, 1962-70; v.p., sr. credit officer Citibank, 1971-73; sr. officer Citibank, Hong Kong, China, Vietnam, 1973-76; investor rels. and problem loan recovery mgmt. Citibank, N.Y.C., 1977-84; pres. Citicorp Holdings, Inc., Citibank Overseas Investment Corp., 1984-96, vice chmn., dir., 1996-98; pres., CEO Citicorp Banking Corp., New Castle, Del., 1984-96, vice chmn., dir., 1996-98; pres. Citibank Del., 1989-96, vice chmn., dir., 1996-98; vice chmn. Far East Bank, Ltd., Hong Kong, 1973-76; bd. dirs. Citicorp Capital Investors Europe Ltd., The Thomas Group, Inc., Irving, Tex.; mem. panel Buenos Aires Group on N.E. Asian Ltd. Nuclear Arms Agreement. Trustee Med. Ctr. of Del.; bd. visitors Nat. Def. U., 1988-93; chmn. Nat. Def. U. Found., 1993—; mem. Gov.'s Coun. on Banking, 1994-97. 1st lt. USAF, 1956-59, maj. gen. USAFR, 1959-93. Decorated D.S.M.; recipient Brooks prize MIT, 1971; Alfred Sloan fellow The Nat. City Found., N.Y.C., 1969. Mem. Nat. Air Force Salute Found. (pres. 1988-90, chmn. 1990-92), Air Force Assn. (Iron Gate chpt. pres. 1988-90, chmn. 1990-92, Ira Eaker fellow 1991, Medal of Merit 1990, Exceptional Svc. award 1989), Coun. on Fgn. Rels., Falcon Found. (trustee), Del. Bankers Assn. (dir., pres. 1992-97), Del. Bus. Roundtable (vice chmn. 1994-96). Episcopalian. Office: PO Box 921 Montchanin DE 19710-0921

FREYTAG, SHARON NELSON, lawyer; b. Larned, Kans., May 11, 1943; d. John Seldon and Ruth Marie (Herbel) Nelson; children: Kurt David, Hillary Lee. BS with highest distinction, U. Kans., Lawrence, 1965; MA, U. Mich., 1966; JD cum laude, So. Meth. U., 1981. Bar: Tex. 1981, U.S. Dist. Ct. (no. dist.) Tex. 1981, U.S. Ct. Appeals (5th cir.) 1982, U.S. Supreme Ct. 1993; cert. civil appellate law. Tchr. English, Gaithersburg (Md.) H.S., 1966-70; instr. English, Eastfield Coll., 1974-78; law clk. U.S. Dist. Ct. for No. Dist. Tex., 1981-82, U.S. Ct. Appeals 5th Cir., 1982; ptnr. appellate sect. Haynes and Boone, Dallas, 1983—, vis. prof. law Southern Meth. U., 1985-86; bd. dirs. State Bar Tex.; faculty Appellate Adv. program NITA. Editor-in-chief Southwestern Law Jour., 1980-81; contbr. articles to law jours. Woodrow Wilson fellow. Recipient John Marshall Constl. Law award, Baird Cmty. Spirit award, 1995. Mem. ABA (mem. litigation sect., chair subcom. on local rules), Fed. Bar Assn. (co-chmn. appellate practice and advocacy sect. 1990-91), Tex. Bar Assn. (mem. appellate coun. 1995-98), State Bar Tex. (bd. dirs. 1997—), Dallas Bar Assn. (mem. appellate coun.), Higginbotham Inn of Ct., Barristers, Order of Coif, Phi Beta Kappa. Lutheran. Office: Haynes & Boone 3100 NationsBank Plz Dallas TX 75202

FRI, ROBERT WHEELER, museum director; b. Kansas City, Kans., Nov. 16, 1935; s. Homer O. and Cora Ruth (Wheeler) F.; m. Jean Landon, Jan. 16, 1965; children—Perry, Sean, Kirk. B.A., Rice U., 1957; M.B.A., Harvard U., 1959. Assoc. McKinsey & Co., Washington, 1963-68; prin. McKinsey & Co., 1968-71, 73-75; dep. adminstr. EPA, Washington, 1971-73; acting adminstr. EPA, 1973; dep. adminstr. ERDA, Washington, 1975-77; acting adminstr. ERDA, 1977; head U.S. delegation to IAEA, 1977; pres. Energy Transition Corp., 1978-86; pres. Resources for the Future, 1986-95, sr. fellow, 1995—; dir. Nat. Mus. Natural History, 1996—; bd. dirs. Am. Electric Power Co., Hagler Bailly, Inc., Sci. Svc., Inc.; mem. Nat. Petroleum Coun. Lt. USNR, 1959-62. Baker scholar. Mem. Phi Beta Kappa, Sigma Xi. Republican. Presbyterian. Home: 6001 Overlea Rd Bethesda MD 20816-2453

FRIAR, JAMES LEWIS, physicist; b. Mansfield, Ohio, June 26, 1940; s. James Harold and Mabelle Louise (Johnson) F.; m. Susan Sommers, Sept. 1, 1962; children: Anne, Robert. BS, Case Inst. Tech., 1962; PhD, Stanford U., 1968. NATO fellow CERN, Geneva, 1967-68; rsch. assoc. U. Wash., Seattle, 1968-70, MIT, Cambridge, 1970-72; asst. prof. physics Brown U., Providence, 1972-76; staff mem. Los Alamos (N.Mex.) Nat. Lab., 1976-86, group leader, 1986-89, lab. fellow, 1989—. Recipient rsch. award for sr. U.S. scientists Alexander von Humboldt Stiftung, 1990. Fellow Am. Phys. Soc. Avocation: running. Home: 493 Brighton Dr Los Alamos NM 87544-3575 Address: Los Alamos National Lab Theory Div T-5 MS B-283 PO Box 1663 # 283 Los Alamos NM 87544-0600

FRIAS, JAIME LUIS, pediatrician, educator; b. Concepción, Chile, Mar. 20, 1933; came to U.S., 1970; s. Luis Humberto and Olga Ana (Fernandez) F.; m. Jacqueline May Steel, Apr. 8, 1961; children: Jaime Arturo, Juan Pablo, Patricio Andres, Maria Josefina. M.D., U. Chile, 1959. Diplomate Am. Bd. Pediatrics, Am. Bd. Human Genetics. Intern Hospital Regional, Concepcion, 1958-59; resident in pediatrics Calvo Mackenna Hosp., Santiago, Chile, 1960-62; clin. genetics and dysmorphology fellow U. Wis.-Madison, 1965-66, U. Wash., Seattle, 1966-67; asst. prof. pediatrics U. Concepcion, 1967-69, prof., 1969-70; asst. prof. pediatrics U. Fla. Coll. Medicine, Gainesville, 1970-74, assoc. prof., 1974-77, prof., 1977-86, chief div. genetics, 1977-86, chmn. med. sch. admissions com., 1983-86; prof. pediatrics U. Nebr. Med. Ctr., Omaha, 1986-91, chmn. dept. pediatrics, 1986-91; prof. pediatrics U. South Fla. Coll. of Medicine, chmn. dept. of pediatrics, 1991—, L.A. Barness prof. pediatrics, 1994—; chmn. Com. for Protection of Human Subjects, 1975-78; chmn. Fla. Com. on Prevention Devel. Disabilities, 1979-82, chmn. infant hearing screening adv. coun., 1982-86; cons. Spanish Collaborative Project on Congenital Malformation, Madrid, 1983—. Author chpts. to books; contbr. articles to profl. jours. Trustee All Children's Hosp; mem. exec. com. Assn. Med. Sch. Pediatric Dept. Chmn., 1993-96. Named Tchr. of Yr. U. Fla. Coll. Medicine, 1978-79, Lewis A. Barness Endowed Chair Pediatrics, 1994. Mem. Am. Acad. Pediatrics (com. genetics 1995—), Am. Pediatric Soc., ACP (affiliate, W.K. Kellogg fellow 1965-67), Am. Soc. Human Genetics, Assn. Clin. Scientists, Tampa Yacht and Country Club, Tampa Club. Democrat. Roman Catholic. Office: U South Fla Dept Pediat 17 Davis Blvd Ste 200 Tampa FL 33606-3438

FRIBERG, GEORGE JOSEPH, electronics company executive; m. Mary Seymour; children: Fane George, Felicia Lynn Friberg Clark. BSME, U. N.Mex., 1962, MBA, 1982, postgrad. Sales engr. Honeywell, L.A., 1962-64; liaison engr. ACF Industries, Albuquerque, 1964-66; quality assurance mgr. data sys. divsn. Gulton Industries Inc., Albuquerque, 1966-72; mgr. mfg. Femco divsn. Gulton Industries Inc., Irwin (Pa.), High Point (N.C.), 1972-77; v.p. mfg. data sys. divsn. Gulton Industries Inc., Albuquerque, 1977-86; pres., CEO Tetra Corp., Albuquerque, 1986-92, also bd. dirs.; pres., CEO Laguna Industries Inc., Albuquerque, 1992-96; dir. programs Tech. Ventures Corp., Albuquerque, 1996—; bd. dirs. Noonday, Inc., 1991—. Mem. editl. bd. N.Mex. Bus. Jour., 1995-97. Mem. N.Mex. R & D Gross Receipts Task Force, 1988-89; mem. Econ. Forum of Albuquerque; bd. dirs. Technet, 1983-97, pres., 1983-84, 88-89; bd. dirs. Lovelace Insts., 1988—, U. N.Mex. R.O. Anderson Bus. Sch. Found., 1988-92, N.Mex. Bus. Innovation Ctr., 1986-92, U. N.Mex. Found., 1999—, Golden Apple Found., 1998, N.Mex. History Mus., 1999—; grad. Leadership N.Mex., 1998. Inducted Anderson Sch. of Bus. Hall of Fame, 1996; recipient Zia award U. N.Mex., 1998, Regents medal U. N.Mex., 1998, Lockweed Martin Nova award, 1998. Mem. Albuquerque C. of C. (bd. dirs. 1985—, polit. action com. 1983-84, chair Buy N.mex. chpt. 1986-87, vice chmn. econ. affairs planning coun. 1987—, chmn. bd. 1990-91), N.Mex. Alumni Lettermen's Club, U. N.Mex. Alumni Assn. (bd. dirs. 1995—, pres.-elect 1997, pres. 1997-98). Home: 13234 Sunset Canyon Dr NE Albuquerque NM 87111-4220

FRIBOURG, MICHEL, international agribusiness executive. With Continental Grain Co., N.Y.C., 1944—, chmn. emeritus, 1994—. Office: Continental Grain Co 277 Park Ave New York NY 10172*

FRIBOURG, PAUL J., grain company executive. Exec. v.p., group pres. commodity mktg. Continental Grain Co., N.Y.C., now chmn., CEO. Office: Continental Grain Co 277 Park Ave New York NY 10172*

FRIBOURGH, JAMES HENRY, university administrator; b. Sioux City, Iowa, June 10, 1926; s. Johan Gunder and Edith Katherine (James) F.; m. Cairdenia Minge, Jan. 29, 1955; children: Cynthia Kaye, Rebecca Jo, Abbie Lynn. Student, Morningside Coll., 1944-47; BA, U. Iowa, 1949, MA, 1949, PhD, 1957; LHD (hon.), Morningside Coll., 1989, DHL (hon.), 1989. Instr. Little Rock Jr. Coll., 1949-56; assoc. prof. biology Little Rock U., 1957-60, prof., chmn. div. life scis., 1960-69; vice chancellor U. Ark., Little Rock, 1969-72, interim chancellor, 1972-73, exec. vice chancellor for acad. affairs, 1973-82, interim chancellor, exec. vice chancellor for acad. affairs, 1982, provost, exec. vice chancellor, 1983—, disting. prof., 1984-94, disting. prof. emeritus, 1994—; cons. in field; assoc. Marine Biol. Lab., Woods Hole, Mass. Contbr. articles to profl. jours. Mem. Ark. Gov.'s Com. on Sci. and Tech., 1969-71; bd. dirs., mem. nat. adv. bd. Nat. Back Found., 1979; vice chmn. NCCJ, 1981-82; div. rep. United Way of Pulaski County, 1980-82; bd. dirs. Ark. Dance Theatre, Little Rock, 1980-82; vestryman Good Shepherd Episcopal Ch.; del. Episcopal Diocese of Ark.; fellow Ark. Mus. Sci. and History, 1987. Fribourgh Hall named in his honor, U. Ark., Little Rock, 1994; NSF fellow History of Sci. Inst., 1959-60. Fellow AAAS, Coll. Preceptors (London), Am. Inst. Fishery Rsch. Biologists, Ark. Mus. Sci. and History; mem. Am. Fisheries Soc. (chmn. com. on internationalism cert. fisheries scientist), AAUP (pres. Ark. conf.), Electron Microscopy Soc. Am., Am. Soc. Swedish Engrs. (corr. mem.), Ark. Acad. Sci. (pres. 1966), Ark. Dean's Assn. (pres. 1982), Am. Assn. State Colls. and Univs., Am. Swedish Inst., Swedish Club (Chgo.), Rotary (Paul Harris fellow), Vasa Order Am. Lodge, Sigma Xi, Phi Kappa Phi. Democrat. Clubs: Swedish, Vasa Order Am. Lodge: Rotary (Paul Harris fellow). Office: U Ark 33rd and University Ave Little Rock AR 72204

FRICK, MR. See GROEBLI, WERNER FRITZ

FRICK, BENJAMIN CHARLES, lawyer; b. Overbrook, Pa., Feb. 23, 1960; s. Sidney Wanning and Marie Pauline (Strickler) F.; m. Stephanie Ann Sears, June 1, 1991; children: Sarah Marie, Anna Elizabeth. BA, Cornell U., 1982; JD, U. Richmond, 1985; LLM in Taxation, Villanova U., 1994. Bar: Pa. 1985. Clerk to Hon. John B. Hannum U.S. dist. court, 1984; trust officer Provident Nat. Bank, Phila., 1985-89; sole practice Haverford, Pa., 1989—. Mem. ABA, S.R. (bd. dirs. Pa. Soc. 1987—, sec. 1991-95, treas. 1995-97, v.p. 1997—), Ardmore Presbyn. Ch. (deacon), Pa. Bar Assn., Phila. Bar Assn., Soc. Mayflower Descendants, Colonial Soc. Pa., Soc. Colonial Wars, Mil. Order Loyal Legion U.S. (sec. 1993-95, v.p. 1995-97, pres. 1997—), The Racquet Club, The Union League of Phila., The Phila. Club, Phi Alpha Delta (pres. local chpt. 1984-85), Alpha Delta Phi. Republican. Presbyterian. Office: 355 Lancaster Ave Haverford PA 19041-1547

FRICK, IVAN EUGENE, college president emeritus, education consultant; b. New Providence, Pa., May 19, 1928; s. Charles George and Lillie Jane (Miller) F.; m. Ruth Hudson, July 16, 1950; children: David Alan, Daniel Eugene, Susan Marie. A.B., Findlay (Ohio) Coll., 1949; B.D., Lancaster Theol. Sem., 1952; S.T.M., Oberlin Coll., 1955; Ph.D., Columbia U., 1959; L.H.D. (hon.), Findlay Coll., 1976. Mem. faculty Findlay Coll., 1953-71, asst. to pres., 1963-64, pres., 1964-71; pres. Elmhurst (Ill.) Coll., 1971-94, pres. emeritus, 1994—; cons. Ivan E. Frick and Assocs., Oak Brook, Ill., 1994—; vice chmn. Fedn. Ind. Ill. Colls. and Univs., 1979-81, chmn., 1983-85; pres., chmn. exec. com. Associated. Colls. of Ill., 1991-93; chmn. West Suburban Regional Acad. Consortium, 1991-92. Mem. Am. Coun. on Edn. Commn. on Govtl. Rels., 1986-89; bd. dirs. United Cmty. Fund Findlay, 1965-71, Lizzadro Mus. Lapidary Art, Elmhurst, Elmhurst YMCA, 1971-84; mem. found. bd. Ray Graham Assn. for People With Disabilities, 1995; chmn. non-pub. adv. com. Ill. Bd. Higher Edn., 1990-94. Danforth Found. fellow, 1959, Paul Harris fellow, 1988; recipient Disting. Alumnus award Findlay Coll., 1964, Outstanding Young Man award U.S. Jr. C. of C., 1964. Mem. Econ. Club Chgo. *Mentors have played a significant role in my life; these mentors have been teachers, older friends, father figures and administrative colleagues. They have supported, challenged and stimulated me and sometimes they have presented an opposite view or role model against which I have reacted. In all, they have helped me immeasurably.*

FRICK, JOHN WILLIAM, health industry executive; b. St. Charles, Mo., Sept. 11, 1951; s. William Lee and Dorothy Ann (Hollingsworth) F.; m. Karen Elizabeth Gercken, Sept. 12, 1987; children: Kathryn Anne, Kerry Kathleen, John William Frick II. Student, U. Mo., Columbia, 1972; BS in Pharmacy, U. Mo., Kansas City, 1975. Lic. pharmacist. Mgr. Adam's Drug, Kansas City, Mo., 1972-77; sec., treas. Drug Depot of Blue Springs (Mo.), Inc., 1978-89; pres. Sam's Prescription Shop, Raytown, Mo., 1983—; pres., founder Home Health Depot, Inc., Kansas City, 1984-92; dir. pharmacy Two Rivers Psychiat. Hosp., Kansas City, 1986—; CEO MedFlex, 1991-93; regional mgr. Curaflex Health Svcs., Inc., 1992-94; pres., CEO Innovative Pharm. Svcs., Inc., 1992—; mem. profl. rels. staff Coram Healthcare Inc. Profl. Rels., 1994-96. Mem. Greater Kansas City Sports Commn., 1986—; adv. mem. St. Joseph Health Care Ctr., 1986—; mem. Spl. Olympics Com., 1988—. Republican. Lutheran. Avocatoins: sailing, flyfishing, collecting sports cars. Office: Innovative Ventures 10 E 9th St Ste G-2 Lawrence KS 66044-2621

FRICK, OSCAR LIONEL, physician, educator; b. N.Y.C., Mar. 12, 1923; s. Oscar and Elizabeth (Ringger) F.; m. Mary Hubbard, Sept. 2, 1954. A.B., Cornell U., 1944, M.D., 1946; M.Med. Sci., U. Pa., 1960; Ph.D., Stanford U., 1964. Diplomate: Am. Bd. Allergy and Immunology (chmn. 1967-72). Intern Babies Hosp., Columbia Coll. Physicians and Surgeons, N.Y.C., 1946-47; resident Children's Hosp., Buffalo, 1950-51; pvt. practice medicine specializing in pediatrics Huntington, N.Y., 1951-58; fellow in allergy and immunology Royal Victoria Hosp., Montreal, Que., Can., 1958-59; fellow in allergy U. Calif.-San Francisco, 1959-60, asst. prof. pediatrics, 1964-67, assoc. prof., 1967-72, prof., 1972—, dir. allergy tng. program, 1964—; fellow immunology Inst. d'Immunobiologie, Hosp. Broussais, Paris, France, 1960-62. Contbr. articles papers to profl. publs. Served with M.C., USNR, 1947-49. Mem. Am. Assn. Immunologists, Am. Acad. Pediatrics (chmn. allergy sect. 1971-72, Bret Ratner award 1982), Am. Acad. Allergy (exec. com. 1972—, pres. 1977-78), Internat. Assn. Allergology and Clin. Immunology (exec. com. 1970-73, sec. gen. 1985—), Am. Pediatric Soc. Club: Masons. Home: 370 Parnassus Ave San Francisco CA 94117-3609

FRICK, ROBERT HATHAWAY, lawyer; b. Cleve., June 28, 1924; s. Claude Oates and Urshal May (Hathaway) F.; m. Lenore M. Maurin, Aug. 16, 1947 (dec. Sept. 1993); children: Elaine D. Frick , Barbara A. Frick Bundick, Catherine L. Frick Cayer. BBA, U. Mich., 1948, JD, 1950; postgrad. Harvard Bus. Sch., 1965. Bar: Mich. 1951, Ill. 1951, Ohio 1952, N.Y. 1962, U.S. Supreme Ct. 1981. Atty., Amoco Corp. (formerly Standard Oil Co. Ind.), Chgo., 1950, 52-60, Paris, 1960-62, N.Y.C., 1962-68, Chgo., 1968-71, assoc. gen. counsel, Chgo., 1972-87; pvt. practice, Cleve., 1951-52. Served with USAAF, 1943-46. Mem. ABA, Am. Soc. Internat. Law, Assn. of Bar of City of N.Y., Ill. Bar Assn., Chgo. Bar Assn., Order of Coif, Westmoreland Country Club, Meadows Country Club, Univ. Club Chgo., Mid Am. Club, Sigma Phi Epsilon. Republican. Home: 921 Westerfield Dr Wilmette IL 60091-1810

FRICKE, HEINZ, conductor; b. Halberstadt, Germany. Mus D, Shenandoah U., 1996. Gen. music dir. Theatre Halberstadt, 1946-48, Weimar, 1948-50, Theatre and Gewandhausorchestre, Leipzig, 1950-60, State Ops., Schwerin, 1960-61, Berlin State Opera, 1961-92; musical dir. Norwegian Nat. Opera, 1984-90, The Wash. Opera, 1993—; guest condr. Deutsche Oper Berlin, Munich Opera Festival, Hamburg State Opera, Deutsche Oper am Rhein, Stockholm, Copenhagen, Cologne, Paris, Madrid, Barcelona, Rome, Turin, Milan, State Vienna, Zurich, Tokyo, Sydney, Australia, Osaka, Rio de Janeiro, Sao Paulo, Santiago, San Diego, Calif., Moscow, Budapest, Prague, Nice (Italy) Teatro, Covent Garden, 1998. Recs. include Strauss's Feuersnot, Lortzing's Zar und Zimmerman, Siegfried Matthus's Graf Mirabeau, Karl-Amadeus Hartmann's Simplicius Simplicissimus, Bellas artes, Mex. City, CD, Operahouse Collogne. Theatre Collogne, Buenos Aires. Office: The Wash Opera JFK Ctr for the Performing Arts Washington DC 20566

FRICKE, MARTIN PAUL, science company executive; b. Franklin, Pa., May 18, 1937; s. Frank Albert and Pauline Jane (Wentz) F.; m. Barbara Ann Blanton, Jan. 3, 1959. BS, Drexel U., Phila., 1961; MS, U. Minn., 1964, PhD, 1967. Program mgr., group leader Gen. Atomics, San Diego, 1968-73; program mgr., divsn. mgr. Sci. Applications Internat. Corp., La Jolla, Calif., 1973-77, v.p., 1977-80, corp. v.p., 1980-84; sr. v.p. Systems Group, The Titan Corp., San Diego, Calif., 1984-87, exec. v.p. Techs Group, 1987-89, sr. v.p. corp. ops., 1989-93; program adminstr. San Diego Supercomputer Ctr., 1995-97; ind. cons., 1997—; mem. cross sect. evaluation working group, Upton, L.I., N.Y., 1970-73, U.S. Nuclear Data Com., Washington, 1970-73. Author pubs. in field. Recipient postdoctoral fellowship U. Mich., Ann Arbor, 1967-68, scholarship Pa. Indsl. Chem. Co., 1956-60; grad. fellow Oak Ridge (Tenn.) Assoc. Univs., 1964-67. Fellow Am. Phys. Soc. (panel on pub. affairs 1982-84); mem. Phi Kappa Phi. Roman Catholic. Achievements include first measurements and theoretical analysis of certain polarization phenomena in nucleon-nucleus inelastic scattering. Home and Office: 109 Whippoorwhill Dr Oak Ridge TN 37820-7233

FRICKE, RICHARD JOHN, lawyer; b. Ithaca, N.Y., Apr. 17, 1945; s. Richard I. and Jeanne L. (Hines) F.; m. Carol A. Borelli, June 17, 1967 (div. 1990); children: Laura, Richard, Amanda; m. Penny Yrizarry, Dec. 29, 1990 (div. 1999); children: Stephanie, Matthew, Tyler. BA, Cornell U., 1967, JD, 1970. Bar: Conn. 1970. Assoc. Gregory & Adams, Wilton, Conn., 1970-73; ptnr. Crehan & Fricke, Ridgefield, Conn., 1973-90; gen. counsel Connex Internat. Inc.; corp. counsel, pres. Safe Alternatives Corp. of Am., Inc.; pres., gen. counsel, dir. T.F.I. Industries, Inc.; gen. counsel Gold Mustache Pub. Corp., Inc.; sec., dir. DXTC.COM, Inc.; dir. Village Bank & Trust Co.; town atty. Town of Ridgefield, 1973-81. Co-patentee low reactive pressure foam, polyurethane foam for cellulostic products. Bd. dirs. Ridgefield Community Ctr., Ridgefield Montessori, Ridgefield Community Kindergarten; founder, pres. Ridgefield Lacross League; constable Town of Wilton, Conn.; mem. Conn. Bar Commn. on Women, 1976. Mem. ABA, Conn. Bar Assn., Danbury Bar Assn. Democrat. Roman Catholic. Address: 440 Main St Ridgefield CT 06877

FRICKLAS, ANITA ALPER, religious organization administrator; b. Perth Amboy, N.J., Nov. 2, 1937; d. William and Dotty (Finkel) Alper; m. Richard Leon Fricklas, Dec. 22, 1957; children: Michael, Kenneth, Susan. A in Comml. Sci., Boston U., 1957; BBA, Upsala Coll., 1959; MA in Religion, Iliff Sch. of Theology, Denver, 1985. Reform Jewish Educator. Instr. Somerset County Coll., Somerville, N.J., 1970-72; dir. edn.-programming Temple Sinai, Denver, 1973-90; prof. Iliff Sch. Theology, 1986-91; exec. dir. Am. Jewish Com., Denver, 1990—. Author: Guide for Interfaith Families, 1993, (chpt.) Jewish Principal's Handbook, 1984. Sec. Hunter Hill Homeowners Assn., Englewood, Colo., 1973-74; mem. Colo. Social Legislation Commn.; rep. Martin Luther King Jr. Meml. Commn., Northwest Coalition Against Malicious Harassment; sec.-treas. Mainstream Colo. Coalition, Cmty. Rls. Coun., Jewish Agy. Exec. Coun.; founder Muslim-Jewish Dialogue and Latino-Jewish Coalition; founding mem. Citizens United Against Hatred. Recipient Disting. Leadership award, 1989-90, Mayor's Cmty. Achievement award, 1999. Mem. ASCD, LWV (pres. Somerset County chpt. 1967, Bridgewatr Twnship. chpt. 1968-70), Nat. Assn. Temple Educators (cons. 1982—, bd. dirs. 1987-91), Jewish Educators Coun. of Denver (pres. 1984-88), Nat. Coun. Jewish Women, Hadassah. Avocations: travel, aerobic walking, weight training. *Respect diversity-but look for more things that unite people than that divide them.*

FRICKS, WILLIAM PEAVY, shipbuilding company executive; b. Byron, Ga., Aug. 14, 1944; s. Walker Nathaniel and Mary (Peavy) F.; m. Deanie Dudley, Aug. 27, 1966; children: Holly Anne, William Peavy, Austin Nathaniel. B.S. in Indsl. Mgmt, Auburn (Ala.) U., 1966; M.B.A. in Fin, Coll. William and Mary, Williamsburg, Va., 1970; A.M.P., Harvard U., 1983. With Newport News Shipbldg. and Dry Dock Co., Va., 1966—; adminstrv. asst. to pres., then contr. and treas. Newport News Shipbldg. and Dry Dock Co., 1979-80, v.p. fin., 1980-83, v.p. tech., 1983-84, v.p. mktg., 1984-85, v.p. human resources, 1985-88, sr. v.p., 1988-92, exec. v.p., 1992-94, pres., COO, 1994-95, pres., CEO, 1995-97, chmn., CEO, 1997—. Office: Newport News Shipbldg 4101 Washington Ave Bldg 86 Newport News VA 23607-9700

FRIDAY, ELBERT WALTER, JR., federal agency administrator, meteorologist; b. DeQueen, Ark., July 13, 1939; s. Elbert Walter and Mary Elizabeth (Ward) F.; m. Karen Ann Hauschild, Nov. 14, 1959; children: Kristine Ann, Kelly Sue. BS in Engring. Physics, U. Okla., Norman, 1961, MS in Meteorology, 1967, PhD in Meteorology, 1969. Commd. 2d lt. USAF, 1961, advanced through grades to col., weather officer, 1961-81, dir. environ. and life scis., Dept. Def., 1978-81, ret., 1981; dep. dir. Nat. Weather Svc., Silver Spring, Md., 1981-87, dir., 1987-97; asst. adminstr. Office Oceanic and Atmospheric Rsch., Silver Spring, 1997-98; dir. Nat. Acad. Scis., 1998—, mem. bd. atmosphere in scis. and climate, 1998; mem. com. on low level wind shear NAS, Washington, 1985-86; U.S. permanent rep. to UN World Meteorol. Orgn., 1988-98, mem. exec. coun., 1988-98; adj. prof. U. Okla., 1998; bd. dirs. Atmospheric Sci. and Climate, NRC, NAS, 1998—. Contbr. articles to prof. jours. Elder Calvary Chrisitan Ch., Burke, Va., 1985-89, trustee, 1989-93, chmn. bd., 1998—. Decorated Bronze Star; recipient Superior Svc. medal Dept. Def., 1981, Presdl. Rank award, 1988, Disting. Achievement award U. Okla., 1992, Fed. Exec. of Yr. award Fed. Exec. Inst. Alumni Assn., 1993. Fellow Am. Meteorol. Soc. (councilor 1988-90, Cleve. Abbe award 1997); mem. AAAS, Nat. Weather Assn., Sigma Xi. Office: National Research Council NOAA/OAR 2101 Constitution Ave NW Washington DC 20418

FRIDAY, GERALD EDMUND, biologist, educator; b. Milw., Mar. 5, 1942; s. Edmund and Marcella F.; m. Angela, June 6, 1964; children: Jeff, Tami. BS, U. Wis., 1964; MS, Mich. State U., 1969. Chemistry educator Bishop Gorman H.S., Las Vegas, 1964-65; biology educator Marquette H.S., Milw., 1966—; cons. Project First, Wis. Acad., Madison, 1997—; water testing com. Riveredge Nature Ctr., Newburg, Wis., 1996—. Mem. Am. Biology Tchrs., Nat. Sci. Tchrs., Wis. Sci. Tchrs. Avocations: walking, hiking, fishing, dancing. Office: Marquette Univ HS 3401 W Wisconsin Ave Milwaukee WI 53208-3842

FRIDAY, GILBERT ANTHONY, JR., pediatrician; b. Pitts., Apr. 16, 1930; s. Gilbert Anthony and Susan Dorothy (Kumer) F.; m. Christina Cecilia McShane, Sept. 12, 1959; children: Martin, Peter, Martha, Timothy, Amy, Anne, Robert. BS, Bucknell U., 1952; MD, Temple U., 1956. Diplomate Nat. Bd. Med. Examiners. Rotating intern Phila. Gen. Hosp., 1956-57; pediatric resident Children's Hosp. of Phila., 1960-62; pediatric resident Children's Hosp. of Pitts., 1962-63, asst. med. dir. ops., 1963-66, preceptorship in allergy/immunology, 1962-67; clin. instr. to asst. prof. U. Pitts., 1963-87, clin. assoc. prof., 1987, prof. pediatrics, 1987—; chmn. bd. dirs. Pa. Blue Shield, Camp Hill, 1992-96; bd. dirs. Highmark Blue Cross Blue Shield, Pitts. Contbr. articles to profl. jours., chpts. to books. Lt. comdr. USN MC, 1956-66. Wyeth Pediatric scholar. Fellow Am. Coll. Allergy, Asthma, and Immunology, Am. Acad. Allery, Asthma, and Immunology, Am. Acad. Pediats.; mem. AMA, Allegheny County Med. Soc. (pres. 1987), Pa. Med. Soc., Pa. Allergy Soc. (pres. 1975), Alpha Omega Alpha. Republican. Roman Catholic. Avocations: skiing, boating, fishing. Home: 1901 Highgate Rd Pittsburgh PA 15241-2210 Office: Children's Hosp of Pitts 3705 5th Ave Pittsburgh PA 15213-2524

FRIDAY, KATHERINE ORWOLL, artist; b. Granite Falls, Minn., Dec. 3, 1917; d. Melvin Sylvester and Anna Elizabeth (Hustvedt) Orwoll; m. Erling Bjarne Struxness, May 8, 1943 (div. 1961); children: John Eric Struxness, Mimi Ann McNicholas, Martha Jane Begin; m. George Edward Friday, Apr. 12, 1969 (dec. Jan. 1997). Student, U. Minn., 1935-36, 40-41, Frederick Mizen Sch. of Art, Chgo., 1941. Designer, illustrator Josten's, Owatonna, Minn., 1936-39, 42-43; layout artist Tempo Inc., Chgo., 1941-42, Voguewright Studios, Chgo., 1943-44; layout, illustration Allan D Parson Advt. Agy., Chgo., 1945, Ad-Art, Wichita, Kans., 1952-54, 63; indsl. designer Harold W. Darr Assoc., Mpls., 1959-61; layout, illustration Lydiard Assoc., Mpls., 1961-64; owner Skyline Studio, Mpls., 1964-66; layout, illustration Comm. Cons., Wilmington, Del., 1971; freelance illustration, med. illustration dept. pathology U. Chgo., Chgo., 1946-48; freelance illustrator Hutchinson, Kans., 1948-58; art dir. SPF Adv., Intermedia, Mpls., 1966-69, Arne Westerman Adv., Portland, Oreg., 1970-71, Battle Advt., Wyncote, Pa., 1971-72; creative dir., owner A'La Carte Advt./Art, Bellevue, Wash., 1973-77; graphic illustration Courseware, Moffat Field, Mountain View, Quantic, Los Altos, Calif., 1978-81; ret., 1981. Exhibited at Westminster Gallery, London, 1995; represented by Northridge Art Gallery, Ridgefield, Conn., Gallery 33, Portland, Rental Sales Gallery, Portland, Portland Art Mus. Recipient Best of Show award Internat. Miniature Art Show, Kirkland, Wash., 1997. Mem. Colored Pencil Soc. Am., Miniature Artists of Am. (hon. signature), Miniature Art Soc. Fla. (1st pl. 1189-90, 97-98, 2d pl. 1994, 95, 99), Ga. Miniature Artist Soc. (1st pl. 1991, 94, 2d pl. and 3d pl. 1990, Merit award 1997), Miniature Painters, Sculptors, Gravers Soc. (assoc. Washington, 1st pl. 1996, 3rd pl. 1990, 1st of show 1998), Cider Painters of Am. (1st in floral 1993, still life 1995, protrait 1995, 98, award of excellence 1992, 93, 94, 97), NorthWest Watercolor Soc. (assoc.), Watercolor Soc. Oreg. (assoc., Award of Achievement spring show 1998), Colored Pencil Soc. Oreg., Main St. Artists, Oreg. Soc. Artists, N.W. Watercolor Soc., Watercolor Soc. Oreg. Avocations: painting, drawing, reading, music.

FRIDAY, WILLIAM CLYDE, university president emeritus; b. Raphine, Va., July 13, 1920; s. David L. and Mary E. (Rowan) F.; m. Ida Howell, May 13, 1942; children: Frances H., Mary H., Ida E. Student, Wake Forest Coll., 1937, LLD (hon.), 1957; BS, N.C. State Coll., 1941; LLB, U. N.C., 1948; DCL (hon.), U. N.C., Chapel Hill and Greensboro, 1988; LLD (hon.), Belmont Abbey Coll., 1957, Duke U., 1958, Princeton U., 1958, Elon Coll., 1959, Davidson Coll., 1961, U. Ky., 1970, Mercer U., 1977, U. N.C., Wilmington, 1992, U. N.C., Wilmington, 1992; DCL (hon.), St. Augustine's Coll., 1986, U. of South, 1976; DPS (hon.), U. N.C., Charlotte, 1986, N.C. State Coll., 1991; DFA (hon.), N.C. Sch. Arts, 1987. Bar: N.C. 1948. Asst. dean student U. N.C., 1948-51, asst. to pres., 1951-55, sec. of univ., 1955-56, acting pres., 1956, pres., 1956-86; Mem. Carnegie Commn. on Higher Edn., Commn. to Study SUNY, So. Regional Edn. Bd.; chmn. President's Task Force on Edn., 1966-67; mem. Commn. White House Fellows, 1965-68. Mem. Nat. Com. for Bicentennial Era, Am. Coun. Edn., Commn. Nat. Changes in Higher Edn.; chmn. Ctr. Creative Leadership, 1981-96, Gov.'s Commn. on Literacy,1987, Regional Literacy Ctr. Commn., 1989-90, So. Growth Policies Bd., 1989—, Knight Found. Nat. Commn. on Intercollegiate Athletics, 1989-93. Mem. Assn. Am. Univs. (pres. 1971, Nat. Humanities medal 1997). Democrat. Baptist. Office: Univ NC The William R Kenan Jr Fund PO Box 3858 Chapel Hill NC 27515-3858

FRIDLEY, ROBERT BRUCE, agricultural engineering educator; b. Burns, Oreg., June 6, 1934; s. Gerald Wayne and Gladys Winona (Smith) F.; m. Jean Marie Griggs, June 12, 1955; children: James Lee, Michael Wayne, Kenneth Jon. BSME, U. Calif., Berkeley, 1956; MS in Agrl. Engring., U. Calif., Davis, 1960; PhD in Agrl. Engring., Mich. State U., East Lansing, 1973; D honoris causa, Universidad Polytecnica de Madrid, 1988. Asst. specialist U. Calif., Davis, 1956-60, prof. agrl. engring., 1961-78, acting assoc. dean engring., 1972, chmn. dept. agrl. engring., 1974-76, dir. aquaculture and fisheries program, 1985-89, exec. assoc. dean agrl. and environ. scis., 1989-94, prof. emeritus, 1994—; dept. mgr. R & D Weyerhaeuser Co., Tacoma, 1977-85; vis. prof. Mich. State U., East Lansing, 1970-71; NATO vis. prof. U. Bologna, Italy, 1975. Co-author: Principles and Practices for Harvesting and Handling Fruits and Nuts, 1973; contbr. articles to profl. jours.; patentee in field. Recipient Charles G. Woodbury award Am. Soc. Hort. Sci., 1966, Alumni citation Calif. Aggie Alumni Assn., 1990. Fellow Am. Soc. Agrl. Engrs. (pres. 1997-98, Young Rschrs. award 1971, Concept of Yr. award 1976, Outstanding Paper awards 1966, 68, 69, 76, 86, Disting. Svc. award 1988, 97, pres. 1997-98, v.p. 1993-96, pres. Found. 1993-96); mem. NAE. Office: U Calif 150 Mrak Hall Davis CA 95616

FRIDLEY, SAUNDRA LYNN, internal audit executive; b. Columbus, Ohio, June 14, 1948; d. Jerry Dean and Esther Eliza (Bluhm) F. BS, Franklin U., 1976; MBA, Golden Gate U., 1980. Accounts receivable supr. Internat. Harvester, Columbus, Ohio, San Leandro, Calif., 1972-80; sr. internal auditor Western Union, San Francisco, 1980; internal auditor II County of Santa Clara, San Jose, Calif., 1980-82; sr. internal auditor Tymshare, Inc., Cupertino, Calif., 1982-84, div. contr., 1984; internal audit mgr. VWR Scientific, Brisbane, Calif., 1984-88, audit dir., 1988-89; internal audit mgr. Pacific IBM Employees Fed. Credit Union, San Jose, 1989-90, Westaff, Inc., Walnut Creek, Calif., 1990—; dir. quality assurance, 1992-98, v.p. audit and investigations, 1998—; owner Dress Fore the 9's, Brentwood, Calif., 1994—; pres., founder Bay Area chpt. Cert. Fraud Examiners, 1990. Mem. NAFE, Friends of the Vineyards, Internal Auditors Speakers Bur., Assn. Cert. Fraud Examiners (founder, pres. Bay area chpt., we. regional gov. 1996-97, Disting. Achievement award 1997, 98), Inst. Internal Auditors (pres., founder Tri-Valley chpt.), Internal Auditor's Internat. Seminar Com., Internal Auditor's Internat. Conf. Com. Avocations: woodworking, gardening, golfing. Home: 19 Windmill Ct Brentwood CA 94513-2502 Office: Western Staff Svcs 301 Lennon Ln Walnut Creek CA 94598-2418 also: Dress Fore The 9's 613 1st St Ste 19 Brentwood CA 94513-1322

FRIDMAN, JOSEF JOSEL, telecommunications company executive; b. Rubcousk, USSR, Dec. 24, 1945; arrived in Can., 1949; s. Moishe and Malka (Hersfeld) F.; m. Georgette Weiss, Aug. 23, 1970; children: Richard Samuel, Kenneth Howard, Michelle Sarah. B Commerce, McGill U., Montreal, Que., Can., 1966, licentiate in acctg., 1968, BCL, 1970. Solicitor Bell Can., Montreal, 1971-74, asst. v.p. taxes, 1974-78, asst. v.p. corp. performance ops., 1978-79, asst. gen. counsel, 1979-83; gen. counsel BCE Inc., Montreal, 1983-85, v.p., gen. counsel, 1985-90, sr. v.p. law and corp. svcs., 1991-93, sr. v.p. law, 1993-94, sr. v.p. law, corp. sec., 1995-98; chief legal officer Bell Can., BCE Inc., Montreal, 1998—; bd. dirs. Telesat Can., Ottawa, TMI Comm. Inc., Ottawa, Alouette Telecom. Inc., Ottawa, Télébec ltée, Montreal, BCE Corp. Svcs., Inc., Montreal. Past pres. Jewish Family Svcs. Social Svcs. Ctr.; past mem. bd. United Talmud Torahs of Montreal, Allied Jewish Community Svcs., Baron de Hirsch Inst. and certain affiliated orgns. Mem. ABA, Internat. Bar Assn., Can. Bar Assn., Montreal Bar Assn., Que. Bar Assn., Can. Inst. Chartered Accts., Can. Tax Found., Inst. Chartered Accts. Ont., Order Chartered Accts. Que., Can. C. of C., Univ. Club Montreal, Elm Ridge Country Club, Inc. Jewish. Avocations: golf, skiing, tennis, reading. Office: Bell Canada and BCE Inc, 1000 de La Gauchetiere St W, Montreal, PQ Canada H3B 4Y7

FRIDOVICH, IRWIN, biochemistry educator; b. N.Y.C., Aug. 2, 1929; s. Louis and Sylvia (Appelbaum) F.; m. Mollie Finkel; children: Sharon E., Judith L. B.S., CCNY, 1951; postgrad., Cornell U. Med. Coll., 1951-52; Ph.D., Duke U., 1955; hon. doctorate, U. Rene Descartes, Paris, 1980. Instr. biochemistry Duke U., Durham, N.C., 1956-58; assoc. Duke U., 1958—; vis. research assoc. Harvard U., Cambridge, Mass., 1961-62; asst. prof. biochemistry Duke U., 1961-66, assoc. prof., 1966-71, prof., 1971—, James B. Duke prof., 1976—, emeritus, 1996—; mem. study sect. Am. Cancer Soc., mem. adv. com. biochemistry and chem. carcinogenesis. Mem. editorial bd. Jour. Biol. Chemistry, Biochemica Biophysica Acta, Archives of Biochemistry and Biophysics, Biochem. Jour., Bioinorganic Chemistry, Biochemistry, Biochem. Pharmacology, Analytical Biochemistry; contbr. articles to sci. jours. Recipient Founders' award Chem. Industry Inst. Toxicology, 1980, Sr. Passano award, 1987, Herty award Ga. sect. Am. Chem. Soc., 1980, Research Career Devel. award NIH, 1959-69, Cressy A. Morrison award N.Y. Acad. Sci., 1984, Townsend Harris medal, 1990; co-recipient Cresson medal, Franklin Inst., 1997, City of Medicine award, Durham, N.C., 1998, Anlyan Lifetime Achievement award Duke Med. Ctr., 1998. Mem. NAS, Am. Acad. Arts and Scis., Am. Soc. Biol. Chemists (pres. 1982), N.C. Acad. Scis., Oxygen Soc. (pres. 1990), Soc. for Free Radical Rsch. Internat., (pres. 1992), Phi Beta Kappa, Sigma Xi. Home: 3517 Courtland Dr Durham NC 27707-5134 Office: Duke U Med Center Box 3711 Durham NC 27710

FRIED, ALBERT, JR., investment banker; b. N.Y.C., Mar. 19, 1930; s. Albert and Rose (Frank) F.; m. Sigrid Walther, Sept. 13, 1964; 1 child, Christina Elaine. BA, Cornell U., 1952, MBA, 1953. Mng. mem. Albert Fried & Co. LLC, N.Y.C., 1955-96; Mng. mem. Buttonwood Specialists, LLC, N.Y.C., 1996—; also bd. dirs. Portec, Inc.; dir. Emcor Group, Inc.; mem. Entrepreneurship and Personal Enterprise Adv. Coun. Cornell U., mem. coll. vet. medicine, equine adv. coun.; trustee N.Y. Racing Assn., Inc. Pres. Fried Found. Inc.; co-founder and dir. Charles A. and Anne Morrow Lindbergh Fund; co-founder, chmn. Centurion Found.; dir. Trooper Found., State of N.Y. Capt. USAF, 1953-55. Hon. commr. N.Y.C. Police Dept. Mem. Confrerie des Chevaliers du Tastevin (commandeur), Thoroughbred Owners and Breeders Assn., Am. Horse Coun., Explorers Club, Sea Space Symposium, Asia Soc., N.Y. Thoroughbred Horsemen's Assn., Statler Club. Home: Buttonwood Farm LLC 2119 State Route 9G Rhinebeck NY 12572-2331 Office: 40 Exchange Pl New York NY 10005-2701

FRIED, ARTHUR, lawyer; m. Kym Vanderbilt. JD magna cum laude, Cornell U., 1975. Bar: N.Y. Law clk. to Hon. John M. Cannella U.S. Dist. Ct. (so. dist.) N.Y., 1975-77; with The Legal Aid Soc. N.Y.C., 1977-90; acting gen. counsel, dep. gen. counsel N.Y.C. Human Resources Adminstrn.; gen. counsel N.Y.C. Dept. Housing Preservation and Devel., to 1995, Social Security Adminstrn., Balt., 1995—. Mem. Order of Coif. Office: Social Security Adminstrn Altmeyer Bldg 6401 Security Blvd Baltimore MD 21235-0001

FRIED, BRUCE MERLIN, health services director. BA, U. Fla., JD. With Fla. Legal Svcs., 1975-81, Nat. Sr. Citizens Law Ctr., 1981-86; exec. dir. Nat. Health Care Campaign, 1986-90; exec. v.p. The Wexler Group, 1990-92; chief coord. Clinton/Gore Campaign's Health Care Adv. Group, 1992; v.p. fed. affairs FHP Internat. Corp.; dir. Office Managed Care, 1995-97; dir. Health Care Fin. Adminstrn. U.S. Dept. Health and Human Svcs., Balt., 1997-99; ptnr. Shawpittan, Washington, 1999—. Office: Shawpittan 2300 N St Washington DC 20037*

FRIED, BURTON DAVID, physicist, educator; b. Chgo., Dec. 14, 1925; s. Albert O. and Bertha (Rosenthal) F.; m. Sally Rachel Goldstein, Aug. 17, 1947; children—Joel Ethan, Jeremy Steven. B.S., Ill. Inst. Tech., 1947; M.S., U. Chgo., 1950, Ph.D., 1952. Instr. physics Ill. Inst. Tech., 1947-52; research physicist Lawrence Berkeley Lab. of U. Calif., 1952-54; sr. staff physicist TRW Systems, Los Angeles, 1954-86; dir. research lab. (Ramo-Wooldridge Computer Div.), Los Angeles, 1961-63; prof. physics UCLA, 1963—. Served with USNR, 1944-46. Fellow Am. Phys. Soc. (chmn. plasma physics div. 1978-79); mem. Sigma Xi. Research and publs. on theoretical elementary particle and plasma physics. E-mail: fried@physics.ucla.edu. Home: 223 Desert Holly Dr Palm Desert CA 92211-7410 Office: UCLA Dept Physics 405 Hilgard Ave Los Angeles CA 90095-9000

FRIED, BURTON THEODORE, lawyer; b. N.Y.C., Feb. 26, 1940; s. Meyer S. and Minnie (Grossberg) F.; m. Gail K. Morgenstern, July 25, 1964; children: Marsha, Howard, Shari. B.S., NYU, 1961; LL.B., Bklyn. Law Sch., 1964. Bar: N.Y. 1964, U.S. Dist. Ct. (ea. and so. dists.) N.Y. 1971. Assoc. atty. H. Bermack, N.Y.C., 1964-66, I. Towbis, N.Y.C., 1966-68; gen. counsel Medispas, Inc., N.Y.C., 1968-72; real estate counsel Michael Industries, Inc., N.Y.C., 1972-74, exec. v.p., gen. counsel and sec., 1974-86; exec. v.p., gen. counsel and sec. The LVI Group, Inc., N.Y.C., 1982-85; vice chmn., gen. counsel, dir. The LVI Group, Inc., 1985-91; pres. The LVI Group Inc., N.Y.C., 1991-93; pres., CEO LVI Environmental Services Group Inc., N.Y.C., 1986—; chmn. LVI Holding Corp., N.Y.C., 1993—; trustee Optometric Ctr. N.Y., 1993—. Vice chmn. sch. bd. Forest Hills Jewish Ctr. Religious Sch., N.Y., 1983-84, chmn. sch. bd., 1984-85, trustee, 1985-88. Lodge: K.P. (Chancellor comdr. 1972-73). Office: LVI Environ Svcs Group Inc 470 Park Ave S New York NY 10016-6819

FRIED, CHARLES, law educator; b. Prague, Czechoslovakia, Apr. 15, 1935; came to U.S., 1941, naturalized, 1948; s. Anthony and Marta (Winterstein) F.; m. Anne Sumerscale, June 13, 1959; children: Gregory, Antonia. AB, Princeton U., 1956; BA, Oxford (Eng.) U., 1958, MA, 1961; LLB, Columbia U., 1960; LLD (hon.), New Eng. Sch. of Law, 1987, Pepperdine U., 1994, Suffolk U., 1996. Bar: D.C. 1961, Mass. 1966. Law clk. to Hon. John M. Harlan U.S. Supreme Ct., 1960; from asst. prof. to prof. law Harvard U., Cambridge, 1961-85, Carter prof. gen. jurisprudence, 1981-85, 89-95, Carter prof. emeritus, disting. lectr. Law Sch., 1995—, Beneficial prof. law, 1999—; assoc. justice Supreme Jud. Ct. Mass., Boston, 1995-99; spl. cons. Treasury Dept., 1961-62; cons. White House office Policy Devel., 1982, Dept. Transp., 1081-82, Dept. Justice, 1983; solicitor gen. U.S., 1985-89. Author: An Anatomy of Values, 1970, Medical Experimentation: Personal Integrity and Social Policy, 1974, Right and Wrong, 1978, Contract as Promise: A Theory of Contractual Obligation, 1981, Order and Law: Arguing the Reagan Revolution, 1991; contbr. legal and philos. jours. Guggenheim fellow, 1971-72. Fellow Am. Acad. Arts and Scis.; mem. Inst. Medicine, Am. Law Inst., Century Assn., Mass. Hist. Soc., Phi Beta Kappa. Office: Harvard Law Sch 1300 New Courthouse Cambridge MA 02138

FRIED, CHARLES A., accountant, financial executive; b. N.Y.C., Jan. 31, 1945; s. Jerome M. and Florence (Silverman) F.; m. Denise Helaine Krafte, Sept. 2, 1965; children: Marc Steven, Shari Lynne. BS in Acctg., Queens Coll., CUNY, 1965. From staff acct. to sr. acct. Klein Hinds & Finke CPAs, N.Y.C., 1965-69; from sr. acct. to mgr. Alexander Grant & Co., N.Y.C., 1969-73; treas. Raybestos-Manhattan, Inc., Trumbull, Conn., 1974-79, v.p., 1979-80; pres. Creative Output, Inc., Milford, Conn., 1980-87; exec. v.p., CFO Home-Med Services Inc., San Diego, 1987-88; asst. v.p. Aetna Life and Casualty, Hartford, Conn., 1988-89; exec. v.p. Avraham Y. Goldratt Inst., New Haven, 1989—; instr. acctg. L.I. U., 1973, Fairfield U., 1977-81. Mem. local bd. Selective Svc. Commn., 1988—; rep., dist. fin. chmn. Fairfield Rep. Town. Commn., 1975-79; chmn., vice-chmn., dir., v.p., treas. Parents and Friends of Retarded Citizens (Kennedy Ctr.), 1975—; campaign worker United Way, 1976-77, United Jewish Appeal, 1976-78; dir., v.p. exec. com. Conn. affiliate Am. Diabetes Assn., 1977—; dir. Fairfield County chpt. Am. Diabetes Assn., 1992—, pres. 1994-95, bd. dirs. ea. region, 1998; chmn. adv. coun. Fairfield U. Bus. Bur., 1978-80; vice-chmn. combined health appeal So. Ctrl. Conn., 1991—, bd. Cmty. Health Charities, 1999—; bd. dirs. N.Am. bd. World Union Progressive Judaism, 1995—; bd. dirs., v.p. N.E. coun. Union of Am. Hebrew Congregations, 1992—, Jewish Fedn. Greater Bridgeport, 1992-95; mem. mktg. com. New Haven United Way, 1994-96; trustee, pres. Congregation B'nai Israel. Mem. AICPA, N.Y. State Soc. CPA's, Conn. Soc. CPA's, Inst. Mgmt. Accts., Risk Ins. Mgrs. Soc., Conn. Bus. and Industry Assn., Probus Club (bd. dirs., various offices local chpt., nat. asst. treas. 1974-86). Jewish. E-mail: cfried@aol.com. Home: 140 Canterbury Ln Fairfield CT 06432-2314 Office: 442 Orange St New Haven CT 06511-6201

FRIED, DANIEL, ambassador; b. Sept. 19, 1952; m. Olga Karpiw; children: Hannah, Sophie. BA in History magna cum laude, Cornell U., 1974; MA, Columbia U., 1977. Fgn. svc. officer, 1977—; jr. officer East-West Trade office Econ. Bus. Bur. State Dept., 1977-79; with Consulate Gen. Office, Leningrad, 1980-81; polit. officer U.S. Embassy, Belgrade, 1982-85; reg. affairs officer Soviet Desk State Dept., Washington, 1985-87; Polish desk officer State Dept., Washington, 1987-89; polit. counselor U.S. Embassy, Warsaw, 1990-93; dir. European affairs NSC, Washington, 1993-95, spl. asst. to pres., sr. dir. ctrl. and Ea. Europe, 1995—; amb. to Poland Warsaw, 1997—. Office: Am Embassy Warsaw Poland Dept of State Washington DC 20521-5010*

FRIED, DONALD DAVID, lawyer; b. N.Y.C., Feb. 28, 1936; s. Fred and Sylvia (Falk) F.; m. Joan Hilbert, Sept. 15, 1963; children: Neil, Derek. BA, CCNY, 1956; JD, Harvard U., 1959. Bar: N.Y. 1959. Assoc. Conboy, Hewitt, O'Brien & Boardman, N.Y.C., 1960-68, ptnr., 1968-86; ptnr. Hunton & Williams, N.Y.C., 1986-88, 92-96; sr. counsel, 1996—; v.p., sec., assoc. gen. counsel Philip Morris Cos., Inc., N.Y.C., 1988-91. Home: 37 W 12th St New York NY 10011-8502 Office: Hunton & Williams 200 Park Ave Rm 4400 New York NY 10166-0091

FRIED, EDWARD R., government official; b. N.Y.C., Apr. 13, 1918. B.A., U. Mich., 1941. Economist, then chief div. research (Far East) Dept. State, 1946-54; chief econ. sect. and dep. prin. officer U.S. consulate Hong Kong, 1955-60; counselor for econ. affairs Am. embassy The Hague, 1960-62; mem. policy planning council Dept. State, Washington, 1962-65; exec. sec. President's Commn. on U.S. Trade Relations with Eastern European Countries and Soviet Union, 1964-65; dep. asst. sec. for econ. affairs Dept. State, 1965-67; sr. staff mem. NSC, 1967-69; exec. dir. President's Task Force on Internat. Devel., 1969-70; sr. fellow Brookings Instn., Washington, 1969-77, 80—; U.S. exec. dir. IBRD, Washington, 1977-79; cons. on internat. energy to White House, 1979-80; sr. fellow Brookings Instn., Washington, 1980—. Served in USAF, 1943-45. Office: 1775 Massachusetts Ave NW Washington DC 20036-2188

FRIED, ELAINE JUNE, business executive; b. L.A., Oct. 19, 1943; grad. Pasadena (Calif.) H.S.; various coll. courses; m. Howard I. Fried, Aug. 7, 1966; children: Donnoven Michael, Randall Jay. Agt., office mgr. Howard I. Fried Agy., Alhambra, Calif., 1975—; v.p. Sea Hill, Inc., Pasadena, 1973-95. Publicity chmn., unit telephone chmn. San Gabriel Valley unit Am. Diabetes Assn., past chmn., vol. lobbyist, mem. patient edn. com. region II Calif. chpt., 1998; past publicity chmn. San Gabriel Valley region Women's Am. Orgn. for Rehab. Tng. (ORT); chmn. spl. events publicity, Temple Beth Torah Sisterhood, Alhambra, membership chmn., 1991-92, v.p. membership, 1991-93; former mem. bd. dirs., pub. relations com., pers. com. Vis. Nurses Assn., Pasadena and San Gabriel Valley; chmn. outside Sisterhood publicity Congregation Shaarei Torah, 1993, pub. rels. chmn., 1993—. Recipient Vol. award So. Calif. affiliate Am. Diabetes Assn., 1974-77, 25 Yr. Vol. Svc. award, 1996, cert. of appreciation, 1987; co-recipient Ner Tamid award Temple Beth Torah. Contbr. articles to profl. jours. Mem. ORT, Hadassah, Greater Pasadena Assn. Life Underwriters (co-v.p. cmty. affairs 1998—). Speaker on psycho-social aspects of diabetes, insurance and the diabetic, ins. medicine. Home: 404 N Hidalgo Ave Alhambra CA 91801-2640

FRIED, HERBERT DANIEL, advertising executive; b. Chgo., May 27, 1928; s. Herbert D. and Beatrice (Frank) F.; m. Ninon Connart, Mar. 7, 1953; children: Bruce M., William F. Student, U. N.Mex., 1946-48, U. Ill., 1948. Account exec. Foote, Cone & Belding, Chgo., 1948-54, Weiss & Geller, Chgo., 1954-55; account exec., gen. mgr. W.B. Doner & Co., Balt., 1955-56; v.p. W.B. Doner & Co., 1956-68, pres., 1968-73, chmn. bd., chief exec. officer, 1973—; bd. dirs. Nat. Advt. Rev. Bd., 1987. Divsn. chmn. Comty. Chest-ARC-United Appeal, 1964, United Fund, 1977; bd. dirs. comm. divsn. United Way, 1978-79; dir. Sinai Hosp., Balt., 1994—, Greater Balt. Com., Balt. Zool. Soc., The Associated, Jewish Comty. Fedn. Balt., 1992—; mem. adv. bd. Ctr. for Advt. History Nat. Mus. Am. History Smithsonian Mus.; bd. dirs. U.S.S. Constellation Fund, 1995—. With USNR, 1946. Recipient award Chgo. Federated Advt. Club, 1949; inducted Advt. Hall of Fame, Advt. Assn. Balt., 1987; named Disting. Marylander of Yr. Advt. and Profl. Club Baltimore, 1991. Mem. Am. Assn. Advt. Agys., Inc. (bd. govs. Chesapeake coun. 1960, regional dir. 1963, chmn. govt. rels. com. 1987-90, bd. dirs. 1987-90), Nat. Advertising Review Bd., Advt. Club Balt., Kappa Sigma. Clubs: Center (Balt.); Suburban of Baltimore County (Pikesville, Md.). Home: Admirals Cove 121 Spinnaker Ln Jupiter FL 33477-4003 Office: W B Doner & Co 400 E Pratt St Baltimore MD 21202-3116

FRIED, JEFFREY MICHAEL, health care administrator; b. Kansas City, Mo., Apr. 9, 1953; s. Harvey J. and SuEllen (Weissman) F.; m. Rosalyn Sue Matz. Student, Drake U., 1971-73; BGS, U. Kans., 1975; MHA, Washington U., St. Louis, 1979. Adminstrv. asst. Rsch. Med. Ctr., Kansas City, Mo., 1979-80; asst. to pres. Rsch. Health Svcs., Kansas City, 1980-81; asst. v.p. Sinai Hosp. Balt., 1981-83, Lancaster (Pa.) Gen. Hosp., 1983-85; v.p., chief oper. officer Lancaster (Pa.) Gen. Svcs. Corp., 1985-86, pres., 1986-88; sr. v.p. Lancaster Gen. Hosp., 1989-91, chief operating officer, 1992-94; pres., CEO Beebe Med. Ctr., Lewes, Del., 1994—; pres., bd. dirs. Lancaster Med. Equipment, Barge Ganse Vena Care; sec., bd. dirs. Preferred Health Care, Lancaster; bd. dirs. Lancaster Diagnostic Imaging, Inc.; v.p., bd. dirs., pres. Welsh Mountain Med. and Dental Ctr., Lancaster, 1989-94; mng. ptnr. Roherstown Imaging Assocs., Lancaster, 1986-94; part-time mem. faculty dept. health adminstrn. and devel. Pa. State U., 1988-94, Coll. of St. Francis, 1988-94; mem. bus. adv. coun. Goodwill Industries, 1989-94; asst. prof. Lebanon Valley Coll., 1994—; mem. MBA program adv. bd. Wilmington Coll., 1996—; adj. faculty Wilmington Coll. Grad. Bus. Program, 1996—. Mem. Leadership Lancaster, 1987-88; pres. bd. dirs. Welsh Mt. Med. and Dental Ctr., 1989-94; pres. bd. dirs. Lancaster chpt. Nat. Commn. for Prevention of Child Abuse, 1986-89; treas., bd. dirs. Lancaster Jewish Fedn., 1986-89; bd. dirs. Lancaster Jewish Cmty. Ctr., 1989-94, Temple Shaarai Shomayim, Clinic for Spl. Children, 1991-94, Pa. Acad. Music, 1994-96, Del. Hospice, 1996—, Rehoboth Art League, 1996—. Fellow Am. Coll. Healthcare Execs. (com. on ethics 1991-93, credentials com. 1995-98); mem. Am. Hosp. Assn. (ho. of dels. 1998-2000), Assn. Del. Hosps. (bd. dirs. 1995—), Lancaster County Bus. Group on Health (legis. com. 1992-94), Ctrl. Pa. Health Care Adminstrs, Young Pres. Orgn. (XPO). Jewish. Avocations: tennis, jogging, cooking, reading. Home: (PO Box 66 Bethany Beach DE 19930-0066 Office: Beebe Med Ctr 424 Savannah Rd Lewes DE 19958-1490

FRIED, JOSEF, chemist, educator; b. Przemysl, Poland, July 21, 1914; came to U.S., 1938, naturalized, 1944; s. Abraham and Frieda (Fried) F.; m. Erna Werner, Sept. 18, 1939 (dec. Nov. 1986); 1 dau., Carol Frances. Student, U. Leipzig, 1934-37, U. Zurich, 1937-38; Ph.D., Columbia U., 1941. Eli Lilly fellow Columbia U., 1941-43; research chemist Givaudan, N.Y., 1943; head dept. antibiotics and steroids Squibb Inst. Med. Research, New Brunswick, N.J., 1944-59; dir. sect. organic chemistry Squibb Inst. Med. Research, 1959-63; prof. chemistry, biochemistry and Ben May Lab. Cancer Research, U. Chgo., 1963—, Louis Block prof., 1973—, chmn. dept. chemistry, 1977-79; mem. med. chem. study sect. NIH, 1963-67, 68-72, chmn., 1971; mem. com. arrangements Laurentian Hormone Conf., 1964-71; Knapp Meml. lectr. U. Wis., 1958. Mem. bd. editors: Jour. Organic Chemistry, 1964-69, Steroids, 1966-86, Jour. Biol. Chemistry, 1975-81, 83-88; contbr. articles to profl. jours. Recipient N.J. Patent award, 1968, Roussel prize 1992, Gregory Pincus medal, 1994. Fellow AAAS, N.Y. Acad. Scis.; mem. NAS, Am. Acad. Scis., Am. Chem. Soc. (award in medicinal chemistry 1974, Alfred Burger award in medicinal chemistry 1996), Am. Soc. Biol. Chemists, Swiss Chem. Socs., Brit. Chem. Socs., Sigma Xi. Patentee in field. Home: 5715 S Kenwood Ave Chicago IL 60637-1742

FRIED, LAWRENCE PHILIP, insurance company executive; b. N.Y.C., Mar. 20, 1938; s. Louis Israel and Gertrude May (Carlin) F.; m. Elaine Lois Raskin, Nov. 28, 1959 (div. 1986); children: Diane, Howard, Elliott; m. Diane Lynn Williford, Nov. 10, 1994. BBA in Mktg., Adelphi U., 1960. Lic. life health ins. and variable annuities agt.; registered rep. Nat. Assn. Securities Dealers; cert. ins. inspector. Prodn. mgr. Verdi Handbags, N.Y.C., 1960-73, Express Handbags, North Bergen, N.J., 1973-74; gen. mgr. Victoria Needlework, Inc., N.Y.C., 1974-79; v.p. sales J&L Hardwood Lumber Sales, Bellmore, N.Y., 1979-81; plant mgr. Jade Handbags and Belts, N.Y.C., 1981-83; mgr. Glamour Glove, Inc., N.Y.C., 1983-87; dir. prodn. Campaign, Inc., Portsmouth, Va., 1987-89; pres. Larry Fried & Assocs., Boca Raton, Fla., 1989-94; sr. v.p. The Philips Group, Inc., Lake Worth, Fla., 1989-93; v.p., ptnr. The Securance Agy., Inc., Roswell, Ga., 1994—; pres. SERVPRO of Chamblee-Dunwoody, Inc., Roswell, Ga., 1994—; area mgr. Broward County Atlantic Plan; cons. Elf Ceations, Inc., Bellmore, 1970-83; regional dir. Eagle Internat. Mktg., Inc., Oklahoma City, 1981-87; lectr. Help Overweight, Inc., Bklyn., 1974-75; bd. dirs. Nassau County Epilepsy Found., 1979-86; active local polit. campaigns, 1979-85. Bd. dirs. Nassau County Epilepsy Found., 1979-86; active local polit. campaigns, 1979, Adelphi U. Alumni adv. coun.; mem. pers. practice com. Jewish Family Svc. Atlanta; mem. Alumni Recruiters Coun. Adelphi U. Life Underwriters Tng. Coun. fellow. Mem. Jewish Geneal. Soc. Ga., Jewish Geneal. Soc. Palm Beach, Bellmore C. of C. (bd. dirs., v.p. 1979-83), Hampton Roads C. of C., Great Neck Power Squadron, U. Mich. Alumni Club Atlanta, Masons, Rotary, Pi Sigma Epsilon (life). Jewish. Avocation: sailing, biking, hiking, recreational motor home traveling. E-mail: larry@ideaplace.com. Home: 620 Brickleberry Ct Roswell GA 30075-3077 Office: SERVPRO Warehouse Office 3788 Green Industrial Way Chamblee GA 30341-1910

FRIED, LOUIS LESTER, information technology and management consultant; b. N.Y.C., Jan. 18, 1930; s. Albert and Tessie (Klein) F.; m. Haya Greenberg, Aug. 15, 1960; children: Ron Chaim, Eliana Ahuva, Gil Ben. BA in Pub. Adminstrn., Calif. State U., Los Angeles, 1962; MS in Mgmt. Theory, Calif. State U., Northridge, 1965. Mgr. br. plant data processing Litton systems, Inc., Woodland Hills, Calif., 1960-65; dir. mgmt. info. systems Bourns, Inc., Riverside, Calif., 1965-68, Weber Aircraft Co., Burbank, Calif., 1968-69; v.p. mgmt. services T.I. Corp. of Calif., Los Angeles, 1969-75; dir. advanced computer systems dept. Stanford Research Inst., Menlo Park, Calif., 1976-85, dir. ctr. for info. tech., 1985-86, dir. worldwide info. tech. practice, 1987-90; v.p. info. tech. cons. Stanford Rsch. Inst., Menlo Park, Calif., 1990-97; spl. advisor to pres. TELUS Corp., Edmonton, Alta., Can., 1997-98; info. tech. mgmt. cons., 1998—; lectr. U. Calif., Riverside, 1965-69, lectr. mgmt. and EDP. Contbr. numerous articles to profl. jours., 2 textbooks. E-mail: LLFRIED@aol.com. Fax: 650-493-8712. Home: 788 Loma Verde Ave Palo Alto CA 94303-4147 also: King George V St 16B 7th Fl #14, Jerusalem 94229, Israel

FRIED, MARVIN PETER, physician; b. N.Y.C., June 10, 1945; s. Otto and Leonore (Schwartz) F.; m. Rita Beth Hyfer, Jan. 25, 1970; children: Jaimie Lisa, Karen Lynn. BS, CUNY, 1961-65; MD, Tufts U. Sch. of Med., Boston, Mass., 1965-69. Diplomate, Am. Bd of Otolaryngology, 1975. Chief of otolaryngology Boston (Mass.) City Hosp., 1977-79; otolaryngolist Beth Israel Hosp., Boston, 1979-92; chief of otolaryngology Beth Israel Deaconess Med. Ctr., 1993-98; otolaryngologist Brigham & Womens Hosp., Boston, 1979-92; chief otolaryngology Brigham & Womens Hosp., 1993-98; otolaryngologist Childrens Hosp., Boston, 1979-98, Mass. Eye and Ear Infirmary, Boston, 1979; prof. otology and laryngology Harvard Med. Sch., Boston, 1997-99; co-dir. Head and Neck Oncology program Dana Farber Cancer Ctr., 1996-98; prof. Otolaryngology Albut Emiten Coll. Medicine; chmn. Dept. Otolaryngology, Montifore Hosp., N.Y., 1999—. Editor: Complications Of Laser Surgery Of The Head And Neck, 1986, Manual of Otolaryngology, 1992, The Larynx, 1995; mem. editl. bd. Ear, Nose & Throat Jour., 1988, Laryngoscope, 1992, Archives of Otolaryngology, 1998. Surgeon (CDR), U.S. Public Health Svc., Norfolk, Va., 1975. Recipient Fowler award, 1984, Mark award, 1994. Fellow Am. Acad. of Otolaryngology, Am. Coll. of Surgeons, Triologic Soc., Am. Laryngological Soc., Am. Bronchoesophagological Soc., Am Soc. for Laser Med. and Surgery (v.p. 1994, pres.-elect 1998), Soc. Univ. Otolaryngology (pres-elect 1998), Phi Beta Kappa, Alpha Omega Alpha. Avocations: travel, music, tennis. Office: Joint Ctr Otolaryngology 333 Longwood Ave Boston MA 02115-5711

FRIED, SAMUEL, lawyer; b. Bklyn., Aug. 16, 1951; s. Zoltan and Helen (Katina) F.; m. Gigi Panush, Dec. 27, 1981; children: Eva M., Orly Z., Jacob J., Molly R., Susanna R. AB, Washington U., St. Louis, 1971; JD, Boston U., 1974, LLM, 1997. Bar: Mass. 1974, Ill. 1983, Mich. 1989; ordained rabbi, 1971. Assoc. Warner & Stackpole, Boston, 1974-77; staff atty. The Bendix Corp., Southfield, Mich., 1977-79, sr. atty., 1979-80, asst. treas., 1980-81; v.p., corp. counsel Clevite Industries, Inc., Glenview, Ill., 1981-83, v.p., sec., gen. counsel, 1983-87; v.p., sec. gen. counsel Exide Corp., Troy, Mich., 1987-91; v.p., gen. counsel The Limited Inc., 1991-99, sr. v.p., gen. counsel, sec., 1999—. Editor: Psychosurgery, 1974. Mem. ABA, Am. Corp. Counsel Assn., Mich. Gen. Counsels Assn., Phi Beta Kappa. Jewish. Avocations: music, reading. Office: The Limited Inc PO Box 16000 3 Limited Pky Columbus OH 43216

FRIED, STEPHEN WILLIAM, English language educator, poet; b. Pitts., Feb. 2, 1946; s. Morris and Frances Helen (Higgins) F.; m. Katrina Faldt-Larsen, May 12, 1970 (div. June 1971); m. Marilyn Diane Kaggen, Mar. 21, 1985; 1 child, Daniel Kaggen Fried. BA, Bucknell U., 1967; MA, Syracuse U., 1972. Tchr. English The Students Sch., St. Thomas, U.S. Virgin Islands, 1971; adj. lectr. English Baruch Coll., CUNY, N.Y.C., 1971-74, 76-77; tchr. English Elizabeth Cleaners St. Sch., N.Y.C., 1972-73; instr. English Bklyn. Coll., CUNY, 1974-76, Coll. New Rochelle, N.Y.C., 1977-79; adj. asst. prof. English L.I. U., Bklyn., 1978-83; lectr. English Coll. Staten Island, CUNY, 1978—; tchr. English Local 1199 Tng. Fund, N.Y.C., 1993—; writer-in-residence Poets in Pub. Svc./Tchrs. and Writers, N.Y.C., 1994—; dir. Bklyn. Poetlink, 1995—; pub. Lunar Offensive Press, Bklyn., 1992—; outreach editor Through the Cracks Mag., N.Y.C., 1992-96. Author (books of poetry): Going Through Doors: NYC EMS Poems, 1993, The Rough Sex Defense for Matricide, 1995, Plackets, 1996; co-author (with Elliot Richman): Women and Men of Air, 1998. Ambulance crew chief North Shore Rescue Squad, Staten Island, 1985-90, Bedford-Stuyvesant Vol. Ambulance, Bklyn., 1991-93; vol. CPR instr. ARC, N.Y.C., 1986-88; EMT, N.Y.C. Emergency Med. Svc., 1988-92. Avocation: woodworking. Office: Coll Staten Island CUNY English Dept 2S-218 2800 Victory Blvd Staten Island NY 10314

FRIED, WALTER, hematologist, educator; b. Frauenkirchen, Austria, Mar. 21, 1935; came to U.S., 1938; s. Alexander and Aurelia (Haberfeld) F.; m. Judith April Weininger, Dec. 13, 1965; children: Deborah, Jennifer. BA, U. Chgo., 1954, MD, 1958. Diplomate Am. Bd. Internal Medicine, Am. Bd. Hematology. Clin. investigator VA Hosp., Chgo., 1965-67; asst. prof. Dept. Med. U. Ill., 1967-70; prof. medicine, dir. hematology U. Ill., Chgo., 1970-76; prof. U. Chgo., 1976-82; prof., assoc. dean med. scis. Rush Med. Coll., Chgo., 1982-92; mem. hematology/oncology divsn. Luth. Gen. Hosp., Park Ridge, Ill., 1995—; Mem. hematology study sect. NIH, Bethesda, Md., 1976-80, 83-87; acting chmn. dept. medicine Michael Reese Hosp., Chgo., 1980-82. Contbr. articles to profl. jours. Vol. Care-Medico, Malaysia, 1963, Am. Dr., Guatemala, 1970; v.p. Ill. divsn. Leukemia Soc., 1982—. Lt. USN, 1959-61. Mem. AMA (house dels. 1989—), Am. Soc. Hematology (del. to AMA 1988—), Internat. Soc. Exptl. Hematology (pres. 1983), Chgo. Soc. Int. Medicine (pres. 1979). Jewish. Home: 3638 Salem Walk Apt Bl Northbrook IL 60062-8435 Office: Luth Gen Hosp Cancer Care 1700 Luther Ln Park Ridge IL 60068-1270

FRIED, WALTER JAY, lawyer; b. N.Y.C., May 27, 1904; s. Joseph and Flora V. (Shamberg) F.; m. Louise E. Goldman, June 8, 1934; 1 son, Michael W.; m. Brita Digby-Brown, July 8, 1948. B.A. magna cum laude, Harvard, 1924; LL.B., Columbia U., 1928. Bar: N.Y. 1929, D.C. 1966. Practiced in N.Y.C., 1929—; former mem. firm, now counsel Fried, Frank, Harris, Shriver & Jacobson; mem. faculty Bklyn. Law Sch., 1931-39; dir. Salant Corp., 1969-93. Former chmn. Am. Chess Found.; hon. trustee Guild Hall, East Hampton, N.Y., chmn., 1974-78; former trustee Southampton Hosp. Served to maj. AUS, 1942-45. Decorated Legion of Merit. Mem. Assn. Harvard Chemists, Phi Beta Kappa. Clubs: Maidstone (East Hampton), Harvard (N.Y.C.), Manhattan Chess (N.Y.C.) (hon. dir.). Home: 14 E 75th St New York NY 10021-2657 also: 18 Lily Pond Ln East Hampton NY 11937 Office: 1 New York Plz New York NY 10004-1901

FRIEDAN, BETTY, author, feminist leader; b. Peoria, Ill., Feb. 4, 1921; d. Harry and Miriam (Horwitz) Goldstein; m. Carl Friedan, June 1947 (div. May 1969); children: Daniel, Jonathan, Emily. AB summa cum laude, Smith Coll., 1942, LHD (hon.), 1975; LHD (hon.), SUNY, Stony Brook, 1985, Cooper Union, 1987; Doctorate (hon.), Columbia U., 1994. Rsch. fellow U. Calif., Berkeley, 1943; lectr. feminism univs., women's groups, bus. and profl. groups in U.S. and Europe; founder NOW, 1st pres., 1966-70, chairwoman adv. com., 1970-72, mem. bd. dirs. legal def. and edn. fund; organizer Nat. Women's Polit. Caucas, 1971, Internat. Feminist Congress, 1973, First Women's Bank, 1973, Econ. Think Tank for Women, 1974; v.p. Nat. Assn. Repeal Abortion Laws, 1970-73; Disting. vis. prof. sch. journalism and studies of women and men in soc., U. So. Calif., 1987; vis. prof. sociology Temple U., 1972, Queens Coll., 1975; vis. lectr. Calhoun Coll., fellow Yale U., 1974; lectr. New Sch. Social Research, N.Y.C., 1971; sr. research assoc. Ctr. Social Scis., Columbia U., N.Y.C., 1979-81; bd. dirs. NOW Legal Defense and Education fund; co-chmn. Nat. Comms. Women's Equality; del. White Ho. Conf. on Family, 1980; del. UN Decade for Women Confs. in Mexico City, Copenhagen, Nairobi; mem. LORAN Commn. Harvard Community Health Plan; vis. scholar U. S. Fla., Sarasota, 1985; Disting. vis. prof. Sch. Journalism and Social Work Sch. U. So. Calif., Cornell U., Ithaca, N.Y., 1998—. Author: The Feminine Mystique, 1963, It Changed My Life: Writings on the Women's Movement, 1976, The Second Stage, 1981, The Fountain of Age, 1993, Beyond Gender: The New Politics of Family and Work, 1998; mem. editl. bd. Present Tense mag.; contbg. editor McCall's mag., 1971-74; contbr. Atlantic Monthly; contbr. articles to New York Times, Cosmopolitan, Saturday Rev., Family Circle, Good Housekeeping, McCall's, Newsweek, American Behavioral Scientist, Social Policy, and others; papers being collected by Schlesinger Libr. Harvard U. Mem. exec. com. Am. Jewish Congress, co-chair nat. commn. women's equality, 1984-85; mem. nat. bd. Girl Scouts USA, 1976-82; mem. N.Y. County Democratic Com. Recipient Humanist of Yr. award, 1974, Eleanor

Roosevelt Leadership award, 1989; Inst. Politics fellow Kennedy Sch. Govt., Harvard U., 1982, rsch. fellow Ctr. Population Studies, Harvard U., 1982-83, Chubb fellow Yale U., 1985, Andrus Ctr. Gerontology fellow U. So. Calif., 1986, guest scholar Woodrow Wilson Ctr. for Internat. Scholars, 1995-96, disting. vis. prof. George Mason U., 1995, Mt. Vernon Coll., 1996; Ford Found. grantee, 1998. Mem. AFTRA, PEN, Author's Guild, Women's Ink, Women's Forum, Mag. Writers, Am. Soc. Journalists and Authors (1st recipient Mort Weisinger award for outstanding mag. journalism 1979, Author of Yr. 1982), Assn. Humanistic Psychology, Am. Sociology Assn., Gerontol. Soc. Am., Cosmos Club, Nat. Press Club, Phi Beta Kappa. Address: 2022 Columbia Rd NW Washington DC 20009-1352*

FRIEDBERG, AARON LOUIS, political science educator; b. Pitts., Apr. 16, 1956; s. Simeon Adlow and Joan Libby (Brest) F.; m. Adrienne Louise Sirken, June 19, 1988; children: Eli, Gideon. BA, Harvard U., 1978, MA, 1986, PhD, 1986. Asst. prof. polit. sci. Princeton (N.J.) U., 1987-93, assoc. prof. polit. sci., 1993—; cons. Nat. Security Coun., Washington, 1979, Dept. Def., Washington, 1979—. Author: The Weary Titan, 1988 (Edward Furniss award, Mershon Ctr., Ohio U., 1989); contbr. articles to pofl. jours. Fellow Ctr. for Internat. Affairs, Harvard U., 1987, Woodrow Wilson Ctr., Smithsonian Inst., 1989, Norwegian Nobel Inst., 1998; recipient Helen Dwight Reid award Am. Polit. Sci. Assn., 1986. Mem. Coun. Fgn. Rels. Office: Princeton U Ctr Internat Studies 321 Bendheim Hall Princeton NJ 08544

FRIEDBERG, BARRY SEWELL, investment banker; b. Atlantic City, Jan. 4, 1941; s. Herbert and Mildred (Salit) F.; m. Charlotte A. Moss, Oct. 10, 1985; children: Benjamin, James. BA, Princeton U., 1962. Trainee Chem. Bank, N.Y.C., 1963-64; with A.G. Becker, N.Y.C., 1964-84, mgr. mergers and acquisitions dept., 1980-83, mng. dir., 1974-84, mgr. investment banking div., 1984; mng. dir. Merrill Lynch & Co., N.Y.C., 1984—; mgr. investment banking div. Merrill Lynch Pierce Fenner & Smith Inc., N.Y.C., 1985-93, chmn. investment banking divsn., 1993—; exec. v.p., mem. exec. com. Merrill Lynch & Co., Inc., 1990—. Bd. dirs. N.Y.C. Ballet Co., 1988-96, 97—, Boys Harbor, Inc. Mem. Princeton Club, Econs. Club. Office: Merrill Lynch & Co World Financial Ctr 250 Vesey St Fl 4 New York NY 10080-0002*

FRIEDBERG, ERROL CLIVE, pathology educator, researcher; b. Johannesburg, South Africa, Oct. 2, 1937; s. Edward and Rena (Berman) F.; children: Malcolm, Andrew, Jonathan, Lawrence. BSc, Witwatersrand U., Johannesburg, 1957, MB BCh, 1961. Intern King Edward VIII Hosp./U. Natal, Durban, South Africa, 1962; resident pathologist Witwatersrand U., 1963-64, Cleve. Met. Gen. Hosp., 1965; postdoctoral fellow dept. biochemistry Case Western Res. U., Cleve., 1966-68; rsch. investigator divsn. nuclear medicine Walter Reed Army Inst. Rsch., Washington, 1969-70; asst. prof. pathology Stanford (Calif.) U., 1971-77, assoc. prof. pathology, 1977-84, prof. pathology, 1984-90; prof., chair dept. pathology U. Tex. Southwestern Med. Ctr., Dallas, 1990—, Senator Betty and Dr. Andy Andujar chair pathology, 1990-93, Senator Betty and Dr. Andy Andujar disting. chair pathology, 1993—; co-organizer symposia and confs. in field. Author: DNA Repair, 1984, Cancer Answers: Encouraging Answers to 25 Questions You Were Always Afraid to Ask, 1992, 93, (with others) DNA Repair and Mutagenesis, 1995, Correcting the Blueprint of Life, 1997, (with others) Sydney Brenner: A Life in Science, 1999; editor or co-editor: DNA Repair Mechanisms, 1978, DNA Repair: A Laboratory Manual of Research Procedures, Vol. 1, 1981, Vol. 2, 1983, Vol. 3, 1988, Cellular Responses to DNA Damage, 1983, Scientific American Reader: Cancer Biology, 1985, Mechanisms and Consequences of DNA Damage Processing, 1988; contbr. numerous articles to profl. publs. Rsch. fellow Andrew W. Mellon Found., 1973-76; recipient Rsch. Career Devel. award USPHS, 1974-79, Merit award USPHS, 1988—; Joshua Macy Jr. Found. faculty scholar, 1978-79. Fellow Royal Coll. Pathology. Office: U Tex Southwestern Med Ctr Dept Path 5323 Harry Hines Blvd Dallas TX 75235-7208

FRIEDBERG, MARVIN PAUL, landscape architect; b. Bklyn., Oct. 11, 1931; s. Morris and Mary (Bennett) F.; m. Esther Louise Hidary, Jan. 21, 1962; children: Mark, Alan Jeffry. B.S. in Landscape Architecture, Cornell U., 1954; LL.D., Ball State U., 1983. Landscape architect with Arthur Hoffman, Hartford, Conn., 1954, Joseph Gangemi, N.Y.C., 1954, 56-58; pres. M. Paul Friedberg and Assocs., landscape architects, N.Y.C., 1960—; vis. critic, lectr. U. Pa., 1967; vis. cirtic, lectr. Syracuse U., 1967, Carnegie Inst. Tech., 1967; vis. critic. lectr. Harvard U., 1966; vis. critic, lectr. 1st Fed. Design Assembly, Washington, 1973, others; mem. faculty Pratt Inst., Columbia U.; mem. New Sch. for Social Research; head urban landscape archtl. program CCNY, 1971—; bd. dirs. Internat. Design Conf., Aspen, Colo., chmn., 1976. Prin. works include, Carver House Plaza, N.Y.C., 1964, Riis Houses Plaza, N.Y.C., 1966, Buchanan Sch., Washington Pub. Sch. 166, N.Y.C., prin. workds include, Bklyn. Bedford-Stuyvesant Superblock, Harlem River Bronx State Park, 1972, prin. works include, Jeannette Plaza, N.Y.C.; landscape architect, Spanish Pavillion, N.Y. World's Fair, 1965, Winter Garden, Niagara Falls, N.Y., 1978, State Street Mall and Concourse, Madison, Wis., 1980, Pershing Park, Washington, 1981, Ft. Worth Cultural Dist., 1983. Del. White House Conf. Natural Beauty, 1965; del. N.Y. State Conf. Natural Beauty, 1966, Urban Am Conf., 1966. Recipient awards Am. Assn. Nurserymen, 1964, 71, 74, 77, 79, 81, 82; recipient Albert S. Bard award, 1965, 67, honor award (2) HUD, 1966, award citation AIA, 1969, honor award AIA, 1967, award Nat. Landscape Assn., 1971, award AIA, 1972, N.Y.C. award for excellence, 1973, I.D.E.A. Downtown Achievement award, 1979, 1st ann. award N.Y.C. Art Commn., 1983. Fellow Am. Soc. Landscape Architects (past v.p. honor awards, Merit awards 1965, 67, 68, 69, 73, 74, 75, 82, v.p.); mem. Assn. N.Y.C., N.Y. Mcpl. Arts Soc. (dir. bronze plaque and merit award, award for Policy Plaza 1974), N.Y.C. Council for Parks and Recreation, Archtl. League. Office: M Paul Friedberg & Ptnrs 41 E 11th St Fl 3 New York NY 10003-4602*

FRIEDBERG, MAURICE, Russian literature educator; b. Rzeszow, Poland, Dec. 3, 1929; came to U.S., 1948, naturalized, 1954; s. Isaac and Ida (Jam) F.; m. Barbara Bisguier, Mar. 18, 1956; children—Rachel Miriam, Edna Sarah. B.S., Bklyn. Coll., 1951; A.M., Columbia U., 1953, Ph.D., 1958; certificate, Russian Inst., 1953. Lectr. Russian Bklyn. Coll., 1952, Middlebury Coll., 1960-61; assoc. Russian Research Center, Harvard U., 1953, Hunter Coll., N.Y.C., 1955-65; prof. Slavic langs. and lits. Ind. U., 1966-75; dir. Russian and East European Inst., Ind. U., 1967-71; prof. Russian lit. U. Ill., Urbana-Champaign, 1975—, head dept. Slavic langs. and lit., 1975-95, 98—, Ctr. for Advanced Study prof., 1995—; vis. asst.prof. Russian lit. Columbia U., 1961-62; lectr. Russian lit. NYU, 1965; Fulbright vis. prof. Russian lit. Hebrew U., Jerusalem, 1965-66; dir. d'etudes invite École des Hautes Études en Sciences Sociales, Paris, 1985; guest scholar Hoover Instn. Stanford U., 1986; fellow Inst. Advanced Study Hebrew U., Jerusalem, 1986-87; cons. Russian lit. and Soviet affairs to pub. radio; mem. acad. coun. Kennan Inst. Advanced Russian Studies, 1985-89; former bd. dirs., mem. selection com. Internat. Rsch. and Exchanges Bd.; juror Nat. Book Award, 1973; sr. univ. scholar U. Ill., 1987—; dir. Russian and East European Ctr., 1996-98. Author: Russian Classics in Soviet Jackets, 1962, The Party and the Poet in the USSR, 1963, A Bilingual Edition of Russian Short Stories, Vol. I, 1964, Vol. II, 1965, The Jew in Post-Stalin Soviet Literature, 1970 (also Portuguese edit), A Decade of Euphoria: Western Literature in Post-Stalin Russia, 1977, Russian Culture in the 1980's, 1985, How Things Were Done In Odessa, 1991, Literary Translation in Russia, 1997; editor: (Leon Trotsky author) The Young Lenin, 1972, The Red Pencil: Artists, Scholars and Censors in the USSR, 1989; deptl. editor: Ency. Judaica, 16 vols, 1971-72, Soviet Society Under Gorbachev, 1987 ; contbr. to scholarly jours. and popular mags. Guggenheim fellow, 1971-81-82; fellow Ctr. for Advanced Study, 1981, 90, NEH fellow, 1990-91. Mem. Polish Inst. Arts and Scis. in U.S. (corr.), Am. Assn. Advancement Slavic Studies (dir.), Am. Assn. Tchrs. Slavic Langs., Russian Acad. of the Humanities. Jewish. Home: 2406 N Nottingham Ct Champaign IL 61821-7017

FRIEDBERG, SIMEON ADLOW, physicist, educator; b. Pitts., July 7, 1925; s. Emanuel B. and Lillian (Adlow) F.; m. Joan Brest, Sept. 4, 1950; children: Elizabeth B., Aaron L., Susan A. A.B., Harvard, 1947; M.S., Carnegie Inst. Tech., 1948, D.Sc., 1951. Fulbright grantee U. Leiden, Netherlands, 1951-52; research physicist Carnegie Inst. Tech., Pitts., 1952-53; mem. faculty Carnegie Inst. Tech., 1953-67, prof. dept. physics, 1962-67; prof. physics Carnegie-Mellon U., Pitts., 1967-93, chmn. dept. physics, 1973-80, emeritus prof. physics, 1993—. Westinghouse fellow, 1950-51; Alfred P. Sloan Found. research fellow, 1957-61; Guggenheim fellow Imperial Coll., London, Eng., 1965-66. Fellow Am. Phys. Soc., AAAS; mem. Sigma Xi, Tau Beta Pi, Phi Kappa Phi, Pi Mu Epsilon. Achievements include studies of magnetic ordering in many compounds of transition series and rare earth metals by magnetic, thermal and neutron scattering methods with emphasis on quasi-one-and two-dimensional spin systems, singlet ground-state systems, magnetic critical phenomena and phase diagrams, and the role of magnons in heat transport. Home: 1220 S Negley Ave Pittsburgh PA 15217-1219

FRIEDBERG, THOMAS HAROLD, insurance company executive; b. N.Y.C., Aug. 25, 1939; s. Henry R. and Ursula J. (Cale) F.; m. Cynthia K. Thisius; children: Donald Henry, Sharon Elizabeth, Linda Lee. Student, Oberlin (Ohio) Coll., 1956-57, Western Res. U., 1959-61; MBA, U. Chgo., 1971. Asst. v.p. CNA Ins. Co., Chgo., 1961-71; v.p. worldwide automobile ins. ops. Am. Internat. Group, N.Y.C., 1971-74; pres., dir. Thurston F & C Ins. Co., Tulsa, 1974-75, Am. Inst. Mktg. Corp., Falls Church, Va., 1975-76; v.p. Hartford Ins. Group, Conn., 1976-79, sr. v.p., 1979-81; sr. v.p. Reliance Ins. Cos., Phila., 1981-83; v.p. Intermediaries of Am., Inc., 1983-85; pres. Transprotection Service Co./Vanliner Ins. Co., Fenton, Mo., 1985-87; exec. v.p. Chase Ins. Enterprises, 1987-93; chmn., pres., chief exec. officer Ranger Ins. Co., 1987-95; chmn., CEO Accel Internat. Corp., Stafford, Tex., 1995—. With AUS, 1957-58. Recipient Disting. Svc. award Park Forest Jaycees, 1967, Jefferson award for pub. svc., 1989, Outstanding Leadership in Edn. award, 1990, Pres.'s award NAACP, 1993, Unity award NAACP, 1994, Hero for Children, Tex. State Dept. of Edn., 1995. Home: 806 Sugar Creek Blvd Sugar Land TX 77478-4031 Office: Accel Internat Corp 12603 Southwest Fwy Stafford TX 77477-3820

FRIEDE, REINHARD L., neuropathologist, educator; b. Jaegerndorf, Czechoslovakia, May 12, 1926; emigrated to U.S., 1957, naturalized, 1962; s. Reinhard and Hilde (Rosner) F.; m. Editha R. Franzen, Dec. 22, 1953; children: Reinhard H., Gerd R. M.D., U. Vienna, 1951. Intern City Hosp., St. Poelten, Austria, 1951-52; resident dept. neurology U. Vienna, Austria, 1953, Clinic of Neurosurgery, Freiburg, Germany, 1953-57; mem. staff Aero. Med. Lab., Wright Air Devel. Center, Dayton, Ohio, 1957-59; faculty U. Mich., Ann Arbor, 1959-65; prof. neuropathology Case Western U., Cleve., 1965-75, U. Zurich, Switzerland, 1975-80, U. Göttingen, Germany, 1981-91; ret., 1991. Author: A Histochemical Atlas of Tissue Oxidation in the Brain Stem of the Cat, 1961, Topographic Brain Chemistry, 1966, Developmental Neuropathology, 1975, 2d edit. 1989; contbr. numerous articles on histochemistry and neuropathology to med. jours. Mem. Am. Assn. Neuropathology. Home: 25 Kehlhofstrasse, 8238 Busingen Switzerland

FRIEDEBERG, PEDRO, painter, sculptor, designer; b. Florence, Italy, Jan. 11, 1937; s. Erwin and Gerda (Landsberg) F. Architecture degree, U. Iberoamericana, Mexico City, 1962. Exhibhied in numerous one man exhbns. including Byron Gallery, N.Y.C., 1964, 66, 67, Souza Gallery, Mexico City, 1962, 64, 66, 68, Misrachi Gallery, Mexico City, 1970, 72, 74, Galerie Pecanins, Barcelona, 1976, Ft. Worth Art Ctr., 1979, Harcourts Gallery, San Francisco, 1980, Needleman Gallery, Chgo., 1981, Llewellyn Gallery, New Orleans, 1985, Museo de Arte Moderno Mex., 1986, Vorpal Gallery, N.Y.C., Museo Biblioteca Pape, Monclova, Mex., 1989, Galeria de Arte Mexicano, Mexico City, 1990; exhibited in numerous group shows including Biennale of São Paulo, 1964, Biennale of Paris, 1964, Labyrinthe, Berlin, 1968, Mus. of Modern Art, Toronto, Ottawa and Montreal, 1973-75, Biennales of San Juan, P.R., 1977-79, Bienal Coltejer, Medellin, Colombia, 1978, Llewellyn Gallery, New Orleans, 1989, Microbienal, Mexico City, Vorpal Gallery, N.Y.C., 1987, Museo de Arte Moderno, Mexico City, 1988, Hokin Galleries, Fla., 1988, 92, R.E.F. Studios, Houston; respresented in numerous mus. in Am., Europe, Argentina, Israel, including Musée Des Arts Decoratifs Du Louvre, Paris, Mus. Contemporary Art, New Orleans, Worcester (Mass.) Art Mus., Brandeis U., Washington and Lee U., Toronto Sci. Mus., Mus. Contemporary Art of Jerusalem and Tel Aviv, Mus. Modern Art of Mexico City, Mus. Modern Art, Bagdad, Iraq, Buenos Aires Mus. Modern Art, Casa de las Americas, Havana, Cuba, Nat. Rsch. Libr., Ottawa, Libr. of Congress, Washington, Museo Marco, Monterrey, Mex., others; Art editor: Mexico This Month, 1960-64; subject of book: Pedro Friedeberg (Ida Rodriguez), 1972, Pedro Friedeberg (A. Neuvillate). Recipient 1st prize Biennale of Córdoba, Argentina, 1967; 2d prize Exposición Solar, Mex., 1968; 1st prize Biennale of San Juan, P.R., 1979; 2d prize Triennale of Buenos Aires, 1979. Mem. Foro de Arte Contemporáneo, Accademia Italia delle Arti e del Lavoro, Gallery La Chinche Mexico City (dir.). Home: Recreo 48, San Miguel Allende, 37700 Guanajuato Mexico Office: Apartado Postal 6-613, 06600 Mexico City Mexico

FRIEDEL, HELEN BRANGENBERG, counselor, therapist; b. Kampsville, Ill., May 16, 1938; d. Carl Morris and Martha Marie (Zipprich) Brangenberg; m. John Laverne Friedel; children: Vincent Joseph, John Francis. BS, So. Ill. U., 1969, MS, 1973. Lic. profl. counselor, Mo. Educator Archdiocese of St. Louis, 1956-87; counselor Diocese of Belleville, Waterloo, Ill., 1988-89, Christian Bros. H.S., St. Louis, 1989—; pvt. practice Florissant, Mo., 1987—. Mem. parents adv. bd. St. Louis Prep. Sem., Florissant, 1973-79; youth moderator Sacred Heart Parish, Florissant, 1967-71, lector and eucharistic min. Named Disting. Lasallion Educator, Midwest Dist. of the Christian Bros., 1998. Mem. ACA, Mo. Counseling Assn. (bd. dirs. 1986-88, 90-93, sec. 1990, pres. 1992, legis. chair 1992-93, Kitty Cole Human Rights award 1993), St. Louis Counseling Assn., Mo. Multicultural Counselors, Mid Rivers Counseling Assn. (pres. 1986), Am. Sch. Counselors Assn., Mo. Sch. Counselors Assn., St. Louis Learning Disabilities Assn. (bd. dirs. 1994), Kappa Delta Pi. Roman Catholic. Avocations: music, drama, history writing. Home: 425 Saint Marie St Florissant MO 63031-5830 Office: Christian Bros Prep HS 6501 Clayton Rd Saint Louis MO 63117-1705

FRIEDEL, JACQUES, physics educator; b. Paris, Feb. 11, 1921; s. Edmond and Jeanne (Bersier) F.; m. Mary Horder, June 2, 1952; children: Jean, Paul. Degree in engring., Ecole Polytechnique, Paris, 1946; post grad., Ecole des Mines, 1948; doctorate, U. Paris., 1954; PhD in Physics., U. Bristol, Eng., 1952; doctorat (hon.), Ecole Polytechnique, Lausanne, Bristol U., Geneva U., Zagreb U., Cambridge U. Engr. Ecole des Mines, Paris, 1948-56; prof. physics U. Paris, 1956-89, ret.; pres. Com. Scientifique France Telecom Paris, 1991-98, Obs. Nat. la Lectr., 1994—; pres. Comite Consultatif de la Recherche Scientifique et Technique, 1979-81. Author: Dislocations, 1956, 64, Graine de Mandarin, 1994; contbr. articles to profl. jours. With French Cavalry, 1944. Decorated grand officer Legion of Honor, comdr. Order Nat. Merit; recipient Gold medals CNRS, Ste. Française Metallurgie Paris, prize Holweck French Soc. Physics and Inst. of Physics, Dannie Heineman prize Acad. Göttingen, von Hippel and Italgas awards. Mem. Acad. des Scis. (past pres.), Swedish Royal Acad. Scis. (hon.), Royal Soc. London (hon.), Am. Acad. Arts and Scis. (hon.), Leopoldina (hon.), Inst. Physics London (hon.), Am. Phys. Soc. (hon.), Nat. Acad. Sci. (hon.), Royal Belgian Acad. Sci. (hon.), Brazilian Acad. Sci. (hon.), European Phys. Soc. (hon.), Max Planck Gesellschaft (hon.). Avocation: gardening. Home: 2 rue Jean-Francois Gerbillon, 75006 Paris France Office: Physique des Solides U, Paris Sud, 91405 Orsay France

FRIEDEL, ROBERT OLIVER, physician; b. Corona, N.Y., Aug. 4, 1936; s. August W. and Denise G. (D'Aoust) F.; m. Susanne Weber, June 30, 1961; children—Christine, Scott, Karin, Linda. B.S., Duke U., 1958, M.D., 1964. Diplomate: Am. Bd. Psychiatry and Neurology. Intern Duke U. Med. Ctr., Durham, N.C., 1964-65, resident in psychiatry, 1967-70, asst. prof. psychiatry and pharmacology dept. psychiatry, 1970-73, assoc. prof. psychiatry and asst. prof. pharmacology, 1973-74; assoc. prof. psychiatry and pharmacology U. Wash. Sch. Medicine, Seattle, 1974-77, dir. div. psychopharmacology, 1974-77, vice chmn., dir. clin. services dept. psychiatry and behavioral scis., 1975-77; prof., chmn. dept. psychiatry Med. Coll. Va.-Va. Commonwealth U., Richmond, 1977-84; prof., chmn. dept. psychiatry, exec. dir. Mental Health Rsch. Inst. U. Mich., Ann Arbor, 1984-85; v.p. psychiat. medicine and rsch. Charter Med. Corp., Macon, Ga., 1985-90, psychiatrist in chief, 1987-90; sr. v.p. clin. svcs. and rsch. Charter Med. Corp., Macon, 1990, physician in chief, 1990, also bd. dirs.; med. dir. Charter Westbrook Hosp., Richmond, 1985-87; prof., chmn. dept. psychiatry U. Ala., Birmingham, 1992—. Author: (with others) Behavioral Science: A Selective View, 1972; mem. editorial bd. Jour. Clin. Psychopharmacology, Hosp. and Community Psychiatry, 1986-92; contbr. book chpts. and articles. Bd. dirs. Nat. Mental Health Assn., 1987-92. Served to lt. comdr. USPHS, 1965-67. Fellow Am. Psychiat. Assn.; mem. Am. Psychopathological Assn., Soc. Biol. Psychiatry, Am. Soc. Pharmacology and Exptl. Therapeutics, Am. Fedn. Clin. Research, Am. Soc. Neurochemistry, AMA, Med. Soc. Va., Am. Coll. Neuropsychopharmacology, Alpha Omega Alpha. Home: 2949 Pump House Rd Birmingham AL 35243

FRIEDEN, CARL, biochemist, educator; b. New Rochelle, N.Y., Dec. 31, 1928; s. Alexander and Evelyn (Gutman) F.; m. Sari Ann Schneider, Dec. 20, 1953; children: Amy, Eric, Karen. B.A., Carleton Coll., 1951; Ph.D., U. Wis., 1955. Mem. faculty biochemistry and molecular biophysics Washington U., St. Louis, 1957—, prof. biol. chemistry, 1963—, interim dept. head, 1986-89, 96—; Alumni Endowed prof., 1994—; dir. med. scientist tng. program Washington U., St. Louis, 1986-91; mem. NIH study sect., biochemistry, 1969-74, cellular molecular basis of disease, 1992-96. Mem. editorial bd.: Jour. Biol. Chemistry, 1963-68, 75-80, Archives Biochemistry and Biophysics, 1973-79, Biochemistry, 1975—. Protein Sci., 1992-96. Fellow AAAS; mem. Nat. Acad. Sci., Am. Soc. Biochemistry and Molecular Biology, Am. Chem. Soc. (St. Louis award 1976), Am. Soc. Cell Biology, Biophys. Soc., Protein Soc., Sigma Xi. Research, publs. on mechanism of enzyme action including correlation of protein structure to catalytic function, protein folding, devel., application of kinetic theory with respect to enzymes; properties of actin. Home: 7452 Wellington Way Saint Louis MO 63105-2926

FRIEDEN, CHARLES LEROY, university library administrator; b. West Bend, Iowa, Feb. 25, 1941; s. Ernest Leo and Loraine Margaret (Klepper) F.; m. Janet Catherine Cronin, Aug. 16, 1969; children—Christopher Charles, Sara Catherine. B.A.B.A., Mankato State U., 1963; M.A. in Polit. Sci., U.Iowa, 1966, M.A. in Library Sci., 1969. Tchr. Lewis-Central Schs., Council Bluffs, Iowa, 1966-68; serials librarian Coe Coll., Cedar Rapids, Iowa, 1969-72; asst. dir. circulation services U. Va., Charlottesville, 1972-77, dir. circulation services, 1978-94, dir. adminstrv. svcs., 1995—. Co-author: Reference/Information Services in Iowa Libraries, 1969. Mem. ALA, Va. Libr. Assn., Greencroft Club (bd. dirs. 1988—, sec. 1988-90, pres. 1990-91, sec. 1991-92), Ivy Farms Neighborhood Assn. (pres. 1994-95). Republican. Roman Catholic. Home: 1903 Stillhouse Rd Charlottesville VA 22901-8837 Office: U Va Alderman Libr Mccormick Rd Charlottesville VA 22904-1000

FRIEDEN, CLIFFORD E., lawyer; b. L.A., Mar. 8, 1949; s. Sidney S. and Norma (Stern) F.; m. Dinah S. Baumring, June 20, 1971; children: Jamie, Kari, Curtis. BA, UCLA, 1971; JD, U. Calif., Berkeley, 1974. Bar: Calif. 1974, U.S. Dist. Ct. (so. dist.) Calif. 1974, U.S. Dist. Ct. (cen. dist.) Calif. 1977. Ptnr. Rutan & Tucker, Costa Mesa, Calif., 1974—. Active Med. Disaster Response, Newport Beach, Calif., 1990-91, Orange County chpt. ARC, 1995—. Mem. Orange County Bar Assn. (del. state conv. 1983-95, chair judiciary com. 1987-88, bd. dirs. 1989-91), Phi Beta Kappa. Avocations: basketball, jogging. Office: Rutan & Tucker PO Box 1950 611 Anton Blvd Ste 1400 Costa Mesa CA 92626-1998*

FRIEDEN, JANE HELLER, art educator; b. Norfolk, Va., Aug. 25, 1926; d. Samuel Ries and Saida (Seligman) Heller; m. Joseph Lee Frieden, Dec. 23, 1950 (dec. 1990); children: Nancy Frieden Crowe, Robert M., Andrew M. AA, Coll. of William and Mary, Norfolk, Va., 1945; BA, Coll. of William and Mary, Williamsburg, Va., 1947; MA, Columbia U., 1950. Lic. pvt. pilot. Tchr. art City of Norfolk Pub. Schs., 1947-48, Hudson Day Sch., New Rochelle, N.Y., 1948-49, Mt. Vernon (N.Y.) Pub. Schs., 1949-50, City of Norfolk Pub. Schs., 1950-51; prof. art Coll. William and Mary Extension, Williamsburg, 1957-72, U. Va. Extension, Norfolk, 1972-78, Community Colls. State of Va., Chesapeake and Hampton, 1978-82, St. Leo Coll., Norfolk, 1982-95; travel agt., 1977-89; tchr. basic drawing Norfolk Sr. Ctr., 1999. Author: (dictionary) A is For Art, 1978-82; artist water color paintings and ink drawings at several shows. Asst. Gen. Douglas MacArthur Meml. Archives, Norfolk, 1945-95; vol. Chrysler Mus. Art, Norfolk, 1991—, Va. Symphony Aux., 1992—, Norfolk Little Theatre Box Office, 1991—, Meals on Wheels, 1962-66, Make a Wish Found., 1996, ARC, 1953-95, Grey Lady project, 1956-62, bloodmobile project, 1966-80, Va. Zool. Soc., 1996; tchr. drawing Ghent Venture, 1993; reader for the visually handicapped Intouch Network WHRO-TV, 1991—; mem. archives com. Ohef Sholom Temple; bd. dirs. Norfolk Little Theatre, 1996; vol. career svcs. Coll. William and Mary, 1992—, drawing tchr. Norfolk Sr. Ctr., 1998. Mem. Ninety-Nines (treas. 1978-85), Tidewater Artists Assn. (bd. dirs. 1975-80, 91—, treas. membership coun.), Tidewater Orchid Soc., Am. Orchid Soc., Norfolk Soc. Arts, United Daus. Confederacy, Hermitage Soc., Norfolk Ex Libris Soc. Coll. William & Mary (mem. steering com. 1993—), Va. Belles (reunion com. 1993—). Republican. Jewish. Avocations: drawing and water color painting, raising orchids, travel. Home: 221 Oxford St Norfolk VA 23505-4354

FRIEDEN, KIT, newspaper editor. State news editor Houston Chronicle, 1992—. Office: Houston Chronicle Pub Co 801 Texas St Houston TX 77002-2996*

FRIEDENBERG, DANIEL MEYER, financial investor, writer; b. Mt. Vernon, N.Y., Feb. 24, 1923; s. Samuel and Rose Abravanel (Klein) F.; BS, U. Pa., 1943; m. Maria del Carmen Joy, May 1, 1956 (div. June 1964); children: Samuel Clark, Danielle Joy; m. June Meredith Daniels, Apr. 12, 1965 (div. May 1986); children: Jay Daniels, Bertrand Russell. With John-Platt Enterprises, Inc., N.Y.C., 1947—, pres., 1957—; curator coins and medals Jewish Mus., N.Y.C., 1962-82; emeritus, 1982—; guest lectr. Columbia U., Yale U., Swarthmore Coll., Hebrew U., Jerusalem. Sec. Young Democrats N.Y.C., 1952; exec. dir. N.Y. County Liberal Party, 1945. Served with AUS, 1943-44. Recipient Spl. Achievement award Loeb mag., 1962, Spl. Achievement award Loeb Newspaper, 1965; Heath Literary award distinguished numismatic achievement, 1969; Nat. Jewish Book award, 1988, 3rd Prize Nat. Libr. of Poetry, 1997. Fellow Am. Numismatic Soc. (life); mem. Am. Numismatic Assn. Author: Great Jewish Portraits in Metal, 1963; Jewish Medals from the Renaissance to the Fall of Napoleon, 1970, Jewish Mint Masters & Medalists, 1976, Medieval Jewish Seals from Europe, 1987, Life, Liberty and the Pursuit of Land, 1992; contbr. articles to newspapers and mags. Home: 79 Byram Shore Rd Greenwich CT 06830-6906 Office: 55 Central Park W New York NY 10023-6003

FRIEDENBERG, RICHARD MYRON, radiology educator, physician; b. N.Y.C., May 6, 1926; s. Charles and Dorothy (Steg) F.; m. Gloria Geshwind, Jan. 22, 1950; children: Lisa, Peter, Amy. A.B., Columbia, 1946; M.D., L.I. Coll. Medicine, 1949. Diplomate: Am. Bd. Radiology. Intern in medicine Maimonides Hosp., Bklyn., 1949-50; resident in radiology Bellevue Hosp., N.Y.C., 1950-51; Nat. Cancer fellow Bellevue Hosp., 1951-52; fellow radiology Columbia-Presbyn. Hosp., 1952-53; cons. radiologist 3d Air Force, London, Eng., 1953-55; asst. prof. radiology Albert Einstein Coll. Medicine, 1955-66, assoc. clin. prof. radiology, 1966-68; dir., chmn. dept. radiology Bronx Lebanon Hosp. Center, 1957-68; prof., chmn. dept. radiology N.Y. Med. Coll., 1968-80; emeritus prof. U. Calif., Irvine, 1992—; dir. radiology Flower Fifth Ave Hosp., Met. Hosp. Ctr., Bird S. Coler Hosp., N.Y.C., Westchester County Med. Ctr., all 1968-80; prof., chmn. dept. radiol. scis. U. Calif., Irvine, 1980-92. Author: (with Charles Ney) Radiographic Atlas of the Genitourinary System, 1966, 2d edit., 1981; Contbr. (with Charles Ney) articles to profl. jours. Fellow Am. Coll. Radiology, N.Y. Acad. Medicine; mem. Assn. Univ. Radiologists, Radiol. Soc. N.Am., Am. Roentgen Ray Soc., N.Y. Acad. Scis., Assn. Am. Med. Colls., AMA, Soc. Chairmen Acad. Radiology Depts. (past pres.), N.Y. Roentgen Soc. (past pres.), Orange CTY Radiology Soc. (past pres.). Home: 18961 Castlegate Ln Santa Ana CA 92705-2801 Office: U Calif Dept Radiology San Diego CA 92103

FRIEDER, GIDEON, computer science and engineering educator; b. Zvolen, Czechoslovakia, Sept. 30, 1937; came to U.S., 1975; s. Armin and Ruzena (Berl) F.; m. Dalia Bogler, Apr. 3, 1960; children—Ophir, Tally, Gony. B.Sc., Israel Inst. Tech., Haifa, Israel, 1959, M.Sc., 1961, D.Sc., 1967. Staff mem. Israel Dept. Def. Research and Devel., Haifa, Israel, 1959-68, dir. computer sci., 1968-70; staff mem. IBM Sci. Ctr., Haifa, Israel, 1973-75; assoc. prof., then prof., chmn. SUNY, Buffalo, 1975-81; prof., chmn. dept. elec. engring. and computer sci. U. Mich., Ann Arbor, 1981-86; dean sch. computer info. science Syracuse (N.Y.) U., 1987-92; dean Sch. Engring. and Applied Sci., A. James Clark prof. George Washington U., 1992-97, A. James Clark chair, prof. engring., applied scis., 1997—; cons. various industries; chief architect computers Nandodata Corp., Buffalo, 1976-80; expert witness patent and copyright cases; lectr. Contbr. articles to profl. jours.; patentee in field of computers, memory and orgn. Mem. Assn. Computing Machinery, IEEE Computer Soc. Office: 8012 Matterhorn Ct Potomac MD 20854-4058

FRIEDERWITZER, FREDDA J(OY), mathematics educator; b. Bklyn., Aug. 18, 1944; d. Daniel and Mildred (Parnes) Kramer; m. Martin Friederwitzer, Oct. 8, 1964; children: Michele, Pnina, Menachem. BA, Bklyn Coll., 1966, MS, 1973; EdD, Rutgers U., New Brunswick, N.J., 1981. Lic. tchr. K-8, math. tchr. 7-12, sch. dist. adminstr., N.Y. Substitute tchr. N.Y.C. Pub. Schs., Bklyn., 1966-71, Bedminster (N.J.) Pub. Schs., 1976-77; adj. prof. Bklyn. Coll., 1973-77, 88-90, Rutgers U., New Brunswick, 1978-79, Coll. Staten Island, N.Y., 1981—; project co-dir. Rutgers U., New Brunswick, 1976-80, Edn. Support Systems Inc., Staten Island, 1981—; math. cons. Edn. Improvement Ctr. N.E., East Orange, N.J., 1980-83, B & F Ednl. Cons., Staten Island, 1978—; spkr., workshop leader Nat. Coun. Tchrs. Math., Reston, Va., 1973—. Author: The Development, Implementation, and Evaluation of a Model Inservice Program in the Teaching of Measurement Concepts to Third and Fifth/Sixth Grade Elementary School Teachers, 1981, Algebra for the Elementary School, 1981; (with B. Berman) Mathematics Through Measurement, 1983, Mathematics: Getting in Touch (Activities With Manipulatives, 1985, Color Tiles, 1986, Connecting Mathematics in the Primary Grades, 1993, Connecting Mathematics Through Measurement, 1994, Metrics With Things, 1978, Inservice Guide to Metrics, 1978, Fractions and Decimals for Junior High School: A Model Integrating Process and Content Skills, 1980, Metric Mini-Course, 1981, Measurement in the Elementary School, 1981, Developing Metric Awareness in the Corporate Environment, 1982, Fraction Circle Activities, 1988. Bd. dirs. Alzheimer's Disease & Related Disorders, Staten Island, 1981-86. Mem. ASCD, Nat. Coun. Tchrs. Math., N.Y. State Tchrs. Math. (mem. ad hoc edn. com. 1984-86, bd. mem. 1975—, county coord. 1994—), N.J. Tchrs. Math., Nat. Coun. Staff Developers, Kappa Delta Pi. Office: B&F Ednl Cons Inc 446 Travis Ave Staten Island NY 10314-6149

FRIEDEWALD, WILLIAM THOMAS, physician; b. N.Y.C., Mar. 7, 1939; s. William Frank and Mary Lucy (Wright) F.; m. Jacquline Jean Judd, Apr. 15, 1967; children: Laura Elizabeth, John Judd, Eric William. BS, U. Notre Dame, 1960; MD, Yale U., 1963; postdoctoral, Stanford U., 1968-69. Intern Yale-New Haven Hosp., 1963-64, resident, 1964-65, 67-68; commd. USPHS, 1965, advanced through grades to capt., 1983; officer Epidemiol. Intelligence Svc. Communicable Disease Ctr., Atlanta, 1965-67; med. officer Nat. Inst. Allergy and Infectious Diseases, NIH, Bethesda, Md., 1965-67, Nat. Heart, Lung and Blood Inst. and NIH, Bethesda, 1967-86; chief cons. sect. biomed. rsch. br. Nat. Heart, Lung and Blood Inst., NIH, Bethesda, 1971-76, br. chief clin. trials br., 1973-79, assoc. dir. clin. applications and prevention program and DHVD, 1979-84, div. dir. div. epidemiology and clin. applications, 1984-86; assoc. dir. Office Disease Prevention Office of Dir., NIH, Bethesda, 1986-89; chief med. dir. MetLife Ins. Co., N.Y.C., 1989-96, sr. v.p., 1991—, head customer svc. orgn., chief med. Adv., 1996—. Democrat. Roman Catholic. Home: 326 W 71st St New York NY 10023-3502 Office: Met Life Ins Co One Madison Ave New York NY 10010

FRIEDHEIM, ERIC ARTHUR, publisher, editor; b. London, Apr. 21, 1910; s. Arthur and Madeleine (Sander) F.; m. Elizabeth Sweeney, Dec. 31, 1951 (dec. 1984); m. Edith Ann Dorsey, Apr. 14, 1990. Student, Am. U., 1928-30. Washington corr. Internat. News Service, 1931-42; combat corr. Air Force mag., 1945-46; also mng. editor Air News mag.; public relations adv. U.S. aviation industry, 1946; public relations and advance rep. Nat. Freedom Train, 1947-49; public relations dir. European Travel Commn., 1951-52; editor, pub. Travel Agt. mag., N.Y.C., 1951-88, chmn., editor in chief, 1989—; pub. Interline Reporter, 1957-85, El Travel Agt. International, 1979-84; assoc. publisher Palm Beach Soc., Fla., 1987-92; travel columnist N.Y. Post, Los Angeles Times; travel adv. com. Dept. Commerce; adv. com. U.S. Travel Service, Congl. Travel and Tourism Caucus, Travel Industry Assn., Govt. Affairs Coun. Author: Fighters Up, an official history of World War II pilots in Europe, 1945, Travel Agents: From Caravans and Clippers to the Concorde. 1992. Co-sponsor with Kennedy Ctr. Performing Arts of Arthur Friedheim ann. competition for best musical works by Am. composers, 1978-85; endowed Eric Friedheim Libr. Nat. Press Club, Johns Hopkins U., Arthur Friedheim Music Libr., Peabody Inst., Eric Friedheim Quadrangle, Am. U.; producing assoc. Country Playhouse, Westport, Conn.; endowed Friedheim Journalism Ctr. Am. U. Served as officer USAAF, 1942-45; col. USAFR; ret. Decorated Air medal; named to Travel Hall of Fame, 1980, Hall of Leaders, Travel Industry Assn., 1987; recipient Jesse Neale award Am. Bus. Press, 1984, Europa award European Travel Commn., 1986. Fellow Inst. Cert. Travel Agts.; mem. Am. Soc. Travel Agts., Soc. Am. Travel Writers (charter), Caribbean Tourist Assn., Pacific Area Travel Assn., Discover Am. Travel Orgns., Confederacione Organiziones Turisticas de la Am. Latina, World Tourism Orgn. Episcopalian. Clubs: Nat. Press (Washington); Skal, Wings (N.Y.C.). Home: 100 Worth Ave Palm Beach FL 33480-6710 also: 860 United Nations Plz New York NY 10017-1810 also: 7 Elwil Dr Westport CT 06880-3706 Office: Travel Agt Mag 801 2nd Ave New York NY 10017-4706

FRIEDHEIM, JERRY WARDEN, museum consultant; b. Joplin, Mo., Oct. 7, 1934; s. Volmer Havens and Billie Alice (Warden) F.; m. Shirley Margarette Beavers, Oct. 17, 1956; children: Daniel Volmer, Cynthia Diane, Thomas Eric. BJ, U. Mo., 1956, AM, 1962. Reporter, editor, editorial writer Neosho (Mo.) Daily News, Joplin (Mo.) Globe, Columbia Missourian, 1956-61; instr. journalism U. Mo., Columbia, 1961-62; aide to Congressman Durward Hall from Mo., Washington, 1962-63; legis. asst., pres. sec., exec. asst. to U.S. Senator John Tower from Tex., Washington, 1963-69; dep. asst. Sec. Def. for Pub. Affairs, U.S. Dept. Def., Washington, 1969-72; asst. Sec. Def. for Pub. Affairs, Washington, 1973-74; v.p. pub. and govt. affairs AMTRAK, 1974-75; exec. v.p., gen. mgr. Am. Newspaper Pubs. Assn. and ANPA Found., Washington, 1975-87, pres., 1987-91; pub. Presstime mag., 1980-90; v.p. pub. affairs The Freedom Forum, Arlington, Va., 1991-95; exec. dir. The Freedom Forum Newseum, 1991-93; dep. dir. The Newseum, Arlington, Va., 1995-97, mem. adv. com., 1998—; bd. dirs. World Press Freedom Com; past chmn. Nat. Press Found. Author: Where are the Voters, 1968. Capt. AUS, 1956-58. Congl. fellow Am. Polit. Sci. Assn.; recipient Disting. Svc. medal Dept. Def., 1972, 74. Mem. Soc. Profl. Journalists, Nat. Press Club. Home: 46865 Grisson St Sterling VA 20165-3575

FRIEDHEIM, STEPHEN BAILEY, public relations executive; b. Joplin, Mo., Nov. 13, 1934; s. Robert Wray and Virginia Grace (Bailey) F.; m. Jan V. Eisenhour, Sept. 1, 1984; children; Neenah Marie, Stephen Bailey II, Robert William. BA, U. Ark., 1956; DBA (hon.), Johnson and Wales U., Providence, 1978; DAM (hon.), Ctrl. New Eng. Coll., Worcester, Mass., 1984. Announcer Sta. KBRS, Springdale, Ark., 1956-57; newsman Sta. KFSB, Joplin, 1957; dir. pub. rels. Am. Pers. and Guidance Assn., Washington, 1961-66; exec. v.p. Am. Soc. Med. Tech., Houston, 1966-76; pres. Assn. Ind. Colls. and Schs., Washington, 1976-84; sr. v.p. Campbell Comm., Bethesda, Md., Dallas, 1984-90; sr. v.p. King Edn. Svcs., 1984-89; pres. Exec. Secretarial Sch., Dallas, 1984—, Am. Edn. Alliance, 1988-90; mng. dir. Nat. Student Records Clearinghouse, 1998—; cons. Profl. Scs., Internat., 1980-82, South-Western Pub. Co., 1984-88, Career Com Corp., 1984-91, Richard D. Irwin, Inc., Paradigm Pub., 1999—, Masters Inst., 1997; bd. dirs. Pvt. Industry Coun. of Dallas, 1992-95, Exec. Comm., 1994-95; maem. task force on transfer credit Coun. on Postsecondary Accreditation, 1977-78, bd. dirs., 1980-82; mem. Nat. Task Force on Image of the Sec., 1980-97. Editor: The Lead Generation, 1984-90, Tex. Times, 1994—. Bd. dirs. St. Aidan's Sch., Alexandria, Va., 1979-82; trustee Dollars for Scholars, 1982-84; vestry man Ascension Ch., Houston, 1973-76, sr. warden, 1976; narrator Minn. Symphony Orch., 1972; founding mem. local county workforce devel. bd. Dallas County, 1996—, vice chmn., bd. dirs., 1999; vice chmn. bd. dirs. CyberTech Inst., 1998—. With U.S. Army, 1957-61. Recipient Freedoms Found. award, 1960, 62, Broadcasting award Am. Legion Aux., 1963. Fellow Australasian Coll. Bio-med. Scientists; mem. Am. Soc. Assn. Execs. (cert.), Nat. Assn. Trade and Tech. Schs. (Outstanding Svc. award 1984), Assn. Ind. Colls. and Schs. (Disting. Svc. award 1991), Washington Soc. Assn. Execs., Work Force Commn. Creative Svc. (1st pl. award 1990, 91), Southwestern Assn. Ind. Colls. and Schs. (bd. dirs. 1985-92, pres. 1989-91), Dallas-Ft. Worth Met. Assn. Career Schs. (bd. dirs. 1985-86, pres. 1999), Assn. Ind. Colls. and Schs. (treas. 1985-89, bd. dirs. 1985-91, chmn. bd. 1990-91), Career Coll. Assn. (bd. dirs. 1991-9, 1st chmn. bd. 1991-94, past chmn. bd. 1994-95), Nat. Ct. Reporters Assn. (strategic alliance com. for edn. 1994—), Nat. Alliance of Bus. Annual Meeting (adv. com. 1994, S.W. regional bd. dirs. 1996—), Career Tng. Found. (bd. dirs. 1992-95, trustee 1995—), Am. Assn. Higher Edn., Am. Vocat. Assn., Nat. Bus. Edn. Assn., Am. Vocat. Assn., Nat. Assn. Execs., Nat. Assn. Concerned Vets., Career Coll. Assn., Career Colls. and Schs. of Tex., U.S. C. of C. (edn., employment and tng. com. 1980-92, adv. bd. 1991-95), Ctr. Workforce Preparation and Quality Edn. Home: 6450 Patrick Dr Dallas TX 75214-2444 Office: 4849 Greenville Ave Ste 200 Dallas TX 75206-4125

FRIEDHOFF, ARNOLD J., psychiatrist, medical scientist; b. Johnstown, Pa., Dec. 26, 1923; s. Abraham M. and Stella (Beerman) F.; m. Frances Wolfe, Feb. 24, 1946; children: Lawrence, Nancy, Richard. B.A., U. Pa., 1944, M.D., 1947. Diplomate: Am. Bd. Psychiatry and Neurology. Intern Western Pa. Hosp., 1947-48; resident psychiatry U.S. Army, 1952-53, Bellevue Hosp., N.Y.C., 1953-55; instr., to Menas S. Gregory prof. psychiatry Sch. Medicine, NYU, N.Y.C., 1956—, head psychopharmacology rsch. unit, 1956-63, co-dir. Ctr. for Study Psychotic Disorders, 1963-69, dir., 1970—, dir. Millhauser Labs., 1970—; mem. clin. projects rsch. rev. com. NIMH, 1970-74, mem., 1977-81; dir. MV/NIMH Mental Health Clin. Rsch. Ctr., 1981—; mem. Mayor's Com. on Prescription Drugs, N.Y.C.; mem. sci. coun. Nat. Alliance for Rsch. in Schizophrenia and Depression, 1986—; mem. rsch. scientist devel. award rev. com., NIMH, 1983-85, mem. nat. adv. mental health coun., 1987—; hon. prof. Basque U., Bilbao, Spain, U. Seoul, Republic of Korea. Co-editor: Yearbook of Psychiatry and Applied Mental Health, 1968-80; assoc. editor Biol. Psychiatry, 1989—, mem. adv. bd., 1969—; contbr. numerous reports on biochem. psychiatry, psychopharmacology. Served to 1st lt. M.C. U.S. Army, 1951-53. Recipient Research Scientist award NIMH, 1967—. Fellow Am. Coll. Neuropsychopharmacology (past councillor and past pres. 1978-79, Paul Hoch Disting. Svc. award 1996), Am. Psychiat. Assn., Am. Soc. Clin. Pharmacology and Therapeutics, Royal Coll. Psychiatrists (Gt. Britain); mem. Am. Chem. Soc., Internat. Soc. Neurochemistry, Assn. for Rsch. in Nervous and Mental Diseases (past asst. sec.-treas.), Am. Psychopath. Assn. (past pres., Samuel B. Hamilton award), Soc. Biol. Psychiatry (past pres., Gold medal 1989, Castilla del Pino Found. prize, Cordoba 1994, George N. Thompson Founder's award 1996). Office: NYU Med Ctr Millhauser Labs 560 1st Ave New York NY 10016-6402

FRIEDKIN, JOSEPH FRANK, consulting engineering executive; b. Bklyn., Oct. 18, 1909; s. Joel and Irene (Hedden) F.; m. Nellie May Berry, Mar. 21, 1937; children: Jonell, Kim. B.S. in Mine Engring., U. Tex., 1932. Registered profl. engr., Calif., Ariz., N.Mex., Tex. Jr. to hydraulic engr. Internat. Boundary and Water Commn.-U.S. and Mexico, El Paso, Tex., 1934-41; resident engr. Internat. Boundary and Water Commn.-U.S. and Mexico, San Diego, 1947-52; prin. engr., supr. Internat. Boundary and Water Commn.-U.S. and Mexico, El Paso, 1952-62, commr., 1962-86; pvt. practice cons. engr. El Paso, 1986—. Contbr. to Internat. U.S. Mex. Treaties: Water Treaty, 1944, Chamizal Boundary Settlement, 1963, Boundary Treaty, 1972, Salinity Agreement, 1972, Border Sanitation Agreement, 1979. Bd. dirs. YMCA, El Paso; mem. steering com. Goals for El. Paso; bd. dirs. El Paso United Fund. Served with C.E. U.S. Army, 1942-46. Recipient Superior Honor award Dept. State, El Paso, 1964, Outstanding Citizen El Paso Bd. Realtors, 1968, Disting. Honor award US. Dept. State, 1986; named Hon. Ambassador by Pres. L.B. Johnson, 1968, Engr. of Yr. Engring. Socs., 1959. Mem. NSPE, ASCE (hon., R.J. Tipton award 1981, Pres.' award 1984), Pan Am. Fedn. Engring. Socs. (U.S. dir. engrs. joint council, Engr. of Yr. award 1979). Lodge: Rotary. Home and Office: 3821 Hillcrest Dr El Paso TX 79902-1706*

FRIEDKIN, THOMAS H., automotive executive; b. 1925. Dir. Pacific Southwest Airlines, San Diego, 1946-87; with Gulf States Toyota, Inc., Houston, 1969—; now chmn. bd. dirs., CEO Gulf States Toyota, Inc. Office: Gulf States Toyota Inc 7701 Wilshire Place Dr Houston TX 77040-5399*

FRIEDKIN, WILLIAM, film director; b. Chgo., Aug. 29, 1939; s. Louis and Rae (Green) F.; m. Sherry Lansing; children: Jack, Cedric. Dir.: (films) Good Times, 1967, The Night They Raided Minsky's, 1968, The Birthday Party, 1968, The Boys in the Band, 1970, The French Connection, 1971 (Acad. award Best Picture 1971, Dirs. Guild of Am. award, Best Dir. Golden Globe award winner), The Exorcist, 1973 (10 Acad. award nominations, Golden Globe award winner), Sorcerer, 1977, The Brinks Job, 1979, Cruising, 1980, Deal of the Century, 1983, To Live and Die in L.A., 1986, The Guardian, 1990, Rampage, 1992, Blue Chips, 1993, Jade, 1995, Twelve Angry Men, 1997, Rules of Engagement, 1999. Mem. Dirs. Guild Am. (dir.), Acad. Motion Picture Arts and Scis. Address: ICM 8899 Beverly Blvd Los Angeles CA 90048-2412 Office: ICM 8942 Wilshire Blvd Beverly Hills CA 90211-1934*

FRIEDL, RANDALL RAYMOND, environmental scientist; b. San Fernando, Calif., Jan. 18, 1957; s. Raymond Joseph and Ione Louise (Anderson) F.; m. Myrna Wijmer, Dec. 20, 1980. BS, UCLA, 1978; MA, Harvard U., 1980, PhD, 1984. From rsch. assoc. to group supr. JPL, Pasadena, Calif., 1984-94, rsch. scientist, 1997—; lead scientist Jet Propulsion Lab., 1998—; project scientist NASA, Washington, 1994-96; co-mission scientist NASA/NOAA/Air Force sponsored field experiement, Atmospheric Chemistry of Compustion Emissions Near the Tropopause, 1999. Assessment chairperson (NASA publ.) Atmospheric Effects of Subsonic Aircraft, 1997; coord. lead author: Intergovernmental Panel on Climate Change Special Report on Aviation and the Global Environment, 1999; contbr. over 30 articles to profl. jours., chpts. to books. Mem. ACS, Am. Geophys. Union, Sigma Xi. Achievements include research on chemistry of importance to understanding anthropogenic impacts on earth's atmosphere. Office: Jet Propulsion Lab Mailstop 183-901 4800 Oak Grove Dr Pasadena CA 91109-8001

FRIEDLAENDER, FRITZ JOSEF, electrical engineering educator; b. Freiburg/Breisgau, Germany, May 7, 1925; came to U.S., 1947, naturalized, 1953; s. Ludwig and Frieda (Murzynski) F.; m. Gisela Triebe, Aug. 7, 1969; 2 children. BS, Carnegie Mellon U., 1951, MS, 1952, PhD, 1955; Dr.-Ing. (E.h.), Ruhr-Universität Bochum, Germany, 1992. Asst. prof. Columbia, 1954-55, Purdue U., West Lafayette, Ind., 1955-59; assoc. prof. Purdue U., 1959-62, prof. elec. and computer engring., 1962—; guest prof. Max-Planck Institut Metallforschung, Tech. U. Stuttgart, Fed. Repubic Germany, 1964-65; Humboldt award and guest prof. Institut für Werkstoffe der Elektrotechnik, Ruhr-Universität, Bochum, West Germany, 1972-73; Japan Soc. for Promotion Sci. fellow and guest prof. Nagoya U., summer 1980; guest prof. U. Regensburg (Fed. Republic Germany), 1981-82; Meyerhoff vis. prof. Weizmann Inst. Sci., Rehovot, Israel, Jan.-June 1990; cons. Gen. Electric Corp., Ft. Wayne, Ind., 1956-58, Components Corp., Chgo., 1959-61, Lawrence Radiation Lab., U. Calif. at Livermore, 1967-69, P.R. Mallory & Co., 1974-78, Oakridge Nat. Lab., 1979-82. Adv. editor Jour. Magnetism and Magnetic Materials, 1975—; co-editor Magnetic Separation News, 1983-91, Magnetic and Electrical Separation, 1991—; mem. editorial bd. Proc. IEEE, 1975-78; contbr. articles to profl. jours. Fellow IEEE (revs. editor trans. Magnetics 1965-67, editorial bd. jour. 1968—, chmn. awards Magnetics Soc. 1966-74, 85—, achievement award Magnetics Soc. 1986, chmn. Intermag 1975, London, program co-chmn. Intermag 1978, Florence, Italy, v.p. Magnetics Soc. 1975-76, pres. 1977-78, chmn. Central Ind. sect. 1979-80, J. Fred Peoples award 1989, disting. lectr. 1991-93, IEEE Magnetics Soc.), fellow Am. Phys. Soc.; mem. Am. Soc. Engring. Edn., Magnetics Soc. of Japan (hon.), Arbeitsgemeinschaft Magnetismus, Sigma Xi, Phi Kappa Phi, Tau Beta Pi, Eta Kappa Nu, Beta Sigma Rho. Achievements include research in magnetics, magnetic devices and memories, high gradient magnetic separation, magnetic bubble dynamics, Vertical Bloch Lines, microwave ferrites, Ni-Fe tape magnetization processes. Home: 150 Colony Rd West Lafayette IN 47906-1209 Office: Purdue U Sch Elec and Computer Engrn 1285 Electrical Engineering West Lafayette IN 47907-1285

FRIEDLAENDER, GARY ELLIOTT, orthopedist, educator; b. Detroit, May 15, 1945; s. Alex Seymour and Eileen Adrianne (Berman) F.; m. Linda Beth Krohner, Mar. 16, 1969; children: Eron Yael, Ari Seth. BS, U. Mich., 1967, MD, 1969; MA (hon.), Yale U., 1984. Diplomate Am. Bd. Orthop. Surgery. Intern, then resident in surgery U. Mich., Ann Arbor, 1969-71; resident in orthop. Yale New Haven Hosp., 1971-74; fellow in musculoskeletal oncology Mass. Gen. Hosp., Boston, 1983; dir. tissue bank Naval Med. Rsch. Inst., Bethesda, Md., 1974-76; instr. surgery Yale U., New Haven, 1974, asst. prof., 1976-79, assoc. prof., 1979-84, prof., chief orthop., 1984-86, prof. chmn. dept. orthop. and rehab., 1986—, Wayne O. Southwick prof. of orthop. and rehab., 1997—; mem. orthopaedics and musculoskeletal study sect. NIH, 1986-89, mem. nat. adv. bd. arthritis and musculoskelegal and skin diseases 1991-95, chmn., 1993-95; mem. blood products adv. com. FDA, 1995-97; mem. adv. coun. Nat. Inst. Arthritis and Musculoskeletal and Skin Diseases, 1998—. Mem. bd. cons. editors Jour. Bone and Joint Surgery, 1981-98; mem. bd. assoc. editors Clin. Orthopaedics and Related Rsch., 1986-97, dep. editor, 1997—; mem. bd. assoc. editors Modern Medicine, 1988—; editor Rheumatology Digest, 1986-95; mem. editl. bd. Transplantation Scis., 1991—, Jour. Oncology, 1994—; dep. editor Clin. Orthopedics and Related Rsch., 1997—; contbr. articles to profl. jours., chpts. to books. Served to lt. comdr. USN, 1974-76. Recipient Kappa Delta Outstanding Rsch. award, 1982, Nicholas Andry award for Outstanding Orthopedic Rsch., 1995. Fellow ACS, Am. Acad. Orthop. Surgeons (chmn. com. biol. implants 1987-93, chmn. com. rsch. 1999—, sec. coun. musculoskeletal splty. socs. 1999); mem. AMA, NIH (orthop. and musculoskeletal study sect. 1986-89, mem. nat. adv. bd. arthritis and musculoskeletal and skin diseases 1991-95, chmn. 1993-95), Am. Assn. Tissue Banks (pres. 1983-85, Disting. Svc. award 1996), Orthop. Rsch. Soc. (pres. 1994-95), Transplantation Soc., Musculoskeletal Tumor Soc., Am. Coun. on Transplantation (pres. 1983-85), Soc. for Surg. Oncology, Am. Soc. Transplant Surgeons, Am. Orthop. Assn., Assn. Bone and Joint Surgeons (2d v.p. 1999), Acad. Orthop. Soc. (pres. 1995-96, chmn. com. rsch. 1999—). Jewish. Home: 15 Old Still Rd Woodbridge CT 06525-1101 Office: Yale U Dept Orthopedics and Rehab PO Box 208071 New Haven CT 06520-8071

FRIEDLAND, BERNARD, engineer, educator; b. Bklyn., May 25, 1930; s. Irving and Beckie (Kissen) F.; m. Zita Isa Silverman, Aug. 16, 1959; children: Barbara, Irene, Shelly. AB, Columbia U., 1952, BSEE, 1953, MSEE, 1954, PhD, 1957. Registered profl. engr., Calif. Instr. Columbia U., N.Y.C., 1953-57, asst. prof., 1957-61; head control lab. Melpar, Inc., Watertown, Mass., 1961-62; prin. scientist Kearfott Guidance and Navigation Corp. (formerly The Singer Co.), Little Falls, N.J., 1962-90; disting. prof. N.J. Inst. Tech., Newark, 1990—; adj. prof. Columbia U., 1965-72, NYU, 1970-73, Poly. U. (formerly Poly. Inst. N.Y.) Bklyn., 1974-90; Lady Davis vis. prof. Technion (Israel Inst. Tech.), 1996-97. Author: Control System Design, 1986, Advanced Control System Design, 1996; co-author: Principles of Linear Networks, 1961, Linear Systems, 1965; contbr. more than 90 articles to profl. jours. Chmn. The Hilary Sch., Newark, 1965. Named to Bklyn. Tech. H.S. Hall of Fame, 1998. Fellow ASME (various offices, Oldenburger medal 1982), IEEE (disting. mem., various offices), AIAA (assoc.; assoc. editor jour.). Democrat. Jewish. Avocations: skiing, swimming, tennis, reading, sculpture. Office: NJ Inst Tech Dept Elec and Computer Engring Newark NJ 07102

FRIEDLAND, LOUIS N., retired communications executive; b. 1913; m. Billie Belenko; children: Eric, Joanne Roberts. BS, Bklyn. Coll., 1934; MA, NYU, 1936. Instr. psychology, 1936-41; chief adminstrn. officer VA, 1946-48; gen. mgr. U.S. Microfilm Co., 1948-52; with MCA, Inc., N.Y.C., 1952—, v.p., 1953, corp. v.p., 1968-86; v.p. MCA, Inc. (MCA TV div., distbr. Universal Studios TV programs), 1953-73; pres. MCA TV div., distbr. Universal Studios TV programs MCA, Inc., 1963-78, chmn. bd. TV div., 1978-86; retired, 1986; Past chmn. Nat. Hemphilia Found. Served as lt. USCG, 1942-46. Recipient citation for bldg. balanced and effective crews, Naval Manning Operation, 12th Naval Dist., USCG, 1946. Home: 10 Steven Ln Great Neck NY 11024-1535

FRIEDLANDER, BERNICE, federal program administrator; b. Middletown, Conn., Aug. 25, 1943; d. Samuel Julius and Masha (Glazer) F. BA, Monmouth Univ., 1964; MA in Pub. Adminstrn., Harvard U., 1983. Legis. asst. Congressman James J. Howard, Washington, 1965-68; legis. rep. Action on Smoking and Health, Washington, 1969-70; adminstrv. asst. Congressman Edwin B. Forsythe, Washington, 1970-72; cons., freelance campaign mgr., 1973-78; pres. sec., sr. legis. asst. Congressman Eugene V. Atkinson, Washington, 1978-82; editor Washington Monitor, Inc., 1984-85; dir. legis. and pub. affairs Autism Soc. Am., Washington, 1985-87; dir. pub. affairs Women's Bur. US Dept. Labor, Washington, 1988-94; dir. US Office Consumer Affairs, Washington, 1994—, dir. divsn. comm., 1996-97; pub. affairs dir. Pres. Clinton's Safety Initiative, 1997-99; outreach coord. for the Pres. Food Safety Initiative Team, 1999—; head U.S. delegation com. on consumer policy OECD, 1995, 96, vice chmn. com. on consumer policy. Dir. Claridge House Coop., Inc., Washington, 1988—, pres. 1992-95. Mem. Harvard Club, Women of Washington. Jewish. Avocations: Celtics, Mystics, astrology, writing. Home: 940 25th St NW Washington DC 20037-2155 Office: US Food & Drug Adminstrn 200 C St SW FOB 8 Rm 3814 Washington DC 20204*

FRIEDLANDER, CHARLES DOUGLAS, space consultant; b. N.Y.C., Oct. 5, 1928; s. Murray L. and Jeane (Sottosanti) F.; m. Diane Mary Hutchins, May 12, 1951; children: Karen Diane, Lauren Patrice, Joan Elyse. BS, U.S. Mil. Acad., 1950; exec. mgmt. program, NASA, 1965; grad., Command and Staff Coll. USAF, 1965, Air War Coll. USAF, 1966. Commd. 2d lt. U.S. Army, 1950, advanced through grades to 1st lt.; officer inf. U.S. Army, Korea, 1950-51; resigned U.S. Army, 1954; mem. staff UN Forces, Trieste, Italy, 1953-54; chief astronaut support office NASA, Cape Canaveral, Fla., 1963-67; space cons. CBS News, Cape Canaveral, Fla., 1967-69; exec. asst. The White House, Washington, 1969-71; v.p. bd. dirs. Internat. Aerospace Hall of Fame, San Diego; space program cons., various cos., Boca Raton, Fla., 1967-69; mem. staff First Postwar Fgn. Ministers Conf., Berlin, 1954; radio/TV cons. space program. Author: Buying & Selling Land for Profit, 1961, Last Man at Hungnam Beach, 1952. V.p. West Point Soc., Cape Canaveral, Fla., 1964. Served to lt. col. USAFR, maj. USAR. Decorated Bronze Star V, Combat Inf. badge; co-recipient Emmy award CBS TV Apollo Moon Landing, 1960; recipient medal of honor N.Y.C., 1951. Mem. Explorer's Club, West Point Soc., Chosin Few Survivors Korea, NASA Alumni League, Nat. Space Soc. Avocations: fishing, travel. *Too many young people think that the exciting and adventurous things in life are out of their reach. When there is a career or vocation that represents something you are good at, and that you would enjoy doing - then do it. Get on a plane, train or bus. Line up at the employment office and take any job just to "get your foot in the door". If you apply yourself, in time you will rise in your chosen field. Always remember: "You can do anything you want to do if you make up your mind to do it!".*

FRIEDLANDER, D. GILBERT, lawyer; b. Hazleton, Pa., Sept. 10, 1946. BA, U. Tex., 1968, JD, 1971. Bar: Tex. 1972, N.Y. 1973. Sr. shareholder, bd. dirs. Johnson & Gibbs, 1973-91; gen. counsel Electronic Data Systems Corp., Plano, Tex., 1991—; sr. v.p., corp. sec., CSU for legal affairs Electronic Data Systems Corp., Plano. Mem. ABA, N.Y. State Bar Assn., State Bar Tex. (corp. com., corp. banking and bus. law sect. 1980—, chmn. com. for rev. corp. tax law 1983-85), Dallas Bar Assn., Dallas Assn. Young Lawyers. Office: Electronic Data Systems Corp Mail Stop H3-3A-05 5400 Legacy Dr Plano TX 75024-3199

FRIEDLANDER, D. GILBERT, lawyer; b. Hazleton, Pa., Sept. 10, 1946. BA, U. Tex., 1968, JD, 1971. Bar: Tex. 1972, N.Y. 1973. Sr. shareholder, bd. dirs. Johnson & Gibbs, 1973-91; gen. counsel Electronic Data Systems Corp., Plano, Tex., 1991—; sr. v.p., corp. sec., CSU for legal affairs Electronic Data Systems Corp., Plano. Mem. ABA, N.Y. State Bar Assn., State Bar Tex. (corp. com., corp. banking and bus. law sect. 1980—, chmn. com. for rev. corp. tax law 1983-85), Dallas Bar Assn., Dallas Assn. Young Lawyers. Office: Electronic Data Systems Corp Mail Stop H3-3A-05 5400 Legacy Dr Plano TX 75024-3199*

FRIEDLANDER, EDWARD JAY, journalism educator; b. Portland, Maine, Apr. 24, 1945; s. Otto and Marguerite Evelyn (Smith) F.; m. Roberta Kay Burford, July 12, 1975; 1 child, Erika Anne. BS, U. Wyo., 1967; MA, U. Denver, 1970; EdD, U. No. Colo., Greeley, 1973. Reporter The Denver Post, 1967-68, U.S. Info. Agy., Washington, 1968-69; publicist Universal Pictures, N.Y.C., 1969-70; mag. editor Daily Times-Call, Longmont, Colo., 1970-71; media coord. Centaurus High Sch., Lafayette, Colo., 1972-73; asst. prof. mass communication Cen. Mo. State U., Warrensburg, 1973-75; asst. prof. dept. journalism U. Ark., Little Rock, 1975-77, assoc. prof. dept.

journalism, 1977-81, prof. dept. journalism, 1981-95, chairperson dept. journalism, 1988-95; dir., prof. U. South Fla. Sch. Mass Comms., Tampa, 1995—; cons. Bur. Indian Affairs, Washington, 1972, The White House, Washington, 1979, Ark. Press Assn., Little Rock, 1980-95; cons., editor FCC, Washington, 1979-81. Author: Excellence in Reporting, 1987, Feature Writing for Newspapers and Magazines, 1988, 3d rev. edit., 1996, Modern Mass Media, 1990, 2nd rev. edit., 1994, Medios de Comunicación Social, 1992. William Robertson Coe fellow U. Wyo., 1973, German Acad. Exch. Svc. fellow, Bonn, 1982, European Acad. fellow, Berlin, 1984. Mem. Assn. Edn. in Journalism and Mass Comm., Assn. Schs. Journalism and Mass Comm. (exec. com. 1997-98, 98—), Soc. Profl. Journalists (officer exec. bd. Ark. profl. chpt. 1986-89, 92-94, v.p. 1989-91, pres. 1991-92), Kappa Tau Alpha. Office: U South Fla Sch Mass Comms CIS # 1040 4202 E Fowler Ave Tampa FL 33620-9951

FRIEDLANDER, EDWARD ROBERT, pathologist; b. Evanston, Ill., Jan. 9, 1952; s. Robert and Joanne (Hiscox) F. AB, Brown U., 1973; MD, Northwestern U., Chgo., 1977. Diplomate Am. Bd. Pathology. Pathologist Kansas City, 1988—; chmn. dept. pathology Univ. of Health Scis.; lectr. in field; operator free disease info. svcs. online. Author: (booklets) Christian Perspectives on Evolution, 1985, William Blake's Visions, 1986. Foster parent Juvenile Corrections, Johnson City, Tenn., 1984-85; bd. dirs. Tenn. Assn. Vols. Criminal Justice, 1983-86; prison vol. Yoke Fellow, Winston Salem, 1982-83. Fellow Coll. Am. Pathologists, Am. Soc. Clin. Pathologists, Lambda Chi Alpha. Home: 7909 Tauromee Ave Kansas City KS 66112-2639 Office: 1750 Independence Ave Kansas City MO 64106-1453

FRIEDLANDER, GERHART, nuclear chemist; b. Munich, Germany, July 28, 1916; came to U.S., 1936, naturalized, 1943; s. Max O. and Bella (Forchheimer) F.; m. Gertrude Maas, Feb. 6, 1941 (dec. 1966); children: Ruth Ann F. Huart, Joan Claire F. Hurley; m. Barbara Strongin, 1983. BS, U. Calif., Berkeley, 1939, PhD, 1942; hon. docorate, Clark U., 1991; hon. doctorate, U. Mainz, Germany, 1992. Instr. U. Idaho, Moscow, 1942-43; staff Los Alamos Sci. Lab., 1943-46; research assoc. Gen. Electric Co. Research Lab., Schenectady, 1946-48; vis. lectr. Washington U., St. Louis, 1948; chemist Brookhaven Nat. Lab., Upton, N.Y., 1948-52; sr. chemist Brookhaven Nat. Lab., 1952-81, 89-91, cons., 1981-89, 91-93, chmn. chemistry dept., 1968-77; chmn. Gordon Rsch. Conf. on Nuclear Chemistry, 1954. Author: (with J.W. Kennedy) Introduction to Radiochemistry, 1949, Nuclear and Radiochemistry, 1955, (with J.M. Miller), 1964, (with E.S. Macias), 1981; editor-in-chief Sci. Spectra, 1993—; editor Radiochimica Acta, 1972-73; assoc. editor Ann. Rev. Nuc. Sci., 1958-67; contbr. articles to profl. jours. Recipient Alexander von Humboldt award Institut für Kernchemie, Mainz, Fed. Republic of Germany, 1978-79, 87, 92, 93. Fellow AAAS; mem. Hungarian Acad. Scis. (hon.), Nat. Acad. Sci., Am. Acad. Arts and Scis., Am. Chem. Soc. (chmn. divsn. nuclear chemistry and tech. 1967, award for nuclear applications in chemistry 1967). Achievements include research on chem. effects of nuclear transformations, properties of radioactive isotopes, mechanisms of nuclear reactions, especially those induced by protons of very high energies, solar neutrino detection, cluster impact phenomena. Home: 5 Lorraine Ct Smithtown NY 11787-1633

FRIEDLANDER, JAMES STUART, lawyer; b. Chgo., Mar. 25, 1942; s. Earle E. and Sally J. (Meyer) F.; m. Sherfunissa Hassen, Sept. 27, 1969; children: Samantha, Melissa, Natasha, Davina. BA, U. Wis., 1963; JD, Harvard U., 1966. Bar: Ill. 1966, D.C. 1979. Internat. legal advisor ministry external affairs Govt. of Malawi, Blantyre, 1968-71; counsel World Bank, Washington, 1972-75; mgr. Citibank, N.A., Nairobi, Kenya, 1975-78; assoc. Duncan, Allen and Mitchell, Nairobi, 1978-80; ptnr. Duncan, Allen and Mitchell, Washington, 1980-88, Mitchell, Friedlander & Gittleman, Washington, 1988-91, Akin, Gump, Strauss, Hauer & Feld, LLP, Washington, 1991—; resident ptnr. Akin, Gump, Strauss, Hauer & Feld, LLP, Moscow, 1994-97; bd. dirs. DAMconsult Ltd., Washington, Internat. Eye Found., Washington, 1990-94. Editor: Malawi Treaty Series, 1964-71, 1971. Vice chmn. Kenya Lawn Tennis Assn., Nairobi, 1981-83; vol. Peace Corps, Blantyre, 1966-68. Mem. ABA, Am. Soc. Internat. Law, Fed. Bar Assn. (chmn., sub-com. on internat. investment 1987-88), Westwood Country Club. Jewish. Avocations: tennis, piano, travel. Office: Akin Gump Strauss Hauer & Feld LLP Ste 400 1333 New Hampshire Ave NW Washington DC 20036-1564

FRIEDLANDER, JEROME PEYSER, II, lawyer; b. Washington, Feb. 7, 1944; s. Mark Peyser and Helen (Finkel) F.; m. Irene Bluethenthal, Apr. 23, 1972; children: Jennifer R., Tyler Weil. BS, Georgetown U., 1965; LLB, U. Va., 1968. Bar: Va. 1968, U.S. Dist. Ct. (ea. dist.) Va. 1968, U.S. Ct. Appeals (4th and D.C. cirs.) 1978, U.S. Supreme Ct. 1978. Ptnr. Friedlander & Friedlander, P.C., Arlington, Va., 1976—; substitute judge Arlington (Va.) Gen. Dist. Ct. Author: Virginia Landlord-Tenant Law, 1992, 2nd edit., 1998, The Limited Liability Company, 1994; co-author: Legal Aspects of Doing Business in North America, 1987; contbr. articles to profl. jours. With U.S. Army, 1969-71. Mem. ABA, FBA (past pres. No. Va. chpt.). Office: Friedlander & Friedlander PC Ste 201 1364 Beverly Rd Mc Lean VA 22101

FRIEDLANDER, JOHN BENJAMIN, mathematics educator; b. Toronto, Oct. 4, 1941; s. Daniel Theodore and Beatrice Adele (Axler) F.; m. Cherryl Lynne Thompson, Sept. 1, 1974; children: Jonathan, Diana, Amanda, Keith. BSc, U. Toronto, 1965; MA, U. Waterloo, Ont., 1966; PhD, Pa. State U., 1972. Asst. to A. Selberg, Inst. Advanced Study, Princeton, N.J., 1972-73, mem. Sch. of Math, 1973-74, 83-84, 95-96, 99-2000; lectr., dept. math MIT, Cambridge, 1974-76; vis. prof. Scuola Normale Superiore, Pisa, Italy, 1976-77; asst. prof. U. Toronto, 1977-79, assoc. prof., 1980-82, prof. math, 1982—, chair dept. math., 1987-91; lectr. U. Ill., Urbana, 1979-80; rsch. prof. Math Sci. Rsch. Inst., Berkeley, Calif., 1991-92; mem. sci. adv. bd. Fields Inst. Rsch. Math. Sci., 1996—; lectr. in field, ICM, 1994; Jeffery-Williams lectr. Can. Math. Soc., 1999. Mem. editl. bd. 4 jours. in field.; contbr. articles to profl. jours. Acad. of Sci. fellow Royal Soc. Can., 1988—. Mem. Am. Math. Soc. Avocations: bridge, chess, sailing, barbecue. Home: 22 Stonemanse Ct, Scarborough, ON Canada M1G 3V3 Office: U Toronto, Dept Math, Toronto, ON Canada M5S 3G3 also: Scarborough Coll, Dept of Math, Scarborough, ON Canada M1C 1A4

FRIEDLANDER, MICHAEL J., neuroscientist, animal physiologist, medical educator; b. Miami, Fla., Jan. 30, 1950; 3 children. BS, Fla. State U., 1972; MS, U. Ill., 1974, PhD, 1977. NIH fellow physiology U. Ill., 1974-77, U. Va., 1977-79; from rsch. asst. prof. anatomy to asst. prof. neurobiology SUNY, Stony Brook, 1979-80; from asst. prof. to assoc. prof. U. Ala., Birmingham, 1980-87, prof. physiology and biophysics, 1987—, prof., chmn. dept. neurobiology, 1987—; co-investigator rsch. project Nat. Eye Inst., 1979-80, Sloan Found. Computer Modeling Award, 1982; prin. investigator Develop. Structure & Function Vis. System, 1981-84, NATO Collaborative Rsch., 1983-87, NSF Devel. Vis. System, 1985—, Effects of Vis. Deprivation on Genicolocortical Pathway, 1984—; sr. inst. rsch. fellow for Australia, 1988. Recipient Sloan Young Neurosci. award; prin. investigator Lucille P. Mashey Found. award for Neurobiology Ctr., 1991-96, C.W. Keck Found. award for Molecular Neurobiology Program Devel., 1994-96; recipient William C. Menninger award for Basic Mental Health Rsch. ACP, 1996; grantee NIH, 1991-96, fellowship Australian Nat. U., 1993-96. Mem. AAAS, Soc. Neurosci., Assn. Rsch. Vis. Ophthalmologists, Sigma Xi. Achievements include rsch. in structural basis of function of individual mammalian brain cells involved in processing visual information in the normal adult brain and during postnatal devel. chem. communication. Office: U Ala Dept Neurobiology 1719 6th Ave S # Circ516 Birmingham AL 35294-0021*

FRIEDLANDER, MICHAEL WULF, physicist, educator; b. Cape Town, South Africa, Nov. 15, 1928; came to U.S., 1956; m. Jessica R. Friedlander; 2 children. BS in Physics, U. Cape Town, 1948, MS with 1st class honors, 1950; PhD in Physics, U. Bristol (Eng.), 1955. Jr. lectr. U. Cape Town, 1950-52; rsch. assoc. U. Bristol, 1954-56; asst. prof. physics Washington U., St. Louis, 1956-61, assoc. prof., 1961-67, prof., 1967—. Author: The Conduct of Science, 1972, Astronomy: From Stonehenge to Quasars, 1985, Cosmic Rays, 1989, At the Fringes of Science, 1995; contbr. articles to Ency. Brit. and profl. jours. Guggenheim Found. fellow, vis. prof. Imperial Coll., London, 1962-63. Mem. AAUP (2d v.p. 1978-80, mem. nat. coun. 1975-78, 86-89), AAAS, Am. Phys. Soc., Am. Astron. Soc., History of Sci. Soc. Achievements include research in elementary particles, cosmic rays, infrared astronomy, and gamma ray astronomy. Office: Washington U Dept Physics One Brookings Dr Saint Louis MO 63130

FRIEDLANDER, MITZI B., artist; b. Louisville, Mar. 31, 1930; d. Charles John Bornwasser and Martha Salome Lehmann-Bornwasser; m. William Perry Friedlander, Sept. 10, 1955; children: Fadel Elizabeth, Eric Charles. BA in English cum laude, U. Louisville, 1952, MA in Theatre Arts, 1971. Singer, actor Iroquois Amphitheater, Louisville, 1948-52; actor Ky. Opera Assn., Louisville, 1952-74; narrator Am. Printing House for the Blind, Louisville, 1963—; adj. faculty Ind. U. S.E., Louisville, 1970-97. Leading role Stephen Foster Story, Bardstown, Ky., 1970, Pioneer Playhouse, Danville, Ky., 1976-80, New Harmony (Ind.) Theatre, 1993-95. Mem. steering com. art and spirituality JB Speed Art Mus., 1960—; active Episcopal Peace Fellowship, 1982—; bd. dirs. Coun. on Peacemaking, Louisville, 1983-96, Bonnycastle Homestead Assn., Louisville, 1995—; bd. dirs., co-founder Interfaith Paths to Peace, Louisville, 1997—. Mem. AFTRA, NOW, ACLU, Actors Equity (ret.). Democrat. Episcopalian. Home: 2040 Bonnycastle Ave #6C Louisville KY 40205

FRIEDLANDER, PATRICIA ANN, marketing professional; b. Chgo., May 9, 1944; d. James Farrell and Therese Mary (Pfeiler) Crotty; m. Daniel B. Friedlander, July 3, 1971 (div. Apr. 1978); children: Michael Derek, David Colin. BA, Cardinal Stritch Coll., 1966; MA, U. Wis., Milw., 1968; post-grad., U. Chgo., 1968-69, U. London, 1968—. Instr. U. Wis., Milw., 1966-68, Chgo. State U., 1968-71, Argo Cmty. H.S., Summit, Ill., 1971-73, Park Dist., Park Forest South, Ill., 1973-77; counselor Will County Mental Health Clinic, Park Forest South, 1977-78; sales rep. Prentice-Hall, Inc., Englewood Cliffs, N.J., 1978-84; nat. sales mgr. Dow Jones-Irwin, Homewood, Ill., 1984-87; dir. mktg. Nat. Textbook Co., Lincolnwood, Ill., 1987-88; mgr. mktg. Scott Foresman & Co., Glenview, Ill., 1988-90; corp. advt. dir. Giltspur, Inc., Itasca, Ill., 1990-96; dir. Mktg. Comms. Exhibitgroup/Gitspur, Roselle, Ill., 1996-98; sales exec. Derse Exhibits, Chgo., 1998-99; pres. Squeaky Wheel Comm., Chgo., 1999—; dir. Printer's Row Bookfair, Chgo., 1985; pub. cons.; spkr. and author in trade show and pub. field; mem. Ctr. for Exposition Rsch. Mktg. Com. Den mother Cub Scouts Am., Park Forest South, 1981-84. Mem. Bus. Mktg. Assn., Midwest Book Travelers (pres. 1983-87), Health Care Conv. & Exhibitors Assn., Trade Show Exhibitors Assn. (pres. Windy City chpt.). Avocations: piano, reading, cycling, swimming. Home: 2320 W Farwell Ave Chicago IL 60645-4735 Office: Derse Exhibits 368 W Ontario St Chicago IL 60610-4017

FRIEDLANDER, SHELDON KAY, chemical engineering educator; b. N.Y.C., Nov. 17, 1927; s. Irving and Rose (Katzewitz) F.; m. Marjorie Ellen Robbins, Apr. 16, 1934; children: Eva Kay, Amelie Elise, Antonia Zoe, Josiah. BS, Columbia U., 1949; SM, MIT, 1951; PhD, U. Ill., 1954. Asst. prof. chem. engring. Columbia U., N.Y.C., 1954-57; asst. prof. chem. engring. Johns Hopkins, Balt., 1957-59, assoc. prof. chem. engring., 1959-62, prof. chem. engring., 1962-64; prof. chem. engring., environ. health engring. Calif. Inst. Tech., Pasadena, 1964-78; prof. chem. engring. UCLA, 1978—, Parsons prof., 1982—, chmn. dept. chem. engring., 1984-88, chmn. steering com. Ctr. for Clean Tech., 1989-92; chmn. EPA Clean Air Sci. Adv. Com., 1978-82. Author: Smoke, Dust, and Haze, 1977. Served with U.S. Army, 1946-47. Recipient Sr. Humboldt prize Fed. Republic of Germany, 1985, Internat. prize Am. Assn. for Aerosol Rsch./Gesellschaft für Aerosolforschung/Japan Assn. for Aerosol Sci. and Tech., Fuchs Meml. award, 1990; Fulbright scholar, 1960-61; Guggenheim fellow, 1969-70. Mem. NAE, Am. Inst. Chem. Engrs. (Colburn award 1959, Alpha Chi Sigma award 1974, Walker award 1979, Lawrence K. Cecil award in environ. chem. engring. 1995), Am. Assn. for Aerosol Research (pres. 1984-86). Office: UCLA Dept Chem Engring 5531 Boelter Hall Los Angeles CA 90095

FRIEDLER, GLADYS, psychiatry and pharmacology educator, scientist; b. Lewiston, Maine; d. Max Herman and Anna Diana (Feld) F. BA in Zoology magna cum laude, U. Maine, 1947; MA in Genetics, U. Pa., 1951; PhD in Pharmacology, Boston U., 1968. Postdoctoral fellow U. Calif. San Francisco Med. Ctr., 1968-70; rsch. fellow in pharmacology Harvard Med. Sch., Boston, 1970-72; rsch. fellow in anaesthesia lying-in divsn. Boston Hosp. for Women, 1970-72; asst. prof. psychiatry Boston U. Sch. Medicine, 1972-81, assoc. prof. psychiatry, 1981—, asst. prof. pharmacology, 1973-81, assoc. prof. pharmacology, 1981—, core faculty behavioral neurosci., 1986—; faculty grad. sch. Boston U., 1973—; mem. admissions com. Boston U. Sch. Medicine, 1984-96, mem. neurosci. steering com., 1986-87; rep. faculty coun. Boston U., 1981-85, 90-92, sec. faculty coun., 1983-84, 92-94, mem. exec. com. faculty coun., 1983-87, 93-95, chair affirmative action/status of women com., 1985-87, acad. freedom com., 1992-97, chair nominating com., 1993-94; ad hoc reviewer March of Dimes, Med. Rsch. Coun. Can., NSF, Nat. Inst. Drug Abuse, Bunting Inst. Sci. Rev. panel, 1993—, various profl. jours. Mem. editl. bd. Neurotoxicology and Teratology, 1997—; contbr. chpts. to books and articles to profl. jours. Mem. Am. Women in Sci.-New Eng. chpt., 1987-93, sec. 1988-89; mem. corp. Marine Biol. Lab., 1989-94; mem. MIT Choral Soc., 1955-68, San Francisco Bach Choir, 1968-70; mem. Cantata Consort, Woods Hole, Mass., 1981—, pres., 1998—; bd. mem., participant Cambridge Cmty. Chorus, 1991—. Sci. scholar Bunting Inst. Radcliffe Coll., Cambridge, 1991-92; grantee Nat. Inst. Drug Abuse, 1975-81, Boston Mental Health Found., 1979-80, March of Dimes Birth Defects Found., 1982-84, Nat. Inst. Alcohol Abuse and Alcoholism, 1986-88. Mem. Am. Soc. Pharmacology and Exptl. Therapeutics, Neurobehavioral Teratology Soc. (constitution and bylaws com. 1984-85, fin. com. 1988-89, chair awards com. 1993-94, publs. com. 1997—), Soc. Inst. Fellows Bunting Inst. (v.p. 1993-95, treas. 1997—), Phi Beta Kappa, Phi Kappa Phi, Sigma Xi. Avocations: music, dance, bicycling, Mayan archeology, travel. Home: 4 Newport Rd Apt 4 Cambridge MA 02140-1588 Office: Boston Univ Sch Medicine 80 E Concord St Boston MA 02118-2307

FRIEDMAN, ALAN E., lawyer; b. N.Y.C., May 5, 1946. BA, Amherst Coll., 1967; JD, Stanford U., 1970. Bar: Calif. 1971. Atty. Tuttle & Taylor, L.A., 1970—. Note editor: Stanford Law Rev., 1969-70. Office: Tuttle & Taylor 355 S Grand Ave Fl 40 Los Angeles CA 90071-1560

FRIEDMAN, ALAN HERBERT, ophthalmologist; b. N.Y.C., 1937; BA in Chemistry with honors, Cornell U., 1959; MD (summer fellow NIH 1960, 62-63), NYU, 1963; m. Sandra Yasser, 1960; children: David, Jonathan, Lisa, Jennifer. Intern in medicine Bellevue Hosp., N.Y.C., 1963-64; resident in ophthalmology NYU Med. Ctr., 1966-69, fellow ophthalmic pathology, 1969-70; research fellow histochemistry Royal Postgrad. Med. Sch., London, 1972; practice medicine specializing in ophthalmology, N.Y.C., 1970—; attending ophthalmologist and pathologist Mt. Sinai Hosp.; attending ophthalmologist Beth Israel Med. Ctr.; clin. prof. ophthalmology and pathology, dir. eye pathology lab. Mt. Sinai Sch. Medicine; assoc. examiner Am. Bd. Ophthalmology; cons. in field. Contbr. numerous articles to profl. publs. With M.C., USAR, 1964-66. Diplomate Am. Bd. Ophthalmology. Fellow ACS, Royal Coll. Ophthalmologists London, Am. Acad. Ophthalmology (Sr. Honor award 1991), N.Y. Acad. Medicine, N.Y. Acad. Scis., Royal Soc. Medicine; mem. AMA, Am. Ophthal. Soc., French Ophthal. Soc., Assn. Rsch. Vision and Ophthalmology, Am. Assn. Ophthalmic Pathologists (pres. 1992—), N.Y. County Med. Soc., Med. Soc. State N.Y., Eastern Ophthalmic Pathology Soc., Pan Am. Assn. Ophthalmology. Address: Mt Sinai Sch Medicine 1 Gustave L Levy Pl # 1183 New York NY 10029-6500 also: 888 Park Ave New York NY 10021-0235

FRIEDMAN, ALAN HOWARD, education educator, writer; b. N.Y.C., Jan. 4, 1928; s. Harry Morris and Mina F.; m. Lenore Ann Helman Friedman, Aug. 1, 1950 (div. July 15, 1967); 1 child, Gregory Lawrence Friedman; m. Kate Miller Gilbert Friedman, Oct. 30, 1977; 1 child, Alexander Nicholas Friedman. BA magna cum laude, Harvard Coll., Cambridge, Mass., 1949; MA, Columbia U., N.Y.C., 1950; PhD, U. Calif. Berkeley, 1964. Asst. prof. Columbia U., N.Y.C., 1965-67; assoc. prof. Swarthmore (Pa.) Coll., 1967-70; vis. assoc. prof. Queens Coll., CUNY, 1973-75; prof. U. Ill. at Chgo., 1978—; exec. bd. mem. Am. Pen Midwest, Chgo., 1985-89. Author: Hermaphrodeity, 1972, The Turn of the Novel, 1966, (book review) N.Y. Times Book Review, 1972-91, (chpt.) The Twentieth Century Mind, 1972. Home: 3530 Monte Real Escondido CA 92029

FRIEDMAN, ALAN JACOB, museum director; b. Bklyn., Nov. 15, 1942; s. George and Eleanor (Goldberger) F.; m. Mickey Thompson, Dec. 26, 1966. BS in Physics, Ga. Inst. Tech., 1964; PhD in Physics, Fla. State U., 1970. Research asst. Ga. Inst. Tech., Atlanta, 1960-64, Fla. State U., Tallahassee, 1964-69; asst. prof. Hiram (Ohio) Coll., 1969-74; dir. astronomy and physics Lawrence Hall of Sci. U. Calif., Berkeley, 1973-84; conseiller scientifique Cite des Scis. et de l'Industrie, Paris, 1982-84; dir. N.Y. Hall of Sci., Corona, 1984—; vis. asst. prof. Am. studies and English Temple U., Phila, 1975; research fellow English dept. U. Calif., Berkeley, 1972-73; vis. lectr. English dept. San Francisco State U., 1974-75. Co-author: Planetarium Educator's Workshop Guide, 1980, Einstein as Myth and Muse, 1985, Planetarium Activities for Student Success, 12 vols., 1993; mem. editorial bd. Jour. Modern Lit. Younger Humanist fellow NEH, 1972-73; recipient Disting. service award Mid-Atlantic Planetarium Soc., 1982, Merit award Astron. Assn. No. Calif., 1983, AAAS award for pub. understanding of sci. and tech., 1996. Fellow AAAS, Internat. Planetarium Soc. (Svc. award 1990); mem. Am. Assn. Physics Tchrs., Internat. Planetarium Soc. (pres. 1985-86), Assn. Sci.-Tech. Ctrs. (bd. dirs. 1989-97), Phi Beta Kappa. Office: NY Hall Sci 47-01 111th St Flushing NY 11368*

FRIEDMAN, ALAN ROY, lawyer; b. N.Y.C., Mar. 18, 1953; s. Oscar B. and Helen (Rosenkrantz) F.; m. Maya Memling, Sept. 3, 1978; 1 child, Charles. AB, Hamilton Coll., 1973; JD, Yale U., 1976. Law clk. to Hon. M. Joseph Blumenfeld U.S. Dist. Ct., Hartford, 1976-77; assoc. Kramer Levin Naftalis & Frankel LLP,, N.Y.C., 1977-84, ptnr., 1984—. Office: Kramer Levin Naftalis & Frankel LLP 919 3rd Ave New York NY 10022-3902

FRIEDMAN, ALAN WARREN, humanities educator; b. Bklyn., June 8, 1939; s. Leon and Anne (Markowitz) F.; m. Elizabeth Butler Cullingford, Nov. 22, 1985; children: Eric Lawrence, Scot Bradley, Lorraine Eve, Daniel Butler. Student, U. Edinburgh, Scotland, 1960-61; BA, Queens Coll., 1961; MA, NYU, 1962; PhD, U. Rochester, 1966. Grad. teaching asst. U. Rochester, 1963-64; instr. English U. Tex., Austin, 1964-66, asst. prof., 1966-69, assoc. prof., 1969-76, prof., 1976—, dir. honors program, 1972-76, chmn. faculty senate, 1987-89; Sr. Fulbright prof. U. Lancaster, Eng., 1977-78, Univ. Coll., Galway, Ireland, 1995; exch. prof. Universite Paul Valery, Montpellier, France, 1985. Author: Lawrence Durrell and the Alexandria Quartet, 1970, Multivalence: The Moral Quality of Form in the Modern Novel, 1978, William Faulkner, 1984, Fictional Death and the Modernist Enterprise, 1995; editor books; contbr. essays and revs. to profl. jours. Chair Dem. Precinct Com.; del. state convs.; founder, 1st pres., chmn. Neighborhood Assn., Austin, 1973-74; bd. dirs. Peace Edn. Ctr., Hillel Found., Austin Hospice, Frontline Theatre Co. Recipient Fulbright Rsch. award, 1995, 1984-85, Travel award France, 1990; NEH fellow, 1970-71. Mem. MLA (del. assembly 1977-79, 82-84, 94-96, exec. com. divsn. on 20th century English lit. 1992-96), AAUP (pres. U. Tex. chpt. 1979-84, nat. coun. 1989-92, exec. com. 1991-92, chair com. governance 1992-95), Tex. Higher Edn. Coord. Bd. (chair faculty adv. com. 1992-95), Tex. Assn. Coll. Tchrs., Nat. Collegiate Honors Coun., Fulbright Alumni Assn. (pres. ctrl. Tex. chpt.), Omicron Delta Kappa. Democrat. Jewish. Office: U Tex Dept English Austin TX 78712

FRIEDMAN, ALVIN, lawyer; b. Bklyn., June 19, 1931; s. Isidor and Freda (Yanuck) F.; m. Maryann Kallison, Mar. 27, 1955; children—Alan K., Margot N. BA with honors in Polit. Sci, Cornell U., 1952; LL.B. cum laude (editor Law Jour. 1956-57), Yale U., 1957. Bar: Tex. 1957, D.C. 1957. Asso. firm Covington & Burling, 1957-63; spl. asst. to gen. counsel Dept. Def., 1963-64, spl. asst. to asst. sec. def. for def. for internat. security affairs, 1964, dep. asst. sec. def. for internat. security affairs Far East and Latin Am., 1964-66; ptnr. Ginsburg & Feldman, Washington, 1966-67, Friedman and Medalie and predecessor firms, Washington, 1967-87; pvt. practice law Washington, 1988—. Served as 1st lt. USAF, 1952-54. Mem. Tex., D.C. bar assns. Office: 700 New Hampshire Ave NW Washington DC 20037-2406

FRIEDMAN, ALVIN EDWARD, investment executive; b. N.Y.C., Aug. 8, 1919; s. Harry and Frances (Levin) F.; m. Pesselle Rothenberg, Feb. 2, 1943; children: Jeffrey F., Joan M. B.B.A., CCNY, 1942; M.B.A., NYU, 1949. Ptnr. Kuhn Loeb & Co., N.Y.C., 1951-78; sr. mng. dir. Lehmann Bros. Kuhn Loeb, N.Y.C., 1978-84; dir. Dillon Read & Co., N.Y.C., 1984-86, sr. advisor, 1986—; bd. dirs. Dreyfus Corp., Avnet, Inc. Pres. Hebrew Arts Sch., N.Y. Served to 1st lt. USAAF, 1943-46, PTO. Home: 101 Del Pond Dr Canton MA 02021-2753 Office: Dillon Read & Co 535 Madison Ave New York NY 10022-4212

FRIEDMAN, ANDREW, director housing and neighborhood preservation; b. N.Y.C., Jan. 29, 1950. BA, Antioch U., 1972; MS, U. Wis., 1984. Asst. dir. ARC, Green Bay, Wis., 1982-86; analyst City of Va. Beach, Va., 1986-89; housing devel. adminstr. City of Va. Beach, 1989-93, dir. housing and neighborhood preservation, 1993—. Mem. allocations com. United Way of S. Hampton Rds., Norfolk. Mem. Va. Assn. Housing and Comty. Devel. Officials (v.p.). Office: City of Va Beach Mcpl Ctr Bldg 18A Virginia Beach VA 23456*

FRIEDMAN, ARNOLD CARL, diagnostic radiologist; b. Bronx, N.Y., Nov. 17, 1951; s. Isidore and Helen and (Lowenthal) F.; children: Jeffrey, Jonathan. BA in Chemistry, Cornell U., 1972; MD, Albert Einstein Coll., 1975. Intern Mt. Sinai Hosp., Hartford, Conn., 1975-76; resident Montefiore Hosp., Bronx, N.Y., 1976-79; asst. prof. Uniformed Svcs. U., Bethesda, Md., 1979-83; assoc. prof. George Washington U., Washington, 1983-84; assoc. prof. Temple U., Phila., 1984-88, prof. radiology, 1989-92; prof. Med. Coll. Pa. Hahnemann U., Phila., 1992-96, acting chmn. radiology scis., 1992-93, chmn. radiology scis., 1993-95; dir. radiology rsch. Med. Coll. Pa. Hahnemann U., Phila., 1996-97; chief radiology svcs. Med. Coll. Pa. Hosp., 1996-97; prof. radiology Allegheny U. of the Health Scis., 1996-97; assoc. chmn. dept. radiology Beth Israel Med. Ctr., N.Y.C., 1997—. Editor: Radiology of Liver, Spleen, Pancreas, Biliary Tract, 1987, Clinical Pelvic Imaging, 1990, Radiology of the Spleen, 1993, Radiology of the Liver Biliary Tract and Pancreas, 1993. Fellow Am. Coll. Radiology; mem. Radiologic Soc. N.Am., Am. Roentgen Ray Soc., Assn. Univ. Radiologists, Assn. Ultrasound in Medicine, Soc. Gastrointestinal Radiology. Avocations: tennis, basketball, ice skating, skiing, fitness. Home: 200 E 94th St Apt 218 New York NY 10128

FRIEDMAN, ARTHUR DANIEL, electrical engineering and computer science educator, investment management company executive; b. Bronx, N.Y., Apr. 24, 1940; s. Henry and Yetta (Pisachowitz) F.; m. Barbara Allyn Bernstein, Mar. 31, 1968; children: Michael Kenneth, Steven David. BA, Columbia U., 1961, BS, 1962, MEE, 1963, PhDEE, 1965. Mem. tech. staff Bell Labs., Murray Hill, N.J., 1965-72; assoc. prof. elec. engring. and computer sci. U. So. Calif., L.A., 1972-77; prof. George Washington U., Washington, 1977-97, dept. chmn., 1980-84, prof. emeritus, 1997—; chmn. bd., co-founder Computer Sci. Press of W.H. Freeman and Co., Rockville, Md., 1974-88, co-editor-in-chief, 1988-89; dir. Gen. Microwave Corp., 1987-94; co-founder, pres. investment mgmt. co. ABF Enterprises, ABF Capital Mgmt.; gen. ptnr. Potomac Ptnrs. L.P., 1991. Author: (with Premanchandra Menon) Fault Detection in Digital Circuits, 1971, Theory and Design of Switching Circuits, 1975, Logical Design of Digital Systems, 1975, Fundamentals of Logic Design and Switching Theory, 1986, (with Melvin Breuer) Diagnosis of Digital Systems, 1976, (with Miron Abramovici and Melvin Breuer) Digital System Testing and Testable Design, 1990, 2d edit., 1995. Pres. Friedman Family Found. Inc.; bd. dirs. men's club Congregation Beth Israel. Fellow IEEE; mem. Market Movers. Avocations: tennis, reading, swimming. Home: 4969 Beauchamp Ct San Diego CA 92130-2742 Office: George Washington U Dept Elec Engring Washington DC 20007

FRIEDMAN, AVNER, mathematician, educator; b. Petah-Tikva, Israel, Nov. 19, 1932; came to U.S., 1956; s. Moshe and Hanna (Rosenthal) F.; m. Lillia Lynn, June 7, 1959; children—Alissa, Joel, Naomi, Tamara. M.Sc., Hebrew U., Jerusalem, 1954, Ph.D., 1956. Prof. math. Northwestern U., Evanston, Ill., 1962-86; prof. math. Purdue U., West Lafayette, Ind., 1984-87, dir. Ctr. Applied Math., 1984-87; prof. math., dir. Inst. Math. and Its Applications U. Minn., 1987-97, dir. Minn. Ctr. for Indsl. Math., 1994—. Author: Generalized Functions and Partial Differential Equations, 1963, Partial Differential Equations of Parabolic Type, 1964, Partial Differential Equations, 1969, Foundations of Modern Analysis, 1970, Advanced Calculus, 1971, Differential Games, 1971, Stochastic Differential Equations and Applications, vol. 1, 1975, vol. 2, 1976, Variational Principles and Free Boundary Problems, 1983, Mathematics in Industrial Problems, 10 vols., 1988-98; contbr. articles to profl. publs. Fellow Sloan Found., 1962-65, Guggenheim, 1966-67; recipient Creativity award NSF, 1983-85, 90-92. Mem. AAAS, NAS, Am. Math. Soc., Soc. Indsl. Applied Math. (pres. 1993, 94, chair bd. math. scis. 1994-97). Office: U Minn Sch Math 206 Church St SE Minneapolis MN 55455-0488

FRIEDMAN, BARRY DAVID, political scientist, educator; b. Meriden, Conn., Sept. 29, 1953; s. Edward Louis and Esia (Baran) F.; m. Cynthia Joy Landis, July 8, 1990. BA in Polit. Sci., U. Hartford, 1976, BS in Engring., 1976; MPA, MBA, U. Conn., 1983, PhD in Polit. Sci., 1991. Forecasting analyst Northeast Utilities, Berlin, Conn., 1976-82; pers. specialist ARC, Fairfax, Va., 1986-87; asst. prof. polit. sci. Valdosta (Ga.) State U., 1987-92; prof. polit. sci. North Ga. Coll. & State U., Dahlonega, 1992—; dir. MPA program North Ga. Coll., Dahlonega; conf. presentations, 1988—. Author: Regulation in the Reagan-Bush Era: The Eruption of Presidential Influence, 1995; contbr. articles to profl. jours. Nat. instr.-trainer ARC 1990-96; chpt. pres. Am. Red Magen David for Israel, West Hartford, Conn., 1980-82. Recipient Outstanding Lt. Gov. award New Eng. dist. Key Club Internat., 1971, Promotion of Excellence in Higher Edn. award, 1999; named Bd. Mem. of Yr., ARC, Valdosta, 1991. Mem. ASPA (life, sec.-treas., pres., editor Ga. chpt. 1994—), Ga. Polit. Sci. Assn. (mem. exec. bd. 1997—), Phi Beta Kappa, Phi Kappa Phi (chpt. pres. 1989-90), Pi Alpha Alpha, Pi Sigma Alpha, Pi Gamma Mu (gov. Ga. 1995—), Beta Gamma Sigma, Alpha Chi, Kappa Mu, Omicron Delta Kappa. Jewish. Office: North Ga Coll & State U Dept Polit Sci Dahlonega GA 30597-1001

FRIEDMAN, BART, lawyer; b. N.Y.C., Dec. 5, 1944; s. Philip and Florence (Beckerman) F.; m. Wendy Alpern Stein, Jan. 11, 1986; children: Benjamin Alpern, Jacob Stein. AB, L.I. U., 1966; JD, Harvard U., 1969. Bar: N.Y. 1970, Mass. 1972. Rsch. fellow Harvard U. Bus. Sch., Cambridge, Mass., 1969-70; assoc. Cahill, Gordon & Reindel, N.Y.C., 1970-72, 77-80, ptnr., 1980—; spl. counsel SEC, Washington, 1974-75, asst. dir., 1975-77; lectr. internat. tax program, Harvard U. Sch. Law, 1971, 85. Mem. vis. com. Harvard U. Grad. Sch. Edn., 1995—, com. on univ. resources, 1996—; trustee Julliard Sch., 1988—, vice chmn., 1994—; trustee Brookings Inst., 1997—, chmn. N.Y. adv. com., 1997—, coun. fgn. rels., 1995—, jt. task force on resources for fgn. affairs; mem. ind. task force on non-lethal weapons; mem., del. to NATO Hdqrs. and Field, 1998; mem. adv. bd. Remarque Inst. NYU, 1997—. Mem. Assn. Bar City of N.Y., Coun. Fgn. Rels., Explorers Club, Down Town Assn. (N.Y.C.), The River Club, City Tavern Club (Washington), The Tuxedo Club, Century Assn. Home: 1172 Park Ave Apt 5B New York NY 10128-1213 Office: Cahill Gordon & Reindel 80 Pine St Fl 17 New York NY 10005-1790

FRIEDMAN, BARTON ROBERT, English educator; b. Bklyn., Feb. 5, 1935; s. Abraham Isaac and Mazie Diana (Cooper) F.; m. Sheila Lynn Siegel, June 22, 1958; children—Arnold, Jonathan, Daniel, Esther. B.A., Cornell U., 1956, Ph.D. (univ. dissertation fellow), 1964; M.A., U. Conn., 1958. Instr. Bowdoin Coll., Brunswick, Maine, 1961-63; from instr. to prof. English lit. U. Wis., Madison, 1963-78; prof. English lit. Cleve. State U., 1978-97, chmn. dept. English, 1978-87, prof. emeritus, 1997—. Author: Adventures in the Deeps of the Mind: The Cuchulain Cycle of W.B. Yeats, 1977, You Can't Tell the Players, 1979, Fabricating History: English Writers on the French Revolution, 1988 (Nancy Dasher award for best scholarly book by mem. Coll. English Assn. Ohio 1989); mem. editl. bd. Irish Renaissance Ann., 1980-84, Lit. Monographs, 1970-76. Recipient William Kiekhofer Teaching Excellence award U. Wis., 1967, Disting. Scholar award Cleve. State U., 1990. Mem. MLA, Am. Com. Irish Studies, Coll. English Assn. Ohio (bd. govs.), Soc. Lit. and Sci. (bibliographer Bibliography of Lit. and Sci. in Configurations), Phi Kappa Phi. Jewish. Home: 2916 E Overlook Rd Cleveland OH 44118-2434 Office: Cleve State Univ Dept English Cleveland OH 44115

FRIEDMAN, BENJAMIN MORTON, economics educator; b. Louisville, Ky., Aug. 5, 1944; s. Norbert and Eva (Lipsky) F.; m. Barbara Allan Cook, Dec. 17, 1972; children: John Norton, Jeffrey Allan. AB summa cum laude, Harvard U., 1966, AM, 1969, PhD, 1971; MSc King's Coll., Cambridge U., 1970. Economist Morgan Stanley & Co., N.Y.C., 1971-72; asst. prof. econs. Harvard U., Cambridge, Mass., 1972-76, assoc. prof., 1976-80, prof., 1980-89, William Joseph Maier prof. polit. economy, 1989—, chmn. dept. of econs., 1991-94; dir. fin. markets and monetary econs. Nat. Bur. Econ. Rsch., Cambridge, 1977-93; dir. Pvt. Export Funding Corp., N.Y.C., 1981—. Author: Economic Stabilization Policy, 1975, Monetary Policy in the United States, 1981, Day of Reckoning, 1988; co-author: Does Debt Management Matter?, 1992; editor: New Challenges to the Role of Profits, 1978, The Changing Roles of Debt and Equity in Financing U.S. Capital Formation, 1982, Corporate Capital Structures in the United States, 1985, Financing Corporate Capital Formation, 1986, Handbook on Monetary Economics, 1990; assoc. editor Jour. Monetary Econs., 1977-95. Trustee Coll. Retirement Equities Fund, N.Y.C., 1978-82, Standish Ayer & Wood Investment, 1989—; dir. Am. Friends of Cambridge U., 1994—. Marshall scholar Cambridge U., 1966-68; Soc. Fellows jr. fellow Harvard U., 1968-71. Mem. Coun. Fgn. Rels., Brookings Panel Econ. Activity, Am. Econ. Assn., Harvard Club N.Y.C. Home: 74 Sparks St Cambridge MA 02138-2238 Office: Harvard U 127 Littauer Center Cambridge MA 02138

FRIEDMAN, BERNARD ALVIN, federal judge; b. Detroit, Sept. 23, 1943; s. David and Rae (Garber) F.; m. Rozanne Golston, Aug. 16, 1970; children: Matthew, Megan. Student, Detroit Inst. Tech., 1962-65; JD, Detroit Coll. Law, 1968. Bar: Mich. 1968, Fla. 1968, U.S. Dist. Ct. (ea. dist.) Mich. 1968, U.S. Ct. Mil. Appeals 1972. Asst. prosecutor Wayne County, Detroit, 1968-71; ptnr. Harrison & Friedman, Southfield, Mich., 1971-78, Lippitt, Harrison, Friedman & Whitefield, Southfield, 1978-82; judge Mich. Dist. Ct. 48th dist., Bloomfield Hills, 1982-88; U.S. dist. judge Ea. Dist. Mich., Detroit, 1988—. Lt. U.S. Army, 1967-74. Recipient Disting. Service award Oakland County Bar Assn., 1986. Avocation: running. Office: US Dist Ct US Courthouse Rm 238 231 W Lafayette Blvd Detroit MI 48226-2702*

FRIEDMAN, B(ERNARD) H(ARPER), writer; b. N.Y.C., July 27, 1926; s. Leonard and Madeline (Uris) F.; m. Abby Noselson, Mar. 6, 1948; children: Jackson, Daisy. BA, Cornell U., 1948. With Cross & Brown Co., 1949-50; v.p., dir. Uris Bldgs. Corp., N.Y.C., 1950-63; lectr. creative writing Cornell U., 1966-67; staff cons., dir. Fine Arts Work Center, Provincetown, Mass., 1968-82; founding mem. Fiction Collective, 1973—; adv. council Cornell U. Coll. Arts and Scis., 1968-83, Herbert F. Johnson Mus., 1972-87. Author: Circles, 1962 (reprinted as I Need to Love, 1963), Yarborough, 1964, Whispers, 1972, Museum, 1974, Almost A Life, 1975, The Polygamist, 1981; (stories) Coming Close, 1982, Between the Flags, 1990, Swimming Laps, 1999; (biographies) Jackson Pollock: Energy Made Visible, 1972, (with Flora Miller Biddle) Gertrude Vanderbilt Whitney, 1978; (plays) In Search of Luigi Pirandello, 1983 (revised as My Small Self, 1998), The Critic, 1986, Beauty Business, 1987, Tony's Case, 1991 (revised as Case History, 1994), Heart of a Boy, 1993 (adapted as screenplay with M. Benderoth, 1997); editor: School of New York, 1959; mem. adv. bd. Cornell Rev., 1977-79; contbr. articles to mags., anthologies and reference vols. Trustee Am. Fedn. Arts, 1958-64, Whitney Mus. Am. Art, 1961—, Broida Mus., 1983-86. With USNR, 1944-46. Recipient awards for short stories, including Nelson Algren award, 1983; fellow Camargo Found., 1991. Mem. PEN, Authors Guild, Dramatists Guild, Century Assn. Club: Century Assn. (N.Y.C.). Home: 439 E 51st St New York NY 10022-6473 also: PO Box 338 Wainscott NY 11975-0338

FRIEDMAN, DANIEL MORTIMER, federal judge; b. N.Y.C., Feb. 8, 1916; s. Henry Michael F. and Julia (Freedman) Friedman; m. Leah Lipson, Jan. 16, 1955 (dec. Dec. 1969), m. Elizabeth Ellis, Oct. 18, 1975. AB, Columbia U., 1937, LLB, 1940. Bar: N.Y. 1941. Practice law N.Y.C., 1940-42; with SEC, Washington, 1942-51; with Justice Dept., Washington, 1951-78, asst. to solicitor gen., 1959-62, 2d asst. to solicitor gen., 1962-68, 1st dep. solicitor gen., 1968-78; chief judge Ct. Claims and U.S. Ct. Appeals, Washington, 1978-89, sr. judge, 1989—. Served with AUS, 1942-46. Recipient Exceptional Service award Atty. Gen., 1969. Office: US Ct Appeals Federal Circuit 717 Madison Pl NW Washington DC 20439-0002

FRIEDMAN, DAVID SAMUEL, lawyer, law review executive; b. Flushing, N.Y., Feb. 21, 1971; s. Stanley and Lita June (Fine) F.; m. Jennifer Katherine Sun. BA magna cum laude, Harvard U., 1993; JD magna cum laude, Harvard Law Sch., 1996. Bar: Mass. 1997, N.Y. 1997, U.S. Dist. Ct. Mass. 1998, U.S. Ct. Appeals (1st cir.) 1999. Editor Harvard Law Rev., Cambridge, Mass., 1994-96, pres., 1995-96; law clerk to Justice John Paul Stevens Supreme Court, 1997-98; law clk. to Judge Michael Boudin First Cir. Ct. Appeals, 1997-98; litigation assoc. Hill & Barlow, Boston, 1998—. Line editor Environ. Law Rev., 1993-94. Harvard Nat. scholar, 1993; named World Univs. Debating Champion, 1993. Mem. Phi Beta Kappa. Democrat. Jewish. Avocations: cooking, tennis, football, basketball. Home: 257 Gramercy Dr Jericho NY 11753-1829

FRIEDMAN, DEBORAH LESLIE WHITE, educational administrator; b. Grand Rapids, Mich., July 5, 1950; d. Edward Charles and Luella Jane (Carr) White; children: Karen Elizabeth, David Edward. BS, Cen. Mich. U., 1972; MBA, U. Toledo, 1980; D in Higher Ednl. Adminstrn., N.C. State U., 1995. Traffic mgr. WTOL-TV, Toledo, Ohio, 1972-74; catering cons. Gladieux Food Svcs., Toledo, 1974-75; mktg. rsch. analyst Owens-Ill., Toledo, 1978; instr. Sampson C.C., Clinton, N.C., 1980-81, chmn. acctg., bus. adminstrn., real estate, 1981-98; divsn. chair bus. and pub. svc. programs Sampson C.C., Clinton, 1998—; pres. faculty senate Sampson C.C., Clinton, N.C., 1983-84; faculty advisor Phi Beta Lambda, 1981-88; adj. trainer N.C. Dept. Community Colls., Raleigh, 1989—; bd. dirs. Sampson County United Way, Inc., 1995-1998, State Employees Credit Union, Clinton br., 1998—. Bd. dirs. Found. for Edn., 1984-89, appropriations chmn., 1984-88, sec., 1988-89; com. mem. Clinton City Schs. Com. on Stds. of Excellence, 1986-87; vol. Girl Scouts Am., Clinton, 1983, 85; mem. N.C. C.C. Leadership Program, 1990; pres. Sunday Sch. Class, 1997-98. Named Outstanding Young Educator, Clinton Jaycees, 1985; recipient Outstanding Svc. award Clinton Student Govt. Assn., 1982, Excellence in Tchg. award N.C. State Bd. C.C., 1989, 98, Cert. of Appreciation, State of N.C. for Vol. Svcs., 1987, EXCEL finalist, 1991, 93-94. Mem. Am. Assn. Women in Cmty. Colls. (membership dir. 1988-89), N.C. Assn. Bus. Chair and Dept. Heads (pres. 1997-99), Am. Bus. Women Assn. (pres. 1983-84, Sampson County Woman of Yr. 1984), Beta Gamma Sigma, Phi Kappa Phi. Avocations: tennis, running, golf. Home: 1603 Shepherds Glade Dr Apex NC 27502 Office: Sampson C C PO Box 318 Clinton NC 28329-0318

FRIEDMAN, DIAN DEBRA, elementary education educator; b. Balt., June 12, 1943; d. Bernard Maurice and Sondra Seletta (Dolgoff) Jacobs; m. Irving Joel Friedman, June 24, 1965; children: Benjamin Aaron, Joshua Jason. AA, Miami (Fla.)-Dade Jr. Coll., 1963; BS in Elem. Edn., Fla. State U., 1965. With contracts and grants Fla. State U., Tallahassee, 1965-66; substitute tchr. Chicopee (Mass.) Sch. Systems, 1965-66; elem. tchr. City of Springfield, Mass., 1966-76; real estate salesperson Gene Kelly Real Estate, Suffield, Conn., 1985-87; ednl. tutor Suffield (Conn.) Sch. Sys., 1987—, mem. curriculum com., 1986-91; tchr. Computer Tots; substitute tchr., tchr. asst. Agawam (Mass.) Jr./Sr. H.S. Bd. dirs. The Village for Families and Children, Inc., Hartford, Conn., 1986-97, pub. issues com., 1994-96; bd. dirs. Child and Family Charities, Inc., Hartford; chairperson Suffield Aux. The Village for Families and Children, Inc., 1978-80, mem. 1973—; mem. Citizens for Suffield, 1990—, Friends of Suffield Libr., 1973—, Springfield Mass. Cyclonauts, Franklin Hampshire Freewheelers Bicycle Clubs. Mem. Mass. Tchr.'s Assn., Fla. State Alumni Club, Suffield Woman's Club, Franklin/Hampshire Free Wheelers, Fla. State Univ. Alumni Assn. Democrat. Jewish. Avocations: skiing, reading, bicycling, jogging, painting. Home: 119 Marbern Dr Suffield CT 06078-1542

FRIEDMAN, EDWARD DAVID, lawyer, arbitrator; b. Chgo.; s. Jacob C. and Bessie (Levison) F.; m. Mary Louise Melia, Nov. 1, 1947 (dec. Feb. 1997); children: Michael, Daniel, Mary Eleanor, Elizabeth. AB with honors, U. Chgo., 1935, JD cum laude, 1937. Bar: Ill. 1937, U.S. Ct. Appeals 1950, D.C. 1969, U.S. Supreme Ct. 1969. Law clk. to fed. master in chancery Chgo., 1937-38; assoc. Rosenberg, Toomin & Stein, Chgo., 1938-39; gen. counsel staff SEC, 1939-42; chief counsel OPA, 1942-43; spl. asst. to dep. solicitor and solicitor Dept. Labor, Washington, 1943-48, dep. solicitor of labor, 1965-68, acting solicitor of labor, 1969; ptnr. Bernstein, Alper, Schoene & Friedman, Washington, 1969-75, Highsaw, Mahoney & Friedman, Washington, 1975-80, Friedman & Wirtz, 1980-90; chief law officer 5th regional office, also asst. gen. counsel NLRB, 1948-60; labor counsel to Senator John F. Kennedy, 1960-61, Senator Wayne Morse, 1961-65, U.S. Senate Labor and Pub. Welfare Com., 1961-65; counsel to majority and minority fl. mgrs. Senators Clark and Case on Civil Rights Bill, 1964; spl. asst. sec. labor fgn. farm labor program, 1965; counsel compaign conduct adminstrv. com. United Steelworkers Am., 1980-89; U.S. del. to OECD, Paris, 1968. Mem. edit. bd. U. Chgo. Law Rev, 1936-37. Mem. town coun., Garrett Park, Md., 1954-58, mayor, 1960-66. U. Chgo. James Nelson Raymond fellow, 1937. Mem. ABA, D.C. Bar Assn., Fed. Bar Assn., Order of Coif, U. Chgo. Alumni Club. Home: 24 Gospel Path PO Box 1123 Truro MA 02666-1123 also: 1300 N Placita Parasol Green Valley AZ 85614-3643

FRIEDMAN, ELI ARNOLD, nephrologist; b. N.Y.C., Apr. 9, 1933; s. Israel and Ida (Gutman) F.; widowed; children: Amy Louise, Rebecca Alicia, Sara Jo. BS, Bklyn. Coll., 1953; MD, SUNY Downstate Med. Center, 1957; DSc (hon.), Maduri Kamaraj U., India, 1985, L.I. U., 1991. Intern in medicine Harvard Med. Sch., 1957-58; resident in medicine Peter Bent Brigham Hosp., Boston, 1960-61; Am. Heart Assn. rsch. fellow Harvard U., 1958-60; mem. faculty, chief divsn. renal disease Downstate Med. Ctr., Bklyn., 1963—; prof. Health Sci. Ctr. SUNY, Bklyn., 1972—, Disting. Tchg. prof., 1992—; bd. dirs. Am. Bur. Med. Aid to China, 1979—, Cleve. Found., 1979—, Bklyn. Nephrology Found., 1978—; Kasperzak lectr. Cleve. Clinic, 1998; alpha Omega Alpha lectr. SUNY Health Sci. Cttr., Bklyn., 1999. Author: Acute Renal Failure, 1973, Strategy in Renal Failure, 1978, Diabetic Renal-retinal Syndrome, 1980, Diabetic Renal-retinal Syndrome 3 Therapy, 1986, Diabetic Nephropathy, 1986, Diabetic Renal-retinal Syndrome 4: Management Strategy, 1987; editor: Journal of Diabetic Complications, 1986—. Lt. comdr. USPHS, 1961-63. Recipient Hoenig award Nat. Kidney Found., 1986, Silver medal U. Bologna, 1988, Disting. Svc. to Black Kidney patients award Howard U., 1989, Physicians award Am. Assn. Kidney Patients, 1989, Alumni medal SUNY Downstate Med. Coll., William Dock Master Tchr. award Alumni Assn. SUNY Health Scis. Ctr., 1992, Recognition award N.Y. Regional Transplant Program, 1994, Am. Kidney Fund Nat. Torchbearer award, 1995, Juvenile Diabetes Found./Bklyn. award honoree, 1995, medal of excellence Am. Kidney Fund, 1996, Torchbearer award Organ Transplantation and Kidney Disease, 1998, Internat. Torchbearer award, India, 1998; grantee NIH, USPHS, N.Y. Kidney Found., N.Y. State Kidney Disease Inst., Am. Kidney Fund, Medal of Excellence award, 1996; named master ACP, 1996. Fellow Explorers Club (1st prize photo competition 1995); mem. ACP (Master 1996), Am. Soc. Nephrology, Internat. Soc. Nephrology, Am. Soc. Artificial Internal Organs (pres. 1987—, editor Transactions 1985—), Am. Soc. Immunology, Transplantation Soc., Assn. Am. Physicians, Internat. Soc. Artificial Organs (pres. 1986), Italian Soc. Nephrology (hon.), Royal Soc. Medicine Belgium (corres. mem.). Achievements include co-invention of suitcase artificial kidney; founding of first federally funded dialysis unit in U.S. Home: 1049 E 17th St Brooklyn NY 11230-4412 Office: 450 Clarkson Ave Brooklyn NY 11203-2056 *Achievement is as much a function of unswerving persistence, which is a learned behavior pattern, as it is of intellectual endowment, over which we have no control. Effective individuals, though often very bright, have learned to stick with it even after initial or repetitive failure. All of us lose some or even most of the time indicating the need to extract maximal joy from our wins no matter how infrequent the event.*

FRIEDMAN, EMANUEL, publishing company executive; b. N.Y.C., June 2, 1919; s. Abraham and Yetta (Jonas) F.; m. Carmel Abelson, July 7, 1940; 1 dau., April. B.S., CCNY, 1938; M.S., U. Md., 1940. Instr. history NYU, N.Y.C., 1947-57, CCNY, 1953-55; sr. editor Collier's Ency., N.Y.C., 1957-67; editor-in-chief Collier's Ency., 1967-85; v.p. Macmillan Pub. Co., 1971-85. Served as 1st lt. Sanitary Corps, Med. Dept. U.S. Army, 1943-46. Mem. Am. Hist. Assn. Home: 486 Tenafly Rd Englewood NJ 07631-1749

FRIEDMAN, EMANUEL A., medical educator; b. N.Y.C., June 9, 1926; s. Louis and Pauline (Feldman) F.; m. E. Judith Salomon, June 6, 1948; children: Lynn Alice, Meryl Ruth, Lee Martin. AB, Bklyn. Coll., 1947; MD, Columbia U., 1951, ScD, 1959; MA, Harvard U., 1969. Diplomate Am. Bd. Ob-Gyn. Intern Bellevue Hosp., N.Y.C., 1951-52; resident Columbia-Presbyn. Hosp., N.Y.C., 1952-57; instr. Columbia Coll. Physicians and Surgeons, 1957-59, asst. prof., 1960-62, assoc. prof., 1962-63; prof., chmn. dept. ob-gyn Chgo. Med. Sch., 1963-69; chmn. dept. ob-gyn Michael Reese Hosp., Chgo., 1963-69; prof. ob-gyn Harvard U., 1969-90, prof. emeritus, 1990—; obstetrician-gynecologist-in-chief Beth Israel Hosp., Boston, 1969-90, obstetrician-gynecologist in chief emeritus, 1990—; prof. health scis. and tech. MIT, 1985-90; prof. ob-gyn Einstein, 1991—. Author: Labor: Clinical Evaluation and Management, 1967, 2d edit., 1978, Rh-Isoimmunization and Erythroblastosis Fetalis, 1969, Lymphatic System of Female Genitalia, 1971, Biological Principles and Modern Practice of Obstetrics, 1974, Blood Pressure, Edema and Proteinuria in Pregnancy, 1976, Pregnancy Hypertension, 1977, Uterine Physiology, 1979, Advances in Perinatal Medicine, 1981, 5th edit., 1986, Obstetrical Decision Making, 1982, 2d edit., 1987, Management of Labor, 1983, 2d edit., 1988, Gynecological Decision Making, 1983, 2d edit., 1987, Labor and Delivery Impact on Offspring, 1987, Legal Principles and Practice in Obstetrics and Gynecology, 1988, Vol. 2, 1990. Served with USNR, 1944-46. Recipient Joseph Mather Smith research prize Columbia U., 1958, Disting. Alumnus award Bklyn Coll., 1964, Bicentennial commemorative silver medallion award Columbia U., 1967. Fellow ACS, Am. Coll. Ob-Gyn, N.Y. Acad. Medicine; mem. N.Y. Acad. Scis., Soc. Exptl. Biology and Medicine, Soc. Gynecologic Investigation, AAUP, AAAS, Alpha Omega Alpha. Office: One Lincoln Pla New York NY 10023

FRIEDMAN, ERNEST HARVEY, physician, psychiatrist; b. Cleve., Jan. 8, 1931; s. Sol and Ann (Nittskoff) F.; m. Anita Rose Bogdanow, Oct. 26, 1962; children: Rachel Samantha, Sarah Ann, Eric Daniel, Jessica Emily. BS, Case Western Res. U., 1952; MD, Ohio State U., 1956. Diplomate Am. Bd. Psychiatry and Neurology. Intern U. Ill. Hosps., Chgo., 1956-57; psychiat. resident U. Hosps. of Cleve., 1957-60; clin. instr. Case Western Res. U., Cleve., 1974-86, asst. clin. prof., 1983—; vis. psychiatrist Mt. Sinai Hosp., Cleve., 1963-70, sr. vis. psychiatrist, 1970—; pvt. practice psychiatry, medicine Cleve., 1962—; owner, computer mfr. Voxaflex Co., East Cleveland, Ohio, 1986—; mem. courtesy staff Laurelwood Hosp., Willoughby, Ohio, 1991—; mem. courtesy staff Huron Hosp., East Cleveland, Ohio, 1971—; chmn. ad hoc com. on stress Am. Heart Assn., Cleve., 1977; cons. psychiatrist Nat. Exercise and Heart Disease Study, Washington, 1972-75. Mem. editorial bd. Heart and Lung, 1974-80; patentee computer software and hardware. Served as lt. comdr. M.C., USNR, 1960-62. Grantee-in-aid Am. Heart Assn., Cleve., 1964, 65, 75. Fellow Am. Psychiat. Assn. Jewish. Avocations: tennis, photography, bicycling. Office: Voxaflex Co 1831 Forest Hills Blvd Cleveland OH 44112-4313

FRIEDMAN, EUGENE STUART, lawyer; b. N.Y.C., Apr. 5, 1941; s. Abe and Etta (Fischer) F.; m. Karin L. Mehlem, Feb. 3, 1968; children: Gabrielle, Douglas, Jason. AB, NYU, 1961; LLB, Columbia U., 1964. Bar: N.Y. 1965, U.S. Supreme Ct. 1979. Atty. NLRB, San Francisco, 1965-67; assoc., ptnr. Cohen, Weiss & Simon, N.Y.C., 1968-86; sr. ptnr. Friedman & Levine, N.Y.C., 1987—; lectr. Ill. Inst. Continuing Legal Edn., Chgo., 1982-84, NYU Conf. Labor & Practicing Law Inst., N.Y.C., 1983-85. Contbr. articles to profl. jours. Active N.Y. State Task Force Plant Closings, N.Y.C., 1984. With USN, 1964-65. Mem. N.Y. State Bar Assn., Assn. of Bar of City of N.Y. (chmn. labor & employment law com. 1987-90), Am. Arbitration Assn. (law com.). Democrat. Jewish. Avocations: scuba diving, tennis. Home: 277 W End Ave New York NY 10023-2604 Office: Friedman & Levine 1500 Broadway New York NY 10036-4015

FRIEDMAN, EUGENE WARREN, surgeon; b. N.Y.C., Mar. 10, 1919; s. Isadore and Dora (Abramowitz) F.; m. Geraldine F. Gewirtz, Nov. 11, 1945; children: John Henry, Robert James. AB, NYU, 1939, MD, 1943. Diplomate: Am. Bd. Surgery, Am. Bd. Laser Surgery (bd. dirs. 1986—). Intern, resident in surgery Morrisania City Hosp., N.Y.C., 1943-45; resident in surgery Mt. Sinai Hosp., N.Y.C., 1947-48, attending surgeon, chief div. head and neck surgery, 1952—, clin. prof. surgery Sch. Medicine, 1967—, Hess Found./Friedman prof. surgical oncology, 1991; resident and fellow in surgery Meml. Hosp., N.Y.C., 1948-52; attending surgeon tumor surgery Manhattan State Hosp., N.Y.C., 1960-72; attending surgeon, co-dir. head and neck surgery French Polyclinic Med. Ctr., N.Y.C., 1965-72; cons. head and neck surgery Bronx-Lebanon Hosp. Ctr., N.Y.C., 1960—, Peninsula Hosp. Ctr., N.Y.C., 1960—, Bronx VA Hosp., N.Y.C., 1960—; attending surgeon Beth Israel Hosp. North (formerly Doctors Hosp.), N.Y.C., 1960—; cons. surgeon Lenox Hill Hosp., N.Y.C., 1976—; lectr. Founding co-editor-in-chief Lasers in Surgery and Medicine, 1980-87; editor-in-chief Jour. Clin. Laser Medicine and Surgery (formerly Laser Medicine and Surgery News and Advances), 1988-97; contbr. chpts. to books and articles in field to profl. jours. Mem. sci. adv. bd. Chemotherapy Found., N.Y.C.; mem. sci. adv. bd. Samuel Waxman Rsch. Fund, Israel Cancer Rsch. Fund; bd. dirs. N.Y. City divsn. Am. Cancer Soc., 1976—; med. dir. Greater N.Y. Area State of Israel Bonds, 1976—; hon. police surgeon, City of N.Y., 1968—. Capt. AUS, 1945-47. Recipient 2nd annaward Israel Cancer Research Fund, 1981m Jacobi medallion Alumni Assn. Mt. Sinai Hosp., N.Y.C., 1988. Fellow ACS, N.Y. Acad. Medicine, Am. Soc. Lasers in Medicine and Surgery; mem. AMA, N.Y. Surg. Soc., N.Y. Cancer Soc., N.Y. Head and Neck Soc., Soc. Head and Neck Surgeons, Soc. Surg. Oncology, Am. Soc. Clin. Oncology, Internat. Soc. Lasers in Surgery and Medicine (sec.-treas. 1980-82), N.Y. County Med. Soc., N.Y. State Med. Soc., Univ. Club, Lotos Club. Democrat. Jewish.

FRIEDMAN, FRANCES, public relations executive; b. N.Y.C., Apr. 8, 1928; d. Aaron and Bertha (Itzkowitz) Fallick; m. Clifford Jerome Friedman, June 17, 1950; children—Kenneth Lee, Jeffrey Bennett. B.B.A., CCNY, 1948. Dir. pub. relations Melia Internat., Madrid, N.Y.C., 1971-73; sr. v.p. Lobsenz-Stevens, N.Y.C., 1973-75; exec. v.p. Howard Rubenstein Assocs., N.Y.C., 1975-83; pres., prin. Frances Friedman Assocs., N.Y.C., 1983-84; pres., chmn. bd. dirs. GCI Group Inc., N.Y.C., 1984-91, pub. rels. and editorial cons., 1991-93; mng. dir. L.V. Power & Assoc., Inc., 1993-97; pub. rels. cons. N.Y.C., 1997—. Bd. dirs. Morris-Jumel Mansion, 1999—, Contemporary Guidance Svcs, 1999, ACRMD- Retarded Children, N.Y.C., 1983-85, City Coll. Fund, N.Y.C., 1970-79; mem. adv. bd. League for Parent Edn., N.Y.C., 1961-65; editor South Shore Democratic Newsletter, North Bellmore, N.Y., 1958-61, press sec. N.Y. State Assembly candidate, 1965, N.Y. State Congl. candidate, 1968; officer Manhasset Dem. Club, N.Y., 1965-69; mem. adv. com. N.Y.C. Council candidate, 1985. U. New Haven Bartels fellow, 1993. Mem. Pub. Relations Soc. Am., Women in Communications (Matrix award for pub. relations 1989), The Counselors Acad., Pride and Alarm, City Club N.Y. Democrat. Jewish. Home: 860 5th Ave New York NY 10021-5856

FRIEDMAN, FRANCES WOLF, political fund raiser; b. Ft. Worth, June 14, 1940; d. Tobian Alexander and Ann (Katz) Wolf; m. Christopher I. Newman (div. 1984); children: Peter A., J. Hope; m. Frederick Friedman Sr., Jan. 3, 1986; stepchildren: Danielle F., David J. BA in Polit. Sci., Tulane U., 1961. Motion picture film prodn. office coord. Columbia Pictures Corp. Paramount Pictures, N.Y.C., 1965-72, Metro Goldwyn Mayer, N.Y.C., 1965-72; dir. vols. Congressman Bill Green, N.Y.C., 1984-86, fin. dir., 1988-92; nat. dir. Modrnpac, N.Y.C., 1993—; bd. dirs. Family Connections, 1998—; domestic violence task force chair Adv. Bd. on the Status of Women-Essex County, Newark, 1997—; mem., co-founder Essex County Coalition on Domestic Violence Svc. Providers, Newark, 1997—. Mem. pub. rels. Concert Artists Guild, N.Y.C., 1982-84, LWV, Millburn-Short Hills, N.J., 1996—; v.p. Rep. Club, Millburn-Short Hills, 1996—; freeholder candidate Rep. Party, Essex County, N.J., 1996, freeholder-at-large, 1996, 99. Avocation: gardening.

FRIEDMAN, FRANK BENNETT, lawyer; b. Newark, May 1, 1940; s. Martin and Gertrude (Tow) F.; m. Esta Kossack, June 2, 1962; children: Amy, Emily. AB, Columbia U., 1962, JD, 1965. Bar: D.C., Pa., Colo., Calif. Atty. FCC, Washington, 1965-67, Dept. Justice, Washington, 1967-70; counsel ATlantic Richfield Co., Phila., 1970-71, Denver, 1971-73, L.A., 1973-78; dir. environ. health and safety ARCO Chem. Co., Phila., 1978-79; mgr. external affairs occupation and environ. protection ARCO Chem. Co., L.A., 1979-81; v.p. health, environ. and safety Occidental Petroleum Corp., L.A., 1981-93; ptnr. McClintock, Weston, Benshoff, Rocheford, Rubalcava &MacCuish, L.A., 1993-94; sr. v.p. health, environ. and safety Elf Atochem N.Am., Phila., 1994—; v.p. health safety and environ. Elf Aquitaine, Inc., Washington, 1998—; mem. exec. com., bd. dirs. Environ. Law Inst., 1979-95,

99—, adv. bd., 1996—. Author: Practical Guide to Environmental Management, 3d edit., 1991, 5th edit., 1993, 6th edit., 1995, 7th edit., 1997. Mem. ABA (natural resources sect. energy and environ. law, chmn. air quality commn. 1975-78, coun. nat. resource energy and environ. law sect. 1978-81, 91-94, internat. environ. law 1989-91), Am. Law Inst., Nat. Environ Devel. Assn. (bd. dirs. 1984-93, 96—), Nat. Safety Coun. (bd. dirs. 1991-93). Office: Elf Aquitaine Inc Ste 800 910 17th St NW Washington DC 20006

FRIEDMAN, GARY DAVID, epidemiologist; b. Cleve., Mar. 8, 1934; s. Howard N. and Cema C. F.; m. Ruth Helen Schleien, June 22, 1958; children: Emily, Justin, Richard. Student, Antioch Coll., 1951-53; BS in Biol. Sci., U. Chgo., 1956, MD with honors, 1959; MS in Biostatics, Harvard Sch. Pub. Health, 1965. Diplomate Am. Bd. Internal Medicine. Intern, resident Harvard Med. Svcs., Boston City Hosp., 1959-61; 2d yr. resident Univ. Hosps. Cleve., 1961-62; med. officer heart disease epidemiology study Nat. Heart Inst., Framingham, Mass., 1962-66; chief epidemiology unit, field and tng. sta., heart disease ctrl. program USPHS, San Francisco, 1966-68; sr. epidemiologist divsn. rsch. Kaiser Permanente Med. Care Program, Oakland, Calif., 1968-76, asst. dir. epidemiology and biostatics, 1976-91, dir., 1991-98; sr. investigator Kaiser Permanente Med. Care Program, Oakland, 1998-99, adj. investigator, 1999—; cons. prof. Dept. Health Rsch. and Policy Stanford U. Sch. Medicine, 1998—; rsch. fellow, then rsch. assoc. preventive medicine Harvard Med. Sch., 1962-66; lectr. dept. biomedical and environ. health scis., sch. pub. health U. Calif. Berkeley, 1968—; lectr. epidemiology and biostatics U. Calif. Sch. Medicine, San Francisco, 1980—, asst. clin. prof. 1967-75, assoc. clin. prof., 1975-92 depts. medicine and family and community medicine; mem. U.S.-USSR working group sudden cardiac death Nat. Heart, Lung and Blood Inst., 1975-82, com. on epidemiology and veterans follow-up studies Nat. Rsch. Coun., 1980-85, subcommittee on twins, 1980—, epidemiology and disease ctrl. study sect. NIH, 1982-86, U.S. Preventive Svcs. Task Force, 1984-88, scientific rev. panel on toxic air contaminants State of Calif., 1988—, adv. com. Merck Found./Soc. Epidemiol. Rsch., Clin. Epidemiology Fellowships, 1990-94; sr. advisor expert panel on preventive svcs. USPHS, 1991-96. author: Primer of Epidemiology, 1974, 2d edit., 1980, 3d edit., 1987, 4th edit., 1994; assoc. editor, then mem. editl. bd. Am. Jour. Epidemiology, 1988-96, 99—; mem. editl. bd. HMO Practice, 1991-98, Jour. Med. Screening, 1997—; contbr. over 250 articles to profl. jours., chpts. to books. Oboist San Francisco Civic Symphony, 1990—, UCSF Orchestra, 1994—, Bohemian Club Band, 1994—; bd. dirs. Chamber Musicians No. Calif., Oakland, 1991-98. Sr. surgeon USPHS, 1962-68. Recipient Roche award for Outstanding Performance as Med. Student; Merit grantee Nat. Cancer Inst., 1987, Outstanding Investigator grantee, 1989, 94; named to Disting. Alumni Hall of Fame Cleve. Heights High Sch., 1991. Fellow Am. Heart Assn. (chmn. com. on criteria and methods 1969-71, chmn. program com. 1973-76, coun. epidemiol.), Am. Coll. Physicians; mem. APHA, Am. Epidemiol. Soc. (mem. com. 1982-86, pres.-elect 1998, pres. 1999), Am. Soc. Preventive Oncology, Internat. Epidemiol. Assn., Internat. Soc. Twin Studies, Soc. Epidemiologic Rsch.(exec. Com., 1998—), Phi Beta Kappa, Alpha Omega Alpha, Delta Omega. Achievements include research on cancer, cardiovascular disease, gallbladder disease, effects of smoking, alcohol and medicinal drugs, evaluation of health screening tests. Office: Stanford U Sch Medicine Dept Health Rsch and Policy Redwood Bldg Rm T210 Stanford CA 94305-5405

FRIEDMAN, GEORGE JERRY, aerospace company executive, engineer; b. N.Y.C., Mar. 22, 1928; s. Sander and Ruth (Oberlander) F.; m. Ruthanne Goldstein, Sept. 7, 1953; children—Sanford, Gary, David. BS, U. Calif.-Berkeley, 1949; MS, UCLA, 1956, PhD, 1967. Registered profl. mech. engr., controls engr., Calif. Mech. engring. assoc. Dept. Water and Power, Los Angeles, 1949-56; devel. engr. Servo Mechanisms, Hawthorne, Calif., 1956-60; v.p. Northrop Corp., Los Angeles, 1960-94; exec. v.p., rsch. dir. Space Studies Inst., Princeton, N.J., 1994—; mem. indsl. adv. group NATO, Brussels, 1977-78; guest lectr. UCLA, 1983—, Calif. State U., Northridge, 1983—, dir. trust fund, 1984-89; cons. to sci. adv. bd. USAF, Washington, 1985—, bd. govs. Aerospace and Elec. Sys. Soc., L.A., 1985—, v.p. publs., 1999; adj. prof. U. So. Calif., L.A., 1994—; pres. Internat. Nat. Coun. on Sys. Engring., 1994, fellow 1998. Contbr. articles to profl. jours. Served as pfc. U.S. Army, 1950-52. Recipient Engring. Excellence award San Fernando Valley Engring. Council, 1983. Fellow IEEE (Baker award 1970), AIAA (assoc.; chmn. planetary def. subcom. 1995-97); mem. Am. Def. Preparedness Assn. (exec. com., preparedness award 1985). Democrat. Jewish. Home and Office: 5084 Gloria Ave Encino CA 91436-1529

FRIEDMAN, GERALD MANFRED, geologist, educator; b. Berlin, July 23, 1921; came to U.S., 1946, naturalized, 1950; s. Martin and Frieda (Cohn) F.; m. Sue Tyler Theilheimer, June 27, 1948; children: Judith Fay Friedman Rosen, Sharon Mira Friedman Azaria, Devorah Paula Friedman Zweibach, Eva Jane Friedman Scholle, Wendy Tamar Friedman Spanier. Student, U. Cambridge, Eng., 1938-39; BSc, U. London, Eng., 1945, DSc, 1977; student, U. Wyo., 1949; MA, Columbia U., 1950, PhD, 1952; Dr rer nat (hon.), U. Heidelberg, Fed. Republic Germany, 1986. Agrl. laborer Eng., 1938-39, baker, 1940-42; internee Brit. Army, 1940; lectr. Chelsea Coll., London, 1944-45; analytical chemist E.R. Squibb & Sons, New Brunswick, N.J., also J. Lyons & Co., London, 1945-49; asst. geology Columbia U., 1950; temporary geologist N.Y. State Geol. Survey, 1950; instr., then asst. prof. geology U. Cin., 1950-54; cons. geologist Sault Ste. Marie, Ont., Can., 1954-56; mem. rsch. dept. Pan Am. Petroleum Corp. (Amoco), Tulsa, 1956-64; sr. rsch. scientist Pan Am. Petroleum Corp. (Amoco), 1956-60, rsch. assoc., 1960-62, supr. sedimentary geology rsch., 1962-64; Fulbright vis. prof. geology Hebrew U., Jerusalem, Israel, 1964; prof. geology Rensselaer Poly. Inst., 1964-84, prof. emeritus, 1984—; prof. geology Bklyn. Coll., 1985-88, Disting. prof. geology, 1988—; prof. earth and environ. scis. Grad. Sch. CUNY, 1985-88, disting. prof. earth and environ. scis., 1988—, dep. exec. officer, 1992-94; pres. Gerry Exploration Inc., 1982-88; rsch. scientist Hudson Labs., Columbia, 1965, 66-69, rsch. assoc. dept. geology, 1968-73; vis. prof. U. Heidelberg, 1967; cons. scientist Inst. Petroleum Rsch. and Geophysics, Israel, 1967-71; lectr. Oil & Gas Cons. Internat., 1968-98; pres. Northeastern Sci. Found. Inc., 1979—; vis. scientist Geol. Survey of Israel, 1970-73, 78; mem. Com. Sci. Soc. Pres., 1974-76; Gerald M. Friedman post-doctoral fellow Inst. Earth Scis., Hebrew U., Israel, 1990—; vis. prof. Martin-Luther-Univ., Halle-Wittenberg, Germany, 1998. Co-author: Principles of Sedimentology (Outstanding Acad. Books, Choice, 1978/79), 1978, Exploration for Carbonate Petroleum Reservoirs, 1982, Exercises in Sedimentology, 1982, Principles of Sedimentary Deposits: Stratigraphy and Sedimentology, 1992; pub. Northeastern Environ. Sci., 1982-90; editor: Jour. Sedimentary Petrology, 1964-70 (Best Paper award 1961, hon. mention 1964, 66), Northeastern Geology (now Northeastern Geology and Environ. Scis.), 1979—, Earth Scis. History, 1982-93, Carbonates and Evaporites, 1986—, 10th Internat. Congress on Sedimentology, 1978, Jour. of the History of the Oil Industry, 1999—; sect. co-editor: Chem. Abstracts (Mineralogical and Geol. Chemistry), 1962-69, abstractor, 1952-69; editl. bd. Jour. Geol. Edn., 1951-55, Sedimentary Geology, 1967-95, Israel Jour. Earth Scis., 1971-76, Coral Reef Newsletter, 1973-75, Jour. Geology, 1977—, GeoJour., 1977-83, Facies, 1987—; mng. editor Sedimentology for Earth Sci. Revs., 1992—; contbg. co-editor: Carbonate Sedimentology in Central Europe, 1968, Hypersaline Ecosystems: The Gavish Sabkha, 1985, editor, contbr.: Depositional Environments in Carbonate Rocks, 1969; co-editor: Modern Carbonate Environments, 1983, Lecture Notes in Earth Scis., 1985—; founding editor: Earth Scis. History, 1982; contbr. articles to profl. jours.; patentee in field. Mem. phys. edn. com., judo instr. Tulsa YMCA, 1958-64, chmn. awards com., 1962-64; adviser, instr. Judo Club, Rensselaer Poly. Inst., 1964-84; bd. dirs. Troy Jewish Community Coun., 1966-72, 74-77; v.p. Temple Beth El, 1986-89, pres., 1989-91, bd. dirs., 1965-76; bd. dirs. Leo Baeck Inst., N.Y.C., 1986—; bd. dirs., chmn. pub. com. Drake Well Found., 1998—. Recipient award for devoted svc. Tulsa YMCA, 1963, Hon. W.Va. award, 1998; named hon. alumnus dept. geology Bklyn. Coll., 1989; grantee Office Naval Rsch., AEC, Dept. Energy, Petroleum Rsch. Fund, N.Y. Gas Assn., N.Y. State Energy Rsch. and Devel. Authority. Fellow AAAS (chmn. geology and geography 1978-79, councillor 1979-80, soc. rep. in geology and geography sect. 1989-97), Mineral. Soc. Am. (mem. nominating com. for fellows 1967-69, awards com. 1977-78), Geol. Soc. Am. (sr., chmn. sect. program com. 1969, candidate sect. chmn. 1969, publs. com. 1980-82, chmn. overseas pub. rels. com. internat. divsn., 1996-97, vice chair history geology divsn. 1997—, awards nom. com. sedimentary geol. divsn. 1999—), Geol. Soc. London (life, chartered geologist, hon. fellow, 1996), Geol. Assn. Can., Soc. Econ. Geologists (sr.) Explorers Club N.Y., N.Y. Acad. Scis. (vice chair geol. scis. sect., 1993-94, 96-97, chmn. 1994-96, 97—); mem. Russian Acad. Nat. Scis. - U.S. sect. (Kapitsa Gold medal of honor, 1996), Am. Inst. Profl. Geologists (cert.), Am. Chem. Soc. (group leader 1962-63), Mineral. Soc. of Gt. Brit. (abstractor mineralogical abstracts 1963-64), Am. Assn. Petroleum Geologists (nat. hon. mem. 1990, Nat. Disting. Svc. award 1988, Disting. Educator award 1996, chmn. carbonate rock com. 1965-69, mem. rsch. com. 1965-71, 76-82, lectr. continuing edn. program 1967—, chmn. Persian Gulf liaison com. 1968-70, mem. marine geology com. 1970-74, adv. coun. 1974-75, Disting. lectr. 1972-73, mem. disting. lectr. com. 1975-78, mem. vis. geologists program com. 1982-85, membership com. 1982-87, ho. of dels. 1977-80, 84-87, 91-93, alt. del. 1980-83, 87-90, 93—, sect. sec. 1979-80, sect. treas. 1980-81, sect. v.p. 1981-82, sect. pres 1982-83, div. profl. affairs rep. from Eastern sect. 1983-84, com. on convs. 1984-85, vice chair standing com. hist. petroleum geology 1997—, nat. v.p. 1984-85, mem. select com. on future petroleum geologist 1985-86, cert. petroleum geologist, vice chmn. history petroleum geology com. 1997—, hon. mem. Eastern sect. 1984, chmn. sect. awards com., 1989-92, John T. Galey Meml. award Medal, 1993, sect. chmn. tech. program com. 1994-95, sect. cert. of merit 1995), Soc. for Sedimentary Geology (nat. v.p. 1970-71, pres. 1974-75, sect. pres. pro tem 1966-67, sect. pres. 1967-68, chmn. Shepard award selection com. 1966-67, nat. hon. mem. 1984, Best Paper award Gulf Coast sect. 1974, Twenhotel medalist, 1997), Paleontological Soc. (hon. mention to Outstanding Paper award Jour. Paleontology 1971), History of the Earth Scis. Soc. (co-founder 1981), Hudson-Mohawk Profl. Geologists Assn. (bd. dirs. 1995—, program com. 1996-97, chmn. program com. 1997—), Capital Dist. Geologists Assn. (chmn. program 1966-73), New Eng. Intercollegiate Geol. Conf. (convenor, editor 1979), Am. Geol. Inst. (governing bd. 1971-72, 74-75), Geologists' Assn. (life), Internat. Assn. Sedimentologists (v.p. 1971-75, pres. 1975-78, past pres. 1978-82, nat. corr. U.S.A. 1971-73, hon. mem. 1986, program com. Internat. Sedimentological Congress 1978, excursion com. Internat. Sedimentological Congress 1982), Geol. Soc. Israel (hon.), Indian Assn. Sedimentologists (mem. governing coun. 1978-82), Geol. Vereinigung, Deutsche Geol. Gesellschaft, Soc. Venezolana Historia Geociencias (internat. corr. mem.), Nat. Assn. Geosci. Tchrs. (nat. treas. 1951-55, chmn. organizing and nominating com. establish east-ctrl. sect. 1952-53, pres. Okla. 1962-63, pres. Ea. sect. 1983-84), subscription and circulation mgr., Jour. of Geosci. Edn., 1953-55. Assn. Earth Sci. Editors (v.p. 1970-71, pres. 1971-72, host 1991, Outstanding Editorial Pub. Contributions award 1993), Geosci. Info. Soc. (mem. membership com. 1983-85, ad hoc com. to devel. criteria for reviewing geosci. jours. 1985-86), N.Y. State Geol. Assn. (pres. 1978-79, bd. dirs. 1979-84), N.Y. State Mus.-N.Y. State Geol. Survey (James Hall medal 1997), Cin. Mineral Soc. (v.p., program chmn. 1953-54), U.S. Judo Fedn. (San Dan, cert. judo tchr.), Okla. Judo Fedn. (pres. 1959-60, v.p. 1961-64), Amateur Athletic Union (Okla., judo com. 1963), Empire State Judo Assn. (v.p. 1975-77, dir. coll. devel. 1972-82), Kodokan (Japan), Sigma Gamma Epsilon (nat. v.p. 1978-82, nat. pres 1982-86, nat. hon. mem. 1986), Sigma Xi (v.p. Rensselaer chpt. 1969-70). Home: 32 24th St Troy NY 12180-1915 Office: Dept Geology Bklyn Coll/Grad Sch CUNY Dept Geology Brooklyn NY 11210

FRIEDMAN, GREGORY H., energy administrator. BBA, Temple U.; MBA, Fairleigh Dickinson U. Sr. auditor U.S. Army Audit Agy., 1968-74; dep. dir. Office of Contingency Planning, FEA, Washington, 1974-80, assoc. dir. Gasoline Rationing Implementation Office, 1980-82; with Office of Insp. Gen. Dept. of Energy, Washington, 1982—, dep. asst. insp. gen. for audit ops., 1985-94, dep. insp. gen. for audit svcs., 1994-97, prin. dep. insp. gen., 1997-98, acting insp. gen., 1998, insp. gen., 1998—; guest lectr. audit matters and govtl. affairs Princeton U., George Washington U. Office: Dept of Energy Insp Gen 1000 Independence Ave SW Washington DC 20585-0002

FRIEDMAN, HAL MARC, history educator; b. Trenton, Mich., Dec. 29, 1965; s. Irving David and Elaine Marion (Ellias) F.; m. Lisa Frances Sampsell, July 23, 1989; 1 child, Jeffrey Francis. BS in Polit. Sci. and History, Ea. Mich. U., 1987; MA in History, Mich. State U., 1991, PhD in History, 1995. Tchg. asst. Mich. State U., East Lansing, 1988-89, 90-91, rsch. asst., 1989-90, history instr., 1995, sci. and tech. studies instr. Lyman Briggs Sch., 1995; adj. instr. history U. Detroit-Mercy, 1991; lectr. dept. history and philosophy, instr. history Ea. Mich. U., Ypsilanti, 1992, tchg. asst. dept. Am. thought and lang., 1993-94; history instr. Henry Ford C.C., Dearborn, 1996—; assoc. grad. faculty mem. Ctrl. Mich. U.-Met. Detroit, 1997—; U.S. history faculty cons. Advanced Placement essay reading program Ednl. Testing Svc., San Antonio, 1997-98; ad hoc C.C. observer Wayne State U., Detroit, 1996. Contbr. articles, revs., abstracts to profl. publs. Den leader Cub Scouts Am., 1997—. With USNR, 1988—. Mich. State U. fellow, 1989, 90, 92, 95, vis. humanities fellow U. Windsor, Ont., Can., 1995; rsch. grantee Harry S. Truman Libr., 1994, 95, Mich. State U. travel grantee, 1993, 94. Mem. Am. Fedn. Tchrs. (del. 1997—), Henry Ford C.C. Fedn. Tchrs., Inst. for Early Am. History and Culture (assoc.), World History Assn., Orgn. Am. History, Phi Kappa Phi, Pi Sigma Alpha, Phi Alpha Theta (hon.). Deist. Avocations: reading, shopping, travel, music, museums. Office: Henry Ford CC Social Sci Divsn 5101 Evergreen Rd Dearborn MI 48128-2407

FRIEDMAN, HANS ADOLF, architect; b. Hamburg, Germany, June 10, 1921; came to U.S., 1939, naturalized, 1942; s. Sally and Erna (Samson) F.; m. Maxine Oppenheimer, May 31, 1952; children: Eric, Katy, John, Paul. B.Arch., Ill. Inst. Tech., 1950. Chief architect DeLeuw, Cather & Co., Chgo., 1951-61; sr. partner Friedman, Omarzu, Zion & Lundgoot, Chgo., 1961; pres. A.M. Kinney Assocs., Inc., Chgo., 1961-87, vice chmn., 1988-92; partner A.M. Kinney Assocs., Cin., 1961-93; cons., pvt. practice Evanston, Ill., 1992—; v.p. Kintech Svcs., Inc., 1975-93; lectr. So. Ill. U., 1959. Editor: Inland Architect, 1958-64. Mem. Evanston (Ill.) Preservation Commn., 1978-85, chmn., 1981-82, Evanston (Ill.) site plan and appearance rev. com., 1996—. Recipient Distinguished Bldg. awards Chemplex Co., Rolling Meadows, Ill., 1969, Distinguished Bldg. awards S.C. Johnson & Sons, Wind Point, Wis., 1969, Distinguished Bldg. awards Quaker Oats Co., Jackson, Tenn., 1973, Disting. Bldg. awards Moore Bus. Forms, Inc., Glenview, Ill., 1973; Lab. of Yr. award Am. Critical Care, 1980; Disting. Pub. Service award City of Evanston, 1985. Fellow AIA (emeritus); mem. Nat. Trust for Historic Preservation, Landmarks Preservation Council of Ill. Home and Office: 1024 Judson Ave Evanston IL 60202-1321

FRIEDMAN, HAROLD EDWARD, lawyer; b. Cleve., Apr. 7, 1934; s. Joseph and Mary (Schreibman) F.; m. Nancy Schweid, Aug. 20, 1961; children: Deborah, Jay, Susan. B.S., Ohio State U., 1956; LL.B., Case Western Res U., 1959. Bar: Ohio 1960. Practiced in Cleve., since 1960; ptnr. Simon, Haiman, Gutfeld, Friedman & Jacobs, 1967-80, Ulmer & Berne, 1981—; chair real property practice group. Sec., trustee Harry K. and Emma R. Fox Charitable Found.; pres. Jewish Vocat. Svcs., Cleve.; pres. Internat. Assn. Jewish Vocat. Svcs.; pres. Cleve. Hillel Found.; vice chmn. endowment fund Jewish Cmty. Fedn. Cleve., bd. dirs.; pres. Metro Health Found.; bd. dirs. Bur. Jewish Edn., Jewish Convalescence and Rehab. Ctr., Big Bros. Greater Cleve., Jewish Cmty. Fedn. Cleve., Jewish Family Svc. Assn., YES, Inc., Bellefaire/Jewish Children's Bur. Recipient Kane Leadership award Jewish Community Fedn. Cleve., 1974. Mem. ABA, Ohio Bar Assn., Cleve. Bar Assn., Oakwood Country Club. Home: 23149 Laureldale Rd Cleveland OH 44122-2101 Office: 900 Bond Ct Bldg Cleveland OH 44114

FRIEDMAN, HARVEY MICHAEL, infectious diseases educator; b. Montreal, May 29, 1944; came to U.S., 1971; s. Sidney and Sybil (Garfinkle) F.; m. Cynthia Diane Mickey, Apr. 12, 1980; children: Lisa, Steven, Julie. BS, McGill U., 1965, MD, 1969. Intern, resident Jewish Gen. Hosp., Montreal, 1969-71; fellow in virology Wistar Inst., Phila., 1971-73; fellow in infectious disease U. Pa. Hosp., Phila., 1973-75; asst. prof., assoc. prof. Med. Sch. U. Pa., Phila., 1975-91, prof. Med. Sch., 1991—; med. dir. Clin. Virology Lab. Children's Hosp., Phila., 1975-96; chief Infectious Diseases U. Pa. Hosp., Phila., 1990—. Contbr. numerous papers and book chpts. Grantee NIH, Found., 1978—. Fellow Infectious Disease Soc. Am.; mem. AAAS, Am. Soc. Clin. Investigation, Assn. Am. Physicians. Achievements include description of novel mechanisms used by herpes simplex virus glycoproteins that favor virus escape from immune attack. Office: U Pa Med Sch 537 Johnson Pavilion Philadelphia PA 19104-6073

FRIEDMAN, HERBERT, physicist; b. N.Y.C., N.Y., June 21, 1916; s. Samuel and Rebecca (Seligson) F.; m. Gertrude Miller, 1940; children—Paul, Jon. BA, Bklyn. Coll., 1936; PhD in Physics, Johns Hopkins U., 1940; DSc (hon.), U. Tübingen, Fed. Republic Germany, 1977, U. Mich., 1979. With U.S. Naval Rsch. Lab., Washington, 1940—, supt. atmosphere and astrophysics div., 1958-63, supt. space sci. div., 1963-80; chief scientist E. O. Hulburt Ctr. Space Rsch. U.S. Naval Rsch. Lab., 1963-80; emeritus, chief scientist U.S. Naval Rsch. Lab., EO Hulburt Ctr. for Space Rsch., 1980—; adj. prof. physics U. Md., 1960-80, U. Pa., 1974-80; vis. prof. Yale U., 1966-68; Martin-Marietta fellow in Space Sci., NASM, 1986-87; mem. space sci. bd. Nat. Acad. Scis.-NRC, 1962-75, 86—, chmn. com. on solar-terrestrial rsch., 1968-71; mem. com. sci. and pub. policy Nat. Acad. Scis., 1967-71, mem. geophysics rsch. bd., 1969-71, chmn., 1976-79, mem. adv. com. internat. orgns. and programs, 1969-77; pres. Interunion Com. on Solar-Terrestrial Physics, 1967-74; pres. spl. com. on solar-terrestrial physics ICSU, 1975-80; chmn. COSPAR working group II, Internat. Quiet Sun Yr.; v.p. COSPAR, 1970-75, 86—; mem. Gen. Adv. Com. on Atomic Energy, 1968-73; mem. Pres.'s Sci. Adv. Com., 1970-73, Advisory Bd. Fermi Lab., 1986-88; chmn. commn. on phys. scis., math and resources NRC, 1984-86. Recipient Disting. Svc. award Dept. Navy, 1945, 80; medal Soc. Applied Spectroscopy, 1957; Disting. Civilian Svc. award Dept. Def., 1959; Disting. Achievement in Sci. award, 1962; Janssen medal French Photog. Soc., 1962; Presdl. medal for disting. fed. svc., 1964; Eddington medal Royal Astron. Soc., 1964; R.D. Conrad medal Dept. Navy, 1964; Rockefeller Pub. Svc. award, 1967; Nat. Medal Sci., 1969; medal for exceptional sci. achievement NASA, 1970, 78; Michelson medal Franklin Inst., 1972; Dryden Rsch. award, 1973; Wolf Found. prize in physics, 1987; Russell award Am. Astron. Soc., 1980; Sci. award Nat. Space Club, 1990; Janssen medal French Astron. Soc., 1990; Massey medal, Royal Soc. London, 1992. Fellow AIAA (hon., Space Sci. award 1963, Internat. Cooperation in Space Sci. medal 1991), Am. Phys. Soc., Am. Optical Soc., Am. Geophys. Union (pres. sect. on solar-planetary relationships 1967-70, Bowie medal 1981), Am. Astronautical Soc. (Lovelace award 1973), AAAS (v.p. 1972); mem. NAS (council 1979-82, chmn. assembly of math. and phys. scis. 1980-83), Am. Acad. Arts and Scis., Internat. Acad. Astronautics, Am. Philos. Soc. (coun. 1992—); hon. mem. Spl. Com. on Solar-Terrestrial Physics, 1984. Club: Cosmos. Achievements include discovery of solar x-ray emission and its role in control of the ionosphere; demonstration of connection between solar flare x-rays and radio fadeout; identification of x-ray star, the crab pulsar and x-ray galaxy. Home: 2643 N Upshur St Arlington VA 22207-4025 Office: Naval Rsch Lab Code # 7690 Washington DC 20375-5352*

FRIEDMAN, HERBERT A., rabbi, educator, fund raising executive; b. New Haven, Sept. 25, 1918; s. Israel and Rae (Aaronson) F.; children from previous marriage: Judith Rae, Daniel Stephen, Joan Michal; m. Francine Bensley, June 28, 1963; children: David Herbert, Charles Edward. BA, Yale U., 1938; MHL, Jewish Inst. Religion, 1943; DD (hon.), Hebrew Union Coll., 1969. Ordained rabbi, 1944. Rabbi Temple Emanuel, Denver, 1943-52, Milw., 1952-55; exec. chmn. Nat. United Jewish Appeal, N.Y.C., 1955-75; pres. Am. Friends of Tel Aviv U., N.Y.C., 1982-85; pres. Wexner Heritage Found., 1985-95, founding pres., 1995—. Author: Collected Speeches, 1971, Roots of the Future, 1999. Chaplain (capt.) U.S. Army, 1944-47, ETO. Mem. Central Conf. Am. Rabbis, Yale Club (N.Y.C.). Home: 500 E 77th St Apt 2519 New York NY 10162-0008 Office: Wexner Heritage Found 551 Madison Ave New York NY 10022-3212

FRIEDMAN, HOWARD MARTIN, financial executive; b. Bronx, N.Y., Apr. 4, 1948; s. Jerome and Dorothy Ray (Patascher) F.; m. Stephanie Sue Grunin, Aug. 4, 1974; children: Peter Mitchell, Jeffrey Douglas. BA, L.I. U., 1970, postgrad., 1975-77; postgrad., NYU, 1972-73. Registered prin. series 24, registered rep. series 7, registered mcpl. prin. series 53, 63, registered associated person Nat. Futures Assn. Asst. Bache & Co., N.Y.C., 1965-67, Thomson & McKinnon, N.Y.C., 1968-73; asst. cashier Winmill Securities, N.Y.C., 1973-74; cashier C.S. McKee & Co., N.Y.C., 1974-76; gen. ptnr. Easton & Co., Fort Lee, N.J., 1976-92; exec. v.p. Hillcrest Fin. Corp., N.Y.C., 1992-94; with Schonfeld Securities, 1995-97, McMahan Securities, 1998—; firm rep. Depository Trust Co., 1976—, Nat. Securities Clearing Corp., 1976—, Options Clearing Corp., 1976—. Allied mem. N.Y. Stock Exch.; mem. Dividend Div. Securities Assn., Reorganization Div. Securities Industry Assn., Barharbour Assocs. Inc. (pres. 1996—). Avocations: travel, baseball, cycling, card collecting. Home: 5 Teal Ct Marlboro NJ 07746-1901 Office: Barharbour Assoc Inc 5 Teal Ct Marlboro NJ 07746-1901

FRIEDMAN, HOWARD SAMUEL, cardiologist, educator, researcher; b. N.Y.C., Dec. 27, 1940; s. Harry and Bella Esther (Israel) F.; m. Maud Tanowitz, June 18, 1961; children: Shawn Marcus, Saroya Danielle, Heather Eve. BA, Bklyn. Coll., 1962; MD, SUNY, Buffalo, 1966. Intern St. Louis City Hosp., 1966-67; asst. resident Barnes Hosp., St. Louis, 1967-68; asst. resident Mt. Sinai Hosp., N.Y., 1968-69, resident cardiology, 1969-70, 72-73; acting chief cardiology VA Hosp., Bronx, N.Y., 1974-76; chief cardiology Bklyn. Hosp. Ctr., 1977-90; chmn. dept. medicine L.I. Coll. Hosp., Bklyn., 1990-97; attending cardiologist NYU Med. Ctr., N.Y.C., 1998—; prof. medicine SUNY Health Sci. Ctr. at Bklyn., 1987-98; attending NYU Med. Ctr., Bellevue Hosp., 1999—; clin. prof. NYU Med. Sch. Contbr. articles to profl. jours. Dir. Am. Heart Assn. N.Y.C. Affiliate Bd., 1985-88; chmn. Coronary Care Com., 1982-88. Fellow Am. Coll. Physicians, Am. Heart Assn., Am. Coll. Cardiology; mem. Am. Physiology Soc., Soc. for Exptl. Biology and Medicine. Democrat. Jewish. Fax: (212) 889-9511. Home: 401 E 84th St New York NY 10028-6268 Office: 3d Fl 650 1st Ave New York NY 10016

FRIEDMAN, HOWARD W., retired real estate company executive; b. Bklyn., Aug. 21, 1925; s. Harry and Bertha (Wang) F.; m. Lee Hazan, Mar. 22, 1952; children—Ira, Debra, Patti, Jane. B.B.A., CCNY, 1945; C.P.A., N.Y. Treas., Amrep Corp., N.Y.C., 1961-68, pres., 1968-77, chmn., chief exec. officer, 1980-91, cons., 1992-94. Mem. N.Y. State Soc. CPAs. Jewish.

FRIEDMAN, IRA HUGH, surgeon; b. N.Y.C., July 17, 1933; s. Leonard Seymour and Ruth (Binder) F.; m. Erika Berger, Oct. 22, 1961; children—Richard Lawrence, Joanne Beth. B.A., NYU, 1953, M.D., 1957. Diplomate Am. Bd. Surgery, Nat. Bd. Med. Examiners. Intern, resident in surgery Beth Isreal Med. Ctr., N.Y.C., 1957-59, 61-63; surg. resident Bellevue Hosp., N.Y.C., 1959-60; practice medicine specializing in surgery N.Y.C., 1963—; attending surgeon Beth Israel Med. Ctr., pres. med. bd., 1981-82; assoc. clin. prof. surgery Albert Einstein Coll. Medicine; med. adv. to N.Y.C. dir. SSS, 1968. Contbr. articles to profl. jours. Bd. dirs. Union Orthodox Jewish Congregations Am., Am. Com. for Shaare Zedek Hosp. of Jerusalem, Yeshiva Sha-alvim, Isreal, P'Tach; co-chmn. bd. dirs. Yeshiva Chofetz Chaim, N.Y.C. Recipient Koach award Israel Bond Orgn., 1977; N.Y. Heart Assn. fellow, 1960-61. Fellow ACS (elected gov. 1996), Am. Coll. Gastroenterology, Am. Soc. Colon and Rectal Surgeons, Royal Soc. Medicine; mem. AMA, N.Y. Acad. Medicine, N.Y. Surg. Soc., Soc. Surgery of Alimentary Tract, Soc. Am. Gastrointestinal Endoscopic Surgeons, Am. Gastroent. Assn., Am. Soc. Gen. Surgeons, Am. Hernia Soc., N.Y. Gastroent. Assn., N.Y. Cancer Soc., N.Y. Soc. Colon and Rectal Surgeons, Collegium Internationale Chirugiae Digestive, N.Y. State Med. Assn., N.Y. County Med. Assn. Home: 1175 Park Ave New York NY 10128-1211

FRIEDMAN, J. ROGER, publisher; b. N.Y.C., Oct. 26, 1933; s. Arnold Darcy and Judith (Scheinberg) F.; m. Patricia Mosle, Dec. 1, 1962; children: Amanda, Randall. BA in English, Williams Coll., 1955. Salesman, Chain Store Age, Drug Editions, N.Y.C., 1957-61; founder, sales mgr. Discount Store News, N.Y.C., 1961-63, publ. dir., 1963-65; v.p. sales Lebhar-Friedman, Inc., N.Y.C., 1965-68, exec. v.p., 1968-70, pres., 1970—; sec. Chain Store Guide, 1970—. Bd. dirs. Upper Pecos Assn., N.Mex., 1971, Brush Ranch Sch., N.Mex., 1974, Students in Free Enterprise, 1977—; pres., bd. dirs. Am. Bus. Press, 1994—; trustee Bus. Press Ednl. Found., McElvain Oil & Gas Co.; hon. trustee Temple Rodeph Shalom, N.Y.C., 1987. Mem. Lotos (pres. 1983-87), Williams (N.Y.C.) (pres. 1991-95, hon. bd. mem.). Office: Lebhar-Friedman Inc 425 Park Ave Ste 501 New York NY 10022-3549

FRIEDMAN, JAMES DENNIS, lawyer; b. Dubuque, Iowa, Jan. 11, 1947; s. Elmer J. and Rosemary Catherine (Stillmunkes) F.; m. Kathleen Marie Maersch, Aug. 16, 1969; children: Scott, Ryan, Andrea, Sean. AB in Polit. Sci., Marquette U., 1969; JD, U. Notre Dame, 1972. Bar: Wis. 1972, U.S. Supreme Ct. 1978, U.S. Ct. Appeals (D.C. cir.) 1973, U.S. Ct. Appeals (7th cir.) 1976, U.S. Ct. Appeals (6th cir.) 1989, Ill. 1996, U.S. Tax Ct. 1997. Pvt. practice Milw., 1972-81; ptnr. Quarles & Brady, Milw., 1981—; presenter in field; mem. legis. coun. spl. study com. on regulation of fin.

instns. State of Wis., 1986-87; bd. dirs. Am. Paper and Packaging Corp., Concours Motors, Inc., Equal Justice Coalition, Inc. Mng. Editor: Notre Dame Law Review, 1971-72; contbr. articles to profl. jours. Alderman 4th and 7th dists. Mequon, Wis., 1979-85, pres. common coun., 1980-82, bd. ethics 1996-98, chair blue ribbon visioning com. 1998—; bd. dirs. Weyenrg. Pub. Libr. Found. Inc., 1983—, pres., 1984—; bd. dirs. Ptnrs. Advancing Values in Edn. Inc., 1987—, Wis. Law Found., 1998—; bd. visitors Marquette U. Ctr. for Study of Entrepreneurship, Milw., 1987-95; bd. dirs. Ozaukee Family Svcs., 1983—, sec., 1993-98; bd. dirs. Notre Dame Club of Milw., 1984-88, sec., 1978, v.p., 1986-88; bd. dirs. Marquette Club of Milw., 1987-88; chair attys. unit United Way Fund Dr. Greater Milw., 1987; mem. St. James Ch., Mequon. Named Outstanding Sr., Coll. of Liberal Arts, Marquette U. Mem. ABA (banking law com. sect. bus. law), State Bar Wis. (chair bd. govs. 1999—, chair exec. com. 1999—, fin. com. 1997-98, strategic planning task force 1997-98, bd. govs. 1996—, exec. com. 1998—, internat. transactions sect. bd. dirs. 1984—, sec. and chair-elect 1988-89, chair 1989-90, del. to ABA Ho. of Dels. 1980-82, standing com. on adminstrn. justice and judiciary 1979-81, legal edn. and bar admissions com. 1984-89, com. on minority lawyers 1992—, chmn. 1997—, bd. dirs. young lawyers divsn. 1978-82, chmn. divsn. bar admission stds. and requirements com. 1979, So. Regional chair 1998-99), Milw. Bar Assn., Wis. Acad. Trial Lawyers (bd. dirs. 1980-82), Wis. Bankers Assn., Milw. Country Club, Sigma Phi Epsilon. Roman Catholic. Avocations: tennis, golf. Office: Quarles & Brady 411 E Wisconsin Ave Milwaukee WI 53202-4409

FRIEDMAN, JAMES MOSS, lawyer; b. Cleve., Aug. 1, 1941; s. Senor I. and Rose L. (Moskowitz) F.; m. Ruth E. Aidlin, Aug. 2, 1964; children: Laura M., Seth M. AB, Dartmouth Coll., 1963; JD, Harvard U., 1966. Bar: Ohio 1966, U.S. Ct. Appeals (6th cir.) 1966, U.S. Dist. Ct. (no. dist.) Ohio 1967. Law clk. U.S. Ct. Appeals, 6th Cir., 1966-67; assoc. Gottfried, Ginsberg, Guren & Merritt, Cleve., 1967-71; chief staff Ohio Gov. John J. Gilligan, Columbus, 1971-72; ptnr. Guren, Merritt, Feibel, Sogg & Cohen, Cleve., 1972-84, Benesch, Friedlander, Coplan & Aronoff, Cleve., 1984—; chmn. Ohio Civil Rights Commn., 1972-74; dir. Overseas Pvt. Investment Corp., Washington, 1978-82; spl. counsel Ohio Atty. Gen., Cleve., 1983-94. Co-author: The Silent Alliance, 1984. Vice chmn. nat. fin. coun. Dem. Nat. Com., 1975-85; pres. Fedn. for Cmty. Planning, Cleve., 1989-92; bd. dirs. United Way Svcs., Cleve., 1989-92, Cuyahoga C.C. Found., 1989-95; bd. dirs. Citizens League Greater Cleve., 1989-95, v.p., 1993-95; pres. Fairmount Temple, 1993-96; mem. Am. Jewish Com., 1981—, pres. Cleve. chpt., 1991-93; mem. nat. bd. trustees Union Am. Hebrew Congregation, 1991—, mem. exec. com., 1997—. Jewish. Office: Benesch Friedlander 2300 BP Town Bldg 200 Public Sq Ste 2300 Cleveland OH 44114-2378

FRIEDMAN, JAMES WINSTEIN, economist, educator; b. Cleve., Sept. 25, 1936; s. Theodore and Gertrude (Winstein) F.; m. Marcia Sherman, Aug. 11, 1957; children: Nancy Elizabeth, Robert U. Student, MIT, 1954-56; BA, U. Mich., 1959; MA, Yale U., 1960, PhD, 1963. Instr., then asst. prof. econs. Yale U., 1963-68; assoc. prof. U. Rochester (N.Y.), 1968-72, prof. econs., 1972-83; prof. Va. Poly Inst., Blacksburg, 1983-85; Kenan prof. U. N.C., Chapel Hill, 1985—; mem. rsch. staff Cowles Found., 1963-68, asst. dir., 1964-66; vis. prof. U. Bielefeld, Fed. Republic Germany, 1976, 87-88, Hebrew U., Jerusalem, 1979, Cath. U. Louvain, Belgium, 1987, 91, 99, U. Paris, 1991, 93, U. Alicante, Spain, 1992, U. Kobe, Japan, 1994. Author: Oligopoly and the Theory of Games, 1977, The Theory of Oligopoly, 1983, Game Theory with Applications to Economics, 1986, 2d edit., 1990; co-author: An Experiment in Noncooperative Oligopoly, 1979; editor: Problems of Coordination in Economic Activity, 1994; assoc. editor Japanese Econ. Rev., 1994—, Regional Sci. and Urban Econs., 1997—, Games and Econ. Behavior, 1998—; contbr. articles to profl. jours. Fellow Econometric Soc. (assoc. editor jour. 1975-81); mem. Am. Econ. Soc. Avocation: hiking. Office: U NC Dept Econs CB# 3305 Chapel Hill NC 27599-3305

FRIEDMAN, JEROME ISAAC, physics educator, researcher; b. Chgo., Mar. 28, 1930; married, 1956; 4 children. A.B., U. Chgo., 1950, M.S., 1953, Ph.D. in Physics, 1956. Research assoc. in physics U. Chgo., 1956-57; research assoc. in physics Stanford U., Calif., 1957-60; from asst. prof. to assoc. prof. MIT, Cambridge, 1960-67, prof. physics, 1967—, dir. lab. nuclear sci., 1980-83, head dept. physics, 1983-88, William A. Collidge prof., 1988-90, instr. prof., 1990—. Recipient Nobel prize in physics, 1990. Fellow AAAS, Am. Phys. Soc. (co-recipient W.H.K. Panofsky prize 1989); mem. NAS, Am. Acad. Arts and Scis. Office: MIT Room 24-502 Dept Physics Cambridge MA 02139*

FRIEDMAN, JOAN M., accounting educator; b. N.Y.C., Nov. 30, 1949; d. Alvin E. and Pesselle Gail (Rothenberg) F.; m. Charles E. Blair III, Sept. 20, 1992. AB magna cum laude, Harvard U., 1971; MA, Courtauld Inst., U. London, 1973; MS with honors, Columbia U., 1974; MAS, U. Ill., 1993. CPA, Ill. Asst. research librarian Beinecke Library, New Haven, Conn., 1974-75; asst. research librarian Yale Ctr. for Brit. Art, New Haven, Conn., 1975-76, curator of rare books, 1976-90; computer cons., teaching asst. dept. accountancy U. Ill., Champaign, 1990-95; vis. asst. prof. acctg. Ill. Wesleyan U., Bloomington, Ill., 1995-99; asst. prof. acctg. Ill. Wesleyan U., Bloomington, IL, 1999—; cons. Johns Hopkins U., Balt., 1983; tchr. Sch. Library Service Columbia U., 1983-88, Sysop WordPerfect Users Forum on CompuServe, 1987—, Sysop, Tapcis Forum on CompuServe, 1988-95. Author: Color Printing in England, 1978; contbr. articles in field. Recipient student achievement award Fedn. Schs. Accountancy, 1993; Nat. Merit scholar Harvard U., 1967; Moss Accountancy fellow U. Ill. 1990. Mem. ALA (chmn. rare books and manuscripts sect. 1982-83), Bibliog. Soc. Am. (coun. 1982-86, sec. 1986-88), Am. Printing History Assn., Phi Beta Kappa, Beta Phi Mu. Jewish. Clubs: Grolier (N.Y.C.); Elizabethan (New Haven). Avocations: microcomputers, bicycling. Office: Ill Wesleyan U Divsn Bus & Econs PO Box 2900 Bloomington IL 61702-2900

FRIEDMAN, JOEL MATTHEW, oral and maxillofacial surgeon, educator; b. Chelsea, Mass., Sept. 20, 1942; s. Abraham and Theda (Epstein) F.; m. Gail Fishman, Dec. 18, 1965 (div. 1981); 1 child, Alison Beth; m. Carole Nadan, May 31, 1981 (dec.); m. Susan K. Shavin, Dec., 1990 (div. 1994); m. Marian G. Faytell, Apr. 9, 1995. BA, Hofstra U., 1964; DDS, Columbia U., 1968. Diplomate Am. Bd. Oral and Maxillofacial Surgery. Intern Bronx Mcpl. Hosp.-Albert Einstein Coll. Medicine, 1968-69, resident in oral and maxillofacial surgery, 1969-71; practice dentistry specializing oral/maxillofacial surgery Bronx, 1971—, Yonkers, N.Y., 1986—; dir. oral and maxillofacial surgery Albert Einstein Coll. Medicine-Bronx Mcpl. Hosp., 1971-78, dir. house-staff edn., 1971-78, dir. oral and maxillofacial surgery, 1978-92; assoc. clin. prof. dentistry Albert Einstein Coll. Medicine, 1976—; asst. dir. oral and maxillofacial surgery Albert Einstein Coll. Medicine-Montefiore Med. Ctr., 1983-92; dir. oral and maxillofacial surgery Yonkers Gen. Hosp., 1988-98; vice-chmn. oral and maxillofacial surgery St. Johns Riverside Hosp., Yonkers; assoc. clin. prof. oral and maxillofacial surgery Columbia U. Sch. Dental and Oral Surgery, 1994—; assoc. attending Presbyn. Hosp., N.Y.C., 1994—. Contbr. articles to profl. jours. Chmn. Bronx Health Sys. Agy. Bd., 1977-78, Montefiore Cmty. Adv. Bd., 1977-90; pres. MMC-CAB, 1981-84; trustee Congregation B'Nai Jeshurun, N.Y.C., 1996—. Fellow Am. Dental Soc. Anesthesiology, Am. Coll. Dentists, Am. Coll. Oral and Maxillofacial Surgeons, Internat. Coll. Dentists; mem. ADA, Am. Soc. Oral and Maxillofacial Surgeons, Am. Dental Soc. Anethesiology (Heidbrink award com.), N.Y. State Dental Soc. (gov. 1998—), N.Y. State Dental Soc. Anesthesiology (pres. 1981), Bronx County Dental Soc. (treas. 1988-90, v.p. 1991-92, pres.-elect 1993-95, pres. 1995-97), Riverdale Dental Study Group, Jarvie Soc., Riverdale Mental Health Assn. (profl. adv. com. 1973—, bd. dirs. 1979—, asst. treas. 1987), Nat. Young Judaea Alumni Assn. (pres. 1990-91), N.Y. State Dental Soc. (gov. 1998—), Hadassah Zionist Youth Commn. N.Y.C. Democrat. Jewish. Avocation: skiing. Home: 185 E 85th St Apt 33B New York NY 10028-2144 Office: 3333 Henry Hudson Pkwy W Bronx NY 10463-3224

FRIEDMAN, JOEL WILLIAM, law educator; b. N.Y.C., Mar. 16, 1951; s. Max Aaron and Muriel (Yudien) F.; m. Vivian Stoleru, Apr. 5, 1987; children: Alexa Erica, Chloe Gabriella, Max Aaron. BS, Cornell U., 1972; JD, Yale U., 1975. Bar: Calif. 1975, U.S. Dist. Ct. (cen. dist.) Calif. 1975. Asst. prof. Tulane U., New Orleans, 1976-79, assoc. prof., 1979-82, prof. law, 1982—, C.J. Morrow prof. law, 1985-86, dir. technology, 1996—; vis. prof. law U. Tel Aviv, Israel, 1983, U. Tex. Law Sch., 1985-86, Chuo Law Sch., Tokyo, 1988, Hebrew U. of Jerusalem Law Sch., 1990; lectr. Fed. Jud. Ctr., Washington, 1987—; cons. La. Ho. of Reps., Baton Rouge, 1982-85, West Group, 1996—; bd. dirs. Ctr. for Computer-Assisted Legal Instrn., 1996; spl. master Pasadena Ind. Sch. Dist., Houston, 1987-93. Editor: Cases and Mat erials on Law of Employment Discrimination, 1983, 4th edit., 1997; contbr. articles to law revs. Pres., bd. dirs. Woldenberg Village, Inc., 1995-97; v.p., bd. dirs. Jewish Fedn. Greater New Orleans, 1995—. Recipient Felix Frankfurter faculty award for disting. tchg. Tulane Law Sch., 1989; Fulbright scholar Israel, 1990. Co-chmn. New Orleans Cmty. Rels. Com., 1984. Mem. Am. Assn. Law Schs. (chair sect. on employment discrimination law 1987-88), Am. Law Inst., B'nai B'rith Hillel Found. (pres. New Orleans 1987-91), Internat. Assn. of Jewish Lawyers and Jurists La. Br. (pres. 1994-95). Democrat. Avocations: running, squash, scuba diving, skiing. Home: 1230 State St New Orleans LA 70118-6027 Office: Tulane Law Sch 6329 Freret St New Orleans LA 70118-6231

FRIEDMAN, JOHN MAXWELL, JR., lawyer; b. N.Y.C., Oct. 31, 1944; s. John M. and Jane (Blum) F.; m. Laurie Suzanne Nevin, July 8, 1973 (div. 1988); children: David, Michael; m. Judith Zuckerman, Mar. 5, 1989; 1 child, Julia. AB, Princeton U., 1966; MA, U. Sussex, Brighton, Eng., 1967; JD, U. Chgo., 1970. Bar: N.Y. 1971, U.S. Ct. Appeals (2d cir.) 1971, U.S. Dist. Ct. (so. and ea. dist.) N.Y. 1972, U.S. Supreme Ct. 1974. Assoc. Dewey Ballantine, N.Y.C., 1970-78, ptnr., 1978-96. Home: 62 Barker Rd New Milford CT 06776-4902

FRIEDMAN, K. BRUCE, lawyer; b. Buffalo, Jan. 1, 1929; s. Bennett and Florence Ruth (Israel) F.; m. Lois G. Rosoff, June 15, 1986. A.B., Harvard U., 1950; LL.B., Yale U., 1953. Bar: N.Y. 1955, D.C. 1956, Calif. 1958. Atty. CAB, Washington, 1955-57; practiced in San Francisco, 1958—; mem. firm Zang, Friedman & Damir, 1969-78, Cotton, Seligman & Ray, 1978-79, Friedman, Olive, McCubbin, Spalding, Bilter, Roosevelt & Montgomery, San Francisco, 1980—; lectr. law U. Calif. Law Sch., Berkeley, 1966-76; Pres. Econ. Roundtable San Francisco, 1964. Bd. dirs. San Francisco chpt. Am. Jewish Com., 1960-76; trustee World Affairs Council No. Calif., San Francisco, 1970-76; pres. San Francisco Estate Planning Council, 1973-74; regional dir. for No. Calif. Asso. Harvard Alumni, 1981-84. Served with U.S. Army, 1953-55. Fellow Am. Coll. Trust and Estate Counsel, Am. Bar Found.; mem. ABA, State Bar Calif., San Francisco Bar Assn., Internat. Acad. Estate and Trust Law (treas. 1996—), Am. Law Inst., San Francisco Com. on Fgn. Rels., U. Calif. San Francisco Found., Univ. Club, Calif. Tennis Club, Commonwealth Club Calif., Harvard Club of San Francisco (pres. 1976-78), Rotary. Jewish. Office: Friedman Olive McCubbin Spalding Bilter Roosevelt & Montgomery 425 California St Ste 2200 San Francisco CA 94104-2207

FRIEDMAN, LAWRENCE M., law educator; b. Chgo., Apr. 2, 1930; s. I. M. and Ethel (Shapiro) F.; m. Leah Feigenbaum, Mar. 27, 1955; children: Jane, Amy. AB, U. Chgo., 1948, JD, 1951, LLM, 1953; LLD (hon.), U. Puget Sound, 1977, CUNY, 1989, U. Lund, Sweden, 1993, John Marshall Law Sch., 1995, U. Macerata, Italy, 1998. Mem. faculty St. Louis U., 1957-61, U. Wis., 1961-68; prof. law Stanford U., 1968—, Marion Rice Kirkwood prof., 1976—; David Stouffer Meml. lectr. Rutgers U. Law Sch., 1969; Sibley lectr. U. Ga. Law Sch., 1976; Wayne Morse lectr. U. Oreg., 1985; Childress meml. lectr. St. Louis U., 1987; Jefferson Meml. lectr. U. Calif., 1994; Higgins vis. prof. Lewis and Clark U., 1998. Author: Contract Law in America, 1965, Government and Slum Housing, 1968, A History of American Law, 1973, 2d edit., 1985, The Legal System: A Social Science Perspective, 1975, Law and Society: An Introduction, 1977, (with Robert V. Percival) The Roots of Justice, 1981, American Law, 1984, Total Justice, 1985, Your Time Will Come, 1985, The Republic of Choice, 1990, Crime and Punishment in American History, 1993; co-editor: (with Stewart Macaulay) Law and the Behavioral Sciences, 1969, 2d edit., 1977, (with Harry N. Scheiber) American Law and the Constitutional Order, 1978, Legal Culture and the Legal Profession, 1996, (with Stewart Macaulay and John Stookey) Law and Society: Readings on the Social Study of Law, 1995, (with George Fisher) The Crime Conundrum, 1997, The Horizontal Society, 1999; contbr. articles to profl. jours. Served with U.S. Army, 1953-54. Recipient Triennial award Order of Coif, 1976, Willard Hurst prize, 1982, Harry Kalven prize, 1992, Silver Gavel award ABA, 1994; Ctr. for Advanced Study in Behavioral Sci. fellow, 1974-75, fellow Inst. Advanced Study, Berlin, 1985. Mem. Law and Soc. Assn. (pres. 1979-81), Am. Acad. Arts and Scis., Am. Soc. for Legal History (v.p. 1987-89, pres. 1990-91), Soc. of Am. Historians. Home: 724 Frenchmans Rd Palo Alto CA 94305-1005 Office: Stanford U Law Sch Nathan Abbott Way Stanford CA 94305-9991

FRIEDMAN, LAWRENCE MILTON, lawyer; b. Chgo., Apr. 2, 1945; s. Armin C. and Mildred T. F.; m. Linda M. Eisenstein, June 25, 1967; children: Benjamin J., David K. BA, U. Ill., 1966; JD, Ohio State U., 1969. Bar: Ill. 1970, U.S. Tax Ct. 1970; CPA, Md., Ill. Ptnr. Coopers & Lybrand, Chgo., 1969-85, Lord, Bissell & Brook, Chgo., 1985—; adj. prof. law IIT Chgo. Kent Coll. Law, Chgo., 1990—, dir., 1980—; mem. adv. bd. Hartford Inst. Ins. Tax, 1995—; spkr. on mergers, aquisitions and taxation. Mem. adv. bd. Ins. Tax Rev., 1987—; contbr. articles to law jours. Sec.-treas., dir. North Shore Performing Arts Ctr. Found. in Skokie, Ill., 1993-97; vice chmn., dir. Jewish Fedn. Met. Chgo., 1992—. Mem. ABA, AICPA, Chgo. Fed. Tax Forum. Office: Lord Bissell & Brook 115 S La Salle St Ste 3200 Chicago IL 60603-3972

FRIEDMAN, LEE GARY, network media solutions architect; b. Oceanside, N.Y., Feb. 21, 1956; s. Seymour Jerome and Naomi Sonia (Mogul) F.; m. Brenda Sue Nannemacher, July 24, 1981; children: Cory, Hannah. BS in Computer Engring., Syracuse U., 1981, MS in Computer Engring., 1983. Cons. Infinite Solutions, Syracuse, N.Y., 1980-84; staff engr. IBM Thomas J. Watson Rsch., Yorktown Heights, N.Y., 1984-86; sr. cons. analyst NCR, Dayton, Ohio, 1986-89; sr. engr. NCR, Atlanta, 1989-91; multimedia technologies mgr. AT&T, Atlanta, 1991-94; chief tech. officer AT&T Human Interface Ctr., Atlanta, 1994-95; chief architect NCR, Atlanta, 1995—; adv. bd. Ga. Tech., Atlanta, 1987-95; CEO Infinite Ideas, Alpharetta, Ga., 1996—; chief tech. ofcr. AT&T Human Interface Ctr., Atlanta, 1994-95; disting. mem. technical staff BellSouth Sci. and Tech., 1997—. Patentee in field. Mem. Assn. Computing Machinery (vis.), IEEE (vis.). Avocations: animation, computer art, photography, scuba diving, hiking. E-mail: LGF@iideasinc.com. Office: Infinite Ideas 10615 Timberstone Rd Alpharetta GA 30022-7519

FRIEDMAN, LOUIS FRANK, lawyer; b. Balt., May 26, 1941; s. Dave Sylvan and Miriam (Sugarman) F.; m. Phyllis Cole, Dec. 25, 1968; 1 son, Samuel. B.S., U. Md., 1963, J.D., 1965; LL.M. in Taxation, Georgetown U., 1968. Bar: Md. 1965. Since practiced in Balt.; ptnr. firm Friedman & Friedman, 1965—; prof. taxation U. Balt. Sch. Bus., 1975-88. Pres. 9400 Ocean Hwy. Condominium, Ocean City, Md., 1976; chmn. young lawyers div. Asso. Jewish Charities, 1975-76. Mem. Md. Bar Assn. (tax counsel 1977-79), Order of Coif, Phi Alpha Delta. Jewish. Lodges: Masons (tax counsel Masonic Charities Md. Inc. 1987—), Amicable. Home: 19 Hambleton Ct Baltimore MD 21208-3333 Office: Merc Bank Bldg 409 Washington Ave Baltimore MD 21204-4920

FRIEDMAN, LYNN JOSEPH, counselor; b. New Orleans, Jan. 12, 1949; d. Leonard Cerf and Paula Rose (Levy) Joseph; children; Rebecca, Naomi. BS, La. State U., 1970; MEd, U. Tex., 1971; PhD, U. New Orleans, 1995. Tchr. Orleans Parish Schs., New Orleans, 1971-73; rehab. counselor L.A. Div. Rehab. Svcs., Metairie, 1973-87, Intracorp, Metairie, 1987-91, GAB Robins/Med Insights, Metairie, 1991—; counselor Metro Battered Women, Metairie, 1990-92; edn. dir. Congregation Gates of Prayer, New Orleans, 1971-75. Contbr. articles to profl. jours. Named Counselor of Yr. Goodall Rehab., 1980; recipient Cert. Appreciation Nat. Assn. Ret. Citizens, 1974, Magnolia Sch., 1976. Mem. ACA (La. Grad. Student of Yr. 1991), Nat. Rehab. Assn. (La. Counselor of Yr. 1979), Chi Sigma Iota (treas. 1990-91, v.p. 1991-92). Democrat. Jewish. Home: 4721 Loveland St Metairie LA 70006-4027 Office: GAB Robins/Med Insights 4721 Loveland St Metairie LA 70006

FRIEDMAN, MARIA ANDRE, public relations executive; b. Jackson, Mich., June 12, 1950; m. Stanley N. Friedman; children: Alexandra, Adam. BA cum laude, U. Md., 1972, MA, 1979; DBA, Nova U., 1993. Writer U.S. Bur. Mines, Washington, 1973-78; head writer Nat. Ctr. Health Svc. Rsch./Healthcare Tech. DHHS, Rockville, Md., 1978-85; chief publs. and info. br. Agy. for Healthcare Policy and Rsch., 1986-89; dir. office pub. affairs Healthcare Fin. Adminstrn., Washington, 1990—, acting assoc. adminstr. for comm., 1992-93; sr. rsch. advisor Healthcare Fin. Adminstrn., Balt., 1994-95, dir. disemination staff ORB, 1995-96, sr. advisor for ins. reform, 1997-99, Y2K outreach coord. for medicaid program, 1999—. Mem. Assn. Health Svcs. Rsch., Acad. of Mgmt. Home: 713 Brandon Green Dr Silver Spring MD 20904-3564 Office: Health Care Fin Adminstrn 7500 Security Blvd Baltimore MD 21244-1849

FRIEDMAN, MARION, internist, family physician, medical administrator, medical editor; b. Onley, Va., Aug. 15, 1918; s. Jacob and Bertha (Bernstein) F.; m. Esther Lerner, May 29, 1941; 1 son, Barry Howard. BS, U. Md., 1938, MD, 1942. Diplomate Am. Bd. Family Practice (charter). Rotating intern U.S. Marine Hosp., Norfolk, Va., 1942-43; asst. health officer Montgomery County, Kans., 1943-44; health officer Cherokee County, Kans., 1944-45; asst. health commr. St. Louis County, Mo., 1945-46; resident internal medicine U.S. Marine Hosp., Balt., 1946-49; fellow medicine Johns Hopkins Sch. Medicine, Balt., 1948-49; pvt. practice in internal medicine and family medicine Balt., 1949-84; asst. medicine U. Md., Balt., 1954-72; chief dept. gen. practice Doctors Hosp., 1952-54; chief dept. family practice N. Charles Gen. Hosp., Balt., 1972-75, med. dir. ambulatory svcs., 1972-86, assoc. chief medicine, 1975-88; pres. med. staff, 1964, 68, chmn. med. exec. com. 1984-85, trustee, 1984-85, physician advisor 1984-91; physician advisor Delmarva Found. for Med. Care, 1984-90, 92-95; instr. Ctr. for Health Edn., 1985; lectr. Md. affiliate Am. Heart Assn., 1986-87; med. dir. Chesapeake Health Plan, 1991-92; task force on improving access to primary care Md.-DC AFL-CIO, 1993-94, consumer-managed care rels. task force, 1996. Contbr. numerous articles to sci. jours. Mem. profl. adv. bd. Patient Care, 1994-96; chmn. cultural com. Liberty Jewish Ctr., 1960-62; mem. Md. High Blood Pressure Coordinating Coun., 1980-82; mem. task force on family physicians Md. Health Resources Planning Commn., Md. State Legislature, 1983-84; trustee Jimmie Swartz Found., 1982-95. With USPHS, 1942-49; lt. col. Md. Def. Force, 1995—. Fellow Am. Acad. Family Physicians (charter), Md. Acad. Family Physicians (chmn. comm. on health care svcs. 1978-83, 84-92, pres. 1983-84, mem. rsch. panel influenza surveillance network 1983, prodn. editor 1984-86, editor 1986—, Chpt. Publ. award 1991, chmn. manpower adv. com. 1992-95, award superb compiling, writing and editing spl. 50th ann. history edit. Md. Family Doctor 1998); mem. AMA, AAAS, Am. Acad. Family Physicians, Balt. City Med. Soc. (alt. del. 1978-82, 93-94, del. 1982-88, profl. edn. com. 1985-87, chmn. 1987-90, nominating com. 1992), Med. and Chirurg. Faculty Md. (lectr. 1983, legis. com. 1985-87, 90-93, pro com. 1989-94, std. benefits tech. adv. com. 1993-94, mem. editl. bd. Md. Med. Jour. 1994-96, co-editor Nov. 1995, editor 1996—, scientific activities com. 1995—, Dr. Henry P. & M. Page Laughlin Dist. Editl. award 1997), World Med. Assn., Pan-Am. Med. Assn., md. Heart Assn., Am. Lung Assn. (mem. planning com. 1994—), Am. Thoracic Soc., Am. Heart Assn., Md. Taxpayers Assn. (bd. dirs. 1994—, sec. 1996-97, mem. exec. com. 1996—), Am. Lung Assn. (Md. chpt.), Phi Kappa Phi (hon. Scholastic Soc. 1938). Democrat. Achievements include contbr. over 60 scientific artiles and notes including first to suggest use of steroid in subacutre deltoid bursis in world lit., 1952. Home: 7906 Terrapin Ct Baltimore MD 21208-3126

FRIEDMAN, MARK JOEL, cardiologist, educator; b. N.Y.C., 1944; s. Hyman and Sylvia (Baumgarten) F.; m. Barbara Lynn Rauch, Oct. 11, 1969; 1 child, Gregory N. BA cum laude, Syracuse U., 1967; MD, N.Y. Med. Coll., 1971. Cert. in internal medicine, specialty in cardiovasc. disease. Intern Mt. Sinai Hosp., N.Y.C., 1971-72, resident in medicine, 1972-74; fellow in cardiology U. Ariz., 1976-78; active staff St. Francis Hosp., Tulsa, 1981—; prof. medicine U. Okla. Tulsa Med. Coll., 1982—. Contbr. articles to profl. jours. Fellow Am. Coll. Cardiology, Am. Heart Assn.; mem. AMA, Alpha Omega Alpha. Office: Springer Clinic Cardi 6151 S Yale Ave Tulsa OK 74136-1900

FRIEDMAN, MARLA LEE, creative services company executive, author; b. Chgo., May 26, 1953; d. Martin P. and Charlotte K. (Beilenson) F. *Grandfather Paul emigrated with his family from Europe to fulfill a dream: "...to own a building built on American soil...". He earned his Civil Engineering degree and learned several languages before departing. During his lifetime, he owned residential buildings in Chicago--a dream fulfilled. Sharing his good fortune, he gifted a homeless man with a free apartment and a job, inspiring Marla's favorite short story. Grandfather Paul's writing advice to Marla: "...always be yourself...a horse can travel the world over, but when he returns home he remains a horse..." His son, Martin, also enjoys creative talents, including writing and woodcrafts.* BSC in Commerce, DePaul U., Chgo., 1977; MBA wih honors, Roosevelt U., Chgo., 1985. Gen. mgr., adminstr. Chgo. Ctr. for Devel. Learning, Inc., 1975-77; dist. health claims adminstrn. analyst Washington Nat. Ins. Co., Evanston, Ill., 1977-80; unit coord. computer resource liaison Luth. Gen. Hosp., Park Ridge, Ill., 1980—; author fiction and nonfiction Glenview, Ill., 1990—; pres., owner Dancing By Candlelight, 1996—; mem. associated writing programs George Mason U. *Marla possesses a highly diverse background, rich in academics and pragmatic experiences. These multicolored threads provide the material to weave words into magical tapestries of stories and articles capturing life's dramatic moments. She has authored a variety of works over the past eight years. Among her most notable works are three novel excerpts, two of which appeared in The Ecphorizer, A Mensa Magazine of Literature and Ideas. She has also formed a creative services company, Dancing By Candlelight, and is launching a new Wedding Division this year, featuring unique invitation ensembles. She also developed a consulting division, known as Beyond Page 2.* Contbr. prose poem Chips Off the Writer's Block, 1992, columnist, 1994; contbr. poem Guided By Voices Anthology, 1998; author short stories, children's stories, novels and articles. Recipient Editors Choice award N.Am. Poetry Open Competition, 1998, awards for nonfiction articles. Fellow Life Mgmt. Soc. (cert. fin. scis.); mem. NAFE, Acad. Am. Poets. Avocations: drama, music, creative cookery. Fax: 847-724-9798. E-mail: BeyondPage2MLF@Compuserve.com.

FRIEDMAN, MARTIN, museum director, arts adviser; b. Pitts., Sept. 23, 1925; s. Israel and Etta (Louik) F.; m. Mildred Shenberg, Sept. 3, 1949; children: Lise, Ceil, Zoe. Student, U. Pa., 1943-45; BA, U. Wash., 1947; MA, UCLA, 1949; postgrad., Columbia, 1956-57, U. Minn., 1958-60; LHD (hon.), U. Minn., 1990, Bates Coll., 1983; DFA (hon.), Macalester Coll., 1983; LHD (hon.), Md. Inst., 1983; DFA (hon.), Hamline U., 1987, Phila. Coll. of Art and Design, 1989. Instr. art, curriculum cons. Los Angeles City Schs., 1949-56; instr. art U. Calif. Extension, Los Angeles, 1950-51; fellow Bklyn. Mus., 1956-57; grantee Belgian-Am. Ednl. Found., Brussels, 1957-58; fellow Am. art U. Minn., 1959-60; curator Walker Art Center, Mpls., 1958-60; dir. Walker Art Center, 1961-90, dir. emeritus, 1990—; mem. mus. adv. com. NEA, 1973-78, adv. coun. internat. exhbns., 1987-91, Nat. Coun. Arts, 1978-84, Smithsonian Coun., 1988-93; adv. Am. Ctr. Paris, 1990-92, Fed. Art Com. Internat. Exhbns., 1987-91; adviser art program Hall Family Found., 1991—, Nat. Gallery Art, Washington, 1991-92, Nelson Atkins Mus. Art, Kansas City, Mo., 1991-92, contemporary art Va. Mus. Fine Arts, Richmond, 1992-93; guest curator Landscape as Metaphor exhbn. Denver Art Mus., 1992-94, Columbus Mus. Art, 1992-94; Am. fine arts commr. São Paulo Bienal, 1963; mem. Nat. Collection Fine Arts Commn., Washington, Commn. on Founds. and Pvt. Philanthropy; hon. mem. commn. Nat. Mus. Am. Art, Washington; mem. adv. bd. on environ. planning Bur. Reclamation, Washington, 1965-69; art adv. com. Japan House Gallery, N.Y.C.; adviser Ind. Curators, Inc., N.Y. Author numerous catalogues on internat. contemporary art, also books, articles; dir. numerous mus. exhbns. Trustee Spring Hill Found., Minn., 1970-81; trustee Am. Fedn. Arts, 1972-85; mem. Internat. Mus. Com., Washington, 1976-78; mem. vis. com. J. Paul Getty Mus., Malibu, Calif., 1990-95. Ford Found. fellow, 1961-62; artist fellow Aspen Inst. Humanistic Studies, 1980, Intellectual Interchange fellow, Tokyo, 1982, Japan Found. fellow, 1991; Asian Cultural Coun. grantee, 1995; recipient Disting. Svc. award Mid-Am. Coll. Art Assn., 1987, Nat. Medal of Arts, White House, 1990, Lifetime Achievement award Internat. Sculpture Ctr., 1999; decorated officer Arts et Lettres (France); honoree DIA Ctr. for the Arts, 1997. Mem. Coll. Art Assn., Assn. Art Mus. Dirs. (pres. 1978-79, trustee 1979-81, citation for disting. svc. 1990), Soc. for Typographic Arts (hon.).

FRIEDMAN, MARTIN BURTON, chemical company executive; b. N.Y.C., June 21, 1927; s. William L. and Ella (Holstein) F.; m. Rita Fleischman, Mar. 19, 1950; children—Jay Edward, Ellen Jane. Student, Mt. St. Mary's

Coll., 1943-44, Cornell U., 1944-45; B.A., Pa. State U., 1949. Mgr. advt. and promotion chems. group Sun Chem. Corp., N.Y.C., 1949-54; mgr. advt. and promotion textile chems. dept. Am. Cyanamid Co., N.Y.C., 1954-58; mgr. advt. and promotion, organic chems. div. Am. Cyanamid Co., 1958-60, gen. merchandising mgr., mgr. fibers div., 1961-64, dir. sales, 1964-65, dir. mktg., 1965-69, asst. gen. mgr. fibers div., 1969-72; v.p. IRC Fibers Co. (subs.), 1969-72; exec. v.p. Formica Corp., Cin., 1972-73; pres. Formica Corp., 1973-80; pres. fibers div. Am. Cyanamid, 1980-84, corp. v.p., 1984-90; chmn. bd. 4th Dist. Fed. Res. Bank, Cin.; adj. prof. Ramapo Coll., 1990-98; chmn. Mgmt. Decision Lab., NYU Grad. Sch. Bus., 1990-98. Author: The Leadership Myth; contbr. articles to textile and tech. publs. Served with USNR, 1945-46. Mem. Am. Chem. Soc., Am. Assn. Textile Chemists and Colorists. Club: Chemists (N.Y.C.). Home: 777 Butternut Dr Franklin Lakes NJ 07417-2281 *Integrity should permeate every discussion of every facet of leadership. Integrity is the basic quality to be sought in consideration of any person's qualifications for assuming a position of trust and responsibility.*

FRIEDMAN, MAURICE STANLEY, religious educator; b. Tulsa, Dec. 29, 1921; s. Samuel Herman and Fanny (Smirin) F.; m. Eugenia Chifos, Jan. 1947 (div. 1974); children: David Michael, Dvora Lisa; m. Aleene Maree Wright Dorn, Sept. 29, 1986. SB in Econs. magna cum laude, Harvard U., 1943; MA in English, Ohio State U., 1947; PhD in History of Culture, U. Chgo., 1950; LLD (hon.), U. Vt., 1961; MA in Psychology, Internat. Coll., 1983; LHD (hon.), Profl. Sch. Psychol. Studies, San Diego, 1986, Hebrew Union Coll., 1998. Prof. philosophy and lit. Sarah Lawrence Coll., 1951-54, prof. philosophy, 1954-64; prof. philosophy and religion Manhattanville Coll. of the Sacred Heart, Purchase, N.Y., 1966-67, Vassar Coll., Poughkeepsie, N.Y., 1967; prof. religion Temple U., Phila., 1966-73, also dir. PhD programs in religion and psychology and religion and lit.; prof. religious studies, philosophy and comparative lit. San Diego State U., 1973-91, ann. Maurice Friedman lectureship in modern Jewish thought, 1992—, prof. emeritus, 1991—; human sci. program dir., faculty Calif. Inst. for Human Sci., San Diego, 1995-97; disting. consulting faculty Saybrook Grad. Sch., 1998—; tutor Internat. Coll., L.A., 1976-86, William Lyon U., 1986-92, Am. Commonwealth U., 1992-95; vis. prof. religious philosophy Hebrew Union Coll.-Jewish Inst. Religion, Cin., 1956, Union Theol. Sem., N.Y.C., 1965, 67, dept. religion U. Hawaii, 1975; mem. faculty New Sch. for Social Rsch., N.Y.C., 1954-66, Washington Sch. Psychiatry, 1957-59, Pendle Hill, Quaker Ctr. for Study, Wallingford, Pa., 1959-60, 64-65, 67-73; guest lectr. William Alanson White Inst. Psychiatry, Psychoanalysis and Psychology, 1958-60; core faculty Calif. Sch. Profl. Psychology, San Diego, 1973-75; univ. rsch. scholar San Diego State U., 1984-85; sr. Fulbright lectr. Hebrew U., Jerusalem, 1987-88; vis. prof. Indira Gandhi Nat. Ctr. for Arts, New Delhi, 1992; fellow com. on the history of culture U. Chgo., 1947-49; co-dir. Inst. for Dialogical Psychotherapy, San Diego. Author: Martin Buber: The Life of Dialogue, 1955, Problematic Rebel: Melville, Dostoievsky, Kafka, Camus, 1963, rev. edit. 1970, The Worlds of Existentialism: A Critical Reader, 1964, To Deny Our Nothingness: Contemporary Images of Man, 1967, Touchstones of Reality: Existential Trust and the Community of Peace, 1972, The Hidden Human Image, 1974, The Human Way: A Dialogical Approach to Religion and Human Experience, 1982, The Confirmation of Otherness: In Family, Community and Society, 1983, Martin Buber's Life and Work: The Early Years 1878-1923, 1982, The Middle Years, 1923-45, 1983, The Later Years 1945-65, 1984 (Nat. Jewish Book award for biography 1985), Contemporary Psychology: Revealing and Obscuring the Human, 1984, The Healing Dialogue In Psychotherapy, 1985 (main selection of Psychotherapy and Social Sci. Book Club, Mar. 1985), Martin Buber and The Eternal, 1986, Abraham Joshua Heschel and Elie Wiesel: "You are my Witnesses", 1987, A Dialogue with Hasidic Tales: Hallowing the Everyday, 1988, Encounter on the Narrow Ridge: A Life of Martin Buber, 1991, Dialogue and the Human Image: Beyond Humanistic Psychology, 1992, Religion and Psychology: A Dialogical Approach, 1992, A Heart of Wisdom: Religion and Human Wholeness, 1992, Encuentro en el Desfiladero: Una Vida de Martin Buber, 1993, Intercultural Dialogue and the Human Image: Maurice Friedman at the Indira Gandhi National Centre for the Arts, 1995; Editor-in-Chief, Martin Buber and the Human Sciences, 1996, The Affirming Flame: A Poetics of Meaning, 1999; contbr. numerous articles to profl. jours. Recipient Outstanding Faculty award San Diego State U., 1980, Humanist Scholar of Yr. award Saybrook Grad. Sch., 1995. Mem. Religious Edn. Assn. (past bd. dirs., past edit. bd.), Am. Philol. Assn., Am. Acad. Religion, Am. Soc. Study Religion, Fellowship of Reconciliation, Jewish Peace Fellowship, Assn. Humanistic Psychology (edit. bd. Jour. Humanistic Psychology and Person-Centered Rev.). Home: 421 Hilmen Pl Solana Beach CA 92075-1318

FRIEDMAN, MENDEL, hospital administration executive; b. Balt., Apr. 30, 1924; s. Hyman and Mamye (Dupkin) F.; m. Phyllis Trabish; children: Roberta, Nancy, Gary, John, Marc, Carla Knoll. Student Pa. State U. With Jolly Co. Inc., Balt., over 40 yrs., now pres., chief exec. officer. Trustee Nat. Jewish Hosp., Denver, 1981—; bd. dirs. Mt. Washington Pediatric Hosp., Balt., 1981—, Deafness Rsch Found.; chmn. Mayor's Ball, City Balt., 1983; fundraiser Ann. Scholar Athlete Awards, Balt., 1978—. Named Man of Yr., Nat. Jewish Hosp., Balt., 1985. Mem. Am. Technion Soc. (Balt. chpt. bd. dirs.), Nat. Trust Hist. Preservation. Clubs: Johns Hopkins, N.Y. Road Runners. Avocations: marathons (10); patron arts; humanitarian; wine connoisseur; reading. Office: Western Regional Rsch Ctr USDA 800 Buchanan St Berkeley CA 94710-1105

FRIEDMAN, MERTON HIRSCH, retired psychologist, educator; b. Boston, Apr. 12, 1925; s. Isadore and Frances (Ponack) F.; m. Judith Lee Freeman, Nov. 27, 1955; 1 child, Eric Lund. BS, Coll. William and Mary, 1945; MA, U. Pa., 1947; PhD, U. Ill., 1952. Lic. psychologist, N.J., Mass. Psychology intern Conn. Valley Hosp., Middletown, 1947-48; postdoctoral intern Dept. Vet. Affairs Mental Health Clinic, Phila., 1952-53; staff psychologist Dept. Vet. Affairs Med. Ctr., Boston, 1953-59; chief psychology svc. Dept. Vet. Affairs Med. Ctr., Providence, 1959-62; chief psychologist Cmty. Mental Health Ctr., Brookline, Mass., 1962-64; dir. clin. svcs. Jewish Vocat. Svc., Milw., 1966-67; clin. assoc. prof. psychiatry U. Medicine and Dentistry N.J., 1968-92; chief psychology svc. Dept. Vet. Affairs Med. Ctr., East Orange, N.J., 1967-96; ret., 1996; vis. lectr. Fulbright program Lund U., Sweden, 1964-66. Contbr. articles to profl. jours. USPHS Rsch. fellow NIMH, U. Ill., 1951-52. Fellow Am. Orthopsychiat. Assn.; mem. APA, Mass. Psychol. Assn., N.J. Psychol. Assn., Sigma Xi (U. Ill. chpt.). Democrat. Jewish. Avocations: piano, hiking, philately, classical music. Home: 79 Falcon Rd Livingston NJ 07039-4414

FRIEDMAN, MEYER, physician; b. Kansas City, Kans., July 13, 1910; s. Joseph and Eva (Werby) F.; m. Mary Alicia Campbell, Sept. 5, 1942 (dec.); children: Joyce, Joseph, Mark. AB, Yale U., 1931; MD, Johns Hopkins U., 1935. Intern Kansas City (Mo.) Gen. Hosp., 1935-36; resident Michael Reese Hosp., Chgo., 1936-38, U. Wis. Gen. Hosp., Madison, 1938-39; dir. Harold Brunn Inst. U. Calif.-San Francisco Mt. Zion Med. Ctr., San Francisco, 1939-75; cons. Riker Labs. of 3M Co., St. Paul; mem. Wilton Park Conf. Center, Wiston House, Sussex, Eng.; Cecil H. and Ida Green vis. prof. Tex. Christian U., 1977; speaker T.W. Samuels Meml. Lecture Series Millikin U. Author: Functional Cardiovascular Disease, 1947; Pathogenesis of Coronary Artery Disease, 1969; (with Ray Rosenman) Type A Behavior and Your Heart, 1974; (with Diane Ulmer) Treating Type A Behavior and Your Heart, 1984, The Medical Diagnosis and Treatment of Type A Behavior, 1996, (with Gerald Friedland) Medicine's 10 Greatest Discoveries, 1998; contbr. articles to profl. jours. Hon. bd. dirs. Meyer Friedman Inst., 1984—. Served with M.C. AUS, 1942-45, PTO. Recipient Disting. Diploma of Honor Pepperdine U., 1982, Heart Rsch. Found. award, 1985, Upjohn Disting. Sci. award, 1993; Meyer Friedman Disting. Prof. established U. Calif., 1997. Mem. Am. Soc. for Clin. Investigation, Western Assn. Physicians, Calif. Acad. Medicine, Am. Physiol. Soc., Am. Heart Assn., Soc. for Exptl. Biology and Medicine, Yale Alumni Assn. of San Francisco, Villa Taverna Club, Family Club. Home: 160 San Carlos Ave Sausalito CA 94965-2046 Office: UCSF Mt Zion Med Ctr 1515 Scott St # 2 San Francisco CA 94115-3511

FRIEDMAN, MICHAEL A., food and drug agency commissioner. BA in English, Tulane U.; MD, U. Tex., Dallas. Diplomate Am. Bd. Internal Medicine, Am. Bd. Med. Oncology. Intern Stanford (Calif.) U.; assoc. prof. dept. medicine U. Calif. San Francisco Med. Ctr., 1975-83, dir. clin. affairs, interim dir. Cancer Rsch. Inst.; chief clin. investigation br. divsn. cancer treatment Nat. Cancer Inst., 1985-88, assoc. dir. cancer therapy evaluation program, 1988-95; dep. commr. ops. FDA, 1995-97, 1997—. Contbr. articles to profl. jours. Recipient Special Achievement award EEO, 1992. Mem. Am. Cancer Soc., Am. Fedn. Clin. Rsch., We. Soc. Clin. Investigation, Phi Beta Kappa, Alpha Omega. Office: FDA 5600 Fishers Ln Rockville MD 20852-1750*

FRIEDMAN, MICHAEL PHILLIP, lawyer; b. N.Y.C., May 26, 1951; s. Jack and Babette (Schapiro) F.; m. Helene Gerstel, Aug. 30, 1981; children: Felice Eva Gerstel, Jaclin Maude Gerstel. Student Alvescot Coll., Oxfordshire, Eng., 1970; BA, CUNY, 1973; JD, New Eng. Sch. Law, 1976. Bar: Mass. 1977, U.S. Dist. Ct. Mass. 1977. Law clk. to chief civil div. U.S. Atty.'s Office, Boston, 1975-76; of counsel Denner & Singer, Cambridge, Mass., 1977-81; prin. Sorett, Friedman & Bielitz, Cambridge, 1981-83; of counsel Brickley, Sears & Sorett, Boston, 1983—; staff atty. Cambridgeport Problem Ctr., Mass., 1976-77. Pres. Trustee's-Beaconsfield Condominium Trust, Brookline, Mass., 1983-86. Mem. Trial Lawyers Assn. Am., Mass. Bar Assn., Mass. Assn. Trial Attys., Boston Bar Assn., Middlesex County Bar Assn. (clin. counselor 1976-82). Named Face to Watch by Boston Mag., 1985. Home: 223 Saint Paul St # 1 Brookline MA 02446-3451 Office: Brickley Sears & Sorett 75 Federal St Boston MA 02110-1913

FRIEDMAN, MILDRED, designer, educator, curator; b. L.A., July 25, 1929; d. Nathaniel and Hortense (Weinsveig) Shenberg; m. Martin Friedman; children: Lise, Ceil, Zoe. BA, UCLA, 1951, MA, 1952; DFA (hon.), Mpls. Coll. Art, 1984; DFA, Hamlin U., 1987. Instr. design L.A. City Coll., 1952-54; archtl. designer Cerny Assocs., Mpls., 1957-69; design curator Walker Art Ctr., Mpls., 1970-90; freelance cons. N.Y.C., 1990—; architecture and design panel Nat. Endowment Arts, 1975-78, policy panel design arts, 1979-82, presdl. design awards jury, 1991; vis. com. sch. architecture and planning MIT, 1985-88, grad. sch. design Harvard U., 1994—; bd. dirs. Internat. Design Conf., Aspen, 1989-91, Chgo. Inst. Architecture and Urbanism, 1990-93, Nat. Inst. Archtl. Edn., 1993—; design jury Am. Acad. Rome, 1991; guest instr. UCLA, 1992; jury to select architect for Whitehall Ferry Terminal, N.Y.C., 1992; vis. instr. Harvard U., 1993; cons. Battery Park City Authority, N.Y.C.; guest curator Bklyn. Mus., 1996—, Can. Ctr. Architecture, 1995—. Editor Design Quar., 1970-91, numerous catalogues. Recipient Outstanding Achievement award YWCA, 1984, Outstanding Svc. award U. Minn., 1991; fellow Intellectual Interchange program Japan Soc., 1982; grantee Nat. Endowment Arts, 1992-93, Graham Found. for Advanced Studies in Fine Arts, 1997; recipient Graham Found grant for Design Quarterly Anthology. Mem. AIA (hon., nat. awards jury 1981, 87, bd. dirs. Minn. chpt. 1984-86, Inst. Honors 1994).

FRIEDMAN, MILES, trade association executive, financial services company executive, university lecturer; b. N.Y.C., Apr. 18, 1950; s. Sol and Rose (Schenkerman) F.; m. Susan Liles, Apr. 26, 1975; children: David Andrew, Diana Leigh. BA in Pub. Affairs, George Washington U., 1971, MA in Polit. Sci., 1972, PhD candidate in Polit. Sci., 1976. Dep. commr. pub. works Town of Ramapo, Suffern, N.Y., 1971; grad. teaching fellow George Washington U., Washington, 1972-75; sr. assoc. Lazar Mgmt. Group, Washington, 1976-77; dir. legis. and policy Nat. Council Urban Econ. Devel., Washington, 1977-80; pres., CEO Nat. Assn. State Devel. Agys., Washington, 1980—; founder, instr. trade specialist tng. program, Phoenix, 1980—, founder, instr. fgn. investment tng. program, 1988-96; instr. Fgn. Svc. Inst., U.S. and Fgn. Comml. Svc. Inst., Georgetown U., Washington, 1991, U. N.C. Basic Econ. Devel. Inst., Chapel Hill, 1984-85; cons. Pres.' Drug Abuse Prevention Office, Washington, 1972; lectr. George Washington U., Washington, 1975-77. Mem. editl. bd., contbg. editor Econ. Devel. Rev., 1991—; contbg. author to several books, directory; contbr. articles to profl. jours. including Wall St. Jour, Area Devel. mag., Export Today mag., others. Mem bd. dirs., sec./treas. Pub. Sector Devel. Found., Washington, 1983—; pres. Am. Devel. Fin., Inc., 1986-95, also bd. dirs.; liaison subcom. Pres.'s Export Council, Washington, 1981-82; Pinewood Forest Council Owners, 1977-78; chmn. Washington Symposium Higher Edn., 1970-71; pres. Coles Little League, 1997-98; chmn. Prince William County Econ. Devel. Coun., 1998—; bd. dirs. Friends of Brentsville Courthouse Hist. Ctr., 1998—. Recipient Pres.'s E award for Excellence in Export Svc., NASDA, 1993. S. C. of C., Am. Soc. Assn. Execs., Nat. Assn. Execs., Tau Kappa Epsilon, Delta Phi Epsilon, Lambda Alpha. Office: Nat Assn State Devel Agys 750 1st St NE Ste 710 Washington DC 20002-4241

FRIEDMAN, MILTON, economist, educator emeritus, author; b. Brooklyn, N.Y., July 31, 1912; s. Jeno Saul and Sarah Ethel (Landau) F.; m. Rose Director, June 25, 1938; children: Janet, David. AB, Rutgers U., 1932, LLD (hon.), 1968; AM, U. Chgo., 1933; PhD, Columbia U., 1946; LLD (hon.), St. Paul's (Rikkyo) U., 1963, Loyola U., 1971, U. N.H., 1975, Harvard U., 1979, Brigham Young U., 1980, Dartmouth Coll., 1980, Gonzaga U., 1981; DSc (hon.), Rochester U., 1971; LHD (hon.), Rockford Coll., 1969, Roosevelt U., 1975, Hebrew Union Coll., L.A., 1981, Jacksonville U., 1993; LittD (hon.), Bethany Coll., 1971; PhD (hon.), Hebrew U., Jerusalem, 1977; DCS (hon.), Francisco Marroquin U., Guatemala, 1978; D honoris causa, Econ. U. Prague, 1997. Assoc. economist Nat. Resources Com., Washington, 1935-37; mem. research staff Nat. Bur. Econ. Research, N.Y.C., 1937-45, 1948-81; vis. prof. econs. U. Wis., Madison, 1940-41; prin. economist, tax research div. U.S. Treasury Dept., Washington, 1941-43; assoc. dir. research, statis. research group, War Research div. Columbia U., N.Y.C., 1943-45; assoc. prof. econs. and statistics U. Minn., Mpls., 1945-46; assoc. prof. econs. U. Chgo., 1946-48, prof. econs., 1948-62, Paul Snowden Russell disting. service prof. econs., 1962-82, prof. emeritus, 1983—; Fulbright lectr. Cambridge U., 1953-54; vis. Wesley Clair Mitchell research prof. econs. Columbia U., N.Y.C., 1964-65; fellow Ctr. for Advanced Study in Behavioral Sci., 1957-58; sr. research fellow Hoover Inst., Stanford U., 1977—; mem. Pres.'s Commn. All-Vol. Army, 1969-70, Pres.'s Commn. on White House Fellows, 1971-74, Pres.'s Econ. Policy Adv. Bd., 1981-88; vis. scholar Fed. Res. Bank, San Francisco, 1977. Author: (with Carl Shoup and Ruth P. Mack) Taxing to Prevent Inflation, 1943; (with Simon S. Kuznets) Income from Independent Professional Practice, 1946; (with Harold A. Freeman, Frederic Mosteller, W. Allen Wallis) Sampling Inspection, 1948, Essays in Positive Economics, 1953, A Theory of the Consumption Function, 1957, A Program for Monetary Stability, 1960, Price Theory: A Provisional Text, 1962; (with Rose D. Friedman) Capitalism and Freedom, 1962, (with R.D. Friedman) Free To Choose, 1980, Tyranny of the Status Quo, 1984, Two Lucky People: Memoirs, 1998; (with Anna J. Schwartz) A Monetary History of the United States, 1867-1960, 1963; (with Schwartz) Monetary Statistics of the United States, 1970, Monetary Trends in the U.S. and the United Kingdom, 1982, Inflation: Causes and Consequences, 1963; (with Robert Roosa) The Balance of Payments: Free vs. Fixed Exchange Rates, 1967, Dollars and Deficits, 1968, The Optimum Quantity of Money and Other Essays, 1969; (with Walter W. Heller) Monetary vs. Fiscal Policy, 1969, A Theoretical Framework for Monetary Analysis, 1972; (with Wilbur J. Cohen) Social Security, 1972, An Economist's Protest, 1972, There's No Such Thing As A Free Lunch, 1975, Price Theory, 1976; (with Robert J. Gordon et al.) Milton Friedman's Monetary Framework, 1974, Tax Limitation, Inflation and the Role of Government, 1978, Bright Promises, Dismal Performance, 1983, Money Mischief, 1992; (with Thomas S. Szasz) Friedman & Szasz on Drugs: Essays on the Free Market and Prohibition, 1992; editor: Studies in the Quantity Theory of Money, 1956; bd. editors Am. Econ. Rev, 1951-53, Econometrica, 1957-69; adv. bd. Jour. Money, Credit and Banking, 1968-94; columnist Newsweek mag, 1966-84, contbg. editor, 1971-84; contbr. articles to profl. jours. Chmn. bd. dirs. Milton and Rose D. Friedman Found. Decorated Grand Cordon of the 1st Class Order of the Sacred Treasure (Japan); recipient Nobel prize in econs., 1976, Pvt. Enterprise Exemplar medal Freedoms Found., 1978, Presdl. medal of Freedom, 1988, Nat. Medal of Sci., 1988, Prize in Moral-Cultural Affairs, Instn. World Capitalism, 1993; named Chicagoan of Yr., Chgo. Press Club, 1972, Educator of Yr., Chgo. Jewish United Fund, 1973, Source award for lifetime achievement The Primary Source, Tufts U., 1997, Robert Maynard Hutchins History Maker award for distinction in edn. Chgo. Hist. Soc., 1997, Templeton Honor Rolls Lifetime Achievement award, 1997, Goldwater award, 1997. Fellow Inst. Math. Stats., Am. Statis. Assn., Econometric Soc.; mem. NAS, Am. Econ. Assn. (exec. com. 1955-57, pres. 1967; John Bates Clark medal 1951), Am. Enterprise Inst. (adv. bd. 1956-79), Western Econ. Assn. (pres. 1984-85), Royal Economic Soc., Am. Philos. Soc., Mont Pelerin Soc. (bd. dirs. 1958-61, pres. 1970-72), Quadrangle Club. Office: Stanford U Hoover Instn Stanford CA 94305-6010

FRIEDMAN, MONROE, psychologist, educator; b. N.Y.C., Oct. 16, 1934; s. Isadore and Pearl Friedman; m. Rita Joyce Shaffer, Sept. 2, 1956; children: Ethan, Mark, Jordan. BS, Bklyn. Coll., 1956; PhD, U. Tenn., 1959. Human factors scientist Sys. Devel. Corp., Santa Monica, Calif., 1959-64; prof. Ea. Mich. U., Ypsilanti, 1964—; dir. Contemporary Issues Ctr., Ypsilanti, 1970-79; vis. prof. Tilburg (The Netherlands) U., 1982-83, U. Leuven, Belgium, 1990-91; cons. NSF, Washington, 1973-75, U.S. Gen. Acctg. Office, Washington, 1973-74, FTC, Washington, 1976-77; presenter in field, Europe, Asia, Latin Am., Australia and U.S.; bd. dirs. Consumer Interest Rsch. Inst., Washington. Author: A Brand New Language, 1991, Consumer Boycotts, 1999; Contbr. Jour. Consumer Affairs, 1998; issue editor Jour. Social Issues, 1991; co-editor: Frontier of Research in the Consumer Interest, 1988; contbr. more than 100 articles to profl. publs.; editl. bd. Jour. Consumer Affairs, Jour. Consumer Rsch., Jour. Consumer Policy; editor: Jour. Consumer Affairs, 1980-84. Pres. Am. Coun. on Consumer Interests, 1989-90. Rsch. grantee AARP Andrus Found., 1990, 92, Mich. Coun. for Humanities, 1975; Congl. fellow Am. Polit. Sci. Assn., 1966-67; recipient Disting. Faculty award Mich. Bd. Regents, 1983. Fellow APA, Am. Psychol. Soc. (charter), Am. Assn. Applied and Preventive Psychology (charter), Am. Coun. on Consumer Interests (disting., Applied Consumer Econs. award, 1991, 97), Soc. for Consumer Psychology, Soc. for the Psychol. Study of Social Issues , Soc. for the Study of Peace, Conflict and Violence; mem. Internat. Assn. for Rsch. in Econ. Psychology (U.S. rep. bd. trustees 1982—), Internat. Assn. Applied Psychology (U.S. rep. bd. trustees econ. psychology divsn. 1988—). Home: 1613 E Stadium Blvd Ann Arbor MI 48104-4452 Office: Ea Mich U Psychology Dept Ypsilanti MI 48197

FRIEDMAN, MORTON LEE, lawyer; b. Aberdeen, S.D., Aug. 4, 1932; s. Philip and Rebecca (Feinstein) F.; m. Marcine Lichter, Dec. 20, 1955; children—Mark, Philip, Jeffrey. Student, U. Mich., 1950-53; A.B., Stanford U., 1954, LL.B., 1956. Bar: Calif. bar 1956. Mem. firm Kimble, Thomas, Snell, Jamison & Russell, Fresno, 1957, Busick & Busick, Sacramento, 1957-59; sr. partner firm Friedman, Collard & Poswall (name now Friedman & Collard), Sacramento, 1959—; lectr. various law schs. and seminars; mem. Calif. Bd. Continuing Edn. Pres. Mosaic Law Congregation, 1977-80, 97—; v.p. Sacramento Jewish Fedn., 1980-82; chmn. Sacramento campaign United Jewish Appeal, 1981; nat. v.p. Am. Israel Pub. Affairs Com.; mem. bd. Calif. State U. Inst., 1995—. 1st lt. USAF, 1956. Recipient Sacramento Businessman of Yr. award Sacramento Met. C. of C., 1991, Best Lawyers in Am. award; Fulbright candidate Stanford Law Sch., 1956. Fellow Am. Coll. Trial Lawyers; mem. ABA, Calif. Bar Assn., Sacramento County Bar Assn. (pres. 1976), Am. Trial Lawyers Assn., Calif. Trial Lawyers Assn. (v.p. 1973-75), Capitol City Lawyers Club (past pres.), Am. Bd. Trial Advocates (adv., pres. 1977, Calif. Trial Lawyer of Yr. 1988), West Sacramento C. of C. (dir.), Order of Coif. Democrat. Home: 1620 Mcclaren Dr Carmichael CA 95608-5936 Office: Friedman & Collard 7750 College Town Dr Ste 300 Sacramento CA 95826-2386

FRIEDMAN, MURRAY, civil rights official, historian; b. N.Y.C., Sept. 15, 1926; s. Benjiman and Eva (Greenspan) F.; m. Eve Rosenfeld, July 23, 1949; children: Oren L., Keith M., Tamima Beth. BA, Bklyn. Coll., 1948; MA, NYU, 1949; PhD, Georgetown U., 1958. Historian Office Chief Mil. History, Washington, 1949-52; asst. to dir. Washington Housing Assn., 1952-53; dir. Va.-N.C. office Anti-Defamation League, Richmond, Va., 1954-59; dir. Mid. Atlantic region Am. Jewish Com., Phila., 1959—; dir. Myer and Rosaline Feinstein Ctr. for Am. Jewish History, Temple U., Phila., 1990—; lectr. USIA, Africa, India, 1974. Author: The Utopian Dilemma, American Judaism and Public Policy: What Went Wrong? The Creation and Collapse of the Black Jewish Alliance, 1995; editor: Overcoming Middle Class Rage, 1971, New Perspectives on School Integration, 1979, Jewish Life in Philadelphia, 1983, Philadelphia Jewish Life, 1986, When Philadelphia Was the Capitol of Jewish America, 1994, (with Nancy Isserman) The Tribal Basis of American Life, 1998; editor: (with A. Chennin) A Second Exodus: The American Movement to Free Soviet Jews. Bd. dirs. Pa. Humanities Coun., Phila., 1984-88, Landmark Legal Found. Ctr. for Civil Rights; bd. dirs., past co-chmn. Greater Phila. Urban Affairs Coalition; vice chmn. U.S. Commn. on Civil Rights, Washington, 1986-89. With USMC, 1945. Mem. Am. Hist. Assn., Am. Jewish Hist. Assn. Democrat. Jewish. Avocation: tennis. Home: 610 Boyer Rd Cheltenham PA 19012-1610 Office: 117 S 17th St Philadelphia PA 19103-5025

FRIEDMAN, MYLES IVAN, education educator; b. Chgo., Apr. 5, 1924; s. Max Edward and Ethel (Goldman) F.; m. Betty Ann McDowell, July 4, 1978; children: Gregg Alan, Myles Ivan Jr. M.A., U. Chgo., 1957, Ph.D., 1959. Real estate, home builder, 1946-58; asst. prof. edn. Northwestern U., 1958-60, assoc. prof., 1960-64; prof. edn. U. S.C., 1964—; vis. prof. U. Calif., Berkeley, summer 1968; cons. in field. Bd. dirs. Head Start Evaluation and Research Center; dir. research Regional Edn. Lab., Carolinas and Va. Author: Rational Behavior, 1975, Teaching Reading and Thinking Skills, 1979; sr. author: Improving Teacher Education, 1979, Human Nature and Predictability, 1981, Teaching Higher Order Thinking Skills to Gifted Students, 1983, The Psychology of Human Control, 1991, Taking Control: Vitalizing Education, 1993, Improving the Quality of Life, 1997, Handboook on Effective Instructional Strategies, 1998; contbr. articles to profl. jours. Served with USAAF, 1942-46. Mem. APA. Home: 1709 Seay Ct Columbia SC 29206-3117 Office: Univ SC Coll Edn Columbia SC 29208 *The harder I work, the luckier I get.*

FRIEDMAN, NATHAN BARUCH, physician; b. N.Y.C., Jan. 30, 1911; s. Emanuel David and Rose (Borgenicht) F.; widower; children: MaryLou, Emily. BS, Harvard U., 1930; MD, Cornell U., 1934. Intern Montefiore Hosp., 1936; resident U. Chgo., 1938-39; instr. Stanford (Calif.) U., 1941; dir. labs. Cedars Hosp., L.A., 1948-69, cons., 1970—; clin. prof. U. So. Calif., L.A., 1950-90, emeritus prof., 1990. Maj. AUS, 1942-46. Home: 15150 Mulholland Dr Los Angeles CA 90077-1619 Office: Cedars-Sinai Med Ctr 8700 Beverly Blvd Los Angeles CA 90048-1865

FRIEDMAN, ORRIE MAX, biotechnology company executive; b. Grenfell, Sask., Can., June 6, 1915; s. Jack and Gertrude (Shulman) F.; m. Marcia Gordon, Sept. 8, 1950 (div. Aug. 1957); 1 child, Mark David; m. Laurel E. Leeder, Jan. 2, 1959; children—Gertrude Jane, Hugh Robert. B.Sc., U. Man., 1935; B.Sc. in Chemistry, McGill U., Montreal, Que., Can., 1941, Ph.D., 1944. Asst. prof. chemistry Harvard U. Med. Sch., Boston, 1952-53; asst. prof., prof., then adj. res. prof. Brandeis U., Waltham, Mass., 1953-70; pres., sci. dir. Collaborative Research Inc., Bedford, Mass., From 1962-82, chmn. bd., 1982—, chief exec. officer, 1986-93, chmn. bd. 1993-94; pres. Grenfell Devel. Corp., 1994—. Contbr. numerous articles to sci. jours. Mem. com. on innovation SBA, 1973-75; mem. corp. Sidney Farber Cancer Inst., Boston, Mus. Sci., Boston; bd. govs. Dana Farber Cancer Inst., Technion, Israel Inst. Tech., Haifa; trustee Barnett Inst. Northeast U., Boston, Beth Israel Hosp., Boston. Recipient many research grants from various U.S. Govt. agys. Fellow AAAS; mem. Am. Chem. Soc., Am. Assn. for Cancer Research, N.Y. Acad. Sci., Sigma Xi. Home: 49 Warren St Brookline MA 02445-5925 Office: Grenfell Devel Corp One Broadway Ste 600 Cambridge MA 02142

FRIEDMAN, PAMELA RUTH LESSING, art consultant, financial consultant; b. N.Y.C., Jan. 15, 1950; d. Fred William and Helen D. (Kahn) Lessing; children: Elizabeth Lessing, Paul Lessing. BA, U. Rochester, 1972; MSLS, U. N.C., Chapel Hill, 1974. Dep. libr. Am. Soc. Internat. Law, Washington, 1974-76; with edn. dept. Nat. Air and Space Mus., Smithsonian Inst., Washington, 1976-84; ind. cons. fin. and art Boulder, Colo., 1984—; pub. C.S.B. Co., Boulder, 1989—; lectr. in fields, 1989—; cons. Denver Art Mus., 1989-91, Asian Art Coordinating Coun., Denver, 1990—; pres. Kylin Resources, Boulder, Colo., 1995—; race ofcl., U.S. Ski Assn., 1998—; chmn. bd. Linking Human Sys. (LINC), 1998—. Author: (reference book) Chinese Snuff Bottles, 1990; editor: (reference book) Flight Service Directory, 1975. Rep. S.E.V.A.B., Smithsonian Instn., 1979-81, mem. exec. bd. docent coun. Nat. Air and Space Mus., 1977-81; mem. trustee coun. U. Rochester, N.Y., 1992, mem. vis. com. coll. of arts and scis. U. Rochester, 1994—; bd. dirs., mem. exec. com. bd., treas. Colo. Music Festival, Boulder, 1983-89; mem. exec. bd. Women's Incentive Fund Colo. U., Boulder, 1988-91; rep. Leadership Boulder, 1986-87; v.p. bd. dirs. Lessing Found., N.Y., 1988—; mem. exec. bd. Interfaith Coun., Boulder, 1987-90; life mem. RAF Mus., 1977—. Recipient Internat. Gold Test Pin award Swiss Skiing Fedn., St. Moritz, 1975. Mem. Internat. Chinese Snuff Bottle Soc., Army and Navy Club

(Washington), Beach Point Club (Mamaroneck, N.Y.), Game Creek Club (Vail, Colo.). Avocations: private aviation, amateur radio, skiing, sailing, scuba diving, collecting. Home and Office: 503 Kalmia Ave Boulder CO 80304-1733

FRIEDMAN, PAUL, chemistry educator; b. Bklyn., Oct. 12, 1931; s. Abraham and Goldie (Wolkoff) F.; m. Ruth Starr, Dec. 19, 1954; children: Dawn, Heather. BS in Chemistry, CCNY, 1953; MA in Chemistry, Bklyn. Coll., 1957; PhD in Chemistry, Stevens Inst. Tech., 1963. Sr. research chemist Evans Research, N.Y.C., 1955-60; instr. in chemistry Newark Coll. Engring., 1960-61; research assoc., instr. U. So. Calif., Los Angeles, 1963-64; asst. prof. to assoc. prof. chemistry Pratt Inst., Bklyn., 1964-70, prof., 1970—; sr. vis. fellow Princeton (N.J.) U., 1986, 86-87, 90-98; cons. Affiliated Engring., Edison, N.J., 1973—. Author chpts. in books; contbr. articles on heterocyclic and theoretical chemistry to profl. jours. Bd. dirs. PLUS Group Homes, Merrick, N.Y., Uniondale, N.Y., 1987—; trustee Pratt Inst., 1985-87. Served with U.S. Army, 1956-57. Mem. Am. Chem. Soc., Royal Soc. Chemistry, N.Y. Acad. Sci., Sigma Xi. Jewish. Avocations: sports, reading, natural history. Home: 2063 Hampton Way Merrick NY 11566-5002 Office: Pratt Inst Dept Of Chemistry Brooklyn NY 11205

FRIEDMAN, PAUL JAY, radiologist, chest radiologist, educator; b. N.Y.C., Jan. 20, 1937; s. Louis Alexander and Rose (Solomon) F.; m. Elisabeth Clare Richardson, June 18, 1960; children: Elizabeth Ruth Coley, Deborah Anne Yeager, Matthew Alexander, Rachel Clare Lentz. BS, U. Wis., 1955; postgrad., Oxford (Eng.) U., 1957-58; MD, Yale U., 1960. Intern Einstein Med. Sch., N.Y.C., 1960-61; resident in radiology Columbia-Presbyn. Hosp., N.Y.C., 1961-64; fellow in pulmonary pathology Yale U., 1966-68; asst. prof., assoc. prof. U. Calif. San Diego Med. Sch., 1968-75, prof. radiology, 1975—, from assoc. dean to dean acad. affairs, 1982-95; cons. VA Hosp.; vis. scholar Inst. Med./NAS, AAMC, 1988-89; adv. com. on rsch. integrity Dept. Health & Human Svcs., 1991-93; cons. 26th and 27th edit. Stedman's Med. Dictionary; specialist in chest radiology and rsch. ethics, tenure and retirement issues; bd. dirs. Am. Coun. Edn., 1996-97. Mem. editl. bd. Investigative Radiology, 1976-87, Am. Jour. Roentgenology, 1986-88; contbr. articles to profl. jours. Bd. dirs. La Jolla Symphony Assn., 1987-92. Lt. comdr. M.C., USNR, 1964-66. Markle scholar acad. medicine, 1969-74; Picker Found. advanced acad. fellow and scholar, 1966-69. Fellow Am. Coll. Chest Physicians, Am. Coll. Radiology; mem. AAUP, Assn. Univ. Radiologists (rep. to coun. acad. socs. Assn. Am. Med. Colls. 1985-97), Fleischner Soc. (pres. 1994-95), Calif. Radiology Soc., Radiol. Soc. N.Am., San Diego Radiology Soc., Roentgen Ray Soc., Soc. Med. Decision Making, Phi Beta Kappa, Alpha Omega Alpha. Avocations: choral singing, computers, gardening. Home: 5644 Soledad Rd La Jolla CA 92037-7048 Office: U Calif Sch Medicine Dept Radiology 200 W Arbor Dr San Diego CA 92103-1911

FRIEDMAN, PAUL LAWRENCE, lawyer; b. Buffalo, Feb. 20, 1944; s. Cecil Alfred and Charlotte (Wagner) F.; m. Elizabeth Ann Zicherman, May 25, 1975. B.A., Cornell U., 1965; J.D. cum laude, SUNY-Buffalo, 1968. Bar: N.Y. 1968, D.C. 1969, U.S. Supreme Ct. 1974. Law clk. to judge U.S. Dist. Ct. D.C., 1968-69, U.S. Ct. Appeals (D.C. cir.), 1969-70; asst. U.S. atty. D.C., 1970-74, asst. to solicitor gen. of U.S., 1974-76; assoc. White & Case, Washington, 1976-79, ptnr., 1979-94; judge U.S. district court, Washington, D.C., 1994—; assoc. ind. counsel Iran-Contra Investigation, 1987-88; adj. prof. Georgetown U., 1973-75; mem. adv. com. procedures U.S. Ct. Appeals (D.C. dir.), 1982-88; mem. grievance com. U.S. Dist. Ct. D.C., 1980-87, chmn. 1984-86; chmn. adv. com. Civil Justice Reform Act, U.S. Dist. Ct., 1991-94; mem. faculty Nat. Inst. Trial Advocacy; mem. D.C. Jud. Nomination Commn., 1990-94, chmn., 1992-94; bd. trustees Pub. Defender Svc. of D.C., 1989-92. Contbr. articles to profl. jours. Pres. Frederick B. Abramson Meml. Found., 1991-93; bd. dirs. Stuart Stiller Meml. Found., Washington Area Lawyers for the Arts, Washington Legal Clinic for the Homeless Inc. Fellow Am. Coll. Trial Lawyers; mem. ABA (standing com. continuing edn. of bar 1982-88, legal aid/indigent defendants 1989-91, ho. of dels. 1985-94, com. on profl. edn. 1988-93, chmn. commn. homeless and poverty 1992-93, commn. on women in profession 1993-94, state del. 1993-94, mem. nominating com. 1993-94), D.C. Bar (gov. 1978-81, 85-88, pres. - elect 1985-86, pres. 1986-87), Am. Law Inst., Am. Judicature Soc. (bd. dirs. 1990-94), Asst. U.S. Attys. Assn. D.C. (pres. 1976-77), Lawyers Club, Cornell Club, Cosmos Club. Jewish. Office: E.Barrett Prettyman U.S.Courthouse Rm 6321 333 Constitution Ave NW Washington DC 20001-2800

FRIEDMAN, PAUL RICHARD, lawyer; b. Washington, Mar. 25, 1944; s. Herbert and Gertrude (Miller) F.; m. Ronna Lee Beck; children: Mali, Luke, Jed. BA, Princeton U., 1965; MA, Trinity Coll., Cambridge U., England, 1967; JD, Yale U., 1970; postgrad., Balt./D.C. Inst. Psychoanalysis, 1971-78. Bar: D.C. 1972, U.S. Ct. Appeals (3d - 1984, 4th - 1979, and D.C. cirs. - 1972), U.S Supreme Ct. 1975. Law clk. to Hon. J. Skelly Wright U.S. Ct. Appeals (D.C. cir.), Washington, 1970-71; fellow Ctr. for Law and Social Policy, Washington, 1971-72; dir. Mental Health Law Project, Washington, 1972-81; mng. ptnr. Ennis, Friedman, Bersoff and Ewing, Washington, 1981-88; pvt. practice Washington, 1988-93, 96—; dep. assoc. atty. gen. Dept. of Justice, Washington, 1993-96; ct.-apptd. mediator and early neutral evaluator, 1988-89; chmn. Practicing Law Inst. Nat. Seminars on Legal Rights of Mentally Disabled Persons, 1979-80; coord. task panel on legal and ethical issues Pres.'s Commn. on Mental Health, 1977-78; mem. adv. com. on procedures U.S. Ct. Appeals (D.C. cir.) 1977-78; mem. steering com. Ctr. for Y2K & Soc., 1998—. Author: The Rights of Mentally Retarded Persons - An American Civil Liberties Handbook, 1976; editor: Legal Rights of Mentally Disabled Persons, 3 vols., 1979; note and comment editor Yale Law Jour., 1969-70, bd. editors 1967-69; contbr. articles to profl. publs. Trustee The Green Door, 1977-83. Nat. Merit scholar, Univ. scholar; Woodrow Wilson fellow, Keasbey fellow. Mem. ABA (mem. comm. on mentally disabled 1981-82), D.C. Bar, Am. Psychoanalytic Assn. (affiliate), 1974-78, Phi Beta Kappa. Avocations: tennis and other racquet sports, computers, photography.

FRIEDMAN, PAULA K., dentist, dental school administrator; b. Wildwood, N.J., June 22, 1948; d. Howard J. and Beatrice E. (Gibbs) Konowitch; m. Emanuel Friedman, Aug. 27, 1972; children: Daniel, Eric, Jeff. BS, U. Mass., 1970; DDS, Columbia U., 1974; MSD, Boston U., 1988. Attending dentist Beth Israel Med. Ctr., N.Y.C., 1975-78, Beth Israel Hosp., Boston, 1978-82; dir. DAU and TEAM program Boston U. Sch. of Dental Medicine, 1980-82, dir. divsn. of O.S. and radiology, 1982-87, asst. dean for adminstrn., 1987-91; coord. GP residency Boston U. Sch. of Denal Medicine, 1980-82; assoc. dean adminstrn., 1991—; chair peer rev. panel HHS, BHPr, 1999; acad. coord. Health Professions Edn. Program, 1998. Chair coun. of faculties AADS, Washington, 1997, adminstrv. bd., cmty. and preventative dentistry, 1990—. Recipient Disting. Alumni award Columbia U. Sch. of Dental and Oral Surgery, 1986. Fellow Am. Coll. Dentists, Internat. Coll. of Dentists; mem. ADA, Fisher Hill Assn. (bd. dirs. 1995—), Gerontol. Soc. of Am. (oral health v.p. 1994-97), Am. Assn. of Women Dentists, Phi Kappa Phi. Fax: 617-638-4729. E-mail: pkf@bu.edu. Office: Boston U Sch of Dental Medicine 100 East Newton St Rm G708 Boston MA 02118

FRIEDMAN, PAULINE POPLIN, civic worker, consultant; b. Scranton, Pa., Apr. 2, 1930; d. Harry and Lillian (Kushner) Poplin; m. Sidney Friedman, Aug. 3, 1952; children: Anne Friedman Glauber, Robert. BS, Pa. State U., 1952. Cons. AID, Washington, 1993—. Trustee Temple Israel, 1985-87, Jewish Cmty. Ctr., 1992—; mem. coun. King's Coll., 1992—; pres. Home Health Svcs.-vis. Nurse Assn., Kingston, Pa., 1987-88, Coun. Family Agys., Harrisburg, Pa., 1987-88, Family Svc. Wyoming Valley, Wilkes-Barre, 1988-90; mentor Leadership Wilkes-Barre; mem. pres.' coun. Wilkes U., 1991—, King's Coll.; v.p. United Way, Interfaith Coun. Wyoming Valley; bd. dirs. Ethics Inst. N.E. Pa., Dallas, 1994—, St. Vincent De Paul Soup Kitchen, Prevent Child Abuse Pa.; bd. alumni coun. Pa. State U.; mem. Jewish Cmty. Bd. Wyoming Valley; chairwoman United Jewish Campaign, Wyoming Valley, 1998-99; chair Speak-Out Day U.S.A., Luzerne County. Recipient Humanitarian award Interfaith Coun. Wyoming Valley, 1989, Phillip Mitchell Cmty. Svc. award Pa. State U., 1990, Woman of Yr. award Family Svc. Wyoming Valley, 1993, Pathfinders award Luzerne County Women's Conf., 1995, Disting. Svc. award B'nai Brith, 1996. Avocations: golf, tennis, travel. Home: 796 Milford Dr Kingston PA 18704-5308

FRIEDMAN, PHILIP, novelist, screenwriter, producer; b. Jan. 8, 1944; s. Samuel N. and Sylvia Friedman. BA in Math., Princeton U.; postgrad., U. Calif., Berkeley, Stanford U.; JD, NYU. Bar: N.Y. Pvt. practice N.Y.C.; screenwriter, assoc. prodr. film Rage; creator, writer TV series The Story of Billy Clay; pres., CEO Sovereign Internat., Inc., High Frontier Co.; Bd. dirs. MaxiVision Cinema Tech., Inc. Author: Rage, Termination Order, Act of Love, Act of War, Wall of Silence, The Pilates Method of Physical and Mental Conditioning (with Gail Eisen), Reasonable Doubt, Inadmissible Evidence, Grand Jury. Bd. dirs. Learning in Focus, Inc. Recipient Am. Jurisprudence award in copyright law; Princeton U. scholar. Mem. Writers Guild Am. West, Authors League, Authors Guild, Mystery Writers Am. (nat. bd. dirs.), Dramatists Guild, Internat. Assn. Crime Writers, N.Y. State Assn. Criminal Def. Lawyers. Office: The William Morris Agy c/o Owen Laster 1325 Avenue Of The Americas New York NY 10019-6026

FRIEDMAN, PHILIP HARVEY, psychologist; b. N.Y.C., Oct. 4, 1941; s. Leonard and Miriam Rosalyn (Solomon) F.; m. Teresa Jean Molinaro, Dec. 22, 1965; 1 son, Mathew Alan. BA, Columbia Coll., 1963; MA, U. Wis., 1965, PhD, 1968. NIMH postdoctoral rsch. fellow Temple U. Med. Sch., 1968-69; clin. psychologist ea. Pa. Psychiat. Inst., Phila., 1969-73; sr. family therapist dept. psychiatry Jefferson U. and Community Mental Health Ctr., Phila., 1973, instr., 1975-77, asst. prof., 1977—, program adminstr., 1978—; exec. dir. Found. for Well-Being, Plymouth Meeting, Pa., 1987—; coord. tng. in marital and family therapy, 1979-81; dir. Friedman Family Circle Assocs., 1980-81; mem. staff Ea. Cons. Assocs., 1980—; asst. prof., sr. supr. Masters in Marital and Family Therapy program Hahnemann Med. Sch., 1982-94; asst. prof. Hahnemann U. and Med. Sch. of Pa., 1995—; dir. Ctr. for Integrative Psychotherapy and Tng., 1983-87; exec. dir. Attitudinal Healing Ctr. Delaware Valley, Plymouth Meeting, Pa., 1983-87; cons. Phila. Bd. Edn., 1978, Ctr. for Study of Adult Devel., 1982; founder, dir. Energy Field Healing and Power Therapy Ctr. Delaware Valley, 1996; founder, moderator Electronic Energy Field Healing and Power Therapy Network, 1997; founder Found. Energy and Spiritual Healing, 1999. Author: Creating Well-Being: The Healing Path to Live, Peace, Self-Esteem and Happiness, 1989, Friedman Well-Being, Scale and Professional Manual, 1994; guest various radio and TV programs, 1980—; cons. to newspapers and mags., 1993—. Guest various radio and TV programs, 1980—. Fellow Pa. Psychol. Assn.; mem. APA, Assn. Transp. Psychologists, Am. Assn. Marriage and Family Therapists, Am. Family Therapy Acad., Phila. Soc. Clin. Psychologists, Internat. Assn. Energy, Spiritual and Power Therapy in Cyberspace (founder). Achievements include research in psychological, emotional, interpersonal and spiritual correlates of well-being. Home: 46 Red Rowan Ln Plymouth Meeting PA 19462-2128 Office: Found for Well-Being PO Box 627 Plymouth Meeting PA 19462

FRIEDMAN, RACHELLE, music retail executive; m. Joe Friedman; children: Jacon, Daryn. Grad., Poly. Inst. N.Y. Co-CEO J & R Music World, N.Y.C. Bd. dirs. Poly. Inst. N.Y., Heritage Trails. Mem. Nat. Assn. Record Merchandisers (mem. retail adv. bd., chmn. bd. dirs., chair conv. San Francisco, host com. Grammy awards). Avocations: travel, boating, working out, reading. Office: J & R Music World 23 Park Row New York NY 10038-2397*

FRIEDMAN, RICHARD BURTRAM, journalist; b. Phila., Nov. 19, 1930; s. Lewis and Ida (Segal) F.; m. Sybil J. Shaw, Sept. 11, 1955; children: Leah Beth Friedman Swetz, Joshua, Jessica, Rachel Friedman Baxter. BS in Journalism, Temple U., 1957. Reporter, photographer Wildwood (N.J.) Leader, 1957-59; assoc. editor Editor & Pub. Mag., N.Y.C., 1959-69; mng. editor Paddock Publs., Arlington Heights, Ill., 1969-71; asst. to pub. Williams Press, Tinley Park, Ill., 1971-77; exec. editor Minuteman Publs., Lexington, Mass., 1978-79; city editor News Tribune, Waltham, Mass., 1980-83; freelance journalist Woburn, Mass., 1983—; adj. prof. photojournalism L.I. U., Bklyn., 1968; cons. Communicate, Woburn, 1983—. Author: (anthology) Responsibilities of the Press, 1964, Beatles: Words Without Music, 1968; co-author: WASPies, 1968; columnist As We Are Mag., 1992-94; contbg. columnist Woburn Adv., 1983—; author of short stories; contbr. articles to profl. jours. With USCG, 1950-53. Named Columnist of Yr., Suburban Press Assn., 1975. Mem. Internat. Soc. Weekly Newspaper Editors, Nat. Writers Union.

FRIEDMAN, RICHARD EVERETT, librarian; b. Cleve., Nov. 24, 1942; s. Harry Martin and Miriam (Zavelson) F. BS, Columbia U., 1966, MA, 1968; MLS, Kent (Ohio) State U., 1984. Asst. curator Met. Mus. Art, N.Y.C., 1968-72; curator Phillips Collection, Washington, 1972-75; pres. Fine Arts Appraisal, Inc., Cleve., 1975-85; collection mgr. U. Akron, Ohio, 1984-86; head librarian Auburn (Ala.) U. Architecture Library, 1986-89; pres. Fine Art Appraisals, Akron, Ohio, 1989—; assoc. prof. Cath. U., Washington, 1973-75. Author: (book) Hundertwasser, 1975. Trustee Cleve. Modern Dance Assn., 1979-83; life fellow Met. Mus. Art; life. mem. Cleve. Mus. Art. Served to cpl. U.S. Army, 1960-63. Fellow Soc. Archtl. Historians; mem. Assn. Coll. and Research Libraries, Art Libraries Socs./N.Am. (v.p. Ohio chpt. 1985-86, devel. com. 1987—), Irish Georgian Hist. Soc., St. Juan de Luz Club (France). Clubs: Walden Golf and Tennis (Aurora, Ohio). Home and Office: Fine Art Appraisals Inc 205 Kenwood Ave Akron OH 44313-6308 Home (summer): Champs Fleuris, Boul D'Augusta, 64200 Biarritz France

FRIEDMAN, RICHARD LEE, lumberyard owner; b. Hammond, Ind., Jan. 28, 1950; s. Arthur and Ida (Ander) F.; m. Carol Smulevitz, May 28, 1972; children: Brett Joseph, Joshua David. BA, Ind. U., 1972. Pers. cons. Murphy Employment Svc., Wheaton, Ill., 1973-74; pers. mgr. Warshawsky and Co., Chgo., 1974-76; pers. mgr. controls div. Singer Co., Crystal Lake, Ill., 1976-79; mgr., owner State Lumber Co., Inc., Calumet City, Ill., 1979—, pres., 1995-97. Bd. dirs. Ind. Jewish Hist. Soc., 1987—, pres., 1995-97. Named Vol. of Yr. N.W. Ind. Jewish Fedn., 1985. Mem. B'nai B'rith (mem. internat. cabinet 1987-91, pres. Ind. state assn. 1990-91, dist. leadership chmn. 1992-93, AZA advisor youth orgn. 1985—, internat. bd. govs. 1992-94, 96-98, dist. pres. 1993-94, nat. disaster relief chair 1997-98, Man of Yr. 1987). Democrat. Avocations: stamps, bowling, racquetball.

FRIEDMAN, ROBERT, broadcast executive; m. Elissa Gertz. BA Psychology, Vassar Coll.; MBA, Columbia U. Grad. Sch. of Bus. Former pres. Playboy Entertainment Group; various pos. ending with sr. VP of Marketing, Promotion & Licensing for MTV & VH1 MTV Networks, New York, 1983-91; pres. New Line Television, New York, 1991—. Office: New Line Television 888 7th Ave 20th Fl New York NY 10106-0001*

FRIEDMAN, ROBERT BARRY, physician; b. Bklyn., Dec. 28, 1953; s. Roy and Bernice (Berger) F. BA, SUNY, Stony Brook, N.Y., 1975; MD, SUNY Health Sci. Ctr., Bklyn., 1980. Bd. Cert. Diplomate Am. Bd. Neurol. Surgery. Gen. med. officer USPHS Indian Health Svc., Sacaton, Ariz., 1981-82; neurosurgeon USAF, Wright Patterson AFB, Ohio, 1989-91, South Broward Neurosurg. Assn., Pembroke Pines, Fla., 1991-95, Cleve. Clinic Fla., Ft. Lauderdale, 1995-97, Spectrum Neurosurg. Specialists, Marietta, Ga., 1997-98, Henry Neurosurg. Specialists, P.C., Stockbridge, Ga., 1998—; med. staff fellow Nat. Inst. Health, Bethesda, Md., 1986-88. Contbr. articles to profl. jours. Maj. U.S.A.F., 1988-91. Recipient Neuroscience award U. Pitts., 1989. Fellow Am. Coll. Surgeons; mem. Am. Assn. Neurol. Surgeons, Congress of Neurol. Surgeons, Southern Med. Assn., Fla. Med. Assn., AMA. Avocation: private pilot. Home: 2403 Carrington Pk Jonesboro GA 30236 Office: c/o Henry Neurosurg Specialists PC 297 Country Club Dr Stockbridge GA 30281

FRIEDMAN, ROBERT LAURENCE, lawyer; b. Mt. Vernon, N.Y., Mar. 19, 1943; s. Alvin S. and Frances (Feinsod) F.; m. Barbara Lander, Dec. 25, 1964; children: Lisa, Andrew. AB, Columbia Coll., 1964; JD, U. Pa., 1967. Bar: N.Y. 1968. Assoc. Simpson, Thacher & Bartlett, N.Y.C., 1967-74, ptnr., 1974-99; sr. mng. dir. The Blackstone Group LP, N.Y.C., 1999—. Office: The Blackstone Group LP 345 Park Ave New York NY 10154

FRIEDMAN, ROBERT LEE, film company executive; b. N.Y.C., Mar. 1, 1930; s. Edward A. and Claire (Seidenberg) F.; m. Marlene Saltz; children: Marc, Lisa. Sales Universal Pictures, N.Y.C., 1948-52, 54-59; exec. v.p., distbn. & mktg. United Artists Corp., N.Y.C., 1959-79; pres., distbn. Columbia Pictures, Burbank, Calif., 1979-82; pres. AMC Entertainment Internat., L.A., 1984-92, pres. motion picture group, 1992—; radio announcer (radio show) The Bob Friedman Hour, 1952-54; cons. RLF Prodns., Beverly Hills, Calif., 1982-84. Exec. prodr., appeared in (motion picture) 9 Deaths of the Ninja, 1984; appeared in (motion picture) Stardust Memories, 1980. Bd. dirs., chmn. Entertainment Industry com. Century City C. of C., L.A., 1988—; chmn. Will Rogers Hosp., 1980-81, also bd. dirs.; bd. dirs. Dare Am.; mem. vision fund The Lighthouse for the Blind. With U.S. Army, 1952-54. Named Man of Yr. N.Y. State Nat. Assn. Theatre Owners, 1981, Va., Md., Washington D.C. Assn. Theatre Owners, 1980. Mem. Acad. Motion Picture Arts & Scis. (bd. dirs. endowment fund, 1979—), Variety Club Am. (L.A.), Motion Picture Pioneers Am., Motion Picture Assocs. Found. (pres. 1970-73), L.A.-Century City C. of C. (Citizen of Yr., 1994). Avocations: going to movies, playing tennis, exercising, photography, spending time with my wife and twin grandchildren. Office: AMC Ent Motion Picture Grp 2029 Century Park E Ste 3945 Los Angeles CA 90067-3025

FRIEDMAN, ROBERT MICHAEL, lawyer; b. Memphis, June 19, 1950; s. Harold Samuel and Margaret (Siegel) F.; m. Elaine Freda Burson, Dec. 21, 1975; children: Daniel Justin, Jonathan Aaron. B.S., U. Tenn., 1973, J.D., 1975; postgrad., Exeter U., Eng., 1974, Nat. Coll. Trial Advocacy, 1985. Bar: Tenn. 1976, U.S. Dist. Ct. (we. dist.) Tenn. 1977, U.S. Dist Ct. (no. dist.) Miss. 1979, U.S. Ct. Appeals (5th cir.) 1979, U.S. Supreme Ct. 1983, U.S. Dist. Ct. (so. dist.) Tex. 1986, U.S. Ct. Appeals (6th cir.) 1986. Assoc. Cassell & Fink, Memphis, 1976-78; pres., sr. ptnr. Friedman & Sissman, P.C., Memphis, 1978-91, Friedman, Sissman & Heaton, P.C., Memphis, 1991—; commr. State of Tenn. Jud. Selection Commn., 1994—; corp. legal/litagation counsel, dir. Tenn. Interpreting Svc. for Deaf, Memphis, 1981-89, Mid-South Hospitality Mgmt. Ctr., Inc., Memphis, 1984-88; legal counsel Moss Hotel Co., Inc., 1986-89, Helena Hotel Co., 1986-89, Charlestown Hotel Co., 1986-89, Jackson Hotel Co., 1986-89, Murfreesboro Hotel Co., 1986-89, Santee Hotel Co., 1986-89, Kingsport Hotel Co., 1986-89, Raleigh Hotel Assocs., Ltd., 1986-89, Ozark Regional Eye Ctr., 1986-90, Brookfield Mortgage Co., Inc., 1987—, Mt. Pleasant Hotel Co., 1987-89, Hattiesburg Hotel Assocs. Ltd., 1987-89, Wright and Assocs. Constrn. Co. Inc., 1987-90, Pro Billiards Tour Assn. Inc., 1996—; legal counsel, pres. Biloxi Hotel Co., Inc., 1986-89; litigation counsel Independence Fed. Bank Batesville, Ark., 1987-88; legal counsel Autorama, Inc., 1988—; bd. dirs./legal counsel Evan R. Harwood Day Tng. Ctr., 1989—; legal/litigation counsel Super D Drugs, Inc., 1989-93, So. Comm. Vols., Inc., WEVL FM Cmty. Radio, 1990-92; mem. staff, contbr. Tenn. Law Rev., 1974-75, recipient cert., 1975; corp. gen., litigation counsel U.S. for Inversiones Tesmo, Sociedad Anonima, Republic of Costa Rica, 1990—; rep. of Tenn. Bar Assn. and State of Tenn. to Nat. Summit Crime and Violence, 1994; legal counsel Pro Billiards Tour Assn., Inc., 1996—. Bd. dirs. Project 1st Offenders, Shelby County, Tenn., 1976-78; bd. dirs., legal counsel Memphis Community Ctr. for Deaf and Hearing Impaired, 1980-81; bd. dirs. Eagle Scout Day, Chickasaw coun. Boy Scouts Am., 1978—, Ea. Dist. committeeman, 1991-93, mem. adv. bd., 1993—, chmn. Eagle Scout recognition day, 1993-98, chaair Silver Beaver Com., 1999; scoutmaster Boy Scouts Am., Memphis, 1991—, mem. nat. bd. dirs. Nat. Eagle Scout Assn., 1998—; mem. U. Tenn. Coll. Law Alumni Adv. Coun., Dean's Cir., 1992—; rep. of Tenn. Bar Assn. and State of Tenn. Nat. Summit Crime and Violence, 1994. With USCG, 1971-77. James E. West fellow, 1996; A.S. Graves Meml. scholar, 1974-75; recipient Outstanding Svc. award and Key, Alpha Phi Omega, 1972, Am. Jurisprudence award Lawyers Co-op. Pub. Co. and Bancroft-Whitney Co., 1973-74, Chancellor's Honor award George C. Taylor Sch. Law, U. Tenn., 1975, Robert W. Richie Outstanding Svc. award Tenn. Assn. Criminal Def. Lawyers, 1993, Order of Arrow, Vigil of Honor, 1994, Nat. award Boy Scouts Am., 1996, Silver Beaver award, 1998. Mem. ABA, ATLA, Tenn. Bar Assn. (ho. dels. 1991-94, bd. dirs. criminal justice sect. 1998—, chmn. criminal justice sect. 1991-94, exec. bd. criminal justice sect. 1998-99, atty./solicitor Tenn Supreme Ct. 1994), Tenn. Jud. Selection Commn. (Tenn. state commr. 1994—), Tenn. Trial Lawyers Assn., Tenn. Assn. Criminal Defense Lawyers (bd. dirs. 1994), Nat. Assn. Criminal Def. Lawyers (vice chmn. law practice mgmt. com. 1990-93, co-chmn. forfeiture abuse task force 1991-93), Memphis and Shelby County Bar Assn., Fed. Bar Assn., Nat. Criminal Justice Assn. (charter 1984—), Alpha Phi Omega, Delta Theta Phi. Democrat. Jewish. Fax: 901-527-3633. Home: 3303 Spencer Dr Memphis TN 38115-3000 Office: Friedman Sissman & Heaton PC 100 N Main St Ste 3400 Memphis TN 38103-0534 *If we fail to vigilantly and aggressively fight to maintain each of our personal rights and liberties, we shall soon have none. If we withhold the full bounty of our individual freedoms from even the most heinous individual, by so doing we shall thereby become enslaved.*

FRIEDMAN, ROBERT SIDNEY, political science educator; b. Balt., Mar. 1, 1927; s. Harry N. and Eva (Cohen) F.; m. Renee Cohen, Aug. 11, 1953; children—Helene, David. BA, Johns Hopkins U., 1948; MA, U. Ill., 1950, PhD, 1953. Research asst. Bur. Govt. Research, Md., 1953-55; instr. govt. and politics U. Md., 1955-56; from instr. to assoc. prof. govt. La. State U., 1956-61; research assoc. Inst. Pub. Adminstrn., U. Mich., 1961-67, acting dir., 1967-68; assoc. prof. polit. sci. U. Mich., 1961-66, prof., 1966-68; prof., head dept. polit. sci. Pa. State U., 1968-78; dir. Center for Study Sci. Policy, Inst. for Policy Research and Evaluation, 1978-88, dir. policy analysis program, 1991-94; prof. emeritus, 1994—; sci. policy cons., 1994—. Co-author: Local Government in Maryland, 1955, Government in Metropolitan New Orleans, 1959, Political Leadership and the School Desegration Crisis in New Orleans, 1963; author: The Michigan Constitutional Convention and Administrative Organization: A Case Study in the Politics of Constitution-Making, 1971; contbg. author: Politics in the American States, 1965, 5th edit., 1990; contbr. articles to profl. jours. Bd. dirs. Pa. Civil Liberties Union, 1969-72; mem. State College (Pa.) Zoning Hearing Bd., 1976-79; chmn. study com. State College Mcpl. Govt., 1991-93; mem. State College Planning Commn., 1996—; mem. safety adv. bd. Three Mile Island-2 Cleanup, 1981-89; Pa. bd. Common Cause, 1998—. With AUS, 1945-46. Recipient McKay Donkin award for disting. service, 1980. Mem. Am., N.E., Midwest, So. polit. sci. assns., Am. Soc. for Pub. Adminstrn., AAAS. Home: 205 Horizon Dr State College PA 16801-8615 Office: Pa State U Burrowes Bldg University Park PA 16802

FRIEDMAN, RODGER, antiquarian bookseller, consultant; b. Detroit, Nov. 10, 1951; s. Stanley B. and Miriam Elizabeth (Levin) F.; m. Kiki Nelson, July 1, 1983. BA, Kalamazoo Coll., 1973; MA, U. N.Mex., Albuquerque, 1979, CUNY, 1987; PhD, CUNY, 1989; MLS, Pratt Inst., 1996. Librarian Century Assn., N.Y.C., 1982-88, Union League Club, N.Y.C., 1989-96. Mem. editl. bd. Ballet Rev., 1983-96; translator: Posthumous People by Massimo Cacciari, 1996; Quar. catalogue of rare books; contbr. articles to profl. jours. Adv. com. Caravan Found. Recipient Frederick II medal U. Naples, 1991. Mem. Am. Printing History Assn., Renaissance Soc. Am., Am. Comparative Lit. Assn. (advisor, exec. com. 1987-89), Assn. Internat. Studi di Lingua Letteratura Italiana, Internat. Assn. for Neo-Latin Studies. E-mail: rf@warwick.net. Home: 1 Mystic Cir Tuxedo Park NY 10987-5027

FRIEDMAN, RONALD MARVIN, cellular biologist; b. Brooklyn, N.Y., Apr. 26, 1930; s. Joseph and Helen (Plotkin) F. B.S., Columbia U., 1960, postgrad. in mammalian and comparative physiology, 1961-63; M.S., NYU, 1967, Ph.D., 1976. Predoctoral fellow Inst. Microbiology, 1968-72, NYU, 1972-76; postdoctoral fellow Dept of Molecular Biochemistry and Biophysics Yale U., 1972-79; vis. fellow Princeton U. Dept. Chemistry, 1978-82; Res. scientist N.Y. State Inst. Basic Rsch. Human Nutrition and Biochemistry, 1979-82; NIH fellow Albert Einstein Coll. Medicine Dept. of Oncology, 1981-82; sr. rsch. scientist dept. infectious diseases Harvard Med. Sch., 1982-95; adv., prof. Chulalongkorn U., Bangkok, Thailand, 1993-95; assoc. rsch. prof. Johns Hopkins U., 1996-99; rsch. scientist Roswell Park Cancer Inst., 1999—; prof. dept. microbiology Changmai Med. Sch., 1999—; research fellow meml. Sloan-Kettering Cancer Center, N.Y.C., N.Y., 1984-85; sr.research assoc. dept. pathology Cath. Med. Ctr., 1983-84; sr. research assoc. inmolecular biology (in collaboration with the U.S. Fish and Wildlife Service) CUNY, 1985-86; research assoc. dept. immunology and biochemistry Roswell Park Meml. Inst., Buffalo, 1986-87; research assoc., infectious disease, Channing Laboratory, Harvard Medical School, Boston, 1987-88; spl. asst. Sec. Gen. U.N. (promoting the philosophy of human dignity and its impact on world peace), N.Y., 1987-88; asst. research prof. CCNY, 1988-89; vis. scientist in molecular biology, Lewis Thomas Labs, Princeton U.1989-1992; vis. prof. Kasetsart U. Bangkok, Thailand, 1992-94, vis. scholar Boston U. 1992-93; scientific cons. U. Rangoon, 1993—, mem. faculty, Johns Hopkins U, 1996; cons. to various university cellular-molecular labs, inspector of Cell Biology Research in Poland and Russia, Citizens Ambassador Program; advisor curriculum research and cell/molecular biology, lectr. cellular and molecular biology. Asst. to Sec. of Agr., 1970-71 serving as spl. liaison to Congress; conducted survey of emergency med. home call service, Bronx County, NY., 1971-72. Knights Templar fellow, 1973-87; NIH fellow, 1981-82; recip. award for meritorious service, Masonic Valley of White Plains, 1996. Mem. Nat. Inst. of Health (alumni member), Harvey Soc., Fedn. Am. Soc. for Exptl. Biology, Am. Soc. Cell Biologists, Sigma Xi. Lodges: Masons, Shriners, K.T. Home: 315 W 232nd St Bronx NY 10463-3841

FRIEDMAN, ROSELYN L., lawyer; b. Cleve., Dec. 9, 1942; d. Charles and Lillian Edith (Zalzneck) F. BS, U. Pitts., 1964; MA, Case Western Res. U., 1967; JD cum laude, Loyola U., Chgo., 1977. Bar: Ill. 1977, U.S. Dist. Ct. (no. dist.) Ill. 1977. Mem. legal dept. No. Trust Co., Chgo., 1979-84, ptnr., 1984-95; ptnr. Sachnoff & Weaver, Ltd., Chgo., 1995—; mem. Loyola U., Chgo. law rev., profl. adv. com. Chgo. Jewish Fedn., chmn., 1999—. Trustee Jewish Women's Found., 1997—. Mem. ABA, Am. Jewish Congress (gov. coun. Midwest region 1995-97), Chgo. Bar Assn. (cert. appreciation continuing legal edn. program 1984, chmn. trust law com. 1989-90), Chgo. Estate Planning Coun. (program com. 1992-94, 98-99, membership com. 1997-98), Chgo. Fin. Exch. (bd. dirs. 1995-97, sec. 1996-97). Office: Sachnoff & Weaver Ltd 30 S Wacker Dr Ste 2900 Chicago IL 60606-7484

FRIEDMAN, RUSSELL PETER, grief recovery educator, restaurant manager; b. Port Chester, N.Y., Jan. 4, 1943; s. Harry and Betty Sybil (Robfogel) F.; m. Jeanne Baier, June 10, 1975 (div. Oct., 1987); 1 child, Kelly Logan. BA, Rollins Coll., 1964. Owner, mgr. Taming of the Stew, L.A., 1970-72, Lost on Larrabee, L.A., 1972-76, Budapest Hungarian, L.A., 1980-86; mgr. Ghengis Cohen, 1986-89; exec. dir. The Grief Recovery Inst., 1989—. Author: Moving Beyond Loss Work Book, 1994; co-author: The Grief Recovery Hand Book, 1988, rev. edit., 1998; contbr. articles to various publs. Co-founder The Grief Recovery Helpline, L.A., 1989, The Grief Recovery Inst. Ednl. Found., 1992. Avocation: golf. Office: Grief Recovery Inst 7906 Santa Monica Blvd Ste 204 Los Angeles CA 90046-5169

FRIEDMAN, SAMUEL SELIG, lawyer; b. N.Y.C., July 25, 1935; s. Nathan and Anne M. (Sobel) F.; m. Maxine E. Goldfarb, Jan. 7, 1961; 1 child, Alison J. BS, MIT, 1956; MBA, U. Pa., 1959; LLB, Columbia U., 1965. Bar: N.Y. 1965, U.S. Dist. Ct. (so. and ea. dists.) N.Y. 1967, U.S. Supreme Ct. 1984. Assoc. Lord, Day & Lord, N.Y.C., 1965-72; ptnr., mem. exec. com. Lord Day & Lord, Barrett Smith and predecessor firm, N.Y.C., 1972-94; ptnr. Morgan, Lewis & Bockius, N.Y.C., 1994—. Vice chmn., dir., mem. exec. com. Times Square Bus. Improvement Dist., 1992-95. 1st lt. U.S. Army, 1959-62. Mem. ABA, N.Y. State Bar Assn., Assn. of Bar of City of N.Y., MIT Club N.Y., The Penn Club, Phi Delta Phi. Avocations: travel, wine, sports. Office: Morgan Lewis & Bockius 101 Park Ave New York NY 10178-0060

FRIEDMAN, SHARON MAE, science journalism educator; b. Phila., Apr. 28, 1943; d. Thomas and Evelyn Eva (Gordon) Berschler; m. Kenneth A. Friedman, July 12, 1963; children: Melissa, Michael. BA in Biology, Temple U., 1964; MA in Journalism, Pa. State U., 1974. Sci. writer/editor Pa. State U., University Park, 1966-67; assoc. info. officer Nat. Acad. Sci., Washington, 1967-70; editor Ctr. for Study of Higher Edn., University Park, 1970-71; adminstrv. and info. officer U.S. Com. for Internat. Biol. Program, State College, Pa., 1971-74; asst. prof., then assoc. prof. journalism Lehigh U., Bethlehem, Pa., 1974-86, dir. sci. writing program, 1977—, prof., 1986—, chmn. dept. journalism, 1986-95, Iacocca prof., 1992—; cons. Pres.'s Commn. on the Accident at Three Mile Island, Washington, 1979, Clement Internat. Corp., Washington, 1988-90, Environ. Unit, UN Econs. and Social Commn. for Asia/Pacific, Bangkok, 1987-89; mem. adv. bd. Environ. Reporting Forum, Radio-TV News Dirs. Found., 1991-93; participant environ. journalism program Found. Am. Comm., 1992-94; mem. bd. trustees Internat. Food Info. Coun. Found., 1992—, vice chairperson, 1995—; Fulbright Disting. lectr., Brazil, 1982, Bosch Found. lectr., Germany, 1984, 92; cons. in field. Co-author: Reporting on the Environment - Handbook for Journalists, 1988; co-editor: Scientists and Journalists: Reporting Science as News, 1986, Communicating Uncertainty: Media Coverage of New and Controversial Science, 1999; assoc. editor: Risk: Health Safety & Environment; mem. editl. bd. Science Communication; contbr. articles to profl. jours., chpts. to books. EPA grantee, 1990, 92, GM grantee, 1986-93, Ctr. for Fgn. Journalists grantee, 1994. Fellow AAAS (sect. Y officer 1991-95, coun. del., 1999—); mem. Sci. Writing Educators Group (chmn. 1985-91), Assn. for Edn. in Journalism and Mass Comm. (mag. divsn. officer 1988-91), Nat. Assn. Sci. Writers Soc. Environ., Soc. Environ. Jounalists. Achievements include research on mass media coverage of science, environment and technology issues, environmental risk communication, coverage of Alar, radon, dioxin, Chernobyl and Three Mile Island radiation issues, and international environmental journalism and training. Office: Lehigh Univ Dept Journalism & Comm 29 Trembley Dr Bethlehem PA 18015-3066

FRIEDMAN, SHELLY ARNOLD, cosmetic surgeon; b. Providence, Jan. 1, 1949; s. Saul and Estelle (Moverman) F.; m. Andrea Leslie Falchook, Aug. 30, 1975; children: Bethany Erin, Kimberly Rebecca, Brent David, Jennifer Ashley. BA, Providence Coll., 1971; DO, Mich. State U., 1982. Diplomate Nat. Bd. Med. Examiners, Am. Bd. Dermatology. Intern Pontiac (Mich.) Hosp., 1982-83, resident in dermatology, 1983-86; assoc. clin. prof. dept. internal med. Mich. State U., 1984-89, adj. clin. prof., 1989—; med. dir. Inst. Cosmetic Dermatology, Scottsdale, Ariz., 1986—; pres. Am. Bd. Hair Restoration Surgery. Contbr. aritcles to profl. jours. Mem. B'nai B'rith Men's Council, 1973, Jewish Welfare Fund, 1973. Am. Physicians fellow for medicine, 1982. Mem. AMA, Am. Osteopathic Assn., Am. Assn. Cosmetic Surgeons, Am. Acad. Cosmetic Surgery, Internat. Soc. Dermatologic Surgery, Internat. Acad. Cosmetic Surgery, Am. Acad. Dermatology, Am. Soc. Dermatol. Surgery, Frat. Order Police, Sigma Sigma Phi. Jewish. Avocations: karate, horseback riding. Office: Scottsdale Inst Cosmetic Dermatology 5206 N Scottsdale Rd Scottsdale AZ 85253-7006

FRIEDMAN, SIDNEY A., financial services executive; b. Bklyn., Mar. 7, 1935; s. Benjamin and Celia (Jacobs) F.; m. Sue Helen Mansbach, May 2, 1965; children: Lori Beth, Wendi Ellen. B.S., NYU, 1957; student, Bklyn. Law Sch., 1958. CLU, ChFC, MSFS; registered health underwriter. Pres. Corp. Fin. Services, Phila., 1970-99, pres., chmn. bd., 1988—; past pres. Phoenix Mut. Adv. Council; motivational speaker, cons. life ins. orgns.; past pres. Top of the Table/25 Million Dollar Forum. Author: How to Make Money Tomorrow Morning, 1991, Success Systems, It's About Time. Bd. dirs. Fight for Sight, 1983; bd. dirs. Phila. Variety Club, 1993. Mem. Million Dollar Round Table; mem. Top of the Table, 25 Million Dollar Forum; recipient Nat. Quality award, 1983, 95. Mem. Am. Coll. Life Underwriters (pres. 1971-72), Health Underwriters, Nat. Assn. Security Dealers (registered investment advisor), Assn. Advanced Underwriters, Phila. Assn. Life Underwriters, Gen. Agts. and Mgrs So. N.J. (past pres.), CLUs So. N.J. (past pres.), Gen. Agts and Mgrs. Assn. Democrat. Office: Corp Fin Svcs Inc 200 S Broad St Fl 4 Philadelphia PA 19102-3803

FRIEDMAN, STANLEY, insect physiologist, educator; b. N.Y.C., Dec. 11, 1925; s. Nathan and Eva (Rothstein) F.; m. Frances Ray Shapiro, May 21, 1955; children: David, Douglas, Catherine, Matthew. Student, CCNY, 1941-43; BA, U. Ill., 1948; PhD, Johns Hopkins U., 1952. Rsch. assoc. U. Ill., 1953-56; biochemist NIH, 1956-58; asst. prof. entomology Purdue U., 1958-62; rsch. fellow London Sch. Hygiene and Tropical Medicine, 1962-63; assoc. prof. entomology Purdue U., 1963-64; assoc. prof. entomology U. Ill., Urbana, 1964-68, prof., 1968-92, prof. emeritus, 1992—, head dept., 1976-92, assoc. dir. Sch. Life Scis., 1989-92. With USN, 1943-46. Fellow AAAS; mem. Am. Soc. Zoology, Am. Soc. Biol. Chemists, Entomol. Soc. Am., Federated Socs. Exptl. Biology and Medicine, Sigma Xi. Office: 320 Morrill Hall 505 S Goodwin Ave Urbana IL 61801-3707

FRIEDMAN, STEPHEN, company executive. Sr. chmn., ltd. ptnr. Goldman Sachs & Co., N.Y.C. Office: Goldman Sachs & Co 85 Broad St New York NY 10004-2456*

FRIEDMAN, STEPHEN JAMES, lawyer; b. Mar. 19, 1938; s. A.E. Robert and Janice Clara (Miller) F.; m. Fredrica L. Schwab, June 25, 1961; children: Vanessa V., Alexander S. AB magna cum laude, Princeton U., 1959; LLB magna cum laude, Harvard U., 1962. Bar: N.Y. 1962, D.C. 1982. Law clk. to justice William J. Brennan Jr. U.S. Supreme Ct., 1963-64; spl. asst. to maritime adminstr. Maritime Adminstrn., Dept. Commerce, 1964-65; assoc. Debevoise & Plimpton, N.Y.C., 1965-70, ptnr., 1970-77, 81-86, 93—; dep. asst. sec. for capital markets policy Dept. Treasury, Washington, 1977-79; commr. SEC, 1980-81; exec. v.p., gen. counsel E.F. Hutton Group Inc., N.Y.C., 1986-88, Equitable Life Assurance Soc., N.Y.C., 1988-93; lectr. law Columbia U., N.Y.C., 1974-77, 82-85. Author: An Affair With Freedom, the Opinions and Speeches of William J. Brennan, Jr., 1967; contbr. articles on legal and policy aspects of fin. inst. to profl. jours. Active Coun. on Fgn. Rels.; trustee, chmn. emeritus Am. Ballet Theatre, N.Y.C.; vice chmn. Overseas Devel. Coun.; dir. United Way N.Y.C.; mem. bd. govs. NASD, 1991-94, Chgo. Bd. Options Exch., 1982-88. With USAR, 1962-68. Mem. ABA, Assn. of Bar of the City of N.Y. (chmn. com. on securities regulation), Univ. Club. Office: Debevoise & Plimpton 875 3rd Ave Fl 23 New York NY 10022-6256

FRIEDMAN, STEVEN H., federal judge. Bankruptcy judge U.S. Bankruptcy Ct. (so. dist.) Fla., West Palm Beach, 1993—. Fax: 561-833-3153. Office: 202 Federal Bldg 701 Clematis St West Palm Beach FL 33401

FRIEDMAN, STEVEN M., textile company executive; b. 1955. Prin., gen. ptnr. Odyssey Ptnrs.; v.p., treas., dir. JPS Holdings, 1988-93; v.p., treas. JPS Textile Group Inc., Greenville, S.C., 1988-93, chmn., CEO, 1993-95; gen. ptnr. EOS Ptnrs., 1995—. Office: JPS Textile Group Inc 555 N Pleasantburg Dr Greenville SC 29607-2194 Office: EOS Ptnrs 320 Park Ave Fl 22 New York NY 10022-6815*

FRIEDMAN, SUE TYLER, technical publications executive; b. Nürnberg, Germany, Feb. 28, 1925; came to U.S., 1938; d. William and Ann (Federlein) Tyler (Theilheimer); m. Gerald Manfred Friedman, June 27, 1948; children: Judith Fay Friedman Rosen, Sharon Mira Friedman Azaria, Devora Paula Friedman Zweibach, Eva Jane Friedman Scholle, Wendy Tamar Friedman Spanier. Student, Beth Israel Sch. Nursing, 1941-43. Exec. dir. Ventures and Publs. Gerald M. Friedman, 1964—; owner Tyler Publs., Watervliet and Troy, N.Y., 1978-86; treas., dir. Northeastern Sci. Found., Inc., Troy, 1979—; treas. Gerry Exploration, Inc., Troy, 1982-88; office mgr. Rensselaer Ctr. Applied Geology, Troy, 1983—. Pres. Pioneer Women/Na'amat, Tulsa, 1961-64, treas., Jerusalem, Israel, 1964, pres., Albany, N.Y., 1968-70; bd. dirs. Temple Beth-El, 1965—, dir. Hebrew Sch., 1965-80; mem. social program com. Internat. Sedimentological. Congress, 1979. Named Hon. Alumna, Dept. Geology, Bklyn. Coll. at CUNY, 1989; Sue Tyler Friedman medal for distinction in history of geology created in her honor Geol. Soc. London, 1988; recipient Disting. Svc. award Temple Beth-El, 1991, Scroll of Honor, State of Israel Bonds, 1981. Mem. Geology Alumni Assn. (hon.). Avocation: world travel. Office: Northeastern Sci Found Inc/Bklyn Coll CUNY Rensselaer Ctr Applied Geology PO Box 746 Troy NY 12181-0746

FRIEDMAN, SUSAN LYNN BELL, non-profit association executive; b. May 23, 1953; d. Virgil Atwood and Jean Loree (Wiggins) B.; m. Frank H. Friedman, July 31, 1976; 1 child, Alex Charles. BA, Purdue U., 1975; MS, Ind. State U., 1981. Asst. dir. pub. rels. Vincennes U. Jr. Coll., Ind., 1977-83; dir. Knox County C. of C., Vincennes, 1983-84; asst. to pres. Am. Assn. Cmty. and Jr. Colls., Washington, 1985-87; owner, pres. SBF Promotions, 1987—; mgr., program developer Family Resources, Inc., 1988-89; partnership coord. Beaufort (S.C.) County Sch. Dist., 1989-90; job tng. coord. Heart of Ga. Tech. Inst., 1990-92, v.p. econ. devel., 1992-96; exec. dir. Tex. Assn. Ptnrs. in Edn., 1996-98; coord. Cmty. Assessment Program, 1999—. Bd. dirs. Women in Need of God's Shelter, Inc., 1991-96, Ga. Common Cause, 1992-96, pres., 1993-95; mem. Dublin-Laurens Leadership Class, 1994-95; Hoosier scholar, 1971, 72; pres. Annandale BPW, Vincennes, Ind., BPW Dublin and Capital City; pres., treas. Brushy Creek Elem. PTA. Mem. NAFE, LWV (v.p. chpt. 1982-84), ACLU, TSAE, TSPRA, NAPE, TAPE, NOW, Kiwanis. Home: 2544 Brandermill Pl Charlottesville VA 22911 Office: 1025 Park St Charlottesville VA 22901-1647

FRIEDMAN, SYDNEY M., anatomy educator, medical researcher; b. Montreal, Que., Can., Feb. 17, 1916; s. Jacob and Minnie (Signer) F.; m. Constance Livingstone, Sept. 23, 1940. B.Sc., McGill U., Montreal, Can., 1938, M.D., C.M., 1940, M.Sc., 1941, Ph.D., 1946. Med. licentiate, Que. Teaching fellow anatomy McGill U., Montreal, Que., Can., 1940-42, asst. prof. anatomy, 1944-48, assoc. prof. anatomy, 1948-50; prof., head dept. anatomy U. B.C., Vancouver, Can., 1950-81, prof. anatomy, 1981-85, prof. emeritus, 1985—; mem. panel on shock Def. Research Bd., Ottawa, Can., 1955-57; sci. subcom. Can. Heart Found., 1962-66, Am. Heart Assn., 1966-68, B.C. Heart Found., Vancouver, founding mem. Author: Visual Anatomy. Served as flight lt. RCAF, 1943-44. Recipient Premier award for rsch. in aging CIBA Found., 1955, Outstanding Svc. award Heart Found. Can., 1981, Disting. Achievement award Can. Hypertension Soc., 1987; Commemorative medal 125th Anniversary Can. Confedn.; Pfizer travel fellow Clin. Rsch. Inst., Montreal, 1971. Fellow Royal Soc. Can.; mem. Am. Anatomical Assn. (exec. com. 1970-74), Can. Assn. Anatomists (pres. 1965-66, J.C.B. Grant award 1982), Coun. High Blood Pressure Research, Internat. Soc. Hypertension, Am. Physiol. Soc., Royal Vancouver Yacht Club, Vancouver Club. Avocation: painting. Home: 4916 Chancellor Blvd, Vancouver, BC Canada V6T 1E1 Office: U BC Dept Anatomy, 2177 Wesbrook Mall, Vancouver, BC Canada V6T 1Z3

FRIEDMAN, VICTOR ALLEN, linguist, eduator; b. Chgo., Oct. 18, 1949; s. Norman Benjamin and Lorraine (Weisman) F. BA, Reed Coll., 1970; MA, U. Chgo., 1971, PhD, 1975; golden plaque (hon.), U. Skopje, Macedonia, 1991. From asst. prof. to prof. U. N.C., Chapel Hill, 1975-93; prof. U. Chgo., 1993—; cons. Internat. Rsch. and Exch. Bd., 1981—; mem. joint com. on Eastern Europe Am. Coun. Learned Socs., 1992-97, fellow, 1986. Author: Grammatical Categories of the Macedonian Indicative, 1977; translator: Macedonian Historical Phonology, 1983; contbr. numerous articles to profl. jours. Fellow NEH, 1980-81; recipient Medal Peoples Republic Bulgaria, 1982. Mem. Am. Com. Slavists (v.p. 1994—), Am. Assn. Southeast European Studies (pres. 1990-92), Soc. Albanian Studies (v.p. 1978-81), Bulgarian Studies Assn. (nominating com. 1984-90), Macedonian Acad. Arts and Scis. Jewish.

FRIEDMAN, VICTOR STANLEY, lawyer; b. N.Y.C., May 9, 1933; s. Harry and Rose (Cohen) F.; m. Sara Ann Riesner, June 21, 1958 (div.); children: Eric H., Diana B., Michael C.; m. Victoria Schonfeld, Mar. 7, 1984; children: Jared D., Rumyana L. A.B., Harvard U., 1954; LL.B., Yale U., 1957. Bar: N.Y. 1958, U.S. Dist. Ct. (so. dist.) N.Y. 1964, U.S. Dist. Ct. (ea. dist.) N.Y. 1966, U.S. Ct. Appeals (2d cir.) 1966, U.S. Ct. Appeals (4th cir.) 1981, U.S. Ct. Appeals (3d cir.) 1972, U.S. Ct. Appeals (8th cir.) 1970, U.S. Ct. Appeals (10th cir.) 1987, U.S. Supreme Ct. 1974. Asst. to dep. atty. gen. Dept. Justice, Washington, 1958-60; assoc. firm Fried, Frank, Harris, Shriver & Jacobson, N.Y.C., 1960-66, ptnr., 1967—. Served with USAR, 1958-59. Mem. ABA, Assn. of Bar of City of N.Y., Am. Coll. Trial Lawyers. Office: Fried Frank Harris 1 New York Plz Fl 22 New York NY 10004-1980

FRIEDMAN, WILBUR HARVEY, lawyer; b. N.Y.C., May 2, 1907; s. Isador Peter and Zara (Sloat) F.; m. Frances Margolis, May 21, 1943. AB, Columbia U., 1927, LLB, 1930. Bar: N.Y. 1931. Law sec. U.S. Supreme Ct. Justice Harlan F. Stone, 1930-31; staff atty. Office of U.S. Solicitor Gen., 1931-32; mem. firm Proskauer Rose Goetz & Mendelsohn (now Proskauer Rose LLP), N.Y.C., 1932-40; ptnr. Proskauer, Rose, Goetz, & Mendelsohn, N.Y.C., 1940—; lectr. Inst. on Fed. Taxation, NYU, 1943-65, lectr. Sch. Gen. Edn., 1955-60, mem. dean's adv. bd. Coll. Dentistry; v.p., bd. dirs. Charter Corp.; bd. dirs., sec. Lawrence M. Gelb Found.; bd. dirs. Cancer Rsch. Inst., 1983—; chmn. exec. com. bd. visitors Law Sch., Columbia U., 1977-91. Contbr. articles to profl. jours. Chmn. bd. overseers Edith C. Blum Art Inst. at Bard Coll., 1985-93; mem. Rockefeller U. Coun., 1986—; mem. med. ctr. adv. bd. N.Y. Hosp.-Cornell Med. Ctr., 1986—. Mem. ABA (mem. ho. dels. 1978-87), N.Y. State Bar Assn. (mem. exec. com. section 1968-76), Assn. of Bar of City of N.Y. (chmn. com. on mgmt. and operation of profl. practice 1981-85), N.Y. County Lawyers Assn. (pres. 1975-77, mem. exec. com. 1977-79, chmn. com. on taxation 1948-54, chmn. com. on group ins. 1960-74, chmn. spl. com. on consumer agreements 1977-83), Lotos Club, Princeton U. Club, Phi Beta Kappa, Phi Beta Kappa Assocs., Tau Delta Phi. Home: 1016 5th Ave Apt 2D New York NY 10028-0132 Office: Proskauer Rose LLP 1585 Broadway New York NY 10036-8200

FRIEDMAN, WILLIAM HERSH, otolaryngologist, educator; b. Granite City, Ill., Aug. 14, 1938; s. Joseph and Lily May (Brody) F.; m. Hillary Lee, Aug. 9, 1974; children: Joseph Morgan, Alexander Lawrence. AB, Washington U., St. Louis, 1960, MD, 1964. Diplomate: Am. Bd. Otolaryngology. Intern Jackson Meml. Hosp., Miami, Fla., 1964-65; resident in surgery and otolaryngology Mt. Sinai Hosp., N.Y.C., 1965-70; NIH fellow Mt. Sinai Hosp., 1966-67; assoc. prof. otolaryngology Mt. Sinai Sch. Medicine, 1974-76, assoc. attending physician, 1973-76; dir. otolaryngology City Hosp. Center, Elmhurst, N.Y., 1971-76; practice medicine specializing in otolaryngology Beverly Hills, Calif., 1976, Boston, 1977; prof. otolaryngology, chmn. dept. St. Louis U. Sch. Medicine, 1977-87; chief otolaryngology Firmin Desloge Hosp., Cardinal Glennon Meml. Hosp. for Children, 1977-87; dir. Park Cen. Inst., 1987—; prof. otolaryngology Columbia U., N.Y.C., 1987-90; dir. dept. otolaryngology St. Luke's/Roosevelt Hosp. 1987-90; chief dept. otolaryngology, head neck surgery Deaconess Hosp., 1988-98; pres. Friedman & Assocs., Inc. Contbr. articles to books and profl. jours. Fellow ACS, Am. Acad. Otolaryngology, Am. Acad. Facial Plastic and Reconstructive Surgery (chmn. forum for surg. excellence, credentials com., Ira J. Tresley Meml. award 1978), Am. Soc. Head and Neck Surgery, Am. Laryngol., Rhinol. and Otol. Soc.; mem. AMA (Hektoen gold medal 1978), Med. Soc. County New York, Soc. Univ. Otolaryngologists, Centurion Club of Deafness Rsch. Found., N.Y. State Soc. Surgeons, Assn. Acad. Depts. Otolaryngology, Mo. Ear, Nose and Throat Club (pres. 1987-88), Westwood Country Club, Mission Hills Country Club, Boothbay Harbor Yacht Club, Phi Beta Kappa, Sigma Alpha Mu. Inventor surg. instruments, including facial plastic instrumentarium. Home: 15 Lake Forest Saint Louis MO 63117-1356 Office: Park Cen Inst 6125 Clayton Ave Saint Louis MO 63139-3265

FRIEDMAN, WILLIAM JOHN, psychology educator; b. May 22, 1950. BA in Psychology with honors, Oberlin Coll., 1972; PhD in Psychology, U Rochester, 1977. Asst. instr. grad. stats. U. Rochester, 1973-74, instr. devel. psychology, 1975-76; trainee in devel. psychology U.S. Dept. Pub. Health, 1972-76; asst. prof. psychology Oberlin (Ohio) Coll., 1976-84, assoc. prof. psychology, 1984-91, prof., 1991—, chair dept. psychology, 1992—; vis. scientist Applied Psychology Unit, Med. Rsch. Coun., Cambridge, Eng., 1983; vis. scientist lab. exptl. psychology U. Grenoble II, 1988-89; vis. scientist U. Canterbury, 1994. Author (book) About Time: Inventing the Fourth Dimension, 1990; editor (book) The Developmental Psychology of Time, 1982; co-editor (book) Time, Action & Cognition, 1992; contbr. articles to profl. jours. Mem. Soc. for Rsch. in Child Devel. Office: Oberlin Coll Dept Psychology Oberlin OH 44074*

FRIEDMANN, E(MERICH) IMRE, biologist, educator; b. Budapest, Hungary, Dec. 20, 1921; came to U.S., 1965; s. Hugo and Gisella (Singer) Friedmann; 1 child, Daphna; m. Roseli Ocampo, July 22, 1974. PhD, U. Vienna, 1951. Instr., lectr. Hebrew U., Jerusalem, 1952-66; assoc. prof. Queens U., Kingston, Ont., Can., 1967-68; assoc. prof. Fla. State U., Tallahassee, 1968-76, prof., 1976—, Robert Lawton Disting. prof., 1991—, dir. Polar Desert Rsch. Ctr., 1985—; concurrent prof. Nanjing U., People's Republic of China, 1987—; vis. prof. Fla. State U., Tallahassee, 1966-67, U. Vienna, 1975. Editor Antarctic Microbiology, 1993; contbr. articles to profl. jours. Recipient Congl. Antartic Service medal NSF, 1979, Alexander v. Humboldt award, 1987, resolution of commendation Gov. of Fla., 1978, Procter & Gamble award Am. Soc. Microbiology, 1998. Fellow AAAS, Linnean Soc. London, Royal Microsc. Soc., Explorers Club; mem. Hungarian Acad. Scis. (fgn.), Am. Soc. Microbiology (Procter and Gamble award in environ. microbiology 1998), Brit. Phycol. Soc., Indian Phycol. Soc., Am. Phycol. Soc., Internat. Phycol. Soc., Soc. Phycol. France, Internat. Soc. for Study of Origins of Life, Hungarian Algological Soc. (hon.). Jewish. Achievements include co-discovery of micro-organism (cryptoendolithic lichens) living in Antarctic rocks, 1976. Home: 692 Duparc Cir Tallahassee FL 32312-1464 Office: Fla State U Dept Biol Sci Tallahassee FL 32306

FRIEDMANN, JEAN MULVEY See VINCENT, EMILY

FRIEDMANN, PATRICIA ANN, writer; b. New Orleans, La., Oct. 29, 1946; d. Werner and Marjorie Sybil (Cahn) F.; m. Robert E. Skinner, Mar. 17, 1979 (div. Nov. 1996); children: Esme Friedmann, Werner Skinner. AB, Smith Coll., 1968; MEd, Temple Univ., 1970; ABD, Univ. Denver, 1975. fiction workshop facilitator, New Orleans, 1994—; reviewer Publishers Weekly Brightleaf, Times-Picayune, 1993—; spkr. in field. Author: Too Smart to Be Rich, 1988, The Exact Image of Mother, 1991, Eleanor Rushing, 1999 (Barnes & Noble Discover Great Writers selection), (play) The Accidental Jew as part of Native Tongues, 1994; short stories. Mem. Authors Guild. Home: 8330 Sycamore Pl New Orleans LA 70118-2941

FRIEDMANN, PAUL, surgeon, educator; b. Vienna, Austria, Dec. 2, 1933; came to U.S., 1938; s. Erich and Rochelle (Behar) F.; m. Janee Armstrong, Apr. 24, 1962; children: Pamela, Cynthia. BA, U. Pa., 1955; MD, Harvard U., 1959. Diplomate Am. Bd. Surgery, Am. Bd. Vascular Surgery. Chmn. dept. surgery Baystate Med. Ctr., Springfield, Mass., 1971-98, sr. v.p. acad. affairs, 1996—; chmn. ad interim dept. surgery, Tufts U. Sch. Medicine, Boston, 1996—; mem. residency rev. com., 1985-91, chmn., 1989-91; chmn. RRC Coun., Accreditation Coun. for Grad. Med. Edn., 1989-91, mem., 1994—. Contbr. articles to profl. jours. Served to capt. USAF, 1961-63. Fellow ACS (bd. govs. 1978-84, 94—, vice chmn., 1998—, pres. Mass. chpt. 1987, exec. com. bd. govs. 1996—, adv. coun. for gen. surgery 1996—); mem. Am. Surg. Assn., Assn. Program Dirs. in Surgery (sec. 1985-87, pres. 1987-89), Coun. Med. Specialty Socs. (bd. dirs. 1993—, sec. 1995-96, pres. elect 1996-97, pres. 1997—98), New Eng. Soc. Vascular Surgery (recorder 1989-90, pres.-elect 1990-91, pres. 1991-92), New Eng. Surg. Soc. (treas. 1991-95, pres.-elect 1995-96, pres. 1996-97), Accreditation Coun. for Grad. Med. Edn. (mem. exec. com. 1995—, chmn. designate 1997—, chmn., 1998—). Office: Baystate Med Ctr 759 Chestnut St Springfield MA 01199-1001

FRIEDMANN, PERETZ PETER, aerospace engineer, educator; b. Timisoara, Romania, Nov. 18, 1938; came to U.S., 1969; s. Mauritius and Elisabeth Friedmann; m. Esther Sarfati, Dec. 8, 1964. DSc, MIT, 1972. Engring. officer Israel Def. Force, 1961-65; sr. engr. Israel Aircraft Industries, Ben Gurion Airport, Israel, 1965-69; research asst. dept. aeronautics and astronautics MIT, Cambridge, 1969-72; asst. prof. mech. and aerospace engring. dept. UCLA, 1972-77, assoc. prof., 1977-80, prof., 1980-98; chmn. dept. mech. and aerospace engring. UCLA, Los Angeles, 1988-91; François-Xavier Bagnoud prof. aerospace engring. dept. U. Mich., Ann Arbor, 1999—. Editor in chief Vertica-Internat. Jour. Rotocraft and Powered Lift Aircraft, 1980-90; contbr. numerous articles to profl. jours. Grantee NASA, Air Force Office Sci. Rsch., U.S. Army Rsch. Office, NSF. Fellow AIAA (recipient Structures, Structural Dynamics and Materials award 1996, Structures, Structural Dynamics and Materials Lectr. award 97); mem. ASME (Structures and Materials award 1984), Am. Helicopter Soc., Sigma Xi. Jewish. Office: U Mich Aerospace Engring Dept 3001 FXB Bldg Ann Arbor MI 48109-2140

FRIEDMANN, THEODORE, physician; b. Vienna, June 16, 1935; s. Eric and Rochelle (Bewar) F.; m. Ingrid Anna Stromberg, Jan. 3, 1965; children: Eric, Carl. BA, U. Pa., 1956, MD, 1960, MA, 1994. Diplomate Nat. Bd. Med. Examiners. Staff scientist NIH, Bethesda, Md., 1965-68; from asst. to full prof. pediatrics U. Calif. San Diego, La Jolla, 1970—, prof. pediatrics, dir. molecular genetics; vis. scientist Salk Inst., La Jolla, 1968-70; Newton Abraham vis. prof., fellow Lincoln Coll., U. Oxford, Eng., 1994; mem. Congrl. Biomed. Ethics Adv. Com., U.S. Congress, Washington, 1989-92; mem. Exptl. Vriology Study Sect./NIH, Washington, 1986-90. Author: (monograph) Gene Therapy: Fact and Fiction, 1993; editor: (book series) Molecular Genetic Medicine, 1989—; patentee in gene therapy. Avocation: music. Office: Univ Calif San Diego Pediatrics Dept-Mail Code 0634 La Jolla CA 92093*

FRIEDMAN PHILLIPS, PAULINE See VAN BUREN, ABIGAIL

FRIEDRICH, PAUL, anthropologist, linguist, poet; b. Cambridge, Mass., Oct. 22, 1927; s. Carl Joachim and Lenore Louise (Pelham) F.; m. Lore

Bucher, Jan. 6, 1950 (div. Jan. 1966); children: Maria Elizabeth, Susan Guadalupe, Peter Roland; m. Margaret Hardin, Feb. 26, 1966 (div. June 1974); m. Deborah Joanna Gordon, Aug. 9, 1975 (div. Nov. 1996); children: Katherine Ann, Joan Lenore; m. Domnica Radulescu, Nov. 10, 1996; 1 child, Nicholas Anton. BA, Harvard Coll., 1950; MA, Harvard U., 1951; PhD, Yale U., 1957. Instr. U. Conn., Storrs, 1956-57; asst. prof. Harvard U., Cambridge, Mass., 1957-58; jr. linguistic scholar Deccan Coll., Poona, India, 1958-59; asst. prof. anthropology U. Pa., Phila., 1959-62; assoc. prof. anthropology U. Chgo., 1962-67, prof. anthropology, linguistics and soc. thought, 1967-96, prof. emeritus, 1996—. Author: Proto-Indo-European Trees, 1970, Agrarian Revolt in a Mexican Village, 1970, The Meaning of Aphrodite, 1978, Bastard Moons, 1979, Language, Context and Imagination, 1979, The Language Parallax, 1986, The Princes of Naranja, 1987; co-editor: Russia and Eurasia-China, 1994, Music in Russian Poetry, 1998. Served to pfc. U.S. Army, 1946-47, Germany. Grantee Wenner-Gren Found., 1955; grantee NIMH, summers 1961-62; fellow Social Sci. Research Council, 1966-67; Guggenheim fellow, 1982-83. Mem. Linguistic Soc. Am. (chmn. program com. 1972, chmn. nominating com. 1975, mem. exec. com. 1981-83), Am. Acad. Arts and Scis. Home: 5500 S South Shore Dr Apt 1609 Chicago IL 60637-1896 Office: U Chgo Dept Anthropology 1126 E 59th St Chicago IL 60637-1580

FRIEDRICH, ROBERT EDMUND, retired electrical engineer, corporate consultant; b. Pitts., July 16, 1918; s. Henry Nicholas and Hildagard Caroline (Schauwecker) F.; m. Mary Ellen Forsell; children: Robert Edmund Jr., Dennis Warren, Norman Theodore. BS in Physics and Engring., U. Pitts., 1940, MS in Physics, 1953. Rsch. asst. Mellon Inst. Indsl. Rsch., Pitts., 1940; advanced devel. engr. Westinghouse Elec. Corp., Pitts., 1940-62, mgr. advanced devel. engring., 1962-75, cons., 1975-80; cons., 1960-70; part-time prof. U. Pitts. Co-author: Circuit Interruption, 1984; contbr. numerous tech. articles to profl. jours.; holder 29 patents. Elder Presbyn. Ch. and Christian Retreat, 1985—, chmn. community com., 1988—. Life fellow IEEE (mem. switchgear com. 1954-85, power cir. breaker com., 1954-89, chmn. power cir. breaker com. 1970-74). Home: Christian Retreat 921 Faith Cir E Lot 27 Bradenton FL 34202-3016

FRIEDRICHS, EDWARD C., architect. BA, Stanford U., 1965; MArch, U. Pa., 1968. Lic. architect Calif., Nev., Utah, Hawaii, N.Y. Architect M. Arthur Gensler Jr. & Assocs., San Francisco, 1969—; dir. projects M. Arthur Gensler Jr. & Assocs., San Francisco, Calif., 1973-76; mng. prin. M. Arthur Gensler Jr. & Assocs., L.A., 1976-95; pres. Gensler, Santa Monica, Calif., 1995—; also bd. dirs., mem. mgmt. com. Gensler, Santa Monica. Pres., bd. govs. West L.A. County coun. Boy Scouts Am. Fellow AIA; mem. Internat. Interior Design Assn., Internat. Facility Mgmt. Assn., Nat. Coun. Archtl. Registration Bds., Urban Land Inst. Office: Gensler 2500 Broadway Ste 300 Santa Monica CA 90404-3062*

FRIEL, BERNARD PRESTON, lawyer; b. St. Paul, Minn., Aug. 23, 1930; s. Bernard Emmett and Janice Virginia (Countryman) F.; m. Damaris Hofer, Jan. 26, 1955; children: Kimberly C., Deirdre Lee, Kevin Scott. BSL, U. Minn., 1954, LLB, 1954. Bar: Minn. 1954, U.S. Dist. Ct. Minn. 1958, U.S. Ct. Appeals (8th cir.) 1959. Asst. judge adv. USAF, Langley AFB, Va., 1954-56; from assoc. to ptnr. Briggs and Morgan, P.A., St. Paul and Mpls., 1956-85, 90—; vice chmn., sec., gen. counsel Hemar Corp., St. Paul, 1985-90; bd. dirs. Lifeworks Inc. Bd. dirs. Voyageur Outward Bound Sch., Minn., 1975-77, Project Environ. Found., 1980-84, Thomas Irvine Dodge Found., St. Paul, 1980-84, Twin Cities Marathon, Inc., 1982-84; bd. dirs., gen. counsel Minn. chpt. Am. Heart Assn., 1973-83; pres. St. Paul Assn. for Retarded Citizens, 1966-67; mem. sch. bd. West St. Paul Mendota Heights, 1967-69; active in Minn Mental Retardation Planning Coun., 1965, Mpls. and St. Paul Met. Aircraft Sound Abatement Coun., 1985-90; mem., chair Minn. Higher Edn. Facilities Authority, 1971-79, and others; bd. trustees Sci. Mus. Minn., 1992-98. 1st lt. USAF, 1954-56. Named among 10 Outstanding Young Men, Minn. Jaycees, 1965; inducted to Hall of Fame St. Paul Cen. High Sch., 1989. Mem. ABA (coun. state and local govt. law sect.), Minn. Bar Assn., Ramsey County Bar Assn., Nat. Assn. Bond Lawyers (pres. 1979-80, honored with creation of Bernard Friel award 1982), Minn. Club (bd. dirs. 1994-99, pres. 1999), N.Am. Nature Photography Assn. (bd. dirs., treas., pres.-elect 1998—). Home: 651 Mohican Ln Saint Paul MN 55120-1633 Office: Briggs and Morgan PA 2200 1st St N Saint Paul MN 55109-3210

FRIEL, BRIAN (BERNARD PATRICK FRIEL), author; b. Omagh, County Tyrone, No. Ireland, Jan. 9, 1929; s. Patrick and Christina (MacLoone) F.; m. Anne Morrison, Dec. 27, 1955; children: Paddy, Mary, Judy, Sally, David. Student, St. Columb's Coll., 1941-46; BA, St. Patrick's Coll., Maynooth, Ireland, 1948; postgrad., St. Joseph's Tchrs. Tng. Coll., Belfast, Ireland, 1949-50; Litt.D. (hon.), Rosary Coll., Chgo., Nat. U. Ireland, New U. Ulster; Trinity Coll., Dublin, Ireland. Tchr. various schs. Derry City, No. Ireland, 1950-60; freelance writer, 1960—; with Tyrone Guthrie Theatre, 1963; co-founder Field Day Theatre Co., Derry, No. Ireland, 1980. Author: (short stories) A Saucer of Larks, 1964, The Gold in the Sea, 1966, The Diviner: Brian Friel's Best Short Stories, 1983, (plays) This Doubtful Paradise, 1960, The Enemy Within, 1962, The Blind Mice, 1963, Philadelphia, Here I Come!, 1964, The Loves of Cass McGuire, 1966, Lovers, 1967, Crystal and Fox, 1968, The Mundy Scheme, 1969, The Gentle Island, 1971, The Freedom of the City, 1972, Volunteers, 1975, Living Quarters, 1977, Faith Healer, 1979, Aristocrats, 1979 (London Evening Standard Best Play award 1988, Best Fgn. Play award N.Y. Drama Critics Circle 1989), Translations, 1980 (Christopher Ewart-Biggs Meml. prize Brit. Theatre Assn. 1981, Plays and Players Best New Play award 1981), American Welcome, 1980, The Communication Cord, 1982, Making History, 1988, Dancing at Lughnasa, 1990 (Tony Best Play award 1992), Wonderful Tennessee, 1993, Molly Sweeney, 1994, Give Me Your Answer, Do!, 1997; (translator) Three Sisters (Anton Chekhov), 1981, Uncle Vanya, 1998; (adaptation) Fathers and Sons (Ivan Turgenev); (screenplay) Philadelphia, Here I Come!, 1970; (version) A Month in the Country; editor: The Last of the Name; contbr. short stories to New Yorker. Mem. Irish Senate, 1987. Recipient Macauley fellow Irish Arts Coun., 1963; hon. fellow U. Coll., Dublin. Fellow Royal Soc. Literature; mem. Nat. Assn. Irish Artists, Am. Acad. Arts and Letters. Office: Drumaweir House, Greencastle, Donegal Ireland

FRIEL, DANIEL DENWOOD, SR., manufacturing executive; b. Queenstown, Md., Aug. 11, 1920; s. Samuel Edward Whiting and Martha Washington (Reynolds) F.; m. Helen June Hennessy, May 1, 1943; children: Barbara Friel Holme, Martha Friel Wilson, Patricia , Daniel D. Jr. BChemE, Johns Hopkins U., 1942. Supr. optical instruments Manhattan Project, U. Chgo., 1943-45; dir. applied physics E.I. du Pont, Wilmington, Del., 1945-61, mgr. investments, 1961-69, dir. electronic products, 1974-77, dir. instrument products, 1977-82; pres. Holotron Corp., Wilmington, 1969-71; pres., chmn. Edgecraft Corp., Wilmington, 1983-91; chmn. bd., chief exec. officer Edgecraft Corp., Avondale, Pa., 1991—; trustee Mt. Cuba Astron. Obs., Wilmington, 1960—. Co-author: Process Instruments and Control, 1960; contbr. articles to profl. jours. Trustee Tatnall Sch., Wilmington, 1967-74. Mem. Phys. Soc. Am., Optical Soc. Am., Instrument Soc. Am., Ams. for Competitive Enterprise System (bd. dirs.), Tau Beta Pi. Achievements include patents for radiation measurement, instruments, and household appliances; invention of radiation detection and analysis devices. Office: Edgecraft Corp 825 Southwood Rd Avondale PA 19311-9765

FRIELING, GERALD HARVEY, JR., specialty steel company executive; b. Kansas City, Mo., Apr. 29, 1930; s. Gerald Harvey and Mary Ann (Coons) F.; m. Joan Lee Bigham, June 14, 1952; children: John, Robert, Nancy. BS in Mech. Engring., U. Kans., 1951. Application engr. Westinghouse Elec. Corp., Pitts., 1951-53; mfg. mgr. Madison-Faessler Tool Co., Moberly, Mo., 1956-60; gen. mgr. wire and tubing Tex. Instruments Inc., Attleboro, Mass., 1960-69; v.p. Air Products & Chems. Co., Allentown, Pa., 1969-79; pres., chief exec. officer, chmn. bd. Nat. Standard Co., Niles, Mich., 1979-89, retired; CEO Tokheim Corp., 1990-91, chmn. bd., 1990-96, vice-chmn., 1997—; bd. dirs. Mossberg Printing Co., CTS; pres. Frieling & Assocs.; instr. Brown U., 1965-68; adj. prof. U. Notre Dame, Grad. Sch. Bus.; mem. adv. bd. U. Kans. Sch. Engring., 1983-96. Author; patentee in field. Served to lt. USNR, 1953-56, Korea. Recipient Wire Assn. medal, 1966, Disting. Engring. Service award U. Kans., 1986. Presbyn. Clubs: Union League (Chgo.), Signal Point Country, Summit.

FRIEMAN, EDWARD ALLAN, academic administrator, educator; b. N.Y.C., Jan. 19, 1926; s. Joseph and Belle (Davidson) F.; m. Ruth Paula Rodman, June 19, 1949 (dec. May 1966); children: Jonathan, Michael, Joshua; m. Joy Fields, Sept. 17, 1967; children: Linda Gatchell, Wendy. BS, Columbia U., 1946, MS in Physics, 1948; PhD in Physics, Poly. Inst. Bklyn., 1952. Prof. astrophys. scis., dep. dir. Plasma Physics Lab. Princeton U., N.J., 1953-79; dir. energy rsch. Dept. Energy, Washington, 1979-81; exec. v.p. Sci. Applications Internat. Corp., La Jolla, Calif., 1981-86; dir. Scripps Instn. Oceanography, La Jolla, 1986-96; vice-chancellor marine scis. U. Calif., San Diego, 1986-96, rsch. prof., dir. emeritus, 1996—; vice-chmn. White House Sci. Coun., 1981-89, Def. Sci. Bd., Washington, 1984-90; mem. Joint Oceanog. Insts., Inc., 1986—, chmn., 1991—; chmn. supercollider site evaluation com. NRC, 1987-89; sci. adv. com. GM, 1987-93, corp. Charles Stark Draper Lab., Inc., 1989—, Sec. Energy Adv. Bd., 1990—, v.p. Space Policy adv. bd., 1992—; bd. dirs. Sci. Applications Internat. Corp.; chmn. NASA Earth Observing Sys. Engring. Rev., 1991-92, v.p.'s space policy adv. bd., 1992—; chmn. Pres.'s Com. on Nat. Medal Sci., 1992-93; chmn. bd. global change NAS/NRC, 1993-94, chmn. bd. on sustainable devel., 1995—; active Joint Oceanog. Insts., Inc., 1986—, chmn., 1991-94; spl. study group NRAC, 1995—; mem. law and policy adv. bd. Ctr. for Oceans, 1994—; mem. Def. Sci. Bd. Task Force on Future Submarines, 1997—. Contbr. articles to profl. jours. With USN, 1943-46, PTO. Recipient Disting. Service medal Dept. Energy, Compass Disting. Achievement Award, Marine Technology Soc., 1995; Disting. Alumni award Poly. Inst. Bklyn.; NSF sr. postdoctoral fellow; Guggenheim fellow. Fellow Am. Phys. Soc. (Richtmyer award); mem. AAAS, NAS, Am. Philos. Soc., Cosmos Club (Washington). Avocations: piano, tennis, literature. Home: 6425 Muirlands Dr La Jolla CA 92037-6310 Office: Univ Calif San Diego Inst Geophys & Plan Physics 9500 Gilman Dr La Jolla CA 92093-5003*

FRIEND, DAVID, publishing executive; b. Chgo., Jan. 31, 1955; m. Nancy Paulsen; children: Sam and Molly (twins). BA summa cum laude, Amherst Coll., 1977. Corr. Life mag., 1978-86, sr. editor, 1987-92; dir. photography and new media Life mag., N.Y.C., 1992-98, dir. photography, asst. mng. editor, 1998; head creative dept. Vanity Fair, 1998—; mem. numerous nat. and internat. photography award juries; co-curator numerous photog. exhbns. including Somalia's Cry; videos include LIFE at Woodstock; prodr. CD-ROM The Face of LIFE, 1936-72; helped place 1st ind. photog. exhbn. on genocide in Bosnia at U.S. Holocaust Meml. Mus., Washington. Author: The Meaning of Life, More Reflections on the Meaning of Life, (juvenile) Baseball, Football, Daddy and Me; contbr. articles to London Sunday Times, Playboy, Nat. Lampoon, Contemporary Lit. Criticism, Life, N.Y. Times Sunday Mag.; editl. dir. LIFE's Web site. Recipient photojournalism editing award Nat. Press Photographers Assn. Mem. Internat. Ctr. Photography (pres. coun.), Overseas Press Club. Office: Vanity Fair Time Life Bldg 350 Madison Ave New York NY 10017*

FRIEND, DAVID ROBERT, chemist; b. Vallejo, Calif., Aug. 10, 1956; s. Carl Gilbert and Roberta (Schwarzrock) F.; m. Carol Esther Warren, Dec. 17, 1983; 1 child, Ian, Michael. BS in Food Biochemistry, U. Calif., Davis, 1979; PhD in Agrl. Chemistry, U. Calif., Berkeley, 1983. Polymer chemist SRI Internat., Menlo Park, Calif., 1984-87, sr. polymer chemist controlled release and biomed. polymers dept., 1987-90, assoc. dir. controlled release and biomed. polymers dept., 1990-92, dir. controlled release and biomed. polymers dept., 1992-93; exec. dir. rsch. and product devel. Cibus Pharm., Burlingame, Calif., 1993-94; v.p. rsch. and product devel. Cibus Pharm., Redwood City, Calif., 1994-96, v.p., chief scientific officer, 1996-98; sr. dir. pharm. ops. Vascular Therapeutics, Mountain View, Calif., 1998—; leader Biopharms. Rsch. Group, 1990; lectr. U. Calif. Sch. Pharmacy, San Francisco. Assoc. editor Jour. Controlled Release, 1991-96, editor, 1996-98; mem. editl. bd. four sci. jours.; contbr. articles to scholarly jours.; patentee in field. Mem. Controlled Release Soc., Am. Assn. Pharm. Sci. Democrat. Jewish. Avocations: piano, swimming. Home: 454 9th Ave Menlo Park CA 94025-1802

FRIEND, EDWARD MALCOLM, III, lawyer, educator; b. Birmingham, Ala., Oct. 12, 1946; s. Edward M. Jr. and Hermione Frances (Curjel) F. BA in History, U. Ala., 1968, JD, 1971. Bar: Ala. 1971. Shareholder Sirote and Permutt, P.C., Birmingham, 1971—, pres., 1991-93; chmn. Birmingham Area C. of C., 1990-91; chmn. dist. bd. dirs. Colonial Bank Ala., Birmingham, 1985—; adj. prof. U. Ala., Birmingham, 1994—. Chmn. Birmingham Area chpt. ARC, 1987-88; chmn. bd. Nat. Conf. Christians and Jews, 1983, nat. bd., 1981-88; pres. coun. U. Ala., Birmingham, 1980-94, Birmingham Jewish Fedn., 1984-89, United Way Ctrl. Ala., 1984-99, chmn., 1993-94, gen. campaign chmn., 1989; bd. dirs. Childrens Hosp. Ala., 1986—; exec. com. Ala. Symphony Assn., 1980-82, bd. dirs., 1982-85, Birmingham Festival Arts, 1978-88, pres., 1984-85, chmn., 1985-86; mem. nat. leadership coun. United Way Am.; pres. Big Bros./Big Sisters Greater Birmingham, 1980, chmn., 1981-83; trustee St. Vincent's Hosp., 1982-86, v.p., 1984-86, Ala. Sch. Fine Arts Found., 1985-91; chmn. Leadership Ala., 1993; bd. dirs. Boy Scouts Am., 1996—. Recipient Brotherhood award Nat. Conf. Christians and Jews, 1987; named to Ala. Acad. of Honor; named Lawyer of Yr., Birmingham Legal Secretarial Assn., 1976, Outstanding Alumnus, U. Ala. Sch. Law, 1984. Mem. So. Inst. Health Law (chmn. 1985-87), Nat. Health Lawyers Assn. (bd. dirs. 1992-95), Farrah Law Soc. (chmn. 1982-84). Office: Sirote and Permutt PC 2222 Arlington Ave S Birmingham AL 35205-4004

FRIEND, HAROLD CHARLES, neurologist; b. Chgo., Nov. 28, 1946; s. Leonard Nathan and Sharlee (Friedman) F.; m. Joyce Friend; children: Reed, Chad. BA, U. Tex., 1968, MD, 1972. Diplomate Am. Bd. Neurology. Resident Upstate Med. Ctr., Syracuse, N.Y., 1972-73, Albert Einstein Coll. Medicine, Bronx, N.Y., 1973-75; mem. staff Boca Raton (Fla.) Community Hosp., 1975—; pres. Neurosci. Ctr., Boca Raton, 1984—; spl. expert witness Fla. Agy. for Health Care Adminstrn.; expert med. advisor divsn. workers compensation Fla. Dept. Labor and Employment Security; bd. dirs. So. Security Bankcorp., Mankrech Transp., 1999—; pres. Puget Sound Yellow Taxi, Inc., 1994-95. Author: Territorial Marking, 1968, Bell's Palsy, 1975, Transient Global Amnesia, 1987. Bd. dirs. Boca Raton Children's Mus., 1989-92; dist. chmn., assoc. lodge advisor Boy Scouts Am., 1980-89, mem. exec. bd., v.p. Gulfstream coun., 1988-93, pres. coun., 1993-95, area I v.p., 1990-92, area IV v.p., 1993-95, area IV pres., 1995-98, mem. so. region exec. bd., 1993—, mem. internat. scouting com., 1998—, chmn. direct svc. coun. exec. bd., 1999—; exec. bd. United Way, Palm Beach County Agy. Rels. Com., 1992-95, mem. allocation com., 1990-92. Recipient Order of Arrow Vigil Honor award Boy Scouts Am., 1983, Dist. Merit award, 1987, Silver Beaver award, 1990, Wood Badge, 1990, Disting. Commr. award, 1991, Disting. Eagle Scout, 1997, Silver Antelope award, 1997; James West fellow, 1993, 1910 Soc., 1998. Fellow Am. Acad. Disability Evaluating Physicians, Am. Acad. Neurology; mem. Am. Soc. Neuroimaging (cert.), So. Clin. Neurol. Soc., Fla. Soc. Neurology, N.Y. Acad. Scis. (life), Sierra Club (life), Palm Beach Med. Svc. (vice chmn. med./legal com.), Rotary (bd. dirs., pres. Boca Raton chpt., dist. world fellowship chmn. 1992-94, 96-97, dist. found. chmn. 1994, chmn. dist. conf. 1995, gov.'s rep. 1994-95, 96-97, dist. gov. 1998-99, chmn. coll. govs. 1999—, Paul Harris fellow, Dist. Found. Svc. award 1992, 95, Pres. Salute Commendation 1993, Internat. Fellowship Running and Fitness Rotarians (internat. chmn. 1992-98, internat. treas. 1998-99, internat. sec. 1999—), Internat. Fellowship Scouting Rotarians (N.Am. sect. chmn. 1995-96, internat. sec. 1996-98, internat. vice chair 1998-99, internat. chair 1999—), Boca Raton Road Runners Club (pres. 1992-93), Phi Beta Kappa, Phi Kappa Phi, Theta Xi, Alpha Phi Omega. Avocation: marathons. Office: 1500 NW 10th Ave Ste 105 Boca Raton FL 33486-1344

FRIEND, HELEN MARGARET, chemist; b. Lyndon, Ohio, Jan. 30, 1931; d. Maurice Chapman and Margaret (Beath) Mossbarger; m. William Warren Friend, Oct. 9, 1982. BA in Chemistry, Coll. of Wooster, 1953. Rsch. chemist Union Carbide Co., Cleve., 1953-56, asst. patent coord. battery products div., 1956-59, patent coord., 1959-86; patent coord. Eveready Battery Co., Westlake, Ohio, 1986-90, tech. patent assoc., 1990-95; ret., 1995; mng. editor JEC Press-Internat. Battery Materials Assn., Cleve., 1978—. Mng. editor Progress in Batteries and Battery Materials, 1978-94, JEC Battery Newsletter, 1987—; tech. editor Electrochem. Soc. Japan, U.S. br., 1975-96; editor-in-chief tech. English divsn. Internat. Tech. Exch. Soc., 1998—. Mem. Am. Chem. Soc., Electrochem. Soc., Phi Beta Kappa. Presbyterian. Avocations: little theater, reading, choral singing. Home: 576 Buckeye Dr Sheffield Lk OH 44054-1615

FRIEND, L. EDWARD, federal judge; b. 1941. BA, W.Va. U., 1963, LLB, 1968; MBA, U. Akron, 1968. Acctg. and bus. instr. W.Va. U., 1966-73; regional counsel IRS, 1968-69; ptnr. Tomasky & Friend, 1973-84; chief bankruptcy judge U.S. Dist. Ct. (no. dist.) W.Va., 1985—, asst. U.S. atty., 1995. Office: US Dist Ct (we dist) Va No Fed Bldg 12th and Chapline Sts Wheeling WV 26003

FRIEND, MIRIAM RUTH, personnel company executive; b. Scranton, Pa., May 19, 1925; d. Benjamin and Etta (Weiss) Loewy; m. Sidney Friend, Aug. 27, 1950. BA, Syracuse U., 1947; cert., Inst. Pub. Welfare Tng. Cornell U., 1950. Social worker Child Placement div. N.Y. State Dept. Welfare, Binghamton and Ithaca, 1948-52; v.p. Office Help Temps., Yonkers, N.Y., 1954-83; pres. Friend & Friend Personnel Agy., Yonkers, N.Y., 1985—. Mem. Eliz Seton Coll. Adv. Council; pres. Pvt. Industry Council, Yonkers, 1981-82, Yonkers Gen. Hosp. Aux., 1983-84, Big Bros./Big Sisters, Yonkers, 1978-80; bd. dirs. Salvation Army, Yonkers, 1977—; publicity chmn. Sen. John E. Flynn Salute, 1986; chmn. breakfast com. Yonkers C. of C., 1978; chmn. Work Opportunities Referral for Kids, Wednesdays Together, 1993—; bd. dirs. Community Planning Council; trustee Yonkers Gen. Hosp., 1978—; coord. mature singles Temple Beth Abraham, 1990—; v.p. Jewish Coun. Yonkers, 1995—. Recipient Disting. Service award United Way, 1983, Community Service award Yonkers Council of Chs., 1984, Woman in Bus. award YWCA, 1986, United Jewish Appeal award, 1996; named Pioneer of Industry Ind. Office Services, Hilton Head, S.C., 1984. Mem. Assn. Bus. Profl. Women, Psi Chi, Soroptimists (pres. 1970-72), Rotary. Home and Office: 11 Abbey Pl Yonkers NY 10701

FRIEND, ROBERT NATHAN, financial counselor, economist, market technician; b. Chgo., Feb. 2, 1930; s. Karl D. and Marion (Wollenberger) F.; AB, Grinnell Coll., 1951; MS, Ill. Inst. Tech., 1953; m. Lee Baer, Aug. 12, 1979; children: Karen, Alan. With K. Friend & Co., Chgo., 1953—, v.p., early 1960's, 1st v.p., 1964—, dir. merger activities with Standard Oil Co. (Ind.), trustee employees' benefit trust, 1958—; active Friend Fin. Svcs.; admissions cons. Grinnell Coll., Ill. Inst. Tech., 1968-70; bd. dirs. Nat. Anorexia Nervosa & Associated Disorders Assn. Mem. ASSA (regional co-chmn. Market Technicians Assn.), Seed Savers Exch. (contbg. assoc.), Carlton Club, Yale Club; fellow So. Finance Assn., Southwestern Fin. Assn., Acad. Internat. Bus., Am. Acad. Polit. and Social Sci., Am. Assn. Individual Investors, Vintage Soc., Renaissance Soc., Sarah Siddons Soc., Art Inst. Chgo. (life), Chgo. Council Fgn. Rels., Am. Econ. Assn., Ea. Fin. Assn., Market Techicians Assn., Acad. Polit. Sci., Phi Kappa Phi. Home: 1300 N Lake Shore Dr Chicago IL 60610-2169 Office: 223 W Jackson Blvd Chicago IL 60606-6908

FRIEND, THEODORE WOOD, III, foundation executive,historian; b. Pitts., Aug. 27, 1931; s. Theodore Wood and Jessica (Holton) F.; m. Elizabeth Groesbeck Pierson, Feb. 20, 1960; children: Theodore Porter, Pierson, Elizabeth Robinson. BA, Williams Coll., 1953, LLD (hon.), 1978; PhD, Yale U., 1958. Mem. faculty SUNY, Buffalo, 1959-73, prof. history, 1966-73; pres. Swarthmore (Pa.) Coll., 1973-82; trustee Eisenhower Exchange Fellowships Inc., 1982—, pres., 1984-96. Author: Between Two Empires, The Ordeal of the Philippines, 1929-46, 65 (Bancroft prize in history 1966), The Blue Eyed Enemy: Japan Against the West in Java and Luzon, 1942-45, 88; (novel) Family Laundry, 1986. Mem. Truman Scholarships Selection Panel, Pa., N.J., Del., 1993—, chmn., 1997—. Fulbright grantee, Philippines, 1957-59; Rockefeller Found. internat. rels. fellow, 1961-62; Nat. Def. Fgn. Lang. postdoctoral fellow, 1966-67; Guggenheim fellow, Indonesia, Philippines, Japan, 1967-68; fellow Woodrow Wilson Internat. Ctr., 1983-84, Bellagio Ctr. for Artists and Scholars fellow, 1988; recipient Dwight D. Eisenhower medal, 1997. Mem. Coun. on Fgn. Rels., Am. Hist. Assn., Soc. Historians Am. Fgn. Rels., Asia Soc., Phila. Com. on Fgn. Rels. (chmn.), Fgn. Policy Rsch. Inst. (sr. fellow), Phila. Club, Franklin Inn Club, Sunday Breakfast Club, Phi Beta Kappa. Presbyterian. Nationally ranked sr. squash player, 1983-93, 97—. Home: 264 S Radnor Chester Rd Villanova PA 19085-1306

FRIEND, WILLIAM BENEDICT, bishop; b. Miami, Fla., Oct. 22, 1931; s. William Eugene and Elizabeth (Paulus) F. Student, U. Miami, 1949-52; cert. in philosophy, St. Mary's Coll., St. Mary, Ky., 1955; cert. of ordination, Mt. St. Mary's Sem., Emmittsburg, Md., 1959; M.A. in Edn., Cath. U. Am., 1965; L.L.D., St. Leo Coll., 1986. Ordained priest Roman Cath. Ch., 1959. Parish priest, educator, counselor, adminstr., 1959-68; ednl. rsch. adminstr. U. Notre Dame, Ind., 1968-71; vicar for edn., supt. schs. Diocese of Mobile, Ala., 1971-76, chancellor adminstrn., vicar for edn., 1976-79; aux. bishop Diocese of Alexandria-Shreveport, La., 1979-83, diocesan bishop, 1983-86; first bishop of Shreveport La., 1986—; chmn. campaign for human devel. Nat. Conf. Cath. Bishops, 1982-85; mem. sci. and human values com. Commn. of Bishops and Scholars, 1983-86, chmn., 1986-92, cons., 1993—; bd. dirs. La. Cath. Conf., 1986-92; mem. Pontifical Coun. for Culture. Editor handbooks and study guides for Cath. edn., 1971-77; editor: (with Ford and Daues) Evangelizing the Cultures in A.D. 2000, 1990, co-editor (with J. Anderson) The Culture of Bible Belt Catholics, 1995; contbr. articles on Cath. edn., Cath. ch. leadership and mgmt., theol. relections to profl. publs. Bd. dirs. S.E. Regional Hispanic Ctr., 1986—, Miami (Fla.) Interchurch Conf., Ctr. for Bioethics and Law, N.W. La.; trustee Notre Dame Sem., 1976, St. Joseph Coll. Sem., New Orleans, 1976—; bd. councillors Shreveport Cmty. Renewal; mem. rsch. oversight com. Biomed. Rsch. Found. N.W. La.; chmn. bd. Ctr. for Applied Rsch. in the Apostolate, 1997—. Decorated Order of Fleur de Lis K.C., 1980, knight comdr. with star Knights of Holy Sepulchre of Jerusalem, 1983; recipient Presdl. award Nat. Cath. Ednl. Assn., 1978, O'Neil D'Amour award Nat. Assn. Bds. Edn., 1982, NCCJ Brotherhood and Humanitarian award, 1987. Mem. AAAS, KC, Am. Acad. Religion, Cath. Acad. Sci., U.S.A., N.Y. Acad. Sci., Soc. for Biblical Lit., World Futures Soc. Avocations: swimming; hiking; art; music; reading. Office: Diocese of Shreveport Catholic Ctr 2500 Line Ave Shreveport LA 71104-3043

FRIEND, WILLIAM L., oil industry executive. MS, U. Del. Mem. staff Lummus Co.; pres., exec. officer J.F. Pritchard; mem. tech. staff Bechtel Group, Inc., Washington, 1977-80; mgr. Bechtel Petroleum, San Francisco, 1980-83; pres., dir. Prin. Oper. Co., 1983-86; gen. mgr. San Francisco & Houston Petroleum divsn., pres. Bechtel Nat., 1986-89; exec. v.p. Bechtel Group Inc., Washington, 1991-96, dir., 1996-98, cons., part-time, 1998—. Fellow AIChE; mem. Nat. Acad. Engrs., Am. Nuclear Soc., Am. Petroleum Inst., Am. Chem. Soc., Sigma Xi. Office: Bechtel Group Inc 1015 15th St NW Ste 700 Washington DC 20005-2612*

FRIENDLY, ED, television producer; b. N.Y.C., Apr. 8, 1922; s. Edwin S. and Henrietta (Steinmeier) F.; m. Natalie Coulson Brooks, Jan. 31, 1952; children: Brooke Friendly-Jones, Edwin S. III. *Natalie Brooks Friendly, wife of Ed Friendly, is a graduate of Friends Acadamy Locust Valley, New York, and Beaver College, Glenside, Pennsylvania. She is the author of two science books for children, both published by Prentice-Hall: Wildlife Teams (1966), and The Miraculous Web (1968). She was a trustee of the New England Genealogical Society from 1997—, and author of genealogical history. The Friendly Family (1998), was published by the Newbury Street Press, a division of the New England Historic Genealogical Society.* Grad., Manlius Sch., 1941. Radio exec., dir. BBD&O, N.Y.C., 1946-49; sales exec. ABC-TV, N.Y.C., 1949-53; ind. producer and packager N.Y.C., 1953-56; producer, program exec. CBS-TV, N.Y.C., 1956-59; v.p. spl. programs NBC-TV, N.Y.C., 1959-67; pres. Ed Friendly Prodns., Los Angeles, 1967—; co-chmn. steering com. Caucus for Producers, Writers and Dirs. Exec. producer: film Little House on the Prairie; Laugh-In; producer: film Peter Lundy and the Medicine Hat Stallion (Emmy nomination); Young Pioneers; mini-series Backstairs at the White House (11 Emmy nominations); also producer motion pictures and TV spls.; exec. producer/producer: Barbara Cartland's The Flame Is Love. Served with inf. U.S. Army, 1942-45, PTO. Recipient Spl. award Internat. Film and TV Festival N.Y., 1967; Emmy award for Laugh-In, 1968; Producer of Yr. award Producers Guild of Am., 1968; Golden Globe award Hollywood Fgn. Press, 1968; Gold medal of honor Internat. Radio and TV Soc., 1970; Christopher award for motion picture, 1975; Western Heritage award Nat. Cowboy Hall of Fame and Western Heritage Center, for Little House on the Prairie, 1975, for Peter

Lundy and the Medicine Hat Stallion, 1978; Scout awards for best weekly series and show of yr. for Laugh-In, 1969. Mem. Calif. Horsemen's Benevolent and Protective Assn. (pres. 1994, former mem. bd. dirs.), Thoroughbred Owners Calif. (founder, pres., chmn. 1993-96, chmn. 1996-97, bd. dirs. 1993—), Nat. Thoroughbred Assn. (vice chmn., bd. dirs. 1996—, founding mem.), Nat. Thoroughbred Racing Assn. (bd. dirs. 1997—). Office: 9000 Wilshire Blvd Ste 455 E Tower Beverly Hills CA 92012-3420

FRIER, BRUCE W., law educator; b. 1943. BA, Trinity Coll., 1964; PhD, Princeton U., 1970. Prof. classics and law U. Mich., 1969—; lectr. Bryn Mawr Coll., Pa., 1968-69. Recipient Goodwin award of merit, 1983. Fellow Am. Acad. of Arts and Scis.; mem. Am. Soc. for Legal Hist., Am. Philol. Assn. Office: U Mich Law Sch 625 S State St Ann Arbor MI 48109-1215

FRIER, RAYMOND EDGAR, telecommunications professional; b. N.Y.C., Apr. 17, 1938; s. Robert Olen and Rosa Mae (Abercrombie) F.; m. Irma Delores DeHaro, Apr. 25, 1965; 1 child, James W. Student, Pace Coll., 1957-58. Overseas clk. GM, N.Y.C., 1956-60; advt./mktg. staff R. Ballantine Beer Co., N.Y.C., 1960-62; ships staff officer, purser Am. Export Lines, N.Y.C., 1962-67; freelance writer, spkr. Frier Assocs., Inc., N.Y.C., 1967—; chairperson adv. bd. N.Y. Hosp./Cornel, N.Y.C., 1982-90. Author: (book, TV script) Bald Eagles, 1994. Mem. Lenox Hill Dem. Club, N.Y.C., 1975-97; tv host cmty. outreach Manhattan Cmty. Bd., N.Y.C., 1985-90; com. mem. Congress Youth Awards Rep. Rangel, N.Y.C., 1986; mem. adv. bd. Times Sq. Sr. Citizens Housing, N.Y.C., 1990-97. Recipient Our Town Thanks You award Our Town News Publ., Manhattan, N.Y.C., 1988, Outstanding Svc. award Sales Assn. of the Graphic Arts, N.Y.C., 1990, Outstanding Achievement Spkr. award Sales Execs. Club N.Y., N.Y.C., 1991. Mem. Toastmasters Internat. (club pres. 1976-77, spkr. 1975, Tri-State Speaking Champion 1975), Internat. Platform Assn., McManus Times Sq. Club, N.Y. Press Club. Roman Catholic. Avocations: reading U.S. history, walking, swimming, collecting political memorabilia. Home: 368 W 46th St New York NY 10036-8308 Office: Frier Assocs Inc 368 W 46th St New York NY 10036-8308

FRIERY, THOMAS P., city treasurer; m. Linda Friery; three children. BS in Acctg., Dyke Coll., 1965; Corp. Cash Mgmt. Cert., Wharton Sch.'s Entrepreneurial, Ctr. Cert. Calif. Mcpl. Treas. Fin. and investment specialist State Auditor Gen., Calif., 1974-76; treasury divsn. mgr. Washington Pub. Power Supply System, Richland, 1976-78; city treas. City of Sacramento, 1978—. Mem. Calif. Mcpl. Treas. Assn. (past prest., chair legis. com.). Avocations: golf, fishing. Office: Office of City Treas 926 J St Ste 300 Sacramento CA 95814-2608*

FRIES, JAMES FRANKLIN, internal medicine educator; b. Normal, Ill., Aug. 25, 1938; s. Albert Charles and Orpha (Loreen) F.; m. Sarah Elizabeth Tilton, Aug. 27, 1960; children: Elizabeth Ann, Gregory James. AB, Stanford U., 1960; MD, Johns Hopkins U., 1964. Diplmate Am. Bd. Internal Medicine. Intern Johns Hopkins Hosp., Balt., 1964-65, resident in medicine, 1965-66, fellow connective tissue disease divsn., 1966-68; resident in medicine Stanford (Calif.) U. Sch. Medicine, 1968-69, instr. in medicine, 1969-71, asst. prof. medicine, 1971-77, assoc. prof. medicine, 1978-93, prof. medicine, 1993—; dir. Arthritis, Rheumatism, Aging Med. Info. Sys., Stanford, 1975—; bd. dirs. Healthtrac Found., Menlo Park, Calif.; chmn. Healthtrac, Inc., 1984—; exec. com. The Health Project, 1992—. Author: Take Care of Yourself, 1975, 6th edit., 1996, Prognosis, 1981, Living Well, 1997, 4th edit., 1999, Taking Care of Your Child, 1999, The Arthritis Helpbook, 5th edit., 1999, Arthritis, 5th edit., 1999; mem. editl. bd. Jour. Rheumatology, Jour. Clin. Rheumatology, Computers Biomed. Rsch. Named Best Med. Specialist in U.S. Town and Country mag., 1984, Best Dr. in U.S. Good Housekeeping mag., 1991, one of Best Drs. in Am. Woodward-White, 1995; recipient C. Everett Koop Nat. Health award, 1994. Fellow ACP, Am. Coll. Rheumatology, Am. Coll. Med. Info. Avocations: running, expedition mountain climbing. Home: 135 Farm Rd Woodside CA 94062-1210 Office: Stanford U Sch Medicine 1000 Welch Rd Ste 203 Palo Alto CA 94304-1808

FRIES, LITA LINDA, school system administrator; b. Merced, Calif., Feb. 16, 1942; d. Alfred Earl and Juanita Lora (Brown) Griffey; m. George Richard Fries, Feb. 3, 1962; 1 child, Damon Brant. BA, U. Calif., Berkeley, 1966; MS, Calif. State U., 1976. Cert. elem. tchr., secondary tchr., ednl. adminstrator, reading specialist. Tchr. Peace Corps, Mwanza, Tanzania, 1963-65; tchr. Oakland (Calif.) Unified Sch. Dist., 1966-74, tchr. spl. assignment, 1974-84, principal, Burckhalter, 1984-85, program mgr., 1985-90, administr., 1990-92, coord. state and fed. programs, 1992-97, dir. elem. edn., 1997—. Mem. Assn. Calif. Sch. Adminstrs., East Bay Reading Assn. (editor 1982-83), Pi Lamda Theta (membership chairperson 1986-88), Delta Kappa Gamma, Phi Delta Kappa. Democrat. Office: Oakland Unified Sch Dist 1025 2nd Ave Oakland CA 94606-2296

FRIES, RAYMOND SEBASTIAN, manufacturing company executive; b. St. Paul, June 19, 1919; s. Jacob H. and Christine Fries; children: Raymond B., John A., Christine. B.S., U. Minn., 1948. Vice pres. Honeywell, Mpls., Los Angeles and Phila., 1944-65; v.p. Varian Assos., Palo Alto, Calif., 1965-67; pres. Esterline Angus, Indpls., 1967-71; v.p. Esterline Corp., N.Y.C., 1969-71; pres. Dietzgen Corp., Chgo., 1971-73; v.p. Allegheny Ludlum Industries, Pitts., 1973-80; exec. v.p. Allegheny Internat., Pitts., 1980-86; also dir. Allegheny Internat.; pres., mgmt. consulting assoc. Chematron Corp., Chgo.; dir. Phila. Corp. Contbg. author: Industrial Engineering Handbook. Mem. ASME, Fries Engrng. Assn., Fossiville Yacht Club (commodore). Clubs: Duquesne, Pitts. Athletic Assn.

FRIES, ROBERT FRANCIS, historian, educator; b. LaCrosse, Wis., Dec. 16, 1911; s. William James and Laura Merlinda (Olsen) F.; m. Frances Katherine Clements, Jan. 2, 1936 (dec. Jan. 1972); children: Mary Ann, Margaret Frances; m. Elizabeth Zevnik Dunne, Dec. 16, 1972. B.E., LaCrosse State Tchrs. Coll., 1933; Ph.M., U. Wis., 1936, Ph.D., 1939. Social sci. tchr. Cashton (Wis.) High Sch., 1933-35; asst. in history U. Wis., 1936-38; asst. prof. history De Paul U., Chgo., 1939-43; asso. prof. De Paul U., 1943-45, prof. history, 1945-80, emeritus prof., 1980—, chmn. dept., 1945-56, 67-76, dean univ. coll., 1955-71; Fellow in history U. Wis., 1938-39. Contbr. to hist. jours.; author: Empire in Pine, the Story of Lumbering in Wisconsin, 1951, rev. edit., 1989; Author: Crown and Parliament in Tudor-Stuart England, 1959, European Civilization: Basic Historical Documents, 1965; editor: Readings in European Civilization, 1956. Recipient Via Sapientiae award, 1980. Mem. AAUP (chpt. sec. 1947-48), Am. Hist. Assn., Orgn. Am. Historians, Wis. Hist. Soc. Home: 2817 Wilmette Ave Wilmette IL 60091-2244

FRIESE, GEORGE RALPH, retail executive; b. Chgo., Feb. 15, 1936; s. George R. and Marie D. (Pilz) F.; m. Patricia J. Brown, Aug. 24, 1957; children: Christine Carol, Kurt Michael. BA, Monmouth Coll., 1956; JD, Chgo. Kent Coll. Law, 1960. Bar: Ill. 1961, U.S. Dist. Ct. Ill. (no. dist.) 1961, U.S. Supreme Ct. 1965. Asst. gen. counsel, v.p. Banner Mut. Ins. Cos., Chgo., 1959-63; ptnr. Madsen & Friese, Park Ridge, Ill., 1963-68; corp. counsel, sec. SCOA Industries, Inc., Columbus, Ohio, 1968-71, v.p. legal, sec., 1971-81, pres., 1981-85; vice chmn., dir. Hills Dept. Stores Inc., Canton, Mass., 1984-95; propietor Portsmouth (N.H.) Athenaeum, 1993—. Bd. dirs. Columbus Symphony Orch., Greater Columbus Art Coun.; chmn., trustee New Eng. Red Cross; trustee Boy Scouts Am., Columbus, 1981-86, Boston Lyric Opera, 1988-95, Strawbery Banke Mus., 1994—, treas., 1996-98; mem., trustee Greater Piscataqua Cmty. Found., 1995—, vice chmn., 1998. Mem. ABA, Ill. Bar Assn., Tau Kappa Epsilon, Phi Delta Phi. Unitarian. Clubs: Athletic (Columbus); Lotos (N.Y.). Home and Office: PO Box 690 New Castle NH 03854-0690

FRIESE, ROBERT CHARLES, lawyer; b. Chgo., Apr. 29, 1943; s. Earl Matthew and Laura Barbara (Mayer) F.; m. Chandra Ullom; children: Matthew Robert, Mark Earl, Laura Moore. AB in Internat. Rels., Stanford U., 1964; JD, Northwestern U., 1970. Bar: Calif. 1972. Dir. Tutor Applied Linguistics Ctr., Geneva, 1964-66; atty. Bronson, Bronson & McKinnon, San Francisco, 1970-71, SEC, San Francisco, 1971-75; ptnr. Shartsis, Friese & Ginsburg, San Francisco, 1975—; pres., bd. dirs. Custom Diversification Fund Mgmt., Inc., 1993—; dir.-co-founder Internat. Plant Rsch. Inst., Inc., San Carlos, Calif., 1978-86. Chmn. bd. suprs. Task Force on Noise Control, 1972-78; chmn. San Franciscans for Cleaner City, 1977; exec. dir. Nob Hill Neighbors, 1972-81; bd. dirs. Nob Hill Assn., 1976-78, Palace Fine Arts, 1992-94, San Francisco Beautiful, 1986—, pres., 1988—; chmn. Citizens Adv. Com. for Embarcadero Project, 1991—; mem. major gifts com. Stanford U.; bd. dirs. Presidio Heights Neighborhood Assn., 1993—, pres., 1996—. Mem. ABA, Assn. Bus. Trial Lawyers (bd. dirs.), Calif. Bar Assn., Bar Assn. San Francisco (bd. dirs. 1982-85, chmn. bus. litigation com. 1978-79, chmn. state ct. civil litigation com. 1983-90, new courthouse com. 1993—), Lawyers Club of San Francisco, Mensa, Calif. Hist. Soc., Commonwealth Club, Swiss-Am. Friendship League (chmn. 1971-79). Office: Shartsis Friese & Ginsburg 1 Maritime Plz Fl 18 San Francisco CA 94111-3404

FRIESECKE, RAYMOND FRANCIS, health company executive; b. Mar. 12, 1937; s. Bernhard P. K. and Josephine (De Tomi) F. BS in Chemistry, Boston Coll., 1959; MSCE, MIT, 1961. Product specialist Dewey & Almy Chem. divsn. W. R. Grace & Co., Inc., Cambridge, Mass., 1963-66; market planning specialist USM Corp., Boston, 1966-71; mgmt. cons. Boston, 1971-74; dir. planning and devel. Schweitzer divsn. Kimberly-Clark Corp., Lee, Mass., 1974-78; v.p. corp. planning Butler Automatic, Inc., Canton, Mass., 1978-80; pres. Butler-Europe Inc., Greenwich and Munich, Conn., Germany, 1980; v.p. mktg. and planning Butler Greenwich Inc., 1980-81; pres. Strategic Mgmt. Assocs., San Rafael, Calif., 1981-96; chmn. Beyond Health Corp., 1994—; corp. clk., v.p. Bldg. R&D, Inc., Cambridge, 1966-68. Host, prodr.: The Ounce of Prevention Show, Sta. KEST, San Francisco, 1994-98, Stas. KBZS and WNN, 1998—, Stas. WRPT and WSRO, 1999—; author: Management by Relative Product Quality, The New Way to Manage; editor: Beyond Health News, 1995—; contbr. articles to profl. jours. State chmn. Citizens for Fair Taxation, 1972-73; state co-chmn. Mass. Young Reps., 1967-69; chmn. Ward 7 Rep. Com., Cambridge, 1968-70; vice-chmn. Cambridge Rep. City Com., 1966-68, Kentfield Rehab. Hosp. Found., 1986-88, chmn., 1988-91; Rep. candidate Mass. Ho. of Reps., 1964, 66; pres. Marin Rep. Coun., 1986-91; chmn. Calif. Acad., 1986-88; sec. Navy League Marin Coun., 1984-91, v.p., 1994—; bd. dirs. The Marin Ballet, 1996-98; bd. dirs. Insts. for Behavioral Physiology, Seattle, 1999—. 1st lt. U.S. Army, 1961-63. Mem. NRA, Nat. Health Fedn., Am. Chem. Soc., Physicians Com. for Responsible Medicine, Marin Philos. Soc. (v.p. 1991-92), Ctr. for Sci. in Pub. Interest, Health Medicine Forum, Orthomolecular Health Medicine Soc., The World Affairs Coun. Home: 141 Convent Ct San Rafael CA 94901-1335 Office: 60 Belvedere St San Rafael CA 94901

FRIESEN, ORIS DEWAYNE, software engineer, historian; b. York, Nebr., Jan. 4, 1940; s. Harry H. and Malita Wanda (Ratzlaff) F.; m. Carey Lea Burbank, May 28, 1964; children: Isabelle Anne, Aric Alan. BS, U. Ariz., 1964, MA, 1966; PhD, Ariz. State U., 1982. Computer sys. analyst Computer Scis. Corp., Richland, Wash., 1967-69; computer sys. designer GE, Phoenix, 1969-70; database sys. designer Honeywell Info. Systems, Phoenix, 1970-84, engring. fellow, database mgmt., 1984-90; engring. fellow, database mgmt. Bull Worldwide Info. Sys., Phoenix, 1990-99; adj. prof. engring. Ariz. State U., Tempe, 1984—; vice chmn. database stds. Am. Nat. Stds. Inst., Washington, 1980-85; rapporteur, database stds. Internat. Stds. Orgn., Geneva, 1984-85; gen. chmn. Internat. Conf. on Deductive and Object-Oriented Databases, Scottsdale, Ariz., 1991-94; treas. Steering Com. for Internat. Conf. on Deductive and Object-Oriented Databases, 1997—; mem. steering com. Advanced Info. and Comms. Infrastructure Found. Group of Ariz. Gov.'s Strategic Partnership for Econ. Devel., 1994-95; mem. indsl. coun. Coll. Engring., No. Ariz. U., Flagstaff, 1995-99; charter mem. Ariz. Telecomms. Info. Coun., Adv. Bd. to Ariz. Telecomms. Policy Office, Found. Group of Ariz. Gov.'s Strategic Partnership for Econ. Devel., 1995—; Ariz. rep. for N.Am. Free Trade Assn., Telecomms. Stds. Subcom. of Office of U.S. Trade Reps., 1994-96; charter mem., vice chair Ariz. Learning Tech. Partnership, 1996—; mem. bd. dirs. ACTC Technologies, Inc., Calgary, Alta., Can., 1996-98; chmn. Ariz. Telecomms. and Info. Coun., 1999—. Author: China Reporting: An Oral History of American Journalism in the 1930s-1940s, 1987; editor Procs. of Phoenix Conf. on Computers and Comms., 1987; contbr. articles to profl. jours. Mem. Phoenix Futures Forum, 1988-91; mem., officer North Tatum Cmty. Homeowners Assn., Phoenix, 1985-88; mem. steering com. for advanced info. comm. Infrastructure Found. of Ariz. Gov.'s Strategic Partnership for Econ. Devel., 1994-96. Mem. IEEE (sr., gen. chmn. Phoenix Conf. on Computers and Communications 1990-91, vice-chmn. Globecom 97 Conf., 1995-97), Assn. for Computing Machinery, Assn. Asian Studies, Am. Hist. Assn., Orgn. Am. Historians. Democrat. Avocation: Chinese language. Home: 5136 E Le Marche Ave Scottsdale AZ 85254-1667 Office: Friesen Info Tech 5136 E Le Marche Ave Scottsdale AZ 85254-1667

FRIESEN, WOLFGANG OTTO, biology educator; b. Elbing, Germany, Oct. 31, 1942; s. Helmuth and Trude (Regier) F.; came to U.S., 1950; m. Lynette Campbell, May 2, 1969; children: Laura, Jonathon. BA, Bethel Coll., 1964; MA, U. Calif., Berkeley, 1966; PhD, U. Calif., San Diego, 1974. Rsch. physicist U. Calif., San Francisco, 1969-70; rsch. assoc. U. Calif., Berkeley, 1974-77; asst. prof. biology U. Va., Charlottesville, 1977-82, assoc. prof., 1982-88, prof., 1988—, chmn. biology dept., 1996—; Thomas Jefferson vis. fellow Downing Coll., Cambridge, Eng., 1993; program dir. NSF, 1995-96. Co-author NeuroDynamix: Computer Models for Neurophysiology, 1994; contbr. articles to profl. jours.; patentee in infant respirator monitor. NIH fellow, 1975-77; Fogarty Sr. Internat. fellow, 1993; grantee NIH, 1978-82, 84-93, NSF 1982-89, 94—. Mem. AAAS, Soc. Rsch. Biol. Rhythms (adv. bd.), Neurosci. Soc., Internat. Soc. Neuroethology. Avocations: hiking, reading, bird watching. Office: U Va Dept Biology Charlottesville VA 22903

FRIESS, DONNA LEWIS, children's rights advocate, writer; b. L.A., Jan. 16, 1943; d. Raymond W. Lewis, Jr. and Dorothy Gertrude (Borwick) McIntyre; m. Kenneth E. Friess, June 20, 1964; children: Erik, Julina, Daniel. BA in Comm., U. So. Calif., 1964; MA in Comm., Calif. State U., Long Beach, 1966; PhD in Psychology, U.S. Internat. U., San Diego, 1993. Cert. tchr., Calif. Prof. human comm. Cypress (Calif.) Coll., 1966—; lectr. survivors of abuse, 1990—, mental health profls., 1990—; CEO Hurt Into Happiness Publishing, 1990—, Hurt Into Happiness Seminars, 1993—; presenter and keynote presenter in field of child abuse, various confs., convs., cmty. groups, workshops, and lawmakers' groups; guest expert (TV shows) Sally Jessy Raphael, 1993, Leeza Gibbons Talk Show, 1994, Sonja: Live, 1994, Oprah Winfrey Show, 1991, many others. Author: Relationships, 1995, Just Between Us: A Guidebook for Survivors of Childhood Trauma, 1995, Cry the Darkness, 1993, European edits. 1995, Danish edit., 1999, Korean edit., 1995, Norwegian edits., 1998, Circle of Love: Secrets to Successful Relationships, 1996, Whispering Waters: The Story of Historic Weesha, 1998; contbr. articles to mags. Recipient Author's award U. Calif. Friends of Libr., 1996, recognition from U.S. Justice Dept. for outstanding efforts to stop child abuse, 1995; nominee for Pres.'s Am. Svc. award, 1996. Mem. Am. Coalition Against Child Abuse (founder), Task Force for ACCA to Educate American Judges on Issues of Sexual Abuse, One Voice, Calif. Psychol. Assn., Western Social Sci. Assn., Child Abuse Listening and Mediating (bd. dirs.), Am. Profl. Soc. on Abuse of Children, Mother Against Sexual Abuse (bd. dirs.), Laura's House for Battered Women (bd. dirs.), Calif. Tchrs. Assn., Faculty Assn. Calif. C.Cs., Speech Communication Assn. of Am., U.S. Internat. U. Alumni Assn. (bd. dirs.). Avocation: painting on porcelain. Office: Cypress College Dept Human Communications Cypress CA 90630

FRIESTEDT, AMÉDÉE CHABRISSON, medical genetics database manager; b. Washington, Aug. 9, 1949; d. Wallace Eugene Danforth and Dorothy Anne (Ball) F. BA in Psychology, George Washington U., 1973; postgrad., Howard U., 1974-79; MS in Physiology and Biophysics, Georgetown U., 1988; postgrad., Walden U., 1993—. Fin. records rep. George Washington U. Hosp., Washington, 1977-84; tech. writer, programmer Computer Scis. Corp., Fairfax, Va., 1984-87; sr. sys. analyst Network Mgmt., Inc., Fairfax, 1987-90; project sys. requirements analyst Unisys Corp., McLean, Va., 1990-92; lead sys. analyst Martin Marietta Tech. Svcs., Lockheed Martin, Inc., Bethesda, Md., 1992-98; sr. mem. SRA Internat., Inc., Bethesda, 1998—; dir. computer ops. dept. physiology and biophysics Georgetown U., Washington, 1986-89; presenter in field. Editor: The Nurture of the Small, 1993, For Every Child, (newsletter) Every Child By Two. Mem. U.S.-China Capital Cities Friendship Coun., Inc., 1985; v.p. D.C. Head Injury Found., 1988-89; career mentor, peer counselor, pro bono computer cons. Epilepsy Found. for Nat. Capital Area, 1997. Recipient cert. of appreciation and letter of commendation Office of Personnel Mgmt., EPA, 1987, letter of commendation Gen. Svcs. Adminstrn., 1988, Office Rsch. and Devel., EPA, 1995. Mem. AAAS, NAFE, AAUW, Nat. Fedn. Bus. and Profl. Women (rec. sec. 1984-89), Women's Caucus for Art (pub. rels., newsletter editor, membership com.). Avocations: music, art, photography, creative writing, self-actualization. Office: NIH/NHGRI Bldg 3C710 Bethesda MD 20892

FRIESZ, MARY LEE, poet, self-employed; b. Little Rock, Ark., Apr. 13, 1940; d. E. Lee and Lala Maurine (Bain) Franklin; m. David Wilson Dubbell, Jan. 28, 1961 (div. Aug. 1982); children: Cheryl Blaine Dubbell Knight, Paul Fremont Dubbell; m. Donald Stuart Friesz; July 5, 1985; children: Mark Allan Friesz, Carol Ann Friesz Leslie. BA in Psychology, U. Ark., 1962. Sec. Stanford U., Palo Alto, Calif., 1962-63; tchr. aide Pedregal Sch., Palos Verdes, Calif., 1974-78; corp. sec. Pel-Freez Biols., Inc., Palos Verdes, Calif., 1978-81; asst. mgr. May Co., Rolling Hills Estates, Calif., 1981-82; investment counselor Am. Savs. & Loan, Redondo Beach, Calif., 1982-84; founder, editor Mustard Seed Poetry, Palos Verdes, 1995—. Author books of poetry. Dir; Poetry By The Sea, Serenos de Point Vicente (televised, 1997-99). Mem. membership com. Assistance League San Pedro/Palos Verdes, 1994—. Recipient Cmty. Svc. award South Bay Panhellenic Coun., 1996. Mem. Palos Verdes Woman's Club (publicity ch.), S.W. Manuscripters, So. Calif. Fedn. Zeta Tau Alpha (pres. 1994-95, pres. local chpt. 1990-91, cert. merit Nat. coun. 1994), Surfwriters (treas. 1994-99), Phi Beta Kappa. Home: 2725 Palos Verdes Dr W Palos Verdes Estates CA 90274-2837 Office: Mustard Seed Poetry PO Box 3842 Palos Verdes Estates CA 90274-9535

FRIGERIO, CHARLES STRAITH, lawyer; b. Detroit, Mar. 8, 1957; s. Louie John and LaVern (Straith) F.; m. Annette Angela Russo, Oct. 18, 1985. BA, St. Mary's U., 1979, JD, 1982. Bar: Tex. 1982, U.S. Ct. Appeals (5th cir.) 1987, U.S. Supreme Ct. 1987; cert. in personal injury trial law. Pros. atty. City Attys. Office, San Antonio, 1982-84; trial atty. City Atty's. Office, San Antonio, 1984—; litigation chief and chief prosecutor City Atty.'s Office, San Antonio, 1995; pvt. practice law enforcement litigation San Antonio, 1995—. Mem. Dem. Nat. Com., San Antonio, 1976; asst. mgr. local campaigns, San Antonio, 1976-84. Mem. ABA, Tex. Bar Assn., Fed. Bar Assn., San Antonio Bar Assn., Assn. Trial Lawyers Am., Cath. Lawyers Assn., Delta Epsilom Sigma. Democrat. Roman Catholic. Home: 317 Cleveland Ct San Antonio TX 78209-5862 Office: Law Offices of Charles Straith Frigerio Riverview Towers 111 Soledad St Ste 840 San Antonio TX 78205-2219

FRIGGENS, THOMAS GEORGE, state official, historian; b. Pontiac, Mich., July 12, 1949; s. Francis G. and Jane E. (Pettit) F.; m. Mary T. Bahra. BA, Albion Coll., 1971; MA, Wayne State U., 1973. Contract historian Mich. Dept. Natural Resources, Fayette, 1973; site historian 07 Mich. Dept. State, History Div., Fort Wilkins Hist. Complex, Copper Harbor, 1974-75, site historian 09, 1975-76, site historian 11, 1976-80, site historian VII, 1980-85; site historian VII Dept. State, Bur. History, Mich. Iron Industry Mus., Negaunee, 1985-87, regional historian VII, 1987-92, regional historian VII supr., 1992-96, historian mgr. XII, 1996-98, history mgr. 13, 1998—; cons. St. Louis County Hist. Soc., Duluth, Minn., 1985, 86. Contbr. articles to jours. in field. Active Hist. Soc. Mich., bd. dirs., 1984-90; active Copper County Heritage Coun., pres., 1982-83; bd. dirs. Marquette County Hist. Soc., 1992-97; mem. Mich. Hist. Preservation Network. Recipient Roy W. Drier award Houghton County (Mich.) Hist. Soc., 1987, Merit award Hist. Soc. Mich., 1983, Disting. Svc. award, 1983. Mem. Am. Assn. State and Local History, Nat. Trust for Hist. Preservation, Phi Alpha Theta. Office: Mich Iron Industry Mus 73 Forge Rd Negaunee MI 49866-9532

FRIIS, ROBERT HAROLD, epidemiologist, health science educator; b. San Jose, Calif., July 15, 1941; s. Harold Hector and Florence Marie (Brant) F.; m. Carol Ann Speer, Oct. 28, 1966; children: Michelle Alanna, Erik Adler. BA, U. Calif., Berkeley, 1964; MA, Columbia U., N.Y.C., 1966, PhD, 1969. Postdoctoral fellow U. Mich., Ann Arbor, 1969-71; asst. prof. Sch. Pub. Health Columbia U., 1971-74, Albert Einstein Coll. Medicine, Bronx, N.Y., 1974-76; assoc. prof. CUNY, Bklyn. Coll., 1976-78; dir. field epidemiology Orange County Pub. Health, Santa Ana, Calif., 1978-79; assoc. clin. prof. U. Calif., Irvine, 1979-93; prof., chairperson dept. health sci. Calif. State U., Long Beach, 1988—; vis. rschr. Karolinska Inst., Stockholm, Sweden, 1993; dir. Joint Studies Inst., Calif. State U. and VA Med. Ctr. Long Beach, 1995—; mem. vol. faculty Coll. Medicine, U. Calif., Irvine, 1993—; ind. cons. epidemiology, Irvine, 1970—. Sr. author: Epidemiology Public Health Practice, 1996, 2d edit. 1999; contbr. articles to sci. jours. Faculty mentor Ptnrs. for Success, Long Beach, 1992—. Grantee, U. Calif., Irvine, 1995, Mexus com. U. Calif., 1988, U. Calif. systemwide, 1988, U. Calif. Tobacco Related Disease Rsch. Program, 1998. Mem. APHA, Am. Statis. Assn. (So. Calif. sect.), Soc. Epidemiol. Rsch., U. Calif. Berkley Alumni Assn., Eta Sigma Gamma. Democratic. Avocations: reading, travel, coin collecting, computers, gardening. Office: Calif State U Long Beach Dept Health Sci 1250 N Bellflower Blvd Long Beach CA 90840-0006

FRIMAN, ALICE RUTH, poet, English educator; b. N.Y.C., Oct. 20, 1933; d. Joseph and Helen (Friedman) Pesner; m. Elmer Friman, July 3, 1955 (div. Dec. 1975); children: H. Richard, Paul Lawrence, Lillian Elaine Friman Wilson; m. Marshall Bruce Gentry, Sept. 24, 1989. BA, Bklyn. Coll., 1954; MA, Butler U., 1971. Lectr., instr. English U. Indpls., 1971-74, asst. prof. English, 1974-81, assoc. prof. English, 1981-90, prof. English, 1990-93, prof. emerita, 1993—; vis. prof. creative writing Ind. State U., Terre Haute, 1982, Ball State U., Muncie, Ind., 1996; writer in residence Curtin U., Perth, Australia, 1989; presenter in field. Author: Reporting from Corinth, 1984, Insomniac Heart, 1990, Driving for Jimmy Wonderland, 1992, Inverted Fire, 1997; editor: Loaves and Fishes: Women Poets of Indiana, 1983; poetry editor The Flying Island, fall/winter 1993, spring/summer 1996; author of poetry; contbr. articles and revs. to profl. jours. Recipient Ezra Pound Poetry award Truman State U., 1998, 1st place internat. poetry contest Abiko Quar., Japan, 1994, award of excellence in poetry Hopewell Rev., 1995, Firman Houghton award New Eng. Poetry Club, 1996, second prize The Anna David Rosenberg award for poems on the Jewish experience, 1996, Ezra Pound poetry award Truman State U., 1998; individual artist fellow Ind. Arts Commn., 1996-97. Mem. MLA (life), Soc. for the Study Midwestern Lit., Associated Writing Programs, Poetry Soc. Am. (Lucille Medwick Meml. award 1993), Writers' Ctr. Indpls. (life, charter). Democrat. Jewish. Avocations: travel, reading. Home: 6312 Central Ave Indianapolis IN 46220-1738

FRIMMER, PAUL NORMAN, lawyer; b. N.Y.C., June 8, 1945; s. William and Irene (Alper) F.; m. Carol S. Zucker, June 9, 1968; children: Tracey, Scott. BS, Queens Coll., N.Y.C., 1966; JD cum laude, Fordham U., 1969. Bar: N.Y. 1969, Calif. 1971. Assoc. Stroock and Stroock, and Lavan, N.Y.C., 1969-71; ptnr. Irell and Manella, L.A., 1971—; panelist Calif. Continuing Edn. of Bar, 1972, co-chmn. various sects. 73, 75, 76, 80, 86; instr. advanced profl. program U. So. Calif., 1977-80; lectr. 6th and 14th Insts. Estate Planning U. Miami Law Ctr., 1972, 80, Practicing Law Inst.-ABA programs, 1973-91, 31st Inst. Fed. Taxation U. So. Calif., 1979, other bar assn. groups on estate planning, probate, taxation, charitable giving and community property. Contbr. numerous articles to profl. jours. Nat. trustee, asst. sec. Leukemia Soc. Am., Inc., 1976-86, 91—, trustee, chmn. planned giving com. L.A. chpt., chpt. pres., 1973-86; trustee L.A. Children's Mus., 1982-86. Fellow Am. Coll. Trust and Estate Counsel, Internat. Acad. Probate and Trust Law; mem. ABA (real property, probate and trust law sect. com. charitable giving, trusts and founds., chmn. disclaimer task force), Calif. Bar Assn. Avocations: tennis, skiing. Office: Irell & Manella 1800 Avenue Of The Stars Los Angeles CA 90067-4276

FRINGS, MANFRED SERVATIUS, philosophy educator; b. Cologne, N. Rhine, Germany, Feb. 27, 1925; came to U.S., 1958; U.S. citizen.; s. Gottfried and Maria (Over) F.; m. Karin Frambach, Dec. 30, 1985; 1 child. PhD, U. Cologne, North Rhine, 1953; postgrad., Staatsexamen, 1956. Sch. master German Higher Edn., North Rhine, 1956-58; asst. prof. philosophy U. Detroit, 1958-62; assoc. prof. philosophy Duquesne U., Pitts., 1962-66; prof. philosophy DePaul U., Chgo., 1966-92, prof. emeritus, 1992—; dir. Max Scheler Archives, Albuquerque; guest prof. U. Cologne, 1979, 83; guest lectr. U. Mainz, Freiburg, Germany, 1980-81; pres. Max Scheler Gesellschaft, 1993-97, hon. pres., 1997—. Author: Max Scheler: A Concise Introduction, 1965, 2d edit., 1996, Person and Dasein, 1969, Zur Phamomenologie der Lebensgemeinschaft, 1971, Philosophy of Prediction and Capitalism, 1987, The Mind of Max Scheler, 1997; editor: The Collected Works of Max

Scheler, Heidegger and the Quest for Truth, 1968, Max Scheler Von der Ganzheit des Menschen, 1991, others; co-editor: Heidegger/Gesamtausgabe, 1976-82; contbr. over 100 publs. to profl. jours. and mags. including Chinese, English, French, German and Japanese translations. Fulbright grantee, 1958, Deutsche Forschungsgemeinschaft of Germany grantee, 1972, 79, 82, 87, Thyssen Found. of Germany grantee, 1983. Mem. Brit. Soc. Phenomenology (corr. 1975-96), Heidegger Conf. in Am. (initiator). Roman Catholic. Avocations: piano, painting, violin. Home: 11809 San Francisco Rd NE Albuquerque NM 87122-1095

FRINK, EUGENE HUDSON, JR., business and real estate consultant; b. Denver, Feb. 6, 1927; s. Eugene Hudson and Maxine Louella (Ingle) F.; m. Catherine Claire Heath, Dec. 27, 1947; children: Douglas Martin, Bryan Clifford, Daniel Neal. BA, Denver U., 1947. Mgr. Frink Creamery Co., Ft. Collins, Colo., 1948-64; co-founder, mgr. ops Aqua-Tec Corp. (Water Pik), Ft. Collins, 1964-66; archtl. designer Gene Frink Designers, Ft. Collins, 1967-84; ptnr. Wakaya Island, Ltd., Fiji, 1968-71; chmn. Beehive Internat., Salt Lake City, 1969-85; prin. Architecture Plus, P.C., Ft. Collins, 1985-88; ptnr. Naindi Plantation, Fiji, 1969—; pres. Ft. Collins Children's Clinic, 1993—; bd. dirs. Conception Tech. Inc., 1996—. Councilman, City of Ft. Collins, 1959-63, mayor, 1961-63; mem. Ft. Collins Regional Planning Bd., 1962-64. Mem. Rotary Club, Pres.'s Seminar. Republican. Episcopalian. Avocations: industrial design, painting, swimming, hiking. Home: 1212 Morgan St Fort Collins CO 80524-3836

FRISBEE, DON CALVIN, retired utilities executive; b. San Francisco, Dec. 13, 1923; s. Ira Nobles and Helen (Sheets) F.; m. Emilie Ford, Feb. 5, 1947; children: Ann, Robert, Peter, Dean. BA, Pomona Coll., 1947; MBA, Harvard U., 1949. Sr. investment analyst, asst. cashier investment analysis dept. 1st Interstate Bank Oreg., N.A., Portland, 1949-52; treas. PacifiCorp, Portland, 1958-60, then v.p., exec. v.p., pres., 1966-73, chief exec. officer, 1973-89, chmn., 1973-94; chmn. emeritus PacifiCorp., Portland, 1994-97; bd. dirs. Wells Fargo Bank. Chmn. bd. trustees Reed Coll.; trustee Safari Game Search Found., High Desert Mus.; mem. cabinet Columbia Pacific coun. Boy Scouts Am.; founder Oreg. chpt. Am. Leadership Forum; mem. exec. com. Oreg. Partnership for Internat. Edn. 1st lt. AUS, 1943-46. Mem. Arlington Club, Univ. Club Multnomah Athletic Club, City Club. Office: 1500 SW 1st Ave Portland OR 97201-5815

FRISBY, JAMES CURTIS, agricultural engineering educator; b. Bethany, Mo., Oct. 22, 1930; s. Jackson Carey and Gladys (Selby) F.; m. Hazel M. Kallenbach, Dec. 20, 1969. BS in Edn., U. Mo., 1952, BSAE, 1956; MS, Iowa State U., 1963, PhD, 1965. Registered profl. engr., Mo. Classromm instr., tech. writer, market analyst Caterpillar Tractor Co., Peoria, Ill., 1956-60; acting mgr. farm services dept. Iowa State U., Ames, 1961-63, instr., 1963-65; asst. prof. agrl. engring. U. Mo., Columbia, 1966-69, assoc. prof., 1969-74, prof., 1974-96, chmn. agrl. engring., 1989-94; prof. emeritus, 1996—. Served to 1st lt. U.S. Army, 1952-54. Recipient award of merit Gamma Sigma Delta, 1976; recipient cert. of appreciation U. Mo. Coll. Engring., 1983, 87. Mem. NSPE (pres. ctrl. chpt. 1995-96), Am. Soc. Agrl. Engrs. (chmn. mid-ctrl. region 1982-83, dir. mid-ctrl. region 1984-86), Am. Soc. Engring. Edn., Nat. Assn. Colls. and Tchrs. Agrl. (tchg. award merit 1994), Mo. Soc. Profl. Engrs. (pres. ctrl. chpt. 1995-96), Am. Aoc. Agrl. Engrs. (mem. of yr. Mo. sect. 1995, Spl. Svc. award MidCentral conf. 1996), Kiwanis Internat. Mem. Ch. of Christ. Home: 1805 Bluff Pointe Dr Columbia MO 65201-6287

FRISCH, ALBERT T., composer; b. Bklyn., Mar. 17, 1916; s. Menyush and Rose Frisch; m. Celia Hirschorn; 1 child, Myra J. Frisch Bennett. Saxophonist in nightclubs, ocean liners, summers resorts; pianist, singer. Author column for Music in Print, Billboard mag.; composer, lyracists for numerous songs, instrumentals, albums, shows, TV spl. materials; recent works include Yourself, A Country Life, If You Should Leave Me, Madame Misia, All the Time in The World, I Love Me, The Way I See It, the Girl in Cabin 54, What Does It Take, Can-Can Rainbow, Where's My Rainbow, To Please the Woman in Me, Grain of the Salt of the Earth, Until the Likes of You, Come Out Wherever You Are, Picture Me, The Morning After, It's A Lonesome Thing, All's Fair in Love and War, Great Company, With One Fell Swoop, Beach Ballet, The Heart's a Wonder, Down the Hatch, Gallant Little Swearers, Be a Hero. With U.S. Army, WWII. Decorated 5 Battle Stars. Mem. ASCAP, Am. Guild Authors and Composers and Dramatists Guild. Avocations: reading, travel, entertaining, singing, piano. Office: Myra Music Co 177 White Plains Rd Apt 33F Tarrytown NY 10591-5511

FRISCH, FRED I., real estate executive; b. Indpls., Oct. 19, 1935; s. Leon and Blanka (Frankovitz) F.; m. Rochelle L. Fein, Sept. 15, 1957; children: Caryn, Susan, Daniel. BBA, U. Miami, Fla., 1957. Lic. real estate broker. Pres. Frisch & Assocs., Indpls., 1976—; pres. Prime Property Investment Group; bd. dirs. Hooverwood Homes, Indpls.; bd. dirs. comml. and indsl. div. Met. Indpls. Bd. Realtors, pres. 1984. Served with USAF, 1960-64. Mem. Real Estate Securities and Syndication Inst. Republican. Jewish. Club: Indpls. Men's (pres. 1966-68). Avocation: reading fiction. Office: 10293 N Meridian St Ste 18 Indianapolis IN 46290-1073

FRISCH, HARRY DAVID, lawyer, consultant; b. N.Y.C., June 5, 1954; s. Isaac and Regina (Rottenberg) F.; m. Sherry Beth Bannerman, 1992; children: Rachel Michele, Michael Elliot. BS, CCNY, 1976; postgrad., Rutgers U., 1976-77; JD, Pace U., 1980. Bar: N.Y 1981, U.S. Dist. Ct. (so. and ea. dists.) N.Y. 1981, U.S. Ct. Appeals (2d cir.) 1984, U.S. Supreme Ct. 1986, U.S. Ct. Appeals (5th cir.) 1987. Law clk. Shearson Hayden Stone, Inc., N.Y.C., 1977-80; assoc. gen. counsel Shearson Loeb Rhoades, Inc., N.Y.C., 1980-82; asst. v.p., asst. corp. sec., assoc. gen. counsel Shearson/Am. Express, Inc., N.Y.C., 1982-85; v.p., sr. litigator, assoc. gen. counsel Shearson Lehman Bros., Inc., N.Y.C., 1985-88; 1st v.p., sr. litigator, assoc. gen. counsel Shearson Lehman Hutton, Inc., N.Y.C., 1988-90, Shearson Lehman Bros., Inc., N.Y.C., 1990-93; 1st v.p., sr. litigator, asst. gen. counsel Smith Barney Shearson Inc., N.Y.C., 1993-94; asst. gen. counsel Gruntal & Co. Inc., N.Y.C., 1994-97, Gruntal & Co., L.L.C., N.Y.C., 1997-99; spl. counsel Lubiner & Schmidt, N.Y.C., 1999—. Contbr. articles to profl. jours. Mem. ABA, N.Y. State Bar Assn., Assn. of Bar of City of N.Y., N.Y. County Lawyers Assn., Fed. Bar Council. Democrat. Jewish. Home: 49 Hudson Watch Dr Ossining NY 10562-2442 Office: Lubiner & Schmidt 111 Broadway 13th Fl New York NY 10006

FRISCH, HENRY JONATHAN, physics educator; b. Los Alamos, Aug. 21, 1944; s. David Henry and Rose Frisch; m. Priscilla Diane Chapman, Mar. 19, 1969; children—Sarah Tenaya, Genevieve Alexandra. B.A., Harvard U., 1966; Ph.D., U. Calif.-Berkeley, 1971. Instr. physics U. Chgo., 1971-73, asst. prof., 1973-77, assoc. prof., 1977-84, prof., 1984—; mem. High Energy Physics Adv. Panel, 1974-77. Fellow Am. Phys. Soc. Fax: 773-702-1914. Home: 1061 Keith Ave Berkeley CA 94708-1604 Office: Univ Chgo Enrico Fermi Inst 5640 S Ellis Ave Chicago IL 60637-1433

FRISCH, IVAN THOMAS, computer and communications company executive; b. Budapest, Hungary, Sept. 21, 1937; came to U.S., 1939, naturalized, 1941; s. Laszlo and Rose (Balog) F.; m. Vivian Scelzo, June 6, 1962; children: Brian, Bruce. B.S., Queens Coll., N.Y., 1958, Columbia U., 1958; M.S., Columbia U., 1958, Ph.D., 1962. Asst. prof. elec. engring. and computer sci. U. Calif., Berkeley, 1962-65; asso. prof. U. Calif., 1965-69; Ford Found. resident engring. practice Bell Labs., Holmdel, N.J., 1965-66; founding mem. Network Analysis Corp., Great Neck, N.Y., 1969—; sr. v.p. Network Analysis Corp., 1971—, gen. mgr., 1978-85; v.p. Contel Bus. Networks, 1985-87; dir. Ctr. on Advanced Tech. in Telecommunications, prof. Poly. U., Bklyn., 1987—; provost Polytech. U., 1992—; adj. prof. computer sci. SUNY, Stony Brook, 1975—, Columbia U., N.Y.C., 1977—; cons. in field. Author: (with Howard Frank) Communication, Transmission and Transportation Networks, 1971; Founding editor-in-chief: Networks, 1971—; contbr. articles to profl. pubs. Guggenheim fellow, 1969. Fellow IEEE (Eric E. Sumner award 1999); mem. N.Y. Acad. Scis., Cable TV Assn. Am., Phi Beta Kappa, Tau Beta Pi, Eta Kappa Nu. Office: Poly U Six Metrotech Ctr Rm JB-555 Brooklyn NY 11201-2907

FRISCH, JOSEPH, mechanical engineer, educator, consultant; b. Vienna, Austria, Apr. 21, 1921; came to U.S., 1940, naturalized, 1946; s. Abraham and Rachel (Lieberman) F.; m. Joan S. Frisch, May 26, 1962; children—Nora Theresa, Erich Martin, Jonathan David. BSME, Duke U., 1946; MS, U. Calif., 1950. Registered profl. engr., Calif. Mem. faculty U. Calif.-Berkeley, 1947—, asst. prof. mech. engring., 1951-57, assoc. prof. mech. engring., 1957—, prof. mech. engring., 1963—, asst. dir. Inst. Engring. Rsch., 1961-63, chmn. div. mech. design, 1966-70, assoc. dean, 1972-75; cons. to indsl. and govtl. labs. Contbr. articles to profl. jours. Fellow ASME (life); mem. Phi Beta Kappa, Sigma Xi, Tau Beta Pi, Pi Tau Sigma. Club: U. Calif.-Berkeley Faculty. Office: U Calif Dept Mech Engring Berkeley CA 94720-1740

FRISCHENMEYER, MICHAEL LEO, sales executive; b. Ottawa, Kans., Feb. 8, 1951; s. Edwin Francis and Patricia Louise (Scheibmeir) F.; m. Helen N. Bright, May 19, 1974; children: Lindsay Patrice, David Edward. BA in Chemistry, U. Mo., 1973, MBA in Mtkg., 1975. Mktg. asst. Mallinckrodt Inc., St. Louis, 1975, asst. product mgr., 1975-77; mgr. tech. services Standard Havens, Inc., Kansas City, Mo., 1977-79, nat. sales mgr., 1979-83; sales engr. Nat. Filter Media Corp., St. Louis, 1983; div. sales mgr. Nat. Filter Media Corp., Memphis, 1983-85, Hamden, Conn., 1986-88; nat. sales mgr. Nat. Filter Media Corp., Memphis, 1985-86, Salt Lake City, 1988-90; v.p., div. mgr. Nat. Filter Media Corp., Memphis, 1991—. Recipient 5 Star Major Advancement award Pollution Engring. mag. 1978, 79. Mem. Air Pollution Control Assn. Avocations: golf, basketball. Home: 2107 Glenalden Dr Germantown TN 38139 Office: 8895 Deerfield Dr Olive Branch MS 38654-3815

FRISCHKNECHT, LEE CONRAD, retired broadcasting executive; b. Brigham City, Utah, Jan. 4, 1928; s. Carl Oliver and Geniel (Lund) F.; m. Sara Jean McCulloch, Sept. 3, 1948; children: Diane Frischknecht Etherington, Jill Frischknecht Taylor, Ellen Frischknecht DePola, Amy Frischknecht Blodgett. BS in Speech, Utah State U., 1951; MA in Radio-TV, Mich. State U., 1957. Announcer sta. KID Radio, Idaho Falls, Idaho, 1951-52; producer-director sta. WKAR-TV, East Lansing, Mich., 1953-57, prodn. mgr., 1958-59, program mgr., 1960-61, gen. mgr., 1962-63; dir. sta. rels. Nat. Ednl. TV, N.Y.C., 1964-67; dir. univ. rels. Utah State U., 1969-70; dir. network affairs Nat. Pub. Radio, Washington, 1971, v.p., 1972, pres., 1973-77; communications cons., 1978—; mgr. ed. telecommunications sta. KAET-TV, Phoenix, Ariz., 1980-86; asst. gen. mgr. sta. KAET-TV, Phoenix, 1987-93; assoc. prof. radio-TV, Mich. State U., 1962-63; assoc. prof. speech Utah State U., 1968-69; lectr. Ariz. State U., 1981-82. Bd. dirs. Nat. Pub. Radio, 1973-78, Ariz. Sch. Svcs. Through Ednl. Tech., 1984-93, PSSC Legacy Fund, 1993—; bd. dirs. Pub. Svc. Satellite Consortium, 1982-90, chmn., 1987-90. Recipient Outstanding Alumnus in Communications award Mich. State U., 1973, Meritorious Svc. award in Communications, Brigham Young U., 1974, Disting. Svc. award Pacific Mountain Network, 1987. Mem. LDS Ch. Home: 8100 E Camelback Rd # 180 Scottsdale AZ 85251-2729

FRISCHLING, CARL, lawyer; b. N.Y.C., Feb. 21, 1937; s. Irving and Anna (Klein) F.; m. Adele Frischling, June 21, 1959; children: William, James, Edward. BA, Columbia U., 1958, JD, 1962, MBA, 1963. Bar: N.Y. 1963, U.S. Dist. Ct. N.Y. 1968. Atty. Am. Stock Exchange, N.Y.C., 1963-65; asst. to chmn. Investors Funding, N.Y.C., 1965-67; exec. v.p. and gen. counsel Am. Gen. Capital Mgmt., N.Y.C., 1968-76; ptnr. Alexander Green, N.Y.C., 1976-79; sr. ptnr. Spengler Carlson Gubar Brodsky Frischling, N.Y.C., 1979-92; ptnr. Reid & Priest, N.Y.C., 1992-94, Kramer Levin, N.Y.C., 1994—; bd. dirs. AIM Mut. Funds, Houston, Lazard Funds, N.Y., Cortland Funds. Office: Kramer Levin 919 3rd Ave Rm 3803 New York NY 10022-3852

FRISCHMUTH, ROBERT ALFRED, landscape planner, filmmaker; b. N.Y.C., Dec. 15, 1940; s. Alfred P. and Emma (Glas) F.; m. Marlis Lowenhagen, July 15, 1967 (div. 1979); children: Bettina, Malissa; m. Ana Berti, June 30, 1995. Student SUNY, Albany, 1958-60; BBA, Pace U., 1973. Cert. nurseryman, N.Y. Statis. analyst N.Y. Central System, N.Y.C., 1961-68; landscape planner Rosedale Nurseries, Hawthorne, N.Y., 1969—; founder RAF Film, 1980—. Producer (films) Gardening: A Brief History, 1979, Tree Transplant, 1980, Florida, 1981, Best of the West, 1982, Kenya Safari, 1983, Of Temples and Tombs, 1984; exhibitor of films, Paramount Ctr., 1987—. Bd. dirs. Paramount Ctr. for the Arts, 1981-87, pres. 1983-85. With U.S. Army, 1963-65. Mem. Am. Film Inst., Info. Film Producers Am. Lutheran. Home: 31 Ogden Ave Cortlandt Mnr NY 10567-4230 Office: Rosedale Nurseries 51 Saw Mill River Rd Hawthorne NY 10532-1508

FRISCO, LOUIS JOSEPH, retired materials science company executive, electrical engineer; b. Patchogue, N.Y., Aug. 21, 1923; s. Anthony Michael and Rose Katherine (Lotito) F.; m. Verona May Kindig, Aug. 20, 1950; children: Richard Samuel, Charles Francis. BSEE, Johns Hopkins U., 1949, MSEE, 1952. Dielectrics lab. dir. Johns Hopkins U., Balt., 1950-64; dielectrics program mgr. GE, Schenectady, N.Y., 1964-65; various tech. and ops. mgmt. positions Raychem Corp., Menlo Park, Calif., 1965-79, dir. corp. product rev., 1979-83, gen. mgr. Wire and Cable div., 1983-89, tech. dir. Electronics Sector, 1989-90; chmn. Conf. on Elec. Insulation, NAS/NRC, 1963-65; U.S. del. tech. com. TC-15 Internat. Electrotech. Commn., 1963-65, 79-82. Editor Digest of Lit. on Dielectrics, NAS/NRC, 1959, 60.; contbr. numerous articles to profl. jours. Fellow IEEE; mem. ASTM, Electrochem. Soc. (chmn. insulation div. 1957-59, bd. dirs. 1957-59, insulation div. editor jour. 1961-64), Tau Beta Pi, Sigma Xi. Roman Catholic.

FRISELL-SCHRÖDER, SONJA BETTIE, opera producer, stage director; b. Richmond, Surrey, Eng., Aug. 5, 1937; d. Bertel and Helena Margaret (Smith) Frisell; m. Rolf Peter Schröder, Feb. 3, 1976. Licentiate, Guildhall Sch. Music and Drama, London, 1958. Asst. dir. Arena Opera, Verona, Italy, summers 1962-65; from asst. dir. to head of regie and prodn. La Scala Opera Co., Milan, Italy, 1964-79; free-lance producer U.S.A., Can., Argentina, Brazil, Italy, France, Austria, Eng. Producer Ballo in Maschera, Paris Opera, 1981, Andrea Chenier, Miami, 1982, Marriage of Figaro, San Francisco, 1982, Khovanscina, San Francisco, 1984, Agrippina, Venice, 1985, Carmen, Teatro Colon, Buenos Aires, 1985, Salome, Seattle, 1986, Aida, Rio de Janeiro, 1986, Ballo, San Francisco, 1986, Ballo, Phila. (with Pavarotti), 1986, Magic Flute, Edmonton, Winnipeg, 1986, Trovatore, Chgo., 1987, Don Carlos, Tulsa, 1987, Marriage of Figaro, Treviso, 1987, Rigoletto, Seattle, 1988, Otello, Barcelona, 1988, Maometto II, San Francisco, 1988, Aida, N.Y.C., 1988, Ballo, Bologna, 1989, Forza del Destino, Washington, 1989, Don Carlos, Chgo., 1989, Daughter of the Regiment, Calgary, Can., 1990, Otello, P.R., 1990, Don Carlos, L.A., 1990, Siege of Calais, Donizetti Festival Bergamo, 1990, Magic Flute, Washington, 1990, Don Giovanni, Cape Town, South Africa, 1991, Don Carlos, Washington, 1991, Forza, San Francisco, 1992, Otello, Washington, 1992, Ballo, Chgo., 1992, Rigoletto, Goteborg, 1993, Trovatore, Chgo., 1993, Lucia diLammermoor, Calgary, 1994, Eugene Onegin, Calgary, 1996, Don Carlos, Chg., 1996, La Gioconda, Milan, 1997, Elena di Feltre, Wexford, 1997, Magic Flute, Washington, 1998, Turandot, Seville, 1998, Turandot Trieste, Cagliari, 1999. Arts scholar Can. Arts Coun., 1960. Mem. Am. Guild Mus. Artists. Avocations: archaeology, walking, dogs, gardening. Office: care CAMI 165 W 57th St New York NY 10019-2201

FRISHMAN, WILLIAM HOWARD, cardiology educator, cardiovasular pharmacologist, gerontologist; b. N.Y.C., Nov. 9, 1946; s. Aaron and Frances (Fishel) F.; m. Esther Rose Sandowsky, Mar. 11, 1971; children: Sheryl Renée, Amy Helene, Michael Aaron. BA, MD, Boston U., 1969. Diplomate Am. Bd. Internal Medicine, Am. Bd. Cardiovascular Medicine, Am. Bd. Critical Care Medicine, Am. Bd. Clin. Pharmacology, Am. Bd. Geriatrics, Am. Bd. Med. Mgmt. Intern Montefiore Hosp., Bronx, N.Y., 1969-70, resident in medicine, 1970-71; resident in medicine Bronx Mcpl. and Einstein Hosps., 1971-72; fellow in cardiology N.Y. Hosp.-Cornell U. Med. Coll., N.Y.C., 1972-74, instr., 1974-76; dir. noninvasive cardiac labs. Einstein Hosp. and Montefiore Hosp., 1976-80, dir. cardiology svc., 1980-82, chief medicine, 1982-91; prof. medicine and epidemiology, assoc. chmn. dept. medicine Albert Einstein Coll. Medicine Yeshiva U., Bronx, 1991-97; prof. medicine and pharmacology, chmn. dept. medicine N.Y. Med. Coll., Valhalla, 1997—; chief of medicine Westchester Med. Ctr., Valhalla, N.Y., 1997—; expert cons. cardiorenal divsn. FDA, Bethesda, Md., 1987—; panel mem. U.S. Pharmacopeial Conv., Rockville, Md., 1990—. Author: Clinical Pharmacology of the Beta-Blocking Drugs, 1980, 2d edit., 1984, Medical Management of Lipid Disorders, 1992; co-author: Calcium Channel Antagonists in Cardiovascular Disease, 1984, Therapy of Angina Pectoris, 1986, Current Cardiovascular Drugs, 1994, 2d edit. 1995, Beta-3 Adrenergic Agonism, 1995, Cardiovascular Pharmacotherapeutics, 1997, Handbook of Cardiovascular Therapeutics, 1998; editor: Year Book of Medicine: Heart Disease; contbr. chpts. to books and articles to profl. jours. Mem. fiscal affairs com. Village of Scarsdale, N.Y., 1991—. Lt. col. M.C., U.S. Army, 1969-90. Named to Boston Collegium of Disting. Alumni, Boston U., 1988, Disting. Alumnus sch. medicine, 1994; teaching scholar Am. Heart Assn., 1979-82; preventive cardiology acad. award Nat. Heart, Lung and Blood Inst., 1980-85; recipient Disting. Tchr. award AAMC-AOA, 1997. Fellow ACP, Am. Coll. Cardiology (bd. govs. 1987-91, pres. N.Y. State chpt. 1991), Am. Coll. Chest Physicians; mem. Am. Soc. for Clin. Pharmacology and Therapeutics (Mckeen Cattell award 1990), Am. Soc. for Clin. Rsch. (assoc. prof. medicine), N.Y. Cardiol. Soc. (pres. 1996-97), Scarsdale Town and Village Club, Alpha Omega Alpha (councillor). Jewish. Avocations: reading, athletic coaching. Home: 7 White Birch Ln Scarsdale NY 10583-7634 Office: Munger Pavilion NY Med Coll Valhalla NY 10595

FRISK, JACK EUGENE, recreational vehicle manufacturing company executive; b. Nampa, Idaho, Jan. 22, 1942; s. Steinert Paul and Evelyn Mildred (Letner) F.; m. Sharon Rose Caviness, Aug. 3, 1959; 1 dau., Toni. With Ideal of Idaho, Inc., Caldwell, purchasing mgr., 1969-75, gen. mgr., sec.-treas., 1975-82; sales mgr. Traveleze Industries div. Thor Industries, Sun Valley, Calif., 1982-88; owner, pres. Crossroads Industry div. Cross Enterprises Inc., Mesa, Ariz., 1988-92; dir. mktg. western divsn. Chariot Eagle, Inc., Ocala, Fla., 1992-95; gen. mgr. Chariot Eagle West, Inc., Phoenix, 1995-96; tool coord. III The Boeing Co., 1996—. Episcopalian. Home: 1430 N Parsell Cir Mesa AZ 85203-3713 Office: The Boeing Co 5000 E Mcdowell Rd # D178 Mesa AZ 85215-9707

FRISMAN, ROGER LAWRENCE, industrial sales executive; b. Cleve., Apr. 30, 1952; s. Al and Elsie (Joseph) F. BA, Kent State U., 1974. Sales rep. Lawyers Title Ins. Corp., Cleve., 1977-80, sales mgr., 1980; asst. v.p. sales Midland Title Security, Cleve., 1983-84, sr. v.p. comml. indsl. sales, 1984-90, sr. v.p., mgr. home builder dept., 1990—; bd. dirs. Ohio Home Builders Assn., mem. exec. com. Advisor YMCA Youth Gov., Stow, 1974; chmn. Nat. Assn. Home Builders Assoc., Build Pac, Wash., 1988—, chmn., 1995, com. vice-chmn., 1996. Recipient Affiliate of the Yr. award Bldg. Industry Assn., 1986, Affiliate of the Yr. award Ohio Home Builders Assn., 1985. Mem. Cleve. Bldg. Industry Assn., Cleve. Bd. Realtors (Affiliate of Yr. award 1982), Mortgage Bankers Assn. Apartment and Home Owners Assn. (Affiliate of Yr. award 1984), Nat. Assn. Home Builders (assocs. com., bd. dirs., exec. com.). Jewish. Avocations: sports watching, playing, softball, baseball, football. Home: 725 Village Club Rd Northfield OH 44067-2333 Office: Midland Title Security Inc IMG Ctr 1360 E 9th St Fl 5 Cleveland OH 44114-1720

FRISON, GEORGE C., education educator. Prof. emeritus of anthropology U. Wyo.; dir. archeol. excavations State of Wyo.

FRISON, PAUL MAURICE, health care executive; b. L.A., Mar. 9, 1937; s. Maurice Michael and Adele (Marion) F.; m. Barbara Louise Hoshaw, Dec. 21, 1957; children: Maryanne, Jill Renee. BA, Occidental Coll., L.A., 1958. V.p. internat. ops. Am. Hosp. Supply Corp., Evanston, Ill., 1962-75; pres., chief operating officer Lifemark Corp., Houston, 1975-84, Computer Craft Corp., Houston, 1984-86; pres., chief exec. officer, chmn. bd. LifeCell Corp., Woodlands, Tex., 1986—; chmn., pres., CEO Houston Tech. Ctr.; bd. dirs. Kanaly Trust Corp., McG Dulworth Corp., Allied Pharmacy Corp., Tex. Inst. for Rsch. and Rehab. Co-chmn. United Way, 1982-84; mem. Pres.'s Coun. on Fitness, 1982-84; bd. dirs. Lions Eye Found. Lt. USCG, 1959-62. Mem. Am. Mgmt. Assn., Houstonian Club, The Forum Club. Republican. Baptist. Home: 102 N Wynden Estates Ct Houston TX 77056-2518 Office: LifeCell Corp 3606 Research Forest Dr The Woodlands TX 77381-4232

FRISON, RICK, agricultural company executive; b. Worland, Wyo., Aug. 22, 1949; s. David T. and Maureen M. (Nelson) F.; m. Nadine M. Van Overbeke; children: Cara M., Jennifer M. BS, Mont. State U., 1977. Salesman ConAgra Mont., Inc., Great Falls, 1977-81, mktg. mgr., 1981-83; div. mgr. ConAgra Fertilizer Co., Billings, Mont., 1983-86; div. mgr. no. region ConAgra Fertilizer Co., Knoxville, Tenn., 1986-89, v.p., gen. mgr. no. region, 1989-91, retail v.p., 1991-92; pres. ConAgra Fertilizer Co., Pekin, Ill., 1994—, Cropmate Co., Pekin, 1992—, United Agri Products, Greeley, Colo., 1993—; mem. editl. adv. bd. Dealer Progress mag., Ballwin, Mo., 1992—; field editor Crop Protection mag., Eugene, Oreg., 1992—. Mem. Fertilizer Inst. (retail coun. 1992—). Office: Cropmate Co PO Box 977 Pekin IL 61555-0977*

FRISQUE, ALVIN JOSEPH, retired chemical company executive; b. Wis., Jan. 27, 1923; s. Henry Louis and Angeline (Thayse) F.; m. Jaye Anzak, June 1, 1950; children: Susan, Alice. B.S., U. Wis., 1948, Ph.D., 1954; M.S., U. Iowa, 1951. Sr. scientist Standard Oil Co. Ind., 1954-61; group leader and research mgr., then v.p. div. research Nalco Chem. Co., 1961-73; corp. v.p. research and devel. Nalco Chem. Co., Oak Brook, Ill., 1973-82, dir. corp. tech., 1982—. Author, patentee in field. Trustee Ill. Benedictine Coll. Served with USAAF, 1943-46. Decorated Air medal; Croix de Guerre France). Mem. Indsl. Research Inst., Am. Chem. Soc., Sigma Xi, Phi Lambda Upsilon. Patentee in field. Home: 129 Acacia Cir Apt 502 Indianhead Park IL 60525-9057

FRIST, THOMAS FEARN, JR., hospital management company executive; b. Nashville, Aug. 12, 1938; s. Thomas Fearn and Dorothy (Cate) F.; m. Patricia Champion, Dec. 22, 1961; children: Trisha, Thomas III, Bill. BS, Vanderbilt U., 1961; MD, Washington U., 1966. Chmn., chief exec. officer Hospital Corp. of Am., Nashville; exec. v.p. Hosp. Corp. Am., Nashville, 1969-77, pres., chief oper. officer, 1977-82, pres., chief exec. officer, 1982-85, chmn., 1985-95; vice chmn. Columbia/ Hosp. Corp. of Am. Healthcare Corp., Nashville, 1995—, chmn., CEO, 1995—; bd. dirs. Columbia Healthcare. Trustee Vanderbilt U., Nashville, 1987, United Way of Am., Alexandria, Va., 1987. Fellow Am. Coll. Healthcare Execs. (hon.); mem. Bus. Roundtable, Bus. Coun., Belle Meade Country Club. Presbyterian. Avocations: marathon running, tennis, skiing, flying. Office: Columbia/HCA Healthcare PO Box 550 Nashville TN 37202-0550*

FRIST, WILLIAM H., senator, surgeon; b. Nashville, Feb. 22, 1952; m. Karyn Frist; children: Harrison, Jonathan, Bryan. AB, Princeton U., 1974; MD, Harvard U., 1978. Resident Mass. Gen. Hosp., 1979-84; chief resident Stanford U. Med. Ctr., 1985; founder, surgeon Vanderbilt Transplant Med. Ctr., 1986—; U.S. senator from Tenn., 1995—; mem. commerce, sci. & transp. com., fgn. rels. com., budget com., labor & human resources com. U.S. Senate, 1995. Republican. Office: US Senate 416 Russell Senate Ofc Bldg Washington DC 20510-4205

FRISWOLD, FRED RAVNDAHL, manufacturing executive; b. Mpls., Jan. 21, 1937; s. Ingolf Oliver and Derrice Ernestine (Anderson) F.; m. C. Marie Martin, Sept. 14, 1957; children—Cynthia, Steven, Barry, Michelle (dec.), Benjamin. BBA with distinction in Fin, U. Minn., 1958. Chartered fin. analyst. With J.M. Dain & Co. (now Dain, Rauscher, Inc.), Mpls., 1958—; exec. v.p. Dain, Bosworth, Inc., 1976-82, pres., CEO, 1982-90, cons., 1990-92; CEO Tonka Equipment Co., Plymouth, Minn., 1992—; Bd. chair, Mpls. Rotary Found., U. Gateway Corp., UMF Investment Advisors. Trustee Metro YMCA, U. Minn. Found.; trustee Univ. Children's Found.; mem. bd. advisors Otologics L.L.C. Mem. Twin City Soc. Security Analysts, Wildwood Lodge, Mpls. Rotary (pres., bd. dirs. 1997—). Methodist. Home: 7033 Comanche Ct Minneapolis MN 55439-1004 Office: Tonka Equipment Co 13305 Water Tower Cir Plymouth MN 55441-3803

FRITCHER, EARL EDWIN, civil engineer, consultant; b. St. Ansgar, Iowa, Nov. 24, 1923; s. Lee and Mamie Marie (Ogden) F.; m. Dorsille Ellen Simpson, Aug. 24, 1946; 1 child, Teresa. BS, Iowa State U., 1950. Registered civil engr., Calif. Project devel. engr. dept. transp. State of Calif., Los Angeles, 1950-74, traffic engr. dept. transp., 1974-87; pvt. practice cons. engr. Sunland, Calif., 1987—; consulting prin. traffic engr. Parsons DeLeuw Inc., 1990—; cons. traffic engr. DeLeuw Cather Internat., Dubai, United Arab Emerates, 1994. Co-author: Overhead Signs and Contract Sign Plans, 1989; patentee in field. Served to 2d lt. USAF, 1942-46, 50-51. Mem. Iowa State U. Alumni Assn. (life). Republican. Methodist. Clubs: Verdugo Hills Numismatic (Sunland), Glendale Numismatic.

FRITH, LYNDA KATHRYN, principal; b. San Antonio, Mar. 11, 1948; d. Ernest, III and Gerladine (Sims) West; m. Lonnie Lee Frith, June 21, 1969; children: Michelle, Becky. BS, S.W. Tex. State, 1969; MEd, Trinity, 1997. Tchr. Brewer Elem., San Antonio, 1969-79, Ball Elem., San Antonio, 1979-96; adminstrv. asst. Burnet Elem., San Antonio, 1996-97, vice prin., 1997-98, prin., 1998—. Trinity U. scholar, 1995-97. Mem. Buzzard Club Am. (sec., treas., bowling league), Alpha Delta Kappa (state officer, historian, scholar 199496), Siemering Lodge Sons of Hermann (fin. adv., Humanitarian award 1984), Order Eastern Star (past matron Havlanadale # 750). Democrat. Methodist. Avocations: bowling, arts and crafts. Home: 16335 Clouded Crest St San Antonio TX 78247-1347 Office: Burnet Elem 406 Barrera St San Antonio TX 78210-1068

FRITH, MICHAEL KINGSBURY, artistic director, illustrator, performing company executive; b. Grand Rapids, Mich., July 8, 1941; s. Alexander J. and Mary Eleanor (Hefferan) F.; m. Kathryn Mullen; children: Calley Allison, Christina Huston, Jonathan Kingsbury. BA, Harvard U., 1963. Art dir., editor-in-chief Random House, Beginner Books, N.Y.C., 1963-75; from art dir. to exec. v.p., dir. creative svcs. Jim Henson Prodns., N.Y.C., 1975-96; founding ptnr. Sirius Thinking Ltd., N.Y.C., 1996—; conceptual designer, creative prodr. Between the Lions; conceptual designer, exec. prodr. Fraggle Rock; creative cons., exec. prodr. Muppet Babies; creative and design cons. The Muppet Show; design cons. five Muppet movies; creative prodr. Little Muppet Monsters; Muppet segment prodr. Free to be...A Family; exec. prodr. Jim Henson's Dog City, Mr. Willowby's Christmas Tree; exec. prodr. The Wubbulous World of Dr. Seuss. Co-author: (with C.B. Cerf) Alligator, 1962; author: I'll Teach My Dog 100 Words, 1973; author, illustrator: (with Dr. Seuss as Rosetta Stone) Because a Little Bug Went Kachoo, 1975, Some of Us Walk, Some Fly, Some Swim, 1971, My Amazing Book of Autographs, 1974, The Early Bermudians, 1985; illustrator (books by Bennett Cerf): Laugh Day, 1965, Treasury of Atrocious Puns, 1968, The Sound of Laughter, 1970, Stories to Make You Feel Better, 1972; illustrator: The World's Largest Cheese, 1968, The Perils of Penelope, 1973, Insomniacs of the World, Goodnight, 1974; illustrator (series) Animals Do the Strangest Things, Birds Do the Strangest Things, Fish Do the Strangest Things, Insects Do the Strangest Things, Reptiles Do the Strangest Things, Prehistoric Monsters Did the Strangest Things, 1964-74. Mem. NARAS, NATAS, Writers Guild Am., Soc. Illustrators, Art Dirs. Club. Office: Sirius Thinking Ltd 146 E 62nd St New York NY 10021-8142

FRITSCH, BILLY DALE, JR., construction company executive; b. Pensacola, Fla., May 10, 1956; s. Billy Dale Fritsch Sr. and Cleta Thiel; children: Mackenzie, Billy Dale III, Jessica. BS, No. Mich. U., 1978. CPA, Ill. Staff acct. Jonet, Fontain, Vande Loo, et al, Green Bay, Wis., 1979; asst. contr. Carpenter Contractors of Am., Pompano Beach, Fla., 1979-81, contr., 1981-84, v.p. fin., 1984-90, exec. v.p., 1990—; cons. Jade Industries, Coral Springs, Fla., 1983-86; mem. team of taxation and acctg. specialists Citizen Ambassador Program, 1988. Mem. AICPA, Fla. Inst. CPAs, Ill. CPA Soc., Constrn. Fin. Mgmt. Assn., Greater Ft. Lauderdale C. of C. (founding trustee 1990), Internat. Platform Assn. Republican. Avocation: squash. Office: Carpenter Contractors Am 941 SW 12th Ave Pompano Beach FL 33069-4610

FRITSCH, DEREK ADRIAN, nurse anesthetist; b. Cuero, Tex., Sept. 12, 1957; s. Adrian Henry and Virginia Emma (Bernshausen) F.; m. Jacqueline Ann Joyce, June 8, 1985; children: Alexander Derek, Adrienne Joyce. AA, Wharton County Jr. Coll., Wharton, Tex., 1978; BSN, U. Tex. Health Sci. Ctr., 1980; CRNA, Harris County Hosp. Dist., Houston, 1983. Cert. registered nurse anesthetist. Anesthesia tng. Ben Taub Gen. Hosp., The Meth. Hosp., VA Hosp., others, Houston, 1979-88; staff anesthetist Anesthesia Specialists of Houston/The Woman's Hosp. Tex., Houston, 1988-94, 95—; freelance staff anesthetist Schick Shadel Hosp., Houston, 1990, Gulf Coast Regional Med. Ctr., Wharton, 1994-95; staff anesthetist, anesthesia specialists of Houston/The Woman's Hosp., Houston, 1995—. Colo. County emergency vol. Ambulance Corps, 1976-78; provider anesthesia internat. eye surgery team, Benovolent Missions Internat., Belize, Boliva, El Salvador, 1993-94, 93-95, gen. surgery team, Guatemala, 1996. Recipient Luth. Brotherhood scholarship, 1979, Rotarian scholarship, Houston, 1979, others. Mem. AANA, Tex. Assn. Nurse Anesthetists, Internat. Anesthesia Rsch. Soc., Gulf Coast Assn. Nurse Anesthetists (bd. dirs. 1987-89, pres. 1988-89), Greater New England Acad. Hypnosis, U.S. Parachute Assn., Phi Theta Kappa (State Recognition award, chpt. pres. 1977-78), Sigma Theta Tau. Lutheran. Avocations: fishing, computers, carpentry, skydiving. Home: 410 Lake Bend Dr Sugar Land TX 77479-5804 Office: Anesthesia Specialists Houston 7800 Fannin St Ste 101 Houston TX 77054-2905

FRITSCH, RICHARD ELVIN, trust company executive; b. Lancaster, Pa., Feb. 3, 1955; s. Elvin Richard and Dolores Audrey (Deppeller) F.; m. Jennifer Lynn Rhodes, June 29, 1996. BS, Elizabethtown Coll., 1977; BA, Lebanon Valley Coll., 1981. Asst. v.p., trust officer First Union Nat. Bank, Lancaster, 1983—. Bd. dirs. Hershey Symphony. Mem. Am. Guild Organists (dean, sub-dean, sec., bd. dirs.), Assn. Luth. Ch. Musicians. Home: 232 Ruby St Lancaster PA 17603-5168

FRITSCHLER, A. LEE, retired college president, public policy educator; b. Schenectady, N.Y., May 5, 1937; s. George A. and Jane E. (Green) F.; m. Aliceann Wohlbruck, Sept. 2, 1961 (div. 1976); children: Craig A., Eric G.; m. Susan Torrence, Dec. 31, 1977. BA, Union Coll., Schenectady, 1959; MPA, Syracuse U., 1960, PhD, 1965; LLD, The Dickinson Sch. of Law, 1993. Asst. prof. Am. U., Washington, 1964-67, prof., 1967-79, acad. dir. Washington semester program, 1964-67, dir. pub. adminstrn. program, 1971-72, dean Coll. Pub. and Internat. Affairs, 1977-79; chmn. U.S. Postal Rate Commn., 1979-81; dir. ctr. pub. policy edn. Brookings Instn., Washington, 1981-87; pres. Dickinson Coll., Carlisle, Pa., 1987-99; guest prof. U. Cologne, Fed. Republic Germany, 1971; vis. prof. Union Coll., 1984; lectr Nat. War Coll., 1969; lectr. on bus.-govt. rels. to exec. devel. programs at IBM Corp., AT&T, GE, Gulf Corp.; co-founder, former chair, treas. The Annapolis Group, 1991—. Author (with B.H. Ross) (textbook) Business Regulation and Government Decision-Making, 1980, (trade book) Executive's Guide to Government: How Washington Works, 1980, Smoking and Politics: Policymaking and the Federal Bureaucracy, 1983, 5th edit., 1996, How Washington Works: The Executive's Guide to Government, 1987; mem. editl. bd. Pub. Adminstrn. Rev., 1976-80, Internat. Jour. Pub. Adminstrn., 1979-88; contbr. numerous articles to profl. jours. Mem. Harrisburg Acad. Cmty. Adv. Bd., 1991-96, Commonwealth Partnership Adv. Bd., 1997—; hon. bd. dirs. Friends of the Joseph Priestly House; mem. exec. com. Am. Collegiate Consortium for East-West Cultural and Acad. Exch., 1993-96. Mem. Am. Soc. Pub. Adminstrn. (nat. pres. 1982-83, bd. dirs. govt.-bus. relations sect.), Nat. Acad. Pub. Adminstrn. (bd. dirs.), Assn. of Governing Bds. Univs. and Colls. (adv. coun. of pres.), Bd. Orgn. Resources Counsellors, Indsl. Rels. Counselors, Inc., Internat. Inst. Adminstrv. Scis. (mem. N.Am. bd. govs. schs. and insts. sect.), Nat. Capital Area Polit. Sci. Assn. (pres. 1975), Nat. Assn. Schs. Pub. Affairs and Adminstrn. (bd. dirs. 1975), Libr. of Congress (coun. scholars), Internat. Assn. Univ. Presidents, Am. Coun. on Edn. (comn. on internat. edn.), Nat. Acad. Found. Acad. Pub. Sbvc. (bd. dirs.), Northeast-Midwest Inst. (bd. dirs.), Ctr. for Regional Policy, Pa. Commn. for Ind. Colls. and Univs. (exec. com.), Assn. Ind. Colls. and Univs. Pa. (bd. dirs. 1997—). Avocations: tennis, furniture repair, golf.

FRITTON, KARL ANDREW, lawyer; b. Olean, N.Y., Mar. 29, 1955; s. William John and Margaret (O'Brian) F.; m. Christine Evelyn Councill, June 9, 1984; children: Katherine Evelyn, Jessica Claire, Rebecca Lee. BS in Econs., SUNY, Albany, 1977; JD, Rutgers U., 1980. Bar: Pa. 1981, N.Y. 1981, U.S. Supreme Ct. 1985. Assoc. Bond, Schoeneck & King, Syracuse, N.Y., 1980-81, Obermayer, Rebmann, Maxwell & Hippel, Phila., 1981-84; assoc. Sprecher, Felix, Visco, Hutchinson & Young, Phila., 1984-86, ptnr., 1987-91; ptnr. Montgomery, McCracken, Walker & Rhoads, Phila., 1991-96, Reed, Smith, Shaw & McLay LLP, Phila., 1996—. Contbr. articles to profl. jours. Active Phila. Vol. Lawyers For Arts, 1981—, Big Brs. Phila., 1981—. Mem ABA (labor law sect.). Democrat. Roman Catholic. Home: 53 Cedarbrook Rd Ardmore PA 19003-1617 Office: Reed Smith Shaw & McLay 2500 One Liberty Pl Philadelphia PA 19103

FRITTS, EDWARD O., broadcast executive; b. Cape Girardeau, Mo., Feb. 21, 1941; m. Martha Dale; children: Kimberley, Timothy, Jennifer. Grad., U. Miss. Pres. Nat. Assn. Broadcasters, Washington, 1982—; past chmn.

joint bd. Nat. Assn. Broadcasters; vice chair U.S. State Dept. Internat. Media Fund. Dir. advt. coun., former trustee Mus. TV and Radio; bd. dirs. Nat. Commn. Against Drunk Driving, Partnership for a Drug-Free Am., Ctrs. for Disease Control's Bus. Responds to AIDS program; cons. U.S. C. of C. Assns. Com.; chair media adv. com. U.S. Bicentennial Commn.; vice chmn. White House Pvt. Sector Initiatives Bd., 1985-88; mem. individual investors adv. com. N.Y. Stock Exch.; active Wolf Trap Found., Arlington Hosp. Found., Nat. Mus. Women in The Arts. Recipient Silver Mike award U. Miss. Mem. Sigma Alpha Epsilon (Highest Effort award). Avocation: golf. Office: Nat Assn Broadcasters 1771 N St NW Ste 200 Washington DC 20036-2891*

FRITTS, HAROLD CLARK, dendrochronology educator, researcher; b. Rochester, N.Y., Dec. 17, 1928; s. Edwin Coulthard and Ava Lee (Washburn) F.; m. Barbara Smith, June 11, 1955 (dec.); children: Marcia L., Paul T.; m. Miriam Colson, July 19, 1982. AB, Oberlin Coll., 1951; MS, Ohio State U., 1953, PhD in Botany, 1956. Asst. prof. botany Eastern Ill. U., Charleston, 1956-60; asst. prof. dendrochronology U. Ariz., Tucson, 1960-64, assoc., 1964-69, prof., 1969-92, emeritus, 1992—; adj. prof. in rsch. Desert Rsch. Inst., U. Nev.; vis. scientist CSIRO forest products divsn., Melbourne, Australia, 1996; owner Dendro-Power, Tucson, 1992—; dir., founder Internat. Tree-Ring Data Bank, 1975-90; NSF faculty, mem. Task Group 3 adv. com. on paleoclimatology, Climate Dynamics Program, 1978-79; lectr. NATO Advanced Study Inst. on Climatic Variability, Sicily, 1980; vis. dir. U. Wyo. Summer Sci. Camp, summer 1956; mem. U. Ariz. del. to People's Republic of China, 1976; participant Nat. Def. U., 1978-79; mem. organizing group internat. conf. on dendroclimatology, Eng., 1980. Author: Tree Rings and Climate, 1976, Reconstructing Large-Scale Climate Patterns from Tree-Ring Data, 1991; mem. editorial adv. bd. Quaternary Rsch., 1977-82; contbr. articles to profl. jours. Mem. local sch. bd., 1971-72. Recipient Dendrochronlogical award of Appreciation Sci. Community, Lund, Sweden, 1990; Grad. fellow Ohio State U., 1954-56, NSF fellow Oreg. Inst. Marine Biology, summer 1957, Guggenheim fellow, 1968-69; grantee NSF 1971-87, U. Calif. Lawrence Livermore Lab., 1978-79, State of Calif., 1979-80, 85-86. Fellow AAAS; mem. Am. Assn. Quaternary Environment (council 1978-82, adv. com. paleonclimatology), Ecol. Soc. Am. (edit. bd. 1964-66, council rep., chmn. paleoecology sect 1984), Am. Inst. Biol. Scis., Tree-Ring Soc., Am. Meteorol. Soc. (Oustanding Achievement in Bioclimatology award 1982). Home: 5703 N Lady Ln Tucson AZ 85704-3905

FRITTS, HARRY WASHINGTON, JR., physician, educator; b. Rockwood, Tenn., Oct. 4, 1921; s. Harry Washington and Hyder (Smith) F.; m. Helen Dyer Goodwin, Aug. 25, 1949; children: John Goodwin, Benjamin Carroll, Patricia Louise. Student, Vanderbilt U., 1941; B.S., Mass. Inst. Tech., 1943; M.D., Boston U., 1951. Diplomate: Am. Bd. Internal Medicine (mem.). Mem. research staff MIT, 1946-47; intern, then resident Univ. Hosp., Boston, 1951-53; vis. fellow Columbia Coll. Physicians and Surgeons, 1953-56, mem. faculty, 1956-73; prof. medicine, 1967-73, Dickinson W. Richards prof. medicine, 1972-73; prof., chmn. dept. medicine Sch. Medicine, State U. N.Y. at Stony Brook, 1973-87, Edmund D. Pellegrino prof. medicine, 1986-87; William Harris vis. prof. Nat. Med. Sch. Taiwan, 1987-88; vis. physician Bellevue Hosp., 1957-68, Presbyn. Hosp., N.Y.C., 1961-73; vis. physician, cons. Manhattan VA Hosp., 1957-68; vis. prof. U. London, 1982; bd. dirs., adv. council research N.Y. Heart Assn.; mem. sci. council Parker Francis Found.; mem. physiology study sect., mem. cardiovascular tng. com. USPHS; mem. council Nat. Heart, Lung and Blood Inst. Author: On Leading a Clinical Department, 1997; assoc. editor: Jour. Clin. Investigation; mem. editl. bd.: Am. Rev. Respiratory Diseases; contbr. articles to profl. jours. Served to lt. (j.g.) USNR, 1943-46. Guggenheim fellow, 1959-60. Fellow ACP; mem. Am. Physiol. Soc., Am. Soc. Clin. Investigation, Assn. Am. Physicians, Am. Clin. and Climatol. Soc., Alpha Omega Alpha. Home: 79 Bevin Rd Northport NY 11768-1133 Office: SUNY at Stony Brook Dept Medicine Stony Brook NY 11794

FRITTS, WILLIAM D., JR., financial executive; b. Cranford, N.J., Nov. 13, 1950; s. William Douglas Fritts Jr. and Mabel Robertson Bovey; children: William D. III, James Robertson, Robertson Charles Hawk, Thomas Bruce Robertson. BA, U. Vt., 1974. Sr. advisor, dir. office security U.S. Dept. Security, Washington, 1990-92; counselor to dept. sec. U.S. Dept. HHS, Washington, 1992-93; mng. dir. U.S. Senator Dave Durenberger, Washington, 1993-94; v.p. Reliastar Fin. Corp., Mpls., 1994—. Presbyterian. Home: 2153 Knapp St Saint Paul MN 55108 Office: Reliastar Fin Corp 20 Washington Ave S Minneapolis MN 55401

FRITZ, BARBARA JEAN, occupational health nurse; b. Helena, Mont., Sept. 16, 1936; d. Marion Caldwell and Clara K. (Bernard) Heffern; m. Bernard John Fritz Sept. 2, 1961; children: Cathleen, Stephen, Elizabeth. Diploma in nursing, Sacred Heart Sch. Nursing, 1957; BS in Nursing, St. Louis U., 1959; postgrad., Oreg. State U., Portland State U., Oreg. Health Scis. U. Cert. occupl. health nurse. Occupl. health nurse Chloride Western Battery, Portland, Oreg., 1984-85, Harder Mech./James River Site, Camas, Wash., 1988; occupl. health nurse unit mgr. Pub. Health Dept. Fed. Occupl. Health, Portland, 1985-86; occupl. health relief nurse James River Corp., Portland, 1986-88; health & safety mgr. Armour Foods, Portland, 1988-90; occupl. health cons. Pacific Rim Occupl. Health & Safety Svcs., Portland, 1990—; occupl. health nurse mgr. Toyota Vehicle Processing, Inc., Portland, 1992-95; med. case mgr. Gates McDonald, Beaverton, Oreg., 1995-96; temp. occupl. health mgr. L.S.I. Logic, Gresham, Oreg., 1997; relief occupl. health cons. Atlas, Copco, Wagner Mining, Portland, 1986—; instr. in field. Chmn. northeast citizen's adv. Portland Planning Commn., 1988, com. historic landmarks, 1988; group mem. Urban Tour Group, Portland, 1995; leadership group Mid-County Sewer Project, 1991-92; historian Columbia River Assn. Occupl. Health Nurses, Portland, 1992-96; vol. Portland Ctr. Performing Arts. Honoree outstanding contbns. at 25th Ann. Urban Tour Group, 1995. Mem. Am. Assn. Occupl. Health Nurses, Columbia River Assn. Occupl. Health Nurses (registered lobbyist, co-chair 1995-96, chair 1996-97, govtl. affairs chair 1996-97, Nat. Govtl. Affairs award 1996, 98). Democrat. Roman Catholic. Achievements include being instrumental in inclusion of occupational health professionals in worksite redesign grant program. Avocation: floral arranging. Home and Office: 4705 NE Ainsworth St Portland OR 97218-1818

FRITZ, BRUCE MORRELL, photographer; b. Madison, Wis., Aug. 13, 1947; s. Marvin Joseph and Jeannette Irene (Morrell) F.; m. Celeste Ann Woodruff, June 7, 1986; 1 child, Julia Woodruff. Student, U. Wis., 1965-69. Staff photographer Capital Times, Madison, Wis., 1969-77; instr. photojournalism U. Wis., 1976-78. One-man shows include 8th Ave. Gallery, Kenosha, Wis., 1972, Focal Point Gallery, Madison, 1974, Madison Art Center, 1975, Sunprint Gallery, Madison, 1977; photographs in Nat. Geog. World, others. With USN, 1967-68. Recipient Disting. Service award in field of news photography Sigma Delta Chi, 1976; named News Photographer of Yr. Madison Press Club, 1974-75. Mem. Nat. Press Photographers Assn., Am. Soc. Media Photographers, Wedding and Portrait Photographers Internat. Address: 4713 Winnequah Rd Monona WI 53716 *I try to remain open and receptive to everything around me. I never compromise when image making; I strive for perfection. I've learned to respect the dignity and wonder of every person and all creatures of Nature. I try to convey that wonder and to capture the awesome beauty of Nature.*

FRITZ, CECIL MORGAN, investment company executive; b. Modoc, Ind., July 30, 1921; s. Kenneth M. and Ruby (Howell) F.; m. Lucile Johnson, June 9, 1946; children: John, Susan, Marcia. BS, Ind. U., 1948, MBA, 1949. With City Securities Corp., Indpls., 1949—, pres., 1980-92, ret., 1994, now dir. Capt. USAAF, 1940-46. Recipient Sagamore of the Wabash-Indiana award. Mem. Masons (32 degree). Republican. Methodist. Home: 8510 Jib Ct Indianapolis IN 46236-9597 Office: City Securities Corp 135 N Pennsylvania St Ste 2200 Indianapolis IN 46204-2462

FRITZ, CHARLES JOHN, artist; b. Mason City, Iowa, Feb. 20, 1955; s. John Walter and Doris Beaunette (Lind) F.; m. Joan Mary Markwardt; children: Isaac John, Erik Charles. BS in Edn., Iowa State U., 1978. Tchr. Boone (Iowa) Cmty. Sch. Dist., 1978-79; artist Billings, Mont., 1980—; guest artist Western Rendezvous of Art, Helena, Mont., 1992, Buffalo Bill Mus. Art Exhibit, Cody, Wyo., 1992—; juror Okla. Art Guild, Oklahoma City, 1996. One-man shows include Turner Art Gallery, Denver, 1988, 90, 92-95, MacNider Art Mus., Mason City, Iowa, 1995; exhibited in group shows at

Miniatures exhibit, Mpls. 1988—, Mus. N.Am. Wildlife, Jackson Hole, Wyo., 1988—, Settlers West Gallery, Tucson, 1988—, Nat. Mus. Wildlife Art, Jackson, Wyo., 1988—, C.M. Russell Mus., Great Falls, Mont., 1989—, Western Heritage Ctr. of Yellowstone County, Billings, 1989, 90-96, Albuquerque Mus. Found., 1990—, Gov.'s Invitational Art Show, Cheyenne (Wyo.) Frontier Days, 1992—, Buffalo Bill Hist. Ctr., Cody, Wyo., 1992—, Thomas Gilcrease Mus., Tulsa, 1992-95, Denver Rotary Club, 1994-96, Nat. Cowboy Hall of Fame, Oklahoma City, 1996, 97, 98, 99, Cin. Mus. Ctr., 1996, C.M. Russell Mus., Great Falls, Mont., 1996; represented in permanent collection Denver Art Mus., Charles H. MacNider Art Mus., Mason City, Buffalo Bill Hist. Ctr., Cody, also pvt. and corp. collections. Rep. bd. St. John's Luth. Home, Billings, 1985-86; chairperson Luth. blood drive United Blood Svcs., Billings, 1993-96; numerous com. and bd. positions Luth. Ch. of Good Shepherd, Billings, 1981-96. Recipient award of merit Wildlife and Western Art Exposition, Mpls., 1987, J. K. Ralston award Western Heritage Ctr. Yellowstone County, Billings, 1989, 90, Dale Hawkins Meml. award Western Heritage Ctr. Yellowstone County, Billings, 1990-95, Juror's Choice-Best of Show, C.M. Russell Art Auction, 1992, 96, Peter Hassrict award of merit Buffalo Bill Hist. Ctr., Cody, 1992, Lee M. Loeb Meml. award for landscape Salmagundi Exhibit, N.Y.C., 1993, Spirit of the West award C.M. Russell Mus. and Art Auction, 1997.

FRITZ, DWAIN ELDON, engineer; b. St. Johns, Ohio, Feb. 26, 1919; s. Karl Kohler and Ada Iona (Rostorfer) F.; m. Carolyn Abraham Fritz, Sept. 21, 1940; children: Robert, Ann. Student, Ohio State U., 1936-37. Cert. profl. elec. engr. Draftsman Westinghouse, Lima, Ohio, 1938-40; design engr. Westinghouse, 1940-43, engring. sec. mgr., 1943-44; chief project engr. Jack & Heintz, Cleve., 1945-50, chief. engr., 1950-53; pres. Avtron Manufacturing, Inc., Cleve., 1953-83, chmn., 1983—. Recipient Meritorious Engring. award IEEE, 1988. Mem. IEEE, Soc. Am. Engrs., Cleve. Engring. Soc. Avocations: target shooting, radio, photography. Home: 8149 Maplegrove Ave N Royalton OH 44133-2068 Office: Avtron Mfg Inc 10409 Meech Ave Cleveland OH 44105-4183

FRITZ, EDWARD LANE, dentist; b. Evansville, Ind., Dec. 15, 1932; s. Edward E. and Virginia B. (Lane) F.; m. Bettye J. Samples, July 31, 1954; children: Mary Ann, Sarah Jane. AB, Ind. U., 1954, DDS, 1957; BS, U. Evansville, 1975, MBA, 1978. Pvt. practice dentistry Evansville, 1959-99, ret.; pres., chmn. bd. Health Resources, Inc., 1986—; corp. bd. dirs. Va. Corp., Evansville, 1962-72, Dynatron, Inc., 1980-87. Editor: The Bulletin of the Am. Assn. of Dental Examiners, 1981-85. Capt. U.S. Army, 1957-59. Named Disting. Alumnus Ind. U. Sch. Dentistry, 1991. Fellow Am. Coll. Dentists, Acad. Gen. Dentistry, Acad. Dentistry Internat., Internat. Coll. Dentists; mem. ADA (continuing edn. com. 1981-83, cons./evaluator 1982), Ind. Dental Assn. (trustee 1983-91, Disting. Svc. award 1996), Vanderburgh County Dental Soc. (pres. 1967, various offices), First Dist. Dental Soc. (pres. 1976-77, various offices), Am. Assn. Dental Examiners (pres. 1989, various offices), Ind. Bd. Dental Examiners (pres. 1982-83, sec. 1980-82), Acad. Operative Dentistry, Internat./Am. Assn. Dental Rsch., Am. Assn. Dental Editors, Acad. Gen. Dentistry, Pierre Fauchard Acad., Sagamores of the Wabash, Phi Kappa Phi. Home: 12200 Edgewater Dr Evansville IN 47720-8169

FRITZ, ETHEL MAE HENDRICKSON, writer; b. Gibbon, Nebr., Feb. 4, 1925; d. Walter Earl and Alice Hazel (Mickish) Hendrickson; m. C. Wayne Fritz, Feb. 25, 1950; children: Linda Sue, Krista Jane. BS, Iowa State U., 1949. Accredited master flower show judge. Dist. home economist Internat. Harvester Co., Des Moines, 1949-50; writer Wallace's Farmer mag., Des Moines, 1960-64; freelance writer, 1960—. Author: The Story of an Amana Winemaker, 1984, Prairie Kitchen Sampler, 1988, The Family of Hy-Vee, 1989. Chmn. Ariz. Coun. Flower Show Judges, 1983-85; medial rels. Presdl. Inaugural Com., 1988. Mem. AAUW, Assn. for Women in Comm. (pres. Phoenix profl. chpt., nat. task force com. 1980-82), Am. Soc. Profl. and Exec. Women, Am. Assn. Family and Consumer Sci., Consumer Sci. Bus. Profls., S.W. Writer's Conf., Ariz. Authors Assn., Phi Upsilon Omicron, PEO Club, Kappa Delta. Republican. Methodist.

FRITZ, EUGENE EARL, university administrator; b. West Reading, Pa., May 15, 1936; s. Eugene Earl and Ethyl Virginia (Bohanon) F.; m. Mary Elizabeth Niebaum, June 14, 1958; children: Jeffrey Eugene, Jean Louise. BS, East Stroudsburg (Pa.) U., 1960; MEd, West Chester (Pa.) U., 1967. Lic. tchr., Pa. Tchr. Schuylkill Valley H.S., Leesport, Pa., 1960-68; prof., dir. campus recreation Millersville (Pa.) U., 1968—; track and cross country coach Millersville (Pa.) U., 1969-85, assoc. dir. athletics, 1986-97. Chmn., vice chmn. Manor Twp. (Pa.) Parka Recreation Bd., 1973-96. Named Coach of Yr. Divsn. II Cross Country Coaches Assn., 1982; recipient Merit award Region I, Nat. Intramural and Recreational Sports Assn., 1994. Mem. Masons, Rotary (sgt. of arms 1995-97). Avocations: raising and training beagles, fly fishing, hunting, gardening. Home: 66 Chestnut Grove Rd Conestoga PA 17516-9316

FRITZ, JACK WAYNE, communications and marketing company executive; b. Battle Creek, Mich., Apr. 22, 1927; s. Charles Lewis and Ruth Marie (Lieb) F.; m. Marilyn Joyce Shingleton, Aug. 26, 1950; children: Jack Wayne II, Dain Thomas, Susan Lynne. B.A., U. Mich., 1949. Sales staff Lever Bros., Mich., 1949-51; with sales staff ABC-owned AM and TV stas., Mich. and Ohio, 1951; product mgr. Pepsodent div. Lever Brothers, N.Y.C., 1951-54; salesman, v.p., sales mgr. v.p., gen. mgr. Blair TV div., N.Y.C., 1954-68; with John Blair & Co., N.Y.C., 1954-87; dir. John Blair & Co., 1968-87, v.p., gen. mgr. broadcasting, 1968-72; pres., chief exec. officer, 1972-87; bd. dirs. Advo, Inc., Hartford, Conn., Fritz Broadcasting, Detroit, Fritz Comms., Warburg-Pincus Funds, N.Y.C. Pres. bd. trustees Nat. Mus. Wildlife Art. Served with AUS, 1945-47. Mem. Internat. Radio and TV Soc. (past dir.), Broadcast Pioneers (past dir.). Republican. Episcopalian. Clubs: Univ. (N.Y.C.), Teton Pines Country Club (Jackson, Wyo.). Address: 2425 N Fish Creek Rd PO Box 1287 Wilson WY 83014-1287

FRITZ, JAMES SHERWOOD, chemist, educator; b. Decatur, Ill., July 20, 1924; s. William Lawrence and Leora Mae (Troster) F.; m. Helen Joan Houck, Apr. 26, 1949 (dec. Oct. 1987); children—Barbara Lisa, Julie Ann, Laurel Joan, Margaret Ellen; m. Miriam Simons Reeves, July 15, 1989. B.S., James Millikin U., 1945; M.S., U. Ill., 1946, Ph.D., 1948. Asst. prof. chemistry Wayne State U., Detroit, 1948-51; asst. prof. Iowa State U., Ames, 1951-55, assoc. prof., 1955-60, prof., 1960-90, disting. prof., 1990—. Author: Acid Base Titrations in Nonaqueous Solvents, 1973; co-author: Quantitative Analytical Chemistry, Ion Chromatography, 1982, 2d edit., 1987; contbr. articles to profl. jours. Recipient Minn. Chromatography Forum award, 1987, Dal Nogare award in chromatography, 1991. Mem. Am. Chem. Soc. (award in chromatography 1976, award in analytical chemistry 1985). Methodist. Avocations: tennis; collecting wall hangings. Home: 2018 Greenbriar Cir Ames IA 50014-7820 Office: Iowa State U 322 Wilhelm Ames IA 50011

FRITZ, JAN MARIE, planning educator; b. Cleve., Nov. 4, 1941; d. Andrew and Julia (Zrencsik) F.; m. Richard Lerner; children: Hyunjin, Karin. BA, Bowling Green State U.; MA, Ohio State U.; PhD, Am. U. Cert. clin. sociologist. Asst. prof. Georgetown U., Washington, 1975-85; sci. assoc. Nat. Cancer Inst., Washington, 1986-89; assoc. prof. Calif. State U., San Bernardino, 1989-93, U. Cin., 1993—. Grantee U.S. EPA, 1996-97, Nat. Gardening Assn., 1996, Kellogg Found. nat. fellow, 1982-85, NEH fellow, 1991-92; recipient Peres-Rabin Peace award, 1999. Mem. Internat. Sociol. Assn. (exec. bd.), Am. Health Planning Assn. (exec. bd.), Sociol. Practice Assn. (Disting. Career award 1992), Assn. Study of Afro-Am. Life and History, Am. Planning Assn., Soc. Profls. in Dispute Resolution.

FRITZ, KRISTINE RAE, secondary education educator; b. Monroe, Wis.. BS in Phys. Edn., U. Wis., LaCrosse, 1970; MS in Phys. Edn., U. N.C., Greensboro, 1978. Softball and fencing program coord. Mequon (Wis.) Recreation Dept., 1970; phys. edn. health and English tchr. Horace Jr. H.S., 1970-81; phys. edn. and health tchr. Sheboygan (Wis.) South H.S., 1982—; basketball and volleyball coach, 1972-89, girls track coach, 1972—; mem. dist. wide curriculum and evaluation coms., 1978—; mem. sch. effectiveness team, 1991-94; sch. evaluation consortium evaluator, 1988—; inbound/outbound coach Sport for Understanding, 1991-96. Contbr. articles to profl. jours. Active Sheboygan (Wis.) Spkrs. Bur., 1987-95, Women Reaching Women. Recipient Nat. H.S. Coaches award for girls track, 1987.

Mem. NEA, AAHPERD (Midwest dist. Tchr. of Yr. 1995, Pathfinder award 1997), Wis. Assn. Health, Phys. Edn., Recreation and Dance (Phys. Edn. Tchr. of Yr. 1993, pres.-elect 1998-99), Nat. Assn. Girls and Women in Sport (Tchr. of Yr. 1995, Pathfinder award 1997), Sheboygan Edn. Assn., Phi Delta Kappa. Home: 1841 N 26th St Sheboygan WI 53081-2008

FRITZ, LEE D., software company executive; b. Sept. 25, 1973. BS in Mktg., Ind. U., 1996. Area tech. mgr. James Martin & Co., Rosemont, Ill., 1996-97; acct. exec. Diversified Software Sys., Lisle, Ill., 1997—. E-mail: lee.fritz@diversifiedsoftware.com. Home: 1504 Fairway Dr #302 Naperville IL 60563

FRITZ, MARK FRANCIS, journalist; b. East Chicago, Ind.; s. Anthony Walter Jr. and Dorothy Frances (Horvath) F.; m. Karyn Vaughn, Oct. 29, 1988. B of Journalism, Wayne State U., 1978. Reporter Kalamazoo Gazette, 1978-83; newsman Associated Press, Detroit, 1984-86; corr. Associated Press, Grand Rapids, Mich., 1986-88; editor, internat. desk Associated Press, N.Y.C., 1988-90; corr. Associated Press, Berlin, 1990-93, Abidjan, Ivory Coast, 1993-94; nat. writer Associated Press, N.Y.C., 1994-96; nat. corr. L.A. Times, N.Y.C., 1998—; vis. faculty Poynter Inst., St. Petersburg, Fla., 1995; spkr. Nat. Writer's Workshop, Ft. Lauderdale, Fla., 1997; cons. ABC News/20-20, N.Y.C., 1997. Author: Lost on Earth: Nomads of the New World, 1999. Recipient Pulitzer prize for internat. reporting, 1995. Avocations: motorcycling, canoeing.

FRITZ, MAURA KATHLEEN, magazine editor; b. Rockville Center, N.Y., Oct. 13, 1957; d. Howard Phillip and Mary Agatha (Noonan) F. BA, St. John's U., 1979; BJ, U. Mo., 1980. Assoc. editor Incentive Mktg., N.Y.C., 1981-82; asst. copy editor Seventeen, N.Y.C., 1983-84, assoc. copy editor, 1984-86; assoc. copy editor GQ, N.Y.C., 1986-89, copy chief, 1989-95; mng. editor Men's Jour., N.Y.C., 1995—. Press aide Dem. Nat. Conv., N.Y.C., 1992. Mem. Am. Soc. Mag. Editors. Home: 519 E 87th St New York NY 10128-7663 Office: Men's Journal 1290 Avenue Of The Americas Fl 2 New York NY 10104-0295*

FRITZ, MELISSA JANE, English educator; b. Bellevue, Ohio, Sept. 28, 1972; d. Louis and Martha (Gerber) F. BS, Bowling Green State U., 1994, MEd in Reading, 1997. English and reading tchr. Willard (Ohio) City Schs., 1994—. Acad. challenge advisor Sophomore Class Advisor, jr. class advisor, 1995. Mem. Nat. Coun. Tchrs. English. Roman Catholic. Avocations: reading, walking, crafts, sporting events. Office: Willard City Schs HS 123 W Whisler Dr Willard OH 44890-1359

FRITZ, NANCY H., educational researcher, administrator; b. Greenfield, Mass., Nov. 21, 1944; d. Gerard Martin and Helen (Cassidy) F. BA in English, Western New Eng. Coll., 1970; EdM in Psychology and Edn., Smith Coll., Northampton, Mass., 1982. Cert. tchr., Mass., N.Y., Vt. Title I reading recovery tchr., dir. Amherst, Mass.; lectr. in field. Contbr. articles to profl. jours. Recipient Eckel Human Rels. Cup, WRA Highest Achievement award. Mem. NEA, AAUW, Internat. Reading Assn., Nat. Coun. Tchrs. English, Nat. Coun. Tchrs. Math., Mass. Reading Assn. Home: The Deerfield Commons South Deerfield MA 01373-9620

FRITZ, RENE EUGENE, JR., manufacturing executive; b. Prineville, Oreg., Feb. 24, 1943; s. Rene and Ruth Pauline (Munson) F.; m. Sharyn Ann Fife, June 27, 1964; children: Rene Scott, Lanz Eugene, Shay Steven, Case McGarrett. BS in Bus. Adminstrn., Oreg. State U., 1965. Sales mgr. Renal Corp., Albany, Oreg., 1965-66, Albany Machine and Supply, 1965-66; pres. Albany Internat. Industries Inc., 1966-85, Wood Yield Tech. Corp., 1972-85, Albany Internat. DISC, 1972-85, Automation Controls Internat. Inc., 1975-85; co-founder, chmn. Albany Titanium Inc., 1981-89; prin. Torwest Capital, 1989; founder, pres. WY Tech. Corp., 1984-89, R. Fritz & Assocs., 1987-89; pres. Chief Execs. Forum, 19789—, Fritz Grup Inc., 1989—; fin. planner, investment banker M&A, Vancouver, Wash., 1991—; chmn. Stormwater Treatment LLC, CSF Treatment Sys.; chmn. NTP, Wilsonville, Oreg., 1999—. Patentee computer controlled machinery. Pres. Oreg. World Trade Coun., 1982—; trustee U.S. Naval Acad. Found., Annapolis, Md., 1988—. Mem. Oreg. State Alumni, Forest Products Rsch. Soc., Young Pres. Orgn., Rotary, Elks. Presbyterian.

FRITZ, ROGER JAY, management consultant; b. Browntown, Wis., July 18, 1928; s. Delmar M. and Ruth M. (Sandley) F.; m. Kathryn Louise Goddard, Oct. 13, 1951; children: Nancy Goddard, Susan Marie. BA in Polit. Sci, Monmouth (Ill.) Coll., 1950; MS in Speech, U. Wis., 1952, PhD in Ednl. Counseling, 1956. Asst. dean men, asst. prof. Purdue U., 1953-56; mgr. pub. relations Cummins Engine Co.; also sec. Cummins Engine Found., 1956-59; sec. John Deere Found.; also mem. pub. relations staff Deere & Co., 1959-65, dir. mgmt. devel. and personnel research; also dir. John Deere Found., 1965-69; pres. Willamette U., 1969-72, Orgn. Devel. Cons., Naperville, Ill., 1972—; bd. dirs. Intelligent Electronics, Inc., List Processing Co., Todays Computers Bus. Ctrs., Entre Computer Ctrs., Inc., Natural Golf, Inc., Quote Me, Inc. Author: A Handbook for Resident Counselors, 1952, The Argumentation of William Jennings Bryan and Clarence Darrow in the Tennesee Evolution Trial, 1952, How Freshmen Change, 1956, The Power of Professional Purpose, 1974, MBO Goes to College, 1975, Practical Management by Objectives, 1976, What Managers Need to Know-A Practical Guide for Management Development, 1978, Performance Based Management, 1980, Productivity and Results, 1981, People Compatibility System, 1983, Rate Yourself as a Manager, 1985, You're in Charge, 1986, Personal Performance Contracts: The Key to Job Success, 1986, Nobody Gets Rich Working for Somebody Else, 1987, Rate Your Executive Potential, 1987, The Inside Advantage, 1987, If They Can-You Can, 1988, Be Your Own Boss, 1988, Managing a Successful Team, 1989, Management Ideas That Work, 1989, Developing A Positive Attitude, 1990, The Entrepreneurial Family, 1991, Think Like a Manager, 1991, How to Export, 1992, How to Get Rich Working for Yourself, 1992, Sleep Disorders-America's Hidden Nightmare, 1993, The Sales Manager's High Performance Guide, 1993, How to Manage Your Boss, 1994, A Team of Eagles, 1994, The Small Business Troubleshooter, 1995, The Field Guide for Boss Types...And How to Deal With Them, 1996, An Idea-A-Day For Promotable People, 1996, Crime Crisis: Bold New Ideas to Fit Punishment with Crimes, 1997, Wars of Succession, 1997, One Step Ahead: The Unused Keys to Success, 1998, Bounce Back and Win, 1999, Fast Track-How to Gain Momentum and Keep It, 1999; also articles, papers; columnmist Entrepreneur mag., New Bus. Opportunity mag., 1989, Benefits and Compensation Solutions Mag., Bus. Start Ups Mag.; mgmt. editor Communication Briefings Newsletter, 1989. Mem. com. preparation coll. tchrs. Ill. Bd. Higher Edn., 1965-67, mem. com. med. edn., 1967-68; edn. com. N.A.M., 1967-69; mem. Iowa-Ill. Indsl. Devel. Group, 1964-69; council contbr. Nat. Indsl. Conf. Bd., 1960-65, council devel., edn. and tng., 1966-69; adv. com. solicitations Nat. Better Bus. Bur., 1964-69; v.p. Oreg. Ind. Colls. Assn., 1969-72; mem. Pres. Johnson's Citizens Adv. Bd. on Youth Opportunity, 1968-69, Gov.'s Personnel Grievance Panel, Ill., 1974-77; trustee Monmouth Coll., 1957-79, chmn., 1961-69; trustee Oreg. Colls. Found., 1969-72, Ind. Coll. Funds Am., N.Y.C., 1972, Internat. Coll. Commerce and Econs., Tokyo, 1970-72, U. Chgo. Cancer Research Found., 1973-78. Mem. Phi Eta Sigma, Omicron Delta Kappa, Tau Kappa Epsilon, Phi Alpha Theta, Sigma Tau Delta, Pi Kappa Delta. Republican. Methodist. Club: Naperville (Ill.) Country. Fax: 630-420-7835. E-mail: r.fritz3800@aol.com. Home: 1113 N Loomis St Naperville IL 60563-2745 Office: 1240 Iroquois Dr Naperville IL 60563-8536

FRITZ, THOMAS VINCENT, association and business executive; b. Pitts., July 6, 1934; s. Zeno and Mary M. (Briley) F.; m. Barbara L. Jacob, Jan. 31, 1959; children: William T., James Z., Juliann W. BBA in Acctg. cum laude, U. Pitts., 1960; JD, Duquesne U., 1964; LLM, NYU, 1966; Advanced Mgmt. Program, Harvard Bus. Sch., 1975. Bar: Pa. 1964, U.S. Supreme Ct. 1969; CPA, Pa. 1962, other states. Ptnr. Ernst & Young (formerly Arthur Young & Co.), Pitts./N.Y.C./Washington, 1970, regional mng. ptnr., vice chmn., 1977-89, vice chmn., 1989-92; pres., CEO Pvt. Sector Coun., Inc., Washington, 1992—; adj. prof. Sch. Law Duquesne U., Pitts., 1966-79; bd. dirs. Pvt. Sector Coun., Washington, Innovative Sys., Inc.; chmn. Alliance for Free Enterprise, Washington. Editor Duquesne U. Law Rev., 1963-64. Active Century Club, Duquesne U.; bd. dirs. Evermay Comty. Assn., pres., 1994-96; bd. dirs. McLean Citizens Assn., 1994-97; co-chmn. U. Pitts. Katz Campaign 3d Century, 1988-91. With U.S. Army, 1955-57. Recipient Gorley award, 1964, Disting. Alumni award U. Pitts., 1981, Advancement Info. Tech. award, 1988, Federal 100 award, 1997. Mem. AICPA, ACBA, D.C. Inst. CPAs, Pa. Inst. CPAs, Harvard Bus. Sch. Assn., Duquesne Club, Met. Club, Rolling Rock Club, Avenel Club, Beta Gamma Sigma, Beta Alpha Psi. Home: 6303 Long Meadow Rd Mc Lean VA 22101-2314 Office: 1101 16th St NW Washington DC 20036-4803

FRITZ, WILLIAM THOMAS, anesthesiologist; b. Pitts., Aug. 14, 1960; s. Thomas V. and Barbara Fritz; m. Mary E. Fritz, Nov. 24, 1979; children: Kristine, Andrea, Mark, Kaitlin. BA in Econs. Biology, Washington and Jefferson U., Washington, Pa., 1982; MD, Hahnemann U., 1986; MBA, U. Pitts., 1996. Cert. in anesthesiology, specialty in pain mgmt. Intern Cooper Hosp.-U. Medicine and Dentistry N.J., Camden, 1986-87; resident in anesthesiology Hahnemann U., Phila., 1987, resident in cardio. anesthesiology, 1989-90; fellow in pediat. anesthesiology St. Christophers Hosp. Children, Phila., 1990; chmn. dept. anesthesia Mercy Med. Ctr., Johnstown, Pa., 1992-97; with Conemaugh Meml. Med. Ctr., Johnstown. Mem. AMA, Am. Soc. Anesthesiologists, Internat. Anesthesia Rsch. Soc., Internat. Assn. for Study of Pain, Soc. Physician Execs., Soc. Cardiovasc. Anesthesiology. Office: AAJ 1086 Franklin St Johnstown PA 15905-4305

FRITZE, JULIUS ARNOLD, marriage counselor; b. Albuquerque, Dec. 30, 1918; s. Martin Herman and Mary (Staerkel) F.; m. Marion Caroline Becker, June 4, 1944; children: Christine, Timothy; m. Anita Carol Dozier, May 18, 1973. Student, St. Paul's Jr. Coll., 1937-39; diploma, Concordia Sem., 1944; BA in Edn., U. N.Mex., 1943; MS, Ctrl. Mo. State Coll., 1969. Nat. cert. counselor; lic. profl. counselor, Tex.; lic. marriage and family therapist, Tex.; ordained to ministry Luth. Ch., 1944. Pastor Corpus Christi, Tex., 1944-48, Higginsville, Mo., 19948-57; exec. dir. Marriage and Parenthood Ctr., 1957-59; pvt. practice marriage counseling, Dallas, 1959—; indsl. psychologist N.Am. Mktg., 1975-76; mgmt. cons. Concord Systems, Inc., 1978—; therapist Procter & Gamble, Dallas, 1991—; cons. Mo. Synod Luth. Ch., St. Louis, 1961, Tex. dist., 1976—; from lectr. to profl. and laymen's insts., 1956—; lectr. Dallas County Jr. Coll. Author: The Essence of Marriage, 1969, Mini Manual for Ministers, 1978, The Essence of Life, 1990; contbr. series of articles to nat. mags. bd. dirs. Dallas area Am. Lung Assn., 1976—. Mem. APA, Am. Assn. Marriage Counselors, Am. Pers. and Guidance Assn., Nat. Vocat. Guidance Assn., Nat. Coun. Family Rels., Southwest Psychol. Assn., Tex. Psychol. Assn., Am. Orthopsychiat. Assn., Internat. Platform Assn. Home: 10532 Castlegate Dr Dallas TX 75229-5101 Office: 3298 Royal Ln Ste 100 Dallas TX 75229-5059

FRITZINGER, REBECCA ANN, English language educator; b. Wilkinsburg, Pa., Sept. 28, 1949; d. Harry Edward Jr. and Pauline Marie (Miller) Myers; m. Darrel Raymond Fritzinger, Oct. 27, 1973; children: Angela Louise, Raymond Michael. AA, C.C. of Allegheny County, 1969; BA, Pa. State U., 1971, Master's equivalency, 1996. Cert. in secondary edn., English and humanities. Tchr. h.s. English Northwestern Lehigh Sch. Dist., New Tripoli, Pa., 1985—; writing cons., trainer Pa. State U., Allentown, 1992—, Lehigh Carbon Intermediate Unit, Schnecksville, Pa., 1992—; adj. tchr. English Lehigh Carbon C.C., Schnecksville, 1990—, Pa. State U., Allentown, 1990—; writing/rsch. cons. Lehigh Valley Writing Project, Allentown. Author: (anthology) Lehigh Valley Writing Project Book, 1990, 92, 95, 96. Nat. writing fellow Pa. State U., 1992; classroom rsch. grantee Lehigh Valley Writing Project, 1993, 94, 96. Fellow Nat. Writing Project; mem. Nat. Coun. Tchrs. of English, Pa. Coun. Tchrs. of English, Northwestern Lehigh Edn. Assn. (pres. 1994, 95). Avocations: camping, traveling. Home: 4804 Five Point Rd New Tripoli PA 18066-3413

FRITZSCHE, HELLMUT, physics educator; b. Berlin, Feb. 20, 1927; came to U.S., 1952; s. Carl Hellmut and Anna (Jordan) F.; m. Sybille Charlotte Lauffer, July 5, 1952; children: Peter Andreas, Thomas Alexander, Susanne Charlotte, Katharina Sabine. Diploma in Physics, U. Göttingen, Fed. Republic Germany, 1952; PhD in Physics, Purdue U., 1954, DSc (hon.), 1988. Instr. physics Purdue U., Lafayette, Ind., 1954-55, asst. prof., 1955-56; asst. prof. U. Chgo., 1957-61, assoc. prof., 1961-63, prof., 1963-96, dir. Materials Rsch. Lab., 1973-77, chmn. dept., 1977-86, Louis Block prof. physics, 1989-96; v.p., bd. dirs. Energy Conversion Devices, Inc., Troy, Mich., United Solar Systems Corp.; mem. adv. com. Encyclopaedia Britannica, 1969-96. Editor: 10 sci. books; assoc. editor Jour. Applied Physics, 1975-80; regional editor Jour. Non-Crystalline Solids, 1987-96; contbr. 270 articles to profl. jours.; patentee in field. Named hon. prof. Shanghai Inst. Ceramics, 1985, Nanjing U., 1987, Beijing U. Astronautics, 1988. Fellow AAAS, Am. Physical Soc. (Oliver Buckley Condensed Matter Physics prize 1989), N.Y. Acad. Scis. (chmn. divsn. condensed matter physics 1979-80). Avocations: the violin, sailing, skiing. Home: 3140 E Camino Juan Paisano Tucson AZ 85718-4206 Office: Energy Conversion Devices Inc 1675 W Maple Rd Troy MI 48084-7197

FRITZSCHE, KATHLEEN (DRAGONFIRE FRITZSCHE), performing arts educator; b. Liverpool, Eng., Apr. 22, 1943; came to U.S., 1964; d. James and Kathleen Honora (Parry) Walker; m. James Dockery, 1966 (div. 1971); 1 child, James Dockery II; m. Francis Frederick Fritzsche, Feb. 14, 1978 (div. 1989); 1 child, Rebecca. Student, L.A. Harbor Coll.; studied with, Lawrence J. Wong, Richard Hatch, Dr. Rodney Oakes. Tchg. staff Angels Gate Cultural Ctr., San Pedro, Calif., 1996—. Writer, composer, performer, artist in various media. Avocation: walking by ocean. Home: 335 Viewland Pl San Pedro CA 90731-1711

FRITZSCHE, R. WAYNE, corporate executive; b. Woodbury, N.J., Jan. 8, 1949; s. Robert Edward and Mae Frances (Geiger) F.; children: Heather Leigh, Allison Anne, Benjamin Robert; m. Kelsey Marie. BA, Rowan U., 1971; MBA, U. San Diego, 1979. Sales rep. Warner Lambert, Morristown, N.J., 1972-74; group product mgr. Hoechst, San Diego, 1974-79; strategic planning Johnson & Johnson, Raritan, N.J., 1978-79; v.p. Cytogen, Princeton, N.J., 1979-80; sr. analyst Channing Weinberg, Inc., N.Y.C., 1980-81; chmn. Fritzsche Pambianchi & Assocs., Inc., Somerville, N.J., 1981-91; founder Fritzsche & Assocs., Bernardsville, N.J., 1991—; founder Immune Response Co., San Diego, 1987—, Cortex Pharm., Irvine, Calif., 1988-90, Med. Bus. Pub. Corp., Sommerville; bd. dirs. CardioCommand, Tampa, Fla., Protein Delivery, Inc., Rsch. Triangle, N.C., Hesed Biomed, Omaha. Mem. N.Y. Acad. Sci., Am. Chem. Soc., Am. Assn. Clin. Chemists. Republican. Baptist. Avocations: piano, running. Office: Fritzsche & Assocs Inc 6413 E Maclaurin Dr Tampa FL 33647-1171

FRIZELIS, KAREN LYNN, adult nurse practitioner; b. Evergreen Park, Ill., July 21, 1959; d. George Walter and Evelyn I. (Wodzin) Halvorsen; m. Edward J. Frizelis, May 22, 1982. Assoc. Nursing cum laude, Moraine Valley Community Coll., 1979; BSN cum laude, Lewis U., 1987; MS in nursing, U. of Akron, 1997. Cert. gerontol. nurse; cert. in staff devel.; cert. ACLS; cert. adult nurse practioner. Staff nurse Palos Community Hosp., Palos Heights, Ill.; asst. head nurse S.W. Gen. Hosp., Middleburg Heights, Ohio; nurse clinician Cleve. Clinic Found.; nurse practitioner Diamont Headach Clinic, Chicago. Mem. Nat. Nursing Staff Devel. Orgn., Am. Academy of Nurse Practitioners, Am.Assn. for the study of headaches, Nat. Headache Found. Sigma Theta Tau. Home: 1023 Thackery Ln Naperville IL 60564-3142

FRIZZELL, GREGORY KENT, judge; b. Wichita, Kans., Dec. 13, 1956; s. D. Kent and Shirley Elaine (Piatt) F.; m. Kelly Susan Nash, Mar. 9, 1991; children: Benjamin Newcomb, Hannah Kirsten, Robert Nash, David Gregory, Elizabeth Piatt, Jubilee Kathryn. BA, U. Tulsa, 1981; JD, U. Mich., 1984. Bar: Okla. 1985, U.S. Dist. Ct. (no., ea. and we. dists.) Okla. 1985, U.S. Ct. Appeals (10th cir.) 1985, U.S. Supreme Ct. 1990. Jud. clk. to judge U.S. Dist. Ct. for No. Dist. Okla., Tulsa, 1984-86; pvt. practice Tulsa, 1986-95; gen. counsel Okla. Tax Commn., 1995-97; dist. judge Tulsa County, 1997—. Counsel bd. dirs. Tulsa Speech and Hearing Assn., 1987-95, pres., 1994-95. Mem. Okla. Bar Assn. (young lawyers rep. to client security fund com. 1990-92), Am. Inns of Ct., Rotary. Avocations: duck hunting, flying. Office: Tulsa County Courthouse 500 S Denver Ave Tulsa OK 74103-3838

FRIZZELL, JOAN PARKER, critical care nurse, educator; b. Phila., July 3, 1947; d. Edwin Spare and Virginia (Murray) Parker; 1 child, Virginia J. BA in Biology, Eastern Bapt. Coll., St. Davids, Pa., 1969; BSN, Temple U., 1978; MSN, U. Pa., 1983, PhD, 1997. RN, cert. critical care nurse, ACLS. Staff nurse Rolling Hill Hosp., Elkins Park, Pa., 1978-86; coord., specialist for med. ICU Grad. Hosp., Phila., 1986-88, coord. critical care edn., 1988-91; lectr. U. Pa., 1991-92; asst. prof. nursing LaSalle U., Phila., 1994—; instr. dept. nursing Ea. Coll., St. Davids, 1983-85; adj. faculty pathophysiology Widener U., Chester, Pa. and LaSalle U., Phila., 1990-94. Contbr. articles to profl. jours. Mem. AACN. Home: 407 Tupelo Grv Ambler PA 19002-5073

FRIZZELL, RICK DALE, corporate creative director; b. Waynesville, N.C., Feb. 6, 1958; s. Theodore Roosevelt Frizzell and Mary Jo (Conard) West. BFA in Design, Western Carolina U., 1980. Art dir. The Mountaineer Newspaper, Waynesville, 1980-82, Lark Comm., Asheville, N.C., 1983-84, Groves Printing, Asheville, 1984-85, U. N.C., Asheville, 1985-88, The Alpha Group, Asheville, 1988-92, Sta. WHNS-TV, Greenville, S.C., 1992-99; corp. creative dir. Eason Publs., Atlanta, 1994—. Illustrator Children's Crafts, 1992. Artist, designer ann. auction Western N.C. AIDS Project., 1990-92. Recipient Addy award Asheville Addy Fedn., 1988-92, Greenville Addy Fedn., 1992-94. Avocations: workout, antique collecting. Office: Eason Publs 750 Willoughby Way NE Atlanta GA 30312-1124

FRIZZELL, WILLIAM KENNETH, architect; b. Knox City, Tex., Dec. 10, 1928; s. Thomas Paul and Kelphia (Williams) F.; children: Jane, John Callender. B.A. magna cum laude in Architecture, Princeton U., 1950; M.A., U. Okla., 1954. Prin. Frizzell Architects, Santa Barbara. Works this country, abroad.; Works include Camelback Inn, Scottsdale, Ariz, Loews Paradise Valley Resort, Paradise Valley, Ariz., Sheraton Hammamet Hotel, Tunisia, Yves St Laurent Boutique, N.Y.C., Becton-Dickenson-Endevco electronics facility, San Juan Capistrano, Calif., Omar Kahyam Hotel, Cairo, Dysan Corp. Bldgs, Santa Clara, Calif., Monarch Hotel, San Francisco, Paradise Valley Hotel, Scottsdale, Ariz., Loews Ventana Canyon Hotel, Tucson, Park Hyatt Hotel, Santa Monica, Calif., Red Lion Hotel, Glendale, Calif., Shutters Hotel, Santa Monica, Calif. Served to lt. (j.g.) USNR. Mem. AIA. Office: 619 Pilgrim Terrace Dr Santa Barbara CA 93101-3928

FRIZZELLE, CHARLES DELANO, JR., military officer, educator; b. Hampton, Va., Sept. 15, 1958; s. Charles Delano Sr. and Betty Ann (Baker) F.; m. Remedios Almanzar Arias, May 5, 1987; children: Robert Thomas, Charles David III. AA, U. Md., Ramstein, Germany, 1978; BSBA, East Carolina U., 1980; MS in Sys. Mgmt., U. So. Calif., 1989; MA in Nat. Security, Georgetown U., 1997; MPA in Pub. Adminstrn., U. So. Calif., 1997, DPA in Pub. Admin., 1998. Cert. master in program mgmt., test and evaluation and comm.-computer sys. Dept. Def. Acquisition Profl. Devel. Program Level III. Commd. 2d lt. USAF, 1980, advanced through grades to maj.; acquisition program mgr., test and devel. dir., air liason officer U.S. Army Spl. Forces Wright Patterson AFB, Dayton, Ohio, 1980-85; comdr. space surveillance ops. crew 17th Surveillance Squadron, San Miguel, The Philippines, 1985-87; chief standardization/evaluation 3d Comms. Squadron, Kapaun Air Sta., Germany, 1987-90; space sys. operational test mgr. AF Operational Test and Evaluation Ctr., Kirtland AFB, Albuquerque, 1990-94; acquisition program dir. Office Asst. Sec. Def. Command, Control, Comm., Intell., Washington, 1994-96; prof. Def. Sys. Mgmt. Coll., Ft. Belvoir, Va., 1996—; assoc. faculty Ga. Inst. Tech., 1997—. Master rescue diver, emergency med. technician Prince George's County, Md.; vol. dive rescue-recovery team Co. 56. Mem. NRA (life), Internat. Test and Evaluation Assn., Jujitsu Am. Profl. Assn. of Dive Instrs., 82d Airborne Assn. (life), Soc. Flight Test Engrs., Sigma Tau Gamma, Phi Alpha Sigma, Pi Alpha Alpha, Omicron Delta Epsilon. Avocations: martial arts, rugby, parachuting, running, scuba diving. Home: 1581 Eglin Way SW Apt F Washington DC 20336-5239 Office: Def Sys Mgmt Coll FD-TE Fort Belvoir VA 22060

FRIZZI, MARY ELIZABETH, rehabilitation specialist; b. Pitts., July 1, 1971; d. John Nicholas and Madeleine Lois (Hill) F. BS, Indiana (Pa.) U., 1993; MEd, U. Pitts., 1995. Cert. rehab. counselor. Rehab. cons. C & F Profl. Disability Svcs., Pitts., 1996—; rehab. specialist United Cerebral Palsy, Pitts., 1997—. Mem. ACA, Nat. Rehab. Assn., Nat. Rehab. Counseling Assn., Pa. Counseling Assn., Keystone Counseling Assn. Avocations: fishing, camping, archery, theatre, art. Office: United Cerebral Palsy 4638 Centre Ave Pittsburgh PA 15213-1596

FROBERG, BRENT MALCOLM, classics educator; b. Balt., Apr. 8, 1943; s. Lawrence Oscar and Ruth Louise (Lindner) F.; m. M. Gail Galloway, Feb. 27, 1970. BA, Ind. U., 1964, MA, 1965; PhD, Ohio State U., 1972. Instr. U. Tenn., Knoxville, 1968-69; asst. prof. U. S.D., Vermillion, 1970-74; assoc. prof. U. S.D., 1974-96. Editor: (newsletter) Nuntius, 1978-96; writer Nat. Greek Exam., ATTIC, Level I, 1998. Pres. Friends of the Libr., Vermillion, 1995-97, sec., 1997-99. Mem. Am. Philol. Assn. (award for excellence in tchg. 1994), Am. Classical League, Vergilian Soc. (membership chmn. 1990-94), Classical Assn. Mid. West & South (Ovatio award 1985, chair Manson Stewart scholarship com. 1998), Eta Sigma Phi (exec. sec. 1978-96). Avocations: crossword puzzles, travel. *

FROCK, TERRI LYN, nursing educator and consultant; b. Uniontown, Pa., Sept. 18, 1953; d. Samuel Edward and Louise Harriet (Hooper) F. BSN, U. Miami, 1975, MS in Nursing, 1980; EdS, Fla. Atlantic U., 1987, EdD, 1994. Asst. head nurse North Broward Med. Ctr., Pompano Beach, Fla., 1976-79; instr. nursing Broward C.C., Ft. Lauderdale, Fla., 1980-85, Fla. Internat. U., Miami, 1994—; asst. prof. nursing Fla. Internat. U., North Miami, 1994—; nursing edn. cons. Fla. Bd. Nursing, 1988-92; camp nurse Kanuga Camp and Conf. Ctr., Hendersonville, N.C., summers 1980-81. Bd. dirs. Am. Heart Assn., Boca Raton; mem. St. Martins-in-the-Fields Episc. Ch., Pompano Beach. Mem. Nat. League for Nursing, Fla. Nurses Assn., Fla. Atlantic U. Alumni Assn. (bd. dirs.), Sigma Theta Tau, Phi Kappa Phi, Kappa Delta Pi, Phi Delta Kappa. Home: 2210 NE 40th Ct Lghthse Point FL 33064-7328

FROEHLICH, FRITZ EDGAR, telecommunications educator and scientist; b. Worms am Rhine, Hesse, Germany, Nov. 12, 1925; came to U.S., 1938; s. Julius and Ida (Heilborn) F.; m. Eileen Karch, Dec. 25, 1949; children: Laurence Alan, Georgine K. Froehlich Scharff, Philip Marc. BS in Physics magna cum laude, Syracuse U., 1950, MS in Physics, 1952, PhD in Physics, 1955. Rsch. asst. Syracuse (N.Y.) U., 1950-54; asst. instr. Utica (N.Y.) Coll., 1952-54; with AT&T Bell Labs., 1954-87; tech. staff Whippany, N.J., 1954-56; supr. data transmission divsn. Murray Hill, N.J., 1956-63; head data theory dept. Holmdel, N.J., 1963-68, head telecommunications and data systems dept., 1968-83; head univ. relations AT&T Info. Systems and Communications, Lincroft, N.J., 1983-87; ret. AT&T (now Lucent Techs.), Holmdel, N.J., 1987; prof. telecommunications U. Pitts., 1987—; mem. adv. bd. Ctr. for Info. and Comm. Scis. Ball State U., Muncie, Ind., 1987-93; nat. telecom. adv. coun. U. Pitts., 1992—. Editor-in-chief Ency. of Telecommunications, 1988—; sr. editor IEEE Trans. on Communications, 1988-94; contbr. articles to profl. jours.; holder 7 patents. Trustee Cong. B'nai Israel, Rumson, N.J., 1970-84, v.p. cong., 1974-76. With U.S. Army, 1944-46. Recipient Hon. Alumnus award Pitts. U., 1992; Ann. Fritz Froehlich award established in his honor Pitts. U. Sch. Info. Sci., 1992. Fellow IEEE (Data Transmission and New Telephone Svcs. award, chmn. tellers com. 1972), Comm. Soc. IEEE (chmn. N.J. Coast sect. 1970, mem. data com., trans. sys. com. 1960—, chmn. comms. terminal com. 1981-84, mem. multimedia, svcs. and terminals com. 1981—, mem. awards bd. 1992-95), Jewish War Veterans, Phi Beta Kappa, Sigma Xi, Sigma Pi Sigma (pres. Syracuse U. chpt. 1949), Pi Mu Epsilon. Home: 10621 NW 71st Ct Tamarac FL 33321-2215 Office: U Pitts 135 N Bellefield St 743 SLIS Bldg Pittsburgh PA 15260

FROEHLICH, HAROLD VERNON, judge, former congressman; b. Appleton, Wis., May 12, 1932; s. Vernon W. and Lillian and (Wohlfeil) F.; m. Sharon F. Ross, Nov. 20, 1970; children: Jeffrey Scott, Michael Ross. BBA, U. Wis., 1959, LLB, 1962. Bar: Wis. 1962. Staff acct. Ruschlien & Stortreon, CPAs, Madison, Wis., 1958-62; practiced in Appleton, 1962-81, judge Circuit Ct., 1981—; dep. chief judge 8th Jud. Dist. Wis., 1983-85, spl. dep. chief judge, 1985-88, chief judge, 1988-94; sec. Wis. Judicial Conf., 1991-97; mem. Wis. Ho. of Reps., 1963-73, speaker, 1967-71, minority floor leader, 1971-73; mem. 93d Congress from 8th Dist., Wis.; v.p. Black Creek Improvement Corp., Outagamie County Family Ct. Commn., 1975-78; chmn. Ctr. Ct. Chief Judges, 1992-94, Com. Chief Judges, 1988-94; chief adminstrn. judge Outagamie County, 1983-88, 94—. Rep. precinct committeeman 19th ward, Appleton, 1956-62; chmn. Outagamie County Rep. Statutory Com., 1958-62; sec. Assembly Rep. Caucus, 1965-66; bd. regents Fox Valley Luth. H.S., Appleton, 1990-93. With USN, 1951-55. Mem. ABA, Am. Judges

Assn. (bd. govs. 1997—, asst. treas. 1998—), Wis. Bar Assn., Outagamie County Bar Assns., Wis. Assn. Trial Judges (pres. 1991—), Am. Legion, VFW (judge adv. 1963-75, 82—), Assn. Trial Judges in Wis. (sec. 1984-91), Midwest Coun. State Govts. (vice-chmn. 1968-69, chmn. 1969-70), Coun. State Govts. (mem. nat. exec. com. 1970-72), Phi Alpha Delta. Home: 1008 E Marnie Ln Appleton WI 54911-1540 Office: 410 S Walnut St Appleton WI 54911-5920

FROEHLKE, ROBERT FREDERICK, financial services executive; b. Neenah, Wis., Oct. 15, 1922; s. Herbert O. and Lillian (Porath) F.; m. Nancy Jean Barnes, Nov. 9, 1946; children: Bruce, Jane, Ann, Scott. LL.B., U. Wis., 1949. Bar: Wis. 1949. Assoc. firm McDonald & MacDonald, Madison, 1949-50; mem. faculty U. Wis. Law Sch., 1950-51; with Sentry Ins. Co., 1951-69; exec. v.p. Sentry Ins. Co., Boston, 1968-69; asst. sec. def. for adminstrn. Washington, 1969-71; sec. of army, 1971-73; pres. Sentry Corp., 1973-75, Health Ins. Assn. Am., 1976-80, Am. Council of Life Ins., 1980-82; chmn. bd. Equitable Life Assurance Soc. U.S., 1983-87; pres. IDS Mutual Fund Group, 1987-93; bd. dirs. ICI Mut. Inc., Burlington, Vt., Marshall Erdman & Assocs., Inc., Madison, Wis.; mem. pub. oversight bd. AICPA, Washington. Mem. bd. Laird Youth Leadership Found.; trustee Inst. for Def. Analyses, Washington; chmn. nat. adv. coun. Marshfield (Wis.) Clinic. Capt. AUS, 1943-46. Mem. Order of Coif, Psi Upsilon. Republican. Presbyterian.

FROELICH, BEVERLY LORRAINE, foundation director; b. Vancouver, B.C., Can., Oct. 23, 1948; came to U.S., 1968; d. Kenneth Martin and Ethel (Seale) Pulham; m. Eugene Leonard Froelich, Dec. 26, 1971; children: Craig, Grant. Cert. in fundraising, U. So. Calif., 1986; profl. designation in pub. rels., UCLA, 1987. Cert. fund raising exec. Contract analyst Universal Studios, Calif., 1968-71; exec. dir. Olive View, UCLA Med. Ctr. Found., Sylmar, Calif., 1987—; pres. Beverly Froelich Pub. Rels., Sherman Oaks, Calif., 1988-90; prin. Tracy Susman & Co., Sherman Oaks, 1986-88. Co-author: (program) Overcoming Chronic Arthritis Pain, 1989; contbg. writer hosp. earthquake preparedness guidelines Hosp. Coun. So. Calif., 1991. Founder San Fernando Valley br. Arthritis Found., Encino, 1983, pres., 1983-87, mktg. com.; bd. dirs. health care com. Valley Industry and Commerce Assn. Recipient Nat. Vol. Svc. award Arthritis Found., 1986, Jane Wyman Humanitarian award Arthritis Found., 1991, Disting. Svc. award Arthritis Found., 1990, Marilyn Magaram award for Cmty. Svc., 1997. Mem. AAUW, Nat. Soc. Fund Raising Execs. (exec. com. San Fernando Valley chpt.), Valley Industry and Commerce Assn., UCLA Alumni Assn. Avocations: hockey, music. Home: 14152 Valley Vista Blvd Sherman Oaks CA 91423-4043 Office: Olive View Med Ctr Found North Annex 14445 Olive View Dr Sylmar CA 91342-1437

FROELICH, WOLFGANG ANDREAS, neurologist; b. Berlin, Apr. 8, 1927; came to U.S., 1955, naturalized, 1960; s. Andreas Ferdinand and Ilse-Gertraud (Schultz-Engelhard) F.; m. Jean Small, Nov. 29, 1959; children: Morna, Leslie, Mark, Stefan, Andrew. MD, Free U., Berlin, 1955. Diplomate Am. Bd. Psychiatry and Neurology. Intern Huron Rd. Hosp., Cleve., 1955-56, resident in surgery, 1956-57; asst. resident in neurology Barnes Hosp., St. Louis, 1957-58, resident in neurology, 1958-59, chief resident, instr. neurology, 1959-60; resident in psychiatry Cleve. Psychiat. Inst., 1960-61; practice medicine specializing in neurology, psychiatry and encephalography, 1961—; chief div. neurology Meridia Huron Hosp., Cleve., 1967—; pres. med. staff Windsor Hosp., Cleve., 1971-73; mem. active staff Huron, Windsor hosps.; cons. staff Geauga Community, Marymount, Meridia Euclid, Meridia Hillcrest hosps. Contbr. articles to med. jours. Served with German Army, 1944-45. Fellow Am. Acad. Neurology; mem. Cleve. Acad. Medicine, Cleve. Soc. Neurology and Psychiatry, Ohio State Med. Assn., Am. Electroencephalographic Soc., Soaring Soc. of Am. Club: Bear Creek Tennis, Bear Creek Golf. E-mail: wolfgang@cwix.com. Home: 38253 Greywalls Dr Murrieta CA 92562-3059

FROELICHER, FRANZ, chemist, geologist, environmental consultant; b. Ridgewood, N.J., Jan. 11, 1936; s. Victor and Helen (Stehli) F.; m. Margarete (Grundmann), Jan. 23, 1976; children: Britta, Niels. BA in Biology, Alaska Meth. U., 1971, BA in Geology, 1972; PhD in Geology, Sedimentology, Paleoecology, Edinburgh U., Scotland, 1977. Researcher, instr. U. Tübingen, Fed. Republic Germany, 1977-79; asst. prof. geology U. So. Miss., Hattiesburg, Miss., 1979-88; dir. European geology field camp U. So. Miss., Hattiesburg, 1980-88; dir. ctr. for coal and coal products rsch. U. So. Miss., Gulfport, 1986-88; chemist nat. monitoring and residue analysis lab. USDA, Gulfport, Miss., 1988-90; v.p. environ. issues DeWitt & Co., Gulfport, Miss., 1990-92; chemist hazardous waste sect. U.S. Army Corps Engrs., Savannah, Ga., 1992—. Author monthly newsletter EcoIssues; contbr. articles to profl. jours., presented papers at profl. meetings. Grantee Miss. Mineral Resources Inst., 1979-86, GCAGS, 1986, TSI, Inc., 1986-87, Army Corps Engrs., 1987, Leaf River Forest Products, Inc., 1987. Mem. Geol. Soc. Am. (coal div.), Miss. Acad. Scis., N.Am. Coal Petrographers, Soc. Organic Petrology, Palaeontologische Gesellschaft, Paleontol. Assn., Sonderforschungsbereich 53, Soc. Organic Petrology Publs. (rev. bd.). Home: 6 Coquena Dr Savannah GA 31410-1331 Office: US Army Corps Engrs Savannah Dist EN-GH Savannah GA 31402

FROEMMING, BRUCE N., umpire; b. Milw., Sept. 28, 1939; m. Rose Marie Loch, May 2, 1959; children: Kevin, Steven. Umpire Nebr. State League, Midwest League, No. League, N.W. League, Tex. League, Pacific Coast League, Nat. League, 1971—; ptnr. umpire sch., Cocoa, Fla. Avocation: golf. Office: Nat League 350 Park Ave New York NY 10022 Office: Umpires Union 1735 Market St Philadelphia PA 19103

FROEMMING, HERBERT DEAN, retail executive; b. Alexandria, Minn., Aug. 19, 1936; s. Herbert Edward and Bertha Anna (Hink) F.; m. Mary Louise Gapinski, Sept. 2, 1961; children—Mark, Traci, Scott. B.B.A., U. Minn., 1959; M.B.A., U. Minn. CPA, Minn. Fin. exec. The Kroger Co., various locations, 1960-69; exec. v.p. E.F. MacDonald Shopping Bag, L.A., 1969-73; also dir.; v.p., treas., dir. Western Auto Supply Co., Kansas City, Mo., 1973-78; sr. corp. v.p., controller Gamble-Skogmo Co., Mpls., 1978-80; exec. v.p. Red Owl Food Stores, Inc., 1980-84; v.p. Sullivan Assocs., Inc., 1985-88; sr. v.p.-adminstr., chief fin. officer Braun's Fashions Inc., Plymouth, Minn., 1989-94, pres., COO, 1994-97, vice chmn., 1997-98; chmn., CEO Millennium Plastics Tech., LLC, El Paso, Tex., 1999—. Served with AUS, 1955-57. Mem. AICPA, Fin. Execs. Inst. Home: 5713 Parkwood Ln Minneapolis MN 55436-1731 Office: Millennium Plastics Tech LLC 5115 El Paso Dr El Paso TX 79905

FROESCHNER, JOHN R., federal judge; b. 1950. BA, Elmhurst Coll., 1972; JD, U. Mo., 1976. Bar: Tex. 1976. Pvt. practice Galveston, Tex., 1976-91; magistrate judge U.S. Dist. Ct. (so. dist.) Tex., Galveston, 1991—. Fax: (409) 5766-3549. Office: US Dist Ct (so dist) Tex 601 Rosenberg 5th Fl Galveston TX 77550

FROGGE, BEVERLY ANN, nurse, consultant; b. Wichita, Kans., Jan. 1, 1943; d. Owen Elba Frogge and Maudie Frances (Gillette) Surber; m. Jake C. Saubers (sept. 5, 1967 (div. May 1989); 1 child, Jeff Lee. Attended, So. Meth. U., 1960-61, St.Mary of Plains Coll., 1961-62; diploma, Wichita-St. Joseph Sch. Nursin, 1964; attended, UCLA, 1965. Registered profl. nurse, Kans.; cert. health facility surveyor. Instr. LPN Program Neosho C.C., 1970-73; pub. health nurse Woodson Co., Yates Ctr., Kans., 1973-75; health facility surveyor Kans. Dept. Health & Environ., Topeka, 1975-77; nursing dir. Neosho Meml. Hosp., Chanute, Kans., 1977-84, Regency Health Care Ctr., Yates Ctr., 1985-89; psychiatric nurse VA Med. Ctr., Topeka, 1989—; dir. Neosho Meml. Hosp. Home Health Agy., Chanute, 1977-84; instr. Disaster Preparedness, Yates Ctr., 1973-75; cons. in field, 1975-77. Author: (textbook) Anatomy & Physiology Medical Treatment, 1965-67; contbg. author: (poetry) National Anthology of College Poetry, 1961; radio presenter weekly broadcast, 1978-84. Founder, dir., instr. Dresser Sch. U.S. Peace Corps, Makele, Ethiopia, 1965-67, spkr., 1967; adv. com. mem. Vocat. Edn. State Kans., Neosho C.C., Chanute, 1980-81. Avocations: music, writing, hiking, canoeing, painting. Home: 910 SW High Ave Topeka KS 66606-1827

FROHLICH, ANTHONY WILLIAM, lawyer, master commissioner; b. Covington, Ky., Dec. 8, 1954; s. Kenneth Raymond and Joan Jude (Laake) F.; m. Candace Powell Robbins, May 31, 1975; children: Kenneth Zane, Matthew Andrew. BS, No. Ky. U., 1976, JD, 1980. Bar: Ky. 1980, U.S. Dist. Ct. (ea. dist.) Ky. 1981. Staff atty. Boone County (Ky.) Child Support Program, 1980-97; city atty. City of Walton, 1980-89; master commr. Boone County Cir. Ct., Burlington, Ky., 1989—; asst. commonwealth atty. 54th Jud. Dist., Burlington, Ky., 1984-89; ptnr. Mathis, Dallas & Frohlich, Florence, Ky., 1980-96, Law Office of Anthony W. Frohlich, Florence, Ky., 1996—; pres. Soccer Tech., Union, Ky., 1994. Bd. dirs. No. Ky. Soccer Club, Florence, 1994, Consumer Credit Counseling Svcs. Greater Cin., 1999; state coach Ky. Youth Soccer, 1994-96; coaching dir. Ky. Olympic Devel. Program Dist. One, Florence, 1992-94; active Union Town Plan Steering Com., 1999. Named Coach of Yr., No. Ky. Soccer Club, 1992. Mem. ABA, ATLA, Ky. Bar Assn., Boone County Bar Assn. (treas. 1980), Ky. Acad. Trial Lawyers. Roman Catholic. Avocations: coaching soccer, basketball. Home: 9253 Us Highway 42 Union KY 41091-9470 Office: Law Office Anthony Frohlich PO Box 396 Florence KY 41022-0396

FROHLICH, EDWARD DAVID, medical educator; b. N.Y.C., Sept. 10, 1931; s. William and May (Zneimer) F.; m. Sherry Linda Fine, Nov. 1, 1959; children: Marjorie, Bruce, Lara. BA, Washington and Jefferson Coll., 1952; MD, U. Md., 1956; MS, Northwestern U., 1963. Diplomate Am. Bd. Internal Medicine. Intern, resident D.C. Gen. Hosp., 1956-58; resident Georgetown U. Hosp., Washington, 1959-60; clin. investigator VA Rsch. Hosp., Chgo., 1962-64; assoc. in medicine Northwestern U., 1963-64; staff mem. rsch. divsn. Cleve. Clinic, 1964-69; prof. medicine, physiology and biophysics U. Okla., Oklahoma City, 1969-76, George Lynn Cross rsch. prof., 1975-76; prof. medicine and physiology La. State U., 1976—; prof. medicine Tulane U., 1976—; cons. FDA, 1971-74, VA, 1972—, NIH, 1972—, WHO, 1975-82, U.S. Pharmacopeia, 1975—, Gov. La. Am. Coll. Cardiology, 1988-91, bd. trustees, 1991-92, 96—; chmn. coun. high blood pressure rsch. Am. Heart Assn., 1988-91. Editor: Pathophysiology—Altered Regulatory Mechanisms in Disease, 1972, 76, 84, Rypins' Medical Licensure Examinations, 1981, 17th edit., 1997, Rypins' Intensive Revs., 13 vols., 1996, Take Heart, 1990, Hypertension: Evaluation and Treatment, 1998; editor-in-chief Jour. Lab. and Clin. Medicine, 1974-76, Hypertension, 1994—; mem. editl. bd. Am. Jour. Cardiology, 1982-91, Circulation, 1978-81, 82-91, Archives of Internal Medicine, 1978-88, Modern Medicine, 1980—, Hypertension, 1980-91, Jour. Hypertension, 1994—; contbr. chpts. to books, numerous articles to profl. jours. Capt. U.S. Army, 1960-62. Cardiovascular rsch. fellow Georgetown U. Hosp., 1958-59; recipient Honors Achievement award Angiology Rsch. Found., 1964, So. Med. Assn. Annual award, 1971, award of Merit Am. Heart Assn., 1986, Lifetime Achievement award Coun. for High Blood Pressure Rsch., Am. Heart Assn., 1994, Okamoto Internat. award for Hypertension Rsch., 1994. Master ACP (laureate 1996); fellow AAAS, Am. Coll. Cardiology, Coun. for High Blood Pressure Rsch. (exec. com. 1972-75, 81-85, vice chmn. 1986-88, chmn. 1989-91); mem. Internat. Soc. Hypertension (sci. coun. 1974-84, treas. 1980-82, v.p. 1982-84), Am. Heart Assn. (Award of Merit 1986, Lifetime Achievement award coun. high blood pressure rsch. 1993, dir. La. 1979-83, Okamoto Internat. award 1993), Am. Soc. Clin. Investigation, Am. Soc. Pharmacology and Exptl. Therapeutics, Am. Soc. Clin. Pharmacology and Therapeutics (past pres.), Am. Physiol. Soc., Am. Soc. Nephrology, Ctrl. Soc. for Clin. Rsch., So. Soc. for Clin. Rsch., Am. Soc. Clin. Investigations, Assn. Am. Physicians, Peruvian Soc. Cardiology, Columbian Soc. Cardiology, Polish Acad. Arst Sci. (faculty medicine), Chi Epsilon Mu, Phi Sigma, Alpha Kappa Alpha. Office: Ochsner Clinic & Med Found Hosp 1516 Jefferson Hwy New Orleans LA 70121-2429

FROHLICH, JACK T., lawyer; b. Bklyn., Feb. 18, 1950; s. Arthur Joseph and Florence Helen (Toppel) F.; m. Gladys Yvette Bravo, Nov. 25, 1971 (div. 1980); m. Susan Anna Christiano, Jan. 17, 1989; 1 child, Arthur William. BA, SUNY, Stony Brook, 1973; cert. labor rels., New Sch. Social Rsch., 1986; JD, N.Y. Law Sch., 1993. Bar: N.Y., 1994, N.J., 1995, Calif., 1995. Class B counterman Pudlin Auto Supply, Bronx, N.Y., 1973-74; trackman N.Y.C. Transit Authority, 1974-80, 82-84, track inspector, 1984-85, safety insp., 1980-81, 86-94; shop steward Internat. Brotherhood Teamsters Local 239, N.Y.C., 1973, Transport Workers Union Local 100, N.Y.C., vice chmn. track divsn., 1980-81, 86-90, dir. ops., 1986-90, rec. sec., 1990-94, adminstrv. dir. union assistance program, 1995-96, staff rep., 1996-98. Exec. bd. Community Free Dems., N.Y.C., 1989-90; commr. deeds office city clk. City of N.Y., 1989-96; v.p. Student Bar Assn., N.Y. Law Sch., 1990-92. Mem. ABA, ACLU, Nat. Lawyers Guild. Jewish. Avocations: science fiction, historical novels. Home: 303 W 66th St Apt 19he New York NY 10023-6326

FROHLICH, KENNETH R., insurance executive; b. Bklyn., Apr. 20, 1945; s. Sol D. and Ruth (Rosen) F.; m. Judith Eileen Singer, June, 1967; children: Eric Alan, Kerri Beth. BA, Lehigh U., 1966; MA, Kent State U., 1968, PhD, 1971. FCAS, ASA, MAAA. Instr., co. dir. Trumbull Computer Ctr. Kent (Ohio) State U., 1968-72; sr. analyst Hartford (Conn.) Ins. Group, 1972-74; from dept. head to sr. v.p. various subs. Cigna Corp., Hartford, Phila., 1974-87; corp. sr. v.p., chief actuarial officer Reliance Ins. Group, Phila., 1987—. Home: 814 Northwinds Dr Bryn Mawr PA 19010-2047 Office: Reliance Ins Co Three Pkwy Philadelphia PA 19102-1376

FROHMAN, LAWRENCE ASHER, endocrinology educator, scientist; b. Detroit, Jan. 26, 1935; s. Dan and Rebecca (Katzman) F.; m. Barbara Hecht, June 9, 1957; children: Michael, Marc, Erica, Rena. M.D., U. Mich., 1958. Diplomate: Am. Bd. Internal Medicine. Intern Yale-New Haven Med. Ctr., 1958-59, resident in internal medicine, 1959-61; asst. prof. medicine SUNY, Buffalo, 1965-69, assoc. prof., 1969-73; prof. medicine U. Chgo., 1973-81; dir. endocrinology Michael Reese Hosp., Chgo., 1973-81; prof., dir. div. endocrinology and metabolism U. Cin., 1981-92; chmn. Dept. Medicine U. of Ill. Chgo., 1992—; dir. Med. Svcs. U. of Ill. Hosp., Chgo., 1992—; dir. Gen. Clin. Rsch. Ctr., 1986-90; mem. sci. rev. com. NIH, Bethesda, Md., 1972-76; mem. sci. rev. bd. VA, Washington, 1979-82; mem. endocrine adv. bd. FDA, Washington, 1982-86; mem. adv. com. Nat. Inst. Diabetes, Digestive and Kidney Diseases, NIH, 1983-94, chmn., 1991-93; mem. sci. adv. bd. Edison Biotech. Inst., Ohio U. Editor: (with others) Endocrinology and Metabolism, 1995; editl. bd. 6 med. and sci. jours., 1970—; contbr. articles to profl. jours. NIH research grantee, 1967-98, Endocrine Soc. Rorer Clin. Investigator award, 1991. Fellow ACP; mem. Endocrine Soc., Assn. Am. Physicians, Am. Soc. Clin. Investigation, Am. Diabetes Assn., Internat. Soc. Neuroendocrinology, Assn. Profs. Medicine, Pituitary Soc. Office: U Ill at Chgo Dept Medicine M/C 787 840 S Wood St Chicago IL 60612-7317

FROHNMAYER, DAVID BRADEN, university president; b. Medford, Oreg., July 9, 1940; s. Otto J. and MarAbel (Fisher) B. F.; m. Lynn Diane Johnson, Dec. 30, 1970; children: Kirsten (dec.), Mark, Kathryn (dec.), Jonathan, Amy. AB magna cum laude, Harvard U., 1962; BA, Oxford (Eng.) U., 1964, MA (Rhodes scholar), 1971; JD, U. Calif., Berkeley, 1967; LLD (hon.), Willamette U., 1988; D Pub. Svc. (hon.), U. Portland, 1989. Bar: Calif. 1967, U.S. Dist. Ct. (no. dist.) Calif. 1967, Oreg. 1971, U.S. Dist. Ct. Oreg. 1971, U.S. Supreme Ct. 1981. Assoc. Pillsbury, Madison & Sutro, San Francisco, 1967-69; asst. to sec. Dept. HEW, 1969-70; prof. law U. Oreg., 1971-81, spl. asst. to univ. pres., 1971-79; atty. gen. State of Oreg., 1981-91; dean Sch. Law U. Oreg., 1992-94, pres., 1994—; chmn. Conf. Western Attys. Gen., 1985-86; chmn. Am. Coun. Edn. Govtl. Rels. commn, 1996-98; bd. dirs. South Umpqua Bank. Mem. Oreg. Ho. of Reps. 1975-81; mem. coun. pub. reps. NIH, 1999—; bd. dirs. Fred Hutchinson Cancer Rsch. Ctr., Nat. Marrow Donor Program, Fanconi Anemia Rsch. Fund, Inc., Tax Free Trust of Oreg. Fund; active Oreg. Progress Bd. Recipient awards Weaver Constl. Law Essay competition Am. Bar Found., 1972, 74; Rhodes scholar, 1962. Mem. ABA (Ross essay winner 1980), Oreg. Bar Assn., Calif. Bar Assn., Nat. Assn. Attys. Gen. (pres. 1987, Wyman award 1987), Round Table Eugene, Order of Coif, Phi Beta Kappa, Rotary. Republican. Presbyterian. Home: 2315 McMorran St Eugene OR 97403-1750 Office: U Oreg Johnson Hall Office of Pres Eugene OR 97403

FROHNMAYER, JOHN EDWARD, lawyer, legal scholar, ethicist, writer; b. Medford, Oreg., June 1, 1942; s. Otto J. and Marabel (Braden) F.; m. Leah Thorpe, June 10, 1967; children: Jason Otto, Jonathan Aaron. BA in Am. History, Stanford U., 1964; MA in Christian Ethics, U. Chgo., 1969; JD, U. Oreg., 1972. Bar: Oreg. 1972, Mont. 1995. Assoc. Johnson, Harrang & Mercer, Eugene, Oreg., 1972-75; ptnr. Tonkon, Torp, Galen, Marmaduke & Booth, Portland, Oreg., 1975-89; 5th chmn. Nat. Endowment for the Arts, Washington, 1989-92; writer, lectr. on art, ethics and politics, 1992—; pvt. practice Oreg., 1972-89, Bozeman, Mont., 1995—; mem. Oreg. Arts Commn., 1978-85, chmn., 1980-84; bd. dirs. Internat. Sculpture Symposium, eugene, 1974; chmn. screening com. Oreg. State Capitol Bldg., 1977. Author: Leaving Town Alive, 1993, Out of Tune: Listening to The First Amendment, 1994; editor-in-chief Oreg. Law Rev., 1971-72; singer; appeared in recital, oratorio, mus. comedy and various other mus. prodns. Trustee Holladay Park Pla.; founding mem. chamber choir Novum Cantorum; bd. dirs. Chamber Music Northwest, Western States Arts Found.; mem. Nat. Endowment for the Arts Opera-Mus. Theater, 1982, 83. With USN, 1966-69. Sr. fellow Freedom Forum, 1993; recipient People for the Am. Way Ann. 1st Amendment award, 1992, Oreg. Gov. Arts award, 1993, Intellectual Freedom award Mont. Libr. Assn., 1997, Citation of Merit, Mu Phi Epsilon, 1998. Fellow Am. Leadership Forum; mem. ABA (com. comml. transactions litigation), Oreg. State Bar Assn. (chmn. bar com. domestic law 1975-76, procedure and practice com. 1984-85), Multnomah County Bar Assn., City Club Portland (bd. dirs.), Sta. L. Rowing Club (sec.), Order of the Coif (legal hon. 1972). Home and Office: 14080 Lone Bear Rd Bozeman MT 59715-6620

FROHOCK, FRED MANUEL, political science educator; b. Perry, Fla., Feb. 7, 1937; s. Fred Clifton and Marie Antonia (Domenech) F.; m. Val Jean Derrick, Sept. 7, 1963; children—Katherine Renee, Christina Marie. B.A., U. Fla., 1960, M.A., 1961; Ph.D., U. N.C., 1966. Asst. prof. polit. sci. Syracuse U., N.Y., 1965-68, assoc. prof., 1968-74, prof., 1974—, chmn. dept. polit. sci., 1985-89; prof. Florence program Syracuse U., Italy, 1969-70; prof., chmn. Madrid program Syracuse U., 1972-74, prof., chmn. London Politics Seminar, 1984—. Author: Nature of Political Inquiry, 1967, Normative Political Theory, 1974, Public Policy, 1979, Abortion: A Case Study in Law and Morals, 1983, Special Care: Medical Decisions at the Beginning of Life, 1986, Rational Association, 1987, Healing Powers, 1992, Public Reason: Mediated Authority in the Liberal State, 1999; contbr. numerous articles to profl. jours. Social Sci. Research Council fellow, 1964-65, 67-68; NEH summer fellow, 1988. Democrat. Roman Catholic. Avocations: tennis, golf, running, watching baseball. Home: 4448 Kasson Rd Syracuse NY 13215-9616 Office: Syracuse U Polit Sci Dept Syracuse NY 13244

FROHOCK, SYLVANUS E., food company executive; b. Rockland, Maine, Sept. 5, 1915; s. Horatio Wilbur and Sarah Ethelyn (Merrill) F.; m. Ernestine Holmes, Apr. 16, 1955; 1 child, Betty Jane. Student, Middlebury Coll., 1937; degree, Wheaton Coll., 1938. Asst. gen. sales mgr. Kraft Foods, Chgo., 1938-55; cons. in food industry sales; career counselor, cons. haldane Assocs., Paris and London, 1965-90. Lt. USNR, 1940-45. Avocations: golf and spectator sports.

FROMAN, SANDRA SUE, lawyer; b. San Francisco, June 15, 1949; d. Jay and Beatrice Froman. AB with honors, Stanford U., 1971; JD, Harvard U., 1974. Bar: Calif. 1974, U.S. Dist. Ct. (cen. dist.) Calif. 1974, U.S. Dist. Ct. (so. dist.) Calif. 1976, U.S. Dist. Ct. (no. dist.) Calif., U.S. Ct. Claims 1979, U.S. Tax Ct. 1984, Ariz. 1985, U.S. Dist. Ct. Ariz. 1985, U.S. Ct. Appeals (9th cir.) 1986, U.S. Supreme Ct. 1986. Assoc. Loeb & Loeb, L.A., 1974-80; ptnr. Loeb & Loeb, 1981-84; assoc. Bilby & Schoenhair, P.C., Tucson, 1985; shareholder Bilby & Schoenhair, P.C., 1986-89; ptnr. Snell & Wilmer, Tucson, 1989-99; vis. asst. prof. law U. Santa Clara, Calif., 1983-85; mem. Pima County Commn. on Trial Ct. Appointments, 1996-98. Trustee Firearms Civil Rights Legal Def. Fund, 1992-98, NRA Found., pres. 1997; bd. dirs., 2d v.p. NRA. Mem. Ariz. Bar Found. (pres. 1996—). Office: Ste 150 200 W Magee Rd Tucson AZ 85704

FROMAN, VERONICA ZASADNI, career officer. BA in Polit. Sci., Seton Hill Coll.; grad., Armed Forces Staff Coll. Commd. U.S. Navy, 1970; advanced through grades to rear admiral, 1995; Naval Air Sta., Milton, Fla., 1970-72, Navy Recruiting Area Four, Columbus, Ohio, 1972-79; exec. officer Personnel Support Activity, Pearl Harbor, Hawaii, 1979-81; with Manpower Planner Joint Staff, 1983-86; commanding officer Personnel Support Activity, Pearl Harbor, 1986-90; Naval Edn. Tng. Support Ctr. Pacific, San Diego, 1981-83; exec. officer Naval Sta., Norfolk, Va., 1986-90; head edn. tng. staff placement Bur. Naval Personnel, Washington, 1990, also head gen. unrestricted line assignment br., 1990-93; commanding officer Naval Sta., Charleston, S.C., 1993-95; dir. manpower personnel Joint Staff, 1995-97; commander Naval Base, San Diego, 1997—. Decorated Def. Disting. Svc. medal, Legion of Merit; named San Diego Press Club Headliner, 1998, San Diego Soroptomists' Woman of Accomplishment, 1998, Adv. of Yr., Nat. Assn. Women Bus. Owners, 1998. Office: 937 N Harbor Dr San Diego CA 92132-5001

FROME, DAVID HERMAN, dentist; b. Richmond, Va., Jan. 22, 1945; married; 3 children. Student, U. Md., 1962-64, 68; DDS, Georgetown U., 1968; MPH, Johns Hopkins U., 1973. Lic. dentist, Md., D.C. Pvt. practice Gaithersburg, Md., 1970—; clin. instr. dental materials Georgetown Sch. Dentistry, 1970-72; clin. instr. pediatric dentistry U. Md., 1970-73; dental dir. Group Health Assn., 1982-86, Md. State Dental Svc. Corp., 1980-81; cons. in field. Contbr. articles to profl. jours. Past pres. Layhill Village East Citizens Assn.; bd. dirs., trustee Hebrew Day Inst., pres., 1986-88; mem. adv. group FDA, 1985, 89-91; bd. dirs. Congregation Har Shalom, 1997-98, fin. sec. 1998—. Capt. AUS, 1968-70, Vietnam. Nat. Inst. Dentistry Rsch. grantee, 1967; Pub. Health fellow; decorated Purple Heart, Bronze Star, Vietnam Svc. Ribbon, Nat. Def. Svc. Ribbon. Master Acad. Gen. Dentistry (chair dental care 1998—); mem. ADA, Md. Dental Assn., So. Med. Dental Soc. Home: 8808 Wooden Bridge Rd Potomac MD 20854-2445 Office: 8 Russell Ave Ste 104 Gaithersburg MD 20877-2962

FROMKIN, AVA LYNDA, management consultant, healthcare risk management services; b. Toronto, Ont., Can., May 3, 1946; d. Joseph and Sara Ann (Hurovitz) F.; came to U.S., 1948, naturalized, 1953; BSN, U. Miami, 1969, cert. adminstrv. scis., 1975, MBA, cert. health adminstrn., 1983. Diplomate Am. Bd. Risk Mgmt. of Healthcare; lic. risk mgr. Nurse, Mt. Sinai Med. Ctr., Miami Beach, Fla., 1970-71, 73-76; dir. surg. svcs. Cedars of Lebanon Health Care Ctr., Miami, 1976-82; adj. prof. intraoperative nursing program Miami (Fla.)-Dade C.C., 1982-83; prin. A. Lynda Fromkin, Inc., Miami, Fla., 1982-94. Mem. ANA, Fla. Nurses Assn., Am. Soc. Post Anesthesia Nurses, Assn. Oper. Rm. Nurses (dir. Miami chpt. 1979-80), F.H.A. Soc. Healthcare Risk Mgmt., Alzheimer's Care Com. Notables, U. Miami Pres. Circle. Home: 555 NE 34th St Apt 2306 Miami FL 33137-4059

FROMKIN, DAVID HENRY, law educator; b. Milw., Aug. 27, 1932; s. Morris and Selma (Strelsin) F. BA, U. Chgo., 1950, JD, 1953; postgrad. diploma in law, U. London, 1958. Bar: Ill. 1953, N.Y. 1959, U.S. Supreme Ct. 1963. Assoc. Simpson Thcher & Bartlett, N.Y.C., 1958-60; pvt. practice N.Y.C., 1960-88; dir. ctr. Internat. Rels. Boston U., 1994-97, prof. internat. rels., history, law, 1994—; bd. dirs. Enhance Reins. Corp., N.Y.C., Asset Guaranty Ins. Corp., N.Y.C. Author: A Question of Government, 1975, The Independence of Nations, 1981, A Peace to End All Peace, 1989 (N.Y. Times Book Rev. Editors' Choice), In the Time of the americans, 1995, others; mem. editl. bd. World Policy Jour., 1997—. Trustee Strelsin Found., N.Y.C., 1964—. 1st lt. JAG U.S. Army, 1954-57. Mem. Coun. Fgn. Rels., Internat. Inst. Strategic Studies, Century Assn. Democrat. Home: 20 Beekman Pl New York NY 10022-8032

FROMKIN, VICTORIA ALEXANDRA, linguist, phonetician, educator; b. Passaic, N.J., May 16, 1923; d. Henry and Rose Lillian (Ravitz) Landish; m. Jack Fromkin, Oct. 24, 1948; 1 child, Mark. BA, U. Calif.-Berkeley, 1944; MA, UCLA, 1963, PhD, 1965. Asst. prof. dept. linguistics UCLA, 1966-69, assoc. prof., 1969-73, prof., 1973—, chmn. dept. linguistics, 1974-77, dean grad. div., vice chancellor grad. programs, 1979-89; mem. communication scis. study sect. NIH, 1981—; mem. com. on basic research behavior and social sci. Nat. Acad. Sci./NRC, 1982—; mem. program in linguistics NSF; vis. fellow Wolfson Coll., Oxford, 1984, 87. Author: (with R. Rodman) An Introduction to Language, 1973, 78, 83, 88, 93, Phonetic Linguistics, 1985; editor: Speech Errors as Linguistic Evidence, 1973, Tone: A Linguistic Survey, 1978, Errors in Linguistic Performance: Slips of the Tongue, Ear, Hand, and Pen, 1980; mem. editorial bd. Brain and Language. Recipient Disting. Tchrs. award UCLA, 1974, Profl. Achievement award UCLA Alumni Assn., 1984. Fellow AAAS (sec. linguistics sect. Z 1993-96, chmn. 1997-98), Acoustical Soc. Am., Am. Psychol. Soc.; mem. Am. Acad. Arts and Scis., Nat. Acad. Sci., N.Y. Acad. Scis., Acad. of Aphasia (chmn., bd.

govs.), Linguistic Soc. Am. (exec. com., sec.-treas. 1979-83, v.p. 1984, pres. 1985), Internat. Phonetics Assn., Am. Assn. Phonetic Sci. (councillor 1982-84), West African Linguistics Soc., Assn. Grad. Schs. (exec. com. 1981-84, pres. 1987-88), Comite Internat. Permanent de Linguistes (U.S. del. 1983—, exec. com., v.p. 1997—), Coun. Grad. Schs. (exec. com. 1985-87). Home: 8508 Lookout Mountain Ave Los Angeles CA 90046-1814 Office: UCLA Los Angeles CA 90046

FROMM, DAVID, surgeon; b. N.Y.C., Jan. 21, 1939; s. Alfred and Hanna F.; m. Barbara Solter, June 13, 1961; children—Marc, Kenneth, Kathleen. BS, U. Calif., Berkeley, 1960, MD, 1964. Intern U. Calif. Hosp., San Francisco, 1964-65; resident in surgery U. Calif., San Francisco, 1965-71; asst. prof. surgery Harvard Med. Sch., Boston, 1973-77; asso. prof. Harvard Med. Sch., 1977-78; prof. chmn. dept. surgery SUNY-Upstate Med. Center, Syracuse, 1978-88; Penberthy prof., chmn. dept. surgery Wayne State U., 1988—; surgeon-in-chief Detroit Med. Ctr., 1988—; chief surgery Harper Hosp., Detroit, 1988. Author: Complications of Gastric Surgery, 1977; editor Gastrointestinal Surgery, 1985; contbr. articles to profl. jours. Trustee Karmanos Cancer Inst. With M.C., U.S. Army, 1971-73. NIH career devel. awardee, 1976-79; grantee, 1974—. Fellow ACS (gov. 1977-83); mem. Soc. Univ. Surgeons, Am. Gastroent. Assn., Soc. Clin. Surgery, Assn. Acad. Surgery, Am. Physiol. Soc., Am. Surg. Assn., Halsted Soc., Soc. Surg. Alimentary Tract (sec. 1994-97, pres. 1998), Am. Bd. Surgery, Detroit Acad. Surgery. Office: 6C Univ Health Ctr 4201 Saint Antoine St Detroit MI 48201-2153

FROMM, ERIKA (MRS. PAUL FROMM), clinical psychologist; b. Frankfurt, Germany, Dec. 23, 1910; came to U.S., 1938, naturalized, 1944; d. Siegfried and Clementine (Stern) Oppenheimer; m. Paul Fromm, July 20, 1938; 1 child, Joan (Mrs. Greenstone). PhD magna cum laude, U. Frankfurt, 1933; postgrad. child care program, Chgo. Inst. for Psychoanalysis, 1949-51. Diplomate: Am. Bd. Examiners in Profl. Psychology, Am. Bd. Examiners Clin. Hypnosis. Rsch. assoc. dept. psychiatry U. Amsterdam, Holland, 1934-35; chief psychologist Apeldoorn State Hosp., Holland, 1935-38, Francis W. Parker Sch., Chgo., 1944-51; supervising psychologist Inst. for Juvenile Rsch., 1951-53; asst. prof. to assoc. prof. med. sch. Northwestern U., 1954-60; prof. U. Chgo., 1960-76, prof. emeritus, 1976—. Author: (with L.D. Hartman) Intelligence - A Dynamic Approach, 1955; (with Thomas M. French) Dream Interpretation: A New Approach, 1964 2d edit., 1986; (with Ronald E. Shor) Hypnosis: Developments in Research and New Perspectives, 1972, 2d. edit., 1979; (with Daniel P. Brown) Hypnotherapy and Hypnoanalysis, 1986; (with Daniel P. Brown) Hypnosis and Behavioral Medicine, 1987; (with Stephen Kahn) Selfhypnosis: The Chicago Paradigm, 1990; (with Michael R. Nash) Contemporary Hypnosis Research, 1992; (with Michael R. Nash) Psychoanalysis and Hypnosis, 1997; also numerous articles in profl. jours.; mem. editl. bd. Jour. Clin. and Exptl. Psychopathology, 1951-59; clin. editor: Internat. Jour. Clin. and Exptl. Hypnosis 1968-97, editl. cons., 1998—; assoc. editor Bull. Brit. Soc. Exptl. and Clin. Hypnosis, 1982-90; mem. bd. cons. editors Psychoanalytic Psychology, 1982-88; mem. adv. bd. editors Imagination, Cognition and Personality: Sci. Study of COnsciousness, 1982—; assoc. editor Hypnos: European Jour. Hypnosis, 1996—. Fellow AAAS, APA (pres. divsn. 30 1972-73, Psychoanalysis award 1985, 97, Hypnosis award for Eminent Enduring Contbns. to Advancement of Profl. Hypnosis 1994); mem. Am. Orthopsychiat. Assn. (dir. 1961-63), Soc. Clin. Exptl. Hypnosis (Best Rsch. Paper award 1965, sec. 1965-67, v.p. 1971-75, pres. 1975-77, Arthur Shapiro award 1973, Best Clin. Paper award 1986, Best Book pub. in Field of Hypnosis award 1987, 91, 93), The Netherlands Soc. for Hypnosis (hon.), Am. Bd. Psychol. Hypnosis (pres. 1971-74, Rollo May award Saybrook Inst. 1997), Ill. Psychol. Assn. (coun. 1951-53, 55-57, bd. examiners 1959-62, v.p. bd. examiners 1960-61), Soc. Projective Techniques, Am. Bd. Examiners in Psychol. Hypnosis (Morton Prince award 1970), Nat. Acad. Practice Psychology (Disting. Practioner in Psychology award 1982), Am. Soc. Clin. Hypnosis (award 1997), Sigma Xi. Home: 5715 S Kenwood Ave Chicago IL 60637-1742 Office: U Chgo Dept Psychology Chicago IL 60637-1742

FROMM, EVA MARIA, lawyer; b. Herne, Germany, May 6, 1956; came to U.S., 1959; d. Georg and Eva (Aust) F. BS in Chem. Engring., Syracuse U., 1978; JD, U. Houston, 1985. Bar: Tex. 1985, U.S. Dist. Ct. (so. dist.) Tex. 1987, U.S. Ct. Appeals (5th cir.) 1997. Engr. Chrysler Corp., Deer Park, Mich., 1978-79; process engr. Mobay Chem. Co., Baytown, Tex., 1980, ETI Engrs. Inc., Houston, 1981-82; engr. Petromas Inc., Houston, 1982-83; sr. chem. engr. NUS Corp., Houston, 1983-84; briefing clk., assoc. Hill Parker Franklin Cardwell & Jones, Houston, 1985-86; assoc. Fulbright & Jaworski LLP, Houston, 1986-93, ptnr., 1994—. Author, editor: Texas Environmental Law Handbook, 1989, 4th edit., 1996, (book chpt.) Environmental Aspects of Real Estate Transactions, 1997. Mem. ABA (co-chair real estate and probate sect., underground storage tank and RCRA com. 1994-95), Houston Bar Assn. (co-chair legal line com. 1988-90; sec. environ. law sect. 1991, vice-chair 1992, chair 1993). Home: 19 Serenity Woods Pl The Woodlands TX 77382-1262 Office: Fulbright & Jaworski LLP 1301 Mckinney St Ste 5100 Houston TX 77010-3031

FROMM, HANNA, educational administrator; b. Nuremberg, W.Ger., Dec. 20, 1913; d. David and Meta (Stiebel) Gruenbaum; m. Alfred Fromm, July 4, 1936; children: David, Caroline Fromm Lurie. Grad. in choreography and music, Folkwang Sch. Dancing and Music, U. Essen, Germany, 1934; D in Pub. Svc. (hon.), U. San Francisco, 1979. Exec. dir., co-founder Fromm Inst. Lifelong Learning U. San Francisco, 1975—. Co-founder Music in the Vineyards, Saratoga, Calif. Bd. dirs. Amnesty Internat., Nat. Coun. of Fine Arts Mus.; former bd. dirs. Young Audiences, Cmty. Music Ctr., Legal Aid to Elderly, San Francisco Chamber Mus. Soc.; coordinating com. geriatric curriculum and program U. Calif.-San Francisco; dir. Nat. Coun. on Aging. Served with ARC, WWII. Recipient Living Legacy award Women's Internat. Ctr., 1990, Laura McBride Power Meml. award Citizens Com. Founding San Francisco, 1991, First Profl. Achievement award San Francisco Alumni Assn., 1993. Mem. Met. Club (San Francisco), Villa Taverna Concordia Club (San Francisco). Jewish. Home: 850 El Camino Del Mar San Francisco CA 94121-1018 Office: 538 University Center 2130 Fulton St San Francisco CA 94117-1080

FROMM, HANS, gastroenterologist, educator, researcher; b. Hagenow, Germany, Aug. 1, 1939; s. Johannes C. and Irene (Biermann) F.; m. Sharon A. Kleiv, June 8, 1968; children: H. Chris, Martin T. MD, Albert Ludwig U., Freiburg, Fed. Republic Germany, 1964. Intern Meml. Hosp., Worcester, Mass., 1966-67; resident Lemuel Shattuck Hosp., Boston, 1967-68, Albany Med. Ctr., 1968-70; fellow Mayo Clinic, Rochester, Minn., 1970-71; resident/fellow Medizinische Hochschule Hannover, Germany, 1971-74; asst. prof. medicine U. Pitts., 1975-80, assoc. prof. medicine, 1980-84, prof. medicine, 1984; prof. medicine George Washington U., Washington, 1984—; dir. divsn. gastroenterology and nutrition George Washington Med. Ctr., Washington, 1984—; mem. numerous grant review coms. including NIH, Med. Rev. Bd. Gastroenterology Med. Rsch. Svc. VA, Washington, 1984-87. Contbr. articles to profl. jours., chpts. to books; mem. editl. bds. Hepatogastroenterology, 1981-88, Hepatology, 1985-88, 1991—. Mem. Am. Soc. Clin. Investigation, Am. Gastroent. Assn. (chmn. com. on admissions 1990-91, chmn. biliary disorders sect. 1997-99, chmn. internat. liaison com. 1995-98), Am. Assn. Study of Liver Diseases (chmn. pubs. com. 1988-90), Orgn. Mondiale de Gastro-Enterologie/World Orgn. Gastroenterology (vice chmn. interamerican edn. com.). Lutheran. Office: George Washington U Med Ctr Ste 3-405 2150 Pennsylvania Ave NW Washington DC 20037-3201

FROMM, HENRY GORDON, retired manufacturing and marketing executive; b. Burlington, Iowa, June 10, 1911; s. Henry Carl and Lillian (Lohmann) F.; m. Elizabeth H. Orthner, July 15, 1936; children—Dan G., Allan P., Martha E., Mark H., Eric C., Lynne M. BSChemE, Iowa State U., 1933; MS (Sloan fellow), MIT, 1950; DHH, Robert Morris Coll., 1998. Gen. plant mgr. Manhattan Soap Co., Bristol, Pa., 1937-44; prodn. mgr. Johnson & Johnson, 1944-55; v.p. ops. Internat. Latex Corp., 1955-61; v.p., gen. mgr. ops. Sun Chem. Corp., N.Y.C., 1961-63; gen. mgr. Crown Cork & Seal Co., Phila., 1963-64; v.p. ops. Marathon Electric Co., Wausau, Wis., 1964-69; pres. Bell & Howell Communications Co., Waltham, Mass., 1969, Bell & Howell Electronics & Instruments Group, Pasadena, Calif., 1969-71; group v.p. Bell & Howell, Chgo., 1971-77; chmn. bd. Ditto, Inc., Chgo., 1977-79; pres. Fromm Services, Inc., Green Bay, Wis., 1973-90, Eau Claire T.A.S., Wis., 1973-89, Gordon Fromm & Assos., Lake Forest, Ill., 1979-87; pres., chief exec. officer Templeton, Kenly & Co., 1979-87, Miller Fluid Power, 1981-87. Mem. gen. council Am. Baptist Conv., Dover (Del.) City Council, 1958-62, Rotary Internat., 1937-87; chmn. Dover City Planning Commn., 1960-62; trustee, treas. Robert Morris Coll., 1982—; mem. Chgo. Exec. Service Corps, 1987—; bd. dirs. Lake Forest Hist. Assn., Lake Forest Sr. Citizens Resources Found. Mem. Midwest Indsl. Mgmt. Assn. (dir.), Am. Mgmt. Assn. (v.p.), Am. Inst. Chem. Engrs., Lake Forest Symphony Assn. (pres. 1988-89), Univ. Club (Chgo.). Home: Lake Forest Pl 1100 Pembridge Dr # 170 Lake Forest IL 60045

FROMM, JEFFERY BERNARD, lawyer; b. Washington, Oct. 9, 1947; s. Seymour Morris and Frances Sylvia (Goldstein) F.; m. Mary Ellen Sommer, Sept. 11, 1971; children: Aaron M., David P. BS in Elec. Engring., BA in Physics, U. Pa., 1970; JD, Widener U., 1981. Bar: Pa. 1982, Calif. 1982, U.S. Ct. Appeals (9th and fed. cirs.) 1982, Colo. 1988. Patent atty. Hewlett-Packard Co., Palo Alto, Calif., 1981-83; sr. patent atty. Hewlett-Packard Co., Palo Alto, 1983-85; mng. patent counsel Hewlett-Packard Co., Andover, Mass., 1985-87; sr. mng. counsel intellectual property Hewlett-Packard Co., Ft. Collins, Colo., 1987—. Asst. scout master Boy Scouts Am., Ft. Collins, 1988-96; asst. coach-umpire Little League, Andover and San Jose, Calif., 1983-87. Mem. ABA, Pa. Bar Assn., Calif. Bar Assn., Colo. Bar Assn., Denver Bar Assn., IEEE, Am. Corp. Counsel Assn. Avocations: skiing, golf. Office: Hewlett-Packard Co 3404 E Harmony Rd Fort Collins CO 80528-9599

FROMM, JOSEPH, retired magazine editor, foreign affairs consultant; b. South Bend, Ind., Jan. 6, 1920; s. Michael M. and Ethel (Mentzel) F.; divorced; children: Margot, Lisa; 1 stepchild, Erik. Student, U. Chgo., 1937-38, Northwestern U., 1938-39. Reporter S. Bend Tribune, 1935-37, Southtown Economist, Chgo., 1937-39; writer UP, Chgo., 1939-40; radio news bur. chief AP, Chgo., 1940-42; mng. editor air edit. Chgo. Sun, 1942; fgn. corr. U.S. News and World Report, 1946-74; dep. editor U.S. News and World Report, Washington, 1974-79; asst. editor U.S. News and World Report, 1979-85, contbg. editor, 1985-88; cons. to think tanks, govt. agys.; lectr. on strategy and internat. rels.; mem. tech. adv. com. Ctr. Naval Analysis, CIA Strategic Adv. Panel. Served with Brit. and Indian armies, 1942-45. Decorated Order Brit. Empire. Fellow Johns Hopkins Fgn. Policy Inst., Internat. Inst. Strategic Studies (mem. exec. com., chmn. U.S. com.), Mem. Coun. on Fgn. Rels., Overseas Writers, Midatlantic Club, Fgn. Corr. Club Japan (pres. 1950), Assn. Am. Corrs. in London (pres. 1967), Fgn. Press Assn. London (dir. 1972-74), Arms Control Assn., Cosmos Club (Washington). Office: PO Box 503 Mc Lean VA 22101-0503

FROMM, PAUL OLIVER, physiology educator; b. Ramsey, Ill., Dec. 2, 1923; s. August Moltke and Edith Marie (Wollerman) F.; m. Mary Magdalene Shaw, June 15, 1947; children: David, Emily. B.S., U. Ill., 1949, M.S., 1951, Ph.D., 1954. Instr. dept. physiology Mich. State U., East Lansing, 1954-58, asst. prof., 1958-62, assoc. prof., 1962-65, prof., 1965-87, prof. emeritus, 1987—; cons. U.S.-Can. Great Lakes Commn., Windsor, Ont., Can., 1981, Nat. Research Council Can., 1983. Contbr. articles to profl. jours. Served with USMC, 1943-46. Fulbright rsch. scholar Musée Oceanographique Monaco, 1963-64. Mem. N.Am. Benthological Soc. (pres. 1958), Am. Soc. Zoologists, Am. Physiol. Soc., Soc. Exptl. Biology and Medicine. Home: 6741 S Lake RR 1 Pentwater MI 49449-9801 Office: Mich State U Dept Physiology East Lansing MI 48824

FROMM, PETER FRANCIS, author; b. Sept. 29, 1958. BS in Wildlife Biology, U. Mont., 1981. Author: The Tall Uncut, 1992, Indian Creek Chronicles, 1993, Monkey Tag, 1994, King of the Mountain, 1994, Dry Rain, 1997, Blood Knot, 1998, Night Swimming, 1999. Recipient Pacific N.W. Bookseller awards (2), 1994, 98, O. Henry prize, 1997. E-mail: petefromm@imt.net.

FROMM, WINFIELD ERIC, retired corporate executive, engineering consultant and investor; b. Haddonfield, N.J., Jan. 18, 1918; s. Niels Ditlev and Julia Gabriella (Svendsen) F.; m. Twanette Chloe Calnen, Nov. 11, 1944; children: Pamela Anne, David Gareth, Karen Elisabeth. BSEE, Drexel U., 1940; MEE, Poly. U., 1948, DEng (hon.), 1974; LHD (hon.), Dowling Coll., 1974. Aircraft radio engr. TWA, Kansas City, Mo., 1940-41; engr. div. war rsch. Columbia U., Mineola, N.Y., 1941-45; engr., supervising engr. Airborne Instruments Labs., Mineola, 1945-58; head dept., dir. div. Airborne Instruments Labs. div. Cutler-Hammer, Inc., Deer Park, N.Y., 1958-64, v.p. rsch. and systems engring. div., 1964, group v.p. Airborne Instruments Labs. div., 1964-68, exec. v.p., 1968-73, pres. of div. and v.p. parent co., 1973-77; group v.p. Cutler-Hammer Inc., 1977-79; v.p. instruments and systems ops. Eaton Corp., Melville, N.Y., 1979-83, ret., 1983; pvt. practice as cons. Fort Myers, Fla., 1983—; dir. LILCO, 1978-83, 84-93, cons. dir., 1983-84, 93-96. Contbr. numerous tech. and mgmt. papers to profl. publs.; patentee electronicals. Trustee, dep. mayor Village of Lloyd Harbor, N.Y., 1961-71; chmn. United Way of L.I., 1975-76; chmn. bd. trustees Dowling Coll., Oakdale, N.Y., 2 yrs., 1970's; corp. mem., fellow Poly. U., Bklyn., 1983-90. Recipient Disting. Citizen award Dowling Coll., 1973, Disting. Alumnus award Poly. U., 1974, Disting. Citizen award Suffolk County Boy Scouts Am., 1978. Fellow IEEE (Outstanding Engring. Mgr. award L.I. sect. 1974), AIAA (assoc.); mem. Phi Kappa Phi, Tau Beta Pi, Eta Kappa Nu. Home and Office: 5802 Turban Ct Fort Myers FL 33908-1668

FROMMELT, JEFFREY JAMES, management consulting firm executive; b. Mpls., July 23, 1940; s. Henry Julius and Inez Vivian (Okins) F.; m. Janet Ruth Parry, Apr. 10, 1965; children: Brian Jeffrey, Craig Henry. BA, Jamestown Coll., 1963; MHA, U. Minn., 1965. Adminstrv. resident R.I. Hosp., Providence, 1964-65; assoc. Herman Smith Assocs., Hinsdale, Ill., 1965-70, prin., 1970-77, pres., 1977-88; ptnr. Coopers & Lybrand, 1988-97; nat. advisor Argus/Arista Assocs., Western Springs, Ill., 1997—; bd. dirs. LaGrange (Ill.) Meml. Health System. Author: Building A Hospital, 1980; contbr. articles to profl. jours. Bd. dirs. Jamestown (N.D.) Coll., 1984—; elder First Presby. Ch., La Grange, Ill., 1981-84; bd. dirs. Cmty. Meml. Found., 1996—. Fellow Am. Assn. Health Care Cons. (treas. 1980-81, chmn. bd. 1982-83); mem. Inst. Mgmt. Cons., Am. Coll. Hosp. Adminstrs. Republican. Lodge: Elks. Home: 4136 Clausen Ave Western Springs IL 60558-1229

FROMSTEIN, MITCHELL S., temporary office services company executive; b. 1928. Grad., U. Wis., 1947. With Krueger Homes Inc., 1948-49; account exec. Mautner Advt. Agy., 1949-53; former pres. TV Parts Inc.; ptnr. Fromstein Assocs.; pres., chief exec. officer, dir. The Parker Pen Co., Janesville, Wis., 1985-86; chmn., pres., chief exec. officer Manpower, Inc., Milw., 1976—. Office: Manpower Inc Box 2053 5301 N Ironwood Ln Milwaukee WI 53217-4982*

FRONCKOWIAK, FELICIA ANN, retired surgical services director; b. Buffalo, Nov. 20, 1934; d. Leo D. and Anne (Sobczak) Koralewski; m. Richard Fronckowiak, Aug. 2, 1958; children: Janet, Paula, Lee Ann. BSN, D Youville Coll., Buffalo, 1956; MSN, SUNY, Buffalo, 1984. Cert. health educator. Clin. instr. Sch. Nursing Buffalo Gen. Hosp., 1980-84; dir. surg. svcs. Griffin Hosp., Derby, Conn., 1985-87, Millard Fillmore Hosp., Buffalo, 1987; dir. surgical svcs. Erie County Med. Ctr., Buffalo, 1987-90; evening supr. Buffalo VA Med. Ctr., 1990-97; ret.; trainer of aides and LPNs, BOCES I, Erie County, N.Y. Intensive Tchr. Tng. Program grantee. Mem. Am. Operating Rm. Nurses, Conn. Exec. RN's, Sigma Theta Tu. Home: 212 Stonehenge Dr Orchard Park NY 14127-2862

FRONTERA, MICHAEL P., municipal official; b. Newburgh, N.Y., May 22, 1969. BA, SUNY, Binghamton, 1991; JD, U. Ariz., 1994. Election specialist City Clk.'s Office City of Tucson (Ariz.), 1993-95; info. dir. Denver Election Commn. City of Denver, 1996-97, exec. dir. Denver Election Commn., 1997-99; client support mgr. Sequoia Pacific, Denver, 1999—. Mem. Election Ctr. 96. Recipient Am. Jurisprudence award in Constl. Law Lawyers Coop. Publishing, 1991. Mem. ABA, Colo. Bar Assn., Denver Bar Assn., Internat. Assn. Clks., Recorders, Election Officials & Treasurers, Colo. State Assn. County Clks. & Recorders. Office: Sequoia Pacific 410 17th St Ste 1950 Denver CO 80202-2617*

FRONTIERE, GEORGIA, professional football team executive; m. Carroll Rosenblum, July 7, 1966 (dec.); children: Dale Carroll, Lucia; m. Dominic Frontiere. Pres., owner L.A. Rams, NFL, 1979—; now mng. ptnr. St. Louis Rams. Bd. dirs. L.A. Boys and Girls Club, L.A. Orphanage Guild, L.A. Blind Youth Found. Named Headliner of Yr., L.A. Press Club, 1981. Office: St Louis Rams 1 Rams Way Earth City MO 63045-1525 also: Transworld Dome 701 Convention Plz Saint Louis C MO 63101*

FRONTUTO, PENELOPE KERR, mental health administrator; b. Rochester, N.Y., May 20, 1945; d. John Francis Kerr and Justine Lorraine (Provost) Emery; m. Joseph Carmen Frontuto, July 16, 1966; children: John K., Stephanie K., J. Justin, Kerrsten E. BS, St. Joseph's Coll., 1980; MPH, Columbia State U., 1997. RN, N.Y. Nurse I Rochester Psychiat. Ctr., 1967-68, nurse II, 1968-79, nurse adminstr. I, 1979-82, asst. DON, 1982, treatment team leader, 1982-91; dir. mental health Newark (N.Y.)-Wayne Cmty. Hosp., 1991-93; team leader, surveyor, psychiat. nursing cons. Behavioral Orgnl. Cons. Assts., Bronx, N.Y., 1991—; dir. mental health Wyoming County Comty. Hosp., Warsaw, N.Y., 1993-98; Palmyra (N.Y.) Group Hom mem. adv. com. Newark Devel. Ctr., 1983-86; mem. Fingerlakes Mentally Ill Chem. Abusers Task Force, 1991-93; commencement speaker Psychiat. Nursing Trends, 1994; pres. Nutcracker Enterprises; cons. in field. Bd. dirs. Wayne County Red Cross, Newark, 1984-86; trustee, dep. mayor Village of Palmyra, 1985-90; v.p. Wayne County (N.Y.) Village Ofcls. Assn., 1989-90; dist. rep. Wayne County Dem. Com., Palmyra, 1982-86. Avocations: gardening, jewelry making, politics, canning and preserving. Office: 258 Cuyler St Palmyra NY 14522-1404

FROSCH, ROBERT ALAN, retired automobile manufacturing executive, physicist; b. N.Y.C., May 22, 1928; s. Herman Louis and Rose (Bernfeld) F.; m. Jessica Rachael Denerstein, Dec. 22, 1957; children: Elizabeth Ann, Margery Ellen. A.B., Columbia U., 1947, A.M., 1949, Ph.D., 1952; DEng (hon.), U. Miami, 1982, Mich. Technol. U., 1983. Scientist Hudson Labs. Columbia U., 1951-53, asst. dir. theoretical div., 1953-54, asso. dir., 1954-56, dir., 1956-63; dir. nuclear test detection Advanced Research Projects Agy., Office Sec. Def., 1963-65; dep. dir. Advanced Research Projects Agy., 1965-66; asst. sec. navy for research and devel. Washington, 1966-73; asst. exec. dir. UN Environment Programme, 1973-75; asso. dir. for applied oceanography Woods Hole (Mass.) Oceanographic Instn., 1975-77; adminstr. NASA, Washington, 1977-81; pres. Am. Assn. Engring. Socs., N.Y.C., 1981-82; v.p. in charge Research Labs. Gen. Motors Corp., Warren, Mich., 1982-93; sr. rsch. fellow Harvard U. John F. Kennedy Sch. Govt., Cambridge, Mass., 1993—; chmn. U.S. del. to Intergovtl. Oceanographic Commn. meetings UNESCO, Paris, 1967, 70. Research and publs. numerous sci. and tech. articles. Recipient Arthur S. Flemming award, 1966, NASA Disting. Service award, 1981, IRI medal Indsl. Rsch. Inst., 1996. Fellow AAAS, AIAA, NAE, IEEE, Acoustical Soc. Am., Am. Astronautical Soc. (John F. Kennedy Astronautics award 1981); mem. Am. Geophys. Union, Seismol. Soc. Am., Am. Acad. Arts and Scis., Soc. Exploration Geophysicists (spl. commendation 1981), Marine Tech. Soc., Nat. Acad. Engring. (sr. fellow), Am. Phys. Soc., Soc. Naval Architects and Marine Engrs., Soc. Automotive Engrs., Engring. Soc. Detroit. Office: Harvard U John F Kennedy Sch Govt CSIA 79 JFK St Cambridge MA 02138-5801

FROSS, ROGER RAYMOND, lawyer; b. Rockford, Ill., Mar. 8, 1940; s. Hollis H. and Dorothy (George) F.; m. Madelon R. Rose, Feb. 14, 1970; 1 child, Oliver. AB, DePauw U., 1962; JD, U. Chgo., 1965. Bar: Ill. 1965. Assoc. Norman and Billick, Chgo., 1965-70; ptnr. Lord, Bissell & Brook, Chgo., 1970—, mng. pntr., 1982-87; bd. dirs. Hyde Park Bank and Trust Co., Chgo., 1975—; pres. Hyde-Park-Kenwood Devel. Corp., 1998—. Bd. dirs. Hyde Park Neighborhood Club, Chgo., 1970—, pres. 1972-73; bd. dirs., mem. exec. com. South East Chgo. Commn., 1978—; mem. Community Conservation Council, Chgo., 1980—; v.p., sec. Hyde Park-Kenwood Local Devel. Corp., Chgo., 1975-95; bd. dirs., sec. Chgo. Metro History Fair, 1991—; bd. dirs. The Joyce Found., 1991—, Lab. Sch. U. Chgo., 1991-94, Citizens Com. of the Juvenile Ct., 1973-96. Rector schlor DePauw U., Greencastle, Ind., 1958-62. Mem. ABA, Ill. Bar Assn., Chgo. Bar Assn. (chmn. com. juvenile delinquents 1972). Office: Lord Bissell & Brook Harris Bank Bldg 115 S La Salle St Ste 3200 Chicago IL 60603-3972

FROST, A. CORWIN, architect, consultant; b. Bronxville, N.Y., Nov. 18, 1934; s. Frederick George Jr. and Gwendolyn Belle (Corwin) F.; m. Rosalie Randolph Halsey, Sept. 26, 1959; children: Frederick Halsey, Anne Randolph. AB, Princeton U., 1956; BS, R.I. Sch. Design, 1959. Registered architect, N.Y., other states. Designer, draftsman Harrison & Abramovitz, N.Y.C., 1959-60; project architect Frederick G. Frost Jr. and Assocs., N.Y.C., 1960-63, assoc., 1963-68; ptnr. Frost Assocs., N.Y.C., 1968-78; assoc. dir. archtl. and engring. services CBS Inc., N.Y.C., 1978-80, dir. planning and design, 1980-86, dir. facilities engring., 1986-88; prin. Frost Assocs. Cons., Bronxville, N.Y., 1988—; dep. dir. dept. design, cons. and mgmt. CUNY, 1992-95; cons. Newark Pub. Schs., 1995—. Chmn. Bronxville Planning Bd., 1990—; trustee Coun. for Arts in Westchester, White Plains, N.Y., 1972-81 (pres. 1974-75), R.I. Sch. Design, 1989-99, Westchester County Hist. Soc., 1998—; trustee, mem. exec. com. Westchester Preservation League, 1989-98; mem. Bronxville Adult Sch., 1982-88, Bronxville Planning Commn., 1977-80. Mem. AIA (exec. com. N.Y. chpt. 1974-76, ethics com. 1978-80, corp. architects com. 1980-82, fin. com. 1981-87), Princeton Club, Bronxville Field Club (pres. 1992-96). Home and Office: Frost Assoc Cons 11 Sunset Ave Bronxville NY 10708-2208

FROST, ANNE, real estate broker, author, publisher; b. Mocksville, N.C., Apr. 1, 1932; d. Ernest Henry and Annie Laurie (Holton) F.; m. Gene T. Wilson, Apr. 20, 1951 (div. 1970); children: Gene, Michelle, Michael, William, Carol. Student, U. N.C., Greensboro, 1948-49; BA in Spanish-English, U. N.C., 1949-52; postgrad., Fla. Atlantic U., 1965, U. Cen. Fla., 1983. Cert. tchr., Fla.; lic. real estate broker, Fla. Tchr. Broward County Schs., Ft. Lauderdale, Fla., 1965-72; assoc. A.J. Richter & Co., Ft. Lauderdale, 1972-76; real estate assoc. G.J. Shirrman & Assocs., Ft. Lauderdale, 1976-79; founder, v.p. The Apartment Guide, Pompano Beach, Fla., 1978; pres., owner, broker Viking Properties, Inc., Lauderdale by the Sea, Fla., 1979-83; pres., owner Anne Frost Real Estate Ctr., Inc., Winter Park, Fla., 1984—; owner Frost Pub., 1989—. Author, pub.: Come Run Away, 1976, Green Grass and Yellow Flowers, 1977, As A Tree Grows, 1986, Footprints in the Sand, 1986, Wings From Above, 1988, Somewhere In Between, 1988, Florida for Sale, 1989; editor, pub. Apartment/Home/Condominium Guide to Rentals in Volusia County, 1979, Jimmy Boy, 1990, Checkmate, 1995, Living Through Florida History, 1996; pub. Frost Quotes greeting cards, 1996. Mem. Nat. Assn. Realtors, Nat. League Am. Penwomen (treas. Winter Park br.), Greater Ft. Lauderdale Bd. Realtors, Greater Orlando Bd. Realtors, Pompano Beach Jaycettes (parliamentarian 1960), Cornelian Soc. Republican. Presbyterian.

FROST, DANIEL ALLEN, financial engineer; b. Salem, Ohio, Jan. 30, 1963; s. Kenneth Robert and Gwendolyn (Wilms) F.; m. Wenlan Hu, Jan. 1, 1998. SBEE, MIT, 1985, SM in Elec. Engring. and Computer Scis., 1987, PhD in EE/Fin., 1993. V.p. Tokai Bank, N.Y.C., 1993-96; v.p. quantitative rsch. Louis Dreyfus Energy Corp., N.Y.C., 1997—. Ednl. counselor MIT, Cambridge, 1997—. Mem. Sigma Xi. Republican. Avocation: amateur radio. Home: 395 S End Ave Apt 7B New York NY 10280-1049

FROST, DAVID, former biology educator, medical editor, consultant; b. Bklyn., Dec. 19, 1925; s. Charles and Regina (Sad) Feivlowitz; m. Ruthann Steinberg, Dec. 24, 1946; children: Michael Joseph, Jane Alice. BS, CCNY, 1945, MED, 1949; MS, NYU, 1952, PhD, 1960. Instr. in biology CCNY, 1946-49; instr. in sci. Rhodes Sch., N.Y.C., 1949-52; asst. prof. biology Rutgers U., Newark, N.J., 1952-59; adj. prof. biology Rutgers U., New Brunswick, N.J., 1960-78; sci. editor Squibb Inst. for Med. Rsch., Princeton, N.J., 1959-75; pvt. practice, Plainfield, N.J., Olmstedville, N.Y., 1975—. Pres. N.J. SANE, 1964-65; co-chmn. Plainfield Joint Def. Com., 1970-85; newsletter editor Cen. Jersey/Masaya, Nicaragua Friendship Cities Project, 1985-97. Mem. Coun. Biology Editors (pres. 1982-83), Schroon Lake Assn. (v.p., 1980—, pres. 1997—). Office: 1229 E 7th St Plainfield NJ 07062-1907 also: PO Box 41B Olmstedville NY 12857-0041

FROST, DAVID, professional golfer; b. Cape Town, South Africa, Sept. 11, 1959. Winner Can. Open, 1993, Hardee's Classic, 1993, Canon Greater Hartford (Conn.) Open, 1994; mem. Pres. Cup Team, 1994; also won 9 over victories worldwide. First player since Johnny Miller in 1975 to repeat a title the week after winning another tournament, 1993. Office: care PGA Tour

112 Tpc Blvd Ponte Vedra Beach FL 32082-3046 Address: PGA America 100 Ave of the Champions PO Box 109601 Palm Bch Gdns FL 33410-9601*

FROST, EDMUND BOWEN, lawyer; b. Pueblo, Colo., Dec. 5, 1942; s. Hildreth and Doris (Bowen) F.; m. Molly Spitzer; children: Julia A., Elizabeth E., Edmund N., Luette S. BA, Dartmouth Coll., 1964; JD magna cum laude, U. Mich., 1967. Bar: Colo. 1967, D.C. 1970, U.S. Supreme Ct. 1980. Assoc. Steptoe & Johnson, Washington, 1969-75; chief legal advisor to commr. ICC, Washington, 1975-76; asst. dir. for gen. litigation Bur. Competition, FTC, Washington, 1976-77; v.p., gen. counsel Chem. Mfrs. Assn., Washington, 1978-82; ptnr. Kirland & Ellis, Washington, 1982-88, Davis, Graham & Stubbs, Washington, 1988-94; sr. v.p. and gen. counsel Clean Sites, Inc., Alexandria, Va., 1994-99; bd. dirs., exec. dir., sec. Ctr. for Land Renewal, Inc., Alexandria, 1996—; shareholder, dir. Leonard Hurt Frost & Lilly, P.C., Washington, 1998—; adv. coun. Environtl. Law Inst., 1998—; bd. dirs., exec. com., sec. Comty. Coun. for Homeless, Washington, 1993—. Contbr. articles to profl. jours. Participant pub. policy dialogs on environ. issues Keystone (Colo.) Ctr., 1980—;guest artisan Washington Nat. Cathedral, 1997—. Capt. U.S. Army, 1967-69. Mem. Cosmos Club Washington. Avocations: sculpture and stone carving, skiing, mountain climbing, tuba and euphonium. Home: 3309 35th St NW Washington DC 20016-3141

FROST, ELIZABETH ANN MCARTHUR, physician; b. Glasgow, Scotland, Oct. 29, 1938; came to U.S., 1963; d. Robert Thomas and Annie M. (Ross) F.; m. Wallace Capobianco, Sept. 4, 1965 (dec. May 1988); children: Garrett, Ross, Christopher, Neil. MBChB, U. Glasgow, 1961. Diplomate Am. Bd. Anesthesiology, Royal Coll. Ob-Gyn., London. Intern in surgery Royal Infirmary, Glasgow, 1961-62; intern in medicine Victoria Infirmary, Glasgow, 1962; intern in obstetrics Royal Maternity Hosp., Glasgow, 1962-63; resident in internal medicine Englewood (N.J.) Hosp., 1963-64; resident in anesthesiology N.Y. Hosp., N.Y.C., 1964-66; instr. in anesthesiology Albert Einstein Coll. Medicine, Bronx, N.Y., 1966-68, asst. prof. to assoc. prof., 1968-81, prof. anesthesiology, 1981-91, mem. dept. history of medicine, 1973-91; prof., chmn. dept. anesthesiology N.Y. Med. Coll., Valhalla, N.Y., 1992—. Book reviewer New Eng. Jour. of Medicine, 1983—; editor Preanesthetic Assessment, Anesthesiology News, 1984—, Gen. Surgery News, 1991; author/contbr. books; contbr. articles to profl. jours. Mem. N.Y. State Soc. Anesthesiologists, Am. Soc. of Anesthesiologists, Assn. of Univ. Anesthesiologists, Soc. of Neurosurg. Anesthesia and Neurologic Supportive Care, Am. Assn. of Neurol. Surgeons, Anesthesia History Assn., Internat. Trauma Anesthesia and Critical Care Soc. Office: NY Medical Coll Macy Pavilion W Room 2389 Valhalla NY 10595

FROST, ELLEN LOUISE, political economist; b. Boston, MA, Apr. 26, 1945; d. Horace Wier and Mildred (Kip) F.; m. William F. Pedersen, Jr., Feb. 2, 1974; 1 son by previous marriage, Jai Kumar Ojha; children: Mark Francis Pedersen, Claire Ellen Pedersen. B.A. magna cum laude, Radcliffe Coll., 1966; M.A., Fletcher Sch. Law and Diplomacy, 1967; Ph.D., Harvard U., 1972. Teaching fellow, instr. Harvard U., Wellesley Coll., 1969-71; legis. asst. Office of Senator Alan Cranston, Washington, 1972-74; fgn. affairs officer Dept. Treasury, Washington, 1974-77; dep. dir. Office of Internat. Trade Policy and Negotiations, 1977; dep. asst. sec. of def. for internat. econ. and tech. affairs Dept. Def., Washington, 1977-81; dir. govt. programs Westinghouse Electric Corp., Washington, 1981-88; corp. dir., internat. affairs United Techs. Corp., Washington, 1988-91; sr. fellow Inst. for Internat. Econs., Washington, 1992-93, 95-98; vis. fellow Inst. for Internat. Econs., Washington, 1998—; counselor to U.S. Trade Rep., Washington, 1993-95. Author: For Richer, For Poorer: The New U.S.-Japan Relationship, 1987, Transatlantic Trade: A Strategic Agenda, 1997. Trustee Aspen Inst. Berlin, 1990-92. NSF trainee, 1967-69. Mem. Internat. Inst. Strategic Studies, Coun. Fgn. Rels., Phi Beta Kappa.

FROST, EVERETT LLOYD, academic administrator; b. Salt Lake City, Oct. 17, 1942; s. Henry Hoag Jr. and Ruth Salome (Smith) F.; m. Janet Owens, Mar. 26, 1967; children: Noreen Karyn, Lysa Lida. BA in Anthropology, U. Oreg., 1965; PhD in Anthropology, U. Utah, 1970. Field researcher in cultural anthropology Taveuni, Fiji, 1968-69; asst. prof. in anthropology Ea. N.Mex. U., Portales, 1970-74, assoc. prof., 1974-76, asst. dean Coll. Liberal Arts and Scis., 1976-78, dean acad. affairs and grad. studies, 1978-80, v.p. for planning and analysis, dean rsch., 1980-91, dean grad. studies, 1983-88, pres., 1991—; cons., evaluator N. Ctrl. Assn. Accreditation Agy. for Higher Edn., 1989—, mem. rev. bd., 1993—; bd. dirs. Quality N.Mex., 1st Savs. Bank of Clovis and Portales, N.Mex., Plains Regional Med. Ctrs., Clovis and Portales; bd. mem. emeritus N.Mex. First; commr. Western Interstate Commn. for Higher Edn., 1993—; pres. Lone Star Athletic Conf. Pres.'s Commn., 1992—; chmn. rsch. com. N.Mex. First, 1989-91. Chmn. N.Mex. Humanities Coun., 1980-88; mem. N.Mex. Gov.'s Commn. on Higher Edn., 1983-86; mem. exec. bd. N.Mex. First, 1987—; bd. dirs. Roosevelt Gen. Hosp., Portales, 1989—; pres. bd. dirs. San Juan County Mus. Assn., Farmington, 1979-82; vice chair Portales Pub. Schs. Facilities Com., 1990—. NDEA fellow, 1969-70; grantee NEW, 1979-80, NSF, 1968-69, Fiji Forbes, Ltd., 1975-76, others. Fellow Am. Anthropol. Assn., Am. Assn. Higher Edn., Soc. Coll. and Univ. Planning, Assn. Social Anthropologists Oceania, Anthropol. Soc. Washington, Sch. Am. Rsch., Western Assn. Grad. Deans, Current Anthropology (assoc.) Polynesian Soc., Phi Kappa Phi.

FROST, HELEN MARIE, writer; b. Brookings, S.D., Mar. 4, 1949; d. Reuben Bernhard and Jean Elizabeth (Timmons) F.; m. Chad Lawrence Thompson, July 23, 1983; 1 child, Glen Andrew Thompson; 1 stepchild, Lloyd Samuel Thompson. BS, Syracuse U., 1971; MAT, Ind. U., 1994. Cert. in elem. edn., Alaska, Ind., Mass. Tchr. Kilquhanity House Sch., Castle Douglas, Scotland, 1976-78; prin., tchr. Telida (Alaska) Sch., 1981-84; tchr. White Cliff Sch., Ketchikan, Alaska, 1990-91; tchr. English, dir. Writing Ctr. Ind. U./Purdue U., Ft. Wayne, 1996-97; freelance writer Ft. Wayne, 1997—; adjudicator panelist Ind. Arts Commn., Indpls., 1994; cons. numerous schs. and orgns., 1990—; mem. Lane Literary Guild, Eugene, Oreg., 1986-89, pres. 1988-89; judge numerous poetry competitions, Alaska, Utah, Wis., Ind., 1985—; resident Cottages at Hedgebrook, Whitby Island, Wash., 1990. Author: (book) Skin of a Fish, Bones of a Bird, 1993 (Women Poets Series award 1993); co-author (play) Why Darkness Seems So Light, 1999; editor: (books) Why Darkness Seems So Light: Young People Speak Out About Violence, 1998, Season of Dead Water, 1990; also 24 nonfiction books for children. Poetry tchr. program for at-risk youth Arts United, Ft. Wayne, 1995-99. Named Outstanding Rural Vol., Akaska Assn. of Comty. Edn., 1983; Mary Anderson fellow, 1993. Mem. Soc. Children's Book Writers and Illustrators, Tchrs. and Writers Collaborative, Poetry Soc. Am. (Robert Winner award 1992, Mary Carolyn Davies award 1993), Acad. Am. poets, Writers Ctr. Indpls. Avocations: crosscountry skiing, gardening, reading. E-mail: frost-thompson@worldnet.att.net. Home and Office: 6108 Old Brook Dr Fort Wayne IN 46835

FROST, J. ORMOND, otolaryngologist, educator; b. Ireland, May 18, 1927; came to U.S., 1952, naturalized, 1963; s. James Patrick and Margaret (O'Loughlen) F.; m. Rita Robert, Oct. 1, 1955; 1 dau., Roberta. M.B.B.Ch., Univ. Coll. Dublin, 1952. House officer Mater Hosp., Dublin, Ireland, 1952; intern Loyola U. Mercy Hosp., Chgo., 1953; resident, asst., assoc. prof. Sch. Medicine NYU, N.Y.C., 1953-74, prof. clin. otolaryngology, 1974-89, clin. prof. otolaryngology, 1989—. Mem. AMA, N.Y. Otologic Soc. (pres. 1983-85), ACS, Am. Acad. Otolaryngology (bd. govs. 1985-88), Am. Otol., Rhinol. and Laryngol. Soc., St. George Soc., Irish-Am. Cultural Inst., W.B. Yeats Soc., Amateur Comedy Club. Roman Catholic.

FROST, JAMES ARTHUR, former university president; b. Manchester, Eng., May 15, 1918; came to U.S., 1926, naturalized, 1942; s. Harry Arthur and Janet (Wilson) F.; m. Elsie Mae Lorenz, Sept. 14, 1942; children: Roger Arthur (dec.), Janet Linda Frost Naleski, Elise Anita Frost Alair. BA, Columbia U., 1940, MA, 1941, PhD, 1949; LLD, So. Conn. State U., 1993. Tchr. Am. history high sch., Nutley, N.J., 1946-47; instr. SUNY Coll.-Oneonta, 1947-49, asst. to pres., 1949-52, dean, 1952-64; assoc. provost acad. planning Cen. Adminstrn., SUNY, 1964-65, exec. dean for four year colls., 1965-68, vice chancellor for univ. colls., 1968-72; exec. dir. Conn. State Colls., New Britain, 1972-83; pres. Conn. State U., 1983-85, pres. emeritus, 1985—; instr. Am. history Columbia U., summers, 1947-48; Smith-Mundt prof. Am. history U. Ceylon, 1959-60; mem. com. on research and devel. Coll. Entrance Exam Bd., 1973-76; mem. adv. bd. Conn. Rev., 1972-76; mem. commn. on higher edn. Middle States Assn. Colls. and Secondary Schs., 1966-72; mem. Nat. Coun. Heads of Systems of Pub. Higher Edn., 1976-85, pres., 1979-80, now hon. mem. Author: Life on the Upper Susquehanna, 1783-1860, 1951; (with David M. Ellis, Harold Syrett, Harry J. Carman) A Short History of New York State, 1957, 2d edit., 1967; (with David M. Ellis and William B. Fink) New York: The Empire State, 1961, 5th edit., 1980; (with R.A. Brown, D.M. Ellis, William B. Fink) A History of the United States: The Evolution of a Free People, 1967, 2d edit., 1969, The Establishment of the Connecticut State University, 1965-85; Notes and Reminiscences, 1991, The Country Club of Farmington, Connecticut, 1892-1995, 1996; mem. editl. bd. SUNY Press, 1964-72; contbr. articles on history and edn. to mags. Trustee Robinson Sch., Hartford, 1973-77; bd. dirs. Conn. State U. Found., Inc., 1983— , treas., 1986-95, pres., 1995-98, investment com. 1995—; sponsor Soc. of Columbia Scholars, 1997—. Maj. AUS, 1941-46, lt. col. USAFR. Rockefeller grantee, 1959. Fellow N.Y. State Hist. Assn.; mem. Country Club of Farmington, Conn. Congregationalist. Home: 17 Neal Dr Simsbury CT 06070-2801 Office: Conn State U 39 Woodland St Hartford CT 06105-2337

FROST, JAMES HAMNER, health facility administrator; b. Beaumont, Tex., Aug. 7, 1934; s. Harvey Newcomb and Velma Veda (Farmer) F.; children: Patricia Eileen, Kenneth Harvey; m. Mary Loonan, May 20, 1995. BA, U. Tex., 1957; MS, Trinity U., San Antonio, 1971. Asst. dir. Hermann Hosp., Houston, 1971-73; asst. adminstr. McAllen (Tex.) Gen. Hosp., 1973-75; chief support svcs. Whittaker Corp. Hosp. Tabuk, Tabuk, Saudi Arabia, 1975-77; hosp. dir. Almana Hosp., Al Khobar, Saudi Arabia, 1977-78; dir. med. svcs. corp. Bechtel Corp., Jubail, Saudi Arabia, 1979-83; CEO Al-Mutabagani Health Svcs., Riyadh, Saudi Arabia, 1983-86; hosp. dir. Asir Cen. Hosp., Abha, Saudi Arabia, 1987-90; dep. project dir. King Fahd Mil. Med. Complex, Dhahran, Saudi Arabia, 1990-98; founder., sr. consulting officer J.H. Frost & Assocs., Beaumont, 1987—; founder, COO, Paramedex Internat. Ltd., Lincoln, Eng., 1989—,. Fellow Am. Coll. Healthcare Execs.; mem. Am. Businessmen's Assn., Internat. Fedn. Hosps., Am. Hosp. Assn., Tex. Hosp. Assn. Republican. Methodist. Avocations: sports fishing, computers, music, reading, rock collecting.

FROST, JERRY WILLIAM, religion and history educator, library administrator; b. Muncie, Ind., Mar. 17, 1940; s. J. Thomas and Margaret Esther (Meredith) F.; m. Susan Vanderlyn Kohler; 1 son, James. B.A., DePauw U., Greencastle, Ind., 1962; postgrad., Yale Div. Sch., 1962-63; M.A., U. Wis.-Madison, 1965, Ph.D., 1968. Instr. Vassar Coll., 1967-68, asst. prof. history, 1968-73; assoc. prof. religion Swarthmore Coll., 1973—, prof. religion, 1980—, Howard M. and Charles F. Jenkins prof. of Quaker history and research, 1981—. Author: The Quaker Family in Colonial America, 1973, Connecticut Education in Revolutionary Era, 1974, A Perfect Freedom: Religions Liberty in Pennsylvania, 1990; co-author: The Quakers, 1988, Christianity: A Social and Cultural History, 1998; editor: The Keithian Controversy in Early Pennsylvania, 1980, Quaker Origins of Antislavery, 1981, Records and Recollections of James Jenkins, 1984, Seeking the Light: Essays in Quaker History, 1987; editor Pa. Mag. of History and Biography, 1981-86; contbr. articles to profl. pubs. Bd. dirs. Friends Hist. Assn., 1973—. John Carter Brown Libr. fellow, 1970, Eugene M. Lang fellow, 1980-81, 97, NEH fellow, 1986; U.S. Inst. of Peace grantee, 1992. Quaker. Home: 512 Elm Ave Swarthmore PA 19081-1115 Office: Swarthmore Coll Friends Hist Libr Swarthmore PA 19081

FROST, JOHN ELLIOTT, minerals company executive; b. Winchester, Mass., May 20, 1924; s. Elliott Putnam and Hazel Lavera (Carley) F.; m. Carolyn Catlin, July 12, 1945 (div. 1969); children: John Crocker, Jeffrey Putnam, Teresa Baird, Virginia Nicholl; m. Martha Hicks, June 6, 1969 (div. 1984); m. Catherine Kearns, July 27, 1985 (dec. Jan. 1997); m. Betty Nelson, Sept. 12, 1997. BS, Stanford U., 1949, MS, 1950, PhD, 1965. Geologist Asarco, Salt Lake City, 1951-54; chief geologist, surface minees supt. Philippine Iron Mines Inc., Larap, Camarines Norte, 1954-60; chief geologist Duval Corp. (Pennzoil Corp.), Tucson, 1961-67; minerals exploration mgr. Exxon Corp., Houston, 1967-71; divsn. minerals mgr. Esso Eastern Inc., 1971-80; sr. v.p. div. Exxon Minerals Co., Houston, 1980-86; pres. Exxon Minerals Internat., Houston, 1980-86, Frost Minerals Internat., Houston, 1986—; v.p. Kalahari Resources, 1996—; bd. dirs. Abitibi Mining Corp., Sedex Mining Corp., UnitedEngring. Trustees, N.Y.C., chmn. real estate com., 1986-89, v.p., 1989-91, pres., 1991-93. *Conceived, designed, built and managed four successful minerals exploration programs for Philippine Iron Mines, Duval-Pennzoil, Exxon U.S.A., and Exxon. Responsible directly, and indirectly as manager, for the discovery of over forty commercial mineral deposits and was the first to conceive and apply successfully the concept of potash zoning to the discovery of a porphyry copper ore body (1961). He conceived and successfully applied a new theory for the occurence of the "strataform" sulfur model to West Texas, and was the first to adapt atomic absorption (AA) to geochemical minerals exploration (1961) and to adapt reverse circulation (RC) drilling to metals exploration (1964).* Mem. adv. bd. Earth Scis., Stanford (Calif.) U., 1983-85; pres. SEG Found., 1984, bd. dirs., 1981-84, 94-98. Served to 1st lt. USAAF, 1943-45, PTO. Fellow Geol. Soc. Am., Soc. Econ. Geologists (pres. 1989-90, councilor 1982-84, program com., chmn. nominating com. 1982); mem. AIME (chmn. edn. com. Soc. Mining Engrs. 1971; Charles F. Rand medal 1984, Disting. Meml. award 1984, Disting. Svc. award 1991), Australian Inst. Mining and Metallurgy, Am. Inst. Profl. Geologists, The Houston Club, Sigma Xi. Republican. Methodist. Home and Office: 60 Sandy Port St Houston TX 77079-2419

FROST, JONAS MARTIN, III, congressman; b. Glendale, Calif., Jan. 1, 1942; s. Jack and Doris (Marwil) F.; children: Alanna Shaw, Mariel Jeanne, Camille Faye; m. Kathryn George. BA, U. Mo., 1964, BJ, 1964; J.D., Georgetown U., 1970. Bar: Tex. 1970. Law clk. U.S. Dist. Ct. Judge Sarah T. Hughes, Dallas, 1970-71; legal commentator Sta. KERA-TV, Dallas, 1971-72; pvt. practice law Dallas, 1972-79; mem. 96th-104th Congresses from 24th Tex. dist., Washington, D.C., 1979—. Del. Dem. Commn. on Congl. Mailing Stds. Nat. Conv., 1976, 84, 88, 92, 96; coord. North Tex. Carter-Mondale Campaign, 1976; chmn. Dem. Caucus. Brig. gen. U.S. Army. Office: US Ho of Reps 2256 Rayburn Office Bldg Washington DC 20515

FROST, JUANITA CORBITT, retired hospital foundation coordinator; b. Rockford, Ill., Aug. 4, 1926; d. Mervin Charles and Eva Marie (Moberg) Corbitt; m. Thomas Tapenden Frost, Jan. 3, 1954; children: Annamarie, Thomas Tapenden. Student, Little Rock U., Ark., 1959-61. Med. sec. asst. clin. pathology lab. VA Hosp., Whipple, Ariz., 1951-54; exec. dir. Camp Fire Girls, Temple, Tex., 1967-73; exec. sec. Scott and White Meml. Hosp. Found., Temple, 1973-82; hosp. found. coordinator, exec. asst. to bd. Scott and White Meml. Hosp., Temple, 1982-98, Scott Sherwood and Brindley Found., Temple, 1982-98; ret., 1998. Vestrywoman Episcopal Ch., Temple, 1985-88, sr. warden, 1987, worship com., 1995-97, search com., 1996-97; active Com. on Bishops Address NW Region Diocese Episcopal Ch., Houston, 1988, Bell County Choral Group, Belton, Tex., 1988-92, Tchr. Literacy Coun., Temple, 1988-93, Temple Civic Theatre Guild, 1997—; mem. St. Francis Ch. Altar Guild. Mem. Am. Hosp. Assn. Exec. Assts., Dau. of the King (sec. St. Clare chpt. 1998—). Avocations: choral singing, playing piano and organ, sailing, needlework, reading. Home: 3001 Las Moras Dr Temple TX 76502-1643

FROST, LINDA GAIL, clergyman, hospital chaplain; b. Louisville, Feb. 26, 1950; d. Halqua Mildon and Christena (Crisp) F. BA, Georgetown (Ky.) Coll., 1972; MDiv, So. Bapt. Sem., Louisville, 1978, DMin, 1982. Ordained to ministry Bapt. Ch., 1978; bd. cert. chaplain. Social worker Dept. Pub. Welfare, Corpus Christi, 1972-76; assoc. to pastor Walnut St. Bapt. Ch., Louisville, 1979-89; chaplain, clin. supr. Koala Hosp., Columbus, Ind., 1989-92; dir. chaplain svcs. Caritas Med. Ctr., Louisville, 1993—; advisor pastoral svcs. Hospice of S.E. Ind., Jeffersonville, 1993—. Author, A Legacy in Missions and Ministry, 1993. Bd. dirs., pres. Neighborhood Devel. Corp., Louisville, 1979-89; mem., sec. Old Louisville Neighborhood Coun., 1979-87.

FROST, MOLLY SPITZER, Chinese culture educator; b. Washington, Nov. 30, 1944; d. John Brumback and Lucy Ohlinger Spitzer; m. Edmund Bowen Frost, June 18, 1966; children: Julia, Elizabeth, Edmund, Luette. BA in English, Wellesley Coll., 1966; PhD in Chinese Linguistics, Georgetown U., 1982. Rsch. assoc., grant proposal writer George Washington U., 1975-93, asst. adj. prof., 1989-90, 93—. Trustee Cleveland Park Club, Washington, 1980-84, 93—; trustee, sec. Internat. Student House, Washington, 1991—; trustee,, pres. Parents Assn. Maret Sch., 1985-87; bd. dirs. Nat. Child Rsch. Ctr., 1982-84. Avocations: aerobics, swimming, travel. E-mail: msf@gwu.edu. Home: 3309-35th Street NW Washington DC 20016 Office: East Asian Langs Dept Rome Hall 462 George Washington U Washington DC 20052

FROST, NORMAN COOPER, retired telephone company executive; b. Nashville, Feb. 6, 1923; s. Norman and Anna Martha (Cooper) F.; m. Katherine McDonald Shapard, Nov. 25, 1948; children: Kathy, Norman Cooper Jr. B.A., Vanderbilt U., 1943, J.D., 1948. Bar: Tenn. 1946, Ga. 1954, N.Y. 1964, D.C. 1965. Practiced in Nashville, 1948-50; trust officer Nashville Trust Co., 1952-53; atty. So. Bell Telephone Co., Atlanta, 1953-61; gen. atty. So. Bell Telephone Co., 1961-62; atty. Am. Tel. & Tel. Corp., N.Y.C., 1962-66; asst. gen. atty. Am. Tel. & Tel. Corp., 1966-67; v.p., gen. counsel South Cen. Bell, Birmingham, Ala., 1968-83; exec. v.p., gen. counsel Bell South Corp., Atlanta, 1983-88. Served with USMCR, 1943-46, 50-52. Mem. ABA, Ga. Bar Assn., Tenn. Bar Assn., N.Y. Bar Assn., D.C. Bar Assn., Order of Coif. Methodist. Home: 9955 Huntcliff Trce Atlanta GA 30350-2717 Office: Bell South Corp 533 Southern Bell Ctr Atlanta GA 30375

FROST, PHILIP, insurance company executive. Chmn., CEO Ivax Corp., Miami, Fla. Office: Ivax Corp 4400 Biscayne Blvd Miami FL 33137-3212*

FROST, ROBERT EDWIN, chemistry educator; b. Gowanda, N.Y., Feb. 1, 1932; s. Sidney Mauthe and Mary Theresa (Bollinger) F.; m. Janice Ruth Young, May 31, 1958; children—Elizabeth Ann, Nancy Lynn, Barbara Jean. B.S., Allegheny Coll., 1953; A.M., Harvard, 1955, Ph.D., 1957. Research chemist B.F. Goodrich Research Center, Brecksville, Ohio, 1957-61; assoc. prof. SUNY at Albany, 1961-64, prof. chemistry, 1964-95, prof. emeritus, 1995; Kettering vis. lectr. U. Ill., Urbana, 1965-66. Mem. Am. Chem. Soc., Phi Beta Kappa, Sigma Xi. Home: 329 W Highland Dr Schenectady NY 12303-5751 Office: SUNY Dept Chemistry Albany NY 12222

FROST, S. DAVID, retired naval officer; b. Southard, Okla., Apr. 21, 1930; s. Chester William and Martha Leah (Weber) F.; m. Dolores Marie Radja, Oct. 17, 1953; children: Kathleen D., David J., Karen T., Mary C. BS, U.S. Naval Acad., 1953; MBA, Stanford U., 1961; student, Naval War Coll., 1964-65. Commd. officer USN, 1953, advanced through grades to rear adm., 1977; jr. officer USS Henrico, 1953-55; with Navy Fin. Center, Cleve., 1956-58; supply officer USS Rankin, 1958-59; asst. planning officer Navy Ordnance Supply Office, Mechanicsburg, Pa., 1961- 64; with Navy Fleet Material Support Office, 1965-68; supply officer USS America, 1968-70; exec. asst. asst. sec. def. (comptroller) Washington, 1970-74; exec. officer Naval Supply Center, Norfolk, Va., 1974-75; comdg. officer Navy Supply Corps Sch., Athens, Ga., 1975-77; dep. comdr. plans, policy and systems devel. Navy Dept., Washington, 1977-78; dep. comptroller of the Navy, 1978-80, comptroller, 1980-81, dep. comptroller, 1981-83; staff dir. for mgmt. Bd. Govs. FRS, 1983—. Pres. Civic League, Virginia Beach, Va., 1969; bd. dirs. N.E. Ga. coun. Boy Scouts Am., 1976-77; bd. dirs. Brent Soc., 1986-92, pres., 1990-91; pres. Oakton Optimist Club, 1986-87, 92-93. Decorated Disting. Service Medal, Legion Merit, Vietnamese Gallantry cross. Mem. Athens C. of C., Optimists Club, Rotary, Knights of Malta, Phi Delta Theta. Roman Catholic. Home: 10870 Meadow Pond Ln Oakton VA 22124-1446 Office: Federal Reserve Bd Washington DC 20551 *My life, both personal and professional, has been guided by allegiance to three primary areas: family, Christian faith, and the nation.*

FROST, WILLIAM LEE, lawyer; b. Larchmont, N.Y., Nov. 5, 1926; s. Charles and Eva (Rodman) F.; m. Judith Spivak, Oct. 18, 1952 (dec. 1961); children—Rebecca, Hannah; m. Susan Lasersohn, June 16, 1966; children—Abigail, Robert. B.A., Harvard U., 1947, M.P.A., 1958; LL.B., Yale U., 1951. Assoc. Sherman & Goldring, N.Y.C., 1951-52; fgn. svc. officer Dept. State, Washington, 1952-59; pvt. practice law N.Y.C., 1959—; exec. Lucius N. Littauer Found., N.Y.C., 1978—, pres., 1985—. Contbr. articles to profl. publs. Mem. Pub. Health Coun. State of N.Y., 1975-96; trustee Collegiate Sch., N.Y.C., 1980-94, Radcliffe Coll., Cambridge, Mass., 1985-89, the Brearley Sch., N.Y.C., 1977-80; chmn. bd. dirs. Jewish Telegraphic Agy., N.Y.C., 1989-93, N.Y. Heart Assn., 1985-87; chair N.Y. State Archives Partnership Trust, 1994-97, Yale Law Sch. Fund, 1994-98. With USN, 1945-46, PTO. Hon. curator of Judaica, Harvard Coll. Libr., 1985-96. Mem. Assn. of Bar of City of N.Y., N.Y. County Bar Assn., N.Y. State Bar Assn., Harvard Alumni Assn. (bd. dirs. 1985), Harvard Club, Yale Club. Avocation: walking. Office: Lucius N Littauer Found 60 E 42nd St Rm 2910 New York NY 10165-2999*

FROST, WINSTON LYLE, lawyer, educator; b. Washington, June 26, 1958; s. Lyle Gooden and Elizabeth Caddell (McLennan) F. BA in Social Sci., U. Calif., Irvine, 1979; JD, O.W. Coburn Sch. of Law, 1982; MBA, Pepperdine U., 1989; LLM in Taxation, Washington U., 1993; MA in Internat. Human Rights, Simon Greenleaf U., 1994; Diplomé Internat. Human Rights, Internat. Human Rights Inst., Strasbourg, France, 1995; MA in Faith and Culture, Trinity Internat. U., 1998; postgrad., Claremont Grad. Schs., 1998—. Bar: Ill. 1982, Calif. 1986, U.S. Dist. Ct. (cen. dist.) Calif. 1987, U.S. Supreme Ct. 1987, D.C. 1989. Pvt. practice Carthage, Ill., 1982-84; adjunct faculty Carl Sandburg Coll., Carthage, Ill., 1982-84; legal editor James Pub. Co., Costa Mesa, Calif., 1985-86; assoc. Law Offices of John Ford, Irvine, Calif., 1986-89, Hunt and Colaw, Inc., Santa Ana, Calif., 1989, Cassidy, Warner, Brown, Combs and Thurber, Santa Ana, Calif., 1989-90; ptnr. Harbin and Frost, Santa Ana, 1990—; prof. Simon Greenleaf U., Anaheim, Calif., 1987-97, asst. dean Sch. Internat. Human Rights, 1994-96; acad. dean Trinity Sch. Law, 1996-97, dean 1997—; arbitrator Orange County Superior Ct., 1992—; judge pro tem Orange County Mcpl. Ct., 1992—; mediator Christian Conciliation Svc., 1995—; columnist Brokers and Agents mag., 1997—. Editor Jour. Christian Juris, 1980-81; editorial staff Athletes in Action mag., 1986-87; columnist Orange County Reporter, 1989-91; editor Orange County Bar Jour., 1991-93. Mem. campaign staff Reagan for Pres., 1980. Recipient Outstanding Achievement award The Travelers, 1987, 88. Mem. ABA, Orange County Bar Assn. (bd. dir. 1988-90, 92-95), Orange County Bar Found. (bd. dirs. 1992-95), Orange County Trial Lawyers Assn., Orange County Barristers (bd. dirs. 1988, pres. 1990), Orange County Ins. Def. Assn. (pres. 1991), Christian Legal Soc., Calif. Trial Lawyers Assn., Peter M. Elliot Inn of Ct., Kiwanis, Toastmasters. Republican. Avocations: collecting books, poetry, community theater, travel. Office: Trinity Law Sch 2200 N Grand Santa Ana CA 92705

FROSTIC, FREDERICK LEE, strategic planning and defense policy consultant; b. Detroit; s. Frederick Ralph and Harriet Julia (Stroh) F.; children by previous marriage: Melinda Ann, Frederick Hollis; m. Dianne Kathleen Hughes, Mar. 15, 1999. BS, USAF Acad., 1963; MS in Engring., U. Mich., 1971. Comml. pilot. Fighter pilot USAF, 1963-89, asst. prof. engring. sci., 1971-74; vice comdr. 50th Tactical Fighter Wing USAF, Hahn Air Base, Germany, 1984-87; comdr. Northeast Air Def. Sector USAF, Griffiss AFB, N.Y., 1987-89; sr. engr., assoc. programming dir. RAND, Santa Monica, Calif., 1989-94; dept. asst. sec. def. Dept. Def., Washington, 1994-97; prin. Booz, Allen & Hamilton, Inc., McLean, Va., 1997—; Mem. Long Range Airpower Panel, 1998—. Author: The New Calculus, 1994. Named Outstanding Young Man Am., 1970. Democrat. Presbyterian. Avocations: sports, reading. Home: 9411 Lee Hwy Apt 1001 Fairfax VA 22031-2000 Office: Allen & Hamilton Inc 8283 Greensboro Dr Mc Lean VA 22102-3802

FROSTIC, GWEN, paper company executive; b. Sandusky, Mich., Apr. 26, 1906; d. Fred Watson and Sara (Alexander) F. A in Teaching, Eastern Mich. U., 1965; BA, Western Mich. U., 1971; LLD (hon.), Ea. Mich. U., 1965; HHD (hon.), Western Mich. U., 1971; DFA (hon.), Mich. State U., 1973; DLitt (hon.), Alma Coll., 1977. Art tchr. Deabron (Mich.) Pub. Schs., 1927-39; tool designer Ford Motor Co., Dearborn, 1940-90; pres. Presscraft Papers, Benzonia, Mich., 1991—; mem. state bd. Bus. and Profl. Women, Wyandotte, 1930-60. Author: My Michigan, 1957, A Walk With Me, 1958, These Things are Ours, 1960, A Place of Earth, 1962, To Those Who See, 1965, Wingborne, 1967, Wisps of Mist, 1969, Beyond Time, 1971, Contemplate, 1973, The Enduring Cosmos, 1976, The Infinite Destiny, 1978, The Evolving Omnity, 1981, The Caprice Immensity, 1983, Multiversality, 1985, Heuristic, 1987, Chaotic Harmony, 1989, Abysmal Acuman, 1991, Aggrandize, 1993, Synthesis, 1995, Ruminate, 1997. Recipient Southwest Mich.

Mensa award, 1981, Franfort C. of C. award, 1981, Ohio Gov.'s Youth Art Exhbn. award, 1981, Huron Valley Mich. Botanical Club award, 1982, Crooked Tree Girl Scout Coun. award, 1982, Mich. Outdoor Edn. Assn. award, 1983, Internat. Assn. Printing House Craftsmen award, 1984, Mich. Capitol Girl Scout Coun. award, 1985, Women's Nat. Farm and Garden Club award, 1986; named to Mich. Womens Hall of Fame, 1986, Jr. Achievment Bus. Hall of Fame, 1991. Mem. Nat. Fedn. Garden Club, PEO, Order Ea. Star, Alpha Delta Kappa, Delta Kappa Gamma, Omicron Nu, Alpha Sigma Tau. Republican. Home and Office: 5140 River Rd Benzonia MI 49616

FROST-KNAPPMAN, (LINDA) ELIZABETH (ELIZABETH FROST KNAPPMAN), publishing company executive; b. Washington, Oct. 1, 1943; d. Edward Laurie and Lorena (Ameter) Frost; m. Edward William Knappman, Nov. 6, 1965; 1 child, Amanda. BA, George Washington U., 1965; postgrad., U. Wis., 1966, NYU, 1966. Editor Natural History Press, N.Y.C., 1967-69, William Collins and Sons, London, 1970-71; sr. editor Doubleday and Co., N.Y.C., 1972-80, William Morrow and Co., Inc., N.Y.C., 1980-82; founder, pres. New Eng. Pub. Assocs. Inc., Chester, Conn., 1982—; lectr. New Eng. colls. and univs. Author: The World Almanac of Presidential Quotations, 1993, The ABC-CLIO Companion to Women's Progress in America, 1994 (Outstanding Acad. Book-Reference of Yr. award ALA); co-author: (under name Elizabeth Frost with David Shrager) The Quotable Lawyer, 1986, 1998, (with Kathryn Cullen-DuPont) Women Suffrage in America: An Eyewitness History, 1992, Courtroom Dramas (with Edward Knappman and Lisa Paddock, 1997; gen. editor: (CD-ROM) American Journey: Women in America, 1994, (with K. Cullen-DuPont) Women's Rights on Trial, 1998. Mem. Assn. Authors Reps., Authors Guild, Am. Soc. Journalists and Authors, Nat. Women's Press Club, Haddam Hist. Soc., Conn. Network of Entrepreneurial Women., Conn. Press Club, Conn. Author's Assn. Avocations: tennis, knitting, singing, reading. Home: 3/59 Parker Hill Rd PO Box 805 Higganum CT 06441-0805 Office: New Eng Pub Assocs Inc PO Box 5 Chester CT 06412-0005

FROTHINGHAM, THOMAS ELIOT, pediatrician; b. Boston, June 21, 1926; s. Channing and Clara Morgan (Rotch) F.; m. Phyllis Mary Steiner, June 12, 1954 (div. 1983); children: Phyllis Eliot, Thomas Dean, Banjamin Rotch, David Griffith; m. Barbara Mathis, Dec. 28, 1987. Student, Harvard U., 1944-46, MD, 1951. Intern Bellevue Hosp., N.Y.C., 1951-52; resident, rsch. fellow in infectious diseases Children's Hosp., Boston, 1955-59; asst. prof. epidemiology Tulane U. Med. Sch., 1959-60; assoc. mem. Pub. Health Rsch. Inst., City of N.Y., 1960-61; asst. prof., then assoc. prof. tropical pub. health Sch. Pub. Health Harvard U., 1961-69; pediatrician Corvallis (Oreg.) Clinic, 1969-73; prof. pediat., family and cmty. medicine Duke U. Med. Ctr., 1973-94, prof. emeritus, 1994—. Contbr. articles to profl. jours. With USNR, 1944-46, 52-55. Mem. Am. Soc. Tropical Medicine and Hygiene, Am. Acad. Pediatrics. Home: 4523 Oak Hill Rd Chapel Hill NC 27514-9732 Office: Ctr for Child and Family Health-NC 3518 Westgate Dr Ste 100 Durham NC 27707-2551

FROULA, JAMES DEWAYNE, national honor society director, engineer; b. Oak Park, Ill., May 17, 1945; s. James Clarence and Helen Barbara (Tanana) F.; m. Barbara Jean Leftwich, June 8, 1968; children: James Matthew, Anna Katherine. BSME, U. Tenn., 1967, MS, 1968. Lic. profl. engr., Tenn. Engr. IBM Corp., Lexington, Ky., 1970-74; engring. mgr. IBM Corp., Boulder, Colo., 1974-82; sec.-treas., editor Tau Beta Pi, Knoxville, Tenn., 1982—; pres. Assn. Coll. Honor Socs., 1991-93. Editor The Bent of Tau Beta Pi, 1982—; patentee magnetic brush roll. 1st lt. U.S. Army, 1968-70, Vietnam. Decorated Bronze Star; fellow Nat. Sci. Found., 1967-68. Mem. ASME, NSPE (bd. dirs. Knoxville chpt. 1988-94, Outstanding Engr. 1994), Coun. Engring. and Sci. Soc. Execs., Tenn. Soc. Profl. Engrs. (chair divsn. profl. engrs. in edn. practice 1993-96), Am. Assn. Engring. Socs. (awards com.). Roman Catholic. Avocations: mountain climbing, hiking. Office: Tau Beta Pi PO Box 2697 Knoxville TN 37901-2697

FROWICK, ROBERT HOLMES, retired diplomat; b. Des Moines, Iowa, Dec. 12, 1929; s. James E. and Hallie M. (Holmes) F.; children: R. Bren, George, Lesley, Brook; m. Ann Louise Powell, Aug. 18, 1975; stepchildren: Kristen, Kirk. BA, Ind. U., 1953, MA, 1957; MA, Yale U., 1959. Vice consul Montreal, Que., Can., 1960-62; 2d sec. Am. Embassy, Bucharest, Romania, 1964-66; 1st sec. Am. Embassy, Paris, 1969-73; dep. chief of mission Am. Embassy, Prague, Czechoslavakia, 1976-79; charge d'affaires Am. Embassy, Prague, 1978-79; polit. counselor Am. Embassy, Rome, 1979-82; polit advisor U.S. Mission to NATO, Brussels, 1982-86; amb., dep. chmn. U.S. del. to Vienna meeting of Conf. on Security and Cooperation in Europe (CSCE), 1986-89; amb., dep. chmn. U.S. del. to negotiations on confidence and security bldg. measures Conf. on Security and Cooperation in Europe (CSCE), Vienna, 1989; amb., exec. sec. N.Y. ministerial meeting to prepare Paris summit Conf. on Security and Cooperation in Europe, 1990, del. to Paris Summit, 1990; amb., head of CSCE Monitor Mission to Macedonia, 1992; exec. sec. Search for Common Ground in Macedonia, 1993-94; amb., head of U.S. del. to CSCE seminar on Early Warning Warsaw, Poland, 1994; amb. head of OSCE Mission to Bosnia and Herzogonia, Foster City, Calif., 1995—; vis. scholar Stanford U., 1989-95; mem. adv. bd. Dean of Coll. of Arts and Scis. Ind. U., 1993—. Contbr. articles on fgn. affairs to jours. Trustee St. Steven's Sch., Rome, 1979-82; chmn. sch. bd. Internat. Sch. of Prague, 1976-79. Served to 1st lt. USAF, 1953-56, to capt. USAFR. Recipient Nat. Def. Svc. medal, 1956, Superior Honor award Dept. State, 1963, 68, 75, 86, 89, Masaryk award Czechoslovak Nat. Coun. of Am., 1988, Disting. Alumni Svc. award Ind. U., 1998; Disting. Citizen fellow Ind. U. Inst. Advanced Study, 1993, Order of Njegos Pres. Plavsic, Republic Srpska, 1997. Home: 3596 Verdi Vista Dr Santa Rosa CA 95404-6235*

FRUCHTER, JONATHAN SEWELL, research scientist, geochemist; b. San Antonio, June 5, 1945; s. Benjamin and Dorothy Ann (Sewell) F.; m. Cecelia Ann Smith, Mar. 31, 1973; children: Diane, Daniel. BS in Chemistry, U. Tex., 1966; PhD in Geochemistry, U. Calif., San Diego, 1971. Research assoc. U. Oreg., Eugene, 1971-74; research scientist Battelle Northwest, Richland, Wash., 1974-79, mgr. research and devel., 1979-87, staff scientist, 1987-91, 94—, tech. group leader, 1991-94. Contbr. numerous articles to profl. jours. Mem. AAAS, Am. Chem. Soc., Phi Beta Kappa, Phi Kappa Phi. Avocations: fishing, skiing, boating. Office: Battelle NW PO Box 999 Richland WA 99352-0999

FRUDAKIS, ANTHONY PARKER, sculptor, educator; b. July 30, 1953. Cert. of completion, Pa. Acad. Fine Arts, 1976; MFA, U. Pa., 1991. tchr. Frudakis Acad. Fine Arts, Phila., 1976, Frudakis Studio, 1976—, Fashion Inst. Tech., N.Y.C., 1982, Atlantic C.C., Mays Landing, N.J., 1990-91; assoc. prof. Hillsdale (Mich.) Coll., 1991—. One-person shows include Ocean City (N.J.) Cultural Ctr., 1992, Sturgis (Mich.) Divic Ctr., 1992; exhibited in group shows NAD, N.Y.C., 1988, 91, Allied Artists Am., N.Y.C., 1982, Renaissance Gallery, Phila., 1988, Gloucester County Coll., Deptford, N.J., 1989, Grand Cen. Art Gallery, N.Y.C., 1990, 92, Toledo (Ohio) Art Mus., 1994, Nat. Scultpure Soc. N.Y., N.Y.C., 1997; represented in permanent collections Brookgreen (S.C.) Gardens Mus.; commd. Atlantic County Libr., Hammanton, N.J., 1983, Bally's Hotel, Atlantic City, N.J., 1986, Cape May Ct. House, N.J., 1989, Athens Sq., N.Y.C., 1993, Hillsdale Coll., 1992, 95 (Bronze award), St. Catherine's, Concord, Mich., 1996, St. Anthony's, Hillsdale, 1996; featured in publs. including Masters of American Sculpture, N.Y. Art Review, Sculpture. Recipient Stewardson prize Pa. Acad. Fine Arts, 1974, 1st prize for sculpture N.J. State Juried Art Show, 1979, M.B. Hexter award Allied Artists of Am., 1982, L. Miselman prize Nat. Sculpture Soc., 1986, Gloria medal, 1983, Gold medal, 1982, Lantz award, 1978, Best Portrait award, 1977; Dolfinger MacMahon tuition scholar Pa. Acad. Fine Arts, 1973; NSS tuition scholar Pa. Acad. Fine Arts, 1974; Harold Bache Found. traveling grantee, 1975. Fellow NAD (Artist Fund prize 1991), Nat. Sculpture Soc. E-mail: tony.frudakis@ac.hillsdale.edu. Studio: 36 Highland St Hillsdale MI 49242

FRUDAKIS, EVANGELOS WILLIAM, sculptor; b. Rains, Utah, May 13, 1921; s. William and Christina (Legerakis) F.; children—Anthony, Jennifer; m. Gerd Hesness, 1982. Student, Greenwich Work Shop, N.Y.C., 1935-39, Beaux Arts Inst. Design, N.Y.C., 1940-41, Pa. Acad. Fine Arts, 1941-42, 45-49, Am. Acad. in Rome, 1950-52. founder, instr. Frudakis Acad. Fine Arts, Phila., 1976-90. One-man shows include Atlantic City Art Center, 1956, 61, Woodmere Art Gallery, 1957, 62, Phila. Art Alliance, 1958, Pa. Acad. Fine Arts, 1962, Briarcliff Coll. Mus. Art, 1975, numerous group shows, 1940—, including, Pa. Acad. Fine Arts anns., N.A.D. anns., Am. Acad. in Rome, Audubon Artists, Phila. Mus. Art, Allied Artists Am., Nat. Arts Club, Pennsylvania Treasures show, Gov.'s Mansion, 1982; represented in permanent collections Pa. Acad. Fine Arts, Lehigh Valley Art Alliance, Woodmere Art Gallery, also pvt. collections; tchr., demonstrator sculpture, Nat. Acad. Design, N.Y.C., 1969-76, sculptor John F. Kennedy meml. monument Atlantic City Conv. Hall, 1964, Statesmen in Medicine Awards; portrait works Brian Brewer Blades, 1969, Melvin R. Laird, 1970, Barnes Woodhall, 1971, Aharon Katzir and Ephraim Katzir for Weizmann Inst., Israel, 1978, Dr. William Feinbloom, Pa. Coll. Optometry, 1989, Stephen E. Hyde, Trump Castle, Atlantic City, 1990; coins and medals Ted Shawn and Ruth St. Denis medal, Jacobs Pillow, Mass., Gemini Space Flights Nat. Commemorative Soc, 1966, Dacron medallion, Dupont, Wilmington, Del., Capt. James Cook medal, Hawaii Festival, Dolly Madison coin, medal Sociéte Commemorative de Femmes Celebres, 1967, Joseph Brant coin, Internat. Fraternal Commemorat Soc., 1968, Paul Lawrence Dunbar medal, Am. Negro Commemorative Soc., 1969, St. Damasus I medal, Cath. Commemorative Soc., Life of Christ series 12 coin medals, 1968-70, Alfred the Great medal, Britannia Commemorative Soc., 1970, Prince of Peace medal, Cath. Commemorative Soc., Scapular medal, Cath. Art Guild, 1970, St. John the 4th Apostle 12 Apostle series, Cath. Commemorative Medal Soc., 1970, John Quincy Adams and Lillian Wald medals, Hall of Fame for Great Ams., 1971, Brian Brewer Blades award medal Statesmen in Medicine, 1970, Richardson Dilworth Meml. Plaque, Phila., 1978, Deng Xioping Portrait Medal, 1979, Fishing Bear fountain, Phila. Zool. Gardens., The Signer, Independence Nat. Hist. Park, Phila., 1982, Naiad Fountain, Phila. Civic Ctr., 1982, Statue of Liberty Greek Relief, Ellis Island, 1986; Welcome Fountain, The Ritten House, Phila., 1989, The Minute Man, Nat. Guard Bld., Washington, 1991, 9' Minute Man, Nat. Guard Readiness Ctr., Arlington, Va., 1995, Reaching Fountain, Brookgreen Gardens, S.C., 1997; mem. coins and medals Art Commn., Atlantic City,. Served with AUS, World War II, ETO. Recipient 2 1st prizes Greenwich Work Shop 1939, Beaux Art Inst. 1941, 1st Julian B. Slevin prize Pa. Acad. Fine Arts 1941, Stimson prize 1947, Stewardson prize 1947, Cresson European scholarship 1947, spl. citation achievement 1948, 1st hon. mention fellowship 1948, Fellowship gold medal 1949, 55, 56, Henry Scheidt Meml. scholarship 1949, 1st hon. mention Prix de Rome 1942, Prix de Rome 1950, 51, Helen Foster Barnett prize N.A.D. 1948, Thomas R. Proctor prize 1957, Eben Demarest Trust Fund prize 1949, Louis Comfort Tiffany scholarship 1949, Sculpture House award Allied Artists Am. 1959, best portrait sculpture award Nat. Sculpture Soc.-Nat. Art Club 1961, John Gregory award Nat. Sculpture Soc. 1963, Nat. Fountain Competition award Little Rock 1965, Elizabeth N. Watrous gold medal N.A.D., N.Y.C. 1968, Dessie Greer prize N.A.D., N.Y.C. 1970, Artists Fund prize 1975, 77, 90, Therese and Edwin H. Richards prize Nat. Sculpture Soc., N.Y. 1972, Gold medal 1972, Francis Keally prize 1974, Herbert Adams Meml. medal 1976), N.S.S. Meiselman prize, 1981; gold medal NAD, 1984. N.A. Fellow Pa. Acad. Fine Arts, Am. Acad. in Rome, Nat. Sculpture Soc. (council), founding mem. Acad. Scis. Phila.; mem. Allied Artists Am.; hon. mem. Am. Inst. Commemorative Art. Address: 312 Valley Dr Kerrville TX 78028-3910

FRUDAKIS, ZENOS ANTONIOS, sculptor, artist; b. San Francisco, July 7, 1951; s. Vasili and Kassiani (Alexis) F.; m. Rosalie Gluchov, Jan. 9, 1976. Student, Pa. Acad. Fine Arts, Phila., 1973-76; BFA, U. Pa., 1982, MFA, 1983. Co-adj. prof. sculpture and drawing Rutgers U., 1984-85, 1993; guest lectr. anatomy and sculpture Med. Coll. Pa., Phila., 1986-87, Scottsdale (Ariz.) Artist's Sch., 1990; invited artist Utsukushi-Ga-Hara Open Air Mus., Japan, 1990. Exhbns include Nat. Sculpture Soc., 1979-97, Allied Artists Am., N.Y.C., 1980-81, NAD, N.Y.C., 1980, 84, 86, 90, 97, Pa. Acad. Fine Arts, 1981, Inst. Contemporary Art, Phila., 1981-83, Rutgers U., 1984-86; numerous commd. works including Irish Wolfhound and Wolf, Brookgreen Gardens, S.C., busts of Sir Paul Girolami, N.C., London, Japan, bust of Martin Luther King Jr. Am. Embassy, Pretoria, South Africa, figure sculpture Nobel Found. Sweden, figure sculptures Utsukushi-ga-hara Open Air Mus. Japan, figure sculptures Capitol Ctr. Pla. Indpls., bas-reliefs Emory Univ. Atlanta, Workers Meml. Bethlehem, Pa., 1991, Fritz Brennan statue Lower Merion, Pa., 1992, Richardson Dilworth Monumental Relief Dilworth Internat. Airport, Phila., Pa., 1992, Richard Tufts statue, Pinehurst Resort N.C., 1993, K. Leroy Irvis, State Mus., Harrisburg, Pa., 1993, Dinah Shore statue Mission Hills Resort, Rancho Mirage, Calif., Mark Twain, Lotos Club, N.Y.C., Father Athenagoras Cavadas, Former Mayor Frank Rizzo, Phila., Anthracite Coal Miner's Meml., Shenandoah,Pa., Gov. Ellis Arnall Ga. State House. Recipient Hakone award, Rodin Grand prize Hakone Open Air Mus., Japan, 1990; inducted into Arnold Palmer, Bobby Jones, Ga. Golf Hall of Fame; devel. grantee Nat. Endowment for Arts, 1985, USIA travelling grantee, 1988-89. Fellow Nat. Sculpture Soc. (bd. dirs. 1988—, Art-in-Architecture award 1990, editor pro-tem Nat. Sculpture Rev. 1991-92); mem. NAD (acad.), Academia Internat. per L'Unita della Cultura (Rome, academician), Lotos Club. Home: 2355 Mount Carmel Ave Glenside PA 19038-4103

FRUEH, BARTLEY RICHARD, surgeon; b. Cleve., Sept. 1, 1937; s. Lloyd Walter and Elizabeth Virginia (Scott) F.; m. Frances Olive Beach, June 10, 1961 (div. Dec. 1976); children: Bartley Christopher, Dylan Beach (dec.), Walter Terry; m. Frances Mallet-Prevost Gaston Sargent, Dec. 31, 1976 (div. July 1997); stepchildren: Eric Winslow Sargent, Laura Elizabeth Sargent. BChemE, Cornell U., 1960; MD, Columbia Coll. Phys./Surgeons, 1964; MS Ophthalmology, U. Mich., 1970. Diplomate Am. Bd. Ophthalmology. Surg. intern N.C. Meml. Hosp., Chapel Hill, N.C., 1964-65; resident in ophthalmology U. Mich., Ann Arbor, 1967-70; fellow eye plastic surgery Alston Callahan, Birmingham, Ala., 1970; asst. prof. ophthalmology, eye plastic surgery U. Mo., Columbia, 1971-72, asst. clin. prof. ophthalmology eye plastic surgery, 1972-76, assoc. clin. prof. ophthalmology eye plastic surgery, 1976-79; pvt. practice, ophthalmology Columbia, 1972-79; assoc. prof. ophthalmology, eye plastic and orbital surgery U. Mich., Ann Arbor, 1979-86, prof. ophthalmology, 1986—; cons. med. staff U. Mo. Med. Ctr., Columbia, 1971-79, Meml. Hosp., Jefferson City, 1971-73, Boone County Hosp., Columbia, 1972-79, Harry S. Truman Meml. Vet.'s Hosp., Columbia, 1971-79; med. staff Columbia Regional Hosp., Columbia, 1974-79, U. Mich. Med. Ctr., 1979—, VA Med. Ctr., 1979—; lectr. in field. Author: Transactions, American Ophthalmological Society, 1984; editor/author: Surgery of the Eye, 1988; editl. bd.: Ophthalmic Surgery, 1980-87, Am. Acad. Ophthalmology Clin. Modules, 1983-86, Ophthalmic Plastic and Reconstructive Surgery, 1984—, Orbit; contbr. articles to profl. jours./publs., books in field. Capt. USAF, 1965-67, Taiwan. Grantee in field. Fellow Am. Acad. Ophthalmology (Wendell Hughes lectr. 1993, Sr. Honor award 1990); mem. Am. Soc. Ophthal. Plastic and Reconstructive Surgery (sec. 1973-74, pres. 1976), Am. Ophthalmol. Soc., Orbital Soc., Ptosis Rsch. Soc. Avocations: pocket billiards, Model T Fords and old Morgans, wine, violin. Office: WK Kellogg Eye Ctr U Mich 1000 Wall St Ann Arbor MI 48105-1912*

FRUEHWALD, KRISTIN G., lawyer; b. Sidney, Nebr., May 15, 1946; d. Chris U. and Mary E. (Boles) Bitner; m. Michael R. Fruehwald, Feb. 23, 1980; children: Laurel Elizabeth, Amy Marie. BS with highest distinction in History, U. Nebr., 1968; JD summa cum laude, Ind. U., 1975. Bar: Ind. 1975, U.S. Dist. Ct. (so. dist.) Ind. 1975. Assoc. Barnes & Thornburg, Indpls., 1975-81, ptnr., 1982—; speaker in field. Contbr. articles to profl. jours. Bd. dirs. Indpls. Parks Found., 1995—, Arts Ind., 1994-98, Ind. Continuing Legal Edn. Forum, 1993—, treas.; bd. dirs. James Whitcomb Riley Meml. Assn., 1995—, asst. treas., 1999—; bd. dirs. Planned Giving Group Ind.; bd. dirs. Ind. Fedn. Cmty. Defenders, Inc., 1993-99; bd. dirs. Indpls. Bar Found., 1992—, chmn., 1997-99; bd. dirs. Ind. affiliate Am. Heart Assn., 1977-81, vice chmn. Marion County chpt., 1981; trustee The Orchard Sch., 1993—, chmn., 1997, 98. Fellow ABA (chmn. distributable net income subcom. 1985-91, sect. taxation, mem. com. adminstrn. decendant's estates, mem. com. significant current legislation, real property, probate and trust sect.), Am. Coll. Trust and Estate Counsel (chmn. Ind. state laws com. 1992-95), Ind. Bar Found., Ind. State Bar Assn. (bd. mgrs. 1989-90, chmn. probate, trust and real property sects. 1987-88, mem. sect. taxation, mem. ho. of dels. 1987—, treas. 1996-97, chair ho. of dels. 1998-99); mem. Indpls. Bar Assn. (pres. 1993, chmn. estate planning and adminstrn. sect. 1982-83, chmn. long range fin. planning com. 1988-89), Indpls. Estate Planning Coun., Internat. Assn. Fin. Planners, Ind. Probate Code Study Commn. Office: Barnes & Thornburg 11 S Meridian St Ste 1313 Indianapolis IN 46204-3519

FRÜHBECK DE BURGOS, RAFAEL, conductor; b. Burgos, Spain, Sept. 15, 1933; s. Guillermo and Estefania (Ochs) F.; m. Maria Carmen Martinez, Dec. 21, 1959; children: Rafael, Gema. Attended, Bilbao Conservatory, Madrid Conservatory, High Sch. for Music, Munich, Germany, U. Munich, Richard Strauss Price, 1958, U. Madrid; dr. honoris causa, U. Navarra, Pamplona, Spain, 1994, U. Burgos, Spain, 1998. Chief condr. Mcpl. Orch., Bilbao, Spain, 1958-62, Nat. Orch., Madrid, 1962-78; gen. musik dir. Düsseldorfer Symphony, Germany, 1966-71; music dir. Montreal Symphony, Can., 1974-76, Vienna Symphony, Vienna, Austria, 1991-96, Deutsche Oper, Berlin, 1992-97, Rundfunk Symphony Orch., Berlin, 1994—; prin. guest condr. Nat. Symphony, Washington, 1980-90, Yomiuri Nippon Symphony Orch., Tokyo, 1980-90, hon. condr. 1991; hon. condr. Nat. Orch., Madrid, 1998. Decorated Encomienda de la Orden de Alfonso X, El Sabio, Gran Cruz de la Orden del Mérito Civil (Spain); Ehrenmedaille in Gold Bürgermeister, Vienna, gold medal to the Civil Merit of Austria; recipient prize of mus. interpretation Larios-CEOE Found., 1992, gold medal Internat. Gustav Mahler Soc., Vienna, 1996, Fundacion Guerrero prize of Spanish Music, Madrid, 1996. Mem. Real Acad. de Bellas Artes de San Fernando (Madrid). Office: care Vitoria, Sagasta 3, 28004 Madrid Spain also: Shaw Concerts Inc 1900 Broadway New York NY 10023-7004 also: care Harold Holt Ltd, 122 Wigmore St, London W1H ODJ, England

FRUIT, J. CURTIS, municipal court clerk; b. Norfolk, Va.. BA, Old Dominion U., 1973; cert. circuit ct. clk., U. Va., 1993. Dep. officer Office of the Clk. of the Circuit Ct., Virginia Beach, Va., 1964-80; circuit ct. clk. City of Virginia Beach, 1980—. Mem. Va. Ct. Clks. Assn. (pres. 1993-94). Office: City of Virginia Beach 2305 Judicial Blvd Virginia Beach VA 23456-9122*

FRUITMAN, FREDERICK HOWARD, investment banker; b. Toronto, Oct. 8, 1950; s. Herbert Lance and Libby (Kamin) F.; m. Marlin Sue Potash, Nov. 21, 1981 (div. Dec. 1996); children: Laura, Hilary; m. Susan Beth Levinsohn, Apr. 19, 1998. SB, MIT, 1972; BA, Oxford (Eng.) U., 1974, MA, 1981; LLB, U. Toronto, 1976; MBA, Harvard U., 1981. Assoc. Davies, Ward & Beck, Toronto, 1976-77, Merrill Lynch White Weld Capital Markets Group, N.Y.C., 1978-79; cons. Bain & Co., Boston, 1981-82; v.p. Investors in Industry Corp., Boston, 1982-84; assoc. E.M. Warburg, Pincus & Co. Inc., N.Y.C., 1984-86; sr. v.p. The Stuart James Co. Inc., N.Y.C., 1986-89; mng. dir. Loeb Ptnrs. Corp., N.Y.C., 1990—; bd. dirs. FIND/SVP, Inc., Micro Warehouse, Inc. Mem. Law Soc. Upper Can., Can. Soc. of N.Y., Harvard Club (N.Y.C). Office: Loeb Ptnrs Corp 61 Broadway New York NY 10006-2701

FRUMKES, LEWIS BURKE, writer, educator; b. Bklyn., May 10, 1939; s. Harry William and Beatrice Teresa (Burke) F.; m. Alana June Martin, Oct. 30, 1965; children: Timothy, Amber. BA, NYU, 1962, MA, 1994. Host Lewis Burke Frumkes show RadionSta. WNWK, N.Y.C., 1987—; Pres. disting. vis. lectr. Marymount Manhattan Coll. Writing Ctr., N.Y.C., 1992—, dir., 1995—; vis. prof. Harvard U., Cambridge, Mass., 1988-91; speaker in field. Author: How to Raise Your I.Q. by Eating Gifted Children, 1983, The Mensa Think-Smart Book, 1986, Name Crazy, 1987, Manhattan cocktail, 1989, Meta- Punctuation,1993, the Logophiles Orgy, 1995; mem. editl. bd. The Writer Mag. Mem. am. soc. Journalists and Authors, PEN, Nat. Arts Club, Harvard Club, Coffee House. Avocations: science, magic. Office: Marymount Manhattan coll 221 E 71st St New York NY 10021-4501

FRUMKIN, ALLAN, art dealer; b. Chgo., July 5, 1926; s. Joseph and Libbie F.; m. Jean Martin; children: Robert, Peter. Ph.B., U. Chgo., 1946. Owner and dir. Allan Frumkin Gallery, Chgo., 1952-80, N.Y.C., 1959-90; pres. Frumkin/Adams Gallery, Inc., N.Y.C., 1990-95; pvt. art dealer N.Y.C., 1995—. Recipient U. Chgo. ALumni Assn. Profl. Achievement award, 1981. Home and Office: 1185 Park Ave New York NY 10128-1308

FRUMKIN, SIMON, political activist and columnist; b. Kaunas, Lithuania, Nov. 5, 1930; came to U.S., 1949; s. Nicholas and Zila (Oster) F.; m. Rhoda Hirsch, June 1953 (div. 1978); children: Michael Alan, Larry Martin; m. Kathy Elizabeth Hoopes, June 22, 1981 (dec. 1994); m. Ella Zousman, Dec. 11, 1995. BA, NYU, 1953; MA in History, Calif. State U., Northridge, 1964. Pres., chief exec. officer Universal Drapery Fabrics, Inc., Los Angeles, 1953-87; chmn. Southern Calif. Council for Soviet Jews, Studio City, 1969—; lectr. Simon Wiesenthal Ctr. for Holocaust Studies, Los Angeles, 1980—; chmn. Union of Councils for Soviet Jews, 1972-73. Columnist Heritage, numerous other So. Calif. newspapers, 1980—; corr. to columnist Panorama, U.S.A. Russian Lang., 1985—; contbr. articles to newspapers. Pres. Media Analysis Found., Los Angeles, 1988; chmn. Ams. for Peace and Justice, 1972-74; mem. Pres.' Senatorial Inner Circle, U.S. Senatorial Club. Honored by Calif. Govt., Los Angeles City Council, Los Angeles Office of City Atty., numerous Jewish orgns. Mem. Assn. Soviet Jewish Emigre's (pres. 1987—), Zionist Orgn. Am., Am. Israel Polit. Action Com., Russian Republican Club, Mensa. Avocations: writing, photography, skiing, fitness. Home and Office: 3755 Goodland Ave Studio City CA 91604-2313

FRUNDT, HENRY JOHN, sociologist, educator; b. Blue Earth, Minn., May 22, 1940; s. John Henry and Mary Ellen (Kane) F.; m. Bette Jule Swatzki, June 13, 1970; children: Michael, Laura, James, Daniel, Janine, Paul. BA, St. Louis U., 1964, MA, PhL, 1967; PhD, Rutgers U., 1975. Tchr. Creighton Prep. Sch., Omaha, 1965-68; program developer U.S. Dept. Labor, Omaha, 1969; instr. sociology U. Wis., Superior, 1969-71; cons. UN, N.Y.C., 1978-85; prof. sociology Ramapo Coll., Mahwah, N.J., 1973—, dir. sch. social sci., assoc. dean, 1989-93; convenor Latin Am. studies Ramapo Coll., Mahwah, 1995—; rsch. assoc. conservation of human resources Columbia U., N.Y.C., 1980-82; rsch. assoc. inter-Am. devel. program Am. U., Washington, 1982-84; Fulbright lectr. U. Rafael Landivar, Guatemala City, 1987-88. Author: Agribusiness Manual, 1978, Refreshing Pauses, 1987, Trade Conditions and Labor Rights, 1998; contbr. articles to profl. jours. Co-chair N.J. Labor Com. on Ctrl. Am., 1987-93; bd. dirs. U.S./Guatemala Labor Edn. Project, 1990—; choral singer N.J. Oratorio Soc., Essex County, N.J., 1994—; commr. commn. on disarmament edn. UN, 1995—. Orgn. Am. States fellow, 1982, Faculty fellow NYU, 1996-97. Mem. Latin Am. Studies Assn., Guatemala Scholars Network, Am. Fedn. Tchrs. (local pres. 1984-87, coun. del. 1997—). Roman Catholic. Office: Ramapo Coll Mahwah NJ 07430

FRUNGILLO, NICHOLAS ANTHONY, JR., accountant; b. Newark, N.J., Sept. 8, 1960; s. Nicholas Anthony and Marie Theresa (Russo) F.; m. Mary Margaret LaMonica, May 11, 1985. BA, Rutgers U., 1982. CPA, N.J. Staff acct. Besser, Colner, Herbst C. Lustbader CPAs, West Orange, N.J., 1981-82, Magla Products Inc, Irvington, N.J., 1982-83; sr. v.p., corp. treas., CFO United Counties Bancorp., Cranford, N.J., 1983-96; CFO Biodynamics Internat. Inc., Parsippany, N.J., 1997-98; sr. v.p., treas., CFO The Town Bank of Westfeield, N.J. Mem. AICPA, Bankers Adminstrn. Inst., N.J. State Soc. CPAs. Roman Catholic. Avocations: archery, golf, swimming, fishing, baseball. Home: 1571 Rising Way Mountainside NJ 07092-1600 Office: Town Bank of Westfield PO Box 220 520 South Ave W Westfield NJ 07090-1402

FRUSETTA, JAMES WALTER, historian; b. Arlington Heights, Ill., June 7, 1971; s. Walter James Frusetta and Joan Ellen Crow-Epps. B History, U. So. Calif., 1992, B Internat. Rels., 1992; M History, Ariz. State U., 1996; postgrad., U. Md., 1996—. Opinion editor State Press, Tempe, Ariz., 1993-95; grad. asst. Ariz. State U., Tempe, 1994-95; fellow U. Md., College Park, 1996-98; rschr. Navigator Pub., Olympia, Wash., 1996-99; Ariz. State U. exch. fellow U. Sts. Cyril and Methodius, 1995-96. Lang. grantee Am. Coun. Learned Socs., 1995, Irex Sead grantee, 1999, Flas grantee, 1998; fellow Nat. Security Edn. Program, 1995-96, 99—. Mem. Am. Assn. for Advancement of Slavic Studies, Internat. Studies Assn., Phi Beta Kappa, Phi Kappa Phi, Phi Alpha Theta. Home: PO Box 801 Sterling AK 99672-0801

FRUSTI, DOREEN KAYE, nursing administrator. BSN summa cum laude, Augustana Coll., 1970; MS in Ednl. Psychology and Counseling, Winona State U., 1979, postgrad., 1988—. RN, Minn. Developer, implementor group therapy program acute psychiat. unit McKennan Hosp., Sioux Falls, S.D., 1970; asst. head nurse gen. surgery Rochester (Minn.) Meth. Hosp., 1970-73, head nurse nephrology and renal transplant, 1973-78, instr. electrocardiology, 1975, asst. DON, 1978-83, mem. facility and program devel. chem. dependence svcs., 1981-83, mem. adminstrv. com., 1983-85, mem. lab. medicine study, 1978, mem. weekened phys. medicine feasibility study, 1978-79, mem. liason com., 1978-80, mem. hospice feasibility study, 1978-82, clin. DIN, 1978-91, mem. mgmt. coun., 1987—, mem. clean air task force com., 1986-87, mem. tornado and disaster coms., 1986-88, mem. nursing info. system steering com., 1987-91, joint head nurse planning com., 1988-91, chair dept. nursing, 1991—; grad. intern supr. Winona (Minn.) State U., 1983-88; co-instr. chem. dependence course Rochester Community Coll., 1985; cons. Meth. Hosp. Indpls., 1989; adj. asst. prof. St. Mary's Coll., Winona, 1986—; mem. cons. com. on alcoholism and drug dependence unit Mayo Clinic, 1980-91, adminstrv. mgmt. com., 1983-88, adolescent chem. dependence unit, 1984-88, mgmt. forum, 1988—, coordinating com., 1988-90, smoking cessation program com. Mayo Med. Ctr., 1985-89, smoke free implementation task force, 1987; cons. Genesee Hosp., Rochester, N.Y., 1989. Mem. hypertension screening program Bethel Luth. Ch., 1976, stewardship com., 1976-78, usher, 1985—, group discussion facilitator, 1985-90, chair, 1986-89, chair pers. and exec. coms., 1987-89, capt., 1988—, lead usher, 1991—; del. dist. conv. Am. Luth. Ch., 1987; del. synodical conv. Evang. Luth. Ch. Am., 1988; chair Outpatient Observation Task Force, 1990-91, steering com. Nursing Ops. Assessment, 1990-91, Incident Report Task Force, 1990-91, Allied Health, 1992—; mem. Bread of the World, 1989—; mem. ops. bd. dirs. Probation Offenders Rehab. and Tng., 1987-90, chair pers. com., 1988-90; supr. Roundtable, 1992—. Mem. Dist. F Orgn. Nurse Execs., Am. Orgn. Nurse Execs., Minn. Orgn. Nurse Execs., Minn. Nurses Assn. (del. 1971, 77, 81, 83, program com. 6th dist. 1973-75, chairperson, 1975-77, adv. bd. com., pres. 1977-79, long range planning com. 1978-79, entry level task force 1981, nursing svc. adminstrn. exec. and legis. coms. 1981-82, nominating com. 1981-83), Sigma Theta Tau (Kappa Mu chpt.). Home: 2100 Valkyrie Dr NW Apt 108 Rochester MN 55901-2451 Office: Rochester Meth Hosp 201 W Center St Rochester MN 55902-3065*

FRY, ALBERT JOSEPH, chemistry educator; b. Phila., May 12, 1937; s. Russell Mayne and Margaret (McCann) F.; m. Melissa Grant Betton, July 30, 1966; children: Anne Margaret, Peter, Jonathan. B.S., U. Mich., 1958; Ph.D., U. Wis., 1963; M.A., Wesleyan U., 1978. Postdoctoral fellow Calif. Inst. Tech., Pasadena, 1963-64; postdoctoral fellow Wesleyan U., Middletown, Conn., 1964-65, asst. prof., 1965-72, assoc. prof., 1972-77; prof. chemistry Wesleyan U., Middletown, 1977—, E.B. Nye prof. chemistry, 1993—. Author: Synthetic Organic Electrochemistry, 1972, 2d edit., 1989; editor: Topics in Organic Electrochemistry, 1986; contbr. articles to profl. jours. Fellow Chem. Soc. London; mem. Am. Chem. Soc., Conn. Acad. Sci. and Engring., Sigma Xi, Alpha Chi Sigma, Phi Lambda Upsilon. Roman Catholic. Home: 116 Maple Shade Rd Middletown CT 06457-5188 Office: Wesleyan Univ Dept Chemistry Middletown CT 06459

FRY, ANNE EVANS, zoology educator; b. Phila., Sept. 11, 1939; d. Kenneth Evans and Nora Irene (Smith) F. AB, Mount Holyoke Coll., 1961; MS, U. Iowa, 1963; PhD, U. Mass., 1969. Instr. Carleton Coll., Northfield, Minn., 1963-65; asst. prof. Ohio Wesleyan U., Delaware, 1969-74, assoc. prof., 1974-80, prof., 1980—. Contbr. articles to profl. jours. Recipient Welch Teaching award Ohio Wesleyan U., 1976. Mem. AAAS, Am. Inst. Biol. Scis., Soc. for Integrative and Comparative Biology, Ohio Acad. Sci., Soc. Devel. Biology, Sigma Xi. Office: Ohio Wesleyan U Delaware OH 43015

FRY, CATHERINE HOWARD, publishing executive; b. Vicksburg, Miss., Jan. 6, 1952; d. Z.B. and Letty (Lassiter) F. BS, La. State U., 1974, MA, 1977. Dir. Baton Rouge Eye Bank, 1977-79; promotion mgr. La. State U. Press, Baton Rouge, 1979-83, mktg. mgr., 1983-89, asst. dir., mktg. mgr., 1989-94, assoc. dir., mktg. dir., 1994-95; dir. U. S.C. Press, Columbia, 1995—; adj. prof. Manship Sch. Mass. Comm. La. State U., 1994; faculty mem. Acad. Scholarly Pub., Charleston, 1996, New Orleans Writers Conf., 1990; spkr. in field. Mem. Assn. Am. Univ. Presses (chair mktg. workshop 1987, mem. mktg. com. 1983-84, chair mktg. com. 1986-87, nominating com. 1992-93, chair equal opportunity com. 1993-95), Pubs. Assn. South (bd. dirs. 1984-87), S.C. Hist. Soc., Thomas Cooper Soc. (program com. 1995-96, bd. dirs. 1997—), S.C. Book Festival (bd. dir. 1997—), Jr. League Columbia (sustaining), Mortar Bd. Alumni Assn., Omicron Delta Kappa, Chi Omega (La. State day chmn. 1980, pres. Baton Rouge Alumni Assn. 1979-80, advisor Phi Gamma chpt.). Democrat. Episcopalian. Office: U SC Press 937 Assembly St Fl 8 Columbia SC 29201-3937

FRY, CHARLES GEORGE, theologian, educator; b. Piqua, Ohio, Aug. 15, 1936; s. Sylvan Jack and Lena Freda (Ehle) F. BA, Capital U., 1958; MA, Ohio State U., 1961, PhD, 1965; BD, Evang. Lutheran Theol. Sem., 1962, MDiv, 1977; DMin, Winebrenner Theol. Sem., 1978. Ordained to ministry Lutheran Ch. U.S.A, 1963. Pastor St. Mark's Luth. Ch. and Martin Luther Luth. Ch., Columbus, Ohio, 1961-62, 63-66; instr. Wittenberg U., 1962-63, 71-72; instr. Capital U., 1963-75, asst. prof. history and religion, 1966-69, assoc. prof., 1969-75; theologian-in-residence North Community Luth. Ch., Columbus, 1971-73; assoc. prof. hist. theology, dir. missions edn. Concordia Theol. Sem., Ft. Wayne, Ind., 1975-84; sr. minister First Congl. Ch., Detroit, 1984-85; Protestant chaplain St. Francis Coll., Fort Wayne, 1982-92; prof. philosophy and theology Luth. Coll. of Health Professions, Ft. Wayne, 1992-98, U. St. Francis, Ft. Wayne, 1998-99; interim min. Arbor Grove Congl. Ch., Jackson, Mich., 1980, hon. minister emeritus 1996, First Presbyn. Ch., Huntington, Ind., 1988-89, St. Luke's Luth. Ch., Ft. Wayne, 1989-90, Mt. Pleasant Luth. Ch., 1990-91, St. Mark's Luth. Ch., 1990-91, Mt. Zion Luth. Ch., Ft. Wayne, 1991-93; interim min. Cmty. Christian Ch., New Carlisle, Ind., 1993-94, First Luth. Ch., Stryker, Ohio, 1994-97, Zion Luth. Ch., West Jefferson, Ohio, 1994-97, Agape Congl. Ch., Bowling Green, Ohio, 1997-98; vis. prof. Damavand Coll., Tehran, 1973-74, bd. dirs., 1976-94; vis. prof. Ref. Bible Coll., 1975-80, Concordia Luth. Sem. at Brock U., summers 1977, 79, Grad. Sch. Christian Min., Huntington (Ind.) Coll., 1986-89, Wheaton Coll., 1987-88; vis. scholar Al Ain U., United Arab Emirates, 1987; theologian-in-residence, tchg. theologian Queentown Luth. Ch., Singapore, 1991, 99; adj. faculty history Ind. U./Purdue U., Ft. Wayne, 1982-98, Winebrenner Theol. Sem., Findlay, Ohio, 1992, Holy Trinity Coll. and Sem., 1999—; pastor-in-residence Wittenberg U., Springfield, Ohio, 1992, Deaconess Cmty. Evang. Luth. Ch. Am., Phila., 1993; min. Zion Luth. Ch., Montpelier, Ohio, 1998—. Author books including Age of Lutheran Orthodoxy, 1979, Lutheranism in America, 1979, Islam, 1980, 2d edit. 1982, The Way, The Truth, The Life, 1982, Great Asian Religions, 1984, Francis: A Call to Conversion, 1988, Brit. edit., 1990, The Middle East: A History, 1988, Congregationalists and Evolution: Asa Gray and Louis Agassiz, 1989, Pioneering a Theology of Evolution: Washington Gladden and Pierre Teilhard de Chardin, 1989, Avicenna's Philosophy of Education: An Introduction, 1990, Explorations in Protestant Theology, 1992, Life's Little Lessons, 1997, Kant's Three Questions, 1997, Four Little Words, 1997, others; co-producer Global Perspectives, IPFW-TV, Ft. Wayne, 1987-97. Bd. dirs. Luth. Liturgical Renewal, 1983-90, 94—; v.p. Internat. Luth. Fellowship, 1995-98, pres., 1998—; consecrated bishop, so. region Internat. Luth. Fellowship, 1996; assoc. St. Augustine's Fellowship, 1996—; bd. dirs. Zwemer Inst., Ft. Wayne, Ind., 1997—. Recipient Praestantia award Capital U., 1970, Concordia Hist. Inst. citation, 1977, Archbishop Robert Leighton award Nat. Anglican Ch., 1997; Regional Coun. for Internat. Edn. rsch. grantee, 1969; Joseph J. Malone postdoctoral fellow Egypt, 1986, Malone postdoctoral fellow, United Arab Emirates, 1987. Fellow Brit. Interplanetary Soc.; mem. Am. Hist. Assn., Am. Acad. Religion, Mid. East Inst. Gen. Soc. War of 1812 (compatriot 1994—, chaplain Ohio chpt. 1996—), Ohio Soc. (chaplain 1996—), Phi Alpha Theta. Democrat. Home: 158 W Union St Circleville OH 43113-1965 Office: Internat Luth Fellowship 387 E Brandon Dr Bismarck ND 58501

FRY, CLARENCE HERBERT, retail executive; b. Pottstown, Pa., June 27, 1926; s. Clarence H. and Rosa B. (Savage) F.; m. Barbara Ruth McGuire, Aug. 28, 1950; children: James Nathan, David Andrew, Joel Timothy, Ann Elizabeth. B.S. magna cum laude, Syracuse U., 1950. C.P.A., Pa. Accountant Peat, Marwick, Mitchell & Co., Phila., 1950-56; supr. Peat, Marwick, Mitchell & Co., 1956-60, mgr., 1960-69; controller Acme Markets, Inc. (now Am. Stores Co.), Phila., 1969-73; chief acctg. officer Am. Stores Group Services, Inc., Phila., 1974-78; controller Am. Stores Group Services, Inc., 1974-75, v.p., 1975-78; v.p., controller Am. Stores Co., Wilmington, Del., 1979; v.p. controller Am. Stores Co., Wilmington, 1979-80; v.p., controller Acme Markets, Inc. subs. Am. Stores Co., Phila., 1980-83, sr. v.p., treas., controller, 1983-87; sr. v.p. fin. Am. Superstores Inc. subs. Am. Stores Co., Wilmington, 1987-89; ret., 1990; mem. food merchandisers LIFO adv. com. Food Mktg. Inst., 1975-82. Served with 69th Inf. Div. AUS, 1944-46. Mem. AICPA, Pa. Inst. CPAs, Chester County Hist. Soc.; pres. Tredyffrin-Easttown History Club, 1992-95, editor quar., 1996—. Presbyterian. Avocations: historical research, motorsports. Home: 519 Daventry Rd Berwyn PA 19312-1740

FRY, DONALD LEWIS, physiologist, educator; b. Des Moines, Dec. 29, 1924; s. Clair V. and Maudie (Long) F.; children—Donald Stewart, Ronald Sinclair, Heather Elise, Laurel Virginia. M.D., Harvard U., 1949. Rsch. fellow Univ Minn Hosp., Mpls., 1952-53; sr. asst. surgeon gen. NIH, Bethesda, Md., 1953-56; surgeon NIH, 1956-57, sr. surgeon, 1957-61, med. dir., 1961-80; prof. Ohio State U., Columbus, 1980—. Contbr. numerous articles and papers on physiology and biophysics of pulmonary mechanics, blood vascular interface, transvascular mass transport and the genesis of atherosclerosis to profl. jours., books. Mem. AAAS, Am. Physiol. Soc., Am. Soc. Clin. Investigation, Biophys. Soc., N.Y. Acad. Scis. Office: Ohio State U Coll Medicine 2025 Wiseman Hall 400 W 12th Ave Columbus OH 43210-1214

FRY, DONALD OWEN, broadcasting company executive; b. Headlee, Ind., Mar. 5, 1921; s. George Mason and Nima E. (Ulrey) F.; m. Phyllis Amy McMillan, Feb. 2, 1947. B.S., Calif. Coll. Commerce, 1953. Chief acct. Philco Dist., Inc., Los Angeles, 1953-58, Pacific Ocean Park (Calif.), 1958-59; controller Eleven-Ten Broadcasting, Pasadena, Calif., 1959-63, Los Angeles Standard, 1963-69; treas. Oak Knoll Broadcasting Corp., Pasadena, 1969—; v.p., gen. mgr. Oak Knoll Broadcasting Corp., 1976-82, pres., chmn. bd., 1982—, dir., 1974—. Trustee, pres., chmn. bd. Broadcast Found. of Calif., Pasadena. Served with U.S. Army, 1940-45. Decorated Bronze star (2). Clubs: Masons, Scottish Rite, Shriners. Home: 966 Regent Park Dr Flintridge CA 91011-4157

FRY, EARL HOWARD, political scientist, educator; b. Oakland, Calif., May 19, 1947; s. Harvey Wallace and Alice (Horlacher) F.; m. Elaine Fisher, May 29, 1971; children: Christopher, Lisa, Leanna, Kimberly, Steven, Kristen. BA, U. Calif., Berkeley, 1967, Brigham Young U., 1971, Brigham Young U., 1971; MA, Brigham Young U., 1972; PhD, UCLA, 1976. Fulbright prof. U. Sorbonne, Paris, 1974-75; asst. prof. Boise State U., Idaho, 1976-79; assoc. prof. SUNY, Plattsburgh, 1979-80; assoc. prof. Brigham Young U., Provo, Utah, 1980-83, prof. dept. Polit. Sci., Endowed prof. Canadian studies, 1989—; spl. asst. Office U.S. Trade Rep., Washington, 1983-84; asst. dir. Brigham Young U.-U Grenoble Semester Abroad Program, 1972; vis. rschr. UN, Geneva, 1974; asst. prof. Boise State U., 1976-79; chmn. BSU Faculty Rsch. com., 1977-78; vis. prof. U. B.C., 1977; prin. investigator Idaho Internat. Trade directory Pacific northwest Regional Commn., 1979; assoc. prof. SUNY Plattsburgh, 1979-80, dir. Internat. Edn., Canadian Studies, 1979-80; vis. prof. U. Montreal, 1989, Ecole des Hautes Etudes en Scis. Sociales, Paris, 1990; review com. Internat. Proposals U.S. Dept. Edn., 1985-88; Utah State Tax Commn. Task Force on Unitary Taxation, 1985; chmn. Canadian Studies, Brigham Young U., 1980—; Univ. rep. Atlantic Coun. U.S., 1987—; fellowship com. Coun. Fgn. Rels., 1989-93, fellow 1983-84; dir. Grad. Studies, Rsch., Publs., David M. Kennedy Ctr. Internat. Studies, 1987-90; Fulbright Commn. review com., 1991; vis. fellow Ams. Soc., N.Y.C., 1991-93; acad. assoc. Atlantic Coun., Washington, 1987—; lectr., cons. and spkr. in field. Author: Financial Invasion of the U.S.A., 1980, Canadian Government and Politics in Comparative Perspective, 1983, The Canadian Political System, 1991, Canada's Unity Crisis: Implications for U.S.-Canadian Economic Relations, 1992; co-author Idaho's Foreign Relations: The Transgovernmental Linkages of an American State, 1978, The Other Western Europe: A Comparative Analysis of the Smaller Democracies, 1980, The Other Western Europe, 1983, America the Vincible: U.S. Foreign Policy for the Twenty-First Century, 1994, The Expanding Role of State and Local Governments in U.S. Foreign Affairs, 1998; co-editor The Canada/U.S. Free Trade Agreement: The Impact on Service Industries, 1988, Investment in the North American Free Trade Area: Opportunities and Challenges, 1992; gen. editor Canadian Studies Curriculum Guide, 1980; contbr. numerous articles to profl. jours. Bd. dirs. Fulbright Assn., 1995—. Recipient Can. Studies Sr. Fellowship award, 1983, Karl G. Maeser Rsch. and Creative Arts award, 1989; rsch. grantee Coll. Family, Home and Social Scis., 1986, 88, 89, 92; rsch. and conf. grantee Can. govt., 1985-92; Fulbright lectr. U. Paris (La Sorbonne), 1974-75; Bissell-Hyde-Fulbright chair U. Toronto, 1995-96; Elliot/Winant Lecture fellow UK, 1993, Coun. Fgn. Rels. Internat. Affairs fellow, 1983, David M. Kennedy Rsch. fellow Brigham Young U., 1985-86, Rsch. grantee, 1987-89; Atlantic Coun. Travel grantee, 1988; Presdl. fellow Am. Grad. Sch. Internat. Mgmt., 1993. Mem. Internat. Polit. Sci. Assn., Assn. Can. Studies in U.S. (Washington v.p. 1989-91, pres. 1991-93, exec. coun. 1985—, Bissell-Hyde Fulbright chair U. Toronto 1995-96), Fulbright Assn. (bd. dirs. 1995-97), Coun. Fgn. Rels. Mem. LDS Ch. Office: Brigham Young U Dept Pol Scis Provo UT 84602

FRY, EDWARD IRAD, anthropology educator; b. Long Branch, N.J., Jan. 7, 1924; s. Wallace Cordiner and Abigail Elizabeth (Hidden) F.; m. Peggy June Crooke, Dec. 23, 1950. BA, U. Tex., 1949, MA, 1950; PhD, Harvard U., 1958. Asst. prof. Antioch Coll., 1955-56; assoc. prof. U. Nebr., Lincoln, 1956-66; prof. anthropology So. Meth. U., Dallas, 1966-87, prof. emeritus, 1987-97; cons. in field, including USAF. Contbr. articles to profl. jours. Served with USAAF, 1942-45. Fulbright fellow N. Z. and South Pacific, 1953-54; Fulbright fellow Hong Kong U., 1963-64. Fellow AAAS (chmn. sect. anthropology 1980), Am. Anthrop. Assn.; mem. Soc. for Study Craniofacial Biology, Internat. Assn. Human Biologists, Human Biology Council, Soc. for Study Human Biology, Am. Assn. Phys. Anthropologists (exec. com., sec.-treas., pres. 1973-75), Sigma Xi. Research on child growth and body composition and human biology especially skeletal aging. Home: 3004 Fondren Dr Dallas TX 75205-1916 *Died June 17, 1999.*

FRY, HEDY, government minister; 3 children. MD, Royal Coll. Surgeons, Dublin, Ireland. Pvt. practice; Mem., sec. of state (multiculturalism) (status of women) Can. Parliament, Ottawa, 1996—; Dr. Hirsh Rosenfeld Disting. Lectr. in family medicine McGill U., 1994; featured on Doctor-Doctor, CBC TV series, 1985-89. Mem. editl. bd. Med. Post. Mem. com. Royal Commn. on Reproductive Technologies.dn. Learning for Living Adv. Bd.; mem. Mayor's Spl. Com. on Urban Natives; bd. dirs. St. George's sch., 1989-91; adv. bd. B.C. Physicians Against Nuclear War; co-chair Liberal Party Health and Social Issues sect., Aylmer Conf., 1992, mem. Leader's Nat. Task For5ce on Women, 1992-93; parliamentary sec. Min. of Health,1 993-96, mem. task force on reform of social security sys., 1994, standing com. on health, 1994, subcom. on AIDS, mem. caucus com. on social policy. Recipient Cmty. Svc. award Commonwealth Caribbean Club, 1991, Black Achievement award, 1994, Congress of Black Women award, 1994. Mem. B.C. Fedn. Med. Women (pres. 1977), Vancouver Women's Network, Vancouver Med. Assn. (pres. 1988-89), B.C. Med. Assn. (pres. 1990-91), Can. Med. Assn. (chair multiculturalism com. 1992-93). Avocations: drama, swimming, racquetball, reading. Office: Constitution Sq Ste 700, 360 Albert St, Ottawa, ON Canada*

FRY, JOHN, magazine editor; b. Montreal, Jan. 22, 1930; s. J. Stevenson and Beatrice (Pratt) F.; m. Marlies Strillinger, Feb. 19, 1965; children—Leslie, William, Nicole. Student, Lower Can. Coll., Montreal, 1936-47; BA, McGill U., 1951. Writer Forster McGuire & Co. Ltd., Montreal, 1951-57; assoc. editor to mng. editor Am. Metal Market, 1957-63; editor-in-chief Ski mag., N.Y.C., 1964-74, editorial dir., 1975-79; editorial dir. Ski Bus., 1964-79, 92—, Golf mag., 1968-71, 77-79, Outdoor Life, 1975-79, Cross Country Ski mag., 1975—; dir. publs. devel. Times Mirror Mags., 1979-83; editorial and publs. cons., 1983—; founding editor Snow Country mag., 1987-98; editor for new mag. devel. N.Y. Times mag. group, N.Y.C., 1995-97; mem. World Cup com. Internat. Ski Fedn., 1970-75. Author: (with Phil and Steve Mahre) No Hill Too Fast, 1985. Bd. dirs. The Riverkeeper, 1989—, Pinchot Inst. for Conservation, 1992—, Beaver Dam Sanctuary. Recipient Lifetime Achievement award Internat. Skiing History Assn., 1996; named to U.S. Nat. Ski Hall of Fame, 1995. Founder Nat. Standard Ski Race. Office: 23 E Lake Dr Katonah NY 10536-3501

FRY, LOUIS EDWIN, JR., architect; b. Prairie View, Tex., Sept. 11, 1928; s. Louis Edwin and Obelia (Swearingen) F.; m. Genelle Wiley, Nov. 7, 1955; children—Jo Nisa, Louis Edwin, Vicki-Lynn, Alexa. A.B., Howard U., 1949; B.Arch., Harvard U., 1953, M.Arch., 1954, M.Arch. in Urban Design, 1962. Registered profl. architect, D.C., Va., Md., Mass., Mich., Ala., Ga., Pa., Calif. Architect McGowan & Johnson, Washington, 1955-59; architect Fry & Welch Assoc. PC, Washington, 1959—; vis. critic Harvard U., Cambridge, Mass., 1970-74; bd. dirs. Mid Atlantic NCARB, Washington, 1979-81; pres. D.C. Arch. Regulation Bd., 1979-84; mem. Redevel. Land Agy., 1978—; mem. design com. Harvard U., 1980—, vis. mem. Grad. Sch. Design. mem. Shepherd Park Community Assn., Washington, Georgia Ave. Profl. and Civic Assn., Washington. Fulbright fellow, Holland, 1954-55. Fellow AIA; mem. Nat. Orgn. for Minority Architects, Omega Psi Phi. Democrat. Avocation: breeding salt-water fish. Home: 7100 Alaska Ave NW Washington DC 20012-1544 Office: Fry and Welch Assocs PC 7100 Alaska Ave NW Washington DC 20012-1544

FRY, MALCOLM CRAIG, retired clergyman; b. Detroit, June 6, 1928; s. Dwight Malcolm and Adrienne (Craig) F.; m. Myrtle Mae Downing, June 5, 1948 (dec.); children: Pamela Mae, Malcolm Craig Jr., Rebecca Fry Gwartney, Matthew Dwight. Student, Bible Bapt. Sem., 1950; Th.B., Am. Div. Sch., Chgo., 1959; student, McNeese State Coll., Lake Charles, La., 1958-61; B.S., Austin Peay State Coll., 1962; M.Ed., U. Ariz., 1969; D. Laws and Letters (hon.), Clarksville Sch. Theology, 1974; D.Ministry, Luther Rice Sem., 1978. Ordained to ministry Free Will Bapt. Ch., 1955. Asst. jewelery store mgr. Sonne Bros., Norwich, N.Y., 1948-50; pastor in Lake Charles, La., 1955-58, 59-61, Bryan, Tex., 1958-59, Ashland City, Tenn., 1961-62; asst. pastor in Royal Oak, Mich., 1962-64; pastor First Free Will Bapt. Ch., Tucson, 1964-71; dir. curriculum and rsch. Bd. Ch. Tng. Svc. Nat. Assn. Free Will Baptists, Nashville, 1971-72; gen. dir., treas. Bd. Ch. Tng. Svc., 1972-78; dir. Nat. Youth Conf., 1972-83, asst. dir. Bd. Sunday Sch. and Ch. Tng., 1978-83; pastor Unity Free Will Bapt. Ch., Smithfield, N.C., 1983-89, Goodlettsville Free Will Bapt. Ch., Goodlettsville, Tenn., 1991-96; ret., 1996; program writer, teen tng. mgr. Nat. Assn. Free Will Bapts., 1963-78, clk., 1965-67, chmn. stewardship commn., 1962-67, editor in chief bd. Sunday Sch. and Ch. Tng., 1989-95. Author: Total Involvement, 1964, Why Worry?, 1967, Precepts for Practice, 1971, Discipling and Developing, 1971, The Teacher-in-Training, 1972, Contemporary Topical Studies, 1973, rev. edit., 1991, The Ministry of Music, 1974, Balancing Christian Education, 1977, Leader's Guide Discipling and Developing, 1979, Leader's Guide the Ministry of Ushering, 1980. Served with AUS, 1946-48; with USAF, 1951-57, Korea. Mem. Evang. Philos. Soc., Kiwanis, Civitan, Phi Delta Kappa.

FRY, MAXWELL JOHN, economist, educator; b. Maidenhead, Eng., Feb. 12, 1944; came to U.S., 1974; s. Thomas Maxwell and Jeanne Mary (Kislingbury) F.; m. Celia Gordon, June 17, 1972; children: Benjamin, Zoe, Jeremy, Caroline. BS, London Sch. Econs., 1965; MA, UCLA, 1966; PhD, London Sch. Econs., 1970. Lectr. Morley Coll., 1966-67; lectr. Middle East Tech. U., Ankara, Turkey, 1967-69; lectr. fin. econs. City U. London, 1969-74; prof. econs. U. Hawaii, Honolulu, 1974-81; vis. prof. Bogazici U., Istanbul, 1977-79, UCLA, 1981-85; prof. econs. U. Calif.-Irvine, 1981-89, chmn. dept., 1983-85; Tokai Bank prof. internat. fin. U. Birmingham, 1989—; dir. Bank of England Ctr. for Ctrl. Banking Studies, 1997—; advisor to min. fin. Govt. of Afghanistan, Kabul, 1972-73, to min. State Econ. Enterprises, Turkey, 1978-79, to gov. Ctrl. Bank Bangladesh, 1984-86, to dir. Bank of Eng., 1990, to min. fin. and govt. Ctrl. Bank Mauritius, 1994-96; cons. to internat. agys., ctrl. banks, AID; vis. fellow Brasenose Coll., Oxford (Eng.) U., 1986; vis. scholar IMF, 1989-90; fellow Inst. S.E. Asian Studies, 1993; sr. Houblon-Norman fellow Bank Eng., 1997. Author: Finance and Development Planning in Turkey, 1972, The Afghan Economy, 1974, Money and Banking in Turkey, 1979, American Money and Banking, 1984, Improving Domestic Resource Mobilization through Financial Development, 1985, Money, Interest and Banking in Economic Development, 1988, 2d edit., 1995, Foreign Direct Investment in Southeast Asia: Differential Impacts, 1993, Central Banking in Developing Countries: Objectives, Activities and Independence, 1996, Emancipating the Banking System and Developing Markets for Government Debt, 1997, Payment Systems in Global Perspective, 1999; contbr. articles to profl. jours.; rsch. on ctrl. banking, monetary policy, domestic resource moblzn., fgn. debt, fgn. direct investment, and balance of payments in developing countries, European monetary union, monetary and exchange rate policies in Ea. Europe. Recipient award Brit. Social Sci. Rsch. Coun., 1971, rsch. award NSF, 1975, 83, award Econ. and Social Rsch. Coun., 1995; Fulbright scholar, 1965. Avocations: playing violin and viola. Home: 6 Farquhar Rd, Birmingham B15 3RB, England Office: Internat Fin Group, Univ Birmingham, Birmingham B15 2TT, England

FRY, MEREDITH WARREN, civil engineer, consultant; b. Bedford, Ind., Mar. 9, 1924; s. Cornelius Alexander and Ruby Estel (Jackson) F.; m. Mary Louise Henley, Dec. 25, 1952; children: James Owen, Robert Dail, Marvin Lee. BSCE, Tri-State U., 1952; MA in Econs., Ball State U., 1985. Registered profl. engr., Mo., Ind., registered land surveyor, Ind. Designer, design squad chief, traffic control designer Mo. State Highway Dept., Jefferson City, 1952-62; project engr., dist. traffic engr. Ind. State Highway Commn., Greenfield, 1962-66; engr. of traffic signs Ind. State Hwy. Commn., Indpls., 1967-69; city traffic engr. City of Muncie, Ind., 1966-67; supt. of planning Ball State U., Muncie, 1969-80, supt. of planning and constrn., 1980-88; civil engr., pres. M.W. Fry, Inc., Chesterfield, Ind., 1988—; cons. Ball State U., 1988—, Muncie Sanitary Dist., 1988-91. Trustee Town Bd., Chesterfield, 1972-76; mem. traffic com. 500 Mile Speedway Race, Indpls., 1962-66, ad hoc com. for handicapped Ball State U., 1963-87, Del.-Muncie planning commn. tech. com., 1963-87; internat. student host family mem. Ball State U., 1979—; mem. The Heritage Found. With USMC, 1944, World War II. Recipient Cert. of Appreciation Ind. Nat. Guard, Indpls., 1965, Disabled Student in Action of Ball State U., 1975, Disting. Svc. award Tri-State U., 1978, Grand Cross of Color, Supreme Assembly-Rainbow for Girls, Oklahoma City, 1961, Outstanding Alumni award Needmore H.S. Alumni Assn., 1995. Mem. NSPE, Inst. Transp. Engrs., Ind. Soc. Profl. Engrs. (pres. Delta chpt. 1979, 92, Engr. of Yr. 1992), Tri-State Alumni (bd. govs. 1992—), First Marine Divsn. Assn. (life), Chesterfield Optimist Club (pres. 1978), Masons (master 1961), Order of Eastern Star. Republican. Mem. Christian Ch. Avocations: travel, music, reading, education. Home and Office: MW Fry Inc 917 Hampton Ln Chesterfield IN 46017-1446

FRY, MICHAEL GRAHAM, historian, educator; b. Brierley, Eng., Nov. 5, 1934; s. Cyril Victor and Margaret Mary (Copley) F.; m. Anna Maria Fulgoni; children: Michael Gareth, Gabrielle, Margaret Louise. B.Sc. in Econs. with honors, U. London, 1956, Ph.D., 1963. Dir. Norman Paterson Sch. Internat. Affairs, Carleton U., Ottawa, Ont., 1973-77; dean, prof. internat. relations Grad. Sch. Internat. Studies, U. Denver, 1978-81; dir., prof. Sch. Internat. Relations, U. So. Calif., Los Angeles, 1981—; vis. prof. Middle East Center, U. Utah, 1979, U. Leningrad, 1976. Author: Illusions of Security: North Atlantic Diplomacy, 1918-1922, 1972, Freedom and Change, 1975, Lloyd George and Foreign Policy, Vol. I, The Education of a Statesman, 1890-1916, 1977, Despatches from Damascus, 1933-39, 1986, History and International Studies, 1987, History, The White House and the Kremlin: Statesmen as Historians, 1991, Power, Personalities and Policies, 1992, The North Pacific Triangle: Canada Japan and the U.S. at Century's End, 1998. NATO rsch. fellow, 1970-71, rsch. fellow Annenberg Program, Washington, 1986-87; grantee Can. Coun. Fellow Royal Hist. Soc.; mem. Soc. Historians Am. Fgn. Rels. Roman Catholic. Home: 1358 Cassins St Carlsbad CA 92009 Office: U So Calif Sch Internat Rels Los Angeles CA 90089

FRY, MORTON HARRISON, II, lawyer; b. N.Y.C., May 15, 1946; s. George Thomas Clark and Louise Magdalen (Cronin) F.; m. Patricia Laylin Coffin, May 29, 1971. AB, Princeton U., 1968; JD, Yale U., 1971. Bar: N.Y. 1973, U.S. Ct. Mil. Appeals 1973, U.S. Dsit. Ct. (so. and ea. dists.) N.Y. 1975, U.S. Ct. Appeals (2d cir.) 1975. Assoc. Cravath, Swaine & Moore, N.Y.C., 1971-72, 75-79; dep. gen. counsel Columbia Pictures Industries, Inc., N.Y.C., 1979-81; v.p., gen. cousnel Warner Home Video Inc., N.Y.C., 1982-83; exec.v.p. Wanrer Electronic Home Svcs., N.Y.C., 1983-84; sr. counsel corp. and new techs. Warner Comms. Inc., N.Y.C., 1984-85; pres., CEO, bd. dirs. The Congress Video Group, Inc., 1985-87; pres., cons. Fry Assocs., 1987-89; ptnr. Marshall, Morris, Bomser & Fry, N.Y.C., 1990-94, rubin, Bailin, Ortoli, Mayer, Baker & Fry, N.Y.C., 1995—. Mem. Dem.

Nat. Fin. Com. Capt. USMC, 1966-75. Democrat. Congregationalist. Home: 41 Barrow St New York NY 10014-3736

FRY, RANDY DALE, emergency medical technician, paramedic; b. Houston, Feb. 3, 1957; s. LeRoy D. Fry and Ardria Faye (Stegall) Boyd; m. Robbie Ruth Rippy, June 4, 1982. Paramedic Panola County Ambulance, Carthage, Tex., 1979-87; cardiac monitor tech. Bossier Med. Ctr., Bossier City, La., 1991—; instr. CPR, PALS Bossier Med. Ctr.; instr. EMS, coord. Panola Jr. Coll., Carthage. Home: RR 1 Box 232 Joaquin TX 75954-9764 Office: Bossier Med Ctr Bossier City LA 75954

FRY, RICHARD E., architectural firm executive. BArch, U. Mich. Registered arch. Mich., Minn., Colo.; cert. Nat. Coun. Archtl. Registered Bds. Pres., prin.-in-charge Fry & Ptnrs. Archs., Inc., Aspen, Col. and Ann Arbor, Mich., 1970—; adj. prof. U. Mich. Coll. Archtl. and Urban Planning; archtl. instr. Washtenaw C.C.; rep. Mich. archs. Nat. AIA Bd., Washington. Prin. works include U. Mich. Vis. Ctr., No. Brewery Office Bldg., Ann Arbor, Mich. League-U. Mich., Ann Arbor Art Assn., U. Mich. Dental Sch. Sindecuse Mus., We. Mich. U. Bookstore, Burns Park Elem. Sch., Ann Arbor Ctrl. Fire Sta., Heydon Wash. St. Properties, Ann Arbor, pvt. residences, others. Past mem. Ann Arbor Planning Commn.; bd. dirs. Bldg. Bd. Appeals; mem. art acquisition com. Washtenaw C.C. Fellow AIA (pres. Mich. chpt., chmn. design awards & recognition com. Mich. chpt., chmn. design retreat com. Mich. chpt., chmn. mid-summer conf. Mich. chpt., regional dir. Mich. chpt., pres. Huron Valley chpt.). Office: Fry & Ptnrs Archs Inc 229 Depot St Ann Arbor MI 48104-1019

FRY, SHIRLEY ANN MILLS, nursing administrator, educator; b. Detroit, Mar. 16, 1955; d. Hersell and Irene F. (Greene) Mills; m. Dwight D. Fry, Aug. 11, 1984; children: Rebecca Esther, Jacob Douglas Mills. BSN with high honors, Berea Coll., 1977; MSN, Med. Coll. Va., 1988. Cert. advanced cardiac life support provider, PALS provider, neonatal resuscitation instr., advanced nursing adminstr.; CPR instr. Commd. 2nd lt. USAF, 1977, advanced through grades to major, 1987; staff nurse adult pediatric surg. unit USAF Hosp., Homestead AFB, Fla., 1978-79, clin. nurse adult and pediatricmed. unit, 1979-80; clin. nurse pediatric unit USAF Regional Med. Ctr., Clark AFB, Philippines, 1980-83; officer in charge emergency rm. and ambulance svcs., nursing ednl. coord. USAF Clinic San Vito dei Normani, San Vito, N.Y., Italy, 1983-84; quality assurance and risk mgmt. officer, nursing ednl. coord. USAF Clinic San Vito dei Normani, APO, N.Y., 1984-85; asst. charge nurse male surgery unit USAF Med. Ctr., Scott AFB, Ill., 1985-86; charge nurse emergency svcs. 97th Med. Group, Eaker AFB, Ark., 1988-91, nursing quality assurance and risk gmgt. coord., 1988-92, charge nurse OB-gyn Clinic, nursing qualityassurance and risk mgmt. coord., 1991-92; coord. outpatient nursing svc., nursing quality improvement/risk mgmt. 90th Med. Group/FE. Warren AFB, Cheyenne, Wyo., 1992-95; nurse mgr. maternal-child unit 90th Med. Group, Ft. Warren, Wyo., 1994-95; ret. USAF, 1995; staff devel. coord. Henry County Med. Ctr., Paris, Tenn., 1995-98, psychiat. clin. nurse, 1998—; staff nurse med.-surg. ward Good Samaritan Hosp., Lexington, Ky., 1977; nurse intern program USAF Med. Ctr., Scott AFB, Ill., 1978. Mem. Nat. Officers Assn.

FRY, TERRY L., English educator; b. Roodhouse, Ill., Oct. 10, 1942; s. Junior Earl and Elizabeth Ann (Nalefski) F.; m. Rochelle Lynne Morris Fry, Aug. 8, 1964; children: Howard Earl, Suzanne Fry Dees. BSEd, Ill. State U., 1965, MS in English, 1969, EdD in Edn., 1976. Tchr. English St. Anne (Ill.) Comm. H.S., 1965-68, Bloomington (Ill.) H.S., 1968—; assoc. prof. English U. Ill., Urbana, 1977-78. Author: (textbook) Public Speaking, 1972. Deacon 2nd Presbyn. Ch., 1994-97; mem. Dem. Nat. Com. Mem. NEA (nat. conv. del. 1965—), Bloomington Edn. Assn. (negotiator, pres. bd. dirs., del. 1968—), Ill. Edn. Assn. (conv. del. 1965—), Moose, Masons. Avocations: vol. hist. interpreting, travel, reading, music, golf. Home: 500 S Blair Dr Normal IL 61761-3110

FRYATT, RICHARD PAUL, import distribution executive; b. Medford, Mass., June 7, 1940; s. Raymond Earnest and Ruth Marrion (Hemmingway) F.; m. Janie Lou Maddock, Aug. 21, 1968 (div. Jan. 1997); children: Troy, Timothy, Todd. A in Bus., Boston U., 1964. Regional sales mgr. M.S. Walker, Inc., Somerville, Mass., 1962—; pres. Boston Wine Exch., Charlstown, Mass., 1985-89. Capt. U.S. Army, 1959-61. Home: 63 Breakwater Dr Chelsea MA 02150-4009 Office: MS Walker Inc 20 3rd Ave Somerville MA 02143-4450

FRYBERGER, ELIZABETH ANN, financial consultant; b. Oakland, Calif., Sept. 7, 1947; d. Marion Raymond Holden and Della Elois Nunley; m. Richard Fryberger, Aug. 19, 1972; 1 child, Laura. BA cum laude, U. Minn., 1987. Registered rep.; accredited investment mgmt. cons.; cert. qualified plans consultant. Investment exec. PaineWebber, Duluth, Minn., 1987-91; trust and investment officer North Shore Bank of Commerce, Duluth, 1991-93; fin. cons. Merrill Lynch, Duluth, 1993-99; registered investment adviser Fryberger Capital Mgmt., Inc. Co-chair Follow Your Dreams Festival, Duluth, 1990; sect. chair United Way, Duluth, 1994; treas. Cmty. Investment Fund, Duluth, 1993-95; v.p. Ind. Sch. Dist. 709 Endowment Fund, Duluth, 1994—; pres. Project SOAR, Duluth, 1991; mem. Jr. League, Duluth, Leadership Duluth, 1990. Mem. NAFE, Second Tuesday Networking Group (founder), Nat. Ctr. for Women and Retirement Rsch., Profl. Women's Network (pres.), Arrowhead Estate Planning Counsel, Greysolon Toastmasters (past pres.). Avocations: reading, traveling, gourmet cooking, golfing. Office: Fryberger Capital Mgmt Inc 3399 Riley Rd Duluth MN 55803

FRYBURGER, LAWRENCE BRUCE, lawyer, mediator, writer; b. Cin., Apr. 7, 1933. BA, U. Cin., 1956; LLB with nat. honors, U. Tex., 1958. Bar: Tex. 1959, U.S. Dist. Ct. (we. dist.) Tex. 1961, U.S. Ct. Appeals (5th cir.) 1962, U.S. Supreme Ct. 1963, U.S. Dist. Ct. (so. dist.) Tex. 1972, U.S. Dist. Ct. (no. dist.) Tex. 1981, U.S. Ct. Appeals (11th cir.) 1981; bd. cert. labor and employment law Tex. Bd. Legal Specialization. Pvt. practice San Antonio, 1959—; spl. prof. labor relations law San Antonio Coll., 1968; originator Tex. Young Lawyer's Inst. Author: Policies, Procedures and People: A Blueprint for Human Resources, 1997; contbr. articles to law jours.; mem. editorial bd. Tex. Lawyers Practice Guide, 1964. Mem. San Antonio Bd. Adjustment, 1969-72; chmn. lawyer's div. United Fund, San Antonio and Bexar County, 1967-68. Sutphin scholar U. Cin., 1956. Mem. ABA, Tex. Bar Assn. (program chmn. current devels. in labor law inst. 1978, mem. coun. labor law sect. 1978-80), San Antonio Bar Assn. (chmn. lawyer reference plan 1970-73), Tex. Young Lawyers Assn. (bd. dirs. 1964-66), San Antonio Young Lawyers Assn. (pres. 1963-64, Outstanding Young Lawyer award 1967), Tex. Assn. of Residential Care Communities (spl. labor law counsel 1996—), Phi Delta Phi, Sigma Chi.

FRYBURGER, VERNON RAY, JR., advertising and marketing educator; b. Cin., June 9, 1918; s. Vernon Ray and Florence Rose (Steding) F.; m. Marjorie Anne Clarke, June 19, 1948; 1 dau., Candace. B.S. in Bus. Adminstrn., Miami U., Oxford, Ohio, 1939; Ph.D. in Econs., U. Ill., 1950. Salesman U.S. Printing & Lithograph Co., 1940-41; instr. mktg. Miami U., 1941-43; assoc. rsch. dir. Nat. Assn. Broadcasters, 1946; asst. prof. journalism U. Ill., 1947-53; faculty Northwestern U., 1953-86, prof. advt. and mktg., chmn. dept. advt., 1959-84, ednl. dir. Inst. Advanced Advt. Studies, 1963-85, prof. emeritus, 1986—; nat. assoc. dean Am. Acad. Advt., 1964-65, nat. dean, 1965-66, chmn. bd.; cons. to bus., 1954—; adviser Advt. Ednl. Found., 1972-84; vis. prof. U. Hawaii, 1965; cons. advt. U.S. Army, 1918-91. Author: (with C.H. Sandage and K. Rotzoll) Advertising Theory and Practice, 12th edit., 1989, (with Boyd and Westfall) Cases in Advertising Management, 1964; editor: (with C.H. Sandage) The Role of Advertising, 1960. Bd. dirs. Lake Forest Library. Served to lt., submarines USNR, 1943-46, PTO. Mem. Am. Mktg. Assn., Internat. Advt. Assn., Assn. Edn. Journalism, Beta Gamma Sigma, Kappa Tau Alpha, Delta Tau Delta, Delta Sigma Pi, Artus. Presbyn. Home: PO Box 62 1921 Shore Acres Dr Lake Bluff IL 60044-1342 Office: Northwestern U Evanston IL 60201

FRYD, VIVIEN GREEN, art history educator, researcher; b. Bklyn., May 14, 1952; d. Herbert and Stefanie (Bier) Green; m. Martin Fryd, June 19, 1983; 1 child, Emma Rene. BA, Ohio State U., 1974, MA, 1977; PhD, U. Wis., 1984. Instr. Pittsburg (Kans.) State U., summer 1978; asst. to the assoc. dean U. Wis., Madison, 1981-84; vis. asst. prof. Ariz. State U., Tempe, 1984-88; asst. prof. art history Vanderbilt U., Nashville, 1985-92, assoc. prof., 1992—. Mem. Am. Studies Assn. (Constance O'Rourke prize com. 1992, program com. 1994, John Hope Franklin prize com. 1994), Coll. Art Assn. Office: Vanderbilt U Nashville TN 37235

FRYDMAN, LUCIO, chemist, researcher, educator; b. Buenos Aires, May 29, 1965; came to U.S., 1990; s. Benjamin J. and Rosalia (Bryks) F.; m. Veronica Frydman, Jan. 11, 1990; children: Clara Rosalie, Uriel David. BS in Chenmistry, U. Buenos Aires, 1986, PhD, 1990. Postdoctoral assoc. U. Calif., Berkeley, 1990-92; asst. prof. chemistry U. Ill., Chgo., 1992-96, assoc. prof., 1996—; vis. rsch. assoc. Argonne (Ill.) Nat. Lab., 1994-96; Meyerhoff vis. prof. Weizmann Inst. Sci., Rehovot, Israel, 1997-98. Author more than 40 articles in chemistry and spectroscopy. Rsch. mentor h.s. undergrad., grad. and postdoctoral students U. Ill., chgo., 1992—. Camille and Henry Dreyfus awardee, 1992, 96, NSF Career awardee, 1995, Bechman Found. grantee, 1996, U. Ill. scholar, 1996, Alfred P. Sloan fellow, 1997, NSF Creativity awardee, 1998. Jewish. Office: U Ill Chgo Dept Chemistry M/C 111 845 W Taylor St Rm 4500 Chicago IL 60607-7056

FRYDMAN, PAUL, real estate broker and developer; b. Yedlinsk, Poland, July 20, 1906; came to U.S., 1933; s. Chaim Jacob and Masha Rachel (Rosenbaum) F.; m. Sarah Weisman, Sept. 11, 1932; children: Harold, Joseph, Gloria, Ronald. Student pub. schs., Poland. Lic. real estate broker and developer, Ohio. Owner street produce bus., Dayton, Ohio, 1934-39, wholesale and retail produce store, Dayton, 1939-48; ptnr. Dybvig & Frydman Realtors, Dayton, 1953-76, Frydman & Assocs., Realtors, Dayton, 1976—; comml. indsl. cons ., Dayton, 1953-96. Active numerous civic orgns., including pres. Beth Jacob Synagogue, Dayton, 1958-59; mem. bldg. com., 1981; chmn. Holocaust Meml. Com., Dayton, 1976-80; former bd. dirs. Jewish Fedn. Greater Dayton, hon. life mem.; gen. chmn. Bonds for Israel, 1968-69; chmn. United Jewish Appeal and Israel Emergency Fund, 1970-71; mem. U. Dayton President's Club, 1974—; active Coun. for Retarded Children Montgomery County; former mem. bldg. com. Hillel Acad. Dayton; mem. Simon Wiesenthal Rsch. Found. Recipient numerous awards, including citation Jewish Cmty. Coun., 1965, tribute Zionist Orgn. Am., 1964, Disting. Svc. award State of Israel Bonds, 1968, David Ben Gurion award, 1973, proclamation Gov. of Ohio, 1984, Mayor, 1984; named hon. citizen Boys Town, 1961; Hillel Acad. bldg. dedicated in name Paul and Sarah Frydman, 1973. Mem. Beth Abraham Synagogue (hon. life), Bar Ilan U. Israel in Fla., Telshe Yeshiva U. Cleve., Covenant House Dayton, Weismann Inst. Israel, Hadassah Hosp. Israel, Shaare Zedek Hosp. Israel, Zionist Orgn. Am., Dayton Area Bd. Realtors, Covenant House Dayton (hon. life), Yeshivot Bnei Akiva, Israel, Red Magen David for Israel, Diskin Orphan Home of Israel, Friends of Israel Disabled War Vets., Gen. Israel Orphans Home for Girls, Home of the Sages of Israel, Keren-Or, Israel, Ner Israel Rabbinical Coll. Balt., Yeshiva U. N.Y. Office: 7271 N Main St Ste 5 Dayton OH 45415-2561

FRYE, BILLY EUGENE, university administrator, biologist; b. Clarkesville, Ga., June 26, 1933. B.S., Piedmont Coll., 1953; M.S., Emory U., 1954, Ph.D. in Biology, 1956. NSF fellow Princeton U., 1956-57; prof. biology Piedmont Coll., 1957-58; vis. asst. prof. U. Va., 1958-61; from asst. prof. to assoc. prof. zoology U. Mich., Ann Arbor, 1961-69, prof., 1969—, assoc. dean Coll. Lit., Sci. and Arts, 1974-75, acting dean, 1974-76, dean, 1976-82, v.p. acad. affairs and provost, 1980-86; v.p. research, dean Grad. Sch. Arts and Scis. Emory U., Atlanta, 1986-87, interim pres., 1993-94, provost, v.p. acad. affairs, 1995-97, chancellor, 1997—. NSF grantee, 1959-60; NIH grantee, 1960—. Mem. AAAS, Am. Soc. Zoologists. Research on metamorphosis; functional and morphological differentiation of the Islets of Langerhans and other embryonic glands; diabetes and pregnancy; developmental biology. Office: Emory Univ Office of Chancellor 474 Woodruff Libr Atlanta GA 30322*

FRYE, CLAYTON WESLEY, JR., financial executive; b. L.A., May 18, 1930; s. Clayton Wesley Sr. and Mary Virginia (Briggs) F.; m. Dorothy Rumsfeld, Jan. 14, 1957; children: Carolyn Frye Halloran, Diane Frye Tanner. AB, Stanford U., 1953, MBA, 1959. Pres., Sutter Hill Devel. Co., Palo Alto, Calif., 1962-69; gen. ptnr. Johnson & Frye Investment Co., San Antonio, 1970-73; sr. assoc. Laurance S. Rockefeller, N.Y.C., 1973—; ptnr. Rockefeller & Assocs. Realty, L.P., San Francisco, Pacific Property Svcs., San Francisco; bd. dirs. Col. Williamsburg (Va.) Hotel Properties, Inc., Times Mirror Co., L.A., King Ranch, Inc., Tex., Woodstock Resort Corp. (Vt.), chmn. Trustee Hist. Hudson Valley, Tarrytown, N.Y.; trustee, chmn. Jackson Hole Preserve, Inc., Woodstock Found., White House Hist. Assn. (bd. dirs.). With USNR, 1948-49. Mem. Urban Land Inst. Office: 30 Rockefeller Plz Rm 5600 New York NY 10112-0002

FRYE, HELEN JACKSON, judge; b. Klamath Falls, Oreg., Dec. 10, 1930; d. Earl and Elizabeth (Kirkpatrick) Jackson; m. William Frye, Sept. 7, 1952; children: Eric, Karen, Heidi; 1 adopted child, Hedy; m. Perry Holloman, July 10, 1980 (dec. Sept. 1991). BA in English with honors, U. Oreg., 1953, MA, 1960, JD, 1966. Bar: Oreg. 1966. Public sch. tchr. Oreg., 1956-63; with Riddlesberger, Pederson, Brownhill & Young, 1966-67, Husband & Johnson, Eugene, 1968-71; trial judge State of Oreg., 1971-80; U.S. dist judge Dist. Oreg. Portland, 1980-95; sr. judge U.S. Dist. Ct., Portland, 1995—. Office: 1107 US Courthouse 1000 SW 3rd Ave Portland OR 97204-2930

FRYE, HENRY E., state supreme court justice; b. Ellerbe, N.C., Aug. 1, 1932; s. Walter A. and Pearl Alma (Motley) F.; m. Edith Shirley Taylor, Aug. 25, 1956; children: Henry Eric, Harlan Elbert. BS in Biol. Scis., A & T U., N.C., 1953; JD with honors, U. N.C., 1959. Bar: N.C. 1959. Asst. U.S. atty. (middle dist.), N.C., 1963-65; prof. law N.C. Central U., Durham, 1965-67; practice law Greensboro, N.C., 1967-83; rep. N.C. Gen. Assembly, 1969-80, N.C. Senate, 1980-82; assoc. justice N.C. Supreme Ct., Raleigh, 1983—; organizer, pres. Greensboro Nat. Bank, 1971-80. Deacon Providence Baptist Ch. Capt. USAF, 1953-55. Mem. ABA, N.C. Bar Assn., Greensboro Bar Assn., Nat. Bar Assn., Am. Judicature Soc. (chair bd. dirs. 1995-97), Kappa Alpha Psi. Office: NC Supreme Ct PO Box 1841 Raleigh NC 27602-1841

FRYE, JUDITH ELEEN MINOR, editor; b. Seattle; d. George Edward and Eleen G. (Hartelius) Minor; student UCLA, 1947-48, U. So. Calif., 1948-53; m. Vernon Lester Frye, Apr. 1, 1954. Acct., office mgr. Colony Wholesale Liquor, Culver City, Calif., 1947-48; credit mgr. Western Distbg. Co., Culver City, 1948-53; ptnr. in restaurants, Palm Springs, L.A., 1948, ptnr. in date ranch, La Quinta, Calif., 1949-53; ptnr., owner Imperial Printing, Huntington Beach, Calif., 1955—; editor, pub. New Era Laundry and Cleaning Lines, Huntington Beach, 1962—; registered lobbyist, Calif., 1975-84. Mem. Textile Care Allied Trade Assn., Calif. Coin-op Assn. (exec. dir. 1975-84, Cooperation award 1971, Dedicated Svc.award 1976), Nat. Automatic Laundry & Cleaning Coun. (Leadership award 1972), Women Laundry & Drycleaning (past pres., Outstanding Svc. award 1977), Printing Industries Assn., Master Printers Am., Nat. Assn. Printers & Lithographers. Office: 22031 Bushard St Huntington Beach CA 92646-8409

FRYE, MARY CATHERINE, prosecutor; b. Amarillo, Tex., Feb. 9, 1950; d. John Gristy and Estelle Angelina (Ashton) F.; m. Irwin Allen Popowsky, Dec. 18, 1977; children: Matthew Frye, Rebecca Susan. AB, Oberlin Coll., 1972; JD, U. Pa., 1977. Bar: Pa. 1977. Law clk. Phila. Orphans' Ct., 1977-79; assoc. Reager, Selkowitz & Adler, Harrisburg, Pa., 1980-89; staff atty. Pa. State Edn. Assn., Harrisburg, 1989-92; chief counsel Pa. Assn. Elem. and Secondary Sch. Prins., Harrisburg, 1992-94; chief civil divsn./asst. U.S. atty. U.S. Atty.'s Office (mid. dist.) Pa., Harrisburg, 1994—; adj. prof. law Widener U., Harrisburg, 1994-94. Author: Sexual Harassment: A Guide for Administrators, 1993. Democrat. Home: 4218 Kirkwood Rd Harrisburg PA 17110-3122 Office: US Atty's Office 228 Walnut St Harrisburg PA 17108-9998

FRYE, RICHARD ARTHUR, lawyer; b. Akron, Ohio, Sept. 3, 1948; s. Virgil Arthur and Margaret (Mullen) F.; children: Kathleen, Emily, Abigail. BA, Wittenberg U., 1970; JD, Ohio State U., 1973. Bar: Ohio 1973, U.S. Ct. Mil. Appeals, 1974, U.S. Dist. Ct. (so. dist.) Ohio 1974, U.S. Ct. Appeals (6th cir.) 1978, U.S. Supreme Ct. 1980, U.S. Ct. Appeals (fed. cir.) 1987, U.S. Ct. Appeals (9th cir.) 1998. Ptnr. Chester, Willcox & Saxbe LLP, Columbus, 1996—. Co-author: Ohio Eminent Domain Practice, 1977, Personal Injury Litigation in Ohio, 1985. Bd. dirs. Am. Heart Assn., Franklin County, Ohio, 1985-87, Legal Aid Soc. Columbus, 1996—, J. Ashburn Youth Ctr., 1996—; chmn. adv. com. on local rules U.S. Dist. Ct. for So. Dist. Ohio, 1990—; reporter adv. group Civil Justice Reform Act, 1992-97, mem. adv. group 1991-95. Fellow Columbus Bar Found., Ohio State Bar Found.; mem. Fed. Bar assn. (pres. Columbus chpt. 1991), Ohio State Bar Assn. (chmn. fed. cts. and practice com. 1988-90), Columbus Bar Assn. (chmn. fed. ct. com. 1988-91). Democrat. Methodist. Office: Chester Willcox & Saxbe LLP 17 S High St Ste 900 Columbus OH 43215-3442

FRYE, ROBERT EDWARD, federal agency administrator; b. Washington, Oct. 11, 1936. BSc, Howard U., 1958; MPA, Am. U., 1970. Geog. data analyst Army Map Svc.; info. sys. project mgr. Wolf R&D Corp.; mgr. Nat. Fire Data Sys. project Nat. Bur. Stds.; dir. injury surveillance divsn. U.S. Consumer Product Safety Commn., Washington, 1973-77, dir. hazard analysis divsn., 1977-96, dir. Office Planning and Evaluation, 1997—. Chmn. Fairfax County Sch. Bd., at-large mem. bd., 1978-85, 89-93, 96—. With U.S. Army. Office: Consumer Product Safety Commn 4330 East West Hwy Bethesda MD 20814

FRYE, ROLAND MUSHAT, literary historian, theologian; b. Birmingham, Ala., July 3, 1921; s. John and Helen Elizabeth (Mushat) F.; m. Jean Elbert Steiner, Jan. 11, 1947; 1 child, Roland Mushat. AB, Princeton U., 1943, MA, 1950, PhD, 1952; postgrad., Princeton Theol. Sem., 1950-52. Instr. English Samford U., 1947-48; from asst. prof. to prof. Emory U., 1952-61; rsch. prof. Folger Shakespeare Libr., Washington, 1961-65; L.P. Stone Found. lectr. Princeton Theol. Sem., 1959, vis. prof., 1963; prof. U. Pa., Phila., 1965-83; emeritus prof. U. Pa., 1983—; trustee, vice-chmn., adv. com. Ctr. Theol. Inquiry, 1979—, chmn., 1989-91. Author: God, Man and Satan: Patterns of Christian Thought and Life in "Paradise Lost," "Pilgrim's Progress" and the Great Theologians, 1960, Perspective on Man: Literature and the Christian Tradition, 1961, Shakespeare and Christian Doctrine, 1963, Shakespeare's Life and Times: A Pictorial Record, 1967, Shakespeare: The Art of the Dramatist, 1970, Milton's Imagery and the Visual Arts: Iconographic Tradition in the Epic Poems, 1978, Is God a Creationist?: The Religious Case Against Creation-Science, 1983, The Renaissance Hamlet: Issues and Responses in 1600, 1984, Language for God and Feminist Language: Problems and Principles, 1988; editor: The Reader's Bible A Narrative: Selections from the King James Version, 1978; contbr. articles to profl. jours. Served to maj. AUS, 1943-46. Decorated Bronze Star; Guggenheim fellow, 1956-57, 73-74; mem. Inst. Advanced Study Princeton, N.J., 1973-74, 79; grantee NEH, 1973-74, Am. Coun. Learned Socs., 1966, 71, 78, Am. Philos. Soc., 1968, 71, 78; vis. scholar Am. Acad. in Rome, 1971; NEH-Huntington Libr. fellow, 1980-81. Mem. Am. Acad. Arts and Scis., Milton Soc. Am. (pres. 1977-78, James Holly Hanford award 1979), Am. Philos. Soc. (sec. 1978-81, John Frederick Lewis prize 1979, Henry Allen Moe prize 1988, Thomas Jefferson medal 1997), Rennaissance Soc. Am. (pres. 1984-85), Cosmos Club (Washington), Merion Cricket Club. Presbyterian. Home: 226 W Valley Rd Wayne PA 19087-2451

FRYE, ROLAND MUSHAT, JR., lawyer; b. Princeton, N.J., Feb. 8, 1950; s. Roland Mushat and Jean (Steiner) F.; m. Susan Marie Pettey, Jan. 23, 1988. AB cum laude, Princeton U., 1972; JD, Cornell U., 1975. Bar: Pa. 1975, D.C. 1978, U.S. Ct. Appeals (D.C. cir.) 1991, U.S. Supreme Ct. 1991. Litigation assoc. White and Williams, Phila., 1975-77; litigation atty. U.S. Dept. Energy, Washington, 1977-79, asst. solicitor, 1979-80; presiding officer Fed. Energy Regulatory Commn., Washington, 1980-83, chief presiding officer, 1983-85, supervisory atty., 1985-88, adv. atty., 1988-91; energy atty. Pepper, Hamilton & Scheetz, Washington, 1991-92; sr. atty. Office Commn. Appellate Adjudication U.S. Nuclear Regulatory Commn., Washington, 1992—; mediator Ctr. for Community Justice, D.C. Superior Ct., 1984-86; bd. editors alumni mag. Sidwell Friends Sch., 1994—. Editor Cornell Law Rev., 1974-75; contbr. articles to profl. jours. Mem. schs. and ann. giving coms. Princeton U., Washington and Phila., 1978-91; arbitrator Better Bus. Bur. Greater Washington, 1983-86, Phila. Ct. Common Pleas, 1975-77. Capt. USAR. Recipient Outstanding Young Man Am. award U.S. Jaycees, 1979. Mem. ABA, D.C. Bar Assn. (fee arbitration panel 1983-89, com. on alt. dispute resolution 1983-87), Fed. Bar Assn., Fed. Energy Bar Assn. (adminstrv. practice com. 1991-92), Sidwell Friends Sch. Alumni Assn. (exec. com. 1985-93, 94—, v.p. 1987-89, pres. 1989-93, Newmyer award), Soc. Cin., St. Andrews Soc., Prettyman-Leventhal Am. Inn of Ct. (barrister 1989-92, master 1992-99, exec. com. 1992-99, program chmn. 1993-95, counsellor 1995-96, pres.-elect 1996-97, pres. 1997-98, nat./emeritus mem. 1999—). Democrat. Presbyterian. Avocations: trout fishing, singing, travel. Home: 207 S Royal St Alexandria VA 22314-3329 Office: US Nuclear Regulatory Commn 11555 Rockville Pike Rockville MD 20852-2739

FRYE, SUSAN CAROLINE, English literature educator; b. Palo Alto, Calif., June 14, 1952; d. Bruce Bradford and Caroline (Reid) Frye; m. Thomas Carlisle Hacker, June 19, 1975 (div. Nov. 1988); 1 child, Elizabeth. BA, Smith Coll., 1974; MA, U. N.Mex., 1981; PhD, Stanford U., 1987. Tchr. English and social studies Sutton (Mass.) H.S., 1974-76, Rio Grande H.S., Albuquerque, 1976-82; asst. prof. English U. Wyo., Laramie, 1986-92, assoc. prof., 1992—. Author: Elizabeth I, 1993; co-editor: Women's Alliances in Early Modern England, 1997. NEH fellow, 1995-96; Folger Shakespeare Libr. grantee, 1995; Wyo. Coun. for Humanities grantee, 1987, 89, 92. Mem. MLA, Rocky Mountain Medieval and Renaissance Assn. (exec. bd., pres. 1986—), Spenser Soc. Am. (exec. bd. 1996—), Soc. for Study of Early Modern Women (nominating com. 1997—), Medieval Feminist Newsletter, Renaissance Soc. Am. Democrat. Jewish. Avocations: skiing, guitar, hiking, theatre, travel. Office: U Wyo Dept English PO Box 3353 Laramie WY 82071-3353

FRYE, WILBUR WAYNE, soil science educator, researcher, administrator; b. Finger, Tenn., Aug. 6, 1933; s. Alfred D. and Lela E. (Rouse) F.; m. Martha Hoskins, Apr. 20, 1957; children: Thomas W., John D. BS, U. Tenn., 1961, MS, 1964; PhD, Va. Tech, 1969. Cert. profl. soil scientist, soil erosion and sediment control specialist; cert. crop advisor. Air traffic controller FAA, Memphis, 1957-58; instr. Tenn. Tech. U., Cookeville, 1963-74; asst. prof. U. Ky., Lexington, 1975-78, assoc. prof., 1978-84, prof., 1984—. Contbr. articles to profl. jours., chpts. to books. Chmn. troop commn. Boy Scouts Am., Lexington, 1976-81; chmn. adminstrv. bd. Trinity Hill United Meth. Ch., Lexington, 1977-79; lay del. to Ky. Conf. United Meth. Ch., 1994-96. Recipient Sci. Faculty Fellowship award NSF, 1967, Master Tchr. award Gamma Sigma Delta, 1978, Great Tchr. award U. Ky. Alumni Assn., 1980, Pres.'s Citation Soil & Water Conservation Soc., 1976, 78; named Danforth Assoc., 1981. Fellow Soil and Water Conservation Soc. (bd. dirs. 1975-79), Soil Sci. Soc. Am. (bd. dirs. 1989-90, assoc. editor Jour. 1990-93, Soil Sci. Edn. award 1995), Am. Soc. Agronomy (Agronomic Resident Edn. award 1995); mem. Coun. for Agrl. Sci. and Tech. (bd. dirs. 1991-99), Internat. Soil Tillage Rsch. Orgn., Assn. Am. Control Ofcls., Assn. Am. Feed Control Ofcls. (bd. dirs. 1995-97). Methodist. Office: U Ky Divsn Regulatory Svcs Lexington KY 40546-0275

FRYE-MOQUIN, MARSHA MARIE, social worker; b. Tecumseh, Mich., Aug. 1, 1950; d. Jesse Roberts Gray and Evelyn Marie Binns Wade; m. Paul Raymond Moquin, Apr. 20, 1990; children: Dawn M. Savidge, James M. Savidge Jr., David R. Frye. AS, Monroe County C.C., Monroe, Mich., 1976; ADN, U. Vt., 1988; BA in Sociology, North Adams (Mass.) State Coll, 1992; MSW, SUNY, Albany, 1994; cert. case mgmt., New Eng. Healthcare Assembly, 1997. Cert. social worker, Mass.; lic. ind. cert. social worker, Mass. Sales clk./cashier Woolworth's dept. Store, Burlington, Vt.; clk./typist New Eng. Telephone, Burlington, 1978-80; unit sec. Prince Georges Hosp., Cheverly, Md., 1969-72, Fairfax Hosp., Falls Church, Va., 1972-73; nurses aide Burlington Convalescent Ctr., 1976-77; EEG technician Med. Ctr. of Vt., Burlington, 1980-88; lab. technician U. Vt., Burlington, 1987-88; staff nurse Berkshire Med. Ctr., Pittsfield, Mass., 1988-90, charge nurse, 1989-90; intern Women's Svcs. Ctr./Battered Women's Shelter, Pittsfield, Mass., 1991, No. Berkshire Health and Human Svcs. Coalition, North Adams, 1992, Hillcrest Ednl. Ctr., Lenox, Mass., 1992-93, Dept. Vet. Affairs Med. Ctr., Northampton, Mass., 1993-94; med. social worker Fairview Hosp., Great Barrington, Mass., 1994—; dir. social svcs., 1995—; nurse, med. social worker Vis. Nurses Assn. No. Berkshire, Williamstown, Mass., 1991-95. Vol. Am. Cancer Soc., 1995—; bd. dirs. United Cerebral Palsy Assn. Berkshire County, Inc. Recipient Clin. Excellence award The Vt. State Nurses Assn., Cert. of Honor for vol. svc. Women's Svc. Ctr., 1991, Cert. of Appreciation, No. Berkshire Health and Human Svcs. Coalition, 1991,

Managerial Excellence award Fairview Hosp., 1997. Mem. NASW, New England Sociological Assn., Alpha Chi. Avocations: concerts, theater, movies. Home: 136 Ingalls Rd Cheshire MA 01225-9731

FRYER, APPLETON, publisher, sales executive, lecturer, diplomat; b. Buffalo, Feb. 25, 1927; s. Livingston and Catherine (Appleton) F.; AB cum laude, Princeton U., 1950; m. Angeline Dudley Kenefick, May 16, 1953; children: Appleton, Daniel Kenefick, Robert Livingston, Catherine Appleton. Head interpreter Hewitt-Robins, Inc., Buffalo, 1950-51; advt. dept. Buffalo Evening News, 1953-55; field rep. Ketchum, MacLeod & Grove, Inc., advt., 1955-56; pres. Duo-Fast of Western N.Y., Inc., Buffalo, 1956-84; pub. Buffalo Bus. Jour., 1984-86; travel cons. Pieper Travel Bur., 1990; hon. consul gen. of Japan, Buffalo, 1979—. Dep. sheriff, Erie County, N.Y., 1954-68; adv. bd. Children's Hosp. of Buffalo; mem. Cmty. Welfare Coun. Buffalo and Erie County; co-chmn. Corp. Div. Episc. Charities, 1988, chmn., 1989; mem. bd. Erie County Sesquicentennial Commn., 1970-71; co-chmn. Erie Bicentennial Commn., 1974-76; adviser City Buffalo Environ. Mgmt. Commn., 1973-75; trustee Theodore Roosevelt Inaugural Nat. Historic Site Found., 1969-87; bd. dirs. Zool. Soc. Buffalo, 1972-78, Buffalo Fine Arts Acad., Albright-Knox Art Gallery, 1973-76; chmn. Buffalo-Kanazawa Sister Cities Com., 1978-79; pres. Arboretum of Met. Buffalo, 1977-78; bd. dirs. Maud Gordon Holmes Arboretum, 1974-88, pres., 1976-78; mem. Buffalo Landmark and Preservation Bd., 1978-87, Erie County Preservation Adv. Bd., 1978-82; mem. coun. Charles Burchfield Ctr., 1974-92; mem. coun. Cen. Erie deanery Diocese Western N.Y., 1970; mem. Erie County Sesquicentennial Commn., 1970-71; mem. com. Young Life on Niagara Frontier, 1971-72; chmn. planning com. Venture in Mission, 1979, mem. campaign exec. com., 1979-80; chmn. N.Y. State sect. ann. giving Princeton U., 1979—, chmn. Western N.Y. annual giving regional com., 1978-79, mem. nat. ann. giving com.; interim exec. dir. Landmark Soc. of Niagara Frontier, 1998—; mem. adv. bd. Erie County Cultural Resources, 1986-92, Concerned Ecumenical Ministry (West Side), 1986—; chmn. devel. com. Crane Cutting Ctr., 1987-90, corp. div. Episc. Charities, 1988-89; comdr. Lorenzo Burrows post Am. Legion, 1988-89; mem. N.Y. State coms. Bicentennial of French Revolution, 1988-90; historian western N.Y. commandery Naval Order U.S., 1991—; patients' rep. Buffalo Gen. Hosp., 1996—. With USNR, 1945-46, to 1st lt. AUS, 1951-52. Recipient Key to the City of Buffalo, Mayor Anthony Masiello, 1996, Buffalo-Kanazawa Sister City Com. award for Long and Dedicated Svc., 1997. Mem. SAR (1st v.p. Buffalo chpt. 1993-94, pres., 1995-96), Niagara Frontier Indsl. Distbrs. Assn., Buffalo Area C. of C. (Buffalo Beautiful Com.), Am. Assn. Mus. (trustee 1978-81), SR (pres. Buffalo Assn. 1966-73), Soc. Mayflower Descs. (regent Buffalo colony 1961-65), Soc. Colonial Wars, Holland Soc. of N.Y. (pres. Niagara Frontier br. 1969-79), Buffalo and Erie County Hist. Soc. (bd. mgrs. 1969—, v.p. 1977-82, pres. 1982-84), Buffalo Soc. Natural Scis., Landmark Soc. Niagara Frontier, Outstanding award 1979 (pres. 1969-73), Old Ft. Niagara Assn. (dir. 1980-90), Order. Colonial Lords of Manors, Princeton Alumni Assn. (chmn. schs. com. Western N.Y. area 1974-77). Episcopalian (warden, licensed lay reader). Clubs: Masons, Rotary of Buffalo (internat. svc. com. 1978-90, bd. dirs. 1983-86); Princeton (N.Y.C.); Princeton of Western N.Y. (pres. 1960), Saturn (vice dean 1963, 86, dean 1990) (Buffalo); Nassau, Univ. Cottage (Princeton, N.J.); Porcupine (gov. 1969-73) (Nassau). Home: 85 Windsor Ave Buffalo NY 14209-1018

FRYER, EDWIN SAMUEL, lawyer; b. St. Louis, Jan. 10, 1947; s. Minot P. and Donne S. Fryer; m. Dorothy S. Perry, July 28, 1990; children: Eliza W., Mary P., Caroline S., Clayton Perry, Kevin Perry. AB cum laude, Brown U., 1969; JD summa cum laude, Wash. U., 1972. Bar: Mo. 1972, U.S. Dist. Ct. (ea. dist.) 1972, U.S. Ct. Appeals (8th cir.) 1974, U.S. Supreme Ct. 1979. Law clk. to Hon. William H. Webster U.S. Dist. Ct., 1971; law clk. to Hon. George J. Moran Ill. Appellate Ct. (5th dist.), 1972; ptnr. Bryan Cave, St. Louis, leader health care group, 1993—. Chancellor Episcopal Diocese Mo.; 1st vice chair Am. Red Cross, 1993—; bd. dirs. United Way Greater St. Louis, 1981-88; trustee Mary Inst./St. Louis Country Day Sch., 1985-91. With U.S. Army, 1971-79. Mem. ABA, Mo. Bar Assn., Bar Assn. Met. St. Louis, St. Louis Country Club, Noonday Club, Deer Creek Club, Order of Coif. Republican. Episcopalian. Home: 25 Foreway Dr Saint Louis MO 63124-1618

FRYER, JUDITH DOROTHY, lawyer; b. N.Y.C., Feb. 14, 1950; d. Jerome M. and Gloria (Abrams) F.; m. Daniel P. Biggs, June 4, 1972; children: Jeremy Fryer-Biggs, Zachary Fryer-Biggs. BA, Washington U., 1972; JD, Hofstra U., 1975. Bar: N.Y. 1976. Assoc. Carro, Spanbock, Fass & Geller, N.Y.C., 1978-82, ptnr., 1982-86; ptnr. Finley & Kumble, N.Y.C., 1987; counsel Kaye, Scholer, Fierman, Hays & Handler, N.Y.C., 1988-89, ptnr., 1989-95; shareholder Greenberg Traurig, N.Y.C., 1995—; Bd. advisers Capital Sources for Real Estate newsletter, 1994—. Author: Roll-up Transactions-The Current Picture, 1992, Taking a REIT Public, 1994, Surprises in Recent REIT and Rollup Offerings, 1994, Integration Issues in Real Estate Securities Offerings, 1995; editor current devels.: Real Estate Securities & Capital Markets newsletter, 1989-90, editor, 1990-92. Fellow Am. Bar Found.; mem. ABA (chair subcom. equipment leasing programs 1988-91, chair subcom. on partnerships & REIT products 1991-96, chair subcom. on partnerships, trusts and unincorporated assns. 1994—, chair women rainmakers interest group 1996—), Nat. Assn. Real Estate Investment Trusts (exec. com. 1994-95, bd. govs. 1994-96). Office: Greenberg Traurig 200 Park Ave New York NY 10166

FRYER, ROBERT SHERWOOD, theatrical producer; b. Washington, Nov. 18, 1920; s. Harold and Ruth (Reade) F. BA, Western Res. U., 1943. Producer: (Broadway plays) (with others) A Tree Grows in Brooklyn, 1951, (with others) By the Beautiful Sea, 1954, Wonderful Town, 1953, The Desk Set, Shangri-La, Auntie Mame, Redhead, There Was a Little Girl, Advise and Consent, A Passage To India, Hot Spot, Roar Like a Dove, Sweet Charity, Chicago, 1975, The Norman Conquests, 1976, California Suite, 1976, On the Twentieth Century, 1977, Sweeney Todd, 1978, Merrily We Roll Along, The West Side Waltz, 1981, Noises Off, 1983, Benefactors, 1985, Wild Honey, 1987, Hapgood, 1989, (films) The Boston Strangler, 1968, Abdication, 1973, Mame, 1973, Great Expectations, 1974, Voyage of the Damned, 1976, The Boys from Brazil, 1978, Prime of Miss Jean Brodie 1969, Travels with My Aunt, 1973, The Shining 1979, Chicago, 1999, artistic dir., 1972-90; cons., 1990—; Ahmanson Theatre, Ctr. Theatre Group, L.A.; author: Professional Theatrical Management New York City, 1947. Bd. dirs. Kennedy Ctr.; trustee, exec. com. John F. Kennedy Ctr., Washington. Served as capt. AUS, 1941-46; maj. Res. Decorated Legion of Merit.; Rockefeller Found. fellow. Mem. Episcopal Actors Guild (v.p.), League of N.Y. Theatres (bd. govs.). Office: Producer Cir Co 200 W 57th St Ste 1403 New York NY 10019-3211 *I am grateful for all God has given me, and I feel an obligation to Him to return goodness and kindness to my fellowman.*

FRYER, THOMAS WAITT, JR., writer and editor; b. Martinsville, Va., Oct. 6, 1936; s. Thomas Waitt and Wilma Pauline (Harp) F.; m. Mary Margaret Allshouse, Jan. 5, 1980; children—Laura Elizabeth, Matthew Thomas, John Anderson. A.A., Mars Hill Coll., 1956; B.A., Wayland Coll., 1958; M.A. (Ford Found. fellow), Vanderbilt U., 1959; Ph.D. (Kellogg Found. fellow), U. Calif., Berkeley, 1968. Instr. in English Daytona Beach Jr. Coll., 1959-61; assoc. dean instrn. Chabot Coll., 1965-67; v.p., chief campus adminstr. Miami-Dade Community Coll., 1967-73; chancellor Peralta Colls., 1973-78; chancellor, dist. supt. Foothill-De Anza Community Coll. Dist., 1978-92; vice chmn. bd. dirs. Am. Council on Edn., 1979-80; vis. prof. U. Calif. at Berkeley, 1988-92; pres. Fla. Assn. Community Colls., 1971-73. Chmn. WASC Accred Com. for Community and Jr. Colls., 1984-86; pres. chief exec. officers Calif. Community Colls., 1986-87; trustee Fla. C.C. Jacksonville, 1999. Recipient Communication and Leadership award Toastermasters Internat., 1977, selected a Young Leader of Acad., 1978; named one of Most Effective Coll. Pres. in Nation Exxon Edn. Found., 1986, one of 50 best community coll. CEO's by U. Tex., Austin, 1988. Mem. Nat. Soc. Study Edn., Am. Assn. Higher Edn. (dir. 1975-78), Assn. for Study of Higher Edn., Phi Delta Kappa. Clubs: Commonwealth of Calif.

FRYKENBERG, ROBERT ERIC, historian; b. India, June 8, 1930; s. Carl Eric and Doris Marie (Skoglund) F.; m. Carol Enid Addington, July 1, 1952; children: Ann Denise Leinis, Brian Robert, Craig Michael. B.A., Bethel Coll., Minn., 1951; M.A., U. Minn., 1953; M.Div., Bethel Theol. Sem., 1955; Ph.D. (Rockefeller fellow 1958-61), London U., 1961. Research asst. U. Calif., Berkeley, 1955-57; instr. Oakland (Calif.) Jr. Coll., 1957-58; Ford and Carnegie research and teaching fellow U. Chgo., 1961-62; mem. faculty U. Wis., Madison, 1962—; prof. history and S. Asian studies U. Wis., 1971-97, emeritus prof. history and South Asian studies, 1997—, chmn. dept., dir. Center S. Asian Studies, 1970-73; vis. prof. U. Hawaii, summer 1968; Radhakrishwan Meml. lectr. Oxford U., 1998. Author: Guntur District, 1978-1848: A History of Local Influence and Central Authority in South India, 1965, History and Belief: The Foundations of Historical Understanding, 1996; editor: Land Control and Social Structure in Indian History, 1969, 77, Land Tenure and Peasant in South Asia: An Anthology of Recent Research, 1977, Studies of South India, 1985, Delhi Through the Ages, 1986, 93; contbr. articles to revs. and profl. publs. Trustee Am. Inst. Indian Studies, 1971-81; dir. summer seminar NEH, 1976. Rsch. fellow Am. Coun. Learned Socs.-Social Sci. Rsch. Coun. 1962-63, 67, 73-74, 83-84, 88-89, Guggenheim fellow, 1968-69, HEW Fulbright Hays sr. fellow, 1965-66, NEH fellow, 1975, fellow Wis. Inst. Rsch. Humanities, 1975, Wilson Ctr., 1986, 91-92, Pew India Rsch. Advancement Projects Dir., 1994-98, 98—, Pew Rsch. fellow, 1997. Fellow Royal Hist. Soc., Royal Asiatic Soc.; mem. Internat. Conf. and Seminars, Soc. S. Indian Studies (pres. 1968-70, 82-84), Am. Hist. Assn. (pres. conf. faith and history 1970-72), Assn. Asian Studies, Inst. Hist. Studies India, Inst. Asian Studies India, Assn. South Asian Studies Australia, Inst. Advanced Christian Studies (dir. 1979-83, 87-91, pres. 1981-83). Office: Univ Wis 4134 Humanities Bldg Madison WI 53706

FRYMAN, VIRGIL THOMAS, JR., lawyer; b. Maysville, Ky., Apr. 9, 1940; s. Virgil Thomas and Elizabeth Louis (Marshall) F. AB cum laude, Harvard U., 1962, LLB, 1966. Bar: N.Y. 1967, U.S. Ct. Appeals (2d cir.) 1967, U.S. Dist. Ct. (so. and ea. dists.) N.Y. 1968, U.S. Supreme Ct. 1970, U.S. Ct. Appeals (6th cir.) 1988, U.S. Dist. Ct. (ea. and we. dist.) Ky. 1988. Assoc. Cravath, Swaine & Moore, N.Y.C., 1966-73; asst. U.S. atty. U.S. Dist. Ct. (so. dist) N.Y., N.Y.C., 1973-78; assoc. gen. counsel Price Waterhouse, N.Y.C., 1978-86; staff counsel U.S. Ho. of Reps. select com. to investigate covert arms transactions with Iran, 1987; mem. Greenebaum Doll & McDonald P.L.L.C., Lexington, Ky., 1988—. Contbr. to Proving Federal Crimes, 6th edit., 1976. Mem. ABA, Assn. Bar City of N.Y., Ky. Bar Assn., Fayette County Bar Assn., Harvard Club, Idle Hour Country Club. Democrat. Episcopalian. Home: Fed Hill Washington KY 41096-0173 Office: Greenebaum Doll & McDonald PLLC 1400 Vine Center Tower PO Box 1808 Lexington KY 40588-1808

FRYMAYER, JOHN W., dean. Dean Vt. Coll. Medicine. Office: U Vt Coll Medicine E 109 85 S Prospect St Burlington VT 05405-1704*

FRYREAR, DONALD WILLIAM, agricultural engineer; b. Haxtun, Colo., Dec. 8, 1936; s. William Alfred and Majorie (Adams) F.; m. Sherry Janice Watson, Sept. 16, 1956; children: Debra Lou, Kenneth William. BSAE, Colo. State U., 1959; MSAE, Kans. State U., 1962. Registered profl. engr., Tex. Engr. USDA-Agrl. Rsch. Svc., Akron, Colo., 1959-60, Manhattan, Kans., 1960-62; rsch. engr. USDA-Agrl. Rsch. Svc., Temple, Tex., 1962-65; rsch. leader USDA-Agrl. Rsch. Svc., Big Spring, Tex., 1965-97; erosion cons. UNESCO, Medmine, Tunisia, 1983, Pretoria, South Africa, 1985; project leader for devel. of Revised Wind Erosion Equation. Contbr. articles to profl. jours. Recipient Appreciation award Howard Coll., 1977; Soil Conservation Soc. Am. fellow, 1982. Mem. Am. Soc. Agrl. Engrs. (assoc. editor 1974, SW Dirs. citation 1996), Soil and Water Conservation Soc. (charter pres. 1972), Am. Soc. Agronomy (state pres. 1977), N.Y. Acad. Sci. Baptist. Achievements include development of graded furrow concept for controlling water erosion, techniques for analyzing field erosion data; design and construction of five wind tunnels; design of first field equipment for measuring wind erosion. Home: 7204 S Service Rd Big Spring TX 79720-0546 Office: Custon Products and Cons 7204 S Service Rd Big Spring TX 79720-0546

FRYT, MONTE STANISLAUS, petroleum company executive, speaker, advisor; b. Jackson, Mich., Aug. 3, 1949; s. Marion S. and Dorothy A. (Fischman) F.; m. Pollyanna Hayes, May 26, 1990. BS in Aerospace Engring., U. Colo., Boulder, 1971; MBA in Mgmt., U. Colo., Denver, 1988. Field engr. Schlumberger Well Svcs., Bakersfield, Calif., 1971-75; computer R & D engr. Schlumberger Well Svcs., Houston, 1975-77; account devel. engr. Schlumberger Well Svcs., L.A., 1977-78; dist. mgr. Schlumberger Well Svcs., Abilene, Tex., 1978-80, Williston, N.D., 1980-81; v.p. ops. Logmate Svcs. Inc., Calgary, Alta., Can., 1981-84; pres. Fryt Petroleum Inc., Denver, 1984-91; mgr. petrophysics Am. Hunter Exploration, Ltd., Denver, 1991-92; prin. Reservoir Evaluations Group, Denver, 1992-99; ptnr., mgr. Monterey Energy LLC, Denver, 1994-98; mgr. tech. Anschutz Exploration Corp., 1995—. Mem. Colo. Rep. Com., 1990—, Rep. Nat. Com., Colo. Rep. Leadership Program, 1992-93; mem. exec. com. Colo. Rep. Bus. Coalition, 1993—, vice-chmn., 1996-97, chmn., 1997-99. Mem. Am. Assn. Petroleum Geologists, Rocky Mountain Assn. Geologists, Elks, Rockies Venture Club, Independence Inst. Roman Catholic. Avocations: mountain climbing, skiing, running, biking, cultural and political reading. Home: 7400 S Curtice Ct Littleton CO 80120-3951 Office: Ste 2400 555 17th St Denver CO 80202-3941

FRY-WENDT, SHERRI DIANE, psychologist; b. Clinton, Mo., Mar. 30, 1958; d. Charles Pierce and Norma Geraldine (Croft) Fry; m. Joseph Otto Wendt, May 24, 1980; children: Benjamin, Ethan, Nathaniel. BSE, Cen. Mo. State U., 1979, MS, 1981; PhD, U. Mo., 1989. Lic. psychologist, Mo.; cert. health svc. provider, Mo. Mental health therapist Wyandot Mental Health Ctr., Kansas City, Kans., 1981-88; EAP contract psychologist Menninger Found., Topeka, 1988-89; contract psychologist Tri-County Mental Health Ctr., Kansas City, 1988-89; pvt. practice Kansas City, 1988—; tng. provider local and state level, 1985—; expert witness State of Kans., 1985—. Youth group sponsor Hillside Christian Ch., Kansas City, 1982-86, children's choir dir., 1983-87, deaconess, 1983-93, dir. vacation bible sch., 1992, 93; deaconess Fairview Christian Ch.; mem. ethics com. Kansas City region Christian Ch. (Disciples of Christ); mem. exec. bd. PTA, pres. 1999-00, youth friend, 1999—. Mem. APA, Greater Kansas City Psychol. Assn., Phi Kappa Phi, Psi Chi. Avocations: piano, guitar, crafts, traveling. Office: 4901 Main St Ste 408 Kansas City MO 64112-2635

FRYXELL, DAVID ALLEN, publishing executive; b. Sioux Falls, S.D., Mar. 8, 1956; s. Donald Raymond and Lucy (Dickinson) F.; m. Lisa Duaine Forman, June 16, 1978; 1 child, Courtney Elizabeth. B.A., Augustana Coll., 1978. Assoc.-sr. editor TWA Ambassador, St. Paul, 1978-80, mng. editor, 1980-81; sr. editor Horizon, Tuscaloosa, Ala., 1981-82; circuit writer Telegraph Herald, Dubuque, Iowa, 1982-85; contbg. editor Horizon mag., 1982-85; dir. publs., exec. editor Pitt mag. U. Pitts., 1985-90; editorial dir. Quad/Creative Group Milwaukee Mag., 1991-92; exec. features editor, dir. new ventures St. Paul Pioneer Press, 1992-95, sr. editor technology and new ventures, 1995-96; sr. editor bus. and tech., 1996; exec. producer Twin Cities Sidewalk Microsoft Corp., 1996-98; mag. editl. dir. F & W Publs., Cin., 1998—; chief judge mags. Golden Quill awards Pitts., 1980; nonfiction columnist Writer's Digest, 1994—. Author: Double-Parked on Main Street, 1988, How to Write Fast While Writing Well, 1992, Elements of Article Writing: Structure and Flow, 1996; contbr. articles to mags. including Travel & Leisure, Playboy, Passages, AAA World, Savvy, Online Access, Diversion, Easy Living, Readers Digest, Link Up, others. Chief writer Anderson for Pres. Com., Minn., 1978. Mem. Am. Assn. Sunday & Feature Editors, Iowa Newspaper Assn. (2d award master columnist 1983, 2d award best feature writing 1983, 2d award best series 1983), Chgo. Art Dirs. Club (Merit award for editing 1981), Coll. and Univ. Pub. Relations Assn. of Pa., Council for Advancement and Support of Edn. (Periodicals Improvement award 1987, 90, 91, Top Ten Mag. award 1990, 91, Articles of Yr. award 1990, Periodical Spl. Issues award 1991, Instl. Rels. Publs. award 1991, Periodical Resource Mgmt. award, 1990, 91), Augustana Coll. Fellows, Augustana Alumni Assn. (Decades of Leadership award 1978), Blue Key, Internat. Assn. Bus. Communicators (Golden Triangle award 1987, 89, best spl. publ. award 1988), Women in Communications (Matrix award 1990, hon. mention 1990, 91), City and Regional Mag. Assn. (Gen. Excellence award 1992, Spl. Sect. award 1992, Commentary award 1992, Investigative Writing award 1992), Mo. Lifestyle Awards (2d Gen. Excellence award 1994, 95). Democrat. Unitarian. Office: F & W Publs 1507 Dana Ave Cincinnati OH 45207-1056

FTHENAKIS, EMANUEL JOHN, diversified aerospace company executive; b. Greece, Jan. 30, 1928; came to U.S., 1952, naturalized, 1956; s. John and Evanthia (Magoulakis) F.; m. Hermione Jane Coates, 1972; children: John, Basil. Diploma mech. and elec. engring., Tech. U. Athens, 1951; MS in Elec. Engring., Columbia U., 1954; postgrad., U. Pa., 1961-62. Mem. tech. staff Bell Tel. Labs., 1952-57; dir. engring. missile and space div. G.E., Phila., 1957-61; v.p., gen. mgr. space and re-entry div. Philco-Ford Co., Palo Alto, Calif., 1961-69; pres. ITT Aerospace Co., L.A., 1969-70; chmn. Am. Satellite Corp., Germantown, Md., 1971-85; v.p. Fairchild Industries, Germantown, 1971-80, sr. v.p., 1980-84, exec. v.p., 1984; pres., chief exec. officer Fairchild Industries, Chantilly, Va., 1985-86, chmn., chief exec. officer, 1986-91; pres., COO Fairchild Corp., Chantilly, 1990-91, also bd. dirs.; chmn., chief exec. officer CEF Corp., Potomac, Md., 1991—; adj. prof. U. Md., 1981-84; mem. Pres.'s Nat. Security Telecomms. Adv. Coun., 1982-91; chmn., CEO, Olympic Airways, 1993. Author: A Manual of Satellite Communications, 1984; patentee in field. Mem. bd. visitors Coll. Engring., U. Md., 1980—; bd. dirs. Challenger Ctr. for Space Sci. and Edn., 1988-96, U. Md. Found., 1989—; chmn. bd. Challenger Ctr. for Space Sci. and Edn., 1994-96; trustee Univs. Rsch. Assn., Inc., 1990—. Named Man of Yr., Electronic & Aerospace Systems Conf., 1982. Fellow IEEE; mem. AIAA (assoc.), The George Town Club. Greek Orthodox. Office: CEF Corp PO Box 59708 Rockville MD 20859-9708

FTHENAKIS, VASILIS, chemical engineer, consultant, educator; b. Chania, Crete, Greece, July 21, 1951; came to U.S., 1976; naturalized, 1986; s. Menelaos and Antonia Korkidis; m. Christina Georgakopoulos, Feb. 6, 1982; children: Antonia, Menelaos. Diploma in Chemistry, U. Athens, 1975; MS in Chem. Engring., Columbia U., 1978; PhD in Fluid Dynamics & Atmospheric Sci., NYU, 1991. Rsch. analyst Columbia U., N.Y.C., project engr.; sr. chem. engr. Brookhaven Nat. Lab., Upton, N.Y., 1980—; cons. in chem. engring., 1986—, semiconductor and photovoltaic cons., 1987—, petroleum and petrochemical cons., specialist on prevention of hazardous gas releases, 1989—; founder, pres. EnviroConsultants Inc., Upton, N.Y., 1991 EnviroEstates Ltd., 1998; amended to EnviroSafety Inc., 1999; chmn. confs.; adj. prof. environ. engring., chem. engring. CCNY, 1992—, Columbia U., 1993—; expert witness on safety and environ. cases, 1997—. Author: Prevention and Control of Accidental Releases of Hazardous Gases, 1993; mem. editl. bd. Progress in Photovoltaics, 1996—, Jour. Loss Prevention, 1998—; contbr. over 130 articles to sci. jours., chpts. to books. Mem. AIChE, Ctr. Chem. Process Safety (panel experts), Semiconductor Safety Assn, Am. Meteorol. Soc. Home: 9 Lucille Ln Dix Hills NY 11746-5848 Office: Brookhaven Nat Lab Environ Waste Tech Ctr Bldg 830 Upton NY 11973

FTOREK, ROBBIE BRIAN (ROBERT BRIAN FTOREK), professional hockey coach; b. Boston, Jan. 2, 1952; s. Stephen Joseph and A. Ruth (Barton) F.; m. Wendy Joan Bray, May 20, 1972; children: Sam, Lucie, Casey, Anna. Grad. high sch., Needham, Mass. Hockey player U.S. Olympic Team, Sapporo, Japan, 1972; profl. hockey player various teams, 1972-81, N.Y. Rangers, N.Y.C., 1982-85; coach New Haven Nighthawks, 1985-87, L.A. Kings, 1987-89; asst coach New Jersey Devils, 89-97, head coach, 97-. Recipient Silver medal U.S. Olympic Com., 1972. Office: New Jersey Devils P.O.Box 504 East Rutherford NJ 07073*

FU, KAREN KING-WAH, radiation oncologist; b. Shanghai, China, Oct. 15, 1940; came to U.S., 1959, naturalized, 1975; d. Ping Sen and Lein Sun (Ho) F. Student, Ind. U., 1959-61; A.B., Barnard Coll., Columbia U., 1963, M.D., 1967. Cert. radiation oncologist. Intern Montreal Gen. Hosp., Que., Can., 1967-68; resident Princess Margaret Hosp., Toronto, Ont., Can., 1968-69, Stanford U. Hosp., Calif., 1969-71; instr. U. Utah, 1971-72; clin. instr. U. Calif., San Francisco, 1972-73, asst. prof., 1973-76, assoc. prof., 1976-82, prof., 1982—, vice chmn., 1994-95, rsch. assoc. Cancer Research Inst., 1973-96. Contbr. articles to profl. jours. Mem. San Francisco Opera Guild, San Francisco Symphony Assn., San Francisco Ballet, Calif. Acad. Sci., De Young Mus. Grantee Am. Cancer Soc., 1982, 86, NIH, 1982, 87. Fellow Am. Coll. Radiology; mem. Am. Soc. Therapeutic Radiologists, Am. Med. Women's Assn., Calif. Radiation Therapy Assn., Calif. Radiol. Soc., No. Calif. Acad. Clin. Oncology, Radiation Research Soc., Am. Soc. Clin. Oncologists, Assn. Women in Sci. Office: U Calif-San Francisco Dept Radiation Oncology Box 0226 San Francisco CA 94143

FU, LEE-LUENG, oceanographer; b. Taipei, Republic of China, Oct. 10, 1950; s. Yi-Chin and Er-Lan (Chen) F.; m. Cecilia C. Liu, Mar. 26, 1977; 1 child, Christine. BS, Nat. Taiwan U., Taipei, 1972; PhD, MIT, 1980. Postdoctoral assoc. MIT, Cambridge, Mass., 1980; mem. tech. staff Jet Propulsion Lab., Pasadena, Calif., 1981-85, tech. group supr., 1986-93, project scientist, 1988—, lead scientist/ocean scis., 1994, sr. rsch. scientist, 1994; chmn. TOPEX/POSEIDON sci. working team NASA, Washington, 1988—, mem. NSCAT sci. working team, 1986—; mem. sci. steering com. U.S. World Ocean Experiment Circulation, 1998—, U.S. Global Ocean Observing System, 1998—. Contbr. articles to profl. publs. Recipient Laurels award Aviation Week and Space Tech., 1993, CNES medal French Space Agy., 1994, Exceptional Scientific Achievement medal NASA, 1996. Mem. AAAS, Am. Geophys. Union, Am. Meteorol. Soc., Oceanography Soc. Office: Jet Propulsion Lab MS 300-323 4800 Oak Grove Dr Pasadena CA 91109-8001

FU, PAUL SHAN, law librarian, consultant; b. Shien-Yang, Liao-Ning, China, Sept. 7, 1932; came to U.S., 1961; s. Mu-Shia and Shih-Wei (Chang) F.; m. Doris S. Ku, Jan. 15, 1963; children: Eugene Y., Vincent Y. LLB, Soochow U., 1960; MCL, U. Ill., 1962; MSLS, Villanova U., 1968. Asst. libr., law lectr. Detroit Coll. of Law, 1968-69; law libr., asst. prof. law Ohio No. U., Ada, 1969-71, law libr., assoc. prof. law, 1971-72; law libr. Supreme Ct. of Ohio, Columbus, 1972—; pres. Asian-Am. Law Librs. Caucus, 1994; dir. Nat. Conf. on State Ct. Librs., Columbus, 1993; cons. Supreme Ct. of Ill. Law Libr., Springfield, 1988, N.H. State Law Libr., Concord, 1987; judge West Pub. Excellence in Law Librarianship Awards Com., 1996. Author: Law Library Handbook of Ohio Supreme Court, 1974; columnist Ohio Lawyer, 1988—; contbr. articles to profl. jours. Recipient Award of Merit Columbus Bar Assn., 1996; U. Ill. fellow, 1961-62. Mem. ALA, Am. Assn. Law Librs. (sec. 1989-93, chair state, ct., and county law librs. sect. 1977-78), Am. Soc. Internat. Law, Univ. Club, Kiwanis (Columbus). Avocations: piano, oil painting, fiction, tennis. Home: 940 Evening St Worthington OH 43085-3051 Office: Ohio State Supreme Ct Law Libr 30 E Broad St Fl 4 Columbus OH 43215-3414

FU, SHOU-CHENG JOSEPH, biomedicine educator; b. Peking, China, Mar. 19, 1924; s. W.C. Joseph and W.C. (Tsai) F.; m. Susan B. Guthrie, June 21, 1951; children: Robert W.G., Joseph H.G., James B.G. BS, MS, Cath. U., Peking, 1944; PhD, Johns Hopkins U., 1949. Postdoctoral fellow Nat. Insts. Health, Bethesda, Md., 1949-51, scientist, 1951-55; Gustav Bissing fellow Johns Hopkins U. at Univ. Coll. London, 1955-56; chief enzyme and bioorganic chemistry lab. Children's Cancer Rsch Found (now Dana Farber Cancer Inst.), 1955-56; rsch. assoc. Harvard U. Med. Sch., Boston, 1955-56; prof., chmn. bd. chemistry Chinese U., Hong Kong, 1966-70, dean sci. faculty, 1967-69; vis. prof. Coll. Physicians and Surgeons Columbia U., N.Y.C., 1970-71; prof. biochemistry and molecular biology U. Medicine and Dentistry of N.J., Newark, 1971—, asst. dean, 1974-77; acting dean Grad. Sch. Biomed. Scis., 1977-78, prof. opthalmology, 1989—. Contbr. articles to profl. jours. Capt. USPHS Res., 1959—. Named Hon. Disting. Prof. and Acad. Advisor Inner Mongolia Med. U., Huthot, Peoples Republic of China, 1988—. Fellow AAAS, Royal Soc. Chemistry (U.K.); mem. Royal Hong Kong Jockey Club, Am. Club Hong Kong, Sigma Xi (chpt. pres. 1976-80, sec. 1974-76, 81-82). Home: 693 Prospect St Maplewood NJ 07040-3105 Office: U of Medicine and Dentistry NJ Med Sch Med Sci Bldg 185 S Orange Ave Newark NJ 07103-2757

FUCALORO, ANTHONY FRANK, dean; b. Bklyn., Apr. 17, 1943; s. Gaetano Atillio and Josepina (Noto) F.; m. Liliane Marie-Louise Rigas, June 25, 1967; children: Nicole Antionette, Cristina Veronique. BS, Poly. Inst., Bklyn., 1964; PhD, U. Ariz., 1969. Assoc. N.Mex. State U., Las Cruces, 1969-71; vis. asst. prof. U. New Orleans, 1971-74; prof. chemistry Claremont (Calif.) McKenna Coll., 1974-93, v.p., pres., dean faculty, 1991—; cons. Occidental Petroleum, Irvine, Calif., Ill. Tool Works, Chgo., Jet Propulsion Lab., Pasadena, Calif. Contbr. articles to profl. jours. Mem. Am. Chem. Soc. (soc. advisor to Congressman David Dreier). Office: Claremont McKenna Coll Bauer Ctr 500 E 9th St Claremont CA 91711-6400*

FUCHS, ALFRED HERMAN, psychologist, college dean, educator; b. Englewood, N.J., Nov. 29, 1932; s. Herman and Wilhemine Katharine (Dieling)

F.; m. Phyllis Elizabeth Rocke, Aug. 27, 1955; children: Christopher Frederick, Jeffrey Alfred, Lisa Marie, Eric William. AB, Rutgers U., 1954; MA, Ohio U., 1958; PhD, Ohio State U., 1960. Psychologist, scientist Gen. Dynamics/Electric Boat Co., 1961-62; asst. prof. psychology Bowdoin Coll., Brunswick, Maine, 1962-66, assoc. prof., 1966-72, prof., 1972-98; prof. emeritus Bowdoin Coll., Brunswick, 1998—; chmn. dept. psychology Bowdoin Coll., Brunswick, Maine, 1965-75, 94-97, dean faculty, 1975-91; summer research participant NSF, 1963, 64. Contbr. articles to profl. jours. NSF grantee, 1963-64, 64-65. Mem. AAAS, APA (pres.-elect divsn. 26 1997-98, pres. 1998—), Ea. Psychol. Assn., Internat. Soc. History Behavioral Scis., Sigma Xi. Democrat. Home: 5 Longfellow Ave Brunswick ME 04011-2535 Office: Bowdoin Coll Dept Psychology Brunswick ME 04011

FUCHS, ANNA-RIITTA, medical educator, scientist; b. Helsinki, Finland, Feb. 8, 1926; came to U.S., 1964; d. Martti Adolf and Rut Ester (Sario) Olsson; m. Fritz Fuchs, May 19, 1948; children: Anneli, Martin, Peter Erik, Lars Frederik. MS in Chemistry with honors, U. Helsinki, 1950; DSc, U. Copenhagen, 1978. Research assoc. Inst. Hygiene Med. Physiology, U. Copenhagen, 1952-62; adj. in reproductive physiology Inst. Med. Physiology, U. Copenhagen, 1962-65; research assoc. bio.-med. div. The Population Council, Rockefeller U., N.Y.C., 1965-71, staff scientist bio.-med. div., 1971-77; faculty mem. pharmacology Cornell U. Med. Sch., N.Y.C., 1973-80, assoc. prof. reproductive biology dept. ob-gyn and dept. physiol. biophysics, 1977-86, prof. reproductive biology dept. ob-gyn and dept. physiology and biophysics, 1986—; vis. scientist dept. ob-gyn. Fed. U. Bahia, Salvador, Bahia, Brazil, 1966; vis. prof. reproductive biology Dept. ob-gyn. Chulalongkorn U., Bangkok, 1972-73, 85; cons. dept. ob-gyn. Dept. Health U.S. Virgin Islands, St. Thomas, 1986; Fogarty sr. internat. fellow Inst. Hormone and Fertility Rsch. U. Hamburg, Germany, 1994-95. Mem. editl. bd. Am. Jour. Physiology: Endocrinology and Metabolism, 1982-85, Clinica e Investigacion en Ginecologica y Obstetrica, Barcelona, Spain, 1977—; guest editor: Directions in Obstetric Perinatology, spl. issue Am. Jour. Perinatology, 1989; editor: (with F. Fuchs and P. Stubblefield) Preterm Birth, 1993; contbr. chpts. to books, more than 200 sci. articles to prof. jours. Elected friend N.Y.C. Commn. on the Status of Women, 1985. Served with Lotta Svard Finnish women's aux., 1939-44. Decorated Medal of Freedom of Finland, 1944. Fellow N.Y. Acad. Sci. (vice chmn., 1988, program chmn. com. for women in sci. 1982-88); mem. AAAS, Soc. for Gynecologic Investigation, Endocrine Soc., Soc. for the Study Reproduction, Soc. for the Study Fertility, Assn. for Women in Sci. (treas. 1978-80), Gynecol. Assn. Finland (hon.). Lutheran. Club: Larchmont (N.Y.) Yacht. Office: Cornell U Med Coll 1300 York Ave Rm S412 New York NY 10021-4805*

FUCHS, ANNE SUTHERLAND, magazine publisher; b. Volta Redonda, Brazil, Apr. 19, 1947; d. Paul Warner and Evelyn Coffman; m. James E. Fuchs, Feb. 6, 1982. Student, U. Paris at Sorbonne, 1967-68, Western Coll. for Women, 1966-67; BA, NYU, 1969. V.p., pub. Woman's Day Spl. Interest Mags.-CBS Mags., N.Y.C., 1980-82, Cuisine Mag., CBS Mags., N.Y.C., 1982-84; v.p., pub. Woman's Day mag. DCI Comm., Inc., N.Y.C., 1985-88; sr. v.p., pub. ELLE mag., N.Y.C., 1988-90, Vogue, N.Y.C., 1990-94; group pub. Harper's Bazaar, N.Y.C., 1994—; chmn. mag. and print com. U.S. Info. Agy., 1989—. Chmn. women's bd. Madison Sq. Boys and Girls Club, N.Y.C.; mem. Com. 200, USIA; bd. dirs. N.Y.C. Partnership, N.Y.C. Partnership Found. Mem. Fin. Women's Assn. N.Y., N.Y. Jr. League, Advt. Women of N.Y., Women in Communications, Women's Forum, Com. of 200, Fin. Women's Assn. N.Y. Club: Economic (N.Y.C.). Office: Harper's Bazaar Hearst Mags 1700 Broadway 28th Fl New York NY 10019-5905*

FUCHS, BETH ANN, research engineer; b. Moberly, Mo., July 22, 1963; d. Larry Dale and Marilyn Sue (Summers) Williams; m. Fred Albano Fuchs Jr., Sept. 30, 1989. AA, Cottey Coll., 1983; BS in Engring., U. N.Mex., 1987. Bookkeeper, chemistry technician U. N.Mex., Albuquerque, 1984-88; rsch. engr. Sandia Nat. Labs., Albuquerque, 1988-97, Ctr. for High Tech. Materials, U. N.Mex., 1997—. Contbr. articles to profl. jours. Republican. Avocations: cooking, counted cross stitch, bowling. Home: 336 Espejo St NE Albuquerque NM 87123-1111 Office: U NMex Ctr for High Tech Materials 1313 Goddard St SE Albuquerque NM 87106-4343

FUCHS, ELAINE V., molecular biologist, educator; b. Hinsdale, Ill., May 5, 1950; d. Louis H. and Viola L. (Lueck) F.; m. David T. Hansen, Sept. 10, 1988. BS in Chemistry with honors, U. Ill., Urbana, 1972; PhD in Biochemistry, Princeton U., 1977. Postdoctoral fellow dept. biology MIT, 1977-80; asst. prof. U. Chgo., 1980-85, assoc. prof., 1985-88, prof. dept. molecular genetics and cell biology, 1989—, Amgen prof. basic scis., 1993—, investigator, Howard Hughes Med. Inst., 1988—. Assoc. editor Jour. Cell Biology, 1993—; contr. numerous articles to profl. jours. Recipient R.R. Benesely award Am. Assn. Anatomists, 1988, Searle Scholar award Chgo. Cmty. Trust, 1981-84, Presdl. Young Investigator award NSF, 1984-89, NIH Merit award, 1993, 98, Wm. Montagna award Soc. Investigative Dermatology, 1995, Keith Porter Lecture award Am. Soc. Cell Biology, 1996, Sr. Woman Achievement award, 1997. Fellow Am. Acad. Arts and Scis., Am. Assn. Microbiology; mem. NAS (elected mem.), Inst. Medicine of NAS, Phi Beta Kappa. Office: U Chgo Howard Hughes Med Inst Dept Molecular Genetics 5841 S Maryland Ave Rm 314N Chicago IL 60637-1463

FUCHS, HANNO, communications consultant, lawyer; b. Karlsruhe, Germany, Dec. 23, 1928; came to U.S., 1941, naturalized, 1950; s. William Werner and Marianne (Hirsch) F.; m. Carol Runyan, Dec. 15, 1962; children—Andrew W., Jessica M., Daniel R., Michael J.; m. Judith Karnes, Dec. 8, 1991. B.S. in Journalism, Syracuse U., 1949; postgrad., Columbia U., 1950, NYU, 1961; JD, Pace U., 1996. Bar: Conn. 1996, N.Y. 1997. With Young & Rubicam, Inc., 1952-69, creative exec., v.p., 1961-69; exec. v.p. Richard K. Manoff, Inc., N.Y.C., 1969-70, pres., 1970-71; v.p. Grey Advt. Inc., N.Y.C., 1971-74; sr. v.p. Needham, Harper & Steers, Inc., 1974-75, Young & Rubicam Inc., N.Y.C., 1975-86; owner Fuchs Comm., Harrison, N.Y., 1987—; pvt. practice Stamford, Conn., 1997—. Bd. assocs. Whitehead Inst., Cambridge, Mass. With U.S. Army, 1951-53. Democrat. Jewish. Home: 301 Birch Ln Irvington NY 10533-2322 Office: 84 W Park Pl Stamford CT 06901-2211*

FUCHS, HENRY, computer science educator; b. Tokaj, Japan, Jan. 20, 1948; came to U.S.; BA, U. Calif., Santa Cruz, 1970; PhD in Computer Sci., U. Utah, 1975. Rsch. asst., tchg. fellow U. Utah, 1970-74; asst. prof. math. sci. U. Tex., Dallas, 1975-78, computer sci. coord., 1977-787; assoc. prof. U. N.C., Chapel Hill, 1978-83, Frederic Gil prof., 1983—; adj. prof. radiation oncology U. N.C.; prin. investor Pixel Flow; bd. dirs. NRC Computer Sci. and Telecom., 1993. Recipient Nat. Computer Graphics Assn. award, 1992, Satava award, 1997. Mem. IEEE, NAE, Assn. Computer Machinery (Computer Graphics Achievement award 1992), Sigma Xi. Office: Univ NC Dept Computer Sci Sitterson Hall Box 3175 Chapel Hill NC 27599*

FUCHS, JEROME HERBERT, management consultant; b. N.Y.C., Jan. 7, 1922; s. Berthold and Fannie (Neuschotz) F.; m. Eleanor May DeRoo, May 26, 1945; children: Jerome S. Taylor, Susan Fuchs Decker, Sandra Fuchs Lombino. BS in Mktg. with honors, Syracuse U., 1950, MBA, 1951. Systems and methods analyst Carrier Corp., 1951-52; supr. systems and methods Lukens Steel, Coatesville, Pa., 1952-54; mgr. systems and methods PennWalt Co., Phila., 1955-57, mgr. systems and methods and office svcs. Amax, Inc., Greenwich, Conn., 1958-60; exec. asst. to pres. Rockbestos Wire & Cable Co., 1960-61; v.p. mfg. United Aircraft Products, Dayton, Ohio, 1970-71; exec. v.p. Bus. Supplies Corp. Am., N.Y.C., 1972; sr. ptnr. Fuchs Assocs., East Meadow, N.Y., 1960—; bd. dirs. Extended Techs. Del Electronics, Advanced Packaging Tech.; indsl. rsch. asst., Syracuse (N.Y.) U., 1949-51; adj. prof. Syracuse U., 1950-52, John Hopkins U., Balt., 1953-54, Drexel, Phila., 1955-57, Queens Coll., N.Y.C., 1963-65, SUNY, Stony Brook, 1987-91, Hofstra U., 1988—. Author: Making the Most of Management Consulting Services, 1975; Managment Consultants in Action, 1975; Computerized Cost Control Systems, 1976; Computerized Inventory Control Systems, 1977; Administering the Quality Control Function, 1979, The Prentice-Hall Illustrated Handbook of Advanced Manufacturing Methods, 1988. Served as 2nd lt. AC, U.S. Army, 1943-46. Mem. Soc. Profl. Mgmt. Cons. (charter, pres. 1977-79), Inst. Mgmt. Cons. (cert., founding mem.), Sigma Iota Epsilon. Home and Office: 1612 Salisbury Park Dr East Meadow NY 11554-5522

FUCHS, JONATHAN M., health care administrator; b. N.Y.C., June 9, 1948; m. Catherine C. Cannan. BA in Psychology, SUNY, Stony Brook, 1970, MS in Health Svcs. Adminstrn., 1975; MA in Coll. and Univ. Adminstrn., Columbia U., 1972. Assoc. dir. Joint Commn. on Accreditation Hosps., Chgo., 1975-78; exec. v.p. San Pedro (Calif.) Peninsula Hosp., 1979-84; asst. v.p. Met. Life Ins., Orange, Calif., 1985-89; v.p. Employers Health Ins., Green Bay, Wis., 1992-96, Preferred Health Network, Long Beach, Calif., 1996-98; CEO, Univ. Mt. Sinai Health System, N.Y.C., 1998—; cons., Long Beach, 1979-85, 89-92; chmn., bd. dirs. Scan Health Plan, Long Beach. Contbr. articles on managed care to profl. jours. Fellow Am. Coll. Healthcare Execs. Office: Univ MSO 1 Park Ave 9th Fl New York NY 10016

FUCHS, JOSEPH LOUIS, retired magazine publisher; b. Bklyn., Nov. 23, 1931; s. Sol and Yetta (Stein) F.; m. Carol Polner, Feb. 7, 1955; children—Beth, Randy, Sheryl. B.A., Baruch Sch., CCNY, 1954. Advt. dir. House and Garden mag., N.Y.C., 1958-73; assoc. pub. House and Garden Guides, N.Y.C., 1973-75; pub. Brides mag., N.Y.C., 1975-77, Mademoiselle mag., 1977-85; v.p. Condé Nast Publs., 1985-87, exec. v.p., 1987-97; ret., 1997. Served with AUS, 1956-58. Mem. Ballen Isles, Engrs. Country Club, Sky Club, Alpha Delta Sigma.

FUCHS, LAWRENCE HOWARD, government official, educator; b. N.Y.C., Jan. 29, 1927; s. Alfred F. and Frances S. (Scheiber) F; m. Betty Corcoran Sept. 12, 1970; 1 adopted child, Carole Hooven; children by previous marriage: Janet Pearl, Frances Sarah, Naomi Ruth. BA, N.Y. U., 1950; PhD, Harvard U., 1955. Teaching fellow Harvard U., Cambridge, Mass., 1950-51; mem. faculty Brandeis U., Waltham, Mass, 1951—, chmn. dept. politics, 1959-60, dean faculty, 1960-61, prof. Am. civilization and politics, chmn. Dept. Am. Studies, 1970-86; on leave as dir. Peace Corps, Phillippines, 1961-63; exec. dir. U.S. Select Commn. on Immigration and Refugee Policy, 1979-81; vice chmn. U.S. Commn. on Immigration Reform, 1992-97; part-time radio-TV news commentator for stas. WCRB and WGBH, Boston, 1951-59. Author: The Political Behavior of American Jews, 1955, Hawaii Pono: A Political and Ethnic History, 1961, John F. Kennedy and American Catholicism, 1967, Those Peculiar Americans: Peace Corps and American National Character, 1967, American Ethnic Politics, 1968, Family Matters, 1972, The American Kaleidoscope: Race, Ethnicity and the Civic Culture, 1990. Former mem. nat. adv. bd. commn. law and social action Am. Jewish Congress; former mem. nat. adv. council Mexican Am. Lega Def. and Edn. Fund; Mass. Cong. Racial Equality; mem. exec. council Am. Jewish Hist. Soc.; vice chmn. Facing History & Ourselves; 1st chmn. Commonwealth Service Corps Commn.; former chmn. exec. com. sch. and soc. program Edn. Devel. Ctr., Inc.; founding pres. Self-Devel. Group, Inc. Served with USNR, 1945-47. Recipient Decade Humanity award Facing History and Ourselves, John Carroll Centennial award, John Hope Franklin award, 1991, Theodore Saloutos award, 1991, Carey McWilliams award, 1992; Woodrow Wilson fellow; grantee Social Scis. Rsch. Coun., East-West Ctr., Rockefeller Found., Ford Found., Exxon Found., Jaffe Found., Sloan Found. Mem. Phi Beta Kappa. Home: 150 Kings Grant Rd Weston MA 02493-2175 Office: Brandeis U Waltham MA 02154

FUCHS, MICHAEL JOSEPH, television executive; b. N.Y.C., Mar. 9, 1946; s. Charles and Sue (Wile) F. BA in Polit. Sci., Union Coll., 1967; JD, NYU, 1971. Bar: N.Y. 1971. Assoc. Marshall, Bratter, Greene, Allison & Tucker, N.Y.C., 1971-74; assoc. Bomser & Oppenheim, N.Y.C., 1974-75; dir. bus. affairs William Morris Agy., N.Y.C., 1975-76; dir. spl. programming Home Box Office, N.Y.C., 1976-77, v.p. spls. & sports, 1977-79, v.p. programming, 1979-80, sr. v.p. programming, 1980-82, exec. v.p. programming, 1982-83, pres. entertainment group, 1983-84, pres., COO, 1984, chmn., CEO, 1984-95; chmn. Home Box Office, New York, N.Y., 1995; chmn., CEO Warner Music Group, New York, N.Y., 1995, Jeffrey Bewkes, 1995—; dir. Turner Broadcasting Sys., Atlanta, 1987-96, Cable Satellite Pub. Affairs Network, Washington, 1984-95, Marvel Entertainment Group, 1992—, exec. com. Tri-Star Pictures, N.Y.C., 1983-87, Columbia Pictures, 1987-89, Time-Life Books, Alexandria, Va., 1982-88; v.p. Time Inc., N.Y.C., 1982-87, exec. v.p., 1987; mem. exec. com. bd. govs. Nat. Cable Acad., Washington, 1985-95; bd. advisors Russian-Am. Press and Info. Ctr., Moscow, 1993—; bd. dirs. IMAX Corp., Auto-By-Tel Corp., Latin Comm. Group. Trustee Simon Wiesenthal Ctr.; bd. dirs. Hebrew Home for Aged at Riverdale, Am. Found. AIDS Rsch., Creative Coalition, Alzheimer's Assn.; chmn. Bryant Park Restoration Corp. recipient Van Guard award NCTA, 1988, Disting. Svc. award Simon Wiesenthal Ctr., 1989, Humanitarian award, 1996, Cable Ace Governors Award, 1994, Nott medal Union Coll., 1995, Spirit of Liberty award People for The Am. Way, 1996; named to Broadcasting & Cable Mag. Hall of Fame, 1994. Mem. Am. Film Inst. (trustee 1982—), N.Y. State Motion Picture and TV Adv. Bd. (bd. dirs. 1984-94), Bklyn. Acad. Music (trustee 1983—), Bronx Mus. Arts (trustee 1983-95), Am. Mus. Moving Image (trustee 1988—), Mus. Modern Art (mem. bus. com.), Met. Mus. Art, Acad. Motion Picture Arts and Scis. (mem. execs. br. 1984—). Democrat. Jewish. Avocations: tennis, travel, reading, art collecting. *

FUCHS, OLIVIA ANNE MORRIS, lawyer; b. Louisville, Ky., May 2, 1949; d. H.H. Morris Jr. and Betty Jean Wills Saltkill; m. Robet Edward Fuchs, Dec. 27, 1969. BA, U. Louisville, 1977; JD cum laude, 1980. Bar: Ky. 1980, Ind. 1987, U.S. Dist. Ct. (we. dist.) Ky. 1985, U.S. Tax. Ct. 1987. Assoc. Brown, Todd & Heyburn, Louisville, 1981-87; mem. Conliffe, Sandmann & Sullivan PLLC, Louisville, 1987-97; pvt. practice Louisville, 1997—. Notes editor Jour. Family Law, 1979-80. Vol. advocate R.A.P.E. Relief Ctr. YWCA, Louisville, 1981-87. Mem. ABA, Ind. Bar Assn., Ky. Bar Assn., Louisville Bar Assn. (probate sect. chmn. 1990, profl. responsibility com., com. chmn. 1988), U. Louisville Law Alumni Coun. (bd. dirs., pres. 1997—), Exec. Club Louisville (pres. 1996-97), Jefferson Club, Citizens for Better Judges, Phi Alpha Delta. Democrat. Presbyterian. Office: 745 W Main St Ste 250 Louisville KY 40202-2647

FUCHS, ROLAND JOHN, geography educator, university science official; b. Yonkers, N.Y., Jan. 15, 1933; s. Alois L. and Elizabeth (Weigand) F.; m. Gaynell Ruth McAuliffe, June 15, 1957; children: Peter K., Christopher K., Andrew K. BA, Columbia U., 1954, postgrad., 1956-57; postgrad., Moscow State U., 1960-61; MA, Clark U., 1957, PhD, 1959, DSc (hon.), 1995. Asst. prof. to prof. emeritus U. Hawaii, Honolulu, 1958—, chmn. dept. geography, 1964-86, asst. dean to assoc. dean coll. arts and scis., 1965-67, dir. Asian Studies Lang. and Area Ctr., 1965-67, adj. rsch. assoc. East West Ctr., 1980—, spl. asst. to pres., 1986; vice rector UN U., Tokyo, 1987-94; dir. Internat. Start Secretariat, 1994—; vis. prof. Clark U., 1963-64, Nat. Taiwan U., 1974; mem. bd. internat. orgns. and programs Nat. Acad. Scis., 1976-81, chmn., 1980-81, mem. bd. sci. and tech. in devel., 1980-85; mem. U.S. Nat. Commn. for Pacific Basin Econ. Coop., 1985-87; sr. advisor United Nations U., 1986. Author, editor: Geographical Perspectives on the Soviet Union, 1974, Theoretical Problems of Geography, 1977, Population Distribution Policies in Development Planning, 1981, Urbanization and Urban Policies in the Pacific-Asia Region, 1987, Megacities: The Challenge of the Urban Future, 1994; asst. editor Econ. Geography, 1963-64; mem. editl. adv. com. Soviet Geography: Rev. and Translation, 1966-85, Geoforum, 1988-96, African Urban Quar., 1987, Global Environ. Change, 1990—, Asian Geographer, 1991-98. Ford Found. fellow, 1956-57; Fulbright Rsch. scholar, 1966-67. Mem. Assn. Am. Geographers, Am. Geophys. Union, Internat. Geog. Union (v.p. 1980-84, 1st v.p. 1984-88, pres. 1988-92, past pres. 1992-96), Assn. Am. Geographers (Hon. award 1982), Am. Assn. Advancement of Slavic Studies (bd. dirs. 1976-81), Pacific Sci. Assn. (mem. coun. 1978—, mem. exec. com. 1986-99, sec. gen-treas. 1991-99), Acad. Europaea (elected fgn. mem.). Home: 1200 N Nash St Arlington VA 22209-3616

FUCHS, VICTOR ROBERT, economics educator; b. N.Y.C., Jan. 31, 1924; s. Alfred and Frances Sarah (Scheiber) F.; m. Beverly Beck, Aug. 29, 1948; children: Nancy, Fredric, Paula, Kenneth. BS, NYU, 1947; MA, Columbia U., 1951, PhD, 1955. Internat. fur broker, 1946-50; lectr. Columbia U., N.Y.C., 1953-54, instr., 1954-55, asst. prof. econs., 1955-59; assoc. prof. econs. NYU, 1959-60; program assoc. Ford Found. Program in Econ. Devel. and Adminstrn., 1960-62; prof. econs. Grad. Ctr., CUNY, 1968-74; prof. community medicine Mt. Sinai Sch. Medicine, 1968-74; prof. econs. Stanford U. and Stanford Med. Sch., 1974-95, Henry J. Kaiser Jr. prof., 1988-95, prof. emeritus, 1995—; v.p. research Nat. Bur. Econ. Research, 1968-78, mem. sr. research staff, 1962—. Author: The Economics of the Fur Industry, 1957; (with Aaron Warner) Concepts and Cases in Economic Analysis, 1958, Changes in the Location of Manufacturing in the United States Since 1929, 1962, The Service Economy, 1968, Production and Productivity in the Service Industries, 1969, Policy Issues and Research Opportunities in Industrial Organization, 1972, Essays in the Economics of Health and Medical Care, 1972, Who Shall Live? Health, Economics and Social Choice, 1975, expanded edit., 1998, (with Joseph Newhouse) The Economics of Physician and Patient Behavior, 1978, Economic Aspects of Health, 1982, How We Live, 1983, The Health Economy, 1986, Women's Quest for Economic Equality, 1988, The Future of Health Policy, 1993, Individual and Social Responsibility: Child Care Education, Medical Care, and Long-term Care in America, 1996.; contbr. articles to profl. jours. Served with USAAF, 1943-46. Fellow Am. Acad. Arts and Scis., Am. Econ. Assn. (disting.; pres. 1995); mem. Inst. Medicine of NAS, Am. Philos. Soc., Sigma Xi, Beta Gamma Sigma. Home: 796 Cedro Way Stanford CA 94305-1032 Office: NBER 204 Alta Rd Stanford CA 94305-8006

FUDENBERG, HERMAN HUGH, immunologist, educator; b. N.Y.C., Oct. 24, 1928; s. Nathan and Frances (Chackowitz) F.; m. Betty Roof, June 1956 (div.); children: Drew, Brooks, David, Haskell. AB, UCLA, 1949; MD, U. Chgo., 1953; MA, Boston U., 1958. Diplomate Am. Bd. Med. Lab. Immunology. Intern U. Utah Hosp., 1953-54; trainee in hematology New Eng. Ctr. Hosp., Tufts U., Boston, 1954-56; resident Mt. Sinai Hosp., N.Y.C., 1956-57, Peter Bent Brigham Hosp., Harvard U., Boston, 1957-58; rsch. assoc. Rockefeller Inst., N.Y.C., 1958-60; asst. prof. medicine U. Calif. Sch. Medicine, San Francisco, 1960-62, assoc. prof. medicine, 1962-66, prof., 1966-75; assoc. prof. immunology U. Calif., Berkeley, 1965-66, prof. bacteriology and immunology, 1966-75; prof., chmn. dept. basic and clin. immunology and microbiology Med. U. S.C., Charleston, 1974-85, prof. medicine, immunology, 1974-88; dir. rsch. NeuroImmunoTherapeutic Rsch. Found., Spartanburg, S.C., 1988—; adj. prof. pub. health U. Calif., Berkeley, 1966-75; adj. prof. epidemiology U. N.C., Chapel Hill, 1977—; vis. prof. at over 50 univs. and rsch. insts. in U.S. and Europe, including Karolinska Inst., Sweden, Middlesex Hosp., Eng., Harvard U., Yale U., Princeton U., NYU, U. Ala., Wayne State U., U. So. Calif., U. Amsterdam, U. Leiden, U. Paris, U. Glasgow, U. Edinburgh, U. P.R., U. Medellin, Colombia, Caracas, Venezuela, U. Innsbruck, Weismann Inst., Israel, Weifang Med. Sch., China, U. Norway, U. Helsinki, also Cancer Rsch. Inst., France, Italy, Russia, and The Netherlands; spkr. in field; mem. nat. adv. coun. Nat. Inst. Allergy and Infectious Diseases, 1981-85; mem. expert adv. panel on immunology WHO, 1962-82; mem. panel biomed. manpower NRC, 1974-78, mem. com. on immunization, 1978-80; mem. nat. task force on multiple myeloma and chronic leukemia NIH, 1966-71; chmn. external evaluation sci. com. U. Merida, Venezuela, 1982-86; mem. sci. adv. bd. UNESCO Internat. Ctr. for Immunology, Lyon, France, 1982-88; chmn. sci. adv. bd. Integra Inst., 1988-92; chmn. bd. sci. direction Inst. Immunology, Weifang Med. Coll., Chandong, China, 1988—; v.p. rsch. Neuro Immunology Therapeutic Rsch. Found. Author: (with others) Basic Immunogenetics, 1972, 3d edit., 1984, Basic and Clinical Immunology, 1974, 4th edit., 1982 (transl. into 12 langs.), Introduction to Medical Immunology, 1986, 2d edit., 1990; editor: (with others) Phagocytic Mechanisms in Health and Disease, 1972, Biomedical Scientists and Public Policy, 1978; editor: Biomedical Institutions, Biomedical Funding, and Public Policy, 1983; past mem. 35 editl. bds. including African Jour. Clin. and Exptl. Immunology, Annals Allergy, Biomedicine and Pharmacotherapy, Clin. and Exptl. Immunology, Folia Allergologica et Immunologica Clinica, Alzheimer's Longevity and Aging, Hosp. Practice, Jour. Irreproducible Results; contbr. over 800 articles to sci. jours.; patentee in field. Mem. nat. adv. coun. Nat. Inst. Allergy and Infectious Diseases, 1981-85; mem. expert adv. panel immunology WHO, 1962-82; mem. panel biomed. manpower Nat. Rsch. Coun., 1974-78, mem. com. on immunization, 1978-80; mem. nat. task force on multiple myeloma and chronic leukemia NIH, 1966-71; chmn. external evaluation sci. com. U. Merida, Venezuela, 1982-86; mem. sci. adv. bd. UNESCO Internat. Ctr. for Immunology, Lyon, France, 1982-88; chmn. sci. adv. bd. Integra Inst., 1988—; chmn. bd. sci. dir. Inst. Immunology, Weifang Med. Coll., Shandong, People's Republic of China, 1988—; v.p. rsch. Neuro Immunology Therapeutic Rsch. Found.; mem. adv. bd. Cambridge Internat. Biog. Centre, 1992; numerous others. Recipient Pasteur medal Inst. Pasteur, 1962, Robert A. Cook medal Am. Acad. Allergy, 1966, Berman medal Am. Acad. Dermatology, 1972, Disting. Svc. award U. Chgo. Med. Alumni, 1973, Petrov Cancer medal Govt. USSR, 1976, Carl Neuberg medal Virchow-Pirquet Med. Soc., 1980, Kioch medal German Soc. Microbiology, 1980, von Behringer medal, 1981, Semmelweis medal Hungarian Soc. Immunology, 1981, Metchnikoff Centennial, 1983, Phagocytosis medal Italian Soc. Immunology, 1983, Danish Cancer Soc., 1988, Castelloa di Pietrarossa award, Italy, 1991, Internat. First Prize, Frontiers in Medicine, Italy, 1992, 1st prize Biomed. Rsch. Italian Acad. Arts and Scis., 1992, 20th Century award rsch. sci. med. rsch. and edn., 1993; decorated Order of San Ciriaco, Italy, 1993; named hon. prof. U. Kuopio, Finland, 1982, U. Claude Bernard, France, 1985, Free Sci. U., Bologna, Italy, 1985, Weifang Med. Coll. Fellow AAAS, Am. Acad. Microbiology; mem. Am. Assn. for Cancer Rsch., Am. Assn. Immunologists (com. for congl. liaison for HEW appropriations, long range planning com.), Am. Rheumatism Assn., Am. Soc. for Clin. Investigation (chmn. com. on pub. info. 1971-74), Am. Soc. Hematology (pres. subdivision on immunohematology and immunogenetics 1970, 74, subcom. rsch in teaching methods 1961-65), Am. Soc. for Human Genetics (exec. coun. 1969-72), Assn. Am. Sch. Microbiology (chmn., pub. affairs com.), Assn. Am. Physicians, Genetics Soc. Am., Internat. Soc. Blood Transfusion (exec. councillor 1965-71), Internat. Soc. Environ. Toxicology and Cancer (bd. councilors), Internat. Soc. Hematology, Internat. Union Immunolog. Socs. (immunoglobin subcom. 1977), Internat. Platform Assn., Midwinter Conf. Immunologists (founder, past pres.), Royal Soc. Medicine (assoc.), Soc. Clin. Immunology, Am. Soc. Med. Labs., Med. Immunology, Sigma Xi. Home: 1070 Hunt Club Ln Spartanburg SC 29301-5479 Office: NeuroImmunoTherapeutics Rsch Found 1092 Boiling Springs Rd Spartanburg SC 29303-2247

FUDGE, ANN MARIE, marketing executive; b. Washington, Apr. 23, 1951; d. Malcolm R. and Bettye (Lewis) Brown; m. Richard E. Fudge, Feb. 27, 1971; children: Richard Jr., Kevin. BA, Simmons Coll., 1973; MBA, Harvard U., 1977; DHL (hon.), Adelphi U., 1995, Howard U., 1998, Simmons Coll., 1998. Manpower specialist GE, Bridgeport, Conn., 1973-75; mktg. asst. Gen. Mills, Mpls., 1977-78, asst. product mgr., 1978-80, product mgr., 1980-83, mktg. dir., 1983-86; assoc. dir., strategic planning Gen. Foods, White Plains, N.Y., 1986-87, mktg. dir., 1987-89, v.p. mktg. and devel., 1989-91, exec. v.p., gen. mgr., 1991-94; exec. v.p. Kraft Foods, 1994-97; pres. Maxwell House Coffee Co., White Plains, N.Y., 1994-97, Maxwell House Coffee and Post Cereal, Tarrytown, N.Y., 1997—; bd. dirs. Catalyst, Fed. Reserve Bank of N.Y., Liz Claiborne, Inc., Allied Signal, Inc.; trustee Thunderbird, The Am. Grad. Sch. of Internat. Mgmt. Bd. dirs. Women's Econ. Devel. Corp., St. Paul, 1984-86; chair allocations panel United Way, Mpls., 1983-86; vol. Big Sisters/Big Bros., Fairfield County, Conn., 1988-90; bd. govs. Boys and Girls Clubs Am. Recipient Leadership award YWCA, Mpls., 1980, Black Achievers award Harlem YMCA, 1988, Candace award Nat. Coalition of 100 Black Women, 1991, 92, Corp. Women's Network award, 1994, She Knows Where She's Going award Girls, Inc., 1994; named Woman of Yr., Glamour Mag., 1995, Ad Woman of Yr., Advt. Women of N.Y., 1995. Mem. Exec. Leadership Coun. (pres. 1994-96), Com. of 200, N.Y. Women's Forum. Office: Kraft Foods 555 S Broadway Tarrytown NY 10591-6301

FUDGE, MARY ANN, vocational school educator; b. Traverse City, Mich., July 21, 1947; d. Thomas C. and Mildred M. (Garey) Moran; m. Lew Fudge, June 28, 1969; children: Brian M., Cheryl M. BS, Cen. Mich. U., 1969; MA, Ea. Mich. U., 1975. Jr. high sch. tchr. math. St. Charles (Mich.) Schs., 1969-71; mid. sch. tchr. Gallatin County Schs., Bozeman, Mont., 1972-73; substitute tchr. Lincoln Consol. Schs., Ypsilanti, Mich., 1973-77; tchr. adult edn. Benton Harbor (Mich.) Area Schs., 1980-82; instr. math. Southwestern Mich. Coll., Dowagiac, 1983-84; high. sch. tchr. math. Coloma (Mich.) Pub. Schs., 1984-86; tchr. adult edn. math. Van Buren Technology Ctr., Lawrence, Mich., 1982-83, math. cons., coord., 1986—. Dep. clk. Hagar Twp., Riverside, Mich., 1987-88. Mem. Nat. Coun. Tchrs. Math., Mich. Coun. Tchrs. Math. Roman Catholic. Home: 25403 63rd Ave Mattawan MI 49071-9594 Office: Van Buren Intermediate Sch Dist 701 S Paw Paw St Lawrence MI 49064-9599

FUENNING, ESTHER RENATE, adult education educator; b. Florence, Mo.; d. Albert Theodore and Elizabeth (Muenzinger) F. BS, U. Nebr.; MA, Columbia U., 1952; doctoral program in recreation, U. Ill., Champaign,

1955-61. Dean of women Carthage (Ill.) Coll., 1949-50; asst. social dir. Ill. Union U., 1955-61; dean of women So. State Tchrs. Coll., Springfield, S.D., 1961-63; asst. dir. student activities Ill. Tchrs. Coll., South Chicago, 1963-64; prof. Wilbur Wright Coll., Chgo., 1964-77; sub. tchr. Chgo. Pub. Schs., 1977-82; tchr. dept. aging and disability Sr. Citizens Ctrs., Chgo., 1980—; dir. pub. relations Wright City Coll., 1964-77; del. Internat. Leisure and Recreation Congress, Krefeld, Germany, World Leisure and Recreation Assn, USSR. Author pamphlets in field; author: Upbeat With Esther, series of materials for sr. citizens, 1993—. Tour guide adults abroad Wright City Coll., 1986—; del. for sr. citizens conf. Wilbur Wright Coll., 1984, organized art fair, 1968—; ofcl. White House Conf. on Aging, Washington, 1955, Ill. White House Conf. on Aging, Springfield, 1990. Recipient Gov. Thompson Sr. Leadership award, Outstanding Svc. award Wright Coll. Alumni, Dedicated and Outstanding Leadership award Wright Coll., 1975, Cert. of Recognition adult edn. activities Wright City Coll., 1988, scholarship Gov.'s Conf. for Aging Network, 1991, Cert. of Life-Time Achievement Women's History Month, 1994, 96; inducted Chgo. Sr. Citizen Hall Fame. Republican. *

FUENTE, DAVID I., office supply manufacturing executive; b. 1946. Prof. Case Western Reserve U., 1970-75; with Gould Inc., Cleve., 1975-79; pres. paint stores group Sherwin-Williams Co., 1979-87; CEO, chmn. bd., dir. Office Depot, Inc., Boca Raton, Fla., 1987—; CEO, chmn. bd., dir., pres. OD Internat., Inc., Delray Beach, Fla. Fax: (800) 937-3600. Office: Office Depot Inc 2200 Old Germantown Rd Delray Beach FL 33445*

FUENTEALBA, VICTOR WILLIAM, professional society administrator; b. Balt., Sept. 1, 1922; s. Manuel Lagos and Antonia (Lengler) F.; m. Viola J. Henderson, Jan. 26, 1952; children: Victoria, Mary Lee, Donna Jean, Patricia. Student, Loyola Coll., 1946-47; JD, U. Md., 1950. Bar: Md. 1950, U.S. Supreme Ct. 1950. V.p. Musicians Union Met. Balt., 1951-53, sec., treas., 1953-58, pres., 1958-78; mem. internat. exec. bd. Am. Fedn. Musicians, N.Y.C., 1967-70, v.p., 1970-78, pres., 1978-87, pres. emeritus, 1987—. Bd. dirs. Hearing and Speech Agy., Balt., 1973-78; mem. Pres.' Com. on Employment of Handicapped; adv. council Ctr. Labor and Indsl. Relations of N.Y. Inst. Tech., Assn. Concert Bands, Van Cliburn Internat. Piano Competition; chmn. bd. Nat. Music Council; v.p. Muscular Dystrophy Assn.; adv. bd. Music Industry Educators Assn. Served with inf. U.S. Army, World War II. Decorated Purple Heart. Mem. Am. Bar Assn., Delta Theta Phi. Democrat. Roman Catholic. Home: 4501 Arabia Ave Baltimore MD 21214-3306 Office: 805 Court Sq Bldg 200 E Lexington St Baltimore MD 21202-3530

FUENTES, CARLOS, writer, former ambassador; b. Mexico City, Mexico, Nov. 11, 1928; s. Rafael Fuentes Boettiger and Berta Macías Rivas; m. Rita Macedo, 1959 (div. 1969); 1 dau., Cecilia; m. Sylvia Lemus, 1973; children: Carlos, Natasha. Ed., U. Mex., Institut des Hautes Etudes Internationales, Geneva; hon. degrees, Columbia Coll., Chgo. State U., Cambridge U., Essex U., Harvard U., Dartmouth Coll., Bard Coll., New Sch., Georgetown U., Washington U., St. Louis, Borwn U. Mem. Mexican del. ILO, Geneva, 1950-52; asst. chief press sect. Mexican Ministry Fgn. Affairs, 1954; asst. dir. cultural dissemination U. Mex., 1955-56; head dept. cultural relations Mexican Ministry Fgn. Affairs, 1957-59; fellow Woodrow Wilson Internat. Center for Scholars, Washington, 1974; Mexican ambassador to France, 1975-77; prof. English and romance langs. U. Pa., 1978-83; prof. comparative lit. Harvard U., 1984-86, Robert F. Kennedy prof., 1987—; prof.-at-large Brown U., Providence, 1995—; Norman Maccoll lectr. Cambridge U., 1977, Simon Bolivar prof., 1986-87; Virgina Gildersleeve prof. Barnard Coll., 1977; Henry L. Tinker lectr. Columbia U., 1978; pres. Modern Humanities Rsch. Assn., 1989—; prof. at large Brown U., 1995—. Author: Los días enmascarados, 1954, La región más transparente, 1958 (ub. as Where the Air Is Clear, 1960), Las buenas conciencias, 1959 (pub. as The Good Conscience, 1961), Aura, 1962, La muerte del Artemio Cruz, 1962 (pub. as The Death of Artemio Cruz, 1964), The Argument of Latin America: Words for North Americans, 1963, Cantar de ciegos, 1964, Zona sagrada, 1967 (pub. as Holy Places, 1972), Cambio de piel, 1967 (pub. as A Change of Skin, 1968; Biblioteca Breve prize Barcelona 1967), Paris: la revolución de mayo, 1968, La nueva novela hispanoamericana, 1969, Cumpleaños, 1969, El mundo de Jose Luis Cuevas, 1969, Casa con dos puertas, 1970, Tiempo mexicano, 1971, Poemas de amor: cuentos del alma, 1971, Cuerpos y ofrendas, 1972, Chac Mool y otros cuentos, 1973, Terra Nostra, 1975 (Rómulo Gallegos prize Venezuela 1977), Cervantes: o, La crítica de la lectura, 1976 (pub. as Don Quixote: or, The Critique of Reading, 1976), La cabeza de la hidra, 1978 (pub. as The Hydra Head, 1978), Una familia lejana, 1980 (pub. as Distant Relations, 1982), Agua quemada, 1981 (pub. as Burnt Water, 1981), High Noon in Latin America, 1983, Juan Soriano y su obra, 1984, Of Human Rights: A Speech, 1984, El gringo viejo, 1985 (pub. as The Old Gringo, 1986; L.A. Times Book award nomination 1986, Rubén Darío prize 1988, Italo-Latino Americano Instituto prize 1988), Latin America: At War with the Past, 1985, Palacio Nacional, 1986, Cristóbal Nonato, 1987 (pub. as Christopher Unborn, 1989), Gabriel Garcia Marquez and the Invention of America, 1987, Myself with Others: Selected Essays, 1988, Constancia, y otras novelas para vírgenes, 1989 (pub. as Constancia and Other Stories for Virgins, 1990), La campaña, 1990 (pub. as The Campaign, 1991), Valiente Mundo Nuevo, 1991, The Buried Mirror: Reflections on Spain and on the New World, 1992, Witnesses of Time, 1992, Return to Mexico: Journeys Beyond the Mask, 1992, El Naranjo, 1993 (pub. as The Orange Tree, 1993), Geografia de la Novela, 1993, Diana the Goddess Who Hunts Alone, 1995, The Crystal Frontier, 1995, La Edad del Tiempo, 1994—, Nuevo Tiempo Mexicano, 1994, Por un Progreso Incluyente, 1997, Retratos en el Tiempo, 1998, Los Anos con Laura Diaz, 1999; (plays) Todos los gatos son pardos, 1970, El tuerto es rey, 1970, Los reinos originarios, 1971, Orquideas a la luz de la luna, 1982 (pub. as Orchids in the Moonlight, 1982; Mexican Nat. award for lit. 1984); screenwriter: (films) Pedro Paramo, 1966, Tiempo de morir, 1966, Los Caifanes, 1967, (TV series) The Buried Mirror, 1991; contbr. to mags. and newspapers including Los Angeles Times, N.Y. Times, Newsweek; editor: Revista Mexicana de Literatura, 1954-58, El Espectador, 1959-61, Siempre, 1960—, Politica, 1960—, Los signos en rotación y otra ensayos, 1971. Trustee N.Y. Pub. Library, mem. Mexican Nat. Commn. Human Rights, 1991—. Recipient Centro Mexicano de Escritores fellowship, 1956-57, Xavier Villaurrutia prize (Mex.), 1975, Alfonso Reyes prize (Mex.), 1979, Miguel de Cervantes Lit. prize Spanish Ministry of Culture, 1987, Medal of Honor for Lit., Nat. Arts Club, N.Y.C., 1988, Rector's medal U. Chile, 1991, Casita Maria medal, 1991, UCLA medal, 1993, Order of Merit (Chile), 1992, French Legion of Honor, 1992, Menéndez Pelayo Internat. award U. Santander, 1992, Picasso medal UNESCO, 1994, Principe de Asturias prize, 1994, Premio Grinzane-Cavour, 1994; named hon. citizen Santiago de Chile, 1993, Buenos Aires, 1993, Veracruz, 1993. Mem. Am. Acad. and Inst. Arts and Letters, Nat. Coll. Mex., Inst. Nat. Strategy (bd. dirs.), ORder of the Southern Cross (Crazil), French Order of Merit.

FUENTEVILLA, MANUEL EDWARD, chemical engineer; b. Havana, Cuba, Feb. 17, 1923; s. Fernando and Edith Agnes (Pira) F.; B.Ch.E., Poly. Inst. Bklyn., 1947; M.S., Drexel U., 1954; m. May Belle Tutwiler, Oct. 18, 1945; children—William F., Diane G., Austin D., Eve J., Inez M. Sr. engr. Catalytic Inc., Phila., 1951-60; chief engr. Stokes Equipment div. Pennwalt Corp., 1960-67; asst. mgr. mfg. Esso Eastern, Tokyo, 1967-69, tech. supt., Okinawa, Japan, 1969-72; project mgr. Jacobs Engring. Co., Cherry Hill, N.J., 1972-75; project mgr. Stauffer Japan Ltd., Tokyo, 1975-77; dir. process devel. Alfa Laval Process, Mt. Laurel, N.J., 1977-79; tech. dir., sr. project mgr. Synergo Inc., Phila., 1979-82; chief mech. engring. Kling/Lindquist Inc., Phila., 1982—, Cerus, Inc., Cherry Hill, N.J., 1986—; process and tech svc. pharm. and chem. applications. Served with USNR, 1943-46. Mem. Am. Inst. Chem. Engrs., Soc. History of Tech., Phi Lambda Upsilon. Club: Cooper River Yacht (Collingswood). Patentee in indsl. processes. Home: 314 Tearose Ln Cherry Hill NJ 08003-3524

FUENTEZ, TANIA MICHELE, copy editor, writer; b. N.Y.C., Nov. 21, 1966; d. C. Pedro Alvarez Carr and E. Kay (Samuels) Queally. BA in Comm. and Rhetorical Studies, Marquette U., 1991; MA in Mass Media Comm., U. Akron, 1996. Asst. rschr. V.I. Legislature, St. Thomas, 1991; reporter V.I. Daily News, St. Thomas, 1993-95; instr. news writing U. Akron, Ohio, 1995-96; copy editor Observer Times, Fayetteville, N.C., 1997, Beacon Jour., Akron, 1997—; adv. bd. diversity com. V.I. Daily News, 1993-95. Contbr. articles to profl. jours. Bd. dirs. U.S. V.I. League of Women Voters, 1994-95; mem. Am. Cancer Soc., 1993-95, mem. St. Thomas Arts Coun., 1992-95. Recipient Cmty. Svc. award Pan African Support Group, 1995; scholar John S. Knight Meml. Fund, 1996, U. Akron, 1995-96. Mem. ESL (asst., participant 1989), Soc. Profl. Journalists, Nat. Assn. Hispanic Journalists, Nat. Assn. Black Journalists, Newspaper Guild (local 1), N.E. Ohio Assn. Black Journalists, Nat. Audubon Soc., Am. Copy Editors Soc., Libr. of Congress, Comm. Workers Am.-AFL-CIO, Cleve. Mus. Art, Smithsonian Instn. Roman Catholic. Avocations: writing, traveling, Chinese martial arts, photography, hiking. Office: Akron Beacon Jour 44 E Exchange St Akron OH 44328-0001

FUERST, RITA ANTOINETTE, management and fundraising consultant; b. Cleve., June 13, 1955; d. Raymond Lawrence and Mary Antoinette (Palumbo) F. BS in Journalism, Ohio U., 1976; MBA, Capital U., Columbus, Ohio, 1984. V.p. The Bill Heim Co., Granville, Ohio, 1980-95; pres. The Bill Heim Co., Granville, 1995-96; dir. devel. Am. Coun. Internat. Edn., Washington, 1996-97; pres. Charitable and Philanthropic Mgmt. Coun., Boston, 1997—; bd. dirs. The Bill Heim Co. Author, editor: What Fundraisers Need to Know About State and Federal Regulation, 1996. Trustee Ohio 4-H Found., 1992-95. Mem. Voluntary Assn. (ARNOVA), CIVICUS, Internatl. Soc. of Third Sector Rsch. (ISTR), Nat. Soc. Fundraising Execs. (cert., trustee Hills of Ohio chpt. 1993-96, pres. 1993-95, gov. rels. com. 1995, Fuerst Outstanding Cmty. Leader award named in her honor 1996), Women in Devel., Nat. Trust for Hist. Preservation. Roman Catholic. Avocations: travel, reading, roller blading, ice skating. Office: Charitable and Philanthropic Mgmt Counsel 213 Commonwealth Ave Ste 7 Boston MA 02116-1714

FUERSTENAU, DOUGLAS WINSTON, mineral engineering educator; b. Hazel, S.D., Dec. 6, 1928; s. Erwin Arnold and Hazel Pauline (Karterud) F.; m. Margaret Ann Pellett, Aug. 29, 1953; children: Lucy (dec.), Sarah, Stephen. BS, S.D. Sch. Mines and Tech., 1949; MS, Mont. Sch. Mines, 1950; ScD, MIT, 1953; Mineral Engr., Mont. Coll. Mineral Sci. and Tech., 1968; hon. doctorate degree, U. Liege, Belgium, 1989. Asst. prof. mineral engring. MIT, 1953-56; sect. leader, metals research lab. Union Carbide Metals Co., Niagara Falls, N.Y., 1956-58; mgr. mineral engring. lab Kaiser Aluminum & Chem. Corp., Permanente, Calif., 1958-59; assoc. prof. metallurgy U. Calif., Berkeley, 1959-62, prof. metallurgy, 1962-86, P. Malozemoff prof. of mineral engring., 1987-93, prof. grad. sch., 1994—; Miller research prof. U. Calif.-Berkeley, 1969-70, chmn. dept. materials sci. and mineral engring., 1970-78; bd. dirs. Homestake Mining Co.; mem. Nat. Mineral Bd., 1975-78; Am. rep. Internat. Mineral Processing Congress Com., 1978-97. Editor: Froth Flotation-50th Anniversary Vol., 1962; co-editor-in-chief: Internat. Jour. of Mineral Processing, 1974—; contbr. articles to profl. jours. Recipient Alexander von Humboldt Sr. Am. Scientist award, Germany, 1984, Frank F. Aplan award The Engring. Found., 1990, Internat. Mineral Processing Congress Lifetime Achievement award, 1995; Rsch. fellow Japan Soc. Promotion Sci., 1993; Douglas W. Fuerstenau professorship established at S.D. Sch. of Mines and Tech., 1998. Mem. NAE, AIChE, Am. Inst. Mining and Metall. Engrs. (chmn. mineral processing divsn. 1967, Robert Lansing Hardy gold medal 1957, Rossiter W. Raymond award 1961, Robert H. Richards award 1975, Antoine M. Gaudin award 1978, Mineral Industry Edn. award 1983, Henry Krumb disting. lectr. 1989, hon. 1989), Soc. Mining Engrs. (bd. dirs. 1968-71, Disting. mem.), Am. Chem. Soc., Russian Fedn. Acad. Natural Scis. (fgn. mem.), Sigma Xi, Theta Tau. Congregationalist. Home: 1440 Le Roy Ave Berkeley CA 94708-1912

FUERSTNER, FIONA MARGARET ANNE, ballet company executive, ballet educator; b. Rio de Janeiro, Apr. 24, 1936; d. Paul G. and Agnes Ethel (Stothard) F.; m. Dane LaFontsee, June 7, 1969 (div. 1992); 1 child, Liana Marie. Studied with San Francisco Ballet, Royal Ballet (London), Ballet Rambert (London) Ballet Theatre Sch. (N.Y.C.), Sch. Am. Ballet (N.Y.C.). With corps de ballet San Francisco Ballet, 1952-55, soloist, 1955-58, prin. dancer, 1958-62; toured with Walter Terry's Am. Dances, 1962-63; prin. dancer Les Grands Ballets Can., Montreal, 1963-64, Am. Choreographer's Co. of N.Y., 1964; prin. dancer Pa. Ballet, 1965-68, prin. dancer, ballet mistress, 1968-74, ballet mistress, instr. co. class, apprentice class, 1974-77, ballet mistress, 1977-78, ballet mistress, instr. co. class, 1978-86; ballet mistress Nashville Ballet, 1986-87, ballet mistress, asst. to artistic dir., 1987-91; ballet mistress Milw. Ballet, 1990-95, asst. to artistic dir. ballet mistress, 1995—; guest dancer Ballet Concerto, Miami, 1967, 68, Erie Civic Ballet, 1969; guest instr. Marsha Woody Dance Acad., Beaumont, Tex., 1974, U. Louisville, 1977-78, co. class San Francisco Ballet, 1985, Tenn. Assn. Dance Nashville Conf., 1988, So. Regional Workshop Chgo., Nat. Assn. Dance Masters in Nashville, 1989, BalletMet, 1991, Memphis Classical Ballet, 1992, 97, Nashville Ballet, 1992; guest ballet mistress BalletMet, 1993; faculty tchr. Sch. of Pa. Ballet, 1977-78, 78-86; organized concert group, ballet mistress, dancer Pa. Ballet, 1971; mem. dance panel Nat. Found. Advancement in the Arts, 1995-98; master tchr. South Eastern Regional Ballet Assn. Festival, 1998. Staged Allegro Brillante, Sch. Pa. Ballet Student Showcase, 1986, Nashville Ballet, 1988, Madrigalesco, Pacific NW Ballet, 1981, (parts) Nutcracker, Nashville Ballet, 1989, Scotch Symphony, Pa. Ballet, 1993, Carmina Burana, Alberta Ballet, 1993, Concerto Barocco, Ballet Omaha, 1994, Ballet Met, 1995, Serenade, Milw. Ballet Sch., 1994, 95, 96, Serenade Milw. Ballet, 1998-99.

FUERTES, RAUL A., psychologist, educator; b. Havana, Cuba, Nov. 4, 1940; came to U.S., 1961; s. Raul and Luisa Elvira (Pichardo) F. BA, U. Miami, 1967, BEd, 1968; MS, Barry U., 1972, EdS, 1992; AA, Miami Dade U., 1977; PsyD, LaSalle U., 1995. Acad. dean, dir. admissions Miami Mil. Acad. (Fla.), 1967-74; sch. psychologist, guidance counselor Dade County Pub. Schs., Miami, 1974—; instr. Miami Dade Community Coll., 1980—; instr., psychology St. Thomas U., 1974; mem. adv. bd. Ednl. Testing Svc., N.J. Mem. Am. Mental Health Counselors Assn., Am. Assn. Counseling and Devel., Nat. Assn. Sch. Psychologists, Nat. Assn. Soccer Coaches, Guidance Counselors Assn. Fla., Republican. Roman Catholic. Home: 1705 SW 125th Ct Miami FL 33175-1413 Office: Miami Palmetto Sr High Sch 7460 SW 118th St Miami FL 33156-4599

FUESS, BILLINGS SIBLEY, JR., advertising executive; b. N.Y.C., Mar. 11, 1928; s. Billings Sibley and Lucile (McNeill) F.; m. Doris Vannoy, July 19, 1952; children: Billings Sibley III, Doris Jr., Frederick, Lucile. AB in Journalism, U. N.C., 1949. Analyst Gallup & Robinson, Princeton, N.J., 1952-53; writer Kenyon & Eckhardt, N.Y.C., 1953-59, Batten, Barton, Durstine & Osborn, N.Y.C., 1959-65; creative dir. Ogilvy & Mather, N.Y.C., 1965-89; pres. Billings S. Fuess Advt., Summit, N.J., 1989—; mem. selection com. N.C. Advt. Hall of Fame award. Author, editor: How to Use the Power of the Printed Word, 1985. Mem. N.Y. Philharmonic Vol. Coun., 1976—. Recipient Grand award Internat. Film and Television Festival N.Y., 1984, Stephen E. Kelly award Mag. Pubs. Assn., N.Y.C., 1983, Gold award Art Dirs. Club N.J., numerous top industry awards; elected to N.C. Advt. Hall of Fame, U. N.C., Chapel Hill, 1995. Mem. Art Dirs. Club of N.J. (bd. trustees 1995—, treas. 1996—). Home: 19 Highland Dr Summit NJ 07901-3108

FUGATE, IVAN DEE, banker, lawyer; b. Blackwell, Okla., Dec. 9, 1928; s. Hugh D. and Iva (Holmes) F.; m. Lois Unita Rossow, June 3, 1966; children: Vickie Michelle, Roberta Jeanne, Douglas B., Thomas P. AB, Pittsburg (Kans.) State U., 1949; LLB, U. Denver, 1952, JD, 1970. Bar: Colo. 1952. Exec. sec., mgr. Jr. C. of C. of Denver, 1950-52; also sec. Colo. Jr. C. of C.; individual practice law Denver, 1954—; chmn. bd., pres. Green Mountain Bank, Lakewood, Colo., 1975-82; chmn., pres. Western Nat. Bank Denver (now Vectra Bank of Colorado); chmn. exec. com. North Valley Bank, Thornton, Colo., 1962—, chmn., pres., 1981—; founder, chmn. emeritus Ind. State Bank of Colo. (now Bankers Bank of West), 1978—, Ind. Bankers of Colo., 1973—; former bd. dirs. Kit Carson State Bank, Colo.; sec. First Nat. Bank, Burlington, Colo.; owner, farms, ranches, Kans., Colo.; instr. U. Denver Coll. Law, 1955-60; mem. Colo. Treas's. Com. Investment State Funds, 1975—. Treas. to Rep. Assos., Colo., 1959-61, trustee, 1959-64. Maj. USAR, 1952-54. Mem. ABA, Colo. Bar Assn., Denver Bar Assn. (trustee 1962-65), Colo. Bankers Assn. (bd. dirs.), Colo. Cattlemen's Assn., Ind. Bankers Assn. Am. (pres. 1978, adminstrv. com., exec. coun. 1976—, bd. dirs. fed. legis. com., chmn. spl. tax com., instr. One Bank Holding Co. seminars 1976—), Denver Law Club, Petroleum Club, Denver Athletic Club, Lakewood Country Club, Phi Alpha Delta. Methodist. Home: 12015 W 26th Ave Lakewood CO 80215-1110 Office: North Valley Bank Bldg PO Box 29429 9001 Washington St Denver CO 80229-4363

FUGATE, WILBUR LINDSAY, lawyer; b. Pulaski, Va., Mar. 27, 1913; s. Jesse Honaker and Elizabeth Gertrude (Brown) F.; m. Barbara Louise Brown, Sept. 19, 1942; m. Cornelia Wolfolk Alfriend, Jan. 2, 1971; children—William, Richard, Barbara, Elizabeth. B.A. cum. laude, Davidson Coll., 1934; LL.B., U. Va., 1937; LL.M., George Washington U., 1951, S.J.D., 1954. Bar: Va. 1937, W.Va. 1938, U.S. Supreme Ct. 1949, D.C. 1971, U.S. Dist. Ct. D.C. 1971, U.S. Ct. Appeals (D.C. cir.) 1971, U.S. Dist. Ct. (ea. dist.) Va. 1979, U.S. Ct. Appeals (5th and 8th cirs.) 1980. Assoc. Campbell & McNeer, Huntington, W.Va., 1937-38; counsel Kanawha Banking & Trust Co., Charleston, W.Va., 1938-42; with antitrust div. Dept. Justice, 1947-73; asst. chief trial sect. Dept. Justice, Washington, 1951-53; chief Honolulu office Dept. Justice, 1960-61; chief fgn. commerce sect. Dept. Justice, Washington, 1962-73; of counsel Glassie, Pewitt, Beebe & Shanks, Washington, 1974-77, Baker & Hostetler, Washington, 1977—; U.S. del. OECD Restrictive Bus. Practices Commn., 1962-73. Author: Foreign Commerce and the Antitrust Laws, 1958, 5th edit., 1997; contbr. articles to legal jours., chpts. to books; bd. advisors Va. Jour. Internat. Law, 1976—. Served to lt. USCG, 1942-45. Mem. ABA (chmn. Antitrust com. internat. law sect. 1975-76, chmn. subcoms. in patents, fgn. antitrust laws sect. antitrust law 1971-77), Fed. Bar Assn., Internat. Bar Assn., Inter-Am. Bar Assn., Cosmos Club, Univ. Club, Army-Navy Country Club. Democrat. Presbyterian. Home: 4800 Fillmore Ave Apt 1152 Alexandria VA 22311-5054 Office: 437 N Lee St Alexandria VA 22314-2301

FUGATE-WILCOX, TERY, artist; b. Kalamazoo. Represented in permanent collections Solomon R. Guggenheim Mus., N.Y.C., Australia Nat. Gallery, Canberra, Mus. Modern Art, N.Y.C., Western Mich. U., J. Hood Wright Park, N.Y.C., J. Patrick Lannan Found. Mus., Palm Beach, Fla., Nat. Shopping Ctrs., Harrisburg, Pa., Prudential Ins. Co., Newark, Damson Oil Co., N.Y.C., N.Y.C. Dept. Parks and Recreations, Princess Gloria von Thurn and Taxis, Regensburg, Germany; sculpture located 7th Ave and Waverly, N.Y.C., City Wall, Lafayette, Houston, N.Y.C., Holland Tunnel Entrance, N.Y.C., 40-ft. sculpture Riverside Dr. and Jay Hoodwright Park, N.Y.C., 30-ft. self-watering sculpture The Prudential Gateway 4, Newark. Address: 7 Worth St New York NY 10013-2925 also: care Fulcrum Gallery 480 Broome St New York NY 10013-2250 *Actual art includes in its statement the long-suppressed dimension of time, in the context of the naturally occurring changes that are part of the life of any material and make it part of the life of the work of art incorporating that material.**

FUGELBERG, NANCY JEAN, elementary music specialist, educator; b. Tarentum, Pa., Mar. 6, 1947; d. Stanley and Mary (Struhar) Homer; m. Darrell Marvin Fugelberg, Aug. 27, 1977. B in Music Edn., Mount Union Coll., 1969; postgrad., Kent State U., 1973-76; EdM in Curriculum and Instrn., Ashland U., 1989. Cert. master piano classes and music lt. Mozarteum, Salzburg, Austria, 1968. Music thcr. Alliance Sch. Dist., Ohio, 1969-70, Minerva Sch. Dist., Ohio, 1970-99; ch. organist First Immanuel United Ch. of Christ, Alliance, Ohio, 1969-85. Pianist for musicals Carnation Players, Alliance, 1969-72; asst. organist, accompanist various chs. Recipient award for working with handicapped children Minerva Sch. Dist., 1981; Alumni Svc. aware Mu Phi Epsilon, 1983, 84; named One of Outstanding Young Women of Am., 1981. Mem. NEA, Minerva Tchrs. Assn., Ohio Edn. Assn., Mu Phi Epislon (chpt. v.p. 1980-82, pres. 1982-84, historian and music therapy chmn. 1984—0. Republican. Avocations:ants, travel, playing, keyboards, giving various musical programs. Address: 345 S Rockhill Ave Alliance OH 44601-2257

FUGGI, GRETCHEN MILLER, education educator; b. Westerly, R.I., Aug. 26, 1938; d. John Louis and Harriet (Scheid) M.; m. William Joseph Fuggi, Aug. 15, 1960; children: Gretchen, Juliann, John, Kristen. BS, So. Conn. State U., 1960, MS, 1969, 6th yr. diploma, 1991, 6th yr. Ednl. Leadership diploma, 1994. Reading cons. Washington Magnet Sch., West Haven, Conn., 1974—; adj. prof. So. Conn. State U., New Haven, 1988—. Pres. Cath. Charity League of Greater New Haven, 1989-90; bd. dirs. New Haven Symphony Aux., 1992—. Mem. AAUP, Internat. Reading Assn., Conn. Reading Assn., Stonington Hist. Soc. of Conn., Delta Kappa Gamma Soc. Internat. Roman Catholic. Home: 19 Westview Rd North Haven CT 06473-2013

FUGIEL, FRANK PAUL, insurance company executive; b. Chgo., Aug. 23, 1950; s. Richard A. and Sally (McKinney) F.; m. Nancy Campbell, Sept. 15, 1973; children: Michele, Rachelle. Student, SUNY, Albany. CLU; cert. managed healthcare profl. Individual underwriter Prudential Ins. Co., Merrillville, Ind., 1971-80, group claims mgr., 1980-82, underwriting mgr., 1982-84; group claims officer Employers Health Ins. Co., Green Bay, Wis., 1984-86, underwriting officer, 1986-88, managed care officer, 1988; 2d v.p. individual health ins. Washington Nat. Ins. Co., 1988-90, v.p. ops., 1990; exec. v.p. Oak Brook (Ill.) group divsn. Aegon U.S.A., 1990-94; exec. v.p. TPA divsn. Centennial Life Ins. Co., Merriam, Kans., 1994-95; v.p. managed care adminstrn. United Chambers HealthCare Corp., Naperville, Ill., 1995-96; v.p. bus. devel. Insurers Adminstrv. Corp., Phoenix, 1996—. Councilman Hobart, Ind. C. of C., 1981. Served as sgt. USMC, 1970-76. Fellow Life Office Mgmt. Inst., Acad. Life Underwriting; mem. Internat. Claims Assn. (assoc. life and health claims), Life Underwriting Edn. Com., Inst. Home Office Underwriters. Home: 22255 N 51st St Phoenix AZ 85054-7126 Office: Insurers Adminstrv Corp VP Bus Devel 10210 N 25th Ave Ste 300 Phoenix AZ 85021-1605

FUHLRODT, NORMAN THEODORE, retired insurance executive; b. Wisner, Nebr., Apr. 24, 1910; s. Albert F. and Lena (Schafersman) F.; student Midland Coll., 1926-28; A.B., U. Nebr., 1930; M.A., U. Mich., 1936; m. Clarice W. Livermore, Aug. 23, 1933; 1 son, Douglas B. Tchr., athletic coach high schs., Sargent, Nebr., 1930-32, West Point, Nebr., 1932-35; with Central Life Assurance Co., Des Moines, 1936-74, pres., chief exec. officer, 1964-72, chmn. bd., chief exec. officer, 1972-74, also dir. Named Monroe St. Jour. Alumnus of Month, U. Mich. Grad Sch. Bus. Adminstrn. Gen. chmn. Greater Des Moines United campaign United Community Service, 1969-70. Former bd. dirs. Des Moines Center Sci. and Industry. Fellow Soc. Actuaries. Home: 760 E Bobier Dr # 116B Vista CA 92084-3806

FUHR, EDWARD J., lawyer; b. N.Y.C., Mar. 8, 1962; s. Joseph Ernest and Erika Joan Fuhr; m. Joy Isabel Cummings, Nov. 6, 1993; children: Anna Isabel, Laura Isabel. BA, U. Va., 1984; JD, U. Chgo., 1987. Jud. clk. hon. Boyce F. Martin Jr. U.S. Ct. Appeals 6th Cir., Louisville, Ky., 1987-88; atty.-advisor Office Legal Counsel, Dept. Justice, Washington, 1988-89; ptnr. Hunton & Williams, Richmond, Va., 1990—; adj. prof. U. Richmond T.C. Williams Law Sch., 1995. Chmn. Henrico County Rep. Com., Richmond, 1992-98, Charitable Gaming Commn., Va., 1995-99; vol. atty. for battered women Women's Shelter Project, Richmond, 1995-96; counsel inagural com. Gov.-elect James S. Gilmore III, Richmond. Named one of Top 40 Under 40, Inside Bus., Richmond, 1997. Mem. ABA, Va. Bar Assn., Richmond Bar Assn. E-mail: efuhr@hunton.com. Fax: 804-788-8218. Office: Hunton & Williams 951 E Byrd St Richmond VA 23219

FUHR, GRANT, professional hockey player; b. Spruce Grove, Alta., Canada, Sept. 28, 1962; m. Corrinee F.; children: Janine, Rochelle. Player Edmonton Oilers, 1981-91, Toronto Maple Leafs, 1991-93; with Buffalo Sabers, 1993-96, St. Louis Blues, 1996—; mem. All-Star first team, 1979-80, 80-81, Stanley Cup Championship teams, 1984, 85, 87, 88, 90; player NHL All-Star game, 1982, 84-86, 88-89. Recipient Vezina Trophy (top NHL goaltender), 1987-88, Stewart (Butch) Paul Meml. trophy, 1979-80, Top Goaltender trophy, 1980-81; named Sporting News All-Star second team, 1981-82, 85-86; mem. NHL All-Star second team, 1981-82; Sporting News All-Star team, 1987-88; mem. NHL All-Star team, 1987-88, All-Star MVP, 1986. Office: St Louis Blues Kiel Ctr 1401 Clark Ave Saint Louis MO 63103-2700*

FUHRER, ARTHUR K., lawyer; b. N.Y.C., Oct. 19, 1926; s. Isidore and Toby (Schorr) Fuhrer; m. Lenore R. Lewis; children: Laura A., Robert A., David A. LL.B., Bklyn. Law Sch., 1949; postgrad. NYU Sch. Law, 1951, 52. Bar: N.Y. 1950, U.S. Dist Ct. (so. dist.) N.Y. 1951, U.S. Supreme Ct. 1977. Assoc. firm Sargoy and Stein, N.Y.C., 1951-52, firm Andrew D. Weinberger, N.Y.C., 1952-54; lawyer William Morris Agy., Inc., N.Y.C., 1954-75, v.p., 1975-95; of counsel Frankfurt, Garbus, Klein and Selz, 1995—; co-chmn. Television and Motion Picture Seminar Practicing Law Inst., 1973. Contbr.:

Lindey on Entertainment and the Law. Office: Frankfurt Garbus Klein and Selz 488 Madison Ave Fl 9 New York NY 10022-5754

FUHRER, LARRY, management consultant, finance company executive; b. Sept. 23, 1939; m. Linda Larsen; 1 child, Lance. AB, Taylor U., 1961; MS, No. Ill. U., 1966, MBA, 1993; MBA, Benedictine U., 1988, MS in Mgmt. and Orgnl. Behavior, 1999; MA, Wheaton Coll., 1999. Founder, chmn. Presdl. Svcs. Ltd., 1965—; founder, pres. Rockford Equities Ltd., 1981—, The L. Führer Co. LLC, 1997—; pubs. mgr. Campus Life Mag., 1962-65, editl. bd., 1966-70; pres. Killian Assocs. Inc., 1973-75; dir. Gamel Broadcasting Inc., WFXW, Geneva, Ill., 1985-88; joint venture ptnr. INEX Trading Co. Ptr. Ltd., Singapore, 1987-89; corp. devel. The Lady D Group Inc., 1987-93; chmn. Mt. Vernon Properties Inc., 1990-91; adj. faculty bus. and social sci. Waubonsee C.C., 1991—, Coll. DuPage Computer Info. Systems, 1999—; adj. prof. mktg. Grad. Sch. Mgmt., Coll. Bus., Lewis U., 1999—; ednl. dir. Haus of Ivy.net. exec. club dir. Youth for Christ, Marion, Ind., 1961-62, dir. devel., 1962; chmn. Washington Conf., 1980; mem. Cmty. Task Force for Econ. Devel. Coll. of DuPage, 1988-89; vol. Pathfinders Bible Studies, 1988—; chmn. Ill. Rsch. & Devel. Corridor Coun., 1988-89; founding chmn. Ill. Assn. of Corridor Coun., 1989-90; vice chmn., co-founder Dakota Ptnrshp., 1989-95; mem. mission & steward com. Presbytery of Chgo., 1990-95, congregational mission planning and strategy coun., 1993-95; pres. Internat. Christian Broadcasters, 1990-95; chmn., co-founder Naperville Conf.; bd. dirs. DuPage Prevention Ptnrshp., 1993; dir. Urban Min. San Marcos, 1997-98. Home: 2808 Willow Ridge Dr Naperville IL 60564-8938

FUHRMAN, CHARLES ANDREW, country club proprietor, real estate management executive, lawyer; b. Milw., June 14, 1933; s. Harry H. and Gertrude (Wynn) F.; m. Ann Marie Brott; children: Anthony Andrew, Nicolas Andrew, Michelle Heather. B.S., U. Wis., 1955, LL.B., 1957. Bar: Wis. 1957, Ohio 1958, Mich. 1964. Pvt. practice Toledo, 1958-62; partner Fuhrman, Gertner, Britz & Barkan, 1963-72; partner Varsity Sq. Apts. Co., Alexian Co., Dundee Co., Tamaron Mgmt. Co.; owner Tamaron Country Club. Served to 2d lt. Transp. Corps, U.S. Army, 1958. Mem. Am., Wis., Mich., Ohio, Toledo bar assns., Phi Delta Phi, Pi Lambda Phi. Republican. Clubs: Masons, Shriners, Jesters, Desert Caballeros. Home: 4778 Springbrook Dr Toledo OH 43615-1164 Office: 2162 W Alexis Rd Toledo OH 43613-2216

FUHRMAN, FREDERICK ALEXANDER, physiology educator; b. Coquille, Oreg., Aug. 13, 1915; s. Cyrus Jacob and Josie (Lyons) F.; m. Geraldine Jackson, Nov. 12, 1942. BS, Oreg. State Coll., 1937, MS, 1939; postgrad., Universität Freiburg im Breisgau, 1937-38, U. Wash., 1939-41; Ph.D., Stanford U., 1943. Univ. fellow in pharmacology U. Wash., 1939-41; research assoc. in physiology Stanford U., 1941-45, instr., 1945-49, asst. prof., 1949-52, assoc. prof., 1952-57, prof. physiology, 1957-61; dir. basic med. scis. labs. Stanford (Med. Sch.), 1959-70, prof. exptl. medicine, 1961-72; prof. physiology Stanford (Sch. Medicine), 1972-80, emeritus, 1981—; physiologist Hopkins Marine Sta., Pacific Grove, Calif., 1972-79; dir. Max C. Fleischmann Labs. of the Med. Scis., 1961-70. Author: Multidiscipline Laboratories for Teaching the Medical Sciences; assoc. editor: Ann. Rev. of Physiology, 1954-62; contbr. articles on metabolism, frostbite, hypothermia, animal toxins and marine pharmacology to profl. jours. Guggenheim fellow, labor of zoophysiology U. Copenhagen, 1951-52; sr. postdoctoral fellow NSF, Inst. Biol. Chemistry, U. Copenhagen and Donner Lab., U. Calif., 1958-59; Commonwealth Fund fellow, 1966-67. Fellow AAAS, N.Y. Acad. Scis.; mem. Am. Physiol. Soc., Am. Soc. Pharmacology and Exptl. Therapeutics, Sigma Xi, Phi Kappa Phi. Active in med. research OSRD, World War II. Home: 2445 Sharon Oak Dr Menlo Park CA 94025-6828

FUHRMAN, GWENDOLYN SUE, secondary school educator; d. Paul Fuhrman; children: Amanda, Curtis. BS in Home Econs. Edn., Mansfield U., 1975, masters equivalency, 1994. Cert. family and consumer scis. tchr., Pa. Famiy and consumer sci. tchr. Conrad Weiser Jr./Sr. H.S., Robesonia, Pa., 1975—. Chair Renaissance Program, Robesonia, 1996—; textiles cons. 4-H, Lebanon County, Pa., 1989-91; leader Girl Scouts U.S., Lebanon County, 1985-93; cub scout leader, mem. com. Boy Scouts Am., Lebanon County, 1994-98, asst. scoutmaster, 1998—. Grantee NEA, 1992, State of Pa., 1998. Mem. Am. Assn. Familly and Consumer Sci., Pa. Assn. Family and Consumer Sci., Pa. State Edn. Assn. (External Comm. grant 1992, Intergroup award 1996, 98), Conrad Weiser Edn. Assn. Office: Conrad Weiser Jr/Sr HS 347 E Penn Ave Robesonia PA 19551

FUHRMAN, RALPH EDWARD, civil and environmental engineer; b. Kansas City, Kans., Sept. 6, 1909; s. Ralph William and Olga (Woinova) F.; m. Josephine Ackerman, Jan. 1, 1935; children—William Edward, Anne Louise. B.S. in Civil Engrng, U. Kans., 1930; M.S. in San. Engrng, Harvard, 1937; D.Eng., Johns Hopkins, 1954. Instr. U. Ka—, 1930-31; Asst. pub. health engr. Mo. Dept. of Health, 1931, 37; city san. engr. Springfield, Mo., 1931-36; asst. supt. D.C. Water Pollution Control Plant, 1937-42, supt., 1942-53; dep. dir. san. engring. D.C. Govt., 1953-54; pres. Water Environ. Fedn., 1950-51, exec. dir., 1955-69; asst. dir. Nat. Water Commn., 1969-71; spl. asst. to dir. municipal wastewater systems div. EPA, 1972-73; mgr. Washington regional office Black & Veatch (Cons. Engrs.), Kansas City, Mo., 1973-78; rep. Black & Veatch (Cons. Engrs.), 1979—; lectr. civil engring. George Washington U., 1941-60. Fellow APHA, ASCE (chmn. exec. com. san. engring. divsn. 1954-55), Chartered Instn. Water and Environ. Mgmt. (Brit., hon.); mem. Chesapeake Water Environ. Assn. (Abel Wolman award 1998), Am. Water Works Assn., Am. Acad. Environ. Engrs., Water Environ. Fedn. (hon.). Episcopalian. Club: Cosmos (Washington). Home and Office: 2917 39th St NW Washington DC 20016-5404

FUHRMAN, RUSSELL L., career officer; b. Shawano, Wis.. BA, West Point Acad., 1968; M in Chem. Engring., Pa. State U. Commd. officer U.S. Army, advanced through grades to maj. gen.; dir. civil works Office of the Chief of Engrs. U.S. Army, Washington, 1996—. Office: Office of the Chief of Engrs US Army 20 Massachusetts Ave NW Washington DC 20314

FUHS, TERRY LYNN, emergency room nurse, educator; b. Gallup, N.Mex., Aug. 21, 1957; d. Louie Rube and Wilda (Boardman) Orr; m. Loren Bruce Fuhs, Dec. 11, 1981; children: Melissa Marincell, Misty Fuhs. ADN, U. N.Mex., Gallup, 1979; BSN, U. N.Mex., 1990. Cert. emergency nurse, TNCC-I, ENPC-I, ACLS-I, PALS-I; RN, N.Mex. Med./surg. staff/chg. nurse Rehoboth McKinley Christian Hosp., Gallup, 1979-83, chg. nurse emergency dept., 1983—, critical care educator, 1992—; affiliate faculty PALS/ACLS, N.Mex. chpt. Am. Heart Assn., 1991—, mem. emergency cardiac care com., 1993—, mem. PALS nat. faculty, 1995-97. Presenter/coord. Emergency Nurses Cancel Alcohol Related Emergencies, Gallup, 1994—, Safe Sitter Program, Gallup, 1994—. Recipient Meritorious award N.Mex. Hosp. Assn., 1994. Mem. ANA, Emergency Nurses Assn. (state coun. mem. 1993—, N.Mex. chpt. trauma com. chmn. 1994—). Democrat. Methodist. Avocations: reading, movies, travel. Home: 1117 Ridgecrest Ave Gallup NM 87301-4980 Office: Rehoboth McKinley Hosp 1901 Redrock Dr Gallup NM 87301-5683

FUIKS, KIMBALL SANDS, neurosurgeon; b. Mar. 13, 1949. BA, Dartmouth Coll., 1972; MD, U. Conn., 1978. Intern Duke U. Med. Ctr., Durham, N.C., 1978-79, resident in neurol. surgery, 1979-80; resident in gen. surgery U. Conn., Hartford, 1980-82; resident in neurology U. N.C., Chapel Hill, 1982-85; resident in neurosurgery U. Tenn., Memphis, 1985-89, fellow in surg. epilepsy, 1989-90; attending neurosurgeon Doylestown and Abington Hosps., Pa., 1990-91; med. dir. Neurosurg. Ctr. Mercy Health Sys., Janesville, Wis., 1991—. Office: Mercy Neurosurgery Ctr Janesville WI 53545

FUJIMOTO, JAMES G., electrical engineering educator; b. Chgo., Sept. 28, 1957; s. Harold H. and Jane S. (Sakoda) F.; m. Carla Helen Milhauser. BSEE, MIT, 1979, MSEE, 1981, PhD, 1985. Asst. prof. MIT, Cambridge, 1985-88, assoc. prof., 1988-94; prof., 1994—; vis. lectr. Harvard Med. Sch., Boston, 1987-91; cons. MIT Lincoln Lab., Lexington, Mass., 1985-96; adj. prof. ophthalmology Tufts U., 1994—. Recipient Presdl. Young Investigator award NSF, 1986, William Baker award NAS, 1990, Award for Initiatives in Rsch., NAS, 1990; traveling lectr. award Lasers and Electro-Optics Soc., 1990. Fellow IEEE; mem. AAAS, Optical Soc. Am., Am. Phys. Soc. Office: MIT Bldg 36-361 Dept Elec Engring-Comp Sci Cambridge MA 02139*

FUJINAMI, ROBERT SHIN, neurology educator; b. Salt Lake City, Dec. 8, 1949. BA, U. Utah, 1972; PhD, Northwestern U., Chgo., 1977. Instr. microbiology and immunology Northwestern U., Chgo., 1973-76; rsch. fellow immunopathology Scripps Rsch. Found., La Jolla, Calif., 1977-80, rsch. assoc. immunopathology, 1980-81, rsch. immunopathologist, 1981-82, asst. mem. immunology, 1981-85, vis. investigator immunology, 1985-89, vis. investigator neuropharm., 1989—; assoc. prof. pathology U. Calif., San Diego, 1985-90; prof. neurology U. Utah, Salt Lake City, 1990—; adj. prof. pathology U. Utah, Salt Lake City, 1991—; mem. neurosci. steering com. U. Utah, 1992-96, chmn. biosafety and PRT coms., 1993-96. Contbr. chpts. to books, 84 articles to profl. jours. Recipient New Investigator award NIH, 1981-83; NIH scholar, 1989-96. Fellow AAAS; mem. Nat. Multiple Sclerosis Soc. (bd. dirs. Utah chpt. 1992—, Harry M. Weaver Neurosci. award 1982-86). Office: Dept Neurology U Utah 50 N Medical Dr Salt Lake City UT 84132-0001

FUJIOKA, JO ANN OTA, educational administrator, consultant; b. Bellflower, Calif., Apr. 30, 1939; d. Richard Masayoshi and Lillian Chiyono (Ihara) Ota; m. Arthur Fujioka, Feb. 19, 1961; 1 child, Dana Kay. BSN, U. Colo., 1961, MSN, 1970; PhD, Colo. State U., 1987. RN; cert. adminstr., supt., spl. edn. dir., sch. nurse, vocat. edn. adminstr., instr. Nurse pub. health, psychiat. Denver Gen. Hosp., Denver Vis. Nurse Svc., 1961-71; sch. nurse Jefferson County Sch. Dist., Golden, Colo., 1971-76; mgr. program, supr. sch. health program Jefferson County Sch. Dist., Golden, 1976-79, mgr. spl. edn. and related svcs., adminstr. elem. bldg., 1979-95; cons. Fujioka Cons., Denver, 1995—; cons. Ctrl. Kans. Bd. Coop. Ednl. Svcs., Salina, 1992, Denver Children's Home, 1996, Colo. Assn. of Family and Children's Agencies, 1997, Colo. Mediation Project, 1998. Contbr. articles to profl. jours. Vice chmn. bd. dirs. Creative Exch., 1997-99, chmn. bd. dirs., 1999—. Mem. NOW, AAUW, Alliance Profl. Cons. (exec. bd.), Japanese Am. Nat. Mus., Am. Assn. Sch. Execs., Univ. Colo. Health Scis. Ctr. Srs. Assn. (bd. dirs., sec. 1997—), Colo. Sch. Health Coun. (pres. 1978-80), Phi Delta Kappa (internat. del. 1993, area coord. 1996—, chpt. pres. 1992-94, chpt. v.p. 1989-91, Doublas County Chpt. Svc. award, 1999, Denver U. Chpt. Svc. award, 1999, Internat. Dist. IV Project Grant Dir., 1993, 99, Fall Conf. Chair, 1993—), Internat. Platform Assn., Jefferson County Adminstrs. Assn. Democrat. Buddhist. Avocations: crossword puzzles, jigsaw puzzles, crocheting, Tai Chi, reading. Home and Office: 540 S Forest St #K Denver CO 80246-8164

FUJITA, BEVERLY YUMI, advertising copywriter; b. Honolulu, Aug. 25, 1963; d. George Shuichi and Kikue (Tomonaga) F. BA in English with highest honors, U. Hawaii Manoa, Honolulu, 1986. Procedure writer Bank of Hawaii, 1986-89; cable guide editor Honolulu Pub., 1989-93, assoc. editor Honolulu Mag., 1991-94; internal comms. writer Bank of Hawaii, Honolulu, 1994-95; asst. dir. mail mgr. Liberty House, Honolulu, 1995—. Bd. dirs. Temari Ctr. for Asian and Pacific Arts, Honolulu, 1994—. Mem. Soc. Profl. Journalists, Asian Am. Journalists Assn., U. Hawaii Alumni Assn., Phi Beta Kappa, Phi Kappa Phi. Avocation: magician's assistant.

FUJITANI, MARTIN TOMIO, software quality engineer; b. Sanger, Calif., May 3, 1968; s. Matsuo and Hasuko Fujitani. BS in Indsl. and Systems Engrng., U. So. Calif., 1990. Sec. Kelly Svcs., Inc., Sacramento, 1987; receptionist Coudert Bros., L.A., 1988; rsch. asst. U. So. Calif., L.A., 1988-89; math. aide Navy Pers. Rsch. and Devel. Ctr., San Diego, 1989; quality assurance test technician Retix, Santa Monica, Calif., 1989-90; software engr. Quality Med. Adjudication, Inc., Rancho Cordova, Calif., 1990-92; test engr. Worldtalk Corp., Los Gatos, Calif., 1993-94; quality engr. Lotus Devel. Corp., Mountain View, Calif., 1994-95, Gen. Magic, Sunnyvale, Calif., 1995-96; software engr. Sun Microsys. Inc., Palo Alto, Calif., 1996—. Assemblyman Am. Legion Calif. Boys State, 1985. Recipient Service Above Self award East Sacramento Rotary, 1986. Mem. Gen. Alumni Assn. U. So. Calif. (life). Avocations: dancing mambo, watching ballet, listening to jazz music, bicycling, windsurfing, cooking. Home: 6890 Avenida Rotella San Jose CA 95139 Office: Sun Microsys Inc MS UMPK 17-204 901 San Antonio Rd Palo Alto CA 94303-4900

FUJITO, WAYNE TAKESHI, international business company executive; b. Stockton, Calif., Nov. 9, 1938; s. Roland Teizo and Helen Toshio F.; m. Kazuko Natori; children: Brian Tomokazu, Joanne Terumi. BA, San Jose State U., 1961; MS, U. So. Calif., 1982. Commd. 2d lt. U.S. Army, 1961, advanced through grades to col., U.S. Army attache to Japan, 1983-87; chief of staff Strategic Def. Command U.S. Army, Arlington, Va., 1988-90; ret. U.S. Army, 1990; v.p. Internat. Tech. & Trade Assocs., Washington, 1990-93, sr. v.p., 1994-95, exec. v.p., 1995—. Vol. advisor CARE Internat., Atlanta, 1993—. Decorated Legion of Merit with oak leaf cluster, Bronze Star, Imperial Order of Scared Treasure, Govt. of Japan. Mem. Army and Air Force Mut. Aid Assn. (bd. dirs. 1994—), Asia Soc., Japan-Am. Soc. of Washington, D.C., Assn. of U.s. Army, Armed Forces Commn. and Electronics Agy., Am. Def. Preparedness Assn. Avocations: skiing, reading, stock market, internet. Home: 1217 Delta Glen Ct Vienna VA 22182-1321 Office: Internat Tech & Trade Assoc 1330 Connecticut Ave NW Ste 210 Washington DC 20036-1726

FUKATSU, TANEFUSA, retired Chinese classics educator; b. Toyota, Aichi, Japan, Apr. 23, 1923; s. Kingo and Shizu (Noba) F.; m. Michiko Kato, Jan. 17, 1954 (dec. 1981); children: Tomonao, Arikata. BA, Tokyo U., 1951. Tchr. Chinese classics Musashi High Sch., Tokyo, 1957-89; asst. prof. Chinese classics Musashi U., Tokyo, 1971-74, prof. Chinese classics, 1974-85; retired, 1989—; lectr. Chinese classics Nisho-Gakusha U., Tokyo, 1967-93, guest prof., 1993—. Author: Juzi Tongbian Jingdianshiwen, 1978, Lunyu Xidu, 1990, Laozi Xidu, 1994, Thought and Life of the Ancient Chinese-Mirror-, 1996, Japanese Culture and Chinese Culture-White Chrysanthemum and Yellow Chrysanthemum, 1997, Studies on the Latent Thought in Chinese Characters and Poetry, 1997, Chinese Thought and Culture, 1998, Studies of the Book of Laozi, 1999. Mem. Nippon-Chugoku-Gakkai, Shibunkai (dir. 1990-93, councilor 1993—). Avocation: hiking. Home: 86-1-501 Konya-Cho, Saiwai-Ku Kawasaki-Shi, Kanagawa-ken 210-0926, Japan

FUKETA, TOYOJIRO, physicist; b. Japan, Feb. 10, 1930; s. Tatsukichi and Fuji (Tsukamoto) Koga; m. Sumiko Fuketa, Oct. 26, 1955; children: Toyoshi, Sachi. BS, Osaka U., Japan, 1953, MS, 1955, DS, 1961. Rsch. physicist Japan Atomic Energy Rsch. Inst., Tokai-Mura, Tokyo, Japan, 1957-93; exec. dir. Japan Atomic Energy Rsch. Inst., Tokyo, 1987-88, v.p., 1989-93; vis. scientist Oak Ridge (Tenn.) Nat. Lab., 1962-63; rsch. assoc. Rensselaer Polytech. Inst., Troy, N.Y., 1963-64; pres. Nuclear Energy Data Ctr., Tokai-Mura, 1993-95, Rsch. Orgn. Info. Sci. & Tech., Tokai-Mura, 1995-97; chmn. Inst. Environ. Sci., Rokkasho-Mura, Aomori-Ken, 1997—; mem. specialist com. Nuclear Safety commn., Tokyo, 1985-93, Atomic Energy commn., Tokyo, 1987-93. Named Hon. Citizen State Of Tenn., 1962, City of Knoxville, 1991. Mem. Atomic Energy Soc. Japan (v.p. 1992-94). Home: 1-19-5 Shoan, Suginami-Ku, Tokyo 167-0054, Japan

FUKS, ZVI Y., medical educator; b. Tel Aviv, Apr. 7, 1936; came to U.S, 1984; married; children: Yaron, Tamar. MD, Hebrew U., Jerusalem, 1960. Am. Bd. Radiology-Radiation Therapy. Intern Hadassah U. Hosp., Jerusalem, Israel, 1961; resident in radiation therapy and med. oncology Hadassah Hosp., Tel Aviv U. Sch. Medicine, Israel, 1964-69; asst. prof. radiology Stanford (Calif.) U., 1969-76; prof., head radiation oncology Hadassah U. Hosp., Jerusalem, 1976-78, prof., chmn. dept. radiation oncology, 1978-84; chmn. dept. radiation oncology Meml. Sloan-Kettering Cancer Ctr., N.Y.C., 1984-98, dep. physician in chief for planning, 1998—. Mem. Am. Coll. Radiology, Am. Soc. Clin. Oncology, Am. Soc. Therapeutic Radiologists, European Soc. Therapeutic Radiol. Oncologists, Nat. Rsch. Coun., Calif. Med. Assn., European Cancer Assn., N.Y. Cancer Soc., N.Y. Roetgen Soc., Radiation Rsch. Soc. Office: Meml Sloan-Kettering Ctr 1275 York Ave New York NY 10021-6007

FUKUDA, SHOHACHI, English language educator; b. Hitoyoshi, Kumamoto, Japan, Jan. 29, 1933; s. Kunihiko and Katsue (Okano) F.; m. Konami Yamamoto, Mar. 30, 1966; children: Komari, Hikaru, Michiru. BA, U. Tokyo, 1956, MA, 1959. Instr. English Kumamoto (Japan) U., 1959-61, lectr. in English, 1961-65, assoc. prof., 1965-78, prof. English, 1978-98; prof. Kyushu Luth. Coll., 1999—; dir. Coun. on English Edn. in Kumamoto, 1970—. Author: The English Teacher Who Can't Speak English, 1979, A History of English and American Literature, 1989, Japan's Linguistic Kaikoku, 1991; co-author: English in Everyday American Life, 1997; editor: Family English, 1997; co-editor: Edmund Spenser: Selected Poems, 1983, The Prince of Poets: Essays on Spenser, 1997; co-translator: The Faerie Queene, 1969 (Best Translation of Yr., Japan Soc. Translators 1970), revised edit., 1997, The Shorter Poems of Spenser, 1980. Recipient Kumanichi award Kumamoto Daily News, 1970, Nishinippon Culture award, Nishinippon Newspaper, Fukuoka, Japan, 1975, Presdl. award of merit U. Mont., Missoula, 1989, Hakuho award Hakuhodo, Tokyo, 1990. Mem. Japan Assn. Coll. English Tchrs. (dir., rep. 1990-94), The Spenser Soc. Japan (dir., pres. 1985—). Buddhist. Avocation: gardening. E-mail: fkds@gpo.kumamoto-u.ac.jp. Home: 1-5-32 Shimizumangoku, Kumamoto 860-0868, Japan

FUKUHARA, HENRY, artist, educator; b. L.A., Apr. 25, 1913; s. Ichisuke and Ume (Sakamoto) F.; m. Fujiko Yasutake, Aug. 18, 1938; children: Joyce, Grace, Rackham, Helen. Student with Edgar A. Whitney, Jackson Heights, N.Y., 1972; student with Rex Brandt, Corona del Mar, Calif., 1974; student with Robert E. Wood, 1975; student with Carl Molno, Woodside, N.Y., 1976; student with Kero Antoyam, 1988. instr. Watercolor Venice (Calif.) Adult Sch., 1991-92, tchr. watercolor. Exhibited in group shows at Friends World Coll., Lloyds Neck, N.Y., 1980, Elaine Benson Gallery, Bridgehampton, N.Y., 1979, 83, Nat. Invitational Watercolor, Zaner Gallery, Rochester, N.Y., 1981, Fire House Gallery, 1982, Parrish Art Mus., 1982, Japan-R.I. Exch. Exhibit, Provincetown, R.I., 1986, Kawakami Gallery, Tokyo, 1986, Setagaya Mus. Art, Tokyo, 1988-91, 5th Ann. Rosoh Kai Watercolor Exhbn., Meguro Mus. Art, Tokyo, 1991, 6th Ann. Rosoh Kai Watercolor Exhbn. Meguro Mus. Art, 1992, 11th ann., 1999, Shinju ku Bunka Ctr., Tokyo, 1993-96, 10th ann., 1997, Stary Sheets Galleries Exhbn., Irvine, Calif., 1992-94, Laguna Beach, 1996—, Living Legends, Mira Mesa Colls., 1994, Miracosta, Coll., 1997; represented in permanent collections at Heckscher Mus., Huntington, N.Y., Abilene Mus. Fine Art, Nassau C.C., SUNY-Stony Brook, L.A. County Mus. Art, Blaine County Mus., Chinook, Mont., Ralston Mus., Sydney, Mont., San Bernardino County Mus., Redlands, Calif., 1984, Riverside Mus. Art, Calif., 1985, Gonzaga U., Spokane, Wash., 1986, Nagano Mus. Art, Japan, 1986, Contemporary Mus. of Art, Hiroshima, 1988, Santa Monica (Calif.) Coll., 1988; subject of profl. publs. Recipient Purchase award Nassau C.C., 1976; Best in Show, Hidden Pond, Town of Islip, 1978, Strathmore Paper Co., 1979, Creative Connections Gallery award Foothills Art Ctr., Golden, Colo., 1984, Judges Choice, Mont. Miniature Art Soc. 7th Ann. Internat. Show, Working with Abandoned Control, 1993, Learn Watercolor Edgar Whitney Way, 1994, Splash 3 and 4 1995/96 in watercolor series, 1996, The Best of Watercolor 2, 1997, The Magic Touch 3, 1999, others. Mem. Nat. Watercolor Soc., Ala. Watercolor Soc., Pitts. Watercolor Soc., Nat. Drawing Assn., Valley Water Color Soc. Address: 1214 Marine St Santa Monica CA 90405-5815

FUKUI, GEORGE MASAAKI, microbiology consultant; b. San Francisco, May 25, 1921; s. Tsunejiro and Kimiko (Wada) F.; m. Yuri Lillyn Kenmotsu, Sept. 23, 1944; children: Lisa Jo, Tenley Kay. BS, U. Conn., 1945, MS, 1948; PhD, Cornell U., 1952. Instr. bacteriology U. Conn., Storrs, 1948-49; lab. instr. Cornell U., Ithaca, N.Y., 1949-52, mem. adv. bd. microbiology dept., 1985-88; asst. br. chief U.S. Army, Frederick, Md., 1952-60; dir. microbiology and immunology Wallace Labs., Cranbury, N.J., 1960-77, Hazelton Labs., Vienna, Va., 1977-78; dir. microbiology Abbott Labs., North Chicago, Ill., 1978-79; rsch. microbiologist Abbott Labs., Irving, Tex., 1979-86; pres. Internat. Cons. in Microbiology, Irving, 1986—. Contbr. articles to sci. jours. Asst. scoutmaster troop 712, Boy Scouts Am., Topaz, Utah, 1943; recruiter Cornell U., Princeton, N.J., 1964-69. With U.S. Army, 1945-46. Recipient commendation Rsch. Soc. Am., 1959, medal for sci. achievement Hiroshima (Japan) U., 1973, Gran Amigo de Mex. commendation Nat. U. Mex., 1982, commendation Tohoku U., Sendai, Japan, 1983. Fellow Am. Acad. Microbiology (charter, diplomate); mem. Am. Soc. for Microbiology, Rutgers Soc. Japan (hon.), Phi Beta Kappa, Sigma Xi. Republican. Episcopalian. Achievements include patents for Non-Allergenic Penicillin; Phenoxypropanediols on Reduction of Penicillin Allergy; Synthetic Penicillin, Non-Allergenic; Suppression of Histamine Release; Salicylates for Quantification of Antibiotics in Sera. E-mail: george.fukui@gte.net. Home and Office: 3813 E Greenhills Ct Irving TX 75038-4819

FUKUI, HATSUAKI, electrical engineer, art historian; b. Yokohama, Japan, Dec. 14, 1927; came to U.S., 1962, naturalized, 1973; s. Ushinosuke and Yoshi (Saito) F.; m. Atsuko Inamoto, Apr. 1, 1954 (dec. 1973); children: Mayumi, Naoki; m. Kiku Kato, Dec. 12, 1975. Diploma, Miyakojima Tech. Coll. (now Osaka City U.), 1949; BS, Tokyo Coll. Sci.; D.Eng., Osaka U., 1961. Rsch. assoc. Osaka City U., 1949-54; engr. Shimada Phys. and Chem. Indsl. Co., Tokyo, 1954-55; sr. engr. to mgr. Sony Corp. semi-condr. div., Tokyo, 1955-61; mgr. engring. div. Sony Corp., 1961-62; mem. tech. staff Bell Telephone Labs., Murray Hill, N.J., 1962-69, supr., 1969-73; v.p. Sony Corp. Am., N.Y.C., 1973; asst. to chmn. Sony Corp., Tokyo, 1973; staff mem. Bell Labs., Murray Hill, N.J., 1973-81; supr. Bell Labs., 1981-83, Lucent Techs. (formerly AT&T Bell Labs.), 1984-89; lectr. Tokyo Met. U. (part-time), 1962. Author: Esaki Diodes, 1963, Solid-State FM Receivers, 1968; contbr. to: Semiconductors Handbook, 1963, GaAs FET Principles and Technologies, 1982; editor: Low-Noise Microwave Transistors and Amplifiers, 1981; contbr. articles to profl. jours.; patentee in field. Fellow IEEE (life; standardization com. 1976-82, edit. bd. IEEE Transactions on Microwave Theory and Techniques 1980—, com. on U.S. competitiveness 1988—); mem. Inst. Electronics, Info. and Comm. Engrs. Japan (Inada award 1959), IEEE Comms. Soc., IEEE Electron Devices Soc., IEEE Lasers and Electro-Optics Soc., IEEE Microwave Theory and Techniques Soc. (Microwave prize 1980, Pioneer award 1990), Electromagnetics Acad., Japan Soc. Applied Physics, Inst. TV Engrs. Japan (tech. steering com. 1973-74), Am. Assn. Museums, Gakushikai, Internat. House Japan. Home: 53 Drum Hill Dr Summit NJ 07901-3141 also: 1-21-16-802 Nakane Meguro, Tokyo 152-0031, Japan

FUKUI, NAOKI, theoretical linguist; b. Tokyo, Oct. 9, 1955; s. Tatsuo and Masako (Kabuyama) F. BA, Internat. Christian U., Tokyo, 1979, MA, 1982; PhD, MIT, 1986. Postdoctoral fellow Ctr. for Cognitive Sci., MIT, Cambridge, 1986-87; asst. prof. Keio U., Tokyo, 1987-89; asst. prof. theoretical linguistics U. Pa., Phila., 1989-90; asst. prof. theoretical linguistics U. Calif., Irvine, 1990-94, assoc. prof., 1994-98, grad. dir. linguistics, 1992—, prof., 1998—. Author: Theory of Projection in Syntax, 1995, Generative Grammar, 1998; mem. edit. bd. Jour. Japanese Linguistics, 1989, The Linguistic Rev., 1992, Jour. East Asian Linguistics, 1992, Linguistic Inquiry, 1995; contbr. articles to profl. jours. Fulbright grantee, 1982-87. Office: U Calif Dept Linguistics 3151 Social Science Plz Irvine CA 92697-5100

FUKUMOTO, GEAL S., investment representative; b. Honolulu, Aug. 22, 1961; d. Alvin J. and Geraldine S. F. BBA, U. Hawaii, 1983. CLU, ChFC. Sales agt. Prudential, Long Beach, Calif., 1986-94; investment rep. Edward Jones, Kaneohe, Hawaii, 1994—; mem. Kaneohe Bus. Group, 1994—, v.p., 1996, pres., 1998; mem. Edward Jones Grass Roots Task Force, 1997—. Bd. dirs. L.A. unit Am. Cancer Soc., 1992-94, chmn. spl. contacts, 1992-94, chmn. gift and estate planning com., 1993-94; vol. Jr. Achievement, 1994—; bd. dirs. Nat. Fedn. Ind. Bus., 1997—; mem. Hawaii Estate Planning Coun., 1996—. Mem. Am. Soc. CLUs (bd. dirs. Harbor chpt. 1992-94, chmn. continuing edn. 1992-93), Am. Bus. Womens Assn. (Ulupono charter chpt. 1994-98), Securities Industry Assn. of Hawaii (dir., govt. affairs chair 1999—), Small Bus. Hawaii, Kaneohe Rotary (chmn. youth svcs. 1996, sec. 1997-98), Investment Soc. Hawaii (bd. dirs. 1997—). Avocations: golf, travel, skiing. Office: Edward Jones 45-1144 Kamehameha Hwy Ste 403 Kaneohe HI 96744-3226

FUKUMOTO, YASUNOBU, American history educator; b. Kobe City, Hyogo, Japan, Apr. 13, 1926; s. Takeji and Kikue (Terada) F.; m. Reiko Tanaka, May 29, 1957; children: Michiko, Yoshiko. BA, Kyushu U., Fukuoka, Japan, 1950; DLitt, Kyushu U., Fukuoka City, Japan, 1972. Asst. faculty literature Kyushu U., 1954-56; instr. literature Seinan Gakuin U., Fukuoka City, 1956-67, asst. prof. literature, 1967-71, prof. literature, 1971-97, ret., hon. prof., 1997. Author: A Study on Lincoln's Slavery-View, 1971, The Making of the Slave Laws, 1983, The Slave Songs, 1988, A Road to the Emancipation Proclamation, 1992, Rise of the Abolitionism, 1997. Mem. Kyushu-Yamaguchi Am. Studies Assn. (editor Jour. Am. Studies 1985—).

Buddhist. Office: Seinan Gakuin U, 6 2 92 Nishijin, Sawara Ku Fukuoka 814, Japan

FUKUSHIMA, BARBARA NAOMI, financial consultant; b. Honolulu, Apr. 5, 1948; d. Harry Kazuo and Misayo (Kawasaki) Murakoshi; m. Dennis Hiroshi Fukushima, Mar. 23, 1974; 1 child, Dennis Hiroshi Jr. BA with high honors, U. Hawaii, 1970; postgrad. Oreg. State U., 1971, 73, U. Oreg., 1972. Intern, Coopers & Lybrand, Honolulu, 1974; auditor Haskins & Sells, Kahului, Hawaii, 1974-77; pres. Book Doors, Inc., Pukalani, 1977-97; pres. Barbara N. Fukushima CPA, Inc., Wailuku. 1979-96; sec. treas. Target Pest Control, Inc., Wailuku, 1979-96; internal auditor, acct. Maui Land & Pineapple Co., Inc., Kahului, 1977-80; auditor Hyatt Regency Maui, Kaanapali, 1980-81; ptnr. D & B Internat., Pukalani, 1980-91; instr. Maui C.C., Kahului, 1982-85; fin. cons. Merrill Lynch, Pierce, Fenner & Smith, Inc., 1986—. Recipient Phi Beta Kappa Book award, 1969. Mem. AICPA, Hawaii Soc. C.P.A.s, C. of C. of Hawaii, Terikyo. Home: 1088 Bishop St Ste 1117 Honolulu HI 96813-3118 Office: 1001 Bishop St Ph Honolulu HI 96813-3429

FUKUSHIMA, TEIICHIRO, obstetrician and gynecologist, educator; b. São Paulo, Brazil, June 20, 1942; came to U.S., 1977; MD, Escola Paulista de Med., Sao Paulo, 1968. Cert. in ob-gyn., specialty in maternal-fetal medicine. Intern King-Drew Med. Ctr., L.A., 1977-78, resident in ob-gyn., 1978-81, fellow in maternal-fetal medicine, 1981-83, chief divsn. obstetrics, 1991-97; assoc. prof. Charles R. Drew Med. Scis., 1993-94, vice chmn., 1994-97, chmn., 1997—. Mem. ACOG, L.A. Ob-Gyn. Soc., Pacific Coast Obstet. and Gynecol. Soc., Soc. Maternal-Fetal Medicine. Office: King-Drew Med Ctr Dept Ob-Gyn 12021 Wilmington Ave Dept Ob Los Angeles CA 90059-3019

FULBRIGHT, HARRIET MAYOR, foundation administrator; b. N.Y.C., Dec. 13, 1933; d. Brantz and Evelyn (Griswold) M.; m. William Watts, Aug. 4, 1954 (div. 1975); children: Evelyn G. Ward, Shelby H. Funk, Heidi H. Mayor; m. J. William Fulbright, Mar. 10, 1990. BA, Radcliffe Coll., Cambridge, Mass., 1955; MFA, George Wash. U., 1975; LLD (hon.), U. Scranton, 1986; LHD (hon.), L.I. U. Chair art dept. Maret Sch., Washington, 1975-80; asst. dir. Congl. Arts Caucus, Washington, 1980-82, Alliance of Ind. Coll. Art, Washington, 1982-84; exec. sec. Internat. Congress Art History, Washington, 1984-87; exec. dir. Fulbright Assn., Washington, 1987-91; pres. The Ctr. for Arts in the Basic Curriculum, Washington, 1991-96; exec. dir. Pres.'s Com. on the Arts and the Humanities, 1997—; vice chair Reves Internat. Ctr., 1994—; mem. J.W. Fulbright Fgn. Scholarship Bd., 1992-98, Acad. for Ednl. Devel., 1995—; pres. Fulbright Internat. Ctr., 1996—; unofficial amb. Fulbright Program's 50th Ann. Author: How To Get Your Own Pre-School Play Group; editor: Fulbrighters Newsletter. Pres. Maret Sch. Bd.; exec. dir. Pres.'s Com. for Arts and Humanities, 1997—;. Honoree, Young Audiences, 1994; recipient El Order de Manuel Amador Querrero (Panama's highest civilian award), 1997. Mem. Nat. Coun. Stds. in the Arts. Fax: 202-682-5668. Office: 1100 Pennsylvania Ave NW Washington DC 20004-2501

FULBRIGHT-BROCK, VIVIAN, supervisory probation officer; b. Paris, Tex., July 30, 1959; d. David Arthur and Dorothy Jean (Fluckus) Fulbright; m. Melvin Brock, Mar. 25, 1989; 1 child, Grace Elizabeth. BA, Austin Coll., 1981; MA in Commerce, Texas A&M U., 1983. Lic. profl. counselor, D.C. Counselor, asst. dir. Vols. of Am., Ft. Worth, 1985-86; outreach counselor Sasha Bruce Youth Walks, Inc., Washington, 1986-88; diagnostic assessor Consortium for Youth Alternatives, Washington, 1988-90; probation officer D.C. Supr. Ct., 1990-96; supr. D.C. Supr. Ct. Juvenile Intake Office, 1996—.

FULCHER, HUGH DRUMMOND, author; b. Lynchburg, Va., Feb. 4, 1945; s. Lewis Page and Frances Louise (Drummond) F.; m. Cheryl Brenn Phelps, July 29, 1972 (div. July 1990); children: Keston Hugh, Kara Brenn. BS in Physics, Math., Va. Poly. Inst. and State U., 1967, MS in Nuclear Engring., 1970. Lic. nuclear reactor operator, Md. Physics instr. Va. Poly. Inst. and State U., Danville, 1968-69, Danville C.C., 1969-71; nuclear engr. supr. Babcock & Wilcox Inc., Lynchburg, 1971-82; nuclear engr. Energy Inc., Richmond, Va., 1982-85; computer engr. Ariz. Pub. Svcs., Phoenix, 1985-90; nuclear engr. Scientech, Inc., Rockville, Md., 1990-91; writer H.D. Fulcher Pubs., Inc., Lynchburg, 1992—; cons. engr. Fla. Power and Light, Miami, 1985, Westinghouse Svannah River, Aiken, S.C., 1991-92. Author: Emotional Mind Modeling (A Possible Cure for Manic-Depression and A Metaphysical Study of God and His Creation), 1995. Argonne Nat. Lab. Grad. Engring. scholar, 1969. Methodist. Avocations: tennis, pool. Home: 1450 Hawkins Mill Rd Lynchburg VA 24503-4952 Office: H D Fulcher Publishers Inc 1450 Hawkins Mill Rd Lynchburg VA 24503-4952

FULCI, FRANCESCO PAOLO, diplomat; b. Messina, Italy, Mar. 19, 1931; s. Sebastiano and Enza (Sciascia) F.; m. Claris Glathar, 1965; children: Sebastiano, Marie Sol, William. LLD, U. Messina, Italy, 1953; M in Comparative Law, Columbia U., 1955; diploma, Acad. Internat. Law, The Hague, The Netherlands, 1956; LLD (hon.), U. Windsor, Ont., Can., 1981. Joined Italian Fgn. Svc., 1956, attache directorate gen. for econ. affairs N.Am. desk, 1956-58, 1st sec. directorate gen. for polit. affairs Soviet and Ea. European desk, 1963-65, liaison officer with Parliament in Cabinet, 1965-68; 1st vice consul Consulate Gen. Italy, N.Y.C., 1958-61; 2nd sec. Italian Embassy, Moscow, 1961-63; counsellor, 1st counsellor Italian Embassy, Paris, 1968-74; min. counsellor Italian Embassy, Tokyo, 1974-76; mem. Italian del. UN Gen. Assembly, N.Y.C., 1965; chief of cabinet to Hon. Amintore Fanfani Italian Senate, Rome, 1976-80; amb. to Can. Ottawa, 1980-85; amb. and permanent rep. of Italy NATO, Brussels, 1985-91; sec. gen. of exec. com. for intelligence and security CESIS, 1991-93; permanent rep. of Italy UN, N.Y.C., 1993—. Decorated Cross of Merit (Germany), officer Legion of Honor (France), comdr. Imperial Order of Rising Sun (Japan), knight Gt. Cross of Order of Merit (Italy), knight Mil. Order of Malta; Fulbright scholar Columbia U., 1954-55. Office: Permanent Mission of Italy UN 2 UN Plaza 24th Fl New York NY 10017-4403*

FULCO, ARMAND JOHN, biochemist; b. L.A., Apr. 3, 1932; s. Herman J. and Clelia Marie (DeFeo) F.; m. Virginia Loy Hungerford, June 18, 1955 (div. July 1985); children: William James, Lisa Marie, Linda Susan, Suzanne Yvonne; m. Doris V.N. Goodman, Nov. 29, 1987. B.S. in Chemistry, UCLA, 1957, Ph.D. in Physiol. Chemistry, 1960. NIH postdoctoral fellow Lipid Labs. UCLA, 1960-61; NIH research fellow dept. chemistry Harvard U., Cambridge, Mass., 1961-63; biochemist, prin. investigator Lab. Nuclear Medicine and Radiation Biology, UCLA, 1963-80; asst. prof. dept. biol. chemistry UCLA (Med. Sch.), 1965-70, assoc. prof., 1970-76, prof., 1976—, prin. investigator lab. biomed. and environ. scis., 1981-93; prin. investigator lab. structural biology/molecular med. UCLA-Dept. of Energy, 1993-95; cons. biochemist VA, Los Angeles, 1968-79; mem. UCLA Molecular Biology Inst., 1991—; co-dir. Lipid-Hormone Core Lab., UCLA, 1989-96; mem. Jonsson Comprehensive Cancer Ctr. UCLA, 1994—. Author: (with J.F. Mead) The Unsaturated and Polyunsaturated Fatty Acids in Health and Disease, 1976; contbr. over 90 articles to sci. jours. Served with U.S. Army, 1952-54. Mem. AAAS, Am. Chem. Soc., Am. Soc. Biochem. and Molecular Biology, Am. Soc. Microbiology, Internat. Soc. for Study of Xenobiotics, Harvard Chemists Assn., Sigma Xi. Office: UCLA Sch Medicine Dept Biol Chemistry 10833 Le Conte Ave Los Angeles CA 90095-1737

FULCO, PAULA, artist; b. Hartford, Conn., May 22, 1966; d. Paul Anthony and Jane Buell (Emerson) F. BFA, Syracuse U., 1989. Portrait artist Syracuse, N.Y., 1985-99; cartoonist The Daily Orange, Syracuse, 1985-87; artist, illustrator Believers Chapel, Cicero, N.Y., 1992-95; freelance illustrator, 1993-97. Author and illustrator: Kingdom Kartoons: The Jesus Story, 1995. Avocations: running, reading.

FULD, GILBERT LLOYD, pediatrician; b. N.Y.C., Aug. 15, 1937; s. Arthur and Goldie (Kiss) F.; m. Alice Kinzler, Feb. 1, 1964; children: Rachel Anne, Sarah Elizabeth. AB, Hamilton Coll., 1958; MD, U. Pitts., 1962. Chief pediatrics Forbes AFB, Topeka, 1965-67; pvt. practice N.Y.C., 1967-71; staff pediatrician Keene (N.H.) Clin., 1971-93, Hitchcock Clin., Keene, 1993—. Mem. Am. Acad. Pediatrics. (bd. dirs. Elkgrove, Ill. 1992-98, chmn. N.H. chpt. 1977-82, alt. chmn. dist. I 1985-91, chair dist. I 1992-98). Office: Hitchcock Clinic 590 Court St Keene NH 03431-1798

FULD, JAMES JEFFREY, retired lawyer; b. N.Y.C., Feb. 16, 1916; s. Gus and Blanche (Weill) F.; m. Elaine Gerstley, Sept. 14, 1942; children: Joan Strauss, James, Nancy Neff. AB, Harvard U., 1937, LLB, 1940. Bar: N.Y. 1940. Mem. firm Proskauer Rose Goetz & Mendelsohn, N.Y.C., 1940-98, mng. ptnr., 1974-84; ret., 1998. Author: The Book of World-Famous Music, 1966, 4th edit., 1995, The Book of World-Famous Libretti, 1994; contbr. to legal and musicol. jours. Bd. dirs. Am. Jewish Com., 1956-60, United Jewish Appeal-Fedn. Jewish Philanthropies of N.Y., N.Y.C., 1974-86; mem. N.Y. State Bd. Social Welfare, Albany, 1973-76; advisor Toscanini Meml. Archives, N.Y. Pub. Library, N.Y.C., 1970—. Served to maj. U.S. Army, 1942-46. Recipient War Dept. citation U.S. Army, 1945; hon. fellow Pierpont Morgan Libr., 1992—. Mem. ABA, Assn. of Bar of City of N.Y., N.Y. County Lawyers Bar Assn. (dir. 1974-77, chmn. corp. law com. 1961-63), Phi Beta Kappa. Republican. Jewish. Club: Sunningdale Country (pres. 1956-58). Home: 1175 Park Ave New York NY 10128-1211 Office: Proskauer Rose 1585 Broadway New York NY 10036-8200

FULD, RICHARD SEVERIN, JR., investment banker; b. N.Y.C., Apr. 26, 1946; s. Richard Severin and Elizabeth (Schwab) F.; m. Kathleen Ann Bailey, Sept. 24, 1978; children: Jacqueline, Christine, Richard S. III. BS, U. Colo., 1969; MBA, NYU, 1973. Mng. dir. Lehman Bros., N.Y.C., 1969-84; vice chmn. Shearson Lehman (merger Shearson and Lehman Bros.), N.Y.C., 1984-90; past CEO, pres. Lehman Bros., N.Y.C., now chmn. bd., CEO, pres.; bd. dirs. Shearson Lehman Mortgage Co.; vice chmn. Shearson Lehman Bros., N.Y.C., 1984—; chmn. Lehman Comml. Paper, N.Y.C., 1984—; mem. PSA Govt. and Fed. Agy. Securities Com. Assoc. trustee Mt. Sinai Hosp., N.Y.C.; trustee Wilbraham (Mass.) & Monson Acad., Mt. Sinai Med. Ctr., Ethical Culture Schs.; chmn. Mt. Sinai Children's Ctr. Found.; bd. dirs. Ronald McDonald House. Avocations: squash, photography. *

FULD, ROBERT O'CONNOR, social worker; b. N.Y.C., Jan. 27, 1947; s. John Joseph Patrick O'Connor and Dorothea (Fuld) MacIntyre; m. Selene Letichevsky, Apr. 1970 (div. June 1979). BSc in Biology and Liberal Arts, Ill. Inst. Tech., Chgo., 1969; M in Social Svc. Adminstrn., U. Chgo., 1973; post master's cert. in social svc. adminstrn., Hunter Coll., 1985. Cert. social worker, N.Y., alcoholism counselor, N.Y. Tchr. physics and remedial scis. Chgo. Bd. Edn., 1968-73; tenant organizer Housing Conservation Coords., N.Y.C., 1974-75; social worker Henry St. Settlement House, N.Y.C., 1975-76; team leader, team IV, dir. youth employment programs Lower East Side Family Union, N.Y.C., 1976-83; dir. juvenile svcs. unit N.Y. Legal Aid Soc., N.Y.C., 1983-87; asst. dir. Stanley and Rita Kaplan Ctr., N.Y.C., 1987-88, social worker, 1989; therapist dept. psychiatry Outpatient Alcoholism Clinic Bellevue Hosp., N.Y.C., 1988-90; pvt. practice psychotherapy N.Y.C., 1989—; bilingual sch. social worker N.Y.C. Bd. of Edn., 1990—. Exhbns. include Cafe des Artistes, Greenwich Village, N.Y., 1998, Bell Cafe, N.Y.C., 1998, Agora Gallery, N.Y.C., 1998, Broome St. Gallery, 1999. Mem. PINS Adv. Bd. Mayor's Office, 1985-87; mem. Mayor's Youth Lit. Task Force, 1981-83. Recipient Excellence Ednl. Initiatives award Group Counseling Program Failing Students, 1999. Mem. NASW, Acad. Cert. Social Workers, Amnesty Internat. Avocations: painting, travel, real estate investment, skiing, dancing. E-mail: RobFuld@aol.com. Home: 217 E 12th St Apt 4F New York NY 10003-9168 Office: 217 E 12th St Apt 1R New York NY 10003-9167

FULD, STEVEN ALAN, financial advisor, insurance specialist; b. Balt., Aug. 20, 1963; s. George Joseph Fuld and Nancy (Morstein) Boltz; m. Julie Michelle Glaser, Jan. 21, 1989; children: Zachary Aaron, Jessica Sydney. Student, Calif. State U., Northridge, 1981-85; postgrad., Am. Coll., 1991—. CLU, ChFC. Agt. Lincoln Nat. Life, Tarzana, Calif., 1984-85; mng. ptnr. The Skyline Group, Encino, Calif., 1985—; mem. extended faculty Am. Coll., 1990-92; lectr. Assn. for Advanced Life Underwriting, The Arthritis Found., Georgetown U., Nat. Assn. Health Underwriters, Nat. Assn. Life Underwriters, Calif. Soc. CPAs, Internat. Soc. Appraisers, March of Dimes, City Nat. Bank, L.A. Bus. Jour., Forth Fin. Network, others; bd. advisors Manulife, 1996-97, chmn. MFP tech. com., 1996-97; co-host TV series: Strategies of the Rich and Smart, 1995—. Contbg. author: Business Insurance Law and Practice, 1989; contbr. articles to profl. jours. Trustee Temple Beth Haverim; bd. trustees, bd. govs. So. Calif. chpt. Arthritis Found., 1995—, mem. planned gift com., mem. exec. com., 1996—, mem. nat. breakthrough century com., chmn. estate planning day, 1996; res. officer L.A. City Police Dept., 1996—; mem. nat. resource devel. com., chair CEO task force, chair major gifts conf., So. Calif. chpt. chair elect Arthritis Found., 1998—. Named Man of Yr., Pacific S.W. Region, Fedn. Jewish Men's Clubs, 1993; recipient Disting. Svc. award Arthritis Found., 1995, Nat. Vol. Svc. citation, 1997. Mem. Am. Soc. CLU and ChFC (lectr., bd. dirs. San Fernando Valley chpt. 1989-92, Disting. Svc. award 1990, 92), Beverly Hills Estate Counselors Forum (bd. dirs. 1992-95), Conejo Valley Estate Counselors Forum (founder), Nat. Assn. Life Underwriters, Assn. for Advanced Life Underwriting, Temple Beth Haverim Men's Club (pres.), Temple Beth Haverim (trustee, v.p. ways and means 1993-95). Office: The Skyline Group Second Fl 15928 Ventura Blvd Encino CA 91436-4401

FULDA, MICHAEL, political science educator, space policy researcher; b. Liverpool, Eng., Apr. 21, 1939; came to U.S., 1962, naturalized, 1966; s. Boris and Catherine (Von Dehn) F.; m. Rosa Bongiorno, July 19, 1970; children: Robert, George. Student, Polytechnique, Grenoble, France, 1956-57, Tech. U., West Berlin, Germany, 1957-58, Karl Eberhardt U., Tubingen, Germany, 1963-66; MA, Am. U., 1968, PhD in Internat. Studies, 1970. Prof. polit. sci. Fairmont State Coll., W.Va., 1971—; internat. rels. specialist NASA, Washington, 1979. Author: Oil and International Relations, 1979; (with other) United State Space Policy, 1985; contbr. articles to profl. jours. Bd. dirs. Fairmont Chamber Music Soc., 1983—; W.Va. state com. chmn., dir. space policy Nat. Unity Campaign for John Anderson, 1980; mem. nat. adv. com. John Glenn Presdl. Com., 1984, space policy group Dukakis/Bentsen Com., 1988; merit badge councilor Boy Scouts Am. With U.S. Army, 1962-66. Fellow NASA Marshall Ctr., Huntsville, Ala., summer 1977, Langley Ctr., Hampton, Va., 1976; Woodrow Wilson Found. fellow, 1969-70; Humanities Found. W.Va. grantee, 1978-80, NASA W.Va. Space Grant Consortium grantee, 1991—; named alt. del. to Aerospace States Assn. by the Gov. of W.Va., 1998. Fellow AIAA (assoc.), Brit. Interplanetary Soc.; mem. Am. Astronautical Soc., Nat. Space Soc. (dir. 1991-93), German Assn. for Luft and Raumfamrt, Soc. Espacial Mexicana, Nat. Space Club, Assn. Argentina Tech. Space, Inst. for Social Sci. Study of Space (pres. 1988—), Fairmont Elks Lodge (edn. com.). Home: 1 Timothy Ln Fairmont WV 26554-1331

FULGHUM, ROBERT L., author, lecturer; b. Waco, Tex., June 4, 1937; s. Lee and Eula (Howard) F.; m. Marcia McClellan, 1957 (div. 1973); children: Christian, Hunter, Molly; m. Lynn Edwards, 1976. Attended, Univ. Colo.; grad., Baylor Bapt. Univ., 1957, Starr King Sch. for the Ministry, Berkeley, Calif. Ordained to ministry Unitarian Ch., 1961. Part time min. Bellingham, Wash., from 1961; part time min. Edmonds Unitarian Ch., Seattle, Wash., 1966-85, min. emeritus, 1985—; instr. art Lakeside Sch., Seattle, Wash., 1971-88; author and lecturer. Author: All I Really Need to Know I Learned in Kindergarten: Uncommon Thoughts on Common Things, 1988, It Was on Fire When I Lay Down on It, 1989, Uh Oh: Some Observations from Both Sides of the Refrigerator Door, 1991, Maybe (Maybe Not): Second Thoughts on a Secret Life, 1993, From Beginning to End: The Rituals of Our Lives, 1995, True Love, 1997. Office: care Random House Inc 31st Fl 201 E 50th St New York NY 10022-7703*

FULGINITI, VINCENT, university dean; b. Phila., 1931. AB in Psychology, Temple U., 1953, MD, 1957, MS in pediatrics, 1961. Intern Phila. Gen. Hosp., 1957-58; resident in pediatrics Christophers Hosp. for Children, 1958-61, chief resident, 1960-61; NIH fellow pediatric infectious diseases U. Colo. Sch. Medicine, Denver, 1961-62, from asst. prof. to assoc. prof. pediatrics, 1962-69; prof., chmn. dept. pediatrics U. Ariz. Coll. Med., Tucson, 1969-85, vice dean for acad. affairs, 1985-89, acting dean, 1988-89; dean Tulane U. Sch. Medicine, New Orleans, 1989-93; chancellor U. Colo. Health Sci. Ctr., Denver, 1993-98, prof. pediats., 1998—. Editor Am. Jour. Diseases of Children, 1983-93. Chmn. Nat. Vaccine Adv. Com., 1990-94. Mem. AAAS, AMA, Am. Pediatric Soc. (pres. 1990), Am . Assn. Physician., Am. Pub. Health Assn., Soc. Pediatric Rsch. Office: U Colo Health Scis Ctr and Children's Hosp 4200 E 9th Ave Denver CO 80220-3706

FULGONI, GIAN MARC, market research company executive; b. Crickhowell, Brecon, England, Jan. 24, 1948; came to U.S., 1970; s. Romeo and Maria F. BSc. in Physics (with honors), Manchester U., 1969; M.A. in Mktg., Lancaster U., 1970. Exec. v.p. Mgmt. Sci. Assocs., Inc., Pitts., 1970-81; pres. Info. Resources, Inc., Chgo., 1981-89, CEO, 1986-98, vice chmn., 1989-90, chmn., 1991-95, bd. dirs.; bd. dirs. Platinum Tech., Inc. Mem. Young Pres. Orgn. Mem. Am. Mktg. Assn. Avocations: scuba diving; jogging; skiing. Home: 65 E Bellevue Pl Chicago IL 60611-1114 Office: Info Resources Inc 150 N Clinton St Chicago IL 60661-1402*

FULK, PAUL FREDERICK, chiropractor; b. Portsmouth, Ohio, Dec. 9, 1935; s. Raymond Tex Fulk and Lettie Marie (Tackett) Butler; m. Brenda Gail Yeary, May 22, 1987; children: Paul Jr., Robert E., Allan, Adam. Student, Olivet Nazarene U., 1954-57, Northwestern U., 1959, So. Meth. U., 1963; D Chiropractic, Palmer U., 1976; FASA, N.Y. Chiropractic Coll., 1999. Founder, v.p., bd. dirs. Liberty Am. Life Ins. Co., Columbus, Ohio, 1963-69; founder, pres., bd. dirs. Am. Liberty Investment Corp., Columbus, 1963-69; founder, chmn., pres., CEO Par Chem. Corp., Columbus, 1969-72; founder, chmn. bd. dirs., CEO Paratech Industries, Inc., Tulsa, 1992—; founder, pres., CEO Valley Chiropractic Ctr., Centerville, Ohio, 1977—; pres. Para Heath Foods, Inc., 1977—; founder, chmn., bd. dirs., CEO Therasys, Inc., Orlando, Fla., 1996—. Formulator non-phosphate indsl. cleaning product, 1969; inventor device to treat carpal tunnel syndrome, tarsal tunnel device, SRD 100-A needle syringe holder. Mem. Nat. Coll. Applied Kinesiologists, Am. Chiropractic Assn., Ohio Coll. Applied Kinesiologists, Ohio State Chiropractic Assn. Republican. Nazarene. Avocations: photography, swimming. Home: 6248 Rivercliff Ln West Carrollton OH 45449-3048 Office: Valley Chiropractic Ctr 7865 Paragon Rd Centerville OH 45459-4027

FULK, ROSCOE NEAL, retired accountant; b. Lebo, Kans., June 23, 1916; s. Roscoe Lloyd and Maude (Calvert) F.; m. Marie Therese Rabbitt, June 15, 1946; children: Thomas, Janet, David, Robert, Kenneth, Howard. B.S., U. Ill., 1940. With Ernst & Ernst, C.P.A.s, Chgo., 1940-76; partner Ernst & Ernst, C.P.A.s, 1957-76; mem. Ill. Bd. Examiners in Accountancy, 1976-79; treas. Exec. Svc. Corps., Chgo., 1978-91, also bd. dirs. Treas. Winnetka (Ill.) Caucus Com., 1956, vice chmn., 1962; chmn. accountants group United Republican Fund Ill., 1958, Met. Crusade of Mercy, 1970; pres. Civic Fedn. Chgo., 1968-70; pres. New Trier Twp. Citizens League, 1961-65; mem. Gov.'s Adv. Council, 1969-73; mem. adv. com. to Coll. Commerce and Bus. Adminstrn., U. Ill., 1970-76; pres., dir. Juvenile Protective Assn., 1970-73; v.p., bd. govs. Chgo. Met. Housing and Planning Council, 1970-75; chmn. Winnetka Zoning Bd. Appeals, 1968-71; mem. Parking Adv. Council Chgo., 1970-74; mem. grand council Am. Indian Center, 1973-76; chmn. pres.'s council bus. assos. Elmhurst Coll., 1969-70; bd. dirs. U. Ill. Found., 1973-79, State Equity Council, 1969-72; pres. United Charities Chgo., 1973-75; v.p. Catholic Charities Chgo., 1973-75, Met. Easter Seal Soc. Chgo., 1973-77; pres.' council U. Chgo., 1973-76; bd. dirs. St. Francis Hosp., Evanston, Ill., 1978-87; trustee, treas. Chgo. Orchestral Assn., 1977-80. Served to lt. USNR, 1942-46. Mem. Am. Inst. C.P.A.s (mem. council 1968-72), Ill. Soc. C.P.A.s (dir. 1963-64, pres. 1969-70), Chgo. Assn. Commerce and Industry (dir. 1975-77). Clubs: Sunset Ridge Country (Winnetka) (dir. 1961-65), Paradise Valley Country (Phoenix). Home: 6820 N 3rd Pl Phoenix AZ 85012-1009

FULKER, EDMUND, management consultant; b. Pittsfield, Mass., June 14, 1927; s. Herbert Ernest Creal Fulker and Albina Archambault; m. Jeanette Ruth Fletcher, July 31, 1948; children: Pamela J. Fulker Leonard, Glenn Herbert. BS, Purdue U., 1950, MS in Psychology, 1951; EdD in Adult Edn., Am. U., 1970. Lic. psychologist, D.C. Instr. Purdue U., Indpls., 1952-54; tng. officer Hdqrs. USAF, Washington, 1954-57, Hdqrs. USDA, Washington, 1957-59; asst. dir. USDA Grad. Sch., Washington, 1959-80, dir., 1980-85; cons. The World Bank, Washington, 1987—; adj. faculty Am. U., Washington, George Washington U., Ctrl. Mich. U., Nat. Cheng Chi U., Taiwan; pres. ASPA, Washington, 1977-78, nat. coun. mem., 1979-81. Contbr. articles to profl. jours. Mgmt. cons. U. Mich., Taipei, Taiwan, 1963, Ford Found., New Delhi, India, Nepal, 1970-71, Ohio State U., Ankara, Turkey, 1993, Egypt Gen. Petroleum Co., Cairo, 1996—. With USNR, 1946-47. Recipient Outstanding Pub. Adminstrn. award USPA, Washington, 1984. Mem. ASTD (pres. chpt. 1964-65, Outstanding Trainer award 1963), APA, Internat. Club Washington. Avocations: boating, golfing, traveling. E-mail: edfulker@aol.com. Home: 15240 San Snead Ln Ft Myers FL 33917

FULKERSON, WILLIAM MEASEY, JR., college president; b. Moberly, Mo., Oct. 18, 1940; s. William Measey and Edna Frances (Pendleton) F.; m. Grace Carolyn Wisdom, May 26, 1962; children: Carl Franklin, Carolyn Sue. BA, William Jewell Coll., 1962; MA, Temple U., 1964; PhD, Mich. State U., 1969. Asst. to assoc. prof. Calif. State U., Fresno, 1981—; asst. to pres. Calif. State U.-Fresno, 1971-73; assoc. exec. dir. Am. Assn. State Colls., Washington, 1973-77; acad. v.p. Phillips U., Enid, Okla., 1977-81; pres. Adams State Coll., Alamosa, Colo., 1981-94, State Colls. in Colo., 1994—; interim pres. Met. State Coll., Denver, 1987-88, Western State Coll., 1996. Author: Planning for Financial Exigency, 1973; contbr. articles to profl. jours. Commr. North Ctrl. Assn., Chgo., 1980—; bd. dirs. Acad. Collective Bargaining Info. Svc., Washington, 1976, Office for Advancement Pub. Negro Colls., Atlanta, 1973-77, Colo. Endowment for Humanities, 1988—, pres., 1998-99. Named Disting. Alumni William Jewell Coll., 1982, Outstanding Alumnus Mich. State U. Coll. Comm., Arts & Scis., 1987. Mem. Am. Assn. State Colls. and Univs. (parliamentarian, bd. dirs. 1992-94), Am. Coun. on Edn. (bd. dirs.), Assn. Pub. Coll.s and Univs. Pres.s (pres. 1994-95), Nat. Assn. Sys. Heads, Alamosa C. of C. (dir., pres. 1984 Citizen Yr. award), Rotary. Office: State Colls in Colo 1580 Lincoln St Ste 750 Denver CO 80203-1505

FULLAGAR, PAUL DAVID, geology educator, geochemical consultant; b. Fort Edward, N.Y., Dec. 19, 1938; s. William Alfred and Evelyn Louise (Hoyt) Fullagar; m. Patricia Ann Kelley, June 6, 1959; children: Scott David, Eric Craig. A.B., Columbia U., 1960; Ph.D., U. Ill, 1963. Asst. prof. Old Dominion Coll., Norfolk, Va., 1963-67; asst. prof. U. N.C., Chapel Hill, 1967-69, assoc. prof., 1969-73, prof. dept. geology, 1973—, chmn. dept., 1979-89, 92-98; analytical geochemist Goddard Space Flight Ctr., Greenbelt, Md., 1964-69; vis. fellow Wolfson Coll., Cambridge U., Eng., 1984-85, 91. Contbr. articles to profl. jours. Gen. Motors scholar Columbia U., 1956-60; fellow U. Ill., 1961; Shell fellow, 1962-63; research grantee NSF, 1964-84, 89-98; grantee N.C. Bd. Sci. and Tech., 1968, So. Regional Ednl. Bd., 1982. Fellow Geol. Soc. Am., Geochem. Soc.; mem. AAAS, AAUP, Am. Geophys. Soc., Nat. Assn. Geology Tchrs. Democrat. Home: 7229 Morrow Mill Rd Chapel Hill NC 27516-7378 Office: U NC Dept Geology CB # 3315 Chapel Hill NC 27599

FULLAGAR, WILLIAM WATTS, lawyer; b. Chgo., July 3, 1914; s. William Watts and Grace (Wilson) F.; m. Doris Virginia Olson, Feb. 11, 1956 (dec. Oct. 29, 1979). B.S., Northwestern U., 1937; LL.B., Chgo. Kent Coll., 1942. Bar: Ill. 1942. With loan dept. First Nat. Bank & Trust Co., Evanston, Ill., 1938-43; assoc., then ptnr. Rooks, Pitts, Fullagar & Poust and predecessor firms, Chgo., 1943-84; of counsel Rooks, Pitts & Poust (and predecessors), 1984—; instr. comml. law Am. Inst. Banking, Chgo., 1947-51. Mem. Am., Ill., Chgo. bar assns., Alpha Delta Phi. Republican. Presbyterian. Club: Union League (Chgo.). Home: 2320 Isabella St Evanston IL 60201-1405 Office: 10 S Wacker Dr Chicago IL 60606-7407*

FULLAM, JOHN P., federal judge; b. Gardenville, Pa., Dec. 10, 1921; s. Thomas L. and Mary Nolan F.; m. Alice Hilliar Freiheit, Apr. 15, 1950; children: Nancy, Sally, Thomas, Jeffrey. B.S., Villanova U., 1942; J.D., Harvard U., 1948. Atty. Bristol, Pa., 1948-60; judge Pa. Ct. Common Pleas, 7th Jud. Dist., 1960-66; judge U.S. Dist. Ct. (ea. dist.) Pa., Phila., 1966—, chief judge, 1986-90; now sr. judge; lectr. in law U. Pa. Law Sch., Phila., Temple U. Law Sch., Phila.; mem. adv. com. Codes of Conduct of Jud. Conf. U.S., mem. adminstrn. magistrates sys., mem. com. to rev. jud. coun. disciplinary and disability orders. Democratic candidate for U.S. Congress, 1954, 56. Mem. Am. Law Inst., Pa. Bar Assn., Bucks County Bar Assn., Phila. Bar Assn. Office: US Courthouse 15614 US Courthouse Ind Mall W 601 Market St Philadelphia PA 19106-1713*

FULLENLOVE, CARMEN (KIT) MILLAY, public relations executive; b. Louisville, Aug. 27, 1959; d. Joseph Claude Millay and Erma Louise

Fleischmann; m. William Burnley Wolfe, Oct. 10, 1981 (div. June 1986); m. James Martin Fullenlove Sr., Sept. 12, 1987; 1 child, Rachel Reneé. BS in Journalism and Polit. Sci., Murray State U., 1980. City editor Mt. Vernon (Ind.) Dem., 1980-81; editor Softball Watch, Marietta, Ga., 1982; reporter, photographer The Sentinel-News, Shelbyville, Ky., 1983-84; editor The Oldham Era, La Grange, Ky., 1984-97; pub. rels. mgr. Bapt. Hosp. East, Louisville, 1997—. Active Oldham County Bd. Edn., La Grange, 1998—. Recipient Sch. Bell award Ky. Edn. Assn., 1997. Mem. Soc. Profl. Journalists (membership chair, pres. 1991-92, Howard Dubin award 1996, Best Column award 1998), Exec. Quality Coun. E-mail: KFullenlove@bhsi.com. Office: Bapt Hosp East 4000 Kresge Way Louisville KY 40207

FULLENWEIDER, DONN CHARLES, lawyer; b. Milw., Jan. 25, 1935; s. Russell Charles and Anne Mae (Murphy) F.; m. Wendy Lattimer; 1 child, Keith Rabon. B.S., U. Houston, 1957, J.D., 1958. Bar: Tex. bar 1958; Cert. in family law and civil trials Tex. Bd. Legal Specialization. Assoc. Fred Parks, Houston, 1958-65; partner Haynes & Fullenweider, Houston, 1965-89; pvt. practice, Houston, 1989-93; ptnr. Fullenweider and Wardell L.L.P., 1993-97, Fullenweider & Assocs., 1997—; Adj. assoc. prof. law U. Houston Bates Coll. Law, 1972-74. Mem. 43d Joint Civilian Orientation Conf., 1973; mem. Tex. Bd. Legal Specialization, 1977-98. Recipient Emison award Tex. Acad. Family Specialists, 1993. Fellow Am. Bar Found., Houston Bar Found., Tex. Bar Found. (dir. 1973-76), Am. Acad. Matrimonial Lawyers (pres. Tex. chpt. 1979-81, bd. dirs. 1981-84, treas. 1985-88, pres.-elect 1988-89, pres. 1990-91); mem. ABA, Am. Bd. Trial Advoacy (advocate), Houston Bar Assn. (treas. 1961-62, 2d v.p. 1962-63, dir. 1971, 73, 1st v.p. 1970-73, Outstanding Svc. award 1974), Am. Coll. Family Trial Lawyers (diplomate 1994—), State Bar Tex. (dir. 1973-76, chmn. bd. 1975-76, exec. com. 1976-77, chmn. litigation sect. 1979-81), Am. Trial Lawyers Assn., Houston Trial Lawyers Assn. (v.p. 1971), Def. Orientation Conf. Assn., Houston C. of C., River Oaks Country Club, Sigma Chi, Phi Delta Phi. Home: 5502 Fieldwood Dr Houston TX 77056-2719 Office: 4265 San Felipe St Ste 1400 Houston TX 77027-2999

FULLER, ANNE ELIZABETH HAVENS, English language and literature educator, consultant; b. Pomona, Calif., Jan. 20, 1932; d. Paul Swain and Lorraine Elizabeth (Hamilton) Havens; m. Martin Emil Fuller, II, June 17, 1961; children: Katharine Hamilton, Peter David Takashi. A.B., Mount Holyoke Coll., 1953; B.A. (Fulbright scholar), Somerville Coll., Oxford U., 1955, M.A., 1959; Ph.D. (Univ. fellow), Yale U., 1958. Instr. English Mount Holyoke Coll., 1957-59; instr. Pomona Coll., 1959-61; asst. prof. U. Fla., Gainesville, 1961-63; lectr. U. Denver, 1964-68, 71-73; assoc. prof., chmn. center for lang. and lit. Prescott (Ariz.) Coll., 1968-70; tchr. Colo. Rocky Mountain Sch., 1970-71; dean of faculty Scripps Coll., Claremont, Calif., 1973-80; prof. English Scripps Coll., 1973-80; spl. asst. to pres., sec. to corp. Claremont U. Center, 1981-83; v.p. for acad. affairs Austin Coll., Sherman, Tex., 1982-84, faculty mem., 1984-96; mem. SW dist. Rhodes Scholar Selection Com., 1975-83. Bd. dirs. Am. Council on Edn., 1979-81. Mem. Assn. Am. Colls. (dir. 1977-81, chmn. 1980-81), Am. Conf. Acad. Deans (dir. 1976-79), Commn. on Women in Higher Edn., Am. Assn. Higher Edn., Modern Lang. Assn. Am. Democrat. Episcopalian. Home: 11304 Pinos Altos Ave NE Albuquerque NM 87111-5701

FULLER, BONNIE, editor. Editor-in-chief Cosmopolitan Hearst Mags., N.Y.C., 1997-98; editor-in-chief Glamour mag., Conde Nast, 1998—. Office: Glamour Mag Conde Nast Bldg 350 Madison Ave New York NY 10017-3704*

FULLER, CASSANDRA MILLER, applications specialist; b. Norwalk, Conn., Dec. 10, 1965; d. George Louis and Bernice (Simmons) Miller; m. David Norman Fuller, Dec. 24, 1988; 1 child, Jessica Ashley. BS, S.C. State Coll., 1987; MBA, U. Bridgeport, 1995. Interior decorator's apprentice Marty Rae Interiors, Orangeburg, S.C., 1984-85; asst. mgr. Dairy Queen, Orangeburg, S.C., 1986-87; day mgr. The Bedford, Stamford, Conn., 1987-88; dept. mgr. Burlington Coat Factory Warehouse, Danbury, Conn.; asst. mgr. Kidstuff, Inc., Orange, Conn., 1989-92; Postage By Phone customer assistance specialist Pitney Bowes, Stamford, Conn., 1992-95, programmer analyst, 1996-98; applications specialist GE Capital Vendor Fin. Svcs., Danbury, Conn., 1998—; cons. Orangeburg Metro Transit 1987. Mem. Nat. Assn. Negro Bus. and Profl. Women's Clubs Inc., Nat. Black MBA Assn., NAFE, African Am. Forum, Kappa Omicron Phi. Democrat. Baptist. Office: GE Capital Corp Vendor Fin Svcs 55 Federal Rd Danbury CT 06810-4045

FULLER, CHARLES H, JR, playwright; b. Phila., Mar. 5, 1939; s. Charles Henry and Lillian (Anderson) F.; m. Miriam A. Nesbitt, Aug. 4, 1962; children: Charles III, David. Student, Villanova U., 1956-58, hon. degree, 1983; student, LaSalle Coll., 1965-67, hon. degree, 1982; hon. degree, Chestnut Hill Coll., 1985. Co-founder, co-dir. Afro-Am. Arts Theatre, Phila., 1967-71; writer, dir. The Black Experience Sta. WIP-Radio, Phila., 1970-71; prof. African-Am. studies Temple U., Phila., until 1993. Plays include The Village: A Party, 1968, rev. as The Perfect Party, 1969, In My Names and Days, 1972, Candidate, 1974, In the Deepest Part of Sleep, 1974, First Love, 1974, The Lay Out Letter, 1975, The Brownsville Raid, 1976, Sparrow in Flight, 1978, Zooman and the Sign, 1981 (Obie award 1981, Audelco award 1981), A Soldier's Play, 1982 (Pulitzer prize in drama 1982, N.Y. Drama Critics award best Am. play 1982, Outer Circle Critics award best off-Broadway play 1982, Audelco award 1982, Theatre Club award 1982), Sons of the Same Lion, 1991; (play series) We Part I "Sally", 1988, Part II "Prince", 1988, Part III "Jonquil", 1989, Part IV "Burner's Frolic", 1990; contbr.: Urban Blight, 1988; writer: (TV miniseries) Roots, Resistance and Renaissance, 1967, (TV series) The Sky is Gray, 1987, (screenplay) A Soldier's Story, 1984 (Academy award nominations best picture and best screenplay adaptation 1984, Edgar Allen Poe Mystery award 1985), (TV movie) A Gathering of Old Men, 1987 (screenplay); dir. (TV movie) Zooman, Showtime, 1995; dir.: The Black Experience, WIP-Radio, 1970-71. Bd. dirs. Adolp Caesar Meml. Fund. Served with AUS, 1959-62. NEA grantee, 1976; Rockefeller Found. grantee, 1976; Guggenheim Found. fellow, 1977-78; recipient Creative Artists Pub. Svc. award, 1974, Hazelitt award Pa. State Coun. Arts, 1984. Mem. PEN (bd. dirs. Am. div.), Writers Guild Am. East, Dramatists Guild, Dramatist Guild Found. Roman Catholic. *I have always sought wisdom and humility, using one to counterbalance the other.**

FULLER, DAVID OTIS, JR., lawyer; b. Grand Rapids, Mich., May 28, 1939; s. David Otis and Virginia Chapin (Emery) F.; m. Isabelle Patrice Gigout, July 5, 1968; children: Thomas Andrew, Christian Scott, Pierre Emery, Margaret Isabelle. BA, Wheaton Coll., 1961; JD, Harvard U., 1964; postgrad. George Washington U., 1963, U. Paris, 1966. Bar: Mich 1964, N.Y. 1967, U.S. Sup. Ct. 1968. Law clk. U.S. Ho. of Reps. Judiciary Com., 1963; assoc. Amberg, Law & Fallon, Grand Rapids, 1964-65; asst. dist. atty. N.Y. County, 1966-72, law sec. to justice, 1972-73; corp. atty. Pan Am. World Airways, Inc., 1973-74; dep. gen. counsel Reader's Digest Assn., Inc., 1974-84; pvt. practice, N.Y.C., 1984-87; ptnr. Baker, Nelson & Williams, N.Y.C., 1987-94, Bosworth, Gray & Fuller, Bronxville, N.Y., 1994—; justice Tuckahoe Village, N.Y., 1986—; lectr. Am. Bar Assn., Practicing Law Inst., Bronx C.C. Warden Episc. Ch., 1991-97. Editor Harvard Jour. on Legislation, 1962-64; contbr. articles to profl. jours. Mem. ABA, Internat. Bar Assn., N.Y. State Bar Assn. (chmn. privacy com. 1982-84), Assn. Bar City N.Y. (communications law com. 1984-87), Am. Arbitration Assn. (arbitrator 1983-96), N.Y. State Magistrates Assn. (dir. 1998—), Westchester County Bar Assn., Westchester County Magistrates Assn. (pres. 1993-94). Republican. Club: Harvard (N.Y.C.). Avocations: fishing, skiing, coins, racquet sports, French. Office: Bosworth Gray & Fuller 116 Kraft Ave Bronxville NY 10708-3810

FULLER, DAVID SCOTT, construction and investment company executive; b. Kansas City, Mo., Sept. 17, 1959; s. Richard Max Fuller and Barbara Jean (Rigdon) Mardis; m. Nancy Kay Baum, June 14, 1983 (div. Feb. 1990). Grad. high sch., Shawnee, Kans. Prin. Fuller Constrn., Shawnee, 1975—, Solar Energy div. Fuller Constrn., Shawnee, 1978-85; founder, pres. Delta Investment Corp., Shawnee, 1984—; owner Sundek, Kansas City, 1994—; mem. Kansas City Chiefs Red Coaters. Admitted to Phase III Wings Program, FAA, 1985-87. Mem. U.S. Pilots Assn., Aircraft Owners and Pilots Assn., Kans. Pilots Assn. Republican. Baptist. Avocations: flight instr., comml. pilot. Home and Office: 12300 W 71st St Shawnee Mission KS 66216-2916

FULLER, DOLORES AGNES, songwriter, actress; b. South Bend, Ind., Mar. 10, 1923; d. Eugene J. and Leonora (Dahms) Eble; m. Donald Fuller (div. June 1952); children: Donald K., Darrel D.; m. Philip Chamberlin. Student, Hunter Coll., 1956-59. Sec. Nat. Artists Found., Las Vegas, Nev. and L.A., 1987-96; guest of honor Munich Internat. Film Festiva, 1995. Star movies Glen or Glenda? (also known as I Led Two Lives), 1953, The Hidden Face (also known as Jailbait), 1954; appeared in Outlaw Women, 1953, The Blue Gardenia, 1953, The Body Beautiful, 1953, Girls in the Night, 1953, Lost Mesa of Women, 1953, College Capers, 1953, The Moonlighter, 1953, Count the Hours, 1953, The Raid, 1954, This Is My Love, 1954, The Playgirl, 1954, Bride of the Monster, 1955, Look Back in Angora, 1994, The Haunted World of Edward D. Wood, Jr., 1996; cameo role in film The Ironbound Vampire, 1997; regular performer TV show Chevrolet Playhouse, with Dinah Shore, 1951-54, Queen for a Day; guest appearances on TV shows include The Danny Thomas Show, The Bob Hope Show, 1951-56, The Tonight Show, The Red Skelton Show, The Dennis Day Show, The Streets of San Francisco, also others; TV movies include Superman, Hollywood Preview, Lineup, It's a Great Life, The Damon Runyon Series, Gildersleeve, Dragnet; songs include (songs sung by Elvis Presley) Rock-a-Hula Baby, Big Love, Big Heartache, Spinout, I Got Lucky I'll Take Love, Steppin' Out of Line, Do the Clam, Have a Happy, Cindy, Cindy, Beyond the Bend, You Can't Say No in Acapulco, Barefoot Ballad, Peggy Lee and Nat "King" Cole, Losers Weepers, Someone To Tell It To, Marriage on the Rocks, Crying Guitar; subject of documentary Diamonds in the Rough, German TV, 1998. Recipient award for contbn. to motion pictures FANEX, ,,, 1996. Mem. ASCAP (winner song writing award for Crossroads of Laredo and Dust of Laredo 1998). Avocations: swimming, photography, chess, golf, dance. Home: 3628 Ottawa Cir Las Vegas NV 89109-3301

FULLER, EDWIN DANIEL, hotel executive; b. Richmond, Va., Mar. 15, 1945; s. Ben Swint and Evelyn (Beal) F.; m. Denise Kay Perigo, July 18, 1970. Student, Wake Forest U., 1965; BSBA, Boston U., 1968; postgrad., Harvard Sch. Bus., 1987. Security officer Pinkerton Inc., Boston, 1965-68; with sales dept. Twin Bridges Marriott Hotel, Arlington, Va., 1972-73; nat. sales mgr. Marriott Hotels & Resorts, N.Y.C., 1973-76; dir. nat. and internat. sales mgr. Marriott Hotels & Resorts, Washington, 1976-78; v.p. mktg. Marriott Hotels & Resorts, 1978-82; gen. mgr. Marriott Hotels & Resorts, Hempstead, N.Y., 1982-83, Marriott Copley Place, Boston, 1983-85; v.p. ops. Midwest region Marriott Corp., Rosemont, Ill., 1985-89; v.p. ops. Western and Pacific regions Marriott Corp., Santa Ana, Calif., 1989-90; sr. v.p., mng. dir. Marriott Hotels & Resorts-Internat., Washington, 1990-93; exec. v.p., mng. dir. internat. lodging Marriott Lodging Internat., Washington, 1994-97, pres., mng. dir., 1997—; chmn. bd. dirs. SNR Reservation Sys., Zurich, Switzerland, 1979-81; bd. dirs. Boston U. Hotel Sch., 1984—, Mgmt. Engrs. Inc., Reston, Va., Barnby Books, Barnaby Books, Honolulu, 1997—; treas. MEI Pacific Honolulu, 1985—; chmn. Fuller Properties, Laguna Hills, Calif., 1990—. Pres. Boston U. Gen. Alumni Assn., 1993—, v.p., 1990-93; v.p. Boston U. Sch. Mgmt. Alumni Bd., 1985—; mem. adv. bd. Boston U. Hospitality Mgmt. Sch., 1985—; trustee Boston U., mem. exec. com. bd. trustees, 1994—. Capt. U.S. Army, 1968-72, Vietnam. Decorated Bronze Star. Mem. Boston U. Alumni Coun. (v.p.), Harvard Sch. Bus. Advanced Mgmt. Program (fund agt.), Sigma Alpha Epsilon, Delta Sigma Pi. Republican. Avocations: real estate, travel, golf, history. Home: 25362 Derbyhill Dr Laguna Hills CA 92653-7835 Office: Marriott Hotels & Resorts 1 Marriott Dr Washington DC 20058-0001

FULLER, ELIZABETH L., writer, playwright; b. Cleve., Sept. 22, 1946; d. Lewis F. and Isabel (Rooney) Brancae; m. John Grant Fuller, Nov. 17, 1978 (dec. Nov. 7, 1990); 1 child, Christopher Lewis; m. Reuel Dorman, Sept. 23, 1996. Student, Ohio State U., 1965-66. Author: My Search for the Ghost of Flight 401, 1978, Poor Elizabeth's Almanac, 1979, 2nd edit., 1980, Having Your First Baby After Thirty, 1983, softcover edit., 1984, Nima: A Sherpa in Connecticut, 1983, The Touch of Grace, 1983, Everyone is Psychic, hardcover edit., 1989, softcover edit., 1990, Me and Jezebel, 1991, Nannies: How I went through eighteen nannies for one little boy before I found perfection in a former Marine Sergeant named Margaret, 1993, When You See the Emu in the Sky, 1997; playwright, actress: Me and Jezebel (play adapted from book), 1992 (nominated Helen Hayes award, nominated Best Play Backstage Mag. award, nominated Drama Best award Best Play); appeared in Entertainment Tonight, news shows on CBS, NBC, ABC, CNN; contbr. articles to major women's mags., N.Y. Times.

FULLER, GLENN STRAITH, minister; b. Tientsin, China, Feb. 17, 1924; came to U.S., 1927; s. Glenn Vincent and Margaret Meldrum (Straith) F.; m. Kathleen Crawford Lester, June 30, 1954; children: Margaret Alicia, Catherine Ann, Mary Wyon. BA, Pomona Coll., 1944; BD, Union Theol. Seminary, 1947, STM, 1961. Sr. pastor Bowen Meml. Meth. Ch., Bombay, 1947-49; various pastor positons worldwide, 1954-69; sr. pastor Seoul (Korea) Union Ch., 1970-73; assoc. pastor Los Altos (Calif.) United Meth. Ch., 1973-76; sr. pastor Almaden Hills United Meth. Ch., San Jose, Calif., 1976-83; assoc. pastor First United Meth. Ch., Palo Alto, Calif., 1983-88; pastor English-Speaking United Meth. Ch., Vienna, 1988-91; chaplain Lytton Gardens, Palo Alto, 1994—; sec. of missions San Jose Dist. Unified Meth. Ch., 1980-88, 92-96; pub. spkr. Gen. Bd. Global Ministries, N.Y.C., 1988—. Mem. World Affairs Coun., San Francisco, 1993—; bd. dirs. United Christian Campus Ministry, Stanford, Calif., 1995—. Mem. Peninsula Dem. Club. Home: 2365 Pine Knoll Dr #7 Walnut Creek CA 94595-3682

FULLER, HARRY LAURANCE, oil company executive; b. Moline, Ill., Nov. 8, 1938; s. Marlin and Mary Helen (Ilsley) F.; m. Nancy Lawrence, Dec. 27, 1961; children: Kathleen, Laura, Randall. BSChemE, Cornell U., 1961; JD, DePaul U., 1965. Bar: Ill. 1965. With Standard Oil Co. (and affiliates), 1961—, sales mgr., 1972-74, gen. mgr. supply, 1974-77; exec. v.p. Standard Oil Co. (Amoco Oil Co. div.), Chgo., 1977-78; pres. Amoco Oil Co., Chgo., 1978-81; exec. v.p. Standard Oil Co. of Ind., Chgo., 1981-83; pres. Amoco Corp., Chgo., 1983-91, chmn., CEO, 1991—, also dir., 1999—; co-chair BP Amoco p.l.c., Chgo., 1999—; bd. dirs. Chase Manhattan Corp., Chase Manhattan Bank N.A., Abbott Labs., Motorola, Inc. Bd. dirs. Chgo. Rehab. Inst.; trustee Orchestral Assn. Mem. Am. Petroleum Inst. (bd. dirs.). Republican. Presbyterian. Clubs: Mid-Am, Chgo. Golf, Chicago. Office: Amoco Corp 200 E Randolph St Chicago IL 60601-6436

FULLER, HOWARD, education educator, academic administrator. Supt. Milw. Sch. Dist.; dist. prof. edn., dir. Inst. Transformation Learning Marquette U., Milw., 1996—. Office: Marquette U Schroedor Complex PO Box 1881 Milwaukee WI 53201-1881

FULLER, JACK WILLIAM, writer, publishing executive; b. Chgo., Oct. 12, 1946; s. Ernest Brady and Dorothy Voss (Tegge) F.; m. Alyce Sue Tuttle, June 2, 1973; children: Timothy, Katherine. BS, Northwestern U., 1968; JD, Yale U., 1973. Bar: Ill. 1974. Reporter Chgo. Tribune, 1973-75, Washington corr., 1977-78, editorial writer, 1978-79, dep. editorial page editor, 1979-82, editorial page editor, 1982-87, exec. editor, 1987-89, v.p. and editor, 1989-93, pres., CEO, 1993-97, pub., 1994-97; pres. Tribune Pub. Co., 1997—; spl. asst. to atty. gen. U.S. Dept. Justice, Washington, 1975-77. Author: Convergence, 1982 (Cliff Dwellers award 1983), Fragments, 1984 (Friends of Am. Writers award 1985), Mass, 1985, Our Fathers' Shadows, 1987, Legends' End, 1990, News Values, 1996. Bd. dirs. McCormick Tribune Found., Field Mus.; mem. Pulitzer Prize Bd.; trustee U. Chgo. With U.S. Army, 1969-70. Recipient Gavel award ABA, 1979, Pulitzer prize for editl. writing, 1986. Fellow Am. Acad. Arts and Scis.; mem. Am. Soc. Newspaper Editors, Newspaper Assn. Am., Inter-Am. Dialogue, Inter-Am. Press Assn. (sec.), Comml. Club of Chgo. Office: Chgo Tribune Co 435 N Michigan Ave Chicago IL 60611-4066

FULLER, JAMES CHESTER EEDY, retired chemical company executive; b. Toronto, Can., June 5, 1927; came to U.S., 1968; s. James Clifford and Marion Winifred (Eedy) F.; m. Doris Shirley Johnson, June 16, 1951 (dec. June 1992); children—Hilary, John; m. Shirley Patricia Honeyman, Feb. 8, 1993. B.S.A., U. Toronto, 1948; M.B.A., U. Western Ont., 1955. Sales and mktg. ofcl. Uniroyal Chem. Co., Man. and Ont., Can., 1948-53, 55-64; with Akzo Chemicals and affiliates, 1964-90; gen. mgr. Armour Indsl. Chems., Toronto, 1964-68; nat. sales mgr., asst. to pres., internat. dir. Armour Indsl. Chems., Chgo., 1968-70; mng. dir. Armour-Hess Ltd., Harrogate, Yorkshire, Eng., 1970-73; exec. v.p. Akzo Chemie Am., Chgo., 1973-74, pres., 1975-87; exec. v.p. Akzo Chemicals B.V., Amersfoort, The Netherlands, 1988-90. Mem. Chem. Inst. Can. Clubs: Farmers (London).

FULLER, JAMES WILLIAM, financial director; b. Rochester, Ind., Apr. 3, 1940; s. Raymond S. and Mildred (Osteimeier) F.; children: Kristen Anne, Glen William. AA, San Bernardino (Calif.) Valley Coll., 1960; BS, San Jose (Calif.) State U., 1962; MBA, Calif. State U., 1967. V.p. Dean Witter, San Francisco, 1967-71, Shields & Co., San Francisco, 1971-74; dir. fin. programs SRI Internat., Menlo Park, Calif., 1974-77; sr. v.p. N.Y. Stock Exch., N.Y.C., 1977-81, Charles Schwab & Co., San Fransico, 1981-85; pres. Bull & Bear Corp., N.Y.C., 1985-87; dir. Bridge Info. Systems, San Fransico, 1987—; bd. dirs. Action Trac Inc., L.A., Current Techs. Inc., Vancouver, B.C., Environ. Scis. Inc., San Diego; chmn. bd. dirs. Pacific Rsch. Inst., 1992—. Dir. Securities Industry Protection Corp., Washington, 1981-87, Global Econ. Action Inst., N.Y.C., 1989—; trustee U. Calif., Santa Cruz. Lt. USN, 1963-66. Mem. The Family Club (San Francisco), Olympic Club (San Francisco), Jonathon Club (L.A.), Univ. Club (N.Y.C.), The Lincoln Club (San Francisco), Polit. Com. for Econ. Growth, Internat. Platform Assn., Newcomer Soc., World Affairs Coun., Coun. on Formulations (San Francisco com.), Commonwealth Club. Republican. Presbyterian. Avocations: tennis, politics, public affairs. Home: 2584 Filbert St San Francisco CA 94123-3318 Office: Bridge Info Systems 555 California St San Francisco CA 94104-1502

FULLER, JANAE, historic site administrator; b. Cedar Falls, Iowa, July 30, 1955. BA, U. No. Iowa, 1978. Dir. Confederate Meml. State Hist. Site, Higginsville, Mo., 1983-86; CEO, site adminstr. Battle of Lexington (Mo.) State Hist. Site, 1986—. Active Lexington Hist. Soc., 1989—, Lexington Tourism Bur., 1993—. Mem. Lexington C. of C. Office: Battle of Lexington State Hist Site PO Box 6 Lexington MO 64067-0006*

FULLER, JANICE MARIE, secondary school educator; b. Flagler, Colo., Feb. 7, 1948; d. William Harrison and Ruth Elsie (Jensen) Martin; m. William Edward Fuller, Sept. 16, 1966; children: James Edward, David William, John Justin. A.Gen. Studies, Pikes Peak C.C., Colorado Springs, Colo., 1982; BS in Biology, Met. State Coll., Denver, 1986. Gen. office mgr. Schmidt Environ. Enterprises, Commerce City, Colo., 1972-77; v.p., sec. Fuller Constrn., Inc., Larkspur, Colo., 1993—; tchr. math. and sci. Douglas County Schs., Castle Rock, Colo., 1988-92; tchr. sci. Christ the King Sch., Denver, 1992-96; tchr. biology Ellicott Jr.- Sr. High Sch., Calhan, Colo., 1996—; tutor math./sci.; coach track, gymnastics, volleyball Castle Rock Jr. H.S., 1990-92; nominated 1st U.S./Russia Joint Conf. on Edn. in Moscow, U. Iowa Citizen Ambassador Program, 1994; mem. dist. accountability com. Ellicott Sch. Dist., 1996—. Mem. dist. accountability commn. Douglas County Sch. Dist., Castle Rock, 1987-91, dist. comm. com., 1990. Mem. ASCD, NAFE, AAUW, Nat. Assn. Student Activity Advisors, Nat. Sci. Tchrs. Assn., Met. State Coll. Alumni Assn. Avocations: cooking, sewing, country living. Office: Ellicott Jr-Sr H S 375 S Ellicott Hwy Calhan CO 80808-8838

FULLER, JOHN GARSED CAMPBELL, food and drug company executive; b. Phila., Dec. 16, 1930; s. William Duncan and Katherine Harper (Campbell) F.; m. Elizabeth Ann Dobbins, Nov. 29, 1969; 1 dau., Sarah. A.B., Harvard U., 1952, M.B.A., 1958. Engaged in mktg. and distbn. Acme Markets, Inc., Phila., 1958-66; asst. treas. Acme Markets, Inc., 1966-69, treas., 1969-73; v.p. finance, treas. Am. Stores Co., 1973—; bd. dirs. Phila. Port Corp. Trustee, Treas. Germantown Hist. Soc.; overseer William Penn Charter Sch. Served with Naval Intelligence USNR, 1952-56. Republican. Episcopalian. Clubs: Harvard (Phila.), Cricket (Phila.). Home: 3910 Vaux St Philadelphia PA 19129-1415 Office: Gibbs Bldg 300 W School House Ln Philadelphia PA 19144-3929

FULLER, JOHN WILLIAM, lawyer; b. San Angelo, Tex., Jan. 1, 1948; s. John Walter and Ann Dorene (Behrend) F.; m. Sara Drucilla Smith, July 1, 1983. BA, Tex. A&M U., 1969; JD, U. Tex., 1976. Bar: Tex. 1977. Copy editor Dallas Morning News, 1972-73; dir. govt. affairs ARA Health Mgmt. Group, Austin, Tex., 1977-79; legis. asst. U.S. Rep. Jim Mattox, Washington, 1980-82, U.S. Rep. Bill Patman, Washington, 1982-85; counsel Jim Mattox Fin. Com., Austin, 1985-86; asst. atty. gen. Atty. Gen. State of Tex., Austin, 1986-91, chief county affairs sect., 1991—. Contbr. articles to profl. jours. Del. state convs. Dem. Party, 1976, 92, 96; vol. Habitat for Humanity, Austin, 1995-96. Capt. USAF, 1969-72. Mem. Soc. Profl. Journalists. Lutheran. Avocations: hiking, photography. Home: 9611 Blue Creek Ln Austin TX 78758-5803 Office: PO Box 12548 Austin TX 78711-2548

FULLER, JOSEPH BARRY, company executive; b. Cambridge, Mass., Mar. 17, 1957; s. Stephen Herbert and Frances (Mulhearn) F.; m. Ruthanne Schwartz, July 30, 1983; children: Christopher Benton, Mark Dylan, David Alan. BA magna cum laude, Harvard U., 1979, MBA., 1981. Cons. Strategic Planning Assocs., Boston, 1981, Bain & Co., Boston, 1981-83; founder, pres., CEO, dir. Monitor Co., Cambridge, Mass., 1983—; bd. dirs. Phillips-Van Hewsen Corp., N.Y.C., 1991—. Charles Warren fellow Harvard U., 1979. Office: Monitor Co 704 Campus Dr # Rains17T Stanford CA 94305-7507

FULLER, KATHRYN HELGESEN, historian, educator; b. Mar. 18, 1960. BA, Agnes Scott Coll., 1982; MA, Johns Hopkins U., 1990, PhD, 1993. Vis. asst. prof. media & am. studies Hampshire Coll., Amherst, Mass., 1992-94; asst. prof. history Va. Commonwealth U., Richmond, 1994—. Author: At The Picture Show, 1996, (with others) Children and the Movies, 1996. E-mail: Kfuller@saturn.vcu.edu. Office: Va Commonwealth U History Dept Richmond VA 23220

FULLER, KATHRYN SCOTT, environmental association executive, lawyer; b. N.Y.C., July 8, 1946; d. Delbert Orison and Carol Scott (Gilbert) F.; m. Stephen Paul Doyle, May 29, 1977; children: Sarah Elizabeth Taylor, Michael Stephen Doyle, Matthew Scott Doyle. BA English, Am. Lit., Brown U., 1968, LHD (hon.), 1992; JD with honors, U. Tex., 1976; postgrad., U. Md., 1980-82; DSci. (hon.), Wheaton Coll., 1990; LLD (hon.), Knox Coll., 1992. Bar: Tex. 1977, D.C. 1979. Rsch. asst. Yale U., New Haven, Conn., 1968-69, Am. Chem. Soc., 1970-71, Harvard U. Mus. Comparative Zoology, Cambridge, Mass., 1971-73; law clerk Devey, Ballantine, Bushby, Palmer & Wood and Vinson & Elkins, N.Y.C., Houston, 1974-76, U.S. Dist. Ct. (so. dist.), Tex., 1976-77; atty., advisor Office Legal Counsel Dept. Justice, Washington, 1977-79, atty. Wildlife and Marine Resources sect., 1979-80, chief Wildlife and Marine Resources sect., 1981-82; exec. v.p., dir. Traffic USA, pub. policy, gen. counsel World Wildlife Fund, Washington, 1982-89, pres., CEO, 1989—. Contbr. articles to profl. jours. Adv. com. Trade Policy and Negotiations; Pres'. Commn. Environ. Quality; bd. dirs. Brown U.; trustee The Ford Found.; mem. World Bank Adv. Com. on Sustainable Devel. Recipient William Rogers Outstanding Grad. award Brown U., 1990, UN Environment Programme Global 500 award, 1990; outstanding woman law student Tex. scholar, 1975. Mem. State Tex. Bar, D.C. Bar (coun. fgn. rels., internat. coun. environ. law, overseas devel. coun.), Zonta Internat. (hon.). Avocations: squash, trekking, scuba diving, gardening, fishing. Office: World Wildlife Fund 1250 24th St NW Washington DC 20037-1124*

FULLER, KENNETH ROLLER, architect; b. Denver, Mar. 7, 1913; s. Robert Kenneth and Nelle Grace (Roller) F.; m. Gertrude Alene Heid, June 16, 1938 (dec. May 1998); children: Robert K. II, Richard H. Student in archtl. engring., U. Colo., 1932-35; student in engring., U. Denver, 1935-36; student in architecture, U. Ill., 1936-37. Registered architect, Colo. Archtl. draftsman Robert K. Fuller, Denver, 1937-40, chief draftsman, 1941-42; architect, engr. U.S. Engrs., Denver and Nebr., 1942-46, architect, 1947-48; ptnr., architect Fuller Fuller & Fuller, Denver, 1949-64; prin. Fuller & Fuller, Denver, 1965-70; pres., owner Fuller Fuller & Assocs., Denver, 1971-81, semi-retired, 1982—; archtl. cons., 1973-76; instr. in architecture U. Colo., Denver, 1947-48. Author: 100 Years of Architecture Roeschlaub-Fuller, 1873-1973, 1973; co-author: Robert S. Roeschlaub—Architect of the Emerging West, 1873-1923, 1987. Recipient Honor award U. Colo. Coll. of Design and Planning, 1983, Award of Merit, Am. Assn. State and Local History, 1989, medal U. Colo. Bd. of Regents, 1995. Mem. AIA (chmn. membership com. Colo. chpt. 1960-63, author history Colo. chpt. 1985-86, Combined Svc. award with Colo. Architects and Denver, North, South and

West chpts. 1980, honored with nat. fellowship 1984, Colo. Architect of Yr. 1989, Pres.'s award 1996), Colo. Soc. Architects-AIA (fellow emeritus 1985, permanent corp. trustee and sec.-treas. ednl. fund 1966—, Disting. Svc. award 1970, Outstanding Svc. Cert. 1974), Colo. Hist. Soc. (hon. curator 1981), Nat. Trust for Hist. Preservation, Grand County Hist. Soc., Lions (bd. dirs. Denver 1964-66, 76-77, 40 Yr. Old Monarch award 1987), Sigma Chi. Republican. Presbyterian. Avocations: hist. archtl. research, hunting, fishing. Mailing Address: 3320 E 2d Ave Denver CO 80206

FULLER, LARRY, choreographer, director; b. Sullivan, Mo., Jan. 22, 1938; s. James Joseph and Alma Lee (Luttrel) F. Student, Marquette U., 1955-56. Dancer numerous Broadway shows including West Side Story, 1957, Music Man, 1958-60, Funny Girl, 1963-64; TV appearances include Ed Sullivan Show, Perry Como Show; choreographer Broadway musicals Evita, Sweeney Todd, On the Twentieth Century, Merrily We Roll Along; dir. off-Broadway prodns. Invitation To the Dance, Oscar Remembered; dir. London West End prodns. Time, Marilyn the Musical; dir., choreographer 1st European prodns. Candide, Girl Crazy, On the Town, On Your Toes (Stuttgart Ballet), Jazz Leggs (Berlin, Friedrichstadtpalast); choreographer Tony Awards show, 1985, 86, Emmy Awards show, 1985, 86; dir. nat. tour Evita, 1992-93, 98; choreographic contbr. films A Little Night Music, The Boarding School. Recipient Los Angeles Drama Critics award, 1980, 2 N.Y. Drama Critics Circle awards, 1979, 80, N.Y. TV Acad. award, 1972. Home and Office: 851 N Kings Rd Apt 106 Los Angeles CA 90069-5930

FULLER, MARGARET JANE, medical technologist; b. Park Rapids, Minn., Jan. 29, 1947; d. Rudolph Kenneth and Jean Ellen (Klenk) Haas; m. Phillip Fuller, Aug. 7, 1970; 1 child, Sharon Dawn. BS in Chemistry, Muhlenberg Coll., 1969; diploma in med. tech., Allentown (Pa.) Hosp., 1972; MPA, Angelo State U., 1988; MS in Microbiology, Tex. Tech. U., 1992. Lab. dir. San Angelo-Tom Green County Health Dept., 1984-89; outpatient lab. supr. Meth. Hosp., Plainview, Tex., 1995-96; lab. mgr. Highland Med. Ctr., Lubbock, Tex., 1996-98; mem. med. adv. bd. Planned Parenthood West Tex., San Angelo, 1987-89; scientist-by-mail, assoc. Children's Mus. Houston, 1991-92; direct patient vol. Hospice of Lubbock, 1993-98. Bd. dirs. El Camino coun. Girl Scouts U.S.A. Recipient Thanks Badge, El Camino coun. Girl Scouts U.S.A., 1986. Mem. Am. Soc. Microbiology, Am. Soc. Clin. Lab. Tech., Am. Soc. Clin. Pathologists (assoc., cert. med. technologist), Tex. Soc. Clin. Lab. Tech. (regional sec. 1985-87), Tex. Pub. Health Assn., Clin. Lab. Mgmt. Assn., Mensa, Beta Beta Beta, Sigma Theta Tau. Episcopalian.

FULLER, MAXINE COMPTON, retired secondary school educator; b. Tiny, Va., Aug. 23, 1921; d. Perry and Lillie (Sutherland) Compton; m. David Thompson Fuller Jr., 1946 (dec. Mar. 1975); children: Davine Miller, Patricia Machen, Shirley Brodeur, Dorothy Brunson, David Thompson III. BS, Longwood Coll., 1943; MA, U. Ala., 1966; AA in Edn., U. Ala., Birmingham, 1980. Receptionist Goodyear Tire and Rubber Co., Richmond, Va., 1943; office mgr. trainee Goodyear Tire and Rubber Co., Selma, Ala., 1943-44; office mgr. Goodyear Service, Bessemer, Ala., 1944-46; sec., ops. mgr. Birmingham So. Coll., 1966; tchr. Manpower-Bessemer State Tech. Coll., 1966-68, McAdory High Sch., 1968-71; bus. edn. coord. Hueytown High Sch., 1971-88, ret., 1988; vis. com. mem. So. Assn. Secondary Schs. and Colls., 1980, 84. Sunday sch. tchr. Pleasant Ridge Bapt. Ch., Hueytown, Ala., 1962-88, pers. com., 1980-83; mem. Hueytown High PTA, 1986-87; liaison officer Adopt-A-Sch. program Hueytown High/Lloyd Noland Hosp., 1987-88; chmn. bus. edn. dept. Hueytown High Sch., 1971-88. Mem. NEA, Am. Vocat. Assn., Nat. Ret. Tchrs. Assn., Ala. Ret. Tchrs. Assn., Longwood Coll. Alumni Assn., former mem., Alpha Delta Kappa (corr. sec. XI chpt. 1982-84), Delta Kappa Gamma (treas. Gamma Lambda chpt. 1976-80), Echo Book Club (Bessemer, pres. 1986-88, sec. 1994-96), Hueytown Culture Club (pres. 1994-96). Baptist.

FULLER, MELVIN STUART, botany educator; b. Livermore Falls, Maine, May 5, 1931; s. George Raymond and Hilda Gordon (Pike) F.; m. Barbara Paul Newman, Apr. 2, 1955; children: Erica Ann, Scott Eliot, Amy Elizabeth. B.S., U. Maine, 1953; M.S., U. Nebr., 1955; Ph.D., U. Calif., 1959; Master's ad eundum, Brown U., 1963. Instr. Brown U., 1959, asst. prof., 1960-63, assoc. prof., 1963-64; asst. prof. U. Calif., 1964-65, assoc. prof., 1965-68; prof. botany U. Ga., 1968—, head dept., 1968-73, 86-89, univ. prof., 1990—; vis. agrl. rsch. biologist Sandoz Ltd., Basel, Switzerland, 1983; vis. rsch. prof. U. Uppsala, Sweden, 1985, 86; adj. prof. botany U. Maine, 1992—; emeritus univ. prof. and emeritus prof. botany U. Ga., 1995—; mem. editorial bd. for publs. in biology McGraw Hill; sec. 2d Internat. Mycol. Congress; organizer Fifth Internat. Fungus Spore Meeting, 1991. Author: The Science of Botany, 1962, Lower Fungi in the Laboratory, 1978, Zoosporic Fungi in Teach. and Research, 1987. Fellow British Mycological Soc.; mem. Bot. Soc. Am., Mycol. Soc. Am. (counselor 1966-68, 70-72, pres. 1975, Disting. Mycologist Award, 1992), Soc. Study of Growth and Devel., Am. Phythopath. Soc., Gulf of Maine Found. (pres. 1997—). Research on growth and devel. aquatic fungi, ultrastructure, mechanism of action of fungicides. Home: PO Box 1449 Damariscotta ME 04543-1449*

FULLER, MILLARD DEAN, charitable organization executive, lawyer; b. Lanett, Ala., Jan. 3, 1935; s. Render and Estin (Cook) F.; m. Linda Caldwell; children: Christopher, Kimberly, Faith, Georgia. BS in Econs., Auburn U., 1957; LLB, U. Ala., 1960; LHD (hon.), Ea. Coll., Pa., 1985, Ottawa U., 1987, Susquehanna U., 1989; D Pub. Svcs. (hon.), DePauw U., 1988; HHD (hon.), Coll. of Wooster, 1989, Wake Forest U., 1990, Mercer U., 1990, Westminster Coll., 1990, Whitworth Coll., 1990, Dallas Bapt. U., 1994, Lynchburg Coll., 1992, North Park Coll., 1992, Tech. U. Nova Scotia, 1992, U. North Ala., 1994, Providence Coll., 1994, Presbyn. Coll., Clinton, S.C., 1995, Bluffton Coll., 1995, Elon Coll., 1995, Nova Southeastern U., 1996. Bar: Ala. 1960, Ga. 1972. Co-founder Fuller and Dees Mktg. Group, Inc., Montgomery, Ala., 1960; pres. Fuller and Dees Mktg. Group, Inc., Montgomery, 1960-65; ptnr. Fuller and Dees (law firm), Montgomery, 1960-65; devel. dir. Tougaloo (Miss.) Coll., 1966-68; dir. Koinonia Ptnrs., Inc. (developer various bus. ops. for Koinonia Christian community), Americus, Ga., 1968-72; dir. devel. Ch. of Christ, Zaire, Equator region Africa, 1973-76; initiator housing project for low-income families, Mbandaka, Zaire Ch. of Christ, Equator region Africa; founder, pres. Habitat for Humanity Internat., Inc., Americus, 1977—. Author: Bokotola, 1977, Love in the Mortar Joints, 1980, No More Shacks!, 1986, The Excitement is Building, 1990, Theology of the Hammer, 1994, A Simple, Decent Place to Live, 1995. Adv. com. Albert Schweitzer Fellowship of Am., 1992. Lt. U.S. Army, 1960. Recipient Kaleidoscope award Creative Ministry Assn., 1985, Outstanding Achievement award Coun. State Housing Agys., 1986, Clarence Jordan Exemplary Chistiran Svc. award So. Bapt. Theol. Sem., 1986, Dr. Marting Luther King, Jr. Humanitarian award, 1987, Disting. chrisitan Svc. in Social Welfare award N.Am. Assn. christians in Social Work, 1988, Internat. Humanity Svc. award Am. Overseas Assn. ARC, 1989, Pub. Svc. Achievement award Common Cause, 1989, M. Justin Herman Meml. award Nat. Assn. Housing and Devel. Ofcls., 1989, The Temple award for Creative Altruism, 1990, Joseph C. Wilson award Rochester Assn. for the UN, 1990, Amicus Certus award Luth. Social Svcs. Ill., Martin Luther Jr. Humanitarian award Ga. State Holiday Commn., 1992, Profl. Achievement award Partnership Affordable Housing, 1993, Harry S. Truman Pub. Svc. award City of Independence, 1994, The McConnell award Truett-McConnell Coll., Ga., 1995, Faithful Servant award Nat. Assn. of Evangelicals, 1996, Spirit of Ga. award, 1996; named Builder of Yr. Profl. Bldr. mag., 1995, Nat. Housing Hall of Fame, 1996, Presdl. Medal of Freedom, 1996, Jefferson award 1999. Mem. Ala. Bar Assn., Ga. Bar Assn., The Am. Works Partnership (bd. dirs.). Democrat. Baptist. Avocations: reading, walking. Office: Habitat for Humanity Internat 121 Habitat St Americus GA 31709-3498*

FULLER, NANCY MACMURRAY, mathematics educator, tutor; b. Great Barrington, Mass., Sept. 19, 1945; d. Robert Wright and Nancy MacMurray (Robinson) F. BA, MacMurray Coll., 1968; postgrad., George Mason U., 1983, U. Va., 1983-95. Cert. tchr., Va. Tchr. Brandon Hall Sch., Dunwoody, Ga., 1969-78, The Scheaffer Sch., Fall Church, Va., 1978-79, Flint Hill Preparatory Sch., Oakton, Va., 1979-87; pvt. tutor Vienna, Va., 1987—; tutor Atlanta area, also Fairfax and Loudon counties, Va., Vienna, Va.; math tutor, Columbus, Ohio, Morrow, Knox and Delaware Counties, Ohio. Asst. dir. cassette ministries and sound depts. Christian Fellowship Ch., Vienna, Va., 1987-91; co-dir. sound, dir. cassette ministry Christian Fellowship Ch. of Leesburg (Va.)/Cornerstone Chapel, 1992-95; mem. Glorybound Singers, 1989-95. Mem. Nat. Coun. Tchrs. Math., No. Va. Learning Disabilities, Coun. for Exceptional Children.

FULLER, NORINE L., lobbyist, educational administrator; b. L.A., Dec. 31, 1952. BA in Sociology, UCLA, 1975. Exec. dir. student fin. svcs. Fashion Inst. Design and Merchandising, Washington, 1977—; sr. cons. Gray and Co., Washington, 1982-84; creator, exec. prodr. EBN Edn. Bus. News, Arlington, Va.; mem. bd. Nat. Adv. Com. on Accreditation and Instnl. Eligibility, Washington, 1986, 88; cons. Office of First Lady, New Orleans, 1984, Dallas, 1988; negotiator negotiated rulemaking com. U.S. Dept. Edn., Washington, 1993. Prodr., writer videos Credit for my Vette, 1985 (1st place pub. rels. award Assn. Ind. Prodrs., 1986, College Costs with Rep. Buck McKeon (R-CA) and Sen. Jim Jeffords (D-VT), 1997; dir., writer counseling video and handbook Default Detours, 1987. Chmn. Rep. Women's Fed. Forum, Washington, 1992. Fax: 202-944-4170. E-mail: nfuller@fidm.com.

FULLER, ORA, nursing administrator, health care executive; b. Brenham, Tex., Nov. 5, 1944; d. Ella Mae Davis; m. Lonnie E. Fuller, Feb. 18, 1989. ADN, Coll. of the Mainland, 1974; BSN, U. Tex., Galveston, 1980, MS in Nursing, 1983. Lic. voc. nurse U. Tex. Med. Branch, Galveston, 1964-68; clinical supvr., charge nurse Meml. Hosp. Galveston County, Texas City, 1968-82; emergency room charge nurse Danforth Meml. Hosp., Texas City, 1982-83; instr. Coll. of the Mainland, Texas City, 1976-83; asst. dir. nursing U. Tex. Med. Branch Hosps., Galveston, 1983-85, dir. nursing, 1986-88; head nurse Emory U. Hosp., Atlanta, 1988-91; dir. case mgmt. South Fulton Med. Ctr., East Point, Ga., 1991—. Adv. com. Grad. Sch. Nursing Mgmt. Tract, 1985-88; bd. dirs. LaMarque Tigers Youth Football Assn., 1980; mem. Galveston Hist. Soc., 1986-88; coord. voter regirstration drives, 1980-92. Nursing scholar Ladies Aux. Mainland Ctr. Hosp., 1973, Pub. Svc. award NAACP, 1982. Mem. ANA, Am. Orgn. Nurse Execs., Ga. Orgn. Nurse Execs., Women Health Care Execs., Nat. Assn. Healthcare Quality, Ga. Assn. Healthcare Quality, Ga. Assn. Healthcare Execs. Home: 190 Morning Springs Walk Fairburn GA 30213-3460 Office: 1170 Cleveland Ave East Point GA 30344-3600

FULLER, PERRY LUCIAN, lawyer; b. Central City, Nebr., Oct. 26, 1922; s. Perry L. and Ruth (Howorth) F.; m. Alice Moorman, Mar. 6, 1948; 1 child, Leslie Ann Fuller. Student, U. Chgo. Law Sch., 1946-47; AB, U. Nebr., 1947, JD, 1949. Bar: Ill. 1950, U.S. Supreme Ct. Mem. staff Chgo. Crime Commn., 1949; sr. ptnr. Hinshaw & Culbertson and predeccessors, Chgo., 1956—; lectr. in law U. Chgo., 1970-76, mem. vis. com., 1991-93. Vice chmn. exec. com. Law in Am. Soc. Found., 1966, chmn., 1967-69, pres., 1969-95; chmn. Cook County CSC, 1967-69; mem. Ill. Law Enforcement Commn., 1971-72; bd. dirs. Winnetka (Ill.) Cmty. Chest, 1966-69; bd. dirs. Ill. Humane Soc., 1978—, pres., 1986; v.p. Fed. Defender, Inc., 1964; trustee Village of Winnetka, 1991-95. 1st lt USMC, 1942-46, capt., 1952-53. Decorated Air medal. Fellow Am. Coll. Trial Lawyers (state chmn. 1972-74), Am. Bar Found., Ill. Bar Found.; mem. ABA (chmn. pub. relations com. 1968-69, gavel awards com. 1974-77, chmn. 1976-78), Ill, Fed., 7th Cir. Chgo. (bd. mgrs. 1967-69) bar assns., Am. Law Inst., Am. Judicature Soc., Internat. Assn. Def. Counsel (chmn. Continuing Legal Edn. bd. 1982-86, exec. com. 1983-86), Soc. Trial Lawyers Ill. (bd. dirs. 1967-68, 73-74, sec. 1975-76, pres. 1977-78), Def. Rsch. Inst. (chmn. insts. com. 1986-90), Scribes, Legal Club, Law Club (pres. 1987-88). Republican. Home: 1093 Fisher Ln Winnetka IL 60093-1503 Office: Hinshaw & Culbertson 222 N La Salle St Ste 300 Chicago IL 60601-1081

FULLER, RENEE NUNI, psychologist, educational publisher; b. Mannheim, Federal Republic of Germany, Apr. 14, 1929; came to U.S., 1938; d. Eric Woldemar and Fridel Gronau (Henning) Stoetzner; widowed. Student, Swarthmore (Pa.) Coll., 1947-49; BA, Hunter Coll., 1951; MA, Columbia U., 1953; PhD, NYU, 1963. Research scientist Letchworth Village N.Y. State Dept. Mental Hygiene, Thiells, 1961-67; project dir. Staten Island (N.Y.) Soc. Mental Health, 1967-68; chief psychol. services Rosewood Hosp. Ctr., Owings Mills, Md., 1968-75; pres. Ball-Stick-Bird Publs. Inc., Colebrook, Conn., 1975—. Author: In Search of the IQ Correlatin, 1977, (reading series) Ball-Stick-Bird; contbr. articles to profl. jours. Recipient Disting. Achievement award Fairleigh-Dickinson U., N.J., 1979. Fellow Am. Psychol. Soc.; mem. APA, Soc. for Rsch. in Child Devel. Office: Ball-Stick-Bird Publs Inc PO Box 13 Colebrook CT 06021-0013

FULLER, ROBERT FERREY, lawyer, investor; b. St. Paul, Aug. 11, 1929; s. Robert Garfield and Gwendolen (Ferrey) F.; m. Marcelle McIntosh, June 6, 1953 (div. 1984); children: Julie, Gordon McIntosh; m. Sheila Nolan Mensing, May 25, 1985; stepchildren: Andrew Mensing, Allison Mensing. AB magna cum laude, Harvard, 1950, JD, 1953. Bar: N.Y. 1956, Conn. 1988, U.S. Dist. Ct. (so. and ea. dists.) N.Y. 1960, U.S. Ct. Appeals (D.C. cir.) 1988, U.S. Ct. Internat. Trade 1988. Assoc. Patterson, Belknap & Webb, N.Y.C., 1955-66; sec., gen. counsel Reuben H. Donnelley Corp., N.Y.C., 1966-68; mng. dir. R.H. Donnelley Internat. Ltd., London, Eng., 1970-73; asst. sec., internat. counsel Am. Can Co., Greenwich, Conn., 1973-86; asst. sec., asst. gen. counsel Am. Can Co. (name changed to Am. Can Packaging Inc. 1986), Greenwich, Conn., 1986-87; ptnr. Bentley, Mosher & Babson, Stamford and Greenwich, Conn., 1987-89, of counsel, 1990-92; underwriting mem. Lloyd's, 1977-97. Active Rep. Town Meeting, Greenwich, 1986-96. Served to lt. (j.g.) USCGR, 1953-55; lt. comdr. Res. ret. Mem. Greenwich Bar Assn., Camp Fire Club Am., Harvard Club N.Y.C., Greenwich Country Club, Loxahatchee Club. Republican. Presbyterian. Avocations: golf, shotgun sports, reading.

FULLER, ROBERT L(EANDER), lawyer; b. N.Y.C., Sept. 8, 1943; s. Robert L. and Elsie V. Fuller; m. Barbara Braverman, Dec. 5, 1973. BS cum laude, SUNY, Stony Brook, 1971; MBA, Columbia U., 1972; JD, Cath. U., Washington, 1977; M. Laws in Taxation, Georgetown U., 1981. Bar: Md. 1977, D.C. 1978; CPA: N.Y. 1974, D.C. 1975; Acct. Ernst & Ernst, N.Y.C., 1972-74; controller Warner-Jenkinson East Inc., N.Y.C., 1974-75, Atomic Indsl. Forum, Inc., N.Y.C., Washington, 1975-76; tax analyst So. Rwy. Co., Washington, 1976-78; asst. tax counsel CACI, Inc., Arlington, Va., 1978-84; tax counsel, mgr. VSE Corp., Alexandria, Va., 1984-87; exec. dir. taxes Ciba Corning Diagnostics Corp., Medfield, Mass., 1988-96; sr. mgr. KPMG Peat Marwick, LLP, Boston, 1997-98; dir. taxes Instron Corp., Canton, Mass., 1998—. With USN, 1961-67. Mem. ABA (tax sect.), AICPA, Mayflower Descendants, SAR, Sigma Pi Sigma. Home: 151 Grove St Wellesley MA 02482-7001 Office: 100 Royall St Canton MA 02021-1009

FULLER, RUTHANN, principal. Prin. Cuntan Mid. Sch. Citation DOE Elem. Sch. Recognition Program, 1989-90. Office: Clinton Middle Sch 75 Chenango Ave Clinton NY 13323-1340*

FULLER, SAMUEL ASHBY, lawyer, mining company executive; b. Indpls., Sept. 2, 1924; s. John L.H. and Mary (Ashby) F.; m. Betty Winn Hamilton, June 10, 1948; children—Mary Cheryl Fuller Hargrove, Karen E. Fuller Wolfe, Deborah R. BS in Gen. Engring, U. Cin., 1946, JD, 1947; cert. fin. planner, Coll. for Fin. Planning, 1989. Bar: Ohio 1948, Ind. 1951, Fla. 1984; cert. fin. planner, 1989. Cleve. claims rep. Mfrs. and Mchts. Indemnity Co., 1947-48; claims supr. Indemnity Ins. Co. N.Am., 1948-50; with firm Stewart, Irwin, Gilliom, Fuller & Meyer (formerly Murray, Mannon, Fairchild & Stewart), Indpls., 1950-85; with firm Lewis Kappes Fuller & Eads (name changed to Lewis & Kappes), Indpls., 1985-89, of counsel, 1990—; pres., dir. Irsugo Consol. Mines, Ltd., 1953-80; dir. Ind. Pub. Health Found., Inc., 1972-84; staff instr. Purdue U. Life Ins. and Mktg. Inst., 1954-61; instr. Am. Coll. Life Underwriters, Indpls., 1964-74; mem. Ind. State Bd. Law Examiners, 1984-96, treas. 1987-88. Bd. dirs. Southwest Social Centre, Inc., 1965-70; pres., dir. Westminster Village North, Inc., 1981-89. Fellow Indpls. Bar Found.; mem. Ind. State Bar Assn. (bd. mgrs. 1986-88), 7th Cir. Bar Assn., Fla. Bar, Sun City Ctr. Golf and Racquet Club, Lincoln Hills Golf Club, Caloosa Golf and Country Club, Masons, Beta Theta Pi. Republican. Roman Catholic. Home: 306 Thornhill Pl Sun City Center FL 33573-5842 Office: Lewis & Kappes 1700 One American Sq PO Box 82053 Indianapolis IN 46282-0003

FULLER, SAMUEL HENRY, III, computer engineer; b. Detroit, June 1, 1946; s. Samuel H. Jr. and Catherine A. (Park) F.; m. Carol Diane Woodbury; children: Amy, Deborah, Matthew. BS in Elec. Engring., U. Mich., 1968; MS, Stanford U., 1969, PhD, 1972. Assoc. prof. computer sci. and elec. engring. Carnegie-Mellon U., Pitts., 1972-78; mgr. systems architecture Digital Equipment Corp., Maynard, Mass., 1978-83, v.p. rsch., 1983-96, v.p., chief scientist, 1996-98; v.p. R&D, Analog Devices, Inc., Norwood, Mass., 1998—; bd. dirs. Nat. Rsch. Initiatives, Reston, VA., Inso Corp.; mem. computer sci. and tech. com. NAS, Washington, 1986-90, employment and tech. panel, 1985-87. Contbr. over 30 tech. papers and articles. Fellow IEEE, AAAS, Assn. Computing Machinery, Am. Acad. Soc.; mem. Nat. Acad. Engring. Office: Analog Devices One Technology Way Norwood MA 02062-9106*

FULLER, STEPHEN HERBERT, business administration educator; b. Columbus, Ohio, Feb. 4, 1920; s. Josiah Allen and Mary Ellen (Quinn) F.; m. Frances Mulhearn, Jun 23, 1951; children: Teofilo M., Rogelio M., Mark B., Joseph B. BA, Ohio U., 1941, PhD, 1977; grad. Indusl. Adminstr., Harvard U., 1941-43, MBA, 1947, D in Bus. Adminstrn., 1958; PhD, Ateneo de Manila, Philippines, 1964, De LaSalle Coll., Manila, 1971, Lawrence Inst. Tech., 1978. From instr. to assoc. prof. in bus. adminstrn. Harvard U., Boston, 1947-61, prof. in bus. adminstrn., 1961-71, assoc. dean. for external affairs, 1964-69; Chua Tiampo prof. in bus. adminstrn. Harvard U., Cambridge, Mass., 1982-85; pres. Asian Inst. Mgmt., Manila, 1969-71; v.p. personnel adminstrn. and devel. staff Gen. Motors Corp., Detroit, 1971-82; chmn., CEO, World Book Inc., Chgo., 1985-92; instr. econs. and labor rels. Ohio U., Athens, 1977, prof. bus. adminstrn., 1992-97. Author: (with others) Problems in Labor Relations, 1950, 3d edit. 1964. Served to capt. AUS, 1943-46. Recipient Presl. Medal Merit, Republic Philippines, 1971. Mem. Internat. Acad. Mgmt., Nat. Mgmt. Assn., Philippine Am. Soc., Phi Beta Kappa, Phi Eta Sigma, Omicron Delta Kappa, Beta Gamma Sigma, Delta Tau Delta, Sigma Iota Epsilon. Republican. Roman Catholic. Clubs: Bald Peak Colony (Melvin, N.H.); Chicago; Harvard (N.Y.C.). Avocations: theatre, travel, reading.

FULLER, THEODORE, retired insurance executive; b. Yonkers, N.Y., Dec. 7, 1918; s. Clarence Wendel and Mary Edgar (Denniston) F. AB cum laude, Princeton U., 1941; LLB, Columbia U., 1948. Bar: N.Y. 1948. With Savs. Bank Life Ins. Fund, N.Y.C., 1948-83, exec. v.p., 1964-65, pres., 1965-83; former mem. N.Y. State Adv. Bd. Life Ins.; cons. Nat. Exec. Svc. Corps, Svc. Corps Retired Execs. Tax counselor Am. Assn. Ret. Persons. Comdr. USNR, World War II, Korea. Mem. Assn. of Bar of City of N.Y., Princeton Club, Univ. Glee Club, Indian Harbor Yacht Club, Retired Men's Assn. (former pres.), Ea. Packard Club, Antique Automobile Club Am., Classic Car Club Am. (former bd. dirs.), Rolls Royce Owners Club, Pierce Arrow Club, Sound Investments Club. Home: 3 Mercia Ln Greenwich CT 06830-7068

FULLER, WAYNE ARTHUR, statistics educator; b. Corning, Iowa, June 15, 1931; s. Loren Boyd and Eva Gladys (Darrah) F.; m. Evelyn Rose Steinford, Dec. 22, 1956; children: Douglas W., Bret E. BS, Iowa State U., 1955, MS, 1957, PhD, 1959. Asst. prof. Iowa State U., Ames, 1959-62, assoc. prof., 1962-66, prof., 1966-83, disting. prof. stats., 1983—; cons. Doane Mktg. Research Inc., St. Louis. Author: Introduction to Statistical Time Series, 1976, 2nd ed. 1996, Measurement Error Models, 1987; also articles. Served as cpl. U.S. Army, 1952-54. Fellow Am. Statis. Assn. (v.p. 1991-93), Inst. Math Stats., Econometric Soc.; mem. Internat. Statis. Inst. Biometric Soc., Royal Statis. Soc., Am. Agr. Econ. Assn. Home: 3013 Briggs Cir Ames IA 50010-4705 Office: Iowa State U Statis Lab 221 Snedecor Hall Ames IA 50010

FULLER, WILLIAM P., president Asia Foundation. BA, Stanford U., 1960, MA in Polit. Sci., 1964, PhD in Devel. Econs. and Edn., 1970; MBA, Harvard U., 1962. Program officer UNICEF, Cairo, Egypt, 1962-64; planning officer and asst. to dep. dir. UNICEF, N.Y.C., 1964-66; regional planning officer UNICEF, Beirut, Lebanon, 1966-67; cons. economist for Nigeria, Ghana, Morocco World Bank/UNESCO Program, Paris, 1970-71; planning and rsch. advisor funded by Ford Found. Nat. Edn. Commn., Bangkok, Thailand, 1971-76; vis. lectr. U. Chgo., 1976; rep. Ford Found., Dhaka, Bangladesh, 1977-81; mission dir. Sr. Fgn. Svc. USAID, Indonesia, 1981-87; dep. asst. adminstr. bur. for Asia and Near East Sr. Fgn. Svc. USAID, Washington, 1987-89; pres. The Asia Found., San Francisco, 1989—; bd. dirs. Overseas Devel. Coun., Washington, Inst. for the Future, Stanford, Calif.; vice chmn. World Affairs Coun. No. Calif., San Francisco. Recipient Pres.'s Meritorious Svc. award, 1985, '87. Fellow Asia Pacific Ctr., Stanford U.; mem. Nat. Com. U.S.-China Rels. Office: The Asia Found 465 California St Fl 14 San Francisco CA 94104-1804*

FULLER, WILLIAM SIDNEY, lawyer; b. Auburn, Ala., Aug. 9, 1931; s. William Melton and Ernestine (Tolbert) F.; m. Joyce Jeffrey, Nov. 5, 1953; children: Jeffrey Melton, Barbara Rush. AB, Auburn U., 1953; LLB, U. Ala., 1956, JD, 1969. Bar: Ala. 1956. Student asst. to dean U. Ala. Law Sch., 1952-53; law clk. to U.S. dist. judge, Montgomery, Ala., 1956-57; practice law Andalusia, 1957—; former city atty. City of Andalusia; dir., sec. Covington County Bank; lectr. Southeastern Trial Inst.; mem. grievance com. Ala. State Bar, 1968-71, mem. bd. commrs., 1979-81; mem. law and contemporary affairs adv. council Auburn U. Author: Personal Injury Treatises. Mem. ABA, Ala., Covington County bar assns., Am. Trial Lawyers Assn., Am. Bd. Trial Advocates, Ala. Plaintiff Lawyers Assn., Ala. Trial Lawyers Assn. (pres. 1968), Phi Delta Phi, Kappa Alpha, Alpha Phi Omega. Presbyterian (elder, trustee, past chmn. bd. deacons Sunday sch. tchr.). Club: Andalusia (dir., pres. 1972), Topsl Beach and Racket (Destin, Fla.). Home: 100 S Ridge Rd Andalusia AL 36420-4214 Office: 28 S Court Sq Andalusia AL 36420-3918

FULLER-MCCHESNEY, MARY ELLEN, sculptor, writer, publisher; b. Wichita, Kans., Oct. 20, 1922; d. Edward Emory and Karen Mabel (Rasmussen) Fuller; m. Robert Pearson, Dec. 17, 1949. AA, U. Calif., Berkeley, 1943. Staff writer Currant; rschr. Archives of Am. Art; publisher Sonoma Mt. Publishing Co. Author: (art book) A Period of Exploration, 1973, Robert McChesney: An American Painter, 1996, also 3 mystery novels, short stories, poems, and articles on art; exhbns. include: (sculpture) Syracuse (N.Y.) Mus., San Francisco Mus., Oakland (Calif.) Mus., Calif. State U. Sonoma, Santa Rosa Civic Ctr., U. Calif. Davis, San Jose (Calif.) State U., U. Calif. Ctr. U. Oaxaca; San Francisco art festivals and many galleries; prin. works include Dos Leones, San Francisco Gen. Hosp., 1974, Children's Scupture Park, Salinas Cmty. Ctr., 1976, Temko Lions, Fresno Ave. Berkeley, Calif., 1976, Falcon, Andrew Hill H.S., San Jose, Calif., 1977, Yuba Totem, Yuba Lion, Dept. Motor Vehicles Bldg., Calif., 1978, Playground, Portsmouth Square, San Francisco, 1982, Olympic Lions, Squaw Valley, Calif., 1983, Stratford Meml. Lion and Bear, Petaluma (Calif.) Libr., 1983, Anshen-Mays Birdbath, Sausalito, Calif., 1984, West Side Pump Sta., San Francisco, 1979; 4 garden sculptures L.A. State Office Bldg., 1987, Walnut Creek Totem, 1992, Seach Park, Santa Cruz, 1993, Utah Arts coun. Bear v Rams, Salt Lake City, 1999. Ford Found. fellow, 1965-66; Nat. Endowment Arts grantee, 1975. Home and Studio: 2955 Sonoma Mt Rd Petaluma CA 94954

FULLERTON, ALBERT LOUIS, JR., bookstore owner; b. Boston, Aug. 25, 1921; s. Albert Louis and Marjorie Hubbard (Durling) F.; m. Mary Siteman, Dec. 27, 1944; children: Albert III, George, Gilbert, Lincoln. AB, Harvard U., 1947; MS, U. Colo., 1951. Sect. head Lincoln Lab. MIT, Lexington, Mass., 1952-54; project leader Melpar Inc., Boston, 1954-59; sect. head GTE Sylvania, Needham, Mass., 1959-61; tech. staff mem. Inst. Naval Studies, Cambridge, Mass., 1961-66; dept. head Sanders Assocs., Nashua, N.H., 1966-78; tech. staff mem. Mitre Corp., Bedford, Mass., 1978-87; proprietor Bernardston (Mass.) Books, 1986—. Annotated and published: (by Dr. John Cook) Voyages and Travels in the Russian Empire in 1770, 3d edit., 1997; publisher: Descendants of John Cook (1679-1780), 1998. With AUS, 1942-46, PTO, ETO. Mem. Mass. and R.I. Antiquarian Booksellers, Harvard Club of Boston. Democrat. Home and Office: 219 South St Bernardston MA 01337-9452

FULLERTON, CHARLES WILLIAM, retired insurance company executive; b. Columbus, Ohio, May 18, 1917; s. Paul O. and Marvina (Groom) F.; m. Anne Hoddy, Jan. 21, 1940; children—Gary, Lynn Fullerton Johnson. B.S., Ohio State U., 1938. C.P.A., Ohio. Dist. financial dir. FSA, Columbus, 1938-40; office mgr. Goodyear Tire & Rubber Co., Huntington, W.Va., 1940-41; chief accountant to v.p. finance Landmark Farm Bur., Columbus, 1941-66; v.p., sec., treas. Nationwide Devel. Co., Columbus,

1966-71; with Nationwide Ins. Affiliates, Columbus, 1971-82; exec. v.p. Nationwide Ins. Affiliates, 1972-73, pres., 1973-82; v.p. Nationwide Ins. Co., 1973-82; dir. Nationwide Devel. Co., Nationwide Communications, Inc., Nationwide Consumer Services, Inc., Heritage Securities, Inc.; bd. govs. Investment Co. Inst., Washington. Mem. steering com. Devel. Com. for Greater Columbus, 1977-79; bd. dirs. Greater Columbus Arts Council, Ohio Dominican Coll., Players Theatre of Columbus; active Downtown Action Com., Capitol Sq. Com. Mem. Am. Inst. C.P.A.'s, Ohio Soc. C.P.A.'s, Treas. Club of Columbus (past pres.), Nat. Soc. Accountants for Coops. (past pres.), Ohio Council Farmer Coops. (v.p.), Columbus Controllers Club. Methodist. Club: Masons. Home: 6861 Hardwood Dr Galloway OH 43119-9077 Office: One Nationwide Plaza Columbus OH 43216 *To achieve the goals and objectives established for a business enterprise, I strive to set tasks and priorities in concert with the persons responsible for the results. This process is carried on in a manner that assists those persons to grow as individuals while the organization becomes stronger through the successful performance of those goals and objectives.*

FULLERTON, DOUGLAS B., sports association adminstrator; b. Hamilton, Mont., Sept. 14, 1946; s. Theodore Hamilton Fullerton and Elizabeth Ann Barlow; m. Cari Gail Cowdrey, Aug. 23, 1986; 1 child, Amanda Gail. BA in Math., Calif. Western U., 1968; MA in Edn., Mont. State U., 1985. Coach, educator Bozeman (Mont.) H.S., 1972-83; flight comdr. Mont. Nat. Guard, Helena, 1983-90; dir. men's athletics Mont. State U., Bozeman, 1985-93, dir. athletics, 1993-94; commr. Big Sky Conf., Ogden, Utah, 1995—. Major U.S. Army, 1969-90. Named Outstanding Grad. in Athletics, Calif. Western U. Athletics Alumnus, San Deigo, 1991; inductee Athletics Hall of Fame, Mont. State U., Bozeman, 1989. Mem. NCAA Football (bd. dirs. 1998—), Nat. Assn. Collegiate Dirs. Athletics, Collegiate Commrs. Assn. (v.p. 1996-99). Republican. Episcopalian. E-mail: FullertonD@earthlink.net. Home: 1789 Shadow Valley Dr Ogden UT 84403 Office: Big Sky Conf Ste 201 2491 Washington Blvd Ogden UT 84401

FULLERTON, ERNEST LEROY, special agent, investigator, educator; b. Erie, Pa., Aug. 17, 1943; s. Ernest Leroy Fullerton Sr. and Marie Patricia (Farina) Fox; m. Christine Trombetta, Dec. 21, 1970; 1 child, Laura Ann Marie. BS in Fin. & Econs., Gannon U., 1968; MS in Adminstrn. Justice, U. Pitts., 1980, PhD Edn. Comm. & Tech., 1983. Cert. law enforcement trainer, Pa. Spl. agent drugs Drug Law Enforcement, Pitts., 1972-74; chief investigator Bur. Cigarette & Revenue, Pitts., 1974; supr. Bur. Cigarette & Revenue, Harrisburg, Pa., 1975; spl. agent Office Criminal Law, Pitts., 1975-96; mgr. Bur. Motor Fuel Taxes Pa. Dept. Revenue, Pitts., 1996—; Dir. tng. Triton Comms. Inc., Pitts., 1986—; coord., instr. Indiana Pa. U. Criminal Justice Tng. Ctr., 1977—; adj. prof. U. Pitts., 1990—. Chmn. Rep. Com. Mt. Lebanon, Pa., 1996—. With USN, 1967-70. Mem. Am. Soc. Law Enforcement Trainers (state dir. 1990—), Pitts. Athletic Assn. Roman Catholic. Avocations: travel, reading. Office: Pa Dept Revenue 875 Greentree Rd Pittsburgh PA 15220-3508

FULLERTON, GAIL JACKSON, university president emeritus; m. Stanley James Fullerton, Mar. 27, 1967; children by previous marriage—Gregory Snell Putney, Cynde Putney Mitchell. B.A., U. Nebr., 1949, M.A., 1950; Ph.D., U. Oreg., 1954. Lectr. sociology Drake U., Des Moines, 1955-57; asst. prof. sociology Fla. State U., Tallahassee, 1957-60; asst. prof. sociology San Jose (Calif.) State U., 1963-67, assoc. prof., 1968-71, prof., 1972-91, dean grad. studies and research, 1972-76, exec. v.p. univ., 1976-78, pres., 1978-91; ret., 1991; bd. dirs. Assoc. Western Univs., Inc., 1980-91; mem. sr. accrediting commn. Western Assn. Schs. and Colls., 1982-88, chmn., 1985-86; mem. Pres.'s Commn. Nat. Collegiate Athletic Assn., 1986-91; bd. dirs. Am. Coll. Assn., 1991. Author: Survival in Marriage, 2d edit, 1977, (with Snell Putney) Normal Neurosis: The Adjusted American, 2d edit, 1966. Carnegie fellow, 1950-51, 52-53; Doherty Found. fellow, 1951-52. Mem. Phi Beta Kappa, Phi Kappa Phi, Chi Omega. *Our lives are the summations of the choices we make, one at a time, by intention or by default. I have tried to choose by deliberate and rational intent, so that even when the choice proves wrong, it is clear to me that I am responsible for myself.*

FULLERTON, JYMIE LUIE, pharmaceutical company executive, consultant; b. Ft. Worth, Oct. 25, 1943; s. Vernon Luie and Ruth (Boyer) F.; m. Martha Jane Smothers; children: Laurie, Patrick, Tammie, Janie, Emily. BBA, Cen. State U., 1971, MBA, 1973. Tchr.-coordinator distributive edn. Stigler (Okla.) High Sch., 1971-72; regional sales rep. Johnson Wax, Racine, Wis., 1973-75; div. sales mgr. Fox-Vliet Retail Computer Service, Oklahoma City, 1975-77; corp. dir. computer services Fox-Vliet Drug Co., Oklahoma City, 1977-78; corp. sales mgr. Foxvliet Drug Co., Oklahoma City, 1978-79; v.p. merchandising Foxmeyer Drug Co., Oklahoma City, 1979-81, v.p. retail ops., 1981-83; v.p. healthmart Foxmeyer Drug Co., Dallas, 1983-84; div. pres. Okla. div. Foxmeyer Drug Co., Oklahoma City, 1985-86, sr. v.p. so. region, 1986-90, sr. v.p. of mktg. and bus. devel., 1990-93; pres. Foxmeyer Internat. Trading Co., 1990-93, A.T.I. Internat. Trading Corp., 1993—; pres., chief exec. Fullerton Properties LLC, Edmond, Okla., 1993—. Served with U.S. Army, 1966-69. Mem. Am. Mgmt. Assn., Nat. Drug Wholesalers Assn. Republican.

FULLERTON, R. DONALD, banker; b. June 7, 1931; married. BA, U. Toronto, 1953. With Can. Bank of Commerce, Vancouver, 1953—; exec. v.p., chief gen. mgr. Can. Bank of Commerce, 1973, elected dir. of bank, 1974, pres., COO, 1976, chmn., CEO, 1984, ret. chmn., CEO, 1992, chmn. exec. com., 1992—; bd. dirs. Westcoast Energy, Inc., George Weston Ltd., Hollinger, Inc., Honeywell, Inc., Asia Satellite Telecomms. Holding, Ltd., Orange plc. Avocations: skiing, golfing. Office: CIBC, Commerce Ct W, Toronto, ON Canada M5L 1A2

FULLINGIM, JOHN POWERS, consulting firm executive; b. Amarillo, Tex., Dec. 10, 1951; s. Jim F. and Wanda (Powers) F.; m. Kristin Kepner, Apr. 27, 1979. BA, Baylor U., 1975; MBA, U. Tex., Dallas, 1979. Broadcaster Sta. KVIL Radio, Dallas, 1976-79; regional sales mgr. Control Data Corp., Dallas, 1979-83; dir. mktg. TOCOM Divsn. Gen. Instrument, Dallas, 1983-87; pres. Addison Mktg. Group, Dallas, 1987—. Author: Professional Services Marketing, 1988, Strategic Value Selling Using Financial Modeling, 1989, Whole Brain Marketing, 1994; contbr. articles to profl. jours.; patentee in field. Bd. dirs., officer 500 Inc., Dallas, 1984-87; v.p. mktg. dir. Allegro Dallas, 1987-90; advisor So. Meth. U. Bus., Dallas, 1988—; bd. dirs. Theatre Three, Dallas, 1991—; grad. Leadership Dallas, 1988; bd. advisors U. North Tex. Coll. of Music, 1997—. Mem. Am. Radio Relay League (asst. sect. mgr. 1997-99), Am. Mktg. Assn. (exec.), Junto II Dallas (founder, sec. 1988-96), Univ. Club of Dallas (chmn. mem. com. 1994-96). Avocations: flying, music, photography, skiing, amateur radio. Office: Addison Mktg Group 15851 Dallas Pky Ste 725 Dallas TX 75248-3360

FULLINGTON, CYNTHIA JANETTE, pediatric nurse; b. Little Falls, N.Y., Nov. 19, 1960; d. Lloyd Douglas and Janette Elizabeth (Trumble) VanAlstine; m. Bruce Fullington, Sept. 8, 1984; children: Scott H., Beth Lindsey. Lic. practical nurse, Otsego Area Occupational Ctr., Milford, N.Y., 1979; AS in Nursing with honors, Fulton-Montgomery Community Coll., Johnstown, N.Y., 1989. RN, N.Y.; cert. BLS, ACLS, PALS; cert. pediatric nurse. Practice nurse surg. med. unit and ICU Mary Imogene Bassett Hosp., Cooperstown, N.Y., 1979-84, practical nurse emergency rm., 1984-89, RN emergency room, 1989-91, pediatric clinic RN-triage nurse, 1991—, part-time allergy nurse, 1996-98. Tchr. Sunday Sch. Mem. Capital Dist. Safe Kids. Home: 1834 Clinton Rd Fort Plain NY 13339-4607 Office: Mary Imogene Bassett Hosp 1 Atwell Rd Cooperstown NY 13326-1394

FULLMER, DANIEL WARREN, psychologist, educator, retired; b. Spoon River, Ill., Dec. 12, 1922; s. Daniel Floyd and Sarah Louisa (Essex) F.; m. Janet Satomi Saito, June 1980; children: Daniel William, Mark Warren. B.S., Western Ill. U., 1947, M.S., 1952; Ph.D., U. Denver, 1955. Post-doctoral intern psychiat. div. U. Oreg. Med. Sch., 1958-61; mem. faculty U. Oreg., 1955-66; prof. psychology Oreg. System of Higher Edn., 1958-66; faculty Coll. Edn. U. Hawaii, Honolulu, 1966-95, retired, 1995, prof. emeritus, 1974—; pvt. practice psychol. counseling; cons. psychologist Grambling State U., 1960-81; founder Free-Family Counseling Ctrs., Portland, Oreg., 1959-66, Honolulu, 1966-74; co-founder Child and Family Counseling Ctr., Waianae, Oahu, Hawaii, Kilohana United Meth. Ch., Oahu, 1992, v.p., sec., 1992; pres. Human Resources Devel. Ctr., Inc., 1974—; chmn. Hawaii State Bd. to License Psychologists, 1973-78. Author: Counseling: Group Theory & System, 2d. edit., 1978, The Family Therapy Dictionary Text, 1991, MANABU, Diagnosis and Treatment of a Japanese Boy with a Visual Anomaly, 1991; co-author: Principles of Guidance, 2d. edit., 1977; author (counselor/cons. training manuals) Counseling: Content and Process, 1964, Family Consultation Therapy, 1968, The School Counselor-Consultant, 1972, Family Therapy as the Rites of Passage, 1998; editor: Bulletin, Oreg. Coop Testing Service, 1955-57, Hawaii P&G Jour., 1970-76; assoc. editor: Educational Perspectives, U. Hawaii Coll. Edn. Served with USNR, 1944-46. Recipient Francis E. Clark award Hawaii Pers. Guidance Assn., 1972, Thomas Jefferson award for Outstanding Pub. Svc., 1993; named Hall of Fame Grambling State U., 1987. Mem. Am. Psychol. Assn., Am. Counseling Assn. (Nancy C. Wimmer award 1963), Masons. Methodist. Office: 1750 Kalakaua Ave Apt 809 Honolulu HI 96826-3725 *I grew up along Spoon River. The people of Spoon River had a principle of life: Improve on what you are. The purpose is to be able to help others help themselves. From here, it is like stepping into a river of life; the deeper you got, the stronger the current. Then, suddenly, here you are nearing the delta. Just ahead lies a beautiful ocean.*

FULLMER, HAROLD MILTON, dentist, educator; b. Gary, Ind., July 9, 1918; s. Howard and Rachel Eva (Tiedge) F.; m. Marjorie Lucile Engel, Dec. 31, 1942 (dec. Apr. 1983); children: Angela Sue, Pamela Rose; m. Shirley Ford Davis, Mar. 28, 1987. B.S., Ind. U., 1942, D.D.S., 1944; hon. doctorate, U. Athens (Greece), 1981. Diplomate: Am. Bd. Oral Pathology. Intern Charity Hosp., New Orleans, 1946-47, resident, 1947-48, vis. dental surgeon, 1948-53; instr. Loyola U., New Orleans, 1948-49, asst. prof., 1949-50, assoc. prof. gen. and oral pathology, 1949-53; cons. pathology VA hosps., Biloxi and Gulfport, Miss., 1950-53; asst. dental surgeon Nat. Inst. Dental Research, NIH, Bethesda, Md., 1953-54; dental surgeon Nat. Inst. Dental Research, NIH, 1954-56, sr. dental surgeon, 1956-60, dental dir., 1960-70; chief sect. histochemistry Nat. Inst. Dental Research, 1967-70, chief exptl. pathology, 1969-70, cons. to dir., 1971-72; mem. dental caries program adv. com. HEW, 1975-79, chmn., 1976-79; dir. Inst. Dental Research; prof. pathology, prof. dentistry, assoc. dean Sch. Dentistry, U. Ala. Med. Center, Birmingham, 1970-87; prof. emeritus, 1987—; sr. scientist cancer research and tng. program, sci. adv. com. Sch. Dentistry, U. Ala. Med. Center (Diabetes Research and Tng. Center), 1977-87; mem. med. rsch. career devel. com. VA, 1977-81; mem. com. grants and allocations Am. Fund for Dental Health, 1977-83. Editor: (with R.D. Lillie) Histopathologic Technic and Practical Histochemistry, 1976; editor in chief, founder Jour. Oral Pathology, 1972-90, Tissue Reactions, 1976-88; assoc. editor Jour. Cutaneous Pathology, 1973-83, Oral Surgery, Oral Medicine, Oral Pathology, 1970. Served to capt. AUS, 1944-46. Recipient Isaac Schour award for outstanding research and teaching in anat. scis. Internat. Assn. Dental Research, 1973, Disting. Alumnus of Yr. award Ind. U. Sch. Dentistry, 1978; Disting. Alumnus of Yr. award, Ind. U., 1981; Disting. Faculty Lectr. award, U. Ala. Med. Ctr., Birmingham, 1989—, Disting. Scientist award Am. Assn. Dental Rsch, 1990. Fellow Am. Coll. Dentists, Am. Acad. Oral Pathology (v.p. 1984-85, pres.-elect 1985-86, pres. 1986-87), AAAS (chmn. sect. 1976-78, sec. sect. 1979-87); mem. ADA (cons. Coun. Dental Rsch. 1973-74), Internat. Assn. Dental Rsch. (v.p. 1974-75, pres. 1976-77, pres. Exptl. Pathology Group 1985-86), Am. Assn. Dental Rsch. (pres. 1976-77), Internat. Assn. Pathologists, Histochem. Soc., Nat. Soc. Med. Rsch. (dir. 1977-79), Biol. Stain Commn. (trustee 1977—), Commd. Officers Assn., Internat. Assn. Oral Pathologists (co-founder, 1st pres. 1979-81, 1st editor 1971-89), Soc. Oral Pathologists, Brit. Soc. Oral Pathologists (hon.), Exchange Club (Birmingham, pres. New Orleans 1952-53). Home: 3514 Bethune Dr Birmingham AL 35223-1418

FULLMER, LEE WAYNE, minister; b. Victor, Iowa, Jan. 12, 1931; s. Joseph Jacob and Hazel Fannie (Carl) F.; m. Hazel June Shook, June 30, 1956; children: Carey Lee, Daniel Ray. Pastoral Dipl., Moody Bible Inst., Chgo., 1954; AB in History, Wheaton (Ill.) Coll., 1956; ThB in Theology, Bapt. Bible Sem., Johnston City, N.Y., 1958. Ordained to ministry Gen. Assn. of Regular Bapt. Chs., 1958. Minister Waneta Lake Bapt. Ch., Hammondsport, N.Y., 1957-61, Panama (N.Y.) Bapt. Ch., 1961-63, Shoaff Park Bapt. Ch., Ft. Wayne, Ind., 1963-69, Mt. Tabor Bapt. Ch., Beckley, W.Va., 1970-79, Norwood Bapt. Ch., Cin., 1979-93; pastor Maranatha Bapt. Ch., Springfield, Ohio, 1993—; tchr. Norwood Bapt. Christian Sch., Cin., 1980-93; trustee Scioto Hills Bapt. Camp, Wheelersburg, Ohio, 1982-93; prof. Appalachian Bible Coll., Bradley, W.Va., part-time, 1970s; min. Philippine Islands, 1998. Republican. Office: Maranatha Bapt Ch 1704 Sunset Ave Springfield OH 45505-4316 *The great need of our troubled society is a return to the Biblical Christianity based upon a renewal of a healthy fear of God.*

FULLMER, PAUL, public relations counselor; b. Evanston, Ill., June 4, 1934; s. Joseph Charles and Marie (Guirsch) F.; m. Sandra Lewars Clifford, Apr. 22, 1961; children: Monica, David. AB, U. Notre Dame, 1955. Newspaper reporter Aurora (Ill.) Beacon News, 1955-57; account exec. Selz/Seabolt Comms., Chgo., 1957-64; v.p. Selz/Seabolt Comms., Inc., Chgo., 1964-72, exec. v.p., 1972-79, pres., 1979-99, chmn., 1999—; bd. dirs. Pinnacle Worldwide, pres. 1990-92, chmn., 1992-93. Pres. Notre Dame Club Chgo., 1964-65, hon. pres., 1992-93; co-chmn. jr. bd. NCCJ, Chgo., 1962; chmn. Amate House, Chgo., 1985-87; chmn. bd. trustees St. Mary's Acad., 1985-88; co-chmn. Bus. Execs. for Econ. Justice, 1992-94; chmn. exec. com. Holy Family Ch., 1989-93. Sgt. USAR, 1957. Fellow Pub. Rels. Soc. Am. (pres. Chgo. chpt. 1988-89); mem. Internat. Pub. Rels. Assn., Union League Club Chgo. Roman Catholic. E-mail: pfullmer@selz.com. Home: 1333 Sleepy Hollow Rd Glenview IL 60025-3043 Office: Selz/Seabolt Communications 221 N La Salle St Chicago IL 60601-1206

FULLMER, STEVEN MARK, systems engineer; b. San Francisco, Mar. 15, 1956; s. Thomas Patrick and Patricia Ann (Carroll-Boyd) F.; m. Rhonda Lynnette Bush, Nov. 8, 1992; children: Wesley Stevenson, Sierra Marin. BA in Chemistry, Willamette U., 1978; BA in Biology, 1978; MBA, Ariz. State U., 1993. Sr. engr., project leader Honeywell Large Computer Products, Phoenix, 1981-86; bank officer, cons., infosecurity cons. First Interstate Bank/Wells Fargo Bank, Phoenix, 1987-96; project mgr. Wells Fargo Bank, 1996; systems engr. AG Comm. Systems, 1996—; cons. J.A. Boyd & Assoc., San Francisco, 1985-96, ImaginInc. Consulting, Phoenix, 1985—. Contbr. articles to profl. jours. Mem. exec. bd. Grand Canyon coun. Boy Scouts Am., scoutmaster, 1983-88, commr., 1988-92, dist. chmn., 1995-96; founder, lt. comdr. Maricopa County Sheriff's Adj. Posse, 1982-93; pres. Heard Mus. Coun., 1995-96; dept. head, lead Liberty Wildlife. Recipient Order of Merit Boy Scouts Am., 1988, Nat. Disting. Commr. award Boy Scouts Am., 1990, Nat. Founder's award Boy Scouts Am., 1991, Silver Beaver award Boy Scouts Am., 1994. Mem. Am. Inst. for Cert. Computer Profls. (cert. data processor 1985), Mensa, KC (membership dir. 1988), Knights Cross (Sovereign Order of St. Stanislas), Phi Lambda Upsilon, Phi Eta Sigma, Kappa Sigma, Alpha Chi Sigma, Sigma Iota Epsilon, Beta Gamma Sigma. Republican. Roman Catholic. Avocations: Am. Indian history, science fiction, scuba diving, hiking, camping. Office: AG Comm Systems 2500 W Utopia Rd Phoenix AZ 85027-4129

FULLMER, TIMOTHY SHAWN, printing company executive; b. Provo, Utah, May 2, 1963; s. Bryan H. and Gertrude LaRee (Andrews) F.; m. Alisa Carole Webb, Aug. 19, 1983; children: Kevin William, Rachel Christine, Brett Harrison, Steven Thomas. AS in Graphic Art, Utah Tech. Coll., 1985; BA in Graphic Communication, Calif. State U., Hayward, 1988, MBA in Ops. Rsch. and Fin., 1990. Prodn. mgr. Advanced Printing, Inc., Pleasanton, Calif., 1981-82, fin. mgr., 1985-91; gen. mgr. The Graphic Shop, Provo, 1982-85; mng. ptnr. Mtn. West Graphics, Orem, Utah, 1983-85; pres. Vista Graphics Inc., Salt Lake City, 1991-93, Vision Internat., Salt Lake City, 1993—; art dir. Escape mag., 1988. Recipient Vocat. Excellence award Utah State Bd. Regents, 1985. Mem. Vocat. Indsl. Clubs Am. (nat. champion graphic comm. 1983, 84, 85), Rotary (club 24). Republican. Mem. LDS Ch. Inventor system for large format digital images. Avocations: collecting vintage guitars, restoration of "muscle" era cars, playing guitar, golfing, playing lacrosse. Home: 1933 Ashley Ridge Rd Sandy UT 84092-4366

FULMER, HUGH SCOTT, physician, educator; b. Syracuse, N.Y., June 18, 1928; s. Herbert C. and Emily (Price) F.; m. Zola M. Jones, July 12, 1952; children: James, Kim, Scott. A.B., Syracuse U., 1948; M.D., SUNY-Syracuse, 1951; M.P.H., Harvard U., 1961. Intern R.I. Hosp., 1951-52; resident internal medicine SUNY-Syracuse, 1954-57; fellow pulmonary medicine SUNY, Syracuse, 1957-58; asst. dir., rsch. assoc. Navajo-Cornell Field Health Research Project, 1958-60; instr. pub. health and preventive medicine Cornell U. Coll. Medicine, 1958-60; asst. prof. community medicine U. Ky. Coll. Medicine, 1960-64, assoc. prof., 1964-66, prof., 1966-68, dir. sr. med. student internat. cross-cultural program, 1964-68, dir. preventive medicine residency program, 1964-68; tech. cons. health Peace Corps, Malaysia, 1968-69; prof., chmn. dept. community and family medicine U. Mass. Med. Sch., 1969-77, asso. dean for clin. edn. and primary care, 1975-79, chief sect. gen. medicine, dept. medicine, 1978-83; dir. ambulatory and community svcs. Carney Hosp., Boston, 1983-88, dir. community-oriented primary care program, 1988-93, dir. preventive medicine residency, 1988-93; exec. dir. Ctr. for Cmty. Reponsive Care, Boston, 1991—, dir. preventive medicine residency & COPC fellowship program, 1991—; adj. prof. sociomed. scis., cmty. medicine and pub. health Boston U. Sch. Medicine and Pub. Health, 1983-96. Served with M.C., USAF, 1952-54. Mem. AMA, APHA, Mass. Med. Soc., Soc. Gen. Internal Medicine, Assn. Tchrs. Preventive Medicine (past pres., Outstanding Tchr. award 1993), Am. Coll. Preventive Medicine (bd. regents 1988-94), Am. Coll. Physician Execs. Achievements include research on community responsive primary care. Home: 61 Cherlyn Dr Northborough MA 01532-1135

FULMER, PHILLIP, university football coach; b. Winchester, Tenn., Sept. 1, 1950; m. Vicky Morey; children: Phillip Jr., Courtney, Brittany, Allison. BA, U. Tenn., 1972. Offensive line coach Wichita (Kans.) State U., 1974, 77-78, linebacker coach, 1975-76; asst. football coach Vanderbilt U., Nashville, 1979; grad. asst. U. Tenn., Nashville, 1972, defensive coord. freshman team, 1973, asst. coach, 1980-91, head coach, 1992—; head coach East-West Shrine Game, 1998; coach Fla. Citrus Bowl, 1993, Orange Bowl, 1997. Led U. Tenn. Vols. to Southeastern Conf. championship, 1997. Mem. Am. Football Coaches Assn. (trustee 1996—, mem. Hall of Fame com., I-A coaches legis. issues com., Kodah Region 2 Coach of Yr. award 1993). Office: care Am Football Coaches Assn 5900 Old McGregor Rd Waco TX 76712*

FULMER, ROBERT M., business educator, management consultant; b. Florence, Ala., Oct. 6, 1939; s. Robert and Reba (Smith) F.; m. Pat Anne Cohen; children: Robert Jeffrey, James Burton. BA, David Lipscomb Coll., 1961; MBA, U. Fla., 1962; PhD, UCLA, 1965. Prof. mgmt. Ga. State U., Atlanta, 1968-73; George R. Brown prof. bus. Trinity U., San Antonio, 1973-79; prof., dir. exec. ed. Emory U., Atlanta, 1979-85; dir. corp. mgmt. devel. Allied-Signal Inc., Morristown, N.J., 1985-87; vis. prof. Columbia U., N.Y.C., 1987-91; W. Brooks George prof. mgmt. Coll. William & Mary, Williamsburg, Va., 1991—; vis. scholar MIT Orgnl. Learning Ctr., Boston, 1993-94; rsch. assoc. Internat. Consortium for Exec. Devel. Rsch., Lexington, Mass., 1994; rschr. Ctr. for Rsch. in Career Strategy, Columbia U., N.Y.C., 1985-86; pres. Inst. for Bus. & Interpersonal Strategies, Morristown, 1986-88; founding exec. dir. Inst. Cert. Profl. Mgrs., 1974-76; sr. fellow Inst. for East West Studies, 1998—; internat. rsch. adv. bd. The Strategic Inst., 1999—. Author: The New Management, 1988; co-author: A Practical Introduction to Business, 1988, Crafting Competitiveness, 1996, Leadership By Design, 1998. Mem. human resource adv. bd. ARC, 1986-89; state sec. Bus. & Indsutry Coun. for Re-election of the Pres., 1972; program dir. Goals for Ga. project, 1971. Named one of Ga.'s Five Outstanding Young Men by Ga. Jr. C. of C., 1972, Atlanta's Outstanding Young Educators by Atlanta Jr. C. of C., 1971. Fellow Acad. Mgmt., So. Mgmt. Assn. (v.p. 1968, pres.-elect 1969, pres. 1970); mem. World Future Soc., Soc. for Advancement of Mgmt. Home: 608 Pollard Park Williamsburg VA 23185-4033 Office: Grad Sch of Business College of William and Mary Williamsburg VA 23185

FULMER, VINCENT ANTHONY, retired college president; b. Alliance, Ohio, Oct. 23, 1927; s. Anthony and Catherine (Long) F.; m. Mary Alma Pineau, Dec. 27, 1950; children: Kevan, Kristine, David, Amy, Charles, Alma Leigh. A.B. cum laude, Miami U., Oxford, Ohio, 1949; postgrad., Harvard U., 1950; S.M., MIT, 1963; LL.D., Suffolk U., 1971; D.Sc., Fla. Inst. Tech., 1982; Ed.D., Hawthorne Coll., 1988. Mem. staff MIT, 1951-86, exec. asst. office chmn., 1960-63, v.p., 1963-73, sec. inst., 1963-85; v.p. adminstrn. William Underwood Co., 1973-75; sec. M.I.T. Corp., 1979-85; v.p., dir. Video Optics Corp., Waltham, Mass., 1985-86; pres. Hawthorne Coll., Antrim, N.H., 1986-88, pres. emeritus, 1988—; bd. dirs. Control Air, Inc., Dia Com Corp., Fiber Spar & Tube, Ind., Tech. Capital Network, Inc.; instr. econs. Williams Coll., 1952. Contbr. chpts. to books and mags. Bd. dirs. Planning Office for Urban Affairs, Archdiocese of Boston, 1968-93; trustee Suffolk U., 1972—, chmn., 1976-81; trustee Hawthorne Coll., 1982-92, chmn., 1985-92; corporator New Eng. Coll. Optometry, 1985-87, trustee, 1987-93; bd. dirs. Sml. Bus. High Tech. Inst., Washington, 1982—; mem. exec. com. MIT Enterprise Forum, 1978—, vice-chmn. 1992-93. With USNR, 1944-46. Mem. Am. Econ. Assn., AAAS, Ops. Research Soc. Am., Inst. Mgmt. Scis., Phi Beta Kappa, Sigma Chi, Omicron Delta Kappa. Home and Office: 26 Kimball Rd Arlington MA 02474-1206 *While individuals may address themselves exclusively to high personal attainments within the existing framework of our institutions, or devote prodigious efforts to improve or restructure those institutions, in the end it is our lifetime example that counts more heavily than all else.*

FULRATH, ANDREW WESLEY, bank executive; b. Rockford, Ill., Jan. 31, 1967; s. Lee Eldon and Susan Mae (Leonard) F.; m. Janelle Ann Edson, Aug. 19, 1989. BA in Religion summa cum laude, Trinity Internat. U., Deerfield, Ill., 1989, MA in Religious Edn. magna cum laude, 1996; Cert. profl. edn., Denver, 1995. CFP licensee. Dir. alumni rels. Trinity Internat. U., 1990-91, dir. devel., 1991-93, dir. gift planning svcs., 1993-97; v.p. trust bus. devel. First Citizens Bank, Wilmington, N.C., 1998—; project vol. Money Mag. Advising Elgin Nat. Project, 1997. Author, editor newsletter Options, 1994-97. Active Willow Creek Cmty. Ch., Good Sense ministry, 1996-97; mem. nominating com. Outstanding Young Women of Am.; exec. vis. vol. Cape Fear United Way Campaign, 1998—; mem. nat. com. on planned giving Cape Fear United Meth. Ch. Wilmington, N.C. Recipient Am. Bible Soc. Outstanding Scholar award, 1989, Lilly Endowment Fund Raising Effectiveness scholarship, 1991; named one of Outstanding Young Men of Am., 1996. Mem. Inst. CFPs, New Hanover County Estate Planning Coun. Avocations: family, personal finance/investment, fitness, jazz/classical music, European and American impressionist art. E-mail: fulrath@msn.com. Office: 315 Market St Wilmington NC 28401-4544

FULRATH, IRENE, corporate marketing executive; b. N.Y.C., Nov. 15, 1945; d. Logan and Grace (Sheehy) F. B.A., Wheaton Coll., Ill., 1967. Media exec. Doyle Dane Bernbach, N.Y.C., 1967-72; account exec., retail sales mgr. Sta. WABC, N.Y.C., 1972-84; account exec. Sta. WABC-TV, N.Y.C., 1984-86; regional sales mgr., Am. Express Co., 1987—. Mem. Fin. Advt. and Mktg. Assn. (bd. dirs. 1981-84, sec. 1984-85, v.p. 1985-86, pres 1986-87). Republican. Presbyterian. Avocation: travel. Home: 150 E 56th St New York NY 10022-3631

FULSHER, ALLAN ARTHUR, lawyer; b. Portland, Oreg., July 5, 1952; s. Rémy Walter and Barbara Lee (French) F.; m. Karen Louise Schmid, Dec. 28, 1974 (dec. Sept. 1990); children: Brian Rémy, Louise Katherine, Elizabeth Alane. BA in Biology, U. Oreg., 1974, BA in Econs., 1976; JD, U. of Pacific, 1979. Bar: Oreg. 1979, Calif. 1980, U.S. Dist. Ct. Oreg. 1980, U.S. Dist. Ct. (ea. dist.) Calif. 1981, U.S. Ct. Appeals (9th cir.) 1982, U.S. Dist. Ct. (no. dist.) Calif. 1985, U.S. Dist. Ct. (so. dist.) Calif. 1986. Assoc. Law Offices of Jacques B. Nichols PC, Portland, 1979-82, Ragen, Roberts, O'Scannlain, Robertson & Neill, Portland, 1982-83; shareholder Bauer, Hermann, Fountain & Rhoades PC, Portland, 1983-87, v.p., 1984-87; shareholder, v.p. Fulsher and Weatherhead PC, Portland, 1987-88, pres., 1988—; gen. counsel Peregrine Holdings, Ltd., Beaverton, Oreg., 1993-97, Peregrine Capital, Inc., Beaverton, 1993—; mgr. Stamford Bridge, LLC, 1995—; pres., mgr. Portland Profl. Soccer, L.L.C., Tigard, Oreg., 1998—; gen. counsel Premier Soccer Alliance, L.L.C., Dallas, 1998—. Mem. Audi Quattro Club U.S.A. Republican. Roman Catholic. Avocations: basketball, automobile racing and restoration, coaching youth and adult sports. Home: 16399 SE Sager Rd Portland OR 97236-5509 Office: Peregrine Capital Inc 9725 SW Beaverton Hillsdale Hw Beaverton OR 97005-3305

FULSON, LULA M., educator; b. Chgo., June 20, 1938; m. Larry E. Fulson, June 9, 1957 (dec. Mar. 1994); children: Darrell, Larry, Daphne, Zachary, Stephanie. BA, Nat.-Louis U., 1983, MEd, 1988. Retention counselor South Suburban Coll., South Holland, Ill., 1984-85, instr., coord., 1985—. Author: Memoirs of a Widow, 1996; co-editor Robbins Bull. Newspaper, 1995—. Sec. Theda Hambright Scholarship, South Holland, 1990—; trustee, treas. William Leonard Pub. Libr., Robbins, Ill., 1995—; corr. sec. Windy City Travelers, Chgo., 1995—; 2d v.p. People's Party, Robbins, 1995—. Named Outstanding County Chairwoman, Mothers Assn. U. Ill., 1993-94, Outstanding Citizen and Bd. Mem., Chgo. Youth Ctr./Robbins, 1996; recipient Living Black History award Harvey (Ill.) Pub. Libr. Youth Svcs., 1988. Mem. Ill. Adult and Continuing Edn. Assn. (jr. dir., sr. dir. 1984-86, co-editor Keeping Pace newsletter 1991-92), Citizens United for Progress. Mem. Ch. of Christ. Avocations: singing, camping, bowling, sports, reading. Home: 3623 Maxey Ct Robbins IL 60472-1936

FULTON, CHERYL LYNN, customer service administrator; b. Chgo., Feb. 21, 1947; d. Theodore Edward and Elsie Amelia Whiffen; m. Richard Lawrence Gniadek, Nov. 15, 1969 (dec. Feb. 1979); m. Richard John Fulton, Sept. 2, 1995. BSBA, Ill. State U., 1969. Prodn. sec. Universal Tng. Systems, Lincolnwood, Ill., 1969-71; exec. sec. Alliance Am. Insurers, Chgo., 1971-78; temp. sec. Kelly Svcs., Grand Rapids, Mich., 1978-79; sec. Honeywell, Inc., Grand Rapids, Mich., 1979-80, sales corr., 1980-81; adminstr. customer quality Honeywell, Inc., Ft. Washington, Pa., 1981-84; rep. customer service Honeywell, Inc., Valley Forge, Pa., 1984-88; fin. acct. Honeywell, Inc., Ft. Washington, 1987-91; br. support supr. Honeywell, Inc., Valley Forge, 1991-92; supr. Regional Customer Svc. Ctr. Honeywell, Inc., Ft. Washington, 1992-95, field svcs. mgr., 1995—. Mem. NAFE, Am. Bus. Women's Assn. (New Directions Charter chpt., pres. 1986, Woman of Yr. 1985), Instrument Soc. Am. (treas., edn. com. Phila. sect., sec., treas., 3d v.p., 2d v.p., 1st v.p., pres. 1994-95). Democrat. Roman Catholic. Avocations: needlework, skiing, reading. Home: 857 Thoreau Ct Warminster PA 18974-2057 Office: Honeywell Inc 1100 Virginia Dr Fort Washington PA 19034-3264

FULTON, KATHERINE NELSON, journalist, consultant; b. Roanoke, Va., Jan. 25, 1955; d. George Henry and Sally Hart (Fishburn) F. BA, Harvard U., 1978. Reporter Greensboro (N.C.) Record, 1979-81; city editor Greensboro Daily News, 1981-82; editor, founder N.C. Ind., Durham, 1983-92; lectr. Duke U., Durham, 1987—; cons. Globa. Bus. Network, 1996—. Contbr. articles to profl. jours. Mem. adv. panel Z. Smith Reynolds Found., Winston-Salem, N.C., 1986-88. Lyndhurst Found. grantee, 1987-89; Nieman fellow Harvard U., 1992-93. Mem. Alternative Newsweeklies (v.p. 1985-87), Inst. for Alternative Journalism (pres. 1994-96). Home: 565 Neilson St Berkeley CA 94707-1502

FULTON, KENNETH RAY, professional association administrator; b. Cleve., Dec. 22, 1948. BS in Social Scis., U. Md., 1973; MS in Mgmt., Am. U., 1977. Mem. staff Nat. Acad. Scis., Washington, 1971-80, dir. membership, 1980-84, spl. asst. to pres., 1984-93; exec. dir. Acad. Scis., Washington, 1993—; mgr. membership and program activities Nat. Acad. Scis., organizer numerous sci. confs. and symposia; mem. U.S. delegation to Codex Alimentarius Commn. UN, 1977-80; coord. Arts at the Acad. program. Publisher Proceedings, Jour. of the Nat. Acad. Scis. With U.S. Navy. Mem. AAAS, Am. Soc. Assn. Execs., Soc. Scholarly Publishers. Office: Nat Acad Scis 2101 Constitution Ave NW Washington DC 20418-0007

FULTON, LEN, publisher; b. Lowell, Mass., May 15, 1934; s. Claude E. and Louise E. (Vaillant) F.; children: Timothy, Brooke. B.A., U. Wyo., 1961; postgrad., U. Calif., Berkeley. Pub. Tourist Topic, Kennebunkport, Maine, also Weekly News, Freeport, Maine, 1957-59; biostatistician Calif. Dept. Public Health, 1962-68; editor, pub. Dustbooks, Paradise, Calif., 1963—; chmn. Com. Small Mag. Editors and Pubs., 1968-71, 73; cons. small presses ALA. Author: The Grassman, 1974, Dark Other Adam Dreaming, 1975; co-author: American Odyssey, 1975; playwright: Dark Other Adam Dreaming, 1985, For the Love of Pete, 1989, Grandmother Dies, 1989, Headlines, 1990, The Court Martial of Paul Revere, 1997. Panelist Calif. Arts Coun., 1975, 85-86, 95, 96, Lit. Program, Nat. Endowment for Arts, 1976-78; supr. Butte County, Calif., 1982-93. With AUS, 1953-55. Grantee Coordinating Coun. Lit. Mags., 1970-73, Nat. Endowment for Arts, 1974, 75. Mem. ABA, PEN. Address: PO Box 100 Paradise CA 95967-0100*

FULTON, NORMAN ROBERT, credit manager; b. L.A., Dec. 16, 1935; s. Robert John and Fritzi Marie (Wacker) F.; AA, Santa Monica Coll., 1958; BS, U. So. Calif., 1960; m. Nancy Butler, July 6, 1966; children: Robert B., Patricia M. Asst. v.p. Raphael Glass Co., L.A., 1960-65; credit adminstr. Zellerbach Paper Co., L.A., 1966-68; gen. credit mgr. Carrier Transicold Co., Montebello, Calif., 1968-70, Virco Mfg. Co., L.A., 1970-72, Superscope, Inc., Chatsworth, Calif., 1972-79; asst. v.p. credit and adminstrn. Inkel Corp., Carson, Calif., 1980-82; corp. credit mgr. Gen. Consumer Electronics, Santa Monica, Calif., 1982-83; br. credit mgr. Sharp Electronics Corp., Carson, Calif., 1983-96; credit mgr. Rocheux Internat. Inc., Carson, 1997—. With AUS, 1955-57. Fellow Nat. Inst. Credit (cert. credit exec.); mem. Credit Mgrs. So. Calif., Nat. Notary Assn. Home: 6437 Kanan Dume Rd Malibu CA 90265-4037

FULTON, SCOTT C., federal agency administrator; b. Nov. 2, 1954. Trial atty. U.S. Dept. Justice, 1982-85, sr. atty., 1985-86, asst. chief environ. enforcement sect., 1986-90; dir. Office Civil Enforcement U.S. EPA, 1990-92, dep. asst. adminstr. Office Enforcement & Compliance, 1992-95, prin. dep. gen. counsel; spl. asst. U.S. Atty., D.C. Office: Environ Protection Agy MC 2311 401 M St SW Washington DC 20460

FULTON, THOMAS, theoretical physicist, educator; b. Budapest, Hungary, Nov. 19, 1927; came to U.S., 1941; s. Michael and Irene (Weisz) F.; m. Babette Pilzer, June 14, 1952; children: Ruth Carol, Judith Pamela. BA, Harvard U., 1950, MA, 1951, PhD, 1954. Frank B. Jewett Found. postdoctoral fellow Inst. Advanced Studies, Princeton, N.J., 1954-55; NSF postdoctoral fellow Princeton, N.J., 1955-56; from asst. prof. to assoc. prof. Johns Hopkins U., Balt., 1956-64, prof., 1964—; rsch. cons. and vis. scientist numerous orgns., 1954—. Author: (with others) Resonances in Strong Interaction Physics, 1963; assoc. editor Jour. Math. Physics, 1968-71; contbr. over 100 articles to profl. jours. Bd. dirs. Shriver Hall Concert Series, Balt., 1981-91. With U.S. Army, 1946-47. John Simon Guggenheim Found. fellow, U. Vienna, 1964-65, Fulbright sr. rsch. fellow, 1964-65; prin. investigator rsch. grantee NSF, Johns Hopkins U., 1960-92. Fellow Am. Phys. Soc.; mem. Archeol. Inst. Am., Sigma Xi. Home: 5600 Roxbury Pl Baltimore MD 21209-4502 Office: Johns Hopkins U Dept Physics And Astro Baltimore MD 21218

FULTON, WILLIAM, mathematics educator; b. Aug. 29, 1939. BA, Brown U., 1961; PhD, Princeton U., 1966. Instr. Princeton (N.J.) U., 1965-66; from instr. to asst. prof. Brandeis U., 1966-69; assoc. prof. Brown U., 1970-75, prof., 1975-87; prof. U. Chgo., 1987-98, Charles L. Hutchinson Disting. Svc. prof., 1995-98; Keeler prof. math. U. Mich., Ann Arbor, 1998—; vis. asst. prof. Princeton U., 1969-70; vis. prof. U. Genoa, 1969, Aarhus U., 1976-77, Orsay, 1987; vis. mem. Inst. des Hautes Etudes Scis., 1981, Inst. Advanced Study, 1981-82, 94, Math. Scis. Rsch. Inst., 1992-93, Ctr. Advanced Study, Oslo, 1994; Erlander prof. Mittag-Leffler Inst., 1996-97; lectr. in field. Author: Intersection Theory, 1984, Introduction to Intersection Theory in Algebraic Geometry, 1984, Introduction to Toric Varieties, 1993, Algebraic Topology, 1995, Young Tableaux, 1997; (with R. MacPherson) A Categorical Framework for the Study of Singular Spaces, 1981; (with S. Lang) Riemann-Roch Algebra, 1985, (with J. Harris) Representation Theory; a first course, 1991; (with S. Bloch and I. Dolgachev, editors) Proceedings of the US-USSR Symposium in Algebraic Geometry, Univ. of Chicago, June-July, 1989, 1991; assoc. editor Duke Math. Jour., 1984-93, Jour. Algebraic Geometry, 1992-93; editor Jour. Am. Math. Soc., 1993-99, mng. editor, 1995-98; mem. editl. bd. Cambridge Studies in Advanced Math., 1994—, Chgo. Lectures in Math., 1994-98. Grantee NSF, 1976—, Sloan Found., 1981-82; Guggenheim fellow, 1980-81; named Erlander prof. Swedish Sci. Found., 1996-97. Mme. AAAS, NAS. Office: U Mich 525 E University Ave Ann Arbor MI 48109-1109

FULTON-QUINDOZA, DEBRA ANN, nurse practitioner; b. Anne Arundel, Md., Dec. 16, 1961; d. William D. and Patricia A. (Rensel) Fulton; m. Stephen S. Quindoza, Nov. 17, 1998; 1 child, William Benjamin Quindoza; 1 stepchild, Costas Quindoza. BSN, U. Tex., Galveston, 1983, MSN, 1986. Advanced RN practitioner, Fla.; cert. profl. nurse practitioner. Clin. nurse specialist Arnold Palmer Hosp. for Childen and Women, Orlando, Fla., 1988; pediatric and internal medicine nurse practitioner Office of Dr. Shirley Nagel, Mt. Dora, Fla., 1990-91; project leader in med. policy-med. rev.-fraud and abuse Medicare of Fla., Jacksonville, 1991-93; med. cons., outreach educator, project mgr. Medicare Fraud Br., Jacksonville, Fla., 1993—; advanced RN practitioner part time Dr. Perry G. Carlos, 1996—; med. cons. in field. Home: 12638 Point Park Dr Jacksonville FL 32225-5508 Office: Medicare Fraud Br 532 Riverside Ave Ste 11 T Jacksonville FL 32202-4914

FULTS, KENNETH WYATT, civil engineer, surveyor; b. Center, Tex., Feb. 20, 1949; s. Raymond Weldon and Dovie Marie (Tindal) F.; m. Carolyn Kay Barnett, Feb. 27, 1971 (div. Aug., 1985); 1 child, Wendy Carol. BS in Civil Engring., Tex. A&M U., 1971. Engring. asst. Tex. Dept. Transp., Crockett, Tex., 1971-73; design engr. Tex. Dept. Transp., Lufkin, Tex., 1973-76; dist. lab. engr. Tex. Dept. Transp., Lufkin, 1976-85, dist. planning engr., 1985-89; bituminous engr. Tex. Dept. Transp., Austin, 1989-90, soils and aggregate engr., 1990-93, dir. pavements, 1993—; chmn. Coll. Curriculum Com., Lufkin, Tex., 1988-89; instr. pavement design, Tex. Dept. Transp., Austin, 1990, asphalt mix design, 1990-91; co-chmn. Joint Spl. Devel. Com., Austin, 1993—. Contbr. reports to Tex. Dept. Transp. Publs. Regional pres. Tex. Pub. Employee Assn., Region II, Tex., 1976; chmn. bd. dirs. Dist. II Credit Union, Lufkin, Tex., 1978-82. Mem. ASCE (v.p. 1989), ASTM, NCHRP, Transp. Rsch. Bd. (presiding officer 2 sessions ann. meeting 1997, presenter peer-reviewed papers), Assn. State Hwy. and Transp. Officials (jt. task force 1993—). Mem. Ch. of Christ. Achievements include research in open graded friction courses; in place recycling of HMA surfaces; sulphur extended asphalts; cement fly-ash stabilization of soils; development of quality control, quality assurance HMA specification;, development of certification program for HMA technicians; development of long-range research plan for pavements; implementation and management oversight of Texas Mobil Load Simulator (TXMLS) accelerated pavement test equipment. Avocations: camping, hiking, reading. Home: 503 Oaklands Dr Round Rock TX 78681-4028 Office: Tex Dept Transp 125 E 11th St Austin TX 78701-2409

FULTZ, BRENT THOMAS, materials scientist, educator, researcher; b. Troy, N.Y., Feb. 24, 1955; s. Stanley Charles and Esther Doris (Richert) F.; m. Colleen Jaye O'Hara, Sept. 30, 1984; children: Emily Elise, Eric Michael, Elissa Katherine. BSc in Physics, MIT, 1975; MSc in Materials Sci., U. Calif., Berkeley, 1978, PhD in Materials Sci., 1982. Staff scientist Lawrence Berkeley (Calif.) Lab., 1982-85; asst. prof. materials sci. Calif. Inst. Tech., Pasadena, 1985-90, assoc. prof., 1991-97, prof., 1997—; prof. U. Udine, Italy, 1992; cons. Everett Charles Technologies, Pomona, Calif., 1986-96, Def. Sci. Study Group, Alexandria, Va., 1994-95, Def. Sci. Bd., Washington, 1996; Los Alamos Nat. Lab., 1997—. Editor 5 books; contbr. over 180 articles to profl. jours.; patentee in field. Recipient Faculty Devel. award IBM, 1986, 87; NSF Presdl. Young Investigator, 1988-93; Xerox Found. grantee, 1986; Wallenberg Found. scholar, 1988. Mem. Am. Soc. Metals (chmn. atomic transport com. 1994-97), Am. Phys. Soc., Minerals Metals Materials Soc. (chmn. chemistry and physics com. 1996—), Internat. Bd. for Applications of Mössbauer Effect, 1998—. Home: 269 S Berkeley Ave Pasadena CA 91107-4734

FULTZ, DAVE, meteorology educator; b. Chgo., Aug. 12, 1921; s. Harry T. and Ora L. (Voyles) F.; m. Jean Laura McEldowney, Apr. 6, 1946; children: Martha M., David L., Katherine R. BS, U. Chgo., 1941, cert. in meteorology, 1942, PhD, 1947. Emergency asst. U.S. Weather Bur., Chgo., 1942; research asst. U. Chgo. and U.S. Weather Bur., 1943-44; mem. faculty U. Chgo., 1945-46, dir. hydrodynamics lab., 1946—, prof. meteorology, 1960-91, prof. emeritus, 1991—; cons. sci. adv. bd. USAF, 1959-64; mem. nat. com. fluid mechanics films Ednl. Services, Inc., Newton, Mass., 1962-71; research grants adv. com. Nat. Air Pollution Control Adminstrn., 1969-72. Contbr. articles to profl. jours. Served with USAAF, 1945. Fellow Guggenheim Found., 1950-51, NSF, 1957-58; recipient Golden Plate award Am. Acad. Achievement, 1968. Fellow Am. Meteorol. Soc. (Meisinger award 1951, C.G. Rossby Research medal 1967), Am. Geophys. Union, AAAS; mem. Royal Meteorol. Soc., Nat Acad. Scis., Phi Beta Kappa, Sigma Xi (sec., treas. Chgo. chpt. 1946, pres. 1975-76). Home: 5550 S South Shore Dr Chicago IL 60637-5051 Office: Univ Chgo Dept of Geophys Scis Chicago IL 60637*

FULTZ, PHILIP NATHANIEL, management analyst; b. N.Y.C., Jan. 29, 1943; s. Otis and Sara Love (Gibbs) F.; m. Anita Neu, Nov. 8, 1998. AA in Bus., Coll. of the Desert, 1980; BA in Mgmt., U. Redlands, 1980, MA in Mgmt., 1982. Enlisted USMC, 1967, advanced through grades to capt., 1972, served in various locations, 1964-78, resigned commn., 1978; CETA coord. County of San Bernardino, Yucca Valley, Calif., 1978-85; contract analyst Advanced Technology, Inc., Twentynine Palms, Calif., 1985-88; spl. transit analyst Omintrans, San Bernardino, Calif., 1988-89; tech. analyst Atlantic Rsch. Corp. (formerly Calculon Corp.), Twentynine Palms, Calif., 1988—; mgmt. analyst Marine Corps Base, Twentynine Palms, Calif., 1991—; adj. asst. prof. mgmt. Chapman U., Orange, Calif., 1992—. Founding dir. Unity Home Battered Women's Shelter, Joshua Tree, Calif., 1982, Morongo Basin Adult Literacy; bd. dirs. Twentynine Palms Water Dist., 1991-95. Mem. Rotary (sec. Joshua Tree chpt. 1983-85). Republican. Home: 73477 Desert Trail Dr Twentynine Palms CA 92277-2218 Office: Morale Walfare & Recreation Marine Corps Base Twentynine Palms CA 92277-2302

FULTZ, ROBERT EDWARD, lawyer; b. Columbus, Ohio, May 24, 1941; s. Clair Ervin and Isabelle (Eichelberger) F.; m. Judith Ann McClannan, June 15, 1963; children: Cynthia, Jennifer, Stephen. BA cum laude, Ohio State U., 1963; JD with distinction, U. Mich., 1965. Ohio 1966, U.S. Supreme Ct. 1970. Assoc. Porter, Wright, Morris & Arthur, Columbus, 1966-70, ptnr., 1971—. Past trustee Columbus Symphony Orch. and Ballet; past trustee, sec. United Cerebral Palsy of Columbus; past trustee, treas. Goodwill Industries; past trustee, pres. Cen. Community House; former advisor, bd. dirs. United Negro Coll. Fund; trustee Columbus Assn. for Performing Arts, Columbus Law Libr. Assn. Mem. Ohio State Bar Assn., Columbus Bar Assn., Phi Beta Kappa, Delta Upsilon (treas.). Home: 4630 Burbank Dr Columbus OH 43220-2806

FULTZ, SARA SPITLER, art educator; b. Staunton, Va., Nov. 11, 1941; d. William Randolph and Mozelle Wilde Spitler; m. Robert Carlton Fultz, Mar. 11, 1989. BS, Madison Coll., 1966. Cert. coll. art educator, Va. Art educator Augusta County Schs., Fishersville, Va., 1966—; living history demonstrator Nat. Pub. Svcs., Washington, 1970-75, asst. site supr., 1975; summer art camp tchr. Staunton/Augusta Art Ctr., 1985. Accident prevention specialist FAA, Washington, 1986-88. Mem. Internat. Women's Pilots Assn. (chmn. 1994—), Mid-Atlantic Sect. 99s (vice chair 1987-89), 99s Internat. Women's Pilot's Assn. Lutheran. Avocations: aviation, travel. E-mail: SaraFultz73043,1627@CompuServe.com. Home: 820 Maple St Staunton VA 24401

FULWEILER, PATRICIA PLATT, civic worker; b. N.Y.C., Mar. 19, 1923; d. Haviland Hull and Marie-Louise (Fearey) Platt; m. Spencer Biddle Fulweiler, Oct. 5, 1946; children: Marie-Louise Fulweiler Allen, Pamela Spencer, Hull Platt, Spencer Biddle. AB cum laude, Bryn Mawr Coll., 1945; MBA, Columbia U., 1950. Jr. copywriter, asst. account exec. Dorland Internat. Pettingell & Fenton, N.Y.C., 1945-46; statistician, fin. staff treas.'s office GM, N.Y.C., 1950-52; asst. account mgr. investment dept. Fiduciary Trust Co., N.Y.C., 1953-61; bd. dirs. Chapin Brearley Exchange, Inc., 1964-74, treas., 1966-71, pres., 1971-73. Bd. dirs. Knickerbocker Greys, 1965—, treas., 1970-75; bd. dirs., treas. City Gardens Club, N.Y.C., 1974-79, chmn. ways and means com., 1974-81; bd. dirs. Nat. Soc. Colonial Dames State N.Y., 1973-82, asst. treas., 1973-82; mem. fin. com. Alumnae Assn. Bryn Mawr Coll., 1970-76; bd. dirs. Daus. of Cin., 1974-81, scholarship adminstr., 1976-81; pres. Ladies Christian Union, 1982-87, chmn. fin. com., 1987-94; rec. sec. Women's Assn. St. James Ch., N.Y.C., 1972-75, co-chmn. Spring Festival, 1974-75, chmn., 1975-76, treas., 1976-81, mem. Altar Guild, 1975—; treas. Churchwomen's League for Patriotic Svc., 1982-86; mem. scholarship com. Youth Found., 1981—, pres., 1990—; membership chmn. Huguenot Soc. Am., registrar, 1986—. Mem. Soc. Sponsors of USN, Alumnae Coun. Spence Sch., 1991-97, Colonial Dames Am. (bd. dirs. 1987-93), Nat. Soc. Colonial Dames (bd. dirs. N.Y. soc. 1984-93, asst. treas. 1973-82), Colony Club, Thursday Evening Club, Wilson Point Beach Assn. Club, Norwalk Yacht Club (hon.). Republican. Address: 3 Hilltop Rd Norwalk CT 06854-5001 also: 158 E 83rd St New York NY 10028-1901

FULWILER, ROBERT NEAL, oil company executive; b. Belton, Tex., Nov. 5, 1937; s. Charles Calvin and Luella (Smith) F.; m. Sylvia Jean Marshall, Dec. 26, 1959; 1 child, Roger Neal. A.A., Temple Jr. Coll., 1959; B.B.A., U. Tex., 1961. Statis. asst. Tex. Eastern Transmission Corp., Houston, 1961-62; adminstrv. asst. subs. LaGloria Oil & Gas, Houston, 1969-76, v.p., 1976; exec. v.p. La Jet, Inc., Houston, 1976-81; pres. La Jet, Inc., 1981-82; chmn. bd. dirs. EnJet Inc., 1982-88; chief exec. officer Trend Energy, Houston, 1989—; bd. dirs. BFC Assocs., Inc. Author: Competition and Growth in American Energy Markets, 1947-1985, 1968. Mem. Aspen Found., Colo. Mem. Knights of Momus., The Aspen Inst. (assoc.). Republican. Mem. Ch. of Christ. Office: Trend Energy 5100 Westheimer Rd Ste 200 Houston TX 77056-5597

FUMERTON, RICHARD ANTHONY, philosopher educator; b. Toronto, Ontario, Can., Oct. 7, 1949; s. Robert Carl and Mabeleine (Reay) F.; m. Patricia C. Rowe, Apr. 18, 1948; children: Tara A., Robert A.; s. Robert Carl and Madeleine (Reay) F.; m. Patricia C. Rowe, Apr. 18, 1948; children: Tara A., Robert A. BA, U. Toronto (Ont.), 1971; MA, Brown U., 1973, PhD, 1974. Asst. prof. philosophy U. Iowa, Iowa City, 1974-79, assoc. prof., 1979-85, prof., 1985—, prof. chmn., 1988—; vis. prof. U. Minn., Mpls., Fall 1978. Author: Metaphysical and Epistemological Problems of Perception, 1985, Reason and Morality, 1990, Metaepistemology and Skepticism, 1995. Recipient Woodrow Wilson fellow, 1971-72, Can. Coun. fellow, Canadian govt., 1973-74. Home: 608 Whiting Ave Iowa City IA 52245-5640*

FUNARI, ROBERT GLENN, health care services executive; b. Pitts., Sept. 20, 1947; s. Mario Ronald and Virginia Alice Funari; m. Marilyn Romcea, July 20, 1970; children: Carla Marie, Michael Anthony. BSME, Cornell U., 1969; MBA, Harvard U., 1975. Dir. distbn. Baxter Internat., Deerfield, Ill., 1977-79, v.p. materials mgmt., 1979-83; pres. Medcom, Inc., Garden Grove, Calif., 1983-86, Paramax Sys. Baxter Internat., Irvine, Calif., 1986-89; corp. v.p. and pres. Pharmaseal divsn. Baxter Internat., Valencia, Calif., 1989-93; exec. v.p., COO Syncor Internat., Woodland Hills, Calif., 1993-96, pres., CEO, 1996—; bd. dirs. Bay Cities Nat. Bank, Redondo Beach, Calif., Cmty. First Group, English, Ind.; chmn. exec. coun. Adaptive Bus. Leaders, Newport Beach, Calif., 1998-99. Trustee Henry Mayo Newhall Hosp., Valencia, 1989-93; bd. dirs. Spl. Children's Found., Valencia, 1990-93. Baker scholar, 1975. Mem. Ctr. for Corp. Innovation, Nat. Coalition for Quality Diagnostic Imaging Svcs. (bd. dirs. 1998—). Home: 25615 Melbourne Ct Calabasas CA 91302 Office: Syncor Internat 6464 Canoga Ave Woodland Hills CA 91367

FUNCHES, JESSE L., financial administrator. BS in Math., Jackson State U.; MS in Math., U. Ill.; MBA, Loyola Coll. Ops. rsch. analyst Office of Sec. of Def., Washington; asst. to chmn. Nuclear Regulatory Commn., Washington, dep. contr., CFO; mem. exec. coun. Nuclear Regulatory Commn. Office: Nuclear Regulatory Commn Washington DC 20555

FUNDERBURK, DAVID BRITTON, consultant, former congressman and ambassador; b. Langley Field, Va., Apr. 28, 1944; married; 2 children. BA, Wake Forest Coll., 1966; MA, Wake Forest U., 1967; PhD, U. S.C., 1974. Instr. Wingate (N.C.) Coll., 1967-69, U. S.C., Columbia, 1969-70; assoc. prof. history Hardin-Simmons U., Abilene, Tex., 1972-78; prof. history Campbell U., Buies Creek, N.C., 1978-81, 85-86; U.S. amb. to Romania Bucharest, 1981-85; cons. U.S. Dept. Edn., 1987-88; mem. Nat. Edn. Com. on Internat. Ednl. Programs, 1987-90, 104th Congress from 2nd N.C. dist., Washington, 1994-96. Candidate for U.S. Senate from N.C., 1986; exec. dir. Conservatives for Freedom Polit. Action Com., 1988-94; chmn. Internat. Romanian Relief Fund, 1990-94; mem. U.S. Congress, 1994-96. Office: Preston Gates Ellis and Rouvelas Meeds 1735 New York Ave NW Washington DC 20006

FUNG, ADRIAN KIN-CHIU, electrical engineering educator, researcher; b. Liuchow, Kwangsi, Republic of China, Dec. 25, 1936; came to U.S., 1960; s. Yum Tien and Man Fan (Chan) F.; m. Jean Lee, Nov. 24, 1966; children: Lindy, Sally, Eula. Ph.D., U. Kans., 1965. Asst. prof. U. Kans., Lawrence, 1965-68, assoc. prof., 1968-72; Jenkins Garrett prof. dept. elec. engring. U. Tex., Arlington, 1984—; dir. Wave Scattering Rsch. Ctr., Arlington, 1984—. Author: Microwave Scattering and Emission Models and Their Applications, 1994; co-author: Microwave Remote Sensing Vol. 1, 1981, Vol. 2, 1982, Vol. 3, 1986. Recipient Halliburton Research award, 1987, Disting. Rsch. award U. Tex., 1989. Fellow IEEE (assoc. editor Oceanic Engrin. 1983-92, Disting. Achievement award 1989); mem. Radio Sci. Assn. (assoc. editor 1983-89, editor Jour. Electromagnetic Wave and Applications 1991—, editorial adv. bd. Remote Sensing Revs. 1993—). Home: 2609 Cedar View Dr Arlington TX 76006-2818 Office: U Texas Elec Engring Dept PO Box 19016 Arlington TX 76019

FUNG, YUAN-CHENG BERTRAM, bioengineering educator, author; b. Yuhong, Changchow, Kiangsu, China, Sept. 15, 1919; came to U.S., 1945, naturalized, 1957; s. Chung-Kwang and Lien (Hu) F.; m. Luna Hsien-Shih Yu, Dec. 22, 1949; children: Conrad Antung, Brenda Pingsi. BS, Nat. Central U., Chungking, China, 1941, MS, 1943; PhD, Calif. Inst. Tech., 1948. Research fellow Bur. Aero. Research China, 1943-45; research asst., then research fellow Calif. Inst. Tech., 1946-51, mem. faculty, 1951-66, prof. aeros., 1959-66; prof. bioengring. and applied mechanics U. Calif., San Diego, 1966—; cons. aerospace indsl. firms, 1949—; prof. (hon.) 15 univs. China. Author: The Theory of Aeroelasticity, 1955, 69, 93, Foundations of Solid Mechanics, 1965, A First Course in Continuum Mechanics, 1969, 77, 93, Biomechanics, 1972, Biomechanics: Mechanical Properties of Living Tissues, 1980, 93, Biodynamics: Circulation, 1984, Biomechanics: Circulation, 1996, Biomechanics: Motion, Flow, Stress and Growth, 1990, Selected Works on Biomechanics and Aeroelasticity by Y.C. Fung, 1997; also papers; editor Jour. Biorheology, Jour. Biomech. Engring. bd. trustees (hon.) Chongqing U.; chair (hon.), bd. trustees Nanjing U., China. Recipient Achievement award Chinese Inst. Engrs., 1965, 68, 93, Landis award Microcirculatory Soc., 1975, Poiseuille medal Internat. Soc. Biorheology, 1986, Engr. of Yr. award San Diego Engring. Soc., 1986, von Karman medal ASCE, 1976, ALZA award Biomed. Engring. Soc., 1989, Borelli award Am. Soc. Biomechanics; Guggenheim fellow, 1958-59, Melville medal Am. Soc. of Mechanical Engineers, 1994. Fellow AIAA, ASME (hon., Lissner award 1978, Centennial medal 1978, Worcester Reed Warner medal 1984, Timoshenko medal 1991, Melville medal 1994); mem. NAS, NAE, Inst. Medicine, Soc. Engring. Sci., Microcirculatory Soc., Am. Physiol. Soc., Nat. Heart Assn., Acad. Sinica, Chinese Acad. Scis. (fgn. mem.), Basic Sci. Coun., Sigma Xi. Home: 2660 Greentree Ln La Jolla CA 92037-1148 Office: Univ Calif Dept Bioengring 9500 Gilman Dr Dept La Jolla CA 92093-5003

FUNK, CARLA JEAN, library association executive; b. Wheeling, W.Va., Sept. 21, 1946; d. David H. and Jean (Duffy) Belt. BA in Psychology, Northwestern U., 1968; MLS, Ind. U., 1973; MBA, U. Chgo., 1985. Libr. adult svcs. Northbrook (Ill.) Pub. Libr., 1973-77; dir. Warren-Newport Pub. Libr. Dist., Gurnee, Ill., 1977-80; cons. Suburban Libr. Sys., Burr Ridge, Ill., 1980-83; dir. automation and tech. svcs., med. student svcs. AMA, Chgo., 1983-92; exec. dir. Med. Libr. Assn., Chgo., 1992—; adj. faculty Dominican U., 1986—; adv. Bicentennial Campaign U. S.C. Coll. Libr. and Info. Sci., Dominican U. Health Sci. com. Contbr. articles to profl. jours. Mem. Internat. Fedn. Libr. Assns. and Insts. (treas., U.S. nat. organizing com.), Am. Soc. Assn. Execs., Ill. Libr. Assn., Assn. Forum of Chicagoland, Beta Phi Mu, Delta Zeta. Home: 6110 Golfview Dr Gurnee IL 60031-4701 Office: 65 E Wacker Place Ste 1900 Chicago IL 60601

FUNK, CYRIL REED, JR., agronomist, educator; b. Richmond, Utah, Sept. 20, 1928; s. Cyril Reed and Hazel Marie (Jensen) F.; m. Donna Gwen Buttars, Feb. 2, 1951; children: Bonnie Arlene, David Christopher, Carol Jean. B.S. (Scholarship A 1955), Utah State U., 1952, M.S., 1955; Ph.D., Rutgers U., 1961; DAgr (hon.), Utah State U., 1994. Mem. faculty Rutgers U., New Brunswick, N.J., 1956—, rsch. prof. turfgrass breeding plant sci. dept., 1969—, also instr. grad. faculty. Author, patentee in field. Served to 1st lt. AUS, 1952-54. Recipient Green Sect. award U.S. Golf Assn., 1980, Achievement award Lawn Inst., 1977. Fellow Crop Sci. Soc. Am., Am. Soc. Agronomy (research award N.E. sect. 1979); mem. AAAS (fellow 1992),

Am. Genetic Assn., Am. Sod Producers Assn. (hon.), Golf Course Supts. Assn. (hon. mem.; Disting. Service award 1979), Internat. Turfgrass Soc., N.J. Turfgrass Assn. (Achievement award 1976, Hall of Fame award 1984), N.J. Golf Course Supts. Assn. (hon.), N.J. Acad. Scis., Sigma Xi, Phi Kappa Phi. Mem. LDS Ch. Developer numerous turfgrasses. Home: 4 Delaware Dr East Brunswick NJ 08816-3255 Office: Rutgers U Cook Coll New Brunswick NJ 08903

FUNK, DAVID ALBERT, retired law educator; b. Wooster, Ohio, Apr. 22, 1927; s. Daniel Coyle and Elizabeth Mary (Reese) F.; children—Beverly Joan, Susan Elizabeth, John Ross, Carolyn Louise; m. Sandra Nadine Henselmeier, Oct. 2, 1976. Student, U. Mo., 1945-46, Harvard Coll., 1946; BA in Econs., Coll. of Wooster, 1949; MA, Ohio State U., 1968; JD, Case Western Res. U., 1951, LLM, 1972; LLM, Columbia U., 1973. Bar: Ohio 1951, U.S. Dist. Ct. (no. dist.) Ohio 1962, U.S. Tax Ct. 1963, U.S. Ct. Appeals (6th cir.) 1970, U.S. Supreme Ct. 1971. Ptnr. Funk, Funk & Eberhart, Wooster, Ohio, 1951-72; assoc. prof. law Ind. U. Sch. Law, Indpls., 1973-76, prof., 1976-97, prof. emeritus, 1997—; vis. lectr. Coll. of Wooster, 1962-63; dir. Juridical Sci. Inst., Indpls., 1982—. Author: Oriental Jurisprudence, 1974, Group Dynamic Law, 1982; (with others) Rechtsgeschichte und Rechtssoziologie, 1985, Group Dynamic Law: Exposition and Practice, 1988; contbr. articles to profl. jours. Chmn. bd. trustees Wayne County Law Library Assn., 1956-71; mem. Permanent Jud. Commn., Synod of Ohio, United Presbyn. Ch. in the U.S., 1968. Served to seaman 1st class USNR, 1945-46. Harlan Fiske Stone fellow Columbia U., 1973; recipient Am. Jurisprudence award in Comparative Law, Case Western Res. U., 1970. Mem. Assn. Am. Law Schs. (sec. comparative law sect. 1977-79, chmn. law and religion sect. 1977-81, sec.-treas. law and social sci. sect. 1983-86), Am. Soc. for Legal History, Pi Sigma Alpha. Republican. Home: 6208 N Delaware St Indianapolis IN 46220-1824

FUNK, DOROTHEA, public health nurse; b. St. Louis, Oct. 26, 1916; d. John Arthur and Pearl M. (Dial) Johnson; m. Frank E. Funk, Jan. 3, 1941 (dec. Jan. 1996). Diploma, Leo N. Levi Meml. Hosp., Hot Springs Nat. Park, Ark. RN, Ark. Asst. dir. nursing svc. Helena (Ark.) Hosp.; nurse-investigator Little Rock Health Dept.; pub. health nurse Clark County Health Dept., Arkedelphia, Ark.; nurse coord. for health manpower recruitment Ark. State Nurses Assn.; patient-coord. and liaison nurse Medi-Ctr. of Am., Inc.; health manpower coord. Ark. Nursing Assn., Little Rock, 1970-73; trustee Ark. Nurses Found., Little Rock, 1996. Vol., field rep. Women's Meml.-Meml. Found. Ind., Arlington, Va.; mem. Ark. Gov.'s Commn. on Status of Women; mem. Spl. Task Force on Delivery of Health Care; active ARC, Ark. Red Cross. Lt. Nurse Corps, U.S. Army, World War II. Recipient Health Planning award in Ark., 1979, Jerome S. Levy award Ctr. Ark. Health Systems Agy., 1983, Lifetime Achievement award Ark. Nurses Coalition, 1994, Disting. Svc. award Ark. Nurses Found., 1998. Mem. ANA, Ark. State Nurses Assn. (charter mem., pres. dist. 10 1971-73, state pres., state treas., chmn. pub. health nursing, trustee 1996-97), Ark. Pub. Health Assn. (charter mem. 1948-98, hon. life mem.), Bus. and Profl. Women's Club (co-dir. S.W. Ark. Fedn., club pres.), Altrusa Internat. (club treas. 1969-71), Am. Bus. Women's Assn., North Little Rock Women's City Club. Home: Lakewood House 701 4801 N Hills Blvd North Little Rock AR 72116-7618

FUNK, FRANK E., retired university dean; b. Jersey City, Feb. 21, 1923; s. Frank and Elsa A. (Bohne) F.; m. Ruth Christy, Feb. 3, 1977; children: Steven Eric, Karen Christine. B.S., Syracuse (N.Y.) U., 1949, M.S., 1952; Ph.D. in Bus. and Indsl. Communication, Purdue U., 1956. Instr. speech, dir. radio workshop Lehigh U., Bethlehem, Pa., 1949-52; grad. teaching asst., then instr. speech Purdue U., 1952-56; mem. faculty Syracuse U., 1956-89; assoc. prof. speech Syracuse U. (Coll. Visual and Performing Arts), 1974-89; chmn. dept. pub. address Syracuse U. (Sch. Speech and Dramatic Art), 1962-65; dean Syracuse U. (Univ. Coll.), 1970-88, dir. continuing edn., 1973-88, prof. emeritus, 1989—; pres. Syracuse U. Theatre Corp., 1973-88, Univ. Council Edn. Pub. Responsibility, 1972-73; adv. bd. WAER, campus FM sta., 1972-73, lectr. U.N.C. Wilmington, 1992-96, vice chancellor search com., 1993. Author articles. Mem. adv. bd. Hendricks Chapel, 1978-83, chmn., 1980-83; bd. dirs. PEACE, Inc., 1969-72; bd. dirs., chmn. coms. Syracuse United Way; v.p. planning allocations Syrause United Way, 1981-83; bd. visitors U. Pitts., 1981-86; bd. dirs. Manlius Pebble Hill Sch., 1984-89, sec. exec. com., 1988-89; mem. com. 1st Presbyn. Ch., Wilmington, N.C., 1992—, elder, 1994-97; narrator Wilmington Symphony Orch., 1993; residential chair Cape Fear Area United Way, 1995; v.p. Alliance for Regional Concert Hall, 1998—. Served as officer USAAF, 1943-45, ETO. Decorated Air medal; fellow Creative Problems-Solving Inst., 1958; fellow Found. Econ. Edn. Bus., summer 1957. Mem. NEA, Assn. Continuing Higher Edn. (dir. 1973-76, regional chmn. 1973-74, chmn. nominating com. 1978, nat. program chmn. 1979, pres. 1981, Leadership award 1988), Nat. Univ. Continuing Edn. Assn. (bd. dirs. 1986-88, chpt. com. chmn., Walton S. Bittner citation 1988), Am. Assn. Adult and Continuing Edn., Sta. WHQR Wilmington N.C. (bd. dirs. 1992-98, pres. 1995-97), Wilmington R.R. Mus. Found. (trustee 1994—, pres. 1996—), Cape Fear Model R.R. Club (treas. 1994—). Democrat. Home: Maritime Sq # 1 622 S 2nd St Wilmington NC 28401-5038

FUNK, JAMES WILLIAM, JR., insurance agency administrator, business owner; b. Vincennes, Ind., May 31, 1947; s. James William and Elizabeth (Bauer) F.; m. Janis Burrell, Aug. 11, 1973; children: Christopher James, Kelly Elizabeth. BA, Butler U., Indpls., 1969. Cert. ins. counselor, 1991. Mem. campaign staff U.S. Senator Birch Bayh, Indpls., 1968; bus. cons. Dun & Bradstreet, Inc., Indpls., 1969-71; dir. ops. Terry Properties, Inc., Springfield, Ill., 1971-72; pers. mgr. Am. Underwriters, Inc., Indpls., 1972-73, adminstrv. asst. to pres., 1973-75, asst. sec., 1975-78, v.p. pub. rels., 1978-79; adminstrv. mgr. Affiliated Agys., Inc., Indpls., 1979-83; ind. agt., v.p., sec. Ctrl. Ins. Assocs., Inc., 1993-98, pres., 1999—; instr. Ins. Edn. A.D. Banker Co., 1997—; owner Bauer Bros. Exploration Co.; lectr., instr. A.D. Banker Co., 1997—. Sec., treas. Ctrl. North Civic Assn., Indpls., 1976, pres. 1977-78; bd. dirs. Ind. Amateur Baseball Assn., 1993—, sec. 1999; active Bishop Chaters H.S. PTO, 1995-97, pres. 1997—. Mem. Ind. Soc. Chgo., Profl. Ins. Agts Ind. (v.p. 1984-85, pres. 1986-87, chmn. legis. com., treas. polit. action com., bd. dirs. 1982-88, 99—, agt. of yr. 1990), Indpls. Children's Mus., Indpls. Zool. Soc., Preussian Benefit Soc., Heimaths Benefit Soc., Butler Univ. Pres.'s Club, K.C. Roman Catholic. Home: 3560 Clearwater Cir Indianapolis IN 46240-2999 Office: 3520 E 96th St Ste A-2 Indianapolis IN 46240-3734

FUNK, JERRY A., federal judge; b. 1945. BA, U. Ga., 1967; LLB, Samford U., 1970. Pvt. practice, 1970-93; bankruptcy judge U.S. Bankruptcy Ct. (mid. dist.) Fla., Jacksonville, 1993—. Active Pine Castle Sch. With USAR, 1968-74. Mem. Fla. Bar Assn., Jacksonville Bar Assn., N.E. Fla. Builders Assn., Jacksonville Assn. Mortgage Brokers, Jacksonville Jewish Ctr., Jacksonville Quarterback Club, C. of C., Scottish Rite, Masons, Morocco Temple. Fax: 904-232-2153. Office: 211 US Courthouse 311 W Monroe St Jacksonville FL 32202

FUNK, JOHN WILLIAM, emergency vehicle manufacturing executive, packaging company executive, lawyer; b. Detroit, Apr. 6, 1937; s. Wilson S. and Myrtle M. (Johnston) F.; m. Carol E. Sutton, June 14, 1958; children: Michael John, Steven John, David John, Susan Elizabeth; m. Helen Rebecca Dutko, July 5, 1980. Student, Gen. Motors Inst., Flint, Mich., 1955-57; BBA, U. Mich, 1959, MBA, JD, 1962. Bar: N.Y. 1962. Assoc. Hodgson, Russ, Andrews, Woods & Goodyear, Buffalo, 1962-66; staff atty. Kroger Co., Cin., 1966-68; counsel Litton Industries, Milw. and Hartford, Conn., 1969-72; gen. counsel, v.p. internat. Jeffrey Galion, Columbus, Ohio, 1972-77; gen. counsel, sec. Wendy's Internat., Inc., Columbus, 1977-80, exec. v.p., chief adminstrv. officer, sec., 1980-86, dir., 1981-87; pres. Vanner, Inc., Columbus, 1986-87, Pressware Internat., Inc., Columbus, 1987-91, Horton Emergency Vehicles Co., Columbus, 1987-97, G-Pax Internat., Columbus, 1990-98; dir. Enzymol Internat., Inc., Hayward Distributing, Co., Shamrock Comms., Inc. Dir. Players Theatre, Columbus, 1991-93. Mem. N.Y. State Bar Assn., Lakes Golf and Country Club, Phi Kappa Phi. Roman Catholic. Avocations: tennis, golf, skiing. Home: 1431 Jewett Rd Powell OH 43065-9735 also: GPAX Internat Inc 3900 Bus Park Dr Columbus OH 43204*

FUNK, SHERMAN MAXWELL, former government official, writer, consultant; b. N.Y.C., Nov. 13, 1925; s. Bernard and Dorothy (Arkin) F.; m. Elaine Myrl Bayer, Mar. 6, 1953 (dec. 1977); children: Katherine Sara, Bernard Eugene; m. Sylvia Grunbaum Straka, June 3, 1978; children Eric, Marc, Paul. A.B., Harvard U., 1950; postgrad., Columbia U., 1956; U. Ariz., 1958. Salesman, sales exec. Bernard Funk Co., N.Y.C., 1950-54; history tchr. Catskill (N.Y.) High Sch., 1954-57; polit. sci. teaching asst. U. Ariz., Tucson, 1957-58; mgmt. intern USAF Hdqrs., Washington, 1958, war planning officer, mgmt. analyst, 1958-63, chief Air Force Mgmt. Improvement Programs Office, 1963-67, chief Air Force Cost Reduction Office, 1967-70; successively asst. dir. adminstrn. and program devel., dir. rsch. and program devel., asst. dir. planning and evaluation Office Minority Bus. Enterprise, Dept. Commerce, 1970-79; spl. asst. for small bus. Dept. Energy, 1979-81; insp. gen. Dept. Commerce, 1981-87; insp. gen. Dept. State, 1987-94, adviser to fgn. govts. on anti-corruption efforts, 1994—; vice chmn. Pres.'s Coun. on Integrity and Efficiency, 1989-90; TV commentator. Contbr. articles to profl. jours., major newspapers. Mem. Bowie City Council, (Md.), 1963-65, chmn. human relations com., 1964-65, chmn. charter rev. com., 1968; pres. Bethesda Jewish Congregation, 1986. Served with inf. AUS, 1943-46. Decorated Purple Heart; recipient Presdl. Unit Citation, spl. award Sec. Air Force, 1968, prizes Washington-Md.-Del Press Assn., 1970, 71, 73, 75, Silver medal Commerce Dept., 1972, Disting. honor award State Dept., 1992. Mem. Fed. Investigators Assn. Office: 5000 Battery Ln Ste 504 Bethesda MD 20814-2658 *My years in government were marked by paradox: I worked with some extraordinarily able people and with important and challenging programs. Yet I increasingly came to doubt the ability of these and other federal programs to solve many national ills. Too many of them are subverted externally by political pork and internally by waste, fraud and don't-rock-the boat thinking. As an Inspector General, under three pres., I tried to fight such abuse, and to help change the poor image of federal service-both appointive and career-which scares off exactly the kind of bright and aggressive talent needed in government. As a private citzen now, free of the constraints levied on appointees, I shall continue this fight with redoubled vigor.*

FUNK, VICKI JANE, librarian; b. Frankfurt am Main, Hesse, Fed. Republic of Germany, Apr. 7, 1951; d. George N. and Maymie Lou Funk; m. David Robert Koble, July 11, 1986. BS, Ind. State U., 1971; MLS, Okla. U., 1975; cert. in comparative libraries, Oxford U., Eng., Summer 1978; cert. in Scottish lit., St. Andrews U., Scotland, Summer 1985. Elem. open concept team tchr. Plainfield (Ind.) Pub. Schs., 1971-72; media specialist, tchr. elem. schs. Enid (Okla.) Pub. Schs., 1972-73, librarian, 1973-74; libr. media specialist Bartlesville (Okla.) Sr. H.S., 1975-96; chmn. library evaluation teams North Cen. Assn., Okla., 1982-86; pres. V.I.E.W. adv. bd. Okla. State Dept. Vocat. Edn., 1980-81; tchr. pub. library continuing adult edn. program, Bartlesville, 1986. Storyteller Ednl. TV Bartlesville Cable, 1975-77, Oral Children's Program Pub. Library, 1985-86; book reviewer Okla. State Dept. Libraries "Gushers and Dusters", 1986-87; mem. book rev. selection com. Bartlesville Pub. Library. V.P. Friends of the Pub. Library, Bartlesville, 1986. Recipient Outstanding Svc. award Okla. Dept. Vocat. Edn., 1981; Emiline Libr. scholar Ind. State U., 1970; Innovative Edn. grantee Bartlesville Pub. Edn. Found., 1990, 91. Mem. NEA, AAUW (edn. officer 1980-81), Okla. Edn. Assn., Bartlesville Edn. Assn., Bartlesville Art Assn., Okla. Libr. Assn., Kappa Kappa Iota (v.p. 1990-91, secd. 1996-98). Democrat. Presbyterian. Avocations: bridge, traveling, skiing, acting, oil painting.

FUNK, WILLIAM HENRY, environmental engineering educator; b. Ephraim, Utah, June 10, 1933; s. William George and Henrietta (Hackwell) F.; m. Ruth Sherry Mellor, Sept. 19, 1964 (dec.); 1 dau., Cynthia Lynn; m. Lynn Bridget Robson, Mar. 30, 1996. B.S. in Biol. Sci, U. Utah, 1955, M.S. in Zoology, 1963, Ph.D. in Limnology, 1966. Tchr. sci., math. Salt Lake City Schs., 1957-60; research asst. U. Utah, Salt Lake City, 1961-63; head sci. dept. N.W. Jr. High Sch., Salt Lake City, 1961-63; mem. faculty Wash. State U., Pullman, 1966-99; assoc. prof. environ. engring. Wash. State U., 1971-75, prof., 1975-99, chmn. environ. sci./regional planning program, 1979-81; dir. Environ. Research Center, 1980-83, State of Wash. Water Research Ctr., 1981-99; cons. U.S. Army C.E., Walla Walla, Wash., 1970-74, Harstad Engrs., Seattle, 1971-72, Boise Cascde Corp., Seattle, 1971-72, Wash. Dept. Ecology, Olympia, 1971-72, ORB Corp., Renton, Wash., 1972-73, U.S. Civil Svc., Seattle, Chgo., 1972-74; mem. High Level Nuclear Waste Bd., Wash., 1986-89; mem. Wash. 2010 Com., 1989; mem. Pure Water 2000 Steering Com., 1990, Inst. Resource Mgmt.; co-founder Terrene Inst., Washington, 1991, pres., 1993—. Author publs. on water pollution control and lake restoration. Served to capt. USNR, 1955-88. Grantee NSF Summer Inst., 1961, U.S. Army C.E., 1970-74, 94-96, 97-98, Office Water Resources Rsch., 1971-72, 73-76, EPA, 1980-83, 93-94, 95-96, U.S. Geol. Survey, 1983-94, 95-96, 97-98, 99-00, Nat. Parks Svc., 1985-87, Colville Confederated Tribes, 1990-92, Nez Pierce Tribe, 1992-95, Wash. Conservation Commn., 1992-95, Clearwater Co., 1992-93, Idaho Dept. Environ. Quality, 1995-96, U.S. Bur. Reclamation, 1995-98; USPHS fellow, 1963; recipient Pres.'s Disting. Faculty award Wash. State U., 1984. Mem. Naval Res. Officers Assn. (chpt. pres. 1969), Res Officers Assn. (U.S. Naval Acad. info. officer 1973-76), N.Am. Lake Mgmt. Soc. (pres. 1984-85, Secchi Disk award 1988), Pacific N.W. Pollution Control Assn. (editor 1969-77, pres.-elect 1982-83, pres. 1983-84), Water Pollution Control Fedn. (Arthur S. Bedell award Pacific N.W. assn. 1976, nat. bd. dirs. 1978-81, bd. dirs. Rsch. Found. 1990-92), Nat. Assn. Water Inst. Dirs. (chair 1985-87, bd. dirs. univ. council on water resources 1986-89), Wash. Lakes Protection Assn. (co-founder 1986, Friend of Lakes award 1999), Am. Water Resources Assn. (v.p. Wash. sect. 1988), Am. Soc. Limnology and Oceanography, Am. Micros. Soc., N.W. Sci. Assn., North Am. Lake Mgmt. Soc. (co-founder 1972), Sigma Xi, Phi Sigma. Home: 330 SW Kimball Ct Pullman WA 99163-2176

FUNKA, THOMAS HOWARD, minister; b. Washington, Pa., July 14, 1946; s. Carl Thomas and Anna Rosella (Deyell) F.; m. Nancy Jane Caldwell, June 14, 1976; children: Andrew B., Gregory T. BA, Bethany Coll., 1968; MDiv, Pitts. Theol. Sem., 1974. Ordained to ministry United Meth. Ch., 1975. Pastor Anne Ashley United Meth. Ch., Munhall, Pa., 1975-79, Emerickville United Meth. Ch., Brookville, Pa., 1979-82, Grace United Meth. Ch., Meadville, Pa., 1982-91, McKean (Pa.) United Meth. Ch., 1991-94, Christ U. Meth. Ch., Bethel Park, Pa., 1995—. Republican. Home: 3675 Maplevue Dr Bethel Park PA 15102-1458 Office: 44 Highland Rd Bethel Park PA 15102-1806 *The individual becomes great only when one realizes his or her dependence on God's power manifested through the Holy Spirit. We accomplish great things when we let God work through us, doing His will and purpose.*

FUNKHOUSER, LAWRENCE WILLIAM, retired geologist; b. Napoleon, Ohio, June 9, 1921; s. Edward A. and Margaret M. (Reinking) F.; m. Jean Garnet Cooper, June 1, 1946; children: Donald W., Thomas E., David P., Karen J. AB in Geology, Oberlin Coll, 1943; MS in Geology, Stanford U., 1948; DSc (hon.), Oberlin Coll., 1990. Geologist, dist. geologist The Calif. Co., New Orleans, 1948-58, div. exploration supt., 1958-61; div. exploration supt., v.p. exploration Standard Oil Co. Tex., Midland and Houston, 1961-66; v.p. exploration Standard Oil Co. Calif., San Francisco, 1968-73, dir., v.p. exploration, 1973-77; dir., v.p. exploration and prodn. Chevron Corp., San Francisco, 1978-86, ret., 1986; v.p., dir. Energy Exploration Mgmt. Co., Houston, 1989-92; mem. Nat. Research Council Commn. on Physical Sci., Math. and Resources, 1987-90. Mem. Am. Assn. Petroleum Geologists (hon., pres.-elect 1986-87, pres. 1987-88), Am. Assn. Petroleum Geologists Found. (chmn. 1991—), Geol. Soc. Am., Phi Beta Kappa, Sigma Xi. Presbyterian. Home: 283 Park Ln Atherton CA 94027-5448 Office: PO Box 1088 Menlo Park CA 94026-1088

FUNKOUSER, MARK, auditor, municipal official; b. New Brighton, Pa., Oct. 4, 1949. BA in Polit. Sci., Thiel Coll., 1971; MSW, W. Va. U., 1976; MBA, Tenn. State U., 1985. Cert. legal auditor. Head performance audit group divsn. of state audit State of Tenn., 1978-88; city auditor City of Kansas City, 1988—. Editor: Local Govt. Auditing Quarterly; contbr. articles to profl. jours. Office: City of Kansas City Office of the City Auditor City Hall 24th Fl 414 E 12th St Kansas City MO 64106-2702*

FUNSETH, ROBERT LLOYD ERIC MARTIN, international consultant, lecturer, retired senior foreign service officer; b. International Falls, Minn., May 10, 1926; s. Martin Emmanuel and Agnes (Guibault) F.; m. Marilyn Ann Schuelke, Mar. 23, 1957; 1 child, Eric Christian. B.A., Hobart Coll., 1948, postgrad., 1950-51; postgrad., Cornell U., 1950, 51, Sch. Advanced Internat. Studies, Johns Hopkins U., 1951-52; M.S., George Washington U., 1969; LL.D, Hobart and William Smith Colls., 1978. Editor Coachella Desert Barnacle, (Calif.), 1948; mng. editor Anaheim Gazette, (Calif.), 1948-50; corr. AP, 1950; resident tutor Hobart Coll., 1950-51; info. officer U.S. Mut. Security Agy., 1952-53; editor USIA, 1953-54; joined U.S. Fgn. Service, 1954; advanced to rank of minister-counselor Career Sr. Fgn. Service; vice consul Tehran, Tabriz, Azerbaijan and Kurdistan, Iran, 1954-56; 3d sec. Am. embassy, Beirut, 1957-59; UN polit. affairs officer Dept. State, 1959-61; Am. consul (Bordeaux), France, 1961-64; Portuguese desk officer Dept. State, Washington, 1964-66; mem. U.S. del. 20th UN Gen. Assembly, 1965; dep. dir. Iberian affairs Dept. State, 1966-68; assigned to Nat. War Coll., 1968-69; dir. mgmt. U.S. diplomatic and consular posts Dept. State, Mex. and Central Am., 1969-70; coordinator Cuban affairs Dept. State, 1970-72, sr. fgn. service insp., 1972-73; counselor Am. embassy, Ottawa, Ont., Can., 1973-74; dep. dept. spokesman and dir. office of press relations Dept. State, Washington, 1974-75, dept. spokesman and spl. asst. to sec. of state for press relations, 1975-77, dir. office No. European affairs, 1977-82; dep. asst. sec. for refugee resettlement Dept. State, 1982-83, sr. dep. asst. sec. Bur. Refugee Programs, 1983-91, cons., 1991—; detailed to U.S. Falkland Island Peace Mission to London and Buenos Aires, 1982; vis. disting. alumni scholar in residence Hobart and William Smith Colls., 1978, Nat. Cathedral Assn.; vis. fellow Woodrow Wilson Found., Princeton U.; lectr. Am. studies U. Tabriz, 1955-56; mem. numerous U.S. Delegations, 1976-89 including NATO Ministerial Meetings in Ottawa, Brussels, Oslo, U.S. China Consultations, Beijing, former Pres. Ford's 1975 visit to Philippines, OECD, Paris, SALT, Moscow, U.S.-So. Africa Initiative, Nairobi, Dar es Salam, Lusaka, Kinshasa, Monrovia, Dakar, UN Trade and Devel. Conf., Kenya, OAS Ministerial Meeting, Santiago, Chile, 1976 econ. summit former Pres. Ford Puerto Rico, 1st U.S. South African Ministerial meeting, Grafenau, Germany, U.S.-Iran Joint Commn., Tehran, U.S. Bilateral Consultations with Afghanistan and Pakistan, 1976 Inauguration Mexican Pres. Lopez-Portillo; head U.S. dels. U.S.-Vietnamese Refugee Consultations, Geneva, Switzerland, 1982-90; head U.S. del., U.S.-Vietnamese negotiations, Resettlement Vietnamese Polit. Prisoners, Hanoi, Vietnam, 1988, 89, 2d internat. conf. Indochinese Refugees, Geneva, 1989. Bd. dirs. Episcopal Ch. Presiding Bishop's Fund for World Relief; bd. govs. Diplomatic & Consular Officers Ret., trustee Diplomatic & Consular Officers Ret.- Bacon House Found.; U.S. observer Internat. Cath. Migration Commn. Conf., Vatican City, 1990; mem. peace commn. Episcopal Diocese of Washington. Served to lt. (j.g.) USNR, 1943-46, PTO. Recipient Outstanding Service commendation Am. Forces Spl. Command, Middle East, 1958, Disting. and Superior Honor Group awards Dept. State, 1959, 61, 70, Superior Honor award Dept. State, 1977, Sesquicentennial award Hobart Coll., 1972, Presdl. honor awards Sr. Fgn. Svc., 1986, 88, 91, Disting. Honor award Dept. State, 1989 , Wilbur Carr disting. svc. award Dept. State, 1991, medal of excellence Hobart Coll. Alumni Assn., 1997. Mem. Am. Fgn. Svc. Assn., Assn. Diplomatic Studies, Hobart Coll. Alumni Assn. (medal of Excellence 1997), Johns Hopkins Alumni Assn. (exec. coun. 1968-70), Sch. Advanced Studies Alumni Assn. (pres., mem. adv. coun. 1969, 70), George Washingon U. Alumni Assn., Nat. War Coll. Alumni Assn., Diplomatic and Consular Officers Retired (Dacor, sec., bd. govs.), Ebenezer Sch. Alumni Assn., West Seneca (N.Y.) Hist. Soc., Mil. Order of Carabao, Phi Sigma Kappa. Club: Dacor-Bacon House, Am. Fgn. Service. Office: 4625 41st St N Arlington VA 22207-2938

FUNSTON, GARY STEPHEN, publishing and advertising executive; b. Phila., July 7, 1951; s. Ralph Gaylord and Adele Rose (DeCintio) F.; m. Nancy Eileen Clark (div. 1974); 1 child, Stephen Blake. Student, DeAnza Coll., 1969-73, San Jose State U., 1973-75, London Bus. Sch., 1995; student exec. devel. program, Cornell U., 1996. Store mgr. Smith & Foley Shoes Inc., Sunnyvale, Calif., 1970-75; sales rep. The Hoover Co., San Jose, Calif., 1975-78, GTE Directories Corp., Santa Clara, Calif., 1978-81; ptnr., sec., treas. Mailco Advt. Inc., Milpitas, Calif., 1981-83; owner, cons. ADCOM, San Jose, 1983-85; dir. sales mgr. Lomar Trans Western Publs., Ft. Lauderdale, Fla., 1985-87; mgr. sales, mktg. Ameritel, San Diego, 1987-89; regional sales dir. United Advt. Publs., San Leandro, Calif., 1989-98; dist. sales mgr. Web Svc. Co., Hayward, Calif., 1998—; sales cons. Republic Telcom, San Jose, 1983-84; mgmt. cons. Norcal Directory Co., San Jose, 1984-85; advt. cons. Yellow Page Programs, San Jose, 1983-85; owner West Coast Aircraft, Hayward, Calif., 1996—. Contbr. articles to profl. jours. Mem. CAP, Mountain View, Calif., 1983-84; com. mem. Housing Ind. Found., San Jose, 1991-97, dinner sponsor, 1991-97, fundraiser, 1991-97. Mem. Calif. Apt. Assn. (suppliers coun. 1990—, chmn. suppliers com. 1993, 95, 96, industry stds. com. 1994, mem. exec. com. 1995, 96, bd. dirs. 1995, 96), Solano-Napa Rental Housing Assn., Tri-County Apt. Assn. (com. mem. 1989—), Rental Housing Owners Assn. So. Alameda County (bd. dirs. 1994, Mem. of Yr. award 1992), Highland Swingers Golf Club (treas. 1990—). Republican. Roman Catholic. Avocations: golf, health club, concerts, dining out, flying. Home: 22135 Sevilla Rd Apt 36 Hayward CA 94541-2861 Office: West Coast Aircraft 21593 Skywest Dr Hayward CA 94541

FUOCO, PHILIP STEPHEN, lawyer; b. Riverside, N.J., Oct. 28, 1946; s. Francis and Mary Helen Fuoco; m. Carol Freeman, June 7, 1969; 1 child. BA in Philosophy, U. Notre Dame, 1968; JD, Villanova (Pa.) U., 1971. Bar: N.J. 1972, U.S. Dist. Ct. N.J. 1972, Pa. 1973, U.S. Dist. Ct. (ea. dist.) Pa. 1975, U.S. Ct. Appeals (3d cir.) 1977, U.S. Supreme Ct. 1980; cert. criminal trial atty. N.J. Supreme Ct. Trial atty. civil rights div. U.S. Dept. Justice, Washington, 1971-75; asst. U.S. atty. U.S. Dist. Ct. (ea. dist.) Pa., Phila., 1975; pvt. practice N.J., 1975—; adj. prof. law Rutgers U., Camden, 1997—. Contbr. articles to profl. jours. and law revs. Bd. dirs. Steininger Ctr., 1990-92, Haddonfield Zoning Bd., 1984-88; mem. Haddonfield Environ. Commn., 1991-93; apptd. mem. com. on model jury charges-criminal N.J. Supreme Ct., 1996, apptd. mem. dist. IV ethics com., 1997, steering com. First Night Haddonfield, 1999—. Fellow NEH, 1978. Mem. ABA, ACLU, Nat. Assn. Dist. Attys., Nat. Assn. Criminal Def. Lawyers, Camden County Bar Assn. (trustee 1986-89), Assn. Criminal Def. Lawyers N.J., N.J. Bar Assn., Camden County Inns of Ct., Lions (Haddonfield pres. 1986-87). Office: 24 Wilkins Ave Haddonfield NJ 08033-2406

FUQUA, CHARLES JOHN, classics educator; b. Paris, France, Oct. 5, 1935; s. John Howe and Gillian Elynor (Quennell) F.; m. Mary Louise Morse, Aug. 26, 1961; children—Andrew Morse, David Reed, Gillian Quennell. B.A. magna cum laude, Princeton, 1957; M.A., Cornell U., 1962, Ph.D., 1964. Instr. classics Dartmouth Coll., Hanover, N.H., 1964; asst. prof. Dartmouth Coll., 1965-66; assoc. prof. classics, chmn. dept. classics Williams Coll., Williamstown, Mass., 1966-72; Garfield prof. ancient langs., chmn. dept. classics Williams Coll., 1972-86; Mem. adv. council Am. Acad. in Rome, 1966, chmn. exec. com., 1974. Served to lt. (j.g.) USNR, 1957-60. Mem. Am. Philol. Assn., Classical Assn. New Eng., Classical Assn. Mass., Vergilian Soc., Phi Beta Kappa, Phi Kappa Phi. Home: 96 Grandview Dr Williamstown MA 01267-2528

FUQUA, JANE BOYD, principal; b. Huntingdon, Tenn., Jan. 1, 1944; d. Joshua Rieff Sr. and Ann Louise Devault Boud; m. C. Mac Fuqua, June 30, 1961; children: Kelly A., Kasey J., Connie L. AS, Kennesaw Coll., 1972; BS, Ga. State U., 1974; MS, U. Tenn., 1981; EdS, Jacksonville State U., 1989. Adminstrv. asst. Oak Ridge (Tenn.) Inst. Nuclear Studies, 1962-63; tchr. Cobb County Schs., Marietta, Ga., 1974-75, 83-85, Oak Ridge Schs., 1975-83, Kennesaw Coll. & State U., Marietta, 1985-87; asst. prin. Cobb County Schs., 1987-94; prin. Nash Mid. Sch., Marietta, 1994-96, North Forsyth Mid. Sch., Cumming, Ga., 1996—; bd. dirs. Ga. Mid. Sch. Assn., reginoal liaison, 1999—. contbr. articles to profl. jours. Com. chair Altrusa Internat. Svc. Orgn., Marietta, 1992-96. Mem. Nat. Assn. Secondary Sch. Prins, Profl. Assn. Ga. Educators, Ga. Assn. Ednl. Leaders, Phi Kappa Phi. Methodist. Avocations: collecting antique art glass & pottery, reading, travel. Office: North Forsyth Mid Sch 3645 Coal Mountain Rd Cumming GA 30040

FURASH, EDWARD E., investment company executive, writer, lecturer; b. Boston, Oct. 31, 1934; s. Moses Harry Furash and Sara (Jacobs) Dorfman; m. Elizabeth Louise Wilson, Jan. 2, 1959; children: Jennifer Lee, Jonathan Wilson, James Shortlidge. AB magna cum laude, Harvard Coll., 1956; MBA, U. Pa., 1958; postgrad., Harvard Bus. Sch., Boston, 1959-67. Rsch. asst. Harvard Grad. Sch. Bus., Boston, 1958-59; asst. editor Harvard Bus. Review, Boston, 1959-62; instr. bus. adminstrn. Harvard Grad. Sch. Bus., Boston, 1961-62; sec. com. on. space Am. Acad. Arts & Scis., Boston, 1962-64; sr. staff assoc., bus. mgr. Arthur D. Little, Inc., Cambridge, Mass., 1964-67; v.p. mktg. Nat. Shawmut Bank Boston, 1967-72, sr. v.p. mktg., 1972-74;

sr. v.p. corp. planning Shawmut Corp. Boston, 1972-78; mng. dir. Golembe Assocs., Washington, 1978-80; chmn. Furash & Co., Washington, 1980-98; vice chmn. dir. Headway Corp. Resources, Inc., N.Y.C., 1995-98; CEO Furash Holdings, Washington, 1994—; chmn. Monument Fin. Group, Alexandria, Va., 1999—; bd. dirs. Pa. Bus. Bank; interviewed on TV ABC, CBS, CNBC, PBS; lectr. Williams Sch. of Banking, 1974-78, Am. Inst. Banking, 1968-98, Stonier Sch. Banking, 1994, 95. Gen. editor: Technology Space & Soc.; contbr. (newspapers, mags.) including Wall St. Jour., Bus. Week, Bankers Mag., Am. Banker, RMA Jour. Credit and Risk Mgmt., and many others; contbr. to profl. jours. Chmn. approp. com. Town of Lexington, Mass., 1967-78; participant Active Lexington Town Meetings, 1969-78; trustee The Carroll Sch., Lincoln, Mass., 1976—. Shell Oil Found. fellow U. Pa., 1957-58. Mem. Nat. Arts Club, City Club Washington, Harvard Club, Nat. Press Club, Harvard Club of Boston, Belle Haven Country Club, The Penn Club, Beta Gamma Sigma. Republican. E-mail efurash@monfin.com. Office: Monument Financial Grp 1199 N Fairfax Ste 800 Alexandria VA 22314

FURBUSH, DAVID MALCOLM, lawyer; b. Palo Alto, Calif., Mar. 25, 1954; s. Malcolm Harvey and Margaret (McKittrick) F. BA, Harvard U., 1975, JD, 1978. Bar: Calif. 1978, U.S. Dist. Ct. (no. dist.) Calif. 1978, U.S. Ct. Appeals (9th cir.) 1987, U.S. Supreme Ct. 1990. Assoc. Chickering & Gregory, San Francisco, 1978-81, Brobeck, Phleger & Harrison, San Francisco, 1981-85; ptnr. Brobeck, Phleger & Harrison, Palo Alto, Calif., 1985—. Office: Brobeck Phleger & Harrison Two Embarcadero Pl 2200 Geng Rd Palo Alto CA 94303-3322

FURCHGOTT, DAVID MAX, cultural programs executive; b. Charleston, S.C., May 24, 1947; s. Max and Marcelle Dorothy (Kleinzahler) F.; m. Adrienne Dorn, Jan. 6, 1972 (div. Nov. 1976); m. Susan Klebanoff, July 10, 1983 (div. May 1987); m. Fetneh Askari Fleischmann, Mar. 31, 1991; 1 child, Shirin Catherine Fleischmann. EdB, U. Miami, 1970; postgrad., Coll. Charleston, 1979. Dir. teen programs Temple Beth Sholom, Miami Beach, Fla., 1968-70; instr., program coord. Coastal Ctr., S.C. Dept. Mental Retardation, Ladson, 1970-71; exec. dir., co-founder Furthur, Inc., Charleston, 1970-72; curator edn., dir. Gallery Sch. Gibbes Mus. Art, Charleston, 1972-74; divsn. dir. cmty. and contemporary arts S.C. Arts Commn., Columbia, 1974-78; pres., exec. dir. Internat. Sculpture Ctr., Washington, 1979-95; pres., CEO, founder Internat. Arts and Artists, Washington, 1995—; cons., panelist Nat. Endowment for the Arts, Washington, 1976-78; cons., spkr. Fuji-Sankei Group, Shiga Prefecture Mus. Art, Otsu City, Shiga, Japan, 1984; cons., advisor Prada! I Pelletieri D'Italia S.p.a., Milan, Italy, 1994-95; visual artistic advisor Spoleto U.S.A., Charleston, 1995-96. Co-initiator Piccolo Spoleto, City of Charleston, 1978; visual arts panelist D.C. Commn. on the Arts, Washington, 1995-99; conscientius objector, 1970-72. Mem. Cosmos Club (art com. 1997). Jewish. E-mail: dfurchgott@aol.com. Home: 3223 Klingle Rd NW Washington DC 20008 Office: Internat Arts & Artists 2nd Fl 3061 M St NW Washington DC 20007

FURCHGOTT, ROBERT FRANCIS, pharmacologist, educator; b. Charleston, S.C., June 4, 1916; married, 1941; 3 children. BS, U. N.C., 1937; PhD in Biochemistry, Northwestern U., 1940; DM (hon.), Autonomous U., Madrid, 1984, U. Lund, 1984; DSc (hon.), U. N.C., 1989, U. Ghent, 1995; postgrad., Mt. Sinai Med. Sch., 1995, Ohio State U., 1996, Med. U. S.C., 1997, Med. Coll. Ohio, 1997, Northwestern U., 1998, U. Coll., London, 1998, Northwe. U., 1998. Rsch. fellow medicine Med. Coll. Cornell U., 1940-43, rsch. assoc., 1943-47, instr. physiology, 1943-48, asst. prof. med. biochemistry, 1947-49; from asst. prof. to assoc. prof. pharmacology Med. Sch. Wash. U., 1949-56; chmn. dept. pharmacology SUNY Health Sci. Ctr., Bklyn., 1956-83, prof., 1956-88, Univ. Disting. prof., 1988—, emeritus prof. pharmacology, 1990—; mem. pharmacol. tng. com. USPHS, 1961-64, mem. pharmacoltoxicol rev. com., 1965-68; Commonwealth fellow, 1962-63; vis. prof. U. Geneva, 1962-63, U. Calif., San Diego, 1971-72, Med. U. S.C., 1980, UCLA, 1980; adj. prof. pharmacology Sch. Medicine, U. Miami, 1989—. Recipient rsch. achievement award Am. Heart Assn., 1990, Bristol-Myers Squibb award for achievement in cariovasc. rsch., 1991, Gairdner Fund Internat. award, 1991, medal N.Y. Acad. Medicine, 1992, Roussel Uclaf prize for rsch. in cell communication and signalling, 1994, Wellcome Gold medal Brit. Pharmacology Soc., 1995, ASPET award for exptl. therapeutics, 1996, Gregory Pincus award for rsch., 1996, Lasker award for med. rsch., 1996, Lucian award, 1997, Nobel prize for medicine, 1998. Mem. AAAS, NAS, Am. Chem. Soc., Am. Soc. Biochemistry, Am. Soc. Pharmacology and Exptl. Therapeutics (pres. 1971-72, Goodman and Gilman award 1984), Harvey Soc., Polish Physiol. Soc. (hon.), Sigma Xi. Office: SUNY Health Sci Ctr Dept of Pharmacology 450 Clarkson Ave # 29 Brooklyn NY 11203-2056

FURCI, JOAN GELORMINO, early childhood education educator; b. Torrington, Conn., Jan. 3, 1939; BS, Western Conn. State Coll., Danbury, 1960; MS, U. Hartford, 1966; Ed.D., Nova U., Ft. Lauderdale, Fla., 1975. Tchr., Conn., 1960-68, dir. Early Childhood Program Univ. Sch., Nova U., 1971-90; asst. prof. Nova Coll., 1990-94, early childhood tchr., N.C. Tng. and Tech. Assistance Ctr., Morganton, 1995—; cons. Early Childhood Program, N.Y., N.C., 1968—; bd. dirs. United Way Child Care Centers, Broward County. Pres. Kids in Distress, 1987-88. Mem. Nat. Assn. for Edn. Young Children, Assn. for Childhood Edn. Internat. Home: 704 Baytree Dr Titusville FL 32780-2310

FURCON, JOHN EDWARD, management and organizational consultant; b. Chgo., Mar. 17, 1942; s. John F. and Lottie (Janik) F.; children: Juliana, Annalisa, Diana; m. Orisha Agatha Kulick, Oct. 28, 1995. BA, DePaul U., 1963, MA, 1965; MBA, U. Chgo., 1970. With Human Resources Ctr. (name formerly Indsl. Relations Ctr.), U. Chgo., 1963-81, project dir., 1966-70, research psychologist, div. dir., 1970-81; with orgn. change practice Harbridge House, Inc., Northbrook, Ill., 1981—, v.p., 1987-93, ptnr., human resource adv. group Coopers & Lybrand, 1993-98; ptnr. Global Human Resource Solutions, Pricewaterhouse Coopers, LLP, 1998—; mem. faculty Traffic Inst., Northwestern U., 1969-84, DePaul U. Sch. for New Learning, 1974-82; cons. bus., ednl. and govt. orgns.; bd. dirs. Bur. of Testing Svcs., 1975-77, Harbridge House, Inc., 1991-97; lectr. in field. Contbr. articles on personnel mgmt. and human resources planning to profl. jours. Active parents bd. Marquette U., 1988-89. Served to lt. AUS, 1963-65. Mem. Soc. Indsl. and Orgnl. Psychology, Indsl. Psychology Assn. Chgo. (chmn. 1973-75), Internat. Assn. Chiefs of Police, Chgo. Coun. Fgn. Rels., World Future Soc., Human Resource Mgmt. Assn. Chgo. Home: PO Box 309 Westmont IL 60559-0309 Office: Global Human Resource Solutions Pricewaterhouse Coopers LLP 203 N La Salle St Chicago IL 60601-1210 Address: PO Box 309 Westmont IL 60559-0309

FUREY, SUSAN MARY, elementary education educator; b. May 13, 1946; d. Thomas James and Elizabeth (Winkelman) Mullan; m. Francis Joseph Furey, Apr., 2, 1977; children: Emmett, Patrick. BS, Cabrini Coll., 1968; MEd, Widener U., 1995, postgrad., 1997—. Cert. elem. tchr., elem. edn. supr. in curriculum and instrn., elem. and secondary prin., asst. supt., Pa. Tchr. S.E. Delco Sch. Dist., Folcroft, Pa., 1968—; bd. dirs. Lower Merion Sch. Dist., 1991-95; expert witness, 1995—. Dir. polit. action Pa. State Edn. Assn., 1993—; v.p. Five County Dem. Women's Coalition, Greater Phila. region, 1996—. Friend Edn. award Lower Merion Edn. Assn., 1995. Mem. Phi Kappa Phi, Kappa Delta Pi. Avocations: aerobics, volunteer work for public education, writing, political action, dancing. Home: 507 Bryn Mawr Ave Bala Cynwyd PA 19004-2526

FURGASON, ROBERT ROY, university president, engineering educator; b. Spokane, Wash., Aug. 2, 1935; s. Roy Elliott and Margaret (O'Halloran) F.; m. Gloria L. Althouse, June 14, 1964; children: Steven Scott, Brian Alan. BSChemE, U. Idaho, 1956, MSCE, 1958; PhD in Chem. Engring., Northwestern U., 1961; postdoctoral, U. Wis., 1961. Registered profl. engr., Idaho. Design engr. Phillips Petroleum Co., Bartlesville, Okla., 1956; rsch. engr. Martin Marietta Co., Denver, 1958; instr. chem. engring. U. Idaho, Moscow, 1957-59, asst. prof., 1961-63, assoc. prof., 1963-67, acting head dept. chem. engring., 1964-65, chmn. dept. chem. engring., 1965-74, prof., 1967-84, dean Coll. Engring., 1974-78, v.p. acad. affairs and rsch., 1978-84; prof., vice chancellor acad. affairs U. Nebr., Lincoln, 1984-90; prof., pres. Tex A&M U.-Corpus Christi, 1990—; NSF advisor scientists and engrs. in econ. devel. program Escuela Politecnica Nacional, Quito, Ecuador, 1973-74, 76; proposal reviewer NSF, 1965-84; program reviewer Clearwater Econ. Devel. Assn., 1978-84; mem. long-range planning commn. Idaho State Bd. Edn., 1978-80, Gov.'s Com. Faculty Salary Equity, 1980, State of Idaho Energy Policy Bd., 1980-84, adv. com. Northwest Power Policy Coun., 1982-84, engring. accreditation commn. Accreditation Bd. Engring. and Tech., 1981-96, exec. bd., 1984-89, vice chmn., 1985-87, chmn., 1988-89, bd. dirs., 1989-95, fellow, 1990, pres., 1993-94; bd. dirs. Hanover Cos.; adv. bd. dirs. NationsBank. Contbr. articles to profl. jours. Chmn. Idaho-Ecuador Ptnrs. of Ams., 1975-77; commr. Moscow Parks and Recreation Commn., 1977-81; mem. charter revision commn. City of Lincoln, 1989-90; chair Nebr. Energy Mgmt. Plan Adv. Com., 1989-90; mem. chem. engring. vis. com. Colo. Sch. Mines, 1989—; mem. exec. adv. bd. Coastal Bend United Way, 1991-93; bd. dirs. S.W. Moscow Cmty. Assn., 1977-84, Am. Festival Ballet, 1978-80, Lincoln Cancer Ctr., 1988-90, Tex. Econ. Edn. Commn., 1991—, Ada Wilson Children's Rehab. Ctr., 1993-96, Tex. State Aquarium, 1994—; adv. bd. Sta. KEDT-TV, Sta. KEDT-FM. Recipient Pub. Svc. award Idaho State Libr. Assn., 1978, Phillip Carrol Nat. award Soc. Advanced Mgmt., 1996, Grinter award Accreditation Bd. Engring. and Tech., 1996; named Citizen of Yr. Kappa Sigma, 1980, Newsmaker of the Yr., Corpus Christi Caller-Times, 1997; Walter P. Murphy fellow. Fellow AIChe (chmn. nat. tech. sessions 1967, sec. dept. heads forum 1971-72, chmn. 1981, nat. vis. lectr. 1977-79, edn. and accreditation com. 1981-92, chair 1989-91, accreditation visitation group 1977—); mem. NSPE, Am. Chem. Soc., Am. Soc. Engring. Edn. (Pacific Northwest coord. effective tchg. 1962-64, bd. dirs. chem. engring. divsn. 1974-77, Centennial medal 1993), Idaho Soc. Profl. Engrs. (No. Idaho chpt. pres. 1970, state pres. 1980, Idaho's Young Engr. of Yr. 1967), Northwest Coll. and Univ. Assn. Scis. (exec. com. bd. dirs. 1976-80, 81-84, chmn. bd. dirs. 1979-80), Corpus Christi C. of C. (bd. dirs. 1990-94), Crucible Club, Wranglers Club, Lions (program chmn., corr. sec., bd. dirs.), Rotary, Sigma Xi, Phi Kappa Phi, Phi Eta Sigma, Sigma Tau. Avocations: piloting, skiing, camping, woodworking. Home: 1334 Sandpiper Dr Corpus Christi TX 78412-3818 Office: Tex A&M U Office of Pres 6300 Ocean Dr Corpus Christi TX 78412-5503

FURGESON, WILLIAM ROYAL, federal judge; b. Lubbock, Tex., Dec. 9, 1941; s. W. Royal and Mary Alyene (Hardwick) F.; m. Marion McElroy, Aug. 15, 1964 (div.); m. Juli Ann Bernat, July 29, 1973; children—Kelly Lynn, Houston, Joshua, Seth, Jill. B.A. in English, Tex. Tech Coll., 1964; J.D. with honors, U. Tex., 1967. Bar: Tex. 1969, U.S. Dist. Ct. (we. dist.) Tex. 1971, U.S. Ct. Appeals (5th cir.) 1974, U.S. Supreme Ct. 1976. Law clk. to presiding justice U.S. Dist. Ct. for No. Dist. Tex., 1969-70; ptnr. Kemp, Smith, Duncan & Hammond, El Paso, Tex., 1970-94; judge U.S. Dist. Ct. (we. dist.) Tex., Midland/Odessa, 1994—. Gen. campaign chmn. El Paso United Way, 1979, 1st v.p., 1980, pres., 1981; mem. Jewish Fedn., El Paso, 1980-86; trustee Baylor U. Coll. Dentistry, 1982-86; chmn. YWCA Capital Devel. Campaign, 1986-87. Served to capt. U.S. Army, 1967-69. Decorated Bronze Star; recipient Service award Social Workers of El Paso, 1982, Faculty award U. Tex. Law Sch., 1983. Mem. El Paso Bar Assn. (pres. 1982-83, Outstanding Young Lawyer award 1972), Am. Law Inst., U. Tex. Law Sch. Assn. (pres. 1978), U. Tex. Law Rev. Assn. (pres. 1982-83), El Paso Legal Assistance Soc. (bd. dirs. 1972-78), NCCJ (chmn. El Paso region 1980), ABA, Fed. Bar Assn. (pres. West Tex. chpt. 1987), Am. Law Inst., Tex. Bar Assn. (sec., treas., chair anti-trust and trade regulation sect. 1985-86), Am. Bar Found., Tex. Bar Found. Democrat. Jewish. Office: US Dist Ct 200 E Wall St Ste 301 Midland TX 79701-5248

FURGIUELE, MARGERY WOOD, vocational educator; b. Munden, Va., Sept. 28, 1919; d. Thomas Jarvis and Helen Godfrey (Ward) Wood; BS, Mary Washington Coll., 1941; postgrad. U. Ala., 1967-68, Catholic U. Am., 1974-76, 80; m. Albert William Furgiuele, June 19, 1943; children—Martha Jane Furgiuele MacDonald, Harriet Randolph. Advt. and reservations sec. Hilton's Vacation Hide-A Way, Moodus, Conn., 1940; sec. TVA, Knoxville, 1941-43; adminstrv. asst., ct. reporter Moody AFB, Valdosta, Ga., 1943-44; tchr. bus. Edenton (N.C.) H.S., 1944-45; tchr. bus., coord. Culpeper (Va.) County High Sch., 1958-82; ret., 1982; tchr. Piedment Tech. Edn. Ctr., 1970—. Co-leader Future Bus. Leaders Am., Culpeper, mem. state bd., 1979-82; state advisor 1978-79, Va. Bus. Edn. Assn. Com. chmn., 1978-79. Certified geneal. record Searcher; author of two books, contbr. articles to profl. jours. Mem. Am. Orchid Soc., African Violet Soc., Country Club (Culpeper). Home: 1630 Stoneybrook Ln Culpeper VA 22701-3336

FURGOL, EDWARD MACKIE, museum curator, historian; b. Utica, N.Y., June 4, 1955; s. Theodore Joseph and Jean Lind (Mackie) F.; m. Mary Theresa Gibbons, Sept. 10, 1981; children: Malcolm John, Katherine Elizabeth, James Philip. BA, Coll. Wooster, 1977; DPhil, U. Oxford, Eng., 1983. Supr., historian Pendle Heritage Centre, Barrowford, Eng., 1982-84; historian Hist. Scotland (formerly Hist. Bldgs. and Monuments Directorate), Edinburgh, Scotland, 1984-86; mus. curator Navy Mus., Washington, 1987—; intern coord. Naval Hist. Ctr., 1995—; vol. cataloguer Nat. Register Archives, Edinburgh, 1984-85; chmn. com. Scottish History Postgrad. Conf., Edinburgh, 1980-81; mem. com. Nat. Covenant Conf., Edinburgh, 1986-88; adviser Women in the Mil., acting dir. Navy Mus., 1997. Author: A Regimental History of the Covenanting Armies, 1639-51, 1990; contbr. articles to profl. jours. DC coord. Md. War of 1812 Initiative, 1997—; mem. bicentennial com. Washington Navy Yard, 1998-99. Grantee Scottish Arts Coun., 1981, Twenty-Seven Found., 1986, Coun. Learned Socs., 1988, Coun. Am. Maritime Mus., 1995; grantee Soc. Antiquaries Scotland, 1983. Fellow Soc. Antiquaries Scotland; mem. Am. Hist. Assn., Soc. History Fed. Govt. Anglican. Avocations: war games, jogging, cooking, gardening. Office: The Navy Mus Washington Navy Yard # 76 Washington DC 20374

FURGURSON, ERNEST BAKER, JR. (PAT FURGURSON), writer; b. Danville, Va., Aug. 29, 1929; s. Ernest Baker and Passie Durham (Ferguson) F.; m. Mary Louise Stallings (div.); children—Ernest Baker III, Elisabeth Glyn; m. Cassie Woodward Thompson, Apr. 21, 1973. Student, Averett Coll., 1948-50; AB, Columbia, 1952, MS, 1953. Reporter Danville comml. appeal Sta. WDVA, 1948-51; with Roanoke (Va.) World-News, 1952, Richmond (Va.) News Leader, 1955-56; reporter, Washington corr. Balt. Sun, 1956-61, chief Moscow bur., 1961-64, White House corr., nat. polit. corr., Saigon corr., nat. affairs columnist, 1964-92, chief Washington bur., 1975-87, assoc. editor, 1987-92; syndicated by L.A. Times Syndicate, 1970-90. Author: Westmoreland: The Inevitable General, 1968, Hard Right: The Rise of Jesse Helms, 1986, Chancellorsville 1963: The Souls of the Brave, 1992, Ashes of Glory: Richmond at War, 1996; contbg. editor Washingtonian mag., 1973-83, Mid-Atlantic Country mag., 1983-96. Dir. Civil War Trust. 1st lt. USMC, 1953-55. Mem. Gridiron Club. Home: 4812 Tilden St NW Washington DC 20016-2330

FURHMAN, HERBERT GARY, police officer; b. Worcester, Mass., May 8, 1952; s. Merton Furhman and Lillian (Moskowitz) Katzenson; m. Liba H. Hekler, June 30, 1974; children: Abby, Michael. BS in Pub. Rels., Boston U., 1974; grad., Conn. Police Acad., 1986. Armed forces asst. field dir. Am. Nat. Red Cross, Ft. Meade, Md., 1974-76; ctr. rep. N.E. Regional Red Cross Blood Program, Boston, 1976-77; pub. info. and devel. officer Waltham (Mass.) Hosp., 1977-79; dir. cmty. rels. and devel. Lynn (Mass.) Hosp., 1979-81; dir. pub. rels. and devel. St. Vincent Hosp., Worcester, Mass., 1981-83; v.p. pub. rels. and devel. New Milford (Conn.) Hosp., 1983-89; police officer Washington (Conn.) Police, 1983—; lt. Conn. State Dept. Corrections, Cheshire, 1991—. Firefighter Gaylordsville Vol. Fire Dept., 1988—, fire police coord., 1997. Recipient Bell Ringer award Publicity Club Boston, 1980, Silver Anvil award Pub. Rels. Soc. Am., 1988. Democrat. Avocations: firearms shooting, hiking, fishing. Home: PO Box 114 Gaylordsville CT 06755-0114 Office: Conn Dept Correction Garner CI Anti Gang Close Custody Unit Newtown CT 06470

FURKA, ÁRPÁD, organic chemist, educator; b. Kristyór, Hunedoara, Romania, Dec. 3, 1931; arrived in Hungary, 1942; s. János and Anna (Petre) F.; m. Erzsébet Szaniszló, Dec. 30, 1959. Diploma in chemistry and physics, U. Szeged, Hungary, 1955, PhD, 1959; DSc (hon.), U. Budapest, Hungary, 1971. H.S. tchr. Áll. Gimnázium, Makó, Hungary, 1955-56; asst. to prof. U. Szeged, 1956-61; rsch. assoc. Peptide Rsch. Group, Budapest, 1961-64; postdoctoral fellow U. Alta., Edmonton, Can., 1964-65; assoc. prof. Eötvös L. U., Budapest, 1966-72, prof. organic chemistry, 1972-95; sr. rsch. fellow Advanced ChemTech Inc., Louisville, 1995—. Author: Organic Chemistry (in Hungarian), 1988; mem. editl. bd. Molecular Diversity, 1995—; patentee in field; contbr. articles to profl. jours. Postdoctoral fellow Nat. Rsch. Coun. Can., 1964; recipient Vinci of Excellence prize Moet Hennessy Louis Vuitton, 1996. Mem. AAAS, Hungarian Chem. Soc., Hungarian Biochem. Soc., European Peptide Soc., N.Y. Acad. Scis., Am. Chem. Soc. Avocations: travel, gardening. Home: 5418 Ye Old Post Rd Louisville KY 40219-2324 Office: Helios Pharms 9800 Bluegrass Pkwy Louisville KY 40299-1906

FURLANE, MARK ELLIOTT, lawyer; b. Joliet, Ill., Aug. 2, 1949; s. Francis Emilio and Tosca (Cipriani) F.; m. Susan M. Keegan, July 4, 1987; children: Gahan Patricia, Michael Keegan. BA magna cum laude, Ctrl. Coll., 1971; JD with honors, George Washington U., 1974; MBA in Finance Specialization, U. Chgo., 1982. Bar: Ill. 1974, U.S. Dist. Ct. (no. dist.) Ill. 1979, U.S. Ct. Appeals (5th, 6th, 7th, 9th and 11th cirs.), U.S. Ct. Mil. Appeals. Ptnr. Gardner Carton & Douglas, Chgo., 1979—. Capt. USMCR. Mem. Fed. Bar Assn. (labor and employment com. 1996—), Chgo. Bar Assn. (chair labor and employment com. 1994-95), GSB Chgo. Club, Rotary One. Democrat. Roman Catholic. E-mail: mfurlane@GCD.com. Office: Gardner Carton & Douglas 321 N Clark St Ste 3200 Chicago IL 60610-4794

FURLAUD, RICHARD MORTIMER, pharmaceutical company executive; b. N.Y.C., Apr. 15, 1923; s. Maxime Hubert and Eleanor (Mortimer) F.; children: Richard Mortimer, Eleanor Jay, Elizabeth Tamsin; m. Isabel Phelps Furlaud. Student, Institut Sillig, Villars, Switzerland; AB, Princeton U., 1944; LLB, Harvard U., 1947. Bar: N.Y. 1949. Assoc. Root, Ballantine, Harlan, Bushby & Palmer, 1947-51; with legal dept. Olin Mathieson Chem. Corp., 1955-56, asst. to exec. v.p. for finance, 1956-57, asst. pres., 1957-59, v.p., 1959-64, gen. counsel, 1957-60, gen. mgr., v.p. internat. div., 1960-64, exec. v.p., 1964-66, now dir., 1964-94; pres., dir. E. R. Squibb & Sons, Inc., 1966-68; pres., chief exec., dir. Squibb Beech-Nut, Inc. (renamed Squibb Corp. 1971), Princeton, N.J., 1968-74; chmn., chief exec., dir. Squibb Corp. (merged with Bristol-Myers Co.), N.Y.C., 1974-89; pres., bd. dirs. Bristol-Myers Co. (renamed Bristol-Myers Squibb Co.), N.Y.C., 1989-91; bd. dirs. Internat. Flavors and Fragrances, Inc. Mem. profl. staff Ho. of Reps. Com. Ways and Means, 1954; chmn. Rockefeller U. Coun.; trustee John M. Olin Found. 1st lt. JAGC U.S. Army, 1951-53. Mem. Assn. Bar City of N.Y., Coun. on Fgn. Rels., Links Club, River Club. Home: PO Box 478 East Hampton NY 11937-0478 Office: Bristol-Myers Squibb Co 150 E 52nd St Fl 12 New York NY 10022-6017

FURLONG, EDWARD V., JR., paper company executive; b. Phila., Feb. 15, 1937; s. Edward V. and Joy (Sadler) F.; m. Rosemary Cerne, Apr. 1968; children: Tracy L., Edward V. III. BA, Princeton U., 1959; MBA, Harvard U., 1963. Successively asst. to pres., treas., exec. v.p. WWF Paper Corp., Bala Cynwyd, Pa., 1963-72, pres., 1972—. Served to lt. j.g. USN, 1959-61. Mem. Nat. Paper Trade Assn. (bd. dirs.), Inst. Dirs. London, Merion Cricket Club, Union League Club, The Ivy Club. Republican. Methodist. Avocations: sailing, tennis, squash. Home: 318 Julip Run Wayne PA 19087-4731 Office: WWF Paper Corp 2 Bala Plz Bala Cynwyd PA 19004-1501*

FURLONG, GEORGE MORGAN, JR., health care foundation executive, retired naval officer; b. Muskogee, Okla., Nov. 23, 1931; s. George M. and Anna (Moore) F.; m. Ryland Hagood Blakey, June 5, 1956; children: Morgan, William. BS in Naval Sci., U.S. Naval Acad., 1956; BS in Aero. Engring., U.S. Naval Postgrad. Sch., 1963. Commd. ensign U.S. Navy, 1956, advanced through grades to rear adm. (upper half), 1981; F-14 program mgr. Comdr. Naval Air Forces, U.S. Pacific Fleet, 1973-74; wing comdr. Attack Carrier Air Wing 14, USS Enterprise, 1974-75; comdg. officer USS Poncantoula, Pearl Harbor, Hawaii, 1975-76, USS Independence, Norfolk, Va., 1977-78; chief of staff U.S. Sixth Fleet, Gaeta, Italy, 1978-80; dir. Air Warfare Systems Analysis Staff, Office Chief of Naval Ops., Washington, 1980-81; comdr. Fighter Airborne Early Warning Wing, U.S. Pacific Fleet, Naval Air Sta., Miramar, San Diego, 1981-83; dep. chief Naval Edn. and Tng., Pensacola, Fla., 1983-85; ret., 1986; exec. v.p. Naval Aviation Mus. Found., Pensacola, 1986-96; dir. devel. Bapt. Health Care Found., Pensacola, 1997—. Decorated Legion of Merit with gold star; recipient John Paul Jones award Nat. Navy League Assn., 1971. Office: Bapt Health Care Found PO Box 17500 Pensacola FL 32522-7500

FURLONG, JAMES CHRISTOPHER, art program administrator, stage director; b. Glen Cove, N.Y., Oct. 12, 1955; s. Richard George and Anne Dolores (Etue) F. BA in Theatre, Trinity Coll., Hartford, Conn., 1976. Dir. spl. projects Soc. Stage Dirs., N.Y.C., 1980-89; staff dir. N.Y. City Opera, N.Y.C., 1986-90; performance coord. Hosp. Audiences, Inc., N.Y.C., 1993-94; dir. arts programs Hudson Guild, N.Y.C., 1994—; stage dir. Bronx (N.Y.) Opera, 1989—, Blue Hill Troupe, N.Y.C., 1992, State Repertory Opera, South Orange, N.J., 1992-96. Editor Jour. Soc. Stage Dirs., 1980-89. Stage dirs. grantee Nat. Inst. Music Theatre, Washington, 1985. Home: 365 W 20th St Apt 11D New York NY 10011-3360

FURLONG, PATRICK DAVID, educator, researcher; b. Cleve., Sept. 27, 1948; s. Harold Joseph and Jean Ann (Blair) F. BS magna cum laude, Lake Erie Coll., Painesville, Ohio, 1975. Staff psychometrist VA Med. Ctr., North Chicago, Ill., 1975-78; psychometrist Northwestern U., Chgo., 1978-80; counselor/coord. vets. affairs Columbia Coll., Chgo., 1980-81; assoc. coord. internat. edn. Roosevelt U., Chgo., 1981-84; dir. accreditation Nat. Commn. on Correctional Health Care, Chgo., 1984-85; sch. counselor/coord. student support svcs. United Edn. and Software, Chgo., 1985-87; psychometrist Northwestern U., Chgo., 1987-93; asst. adminstr. Assessment Sys., Inc., Chgo., 1993-94; lead ctr. adminstr. Sylvan Learning Sys., Inc., Chgo., 1994-96; benefit analyst Dept. Health and Human Svcs., Chgo., 1996—. With USN, 1967-71, Vietnam. Decorated Navy Achievement medal with combat V. Mem. AACD, APA, Psi Chi. Home: 1233 W Winnemac Ave Chicago IL 60640-2911

FURLONG, PATRICK J., historian, educator, university administrator; b. Lexington, Ky., Feb. 7, 1940; s. Dennis A. and Anna (Corollo) F.; m. Gertrude Alice Griffin, Aug. 2, 1965; children: Elizabeth, Joseph. AB, U. Ky., 1961; MA, Northwestern U., 1962, PhD, 1966. Prof. history Ind. U., South Bend, 1967—, dir. MLS program, 1995—, chmn. dept. history, 1997—. Author: Indiana: An Illustrated History, 1985; rsch. dir. TV documentary Studebaker: Less Than They Promised, 1983; contbr. articles to profl. jours. Bd. dirs. Southold Preservation, Inc., South Bend, 1965-91, 93-98, Discovery Hall Aassocs., Inc., South Bend, 1977-85. Recipient Lundquist award Ind. U. South Bend, 1988. Mem. Am. Hist. Assn., Orgn. Am. Historians. Avocation: travel. Home: 1320 Sunnymede Ave South Bend IN 46615-1018 Office: Ind U South Bend PO Box 7111 South Bend IN 46634-7111

FURLONG, PATRICK LOUIS, health science association administrator; b. Albany, N.Y., Jan. 13, 1940; s. Patrick Anthony and Alice Mary (Condon) F.; m. Rebecca Jane Weist, Feb. 15, 1964; children: John Patrick, Kevin David. BBA in Acctg., Siena Coll., 1965; postgrad., SUNY, Albany, 1973-74. Examiner mcpl. affairs audit and control dept. State of N.Y., Albany, 1965-66, internal auditor Thruway Authority, 1966-69, internal auditor dept. mental hygiene, 1969-72, chief budget analyst dept. mental hygiene, 1972-74, asst. dir. rsch. adminstrn. dept. mental hygiene, 1974-78, dir., fin. mgmt. office mental hygiene, 1978-80; mng. dir. Rsch. Found. Mental Hygiene, Inc., Albany, 1980-96; dep. dir. for adminstrn. Nathan Kline Inst. Psychiatric Rsch., Orangeburg, N.Y., 1996—. Treas. Cub Scouts, Woorheesville, N.Y., 1970-72; coach Little League, Voorheesville, 1972-73. With USN, 1959-61. Recipient Rsch. Svc. award N.Y. State Inst. Basic Rsch., 1993. Mem. Nat. Coun. Univ. Rsch. Adminstrs., Soc. Rsch. Adminstrs., Normanside Country Club. Avocations: golf, skiing, photography, carpentry. Office: Nathan Kline Inst 140 Old Orangeburg Rd Orangeburg NY 10962-1157*

FURLONG, THOMAS CASTLE, newspaper editor; b. Chgo., Oct. 23, 1945; s. Thomas Raphael and Winifred Harrison (Castle) F.; m. Susan Howlett, Dec. 1, 1985; children: Brendan Howlett, Castle Christina, Cameron Thomas. BA, Denison U., 1967. Reporter City News Bur., Chgo., 1971-72; reporter, editor Pioneer Press, Wilmette, Ill., 1972-75, Chgo. Daily News, 1976-78; reporter Long Beach Press-Telegram, Calif., 1978-79; reporter, editor Chgo. Sun Times, 1979-81; reporter L.A. Times, 1981-92, asst. bus. editor, 1993-96, dep. bus. editor, 1996-98, dep. nat. editor, 1998—. Lt. USN, 1967-71. Recipient Best Bus. Articles award L.A. Press Club, 1988. Avocations: physical fitness, reading, book research. Office: LA Times Times Mirror Sq Los Angeles CA 90053

FURLOTTI, ALEXANDER AMATO, real estate development company executive; b. Milan, Italy, Apr. 21, 1948; came to U.S., 1957; s. Amato and Polonia Concepcion (Lopez) F.; m. Nancy Elizabeth Swift, June 27, 1976; children: Michael Alexander, Patrick Swift, Allison Nicole. BA in Econs., U. Calif. Berkeley, Berkeley, 1970; JD, UCLA, 1973. Bar: Calif. 1973, U.S. Dist. Ct. (9th cir.) 1973. Assoc. Alexander, Inman, Kravetz & Tanzer, Beverly Hills, Calif., 1973-77, ptnr., 1978-80; ptnr. Kravetz & Furlotti, Century City, Calif., 1981-83; pres. Quorum Properties, L.A., 1984—; dir., CEO Transmar N.V., Netherland Antilles, 1984—. Trustee Harvard-Westlake Sch., L.A., 1989-97, Yosemite Nat. Inst., San Francisco, 1990-92. Recipient Grand award Pacific Coast Bldrs. Conf., 1993, 98, Golden Nugget award, 1993, 98, Grand award Nat. Assn. Home Builders, 1993, Platinum award, 1997, Best Attached Housing award, 1998, Residential Project of Yr., 1998. Mem. Am. Bar Assn., Urban Land Inst., The Beach Club. Republican. Episcopalian. Office: Quorum Properties 1875 Century Park E Los Angeles CA 90067

FURLOW, MACK VERNON, JR., retired financial executive, treasurer; b. Summit, Miss., Aug. 20, 1931; s. Mack Vernon and Trudie Dena (Ratcliff) F.; m. Barbara Elaine Rolfs, Mar. 20, 1954 (div. Dec. 1985); children—David Wayne, Kevin Rolfs. B.S., La. State U., 1953; grad., advanced mgmt. program Harvard, 1968. Financial and systems analyst Humble Oil & Refining Co., Baton Rouge, 1957-61; asst. controller Skyland Internat. Corp., Chattanooga, 1961-65; v.p., corp. controller Blount, Inc., Montgomery, Ala., 1965-71; pres. Pipeco Steel Co., Inc., Wilmington, Del., 1971-73; v.p. fin., treas. Huber, Hunt & Nichols, Inc., Indpls., 1973-96; dir. Huber, Hunt & Nichols, Inc., 1977-96; Asst. treas. 54th Advanced Mgmt. Program class Harvard Bus. Sch., 1968—. Served to 1st lt. AUS, 1953-57. Mem. La. State U. Alumni Assn. (mem. adv. com. Montgomery chpt. 1967-71), Nat. Assn. Accts. (nat. bd. dirs. 1976-78), Fin. Execs. Inst. (nat. bd. dirs. 1994-97). Republican. Lutheran. Home: 7322 Lions Head Dr Indianapolis IN 46260-3440 *The creation of a management climate or environment which causes people to want to excel and perform to their fullest capabilities is a far superior approach than is a management style which causes people to perform because they are constantly afraid of the consequences of failing to perform.*

FURLOW, MARY BEVERLEY, English language educator; b. Shreveport, La., Oct. 14, 1933; d. Prentiss Edward and Mary Thelma (Hasty) F.; divorced, 1973; children: Mary Findley, William Prentiss, Samuel Christopher; m. William Peter Cleary, Aug. 1, 1989. BA, U. Tenn., 1955, MEd, 1972; MA, Governors State U., 1975; cert. advanced study, U. Chgo., 1987. Mem. faculty Chattanooga State C.C., 1969-73, Moraine Valley C.C., Palos Hills, Ill., 1974-78; mem. English faculty Pima C.C., Tucson, 1978—; cons. in field. Contbr. author: Thinking on the Edge, 1993. Named one of Outstanding Educators of Am., 1973. Fellow Internat. Soc. Philos. Enquiry; mem. DAR, Internat. Soc. Appraisers, Internat. Soc. Philos. Enquiry, Ariz. Antiquarian Guild, Cincinatus Soc., Jr. League, Mensa, Holmes Socs., Clan Chattan Soc., Daus. of Confederacy, Alpha Phi Omega (Tchr. of Yr. 1973), Pi Beta Phi. Democrat. Episcopalian. Home: 1555 N Arcadia Ave Tucson AZ 85712-4010 Office: Pima CC 8202 E Poinciana Dr Tucson AZ 85730-4645

FURLOW, THOMAS WILLIAM, JR., neurologist; b. Orange, Calif., Sept. 11, 1946; s. Thomas William and Tweet Fentress Furlow; m. Leslie Anna Levitt; children: Christopher Thomas, Elisabeth Fentress, Gregory Scott. BA, George Washington U., 1968, MD, 1971. Diplomate Am. Bd. Psychiatry and Neurology. Intern Vanderbilt U. Hosp., Nashville, 1971-72; resident in neurology U. Va. Hosp., Charlottesville, 1972-75; prof. neurology U. Ala., Birmingham, 1978-83; dir. opers. Neurotechnics, Inc., Arnold, Md., 1985-95; clin. prof. neurology U. Md. Sch. Medicine, Balt., 1991—; col. U.S. Army/Walter Reed Army Med. Ctr., Washington, 1984—; rsch. officer Navy Med. Rsch. Inst., Bethesda, Md., 1977-78. Co-designer intraoperative monitoring electrodes and prosthetic vertebral device; contbr. numerous articles to profl. jours. Col. USAR, 1975-78, 84-89, 94—. Mem. Phi Beta Kappa, Alpha Omega Alpha. Episcopalian. Avocations: photography, digital imaging, precision metalworking, classic motorcycles. E-mail: tfurlow@erols.com.

FURMAN, ANTHONY MICHAEL, public relations executive; b. L.A., Nov. 5, 1934; s. LeRoy S. and Geraldine P. F.; B.A., Bethany (W.Va.) Coll., 1957; postgrad. Columbia U. 1957-58; m. Betty Gayle Morgan, Nov. 1, 1970; 1 child, Michael Jason. Asst. account exec. Jules Beitler, Pub. Relations, Newark, 1958; account exec. Barber & Baar Pub. Rels. Corp., N.Y.C., 1959-60; account exec., media dir. Sydney S. Baron & Co., Inc., N.Y.C., 1961-66; pres. Anthony M. Furman, Inc., N.Y.C., 1966-81; v.p., mng. dir. sports devel. div. Hill & Knowlton, Inc., 1981-85; pres., Dorf and Stanton Sports Mktg., 1985-86, pres. Anthony M. Furman, Inc., N.Y.C., 1986—; adj. prof. L.I. U., 1986-91; guest lectr. NYU, 1989, adj. prof., 1992—; bd. dirs. FKP Assocs., Lake Placid, N.Y. Recipient Outstanding Alumnus award Bethany Coll., 1987. Served with M.C., U.S. Army, 1957-58. Mem. Pub. Rels. Soc. Am. Democrat. Jewish. Exec. producer film: Floating Free, 1977 (1978 Acad. award nominee). Office: 250 W 57th St Ste 1501 New York NY 10107-1699

FURMAN, JAMES HOUSLEY, lawyer; b. Charlotte, N.C., Oct. 9, 1946; s. Henry Jones and Nell (Housley) F.; m. Susan Marie Barnett, Mar. 12, 1969; children: James Housley Jr., Jason Haynsworth. BS in Aero. Sci., Embry-Riddle Aero. U., 1972; MBA, U. North Fla., 1977; JD, U. Tex., 1980. Bar: Tex. 1981, U.S. Dist. Ct. (we. and so. dists.) Tex. 1983, U.S. Ct. Appeals (5th cir.) 1984, U.S. Dist. Ct. (no. dist.) Tex. 1993; bd. cert. personal injury trial law Tex. Bd. Legal Specialization. Briefing atty. Supreme Ct. Tex., Austin, 1981-82; assoc. Byrd, Davis & Eisenberg, Austin, 1982-87, ptnr., 1988—. Mem. coun. Boy Scouts Am., Austin. With U.S. Army, 1966-71, Viet Nam; with USAR, ARNG, 1971-87. Decorated Bronze Star, Army Commendation medal, Purple Heart. Mem. Coll. State Bar Tex. (coun. mem. aviation sect.), Lawyer Pilots Bar Assn., Am. Trial Lawyers Assn. (chair, vice chmn. aviation sect., sec.), Tex. Trial Lawyers Assn. Presbyterian. E-mail: jamesfurman@compuserve.com. Home: 6301 Royal Birkdale Overlook Austin TX 78746-6141 Office: Byrd Davis & Eisenberg LLP 707 W 34th St Austin TX 78705-1204

FURMAN, JOHN ROCKWELL, wholesale lumber company executive; b. Wellsville, N.Y., June 25, 1917; s. Harry Brennan and Helen (Rockwell) F.; m. Mary Hale Sutton, Aug. 2, 1941; children: John Rockwell Jr., Margery, Harry S. BA in Econs., Cornell U., 1939. New Eng. mgr. Dant and Russell, Inc., Portland, Oreg., 1948-56; founder, pres., chief exec. officer Furman Lumber, Inc., Boston, 1956—. Trustee Northeast Growth Fund, Boston, 1980—, Tilton (N.H.) Sch., 1963—. Lt. Comdr. USNR, 1941-46. Mem. N.Am. Wholesale Lumber Assn. (bd. dirs. 1967-75), Comml. Club. also: Furman Lumber Inc PO Box 130 Nutting Lake MA 01865-0130

FURMAN, MARK EVAN, human performance scientist; b. Bronx, Mar. 14, 1962; s. Edward and Charlotte F.; m. Beth Ann Schad, Aug. 9, 1987; children: Lauren Ashley, Jonathan Cyle. BA in Behavioral Scis./Psychology, Coll. of S.I., 1984. Cert. practitioner of neuro-linguistic programming. Dir. edn. and rsch. Assoc. Schs. Music, Inc., Cooper City, Fla., 1988-97; spkr., author, human performance cons., 1990—; founder, exec. dir. Furman Rsch. Assocs., Pompano Beach, Fla., 1987—; dir. edn. and rsch. The Keys to Success, Inc., Coral Springs, Fla., 1992—, Ozone Park, N.Y., 1992—; lectr. in field of neurosci.; founder, exec. dir. Furman Rsch. Assocs.; designer comm. program Jewish Ednl. Found. of Am., theoretical tng. model Syntonics Ednls., Switzerland; cons. Keys to Success Music Sch., N.Y., Century 21, Fla.; founder Internat. Soc. for Edn. Neurosci.; developer Intelligent Learning Systems, neuroprint, Human Performance Modeling & Engineering; numerous others bus. Author: (book) Mind in Motion, The Human Performance Technology for the Next Millenum, 1996; author: Jour. for the Soc. of Neuro-Linguistic Programming, 1995-97, The Neurophysics of Human Behavior: Explorations at the Interface of Brain, Mind and Behavior, 1999; contbr. articles to profl. jours. Mem. AAAS, APA (affiliate, divsn. 48, divsn. peace psychology), Internat. Soc. for Epistemiol. Neurophysics (founder), Soc. for Study of Peace, Conflict and Violence. Achievements include developing intelligent learning systems (ILS); currently pioneering coordinated research of develpement efforts in the field of education neuroscience, studying the neurophysics of human information processing and its application to the field of human education; advanced standard theory: Pattern-Entropy dynamics of matter and energy interaction. Avocations: developing brain-based human performance technologies and applications. Home: 3370 Beau Rivage Dr Pompano Beach FL 33064-2057 Office: The Keys to Success Inc 10758 Wiles Rd Coral Springs FL 33076-2009

FURMAN, ROY L., investment banker, theatrical executive; b. N.Y.C., Apr. 19, 1939; s. Joseph M. and Frances L. (Kurlander) F.; m. Frieda Anne Bueler, Nov. 7, 1965; children: Jill Tracy, Stephanie Gail. A.B., Bklyn. Coll., 1960; LL.B., Harvard U., 1963. Civy. Western Electric Co., N.Y.C., 1964-67; v.p. Continental Tel. Supply Co., N.Y.C., 1967-68; with Seiden & de Cuevas, Inc., N.Y.C., 1968-73, pres., 1972-73; co-founder, pres. Furman Selz LLC, N.Y.C., 1973-98, also bd. dirs., 1973-98; chmn., CEO Livent Inc., N.Y.C., 1998; vice chmn. Furman Selz LLC, N.Y.C., 1997—; former nat. fin. chmn. Dem. Nat. Com.; past chmn. splty. firms adv. com. N.Y. Stock Exch.; bd. dirs. Westfield Am. Chmn. Film Soc., Lincoln Ctr.; v.p. N.Y.C. Opera; vice chmn. Lincoln Ctr. for Performing Arts; past nat. chmn. Harvard Law Sch. Fund; trustee Bklyn. Coll. Found., 1983-97; vice-chmn. dean's adv. bd. Harvard Law Sch. Office: Livent Inc 214 W 43rd St New York NY 10036

FURMAN, THOMAS D., JR., engineering company executive; b. Edgefield, S.C., Feb. 6, 1943. BS in Civil Engring., U. Fla., 1966, M in Engring., 1967. With Camp Dresser & McKee, Inc., Cambridge, Mass., 1968-73, pres., CEO, 1973—. Office: Camp Dresser & McKee Inc 1 Cambridge Ctr Ste 11 Cambridge MA 02142-1603*

FURMANSKI, PHILIP, cancer research scientist; b. Germany, July 26, 1946; came to U.S., 1947, naturalized, 1954; s. Ed and Rose (Warsawski) F.; m. Susan Wheeler; children: Lisa Anne, Jonathan David. BA, Temple U., 1966, PhD, 1969. Research assoc. Albert Einstein Med. Ctr., Phila., 1970; research assoc., instr. Dartmouth Coll. Med. Sch., Hanover, N.H., 1970-72; chmn., asst. dir. Mich. Cancer Found., Detroit, 1974-81; asst. prof., then assoc. prof. Wayne State U. Sch. Med., Detroit, 1974-81; assoc. dir., sci. dir. AMC Cancer Research Ctr., Denver, 1981-90; prof., chmn. dept. biology NYU, 1990—, interim dean Coll. Arts & Scis., 1993-95, dean faculty arts and scis., 1995—; assoc. mem. cancer ctr., prof. dept. pathology NYU Med. Sch., 1992—; mem. virus working group WHO/Food and Agr. Orgn., 1977-80; mem. rev. com. Nat. Cancer Inst., Bethesda, Md., 1981—; cons. indsl. and acad. concerns, 1975—; adj. prof., full mem. Cancer Ctr. U. Colo., 1988-90. Editor: Biological Carcinogenesis, 1982, Understanding Breast Cancer, 1983, RNA Tumor Viruses, Oncogenes, Human Cancer, and AIDS, 1985; mem. editl. bd. In Vivo, 1987—, Cancer Rsch., 1990—, Molecule Cell Differentiation, 1992—, Am. Jour. Pathology, 1994—; also articles. Damon Runyon Meml. fellow NIH, 1967-72; Nat. Cancer Inst. grantee, 1969—. Mem. Internat. Soc. Exptl. Hematology, Internat. Assn. Breast Cancer Research, Am. Soc. Cell. Biology, AAAS, Am. Assn. Cancer Research. Office: NYU Dept Biology Main Bldg Rm 1009 New York NY 10003

FURNAD, V. R. (BOB FURNAD), television news executive. BA in Radio/TV, American U. Fl. dir., film editor, assoc. dir., prodr. Sta. WMAL-TV, Washington; with ABC News, 1964-68, 69-83; from polit. news dir. to exec. v.p. and sr. exec. prodr. CNN, 1983—, now pres. Headline News network, 1997—. Recipient George Foster Peabody award, Acad. for cable Excellence GoldenACE, Emmy award, Overseas Press Club award, Alfred I. duPont award. Office: CNN Headline News One CNN Ctr PO Box 105366 Atlanta GA 30348-5366*

FURNAS, DAVID WILLIAM, plastic surgeon; b. Caldwell, Idaho, Apr. 1, 1931; s. John Doan and Esther Bradbury (Hare) F.; m. Mary Lou Heatherly, Feb. 11, 1956; children: Heather Jean, Brent David, Craig Jonathan. AB, U. Calif.-Berkeley, 1952, MS, 1957, MD, 1955. Diplomate Am. Bd. Surgery, Am. Bd. Plastic Surgery (dir. 1979-85, sr. examiner 1986—), Royal Coll. Surgeons Found. (trustee 1995—). Intern U. Calif. Hosp., San Francisco, 1955-56, asst. resident in surgery, 1956-57; asst. resident in psychiatry, NIMH fellow Langley Porter Neuropsychiat. Inst. U. Calif., San Francisco, 1959-60; resident in gen. surgery Gorgas Hosp., C.Z., 1960-61; asst. resident in plastic surgery N.Y. Hosp., Cornell Med. Center, N.Y.C., 1961-62; chief resident in plastic surgery Cornell U. Svc., VA Hosp., Bronx, N.Y., 1962-63; registrar Royal Infirmary and Affiliated Hosps., Glasgow, Scotland, 1963-64; assoc. in hand surgery U. Iowa, 1964-68, sr. resident, faculty assoc. in surgery, 1964-65, asst. prof. surgery, 1966-68, assoc. prof., 1968-69; assoc. prof. surgery, chief div. plastic surgery U. Calif., Irvine, 1969-74, prof., chief div. plastic surgery, 1974-80, clin. prof., chief div. plastic surgery, 1980—; surgeon East Africa Flying Drs. Svc., African Med. and Rsch. Found., Nairobi, Kenya, 1972-73; plastic surgeon S.S. Hope, Nicaragua, 1966, Sri Lanka, 1968; mem. Balakbayan med. mission Mindanao and Sulu, The Philippines, 1980, 81, 82; overseas vis. prof. plastic surgery Ednl. Found., 1994. Contbr. chpts. to textbooks, articles to med. jours.; author, editor 6 textbooks; assoc. editor Jour. Hand Surgery, Annals of Plastic Surgery, Jour. Craniofacial Surgery. Expedition leader Explorer's Club Flag 171 Skull Surgeons of the Kisii Tribe, Kenya, Flag 44 Skull Surgeons of the Marakwet Tribes, Kenya, 1987. Capt. Med. Corps, USAF, 1957-59; col. Med. Corps., USAR, 1989-92, ret. Recipient Golden Apple award for teaching excellence U. Calif.-Irvine Sch. Medicine, 1980, Kaiser-Permanente award U. Calif.-Irvine Sch. Medicine, 1981, Humanitarian Service award Black Med. Students, U. Calif. Irvine, 1987, Sr. Research award (Basic Sci.) Plastic Surgery Ednl. Found., 1987; named Orange County Press Club Headliner of Yr., 1982, Physician of the Year, Orange County Med. Assn., 1998. Fellow ACS, Royal Coll. Surgeons Can., Royal Soc. Medicine, Explorers Club, Royal Geog. Soc.; mem. AMA, Calif. Med. Assn., Orange County Med. Assn. (Physician of Yr. 1998), Am. Soc. Plastic and Reconstructive Surgeons (bd. dirs. 1970-73), Am. Soc. Reconstructive Microsurgery, Soc. Head and Neck Surgery, Am. Cleft Palate Assn., Am. Soc. Surgery of Hand, Soc. Univ. Surgeons, Am. Assn. Plastic Surgeons (trustee 1983-86, treas. 1988-91, v.p. 1993-94, pres.-elect 1994, pres. 1995), Am. Soc. Aesthetic Plastic Surgery, Am. Soc. Maxillofacial Surgeons, Assn. Acad. Chairmen Plastic Surgery (bd. dirs. 1986-89), Assn. Surgeons East Africa, Assn. Plastic & Reconstructive Surgeons So. Africa (hon.), Pacific Coast Surg. Assn., Internat. Soc. Aesthetic Plastic Surgery, Internat. Soc. Reconstructive Microsurgery, Internat. Soc. Craniomaxillofacial Surgery, Pan African Assn. Neurol. Sci., African Med. and Rsch. Found. (bd. dirs. U.S.A. 1987—), Muthaiga Club, Ctr. Club, Club 33, Univ. Club, Phi Beta Kappa, Alpha Omega Alpha. Office: U Calif Div Plastic Surgery Irvine Med Ctr 101 City Dr S Orange CA 92868-3201 *A crisis, at the outset, usually augurs nothing but ill. In the long run, however, my crises have more often than not marked a new course for my life, which is more fulfilling, and more exciting than anything in the past. Yes, a bit of good luck is needed, but the special feature of a crisis is that you are suddenly cut off from past patterns, habits, and interdependencies. Along with the distress and pain is freedom! Freedom to build again, with a new foundation and modern structure, using wisdom you didn't have the last time you built.*

FURNAS, HOWARD EARL, business executive, educator, retired government official; b. Battle Creek, Mich., Jan. 29, 1919; s. Howard Earl and Dorothy Anna (Collings) F.; m. Gail Abbott, May 14, 1942; children: Howard Earl III, Paul Abbott, Christopher Collings. AB, Hillsdale (Mich.) Coll., 1940; postgrad., Harvard U., 1945-47. Joined Fgn. Svc. Dept. State, 1947; assigned to embassy New Delhi, 1948-49; asst. to spl. asst. to sec. state for intelligence, 1949-52, 54-57; assigned to U.S. mission to NATO, Paris, 1952-54; mem. policy planning staff, also alternate Dept. State rep. to plannning bd. NSC, 1957-61; dep. spl. asst. to sec. state for atomic energy and outer space, 1961-62; dept. exec. sec. Dept. State, 1962-63; del. 2d Nat. Conf. Peaceful Uses Space, Seattle, 1962; dep. spl. asst. to sec. state for multilateral force negotiations, 1963-64, spl. asst. to sec. state, 1964-65, mem. VIII sr. seminar in fgn. policy, 1965-66; assigned Office Undersec. State Polit. Affairs, 1966-69; spl. asst. to dir. ACDA, 1969-71, spl. adviser to chmn. gen. adv. com. on arms control and disarmament, 1969-71; prof. internat. rels. Windham Coll., Putney, Vt., 1971-76, also trustee; pres. Unipro Tennis Svcs., Howard Furnas Assocs., Windsor, Vt., 1974—, Chuckle Hill, Ltd., 1975-76; pres. The Vermont Group, Internat. Cons., 1989-90. Contbr. articles to profl. jours. and newspaper columns. Bd. dirs. Montgomery County (Md.) Scholarship Fund, 1954-60; trustee Woodstock (Vt.) Country Sch., 1973-75; vestryman St. James Ch., Woodstock, Vt.; justice of peace West Windsor, Vt., 1986-95. Maj. USAAF, 1942-45, ETO. Recipient Alumni Achievement award Hillsdale Coll., 1957. Mem. Kenwood Golf and Country Club (Washington), Woodstock Country Club, Twin States Valley Club, The Round Table, Delta Tau Delta. Episcopalian. Home and Office: 1360 Sheddsville Rd Windsor VT 05089-9664

FURNAS, JOSEPH CHAMBERLAIN, writer; b. Indpls., Nov. 24, 1905; s. Isaiah George and Elizabeth (Chamberlain) F. A.B., Harvard, 1927. Author: The Prophet's Chamber, 1937, Many People Prize It, 1938, So You're Going to Stop Smoking, 1939, Anatomy of Paradise, 1948 (Anisfield-Wolff non-fiction award), Voyage to Windward; The Life of Robert Louis Stevenson, 1951; Collaborator: (with Ernest M. Smith) Sudden Death and How to Avoid It, 1935, How America Lives, (with editorial staff of Ladies' Home Jour.), 1941; author: Goodbye to Uncle Tom, 1956, The Road to Harpers Ferry, 1959, The Devil's Rainbow, 1962, The Life and Times of the Late Demon Rum, 1955, Lightfoot Island, 1968, The Americans, 1969, Great Times, 1974, Stormy Weather, 1977, Fanny Kemble, 1981 (George Freedley award 1982), My Life in Writing: Memoirs of a Maverick, 1989. Mem. Phi Beta Kappa. Club: Harvard. Address: c/o Brandt & Brandt 150 Broadway New York NY 10036

FURNESS, PETER JOHN, lawyer; b. Providence, Jan. 30, 1956; s. Robert I. and Elsie R. (Mooradian) F.; m. Anne Marie Tommasiello, June 7, 1981; children: Lindsey Elizabeth, Jonathan Peter. BA, U. R.I., 1979; JD, U. Pitts., 1982. Bar: Pa. 1982, U.S. Dist. Ct. (we. dist.) Pa. 1982, R.I. 1987, Mass. 1989, U.S. Dist. Ct. Mass. 1989. Atty. Mazzotta & Winters, Pitts., 1984-86, Hinckley, Allen, Snyder & Comen, Providence, 1986-91; ptnr. Nixon Peabody LLP, Boston/Providence, 1991—; lectr. Nat. Bus. Inst., Inc., 1986—. Author: (seminar books) NBI Foreclosure in Rhode Island, 1986, NBI Basic Bankruptcy in Rhode Island, 1988, NBI Protection of Secured Interests in Bankruptcy, 1989. Bd. dirs. R.I. Chpt. for Prevention of Child Abuse. Mem. ABA, Am. Bankruptcy Inst., Fed. Bar Assn., Pa. Bar Assn., R.I. Bar Assn., Mass. Bar Assn., Comml. Law League, Phi Beta Kappa, Phi Kappa Phi. Avocations: photography, golf, fishing, vol. work with nonprofit orgns. Office: Nixon Peabody LLP 1 Citizens Plz Providence RI 02903-1344

FURNEY, LINDA JEANNE, state legislator; b. Toledo, Sept. 11, 1947; d. Robert Ross and Jeanne Scott (Hogan) F. BS in Edn., Bowling Green State U., 1969; postgrad., U. Toledo. Tchr. Washington Local Schs., Toledo, 1969-72, Escola Americano do Rio de Janiero, 1972-74, Springfield Schs., Holland, Ohio, 1977-83; council mem. City of Toledo, 1983-86; mem. Ohio State Senate, Columbus, 1987—, mem. edn. com., rules com., reference and oversight com., fin. com., asst. minority leader, 1997-99. Dem. precinct committeewoman Toledo, 1980-90; mem. Toledo Bd. Edn., 1982-83. Recipient Citizen award Ohio Assn. Edn. Young Children, Stanley K. Levinson award Planned Parenthood Northwest Ohio, Educator of Yr. award Phi Delta Kappa. Mem. NOW, AAUW, NAACP, ACLU (Found. award), Toledo Mus. Art, Toledo Zoo. Congregationalist. Home: 2626 Latonia Blvd Toledo OH 43606-3620 Office: Ohio Senate Senate Bldg Rm 228 Columbus OH 43215*

FURNISS, KEITH RICHARD, educational administrator; b. Bristol, Conn., June 10, 1969; s. Richard Marsh and Elaine (Jabs) F.; m. Jacquelyn Letizia, June 8, 1996. BA, U. Conn., 1991; MA in Counseling Psychology, Northeastern U., 1994. Clin. case coord. Waterford (Conn.) Country Sch., 1995—. Home: 128 Laurel St Bristol CT 06010-5706

FURNIVAL, GEORGE MITCHELL, petroleum and mining consultant; b. July 25, 1908; s. William George and Grace Una (Rothwell) F.; m. Marion Marguerite Fraser, Mar. 8, 1937; children: William George, Sharon (Mrs. John M. Roscoe), Patricia M., Bruce A. BSc, U. Man., Can., 1929; MA, Queens U., Can., 1933; PhD, MIT, 1935. Field geologist Man., Ont., NWT, Que., 1928-36; asst. mine supt. Cline Lake Gold Mines, Ltd., 1936-39; geologist Geol. Survey Can., Sask., 1939-42; with Std. Oil Co. Calif. (Chevron) subs., 1942-70; dist. geologist Std. Oil Co. Calif. (Chevron) subs., Calgary, Alta., 1942-44, asst. to chief geologist, 1944-45, field supt. So. Alta., 1945-46, mgr. land and legal dept., 1948-50, v.p. land and legal, dir., 1950-52, v.p. legal, crude oil sales, govt. rels., dir., 1952-55; pres., dir. Dominion Oil, Ltd., Trinidad and Tobago, 1952-60; v.p. exploration, dir. Calif. Exploration Co. (Chevron Overseas Petroleum), Inc., San Francisco, 1955-63; staff asst. land to corp. v.p. exploration and land Std. Oil Co. of Calif., 1961-63; chmn. bd., mng. dir. West Australian Petroleum Pty., Ltd. (Chevron operated), Perth, 1963-70; ret., 1970; dir. mines Dept. Mines and Natural Resources, Man., 1946-48; v.p., dir. Newport Ventures, Ltd., Calgary, 1971-72; v.p. ops., dir., mem. exec. com. Brascan Resources subs. Brascan Ltd. (formerly Brazilian Traction Ltd.), Calgary, 1972-75, sr. v.p., dir., 1975-77, sr. cons. 1977-78; pres., CEO, dir. Western Mines Ltd. (Brascan), 1978-80, exec. v.p., divsn. gen. mgr. Westmin Resources Ltd. (Brascan), also dir., mem. exec. com., 1981-82; pres., acting gen. mgr. Coalition Mining Ltd.; pres., COO, dir. Lathwell Resources Ltd., 1983-84; cons. petroleum and mining, 1985—; founder Man. Geol. Survey, 1946; dir. Cretaceous Pipe Line Co., Ltd., Austen & Butta Pty., Ltd., Western Coal Holdings, Inc., Quest Explorations Ltd., San Antonio Resources Inc.; del. Interprovincial Mines Mins. Conf.; sec. Winnipeg Conf., 1947. Author numerous govt. and co. papers, reports, reference texts, also sci. articles to profl. jours. Elected to Order of Can., 1983; scholarship in mining geology named in his honor U. B.C., Can. Fellow Royal Soc. Can., Geol. Soc. Am., Geol. Assn. Can., Soc. Econ. Geologists, Am. Assn. Petroleum Geologists (hon. life); mem. Engring. Inst. Can., Can. Inst. Mining, Metallurgy and Petroleum (hon. life, past br. chmn., dist. councillor, v.p., chmn. petroleum divsn., Disting. Svc. award 1974, Selwyn G. Blaylock Gold medal 1979), Australian Petroleum Producing Exploration Assn. (hon. life, chmn. com. West Australian petroleum legislation, councillor, state chmn. for Western Australia), Assn. Profl. Engrs., Geologists and Geophysicists of Alta. (hon. life, Centennial award 1985), Coal Assn. of Can. (bd. dirs.), Calgary Golf and Country Club, Calgary Petroleum Club, Ranchmen's Club. Fax: (403) 255-5322. Home: 1315 Baldwin Cres SW, Calgary, AB Canada T2V 2B7

FURRER, JOHN RUDOLF, retired manufacturing business executive; b. Milw., Dec. 2, 1927; s. Rudolph and Leona (Peters) F.; m. Annie Louise Waldo, Apr. 24, 1954; children: Blake Waldo, Kimberly Louise. BA, Harvard U., 1949. Spl. rep. ACF Industries, Madrid, 1949-51; asst. supr. thermonuclear devel. and test Los Alamos, Eniwetok Atoll, 1952-53; dir. product devel. ACF Industries, N.Y.C., 1954-59; dir. machinery, systems group, central engring. labs. FMC Corp., San Jose, Calif., 1959-68, gen. mgr. engineered systems div., 1968-70; v.p. in charge planning dept., cen. engring. labs. and engineered systems div. FMC Corp., Chgo., 1970-71; v.p. material handling group FMC Corp., Chgo., 1971-77, v.p. corp. devel., 1977-88, sr. v.p., 1988-90. Patentee in field. Trustee Ravinia Festival, 1986-90. Served with USN, 1945-46. Mem. ASME, Coun. Planning Execs. (chmn. conf. bd. 1986-87), Harvard Club N.Y.C., Riomar Bay Yacht Club, Mid-Am. Club, Ocean Reef Club. Home: 203 Spinnaker Dr Vero Beach FL 32963-2953 also: PO Box 10849 Jackson WY 83002-0849

FURSE, ELIZABETH, former congresswoman, small business owner; b. Nairobi, Kenya, 1936; came to U.S., 1958, naturalized, 1972; m. John Platt; 2 children (from previous marriage). BA, Evergreen State Coll., 1974; postgrad., U. Wash., Northwestern U., Lewis & Clark Coll. Dir. Western Wash. Indian program Am. Friends Svc. Com, 1975-77; coord. Restoration program for Native Am. Tribes Oreg. Legal Svc., 1980-86; co-owner Helvetia Vineyards, Hillsboro, Oreg.; mem. 103rd-105th Congresses from 1st Oreg. dist., 1993-98, mem. commerce, fin. and hazardous materials, health and environment, energy and power coms., mem. telecomm. and finance com. Co-founder Oreg. Peace Inst., 1985. Address: PO Box 4143 Portland OR 97208*

FURSLAND, RICHARD CURTIS, international business executive; b. London, Feb. 25, 1948; came to U.S., 1981; s. Albert Samuel and Irene Alice (Haggett) F.; m. Mary Jo Territo, May 5, 1984; 1 child, Emma Jane. BA, Cambridge U., 1969, MA, 1973; Chinese lang. advanced cert., Hong Kong U., 1973. 2nd sec., trade rep. Brit. Trade Commn., Hong Kong, 1970-73, Brit. Embassy, Beijing, China, 1973-76; dir. Chinese and South Asian Affairs Brit. Fgn. Office, London, 1976-80; 1st sec., U.K. rep. U.K. Mission to U.N., 1981-85; v.p. Gavin Anderson & Co., N.Y.C., 1985-88; exec. v.p., mng. dir. internat. bus. GCI Group, N.Y.C., 1988-95; exec. dir. Internat. Peace Acad., N.Y.C., 1995-97; mng. dir. Brit. Am. C. of C., N.Y.C., 1997—; exec. dir. Brit. Am. Bus. Coun., N.Y.C., 1997—. Henry fellow Harvard U., 1970-71. Home: 23 Wiltshire Pl Bronxville NY 10708-1113 Office: Brit Am C of C 52 Vanderbilt Ave New York NY 10017-3808

FURST, ALEX JULIAN, thoracic and cardiovascular surgeon; b. Augusta, Ga., Aug. 21, 1938; m. George Alex and Ann (Segall) F.; m. Elayne Kobrin, Aug. 11, 1962; children: James Andrew, Jeffrey Michael, Joseph Robert. Student, U. Fla., 1963; M.D., U. Miami, 1967. Intern U. Miami Hosp., 1967-68, resident, 1968-72, clin. instr. dept. surgery, 1974-91; chief resident in thoracic and cardiovascular surgery Emory U. Hosp., Atlanta, 1972-73, sr. surg. registrar of thoracic unit, 1972-73; sr. surg. registrar of thoracic unit Hosp. for Sick Children, London, 1973-74; practice medicine specializing in thoracic and cardiovascular surgery Miami, Fla.; assoc. prof. surgery and cardiology, chief surg. svc. Miami VA Med. Ctr., 1991—, prof., surgery and medicine; chief thoracic surgery, pres. med. staff Mercy Hosp.; mem. staff Bapt. Hosp., South Miami Hosp., Doctor's Hosp. (all Miami), North Ridge Gen. Hosp., Ft. Lauderdale. Served with U.S. Army, 1958-60. Fellow Am. Coll. Cardiology, Am. Coll. Chest Physicians, A.C.S.; mem. Dade County Med. Assn., Fla. Med. Assn., Heart Assn. Greater Miami, Soc. Thoracic Surgeons, So. Thoracic Surg. Assn. Home: 8802 Arvida Dr Miami FL 33156-2302

FURST, ARTHUR, toxicologist, educator; b. Mpls., Dec. 25, 1914; s. Samuel and Doris (Kolochinsky) F.; m. Florence Wolovitch, May 24, 1940; children: Carolyn, Adrianne, David Michael, Timothy Daniel. AA, L.A. City Coll., 1935; AB, UCLA, 1937, AM, 1940; PhD, Stanford U., 1948; ScD, U. San Francisco, 1983. Mem. faculty, dept. chemistry San Francisco City Coll., 1940-47; asst. prof. chemistry U. San Francisco, 1947-49, assoc. prof. chemistry, 1949-52; assoc. prof. medicinal chemistry Stanford Sch. Medicine, 1952-57, prof., 1957-61; with U. Calif. War Tng., 1943-45, San Francisco State Coll., 1945; rsch. assoc. Mt. Zion Hosp., 1952-82; clin. prof. pathology Columbia Coll. Physicians and Surgeons, 1969-70; dir. Inst. Chem. Biology; prof. chemistry U. San Francisco, 1961-80, prof. emeritus, 1980—, dean grad. div., 1976-79; vis. fellow Battelle Seattle Research Center, 1974; Michael vis. prof. Weizmann Inst. Sci., Israel, 1982; cons. toxicology, 1980—; cons. on cancer WHO; mem. com., bd. mineral resources NRC; sr. mem. scientific advisory bd., GNLD, Internat. Author: Toxicologist as Expert Witness, 1997; contbr. over 300 articles to profl. and ednl. jours. Recipient Klaus Schwartz Commemorative medal Internat. Toxological Congress, Tokyo, 1986, Profl. Achievement award UCLA Alumni Assn., 1992, Henry Hall Clay award U. San Francisco, 1977. Fellow Acad. Toxicological Scis. (diplomate), AAAS, Am. Coll. Nutrition, Am. Coll. Toxicology (nat. sec., pres. 1985), N.Y. Acad. Scis., Am. Inst. Chemists; mem. Am. Soc. Pharmacology and Exptl. Therapeutics, Am. Soc. Pharmacology and Exptl. Therapeutics, Am. Chem. Soc., Am. Assn. Cancer Research, Soc. Toxicology, Sigma Xi, Phi Lambda Upsilon. Research activities on organic synthesis, chemotherapy cancer, carcinogenesis of metals and hydrocarbons. Home: 23500 Cristo Rey Dr Cupertino CA 95014-6503 Office: U San Francisco Inst Chem Biology San Francisco CA 94117-1080

FURST, DAN (DANIEL CHRISTOPHER FURST, III), producer, writer, actor; b. N.Y.C., Sept. 14, 1944; s. Daniel Christopher and Mary Ann Monica (Dolan) F.; m. Kimie Yoshimura, Dec. 17, 1986. BA, Rockhurst Coll., 1966; MA, Columbia U., 1967, PhD, 1974. developer, tchr. intensive courses in English Nippon Steel, Kawasaki Heavy Industries, Kubota Engring., others, 1985-91; guest lectr. Japanese theatre U. Hawaii, New Sch., N.Y.C., 1991; workshop leader Movement, Intuition and Silence, Kyoto, 1992; tchr. multimedia courses Kyoto U., 1993-95; announcer, emcee The Kyoto Global Forum, 1993, The Conf. on Ecol. Responsibility, New Delhi, 1993; artist mgr. Asia Pacific Wave concerts, Osaka, 1993, Count Basie Orch. Japan tour, 1994. Columnist: Mainichi Daily News, Asahi Evening News, Kansai Time Out Mag., Japan Times, Daily Yomiuri, 1985-95; contbr. articles to Edinburgh Internat. Festival Souvenir, Am. Theatre, High Performance, Asia Times, others; actor, fight dir. King Lear, 1987, Macbeth, 1989, Just Between the Three of Us, 1989, f/F Parasite, 1989, Bau Talkie, 1989; appeared in (films) Geisha, 1988, As Is, 1990, Cosmic Itch, 1991, Curious Fish, 1993, City Life White Paper, 1994, Undesirable Elements, 1995; founder, artistic dir. Sirius Prodns. theater co., Kyoto, 1988-95, The Play of Freedom, 1995-98. Home: 2355 Orchid St Honolulu HI 96816-3117

FURST, E. KENNETH, accountant; b. Oct. 11, 1946. BS in Econs., U. Pa., 1968, MS in Acctg., 1969. CPA, N.J. V.p. fin. Sealand Corp., Edison, N.J., 1971-89; CFO, dir., owner Toledo, Peoria (Ill.) & Western R.R., 1989-96; CFO, v.p. Golden Eagle Network, Bethel, Conn., 1996-97; owner E. Kenneth Furst, CPA, Short Hills, N.J., 1997—. Mem. N.J. Soc. CPAs (trustee, 1997-99, pres. Essex chpt., 1995-96), U. Penn. Club Metro. N.J. (pres., 1995-96). E-mail: furst@worldnet.att.net.

FURST, RAYMOND BRUCE, engineer, consultant; b. Los Nietos, Calif., Aug. 20, 1924; s. Guy Thomas and Mary Erma (Bruckman) F.; m. Patricia Sheila Fitzgerald, Oct. 28, 1996; children: Christopher, Colleen, Janice, Sheila, Erin, Robert, Patricia. AA, Fullerton (Calif.) Jr. Coll., 1943; student, Calif. Inst. Tech., 1943-44; BSME, U. Calif., Berkeley, 1948; MSME, U. So. Calif., 1957; bus. cert., UCLA, 1983. Project engr. C.F. Braun & Co., Alhambra, Calif., 1948, AiResearch Mfg. Co., L.A., 1949-58; mgr. fluid mechs. Rocketdyne, Canoga Park, Calif., 1958-86; cons. Propulsion Assocs., Vernon, France, 1986-90, R. Furst & Assocs., Dana Point, Calif., 1990—. Author: Liquid Rocket Engine Centrifugal Flow Turbopumps, 1973; co-author: Centrifugal Pump Design and Performance, 1997; also numerous inventions. Served with USN, 1943-46. Recipient Certs. of Recognition NASA, 1983, 87, Apollo award NASA, 1968, 69. Fellow Inst. for Advancement of Engring.; mem. ASME (chmn. San Fernando Valley chpt. 1976-77, Worthington medal for contbns. to pump industry 1989). Avocations: sailing, photography, tennis, gardening. Home and Office: 23822 Salvador Bay Dana Point CA 92629-4207

FURST, WARREN ARTHUR, retired holding company executive; b. Chgo., May 2, 1924; s. Joseph and Elizabeth (Pratscher) F.; B.S., Ill. Inst. Tech., 1944; J.D., John Marshall Law Sch., 1950; M.B.A., U. Chgo., 1962; m. Billie L. Arvidson, Dec. 1, 1951; children—Ronald, Jeanette, Shirley, Mary, Kathryn. Mgr. indsl. relations Am.-Marietta/Martin Marietta, Chgo., 1952-65; v.p. Wedron Silica Sand Co., Chgo., 1965-68; mgr. indsl. relations MSL Industries, Chgo., 1968; v.p. indsl. relations Consol. Packaging Corp., Chgo., 1969; v.p., sec. Katy Industries, Inc., Elgin, Ill., 1970-93, ret., 1993. Served to lt. (j.g.) USNR, 1943-46. Mem. Ill. Bar Assn. Republican. Presbyterian. Home: 277 Otis Rd Barrington IL 60010-5123

FURSTE, WESLEY LEONARD, II, surgeon, educator; b. Cin., Apr. 19, 1915; s. Wesley Leonard and Alma (Deckebach) F.; m. Leone James, Mar. 28, 1942; children: Nancy Dianne, Susan Deanne, Wesley Leonard III. A.B. cum laude (Julius Dexter scholar 1933-34); Harvard Club scholar 1934-35), Harvard U., 1937, M.D., 1941. Diplomate: Am. Bd. Surgery. Intern Ohio State U. Hosp., Columbus, 1941-42; fellow surgery U. Cin., 1945-46; asst. surg. resident Cin. Gen. Hosp., 1946-49; sr. asst. surg. resident Ohio State U. Hosps., 1949-50, chief surg. resident, 1950-51; limited practice medicine specializing in surgery Columbus, 1951—; instr. Ohio State U., 1951-54, clin. asst. prof. surgery, 1954-66, clin. assoc. prof., 1966-74, clin. prof. surgery, 1974-85, clin. prof. emeritus, 1985—; mem. surg. staff Mt. Carmel Med. Center, chmn. dept. surgery, 1981-85, dir. surgery program, 1981-82; mem. surg. staff Children's, Grant Med. Ctr., Univ., Riverside, Meth. Hosps., St. Anthony Med. Ctr., Park Med. Ctr. (all Columbus); surg. cons. Dayton (Ohio) VA Hosp., Columbus State Sch., Ohio State Penitentiary, Mercy Hosp., Benjamin Franklin Hosp., Columbus, Columbus Cmty. Hosp.; regional adv. com. nat. blood program ARC, 1951-68, chmn., 1958-68; invited participant 2d Internat. Conf. on Tetanus, WHO, Bern, Switzerland, 1966, 3d, São, Paulo, Brazil, 1970, 4th, Dakar, Sénégal, 1975, 5th, Ronneby Brunn, Sweden, 1978, 6th, Lyon, France, 1981, 7th, Copanello, Italy, 1984, 8th, Leningrad, USSR, 1987, 9th, Granada, Spain, 1991; invited rapporteur 4th Internat. Conf. on Tetanus, Dakar, Sénégal, 1975; mem. med. adv. com. Medic Alert Found. Internat., 1971-73, 76-80, bd. dirs., 1973-76; Douglas lectr. Med. Coll. of Ohio, Toledo; founder Digestive Disease Found; lectr. U.S. Army M.C. on WWII Chinese activities during 1943-46; invited orator for new citizens at naturalization ceremonies U.S. Dist. Ct. (so. dist.) Ohio. *Wesley L. Furste, II has had as his aim for his entire professional career the best possible surgical care of patients. He has been greatly influenced by the Halsted concept of the 24-hour care of the sick and wounded. As a surgeon in the United States Army 22nd Field Hospital in China from 1943 to 1946, he cared for sick Chinese civilians and wounded Chinese men and officers. Greatly influenced by the overwhelming infections of tetanus and gas gangrene, he continued to conduct research and publish about these problems throughout his entire professional career. He has been particularly pleased that only 34 cases of tetanus were reported, during 1998 (for the approximately one-quarter billion individuals in the U.S.), to the U.S. Department of Health and Human Services Centers for Disease Control and Prevention.* Prime author: Tétanos; Tetanus: A Team Disease; contbg. author: Advances in Military Medicine, 1948, Management of the Injured Patient, Immediate Care of the Acutely Ill and Injured, 1978, Anaerobic Infections, 1989, Procs. of Internat. Tetans Confs. in Switzerland, Brazil, Sweden, Sénégal, France, Italy, USSR, Current Therapy in Emergency Medicine, Surgical Infectious Diseases (3 edits.), Currenty Emergency Therapy, Surgical Infections, Current Diagnosis (multiple edits.), Current Therapy (multiple edits.), Surgical Infections, 5 Minute Clinical Consult, 6 edits. (4 and 5 CD-Rom, Internet), Medical Microbiology and Infectious Diseases, editor Surgical Monthly Review; contbr. articles to profl. jours. Mem. Ohio Motor Vehicle Med. Rev. Bd., 1965-67, Pres. Club, Ohio State Univ.; bd. dirs. Am. Cancer Soc. Franklin County, pres., 1964-66. Served to maj., M.C. AUS, 1942-46, CBI, 1951-53. Recipient China Liberation medal, 2 commendations for surg. service in China U.S. Army; cert. of merit Am. Cancer Soc.; award for outstanding achievement in field clostridial infection dept. surgery Ohio State U. Coll. Medicine, 1984, Outstanding Service award, 1985; award for outstanding and dedicated service Mt. Carmel Med. Ctr., 1985; award for over 25 yrs. service St. Anthony Med. Ctr., U.S.A. Nat. Softball Squash Champion for age group, (75+), Houston, 1992, (80+), Denver, 96. Mem. AMA, AAAS, APHA, Cen. Surg. Assn., Surgical Infection Soc., Internat. Biliary Assn., Shock Soc., Soc. Am. Gastrointestinal Endoscopic Surgeons (com. on stds. of practice, resident and fellow edn., com. legis. review), Soc. Surgery of Alimentary Tract, A.C.S. (gov.-at-large, chmn. Ohio com. trauma; nat. subcom. prophylaxis against tetanus in wound mgmt., Ohio chapter Disting. Service award 1987; regional credentials com.), Am. Assn. Surgery of Trauma, Ohio Surg. Assn., Columbus Surg. Assn. (hon. mem.; pres. 1983), Am. Trauma Soc. (founding mem., dir.), Ohio Med. Assn., Acad. Medicine Columbus and Franklin County (Award of Merit for 17 yrs. service, chmn. blood transfusion com., 50 Year Svc. award), Acad. Medicine Cin., Am. Med. Writers Assn., Grad. Surg. Soc. U. Cin., Robert M. Zollinger Surg. Ohio State U. Surg. Soc., Mont Reid Grad. Surg. Soc., Am. Geriatrics Soc., N.Y. Acad. Scis., Assn. Program Dirs. in Surgery, Assn. Physicians State of Ohio, Collegium Internationale Chirurgiae Digestivae, Assn. Am. Med. Colls., Internat. Soc. Colon and Rectal Surgeons, Soc. Internat. de Chirurgie, Am. Assn. Sr. Physicians, Société Internationale sur le Tétanos, Am. Physicians Art Assn., Am. Assn. Retired Persons (bd. dirs. Franklin County Unit), China-Burma-India Vets., Assn. Columbus Basha (vice comdr. 1992-93, comdr. 1993-94, V-J Day coord., surgeon gen. 1994—), Am. Legion NW Post # 443, Am. Med. Golfing Assn., Internat. Brotherhood Magicians, Soc. Am. Magicians, N.Y. Cen. System Hist. Soc., U.S. Squash Racquets Assn. (mem. ranking com., med. adv. com.), Am. Platform Tennis Assn., Columbus Squash Racquets Assn. (bd. dirs.), VFW of U.S. (lectr.), Pres.'s Club (Ohio State U.). Presbyterian. Fax: (614) 457-5119. E-mail: wfursteII@aol.com. Home and Office: Ohio State Univ 3125 Bembridge Rd Columbus OH 43221-2203

FURTAK, THOMAS ELTON, physicist, educator, author, consultant; b. Ord, Nebr., May 23, 1949; s. Sylvester B. and Elsie L. (Pecenka) F.; m. Carolyn Kay Furtak, Jan. 30, 1971; children: Rick Anthony, Erin Marie, Mark Lim. BS, U. Nebr., 1971; PhD, Iowa State U., 1975. Postdoctoral fellow Ames (Iowa) Lab., 1975-77, assoc. physicist, 1977-80; assoc. prof. Rensselaer Poly. Inst., Troy, N.Y., 1980-86; prof. physics Colo. Sch. Mines, Golden, 1986—. Co-author: (textbook) Optics, 1986; co-editor: Surface Enhanced Raman Scattering, 1982; adv. editor Chem. Physics Letters, 1983-93. Mem. Am. Phys. Soc., Optical Soc. Am., Electrochem. Soc., Am. Chem. Soc., Materials Rsch. Soc., Am. Vacuum Soc., Phi Beta Kappa, Sigma Xi, Pi Mu Epsilon. Democrat. Roman Catholic. Avocations: skiing, hiking, baseball, piano, guitar. Office: Colo Sch Mines 16th and Illinois Sts Golden CO 80401

FURTH, FREDERICK PAUL, lawyer; b. West Harvey, Ill., Apr. 12, 1934; s. Fred P. and Mamie (Stelmach) F.; children: Darby, Ben Anthony, Megan Louise; m. Peggy Wollerman, July 19, 1986. Student, Drake U., 1952-53; BA, U. Mich., 1956, JD, 1959; postgrad., U. Berlin, 1959, U. Munich, Fed. Republic Germany, 1960. Bar: Mich. 1959, N.Y. 1961, D.C. 1965, U.S. Supreme Ct. 1965, Calif. 1966. Assoc. Cahill, Gordon, Reindel & Ohl, N.Y.C., 1960-64; with Kellogg Co., Battle Creek, Mich., 1964-65; assoc. Joseph L. Alioto, San Francisco, 1965-66; sr. ptnr. Furth, Fahrner & Mason, San Francisco, 1966—; bd. dirs. Robert Half Internat.; chmn., propr. Chalk Hill Winery. Trustee, chmn. bd. Furth Family Found., San Francisco; bd. dirs. Franklin and Eleanor Roosevelt Inst., 1996—, The Ctr. for Democracy, Washington; chmn. Internat. Jud. Conf., Strasbourg, France. Mem. ABA, Internat. Bar Assn., N.Y. Bar Assn., San Francisco Bar Assn., State Bar Calif., Assn. of Bar of City of N.Y., St. Francis Yacht Club, Olympic Club. Office: Furth Fahrner & Mason 201 Sansome St San Francisco CA 94104-2303

FURTH, GEORGE, actor, playwright; b. Chgo., Dec. 14, 1932; s. George R. and Evelyn (Tuerk) Schweinfurth. BS in Speech, Northwestern U., 1954; postgrad., Columbia U., 1955. Actor, playwright various studios, N.Y.C., 1956—; mem. faculty drama dept. U. So. Calif., Los Angeles. Actor numerous feature films including The Best Man, 1964, The New Interns, 1964, A Very Special Favor, 1965, Games, 1967, The Cool Ones, 1967, How to Save a Marriage (And Ruin Your Life), 1968, The Boston Strangler, 1968, Butch Cassidy and The Sundance Kid, 1969, Myra Breckinridge, 1970, Blazing Saddles, 1974, Shampoo, 1975, Oh, God!, 1977, Airport '77, 1977, Hooper, 1978, American Raspberry, 1980, Young Doctors in Love, 1982, Megaforce, 1982, Doctor Detroit, 1983, The Man with Two Brains, 1983, Bulworth, 1998, also major TV shows; writer: (Broadway mus.) Company, 1969 (Tony award, N.Y. Drama Critics Circle award, Drama Desk award, Outer Critics Circle award 1970), The Act, 1977; Twigs, 1971, The Supporting Cast, Merrily We Roll Along, Precious Sons, Getting Away With Murder, 1996; actor (TV) Fame is the Name of the Game, 1966, Sam Hill: Who Killed Mr. Foster?, 1971, Let's Switch, 1975, The Scarlett O'Hara War, 1980; TV guest appearances include Batman, 1966, The Odd Couple, 1970, Honey West, 1965, The Monkees, 1966, F Troop, 1965, Bonanza, 1959, I Dream of Jeannie, 1965, Night Gallery, 1970, All in the Family, 1971, Little House on the Prairie, 1974, Murder, She Wrote, 1984, Dr. Quinn, Medicine Woman, 1993. Served with USNR, 1958-62. Recipient Drama-Logue award, Evening Standard award. Mem. Actors Studio. Home: 9200 Sunset Blvd Ste 701 Los Angeles CA 90069-3602*

FURTH, JOHN JACOB, molecular biologist, pathologist, educator; b. Phila., Jan. 25, 1929; s. Jacob and Olga (Berthauer) F.; m. Mary Autry, June 24, 1959; children: Karen, Susan, Robin. BA, Cornell U., 1950; student, Yale Law Sch., 1950-51; MD, Duke U., 1958; MA (hon.), U. Pa., 1972. Intern Bellevue Hosp., N.Y.C., 1958-59; resident in pathology NYU Sch. Medicine, N.Y.C., 1959-60, postdoctoral fellow dept. microbiology, 1960-62; mem. faculty dept. pathology U. Pa. Med. Sch., Phila., 1962—, prof., 1978—. Contbr. articles to profl. jours. Bd. dirs., chmn. hist. sites com. Darby Creek Valley Assn., 1984-96, 1st v.p. 1997—; bd. dirs., founder Friends of the Swedish Cabin (constructed circa 1654), Upper Darby, Pa., 1987; bd. dirs. Fair Housing Coun. of Suburban Phila., 1995—, 2d dist. leader Upper Darby Democratic Party, 1994—. 2d lt. Q.M.C., U.S. Army, 1951-53. Recipient Hoffman LaRoche award, 1958; Eleanor Roosevelt fellow, 1977-78. Mem. AAAS, Am. Soc. Biol. Chemists and Molecular Biologists, Am. Assn. Cancer Rsch., Am. Assn. Pathologists. Democrat. Mem. Soc. of Friends. Achievements include codiscovery of RNA polymerase. Home: 43 Roselawn Ave Lansdowne PA 19050-2317 Office: U Pa Sch Medicine Dept Pathology and Lab Med Philadelphia PA 19104-6082

FURTH, KAREN J., artist, art educator. BA in Am. History, U. Pa., 1983; MA in Photography, NYU, 1988. Biomed. photographer Rockefeller U., 1988-89; photographer Smithsonian Instn., 1989-94; tchr. Trinity Sch., 1990; freelance photographer, 1994—; tchr., cons. Ctr. Urban Cmty. Svcs. The Times Sq., 1994—; tchr. Internat. Ctr. Photography at The Point, N.Y.C., 1998—. One-woman shows include Washington Sq. East Galleries, N.Y.C., 1988, 494 Gallery, N.Y.C., 1991, 92, 94, Pulse Art Gallery, N.Y.C., 1997; exhibited in group shows at Oswego Civic Art Ctr., N.Y.C., 1988, 494 Gallery, N.Y.C., 1991, 92, Synchronicity Space, N.Y.C., 1995, Pulse Art Gallery, N.Y.C., 1996, Golin/Harris, N.Y.C., 1998, others; curatorial projects include The Times Sq. Photography Project, Met. Transp. Authority, 1999; presenter in field; contbr. articles to profl. jours; represented in permanent collections JP Morgan, Mt. Sinai Hosp., others. Recipient Gilbert Graphic Paper award, 1993; Faculty scholar U. Pa., 1979-83; Internat. Outreach grantee, 1993, 94; Open Soc. Inst. Individual Project fellow Soros Found., 1997.

FURTH, YVONNE, advertising executive. Pres. Draft Worldwide, Chgo. Office: Draft Worldwide 142 E Ontario St Chicago IL 60611-2818*

FURUBOTN, EIRIK GRUNDTVIG, economics educator; b. N.Y.C., Apr. 18, 1923; s. Konrad Martin and Caroline (Grundtvig) F.; m. Florence Birkby Duckworth; children—Karin Florence, Erik Grundtvig, Kristian George. BA, Brown U., 1948; MA, Columbia U., 1950, PhD, 1959. Instr. Wesleyan U., Middletown, Conn., 1953-55; asst. prof. Lafayette Coll., Easton, Pa., 1958-60; assoc. prof. Emory U., Atlanta, 1960-63; prof. SUNY, Binghamton, 1963-67, Tex. A&M U., College Station, 1967-82; James L. West prof. econs. U. Tex., Arlington, 1982-96; rsch. assoc. pvt. enterprise rsch. ctr. Tex. A&M U., College Station, 1996—; com. mem. Tex. A&M Univ. Press, College Station, 1974-82; co-dir. Ctr. for Study of New Instl. Econs., U. Saarland, W.Ger., 1986—. Co-author: (with R. Richter) Neue Institutionen Okonomik, 1996, The Evolution of Modern Demand Theory, 1972; co-editor: The Economics of Property Rights, 1974, The New Institutional Economics: An Assessment, 1991, Institutions and Economic Theory, 1997; mem. editl. bd. Applied Econs., London, 1971-72; mem. bd. editors So. Econ. Jour., 1979-81, Zeitschrift für die gesamte Staatswissenschaft, 1984—; contbr. articles to profl. jours. Trustee Allen Acad., Bryan, Tex., 1974-76; mem. adv. coun. Polit. Economy Rsch. Ctr., Bozeman, Mont., 1984-92; mem. nat. adv. bd. Nat. Ctr. for Privatization, Wichita, Kans., 1985-95. Cpl. U.S. Army, 1942-46, ETO. Francis Wayland scholar Brown U., 1948; named Honorarprofessor für Volkswirtschaftslehre U. Saarland, Fed. Republic of Germany. Mem. Am. Econ. Assn., So. Econ. Assn. (exec. com. 1975-77), Can. Econ. Assn., Phi Beta Kappa, Omicron Delta Epsilon, Beta Gamma Sigma, Omega Rho. Republican. Episcopalian. Avocations: antiques; travel. Home: 750 N Rosemary Dr Bryan TX 77802-4307 Office: Tex A&M U Pvt Enterprise Rsch Ctr PO Box 3327 College Station TX 77841-3327

FURUYAMA, RENEE HARUE, association executive; b. Honolulu, Feb. 15, 1957; d. Walter Tadashi and Jane Machie (Kamada) F.; m. Joel Fischer, Oct. 31, 1991; children: Lisa, Nicole. Grad., Tohoku U., Sendai, Japan, 1984; MSW, U. Hawaii, 1988, M.Urban and Regional Planning, 1993. Lic. social worker, Hawaii. Geriatric case mgr. Dept. Human Svcs., Honolulu, 1992-95; pub. policy dir. Mental Health Assn. Hawaii, Honolulu, 1995-98; instr. U. Hawaii Sch. Social Work, 1998—; lectr., spkr. in field. Bd. dirs. Waianae Clubhouse, Miyagi Kenjinkai, Am. Friends Svc. Com.; mem. Unity Organizing Com.; chmn. Hawaii Commn. for Africa. Tohoku U. scholar; recipient numerous scholarships and awards. Mem. NASW, UN Assn. Hawaii (treas. 1988-91). Democrat. Avocation: Buddhist sculpture. Home: 1371-4 Hunakai St Honolulu HI 96816-5501

FURYK, JAMES MICHAEL, professional golfer; b. West Chester, Pa., May 12, 1970. Grad. in Gen. Bus., U. Ariz., 1992. Profl. golfer, 1992—; mem. Ryder Cup team, 1997. Winner Nike Miss. Gulf Coast Classic, 1993, Las Vegas Internat., 1995, United Airlines Hawaiian Open, 1996, Argentine Open, 1997, Las Vegas Invitational, 1998; 2d pl. Meml. Tournament, 1997, The Tour Championship, 1997. Avocation: sports. Office: c/o PGAAmerica Box 109601 100 Ave of Champions Palm Beach Gardens FL 33410*

FUSARO, RAMON MICHAEL, dermatologist; b. Bklyn., Mar. 6, 1927; s. Angelo and Ida (Pucci) F.; m. Lavonne Johnsen, Nov. 6, 1971; children: Lisa Ann, Toni Ann; stepsons: Jeff, Scott. BA, U. Minn., 1949, BS, 1951, MD, 1953, MS, 1958, PhD, 1965. Diplomate Am. Bd. Dermatology. Intern Mpls. Gen. Hosp., 1953-54, resident in internal medicine, 1954-57; from instr. to assoc. prof. U. Minn., 1957-70, dir. outpatient dermatology clinic, 1962-70; prof., chmn. dept. dermatology U. Nebr. Med. Center, Omaha, 1970-82; prof. dermatology sect. dept. internal medicine U. Nebr. Med. Ctr., Omaha, 1982-91, acting chief sect. dermatology, 1991-94; prof., chmn. dept. dermatology Creighton U., Omaha, 1975-87; prof. dermatology dept. internal medicine Creighton U. Sch. Medicine, Omaha, 1983-89; prof. Creighton U., Omaha, 1989—; dir. dermatology residency program Creighton/Nebr. Univs. Health Found., 1975-83; prof. dept. pub. health and preventive medicine Hereditary Cancer Inst., Creighton U., 1984—. Contbr. over 300 articles to profl. jours., chpts. in books. With USN, 1944-46. Mem. Am. Acad. Dermatology, Soc. Investigative Dermatology, Am. Soc. Photobiology, Sigma Xi. E-mail: rmfusaro@Creighton.edu. Home: 908 Beaver Lake Blvd Plattsmouth NE 68048-4500 Office: 984360 Nebr Med Ctr Omaha NE 68198-4360 also: Creighton U Med Sch Criss III Dept Prev Med 2500 California Plz Omaha NE 68178-0001

FUSCIARDI, KATHERINE, nursing administrator; b. Highland Park, Mich., Aug. 15, 1965; d. William Charles and Geraldine May (Revoldt) Freigruber; m. Antonio Fusciardi, July 11, 1987; children: Samantha Nicole, Michael Antonio. BSN, Oakland U., Rochester, Mich., 1987. Cert. BCLS instr., NALS instr. Staff nurse William Beaumont Hosp., Royal Oak, Mich.; staff nurse, head nurse Shady Grove Adventist Hosp., Rockville, Md.; staff nurse, asst. clin. mgr. St. Joseph's Mercy Hosp., Mt. Clemens, Mich.; staff nurse Mercy Hosp. South, Charlotte, N.C.; mem. clin. faculty Salisbury (Md.) State U., fall 1994; staff nurse Penninsula Regional Med. Ctr., Salisbury, 1995-96; per diem nurse Queen of Valley Hosp., West Covina, Calif., 1996—. Mem. NAACOG, Sigma Theta Tau.

FUSCO, ANDREW G., lawyer; b. Punxsutawney, Pa., Jan. 11, 1948; s. Albert G. and Virginia N. (Whitesell) F.; m. Deborah K. Lucas; children: Matthew, Geoffrey, David. BS in Bus. Adminstrn. and Fin., W.Va. U., 1970, JD, 1973. Bar: W.Va. 1973, U.S. Ct. Appeals (4th cir.) 1974, U.S. Supreme Ct. 1977, U.S. Ct. Appeals (fed. cir.) 1985, U.S. Tax Ct. 1995. Pvt. practice Morgantown, W.Va., 1973-85; prin. The Fusco Legal Group, L.C., Morgantown, 1998—; pros. atty. Monongalia County, W.Va., 1977-81, 1977-81; instr. Coll. Bus. and Econs., Law Ctr. W.Va. U., 1975-76, instr. Sch. Journalism, 1997—; pros. atty. Monongalia County, W.Va., 1977-81; instr. Coll. Bus. and Econs., Law Ctr., W.Va. U., 1975-76, sch. journalism, 1997—; dir. Pitts. Environ. Systems Inc., 1983-86; adj. prof. W.Va. U. Sch. Journalism, 1997. Author: Antitrust Law (West Virginia Practice Handbook), 1991; editor, contbg. author: Twenty Feet From Glory (John R. Goodwin), 1970, Business Law (John R. Goodwin), 1972, Beyond Baker Street (Michael Harrison), 1976. Bd. dirs. W.Va. Career Colls., 1971-76; mem. profl. adv. bd. Childbirth and Parent Edn. Assn., 1975-82, Rape and Domestic Violence Info. Ctr., 1977-81; mem. W.Va. Sec. State's Tribunal on Election Reform, 1977-81; chmn. Monongalia County Drug Edn. Task Force, 1978-80; mem. bd. advisors Nat. Smokers Alliance, 1998—. Recipient Am. Jurisprudence award Bancroft-Whitney Publ. Co., 1971; named Outstanding Young Man of Morgantown, 1979. Mem. ABA, ATLA, Monongalia County Bar Assn., Am. Judicature Soc., W.Va. Bar Assn., Baker St. Irregulars of N.Y., Sherlock Holmes Soc. London, Nat. Dist. Attys. Assn., Son of Italy, W.Va. Law Sch. Assn., Monongalia Arts Ctr. (pres., treas., trustee). Democrat. Roman Catholic. E-mail: andyfusco@aol.com. Fax: 304-594-1181. Home: 20 Harewood Mnr Morgantown WV 26508-9108 Office: The Fusco Legal Group LC 2400 Cranberry Sq Morgantown WV 26508-9209

FUSCO, BARBARA LEIGH, communications executive, editor; b. Albany, N.Y., Jan. 31, 1974. BA in Religion & Anthropology cum laude, Williams Coll., 1996. News asst. Williams Coll., Williamstown, Mass., 1994-96; sr. rsch. assoc. Adv. Bd. Co., Washington, 1996-97; rsch. assoc. The Communitarian Network, Washington, 1997-99; comm. mgr. Assn. Sales & Mktg. Cos., Reston, Va., 1999—. Contbr. Limits of Privacy by Amitai Etzioni, 1999; columnist The Responsive Community, 1997-99. Active, donor Leukemia Soc. Am., 1998, Whitman-Walker Clinic of D.C., 1996—; vol. Arlington Agy. on Aging, 1997—. Mem. Washington RunHers (treas. 1998—), Internat. Assn. Bus. Comm. Avocations: marathon running, reading, swimming, tennis. E-mail: bfusco@asmc.org. Office: Assn Sales & Mktg Cos 2100 Reston Pky Ste 400 Reston VA 20191

FUSELIER, HAROLD ANTHONY, JR., physician, urologist; b. Abbeville, La., Dec. 1, 1942; s. Harold Anthony and May Elizabeth (Fowler) F.; m. Ann Valentino, May 17, 1968; children: Harold Anthony III, F. Scott, J.

Prentice, Mims Michael. BS, La. State U., Baton Rouge, 1964; MD, La. State U., New Orleans, 1967. Diplomate Am. Bd. Urology. Internship Charity Hosp., New Orleans, 1967-68; residency urology Alton Ochener Medical Found., 1970-74; mem. dept. urology Ochsner Clinic, New Orleans, 1974-89, chmn. dept. urology, 1989—; med. dir. surgery Ochsner Found. Hosp., New Orleans, 1990—; clin. prof. urology Tulane U. Med. Ctr., New Orleans, 1988—, La. State U. Med. Ctr., New Orleans, 1990—; program dir. La. State U./Ochsner Urology Tng. Program, 1991—. Contbr. articles to profl. jours. Capt. USAF, 1968-70. Fellow ACS; mem. Am. Urol. Assn., Soc. Internat. d'Urologie, Soc. for Study of Impotence, Soc. Univ. Urologists. Roman Catholic. Avocations: golf, hunting, fishing. Office: Ochsner Clinic 1514 Jefferson Hwy New Orleans LA 70121-2483

FUSELIER, LOUIS ALFRED, lawyer; b. New Orleans, Mar. 26, 1932; s. Robert Howe and Monica (Hanemann) F.; m. Eveline Gasquet Fenner, Dec. 27, 1956; children: Louis Alfred, Henri de la Claire, Elizabeth Fenner. B.S., La. State U., 1953; LL.B., Tulane U., 1959. Bar: La. 1959, Miss. 1964, U.S. Supreme Ct. 1965. Trial atty. NLRB, New Orleans, 1959-62; pres., ptnr. Fuselier, Hector, Robertson & Ott and successor firms, 1969-94; v.p., ptnr. Young, Williams, Henderson & Fuselier, P.A., Jackson, Miss., 1994—. Capt. USAF, 1953-56. Fellow Am. Acad. Hosp. Attys., Am. Coll. Labor and Employment Lawyers, The Am. Employment Laws Coun., Am. Law Inst.; mem. ABA (practice and procedure com. of labor law sect.), La. Bar Assn. (past chmn. labor law sect.), Miss. Bar Assn., Hinds County Bar Assn., Miss. Bar Found., Miss. Def. Lawyers, Miss. Wildlife Fedn. (pres. 1975-76), Newcomen Soc., Soc. Human Resource Mgmt. (accredited pers. diplomate), Miss. Econ. Coun. (dir. 1996-97), Miss. Mfrs. Assn., Boston Club (New Orleans), Country Club of Jackson, Univ. Club (Jackson), Rotary (Paul Harris fellow). Home: 3804 Old Canton Rd Jackson MS 39216-3521

FUSFELD, DANIEL ROLAND, economist; b. Washington, May 23, 1922; s. Irving Sidney and Cecile (Leban) F.; m. Harriet Miller, Aug. 30, 1947; children: Robert, Sarah, Yaakov Sadeh. BA, George Washington U., 1941; MA, Columbia U., 1947, PhD, 1953. Instr. Hofstra Coll., Hempstead, N.Y., 1947-53, asst. prof., 1953-56; asst. prof. Mich. State U., East Lansing, 1956-60; assoc. prof. U. Mich., Ann Arbor, 1960-64, prof., 1964-87, prof. emeritus, 1987—; lectr. USAF Inst. Tech., Dayton, Ohio, 1958-59; vis. assoc. prof. Columbia U., N.Y.C., 1960; bd. dirs. Spectrum Human Svcs., 1992-98, Avalon Housing, Inc. Author: Economic Thought of Franklin D. Roosevelt, 1956, The Age of the Economist, 1966, 8th edit. 1998, Economics, 1972, The Basic Economics of the Urban-Racial Crisis, 1973, Rise and Repression of Radical Labor, 1877-1918, 1985; co-author: The Political Economy of the Urban Ghetto, 1984; co-editor: The Soviet Economy, 1962; also articles. With U.S. Army, 1943-46. Mem. Am. Econ. Assn., Assn. for Evolutionary Econs. (v.p. 1970, pres. 1971), Internat. Network for Econ. Method (chmn. 1989-92), Hist. Econ. Soc. Home: 3975 Ridgemaar Sq Ann Arbor MI 48105-3046 Office: U Mich Dept Econs Ann Arbor MI 48109

FUSILLO, THOMAS VICTOR, environmental engineer; b. Bklyn., Feb. 17, 1953; s. Pat and Catherine (Notarnicola) F.; m. Michele Fran Lipman, June 24, 1979; children: Jennifer Lynn, Steven Joseph, Alyssa Nicole. BS in Environ. Sci., Rutgers U., 1975, MS in Agrl. Engring., 1977. Cert. groundwater profl. Rsch. intern Rutgers U., New Brunswick, N.J., 1975-77, adj. instr., 1976-77; hydrologist U.S. Geol. Survey, Trenton, 1977-87, dist. geochemistry specialist, 1983-87; sr. assoc. Environ Corp., Princeton, N.J., 1987-89, project mgr., 1989-91, mgr., 1991-94, prin. 1994—. Mem. Am. Geophys. Union, Assn. Ground Water Scientists and Engrs., Sigma Xi, Alpha Zeta. Home: 1228 Bridle Estates Dr Yardley PA 19067-3957 Office: 214 Carnegie Ctr Princeton NJ 08540-6237

FUSSELL, KEITH BAUGUS, minister; b. Dickson, Tenn., Apr. 23, 1961; s. Herman Clyde Jr. and Carey Alberta (Baugus) F.; m. Kimberly Diane McDowell, June 29, 1985; children: Joshua Keith, Joanna Hillary, Joel McDowell. BA, David Lipscomb U., 1983; MA in Religion, Harding U., 1990. Lic. profl. counselor, Tenn.; cert. Nat. Bd. for Cert. Counselors. Assoc. minister Sunset Ch. of Christ, Miami, Fla., 1983-87; minister Kiski Valley Ch. of Christ, Apollo, Pa., 1987-88; asst. campus minister Highland St. Ch. of Christ, Memphis, 1989-90; lead geriatric counselor N.E. Mental Health Ctr., Memphis, 1990-92; family life minister Sycamore View Ch. of Christ, Memphis, 1993—. Mem. Am. Assn. Christian Counselors, Am. Assn. Marriage and Family Therapy (assoc.), Psi Chi. Office: Sycamore View Ch of Christ 1910 Sycamore View Rd Memphis TN 38134-6634

FUSSELL, PAUL, author, English literature educator; b. Pasadena, Calif., Mar. 22, 1924; s. Paul and Wilhma Wilson (Sill) F.; m. Betty Ellen Harper, June 17, 1949 (div. 1987); children: Rosalind, Samuel; m. Harriette Behringer, Apr. 11, 1987. BA, Pomona (Calif.) Coll., 1947, LittD (hon.), 1981; MA, Harvard U., 1949, PhD, 1952; MA (hon.), U. Pa., 1983; LittD (hon.), Monmouth Coll., N.J., 1985. Instr. English, Conn. Coll., 1951-55; mem. faculty Rutgers U., 1955—, John DeWitt prof. English lit., 1976-83; Donald T. Regan prof. English lit. U. Pa., Phila., 1983-94, prof. emeritus, 1994—; cons. editor Random House, 1963-64; lectr. Am. univs., 1965—; vis. prof. Kings Coll., London, 1990-92. Author: The Rhetorical World of Augustan Humanism, 1965, Poetic Meter and Poetic Form, 1965, rev., 1979, Samuel Johnson and The Life of Writing, 1971, The Great War and Modern Memory (Nat. Book Critics Circle award 1975, Nat. Book award 1976), Abroad: British Literary Traveling Between the Wars, 1980, The Boy Scout Handbook & Other Observations, 1982, Class: A Guide through the American Status System, 1983, Thank God for the Atom Bomb & Other Essays, 1988, Wartime: Understanding and Behavior in the Second World War, 1989; BAD: or The Dumbing of America, 1991, The Anti-Egoist: Kingsley Amis, Man of Letters, 1994, Doing Battle: The Making of a Skeptic, 1996; contbg. editor Harper's, 1979-83, The New Republic, 1979-85. Served with AUS, 1943-46. Decorated Purple Heart, Bronze Star; recipient James D. Phelan award Phelan Found., 1964; Lindback Found. award, 1971; Ralph Waldo Emerson award Phi Beta Kappa, 1976; sr. fellow Nat. Endowment Humanities, 1973-74; Guggenheim fellow, 1977-78; Rockefeller Found. fellow, 1983-84. Fellow Royal Soc. Lit., Soc. Am. Historians; mem. MLA, Acad. Lit. Studies. Home: 2020 Walnut St Philadelphia PA 19103-5635

FUSSELL, ROBERT F., federal judge. BA, U. Ark., 1960, LLB, 1965. With NLRB, 1965-67; asst. U.S. atty. Eastern Dist. Ark., U.S. Dist. Justice, Little Rock, 1968-76; pvt. law practice, 1976-82; bankruptcy judge U.S. Dist. Ct. (ea. and we. dists.) Ark., Little Rock, 1983—. Served with U.S. Army, 1960-62. Mem. ABA, Ark. Bar Assn., Nat. Conf. Bankruptcy Judges. Office: US Bankruptcy Ct 300 W 2d St Little Rock AR 72201

FUSTÉ, JOSÉ ANTONIO, federal judge; b. San Juan, Puerto Rico, Nov. 3, 1943. BBA, U. P.R., San Juan, 1965, LLB, 1968. Ptnr. Jimenez & Fuste, Hato Rey, P.R., 1968-85; judge U.S. Dist. Ct. P.R., San Juan, 1985—; prof. U. P.R., 1972-85. Roman Catholic. Office: US Courthouse CH-133 150 Ave Carlos Chardon Hato Rey San Juan PR 00918-1703*

FUSTER, JAIME B., supreme court justice; b. Guayama, P.R., Jan. 12, 1941; s. Jaime L. and Maria Luisa (Berlingeri) F.; m. Mary Jo Fuster, Dec. 19, 1966; children: Maria Luisa, Jaime. BA, Notre Dame U., 1962; JD, U. P.R., 1965; LLM, Columbia U., 1966; SJD, Harvard U., 1974; LLD(hon.), Temple U., 1985. Bar: P.R. Prof. law U. P.R., 1966-73, 78-80, project dir. Study on Legal Profession of P.R., Ctr. Social Research, 1970-73, dean Law Sch., 1974-78; ednl. cons. Office of Cts. Adminstrn. Govt. of P.R., 1978-80; dep. asst. atty. gen. U.S. Dept. Justice, Washington, 1980-81; pres. Cath. U. P.R., 1981-84; mem. Congress from P.R., Washington, 1984-92; resident commr. Commonwealth of P.R., 1984-92; assoc. justice P.R. Supreme Ct., 1992—; cons., lectr. in field. Author: Political and Civil Rights in Puerto Rico, 1968, The Duties of Citizens, 1973, The Lawyers of Puerto Rico: A Sociological Study, 1974, Law and Problems of Elderly People, 1978; editor-in-chief U. P.R. Law Rev., 1964-65; contbr. chpts. to books, articles to profl. jours. Named One of Outstanding Young Men of Am., U.S. Jr. C. of C., 1978. Mem. Assn. Am. Colls. (adv. bd. 1980-84), Interam. Bar Found. (bd. dirs. 1975-79). Democrat. Roman Catholic. Avocation: tennis. Office: PO Box 2392 San Juan PR 00902-2392

FUSTER, VALENTIN, cardiologist, educator; b. Barcelona, Spain, Jan. 20, 1943; s. Joaquin and Pilar Fuster; m. Angela-Maria Guals, Sept. 3, 1968; children: Pablo, Silvia. Baccalaurate, Colegio Jesuitas, Barcelona, 1961; MD, Barcelona U., 1967. Diplomate Am. Bd. Internal Medicine (mem. com. subsplty. bd. cardiovas. disease), Am. Bd. Cardiology. Intern Hosp. Clinico, Barcelona, 1967-68; rsch. fellow U. Edinburgh, Scotland, 1968-71; fellow in medicine and cardiovasc. diseases Mayo Grad. Sch. Medicine, Rochester, Minn., 1971-74; asst. prof. medicine Mayo Med. Sch., Rochester, 1974-77, assoc. prof. medicine, 1978-81, assoc. prof. pediat., 1980—, prof. medicine and cardiovasc. diseases, 1981-82; Arthur A. and Hilda M. Master prof. medicine Mt. Sinai Sch. Medicine, N.Y.C., 1982-91, chief divsn. cardiology, 1982-91; head cardiology unit Mass. Gen. Hosp., 1991-93; Mallinckrodt prof. medicine Harvard Med. Sch., Boston, 1991-93; dir. Cardiovasc. Inst. Mt. Sinai Med. Ctr., N.Y.C., 1993—; mem. cardiology adv. com. NIH; mem. com. Am. Bd. Cardiology; hon. lectr. numerous orgns.; mem. adv. coun. Nat. Heart, Lung and Blood Insts., 1997. Mem. editl. bd. Am. Jour. Cardiology, 1982, Arteriosclerosis, 1982, Jour. The Am. Coll. Cardiology, 1987, Circulation, 1988, consulting editor, 1992, circulation rsch. consulting editor, 1997; contbr. over 400 articles to profl. jours. Recipient 30 rsch. and tchg. awards including Gruntzig award European Soc. Cardiology, 1992, Disting. Sci. award Am. Coll. Cardiology, 1993, Disting. Conner Lectr. award Am. Heart Assn., 1993, Principe de Asturias award for sci. and tech. Found. Principe de Asturias, Oviedo, Spain, Principe de Asturias award for sci. and tech. U. Asturias in conjunction with Royal Family of Spain, 1996. Fellow Am. Coll. Cardiology (chair tng. dirs. com. 1997, Disting. Bishop Lectr. award 1994), Royal Coll. Physicians; mem. Am. Heart Assn. (chmn. pub. com., bd. dirs. 1994, pres.-elect 1997, pres. 1998—), Am. Soc. Clin. Investigations, European Soc. Clin. Investigation, Brit. Cardiac Soc. (corr.). Office: Mt Sinai Med Ctr 1 Gustave L Levy Pl # 1030 New York NY 10029-6500

FUSTON, ANDREW D., interior designer, educator, speaker, writer, environmentalist; b. Kansas City, Kans., Dec. 27, 1963; s. Donald Max and Margaret G. Fuston. BFA, U. Kans., 1989. Interior designer Brennan Beer Gorman Monk, N.Y.C., 1989-91, Silberstang Architects, N.Y.C., 1991-92; sr. interior designer Rockwell Group, N.Y.C., 1992-94, Gruzen Samton, N.Y.C., 1994-1998; adj. prof. Fashion Inst. Tech., N.Y.C., 1996—; adj. asst. prof. NYU, N.Y.C., 1991—; sr. project designer Pembrooke and Ives, N.Y.C., 1998-99; interior designer Mancini Duffy, N.Y.C., 1999—; chair Green October, N.Y.C., 1992, Green Design New York, N.Y.C., 1993-95, IBD/N.Y. Coun. on the Environment, N.Y.C., 1989-92. Co-author: The Green Pages, 1991, 93, 95; contbr. to book and newsletters; designer restaurant Nobu, 1994. Mem. Orgn. Lesbian and Gay Archs. and Designers, Internat. Interior Design Assn. (profl. mem.; v.p.). Avocations: European travel, ecotourism. Home: 45 E 25th St 8th Fl New York NY 10010-2940 Office: Mancini Duffy 2 World Trade Ctr New York NY 10048

FUTCH, ARCHER HAMNER, retired physicist; b. Monroe, N.C., Mar. 21, 1925; s. Archer Hamner and Emma Lee (Covington) F.; m. Patricia West, June 13, 1953; children: Lisa Stewart, Jacqueline Lee, Tina Corine. BS, U. N.C., 1949, MS, 1951; PhD, U. Md., 1955. Physicist E.I. Du Pont de Nemours Co., Aiken, S.C., 1955-58, Lawrence Livermore (Calif.) Nat. Lab., 1959-91. Mem. Livermore Planning Commn., 1968-72, Livermore City Coun., 1972-76; mayor City of Livermore, 1976; bd. dirs. Alameda County Water Dist., 1976-80, South Livermore Valley Agric. Land trust, 1995—. Mem. Am. Phys. Soc., Phi Beta Kappa, Sigma Xi, Sigma Pi Sigma. Republican. Home: 1252 Westbrook Pl Livermore CA 94550-6430 Office: Lawrence Livermore Nat Lab Livermore CA 94550

FUTCH, WILLIAM STEWART, JR., gastroenterologist; b. Charlotte, N.C., Oct. 21, 1957; s. William Stewart and Norma Anne (Blue) F.; m. Lucy Nan Wright, Dec. 16, 1989; children: William Stewart III, John Harrison. BS in Biology, U. Richmond, 1980; MS in Microbiology and Immunology, Va. Commonwealth U., 1985; MD, Eastern Va. Med. Sch., Norfolk, 1990. Intern in internal medicine Eastern Va. Grad. Sch. Medicine, 1990-91, resident in internal medicine, 1991-93; fellow in gastroenterology Med. Coll. Va., Richmond, 1993-96; staff physician Virginia Beach (Va.) Free Clinic, 1991-92, clin. instr. of med., Bowman-Gray Sch. of Med., 1997—, pvt. prac. in gastroenterology with Carolina Phys., New Bern, N.C., staff phys., Craven Regional Med. Ctr., New Bern, N.C. Contbr. articles to profl. jours. Vol. Big. Bros. Am., 1978-80, Pi Kappa Alpha hwy. cleanup program, 1979, 80. Mem. AGA, ACG, Med. Soc. of North Carolina, Am. Soc. Microbiology, Med. Soc. Va., Sigma Xi. Avocations: tennis, biking, photography. Office: 700B McCarthy Blvd New Bern NC 28562

FUTCHER, PALMER HOWARD, physician, educator; b. Balt., Sept. 13, 1910; s. Thomas Barnes and Gwendolen Marjorie (Howard) F.; m. Mary Viola Rightor, Nov. 21, 1942 (dec. Mar. 1985); children: Marjorie Rightor, Jane Pillow. AB, Harvard U., 1932; MD, Johns Hopkins U., 1936. Diplomate Am. Bd. Internal Medicine (exec. dir. 1967-75). Intern, then asst. resident and chief resident Johns Hopkins Hosp., 1936-39, 41; asst. resident Rockefeller Inst. Hosp., 1939-41; asst. prof. medicine Washington U., St. Louis, 1946-48; assoc. prof. medicine Johns Hopkins U., Balt., 1948-66; assoc. prof. medicine U. Pa., Phila., 1967-89, prof., 1989-94, asst. dean John Hopkins U. Sch. Medicine, 1959-62, dir. health svcs. med. instns., 1962-66; physician in charge pvt. outpatient svc. Johns Hopkins Hosp., 1948-57. Author: Giants and Dwarfs, 1933; contbr. numerous articles to profl. jours. Comdr. M.C., USN, 1941-46. Fellow Coll. Physicians Phila.; mem. Am. Soc. Clin. Investigation, Endocrine Soc., Am. Diabetes Assn., Am. Clin. and Climatol. Assn., Am. Osler Soc., World Federalist Assn., 14 West Hamilton St. Club (Balt.), Phi Beta Kappa. Democrat. Episcopalian. Avocations: tennis, golf, sailing, fishing, world peace affairs. Home: 13801 York Rd Apt D11 Cockeysville Hunt Valley MD 21030

FUTEY, BOHDAN A., federal judge; b. 1939. BA, Case Western Reserve U., 1962, MA, 1964; JD, Cleve. State U., 1968. Ptnr. Futey & Rakowsky, Cleve., 1968-72; chief asst. police prosecutor Cleve., 1972-74; exec. asst. Mayor of Cleve., 1974-75; ptnr. Bazarko, Futey and Oryshkewych, Cleve., 1975-84; chmn. U.S. Foreign Claims Settlement Commn., 1984-87; judge U.S. Claims Ct., Washington, 1987—. Mem. ABA, Parma Bar Assn., Ukrainian Am. Bar Assn., Cleve. Bar Assn., D.C. Bar Assn. Office: US Claims Ct 717 Madison Pl NW Washington DC 20005*

FUTRELL, JOHN WILLIAM, legal association administrator, lawyer; b. Alexandria, La., July 6, 1935; s. J.W. and Sarah Ruth (Hitesman) F.; m. Iva Macdonald, Aug. 13, 1966; children: Sarah, Daniel. BA, Tulane U., 1957; postgrad., Free U. Berlin, 1958; LLB, Columbia U., 1965. Bar: La. 1966. Atty. Lemle & Kelleher, New Orleans, 1966-71; prof. law U. Ala., 1971-74, U. Ga., 1974-80; pres. Environ. Law Inst., Washington, 1980—; lectr. USIA, Japan and India, 1978, Austria, 1979, Sweden, Germany, U.K. and Ireland, 1980, Argentina, 1988, Brazil, 1991, Mex., 1992, Germany and Chile, 1993, India, 1997; Woodrow Wilson fellow Smithsonian Instn., Washington, 1978-80. Co-author: Sustainable Environmental Law, 1993. Pres. Sierra Club, San Francisco, 1977-78, nat. bd. dirs., 1971-81; del. UN Conf. on Water, 1977, White House Conf. Inflation, 1974. Capt. USMC, 1957-62. Fulbright scholar, 1958. Mem. ABA, AAAS, Am. Law Inst., Phi Beta Kappa, Order of Coif. Club: Cosmos. Home: 4600 7th St N Arlington VA 22203-2011 Office: Environ Law Inst 1616 P St NW Washington DC 20036-1434

FUTRELL, ROBERT FRANK, military historian, consultant; b. Waterford, Miss., Dec. 15, 1917; s. James Chester and Sarah Olivia (Brooks) F.; m. Marie Elizabeth Grimes, Oct. 8, 1944 (dec. 1978); m. JoAnn McGowan Ellis, Dec. 15, 1980. BA with distinction, U. Miss., 1938, MA, 1939; PhD in History, Vanderbilt U., 1950. Spl. cons. U.S. War Dept., Washington, 1946; historian USAF Hist. Office, Washington, 1946-49; assoc. prof. mil. history Air U., Maxwell AFB, Ala., 1950-51, prof., 1951-71, sr. historian, 1971-74, prof. emeritus mil. history, 1974—; professorial lectr. George Washington U., 1963-68; guest lectr. Air U. Squadron Officer Sch., Air Command and Staff Coll., Air War Coll., Air Force Acad., Army War Coll., Militärgeschichtliches Forschungsamt, German Fed. Republic, 1951—, Sch. Advanced Airpower Studies; participant Air Force Acad. Mil. History Symposia, 1968—, Militärgeschichtliches Forschungsamt, Freiburg, German Fed. Republic, 1988; vis. prof. mil. history Airpower Rsch. Inst., Ctr. for Aerospace Doctrine Rsch. and Edn., Air U., 1982-85, hist. advisor to USAF project Corona Harvest, 1969-74; cons. East Aviation Svcs. & Tech., Inc., Chantilly, Va.; hist. advisor Lafayette Mus. Found., Air Force Acad., 1990. Author: Ideas, Concepts, Doctrine: A History of Basic Thinking in the United States Air Force, 1907-1964, 1971, rev. edit., 1907-84, 2 vols., 1989, The United States Air Force in Korea, 1950-1953, 1961, rev. edit., 1983, The United States Air Force in Southeast Asia: The Advisory Years to 1965, 1981, (with Wesley Frank Craven, James L. Cate) The Army Air Force in World War II, 1948-1958; contbr. chpts. to hist. books, articles to scholarly publs. Served to capt. USAAF, 1941-45, lt. col. USAF Res., ret. Recipient Meritorious Civilian Svc. award USAF, 1970, Exceptional Civilian Svc. decoration Sec. of USAF, 1973. Mem. Ala. Hist. Assn., The Ret. Officers Assn., SAR (pres. Montgomery County chpt. 1971-74), So. Hist. Assn., Air Force Hist. Found. (mem. editorial advisors 1969-81, trustee 1985—), Inst. Mil. Affairs, Montgomery Capital City Club, Kiwanis Club of Montgomery, Phi Eta Sigma, Pi Kappa Pi. Methodist. Address: 908 Lynwood Dr Montgomery AL 36111-2514

FUTTER, ELLEN VICTORIA, museum administrator; b. N.Y.C., Sept. 21, 1949; d. Victor and Joan Babette (Feinberg) F.; m. John A. Shutkin, Aug. 25, 1974; children—Anne Victoria, Elizabeth Jane. Student, U. Wis., 1967-69; AB magna cum laude, Barnard Coll., 1971; JD, Columbia U., 1974, LLD (hon.), 1984; LLD (hon.), Hamilton Coll., 1985, N.Y. Law Sch.; DHL (hon.), Amherst Coll., Hofstra U., 1994, CCNY, 1996, L.I. City Coll., 1995. Bar: N.Y. 1975. Assoc. Milbank, Tweed, Hadley & McCloy, N.Y.C., 1974-80; acting pres. Barnard Coll., N.Y.C., 1980-81, pres., 1981-93; president American Museum of Natural History, New York, NY, 1993—; bd. dirs. Bristol Myers Squibb, Am. Internat. Group, J.P. Morgan, Consol. Edison of N.Y.; trustee Am. Mus. Natural History. Ptnr. N.Y.C. Partnership; bd. dirs. The Am. Assembly. Recipient Spirit of Achievement award Albert Einstein Coll. Medicine/Yeshiva U., Abram L. Sachar award Brandeis U., Elizabeth Cutter Morrow award YWCA, Distinction medal Barnard Coll., Excellence medal Columbia U. Mem. ABA, Am. Acad. Arts and Scis., N.Y. State Bar Assn., Assn. Bar City N.Y., Nat. Inst. Social Scis., Coun. Fgn. Rels., Cosmopolitan Club, Century Club, Phi Beta Kappa. Office: Am Mus Natural History Central Park West at 79th New York NY 10024*

FUTTER, JOAN BABETTE, former school librarian; b. N.Y.C., Nov. 15, 1921; d. Samuel S. and Helen (Mosher) Feinberg; m. Victor Futter, Jan. 26, 1943; children: Jeffrey Leesam, Ellen Victoria Futter Shutkin, Deborah Gail Futter Cohan. AB, NYU, 1941; MS, L.I. U., 1966. Sch. libr. Carrie Palmer Weber Jr. High Sch., Port Washington, N.Y., 1966-91. Mem. LWV, AAUW, L.I. Sch. Media Assn., C.W. Post Libr. Assn., Cold Spring Harbor Beach Club, Manhasset Bay Yacht Club. Home: 17 Sunnyvale Rd Port Washington NY 11050-4519

FUTTER, VICTOR, lawyer; b. N.Y.C., Jan. 22, 1919; s. Leon Nathan and Merle Caroline (Allison) F.; m. Joan Babette Feinberg, Jan. 26, 1943; children: Jeffrey Leesam, Ellen Victoria Futter Shutkin, Deborah Gail Futter Cohan. AB in Govt. and English with honors, Columbia U., 1939, JD, 1942. Bar: N.Y. 1942, U.S. Supreme Ct 1948. Assoc. firm Sullivan & Cromwell, 1946-52; with Allied Corp. (now Allied Signal Inc.), Morristown, N.J., 1952-84, assoc. gen. counsel, 1976-78, v.p., sec., 1978-84; dir. Allied Chem. Nuclear Products, 1977-84; gen. counsel, sec. to bd. trustees Fairleigh Dickinson U., 1984-85; spl. prof. law Hofstra Law Sch., 1976-78, 88-89, 94—, spl. cons. to the dean, 1997—; lectr., seminar on corp. in modern soc. Columbia U. Law Sch., 1986-98. Editor: Columbia Law Rev; gen. editor Nonprofit Governance: An Executive's Guide, 1997; contbr. articles to profl. jours. Trustee, dep. mayor Village of Flower Hill, N.Y., 1974-76; mem. senate Columbia U., 1969-75; chmn. bd. Columbia Coll. Fund, 1970-72; pres. parents and friends com. Mt. Holyoke Coll., 1978-80; pres. Flower Hill Assn., 1968-70; bd. dirs. N.Y. Young Dems., 1948-52, Nat. Exec. Svc. Corps, 1997—, Soc. Columbia Grads., 1998—; co-chmn. fund drive Port Washington Cmty. Chest, 1965-66, bd. dirs., 1965-75; mem. coun. overseers C.W. Post, 1984-85; bd. dirs. Acad. Polit. Sci., 1986-94; bd. dirs. Greenwich House, 1985—, sr. vice chair, 1991—; bd. dirs. Nat. Assn. Local Arts Agys.-Arts for Am., 1989-91, Am. Soc. Corp. Secs., 1987-90, pres. N.Y. chpt., 1983-84; chmn. Com. on Nonprofits, 1992-97; bd. dirs. Justice Resource Ctr., 1992-97; chair ad hoc Lunch Group for Nonprofits, 1993—. Maj. AUS. Recipient Alumni medal Columbia U., 1970, Disting. Svc. award Am. Soc. Corp. Secs., 1994; James Kent scholar. Fellow Am. Bar Found.; mem. ABA (bd. govs. 1999—, coun. sr. lawyers divsn. 1989-97, chair 1995-96, chair Editl. Bd. Experience, 1989-95, liaison to ABA CEELI program 1990—, sec. on bus. law, corp. laws com., com. on non-profit corps., sect. on internat. law and practice 1990—), Assn. of Bar of City of N.Y. (com. on internat. human rights 1983-85, com. on 2d century 1985-89, sr. lawyers com. 1989—, chair 1992-95, nonprofit com. 1995-96, Disting. Svc. award Individual Mentor Program 1995), Am. Law Inst. (consultative group for restatement of law governing lawyers 1987-98), Nat. Assn. Corp. Dirs. (pres. N.Y. chpt. 1988-89), Nat. Assn. Coll. Univ. Attys. (sec. on personal rels., tenure and retirement programs 1984-86), Am. Judicature Soc., N.Y. Lawyers Alliance for World Security, Columbia Coll. Alumni Assn. (pres. 1972-74), The Supreme Ct. Hist. Soc., Dramatists Guild, Playwrights First, U.S. Lawn Tennis Assn., Am. Philatelic Soc., Univ. Club (coun. 1996-99, chair spl. events com. 1993—, chair club activities com. 1996-99), Manhasset Bay Yacht Club, Cold Spring Harbor Beach Club, Village Club of Sands Point, Phi Beta Kappa.

FUZESI, STEPHEN, JR., lawyer, communications executive; b. Budapest, Hungary, Hungary, Aug. 3, 1948; came to U.S., naturalized, 1963; s. Stephen, Sr. and Marta (Jancso) F; m. Nancy J. Steinhardt, Apr. 5, 1975; children—Stephen Joseph, Timothy Roger. A.B., Princeton U., 1970; J.D., U. Pa., 1974. Bar: N.Y. 1975, D.C. 1982. Atty. Davis, Polk & Wardwell, N.Y.C., 1974-82; ptnr./of counsel Reid & Riege, PC, Hartford, Conn., 1982-83; 1st. sr. v.p., gen. counsel and sec. Am. Savings Bank, FSB, N.Y.C., 1984-87; sr. v.p., gen. counsel, sec. Stamford Capital Group, Inc., 1987-90; of counsel White & Case, N.Y.C., 1990-94; v.p., sec., chief counsel Newsweek, N.Y.C., 1994—. Contbr. articles to jours., newspapers. Term mem. Coun. Fgn. Rels., N.Y., 1976-81; mem. Am. Coun. on Germany, 1977-80; mem. Greenwich (Conn.) Bd. Edn., 1987-91; candidate 36th dist. Conn. State Senate, 1986; mem. Greenwich Dem. Town Com., 1985-94; bd. dirs. Greenwich Soccer Assn., 1989-94. Recipient Keedy Law Rev. award U. Pa. Law Sch., 1974. Mem. Assn. of Bar of City of N.Y. (com. internat. human rights 1979-81, banking law com. 1987-90, com. on comms. and media law 1994—), Mag. Pub. Assn. (legal affairs com. 1994—, chmn. bus. affairs subcom. 1995—), Copyright Soc. U.S.A., Burning Tree Country Club. Office: Newsweek 251 W 57th St New York NY 10019-1802

FYBEL, RICHARD D., lawyer; b. Apr. 7, 1946. AB, UCLA, 1968, JD, 1971. Atty. Morrison & Foerster, LLP, Irvine, Calif., mng. ptnr., 1988-93; judge pro tempore L.A. County Superior Ct., 1988—, L.A. County Mcpl. Ct., 1979—; chair L.A. County Profl. Responsibility and Ethics Com., 1990-91. Staff UCLA Law Review, 1969-71. Mem. UCLA Law Alumni Assn. (v.p. 1997), Order of Coif. Office: Morrison & Foerster 12th Fl 19900 MacArthur Blvd Irvine CA 92715*

FYE, W. BRUCE, III, cardiologist; b. Meadville, Pa., Sept. 25, 1946; s. W. Bruce Jr. and Anne Elizabeth (Schreck) F.; m. Lois Eileen Baker, May 10, 1969; children: Katherine Anne, Elizabeth Jane. AB, Johns Hopkins U., 1968, MD, 1972, MA in Med. History, 1978. Diplomate Am. Bd. Internal Medicine, Am. Bd. Cardiovascular Diseases. Intern N.Y. Hosp.—Cornell Med. Ctr., N.Y.C., 1972-73, asst. resident, 1973-74, sr. asst. resident, 1974-75, fellow cardiology, 1975; fellow in cardiology Johns Hopkins U. Sch. Medicine, Balt., 1975-77, postdoctoral fellow in med. history, 1976-78, instr. in medicine, 1977-78; dir. cardiographics lab. Marshfield (Wis.) Clinic, 1978-99, chmn. dept. cardiology, 1981-99, dir. noninvasive cardiology, 1999; assoc. prof. medicine Med. Coll. Wis., Milw., 1988—; vice chief of staff St. Joseph's Hosp., Marshfield, 1989-99, exec. com., bd. dirs., 1994-97; clin. prof. medicine, adj. prof. history of medicine U. Wis., Madison, 1990—. Author: The Development of American Physiology, 1987; editor: William Osler's Collected Papers on the Cardiovascular System, 1985, Classic Papers on Coronary Thrombosis and Myocardial Infarction, 1991; editor-in-chief: Classics of Cardiology Library, 1985—; author: American Cardiology: The History of a Specialty and Its College, 1996; mem. editl. bd. Marshfield Med. Bull., 1985-95, Am. Jour. Cardiology, 1990—, Clin. Cardiology, 1994—. Fellow Am. Coll. Cardiology (chmn. libr. com. 1991, historian 1991—, gov. Wis. chpt. 1993-96, steering com. bd. govs., 1994—, nominating com., 1994-96, chair govt. rels. com. 1996-99, trustee 1997—); mem. Am. Assn. for History of Medicine (program chair 1987), State Med. Soc. Wis. (alt. del. 1990-94), Am. Hist. Assn., Am. Osler Soc. (pres. 1988-89), Am. Heart Assn. (exec. com. coun. on clin. cardiology 1991-97, chmn. membership com. coun. on clin. cardiology 1994-97, chair credentials com. coun. on clin. cardiology 1994-97), Inst. for Study of Cardiovascular Medicine (bd. dirs. 1994—), Phi

Beta Kappa, Alpha Omega Alpha, Grolier Club. Presbyterian. Avocation: collecting and selling antiquarian medical books. Home: 1607 N Wood Ave Marshfield WI 54449-1255 Office: Marshfield Clinic 1000 N Oak Ave Marshfield WI 54449-5702

FYFE, ALISTAIR IAN, cardiologist, scientist, educator; b. Hobart, Tasmania, Australia, Sept. 5, 1960; came to U.S., 1991; s. Ian John and Merrill Millicent (Faragher) F.; 1 child, Alexander Jonathan. B of Med. Sci., U. Tasmania, 1980, B of Med. Sci. with honors, 1981, MBBS, 1984; PhD in Molecular Biology, UCLA, 1995. Diplomate Am. Bd. Internal Medicine and Cardiovasc. Disease. Intern Royal Hobart Hosp., 1985-86; resident in internal medicine U. B.C., Vancouver, Can., 1986-89; cardiology fellow U. Toronto, Ont., Can., 1989-91; cardiac rsch. fellow UCLA, 1991-95, asst. prof. medicine and cardiology, 1995-99, dir. Ctr. for Cholesterol and Lipid Mgmt., 1995-98, assoc. mem. Molecular Biology Inst., 1996-98; dir. clin. rsch. Heart Place, Dallas, 1999—. Author: (with others) Progress in Pediatric Cardiology, 1993; contbr. articles to profl. jours. Recipient Fellowship Clinician Scientist award Med. Rsch. Coun., Can., 1992. Fellow Royal Coll. Physicians Can., Am. Coll. Cardiology, Coun. Arterial Sclerosis; mem. Internat. Heart Transplant Soc., Am. Heart Assn. (fellow arteriosclerosis coun., reviewer 1993—, Young Investigator award, 1993, 95), Am. Soc. Clin. Investigation, Am. Diabetes Assn. Achievements include first demonstration of genetic modification of solid organ transplants. Office: Heart Place Ste A341 7777 Forest Ln Dallas TX 75230

FYFE, WILLIAM SEFTON, geochemist, educator; b. New Zealand, June 4, 1927; s. Colin Alexander and Isabella Fyfe; m. Patricia Walker, Feb. 27, 1981; children: Christopher, Catherine, Stefan. BSc, U. Otago, New Zealand, 1948, MS, 1949, PhD, 1952; DSc (hon.), Meml. U., Lisbon, Portugal, 1989, 90, Lakehead U., 1992, Guelph U., 1994, St. Mary's U., Otago, New Zealand, 1994, Otago U., New Zealand, 1995, U. Western Ont., 1995. Prof. chemistry in N.Z., 1955-58; prof. geology U. Calif., Berkeley, 1958-66; research prof. Manchester U. and Imperial Coll., London, 1966-72; chmn. dept. geology Western Ont. U., 1972-84, prof. dept. geology, 1984-92, prof. emeritus dept. earth sci., 1992—, dean faculty sci., 1986-90. Decorated companion Order of Can.; Commemorative medal (New Zealand), Commemorative medal (Canada); recipient Logan medal Geol. Assn. Can., Arthur Holmes medal European Union of Geoscis., Can. Gold medal for Sci. and Engring., 1991; Guggenheim fellow, 1964, 83; named hon. prof. U. Beijing. Fellow Geol. Soc. London (hon.), Royal Soc. London, Geol. Soc. Am. (hon. life, Day medal), Mineral Soc. Am. (Roebling medal); mem. Internat. Union Geoscis. (pres. 1992-96, Grand Cross Ordem Nacional do Merito Cientifico, Brazil, 1996), Nat. Sci. and Engring. Rsch. Coun. Can., Royal Soc. Can., Acad. Sci. Brazil, Brit. Chem. Soc., Russian Acad. Sci., Indian Acad. Sci., Chinese Acad. Sci. Home: 1197 Richmond, London, ON Canada N6A 3L3 Office: U Western Ont, Dept Earth Scis, London, ON Canada N6A 5B7

FYGI, ERIC J., federal government lawyer; m. Mary Hyllis Denninger. BA, Va. Mil. inst.; JD, U. Calif. Hastings Coll. Law. Asst. gen. counsel for gen. law and legis. Fed. Energy Office, 1974-75; dep. gen. counsel Fed. Energy Adminstrn., 1975-77, 82—; acting gen. counsel Dept. Energy, Washington, 1977—. Office: Department of Energy 1000 Independence Ave SW Washington DC 20585-0002*

FYKE, JAMES H., city official; b. Old Hickory, Tenn.. Grad., George Peabody Coll. With Metro Bd. Parks and Recreation, Nashville, 1964—, sports adminstr., supt. adminstrn. and spl. svcs., dir., 1978—; chmn. local host. com. Tenn. Sportsfest Finals, 1993; regent Revenue Sources Mgmt. Sch.; chmn. bd. regents Sports Mgmt. Sch., N.C. State U. and Nat. Recreation and Park Assn.; past pres. Tenn. Am. Amateur Baseball Congress; past bd. mem. Nashville Area Athletic Club; bd. mem. Nashville Sports Coun. Bd. mem. Charles Davis Found. Recipient fellow award for outstanding svc. and contbn. to parks and recreation profession State of Tenn., 1982. Mem. Tenn. Recreation and Park Assn. Avocations: sports, golf, Braves. Office: Met Bd Parks & Recreation Centennial Park Office Nashville TN 37201*

FYLER, CARL JOHN, dentist; b. Spearville, Kans., May 14, 1921; s. John Henry and Helen Elsie (Parthie) F.; m. Marguerite E. Burris, Feb. 14, 1946. DDS, U. Mo., Kansas City, 1950. Practice dentistry Topeka, Kans., 1950-92; ret., 1992. Author: Staying Alive. Served to maj. USAF, 1942-46, ETO. Decorated Purple Heart, 5 Air Medals, Distinguished Flying Cross, E.T.O medal with 3 battle stars, Prisoner of War medal. Mem. ADA (life), Kans. Dental Assn., Shawnee County Dental Assn., Internat. Fedn. Dentists, Am. Ex-Prisoners of War (nat. dir. 1974-85, nat. jr. vice comdr. 1984-85), Kans. Ex-Prisoners of War (Gov.'s adv. com. 1978-86), 303d H.B.G. Assn. (pres. 1987-89), Eighth Air Force Hist. Soc. (bd. dirs. 1989-92, heavy bomb group), Mil. Order of World Wars (pres. Topeka chpt. 1996—), Distinguished Flying Cross Soc., Am. Legion, D.A.V., Am. Vets. Republican. Presbyterian. Avocations: flying, lapidary, rock hunting. Home: 300 SW Yorkshire Rd Topeka KS 66606-2260

FYLER, JOHN MORGAN, English language educator; b. Chgo., Sept. 17, 1943; s. Earl Harris and Harriet (Morgan) F.; m. Julia Ann Genster, Aug. 5, 1978; children: Amanda, Lucy. AB, Dartmouth Coll., 1965; MA, U. Calif., Berkeley, 1967, PhD, 1972. Asst. prof. Tufts U., Medford, Mass., 1972-78, assoc. prof., 1978-88, prof., 1988—. Author: Chaucer and Ovid, 1979; contbg. editor: Riverside Chaucer, 1986. ACLS fellow, 1975-76, Guggenheim fellow, 1982-83. Home: 126 Central St Concord MA 01742-2911 Office: Dept English Tufts U Medford MA 02155

FYNAARDT, TAMARA DIANNE, public relations professional, educator; b. Rapid City, S.D., July 27, 1968; d. Duane Myron and Diane Yvonne (Meyer) Mulder; m. Keith Edward Fynaardt, May 25, 1990. BA, Dordt Coll., 1990; postgrad., Iowa State U., 1990-91; MA, No. Ill. U., 1992. Admissions counselor Evang. Health Sys., DeKalb, Ill., 1992-93; pub. rels./mktg. dir. EHS Extended Care Divsn. (now Advocate Health Care), Downers Grove, Ill., 1993-95; English instr. Northwestern Coll., Orange City, Iowa, 1995, Dordt Coll., Sioux Center, Iowa, 1996; assoc. pub. rels. dir. Northwestern Coll., Orange City, 1996—; comms. instr. Northwestern Coll., Orange City, 1997. Bd. dirs. Northwestern Coll. Theatre Patrons, Orange City, 1996—, pres. 1997—. Democrat. Mem. Reformed Church in America. Avocations: reading, fiction writing, interior decorating. Home: 703 Arizona Ave NW Orange City IA 51041-2044 Office: Northwestern Coll 101 7th St SW Orange City IA 51041-1923

GAAL, JOHN, lawyer; b. Flushing, N.Y., Oct. 10, 1952; s. Stephen Alfred and Marjorie (Lappin) G.; m. Barbara Jeanne Zacher, Aug. 5, 1973; children: Bryan A., Adam C., Benjamin Z. BA cum laude, U. Notre Dame, 1974, JD magna cum laude, 1977. Bar: N.Y. 1978, U.S. Ct. Appeals (D.C. cir.) 1978, U.S. Dist. Ct. (no. dist.) N.Y. 1979, U.S. Supreme Ct. 1986. Law clk. to judge U.S. Ct. Appeals (D.C. cir.), Washington, 1977-78; assoc. Bond, Schoeneck & King, Syracuse, N.Y., 1978-85, ptnr., 1986—; bd. dirs. Legal Svcs. of Ctrl. N.Y., Syracuse, 1981-87, 94—, pres. 1999—; adj. prof. Syracuse U., 1989-92. Editor: Senior Citizens Handbook, 1988; contbg. author: Public Sector Labor and Employment Law, 1988; mem. editl. bd. Jour. Coll. and Univ. Law, 1998—; columnist The Bus. Jour., 1998—; contbr. articles to profl. publs. Fellow Am. Bar Found.; mem. ABA (labor and employment law sect.), N.Y. State Bar Assn. (labor and employment law sect., chair young lawyer sect. 1989-90, spl. com. on AIDS and the law 1988, spl. com. on mandatory pro bono svc. 1989, ho. of dels. 1987-89, 90-91, co-chair adhoc com. ethics 1999—). Democrat. Roman Catholic. Home: 6732 Serah Ln Jamesville NY 13078-9690 Office: Bond Schoeneck & King 1 Lincoln Ctr Fl 18 Syracuse NY 13202-1324

GABARRA, CARIN LESLIE, professional soccer player; b. East Orange, N.J., Jan. 9, 1965; m. Jim Gabarra. Degree in bus. mgmt., U. Calif., Santa Barbara, 1987. Mem. U.S. Nat. Women's Soccer Team; mem. U.S. Olympic World Festival team, 1986-89; women's soccer U.S. Naval Acad., 1993. Ranked as 3d-leading goal scorer in U.S. women's history; mem. CONCACAF Championship team, 1993, 94; named U.S. Soccer's Female Athlete of Yr., 1987, 92, Golden Ball, FIFA Women's World Championship, China, 1991; named to U. Calif.-Santa Babara Athletic Hall of Fame. Office: c/o US Soccer Fedn 1801 S Prairie Ave # 1811 Chicago IL 60616-1357

GABAY, DONALD DAVID, lawyer; b. Bklyn., Apr. 25, 1935; s. Harry I. and Rachel Gabay. B.B.A., CCNY, 1956; LL.B., Bklyn. Law Sch., 1961. Bar: N.Y. 1962. Pvt. practice law, N.Y.C., 1962-75; chief counsel N.Y. State Assembly Com. on Ins., Albany, 1975-78; 1st dep. supt. N.Y. State Ins. Dept., N.Y.C., 1978-84; ptnr. Stroock & Stroock & Lavan, N.Y.C., 1984—; pres. Ins. Fedn. N.Y., 1994-98, pres., 1999—, chmn., Ins. Fedn., NY. Served with U.S. Army, 1956-58. Named Ins. Man of Yr., Ind. Ins. Brokers Assn., 1973; Pub. Service award Bklyn. Ins. Brokers Assn., 1977; ann. achievement award Council Ins. Brokers, 1981; Outstanding Achievement award, CCNY Alumni Assn., 1981, Pub. Service award Ind. Ins. Agts. Assn., 1984; Torch of Liberty award ins. div. Anti-Defamation League, 1984. Office: Stroock Stroock & Lavan LLP 180 Maiden Ln New York NY 10038-4925

GABBARD, (JAMES) DOUGLAS, II, judge; b. Lindsay, Okla., Mar. 27, 1952; s. James Douglas and Mona Dean (Dodd) G.; m. Connie Sue Mace, Dec. 30, 1977 (div. Feb. 1979); m. Robyn Marie Kohlhaas, June 18, 1981; children: Resa Marie, David Ryan, James Douglas III, Michael Drew. BS, Okla. U., 1974, JD, 1977; grad., Nat. Jud. Coll., 1987; U. Kans. Law Orgnl. Econs., 1997. Bar: Okla. 1978. Ptnr. Stubblefeild & Gabbard, Atoka, Okla., 1978; sole practice Atoka, 1979; asst. dist. atty. State of Okla., Atoka, 1979-82; 1st asst. dist. atty. State of Okla., Atoka, Durant and Coalgate, 1982-85; dist. judge 25th Jud. Dist. State of Okla., Atoka and Coalgate, 1985—; presiding judge South East Adminstrn. Dist., Okla., 1992—, State Ct. Tax Review, Okla., 1992—; presiding judge of emergency panel of State Ct. Criminal Appeals, State Ct. on Judiciary (Trial divsn.), 1997—; dir. Okla. Trial Judges Assn., 1996—; mcpl. judge City of Atoka, 1978-79;. Mem. Bryan County/Durant Arbitration Com., 1984; negotiator Bryan Meml. Hosp. Bd., Durant, 1984-85. Mem. Okla. Bar Assn. (legal ethics com. 1988-90, jud. adminstrv. com. 1988-90, resolutions com., 1998—, long range planning com. 1999—, bench and bar com. 1999—), Okla. Jud. Conf., Am. Judges Assn., Masons. Democrat. Methodist. Avocations: painting, tennis, reading, jogging. Home: 1401 S Walker Dr Atoka OK 74525-3611 Office: County Ct House Atoka OK 74525

GABBARD, GLEN OWENS, psychiatrist, psychoanalyst; b. Charleston, Ill., Aug. 8, 1949; s. Earnest Glendon and Lucina Mildred (Paquet) G.; children: Matthew, Abigail, Amanda, Allison; m. Joyce Eileen Davidson, June 14, 1985. BS, Eastern Ill. U., 1972; MD, Rush Med. Coll., 1975; degree in psychoanalytic tng., Topeka Inst. for Psychoanalysis, 1984. Diplomate Am. Bd. Psychiatry and Neurology. Resident in psychiatry Menninger Sch. Psychiatry, Topeka, 1975-78, mem. faculty, 1978—; staff psychiatrist C.F. Menninger Hosp., Topeka, 1978-83, sect. chief, 1984-89; med. dir., 1989-94; tng. analyst Topeka Inst. for Psychoanalysis, 1989—, dir., 1996—; v.p. for adult svcs. Menninger Clinic, 1991-94; clin. prof. psychiatry U. Kans. Med. Sch., 1991—; Callaway Disting. prof. Menninger Clinic and Karl Menninger Sch. Psychiatry. Author: With the Eyes of the Mind, 1984, Psychiatry and the Cinema, 1987, Medical Marriages, 1988, Sexual Exploitation in Professional Relationships, 1989, Psychodynamic Psychiatry in Clinical Practice, 1990, 2d edit., 1994, Treatments of Psychiatric Disorders: the DSM-IV Edition, 1995; contbr. articles to profl. jours. V.p. Topeka Civic Theatre, 1981-82, pres. 1982-83, bd. dirs. 1981-83. Named one of Outstanding Young Men in Am. U.S. Jaycees, 1984. Mem. AAAS, Am. Psychoanalytic Assn. (assoc. editor jour.), Am. Psychiat. Assn. (Falk fellow 1976), Sch. Psychotherapy Rsch., Menninger Sch. Psychiatry Alumni Assn. (pres. 1982-83), Alpha Omega Alpha. Avocations: theater, music. Home: 5410 SW Mission Ave Topeka KS 66610-9405 Office: Menninger Clinic PO Box 829 Topeka KS 66601-0829

GABBE, STEVEN GLENN, physician, educator; b. Newark, Dec. 1, 1944; s. Charles Paul and Marcia May Gabbe; m. Jessica Gabbe, June 26, 1966 (div. 1980); children: Amanda, Daniel; m. Patricia Temple, July 26, 1981. BA, Princeton U., 1965; MD, Cornell U., 1969; MA (hon.), U. Pa., 1983. Diplomate Am. Bd. Ob-Gyn (examiner 1980—), Am. Bd. Maternal-Fetal Medicine (examiner 1979-89). Intern in medicine N.Y. Hosp., N.Y.C., 1969-70; rsch. fellow reproductive medicine Boston Hosp. for Women, 1970-71, resident in ob-gyn, 1972-74; rsch. fellow in biol. chemistry Harvard Med. Sch., Boston, 1970-71, clin. fellow ob-gyn., 1972-74; asst. prof. ob-gyn U. So. Calif., L.A., 1975-77; assoc. prof. U. Colo. Sch. Medicine, Denver, 1977-78; assoc prof. ob-gyn. and pediatrics U. Pa. Sch. Medicine, Phila., 1978-87, prof. radiology, 1987; mem. staff Hosp. of U. Pa., Phila., 1978-87, dir. Jerrold R. Golding div. fetal medicine, 1978-87, mem. med. bd. and numerous coms., 1984-87; prof. U. Pa. Sch. Nursing, Phila., 1982-87; prof., chmn. dept. ob-gyn Ohio State U. Coll. Medicine, Columbus, 1987-96; prof., chmn. dept. ob/gyn. U. Wash. Sch. Medicine, Seattle, 1996—; dir. Jerrold R. Golding div. fetal medicine Hosp. of U. Pa., Phila., 1978-87, mem. med. bd. and numerous coms., 1984-87; vis. prof. ob-gyn King's Coll. Hosp., London, 1985-86; dir. maternal and infant care program Phila. Dept. Health, Disease Prevention and Health Promotion, 1982-87; mem. maternal and infant care adv. coun. Dept. Pub. Health, Phila., 1983-87; mem. subcom. on pregnancy and weight gain NRC, NAS, 1981; mem. internat. sci. bd. Reproductive Toxicology Ctr., 1984—; bd. dirs., med. adv. bd. Diabetes Treatment Ctrs. Am., 1984, others; mem. Coun. Univ Chairs of Ob-Gyn., 1996—. Author: Clinical Obstetrics and Gynecology: Diabetes and Pregnancy, 1985, Clinical Obstetrics and Gynecology: Obstetric Ultrasound Update, 1988; (with J.R. Niebyl and J.L. Simpson) Obstetrics: Normal and Problem Pregnancies, 1986, 2d edit., 1991; contbr. numerous articles to profl. jours. and chpts. to books; editor i chief Am. Jour. Perinatology, 1983—; mem. numerous editorial bds. Mem. Pa. Diabetes Task Force, 1981-87, Ohio Diabetes Task Force, 1987—; bd. dirs. UNITE, Jeanes Hosp., 1980-87. Recipient Sr. Resident's award for Excellence in Tng., L.A. County Women's Hosp., 1976, Disting. Tchr. award from Graduating Class, U. Wash., 1999; grantee Juvenile Diabetes Found., 1981, HHS, 1984, 1985, Diabetes Treatment Ctrs. Am., 1986. Fellow Am. Coll. Obstetricians and Gynecologists (mem. PROLOG self assessment program task force 1981-82, chmn. 1986, mem. PROLOG subcom. 1986—); mem. Am. Gynecol. and Obstet. Soc., Am. Inst. Ultrasound in Medicine, Perinatal Rsch. Soc., Soc. Gynecologic Investigation, Soc. Perinatal Obstetricians (v.p. 1986, pres. 1987-88, bd. dirs. 1983-88, chmn. credentials, constn. and by-laws com. 1983-87), Am. Diabetes Assn. (mem. nat. rsch. bd. 1981-83, chmn. coun. on diabetes in pregnancy 1985, com. on food and nutrition 1976-80), Juvenile Diabetes Found. (mem. med. sci. rev. com., med. sci. adv. bd. 1981-83), Phila. Neonatal Soc., Obstet. Soc. Phila. (program chmn. 1986-87), Phila. Perinatal Soc. (pres. 1982-84), Columbus Ob-Gyn Soc., Pa. Diabetes Acad. (acad. steering com. 1986—, editorial rev. com. 1986—), Union League (Phila.), Phi Beta Kappa, Alpha Omega Alpha. Avocations: sports, running. Home: 4547 W Laurel Dr NE Seattle WA 98105-3840 Office: U Wash Dept of Ob-Gyn Box 356460 Seattle WA 98195-6460*

GABBOUR, ISKANDAR, city and regional planning educator; b. Mansura, Egypt, Feb. 6, 1929; s. Iskandar Gabbour and Mathilde Louli; m. Amy Surur, Feb. 4, 1956; children: May, Tamer, Rami. B.Arch. with honors, Cairo U., 1953; M.Arch., M.C.P., U. Pa., 1963, Ph.D., 1967. Architect, chief design Devel. & Popular Housing Co., Cairo, 1954-61; research assoc. U. Pa., Phila., 1966-67; prof. city and regional planning U. Montreal, Que., Can., 1967-97, vice dean acad. affairs faculty environ. design, 1993-97, hon. prof., 1997—; cons. UN Ctr. for Human Settlements, Nairobi, Kenya, 1985; vol. advisor Tech. Studies and Devel. Office, Abidjan, Ivory Coast, 1998. Contbr. numerous articles to profl. jours. Mem. Am. Planning Assn. (charter), Am. Inst. Cert. Planners (charter), Can. Inst. Planners, Royal Archtl. Inst. Can., Assn. Collegiate Schs. Planning, Order Urbanists of Que. Fax: (514) 484-8245. E-mail: gabbour@magellan.umontreal.ca. Home: 5510 Ashdale Ave, Montreal, PQ Canada H4W 3G4

GABEL, CREIGHTON, retired anthropologist, educator; b. Muskegon, Mich., Apr. 5, 1931; s. Kenneth Alonzo and Edith Myrtle (Creighton) G.; m. Jane Whitfield, Sept. 6, 1952; children: James, Anne, Molly. B.A., U. Mich., 1953, M.A., 1954; Ph.D., U. Edinburgh, Scotland, 1957. Instr. Northwestern U., 1956-58, asst. prof., 1958-63; asso. prof. Boston U., 1963-69, prof., 1969-96, prof. emeritus, 1996—; research assoc. Boston U. African Studies Center, 1963-96, chmn. anthropology dept., 1970-72, 76-79. Author: Stone Age Hunters of the Kafue, 1965, Analysis of Prehistoric Economic Patterns, 1967; editor: Man Before History, 1964; editor: Reconstructing African Culture History, 1967, Jour. Field Archaeology, 1985-95. NSF grantee, 1960-61, 66-67; Fulbright grantee, 1973; Social Sci. Research Council grantee, 1963-64. Mem. Comm. Internat. Exchange of Scholars (chmn. discipline screening com. in archaeology 1985-88).

GABEL, KATHERINE, academic administrator; b. Rochester, N.Y., Apr. 9, 1938; d. M. Wren and Esther (Conger) G.; m. Seth Devore Strickland, June 24, 1961 (div. 1965). AB, Smith Coll., Northampton, Mass., 1959; MSW, Simmons Coll., 1961; PhD, Syracuse U., 1967; JD, Union U., 1970; bus. program, Stanford U., 1984. Psychol. social worker Cen. Island Mental Health Ctr., Uniondale, N.Y., 1961-62; psychol. social worker, supt. Ga. State Tng. Sch. for Girls, Atlanta, 1962-64; cons. N.Y. State Crime Control Coun., Albany, 1968-70; faculty Ariz. State U., Tempe, 1972-76; supt. Ariz. Dept. of Corrections, Phoenix, 1970-76; dean, prof. Smith Coll., 1976-85; pres. Pacific Oaks Coll. and Children's Sch., Pasadena, Calif., 1985-98; we. regional leader Casey Family Program, Pasadena, 1998—; advisor, del. UN, Geneva, 1977; mem. So. Calif. Youth Authority, 1986-91. Editor: Master Teacher and Supervisor in Clinical Social Work, 1982; author report Legal Issues of Female Inmates, 1981, model for rsch. Diversion program Female Inmates, 1984, Children of Incarcerated Parents, 1995. Vice chair United Way, Northampton, 1982-83; chair Mayor's Task Force, Northampton, 1981. Mem. Nat. Assn. Social Work, Acad. Cert. Social Workers, Nat. Assn. Edn. Young Children, Western Assn. Schs. and Colls., Pasadena C. of C., Athenaeum, Pasadena Rotary Club. Democrat. Presbyterian. Avocations: collecting, S.W. Indian art, aviary.

GABELER-BROOKS, JO, artist; b. Baton Rouge, Feb. 14, 1931; d. Gustav Adolph Jr. and Ruth Adelaide Stein; m. Charles Pierce Gabeler Jr., Feb. 17, 1951 (div. Feb. 1973); children: Ann Speed, Charles Pierce III, T. Dolph, Caroline Hart; m. Ralph Brooks, Aug. 8, 1990. BA, Stephens Coll., 1950; studied with Edward Betts, Judi Betts,, Al Brouillete, Jeanne Dobie, Ray Ellis,, Dong Kingman, Fred Messersmith, John, Pike, Tony Van Hasselt, Millard Wells. Illustrator: (with others) The Golf Courses at the Landings on Skidaway Island, 1993, The Galley Collection, 1998. Currently showing at John Tucker Fine Arts, Savannah, Ga.; one-woman shows include Elliott Mus., Stuart, Fla., 1986, Scarborough House, Savannah, 1988; exhbns. include Fla. Watercolor Soc., Mus. Arts and Scis., Daytona, Fla., 1978, Brevard Art Ctr. and Mus., Melbourne, 1981, State Capitol, Tallahassee, 1982, Boca Raton Mus. Art, 1984, 86, Houston Pub. Libr., 1981, Galveston (Tex.) Art League, 1983; represented in permanent collections The Moody Found., Elliott Mus., The Rosenberg Libr., Transco Energy Co. Houston, Allied Bank of Seabrook, Tex. Mem. Fla. Watercolor Soc. (Pres.'s award 1981, 82, Purchase award 1986, signature life mem.), Salmagundi Club, Galveston Art League (pres. 1981-82, Purchase award 1982), Profl. Artist Guild, Landings Art Assn. (pres. 1990). Home: 11 Mainsail Xing Savannah GA 31411-2723

GABELNICK, HENRY LEWIS, medical research director; b. Boston, May 10, 1940; s. Murray and Lillian G.; m. Faith Schectman, June 17, 1962; children: Deborah Anne, Tamar Miriam; m. Clare Ann Donaher, May 22, 1987. BS, MIT, 1961, MS, 1962; PhD, Princeton U., 1966. Sr. chem. engr. Monsanto Co., Springfield, Mass., 1966-68; biomed. engr. NIH, Bethesda, Md., 1968-1986; dir. extramural rsch. CONRAD Program Ea. Va. Med. Sch., Arlington, 1986-89, dep. dir. CONRAD Program, 1989-90, dir. CONRAD Program, 1990—; pres. Reprodn. Rsch. Inst., 1997—; tech. advisor WHO, Geneva, 1977—; tech. expert UN Devel. Program, Haifa, Israel, 1973. Editor: Rheology of Biological Systems, 1973, Drug Delivery Systems, 1976, Heterosexual Transmission of AIDS, 1990, Barrier Contraceptives, 1993, Biology, Pharmacology, and Clinical Applications of Androgens, 1996. Fellow Textile Research Inst.; mem. APHA, N.Y. Acad. Scis., Am. Chem. Soc., Controlled Release Soc., Sigma Xi. Avocation: nature photography. Home: 11612 Danville Dr Rockville MD 20852-3716

GABERINO, JOHN ANTHONY, JR., lawyer; b. Tulsa, Aug. 6, 1941; s. John A. Sr. and Elizabeth (McCafferty) G.; m. Marjory Ann Diamond, Aug. 21, 1965; children: Christina M., Megan E., Courtney L., John A. III, Kathleen A. AB cum laude, Georgetown U., 1963, JD, 1966. Bar: Okla. 1966, U.S. Dist. Co. (no. and we. dists.) Okla. 1968, U.S. Ct. Appeals (10th cir.) 1968, U.S. Tax Ct. 1968, U.S. Supreme Ct. 1994. Assoc. Huffman, Arrington & Kihle, Tulsa, 1968-75; ptnr. Arrington, Kihle, Gaberino & Dunn, Tulsa, 1975-87, also bd. dirs., 1987-97; sr. v.p., gen. counsel ONEOK, Inc., 1998—; counsel, bd. dirs. St. Francis Health Sys., Inc., Tulsa, 1989-97. Chmn. Georgetown U. Law Ctr. Alumni Bd., 1990-92; bd. govs. Georgetown U., 1990—; pres. Georgetown U. Club Okla.; chmn. Georgetown U. AAP for Okla.; past chmn. Christ the King Bd. Edn.; past pres. bd. trustees Monte Cassino Sch.; chmn. bd. trustees Monte Cassino Sch. Endowment Fund; bd. dirs. W.K. Warren Found., Tulsa Area United Way; chmn. bd. dirs. Operation Aware, Inc., 1991. Capt. U.S. Army, 1966-68. Recipient John Carroll medal Georgetown U., 1993. Fellow ABA; mem. NCCJ (bd. dirs. Tulsa chpt., pres. 1993-95), Okla. Bar Assn. (mem. bd. govs. 1990-92, 95, 97-99, v.p. 1995, pres. 1998), Tulsa Bar Assn. (chmn. constrn. and bylaws com., bd. dirs. 1989, 91-94, sec. 1988, pres. 1993), Tulsa County Bar Found. (bd. dirs. 1993—, pres. 1994), Knights Holy Sepulchre (hon. soc. Cath. ch.), So. Hills Country Club (mem. bd. govs. 1990-95, 1st v.p. 1991-93, pres. 1994), Met. Tulsa C. of C. (bd. dirs.), Phi Beta Kappa. Democrat. Roman Catholic. Avocations: golf, tennis. Office: ONEOK Inc 100 W 5th St Tulsa OK 74103-4240

GABERMAN, HARRY, lawyer, economic analyst; b. Springfield, Mass., May 6, 1913; s. Nathan and Elizabeth (Binder) G.; m. Ingeborg Luise Gruda, Sept. 24, 1953; children: Claudia, Natalie Gaberman Razzook, Victor Lucius. JD, George Washington U., 1941; LLM, Cath. U. Am., 1954. Bar: D.C. 1942. Atty.-investigator, atty-advisor U.S. Mil. Govt. and U.S. High Commn. for Germany, Berlin, Frankfurt, Bonn; indsl. specialist, bus. economist U.S. Mil. Govt. and U.S. High Commn. for Germany, Berlin, Frankfort, Bonn; dep. U.S. agt. before Italian-U.S. Conciliation Commn.; legal and intercorp. rels. analyst U.S. Mil. Govt. and U.S. High Commn. for Germany, Berlin, Frankfort, Bonn, 1945-53, asst. chief industry control sect., 1945-53; asst. legal advisor, attache Am. Embassy, Rome, 1953; pvt. practice Washington, 1953-55; intelligence analyst Army Transp. Intelligence Agy., Gravelly Point, Va., 1955-56; supervisory atty.-advisor, atty.-advisor Air Force Sys. Command, Andrews AFB, Md., 1956-75; asst. to U.S. mem. Four-power liquidation of German War Potential Com., Berlin, 1946; chief deconcentration br. U.S. High Commn., Frankfurt, 1949; acting dep. U.S. mem. law com. Allied Kommandatura, Berlin, 1951; U.S. mem. 3-power Film Reorgn. Com., Bonn, 1949-50. *Mr. Gaberman's responsibilities include overseeing 14 substantive law councils containing 83 constituent comittees.* Contbr. articles to profl. jours. Recipient Profl. Achievement award George Washington U. Law Alumni, 1983. Mem. Fed. Bar Assn. (dep. coun. and com. coord. 1982, coun. and com. coord. overseeing 14 substantive law couns. containing 83 constituent coms. 1983, chmn. coun. on govt. contracts 1970-75, 80-81, chmn. internat. procurement com. 1977-79, dep. chmn. sect. on internat. law and its newsletter editor 1984-97, dep. chmn. sect. on internat. law and its newsletter contbg. editor 1998-99, numerous Disting. Svc. awards, others), D.C. Bar Assn. (chmn. govt. contracts com. 1964-66), Diplomatic and Consular Officers Ret. (charter mem.), Am. Fgn. Svcs. Assn., Air Force Assn. Avocations: walking, reading, listening to classic and semi-classic music. Address: 5117 Overlook Park Annandale VA 22003-4361

GABINSKI, THERI, city official; b. Nov. 30, 1938. BA, No. Ill. U., MA. H.s. tchr., 1962-64, spl. edn. instr., 1966-68; mem. Chgo. City Coun.; alderman Chgo., 1969-98; chmn. sts. and alleys com., mem. beautification and recreation, bldg. and fin. coms. Coord. Kettering Found., 1964-66; aide U.S. Rep. Daniel Rostenkowski, 1968-71. Office: 2148 N Damen Ave Chicago IL 60647-4562*

GABLE, CARL IRWIN, business consultant, private investor, lawyer; b. Charleston, S.C., Aug. 7, 1939; s. Carl Irwin and Charlotte Belle (Kersey) G.; m. Sarah Alice Bogle, June 6, 1964; children: Ashley Grinnell, Carl Irwin III, James Kersey. BA, Harvard U., 1961; JD, Harvard, 1964. Bar: Ga. 1964, D.C. 1976. Assoc. Kilpatrick & Cody, Atlanta, 1964-70, ptnr., 1970-84; pres. Interface Inc., Atlanta, 1984-85; vice chmn. Intermet Corp., Atlanta, 1985-90, also bd. dirs.; ptnr. Booth, Owens & Jospin, 1992-96; of counsel Troutman Sanders L.L.P., Atlanta, 1996-98; pres. Boglewood Corp., Kiev, Ukraine, 1993—; bd. dirs. Interface, Inc., 1984—. Contbr. articles on internat. law to profl. jours.; inventor interlocking modular carpet. Bd. dirs. Atlanta Coun. Internat. Visitors, Inc., 1987-93, Atlanta Opera, Inc., 1980—, Michael Carlos Mus. of Emory U., 1994—; bd. dirs. Spoleto Festival USA, Inc., 1993—, treas., 1993-95; founder, chmn. Atlanta Opera Endowment, Inc., 1986—. Fellow Am. Coll. Investment Counsel; mem. ABA., Atlanta

Bar Assn., Internat. Bar Assn., Capital City Club, Atlanta Lawyers Club. Avocation: Italian studies.

GABLE, CAROL BRIGNOLI, health economics researcher; b. N.Y.C., Dec. 28, 1945; d. Peter Joseph and Frances Veronica (Guma) Abatemarco; m. Frank Giovanni Brignoli, May 19, 1968 (div. Nov. 1981); children: Barbra, James; m. Raymond Lewis Gable, Jan. 8, 1983; 1 child, Matthew. BS, CUNY, 1968; PhD in Chemistry, U. Md., 1973, MA in Statistics, 1986. Chemist N.Y. Rsch. Inst., N.Y.C., 1967-68; grad. asst. U. Md., College Park, 1968-73; lectr. Montgomery Coll., Takoma Park, Md., 1972-75; rsch. assoc. USDA/CFEI, Hyattsville, Md., 1974-76; chemist FDA, Washington, 1977-89; rsch. dir. pharmacoepidemiology Systemetrics/McGraw Hill, Washington, 1989-92; project dir. Degge Group Ltd., Arlington, Va., 1992-93; dir. Health Econs. State and Fed. Assocs., Alexandria, Va., 1994-96, v.p., 1996; dir. outcomes rsch. Pfizer, Inc., U.S. Pharms. Group (PPG), N.Y.C., 1996—. Contbr. articles to profl. jours. including Biophys. Chemistry, Nutrition, Risk Assessment, Pharmacoepidemiology, Pharmacoeconomics, Jour. AMA. N.Y. State Regents scholar, 1963-67; recipient NSF traineeship, 1969-73. Mem. Am. Chem. Soc., Am. Assn. Pharm. Scis. (mem. econ. mktg. and mgmt. sect., vice chmn. 1992-93, chmn.-elect 1993-94, chmn. 1994-95), Soc. for Risk Analysis, Internat. Soc. for Pharmacoepidemiology, Drug Infos. Assn., Assn. Health Svcs. Rsch., Assn. Pharms. Outcomes Rsch. Democrat. Methodist. Avocation: jogging. Office: Pfizer US Pharmaceuticals Group 235 E 42nd St New York NY 10017-5755

GABLE, CATE M., communications company executive; b. Oct. 17, 1949. BA, U. Pa., 1972; MA, U. Wash., 1974. Co-publisher Common Ground, Kamuela, Hawaii, 1979-80; chair English dept. Hawaii Prep. Acad., Kamuela, 1974-80; counselor Family Crisis Ctr., Yakima, Wash., 1980-81; creative writing instr. State Dept. Edn., Wash., Calif., Hawaii, 1981-84; dir. pub. info. U.S. Fed. Res. Bank, San Francisco, 1984-89; mktg. mgr. Citibank Calif., Oakland, 1989-91; dir. pub. info. Ohlone Coll., Fremont, Calif., 1991-96; pres. Axioun Comms. Internat., Berkeley, Calif., 1992—. Home: 3035 Ellis Berkeley CA 94703

GABLE, EDWARD BRENNAN, JR., lawyer; b. Shamokin, Pa., Mar. 15, 1929; s. Edward Brennan and Kathleen (Welsh) G.; BS, Villanova U., 1953; J.D., Georgetown U., 1957; m. Judy Lipshy July 17, 1981; children by previous marriage: Karen Lynn, Kimberly Ann, Katherine Rebel; stepchildren: Steven H., Karen Sue, Scott Michael. Bar: D.C. 1957, U.S. Dist. Ct. D.C. 1957, U.S. Ct. Appeals (D.C. cir.) 1957, U.S. Ct. Customs and Patent Appeals, 1959, U.S. Customs Ct. , 1961, U.S. Ct. Mil. Appeals, 1966, U.S. Supreme Ct., 1967, U.S. Ct. Appeals (fed. cir.) 1982. With U.S. Customs Svc., Treasury Dept., Washington, 1958-88, chief documentation br., 1965-66, chief carrier rulings br., 1966-76, chief penalties br., 1976-78, spl. asst. to asst. commr. Office of Regulations and Rulings, 1978-82, dir. carriers, drawback and bonds div., 1983-88, legal cons. in martime law, Washington, 1988—; mem. U.S. del. Intergovtl. Maritime Cons. Orgn., London, 1972-75, U.S. rep., inter-sessional meeting, Hamburg, Fed. Republic Germany, 1973. Pres., Customs Fed. Credit Union, 1967-69. Recipient Superior Performance award Treasury Dept., 1962, commendation letter from asst. sec. treasury, 1964, Customs Outstanding Performance award, 1983, Customs Cash Performance award, 1984, 85. Mem. Customs Lawyers Assn. (pres. 1965-66), Fed. Bar Assn., Propeller Club U.S., United Seamen's Svc. (council of trustees 1986-88), Natl. Lawyers Club, Elks, Delta Pi Epsilon, Delta Theta Phi. Roman Catholic. Home and Office: 955 26th St NW Washington DC 20037-2009

GABLE, G. ELLIS, retired lawyer; b. Kerens, Tex., Mar. 7, 1905; s. George Warren and Sue Ethel (Collins) G.; m. Frances Doyle, Dec. 30, 1933; children: Richard Warren, Thomas Doyle. Tchrs. cert., Northeastern Okla. State U., Tahlequah, 1922; JD, Okla U., 1926. Bar: Okla. 1926. Pvt. practice Tulsa, 1926-93; of counsel Gable & Gotwals, 1993; judge pro-tem Tulsa County, 1938-39. Past mem. Tulsa Bd. Edn., pres., 1956-57; mem. Okla. State Regents for Higher Edn., 1958-76. Mem. ABA (mem. fellows), Okla. Bar Assn. (pres. 1954), Tulsa County Bar Assn. (pres. 1949), Masons (Shriner, Jester), Rotary (pres. 1961-62), Phi Delta Phi. Methodist. Home: 5813 S Indianapolis Ave Tulsa OK 74135-7801 Office: 2000 NationsBank Ctr 15 W 6th St Tulsa OK 74119-5415 *Every lawyer owes a part of his time to his profession and community.*

GABLE, ROBERT ELLEDY, real estate investment company executive; b. N.Y.C., Feb. 20, 1934; s. Gilbert E. and Paulina (Stearns) G.; m. Emily Brinton Thompson, July 5, 1958; children: James, Elizabeth, John. BS, Stanford U., 1956. With The Stearns Co. Ltd. (formerly Stearns Coal & Lumber Co. Inc.), Lexington, Ky., 1958—, asst. to pres., 1958-60, sec., 1960-70, treas., 1961-62, v.p., 1962-70, chmn. bd., 1970—, pres., 1975-78, also dir.; former chmn. bd., dir. Ky. & Tenn. Ry., Lexington; former chmn. bd. Lumber King Inc., Lexington; former dir., mem. audit com. Kuhn's-Big K Stores Corp., Nashville, 1979-81; dir. emeritus Blue Cross and Blue Shield Ky.; former dir. Bank of McCreary County. Commr. Ky. Dept. Parks, 1967-70; mem. pub. lands com. Interstate Oil Compact Commn., 1968-70; mem. adv. com. Ky. Ednl. TV, 1971-75; former mem. Breaks Interstate Park Commn.; past pres., past dir. McCreary County Indsl. Devel. Corp.; former trustee Stearns Recreational Assn., Inc.; mem. S.E. regional adv. com. Nat. Park Service, 1973-78, sec., 1977-78; former bd. dirs. Ky. Mountain Laurel Festival Assn., v.p., 1974-75; mem. McCreary County Air Bd., 1967-81; mem. adv. bd. U. Ky. for Somerset Community Coll., 1965-73. Republican candidate for U.S. Senate from Ky., 1972; Ky. co-chmn. Finance Com. for Re-election of Pres., 1972; mem. Rep. Nat. Com., 1986-94, mem. budget com., 1989; mem. Rep. Nat. Finance Com., 1971-76; Rep. state finance chmn., 1973-75, 86; mem. Ky. Rep. Central Com., 1974-94; state chmn. Rep. Party Ky., 1986-94; Rep. nominee for gov. Ky., 1975; trustee George Peabody Coll. for Tchrs., Nashville, 1970-79, mem. exec. com., 1976-79, chmn. bd., 1979; former trustee Capital Day Sch., Frankfort, Ky.; bd. dirs., past chmn., past pres., founder Ky. Council on Econ. Edn., Inc.; mem. bd. founders Nat. Coun. Econ. Edn. (formerly Joint Coun. Econ. Edn.) N.Y.C., 1982—; trustee Ky. State U. Found., 1979-82; trustee Vanderbilt U., Nashville, 1979-87, former mem. budget com.; past mem. bd. dirs. Ky. Better Roads Council, Inc., vice chmn., 1976-79; former mem. missions bd. Episcopal Diocese of Lexington; bd. dirs. Lexington Conv. and Tourist Bur., 1982-85, Ky. Opera Assn., 1982—, Rehab. Found., Inc., Louisville, 1982-84, Headley-Whitney Mus., Lexington, 1985-90; founding bd. Lexington Fund for the Arts, 1984-86; treas., state chmn. So. Assn. Rep., 1989-91, chmn., 1991-94; appointed Pres. Adv. Com. Arts, 1992-93; mem. Nat. Com. for Performing Arts, John F. Kennedy Ctr. for Performing Arts, Washington, 1993—, pres., CEO, 1993-97; mem. nat. leadership coun. Rep. Exchange Satellite Network, Nashville, Tenn., 1993-95. Served to lt. (j.g.) USNR, 1956-58. Named Ky. Col., Mr. Coal of Ky., 1970. Mem. Ky. Coal Assn. (dir. 1972-86, exec. com. 1974-78, sec. 1979-86); Ky. C. of C. (regional v.p., 1971-72, 76-80, exec. com. 1971-72, 76-80, dir. 1971-80, fin. com. 1978-79), Lexington C. of C. (dir. 1982, 84-87), Frankfort Country Club, Keeneland Club, Lafayette Club, Thoroughbred Club, Bluegrass Auto Club (former bd. dirs.), Pendennis Club, River Valley Club, Capitol Hill Club, Tau Beta Pi, Alpha Kappa Lambda (past chpt. pres.). Home: 1715 Stonehaven Dr Frankfort KY 40601-8624 Office: 410 W Vine St Lexington KY 40507-1616

GABLE, ROBERT WILLIAM, JR., aerospace engineer; b. Clarinda, Iowa, Nov. 20, 1939; s. Robert William and Elsie Gable; m. Karen Elaine Clay, Feb. 4, 1961; children: Susan, Barbara, Robert. BS, Iowa State U., 1963. Engr. Boeing, Seattle, 1963; engr. GM, Indpls., 1964-71, Phoenix, 1971-73; engr., project mgr. GM, Indpls., 1973-93; systems engr. Allison Engine Co., 1993-94; tech. control officer, bus. mgr. Allison Advanced Devel. Co., 1995—. Home: 460 N County Road 450 E Danville IN 46122-8020 Office: Allison Advanced Devel Co Speed Code X12 PO Box 7162 Indianapolis IN 46207-7162

GABLER, LEE, talent agency executive. Co-chmn. Creative Artists Agy. Office: Creative Artists Agy 9830 Wilshire Blvd Beverly Hills CA 90212-1825*

GABLIK, SUZI, art educator, writer; b. N.Y.C., Sept. 26, 1934; d. Anthony Julius and Geraldine (Schwartz) G. BA, Hunter Coll., 1955. Vis. prof. art Sydney Coll. Arts, 1980, U. of the South, Sewanee, Tenn., 1982, 84, U. Calif., Santa Barbara, 1985, 86, 88, Va. Commonwealth U., Richmond, 1987, Va. Tech., Blacksburg, 1990, U. Colo., Boulder, 1990; endowed lectr. U. Victoria, B.C., 1983, Colo. Coll., 1983, U. Santa Barbara, 1985, Va. Tech., 1989. Author: Magritte, 1979, Has Modernism Failed?, 1984, The Reenchantment of Art, 1991, Conversations Before the End of Time, 1995. Home: 3271 Deer Run Rd Blacksburg VA 24060-9075

GABOR, FRANK, insurance company executive, management consultant; pres. Gabor & Co., Inc., 1948-83, Anglo-Am. Agrl. Underwriters, Inc., Havana, Cuba, 1950-52; v.p., dir. Wilson Nat. Life, 1957-73; pres. Fla. Assn. of Health Unds., 1960-66, Variable Income Planning Co., 1966, Bent Tree Farm, Inc., 1971—; dir., mem. exec. com. Stanwood Corp., Charlotte, N.C, 1975-88; pres. Gabor Reins, Mgmt. Corp., 1975-93, Ins. Svc. Agy. of Fla. Inc., Miami, 1983—; mng. dir. Gabor Mgmt. Svcs., Inc.; chmn. The Gabor Agy., Inc., 1983—; bd. dirs. Am. Reliance Ins. Co. of N.J.; underwriter mgr., cons. Life Disability, Property & Casualty Ins. Co's. With USNR, 1944-46. Mem. Internat. (dir. 1964-68), Fla. Assns. Health Underwriters (pres. 1960-66), Internat. Assn. Health Underwriters (dir., 1960-66), Masons (Shriner). Home: 600 Biltmore Way Miami FL 33134-7541 Office: 3901 NW 79th Ave Miami FL 33166-6554

GABOR, JEFFREY ALAN, insurance and financial services executive; b. Cambridge, Mass., July 7, 1942; s. Frank and Selma (Cluck) G.; m. Ann Steinholtz, June 15, 1963; children: Elissa, Andrea, William. Student, U. Miami, 1960-64. Cert. fin. planner, chartered life underwriter. Pres. The Gabor Agy., Inc., Tallahassee, Fla., 1964—, Gabor Settlements Inc., Tallahassee, 1994—. Mem. Nat. Assn. Life Underwriters, Tallahassee Life Underwriters Assn. (bd. dirs. 1985—), Inst. CFP, Nat. Structured Settlements Trade Assn., Gen. Agts. and Mgrs. Assn. (pres. 1983-84), Million Dollar Round Table (life). Home: 3050 Fermanagh Dr Tallahassee FL 32308-3333 Office: Gabor Cos 3534 Thomasville Rd Tallahassee FL 32308-3413

GABOVITCH, STEVEN ALAN, lawyer, accountant; b. Newton, Mass., Feb. 7, 1953; s. William and Annette (Richman) G.; m. Rhonda Merle Kitover, Aug. 6, 1978; childre: Daniel J., Lindsey D. BS in Acctg., Boston Coll., 1975, JD, 1978; LLM in Taxation, Boston U., 1982. Bar: Mass. 1978, R.I. 1979, U.S. Dist. Ct. R.I. 1979, U.S. Tax Ct. 1980, U.S. Ct. Appeals (1st cir.) 1980, U.S. Dist. Ct. Mass. 1981, U.S. Ct. Appeals (fed. cir.) 1982, U.S. Supreme Ct. 1983. Tax specialist Peat, Marwick, Mitchell & Co., Providence, 1978-80; prin. William Gabovitch & Co., Boston, 1980-97; lectr. on bankruptcy taxation. Contbr. articles to profl. jours. Mem. R.I. Bar Assn., Mass. Bar Assn., Boston Bar Assn., Beta Gamma Sigma. Office: 378 Page St 3 Deerfield Corp Ctr Stoughton MA 02072

GABOVITCH, WILLIAM, lawyer, accountant; b. Boston, June 18, 1922; s. Ezra and Lena Ruth (Elkins) G.; m. Annette Richman, Sept. 19, 1925; children: Steven A., Ellis. BSBA, Boston U., 1943; JD, Boston Coll., 1949; LLM in Taxation NYU, 1950. Bar: Mass. 1949, U.S. Dist. Ct. Mass., U.S. Dist. Ct. R.I., U.S. Ct. Appeals (1st cir.), U.S. Tax Ct., U.S. Ct. Claims, U.S. Ct. Appeals (fed. cir.), U.S. Supreme Ct.; C.P.A., Mass. Sr. ptnr. William Gabovitch & Co., C.P.A.s, Boston, 1962—; lectr. in legal acctg. and taxation Boston Coll. Law Sch., 1959-70; examiner and trustee in bankruptcy, state ct. receiver. Campaign treas. Congressman Robert F. Drinan, 1970-84. Lt. (s.g.) USNR, 1943-46. Mem. ABA, Am. Inst. CPA's, Mass. Soc. CPA's, Mass. Bar Assn., Boston Bar Assn., Mensa, Masons. Home: 33 Old Nugent Farm Rd Gloucester MA 01930-3169 Office: 148 State St Boston MA 02109-2506

GABOW, PATRICIA ANNE, internist; b. Starke, Fla., Jan. 8, 1944; m. Harold N. Gabow, June 21, 1971; children: Tenaya Louise, Aaron Patrick. BA in Biology, Seton Hill Coll., 1965; MD, U. Pa. Sch. Medicine, 1969. Diplomate Am. Bd. Internal Medicine, Am. Bd. Nephrology, Nat. Bd. Med. Examiners; lic. Colo. Internship in medicine Hosp. of U. of Pa., 1969-70; residency in internal medicine Harbor Gen. Hosp., 1970-71; renal fellowship San Francisco Gen. Hosp. and Hosp. of U. Pa., 1971-72, 72-73; instr. medicine divsn. renal diseases, asst. prof. U. Colo. Health Scis. Ctr., 1973-74, 74-79, assoc. prof. medicine divsn. renal diseases, prof., 1979-87; chief renal disease, clin. dir. dept. medicine Denver Gen. Hosp., 1973-81, 76-81, dir. med. svcs., 1981-91; CEO, med. dir. Denver Health and Hosps., 1992—; intensive care com. Denver Gen. Hosp., 1976-81, med. records com., 1979-80, ind. rev. com., 1978-81, continuing med. edn. com., 1981-83, animal care com., 1979-83; student adv. com. U. Colo. Health Scis. Ctr., 1982-87, faculty senate, 1985, 86, internship adv. com., 1977-92; exec. com. Denver Gen. Hosp., 1981—, chmn. health resources com., 1988-90, chmn. pathology search com., 1989, chmn. faculty practice plan steering com., 1990-92. Mem. editorial bd. EMERGINDEX, 1983-93, Am. Jour. of Kidney Disease, 1984-96, Western Jour. of Medicine, 1987—, Annals of Internal Medicine, 1988-91, Jour. of the Am. Soc. of Nephrology, 1990-97; contbr. numerous articles, revs. and editorials to profl. publs., chpts. to books. Mem. Mayor's Safe City Task Force, 1993; mem. sci. adv. bd. Polycystic Kidney Rsch. Found., 1984-96, chmn., 1991; mem. sci. adv. bd. Nat. Kidney Found., 1991-94; mem. Nat. Pub. Health and Hosps. Inst. Bd., 1993—. Recipient Sullivan award for Highest Acad. Average in Graduating Class, Seton Hill Coll., 1965, Pa. State Senatorial scholarship, 1961-65, Kaiser Permanente award for Excellence in Teaching, 1976, Ann. award to Outstanding Woman Physician, 1982, Kaiser Permanente Nominee for Excellence in Teaching award, 1983, Seton Hill Coll. Disting. Alumna Leadership award, 1990; named one of The Best Doctors in Am., 1994-95; grantee Bonfils Found., 1985-86, NIH, 1985-90, 91-96, 96—. Mem. Denver Med. Soc., Colo. Med. Soc., Am. Soc. Nephrology, Internat. Soc. Nephrology, Am. Coll. Physicians, Am. Fedn. Clin. Rsch., Am. Physiol. Soc., Polycystic Kidney Disease Rsch. Found. (sci. advisor 1984-96), Western Assn. Physicians, Nat. Kidney Found. (sci. adv. bd. 1987-91), Women's Forum of Colo., Inc., Assn. Am. Physicians. Roman Catholic. Office: Denver Health 660 Bannock St Denver CO 80204-4506

GABRIA, JOANNE BAKAITIS, health and education volunteer, former information processing systems equipment company executive; b. Washington, Pa., Jan. 16, 1945; d. Vincent William and Mary Jo (Cario) Bakaitis. BA in English, U. Dayton, 1965, MA in Mktg. Communications, 1973, MBA, 1979. Advt. writer Dancer-Fitzgerald-Sample, Dayton, Ohio, 1969-72; advt. coord. Monarch Marking Systems, Dayton, 1972-73; product tech. editor Frigidaire div. GM, Dayton, 1973-77; dir. tech. communications Mead Tech. Lab., Dayton, 1977-79; publs. mgr. NCR Corp., Dayton, 1979-81, internat. product mgr., 1981-86, mgr. internat. market analysis, 1986-87, mgr. internat. market rsch., 1987-93; mgr. european information resources, 1993-94. Author: Microwave Cooking in 3 Speeds, 1976, Communications Standards, 1978, Retail Operations, 1982; editor: Ivy Jour., 1980-82. Chair numerous coms. St. Leonard Community, Centerville, Ohio, 1978-88; telephone vol. Contact-Dayton Crisis Intervention, 1982-86; big sister Big Bros./Big Sisters, Dayton, 1985-86; bd. dirs. Miami Valley chpt. Nat. Kidney Found. of Ohio, 1987-91, spkrs. bur., 1995—; mem. Ohio Patient adv. com. Renal Network, Inc., 1989-91, Patient Leadership Com., Renal Network, 1997—; bd. dirs. Contact-Dayton, 1984-85; local coord. Friends of Polycystic Kidney Rsch. Found., 1994—; tutor Miami Valley Literacy Coun. Literacy Vol. Am., Inc., 1997—. Recipient Disting. Achievement award Contact-Dayton, 1985, Outstanding Service award Miami Valley chpt. Nat. Kidney Found. of Ohio, 1988, Edn. award, 1990. Mem. Dayton Soc. Natural History, Marianist Affiliates (co-chmn. 1981-86), Leo Meyer Soc. Democrat. Roman Catholic. Avocations: nature, classical music.

GABRIEL, DONALD EUGENE, science educator; b. Brush, Colo., May 24, 1944; s. Max and Vera Ellen (Coleman) G.; m. Evonne Kay Asheim, Sept. 27, 1964; children: Shawn Lee, Dawn Kay. AA, Northeastern Jr. Coll., Sterling, Colo., 1964; BA, Colo. State Coll., 1967; MA, U. No. Colo., 1972. Cert. secondary chemistry tchr. Tchr. sci. and math. Brush (Colo.) H.S., 1967—; adv. bd. mem. Colo. Sci. and Engring. Fair, Fort Collins, 1980—; ea. zone chairperson Colo.-Wyo. Jr. Acad. Sci., Fort Morgan, Colo., 1980—; co-dir. Morgan-Washington BiCounty Sci. Fair, Fort Morgan, 1975—. Contbr. articles to profl. jours. Pres. South Platte Valley BOCES, Fort Morgan, 1993-99, v.p., 1991-93; Eagle Scout reviewer Boy Scouts Am., Fort Morgan, 1990—; sec., treas. Brush Pub. Schs., 1995-99. Grantee Tandy Corp., 1989, Joslin Needhams Found., 1990; recipient Presdl. award NSF, 1994; named Milken Nat. Educator, Milken Found., 1991, Tandy Tech. Scholars Outstanding Tchr., 1994-95, Pub. Svc. Co. of Colo. Classroom Connection awards, 1993-99, S. Platte Valley Bd. of Coop. Ednl. Svcs. grants, 1995-98. Mem. Nat. Sci. Tchrs. Assn. (Presdl. award 1994), Colo. Assn. Sci. Tchrs. (regional dir. 1993-96, Outstanding Tchr. 1990). Republican. Lutheran. Avocations: arrowhead hunting, rock hounding. Home: 26137 MCR S 2 Brush CO 80723 Office: Brush HS PO Box 585 Brush CO 80723-0585

GABRIEL, EARL A., osteopathic physician; b. Phila., Aug. 13, 1925; s. John and Rose (Cohen) G.; m. Fredelle, Feldman, Dec. 19, 1948; children: Debra Mae, Barbara Lynn, Sheri Ann, Michael David. *Father John Gabriel born in Ukraine 1887, Master Machinist, Tool and Dye Maker, Inventor. Patent given by U.S. Navy (repair of ball bearings in propellers of fighter planes). Invented mechanical fish scaler. Father-in-law George Feldman, Executive Director of Jewish Federation of Allentown, Pennsylvania. Member of Allentown Charter Commission; established guidelines for mayor-council form of government. Attended college at Muhlenberg, varsity baseball, basketball, football captain, 1920. Wife is Annette Pearlman Feldman.* B.S., Muhlenberg Coll., 1950; D.O., Phila. Coll. Osteo. Medicine, 1954. Gen. practice osteo. medicine Allentown, Pa., 1955-78; chief of staff Allentown Osteo. Hosp., 1967-68, chmn. intern tng., 1956-58; prof., chmn. family practice medicine, assoc. dean clin. affairs Coll. Osteo. Medicine of Pacific, Pomona, Calif., 1978-88, assoc. dean clin. affairs for postdoctoral tng., 1983-88; med. dir. clinics, 1986-88, ret., 1988; pvt. practice gen. medicine Claremont, Calif., 1988-90, Rancho Cucamonga, Calif., 1990-94; dir. med. edn. San Bernardino (Calif.) County Med. Ctr., 1994—; mem. Pa. Gov.'s Sci. Adv. Com. on Health Care Delivery, 1970, 71; preceptor in gen. practice Phila. Coll. Osteo. Medicine; mem. ad hoc profl. group FDA, HEW, 1976-77; mem. Pa. Profl. Services Rev. Orgn. Council, 1977. Editorial adviser Family Practice News, 1976—. Active Lehigh Valley Cancer Soc. Served with USNR and USMCR, 1943-46, PTO, CBI. Recipient cert. of honor Phila. Coll. Osteo. Medicine, 1981, Alumni Achievement award Muhlenberg Coll., 1983; elected Physicians Hall of Fame John Shankwiler Soc. Muhlenberg Coll., 1995; Shankweiler fellow, 1995. Fellow Am. Coll. Gen. Practice in Osteo. Medicine and Surgery (cert., pres. div. 1959, Disting. Svc. award, life mem. Pa. div. 1978); mem. Lehigh Valley Osteo. Soc. (pres. 1959-60), Pa. Osteo. Med. Assn. (pres. 1970, Disting. Svc. award 1975), Am. Osteo. Assn. (cert., ho. dels. 1966—, trustee 1970—, pres. 1975-76, cons. family gen. practice com. on osteo. colls. and bur. profl. edn. 1988), Osteo. Physicians and Surgeons of Calif. (trustee 1981—, pres. 1985), Calif. Bd. Osteo. Examiners, Phi Epsilon Pi (pres. 1950), Sigma Sigma Phi. Republican. Jewish. Clubs: Masons, Shriners, Jester, Lions (Host Pomona), Lehigh Valley. Address: 1551 Marjorie Ave Claremont CA 91711-3545

GABRIEL, JEANETTE HANISEE, curator, art historian; b. Long Beach, Calif., Jan. 12, 1940; d. William Edward and Lorena (Mansell) Lester; m. Robert Maxwell Hanisee, Sept. 28, 1973 (div. 1986); children: Robb Andrew Hanisee, Michele Alpoente Hanisee, Leigh Mathilde Hanisee, Caleb Joseph Hanisee, Patricia Lorena Hanisee, Molly Beverly Hanisee; m. Angelo Julius Gabriel, Oct. 1, 1992. BS, Calif. State U., Northridge, 1978, MS, 1978; MA, U. Calif., Santa Barbara, 1988. Instr. Ventura (Calif.) Coll., 1979-81; dir., founder Adoptions Unltd., Ontario, Calif., 1981-83; curator L.A. County Mus. Art, 1988-92, Gilbert Collection aka Gilbert Collection at Somerset House, L.A. and London, 1994—. Author: The Gilbert Collection of Mosaics, 1999; co-author: By Judgement of the Eye: The Varya and Hans Cohn Collection at the Los Angeles County Museum of Art, 1991, The World of Jade, 1992. Mem. Internat. Churchill Soc., The Churchill Ctr. (founding mem., Clementine Churchill assoc. 1998), Reform Club London. Avocations: antique collecting, movie memorabilia and autographs, gardening. FAX: 310-271-1854. Office: Arthur and Rosalinde Gilbert Collection 9536 Wilshire Blvd #420 Beverly Hills CA 90212

GABRIEL, JOHN, sports team executive; b. Feb. 17; m. Dorothy; children: Amelia, Meredith. Graduate, Kutztown State U. Asst. coach Trinity High Sch., Harrisburg, Pa.; asst. coach, scout, front office exec. Phila. 76ers, 1982-87; from asst. coach to gen. mgr. Orlando (Fla.) Magic, 1987-95, gen. mgr., 1995—. Office: Orlando Magic One Magic Pl 2701 Maitland Summit Blvd Orlando FL 32801*

GABRIEL, MICHAEL, psychology educator; b. Phila., May 5, 1940; s. Michael and Josephine (Alesio) G.; m. Linda Prinz, June, 1967 (div.); 1 child, Joseph Michael; m. Sonda S. Walsh, 1984. AB in Psychology, St. Joseph's Coll., 1962; MA, U. Wis., 1965, Ph.D., 1967. Asst. prof. Pomona Coll., Claremont, Calif., 1967-70; staff psychologist Pacific State Hosp., Pomona, Calif., 1968-70; NIMH sr. postdoctoral fellow U. Calif.-Irvine, 1970-72; asst. prof. U. Tex.-Austin, 1973-77, assoc. prof., 1977-82; prof. psychology U. Ill., Urbana, 1982—; appointee Ctr. for Advanced Study U. Ill., 1990-91; area chmn. Biol. Psychology Program, U. Tex., Austin, 1979-82; mem. rev. panel in behavioral and neural scis. NSF, 1988-91, prin. investigator database system for neuronal pattern analysis project, 1992—, ad hoc mem. biopsychology rev. panel, 1997-98; faculty Beckman Inst., U. Ill., Urbana, 1989—; chmn. Neuronal Pattern Analysis Group, Beckman Inst. Co-editor: (with J. Moore) Learning and Computational Neuroscience: Foundations of Adaptive Networks, 1989, (with B. Vogt) Neurobiology of Cingulate Cortex and Limbic Thalamus, 1993. grantee NIMH, 1978-88, 98—, NIH, 1988—, Air Force Office Sci. Rsch., 1988-91, NSF, 1992—, NIDA, 1996—. Fellow Am. Psychol. Soc., Internat. Behavioral Neurosci. Soc.; mem. Sigma Chi. Office: U Ill Beckman Inst 405 N Mathews Ave Urbana IL 61801-2325

GABRIEL, MORDECAI LIONEL, biologist, educator; b. N.Y.C., Mar. 18, 1918; s. Joseph and Bertha (Fram) G.; m. Elinor Rosenstein, Nov. 11, 1945; children—Alisa, Jessica. A.B., Yeshiva U., 1938; M.A., Columbia, 1938, Ph.D., 1944. Instr. genetics U. Conn., 1943-45; mem. faculty Bklyn. Coll., 1945—, prof. biology, 1963—, chmn. dept., 1965-71; dean Bklyn. Coll. (Sch. Sci.), 1971-76, acting v.p. for acad. affairs, 1981-82; assoc. provost Bklyn. Coll., 1982-88, assoc. provost emeritus, 1988—; vis. prof. Columbia, 1956; Fulbright lectr., vis. prof. U. Tel Aviv, 1959-60; mem. Marine Biol. Lab., Woods Hole, Mass., 1950—. Author: (with S. Fogel) Great Experiments in Biology, 1956. Ford Found. faculty fellow, 1955-56. Fellow AAAS; mem. Am. Soc. Zoologists, Am. Assn. Anatomists, N.Y. Acad. Scis., Soc. Study Evolution, Vertebrate Paleont. Soc., AAUP (pres. Bklyn. Coll. chpt. 1964-66), Phi Beta Kappa, Sigma Xi. Home: 120 Old Mill Rd Great Neck NY 11023-1936 Office: Brooklyn Coll Brooklyn NY 11210

GABRIEL, RENNIE, financial planner; b. L.A., July 27, 1948; s. Harry and Milly (Broder) Goldenhar; m. Judi Robbins, Nov. 24, 1968 (div. Feb. 1989); children: Ryan, Davida; m. Lesli Gilmore, May 5, 1990 (div. Aug. 1998). BA, Calif. State U., Northridge, 1971; CLU, Am. Coll., 1979, Cert. Fin. Planner, 1988. Ins. agt. Prudential and Provident Mutual, Encino, Calif., 1972-78; pension cons. Shadur LaVine & Assocs., Encino, 1978-81; owner Artist Corner Gallery Inc., Encino, 1977-82; pension and fin. planner Gabriel Tolleson & Stroum, Tarzana, Calif., 1983-87; pension cons., fin. planner Shadur LaVine/Integrated Fin., Encino, 1987-90; dir. pensions U.S. Life of Calif., Pasadena, Calif., 1983; fin. planner Pension Alternatives, Encino, 1990-92, The Fin. Coach Inc., Encino, 1993—; instr. UCLA, 1992—; pub. Gabriel Publs., 1996—. Contbr. articles to fin. publs. Mem. Internat. Assn. Fin. Planning (pres. San Fernando Valley chpt. 1992), Nat. Assn. Life Underwriters (Achievement award 1974, Nat. Quality award 1975, Million Dollar Round Table 1990), Internat. Assn. Fin. Planning, CLUs, Inst. Cert. Fin. Planners, Employee Assistance Profls. Assn. (treas. San Fernando Valley chpt. 1992), Apt. Assn. San Fernando Valley-Ventura County (bd. mem. 1992). Avocations: jogging, skiing, real estate management, psychology.

GABRIEL, RICHARD WEISNER, lawyer; b. Greensboro, N.C., Nov. 2, 1949; s. George Deeb and Lillian (Weisner) G.; m. Elizabeth Diane Burton, June 23, 1979; children: Margaret Elizabeth, Richard Weisner Jr. AB, Duke U., 1971; MBA, U. N.C., Greensboro, 1977; JD, Wake Forest U., 1975. Bar: N.C. 1975, U.S. Supreme Ct. 1978, U.S. Tax Ct. 1981, U.S. Dist. Ct. (mid. dist.) N.C. 1975. Pvt. practice Greensboro, 1975-77; mng. ptnr. Gabriel, Berry & Weston LLP, Greensboro, 1978—; vis. lectr. Guilford Coll., Greensboro, 1977-81; counsel Internat. Home Furnishings Reps. Assn., High Point, N.C., 1988—. Co-author: (manuals) Proving Damages in North Carolina, 1989, Trial Advocacy in North Carolina, 1990, Trying the Automobile Injury Case in North Carolina, 1992, 93, 95, Counseling the Small Business Client in North Carolina, 1996, Negotiating and Drafting Acquisition Agreements in North Carolina, 1999; contbg. author Contact Mag., 1988—; editor-in-chief Wake Forest Jurist, 1975. With N.C. Army

N.G., 1971-77. Recipient award for exemplary svc. Upjohn Health Care Svcs., 1988, Presdl. Citation, IHFRA, 1991. Office: Gabriel Berry & Weston LLP 214 Commerce Pl Greensboro NC 27401-2427

GABRIEL, ROGER EUGENE, management consulting executive; b. Rock Island, Ill., Oct. 11, 1929; s. Walter Paul and Annabele (Darling) G.; m. Dixie Fay Duteil, Mar. 29, 1952; children: Michele Kelly, Dawn, Scott. BS in Behavioral Scis., George Williams Coll., Chgo., 1952. Mgr. pers. RCA, Cin., 1953-59; mgr. pers. devel. Martin Marietta, Cocoa Beach, Fla., 1959-66; v.p. ops. Argyle Pub. Corp., N.Y.C., 1966-68; v.p. orgn. devel. Pan Am. World Airways, N.Y.C., 1968-72; corp. dir. mgmt. devel. Rockwell Internat., El Segundo, Calif., 1972-77; v.p. adminstrn. Kaiser-Aetna, Oakland, Calif., 1977-80; v.p. Marshall Industries Corp., El Monte, Calif., 1980-82; v.p., ptnr. Paul R. Ray & Co., L.A., 1982-87; pres. Indian River Cons. Group, Inc., Melbourne, Fla., 1987—; bd. dirs. Bell Electric Supply, San Jose, Calif., Debenham Elec. Supply, Anchorage, C.B. Sullivan Co., Manchester, N.H., Child Welfare Inst.; tchr. first course on creative thinking U. Cin., 1958; speaker creative thinking to 100 orgns. in U.S., 1955-65. Pres. Rep. Club, Green Hills, Ohio, 1956, PTA, Indian Harbor Beach, Fla., 1958. With USNR, 1948-53. Republican. Home: 230 Country Club Dr Melbourne FL 32940-7624 Office: Indian River Cons Group Inc 104 S Harbor City Blvd Ste A Melbourne FL 32901-1373

GABRIEL, RONALD SAMUEL, child neurologist; b. Monterey, Calif., Mar. 19, 1937; s. Philip Louis and Theresa Shaheen Gabriel; children: Philip Louis III, Paula Shaheen, Matthew William. BA with honors, Yale U., 1959; MD, Boston U., 1963. Diplomate Am. Bd. Psychiatry and Neurology (examiner 1978-88), Am. Bd. Pediatrics. Intern, resident in pediatrics Los Angeles County Gen. Hosp., 1963-66; fellow in neurology and pediatric neurology UCLA med. ctr., 1966-68, 70-71; head physician, cons. Calif. Children's Svcs., 1970—; clin. prof. neurology/pediatrics UCLA Sch. Medicine, 1971—, dir. pediat. neurology/outpatient, 1971-76; cons. Regional Ctr.-Calif., 1971—; vis. prof. Prince of Wales, Royal Children's Hosp., Sydney and Melbourne, Australia, 1978; mem. expert panel L.A. Superior Ct., 1992—; founding and mng. gen. ptnr. Med. Imaging of So. Calif., L.A., 1980-94; mng. dir. GFA Cattle and Farm Co. Author: The 410 Shotgun, 1999, Diary of a Mountain Hunter, 1999, co-author: Textbook of Child Neurology, 1974, 4th edit., 1990, Difficult Diagnoses in Pediatrics, 1990, Founders of Child Neurology, 1990. Mng. dir. GFF Natural History Mus. Maj. U.S. Army, 1968-70. Spl. fellow Nat. Inst. Neurol. Disease/Stroke, 1966-68, 70-71. Fellow Am. Acad. Pediatrics, Am. Acad. Neurology; mem. Calif. Med. Assn. (mem. sci. adv. panel 1987-94, chmn. sci. adv. com. 1989-90). Roman Catholic. Avocations: writing, mountaineering, hunting. Fax: (310) 277-9285. Office: Neurology-Pediat Neurology Assocs 2080 Century Park E Ste 203 Los Angeles CA 90067

GABRIELE, MARK DAVID, policy analyst; b. Sept. 9, 1963. BS in Computer Engring., U. Mich., 1985; MS in Computer Sci., U. Toronto, 1991; PhD in Policy Analysis, RAND Grad. Sch., 1997. Sys. evaln. expert Dept. of Def., Ft. Meade, Md., 1985-89; mem. tech. staff The Aerospace Corp., El Segundo, Calif., 1991-93; policy analyst The RAND Corp., Santa Monica, Calif., 1993—. E-mail: gabriele@rand.org.

GABRIELSEN, CAROL ANN, employment consulting company executive; b. Oak Park, Ill., Aug. 8, 1951; d. George Kenneth and Marijo (Martin) G.; children: Sean Martin, Zachary George. Student, Harper Jr. Coll., 1970-71. Regional mgr. Reed Roberts Assn., Ill., Wis., Pa., 1972-79; account rep. The Gibbens Co., Schiller Park, Ill., 1980-81; CEO Unemployment Consultants, Inc., Arlington Heights, 1981-94; tech. advisor Gov. Edgar Unemployment Task Force, 1990-96. Author: Manufacturer's Guide to the New Unemployment Law, 1987, rev. edit., 1992. Vol. Bush/Quayle campaign, Arlington Heights, 1988; chairwoman golf outing Spl. Leisure Svcs. Found., 1992-99; legis. com. Greater Ohare Assn., 1992-98, PAC chair, 1997, bd. dirs., 1999. Mem. Assn. Unemployed Tax (v.p. 1989, pres. 1990), Ill. Mfrs. Assn., Employers Assn. Ill., Our Lady of the Wayside Alumni Assn. (pres. 1990-92), Arlington Heights C. of C. (bd. dirs. 1987-92, v.p. 1991), Arlington Heights Rotary (chair youth exch. 1987-94, chair membership com. 1994-98, GSE sect. chair, 1995). Roman Catholic. Avocations: traveling, reading, golfing. Office: Unemployment Consultants 55 S Vail Ave Apt 1102 Arlington Heights IL 60005-1874

GABRIELSON, CHARLES, publishing executive. Pub. USA Weekend Gannett Co., Inc., Arlington, Va. Office: Gannett Co Inc 535 Madison Ave Fl 21 New York NY 10022-4216*

GABRIELSON, IRA WILSON, physician, educator; b. N.Y.C., Nov. 27, 1922; s. Benjamin and Lily (Baran) G.; m. Mary Putnam Oliver, Sept. 4, 1948; children: Deborah Anne, David Dwight, Hugh Wilson, Carl Oliver. BA, Columbia U., 1944, MD, 1949; MPH, Johns Hopkins U., 1959. Diplomate: Am. Bd. Pediatrics, Nat. Bd. Med. Examiners. Adminstrv. asst., asst. dir. Johns Hopkins Hosp., 1953-57; dir. community program retarded children New Haven, 1959-61; asst. attending pediatrician Yale-New Haven Community Hosp., 1959-68; asst. prof. public health Yale, 1961-68, exec. officer dept. epidemiology and public health, 1962-67; clin. prof. U. Calif., Berkeley, 1968-71; prof., chmn. dept. community and preventive medicine Med. Coll. Pa., 1971-89, prof. pediatrics, 1987-90, prof. emeritus, 1990—; adj. prof., exec. dir. physician asst. program Springfield (Mass.) Coll., 1994-97; cons. in field. Editor Medicine Looks at the Humanities, 1987. With AUS. Fellow Nat. Found., 1958. Fellow Am. Acad. Pediatrics, Am. Public Health Assn., Coll. Physicians Phila. (pub. health com. 1976-90); mem. Phila. Pediatric Soc. (chmn. sch. health com. 1983-90—), Assn. Tchrs. of Preventive Medicine, Sigma Xi, Delta Omega. Club: Appalachian Mountain (Boston). Avocations: photography, hiking. Home: 85 Old Goshen Rd Williamsburg MA 01096-9707 Office: Med Coll Pa Dept Cmty & Preventive Med 1505 Race St # Ms644 Philadelphia PA 19102-1119

GABRIELSON, SHIRLEY GAIL, nurse; b. San Francisco, Mar. 17, 1934; d. Arthur Obert and Lois Ruth (Lanterman) Ellison; m. I. Grant Gabrielson, Sept. 11, 1955; children: James Grant, Kari Gay. BS in Nursing, Mont. State U., 1955. RN, Mont. Staff and operating room nurse Bozeman (Mont.) Deaconess Hosp., 1954-55, 55-56; staff nurse Warm Springs State Hosp., 1955; office nurse, operating room asst. Dr. Craft, Bozeman, 1956-57; office nurse Dr. Bush, Beach, N.D., 1957-58; pub. health nurse Wibaux County, 1958-59; staff and charge nurse Teton Meml. Hosp., Choteau, Mont., 1964-65; staff pediatric and float nurse St. Patrick Hosp., Missoula, Mont., 1965-70; nurse, insvc. dir. Trinity Hosp., Wolf Point, Mont., 1970-79; ednl. coord. Community Hosp. and Nursing Home, Poplar, Mont., 1979-96; coord. staff devel. Faith Luth. Home, Wolf Point, 1980-81; risk mgr. Northeast Mont. Health Svcs., Inc., Poplar, 1996—; CPR instr. ARC, Am. Heart Assn., Great Falls, Mont., 1979-97; condr. workshops and seminars; program coord., test proctor for cert. nursing assts., 1989-96; risk mgr. N.E. Mont. Health Svcs., Poplar, Wolf Point, 1996—; preceptor for student nurses in rural health nursing clin. U. N.D., 1993-96. Author: Independent Study for Nurse Assistants, 1977. Former asst. camp leader Girl Scouts U.S.A.; former mother advisor, bd. dirs. Rainbow Girls; pres. Demolay Mothers Club, 1977; bd. dirs. Mont. div. Am. Cancer Soc., 1984-90, mem. awards com., 1986-89; founder Tri-County Parkinson's Support Group, N.E. Mont. Recipient Lifesaver award Am. Cancer Soc., 1987, Svc. award ARC, 1989, Health and Human Svcs. award Mont. State Dept., 1990, U.S. Dept. Health award, 1990, Outstanding award, U.S. HHS, Mont. Health Promotion award Dept. Health and Environ. Scis. Mem. ANA, Mont. Nurses Assn. (mem. commn. on continuing edn. 1977-91, chmn. 1984-86), Order Eastern Star (Worthy grand matron 1995-96), Alpha Tau Delta (alumni pres. 1956). Presbyterian. Avocations: music, travel, writing prose and poetry. Home: 428 Hill St Wolf Point MT 59201-1244 Office: NE Mont Health Svcs Inc PO Box 38 Poplar MT 59255-0038

GABRILOVE, JACQUES LESTER, physician; b. N.Y.C., Sept. 21, 1917; s. Benjamin and Pauline (Levine) G.; m. Hilda R. Weiss, May 19, 1946; children: Sandra Leslie Saltzman, Janice Lynn Gabrilove Dirzulaitis. BS magna cum laude, CCNY, 1936; MD, NYU, 1940. Diplomate Am. Bd. Internal Medicine. Intern Mt. Sinai Hosp., N.Y.C., 1940-41; rotating intern Mt. Sinai Hosp., 1941-43, vol. radiology, 1943, resident medicine, 1943-44, Blumenthal fellow medicine, 1946-48, research asst. medicine, 1949-51, asst. attending physician, 1952-60, assoc. attending physician, 1960-68, attending physician, 1969—; chief endocrine clinic, clin. prof. medicine Mt. Sinai Sch. Medicine, 1969-82, Baumritter prof., 1982-90, Baumritter prof. emeritus, 1990—, prof., 1995—, cting dir. divsn. endocrinology, 1985, assoc. dir. divsn., 1986—, dir. endocrine fellowship program, 1986—; Libman fellow in medicine Yale U., 1945; clin. asst. prof. SUNY Coll. Medicine, N.Y.C., 1957-59, clin. assoc. prof., 1959-66, clin. prof., 1966-69, professorial lectr., 1969—; cons. endocrinology VA Hosp., East Orange, N.J., 1958-66, Elizabeth A. Horton Hosp., Middletown, N.Y., 1961—, VA Hosp., Bronx, N.Y., 1969—, Norwalk (Conn.) Hosp., 1974—, Elmhurst (N.Y.) City Hosp., St. Francis Hosp., Port Jervis, N.Y.; mem. panel on metabolic and rheumatoid diseases U.S. Pharmacopeia, 1956; mem. spl. com. on rsch. tng. grants in diabetes, endocrinology and metabolism NIH, 1976-79, mem. com. on diabetes rsch. and tng. ctrs., 1977-79; Saltzman lectr. Mt. Sinai Hosp., Cleve., 1974; cons. Jour. Urology, 1984-89. Author, contbr. to books in field, also articles to med. jours.; mem. editl. bd. Mt. Sinai Jour. Trustee, v.p. area Jewish synagogue. Recipient Globus prize Mt. Sinai Jour., Townsend Harris medal CCNY Alumni Assn., 1998; J. Lester Gabrilove award established in his honor, 1988. Fellow ACP, Am. Coll. Endocrinology (Disting. Clin. Endocrinologist award 1996), N.Y. Acad. Medicine; mem. AMA, AAAS, Am. Assn. Clin. Endocrinologists, Am. Diabetes Assn., Harvey Soc., Endocrine Soc., Royal Soc. Medicine, Pan Am. Med. Assn. (v.p. N.Am. endocrinology), Peruvian Endocrine Soc. (hon.), N.Y. Acad. Scis., N.Y. County Med. Soc., N.Y. Diabetes Assn., Mt. Sinai Alumni Assn. (pres. 1970, Jacobi medallion), Lotos Club (bd. dirs.), Phi Beta Kappa, Phi Beta Kappa Assocs., Alpha Omega Alpha (prize). Achievements include research in delineaton of hyperfunctioning and hypofunctioning endocrine disorders of the adrenal cortex and gonads; mechanism of gynecomastia; medical treatment of thyrotoxicosis; med. treatment of benign prostatic hyperplasia. Home: 25 E 86th St New York NY 10028-0553

GABRIS, GEORGE STEVEN, sculptor, welder; b. N.Y.C., Jan. 2, 1953; s. Stephen John and Kveta (Rybička) G.; m. Stephanie Anne Mazanek, Dec. 30, 1989. Cert. in Welding, Albuquerque Tech. Vocat. Inst., 1979. Tchr. art, recreation instr. N.Y.C. Housing Authority, 1975-76; artist, 1977; prodn. welder Environ. Bldg. Products, Albuquerque, 1979-81, H&L Iron Works, Albuquerque, 1982, Hemisphere Steel Co., Bklyn., 1984-85; test welder R&D Eutectic Corp. of Eutectic and Castolin Inc. Internat., Flushing, N.Y., 1985-88; car maintainer in train overhaul shop N.Y.C. Transit Authority, 1988—. Group exhbns. include Lever House, N.Y.C., 1975, A.S.A. Gallery, Albuquerque, 1981, 82, Gelabert Studios, N.Y.C., 1992, Abney Gallery, N.Y.C., 1992, Crossland Svs. Bank, L.I. and Manhattan, N.Y., 1993, Limner Gallery, N.Y.C., 1993, 94, Westbeth Gallery, N.Y.C., 1994, 97, Art Initiatives, N.Y.C., 1996, Broome St. Gallery, N.Y.C., 1996, Stephen Gang Gallery, N.Y.C., 1997, (website) Internat. Artists Interface, 1996—, Americas Towers Lobby, 1998-99; represented in numerous pvt. collections. Vol. dept. social and cmty. svcs. N.Y.C. Housing Authority, 1974, 75; youth project coord. Visions/Urban Youth Project, N.Y.C., 1976. Recipient Critics' Pix award Manhattan Arts Internat. Mag., 1994, Showcase award, 1996, 98, 1st prize Internat. Art League, 1998. Mem. Nat. Sculpture Soc., Am. Welding Soc. (cert.), Orgn. Ind. Artists, Transit Workers Union (local 100). Democrat. Avocations: art collector, bread baker, gourmet cook, exotic birds, "good" cigars. E-mail: gssculp@aol.com. Home: 59 E 2nd St Brooklyn NY 11218-1019

GAC-ARTIGAS, PRISCILLA, foreign language educator, publisher; m. Gustavo Gac-Artigas; children: Melina, Alejandro. BA, U. P.R., Río Piedras, 1977; MA, Middlebury (Vt.) Coll., 1978; PhD, U. Franche-Comté, France, 1994. Asst. prof. fgn. langs. Monmouth U., West Long Branch, N.J., 1995—. Author: Critical Study of Latin American Popular Theater in the Sixties, 1996 (Elena Rale award 1994); co-author: Spanish for English Speakers, 1996, French for English Speakers, 1996, To the Point: English for Spanish Speakers, 1996.

GACEM, DEBRA ANN, critical care nurse; b. St. Louis, Aug. 19, 1955; d. Roy Leo and Nina Lee (Sutton) Case; 1 child, Sam Gacem. Diploma, Barnes Hosp. Sch. Nursing, St. Louis, 1975. Cert. critical care nurse. Staff nurse Barnes-Jewish Hosp., St. Louis; asst. head nurse post-anesthesia care unit Barnes Hosp., St. Louis, staff nurse post-anesthesia care unit, unit based clin. educator for cardiothoracic post-anes care. Mem. Am. Soc. Post Anesthesia Nurses, Ill. Soc. Post Anesthesia Nurses, Barnes Hosp. Sch. Nursing Alumni Assn. Home: 3210 Yorkchester Dr Saint Louis MO 63129-1736

GACKLE, DONALD CHRISTOPH, publisher; b. Kulm, N.D., Apr. 12, 1929; s. Otto and Alice Irene (Higdem) G.; m. Phyllis Darlene King, Jan. 28, 1951; children: Michael William, Cynthia Alice. PhB in Journalism, U. N.D., 1951. Pub. affairs dir. Greater N.D. Assn.-N.D. State C. of C., 1953-63; editor, owner McLean County Ind., 1963—; founder, pub. BHG, Inc, Garrison, N.D., 1971—. With U.S. Army, 1951-53. Mem. N.D. Newspaper Assn. (pres. 1976), Am. Legion, Masons (master 1974), Elks. Avocations: trail biking, bicycling, golf. Home: Box 1056 103 1st St Garrison ND 58540 Office: BHG Inc Box 309 91 N Main St Garrison ND 58540-7166

GAD, LANCE STEWART, investment advisor, lawyer, private investor; b. Peekskill, N.Y., Dec. 11, 1945; s. Martin Harold and Claire (Entner) G.; m. Helen Alexandra Grevey, Jan. 14, 1972 (div. 1978); m. Janiece Lee Feiden, Feb. 14, 1987. BA cum laude, SUNY, Stony Brook, 1967; JD, Cornell U., 1970, MBA, 1971; LLM in Taxation, NYU Law Sch., 1975. Assoc. Spear & Hill, N.Y.C., 1971-72, Wien, Malkin & Bettex, N.Y.C., 1972-74; mgr. Wheelabrator-Frye, N.Y.C., 1974-75, Citicorp, N.Y.C., 1975-86; mgr. Citibank N.A., N.Y.C., 1975-77, asst. v.p., 1977-79, v.p., 1979-86; v.p., gen. counsel and sec. Citicorp Services, Inc., N.Y.C., 1980-85; v.p. Citicorp Investment Bank, N.Y.C., 1985-86; investment advisor WR Family Assocs., N.Y.C., 1986-90, Am. Securities Corp., N.Y.C., 1986-90; chmn., mng. dir., chief investment officer Greenfield Hill Capital Mgmt., 1991—; chmn., pres., treas., dir. The Lance and Janiece Gad Found., Inc., 1987—. Mem. N.Y. State Bar Assn., Cornell Law Assn., Johnson Sch. Mgmt. Alumni Assn., NYU Grad. Sch. Law Alumni Assn., Cornell Club of N.Y. Home and Office: 1250 Fence Row Dr Fairfield CT 06430-7025 also: 14 N Hollow Dr East Hampton NY 11937 also: 6 Peter Cooper Rd Apt 8F New York NY 10010-6709

GADACZ, THOMAS ROMAN, surgery educator; b. South Bend, Ind., Nov. 23, 1940; m. Judith Gadacz; children: Audrey, Emily, Alissa, Nicholas. BS in Biology, U. Notre Dame, 1962; MD, St. Louis U., 1966. Diplomate Am. Bd. Surgery. Intern in surgery U. Chgo., 1966-67, resident in surgery, 1967-68; mem. staff Naval. Hosp., San Diego, 1968-69; resident in surgery U. Calif., San Francisco, 1971-74, chief resident in surgery, 1973-74; staff surgeon, chief surg. rsch. Balt. VA Med. Ctr., 1975-78, chief surg. svc., 1978-91; asst. prof. surgery U. Md. Sch. of Medicine, 1979-84, assoc. prof. surgery, 1984-91; asst. prof. surgery Johns Hopkins Hosp., 1975-78, assoc. prof. surgery, 1979-88, prof. surgery, 1988-91, lectr. surgery, 1992-94, 96-97; prof., chmn. dept. surgery Med. Coll. Ga., Augusta, 1991—; vis. surgeon Francis Scott Key Med. Ctr., Balt., 1975-91; rschr. in G.I. physiology U. Calif., San Francisco, 1970-71; clin. rschr. gastro-intestinal absorption and bile acid metabolism Mayo Clinic, 1974-75; mem. numerous coms. VA, Johns Hopkins U., Med. Coll. Ga. Mem. editl. bd. Jour. Gastrointestinal Surgery, Laparoscopic Surgery; guest editor Surg. Rounds. With USN, 1968-70. Rsch. fellow Am. Cancer Soc.; Surgery Tng. grantee NIH, 1970-73. Fellow ACS (Young Surgeon rep. Md. 1980, sec. Md. chpt. 1983-85, v.p. 1985-87, pres. 1987-89, com. surg. edn. in med. schs., continuing edn. com. 1996—), Am. Soc. Laser Medicine and Surgery; mem. Am. Assn. Study of Liver Disease, Am. Gastroenterol. Assn., Am. Pancreatic Study Group, Am. Surg. Assn., Assn. Acad. Surgery (nominating com. 1978-81, coun. 1985-87), Assn. Am. Med. Colls., Assn. VA Surgeons, Balt. Acad. Surgery Balt. Liver Group, Ga. Gastroenterol. and Endoscopic Soc., Internat. Soc. Surgery, Johns Hopkins Med. Soc., Mayo Alumni Assn., Moretz Surg. Soc., Naffziger Surg. Soc., Nat. Assn. Biomed. Rsch., Nat. Assn. VA Physicians, Soc. Univ. Surgeons, Soc. Med. Conss. to Armed Forces, Soc. Surgeons of Alimentary Tract (rep. to Nat. Soc. Med. Rsch. 1987—, chmn. patient care com. 1995-98), Southeastern Surg. Congress (fin. com. 1995-96, exec. com. 1994-96, 96—, patient guidelines com., councillor-at-large nominating com., 1993-96, 96—), So. Med. Assn., So. Surg. Assn., World Assn. Hepato-Pancreatic Biliary Surgery, Phi Beta Pi. Fax: (706) 721-2063. E-mail: tgadacz@mailmcg.edu. Office: Med Coll Ga Dept Surgery 1120 15th St Dept Surgery Augusta GA 30912-0006*

GADAPEE, BRETT RONALD, English language educator, coach; b. Berlin, Vt., Feb. 3, 1970; s. Richard H. and Patsy (Fleming) G.; m. Amy Katherine Adams, Aug. 1, 1997. BA in English, U. Fla., 1992, MA in Secondary English. Edn., 1993. Cert. secondary tchr., Fla. English language tchr. Astronaut H.S., Titusville, Fla., 1993-96, Orange Park (Fla.) H.S., 1996—; head coach jr. varsity football, Astronaut H.S., Titusville, Fla., 1993-96, jr. varsity basketball, 1993-95, jr. varsity baseball, 1996, girls softball, Orange Park (Fla.) H.S., 1997, asst. varsity football, 1997, 98, head jr. varsity softball, 1997, 98. Methodist. Avocations: reading, coaching. Home: 1530 Slash Pine Ct Orange Park FL 32073 Office: Orange Park HS Kingsley Ave Orange Park FL 32073

GADBERRY, VICKI LYNN HIMES, librarian; b. Frederick, Md., Jan. 3, 1950; d. Guilford Swisher and Eloise Alberta (Twentey) Himes; m. Eric Brett Gadberry, Aug. 15, 1971. BS, U. Md., 1971; MLS, U. S.C., 1974; postgrad., Penland Sch. Crafts, 1989, 96, Sul Ross State U., 1997-98. Cert. media coord. N.C. Dept. Pub. Instrn. Media coord. N.C. Pub. Schs., Fayetteville, 1976-78, Hendersonville, 1980-85, Asheville, 1985-88; pub. svcs. coord. Mars Hill (N.C.) Coll., 1990-92, reference svcs. libr., 1992-97; asst. exec. dir. Fort Davis (Tex.) C. of C., 1998—; on-site dir. Children's Art in the Mountains Program, Marshall, N.C., summer 1992, tchr. fiber art, summer 1990; artist-in-residence Mountain Arts Program, Waynesville, N.C., 1990. Project designer book: Molas!, 1998; contbr. articles, revs., index to profl. publs. Mem. planning com. Beacon Handloom Weaving Show, Asheville, N.C., 1988, 90-92, chair, 1989; bd. dirs. Children's Art in the Mountains Program, Marshall, N.C., 1991-93. Mem. Handweaver's Guild Am. (orgnl. C.O.E. com. co-chair 1992-94). Avocations: weaving, photography. E-mail: vgadberry@hotmail.com. Home: PO Box 393 Fort Davis TX 79734

GADDES, RICHARD, performing arts administrator; b. Wallsend, Northumberland, Eng., May 23, 1942; s. Thomas and Emilie Jane (Rickard) G. L.T.C.L. in piano, L.T.C.L. for sch. music; G.T.C.L., Trinity Coll. Music, London, 1964; D. Mus. Arts (hon.), St. Louis Conservatory, 1983; D.F.A. (hon.), U. Mo.-St. Louis, 1984; D.Arts (hon.), Webster U., 1986. Founder, mgr. Wigmore Hall Lunchtime Concerts, 1965; dir. Christopher Hunt and Richard Gaddes Artists Mgmt., London, 1965-66; bookings mgr. Artists Internat. Mgmt., London, 1967-69; artistic adminstr. Santa Fe Opera, 1969-78, assoc. gen. dir., 1995—; gen. dir. Opera Theatre of St. Louis, 1975-85, bd. dirs., 1985—; bd. dirs. Grand Ctr., Inc., 1988—, pres., 1988-95; bd. dirs. William Matheus Sullivan Found. Mem. bd. advisors Royal Oak Found. Recipient Lamplighter award, 1982, Mo. Arts award, 1983, St. Louis award, 1983, Human Relations award Jewish-Am. Com., St. Louis, 1985, Nat. Inst. for Music Theatre award, 1986, Cultural Achievement award Young Audiences, 1987. Office: Santa Fe Opera PO Box 2408 Santa Fe NM 87504-2408*

GADDIE, RONALD KEITH, political science educator, writer; b. Louisville, Jan. 23, 1966; s. James Ronald and Rita Harrod Gaddie; m. Kimberly Conrad, June 8, 1991; children: Collin, Alec. BS in Polit. Sci., Fla. State U., 1987; MA in Polit. Sci., U. Ga., 1989, PhD in Polit. Sci., 1993. Programmer, analyst Electoral/Demographics, Athens, Ga., 1987-92; postdoctoral fellow Tulane U., New Orleans, 1992-94; rsch. prof. Tulane Sch. Pub. Health and Tropical Medicine, New Orleans, 1994-96; prof. U. Okla., Norman, 1996—; cons. to Mayor of New Orleans, 1994, Electoral/Demographics, Athens, 1992—. Author: The Economic Realities of Political Reform, 1995, Regulating Wetlands Protections: Environmental Federalism and the States, 1999; author, editor: (serial book) The Almanac of Oklahoma Politics, 1998, 99; editor: David Duke and the Politics of Race in the South, 1995. Campaign mgr. Chuck Pardue for Congress, Augusta, Ga., 1992; vol. Habitat for Humanity, New Orleans, 1993-96; organizer/donor rep. The Charles S. Bullock III Fellowship, U. Ga., 1998—. Recipient Freeport-McMoRan Environ. Policy fellowship Tulane U., 1992-94, Coca-Cola Faculty mentor Tulane U., 1995. Mem. Am. Polit. Sci. Assn., So. Polit. Sci. Assn., Southwestern Polit. Sci. Assn., Pi Sigma Alpha, Phi Kappa Tau. Episcopalian. Avocations: biking, writing, snorkling. E-mail: KGaddie@worldnet.att.ent. FAX: 405-325-0718. Home: 4112 Kent St Norman OK 73072 Office: Univ Okla Dept Polit Sci Norman OK 73019

GADDIS, EVAN R., career officer. Commd. officer U.S. Army, advanced through grades to maj. gen.; commdg. gen. Recruiting Command U.S. Army, Ft. Knox, Ky., 1998—. Office: US Army Recruiting Command Ft Knox KY 40121-2726

GADDIS, JOHN LEWIS, history educator; b. Cotulla, Tex., Apr. 2, 1941. BA, U. Tex., 1963, MA, 1965, PhD, 1968. Asst. prof. Ind. U. S.E., Jeffersonville, 1968-69; asst. prof. history Ohio U., Athens, 1969-71, assoc. prof., 1971-76, prof., 1976-83, disting. prof. history, 1983-97, dir. Contemporary History Inst., 1987-93; Robert Lovett prof. history Yale U., New Haven, 1997—; vis. prof. Naval War Coll., 1975-77; Bicentennial prof. Am. history, U. Helsinki, 1980-81; vis. prof. politics Princeton U., 1987; Harmsworth prof. Am. History Oxford U., 1992-93. Author: The United States and the Origins of the Cold War, 1941-47, 1972, Russia, the Soviet Union, and the United States: An Interpretive History, 1978, 2d edit., 1990, Strategies of Containment: A Critical Appraisal of Postwar American National Security Policy, 1982, The Long Peace: Inquiries into the History of the Cold War, 1987, The United States and the End of the Cold War, 1992, We Now Know: Rethinking Cold War History, 1997. Fellow Woodrow Wilson Ctr., 1995-96; recipient Bancroft prize, 1973, Stuart L. Bernath prize, 1973, Nat. Hist. Soc. prize, 1973. Mem. Am. Hist. Assn., Orgn. Am. Historians, Soc. for Historians of Am. Fgn. Rels., Coun. on Fgn. Rels.

GADDIS, M. FRANCIS, mechanical and marine engineer, environmental scientist; b. Boston, July 27, 1920; s. Michael Joseph and Catherine Agnes (Lavelle) G.; m. Marie B. Leen, Nov. 22, 1946 (dec. Feb. 1979); children: Robert L., Paul L.; m. Jeanne Bowen Crites, Oct. 27, 1990. BS, U. Ala., 1945; BA, Adelphi U., 1977, MSc, 1979, cert. environ. mgmt., 1979; MPhil, Columbia U., 1981, PhD, 1988. Chief marine engr. U.S. Army, Port of N.Y., 1944-45; svc. engr. Garlock Inc., Boston, 1946-47; ter. mgr. Garlock Inc., N.Y.C., 1947-61; pres., chief engr. Gaddis Engring. Co., Port Washington, N.Y., 1961—; seals edn. workshop com. Dept. Energy, Office Naval Rsch., Am. Soc. Lubrication Engrs., ASME, 1979-80; naval arch. and marine engring. com. People to People Delegation to China, 1986, Delegation to Bicentennial Maritime Symposium, Australia, 1988, ASME Delegation to S.Am., 1989; engr. cons. Gaddis, Inc., Hilton Head Island, S.C., 1994—. Author: Awareness of Environmental Hazards in Risk Management, 1979, Siting Criteria in Hazardous Waste Disposal, 1987, The Politics of Waste Disposal, 1989, Environmental Awareness, 1990. Recipient Disting. Alumni medal Adelphi U., 1984. Mem. ASME, Am. Soc. Naval Engrs. (Pres. Club), Am. Soc. Tribologists and Lubrication Engrs. (emissions com. 1980-84), Nat. Assn. of Environ. Profls., Environ. Law Inst., Pacific Basin Consortium for Hazardous Waste Rsch., East-West Inst., Soc. Naval Architects and Marine Engrs., Assn. Environ. Profls (Calif.), Marine Tech. Soc., N.Y. Acad. Scis., Soc. for Risk Analysis, John Henry Newman Hon. Soc., Columbia (N.Y.C.) Club, North Shore Yacht (Port Washington) Club, Adelphi U. Alumni Assn. (v.p. 1999—), Delta Tau Delta (MIT chpt. adviser 1946-47). Achievements include research in hydrogeological environmental considerations in toxic waste disposal facility siting, materials and systems in mechanical sealing and containment; co-development of cryogenic vapor barrier. Home: PO Box 411 Locust Valley NY 11560-0411 Office: Gaddis Engring Co PO Box 689 Port Washington NY 11050-0215

GADDIS ROSE, MARILYN, comparative literature educator, translator; b. Fayette, Mo., Apr. 4, 1930; d. Merrill Elmer and Florence Georgia (Lyon) G.; m. James Leo Rose, Dec. 23, 1956 (div. 1966); m. Stephen David Ross, Nov. 16, 1968; 1 son, David Gaddis. B.A., Central Meth. Coll., 1952; M.A., U. S.C., Columbia, 1954-55; Ph.D., U. Mo., 1958; L.H.D., Cen. Meth. Coll., 1987. Instr. Stephens Coll., Columbia, Mo., 1958-68; assoc. prof. Ind. U., Bloomington, 1968; prof. comparative lit. SUNY, Binghamton, 1968—, disting. svc. prof., 1991—; dir. translation program SUNY, 1973—. Translator: Axel, 1970, 86, Lui: A View of Him, 1986, Eve of the Future Eden, 1981, Adrienne Mesurat, 1991, Volupté, The Sensual Man, 1995, Translation Horizon, 1996, Translation as Literary Criticism, 1998; editor, contbr.: Translation Spectrum, 1981; editor Translations Perspectives; contbr. articles in field to profl. jours. Fulbright fellow U. Lyon, France, 1953-54; Humanities Research Centre sr. fellow Australian Nat. U., 1977. Mem. MLA (pres. N.E. sect. 1975-76, del. assembly 1974-78, 84-87), PEN N.Y., Am. Lit.

Translators (sec.-treas. 1981-83), Am. Translators Assn. (mng. editor Series 1986—, bd. dirs. 1986-88, Alexander Gode award 1988, Spl. Svc. award 1995). Home: 4 Johnson Ave Binghamton NY 13905-4312

GADDY, JAMES LEOMA, chemical engineer, educator; b. Jacksonville, Fla., Aug. 16, 1932; s. Leoma Ithama and Mary Elizabeth (Edwards) G.; m. Betty Maricella, Sept. 7, 1952; children: James, Teresa. BSChemE, La. Poly. U., 1955; MSChemE, U. Ark., 1968; PhDChemE, U. Tenn., 1972. Registered profl. engr., Ark. Process engr. Ethyl Corp., Baton Rouge, 1955-60; project mgr., engring. supr. Ark.-La. Gas, Shreveport, La., 1960-66; assoc. prof. chem engring. U. Mo., Rolla, 1972-79, prof., dir. rsch. ctr., 1979-80; prof., head chem. engring. U. Ark., Fayetteville, 1980-88, disting. prof., 1988-91, emeritus disting. prof., 1991—; pres. Bioengring. Resources, Fayetteville, 1984—; cons. to 15 orgns.; tchr. numerous short courses in chem. engring. for industry; adminstr. rsch. contracts various cos. Mem. editl. bd. Biomass and Biofuels, Chem. Engring. R & D; contbr. to numerous presentations and publs. Faculty fellow Swiss Fed. Inst. Tech. Zurich, 1978. Mem. AIChE(mem. spkrs. bur.), Am. Chem. Soc., Am. Soc. Engring. Edn., AAAS, Tau Beta Pi (Eminent Engr. 1976), Alpha Chi Sigma, Omega Chi Epsilon. Baptist. Home: 2207 Tall Oaks Dr Fayetteville AR 72703-6126 Office: Bioengring Resources 1650 Emmaus Rd Fayetteville AR 72701-7283

GADDY, NORMA SMITH, nursing administrator; b. Cleve., Apr. 11, 1950; d. Norman N. and Betty F. (Curtis) Smith; m. Larry J. Gaddy, Aug. 7, 1970; children: Jeffrey Allan, Tara Michelle. AS, Polk C.C., Winter Haven, Fla., 1974; BSN, Fla. So. Coll., 1985; MSN, U. Fla., 1992. RN, Fla.; cert. RN in inpatient obstetrics, neonatal resuscitation program. Staff nurse Tallahassee Meml. Hosp., 1977-80; staff nurse Lakeland (Fla.) Regional Med. Ctr., 1974-77, staff nurse, charge nurse, 1980-85, asst. dept. mgr., 1985-87, dept. mgr., 1987-91, dir. nursing, 1991—; cons. Healthy Start Coalition, Winter Haven, 1993-94; expert panel mem. Fetal Infant Mortality Review Bd., Winter Haven, 1994. Mem. Nat. Perinatal Assn., Fla. Assn. Neonatal Nurses, Fla. Orgn. Nurse Execs., Fla. Nurses Assn. (2d v.p. chpt. 12 1992-93), Assn. Women's Health, Obstetrics, Neonatal Nursing, Sigma Theta Tau (Alpha Theta chpt.). Office: Lakeland Regional Med Ctr PO Box 95448 Lakeland FL 33804-5448

GADDY, OSCAR LEE, electrical engineering educator; b. Republic, Mo., July 18, 1932; s. Oscar Franklin and Ruth Winnie (Cowart) G.; m. Mary Margaret Vaeth, Aug. 8, 1953; children: Oscar Franklin, John Anton, William Lee. BS, U. Kans., 1957, MS, 1959; PhD, U. Ill., 1962. Rsch. asst., instr. dept. elec. engring. U. Kans., Lawrence, 1957-59; rsch. asst. dept. elec. and computer engring. U. Ill., Urbana, 1959-62, asst. prof., 1962-65, assoc. prof., 1965-69, assoc. head, 1971-84, prof. dept. elec. and computer engring., 1969-93, prof. emeritus, 1993—. Contbr. articles to profl. jours. Fellow IEEE. Avocations: skeet and trap shooting, antique firearm restoration. Home: 609 E Evergreen Ct Urbana IL 61801-5930 Office: U Ill Dept Elec & Computer Enging 1406 W Green St Urbana IL 61801-2918

GADE, MARVIN FRANCIS, retired paper company executive; b. Clinton, Iowa, Nov. 10, 1924; s. Bernhardt Henry and Anna Mae (Jessen) G.; m. Lorraine F. McDonald, Dec. 2, 1944 (dec.); children: Michael David, Patricia Ann Gade Conn, Steven Dennis, Laura Jean Gade Walls, Mary Kay Gade Brock, Karen Lynn Gade Murphy, Jeffrey Scott; m. Carmell M. Clayton, July 16, 1995. BS in Engring., U. Iowa, 1952; postgrad. exec. program, UCLA, 1960-61. Process instrumentation engr. Standards Brands Co., Clinton, 1946-50; with Kimberly-Clark Corp. (hdqrs.), Neenah, Wis., 1952-88; sr. v.p., group exec. Kimberly-Clark Corp. (hdqrs.), 1974-77; exec. v.p. Kimberly-Clark Corp. (hdqrs.), Coosa Pines, Ala., 1977-88; also dir. Kimberly-Clark Corp.; pres. Kimberly Clark Health Care, Paper and Spltys. Cos., 1981-88, vice chmn. bd., 1983-88; dir. First Bank of Childersburg, Ala. Bd. dirs. Calif. Water Quality Control Bd., 1964-67, S.C. Tech. Edn. Bd., 1968-70; bd. dirs., sec. Children's Harbor, Alexander City, Ala.; chmn. bd. adv. com. St. Jude's Hosp., Fullerton, Calif., 1962-67; trustee Fulton County Ga. Hosp. Authority, Northside Hosp., Oglethorpe U., Atlanta, Wesley Woods Hosp., Atlanta, Woodruff Art Alliance; bd. visitors Emory U., Atlanta. Served as aviator USNR, 1943-46. Home: 514 Fairway Dr Alexander City AL 35010-6225 *In my lifetime of managing operations and administration I never met a "small" person - just small jobs.*

GADEN, ELMER LEWIS, JR., chemical engineering educator; b. Bklyn., Sept. 26, 1923; s. Elmer Lewis and Gertrude Estelle (McClellan) G.; m. Jennifer Marie Soley, Mar. 28, 1964; children: David Andrew, Paul Alexander; 1 dau. by previous marriage, Barbara Joan. BS, Columbia U., 1944, MS, 1947, PhD, 1949; DEngring (hon.), Rensselaer Poly., 1987. Rsch. engr. Pfizer Inc., 1948-49; mem. faculty Columbia, 1949-74, prof. chem. engring., 1958-74, chmn. dept., 1960-69, 71-74; dean Coll. Engring. Math. and Bus. Adminstrn., U. Vt., Burlington, 1975-79; Wills Johnson prof. chem. engring. U. Va., Charlottesville, 1979-94, prof. emeritus, 1994—, chmn. dept., 1985-88. Editor: Biotech. and Bioengring. jour., 1959-83. Served with USNR, 1943-46. Mem. NAE, AIChE, Am. Chem. Soc., Am. Soc. Engring. Edn. Home: 3400 Rodman Dr Charlottesvle VA 22901-9450 Office: U Va Dept Chemical Engineer Charlottesville VA 22903

GADOLA, PAUL V., federal judge; b. 1929. AB, Mich. State U., 1951; JD, U. Mich., 1953. Diplomate Nat. Bd. Trial Advocacy; Bar: Mich. Atty. Hoffman and Rubenstein, Flint, Mich., 1955-60; pvt. practice Flint, 1960-88; judge U.S. Dist. Ct. (ea. dist.) Mich., Detroit, 1988—; mem. bd. dirs. Mackinac Ctr. for Pub. Policy Rsch.; past trustee, chmn. bd. dirs. Mott Coll. With U.S. Army, 1953-55. Fellow Am. Trial Lawyers Found. (life), Roscoe Pound Found. (life), Mich. State Bar Found.; mem. Mich. State Bar Assn., U. Mich. Alumni Assn., Mich. State U. Alumni Assn., Soc. Irish/Am. Lawyers (pres.), Hannah Soc. and Pres.'s Club of Mich. State U., Federalist Soc., Flint Coll. and Cultural Fund Committed of Sponsors, Phila. Soc., Econ. Club of Detroit. Address: Federal Building 600 Church St Rm #140 Flint MI 48502-1214*

GADOMSKI, ROBERT EUGENE, chemical and industrial gas company executive; b. Chgo., Mar. 24, 1947; s. Chester and Adeline (Carpinelli) G.; m. Susan Freed, Aug. 12, 1972; children: Stephen, Andrew, Elizabeth. BS, Purdue U., 1969, MS in Indsl. Adminstrn., 1970; grad. advanced mgmt. program, Harvard U., fall 1990. Amines bus. mgr. indsl. chems. div. Air Products and Chems., Inc., Allentown, Pa., 1974-77, gen. sales mgr. indsl. chems. div., 1977-78, asst. gen. mgr. indsl. chems. div., 1978-81, mgr. chems. group mfg. div., 1981-83, gen. mgr. chems. group mfg. div., 1983-84, v.p., gen. mgr. chems. group mfg. div., 1984-86, v.p., gen. mgr. indsl. chems. div., 1986-88, v.p., gen. mgr. process systems group, 1988-90, mgmt. com., 1988—, group v.p. process systems group, 1990-92, group v.p. chems. group, 1992-96, exec. v.p., mem. corp. exec. com., 1996-98, exec. v.p. chems., Asia and Latin Am.; bd. dirs. Process Systems, Inc., Memphis. Bd. dirs. South Whitehall Planning Commn., Allentown, 1984-89, Lehigh Valley United Way, Allentown, 1991-94; chmn. March of Dimes Walkathon, Allentown, 1985; bd. dirs. Kemerer Mus. Decorative Arts, 1991-94, St. Luke's Hosp., Bethlehem, Pa., 1994-99; bd. dirs. Hist. Bethlehem Partnership, 1993—; v.p. Minsi Trails Coun. Boy Scouts Am. Named Disting. Alumnus, Krannert Sch. Mgmt., Purdue U., 1988, Sch. Engring., 1992. Mem. AIChE; mem. Nat. Petroleum Refiners Assn. (bd. dirs. 1986-93). Roman Catholic. Avocations: golf, fine dining. Office: Air Products & Chems Inc 7201 Hamilton Blvd Allentown PA 18195-1526

GADSBY, ROBIN EDWARD, chemical company executive; b. St. Leonards on Sea, Eng., Mar. 22, 1939; came to U.S., 1977, naturalized, 1988; s. John Ernest and Emily Louisa (Burt) G.; m. Olwyn Diane Bowen, Aug. 5, 1961 (div. 1981); children: Tricia Clare, Tracey Carolyn; m. Margaret Alice Fuessel, Dec. 29, 1983. MA in Natural Scis., Cambridge U., Eng., 1960, MEng, 1961; MBA, U. Chgo., 1982. CFA. Chem. engr. ICI Billingham (Eng.) div., 1961-62, corp. planner, 1962-65; plant mgr. ICI PLC Agrl. div., Heysham, Eng., 1965-67; chem. engring. mgr. ICI PLC Agrl. div., Billingham, 1967-70, process tech. mgr., 1970-76, research group mgr., 1976-77; pres. Katalco Corp., Oak Brook, Ill., 1978-83; gen. mgr. Rubicon Chems. Inc., Wilmington, Del., 1984-86; pres. polyurethanes group div. ICI Ams., Inc., Wilmington, 1986-90, pres. chems. and polymers group, 1990-97, also bd. dirs.; ptnr. Venture Catalysts, Inc., Spring House, Pa.; bd. dirs., cons. Callard, Madden & Assocs., Inc., Chgo.; mem. Callard-Ogden Investment Mgmt., L.L.P. Dir. alumni bd. U. Chgo. Grad. Sch. Bus., 1985—. Mem. AIChE, Assn. for Investment Mgmt. and Rsch., Inst. Chem. Engrs. (U.K. editl. bd. 1976-77), Internat. Isocynates Inst. (pres. 1990-91), Fin. Analysts Soc. Phila., Concord Country Club (Pa.), Classics Country Club (Fla.), Beta Gamma Sigma. Fax: 610 399-9551. Home and Office: 455 Fox Meadow Ln West Chester PA 19382-8464

GADSDEN, CHRISTOPHER HENRY, lawyer; b. Bryn Mawr, Pa., Aug. 7, 1946; s. Henry White and Patricia (Parker) G.; m. Eleanore R.B. Hoeffel, July 27, 1968; children: William C., Eleanore P., Patricia C. BS, Yale U., 1968, JD, 1973. Bar: Pa. 1973, U.S. Dist. Ct. (ea. dist.) Pa. 1973. Assoc. Drinker Biddle & Reath, Phila., 1973-80, ptnr., 1980-98; mng. ptnr. Drinker Biddle & Reath, 1998—; lectr. law U. Pa. Law Sch., Phila., 1986-89, 93. Author: Pennsylvania Estate Planning, 1996; contbg. author: Local Public Finance and the Fiscal Squeeze, 1977; co-editor: Administration of Estates, 1983. Mem. vestry St. Thomas Ch., Whitemarsh, Ft. Washington, Pa., 1980-82; trustee Abington (Pa.) Meml. Hosp., 1980—, chair bd. trustees, 1994-98; pres. bd. trustees Germantown Acad., Ft. Washington, 1987-90. With U.S. Army, 1968-70. Fellow Am. Coll. Trust and Estate Counsel; mem. Phila. Bar Assn. (probate and trust law sect., chair 1994), Phila. Cricket Club. Democrat. Avocations: squash, tennis, gardening. Home: 140 W Chestnut Hill Ave Philadelphia PA 19118-3702 Office: Drinker Biddle & Reath 1000 Westlakes Dr Ste 300 Berwyn PA 19312-2409

GAEDE, JAMES ERNEST, physician, medical educator; b. Calgary, Alta., Can., July 2, 1953; s. John Ernest and Florence Eleanor (Hilmer) G.; married, Dec. 23, 1994; children: Graham, Jason, Nikki, Mary Frances, Sydney. BA, Augustana Coll., 1975, MA, 1976; MD, U. S.D., 1980. Diplomate Am. Bd. Family Practice. Staff physician Queen of Peace, Mitchell, S.D., 1983—; chief of staff Queen of Peace, Mitchell, 1988, med. dir., 1988-89; med. dir. St. Joe's Med. Assn., Howard, S.D., 1988—, Women's Health Clinic, Mitchell, S.D., 1983—; assoc. prof. U. of S.D. Sch. Medicine; presenter U.S. Senate, Washington, 1991. Contbr. articles to profl. jours. Bd. dirs. Dakota Weslayan U., Mitchell, 1986-89, Dakota Mental Health, Mitchell, 1988-90; mem. Commn. 2000 S.D., Sioux Falls, 1988—; pub. health officer City of Mitchell, 1983—. Fellow Am. Acad. Family Practice (Active Tchrs. award 1984—); mem. AMA, S.D. Assn. Family Practice, S.D. State Med. Assn. (del. 1983—), Mitchell C. of C., Mayo Alumni Assn., Doctors Mayo Soc. Avocations: sailing, music, auto restoration. Home: 210 N Harmon Dr Mitchell SD 57301-6245 Office: Sixth Ave Family Practice 1200 E 6th Ave Mitchell SD 57301-2922*

GAEDE, JANE TAYLOR, pathologist, educator; b. Washington, July 8, 1941; d. Raleigh Colston and Margaret (Lamb) Taylor; m. William Hanks Gaede, Feb. 12, 1966; children: Geoffrey Terence, Bruce Lucas. BA, U. Miss., 1962; MD, Duke U., 1966. Diplomate Am. Bd. Pathology. Intern in surgery N.C. Bapt. Hosp., Winston-Salem, N.C., 1966-67; resident in pathology Duke Med. Ctr., Durham, N.C., 1967-71, asst. prof. pathology, 1974—; asst. prof. pathology Med. U. S.C., Charleston, 1971-74; staff pathologist VA Med Ctr., Durham, 1974—. Author: Clinical Pathology for the House Officer, 1982. Fellow Am. Soc. Clin. Pathologists; mem. DAR (1st vice regent local chpt. 1992-94, regent 1996-98), N.C. Soc. Pathologists. Presbyterian. Avocations: aerobic exercise, weight training, gardening. Office: Duke Univ Med Ctr Dept Pathology PO Box 3712 Durham NC 27710

GAEDE, RUTH ANN, nursing manager; b. Waverly, Iowa, July 20, 1952; d. Ruben and Lucynda (Niemeyer) Engert; m. Steven A. Gaede, Aug. 19, 1973; children: Erica, Stephanie. Diploma in practical nursing, Hawkeye Inst. Tech., 1971; diploma, Allen Sch. Nursing, 1977; BSN cum laude, U. Dubuque, 1986; MSN, Drake U., 1993. RN, Iowa. Diabetic nurse cons. Internat. Diabetes Ctr. N. Iowa Affil. Allen Meml. Hosp., Waterloo, 1990-92; nursing mgr. emergency svcs. Sartori Meml. Hosp., Iowa, 1992-94; occupational health and safety nurse Viking Pumps, Inc., 1994—; presenter in field. Nat. Hwy Traffic Safety Assn. grantee, 1987. Mem. Iowa Nurses Assn. (2nd v.p., mem. state practice com., grantee 1987), Emergency Nurses Assn. (mem. state trauma nursing com., grantee 1987), Sigma Theta Tau.

GAENGLER, PETER WOLFGANG, dentist, researcher; b. Meissen, Saxony, Germany, Oct. 30, 1941; s. Wolfgang Ernst-Otto and Dorothea Friedericke (Moebius) G.; m. Sabine Gertrud Ahlborn, Nov. 6, 1970; children: Felix Peter, Beate Petra. Stomatology Diploma, Faculty of Dental Medicine, Leningrad, Russia, 1965; DrMedDent, Sch. Dental Medicine, Dresden, Germany, 1967, PhD, 1974. Diplomate in dentistry. Dentistry Community Hosp., Wittenberge, Germany, 1965-66; asst. prof. Sch. Dental Medicine, Dresden, 1966-75; prof., chmn. Sch. Dental Medicine, Erfurt, Germany, 1975-92; dean Faculty of Dental Medicine, Witten, Germany, 1992Ö; mem. FDI/WHO Joint Working Group 1/10, Geneva, 1979; mem. IADR Com. on Membership and Recruitment, Washington, 1989-93. Author: Lehrbuch der Konservierenden Zahnheilkunde, 3d edit., 1995; editor Medizin aktuell, 1975-90. Recipient Humboldt medal Ministry Higher Edn., Berlin, 1978; grantee in field. Mem. Assn. Conservative Dentistry (pres. 1978-87), Assn. Stomatology (v.p. 1988-90, Philip-Pfaff medal 1988), Polish Assn. Dentistry (hon.), Hungarian Assn. Dentistry (hon.; Semmelweis medal 1993), Assn. Dental Edn. Europe (exec. com. 1997—, bd. dirs. 1997—). Avocations: literature, sailing, skiing. Home: Waldweg 9, D-58313 Herdecke Germany Office: U Witten/Herdecke, Faculty Dental Medicine, D-58448 Witten Germany

GAERTNER, DONELL JOHN, retired library director; b. St. Louis, Sept. 30, 1932; s. Elmer Henry and Norine Helen (Colomb) G.; m. Darlene Oberbeck, Mar. 17, 1956; children: Karen Elaine, Keith Alan. A.B. in Econs., Washington U., 1954; M.L.S., U. Ill., 1955. Adminstrv. asst. St. Louis County Library, 1957-64, asst. dir., 1964-68, dir., 1968-97; ret., 1997. Bd. dirs. Emmaus Homes Inc. (for adult mentally retarded). Served to 1st lt. U.S. Army, 1955-57. Mem. ALA, Mo. Library Assn., Spl. Library Assn., Phi Beta Mu, Omicron Delta Gamma. Mem. United Church of Christ. Lodges: Masons, Order Eastern Star.

GAERTNER, GARY M., judge; b. St. Louis; m. Maureen; children—Gary M., Lisa, Mark. Student in polit. sci. St. Louis U., JD, Sch. Law; grad. Nat. Jud. Coll., U. Nev., Mo. Trial Judges Coll., Am. Acad. Jud. Edn., U. N.H., Sch. Law U. Va., Stanford U. Law Sch., Harvard U. Sch. Law; attended Oxford (Eng.) U. Bar: Mo., Ill., U.S. dist. ct., U.S. Ct. Appeals, U.S. Supreme Ct. After pvt. practice law, served as asst. city counselor City of St. Louis, until 1964, assoc. city counsel, 1964-67, city counselor, 1967-69; former judge 22d Jud. Cir. Mo., 1969-85, including presiding judge criminal divs., juvenile judge, asst. presiding judge and presiding judge and chief adminstrv. officer 22d Jud. Cir. Mo.; chief judge Ct. Appeals (ea. dist.) Mo., 1985; past pres. Mo. Council Juvenile Ct. Judges; former chmn., former chmn. juvenile subcom. Mo. Council Criminal Justice, region 5; former mem. St. Louis Commn. on Crime and Law Enforcement. Bd. dirs. Boys Town Mo.; v.p. Khoury Internat. Leagues, Policeman and Fireman's Fund of St. Louis, Shared Resource Enterprises Inc.; former dist. chmn., now dist. vice-chmn. Tomahawk dist. Boy Scouts Am.; past mem. exec. bd. St. Louis Area council Boy Scouts Am. Served with USCG. Recipient awards, including Judiciary award St. Louis Grand Jury Assn., Man of Yr. award George Khoury Internat. Assn., Spl. Act. award U.S. Assn. Fed. Investigators; named an Outstanding Young St. Louisian, St. Louis Jaycees; recipient diploma Jud. Skills Am. Acad. Jud. Edn. Mem. ABA, Mo. Bar Assn., Mo. Assn. Trial Attys., Bar Assn. Met. St. Louis, Lawyers Assn. Met. St. Louis, Am. Judicature Soc., Phi Delta Phi. Office: 111 N 7th St Saint Louis MO 63101-2100

GAETTI, GARY, baseball player; b. Centralia, Ill., Aug. 19, 1958; m. Debby Duncan; children: Joseph, Jacob. Student, N.W. Mo. State U. Baseball player Minn. Twins, 1981-91, Kansas City Royals, 91-94, St Louis Cardinals, 95-98; baseball player 3B Chicago Cubs, 98-; mem. World Series Champions, 1987, Am. League All-Star Team, 1988. Office: Chicago Cubs 1060 W Addison St Chicago IL 60613-4397

GAFF, ALAN DALE, writer; b. Ft. Wayne, Ind., Sept. 25, 1948; s. Kenneth E. and Mona (Traxler) G.; m. Maureen Ann Oxley, Dec. 27, 1969; children: Donald Hugh, Jeffrey John. BA in History, Ind. U., 1979; MA in Am. History, Ball State U., 1980. Pres. Richmond City Greys, Ft. Wayne, 1984—, Hist. Investigations, Ft. Wayne, 1996—. Author: Brave Men's Tears, 1988, If This Is War, 1991, Our Boys, 1996, On Many A Bloody Field, 1997. Vol. Allen County Pub. Libr., Ft. Wayne, 1981—. Sgt. U.S. Army, 1969-71. Mem. DAV (life), Ind. Hist. Soc., Sons of Union Vets., State Hist. Soc. Wis., Ind. U. Alumni Assn. Avocation: golf. Home: 2812 Overlook Dr Fort Wayne IN 46808-1848 Office: US Postal Svc Centennial Sta 2525 Independence Dr Fort Wayne IN 46808-4418

GAFF, BRIAN MICHAEL, attorney, electrical engineer; b. Boston, Mar. 14, 1962; s. Gilbert Gerard and Josephine Claire (Franklin) G. BSEE magna cum laude, U. Mich., 1983, MSEE, 1984; JD magna cum laude, Suffolk U., 1999. Bar: Mass., U.S. Patent Office; registered profl. engr., Mass., Calif., N.H. Engr. GTE Communications Products Corp., Westborough, Mass., 1984; mem. tech. staff Draper Lab., Cambridge, Mass., 1984-88; engring. specialist GPT Stromberg-Carlson, Lake Mary, Fla., 1989-90; safety mgr. imaging sys. divsn. Hewlett-Packard Med. Products Group, Andover, Mass., 1990—; pvt. practice, 1999—; founder, prin. Solid-State Cons., Swampscott, Mass., 1983—, SSC Constrn., Swampscott, 1991—. Mem. IEEE (sr.), NSPE, ABA, Am. Phys. Soc., Am. Mgmt. Assn. Semiconductor Equipment and Materials Internat., Am. Vacuum Soc., Am. Intellectual Property Law Assn., Am. Inst. Steel Constrn., Mensa, Mass. Soc. Profl. Engrs., Mass. Bar Assn., Boston Patent Law Assn., Boston Bar Assn. Republican. Roman Catholic. Avocation: photography. Home: PO Box 166 Swampscott MA 01907-0266 Office: Hewlett-Packard Med Products Group 3000 Minuteman Rd Andover MA 01810-1099

GAFF, JERRY GENE, academic administrator; b. DeKalb County, Ind., Feb. 5, 1936; s. Kenneth E. and Mona F. (Traxler) G.; m. Julia Friedman; children: David B., Amy E. Ringo, Kathryn Friedman. AB, DePauw U., 1958; PhD, Syracuse U., 1965. Asst. research prof. U. Calif., Berkeley, 1967-72; project dir., vis. prof. Calif. State U.'s and Colls., 1972-75; project dir. Soc. Values in Higher Edn., Washington, 1975-81; dir. curriculum devel. Assn. Am. Colls., Washington, 1981-83; dean coll. liberal arts Hamline U., St. Paul, 1983-87, acting pres., 1987-88, v.p. for planning, 1988-89; sr. fellow U. Minn., 1989-91; v.p. Assn. Am. Colls. and Univs., 1991—; cons. to colls., univs. and founds., 1970—. Author: The Cluster College, 1970, Toward Faculty Renewal, 1975, Professional Development, 1978, General Education Today, 1983, New Life for the College Curriculum, 1991, Handbook of the Undergraduate Curriculum, 1996, Building the Faculty We Need, 1999. Recipient Acad. Leadership award Coun. of Ind. Colls., 1989, Joseph Katz award Assn. Gen. and Liberal Studies, 1992; Exxon Edn. Found. grantee, 1972-74, 78-81, 88-89, U.S. Govt. grantee, 1975-81, Lilly Endowment grantee, 1989-92, Pew Charitable Trusts grantee, 1993—, Natl. Sci. FOund. grantee, 1998. Mem. Am. Assn. for Higher Edn. (trustee 1985-88), Soc. for Values in Higher Edn., Assn. Gen. & Liberal Studies. Avocations: theatre, social analysis, athletics, gardening, fishing. Home: 4301 39th St NW Washington DC 20016-2247 Office: Assn Am Colls and Univs 1818 R St NW Washington DC 20009-1604

GAFFEY, THOMAS MICHAEL, JR., retired consumer products executive; b. Elmira, N.Y., Mar. 1, 1934; s. Thomas Michael and Alice (Faul) G.; m. Constance R. Watkins, May 23, 1964. B.S. in Acctg., Syracuse (N.Y.) U., 1956. CPA, N.Y. Auditor, cons. Lybrand Ross Bros. & Montgomery (C.P.A.s), N.Y.C., 1956, 58-64; with Liggett Group Inc., 1964-83, asst. contr., then contr., 1969-76; treas. Liggett Group Inc., Durham, N.C. and Montvale, N.J., 1976-80; v.p., treas. Liggett Group Inc., 1980-82, sr. vp., CFO, dir., 1982-83; with GrandMet USA, Inc. (formerly Liggett Group Inc.), 1983-88, sr. v.p., CFO, dir., 1983-86, exec. v.p., 1987-88, ret., 1988; dir. Durham City bd. N.C. Nat. Bank, 1972-76; mem. adv. bd. Arkwright-Boston Ins. Co. Mem. N.Y. County Republican Com., 1965-67. Served with U.S. Army, 1956-58. Mem. AICPA, Fin. Execs. Inst. (pres. N.C. chpt. 1977-78, chmn. admissions com. 1983-85), N.Y. State Soc. CPAs. Roman Catholic. Clubs: Ridgewood (N.J.) Country; Union League (N.Y.C.); Pine Tree Golf (Boynton Beach, Fla.), The Delray Beach Club. Home: 2150 S Ocean Blvd Apt 7I Delray Beach FL 33483-6450*

GAFFIN, JOAN VALERIE, secondary school educator; b. N.Y.C., Nov. 25, 1947; d. William John and Louise Eleanor (Liebig) Philibert; m. Ira Martin Gaffin, May 7, 1981. BS in Bus. Edn., Rider U., 1971; MA in Student Personnel Svcs., Montclair State U., 1978. Cert. coop. bus. edn. coord., bus. edn. adminstr. and coord. Bus. edn. instr., coord. Econ. Manpower Corp., N.Y.C., 1971-72; bus. edn. coord., educator Northern Valley Regional H.S., Old Tappan, N.J., 1972—; gymnastics instr. Twp. of Teaneck, N.J., 1985—; adj. grad. prof. Montclair State U., Upper Montclair, N.J., 1994—. Recipient N.J. Gov.'s Outstanding Tchr. of Yr. award, 1986. Mem. NEA, Nat. Bus. Edn. Assn., N.J. Bus. Edn. Assn. (legis. com. mem. 1990-92, bd. dirs. 1991—, chmn. critical issues task force 1991-95, N.J. bus. tchr. of yr. 1993), N.J. Edn. Assn., Eastern Bus. Edn. Assn. (educator of yr. 1993), N.J. Cooperative Bus. Edn. Coord.'s Assn. (Bergen sector sec. and pres., coord. of yr. 1993), Northeast Bergen Ind. Assn. (treas., bd. dirs. 1978—), Northern Valley Edn. Assn. (sec. 1978-80, 85-86, 91-92, tchr. recognition award 1990-91). Avocations: traveling, reading, cooking, exercising, antiquing. Home: 852 W Crescent Ave Allendale NJ 07401-2129 Office: Northern Valley Regional HS Central Ave Old Tappan NJ 07675

GAFFNEY, DONALD LEE, lawyer; b. Phoenix, July 7, 1952; s. Leroy H. and Myriam (Brazeal) G.; m. Debby Dunn, May 31, 1974; children: Brian, Colin, Caitlin. BA, Austin Coll., 1974; JD, U. Tex., 1977. Bar: Ariz. 1979, U.S. Ct. Appeals (9th cir.) 1979, U.S. Ct. Appeals (10th cir.) 1984, U.S. Supreme Ct. 1984. Ptnr. Streich & Lang, Phoenix, 1977-89, Snell & Wilmer, Phoenix, 1988—; adj. prof. Ariz. State U. Law Sch., Tempe, 1983-84. Co-author: Bankruptcy, 1987; note comment and book review editor: Tex. Law Review 1976-77; contbr. to profl. jours. Mem. Gov.'s Task Force Ctrl. Ariz. Project, 1993. Austin scholar. Mem. ABA, Am. Arbitration Assn. (com. panel), Comml. Law League of Am. (bankruptcy com. 1980-84), State Bar Ariz. (chmn. bankruptcy sect., 1982-84, com. on bankruptcy rules 1979-81, uniform comml. code com. 1980—) , Phi Delta Phi. Democrat. Presbyterian. Office: Snell and Wilmer 1 Arizona Ctr Phoenix AZ 85004-0001*

GAFFNEY, EDWARD MCGLYNN, law educator, university administrator; b. San Francisco, Aug. 18, 1941; s. Edward McGlynn and Mary Catherine (Wright) G.; m. Jane Ann Mullen, Feb. 1972 (div. Feb. 1982); children: Margaret Mairead, Elizabeth Atkins; m. A'ine O'Healy, May 29, 1982; children: Deirdre, Miriam. BA, St. Patrick's Coll., 1963; STL, Gregorian U., Rome, 1967; JD, MA in History, Cath. U., 1975; LLM, Harvard U., 1976. Bar: Calif. 1990, U.S. Ct. Appeals (D.C. cir.) 1975, U.S. Ct. Appeals (7th cir.) 1980, U.S. Ct. Appeals (5th and 11th cirs.) 1981, U.S. Ct. Appeals (9th cir.) 1983, U.S. Ct. Appeals (2d cir.) 1985, U.S. Dist. Ct. (ctrl. dist.) Calif. 1990, U.S. Dist. Ct. (so. dist.) Ind. 1992, U.S. Supreme Ct. 1980. Assoc. dir. Nat. Conf. Cath. Bishops Ecumenical and Interreligious Com., Washington, 1970-72; atty. advisor Office of Atty Gen. U.S. Dept. of Justice, Washington, 1976-77; assoc. dir. Ctr. for Constitutional Studies, Notre Dame, Ind., 1977-81; dir. Ctr. for Constitutional Studies, Notre Dame, 1981-83; Bradley prof. constitutional law Loyola Law Sch., L.A., 1983-85, assoc. prof., 1985-89; scholar in residence Stanford Law Sch., Palo Alto, Calif., 1989-90; dean and prof. law Valparaiso (Ind.) U. Sch. of Law, 1990-97; scholar-in-residence Pepperdine U. Sch. of Law, Malibu, Calif., 1997-98; prof. law Valparaiso U. Sch. of Law, Ill., 1998—; mem. bd. editors Jour. Law and Religion, St. Paul, 1980—; edtl. cons. Williamsburg Ctr. Found., Washington, 1987-89; bd. dirs. Ctr. for Constitutional Studies, Waco, Tex., 1990—, Christian Legal Soc., Annandale, Va., 1992-98, Ind. Bar Found., Ind. Continuing Legal Forum. Author: Government and Campus, 1980, State and Campus, 1982, Ascending Liability in Religious and Non-Profit Organizations, 1983, Church and Campus, 1989; editor: Public Schools and the Private Good, 1981. Recipient Champion of Justice award Am. Forum for Jewish-Christian Cooperation, Washington, 1981. Fellow Ctr. for Ch.-State Studies, Internat. Acad. for Freedom of Religion and Belief; mem. ABA, Am. Law Inst., Assn. Am. Law Schs. (chmn. sect. on law and religion, sect. on law and edn. 1981-83). Democrat. Roman Catholic. Office: Valparaiso U Sch of Law Wesemann Hall Valparaiso IN 46383

GAFFNEY, KATHLEEN MARY, writer, videographer; b. Queens, N.Y., Aug. 22, 1959; d. Joseph Frances and Margaret Ann (Denza) G. B in Comm. magna cum laude, Adelphi U., 1981. Videographer Town of Hempstead (N.Y.) Cablevision Long Island, 1983-94; lectr., guest spkr. Adult Learning Inst., Columbia-Greene Coll., Hudson, N.Y., 1995; televised guest lectr. Columbia-Greene Coll. at Mid-Hudson Cablevision, Catskill, N.Y., 1995; videographer and editor monthly program Cablevision of L.I.; instr., lectr. broadcast/prodn. videography classes on L.I. Prodn. asst. (pub. svc. announcement) U.S. Pres. Coun. on Phys. Fitness, 1982; videographer, editor (pub. svc. announcement) Hempstead L.I. Animal Shelter, 1985; contbr. articles to profl. jours. and newspapers. Active Town of Cairo (N.Y.) Task Force, 1993—. Mem. Wallace Nutting Collector's Club. Democrat. Roman Catholic. Avocations: writing children's books, screen and tele-play writing, cartoon illustrating, antique collecting. Home: HCI Box 85C-1B Acra NY 12405

GAFFNEY, PAUL COTTER, retired physician; b. DuBois, Pa., May 12, 1917; s. John Charles and Anna Catherine (Cotter) G.; m. Lois G. Brown, Oct. 14, 1944; children: Louise A., Paul Cotter, William J., Maureen E., Mary Ellen, Frances J., Michael B. B.S. magna cum laude, U. Pitts., 1940, M.D., 1942. Intern St. Francis Hosp., Pitts., 1942-43; resident in pathology St. Francis Hosp., 1946-48; resident in pediatrics Children's Hosp., Pitts., 1948-50; mem. staff Children's Hosp., 1951-95, med. dir., 1978-81, trustee, 1981—; ret., 1995; fellow hematology Children's Hosp., Detroit, 1950-51; practice medicine specializing in pediatrics and hematology, Pitts., 1951-63; mem. med. faculty U. Pitts., 1961-93, prof. emeritus pediatrics, 1993—; assoc. dean, dir. admissions U. Pitts. Sch. Medicine, 1977-78; exec. dir. Med. Alumni Assn. Sch. Medicine U. Pitts Sch. Medicine, 1980-90; mem. staff Magee-Women's Hosp., Pitts., 1951-80; mem. med. adv. com. Comprehensive Health Planning Assn. Allegheny County, 1968-76; bd. dirs. Cen. Blood Bank Pitts., 1969-76; med. dir. Childrens Hosp. Pitts., 1978-81; chmn. bd. trustees Cancer Support Network Pitts., 1992-96. Served to maj., M.C. U.S. Army, 1943-46. Decorated Bronze Star with oak leaf cluster; named Man of Yr. in Medicine, Pitts. Acad. Medicine, 1978; recipient Phillip S. Hench Disting. Alumnus award U. Pitts. Sch. Medicine, 1980; Children's Hosp. of Pitts. established the Paul C. Gaffney Chair in Pediatric Hematology-Oncology, 1993. Fellow Am. Acad. Pediatrics; mem. AMA, Pa. Med. Soc., Allegheny Med. Soc. (dir. 1973-76, 81-84), Am. Pediatric Soc. (Golden Apple teaching award 1967, 71, 75), Pediatric Travel Club, Phi Beta Pi. Republican. Roman Catholic. Research on treatment of childhood leukemia. Home: 5540 Elgin St Pittsburgh PA 15206-1433

GAFFNEY, PAUL GOLDEN, II, military officer; b. Attleboro, Mass., May 30, 1946; s. Paul G. and Elfrieda L. (Piepenstock) G.; m. Linda L. Myers; 1 child, Crista L. BS, U.S. Naval Acad., 1968; MS in Engring., Cath. U. Am., 1969; grad. with highest distinction, Naval War Coll., Newport, R.I., 1979; MBA, Jacksonville U., 1986. Commd. ensign USN, 1968, advanced through grades to rear adm., 1994; ops. officer USS Whipporwill USN, Sasebo, Japan, 1969-71; advisor Vietnamese Combat Hydrog. Survey Team USN, Vietnam, 1971-72; ocean svcs. officer Fleet Weather Cen. USN, Rota, Spain, 1972-75; exec. asst. Office of Oceanographer USN, Alexandria, Va., 1975-78; rsch. fellow Naval War Coll Ctr. Advanced Rsch. USN, Newport, R.I., 1978-79; comdg. officer Oceanographic Unit 4 USN, Indonesia, 1979-80; dir. Arctic and Earth Scis. Rsch. Office Naval Rsch. USN, Arlington, VA, 1980-81; mil. asst. internat. security affairs to Asst. Sec. Def. Washington, 1981-83; comdg. office Oceanography Command Facility USN, Jacksonville, Fla., 1983-86; dir. resources Office of Oceanographer USN, Washington, 1986-89; asst. chief, Office Chief of Naval Rsch. USN, Arlington, Va., 1989-91; comdg. officer Naval Rsch. Lab. USN, Washington, 1991-94; commdr. Naval Meteorology and Oceanography Command USN, Stennis Space Ctr., Miss., 1994-97; chief of naval rsch. USN, Arlington, Va., 1996—, dir. naval test and evaluation and tech. requirements, 1998—; grad. rsch. asst. Cath. U. Am., Washington, 1968—. Author: Soviet Navy, 1979 (Middendorf prize 1979); mem. policy com. Jour. Def. Rsch., 1989-91. Decorated Def. Superior Svc. medal, Legion of Merit with three gold stars, Bronze Star with V. Fellow Am. Meteorol. Soc., Explorer's Club; mem. Naval Acad. Alumni Assn., Sigma Xi. Republican. Roman Catholic. Avocations: running, track and field and cross country announcing and officiating. Office: Chief of Naval Rsch 800 N Quincy St Ste 907 Arlington VA 22203-1906

GAFFNEY, SUSAN, federal official. BA, Wilson Coll., 1965; MA in Advanced Internat. Studies, John Hopkins. Staff analyst to dep. commr. Dept. Housing Preservation and Devel., City of N.Y., 1970-79; dir. policy, plans and programs Office of Inspector Gen., Agy. for Internat. Devel., 1979-82; asst. inspector gen. Gen. Svcs. Adminstrn., 1982-87, dep. inspector gen., 1987-91; chief mgmt. integrity br. Office of Mgmt. and Budget, 1991-93; inspector gen. Dept. Housing and Urban Devel., 1993—. Recipient Presdl. Meritorious Rank award, Disting. Honor award, Disting. Leadership award Joint Fin. Mgmt. Improvement Program. Office: HUD Office of the Inspector General 451 7th St SW Rm 8256 Washington DC 20410-0001

GAFFNEY, THERESA ADCOCK, nursing administrator; b. June 4, 1959. BSN, Med. Coll. Va., 1981; MPA, Va. Tech, 1997. RN, D.C. Asst. dir. gov. rels. Paralyzed Vets. Am., Washington, 1989-91; field rep. ANA, Washington, 1991-95, dir. state govt. rels., 1995-98; dir. Am. Acad. Nursing, Washington, 1998—. E-mail: TAGAFFNEY@EROLS.COM. Home: 5521 Kempton Dr Springfield VA 22151

GAFFNEY, THOMAS, banker; b. San Francisco, Sept. 22, 1915; s. John and Hannah (Doherty) G.; m. Claire Bastian, Dec. 15, 1945; children: Bruce Edward, Bryan Keith. Cert., Am. Inst. Banking, 1940. Bank insp. Bank of Am., 1935-50; asst. cashier First Nat. Trust and Savs. Assn., Santa Barbara, Calif., 1950-51; asst. cashier, asst sec. Oakland Central Bank, Calif., 1951-53; chief insp. Transamerica Corp., San Francisco, 1953-55; v.p., auditor First Western Bank, San Francisco, 1955-61; v.p. New First Western Bank, Los Angeles, 1961-74; v.p. and auditor Lloyds Bank Calif., Los Angeles, 1974-80; pres. Golden Gate chpt. Bank Adminstrn Inst., San Francisco, 1961, nat. bd. dirs., 1965-67, gen. chmn. conv., L.A., 1967, speaker bank convs., nationwide; chmn. crime deterrant com. Calif. Bankers Assn., 1977-79; banking cons., 1980—. Mem. Ad Hoc Com. City of L.A. to study and recommend controls on all city depts., 1977—. Lodge: Elks (bd. dir. Locker Room 67 club San Francisco 1960).

GAFFNEY, THOMAS EDWARD, retired physician; b. East St. Louis, Ill., Nov. 5, 1930; s. John V. and Leola (Heisner) G.; m. Edith Ann Heitholt, June 12, 1954; children—John, David, Michael. A.B., U. Mo., 1951, M.S., 1953; M.D., U. Cin., 1957. Intern Harvard Med. Service of Boston City Hosp., 1957-58; resident medicine Mass. Gen. Hosp., 1958-59; instr. pharmacology, asst. medicine U. Cin., 1959-60; clin. assoc. Nat. Heart Inst., 1960-62; assoc. prof. pharmacology U. Cin., 1962-67, asst. prof. medicine, 1962, dir. div. clin. pharmacology, 1962-72, prof. pharmacology, 1967-72, prof. medicine, 1969-72; prof., chmn. dept. pharmacology, prof. medicine Med. U. S.C., 1972-90, disting. prof., 1986-90; vis. scientist Merck Sharp & Dohme Rsch. Labs., Rahway, N.J., 1989-93; ret., 1993; vol. clinician Buncombe County Health Dept., 1998—; mem. cardiovascular panel NAS Drug Efficacy Study, 1967-70; mem. pharmacology and exptl. therapeutics study sect. Nat. Heart Inst., 1967-69; mem. med. adv. bd. Coun. High Blood Pressure Rsch., 1969—; mem. Coun. on Basic Scis. of Am. Heart Assn., 1969—, mem. cardiovascular A study sect., 1972; mem. program rev. com. pharmacology and toxicology Nat. Inst. Gen. Med. Scis., 1971-75, chmn. 1973-75; mem. tech. adv. bd. S.C. Rsch. Authority, 1986-89. Mem. editorial bd. Jour. Pharmacology and Exptl. Therapeutics, 1965-77, Ann. Rev. Pharmacology and Toxicology, 1986-91. Served with USPHS, 1960-62. Recipient research career devel. award Nat. Heart Inst., 1962, 67, 72; Myrtle Wreath award for research Hadassah, 1980; NIH sr. rsch. fellow, 1989. Mem. Am. Fedn. Clin. Rsch., Am. Soc. Pharmacology and Exptl. Therapeutics, Ctrl. Soc. Clin. Rsch., Am. Soc. Clin. Investigation, Alpha Omega Alpha. Home: 348 Sugar Hollow Rd Fairview NC 28730-9560

GAFFNEY, THOMAS FRANCIS, investment company executive; b. Rockford, Ill., Aug. 29, 1945; s. Francis William and Catherine Zeta (Haeberle) G.; m. Donna Lee Gottfried, Apr. 17, 1971; 1 child, Cory. BA, Brown U., 1967; MBA, U. Chgo., 1969. CPA, Ill. Fin. cons. Duff and Phelps, Inc., Chgo., 1969-70; dir. adminstrn. Masury-Columbia Co. subs. Alberto-Culver Co., Melrose Park, Ill., 1970-75; exec. v.p., dir. Guardian Industries Corp., Northville, Mich., 1975-87; chmn. bd. The Oxford Investment Group, Bloomfield Hills, Mich., 1985-90; chmn. bd., CEO Automotive Plastic Techs., Inc., Sterling Heights, Mich., 1990-92; chmn. Ashland Products, Inc., Chgo., 1992-95; mng. dir. Raymond James Captial, Inc., St. Petersburg, FL, 1997—; bd. dirs. Am. Life Holdings, Inc. Decorated Chevalier de L'Orde Grand Ducal de le Couronne de Chene Grand Duchy Luxembourg, 1983. Mem. AICPA. Home: 2091 Oceanview Dr Tierra Verde FL 33715-2512

GAFNEY, HARRY D., chemistry educator; b. Springfield, Mass., Apr. 21, 1943; s. Harry Dabol and Ruth (Fitzgerald) G.; m. Patricia Jane Sattler, Sept. 9, 1967; children: David, Brian. BS, U. Mass., 1966; PhD, Wayne State U., 1970. Fellow U. So. Calif., L.A., 1970-72, Northwestern U., Evanston, Ill., 1972-73; asst. prof. chemistry Queens Coll., CUNY, Flushing, 1973-77, assoc. prof., 1978-81, prof., 1982—; vis. scientist, Dow Chem. Co.; cons. Dow Chem. Co., Midland, Mich., 1977-83, Corning (N.Y.), Inc., 1978—, fiber optics fabricator, 1994—; program officer, NSF, 1977-98. Author: (with others) Photochem of Metal Carbonyls on Porous Glass, 1989. Pres. North Woodbury (N.Y.) Civic Assn., 1976—. Recipient Teaching award Dupont Co., 1968; fellow Mellon Found., 1982-84. Mem. Am. Chem. Soc., N.Y. Acad. Sci., Materials Rsch. Soc., Sigma Xi, Phi Lambda Upsilon. Achievements include research in excited state redox and acid-base chemistry of Ru(II) diimines, enhanced charge separation on porous vycor glass, luminescent Ru(II) dimers, a photochemical approach to integrated optics, photolithographic metal deposition in glass. Office: Queens Coll CUNY Dept Chemistry Kissena Blvd Flushing NY 11367

GAGARIN, DENNIS PAUL, advertising agency executive; b. Long Beach, Calif., July 9, 1952. BS in Graphic Design, San Jose State U., 1976. Art dir. Brower, Mitchell, Gum Advt., Los Gatos, Calif., 1976-79, Offield & Brower Advt., Los Gatos, 1979-82; sr. art dir. Tycer, Fultz, Bellack Advt., Palo Alto, Calif., 1982-85; head art dir. TFB/BBDO Advt., Palo Alto, 1985-87; creative dir. Lena Chow Advt., Palo Alto, 1987-90; prin., ptnr. Gagarin/McGeoch Advt. and Design, Redwood City, Calif., 1989—; prof. San Jose (Calif.) State U., 1987-90, now guest lectr.; guest art dir. Western Art Dirs. Club, Palo Alto. Recipient awards for graphic design, art direction. Office: Gagarin/McGeoch Advt-Design 493 Seaport Ct Ste 102 Redwood City CA 94063-2788

GAGE, BEAU, artist; b. Rye, N.Y., Dec. 3, 1945; d. John Alden and Frances (Johnston) G.; m. Glenn A. Ousterhout, May 24,1980. BA, St. John's Coll., Santa Fe and Annapolis, Md., 1971; student, Internat. Ctr. Photography, N.Y.C., 1981-82, 82-83, Art Students League N.Y., 1983-87, The Sculpture Ctr. Sch., N.Y.C., 1985-87, Nat. Acad. Design, 1988-89. Staff asst. to the pres. The White House, Washington, 1972-73; key accounts mgr. Sterling Drug, Inc., Montvale, N.J., 1975-79. Works exhibited at Internat. Ctr. Photography, 1981-83, Art Students League, 1984-87, The Sculpture Ctr., 1985-87, Westbeth Gallery, N.Y.C., 1984, 86, Sotheby's Auction House, 1990, others; permanent pub. sculpture Jacksonville (Fla.) Jaguars, Inc. Supporter, guild mem. Martha Graham Dance Co., N.Y.C., 1989—; garden patron N.Y. Botanical Gardens, Bronx, 1999—. Fellow Mus. Modern Art; mem. Met. Mus. Art, Internat. Ctr. Photography, Orgn. Ind. Artists, The Nature Conservancy, Mass. Soc. Mayflower Descendants. Avocations: astronomy, sailing, yoga. Home: 320 E 46th St Apt 34E New York NY 10017-3057

GAGE, CHARLES QUINCEY, lawyer; b. Bluefield, W.Va., Jan. 20, 1946; s. Everett Lyle and Mary Isabella (Sloatman) G.; m. Karen Sue Wright, July 9, 1966; children: Charles Quincey III, Katherine Marshall, Geoffrey Maxwell. BSBA, W.Va., 1967, JD, 1970. Bar: W.Va. 1970, U.S. Dist. Ct. (so. dist.) W.Va. 1970, U.S. Dist. Ct. (no. dist.) W.Va. 1972, U.S. Ct. Appeals (4th cir.) 1972, U.S. Supreme Ct. 1974. Assoc. Jackson & Kelly, Charleston, W.Va., 1970-76, ptnr., 1977—. Mem. Cosmos Club Charleston (pres. 1978-79), Rotary, Shriner, Masons. Republican. Presbyterian. Avocations: golf, hunting, skiing. Home: 31 Quarry Rdg Charleston WV 25304-1052 Office: Jackson & Kelly PO Box 553 Charleston WV 25322-0553*

GAGE, EDWIN C., III (SKIP GAGE), travel and marketing services executive; b. Evanston, Ill., Nov. 1, 1940; s. Edwin Cutting and Margaret (Stackhouse) G.; m. Barbara Ann Carlson, June 26, 1965; children—Geoff, Scott, Christine, Richard. B.S. in Bus. Adminstrn., Northwestern U., 1963, M.S. in Journalism, 1965. Account exec. Foote, Cone and Belding, 1965-68, dir. mktg. devel. & rsch., 1968-70; v.p. direct mktg. Carlson Mktg. Group of Carlson Cos., Mpls., 1970-75, exec. v.p., 1975-77, pres., 1977-83, also bd. dirs.; exec. v.p., COO Carlson Cos. Inc., Mpls., 1983, pres., CEO, 1984-89, pres., chief exec. officer, 1989-91; now chmn., CEO Gage Marketing Group, Mpls.; bd. dirs. Gage Mktg. Group, Carlson Holdings Inc., Carlson Real Estate, Carlson Real Estate Co., Inc., Supervalu Stores Inc., Fingerhut Cos., Kellogg adv. bd. Northwestern U., Minn. Coun. Quality, Mpls. Inst. Arts. Lt. USN. Mem. Young Pres. Orgn., Minn. Execs. Orgn. Avocations: music folk and popular, tennis, golf, hunting, fishing. Office: Gage Marketing Group 10000 Highway 55 Ste 100 Minneapolis MN 55441-6365*

GAGE, FRED KELTON, lawyer; b. Mpls., June 20, 1925; s. Fred K. and Vivian L.; m. Dorothy Ann, Sept. 7, 1974; children: Deborah, Penelope, Amy, Lawrence. BS, U. Minn., 1948, LLB, 1950. Bar: Minn. 1950. Assoc. Wilson, Blethen & Ogle, Mankato, 1950-55; ptnr. Blethen, Gage, Krause, Blethen, Corcoran, Berkland & Peterson and predecessor firms, Mankato, 1955-90, of counsel, 1991—; mem. State Bd. Profl. Responsibility, Minn. Supreme Ct., 1974-82, mem. legal svcs. adv. com., 1996—. Mem. Mankato Sch. Bd., 1957-66, Minn. State Coll. Bd., 1960-64; mem. Minn. Senate from 11th Legis. Dist., 1966-72; Mem. Minn. Sports Facilities Commn., 1976-84. Served with USN, 1943-46. Named Mankato Outstanding Young Man of Yr., 1956, Outstanding Man of Minn., Mankato Jr. C. of C., 1958. Fellow Am. Bar Found.; mem. ABA (assembly del. 1980-86), Minn. Bar Assn. (chmn. tax sect. 1956-58, pres. 1977-78), Order of Coif. Republican. Methodist. Office: Blethen Gage & Krause PO Box 3049 127 S 2nd St Mankato MN 56001-3658

GAGE, GEORGE H(ENRY), retired high technology company executive; b. Rochester, N.Y., Oct. 1, 1924; s. George Henry and Ethel (Morley) G.; m. Frances Irvine, Dec. 21, 1946; children: Betsey Gage La Breche, James George, Nancy Gage Mandeville. BSEE, Rensselaer Poly. Inst., 1948. Application engr. GE, Owensboro, Ky., 1948-56, comml. engr., Syracuse, N.Y., 1957-58; mgr. product planning CBS Electronics, Danvers, Mass., 1959-61; dir. planning EG&G, Inc., Bedford, Mass., 1962-75, v.p., Wellesley, Mass., 1975-83, sr. v.p., 1983-86; dir. Adams Russell Co., Inc., Waltham, Mass., 1979-89; gov. Newell Health Corp., Newton-Wellesley Hosp., 1979-87. Contbg. author: Industrial Electronics Handbook, 1957; Implementation of Strategic Planning, 1982. Staff sgt. U.S. Army, 1943-46, PTO. Mem. Sigma Xi (assoc.), Tau Beta Pi, Eta Kappa Nu. Avocations: computer simulations, reading, walking. Home: 23 Fiddlers Green Lansing NY 14882-8877

GAGE, NATHANIEL LEES, psychologist, educator; b. Union City, N.J., Aug. 1, 1917; s. Hyman and Rose (Lees) Gewirtz; m. Margaret Elizabeth Burrows, June 27, 1942; children: Elizabeth, Thomas Burrows, Sarah, Anne. A.B. magna cum laude, U. Minn., 1938; Ph.D., Purdue U., 1947, Litt.D. (hon.), 1978. Asst. prof. div. ednl. reference Purdue U., 1947-48; prof. edn. U. Ill., Urbana, 1948-62; prof. edn. and psychology Stanford U., 1962-87, Margaret Jacks prof. edn., 1981-87, prof. emeritus, 1987—; Sachs vis. prof. Tchrs. Coll., Columbia U., 1977; lectr. U. Hamburg, 1978, Taipei, 1989, Madrid, 1992, U. Ill., 1994, numerous others; vis. fellow Brasenose Coll., Oxford U., 1983; vis. prof. NYU, 1959, Harvard U., 1984, SUNY, Albany, 1988; mem. rsch. adv. com. Am. Coun. Edn., 1967-73, chmn., 1972-73; mem. Nat. Adv. Com. on Edn. Labs, 1966-69; cons. Internat. Inst. Ednl. Planning, Paris, 1973-74; chmn. exec. bd. Stanford Ctr. Rsch. and Devel. in Tchg., 1968-76, founding co-dir., 1965-68; also dir. program on teaching effectiveness Ctr. for Ednl. Rsch., Stanford, 1972-83; vis. scholar, chmn. planning conf. on studies in teaching Nat. Inst. Edn., 1974; chmn. project coun. internat. classroom environ. study Internat. Assn. for Evaluation of Ednl. Achievement, 1979-81; Fulbright lectr., Brazil, 1985; mem. final selection com. Spencer Found. Dissertation Yr. Fellowships, 1987, 88; participant U. S. Dept. Edn. Conf. on School-Linked Comprehensive Svcs. for Children and Families, 1994. Author: Teacher Effectiveness and Teacher Education, 1972, Scientific Basis of the Art of Teaching, 1978, Hard Gains in the Soft Sciences: The Case of Pedagogy, 1985; co-author: Educational Measurement and Evaluation, 1943, 2d edit., 1955, A Practical Introduction to Measurement and Evaluation, 1960, 2d edit., 1965, Educational Psychology, 1975, 6th edit., 1998; editor: Handbook of Research on Teaching, 1963, Mandated Evaluation of Educators, 1973, Psychology of Teaching Methods, 1976; founding editor Teaching and Teacher Education: An Internat. Jour. Rsch. and Studies, 1983-86; co-editor: Readings in the Social Psychology of Education, 1963; cons. editor Jour. Ednl. Psychology, numerous other jours. Served with USAAF, 1943-45. Recipient Creative Leadership award NYU Sch. Edn., 1980, Outstanding Writing award Am. Assn. Colls. Tchr. Edn., 1986, Disting. Alumnus award Purdue U., 1994; fellow Ctr. for Advanced Study in Behavioral Scis., 1965-66, 87-88, USPHS, 1965-66, Guggenheim fellow, 1976-77. Fellow APA (pres. divsn. ednl. psychology 1961-62, Thorndike award 1986), Am. Psychol. Soc. (charter fellow); mem. Am. Ednl. Rsch. Assn. (pres. 1963-64, Disting. Contbns. award 1988), Nat. Soc. Study Edn. (bd. dirs. 1970-80, chmn. 1972, 74, 78), Nat. Acad. Edn., Phi Beta Kappa, Sigma Xi, Phi Delta Kappa (award for meritorious contbns. to edn. 1981). Home: 85 Peter Coutts Cir Stanford CA 94305-2512

GAGE, (LEONARD) PATRICK, research company executive; b. Endicott, N.Y., May 4, 1942; s. Leonard Augustine and Mary Margaret (O'Brien) G.; m. Nancy Virginia Graffius, Aug. 7, 1965 (div. Mar. 1985); children: Darren, Cynthia; m. Evelyn Anne Devine, June 29, 1985; children: Christopher, Devin. BS, MIT, 1964; PhD, U. Chgo., 1969. NIH postdoctoral fellow Carnegie Inst., Washington, 1969-71; mem. dept. cell biology Roche Inst. Molecular Biology, 1971-80; dir. lab. for recombinant DNA rsch. Roche Inst. Molecular Biology, Nutley, N.J., 1980-81, dir. dept. molecular genetics, 1981-83; v.p. biol. R & D Roche Inst. Molecular Biology, 1983-84; v.p. exploratory rsch. Hoffmann-La Roche Inc., Nutley, N.J., 1984-89; exec. v.p. Genetics Inst. Inc., Cambridge, Mass., 1989-93; chief oper. officer Genetics Inst., Inc., Cambridge, Mass., 1993-97, pres., 1997-98; pres. Wyeth-Ayerst Rsch. (Amer Home Products Corp.), 1998—; trustee The Jackson Lab., 1993—; bd. dirs. Mass. Biotech. Coun., Biotech. Industry Orgn., ArQule, Inc. mem. adv. bd. Life Sci. Rsch. Found., 1988—. Roman Catholic. Avocations: skiing, tennis. Office: Wyeth-Ayerst Rsch 555 E Lancaster Ave Saint Davids PA 19087-5109

GAGE, ROBERT CLIFFORD, minister; b. Beverly, Mass., Nov. 20, 1941; s. George V. and Elizabeth B. (May) G.; m. Mary Neefe, June 17, 1961; children: Joanna, Jonathan, Judith, Joshua, Joy. Student, Tenn. Temple U., 1961-62; BA, Phila. Coll. of Bible, 1964; postgrad., Ea. Bapt. Theol. Sem., 1966-67, New Sch. Soc. Rsch., 1975-76; D of Religion, Newport U., 1983. Ordained to ministry Gen. Assn. Regular Bapt. Chs., 1964. Pastor Whitehall Bapt. Ch., Phila., 1964-65, Glencroft Bapt. Ch., Glenolden, Pa., 1966-68; pastor 1st Bapt. Ch., Newfield, N.J., 1969-70, Hackensack, N.J., 1971-79; pastor Wealthy St. Bapt. Ch., Grand Rapids, Mich., 1979-88; evangelist, 1988-91; pastor Haven Bapt. Ch., Winter Haven, Fla., 1991—, adminstr., 1996—; radio min., 1965-88; adminstr. Haven Christian Acad. Author: The Birthmarks of the Christian Life, 1976, Our Life in Christ, 1978, The Pastor's Counseling Workbook, 1983, The Pre-Marriage Counseling Workbook, 1984, Discipleship Evangelism, 1985, Cultivating Spiritual Fruit, 1986, basic Discipleship, 1987, Why Me, Lord, 1988, The Unveiling, 1990; editor sword and Shield, 1969—; contbr. sermons to ch. publs.; weekly columnist Pers. Pub. Clinics, Winter Haven News Chief. Home: 1388 Avenue H SW Winter Haven FL 33880-2608 Office: 2105 King Rd Winter Haven FL 33880-1753 *Lord Jesus Christ, the work is Thine, not ours but Thine alone, and prospered by thy power Divine, can never be overthrown.*

GAGE, TOMMY WILTON, pharmacologist, dentist, pharmacist, educator; b. Stamford, Tex., Oct. 6, 1935; s. Carl and Mildred (Hughes) G.; m. Loyce M. Voss, June 2, 1956; children—Sharon, Stephen, Susan, Stacey. B.S., U. Tex., Austin, 1957; D.D.S., Baylor U., 1961, Ph.D., 1969. Gen. practice dentistry Munday, Tex., 1963-66; mem. faculty Baylor Coll. Dentistry, Dallas, 1969—; prof. pharmacology Tex. A&M U. Sys. at Baylor Coll. Dentistry, 1972—, chmn. dept., 1969-92, vice chmn. dept. oral and maxillofacial surgery and pharmacology, 1992—. Author papers in field, chpts. in books. Served with USAR, 1961-63. Nat. Inst. Dental Research postdoctoral fellow, 1966-69. Fellow Am. Coll. Dentists; mem. ADA, Am. Soc. Pharmacology and Exptl. Therapeutics, Am. Assn. for Dental Rsch., Internat. Assn. Dental Rsch., Am. Assn. Dental Schs., Tex. Dental Assn. (Cooley Trophy 1976), S.W. Soc. Oral Medicine, Dallas County Dental Assn., Rho Chi, Omicron Kappa Upsilon. Methodist. Office: 3302 Gaston Ave Dallas TX 75246-2013

GAGEL, BARBARA JEAN, health insurance administrator; b. Celina, Ohio, Nov. 19, 1943; d. Vincent James and Theresa Barbara (Goettermoeller) G. BA, Miami U., 1965; MBA, U. Chgo., 1977. Asst. dir. for internat. trade State of Ill., Chgo., Brussels, Hongkong and Sao Paulo, Brazil, 1973-76; dir. office of mgmt. and planning Office Human Devel. Svcs., Chgo., 1976-79; dep. regional adminstr. Health Care Financing Adminstrn., Chgo., 1979-82, regional adminstr., 1982-87; dir. bur. of prog. ops. Health Care Financing Adminstrn., Balt., 1987-92; dir. health stds. and quality bur. Health Care Fin. Adminstrn., Balt., 1992-96; pres., CEO AdminaStar, Inc., Indpls., 1996—. Recipient Presdl. Disting. Rank award 1988, 94, Presdl. Meritorious Rank award 1987, 92; named Fed. Exec. of Yr., 1987. Home: 10461 Spring Highland Dr Indianapolis IN 46290-1103 Office: AdminaStar Inc 8085 Knue Rd Indianapolis IN 46250-1921

GAGEN, J. WILFRID, business owner, marketing and public relations executive, consultant; b. N.Y.C.; s. John Ruger and Mary (Noonan) G.; children: Melissa, Carter; m. Barbara Jean Clendenon, Dec. 1997. BS, Villanova U. Producer/dir. radio show Naval Hosps., Bethesda, Md.; reporter Voice of Am. Radio Show, N.Y.C.; ind. producer/dir. Paramount and Universal Pictures; producer/dir./writer for the fashion/cosmetics industry U.S. exhibition U.S. State Dept., Moscow, USSR; pres. Gagen Assocs., Mktg. Comms., N.Y.C., 1960—; exec. dir. Found. Technol. Edn., Inc., Sarasota, Fla.; exec. prodr. Kaleidoscope; adj. prof. broadcast mktg. Marymount Manhattan Coll., Fashion Inst. Tech., N.Y.C., 1978-86; v.p. mktg. Jordache Enterprises, N.Y.C., 1979-82; guest lectr. foot wear industry in U.S. and Can. Harvard U., Columbia U., Wharton Sch., N.Y. Sales Exec. Club; appeared in video as one of ten top marketers The Marketing Wars, Prentice-Hall; expert witness mktg. comms.; guest lectr. cruises; cons. Sarasota Schs. Multimedia Program. Exec. prod. various tv films including The Road Back, WOR-TV, 1973, Allergy Alert, PBS, 1977 (radio shows) Medical Update, Celebrity Lifestyle, UPI radio network, 1975-91; columnist Sarasota Breeze; contbr. short stories to popular mags. Pres. Found. Prevention Addictive Diseases, N.Y.C., 1975-78, Internat. Youth Achievement Awards, N.Y.C., 1980-85; active Jerusalem Mental Health Ctr., N.Y.C., 1986. Served to 1st Lt. USMCR, 1944-46. Decorated Purple Heart with oak leaf cluster. Recipient Nat. Retail Merchants Assn. award, 1974, N.Y.C. Intern. Film Festival award, 1975, 85, Safety Article award McCall's Mag., 1975, George Washington Honor medal Freedoms Found. Valley Forge, Pa., Am. Silver Anvil award Pub. Rels. Soc., Golden Shovel award Pres. of Peru, Lectr. award Harvard Bus. Sch.; hon. N.Y. Met # 39; recorded for largest live fashion show Guiness Book of Records. Patentee spillproof nail polish bottle. *

GAGGIOLI, RICHARD ARNOLD, mechanical engineering educator; b. Highwood, Ill., Dec. 3, 1934; s. Gustavo and Constantina Lucille (Mordini) G.; m. Anita Catherine Sage, Nov. 9, 1957; children: Catherine Anne, Michael James, Daniel Richard, Edward Thomas, Mary Esther. BME, Northwestern U., 1957, MS (NSF fellow), 1958; PhD (Gen. Electric, NSF fellow), U. Wis., 1961. Registered profl. engr., Wis. Coop. student engr. Abbott Labs. (pharms.), North Chicago, Ill., 1954-58; asst. prof. mech. engring. U. Wis., Madison, 1962-66, assoc. prof., 1966-69; prof., chmn. dept. mech. engring. Marquette U., Milw., 1969-72, prof., 1969-81, 90—; dean engring. and architecture Cath. U. Am., Washington, 1981-84; prof. mech. engring. U. Mass., Lowell, 1985-89; mem. U.S. Army Math. Research Ctr., Madison, 1964-66; NSF-Soc. Indsl. and Applied Math. vis. lectr., 1969-72, engring. cons., 1970—. Author: (with E.F. Obert) Thermo-dynamics, 1963; editor: Thermodynamics-Second Law Analysis, Vol. 1, 1980, Vol. 2, 1983, Analysis of Energy Systems, 1985, Computer-Aided Engineering of Energy Systems, 1986; (with M.J. Moran) Analysis and Design of Advanced Energy Systems: Fundamentals, 1987; (with G. Tsatsaronis) Fundamentals of Thermodynamics and Energy Analysis, 1990; (with G.M. Reistad) Thermodynamics and Energy Systems: Fundamentals, 1991, (with R.F. Boehm et al.) Thermodynamics and the Design of Energy Systems, 1992; hon. editor Internat. Jour. Applied Thermodynamics, 1998—; contbr. articles to profl. jours. Chmn. bd. trustees Montrose Sch., Westwood, Mass., 1987-89. Recipient Emil H. Steiger Meml. Teaching award U. Wis., 1965, Pere Marquette award for faculty excellence Marquette U., 1976, Best Paper award Am. Chem. Soc. Chem. Tech. jour. 1977; NSF postdoctoral fellow chem. engring. U. Wis., 1961-62; vis. fellow Battelle Meml. Inst., 1968-69; invited lectr., Rome, 1987, 95, Beijing 1986, 89, 97, Zaragoza 1993, Florence, 1989, Athens, 1991, Istanbul, 1995, Krakow, 1994, 98, Tokyo, 1999, others. Fellow ASME (James Harry Potter gold medal 1988, award advanced sys.

divsn. 1991); mem. ASHRAE, AIChE, Summit Edn. Assn. (treas., trustee 1993—), Sigma Xi, Pi Tau Sigma, Tau Beta Pi. Roman Catholic. Home: 5239 S Gurin Pass New Berlin WI 53151-8138 Office: Marquette U Dept Mech Engring Milwaukee WI 53233-2286

GAGLIANO, ALFONSO, Canadian government official; b. Siculiana, Italy, Jan. 25, 1942; s. Vincenzo and Maria (Augello) G.; m. Ersilia Gidaro, July 3, 1965; children: Vincenzo, Maria, Immacolata. Cert. gen. acctg., George Williams U., Montreal. Sch. commr. Jérôme LeRoyer Sch. Bd., Montreal, Quebec, Can., 1977-83; pres. Jérôme-LeRoyer Sch. Commn., Montreal, 1983-84; MP St. Leonard Anjou Riding Can. Parliament, Ottawa, 1984-88, MP St. Leonard Riding, 1988-94; sec. state parliamentary affairs, dep. leader of govt. Can. Parliament House of Commons, Ottawa, 1994-96; min. of labour and dep. govt. house leader Can. Govt. House of Commons, Ottawa, 1996-97, min. pub. works and govt. svcs., 1997—; official opposition critic for small bus., rev. Canada and Canada Post Corp., 1984-91; opposition critic for industry dept., mem. permanent com. on fin. Can. House of Commons, 1988-91; opposition critic for immigration 1990-91; chair Quebec Liberal Caucus, 1988-91; chief govt. whip, 1993-94; chair electoral commn. Liberal Party of Canad (Quebec), 1994—. Office: Office Pub Works/Govt Svcs, Ottawa, ON Canada K1A OS5*

GAGLIANO, FRANK JOSEPH, playwright; b. Bklyn., Nov. 18, 1931; s. Francis Paul and Nancy (La Barbera) G.; m. Sandra Renee, Jan. 18, 1958; 1 child, Francis Enrico. BA, U. Iowa, 1954; MFA, Columbia U., 1957. Freelance copywriter N.Y.C., 1958-61; promotion copywriter text-film divsn. McGraw-Hill Co., N.Y.C., 1962-65; asst. prof. drama Fla. State U., 1969-72; lectr. in playwriting, dir. E. P. Conkle Workshop for Playwrights, U. Tex., Austin, 1972-75; Benedum prof. theater W.Va. U., 1976—; disting. vis. alumni prof. U. R.I., 1975; artistic dir. Showcase of New Plays, Carnegie-Mellon U., 1987-98, artistic dir. Festival of New Works, U. Mich., 1999—. Author: (plays) Conerico Was Here to Stay, 1965, Paradise Gardens East, 1966, Night of the Dunce, 1966, Father Uxbridge Wants to Marry, 1967, The Hide-and-Seek Odyssey of Madeleine Gimple, 1968, Big Sur, 1969, The Prince of Peasantmania, 1970, The Commedia World of Lafcadio B, 1973, In the VooDoo Parlour of Marie Laveau, 1974, The Resurrection of Jackie Cramer, 1976, Congo Square, 1979, rev. edit., 1989, The Total Immersion of Madeleine Favorini, 1981, (cantata) San Ysidro, 1985, (novel) Anton's Leap, 1986, rev. edit., 1991, From the Bodoni County Songbook Anthology, 1986, (musical version), 1987, rev. edit., 1989, 90, 91, 95, My Chekhov Light, 1987, rev. edit., 1983, 92, (for German pub.) 98, Hanna-A Run on Odyssey, 1990-92, The Farewell Concert of Irene and Vernon Palazzo, 1995, And the Angels Sing (musical), 1996, Piano Bar (musical), 1998. With U.S. Army, 1954-56. Wesleyan U.-O'Neill Found. fellow, 1967; Guggenheim fellow, 1975; Rockefeller grantee, 1965, 66; Nat. Endowment for Arts grantee, 1973; Penn. Coun. Playwriting fellow, 1989. Mem. ASCAP, Dramatists Guild, Writers Guild Am., East, New Dramatists (alumnus). Office: WVa U Creative Arts Ctr Morgantown WV 26506

GAGLIARDI, LEE PARSONS, federal judge; b. Larchmont, N.Y., July 17, 1918; s. Frank M. and Mary F. (DeCicco) G.; m. Marian Hope Selden, Aug. 5, 1943; children: Elizabeth G. (Mrs. Charles J. Tobin III) Marian S. (dec.). Grad., Phillips Exeter Acad.; B.A., Williams Coll., 1941; J.D., Columbia U., 1947. Bar: N.Y. 1948. Asst. to gen. atty. N.Y. Central R.R. Co., N.Y.C., 1948-55; partner Clark, Gagliardi, Gallagher & Smyth, N.Y.C., 1955-72; judge U.S. Dist. Ct. (so. dist.) N.Y., 1972—, now sr. judge. Chmn. Bd. Police Commrs., Mamaroneck, N.Y., 1970-72; sec. Westchester County Caddie Scholarship Com., 1964-72; bd. govs. New Rochelle Hosp. Med. Ctr., N.Y., 1975-85; bd. dirs. Sherman Fairchild Found., Inc., 1979-93. Mem. Dorset (Vt.) Field Club, Wilderness Country Club (Naples, Fla.). Office: US Dist Ct So Dist PO Box 768 Historic Rt 7A Manchester VT 05254-0768*

GAGLIARDI, RAYMOND ALFRED, physician; b. New Haven, Nov. 20, 1922; s. Carl Albert and Carmela (Esposito) G.; m. Patricia DeTuncq, Apr. 6, 1946; children: Laura E. Quigley, John Bell. BS, Yale U., 1943, MD, 1945. Pvt. practice radiology Pontiac, Mich., 1951-92; chmn. dept. radiology St. Joseph Mercy Hosp., Pontiac, 1976-91, chmn. emeritus, 1991—. Author: The Golf Story: An Anecdotal History of Golf, 1999; editor-in-chief History of the Radiological Sciences, 1995; contbr. articles to profl. jours. Capt. U.S. Army, 1946-48; PTO. Fellow Am. Coll Radiology; mem. Am. Roentgen Ray Soc. (pres. 1987-88, Gold Medal award 1989, Hartman medal 1995), Mich. Radiol. Soc. (pres. 1972), Mich. Med. Soc. (Disting. Svc. award 1988), Oakland Hills Country Club, Royal Palm Yacht and Country Club (past commodore 1994). Republican. Avocation: golf. Home: 2100 Queen Palm Rd Boca Raton FL 33432-7932 also: 789 Uper Scotsborough Way Boca Raton FL 33432

GAGLIARDI, UGO OSCAR, systems software architect, educator; b. Naples, Italy, July 23, 1931; came to U.S., 1956; s. Edgardo and Lina (Valenzuela) G.; m. Anna Josephine Italiano, July 7, 1954 (div. May 1972); children: Oscar Marco, Alex Piero. Diploma in Math. and Physics, U. Naples, Italy, 1951; DEng in Elec. Engring., U. Naples, 1954. Chief scientist U.S. Air Force, Hanscom AFB, Mass., 1965-66; rsch. fellow Harvard U., Cambridge, Mass., 1965-66; v.p. tech. ops. Interactive Scis., Inc., Braintree, Mass., 1968-70; dir. engring. Honeywell Info. Systems, Waltham, Mass., 1970-75; lectr. Harvard U., Cambridge, Mass., 1966-74, prof. practice computer engring., 1974-83, Gordon McKay prof. practice computer engring., 1983—; pres. Gen. Systems Group, Inc., Salem, N.H., 1975—; chmn. Ctr. for Software Tech., Inc.; mem. NAS rsch. coun. panel Nat. Computer Systems Lab. (formerly Inst. Computer Scis. and Tech.), Nat. Inst. Standards and Tech. (formerly Nat. Bur. Standards), 1985-91, chmn., 1988-91. Fulbright scholar Columbia U., 1955-56. Office: Harvard U 40 Oxford St Cambridge MA 02138-1903

GAGNE, ANN MARIE, special education educator; b. Elmont, N.Y., Feb. 21, 1956; d. Wilfred Alfred and Anita Agnes (Henne) G. BA in Edn., U. Miss., 1978, MEd, 1979; postgrad., Nicholl State U., 1982-85, U. Memphis, 1989-92. Tchr. learning disabled So. Elem. Sch., Southaven, Miss., 1979-82; tchr. spl. edn. Labodieville (La.) Elem. Sch., 1982-84, Bayou Bay (La.) Elem. Sch., 1984-86; tchr. physically disabled and medically fragile Shrine Sch., Memphis, 1986-97; tchr. comprehensive devel. class primary class Knight Rd. Sch., Memphis, 1997—; career ladder III tchr. 21st century classroom tchr.; athletic sports coach Spl. Olympics, wheelchair events dir.; parent contract advisor Tenn. Infant Parent Svcs., 1997—. Active human rights com. Open Arms Corp.; mem. tech. adv. panel United Cerebral Palsy; mem. assistive tech. adv. panel U. Memphis. Mem. Coun. Exceptional Children, Friends of Orpheum, Open Arms Corp. Human Rights Com., Delta Kappa Gamma. Roman Catholic. Avocations: cross-stitch, reading, walking. Home: 6850 Club Ridge Cir Apt 97 Memphis TN 38115-5385

GAGNE, DAVID WARD, music educator; b. June 3, 1949. BA, Columbia U., 1971; MA, CUNY, 1980, PhD, 1988. Assoc. music dir. Dance Theatre of Harlem, N.Y.C., 1971-77; faculty Munnes Coll. Music, N.Y.C., 1978—; assoc. prof. Queens Coll., CUNY, 1988—. Home and Office: 211 W 106th St Apt 14B New York NY 10025

GAGNE, MARGARET LEE, accounting educator; b. Miller, S.D., June 23, 1953; d. E.A. and Helen A. (Simonds) Andersen; m. Ronald W. Gagne, Jan. 2, 1988. B summa cum laude, Huron Coll., 1975; MBA, U. S.D., 1979; PhD, Ind. U., 1989. Tchr. Hitchcock (S.D.) Ind. Schs., 1975-77; staff auditor Banco, Inc., Sioux Falls, S.D., 1979-81; instr. acctg. U. S.D., Vermillion, 1981-83; from instr. to asst. prof. U. Colo., Colorado Springs, 1987-96, assoc. prof., 1996—; cons. Walter Drake, Colorado Springs, 1994, Johns Manville, Denver, 1998. Contbr. articles to profl. jours. Treas. St. Luke's Luth. Ch., Colorado Springs, 1987-88; vol. Ecumenical Social Ministries, Colorado Springs, 1995-96. Ind. U. fellow, 1983-86. Mem. Am. Acctg. Assn., Inst. Internal Auditors (bd. govs. 1980-81). Republican. Avocations: reading, walking, crocheting. Office: U Colo at Colorado Springs 1420 Austin Bluffs Pkwy Colorado Springs CO 80918-3733

GAGNE, MARY, secondary school principal. Prin. Monsignor Kelly High Sch., Beaumont, Tex. Recipient Blue Ribbon award U.D. Dept. Edn., 1990-91. Office: Monsignor Kelly High Sch 5950 Kelly Dr Beaumont TX 77707-3503*

GAGNON, CRAIG WILLIAM, lawyer; b. St. Cloud, Minn., Dec. 19, 1940; s. Marvin Sylvester and Signa Gunhild (Johnson) G.; m. Judith, 1964; children: Nicole, Jeffrey, Camille; m. Pam Peglow Nov. 8, 1980; children: Claire, Jillian, Jane. BA, U. Minn., 1964; JD magna cum laude, William Mitchell Coll. Law, 1968. Bar: Minn. 1968, U.S. Dist. Ct. Minn. 1968, U.S. Tax Ct. 1972, U.S. Supreme Ct. 1970. Ptnr. Oppenheimer, Wolff & Donnelly, Mpls., 1968—. Trustee William Mitchell Coll. Law, St. Paul. 1989—, chmn. bd., 1999—. Named Alumnus of Notable Achievement, U. Minn. Fellow Am. Coll. Trial Lawyers; mem. U.S. Supreme Ct. Hist. Soc., Metro Breakfast Club (pres. 1993). Avocations: hunting, fishing, golf. Home: 4807 Sunnyside Rd Edina MN 55424-1109 Office: Oppenheimer Wolff & Donnelly 45 S 7th St Ste 3400 Minneapolis MN 55402-1609

GAGNON, EDITH MORRISON, ballerina, singer, actress; b. Chgo., Apr. 8; grad. Chalif Sch. Dancing, N.Y.C.; student Northwestern U.; voice student Forest Lamont of Chgo. Opera Co.; grad., trained with Ivan Tarasoff Chalif Sch. of N.Y.; m. Alfred Gagnon, Feb. 3, 1977; children by previous marriage—Joyce, Morton. Premiere ballerina Pavley and Oukrainsky Russian Ballet of Chgo., performer with Chgo., Met., Ravinia Opera Cos.; appeared Birthday of Infanta, Greenwich Follies, The Five O'Clock Girl; founder, dir., instr. Sch. of Dance, St. Louis; singer in concert, Carnegie Hall; commentator radio programs Women on the Home Front, Sta. KSD, St. Louis, and CD program Sta. WEW, St. Louis U.; voice coach, producer, performer benefit performances, St. Louis, San Francisco area. Pres. Pets Unlimited, San Francisco; bd. dirs. Artists Embassy. Mem. Pacific Musical Soc. (v.p. San Francisco), Equity Guild. Clubs: Burlingame Country; International Embassy, Francisca

GAGNON, EDOUARD CARDINAL, ecclesiastic; b. Port Daniel, Que., Can., Jan. 15, 1918. Ordained priest Roman Catholic Ch., 1940, consecrated bishop, 1969. Bishop St. Paul, Alberta, Can., 1969-72; rector Can. Coll., Rome, 1972-77; v.p., sec. Vatican Com. for Family, 1973-80; titular archbishop of Guistiniana Prima, 1983; pro-pres. Pontifical Council for the Family, 1983-85, pres., 1985-90; pres. Pontifical Com. Internat. Eucharistic Congresses, 1991—; elevated to Sacred Coll. of Cardinals, 1985. Office: Pontifical Com Internat Eucharistic Congr, Piazza San Calisto 16, 00153 Rome Italy*

GAGNON, JOHN HARVEY, psychotherapist, educator; b. Derby, Conn., Dec. 16, 1946; s. Ernest John and Pauline Stella (Dziedulonis) G.; m. Eleanor Moser, Apr. 22, 1995; 1 child, Isabelle Eleanor. BS, Fairfield U., 1969; MS, Western Conn. State Coll., 1976; PhD, Union Inst., 1982. Diplomate Am. Bd. Psychothrapy (fellow); lic. marriage and family therapist, EMT, Conn.; cert. family life educator; bd. cert. in med. hypnosis, clin. hypnotherpy and hynoanesthesiology. Counselor in tng. Conn. Valley Hosp., 1972-73; counselor Whiting Forensic Inst., 1973; coord., dir. Danbury Hosp. Day Treatment Program, 1973-77; pvt. practice, 1977-80; psychotherapy intern Counseling Ctr. and N.Y. Inst. for Gestalt Therapy, 1981-83; pvt. practice, 1983—; rsch. cons. Newtown Counseling Ctr., 1987-89; instr. N.Y. Inst. for Gestalt Therapy, 1983-89; lectr. Yale U., 1983; adj. prof. Western Conn. State U., 1983-86, U. Bridgeport, 1988-90; adj. lectr. U. Conn., 1990-93; cons. dept. psychology Fairfield U., 1994-95. Author: Gagnon's Directory, 1986, Wounded Healer, 1993; contbr. articles to profl. jours. Ofcl. emergency sta. Am. Radio Relay League, 1992—; chmn. adult program Unitarian-Universalist Soc. North Fairfield County, West Redding, Conn., 1990-91, tchr. religious edn., 1984-86; judge sr. divsn. Conn. State Fair, 1986—; bd. trustees Unitarian-Universalist Ch. of Stamford, 1996-98. Fellow Internat. Coun. for Sex Edn. and Parenthood; mem. ACA, AAUP, Assn. for Counselor Edn. and Supervision, Am. Soc. for Group Psychotherapy and Psychodrama, Am. Acad. Psychotherapists, Am. Assn. for Marriage and Family Therapy, Am. Bd. Hypnotherapy & Hypnotic Anesthesiology, Assn. for Humanistic Psychology, Internat. Assn. Marriage and Family Counselors, Nat. Coun. Family Rels., Phi Delta Kappa. Democrat. Office: 270 Greenwich Ave Ste 26 Greenwich CT 06830

GAGNON, MONIQUE FRANCINE, pediatrician; b. Detroit, Apr. 16, 1963; d. Alden George and Francine Marie-Paule (MArchand) G.; m. Tomas Jose Vietorisz, May 30, 1992. BA, Mt. Holyoke Coll., 1985; MD, Mt. Sinai Sch. Medicine, 1989. Diplomat Am. Bd. Pediatrics. Intern, resident New Eng. Med. Ctr., Boston, 1989-92; pediatrician Stamford (Conn.) Hosp., 1993-94, pvt. practice, Stamford, 1994—. Fellow Am. Acad. Pediatricians; mem. Conn. Med. Soc., Soc. Adolscent Medicine. Office: The Pediatric Ctr 126 Morgan St Stamford CT 06905-5431*

GAGNON, PAUL MICHAEL, lawyer, former county attorney; b. Manchester, N.H., July 9, 1949; s. Raymond Charles, Sr. and Mary Elizabeth (Mullen) G.; m. Catherine Mary McBride, June 5, 1976; children—Nicole Marie, Amy Catherine. B.A., U. N.H., 1971; J.D., Suffolk U., 1977. Bar: N.H. 1977, U.S. Dist. Ct. N.H. 1977, U.S. Supreme Ct. 1984. Asst. county atty. Hillsborough County, Manchester, 1977-79, county atty., 1982-86; assoc. Malloy & Sullivan, 1979-81; sole practice, Manchester, 1981—; now U.S. atty. N.H. Dept. Justice, Concord; criminal law instr. St. Anselm's Coll., 1985-86. Bd. dirs. Hillsborough County Task Force Crimes Against Children, 1984-86; advisor Law Explorer post Boy Scouts Am., Manchester, 1981; committeeman Nat. State Democratic Com., 1984-86; Dem. candidate for gov., N.H., 1986. Served to 1st lt. USAF, 1971-74, N.H. Air N.G., 1975—. Mem. N.H. Bar Assn. (chmn. com. 1981-83), Manchester Bar Assn., ABA, Am. Trial Lawyers Assn., N.H. Assn. County Prosecutors. Democrat. Roman Catholic. Office: US Atty's Office James C Cleveland Fed Bldg 55 Pleasant St Rm 352 Concord NH 03301-3939*

GAGNON, ROBERT JAMES, JR., manufacturing engineer; b. Derby, Conn., Nov. 21, 1969; s. Robert James Sr. and Marguerite Anne (Cammarata) G.; m. Monika Mosiej, July 12, 1997. BS in Mech. Engring., Marquette U., Milw., 1991. Engring. technician United Illuminating, New Haven, 1989, Lacey Mfg. Co., Bridgeport, Conn., 1992-96; mfg. engr. Hubbell Inc., Bridgeport, 1996—. Vol. recruiter students Marquette U., Milw., 1991—. Democrat. Roman Catholic. Avocations: running, travel, music, reading, foreign languages. Office: Hubbell Inc Wiring Device-Kellens 1613 State St Bridgeport CT 06605-2000

GAGNON, ROBERT MICHAEL, engineering executive, educator; b. Washington, Oct. 25, 1948; s. Robert James and Martha (Proctor) G.; m. Martha Ellen Mason, Aug. 1, 1975; 1 child, Rebecca Jane Gagnon-Tacchetti. BA in Math., Western Md. Coll., 1971; BS in Fire Protection Engring., U. Md., 1990, MS in Fire Protection Engring., 1995. Registered profl. engr., Md., Va., Pa., N.C., D.C.; cert. level IV Nat. Inst. for Cert. Engring. Technicians. Dist. design mgr. Automatic Sprinkler Corp., Washington, 1970-77; project mgr. Fireguard Corp., Washington, 1977-83; regional spl. hazards design mgr. Automatic Sprinkler Corp., Balt., 1983-91; pres., prin. engr. Gagnon Engring. Corp., Ellicott City, Md., 1991—; adj. prof. applied techs. Montgomery Coll., Gaithersburg, Md., 1992—; adj. prof. fire protection engring. U. Md., College Park, 1993—, mentor to engring. students Coll. Engring., 1993—. Author: A Consulting Guide to Ultra High Speed Deluge Protection Systems, 1990, Design of Water-Based and Special Hazard Systems, 1996; contbr. articles to profl. jours. Founder Robert J. Gagnon Meml. Nurses Tng. Scholarship, Am. Legion, 1986—, Gagnon Engring. Corp. Scholarship U. Md., 1993—. Capt. U.S. Army-Infantry, 1971. Recipient Eagle Scout medal Boy Scouts Am., 1964; Senatorial scholar Md. State Senate, Western Md. Coll., 1968-71. Mem. NSPE (v.p. Howard County chpt. 1993—, pres. 1995—), Am. Fire Sprinkler Assn. (prin. NFPA 15 com. 1993—, NFPA 16, NFPA 11, NFPA 24 and NFPA 214 coms. 1994—), Soc. Fire Protection Engrs. (exec. com. 1992—, v.p. 1995-96, pres. 1997—), Salamander Fire Protection Engring. Honor Soc., La Societe Des Quarante Hommes et Huit Chevaux (scholarship chmn. 1986—), U. Md. Emngring Alumni Assn. (exec. com. 1993-97, pres. 1998—), Md. Soc. of Profl. Engrs. (pres. 1998—), Tau Beta Pi (pres. alumni chpt. 1994—, scholarship chmn. 1993—). Republican. Methodist. Avocations: collecting music of the 1950's and 1960's, world travel. Home and Office: Gagnon Engring Corp 10110 Labelle Ct Ellicott City MD 21042-6203

GAGOSIAN, ROBERT B., chemist, educator; b. Medford, Mass., Sept. 17, 1944; m. Susan Gagosian; children: Travis, Alex. SB in Chemistry, MIT, 1966; PhD in Organic Chemistry, Columbia U., 1970. Asst. scientist Woods Hole Oceanographic Instn., 1972-76; assoc. scientist Woods Hole (Mass.) Oceanographic Inst., 1976-82; sr. scientist Woods Hole Oceanographic Instn., 1982—, chmn. dept. chemistry, 1982-87, assoc. dir. rsch., 1987-92, sr. assoc. dir., dir. rsch., 1992-93; acting dir., 1993-94; dir. Woods Hole Oceanographic Inst., 1994—; vis. lectr. dept. geology and geophysics Yale U., 1975, cons., lectr. in field; mrm. numerous vis. coms. and rsch. panels NSF, Office Naval Rsch., univs. and rsch. orgns. in U.S. and fgn. countries; regional bd. dirs. BankBoston; mem. corp. Bermuda Biol. Sta. for Rsch., Sea Edn. Assn. Contbr. chpts. to books, articles to profl. jours. Grantee and fellow numerous profl. and ednl. instns. including vis. scholar U. Wash., 1983, Australian Inst. Marine Scis., 1983; vis. fellow Australian Nat. U., 1983; William Evans fellow, U. Otago, Dunedin, New Zealand, 1987. Mem. Am. Chem. Soc., AAAS, Geochem. Soc. Am., Am. Geophys. Union, European Assn. Organic Geochemists, Sigma Xi. Office: Woods Hole Oceanographic Inst Woods Hole MA 02543

GAGUINE, BENITO, lawyer; b. Paris, Apr. 28, 1912; came to U.S., 1920, naturalized, 1926; s. Silvio Alexander and Rose (Braun) G.; m. Frances Cass Crouse, July 15, 1944; children—John Benedict, Bruce Alexander. A.B., Columbia U., 1932, LL.B., 1934; LL.M., George Washington U., 1940. Bar: N.Y. 1934. Atty., judge adminstrv. law various U.S. Govt. agys., Washington, 1935-53; ptnr. Fly, Shuebruk, Gaguine, Boros & Braun, Washington, 1953-88; of counsel Bechtel & Cole, Washington, 1988-91, Reddy, Begley & Martin, Washington, 1991-92; pvt. practice Washington, 1992—; Adviser U.S. dels. internat. confs.; mem. juridical com. Interam. Broadcasters Assn. Contbr. articles to legal jours. Served to lt. col. AUS, 1943-47. Mem. ABA, Fed. Bar Assn., Fed. Communications Bar Assn., D.C. Bar Assn. Democrat. Club: University (Washington). Home: 8100 Connecticut Ave Apt 809 Chevy Chase MD 20815-2816 Office: 2300 M St NW Ste 900 Washington DC 20037-1434*

GAHAGAN, JAMES EDWARD, JR., artist; b. Bklyn., Sept. 20, 1927; s. James Edward and Anna (Biondi) G.; m. Patricia De Gogorza, Apr. 18, 1963; children: Paulo, Sharon. BA, Goddard Coll., 1951; postgrad., Hans Hofmann Sch. Fine Art, N.Y.C., 1952-58. Asst. dir. Hans Hofmann Sch. Fine Arts, 1954-58; art tchr. Adult Workshop, SUNY, Great Neck, L.I., 1955-62; tchr. painting, drawing Pratt Inst., Bklyn., 1965-71; lectr. arts Columbia U. Grad. Sch. Arts, N.Y.C., 1968-71; mem. art faculty, chmn. faculty, acting dean, art dept. chmn. Goddard Coll., Plainfield, Vt., 1971-79; tchr. Lesley Coll. Grad. Sch., Cambridge, Mass., 1981; field faculty grad. program Vt. Coll., Montpelier, 1983—; faculty Vt. Studio Sch., Johnson, 1984—; artist, tchr. Internat. Artist Workshop, New Zealand, 1991, 92; mem. Artist Tenants Assn., N.Y.C., 1960-71, pres., 1960-62, 65-66. Co-pub./editor: N.Y. Element newspaper, 1968-71; 18 one-man shows, 1954-81, Tirca Karlis Gallery, Provincetown, Mass., annually, 1980-86; exhibited in numerous group shows; represented in permanent and pvt. collections; chief asst. to Hans Hofmann on 2 Mosaic-mural projects, N.Y.C., 1956, 57; represented by Feingarten Galleries, L.A., 1990—, Clarke Galleries, Stowe, Vt., 1993—, C. Carr Gallery, N.Y.C., 1997—. Mem. N.Y.C. Mayor's Com. on Cultural Affairs, 71965-66, health officer, Woodbury, 1975-90, justice of peace, Woodbury, Vt., 1975-77, 80—, selectman, 1990—; bd. trustees H&T Burkhardt Found., L.A., 1996—. Recipient Cape Cod Art Assn. award, 1957; Longview Found. grantee, 1958; Adolph and Esther Gottlieb Found. grantee, 1984. Mem. AAUP, ACLU, Art Resource Assn. Vt. (chmn. bd. dirs. 1975—), Am. Fedn. Tchrs., Printmaking Workshop N.Y.C., Artworkers Found. for Community of Artists N.Y.C., Provincetown (Mass.) Art Assn., Vt. Council Arts. Democrat. Address: RFD 1 RR 1 Box 116 East Calais VT 05650-9508 *If I had my life to live over, I would again choose to spend it as a creative, visual, fine artist. It is a constructive, nonviolent, life-affirming commitment to explore reality.*

GAHAGAN, PATRICIA DE GOGORZA, sculptor; b. Detroit, Mar. 17, 1936; d. Maitland and Julia Harlow (Brodt) de G.; m. Dadi Wirz, Aug. 7, 1958 (div. Dec. 1962); 1 child, Paulo; m. James Edward Gahagan, Apr. 18, 1963; 1 child, Sharon. BA, Smith Coll., 1958; MA, Goddard Coll., 1975. Asst. prof. art Bard Coll., Annandale, N.Y., 1966-69; drawing instr. U. Vt., Burlington, 1980-81; instr. Vt. Studio Ctr., Johnson, 1984—; sculpture instr. The Carving Studio, West Rutland, Vt., 1987—, Johnson State Coll., 1996, Arts Workshop, Akaroa, New Zealand, 1999; chair sculpture dept. Goddard Coll., Plainfield, Vt., 1973-74, 78-79; faculty MFA program Vt. Coll., Montpelier, 1992-93; instr. Vt. Clay Studio, Montpelier, 1994-97, Arts Workshop, Akaroa, New Zealand, 1999. Solo shows sculpture include Sculpin Gallery, Martha's Vineyard, 1973, Bundy Mus., Waitsfield, Vt., 1982, Dibden Gallery, Johnson State Coll., Johnson, Vt., 1984, Moonbrook Gallery, Rutland, Vt., 1985, A.V.A. Gallery, Hanover, N.H., 1985, Wood Art Gallery, Montpelier, 1988, Hillyer Gallery, Smith Coll., Northampton, Mass., 1989, Brown Libr., Craftsbury, Vt., 1999; group shows include Carving Studio Sculptors in Vt., 1988-97, Helen Day Art Ctr., Stowe, Vt., 1986-98, So. Vt. Art Ctr., Manchester, 1993-97, West Branch Sculpture Gardens, Stowe, 1994-98, Akaroa Mus., New Zealand, 1999; works in permanent collectins include Sun/Moon Cycle granite sculpture Johnson State Coll., 1989, Riverbirds marble sculpture Marble St. Sculpture Park, West Rutland, 1991, Pegasus, marble sculpture Burlington City Bike Path, 1992, Mermaid, Merman and Dolphin, 2 marble sculptures 1993, Tree of Life, State of Vt., Pavilion Bldg., Montpelier, 1995, numerous pvt. collections. Bd. dirs., pres. Art Resource Assn., Montpelier, 1976-84; chair Dem. Party, Woodbury, Vt., 1982—; art organizer, tchr. Rural Sch. Devel. Program, Woodbury, 1972-74; violinist I Vt. Philharm. Orch., 1979-99, Montpelier Chamber Orch., 1997-99. Mem. Internat. Sculpture Ctr., Art Resource Assn., Carving Studio. Democrat. Avocations: violin, gardening. Home and Office: 1580 Dog Pond Rd East Calais VT 05650-8134

GAIBER, LAWRENCE JAY, financial company executive; b. Chgo., Mar. 20, 1960; s. Sy Bertrym and Mildred (Dickler) G. BS in Econ., U. Pa., 1982. Mgmt. intern Eisai Co. Ltd, Tokyo, 1980; dept. mgr. Anglo Am. Corp., Johannesburg, Republic of South Africa, 1982-84; pres. Sandton Fin. Group, L.A., 1984—; pres. Swellendam Fin. Group, Studio City, Calif., 1984—, also bd. dirs.; bd. dirs. Lawrand Ltd, Satellite Telecommunication, Inst. Cellular Nutritional Immunology, Introlagater, Gaiber, Introlagater, L.A. Greetings; chmn. Mechanics Express Inc. Contbr. articles to profl. jours and mags. Mem. South Africa Found., Johannesburg, 1984—, Town Hall Calif., 1986; bd. dirs. Brentwood Arts Coun.; vice chmn. western region 1986 Pres.' dinner Rep. Nat. Com., Washington. Recipient Most Active Vol. award S. African Inst. Internat. Affairs, 1983; honoree for contbns. to aspiring entrepreneurial women Mayor Tom Bradley's Office and Nat. Network of Hispanic Women, L.A., 1986. Mem. L.A. Venture Assn., L.A. C. of C., L.A. Jr. C. of C., Van Nuys C. of C., L.A. County Rep. Lincoln Club, L.A. County Young Reps., Brentwood Rep. Club (Pres. 1984—). Clubs: Wharton Bus. Sch., Calif. Yacht. Avocation: world travel.

GAIL, MITCHELL H., science foundation executive; b. Lexington, Ky., July 10, 1941; married. BA magna cum laude, Harvard U., 1962, MD cum laude, 1968; MS in Math. Statistics, George Washington U., 1973, PhD in Math. Statistics, 1977. Rsch. dept. biochemistry Harvard U. Sch. Medicne, Boston, 1964-65; Knox fellow Cambridge (Eng.) U., 1962-63; intern Beter Bent Brigham Hosp., Boston, 1968-69; rsch. assoc. in cell biology NIH, Nat. Cancer Inst., 1969-72; rschr. lab. for computer scis. Mass. Gen. Hosp., Boston, 1968; med. statis. investigator clin. and diagnostic trials sect. NIH, Nat. Cancer Inst., 1972-85, head epidemiol. methods sect., 1985—, chief biostatistics br. divsn. cancer etiology, 1994-95, chief biostatistics br. divsn. cancer epidemiology/genetics, 1995—; chmn. adv. com. to editors of Jour. of Controlled Clin. Trials, 1989, mem. editorial bd. 1987-94; vis. lectr. U. Pitts., 1991; vis. prof. internal medicine, U. Va., 1989; adj. prof. dept. biostatistics, Johns Hopkins U., 1988—; mem. external adv. bd. to Ctr. for AIDS Rsch., U. Wash., 1989-93; mem. adv. bd. biostatistics dept. Harvard U., Sch. Pub. Health, 1995; Charles Odoroff Meml. lectr., U. Rochester, 1996. Mem. editorial bd. Jour. AIDS, 1988—; contbr. articles to profl. jours. Fellow AAAS, Am. Statis. Assn. (chmn. biostatistiacs sect. 1986, bd. dirs. 1994-96); mem. Internat. Statis. Inst., Am. Soc. for Clin. Investigation. Soc. for Clin. Trials (chmn. program com. 1981, bd. dirs. 1981-85), Soc. for Epidemiol. Rsch., Biometric Soc. (regional adv. bd. 1981-84), Washington Statistical Soc. (chmn. biostatistics program 1982), Internat. Statis. Inst., Internat. Chinese Statis. Assn. (hon.), Phi Beta Kappa. Office: NCI Divsn Cancer & Epidemiology EPS 8032 Bethesda MD 20892*

GAILEY, THOMAS CHANDLER, professional football coach; b. Gainesville, Ga., Jan. 5, 1952. BS in Phys. Edn., U. Fla., 1974. Grad. asst. U. Fla., 1974-75; defensive backfield coach Troy State U., 1976-79, head coach,

1983-84; defensive backfield coach Air Force, 1979-82; asst. coach Denver Broncos, NFL, 1989-90, offensive coord., wide receivers coach, 1989-90; head coach Birmingham Fire, WFL, 1991-92, Samford U., 1993; wide receivers coach Pitts. Steelers, NFL, 1994-95, offensive coord., 1996-98; coach Dallas Cowboys, 1998—. Office: care Dallas Cowboys One Cowboys Pkwy Irving TX 75063*

GAILIUS, GILBERT KEISTUTIS, manufacturing company executive; b. Boston, June 21, 1931; s. Joseph B. and Mary K. G.; B.S. in Bus. Adminstrn., Suffolk U., 1958; M.B.A., Boston Coll., 1962; m. Lillian P. Romanskis, Sept. 6, 1954; children—Gregory, Laura, Louise, Gilbert, Linda, Gary. Plant controller, staff asst. corp. controller Continental Group, N.Y.C., 1954-66; v.p. fin. Foster Grant Co., Inc., Leominster, Mass., 1966-77, Midland Glass Co., Cliffwood, N.J., 1977-78, Am. Biltrite Inc., Wellesley Hills, Mass., 1978—, also bd. dirs. Served with U.S. Army, 1952-54. Mem. Fin. Execs. Inst. Home: 616 Hayward Mill Rd Concord MA 01742-4609 Office: Am Biltrite Inc 57 River St Wellesley MA 02481-2006

GAILLARD, GEORGE SIDAY, III, architect; b. Miami, Fla., Apr. 24, 1941; s. George Siday and Sarah Margaret (Crawford) G.; m. Charlalee Bailey, 1965 (div. 1969); m. Sylvia Gayle Bridgewater, July 18, 1977; 1 child, Barron Matthew. B.S., Ga. Inst. Tech., 1965; postgrad., Ga. State U. Registered architect Ga. Sole propr. Fox Magnanimus, Atlanta, Ga., 1971-78, Gaillard & Assocs., Atlanta, 1978-81, 1983—; mgr. design dept. Deca Inc., Miami, 1982. Sculpture exhibited in group shows at Piedmont Arts Festival, 1971, 73. Cubmaster Cub Scouts Am., Stone Mountain, Ga., 1988-89. With USMCR, 1962-68. Mem. AIA (chmn. liason com. So. Coll. Tech. for Atlanta chpt. 1989-90), Huguenot Soc. S.C., Clan Lindsay Assn. U.S.A. Inc. (Ga. rep. 1989-95), St. Andrew's Soc. Atlanta (bd. dirs. 1996-98). Avocations: reading, camping, constructing and competing with blackpowder rifles.

GAILLARD, JOHN PALMER, JR., former government official, former mayor; b. Charleston, S.C., Apr. 4, 1920; s. John Palmer and Eleanor Ball (Lucas) G.; m. Lucy Huguenin Foster, July 15, 1944; children: John Palmer III, William Foster, Thomas Huguenin. LLD, The Citadel, 1975. Alderman City of Charleston, 1951-59, mayor, 1959-75; dep. asst. sec. for res. affairs Dept. Navy, Washington, 1975-77; v.p. Ruscon Corp., Charleston, S.C., 1977-86; bd. dirs. Home Fed. Savs. Bank (now South Trust Bank), Charleston. Pres. Mcpl. Assn. S.C., 1964-65. Lt. USNR, 1941-45. Mem. C. of C., St. Andrews Soc., U.S. Conf. Mayors (adv. bd. 1969, trustee), Am. Legion, Carolina Yacht Club, Hibernian Club, Charleston Club, Elks. Episcopalian. Home: 77 Montagu St Charleston SC 29401-1238

GAILLARD, MARY KATHARINE, physics educator; b. New Brunswick, N.J., Apr. 1, 1939; d. Philip Lee and Marion Catharine (Wiedemayer) Ralph; children: Alain, Dominique, Bruno. BA, Hollins (Va.) Coll., 1960; MA, Columbia U., 1961; Dr du Troiseme Cycle, U. Paris, Orsay, France, 1964, Dr-es-Sciences d'Etat, 1968. With Ctr. Nat. Rsch. Sci., Orsay and Annecy-le-Vieux, France, 1964-84; head rsch. Ctr. Nat. Rsch. Sci., Orsay, 1973-80; head rsch. Ctr. Nat. Rsch. Sci., Annecy-le-Vieux, 1979-80, dir. rsch., 1980-84; prof. physics, sr. faculty staff Lawrence Berkeley lab. U. Calif., Berkeley, 1981—; Morris Loeb lectr. Harvard U., Cambridge, Mass., 1980; Chancellor's Disting. lectr., U. Calif., Berkeley, 1981; Warner-Lambert lectr. U. Mich., Ann Arbor, 1984; vis. scientist Fermi Nat. Accelerator Lab., Batavia, Ill., 1973-74, Inst. for Advanced Studies, Santa Barbara, Calif., 1984, U. Calif., Santa Barbara, 1985; group leader L.A.P.P., Theory Group, France, 1979-81, Theory Physics div. LBL, Berkeley, 1985-87; sci. dir. Les Houches (France) Summer Sch., 1981; cons., mem. adv. panels U.S. Dept. Energy, Washington; cons. Nat. Sci. Bd., 1996-97, bd. dirs., 1997—. Co-editor: Weak Interactions, 1977, Gauge Theories in High Energy Physics, 1983; contr. articles to profl. jours. Recipient Thibaux prize U. Lyons (France) Acad. Art & Sci., 1977, E.O. Lawrence award, 1988, J.J. Sakurai prize for theoretical particle physics, APS, 1993; Guggenheim fellow, 1989-90. Fellow Am. Acad. Arts and Scis., Am. Physics Soc. (mem. various coms., chairperson com. on women, J.J. Saburai prize 1993); mem. AAAS, NAS, Nat. Sci. Bd. Office: U Calif Dept Physics Berkeley CA 94720

GAINER, BARBARA JEANNE, radiology educator; b. Omaha, Dec. 9, 1938; d. Merrill Lester and Ressie (Kirby) Steele; m. Glenn Thomas Gainer, Oct. 26, 1968; 1 child, Kelly Jeanne Gainer. BA, Austin Coll., 1960; MD, U. Tex. Southwestern, 1966. Diplomate Am. Bd. Radiology. Rotating intern Meth. Hosp. Dallas, 1966-67, resident in diagnostic radiology, 1967-70; chief radiology RE Thomason Gen. Hosp., El Paso, Tex., 1971-77; pvt. practice Radiology Cons., El Paso, 1977-78; from asst. to assoc. prof. radiology Tex. Tech. Health Scis. Ctr., El Paso, 1978-90, prof., 1990—; med. advisor radiologic tech. program El Paso C.C., 1979—; chief med. staff Thomason Gen. Hosp., 1989-90. Bd. dirs. Planned Parenthood, El Paso, 1983-86. Mem. AMA, Am. Coll. Radiology (councilor), Radiol. Soc. N.Am., Tex. Radiol. Soc., Tex. Med. Assn., Assn. Univ. Radiologists. Republican. Presbyterian. Avocations: travel, stained glass, needlework, reading. Home: 8727 Marble Dr El Paso TX 79904-1709 Office: Tex Tech Health Scis Ctr at El Paso 4800 Alberta Ave El Paso TX 79905-2709*

GAINER, RONALD LEE, lawyer; b. Lansing, Mich., Aug. 7, 1934; s. Asher Leroy and Gladys Irene (Harvey) G.; m. Alice Louise Sherwood, June 15, 1957; children—Gregory Sherwood, Geoffrey Scott. B.A., Mich. State U., 1956; J.D., U. Mich., 1959. Bar: N.Y. 1960, D.C. 1963, U.S. Supreme Ct. 1963. Atty. appellate sect., criminal div. Dept. Justice, Washington, 1963-69; dep. chief legis. and spl. projects Dept. Justice, 1969-73, chief legis. and spl. projects, 1973-75, dir. Office of Policy and Planning, 1975-77; dep. asst. atty. gen. Office for Improvements in Adminstrn. of Justice, 1977-81; dep. asst. atty. gen. Office of Legal Policy, 1981-83, dep. assoc. atty. gen., 1984-85, assoc. dep. atty. gen., 1985-86, dep. assoc. atty. gen., 1986-89; ptnr. Gainer, Rient and Hotis, Washington, D.C., 1990—; U.S. expert mem. UN Com. on Crime Prevention and Control, 1979-92; designated mem. U.S. Sentencing Commn., 1985-88; bd. dirs., mem. adv. com. Internat. Centre Criminal Law Reform and Criminal Justice Policy, 1992—. Editorial bd.: Criminal Law Forum, 1989—. Bd. dirs. Found. Justice and Democracy in L.Am., 1997—.Served to capt. U.S. Army, 1960-63. Recipient Disting. Service award U.S. Atty. Gen., 1973. Mem. Am. Law Inst., Am. Soc. Internat. Law, Internat. Soc. for Reform of Criminal Law (bd. dirs., mem. mgmt. com., 1989—), Internat. Assn. Penal Law, D.C. Bar Assn. Home: 3000 N Monroe St Arlington VA 22207-5371 Office: Gainer Rient and Hotis Ste 690 1875 Connecticut Ave NW Washington DC 20009

GAINER, TERRANCE W., police official; m. Irene Gainer; 6 children. M in Mgmt. and Pub. Svc., DePaul U., JD. Patrolman, homicide detective, sgt. Chgo. Police Dept., 1968, chief legal officer, police trainer, adminstr.; spl. asst. U.S. Sec. Transp., 1989-91; dep. dir. Ill. State Police, Springfield, 1987-89, dir., 1991-98; asst. chief Met. Police Dept., Washington, 1998—. Capt USNR. Office: Met Police Dept 300 Indiana Ave NW Washington DC 20001*

GAINES, ANNE FARLEY, artist, art educator; b. Grand Rapids, Mich., May 19, 1954; d. Ralph Clay and Nancy Bogue (Farley) G. BA magna cum laude, Principia Coll., 1976; MA, Bowling Green State U., 1980, MFA, 1980. Instr. in color theory Internat. Acad. of Merchandising and Design, Chgo., 1987-92; commd. muralist Sara Lee Bakery Headqtrs., Chgo., 1992-93; artist in residence Chgo. Jr. Sch., Elgin, Ill., 1993-94; art tchr. grades 1-8 Chgo. Jr. Sch., Elgin, 1994-95; vis. asst. prof. art Ripon (Wis.) Coll., 1995-97; adj. prof. of art and humanities Moraine Valley C.C., Palos Hills, Ill., 1997—; vis. scholar Principia Coll., Elsah, Ill., 1989; owner, artist Pilsen Screens, Chgo., 1990—; mem. adv. bd. Collegiate Press, 1998—; instr. at art workshops, Chgo., Mich., Fla. Illustrator: (book) From Greek to Graffiti, English Words that Survive and Thrive, 1981; artist solo exhbns. include Lighthouse Gallery, Tequesta, Fla., 1983, South Haven (Mich.) Ctr. for Fine Arts, 1990, Wilderness at A.R.C. Gallery, Chgo., 1995, Strange Yards and Other Eulogies, Harper Coll., Palatine, Ill., Outer Depictions/Inward Questions, De Caprio Gallery, Moraine Valley C.C., Palos Hills, Ill., 1997; selected group exhbns.: Stockton State Coll., Pomona, N.J., 1985, Ill. State Mus., Springfield, 1985, Ukranian Inst. Art, Chgo., 1988, Alice and Arthur Baer Juried Competition, Beverly Art Ctr., Chgo., 1989, Quincy (Ill.) Art Ctr., 1989, Watercolor Alternatives -4 Chgo. artists- South Bend Art Ctr., Women's Art League Gallery, 1990, Botanics Gallery 10, Rockford, Ill. (1st place), 1991, Sacred Arts, Billy Graham Ctr. Mus., Wheaton (Ill.) Coll., 1992, Chgo. Botanic Gardens, Glencoe, Ill., 1992, Barrington (Ill.) Area Arts Coun. Gallery, 1993, Coll. Lake County, Grays Lake, Ill., 1993, Caestecker Gallery, Ripon (Wis.) Coll., 1995, P.E.A.C.E. Gallery, Chgo., 1996, Mus. Sci. and Industry, Chgo., 1996, Jacqueline Ross Gallery, Chgo., 1998; works in pub. collections: Am. Nat. Bank, Chgo., Borg Warner, Chgo., Bowling Green (Ohio) State U., G.A.T.X. Corp., Chgo., Nat. Soc. Am. Colls. and Univs., Washington, Rockford Art Mus., Sara Lee Bakery, Chgo.; major commns. include 21 x 8 mural, Conf. Rm., Bowling Green (Ohio) State U., 1979, 4 20 x 12 painted solar fabric murals, Sara Lee Bakery, Chgo., 1992-93, mixed media installation and watercolors, office suite, Fox Valley Neurosurger, McHenry Ill., 1995, 4 mixed-media panels Valley Hosp., Ridgewood, N.J., 1990. Lectr. com. chmn. 17th Ch. of Christ, Scientist, Chgo., 1996-98. Named Accomplished Gradn. Honoree in Fine Arts, Bowling Green (Ohio) State U., 1992; grantee: Ill. Arts Coun., Chgo., 1986, Ripon (Wis.) Coll., 1995, 96. Mem. Coll. Art Assn., Women's Caucus for Arts, Cgo. Artists Coalition, A.R.C. Gallery (grant chmn., chair self-portrait show 1984-86), Pilsen Artists (chair open house 1981, 90, fund raising 1991-95). Avocations: playing classical piano, choral singing, gourmet cooking, rehabbing Victorian house. Home: 713 W 19th St Chicago IL 60616-1023 Office: Pilsen Screens 1839 S Halsted St Chicago IL 60608-3455

GAINES, BARRY JOSEPH, English literature educator; b. Chgo., May 4, 1942; s. Gregory and Miriam (Davis) G.; m. Janet Colee Howe, Mar. 15, 1974; children: Gwendolyn Loren, Jason Micah Howe. BA, Rice U., 1965; MA, U. Wis., 1966, PhD, 1970. Prof. English lit. U. Tenn., Knoxville, 1970-79, U. N.Mex., Albuquerque, 1979—. Author: (book) Sir Thomas Malory: An Anecdotal Bibliography of Editions, 1990; co-editor: (book) A Yorkshire Tragedy, 1986; assoc. editor: Shakespeare Studies, 1974-93; mem. editl. bd.: Medieval and Renaissance Drama in England, 1983—; contbr. articles to lit. jours. Pres. Congregation Albert, Albuquerque, 1989-90. Recipient Disting. Educators award Pub. Svc. Co. of N.Mex. Found., 1992; Fulbright-Hays exch. scholar, 1987. Mem. MLA (chair del. assembly steering com. 1984-85), Shakespeare Assn. Am. (various offices), Phi Eta Sigma (Excellence in Tchg. award 1975), Phi Kappa Phi (hon., pres. 1997-98). Jewish. Home: 12809 Northern Sky NE Albuquerque NM 87111 Office: U NMex Dept English Albuquerque NM 87131

GAINES, EDWARD R., federal judge; b. 1940. BA, Miss. U., MA, JD, 1968. Ptnr. Palmer & Gaines, 1968-86; bankruptcy judge U.S. Dist. Ct. (so. dist.) Miss., 1986—; pros. atty., Gulfport, Miss. Office: US Dist Ct (so dist) Miss 725 Washington Loop Rm 117 Biloxi MS 39530-2448

GAINES, FRANCIS PENDLETON, III, lawyer; b. Lexington, Va., Sept. 24, 1944; s. Francis Pendleton Jr. and Dorothy Ruth (Bloomhardt) G.; m. Mary Chilton, Dec. 19, 1967 (div. Aug. 1992); children: Elizabeth Chilton, Edmund Pendleton, Andrew Cavett. BA in Hist., U. Ariz., 1967; LLB, U. Va., 1969. Bar: U.S. Dist. Ct. (Ariz.) 1969, Ariz. 1969, U.S. Ct. Appeals (9th cir.) 1972, U.S. Supreme Ct. 1975. Assoc. Evans, Kitchel & Jenckes, Phoenix, 1969-75, ptnr., 1975-89; ptnr. Fennemore Craig, Phoenix, 1989—; mem. panel arbitrators N.Y. Stock Exch., 1984—, NASD, 1984—; judge pro tem Ariz. Ct. Appeals, 1994-95, Maricopa County (Ariz.) Superior Ct., 1994—; mem. State Bar Disciplinary Hearing Com., 1991—, chair, 1995-97; mem. nat. litig. panel U. Va. Sch. Law; lectr. and panelist various CLE programs. Author: Punitive Damages-A Railroad Trial Lawyers Guide, 1985. Sr. warden All Saints' Episcopal Ch., 1994-97, parish chancellor, 1997—; mem. standing com. Episcopal Diocese of Ariz., 1997—; chmn. bd. govs. All Saints' Day Sch., Phoenix, 1990-91; chmn. Phoenix planned giving subcom. U. Ariz., 1985. Fellow Am. Bar Found., Ariz. Bar Found.; mem. ABA, State Bar Ariz., Maricopa County Bar Assn., Nat. Assn. Railroad Trial Coun. (exec. com. Pacific region, v.p. 1997-98), Ariz. Assn. Def. Coun., Securities Industry Assn. (law and compliance divsn.), Univ. Club, Internat. Wine & Food Soc. (Phoenix br.). Republican. Episcopalian. Office: Fennemore Craig 3003 N Central Ave Ste 2600 Phoenix AZ 85012-2913

GAINES, HOWARD CLARKE, retired lawyer; b. Washington, Sept. 6, 1909; s. Howard Wright and Ruth Adeline-Clarke Thomas Gaines; m. Audrey Allen, July 18, 1936; children: Clarke Allen, Margaret Anne. J.D., Cath. U. Am., 1936. Bar: D.C. bar 1936, U.S. Supreme Ct. bar 1946, U.S. Ct. Claims bar 1947, Calif. bar 1948. Individual practice law Washington, 1938-43, 46-47, Santa Barbara, Calif., 1948-51; assoc. firm Price, Postel & Parma, Santa Barbara, 1951-54; partner Price, Postel & Parma, 1954-88; of counsel, 1989-94, ret., 1994; chmn. Santa Barbara Bench and Bar Com., 1972-74. Chmn. Santa Barbara Police and Fire Commn., 1948-52; mem. adv. bd. Santa Barbara Com. on Alcoholism, 1956-67; bd. dirs. Santa Barbara Humane Soc., 1958-69, 85-92; bd. trustees Santa Barbara Botanic Garden, 1960—, v.p., 1967-69; bd. trustees Cancer Found. Santa Barbara, 1960-77; dir. Santa Barbara Mental Health Assn., 1957-59, v.p., 1959; pres. Santa Barbara Found., 1976-79, trustee, 1979—. Fellow Am. Bar Found.; mem. ABA, Bar Assn. D.C., State Bar Calif. (gov. 1969-72, v.p. 1971-72, tres. 1971-72), Santa Barbara County Bar Assn. (pres. 1957-58), Am. Judicature Soc., Santa Barbara Club. Republican. Episcopalian. Home: 1306 Las Alturas Rd Santa Barbara CA 93103-1600 *Strive for a career in productive work you truly enjoy. Give due respect to others and their opinions. Learn to listen before voicing criticism or giving constructive advice. Season your life with a little humor.*

GAINES, IRVING DAVID, lawyer; b. Milw., Oct. 14, 1923; s. Harry and Anna (Finkelman) Ginsburg; m. Ruth Rudolph, May 22, 1947 (dec. Apr. 5, 1979); children: Jeffrey S., Howard R., Mindy S. Gaines Pearce; m. Lois Shier, Nov. 25, 1979. BA, U. Wis., Madison, 1943; JD, 1947; postgrad., U. Pa., 1943-44. Bar: Wis. 1947, Fla. 1971, U.S. Dist. Ct. (ea. dist.) Wis. 1947, U.S. Dist. Ct. (we. dist.) Wis. 1970, U.S. Dist. Ct. (so. dist.) Fla. 1972, U.S. Dist. Ct. (mid. dist.) Fla. 1976, U.S. Ct. Appeals (7th cir.) 1954, U.S. Ct. Appeals (11th cir.) 1981, U.S. Supreme Ct. 1954. Sole practice Milw., 1947-72; ptnr. Gaines & Saichek, S.C. (and predecessor firm), Milw., 1972-78; sr. ptnr. Gaines Law Offices, S.C., Milw., 1979—; arbitrator N.Y. Stock Exchange, Nat. Assn. Securities Dealers, Am. Stock Exchange, Am. Arbitration Assn. 1988—. Mem. bd. visitor U. Wis. Law Sch., 1987-96, Cir. Ct. Commn., 1997—. Served with AUS, 1943-46. Mem. ABA (various coms.), Fla. Bar Assn. (past mem. exec. com., cts. com., econs. law com., past chn. unauthorized practice of law com., past chmn. negligence sect., lectr. programs, seminars), State Bar Assn. Wis. (bd. govs. 1982-85, comms. com. 1981-85, 88-91), 7th Fed. Cir. Bar Assn., Wis. Acad. Trial Lawyers (pres. 1958-59, 70-71). Home: 7821 N Mohawk Rd Milwaukee WI 53217-3123 Office: 312 E Wisconsin Ave Ste 208 Milwaukee WI 53202-4305

GAINES, JAMES EDWIN, JR., retired librarian; b. Dalton, Ga., Feb. 21, 1938; s. James Edwin and Olivia (McCarty) G.; m. Sally Martin, Nov. 27, 1965 (div. May 29, 1985); chiildren: Thomas Martin, Robin Jeannette, Steven McCarty; m. Elizabeth Hood, July 28, 1990. AB, Emory U., 1961, MLS, 1964; PhD, Fla. State U., 1977. Tchr. English Marist Coll. H.S., Atlanta, 1961-62; grad. library asst. Emory U., Atlanta, 1962-64; asst. to head of pub. services U. Cin., Cin., 1964-65; asst. cataloger Antioch Coll., Yellow Springs, Ohio, 1965-68; dir. library Birmingham-So. Coll., Birmingham, Ala., 1968-74; head librarian Va. Mil. Inst., Lexington, 1976-93; ret., 1994. Contbr. articles to profl. jours. Mem. Com. on Fgn. Rels., Charlottesville, Va., 1982-91; sec. ARC, Rockbridge County, Va., 1993-98, Rockbridge Disability Svcs. Bd., 1993—. Mem. ALA, Va. Libr. Assn. (chmn. coll. and univ. sect. 1979-80), So. Assn. Colls. and Schs. (vis. committeeman 1969-98), Kiwanis (sec. 1985-92). Democrat. Presbyterian. E-mail: Gainesje@vmi.edu. Home: 9 Edmondson Ave Lexington VA 24450-1903

GAINES, JAMES RUSSELL, magazine editor, author; b. Dayton, Ohio, Aug. 11, 1947; s. Robert William and Harriet Elizabeth (Fenner) G.; m. Leslie Friedman, May 23, 1971 (div. 1978); 1 child, Allison; m. Pamela Butler, July 9, 1983 (div. 1989); m. Karen Lipton, Feb. 9, 1992; children: Nicolas L., William S., Lillian B. B in Gen. Studies, U. Mich., 1970. Editor The Herald, N.Y.C., 1971-72; assoc. editor Saturday Rev., N.Y.C. and San Francisco, 1972-73, Sta. WNET/13—The 51st State, N.Y.C., 1973-74, Newsweek, N.Y.C., 1974-76; assoc. editor People Mag., N.Y.C., 1977-78, sr. editor, 1979-82, asst. mng. editor, 1982-86, exec. editor, 1986-87, mng. editor, 1987-89; mng. editor and publisher Life, N.Y.C., 1989-92; mng. editor Time Mag., N.Y.C., 1993-95; corp. editor Time Inc., N.Y.C., 1996-97; editor-in-chief Travel & Leisure/Golf mag., Boulder, 1998—. Author: Wit's End: Days and Nights of the Algonquin Round Table, 1977; author, editor: The Lives of the Piano, 1981. Office: 1942 Broadway St Ste 201 Boulder CO 80302-5213*

GAINES, JERRY LEE, secondary education educator; b. Seminole, Okla., Feb. 18, 1940; s. Frank Gaines and Jane M. (Crowe) Gring; m. Lorraine Louise Paulson, Oct. 7, 1961; children: Paul Martin, Mark Edwin. AA, Pasadena City Coll., 1960; BA, Calif. State U., L.A., 1964; MA, Calif. State U., Long Beach, 1969. Tchr. bus. Rolling Hills High Sch., Rolling Hills Estates, Calif., 1965-91, Palos Verdes Peninsula High Sch., Rolling Hills Estates, 1991—; coord. driver edn. Palos Verdes Peninsula Unified Sch. Dist., Palos Verdes Estates, Calif., 1970-91, mentor tchr., 1984-93. Co-author driver edn. workbook; contbr. articles to traffic safety publs. Chmn. San Pedro (Calif.) Citizens Adv. Com., 1985-88; pres. South Shores Homeowners Assn., San Pedro, 1986-90, 95-96, San Pedro and Peninsula Homeowners Coalition, 1990-93; commr. City of L.A. Charter Reform Commn., 1997-99. With USN, 1960-62. Mem. NEA, Calif. Tchrs. Assn., Palos Verdes Faculty Assn., Nat. Bus. Edn. Assn., Calif. Bus. Edn. Assn., Am. Driver and Traffic Safety Edn. Assn. (bd. dirs. 1982-88), Calif. Assn. Safety Edn. (pres. 1982-83, 98—), Elks, Phi Delta Kappa. Avocations: travel, model railroading. Home: 2101 W 37th St San Pedro CA 90732-4707 Office: Palos Verdes Peninsula High Sch 27118 Silver Spur Rd Palos Verdes Peninsula CA 90274-2300

GAINES, LA DONNA ADRIAN See **SUMMER, DONNA**

GAINES, MICHAEL JOHNSTON, parole commissioner. Grad., U. Ark., 1973, JD, 1977. Bar: Ark. 1977, U.S. Dist. Ct. Ark. 1977, U.S. Supreme Ct. 1977. Pvt. practice law, 1977-78; parole hearing examiner Ark. Dept. Correction, 1978-83; criminal justice liaison and pardon and extradition counsel Gov. Bill Clinton, 1983-86; exec. dir. Ark. Supreme Ct. Com. on Profl. Conduct, 1986-89; mem. Ark. Bd. Parole, 1986-89, chmn., 1989; chmn. U.S. Parole Commn., 1994—; mem. staff Gov. Dale Bumpers, Gov. David Pryor; mem. Bd. Correction, Gov.'s Corrections Resources Commn., Gov.'s Task Force on Crime. Mem. ABA (corrections and sentencing com., criminal justice sect.), Assn. Paroling Authorities Internat. (coun. of chairs), Am. Correctional Assn., Am. Probation and Parole Assn. FAX: 301-492-5307. Office: US Parole Commn 5550 Friendship Blvd Chevy Chase MD 20815-7256

GAINES, PETER MATHEW, lawyer; b. N.Y.C., Mar. 5, 1951; s. Dan M. and Ellen M. Gaines; m. Jane Lausch, July 14, 1972; children: Matthew P., Elizabeth C., Carolyn E. BA, U. Wis., 1972, JD, 1975. Bar: Ill. 1975; N.Y. 1988. Assoc. Mayer, Brown & Platt, Chgo., 1975-81, ptnr., 1982-90; ptnr. Mayer, Brown & Platt, London, 1990-95, Baker & McKenzie, London, 1995—. Note and comment editor U. Wis. Law Rev., 1975. Mem. ABA. Office: Baker & McKenzie, 100 New Bridge Sheet, London EC4V 6JA, England

GAINES, ROBERT DARRYL, lawyer, food services executive; b. Kansas City, Mo., May 27, 1951; s. Ralph Robert and Betty June (Crawford) G.; m. Shanette Carrol Kirch, Aug. 14, 1977; 1 child, Ariel Kirch. BA, U. Ariz., 1972; MBA, Mich. State U., 1973; JD, U. Mo., Kansas City, 1983. Bar: Mo. 1983, Ariz. 1983. Pvt. practice law Kansas City, 1983—; pres. Colony Lobster Pot Co., Kansas City, 1984—, Colony Pla Co., Kansas City, 1985—. Mem. ABA, Mo. Bar Assn., Ariz. Bar Assn., Kansas City Bar Assn., Nat. Restaurant Assn., Mo. Restaurant Assn., Phi Delta Phi (treas. 1982-83). Avocations: flying, racquetball. Home: 11201 Madison Ave Kansas City MO 64114-5238 also: 8821 State Line Rd Kansas City MO 64114-2704

GAINES, ROBERT MARTIN, lawyer; b. Hartford, Conn., Nov. 27, 1931; s. Charles Edward and Ellen Marie (Hammerstrom) G.; m. Joan Isabel Sanderson, May 20, 1961 (div. Oct. 1983); children: Todd, Dayna; m. Julie Ann Ramsdell, May 11, 1985. AB, U. Conn., 1953, JD, 1956. Bar: Conn. 1956, U.S. Ct. Mil. Appeals 1959, U.S. Dist. Ct. Conn. 1961, U.S. Tax Ct., 1994. Assoc. Regnier & Moller, Hartford, 1960-62; asst. counsel Pratt & Whitney, East Hartford, Conn., 1962—. Mem. Somers (Conn.) Bd. Edn., 1968-70. With USAF, 1957-60. Mem. Am. Corp. Counsel Assn. Republican. Roman Catholic. Avocations: sports, music. Home: 44163 S Main St Manchester CT 06040

GAINES, RUTH ANN, educator. BA in Drama and Speech, Clarke Coll.; MA in Dramatic Art, U. Calif., Santa Barbara. Drama tchr. East High Sch., Des Moines; host Classroom Connection Cable TV; former TV/radio prodr., talk show host TCI of Ctrl. Iowa, WHO; facilitator Heartland Area Edn. Agy., Des Moines. Bd. dirs. Very Spl. Arts, Hospice of Ctrl. Iowa, Westminster Ho.; former bd. dirs. YWCA of Greater Des Moines, Polk County Mental Health Assn., Drama Workshop, Des Moines Tutoring Ctr.; vice chair City Wide Strategic Plan, 1994-95; state senate candidate, 1994; racial justice coord. YWCA, 1992-93; chair Cross Cultural Rels., Des Moines Area Religious Coun., 1988-89; dir. religious edn. St. Ambrose Cathedral, 1981-83; grad. Leadership Iowa Class of 1997. Recipient Wal-Mart Tchr. of Yr., 1998, Iowa Tchr. of Yr., 1998. Mem. Des Moines and Iowa State Ednl. Assns., Delta Kappa Gamma, Phi Delta Kappa, Delta Sigma Theta. Home: 3501 Oxford Des Moines IA 50313 Office: East High Sch 815 East 13th St Des Moines IA 50316

GAINES, TYLER BELT, lawyer; b. Omaha, Oct. 21, 1924; s. Francis S. and Dorothy Tyler (Belt) G.; m. Elizabeth Bush Caldwell, Feb. 24, 1951; children: Katherine C., Elizabeth D., David T., Sarah B., Mary C.; m. Agneta Margareta Anderhagen, Nov. 27, 1977; stepchildren: Anna C., Anders C. Student Yale U., 1942-43, U. Omaha, 1946; LLB, Nebr. U., 1949. Bar: Nebr. 1949, U.S. Supreme Ct. 1964, U.S. Ct. Appeals (8th cir.) 1953, U.S. Dist. Ct. Nebr. 1949, U.S. Tax Ct. 1970. Ptnr., Gaines, Mullen, Pansing & Hogan and predecessor firms, Omaha, 1960—. Bd. dirs. Gilbert and Martha Hitchcock Found., 1970—, Kirkpatrick Charity Found., 1991—, Brownell Talbot Sch. Found., 1994—, Forest Lawn Cemetary, 1960—. Served with USNR, 1943-45. Mem. Am. Coll. Probate Counsel, Nebr. Bar Assn., Omaha Bar Assn. (pres. 1982-83). Republican. Episcopalian. Clubs: Omaha Country, Omaha. Office: Gaines Mullen Pansing & Hogan 10050 Regency Cir Ste 200 Omaha NE 68114-3721

GAINES, WEAVER HENDERSON, lawyer; b. Ft. Meade, S.D., Aug. 31, 1943; s. Weaver Henderson and Bertha Louise (Harris) G. AB in Philosophy, Dartmouth Coll., 1965; LLB, U. Va., 1968. Bar: N.Y. 1969, Pa. 1979, U.S. Dist. Ct. (so. dist.) N.Y. 1973, U.S. Dist. Ct. (ea. dist.) N.Y. 1975, U.S. Ct. Appeals (2d cir.) 1975. Assoc. Dewey, Ballantine, Bushby, Palmer & Wood, N.Y.C., 1970-79; sr. staff counsel INA Corp., Phila., 1979; asst. gen. counsel, sec. Thyssen-Bornemisza Inc., N.Y.C., 1979-82, v.p. strategic projects, 1982-85; v.p., dep. gen. counsel Mut. of N.Y., N.Y.C., 1985-86, sr. v.p., gen. counsel, 1986-90, exec. v.p., gen. counsel, 1990-92; pres. Unified Mgmt. Corp., 1989-90; chmn., CEO Ixion Biotechnology, Inc., Alachua, Fla., 1993—; bd. dirs. First ING Life Ins. Co. of N.Y., Unified Fin. Svcs., Inc., Voyetra Turtle Beach, Inc., Ixion Biotechnology, Inc., BIO Fla. Inc., North Fla. Tech. Inovation Corp., Dance Alive!. Bd. dirs. N.Y. Lawyers for Nixon, 1972; sr. advisor Bush/Quayle '92. Capt. U.S. Army, 1968-70, Vietnam. Decorated Bronze Star. Mem. ABA, Assn. of Bar of City of N.Y., Am. Corp. Counsel Assn., Assn. Life Ins. Counsel, N.Y. Athletic Club, Haile Plantation Golf and Country Club. Republican. Episcopalian. Office: Ixion Biotechnology Inc 13709 Progress Blvd Box 13 Alachua FL 32615-9495

GAINES, WILLIAM CHESTER, journalist; b. Indpls., Nov. 1, 1933; s. Philip Damon and Georgia Agnes (Smith) G.; m. Nellie Gilyan; children: Michael, Michelle, Matthew. BS in Broadcasting, Butler U., 1956. TV announcer Sta. WKZO-TV, Kalamazoo, 1958-59; reporter Sta. WWCA Radio, Gary, Ind., 1959-60, Sta. WJOB Radio, Hammond, Ind., 1960-63; pres. Sta. WAMJ Radio, South Bend, Ind., 1983-88; from reporter to investigative reporter Chgo. Tribune, 1963—; instr. Columbia Coll., Chgo., 1974-98; bd. advisors Fund for Investigative Journalism, Inc. Author: Investigative Reporting in Print and Broadcast, 1992. Recipient Pulitzer prize in Journalism, Columbia U., N.Y.C., 1976, 1988, Peter Lisagor award Chgo. Headline Club, 1986, 87. Office: Chgo Tribune 435 N Michigan Ave Chicago IL 60611-4066*

GAINES NELSON, TAMI CAMARI, management consultant; b. Boston, Nov. 29, 1967; d. Richard Denis and Camari Lea (Tomlin) Gaines; m. Bruce Philip Nelson, Aug. 28, 1995; 1 child, Haili Sage. BA, Tufts U., 1989; MBA, Columbia U., 1993. Account exec. Lehman Advt., N.Y.C., 1989-90; consumer affairs rep. Colgate Palmolive Co., N.Y.C., 1990-91, ethnic mktg. asst., 1992-93, assoc. product mgr., 1993-94; mktg. mgr. Martin Hummel, Inc., N.Y.C., 1994-95; dir. mktg. Am. Safety Razor, Charlottesville, Va., 1995-97; pres. G2 Consulting, Inc., Montclair, N.J., 1997—; founding ptnr. Agnes' Very Very Bagels, Charlottesville, Va.; adv. bd. The Marketplace, Richmond, Va., Work@Home Mag., Rancho Sante Fe, Calif.; lectr. U. Va., Charlottesville, 1997. Literacy vol. Literacy Vols. of Am., N.J., 1991-95; mentor Yang Entrepreneurs Club, N.Y.C., 1991-93. Mem. NAFE, Am. Mktg. Assn., Am. Mgmt. Assn., C. of C. Episcopalian. Avocations: creative fiction writing, sports, cooking without recipes. Office: G2 Consulting Inc 41 Watchung Plz Ste 341 Montclair NJ 07042-4117

GAINEY, ROBERT MICHAEL, professional hockey coach, former player; b. Peterborough, Ont., Can., Dec. 13, 1953. Hockey player Montreal Canadiens, 1973-89; coach, player Les Ecureuils, Epinal, France; head coach, gen. mgr. Minn. North Stars, NHL, 1990—; now v.p., gen. mgr. Dallas Stars. Recipient Frank J. Selke award as Best Defensive Forward, 1977-78, 78-79, 79-80; Conn Smythe trophy as Most Valuable Player Nat. Hockey League Playoffs, 1978-79; elected to Hockey Hall of Fame, 1992. *

GAINOR, THOMAS EDWARD, banker; b. St. Paul, Oct. 13, 1933; s. Joseph Paul and Teresa Cecilia (Whelan) G.; m. Janan Rose Nolan, Aug. 8, 1964; children: Mary, Michael, John, Daniel. B.S., Marquette U., 1955; postgrad., Stonier Grad. Sch. Banking, Rutgers U., 1965-67, Stanford U. Exec. Program, 1977. With Fed. Res. Bank of Mpls., 1958-93, asst. v.p., 1967-72, v.p., 1972-75, sr. v.p. ops., 1975-78, 1st v.p., 1978-93. Bd. dirs. Mpls. United Way, 1974-83, v.p., 1974-77; bd. dirs. Vis. Nurse Svc., 1967-75, pres., 1971-72; trustee Visitation Sch., 1983-89, v.p., 1985, chmn., 1986-88; mem. Commn. Archdiocesan Programs, 1983-89, chmn., 1986-87; trustee St. Joseph's Ch., 1985—; trustee St. Thomas Acad., 1989-98, chmn., 1992-98; bd. dirs. St. John Vianney Sem., 1986—, Cath. Charities, 1990-96; pres. Cath. Cmty. Found., 1994—; internat. adv. coun. Am. Grad. Sch. Internat. Rels. and Diplomacy, Paris, 1997—; bd. dirs. Total Life Care Ctrs., 1998—. Served as officer USNR, 1955-58. Mem. Stanford Alumni Assn., Marquette U. Alumni Assn., Naval Res. Assn. Roman Catholic. Club: Six o'Clock (pres. 1982).

GAINSBURG, ROY ELLIS, publishing executive; b. Bklyn., May 1, 1932; s. Herbert Harry Gainsburg and Etta (Stein) Kornfeld; m. Vicki Bloye, July 12, 1957; children: Julie, Jeanne. AB, Brown U., 1954; LLB, Harvard U., 1957. Bar: N.Y. 1957. From assoc. to ptnr. Szold & Brandwen, N.Y.C., 1957-87; exec. v.p. St. Martin's Press Inc., N.Y.C., 1987, pres., 1987-97, part-time v.p. adminstrn., 1997—; bd. dirs. Grove's Dictionaries, Inc. Treas., bd. dirs. The Partnership for the Homeless, N.Y.C. Democrat. Home: 157 Ralston Ave South Orange NJ 07079-2344 Office: St Martin's Press Inc 175 5th Ave Fl 4 New York NY 10010-7848

GAINTNER, RICHARD J., health facility administrator; b. Lancaster, Pa., Feb. 18, 1936. MD, John Hopkins U., 1962. CEO Shands Hosp., Gainesville, Fla., 1997—. Mem. Gainesville Country Club, Havard Club, Duxbury Yacht Club. Office: 1600 SW Archer Rd Gainesville FL 32610

GAIPA, NANCY CHRISTINE, pharmacist; b. Benton Harbor, Mich., Oct. 11, 1949; d. Frank Thomas and Anne Marie (Scardina) G. BS, Marygrove Coll., Detroit, 1971; BS in Pharmacy, Wayne State U., 1992; postgrad., Ferris State U., 1996. Registered pharmacist, Mich.; cert. secondary educator, Mich. Educator Regina H.S., Harper Woods, Mich., 1971-88; staff pharmacist Perry Drugs, Northville, Mich., 1993, Meijers, Inc., Westland, Mich., 1993-97, F&M Drug Emporium, Bloomfield Hills, Mich., 1997-98, Walgreen's, Livonia, Mich., 1998—, Providence Hosp. and Med. Ctrs., Southfield, Mich., 1998. Vol. Detroit Welfare Reform Coalition, 1989-91, Maral, Southfield, Mich., 1991. State of Mich. scholar, 1967-71. Mem. AAUW, NOW, Detroit Area Women's Network, Am. Pharm. Assn., Mich. Pharmacists Assn. (mem. ho. of dels.), Oakland County Pharmacists Assn., Southeastern Mich. Soc. Health-System Pharmacists, Golden Key Nat. Honor Soc., Women Matter, Iota Gamma Alpha, Rho Chi. Office: Providence Hosp and Med Ctrs 37595 Seven Mile Rd Livonia MI 48152-1003

GAIR, KEVIN LINDSEY, learning director, educator; b. Baldwin Park, Calif., Dec. 21, 1958; s. Robert Corrington and Nora Linda (Lindsey) G.; m. Beverly Helen Wood, May 1, 1982; children: Stephanie Renee, Cristine Nicole. BA, Calif. State Poly. U., 1984; MEd in Adminstrn., Point Loma Nazarene Coll., 1990; PhD, LaSalle U., 1996; JD, Northwestern Calif. U., 1999. Clear credential, Calif. Dept. Edn. Police officer Glendora (Calif.) Police Dept., 1981-83; security host Disneyland, Anaheim, Calif., 1983-84; history, computer and sci. tchr. Baldwin Park Unified Sch. Dist., 1984-91; history tchr. Fowler (Calif.) Unified Sch. Dist., 1991-94, mentor tchr., 1994-95; learning dir. Kings Canyon Unified Sch. Dist., Reedley, Calif., 1995—; mem. various sch. coms. including chair history dept., mem. tech. com. Fowler H.S., 1993-95; chair tech. com., mem. Parent Tchr. Club and sch. site coun. Dunlap Sch., 1995-96; adj. prof. edn. Nat. U., Fresno, 1996-99. Author: Dark Descent, 1993, Dark Descent II, 1995; editor-in-chief Baldwin Park Press, 1988; author of short stories. Mem. Shannon Valley Property Owners, Squaw Valley, Calif., 1991-96, Squaw Valley Coun., 1995-96; vol. firefighter Mountain Valley Fire Dept., Dunlap, Calif., 1995—. Recipient Cert. of Merit, Calif. State Senate, 1990. Mem. Free and Accepted Mason. Avocations: music, aerobics, reading. Home: 33088 Coyote Ln Squaw Valley CA 93675-9733 Office: Dunlap Sch PO Box 100 Dunlap CA 93621-0100

GAISSER, JULIA HAIG, classics educator; b. Cripple Creek, Colo., Jan. 12, 1941; d. Henry Wolseley and Gertrude Alice (Lent) Haig; m. Thomas Korff Gaisser, Dec. 29, 1964; 1 child, Thomas Wolseley. AB, Brown U., 1962; MA, Harvard U., 1966; PhD, U. Edinburgh, Scotland, 1966. Asst. prof. Newton (Mass.) Coll., 1966-69, Swarthmore (Pa.) Coll., 1970-72, Bklyn. Coll., 1973-75; assoc. prof. dept. Latin Bryn Mawr (Pa.) Coll., 1975-84, prof., 1984—. Author: Catullus and his Renaissance Readers, 1993; editor Bryn Mawr Latin Commentaries, 1983—. Mem. Mid-East sel. com. Marshall Scholarships, Washington, 1975-89, chmn., 1984-89; mem. mng. com. Intercollegiate Ctr. for Classical Studies in Rome, Stanford, Calif., 1984-92, chmn., 1988-92. Decorated MBE; MArshall scholar U. Edinburgh, 1962-64, NEH summer stipend, 1977, Phi Beta Kappa Vis. scholar, 1996-97; rsch. grantee Am. Philos. Soc., 1980, 93, ACLS Trael grantee, 1985, fellow, 1989-90; NEH sr. fellow, 1985-86, 93-94, 99. Mem. Am. Philos. Assn. (dir. 1985-88), Renaissance Soc. Am., Intenrat. Neo Latin Soc. Office: Bryn Mawr Coll Dept Latin Bryn Mawr PA 19010

GAITAN, FERNANDO J., JR., federal judge; b. 1948. Student, Kansas City (Kans.) C.C., 1966-67, Donnelly Coll., 1967-68, Pittsburg State U., 1968-70; JD, U. Mo., Kansas City, 1974. Atty. Southwestern Bell Telephone Co., 1974-80; judge 16th jud. cir. Jackson County Cir. Ct., 1980-86; judge Mo. Ct. Appeals (we. dist.), 1986-91; fed. judge U.S. Dist. Ct. (we. dist.) Mo., Kansas City, 1991—. Past pres. bd. dirs. De La Salle Edn. Ctr., Inc., 1985-87, active, 1983—; active Kansas City Mus., 1988—, St. Luke's Hosp., Kansas City, 1984—, NAACP, 1982—, NCCJ, 1984—. Mem. ABA, Mo. Bar Assn., Kansas City Met. Bar Assn., Lawyers' Assn., Jackson County Bar Assn., Univ. Club, Hillcrest Country Club, U. Mo. Kansas City Law Found., KCMC Child Devel. Corp., Kappa Alpha Psi. Office: US Dist Ct 7952 US Cthouse 400 E Ninth St Kansas City MO 64106-1904*

GAITHER, GEORGE MANNEY, marketing consultant; b. Mineola, N.Y., Sept. 21, 1930; s. Roscoe Bradley and Frances Bullitt (Williams) G.; m. Dorothy Wineman Streater, Apr. 4, 1953; children: Neal, George, Anne, Emee, Bruce. *A pioneer in international marketing and political research, he is a 12th generation descendant of John Gaither, who emigrated from England to Jamestown, Virginia, in 1620, and a descendant on his maternal side from Jeremiah Routh, one of the First Families of Mississippi (1699-1817). Wife Dorothy is one of the trademark "Three Little Girls" of Daytona Beach, Florida, and years later in 1950 was legally adopted at age 18 by that city.* B in Journalism, U. Mo., 1952. From gen. mgr. to pres. Internat. Rsch. Assocs., Inc., N.Y.C., 1955-71; pres., founder Gaither Internat., Inc., Stamford, Conn., 1971-96; pres. cons. GMG Cons., Winchester, Va., 1997—. Lt. U.S. Army, 1952-55, Korea. Mem. Market Rsch. Coun. Republican. Avocation: writing. Home: 2628 Windwood Dr Winchester VA 22601-6418

GAITHER, JAMES C., lawyer; b. Oakland, Calif., Sept. 3, 1937; s. Horace Rowan Jr. and Charlotte Cameron (Castle) G.; m. Susan Good, Apr. 30, 1960; children: James Jr., Whitaker, Reed, Kendra. BA in Econs., Princeton U., 1959; JD, Stanford U., 1964. Bar: Calif. 1964, U.S. Dist. Ct. D.C. 1965, U.S. Dist. Ct. (no. dist.) Calif. 1965, U.S. Ct. Appeals (D.C. cir., 7th cir., 9th cir.), 1965, U.S. Supreme Ct. Law clk. to chief justice Earl Warren, Washington, 1964-65; spl. asst. to asst. atty. gen. John W. Douglas, Washington, 1965-66; staff asst. Pres. Lyndon B. Johnson, Washington, 1966-69; atty. Cooley Godward LLP, San Francisco, 1969-71, ptnr., 1971—, mng. ptnr., 1984-90; cons. to sec. HEW, 1977, chmn. ethics adv. bd., 1977-80; bd. dirs. Basic Am. Inc., San Francisco, Levi Strauss & Co., San Francisco, Amylin Pharms., Inc., San Diego, Siebel Sys., San Mateo; mVidia Corp., Santa Clara; chmn. James Irvine Found.; vice chair Carnegie Endowment for Internat. Peace; dir. Hewlett Found.; trustee The RAND Corp. Note editor Stanford Law Rev., 1963-64. Former pres. bd. trustees, Stanford (Calif.) U.; mem. exec. com. bd. vis. Sch. Law Stanford U.; former chmn. bd. trustees Branson Sch., Ross, Calif., Ctr. for Biotech. Rsch. San Francisco; past trustee Family Svc. Agy. San Francisco, St. Stephens Parish Day Sch., Belvedere, Calif., The Scripps Rsch. Inst.; past trustee, chmn. protem Marin Cmty. Found. Marin County, Calif.; past pres. bd. trustees Marin County Day Sch., Corte Madera; past pres. bd. trustees Marin Ednl. Found., San Rafael; past treas., trustee Rosenberg Found.; past v.p., trustee, vice chmn. San Francisco Devel. Fund; past chmn. Dean's Adv. Coun. Stanford Law Sch., chmn. capital campaign; Inst. Capt. USMC, 1959-61. Recipient Disting. Pub. Svc. award HEW, 1977, Stanford Assocs. award Stanford U., 1989, 97; named Entrepreneur of Yr. Harvard Bus. Sch., 1979. Fellow Am. Acad. Arts and Scis.; mem. ABA, Calif. Bar Assn., San Francisco Bar Assn., Order of Coif, Phi Delta Phi (province 12). Democrat. Presbyterian. Avocations: tennis, hiking, camping, fishing, photography. Office: Cooley Godward LLP 1 Maritime Plz Fl 20 San Francisco CA 94111-3404

GAITHER, JOHN F., lawyer; b. Evansville, Ind., Mar. 31, 1949; s. John F. and Marjilee G.; m. Christine Luby, Nov. 26, 1971; children: John F. III, Maria Theresa. BA in Acctg., U. Notre Dame, 1971, JD, 1974. Bar: Ind. 1974, Ill. 1975, U.S. Ct. Appeals (7th cir.) 1975, U.S. Ct. Mil. Appeals 1977. CPA, Ind. Law clk. to Hon. Wilbur F. Pell, Jr. Ct. of Appeals 7th Cir., Chgo., 1974-76; assoc. atty. Bell, Boyd & Lloyd, Chgo., 1979-82; sr. atty. Baxter Healthcare Corp., Deerfield, Ill., 1982-83, asst. sec., sr. atty., 1983-84, asst. sec., asst. gen. counsel, 1984-85; sec., assoc. gen. counsel Baxter Internat. Inc., Deerfield, 1985-87, sec., dep. gen. counsel, 1987-91; v.p. law/devel. Baxter Diagnostics Inc., Deerfield, 1991-92; v.p. law, strategic planning Baxter Global Businesses, Deerfield, 1992-93; dep. gen. counsel, v.p. strategic planning Baxter Internat. Inc., Deerfield, 1993-94, corp. v.p., corp. devel., 1994—. Editor-in-chief Notre Dame Lawyer, 1973-74; contbr. articles to profl. jours. Lt. comdr. USNR, 1976-79. Mem. ABA, Ill. Bar Assn., Ind. Bar Assn., Chgo. Bar Assn., Ind. Assn. CPAs. Avocations: sailing, skiing. Office: Baxter Internat Inc 1 Baxter Pkwy Deerfield IL 60015-4625

GAITHER, JOHN STOKES, chemical company executive; b. Boston, Apr. 20, 1944; s. Perry Stokes and Elizabeth (Hamlin) G.; m. Shirley Anne Anderson, July 10, 1982; children: Christina Elizabeth, Laura Anne. BA in Econs., U. Pa., 1967; MBA, European Inst. Bus. Adminstrn., Fountainebleau, France, 1973. With Reichhold Chems., Inc., 1967—; v.p. internat. sales and mktg. Reichhold Chems., Inc., White Plains, N.Y., 1978-79; sr. v.p. internat. Reichhold Chems., Inc., 1980-83, v.p. resins and binders div., 1984-85, pres. reactive polymers div., 1986-89, pres. emulsion polymers divsn., 1989-92; pres. coatings divsn. Reichold Chems. Inc., Research Triangle Park, N.C., 1992-95, exec. v.p., exec. leadership team, 1996—; bd. dirs. Reichhold Quimica de Mex., Resimon, Venezuela; pres., bd. dirs. Reichhold Ltd., Can. Mem. Soc. Plastics Industry, Nat. Paint and Coatings Assn. (bd. dirs. 1992-94). Republican. Episcopalian. Office: Reichold Chems Inc PO Box 13582 Research Triangle Park NC 27709

GAITHER, NINA DENISE, special education educator; b. Balt., July 9, 1973; d. William Thomas and Mary (Riles) G. BS, U. Md. Eastern Shore, Princess Anne, 1995, MEd, 1997. Cert. spl. edn. tchr., Md. Spl. edn. tchr. Anne Arundel County Pub. Schs., Annapolis, Md., 1997—. Avocations: singing, dancing, reading. Home: 7654 Spencer Rd Glen Burnie MD 21060

GAITHER, WILLIAM SAMUEL, civil engineering executive, consultant; b. Lafayette, Ind., Dec. 3, 1932; s. William Marcius and Susan Frances (Kirkpatrick) G.; m. Robin Cornwall McGraw, Aug. 1, 1959; 1 dau., Sarah Curwen. Student, Purdue U., 1950-51; B.S. in Civil Engring, Rose Poly. Inst., 1956; M. Sci. Engring. (Arthur Le Grand Doty fellow), Princeton, 1962, M.A. (Ford Found. fellow), 1963, Ph.D. (Ford Found. fellow), 1964. Registered profl. engr., Alaska, Calif., Del., Fla., Penn., Wis. Engr. Dravo Corp. (marine constrn.), Pitts., 1956-60; supt. Myer Corp., Neenah, Wis., 1960-61; supervising engr., chief engr. port and coastal devel., pipeline div. Bechtel Corp., San Francisco, 1965-67; assoc. prof. coastal engring. dept. U. Fla. at Gainesville, 1964-65; mem. faculty U. Del. at Newark, 1967-84, assoc. prof. civil engring., 1967-70, prof. civil engring., 1970; prof., dean U. Del. at Newark (Coll. Marine Studies), 1970-84, also dir. sea grant coll. program; pres., prof., trustee Drexel U., Phila., 1984-87, Weston Inst., West Chester, Pa., 1988-93; Inner City Consortium, Inc., 1993-94; mng. prin. Gaither & Assocs., Phila., 1993—; trustee Mut. Assurance Co., 1985-96; mem. marine bd. NRC, 1975-81; chmn. Gov.'s Oil Transp. Study Com., 1971-73; mem. Gov.'s Task Force Marine and Coastal Affairs, 1970-72, Gov.'s Coun. Sci. and Tech., Del., 1970-72; mem. ocean affairs adv. com. U.S. Dept. State; mem. Commn. on the Future, Rose-Hulman Inst. Tech., 1991-93; mem. Cyberfab.net. LLC, 1999—. Chmn. adv. coun. dept. civil engring. Princeton U., 1973-84; bd. dirs. University City Sci. Ctr., 1984-93, Penjurdel Coun., 1984—, Ednl. Found. of Chester County, 1989-92; pres., dir. Soc. John Gaither Desc., Inc., 1984-87; port warden Phila. Maritime Mus., 1987-93; founding dir., sec. Internat. Consciousness Rsch. Labs., 1996—; vestryman Ch. St. Andrew and St. Monica, 1987-93, chmn. fin. com. 1991-96; bd. dirs., mem. exec. com. Phila. H.S. Acads., Inc., 1988-93; chmn. bd. govs. Environ. Tech. Acad., 1988-93, active, 1988-94; prin. sponsor Delaware Valley Sci. Fairs, 1990-93. Recipient Disting. Achievement award Rose Poly. Inst., 1975, Disting. citizenship award News Jour. Papers, Del., 1975, Norman Sollenberger award Princeton U., 1983; named to Lambda Chi Alpha Alumni Hall of Fame, 1996; named hon. citizen of Lewes, Del., 1980. Fellow ASCE (chmn. offshore policy com. 1979-84); mem. Del. Acad. Sci. (pres. 1971-72), Soc. Naval Architects and Marine Engrs., Marine Tech. Soc., Am. Geophys. Union, Assn. Sea Grant Program Instns. (pres. 1973-74), Acad. Sci. Phila. (bd. dirs. 1989-92), Nat. Water Rsch. Inst. (rsch. adv. bd. 1991—), Cosmos Club (Washington), Wilmington Club (Del.), Germantown Cricket Club, Sunday Breakfast Club (Phila.). Home and Office: 3601 Baring St Philadelphia PA 19104-2332

GAJARSA, ARTHUR J., judge; b. Norcia, Italy, Mar. 1, 1941; came to U.S., 1949; m. Melanie E. Martinelli. BSEE, Rensselaer Polytech Inst, 1962; JD, Georgetown U., 1967; MA in Econs., Cath. U., 1968. Bar: U.S. Patent Office 1963, D.C. 1968, U.S. Dist. Ct. D.C. 1968, U.S. Ct. Appeals (D.C. cir.) 1968, Conn. 1969, U.S. Supreme Ct. 1971, U.S. Superior Ct. 1972, U.S. Ct. Appeals (D.C. cir.) 1972, U.S. Ct. Appeals (9th cir.) 1974, U.S. Dist. Ct. (no. dist.) N.Y. 1980. Patent examiner U.S. Patent Office, Dept. Commerce, 1962-63; patent adviser USAF, Dept. Def., 1963-64, Cushman, Darby & Cushman, 1964-67; law clk. to Judge Joseph C. McGarraghy U.S. Dist. Ct. (D.C.), Washington, 1967-68; atty. office gen. counsel Aetna Life and Casualty Co., 1968-69; spl. counsel, asst. to commr. Indian affairs Bur. Indian Affairs, Dept. Interior, 1969-71; assoc. Duncan and Brown, 1971-72; ptnr. Gajarsa, Liss & Sterenbuch, 1972-78, Gajarsa, Liss & Conroy, 1978-80, Wender, Murase & White, 1980-86; ptnr., officer Joseph, Gajarsa, McDermott & Reiner, P.C., 1987-97; judge U.S. Ct. Appeals Fed. Cir., Washington, 1997—; bd. dirs. Eyring Corp., 1992-96. Contbr. articles to profl. jours. Trustee Rensselaer Neuman Found., 1973—, Found. Improving Understanding of Arts, 1982-96, Outward Bound, 1987-96, Rensselaer Polytech Inst., 1994—; gov. John Carroll Soc., 1992—; regent Georgetown U., 1995—. Recipient Sun and Balance medal Rensselaer Polytech Inst., 1990, Rensselaer Key Alumni award, 1992, Gigi Pieri award Camp Hale Assn., 1992, 125th Anniversary medal Georgetown U. Law Ctr., 1995, Order of Commendatore, Republic Italy, 1995, Alumni Fellows award Rensselaer Alumni Assn., 1996. Mem. FBA, ABA, Fed. Cir. Bar Assn., Nat. Italian Am. Found. (bd. dirs. 1976—, gen. counsel 1976-89, pres. 1989-92, vice-chair 1993-96), D.C. Bar Assn., Am. Judicature Assn. Office: US Ct Appeals Fed Cir 717 Madison Pl NW Washington DC 20439-0002

GAJEWSKI, RONALD S., consulting and training company executive; b. Chgo., Feb. 3, 1954; s. Stanley B. and Irene M. (Onak) G.; m. D. June Easley, Nov. 22, 1980; 1 child, Mary Anne. BSEE summa cum laude, DeVry Inst., Irving, Tex., 1977; MBA summa cum laude, U. Dallas, Irving, 1981. Product mgr. Docutel Corp., Irving, 1975-82; v.p. Automated Banking, Dallas, 1983-85; asst. v.p. MTech subs. MBank, Dallas, 1986-87; dir. bus. devel. Uccel Corp., Dallas, 1987-89; dist. sales mgr. Goal Systems Internat., Dallas, 1989-90; v.p., gen. mgr. Acclivus Corp., Dallas, 1991—. Editor: (sales skills handbook) Building on the Base, 1995; mem. editl. adv. com. Sales and Mktg. Mgmt., 1996-97. Bd. dirs. Hickory Creek (Tex.) Property and Zoning Bd., 1995—. Mem. ASTD, Instructional Systems Assn. (rsch. com. 1993—). Roman Catholic. Avocation: building period antique furniture reproductions. Office: Acclivus Corp 14500 Midway Rd Dallas TX 75244-3109

GAJL-PECZALSKA, KAZIMIERA J., surgical pathologist, pathology educator; b. Warsaw, Poland, Nov. 15, 1925; came to U.S., 1970; d. Kazimierz Emil and Anna Janina (Gervais) Gajl; widowed; children: Kazimierz Peczalski, Andrew Peczalski. Student, Jagiellonian Univ., Cracov, Poland, 1945-47; MD, Warsaw U., Poland, 1951, PhD in Immunopathology, 1964. Diplomate Polish Bd. Pediatrics, Polish Bd. Anatomic Pathology, Am. Bd. Pathology. Attending pediatrician Children's Hosp. for Infectious Diseases, Warsaw, Poland, 1953-58, head, pathology lab., 1958-65; adj. prof. Postgrad. Med. Sch., Warsaw, Poland, 1965-70; fellow U. Minn., Mpls., 1970-72, asst. prof. dept. pathology, 1972-75, assoc. prof. dept. pathology, 1975-79, prof. dept. pathology, 1979—, dir. immunophenotyping and flow lab., 1974—, dir. cytology dept. pathology, 1976-95. Author chpts. to book; contbr. of numerous papers to profl. jours. Fellow WHO, Paris, 1959, London, 1962, Paris, 1967, U.S. Pub. Health Svcs. fellow, 1968-69; recipient Scientific Com. award Polish Ministry of Health and Social Welfare, 1964. Mem. Am. Soc. Experimental Pathology, Am. Soc. Cytology, Internat. Acad. Pathology, British Soc. Pediatric Pathology, Polish Soc. Pathology, Polish Soc Pediatricians. Roman Catholic. Avocations: music, skiing. Office: U Minn Dept Pathology U Health Ctr PO Box 609 Minneapolis MN 55455

GAL, RICHARD JOHN, industrial engineer; b. Youngstown, Ohio, Oct. 30, 1957; s. John and Maria (Hesch) G.; m. Connie Marie Norton, 1996; children: Stephanie, Kristin, Richard John Jr. B in Engring., Youngstown State U., 1979; MBA, Ea. Mich. U., 1981. Indsl. engr. trainee Nat. Steel, Ecorse, Mich., 1979-81; indsl. engr. Republic Steel, Massillon, Ohio, 1981-84; div. indsl. engr. Avery, Painesville, Ohio, 1984-87; assoc. prin. engr. Sverdrup Tech., Niceville, Fla., 1987-94; quality dir. Sverdrup Tech., Elgin AFB, Fla., 1995-98; quality officer Sverdrup Tech., Cape Canaveral, Fla., 1998—; examiner Malcolm Baldrige Nat. Quality award, 1998, 99; sr. examiner F.L. Sterling Award, 1995, 96, 97, 98, 99; chmn. Fla. Sch. to Work Program, 1998. Contbr. articles to profl. jours. Advisor Jr. Achievement, Canton, Ohio, 1981-82. Mem. Inst. Indsl. Engrs. (sr.), Am. Soc. Quality Engrs. Home: 1180 Grand Cayman Dr Merritt Island FL 32952 Office: 1613 Sab Rd Rm 18 Patrick A F B FL 32925

GALAMBOS, JOHN THOMAS, medical educator, internist; b. Budapest, Hungary, Oct. 29, 1921; came to U.S., 1947; m. Eva G. Cohn; children: Sharon Tobae Galambos McDuff, John Douglas, Michael Robert. BS, U. Ga., 1948; MD, Emory U., 1952. Diplomate Nat. Bd. Med. Examiners, Am. Bd. Internal Medicine, Am. Bd. Gastroenterology. Intern Barnes Hosp., St. Louis, 1952-53; resident U. Chgo. Clinics, 1953-55; dir. gastroenterology teaching program Emory U. Sch. Medicine, Atlanta, 1957-92, dir. gastroenterology labs., 1958-92, dir. div. digestive diseases, 1966-92; dir. Gastroenterology Clinic Grady Hosp., Atlanta, 1957-92; mem. adv. bd. Nat. Inst. Digestive Diseases, NIH, Washington, 1985-88. Author: Cirrhosis, 1979, Digestive Diseases, 1983; author or co-author 36 book chpts.; contbr. 165 articles to profl. jours. Fellow ACP, Am. Coll. Gastroenterology (pres. 1975), Am. Gastroenterol. Assn., Am. Assn. for Study Liver Diseases, Internat. Assn. for Study Liver Diseases, Alpha Omega Alpha. Republican. Jewish. Avocation: sailing. Office: 95 Collier Rd NW Ste 4075 Atlanta GA 30309-1751

GALAMBOS, THEODORE VICTOR, civil engineer, educator; b. Budapest, Hungary, Apr. 17, 1929; s. Paul and Magdalena (Potzner) G.; m. Barbara Ann Asp, June 25, 1957; children: Paul, Ruth, Ronald, John. BSCE, U. N.D, 1953, MSCE, 1954; PhD in CE, Lehigh U., 1959; Dr. Honoris Causa, Tech. U., Budapest, 1982; PhD (hon.), U. N.D., 1998. Registered profl. engr., Pa., Minn., Mo. From asst. to assoc. prof. civil engring. Lehigh U., Bethlehem, Pa., 1959-65; prof. Washington U., St. Louis, 1965-81, head dept., 1970-78; prof. U. Minn., Mpls., 1981-96, emeritus prof., 1997—; cons. engr. Steel Joist Inst., Myrtle Beach, S.C., 1965—; vis. prof. U.S. Mil. Acad., West Point, 1990. Author, co-author 4 books in field; editor 1 book; contbr. over 100 articles to profl. jours. Served with U.S. Army, 1954-56. Recipient T.R. Higgins award Am. Inst. Steel Constrn., 1981. Mem. ASCE (hon., Norman medal 1983, Shortridge Hardesty award 1988, E.E. Howard award 1992), NAE, Internat. Assn. Bridge and Structural Engrs. Democrat. Baptist. Avocation: photography. Home: 4375 Wooddale Ave Minneapolis MN 55424-1060 Office: U Minn Civil Engring Dept Minneapolis MN 55455

GALANDIUK, SUSAN, colon and rectal surgeon, educator; b. N.Y.C., Mar. 6, 1957; d. Joseph and Dora (Neu) G.; m. Hiram C. Polk Jr., Dec. 22, 1991. BS cum laude, SUNY, Albany, 1976; MD summa cum laude, Julius Maximilians U., Wuerzburg, Germany, 1982. Diplomate Am. Bd. Surgery, Am. Bd. Colon and Rectal Surgery. Surg. intern Chirurgische Univ. Klinik, Julius Maximilians U., Wuerzburg, Germany, 1982-83; surg. intern Cleve. Clinic Found., 1983-84, surg. resident, 1984-88; Price fellow in surg. rsch., dept. surgery U. Louisville, 1988-89, instr. dept. surgery, 1990-91, asst. prof. dept. surgery, 1991-96, assoc. prof., 1996—; colon and rectal surgery fellow Mayo Clinic, Rochester, Minn., 1989-90; presenter in field. Assoc. editor Digestive Surgery; contbr. chpts. to books, articles to profl. jours. Chmn. fund raising com. ARC, Louisville, 1993, 95-97, bd. dirs., 1997-98; bd. mem. Fund for the Arts, 1996-99; chair med. adv. com. Ky. chpt. Crohn's and Colitis Found. Am., Louisville, 1993-97. William E. Lower Fellow Thesis prize Cleve. Clinic Found., 1986. Fellow ACS, AAUP, Am. Soc. Colon and Rectal Surgeons (mem. chmn. rsch. found. young rschrs. com. 1996—, mem. program com. 1994-96); mem. AMA, Am. Med. Women's Assn., Am. Soc. Microbiology, Assn. Acad. Surgery, Assn. Surg. Edn., Assn. Women Surgeons, Collegium Internat. Chirurgiae Digestivae, Jefferson County Med. Soc., Ky. Med. Assn. (mem. cancer com.), Louisville Surg. Soc., Hiram C. Polk Jr. Surg. Soc., Ohio Valley Soc. Colon and Rectal Surgeons, Priestly Soc., Soc. Surgery of Alimentary Tract, Soc. Am. Gastrointestinal Endoscopic Surgeons, Soc. Surg. Oncology (mem. com. rels. and issues, govt. affairs coms.), Southea. Surg. Congress (councillor 1997-99), Surg. Infection Soc., Soc. Univ. Surgeons, Am. Soc. Gastrointestinal Endoscopists, Ctrl. Surg. Assn., Western Surg. Assn., Am. Gastroent. Assn. Greek Catholic. Office: U Louisville Dept Surgery 550 S Jackson St Louisville KY 40202-1622*

GALANE, MORTON ROBERT, lawyer; b. N.Y.C., Mar. 15, 1926; s. Harry J. and Sylvia (Schenkelbach) G.; children: Suzanne Galane Ash, Jonathan A. B.E.E., CCNY, 1946; LL.B., George Washington U., 1950. Bar: D.C. 1950, Nev. 1955, Calif. 1975. Patent examiner U.S. Patent Office, Washington, 1948-50; spl. partner firm Roberts & McInnis, Washington, 1950-54; practice as Morton R. Galane, P.C., Las Vegas, Nev., 1955—; spl. counsel to Gov. Nev., 1967-70. Contbr. articles to profl. jours. Chmn. Gov.'s Com. on Future of Nev., 1979-80. Fellow Am. Coll. Trial Lawyers; mem. IEEE, ABA (council litigation sect. 1977-83), Am. Law Inst., State Bar Nev., State Bar Calif., D.C. Bar. Home: 2019 Bannie Ave Las Vegas NV 89102-2208 Office: 302 Carson Ave Ste 1100 Las Vegas NV 89101-5909

GALANOS, JAMES, fashion designer; b. Phila., Sept. 20, 1924; s. Gregory D. and Helen (Gorgoliatos) G. With Hattie Carnegie, 1944; asst. to designer Columbia Pictures Corp., Hollywood, Calif., 1946-47; trainee Robert Piguet, Paris, France, 1947-48; founder, designer Galanos Originals, L.A., 1951—.

Exhbns. include restrospectives Costume Council of Los Angeles County Mus. Art, 1974, Fashion Inst. Tech., 1976, Costume Inst. Mus. Fine Arts, Houston, 1987, Galanos Retrospective, 1951-92, 1997, Cleve. Hist. Soc., 1996, 45 yr. career retrospective Los Angeles County Mus. Art, 1997. Recipient award for distinguished service in field of fashion Neiman-Marcus, 1954; Am. Fashion Critics award Met. Mus. Art, Costume Inst., 1954; Return award, 1956; Hall of Fame, 1959; Creativity award Internat. Achievements Fair, 1956; Filene's Young Talent design award Boston, 1958; Cotton Fashion award, 1958; Lifetime Achievement award Council Fashion Designers Am., 1985; Stanley award Fashion Collectors of Dallas Hist. Soc., 1986; Otis-Parsons Design Achievement award, 1987, first Annual award for Design Excellence Costume Com. Chgo. Hist. Soc., 1992; Recognition award outstanding contbn. to the World of Fashion. Office: 2254 S Sepulveda Blvd Los Angeles CA 90064-1812

GALANT, HERBERT LEWIS, lawyer; b. N.Y.C., Oct. 16, 1928; s. Charles A. and Bertha (Rosenberg) G.; m. Fern Judith Laikin, Feb. 10, 1957; children: Peter B., John M., Amy E. BA cum laude, U. Wis., 1949; LLB magna cum laude, Harvard U., 1952; LLM, NYU, 1960. Bar: N.Y. 1955, U.S. Dist. Ct. (so. dist.) N.Y. 1956, U.S. Ct. Appeals (2d cir.) 1959. Assoc. Fried, Frank, Harris, Shriver & Jacobson, N.Y.C., 1955-61, ptnr., 1962-95, co-chair, 1992-95, of counsel, 1995—. Editor: Harvard U. Law Rev., 1950-52. Mem. Tenafly Twp. (N.J.) Bd. Ethics, 1978-88, Tenafly Twp. Planning Bd., 1997—. 1st lt. USAF, 1952-54. Mem. Assn. of Bar of City of N.Y., Harvard U. Club (N.Y.C.). Democrat. Jewish. Home: 150 Tekening Dr Tenafly NJ 07670-1219 Office: Fried Frank Harris Shriver & Jacobson 1 New York Plz Fl 22 New York NY 10004-1980

GALANTE, JORGE OSVALDO, orthopedic surgeon, educator; b. Buenos Aires, Dec. 18, 1934; came to U.S., 1958; m. Sofija; 1 child, Charles. BA, Colegio Nacional de Buenos Aires, 1952; MD, U. Buenos Aires, 1958; DMSc, U. Goteborg, Sweden, 1967. Diplomate Am. Bd. Orthopedic Surgery. Resident in orthopaedics U. Ill., Chgo., 1960-64; assoc. investigator bioengineering lab. U. Goteborg, 1964-67; asst. prof. orthopedic surgery U. Ill. Med. Ctr., Chgo., 1967-70, assoc. prof., 1970-72; lect. in orthopedics U. Ill. Abraham Lincoln Sch. Medicine, Chgo., 1972—; adj. rsch. prof. U. Ill. Circle, Chgo., 1972—, mem. graduate faculty, 1974—; prof., chmn. dept. orthopedic surgery Rush-Presbyn.-St. Luke's Med. Ctr., Chgo., 1972-94; prof. anatomy Rush Med. Coll., Chgo., 1977—; dir. Rush Arthritis and Orthopedic Inst., 1994—; assoc. prof. exptl. orthopedics. U. Goteborg, 1969—. Contbr. articles to profl. jours. Recipient Kappa Delta award Am. Acad. Orthopedic Surgery, 1970, Clemson (S.C.) U. award, 1975, Steindler award Orthopedic Rsch. Soc., 1990, Zimmer Award for Disting. Achievement in Orthopedic Rsch. Bristol-Myers Squibb, 1996. Office: Rush-Presbyn-St Luke's Med Ctr 1653 W Congress Pkwy Chicago IL 60612-3833

GALANTE, JOSEPH A., bishop; b. Philadelphia, PA, July 2, 1938. BA, St. Charles Seminary, Phila.; JCD, Lateran U., Rome, Italy; MA Spiritual Theology, U. of St. Thomas (Angelicum), Rome, Italy. Ordained priest, 1964; ordained bishop, 1992. Asst. pastor Our Lady of Consolation Parish, 1964-65, St. John of the Cross, Roslyn, 1965; Bishop's secretary & Diocesan Master of Ceremonies Diocese of Brownsville, Tex., 1968-72; vicar for religious & Diocesan newspaper editor Diocese of Brownsville, 1969-72; asst. vicar for religious Archdiocese of Phila., 1972-79; resident Good Shepherd Parish, 1972-73; defender of The Bond Archdiocesan Tribunal, Phila., 1972-74; chaplain Catholic Home for Girls, St. Vincent's Residence, 1973-81; prof. Canon Law St. Charles Seminary, 1974-77, Mary Immaculate Seminary, Northampton, Pa., 1975-78; vicar for religious Archdiocese of Phila., 1979-87; chaplain Convent of the Handmaids of the Sacred Heart, Haverford, Pa., 1981-87; undersec. Congregation for Institutes of Consecrated Life & Societies of Apostolic Life, Rome, Italy, 1987-92; aux. bishop Diocese of San Antonio, 1992-94; bishop Diocese of Beaumont, Tex., 1994—; pres. Nat. Conf. for Vicars of Religious, 1976-80; mem. religious affairs com. Canon Law Soc. Contbr. to Procs. of Nat. Conf. of Vicars for Religious and Canon Law Soc. Am. Office: Dicesan Pastoral Office PO Box 3948 Beaumont TX 77704-3948*

GALANTE, JOSEPH ANTHONY, JR., computer programmer; b. Yonkers, N.Y., July 15, 1947; s. Joseph Anthony Sr. and Lavinia (Brue) G. BS in secondary edn., physics, U. Md., 1971; MS in Tech. Mgmt., Am. U., 1974. Programmer UNISYS, Green Belt, Md., 1971-76; programmer analyst N.Y. Tel., White Plains, 1976-79, Telic Corp., Darien, Conn., 1978-81; assoc. mgr. N.Y. Tel., N.Y.C., 1981-85; sr. systems specialist Telesector Resources Group, Pearl River, N.Y., 1985--. Pres. Communicators Westchester, Hasting, N.Y., 1979; chmn. by law com. Masthope Rapids Property Owners Coun., Lackawaxen, Pa., 1977-79; bd. dirs. Mast Hope Mountain Property Owners Coun., 1996—; pres. West Colang Lake Assn., 1996—; mem. Pike County Pa. Visioning Com., 1998, Land Use Task Force, 1998. Recipient Apollo 11 Team Medallion NASA, 1971, Apollo 17 Personal Contribution plaque, 1975, First Annual Bell Atlantic Leaders in Excellence award for participation in the design and devel. of the Amdahl EnView Software product, 1998; N.Y. State scholar, 1965. Mem. Masthope Rapids Assn. (bd. dirs. 1996—), Westcolang Lake Assn. (pres. 1996-97), Masthope Rapids Prop. Owners Coun. (com.chmn. 1977-79), Kappa Delta Pi. Roman Catholic. Achievements include development of data conversion techniques for information interchange between UNISYS and IBM using ASCII COBOL; conversion of real time basic assembly lang. program complex from SVS to MVS. Office: NYNEX TRG 2 Blue Hill Plz Fl 4 Pearl River NY 10965-3101

GALANTER, MARC, psychiatrist, educator; b. N.Y.C., Sept. 17, 1941; s. Jacob and Ada (Simms) G.; m. Wynne L. Roberts, June 7, 1964; children—Cathryn, Margit. B.A., Columbia U., 1963; M.D., Albert Einstein Coll. Medicine, 1967. Diplomate Am. Bd. Psychiatry and Neurology with added qualifications in addiction psychiatry; cert. Am. Soc. Addiction Medicine. Intern UCLA Hosp., 1967-68; resident in psychiatry Albert Einstein Coll. Medicine-Bronx Mcpl. Hosp. Ctr., 1968-71, fellow in community psychiatry, 1972-73, clin. instr., 1972-74, dir. Drug and Alcohol Cons. Service, 1972-75, career tchr. drug abuse and alcoholism Nat. Inst. on Alcohol Abuse and Alcoholism, Nat. Inst. Drug Abuse, 1973-76, asst. prof., 1974-78, dir. div. alcoholism and drug abuse, 1975-87, assoc. prof., 1978-83, prof. dept. psychiatry, 1983-87; prof. psychiatry, dir. div. alcoholism and drug abuse NYU Sch. Med., 1987—; dir. addiction divsn., rsch. scientist Collaborating Ctr. WHO, 1987-98, dep. dir. Collaborating Ctr., 1998—; clin. assoc. Lab. Clin. Psychopharmacology, NIMH, Washington, 1970-72; instr. psychiatry residency program St. Elizabeth's Hosp.; presenter at profl. confs. U.S., Can., Thailand, Germany, Japan, India, Kenya and Italy; chmn. Nat. Conf. on Alcohol and Drug Abuse Edn., 1977; program chmn. Internat. Conf. Med. Edn. in Alcohol and Drug Abuse, WHO and Assn. Med. Edn. and Rsch. in Substance Abuse, 1982, founder, pres., 1976-77; dir. Lab. Alcoholism and Drug Abuse WHO. Editor: Ofcl. Sci. Procs. of Nat. Coun. on Alcoholism, 1978-80, Alcohol and Drug Abuse in Medical Education, 1980, (book series) Currents in Alcoholism, 1979, 80, 81, Recent Developments in Alcoholism; mem. editl. bd. Am. Jour. Drug and Alcohol Abuse, 1978—; assoc. editor jour. Alcoholism Clin. and Exptl. Rsch., Am. Jour. of Addictions, 1979, Jour. Substance Abuse Treatment, 1995—; co-editor: Advances in the Psychosocial Treatment of Alcoholism, 1984; editor-in-chief Substance Abuse Jour., 1978—; author: Network Therapy for Alcohol and Drug and Abuse, 1993, 2nd edit., 1999, Cults: Faith, Health and Coercion, 1989, 2nd edit., 1999. Recipient Psychopharmacology award Am. Psychol. Assn., 1972; Career Tchr. award in drug abuse and alcoholism NIMN, 1973-77, Organon Tchg. awad Am. Psychiat. Assn., 1999; ann. Book award Commonwealth Fund, 1978-82, Macarthur medal Assn. Med. Edn. and Rsch., 1994. Fellow Am. Psychiat. Assn. (chmn. panel on alcoholism, nat. task force on psychiat. treatment 1983—, mem. task force on cults 1977-80, mem. com. on alcoholism, chmn. com. on addiction edn. 1992—, chmn. com. on religion 1985-90, Gold Achievement award 1993); mem. AAAS, Am. Soc. of Addiction Medicine (bd. dirs. 1986—, sec. 1995-97, pres. elect 1997-99, pres. 1999—), Am. Bd. Psychiatry and Neurology (vice chair com. om added qualifications in addictino psychiatry 1992-98), Rsch. Soc. on Alcoholism (sec. 1983-85), N.Y. Acad. Medicine (addiction com. 1985—), N.Y. State Task Force on Dual Psychiat. and Addictive Disorders (task force chmn. 1986-89, 93), N.Y. Psychiat. Soc., Am. Acad. Addiction Psychiatrists (v.p. 1987-89, pres. 1991-93, bd. dirs. 1986—), Nat. Inst. Alcohol Abuse and Alcoholism (Nat. Adv. Coun. 1997—). Office: 285 Central Park W New York NY 10024-3006

GALANTER, RUTH, city official. Grad., U. Mich.; MA, Yale U. Chair South Coast Regional Coastal Commn.; city coun. 6th dist. L.A., 1987—. Mem. Am. Pub. Health Assn. Office: City Hall 200 N Main St Rm 515 Los Angeles CA 90012-4103*

GALARRAGA, ANDRES JOSE, professional baseball player; b. Caracas, Venezuela, June 18, 1961; m. Eneyda G., Feb. 18, 1984; 1 child, Andria. First baseman Montreal Expos, 1979-91, St. Louis Cardinals, 1991-92, Colorado Rockies, 1992-97, Atlanta Braves, 1997—. Named to Nat. League All-Star Team, 1988, 93; recipient Gold Glove award, 1989-90, Silver Slugger award, 1988, 96; Nat. League Batting Champion, 1993; named Comeback Player of Yr., 1993, MVP So. League. 1984. Office: Atlanta Braves Turner Field PO Box 4064 Atlanta GA 30302-4064*

GALASK, RUDOLPH PETER, obstetrician and gynecologist; b. Fort Dodge, Iowa, Dec. 23, 1935; s. Peter Otto and Adeline Amelia (Maranesi) G.; m. Gloria Jean Vasti, June 19, 1965. BS, Drake U., 1959; MD, U. Iowa, 1964, MS, 1967. Diplomate Am. Bd. Obstetrics and Gynecology. Research fellow in microbiology U. Iowa, Iowa City, 1965-67, resident in ob-gyn., 1967-70, asst. prof., 1970-74, asst. prof. microbiology, 1973-74, assoc. prof. obstetrics and gynecology microbiology, 1974-78, prof., 1978—; chmn. exec. com. Coll. Medicine, 1992-93; cons. various pharm. and diagnostic cos. Editor: Infectious Diseases in the Female Patient, 1986-89; contbr. numerous articles to profl. jours. Served to staff sgt. USNG, 1954-64. Recipient I.D.S.O.G./Ortho McNeil award for outstanding contbns. to field of infectious diseases in ob-gyn.; numerous grants to study the efficacy of various antibiotics and chemotherapeutics. Fellow Am. Gynecol. and Obstet. Soc., Am. Coll. Obstetricians and Gynecologists (Resident Tchr. of Yr. 1997), Infectious Disease Am.; mem. AAAS, Cen. Assn. for Obstetricians and Gynecologists, Infectious Disease Soc. for Ob-Gyn. (pres. 1982-84, founding mem.), Soc. Gynecol. Investigation (coun. 1987-90), Queens Gynecol. Soc. (hon.), Tex. Assn. Obstetricians and Gynecologists (hon.), Am. Soc. Microbiology, Izaac Walton League, Ducks Unltd. Club (sponsor), Sigma Xi. Roman Catholic. Office: Univ Iowa Hosps Dept Ob-Gyn Iowa City IA 52242 *Power is a perception that lasts a moment but respect is a legacy that lasts forever.*

GALASSI, JONATHAN WHITE, book publishing company executive; b. Seattle, Nov. 4, 1949; s. Gerard Goodwin and Dorothea Johnston (White) G.; m. Susan Grace, June 21, 1975; children: Isabel Grace, Beatrice Grace. AB, Harvard U., 1971; MA, Cambridge (Eng.) U., 1976. Editor Houghton Mifflin Co., Boston, N.Y.C., 1973-81; sr. editor Random House, Inc., N.Y.C., 1981-86; exec. editor, v.p. Farrar, Straus & Giroux, Inc., N.Y.C., 1986-87, editor in chief, sr. v.p., 1988-93, exec. v.p., editor-in-chief, 1993—. Author: Morning Run: Poems, 1988; editor, translator: The Second Life of Art: Selected Essays of Eugenio Montale, 1982, Otherwise: Last and First Poems of E. Montale, 1986, Collected Poems 1920-1954, 1998; poetry editor Paris Rev., 1978-88. Recipient Roger Klein award for editing PEN, 1984; Marshall scholar Brit. Marshall Commn., London, 1971-73; Guggenheim fellow, 1989. Mem. Acad. Am. Poets (bd. dirs. 1990—, pres. 1994—). Home: 239 Sackett St Brooklyn NY 11231-3604 Office: Farrar Straus & Giroux Inc 19 Union Sq W Fl 4 New York NY 10003-3304*

GALASSO, FRANCIS SALVATORE, materials scientist; b. Monson, Mass., Apr. 26, 1931; s. Paul and Rubino (Cirillo) G.; m. Lois E. Wood; children: Cynthia Egolf, Gary Galasso. B.S., U. Mass., 1953; M.S., U. Conn., 1957, Ph.D., 1960. Chief materials United Technologies Research Ctr., East Hartford, Conn., 1960-74, prin. scientist, 1974-77, sr. material scientist, 1977-85, mgr., 1985-91; with Galasso Tech. Assocs., Manchester, Conn., 1991—; mem. adv. bd. Chem. Rubber Co., 1971—; cons. in space experiments NASA, Huntsville, Ala., 1971-77; vis. prof. U. Conn., Storrs, 1985—. Author 6 books; contbr. articles to profl. jours.; patentee in field. Coach Manchester Little League, Conn., 1960-75, v.p., 1970-84, pres., 1984-88, bd. govs. adv. com. on accreditation, 1988-90. Served to 1st lt. USAF, 1953-55. Recipient Outstanding Achievement award United Technologies, 1983, 90. Fellow Am. Ceramic Soc.; mem. Am. Chem. Soc., AIME, Sigma Xi. Democrat. Roman Catholic. Clubs: Army-Navy, Am. Legion. Office: 13 Green Manor Rd Manchester CT 06040-3342

GALASSO, MARTIN JOHN, communications consultant, writer; b. Pitts., June 10, 1958; s. Joseph Anthony and Marie Frances (Tripoli) G. BA in English, Westminster Coll., New Wilmington, Pa., 1980. Writer Westinghouse Electric Co., Pitts., 1981-85, Blue Cross/Blue Shield, N.Y.C., 1985-87; comm. mgr. MetLife, N.Y.C., 1987-94; cons., writer M.G. Bus. Comm., N.Y.C., 1994—. Trustee Big Bros. and Big Sisters N.Y.C., 1992-95. Recipient silver medal Internat. TV and Video Assn., 1994. Mem. Internat. Assn. Bus. Communicators (Silver Quill award 1994). Republican. Roman Catholic. Avocations: bicycling, music, travel, reading. Office: MG Bus Comm 310 E 46th St New York NY 10017-3002

GALATI, MICHAEL BERNARD, lay church worker; b. Chgo., Sept. 4, 1931; s. Anthony Kenneth and Ingeborg Marie (Flugum) G.; m. Mary Jeanne Kelsey, Apr. 19, 1952 (dec.); children: Anna Marie Galati Logsdon, Anthony K., Peter M., Joseph S. BS in Edn., No. Ill. U., 1953, MS, 1956, EdD, 1985. Mem. bd. Christian social concerns Rock River Conf., United Meth. Ch., 1965-67, mem. coun. ministries No. Ill. Conf., 1971-76, 83-94, vice chmn. Aurora dist. coun. ministries, 1974-76; chmn. dept. lang. arts and social scis., dir. student tchg. program Lemont (Ill.) Twp. High Sch., 1956-81, head humanities divsn., 1981-94; sr. editor Lemont Met., 1982-83, 94-95; adj. instr. Joliet Jr. Coll., 1995-98, No. Ill. U., 1998—; bd. dirs. John Wesley Theol. Inst. Author: Love Me a Village; contbr. poems and articles to mags. and jours. Trustee Village of Lemont, 1963-69. Recipient Freedom's Found. at Valley Forge Tchr. medal, 1971, Rosicrucian Order Humanitarian award Ancient and Mystical Order Rosae Crucis, 1973, Pride in Excellence award Lemont Twp. H.S., 1989. Mem. Ill. Poetry Soc., Chgo. Poets Club, Poets and Patrons, Lemont Writers Club. Democrat. Home: 21 Norton Ave Lemont IL 60439-3944 Office: 800 Porter St Lemont IL 60439-3777 *In doing the work of the Kingdom, love and faith and caring have an efficacy that legal force and political power and the gaining of prestigious positions cannot ever equal. This applies to work done in the world as well as to work done within the church.*

GALATIANOS, GUS A., computer executive, information systems consultant, educator; b. Hermoupolis, Siros, Greece, Jan. 18, 1947; came to U.S., 1973; s. Athanassios Constantine and Despina Athanassios (Stefanou) G.; m. Katerina E. Saridis, Sept. 29, 1974; children: Athanassios, Deborah. BSEE, N.Y. Inst. Tech., 1974; MSEE, Columbia U., 1977; MS in Computer Sci., Stevens Inst. Tech., 1977; PhD in Computer Sci., Poly. U., N.Y.C., 1986. Mgr. ops. Solomos Bus. Machines, Athens, Greece, 1970-73; computer cons. Univ. Computer Ctrs., N.Y.C., 1973-77; tech. dir. Computer Dynamics Corp., N.Y.C., 1977-79; assoc. prof., chmn. dept. computer sci. SUNY, Old Westbury, 1979-93, prof., 1993—, chmn. dept. computer sic., 1995—; computer cons. Keane Inc., N.Y.C., 1980-81, Ins. Svcs. Office, N.Y.C., 1981-82, Computer Corp. Am., N.Y.C., 1983-84; mgr. fin. systems Singer/Electronic Systems Div., Little Falls, N.J., 1984-87; pres. Advanced Computer Cons. Internat., N.Y.C., 1988—; pres. ACCI Properties, Inc., N.Y.C., 1988. Author: Principles of Software Engineering, 1986, Principles of Database Systems, 1986; contbr. articles to profl. jours. Mem. Statue of Liberty Found. Inc., N.Y.C., 1984, Nat. Fedn. Blind, Balt., 1988, Rep. Presdl. Task Force, Washington, 1984—, Greater Whitestone Taxpayers Civic Assn., N.Y.C., 1984—. Served with Greek Air Force, 1965-67. Mem. IEEE, AAAS, Assn. Computing Machinery, N.Y. Acad. Scis., Am. Mgmt. Assn., Am. Assn. Artificial Intelligence, Am. Cons. League, Hellenic Univ. Club (N.Y.C.). Republican. Greek Orthodox. Avocations: music, hunting, travel, reading. Home: 17-24 Parsons Blvd Whitestone NY 11357-3041 Office: SUNY Dept Computer Sci Old Westbury NY 11568

GALATY, CAROL POPPER, health policy administrator; b. Buffalo, Mar. 31, 1943; d. David Henry and Florence Popper; m. David Holt Galaty, June 21, 1965 (div. Apr. 1975); children: Mara, Elise; m. James Hill, June 25, 1978; children: Andy, Bruce. BA in Zoology, Pomona Coll., 1964. Vol. Peace Corps, Ghana, West Africa, 1964-66; various positions HEW, 1966-68; founder, mem., bd. dirs. Planned Parenthood of Green Bay, Wis., 1969-74; assoc. dir. Com. for Nat. Health Ins., Washington, 1975-76; Office of Child Health in Office of Asst. Sec. for Health, HEW, Washington, 1976-78; exec. dir. Fed. Internat. Yr. of the Child, Dept. HHS, Washington, 1978-80; dir. CHAMPUS Liaison Office, Washington and Aurora, Colo., 1981-83; dir. health benefits Office Asst. Sec. Def., DOD, Washington, 1983-90; spl. asst. ops. spl. projects Def. Med. Systems Support DOD, Falls Church, Va., 1990-91; dir. office of program devel., maternal/child health bur. Dept. HHS, Rockville, Md., 1991—; cons. Chilean Health Systems, Santiago, 1976-77; mem. HRSA managed care group Dept. HHS, 1994—, mem. steering com. for state child health ins. program, 1995—; mem. health care reform team White House, 1993. Bd. dirs. Returned Peace Corps Vols., 1989-91; mem. adv. group Nat. Women's Polit. Caucus, Washington, 1975-78; mem. Office Sec. Def. Sr. Exec. Women, Washington, 1981-91. Mem. Northeastern Wis. Health Planning Coun. (econ. task force 1973-75), Milw. Planned Parenthood (bd. dirs. 1970-73), Wis. Family Planning Coordinating Coun. (bd. dirs. 1970-72). Democrat. Jewish. Avocations: art, tennis, travel, camping, theater. Office: Parklawn Bldg 5600 Fishers Ln Rockville MD 20852-1750

GALATZ, HENRY FRANCIS, lawyer; b. N.Y.C., Feb. 5, 1947; s. Julius D. and Dorothy (Kirschen) G.; m. Colleen Prager, Aug. 19, 1973; children: Benjamin Chase, Brandon Kyle. BA, U. Ariz., 1970, MEd, MA with honors, 1973; JD, U. the Pacific, 1979. Bar: Ill. 1981, U.S. Dist. Ct. (no. dist.) Ill. 1982, U.S. Dist. Ct. (ea. dist.) Mich. 1982, U.S. Dist. Ct. (ea. dist.) Mo. 1985, U.S. Dist. Ct. Mont. 1986, U.S. Dist. Ct. (we. dist.) Tex. 1987, U.S. Ct. Appeals (7th cir.) 1981, U.S. Ct. Appeals (6th cir.) 1982, U.S. Supreme Ct. 1985, U.S. Dist. Ct. (no. dist.) Calif. 1992, U.S. Dist. Ct. Nebr. 1993, U.S. Dist. Ct. (no. dist.) Ohio 1997; cert. coach and referee U.S. Soccer Fedn. Cons. labor rels. Phoenix Closures, Chgo., 1974-75, Galatz Elec. Corp., Las Vegas, Nev., 1975-80; labor counsel W.W. Grainger, Inc., Skokie, Ill., 1980—; pvt. practice Olympia Fields, Ill., 1981—; hearing officer Ill. State Bd. Edn., Chgo., 1982—: atty. Chgo. Legal Svcs. Found., 1983—, Ill. Inst. for Dispute Resolution, 1992—; mem. com. Employment Law Inst., Northwestern U., Evanston, Ill. Pres., coach Homewood-Flossmoor (Ill.) Soccer Club, 1985—, Intercollegiate Varsity Athletics (soccer and lacrosse); co-chair soccer Ill. Prairie State Games, 1992; pres. P.O.P.S. Homewood-Flossmoor H.S., 1996—; mem. bd. edn., pers. com. Homewood-Flossmoor H.S., 1998—. Recipient Judge Mason Rothwell Award, 1979, Cert. of Merit Chgo. Legal Services Found., 1983. Mem. ABA, ATLA, Am. Corp. Counsel Assn. (labor and employment sect.), Ill. Bar Assn., Chgo. Bar Assn., Am. Arbitrators Assn. (arbitrator), Am. Judicature Soc., Ill. Trial Lawyers Assn., North Shore (Ill.) Labor Counsel Assn., Phi Delta Phi, Alpha Epsilon Pi. Democrat. Jewish. Avocations: soccer, lacrosse. Home: PO Box 374 Flossmoor IL 60422-0374 Office: W W Grainger Inc 455 Knightsbridge Pkwy Lincolnshire IL 60069-3620

GALAZKA, JACEK MICHAL, publishing company executive; b. Wilno, Poland, Apr. 28, 1924; s. Michal J. and Zofia Galazka; m. Jacoba J.M. Jansen, July 22, 1958. B.Com., U. Edinburgh, 1948. Dir. sales and promotion St. Martin's Press, N.Y.C., 1955-63; mgr. reference dept. Charles Scribner's Sons, N.Y.C., 1963-67; dir. mktg. Charles Scribner's Sons, 1967-74, dir. trade pub., 1974-78, exec. v.p., 1978-83, pres., 1983-85; pub. spl. interest books Macmillan Pub. Co., 1985-86, v.p., 1986; pub. The Polish Heritage Publ., 1987—, Hippocrene Books, N.Y.C., 1988—. Author 2 books; translator 2 books. Served with Polish Forces, 1942-45, U.K. Home: 130 E 24th St New York NY 10010-3618 Office: Hippocrene Books Inc 171 Madison Ave New York NY 10016-5110

GALBRAITH, EVAN GRIFFITH, investment banker; b. Toledo, July 2, 1928; s. Evan Griffith and Nina (Allen) G.; m. Nancy Burdick, July 23, 1955 (div. 1962); 1 dau., Alexandra; m. Marie Helene Rockwell, Dec. 4, 1964; children: Evan, Christina, John. B.A., Yale U., 1950; LL.B, Harvard U., 1953. Bar: D.C. 1953, N.Y. 1957. Assoc. firm Shearman & Sterling, N.Y.C., 1957-60; spl. asst. to sec. Dept. Commerce, Washington, 1960-61; v.p. Morgan Guaranty Trust Co., N.Y.C. and Paris, 1961-69; chmn. Bankers Trust Internat., 1969-75; mng. dir. Dillon, Read & Co., London and N.Y.C., 1975-81; U.S. ambassador to France Paris, 1981-85; adv. dir. Morgan Stanley, 1985—; chmn. LVMH Moet Hennessy Louis Vuitton Inc., 1985-98; chmn. bd. Nat. Rev. mag., N.Y.C. Co-author: The German Stock Corporation, 1966; author: Ambassadeur du Choc, 1986, Ambassador in Paris, 1987, Operation Ventd'Quest, 1997; contbr. articles to fin. jours. Served with USNR, 1953-57, CIA. Mem. Coun. on Fgn. Rels., Yale Club. Home: 133 E 64th St New York NY 10021-7045

GALBRAITH, FRANCES LYNN, educational administrator; b. Phila., Jan. 16, 1950; d. Noble Galbraith and Frances J. Griffin; divorced; 1 child, Frances Lynn Witucki; m. Spencer McPherson Kuhn, June 23, 1989, (div.); children: Arthur McPherson, Edward James. BA, Rutgers U., Camden, N.J., 1974; EdD, Rutgers U., New Brunswick, N.J., 1986; MA, Glassboro State Coll., 1977. Tchr. of English Lenape Regional H.S., Medford, N.J., 1974-90, cmty. rels. coord., 1977-90, supr. curriculum, 1990-94; tchr. English Shawnee H.S., 1994-96; dir. adult and continuing edn. Lenape Regional H.S. Dist., 1996—; adj. prof. Rutgers U., New Brunswick, 1981—; chmn. writing com., test devel. N.J. Dept. Edn., Trenton, 1982-94, cons. N.J. Div. Gen. Acad. Edn.; reader, table leader, Ednl. Testing Svc., Princeton, N.J., 1981—; mem. reading and writing adv. coun. N.J. Dept. Higher Edn., 1980-81; manuscript reviewer Harcourt, Brace, Jovanovich; test devel. cons., item developer, Nat. Evaluation Systems, Westinghouse/Am. Coun. on Edn.; cons., workshop presenter Ednl. Info. Resource Ctr. South, 1987—; presenter in field. Mem. Nat. Coun. Tchrs. English (mem. commn. on composition 1986-90, writing achievement awards adv. com. 1984-87; chmn. numerous confs., asst. editor Quarterly Rev. of Doublespeak, 1980-84, other), N.J. Coll. English Assn. (presenter 1983 spring conf.), NEA (presenter conf. 1983), N.J. Edn. Assn., N.J. Assn. Learning Cons., N.J. Assn. Supervision and Curriculum Deve. (exec. bd. 1980-81, editor FOCUS newsletter 1980-81, other offices), Assn. South Jersey English Depts. Home: 118 Sheridan Dr Cape May NJ 08204-3833 Office: Lenape Regional High Sch 235 Hartford Rd Medford NJ 08055-4001

GALBRAITH, JAMES MARSHALL, lawyer, business executive; b. Iowa City, Oct. 4, 1942; s. John Semple and Laura (Huddleston) G.; m. Margaret Rodi, Aug. 19, 1966; children: Margaret Laura, Katherine Lou, Robert James. BA, Pomona Coll., 1964; JD, Stanford U., 1967. Bar: Calif. 1968. Assoc. Gibson, Dunn & Crutcher, Los Angeles, 1967-68; ptnr. Rodi, Pollock, Pettker, Galbraith & Cahill, Los Angeles, 1968-84, of counsel, 1984—; pres. Bell Helmets Internat., Inc., San Marino, Calif., 1980-84; ptnr. Palm Properties Co., San Marino, Calif., 1979—; pres., dir. Van de Kamp's Bakers, Inc., San Marino, 1985-87; ptnr. Huntington Hotel Assocs., San Marino, 1986-95; pres. Crestmont Fin. Svcs., Inc., 1991—, Crestmont Industries, LLC, 1996—. Author: In the Name of the People, 1977, The Money Tree, 1982, Fear of Failure, 1993, Patient Power, 1995; mem. bd. editors Stanford Law Rev., 1965-67. Trustee Pomona Coll., 1987-89, hon. trustee, 1989—; trustee, mem. exec. com. Children's Hosp. L.A., 1986-91, hon. trustee, 1991—; mem. Soc. of Fellows, Huntington Libr. Art Gallery and Bot. Gardens, 1982—; mem. Young Pres. Orgn., 1979-93. Mem. State Bar Calif., Phi Beta Kappa. Episcopalian. Clubs: California (L.A.), Valley Hunt (Pasadena). Home: 1640 Oak Grove Ave San Marino CA 91108-1109 Office: 2600 Mission St San Marino CA 91108-1676

GALBRAITH, JOHN KENNETH, retired economist; b. Iona Station, Ont., Can., Oct. 15, 1908; s. William Archibald and Catherine (Kendall) G.; m. Catherine Atwater, Sept. 17, 1937; children: Alan, Peter, James. BS, U. Guelph, 1931, LLD (hon.); MS, U. Calif., 1933, PhD, 1934; postgrad., Cambridge (Eng.) U., 1937-38; LLD (hon.), Bard Coll., U. Calif., Miami U., U. Mass., U. Mysore, Brandeis U., U. Toronto, U. Sask., U. Mich., U. Durham, R.I. Coll., Boston Coll., Hobart and William Smith Colls., Albion Coll., Tufts U., Adelphi Suffolk Coll., Mich. State U., Louvain U., Oxford U., U. Paris, Carleton Coll., U. Vt., Queens U., Moscow State U., Harvard U., Smith Coll., others. Research fellow U. Calif., 1931-34; instr. and tutor Harvard U., 1934-39; asst. prof. econs. Princeton U., 1939-42; econ. adviser Nat. Def. Adv. Commn., 1940-41; asst. adminstr. in charge price div. OPA, 1941-42, dep. adminstr., 1942-43; mem. bd. of editors Fortune Mag., 1943-48; lectr. Harvard U., 1948-49, prof. econs., 1949-75, Paul M. Warburg prof. econs., 1959-75, ret., 1975; hon. fellow Trinity Coll., Cambridge U.; hon. prof. U. Geneva; U.S. ambassador to India, 1961-63. Author: numerous books including American Capitalism, 1952, A Theory of Price Control, 1952, The Great Crash, 1955, The Affluent Society, 1958, The Liberal Hour, 1960, Economic Development, 1963, The Scotch, 1964, The New Industrial State, 1967, Indian Painting, 1968, Ambassador's Journal, 1969, Economics,

Peace and Laughter, 1971, A China Passage, 1973, Economics and the Public Purpose, 1973, Money: Whence It Came, Where It Went, 1975, The Age of Uncertainty, 1977, (with Nicole Salinger) Almost Everyone's Guide to Economics, 1978, Annals of an Abiding Liberal, 1979, The Nature of Mass Poverty, 1979, A Life in Our Times, 1981, The Anatomy of Power, 1983, The Voice of the Poor: Essays in Economic and Political Persuasion, 1983, A View From the Stands, 1986, Economics in Perspective: A Critical History, 1987, (with Stanislav Menshikov) Capitalism, Communism and Coexistence, 1988, (novel) The Triumph, 1968, A Tenured Professor, 1990, The Culture of Contentment, 1992, A Journey Through Economic Time, 1994, A Short History of Financial Euphoria, 1993, The Good Society, 1996; contbr. to econ. and sci. jours. Dir. U.S. Strategic Bombing Survey, 1945; dir. Office of Econ. Security Policy, State Dept., 1946. Fellow Social Sci. Research Council, 1937-38; Recipient Medal Freedom, 1946. Fellow Am. Acad. Arts and Letters (pres. 1984-87); mem. AAAS, Am. Econ. Assn. (pres. 1972), Am. Agrl. Econ. Assn., Ams. for Dem. Action (chmn. 1967-68). Clubs: Century, Saturday. Home: 30 Francis Ave Cambridge MA 02138-2010 Office: Harvard U 206 Littauer Ctr Cambridge MA 02138

GALBRAITH, JOHN ROBERT, insurance company executive; b. Portland, Oreg., Oct. 18, 1938; s. Maurice Kerr and Margaret Ione (Veach) G.; m. Maureen McKovich, Oct. 2, 1971 (div. Mar. 1978); children: Margaret Maureen, Marc Ryan; m. Betty Jean Irelan, Dec. 11, 1987. BA, Willamette U., 1960; MBA, U. Washington, 1962. CPA, Oreg. Staff acct. Ernst & Young, Portland, 1962-65; treas. First Pacific Corp., Portland, 1965-71; v.p., treas. Geo McKovich Cos., Palm Beach, Fla. and L.A., 1971-80; v.p., chief fin. officer SAIF Corp., Salem, Oreg., 1980-82; exec. v.p., CFO Liberty N.W. Ins. Corp., Portland, 1983—, bd. dir.; bd. dir. Helmsman Mgmt. Svcs. N.W., Inc., Portland, 1987—. Bd. dirs. Liberty Health Plan, Inc., Portland, 1992—. With Army N.G., 1957-66. Mem. AICPAs, Fin. Exec. Inst., Fla. Ins. CPAs, Calif. Soc. CPAs, Oreg. Soc. CPAs, Multnomah Athletic Club. Republican. Home: 3025 NE Dunckley St Portland OR 97212-1729 Office: Liberty NW Ins Corp One Liberty Ctr Portland OR 97232-2038

GALBRAITH, JOHN SEMPLE, history educator; b. Glasgow, Scotland, Nov. 10, 1916; came to U.S., 1925, naturalized, 1931; s. James M. and Mary (Marshall) G.; m. Laura Huddleston, Aug. 22, 1940; children: James M., John H., Mary P. BA, Miami U., Oxford, Ohio, 1938; MA, U. Iowa, 1939, PhD, 1943; LLD, Mount Union Coll., 1968. Prof. Brit. Empire history UCLA, 1948-64, 69-84, chmn. dept., 1954-58; chancellor U. Calif., San Diego, 1964-68, prof. history, 1984—; Smuts vis. fellow Cambridge (Eng.) U., 1968-69. Served as officer AUS, 1943-46. Mem. AAUP, Royal Hist. Soc., Am. Hist. Assn. (pres. Pacific Coast br. 1965), Can. Hist. Assns., Soc. Am. Historians, African Studies Assn., Athenaeum Club (London), Phi Beta Kappa. Author: The Establishment of Canadian Diplomatic Status in Washington, 1951; The Hudson's Bay Company as an Imperial Factor, 1957; Reluctant Empire, 1963; Mackinnon and East Africa, 1972; Crown and Charter, 1974; The Little Emperor, 1976.

GALBRAITH, JOHN WILLIAM, securities company executive; b. Kansas City, Mo., Aug. 8, 1921; s. Harvey C. and Honora E. (Coughlin) G.; m. Rosemary P. Loveless, Sept. 11, 1948; children: Rachel Leah Galbraith Watson, Rebecca Louise. BSBA, U. Mo., Columbia, 1941. CPA, Kans. V.p. United Internat. Fund Inc., Hamilton, Bermuda, 1961-63, United Funds Mgmt., Toronto, Ont., Can., 1963-69, Waddell & Reed Inc., Kansas City, Mo., 1969-70; pres. Lexington Mgmt. Corp., Englewood, N.J., 1970-74; pres., chmn. Templeton Funds Mgmt. Inc., St. Petersburg, Fla., 1974-91; vice chmn. Templeton, Galbraith & Hansberger, Ltd., Nassau, The Bahamas, 1986-92; pres. Galbraith Properties, Inc., 1991—; bd. dirs. Templeton Mut. Funds, Gulf West Banks. Bd. govs. Contractual Plan Sponsors, N.Y.C., 1971-74; chmn. adminstrn. com. Can. Mut. Fund Assn., Toronto, 1964-67; councilman Borough of Saddle River, N.J., 1977; trustee Eckerd Coll., St. Petersburg, 1983—, chmn. bd. trustees, 1990-92; chmn. Fla. Internat. Mus., Inc., 1992-98. Mem. AICPA, Nat. Assn. Securities Dealers (fin. prin., investment cos. com. 1980-84), Investment Co. Inst. (bd. govs. 1985-88, 89-91), St. Petersburg Yacht Club, Yale (N.Y.C.) Club, Mid-Ocean (Bermuda) Club. Republican. Roman Catholic. Office: 360 Central Ave Ste 1300 Saint Petersburg FL 33701-3838

GALBRAITH, NANETTE ELAINE GERKS, forensic and management sciences company executive; b. Chgo., June 15, 1928; d. Harold William and Maybelle Ellen (Little) Gerks; m. Oliver Galbraith III, Dec. 18, 1948; children: Craig Scott, Diane Frances. BS with high honors with distinction, San Diego State U., 1978. Diplomate Am. Bd. Forensic Document Examiners. Examiner of questioned documents San Diego County Sheriff's Dept. Crime Lab., San Diego, 1975-80; sole prop. Nanette G. Galbraith, Examiner of Questioned Documents, San Diego, 1980-82; pres., examiner of questioned documents Galbraith Forensic & Mgmt. Scis., Ltd., San Diego, 1982-97; cons., 1997—; one of keynote speakers Internat. Assn Forensic Scis., Adelaide, South Australia, 1990. Contbr. articles to profl. jours. including Jour. Forensic Scis., Forensic Sci. Internat., Internat. Jour. Forensic Document Examiners. Fellow Am. Acad. Forensic Scis. (questioned documents section, del. to Peoples Rep. of China 1986, USSR, 1988); mem. Am. Soc. Questioned Document Examiners, Southwestern Assn. Forensic Document Examiners (charter), U. Club Atop Symphony Towers, Phi Kappa Phi. Republican. Episcopalian.

GALBRAITH, RICHARD ANTHONY, physician, hospital administrator; b. Valetta, Malta, Oct. 6, 1950; came to U.S., 1978; s. Robert Edward and Marjorie Dorothy (Ralph) G. BS, Kings Coll., London, 1971, MD, 1974; PhD, Med. U. S.C., 1981. Diplomate English Bd. Internal Medicine, subspecialty endocrinology Am. Bd. Med. Mgmt.; lic. physician, S.C., N.Y. Vt. Intern, house officer pediatrics, house officer surgery King's Coll. Hosp., St. Nicholas Hosp., London, 1975-76; resident gen. internal medicine St. Nicholas Hosp., London, 1976-77, med. registrar, 1977-78; fellow endocrinology Med. U. S.C., Charleston, 1978-80, attending physician Charleston Meml. & Charleston VA hosps., 1980-83; assoc. physician The Rockefeller U. Hosp., N.Y.C., 1983-88, physician, 1988-95; program dir. Gen. Clin. Rsch. Ctr. U. Vt., Burlington, 1995—, assoc. dean for patient-oriented rsch., 1995—; med. dir., adminstr. The Rockefeller U. Hosp., N.Y.C., 1990-95; coattending physician N.Y. Hosp., 1984-95; dir. patient oriented rsch. U. Vt. Med. Ctr., Burlington, 1995—; instr. medicine Med. U. S.C., 1980-81, asst. prof. medicine, grad. sch. faculty, 1981-83; asst. prof. The Rockefeller U., 1983-90, assoc. prof., 1990-95; adj. asst. prof. medicine Cornell U. Med. Coll., 1984-90, adj. assoc. prof. medicine, 1990-95; co-attending physician N.Y. Hosp., N.Y.C., 1984-95; dir. introduction clin. rsch. for MD, PhD students Rockefeller U./Cornell Med. Sch., N.Y.C., 1988-95; preceptor in advanced biochemistry for chemistry students Rockefeller U., N.Y.C., 1989-95; prof. medicine U. Vt., Burlington, 1995—. Contbr. over 70 articles to profl. jours.; patentee in field. Bd. dirs. Am. Porphyria Found., Chgo., 1988—, Internat. Com. on Porphyrinogenicity of Drugs, 1987—. Hartford fellow, Surdna Found. fellow. Fellow Am. Soc. Clin. Nutrition, Royal Coll. Physicians; mem. ACP, Brit. Med. Assn., Royal Coll. Physicians U.K., Am. Fedn. Clin. Rsch., N.Am. Soc. Study Obesity, Am. Coll. Physician Execs., Royal Soc. Medicine, Am. Soc. Clin. Investigationi, Am. Inst. Nutrition. Office: U Vt Med Ctr Baird 795 Burlington VT 05406

GALBRAITH, RICHARD FREDERICK, physician, neurologist; b. Seattle, Apr. 8, 1931; s. Maurice Frederick and Florence Evelyn (Smith) G.; m. Margaret Jean Patten, July 30, 1955; children: Deborah, Mark, Christine, Kevin. BS, Seattle U., 1952; MD, St. Louis U., 1956. Diplomate Am. Bd. Psychiatry and Neurology (examiner 1970-85). Intern St. John's Hosp., St. Louis, 1956-57; resident in medicine and neurology Mayo Grad. Sch. Medicine, Rochester, Minn., 1959-64; physician, neurologist Mpls. Clinic Neurology, 1965-96, Minn. Neurologic Evaluations Ltd., St. Louis Park, 1996—; pres., chmn. Found. Health Care, 1979-81. Lt. Med. Svc. Corps, USN, 1957-59. Fellow Am. Acad. Neurology, AMA, Hennipen County Med. Soc. Fax: 612-925-0809. Home: 6228 Sandpiper Ct Edina MN 55436-1926 Office: Minn Neurol Evauations Ltd Norwest Bank Bldg Ste 304 3601 Park Center Blvd Saint Louis Park MN 55416-2525

GALBRAITH, RUTH LEGG, retired university dean, home economist; b. Lecompte, La., Nov. 5, 1923; d. Byron S. and Dora Ruth (Lindley) Legg; m. Harry W. Galbraith, June 16, 1950; 1 son, Allan Legg. B.S., Purdue U., 1945, Ph.D., 1950. Chemist E.I. duPont de Nemours, Waynesboro, Va., 1945-46; textile chemist Gen. Electric Co., Bridgeport, Conn., 1946-47; teaching asst. Purdue U., 1947-48, research fellow, 1948-50; prof. textiles and clothing U. Tenn., Knoxville, 1950-55; asso. prof. U. Ill., Urbana, 1956-64; prof. U. Ill., 1964-70, chmn. textiles and clothing div., 1962-70; prof., head consumer affairs dept. Auburn (Ala.) U., 1970-73; dean Sch. Home Econs., head home econs. research, 1973-85; mem. task force on quality of living Dept. Agr., 1967-68; mem. nat. adv. com. Flammable Fabrics Act, 1971-73; mem. U.S. Dept. Agr. Com. of Nine, 1981-83, chmn., 1983. Mem. editorial bd.: Research Jour. Home Econs., 1973-77, chmn. policy bd., 1978-80; contbr. articles to profl. jours. Recipient Disting. Alumni award Purdue U., 1970. Fellow Am. Inst. Chemists; mem. Am. Home Econs. Assn. (chmn. agy. mem. unit 1975-76, chmn. research sect. 1978-80, Outstanding Home Economist award 1984), Ala. Home Econs. Assn. (pres. 1983-84), Am. Assn. Textile Chemists and Colorists, Am. Chem. Soc., ASTM (3d v.p. com. D-13 textiles 1975-79), Assn. Adminstrs. Home Econs., Nat. Council Adminstrs. Home Econs., AAUW, Sigma Xi, Omicron Nu, Phi Kappa Phi, Delta Kappa Gamma. Home: 368 Singleton St Auburn AL 36830-6317

GALBRAITH, WILLIAM BRUCE, physician, educator; b. Romeo, Mich., Oct. 21, 1930; s. Bruce McKenzie and Helen Athelene (Stringham) G.; m. Jo Anne Fetterly Ames, June 27, 1953; children: Elise, Susan, Scott. BS, Ariz. State U., 1953; MD, George Washington U., 1957. Diplomate Am. Bd. Internal Medicine. Internship Good Samaritan Hosp., Phoenix, 1957-58; residency U. Iowa Hosps. and Clinics, Iowa City, 1958-61; instr. internal medicine U. Iowa Coll. Medicine, Iowa City, 1961-63, asst. prof., 1963-65, dir. gen. medicine tng. program, 1994-96, assoc. internal medicine, 1994-95; prof. clin. internal medicine U. Iowa, Iowa City, 1995-97, prof. emeritus, 1998—; owner Internists P.C., Cedar Rapids, Iowa, 1965-93, pres., 1986-93; bd. dirs. Am. Bd. Internal Medicine, Phila., 1992-96. Fellow ACP (gov. for Iowa 1979-83, Laureate award 1988, master 1997); mem. Iowa Clin. Soc. Internal Medicine (Internist of Yr. 1994), Alpha Omega Alpha. Avocations: flyfishing, photography, birding.

GALDA, DWIGHT WILLIAM, financial company executive; b. Bklyn., Dec. 19, 1942; s. Fred C. and Audrey D. G.; m. Margaret L., Mar. 21, 1992; children: Cynthia A., Gregory J. BA, Widener U., 1964; postgrad., Am. U., 1965-67, Tex. Christian U., 1997—. Cert. Nat. Assn. Securities Dealers; registered prin. and Natl. Panal Arbitration. Rep. United Svcs. Planning Assn. and Ind. Rsch. Agy., Ft. Worth, 1983-86; dist. exec. USPA and IRA, Ft. Worth, 1986-92, regional exec., 1992-96, prin., 1990-96; prin. Carefree (Ariz.) Capital Mgmt. and Rsch., Carefree, Ariz., 1997—; ind. cons. Dwight W. Galda Consultancy, 1985—; spkr. in field. Contbr. articles profl. jours.; creator U.S. Army Opposing Force Program, 1976. Lt. col. U.S. Army, 1964-82; Army attache U.S. Embassy, Cambodia, 1973-75. Recipient Pace award Dept. of Army, 1976, 77, Legion of Merit, Bronze star, Meritorious Svc. medal, air medal, Vietnamese Cross of Gallantry with Silver star, Cambodian Nat. Def. Svc. medal. Fellow Assn. Investment Mgmt. and Rsch. (adv. advocacy com.), Phoenix Soc. Investment Analysts. Episcopalian. Avocations: running, chamber music, travel. Home: 2741 Manorwood Trl Fort Worth TX 76109-5589 Office: Drawer 1168 100 Easy St Carefree AZ 85377-0180

GALDI-WEISSMAN, NATALIE ANN, secondary education educator; b. N.Y.C., Nov. 28, 1948; d. Alphonse Vincent and Jean (Banek) Galdi; m. David Allen Weissman, Feb. 7, 1987; 1 child, Adam Justin Weissman. BA, Adelphi U., 1970, MA, 1971; PhD, NYU, 1978. Tchr. Jr. High Sch. 101, N.Y.C., 1971-81, Evander Child High Sch., N.Y.C., 1981-82, South Bronx High Sch., N.Y.C., 1982—; adj. prof. Mercy Coll., Dobbs Ferry, N.Y., 1976-88; prep. coord. South Bronx High Sch., acad. olympics coach, 1985-87. Mem. Union Fedn. Tchr. Avocations: gardening, environmental wildlife affairs, needlepoint, knitting, dog training.

GALE, ARNOLD DAVID, pediatric neurologist, consultant; b. Chgo., Nov. 2, 1949; s. Benjamin and Revelle Frances (Steinman) G. AB summa cum laude, Stanford U., 1971; MD, Johns Hopkins U., 1976. Diplomate Am. Bd. Pediatrics, Nat. Bd. Med. Examiners; med. lic., Calif. Resident in pediatrics Mass. Gen. Hosp., Boston, 1976-78; postdoctoral fellow Johns Hopkins Hosp., Balt., 1978-79, resident in neurology, 1979-82; asst. prof. pediatrics and neurology George Washington U. Sch. Medicine, Washington, 1982-89; dir. neurology tng. program Children's Hosp. Nat. Med. Ctr., Washington, 1982-89; med. info. officer Muscular Dystrophy Assn., Tucson, 1992—; consulting neurologist Vaccine Injury Program U.S. Dept. HHS, Rockville, Md., 1989—, Inst. Vaccine Safety Sch. Hygiene and Pub. Health Johns Hopkins U., Balt., 1998—; adv. panel FDA, Rockville, 1983-89; reviewer Am. Jour. Diseases of Children, 1991, New Eng. Jour. Medicine, 1986. Author: Pediatric Emergency Medicine, 1989; contbr. articles to profl. jours. Support group coord. Muscular Dystrophy Assn., San Jose, Calif., 1989—; mem. Pres.'s Com. Employment of People Disabilities, Washington, 1992—; med. adv. bd. Multiple Sclerosis Soc., Santa Clara, Calif., 1990—; v.p. Muscular Dystrophy Assn., Tucson, 1992-94, bd. dirs., 1993-96. Recipient Nat. Rehab. award Allied Svcs., Scranton, Pa., 1994. Fellow Am. Acad. Pediatrics; mem. Am. Acad. Neurology, Am. Soc. Neurol. Investigation (founding mem.), Child Neurology Soc., Nat. Alumni Coun. (Johns Hopkins U.), Phi Beta Kappa, Alpha Omega Alpha. Jewish. Avocations: writing, travel. Office: 335 Elan Village Ln Unit 107 San Jose CA 95134-2540

GALE, EDWIN JOHN, prosecutor; b. Brattleboro, Vt., Apr. 8, 1943; s. Richard Ephriam and Florence (Mead) G.; children: Karen Elizabeth, Brian Paul. BS, U.S. Naval Acad., 1965; JD, U. Santa Clara, 1972. Bar: Calif. 1972, R.I. 1979, U.S. Dist. Ct. R.I., U.S. Dist. Ct. (no. dist.) Ohio, U.S. Dist. Ct. Mass., U.S. Dist. Ct. (cen. dist.) Calif., U.S. Ct. Appeals (1st cir.). Atty. organized crime and racketeering sect. U.S. Dept. Justice, Cleve., Washington and Providence, 1972-85; chief L.A. strike force organized crime and racketeering sect. U.S. Dept. Justice, 1985-87; 1st asst. U.S. Atty.'s Office, Providence, 1987-93; U.S. atty. U.S. Dept. of Justice, Providence, R.I., 1993-94; Fed. Bar Examiner, 1995—. Mem. R.I. Ho. of Dels., 1997—. Capt. USNR, ret. Home: 215 King's Ridge Rd Wakefield RI 02879 Office: Office of US Atty 50 Kennedy Plz Providence RI 02903-2393

GALE, FOURNIER JOSEPH, III, lawyer; b. Mobile, Ala., Aug. 3, 1944; s. Fournier J. Jr. and Clara (Beckham) G.; m. Louise Smith, Aug. 7, 1965; children: Carolyn, Jeanette. BA, U. Ala., 1966, JD, 1969; postgrad., Oxford U., summer 1968. Bar: Ala. 1969. From assoc. to ptnr. Cabaniss, Johnston, Gardner, Dumas & O'Neal, Birmingham, Ala., 1969-84; ptnr. Maynard, Cooper & Gale, PC, Birmingham, 1984—; bd. dirs. McWane, Inc., Birmingham; gen. counsel, bd. dirs. Bus. Coun. Ala., Birmingham, 1977—; mem. Ala. Permanent Study Commn. on Judiciary, 1977-83; mem. Jefferson County Jud. Nominating Commn., 1993—; chmn. Ala. Commn. on Higher Edn., 1998—; spl. counsel to Gov. Don Siegelman, 1999—. Mem. Leadership Birmingham, 1986-87; pres. U. Ala. Law Sch. Found., 1987—. Mem. ABA (standing com. on environ. law, standing com. on fed. judiciary), Birmingham Bar Assn. (pres. 1989), Ala. Young Lawyers Assn. (pres. 1976-77), Am. Judicature Soc. (bd. dirs. 1980-85), Jud. Conf. Ala., Am. Bar Found., Kiwanis. Roman Catholic. Home: 2937 Southwood Rd Birmingham AL 35223-1232 Office: Maynard Cooper & Gale PC 2400 Amsouth Harbert Plz Birmingham AL 35203

GALE, JOSEPH H., federal judge; b. Smithfield, Va., 1953; s. Robert Whitfield and Charlotte H. G. AB, Princeton U., 1976; JD, U. Va., 1980. Atty. Dewey, Ballantine, Bushby, Palmer & Wood, N.Y.C., Washington, 1980-83, Dickstein, Shapiro & Morin, Washington, 1983-84; legis. counsel Senator Daniel P. Moynihan, Washington, 1985-88; adminstrv. asst. and tax counsel Hon. Daniel P. Moynihan, Washington, 1989, chief counsel, 1990-92; chief tax counsel Senate Finance Com., Washington, 1993-94, minority chief of staff, 1995; judge U.S. Tax Ct., Washington, 1996—. Dillard fellow U. Va. Office: US Tax Court 400 2nd St NW Washington DC 20217-0002

GALE, MARLA, social worker; b. Uniontown, Pa., July 20; d. Saul and Sarah (Lisowitz) Krongold; m. Edward Gale, June 12, 1954; children: Jeffrey, Wendy, Lori. AB magna cum laude, U. Miami, 1970; MSW, Barry Coll., 1972. Diplomate Am. Bd. Clin. Social Work; cert. family mediator. Clin. assoc. prof. Barry U., Miami Shores, Fla.; rsch. social worker VA Hosp., Miami, Fla., 1971; caseworker Jewish Family Svc. Broward County, Hollywood, Fla., 1971-81, supr. profl. staff, 1981-88; pvt. practice Boca Raton, Fla., 1992—; v.p. Coun. for Marriage Preservation and Divorce Resolution. Author: A Toolbox of Relationship Skills, 1992, Dirty Dishes and Other War Stories, 1998, Communication Solutions at Home, At Work, At Play, 1999. Mem. NASW (diplomate), Acad. Cert. Social Workers. Democrat. Jewish. Office: 5301 N Federal Hwy Boca Raton FL 33487-4917

GALE, MICHAEL JONATHAN, entrepreneur; b. Adelaide, Australia, Oct. 27, 1962; s. Milton Ewart and Gwendoline Fay (Gilding) G.; m. Annette Francis Carr; 1 child, Kirsty Ellen; m. Allison Diane Owens; children: Matthew Jonathan, Cameron David. Prin. The Harbor Book Shop, Adelaide, 1982-86; bus. devel. mgr. Computer Power Group, Melbourne and Sydney, Australia, 1986-90; mng. dir. Macromedia Pacific, San Francisco and Sydney, 1990-93; CEO Double Impact, San Francisco, 1993—; bd. dirs. Double Impact Capital, Melbourne, Tradewind, Inc., Boston, Haht Asia, San Francisco, Voteglobal.com, San Francisco. Office: Double Impact 10th Fl 78S Market St San Francisco CA 94103-2033

GALE, NEIL JAN, internet consultant, computer consultant; b. Chgo., Jan. 12, 1960; s. Jack and Adele (Field) G. AA in Computer Sci., Wright Coll., 1980; D of Bus. Mgmt. (hon.), London Inst. Applied Rsch., 1993; diploma, Academia Argentina de Diplomacia, 1994; diploma (hon.), Institut Des Affaires Internationales, Paris, 1994; D of Bus. Mgmt. (hon.), World Acad., Monchengladbach, Germany, 1994. Mgr. Gen. Fin. Co., Chgo., 1980-84; mktg. mgr. Midland Fin. Co., Chgo., 1984-85; mktg. dir. Diamond Mortgage Corp., Chgo., 1985-86; sr. fin. analyst McKay Mazda-Nissan, Evanston, Ill., 1987-88; pres., CEO, Nat. Consumer Credit Cons., Chgo., 1988—; webmaster Everything Internet (merger with Millenium Techs. Inc. 1998), Bloomingdale, IL, 1996-98; pres. DrGale.com, Bloomingdale, Ill., 1998—; hon. prof. bus. mgmt. Inst. des Hautes Etudes Econs. et Sociales, Brussels, 1993; hon. prof. fin. Australian Inst. Coordinated Rsch., 1994; mem. adv. coun. Internat. Biog. Ctr., Cambridge, Eng.; mem. bd. govs., dep. gov. Am. Biog. Inst., 1990—, mem. rsch. bd. advisors, 1989—; notary pub. Ill., 1986-90. Contbr. articles to profl. jours. First aid chmn. Walk with Israel, 1977; notary pub., Ill., 1986-90. Decorated Knight of Order of San Ciriaco; recipient Bus. in Urban Environment award Chgo. Bd. Edn. and Ill. Bell Tel. Co., 1978, Outstanding Achievement award Chgo. Pub. Libr., 1979. Mem. Auto Credit (hon.), Friendship Cir. Club (treas. 1976-78). Avocation: antique Chgo. postcard and book collection. Home and Office: DrGale.com 780 W Army Trail Rd Ste 208 Carol Stream IL 60188*

GALE, ROBERT L., educational association administrator, consultant; b. St. Cloud, Minn., Jan. 13, 1927; s. John Henry and Helen (Andrews) G.; m. Barbara Carr Davis, Oct. 19, 1951; children: Jennifer Gale Dunkin, Robert L. Gale, Jr., Morgan Andrews. Midshipman, U.S. Naval Acad., 1945-46; BA, Carleton Coll., 1948; DHL, U. N.C., Asheville, 1989. Editor-in-chief Maco Mag. Corp., N.Y.C., 1954-57; v.p. Carleton Coll., Northfield, Minn., 1957-63; dir. recruiting Peace Corps, Washington, 1963-65; dir. pub. affairs EEOC, Washington, 1965-66; chmn., ceo Gale Assocs., Washington, 1966-74; pres. Assn. Governing Bds. Univs. and Colls., Washington, 1974-92, pres. emeritus, 1992—; bd. trustees Carleton Coll., Northfield, 1972—; bd. dirs. Nat. Peace Corps Assn., Washington, Nat. Ctr. Nonprofit Bds., Washington, Nat. Exec. Svcs. Corps, N.Y.C., CARE, Inc., Atlanta, 1982-96, U. Pretoria Fund. Chmn. bd. Nat. Peace Garden Monument, Washington, 1995—. With U.S. Navy, 1944-45. Democrat. Episcopalian. Avocations: tennis, travel, volunteering. Home: Rte 1 Bethany Beach DE 19930-9801

GALE, ROBERT LEE, retired American literature educator and critic; b. Des Moines, Dec. 27, 1919; s. Erie Lee and Miriam (Fisher) G.; m. Maureen Dowd, Nov. 18, 1944; children: John Lee, James Dowd, Christine Ann. BA, Dartmouth Coll., 1942; MA, Columbia U., 1947, PhD, 1952. Lectr. Columbia U., N.Y.C., 1947-48; instr. U. Del., Newark, 1949-52; asst. prof. U. Miss., Oxford, 1952-56, assoc. prof., 1956-59; asst. prof. U. Pitts., 1959-60, assoc. prof., 1960-65, prof. Am. lit., 1965-87, ret., 1987; Fulbright prof. Istituto Universitario Orientale, Naples, Italy, 1956-58, U. Helsinki, Finland, 1975. Author numerous books, including: Thomas Crawford, 1964, The Caught Image: Figurative Language in Henry James, 1964, Richard Henry Dana, Jr., 1969, Francis Parkman, 1973, Plots and Characters in Mark Twain, 1973, John Hay, 1978, Luke Short, 1981, Will Henry, 1984, Louis L'Amour, 1985, rev. edit., 1992, A Henry James Encyclopedia, 1989, Matt Braun, 1990, A Nathaniel Hawthorne Encyclopedia, 1991, The Gay Nineties: A Cultural Dictionary of the 1890s in the U.S., 1992, A Cultural Encyclopedia of the American 1850s, 1993, A Herman Melville Encyclopedia, 1995, An F. Scott Fitzgerald Encyclopedia, 1998; contbr. numerous articles, book chpts. and revs. Served with U.S. Army, 1942-46, ETO. Mem. MLA, Phi Beta Kappa. Home: 131 Techview Ter Pittsburgh PA 15213-3820

GALE, ROBERT PETER, physician, scientist, researcher; b. N.Y.C., Oct. 11, 1945; s. Harvey Thomas and Evelyn (Klein) G.; m. Tamar Tishler, June 2, 1976; children: Tal, Shir, Elan. BA, Hobart Coll., 1966; MD, SUNY, Buffalo, 1970; PhD, UCLA, 1976; DSc (hon.), Albany Med. Coll., 1987; LHD (hon.), Hobart Coll., 1987; D of Pub. Svc. (hon.), MacMurray Coll., 1988. Diplomate Am. Bd. Internal Medicine, Am. Bd. Med. Oncology, Am. Bd. Hematology. Resident in hematology and oncology UCLA, 1972-74, prof. medicine, 1974—; dir. bone marrow and stem cell transplantation Salick Health Care, Inc., 1993—; chmn. Internat. Bone Marrow Transplant Registry, Milw., 1982—; pres. Armand Hammer Ctr. for Advanced Studies in Nuc. Energy and Health; sci. dir. Ctr. for Advanced Studies in Leukemia, L.A.; mem. Am. Com. on U.S.-Soviet Rels. Author 20 books, 700 articles on hematology, oncology, immunology and transplantation. Recipient Presdl. award N.Y. Acad. Scis., 1986, Olender Peace prize, 1986, Emmy award NATAS, Scientist of Distinction award Weizmann Inst. Sci., 1988; Bogart fellow and scholar Leukemia Soc. Am., 1976-81. Fellow ACP; mem. Transplantation Soc., Am. Soc. Hematology, Am. Assn. Immunology, Internat. Soc. Hematology, Soc. Exptl. Hematology, Am. Soc. Clin. Oncology, Am. Assn. Cancer Rsch., Russian Acad. Med. Sci. (hon.). Home: 2316 Donella Circle Los Angeles CA 90077-1801 Office: 8201 Beverly Blvd Los Angeles CA 90048-4505

GALE, THOMAS MARTIN, university dean; b. Green Bay, Wis., May 16, 1926; s. Thomas Griswold and Carrie (Danz) G.; m. Mary Margaret Hardman, May 28, 1960; children—Thomas Hardman, John Martin. B.A., U. Calif. at Berkeley, 1949, M.A., 1950; Ph.D., U. Pa., 1958. Dean Coll. Arts and Scis. N.Mex. State U., 1971-91, bd. dirs. Acad. for Learning in Retirement, 1991-96, ret., 1991; with Border Books Festival, 1996—. Chmn. N.Mex. Humanities Coun., NEH, 1972-77; chmn. Las Cruces Am. 2000 Task Force, 1991—; vice-chmn. N.Mex. Commn. on Higher Edn.; bd. dirs. exec. com. N.Mex. State U. Found. With AUS, 1944-46. Social Sci. Research fellow, 1952-53, 53-54; Huntington Library fellow, 1959; Fulbright fellow Peru, 1960. Mem. Phi Beta Kappa, Phi Alpha Theta. Club: Rotarian. Home: 3115 Majestic Rdg Las Cruces NM 88011-4603

GALEAZZO, CONSTANCE JANE, neonatal nurse practitioner; b. Daytona Beach, Fla., Dec. 3, 1946; d. O.D. and Ruth (Centers) Bales; m. James Guy Galeazzo, Oct. 8, 1966; children: James Bryan, Amy Caroline, Rebecca Jane. BA, Wesleyan Coll., Macon, Ga., 1987; BSN, Ga. Coll., Milledgeville, 1990; MSN, U. South Ala., 1996. RN; cert. nurse practitioner. Program coord. Rape Crisis Line Macon-Bibb County, Ga.; mental health technician, neonatal nurse, staff nurse orthopaedics Med. Ctr. Ctrl. Ga., Macon, nurse extern; neonatal nurse practitioner, 1996—. R.A. Bowen scholar, Whitehead Found. scholar. Mem. Nat. Assn. of Neonatal Nurses, Sigma Theta Tau, Psi Chi, Gamma Beta Phi. Home: 208 Governors Walk Kathleen GA 31047-2130

GALES, ROBERT ROBINSON, judge; b. N.Y.C., Feb. 15, 1941; s. Arthur S. and Gertrude L. (Robinson) G.; m. Karen A. Terry, Nov. 25, 1986; children: Laurie Ann, Thomas Michael, Robert Robinson II, Brian Timothy, Victoria Marie. BA in History and Geography, Ohio Wesleyan U., 1962; JD, Syracuse U., 1965; LLM, George Washington U., 1966; postgrad. U. Philippines, 1969, Indsl. Coll. Armed Forces, 1971, Air U., 1977, 89. Bar: N.Y. 1966, U.S. Dist. Ct. (so. and ea. dists.) N.Y. 1967, U.S. Dist. Ct. (we. dist.) Wash. 1967, U.S. Ct. Appeals Armed Forces 1967, U.S. Ct. Claims 1967, U.S. Ct. Appeals (9th cir.) 1968, D.C. 1973, U.S. Dist. Ct. (ea. dist.) Va. 1973, U.S. Ct. Appeals (4th cir.) 1973, U.S. Ct. Appeals (2d cir.) 1975, U.S. Customs Ct. 1977, U.S. Ct. Customs and Patent Appeals 1978, Ill. 1978, U.S. Ct. Internat. Trade, 1980, U.S. Ct. Appeals (Fed. cir.) 1982, U.S. Ct. Appeals (7th cir.) 1983, U.S. Dist. Ct. (no. dist.) Ill. 1983, U.S. Dist. Ct. (so. dist.) Ill. 1984. Travel cons. ESSO Touring Svc., N.Y.C., 1960; dep. dir. internat. law 13th Air Force, Philippines, 1969-71; asst. legal advisor U.S.

del. Renegotiation of Philippines-U.S. Status of Forces Agreement, 1969-71; chief civil law Tactical Air Command, USAF, Hampton, Va., 1971-72, chief adminstrv. law, 1972-73; assoc. Herzfeld & Rubin, P.C., N.Y.C., 1973-77; task force coord. Volkswagen of Am., Inc., Englewood Cliffs, N.J., 1977; sr. atty. Velsicol Chem. Corp., sec. fgn. subsidiaries, 1977-80; asst. atty. gen. Consumer Protection div. Office of Ill. Atty. Gen., Bensenville and Joliet, 1981-83; chief Utility and Acquisition Law, 375th Air Base Group, Scott AFB, Dept. Air Force, Belleville, Ill., 1984-87; dept. counsel Def. Legal Services Agy., Directorate for Indsl. Security Clearance Rev., Arlington, Va., 1987-88, mem. appeal bd., 1988-90, chief adminstrv. judge, 1990-94; chief adminstrv. judge Def. Legal Svcs. Agy., Def. Office Hearings and Appeals, 1994—; mobilization asst. to dir. Judiciary USAF, 1987-89; dir. Civil Law Office of Judge Adv. Gen., 1989-91; sr. res. advisor to staff judge adv. Air Force Dist. of Wash., 1991-92; vis. adj. lectr. Manhattan Coll., 1973-77, N.J. Inst. Tech., 1975-77, Ill. Inst. Tech., 1978-84, So. Ill. Univ., Carbondale, 1984-86. Contbg. editor, writer to newspapers. Mem. Wash. State Soccer Commn., 1967-68; chmn. exploring com. Far East council Philippine dist. Boy Scouts Am., 1969-71; dist. judge adv. Va. VFW, 1972-73; pres., chmn. exec. com. Briarcliff Citizens for Responsive Govt., 1973-74; bd. dirs. Ossining (N.Y.) Area Jaycees, 1973-74, sec., 1974-75; pres. Ossining Hist. Soc., 1974-76; Rep. dist. leader Town of Ossining, 1974-78; dir. Soc. Prevention of Cruelty to Animals of Westchester, 1974-77; bd. dir. Briarcliff-Ossining-Scarborough br. ARC, 1975-76; mem. Westchester County Rep. Com., 1975-78; commr. Wayne Twp. (Ill.) Soccer, 1979-83; Rep. precinct committeeman Wayne Twp., 1979-82; adv. bd. Elgin (Ill.) High Sch., 1979-83; trustee Wayne Twp., 1979-85; pres. Melstone neighborhood bd. Little Rocky Run Homeowners Assn., 1987-92. Ret. col. USAFR, Vietnam. Decorated Legion of Merit, Bronze Star, Meritorious Service medal with 3 oak leaf clusters, Air Force Commendation medal with 3 oak leaf clusters, Air Force Achievement medal (U.S.) Air Force Recognition Ribbon; various medals Republic of Vietnam, Outstanding Contribution to Contracting award USAF, 1986, N.Y. State Conspicuous Svc. Cross with 2 silver devices, 1997; Master of the Bench and mem. Prettyman-Leventhal Am. Inn of Court, 1996—. Mem. Am. Judges Assn., Nat. Assn. Adminstrv. Law Judges, mem. bd. advs. to the Journal of The Nat. Assn. of Adminstn. Law Judges, 1995—. Vietnam Vets. Bar Assn. (air force judge adv.), Arnold Air Soc., Delta Phi Epsilon, Phi Alpha Delta. Republican. Contbr. articles to profl. jours. Avocations: sports, travel, collecting model soldiers, dining, writing. Home: 6638 Rockland Dr Clifton VA 20124-2501

GALES, SAMUEL JOEL, retired civilian military employee, counselor; b. Dublin, Miss., June 14, 1930; s. James McNary McNeil and Alice Francis (Smith) Broadus-Gales; m. Martha Ann Jackson (div. Jan. 1978); children: Samuel II (dec.), Martha Diane Townsend, Katherine Roselein, Karlmann Von, Carolyn B. Ratcliff, Elizabeth Angelica McCain. BA, Chapman Univ., 1981, MS, 1987. Ordained Eucharist minister, Episcopal Ch., 1985; cert. tchr., Calif. Enlisted U.S. Army, 1948, advanced through grades to master 1st sgt., 1969, ret., 1976; tchr. Monterey (Calif.) Unified Sch. Dist., 1981-82; civilian U.S. Army Directorate of Logistics, Ft. Ord, Calif., 1982-93; collateral EEOC counselor Dept. Def., U.S. Army, 1987-93; peer counselor, 1982-84. Active Family Svc. Agy., Monterey, 1979-85; rep. Episc. Soc. for Ministry on Aging, Carmel, Calif., 1980-86, Task Force on Aging, Carmel, 1983-87, vestryman, 1982-85, 91-94; ombudsman Monterey County Long-Term Care Program, Calif. Dept. for the Aging, 1993-97; vol. guide Monterey Bay Aquarium Found., 1994—, vol. docent Bay Net, Ctr. for Marine Conservation, Monterey Bay Nat. Marine Sanctuary, 1997—. Decorated Air medal. Mem. Nat. Assn. Ret. Fed. Employees (pres. chpt. 579 1999—), Am. Legion (post comdr. 1973-74), Forty and Eight (chef-de-gare 1979, 80), Monterey Chess Club, Comdr.'s Club Calif. (pres. Outpost 28 1981-82). Republican. Avocation: classical music. Home: PO Box 919 1617 Lowell St Seaside CA 93955-3811

GALIARDO, JOHN WILLIAM, lawyer; b. Elizabeth, N.J., Dec. 28, 1933; s. Joseph A. and Genevieve A. (Luxich) G.; m. Joan A. DeTurk, Aug. 26, 1961; children: Richard C., Christopher D., Elizabeth A. BS, U. Md., 1956; LLB, Columbia U., 1962. Bar: N.Y. 1962. Assoc. Dewey, Ballantine, Bushby, Palmer & Wood, N.Y.C., 1962-71; asst. gen. counsel E.R. Squibb & Sons, Inc., Princeton, N.J., 1971-77; v.p., gen. counsel Becton Dickinson and Co., Franklin Lakes, N.J., 1977-94, vice chmn. bd. dirs., gen. counsel, 1994—; trustee Com. for Econ. Devel., 1994—, HealthCare Inst. N.J., 1998—; mem. Healthcare Leadership Coun., 1994, trustee, 1995—; bd. dirs. VISX, Inc., N.J. Mfrs. Inst. Cos., Gynetics, Inc. Treas. Charter Study Commn., Scotch Plains, N.J., 1970-71; mem. Joint Consol. Com., Princeton, N.J., 1973-76; mem. legal adv. coun. Atlantic Legal Found., N.Y.C., 1986-92, trustee, 1992—; trustee Ind. Coll. Fund N.J., Summit, 1986-93, chmn., 1992; trustee Fairleigh Dickinson U., 1993—; bd. dirs. Project Hope, 1995—. Mem. ABA, N.Y. State Bar Assn., Assn. Bar of City of N.Y., Health Industry Mfrs. Assn. (bd. dirs. 1995—, chmn. 1998—), N.J. Bus. & Industry Assn. (trustee 1995—). Home: 56 Crooked Tree Ln Princeton NJ 08540-2950 Office: Becton Dickinson & Co 1 Becton Dr Franklin Lakes NJ 07417-1880*

GALILEY, C. JEROME, secondary education educator; b. Bklyn., Aug. 22, 1948; s. Jerome Clemence and Marion (Szymborski) G.; m. Diane Lynn Nichols, June 10, 1970 (div. June 1975). BA Applied Arts/Scis. with distinction, San Diego State U., 1970, MA in Edn., 1974; student, U. Calif., San Diego, 1992. Cert. vocat. subjects supr. and coord., Calif. Regional occupl. instr. San Diego County Regional Occupl. Program, Poway, Calif., 1970-71; tchr. San Dieguito Union H.S. Dist., Encinitas, Calif., 1971—; cons. Poway Unified Sch. Dist., 1971, 77; mem. vocat. adv. com. Mira Costa C.C., Oceanside, Calif., 1992—. Critical reviewer: Automotive Technology Today, 1989. Mem. Calif. Automotive Tchrs. Assn., Calif. Indsl. and Tech. Edn. Assn., Automotive Svc. Coun. Avocations: surfing, snow skiing, water skiing, mountain-biking, backpacking/hiking. Home: 4707 Norma Dr San Diego CA 92115-3137 Office: San Dieguito Union High Sch Dist 710 Encinitas Blvd Encinitas CA 92024-3357 also: Torrey Pines HS 3710 Del Mar Heights Rd San Diego CA 92130-1316

GALIN, MILES A., ophthalmologist, educator; b. N.Y.C., Jan. 6, 1932; s. Albert and Freda (Simkowitz) G.; m. Glenda Goldenberg, June 27, 1953; children—Amy, Elizabeth, Scott, Jonathan. A.B. in Math. cum laude, NYU, 1951, M.D., 1955. Diplomate Nat. Bd. Med. Examiners, Am. Bd. Ophthalmology. Intern Mt. Sinai Hosp., 1955-56; asst. resident surgery N.Y. Hosp., N.Y.C., 1956-58; resident surgeon N.Y. Hosp., 1958-59, surgeon to out-patients, 1959-61, asst. attending surgeon, 1961-64, assoc. attending surgeon, 1964-66; practice medicine, specializing in ophthalmology N.Y.C., 1959—; cons. ophthalmology Meml. Hosp., 1960-66; attending ophthalmologist Flower and Fifth Ave. Hosp., 1966-79, Met. Hosp., Bird S. Coler Hosp., 1966-79, Cath. Med. Ctr. Bklyn. and Queens, 1976—, Cabrini Med. Ctr., N.Y., 1982—, Westchester County Med. Ctr., 1975-79, Blythedale Children's Hosp., Valhalla, N.Y., 1968-73, Med. Arts Ctr. Hosp., N.Y.C., 1978—, Meadowlands Hosp., 1984—; asst. in surgery ophthalmology Cornell U. Med. Coll., N.Y.C., 1956-58, instr. surgery, 1958-61; clin. asst. prof., 1961-63, asst. prof., 1963-66; prof. N.Y. Med. Coll., 1966-79, chmn. dept. ophthalmology, 1966-73, dir. rsch., also dir. planning dept. ophthalmology, 1973-79; adj. prof. polymer sci. U. Lowell (Mass.), 1982—; exchange scientist to USSR, U.S.-Soviet Health Exchange, 1969, 71, 74; cons. FAA, Mt. Vernon Hosp., Nat. Multiple Sclerosis Found.; tech. cons. Regional Med. Program; mem. med. adv. com. Quality Vision Care; tech. adv. com. ophthalmology Bur. for Handicapped Children; mem. spl. mediation panel Supreme Ct. Appellate Div. 1st Dept.; mem. adv. bd. govs. Internat. Glaucoma Congress; bd. dirs. Better Vision Inst.; prin. investigator and co-investigator Nat. Soc. for Prevention Blindness, Cornell U., 1959-66, N.Y. Med. Coll., 1966-67, Nat. Coun. to Combat Blindness, Cornell U., 1955-66, N.Y. Med. Coll., 1966-67, USPHS, Cornell U. Med. Coll., 1959-66, N.Y. Med. Coll., 1966-77, NIAID, N.Y. Med. Coll., 1966-77 ; career scientist Health Rsch. Coun., N.Y.C., 1963-66; Dr. Henry Balconi Meml. lectr. Rochester, N.Y., 1967; Culler Meml. lectr. Columbus, Ohio, 1967; Edward A. Weisser Meml. lectr. Pitts., 1976; Binkhorst Meml. lectr., 1978, Rayner Found. lectr. U.K. Intraocular Implant Soc., 1979. Co-editor: Seminars in Ophthalmology; U.S. editor Annali de Ottalmologia, 1967—; mem. editorial bd. Metabolic Ophthalmology, Annals of Ophthalmology, Glaucoma; contbr. more than 300 articles to profl. jours., chpts. to textbooks. Trustee Upsala Coll., 1990-95. Guild of Prescribing Opticians scholar, 1956-59; Health Rsch. Coun. career scientist fellow, 1963-66; recipient William Warner Hoppin award N.Y. Acad. Medicine, 1965, Temoignange d'Honneur Can. Implant Assn., 1975, Binkhorst award Am. Intra-Ocular Implant Soc., 1978; Dr. P. Siva Reddy gold medal Global Intraocular Lens Implant Workshop, Hyderbad, India, 1982. Fellow Internat. Coll. Surgeons (vice regent 1984—); mem. AAAS (Sr. Honor award 1984), AMA, Am. Chem. Soc., Am. Acad. Ophthalmology and Otolaryngology (award of merit 1967), Am. Inst. Ultrasound in Medicine, Am. Soc. Microbiology, N.Y. Acad. Medicine, N.Y. Acad. Scis., N.Y. Soc. for Clin. Ophthalmology, Royal Soc. Health, Royal Soc. Medicine, Surg. Soc. N.Y. Med. Coll., Assn. Career Scientists N.Y.C., Assn. U. Profs. Ophthalmology, Assn. for Rsch. in Vision and Ophthalomology, Am. Soc. Cataract and Retractive Surgery (chmn. intra-ocular lens fellowship com., chmn. sci. adv. bd., v.p., pres.), Internat. Glaucoma Congress (hon. charter), Internat. Soc. Metabolic Diseases, Metabolic Ophthalmology Soc., Internat. Strabismological Assn., French, Israel ophthalmol. socs., Instituto Barraquer, N.Y. State Soc. Med. Rsch., Ophthalmol. Soc. U.K., Oxford Congress, Pan Am. Assn. Ophthalmology (hon.), Argentine, Peruvian assns. ophthalmology, Colo. Ophthalmol. Soc., Ga. Soc. Ophthalmology and Otolaryngology, Oklahoma City Clin. Soc., Pacific Coast Oto-Ophthalmology Soc., Pa. Acad. Opthalmology and Otolaryngology, Am. Intraocular Implant Soc. (pres. 1979), Pan-Am. Implant Assn. (bd. dirs. 1985—), Plastics and Rubber Inst., Phi Beta Kappa, Alpha Omega Alpha; hon. mem. numerous other profl. socs. Jewish. Clubs: Friars, DAC (N.Y.C.). Office: 345 E 37th St Fl 3D New York NY 10016-3256

GALINAT, NICOLE See **PALAUSI, NICOLE**

GALINAT, WALTON CLARENCE, research scientist; b. Manchester, Conn., Dec. 9, 1923; m. Elizabeth Ruth Warren, 1945; children: David W., Alice R. BS with honors, U. Conn., 1959; MS, U. Wis., 1951, PhD, 1953. Asst. in genetics Conn. Agrl. Experiment Sta., 1946-50; asst. in agronomy Wis. Agrl. Experimenbt Sta., 1950-53; rsch. fellow, rsch. assoc. Bussey Inst. Harvard U., 1953-64; assoc. prof. Waltham Field Sta. U. Mass., 1964-68, prof. Suburban Experiment Sta., 1968-90, prof. emeritus plant and soil scis., 1990—. With USCG, 1943-46. Recipient Disting. Econ. Botanist award Soc. Econ. Botany, 1994. Fellow AAAS. Office: Suburban Experiment Sta U Mass 240 Beaver St Waltham MA 02452-8096

GALINSKY, DEBORAH JEAN, county official; b. Oakland, Calif., Jan. 22, 1951; d. Jerome James and Barbara Ann (Ball) G.; m. William H. Furr III, Sept. 27, 1997; 1 child by previous marriage, Lauren Rachel Lipscomb. BSW, Bowie State U., 1978. Cert. housing counselor. Substitute tchr. Anne Arundel County Schs., Ft. Meade, Md., 1972-74; addictions counselor Dept. of Health, Ellicott City, Md., 1977-78; coord. dept. Citizens Svcs., housing program specialist Housing and Cmty. Devel., Ellicott City, 1979; coord. youth teen devel. County of Howard, Ellicott City, 1978—; tchr. Rapides Parish Sch. Bd., Pineville, La., 1996—, arts and crafts youth tchr., 1997; rep. Inter-Agy. Com., Ellicott City, 1990-93; computer instr. Aerie; tchr. Cabrini Sch., Alexandria, La. Author homeownership programs. Vol. Bethany United Meth. Ch., Ellicott City, 1987; tchr. Woodland Presbyn. Ch., Pineville. Fellow Nat. Assn. Housing and Revel. Ofcls.; mem. Nat. Fedn. Housing Counselors, Assn. Cmty. Svcs. (counselors rep.). Democrat. Avocations: dance choreographing, creative art crafts, water aerobics, bicycling, camping. Home: 2228 Marye St Alexandria LA 71301 Office: County of Howard Housing & Comm Devel Dept 3450 Court House Dr Ellicott City MD 21043-4330

GALINSKY, GOTTHARD KARL, classicist, educator; b. Strassburg, Alsace, Feb. 7, 1942; came to U.S., 1961, naturalized, 1971; s. Hans Karl and Edith (Margenburg) G.; m. Harriet Eileen Harris, June 29, 1986; children by previous marriage—Robert Charles, John Anthony. B.A., Bowdoin Coll., 1963; M.A., Princeton U., 1965, Ph.D., 1966. Instr. classics Princeton U., 1965-66; mem. faculty U. Tex., Austin, 1966—; prof. classics U. Tex., 1972—, chmn. dept., 1974-90, Armstrong Centennial prof., 1985-91, Cailloux Centennial prof., 1991—, chmn. grad. assembly, 1977-79, chmn. faculty senate, 1981-82; dir. summer seminars NEH, 1975, 76, 83-85, 97; dir. residential seminar, 1977-78, dir. Collaborative Sch. Project, 1987-89, cons., 1976-78, 80—; classicist-in-residence Am. Acad. Rome, 1972-73, vis. scholar, 1991; mem. adv. coun. Classical Sch., 1967—, chmn., 1982-85, mem. classical jury, 1970-71; lectr. U.S.-U.K. Edn. Commn., 1973; regional chmn. Mellon Humanities Fellowships, 1982-90; nat. lectr. Phi Beta Kappa, 1989-90; vis. Mellon prof. Tulane U., 1995; vis. prof. U. Nacional de La Plata, 1997; vis. prof. Gutenberg U. Mainz, Germany, 1998. Author: Aeneas, Sicily and Rome, 1969, Tibulli Carmina, 1971, The Herakles Theme, 1972, Perspectives of Roman Poetry, 1974, Ovid's Metamorphoses, 1975, The Interpretation of Roman Poetry, 1992, Classical and Modern Interactions, 1992, Augustan Culture, 1996; mem. editorial bd. Classical World, 1973-76, Vergilius, 1973—, Classical Jour., 1991-98, Auster, 1996—. Mem. Leadership Austin, 1983-84. Fellow Am. Coun. Learned Socs., 1968-69, Fulbright fellow, 1972-73, Guggenheim fellow, 1972-73, NEH fellow, 1993-94; recipient Teaching Excellence award U. Tex., 1970, 76, Robert W. Hamilton Author award U. Tex., 1997; Humboldt Found. sr. rsch. award, 1993, reinvitation award, 1998. Mem. Am. Philol. Assn. (Teaching Excellence award 1979, dir. 1980-83), Archaeol. Inst. Am., Classical Assn. Midwest and South (pres. 1980-81), Vergilian Soc. Am. (trustee 1972-76, v.p. 1976-77), Assn. Depts. Fgn. Langs. (exec. com. 1980-83, pres. 1983). Home: 4508 Edgemont Dr Austin TX 78731-5224 Office: U Tex Dept Classics Austin TX 78712-1181

GALIPEAU, PETER ARMAND, video producer, advertising account executive; b. Willimantic, Conn., July 26, 1963; s. Joseph Dennis and Theresa Dorothy (Gratton) G.; m. Susan Lynn Arbogast, June 23, 1990; 1 child, Jennifer Lynn. BS magna cum laude, Ea. Conn. State U., 1989. Regional mktg. mgr. Tele-Media Corp., Willimantic, 1989-91; advt. account exec. Media One Advt., Norwalk, Ohio, 1991—; owner Seneca Video Prodns., Tiffin, Ohio, 1992—; mem. mktg. leadership panel The Myers Report, Pine Brook, N.J., 1998—. City councilman at large Tiffin City Coun., Ohio, 1998—; chmn. Materials and Equipment Com., Tiffin, 1998—; mem. Law and Comty. Planning Com., Tiffin, 1998—, Fin. Com., Tiffin, 1998—, Tiffin Parks and Recreation Bd., 1993-94, Hebron (Conn.) Rep. Town Com., 1990-91; softball coach Tiffin Ponytail Softball League, 1993—; v.p. Seneca County (Ohio) Young Reps., 1992-94. With USAF, 1982-87. Mem. Nat. Youth Sports Coaches Assn., Cable Advt. Bur., Ohio Cable TV Assn., Kodak Profl. Network, Nikon Profl. Svcs., Elks, KC (3d degree). Roman Catholic. Avocations: genealogy, home renovations, gardening, drumming, playing bass guitar. Home: 108 Clinton Ave Tiffin OH 44883-1620 Office: Seneca Video Prodns 108 Clinton Ave Tiffin OH 44883-1620

GALISON, PETER LOUIS, history of science educator; b. N.Y.C., May 17, 1955; m. Caroline A. Jones, 1954; two children. BA, MA, Harvard U., 1977, PhD in Physics and History of Sci., 1983; MPhil, Cambridge U., 1978. From asst. prof. to prof. philosophy and physics Stanford U., 1983-92, chmn. dept. history of sci., 1993-97; Mallinckrodt prof. history of sci. and physics Harvard U., 1994—; Howard Found. fellow, 1985; vis. asst. prof. dept. history, Princeton U., 1985; fellow Ctr. for Advanced Study Behaviorial Sci., 1989-90, co-chmn. program history of sci., 1990-92; bd. dirs. Ctr. Philosophy and History of Sci., Boston U., 1993-96; visitor Inst. Advanced Study, 1994-95. Recipient Presidential Young Investigator award, NSF, 1986-91; named Marta Sutton Weeks faculty scholar in humanities, 1989-92; fellow John D. and Catherine T. Mac Arthur Found., 1997. Fellow AAAS, Am. Acad. Arts and Scis.; mem. Nat. Aad. Sci., Am. Phys. Soc., Insternat. Soc. History of Sci., History of Sci. Soc. (mem. coun. 1993-95), Sigma Xi.

GALITELLO-WOLFE, JANE MARYANN, artist, writer; b. Torrington, Conn., Aug. 27, 1942; d. Morris D. and Rose A. (Abate) Galitello; children: Henry Berg III, Jason Sterling, Marissa Tracy. Student, Ward Sch. Elec., 1961, Porter-Chester Coll., 1982. Nurse aide Palm Bay, Fla., 1989; decorator, designer Waterbury, Conn.; electronic engr. Torrington, Conn.; sales rep. Thomaston, Conn.; dance tchr. San Jose, Calif.; freelance artist, writer Torrington. Author: Your Gift of Life, 1991 (award 1993), Snow Bird Melt, 1991, Tody, Heart Desire; published 3 songs including Shadow of Love. Faith healer; active Govt. for Abuse Through Nation and Unity of Nation; advocate for the homeless; active Untied We Stand in Love; min. Your Gift of Life, WBCC-CoCo Radio. Home: PO Box 61851 Palm Bay FL 32906-1851

GALITZ, ROBERT WALTER, art broker, dealer; b. Wisconsin Dells, Wis., Oct. 19, 1935; s. Robert William Galitz and Gertrude Ann Welk; m. Eleanor Jane McFarlin, Nov. 22, 1958; children: Michele Rae, Robert Cliff. Bus. degree, Aurora Coll. Art salesperson, buyer, broker. Mem. Art Inst. Chgo. Fox Valley Arts Coun., Mus. Contemporary Arts, Shriners, Masons. Avocations: snow and water skiing, gun target, art expos and fairs, traveling. Home: 166 Hilltop Ln Sleepy Hollow IL 60118

GALKIN, ROBERT THEODORE, company executive; b. Providence, Sept. 18, 1926; s. Athur Sherman and Shirley (Mann) G.; m. Wini Blacher, Nov. 2, 1952; children: Ellen Lee Kenner, Jane S. Litner, Debra L. Krim. BA, Brown U., 1949; postgrad., Oxford U., 1950. Sales mgr. Natco Products Corp., West Warwick, R.I., 1949-60; v.p. Natco Products, West Warwick, 1960-75, pres., 1975-94; chmn. bd., 1994—; pres. Natco Home Fashions, 1994—, Norwood Devel. Corp., 1965—, Valley Industries, 1970—, Valley Hydro, 1984—, Arctic Devel., 1965—, New England Warehouse Co., 1984—, NPC South, Dalton and Chatsworth, Ga., 1985; active devel. of low power hydroelectric in R.I., leader in recycling industry, R.I., Ga., 1975—. City coun. Good Govt. Candidate, Cranston, 1956; mem. adv. bd. Bryant Coll. Inst. Family Enterprise. With USN, 1944-45. Recipient Williams award for outstanding contbns. to Brown U. Mem. Naval War Coll. Assn., Ledgemont Country Club, Goat Island Yacht Club, Brown Club, R.I. Commodores., Pres.'s Cir. Brown U. Office: Natco Products Corp 155 Brookside Ave West Warwick RI 02893-3802

GALKIN, SAMUEL BERNARD, orthodontist; b. Newark, Feb. 9, 1933; s. Saul J. and Mollie (Kleinberg) G.; children from previous marriage: Jamie Michelle, Richard Stewart; m. Gail Beth Elkin, Feb. 26, 1972; children: Scott David, Seth Paul. Student, U. Conn., 1951-54; DDS, Temple U., 1958; MS in Histology, U. Ill., 1963, cert. grad. orthodontics, 1963; cert. in craniomandibular disorders, U. Medicine and Dentistry of N.J., 1989. Diplomate Am. Bd. Orthodontics. Group practice orthodontics Woodbridge, N.J., 1963—; staff orthodontist J.F.K. Community Hosp., Edison, N.J., 1966—, with cleft palate com., 1971—, dir. dental dept., 1979—; staff Woodbridge Health Ctr., 1967—, with dental adv. com., 1971—; dir. dept. dentistry John F. Kennedy Med. Ctr., Edison, 1979-81; staff orthodontist Perth Amboy (N.J.) Gen. Hosp., 1986—, dir. dept. dentistry, 1990—; staff orthodontist Rahway Hosp., N.J., 1986—; asst. prof. orthodontics N.J. Coll. Medicine and Dentistry, Jersey City, 1963-73; mem. panel physicians N.J. Crippled Children Program, 1971—; dentist Woodbridge Twp. Sch., 1989—. Chmn., Woodbridge Twp. Debutante Ball, 1970; bd. dirs. Woodbridge Twp. YMCA. Lt. Dental Corps, USN, 1958-61. Mem. ADA, Mid. Atlantic Soc. Orthodontists (chmn. clinics 1969-72), N.J. Dental Soc., Middlesex County Dental Soc., Am. Soc. Dentistry for Children, Am. Assn. Orthodontists, Am. Lingual Orthodontic Assn. (charter), Am. Assn. Dental Schs., Am. Acad. Head, Neck, Facial Pain and TMJ Orthopedics, N.E. Craniomandibular Soc., N.J. Craniomandibular soc. (charter), Am. Acad. Orofacial Pain, Am. Acad. Oral Medicine, Alpha Omega (chpt. v.p. 1969—), Omicron Kappa Upsilon. Home: 3 Dorset Rd Colonia NJ 07067-3101 Office: 711 Amboy Ave Woodbridge NJ 07095-3139 also: 233 Madison Ave Perth Amboy NJ 08861-4306

GALL, BETTY BLUEBAUM, office services company executive; b. Williamson, W.Va., June 11, 1944; d. Thomas Jefferson Bluebaum and Ollie Mae (Moore) Bluebaum Walker; Charles B. Walker (stepfather); 1 child, Thomas Ethan. Ptnr., dir. Chicagoland Register, dating svc., Chgo., 1974-84; cooking instr. Elizabeth Benson Internat. Cooking Lessons, 1978-84; owner Ethnic Party People Catering, 1981-92, Phone-A-Friend Dating Svc., Chgo., 1984-90, Betty Gall Office Svcs., Chgo., 1991—; office mgr. Myers & Assocs., 1998—. Contbr. poetry to Nat. Libr. Poetry, 1997, 98. Mem. comm. dept. Little City Found., 1989-91. Home: 6314 N Troy St Chicago IL 60659-1414

GALL, DONALD ARTHUR, minister; b. Edgely, N.D., Apr. 30, 1936; s. Arthur Fred and Luella Sara (Weidenbach) G.; m. Shirley Ann Stevenson, Aug. 19, 1956 (div. Aug. 1972); children: Deborah Sue, Craig Donald, Matthew Allan; m. Patricia E. deJong, Dec. 29, 1984. BA, Yankton Coll., 1958; MDiv., MA in Religious Edn., Hartford Sem., 1962; D in Ministry, Eden Theol. Sem., 1983. Ordained to ministry United Ch. of Christ. Pastor 1st Congl. Ch., Whiting, Iowa, 1962-65; assoc. conf. minister Nebr. Conf. United Ch. Christ, Lincoln, 1965-70; dir. leadership devel. Presbyns. Associated for Common Tasks, Eugene, Oreg., 1970-72; assoc. min. 1st Congrl. Ch. United Ch. Christ, Eugene, 1972-75; assoc. conf. minister Fla. Conf. United Ch. Christ, Miami, 1975-79; program exec. Bd. Homeland Ministry, N.Y.C., 1979-86; conf. min. Iowa Conf. United Ch. Christ, Des Moines, 1986-94; sr. min. Eden United Ch. Christ, Hayward, Calif., 1995—; bd. dirs. Iowa Interch. Forum, Des Moines; pres. Iowa conf. United Chs. Christ Inc., Des Moines, 1986-94; chair Agy. for Peace and Justice, Des Moines, 1988-91; trustee United Theol. Sem., New Brighton, Minn., 1991; mem. Coun. Conf. Mins., 1986-94, Gen. Synod Com. on Structure, 1989-95; mem. exec. coun. United Ch. Christ, 1989-91. Author: THe Eleventh Hour, 1979; also articles. Bd. dirs. Mayflower Homes Inc., Grinnell, Iowa, 1986-94; pre. Emergency Family Shelter House, Eugene, Oreg., 1972-74, Fla. IMPACT, Tallahassee, 1977-79; vol. Oreg. Dem. Campaign, 1974. Named a Community Leader of Am., Community Leaders of Am., Inc., 1968. Avocations: writing, skiing, golfing, wood working. Home: 1338 Grizzly Peak Blvd Berkeley CA 94708-2130

GALL, ERIC PAPINEAU, physician, educator; b. Boston, May 24, 1940; s. Edward Alfred and Phyllis Hortense (Rivard) G.; m. Katherine Theiss, Apr. 20, 1968; children: Gretchen Theiss Gall, Michael Edward. AB, U. Pa., 1962, MD, 1966. Asst. instr. U. Pa., Phila., 1970-71, post doctoral trainee, fellow, 1971-73; asst. prof. U. Ariz., Tucscon, 1973-78, assoc. prof., 1978-83, prof. internal medicine, 1983-94, prof. surgery, 1983-94, prof. family/community medicine, 1983-94, chief rheumatology allergy and immunology, 1983-93, dir. arthritis ctr., 1986-94; Herman Finch Univ. of Health Scis. prof. of medicine The Chgo. Med. Sch., North Chicago, Ill., 1994—, prof. microbiology and immunology, 1994—, chmn. dept. medicine, 1994—, chief rheumatology sect., 1994-98, assoc. dean clin. affairs, 1996-97; dir. metabolic bone unit The Chgo. Med. Sch., North Chicago, 1997—. Author, editor: Rheumatoid Arthritis: Illustrated Guide to Path DX and Management of Rheumatoid Arthritis, 1988, Rheumatic Disease: Rehabilitation and Management, 1984, Primary Care, 1984; editor Clin. Care in The Rhematic Diseases, 1996; contbr. numerous articles to profl. jours. Chmn. med. and scientific com. Arthritis Found., Tucson, 1979-81. Maj. M.C., U.S. Army; Vietnam. Decorated Bronze Star; recipient Addie Thomas Nat. Svc. award Arthritis Found., 1988. Fellow ACP (coun. Ill. chpt. 1995—), Am. Coll. Rheumatology (founding chair ednl. materials com. 1986-89, bd. dirs. 1992-95, chmn. rehab. sect. 1992-95); mem. AMA (rep. sect. on med. schs. 1995—), Arthritis Health Professions Assn. (nat. pres. 1982-83), Am. Assn. Med. Colls., Am. Fedn. Clin. Rsch., Ctrl. Soc. Clin. Investigation, Arthritis Found. (nat. vice chmn. 1982-83, chmn. profl. edn. com. 1996—, chmn. ednl. materials com. 1991-96, blue ribbon com. on qualty of life, bd. trustees Greater Chgo. chpt. 1997—, exec. com. 1998—), Assn. Profs. Medicine (bd. dirs.), Ill. Med. Soc., Lake County Med. Soc. (treas. 1998—), Sigma Xi, Alpha Omega Alpha (regional counselor 1998—), Alpha Epsilon Delta. Avocations: photography, fishing. Office: The Chgo Med Sch Dept Medicine 3333 Green Bay Rd North Chicago IL 60064-3037 *Academic medicine provides the ideal opportunity to help patients, help touch and shape the lives of hundreds of students and trainees, and to add to the fund of knowledge in one's world.*

GALL, JOSEPH GRAFTON, biologist, researcher, educator; b. Washington, Apr. 14, 1928; s. John Christian and Elsie (Rosenberger) G.; m. Dolores Marie Hogge, Sept. 17, 1955 (div. 1982); children: Lawrence, Barbara.; m. Diane Marie Dwyer, July 17, 1982. B.S., Yale, 1949, Ph.D., 1952. Faculty U. Minn., 1952-63, prof., 1963; prof. biology and molecular biophysics Yale, 1963-83; staff dept. embryology Carnegie Instn., Balt., 1983—; Am. Cancer Soc. prof. developmental genetics Carnegie Instn., 1984—; mem. cell biology study sect. NIH, 1963-67, chmn., 1972-75; chmn. bd. sci. counselors Nat. Inst. Child Health and Human Devel., NIH, 1986-90; mem. Yale Corp., 1989-95. Contbr. articles profl. jours. Recipient E.B. Wilson award Am. Soc. Cell Biology, 1983, Wilbur Cross medal Yale U., 1988, V.D. Mattia award Roche Inst. Molecular Biology, 1989. Mem. AAAS (Mentor award for lifetime achievement 1996), Am. Soc. Cell Biology (past pres.), Genetics Soc. Am., Nat. Acad. Scis., Am. Acad. Arts and Scis., Am. Philos. Soc., Accademia Nazionale dei Lincei, Soc. Developmental Biology (pres. 1984-85). Home: 107 Bellemore Rd Baltimore MD 21210-1314 Office: Carnegie Instn Dept Embryology 115 W University Pkwy Dept Baltimore MD 21210-3399

GALL, KEITH M., director. Dir. Enterprise Village, Largo, Fla. Office: Enterprise Village 12100 Starkey Rd Largo FL 33773-2729*

GALL, LINDA LEE, artist, administrator; b. Columbus, Ohio, Nov. 18, 1949; d. Charles William and Ruth Ann (Cleaveland) Zimmerman; m. Ronald Joseph Gall, Oct. 6, 1973; children: James Aaron, Joshua, Noah. BFA, Rutgers U., 1979, MFA, 1981. Adminstr. Ohio Art League, Columbus, 1994—. Artist numerous exhbns. Sec., bd. trustees, founding mem. Zanesville (Ohio) Appalachian Arts Project, 1996—; bd. dirs. Zanesville Art Ctr., 1998—. Democrat. E-mail: lgall@prodigy.net. Home: 2300 Arch Hill Rd Zanesville OH 43701 Office: Ohio Art League 765 Summit St Columbus OH 43215

GALL, MARY SHEILA, federal agency administrator; 2 children. BA, Rosary Hill Coll., 1971; MEd, Old Dominion U., 1998. Staff mem. various mems. of Senate and Ho. of Reps., 1971-79; sr. legis. analyst study com. Ho. of Reps., 1980-81; dep. domestic policy adviser Office of V.P. of U.S., 1981-86; counselor to dir. U.S. Office Pers. Mgmt., 1986-89; asst. sec. human devel. svcs. HHS, Washington, 1989-91; commr. U.S. Consumer Product Safety Commn., Washington, 1991—; chair Pres.'s Task Force on Adoption, 1987-89. Dir. rsch. George Bush for Pres. campaign, 1979-80; mem. Reagan-Bush Presdl. campaign and transition team, 1980-81; tchr. Sunday sch. Office: US Consumer Product Safety Commn Washington DC 20207

GALL, MEREDITH DAMIEN (MEREDITH MARK DAMIEN GALL), education educator, author; b. New Britain, Conn., Feb. 18, 1942; s. Theodore A. and Ray (Ehrlich) G.; m. Joyce Pershing, June 12, 1968; 1 child, Jonathan. AB, Harvard U., 1963, EdM, 1963; PhD, U. Calif., Berkeley, 1968. Sr. research assoc. Far West Lab. for Ednl. Research and Devel., San Francisco, 1968-75; assoc. prof. edn. U. Oreg., Eugene, 1975-79, prof., 1980—, dir. grad. studies, 1997—. Author: Handbook for Evaluating and Selecting Curriculum Materials, 1981, (with K.A. Acheson) Techniques in the Clinical Supervision of Teachers, 4th edit., 1997, (with J.P. Gall) Making the Grade, rev. 2d edit., 1993, (with W.R. Borg and J.P. Gall) Educational Research: An Introduction, 6th edit., 1996, (with J.P. Gall, D.R. Jacobsen, and T.L. Bullock) Tools for Learning: A Guide to Teaching Study Skills, 1990, (with W.R. Borg and J.P. Gall) Applying Educational Research, 4th edit., 1999; editor: (with B.A. Ward) Critical Issues in Educational Psychology, 1974; cons. editor Jour. Ednl. Rsch., Jour. Rsch. in Rural Edn., Forum for Reading, Jour. Exptl. Edn. USPH fellow, 1963-64. Fellow Am. Psychol. Assn.; mem. ASCD, Am. Ednl. Research Assn., Oreg. Ednl. Research Assn. (pres. 1985-86), Phi Delta Kappa (Dist. I Meritorious award 1978). Home: 4810 Mahalo Dr Eugene OR 97405-4609 Office: U Oreg Coll Edn Eugene OR 97403

GALL, MICHAEL LOUIS, educator; b. Perth Amboy, N.J., May 3, 1947; s. Michael Louis and Anna (Mizerak) G.; m. Kathleen Kalita, May 1, 1971. BS, Mt. St. Mary's Coll., 1969; MA, Jersey City State, 1975; EdD, Nova U., 1990. Tchr. Brick (N.J.) Bd. Edn., 1969—, staff developer, 1983—, dir. adult edn., 1994—; prof. Middlesex County Coll., Edison, N.J., 1988—; cons. East Coast Cons., Colts Neck, N.J., 1984—, bd. dirs., 1985—; adj. prof. Temple U., Phila., Monmouth U., West Long Branch, N.J. Mem. Nat. Edn. Assn., N.J. Edn. Assn., Brick Twp. Edn. Assn. Republican. Roman Catholic. Avocations: golf, running, gardening, reading, naturalism. Home: 8 Colonial Ter Colts Neck NJ 07722-1207

GALL, STANLEY ADOLPH, physician, immunology researcher; b. Bismarck, N.D., May 31, 1936; s. Adolph and Wilma Thelma (Nickisch) G.; m. Florence Marie Ketterling, Aug. 17, 1958; children: Stanley, Kathryn Louise, Mark Allan, Thomas Andrew. BA, U. Minn., 1958, MD, 1962. Diplomate Am. Bd. Ob-Gyn. Intern U. Oreg. Hosp., Portland, 1962-63; resident in ob-gyn U. Minn. Hosps., Mpls., 1963-66; asst. prof. ob-gyn U. Miami, Fla., 1968-73; assoc. prof. ob-gyn Duke U. Med. Ctr., Durham, N.C., 1973-78, prof., 1968—, dir. divsn. perinatal medicine; prof. ob-gyn, assoc. head dept. ob-gyn U. Ill. Coll. Medicine, 1985-89; prof., chmn. dept. ob-gyn U. Louisville, 1989—. Contbr. articles to profl. jours. Capt. U.S. Army Med. Corps, 1966-68. Fellow ACOG; mem. Soc. Gynecol. Oncology, Soc. Gynecol. Investigations, Infectious Diseases Soc. Ob-Gyn, Ctrl. Assn. Obstetricians and Gynecologists, Soc. Perinatal Obstetricians. Lutheran. Office: U Louisville Dept Ob-Gyn 550 S Jackson St Louisville KY 40202-1622

GALLAGER, ROBERT GRAY, electrical engineering educator; b. Phila., May 29, 1931; s. Jacob Boon and May (Gray) G.; m. Ruth Atwood, Oct. 19, 1957 (div. July 1981); children: Douglas, Ann, Rebecca; m. Marie Tarnowski, July 18, 1981. BEE, U. Pa., 1953; MEE, MIT, 1957, ScD, 1960. Mem. tech. staff Bell Telephone Labs., Murray Hill, N.J., 1953-54; rsch. asst. MIT, Cambridge, Mass., 1956-60, asst. prof., 1960-64, assoc. prof., 1964-67, prof., 1967—; co-dir. Lab. Info. and Decision Systems, 1986—; chmn. adv. com. NSF Div. on Networking and Comm. Rsch. and Intrastructure, Washington, 1989-92; mem. adv. coun. Elec. Engring. Dept., U. Pa., 1991—. Author: Information Theory and Reliable Communication, 1968, Discrete Stochastic Processes, 1995; co-author Data Networks, 1987, 2d edit. 1992; patentee in field. Recipient Gold medal Moore Sch., U. Pa., 1973; Guggenheim fellow, 1978. Fellow IEEE (Baker prize 1966, Medal of Honor 1990); mem. AAAS, NAS, NAE, Infor. theory Soc. of IEEE (bd. govs. 1965-72, 79-88, pres. 1971). Avocations: piano, skiing, windsurfing. Home: 3 Hawthorne Ln Gloucester MA 01930-4128 Office: MIT Dept Elec Eng/Comp Sci Rm 35-206 Cambridge MA 02139

GALLAGHER, ANNE PORTER, business executive; b. Coral Gables, Fla., Mar. 16, 1950; d. William Moring and Anne (Jewett) Porter; m. Matthew Philip Gallagher, Jr., July 31, 1976 (div. July 1998); children: Jacqueline Anne, Kevin Sharkey. BA in Edn., Stetson U., 1972. Tchr. elem. schs. Atlanta, 1972-74; sales rep. Xerox Corp., Atlanta, 1974-76, Rosslyn, Va., 1976-81; sales rep. No. Telecom Inc., Vienna, Va., 1981-84, account exec., 1984-85, sales dir., 1985-94, mktg. dir., 1995-96; v.p. Fed. Pub. Sector Timeplex Fed. Sys., Inc., Fairfax, Va.; bus. devel. dir. Informix Software, Vienna, 1996-97; sr. v.p. Tricor Industries Inc., Alexandria, Va., 1997-98; v.p. fed. sys. Metromedia Fiber Network, McLean, Va., 1999—. Bd. dirs. Make a Wish Friends. Mem. Info. Tech. Assn. of Am. (bd. dirs.), Armed Forces Comm. and Electronics Assn., Pi Beta Phi. Episcopalian. Avocations: skiing, joggin. Home: 4643 Kirkland Pl Alexandria VA 22311-4949 Office: Metromedia Fiber Network 8201 Greensboro Dr Mc Lean VA 22102

GALLAGHER, BRIAN JOHN, lawyer; b. Bklyn., Oct. 24, 1939; s. John Joseph and Margaret R. (Smith) G.; m. Mary Loughney, Sept. 10, 1966; children—Amanda, Ian. B.S.S., Fairfield U., 1961; J.D., Fordham U., 1964; postgrad. NYU Law Sch., 1969-70. Bar: N.Y. 1965, U.S. Dist. Ct. (so. dist.) N.Y. 1967, U.S. Dist. Ct. (ea. dist.) N.Y. 1974, U.S. Ct. Appeals (2d cir.) 1971, U.S. Ct. Appeals (11th cir.) 1982, U.S. Ct. Appeals (D.C. cir.) 1986. Ptnr., Kronish, Lieb, Weiner & Hellman, LLP, N.Y.C., 1976—; asst. U.S. Atty. So. Dist. N.Y., 1967-71. Mayor, Village of Pelham Manor, N.Y., 1995-97, trustee, 1989-95. Mem. ABA, N.Y. State Bar Assn., Assn. Bar City N.Y., Fed. Bar Coun., Larchmont (N.Y.) Yacht Club. Office: 1114 Avenue Of The Americas New York NY 10036-7703

GALLAGHER, CYNTHIA, artist, educator. BFA, Phila. Coll. Art, 1972; MFA, Queens Coll., 1974. Critic NYU, N.Y.C., 1974-75; instr. N.Y. Inst. Tech., N.Y.C., 1974-88, CUNY, Queens Coll., N.Y.C., 1974-89, Phila. Coll. Art, 1976-77, Yale U., Norfolk, Conn., 1980, Fashion Inst. Tech., N.Y.C., 1988—, Parsons Sch. Design, 1995—; critic Brown U., 1994, R.I. Sch. Design, 1994, Cooper Union for Advancement of Sci. and Art, 1994; selection com. vis. artists Fashion Inst. Tech., 1992-93; graphics cons. N.Y. State Found. Arts, 1978. One-woman shows include 55 Mercer St., N.Y.C., 1978, Grace Borgenicht Gallery, N.Y.C., 1981, Luise Ross Gallery, N.Y.C., 1988, Edward Thorden Gallery, Gothenborg, Sweden, 1989, Charles More Gallery, Phila., 1990, 91, Mary Ryan Gallery, N.Y.C., 1992, Espace Crois, Barangnon, Toulouse, France, 1993, Johnson & Johnson, New Brunswick, N.J., 1998; two-woman shows include Weatherspoon Mus., Greensboro, N.C., 1982, Castelli Graphics, N.Y.C., 1983, Bess Cutler Gallery, N.Y.C., 1984, Parrish Art Mus., Southampton, L.I., N.Y., 1991, Tiffany's, N.Y.C., 1993, Critical Perspectives, N.Y.; represented in permanent collections at Met. Mus. Art, N.Y.C., Best Inc., Citibank, 1st Nat. Bank Chgo., Home Ins. Co., Owens Corning Corp., Salomon Bros., Shearson-Lehman Am. Express, N.Y.C., San Francisco, Skadden, Arts, Slate, Meagher and Flom, Johnson & Johnson, Nat. Mus. Woman in Arts, others; Reprodn.: Oil Pastel, 1990; contbr. articles to profl. publs. Mem. adv. bd., bd. dirs. YWCA Elsa Mott Ives Gallery, 1992, curator, 1993. Creative Artists Pub. Svc. Program grantee, 1981-82, NEA grantee, 1983-84, 89-90, N.Y. Found. for Arts, 1989-90.

GALLAGHER, DENNIS JOSEPH, municipal official, state senator, educator; b. Denver, July 1, 1939; s. William Joseph and Ellen Philomena (Flaherty) G.; BA, Regis Coll., 1961; MA, Cath. U. Am., 1968; postgrad. (Eagleton fellow) Rutgers U., 1972, 86; children: Meaghan Kathleen, Daniel Patrick. With locals of Internat. Assn. Theatrical and Stage Employees, Denver and Washington, 1956-63; tchr. St. John's Coll. H.S., Washington, 1964-66, Heights Study Ctr., Washington, 1965-67, Regis U., 1967; mem. Colo. Ho. of Reps. from 4th Dist., 1970-74; mem. Colo. Senate, 1974-95, councilman dist. 1, Denver, 1995—; chmn. Dem. Caucus, 1982-84, Dem. Whip, 1985-87. Mem. Platte Area Reclamation Com., 1973-75; mem. Denver Anti-Crime Coun., 1976-77; trustee Denver Art Mus.; bd. dirs. Cath. Cmty. Svcs.; past mem. Colo. Commn. on Aging; past mem. Colo. State Adv. Coun. on Career Edn.; mem. Victim Assistance Law Enforcement Bd., Denver, 1984-88; bd. dirs. Denver Am. Ireland Fund. Named Gates Found. fellow Harvard U. Mem. Colo. Fedn. Tchrs. (pres. local 1333, 1972-74), Colo. Calligrapher's Guild, Colo. History Group, James Joyce Reading Soc. Mem. Speech Comm. Assn. Colo., Western States Comm. Assn. Democrat. Roman Catholic. E-mail: dgallagh@regis.edu. Fax: 303-640-2636. Home: 5097 Meade St Denver CO 80221-1033 Office: Regis U Dept Comm 3333 Regis Blvd Dept Comm Denver CO 80221-1099 also: 458 City and County Bldg Denver CO 80202 also: 4404 Lowell Blvd Denver CO 80211-1367

GALLAGHER, EDWARD PETER, foundation administrator; b. San Francisco, Mar. 23, 1951; s. Edward Owen and Virginia Anne (Scully) G. BA, U. Calif., 1976; MBA, Columbia U., 1982. Dir. comm. Wolf Trap Farm Pk. for Performing Arts, Vienna, Va., 1977; program mgr. Smithsonian Instn., Washington, 1977-79; sr. program mgr. Smithsonian Inst., Washington, 1979-81; dir. membership Mus. Modern Art, N.Y.C., 1983-90, dir. devel., 1986-87; dir. NAD, N.Y.C., 1990-96; pres. Am.-Scandinavian Found., N.Y.C., 1996—; also trustee; cons. Cooper Hewitt Mus., N.Y.C., 1982-83; bd. dirs. Ireland Am. Arts Exch., Washington, Yorkville Common Pantry, N.Y.C.; knight 1st class Norwegian Royal Order of Merit. Mem. Internat Commn. Mus., Am. Assn. Mus. Home: 666 W End Ave # 21 F New York NY 10025-7357

GALLAGHER, ELLEN, artist; b. Providence, 1965. Student, Sch. Mus. Fine Art, Boston, 1992, Skowhegan Sch. Art, 1993. One-person shows include Akin Gallery, Boston, 1992, Mario Diacono Gallery, Boston, 1994, Mary Boone Gallery, N.Y., 1996, Anthony d'Offay Gallery, London, 1996, Gagosian Gallery, N.Y., 1998, Ikon Gallery, Birmingham, 1998, Galerie Max Hetzler, Berlin, 1999; exhibited in group shows at Brandeis U., Waltham, 1993, Mus. Fine Arts, Boston, 1993, Inst. Contemporary Art, Boston, 1994, 96, Mus. Fine Arts, Boston, 1995, Whitney Mus. Am. Art, N.Y., 1995, Whitechapel Art Gallery, London, 1996, Mario Diacono Gallery, Boston, 1997, De Beyerd Ctr. Contemporary Art, Breda, The Netherlands, 1998, others; represented in permanent collections Mus. Modern Art, N.Y., Whitney Mus. Art, N.Y., Met. Mus. Art, N.Y., Guggenheim Mus., N.Y., Mus. Fine Art, Boston, Mus. Contemporary Art, L.A., Denver Mus. Art, Moderna Museet, Stockholm; featured in numerous articles and reviews. Ann Gund fellow, 1993; Provincetown Fine Arts Work Ctr. fellow, 1995; Joan Mitchell fellow, 1997. Office: care Mario Diacono Gallery 207 South St Boston MA 02111

GALLAGHER, GEORGE R., judge. Sr. judge D.C. Ct. Appeals. Office: 500 Indiana Ave NW Ste 6000 Washington DC 20001-2131

GALLAGHER, GERALD RAPHAEL, venture capitalist; b. Easton, Pa., Mar. 17, 1941; s. Gerald R. and Marjorie A. G.; m. Ellen Anne Mullane, Aug. 8, 1964; children: Ann Patrice, Gerald Patrick, Megan Ann. B.S. in Aero. Engring., Princeton U., 1963; M.B.A. (Exec. Club Chgo. fellow 1969), U. Chgo., 1969. Dir. strategic planning Metro-Goldwyn-Mayer, N.Y.C., 1969; v.p. Donaldson, Lufkin & Jenrette, N.Y.C., 1969-77; from v.p. to sr. v.p. planning and control Dayton Hudson Corp., Mpls., 1977-79; exec. v.p., chief adminstrv. officer subs. Mervyn's, Hayward, Calif.; then vice chmn., chief adminstrv. officer, 1979-85, vice chmn., chief adminstrv. office parent co., 1985-87, also dir.; gen. ptnr. Oak Investment Ptnrs., Mpls., 1987—; bd. dirs. AutoChoice, Caribou Coffee, Dick's Clothing and Sporting Goods, Garden Escape, Jamba Juice, La Madeleine, P.F. Chang's China Bistro, Sweet Factory, Zany Brainy, World Wrapps. Mem. Fairview Hosp. and Healthcare Svcs. With USN, 1963-67. Mem. N.Y. Soc. Security Analysts, Mpls. Club, Interlachen Country Club, Beta Gamma Sigma. Roman Catholic. Office: Oak Investment Ptnrs 4550 Norwest Ctr 90 S 7th St Minneapolis MN 55402-3903

GALLAGHER, HUBERT RANDALL, government consultant; b. Salida, Colo., Jan. 8, 1907; s. Hugh and Margaret (Dinsmore) G.; m. Luthera Wakefield, July 29, 1930; children: Hugh, Janet. AB, Stanford U., 1929; MS, Syracuse U., 1930. Instr. Syracuse (N.Y.) U., 1930-32; asst. prof. Stanford U., 1932-33; rsch. cons., later assoc. dir., coun. of state govts., 1933-50; assoc. dir. state divsn. Nat. Def. Commn., 1940-45; chmn. Internat. Bd. of Inquiry for Great Lakes Fisheries, 1940-41; office dir. Am. Mission Aid to Greece-AMAG, 1947-48; presdl. staff asst. OCDM and Office Emergency Planning (Exec. Office of Pres., White House), Washington, 1950-69; v.p. Wakefield Farm Co., 1976—; alt. del. NATO Civil Emergency Com., 1962-64. Author: Crime Prevention, Syracuse U., 1930, Report of International Board of Inquiry for the Great Lakes Fisheries, U.S. Govt., Dept. of State, 1943; editor: The Book of the States, Coun. of State Govts., 1943-44; contbr. articles to profl. mags. Assoc. fellow Harry S. Truman Libr. Inst. Nat. and Internat. Affairs. Mem. Am. Soc. Pub. Adminstrn. (past pres. Washington 1955-56, chmn. com. emergency mgmt. disaster assistance 1983-84), Delta Tau Delta. Presbyterian. Home: 5416 Burling Rd Bethesda MD 20814-1214

GALLAGHER, HUGH GREGORY, government affairs author, consultant; b. Palo Alto, Calif., Oct. 18, 1932; s. Hubert Randall and Luthera (Wakefield) G. BA magna cum laude, Claremont Men's Coll., 1956; BA, MA, Oxford (Eng.) U., 1959; PhD (hon.), CUNY, 1996. Legis. asst. to Senator John. A. Carroll, 1959-62; adminstrv. asst. to Senator E.L. Bartlett Washington, 1962-68; legis. coord. Bur. Budget, Exec. Office Pres. of U.S., 1966-67; Washington rep. British Petroleum, 1968-74; writer, consultant govtl. affairs, 1974—; policy cons. European/Australian cos., Washington, 1974-91; cons. U.S. Senate, 1976, Libr. of Congress, 1989-91; vis. fellow Woodrow Wilson Internat. Ctr. for Scholars, Washington, 1981-82. Author: National Architectural Barriers Act, 1968, Advise and Obstruct: The Role of United States Congress in Foreign Policy Decision, 1969, Etok, A Story of Eskimo Power, 1974, FDR's Splendid Deception, 1994, By Trust Betrayed: Patients, Physicians, and the License to Kill in the Third Reich, 1995, Black Bird Fly Away: Disabled in an Able Bodied World, 1998; contbr. articles to N.Y. Times, Washington Post. Campaign mgr. Senator Bartlett reelection, Alaska, 1966; state coord. Humphrey Presdl. Campaign, Colo., 1968. Marshall scholar Oxford U., 1986-89, Kennedy Inst. Bioethics scholar, 1964-65, Congl. fellow Am. Polit. Sci. Assn., 1966-67. Mem. Cosmos Club. Democrat. Roman Catholic. Home: 7600 Cabin Rd Cabin John MD 20818-1405

GALLAGHER, JOHN FRANCIS, education educator; s. John Charles Edward and Marion (McKeon) G.; m. Georgiana Frances Cole; children: Kristen Marie, John David. BA in Philosophy, Mary Immaculate Coll.; STD in Theology, U. Fribourg, Switzerland; MS in Indsl. Rels., Rutgers U., EdD. Instr. Mary Immaculate Coll., Northampton, Pa., 1962-65; asst. prof. Coll. St. Vincent De Paul, Boynton Beach, Fla., 1965-69; pres. Coll. St. Vincent De Paul, Boynton Beach, 1966-70, assoc. prof., 1969-70; advisor instructional resources SUNY, Plattsburgh, 1970-71; dean humanities Brookdale Community Coll., Lincroft, N.J., 1971-73, v.p. acad., 1973-81; dir. Rockland Campus Iona Coll., New Rochelle, N.Y., 1981-83, dean Sch. Gen. Studies, 1983-89, provost, v.p. acad. affairs, 1989-95, prof. edn., 1995—; coll. evaluation team mem. N.J. Dept. Higher Edn., Trenton, 1975-77, N.Y. State Edn. Dept., Albany, 1980—. Chair County Arts Festival, Monmouth County, N.J., 1972; trustee Monmouth County Arts Coun., Red Bank, N.J., 1973-76. Mem. ASCD, Am. Ednl. Studies Assn., Philosophy of Edn. Soc., Soc. for History of Edn., Mid. States Assn. Colls. and Scis. (coll. evaluation team 1976—), Phi Delta Kappa. Avocations: photography, classical music, tennis. Office: Iona Coll Dept Edn New Rochelle NY 10801

GALLAGHER, JOHN PAUL, association administrator; b. Chgo., Aug. 14, 1961; s. Wayne and Phyllis (Lehn) G. AS, Northwestern Bus. Coll., 1982; BS, DeVry Inst. Technology, Chgo., 1985. Adminstr.-treas. PREVAIL, Inc., Madison, Wis., 1991-96; exec. dir. Cordial Unltd., Inc., Madison, 1996—; adminstrv. asst. Wis. Mental Health Consumer/Survivor Work Group, Madison, 1994-96; bd. dirs. M.C. Video Prodns., Inc. Co-author: Stress Kit Workbook, 1996, Gaining Access: Financial Benefits for the Disabled, 1997; co-editor: The ADA, 1997, Managed Care and You, 1997.

GALLAGHER, JOHN PIRIE, retired corporation executive; b. Chgo., Oct. 12, 1916; s. Edward and Elsie (Pirie) G.; m. Penny Boyer, Sept. 13, 1940; children: David A., Kathe L. Dugan, Laurie S., Steven R. Student, Northwestern U., 1934-40; MBA, U. Chgo., 1947; LLD (hon.), Elmhurst Coll., 1975. With Commonwealth Edison Co., Chgo., 1934-46; partner, v.p. Booz, Allen and Hamilton, Inc., Chgo., 1946-63; dir. McKinsey and Co., Chgo., 1963-68; pres., chmn., CEO Chemetron Corp., Chgo., 1968-77; ret. Chemetron subs. Allegheny Ludlum Industries, Inc., 1981; exec. cons. to Chemetron Corp., 1978-81; sr. lectr. Grad. Sch. Bus., U. Chgo., 1979-93. Trustee Glenwood Sch. for Boys. Mem. Comm. Club, Hinsdale Golf Club, Beta Gamma Sigma. Mem. Hinsdale Union Ch. Home: 420 E 3rd St Hinsdale IL 60521-4225

GALLAGHER, JOHN ROBERT, JR., county official; b. Berwyn, Ill., May 6, 1941; s. John Robert and Marion Catherine (Banker) G. AB in Govt., Georgetown U., 1963; MA in Pub. Adminstrn., Govs. State U., University Park, Ill., 1977; grad., Armed Forces Staff Coll., 1974; grad. Econ. Devel. Inst., U. Okla., 1985. Adminstrv. asst. City of Joliet, Ill., 1977-78, asst. personnel dir., 1978-79, dep. city mgr., 1979-82; devel. dir. County of Will, Joliet, 1982-86, personnel dir., 1986-92, dep. county adminstr., 1989-92; county adminstr. County of Whiteside, Morrison, Ill., 1992—; instr. polit. and mil. sci. U. Conn., West Hartford, 1970-72; cons. Joliet, 1977-92, Sterling, Ill., 1992—. Mem. citizens adv. bd. No. Ill. RTA Met. Rail, Chgo., 1987-92. With USNG, 1959-61, 84-91, USAR, 1961-63, 75-84, U.S. Army, 1963-75; brig. gen. N.G. ret. Mem. Am. Soc. for Pub. Adminstrn., Internat. City Mgmt. Assn., Ill. City Mgmt. Assn., Will County Mgrs. and Adminstrs. Assn., Assn. U.S. Army, Soc. 1st Inf. Div., 2d U.S. Inf. Regt. Assn., Am. Legion, VFW, Georgetown U. Alumni Assn., Governors State U. Alumni Assn., U. Okla. Alumni Assn. Roman Catholic. Avocations: horseback riding, swimming, camping, biography and hist. novels. Office: County of Whiteside 200 E Knox St Morrison IL 61270-2809

GALLAGHER, JOSEPH FRANCIS, marketing executive; b. N.Y.C., May 15, 1926; s. Joseph O'Neil and Nora (Shea) G.; m. Anne Decker, June 17, 1950; children: June, Virginia, Aline. Student, U. Va., 1947-50. Advanced to pres., dir. Erwin Wasey, Inc., Los Angeles, 1968-80; pres. JFG, Inc., Oildale, Calif., 1981—. Served with USNR, 1944-46. Mem. Phi Gamma Delta, Delta Sigma Rho. Home: 5088 Ovalo Laguna Hills CA 92653-1801 Office: JFG Inc Oildale CA 93388-5841

GALLAGHER, LINDY ALLYN, banker, financial consultant; b. Kalamazoo, Sept. 27, 1954; d. Karl P. Joslow and Audrey S. Phillips; m. Thomas J. Gallagher, Nov. 29, 1975; children: James Allyn Buckley, Phillip Graham, Charles Bedloe. BS, U. Pa., 1975; MBA, Columbia U., 1982. Mem. faculty, rschr. U. Pa., Phila., 1976-80; corp. banking officer Bank of Montreal, N.Y.C., 1982-84; v.p. Citibank NA, N.Y.C., 1984-89; v.p., mgr. Chase Manhattan Bank, N.Y.C., 1989-90; pres. The Allyn Co., New Canaan, Conn., 1990-99; princ. State Street Global Advs., 1999—; treas., dir. 957 Lexington Corp., 1981-87. Editor Columbia Jour. World Bus., 1980-82. Mem. Women's Nat. Rep. Club, 1986—; commr. Town of New Canaan, 1991-99; treas., sec. Young Women's League New Canaan, Inc., 1992-94. Mem. Stanwich Club, The Penn Club (N.Y.C.). Republican. Episcopalian.

GALLAGHER, MATTHEW PHILIP, JR., advertising agency executive; b. Providence, June 17, 1944; s. Matthew Philip and Roberta Marie (Tierney) G.; m. Anne Weathers Porter, July 31, 1976; children: Jacqueline Anne, Kevin Sharkey. BA, St. Bonaventure U., 1966. Systems engr. IBM Corp., Arlington, Va., 1967-71; sales rep. Xerox Corp., Silver Spring, Md., 1971-75; dir. mktg. Taft Corp., Washington, 1976-78; dir. devel. World Wildlife Fund, Washington, 1978-79; pres. advt. agy. Gallagher & Assocs., Inc., Alexandria, Va., 1979—; songwriter, entertainer, Atlanta, 1975-76. Author: Hans and the Gold Nugget, 1993; cons. editor: Corporate Foundation Directory. Bd. dirs. Alexandria Sheltered Enterprises, 1980-89, ARC Found. of No. Va., 1991-95. 1st lt. USAFR, 1966-71. Mem. Direct Mktg. Assn. Washington (Internat. Dir. Mktg. Leader award 1983). Avocations: skiing, tennis, golf. Home: # 201 4965 Americana Dr Annandale VA 22003 Office: Gallagher & Assocs Inc 6564 Loisdale Ct Ste 320 Springfield VA 22150

GALLAGHER, MICHAEL ROBERT, consumer products company executive; b. Cedar Rapids, Iowa, Jan. 21, 1946; s. John Robert and Mabel Helen (Slaymaker) G.; m. Linda Katherine Nebb, Oct. 25, 1975; children: Megan Elizabeth, John William, Edward Michael. BS, U. Calif., Berkeley, 1967, MBA, 1968. Brand mgr. Procter & Gamble Co., Cin., 1968-72; various positions Clorox Co., Oakland, Calif., 1972-77; pres., gen. mgr. Clorox Can., Vancouver, B.C., advt. mgr. household products div., 1980-81, gen. mgr. household products div., 1982-84; pres. consumer products div. Lehn & Fink/Sterling Drug, Montvale, N.J., 1984-85; sr. v.p. Lehn & Fink Products, Montvale, N.J., 1985-87, exec. v.p., 1987-88; pres., chief exec. officer L&F Products Inc. (formerly Lehn & Fink), Montvale, N.J., 1989-95; pres., CEO Reckitt & Colman Inc., Montvale, 1995; CEO Playtex Products Inc., Westport, Conn., 1995—; bd. dirs. Nat. Westminster Bancorp., 1994-96, Fleet Bank N.A., 1996-98, Allergan, 1998—. Vice chmn. United Way Bergen County, N.J., 1985-87, bd. dirs., 1989-96, chmn. bd. dirs. 1993-95, chmn. Golden Ball, 1990; sports chmn. Cancer Care of Am., 1989; mem. exec. coun. Boy Scouts Am., Bergen County, 1990-95, bd. dirs. Fairfield County; bd. trustees St. Luke's Sch., 1998—. Mem. Soap and Detergent Assn. (bd. dirs. 1992-95), Grocery Mfrs. Assn. (bd. dirs. 1997—). Home: 37 Fanton Hill Rd Weston CT 06883-2407 Office: Playtex Products Inc 300 Nyala Farms Rd Westport CT 06880-6268

GALLAGHER, MORTIMER ANTHONY, surgeon; b. Providence, Sept. 19, 1921; s. Henry Joseph and Eliza Mary (Dougan) G.; m. Nina Fay Knight, Feb. 6, 1951; children: Warren, Christopher, Mark, Douglas, Nancy. AB, Brown U., 1943; MD, Harvard U., 1945. Diplomate Am. Bd. Surgery; lic., R.I., Ohio. Surgeon dept. surgery Akron (Ohio) Clinic, 1954-88; staff surgeon Akron Gen. Med. Ctr., 1954-88, chief of staff, 1972-73, hon. staff, 1988—; asst. to assoc. prof. surgery N.E. Ohio Univs. Coll. Medicine, Rootstown, 1972-88. Capt. AUS M.C., 1946-48. Fellow Soc. Disting. Physicians; mem. Phi Beta Kappa, Sigma Xi. Republican. Episcopalian. Avocation: sailing. Home: 962 Newport Rd Akron OH 44303-1373

GALLAGHER, PATRICK FRANCIS XAVIER, public relations executive; b. Cleve., Feb. 9, 1952; s. Patrick Francis and Eileen (Brennan) G.; m. Anne Platek, May 3, 1980; children: Molly Anne, Kate Louise. Student, Holy Cross Coll., Worcester, Mass., 1970-72; BA, U. Pa., 1974; MBA, Cleve. State U., 1991. Accredited in pub. rels. Staff editor Penton Pub. Co., Cleve., 1975-80, editor, 1980-83; mgr. corp. communications Leaseway Transp. Corp., Cleve., 1983-84, dir. pub. rels., 1984-85; sr. account exec. Edward Howard & Co., Cleve., 1985-89, v.p., 1990-94, sr. v.p., 1994—. Mem. Pub. Rels. Soc. Am., Nat. Investor Rels. Inst. (bd. dirs. Cleve.-Akron chpt.), Cleve. Soc. Security Analysts-Assn. for Investment Mgmt. and Rsch. Office: Edward Howard & Co 7th Fl One Erieview Plz Cleveland OH 44114

GALLAGHER, PAULA MARIE, real estate appraiser; b. Omaha, Nov. 10, 1959; d. Kenneth Leroy and Phyllis Virginia (Stopak) G. Diploma, Nebr. Coll. Bus., 1978-79; student, Met. Tech. Community Coll., Omaha, 1979-81, U. Nebr., Omaha, 1981-85, 91, Coll. St. Mary, Omaha, 1986-90; BS, Bellevue U., 1993. Lic. real estate appraiser and broker, Nebr. Legal sec. McCormick Cooney Mooney & Hillman P.C., Omaha, 1979; word processor Firstier Bank, Omaha, 1979-83, staff asst., 1983-84; sec. Morrissey Appraisal Svcs., Omaha, 1984; appraiser trainee Morrissay Appraisal Svcs., Omaha, 1985-88, real estate appraiser, 1988—; residential mem. Am. Inst. Real Estate Appraisers. Mem. Appraisal Inst. (sr. residential appraiser), Am. Bus. Women's Assn. (rec. sec. 1984-85, treas. 1988-89, Women of Yr. award 1989), Omaha Women's C. of C. (pres.-elect 1996, pres. 1997, mem. edn. com. 1990-92, mem. fin. com. 1991, dir. cmty. recognition 1992, dir. edn. 1993, chmn. fin. style show 1995, immediate past pres. 1998). Roman Catholic. Avocations: needlepoint, counted cross stitch, sewing, reading. Home: 10321 N 186th Ave Bennington NE 68007-6165 Office: Morrissey Appraisal Svcs 13825 P St Omaha NE 68137-2701

GALLAGHER, PETER, actor; b. N.Y.C., Aug. 19, 1955; m. Paula Harwood; children: James, Kathryn. Broadway appearances include Hair, 1977, Grease, 1978, A Doll's Life, 1982, The Corn in Green, 1983, The Real Thing, 1984, Long Day's Journey Into Night, 1986, Guys and Dolls, 1992; regional appearances include Caligula, 1978, Romeo and Juliet, 1980, Another Country, 1982, Pride and Prejudice, 1985, Pal Joey, City Ctr., N.Y.C., 1995; TV appearances include Skag, 1980, The Big Knife, 1988, The Caine Mutiny Courtmartial, 1988, The Murder of Mary Phagan, 1988, I'll Be Home for Christmas, 1988, Love and Lies, 1990, (Showtime) The Quiet Room, 1994, Fallen Angels, Frightening Frammis, 1994, (HBO) White Mile, 1994; films include The Idolmaker, 1980, Summer Lovers, 1982, Dreamchild, 1983, My Little Girl, 1987, High Spirits, 1988, Sex, Lies and Videotape, 1989, Tune in Tomorrow, 1990, The Cabinet of Dr. Ramirez, 1991, Late for Dinner, 1991, The Player, 1992, Bob Roberts, 1992, Watch It, 1993, Short Cuts, 1993, Malice, 1993, Mother's Boys, 1994, The Hudsucker Proxy, 1994, Dorothy Parker's The Vicious Circle, 1994, The Underneath, 1995, While You Were Sleeping, 1995, Cannes Man, 1996, Last Dance, 1996, To Gillian on Her 37th Birthday, 1996, The Man Who Knew Too Little, 1997, Johnny Skidmarks, 1998, House on the Haunted Hill, 1999, American Beauty, 1999. *

GALLAGHER, RICHARD S., lawyer; b. Minot, N.D., May 10, 1942; s. J.W.S. and Esther T. (Tappon) G.; m. Ann Rylands Larson, June 24, 1972; children: Elizabeth, Catherine. BSBA, Northwestern U., 1964; JD, Harvard U., 1967. Ptnr. Foley & Lardner, Milw., 1967—; bd. dirs. Badger Meter Found., Milw. Bd. chmn. Milw. Youth Symphony Orchs., Milw., 1980-82; bd. chmn. Milw. County Performing Arts Ctr., Milw., 1986-91; dir. Curative Rehab. Ctr., Milw., 1988-93, United Performing Arts Fund, 1991—; pre. Donors Forum of Wis., 1997—. Lt. comdr., USN, 1967-69, Vietnam. Fellow Am. Coll. Tax Counsel, Am. Coll. of Trust and Estate Coun., Am. Law Inst.; mem. ABA (chmn. exempt orgns. com., sect. of taxation 1989-91, chmn. com. on adminstrn. of trusts and estates, sect. probate and trust law 1996-98). Office: Foley & Lardner Firstar Ctr 777 E Wisconsin Ave Milwaukee WI 53202

GALLAGHER, ROBERT P., JR., bank executive; b. N.Y.C., Dec. 31, 1964; s. Robert P. Sr. and Renata Dohrenwend Gallagher. BA in Econs., Williams Coll., 1988; MBA in Fin., NYU, 1992. Lending officer Scotiabank, N.Y.C., 1992-94; v.p. mktg. Dai Ichi Kangyo Bank, Ltd., N.Y.C., 1994—. Contbg. editor NYU MBA Rev., 1990, 91, 91, 93. Active Kips Bay Boys & Girls Club, N.Y.C., 1994-99, Netherland-Am. Found., N.Y.C., 1998. Mem. Chelsea Racquet Club. Republican. Roman Catholic. Avocations: squash, golf, tennis, opera. E-mail: rgallagher@dkb.com. Fax: 212-524-0579. Office: Dai Ichi Kangyo Bank Ltd 1 World Trade Ctr New York NY 10048

GALLAGHER, SHAUN ANDREW, philosophy educator, writer; b. Phila., Oct. 3, 1948; s. John and Bridget (McBride) G.; m. Elaine DeBenedictis, May 29, 1983; children: Laura, Julia. MA, Villanova U., 1976; PhD, Bryn Mawr Coll., 1980; MA, SUNY, Buffalo, 1987. Asst. prof. Gwyneed(Pa.)-Mercy Coll., 1980-81; from asst. to assoc. prof. Canisius Coll., Buffalo, 1981-93, prof. philosophy, 1993—, dir. cognitive sci. program, 1996—; vis. scientist cognition and brain scis. Med. Rsch. Coun., Cambridge, Eng., 1994; editl. bd. The Personalist Forum, 1996—. Author: Hermeneutics and Education, 1992, The Inordinance of Time, 1998, Models of the Self, 1999; editor: Hegel, History and Interpretation, 1996; co-editor: Merleau-Ponty, Hermeneutics and Post-Modernism, 1992, Models of the Self, 1999. Bd. dirs. Audubon Devel. Corp., Amherst, N.Y., 1988-90; chair Audubon Archtl. Com., Amherst, 1985-96; bd. dirs. Audubon Assn., Amherst, 1986-90. Fellow Whiting Found., Louvain, Belgium, 1979, NEH, 1994, 98. Mem. Am. Philos. Assn., Internat. Forum on Persons, Merleau-Ponty Soc. (bd. advisors 1989—). Avocations: Irish music, British mysteries, travel. Office: Canisius Coll Churchill Tower Buffalo NY 14208

GALLAGHER, TERENCE JOSEPH, lawyer; b. N.Y.C., Apr. 12, 1934; s. Terence Moran and Nora Maureen (Buckley) G.; m. Barbara Wogan, Oct. 7, 1961; children: Mary Elizabeth, Anne Marie, Terence, Robert. BA, Manhattan Coll., 1955; JD, Harvard U., 1958; LLM in Taxation, NYU, 1966. Bar: N.Y. 1959, U.S. Ct. Appeals (2d cir.) 1968, U.S. Supreme Ct. 1966. Asst. staff judge adv. USAF, Amarillo, Tex., 1958-60; atty. Eltra Corp., N.Y.C., 1960-65, sr. atty., 1966; atty. Pfizer Inc., N.Y.C., 1966—, v.p. legal adminstrn., 1987-93, v.p. corp. governance, 1993—; bd. dirs. Pfizer Found., N.Y.C., Calvary Hosp. Fund, N.Y.C. Served to capt. USAF, 1958-60. Mem. ABA, Am. Soc. Corp. Secs. (bd. dirs.), N.Y. State Bar Assn. (editor corp. counsel newsletter), Bus. Adv. Council on Fed. Reports (trustee). Roman Catholic. Home: 22 Hewitt Ave Bronxville NY 10708-2329 Office: Pfizer Inc 235 E 42nd St New York NY 10017-5755*

GALLAGHER, TERRENCE VINCENT, editor; b. Phila., Nov. 22, 1946; s. Harold John and Marie Elizabeth (Kershaw) G.; m. Eileen Rose Small, Dec. 26, 1971; children: Sean Terrence, Elizabeth I. B.S. in Journalism, Temple U., 1971. With Chilton Co., Radnor, Pa., 1971-94; asst. editor Product Design and Devel. mag, 1971-73; mng. editor Internat. Product Digest, 1973-74; editor-in-chief Instrument and Apparatus News mag., 1974-84, Hardware Age mag., 1984-94, Decorative Products World, 1989-94, Outdoor Power Equipment Mag, 1989-94, Garden Supply Retailer mag., 1989-94; editorial dir. Chilton's Home and Yard Care Group, 1989-94; chmn. editorial bd. Chilton Co., 1980-83; contbg. editor Tennis U.S.A., 1974-75; pres. Gallagher Communications, 1994—. Served to 1st lt. U.S. Army, 1966-69, Vietnam. Decorated Bronze Star with 2 V devices; Vietnamese Cross of Gallantry. Home: 6 Calvert Cir Paoli PA 19301-1001

GALLAGHER, THOMAS FRANCIS, physicist; b. Bronxville, N.Y., Nov. 19, 1944; s. Thomas Francis and Margaret Ann (Sheekey) G.; m. Betty Barbara Cassiman, Sept. 21, 1974; 1 child, Thomas Francis. AB, Williams Coll., Williamstown, Mass., 1966; PhD, Harvard U., 1971. Rsch. assoc. U. Utah, Salt Lake City, 1971-72; postdoctoral physicist SRI Internat., Menlo Park, Calif., 1972-73, physicist, 1973-79, sr. physicist, 1979-83, program mgr., 1983-84; prof. physics U. Va., Charlottesville, 1984-91, Jesse Beams prof. physics, 1991—. Author: (monograph) Rydberg Atoms; assoc. editor Optics Letters, 1985-89; div. assoc. editor Phys. Rev. Letters, 1988-91; mem. bd. editors Physics Reports, 1996—; mem. editl. bd. Review of Scientific Instruments, 1999—; contbr. more than 200 articles to profl. jours. Named Outstanding Scientist of Va., 1997. Fellow Am. Phys. Soc. (Davisson-Germer Prize in Atomic or Surface Physics 1996), Optical Soc. Am. Roman Catholic. Achievements include patents in field; research on laser spectroscopy of atoms and small molecules, properties of highly excited atoms. Office: Univ of Va Dept Physics Charlottesville VA 22901

GALLAGHER, THOMAS JOSEPH, banker; b. Elizabeth, N.J., Jan. 21, 1949; s. T. Stanley and Madeline (Buckley) G.; m. Lindy Allyn Joslow, Nov. 29, 1975; children: James Allyn Buckley, Philip Graham, Charles Bedloe. BA magna cum laude, U. Pa., 1973, MBA, 1975. V.p. PNC Fin. Corp., Phila., 1975-79, Bank of Am. Nat. Trust & Savs. Assocs., San Francisco, 1979-83; v.p. fin., CFO Page Am. Group, Inc., N.Y.C., 1984-85; v.p. investment banking dept. Bankers Trust Co., N.Y.C., 1983-88; sr. v.p., group exec. The Chase Manhattan Bank N.A., N.Y.C., 1988-96; mng. dir., global aerospace exec. CIBC Oppenheimer Corp., N.Y.C., 1996—; adj. prof. NYU, 1996—. Author: (with Darryl Jenkins) The Handbook of Airline Economics, 1995, (with Gail Butler) Handbook of Airline Marketing, 1998; advisor Jour. of European Bus. Commr. utilities Town of New Canaan, chmn. 1991—. Mem. The Blue Hill Troupe, The Penn Club (N.Y.C.), Stanwich Club, The Wings Club (N.Y.C.), Lawrenceville Club (N.Y.C.), Phi Beta Kappa. Republican. Episcopalian. Home: 596 Silvermine Rd New Canaan CT 06840-4323 Office: CIBC Oppenheimer 425 Lexington Ave New York NY 10017-3903

GALLAGHER, THOMAS M., city official Jersey City; b. Hoboken, N.J., July 27, 1969. BA in Polit. Sci, U. Fla., 1990; MA in Pub. Policy, Harvard U., 1993. Dir. dept. housing, econ. devel. and commerce City of Jersey City, N.J., 1997—. Home: 280 Grove St Jersey City NJ 07302*

GALLAGHER, TIM, parks and recreation director; b. Burbank, Calif., Jan. 30, 1953. BS, UCLA, 1974; MS, Calif. State U., 1977. Dir. parks and recreation City of Yreka (Calif.), 1979-85; mgr. parks and open spaces County of San Luis Obispo (Calif.), 1985-97; dir. parks and recreation City of Stockton (Calif.), 1997—. Office: City of Stockton 6 E Lindsay St Stockton CA 95202-1912

GALLAGHER, TONYA MARIE, family support specialist; b. Great Falls, Mont., Aug. 2, 1971; d. Ronald A. and Sherry E. (Morris) G. BA in Psychology, U. Mont., 1994, BA in Comm. Studies, 1994, MIS, 1998. Project asst./resource coord VVCAP, Missoula, Mont., 1993-96; grad. asst. dept. psychology U. Mont., Missoula, 1996-97; family support specialist Western Mont. Comprehensive Devel. Ctr., Missoula, 1997—; Mem. coun. Youth in Crisis Coalition, 1995—. Vol. coord. AmeriCorps, Missoula, 1996—; crisis vol. YWCA Domestic Violence Assistance Program, 1992-95. Recipient Children And Youth scholarship award Am. Legion, 1993, Heisey award Mont. Cascade Coun., 1992; Mountain West Regional scholar Golden Key Nat. Honor Soc., 1994-95; Early Intervention scholar, 1994-97. Mem. AAUW, Grad. Student Assn., Psi Chi, Alpha Phi (treas. 1989). Lutheran. Avocations: stamp collecting, poetry, skiing, hiking, dance. Home: 1315 E Broadway St Apt 11 Missoula MT 59802-4919 Office: Western Mont Comprehensive Devel Ctr T-214 Fort Missoula Rd Missoula MT 59804-7254

GALLAGHER, VICKI SMITH, real estate agent; b. Norfolk, Va., Dec. 6, 1950; d. James Colan and Margaret Helen (Brewer) Smith; m. Steven Robert Gallagher, Nov. 19, 1977. BS in Music Performance, Old Dominion U., 1973. Agt. GSH Residential, Chesapeake, Va., 1979-84, Realty Cons., Virginia Beach, Va., 1984-90, Leading Edge Realty, Virginia Beach, 1990—. Recipient Million Dollar Sales award Nat. Assn. Home Builders, 1993, Internat. Cat Assn. Mid-Atlantic Region Humanitarian of Yr., 1996. Mem. Tidewater Bd. Realtors (Million Dollar Sales Club Gold award 1993, Silver award 1994, 96, others), Tidewater Builders Assn. (Million Dollar Sales Club 1993, 1998, Silver Hammer award Million Dollar Sales Circle 1994, Million Dollar Circle 1995-97, Pres.'s award 1996, others), Va. Assn. Realtors, Tidewater Assn. Realtors (Million Dollar Club 1995, 1998, Million Dollar Sales Club 1996-97), Leading Edge Realty Achievers Club (Listing Agt. of Yr. 1995), TAR Million Dollar Club, 1998, TB. Avocation: showing cats. Home: 2236 Crossroad Trl Virginia Beach VA 23456-3538 Office: Leading Edge Realty Expressway Ctr 4772 Euclid Rd Ste B Virginia Beach VA 23462-3800

GALLAHER, WILLIAM MARSHALL, dental laboratory technician; b. Philipsburg, Pa., June 10, 1952; s. Marshall William and Florence Marie (Millner) G. Degree in Dental Tech., Hiram G. Andrews Ctr., 1971; BS, Rutgers U., 1979. Cert. dental technician in full dentures. Dental lab. technician to pvt. practice dentist Osceola Mill, Pa., 1971-72; dental lab. technician Profl. Dental Lab., South Amboy, N.J., 1972-79; instr. dental lab. tech. Union Tech. Inst., Neptune, N.J., 1979-84, Hiram G. Andrews Ctr., Johnstown, Pa., 1980-91; owner Gallaher's Dental Lab., Asbury Park, N.J., 1982-90; sr. dental lab. technician Denture Walk-In Ctr., Harrisburg, Pa., 1991—; adv. bd. Union Tech. Inst., 1984-90, Hiram G. Andrews Ctr., 1991-92; founder, pres. Person Enjoying New and Innovative Software User Group, Asbury Park, 1985-90. Author instrnl. manuals. Vol. deaf svcs. Monmouth County Deaf Group, Asbury Park, 1976-77; publicity chmn. Neighbor Preservation Program, Asbury Park, 1979-82. Mem. Nat. Dental Lab. Assn., Nat. Denturist Soc., N.J. Denturist Soc., Pa. Denturist Assn., Indian Tribal Denturity Assn., Internat. Brotherhood Magicians, Internat. Magicians Soc. (life), Masons (sr. master of ceremonies 1982—). Achievements include research on low-cost denture procedures, cleft palate and post cancerous intra-oral appliances. Home: 1912 N 3rd St Harrisburg PA 17102-1855 Office: Denture Walk In Ctr 2023 N 2nd St Harrisburg PA 17102-2103

GALLAMORE, BETTY LOU, nurse; b. Poplar Bluff, Mo., Nov. 23, 1951; d. Virgil Luther and Alta Elaine (Dickerson) Groves; m. James Dewey Gallamore, June 27, 1970 (div. 1979); 1 child, Deborah Lynn; m. Jerry L. Capes, May 28, 1988 (div. 1993). AAS, Belleville Area Coll., Ill., 1979; BSN, St. Mary Coll., Leavenworth, Kans., 1987; MS in Nursing, U. Mo., Kansas City, 1991. RN, Kans.; cert. ARNP; clin. nurse specialist in gerontology. Office nurse Met. Orthopedics Ltd., St. Louis, 1973-81; dir. nursing Gardner (Kans.) Skilled Facility, 1982-84; staff nurse Bethany Med. Ctr., Kansas City, Kans., 1984-88; staff nurse-ICU Munson Army Hosp., Ft. Leavenworth, 1985-88; nurse coordinator VA Hosp., Leavenworth, 1988-90; staff nurse Bethany Med. Ctr., Kansas City, Kans., 1989-93, Trinity Luth. Hosp., Kansas City, Mo., 1990-95; edn. coord. Kansas City Presbyn. Manor, 1991-95; nurse Coffeyville (Kans.) Regional Med. Ctr., 1993-95; nurse Mercy Hosp., Independence, Kans., 1993-94, traveling nurse, 1995—; adminstrv. supr. Lafayette-Grand Hosp., St. Louis, 1996—; staff nurse Woodriver Twp. Hosp., Woodriver, Ill., 1997—, Jefferson Meml. Hosp., Crystal City, Mo., 1998—; conductor workshop in field; affiliate faculty U. Mo., Kansas City, 1992—. Mem. Kans. Nurses Assn., Eagles, Nightingale Nursing Honor Soc. (fellow in nursing sci.), Sigma Theta Tau. Home: 201 Kroeger Ave Dupo IL 62239-1303

GALLANT, GEORGE WILLIAM, political scientist; b. Boston, Nov. 14, 1931; s. George William and Gladys Mary (Dalby) G.; m. Joan Cornelia Crimmins, Nov. 6, 1954; children: Julith Cornelia, Nicole Marie. AB cum laude, Boston Coll., 1952; MA, Georgetown U., 1965; PhD, Fordham U., 1971; grad., various specialized mil. schs. Commd. 2d lt. U.S. Army, 1952, advanced through grades to col., 1975; svc. in Eng., Fed. Republic Germany and Vietnam; asst. prof. U.S. Mil. Acad., West Point, N.Y., 1967-70; head Soviet and Asian communist rsch. sects. and divsns. Dept. Def., 1970-75; Soviet cons. and translator, 1975—; adj. faculty mem. polit. sci. Stonehill Coll., North Easton, Mass., 1977-85, asst. prof., 1985-91, assoc. prof., 1991-97, dir. Stonehill Coll.-Yaroslavl State U. (Russia) Exch. Program, 1993-97, ret., 1997. Contbr. articles to profl. jours.; creator TV programs. Rep. Stoughton Town Meeting, 1975—, chmn. mcpl. ops. com. Decorated Legion of Merit (2), Bronze Star. Mem. Am. Assn. for Advancement Slavic Studies, Am. Polit. Sci. Assn., Assn. U.S. Army, Ret. Officers Assn., Cape Cod Ret. Officers Assn., Boston Coll. Alumni Club, Sigma Iota Rho, Phi Beta Kappa, Alpha Lambda Sigma (hon. mem. Beta Xi chpt.). Address: 303 Morton St Stoughton MA 02072-3239

GALLANT, MAVIS, author; b. Montreal, Que., Can., Aug. 11, 1922. Hon. doctoral degree, U. St. Anne, N.S., Can., 1984, York U., Toronto, 1984, U. Western Ont., 1990; hon. doctoral degree, Queen's U., 1992, U. Montreal, 1995, Bishop's U., 1995. Writer-in-residence U. Toronto, 1983-84. Author: Green Water, Green Sky, 1959, 60, A Fairly Good Time, 1970; short stories The Other Paris, My Heart Is Broken: 8 Stories and a Short Novel (Brit. title An Unmarried Man's Summer), 1964, The Affair of Gabrielle Russier; introductory essay, 1971; The Pegnitz Junction, a Novella and Five Short Stories, 1973, The End of the World and Other Stories, 1974; short stories From the Fifteenth District, 1979, Home Truths, 1981, Overhead in a Balloon, 1985; play What Is To Be Done? (produced Toronto 1982), 1984, Paris Notebooks: Essays and Reviews, 1986, (short stories) In Transit, 1989, (short stories) Across the Bridge, 1993; The Moslem Wife and other stories, 1994, Collected Stories, 1996; contbr. to New Yorker, 1951—. Decorated Order of Can.; recipient Gov.-Gen.'s Lit. award, 1982, Molson award, 1997, Medaille de la Ville de Paris, 1999. Fellow Royal Soc. Lit.; fgn. hon. mem. Am. Acad. and Inst. Arts and Letters. Home: 14 rue Jean Ferrandi, Paris 75006, France

GALLANTZ, GEORGE GERALD, lawyer; b. N.Y.C., Apr. 23, 1913; s. Samuel and Gussie (Safir) G.; m. Lillian Kolko, Nov. 12, 1939; children—Michael, Judith Coven. B.S., CCNY, 1932; LL.B. cum laude, Bklyn. Law Sch., 1935. Bar: N.Y. 1935. Atty. N.Y.C. Corp. Counsel's Office, 1939-42; clk. to judge N.Y. State Ct. Appeals, 1943-45; assoc. firm Simpson Thacher & Bartlett, N.Y.C., 1946-56; partner firm Colton, Gallantz & Fernbach, N.Y.C., 1958-63; Proskauer Rose Goetz & Mendelsohn, 1963-94; ret. Trustee Bklyn. Law Sch., 1983-97. Mem. Am. Bar Assn., Assn. Bar City N.Y. (chmn. exec. com. 1974-75). Home: 37 W 12th St New York NY 10011-8502

GALLAR, JOHN JOSEPH, mechanical engineer, educator; b. Poland, July 3, 1936; came to U.S., 1981; s. Joseph and Sophie (Gallar) Filipecki; m. Christina B. Wilczynski, June 30, 1962; 1 child, Darek A. BSME, State U. Poland, 1957, MSME, 1958; PhD in Tech. Scis., M & M Acad., 1966; professorship, Ahmadu Bello U., Zaria, Nigeria, 1980. Dir., prof. engring. Acad. State U., Poland, 1957-72; dir., prof. engring. Ahmadu Bello U., 1973-81, dir. postgrad. studies, 1976-81; with module design Timex Co., Cupertino, Calif., 1981-82; mgr. mfg. Computer Research Co., Santa Clara, Calif., 1982-84; mgr. hardware devel. Nat. Semiconductor Co., Santa Clara, 1984-85; chief robotics engr. Varian Corp., Palo Alto, Calif., 1986-93; pres., owner Frontier Engring., San Jose, Calif., 1994—; dep. vice-chancellor State U., Poland, 1970-71; cons. Enplan Corp., Kaduna, Nigeria, 1980-81, Criticare Tech., Sparks, Nev., 1985-86, also bd. dirs.; mgr. mfg. engring. Retro-Tek Co., Santa Clara, 1986. Contbr. poetry to Nat. Libr. of Poetry; contbr. articles to profl. jours.; patentee in field. Trustee, charter life mem. Presdl. Task Force, Washington, 1984; mem. Nat. Conservative Polit. Action Com., Washington, 1981. Recipient U.S. Ceremonial Flag Presdl. Task Force; Medal Merit from Pres. Ronald Reagan, Washington, 1985. Mem. NRA, Internat. Soc. Poets (life). Roman Catholic. Avocations: writing poetry, listening to country-western music. Home: 5459 Entrada Cedros San Jose CA 95123-1418 Office: Frontier Engring 5459 Entrada Cedros San Jose CA 95123-1418

GALLAS, JAMES S., federal judge; b. 1928. AB, Bethany U., 1949; LLB, Cleve. State U., 1953. Pvt. practice, claims adjuster, 1953-63; asst. atty. gen. State of Ohio Atty. Gen. Office, 1964-71; clk. of ct. U.S. Dist. Ct. (no. dis.) Ohio, 1977-91; magistrate judge U.S. Dist. Ct. (no. dist.) Ohio, Akron, 1991—. With U.S. Army, 1946-47. Fax: (216) 375-5536. Office: US Dist Ct No Dist Ohio 480 US Courthouse 209 S High St Akron OH 44308

GALLEA, ANTHONY MICHAEL, portfolio manager; b. Rochester, N.Y., Aug. 5, 1949; s. Frank and Josephine (Battaglia) G.; m. Bonita Anderson, Mar. 28, 1970; children: Christopher, Michelle, Lisa. BA, U. Rochester, 1973. Gen. mgr. Gallea, Inc., Rochester, 1974-80; fin. con. Shearson Lehman Bros., Rochester, 1980-82; 2d v.p., cons. Shearson Lehman Hutton, Rochester, 1982-83, v.p., fin. cons., 1983-86, 1st v.p., fin. cons., 1986-88, sr. v.p., portfolio mgr., 1988—; mem. dir.'s coun. Shearson Lehman Bros., N.Y.C., 1989-93; sr. portfolio mgr. Smith Barney, 1993-96, sr. portfolio mgmt. dir., 1996—; arbitrator N.Y. Stock Exch., N.Y.C., 1987—. Author: The Lump Sum Handbook: Investment and Tax Strategies For A Secure Retirement, 1993, Contrarian Investing, 1996, The Lump Sum Advisor, 1999. Trustee Henrietta Pub. Libr., Rochester, 1985-88. Mem. Phila. Bd. Trade. Avocations: music, sailing, mountain climbing. Office: Salomon Smith Barney 71 Monroe Ave Pittsford NY 14534-1312

GALLEGLY, ELTON WILLIAM, congressman; b. Huntington Park, Calif., Mar. 7, 1944; married; four children. Attended, Calif. State U., L.A. Businessman, real estate broker Simi Valley, Calif., from 1968; mem. Simi Valley City Coun., 1979; mayor City of Simi Valley, 1980-86; mem. 100th-106th Congresses from the 21st (now 23d) Calif. dist., 1986—; chmn. internat. rels. subcom. on the western hemisphere, mem. judiciary com., mem. resources com.; mem. exec. com. U.S. Ho. Reps. Rep. Study Com.; mem. Congl. Human Rights Caucus, Congl. Fire Svcs. Caucus; formerly vice-chmn., chmn. Ventura County Assn. govts., Calif. Bd. dirs. Moorpark Coll. Found. Office: US Ho of Reps 2427 Rayburn HOB Washington DC 20515

GALLEGOS, LARRY DUAYNE, lawyer; b. Cheverly, Md., Mar. 23, 1951; s. Belarmino R. and Helen (Schlotthauer) G.; m. Claudia M. King, Oct. 1, 1994; 1 child, Will Adam. BS summa cum laude, U. Puget Sound, 1978; JD, Harvard U., 1981. Bar: Colo. 1981, U.S. Dist. Ct. Colo. 1981, U.S. Tax Ct. 1989. Assoc. Pendleton & Sabian, Denver, 1981-83; assoc. O'Connor & Hannan, Denver, 1983-86, ptnr., 1986-89; ptnr. Rossi & Judd, P.C., Denver, 1989-92, Berliner Zisser Walter & Gallegos, P.C., Denver, 1992—. Served with U.S. Army (ARCOM), 1972-74. Mem. ABA (real property, probate and trust law sect.), Colo. Bar Assn., Colo. Trial Lawyers Assn., Denver Bar Assn., U.S. Golf Assn. Avocations: tennis, golf. Office: Berliner Zisser Walter & Gallegos PC 1700 Lincoln St Ste 4700 Denver CO 80203-4547

GALLEGOS, LOU, federal agency administrator. Student, U. Md., W.M. Highlands U. Dir. field ops. for Sen. Pete V. Domenici, 1977-84; exec. dir. Rep. Party N.Mex., 1985; state dir. N.Mex. FHA USDA, 1985-86; cabinet sec. human svcs. dept. for Gov. Garrey E. Carruthers, N.Mex., 1987-89; asst. sec. policy budget and adminstrn. Dept. Interior, Washington, 1989—; candidate for U.S. Congress, 1984. Office: Dept Interior Policy Budget & Adminstrn 18th & C Sts NW Washington DC 20240

GALLENKAMP, CHARLES, writer; b. Dallas, Apr. 13, 1930; s. Charles O. and Norma (Benton) G.; m. Karen L. Wright, May 19, 1994. Student, U. Tex.; BA in Anthropology and Art History, U. N.Mex., 1954. Asst. dir. Mus. Anthropology, U. N.Mex., 1949-52; asst. curator anthropology Houston Mus. Natural Sci., 1954-57; dir. Maya Rsch. Fund, Interam Found., North Tex. State U., Denton, 1957-62; owner-dir. Janus Gallery, Santa Fe, 1970-78; exhbn. coord. Albuquerque Mus., 1980-87. Author: (juvenile) The Pueblo Indians in Story, Song, and Dance, 1955, 2nd edit., 1980, Finding Out About the Maya, 1963, (with Carolyn Meyer) The Mystery of The Ancient Maya, 1985 (one of Best Books of Yr. Sch. Libr. Jour.); author: Maya: The Riddle and Rediscovery of a Lost Civilization, 1959, 2nd edit., 1976, 3rd edit., 1985; editor: Maya: Treasures of An Ancient Civilization, 1985; contbr. articles to profl. jours. Grantee Interam Found., 1957, Helene Wurlitzer Found., 1962-63, Chapelbrook Found., 1965, Sch. Am. Rsch., 1978-79, Earhart Found., 1992, Ludwig Vogelstein Found., Edward Ewing Barrow Found. Mem. Soc. Am. Archaeology, Archaeol. Inst. Am., Sch. Am. Rsch. (rsch. assoc. 1976-79, 91-93, 98), Explorers Club (emeritus). Home: PO Box 9275 Santa Fe NM 87504-9275

GALLERANO, ANDREW JOHN, lawyer; b. Houston, Dec. 2, 1941; s. Andrew H. and Victoria J. (LaNasa) G.; m. Evelyn Cornelius, June 6, 1964; children: Kelly Lynn, Wendy Michelle. BA, U. Tex., Austin, 1964; JD, South Tex. Coll. Law, 1968. Bar: Tex. 1968, U.S. Supreme Ct. 1973. Asst. atty. gen. State of Tex., 1968-71; regional atty. Montgomery Ward & Co., 1971-72; v.p. Foley's, div. Federated Dept. Stores Inc., 1972-79; v.p., gen. counsel, sec. Nat. Convenience Stores Inc., Houston, 1979-89; sr. v.p., gen. counsel, sec. Nat. Convience Stores Inc., Houston, 1989-96; ptnr. Baker, Boldt & Gallerano, Dripping Springs, Tex., 1996—; adj. prof. South Tex. Coll. Law, 1973-75; mem. adv. coun. U. Tex. Coll. Bus., 1993-98. Pres. S. Tex. Hosp. Fin. Agy., 1979—; mem. devel. bd. U. Tex. Health Sci. Ctr., Houston, 1978-93; bd. dirs. YMCA, 1973-86, 90-92, Assn. Cmty. TV, 1974-80; chmn. bd. trustees Star of Hope Mission, 1990-96. Mem. Tex. Bar Assn. (grievance com. 1986-89), U. Tex. Ex-Students Assn., Houston Retail Mchts. Assn. (bd. dirs. 1973—, pres. 1976-78), Tax Rsch. Assn. (bd. dirs. 1975-92). Home: PO Box 1159 Dripping Springs TX 78620-1159 Office: Baker Boldt & Gallerano PO Box 718 Dripping Springs TX 78620-0718

GALLERT, BARBARA LYNN, communications executive; b. Pasadena, Calif., June 18, 1957; d. Horst Gerhard and Annerose Gertrud Gallert. BA in History, Calif. State Poly. U., Pomona, 1981, BS in Comm. Arts, 1981; MPA, Calif. State U., San Bernardino, 1999. Linehaul dispatcher Roadway Express, Inc., Adelanto, Calif., 1982-85; cmty. rels. rep. Walnut (Calif.) Valley Water Dist., 1986-88; comm. specialist Western Mcpl. Water Dist., Riverside, Calif., 1988—; mem. dept. water resources Water Edn. Adv. Coun., Sacramento, 1988—; chair Water Edn. Adv. Coun. Western Riverside County, 1995—; presenter in field. Contbr.: Water Conservation Garden Activity Book, 1992. Dir. Greater Riverside C. of C., 1991-93; vice chair Riverside Mcpl. Mus. Bd., 1994-97; vol. Riverside Humane Soc., 1998—; mem. Leadership Southern Calif., Leadership Riverside. mem. ASPA, L.A. Conservancy. Avocations: travel, antiques, volunteer work, movies, hiking.

GALLETTI, MARIE ANN, English language and linguistics educator; b. N.Y.C., Nov. 25, 1944; d. Fidel G. and Marie Theresa (Chaumard) G.; m. Wayne Lee Mitchell. BA cum laude, Queens Coll. CUNY, 1965; MA, Hunter Coll. CUNY, 1971; M in Counseling, Ariz. State U., 1981. Prof. English Glendale (Ariz.) Cmty. Coll. Maricopa Cmty. Coll. Dist., 1975—.

Co-editor: (anthologies) Native American Substance Abuse, 1982, American Indian Families: Developmental Strategies, 1982. Mem. Nature Conservancy, 1984—, World Wildlife Fund, 1984—, Humane Soc. of U.S., 1984—, Ellis Island Found., 1986—; founding mem. 390th Meml. Mus. Found., Tuscon, 1994. Recipient Regents' scholarship N.Y. State Bd. Regents, 1961. Mem. AAUP, Phi Beta Kappa (founding v.p. Phoenix met. area chpt. 1981-83), Phi Delta Kappa. Office: Glendale Cmty Coll 6000 W Olive Ave Glendale AZ 85302-3006

GALLI, DARRELL JOSEPH, management consultant; b. Ft. Bragg, Calif., Nov. 10, 1948; s. Joseph Germain and Esther Edith (Happajoki) G.; B.A. in Transp./Internat. Bus., San Francisco State U., 1975; BS in Computer Info. Systems, 1985; MBA Golden Gate U., 1980; m. Rondus Miller, Apr. 23, 1977 (div. 1981); 1 dau., Troyan Hulda. With Pacific Gas & Electric Co., Santa Cruz, Calif., 1972-73; with Calif. Western R.R., Ft. Bragg, 1975-77, Sheldon Oil Co., Suisun, Calif, 1978-80; mgr. House of Rondus, Suisun, 1974-79; mgmt. cons., Suisun City, 1979—; instr. Solano Coll., 1979-81, Golden Gate U., 1981; mem. faculty U. Md. European div., Heidelberg, W.Ger., 1982-88; owner, mgr. Old Stewart House Bed and Breakfast, Fort Bragg, Calif., 1990—; lectr. Coll. Redwoods, Ft. Bragg, 1989—; coord. Small Bus. Mgmt. Seminar, 1980. Asst. coordinator Sr. Citizens Survey for Solano Coll. and Sr. Citizens Center, 1980; mem. Ft. Bragg City Coun., 1994—. Served with U.S. Army, 1969-71. Lic. Calif. real estate agt. Mem. Am. Assn. M.B.A. Execs., World Trade Assn., Bay Area Elec. R.R. Assn. Democrat. Episcopalian. Club: Odd Fellows. Home and Office: 511 Stewart St Fort Bragg CA 95437-3226

GALLIAN, RUSSELL JOSEPH, lawyer; b. San Mateo, Calif., Apr. 24, 1948; s. Phillip Hugh and Betty Jane (Boulton) G.; m. Marian Barbara Howard, Sept. 21, 1969; children: Lisa, Cherie, Joseph, Russell, Yvette, Jason, Ryan. BS, U. San Francisco, 1969, JD with honors, 1974. Bar: Calif. 1974, Utah 1975, U.S. Ct. Appeals (10th cir.) 1975, U.S. Supreme Ct. 1990; CPA, Calif. Staff acct. Arthur Andersen & Co., CPAs, San Francisco, 1969-71; treas., contr. N.Am. Reassurance Life Svc. Co., Palo Alto, Calif., 1972-74; assoc. VanCott Bagley Cornwell & McCarthy, Salt Lake City, 1975-77; sr. ptnr. Gallian & Westfall, Wilcox & Wright LC, St. George, Utah, 1977—; chmn. bd. dirs. Dixie Title Co., St. George. Chmn. Tooele (Utah) City Planning Commn., 1978; atty. City of Tooele, 1978-80, Town of Ivins, Utah, 1982—, Town of Springdale, Utah, 1987-90, Town of Rockville, Utah, 1987, Town of Virgin, 1995—; commr. Washington County, 1993-96; chmn. Washington County Econ. Devel. Coun., 1993-96; bd. dirs. Dixie Ctr., 1993-96; active Habitat Conservation Plan Steering Com. Mem. ABA, Utah State Bar Assn., Tooele County Bar Assn. (pres. 1978-79), So. Utah Bar Assn. (pres. 1986-87). Republican. Mormon. Office: Gallian & Westfall Wilcox & Wright LC 59 S 100 E Saint George UT 84770-3422

GALLICK, HAROLD LYNN, cardiac surgeon; b. Lansing, Mich., Dec. 12, 1955; s. Harold and Mary Catherine (McMillion) G.; m. Marilynn Sultana Gallick, Mar. 27, 1982; children: Karista Lynn, Nicholas Alexander, Matthew Tyler. BS with high honors/high distinction, U. Mich., 1978; MD, Wayne State U., 1982. Diplomate Nat. Bd. Med. Examiners, Am. Bd. Surgery, Am. Bd. Thoracic Surgery. Intern and resident in gen. surgery Wayne State U., Detroit, 1982-87, resident in cardiothoracic surgery, 1987-90; cardiac surgeon St. John Hosp., Detroit, 1990—; pvt. practice Detroit; clin. instr. surgery Wayne State U., Detroit, 1990-95, clin. asst. prof., 1995-97. Contbr. articles to profl. jours., chpts. to books. Fellow ACS, Am. Coll. Chest Physicians, Am. Coll. Cardiology; mem. Soc. Thoracic Surgeons, Wayne County Med. Soc. (del. 1995), Mich. State Med. Soc. Office: Cardiovas Surgeons Met Det 22151 Moross Rd Ste 20 Detroit MI 48236-2114

GALLICK, SARAH PATRICIA, editor, writer; b. N.Y.C.; d. Joseph Paul and Mary Katherine (Elliott) G. BA in English, Hofstra U., 1973; MBA, Pace U., 1979. Editor Doubleday Direct, N.Y.C., 1997—. Author: Secrets, 1985, Born to Be Rich, 1990, Oprah! Up Close and Down Home, 1993, Barbra Streisand: The Untold Story, 1994, The Kennedy Men, 1996, The Real Ally McBeal, 1999, Ronald Reagan: A Pictorial Biography, 1999. Mem. Romance Writers Am., Women's Media Group, Novelists, Inc. Roman Catholic. Avocation: art collecting. Home: 51 W 81st St New York NY 10024-6004

GALLIENNE, ROBERT LEE, nursing educator; b. Bronxville, N.Y., Jan. 9, 1967; s. Robert James and Trudy Louise (Biesecker) G. BA in Biology, Wittenberg U., 1989; D Clin. Nursing, Case Western Res. U., 1992. Cert. critical care nurse; RN, Ohio. Nurse technician VA Med. Ctr., Cleve., 1990-91; nurse extern Univ. Hosp. of Cleve., 1991, clin. nurse, 1992-97, nursing instr., 1997—; instr. Am. Heart Assn., Cleve., 1990—. Chair social concerns com. Christ Luth Ch., Willoughby, Ohio, 1995-97; sec. alumni bd. Frances Payne Bolton Sch. Nursing, Cleve., 1997-99. Mem. AACN, Soc. Critical Care Medicine, Sigma Theta Tau. Avocations: hiking, writing. Home: 20110 Lorain Rd Apt 506 Fairview Park OH 44126-3435 Office: Univ Hosps Cleve 11100 Euclid Ave Cleveland OH 44106-1736

GALLIMORE, MARGARET MARTIN, poet; b. Winston Salem, Mar. 20, 1947; d. Holland Henry and Dallas Cornell (Robbins) Martin; m. Elmer Harold Holden Jr., Feb. 14, 1965; children: Andrew Harold, Amy Darlene, John Alan; m. Timothy Milton Gallimore, May 9, 1986. Student, High Point (N.C.) Coll., 1988. Lic. real estate broker, N.C. With AT&T Network Sys., Winston-Salem, 1965-69, 73-75, prodn. operator, 1979-89; real estate salesperson Lambe-Young Real Estate Co., Kernersville, N.C., 1975-79; leasing cons. Vinyard Gardens Apts./S.E. Atlantic Properties, Winston-Salem, 1994-95; comm. assoc. AT&T Phone Ctr., Winston-Salem, 1995-96; real estate salesperson Triad Piedmont Properties, Kernersville, 1996; real estate broker Winston-Salem, 1996—; asst. cmty. mgr. Lindsey Manor Apts./Steven D. Bell & Co., Kernersville, 1997; ret., 1997. Author poetry. Recipient Editors Choice awards (2) Nat. Libr. of Poetry, 1995, 97; named to Internat. Poetry Hall of Fame, Nat. Libr. Poetry, 1996. Mem. Internat. Soc. Poets (Disting. mem.). Home: 2534 Union Cross Rd Winston Salem NC 27107-4420

GALLINA, CHARLES ONOFRIO, nuclear scientist; b. New Brunswick, N.J., Oct. 10, 1943; s. Matthew Salvatore and Mary (Piazza) G.; m. Ellen Mary Romano, Oct. 10, 1976; children: Mary Catharine, Matthew Charles, Maria Christine. BS, Fordham U., 1965; MS, Rutgers U., 1967, PhD, 1971. Environ. radiation specialist Consol. Edison N.Y., N.Y.C., 1971-72; radiation specialist AEC, Newark, 1972-73; sr. radiation specialist Nuclear Regulatory Commn., King of Prussia, Pa., 1973-76, sr. duty officer, 1973-82, investigation specialist, 1976-80, coord. emergency preparedness, 1980-82; sr. emergency preparedness engr. Tera Corp., King of Prussia, 1982; sr. radiol. engr. Hydro Nuclear Svcs., Marlton, N.J., 1982-84, dir. tech. mktg., 1984-85; mgr. bus. devel. Westinghouse Electric Corp., Moorestown, N.J., 1985-87; mgr. tech. program devel. Westinghouse Radiological Svcs., Moorestown, N.J., 1987-89; sr. nuclear scientist Dept. Nuclear Safety State of Ill., Springfield, 1990—; pres., CEO Springfield STOPP, Inc., 1994—; exec. cons. Profl. Nuclear Assocs., Springfield, Ill., 1990—; mem. bd. sci. and policy advisors Am. Coun. on Sci. and Health, 1991—; spl. tech. cons. to U.S. Def. Nuclear Agy.; tech. expert in area of emergency preparedness, radiation safety environ. monitoring and reactor health physics IAEA. Tech. reviewer, contbr. Radiation Protection Management Mag., Health Physics Soc. Jour.; contbr. articles to Health Physics Soc. Jour. Pres. Providence Force Condominium Assn., 1973-77; pres., CEO STOPP (Stop Planned Parenthood) of Ill., Inc., 1993—. AEC fellow, 1968-70, USPHS fellow, 1967, fellow Fed. Water Pollution Control Assn., 1971. Mem. Am. Nuclear Soc. (vice chmn., chmn.-elect Midwest Ill. chpt. 1991-93), Delaware Valley Soc. Radiation Protections, Health Physics Soc. (charter mem. Prairie State chpt. 1990—, bd. dirs. Prairie State chpt. 1993—), Am. Coun. of Sci. and Health (bd. sci. and policy advisors 1991—). E-mail: cgallina@fgi.net. Fax: 217-793-5078. Home: 3505 Bluff Rd Springfield IL 62707-7954 Office: 1035 Outer Park Dr Springfield IL 62704-4462

GALLINARO, NICHOLAS FRANCIS, business executive; b. Somerville, Mass., Feb. 25, 1930; s. Joseph Michael and Mary Marie (Valerio) G.; B.A., Boston Coll., 1952, M.B.A., 1964; B.S. in Mech. Engring., Notre Dame U., 1953; m. Inez Hanken, July 27, 1957; children—Michael J., James J., Stephen P., Robert N. With Clark Equipment Corp, Battle Creek & Benton Harbor, Mich., 1951-53; v.p., Harnischfeger Internat, Corp., Milw., Wis., 1953-63; v.p., dir. McLaughlin Equipment Corp., N.Y.C., 1963-71; v.p., dir. Prudential Internat. Corp., N.Y.C., 1971-72; chmn., chief exec. officer GAR Internat. Corp., Red Bank, N.J., 1972—; chmn. bd. CIMAT S.r.1., Milan Italy, GAR Internat. SA, Lima, Peru, GAR Internat. C.A., Caracas, Venezuela. Trustee, Christian Brothers Acad. With USMC, 1949-51. Mem. Soc. Am. Mil. Engrs., N.Y. World Trade Assn., Pan Am. Soc., Am. Mining Congress, Associated Equipment Distbrs., Internat. Road Fedn. USA (dir.). Republican. Roman Catholic. Clubs: K.C., Navesink Country. Home: 79 Rolling Hills Ct Holmdel NJ 07733 Office: GAR Internat Corp 3315 Commerce Pkwy Miramar FL 33025-3954

GALLINAT, MICHAEL PAUL, fisheries biologist; b. Flint, Mich., Nov. 1, 1962; s. Paul John Richard and Myrna Mae (Dingman) G.; m. Carol Ann Koshko, Sept. 8, 1989; children: Nathan Michael, Adam Andrew. BS in Fisheries and Wildlife Mgmt., Lake Superior State U., Sault Ste. Marie, Mich., 1985; MS in Fisheries Biology, Ball State U., 1987. Grad. rsch. asst. Ball State U., Muncie, Ind., 1985-87; pvt. aquatic contractor, Flushing, Mich., 1987-88; rsch. asst. U. Mich., Ann Arbor, 1988; fisheries biologist, program adminstr. Red Cliff Band of Lake Superior Chippewa, Bayfield, Wis., 1988—; mem. Wis. Coastal Mgmt. Coun., Madison, 1991—, Native Peoples Fisheries Com., 1990-92; adj. mem. Lake Superior Tech. Com., 1988—, mem. steelhead, walleye and brook trout subcoms.; adj. faculty Envirovet Program U. Ill., 1991-95. Mem. Am. Fisheries Soc., Sigma Xi (assoc.). Achievements include research in the biology, life history and food habits of lake trout and lake whitefish in Lake Superior. Home: 1012 3rd Ave W Ashland WI 54806-3107 Office: Red Cliff Fisheries Dept PO Box 529 Bayfield WI 54814-0529

GALLINGER, LORRAINE D., prosecutor; b. Sept. 2, 1948. BS, U. Wyo., 1970; JD, Cath. U. Am., 1975. Bar: D.C., Mont. 1st asst. U.S. atty. Dept. Justice, Billings, Mont., 1976-85, 91, sr. litigation counsel, chief civil divsn., 1985-91, acting U.S. atty., 1991-93; first asst. U.S. Attys. Office, Billings, Mont., 1993—; instr. Atty. Gen. Advocacy Inst. Recipient Dir.'s Superior Performance award AUSA, 1988. Office: US Attys Office PO Box 1478 Billings MT 59103-1478*

GALLINOT, RUTH MAXINE, educational consultant; b. Carlinville, Ill., Feb. 16, 1925; d. Martin Mike and Augusta (Kumpus) G. BS, Roosevelt U., Chgo., 1971, MA with honors, 1974; PhD, The Union Inst., Cin., 1978. Adminstrv. asst., exec. sec. Karoll's Inc., Chgo., 1952-66; asst. dean Cen. YMCA Community Coll., Chgo., 1966-81, dir. life planning inst., 1979-80; pres. Gallinot & Assocs., Chgo., St. Louis and Bethalto, Ill., 1980—; mem. task force Office Sr. Citizens and Handicapped, City of Chgo., 1971-79; mem. criteria and guidelines com. Internat. Assn. for Continuing Edn. and Tng., 1983-86, survey and rsch. com., 1984-88; team chair accreditation evaluation team Accrediting Commn. Ind. Colls. and Schs., Washington, 1983-88; instr. Grad. Sch., USDA, 1984—, Coun, Rehab. Affiliates, Chgo., 1985—. Developer leisure time adult edn. series for elderly Uptown model cities area dept. human resources City of Chgo., 1970; editor: Certified Professional Secs. Rev., 1983; reporter Greater Alton Pub. Co., 1987-89; contbr. articles to profl. jours. Chmn. Commn. Status of Women in State of Ill., 1963-68; del. White House Conf. on Equal Pay, 1963, White House Conf. on Civil Rights, 1965, City of Chgo. White House Conf. on Info. and Libr., 1976, State of Ill. White House Conf. Info. Svcs. and Libr. Svcs., 1977; life mem. Mus. Lithuanian Culture, Chgo., 1973—; pub. mem. Fgn. Svc. Selection Bd. U.S. Dept. State, 1984; bd. dirs. Luths. for Chgo., 1978-83, also founding member; member adv. edn. com. Chgo. Commn. Human Rels., 1968-75 fundraising chmn. Bethalto (Ill.) Sr Citizens new bldg. furnishings, 1990-91, pres. 1995-97; mem. dist. adv. com. Bethalto (Ill.) Cmty. Unit Sch. Dist. # 8, 1997—. Recipient Leadership in Civic, Cultural and Econ. Life of the City award YWCA, Chgo., 1972, Achievement in Field Edn. award Operation P.U.S.H., Chgo., 1975. Mem. Internat. Assn. Adminstrv. Profls. (past pres., ednl. cons. 1980-84), Edn. Network Older Adults (v.p., sec. 1979-86), Assn. Cert. Profl. Secs., Nat. Assn. Parliamentarians (Ill. and Chgo. chpts.), Literacy Coun. Chgo. (bd. dirs. 1979-86), Zonta of Alton (treas. Chgo. club 1965-66). Lutheran. Home and Office: Gallinot & Assocs 210 James St Bethalto IL 62010-1318

GALLIS, CAROLE CAMPBELL, secondary education educator; b. Darby, Pa., Dec. 3, 1944; d. Jack Henry and Marion Alice (McCrea) Campbell; m. John Nicholas Gallis, June 17, 1967; children: John Christopher, Robin Noel Talbot. BS in Edn., Millersville U., 1966; MEd, Pa. State U., Great Valley, 1994. Cert. tchr. English and French, Pa. Tchr. Garden Spot H.S., New Holland, Pa., 1966-67, asst. girls basketball coach, 1966; substitute tchr. Upper Merion Area Sch. Dist., King of Prussia, Pa., 1977-84, tchr., 1984—; girls winter track coach Upper Merion Area Sch. Dist., 1984-88; advisor H.S. newspaper, 1994—, lit. mag., 1997—; receptionist, tchr., Phebe Anna Thome Sch., Bryn Mawr (Pa.) Coll., 1979-81; historic interpreter Mystic (Conn.) Seaport, 1976. Brownie leader, Freedom Valley Girl Scout Coun., Valley Forge, Pa., 1977-79, Brownie coord., 1979-80. Mem. NCTE, NEA, Am. Assn. Tchrs. Fgn. Lang., Pa. State Edn. Assn., Upper Merion Area Edn. Assn., Kappa Sigma Delta (pres. 1987-89). Methodist. Home: 727 Suellen Dr King Of Prussia PA 19406 Office: Upper Merion Area Sch Dist 435 Crossfield Rd King Of Prussia PA 19406

GALLIS, JOHN NICHOLAS, naval officer, healthcare executive; b. Pitts., Dec. 18, 1944; s. John Vincent Glade and Sylvia Delores (Rizzo) Friedman; m. Carole Campbell, June 17, 1967; children: J. Christopher, Robin Noel. AS in Edn., No. Va. C.C., 1975; BS in Healthcare Adminstrn., George Washington U., 1977; MPA, Pa. State U., 1980. Enlisted USN, 1962, advanced through grades to capt., 1995; outpatient svcs. officer Submarine Med. Ctr., New London, Conn., 1974-76; patient adminstrn. officer Naval Hosp., Phila., 1977-80; officer-in-charge Naval Med. Clinic, Willow Grove, Pa., 1980-82; hosp. corpsman/dental technician rating assignment officer Bur. Naval Pers., Arlington, Va., 1982-85; dir. for adminstrn. Naval Hosp., Phila., Va., 1985-88; dir. leadership course Naval Sch. Health Scis., Bethesda, Md., 1988-91; assignment officer Med. Svc. Corps, Arlington, Va., 1991-93; exec. officer Naval Acad. Med. Clinic, Annapolis, Md., 1993-96; leadership and splty. tng. Naval Sch. Health Scis., Bethesda, 1996-98; cons., instr. Naval Med. Quality Inst., Bethesda, 1999—. Recipient Meritorious Svc. medal (2 awards), Navy Achievement medal, Navy Commendation medal (5 awards), Submarine Svc. badge. Fellow Am. Coll. Healthcare Execs. Republican. Roman Catholic. Avocations: teaching, workshop. Home: 727 Suellen Dr King Of Prussia PA 19406

GALLIVAN, JOHN WILLIAM, publisher; b. Salt Lake City, June 28, 1915; s. Daniel and Frances (Wilson) G.; m. Grace Mary Ivers, June 30, 1938; children: Gay, John W. Jr., Michael D., Timothy. B.A., U. Notre Dame, 1937. With Salt Lake Tribune, 1937—, promotion mgr., 1942-48, asst. pub., 1948-60, pub., 1960-84; pres. Kearns-Tribune Corp., 1960-86, chmn. bd., 1984-89; dir., exec. com. Tele-Communications, Inc., 1989—; pres. Silver King Mining Co., 1960—. Pres. Utah Symphony, 1964-65. Mem. Sigma Delta Chi, Bohemian Club (San Francisco). Clubs: Nat. Press (Washington); Alta (Salt Lake City), Salt Lake Country (Salt Lake City), Rotary (Salt Lake City). Home: 17 S 12th E Salt Lake City UT 84102-1607 Office: Kearns-Tribune Corp 143 S Main St Salt Lake City UT 84111-1924

GALLMAN, CLARENCE HUNTER, textile executive; b. Rock Hill, S.C., Jan. 3, 1922; s. Clarence Calhoun and Hattie (Wood) G.; m. Beatrice Byers; children: Martha Gallman Alewine, Thomas Clarence. BS in Textile Engring., Clemson U., 1943. Various positions with J.P. Stevens, Greenville, S.C. and N.Y.C., 1943-80; sr. v.p. corp. mfg. M. Lowenstein Corp., N.Y.C., 1980-87; group v.p. domestics mfg. Springs Industries, Ft. Mill, S.C., 1987-88, ret., 1988; pres. C. Hunter Gallman Mgmt. Svcs., Greer, S.C., 1988—; bd. dirs. Textile Hall, Greenville. Mem. J.E. Sirrine Textile Found., Greenville. Served to capt. U.S. Army. Recipient Exec. of Yr. award Assn. Textile Indsl. Engrs., 1982, Chapman award So. Textile Assn., 1985. Mem. S.C. Textile Mfg. Assn. (pres. 1985-86, textile leader of yr. award 1984), Nat. Air Craft Owners & Pilots Assn. Baptist. Clubs: Greenville Gun, Beechcraft Aero. Lodges: Rotary, Masons, Elks. Avocations: golf, flying, hunting, skeet shooting. Office: C Hunter Gallman Mgmt Svcs 125 E Poinsett St PO Box 929 Greer SC 29652-0929

GALLO, ADRIENNE ARLINE, librarian; b. Providence, June 1, 1969; d. Richard A. and Marlene D. G. BS, U. R.I., 1991; MA, Emerson Coll., 1993; MLS, U. R.I., 1996. Grad. asst. Emerson Coll. Libr., Boston, 1992-93; rsch. asst. Boston Pub. Libr., 1992; interim circulation coord. Emerson Coll., 1993, Lesley Coll. Libr., Cambridge, Mass., 1994-95; grad. asst. U. R.I., Kingston, 1996; libr. asst. Cranston (R.I.) Pub. Libr., 1987-96, youth svcs. libr., 1999—; libr. dir. Blackstone (Mass.) Pub. Libr., 1996-99. Vol. religious edn. Immaculate Conception Ch., Cranston, R.I., 1998—. Mem. ALA, R.I. Libr. Assn., Beta Phi Mu, Sigma Iota Epsilon, Phi Eta Sigma. Roman Catholic. Avocations: sports, music, recreational bicycling. Office: Cranston Pub Libr 140 Sochanosset Cross Rd Cranston RI 02920

GALLO, ANTHONY ERNEST, economist, agribusiness author; b. Vandergrift, Pa., Feb. 3, 1939; s. Dominic and Sara (Raso) G.; divorced; 1 child, Thomas Augustus. BA, Coll. William and Mary, 1961; MBA, U. Pa., 1963; postgrad., U. Pitts., 1966-70. Investment analyst Pitts. Nat. Bank, 1963-66; instr. mktg. and stats. Duquesne U., Pitts., 1964-69; instr. mktg. U. Pitts., 1965-69; instr. money and banking St. Vincent Coll., Latrobe, Pa., 1966-69; asst. prof. econs. Allegheny C.C., Pitts., 1966-70; econ. cons. SBA, Washington, 1967—; bus. economist Bur. Econ. Analysis/U.S. Dept. Commerce, Washington, 1970-71; sr. economist Econ. Rsch. Svc./USDA, Washington, 1971—; propr. Capitol Hill Victorian Restorations, Washington, 1970-90. Econs. editor U.S. Food Mktg. Rev., 1984—; contbr. more than 400 articles to profl. and govt. jours. include Food Mktg. Sys., Impact of Race on Consumer Food Expenditures, Sr. Citizens, Food Expenditures and Assistance, Couponings Growth in Food Marketing. Mem. Capitol Hill Restoration Soc., Washington, 1972—, mem. endowment bd., 1999; mem Capitol Hill Garden Club, Washington, 1972—; commr. Vandergrift Mcpl. Authority, 1965-67; pres. Civic League, Vandergrift, 1965-70; mem. governing coun., endowment bd. Holy Rosary Ch. With U.S. Army, 1963. Named Outstanding Civic Leader, Jaycees, Vandergrift, 1967. Mem. Am. Agrl. Econs. Assn., Cosmos Club (endowment advisor 1996—), Arts Club Washington (endowment bd. 1996-99), Cheverly Swim and Racquet Club, John Carroll Soc., Thomas Merton Soc., Red Circle, U.S. Food Distbn. Rsch. Soc. (bd. dirs. 1994-97), Wharton Sch. Club (bd. dirs. 1991—), Italian Cultural Soc. (bd. dirs. 1994-97). Roman Catholic. Avocations: reading, gardening, soccer-volleyball, historic preservation, bridge. Home: PO Box 15414 Washington DC 20003-0414 Office: Econ Rsch Svc 1800 M St NW Washington DC 20036-5802

GALLO, DONALD ROBERT, retired English educator; b. Paterson, N.J., June 1, 1938; s. Sergio and Thelma Mae (Lowe) G.; m. C.J. Bott, Feb. 14, 1997; 1 child, Brian Keith; 1 stepchild, Christian Perrett. BA in English, Hope Coll., 1960; MAT in English Edn., Oberlin Coll., 1961; PhD in English Edn., Syracuse U., 1968. English tchr. Bedford Jr. High Sch., Westport, Conn., 1961-65; rsch. assoc. Syracuse (N.Y.) U., 1965-67; from asst. prof. to assoc. prof. edn. U. Colo., Denver, 1968-72; reading specialist Golden Jr. High Sch., Jefferson County Pub. Schs., Colo., 1972-73; prof. English Cen. Conn. State U., New Britain, 1973-97; instr. composition Onondaga C. C., Syracuse, 1967; vis. faculty grad. liberal studies program Wesleyan U., 1983; staff writer reading assessment Nat. Assessment Ednl. Progress, Denver, 1972-73; speaker in field; cons. to schs. and librs. Mem. editl. bd. Nat. Coun. Tchrs. English, 1985-88; compiler, editor: Speaking for Ourselves, 1990, Speaking for Ourselves, Too, 1993; editor: Connections: Short Stories by Outstanding Writers for Young Adults, 1989, Visions: Nineteen Short Stories by Outstanding Writers for Young Adults, 1987, Center Stage: One-Act Plays for Teenage Readers and Actors, 1990, Sixteen: Short Stories by Outstanding Writers for Young Adults, 1984, Books for You, 1985, Authors' Insights: Turning Teenagers into Readers and Writers, 1992, Short Circuits: Thirteen Shocking Stories by Outstanding Writers for Young Adults, 1992, Within Reach: Ten Stories, 1993, Join In: Multiethnic Short Stories by Outstanding Writers for Young Adults, 1993, Ultimate Sports: Short Stories by Outstanding Writers for Young Adults, 1995, No Easy Answers: Short Stories About Teenagers Making Tough Choices, 1997, Time Capsule: Short Stories About Teenagers Throughout the Twentieth Century, 1999; author: Presenting Richard Peck, 1989, Bookmark Reading Program, Seventh and Eighth Grade Texts and Workbooks, 1979, Heath Middle Level Literature, 1995; co-author: (with Sarah K. Herz) From Hinton to Hamlet: Building Bridges Between Young Adult Literature and the Classics, 1996. Recipient Disting. Svc. award Conn. Coun. Tchrs. English, 1989, ALAN award Assembly on Lit. for Adolescents of the Nat. Coun. Tchrs. English, 1992, Cert. of Merit award Cath. Libr. Assn., 1995. Mem. Nat. Coun. Tchrs. English, Assembly on Lit. for Adolescents, Internat. Reading Assn., Conf. on English Edn., Ohio Coun. Tchrs. English Lang. Arts, Conn. Coun. Tchrs. English, Soc. Children's Book Writers and Illustrators, Authors Guild. Avocations: gardening, cooking, traveling, photography. Address: 34540 Sherbrook Park Dr Solon OH 44139-2046

GALLO, ERNEST, vintner; b. 1909; widowed. Co-owner, chmn. bd. dirs. E & J Gallo Winery, Modesto, Calif., 1933—. Office: E & J Gallo Winery PO Box 1130 600 Yosemite Blvd Modesto CA 95354-2760*

GALLO, JOAN ROSENBERG, city attorney; b. Newark, Apr. 28, 1940. BA in Psychology, Boston U.; postgrad. studies in Counseling, We. Md. Coll.; postgrad studies in Clin. Pyschology, We. Grad. Sch. Psychology; JD magna cum laude, U. Santa Clara, 1975. Bar: Calif. 1975. Assoc. with Cynthia Mertens U, Santa Clara, Calif., 1975-76; sr. law clk. U.S. Dist. Ct., Calif., 1976-78; assoc. Decker and Collins, San Jose, Calif., 1978-79; from dep. city atty. to city atty. City of San Jose, 1979—. Mem. Psi Chi. Office: City of San Jose Office City Atty 151 W Mission St San Jose CA 95110-1710

GALLO, JON JOSEPH, lawyer; b. Santa Monica, Calif., Apr. 19, 1942; s. Philip S. and Josephine (Sarazan) G.; m. Jo Ann Broome, June 13, 1964 (div. 1984); children: Valerie Ann, Donald Philip; m. Eileen Florence, July 4, 1985; 1 child, Kevin Jon. BA, Occidental Coll., 1964; JD, UCLA, 1967. Bar: Calif. 1968, U.S. Ct. Appeals (9th cir.) 1968, U.S. Tax Ct. 1969. Assoc. Greenberg, Glusker, Fields, Claman & Machtinger, L.A., 1967-75, ptnr., 1975—; bd. dirs. USC Probate and Trust Conf., L.A., 1980—, UCLA Estate Planning Inst., chmn. 1992—. Contbr. articles to profl. jours. Fellow Am. Coll. Trust and Estate Counsel; mem. ABA (chair Generation Skipping Taxation com. 1992-95, co-chair life ins. com. 1995—), Internat. Acad. Estate and Trust Law, Assn. for Advanced Life Underwriting (assoc. mem.). Avocation: photography. Office: Greenberg Glusker Fields Claman & Machtinger LLP Ste 2100 1900 Avenue Of The Stars Los Angeles CA 90067-4502

GALLO, LOUIS, historian, educator; b. Red Bank, N.J., Sept. 5, 1966; s. George Washington and Theresa Florence (McBride) G. BA, Coll. N.J., 1989; MS, U. Tenn., 1993. Social studies tchr. West H.S., Knoxville, Tenn., 1994—. Mem. Profl. Educators Tenn., Foothills Coun. Social Studies. Republican. Roman Catholic. Avocations: reading, snow skiing, travel, history. Home: 4404 Warbler Rd Knoxville TN 37918-1525 Office: West HS 3300 Sutherland Ave Knoxville TN 37919-4544

GALLO, MARK ALLEN, microbiology educator; b. Jeanette, Pa., Dec. 28, 1959; s. Saverio Seraphino and Phyllis (Vaglia) G.; m. Jean Carol Adsit, July 2, 1989; children: Mary Catherine, Angela Nicole. BS in Biochemistry, Pitt U., 1982, MS in Biochemistry, 1985; PhD in Microbiology, Cornell U., 1991. Postdoctoral fellow U. Wis., Madison, 1991-95; asst. prof. Niagara U., Lewiston, N.Y., 1995—. Co-author: Evolution of Metabolic Pathways, 1991; contbr. articles to profl. jours. Vol. Habitat for Humanity, Niagara Falls, N.Y., 1997-98; webmaster A Festival of Lights, Niagara Falls, 1997-98. Math. and sci. summer camp grantee GTE, 1997-98. Mem. AAAS, Am. Soc. Microbiology, Soc. Indsl. Microbiology. Achievments include isolation of genes for the biosynthesis of daunorubicin from streptomyces peucetius. Home: 230 N 4th St Lewiston NY 14092-1240 Office: Niagara U Dept Biology Lewiston NY 14109

GALLO, PIA, art historian; b. N.Y.C., May 10, 1956; d. Thomas Joseph and Maria Dolores (Daniele) Gallo; m. Peter Van Wagner, Sept. 2, 1989; 1 child, Annalisa Van Wagner. Student, John Cabot Coll., Rome, 1974-76; BA in English, Hiram (Ohio) Coll., 1978; postgrad., U. Chgo. Pvt. art dealer specializing in old master and modern prints Chgo., 1981—, N.Y.C., 1995—. Author catalogues: American Prints, 1981, Herman Armour Webster, 1983, Recent Acquisitions, 1986, Pietro Testa, 1989, Venice and Venetians, 1997, The Landscape in Europe, 1531-1913, 1998, Angels on Paper, 1999. Mem. Internat. Fine Print Dealers Assn., Arts Club of Chgo., Pvt. Art Dealers Assn. Office: PO Box 6726 New York NY 10128

GALLO, ROBERT CHARLES, research scientist; b. Waterbury, Conn., Mar. 23, 1937; s. Francis Anton and Louise Mary (Ciancuilli) G.; m. Mary Jane Hayes, July 1, 1961; children: Robert Charles, Marcus. BA, Providence Coll., 1959, DSc (hon.), 1974; MD, Jefferson Med. Coll., 1963; 13 hon. degrees from univs. in U.S., Belgium, Italy, Israel, Sweden. Intern, resident medicine U. Chgo., 1963-65; clin. assoc. med. br. Nat. Cancer Inst. NIH, Bethesda, Md., 1965-68, sr. investigator human tumor cell biology br., 1968-69, head sect. cellular control mechanisms, 1969-72, chief lab. tumor cell biology, 1972-93; dir., prof. medicine and microbiology Inst. Human Virology U. Md., Balt., 1993—; adj. prof. genetics George Washington U.; adj. prof. biology Johns Hopkins U., Balt., hon. prof. biology, 1985—; hon. prof. medicine Karolinska Inst., Stockholm, 1998—, hon. prof. Karolinska Inst., Stockholm, 1998—, U.S. rep. to world com. Internat Comparative Leukemia and Lymphoma Assn., 1981—; mem. bd. govs. Franco Am. AIDS Found., 1987, world AIDS Found., 1987. Author: Virus Hunting, 1991, author or co-author of more than 1,100 scientific papers. With USPHS, 1965-68. Recipient Dameshek award Am. Hematol. Soc., 1974, CIBA-GEIGY award in biomed. sci., 1977, 88, Superior Svc. award USPHS, 1979, Meritorious Svc. medal, 1983, Stitt award, 1983, Disting. Svc. medal, 1984, First F. Stohlman of Am. Soc. Hem lecture award, 1979, Lasker award for basic biomed. rsch., 1982, 86, Abraham White award in biochemistry George Washington U., 1983, 1st Otto Herz award for cancer rsch. Tel Aviv U., 1982, Griffuel prize Assn. for Cancer Rsch., France, 1983, GM award in cancer rsch., 1984, Gruber prize Am. Soc. Investigative Dermatology, 1984, Lucy Wortham prize in cancer rsch. Soc. for Surg. Oncology, 1984, Gold medal Am. Cancer Soc., 1984, Birla Internat. Sci. prize, India, 1985, Hammer prize for Cancer Rsch., 1985, Gairdner prize for Biomed. Rsch., Can., 1987, spl. award Am. Soc. Infectious Disease, 1986, Gold Plate award Am. Acad. Achievement, Lions Humanitarian award, 1987, Japan prize in Sci. and Tech., 1988, Ciba Corning award, 1993, 1st Dale McFarlin award for rsch. Internat. Soc. Human Retrovrology, 1994, 1st Gustav Embden award U. Frankfurt, 1996, Pomesa award, 1996, 1st award Internat. Soc. of Blood Transfusion, 1997, Nomura prize Japan for AIDS and Cancer Rsch., 1998, Warren Alpert prize Harvard U., 1998, Paul Erlich award, Germany, 1998. Mem. NAS, Inst. Medicine, Internat. Soc. Hematology, Am. Soc. Clin. Investigation, Am. Soc. Biol. Chemists, Am. Microbiology Soc., Biochem. Soc., Am. Assn. Cancer Rsch. (Rosenthal award 1993), Am. Soc. Microbiology, Am. Fedn. Clin. Rsch., Fedn. for Advanced Edn. in Scis., Royal Soc. Physicians of Scotland (hon.), Royal Soc. Medicine (hon.), Royal Soc. of Medicine (Belgium), Alpha Omega Alpha (hon.). Achievements include research on viruses, AIDS, and Leukemia; co-discoverer of AIDS virus; discovery of first and second human retroviruses.

GALLO, VINCENT JOHN, financial planner; b. N.Y.C., Aug. 13, 1943; s. Nicholas and Catherine (Vitiello) G.; m. Blanche Marie Poplin, Apr. 15, 1972; children: Steven, Mark. BA, U. Dayton, 1965. Registered fin. planner; CLU; Chartered Fin. Cons. Mgr. methods engring. Daniel Internat. Corp., Greenville, S.C., 1971-75; exec. v.p. Am. Ind. Elec. Contractors Assn., Arlington, Tex., 1975-77; pres. Vincent J. Gallo & Assocs., Inc., Winston-Salem, N.C., 1977—; adj. instr. Am. Coll., Bryn Mawr, Pa., 1984-86. Capt. USAF, 1966-71. Served to capt. USAF, 1966-71. Mem. Am. Soc. CLUs and Chartered Fin. Cons. (continuing edn. chmn. 1984, pres. 1988-89), Internat. Assn. Fin. Planners, Nat. Assn. Securities Dealers, Nat. Soc. Pub. Accts., N.C. Planned Giving Coun. (pres. 1997—, accredited estate planner), Winston-Salem Estate Planning Coun. (v.p.), Am. Soc. Pension Actuaries, N.C. Soc. Accts., Mensa, Million Dollar Round Table. Avocations: tennis, reading, gourmet cooking, skiing. Home: 8800 Harwick Ct Clemmons NC 27012-9737 Office: 3775 Vest Mill Rd Ste C Winston Salem NC 27103-2990

GALLO, WILLIAM VICTOR, cartoonist; b. N.Y.C., Dec. 28, 1922; s. Francisco and Henrietta (Caballero) G.; m. Dolores Rodriguez, Mar. 13, 1950; children: Gregory, William. With N.Y. Daily News, 1941—, sports cartoonist, sports columnist, 1960—, assoc. sports editor, 1984—. One-man show, Spectrum Fine Arts Gallery, N.Y.C., 1981; works represented in permanent collection, Baseball Hall of Fame, Cooperstown, N.Y., Syracuse U. archives. Served with USMC, 1942-45. Recipient 19 Page One awards N.Y. Newspaper Guild, 1965-86; Elzie Segar award,, 1976, Alumni Achievement award Sch. Visual Arts, 1977, Power of Printing award, 1977; named best sports cartoonist Nat. Cartoonist Soc., 1969-73, 84-86; named to Yonkers Hall Fame, 1984, Westchester Hall Fame, 1984. Mem. N.Y. Boxing Writers (pres.), Nat. Cartoonists Soc. (pres., Milt Caniff Lifetime Achievement award 1999), Baseball Writers, Profl. Football Writers, Turf Writers, N.Y. Press Assn., (award 1986), Soc. Silurians, Soc. Illustrators. Home: 1 Mayflower Dr Yonkers NY 10710-3801 Office: NY News Inc 450 W 33rd St New York NY 10001-2603 *Everything has to start with a dream. First the dream, and then the chasing of it. I pity the person who doesn't own a dream.*

GALLON, DENNIS P., college president; b. Monticello, Fla.. BS, Edward Waters Coll.; MS, Ind. U.; PhD, U. Fla., EdS. Bus. instr.; assoc. v.p. of instrn. Fla. C.C., Jacksonville, dist. dean of liberal arts and scis., dean of occupl., adult and continuing edn., campus bus. mgr., pres. Kent campus; pres. Palm Beach C.C. Office: Palm Beach Cmty Coll 4200 Congress Ave Lake Worth FL 33461

GALLOP, JANE (ANNE), women's studies educator, writer; b. Duluth, Minn., May 4, 1952; d. Melvin Gordon and Eudice Zelda (Titch) G.; children: Max Blau Gallop, Ruby Gallop Blau. BA, Cornell U., 1972, PhD, 1976. Lectr. French Gettysburg (Pa.) Coll., 1976; asst. prof. Miami U., Oxford, Ohio, 1977-81, assoc. prof., 1981-85; prof. women's studies Rice U., Houston, 1985-87, Autrey prof., 1987-90; prof. English U. Wis., Milw., 1990-92, Disting. prof., 1992—; NEH vis. prof. Emory U., Atlanta, 1984-85; Hill vis. prof. U. Minn., Mpls., 1987; dir. seminar for coll. tchrs. NEH, Milw., 1985, 88; instr. Sch. of Criticism and Theory, Dartmouth Coll., 1991. Author: Intersections, 1981, The Daughter's Seduction, 1982, Reading Lacan, 1985, Thinking Through the Body, 1988, Around 1981, 1992, Feminist Accused of Sexual Harassment, 1997; editor: Pedagogy, 1995. Guggenheim fellow, 1983-84. Mem. MLA. Office: U Wis PO Box 413 Milwaukee WI 53201-0413

GALLOPOULOS, NICHOLAS EFSTRATIOS, chemical engineer; b. Athens, Apr. 5, 1936; came to U.S., 1953; s. Efstratios C. and Lucia N. (Romanides) G.; m. Mary Frances Veale, Oct. 25, 1958; children: Gregory S., Lucia Anne. BS in Chem. Engring., Tex. A&M U., 1958; MS in Chem. Engring., Pa. State U., 1959. Tech. specialist Humble Oil & Refining Co. (Exxon), Houston, 1967-68; rsch. engr. Gen. Motors Rsch. Labs., Warren, Mich., 1959-67, 68-75, asst. dept. head fuels and lubricants, 1975-85, head dept. environ. sci., 1985-89, head dept. engine rsch., 1989—; mem. Coordinating Rsch. Coun., Atlanta, 1974-89. Author: Future Automotive Fuels, 1977; contbr. chpts. to books, articles to Sci. American, Indsl. and Engring. Chemistry. Mem. Econ. Devel. Corp., Rochester Hills, Mich., 1978-91; mem., chmn. Planning Commn., Rochester Hills, 1982-92. Fellow Soc. Automotive Engrs.; mem. AAAS, Am. Chem. Soc., Sigma Xi. Achievements include research on the chemical mechanism of action of various lubricating oil additives, alternative fuels and their role in automotive transportation; co-founding (with R. A. Frosch) of the field of Industrial Ecology. Home: 1565 Hampstead Ln Rochester Hls MI 48309-2948 Office: Gen Motors Rsch Box 9055 30500 Mound Rd Warren MI 48092-2031

GALLOWAY, BRENDA MABREY, school system administrator; b. Logan, W.Va., Apr. 27, 1949; d. Raymond Brenton and Esther Emma (Bergman) Mabrey; m. Charles H. Galloway, Aug. 21, 1971; children: Heather, Heath. AS in Edn., Andrew U., 1969; BS in Edn., Ga. So. U., 1972; MS in Edn. Leadership, U. West Fla., 1982. Sch. sys. supt. Franklin County Sch. Bd., Apalachicola, Fla. Mem. Phi Theta Kappa, Delta Kappa Gamma. Episcopalian. Avocation: reading. Office: Franklin County Sch Bd 155 Avenue E Apalachicola FL 32320-2069

GALLOWAY, DANIEL LEE, investment executive; b. Columbia, Mo., Apr. 16, 1958; s. Robert Eugene and Lilie Ann (Riechard) G.; m. Wanda Sue Wegener, June 22, 1979; 1 child, Rob. BA, William Jewell Coll., Liberty, Mo., 1979; postgrad., Wolfson Coll., Cambridge, Eng., 1979-80. Asst. to pres. Galloway Limestone Co., Inc., Bowling Green, Mo., 1980-81; v.p. Galloway Limestone Co., Inc., 1981-90; pres., investment adviser Galloway & Galloway, Inc., 1989—; treas., chair fin. com. bd. dirs. Hannibal Regional Healthcare Sys., 1994-97, vice chair, 1997-99, chair, 1999—; cons. Cecil C. Daffron & Assocs., Bowling Green, 1987-96; mem. adv. bd., bd. dirs. Kids' Wall Street News, Inc., 1997—. Bd. dirs. Mo. State Sch. Bds. Assn. Region 6, 1989, 90; sec. Bowling Green R-1 Sch. Bd., 1989-92, First Presbyn. Ch. Bd. of Session, 1983-86; diaconate First Christian Ch., Hannibal, 1995-96; mem. steering com. Hannibal Accelerated Mid. Sch. Program, 1995-98, mem. tech. adv. com., 1996-97. Mem. Mo. Limestone Producers Assn. (bd. dirs. 1982-85), Mo. State Sch. Bd. Assn. (edn. com. 1989-90). Avocations: reading, computers. Home: 15 Riverpoint Rd Hannibal MO 63401-2019 Office: Galloway & Galloway Inc PO Box 1256 Hannibal MO 63401

GALLOWAY, DAVID ALEXANDER, publishing company executive; b. Toronto, Ont., Can., Nov. 1, 1943; s. Robert and Dorothy Elizabeth (Kennedy) G.; m. Judy K. Clarkson, June 10, 1966; children: Andrew, Stephanie. BA, U. Toronto, 1966; MBA, Harvard U., 1968. Mktg. profl. Gen. Foods Corp., Toronto, 1968-71; ptnr. Can. Consulting Group, Toronto, 1971-80; v.p. corp. devel. Torstar Corp., Toronto, 1980-81, exec. v.p., 1981-82; pres., CEO Harlequin Enterprises, Ltd., Toronto, 1983-88, chmn., 1990-97; pres. Torstar Book Pub. and Direct Mktg. Div., Toronto, 1984-86; pres., bd. dir., CEO Torstar Corp., Toronto, 1988—; bd. dirs. Westburne Inc., Montreal, Clearnet Inc., Scarborough, Bank of Montreal, Toronto. Bd. govs., faculty of adminstrv. studies York U.; trustee Hosp. for Sick Children. Clubs: Badminton & Racquet, Devil's Pulpit Golf, Caledon, Toronto. Avocations: running, golf, tennis. Home: 82 Cluny Dr. Toronto, ON Canada M4W 2R3 Office: Torstar Corp, 1 Yonge St, Toronto, ON Canada M5E 1P9

GALLOWAY, ETHAN CHARLES, technology development executive, former chemicals executive; b. Howell, Mich., Oct. 31, 1930; s. Almon Fred and Rose Marie (Hodkinson) G.; m. Patricia Winner, Dec. 23, 1973. B.S.C., Mich. State U., 1951; Ph.D., U. Calif., Berkeley, 1954. With Dow Chem. Co., Midland, Mich., 1954-62; dir. research plastics div. Nopco Chem. Co., North Arlington, N.J., 1962-65; successively v.p. research, exec. v.p., corp. dir. Stauffer Chem. Co., Westport, Conn., 1965-85; exec. v.p. Chesebrough-Pond's Inc., 1985-88; pres. new bus. devel. Loctite Corp., Hartford, Conn., 1988-89; pres. Edison Polymer Innovation Corp., Brecksville, Ohio, 1989-95; ret., 1995. Fellow Poly. Inst. N.Y.; mem. Indsl. Research Inst. (pres. 1978-79), Chem. Industry Inst. Toxicology (past dir.), Food Safety Council (former trustee), Council for Chem. Research (past chmn.), Conn. Acad. Sci. and Engring., Sigma Xi. Home: 6549 Thornbrook Cir Hudson OH 44236-3552

GALLOWAY, JANICE, writer, editor; b. Kilwinning, Scotland, Dec. 2, 1956; d. James and Janet (McBride) G.; 1 child, James Alexander Galloway McNaught. MA, Glasgow U., 1978. Tchr. Strathclyde Regional Coun., Ayrshire, Scotland, 1980-90; music critic. Editor: (with Hamish Whyte) New Writing Scotland, 1990, 91, 92; author: The Trick Is to Keep Breathing, 1990 (Scottish Arts Coun. Book award 1990, MIND Book of Yr.-Allan Lane award Book Trust 1991), Blood, 1991 (Scottish Arts Coun. Book award 1991), Foreign Parts, 1994, Where You Find It, 1996; librettist: (concert operas) Clara, 1994, Monster, 1996. Recipient Cosmopolitan/Perrier award, 1991, E.M. Forster award in lit. Am. Acad. Arts and Letters, 1994, McVitie's prize for Scottish Writer of the Yr., 1994. Home: 24 Circus Dr, Dennistoun Glasgow G31 2JH, Scotland Office: care Jonathan Cape, 20 Vauxhall Bridge Rd, London SW1 6RB, England also: care Derek Johns AP Watt Agy, 20 John St, London WC1N 2DR, England

GALLOWAY, JOHN W., JR., lawyer; b. Rockwood, Tenn., Mar. 4, 1954; s. John W. and Avilee (Garrett) G.; m. Pamela A. Kissel, June 5, 1980; children: Laura K., Amanda K. BS, Tenn. Tech. U., 1975; JD, U. Tenn., 1978. Bar: Tenn. 1978. Asst. dist. atty. gen. 8th Jud. Dist., Huntsville, Tenn., 1982—. Capt. U.S. Army, 1978-82. Democrat. Methodist. Avocations: farming. Office: Dist Atty Gen Office PO Box 10 Huntsville TN 37756-0010

GALLOWAY, JOSEPH LEE, JR., writer, journalist; b. Bryan, Tex., Nov. 13, 1941; s. Joseph L. and Marian D. (Dewvall) G.; m. Theresa Magdalene Null, Sept. 9, 1966 (dec. Jan. 1996); children: Lee T., Joshua J.; m. Karen Metsker McCray, Oct. 24, 1998; children: Alison, Abigail, Thomas. Grad., Refugio, Tex., 1959. Reporter Victoria (Tex.) Advocate, 1959-61, United Press Internat., Kansas City, Mo., 1961; bureau chief United Press Internat., Topeka, Kans., 1962-64; war correspondent United Press Internat., South Vietnam, 1965-66; correspondent United Press Internat., Tokyo, 1966-68; bureau chief United Press Internat., Jakarta, Indonesia, 1968-73; mgr. South Asia United Press Internat., New Delhi, India, 1973-74; mgr. southeast Asia United Press Internat., Singapore, 1974-75; bureau chief United Press Internat., Moscow, 1976-80, L.A., 1980-82; west coast editor U.S.News & World Report, L.A., 1982-84; assoc. editor U.S. News, Washington, 1984-86, sr. editor, 1986-90, sr. writer, 1990—. Co-author: Triumph Without Victory, 1992, We Were Soldiers Once... and Young, 1992. Dir. No Greater Love, Washington, 1990—; bd. adv. Vietnam Vets. Meml. Fund,. Decorated Bronze Star with V device; Recipient Nat Mag. award Am. Soc. Mag. Editors, 1991, Nat. News Media award Vet. of Fgn. Wars of U.S.A., 1992. Mem. Soc. Profl. Journalists, Overseas Press Club, 7th Cavalry Assn., 1st Cavalry Divsn. Assn. Avocations: travel, gardening. Home: PO Box 6222 Falls Church VA 22040-6222 Office: U S News & World Report 1050 Thomas Jefferson St NW Washington DC 20007

GALLOWAY, KENNETH FRANKLIN, engineering educator; b. Columbia, Tenn., Apr. 11, 1941; s. Benjamin F. and Carrie (Dowell) G.; m. Dorothy Elise Lamar; children: Kenneth Jr., Carole A. BA, Vanderbilt U., 1962; PhD, U. S.C., 1966. Rsch. assoc. Ind. U., Bloomington, 1966-67, asst. prof., 1967-72, assoc. prof., 1972; rsch. physicist Naval Weapons Support Ctr., Crane, Ind., 1972-74; tech. staff Nat. Bur. Standards, Gaithersburg, Md., 1974-77; chief sect. Nat. Bur. Standards, Gaithersburg, 1977-79, chief div., 1980-86; prof. elect. engring. U. Md., 1980-86; prof., dept. head elect. and computer engring. U. Ariz., Tucson, 1986-96; dean engring., prof. elec. engring. Vanderbilt U., Nashville, 1996—. Contbr. articles to profl. jours. Sci. and Tech. fellow U.S. Dept. Commerce, 1979-80. Fellow IEEE (gen. chmn. Nuclear and Space Radiation Effects Conf. 1985, v.p. Nuclear and Plasma Sci. Soc. 1990, chmn. radiation effects com. 1991-94, chmn. engring. rsch. and devel. policy com. 1994, gen. chmn. Internat. Electron Devices Meeting 1997), AAAS; mem. Electrochem. Soc., Am. Phys. Soc., Am. Soc. Engring. Edn., Sigma Xi, Eta Kappa Nu, Tau Beta Pi. Office: Vanderbilt U Sch Engring Box 1826 Station B Nashville TN 37235

GALLOWAY, LILLIAN CARROLL, modeling agency executive, consultant; b. Hazard, Ky., Sept. 23, 1934; d. William Zion and Clemma (Lewis) Carroll; m. Thomas Roddy Galloway, Dec. 21, 1957; children: David Junkin, Scott Thomas, Donald Lewis. Student, Cumberland Coll., 1955, Ea. U., Richmond, Ky., 1956, U. Cin., 1958, John Robert Powers Sch., Cin., 1958. Tchr. Vandalia (Ohio) Elem. Sch., 1954-56, Kenwood Elem. Sch., Louisville, 1956-57, Cin. Pub. Schs., 1957-64; founder, pres. Fairfax Model Agy., Washington, 1964-67, Cin. Model Agy. Internat., 1967—, Lillian Galloway Modeling Acad., Cin., 1971—, Children Model Agy. Internat., Cin., 1985—, Lillian Galloway Fashion Show Prodn. Co., 1998—; cons., co-owner John Robert Powers Modeling Sch., Cin., 1957-64; pres. Student Model Bds., Cin., 1984—; dir. Career Day, Cin., 1967—. Mem. Cin. Better Bus. Bur., 1967—; trustee Knox Presbyn. Ch., Cin. Named Cin.'s Outstanding Bus. Woman, Sta. WCPO-TV, 1985, Outstanding Alumni, Cumberland Coll., 1988. Mem. DAR, Modeling Assn. Am. (chmn. convs. 1975-77), Am. Modeling Assn. Internat. (pres. 1976-77), Cin. Advertisers Club (membership and program coms., Outstanding Bus. Woman award 1985), Exec. Women Internat. (program com., chmn. bd. dirs. 1986, Woman of Achievement award 1986), Cin. C. of C., Cumberland Coll. Alumni Assn. (pres. 1982), English Speaking Union, Order Ky. Cols., Cin. Woman's Club (bd. dirs. 1992—, lecture/entertainment chmn. 1992-95), Town Club (bd. dirs. 1988—), Order Ea. Star (organist 1953—). Republican. Avocations: art, French antiques, gardening, music, travel. Home: 6027 Stirrup Rd Cincinnati OH 45244-3917 Office: 6047 Montgomery Rd Cincinnati OH 45213-1611

GALLOWAY, SISTER MARY BLAISE, mathematics educator; b. Mendota, Ill., June 30, 1933; d. Otto William and Rita Irene (Cannon) G. BS in Math., St. Joseph's Coll., 1965; MS in Math. Edn., U. Ill., 1970; MS in Adminstrn., U. Notre Dame, 1985. Tchr. elem. edn. St. Augustine Sch., Richmond, Mich., 1952-58, Holy Rosary Sch., Duluth, Minn., 1958-65; asst. prin. Sacred Heart Acad., Springfield, Ill., 1983-85, co-prin., 1985-87; instr. math. Marian Cath. H.S., Chicago Heights, Ill., 1965-75, 90—, instr. math., chair math. dept., 1975-83, asst. prin., 1987-90; mem. curriculum com., adv. bd., registrar Marian Cath. H.S., Chicago Heights, 1987-90, faculty coun., 1994—. Grantee Ill. State U., 1992, 95, Ohio State U., 1992, U. Ill., 1990. Mem. Nat. Coun. Tchrs. Math., Ill. Coun. Tchrs. Math., Math. Tchrs. Assn. Chgo. (Master Tchr. 1994, pres. 1996-98). Roman Catholic. Avocations: gardening, music, reading. Home and Office: 700 Ashland Ave Chicago Heights IL 60411-2073

GALLOWAY, PATRICIA KAY, systems analyst, ethnohistorian; b. Bloomington, Ind., Sept. 7, 1945; BA in French with honors, Millsaps Coll., 1966; MA, U. N.C., Chapel Hill, 1968, PhD, 1973. Instr. French, German, U. N.C., Wilmington, 1971-72; archaeol. finds supr. Norway and Eng., 1973-77; humanities programming advisor computer unit Westfield Coll., U. London, 1977-79; editor, adminstrv. asst., spl. projects officer Miss. Dept. Archives and History, Jackson, 1979—; pres. S.E. Archeol. Conf., 1995-96. Woodrow Wilson fellow, 1966-67; U. N.C. career teaching fellow, 1967-68. Mem. Assn. for Computing Machinery, French Colonial Hist. Soc., Soc. for Am. Archaeology. Democrat. Author: Choctaw Genesis 1500-1700, 1995 (Erminie Wheeler-Voegelin prize for ethnohistory 1996, James Mooney award for southern anthropology 1996); editor: La Salle and His Legacy, Mississippi Provincial Archives: French Dominion, Vols. IV and V (Chinard prize for French hist. studies 1985), Southeastern Ceremonial Complex, The Hernando de Soto Expedition; contbr. articles to profl. jours. Office: 100 S State St PO Box 571 Jackson MS 39205-0571

GALLOWAY, RANDY, newspaper sports columnist. Sports columnist Dallas Morning News, 1976—. Office: The Dallas Morning News 508 Young St Dallas TX 75202-4828*

GALLOWAY, RICHARD H., lawyer; b. Pittston, Pa., Feb. 2, 1940; s. Hollie M. and Blanche Thelma (Lewis) G.; m. Janice Ann Clelland, Dec. 21, 1963; children: Lisa Sue, Richard Miles. BA, Lehigh U., 1962; JD, U. Pitts., 1965. Bar: Pa. 1965, U.S. Dist. Ct. (we. dist.) Pa. 1965, U.S. Ct. Appeals (3d cir.) 1966, U.S. Ct. Appeals (6th cir.) 1967, U.S. Supreme Ct. 1977. Assoc. McArdle, Harrington, Feeney & McLaughlin, Pitts., 1965-68; ptnr. Ackerman & Galloway Law Office, Greensburg, Pa., 1968-80; chief exec. officer Richard H. Galloway & Assocs. P.C., Greensburg, 1980-89, Galloway, DeBernardo, Antoniono, McCabe and Davis, P.C., Greensburg, 1989-91, Quatrini, Rafferty, Galloway, Greensburg, 1991—. Solicitor, Delmont (Pa.) Borough, 1978-85; pres. Delmont PTA, 1973-75; Dem. candidate for Pa. Ho. of Reps., 1972. Mem. ATLA, Pa. Trial Lawyers (bd. govs. 1987-90), We. Pa. Trial Lawyers (bd. govs. 1985-87, v.p. 1987-88, pres. 1989-90), Westmoreland Acad. Trial Law (bd. govs. 1986-88, v.p. 1988-90, pres. 1992-94), Pa. Bar Assn. (ho. of dels. 1991-94, bd. govs. 1994-97), Westmoreland County Bar Assn. (exec. bd. 1986-88, v.p. 1988-89, pres. 1990-91). Democrat. Presbyterian. Avocations: sailing, skiing, scuba. Office: Underwood Ctr 550 E Pittsburgh St Greensburg PA 15601-2674

GALLOWAY, SHARON LYNNE, special education educator; b. Pensacola, Fla., Jan. 2, 1951; d. Richard Earl and Beatrice Kathlyn (Stone) G. AA, Pensacola Jr. Coll., 1995; BA, U. West Fla., 1998, postgrad., 1998—. Travel counselor, trainer Gulf Breeze (Fla.) Travel, 1985-95; sign lang. interpreter Pensacola Jr. Coll., 1995-97; tchg. intern Sherwood Elem., Pensacola, 1997-98; tchr. Sherwood Elementary, Pensacola, FL, 1998—. Coord. deaf ministries Gulf Breeze United Meth. Ch., 1995—, interpreter, 1995—, youth counselor anchor program, 1996-98; vol. Habitat for Humanity, Gulf Breeze, Pensacola, 1994-96, Gulf Coast Sports Ability Games, 1996; interpreter Ala.-West Fla. Annual Conf. United Meth. Ch., Montgomery, Ala., 1996—; server, cleanup com. Loaves and Fishes, Pensacola, 1996-97; reading camp tchr. U. West Fla., Pensacola, 1997. Mem. NEA, Internat. Reading Assn., Fla. Registry Interpreters for Deaf (bd. dirs., treas. 1991-97), Student Coun. Exceptional Children (mem. chair 1996-98) Golden Key Nat. Honor Soc. (chpt. webmaster, chpt. treas. 1998), Coun. for Exceptional Children, Coun. for Children with Behavioral Disorders. Alpha Sigma Lambda, Phi Kappa Phi, Phi Delta Kappa. Avocations: gardening, carpentry, interior desighn, webpage design. Home: 3367 Crestview Ln Gulf Breeze FL 32561-2739 Office: Sherwood Elem Sch 501 Cherokee Trl Pensacola FL 32506

GALLOWAY, THOMAS D., dean. Dean coll. architecture Ga. Inst. Tech., Atlanta, 1992—. Office: Ga Inst Technology Coll Arch 247 4th St Atlanta GA 30332-0155*

GALLOWAY, WILLIAM JEFFERSON, former foreign service officer; b. Throckmorton, Tex., Oct. 21, 1922; s. James Thomas and Ottis Virgil (Marrs) G.; m. Elizabeth Alice Cox, June 3, 1950; children—Jeff, Mary Elizabeth. B.S., Tex. A. and M. U., 1943. Fgn. affairs officer Dept. State, 1948-50; spl. asst. to U.S. ambassador to NATO, London, Paris, 1950-53; spl. asst. to counselor Dept. State, 1953-56; 1st sec. Vienna, 1956-59; spl. asst. to dir. gen. fgn. service Dept. State, Washington, 1959-64; assigned Nat. War Coll., 1964-65; 1st sec., counselor polit. affairs Am. embassy, London, Eng., 1965-74; exec. asst. to under sec. state Dept. State, Washington, 1974-80; cons. Dept. State, 1980—. Served to capt. AUS, 1943-48. Home: 1430 Colleen Ln Mc Lean VA 22101-3104 Office: Dept State Washington DC 20520

GALLOWAY-MCQUITTER, LIZ, university head basketball coach; b. Rockdale; 1 child, William. AA in Sociology, Temple Jr. Coll., 1975; BS in Phys. Edn., UNLV, 1978. Adminstrv. asst. Pro Sports Promotion, 1980-81; basketball supr. East Bank Club, Chgo., 1981-83; asst. scouting Northwestern, 1983-84; head coach Mundelein Coll., 1984-86; asst. coach, recruiting coord. Dartmouth Coll., 1986-89, DePaul U., 1989-91; head coach Lamar U., 1991-94, No. Ill. U., 1994-98; head asst. coach basketball, recruiting coord. Tex. A&M U., College Station, 1998—. Named as 100 Women Making a Difference in the 1990's Today's Chgo. Woman mag., 1990. Mem. Black Coaches Assn. (bd. dirs., orgn. rep. 1993). Office: Tex A&M U Woman's Basketball PO Box 30017 College Station TX 77842-3017*

GALLUCCI, MICHAEL A., lawyer; b. Jersey City, Nov. 26, 1966; s. Michael J. and Marilyn A. (Christiano) G.; m. Catherine Jane Branch, June 17, 1995. BA, Catholic U., 1988, JD, 1991. Bar: N.J. 1991, U.S. Dist. Ct. N.J. 1991. Legis. aide Bergen County Freeholders, Hackensack, N.J., 1992-93; assoc. Nowell Amoroso, Hackensack, 1996—. Sec. Teaneck (N.J.) Hist. Preservation, 1992-95; com. liaison Teaneck Econ. Devel. Corp., 1996-97, Teaneck Planning Bd., 1997—; nominating com. chmn. Bergen County (N.J.) Boy Scouts, 1997—; dep. mayor Teaneck, 1996—, coun., 1995—. Mem. N.J. State Bar Assn., Bergen County Bar Assn. Avocations: golf, travel, skiing. Home: 112 Johnson Ave Teaneck NJ 07666-4216 Office: Nowell Amoroso 155 Polifly Rd Hackensack NJ 07601-1749

GALLUCCI, ROBERT LOUIS, diplomat, federal government official; b. Bklyn., Feb. 11, 1946; m. Jennifer Emily Sims, Dec. 27, 1976. BA, SUNY, Stony Brook, 1967; MA, Brandeis U., 1968, PhD, 1973. Cons. USAF, 1970; Rockefeller Found. fellow Washington Ctr. for Fgn. Policy Rsch., 1973-74; fgn. affairs officer U.S. Arms Control and Disarmament Agy., 1974-76; rsch. fellow program for sci. and internat. affairs Harvard U., 1977; rsch. assoc. Internat. Inst. Strategic Studies, London, 1977; chief nuclear and sci. divsn. Bur. Intelligence and Rsch., Dept. State, Washington, 1978-79; mem. policy planning staff Dept. State, Washington, 1979-81; dep. dir. office of non-proliferation and nuclear export policy Bur. Oceans and Internat. Environ. and Sci Affairs, Dept. State, Washington, 1981-82; dir. office of regional affairs Bur. Near Eastern and South Asian Affairs, Dept. State, Washington, 1982-83; dir. office of regional security affairs Bur. Politico- Mil. Affairs, Dept. State, Washington, 1983-84; dep. dir. gen. Multinational Force and Observers, Rome, 1984-88; prof. nat. security policy Nat. War Coll., 1988-91; dep. exec. chmn. UN Spl. Commn. on Iraq, 1991-92; sr. coord. Office of Dep. Sec. of State, Washington, 1992; asst. sec. Bur. Polit. Mil. Affairs, Dept. State, 1992-94; ambassador at large Office of Sec. of State, 1994-96; dean Sch. of Fgn. Svc. Georgetown U., Washington, 1996—. Author: Neither Peace Nor Honor: The Politics of American Military Policy in Viet-Nam, 1975; contbr. articles to profl. jours. Recipient Outstanding Civilian Svc. award Dept Army, 1991; Woodrow Wilson fellow Brandeis U., 1967-68, rsch. fellow Brookings Instn., 1970-71, Fgn. Affairs fellow Coun. Fgn. Rels., 1977. Mem. Coun. Fgn. Rels.

GALLUCCI, ROBERT R., librarian; b. July 3, 1953. BA, So. Conn. State U., 1975, MLS, 1977. Asst. libr. Watertown (Conn.) Libr. Assn., 1977-79; libr. dir. Prospect (Conn.) Pub. Libr., 1979-81, Seymour (Conn.) Pub. Libr., 1981-86, The Brookfield (Conn.) Libr., 1986—.

GALLUP, DONALD CLIFFORD, bibliographer, educator; b. Sterling, Conn., May 12, 1913; s. Carl Daniel and Lottie Elizabeth (Stanton) G. AB, Yale U., 1934, PhD, 1939; LittD, Colby Coll., 1971. Instr. English So. Meth. U., Dallas, 1937-40, 41-42; cataloguer library Yale U., 1940-41; asst. prof. bibliography, curator collection Am. lit., editor Library Gazette; fellow Jonathan Edwards Coll., 1947-80. Author: Ezra Pound Bibliography, 1983, T.S. Eliot Bibliography, 1969, T. S. Eliot & Ezra Pound, 1970, On Contemporary Bibliography, 1970, A Curator's Responsibilities, 1976, Pigeons on the Granite, Memories, 1988, What Mad Pursuits! More Memories, 1998, Eugene O'Neill and His Eleven-Play Cycle, 1998; editor: The Flowers of Friendship, 1953, Eugene O'Neill, Inscriptions, 1960, Eugene O'Neill, More Stately Mansions, 1964, Gertrude Stein, Fernhurst, Q.E.D., and Other Early Writings, 1971, Thornton Wilder, The Alcestiad, 1977, Eugene O'Neill, Poems, 1979, Thornton Wilder, American Characteristics, 1979, Eugene O'Neill, Work Diary, 1981, Eugene O'Neill, The Calms of Capricorn, 1981, Kathryn Hulme, Of Chickens and Plums, 1982, Thornton Wilder, The Journals, 1985, Ezra Pound, At the Circulo de Recreo, 1985, Ezra Pound, Plays Modelled on the Noh, 1987, Thornton Wilder, The Collected Short Plays, 1997-98. Served as lt. col. AUS, 1941-46. Decorated Bronze Star medal, French Croix de Guerr avec etoile de vermeil, 1945; recipient Tao House award for svcs. to Am. theater Eugene O'Neill Found., 1994, Eugene O'Neill Soc. medal, 1995; Guggenheim fellow, 1961, 68. Mem. Bibliog. Soc. Am., Elizabethan Club (New Haven), Grolier Club (N.Y.C.), Grad. Club (New Haven), Phi Beta Kappa. Home: 216 Bishop St Apt 201 New Haven CT 06511-3742

GALLUP, JAMES DONALD, physician; b. Miles City, Mont., Oct. 15, 1935; s. Warren Albert and Olive Madelyn (De Castro) G.; m. Maxine R. Keyes, Apr. 2, 1960 (div. Feb. 1995); children: Timothy Tyler, Derek De Willerdee. BS, U. Wyo., 1957; MD, U. Rochester, 1961. Bd. cert. anatomic and clin. pathology. Sr. med. officer USN Naval Air Sta., Grosse Ile, Mich., 1963-65; resident NIH, Bethesda, Md., 1966-69; chief clin. chemistry and emergency room svcs. St. Joseph Mercy Hosp., Pontiac, Mich., 1969-74; chief anatomic and clin. lab. Honolulu Med. Group, 1974-86; consultation svc. attending flight surgeon Brooks AFB, San Antonio, 1986-89, chief lab. svcs., 1987-89; chief aeromed. svcs. Mather AFB, Sacramento, 1989-92; work star occupl. health dir. corp. fitness St. Francis Hosp. West, Ewa Beach, Hawaii, 1992-95; staff physician Hawaii Ueno Med. Clinic, Honolulu, 1995—; med. legal cons., Honolulu, 1974-86, 92—; asst. clin. prof. pathology U. Hawaii Med. Sch., Honolulu, 1975-86; state air surgeon Hawaii Air Nat. Guard, Honolulu, 1981-86; asst. med. dir. varsity sports U. Hawaii, Honolulu, 1985-86. Author: Automation and Data Processing in the Clinical Laboratory, 1970; contbr. articles to profl. jours. Student senator liberal arts U. Wyo., Laramie, 1955-56; bd. mem., sec.-treas. Diamond Head Landing Assn., 1993—; race dir. Opportunities for the Retarded, Honolulu, 1997; bd. dirs. Am. Cancer Soc., Honolulu, 1997—, mem. tobacco ctrl. bd., 1997—. Col. USAF, 1986-92. Named Nat. AAU Marathon champion, Honolulu, 1976, Athlete of Yr., Honolulu Quarterback Club, 1985; State of Wyo. scholar U. Wyo., Laramie, 1953-56, Katherine Hoyt Whipple scholar U. Rochester Sch. Medicine, N.Y., 1956-58. Mem. Phi Beta Kappa, Omicron Delta Kappa. Avocations: running, chess, tennis, stamp and coin collecting, racquetball. Home: 2937 Hibiscus Pl Honolulu HI 96815-4727 Office: Hawaii Ueno Med Clinic 1777 Ala Moana Blvd Honolulu HI 96815-1606

GALLUP, JANET LOUISE, human resources development executive; b. Rochester, N.Y., Aug. 11, 1951; d. John Joseph and Mildred Monica (O'Keefe) VerHulst; 1 son, Jason Hicks. BA, Hofstra U., 1973; MA, Calif. State U., 1979. Asst. trader E.F. Hutton, N.Y.C., 1975; instr. Calif. State U., Long Beach, 1978-79, grad. asst., 1979; fin. analyst Rockwell Internat., Seal Beach, Calif., 1979-85; coord. mgmt. and exec. devel. and succession planning, 1985-91; mgr. orgn. and employee devel. activities Hughes Aircraft, 1991-95; mgr. tng. ops. Smart & Final Co., L.A., 1995-98; mgr. human resources devel. Yons-A Safeway Co., Arcadia, Calif., 1998—. Vol. Cedar House Ctr.-Child Abuse, Long Beach, 1976. Democrat. Roman Catholic. Office: Vons—A Safeway Co 618 Michillinda Ave Arcadia CA 91007

GALLUP, JOHN GARDINER, retired paper company executive; b. Bridgeport, Conn., Oct. 31, 1927; s. Prentiss Brownell and Evelyn (Crocker) G.; m. Paula Burgee, June 10, 1951; children: Susan, Paula, Bruce. A.B., Dartmouth Coll., 1949; William Pynchon hon. degree in Humanics, Springfield Coll., 1998. Dept. mgr. J.B. White Co., Greenville, S.C., 1951, Castner Knott Dept. Store, Nashville, 1951-52; asst. store mgr. A.T. Gallup, Inc., Holyoke, Mass., 1952-55; with Strathmore Paper Co., Westfield, Mass., 1955-92; prodn. mgr. Strathmore Paper Co., 1968-70, pres., div. mgr., 1970-92; dir. Bank of New Eng.-West, Springfield, Mass.; chmn. Mass. Ventures, Inc. Mem. George Bush Campaign Com., 1979; chmn. Baystate Med. Center, Springfield, 1979-82; chmn. Baystate Health Systems, Inc., 1982-83; bd. dirs. Jr. Achievement Western Mass., 1979; trustee Springfield Coll., 1979-91; chmn. Valley 2,000; trustee Community Found. W. Mass., Beveridge Found; commr. Mass. Commn. Jud. Conduct; trustee St. Andrew's Ch. Longmeadow. Served with USMC, 1945-47. Mem. Boston Paper Trade Assn. (pres. 1979), Am. Paper Inst. (exec. com. cover and text paper group 1979-91), Greater Springfield C. of C. (vice chmn. 1985-88, chmn. 1988-91, vol. econ. devel.), Visiting Nurses Assn. (bd. dirs.), Corp. fur Bus., Work and Learning (bd. dirs.), Cmty. Svc. Learning (bd. dirs.), World Affairs Coun. (bd. dirs.), Springfield Orch. Assn. (pres.), Associated Industries Mass. (hon. dir.), Century Club. Episcopalian. Club: Longmeadow (Mass.) Country, Colony (Springfield). Home: 64 Cambridge Cir Longmeadow MA 01106-2828 Office: 1350 Main St Ste 3 Springfield MA 01103-1627

GALLUP, PATRICIA, computer company executive. Chair, pres., CEO PC Connection, Inc., Milford, Mass. Office: PC Connection Inc 730 Milford Rd Merrimack NH 03054-4631*

GALLUPS, VIVIAN LYLAY BESS, federal contracting officer; b. Vicksburg, Miss., Jan. 14, 1954; d. Vann Foster and Lylay Vivian (Stanley) Bess; m. Ordice Alton Gallups, Jr., July 12, 1975. BA, Birmingham So. Coll., 1975, MA in Mgmt., 1985; MA in Edn., U. Ala., Birmingham, 1975. Cert. purchasing mgr. Nat. Assn. Purchasing Mgmt. Counselor Columbia (S.C.) Coll., 1975-76; case mgr. S.C. Dept. Social Services, Lexington, 1976; benefit authorizer, payment determination specialist then recovery reviewer Social Security Adminstrn., Birmingham, 1977-85; adminstrv. contracting officer U.S. Dept. Def., Birmingham, Ala., 1992-94; supr. contract adminstr. Def. Logistics Agy. U.S. Dept. Def., Ft. Belvoir, Va., 1994-95; contract adminstr., supervisory contract adminstr. Def. Logistics Agy., Ft. Belvoir, Va., 1995-97; contract specialist U.S. Coast Guard, Washington, 1997-98; chief of contracting ops. U.S. Coast Guard Engring. Logistics Ctr., Balt., 1998—. Hospice vol. Bapt. Med. Ctr.-Montclair, Birmingham, 1982; trustee, treas. Resurrection House, Birmingham, 1984-85; vol. counselor Cathedral Ch. of Advent, Birmingham, 1987; organist St. Thomas' Parish, Upper Marlboro, Md., 1998—. Mem. Nat. Contract Mgmt. Assn. (cert. profl. contracts mgr., chpt. sec. 1987, pres. 1990-93, nat. dir. 1993-94), Assn. of Luth. Ch. Musicians. Lutheran. Avocations: music, dance. E-mail: VGallups@elcbalt.uscg.mil. Home: 14144 Reverend Rainsford Ct Uppr Marlboro MD 20772-5986 Office: US Coast Guard 2401 Hawkins Point Rd Baltimore MD 21226-5000

GALLUS, CHARLES JOSEPH, journalist; b. Havre, Mont., Jan. 24, 1947; s. Raymond Charles and Anna Jo (Mack) G. BA in Polit. Sci. cum laude, Carroll Coll., 1969; MA in Polit. Sci., U. Mont., 1972. Bookkeeper's asst. Ellen Solem, CPA, Chinook, Mont., 1972; circulation asst. Havre Daily News, 1972-73, wire editor, reporter, photographer, 1973-97. Mem. 2 study comms. Havre local govt., 1974-77, 84-86; mem. Hill County Dem. Ctrl. Com., Havre, 1974—. Mem. AP, Glacier Natural History Assn., Northwinds Athletic Club, Soc. Profl. Journalists, KC, Sigma Delta Chi. Roman Catholic. Avocations: outdoor recreation, travel, reading, dancing. Home: 112 3rd St # 746 Havre MT 59501-3532

GALOTTI, RONALD A., magazine publisher. Pub. Vogue mag., 1998—; pres. Talk Media, Inc., N.Y.C., 1998—. Office: Talk Media Inc Conde Nast Publs 152 W 57th St New York NY 10019*

GALOWICH, RONALD HOWARD, real estate investment executive, venture capitalist; b. Peoria, Ill., Feb. 18, 1936; s. Louis J. and Leah (Kahn) G.; m. Eleanor Bernstein, June 16, 1957 (div. Aug., 1977); children: Jeffrey, Robert, Pamela; m. Susan E. Loggans, Sept. 11, 1977 (div. Apr. 1988). BS in Commerce and Law, U. Ill., 1957, JD, 1959. Bar: Ill. 1959, U.S. Supreme Ct. 1963. Pres. Twin Oaks-Burr Oaks Realty, Joliet, Ill., 1961-81; ptnr. Galowich & Galowich, Joliet, Ill., 1960-81; dir. real estate ops. Pritzker & Pritzker, Chgo., 1981-90; chmn. Madison Realty Group, Inc., Chgo., 1985—; Madison Group Holdings, Inc., Chgo., 1990—; founder, chmn. CEO Madison Info. Technologies, Inc., Chgo., 1994—; co-founder, sec., dir. First Health Group Corp. (formerly Health Care Compare Corp.), Downers Grove, Ill., 1982—; commr. Ill. Supreme Ct., 1968-70. Bd. visitors U. Ill. Coll. Law, 1996—, pres., 1999—; mem. leadership com. Cancer Inst., Rush-Presbyn. St. Lukes Med. Ctr., Chgo., 1993—; bd. dirs. Athletes Against Drugs, 1992—; bd. mgrs. Riverside Hosp. Cancer Ctr., Kankakee, Ill., 1999—. Fellow Am. Judicature Soc., Ill. Bar Found.; mem. ABA, Ill. Bar Assn., Urban Land Inst., Chgo. Bar Assn. Jewish. Avocation: lic. airline transport pilot. Home: 1248 N Astor St Chicago IL 60610-2308 Office: Madison Group Holdings Inc 200 W Madison St Chicago IL 60606-3414

GALSON, STEVEN KENNETH, preventive medicine specialist; b. Syracuse, N.Y., July 5, 1956; s. Edgar Leon and Eva Charlotte Galson; married; three children. BS, SUNY, Stony Brook, 1978; MD, Mt. Sinai, 1983; MPH, Harvard U., 1990. Diplomate Am. Bd. Preventive Medicine. Supr. med. officer Nat. Inst. Occpl. Safety and Health/Ctrs. Disease Ctrl., Cin., 1990-91, deputy dir. divsn. stds. devel. and tech. transfer, 1993-94; chief med. sect. Nat. Inst. Occupl. Safety and Health, Cin., 1991-93; chief med. officer office environ., safety & health U.S. Dept. Energy, Washington, 1994-96, chief med. office, counselor office sec., 1996-97; sci. dir., advisor to the adminstr. U.S. EPA, Washington, 1997-98, dir. Office of Sci. Coord. and Policy, 1998—; reviewer Jour. Am. Med. Assn., 1994—; liaison mem. bd. health sci. policy Inst. of Medicine; mem. com. environ. health policy U.S. Dept. HHS. Contbr. article to Lancet. Capt. USPHS. Recipient Achievement award Pub. Health Svc., 1991, unit commendation award, 1991, foreign duty svc. ribbon, 1993. Office: US EPA Sci Coord and Policy # 7201 401 M St SW Washington DC 20024-2610

GALSTER, RICHARD W., engineering geologist; b. Seattle, May 13, 1930. BS in Geology, U. Wash., 1951, MS, 1956. Geologist Grant County (Wash.) Pub. Utilities Dist., 1954-55; geologist Seattle dist. U.S. Army Corps. Engrs., 1955-85; dist. geologist, 1973-85, consulting engring. geologist, 1985—. Recipient Dept. of Army Decoration for Meritorious Civilian Svc., 1985, Claire P. Holdredge award Assn. Engring. Geologists, 1991. Fellow Geol. Soc. Am. (chmn. engring. geology divsn. 1978-79, E.B. Burwell award 1993, Disting. Practice award 1995), Assn. Engring. Geologists (hon., pres. 1982-83). Home and Office: PO Box 908 Edmonds WA 98020-0908

GALSTON, ARTHUR WILLIAM, biology educator; b. N.Y.C., Apr. 21, 1920; s. Hyman and Freda (Zaks) G.; m. Dale Judith Kuntz, June 27, 1941; children: William Arthur, Beth Dale. B.S., Cornell U., 1940; M.S., U. Ill., 1942, Ph.D., 1943. Rsch. plant physiologist emergency rubber project Calif. Inst. Tech., 1943-44, sr. rsch. fellow, 1947-50, assoc. prof. biology, 1951-55; instr. Yale U., 1946-47, prof. plant physiology, 1955-65, prof. biology, 1965-72, Eaton prof. botany, 1973-90, emeritus prof., 1990, dir. div. biol. scis., 1965-66, sr. rsch. biologist, 1990—, chmn. dept. botany, 1961-62, chmn. dept. biology, 1985-88; cons. ctrl. rsch. dept. E.I. duPont de Nemours & Co., 1956-78, Plant Resources Venture Funds, 1983-89; NASA, 1988-94; mem. divsn. biology and agr. NRC, 1963-66, 85-88, mem. com. on space biology and medicine, 1983-86; Einstein prof. Faculty Agr. Hebrew U., Jerusalem, 1980; vis. scientist Plant Breeding Inst., Cambridge, Eng., 1983; vis. fellow Wolfson Coll., Cambridge U., 1983; vis. scholar Riken Inst., Japan, 1988-89. Author: Life of the Green Plant, 1961, 3d edit. (with Peter J. Davies and Ruth L. Satter) 1980, (with James Bonner) Principles of Plant Physiology, 1952 (with Peter J. Davies) Control Mechanisms in Plant Development, 1970, Daily Life in People's China, 1973, Green Wisdom, 1981, Life Processes in Plants, 1994; mem. editorial adv. bd.: World Book Science Year, 1976-78, Pesticide Physiology and Biochemistry, 1978-88, Plant Growth Regulation, 1983-93, Chem. Engring. News, 1977-78, Environment, 1979-83; contbr. sci. articles. Served as ensign USNR, 1944-46; mil. govt. Okinawa. Guggenheim fellow Stockholm, Paris, Sheffield, Eng., 1950-51; Fulbright fellow Canberra, Australia, 1960-61; Sci. Faculty fellow NSF, London, 1967-68. Fellow AAAS (chmn. com. on meetings 1956-59, life mem.); mem. Am. Soc. Plant Physiologists (sec. 1955-57, v.p. 1957-58, pres. 1963-64), Internat. Assn. Plant Physiology (sec.-treas. 1961-67), Bot. Soc. Am. (editl. bd. 1959-61, 72-76, pres. 1967-68), Fedn. Am. Scientists (coun. 1973-76), Am. Soc. Biochemists, Molecular Biol., Am. Soc. Photobiology, Am. Inst. Biol. Scis., Am. Acad. Arts & Scis. Home: 307 Manley Heights Rd Orange CT 06477-3028 Office: Molecular Cellular & Devel Dept Biology Yale U New Haven CT 06520-8103

GALSTON, WILLIAM ARTHUR, political scientist, educator; b. Bklyn., Jan. 17, 1946; s. Arthur William and Dale Judith (Kuntz) G.; m. Miriam, Sept. 15, 1968; 1 child, Ezra Moses. BA, Cornell U., 1967; MA, U. Chgo., 1969, PhD, 1973. Asst. prof. dept. govt. U. Tex., Austin, 1973-80, assoc. prof. dept. govt., 1980-82; issues dir. Mondale Pres. Campaign, Washington, 1982-84; dir. econ. and social programs Roosevelt Ctr. Am. Policy Studies, Washington, 1985-88; prof. sch. pub. affairs U. Md., College Park, 1988—; dep. asst. to pres. domestic policy The White House, Washington, 1993—; vis. fellow Instn. Social and Policy Studies, Yale U., 1980-81; cons. Temple for Gov. Campaign, 1982; mem. adv. bd. Ford/Aspen-Wye Rural Econ. Policy Project, 1989-92; mem. selection com. rural policy fellowships Woodrow Wilson Nat. Fellowship Found., 1989-91; cons. and spkr. in field. Author: Kant and the Problem of History, 1975, Justice and the Human Good, 1980, A Tough Row to Hoe: The 1985 Farm Bill and Beyond, 1985, Liberal Purposes, 1991 (Spitz prize 1993), Rural Development in the United States, 1995; editor Virtue, 1992; mem. editl. bd. Ethics, 1991—, Nomos, 1991—; contbr. numerous articles to profl. jours. Advisor Gore for Pres. Campaign, Washington, 1988; chief speechwriter John Anderson Nat. Unity Campaign, Washington, 1980; mem. working group on bicentennial bill of rights Wilson Ctr., 1990-91. Sgt. USMC, 1969-70. Fellow Danforth Found., 1967-68, NEH, 1980-81, Woodrow Wilson Ctr., 1991-92. Mem. Am. Polit. Scis. Assn. (program chmn. nominative polit. theory sect. 1992), Conf. Study Polit. Thought, Am. Soc. Polit. and Legal Philosophy (program chmn. ann. mtng. 1989), Phi Beta Kappa. Democrat. Jewish. Home: 5616 Durbin Rd Bethesda MD 20814-1014

GALT, JOHN WILLIAM, actor, writer; b. Jackson, Miss., Apr. 4, 1940; s. William Neal and Lyndel Janes (Fortenberry) G.; m. Anna Marie Kolenovsky, Dec. 14, 1965 (div. 1973); children: Joseph William, Edward Wayne; m. 2d Diane Renee Wallace, June 6, 1981; children: Christopher Wallace, Geoffrey Warren. Student, U. Md. at Munich (Germany), 1960-61; BA, Univ. Scis. Am., L.A., 1992. toured as folksinger U.S.A. and Europe, 1960-62; voice talent on numerous radio and TV commls., Dallas, 1965-78, 80—, L.A., 1978-80; 31 film appearances as actor; looped characters in 4 movies; voice of Lyndon B. Johnson in Oliver Stone's JFK, 1992, Forrest Gump, 1994; writer film script Iceman, 1976; contbg. writer For The Love of Benji, 1977; writer screenplay Step Back From Anger, 1986, The Guardians, 1987; contbg. writer The Internal Affair, 1988; v.p. Tex. Ind. Feature Prodns., Inc., 1981—, Jackson Galt Creative Enterprise Inc. 1991-99. Co-author numerous short fictions. With USAF, 1957-62. Recipient Dallas Citizen's Cert. Merit, 1973, Clios (26), Tellys (25), N.Y. Film Festival Silver, Addys (43), CHA Gold Spirit award; several Tops in advt. awards. Mem. NATAS (Heartland chpt.), Actor's Equity Assn., Screen Actor's Guild, AFTRA, Writers Guild of Am., Acad. for Preservation of Talking Pictures. Avocations: martial arts (2d degree black belt Tae Guek Kwan Kung Fu 1993, advanced oriental broad sword combat forms, brown belt Hapkiko OHTC 1989). Office: care Sylvia Gill Kim Dawson Agy 7210 Stemmons Twp N Dallas TX 75200

GALT, MARGOT FORTUNATO, writer; b. Pitts., Sept. 4, 1942; d. Leonard Henry and Maxine Wipperman Fortunato; m. Robert L. Kriel, Jan. 1964 (div. Apr. 1982); 1 child, Helena; m. Francis E. Galt, May 25, 1985. BA, Goucher Coll., 1963; MA, Columbia U., 1965; PhD, U. Minn., 1976. Program dir. The Loft, Mpls., 1981-82, edn. dir., 1991-92; writer-in-the-schs. COMPAS, Minn. State Arts Bd., St. Paul, 1978—; adj. assoc. prof. Hamline U. Grad. Sch., St. Paul, 1991—; cons. Minn. Humanities Commn., St. Paul, 1990—; writer, cons. Women's Arts Registry of Minn., Mpls., 1995-96; pres. bd. dirs. The Loft, Mpls.; mem. grants bd. cmty. arts fund COMPAS, St. Paul, 1986-88. Author: The Story in History, 1992, The Country's Way with Rain, 1994, Up to the Plate, 1995; co-author: Turning the Feather Around, 1998. Newsletter writer Lex-Ham Coun., St. Paul, 1995—. Rsch. grant Minn. Hist. Soc., 1994, grantee Ctr. for Arts Criticism, 1993, 95, travel grant Jerome Found., 1990, poetry grant Minn. State Arts Bd., 1980. Mem. Grand Marais Art Colony, Acad. of Am. Poets. Avocations: bird watching, bird feeding, gardening, travel. Home: 1177 Laurel Ave Saint Paul MN 55104-6926

GALTERIO, LOUIS, healthcare information executive; b. N.Y.C., Apr. 20, 1951; s. Elio and Angelina (Mattina) G.; m. Elizabeth Anne Coddington, May 2, 1971; children: Jason, Heather. Student, CCNY, 1969-70, Baruch Coll., 1970-75; BS in Mgmt. summa cum laude, Mercy Coll., 1978; MBA in Fin., L.I. U., 1980. Asst. mgr. Mfrs. Hanover Trust, N.Y.C., 1971-82; v.p. Bankers Trust Co., N.Y.C., 1982-87; CIO Mortgage Backed Securities Clearing Corp., N.Y.C., 1987-88; sr. cons. capital markets Digital Equipment Corp., N.Y.C., 1988-90, integration exec., 1990-91; chief info. officer healthcare Health and Hosps. Corp. NYC, 1991-93; dir. clin. info. sys. Soc. of N.Y. Hosp., N.Y.C., 1993—; mgmt. cons., cert. neurofeedback practitioner Galterio Cons., N.Y.C., 1987—. Mem., sect. capt. Throgs Neck (N.Y.) Estates, 1988. Mem. IEEE (assoc.), Bankers Trust Alumni Orgn., Am. Hosp. Assn., Coll. Healthcare Info. Mgmt. Execs., Healthcare Info. & Mgmt. Systems Soc., Alpha Chi. Independent. Home: 2453 Nimbus Dr North Port FL 34287 also: The NY Hosp 525 E 68th St # 151 New York NY 10021-4873

GALTON, STEPHEN HAROLD, lawyer; b. Tulare, Calif., Dec. 23, 1937; s. Harold Parker and Marie Rose (Tuck) G.; m. Grace Marilyn Shaw, Aug. 15, 1964; children—Mark, Bradley, Jeremy, Elisabeth. B.S., U. So. Calif., 1966, J.D., 1969. Bar: Calif. 1970, U.S. Ct. Appeals (9th cir.) 1973, U.S. Dist. Ct. (no. dist.) Calif. 1973, U.S. Dist. Ct. (cen. dist.) Calif. 1970, U.S. Dist. Ct. (ea. and so. dists.) Calif. 1973. Assoc. Martin & Flandrick, San Marino, Calif., 1970-71, ptnr., 1971-72; assoc. Booth, Mitchel, Strange & Smith, Los Angeles, 1973-77, ptnr., 1978-85; ptnr. Galton & Helm, Los Angeles, 1986—. Mem. ABA (litigation, tort, insurance sects.), Am. Bd. Trial Advs. (assoc.), Calif. State Bar Assn. (del. 1974-81, chair fed. cts. com.), Wilshire Bar Assn. (pres. 1986-87), Los Angeles County Bar Assn. (bd. of trustees 1987—). Republican. Presbyterian. Contbr. articles to profl. jours. Office: Galton & Helm 500 S Grand Ave Ste 1200 Los Angeles CA 90071-2624

GALTON, VALERIE ANNE, endocrinology educator; b. Louth, Eng., May 6, 1934; came to U.S., 1959; d. Wilfrid and Eileen (Watson) Hamilton; m. Michael Galton, Aug. 26, 1956 (dec. 1968); children: Ian Andrew, Kenneth Anthony. BSc with honors, U. London, 1955, PhD, 1958, 1967-75; Research assoc. Nat. Inst. Med. Research, Mill Hill, London, 1955-58; research assoc. Med. Sch., Harvard U., Boston, 1959-61; instr., then asst. prof. Dartmouth Med. Sch., Hanover, N.H., 1961-66, assoc. prof., 1968-75, prof., 1975—; cons. NIH, Bethesda, Md., 1973-98. Mem. editl. bd. Endocrinology, 1982-85, Am. Jour. Physiology, 1982-85, 95—; contbr. articles to profl. jours. NIH grantee, 1962—. Mem. Am. Thyroid Assn., Endocrine Soc. Home: 57 Jenkins Rd Lebanon NH 03766-2002 Office: Dartmouth Med Sch Lebanon NH 03756

GALUCKI, FRANCES JANE, nursing educator, medical/surgical nurse; b. Waverly, N.Y., May 5, 1925; d. Clarence Watson and Edith Agnes (LaFever) McCray; m. Edward W. Galucki, Feb. 17, 1947; children: Clarence W., Linda S. Galucki Schmidt, Edward F., Alan J., Donna J. Galucki Plewes. RN, Buffalo (N.Y.) Gen. Hosp., 1947. Staff nurse Buffalo Gen. Hosp., 1949-52, 58-63, 73-76, acting head nurse, 1963-64, insvc. instr., 1964-69, supr. blood team, ward clks., 1965-69; staff nurse Kimberly Quality Care, St. Petersburg, Fla., 1986-93; ret., 1994. Mem. N.Y. State Nurses Assn. (dist. 1), ANA, Nurses Official Registry of Buffalo (nomination com., past chmn. grievance com.). Office: 10901 Roosevelt Blvd N Ste 100 Saint Petersburg FL 33716-2305

GALVAN, ELIAS GABRIEL, bishop; b. San Juan Acozac, Puebla, Mexico, Apr. 9, 1938; came to U.S., 1956; s. Elias and Olga (Peralta) G.; m. Zoraida Freytes, July 12, 1986, 1 child, Elias Gabriel. BA, Calif. State U., Long Beach; D in Religion, Sch. Theology Claremont. Ordained deacon United Meth. Ch., 1964, ordained elder, 1970. Asst. pastor Asbury United Meth. Ch., L.A., 1964-66; pastor City Ter. United Meth. Ch., L.A., 1966-69, All Nations United Meth. Ch., L.A., 1969-71; exec. dir. ethnic planning dept. United Meth. Ch., L.A., 1971-74, dist. supt. Santa Barbara Dist., 1974-80, coun. dir. Pacific and Southwest Conf., 1980-84, bishop United Meth. Ch., Phoenix area, 1984-96, now bishop, Seattle. 1st Hispanic bishop elected by United Meth. Ch. Avocation: tennis. Office: 2112 3rd Ave Seattle WA 98121-2310

GALVAN, JOE H., federal judge. Bar: N.Mex. Magistrate judge for N.Mex., U.S. Magistrate Ct., Las Cruces, 1991—. Office: US Magistrate Ct B-201C US Courthouse 200 E Griggs Ave Las Cruces NM 88001-3523

GALVANI, CHRISTIANE MESCH, English as a second language educator, translator; b. Kiel, Federal Republic of Germany, Jan. 19, 1954; came to U.S., 1977; d. Edgar and Elisabeth (Depken) Mesch; m. Paul Andrew Galvani, Dec. 19, 1979; 1 child, Jacqueline. BA, U. London, 1977; MA, Rice U., 1986. Freelance translator Houston, 1979—; instr. English, German, French Berlitz Sch. Langs., Houston, 1981-82, interpreter, translator, 1981-84, prodn. coord., 1982-84; lead ESL instr. Tex. So. U., Houston, 1989—; instr. Rice U., Houston, 1990 (summer). Translator: The Flowing Light of the Divinity, 1991. Named to Outstanding Young Women of Am., 1986. Mem. MLA, Am. Translators Assn., Am. Lit. Translators Assn., Houston Profl. Translators Forum (dir. 1982-83), Houston Interpreter's and Translator's Assn., Houston Humane Soc. Guild. Avocations: music, playing the recorder, reading. Home: 2926 Fairway Dr Sugarland TX 77478-4023 Office: Tex So Univ 3100 Cleburne St Houston TX 77004-4501

GALVANI, PAUL B., lawyer; b. Nov. 28, 1938; s. John L. and Helen (Bransfield) G.; m. Sheila Dacey, June 24, 1967; children: Jill D., Susan D. BA, Williams Coll., 1960; JD, Harvard U., 1964. Bar: Mass. 1964, N.Y. 1965, U.S. Tax Ct. 1965, U.S. Dist. Ct. (so. and ea. dists.) N.Y. 1966, U.S. Dist. Ct. Mass. 1970, U.S. Dist. Ct. Nebr. 1978, U.S. Dist. Ct. Calif. (no. dist.) 1992, U.S. Ct. Appeals (2d cir.) 1966, U.S. Ct. Appeals (1st cir.) 1970, U.S. Ct. Appeals (9th cir.) 1993, U.S. Supreme Ct. 1981. Law clk. U.S. Dist. Ct. (so. dist.) N.Y., N.Y.C., 1964-66, asst. U.S. atty., 1966-70; assoc. Ropes & Gray, Boston, 1970-75, ptnr., 1975—. Fellow Am. Coll. Trial Lawyers; mem. ABA, Am. Law Inst., Boston Bar Assn. Office: Ropes & Gray One International Pl Boston MA 02110-2624

GALVAO, LOUIS ALBERTO, import and export corporation executive, consultant; b. Ponta Delgada, Sao Miguel, Portugal, July 5, 1949; came to U.S., 1969; s. Jeremias B. and Margarida M. G.; m. Antonieta A. Galvao, Oct. 26, 1966 (div. 1984); children: Marlene, Vanessa. Degree in Bus. Mgmt., Indsl. & Commerce Sch., Azores, Portugal, 1968; Dr. Universal Life (hon.), Universal Life Ch., 1991. Asst. mgr. sales J.B. Galvao Imports, Azores, 1964-68; asst. supr. Union Carbide Corp., Peabody, Mass., 1969-70, Container Corp. Am., Wakefield, Mass., 1970-73; sales dir. McCulloch Oil Corp., Lake Havash City, Ariz., 1972-74; pres. Sunset Investments Corp., Phoenix, 1974—; v.p. United Universal Enterprises Corp., Phoenix, 1985—; pres. Universal Imports, Inc., Phoenix, 1977—; dir. Global Savings & Loan Ltd., London, 1990—. mem. Nat. Rep. Congl. Com., Washington, 1982—(cert. recognition 1981, 84, 85, Campaign Kickoff award 1984, cert. merit 1992), Rep. Presdl. Task Force, Washington, 1984— (Am. flag dedicated in his honor at Rotunda of U.S. Capital bldg. 1986, life mem., mem. presdl. election registry 1992), Rep. Nat. Com. (cert. recognition 1990, 92), European Movement, U.K., 1990—, Social Dem. Party, Portugal, 1990—, Washington Legal Found.; charter mem. U.S. Def. Com.; del. The Presl. Trust, Washington, 1992. Recipient award U.S. Def. Com., 1984; inducted to Rep. Nat. Hall Honor Rep. Nat. Candidate Trust, 1992. Mem. Am. Mgmt. Assn., Nat. Assn. Export Cos., Profl. Fin. Assts., Heritage Bus. Club,

Senatorial Club, Universal Life Ch. Roman Catholic. Avocations: reading, traveling, biking, movies.

GALVEZ-JIMENEZ, NESTOR, neurologist; b. Panama City, Aug. 28, 1957. MD, U. San Carlos, Guatamala City, 1983. Diplomate Am. Bd. Neurology, Am. Bd. Internal Medicine. From intern to resident in internal medicine Booth Meml. Hosp., N.Y., 1986-90; resident in neurology Cleve. Clin. Found., 1991-94; fellow U. Toronto, 1994-96; dir. movement disorders program, cons. neurology Cleveland Clin. Fla., Ft. Lauderdale. Mem. Am. Acad. Neurology, Movement Disorder Soc. Office: Cleve Clin Fla Hosp Dept Neur Move Disord Prgm 3000 W Cypress Creek Rd Fort Lauderdale FL 33309-1710

GALVIN, CHRISTOPHER B., electronics company executive; b. 1951. Bachelors, Northwestern U., MBA, 1977. With Motorola, Inc., 1973—; sr. exec. v.p., asst. COO Motorola, Inc., Schaumberg, Ill., 1989-95, pres., COO, 1995—, now CEO. Office: Motorola Inc 1303 E Algonquin Rd Schaumburg IL 60196-1079*

GALVIN, JOHN ROGERS, educator, retired army officer; b. Wakefield, Mass., May 13, 1929; s. John James and Mary Josephine (Logan) G.; m. Virginia Lee Brennan, June 5, 1961; children: Mary Jo, Elizabeth Ann, Kathleen Mary, Erin Elizabeth. BS, U.S. Mil. Acad., 1954; MA, Columbia U., 1962; postgrad., U. Pa., 1964-65; grad., Command and Gen. Staff Coll., 1966. Commd. 2d lt. U.S. Army, 1954, advanced through grades to gen.; mil. asst. to Supreme Allied Comdr. Europe, 1974-75; comdr. DISCOM, chief of staff 3d Infantry div., Germany, 1975-78; asst. div. comdr. 8th Infantry div., 1978-80; comdg. gen. 24th Infantry div., Ft. Stewart, Ga., 1981-83, also post comdr.; comdg. gen. VII U.S. Corps, Stuttgart, Fed. Republic Germany, 1983-85; comdr. in chief U.S. So. Command, Quarry Heights, Panama, 1985-87; supreme allied comdr. Europe, comdr.-in-chief U.S. European Command, 1987-92; ret., 1992; Olin disting. prof. nat. security studies U.S. Mil. Acad., West Point, N.Y., 1992-93; disting. vis. policy analyst The Mershon Ctr., Ohio State U., 1994-95; dean Fletcher Sch. Law and Diplomacy, Tufts U., Boston, 1995—; bd. dirs. Raytheon. Author: The Minute Men, 1967, Air Assault, 1969, Three Men of Boston, 1976. Former bd. dirs. Wesleyan Coll. Fletcher Sch. of Law and Diplomacy fellow, 1972-73; decorated Silver Star, Legion of Merit, DFC, Bronze Star. Mem. Coun. Fgn. Rels., Ctr. for Creative Leadership (bd. govs.), Seligman (bd. dirs.), Am. Coun. on Germany (chmn. emeritus bd. dirs.), Inst. for Def. Analyses (trustee). Roman Catholic. Home: 114 South St Medford MA 02155-7121

GALVIN, KATHLEEN MALONE, communications educator; b. N.Y.C., Feb. 9, 1943; d. James Robert and Helen M. (Sullivan) G.; m. Charles A. Wilkinson, June 19,1973; children: Matthew, Katherine, Kara. BS, Fordham U., 1964; MA, Northwestern U., 1965, 80, PhD, 1968. Tchr. Evanston (Ill.) Township High Sch., 1967-72; asst. prof. Northwestern U., Evanston, 1968-73, assoc. prof., 1973-78, prof., 1978—, assoc. dean, 1988—; presenter workshops in field. Author: Listening by Doing, 1986; sr. author: Family Communication, 5th edit., 2000; co-author: Person to Person, 5th edit., 1996, Basics of Speech, 3d edit., 1998; co-editor: Making Connections, 1996, 2d edit., 1999; contbr. articles to profl. jours.; developer, instr. 26-video series on Family Communication (PBS Adult Satellite Sys.). Office: Northwestern U Sch Speech 206 Am Swift Hall Evanston IL 60208-2260

GALVIN, MATTHEW REPPERT, psychiatry educator; b. Seattle, July 24, 1950; s. Ralph B. and Virginia (Reppert) G.; children: Joseph, Sarah. AB with honors, Ind. U., 1975, MD, 1979. Diplomate Am. Bd. Adolescent Psychiatry, Am. Bd. Psychiatry and Neurology. Asst. prof. Ind. U. Med. Ctr., Indpls., 1984-95, clin. assoc. prof., 1995—; child psychiatrist Pleasant Run Children's Home/Hamilton Ctr. Joint Venture, Indpls., 1998—; staff psychiatrist Larue Carter Meml. Hosp., Indpls., 1984-88, assoc. dir. youth svcs., 1988, acting dir., 1988-90; child psychiatrist Riley Child Psychiatry Svcs., Indpls., 1990-98, Pleasant Run/Hamilton Ctr. Alliance Family Svcs., 1998—; vol. faculty Riley Child Psychiatry and Ind. U. Med. Ethics Program. Author: Ignatius Finds Help, A Story about Psychotherapy, 1988, Otto Learns About Medicine, A Story About Grown-ups Helping Children, 1988, Clouds and Clocks, A Story for Children Who Soil, 1989; co-author: Sometimes Y, A Story for Families with Gender Identity Issues, 1993, The Conscience Celebration, 1998; contbr. articles to profl. jours. With M.C., U.S. Army, 1970-73, Vietnam. Fellow Am. Psychiat. Assn.; mem. Am. Acad. Child Adolescent Psychiatry, Am. Soc. Adolescent Psychiatry, Nat. Alliance Against Mental Illness (affiliate), Ind. Coun. Child and Adolescent Psychiatry (treas. Indpls. chpt. 1986-89, pres. elect 1989-90, pres. 1990-91). Office: Pleasant Run/Hamilton Ctr Alliance Family Svcs 2400 N Tibbs Ave Indianapolis IN 46202

GALVIN, MICHAEL JOHN, JR., lawyer; b. Winona, Minn., July 8, 1930; s. Michael John Sr. and Margaret Elizabeth (O'Donohue) G.; m. Frances Dennis Culligan, Sept. 7, 1957; children: Sean, Kevin, Kathleen, Nora, Mary, Margaret, Patricia. BA, U. St. Thomas, 1952; LLB, U. Minn., 1957. Bar: Minn. 1957, U.S. Dist. Ct. Minn. 1957, U.S. Supreme Ct. 1961. With sales and svc. Badger Machine Co., Winona, 1950-56; mgr. Oaks Hotel Inc., Winona, 1950-56; ptnr. Briggs & Morgan, P.A., St. Paul, 1957—. Pres. St. Paul Winter Carnival Assn., 1970; sec. St. Paul Area C. of C., 1968-71; trustee U. St. Thomas, 1978-85. Lt. USAF, 1952-54, USAFR, 1954-60. Recipient Disting. Alumnus award Univ. St. Thomas, 1983; named Outstanding Young Man, City St. Paul, 1964, Boss of Yr., St. Paul Jaycees, 1990. Mem. ABA (labor and employment law sect. 1957—), Minn. Bar Assn. (treas. 1991-93, pres.-elect 1993, pres. 1994-95, labor and employment law sect. 1957—), Ramsey County Bar Assn. (exec. coun. 1965-68, 83-86, pres. 1984-85), Minn. Vol. Attys. Corp. (pres. 1993-94), Univ. Club (pres. 1962), Minn. Club (pres. 1971), St. Paul Athletic Club (pres. 1986), St. Paul Area C. of C. (bd. dirs. 1995—, chair 1997-98). Republican. Roman Catholic. Office: Briggs & Morgan 2200 1st St N Saint Paul MN 55109-3210

GALVIN, ROBERT J., lawyer; b. New Haven, Dec. 10, 1938; s. Herman I. and Freda (Helfand) G.; m. Susan I. Goldstein, Oct. 15, 1960 (div.); children: David B., Peter J. A.B., Union Coll., Schenectady, N.Y., 1961; J.D., Suffolk U., Boston, 1967. Bar: Mass. 1967, U.S. Dist. Ct. Mass. 1967, U.S. Supreme Ct. 1988. Pvt. practice law, Boston, 1967-78; ptnr. Lippman & Galvin, Boston, 1978-84; of counsel Gage, Tucker & Vom Baur Boston, 1984-86; ptnr. Davis, Malm & D'Agostine, Boston, 1986—; lectr. Boston Ctr. Adult Edn., 1972-89, Northeastern U., Boston, 1977-78. Real estate columnist Boston Ledger, 1981. Co-author, editor Massachusetts Condominium Law, 1988, 91, 93, 96, 97, 98; contbg. author: Crocker's Notes on Common Forms, 1995, 96; contbr. numerous articles to profl. jours. Bd. dirs., v.p. Rental Housing Assn. div. Greater Boston Real Estate Bd., 1974, Boston Ctr. Adult Edn., 1979—, chmn. fin. com., 1985-86, pres., 1987-91; bd. dirs. Thoreau Soc., Inc., 1993—, chmn. fin. com.; bd. dirs. Beech Hill Found., Inc., 1989—, pres., 1989—. Fellow Mass. Bar Found. (life mem., Greater Boston 3 grantmaking adv. com. 1997, 98, 99); mem. Mass. Bar Assn. (coun. mem. property law sect. 1977-80, chmn. condominium com. 1979-91), Mass. Continuing Legal Edn. (real estate curriculum adv. com. 1983-87), Am. Arbitration Assn. (comml. arbitration panel), Mass. Conveyancers Assn., Community Assns. Inst. (atty's. com. New Eng. chpt.), Soc. for Censure, Reproof and Arraignment of Pub. Error. Home: 344 Pond St Jamaica Plain MA 02130-2447 Office: Davis Malm & D'Agostine PC One Boston Pl Ste # 3700 Boston MA 02108

GALVIN, ROBERT W., electronics executive; b. Marshfield, Wis., Oct. 9, 1922. Student, U. Notre Dame, U. Chgo.; LL.D. (hon.), Quincy Coll., St. Ambrose Coll., DePaul U., Ariz. State U. With Motorola, Inc., Chgo., 1940—, exec. v.p., 1948-56, former pres., from 1956, chmn. bd., 1964-90, now chmn. exec. com., 1990—, chief exec. officer, 1964-86, also dir.; chmn. bd. Semantech Inc., Austin, Tex. Former mem. Pres.'s Commn. on Internat. Trade and Investment.; chmn. industry policy adv. com. to U.S. Trade Rep.; mem. Pres.'s Pvt. Sector Survey; chmn. Pres.'s Adv. Council on Pvt. Sector Initiatives; chmn. Ill. Inst. Tech., U. Notre Dame; bd. dirs. Jr. Achievement Chgo. Served with Signal Corps, AUS, World War II. Recipient Nat. medal Tech. U.S. Dept. Commerce Tech. Adminstrn.; named Decision Maker of Yr. Chgo. Assn. Commerce and Industry-Am. Statis. Assn., 1973; Sword of Loyola award Loyola U., Chgo.; Washington award Western Soc. Engrs., 1984. Mem. Electronic Industries Assn. (pres. 1966, dir., Medal of Honor 1970, Golden Omega award 1981). Office: Motorola Inc 1303 E Algonquin Rd Schaumburg IL 60196-1079*

GALVIN, THOMAS JOHN, information science policy educator, librarian, information scientist; b. Arlington, Mass., Dec. 30, 1932; s. Thomas John and Elizabeth (Rossiter) G.; m. Marie C. Schumb, Nov. 24, 1956; 1 child, Siobhan Marie Wee. AB, Columbia U., 1954; SM, Simmons Coll., Boston, 1956; PhD, Case Western Res U., 1973. Reference libr. Boston U., 1954-56; dir. Abbot Pub. Libr., Marblehead, Mass., 1956-59; asst. dir. Simmons Coll. Libr., 1959-62; assoc. dir., prof. Sch. Libr. Sci., 1962-74; dean, prof. Sch. Libr. and Info. Sci., U. Pitts., 1974-85; exec. dir. Am. Libr. Assn., Chgo., 1985-89; prof. info. sci. and policy, dir. info. sci. doctoral program SUNY at Albany, 1989-99, prof. emeritus, 1999—; grad. fellow Case Western Res U., 1965-66; external examiner U. Ibadan, Nigeria, 1976-78; trustee Thayer Pub. Libr., Braintree, Mass., 1973-74; faculty fellow Ctr. for Tech. in Govt. SUNY, Albany. Author: Library Resource Sharing, 1977, Problems in Reference Service, 1965, Current Problems in Reference Service, 1971, The Case Method in Library Education, 1973, The On-Line Revolution in Libraries, 1978, The Structure and Governance of Library Networks, 1979, Excellence in School Media Programs, 1980, Information Technology, 1982, Priorities for Academic Libraries, 1982, Navigating the Networks, 1994, Smart IT Choices, 1996; also articles. Recipient Alumni Achievement award Simmons Coll. Sch. Libr. Sci., 1978, Disting. Alumnus award Case Western Res. U., 1979, Disting. Svc. award Pa. Libr. Assn., 1985, Ida and George Eliot prize Med. Libr. Assn., 1988, award contbr. to edn. Assn. for Libr. Info. Sci. Edn., 1993. Mem. ALA (pres. 1979-80, exec. bd., coun.; past pres. libr. edn. div., Isadore Gilbert Mudge award 1972), Assn. for Libr. and Info. Sci. Edn., Am. Soc. for Info. Sci., Phi Beta Kappa, Beta Phi Mu. Democrat. Roman Catholic.

GALVIN, WILLIAM FRANCIS, secretary of state, lawyer; b. Brighton, Mass., Sept. 17, 1950; m. Eileen Galvin. Degree cum laude, Boston Coll., 1972; JD, Suffolk U., 1975. Bar: Mass., Fed. Aide Gov.'s Coun., 1972; state rep. Mass. Gen. Ct., 1975-91; vice-chmn. Congl. Redistricting Com., 1981-83; chmn. Govt. Regulations Com., 1983-91; state legislator Commonwealth of Mass.; sec. of the Commonwealth of Mass., 1995—. Address: 20 Linden Glen Rd Canton MA 02021-4226 Office: 337 State House Boston MA 02133-1001*

GALWAY, JAMES, flutist; b. Belfast, Northern Ireland, Dec. 8, 1939; s. James Galway and Ethel Stewart (Clarke) G.; m. 1965 (div.), 1 son; Anna Christine Renggli, 1972 (div.), 1 son, 2 daughters; m. Jeanne Cinnante, 1984. Student, Royal Coll. Music, Guildhall Sch. Music, London, Conservatoire National Superieur de Musique, Paris; MA (hon.), Open U., Eng., 1979; MusD (hon.), Queen's U., Belfast, 1979, New Eng. Conservatory Music, 1980. First post wind band of Royal Shakespeare Theatre, Stratford-on-Avon. Flutist, Wind Band of Royal Shakespeare Theatre, Sadler's Wells Orch., 1960-65, Royal Opera House Orch., BBC Symphony Orch.; prin. flutist London Symphony Orch., 1966, Royal Philharm. Orch., 1967-69; prin. solo flutist Berlin Philharm. Orch., 1969-75; now solo performer and condr.; U.S. debut, 1978; recs. includes works of C.P.E. Bach, J.S. Bach, Beethoven, Corigliano, Danzi, Dvorak, Feld, Franck, Mozart, Quantz, Prokofiev, Nielsen, Reinecke, Rodrigo, Stamitz, Telemann, Vivaldi, Khachaturian; recordings include Annie's Song, The Classical James Galway, The Concerto Collection, Dances for the Flute, The Enchanted Forest: Melodies from Japan, Galway at the Movies, Greatest Hits Vol 1, Vol. 2, Vol. 3, James Galway and the Chieftains In Ireland, Galway at 50: A Portrait of James Galway, Winter's Crossing, 1998, James Galway Plays Lowell Liebermann, 1998. Author: James Galway: An Autobiography, 1978, Flute, 1982, James Galway's Music in Time, 1983, Masterclass, 1987; several TV appearances including The Tonight Show, Good Morning America, CBS This Morning, Live with Regis and Kathie Lee, Sesame Street, Live from Lincoln Center. Decorated officer Order Brit. Empire, 1977; recipient Grand Prix du Disque, 1976, Order of the British Empire award, 1979; Record of Yr. award Cash Box and Billboard mags.; named Musician of Yr., Musical Am., 1997. Fellow Royal Coll. Music, Birmingham Schs. Music. Avocations: swimming, walking, films, theatre, computers. Office: RCA care BMG 1540 Broadway New York NY 10036-4039 Address: care IMG Artists Europe-Media House, 3 Burlington Ln, Chiswick London W4 2TH, England also: IMG Artists NA 420 W 45th St New York NY 10036-3503*

GALYA, THOMAS ANDREW, geologist; b. New Brunswick, N.J., July 11, 1947; s. Andrew Peter and Geraldine Rose Galya; m. Lanora Lucille Bucklew, Jan. 8, 1970. BS, W.Va. U., 1971; MS, N.E. La. U., 1975; PhD, Miami U., Oxford, Ohio, 1983. Geologist Sewell Coal Co.-Pittston Co., Nettle, W.Va., 1972; chief geologist Clinchfield Coal Co.-Pittston Co., Dante, Va., 1978-82; sr. coal geologist, head coal quality group Exxon Coal Resources USA, Inc., Houston, 1982-86; staff geologist Exxon Coal and Minerals Co., Houston, 1986-89; owner, pres. Galya & Assocs., Katy, Tex., 1989; sr. geologist Occidental Petroleum-Island Creek Coal Corp., 1989-91; geologist III W.Va. Divsn. Environ. Protection, Logan, 1991-96; lead geologist so. ops. W.Va. Divsn. Environ. Protection, 1996-98, lead geologist statewide, 1998—; tchg. asst. N.E. La. U., Monroe, 1973-75; tchg. fellow Miami U., Oxford, Ohio, 1975-77, fellow, 1977-78. Mem. Am. Inst. Profl. Geologists, Am. Assn. Petroleum Geologists, Soc. Sedimentary Geology, Geol. Soc. Am., Sigma Xi, Sigma Gamma Epsilon. Democrat. Roman Catholic. Home: 65 Dogwood Ln Madison WV 25130-1268 Office: WWV Divsn Environ Protection 525 Tiller St Logan WV 25601-3438

GALYEAN, TAG, architect; b. Huntington, W.Va., Sept. 28, 1941; s. Tinsley Azariah and Jane Elizabeth (Elliott) G.; m. Ann Taylor, June 21, 1962 (div. May 1986); children: Tinsley, Taylor; m. Annabelle Galyean, Oct. 31, 1993. Student, Stanford U., 1960-62; BArch, Pratt Inst., 1966. Registered architect, W.Va., N.Y., Col., Fla., Ky., Vt., Mich., Va., Wy., D.C. Designer Richar dKaplan, N.Y.C., 1966-70; v.p. design WVHDF, Charleston, W.Va., 1970-72; pres. TAG Architects, Charleston, Washington, 1973-86; prin. The TAG Studio, Lewisburg, W.Va., 1986—. Recipient Platnium Circle award Hospitality Design, 1998. Republican. Presbyterian. E-mail: tagstudio@nearlife.com. Office: The TAG Studio 219 E Washington St Lewisburg WV 24901-1322

GALYSH, ROBERT ALAN, information systems analyst; b. Cleve., Apr. 4, 1954; s. Fred Theodore and Jennie Catherine (Masiglowa) G.; m. Nanette Marie Kappus, Mar. 3, 1984; children: Joanna Marie, Matthew Glenn. BA in Econs., Cleve. State U., 1976, MA in Econs., 1982. Savs. officer Cleve. Fed. Savs., 1977-79; v.p., systems and procedures analyst Continental Fed. Savs. (formerly Cleve. Fed. Savs.), Cleve, 1979-84; data processing officer, mgr. systems and procedures Continental div. Dollar Bank FSB, Cleve, 1984-86; systems analyst Cleve. Met. Gen. Hosp., 1986-87, sr. systems analyst, 1987-90; project leader info. systems MetroHealth Sys. (formerly Cleve. Met. Gen. Hosp.), 1990-95, group mgr. info. svcs., 1995-97; project mgr. info. svcs. Fairview Health Sys., Cleve., 1997—; info. sys. tech. cons. to MetroHealth Sys., 1997—. Mem. Nat. Warplane Mus. Mem. Omicron Delta Epsilon. Presbyterian. Avocations: aviation history, home computing, photography, travel. Home: 26602 Sudbury Dr North Olmsted OH 44070-1844

GAMACHE, KATHLEEN SMITH, retired psychotherapist; b. Jersey City, Sept. 13, 1936; d. Robert George and Evelyn Veronica (Kaiser) Smith; m. R. Donald Gamache, Nov. 22, 1958; children: Nanette Campbell, Lisette Becker. BS, State Coll. N.J., 1958; MS, U. Bridgeport, 1972; postgrad., Yale U., 1986-88, Boston U., 1985. Pub. health nurse City of Jersey City, 1958-59; social worker Park City Hosp., Bridgeport, Conn., 1972-74; psychotherapist Dept. Children Youth Svcs., Bridgeport, 1979-81, City of Balt., 1958-59, Yale Behavioral Med. Clinic, New Haven, 1986-90, Fairfield Behavioral Medicine, 1989-90, Conn. Ctr. Behavioral Medicine Bio-feedback, Norwalk; ret., 1990; part time pub. health nurse Fairfield, Conn., 1966-76. Bd. dirs. Enfield (N.H.) Shaker Mus. Recipient Best Bedside Nursing award Jersey Med. City, 1958. Mem. Soc. Behavioral Medicine. Home: 33 Chosen Vale Ln Enfield NH 03748-2421

GAMACHE, RICHARD DONALD, retired business development executive; b. Fall River, Mass., Aug. 30, 1935; s. Armand Wilfred and Imelda (Gagnon) G.; m. Kathleen Florence Smith, Nov. 22, 1958; children: Mariette, Nanette Campbell, Lisette Becker. BS, St. Peter's Coll., 1958. Account exec. Harold Shore Assocs., N.Y.C., 1965-67; v.p. Van Dyck Corp., Southport, Conn., 1967-69; pres. Shippan Corp., Stamford, Conn., 1969; pres. INNOTECH. Corp., Trumbull, Conn., 1969-86, chmn., 1985-94; ret., 1994. Contbg. author Handbook for Creative and Innovative Managers, 1988, New Directions in Creative and Innovative Management, 1988; author: The Creativity Infusion, 1989; contbr. numerous articles to profl. jours. Active Charleston (S.C.) Symphony Orch., Sea Island Habitat for Humanity, United Way Upper Valley, Lebanon, N.H. Avocations: music, baking, gardening. Home (summer): 29 Chosen Vale Ln Enfield NH 03748-2421

GAMBACCINI, LOUIS JOHN, transportation executive, educational; b. New Haven, May 6, 1931; s. Basilio Augusto and Pierina Malerba G.; m. Annette Bush, Aug. 24, 1954 (dec. Mar. 1994); children: Mark, Claire, Beth, Paul, Sue, Jill. BS in Govt., U. Conn., 1952; MPA, Syracuse U., 1956. Asst. exec. dir., v.p., gen. mgr. Path, dir. rail dept. N.Y. and N.J. Pub. Authority, Port Authority, 1956-78, 81-88; commr. transp., chmn. N.J. Transit Corps State N.J., 1978-81; gen. mgr. S.E. Pa. Transp. Authority, Phila., 1988-97; dir. Nat. Transit Inst. Rutgers U., New Brunswick, N.J., 1998—; founder N.J. Transit, Newark, 1979, Transcom, Jersey City, N.J., 1986, Transit Ctr., N.Y.C., 1986. Founder Coun. Excellence in Govt., prin., 1983-87. With U.S. Army, 1952-55. Recipient Turner award Am. Soc. Civil Engrs., 1993. Fellow Nat. Acad. Pub. Adminstrn.; mem. Am. Pub. Transit Assn. (chmn. 1992-93), Am. Soc. Pub. Adminstrn. (pres. N.Y. chpt. 1964), Transp. Rsch. Bd. (chmn. 1990). Roman Catholic. Avocations: traveling, reading. Office: Nat Transit Inst 120 Albany St Ste 705 New Brunswick NJ 08901

GAMBARDELLA, ROSEMARY, federal judge. BA, JD, Rutgers U. Admitted to bar, 1980. Chief judge U.S. Bankruptcy Ct. for Dist. N.J., Newark. Office: US Bankruptcy Ct M L King Jr Fed Bldg 50 Walnut St Ste 5 Newark NJ 07102-3550

GAMBEE, ROBERT RANKIN, investment banker; b. N.Y.C., Aug. 26, 1942; s. Sumner and Eleanor Elizabeth (Brown) G.; m. Elizabeth Gregory Heard, 1991; children: Robert Gregory, Claire Elizabeth Fay. Grad., Phillips Exeter Acad.; AB, Princeton U., 1964; MBA, Harvard U., 1966. Assoc. corp. fin. White, Weald & Co., N.Y.C., 1966-71, v.p., 1971-73; v.p. Schroder Capital Corp. affiliate J Henry Schoder Wagg-London, N.Y.C., 1973-78, Atlantic Capital Corp. affiliate Deutsche Bank AG, Frankfurt, Germany, 1978-84; 1st v.p. Deutsche Bank Securities Inc., 1985-91, dir., 1991—, dir., COO German fund; v.p. Apollo, Atlas, Hercules, Hermes, Mercury, Olympus, Orion, Pegasus, Taurus, Titan and Zeus Instl. Investments, Inc., 1984-92; COO, sec. Germany Fund, Inc., 1986—, The New Germany Fund, Inc., 1990—, The Future Germany Fund, Inc, 1990-96, The Ctrl. European Equity Fund, Inc., 1995—; v.p., sec. Deutsche Funds Inc.; corp. sec. Deutsche Bank Securities Asset Mgmt. Inc. Author, photographer: Nantucket Island, 1973, rev. edit., 1974, 81, paper edit., 1978, 87, 89, color edits., 1986, 88, Manhattan Seascape: Waterside Views Around New York, 1975, Exeter Impressions (intro. by Nathaniel Benchley), 1980, Princeton in Color (intro by Robert F. Goheen), 1987, peper edit., 1988, 2d rev. edit., 1993, 98, A Wall Street Christmas, 1989, rev. edit., 1990, Nantucket in Color, 1992, 94, 96, paperback edit., 1996, Wall Street-Financial Capital, 1998. Trustee Dwight-Englewood Sch., 1978-85, Elizabeth Morrow Sch., 1990—, Rye (N.Y.) Art Ctr., 1993—, Rye Presbyn. Ch., 1998—. Mem. Soc. Colonial Wars, Princeton Alumni Assn. Nantucket (v.p., sec.), Princeton Alumni Rye (pres.), Princeton Club, Nantucket Yacht Club, Univ. Club. Republican. Presbyterian. Home: Wendover Rd Rye NY 10580*

GAMBERT, STEVEN ROSS, geriatrician, internist; b. N.Y.C., Aug. 22, 1949; s. Lawrence and Mildred (Engel) G.; m. Gry Magdalene Biong, Oct. 15, 1972; children: Christopher, Iselin. AB, NYU, 1971; MD, Columbia U., 1975. Diplomate Am. Bd. Internal Medicine. Assoc. prof. Med. Coll. Wis., Milw., 1979-83; assoc. dean, prof. medicine N.Y. Med. Coll., Valhalla, 1983-97; prof. medicine, vice-chmn. acad. affairs UMDNJ-NJUS, Newark, N.J., 1997-98; chair dept. med. Sinai Hosp. Baltimore (Md.) Johns Hopkins U., 1998—. Pres. Byram Hills Sch. Bd., North Castle, N.Y., 1994-95. Fellow Am. Geriatrics Soc., Gerontol. Soc. Am., Am. Coll. Physicians, Med. Rsch. Assn. (pres. 1993-96), Med. Bus. Assn. (pres. 1993-96). Avocations: watercolor painting, photography. Home: 220 Wendover Rd Baltimore MD 21218-1837 Office: Sinai Hospital Baltimore Dept Medicine 2401 W Belvedere Ave Baltimore MD 21215-5269

GAMBESCIA, STEPHEN FRANCIS, higher education administrator; b. Phila., Dec. 7, 1957; s. Joseph M. and Mary E. (Botto) G.; m. Susan Rice, May 8, 1982; children: Stephanie, Stephen J. BS in Sociology, St. Joseph's U., 1980; diploma in journalism and pub. rels. cum laude, Charles Morris Price Sch. Adv. and Journalism, 1984; MEd in Curriculum and Instrn., Pa. State U., 1985; PhD in Polit. Sci., Temple U., 1996. Cert. health edn. specialist. Bookroom mgr., coach Sch. of Holy Child Jesus, Rosemont, Pa., 1980-81; health educator community health dept. St. Agnes Med. Ctr., Phila., 1981-83; coord. workplace cancer control Am. Cancer Soc., Phila., 1984-86, asst. dir. pub. edn., 1986-89, dir. corp. rels., 1990, v.p. corp. rels., 1990-92; v.p. ednl. programs and rsch. Am. Heart Assn., Phila., 1992-98; asst. to the pres. Neumann Coll., Aston, Pa., 1999—; bd. govs. St. Joseph's U.; presenter in field. Assoc. editor Health Promotion Practice Jour.; contbr. articles to profl. jours. Carrie May Price Trust scholar Charles Morris Price Sch. Advt. and Journalism, 1984, NCAA Athletic scholar St. Joseph's U., 1980, Carr Alumni scholar St. Joseph's U., 1980; recipient Gov.'s Letter of Commendation, 1996. Fellow Soc. for Pub. Health Edn. (pres. Pa. chpt. 1988-89, 92-93, chmn. comms. com., nat. del. 1997-99, nat. treas. 1998—); mem. APHA, Pa. Pub. Health Assn. (planning com. ann. meetings 1991, 92, 93, 98), Coalition for Tobacco Free Pa. (pres. 1993-95, chmn. bus. awards com.), Delaware Valley Healthcare Coun., Pa. State Alumni Assn. (life mem.), Phila. Coll. Physicians, St. Joseph's U. Alumni Track Club, Order Sons of Italy in Am., Men of Malvrern Retreat League (capt.). Office: Neumann Coll One Neumann Dr Aston PA 19014-1298

GAMBILL, C. CLEVELAND, federal judge; b. 1945. AB, Transylvania U., 1968; MBA, George Washington U., 1972; JD, Duke U., 1975. Asst. U.S. atty. ea. dist. Ky. U.S. Atty. Gen.'s Office, 1976-83, asst. U.S. atty. we. dist. Ky., 1984-91; asst. solicitor U.S. Dept. Interior, 1983-84; magistrate judge U.S. Dist. Ct. (we. dist.) Ky., Louisville, 1991—. Mem. Fed. Bar Assn., Ky. Bar Assn. Fax: (502) 582-5793. Office: US Dist Ct We Dist Ky 200 Gene Snyder Courthouse 601 W Broadway Louisville KY 40202

GAMBILL, JAN-MICHAEL, professional tennis player; b. Spokane, Wash., June 3, 1977. Professional tennis player, 1996—; team player Davis Cup, 1997. Office: c/o USTA 70 W Red Oak Ln White Plains NY 10604*

GAMBINO, JEROME JAMES, nuclear medicine educator; b. N.Y.C., Sept. 13, 1925; m. Jacquelyn Ann Mazzola, Mar. 27, 1948; children: Charles, John, Mary Ellen, Jacquelyn. BA, U. Conn., 1950, MS, 1952; PhD, U. Calif., 1957. Asst. prof. natural scis. SUNY, New Paltz, 1957-59; research radiobiologist UCLA, 1959-61; mem. research staff Northrop Corp., Hawthorne, Calif., 1961-69; dir. edn. nuclear medicine dept. VA Med. Ctr., Los Angeles, 1969-96; rsch. cons. VA Med. Ctr., L.A., 1996—; lectr. anatomy U. So. Calif., L.A., 1963-89, radiol. scis. UCLA, 1978—. Mem. Radiation Research Soc., Soc. Nuclear Medicine (pres. So. Calif. chpt. 1981-82). Avocations: watercolor painting, pen and pencil sketching. Office: West LA VA Med Ctr Nuclear Medicine 115 11301 Wilshire Blvd Los Angeles CA 90073-1003

GAMBINO, S(ALVATORE) RAYMOND, medical laboratory executive, educator; b. N.Y.C., Oct. 13, 1926; s. Salvatore Benedict and Rose (Ragona) G.; m. Madeline Russo, Apr. 5, 1953; children: Catherine Rose Garroni, Stephen Raymond. BS, Antioch Coll., 1948; MD, U. Rochester, 1952. Diplomate Am. Bd. Pathology. Labs. dir. Englewood (N.J.) Hosp., 1961-68; prof. pathology Columbia U., N.Y.C., 1968-82; dir. chemistry labs. Presbyn. Hosp., N.Y.C., 1968-77; labs. dir. St. Luke's-Roosevelt Hosp., 1978-82; chief med. officer, exec. v.p. MetPath, Inc., Teterboro, N.J., 1983-94, exec. v.p., chief med. officer emeritus, 1994—; adj. prof. pathology Columbia U., N.Y.C., 1983—; mem. Corning (N.Y.) Mgmt. Group, 1984-94; bd. dirs. Ciba-Corning, 1988-94. Co-author: Beyond Normality, 1975; editor: (newsletter) Lab Report for Physicians, 1979-98. Mem. Englewood Cliffs (N.J.) Sch. Bd., 1966-69. Served with USN, 1945-46. Mem. Am. Soc. Clin. Pathologists (editor check sample program 1968-93), Alpha Omega Alpha.

Roman Catholic. Avocations: walking, writing, travel. Office: Quest Diagnostics Inc One Malcolm Ave Teterboro NJ 07608

GAMBLE, DOUGLAS IRVIN, state official, educator; b. Wheeling, W.Va., Dec. 27, 1953; s. Wiley Irvin and Myrtle Stewart (Yeater) G.; m. Lois Winifred Betz, June 26, 1976; children: Rebekah Winifred, Mary Amelia, Martha Suzanne, Rachel Emma, Michael Irvin, Katrina Ruth. Student, Archtl. Assn. Sch. Architecture, London, 1975; B in Environ. Design, Miami U., Oxford, Ohio, 1976; MArch, U. Ill., 1979. Lic. asbestos worker, insp., mgmt. planner and supr. Draftsman G.T. Hardwick & Assocs., Champaign, Ill., 1976-77, Glenn G. Frazier & Assocs., Urbana, Ill., 1977; rsch. asst. Small Homes Coun.-Bldg. Rsch. Coun., Urbana, 1977-79; archtl. designer Carl Fischer & Assocs., Springfield, Ill., 1979-80; archtl. programmer Sarti-Huff Archtl. Group, Springfield, 1980-82, Huff Archtl. Group, Springfield, 1982-86; project mgr., accessiblty specialist Capital Devel. Bd. State of Ill., Springfield, 1986—; instr. Parkland Coll., Champaign, 1978-79, U. Ill. Midwest Tng. Ctr., Chgo., 1987—, Lincoln Land Coll, Springfield, 1991—. Testifier elem. and secondary edn. com. on asbestos Ill. Senate, 1984; v.p. Faith Luth. Ch., Springfield, 1988-89. Miami U. rsch. grantee, 1975. Mem. AIA (assoc.), Constrn. Specificiations Inst. (pres. Cen. Ill. chpt. 1990-92, membership chair North Cen. region 1992-93, dir. North Cen. region 1996-97, mem. nat. spkrs. bur. 1988-96, Pres. cert. of appreciation Cen. Ill. chpt. 1988, North Cen. region mem. commendation award 1989, Inst. Commendation award 1990, North Cen. Region Dirs. Cert. award 1991), Nat. Asbestos Coun. (spkr. nat. conv. 1992), On My Own Time Art Competition, Geneal. Inst. Mid-Am., Nat. Geneal. Soc., Ill. State Geneal. Soc., Springfield Civil War Roundtable, Hon. Order Ky. Cols. Avocations: genealogy, music, photography. Home: 1425 S Whittier Ave Springfield IL 62704-3744 Office: Ill Capital Devel Bd 3d Fl 401 S Spring St Springfield IL 62706-4050

GAMBLE, E. JAMES, lawyer, accountant; b. Duluth, Minn., June 1, 1929; s. Edward James and Modesta Caroline (Reichert) G.; m. Lois Kennedy, Apr. 3, 1954; children: John M., Martha M., Paul F. AB, U. Mich., 1950, JD, 1953. Bar: Mich. 1953, D.C. 1980; CPA, Mich. Tax acct. Ernst & Ernst, Detroit, 1957-59; assoc. Dykema, Gossett, Spencer, Goodnow & Trigg, Detroit, 1959-67; ptnr. Dykema Gossett, Detroit, 1967-94, Gamble, Rosenberger & Joswick LLP, Bloomfield Hills, 1994—; adj. prof. law Wayne State U., Detroit, 1964-79; adj. lectr. law U. Mich., Ann Arbor, 1979-81, 93; co-reporter Uniform Principal and Income Act (1997); mem. adv. com. Restatement of the Law, 3rd, Property, Wills and Other Donative Transfers, Restatement of the Law, 3rd, Trusts; counsel Mich. State Bd. Accountancy, Lansing, 1973-77; dir. Ernst Concrete and Supply Co., Warren, Mich. Author: (handbook) The Revised Uniform Principal and Income Act, 1966; contbr. articles to profl. jours. Trustee Rehab. Inst., Inc., Detroit, 1961-84, chmn. bd. trustees, 1974-77; bd. dirs., sec. Jr. Achievement Southeastern Mich., 1973-86; trustee Walsh Coll. Accountancy and Bus. Adminstrn., Troy, Mich., 1975-87, Alma (Mich.) Coll., 1981-91; mem. Fin. and Estate Planning Coun. Detroit, bd. dirs., 1969-76, pres., 1975. Lt. USN, 1953-57. Recipient Bronze Leadership award Jr. Achievement, Inc., 1985. Fellow Am. Coll. Tax Counsel, Am. Coll. Trust and Estate Counsel (mem. bd. regents 1988—, chmn. estate and gift tax com. 1989-92, mem. exec. com. 1990-93, treas. 1994-96, v.p. 1996-97, pres.-elect 1997-98, pres. 1998-99, immediate past pres. 1999—), Academician, Internat. Acad. Estate and Trust Law, Am. Bar Found. (life), Mich. State Bar Found.; mem. ABA (mem. spl. com. on profl. rels. with AICPA 1968-70), Mich. Bar Assn. (mem. various coms.), Detroit Bar Assn. (chmn. taxation com. 1968-74), Detroit Bar Assn. Found. (trustee, treas. 1973-79), Birmingham Athletic Club, Leland Country Club. Presbyterian.

GAMBLE, HARRY T., professional football team executive. Pres., COO Phila. Eagles; now coord. football operations/club relations NFL.

GAMBLE, MARY G(RACE), marketing and quality professional; b. Evanston, Ill., Feb. 23, 1950; d. John D. and Bertha E. (Flynn) G.; m. John P. Kondrotas. BA with honors, U. Fla., 1971, MBA, 1993. Mgr. maj. market Gillette Co., Chgo., 1977-83; asst. regional sales mgr. Atlanta, 1983-85; v.p. sales and mktg. Hemochek Corp., Gainesville, Fla., 1985-89; div. mgr. Environ. Sci. & Engring., Gainesville, Fla., 1989-93; v.p., chief quality officer Hellmuth, Obata & Kassabaum, St. Louis, 1993-99, cons., 1999—; judge Fla. Quality Sterling Award. Bd. mem. Gov.'s Sterling Coun., 1989—, United Way of Alachua County, 1990-93, United Way of Hillsborough County, 1994—; bd. examiners Malcolm Baldridge Nat. Quality Award. Mem. Am. Soc. Quality, Assn. Jr. Leagues, Univ. Club, Rotary. Republican.

GAMBLE, STEVEN G., academic administrator. Pres. Southern Ark. U., Magnolia. Office: Southern Arkansas U Office of The President PO Box 9392 Magnolia AR 71753-5000*

GAMBLE, THEODORE ROBERT, JR., investment banker; b. St. Louis, Sept. 18, 1953; s. Theodore Robert and Rispah Adele (Dowse) G.; m. Susan Lee Stupin, Mar. 3, 1984. AB, Princeton U., 1975; MArch, Harvard U., 1977, MBA, 1979. Assoc. Morgan Stanley & Co., Inc., N.Y.C., 1979-84, v.p., 1984-86, prin., 1986-87; pres. The Prescott Group Inc., N.Y.C., 1987—; mng. dir. Transwestern Commercial Svcs., LLC, N.Y.C., 1999—. Co-chmn. adv. com. real estate devel.; chmn. vis. com. Grad. Sch. Design Harvard U.; mem. bus. and vis. coms. Met. Mus. Art; mem. vestry St. Thomas Ch., N.Y.C.; bd. dirs., exec. v.p. Greater N.Y. coun. Boy Scouts Am.; bd. dirs. N.Y. Hist. Soc., Coll. of Arms Found.; vice chancellor, bd. govs. Am. Soc., Order St. John of Jerusalem. Mem. Internat. Coun. Shopping Ctrs., Urban Land Inst. (comml. and retail devel. coun., internat. com.), Nat. Assn. of Real Estate Investment Trusts, Internat. Assn. Corp. Real Estate Execs., Real Estate Bd. N.Y., Young Mortgage Bankers Assn., River Club, Racquet and Tennis Club, Univ. Club, Knickerbocker Club, Links Club, Brook Club, Doubles Club, Met. Opera Club, Princeton Club (bd. govs., exec. com., v.p. fin.), Harvard Club (N.Y.C. and Boston), City Club (Miami), Coral Beach and Tennis Club (Bermuda). Republican. Episcopalian. Home: 860 UN Pla New York NY 10017 Office: Transwestern Commercial Svcs LLC The Prescott Group Inc 666 5th Ave New York NY 10103-0001

GAMBLE, THOMAS ELLSWORTH, academic administrator; b. Chgo., Nov. 14, 1941; s. Slade LeBlount and Anna Marie VanDuzer G.; m. Donna Kay Dersch, Nov. 3, 1973; children: Brendan, Shari, Oscar, Rebecca, Slade, Aubrey, David, Donna. BA in Biology, Northwestern U., 1964; MEd in Ednl. Psychology, U. Ill., 1970, PhD in Higher Ednl. Adminstrn., 1973. Asst. to dean student pers. U. Ill., Urbana-Champaign, 1968-71, asst. prof. edn., 1972-77, asst. dean Coll. Medicine, 1971-76; assoc. prof. Coll. Medicine U. Ill., Chgo., 1977-83; exec. asst. to chancellor U. Ill. Med. Ctr., Chgo., 1976-78, asst. chancellor, 1978-83; dean intercampus affairs Ill. Ea. C.C., Olney, 1983-84; dean of instrn. Wabash Valley Coll., Mt. Carmel, Ill., 1984-89, dean of coll., 1989-90; pres. Dodge City (Kans.) C.C., 1990-95, Joliet (Ill.) Jr. Coll., 1995-98; dist. pres. Brevard C.C., Coco, Fla., 1998—; asst. prof. U. Ill. Coll. Edn., 1972-77; assoc. prof. U. Ill. Coll. Medicine, 1982-83; pres. Kans. Jayhawk C.C. Athletic Conf., 1993-94, Ill. N4C C.C. Athletic Conf., 1996—. Contbr. articles to profl. jours. Bd. dirs. St. Joseph's Med. Ctr., Joilet, The Salvation Army, Joilet, Partnership for Health Comm., Kans. Newman Coll., Wichita, 1994-96. Capt. USNR, 1964-87, ret. Mem. VFW (life), Am. Assn. Cmty. Colls., Am. Assn. Higher Edn., Ill. Coun. Cmty. Coll. Pres., U. Ill. Coll. Edn. Alumni Assn. (life, sr. advisor, pres. 1988-90), Will County C. of C. (bd. dirs. 1996—), Joliet Area C. of C. (legis./transp. com. 1996—), Rotary Joliet, Beta Beta Beta, Chi Gamma Iota, Kappa Delta Pi, Phi Delta Kappa, Phi Kappa Phi. Avocations: non-fiction reading, children, classical music, naval science. Office: Brevard CC Office of Pres 1519 Clearlake Rd Cocoa FL 32922*

GAMBLE, VANESSA N., historian; b. May 20, 1953. BA, Hampshire Coll., 1974; MD, U. Pa., 1983, PhD, 1987. Asst. prof. history of medicine, science and family medicine U. Wis., Madison, 1989-93, assoc. prof., 1994—; dir. Ctr. for the Study of Race and Ethnicity in Medicine U. Wis. Sch. of Medicine, Madison, 1996—. Office: Ctr for Study of Race/Ethnicity in Medicine U Wis 1300 University Ave Madison WI 53706-1532

GAMBLIN, JAMES E., quality assurance specialist; b. St. Louis, Nov. 10, 1954; s. Donald Burton and Bette Sue (Welch) G. AA, Johnson County Community Coll., 1978; BA in Math. cum laude, Avila Coll., 1979; MS in Ops. Mgmt. summa cum laude, U. Ark., 1991; postgrad., Kennesaw State Coll., 1996—. Lic. pilot, FAA. Instr. U. Ark., Fayetteville, Ark., 1979-80; quality assurance specialist Def. Logistics Agy., Wichita, 1980-86, St. Louis, 1986-89; chief quality assurance specialist Def. Logistics Agy., Camden, Ark., 1989-91, Warner Robins, Ga., 1991-94; indsl. property/plant clearance officer Def. Logistics Agy., Marietta, Ga., 1994-98; quality assurance sr. functinal advisor Def. Logistics Agy., Boston and Marietta, Ga., 1998—; instr. quality Def. Logistics Agy., St. Louis, 1984-89; site adminstr. Def. Contract Mgmt. Command Atlanta World Wide Web, 1996-97. Frequent contbr. articles to Def. Contract Mgmt. Command, Atlanta Total Quality Eagle, Def. Contract Mgmt. Dist. South Southern Exposure, and other publs. Editor Singles' newsletter First Bapt. Ch., Canton, Ga., 1994-96. Mem. Am. Soc. Quality (sr.; mid. Ga. sect. treas. 1993-94, vice chmn. 1994-95), U. Ark. Alumni Assn. (life), Aircraft Owners and Pilots Assn., NRA (life), Good Sam Club (life), Shriners, York Rite, Scottish Rite, Masons (32d degree). Baptist. Avocations: woodworking, backpacking, hiking, canoeing, clock making. Office: US Govt Def Logistics Agy 805 Walker St SE Ste 1 Marietta GA 30060-2731

GAMBOA, GEORGE CHARLES, oral surgeon, educator; b. King City, Calif., Dec. 17, 1923; s. George Angel and Martha Ann (Baker) G.; m. Winona Mae Collins, July 16, 1946; children: Cheryl Jan Gamboa Granger, Jon Charles, Judith Merlene Gamboa Hiscox. Pre-dental cert., Pacific Union Coll., 1943; DDS, U. Pacific, 1946; MS, U. Minn., 1953; AB, U. So. Calif., 1958, EdD, 1976. Diplomate Am. Bd. Oral and Maxillofacial Surgery. Fellow oral surgery Mayo Found., 1950-53; clin. prof. grad. program oral and maxillofacial surgery U. So. Calif., L.A., 1954—; assoc. prof. Loma Linda (Calif) U., 1958-99, chmn. dept. oral surgery, 1960-63; pvt. practice oral and maxillofacial surgery San Gabriel, Calif., 1955-93; dir. So. Calif. Acad. Oral Pathology, 1995—. Mem., past chmn. first aid com. West San Gabriel chpt. ARC. Fellow Am. Coll. Dentists, Am. Coll. Oral and Maxillofacial Surgeons (founding fellow), Pierre Fauchard Acad., Am. Inst. Oral Biology, Internat. Coll. Dentists, So. Calif. Acad. Oral Pathology; mem. Am. Assn. Oral and Maxillofacial Surgeons, Internat. Assn. Oral Surgeons, So. Calif. Soc. Oral and Maxillofacial Surgeons, Western Soc. Oral and Maxillofacial Surgeons, Am. Acad. Oral and Maxillofacial Radiology, Marsh Robinson Acad. Oral Surgeons, Profl. Staff Assn. Los Angeles County-U. So. Calif. Med. Ctr. (exec. com. 1976—), Am. Cancer Soc. (Calif. div., profl. edn. subcom. 1977-90, pres. San Gabriel-Pomona Valley unit 1989-90), Am. Dental Assn. (sci. session chmn. sect. on anesthesiology, 1970), Calif. Dental Soc. Anesthesiology (pres. 1989-94), Calif. Dental Found. (pres. 1991-93), Calif. Dental Assn. (jud. coun. 1990-96), San Gabriel Valley Dental Soc. (past pres.), Xi Psi Phi, Omicron Kappa Upsilon, Delta Epsilon. Seventh-Day Adventist. Home: 1102 Loganrita Ave Arcadia CA 91006-4535

GAMBONE, KENNETH F., secondary education educator, English educator; b. Norristown, Pa., Feb. 16, 1926; s. Mitchell and Eva Marie (DeMarco) G.; m. Joan P. Opielski, June 21, 1958; children: Lynne J. Gambone Cohen, Kenneth G. BS in Edn. and English, West Chester U., 1951; MA in English, Pa. State U., 1953, EdD, 1972. Cert. English tchr., prin., Pa., N.Y. English tchr. Saltsburg (Pa.) Schs., 1952-55, Pottsgrove (Pa.) Pub. Schs., 1955-57, West Chester (Pa.) Pub. Schs., 1957-64; English supr. Oyster Bay (N.Y.) Schs., 1964-88; adj. prof. English C.W. Post Grad. Sch., Greenvale, N.Y., 1964-70, Nassau C.C., Garden City, N.Y., 1971-91, St. John's U., Jamaica, N.Y., 1997—; founder, dir. L.I. Writing Conf., Garden City, 1973-83; chair Nat. English Conf., N.Y.C., 1977; staff rschr. Dictionary of Am. Regional English, Madison, Wis., 1965-67. Author: LP Recordings in English, 1963, Blueprints for Mother Tongue, 1968, (essays) Remembering Walt Whitman, 1992, (children's lit.) Tales for Tyler, 1995. Trustee Oyster Bay Hist. Soc., 1985-88, editor Candlelight, 1985-88. Cpl. USAAF, 1944-46, ETO. Recipient Meritorious Svc. award N.Y. State English Coun., 1973, Outstanding Svc. award, 1980, Fellows award, 1994, Writing award L.I. Writing Coun., 1986. Mem. Nat. Coun. Tchrs. English (life), Coll. English (life), N.Y. State United Tchrs. (life). Avocations: books, researching watermarks and pianos, photography, building eighteenth century furniture reproductions. Home: 9 Francesca Dr Oyster Bay NY 11771-3711

GAMBONE, PHILIP ARTHUR, English language educator; b. Melrose, Mass., July 21, 1948; s. Arthur Louis and Nancy G. (DeVita) G. AB, Harvard U., 1970; MA, Episcopal Divinity Sch., Cambridge, Mass., 1976. Faculty Sunset Hill Sch., Kansas City, Mo., 1970-73, Park Sch., Brookline, Mass., 1977—, Harvard Ext. Sch., Cambridge, 1989—; resident MacDowell Colony, Peterborough, N.H., 1986, Helene Wurlitzer Found., Taos, N.Mex., 1996. Author: The Language We Use Up Here, 1991, Something Inside: Conversations with Gay Fiction Writers, 1999; book reviewer: N.Y. Times, 13—. Fellow NEH, 1985. Mem. PEN.

GAMBONE, VICTOR EMMANUEL, JR., internist; b. Phila., Aug. 28, 1949; s. Victor Emmanuel and Eleanor Joyce (Porambo) G. BS, Pa. State U., 1971, MD, 1975. Diplomate Am. Bd. Quality Assurance and Utilization Rev. Physicians, Am. Bd. Internal and Geriatric Medicine; cert. med. dir. in long term care. Intern then resident in internal medicine U. S.Fla., Tampa, 1975-78; practice medicine internal medicine and geriatrics U. S.Fla., Dunedin, Fla., 1978—; coord. geriat. medicine curriculum Morton Plant Mease U. S.Fla. Family Practice Residency Program, 1996—; med. dir. Hospice Care, Inc., Pinellas County, 1982-86, Stratford Ct. Marriott Health Ctr., Palm Harbor, Fla., 1991—, St. Mark Village, Palm Harbor, 1993—, Mease Continuing Care, Dunedin, Fla., 1993—, Manor Care Nursing Ctr., Dunedin, 1994—, Spanish Gardens Nursing Ctr., Dunedin, 1994-98, Regency Oaks Nursing Ctr., Clearwater, 1996—, Bayview Nursing Pavillion, Clearwater, 1996—, Mariner Health of Clearwater, 1996—, EverCare (United Healthcare) HMO, Tampa, Fla., 1996-, Arbors of Safety Harbor, Fla., 1997-98, Mariner Health Belleair, Clearwater, 1997-98, Sabal Palms Health Care Ctr., Largo, Fla., 1997-99, Morton Plant Rehab. Ctr., 1998—, Drew Village Rehab. and Nursing Ctr., Clearwater, Fla., 1998—; med. dir. Beverly Healthcare, Largo, Fla., 1999—; chmn. dept internal medicine Mease Health Care, Dunedin, Fla., 1989; bd. dirs. Morton Plant Mease Physician Hosp. Orgn., 1997—. Author: Post Operative Recall of Intra-Operative Events, 1975 (rsch. award U. Miami Med. Sch.). Mem. AMA, ACP, Am. Med. Dirs. Assn., Am. Geriatrics Soc., Am. Soc. Internal Medicine, Am. Coll. Physician Execs. Office: 601 Main St Dunedin FL 34698-5848

GAMBONI, CIRO ANTHONY, lawyer; b. Bklyn., Aug. 16, 1940; m. Gail Pollack, Aug. 1, 1965; children: Dina, Lee. BBA cum laude, CCNY, 1963; LLB cum laude, NYU, 1965; LLM in Taxation, Georgetown U., 1969. Bar: N.Y., U.S. Dist. Ct. (so. dist.) N.Y., U.S. Tax Ct. Ptnr. Cahill, Gordon & Reindel, N.Y.C. Mem. patron com. Lincoln Ctr. Theatre, N.Y.C. Served to capt. JAGC, U.S. Amry, 1966-69. Mem. N.Y. State Bar Assn. (tax. sect.), NYU Law Review, Order of Coif, Beta Gamma Sigma, Beta Alpha Psi. Clubs: Downtown Assn., Lotos (N.Y.C.). Avocation: non-profit theater. Office: Cahill Gordon & Reindel 80 Pine St Fl 17 New York NY 10005-1790

GAMBRELL, DAVID HENRY, lawyer; b. Atlanta, Dec. 20, 1929; s. E. Smythe and Kathleen (Hagood) G.; m. Luck Coleman Flanders, Oct. 16, 1953; children: Luck Coleman, David Henry, Alice Kathleen Hagood, Mary Latimer. BS, Davidson Coll., 1949; JD cum laude, Harvard U., 1952. Bar: Ga. 1951. Pvt. practice Atlanta, 1952-54, 56—; teaching fellow Harvard Law Sch., 1954-55; partner firm Gambrell & Stolz, 1963—; U.S. senator from Ga. to succeed Richard B. Russell Coms. on Banking and Space, 1971-72. Bd. editors: Am. Bar Assn. Jour, 1969-70. Chmn. Ga. Gov.'s Com. on Postsecondary Edn., 1978-79; trustee Met. Atlanta Crime Commn., 1966-68; bd. dirs. Nat. Legal Aid and Defender Assn., 1965-69; chmn. Dem. Party of Ga., 1970-71. Mem. ABA (ho. of dels. 1975), Atlanta Bar Assn. (pres. 1965-66), State Bar Ga. (pres. 1967-68, trustee Fellows Found.), Lawyers Club Atlanta, Ga. C. of C. (bd. dirs. 1989-92), N.C. Soc. Cin., Ga. Hist. Soc. (bd. curators 1999—), Met. Club (Washington), Piedmont Driving Club, Commerce Club, Capital City Club, Peachtree Golf Club, Sigma Alpha Epsilon, Omicron Delta Kappa. Democrat. Presbyterian. Home: 3205 Arden Rd NW Atlanta GA 30305-1918 Office: Gambrell & Stolz 303 Peachtree St NE Ste 4300 Atlanta GA 30308-3254

GAMBRELL, JAMES BRUTON, III, lawyer, educator; b. Rochester, Minn., Jan. 17, 1926; s. James Bruton and Martha Judson (Corley) G.; m. Helen Jeanette Roddy, Aug. 12, 1950; children: Jamey, Gretchen, James Bruton IV. Student, UCLA, 1943-44; B.S. in Mech. Engring, U. Tex., 1949; M.A. in Econs, Columbia U., 1950; LL.B., N.Y. U., 1957. Bar: D.C. 1957, Okla. 1958, Calif. 1961, N.Y. 1967, Tex. 1976. Mem. staff Tex. Legis. Council, Austin, 1950; instr. econs. Baylor U., Waco, Tex., 1950-51; mem. tech. staff (engr.) Bell Telephone Labs., Murray Hill, N.J., 1951-53; mem. patent staff Bell Telephone Labs., N.Y.C., 1953-57; admitted to practice before U.S. Patent Office, 1954; asst. patent atty. Well Surveys, Inc., Tulsa, 1957-59; assoc. Townsend & Townsend, San Francisco, 1959-61; spl. asst. to commr. patents, dir. office legis. planning U.S. Patent Office, Washington, 1961-63; ptnr. firm Fowler, Knobbe & Gambrell, Santa Ana, Calif., 1963-66; prof. law N.Y. U., N.Y.C., 1966-76; patent counsel N.Y. U., 1967-76; prof. law U. Houston, 1976-82; ptnr. firm Pravel, Gambrell, Hewitt, Kimball & Krieger, Houston, 1976-92; ptnr. Gambrell, Wilson & Hamilton, Austin, Tex., 1993-95, Akin, Gump, Strauss, Hauer & Feld L.L.P., Austin, Tex., 1995—; cons. to Practicing Law Inst., N.Y.C., 1966-71, Commn. Revision Fed. Ct. Appellate System, 1974, Energy and Rsch. Adminstrn., 1976; commr. patents Patent Adv. Com., 1968-72; adj. prof. Law U. Tex., Austin, 1974. Author: Patent Law Perspectives, 2d edit., 6 vols., 1970-88; editor: Orange County Bar Bull., 1965-66; mem. adv. bd.: Patent, Trademark and Copyright Jour., 1972-86, 94—. Served to lt. (j.g.) USNR, 1943-46. Mem. ABA, Calif. Bar Assn., Tex. Bar Assn., Assn. Bar City N.Y., Am. Intellectual Property Law Assn. (bd. mgrs. 1977-80), N.Y. Patent Law Assn., Licensing Execs. Soc., Internat. Trademark Assn., Copyright Soc., Intellectual Property Panel of Experts, Am. Arbitration Assn., Ctr. for Pub. Resources. Home: 3801 Cima Serena Dr Austin TX 78759-8229 Office: 816 Congress Ave Ste 1900 Austin TX 78701-2443

GAMBRELL, RICHARD DONALD, JR., endocrinologist, educator; b. St. George, S.C., Oct. 28, 1931; s. Richard Donald and Nettie Anzo (Ellenburg) G.; m. Mary Caroline Stone, Dec. 22, 1956; children: Deborah Christina, Juliet Denise. BS, Furman U., 1953; MD, Med. U. S.C., 1957. Diplomate Am. Bd. Obstetrics and Gynecology, Diplomate Div. Reproductive Endocrinology. Intern Greenville Gen. Hosp., S.C., 1957-58, resident, 1961-64; commd. USAF, 1958, advanced through grades to col.; chmn. dept. ob-gyn, cons. to surgeon gen. USAF Hosp. USAF, Wiesbaden, Germany, 1966-69; chief gynecologic endocrinology Wilford Hall USAF Med. Ctr. USAF, Lackland AFB, Tex., 1971-78; ret. USAF, 1978; clin. prof. ob-gyn and endocrinology Med. Coll. Ga., Augusta, 1978—; practice medicine specializing in reproductive endocrinology Augusta, 1978—; fellow in endocrinology Med. Coll. Ga., 1969-71; mem. staff Westlawn Bapt. Mission Med. Clinic, San Antonio, 1972-78; assoc. clin. prof. U. Tex. Health Sci. Ctr., San Antonio, 1971-78; internat. lectr.; mem. ob-gyn. adv. panel U.S. Pharmacopeial Conv., 1986-90; mem. sci. adv. bd. Nat. Osteoporosis Found., 1988-91. Co-author: The Menopause: Indications for Estrogen Therapy, 1979, Sex Steroid Hormones and Cancer, 1984, Unwanted Hair: Its Cause and Treatment, 1985, Estrogen Replacement Therapy, 1987, Hormone Replacement Therapy, 3rd edit., 1992, 4th edit., 1995, 5th edit., 1997, Estrogen Replacement Therapy Users Guide, 1989, 2d edit., 1997; mem. editl. bd. Jour. Reproductive Medicine, 1982-85, Maturitas, 1982-99, The Female Patient, 1992—, Menopause: Jour. of the N.Am. Menopause Soc., 1995—; mem. editl. bd. Internat. Jour. Fertility, 1986-91, assoc. editor, 1988-91; contbr. articles to med. jours., chpts. to books. Deacon, Sunday sch. tchr. Baptist Ch., 1971—; mem. sci. adv. bd. Nat. Osteoporosis Found., 1988-91. Recipient Chmn.'s Best Paper in Clin. Rsch. from Tchg. Hosp. award Armed Forces Dist. Am. Coll. Ob-Gyn., 1972, 88, Host award, 1977, Chmn.'s award, 1978, Purdue-Frederick award, 1979, Outstanding Exhibit award Am. Fertility Soc., 1983, Am. Coll. Obstetricians and Gynecologists award, 1983, Thesis award South Atlantic Assn. Ob-Gyn., Winthrop award Internat. Soc. Reproductive Medicine, 1985, Chmn.'s Best Paper award Pan Am. Soc. for Fertility, 1986, Outstanding Sci. exhibit award Am. Acad. Family Physicians, 1986, 87, 92, Boston, 1994, New Orleans, 1996, Merit award ACS, 1994, Cert. of Appreciation for Sci. Exhibit, 1995, Best Doctors for Women award Good Housekeeping, 1997; named to Hall of Fame, Lloyd Meml. H.S., Erlanger, Ky., 1996. Fellow ACOG (mem. subcom. on endocrinology and infertility 1983-86); mem. Pacific N.W. Ob-Gyn Soc. (hon.), So. Med. Assn. (2nd place Sci. Exhibit award 1992), Am. Fertility Soc., Ga. Obstetric and Gynecologic Soc., Tex. Assn. Ob-Gyn., Augusta Obstetric and Gynecologic Soc., San Antonio Ob-Gyn. Soc. (v.p. 1975-76), Chilean Soc. Ob-Gyn. (hon.), South Atlantic Assn. Obstetricians and Gynecologists (v.p. 1997-98, pres.-elect 1998-99, pres. 1999—), Soc. Obstetricians and Gynecologists of Can. (hon.), Internat. Family Planning Rsch. Assn., Internat. Menopause Soc. (mem. exec. com. 1981-84), Internat. Soc. for Reproductive Medicine (program chmn. 1980, pres. 1986-88), Am. Assn. of Pro-Life Obs. and Gyn. (exec. bd. 1995—), Am. Geriat. Soc. (mem. editl. bd. 1981-83), Nat. Geog. Soc., Phi Chi, Alpha Epsilon Delta. Home: 3542 National Ct Augusta GA 30907-9517 Office: 903 15th St Augusta GA 30901-2607

GAMBRELL, SARAH BELK, retail executive; b. Charlotte, N.C., Apr. 12, 1918; d. William Henry and Mary (Irwin) Belk; BA, Sweet Briar Coll., 1939; D in Humanities (hon.), Erskine Coll., 1970, U. N.C.-Asheville, 1986, Furman U., 1997; m. Charles Glenn Gambrell (dec.); 1 child, Sarah Belk Gambrell Knight. Dir., Belk Inc., 1947—. Hon. trustee emeritus Princeton (N.J.) Theol. Sem.; trustee Johnson C. Smith U., Charlotte, N.C., Warren Wilson Coll., Swannanoa, N.C., Hezekiah Alexander Found., Charlotte, Furman U., Greenville, S.C., (hon.) Cancer Rsch. Inst.; trustee nat. bd. YWCA; bd. dirs. Parkinson's Disease Found., N.Y.C., N.C. Cmty. Found., Raleigh, Charlotte Philharmonic Orch., Cmty. Sch. of the Arts, Charlotte, (hon.) bd. dirs. YWCA, N.Y.C. Mem. Fashion Group, Inc., Jr. League Charlotte, Nat. Soc. Colonial Dames, DAR. Home: 300 Cherokee Rd Charlotte NC 28207-1908 Office: Belk Stores Svcs Inc 2801 W Tyvola Rd Charlotte NC 28217-4525

GAMBRELL, THOMAS ROSS, investor, retired physician, surgeon; b. Lockhart, Tex., Mar. 17, 1934; s. Sidney Spivey and Nora Katherine (Rheinlander) G.; m. Louise Evans, Feb. 23, 1960. Student summa cum laude, U. Tex., 1953, MD, 1957. Intern Kings County Hosp., Bklyn., 1957-58; company physician Hughes Aircraft, Fullerton, Calif., 1958-65, Chrysler Corp., Anaheim, Calif., 1962-65, L.A. Angels Baseball Team, Fullerton, 1962-64; pvt. practice medicine Fullerton, 1958-91; with St. Jude Hosp., Anaheim Meml. Hosp., Fullerton Cmty. Hosp., Martin Luther Hosp.; mem. utilization rev. com. St. Mary's Convalescent Hosp., Fullerton Convalescent Hosp., Sunhaven and Fairway Convalescent Hosp.; owner Ranching (Citrus) & Comml. Devel., Ariz., Tex., N.Y., 1962-94. Contbr. articles to profl. jours. Organizer of care for needy elderly, North Orange County, 1962-65; sponsor numerous charity events. Fellow Am. Acad. Family Physicians; mem. AMA, Am. Geriats. Soc., Calif. Med. Assn., Tex. Med. Assn., Tex. Alumni Assn., Orange County Med. Assn., Mayflower Soc., Plantagenet Soc., Sons of Confederacy, SAR, Order Royal Descendants Living in Am. (col., listed in Living Descendants of Blood Royal), Order Crown (col.), Baronial Order Magna Carta, Order of Aesculaepius, Phi Eta Sigma, Delta Kappa Epsilon, Phi Chi. Avocations: collecting, travel, history. Office: PO Box 6067 Beverly Hills CA 90212-1067

GAMET, DONALD MAX, appliance company executive; b. Mapleton, Kans., Feb. 21, 1916; s. Carl Adolph and Pearl May (McClanahan) G.; m. L. Pauline Fleming, Apr. 14, 1938 (dec. Dec. 1981); children: Merilyn Kay Gamet Paris, Carleton Lenoir, Kathy Lynn Gamet Stephenson; m. Marilyn Lang, Jan. 15, 1983. BBA, Ft. Hays State Coll., 1938; MBA, U. Kans., 1939, JD, 1942. CPA, Mo. Staff acct. Arthur Andersen & Co., Kansas City, Mo., 1942-46, mgr., 1946-54, ptnr., 1954-78, mng. ptnr. Kansas City office, 1956-70; vice chmn. tax practices Arthur Andersen & Co., Chgo., 1970-77, sr. ptnr., 1977-78; cons. Kansas City, 1978-84; v.p.-treas. Chgo. Pacific Corp. (merged with Maytag 1989), 1984-85, exec. v.p. fin., 1985-87, spl. cons. to chief exec. officer, 1987-89, ret., 1989; bd. dirs. ANUHCO, Inc., Overland Park, Kans. Pres., chmn. bd. dirs. Heart Am. United Funds, Met. Kansas City, 1967-68, chmn. spl. reorgn. study com., 1980-84; mem. adv. bd. Salvation Army Kansas City, 1982-84; mem. personnel com. Village United Presbyn. Ch., 1982-84; pres., bd. dirs. Estate Planning Council Kans., 1962-63, Minority Supplier's Devel. Council Kansas City, 1983-84; bd. dirs., mem. exec. com., treas. Civic Council Kansas City, 1967-70; bd. dirs., chmn. long range planning com. Geriatic Resources Corp. Kansas City, 1982-84; bd. dirs. Metro Kansas City C. of C., 1962-70, pres., 1969-70; bd. dirs. Kansas City Indsl. Found., 1968-70, Jr. Achievement Kansas City, 1960-65. Named Boss of Yr., Met. Kansas City Jaycees, 1962; recipient Alumni Achievement award Ft. Hays State Coll., 1969. Mem. AICPA, Kansas City Club. Republican. Home: 5220 W 121st St Shawnee Mission KS 66209-3501

GAMMAGE, ROBERT ALTON (BOB GAMMAGE), lawyer; b. Houston, Mar. 13, 1938; s. Paul and Sara Ella (Marshall) G.; m. Judy Ann Adcock,

Aug. 3, 1962 (div. 1979); children: Terry Lynne, Sara Noel, Robert Alton Jr.; m. Lynda Ray Hallmark, July 4, 1980; 1 child, Samuel Paul. AA, Del Mar Coll., Corpus Christi, Tex., 1958; BS, U. Corpus Christi, (now Tex. A&M U.), 1963; MA, Sam Houston State U., 1965; JD, U. Tex., 1969; LLM, U. Va., 1986. Bar: Tex. 1969, U.S. Dist. Ct. (so. dist.) Tex. 1970, U.S. Ct. Appeals (5th cir.) 1970, U.S. Supreme Ct. 1973, U.S. Ct. Appeals (11th cir.) 1981, U.S. Dist. Ct. (we. dist.) Tex. 1983, U.S. Ct. Mil. Appeals 1986, U.S. Ct. Appeals (D.C. cir. 1993). Tchg. fellow, dir. fraternities Sam Houston State U., Huntsville, Tex., 1963-65; dean of men, dir. student activities U. Corpus Christi, 1965-66; property mgr. Harrison-Wilson-Pearson, Austin, Tex., 1966-69; pvt. practice law Houston, 1969-79; mem. Tex. House of Reps., Austin, 1971-73, Tex. Senate, Austin, 1973-76; del. Tex. Constl. Conv., Austin, 1974; mem. U.S. House of Reps., Washington, 1977-79; asst. atty. gen. State of Tex., Austin, 1979-80; pvt. practice Austin, 1980-82; spl. cons. U.S. Dept. of Energy, 1980; justice Tex. Ct. Appeals, Austin, 1982-91, TX State Supreme Ct, Austin, TX, 1991-95; pvt. practice Austin, 1995—; of counsel Steven E. Rogers, Dallas; mem. Tex. Jud. Budget Bd., Austin, 1983-88, Supreme Ct. Jud. Edn. Exec. Com., 1985-93, Tex. Jud. Coun., Austin, 1986-93, Jud. Com. on Ct. Funding, Austin, 1988-91; instr. govt. San Jacinto Coll., Pasadena, Tex., 1969-70; adj. prof. South Tex. Coll. Law, Houston, 1971-73; vis. prof. polit. sci. Sam Houston State U., Huntsville, Tex., 1996-97; vis. prof. pub. adminstrn. Tex. A&M U., Corpus Christi, 1997. With U.S. Army, 1959-60, USAR, 1960-64, USNR, 1965-95. Named Outstanding Sen. Tex. Intercollegiate Students Assn., 1973; recipient Disting. Svc. award Alcoholism Coun. Tex., 1976. Mem. ABA, State Bar Tex. (Disting. Svc. award 1975, vice chmn. funding judiciary com. 1988-91), Am. Judicature Soc., Inst. Jud. Adminstrn., Tex. Ctr. Legal Ethics and Professionalism, Democrat. Baptist. Avocations: skiing, water sports, teaching, writing, jogging. Office: 611 W 15th St Austin TX 78701-1513 also: PO Box 400 Plano TX 78643

GAMMELL, GLORIA RUFFNER, professional association administrator; b. St. Louis, June 19, 1948; d. Robert Nelson and Antonia Ruffner; m. Doyle M. Gammell, Dec. 11, 1973. AA in Art, Harbor Coll., Harbor City, Calif., 1969; BA in Sociology, Calif. State U., Long Beach, 1971. Cert. fin. planner. Bus. analyst Dun & Bradstreet, Los Angeles, 1971-81; sales rep. Dun & Bradstreet, Orange, Calif., 1971-93; rep. sales Van Nuys, Calif., 1981-90; pres. sec. Gammell Industries, Paramount, Calif., 1993-95, also bd. dirs.; regional v.p. Am. Mgmt. Assn., 1995—. Mem. Anne Banning Assistance League, Hollywood, Calif., 1981-82; counselor YWCA, San Pedro, Calif., 1983-84; fundraiser YMCA, San Pedro, 1984-85; mem. womens adv. com. Calif. State Assembly, 1984-89. Recipient Best in the West Presdl. Citation, 1981-86, 89, 90. Home: 991 W Channel St San Pedro CA 90731-1415

GAMMILL, LEE MORGAN, JR., insurance company executive; b. N.Y.C., Mar. 25, 1934; s. Lee Morgan and Blanche (Reeves) G.; m. Jane Houchin, Apr. 2, 1960; children: Christopher Morgan, Sarah Louise. BA, Dartmouth Coll., 1956. CLU. Mgmt. trainee N.Y. Life Ins. Co., San Francisco, 1957-58, field underwriter, 1958-60, sales mgr., 1960-64, gen. mgr., 1965-71, regional supt., 1971-75, gen. mgr., 1975-86, sr. v.p., 1986-89; exec. v.p. N.Y. Life Ins. Co., N.Y.C., 1989-95, vice chmn. bd. dirs., 1995—; pres. N.Y. Life and Annuity Corp., N.Y.C., 1987—; bd. dirs. N.Y. Life Securities Corp., N.Y.C., N.Y. Life Equity Corp., N.Y.C., N.Y. Life Realty Corp., N.Y.C., N.Y. Life Ins. Co.; chmn. bd. Life Ins. Mktg. and Rsch. Assn. Internat.; bd. dirs., mem. exec. com. Life Underwriters Tng. Coun. Dir. The Am. Coll.; chmn. Town Recreational Adv. Bd., Ross, Calif., 1977; trustee Ross Sch. Dist., 1978-84; trustee The Am. Coll. Mem. Gen. Agts. and Mgrs. Assn. (pres. San Francisco chpt. 1985), Nat. Assn. Life Underwriters, CLU Assn., MIll Valley Tennis Club (pres. 1972-73), Lagunitas Country Club, Pacific Union Club, Bohemian Club, The Links Club, Lyford Cay Club. Republican. Presbyterian. Avocation: tennis. Office: NY Life Ins Co 51 Madison Ave New York NY 10010-1603

GAMMON, JAMES ALAN, lawyer; b. Keokuk, Iowa, Jan. 30, 1934; s. Tench Temme and Helen Dolores Gammon; m. Joanne Mott, Aug. 31, 1957; children—Daniel, Thomas, Matthew, Kelly, Timothy. BS in Commerce cum laude, U. Notre Dame, 1956; JD, Georgetown U., 1959. Bar: D.C. 1959. Assoc. McGrath & McGrath, Washington, 1959-62; ptnr. Molnar & Gammon, Washington, 1962-72; sole practice Washington, 1972-76; ptnr. Gammon & Tierney, Washington, 1976; ptnr. Gammon & Grange, Washington, 1977-89, of counsel, 1989—; pres. Gammon Media Brokers, Washington, 1981—. Mem. Am. Bar Assn., Fed. Communications Bar Assn., Christian Legal Soc., Nat. Assn. Media Brokers (pres. 1989-91). Democrat. Roman Catholic. Avocation: body building. Office: 8280 Greensboro Dr Fl 7 Mc Lean VA 22102-3807

GAMMON, JAMES EDWIN, SR., clergyman; b. San Diego, Jan. 23, 1944; s. Jack Albert and Thalia Gammon; BA, Tex. Christian U., 1970, postgrad., 1970-72; m. Sharon Elaine Head, June 27, 1965; children: John Paul, James Edwin, Jeffrey David. Ordained to ministry Ch. of Christ, 1966; minister Carter Park Ch., Ft. Worth, 1966-69; Scotland Hills Ch., Ft. Worth, 1969-70, Northside Ch., Dallas, 1970-73, Central Ave Ch., Valdosta, Ga., 1973-78; debate coach Christian Coll. S.W., Dallas, 1971-73; pres. So. Bible Inst., Valdosta, 1977-78; minister Trinity Oaks Ch. of Christ, Dallas., 1978-80, Parkview Ch. of Christ, Sherman, Tex., 1980-85; pres. Texoma Bible Inst., 1980-85; minister Eisenhower Ch. of Christ, Odessa, Tex., 1985-86; minister Cen. Ch. of Christ, McMinnville, Tenn., 1986—; pres. Eagle Trust, 1994; chmn. Warren County Hist. Commn., 1995-98. Author: Notes on the Acts, 1983, Notes on I, II Corinthians, 1984, Thessalonians, 1985, Notes on James, 1985, Notes on Romans, 1988, Notes on the Beatitudes, 1989, Notes on II Peter, 1994. With U.S. Army, 1963-66. Republican. Home: 203 S Arrowhead Dr Mc Minnville TN 37110-2934 Office: Court Sq PO Box 536 Mc Minnville TN 37111-0536

GAMMON, MALCOLM ERNEST, SR., surveying and engineering executive; b. Chattanooga, Tenn., Sept. 7, 1947; s. George A. and Frances Helen (Conway) G.; m. Glenna Dee Shirk, June 5, 1971; children: Malcolm Ernest Jr., Christopher Brian. BS, Miss. State U., 1970. Ops. mgr. Pyburn & Odom, Inc., Baton Rouge, 1970-84; chief exec. officer, prin. owner Hydro Cons., Inc., Baton Rouge, 1984—. Tech. contbr. (textbook) 4567 Review Questions for Surveyors, 11th edit., 1985, Elementary Surveying, 8th edit., 1989. State chmn. La. Trig Star Program, Baton Rouge, 1988-89; mem. adv. bd. La. Math. Coalition. Mem. La. Soc. Profl. Surveyors (registered, pres. 1990), Miss. Assn. Land Surveyors (registered), Nat. Soc. Profl. Surveyors (profl. mem., bd. govs.), Am. Congress on Surveying and Mapping (profl. mem., cert. hydrographer), Ark. Soc. Profl. Surveyors (registered), Ala. Profl. Land Surveyors (registered). Home: 19021 St Clare Dr Baton Rouge LA 70810 Office: Hydro Cons Inc 10275 Siegen Ln Baton Rouge LA 70810-4926

GAMMON, SAMUEL RHEA, III, association executive, former ambassador; b. Tex., Jan. 22, 1924; m. Mary Renwick. B.A., Tex. A. and M. U., 1946; A.M., Princeton U., 1948, Ph.D., 1953. Instr. Emory U., 1952-54; joined Fgn. Service, Dept. State, 1954; served in Milan and Palermo, Italy, 1954-58; with Dept. of State, 1959-63; detailed fgn. affairs aide to Vice Pres. Lyndon Johnson, 1963; consul gen. Asmara, Ethiopia, 1964-67; counselor for polit. affairs Rome, 1967-70; detailed USIA dep. asst. dir. for W. Europe, 1970-71, exec. asst. to undersec., 1971-73; dep. exec. sec. State Dept., 1973-75; minister counselor Am. Embassy, Paris, 1975-78; ambassador to Mauritius Port Louis, 1978-80; exec. dir. Am. Hist. Assn., 1981-94. Pres. Nat. Humanities Alliance, 1986-88; bd. dirs. Consortium Social Sci. Assns., 1981-94, Truman Libr. and Inst., 1982-94, Assn. for Diplomatic Studies, 1986—. Served to Capt. AUS, 1943-46, 1950-52. Mem. Am. Fgn. Svc. Protective Assn. (bd. dirs. 1991—, pres. 1992—).

GAMMONS, PETER, columnist; b. Boston, Apr. 9, 1945; s. Edward Babson and Betty (Allen) G.; m. Gloria Fay Trowbridge, Aug. 24, 1968. BA, U. N.C. 1969. Writer, columnist Boston Globe, 1969-86; sr. writer Sports Illustrated, 1982-90; Major League Baseball studio analyst ESPN, 1988—, columnist, 1990—. Home: 36 Glen Rd Brookline MA 02445-7721 Office: ESPN Sports Television 935 Middle St Bristol CT 06010-1099*

GAMPEL, ELAINE SUSAN, investment management analyst and consultant; b. New Haven, Apr. 12, 1950; d. Stanley Irwin and Marion (Levine) G.; m. Alan Joseph Tedeschi, Sept. 9, 1984; children: Zachary Joseph Gampel Tedeschi, Matthew Samuel Gampel Tedeschi. BS in Spl. Edn.,

Boston U., 1972; MS in Counseling, So. Conn. State U., New Haven, 1975; cert. investment mgmt. analyst, Wharton Sch. Bus. Spl. edn. tchr. Ansonia (Conn.) Pub. Schs., 1972-77; v.p., investment mgmt. cons. Paine Webber Inc., Denver, 1977-89; v.p. investments Dean Witter Reynolds, Denver, 1989-93, 1st v.p. investments, sr. cons., 1993—; bd. dirs. the Denver Nuggets (bd. 1992-95). Bd. dirs. United Cerebral Palsy of Denver, 1984-93; mem. outside editorial bd. Denver Post, 1991-96; chair investment com. Women's Found. Colo., Denver, 1995-97, treas., bd. dirs., 1998—, chair fin. com. Women's Found. Colo., 1998—. Mem. Investment Mgmt. Cons. Assn. (cert., cert. com. 1990—), Women's Found. Colo. Avocations: tennis, running, biking. Office: Morgan Stanley Dean Witter 370 17th St Ste 5100 Denver CO 80202-5651

GAMROTH, ARTHUR PAUL, small business owner; b. Independence, Wis., Jan. 1, 1930; s. George Dominic and Frances Kathleen (Sylla) G.; m. Arline Hellen Leipski, Feb. 14, 1953; children: Shawne HCF, Bradley Paul, Todd Arthur, Timothy Curtis, Gary Mac. Diploma, Milw. Area Tech. Ctr., 1950. Mechanic Bonded Heating, Elm Grove, Wis., 1949-55; real estate salesman Anchor Realty, Waukesha, Wis., 1959-70; v.p. Ablenc, Inc., Waukesha, Wis., 1967—; pres. Energy Mgmt. of Wis., Waukesha, 1977—; cons. E.M.O.W., Waukesha, 1977—. Designer Sophisticated Mcpl. Recycling Facility with composting capabilities; patentee biomass burner. Lobbyist RDF, Wis., 1987—. With U.S. Army, 1950-52, Korea. Recipient Spl. Recognition award U. Wis., 1986. Mem. Am. Contract Bridge League, Waukesha Bridge Club Am. Republican. Lodge: Eagles.

GAMS, AARON JOSEPH, lawyer; b. N.Y.C., Apr. 5, 1959; s. Theodore Charles and Alma Raphel (Gianea) G.; m. Zinora Ann Koven; children: Theodore Cameron, Brennan, Megan Ann Khan Karen; 1 step child, Megan Ann. BA, Boston Coll., 1980; JD, Boston U., 1983, MBA, 1983; PhD, Columbia State U., 1997. Bar: N.Y. Ptnr. The Ogden Group Inc., Northbrook, Ill., 1984-95; sr. ptnr. Davis Gams and Peterson Inc., N.Y.C., 1995—; sr. advisor Legal Aide for Disadvantaged, N.Y.C. Author: A Dangerous Year, 1997. Vol. Neon Light Shelter for the Homeless, Chgo., 1991-95, Amnesty Internat., London, 1991—; asst. dir. Habitat for Humanity Internat., 1997—. British Formula Ford champion Royal Auto. Club, 1982; recipient Winfield award Ecole Pilotage Winfield, Toulon, France, 1984. Mem. ABA, ATLA, N.Y. Bar Assn., N.Y. Trial Law Assn., Conn. Bar Assn., Pa. Bar Assn., Fed. Bar Assn., Atlanta Bar Assn., Univ. Club. Avocations: motor racing, blue-water sailing, skeet shooting, tennis. E-Mail: welitagate@aol.com. Office: March Grp Inc 244 Fifth Ave New York NY 10001

GAMSKY, NEAL RICHARD, university administrator, psychology educator; b. Menasha, Wis., Feb. 17, 1931; s. Andrew P. and Lillian G.; m. Irene Janet Jimos, Aug. 16, 1956; children—Elizabeth, Patricia. BS, U. Wis., 1954, MS, 1959, PhD, 1965. Counselor, Appleton Pub. Schs. (Wis.), 1959-62; ednl. and counseling cons. Wis. Div. Mental Hygiene, 1967. dir. ednl. services Wis. Diagnostic Ctr., Madison, 1962-67; dir. rsch. pupil pers. svcs. Coop. Edn. Svc. Agy., Waupun, Wis., 1967-70; dir. student counseling ctr. Ill. State U., Normal, 1970-73, v.p. student affairs, prof. psychology, 1973-91; Served with U.S. Army, 1954-56. Mem. Am. Psychol. Assn., Am. Assn. Counseling and Devel., Nat. Assn. Student Pers. Adminstrs., Am. Assn. Higher Edn., Am. Coll. Pers. Assn., Am. Orthopsychiat. Assn. Author: (with G.F. Farwell and B. Mathieu-Coughlan) The Counselor's Handbook, 1974; contbr. 26 articles in field to profl. jours.

GAMST, FREDERICK CHARLES, anthropology educator; b. N.Y.C., May 24, 1936; s. Rangvald Julius and Aida (Durante) G.; m. Marilou Swanson, Jan. 28, 1961; 1 child, Nicole Christina. AA, Pasadena City Coll., 1959; AB, UCLA, 1961; PhD, U. Calif., Berkeley, 1967. Instr. anthropology Rice U., Houston, 1966-67, asst. prof., 1967-71, assoc. prof., 1971-75; prof. dept. anthropology U. Mass., Boston, 1975—, chmn. dept. anthropology, 1975-78, assoc. provost for grad. studies, 1978-83; cons. in social rels., human factors and ops. to R.R. industry, 1970—; acting dir. Houston Inter-Univ. African Studies Program, 1969-71, Behavioral Sci. Grad. Program, Rice U., 1974-75; mem. Joint Internat. Observer Group (for observation of Ethiopian elections), 1992. Author: Travel and Research in Northwestern Ethiopia, 1965, The Qemant: A Pagan-Hebraic Peasantry of Ethiopia, 1969, Peasants in Complex Society, 1974, The Hoghead: An Industrial Ethnology of the Locomotive Engineer, 1980, Highballing with Flimsies: Working under Train Orders, 1990; editor: Studies in Cultural Anthropology, 1975, Letters from the United States of North America on Internal Improvements, Steam Navigation, Banking, Etc., 1990, Anthropology Quar., Golden Anniversary Spl. Issue on Indsl. Ethnology, 1977, (with Edward Norbeck) Ideas of Culture: Sources and Uses, 1976, Meanings of Work: Consideration for the Twenty-First Century, 1995, Early American Railroads: Franz Anton Ritter von Gerstner's Die Innern Communicationen (1842-1843), 2 vols., 1997, (video documentary) T-Time: The History of Mass Transit in Boston, 1984; contbr. articles and revs. to profl. publs., chpts. to books. Mem. adv. com. Quincy Quarries Hist. Site, Met. Dist. Commn. Mass., 1987—. N.Y. State Regents scholar 1954-58, UCLA scholar 1959-60, Haynes Found. scholar 1960-61; Woodrow Wilson Nat. fellow 1961-62, Ford Found. Fgn. Area fellow 1962-63, Social Sci. Research Council & Am. Council of Learned Socs. Fgn. Area fellow 1963-66; Rice U. research grantee 1967, NSF grantee 1970-72, NIMH grantee 1972-74, others. Fellow AAAS, Am. Anthrop. Assn. (Conrad Arensberg award 1995), Soc. Applied Anthropology, Royal Anthrop. Inst. Gt. Britain and Ireland; mem. Sci. Rsch. Soc., Ry. and Locomotive Hist. Soc. (dir., editor 4 vol. Franz Anton Ritter von Gerstner project 1988—), Indsl. Rels. Rsch. Assn., Soc. for History Tech., Lexington Group in Transp. History, Northeastern Anthrop. Assn., Brotherhood Locomotive Engrs., Ry. Fuel and Operating Officers Assn., Am. Assn. R.R. Supts., Transp. Rsch. Bd., Soc. Anthrop. Work (pres. 1984-87, bd. dirs. 1987-90), Internat. Union Anthrop. and Ethnol. Scis. (chmn. curriculum com. Commn. Study of Peace 1983-86), Assn. for Study Lang. in Prehistory (bd. dirs. 1988—). Home: 73 Forest Ave Cohasset MA 02025-1335 Office: U Mass Harbor Campus Boston MA 02125-3393

GANAS, PERRY SPIROS, physicist; b. Brisbane, Australia, June 20, 1937; came to U.S., 1968, naturalized, 1975; s. Arthur and Lula (Grivas) G. B.S., U. Queensland, Australia, 1961; Ph.D., U. Sydney, 1968. Postdoctoral research assoc., instr. U. Fla., 1968-70, vis. asst. research prof., 1972, vis. assoc. prof. physics, 1978, vis. assoc. research prof., 1979-80; prof. physics Calif. State U., Los Angeles, 1970—; lectr. U. So. Calif., 1985-86, East L.A. Coll., 1988—; vis. prof. physics UCLA, summer 1987, 91, 92; referee Phys. Rev., Phys. Rev. Letters. Contbr. articles to profl. jours. Mem. AAUP, Congress of Faculty Assns., Am. Phys. Soc., Sigma Xi. Home: 11790 Radio Dr Los Angeles CA 90064-3615 Office: Calif State U Physics Dept Los Angeles CA 90032

GANASSI, CHIP, professional race car executive, owner; b. Pitts., May 24, 1958; m. Cara Ganassi; 1 child, Tessa. BA in Fin., Duquesne U., 1982. Exec. v.p. FRG Group, Pitts.; ptnr. Pitts. Pirates; promoter, co-mgr. Chgo. Motor Speedway; co-owner Target/Chip Ganassi Racing, 1990—; former profl. race car driver, fastest of 9 rookies at Indpls. 500, 1982; 8 top-10 finishes in 28 Indy car appearances, 1986; ret. 1986; co-owner Patrick Racing, 1988-89; established Reynard N.Am., Indpls., 1993. Office: c/o Target/Chip Ganassi Racing 3821 Industrial Blvd Indianapolis IN 46254*

GANAWAY, GEORGE KENNETH, psychiatrist, psychoanalyst; b. Davenport, Iowa, Mar. 22, 1946; s. Kenneth Joseph and Elizabeth Earl (Baker) G.; m. Elzada Lawson, Dec. 27, 1969; children: Heather, Erin. BS in Clin. Psychology, Duke U., 1968; MD, Emory U., 1973. Diplomate Am. Bd. Psychiatry and Neurology; lic. physician, Ga. Resident in psychiatry Emory Affiliated Hosps., Atlanta, 1973-76; candidate Emory Psychoanalytic Inst., 1993—; pvt. practice in gen. adult and adolescent psychiatry Atlanta, 1976—; regional med. advisor Social Security Disability Program, 1997—; founder, program dir. Ridgeview Ctr. for Dissociative Disorders, Smyrna, Ga., 1987-96; med. cons. dissociative disorder Ridgeview Inst., 1996—; asst. prof. psychiatry Emory U. Sch. Medicine, Atlanta, 1976-80, clin. asst. prof. psychiatry, 1981—; clin. asst. prof. psychiatry Morehouse Sch. Medicine, Atlanta, 1990—; tchg. faculty Emory Psychoanalytic Inst., 1997—; regional med. advisor Social Security Disability Program, 1997—; psychiat. cons. Disability Adjudication br. Social Security Adminstrn., Atlanta, part-time, 1980-87, Douglas County Mental Health Clinic, Douglasville, 1977-81, South Cobb Mental Health Ctr., Austell, Ga., 1978-80, Atlanta Depression

Clinic of Ctr. Metabolic Studies, 1976-77, others; ann. chmn. S.E. Regional Conf. Dissociative Disorders, 1987-96; courtesy staff Ridgeview Inst.; cons. staff Kennestone Hosp., Marietta. Asst. editor Dissociation: Progress in Dissociative Disorders, 1988-98; assoc. editor Internat. Jour. Clin. and Exptl. Hypnosis, 1995-96; mem. editl. adv. bd. Insight mag.; editl. reviewer Am. Jour. Psychiatry, Child Abuse and Neglect: The Internat. Jour., Jour. Psychology and Theology, Jour. Nervous and Mental Disease. Dissociation: Progress in the Dissociative Disorders; contbr. articles to profl. jours., chpts. to textbooks of psychiatry. Sci. adv. bd. False Memory Syndrome Found., 1992—. Fellow Internat. Soc. for Study of Dissociation (task force on stds. of practice 1991-96), Am. Psychiat. Assn.; mem. Ga. Psychiat. Physicians Assn. So. Med. Assn. Avocations: breeding and riding horses, collecting maritime antiques. Office: D-201 5064 Roswell Rd NE Ste 201D Atlanta GA 30342-2266

GANCHROW, MANDELL I., surgeon; b. Bklyn., Feb. 6, 1937; s. Morris S. and Kate (Wallach) G.; m. Sheila Weinreb, Dec. 29, 1940; children: Marcia, Ari, Elliot. BA, Yeshiva U., 1958; MD, Chgo. Med. Sch., 1962. Intern Beth-el Hosp., Bklyn., 1962-63; surg. resident Montefiore Hosp., Bronx, N.Y., 1963-64, Brookdale Hosp., Bklyn., 1964-67; colon-rectal resident Ferguson Clinic, Grand Rapids, Mich., 1969-70; surgeon Good Samaritan Hosp., Suffern, N.Y., 1970—; cons. NYack (N.Y.) Hosp., 1970—; clin. assoc. prof. surgery N.Y. Med. Sch., 1984—. Contbr. articles to profl. jours. Pres. Hudson Valley Polit. Action Commn., Spring Valley, N.Y., 1982-94; pres. Adolph Schreiber Hebrew Acad., Monsey, N.Y., 1982-83, Cmty. Synagogue of Monsey, 1979-80, Union Orthodox Jewish Congregations of Am.; chmn. Inst. for Pub. Affairs; bd. dirs. Am. Israel Pub. Affairs Commn., Washington, 1985-90. Fellow Am. Coll. Surgeons, Am. Soc. Colon and Rectal Surgeons, Am. Coll. Gastroenterology, N.Y. Colon and Rectal Surgeons, N.J. Colon and Rectal Surgeons, Soc. Am. Gastroenterologic Endoscopic Surgeons. Home: 12 Miriam Ln Monsey NY 10952-2007 Office: Hudson Valley PAC 100A Schoolhouse Rd Spring Valley NY 10977

GANCZARCZYK, JERZY JOZEF, civil engineering educator, wastewater treatment consultant; b. Tarnow, Poland, May 25, 1928; emigrated to Can., 1969; s. Kazimierz G. and Franciszka (Adamczyk) Ganczarczyk; m. Elizabeth B. Sawczynska, Aug. 7, 1956; 1 dau., Magdalena-Lynn Ganczarczyk Hamilton. M.A. Sci. in Engring., Silesian Tech. U., Gliwice, Poland, 1950, D.Sc. in Engring., 1956; Habilitation, Warsaw Tech. U., Poland, 1962. Diplomate: registered profl. engr., Ont. Research engr. Silesian Tech. U., 1951-56, sr. lectr., 1956-63; head tech. lab. Hydroproject Cons., Gliwice, 1956-63; v.p., research prof. Water Mgmt. Research Inst., Warsaw, 1964-69; prof. civil engring. U. Toronto, 1969—; cons. Bio-San Cons., Warsaw, 1968-69; mem. panel of experts WHO, Geneva, 1966-72; pres. J. Ganczarczyk & Assocs., Toronto, 1975—. Author: Activated Sludge Treatment, 1966, 1969, 1983; inventor utilization of desulfurization slag, 1983, controlled inhibition of nitrification, 1988. Recipient award Ministry of Constrn., Warsaw, 1968; recipient Polish State award, Warsaw, 1969. Fellow Royal Soc. Health; mem. Water Environ. Fedn., Internat. Assn. Water Quality, Assn. Environ. Engring. Profs. Roman Catholic. Home: 83 Edenbridge Dr, Islington, ON Canada M9A 3G5 Office: U Toronto, Dept Civil Engring, Toronto, ON Canada M5S 1A4

GANDARA, DANIEL, lawyer; b. L.A., July 7, 1948; s. Henry and Cecilia (Contreras) G.; m. Juleann Cottini, Aug. 26, 1972; children: Mario, Enrico. BA, UCLA, 1970; JD, Harvard U., 1974. Bar: Calif. 1974, Wash. 1978. Asst. city atty. City of L.A., 1974-77; staff atty. FTC, Seattle, 1977-79; ptnr. Lane, Powell, Moss & Miller, Seattle, 1979-87, Graham & Dunn, Seattle, 1987-93, Vandeberg, Johnson & Gandara, Seattle, 1993—. Mem. ABA, Wash. State Bar Assn., King County Bar Assn., Hispanic Nat. Bar Assn., Wash. State Hispanic C. of C., Seattle Athletic Club. Democrat. Roman Catholic. Home: 2010 E Lynn St Seattle WA 98112-2620 Office: Vandeberg Johnson & Gandara 600 Union St Seattle WA 98101

GANDER, JOHN EDWARD, biochemistry educator; b. Roundup, Mont., Mar. 9, 1925; s. Loren Dwight and Blanche Lenore (Mackay) G.; m. Dorothy Alice Hoffman, Jan. 1, 1951; children: Sharon Lee, Peggy Corinne, Linda Kay. B.S. in Agr, Mont. State U., 1950; M.S. in Biochemistry, U. Minn., 1954, Ph.D., 1956. Asst. prof. chemistry Mont. State U., Bozeman, 1955-58; asst. prof. agrl. biochemistry Ohio State U., Columbus, 1958-62; assoc. prof. Ohio State U., 1962-64, U. Minn., St. Paul, 1964-68; prof. biochemistry U. Minn., 1968-84; prof., chmn. dept. microbiology and cell sci. U. Fla., 1984-89, prof., 1989-97, prof. emeritus, 1997—; mem. external site visit rev. teams for Dept. Energy, USDA, NIH, 1979-93. Contbr. chpts. to books, articles to profl. jours. and encys. Served with USAAF, 1943-46. Recipient Research Career award NIH, 1966-71; research grantee USPHS, 1960-69, 74-87; research grantee NSF, 1957-75, 80-84. Mem. AAAS, Am. Soc. Biochemistry and Molecular Biology, Am. Chem. Soc., Am. Soc. Microbiology, Sigma Xi. Presbyterian. Lodge: Masons. Home: 4219 Rancho Grande Pl NW Albuquerque NM 87120-5337

GANDHI, OM PARKASH, electrical engineer; b. Multan, Pakistan, Sept. 23, 1934; came to U.S., 1967, naturalized, 1975; s. Gopal Das and Devi Bai (Patney) G.; m. Santosh Nayar, Oct. 28, 1963; children: Rajesh Timmy, Monica, Lena. BS with honors, Delhi U., India, 1952; MSE, U. Mich., 1957, Sc.D., 1961. Rsch. specialist Philco Corp., Blue Bell, Pa., 1960-62; asst. dir. Cen. Electronics Engring. Rsch. Inst., Pilani, Rajasthan, India, 1962-65, dep. dir., 1965-67; prof. elec. engring., rsch. prof. bioengring. U. Utah, Salt Lake City, 1967—; chmn. elec. engring., 1992—; cons. U.S. Army Med. R & D Command, Washington, 1973-77; cons. to microwave and telecom. industry and govtl. health and safety orgns.; mem. Commns. B and K, Internation Union Radio Sci.; mem. study sect. on diagnostic radiology NIH, 1978-81. Author: Microwave Engineering and Applications, 1981; editor: Engineering in Medicine and Biology mag., 1987, Electromagnetic Biointeraction, 1989, Biological Effects and Medical Applications of Electromagnetic Energy, 1990; contbr. over 200 articles to profl. jours. Recipient Disting. Rsch. award U. Utah, 1979-80; grantee NSF, NIH, EPA, USAF, U.S. Army, USN, N.Y. State Dept. Health, others. Fellow IEEE (editor spl. issue Procs. IEEE 1980, co-chmn. com. on RF safety stds. 1988-97, Tech. Achievement award Utah sect. 1975, Utah Engr. of Yr. 1995), Am. Inst. for Med. and Biol. Engring.; mem. Electromagnetics Acad., Bioelectromagnetics Soc. (bd. dirs. 1979-82, 87-90, v.p., pres. 1991-94, d'Arsonval award 1995). Office: Univ Utah Dept Elec Engring 3280 Merrill Engring Salt Lake City UT 84112

GANDOLF, RAYMOND L., media correspondent; b. Norwalk, Ohio, Apr. 2, 1930; s. Raymond L. Gandolf and Rose (Brenner) Gandolf Neller; m. Blanche Haywood Cholet, Oct. 13, 1956; children—Alexandra, Jessica, Victoria, Amanda, Susanna. B.S in Speech, Northwestern U., 1951. Actor, 1951-62; writer, producer WCBS-TV, N.Y.C., 1963-65; writer, corr. CBS News, N.Y.C., 1965-82; corr. ABC News-Sports, N.Y.C., 1982-92, host Our World, 1986-87. Panel mem. Dictionary of Contemporary Usage, 1985. Recipient Peabody award U. Ga., 1980, Dupont award Columbia U., 1981, Emmy award, 1987. Mem. AFTRA, Writers Guild Am. Office: ABC News 7 W 66th St New York NY 10023-6294

GANDOLFO, LUCIAN JOHN, minister, federal official; b. Chgo., Aug. 28, 1954; s. Michael and Elda (Campi) G.; m. Lisa Mary Thornton, Aug. 24, 1985; children: Landon, Lindsay, Lauren, Lucian-Michael. AA, John Jay Coll. Criminal Justice City N.Y., 1979; AS, SUNY, Albany, 1978; BS, SUNY, Briarcliff Manor, 1980; MS, L.I. U., 1982; DD (hon.), So. Calif. Grad. Sch. Theology, 1996. Ordained to ministry Christian Ch. of N.Am., 1996. Spl. agt. FBI, New Orleans, 1984-86, N.Y.C., 1986-95; supervisory spl. agt. FBI, Washington, 1995-97; supervisory sr. resident agt. FBI, Scranton, Pa., 1997—; pres. ea. dist. Christ Crusaders Christian Ch. N.Am., 1988-94; min. Italian Christian Ch., Astoria, N.Y., 1991-95, asst. pastor, 1991-94, interim pastor, 1994-95, distr. presbyter, 1996—; nat. edn. dir. Christian Ch. N.Am., 1997—. *The greatest accomplishment in one's life is to be found in right relationship with his Creator. The Greatest honor and fulfillment a person can ever experience is to receive and obey the call of God in his (her) life.*

GANDRUD, ROBERT P., fraternal insurance executive; b. 1943. Mem. actuarial staff Lutheran Brotherhood, Mpls., 1965-75, asst. v.p., 1975-76, v.p., 1976-80, sr. v.p., 1980-86, sr. exec. v.p., COO, 1986-87; pres., CEO &,

Mpls., 1987—. Office: Lutheran Brotherhood 625 4th Ave S Ste 100 Minneapolis MN 55415-1665*

GANDY, BONNIE SERGIACOMI, oncological and intravenous therapy nurse; b. Bridgeton, N.J., July 12, 1952; d. Albert A. and Jean (Goodwin) Sergiacomi; m.Robert H. Gandy, Aug. 15, 1981 (dec.); 1 child, Anthony Robert. BA, Glassboro (N.J.) State Coll., 1974; ADN, Cumberland County Coll., Vineland, N.J., 1985; BSN, U. Winston-Salem, 1999. RN, N.J., N.C., S.C., Va.; cert. tchr., N.J.; cert. oncology nurse, intravenous nurse. Staff nurse, charge nurse William B. Kessler Meml. Hosp., Hammonton, N.J., 1985-86; supr. med. outpatient unit South Jersey Hosp. System-Millville (N.J.) Div., 1986-93; dir. home care nursing Med IV Home Health Svcs., Hickory, N.C., 1994-95; IV nurse cons., IV therapist Am. Pharm. Svcs., Hickory, N.C., 1995—. Mem. Intravenous Nurse's Soc., Oncology Nursing Soc., Phi Theta Kappa.

GANDY, H. CONWAY, judge, state official; b. Washington, Nov. 3, 1934; s. Hoke and Anne B. (Conway) G.; m. Carol Anderson, Aug. 29, 1965; children: Jennifer, Constance, Margaret. *Earliest ancestor, Edwin Conway, came to Virginia circa 1640, as the recipient of a colonial land grant. His grandson, also name Edwin, married Anne Ball whose sister, Mary Ball, was the mother of George Washington. A great granddaughter of the first Edwin Conway was Eleanor Rose Conway, mothe rof President James Madison, who was born at the Conway family plantation, Belle Grove, Port Conway, Virginia. Great Grandfather, Robert Moncure Conway, served in the Confederate Army during the Civil War with Terry's Texas Rangers, while his brother, Moncure Daniel Conway, was an abolitionist whose biography is entitled Southern Emancipator.* BA, Colo. State U., 1962; JD, U. Denver, 1968. Bar: Colo. 1969, U.S. Dist. Ct. Colo. 1969. Pvt. practice Ft. Collins, Colo., 1969-81; adminstrv. law judge divsn. adminstrv. hearings State of Colo., Denver, 1981—. Bd. dirs. Foothills-Gateway Rehab. Ctr., 1970-80, Colo. State Bd. Dental Examiners, 1976-81; Dem. candidate for Colo. Senate, 1974, dist. atty., 1976; trustee Internat. Bluegrass Music Assn. Trust Fund, 1990—. With USN, 1954-58. Mem. Nat. Assn. Adminstrv. Law Judges (pres. Colo. chpt. 1985-86), Sertoma (Centurion award 1973, Tribune award 1975, Senator award 1977, 79, sec. Honor club 1977-78, pres. Ft. Collins club 1978-79, pres. Front Range club 1988-89). Home: 724 Winchester Dr Fort Collins CO 80526-2636

GANDY, JAMES THOMAS, meteorologist, entrepreneur; b. Memphis, Tenn., Nov. 25, 1952; s. Thomas Marion and Sible Christaline (McBride) G.; m. Ann Cuppia, Apr. 12, 1986. BS, Fla. State U., 1974; postgrad., U. S.C. Meteorologist Sta. WREG-TV (CBS affiliate), Memphis, 1975-77; staff meteorologist Sta. KTVY-TV (NBC affiliate), Oklahoma City, 1977-82; dir. ops. Weather Data, Inc., Wichita, Kans., 1982-84; meteorologist Kans. State Network (NBC affiliate), Wichita, 1982-84; chief meteorologist Sta. WIS-TV (NBC affiliate), Columbia, S.C., 1984-98; pres. JAG Corp. of S.C. dba Cartoon Connection, 1997—; cons. meteorologist Gannett TV, Arlington, Va., 1998—; writer, cons. The State Newspaper, Columbia, S.C., 1999—; guest lectr. U. S.C., Columbia, 1991, 95, 98; writer, cons. The State Newspaper, Columbia, S.C., 1999—. *With over 24 years of experience in the television industry, Jim Gandy built and directed the weather coverage at WIS Television. His most outstanding forecasts were the snowstorm of 1989 and Hurricane Hugo later that year. His forecast of Hugo gave state officials the needed time to prepare for the storm's arrival. He helped WIS coordinate coverage of the Superstorm in 1993, the tornado outbreak of 1994, and of hurricanes Bertha and Fran in 1996. Many came to rely on his forecasts in critical weather situations.* Named Best TV Weather Forecaster, The State Newspaper, Columbia, S.C., 1993, Best TV Weather Personality, Columbia Met. Mag., 1994, 95, 96, 97, 98. Mem. AAAS, Am. Meteorol. Soc. (TV Seal of Approval 1985, Memphis chpt. sec. 1976-77, chmn. 1977, Ctrl. Okla. chpt. sec.-treas. 1979, 82, pres. 1980, Palmetto chpt. v.p. 1988-89, 97-98, pres. 1989-90, 98-99), Nat. Weather Assn., Planetry Soc. (charter mem.), N.Y. Acad. Scis., Order Internat. Fellowship (charter). Home and Office: 101 W Ashford Way Irmo SC 29063-8325

GANGAROSA, RAYMOND EUGENE, epidemiologist, engineer; b. Rochester, N.Y., July 1, 1951; s. Eugene John and Rose Christine (Salamone) G. BA, Emory U., 1972; MSEE, Ga. Inst. Tech., 1976; MD, Med. Coll. Ga., 1980; M in Pub. Health, Emory U., 1991. Diplomate Am. Bd. Internal Medicine. Rsch. technician Electromagnetic Scis., Inc., Altanta, 1973-74; med. resident U. Md., Balt., 1980-81; clin. scientist Picker Internat., Cleve., 1981-88; vis. scientist Ctrs. for Disease Control, Atlanta, 1990—; doctoral candidate Emory U., Atlanta, 1990—; rsch. fellow Emory U. Ethics Ctr., 1994—; med. epidemiologist Ga. Divsn. Pub. Health, 1995-97; coord. Instl. Rev. Bd., Cleve., 1982-84, 86-87; cons. Novel Imager Design Team, Cleve., 1987-88. Editor Picker Internat. Newsletter, 1985-87; coord. audiovisual tng. courses for magnetic resonance imaging, 1982-84; contbr. articles to profl. and law jours. Campaign dir. David Drexel for State Senate, Chapel Hill, N.C., 1972; sculptor Toys on Request, 1982—; coord. Control Alcohol, Tobacco and Drug Use, Atlanta, 1989—. Mem. AAAS, Am. Pub. Health Assn., N.Y. Acad. Scis., Soc. for Epidemiologic Rsch. Achievements include patents in magnetic resonance imaging cardiac/respiratory gating system; in integrated expert system for medical imaging scan, setup, scheduling; in reduced weight iron core magnetic resonance scanner; invented reduced weight magnet return path using correction fields, horizontal field iron core magnetic resonance scanner, litigation strategies against tobacco companies to recover health care costs, surveillance of infant mortality and child abuse, systems approach to infant mortality and addiction.

GANGEMI, GAETANO TOMMASO, SR., computer company executive; b. Phila., Jan. 26, 1946; s. Anthony Theodore and Louise Bridget Gangemi; m. Anna Katherine Yocum, Nov. 5, 1966; children: Robina Ann Gangemi Slupski, Gaetano Tommaso Gangemi, Jr. Grad. Program for Sr. Execs. in Security, Harvard/JFK Sch. of Govt., Boston, 1990. Cert. info. system security profl., Internat. Info. Systems Security Cert. Consortium, Inc. Profl. in customer svc. orgn., rsch. and devel. Wang Labs., Inc., Lowell, Mass., 1971-97; pres., CEO CYCOMM Secure Solutions, Sebastian, Fla., 1997—; mem. Dept. Commerce Computer Systems Security and Privacy Adv. Bd., Washington. Author: Computer Security Basics, 1991. Cem. master plan adv. bd. City of Chelmsford, Mass., 1982, marine patrol aux., N. H. Divsn. Safety Svcs., Concord, N.H., 1992—. Staff sgt. U.S. Army, 1965-71. Recipient Achievement award Soc. for Tech. Publs., 1991. Mem. Internat. Systems Security Assn., Am. Soc. for Indsl. Security, Security Affairs Support Assn. Republican. Roman Catholic. Avocations: pilot, boating, pistol team. Office: CYCOMM Secure Solutions 10305 102d Ter Sebastian FL 32958

GANGEMI, J(OSEPH) DAVID, microbiology educator, biomedical researcher, research administrator, hospital administrator; b. Wilmington, Del., July 3, 1947; s. Joseph C. and Lavern (Wagener) G.; m. Nancy Elizabeth Thompson, Aug. 22, 1970; children: Stephanie Elizabeth, Alyssa Lavern, Jennifer Anne. BS, Clemson U., 1969; PhD, U. N.C., 1973. Commd. 2nd lt. U.S. Army, 1969; rsch. virologist U.S. Army, Frederick, Md., 1973-78; ret. U.S. Army, 1978; asst. prof. microbiology, immunology Sch. Medicine U. S.C., Columbia, 1978-82, assoc. prof. Sch. Medicine, 1982-90, assoc. dir. tech. transfer, 1989-92, dir. tech. transfer, 1991-92, prof. microbiology, immunology Sch. Medicine, 1991-92; sabbatical Ciba-Geigy, Basel, Switzerland, 1987-88; prof. microbiology Clemson (S.C.) U., 1991—, dir. Greenville Hosp. System/Clemson U. Biomed. Coop., 1992—; rsch. cons. Charles Pfizer Labs., Groton, Conn., 1980-83, Ciba-Geigy, Basel, 1986—, Drug Innovation and Design, Inc., Newton, Mass., 1990—; mem. tech. adv. bd. S.C. Rsch. Authority, 1996—. Contbr. articles to profl. jours.; editl. bd. Letters in Applied Microbiology, 1988—. Capt. USAR, 1978, lt. col., 1989. Mem. AAAS, Internat. Soc. Antiviral Rsch., Am. Soc. Tropical Medicine and Hygiene, Am. Thoracic Soc., S.C. Acad. Sci., S.C. br. Am. Soc. Microbiology (pres. 1983-85, Outstanding Microbiologist 1993). Roman Catholic. Avocations: hiking, fishing. Office: Clemson Univ 445 Brackett Hall Clemson SC 29634

GANGLOFF, LINDA LEE, secondary education educator, underwater photographer, writer; b. Tarentum, Pa., Aug. 8, 1942; d. Albert Carl and Mary Donna (Stennett) G. BS, Bucknell U., 1964; MA, Montclair State Coll., 1975. Cert. secondary biol. sci. and English tchr., N.J. Tchr. biology Morris Sch. Dist., Morristown, N.J., 1964-97, staff asst. sci. dept., 1974-78; ret., 1997; biology text critic reader Silver Burdett Pub. Co., Morristown, 1979; presenter N.J. Sci. Conv., 1986, Expanding Your Horizons Conf., 1993. Author, photographer (slide-cassette program) Underwater Photography, 1988-89. Vol. N.Y. Aquarium, Bklyn., 1985-87. Recipient J. Burton Wiley Scholar award Morris Sch. Dist., 1988; grantee Geraldine R. Dodge Found., 1988, Morris Sch. Dist. Ednl. Found., 1993. Mem. NEA, Nat. Assn. Biology Tchrs., Nat. Marine Educators Assn., Am. Littoral Soc., Underwater Soc. Am., Internat. Oceanographic Found., N.J. Assn. Biology Tchrs., AAUW, Alpha Phi. Lutheran. Avocation: scuba diving. Home: 17 Clairview Rd Denville NJ 07834-3301

GANGOPADHYAY, NIRMAL KANTI, mining company executive; b. Dacca, Bengal, India, Apr. 23, 1943; came to U.S. 1970; s. Madhusudan and Sudha Rani (Chakravarty) G.; children: Molly, Dolly. B.Engring., U. Calcutta, India, 1965; M.Tech., Indian Inst. Tech., Kharagpur, India, 1968; MS, U. Idaho, 1971. Registered profl. engr., Ky., Pa., Va., W.Va. Office engr. Mt. State Constrn., Charleston, W.Va., 1971-73; project engr. The Pioneer Constrn. Co., Charleston, 1973-75; chief engr. Perry & Hylton, Inc., Beckley, W.Va., 1975-87; v.p. engring. WRM, Inc., Perry & Hylton, Inc., Beckley, 1987—. Contbr. articles to profl. jours. Fund raiser Raleigh County Bus. Coalition com., Beckley, 1986. Dept. Civil Engring., U. Idaho research fellow, 1970. Mem. W.Va. Mining and Reclamation Assn. (tech. com.). Republican. Hinduism. Avocations: stamp collecting, world travel, tennis. Home: PO Box 93 Mabscott WV 25871-0093

GANGOPADHYAY, PARTHA, management educator; b. India, Mar. 19, 1961; s. Haraprasad and Mary (Mukherjee) Ganguly; m. Nabaneeta Mukherjee, May 24, 1990; children: Ankan, Arjun. BA with honors, Jadavpur U., India, 1981; MA, U. Iowa, 1991, PhD, 1993; Diploma in Mgmt., Indian Inst. Mgmt. Asst. to v.p. Blue Star Ltd., India, 1984-85; instr., grad. asst. U. Iowa, Iowa City, 1987-92; asst. prof. St. Cloud (Minn.) State U., 1992-95, assoc. prof., 1995—; cons. Kennedy Western U., Cheyenne, Wyo., 1998—. Referee Fin. Rev., Internat. Rev. of Econs. and Fin., Quar. Jour. Bus. and Econs., Jour. Econs. and Bus.; contbr. articles to profl. jours. Participant, St. Cloud Leadership Program, 1996-97. Recipient Gold medal Jadavpur U., 1981; Govt. of India Nat. Merit scholar, 1976. Mem. Fin. Mgmt. Assn., Midwest Fin. Assn., So. Fin. Assn., Southwestern Fin. Assn., Delta Sigma Pi, Beta Gamma Sigma. Avocations: chess, music, karate. Home: 2712 Stearns Way Saint Cloud MN 56303-1371 Office: St Cloud State U Coll Bus Fin/Ins/Real Estate 720 4th Ave S Saint Cloud MN 56301-4442

GANGSTAD, JOHN ERIK, lawyer; b. New Brunswick, N.J., May 16, 1948; s. Edward Otis and Ruth Margaret (Fletcher) G.; m. Cynthia Diane Coffman, July 5, 1974; children: Allison, Erik, Amy. BA, U. Tex., 1970, JD, 1974. Bar: Tex. 1974, U.S. Dist. Ct. (no. dist.) Tex. 1974. Assoc. Turner, Hitchins, McInnery, Webb & Hartnett, Dallas, 1974-76, ptnr., 1977-81; ptnr. Brown McCarroll & Oaks Hartline, L.L.P., Austin, Tex., 1982—; partnership com. State Bar Tex., 1981-98. Bd. dirs. Found. for the Homeless, Austin, 1988—. With USNG. Mem. ABA, Tex. Bar Assn., Order of Coif. Presbyterian. Avocations: golf, reading. Home: 3106 Eaneswood Dr Austin TX 78746-6717 Office: Brown McCarroll & Oaks Hartline LLP 1400 Franklin Pla 111 Congress Ave Ste 1200 Austin TX 78701-4049

GANGULY, ANANDA ROOP, business management educator; b. Calcutta, India, Oct. 19, 1963; came to U.S., 1988; s. Purna Nanda and Kalyani Ganguly. B Comm. with honors, U. Calcutta, 1985; PhD, U. Pitts., 1995. Part-time lectr. U. Pitts., 1991-95; lectr. U. Ill., Champaign/Urbana, 1995, asst. prof., 1995—; mem., cons. Round Table Group, 1997—; session chair, conf. organizer in field; ad-hoc reviewer Am. Acct. Assn., Contemporary Acctg. Rsch., 1996—; faculty advisor undergrad. case-study competitions Deloitte and Touche, 1996—. *Ph.D. major was in accounting, with a minor in economic decision-making. Research focuses on the interface between single-person decision-making and multi-person (group or market) outcomes in accounting, auditing and financial market settings. Research methodology includes computer simulations and laboratory experimentation with human subjects. Award winning teacher of accounting. Current accounting courses include strategic and economic analyses and the use of several active-learning techniques not common in traditional accounting courses. Involved with several joint activities with financial professionals, notably with Caterpillar, Inc., Deloitte & Touche, and the Assurance Services group at KPMG Peat Marwick.* Mem. focus groups Deloitte Touche Tohmatsu, Pitts., 1994; faculty mentor summer rsch. opportunities program for minority students U. Ill., 1997. Grantee/fellow Case Devel., 1993, Arthur Andersen & Co. Found., 1994, U. Pitts., 1996, U. Ill., 1997, Caterpillar Inc., 1998. Mem. Am. Acctg. Assn. (doctoral consortium fellow 1994), Am. Econ. Assn., Soc. for Computational Econs., Soc. for Judgment and Decision Making. Avocations: creative writing, computers, chess, photography, target shooting. Fax: (217) 244-0902. E-mail: aganguly@uiuc.edu. Office: U Ill Dept Accountancy MC-706 Champaign IL 61820

GANI, JOSEPH MARK, statistics educator, administrator, researcher; b. Cairo, Dec. 15, 1924; came to U.S., 1981; s. Mark Joseph and Lucie (Israel) G.; m. Ruth Stephens, Sept. 3, 1955 (dec. Jan. 1997); children: Jonathan, Miriam, Matthew, Sarah. BSc, London U., 1947; diploma, Imperial Coll., 1948; PhD, Australian Nat. U., Canberra, 1955; DSc, London U., 1970; DSc (hon.), Sheffield U., 1989, Wollongong U., 1991. Lectr. math stats. U. Western Australia, Perth, 1953-57, sr. lectr., 1957-59, reader, 1959-60; sr. fellow Australian Nat. U., 1961-64; prof. U. Sheffield, Eng., 1965-74; chief divsn. math. and stats. Commonwealth Sci. and Indsl. Research Orgn., Canberra, 1974-81; prof. stats., chmn. dept. U. Ky., Lexington, 1981-85; prof. dept. stats. U. Calif., Santa Barbara, 1985-94; ret., 1994; hon. vis. fellow Australian Nat. U., 1995-97, fellow, 1998—. Author: The Condition of Science in Australian Universities, 1963; editor: Perspectives in Probability and Statistics, 1975, The Making of Statisticians, 1982, The Craft of Probabilistic Modelling, 1986, (with D.J. Daley) Epidemic Modelling: An Introduction, 1999; mng. editor: Applied Probability Jours., 1964—; advisor: Springer-Verlag Series in Statistics, 1976-95. Gov. High Storrs Sch., Sheffield, 1971-74; founder mem. South Yorkshire Family Housing Assn., Sheffield, 1972. Nuffield Found. fellow, 1956; Australian Acad. Sci. fellow, 1976, recipient Pitman medal Statis. Soc. Australia, 1994. Fellow Inst. Math. Stats., Royal Statis. Soc., Am. Statis. Assn., mem. Am. Math. Soc., Internat. Statis. Inst., Australian Math. Soc. (pres. 1978-80). Office: Australian Nat U, Sch Math Scis, Canberra ACT 0200, Australia

GANLEY, BEATRICE, English educator, writer; b. Oct. 21, 1932. BS in Edn., Nazareth Coll., 1958, BA in English, 1964; MA in English, SUNY, Brockport, 1994. Tchr. elem. schs. Diocese of Rochester (N.Y.), 1955-66; tchr. English dept. Nazareth Acad. High Sch., Rochester, 1967-82; dir. comms. Sisters of St. Joseph, Rochester, 1984-89; lectr. English Nazareth Coll., Rochester, 1989—. Office: 4095 East Ave Rochester NY 14618-3732

GANLEY, JAMES POWELL, ophthalmologist, educator; b. Altadina, Calif., Apr. 25, 1937; s. Joseph Harrington and Ruth Alice (Carr) G.; m. Anne Hay Hunter, Aug. 7, 1965; children: Anne Hay, Susan Powell, Katherine Carr, Elizabeth Pearson. BS in Biology, Mt. St. Mary's Coll., 1959; MD, Georgetown U., 1963; MPH, Johns Hopkins U., 1969, DPH, 1972. Diplomate Am. Bd. Med. Examiners, Am. Bd. Preventive Medicine (fellow), Am. Bd. Ophthalmology (fellow). Intern Washington Hosp. Ctr., 1963-64; resident in ophthalmology SUNY Upstate Med. Ctr., Syracuse, 1965-68; resident in preventive medicine Johns Hopkins U., Balt., 1969-71; sr. staff fellow Nat. Eye Inst., NIH, Bethesda, Md., 1971-74; asst. prof. ophthalmology U. Ariz. Med. Ctr., Tucson, 1974-80; assoc. prof., dept. head La. State U. Med. Ctr., Shreveport, 1980-82, asst. dean clin. affairs, 1981-87, prof., head dept., 1982-97, prof., 1998—; mem. sci. adv. panel Onchocerciasis Control Program, WHO, Geneva, Switzerland, 1974-79; med. adv. bd., Internat. Eye Found., Bethesda, 1974-77; ophthalmic drugs adv. com. FDA, HEW, Rockville, Md., 1976-82; mem. epidemiol. and disease control study sect. NIH, 1982-86. Author: book chpts., procs.; editor Ophthalmic Epidemiology, 1993—; mem. editorial bd. Sightsaver, Nat. Soc. to Prevent Blindness, 1982-86. Bd. dirs. Northwest Lions Eye Bank, Shreveport, 1987. Lt. USN, 1964-65. Mem. Am. Coll. Preventive Medicine, Am. Acad. Ophthalmology (com. rsch. regulatory agys. and fed. sys. 1986-91, chmn. 1990-91), Internat. Soc. Geog. Ophthalmology (pres. 1982-88, treas. 1988—, exec. bd. 1988—), Am. Coll. Epidemiology, La. Assn. Blind (bd. dirs. 1980-96, 1st vice chmn., sec. exec. bd. 1989-91, chmn. bd. 1992-93), Shreveport Med. Soc. (bd. dirs. 1990-96, 2d v.p. 1993, 1st v.p. 1994, pres. 1995), Assn. Rsch. in Vision and Ophthalmology (program planning com. 1993-96), Revs. Rsch. NIH. Republican. Roman Catholic. Avocations: tennis, swimming, sailing. Office: La State Univ Med Ctr 1501 Kings Hwy Shreveport LA 71103-4228

GANLEY, OSWALD HAROLD, university official; b. Amsterdam, The Netherlands, Jan. 28, 1929; came to U.S., 1947, naturalized, 1952; s. Eric Harold and Emily (Auerbach) G.; m. Gladys Dickens, Sept. 3, 1950; children: Robert C., Delia A. AB, Hope Coll., 1950; MS, PhD, U. Mich., 1953; MPA, Harvard U., 1965. Cert. physician asst. Rsch. asst. Walter Reed Inst., 1953-55; rsch. assoc. Merck Inst. Therapeutic Rsch., Rahway, N.J., 1955-60; asst. dir. internat. rels. Merck, Sharp and Dohme Rsch. Labs., Rahway, 1960-64; head tech. div. Bur. Internat. Sci. and Tech. Affairs, State Dept., 1965-66, head European affairs, 1966-69; sci. attaché Am. Embassy, Rome and Bucharest, 1969-73; dir. Soviet and Eastern European sci. and tech. affairs State Dept., Washington, 1973-75; diplomatic sci. adv. to pres. Washington, 1973-78; dep. asst. sec. for tech. affairs State Dept., Washington, 1975-78; rsch. assoc. John F. Kennedy Sch. Govt. Harvard U., Cambridge, Mass., 1978-80; exec. dir. Harvard Program Info. Resources Policy, 1980-94; ret., 1994; lectr. in pub. policy, Harvard U. 1980-94, Cardiology Assocs., Duke U. Med. Ctr., 1997—. Author: To Inform or to Control?, 1982, 2d edit., 1989, The Global Political Impact of VCRs, 1987; contbr. articles to sci. jours. Bd. dirs. Jaycees, 1958-60, Am. Hosp., Rome, Fulbright Commn., Ctr. Info. Policy Rsch., 1992—; dir. pub. rels. Civil Def., Plainfield, N.J., 1962-64. Served with AUS, 1953-55, USPHS Res., 1956-84. Sci. and Pub. Policy fellow Harvard U., 1964-65. Fellow Am. Acad. Physician Assts., Am. Acad. Microbiology; mem. Am. Physiol. Soc., Am. Soc. Microbiology, Assn. Mil. Surgeons, Sigma Xi. Clubs: Circolo Catoniere Tevereremo (Rome); Cosmos; Harvard (N.Y.C.). Home: 408 N Estes Dr Chapel Hill NC 27514-7629

GANN, BENARD WAYNE, air force officer; b. Nacogdoches, Tex., Dec. 28, 1939; s. Ewell Benard and Lois Marquerite (Heaberlin) G.; m. Genelle Lynn Amason, Oct. 8, 1944; children: Scott, Mason, Ashley. BBA in Fin., Baylor U., 1962; MS in Counseling, Troy State U., 1975; grad., Air Command and Staff Coll., Montgomery, Ala., 1975, Indsl. Coll. of the Armed Forces, 1977, Air War Coll., Montgomery, Ala., 1983. Commd. 2d lt. USAF, 1963, advanced through grades to brig. gen., 1989; chief aircrew assignments AF Manpower and Pers. Ctr., Randolph AFB, Tex., 1977-81; comdr. 51st Bomb Squadron, Seymour Johnson AFB, N.C., 1981-82; chief aircrew tng. Hdqrs. Strategic Air Command, Offutt AFB, Nebr., 1983-84; dir. ops. 43 Strategic Wing, Andersen AFB, Guam, 1984-85, vice comdr., 1985-86; comdr. 5 Bomb Wing, Minot AFB, N.D., 1986-88, 43 Bomb Wing, Andersen AFB, Guam, 1988-89; dir. strategy and policy Hdqrs. U.S. So. Command, Quarry Heights, Panama, 1989-91; dep. comdr. Can. NORAD Region, North Bay, 1991-1993; fin. cons. Merrill Lynch, Inc., 1994-97; prin. Everen Securities, Inc., 1997—. Contbr. articles to profl. jours. Decorated Bronze Star, Legion of Merit, Def. D.S.M. Mem. Air Force Assn., Daedalians, Tryon Coterie (pres. Baylor U. chpt. 1962). Republican. Avocation: golf. Office: 110 N College Ave Ste 100 Tyler TX 75702-7229

GANN, PAMELA BROOKS, academic administrator; b. 1948. BA, U. N.C., 1970; JD, Duke U., 1973. Bar: Ga. 1973, N.C. 1974. Assoc. King & Spalding, Atlanta, 1973, Robinson, Bradshaw & Hinson, P.A., Charlotte, N.C., 1974-75; asst. prof. Duke U. Sch. Law, Durham, N.C., 1975-78, assoc. prof., 1978-80, prof., 1980-99, dean, 1988-99; pres. Claremont McKenna Coll., Claremont, Calif., 1999—; vis. asst. prof. U. Mich. Law Sch., 1977; vis. assoc. prof. U. Va., 1980. Author: (with D. Kahn) Corporate Taxation and Taxation of Partnerships and Partners, 1979, 83, 89; article editor Duke Law Jour. Mem. Am. Law Inst., Coun. Fgn. Rels., Order of Coif, Phi Beta Kappa. Office: Claremont McKenna Coll Office of the Pres 500 E 9th St Claremont CA 91711-6400

GANNON, SISTER ANN IDA, retired philosophy educator, former college administrator; b. Chgo., 1915; d. George and Hanna (Murphy) G. A.B., Clarke Coll., 1941; A.M., Loyola U., Chgo., 1948, LL.D., 1970; Ph.D., St. Louis U., 1952; Litt.D., DePaul U., 1972; L.H.D., Lincoln Coll., 1965, Columbia Coll., 1969, Luther Coll., 1969, Marycrest Coll., 1972, Ursuline Coll., 1972, Spertus Coll. Judaica, 1974, Holy Cross Coll., 1974, Rosary Coll., 1975, St. Ambrose Coll., 1975, St. Leo Coll., 1976, Mt. St. Joseph Coll., 1976, Stritch Coll., 1976, Stonehill Coll., 1976, Elmhurst Coll., 1977, Manchester Coll., 1977, Marymount Coll., 1977, Governor's State U., 1979, Seattle U., 1981, St. Michael's Coll., 1984, Nazareth Coll., 1985, Holy Family Coll., 1986, Keller Grad. Sch. Mgmt., Our Lady of Holy Cross Coll., New Orleans, 1988. Mem. Sisters of Charity, B.V.M.; tchr. English St. Mary's High Sch., Chgo., 1941-47; residence, study abroad, 1951; chmn. philosophy dept. Mundelein Coll., 1951-57, pres., 1957-75, prof. philosophy, 1975-85, emeritus faculty, 1987—, archivist, 1986—. Contbr. articles philos. jours. Mem. adv. bd. Sec. Navy, 1975-80, Chgo. Police Bd., 1979-89; bd. dirs. Am. Coun. on Edn., 1971-75, chmn., 1973-74; nat. bd. dirs. Girl Scouts USA, 1966-74, nat. adv., 1976-85; trustee St. Louis U., 1974-87, Ursuline Coll., 1978-92, Cath. Theol. Union, 1983-89, DeVry, Inc., 1987-98, Duquesne U., 1989-91, Montay Coll., 1993-95; bd. dirs. Newberry Libr., 1976—, WTTW Pub. TV, 1976—, Parkside Human Svcs. Corp., 1983-89. Recipient Laetare medal, 1975, LaSallian award, 1975, Aquinas award, 1976, Chgo. Assn. Commerce and Industry award, 1976, Hesburgh award, 1982, Woman of Distinction award Nat. Conf. Women Student Leaders, 1985, Outstanding Svc. award Coun. Ind. Colls., 1989, Woman of History award for edn. AAUW, 1989; named One of 100 Outstanding Chgo. Women, Culture in Action, 1994. Mem. Am. Cath. Philos. Assn. (exec. coun. 1953-56), Assn. Am. Colls. (bd. dirs. 1965-70, chmn. 1969-70), Religious Edn. Assn. Am. (pres. 1973, chmn. bd. 1975-78), North Cen. Assn. (commn. on colls. and univs. 1971-78, chmn. exec. bd. 1975-77, bd. dirs.), Assn. Governing Bds. Colls. and Univs. (bd. dirs. 1979-88, hon. bd. dirs. 1989-92), Alpha Sigma Nu. Office: Loyola U Office Archives Sullivan Ctr 6525 N Sheridan Rd Chicago IL 60626-5344 Home: Loyola U Coffey Hall 6525 N Sheridan Rd Chicago IL 60626-5311

GANNON, JAMES PATRICK, newspaper editor; b. Mpls., July 6, 1939; s. Lawrence Patrick and Nora G.; m. Joan Dorothy Ring, Aug. 12, 1961; children: Julia, Michael, Elizabeth, Virginia, Christopher, Marcella. B.A., Marquette U., Milw., 1961. With Wall St. Jour., 1961-78, chief econ. writer, 1973-76, polit. writer, 1976-78; exec. editor, v.p. Des Moines Register and Tribune, 1978-82, editor, 1982-89; Washington Bur. chief, columnist The Detroit News, 1989-94; nat. affairs columnist Gannett News Svc., Washington, 1989-95; freelance writer, civil war historian Castleton, Va., 1995—. Mem. Nat. Press Club. Roman Catholic. *

GANNON, JOHN SEXTON, lawyer, management consultant, arbitrator/mediator; b. East Orange, N.J., Apr. 7, 1927; s. John Joseph and Agnes (Sexton) G.; m. Diane Ditchy, Aug. 11, 1951; children: Mary Catherine, John, Laine Elizabeth, James. BA, U. Mich., 1951; JD, Wayne State U., Detroit, 1961. Bar: Mich. 1962, Tenn. 1971, U.S. Ct. Appeals (6th cir.) 1977, U.S. Dist. Ct. (mid. dist.) 1989; approved mediator Tenn. Supreme Ct. Labor negotiator, mgr. employee rels. Chrysler Corp., Highland Park, Mich., 1951-61; labor counsel, mgr. employee rels. Ex-Cell-O Corp., Highland Park, 1961-65; assoc. Constangy & Powell, Atlanta, 1966; v.p. employee rels., labor counsel Werthan Industries, Nashville, 1967-80; ptnr. Dearborn & Ewing, Nashville, 1980-90; pvt. practice Nashville, 1991—; mem. adj. faculty Owens Sch., Vanderbilt U., Nashville, 1975-85; instr. Soc. Human Resource Mgmt. Profl. cert. program Mid. Tenn. State U., 1993—; pres. Employee Rels. Svcs., Inc., Nashville, 1987—. Contbr. articles to profl. jours. Mem. Birmingham (Mich.) Bd. Zoning Appeals, 1963-66; mem. Human Rels. Commn., Nashville, 1979-89; chmn. Tenn. Citizens for Ct. Modernization, Nashville, 1979-80; mem. Pvt. Industry Coun., Nashville, 1986-95. With USN, 1945-47. Mem. ABA, FBA (chmn. sr. lawyers divsn. mediatin and arbitration com.), Tenn. Bar Assn., Mich. Bar Assn., Nashville Bar Assn., Soc. Human Resource Mgmt., Am. Arbitration Assn. (panel employment mediators and arbitrators), Univ. Club, Hillwood Country Club, Kiwanis. Home: 216 Jackson Blvd Nashville TN 37205-3300

GANNON, ROBERT HAINES, writing educator, writer; b. White Plains, N.Y., Mar. 5, 1931; s. John Albert and Dorothy Belle (Merrick) G.; m. Melady Kehm, Oct. 25, 1991. Student, Miami U. Ohio, 1949-53, Columbia U., 1955, NYU, 1958. Assoc. prof. English Pa. State U., University Park, 1974—; freelance writer, 1959—. Author: Hellions of the Deep; The

Development of American Torpedoes in World War II, 1996, Best Science Writing; Readings and Insights, 1991, Article Writing, 1989, Half Mile Up Without an Engine--the Excitement, the Essentials of Soaring, 1982, Why Your House May Endanger Your Health, 1980, Pennsylvania Burning, 1976, Great Survival Adventures, 1973, What's Under a Rock?, 1971, Time is Short and the Water Rises, 1967, The Complete Book of Archery, 1963; contbg. editor Popular Sci. Mag., 1965—; contbr. articles to profl. jours. Home: 334 E Howard St Bellefonte PA 16823-1814 Office: Pa State Univ English Dept 103 Burrowes Bldg University Park PA 16802-6200

GANOE, CHARLES STRATFORD, banker, consultant; b. Abington, Pa., July 16, 1929; s. Robert L. and Leonette (Rehfuss) G.; m. Frances-Sue Williams, Apr. 2, 1960; children: F. Hemsley, Alice N. BA, Princeton U., 1951; MBA, U. Pa., 1952. With Fidelity-Phila Trust Co. (now 1st Union Bank), 1952—; asst. treas., 1956-60; asst. v.p. Fidelity-Phila Trust Co. (now 1st Union Bank), 1960-61, v.p., 1961-66, sr. v.p., 1966-69, exec. v.p. charge internat. dept., 1969-75, sr. exec. v.p., dir., 1975-79; exec. v.p. N.Y. Bank for Savs., N.Y.C., 1979-82; sr. v.p. Am. Express Internat. Banking Corp., N.Y.C., 1982-84, 1st Am. Bank of N.Y., N.Y.C., 1984-91; mng. dir. FMS Group inc., Blue Bell, Pa., 1991-94; pres. Ganoe Assocs., Inc., Princeton, N.J., 1995—; v.p. Co. for Investing Abroad (became Fidelity Internat. Corp., merged into Fidelity Internat. Bank 1972), 1963-65, pres., bd. dir., 1965-72; bd. dir., chmn. exec. com. Fidelity Internat. Bank, N.Y.C., 1970-79; mem. adv. com. Export-Import Bank U.S., 1973-74. Co-author: Offshore Lending by U.S. Commercial Banks; contbr. articles to profl. jours. Class agt. Class of 1951 Princeton U., 1954-56, treas., 1956-61, v.p., 1981-85, pres., 1985-86; bd. dirs. Phila. Coun. for Internat. Visitors, 1963-69, chmn., 1969-73; mem. Phila. Dist. Export Coun., 1966-75. Mem. Bankers Assn. for Fgn. Trade (bd. dirs. 1969—, v.p. 1971-72, exec. v.p. 1972-73, pres. 1973-74), Robert Morris Assocs. (past pres. Phila. chpt., Duning Meml. awards 1962, 65, 68), Greater Phila. C. of C. (sec. 1960-64, treas. 1960-70, bd. dirs. 1960-73, mem. adminstrv. com.), Wharton Grad. Sch. Alumni Assn. (past pres.), Coun. Fgn. Rels., Merion Cricket Club (Haverford, Pa.), Princeton Club (N.Y.C.), Princeton (N.J.) Elm Club, Ausable Club (St. Huberts, N.Y.), Delta Psi. Home: 23 Constitution Hl Princeton NJ 08540 Office: Ganoe Assocs 475 Wall St Princeton NJ 08540-1509

GANONG, WILLIAM F(RANCIS), physiologist, physician; b. Northampton, Mass., July 6, 1924; s. William Francis and Anna (Hobbet) G.; m. Ruth Jackson, Feb. 22, 1948; children: William Francis III, Susan B., Anna H., James E. AB cum laude, Harvard U., 1945, MD magna cum laude, 1949; DSc (hon.), Med. Coll. Ohio, 1995. Intern, jr. asst. resident in medicine Peter Bent Brigham Hosp., Boston, 1949-51; asst. in medicine and surgery Peter Bent Brigham Hosp., 1952-55; research fellow medicine and surgery Harvard U., 1952-55; asst. prof. physiology U. Calif., San Francisco, 1955-60; assoc. prof. U. Calif., 1960-64, prof., 1964-82, Jack D. and Deloris Lange prof., 1982-91, Lange prof. emeritus, 1991—, faculty research lectr., 1968, vice chmn. dept., 1963-68, chmn., 1970-87; cons. Calif. Dept. Mental Hygiene. Author: Review of Medical Physiology, 19th edit., 1999, Physiology: A Study Guide, 3d edit., 1989; editor: (with L. Martini) Neuroendocrinology, vol. I, 1966, vol. II, 1967, Frontiers in Neuroendocrinology, 1969, 71, 73, 76, 78, 80, 82, 84, 86, 88, (with S. McPhee, V. Lingappa and J. Lange) Pathophysiology of Disease, 1995, 3d edit., 1999; editor-in-chief Neuroendocrinology, 1979-84; co-editor Frontiers in Neuroendocrinology, 1990—. Served with U.S. Army, 1943-46; served to capt. M.C. 1951-52. Recipient Boylston Med. Soc. prize Harvard U., 1949, A.A. Berthold medal, 1985, Lifetime Achievement award High Blood Pressure Rsch. Coun., Am. Heart Assn., 1995; named Disting. Svc. mem. Assn. Med. Colls., 1988. Felow AAAS; mem. Am. Physiol. Soc. (pres. 1977-78), Assn. Chairmen Depts. Physiology (pres. 1976-77), Am. Soc. for Gravitational and Space Biology (bd. dirs. 1984-87), Soc. Exptl. Biology and Medicine (councillor 1989-93), Endocrine Soc., Chilean Endocrine Soc. (corr.), Internat. Brain Rsch. Orgn., Soc. for Neurosci., Internat. Soc. Neuroendocrinology (hon., v.p. 1976-80). Home: 710 Hillside Ave Albany CA 94706-1022 Office: U Calif Dept Physiology San Francisco CA 94143-0444

GANS, CARL, zoologist, educator; b. Hamburg, Germany, Sept. 7, 1923; came to U.S., 1939, naturalized, 1945; s. Samuel S. and Else Hubertine (Leeser) G.; m. Kyoko Andow, Nov. 18, 1961. BME, NYU, 1944; MS, Columbia U., 1950; PhD in Biology, Harvard U., 1957; PhD (hon.), U. Antwerpen, Belgium, 1985. Contract and svc. engr. Babcock & Wilcox Co., 1947-55; from asst. prof. to prof. biology, chmn. dept. biology SUNY, Buffalo, 1958-71; prof. zoology U. Mich., Ann Arbor, 1971-98; chmn. dept. U. Mich., 1971-75; prof. emeritus U. Mich., MI, 1998—; adj. prof. zoology U. Tex., Austin; rsch. assoc. Carnegie Mus., 1953—, Am. Mus. Natural History, 1958—; prof. lab. comparative anatomy Nat. Mus. Natural History, Paris, 1985, assoc., 1989—; guest prof. biology U. Antwerpen, 1985-86; sec., bd. dirs. Zool. Soc. Buffalo, 1961-71; mem. adv. coun. Detroit Zool. Pk., 1973-90; cons. in field; vis. prof. univs. and colls.; rsch. assoc. Mus. Zool. Kans., 1982—. Author: Biomechanics, 1974, Reptiles of the World, 1975; co-author: Photographic Atlas of Shark Anatomy, 1964, Electromyography for Experimentalists, 1986; gen. editor Biology of the Reptilia, 19 vols., 1969-91; editor Jour. Morphology, 1968-95. Internat. adv. coun. Nat. Collections Natural History Hebrew U., Jerusalem, 1997—. Served with AUS, 1944-47. Guggenheim fellow, 1953, 77; NSF predoctoral fellow, 1956-57; postdoctoral fellow U. Fla., Gainesville, 1957-58; grantee NSF, NIH; recipient Gold medal Royal Zool. Soc., Antwerpen, 1985. Fellow N.Y. Zool. Soc., Zool. Soc. London, AAAS, Animal Behavior Soc., Zool. Soc. India, Acad. Zoology India; mem. Am. Soc. Zoologists (pres. 1977), ASME, Soc. Study Evolution (v.p. 1971), Am. Soc. Ichthyology and Herpetology (gov. 1961, 70, 76, pres. 1979), Am. Inst. Biol. Scis. (gov. bd. 1975-78), Soc. Study Amphibians and Reptiles (pres. 1983), Am. Assn. Anatomists, Soc. Exptl. Biology, Am. Physiol. Soc., Senckenberg. Naturforsch. Gesellschaft (corr.). Achievements include 1 U.S. patent and 1 German patent. Home: 2501 Slow Turtle Cv Austin TX 78746-2317 Office: Univ Tex Dept Zool Austin TX 78712

GANS, CURTIS B., think tank administrator. AB, U. N.C., 1959. Dir., v.p. Com. for the Study of the Am. Electorate, 1977—; reporter Miami News, UPI; dir. Com. Study of the Am. Electorate; cons. Woodrow Wilson Ctr. Internat. Scholars, Nat. Com. for Effective Congress. Contbr. articles to reviews including The Atlantic, Public Opinion, The Washington Monthly, The Nation, The New Republic, Social Policy, The N.Y. Times Book Rev., Book World, books and anthologies; guest Today, Good Morning Am., All Things Considered, The McNeil-Lehrer Report. Served with USMC Res. Avocations: baseball. Office: Com Study of Am Electorate 421 New Jersey Ave SE Washington DC 20003-4007*

GANS, DENNIS JOSEPH, information technology solutions specialist; b. Yokohama, Japan, Sept. 7, 1949; came to U.S., 1951; s. Harry Leo and Hope Lorene (Everett) G.; m. Carolyn Johnson O'Grady, 1986; 1 child, Erik Christopher. BS in Bldg Constrn. (Engrng./Mgmt.), Tex. A&M U., 1971. Project mgr. D.C.B., Inc., 1972-73, 78-79, 86-87; quality control engr. Martin Zachry, Kwajalein, Marshall Islands, 1975-76; co-owner B.G.S.Y. Enterprises, Denver, 1975; project mgr. State of Colo., 1977-78, 79-80; co-owner Denver Skatewear, 1978-80; mgr. scheduling Morrison Knudsen, Zaire, 1980-82; constrn. engr. Bechtel Internat., Jubail, Saudi Arabia, 1982; project mgr. Village at Breckenridge (Colo.) Resort, 1984-86; sr. buyer Hewlett Packard Co, Roseville, Calif., 1988-91, bus. analyst, 1991-95, info. tech. specialist, 1995-98, info. tech. solutions specialist, 1998—. Deacon, Presbyn. Ch. U.S.A.; mem. Comty. Archtl. Com.; vis. scientist elem. schs. Mem. Tex. A&M U. Assn. Former Students, Sierra Club. Republican. Avocations: golf, personal computers, photography, model rocketry. Home: 4611 Nassau Ct Rocklin CA 95765-5210

GANS, EUGENE HOWARD, cosmetic and pharmaceutical company executive; b. N.Y.C., Dec. 17, 1929; m. 1953; 2 children. BS, Columbia U., 1951, MS, 1953; PhD, U. Wis., 1956. Lab. asst. Columbia U., 1951-53; sr. scientist group leader Hoffman-LaRouche, Inc., N.J., 1956-60; head new product devel. sect. Vick Div. Research and Devel. Labs. Richardson-Merrell, N.Y., 1960-64, asst. dir. devel., 1964-67, dir., 1967-71; assoc. dir. Alza Inst. Pharm. Chemistry, 1971-72; dir. research Vicks Personal Care div. Richardson-Vicks div. Proctor-Gamble, Shelton, Conn., 1972-76, v.p., dir. research and devel., 1976-87; pres. Hastings Assocs., Westport, Conn., 1987—, Lincoln Techs., Westport, Conn., 1989—; chmn. ctrl. rsch. Medicis Pharm. Co., Phoenix, 1992—; chmn. proprietary drug task group FDA, 1976-86, chmn. non-prescription drug mfg. assn. task group, 1996—; chmn. sci. adv. com. Cosmetic, Toiletry and Fragrance Assn., Washington, 1984-86. Mem. Am. Pharm. Assn., Am. Chem. Soc., Am. Acad. Dermatology, Soc. Investigative Dermatology, Sigma Xi. Office: 5101 N Casa Blanca Dr #223 Scottsdale AZ 85253-6988

GANS, HERBERT J., sociologist, educator; b. Cologne, Germany, May 7, 1927; came to U.S., 1940, naturalized, 1945; s. Carl M. and Elise (Plaut) G.; m. Louise Gruner, Mar. 19, 1967; 1 son, David. PhB, U. Chgo., 1947, MA, 1950; PhD, U. Pa., 1957. Planner pvt. and pub. planning agys. Chgo. and Washington, 1950-53; from lectr. to asso. prof. urban studies and planning U. Pa., 1953-64; from asso. prof. to adj. prof. sociology Tchrs. Coll., Columbia, also sr. staff scientist Center Urban Edn., 1964-69; prof. sociology and planning Mass. Inst. Tech., also Mass. Inst. Tech.-Harvard Joint Center for Urban Studies, 1969-71; prof. sociology Columbia (Ford Found. Urban chair), 1971—; Robert S. Lynd prof. sociology Columbia U., 1985—; sr. fellow Gannett Ctr. for Media Studies, falls 1985, 86, Media Studies ctr., 1996-97; vis. scholar Russell Sage Found., 1989-90; film critic Social Policy mag., 1971-78; cons. Ford Found., HEW, Nat. Adv. Commn. Civil Disorders. Author: The Urban Villagers, 1962, 2d edit., 1982, The Levittowners, 1967, 82, People and Plans, 1968, More Equality, 1973, Popular Culture and High Culture, 1974, Deciding What's News, 1979 (Theatre Library Assn. award 1979, 1980 Book award Nat. Assn. Ednl. Broadcasters), Middle American Individualism, 1988, 91, People, Plans and Policies, 1991, 94, The War Against the Poor, 1995, 96 (Pass award Nat. Coun. Crime and Delinquency 1996, Gustavus Myers award on human rights 1996, Choice Outstanding Acad. Book 1996), Making Sense of America, 1999; Popular Culture and High Culture, revised and updated edit., 1999; co-editor: On the Making of Americans, 1979; editor: Sociology in America, 1990; adv. editor Jour. Am. Inst. Planners, 1965-75, Urban Life (name now Jour. Contemporary Ethnography), 1971—, Am. Jour. Sociology, 1972-74, Society, 1971-76, Social Policy, 1971—, Pub. Opinion Quar., 1972-86, Jour. Comms., 1974-91, Ethnic and Racial Studies, 1977-89, 95—, Internat. Ency. Comms., 1984-88, The Am. Sociologist, 1991-95, Georgetown Jour. Fighting Poverty, 1992—, Critical Studies in Mass Communication, 1992—. Bd. dirs. Ams. for Dem. Action, 1969-75, Met. (formerly Suburban) Action Inst., 1974-85, Human Serve Inst., 1987—, Workers Def. League, 1992—, Working Today, 1995—, Rsch. Coun. Jt. Project on Equality, 1996—, Nat. Jobs for All Coalition, 1996. With AUS, 1945-46. Recipient Excelsior award SUNY, Albany, 1987, award for disting. contbn. to media and media studies Freedom Forum Media Studies Ctr., 1995; Guggenheim fellow, 1977-78, rsch. fellow German Marshall Fund, 1984. Fellow Am. Acad. Arts and Scis.; mem. Am. Sociol. Assn. (exec. coun. 1968-71, pres. 1988, Lynd award for lifetime contbn. to rsch. cmty. and urban sociology sect.), Ea. Sociol. Soc. (pres. 1972, Merit award, 1995), Sociol. Rsch. Assn., German Sociol. Assn. (hon.). Office: Columbia U 404 Fayerweather Hall New York NY 10027

GANS, ROGER FREDERICK, mechanical engineering educator; b. N.Y.C., May 5, 1941; s. Frederick Charles and Priscilla (Bacon) G.; m. Janet Hana Slavens, Aug. 25, 1971. BS in Earth Sci., MIT, 1963; MS in Geology, UCLA, 1968, PhD in Geology, 1969. Registered profl. engr., N.Y. Rsch. assoc. in geol. scis. Calif. Inst. Tech., Pasadena, 1969-71; instr. in applied math. MIT, Cambridge, 1971-73, rsch. assoc. in aerospace/astronautics, 1973-74; asst. prof. to prof. mech. engrng. U. Rochester, N.Y., 1974—, chmn. dept., 1984-92. Contbr. to textbook, numerous sci. and tech. articles to profl. jours. Fellow Woods Hole Oceanographic Inst., summer 1969. Mem. ASME, Am. Phys. Soc., Am. Geophys. Union, Sigma Xi. Avocations: stage acting, emergency medicine. Office: U Rochester Dept Mech Engrng Rochester NY 14627

GANS, SAMUEL MYER, temporary employment service executive; b. Phila., June 10, 1925; s. Arthur and Goldie (Goldhirsh) G.; grad. in acctg. Peirce Jr. Coll., 1946-49; m. Ada S. Zuckerman, Aug. 1, 1948; children: Gary M., Jeffrey R. Public acct., 1949-55; sales exec., 1955-58; franchise owner, pres., chief exec. officer Manpower, Inc. Delaware Valley, Pennsauken, N.J., 1958-86; owner Micrographic Services Inc., Pennsauken, 1975—; with All-state Services Inc., County Maintenance Corp., Affiliated Personnel Svc.; owner Antique & Classic Cars Storage Garage Inc., Voorhees, N.J. ; franchise cons.; instr. motivation courses. v.p., exec. bd. United Fund Camden County; v.p., bd. dirs. So. N.J. Devel. Coun., ARC Camden County, Nat. Conf. of Christian and Jews; bd. mgrs. Am. Cancer Soc. Camden County; active Boy Scouts Am., Employer Legis. Com., Camden County Bicentennial Com., Score and Ace programs, Camden, YMCA, Allied Jewish Appeal, World Affairs Coun.; mem. N.J. Gov.'s Mgmt. Commn., 1971; trustee Camden County Heart Assn., Camden County Mental Health Assn.; exec. bd., founder Big Bros. Assn. Camden County; pub. rels. com. U.S. Savs. Bonds, Camden and Trenton. Served with USNR, 1943-46. Mem. Nat. Assn. Temp. Services (chpt. relations com. 1973), Nat. Soc. Public Accts., Camden County C. of C., S. Jersey Public Relations Assn. (pres. 1967), S. Jersey Mfg. Assn. (exec. bd., treas.), S. Jersey Personnel Assn. (treas.), Cherry Hill C. of C. (bd. dirs., v.p.), Better Bus. Bur. Camden County, Adminstrv. Mgmt. Soc., N.J. Assn. Temp. Services (pres. 1970-72, bd. dirs.), South Jersey Purchasing Agts. Assn., Assn. of Manpower Franchise Owners, Jewish War Veterans; Jewish (exec. bd. dirs. congregation). Club: Dolphin Beach Condo. Lodges: Masons, Lions (pres. Camden 1972-73, Lion of Year 1977), Shriners, B'Nai B'Rith. Home: 4 N Derby Ave Ventnor City NJ 08406-2356 Office: 3801 Marlton Pike Camden NJ 08105-3312

GANSKE, J. GREG, congressman, plastic surgeon; b. New Hampton, Iowa, Mar. 31, 1949; s. Victor Wilber and Mary Jo (O'Donnell) G.; m. Corrine Mikkelson, 1976; children: Ingrid, Briget, Karl. BA, U. Iowa, 1972, MD, 1976. Diplomate Am. Bd. Plastic Surgery, Am. Bd. Surgery. Intern in gen. surgery U. Colo. Med. Ctr., Denver, 1976-78; resident in gen. surgery U. Oreg. Health Sci. Ctr., Portland, 1978-81, chief resident in gen. surgery, 1981-82; resident in plastic surgery Harvard Med. Sch., Boston, 1982-84; chief resident plastic surgery Brigham and Women's Hosp. and Children's Hosp., 1983-84; pvt. practice plastic/reconstructive surgeon Des Moines, 1984-94; mem. 105th-106th Congresses, Washington, 1994—; mem. commerce com.; mem. staff Iowa Luth. Hosp., Iowa Meth. Med. Ctr., Mercy Hosp. Med. Ctr., Vets. Hosp., Charter Cmty. Hosp., Des Moines Gen. Hosp. Lt. col. M.C., USAR, 1984—. Fellow ACS, Am. Soc. Plastic and Reconstructive Surgeons; mem. AMA, Am. Assn. Plastic Surgeons, Iowa Med. Soc., Polk County Med. Soc., Iowa Soc. Plastic and Reconstructive Surgeons, Am. Assn. Hand Surgery, Midwestern Assn. Plastic Surgeons, Am. Soc. for Surgery of the Hand, Iowa Acad. Surgery, Am. Cleft Palate-Craniofacial Assn. Republican. Roman Catholic. Home: 5206 Waterbury Rd Des Moines IA 50312-1922 Office: US Ho of Reps 1108 Longworth HOB Washington DC 20515-1504*

GANSKE, VICKI SMITH, lawyer; b. Lubbock, Tex., Sept. 16, 1947; d. Richard Claire Smith and Virginia (Collier) Frances; m. Frederick C. Ganske, Dec. 27, 1969; children: Richard F., Charles D. BA in Speech, Tex. Tech. U., 1969, JD, 1977. Bar: Tex. 1977; cert. residential real estate Tex. Bd. Legal Specialization. Tchr. English J.F. Kennedy H.S., Agana, Guam, 1973-74; briefing atty. Ct. of Civil Appeals, Ft. Worth, 1978-80; staff atty. Tandy Corp., 1980-82; sole practice Ft. Worth, 1982-87; v.p., corp. counsel Foster Mortgage Corp., 1987-92; of counsel Hunter & Cameron, Ft. Worth, 1992—. Author, editor: Residential Loan Origination State Disclosures & Regulations, 1994. Mem. Tarrant County Young Lawyers (pres. 1982), Tarrant County Women's Bar Assn. (pres., archivist), Tarrant County Bar Assn., Consumer Credit Counseling Svc. Greater Ft. Worth (chair). Home: 2225 Goldenrod Ave Fort Worth TX 76111-1610 Office: Hunter & Cameron Ste 1115 1701 River Run Fort Worth TX 76107-6579

GANSLER, JACQUES SINGLETON, executive in acquisition and technology; b. Newark, Nov. 21, 1934. BE, Yale U., 1956; MSEE, Northea. U., 1959; MA in Polit. Econ., New Sch. for Social Rsch., 1972; PhD in Econs., Am. Coll., 1978. V.p. program mgmt. Singer Corp.; v.p. ITT Corp., 1970-72; dep. asst. def. sec. U.S. Govt.; engrng. mgmt. dir. Raytheon Corp.; exec. v.p, dir. TASC, Inc., 1977-97; undersec. of def. for acquisition and tech. U.S. Govt.; vis. scholar at Kennedy Sch. of Govt. Harvard U.; hon. prof., Indsl. Coll. of Armed Forces; vis. prof. U. Va. Author: The Defense Industry, 1980, Affording Defense, 1989, Defense Conversion: Transforming the Arsenal of Democracy, 1995; contbr. author to 12 books on nat. security, rsch. and devel. mgmt. and pub. adminstr.; contbr. articles to profl. jours. Office: Under Sec of Def Acquisition and Tech 3D933 Defense Pentagon Washington DC 20301-3010

GANSLER, ROBERT, professional soccer coach; b. Mucsi, Hungary, July 1, 1941; came to U.S., 1952; m. Nancy Gansler; children: Robert, MIchael, Peter, Daniel. Grad., Marquette U., 1964. Head coach Kansas City Wizards/MLS, 1999—. Office: care Kansas City Wizards 706 Broadway Ste 100 Kansas City MO 64105*

GANT, DONALD ROSS, investment banker; b. Long Branch, N.J., Oct. 5, 1928; s. Raymond LeRoy and Evelyn (Ross) G.; m. Jane Harriet Taylor, Sept. 12, 1953; children: Laura R., Christopher T., Sarah R., Alison A. B.S., U. Pa., 1952; M.B.A., Harvard U., 1954. Assoc. Goldman, Sachs & Co., N.Y.C., 1954-64, ptnr., 1965-90, ltd. ptnr., 1990—; bd. dirs. Diebold, Inc., Canton, Ohio, Am. Air Liquide, Inc., Houston, Stride Rite Corp., Cambridge, Mass., ABC Rail Products Corps., Chgo.; mem. vis. com. Harvard Bus. Sch., 1991-97. Served with U.S. Army, 1946-48. Republican. Presbyterian. Home: PO Box 83 New Vernon NJ 07976-0083 Office: Goldman Sachs & Co 85 Broad St New York NY 10004-2456

GANT, NORMAN FERRELL, JR., obstetrician, gynecologist; b. Wichita Falls, Tex., Feb. 16, 1939; s. Norman Ferrell and Eleanor (Taylor) G. BA, North Tex. State U., Denton, 1962; MD, U. Tex., 1964. Diplomate: Am. Bd. Obstetrics and Gynecology (exec. dir.). Intern Parkland Meml. Hosp., Dallas, 1964-65; resident Parkland Meml. Hosp., 1965-68; mem. faculty U. Tex. Southwestern Med. Sch., Dallas, 1968—; prof. obstetrics and gynecology U. Tex. Southwestern Med. Sch., 1976—, chmn. dept., 1977-83; exec. dir. Am. Bd. Ob-Gyn., Inc., 1993—; v.p. Internat. Soc. for Study of Hypertension in Pregnancy, 1992-94. Co-author: Williams Obstetrics; editor, sec./treas. Clin. Jour. of Hypertension; contbr. articles to med. jours. Recipient Outstanding Alumnus award U. North Tex., 1998. Fellow Royal Coll. Obstetricians and Gynecologists, Am. Coll. Obstetricians and Gynecologists; mem. AMA (resident rev. com. of Accreditation Coun. of Grad. Med. Edn.), Soc. Gynecologic Investigation (pres. 1991), Am., Tex., Dallas County Med. Assns., Tex. Assn. Obstetricians and Gynecologists, Dallas-Ft. Worth Obstet. and Gynecol. Soc., Am. Bd. Obstetrics and Gynecology (Maternal-Fetal Medicine, examiner for obstetrics and gynecology and maternal-fetal medicine bds., mem. exec. com., credentials com.), Southwestern Gyn. Assembly (pres. 1993). Address: Am Bd Ob-Gyn 2915 Vine St Dallas TX 75204-1045

GANT, RON (RONALD EDWIN GANT), professional baseball player; b. Victoria, Tex., Mar. 2, 1965. With Atlanta Braves, 1983-94, Cin. Reds, 1994-95, St. Louis Cardinals, 1996-98; outfielder Phila. Phillies, 1999—. Mem. Nat. League All-Star Team, 1992; named to Sporting News All-Star team, 1991, recipient Silver Slugger award, 1991. Office: Phila Phillies Vets Stadium 3501 S Broad St Philadelphia PA 19101*

GANTER, GARLAND, radio station executive. Gen. mgr. KPFT-FM, Houston, 1994—. Home: KPFT-FM 419 Lovett Blvd Houston TX 77006*

GANTMAN, GERALDINE ANN, marketing executive, consultant; b. N.Y.C., Jan. 14, 1945; d. Robert Marquette and Mary (Terrazzi) Rhynus. BA in History, CUNY, 1965. Project dir. Audits & Surveys, Inc., N.Y.C., 1966-68; sr. v.p. CCI, Inc., N.Y.C., 1968-80; v.p., account supr. N.W. Ayer, Inc., N.Y.C., 1980-83; exec. v.p. Tel. Mktg. Resources, Inc., N.Y.C., 1983-88; co-founder, sr. ptnr. Oetting & Co., Inc., N.Y.C., 1983—. Mem. Direct Mktg. Assn. (chmn. tel. mktg. coun. 1987-89), Am. Telemarketing Assn. Office: Oetting & Co Inc 1995 Broadway New York NY 10023-5882

GANTMAN, LEWIS I., real estate company executive. BS in Acctg. and Fin. summa cum laude, U. Pa., JD. Lic. real estate broker, Pa. Assoc. Wolf, Block, Schorr & Solis-Cohen; gen. counsel Kravco Co., King of Prussia, Pa., 1983-90, exec. v.p., 1990-95, pres., COO, 1995—. Editor U. Pa. Law Rev. Bd. dirs. Penjerdel Coun. Mem. Internat. Coun. Shopping Ctrs., King of Prussia C. of C., Greater Phila. Fedn. Jewish Agys. Office: Kravco Co 234 Mall Blvd King Of Prussia PA 19406

GANTT, ELISABETH, plant biology educator, researcher; b. Gakovo, Yugoslavia, Nov. 26, 1934; m. R. Raymond, 1958; 1 child. BA, Blackburn Coll., 1958; MSc, Northwestern U., 1960; PhD in Biology, 1963. NIH rsch. assoc. microbiology Dartmouth Coll. Med. Sch., 1963-66, Smithsonian Inst. Radiation Biology Lab., 1966-88; prof. plant biology U. Md., 1988—; co-dir. MOCB; mem. bd. fellows and assocs. Nat. Rsch. Coun., 1973-76. Recipient Darbaker prize Botany Soc., 1981, G.M. Smith medal NAS, 1994. Fellow AAAS, Am. Inst. Biological Sci., Am. Soc. Photobiology, Am. Soc. Plant Physiologists (v.p. 1988, pres. 1989), Phycol. Soc. Am. (v.p. 1977, pres. 1978), Japan Soc. Plant Physiologists, Nat. Acad. Sci. Research in structure of photosynthetic apparatus; characterization of carotenoids and photosynthetic membrane structure. Office: U Md Rm 1109 Cell Biol and Molecular Gen Dept College Park MD 20742*

GANTT, HARVEY B., former mayor; b. Charleston, S.C., Jan. 14, 1943; m. Lucinda Brawley; four children. Student, Iowa State U., 1960-62; B.Arch., Clemson U., 1965; M.A., MIT, 1970. Lectr. U. N.C., Chapel Hill, 1970-72; vis. critic Clemson U., S.C., 1972-73; mem. Charlotte City Council, N.C., 1975-79; mayor pro tem City of Charlotte, 1981-83, mayor, 1983-91; chmn. Nat. Capital Planning Commn. Life mem. NAACP; bd. dirs. 100 Black Men of Charlotte, Ctrl. Piedmont Coll. Found., Am. Archtl. Found.; former bd. dirs. YMCA, Afro-Am. Cultural Ctr., Found. for the Carolinas, Charlotte C. of C., Urban League, United Negro Coll. Fund; choir mem. Friendship Bapt., former bd. trustees. Named Citizen of Yr., Charlotte chpt. NAACP, 1975, 84. Mem. AIA, Am. Planning Assn., N.C. Design Found. Avocations: tennis, reading. Office: Nat Capital Planning Commn 801 Pennsylvania Ave NW Ste 301 Washington DC 20004-2682

GANTT, JAMES RAIFORD, thoracic surgeon; b. Texarkana, Mar. 5, 1930; s. James Emmett and Nettie Ruth (Raiford) G.; m. Joan Maire Durstine, Aug. 18, 1968. BA, Baylor U., 1953; MD, Johns Hopkins U., 1957. Diplomate Am. Bd. Surgery, Am. Bd. Thoracic Surgery. Rotating intern Charity Hosp., New Orleans, 1957, resident internal medicine, 1958, resident in surgery, 1962-64, resident in thoracic surgery, 1965; NIH rsch. fellow Tulane U., New Orleans, 1959; resident in thoracic surgery Kans. U., Kansas City, 1966; pvt. practice Dallas, 1966-84, James R. GanttProfl. Assocs., 1971-84, Irving, Tex., 1978-84; chief of surgery Irving Cmty. Hosp., Irving, Tex., 1980—. Lt. USN, 1960-62. Fellow ACS; mem. AMA, So. Thoracic Assn., Am. Coll. Chest Physicians, Tex. Med. Assn. Republican. Presbyterian. Avocations: hunting, fishing, training my dog. Home: 3512 Lexington Ave Dallas TX 75205-3915

GANTT, MICHAEL DAVID, business executive; b. Columbia, S.C., Oct. 21, 1951; s. Richard F. Jr. and Dolores Sybil (Hebert) G.; m. Janie Peden, May 20, 1972; children: Jennifer, Jason, Jessica, Jonathan. BBA, U. S.C., 1972; MDiv, Covenant Theol. Sem., 1986; DMin, Fuller Theol. Sem., 1992. Ordained to ministry, 1982; chartered property and casualty underwriter. Asst. v.p. Seibels, Bruce & Co., 1972-78; youth dir. Kirk of the Hills Presbyn. Ch., St. Louis, 1980-82; pastor Ch. on the Hill, Florissant, Mo., 1982-86, Established Westport Ch., St. Louis, 1986-94; v.p. PMSC, Columbia, S.C., 1995, chief quality officer, 1996, chief tech. officer, 1997-98, sr. v.p., 1998—. Author: Computers in Insurance, 1979, A Non Churchgoers Guide to the Bible, 1995, Crash Course on the Bible, 1997. Home: 310 Lost Spring Rd Lexington SC 29072-9683 Office: PMSC PO Box 10 Columbia SC 29202-0010

GANTZ, BRUCE JAY, otolaryngologist, educator; b. N.Y.C., May 18, 1946; m. Mary Katherine DeJong; children: Ellen Katherine, Jessica Rose, Jay Alexander. BS in Gen. Sci., U. Iowa, 1968, MD, 1974, MS in Otolaryngology, 1980; fellow neurotology, U. Zürich, Zurich, 1981-82. Asst. prof. dept otolaryngology U. Iowa Coll. Medicine, Iowa City, 1980-84, assoc. prof., 1984-87, prof., 1987—; interim head dept. otolaryngology head & neck surgery U. Iowa Hosps. & Clinics, Iowa City, 1993-95, head dept. otolaryngology head & neck surgery, 1995—; mem. adv. bd. Deafness Research Found. Sci., 1988—. Mem. editl. bd. Am. Jour. Otology, Laryngoscope, Skull Base Surgery, Operative Techniques in Otolaryngology-Head and Neck Surgery, Anales De Otolarnolaringo-logica Mexicana, Annals Otolaryngology, Rhinology and Laryngology; contbr. articles to profl. jours. Recipient Tchr.-Investigator Devel. award Pub. Health Svc., 1981-86, Program Project award NIH, 1985—; clin. rsch. ctr. grantee NIDCD, 1990, 95. Mem. AMA, Assn. for Rsch. in Otolaryngology (pres. 1995), Deafness Rsch. Found. (state chmn. 1985—), Am. Acad. Otolaryngology-Head and Neck Surgery, Soc. Univ. Otolaryngologists, Am. Neurotology Soc. (v.p. 1994-96, pres.-elect 1996-97, pres. 1997—), Am. Otological Soc., Collegium Oto-Rhino-Laryngologicum Amictuae Sacrum. Office: U Iowa Hosps & Clinics 200 Hawkins Dr Iowa City IA 52242*

GANTZ, CARROLL MELVIN, industrial design consultant, consumer product designer; b. Sellersville, Pa., Sept. 9, 1931; s. Melvin Charles G. and Leona Alberta (Hornberger) Barner; m. Lorraine Sachs, Mar. 5, 1955; children: Erika Christine, Mitchell Allen. B.F.A., Carnegie Mellon U., 1953. Head indsl. design Hoover Co., North Canton, Ohio, 1956-72; mgr. indsl. design Black & Decker, Inc., Towson, Md., 1972-81; dir. indsl. design household products group Black & Decker (U.S.), Inc., Shelton, Conn., 1981-86; prof., head dept. design Carnegie-Mellon U., Pitts., 1987-92; established Carroll Gantz Design, 1992; designer canal boat St. Helena II, Canal Fulton, Ohio, 1967-70; dir. Am. Canal Soc., York, Pa., 1974-79. 28 patents in field of design for consumer products. Bd. dirs. Stark County Hist. Soc., 1970. Served with Security Agy. U.S. Army, 1953-56. Recipient Design award Indsl. Designers Inst., 1961, Indsl. Design Excellance award, 1995; Brashear scholar, 1949. Fellow Indsl. Designers Soc. Am. (pres. 1979-80, chmn. bd. 1981-82); mem. SAR, Omicron Delta Kappa, Tau Sigma Delta. Republican.

GANTZ, DAVID ALFRED, lawyer, university official; b. Columbus, Ohio, July 30, 1942; s. Harry Samuel and Edwina (Bookwalter) G.; m. Susan Beare, Aug. 26, 1967 (div. Feb. 1989); children: Stephen David, Julie Lorraine; m. Catherine Fagan, Mar. 28, 1992. AB, Harvard U., 1964; JD, Stanford U., 1967, M in Jud. Sci., 1970. Bar: Ohio 1967, D.C. 1971, Ariz. 1995, U.S. Ct. Internat. Trade 1983, U.S. Ct. Appeals (9th cir.), U.S. Supreme Ct. 1972. Asst. prof. law U. Costa Rica, San Jose, 1967-69; law clk. U.S. Ct. Appeals, San Francisco, 1969-70; asst. legal advisor U.S. Dept. State, Washington, 1970-77; ptnr. Cole & Corrette, Washington, 1977-83, Oppenheimer Wolff & Donnelly, Washington, 1983-90; ptnr. Reid & Priest, Washington, 1990-93, of counsel, 1993-97; of counsel Dorsey & Whitney, 1997—; prof. law, dir. grad. studies U. Ariz. Coll. Law, Tucson, 1993—; assoc. dir. Nat. Law Ctr. for Inter-Am. Free Trade, 1993—; panelist U.S.-Can. Free Trade Agreement, 1989-92, Am. Arbitration Assn., 1996—, NAFTA, 1994—; judge OAS Adminstrv. Tribunal, 1987-95; adj. prof. Georgetown U. Law Ctr., 1982-93. Contbr. numerous articles on internat. law to profl. jours. Pres. Potomac River Sports Found., 1992-94. Mem. ABA, Am. Soc. Internat. Law, Potomac Boat Club (Washington, bd. dirs. 1986-93). Home: 7112 N Corte Del Anuncio Tucson AZ 85718-7333 Office: Ariz Coll Law 1201 E Speedway Blvd Tucson AZ 85719

GANTZ, NANCY ROLLINS, nursing administrator, consultant; b. Buffalo Center, Iowa, Mar. 7, 1949; d. Troy Gaylord and Mary (Emerson) Rollins. Diploma in Nursing, Good Samaritan Hosp. and Med. Ctr., Portland, Oreg., 1973; BSBA, City U., 1986; MBA, Kennedy-Western U., 1987, PhD, 1991. Nurse ICU, Good Samaritan Hosp., 1973-75; charge nurse Crestview Convalescent Hosp., Portland, 1975; dir. nursing svcs. Roderick Enterprises, Inc., Portland, 1976-78, Holgate Ctr., Portland, 1978-80; nursing cons. in field of adminstrn., 1980-84; coord. CCU; mgr. ICU/CCU Tuality Community Hosp., Hillsboro, Oreg., 1984-86; head nurse intensive care unit, cardiac surgery unit, coronary care unit, Good Samaritan Hosp. & Med. Ctr., Portland, 1986-88, mgr. critical care units, 1988-92, asst. v.p. patient care svcs., 1992-93, dir. heart ctr. Deaconess Med. Ctr., Spokane, Wash., 1992-93; asst. exec. dir. King Faisal Specialist Hosp. and Rsch. Ctr., Children's Cancer Ctr., Riyadh, Saudi Arabia, 1994—; mem. speakers bur. Nurses of Am.; mem. task force Oreg. State Health Div. Rules and Regulations Revisions for Long Term Health Facilities and Hosps., 1978-79; numerous internat. and nat. speaking presentations. Contbr. chpts. to books and articles to profl. jours. Mem. Am. Nuses Assn. (cert.), Nat. League Nursing, Am. Assn. Critical Care Nurses (pres. elect greater Portland chpt. 1985-86, pres. 1986-87, bd. dirs. 1985—), Am. Heart Assn., Oreg. Heart Assn., Geriatric Nurses Assn. Oreg. (founder, charter pres.), Clackamus Assn. Retarded Citizens, AACN (chpt. cons. region 18 1978-89, mgmt. SIC region 18 1990-92), AONE Coun. Nurse Mgrs. (bd. dirs. Region 9 1991-92), Sigma Theta Tau. Seventhday Adventist. Fax: (503) 873-0604. Home: 401 Charles Ave Silverton OR 97381-2006

GANTZ, RICHARD ALAN, museum administrator; b. Ft. Wayne, Ind., July 28, 1946; m. Ruth Ann Kennell; 1 child, Sally Elizabeth. BS in Edn. with honors, Ball State U., 1968; MA, George Washington U., 1971; PhD, Ind. U., 1986. Social studies tchr. Ft. Wayne (Ind.) Community Schs., 1969-73; Nat. Park Svc. seasonal hist. Homestead Nat. Monument, Beatrice, Nebr., 1972; assoc. instr. Ind. U., Bloomington, 1975-76; asst. state hist. preserv. officer dept. natural resources State of Ind., 1976-90, asst. dir. divsn. mus. and memls., 1978-81, acting dir., 1982-83, dir. divsn. hist. preservation and archeology, 1981-90, acting dir. divsn. state mus. and hist. sites, 1989, dir. divsn. state mus. and hist. sites and Ind. State Mus., 1990—; mem. adj. faculty history dept. Butler U., Indpls., 1988—; mem. steering com. Dept. Commerce Heritage, Tourism and Edn., 1991-94; mem. project com. Ind. Heritage Trust, 1992—; chmn. Ind. Hist. Exchange Coun., 1984-91, Ind. Hist. Bridge Com., 1984-90. Contbr. articles to profl. jours. Active Ind. Main State Coun., 1985—; sec. New Harmony State Commn., 1989—; mem. White River State Park Commn., 1993—, Ind. Gov.'s Millennium Task Force, 1998—, Ind. Gov.'s Residence Adv. Com., 1998—. Mem. Orgn. Am. Hists., Nat. Trust Hist. Preservation, Ind. Assn. Hists., Ind. State Mus. Soc., Assn. Ind. Mus., Midwest Mus. Conf. Office: Ind State Mus and Hist Sites 202 N Alabama St Indianapolis IN 46204-2101*

GANULIN, JUDY, public relations professional; b. Chgo., May 2, 1937; d. Alvin and Sadie (Reingold) Landis; m. James Ganulin, June 23, 1957; children: Stacy Ganulin Clark, Amy Ganulin Lowenstein. BA in Journalism, U. Calif., Berkeley, 1958. Copywriter-sec. Joe Connor Advt., Berkeley, 1958; exec. sec. Prescolite Mfg. Co., Berkeley, 1958-59; info. officer Office of Consumer Counsel, Sacramento, 1959-61; pub. rels. positions various polit. campaigns, Fresno, Calif., 1966; adminstrv. asst., editor, mktg. Valley Pubs., Fresno, 1971-80; staff asst. to county supr. Bd. Suprs., Fresno, 1980-82; field rep. Assemblyman Bruce Bronzan, Fresno, 1982-84; prin. Judy Ganulin Pub. Rels., Fresno, 1984—; speaker new bus. workshop SBA/Svc. Corps Ret. Execs., Fresno, 1990—. Active Hadassah, Fresno, 1975—; pres. Temple Beth Israel Sisterhood, Fresno, 1976; panelist campaign workshop Nat. Women's Polit. Caucus, Fresno, 1994; bd. dirs. Temple Beth Israel, Fresno, 1972-75, Planned Parenthood Ctrl. Calif., Fresno, 1986-91. Mem. Pub. Rels. Soc. Am. (accredited pub. rels. practitioner, pres. Fresno/Ctrl. Valley chpt. 1994), Am. Mktg. Assn. (pres. ctrl. Calif. chpt.-ctrl. 1987-88), Calif. Press Women, Fresno Advt. Fedn., Pub. Rels. Roundtable (v.p., pres. 1991-93), Fresno C. of C. (mem. mktg. com. 1988—). Democrat. Avocations: traveling, reading, cooking. Office: Judy Ganulin Pub Rels 1117 W San Jose Ave Fresno CA 93711-3112

GANZ, CHARLES, laboratory executive. Pres. En-Cas Analytical Lab., Winston-Salem, N.C., 1976—. Office: En-Cas 2359 Farrington Point Dr Winston Salem NC 27107-2457*

GANZ, DAVID L., lawyer; b. N.Y.C., July 28, 1951; s. Daniel M. and Beverlee (Kaufman) G.; m. Barbara Bondanza, Nov. 3, 1974 (div. 1978); m. Sharon Ruth Lamnin, Oct. 30, 1981 (div. 1996); children: Scott Harry, Elyse Toby, Pamela Rebecca; m. Kathleen Ann Gotsch, Dec. 28, 1996. BS in Fgn. Svc., Georgetown U., 1973; JD, St. John's U., 1976. Bar: N.Y. 1977, D.C. 1980, N.J. 1985. Assoc. Regan, Dorsey & De Riso, Flushing, N.Y., 1977-79; ptnr. Durst & Ganz, N.Y.C., 1979-80; mng. ptnr. Ganz, Hollinger & Towe, N.Y.C., 1981-98, Ganz & Hollinger, N.Y.C., 1999—; exec. com. Industry Coun. Tangible Assets, Washington, 1983—, bd. dirs.; cons. in field. Author: A Critical Guide to the Anthologies of African Literature, 1973, A Legal and Legislative History of 31 USC Sec 342d-324i, 1976, The World of Coin Collecting, 1980, 3d edit., 1998, The 90 Second Lawyer, 1996, The 90 Second Lawyer's Guide to Selling Real Estate, 1997, How to Get an Instant Mortgage, 1997, Planning Your Rare Coin Retirement, 1998, Guide Commemorative Coin Values, 1999; corr. Numis. News Weekly, 1969-73, asst. editor, 1973-74, spl. corr., 1974-75, columnist, 1969-76, 96—; contbg. editor, columnist COUNage Mag., 1974—; columnist Coun World, 1974-96, COINS Mag., 1973-83; contbr. articles to profl. jours. Mem. U.S. Embassy Commn., 1974; bd. dirs. Georgetown Libr. Assocs., Washington, 1982—; mem. N.Y. County Draft Bd., 1984, Bergen County, N.J., 1985—, vice chair, 1996—; sec., mem. Zoning and Adjustment Bd., Fair Lawn, N.J., 1988-92, chmn., 1993-97; elected mem. Dem. County Com. Bergen County, 1988-96, borough coun. Borough of Fair Lawn, 1998—, mayor, 1999—. Decorated Order of St. Agatha (Republic of San Marino). Fellow Am. Numis. Soc. (life); mem. Am. Numis. Assn. (life, legis. coun. 1978-81, 83-95, elected bd. govs. 1985-95, v.p. 1991-93, pres. 1993-95), Assn. of Bar of City of N.Y. (com. on state legis. 1987-90), N.Y. State Bar Assn. (mem. civil practice com., chmn. subcom. 1978-84), Profl. Numis. Guild Inc. affiliated mem. 1989—, gen. coun. 1981-92), Am. Soc. Internat. Law, Nat. Assn. Coin and Precious Metals Dealers (asoc. mem., gen. coun. 1981-85), Flushing Lawyers Club (pres. 1982-83). Democrat. Jewish. Avocation: numismatic. Office: Ganz Hollinger & Towe 1394 3rd Ave New York NY 10021-0467

GANZ, HOWARD LAURENCE, lawyer; b. N.Y.C., Apr. 3, 1942; s. Myron and Beatrice (W.) G.; children: Beth, David. BA, Colgate U., 1963; LLB, Columbia U., 1966. Bar: N.Y. 1966, U.S. Dist. Ct. (so. dist.) N.Y. 1968, U.S. Dist. Ct. (ea. dist.) N.Y. 1969, U.S. Dist. Ct. (no. dist.) Calif. 1984, U.S. Ct. Appeals (3d cir.) 1974, U.S. Ct. Appeals (4th cir.) 1985, U.S. Dist. Ct. (9th cir.) 1984, U.S. Dist. Ct. (D.C. cir.) 1986, U.S. Supreme Ct. 1986. Law clk. to Hon. Marvin E. Frankel U.S. Dist. Ct., N.Y.C., 1966-68; assoc., ptnr. Proskauer Rose LLP, N.Y.C., 1968—, assoc. ptnr., mem. exec. com. Named One of 100 Best Lawyers in N.Y., N.Y. Mag., 1995, One of Best Lawyers in America, 1997. Mem. Fed. Bar Coun., N.Y. State Bar Assn., N.Y. County Lawyers Assn., Assn. of Bar of City of N.Y. Office: Proskauer Rose LLP 1585 Broadway New York NY 10036-8200

GANZ, SAMUEL, human resource and management professional; b. Bklyn., Nov. 12, 1911; s. Emanuel and Dora (Zahalsky) G.; m. Helen Lichtig, June 26, 1938; children: Edward, Jeffrey. BS, MS, CCNY, 1932; postgrad., NYU, 1941-43. Exec. in men's clothing industry, 1932-36; with N.Y. State Dept. Labor, 1936-40; with U.S. Dept. Labor, Washington, 1940-66, asst. to adminstr. wage and hour and pub. contracts div., 1947-57, asst. adminstr., 1957-62; asst. dir. manpower, automation R&D Office of Manpower, Automation and Tng., Washington, 1962-64, dep. manpower adminstr., 1964-66; commr. Manpower and Career Devel. Agy., City of N.Y., 1966-69; chmn., pres. Econ. and Manpower Corp., N.Y.C., 1969-79; mem. rsch. subcom. Nat. Manpower Adv. Com. to Secs. Labor and Health, Edn. and Welfare, 1966-69; mem. faculty New Sch. for Social Rsch.; adj. prof. Pace U., N.Y.C., 1971-74; prof. C.W. Post Ctr., L.I. U., 1974-76, faculty adviser Iranian Students Forum; adj. prof., in charge program devel., cons. to coop. edn. and internship program Queens Coll., CUNY, 1988—; asst. to provost for spl. programs and adj. prof. human resources, dir. coop. edn., N.Y. Inst. Tech., adv. coun. Ctr. for Labor and Indsl. Rels., from 1977; industry coord. Nassau-Suffolk Health System Agy., 1983-84; exec. com. Inst. Econ. Action; cons. in field. Contbr. articles to profl. publs. Mem. N.Y. Gov.'s Task Force on Manpower and Unemployment, Task Force on Econ. Devel.; chmn. Gov.'s Subcom. on Pub. Svc., Gov.'s Com. on Human Resources; mem. adv. com. Corsi Inst. Labor-Mgmt. Rels., Pace U.; trustee chmn. manpower com. Am. Found. for the Blind, 1976-79; dir., v.p. Greater N.Y. Safety Coun., 1976-79; dir. Forum for Greater L.I., 1982. Recipient commendation Mayor of N.Y.C., 1966, cert. merit Minority Bus. Enterprise, Disting. Svc. award U.S. Dept. Labor, 1961, 66. Mem. Indsl. Rels. Rsch. Assn., Am. Soc. for Pub. Adminstrn., Am. Econ. Assn., Am. Vocat. Assn., N.Y. C. of C. and Industry (spl. com. on environment 1972, manpower devel. com. 1970-75, chmn. subcom. employment svc. 1974-75), N.Y. State Coop. and Exptl. Edn. Assn. (v.p., pres.-elect 1982), Coop. Edn. Assn. Jewish. Home: 7031 Summer Tree Dr Apt 202 Boynton Beach FL 33437-6103 *I believe each human being should be given the opportunity and assistance to reach his or her optimum potential in a peaceful world, one in which its environment is protected and its natural and human resources are employed for the advancement of society. These goals can be achieved best through a harmonious, cooperative working relationship between the private, non-profit and public sectors.**

GANZ, WILLIAM ISRAEL, radiology educator, medical director, researcher; b. Munich, Jan. 2, 1951; s. Lazar and Jean Ganz; m. Susan Rebecca Sirota, June 22, 1980; children: Tova, Debora, Harry. BA, Adelphi U., 1972; MS and MD, Albert Einstein Coll. Medicine, Medicine, 1979. Diplomate Am. Bd. Nuclear Medicine. NIH med. scientist trainee Albert Einstein Coll. Medicine, Bronx, N.Y., 1972-78, pharmacology rsch. fellow, 1978-79, NIH cardiovasc. fellow, 1979-80, radiology resident, 1980-83; radiology/nuc. medicine fellow Barnes Hosp./Inst. Radiology, St. Louis, 1983-85; asst. prof. Sch. Medicine U. Miami, Fla., 1985-90, assoc. prof., 1990-97, coord. nuc. medicine tchg. program, 1990-97; radiation safety officer, coord. clin. nuc. medicine South Shore Hosp., 1994-97; dir. nuc. medicine Animal Rsch. Lab., 1995-97; med. dir. PET/Nuc. Medicine Ctr., Metabolic Imaging of Boca Raton, Fla., 1996-98; instr. radiology, nuc. medicine Mt. Sinai Med. Ctr., Miami Beach, Fla., 1998-99; staff cons. cardiovasc. nuc. medicine Cedars Med. Ctr., 1985—; medical dir. Imaging Ctr. and Dignostic Testing Group, Miami, 1996—; staff South Shore Hosp., 1994—; prof. panel Pfizer Pharms., Miami, 1986-95; guest editor Nuc. Medicine Ednl. Review, 1996—; med. dir. Diagnostic Testing Ctr. and Imaging Ctr., Atlantis, Fla., 1998—; staff physician nuclear medicine Holy Cross Hosp., Ft. Lauderdale, Fla., 1999—, Clin. Neurosci. Inst. Brain Rsch. Group, 1999—. Reviewer Jour. Nuc. Medicine; exhibitor in field; contbr. articles to profl. jours. Recipient NIH Svc. awards 1975-78, NSF award 1976, others. Mem. AMA, Am. Coll. Nuc. Physicians, Am. Coll. Cardiology, Radiol. Soc. N.Am., Soc. Nuc. Medicine, Soc. Magnetic Resonance Imaging, Am. Soc. Orthodox Jewish Scientists. Democrat. Jewish. Home: 4333 Adams Ave Miami FL 33140-2927

GANZI, VICTOR FREDERICK, lawyer; b. N.Y.C., Feb. 14, 1947; s. Walter John and Gertrude (Meyer) G.; m. Patricia Frances Martin, July 10, 1971; children: Danielle Martin, Victoria Louise. BS, Fordham U., 1968; JD, Harvard U., 1971; LLM in Taxation, NYU, 1981. Bar: N.Y. 1973, U.S. Dist. Ct. (so. and ea. dists.) N.Y. 1975, U.S. Ct. Appeals (2d cir.) 1975, U.S. Tax Ct. 1975; CPA, Colo. Tax acct. Touche Ross & Co., Denver, 1971-73; assoc. Rogers & Wells, N.Y.C., 1973-78; ptnr. Rogers & Wells, 1978-86, mng. ptnr., 1986-90; v.p., sec., gen. counsel Hearst Corp., N.Y.C., 1990-92, CFO, chief legal officer, sr. v.p., 1992-94, also bd. dirs.; exec. v.p., pres. Hearst Books/Bus. Pub. Group, 1997—, COO, 1998—; speaker various insts.; bd. dirs. Palm Mgmt. Corp., N.Y.C., PGA Tour, Inc., ESPN, N.Y.C., IMI Sys. Inc., N.Y.C., N.Y.C. Econ. Devel. Corp., Olsten Corp.; mem. Coun. future of Law Sch., NYU Sch. Law. Mem. ABA, AICPA, Colo. Soc. CPAs, Sky Club, Cherry Valley Club (Garden City, N.Y.). Home: 303 Captains Way Bay Shore NY 11706-8106 Office: The Hearst Corp 959 8th Ave New York NY 10019-3795

GAPE, SERAFINA VETRANO, decorative artist and designer; b. Villa Franco, Sicily, Italy, Oct. 4, 1945; came to U.S., 1947; d. Augustino and Maria (Tramuta) Vetrano; m. William Evan Gape, Jan. 27, 1965; children: William Edward, Andrea Marie. BA cum laude, SUNY, Utica, 1982. Apprentice/journeyman/master Augustino Vetrano, New Hartford, N.Y., 1955-70; artist N.Y., 1970—; owner, designer Decorative Painting/Lit. Restoration Co., N.Y., 1980—; art tchr. Mohawk Valley C.C., Utica, N.Y., 1988; decorative arts guide Fountain Elms/Hist. HouseMus., Utica, 1985—; cons., lectr. various chs., businesses, art orgns. Exhibited in group and one-woman shows including Italian Cultural Ctr., Utica, 1987, Ctrl. N.Y. Cmty. Arts Coun., N.Y.C., 1985 (awarded in a variety of mediums including oil, watercolor, acrylic and pastels); represented in pvt. collections in U.S., Can., Eng.; works include restoration and redesign of interiors of numerous chs. throughout Ctrl. N.Y. State, includes Mohawk Valley C.C., Utica, N.Y., St. Mary of Mt. Carmel Ch., Utica, Holy Trinity, Our Lady of Lourdes, Utica, St. Paul, Oxford, N.Y., St. Casmir, Elmira, N.Y., Columbus (N.Y.) Comty. Ch., St. Peter, Passaic, N.J., St. Paul, Passaic, others. Recipient 2d pl. mixed media award Rural Show, SUNY, 1995, 2d pl. oil award Rome (N.Y.) Comty. Art, 1994, Best in Show pastel award Utica Pub. Libr., 1994, Painting of the Month award Utica Art Assn., 1995. Mem. Munson-Williams-Proctor Inst., Kirkland Art Ctr., Utica Art Assn. (pres. 1984-87), Italian Cultural Ctr., Leatherstocking County Stencillers (v.p. 1990-91, pres. 1993-94), Stencil Artisans League. Avocations: reading, travel, antiques, silk ribbon embroidery. Home: 652 Daytona St Utica NY 13502-1110

GAPPA, JUDITH M., university administrator. Student, Wellesley Coll., 1957-60; BA in Music, George Washington U., 1968, MA in Musicology, 1970; EdD in Ednl. Adminstrn., Utah State U., 1973; cert. Inst. for Ednl. Mgmt., Harvard U., 1980. Lectr. George Washington U., Washington, 1968-69; dir. fine arts program The York Sch., Monterey, Calif., 1970; program cons. Western Interstate Commn. for Higher Edn., Boulder, Colo., 1973; coord. affirmative action program Utah State U., Logan, 1973-75, dir. affirmative action/equal opportunity programs, asst. prof., 1975-77, 78-80, project dir., 1979-81; sr. staff assoc. Nat. Ctr. for Higher Edn. Mgmt. Systems, Inc., Boulder, 1977-78; assoc. v.p. for faculty affairs, dean of faculty, prof. San Francisco State U., 1980-91; sr. assoc. Am. Assn. Higher Edn., 1995-97; prof. Purdue U., West Lafayette, Ind., 1991—, v.p. human rels., 1991-98; served on numerous coms., couns. Utah State U., San Francisco State U.; cons. Assn. Governing Bds., 1994, U. Mich., Duluth, 1992, Calif. State U. Human Resources Mgmt. Office, 1992, Am. U., Washington, 1987, No. Rockies Consortium for Higher Edn. Conf., 1985, So. Utah State Coll., 1982, Nat. Ctr. for Rsch. in Vocat. Edn., 1980-81, Hood Coll., 1982-84, Am. Insts. for Rsch. in Behavioral Scis., 1980-81; condr. workshops on edn. Coauthor: The Invisible Faculty, 1993; mem. editl. bd. Rev. of Higher Edn., 1994-97; contbr. numerous articles to profl. jours. Grantee Lilly Endowment, 1995, United Techs. Corp., 1992, TIAA-CREF/Lilly Endowment, 1990, Calif. State U., 1985, San Francisco State U., 1981, HEW, 1979-81, Nat. Inst. Edn., 1977, Utah State U., 1977, Fed. workshop grant, 1976, State of Utah, 1975, 76. Mem. Western Assn. Schs. and Colls. (accreditation team mem. Calif. State U.-L.A. 1990), Am. Assn. for Higher Edn. (sr. assoc. Washington chpt. 1995-97), Assn. for Study of Higher Edn. (nat. adv. bd. ASHE-ERIC Higher Edn. Report Series 1990-91, editl. bd. Rev. of Higher Edn. 1994-97, nominating com. 1986-87, program com. for 1986 nat. conf., membership com. 1982-84, conf. com. 1983, editl. bd. Rev. of Higher Edn. 1994-97), Am. Coun. on Edn. Nat. Identification Program (No. Calif. state coord. 1988-91). Office: Purdue Univ Sch Edn 1446 Liberal Arts Rd West Lafayette IN 47907-1075*

GARABEDIAN, CHARLES, artist; b. Detroit, 1923. MFA, UCLA, 1961. Solo shows include LaJolla (Calif.) Mus. Art, 1966, CeJee Gallery, N.Y., 1966, 67, Eugenia Butler Gallery, L.A., 1970, Newspace Gallery, L.A., 1974, Whitney Mus. Am. Art, N.Y.C., 1976, Broxton Gallery, L.A., 1976, L.A. Louver Gallery, Venice, Calif., 1979, 83, 86, 89, 90, 92, 94, 96, LaJolla Mus. Contemporary Art, 1981, Ruth S. Schaffner Gallery, Santa Barbara, Calif., 1982, Rose Art Mus., Waltham, Mass., 1983, Hirschl & Adler Modern Mus., N.Y.C., 1984, Gallery Paule Anglim, San Francisco, 1985, 93, 98, numerous others; exhibited in group shows at numerous mus. including Rose Art Mus., The High Mus., Atlanta, 1980, Emanuel Walter Gallery, San Francisco, 1981, LaJolla Mus. Contemporary Art, 1981, Mizumo Gallery, L.A., 1981, Mandeville Art Gallery, San Diego, Oakland Mus. Art, 1981, Brooke Alexander Gallery, N.Y., 1982, Kunst Mus., Luzern, 1983, Fresno Art Ctr., 1983, Tibor de Nagy Gallery, N.Y.C., 1983, Hirshhorn Mus. and Sculpture Garden, Smithsonian Instn., Washington, 1984, Newport Harbor Art Mus., Calif., 1984, El Museo Rufino Tamayo, Mexico City, 1984, L.A. Mcpl. Art Gallery, 1984, L.A. Louver, Venice, 1985, Whitney Mus. Art, 1986, Di-Laurenti Gallery, N.Y., 1986, R.C. Erpf Gallery, N.Y., 1987, N.Y. State Mus., Albany, 1987, Richard Green Gallery, 1988, Bklyn. Mus. Art, 1989, James Corcoran Gallery, 1991, Riva Yares Gallery, Scottsdale, Ariz., 1994, Hirschl & Adler Mus., 1996, Mcpl. Art Gallery L.A., 1997; pub. collections include Met. Mus. Art, N.Y.C., Whitney Mus. Am. Art, Mus. Contemporary Art, L.A., Rose Art Mus., San Diego Mus. Contemporary Art, L.A. County Mus. Art. Staff sgt. USAF, 1942-45. John Simon Guggenheim Meml. Found. fellow, 1979, Nat. Endowment for the Arts fellow, 1977. Office: L A Louver 45 Venice Blvd Venice CA 90291

GARABEDIAN, CHARLES, JR., mathematics educator; b. Whitinsville, Mass., July 16, 1943; s. Charles and Sadie (Madanjian) G.; m. Manoushag Manougian. BS, Worcester State Coll., 1965; MEd, Framingham State Coll., 1970; PhD, U. Conn., 1981. Cert. secondary tchr., Mass. Math. tchr. Holliston (Mass.) High Sch., 1965—; assoc. prof. math. Framingham (Mass.) State Coll., 1971-75, 84—; math. tchr. Ea. Conn. State Coll., Willimantic, 1976; cons., math. instr. Huntington Learning Ctr., Shrewsbury, Mass., 1993—. Recipient Presdl. Disting. Tchr. award, Harvard U. Practitioner award, 1988, Disting. Tchr. award White House Commn. on Presdl. Scholars, 1991, Christa Corrigan McAuliffe award Christa McAuliffe Ctr. for Edn. and Tchg. Excellence, 1996. Mem. Nat. Coun. Tchrs. of Math., ASCD, N.E. Assn. Tchrs. of Math., Mass. Assn. Tchrs. of Math., Mass. Assn. Supervision and Curriculum Devel., Mass. Assn. RR Passengers, Nat. Assn. RR Passengers, Knights of Vartan, Phi Delta Kappa. Mem. Armenian Evangelical Ch. Avocations: music, photography, model railroads, cooking, reading. Home: PO Box 452 Shrewsbury MA 01545-0452

GARABEDIAN-URBANOWSKI, MARTHA ANN, foreign language educator; b. Whitinsville, Mass., Dec. 8, 1953; d. Charles and Sadie (Madanjian) G.; m. William John Urbanowski, Jr., June 8, 1991. BA summa cum laude, Worcester State Coll., 1975; MA, U. Conn., 1978, PhD, 1984. Grad. tchg. asst. in Spanish U. Conn., Storrs, 1975-79; vis. asst. prof., lectr. Spanish Assumption Coll., Worcester, Mass., 1984-90; assoc. prof. Spanish Western New Eng. Coll., Springfield, Mass., 1990—; adj. prof. Spanish, Worcester State Coll., fall 1985. Contbr. articles to profl. jours. Mem. Am. Evang. Ch. The Josefina Romo-Arregui Meml. scholar U. Conn., Storrs, 1983. Mem. MLA, N.E. MLA, Am. Coun. on the Tchg. Fgn. Langs., Am. Assn. Tchrs. Spanish and Portuguese, Mass. Fgn. Lang. Assn., Worcester Art Mus., The Smithsonian, Libr. Congress, Phi Kappa Phi, Kappa Delta Pi. Armenian Evangelical. Avocations: golf, music, art, reading, travel. Home: 21 Pine Ridge Rd Southbridge MA 01550-2139 Office: Western New Eng Coll 1215 Wilbraham Rd Springfield MA 01119-2612

GARAGIOLA, JOE, sports broadcaster; b. St. Louis, Feb. 12, 1926; s. John and Angelina (Garavaglia) G.; m. Audrie Dianne Ross, Nov. 5, 1949; children: Joseph, Stephen, Gina. Ed. parochial schs. Profl. baseball player with St. Louis Cardinals, Pitts. Pirates, Chgo. Cubs and N.Y. Giants, 1946-54; engaged in radio-TV, 1955—. Broadcaster: All Star Baseball games, World Series and Game of the Week, N.Y. Yankee games; appeared on Jack Paar Show, Tonight Show; host Orange Bowl Parade, Tournament of Roses Parade; regular mem. cast, now correspondent-at-large: Today Show, 1969-73, 90—; broadcaster: NBC Sports, 1961-88; commentator NBC Radio and TV programs; host own radio and TV show from 1963; host: Sale of Century, He Said-She Said, To Tell the Truth, Strike it Rich; author: Baseball is a Funny Game, 1960, It's Anybody's Ballgame, 1988. Pres. Baseball Assistance Team. Served with AUS, World War II. Recipient George Foster Peabody award for TV show The Baseball World of Joe Garagiola, 1974, Freedoms Found. award. Office: care Major League Baseball 350 Park Ave New York NY 10022-6022*

GARAGIOLA, JOE, JR., baseball team executive; m. Noel Garagiola; children: Meredith, Valerie, Natalie, Christopher. BA cum laude, U. Notre Dame, 1972; JD, Georgetown U., 1975. Bar: Ariz., Calif., N.Y. Gen. counsel, asst. to pres. N.Y. Yankees, N.Y.C.; ptnr. Gallagher and Kennedy, Phoenix, 1982—; chmn. bd. dirs. Phoenix Met. Sports Found., 1985-87; v.p., gen. mgr. Ariz. Diamondbacks (profl. baseball expansion team), 1995—; vice chmn. Gov.'s Cactus League Task Force, Phoenix, mem. Mayor's profl. baseball com.; chmn. Maricopa County (Ariz.) Sports Authority, Ariz. Baseball Commn. Bd. dirs. Am. West Airlines Ednl. Found., Phoenix Meml. Hosp. Recipient Inst. Human Rels. award, Am. Jewish Com., 1998. Office: c/o Ariz Diamondbacks 401 E Jefferson Phoenix AZ 85003*

GARAHAN, PETER THOMAS, software company executive; b. Queens, N.Y., Sept. 6, 1946; s. Thomas Hugh and Catherine Amelia (Slavin) G.; m. Maryam Aminzadeh, Jan. 26, 1985. B.A. in History and Polit. Sci, SUNY, Stony Brook, 1971; M.B.A., Cornell U., 1977. Real estate salesman Martin Assocs., Killington, Vt., 1972-75; asst. to pres., asst. to bd. dirs. United Nuclear Corp./UNC Resources, Falls Church, Va., 1977-79, treas., 1979-83, v.p., 1980-83; v.p., chief fin. officer Sage Systems Inc., Rockville, Md., 1984-88; exec. v.p., chief oper. officer Chartway Techs., Rockville, 1988-92; pres., chief exec. officer Med. Claims Rev. Svc., 1992-94; pres., CEO Mitchell Med., 1994-97; exec. v.p. sales and mktg. Mitchell Internat., 1995-97; bd. dirs. Amteva Techs.; COO, dir. Amteva Techs., 1997—; prin. The Ryegate Group, 1997—. Bd. dirs. Falls Church Jr. Achievement, 1980-83. Served with USNR, 1965-67.

GARAN, D. G. See GARANCE, DOMINICK

GARANCE, DOMINICK (D. G. GARAN), lawyer, author; b. Varaklani, Latvia, Oct. 14, 1912; came to U.S., 1950, naturalized, 1955; s. John and Virginia (Cakuls) Garans. LL.M., U. Riga, Latvia, 1935; J.U.D., U. Freiburg, Germany, 1945; LL.D., U. Paris, France, 1947; Ph.D., U. London, Eng., 1949. Bar: N.Y. 1958. Atty.-at-law, legal counsel Ministry of Welfare, Riga, 1936-42; law sec. French Mil. Govt. in Germany, Freiburg, 1945-46; documentary officer Harvard Law Sch. Internat. Program of Taxation, 1952-57; pvt. practice law N.Y.C., 1958—. Author: The Paradox of Pleasure and Relativity, 1963, Relativity for Psychology, A Causal Law for the Modern Alchemy, 1968, The Key to the Sciences of Man, 1975, Against Ourselves: Disorders from Improvements under the Organic Limitedness of Man, 1979, Our Sciences Ruled by Human Prejudice, 1987. Mem. ABA, N.Y. State Bar Assn., N.Y. State Trial Lawyers Assn., N.Y. Acad. Sci., Philosophy of Sci. Assn., Am. Assn. Advancement Sci., Lacuania. Address: 2926 E 196th St Bronx NY 10461-3804 *All our positive motivations and capacities, like love and interests, are satisfactions or pleasures. But satisfaction can come only from an equal need, that is nonsatisfaction; and pleasure release without equal restrictions leads to exhaustion or stress—because of our organic limitedness. Otherwise, everybody would increase only the positive, pleasant capacities.*

GARAUFIS, NICHOLAS G., federal official; b. Paterson, N.J., Sept. 28, 1948; widower; children: James, Matthew.; AB, Columbia Coll., 1969; JD, Columbia U., 1974. Assoc. Chadbourne & Parke, 1974-75; asst. atty. gen. N.Y. State, 1975-78; counsel to Hon. Claire Shulman/Pres. of Borough of Queens, N.Y.C., 1978-86; pvt. practice Queens, N.Y.; chief counsel FAA, Washington, 1995—. Office: US Dept Transp FAA/Office Chief Counsel 800 Independence Ave SW Washington DC 20591-0001

GARAVELLI, JOHN STEPHEN, biochemistry research scientist; b. Memphis, Sept. 7, 1947; s. Daniel and Frances Louise (Chambers) G. BS, Duke U., 1969; PhD, Wash. U., St. Louis, 1975. Postdoctoral fellow Duke Marine Lab., Beaufort, N.C., 1975-76; postdoctoral fellow, lectr. U. Del., Newark, 1976-80; rsch. assoc., lectr. Tex. A&M U., College Station, 1980-83; sr. rsch. fellow NASA Ames Rsch. Ctr., Moffett Field, Calif., 1983-85; rsch. assoc., dir. computer ops. Agouron Inst., La Jolla, Calif., 1986; dir. computer ops. Biomolecular Analysis Facility U. Ill., Chgo., 1986-88; sr. rsch. scientist, assoc. dir. Nat. Biomed. Rsch. Found. Protein Info. Resource, Washington, 1989-96, assoc. dir., 1996—. Contbr. articles to profl. jours. Candidate Tenn. Ho. of Reps., Shelby County 13th Dist., 1970. With U.S. Army, 1970-72. Proctor & Gamble Acad. scholar, 1965-68; grantee Tenn. Acad. Sci. Rsch., 1964-65, NSF Undergrad. Rsch. Tng., 1968-69, NIH Predoctoral Trainee, 1969-70, 71-75, NASA Rsch. Assoc., 1982-83; fellow NASA, summers 1982, 83, NRC Sr. Rsch., 1983-85. Mem. AAAS, Am. Chem. Soc., Am. Philatelic Soc., Am. Soc. Gravitational and Space Biology, Internat. Soc. Study of Origin of Life, Internat. Union of Pure and Applied Chemistry, Commn. on Profls. in Sci. and Tech., Protein Soc., Am. Uniform Assn., Washington Philos. Soc. (pres. 1999). Democrat. Home: PO Box 3783 Washington DC 20007-0283 Office: Nat Biomed Rsch Found 3990 Reservoir Rd NW Washington DC 20007-2126

GARBA, EDWARD ALOYSIUS, financial executive; b. Newark, Sept. 26, 1921; s. Edward Victor and Ludmila (Krcah) G.; m. Martha Rheinlander, Aug. 29, 1953; 1 dau., Darina (Mrs. Gerald Kreitschitz). Diploma Engr., U. Commerce, Bratislava, Czechoslovakia, 1946; M.S., Columbia U., 1953. Mgr. Slovak Textile Works, Czechoslovakia, 1946-48; treas. Alltex Service Corp., N.Y.C., 1949-53; pub. accountant Peat, Marwick, Mitchell & Co., 1953-57; chief accountant internat. operations McCann-Erickson, Inc., 1957-60, asst. to treas., 1960-62; treas. McCann-Erickson Corp. Internat., hdqrs. internat. operations Interpub. group, Geneva, Switzerland, 1962-65; v.p., treas. internet. operations Interpub. Group McCann-Erickson Corp. Internat., Geneva, 1965-67; v.p., asst. treas. Interpub. Group Cos., Inc., N.Y.C., 1967-73; sr. v.p., treas. Interpub. Group Cos., Inc., 1973—. Chmn. Slovak-Am. Cultural Center, N.Y.C. Mem. N.Y. Credit and Financial Mgmt. Assn. Roman Catholic. Club: New York Athletic. Home: 125 Carleon Ave Larchmont NY 10538-3222 Office: 1271 Avenue Of The Americas New York NY 10020-1300

GARBACIAK-BOBBER, JOYCE KATHERINE, news anchor; b. Chgo., July 9, 1962; d. John Anthony and Irene Helen (Mroz) Garbaciak; m. Bernard John Bobber, Apr. 8, 1989; children: Caitlin Elizabeth, Meredith Grace, Grace Carolyn. BS in Journalism, Northwestern U., 1984, MS in Journalism, 1985. Reporter, anchor WSAW-TV, Wausau, Wis., 1985-87, WTVF-TV, Nashville, 1987-88, WITI-TV, Milw., 1988—; guest spkr. in field. Telethon advisor Muscular Dystrophy Assn., Milw., 1989-97; hon. UNICEF month chair UN Children's Fund, Milw., 1992-95; debate moderator Assn. for Women Lawyers, 1995-98. Recipient various honors Milw. Press Club, 1989-99, Excellence in Journalism award State Bar Wis., Madison, 1989, 90, 93, 99, Best News Series award AP, Wis., 1990, Best News Series award Wis. Broadcasters Assn., Madison, 1990, 91, 93, Best Hard News and Reporting and Best Svc. to Children, 1998, Profl. Communicator of Yr. award Alverno Coll. chpt. Women in Comm., 1996, Emmy award for excellence in news anchoring Chgo. chpt. NATAS, 1997, others. Mem. Radio and TV News Dirs. Assn. Office: WITI-TV 9001 N Green Bay Rd Milwaukee WI 53209-1297

GARBACZ, GERALD GEORGE, information services company executive; b. San Francisco, Oct. 12, 1936; s. George and Violette (Derbeck) G.; m. Jane E. Snyder, July 1, 1961; children: Geoffrey, Gregory. Student, Dartmouth Coll., 1954-55, M.B.A., 1965; B.S., U.S. Naval Acad., 1959; postgrad., U.S. Naval War Coll., 1978. Asst. to v.p. corp. planning Cummins Engine Co., Columbus, Ind., 1965-66; exec. dir. fin. planning and analysis Cummins Engine Co., 1967; asst. to sec. defense (White House fellow), 1968-69; dir. corp. planning Boise Cascade Corp., Idaho, 1970-72; v.p. finance, treas. Phillips Industries, Dayton, Ohio, 1972-74; ops. asst. W.R. Grace & Co., N.Y.C., 1974-75; v.p. W.R. Grace & Co., 1975-80, pres. Baker & Taylor div., 1980-83, sr. v.p., 1983-86, exec. v.p., 1986-92; chmn., chief exec. officer Baker & Taylor, Inc., 1992-94; chmn., CEO Nashua (N.H.) Corp., 1996—; bd. dirs. So. N.H. Regional Med. Ctr.; chmn. bd. dirs. Cerion Techs., 1996-98; instr. Ind. U., 1967-68, UCLA, 1972-74; cons. Dept. Def., 1969-70; regional selection panelist Pres.'s Commn. on White House Fellows, 1971, 72, 79-81, 84-86; endowment trustee Am. Libr. Assn., 1994-97; trustee Gettysburg Coll., 1995—; dir. White House Fellows Found., 1995—, chmn., 1997-98; mem. Pres.'s Commn. on White House Fellows, 1997. Chmn. Idaho steering com. Common Cause, 1972; bd. overseers Amos Tuck Sch. Bus. Adminstrn., Dartmouth, 1970-76; elder Boise (Idaho) Presbyn. Ch., 1967-69, Southwestern Presbyn. Ch., Centerville, Ohio, 1971-72, Wilton (Conn.) Presbyn. Ch., 1978-81; pres., bd. trustees Presbytery of So. New Eng., 1995-96. Maj. USMCR, 1959-82. Mem. Bus. and Indsl. Assn. N.H. (bd. dirs. 1997—), U.S. Naval Acad. Alumni Assn. Club: Dartmouth (N.Y.). Office: Nashua Corp 44 Franklin St Nashua NH 03060-2665

GARBACZ, PATRICIA FRANCES, school social worker, therapist; b. Hamtramck, Mich., Nov. 26, 1941; d. Stanley and Frances (Harubin) G. BS, Siena Heights Coll., 1969; M. Pastoral Counseling, St. Paul U., Ottawa, Can., 1972; ThM, St. John Provincial Sem., 1983; MSW, Wayne State U., 1989. Cert. social worker Acad. Cert. Social Workers; cert. sch. social worker; lic. marriage and family therapist; cert. addictions counselor level I. Assoc. dir. vocations Archdiocese of Detroit, 1975-77; co-dir. of inst. for women Archdiocese of Lusaka (Zambia), 1977-78; pastoral minister Archdiocese of Detroit, 1979-80, assoc. dir. preformation, 1980-84; tchr., ministry coord. Bishop Borgess High Sch., Redford, Mich., 1984-86; tchr., dept. chair Aquinas High Sch., Southgate, Mich., 1986-88; therapist Community Coun. on Drug Abuse/Livonia (Mich.) Counseling, 1988-89; substance abuse therapist Oxford Inst., St. Clair Shores, Mich., 1989-91; sch. social worker Lakeshore Pub. Schs., St. Clair Shores, 1990—; therapist Macomb Child Guidance, 1989-96. Mem. NASW, Am. Assn. Marriage and Family Therapists, Mich. Assn. Sch. Social Workers. Avocations: reading, walking, piano, dulcimer, spinning and weaving.

GARBACZ, STEPHEN LAWRENCE, financial director; b. Huntsville, Ala., Jan. 6, 1959; arrived in Poland, 1996; s. Michael Lawrence and Mary Lee (Withers) G.; m. Ineke Prins. BS in Econs., George Mason U., 1981; MBA, NYU, 1986; German lang. cert., Goethe-Inst., Frankfurt, Germany, 1990. Rsch. asst. Brookings Instn., Washington, 1981-82; cons. ICF Inc., Washington, 1982-84; mergers and acquisitions staff Kraft Internat., Rye, N.Y., 1986-89; fin. contr. Kraft Jacobs Suchard, Bremen, Germany, 1989-92; fin. mgr. Kraft Jacobs Suchard, Zürich, 1992-96; fin. dir. Kraft Jacobs Suchard, Warsaw, 1996—. Mem. Am. C. of C. Poland, Beta Gamma Sigma, Alpha Chi, Omicron Delta Epsilon.

GARBARINO, JOSEPH WILLIAM, labor arbitrator, economics and business educator; b. Medina, N.Y., Dec. 7, 1919; s. Joseph Francis and Savina M. (Volpone) G.; m. Mary Jane Godward, Sept. 18, 1948; children: Ann, Joan, Susan, Ellen. B.A., Duquesne U., 1942; M.A., Harvard U., 1947, Ph.D., 1949. Faculty U. Calif., Berkeley, 1949—; prof. U. Calif., 1960-88, dir. Inst. Bus. and Econ. Research, 1962-88, prof. emeritus, 1988—; vis. lectr. Cornell U., 19S9-60, UCLA, 1949, SUNY, Buffalo, 1972; Fulbright lectr. U. Glasgow, Scotland, 1969; vis. scholar U. Warwick; mem. staff Brookings Instn., 1959-60; vis. lectr. U. Minn., 1978; labor arbitrator. Author: Health Plans and Collective Bargaining, 1960, Wage Policy and Long Term Contracts, 1962, Faculty Bargaining: Change and Conflict, 1975, Faculty Bargaining in Unions in Transition. Served with U.S. Army, 1942-45, 51-53. Decorated Bronze Star. Democrat. Roman Catholic. Home: 7708 Ricardo Ct El Cerrito CA 94530-3344

GARBARINO, ROBERT PAUL, retired administrative dean, lawyer; b. Wanaque, N.J., Oct. 6, 1929; s. Attillio and Theresa (Napello) G.; m. Joyce A. Sullivan, June 29, 1957; children: Lynn, Lisa, Mark, Steven. BBA cum laude, St. Bonaventure U., 1951; JD with highest class honors, Villanova U., 1956. Bar: Pa. 1956, U.S. Dist. Ct. (ea. dist.) Pa. 1956, U.S. Ct. Appeals (3d cir.) 1962, U.S. Supreme Ct. 1962, U.S. Tax Ct. 1966, U.S. Ct. Internat. Trade 1966. Law clk. U.S. Dist. Ct. (ea. dist.) Pa., Phila., 1956-57; asst. counsel Phila. Electric Co., Phila., 1957-60, asst. gen. counsel, 1960-62; ptnr. Kania & Garbarino & predecessor firm, Phila. and Bala Cynwyd, Pa., 1962-81; assoc. dean adminstrn. Sch. Law Villanova (Pa.) U., 1981-96; right-of-way cons. Edison Electric Inst., N.Y.C., 1960-62; trustee reorgn. Tele-Tronics Co., Phila., 1962-64; mem. bd. consultors Law Sch. Villanova U., 1967-81, chmn., vice chmn. bd. consultors, 1971-96, chmn. Profl. Sports Career Counseling Panel Villanova U.; mem pres.'s adv. coun. St. Bonaventure U., N.Y., 1975-86, chmn., 1976-78. Contbr. articles to profl. jours. Mem. community leadership seminar Fels Inst. Local and State Govt., 1961. Staff sgt. USMC, 1951-53. Mem. ABA, Phila. Bar Assn., Order of Coif. Home: 120 Ladderback Ln Devon PA 19333-1815

GARBATY, THOMAS JAY, retired English language educator; b. Jan. 10, 1930. BA, Haverford Coll., 1951; MA, U. Pa., 1954, PhD, 1957. Asst. prof. English Dept. Clemson U., 1957-60; mem. faculty dept. English, U. Mich., Ann Arbor, 1960-93, prof., 1962-1993, prof. emeritus, 1993—; vis. prof. U. Bern, Switzerland, 1970-80; TV commentator, PBS. Contbg. author Variorum Chaucer, 1970-90; asst. editor: Middle English Dictionary, 1960-61; mem. editl. bd. Genre, Envoi; contbr. to Medieval Englan, an Encyclopedia and Modern Language Assn. Approaches to Teaching the Canterbury Tales; reviewer, contbr. articles to profl. jours. Recipient Amoco Teaching award, 1968, State of Mich. Teaching Excellence award, 1990. Mem. MLA (life, chmn. divsn. on Chaucer 1976), Medieval Acad., New Chaucer Soc., Phi Beta Kappa. E-mail: tgarbaty@umich.edu. Home: 2981 Hickory Ln Ann Arbor MI 48104 Office: U Mich Dept English Ann Arbor MI 48109

GARBER, BARRY L., magistrate judge; b. Phila., May 16, 1930; s. Morris and Mollye Lorraine (Greenberg) G.; m. Barbara Lee Kagan, Apr. 4, 1954; children: Lisa, Terri. BA, Emory Univ., Atlanta, 1951; JD, Univ. Miami, Fla., 1954. Bar: Fla. 1954, U.S. Dist. Ct. (so. dist.) Fla. 1954, (so. dist. trial bar) Fla. 1983, U.S. Ct. Appeals (5th cir.) 1968, (11th cir.) 1989, U.S. Supreme Ct. 1967. Assoc. Dubbin, Blatt & Schiff, Miami, Fla., 1954-57; asst. state atty. Dade State Atty's Office, Miami, Fla., 1957-59; ptnr. Garber & Chadroff, Miami, Fla., 1959-71, Garber & Buoniconti, Miami, Fla., 1972-86, Dubbin, Berkman, Garber, Miami, Fla., 1986-91; magistrate judge U.S. Dist. Ct. (so. dist.) Fla., 1991—. Bd. trustee Project to Cure Paralysis, Miami, Fla., 1986—. Recipient James L. Kind award, 1998. Mem. ABA, The Fla. Bar, Am. Inns of Court. Democrat. Jewish. Avocation: music. Office: US Courthouse 300 NE 1st Ave Miami FL 33132-2126

GARBER, DANIEL ELLIOT, philosophy educator; b. Schenectady, N.Y., Sept. 26, 1949; s. William and Laura Sarah (Coplon) G.; m. Susan McClary, 1972 (div. 1982); m. Susan Joyce Paul, 1982; children: Hannah Laura, Elisabeth Sarah. AB, Harvard U., 1971, AM in Philosophy, 1974, PhD in Philosophy, 1975. Asst. prof. U. Chgo., 1975-82, assoc. prof., 1982-86, prof. dept. philosophy, 1986—, chair dept., 1987-94, chair Conceptual Found. of Sci., 1994-95, 99—, Lawrence Kimpton Disting. Svc. prof., 1995—, assoc. provost rsch. and edn., 1995-98; vis. asst. prof. U. Minn., Mpls., 1979, Johns Hopkins U., Balt., 1980-81, Princeton (N.J.) U., 1982-83; mem. Inst. Advanced Study, Princeton, 1985-86. Author: Descartes' Metaphysical Physics, 1992; co-editor: The Cambridge History of 17th Century Philosophy, 1998, The Yale Leibniz; co-translator, editor: Leibniz: Philosophical Essays, 1989; contbr. articles to profl. jours. Fellow Am. Coun. Learned Socs., 1985-86; grantee NEH, 1986-94, NSF, 1991-94. Mem. Am. Philos. Assn., History of Sci. Soc., Philosophy of Sci. Assn. (bd. govs. 1990-93), Brit. Soc. for History of Philosophy, Internat. Berkeley Soc. (bd. officers), Leibniz Soc. Am. (pres.). Office: U Chgo Dept Philosophy 1050 E 59th St Chicago IL 60637-1512

GARBER, HAROLD DAVID, school system superintendent, columnist; b. Petersburg, W.Va., Mar. 17, 1941; s. E.C. and Charlotte V. (Dean) G.; m. Irma Bergdoll Bauer, July 4, 1976; stepchildren: Yvonne, Sonja, Michelle, Germaine, Darwin. BA, Bridgewater (Va.) Coll., 1963; MEd, James Madison U., 1978; postgrad., U. Md., 1984-87. Cert. supt., W.Va. Instr. social studies Petersburg H.S., 1966-71, asst. prin., 1971-78, prin., 1978-85; adminstrv. asst. Grant County Bd. of Edn., Petersburg, 1985-96, supt., 1996—. Editor: Grant County, Our Heritage, 1994; columnist A Backward Look, 1985—; sportscaster WELD Radio, Fisher, W.Va., 1970—. Part-time minister Oak Dale Ch. of the Brethren, Petersburg, 1987-97; mem. State of W.Va. Archives and History Commn., Charleston, 1986-88. Mem. NEA, ASCD, Am. Numismatic Assn. (life), Am. Philatelic Assn. (life), W.Va. Edn. Assn., W.Va. Assn. Sch. Adminstrs., Kiwanis (pres. Petersburg chpt. 1974, lt. gov. 1994). Avocations: writing, broadcasting, hunting, travel, genealogy. Home: PO Box 665 Petersburg WV 26847-0665

GARBER, PAUL WILLIAM, lawyer; b. Boston, Nov. 16, 1934; s. Rubin Elias and Sarah Rose Garber. AB in Medieval History magna cum laude, Harvard Coll., 1956, JD, 1961; diploma in Command and Staff, U.S. Naval War Coll., 1967, diploma in Naval Warfare, 1970. Registered Land Court Title Examiner, 1966. Atty. Garber and Garber, Esqs., Boston, 1961-76, pres., 1976—; consul. Consulate of Chile, Boston, 1974—. Author: (with Philip C. Garber) The Political Constitution of Chile-An English Translation, 1984; contbr. articles to profl. jours. Pres. Constn. Naval Res. Assoc., 1973-75, Navy Chpt. 5 Res. Officers Assn., 1979, First Region Naval Res. Assn., 1980, exec. v.p. 1971-72, Club Chileno, hon. pres., 1974-80, dir. Alumni Assoc., West End House, 1963-99, Scholarship Com., 1976-99, bd. dirs. Eastern Mass. chpt. Navy League U.S., 1976-85; judge Adv. Mass. Bay Coun., NLUS, 1985-99, dir. emeritus, 1999—. Capt. USNR, 1956-86. Decorated Navy Commendation medal, USN; knight comdr. order Bernardo O'Higgins, Govt. Chile. Mem. Res. Officers Assoc., USN Inst., Medieval Acad. Am., Navy League of the U.S., USS Const. Mus., Surface Warfare Assoc., Naval War Coll. Found., Boston Athenaeum, Harvard Club of Boston, Wardroom Club, Caleuche Litoral Valparaiso. Avocations: gardening, reading, antiquarian research. E-Mail: conchile@bitwise.net. Office: Consulate of Chile 79 Milk St Suite 600 Boston MA 02109

GARBER, ROBERT EDWARD, lawyer, insurance company executive; b. N.Y.C., Jan. 4, 1949; s. Edward Robert and Estelle (Rosenberg) G.; m. Mary Ellen Roche, Jan. 17, 1981; 1 child, Edward Thomas. A.B., Princeton U., 1970; J.D., Columbia U., 1973. Bar: N.Y. 1974. Law clk. U.S. Dist. Ct. (so. dist.), N.Y.C., 1973-75; assoc. Debevoise, Plimpton, Lyons & Gates, N.Y.C., 1976-79; assoc. counsel, v.p. Irving Trust, N.Y.C., 1979-82, sr. v.p., 1982-87; gen. counsel Irving Bank Corp. and Irving Trust Co., N.Y.C., 1987-89; sr. v.p., dep. gen. counsel Equitable Life Assurance Soc. U.S., N.Y.C., 1989-93; sr. v.p., gen. counsel Equitable Cos., Inc. and Equitable Life Assurance Soc. U.S., 1993-94, exec. v.p., gen. counsel, 1994—; dir. Am. Arbitration Assn. Served to capt. USAR, 1970-78. Mem. Assn. of Bar of City of N.Y. Home: 45 Sturgis Rd Bronxville NY 10708-5012 Office: Equitable Life Assurance Soc US 1290 Avenue Of The Americas New York NY 10104

GARBER, SAMUEL BAUGH, lawyer, retail company executive; b. Chgo., Aug. 16, 1934; s. Morris and Yetta G.; m. Marietta C. Bratta; children: Debra Lee, Diane Lori. JD, U. Ill., 1958. MBA, U. Chgo., 1968. Bar: Ill., 1958. Ptnr. Brown, Dashow and Langluttig, Chgo., 1960-62; corp. counsel Walgreen Co., 1962-69; v.p., gen. counsel, exec. asst. to the pres. Carlyle & Co., 1969-73; dir. legal affairs Stop & Shop Co., Inc., 1973-74; gen. counsel Goldblatt Bros., Inc., 1974-76; v.p., sec., gen. counsel, dir. Evans, Inc., 1976—; prof. mgmt. DePaul U., 1975—; adj. prof. bus. law grad. sch. bus. U. Chgo., 1993; arbitrator N.Y. Stock Exch., 1996, Chgo. Merc. Exch., 1996, Am. Stock Exch., 1997, Nat. Futures Assn., 1997. Columnist Gardner's Gurus Tribune Media Svcs. With U.S. Army, 1958-60. Mem. ABA, NYSE (arbitrator 1996—), Am. Arbitration Assn. (arbitrator 1993—), Nat. Retail Fedn., Il!. Retail Mchts. Assn. Home: 2626 N Lakeview Ave Chicago IL 60614-1809 Office: Evans Inc 36 S State St Ste 600 Chicago IL 60603-2691

GARBER, VICTOR, stage and film actor; b. London, Ont., Can., Mar. 16, 1949. Appeared in films Liberace: Behind the Music, 1988, Light Sleeper, 1991, Sleepless in Seattle, 1993, Life with Mikey, 1993, Mixed Nuts, 1994, First Wives Club, 1996, Titanic, 1997, others; TV films include Grand Larceny, 1991, First Circle, 1991, Dieppe, 1991, Queen, 1993, Let Me Call You Sweetheart, 1997, Invisible Child, 1999; TV appearances include Days and NIghts of Molly Dodd, 1987, I'll Fly Away, 1991, E.N.G. intermittently, Kung Fu: The Legend Continues, 1992, Law and Order, 1990, Outer LImits, 1996; appeared on stage on Broadway in Sweeney Todd, revival of Damn Yankees, others. Office: care The Gersh Agy 232 N Canon Dr Beverly HIlls CA 90210*

GARBERDING, LARRY GILBERT, utilities companies executive; b. Albert City, Iowa, Oct. 29, 1938; s. Gilbert D. and Lavern Marie Garberding; m. Elizabeth Ann Hankens, Aug. 20, 1961; children: Scott Richard, Kathryn Ann, Michael John. BS, Iowa State U., 1960. CPA, Nebr. Ptnr. Arthur Andersen & Co., Chgo., 1960-71; chief fin. officer Kans.-Nebr. Natural Gas Co., Inc., Hastings, Nebr., 1971-81; chief fin. officer Tenn. Gas Transmission, Houston, 1981-83, exec. v.p., 1983-87; pres. Tenn. Gas Mktg., Houston, 1987-88, NICOR Inc., Naperville, Ill., 1988-90; exec. v.p., chief fin. officer Detroit Edison Co., 1990—. With U.S. Army, 1961. Mem. AICPA. Republican. Lutheran. Office: The Detroit Edison Co 2000 2nd Ave Detroit MI 48226-1279

GARBIN, ALBENO PATRICK, sociology educator; b. Girard, Ill., June 20, 1932; s. Cipriano and Angelina (Sommavillia) G.; m. Carol Townsend Nichols, Sept. 3, 1969; children—Angela Marie, Tina Ann, A. Patrick, Carol Anne. A.B., Blackburn Coll., 1956; M.A., La. State U., 1959, Ph.D., 1963. Instr., asst. prof. sociology U. Omaha, 1961-64; asst. prof. Fla. State U., Tallahassee, 1964-66; assoc. prof., specialist occupation edn. Ohio State U., Columbus, 1966-68; prof. sociology U. Ga., Athens, 1968-97, prof. emeritus, 1997—, chmn. dept., 1982-90. Contbr. articles to profl. jours., chpts. to books. Served with U.S. Army, 1954-56. Recipient Research award Am. Personnel and Guidance Assn., 1977, Excellence in Undergrad. Teaching award U. Ga., 1978, Meritorious Svc. award Ga. Soc. Assn., 1991. Mem. Am. Sociol. Assn., So. Sociol. Soc., Ga. Sociol. Assn. (v.p. 1984-85, pres. 1986-87). Democrat. Roman Catholic. Avocations: gardening, photography. Home: 85 Timberland Trail Arnoldsville GA 30619-2216 Office: U Ga Dept Sociology Athens GA 30602 *Hard work is a requisite, but luck can be very helpful! A loving wife and family make it all worthwhile.*

GARBIS, MARVIN JOSEPH, judge; b. Balt., June 14, 1936; s. Samuel and Adele E. (Warshaw) G.; m. Phyllis Lorraine Zaroff, Aug. 27, 1961; children: Kendall Rose, Jason Anders, Kerri Jill. BES., Johns Hopkins U., 1958; JD, Harvard U., 1961; LLM, Georgetown U., 1962. Bar: D.C. 1961, Md. 1962. Trial atty. Tax Div., Dept. Justice, Washington, 1962-67; sole practice Balt., 1967-71; ptnr. Garbis, Marvel & Junghans, Balt., 1971-86, Melnicove, Kaufman, Weiner, Smouse & Garbis, Balt., 1986-88, Johnson & Gibbs, Washington, 1988-89; judge U.S. Dist. Ct. Md., 1989—; lectr. U. Md. Law Sch., 1970-85, NYU Fed. Tax Inst., 1970, 74, 79, 87-88; adj. prof. Georgetown U. Law Sch., 1978-80, U. Balt. Law Sch., 1982—; adviser on tax procedure study, jud. com. U.S. Senate, 1969-70; mem. adv. commr. to commr. IRS, 1982; mem. adv. coun. U.S. Claims Ct., 1982—; mem. Md. Inst. for Continuing Profl. Edn. for Lawyers, 1978-80, pres., 1980-82. Author: (with Frome) Procedures in Federal Tax Controversy, 1968, (with Schwait) Tax Refund Litigation, 1971, Tax Court Practice, 1974, (with Struntz) Cases and Materials on Federal Tax Procedure, Civil and Criminal, 1981, (with Junghans and Struntz) Federal Tax Litigation, 1985, (with Struntz and Rubin) Cases and Materials on Tax Procedure and Tax Fraud, 2d edit., 1987, (with Rubin and Morgan) Cases and Material on Tax Procedure and Tax Fraud, 3d edit., 1991; contbr. articles to profl. jours. Recipient Jules Ritholz Meml. Merit award, 1996; E. Barrett Prettyman fellow Georgetown Law Sch., 1961-62; named hon. justice Fed. Ct. Australia, 1998. Mem. Fed. Bar Assn. (pres. Balt. chpt. 1972-73, nat. vice chmn. tax com. 1974-76), Md. Bar Assn. (chmn. tax sect. 1970-71, chmn. continuing legal edn. 1973-80), ABA (chmn. ct. procedure com., tax sect. 1975-77), Balt. Bar Assn. (bd. govs. 1974-79), Fed. Cir. Bar Assn. (bd. dirs. 1985—). Am. Law Inst., Md. Inst. Continuing Profl. Education Lawyers (pres. 1981-82). Office: US Dist Ct 101 W Lombard St Ste 404 Baltimore MD 21201-2626

GARCETTI, GILBERT I., prosecutor. BS, U. So. Calif., L.A.; JD, UCLA, 1968. Dist. atty. County of Los Angeles, 1983—. Office: County of Los Angeles Dist Attys Office 210 W Temple St Rm 18-709 Los Angeles CA 90012-3210*

GARCHIK, LEAH LIEBERMAN, journalist; b. Bklyn., May 2, 1945; d. Arthur Louis and Mildred (Steinberg) Lieberman; m. Jerome Marcus Garchik, Aug. 11, 1968; children—Samuel, Jacob. B.A., Bklyn. Coll., 1966. Editorial asst. San Francisco Chronicle, 1972-79, writer, editor, 1979-83, editor This World,, 1983-84, columnist, 1984—; also author numerous book and movie reviews, features and profiles; Author: San Francisco; the City's Sights and Secrets, 1995; panelist (radio quiz show) Mind Over Matter; gossip reporter Bay TV; contbr. articles to mags. Vice pres. Golden Gate Kindergarten Assn., San Francisco, 1978; pres. Performing Arts Workshop, San Francisco, 1977-79; bd. dirs. Home Away From Homelessness, 1994—. Recipient 1st prize Nat. Soc. Newspaper Columnists, 1992. Mem. Deutsche Music Verein, Newspaper Guild. Democrat. Jewish. Home: 156 Baker St San Francisco CA 94117-2111 Office: San Francisco Chronicle 901 Mission St San Francisco CA 94103-2905

GARCIA, ADOLFO RAMON, lawyer; b. Havana, Cuba, Nov. 5, 1948; came to U.S., 1961; s. Adolfo Damian and Luz I. (Garcia) G.; m. Elizabeth Ensor, July 17, 1971; children: Andrew, Laurence. AB magna cum laude, Harvard U., 1971; JD, Georgetown U., 1974. Bar: N.Y. 1975, Mass. 1981. Assoc. Cahill Gordon & Reindel, N.Y.C., 1974-79, Choate, Hall & Stewart, Boston, 1979-82; sr. ptnr. McDermott, Will & Emery, Boston, 1982—, mem. mgmt. coms., 1993—, sr. coord. Spanish-speaking countries/transactions area, 1991—; bd. dirs. Carboclor Industrias. Sec., co-chmn. legal affairs com., bd. dirs. Internat. Bus. Ctr. New Eng. Inc., Boston, 1983-87; past chmn. and pres., bd. dirs. Boston Ctr. for Internat. Visitors, 1981-86; mem. Mass. Internat. Trade Coun., Boston, 1984-86; v.p., dir. New Eng.-Latin Am. Bus. Coun. Mem. Internat. Bar Assn., Boston Bar Assn. (co-chmn. pvt. internat. law sect. 1982-86), InterAm. Bar Assn., Essex County Club, Manchester (Mass.) Yacht Club. Republican. Home: October Hill Prides Crossing MA 01965 Office: McDermott Will & Emery 28 State St 33rd Flr Boston MA 02109-1775

GARCIA, ALEXANDER, orthopedic surgeon; b. N.Y.C., July 3, 1919; s. Alexander and Pilar (Prieto) G.; m. Helen Ann Proskey, June 12, 1943; 1 son, Alexander, III. B.S., CCNY, 1940; M.D., L.I. Coll. Medicine, 1943. Diplomate: Am. Bd. Orthopaedic Surgery. Intern Syracuse (N.Y.) U. Med. Center, 1944, asst. resident in gen. surgery, 1944-45, chief resident, 1945-46; resident in gen. surgery Nassau Hosp., Mineola, N.Y., 1948; asst. resident in orthopaedic surgery N.Y. Orthopaedic Hosp., N.Y.C., 1948-50; resident, jr. Annie C. Kane fellow N.Y. Orthopaedic Hosp., 1950-51, acting dir. orthopaedic service, 1976-77, hosp. dir., 1977-83, dir. emeritus, 1983—; chief orthopaedic surg. sect. North Shore Hosp., Manhasset, N.Y., 1957-70, cons.,

1970—; mem. faculty Columbia U. Coll. Phys. and Surg., 1952—, prof. orthopaedic surgery, 1972—, chmn. dept., 1977—, Frank E. Stinchfield prof., 1978-83, Frank E. Stinchfield prof. emeritus, 1983—; pres. med. bd. Presbyn. Hosp.-Columbia Presbyn. Med. Ctr., N.Y.C., 1979-82; cons. numerous area hosps. *In celebrating its tenth anniversary, Orthopaedic Review examined the past and looked into the future. It was the consensus of the Editorial Board and publisher that we should move ahead in disseminating orthopaedic information to the practicing orthopaedic surgeon and reinforce the review system to assure high quality articles in the Journal. With these goals in mind, I have been invited to be Editor-In-Chief of Orthopaedic Review. I am honored and hope to devote the time to the development and supervision of the editorial content.* Editor-in-chief Orthopedic Review; mem. editoral bds. profl. jours. Served as officer M.C. AUS, 1946-48. Mem. Internat. Soc. Orthopaedic Surgery and Traumatology, A.C.S., AMA, Am. Acad. Orthopaedic Surgeons, Am. Assn. for Surgery of Trauma, Pan Am. Med. Assn., Assn. Bone and Joint Surgeons, Am. Orthopaedic Assn., N.Y. State Med. Soc., N.Y. Acad. Medicine, N.Y. Acad. Scis., N.Y. State Soc. Orthopaedic Surgeons, Soc. Ortopedia y Traumatologia Dominicana. Democrat.

GARCIA, ANDREW B., chemical engineer; b. Las Cruces, N.Mex., Apr. 22, 1949; s. Rudolf A. and Margaret (Rivera) G.; m. Katherine D. Montano, July 5, 1974 (dec. Aug. 1996); children: Lauren, Alexandra. BS in Chem. Engrng. with honors, N.Mex. State U., Las Cruces, 1972; MBA, St. Mary's Coll., Moraga, Calif., 1979; postgrad., U. Calif., Berkeley, 1994. Registered environ. assessor; cert. hazardous materials mgr. Design engr. Gen. Electric Co., San Jose, Calif., 1972-75; chem. engr. Chevron Chem. Co., Richmond, Calif., 1975-78; supr. Chevron Corp., San Francisco, 1978-80; supply product mgr. Chevron USA Inc., Walnut Creek, Calif., 1980-89; project mgr. Chevron Land & Devel. Co., San Francisco, 1989-93; environ. project mgr. Alameda County, Oakland, Calif., 1993-95; environ. support mgr. Computer Scis. Corp., Edwards AFB, Calif., 1995—. Park and recreation commr. City of Martinez, Calif., 1984-89; mem. citizens adv. bd. City of Martinez, 1989-91. Mem. AIChE, Project Mgmt. Inst. Roman Catholic. Achievements include reputation for being expert on the cleanup and remediation of rural, industrial and urban properties; successful management of multimillion dollar environmental projects. Home: 28420 N Rock Canyon Pl Santa Clarita CA 91350-5227 Office: Computer Scis Corp PO Box 446 Edwards CA 93523-0446

GARCIA, ANDY, actor; b. Havana, Cuba, Apr. 12, 1956. Student, Fla. Internat. U., U. Miami. Actor: (films) The Mean Season, 1985, 8 Million Ways to Die, 1986, The Untouchables, 1987, Stand and Deliver, 1987, American Roulette, 1988, Black Rain, 1989, Internal Affairs, 1990, The Godfather III, 1990 (Oscar nominee best supporting actor), Dead Again, 1991, Hero, 1992, Jennifer 8, 1992, When a Man Loves a Woman, 1994, Steal Big Steal Little, 1995, Things to Do in Denver When You're Dead, 1996, Night Falls on Manhattan, 1997, Lorca, 1997, Hoods, 1997, Desperate Measures, 1997 (TV) Swing Vote, 1999; actor, prodr.: (film) Just the Ticket, 1999; dir., prodr.: (films) Cachao, Like His Rhythm There Is No Other; music prodr.: (album) Cachao Master Sessions, vol. I (Grammy award 1994), Cachao Master Sessions, Vol. II (Grammy nominee 1995), Just the Ticket soundtrack. Office: Paradigm 10100 Santa Monica Blvd Fl 25 Los Angeles CA 90067-4003

GARCÍA, CELSO-RAMÓN, obstetrician and gynecologist; b. N.Y.C., Oct. 31, 1921; s. Celso García y Ondina and Oliva Menéndez (del Valle) G.; m. Shirley Jean Stoddard, Oct. 14, 1950; children: Celso-Ramón, Sarita Stoddard. BS, Queens Coll., 1942; MD, SUNY Downstate Med. Ctr., 1945; MA (hon.), U. Pa. Intern Norwegian Hosp., Bklyn., 1945-46; resident, rsch. fellow in gynecology Cumberland Hosp., Bklyn., 1949-50; assoc. in ob-gyn. U. P.R., San Juan, 1953-54; asst. prof. ob-gyn. Sch. Medicine and Tropical Medicine, San Juan, 1954-55; co-dir. Rock Reproductive Study Ctr.; asst. obstetrician and gynecologist Boston Lying-In Hosp.; assoc. surgeon Free Hosp. for Women, Brookline, Mass., 1955-65; sr. scientist, dir. tng. program in physiology reprodn. Worcester Found. for Exptl. Biology, Shrewsbury, Mass., 1960-62; asst. surgeon, chief Infertility Clinic, Mass. Gen. Hosp.; from asst., instr. to clin. assoc. ob-gyn. Harvard Med. Sch., 1962-65; prof. obstetrics and gynecology U. Pa., Phila., 1965-92; William Shippen, Jr. prof. human reprodn. U. Pa., 1970-92, William Shippen, Jr prof emeritus, 1992—, dir. infertility and reproductive endocrinology and surgery, 1987-95; extraordinary prof. U. San Luis Potosi, Mex., 1974; rapporteur com. of experts on clin. aspects oral gestogens WHO, Geneva, 1965; mem. ad hoc adv. com. contraceptive devel., contract program Nat. Inst. Child Health and Human Devel., 1971-75; mem. original team which developed clin. application of 1st FDA approved progestagen-estrogen combinations for oral contraception (the Pill); developer, dir. first formal tng. program in physiology of reprodn. in U.S.; innovator surg. approach to infertility of women; cons. Pa. Hosp., 1973-94; asst. staff Faulkner Hosp., Jamaica Plain, Boston; courtesy staff Glover Meml. Hosp., Needham, Mass.; adv. bd. Global Alliance for Women's Health, 1995—. Chmn. nat. med. adv. com. Planned Parenthood World Population, 1971-74; mem. nat. adv. child and human devel. coun. Nat. Inst. Child Health and Human Devel., 1981-84. With AUS, 1943-48. Recipient Carl G. Hartman award Am. Soc. Study of Sterility, 1961, MD Master Tchg. award Alumni Assn. SUNY, 1989, Recognition award APGO Wyeth-Ayerst, 1993, Frank L. Babbott award SUNY, 1995; Sidney Graves fellow in gynecology Harvard Med. Sch., 1955. Fellow ACS, ACOG, Coll. Physicians Phila.; mem. AMA, Global Alliance Women's Health (adv. bd. 1994—, rep. to U.N. Economic and Social Coun. 1998), Am. Soc. Gynecol. Surgeons, Am. Gynecol. and Obstet. Soc., Am. Physiol. Soc., Assn. Planned Parenthood Physicians (past pres.), Soc. Reproductive Surgeons (founding pres.), Am. Soc. Reprodn. Medicine (bd. dirs., past pres.), Phila. Obstet. Soc., Boston Obstet. Soc. (emeritus), Fedn. Columbian Socs. Ob-Gyn. (hon.), Cuban Soc. Ob-Gyn. (in exile, hon.), Masons, Sigma Xi. Republican. Presbyterian. Home: 109 Merion Rd Merion Station PA 19066-1734 Office: 3400 Spruce St Philadelphia PA 19104-4204

GARCIA, DANIEL P., real estate manager. BBA, Loyola U., L.A.; MBA, U. So. Calif.; JD, UCLA. Ptnr. Munger, Tolles & Olson, L.A.; sr. v.p., worldwide corp. real estate Warner Bros., 1991—; sr. v.p., corp. real estate Warner Music Group, 1996—. Contbr. articles on urban policy issues including land use, housing, development and urban planning to profl. jours. Hearing examiner L.A. City Police Commn., 1975-76; pres. L.A. Planning Commn., 1978-88; mem. L.A. Bd. Police Commrs.; apptd. 1993 by Mayor Riordan to Airport Commn.; transferred 1994 to Bd. Commns. L.A. Cmty. Redevel. Agy. (chmn.); transferred back to Airport Commn., 1995 (pres.); trustee Rockefeller Found.; mem. nat bd. dirs. Kaiser Found. Hosps. and Health Plans. Platoon sgt. combat infantry U.S. Army, 1967-69, Vietnam. Decorated Purple Heart with 2 oak leaf clusters, Silver Star, Bronze Star with oak leaf cluster, Air medal. Planning Assn. regional, state, nat. awards for excecellence in pub. planning. Office: Warner Bros 4000 Warner Blvd Bldg 137 Burbank CA 91522-0002*

GARCIA, DAVID P., construction company executive; b. Alice, Tex., Jan. 28, 1952; s. Reyes and Idalia (Ruiz) G.; m. Irma Mejia, Dec 23, 1971; children: Dave, Matthew, Michael. BBA in Acctg., Tex. A&I, Kingsville, 1975. Auditor I State of Tex., Corpus Christi, 1976-77; auditor II State of Tex., McAllen, 1977-80; v.p., controller US Home Corp., McAllen, 1980-96, exec. v.p., 1997—. Coach Boys and Girls Club, McAllen, Tex., 1990—, Nat. Youth Soccer Assn., McAllen, 1990—. Mem. Rio Grande Valley Builders Assn. (v.p. 1990-96, pres. 1991-97 Builder of Yr. 1990, 96). Avocations: golf, walking, coaching. Home: 6409 N First Ln Mcallen TX 78504 Office: US Home Corp 6521 N 10th Mcallen TX 78504

GARCIA, EDWARD J., federal judge; b. 1928. AA, Sacramento City Coll., 1951; LLB, U. Pacific, 1958. Dep. dist. atty. Sacramento County, 1959-64, supervising dep. dist. atty., 1964-69, chief dep. dist. atty., 1969-72; judge Sacramento Mcpl. Ct., 1972-84; judge U.S. Dist. Ct. (ea. dist.) Calif., Sacramento, 1984-96, sr. judge, 1996—. Served with U.S. Army Air Corps, 1946-49. Office: US Dist Ct US Courthouse Clerk Office 501 I St Rm 4-200 Sacramento CA 95814-4707

GARCIA, F. CHRIS, academic administrator, political science educator, public opinion researcher; b. Albuquerque, Apr. 15, 1940; s. Flaviano P. and Crucita A. Garcia; m. Sandra D. Garcia; children: Elaine L., Tanya C. BA, U. N.Mex., 1961, MA in Govt., 1964; PhD in Polit. Sci., U. Calif., Davis, 1972. Asst. prof. polit. sci. U. N.Mex., Albuquerque, 1970-74, assoc. prof., 1974-78, prof., 1978—, asst. dir. divsn. govt. rsch., 1970-72, assoc. dean Coll. Arts and Scis., 1975-80, dean Coll. Arts and Scis., 1980-86, v.p. acad. affairs, 1987-90, provost, 1993, 98—; founder Zia Rsch. Assocs., Inc., Albuquerque, 1973-94, also chmn. bd. dirs.; cons.-evaluator North Ctrl. Assn., 1994—. Author: Political Socialization of Chicano Children, 1973, La Causa Politica, 1974, The Chicano Political Experience, 1977, State and Local Government in New Mexico, 1979, New Mexico Government, 1976, 81, 94, Latinos and the Political System, 1988, Latino Voices, 1992, Pursuing Power, 1997. Mem. edn. com. Good Govt. Group; mem. charter rev. com. City of Albuquerque, 1999—. Mem. Western Polit. Sci. Assn. (pres. 1977-78), Am. Polit. Sci. Assn. (v.p. 1994-95, mem. exec. coun. 1984-86, sec. 1992-93), Am. Assn. Pub. Opinion Rsch., Coun. Colls. of Arts and Sci. (bd. dirs. 1982-85), Nat. Assn. State Univs. and Land Grant Colls. (mem. coun. acad. affairs 1987-90, mem. exec. com. 1989), Western Social Sci. Assn. (mem. exec. coun. 1973-76), Phi Beta Kappa, Phi Kappa Phi, Gold Key. Home: 1409 Snowdrop Pl NE Albuquerque NM 87112-6331 Office: U N Mex Polt Sci Dept Social Scis Bldg 2059 Albuquerque NM 87131

GARCIA, FRIEDA, community foundation executive. BA, New Sch. Social Rsch., 1964; AA (hon.), Roxbury C.C., 1987. Social worker Roxbury (Mass.) Multi-Svc. Ctr., 1966-71; exec. dir. La Alianza Hispana Inc., 1971-73; cmty. fellow MIT, Boston, 1974; spl. asst. to gov. Commonwealth of Mass., Boston, 1974-75; dir. consultation and edn. Solomon Carter Fuller Mental Health Ctr., Boston, 1975-81; pres. United South End Settlements, Boston, 1981—; bd. dirs. Local Initiatives Support Corp. Chair Boston Found.; bd. dirs. Lincoln Filene Ctr. for Citizenship & Pub. Affairs, Associated Grantmakers of Mass.; trustee Isabella Gardner Mus. Recipient Drum Maj. for Peace award Martin Luther King Jr. Ann. Breakfast, 1981, Abigail Adams award Mass. Women's Polit. Caucus, 1993, Mass. Legis. Black Caucus award, 1995. Mem. The Boston Panel of Agy. Execs., Boston Pvt. Industry Coun. (bd. dirs.), Coun. of Foundations, Women & Founds./Corp. Philanthropy, Hispanics in Philanthropy. Office: United South End Settlements Harriet Tubman House 566 Columbus Ave Boston MA 02118-1181*

GARCIA, HECTOR DAVID, toxicologist; b. Rio Grande City, Tex., Aug. 26, 1946; s. Toribio and Lilia Emma Garcia; m. Martha Rita Maldonado, Apr. 14, 1974; children: Mary Catharine, Christina, David. BA, U. St. Thomas, Houston, 1968; MS, U. Tex., Houston, 1975, PhD, 1979. Postdoctoral fellow Chem. Industry Inst. Toxicology, Research Triangle Park, N.C., 1979-81; rsch. scientist Philip Morris U.S.A., Richmond, Va., 1981-87; cons. Functional Mgmt. Inst., McLean, Va., 1987-89; v.p. Advanced Tech. Innovations, McLean, 1989-90; sr. rsch. scientist Krug/Wyle Labs., Life scis. Sys. and Svcs., Houston, 1990—. Author: Banbury Report 13, 1982, Spacecraft Maximum Allowable Concentrations of Selected Airborne Contaminants, Vol. 1 and 2, 1994, vol. 3, 1996. Sgt. U.S. Army, 1969-71. Mem. KC. Roman Catholic. Avocations: guitar, piano. Home: 8214 Buffalo Speedway Houston TX 77025-2507 Office: Wyle Life Scis 1290 Hercules Dr Ste 120 Houston TX 77058-2769

GARCIA, HENRY FRANK, finance and administration executive; b. San Antonio, Aug. 29, 1943; s. Henry V. and Lucia (Dominguez) G.; m. Rose Lozano, Feb. 28, 1970; children: John Henry, Rebecca. BA in Psychology, St. Mary's U., San Antonio, 1969, MA in Econs., 1974. Cert. purchasing mgr., Tex. Buyer purchasing Southwest Research Inst., San Antonio, 1967-70, asst. mgr. purchasing, 1970-74, mgr. purchasing, 1974-78, asst. dir. materials mgmt., 1978-80, dir. corp. travel, 1980-87, dir. materials mgmt., 1980-87; dir. fin. and adminstrn. Ctr. for Nuclear Waste Regulatory Analyses, San Antonio, Tex., 1987—; instr. U. Tex., San Antonio, 1976-77; instr. materials mgmt. and econs., San Antonio Coll., 1975-83; instr. econs. St. Marys U., San Antonio, 1976-81; adj. prof. econs. Webster U., San Antonio, 1980—. Contbr. articles to profl. jours. Chmn. San Antonio Regional Minority Purchasing Council, 1983. Mem. Nat. Purchasing Inst. (pres. 1979-80, Outstanding Svc. award 1986), Nat. Assn. Purchasing Mgmt. (cert., v.p. dist. II 1987-89, Pro-D Man of Yr. award 1985, Congrove Outstanding Mem. award 1991, President's award 1994), Purchasing Mgmt. Assn. San Antonio (pres. 1981-82, Conway L. Holmes award 1984, J.Shipman Gold Medal award 1998), Nat. Bus. Travel Assn. (v.p. 1985-86), Nat. Assn. Bus. Economists (pres. local chpt. 1978), Project Mgmt. Inst. Democrat. Roman Catholic. Office: Ctr Nuclear Waste Regulatory Analyses 6220 Culebra Rd San Antonio TX 78238-5166

GARCIA, HIPOLITO FRANK (HIPPO GARCIA), federal judge; b. San Antonio, Dec. 4, 1925; s. Hipolito and Francisca G. LLB, St. Mary's U., San Antonio, 1951. Bar: Tex. 1952. Dep. dist. clk. Bexar County, Tex., 1950-52; asst. criminal dist. atty. Dist. Atty's Office, San Antonio, 1952-63; with Garcia, Chavarria & Reeder, 1963-64; judge County Ct. at Law, 1964-74, Tex. Dist. Ct. Dist. 144, 1975-79, U.S. Dist. Ct. (we. dist.) Tex., San Antonio, 1980—. Served U.S. Army, 1943-45. Recipient cert. of Merit Am. Legion. Mem. San Antonio Bar Assn., Am. Bar Assn., Delta Theta Phi. Democrat. Office: US Courthouse 1st Fl 655 E Durango Blvd San Antonio TX 78206-1102*

GARCIA, JOHN, psychologist, educator; b. Santa Rosa, Calif., June 12, 1917; married; 3 children. BA, U. Calif., Berkeley, 1948, MA, 1949, PhD, 1965. Teaching asst. U. Calif., Berkeley, 1949-51; psychologist U.S. Naval Radiol. Def. Lab., San Francisco, 1951-58; tchr. biol. sci. Oakland (Calif.) Pub. Schs., 1958-59; asst. prof. psychology Calif. State Coll., Long Beach, 1959-65; assoc. biologist, neurosurg. svc. Mass. Gen. Hosp., Boston, 1965-68; prof. psychology, chmn. psychobiology program SUNY, Stony Brook, 1968-71, chmn. dept., 1971-72; prof. U. Utah, Salt Lake City, 1972-73; prof. psychology and psychiatry UCLA, 1973-87, emeritus prof. psychology and psychiatry, 1987—. Recipient Lifetime Achievement award for neurosci., Soc. for Neurosci., 1998—. Fellow Soc. Exptl. Psychologists (Howard Crosby Warren medal 1978); mem. AAAS, APA (Disting. Sci. Contbn. award 1979), Nat. Acad. Scis., Am. Psychol. Soc. (William James fellow), N.Y. Acad. Scis., Western Psychol. Assn. (pres. 1991—), Sigma Xi. Address: 19442 Best Rd Mount Vernon WA 98273-9215*

GARCIA, JUNE MARIE, library director; b. Bryn Mawr, Pa., Sept. 12, 1947; d. Roland Ernest and Marion Brill (Hummel) Traynor; m. Teodosio Garcia, July 17, 1928; children: Gretchen, Adrian. BA, Douglass Coll., 1969; MLS, Rutgers U., 1970. Reference libr. New Brunswick (N.J.) Pub. Libr., 1970-72, Plainfield (N.J.) Pub. Libr., 1972-75; br. mgr. Phoenix Pub. Libr., 1975-80, extension svcs. adminstr., 1980-93; dir. San Antonio Pub. Libr., 1993-99; CEO CARL Corp., Denver, 1999—. Recipient Productivity Innovator award City of Phoenix, 1981. Mem. ALA (life, coun. 1986-90, 93—, pres. Pub. Libr. Assn. 1991-92, new stds. task force 1983-87, goals, guidelines and stds. com. 1986-90, chairperson 1987-90, resource allocation com. 1998—, resource allocation com. 1998-99, Libr. Adminstrn. and Mgmt. Assn., Assn. Libr. Svc. Children, Young Adult Svcs. Divsn.), REFORMA, Tex. Libr. Assn., Freedom Read Found. (bd. dirs.), Ariz. State Libr. Assn. (pres. 1984-85, Libr. of Yr. award 1986, Pres.'s award 1990), Beta Phi Mu. Office: CARL Corp Ste 300 3801 E Florida Denver CO 80210

GARCIA, KATHERINE LEE, comptroller, accountant; b. Portland, Oreg., Nov. 4, 1950; d. Gerald Eugene and Dolores Lois (Erickson) Moe; m. Buddy Jesus Garcia; Nov. 19, 1977; children: Kevin, Brett, Rodd. BS cum laude, U. Nev., 1976. CPA, Idaho, Nev. Retail clk. Raleys, Food King, Reno, 1968-76; sr. acct. Pieretti, Wilson and McNulty, Reno, 1976-78, Deloitte Haskins and Sells, Boise, Idaho, 1979-81; sr. acct. Washoe County, Reno, 1981-83, chief dep. comptr., 1983-94, comptroller, 1994—. Treas., bd. dirs. Friends of 4 (pub. TV), Boise, 1979-81; tutor RAD program, 1995-97; treas. Sierra Miners, 1998—. Recipient Cert. of Excellence in Fin. Reporting, Govt. Fin. Officer's Assn., 1982—. Mem. AICPA, Nev. Soc. CPAs (chmn. state and local govt. com. 1992-93, 98—), Govt. Fin. Officers Assn. (mem. spl. rev. com. 1989-97, state rep.), Nev. Govt. Fin. Officers Assn. (treas. 1989-91). Republican. Avocations: jogging, sewing, biking, reading. Home: 655 Joy Lake Rd Reno NV 89511-5766 Office: Washoe County PO Box 11130 Reno NV 89520-0027

GARCIA, LORENZO F., federal judge; b. 1947. BA with honors, Coll. of Santa Fe, 1969; JD, U. N.Mex., 1973. Bar: N.Mex. Judge N.Mex. Dist. Ct., Santa Fe, N.Mex. Ct. Appeals, Santa Fe; designated justice N.Mex. Supreme Ct.; magistrate judge for N.Mex., U.S. Dist. Ct., Albuquerque, 1992—. Editor N.Mex. Law Rev. With U.S. Army. Office: US Dist Ct US Courthouse 333 Lomas NW Albuquerque NM 87103

GARCIA, MARIA LUISA, biochemist, researcher; b. Valladolid, Spain, Oct. 9, 1953; came to U.S., 1979; d. Baldomero and Dolores (Garcia) G.; m. Gregory Kaczorowski, June 21, 1982. PhD, Autonoma U., Madrid, 1979. Sr. rsch. biochemist Merck & Co., Rahway, N.J., 1985-87; rsch. fellow Merck & Co., Rahway, 1987-91, sr. rsch. fellow, 1991-97, sr. investigator, 1997—; invited speaker, presenter papers in field. Contbr. numerous articles and revs. to profl. jours.; patentee in field. Mem. AAAS, Am. Soc. Biol. Chemists, Biophys. Soc., N.Y. Acad. Sci. Home: 5 Ashbrook Dr Edison NJ 08820-4318 Office: Merck Rsch Labs PO Box 2000 Rahway NJ 07065-0900

GARCÍA, MARY ELIZABETH, Spanish and English as second language educator; b. Winter Haven, Fla., Mar. 3, 1931; d. Walter Roberts and Mary Elmira (Williams) Rozier; m. Guillermo García, Sept. 21, 1957; children: Mary Leonor, Guillermo Clyde. BA, U. Fla., 1956; MA, Maryville Coll., 1983. Cert. tchr. Spanish, ESL, bilingual lang. edn., Fla. Tchr. Spanish and civics Palatka (Fla.) Sr. H.S., 1956-58; tchr. ESL Centro Colombo-Americano, Bogotá, Colombia, 1959, Medellín, Colombia, 1960-65, Cali, Colombia, 1965-66; tchr. English and history The Internat. Sch., Maracay, Venezuela, 1969-71; area head in lit. U. Venezuela, Maracay, 1975-85; dir. bilingual program Price Mid. Sch., Interlachen, Fla., 1985-88; chair fgn. lang. Crescent City (Fla.) H.S., 1988-95; tchr. ESOL courses for tchrs. Putnam County, Palatka, 1991-96; adj. prof. Spanish Stetson U., Deland, Fla., 1995-97; Venezuelan del. 1st Caribbean Conf., Santo Domingo, Dominican Republic, 1995; spkr. 2d ann. TESOL Conf., Caraballeda, Venezuela, 1994, TESOL Conf., U. Met. Caracas, Venezuela, 1985. Mem. TESOL, Hon. Spanish Soc. (sponsor 1988-95), Am. Assn. Tchrs. of Spanish and Portuguese, Venezuelan TESOL (founding mem., state rep. 1988-85), Phi Beta Kappa, Phi Kappa Phi. Democrat. Roman Catholic. Avocations: reading, cooking, growing orchids. Home: PO Box 639 120 Parkin Rd Pomona Park FL 32181

GARCIA, MICHAEL JOSEPH, telecommunications company executive; b. Alameda, Calif., July 23, 1949; s. Manuel Oliviera and Mary (Gonzales) G.; m. Patti Ann Tognetti, July 22, 1972; children: Michael Joseph II, Jennifer Anne. Degree in maths., econs., U. Calif., Berkeley, 1971. Cert. employee benefits specialist. From dir. customer billing to dir. benefit adminstrn. Pacific Tel., San Francisco, 1971-87; dir. fin. mgmt. Pacific Telesis, San Francisco, 1987-89; from exec. dir. info. sys. to exec. dir. technology svcs. Pacific Bell, San Francisco, 1989—; chmn. adv. bd. Contra Costa Health Plan, Martinez, Calif., 1985-95. Chmn. bd. dirs. Managed Care Commn., Martinez, 1997. Col. USANG, 1967—. Mem. Am. Mgmt. Assn., Nat. Guard Assn., Air Force Assn. Roman Catholic. Avocations: golf, reading, gardening. Home: 2409 Saddleback Dr Blackhawk CA 94506-3112 Office: Pacific Bell #1E501 2600 Camino Ramon San Ramon CA 94583

GARCIA, MICHAEL RALPH, funeral director; b. Albany, Oreg., June 27, 1942; s. Modesto Huerta and Maria Dolores (Mireles) G.; m. Carol Gene Couchman, Dec. 27, 1963; children: Kimberly E., Kelly J. Student, Linfield Coll., McMinnville, Oreg., 1960-62; grad., San Francisco Coll. Mortuary, 1964. Funeral dir., embalmer Whitaker Funeral Home, Albany, Oreg., 1965-69, Chapel of the Gardens, Salem, Oreg., 1970—; dir. Pioneer Trust Bank, Salem. Mem. City of Salem Human Rights Commn., 1985-91; mem. equity issues com. Salem-Keizer Sch. Dist., 1991-95; bd. dirs. Chemeketa C.C., Salem, 1993—; mem. instnl. rev. bd. Salem Hosp., 1994—; chair Strengthening Families (Father in Father), 1996—. Recipient Disting. Svc. award C. of C., Salem, 1991, Willard C. Marshall award City of Salem, 1991. Mewm. Oreg. Funeral Dirs. Assn. (mem. ethics and stds. com. 1996, Employee of Yr. 1995), Capital Area Sunrise Rotary (vocat. dir. 1996—). Democrat. Avocations: wood carver, reading, travel. Home: 3760 Augusta National Dr S Salem OR 97302-3771 Office: City View Funeral Homes and Cemetery 390 Hoyt St S Salem OR 97302-4295

GARCIA, OFELIA, dean; b. Havana, Cuba, Feb. 12, 1941; d. Ramon Garcia-Castro and Nieves (Gomez de Molina) Garcia. Student, Escuela de Bellas Artes, Havana, 1958-60; BA, Manhattanville Coll., 1969; MFA, Tufts U., 1972; postgrad., Duke U., 1973-75; D. Fine Arts (hon.), Atlanta Coll. Art, 1991. Asst. prof., art dept. chair, div. dir. humanities and fine arts Newton (Mass.) Coll., 1969-75; dir. studio art Boston Coll., Chestnut Hill, Mass., 1975-76; exec. dir. The Print Club, Phila., 1978-86; critic Pa. Acad. Fine Arts, Phila., 1982-86; pres. Atlanta Coll. Art, 1986-91, Rosemont (Pa.) Coll., 1991-96; sr. fellow Am. Coun. on Edn., 1996-97; dean, coll. arts and comm., prof. William Paterson U., 1997—; visual arts panelist State Coun. of the Arts, Pa. and N.J., 1985-86, Ga., 1990-91; mem. vis. com. dept. art and architecture Lehigh (Pa.) U., 1990-96; bd. mgrs. H averford Coll., 1992—; external reviewer Mid. States Assn. Colls. and Schs. Artist exhibitions of prints and drawings; curator, juror numerous nat. and internat. or regional art exhibitions. Nat. pres. Women's Caucus for Art, 1984-86; bd. dirs. Am. Coun. on Edn., 1993-96; co-chair M ayor's Commn. for Women, City Phila., 1992-97; Arts Adv. Com. Barnes Found. Bd., 1992-95. Recipient Am. Bookbuilders prize Boston Mus. Sch., 1969, Park Found. award, 1974; Kent fellow Danforth Found., 1975-80. Fellow Soc. for Values Higher Edn.; mem. Coll. Art Assn. Am. (bd. dirs. 1986-90, bd. coms. 1986-92), Commn. on Women in Higher Edn., Am. Coun. on Edn. (chair 1990-91), So. Assn. Colls. and Schs. (accreditation evaluator 1990-91), ArtTable, Inc. Roman Catholic. Office: William Paterson U 300 Pompton Rd Wayne NJ 07470-2152

GARCIA, ORLANDO LUIS, judge; b. 1952. BA, U. Tex., 1975, JD, 1978. Legis. aide to Hon. Matt Garcia and Ernestine Glossbrenner Tex. Ho. of Reps., 1974-83; atty. Law Offices of Matt Garcia, 1978-85; mem. Tex. Ho. of Reps., 1983-91; atty. Heard, Goggan, Blair & Williams, 1985-90; judge 4th Ct. of Appeals, San Antonio, 1991-94, U.S. Dist. Ct. (we. dist.) Tex., San Antonio, 1994—. Vol. San Antonio State Hosp. Vol. Coun., San Antonio Pro Bono Project. Named One of Ten Best Legislators of 70th Tex. Legislature, State Bar Tex., 1987, Outstanding State Rep. of Yr., Tex. Youth Commn., 1990, Legislator of Yr., Tex. Pub. Employees Assn., 1989, Tex. Alliance for Mentally Ill., 1990,. Mem. State Bar Tex., Tex. Bar Found., San Antonio Bar Assn., Tex. Jud. Coun. Office: US Dist Ct US Courthouse 1st Fl 655 E Durango Blvd San Antonio TX 78206-1102*

GARCIA, OSCAR NICOLAS, computer science educator; b. Havana, Cuba, Sept. 10, 1936; s. Oscar Vicente and Leonor (Hernandez) G.; m. Diane Ford Journigan, Sept. 9, 1962; children: Flora, Virginia. BSEE, N.C. State U., 1961, MSEE, 1964; PhDEE, U. Md., 1969. Engr. IBM Corp., Endicott, N.Y., 1962-63; asst. prof. Old Dominion U., 1963-66, assoc. prof., 1969-70; research asst., instr. U. Md., 1966-69; assoc. prof. U. South Fla., Tampa, 1970-75; prof. computer sci., chmn. dept. U. South Fla., 1975-85; prof. dept. elec. engrng. and computer sci. George Washington U., Washington, 1985-95; NCR prof. Wright State U., Dayton, Ohio, 1995—; chmn. dept. computer sci. and engrng. Wright State U., 1995—; dir. interactive sys. program in info., robotics and intelligent sys. divsn. Computer and Info. Sci. and Engrng. Directorate, Intergovtl. Pers. Act, NSF, Washington, 1992-94; cons. and lectr. in field. Author: (with Y.T. Chien) Knowledge-Based Systems: Fundamentals and Tools, 1991. Fellow IEEE (bd. dirs. 1984-85, mem. U.S. activities bd. 1984, Profl. Leadership award 1991, Richard M. Emberson award 1994), Computer Soc. of IEEE (pres. 1981-83, Richard E. Merwin Disting. Svc. award 1988, Meritorious Svc. award 1991), AAAS; mem. Assn. Computing Machinery, Am. Soc. Engrng. Edn., Am. Assn. Artificial Intelligence, Sigma Xi, Eta Kappa Nu, Phi Kappa Phi, Tau Beta Pi. Home: 1917 S Highgate Ct Beavercreek OH 45432-1880 Office: Russ Center Rm 303 Dept Comp Sci & Engrng Wright State Univ Dayton OH 45435

GARCIA, PATRICIA A., lawyer; b. New Orleans, Feb. 18, 1956; d. Martin F. and Shirley (Polders) G. BA in History, U. New Orleans, 1976; JD, Loyola U., New Orleans, 1980. Bar: La. 1980, U.S. Tax Ct. 1982, U.S. Dist. Ct. (ea. dist.) La. 1984, U.S. Dist. Ct. (mid. dist.) La. 1986. Staff atty. office of chief counsel IRS, Washington, 1980-82; law clk. U.S. Ea. Dist. Ct. of La., New Orleans, 1983-86; assoc. Law Office of Eric A. Holden, New Orleans, 1986-89, Holden & Garcia, New Orleans, 1990—; bd. dirs. La. Ctr. for Law and Civic Edn., 1992-96, pres., 1994-95, New Orleans Legal Assistance Corp., 1995—. Co-chair No/AIDS Task Force, 1997—, sec./treas., 1994-97. Mem. ABA (comm. chair, exec. com. young lawyers divsn. 1990-91, gen. practice sect. gen. practice link conf. team 1994—, vice chair sole practitioners and small firms com. 1990—, vice chair law students com. 1991—, vice chair law sch. curriculum com. 1991—, La. dist. gov. 1979-80, project dir. model project for effective delivery of law-related edn. to low income families 1985—, project dir. com. on substance abuse, chmn. delivery of legal svcs. com. young lawyers divsn. 1987, chmn. law student outreach com. 1988-91, asst. editor Affiliate mag. 1988-90, liaison to law student divsn. 1987-91, recipient Gold Key award 1980, regional coord. state and local bar liaison com. 1992-98, standing com. on Gavel awards 1994-97, project dir. com. on substance abuse 1994—, ann. mtg. 1994 host com., ho. dels. 1994, 97—), La. Bar Assn. (chmn. law week 1986, mem. young lawyers sect. 1986-92, Achievement award 1985, 86, 87, mem. local and splty. bars com. 1992-98), New Orleans Bar Assn. (1st v.p. 1990-91, pres.-elect 1991-92, pres. 1992-93, chmn. TV com. 1992-98, com. on drugs and violence 1992-96, vice chmn. young lawyers sect. 1984-86, chmn. 1987-88, chmn. membership com. 1988-91, exec. com. 1988-94, vice chmn. increasing membership com. 1986-87, pub. rels. com. 1984-92, project grantee 1985-87), La. Ctr. for Law and Civic Edn. (pres. 1994-95, v.p. 1993-94, bd. dirs. 1992-96). Democrat. Roman Catholic. Home: 7008 Milne Blvd New Orleans LA 70124-2342 Office: Holden & Garcia Ste 303 990 N Corporate Blvd New Orleans LA 70123

GARCIA, RAFAEL JORGE, retired chemical engineer; b. Havana, Cuba, July 2, 1933; came to U.S., 1962; s. Rafael and Martha Teresa (Suarez) G.; m. Amelia Fernandez, Feb. 23, 1958; children: Amelia Maria, Rafael Jorge Jr. *Rafael and wife Amelia left Communist Cuba in 1962 and came to the U.S. Daughter Amelia Maria is a 1985 graduate of the Uniformed Services University of the Health Sciences School of Medicine and is currently a pediatrician in private practice in Arizona. Son Rafael Jorge Jr. is a graduate (1982) of the United States Military Academy at West Point. He served with the 101st Air Assault Division in the Gulf War, where he commanded an attack helicopter company, and was awarded a bronze star and an air medal with "V" (for valor) device.* BA, Columbia Coll., 1954; BS in Chem. Engring., La. State U., 1957; MS in Environ. Engring., Johns Hopkins U., 1975. Registered profl. engr., Ind., Ky., La., Md.; registered environ. mgr. Chem. engr. Freeport Sulphur Co., New Orleans, 1957-58; prodn. supt. Litografia Garcia Muniz, Havana, 1958-62; chem. engr. The Am. Sugar Refining Co., Balt., 1962-63, The House of Seagram, Balt., 1963-80; chief ecology engr. The House of Seagram, Louisville, 1981-97; cons. environ. regulatory affairs, 1998—; pres. Garcia Environ. Mem. Am. Inst. Chem. Engrs., Instrument Soc. Am., St. Matthews Lions (pres. 1986-87). Republican. Roman Catholic. Home: 912 Lake Forest Pkwy Louisville KY 40245-5126

GARCIA, RAYMOND LLOYD, dermatologist; b. Paterson, N.J., Jan. 24, 1942; s. Raymond and Ruth Elaine (De Graff) G.; m. Cynthia Ruth Towne (div.); m. Toy Ping Woo, Dec. 22, 1984; 1 child, Christopher Drew. BA cum laude, Drew U., 1963; MD, Temple U., 1967. Diplomate Am. Bd. Dermatology, Am. Bd. Dermatology-Pathology. Commd. Col. USAF, 1966; intern Wilford Hall USAF Med. Ctr., San Antonio, 1967-68; dermatology resident, 1969-72; vice-chmn. residency tng. program Wilford Hall USAF Med. Ctr., San Antonio, 1972-82; asst. chief aerospace medicine USAF Acad., Colorado Springs, Colo., 1968-69; chief dermatology Carswell USAF Hosp., Ft. Worth, 1982-86; pvt. practice Irving, Tex., 1986—; asst. prof. U. Tex. Med. Sch., San Antonio, 1972-82; assoc. prof. Tex. Coll. Osteo. Medicine, Ft. Worth, 1982-92; cons. to surgeon gen. USAF, 1979-86. Editor: Jour. the Assn. Mil. Dermatologists, 1978-86, Handbook of Dermatology, 1980; contbr. over 50 articles to profl. jours. Decorated Nat. Defense medal USAF, 1972, Meritorious Svc. medal 1982. Fellow Am. Acad. Dermatology (legis. liaison com. 1972-78); mem. Assn. Mil. Dermatologists (sec., treas. 1973-75, v.p. 1977-78, pres. 1980), Tex. Med. Assn., Tarrant County Med. Soc., Babcock Surg. Soc. of Temple U. Med. Sch., Tex. Dermatol. Soc., Biol. Honor Soc. of Drew U., Alpha Kappa Kappa, Beta Beta Beta. Republican. Baptist. Avocations: collecting coins, sports memorabilia, antique gun and flag collecting. Home: 1110 San Juan Ct Arlington TX 76012-2750 Office: Dermatology Center 2015 W Park Dr Irving TX 75061-2197

GARCIA, RICHARD RAUL, major league umpire; b. Key West, Fla., May 22, 1942; s. Eloy Garcia and Griselda Garcia Janesek; m. Sheryl Lynn Rivard, Oct. 29, 1977; children: Richard Daniel, Dina Ann, Lisa Marie Garcia Egan, Stephanie Lynn. Student umpire sch., St. Petersburg, Fla. Profl. umpire Am. League of Baseball, 1975—; umpired Am. League playoffs, 1978, 82, 86, 90, World Series games, 1981, 84, 89, All-Star games, 1980-91. With USMC, 1960-64. Republican. Roman Catholic. Avocation: golf. Office: Major League Umpires Assoc 1735 Market St Ste 3420 Philadelphia PA 19103-7509*

GARCIA, RUDOLPH, lawyer; b. Phila., June 22, 1951; s. Rudolph Sr. and Assunta Rita (Marrara) G.; m. Randi Ellen Pastor, Aug. 3, 1980; 1 child, Jonathan P. BA magna cum laude, Temple U., 1974, JD cum laude, 1977. Bar: Pa. 1977, U.S. Dist. Ct. (ea. dist.) Pa. 1977, U.S. Ct. Appeals (3d cir.) 1982, U.S. Supreme Ct. 1982. Assoc. Wright, Thistle & Gibbons, Phila., 1977-78; assoc. Saul, Ewing, Remick & Saul, Phila., 1978-84, ptnr., 1984—. Judge pro tem Phila. Ct. Common Pleas. Fellow Acad. of Adv.; mem. ABA, Pa. Bar Assn., Phila. Bar Assn. (chmn. local rules subcom. 1988-92, chmn. state civil com. 1999), Phila. Assn. Def. Counsel, Justinian Soc., Phi Beta Kappa. Avocations: computers, photography, golf. Home: 235 Lloyd Ln Wynnewood PA 19096-3323 Office: Saul Ewing Remick & Saul 3800 Centre Sq W Philadelphia PA 19102-2174

GARCIA, SERAFIN MONTEALTO, physician; b. Sariaya, Philippines, Nov. 12, 1943; came to U.S., 1962; s. Zacarias and Roberta (Montealto) G.; children: John, Linda, Kimberly. BS, Columbia Union Coll., 1969; MD, Loma Linda U., 1973. Diplomate Am. Coll. Physicians. Chmn. bd. dirs. Covina Valley Cmty. Hosp., 1978-98; pres., adminstr. Glendale (Calif.) Home Health Care, 1988—; pres. Calif. Mobile X-Ray, Glendale, 1988—; chmn. bd. dirs. Thompson Meml. Med. Ctr., 1993-95. Bd. dirs. ARC, Glendale, 1996—. Avocations: tennis, golf, bicycling, skiing. Office: Glendale Home Health Care 601 E Glenoaks Blvd Ste 108 Glendale CA 91207-1760

GARCIA, STEPHANIE BROWN, aerospace company pricing manager; b. San Jose, Calif., July 18, 1959; d. Thomas Francis III and Martha Caroline (Bramer) B.; m. Markcos Mario Garcia, Apr. 5, 1986; children: Ryan Markcos, Jason Thomas, Corey Lawrence. BBA, James Madison U., 1981; MBA, U. San Diego, 1986. Adminstrv. assoc. Gen. Dynamics Corp., San Diego, 1981-82, estimator, 1982-84, sr. estimator, 1984-85; prin. fin. rep. Sundstrand Corp., San Diego, 1985-87, pricing mgr., 1987-93, 96—, contract compliance and estimating mgr., 1993-96. Fund raiser United Way, San Diego, 1990-93; active Tecolote Youth Baseball Assn., San Diego, 1991—. Mem. Nat. Contract Mgmt. Assn. (dir. youth and civic activities 1983-85), U. San Diego Grad. Bus. Alumni Assn., Phi Beta Kappa, Beta Gamma Sigma. Republican. Roman Catholic. Avocations: hiking, camping, biking, antiques. Home: 2853 Denver St San Diego CA 92117-6126 Office: Sundstrand Power Sys PO Box 85757 4400 Ruffin Rd San Diego CA 92123-1665

GARCIA-BUÑUEL, LUIS, neurologist; b. Madrid, Feb. 24, 1931; came to U.S., 1955; s. Pedro Garcia and Concepcion Buñuel; m. Virginia May Hile, June 30, 1960. BA, BS, U. Zaragoza, Spain, 1949; MD, U. Zaragoza, 1955. Diplomate Am. Bd. Psychiatry and Neurology. Resident neurology Georgetown U., Washington, 1955-59; postdoctoral fellow Washington U., St. Louis, 1959-61; asst. prof. neurology Thomas Jefferson U., Phila., 1961-67; assoc. prof. U. N.Mex., Albuquerque, 1967-72, U. Oreg. Health Scis. Ctr., Portland, 1972-84; chief neurology svc. Portland VA Med. Ctr., 1972-84; pvt. practice, Phoenix, 1984—; chief staff Carl T. Hayden VA Med. Ctr., Phoenix, 1984-96. Contbr. articles to sci. jours., including Nature, Sci., Neurology, Jour. Neurol. Sci. Lt. Spanish Air Force, 1952-55. Fellow Am. Acad. Neurology (sr. mem.), Sigma Xi. Unitarian. Avocations: painting, computer art, steel-welded sculpture. Home and Office: 5939 E Orange Blossom Ln Phoenix AZ 85018

GARCIA C., ELISA DOLORES, lawyer; b. Bklyn., Nov. 8, 1957; d. Vincent Garcia, Jr. and Dolores Elizabeth (Canedo) Marmo; m. John Jay Hasluck, Feb. 28, 1987; children: Brooke Elisabeth, John Neville. BA, MS, SUNY, Stony Brook, 1980; JD, St. John's U., 1985. Bar: N.Y. 1986. Cons. Energy Devel. Internat., Pt. Jefferson, N.Y., 1980-83; assoc. Willkie Farr & Gallagher, N.Y.C., 1985-89; sr. counsel GAF Corp./Internat. Specialty Products, Wayne, N.J., 1989-94; regional counsel for L.Am., Philip Morris Internat., Rye Brook, N.Y., 1994—. Mem. Glen Rock (N.J.) Planning Bd., 1992-95, chmn., 1994-95. Mem. ABA, N.Y. State Bar Assn. Roman Catholic. Avocations: gardening, scuba diving. Office: Philip Morris Internat 800 Westchester Ave Rye Brook NY 10573-1322 Home: 52 Old Lyme Rd Chappaqua NY 10514-3806

GARCÍA-GODOY, CRISTIÁN, historian, educator; b. Mendoza City, Argentina, June 3, 1924; came to the U.S., 1963; s. Cristián García Pontis and Renee Godoy Ponce; children: María Celina Heeter, María Inés García Robles, María Susana García Robles. Degree in law, U. Buenos Aires, 1950; diploma, U. Nacional de Cuyo, 1952; postgrad., Washington U., 1969, Cath. U., 1971. Official various banks, Argentina, 1941-62; sec. gen. Secretaria de Comercio de la Nación, Argentina, 1958-59; cabinet mem. Ministro de Economía, Río Negro, Argentina, 1959-60; pres.-organizer Banco de la Provincia de Río Negro, Argentina, 1960; internat. civil servant GS/OAS, 1962-89; prof. history Argentine Sch., Washington, 1981—. Author: Asociados Eminentes de San Martin, 1998, San Martin en el Reino Unido, 1996, Jefes Espanoles en la Formacion Militar de San Martin, 1995, Correspondencia Inedita de Tomas Godoy Cruz con su Padre Clemente Godoy y Videla, 1993, The Essential San Martin, 1993-94, Tomas Godoy Cruz: Su tiempo, su vida, su drama, 1991, Tomas Godoy Cruz, Dictamen Federalista, Introduccion y estudio, 1991, Los XII Presidentes 1850-1910, 1989, The San Martin Papers, 1988, Selected U.S. Supreme Court Decisions Related to Constitutional Law, 1986, San Martin y Unanue en la Liberacion del Peru, 1983, Evolucion Historica y Constitucional de la Argentina, 1982, San Martin, Selected Bibliography, 1978, Ampliación y Actualización 1978/96, Tribute to the Liberator General San Martin, 1978; contbr. articles to profl. jours. Lt. Argentine Army, 1946. Mem. Academia Nacional de la Historia, Premio Republica Argentina, Soc. Argentina de Historiadores Buenos Aires, Nat. Geneal. Soc. USA, Inst. Argentino de Ciencias Genealogicas, Inst. Bonaerense de Numismatica y Antiguedades, Acad. Nacional Sanmartiniana Buenos Aires, Junta de Estudios Historicos Mendoza, Inst. de Estudios Ibericos Buenos Aires, Internat. Inst. Pub. Adminstrn. (U.K.), Acad. Polit. Sci. USA, Am. Soc. Internat. Law, Washington Fgn. Law Soc. USA, San Martin Soc. (pres.), Hermandad Ysabel la Catolica (chancellor). Avocations: collecting art, rare books, maps, antiques and military decorations and historical medals. E-mail: cggodoy@email.msn.com. Home: 1128 Balls Hill Rd Mc Lean VA 22101-2653 Office: San Martin Soc PO Box 33 Mc Lean VA 22101-0033

GARCIA-GUZMAN, BARBARA MARI, secondary education educator; b. Aug. 13, 1965. MA, Calif. State U., Long Beach, 1990. Tchr., chair dept. St. Anthony H.S., Long Beach, 1991-95; tchr. Fairmont H.S., Anaheim, Calif., 1995-96, Pacific H.S., West Hollywood, Calif., 1996-98.

GARCIA-HERAS, JAIME, clinical cytogeneticist, researcher; b. Caracas, Venezuela, Dec. 10, 1951; came to U.S., 1988; s. Napoleon Garcia-Zelada and Maria Esther Heras. MD, La Plata U., Argentina, 1977, PhD in Medicine, 1986. Diplomate Am. Bd. Med. Genetics. Clin. rsch. fellow Children's Hosp., Buenos Aires, 1980-85; staff cytogeneticist Nat. Acad. Medicine, Buenos Aires, 1985-88; post doctoral fellow Inst. Molecular Genetics Baylor Coll. Medicine, Houston, 1988-90; postdoctoral fellow in clin. cytogenetics U. Md., Balt., 1990-92; dir. cytogenetics genetic testing ctr. Tex. Dept. Health, Denton, 1992—. Contbg. editor, reviewer Jour. Assn. Genetic Technologists, 1997—. Avocations: dancing, travelling, folk music, outdoor activities. Home: 18880 Marsh Ln Apt 305 Dallas TX 75287-2207 Office: Tex Dept Health Genetic Testing Ctr 3600 E Mckinney St Denton TX 76201-6431

GARCIA-MELY, RAFAEL, retired education educator; b. N.Y.C., Dec. 28, 1921; s. Rafael and Vivian (Mely) G.; m. Lucy ortiz, Mar. 2, 1951 (div. Dec. 1968); children: Martin, Christine. B.S. in Social Sci., CCNY, 1946; BD, Yale U., 1949, MDiv, 1972; MA, NYU, 1951, PhD, 1959; LHD (hon.), World U. (P.R.), 1975. Ordained to ministry United Ch. of Christ U.S.A., 1949. Dir., cmty. coord. Brownsville Houses Cmty. Ctr., N.Y.C. Housing Authority, 1949-51; assoc. pastor, assoc. dir. Ch. of the Good Neighbor and Cmty. Ctr., N.Y.C., 1951-53; dir. New Neighbors Project, Hudson Guild, N.Y.C., 1953-54; youth min. First Reformed Ch., Schenectady, 1954-56; prof. edn. Inter-Am. U., San German, P.R., 1957-65, dean co-campus programs, 1962-63, dean adminstrn., 1963-65, prof. grad. edn. program metro campus, 1984-94; ret., 1994; dep. gen. sec. World Council Christian Edn., Geneva, 1966-68; dean of acad. affairs World U., San Juan, P.R., 1969-78; dean grad. program Internat. Inst. World U. Am. San Juan, 1978-83; adj. prof. Caribbean Residence Ctr. Dowling Coll., San Juan; dean U. of the Air, 1985-86. Editor Jour. World Christian Edn., 1966-68. Sec., bd. gov. World Univs., San Juan, 1968-83; v.p., treas. Latin Am. Evang. Council Christian Edn., Lima, Peru, 1968-81; bd. dirs., co-founder World Univs., Inc., San Juan, 1965-83; bd. dirs. govs. World Council Christian Edn., Geneva, 1968-71; regional sec. Scholarship Commn. World Council of Chs., Geneva, 1971-80; co-founder Fomento de la Opera, San Juan, 1977. Mem. ASCD, Am. Assn. Higher Edn., Am. Sociol. Assn., Religious Edn. Assn., Adult Edn. Assn., Phi Epsilon Chi, Phi Delta Kappa. Avocations: music, educational activities, sports.

GARCIAPARRA, NOMAR (ANTHONY NOMAR GARCIAPARRA), professional baseball player; b. Whittier, Calif., July 23, 1973. Student, Ga. Tech. Shortstop Fla. St. League, Sarasota, 1994, Eastern League, Trenton, 1995, Internat. League, Pawtucket, 1996, G. C. Red Sox, 1996; shortstop, designated hitter, 2d baseman Boston Red Sox, 1996, shortstop, 1997—; mem. U.S. Olympic baseball team, 1992. Named Am. League Rookie Player of the Yr. The Sporting News, 1997, Player's Choice Am. League Outstanding Rookie; named Am. League Rookie of the Yr. Baseball Writers' Assn. Am., 1997, recipient Thomas A. Yawkey award (team Most Valuable Player). Office: care Boston Red Sox Fenway Pk 4 Yawkey Way Boston MA 02215-3409

GARCIA-RILL, EDGAR ENRIQUE, neuroscientist; b. Caracas, Venezuela, Oct. 31, 1948; came to U.S., 1973; s. Juan Garcia and Aracelis (Rill) Ramirez; m. Sherrie Hunt, Oct. 2, 1978 (div.); children: Sarah Thais; m. Susan Gene Ebel, May 13, 1984 (div.); m. Catherine Cagan, July 3, 1998. BA, Loyola of Montreal, 1968; PhD, McGill U., 1973. Rsch. asst. dept. psychiatry McGill U., Montreal, 1972-73; postdoctoral fellow UCLA, 1973-78; asst. prof. anatomy U. Ark. for Med. Scis., Little Rock, 1978-82, assoc. prof., 1982-87, prof., 1987—, prof. psychiatry, 1990—; dir. NSF Exptl. Program to Stimulate Competitive Rsch., Ark. Neurobiology Rsch. Ctr., 1989—; mem. biomed. rsch. study sect. NIAAA, Washington, 1983-87, biopsychology study sect. NIH, Washington, 1988-93; chmn. biopsychology rev. com. NIH, 1991-93; reviewer several neurosci. jours., 1979—, small bus. innovative rsch. study sect. NIH, 1988-92; exec. office of pres. Office of Sci. and Tech. Policy Forum, 1994. Editor: (videotape) The Basal Ganglia and the Locomotor Regions, 1986; patentee in field. V.p., bd. dirs. Morris Found., Little Rock, 1985—. Postdoctoral fellow Que. Med. Rsch. Coun., 1973; grantee NSF, 1980-85, 88—, NIH, 1983—. Mem. Soc. for Neurosci. (chpt. com. 1991-93), Am. Assn. Anatomists. Avocation: golf. Office: U Ark for Med Scis 4301 W Markham St Little Rock AR 72205-7101

GARCIA Y CARRILLO, MARTHA XOCHITL, pharmacist; b. Austin, Tex., Dec. 7, 1919; d. Alberto Gonzalo and Guadalupe Eva (Carrillo) Garcia; m. Jerjes Jose Rodriguez, Oct. 9, 1943 (dec. 1987); children: Marie Eugenia, Jerjes Alberto, Nicanor Francisco. *Alberto Gonzalo Garcia (1889-1962), son of a Mexican cobbler, and his wife, Eva Carrillo y Gallardo (1888-1979), a California born descendent of Spanish aristocracy, were early fighters for the civil rights of Mexican Americans in Texas during much of the twentieth century. Alberto and his future wife were trained as physician and missionary nurse at the world renowned Battlecreek Sanitorium of Dr. John Harvey Kellogg, a physician, nutritionist, writer, and inventor of the cornflake. As one of forty two adopted children of Dr. Kellogg, Alberto was exposed to many of the worlds leading thinkers, politicians, and businessmen who visited the sanitorium. Eva was an early social activist involved in the Suffragette and Women's Temperance movements in turn of the century Chicago, with training at the famed Hull House. After graduating from Tulane University Medical School and subsequently experiencing the strife of revolution in Mexico, the Garcias settled in Austin, Texas in 1915. He was the first Mexican American physician to set up practice in Austin. Eva and Alberto stood up to social injustices as leaders in the Mexican American community.* BS in Pharmacy, U. Tex., 1944. RPh, Tex. Retail pharmacist Ward Drug Store, Austin, Tex., 1952-57, Sommer's Drug Store, San Antonio, 1957-62, Skillern's Drug Store, Dallas, 1962-66; hosp. pharmacist Brackenridge Hosp., Austin, 1968-75; retail pharmacist Thorp Lane Pharmacy, San Marcos, Tex., 1975-77, The Pharmacy, San Marcos, 1975-79, MHMR Pharmacy, Austin, 1975-78, Ace Drug Co., Austin, 1979-82; ret. Contbg. author: The New Handbook of Texas, 1996. Recipient Citation of Achievement Tex. State Bd. Pharmacy, 1996. Mem. Am. Pharm. Assn., Tex. Pharmacy Assn., Capitol Area Pharmacy Assn., Tex. State Hist. Assn., Ex-Students Assn. U. Tex. (life, Golden Anniversary cert. 1994). Republican. Avocations: reading, playing piano, current events, pharmacy medicine. Home: 21107 Ridgeview Rd Lago Vista TX 78645-4617

GARD, CAROL LEE, nurse educator; b. Loveland, Colo., Sept. 4, 1939; d. Oscar V. and Anna W. Gard. Diploma in nursing, Carroll Coll., 1960; BSN, Mont. State U., 1963, MN, 1965. RN. Staff nurse St. Vincent's Hosp., Billings, Mont., 1960-62; instr. N.E. La. State Coll., Monroe, 1965-66; staff nurse Yavapai Cmty. Hosp., Prescott, Ariz., 1967-68; instr. No. Ariz. U., Flagstaff, 1968-73; asst. prof. Lewis U., Romeoville, Ill., 1973-74, Bradley U., Peoria, Ill., 1974—. Vol. Am. Heart Assn. Mem. Am. Nurses Assn. (dist. recording sec. 1994-98, corr. sec. 1998—), Nat. League Nursing, AAUP, Coun. Grad. Educators in Nursing Adminstrn., Sigma Theta Tau. Lutheran. Avocations: reading, cross stitch, needlework. Office: Bradley U 1501 W Bradley Ave Peoria IL 61625

GARD, JUDY RICHARDSON, artist, educator; b. Woodward, Okla., Mar. 11, 1938; d. Russell Eugene and Bertie Easter (Bailey) Richardson; m. Robert Lee Gard, Aug. 31, 1958; children: Michael Cameron, Matthew Davis. Attended, U. Okla., 1956, 57, Volkshochschule, Wiesbaden, Germany, 1963, Am. U., 1967. Tchr. Watercolor Art Soc., Houston, 1983-90, Arrowmont Sch. Arts and Crafts, Gatlinberg, Tenn., 1992, Okla. Art Workshops, Tulsa, 1992-96; demonstrator Elrod Elem. Sch., Houston, 1975, 78-79, U. Houston, 1986; juror Soc. Layerists in Multimedia, Albuquerque, 1992, San Antonio Art League, 1992, EXPO Photog. Soc., Tulsa, 1994; critic, demonstrator Okla. Art Workshops, 1994-95; lectr. Charles Page H.S., Sand Springs, Okla., 1994. Featured artist in book, The New Spirit of Watercolor, 1989. Named Best of Show, Western Fedn. Watercolorists Tucson, 1975, Art League Houston, 1979, Tex. Watercolor Soc., 1977, 80; recipient Honor award Watercolor USA Honor Soc., 1993. Mem. Am. Watercolor Soc. (Washington Sch. of Art award 1976, High Winds medal 1987), Tulsa Artists Guild, Tex. Watercolor Soc. Avocations: cooking, gardening.

GARD, RICHARD ABBOTT, religious institute executive, educator; b. Vancouver, B.C., Can., May 29, 1914; parents U.S. citizens; s. Charles Ned and Clara Edna (Abbott) G.; m. Tatiana Ruzena Kristina Moravec, Nov. 1, 1952; children: Alan Moravec, Anita Nadine. B.A., U. Wash., 1937; M.A., U. Hawaii, 1940; postgrad. U. Pa., 1945-47; Ph.D., Claremont Grad. Sch., 1951; postgrad. Otani U. and Ryukoku U., Kyoto, Japan, 1953-54; D.H.L. (hon.), Monmouth Coll., 1963. Dir. plans dept. Asia Found., San Francisco, 1954-56, spl. adviser to pres., San Francisco and Tokyo, 1956-59, cons. Buddhist affairs, San Francisco, 1959-63; cultural affairs officer USIA, Washington, 1963-64; Buddhist affairs officer Dept. State, Washington and Hong Kong, 1964-69; librarian Inst. for Advanced Studies of World Religions, SUNY-Stony Brook, 1971-73, dir. inst. services, 1971-84, pres., 1985-89; v.p. for U.S., World Fellowship of Buddhists, Bangkok, Thailand, 1961-64, asst. sec. gen., 1971-75; vis. assoc. prof. Yale U., New Haven, 1959-63; adj. prof. Asian Studies St. John's U., Jamaica, N.Y., 1974-78; vis. prof. Asian studies Wittenberg U., Springfield, Ohio, 1970, Grad. Inst. Oriental Humanities Hua Fan Coll. Humanities and Tech., Taipei, Taiwan, 1994—; cons. Asian Buddhism Inst. Sino-Indian Buddhist Studies, Taipei, Taiwan, 1981-93, also rsch. fellow, 1993— , Inst. for Advanced Studies of World Religions, Carmel, N.Y., 1989-92, also rsch. fellow, 1993-95. Editor-in-chief series: Great Religions of Modern Man, 1961; editor, contbg. author: Buddhism, 1961; editor Buddhist Text Info., 1974-95, Buddhist Rsch. Info., 1979-84; editor-in-chief Asian Religious Studies Info., 1987-90; contbr. articles to acad., religious jours, Asia, U.S. Sec. 3 Village Men's Garden Club, Setauket, N.Y., 1980-84. Served to lt. col. USMCR, 1941-46; PTO. Japanese Buddhist okesa Jodo-shu, Phila., 1946, Japanese Buddhist okesa Shingon-shu, Los Angeles, 1950; recipient Thai Buddhist Theravada award Mahamakuta Found., Bangkok, 1956, Burmese Buddhist Theravada award Shwedagon, Rangoon, 1957, Korean Buddhist Mahayana award Cho-gye-jong, Pom-o-sa, Republic of Korea, 1965; Rockefeller Found. Rsch. fellow U. Pa., Phila., 1946-47; Ford Found. grantee Wittenberg U., 1970. Mem. Assn. Asian Studies (pres. Mid-Atlantic region 1974-75), Tibet Soc. (bd. dirs. 1978-83, 87-89, 91-93), Internat. Assn. Buddhist Studies (bd. dirs. 1982-86, 87-94), Am. Soc. for Study Religion (exec. com. 1983-86). Buddhist. Avocations: landscape gardening, mountain hiking, chamber music. Address: PO Box 2866 Setauket NY 11733-0866

GARDE, ANAND MADHAV, materials scientist; b. Sangli, India, Jan. 1, 1945; came to U.S., 1968; s. Madhav Moreshwar and Malati Madhav (Javadekar) G.; m. Vandana Mukund Joshi, Jan. 22, 1972; children: Vinaya, Preeti. B in Tech., Indian Inst. Tech., Bombay, 1967; MS, Syracuse U., 1970; PhD, U. Fla., 1973. Asst. metallurgist Argonne (Ill.) Nat. Lab., 1974-79; prin. engr. Combustion Engring., Windsor, Conn., 1979-88; consulting engr. ABB Combustion Engring., Windsor, 1989-96; sr. cons. engr. ABB Combustion Engring., Hematite, Mo., 1996—; adj. lectr. Hartford (Conn.) Grad. Ctr., 1989-99; adj. assoc. prof. REnsselaer at Hartford, 1999—; symposium chmn. 10th Internat. Symposium on Zirconium in the Nuclear Industry, Balt., 1993. Contbr. over 35 articles, 32 tech. reports and 20 abstracts to profl. jours. Pres. India Assn. of Greater Hartford, 1982; program coord. India Festival of Sci., West Hartford, 1988-89. Recipient ASTM Schemel award, 1996. Mem. AIME (nuclear metallurgy com. 1984—), ASTM (B10, G1 coms. 1985—, tech. editor spl. tech. publs. 1132 & 1245, 1991, 94), Am. Soc. Metals Internat., Indian Inst. Metals. Republican. Hindu. Achievements include 9 patents for Ductile Irradiated Zirconium Alloys and Corrosion Resistant Zirconium Alloys, patents pending. Office: ABB Combustion Engring 2000 Day Hill Rd Windsor CT 06095-1565

GARDE, JOHN CHARLES, lawyer; b. Lyndhurst, N.J., Aug. 17, 1961; s. John Charles and Jean (Sheperd) G.; m. L. Allison Ghenn, Aug. 9, 1986. BA, Drew U., 1983; JD, William and Mary, 1986. Bar: N.J. 1986, U.S. Ct. N.J. 1986, U.S. Ct. Appeals (2nd, 3rd and 7th cirs.) 1990. Law sec. to presiding judge Superior Ct Appellate div., Hackensack, N.J., 1986-87; assoc. McCarter & English, Newark, 1987-94, ptnr., 1995—. Contbr. William and Mary Law Rev. Warden St. Thomas Epis. Ch., 1987—; trustee St. Phillip's Acad., 1996—. Mem. ABA, N.J. State Bar Assn., Essex County Bar Assn., Order of the Coif, Phi Beta Kappa. Republican. Episcopalian. Office: McCarter & English 100 Mulberry St Newark NJ 07102-4004

GARDEBRING, SANDRA S., academic administrator. Grad., Luther Coll., Decorah, Iowa; JD, U. Minn. Dir. Region 5 U.S. EPA; commr. Minn. Pollution Control Agy., Minn. Dept. Human Svcs.; judge Minn. Ct. Appeals; assoc. justice Minn. Supreme Ct., 1991-98; v.p. U. Minn., 1998—; chmn. bd. regional planning agy. Met. Coun. Mem. Ctr. Victims of Torture; mem. Minn. Advocates, LWV; past bd. dirs. St. Paul United Way, Camp DuNord, Project Environment Found., Clean Sites. Office: U Minn 11 Morris Hall 100 Church St SE Minneapolis MN 55455-0110

GARDENOUR, DIANE LESLIE, library director; b. Haverhill, Mass., Nov. 11, 1950; d. Frank and Priscilla May Leslie; m. Larry Lee Gardenour, Sept. 26, 1970; children: Jeffrey Michael, Lori Beth. Libr. aide Mastricola Mid. Sch., Merrimack, N.H., 1980-88; children's libr. Ingalls Meml. Libr., Rindge, N.H., 1988-90, libr. dir., 1990—. Cmty. chmn. Girl Scouts Am., Merrimack, 1985, 86. Mem. N.H. Libr. Assn. Avocations: crafts, archery. E-mail: ingallslib@top.monad.net. Office: Ingalls Meml Libr Main St Rindge NH 03461-0224

GARDIN, JOHN GEORGE, II, psychologist; b. Renton, Wash., Jan. 5, 1949; s. John George and Charlotte (Larabee) G.; m. Dana Rothrock, Oct. 22, 1986; children: Greg, Gina, Bret; 1 stepchild, Angie West. BS in Chemistry, Seattle U., 1971; BS in Psychology, U. Wash., 1972; MS in Psychology, Portland State U., 1975; PhD in Psychology, U. Tenn., 1986. Lic. psychologist. Clinician Luth. Family Svcs., Portland, Oreg., 1978-80;

mental health specialist Probation Dept. Oreg. State, Roseburg, 1980-81; exec. dir. ADAPT, Roseburg, 1981-85; psychologist, ptnr. South Coast Psychol., Irvine, Calif., 1986-91; assoc. prof. psychiatry U. Calif. Irvine, Dana Point, Calif., 1988-90; med. dir. Chem. Dependency Charter Hosp., Corona, Calif., 1990-91; ptnr. LifeOne, Irvine, 1991-92; pvt. practice psychology San Juan Capistrano, Calif., 1985—; cons. Real World TV Show, Bunim-Murray Prodns., 1993-97, Flagship Healthcare, 1994-95, Orange County Youth Ctrs., 1996-97; v.p. Pacific Hills Treatment Ctrs., Inc., 1997—; mem. exec. com. CALNET, 1998—. Pres. Alcohol/Drug Program Dirs. of Oreg., 1984; bd. dirs. Oreg. State Coun. on Alcoholism, 1983; mem. Counselors Credentials Task Force, Oreg., 1984. Mem. APA, Calif. State Psychol. Assn., Am. Athletic Union, Japan Karate-Do Fedn., Martial Arts Fedn., Christian Assn. Psychol. Svcs., Assn. of Christian Therapists, Am. Coll. Advanced Practice Psychologists (founding fellow). Avocations: martial arts, scuba diving, boating, travel. Office: 3151 Airway Ave Ste D1 Costa Mesa CA 92626-4622

GARDIN, JULIUS MARKUS, cardiologist, educator; b. Detroit, Jan. 14, 1949; s. Abram and Fania (Toba) G.; m. Susan Deanne Kelemen, Dec. 19, 1982; children: Adam Lev, Tova Michal, Margot Anne. BS with high distinction, U. Mich., 1968, MD cum laude, 1972. Diplomate Am. Bd. Internal Medicine; cert. cardiovascular diseases. Intern then resident in medicine U. Mich., Ann Arbor, 1972-75; fellow in cardiology Georgetown U., Washington, 1975-77; dir. cardiology noninvasive lab., staff cardiologist Lakeside VA Med. Ctr., Chgo., 1977-79; staff cardiologist, asst. prof. Med. Sch. Northwestern U., Chgo., 1978-79; dir. cardiology noninvasive lab. Irvine Med. Ctr. U. Calif., Orange, 1979—, from asst. prof. to assoc. prof. Irvine Med. Ctr., 1979-89, prof., 1989—; chief cardiology U. Calif., Irvine, 1994-99; acting chief cardiology Long Beach (Calif.) VA Med. Ctr., 1982-84. Co-editor: Textbook of Two-Dimensional Echocardiography, 1983; editor: Update on Cardiovascular Diagnostics, 1982; assoc. editor Am. Jour. Cardiac Imaging, 1985-97; mem. editl. bd. Archives of Internal Medicine and Chest, 1978-88, Am. Jour. Noninvasive Cardiology, 1985—, Am. Jour. Cardiology, 1987-94, 96—, Cardiovascular Imaging, 1988—, Echocardiography, 1985—, Jour. Am. Coll. Cardiology, 1990-94; cardiovasc. area editor Jour. Clin. Ultrasound, 1989-94, Jour. Am. Soc. Echocardiography, 1992—; contbr. articles to profl. jours. Maj. Med. Svc. Corps, USAR. Grantee Am. Heart Assn., 1980-82, 83-84, 99—, Nat. Heart Lung and Blood Inst., 1988—. Fellow ACP, Am. Coll. Cardiology (physician workforce adv., health care reform and echocardiography coms.), Am. Heart Assn. (fellow coun. clin. cardiology, coun. epidemiology and coun. cardiovascular radiology), Soc. Geriatric Cardiology (v.p. 1990-92, pres. 1992-93); mem. Internat. Cardiac Doppler Soc. (sec., bd. dirs., chmn. Pan-Am. sect. 1984—, v.p. 1988-90, pres. 1990-92), Am. Soc. Echocardiography (bd. dirs., treas. 1989-91, v.p. 1991-93, pres. 1993-95, chmn. nomenclature and stds. 1991-95, chmn. task force on standardized echo report), U. Mich. Med. Ctr. Alumni Assn. (bd. govs. 1979-81), Phi Beta Kappa, Alpha Omega Alpha, Phi Delta Epsilon. Jewish. Office: U Calif Irvine Med Ctr Div Cardiology 101 The City Dr S Bldg 53 Rt 81 Orange CA 92868-3201

GARDINER, DAVID, federal agency administrator; married; 3 children. BA in History with honors, Harvard U. Legis. dir. Sierra Club, Washington; asst. adminstr. for policy, planning and evaluation U.S. EPA, Washington, 1993—. Office: Environmental Protection Agency Policy Planning & Evaluation 401 M St SW Washington DC 20460-0003*

GARDINER, E. NICHOLAS P., executive search executive; b. Boston, June 19, 1939; s. John Pennington and Juliana (Geszty) G.; m. Judith Beck, Jan. 19, 1975 (div. Sept. 1981); m. Sigrid Becker Bron, Mar. 19, 1987; stepchildren: Christian Bron, Eric Edouard Bron. BA, Yale U., 1961; PMD, Harvard Bus. Sch., 1971. Gen. mgr. W.R. Grace & Co., N.Y.C., 1965-70, Envases Sanmarti div. W.R. Grace & Co., Lima, Peru, 1967-70; dir. corp. devel., N.Y. Internat. Basic Economy Corp., 1970-72, v.p., N.Y., 1974-78; v.p. Cen. Nat. Corp., 1973; v.p. Boyden Assocs., N.Y.C., 1979-80, ptnr., 1980-83, sr. v.p., 1982-83; pres., chief exec. officer Haley Internat. Inc., N.Y.C., 1984-87; mng. dir. Gardiner Stone Hunter Internat. Inc., N.Y.C., 1987-92; exec. Paul Ray & Co., N.Y.C., 1992-93; pres. Eric Salmon & Ptnrs. Inc., N.Y.C., 1993-95, Gardiner Internat., N.Y.C., 1995—, Gardiner, Townsend & Assocs., N.Y.C., 1998—. Pres. Radio Free Europe/Radio Liberty Fund.; dir. Am. Coun. on Germany, French-Am. Found. Served to 1st lt. USMCR, 1961-64. Mem. The Japan Soc., Inst. Francais des Rels. Internat., Royal Inst. Internat. Affairs, The European Inst., The Soc. Cin., The Brook, Racquet and Tennis Club, Jesters Club, Polo Club (Paris). Republican. Episcopalian. Home: West Lake Stable Road Tuxedo Park NY 10987-9999 Office: Gardiner Townsend & Assocs 101 E 52nd St New York NY 10022-6018

GARDINER, GEOFFREY ALEXANDER, JR., radiologist, educator; b. L.A., Aug. 28, 1949; s. Geoffrey Alexander and Doris Joyce (Engelhard) G.; children: Bryan Scott, Brent Michael. MD, Loma Linda U., 1973. Diplomate Am. Bd. Radiology. Intern Fla. Hosp., Orlando, 1974-75; resident in diagnostic radiology Loma Linda (Calif.) U. Med. Ctr., 1975-78; pvt. practice Portland, Oreg., 1978-84; fellow in cardiovascular and interventional radiology Brigham and Women's Hosp.-Harvard U. Med. Sch., Boston, 1984-85; instr. med. sch. Harvard U. Med. Sch., 1985-86; dir. cardiovascular and interventional radiology Thomas Jefferson U. Hosp., Phila., 1986—; asst. prof. radiology Thomas Jefferson U. Med. Coll., 1986—; assoc. prof. radiology, 1990. Cons. editor Cardiovascular and Interventional Radiology, 1986—; assoc. editor Jour. Vascular and Interventional Radiology, 1990—, Radiology, 1991—; contbr. articles to med. jours., chpt. to book. Mem. Am. Coll. Radiology, Assn. Univ. Radiologists, Soc. Cardiovascular and Interventional Radiology, Radiol. Soc. N.Am. Presbyterian. Home: 206 Homestead Rd Wayne PA 19087-2430 Office: Thomas Jefferson U Hosp Ste 4200 Gibbon Bldg 111 S 11th St Philadelphia PA 19107-5084*

GARDINER, JOHN JACOB, leadership studies educator, author, philosopher; b. Tel Aviv, Feb. 6, 1946; came to U.S., 1952; s. Leon and Zipora (Shalev) Zucker; m. Joanna Meredith Winslow, Dec. 24, 1967; children: James, Katharine. BA, U. Fla., 1967, PhD, 1973; postgrad., U. Oreg., 1978, Stanford U., 1983. Tchr., dept. chair Keystone Heights (Fla.) Sch., 1968-72; instr., asst. to v.p. acad. affairs U. Fla., Gainesville, 1973-75; asst. prof. edn. The Citadel, Charleston, S.C., 1975-77; prof., dept. chair Okla. State U., Stillwater, 1979-91, Seattle U., 1991—; assoc. in edn. Harvard U., 1985; vis. asst. prof. Fla. State U., Tallahassee, 1977-78, U. Oreg., Eugene, 1978-79; chair bd. Pacific N.W. Postdoctoral Inst., Seattle, 1995—. Co-author: UNESCO Guide, 1991, Insights on Leadership, 1998. Permanent fund chair dist. 5030 Rotary, Seattle, 1996—. Recipient Svc. to State award Gov. and Ho. of Reps., 1991; fellow W. K. Kellogg Found., 1972-73; grantee James McGregor Burns Leadership Acad. Ctr. for Advanced Study of Leadership, 1999. Mem. Am. Coun. Edn. (bd. dirs. Nat. Leadership Group 1985-96), Assn. Study of Higher Edn. (bd. dirs. 1983-85), Am. Ednl. Rsch. Assn. (bd. dirs. divsn. J 1983-85), Vashon Island Club (bd. dirs. 1995—). Episcopalian. Avocations: walking, reading, gardening, public speaking. Office: Seattle U 510 Loyola Hall Broadway and Madison Seattle WA 98122

GARDINER, JUDITH KEGAN, English language and women's studies educator; b. Chgo., Dec. 17, 1941; d. Albert and Esther (Oswianza) Kegan; divorced; children: Viveca, Carita. BA, Radcliffe Coll., 1962; MA, Columbia U., 1964, PhD, 1968. Prof. English and women's studies U. Ill., Chgo., 1969—, acting dir. women's studies, 1989, 91. Author: Rhys Stead Lessing, 1989; editor: Provoking Agents, 1995; editor Feminist Studies, 1989—; also articles. Organizer Newberry Libr. Feminist Lit. Criticism Group, Chgo., 1985-95. Fellow NEH, 1988. Office: U Ill Dept English M/C 162 601 S Morgan St Chicago IL 60607-7120

GARDINER, LESTER RAYMOND, JR., lawyer; b. Salt Lake City, Aug. 20, 1931; s. Lester Raymond and Sarah Lucille (Kener) G.; m. Janet Ruth Thatcher, Apr. 11, 1955; children: Allison Gardiner Bigelow, John Alfred, Annette Gardiner Weed, Leslie Gardiner Crandall, Robert Thatcher, Lisa Gardiner West, James Raymond, Elizabeth, David William, Sarah Janet. BS with honors, U. Utah, 1954; JD, U. Mich., 1959. Bar: Utah 1959, U.S. Dist. Ct. Utah 1959, U.S. Ct. Apls. (10th cir.) 1960. Law clk., U.S. Dist. Ct., 1959; assoc. then ptnr. Van Cott, Bagley, Cornwall & McCarthy, Salt Lake City, 1960-67; ptnr. Gardiner & Johnson, Salt Lake City, 1967-72; ptnr. Christensen, Gardiner, Jensen & Evans, 1972-78; ptnr. Fox, Edwards, Gardiner & Brown, Salt Lake City, 1978-87, ptnr. Chapman & Cutler, 1987-89, ptnr. Gardiner & Hintze, 1990-92; CEO and pres. Snowbird Ski and Summer Resort, Snowbird Corp., 1993-97, prin., mgmt. cons. Ray Gardiner Assocs., 1998—; reporter, mem. Utah Sup. Ct. Com. on Adoption of Uniform Rules of Evidence, 1970-73, mem. com. on revision of criminal code, 1975-78; master of the bench Am. Inn of Ct. I, 1980-90; mem. com. bar examiners Utah State Bar, 1973; instr. bus. law U. Utah, 1965-66; adj. prof. law Brigham Young U., 1984-85. Mem. Republican State Central Com. Utah, 1967-72, mem. exec. com. Utah Rep. Party, 1975-78, chmn. state convs., 1980, 81; mem. Salt Lake City Bd. Edn., 1971-72; bd. dirs. Salt Lake City Pub. Library, 1974-75; trustee Utah Sports Found., 1987-91; bd. dirs. and exec. com. Salt Lake City Visitors and Conv. Bur., 1988-91, 93-98. Served to 1st lt. USAF, 1954-56. Mem. Utah State Bar Assn., Sons of Utah Pioneers, Utah Ski Assn. (bd. dirs. 1994-97), Nat. Ski Areas Assn. (mem. pub. lands com. 1994-97, gov. affairs com. 1994-97), Rotary. Mormon. Office: Ray Gardiner Assocs 93 Laurel St Salt Lake City UT 84103-4349

GARDINER, STEPHANIE JOANN, staff office nurse, endoscopy nurse; b. Columbus, Ohio, Feb. 6, 1956; d. Elton Clarence and Frieda Louise (Baas) Renner; m. Jay Vernon Gardiner, Dec. 23, 1978; children: Nickalas, Tiffany, Timothy. Diploma, Springfield Hosp. Sch. Nursing, 1978. RN, Ohio. Staff nurse Meml. Hosp., Marysville, Ohio, 1978-80, Newport (R.I.) Hosp., 1980; charge nurse Long Lake Manor, Port Orchard, Wash., 1984; float nurse to staff nurse Palomar Meml. Hosp., Escondido, Calif., 1986-87; staff nurse, drs. endoscopy call nurse Gastroenterology Ltd., Virginia Beach, Va., 1991-95; endoscopy staff nurse Virginia Beach Gen. Hosp., 1991-95, endoscopy call nurse, 1993-95; charge nurse Alzheimers Specialty Ctr.; endoscopy call nurse Virginia Beach Gen. Hosp., 1993-95. Active English handbells Stow Presbyn. Ch. Mary Bells, Stow Heritage Ringers; dir. youth handbell choir Stow Presbyn. Ch. Mem. Ea. Stars, Soc. of Gastroenterology Nurses and Assocs., Inc., Providence Presbyn. Handbells, Providence Presbyn. Youth Handbells. Republican. Avocations: sewing, needle work, collecting stamps, playing English handbells, gardening. Home: 5653 Williamsburg Cir Hudson OH 44236-3761

GARDINER, SUSAN NIVEN, purchasing executive; b. N.Y.C., Aug. 28, 1956; d. Robert MacPherson Gardiner and Janet (Eaton) Gardiner Glover; m. René Raul Trespalacios, Oct. 12, 1991. BA in French Lang. and Lit., Smith Coll., 1978. Prodn. mgr. Wunderman, Ricotta & Kline, N.Y.C., 1978-79; prodn. supr. Random House Enterprises, N.Y.C., 1979-81; print svcs. mgr. Esquire Mag., N.Y.C., 1981-82; purchasing agt. Playtex, inc., Stamford, Conn., 1982-84; purchasing buyer Gen. Foods Corp., White Plains, N.Y., 1984-86; asst. v.p. promotional purchasing Lancome, Inc., N.Y.C., 1986—. Mem. Assn. Graphic Arts (judge 1991—). Home: 8 Brandywine Ter Morristown NJ 07960-3503 Office: Lancome Inc 575 Fith Ave New York NY 10017

GARDINER, T(HOMAS) MICHAEL, artist; b. Seattle, Feb. 5, 1946; s. Thomas Scott Gardiner and Carolyn Virginia (Harmer) Bolin; m. Kelly Michelle Floyd, Mar. 7, 1981 (div. Dec. 1983); m. Diana Phyllis Shurtlieff Rainwater, Sept. 26, 1986; children: Rita Em, Nigel Gus. BA in Philosophy, Sulpician Sem. N.W., Kenmore, Wash., 1969; student, Cornish Inst. Arts, 1971-73. Seaman Tidewater Barge, Camas, Wash., 1969; pari-mutuel clk. Longacres Racetrack, Renton, Wash., 1969-92; dock worker Sealand, Inc., Seattle, 1970; tchr. Coyote Jr. H.S., Seattle, 1989-95, Sch. Visual Concepts, Seattle, 1990-95; tchr., vis. artist Ctrl. Wash. U., Ellensburg, 1991. Represented in permanent collections Seattle Water Dept., Nordstrom, Seattle City Light, Sultan (Wash.) Sch. Dist., King County Portable Works Collection, SAFECO Ins. Co., Seattle, City of Portland Collection, 1988, Highline Sch. Dist., Seattle; commns. include ARTp Metro Art Project, Seattle, interior painting Villa del Lupo restaurant, Vancouver, B.C., Can.; illustrations included in The New Yorker Mag., Am. Illustration 13, The Seattle Times. Recipient Best Design award Print Mag., 1985; Nat. Endowment for Arts Fellowship grantee, 1989. Democrat. Roman Catholic. Home and Office: 3023 NW 63rd St Seattle WA 98107-2566

GARDINER, WILLIAM CECIL, JR., chemist, educator; b. Niagara Falls, N.Y., Jan. 14, 1933; s. William Cecil and Annie Charlotte (Hicks) G.; children—Grace, Charlotte, Amy Louise; m. Regina R. Monaco, July 15, 1991. AB, Princeton U., 1954; postgrad., U. Heidelberg, 1954-55, U. Göttingen, 1955-56; PhD, Harvard U., 1960. Instr. chemistry U. Tex., Austin, 1960-62; asst. prof. U. Tex., 1962-66, assoc. prof., 1966-72, prof., 1972—; cons. on chemistry of combustion reactions to govtl. agencies. Contbr. articles on rates of chem. reactions to tech. jours. Fulbright fellow, 1954-55, 75-76; Guggenheim fellow, 1975-76; Humboldt fellow, 1979, 82; Thyssen fellow, 1983; Lady Davis prof., 1985. Fellow Japan Soc. for Promotion Sci; mem. Am. Chem. Soc., Am. Phys. Soc., AAAS, Combustion Inst., Phi Beta Kappa, Sigma Xi. Home: PO Box 8230 Austin TX 78713-8230 Office: Univ Tex Dept Chemistry/Biochemistry WEL 2.406 MC A5300 Austin TX 78712

GARDINER, WILLIAM DOUGLAS HAIG, bank executive; b. Chatham, Ont., Can., Apr. 21, 1917; s. William Henry and Elsie May (Armstrong) G.; m. Jean Elizabeth Blatchford, Sept. 5, 1945; children: Donald W. B., Campbell D., Gregory F. Grad., Kennedy Collegiate Sch., Windsor, Ont. Asst. gen. mgr. Royal Bank of Can., Montreal, 1961-64, Vancouver, 1964-67; v.p., dist. gen. mgr. Royal Bank of Can., 1967-73; dep. chmn., exec. v.p. Royal Bank of Can., Toronto, 1973-77, vice chmn., dir., 1977-80; pres. W.D.H.G. Fin. Assocs. Ltd., Vancouver. Served to lt. comdr. RCNVR. Decorated Order of Canada. Presbyterian. Clubs: York; Vancouver, Shaughnessy Golf, Eldorado Golf. Home: 3115 W 49th Ave, Vancouver, BC Canada V6M 3T3

GARDINO, VINCENT ANTHONY, broadcasting executive; b. N.Y.C., Sept. 19, 1953; s. Anthony John and Carmelina Mary (Boglia) G. BA magna cum laude in History, St. Francis Coll. V.p. N.Y. sales mgr., dir. spl. programming and sales Metro Radio Sales, N.Y.C., 1976-79; acct. exec. WABC Radio, N.Y.C., 1979-81; dir. ABC Radio Network, N.Y.C., 1981-85, ABC Direction and Entertainment Radio Networks, 1981-85; pres., chief ops. officer Selcom Radio, N.Y.C., 1985—; v.p., gen. sales mgr. Sta. WOR-AM, N.Y.C., 1985-95; v.p. ea. sales CNBC, 1995-98; dir. corp. underwriting sales Sta. WNYC-FM, Sta. WNYC-AM, 1998—. Mem. Mus. Broadcasting, Internat. Radio and TV Soc., Famija Piemonteisa (bd. dirs.), NYU Med. Ctr. (Kaplan Cancer Ctr., bd. dirs.) St. Francis Coll. Alumni Assn. (bd. dirs.), N.Y. Athletic Club, Columbus Citizens Found., Inc. Roman Catholic. Avocations: tennis, golf, skiing, historical autograph collecting. Office: WNYC AM/FM 1 Centre St New York NY 10007-1602

GARDNER, ADRIENNE MOORE, public relations specialist; b. Seattle, Mar. 24, 1976; d. Donald Ray and Lorraine Hatcher M.; m. Vincent Demetris Gardner, June 3, 1998. BS in Pub. Policy & Mgmt., U. So. Calif., 1998. Reader U. So. Calif. Readers Program, L.A., 1996-97, comm. coord., 1997-98; devel. asst. Northpointe Achievement Agy., Zion, Ill., 1998—. Tutor Upward Bound Program, L.A., 1995; mentor Joint Ednl. Project, L.A., 1994-95. Mem. Am. Soc. Pub. Adminstrn. Democrat. Baptist. Avocations: scrapbooking, Winnie-the-Pooh collectibles. Office: 3441 Sheridan Rd Zion IL 60099

GARDNER, ANNE LANCASTER, lawyer; b. Aug. 19, 1942; d. Jack Quinn and DeWitte (Benton) Lancaster; m. Terry Gardner; 1 child, Travis Gregory. BA, U. Tex., 1964, LLB, 1966. Bar: Tex. 1966. Asst. dir. CLE State Bar Tex., 1966-67; law clk. to U.S. Dist. Ct. judge, 1967-71; ptnr. Simon, Peebles, Haskell, Gardner & Betty, Ft. Worth, 1971-85, McLean, Sanders, Price, Head & Ellis, P.C., Ft. Worth, 1985-88; ptnr. Shannon, Gracey, Ratliff & Miller, Ft. Worth, 1988—, chair appeals sect.; mem. adv. commn. State Bd. Legal Specialization Appellate Civil Law, chair, 1993-94; mem. Tex. Supreme Ct. adv. com., 1993—; chair merit selection Panel for U.S. Magistrate Judges, no. dist. Tex., 1995. Editor legal jours. Fellow Tex. Bar Found. (life); mem. ABA, Tarrant County Bar Assn. (dir., v.p., pres.-elect 1993, pres. 1994), Tex. Assn. Def. Counsel (bd. dirs.).

GARDNER, ARNOLD BURTON, lawyer; b. N.Y.C., Jan. 3, 1930; s. Harry P. and Ruth G. (Gutfreund) G.; m. Sue Shaffer, Aug. 24, 1952; children—Jonathan H., Diane R. B.A. summa cum laude, U. Buffalo, 1950; LL.B., Harvard U., 1953. Bar: N.Y. State bar 1954. Assoc. firm Kavinoky & Cook (and predecessor), Buffalo, 1953-58, ptnr., 1958—; sr. ptnr. Kavinoky & Cook (and predecessor), 1977—. Mem. Buffalo Bd. Edn., 1969-74, pres., 1971-72; mem. nat. bd. govs. Am. Jewish Com., 1972-95, nat. v.p., 1986-89; chmn. N.Y. State Edn. Dept. Task Force on Tchr. Edn. and Certification, 1975-77; trustee SUNY, 1980-99, vice chmn., 1991-95; bd. govs. Hebrew Union Coll., Jewish Inst. Religion, Cin., 1981-87; trustee N.Y. State Archives, 1994—; mem. N.Y. State Bd. Regents, 1999—. With U.S. Army, 1954-56. Recipient Community Service award NCCJ, 1974, 88, Lawyer of Yr. U. Buffalo Sch. of Law, 1994. Mem. ABA, N.Y. State Bar Assn., Erie County Bar Assn., Am. Law Inst. Club: Buffalo. Home: 89 Middlesex Rd Buffalo NY 14216-3617 Office: Kavinoky & Cook 120 Delaware Ave Rm 600 Buffalo NY 14202-2793

GARDNER, BARBARA ROGERS, humanities educator, writer; b. St. Louis, June 12, 1935; d. William Houston and Jean (Cadman) Jack; m. David Rogers, Sep. 4, 1952 (div. Apr. 1977); children: Jean, Steven, John; m. Mark Gardner, June 13, 1983. BA, Syracuse U., 1955; MA, U. Iowa, 1986; PhD, Rutgers U., 1971. Prof. Ramapo Coll., Mahwah, N.J., 1972-84; prof. mythol. studies, psychology and lit. Pacifica Grad. Inst., Carpinteria, Calif., 1989-97. Author: The Doomsday Scroll, 1980, Jung and Shakespeare, 1992, (play) Isadora, 1988, The Sai Prophecy, 1999; exhibited in group show Rannells Art Gallery, 1996. Mem. Sculpture Guild, Santa Barbara Screenwriters Assn. (prize 1996). Democrat. Episcopalian. Avocations: choir, Irish harp, ceramic sculpture.

GARDNER, BRIAN E., lawyer; b. Des Moines, July 13, 1952; s. Lawrence E. and Sarah I. (Hill) G.; m. Rondi L. Veland, Aug. 7, 1976; children: Meredith Anne, Stephanie Lynn, John Clinton. BS, Iowa State U., 1974; JD, U. Iowa, 1978. Bar: Iowa 1978, Mo. 1978, Kans. 1979, U.S. Ct. Appeals (10th cir.) 1980, U.S. Dist. Ct. Kans. 1979, U.S. Dist. Ct. (we. dist.) Mo. 1978. Assoc. Morrison, Hecker, Curtis, Kuder & Parrish, Kansas City, Mo., 1978-80, Parker & Handsaker, Nevada, Iowa, 1980-81, Morrison, Hecker, Curtis, Kuder & Parrish, Overland Park, Kans., 1981-83; ptnr. Morrison & Hecker, Kansas City, Mo., 1983—, mng. ptnr., 1990-93, 96—; city atty. Mission Hills, Kans., 1992—. Bd. dirs. Overland Park Conv. and Visitors Bur., 1985-97, chmn., 1988-90; dir., mem. exec. com. Johnson County C.C. Found., Overland Park, 1990—, pres., 1997—; bd. dirs. KCPT, 1993—, chmn., 1997-98; active Kansas City Area Devel. Coun., 1992—, Civic Coun. Greater Kansas City, 1998—. Mem. Kans. Bar Assn., Kans. Assn. Def. Counsel, Kansas City Met. Bar Assn., Mo. Bar Assn., Johnson County Bar Assn., Blue Hills Country Club, Cardinal Key, Phi Beta Kappa. Lutheran. Avocation: golf. Office: Morrison & Hecker LLP 2600 Grand Blvd Kansas City MO 64108-4606

GARDNER, CAROL ELAINE, elementary school educator; b. Savannah, Ga., Dec. 12, 1958; d. Marshall Lee and Lillie Mary (Brown) Williams; m. Jacky Lee Gardner, Sept. 29, 1979; children: Brian Alexander, Brandon Lee, Brent Matthew. BE, Cameron U., Lawton, Okla., 1979. Cert. elem. tchr., Okla. Tchr. grade 4 Swinney Elem. Sch., Lawton, 1980; tchr. grade 1 Swinney Elem. Sch., 1980—; Lawton Sch. Dist curriculum adv. bd., 1990-91; rep. Profl. Planning Devel. Coun., 1992—, chmn. fin. com., 1996-97; mem. Bldg. Leadership Team, 1991—; mentoring tchr. Cameron U., Fall, 1995. Recipient Environ. award Pub. Svc. Co. Okla., 1996. Mem. NEA, Lawton Reading Coun., Profl. Educator Assn. Lawton, Tchrs. Applying Whole Lang. Jehovah's Witness. Avocations: reading, biking, hiking, coin collecting. Home: 2306 NW 72nd St Lawton OK 73505-1007

GARDNER, CHARLES CLIFFORD, JR., colorectal surgeon; b. Cleve., Dec. 19, 1946; s. Charles Clifford and Ann Julia (Marolt) G.; m. Martha Carroll Porter, Aug. 9, 1969; children: Tiffany Ann, Kelley Elizabeth. BA in Biology, St. Mary's U., San Antonio, 1972; MD, U. Tex. Health Sci. Ctr., 1976. Diplomate Am. Bd. Surgery, Am. Bd. Colon Rectal Surgery. Resident in gen. surgery Wilford Hall Med. Ctr., Lackland AFB, Tex., 1976-81; fellow colon rectal surgeon Cleve. Clinic, 1981-82; colorectal surgeon in pvt. practice Dayton, Ohio, 1987—; mem. colon rectal adv. bd. Ethicon, Inc., Cin., 1982-93; chmn. dept. surgery St. Elizabeth Med. Ctr., Dayton, 1994-95, 98—. Lt. col. USAF, 1972-87. Fellow ACS, Am. Soc. Colon Rectal Surgeons (self-assessment com. 1987-88); mem. AMA, Ohio Valley Colon Rectal Soc., Dayton Surg. Soc. (treas. 1987-88, pres. 1989-90), Alpha Omega Alpha. Republican. Roman Catholic. Avocations: fishing, hunting, sports. Office: 627 S Edwin C Moses Blvd Ste N Dayton OH 45408-1461

GARDNER, CHARLES OLDA, plant geneticist and breeder, design consultant, analyst; b. Tecumseh, Neb., Mar. 15, 1919; s. Olda Cecil and Frances E. (Stover) G.; m. Wanda Marie Steinkamp, June 9, 1947; children—Charles Olda, Jr., Lynda Frances, Thomas Edward, Richard Alan. B.S., U. Nebr., 1941, M.S., 1948; M.B.A., Harvard U., 1943; Ph.D., N.C. State U., 1951. Asst. extension agronomist U. Nebr., Lincoln, 1946-48, assoc. prof., 1952-57, chmn. statis. lab., 1957-68, prof., 1957-70, regents prof., 1970-89, prof. emeritus, 1989—, interim head Biometrics Ctr., 1988-89; asst. statistician N.C. State U., Raleigh, 1951-52; vis. prof. U. Wis., 1962-63; cons. CIMMYT and Rockefeller Found., Mex., Latin Am., 1964—, cons., CIBA-GEIGY, Eastern half of U.S., 1983; cons., lectr. Dept. Agr., Queensland, Australia, 1977; cons., lectr. maize program Kasetsart U. and Ministry of Agr., Bangkok, 1990; spl. lectr. advanced maize breeding course for leaders of nat. maize programs in developing countries Internat. Ctr. for Maize and Wheat Improvement, El Batan, Mex., 1989, 91, 93. Contbr. articles to profl. jours. Elder, Eastridge Presbyterian Ch.; pres. Eastridge PTA. Served to capt., U.S. Army, 1943-46. Recipient Outstanding Research and Creativity award U. Nebr., 1981, USDA Disting. Service award, 1988, Award of Merit U. Nebr. Alumni Assn., 1996. Fellow Am. Soc. of Agronomy (pres. 1982, agronomic service award, 1988), Crop Sci. Soc. of Am. (pres. 1975, recipient Crop Sci. award, 1978, DeKalb-Pfizer Crop Sci. Disting. Career award 1984), AAAS (chmn. sect. O com. 1987); mem. Am. Genetic Assn., Genetic Soc. of Am., Biometric Soc. (mem. regional com.), Sigma Xi, Gamma Sigma Delta (Internat. Disting. Svc. Agr. 1977). Republican. Presbyterian. Avocations: photography; golf; fishing; gardening. Home: 5835 Meadowbrook Ln Lincoln NE 68510-4026 Office: U Neb Dept Biometry Lincoln NE 68583-0712

GARDNER, CLYDE EDWARD, healthcare executive, consultant, educator; b. Steubenville, Ohio, Oct. 8, 1931; s. Peter D. and Louella Mary (Gillespie) G.; m. Patricia Jackson, Oct. 4, 1953 (div. Dec. 1977); 1 child, Bruce Stephen. BA, San Francisco State U., 1969, MS, 1971. Adminstr. Gardner Convalescent Hosp., Napa, Calif., 1955-68; exec. dir. Haight Ashbury Free Med. Clinic, San Francisco, 1970-71; lectr. San Francisco State U., 1969-71; dir. planning and rsch. divsn. N. Country Com. on Area Wide Health Planning, Canton, N.Y., 1971-77; prof. Gov.'s State U., University Park, Ill., 1977-83; sr. ptnr. Health Care Cons., Park Forest, Ill., 1983-86; exec. dir. Mahoning Shenango Area Health Edn. Network, Youngstown, Ohio, 1986-90; pres., CEO Mahoning Edn. and Tng. Network, Youngstown, Ohio, 1990-92, Health Sci. Assocs., Tucson, 1992—; adj. prof. SUNY, Canton, 1975-76, Youngstown State U., 1987-90; bus. rep. Apollo Coll., 1994-95; rschr. FMR Rsch., 1996-97; lectr. San Francisco State U., 1969-71. Author: Data Book for Health and Institutional Planning, 1981; author of numerous pub. health planning, health edn. studies and funded pvt., state and fed. health care grants, 1971-90. Pres. Found. I Ctr. for Human Devel., Harvey, Ill., 1978-83, U. Profls. of Ill., Chgo., 1982-83; bd. dirs. Blue Cross/Blue Shield Drug and Alcohol Benefit Study, Chgo., 1980-83; coord. pub. rels. and resource devel. VISTA; vol. Habitat for Humanity, Vista Leadership Corp, Tucson, 1997-98. Recipient Recognition award Ill. Dangerous Drugs Commn., 1980, 81, Outstanding Svc. award U. Profls. Ill., 1983-84, Outstanding Svc. award Ill. Fedn. Tchrs., 1983. Mem. Disabled Artist Assn. (bd. dirs., chair resource devel. com. 1992-93). Democrat. Avocations: painting, writing.

GARDNER, DALE RAY, lawyer; b. Broken Arrow, Okla., May 8, 1946; s. Edward Dale and Dahlia Faye (McKeen) G.; m. Phyllis Ann Weinschrott, Dec. 27, 1969. BA in History, So. Ill. U., 1968; MA in History, St. Mary's U., San Antonio, 1975; JD, Tulsa U., 1979. Bar: Okla. 1979, Colo. 1986, Tex. 1991, U.S. Ct. Mil. Appeals 1988, U.S. Ct. Claims 1989, U.S. Dist. Ct. (no. dist.) Okla. 1981, U.S. Dist. Ct. Colo. 1986, U.S. Dist. Ct. (so. dist.) Tex. 1992, U.S. Ct. Appeals (10th cir.) 1986. Pvt. practice Sapulpa, Okla., 1979-80, 94—; asst. dist. atty. child support enforcement unit 24th Dist. Oklahoma, Sapulpa, 1980-86, 94-95; pvt. practice Aurora, Colo., 1986-91, Houston, 1991-94; mng. atty. Hyatt Legal Svcs., Aurora, 1988-89; city atty. City of Sapulpa, Okla., 1996—. Author: Immigration Act of 1965: The Preliminary Results, 1974, Teapot Dome: Civil Legal Cases that Closed the Scandal, 1989. Mem. Child Support Enforcement, Sapulpa, 1980-86, 94-96;

trustee United Way, Sapulpa, 1985, 95; Domestic Violence Counsel, Sapulpa, 1985; chmn. bd. trustees 1st Presbyn. Ch., Sapulpa, 1985. Capt. U.S. Army, 1969-75, Vietnam., lt. col Res., judge adv. Mem. Okla. Bar Assn., Tex. Bar Assn., Creek County Bar, Gold Coat Club (pres.), Sertoma (pres. Sapulpa 1985, pres. Collumbine 1988, 90, Sertoman of Yr. 1985). Democrat. Avocations: fishing, post card collecting. Home: 1533 Terrill Cir Sapulpa OK 74066-2567 Office: 7 S Park St Sapulpa OK 74066-4219

GARDNER, DAN NOBLES, deacon, church official; b. Austin, Tex., July 30, 1942; s. Dan B. and Virginia (Nobles) G.; m. Mary K. Gardner, Apr. 15, 1965; children: Ginger L., Dan B. BBA, U. Tex., 1966. Deacon Hyde Park Bapt. Ch., Austin, 1965—, bus. coord., 1975—; instr. ch. mgmt. Austin C.C., 1988-90; tchr. Hyde Park Bapt. Sch., Austin, 1990-91; high sch. baseball coach, 1990-93. Contbg. author: Church Administration, 1985. Lt. col. U.S. Army, Vietnam, 1966-67, mem. Res. Recipient Faith in God award Austin Jaycees, 1969, Good Shepherd award Boy Scouts Am., 1990. Mem. Nat. Assn. Ch. Bus. Adminstrs., Am. Assn. Baseball Coaches, Tex. High Sch. Coaches Assn. Home and Office: Hyde Park Bapt Ch 3901 Speedway Austin TX 78751-4625

GARDNER, DAVID CHAMBERS, education educator, psychologist, business executive, author; b. Charlotte, N.C., Mar. 22, 1934; s. James Raymond and Jessica Mary (Chambers) Bumgardner m. Grace Joely Beatty, 1984; children: Joshua Avery, Jessica Sarah. BA, Northeastern U., 1960; MEd, Boston U., 1970, EdD, 1974; PhD, Columbia Pacific U., 1984. Diplomate Am. Bd. Med. Psychotherapists. Mgr. market devel. N.J. Zinc Co., N.Y.C., 1961-66, COMINCO, Ltd., Montreal, Que., Can., 1966-68; dir. Alumni Ann. Giving Program, Northeastern U., Boston, 1968-69; dir. career and spl. edn. Stoneham (Mass.) Pub. Schs., Boston, 1970-72; assoc. prof. div. instructional devel. and adminstrn. Boston U., 1974—; sr. ptnr. Gardner Beatty Group, 1990—; chmn. bd. CyberHelp, Inc., 1995—; v.p. for edn. and mktg. Kaleidoscope Software, Inc., 1997-98; exec. v.p. ISMChina, Ltd., Rancho La Costa, Calif., 1998—; coord. program career vocat. tng. for handicapped, 1974-82, chmn. dept. career and bus. edn., 1974-79, also dir. fed. grants, 1975-77, 77-79; co-founder Am. Tng. and Rsch. Assocs., Inc., chmn. bd., 1979-83, pres., chief exec. officer, 1984—; dir. La Costa Inst. Lifestyle Mgmt., 1986-87. Author: Careers and Disabilities: A Career Approach, 1978; co-author: (with Grace Joely Beatty) Dissertation Proposal Guidebook: How to Prepare a Research Proposal and Get It Accepted, 1980, Career and Vocational Education for the Mildly Learning Handicapped and Disadvantaged, 1984, Stop Stress and Aging Now, 1985, Never Be Tired Again, 1990; co-author: The Visual Learning Guide Series, 1992, 93, 94, 95, 96, 97, Internet for Windows: America Online Edition, 1995, Cruising America Online for Windows, 1995, Windows 95: The Visual Learning Guide, 1995, Quicken 5 for Windows, 1995, The Visual Learning Guide, 1995, Excel for Windows 95: The Visual Learning Guide, 1995, Word for Windows 95, The Visual Learning Guide, 1995, Windows NT 4.0 Visual Desk Reference, 1997, Discover Netscape Communicator, 1997, Discover Internet Explorer, 1997; editor Career Edn. Quar., 1975-81; contbr. articles to profl. jours. With AUS, 1954-56. U.S. Office Edn. fellow Boston U., 1970, U.S. Office Edn.-Univ. Boston rsch. fellow, 1974. Fellow Am. Assn. Mental Deficiency (Ann. Profl. Tchr. and Rsch. award Region X 1979); mem. Nat. Assn. Career Edn. (bd. dirs., past pres.), Coun. for Exceptional Children, Ea. Ednl. Rsch. Assn. (founding dir.), Am. Vocat. Assn., Phi Delta Kappa, Delta Pi Epsilon. Home and Office: 7618 Nueva Castilla Way Carlsbad CA 92009-8137

GARDNER, DAVID JOHN, communications executive, recording engineer; b. Binghamton, N.Y., Jan. 8, 1953; s. Daniel Sparrow and Anne Mae (Worthing) G.; m. Nancy Tipton Peacock, 1992; 1 child, Deborah Anne. AA, Broome Community Coll., Binghamton, 1973; BA, Hofstra U., 1975. Prodn. control analyst IBM, Systems Mfg. Div., Endicott, N.Y., 1971-73; rec. engr. Eye-Full Films, San Francisco, 1972-78; gen. mgr. J.K. Theater Corp., Binghamton, 1975-77; rec. engr. The Image Works, Binghamton, 1977-80; audio/video engr. Sta. WBNG, Binghamton, 1977-78; media technician Nat. Sci. Found., Washington, 1978-79; tech. ops. RCA Americom Svcs., Inc., Princeton, N.J., 1980-84, supr. ops., 1984-86; mgr. network ops. ctr. GE Americom, Inc., Princeton, 1986-90, mgr. Vernon Valley tech. ops., 1990-92, mgr., customer svcs. and ops., 1992-95; dir. media svcs. Loral Skynet, Bedminster, NJ, 1995—; owner, pres., rec. engr. Ind. Sound, Binghamton, 1963—; bd. dirs. New Orleans Rec. Co., 1980—, Street Rhythm Prodns., Bklyn., 1980—. Mem. Soc. Broadcast Engrs., Soc. Motion Picture and TV Engrs. Episcopalian. Lodge: Order of DeMolay. Avocations: tennis, basketball, audio/video recording. Home: 4405 Rex Pl Rockville MD 20853-1255 Office: Loral Skynet 2440 Research Blvd Rockville MD 20850-3238

GARDNER, DAVID WALTON, educational administration educator; b. Galveston, Tex., Apr. 30, 1950; s. Walton Blaylock and Ruth (Pittman) G. BA, U. Houston, 1972; EdM, Tex. A&M U., 1976, PhD, 1979. Rsch. asst. Tex. A&M U., College Station, 1976-79, vis. prof., 1985; dir. MS program and grad faculty mem. Hofstra U., Hempstead, N.Y., 1980-85; program dir. univs. and rsch. coord. bd. Tex. Coll. and Univ. Sys., Austin, 1985-87; planning dir. higher edn. coord. bd. State of Tex., Austin, 1987-91, asst. to commr., 1988-91, dep. asst. commr. for rsch., planning and fin., 1991—, dir. Tex. advanced rsch. and advanced tech. programs., 1991-97. Contbr. articles to profl. jours., chpts. to books. Mem. Am. Assn. Sch. Adminstrs. (edtl. bd. AASA Professor 1984-87), Acad. Mgmt., Am. Ednl. Rsch. Assn., Nat. Conf. Profs. of Ednl. Adminstrn. (convenor 1985-90), Soc. for Coll. and Univ. Planning, Phi Delta Kappa, Phi Kappa Theta (v.p. 1971-72). Office: State of Tex Higher Edn Coordinating Bd PO Box 12788 Austin TX 78711-2788

GARDNER, DONALD ANGUS, architect; b. Portchester, N.Y., June 3, 1944; s. Angus John and Mercedes (Speedie) G.; m. Gloria Orr, Dec. 27, 1966; children: Angela Renee, Donald Angus, Sonia Dale. BArch., Clemson U., 1968. Draftsman J.B. Lindsay, Clemson, S.C., 1970-74; project architect Vickery Allen Bashor, Greenville, S.C., 1974-75; ptnr. Gardner, Edelbut & Assocs., Seneca, S.C., 1975-76; project architect Daniel Internat./Daniel Engrs., Greenville, 1976-79, Lockwood Greene Engrs., inc., Spartanburg, S.C., 1979-82; project mgr. Enwright Assocs., Inc., Greenville, 1982-84; pres., dir. Donald A. Gardner Architects, Inc., Greenville, 1978—, Donald A. Gardner Builders, Inc., Greenville, 1994—, Donald A. Gardner, Inc., Greenville, 1998—, Donald A. Gardner Interactive LLC; draftsman J.B. Lindsay, Clemson, S.C., 1970-74. Served to 1st lt. C.E., U.S. Army, 1968-70. Decorated Army Commendation medal. Mem. AIA, Nat. Assn. Home Builders, Urban Land Inst. Methodist. Home: 9 Rocky Creek Ln Greenville SC 29615-5819 Office: PO Box 26178 Greenville SC 29616-1178

GARDNER, ELLA HAINES, artist; b. Montfort, Wis.; d. Robert Daniel and Gena Helena (Helgeson) Haines; m. Russell Robert Gardner, June 1, 1937; children: Russell R., Wayne, Keith. One-woman shows include Bank of Granton, Wis., 1977—, Marshfield (Wis.) Living Ctr., 1985—, First Nat. Bank, Neillsville, Wis., 1982-84, Dept. Industry, Labor and Human Rels., Madison, Wis., 1987, Marshfield Libr., 1990, 91, The Mabel Tainter Meml. Mus., Menomonie, Wis., 1996, McMillan Meml. Gallery, Wisconsin Rapids, Wis., 1997, Lucille Tack Ctr. for the Arts Mus., Spencer, Wis., 1998; two-woman shows include Jail Mus., Neillsville, 1985; exhibited in group shows at Rahr West Mus., Manitowoc, Wis., 1982, gov.'s Office, Madison, 1983, 88-89, King (Wis.) Treatment Ctr., 1983, Tuffs Mus., Neillsville, 1983, Gray Owl Exhibit, Athens, Wis., 1988, Silverman Gallery, Spring Green, Wis., 1989, New Visions Gallery, Marshfield, 1989, 90, Art for Faith, Janesville, 1990, Wis. Ctr., Madison, 1997, Porter Bulls Gallery, Meml. Union, Madison, 1998; represented in numerous pvt. collections; author: A Celebration of Life, 1998. Charter mem. Nat. Mus. Women in the Arts. Recipient K & M Kuemmerlin award, 1986, Grumbacher Bronze award, 1987, Northwood Art Assn. award, 1987, Traveling Show award, 1987, 97-98, Obermiller Edn. award, 1993, Ctrl. Wis. State Fair award, 1973-98, State exhibit award 1998, Kenneth Kummerlein Meml. award, 1998. Mem. Wis. Regional Artists Assn. (Meml. award 1988, Contour award 1978, 81, 84, 85, 86, 87, 88, 91, 93), Wis. Women in the Arts. Avocations: sewing, gardening. Home: 10598 Hwy H Marshfield WI 54449

GARDNER, EVERETTE SHAW, JR., information sciences educator, consultant, author; b. Osceola, Ark., Oct. 3, 1944; s. Everette Shaw and Evelyn (Fletcher) G.; m. Mary Ann Sihelnik, May 28, 1966; children: Cynthia Anne, Stacey Diane. BBA, Memphis State U., 1966; MBA, U. N.C., 1974, PhD, 1978. Commd. ensign USN, 1966, advanced through grades to comdr., 1980, ret., 1986; assoc. prof. U. Houston, 1987-88, chmn. dept. of decision and info. scis., 1988-95, prof., 1989—, dir. Ctr. Global Mfg., 1991—; bd. dirs., pres. Gardner Rsch., Inc., Sugar Land, Tex., 1987—; cons. NASA Johnson Space Ctr., Houston, 1988-89, Shell Oil Co., Houston, Continental Airlines, Houston, 1993—, Continental Micronesia, Guam, Delta Airlines, Atlanta, 1997—, Texaco, Houston, Pennzoil, Houston, Arthur Andersen, Houston, Exxon Co. USA, Houston, Compaq Computers, Houston, Frito-Lay, Dallas, Southwestern Bell, Houston, Centel Comm., Houston, Sys. Evolution, Houston, Tenneco, Houston, Spring Comm., L.A., Alamo Water Refiners, San Antonio, Houston Livestock Show and Rodeo, 1992—, APS Holding Corp., Houston, Oil and Gas Consultants Inc., Tulsa, 1996—, Telecheck Svcs. Inc., Houston, 1997—, Randalls Food Markets, Inc., Houston, 1997-99, Trees Inc., Houston, 1999—. Co-author: Quantitative Approaches to Management, 1993; author: (software) Autocast: Business Forecasting System, 1992, The Spreadsheet Forecaster, 1994, The Spreadsheet Quality Manager, 1993; assoc. editor Internat. Jour. of Forecasting, 1985-87, Mgmt. Sci., 1987-91, Interfaces, 1987-92; contbr. articles to profl. jours.; columnist Lotus mag., 1986-92. Bd. dirs. Women's Home Houston, 1992-97; mem. Republican Nat. Com. Mem. NRA, La. Shooting Assn., Tex. State Rifle Assn., Internat. Inst. Forecasters (pres. 1990-92, dir. 1987-94), Inst. for Ops. Rsch. and Mgmt. Scis., Operational Rsch. Soc., U.S. Naval Inst., Am. Prodn. and Inventory Control Soc. (bd. dirs. Houston chpt. 1997-98), La. Hist. Assn., Ret. Officers Assn., Sons. of Confederate Vets., 100 Club of Houston. Presbyterian. Avocations: competitive pistol shooting, tennis, gardening, Civil War history. Office: U Houston 4800 Calhoun Rd Houston TX 77204-6282

GARDNER, FREDERICK BOYCE, library director; b. Hopkinsville, Ky., Mar. 12, 1942; s. Boyce and Alleen Louise (Brown) G. BA, U. Ky., 1964; MA, Ind. U., Bloomington, 1966. Head librarian U. Ky. Hopkinsville Community Coll., Hopkinsville, 1966-69; head, readers service CUNY, Manhattan Community Coll., N.Y.C., 1969-71; reference librarian Calif. Inst. of the Arts, Valencia, Calif., 1971-84; head, pub. svcs. Calif. Inst. of the Arts, Valencia, 1974-87, dir. computer svcs., 1984-87, acting dir., 1987-88, dean of the library, 1988—; del. Calif. Conf. on Networking, Pomona, 1985; mem. Calif. Networking Task Force, 1990-95. Sec. Sequoia String Quartet Found., L.A., 1977-87. Capt. USAF, 1968-69. Mem. ALA, Assn. Coll. and Rsch. Librs., Santa Clarita Interlibr. Network (pres. 1989-91), Calif. Pvt. Acad. Librs. (exec. bd. 1988-91, 96—, chmn. 1990), Total Interlibr. Exch. (v.p. 1980-81, pres. 1981-82, chmn. 1983-86, cons. 1983-85), Calif. Libr. Assn., Performing Arts Librs. Network (chmn. 1991), West Hollywood Chorale (exec. com. 1997—). Avocations: music, computers, hiking. Office: Calif Inst Arts 24700 McBean Pky Santa Clarita CA 91355-2397*

GARDNER, GARY EDWARD, lawyer; b. Windsor, Ont., Can., Oct. 21, 1952; s. Edward Thomas and Antonionette Ursla (Urbanski) G.; m. Sheila Mary Hand, Oct. 5, 1984. BA, Mich. State U., 1975; JD, U. Detroit, 1981. Mktg. officer Ford Motor Co. Australia, Melbourne, 1975-77; analyst Ford Motor Co., Dearborn, Mich., 1977-79; asst. to gen. counsel Ford Motor Co. Australia, Melbourne, 1979-80; assoc. James R. Shively, P.C., Detroit, 1980-82; instr. law Detroit Coll. of Bus., Dearborn, Mich., 1982-84; ptnr. Shively, McCloskey, Corriveau & Gardner, Mich., 1984-86; pvt. practice Dearborn, 1986-90; ptnr. Gardner & Doyle, 1990-94, Gary Edward Gardner, P.C., Dearborn, Mich., 1995—; atty. pvt. practice, Dearborn, Mich., 1995—. Candidate Judge of Ct. of Appeals S.E. Mich., 1988; candidate Judge 19th Dist. Ct., 1992, 94, Judge Wayne County Cir. Ct., 1998; bench-bar liaison com. Wayne County Cir. Ct., 1999. Mem. ABA, Mich. Bar Assn. (com. domestic violence 1993-99), Dearborn Bar Assn. (pres. 1996-97), Wayne County Family Law Bar Assn. (founding mem., pres. 1997-99), Fairlane Club, Detroit Coll. Rugby Club, Kiwanis Club Dearborn. Republican. Roman Catholic. Home: 246 River Ln Dearborn MI 48124-1047 Office: 25121 Ford Rd Dearborn MI 48128-1058

GARDNER, GUY S., government official; b. Altavista, Va., Jan. 6, 1948; m. Linda Gardner; children: Jennifer, Sarah, Jason. BS in Aeronautics, Math. & Engring Sci., USAF Acad., 1969; MS in Aeronautics and Astronautics, Purdue U., 1970. Pilot astronaut NASA, 1980-91; program dir. joint U.S. and Russian Shuttle-Mir Program NASA, Washington, 1992-94; dir. quality assurance divsn. Office Safety and Mission Assurance, NASA, 1994-95; dir. William J. Hughes Tech. Ctr. FAA, Atlantic City, N.J., 1995-96; assoc. adminstr. regulation and certification FAA, Washington, 1996-98; retired, 1998. With USAF, 1971-76, 91-92. Decorated Legion of Merit, Def. Superior Svc. medals (2), Def. Disting. Svc. medal, DFC (3), Air medals (14). *

GARDNER, HOWARD ALAN, travel marketing executive, travel writer and editor; b. Rockford, Ill., June 24, 1920; s. Ellis Ralph and Leanor (Roseman) G.; m. Marjorie Ruth Klein, Sept. 29, 1945; children: Jill, Jeffrey. B.A., U. Mich., 1941. With advt. dept. Chgo. Tribune, 1941-43; mgr. promotion dept. Esquire mag., 1943-46; advt. mgr. Mrs. Klein's Food Products Co., 1946-48; pres. Sales-Aide Service Co., 1948-56, Gardner & Stein, 1956-59, Gardner, Stein & Frank, Inc., Chgo., 1959-83, Fun-derful World, Chgo., 1983—. Mem. Travel Industry Assn. Am., Confrerie de la Chaine des Rotisseurs (bailli hon., officier commandeur), Am. Geog. Soc., Nat. Geog. Soc., Connoisseurs Internat. (bd. dirs.), Phi Beta Kappa. Clubs: Travelers' Century, Carlton, International. Home: 100 E Bellevue Pl Chicago IL 60611-1157 Office: Fun-derful World 100 E Bellevue Pl Chicago IL 60611-1157

GARDNER, HOWARD EARL, psychologist, author; b. Scranton, Pa., July 11, 1943; s. Ralph and Hilde (Weilheimer) G.; m. Ellen Winner; children: Kerith, Jay, Andrew, Benjamin. AB summa cum laude, Harvard U., 1965, PhD, 1971; hon. degree, Curry Coll., 1992, New Eng. Conservatory of Music, 1993, Ind. U., 1995, Moravian Coll., 1996, Cleve. Inst. of Music, 1996, Salem State Coll., 1996, L.I. U., 1997, Macalester Coll., 1997, Tel-Aviv U., 1998, Princeton U., 1998, Pa. State U., 1998, Ithaca Coll., 1999, Conn. Coll., 1999, McGill U., 1999. Lectr. edn. Harvard U., 1971-86, co-dir. Project Zero, 1972—, prof. edn., 1986—, affiliated prof. psychology, 1987—; prof. neurology Boston U. Sch. Medicine, 1984-87, adj. prof. neurology, 1987—; rsch. psychologist Boston VA Med. Ctr., 1978-93. Author: The Shattered Mind, 1975, Art, Mind and Brain, 1982, Frames of Mind, 1983 (Best Book award Am. Psychol. Assn. 1984), The Mind's New Science, 1985 (William James award 1988), To Open Minds, 1989, The Unschooled Mind, 1991, Multiple Intelligences, 1993, Creating Minds, 1993, Leading Minds, 1995, Extraordinary Minds, 1997, The Disciplined Mind, 1999, Intelligence Reframed, 1999. Recipient Grawemeyer award in edn., 1990, Disting. Svc. medal Columbia U. Tchr.'s Coll., 1994, Pa. Gov.'s award in humanities, 1994, McGovern award Smithsonian, 1998, Walker prize Boston Mus. of Sci., 1999; MacArthur Prize fellow, 1981; rsch. grantee numerous govtl. and pvt. founds. Fellow AAAS; mem. Am. Acad. Arts and Scis., Nat. Acad. Edn. (v.p.), Phi Beta Kappa. Office: Harvard U Grad Sch Edn Larsen Hall Cambridge MA 02138

GARDNER, HOWARD GARRY, pediatrician, educator; b. Gary, Ind., Oct. 5, 1943; s. Oscar and Anita (Arenson) G.; m. Judith (Green), June 21, 1986; children: Molly, Joseph. BA, Ind. U., 1965, MD, 1968. Intern, resident St. Louis U., 1969-73; pvt. practice Hinsdale (Ill.) Pediatrics, 1973-79, DuPage Pediatrics, Darien, Ill., 1979—; attending staff Hinsdale Hosp., 1973—, Loyola U. Med. Ctr., Maywood, Ill., 1973—; courtesy staff Childrens Meml. Hosp., Chgo., 1988—; clin. prof. Dept. Pediatrics Loyola U. Sch. of Medicine, Maywood, 1983—; chmn. Dept. of Pediatrics Hinsdale Hosp., 1983-85; med. adv. bd. YMCA of the USA, Chgo., 1989—. Mem. editl. bd. Pediatric News, 1990—; contbr. articles to profl. jours. Co-chmn. med. adv. bd. DuPage Easter Seal Ctr., Villa Park, Ill.; past, founding mem. bd. dirs. Loyola Ronald McDonald House; co-founder, past pres. Ill. Child Passenger Safety Assn.; pediatric program dir. Des Plaines Valley Health Ctr., Argo, Ill.; mem. med. adv. bd. Pathways Awareness Found.; officer, steering com. DuPage Interagy. Coun. on Early Intervention. Lt. USN, 1969-71. Recipient Outstanding Clin. Tchr. award Loyola Med. Sch., 1978, Tchr. of Yr. Hinsdale Hosp. Family Practice Residency, 1981, Chgo. Caring Physician's award Met. Chgo. Health Care Coun., 1987, Buckle Up Am.! award Ill. Coalition for Safety Belt Use, 1991, Parent and Child Edn. Soc. 20th Anniversary Achievement award, 1992. Fellow Am. Acad. Pediat. (past pres. Ill. chpt., past mem. nat. nominating com., instnl. rev. bd., Pisani Pediatrician of Yr. award 1986); mem. Chgo. Pediat. Soc. (past pres., Archibald Hoyne Pediatrician of Yr. 1994), Ill. Maternal and Child Health Coalition (bd. dirs., Advocacy award 1996), DuPage County Med. Soc. (bd. dirs.). Democrat. Jewish. Avocations: reading, skiing, photography. Office: DuPage Pediatrics 1306 Plainfield Rd Darien IL 60561-5038

GARDNER, J. STEPHEN, lawyer; b. Dayton, Ohio, May 10, 1944; s. David L. and Mary (Webb) Gardner; m. Sandra Ellen Ott, Dec. 23, 1967; children: Stephen, Truett, P.J. BA in Math., U. Fla., 1966, JD, 1969. Bar: Fla. 1969, U.S. Dist Ct. (mid. dist.) Fla. 1971. Co-founder, ptnr. Ott & Gardner, Tampa, Fla., 1971-72, Bucklew, Ramsey, Ott & Gardner, Tampa, 1972-75; ptnr. Trinkle & Redman, Brandon, 1976-81; co-founder, shareholder Bush Ross Gardner Warren & Rudy, P.A., Tampa, 1981—; mem. adv. bd. SouthTrust Bank, 1986, South Hillsborough Cmty. Bank, 1988-92. Past chmn. Tampa Downtown Partnrship; past pres. Davis Islands Civic Assn.; bd. dirs. Young Life Tampa, 1972, 88; bd. dirs. F.L.O.A.T., Inc., 1986-87, v.p. 1987; mem. Leadership Tampa Class of 1980; mem. bd. counelors U. Tampa, 1976-84; chmn. pastor-parish com. Hyde Park United Meth. Ch., 1982, chmn. ch. and society com., 1975, chmn. budget raisning com., 1984, lay leader, 1985, Sunday sch. supt., 1986-87, Sunday sch. tchr., 1973-86, mem. adminstrv. bd., 1974-87, chmn., 1976, co-chmn. capital campaign com., 1997. 1st lt. U.S. Army, 1969-71, Vietnam; capt. USAR, 1972-75. Decorated Bronze star with oak leaf cluster. Mem. AMA, Fla. Bar Assn. (probate rules com. 1985-87), Hillsborough County Bar Assn., Tampa Tennis Assn. (past pres.), Ye Mystic Krewe Gasparilla, Tampa Yacht and Country Club (past commodore), Exch. Club (past pres. Tampa), Univ. Club Tampa (bd. dirs., past pres.). Methodist. Office: Bush Ross Gardner Warren & Rudy PA 220 S Franklin St Tampa FL 33602-5330

GARDNER, JAMES, recreational management executive, personal care industry executive; b. Ridgeland, S.C., May 27, 1953; s. Shirley Mae Gardner; m. Cathy Brantley, Dec. 27, 1986; 1 child, Jasmine Charese. BA, St. Augustine's Coll., 1975. Med. lab. technician Beaufort-Jasper Comprehensive Health Svcs., Ridgeland, S.C., 1975-76; asst. mgr. Liberty Loans Inc., Hampton, S.C., 1976-77; sr. asst. mgr. Household Fin. Corp., Beaufort, S.C., 1977-79; nigh auditor Hyatt Hotels Corp., Hilton Head, S.C., 1979-80; machinist Gen. Carbide Corp., Jasper, 1979-80; chem. unloader/machinist apprentice St. Regis Paper Co., Jacksonville, Fla., 1981-82; night auditor/mgr., front desk clk. Holiday Inn, Jacksonville, Fla., 1982; owner, operator Gardner's Barber Styling Salon, Ridgeland, S.C., 1984—; parks and recreation dir. Jasper County Coun., Ridgeland, 1992—; dist. dir. Am. Youth Basketball Tour, 1999. Mem. Ridgeland Mid. Sch. Improvement Coun. 1992; bd. dirs. Jasper County Dept. Social Svcs., 1991, Beaufort-Jasper Comprehensive Health Svcs.; mem. recreation task force Jasper County Coun., 1991; pres., dir. Low Country Amateur Athethics, Inc. 1993; pres. Southeastern Pro-Am Basketball Assn.; active Ridgeland Mid. Sch. Youth Basketball Program; youth program coord. Rep. Juanita White's Campaign Com., Ridgeland, 1980. Mem. NAACP, Citizen's Organized for Pub. Svc. Home: PO Box 399 Ridgeland SC 29936-0399

GARDNER, JAMES HARKINS, venture capitalist; b. Evanston, Ill., July 15, 1943; s. James Floyd and Charlotte (Hoban) G.; m. Shirley Jane Bisset, June 22, 1968 (div. 1980); 1 child, Warren Lee; m. Shannon Lee Greer, Nov. 19, 1982; 1 child, Charlotte Greer. BS, Purdue U., 1965; MBA, Harvard U., 1968. V.p. Geomet, Inc., Rockville, Md., 1970-78; pres. Risk Mgmt. Resources, Inc., San Francisco, 1979-91; COO KinderCare Learning Ctrs., Inc., Montgomery, Ala., 1991-93; pres., COO, dir., Discovery Zone, Inc, 1994-95; mng. gen. ptnr., Media Venture Ptnrs., 1995—; CEO HBS Funding, Inc. dba Great City Traders, 1998—; del. White House Conf. on Small Bus., 1986; treas. No. Calif. With USPHS, 1968-70. Mem. Nat. Fedn. Ind. Bus. (Calif. guardian coun., dir. Calif. polit. action com., fed. liaison 1988-91), Ind. Adminstrs. Assn. (bd. dirs. 1989-91, v.p. 1991), Commonwealth Club Calif. (San Francisco), Masons, Sigma Nu. Office: Great City Traders PO Box 885166 San Francisco CA 94188-5166

GARDNER, JANET PAXTON, journalist, video producer; b. Dayton, Ohio, Sept. 6, 1940; d. Edward Tytus and Mary Elizabeth (Paxton) G.; m. George Karl Debreczeny, Sept. 10, 1964 (div. Feb. 1970); 1 child, Karl Philip; m. George Edward Bradshaw Morren, Jr., Nov. 6, 1980. BFA in Art and Architecture, Cooper Union, 1965; MFA in Film Prodn., NYU, 1971; postgrad., Columbia U., 1976. Film editor, assoc. prodr. Sta. WRC-TV, NBC, Washington, 1972; asst. film editor NBC News, N.Y.C., 1973-74; newswriter, field prodr. NewsCenter4 NBC, N.Y.C., 1974-75; freelance film editor CBS News, N.Y.C., 1976-79; staff reporter, feature writer The Plain Dealer, Cleve., 1979-81; edn. columnist, editor Glamour mag., 1981-82; staff writer Asbury Park Press, Neptune, N.J., 1985-86; press officer UN, 1989; owner, mgr. prodr. The Gardner Group, N.Y.C., 1991—; mem. adj. faculty journalism Univ. Coll., Rutgers U., Newark, 1988-92, Montclair State Coll., Upper Montclair, N.J., 1992; mem. L.A. Times pub.-prof. exch. program, 1989. Prodr., dir., writer documentary videos The United Nations: It's More Than You Think, 1991, Vietnam: Land of the Ascending Dragon, 1993, Children of the Night & Starting Over, 1994, A World Beneath The War, 1996, Dancing Through Death: The Monkey Magic & Madness of Cambodia, 1999; editor CBS News documentary film The Black Robes, 1978; prodr. Preparing To Give Birth, 1977, Choices in Childbirth, 1977, (film) Inside Ladies Home Jour., 1970; contbr. to N.Y. Times, Phila. Inquirer, Boston Globe, Newsday, The Nation, Glamour, Working Women, New Woman, Diversion, Health Week, Indochina Newsletter, N.J. Monthly, W, also others. Co-chair peace and social order com. Religious Soc. of Friends, Princeton, N.J., 1994; participant U.S.-Indochina Reconciliation Project Del. to Vietnam, 1987, to Cambodia, 1990. Recipient spl. citation Edn. Writers Assn., 1983, 2d place award for news reporting N.J. Press Women, 1990, 1st place award for newspaper feature writing, 1990, cert. of merit Media & Methods mag., 1992, Lowell Thomas award for video on Vietnam, Soc. Am. Travel Writers Found., 1993, Bronze Apple award Nat. Edn. Film and Video Festival, 1993, Golden Eagle award CINE, 1994, Silver Apple award Nat. Edn. Film & Video Festival, 1997, Best Feature Reporting TV, Soc. Profl. Journalists N.Y. chpt. Deadline Club, 1997; Woolrich writing fellow Columbia U. Sch. Gen. Studies, 1976; nominee Emmy award Outstanding Hist. Programming Nat. Acad. Arts and Scis., 1997. Mem. Soc. Profl. Journalists (juror nat. mag. awards 1985, scholastic press awards 1986, chief juror editl. writing awards 1988), Investigative Reporters a nd Editors, Internat. Documentary Assn., North Jersey Press Club (2d place award for bus. feature writing 1990, 1st place award 1991, 1st place award for best documentary 1992, 2d place award for feature photography 1993), N.Y. Women in Film and TV. Avocation: travel. Home: PO Box 166 118 Washington St Rocky Hill NJ 08553 Office: 330 W 42nd St Ste 1510 New York NY 10036-6902

GARDNER, JANETTE LYNN, critical care nurse, educator; b. Easton, Pa., Nov. 20, 1955; d. William H. and Sylvia J. (Fritts) Weller; m. Richard D. Gardner, Jan. 26, 1980; children: Kristen, Daniel, Stephanie. Diploma in nursing, Abington (Pa.) Meml. Hosp., 1977; BS, St. Joseph's Coll., North Windham, Maine, 1989. RN, Pa.; cert. in chemotherapy, BCLS, ACLS, trauma nursing. Critical care educator Easton Hosp., 1980-89, preceptor, staff nurse surg. ICU, 1989-94; ECU nurse, 1994—. Contbr. articles to profl. journs. Mem. Pa. Nurses Assn., Lehigh Valley Profl. Educators. Address: 170 Anderson Rd Asbury NJ 08802-1041

GARDNER, JERRY DEAN, dentist, military officer; b. Taylorville, Ill., Feb. 11, 1939; s. Lavern Y. and Helyn R. (Clements) G.; m. Judith M. Waud, June 17, 1961; children: Mark A., Jeffrey S., Jennifer A. BS, U. Ill., Chgo. 1961, DDS, 1964; MS, Boston U., 1972. Diplomate Am. Bd. Prosthodontics. Commd. officer Dental Corps USAF, 1964, advanced through grades to brig. gen., gen. dental officer, 1964-72, prosthodontist, 1972-82, dir. dental services, 1982-85, command dental surgeon, 1985-89, dir. dental svcs. WHMC, 1989-90, dep. asst. surgeon gen. for dental svcs., 1990-93, asst. surgeon gen. dental svcs., 1993-95, cons. to surgeon gen., 1979-95, cons. fixed prosthodontics, 1979-81, chief Dental Corps, 1993-95, ret., 1995. Decorated Bronze Star, Legion of Merit, Disting. Svc. medal; recipient U. Ill. Alumni Achievement award, 1996. Fellow Am. Coll. Prosthodontics (life), Internat. Coll. Dentistry; mem. ADA. Avocations: oil painting, fishing, woodworking. Home: 3606 Willow Rd Taylorville IL 62568-9057

GARDNER, JOAN, medical, surgical nurse; b. Ft. Worth, Oct. 5, 1950; d. Bert and Pearl (Sandgarten) G. BS in Edn., U. Tex., 1972, BS in Communication, 1976; diploma, Brackenridge Hosp., 1982. RN, Tex. Trust asst. Austin (Tex.) Nat. Bank; tchr. English and reading Columbus (Tex.) Ind. Schs.; staff orthopedics nurse Seton Med. Ctr., Austin, 1982-83, staff nurse gyn. surgery and post partum, 1983-84, staff nurse post partum, 1984-85, staff nurse gyn. surgery and ear, nose, throat, and eye, 1986, charge nurse gen. surgery, 1988-92, staff nurse short-term surgery, 1992-99; radiology charge nurse South Austin Hosp., 1999—. Home: 1602 Leigh St # A Austin TX 78703-2452 Office: 1201 W 38th St Austin TX 78705-1006

GARDNER, JOEL ROBERT, writer, historian; b. N.Y.C., May 12, 1942; s. Stephen H. and Diana (Schneider) G.; m. Holly Alpine Phelps, July 7, 1980. BA, Tulane U., 1962; MA, UCLA, 1966. Assoc. editor The Riverdale (N.Y.) Press, 1966-68; oral historian UCLA Oral History Program, 1971-80, La. State Archives, 1980-82; asst. dir. La. Divsn. of the Arts, 1983-85; dir. Perkins Ctr. for the Arts, 1985-87; pres. Gardner Assocs., Cherry Hill, N.J., 1987—; cons. The Pew Charitable Trusts, 1988-94, Robert Wood Johnson Found., 1991—, John D. and Catherine T. MacArthur Found., 1994—. Author: Oral History for Louisiana, 1980, 75 Years of Good Taste: A History of the Tasty Baking Company, 1990, A History of the Pew Charitable Trusts, 1991, (with others) In the Company of Writers, 1991, Neighbor Caring for Neighbor, 1996; editor: Built in Louisiana, 1985, Oral History and the Law, 1985. Bd. dirs. N.J. Com. for the Humanities, 1991-94, sec., 1993-94. Mem. Oral History Assn. (bd. dirs. 1982-83), Oral History for Middle Atlantic Region (v.p. 1991-92, pres. 1992-93), Rotary (Garden State club 1998—). Democrat. Jewish. Office: 1060 Kings Hwy N Ste 315 Cherry Hill NJ 08034-1910

GARDNER, JOHN HOWLAND, III, neurologist; b. New Haven, Conn., Oct. 1, 1931; s. John Howland Jr. and Ruth (Huntley) G.; m. Anne Kates Larkin, Apr. 23, 1960; children: Elizabeth Larkin Gardner Milgram, Helen Douglass Gardner Hornblower, Sarah Stewart Gardner. Student, Harvard U., 1949-52; MD, Yale, 1956. Diplomate Am. Bd. Psychiatry and Neurology. Intern Stanford, 1956-57; asst. to assoc. resident in medicine Strong Mem. Hosp., Rochester, N.Y., 1957-59; resident in neurology Boston City Hosp., 1959-61; resident in neuropathology Strong Mem. Hosp., Rochester, N.Y., 1961-62; officer in charge in neurology USAF Hosp. Keesler AFB, Biloxi, Miss., 1962-64; asst. prof. Case Western Res. U. Sch. Med., Cleve., 1965-67; asst. clin. prof. Case Western Res. U. Sch. Medicine, Cleve., 1967-83, assoc. clin. prof., 1983-98, emeritus assoc. prof. neurology, 1998—; chief of neurology St. Luke's Hosp., Cleve., 1967-85; neurologist U. Suburban Health Care Ctr., Cleve., 1975-96; pres. Greater Cleveland Chpt. Epilepsy Fdn. Am., 1973-75; chmn. Mediation Comm. Acad. Med. Cleveland, 1982-84. Vestryman, St. Paul's Episcopal Church, Cleveland Hts., 1980-82. Capt. USAF, 1962-64. Decorated Commendation Medal, USAF. Fellow Am. Acad. Neurology; mem. AMA, Acad. Med. Cleveland, Ohio State Med. Assn., Yale Alumni Assn. (v.p. Cleve. 1988—). Republican. Avocations: skeet shooting, photography, hunting, music, sailing.

GARDNER, JOHN WILLIAM, writer, educator; b. Los Angeles, Oct. 8, 1912; s. William and Marie (Flora) G.; m. Aida Marroquin, Aug. 18, 1934; children: Stephanie Gardner Trimble, Francesca Gardner. A.B., Stanford U., 1935; Ph.D., U. Calif., 1938, LL.D. (hon.), 1959; hon. degrees from various colls., univs.; hon. fellow, Stanford U., 1959. Teaching asst. in psychology U. Calif., 1936-38; instr. psychology Conn. Coll., 1938-40; asst. prof. psychology Mt. Holyoke Coll., 1940-42; head Latin-Am. sect. FCC, 1942-43; mem. staff Carnegie Corp. of N.Y., 1946-47, exec. assoc., 1947-49, v.p., 1949-55, pres., 1955-65, cons., 1968-77; pres. Carnegie Found. Advancement of Teaching, 1955-65; sec. U.S. Dept. Health, Edn. and Welfare, 1965-68; chmn. Urban Coalition, 1968-70; founder and chmn. Common Cause, 1970-77; chmn. Pres.'s Commn. on White House Fellowships, 1977-80; co-founder, chmn. Independent Sector, 1980-83, dir. leadership studies program, 1984-89; Miriam and Peter Haas prof. pub. svc. Stanford (Calif.) U., 1989-96; cons. prof. Stanford Sch. Edn., 1996—; mem. Pres. Kennedy's Task Force on Edn., 1960; chmn. U.S. Adv. Commn. International. Ednl. and Cultural Affairs, 1962-64, Pres. Johnson's Task Force on Edn., 1964, White House Conf. Edn., 1965; dir. N.Y. Telephone Co., 1961-65, Shell Oil Co., 1962-65, Am. Airlines, 1968-71, Time, Inc., 1968-72. Author: Excellence, 1961, rev. edit., 1984, Self-Renewal, 1964, rev. edit, 1981, No Easy Victories, 1968, The Recovery of Confidence, 1970, In Common Cause, 1972, Know or Listen to Those Who Know, 1975, Morale, 1978, Quotations of Wit and Wisdom, 1980, On Leadership, 1990; Editor: To Turn the Tide (John F. Kennedy). Chmn. Nat. Civic League, 1994-96; trustee N.Y. Sch. Social Work, 1949-55, Met. Mus. Art, 1957-65, Stanford U., 1968-82, Rockefeller Bros. Fund, 1968-77, Jet Propulsion Lab., 1978-82, Enterprise Found., 1982-91. Recipient USAF Exceptional Services award, 1956; Presdl. Medal of Freedom, 1964; Nat. Acad. Scis. Pub. Welfare medal, 1966; U.A.W. Social Justice award, 1968; Democratic Legacy award Anti-Defamation League, 1968; AFL-CIO Murray Green medal, 1970. Office: Stanford Sch Edn Stanford CA 94305-3084

GARDNER, JOSEPH LAWRENCE, editor, writer; b. Willmar, Minn., Jan. 26, 1933; s. Elmer Joseph and Margaret Eleanor (Archer) G.; m. Sadako Miyasaka, Feb. 25, 1967; children: Miya Elise, Justin Lawrence. Student, U. Portland, Oreg., 1951-52; B.A. summa cum laude, U. Oreg., 1955; M.A. (Woodrow Wilson fellow), U. Wis., 1956. Researcher, writer, asst. editor; mng. editor Am. Heritage Books div. Am. Heritage Pub. Co., Inc., N.Y.C., 1959-65; editor Am. Heritage Jr. Library and Horizon Caravel Books, 1965-68; mng. editor Newsweek Books div. Newsweek Inc., N.Y.C., 1968-70, editor, 1971-76; sr. staff editor Reader's Digest Gen. Books, N.Y.C., 1976-81, group editor gen. reference, 1982-84; dir. internat. book pub. Reader's Digest Assn., Inc., 1984-88; pres., editorial dir. Gardner Assocs., 1989—. Author: Labor on the March, 1969, Departing Glory, Theodore Roosevelt as Ex President, 1973; editor: Newsweek Condensed Books and book series, including Wonders of Man, Milestones of History, The Founding Fathers, World of Culture, 1971-76, The World's Last Mysteries, 1978, Reader's Digest Wide World Atlas, 1979, Reader's Digest Atlas of the Bible, 1981, Eat Better, Live Better, 1982, Mysteries of the Ancient Americas, 1986, Reader's Digest Atlas of the World, 1987, Great Mysteries of the Past, 1991, The Story of Jesus, 1993, Who's Who in the Bible, 1994, Complete Guide to the Bible, 1998; contbg. editor Through Indian Eyes, 1996. Bd. dirs. Friends of Scarsdale Library, 1976-81, v.p., 1979-81; trustee Scarsdale Adult Sch., 1978-84, treas., 1981-83; trustee Scarsdale Pub. Library, 1983-84, 86-91, pres., 1989-91. Served with AUS, 1956-58. Mem. PEN, Phi Beta Kappa, Sigma Delta Chi, Phi Kappa Psi. Home and Office: 10 E End Ave Apt 15C New York NY 10021-1122

GARDNER, JUDITH ANN, secondary school and university educator; b. Sept. 25, 1949. BA, Wilkes U., 1971, MS, 1975; PhD, U. Pa., 1993. Instr. Luzerne County C.C., Nanticoke, Pa., 1976-83, Wilkes U., Wilkes-Barre, Pa., 1986—; tchr. N.W. Area Sch. Dist., Shickshinny, Pa., 1984—. Home: 65 Tilbury Ave West Nanticoke PA 18634

GARDNER, JUDITH STURGEN, nursing administrator, educator; b. Harrisburg, Pa., Nov. 28, 1939; d. George W. Sr. and Gladys E. (Lenker) Sturgen; children: Scott, Alan, Wendy. Student, Fayetteville Community Coll., 1974; BS, Pa. State U., Middletown, 1986. Cert. CPR and BLS instr. Head nurse Aspen Ctr., Dauphin County, Harrisburg, Pa., 1979-81; instr. Acad. Med. Arts, Harrisburg, 1982-84; asst. dir. First Step program Goodwill Industries of Cen. Pa., Inc., Harrisburg, 1986-92; case mgr. physicians health program Ctr. and Sci. Trust of the Pa. Med. Soc., Harrisburg, 1992-94; case mgr. job health program Cmty. Gen. Osteo. Hosp., Harrisburg, Pa., 1994; managed care analyst Pa. Highmark Blue Shield, Harrisburg, 1994—. Mem. United Way Cabinet. Mem. Pa. Nurses Assn. (past bd. mem.). Home: 3211 Elm St Harrisburg PA 17109-5746

GARDNER, KATHLEEN D., gas company executive, lawyer; b. Fayetteville, Ark., July 14, 1947; d. Harold Andrew and Bess (Gunn) Dulan; m. Robert Gardner, June 7, 1969 (dec. Sept. 1974); m. Cecil Alexander, Feb. 4, 1995; 1 child, Christina Ann. BS, U. Ark., 1969, JD, 1978; MA, U. Ala., 1972. Atty., corp. officer SW Energy Co., Fayetteville, 1978-85; asst. gen. counsel, asst. v.p. Reliant Energy Akrla a divsn. of Reliant Energy Resources, Little Rock, 1985-86, gen. counsel, v.p., 1986—; chmn. Regional Tng. Program, Birmingham, Ala., 1972-75. Bd. dirs. the New Sch. Fayetteville, 1978-79, Robert K. Gardner Meml. Fund, Fayetteville; past bd. dirs. Keep Ark. Beautiful Commn., Ballet Ark., Ark. Mus. Sci. and History, Vis. Nurse Corp. Named Outstanding Young woman Fayetteville Jaycettes, Ark. Jaycettes, recipient Woman of Achievement in Energy award, 1990; named to Top 100 Women in Ark., Ark. Bus. Newspaper, 1995, 96, 97, 98. Mem. ABA, Ark. Bar Assn. (sec. natural resources sect. 1981), Pulaski County Bar Assn., Am. Gas Assn., DAR, Ark. Assn. Def. Counsel, Am. Arbitration Assn. (Ark. adv. coun.), Alpha Delta Pi. Episcopal. Office: ARKLA divsn NorAm Energy Corp 400 E Capitol Ave Little Rock AR 72202-2465

GARDNER, KERRY ANN, librarian; b. Honolulu, May 19, 1955; d. Byron Patton and Claire (Teig) G. BA in Polit. Sci. magna cum laude, Temple U., 1976; MA in Latin Am. Studies, U. Ariz., 1983, MLS, 1990. Documents libr. FMC Corp., Chgo., 1977-78; grad. rsch. asst. U. Ariz., Tucson, 1983-86; rsch. cons. Tucson, 1983-92; libr. asst. I Phoenix Pub. Libr., 1988-89; project mgr. U. Ariz., 1990-92; mgr. faculty resource libr. U. Ariz. Ctr. English as 2d Lang., 1989-90, 91-92; pub. svcs. libr. Bryan Wildenthal Meml. Libr., Sul Ross State U., Alpine, Tex., 1992-95; libr. dir. Am. U., Dubai, United Arab Emirates, 1995-96; literacy libr. Sterling Mcpl. Libr., Baytown, Tex., 1996-98; libr. Valle Verde campus El Paso C.C., 1998—; indexer Hispanic Am. Periodicals Index, 1995; maintain GPO Access Web site, 1998—. Contbr. articles to profl. publs. Tchr. English Literacy Vols. Am., 1991-92, 96-98. Grad. scholar U. Ariz., 1976-77, 81-82. Mem. ALA, Assn. Coll. and Rsch. Librs., Tex. Libr. Assn. (legis. com. coll. and univ. librs. divsn. 1993-94), SALALM (marginalized peoples and ideas subcom. acquisitions com. 1995-98, elec. resources com. 1995-98), Border Libr. Assn. (chair publicity com. 1999—), Assn. Borderlands Scholars, Beta Phi Mu. Avocations: travel, birding, languages. Office: El Paso C C Valle Verde Campus PO Box 20500 El Paso TX 79998-0500

GARDNER, LEE ROBBINS, psychiatrist; b. Balt., June 6, 1934; d. Bernard S. and Lee (Fraidin) Robbins; m. Robert Williams, Oct., 1990 (dec. Oct. 1997); children: Andrew, Nancy, Julie. BA, Barnard, 1955; MD, Columbia U., 1959, cert. adult psychoanalysis, 1979, cert. child psychoanalysis, 1981. Intern St. Luke Hosp., 1959-60; resident N.Y. State Psychiat. Inst., N.Y.C., 1962-66; attending psychiatrist N.Y. State Psychiat. Inst., 1966—; asst. clin. prof. psychiatry Columbia Coll. Physicians and Surgeons, N.Y.C., 1982—; faculty Columbia Psychoanalytic Ctr., Columbia U., 1980—; bi-annual lectr. N.J. Coll. Medicine & Dentistry. Jewish.

GARDNER, LEONARD BURTON, II, retired industrial automation engineer; b. Lansing, Mich., Feb. 16, 1927; s. Leonard Burton and Lillian Marvin (Frost) G.; m. Barbara Jean Zivi, June 23, 1950; children: Karen Sue, Jeffrey Frank. B.Sc. in Physics, UCLA, 1951; M.Sc., Golden State U., 1953, Sc.D. in Engring., 1954; M.Sc. in Computer Sci, Augustana Coll., Rock Island, Ill., 1977. Registered profl. engr.; cert. mfg. engr. Instrumentation engr. govt. and pvt. industry, 1951-89; prof. and dir. Ctr. for Automated Integrated Mfg., 1982—; with computerized systems Naval Electronic Systems Engring. Ctr., San Diego, 1980-82; founder, dir. Automated Integrated Mfg., San Diego; cons. govt. agys. and industry, lectr., adj. prof. vaious univs. and colls., sci. advisor state and nat. legislators, 1980—, speaker in field. Author: Computer Aided Robotics Center; editor: Automated Manufacturing. Contbg. author: Instrumentation Handbook, 1981; contbr. numerous articles to tech. jours. Recipient award U.S. Army. Fellow IEEE; sr. mem. Soc. Mfg. Engrs. (Pres.'s award 1984); mem. ASTM, Nat. Soc. Profl. Engrs., Calif. Soc. Profl. Engrs., Sigma Xi. Home: 416 Sugar Maple Ln Cincinnati OH 45246-4147 *I believe in professional development through continuing education and participation in technical societies. I am committed to do my fair share and believe if everyone discharged this responsibility, no one person would become burdened and mankind would benefit immeasurably.*

GARDNER, LLOYD CALVIN, JR., history educator; b. Delaware, Ohio, Nov. 9, 1934; s. Lloyd Calvin and Hazel Belle (Grove) G.; m. Nancy Jean Wintermute, June 3, 1956; children: Rebecca, Erin, Timothy. B.A., Ohio Wesleyan U., 1956; M.S., U. Wis., 1957, Ph.D., 1960. Instr. Lake Forest (Ill.) Coll., 1959-60; faculty history dept. Rutgers U., New Brunswick, N.J., 1963—; asst. prof. Rutgers U., 1963-64, asso. prof., 1964-67, prof., 1967—, chmn. history dept., 1970-73, prof. II, 1977—, Charles A. Mary R. Beard prof. history, 1986—; adv. com. Franklin D. Roosevelt Library, Hyde Park, N.Y., 1972-73, Fgn. Relations U.S. publ. State Dept., 1975—, chmn., 1977-78; Fulbright prof., Eng., 1975-76, Fulbright Bicentennial prof., Helsinki, 1983-84. Author: Economic Aspects of New Deal, 1964, Architects of Illusion, 1970, (with William O'Neill) Looking Backward, 1972, Imperial America, 1976, A Covenant with Power, 1983, Safe for Democracy, 1984; editor: Redefining the Past, 1987, Approaching Vietnam, 1988, Shperes of Influence, 1993, Pay Any Price: Lyndon Johnson and the Wars for Vietnam, 1995; co-editor: Vietnam: The Early Decisions, 1997. Served with USAF, 1960-63. Social Sci. Research Council fellow, 1965-66; Guggenheim fellow, 1973-74. Fellow Soc. Am. Historians; mem. Am. Hist. Assn., Orgn. Am. Historians, Soc. Historians of Am. Fgn. Rels. (v.p. 1987, pres. 1988), AAUP. Home: 134 S Mill Rd Princeton Junction NJ 08550-2006 Office: Rutgers U History Dept New Brunswick NJ 08901

GARDNER, MARVIN ALLEN, JR., pastoral and clinical psychologist; b. Washington, Mar. 15, 1943; s. Marvin Allen and Lillian Gertrude (McCracken) G.; m. Donna Frances Craven, Mar. 16, 1962 (div. 1987); children: Stephen Gregory, Sarah Elizabeth; m. Laura Churchill Mink, May 21, 1988; children: Charles Treadway, Laura Faith. BA with honors, U. Md., 1964; MDiv cum laude, Va. Theol. Sem., 1967; DMin, Wesley Theol. Sem., Washington, 1979; PhD, The Union Inst., Cin., 1991. Lic. profl. couselor, lic. clin. psychologist, diplomate Am. Assn. Pastoral Counselors, D.C.; ordained priest Anglican Cath. Ch. Curate Ascension Epsicopal Ch., Mt. Vernon, N.Y., 1967-69; rector St. Paul's Episcopal Ch., Waldorf, Md., 1969-76; pastoral counselor Pastoral Counseling and Cons. Ctrs. of Greater Washington, Oakton, Va., 1976-81; co-dir. Marriage and Family Inst., Washington, 1981-84; dir. Family & Marriage Assocs., La Plata, Md., 1984-86, Capital Hill Ctr. of Pastoral Counseling & Cons. Ctrs., Oakton, 1986-94; faculty and supr. Inst. for Pastoral Psychotherapy, Oakton, 1993-97; rector Holy Family Anglican Ch., Gaithersburg, Md., 1993-96, St. Thomas of Canterbury Anglican Cath. Ch., Roanoke, Va., 1997—; pvt. practice pastoral and clinical psychology Washington, 1994-96; dir. The Pastoral Inst. of Greater Roanoke, 1997—; mem. Bd. Profl. Counseling, Washington, 1993-95; adj. asst. prof. pastoral counseling Loyola Coll., Columbia, Md., 1993-96; cert. med. expert The Office of Hearings and Appeals Social Security Adminstrn., 1999—. Author: Pastoral Excellence in Pastoral Counselor Education and Training, 1991; contbr. articles to profl. jours. Mem. APA, Am. Assn. Pastoral Counselors (diplomate, chmn. bd. govs. rsch. com. 1992-95, Writing and Rsch. award 1991), Am. Assn. Marriage and Family Therapy, Am. Assn. Christian Counselors. Home and Office: 1725 Wilbur Rd SW Roanoke VA 24015-3627

GARDNER, MARY ADELAIDE, retired journalism educator; b. Kingston, Ohio, July 20, 1920; d. J.P. and Wyland (Davis) G. AA, Stephens Coll., Columbia, Mo., 1942; BA in Bacteriology, Ohio State U., 1944, MA in Journalism, 1954; PhD in Journalism, U. Minn., Mpls., 1969. Asst. prof. journalism U. Tex., Austin, 1963-65, U. Mich. State, Lansing, Mich., 1970-71; assoc. prof. U. Mich. State, Lansing, 1971-76, prof., 1976-91, prof. emeritus, 1991—; newspaper work on El Norte, Mex., 1970-90 summers; sabbatical year in Lima, Peru, Guatemala studying mags. and newspapers. Contbr. articles on Latin Am. Press to profl. jours. Vol. worker Dem. party, N.Y. (Emily List). Officer U.S. Army 1944-46. Recipient Inter Am. award, Govt. of Brazil, 1976; elected Disting. Faculty Mem. by Mich. State Faculty, 1976. Mem. NOW (Mich. chpt.), Assn. of Edn. for Journalism and Comm. (International. award 1994, Women's award 1996), Mich. Studies Assn., Cmty. Vols. for Internat. Programs, Fast Break Club, Kappa Tau Alpha, Kappa Alpha Theta. Avocations: swimming, walking. Home: 6217 Cobblers Ct East Lansing MI 48823-7829

GARDNER, MURRAY BRIGGS, pathologist, educator; b. Lafayette, Ind., Oct. 5, 1929; s. Max William and Margaret (Briggs) G.; m. Alice E. Danielson, June 20, 1961; children: Suzanna, Martin, Danielson, Andrew. B.A., U. Calif., Berkeley, 1951; M.D., U. Calif., San Francisco, 1954. Intern Moffitt Hosp., San Francisco, 1954-55; resident in gen. practice Sonoma County Hosp., Santa Rosa, Calif., 1957-59; resident in pathology U. Calif. hosps., San Francisco, 1959-63; faculty U. So. Calif. Sch. Medicine, Los Angeles, 1963-81; prof. pathology U. So. Calif. Sch. Medicine, 1973-81; prof. pathology U. Calif., Davis Sch. Medicine, 1981—, chmn. dept. pathology, 1982-90. Contbr. chpts. to books, numerous articles in field to profl. jours. Served to lt. M.C. USNR, 1957-59. NIH grantee, 1968—. Mem. Coll. Am. Pathologists, Internat. Acad. Pathology. Home: 8313 Maxwell Ln Dixon CA 95620-9662 Office: U Calif-Davis Med Sch # Ms-1 Davis CA 95616

GARDNER, NANCY BRUFF, writer; b. Fairfield County, Conn., Nov. 15, 1909; d. Austin Bruff and Alice (Birdsall) Weeks; m. Thurston Clarke Mar. 11, 1939 (dec. May 1962); children: Thurston B., Penelope; m. Esmond Brown Gardner July 20, 1963 (dec. June 1996). Student, U. Paris, 1932-36. Author: (novels) The Manatee, 1945, cider from Eden, 1947, Beloved Women, 1949, Love is Not Love, 1950, The Fig Tree, 1965, The Country Club, 1969, The Mist Maiden, 1975; (poetry) My Talon in Your Heart, 1946, Walk Lightly on the Planet, 1985; co-editor (anthology) Five Great Healers Speak Here, 1982, (plays) Cast Iron Smile, 1989, Mrs. Hollister's Trojan Horse, 1996. Mem. Poetry Soc. Am., Authors League, Authors Guild, Dramatists Guild, Mayflower Soc., Colonial Dames Am., Huguenot Soc. Episcopalian. Club: Cosmopolitan (N.Y.C.).

GARDNER, NORD ARLING, management consultant administrator; b. Afton, Wyo., Aug. 10, 1923; s. Arling A. and Ruth (Lee) G.; BA, U. Wyo., 1945; MS, Calif. State U., Hayward, 1972, MPA, 1975; postgrad. U. Chgo., U. Mich., U. Calif.-Berkeley; m. Thora Marie Stephen, Mar. 24, 1945; children: Randall Nord, Scott Stephen, Craig Robert, Laurie Lee. With U.S. Army, 1941 Commd. 2d lt., 1945, advanced through grades to lt. col., 1964; ret., 1966; personnel analyst Univ. Hosp., U. Calif.-San Diego, 1966-68; coordinator manpower devel. U. Calif.-Berkeley, 1968-75; univ. tng. officer San Francisco State U., 1975-80, personnel mgr., 1976-80; exec. dir. CRDC Maintenance Tng. Corp., non-profit community effort, San Francisco, 1980-85; pres., dir. Sandor Assocs. Mgmt. Cons., Pleasant Hill, Calif., 1974-86, 91-96; gen. mgr. Vericlean Janitorial Service, Inc.; in-charge bus. devel. East Bay Local Devel. Corp., Oakland, Calif., 1980-85; incorporator and pres. Indochinese Community Enterprises, USA, Ltd., Pleasant Hill, Calif., 1985-87; freelance writer, grantsmanship cons., 1987—; ptnr. Oi Kit Bldg. Maint. Svc., 1988-91; dir. univ. rels. Internat. Pacific U., San Ramon, Calif., 1990—, exec. dir., bd. dirs. Internat. Pacific Inst., 1994— ; cons. Phimmasone International. Import-Export, Richmond, Calif., Lao Lanx-Xang Assn., Oakland Refugee Assn., 1988-90; instr. Japanese, psychology, supervisory courses, 1977-78; bd. dirs. New Ideas New Imports, Inc. Author: To Gather Stones, 1978. Adv. council San Francisco Community Coll. Dist. Decorated Army Commendation medal. Mem. Ret. Officers Assn., Am. Soc. Tng. and Devel., No. Calif. Human Resources Council. Am. Assn. Univ. Adminstrs., Internat. Personnel Mgrs. Assn., Coll. and Univ. Personnel Assn., Commonwealth Club of Calif., U. Calif.-Berkeley Faculty Club, San Francisco State U. Faculty Club, Army Counter Intelligence Corp Vets., Inc. Republican. Home: 2995 Bonnie Ln Pleasant Hill CA 94523-4547 Office: Internat Pacific Inst 2995 Bonnie Ln Pleasant Hill CA 94523-4547

GARDNER, PETER JAGLOM, publisher; b. N.Y.C., 1958; s. Ralph David and Natalie (Jaglom) G.; m. Victoire Taittinger, 1984; children: Evan, Emma, Nadya, Parker. BA, Middlebury (Vt.) Coll., 1980; JD magna cum laude, Vt. Law Sch., 1999. Pres. Transatlantic Comml. Svcs. Corp., 1982-90; pub. Northern Centinel, Kinderhook, N.Y., 1991—; pres., CEO Centinel Co., 1991—. Mem. Overseas Press Club, Frank Rowe Kenison Inn of Ct. (treas. 1999—), NH Internat. Trade Assn. Office: Stebbins Bradley Wood & Harvey 41 S Park St Hanover NH 03755

GARDNER, RALPH DAVID, advertising executive; b. N.Y.C., Apr. 16, 1923; s. Benjamin and Myra (Berman) G.; m. Nellie Jaglom, Apr. 9, 1952; children: Ralph David, John Jaglom (dec.), Peter Jaglom, James Jaglom. Diploma in journalism, NYU, 1942; diploma in mil. adminstrn., Colo. State Coll., 1943. With N.Y. Times, 1942-55; copy boy, city desk, fgn. corr., started internat. edit. N.Y. Times, Paris, 1949; bur. mgr. for Germany and Austria, Frankfurt N.Y. Times, 1950, resigned, 1955; pres. Ralph D. Gardner Advt., N.Y.C., 1955—; dir. Gardner Internat. Corp.; Quality Irish Food Export (Dublin) Ltd.; dir. various other U.S. and fgn. corps.; writer, book reviewer, lectr., bibliographer 19th Century Am. lit.; Mary C. Richardson lectr. SUNY-Geneseo, 1974; vis. prof. U. Wyo., Baylor U., others; mem. faculty Georgetown U. Writers Conf., 1976, 80; Hess research fellow U. Minn., 1979; book reviewer, host Ralph Gardner's Bookshelf, WVNJ-N.Y., other radio stas., 1974-87. Author: Horatio Alger, or The American Hero Era, 1964, 78, 90, Road to Success: The Bibliography of the Works of Horatio Alger, 1971, Introduction to Silas Snobden's Office Boy, 1973, Introduction to Cast Upon the Breakers, 1974, History of Street & Smith, in Publishers for Mass Entertainment in 19th Century America, 1980, Introduction to a Fancy of Hers, 1981, The Disagreeable Woman, 1981 (English-Speaking Union selection 1981), Struggling Upward, 1984, Writers' Talk to Ralph D. Gardner, 1989, others; contbr. to: N.Y. Times Book Rev., Sat. Eve. Post, No. Centinel, 1st Printings of Am. Authors, vol. 5, 1987; syndicated newspaper columnist Maturity News Svc., 1987—. Mem.-at-large Greater N.Y. council Boy Scouts Am., 1950-60; bd. dirs. Fresh Air Council, 1964-66; mem. hon. exec. com. Nat. Citizens for Public Libraries. Served as newswriter with Air Corps and Inf. AUS, 1943-46, ETO; field Corr. Yank Mag. Recipient award for lit. Horatio Alger Soc., 1964, 72, 81, 85, 91; spl. citation scroll Horatio Alger Assn. Disting. Ams., 1978. Mem. Manuscript Soc., Bibliog. Soc. Am., Childrens Lit. Assn., Friends of Princeton U. Libr., Syracuse U. Libr. Assocs. (hon.), Brandeis U. Bibliophiles (hon.), Overseas Press Club of Am. (chmn. best book on fgn. affairs awards com., bd. govs. 1987-88, 92-94, v.p. 1988-92), Frankfurt Press Club, Nat. Book Critics Cir., Soc. Silurians, PEN, Grolier Club, Baker St. Irregulars, Alpha Epsilon Pi. Home: 135 Central Park W New York NY 10023-2413

GARDNER, RICHARD ALAN, psychiatrist, writer; b. Bronx, N.Y., Apr. 28, 1931; s. Irving and Amelia (Weingarten) G.; m. Lee Robbins, Apr. 14, 1957 (div. Nov. 1984); children: Andrew Kevin, Nancy Tara, Julie Anne; m. Patricia Lefevere, July 4, 1987 (div. Apr. 1998). AB, Columbia U., 1952; MD, SUNY Downstate Med. Ctr., 1956; cert. psychoanalysis, William A. White Psychoanalytical Inst., 1966. Diplomate Am. Bd. Psychiatry and Neurology, Am. Bd. Child Psychiatry. Intern Montefiore Hosp., N.Y.C., 1956-57, resident child psychiatry, 1959-60, 62-63; dir. child psychiatry U.S. Army Hosp., Frankfurt, Federal Republic of Germany, 1960-62; mem. attending staff Presbyn. Hosp., N.Y.C., 1963—; pvt. practice specializing in psychiatry, child psychiatry and psychoanalysis Cresskill, N.J., 1963—; instr. child psychiatry Columbia Coll. Physicians and Surgeons, N.Y.C., 1963-70, assoc. child psychiatry, 1970-72, asst. clin. prof. child psychiatry, 1972-76, assoc. clin. prof. child psychiatry, 1976-83, clin. prof. child psychiatry, 1983—; vis. prof. child psychiatry, U. Louvain, Belgium, 1981-83, U. St. Petersburg, Russia, 1990-97; mem. faculty William A. White Psychoanalytic Inst., 1967-83. Author: The Child's Book about Brain Injury, 1966, The Boys and Girls Book about Divorce, 1970, Therapeutic Communication with Children: The Mutual Storytelling Technique, 1971, Dr. Gardner's Stories about the Real World, Vol. I, 1972, MBD: The Family Book about Minimal Brain Dysfunction, 1973, Understanding Children: A Parent's Guide to Child Rearing, 1973, Dr. Gardner's Fairy Tales for Today's Child, 1974, Psychotherapy with Children of Divorce, 1976, The Parent's Book about Divorce, 1977, Dr. Gardner's Modern Fairy Tales, 1977, The Boys and Girls Book about Stepfamilies, 1981, Family Evaluation in Child Custody Litigation, 1982, Dr. Gardner's Stories about the Real World, Vol. II, 1983, Separation Anxiety Disorder: Psychodynamics and Psychotherapy, 1984, Child Custody Litigation: A Guide for Parents and Mental Health Professionals, 1986, The Psychotherapeutic Techniques of Richard A. Gardner, 1986, Hyperactivity, The So-Called Attention Deficit Disorder and The Group of MBD Syndromes, 1987, The Parental Alienation Syndrome and the Differentiation between Fabricated and Genuine Child Sex Abuse, 1987, Psychotherapy with Adolescents, 1988, Family Evaluation in Custody Mediation, Arbitration and Litigation, 1989, The Girls and Boys Book about Good and Bad Behavior, 1990, Sex Abuse Hysteria: Salem Witch Trials Revisited, 1991, The Parents Book About Divorce, 2d edit., 1991, The Parental Alienation Syndrome: A Guide for Mental Health and Legal Professionals, 1992, Self-Esteem Problems of Children: Psychodynamics and Psychotherapy, 1992, The Psychotherapeutic Techniques of Richard A. Gardner, 2d edit., 1992, True and False Accusations of Child Sex Abuse: A Guide for Legal and Mental Health Professionals, 1992, Conduct Disorders of Childhood: Psychodynamics and Psychotherapy, 1994, Protocols for the Sex Abuse Evaluation, 1995, Psychogenic Learning Disabilities: Psychodynamics and Psychotherapy, 1996, Testifying in Court: A Guide for

Mental Health Professionals, 1995, Psychotherapy with Victims of Child Sexual Abuse: True, False, and Hysterical, 1996, Dream Analysis in Psychotherapy, 1996, The Parental Alienation Syndrome, 2d edit., 1998, The Utilization of the Gardner Children's Projective Battery, 1999, Sex Abuse Trauma? or Trauma From Other Sources?, 1999; editor in chief Internat. Jour. Child Psychothrapy, 1972-73. Capt. M.C., USAR, 1960-62. Fellow Am. Acad. Psychoanalysis, Am. Acad. Child and Adolescent Psychiatry, Am. Psychiat. Assn. (life). Home: 24 Mackay Dr Tenafly NJ 07670-2420 Office: 155 County Rd Cresskill NJ 07626-2200

GARDNER, RICHARD EUGENE, landscape architect; b. Monterey, Calif., Jan. 4, 1944; s. Lawrence E. and Sarah I. (Hill) G.; m. Mary Rosalee Kaldenberg, Sept. 3, 1966; children: Grant E., Molly J., Charles D. BS in Landscape Architecture, Iowa State U., 1967, M Landscape Architecture, 1969. Lic. landscape architect, Iowa, Nebr. Landscape architect Crose Gardner Assocs., Des Moines, 1969-73, ptnr., 1973-95; pres. Rdg Crose Gardner Shukert, Des Moines and Omaha, 1995—. Mem. Bd. Appeals, Urbandale, Iowa, 1992—, Design Adv. Team, Des Moines, 1992—; bd. dirs. Living History Farms, Urbandale, 1995—. Mem. Am. Soc. Landscape Architects, Orgn. Profls. and Execs. (pres. 1995), Greater Des Moines Bus. Exch. (pres. 1990). Office: Rdg Crose Gardner Shukert 414 61st St Des Moines IA 50312-1407

GARDNER, RICHARD HARTWELL, oil company executive; b. Cambridge, Mass., Oct. 9, 1934; s. Richard Hosmer and Marjorie Georgine (Pierce) G.; m. Helen Carolyn McIntyre, Oct. 11, 1957; children—Pamela, Hartwell. A.B., Colgate U., 1956; M.B.A., Harvard U., 1961. Treas. Mobil Latin Am. Inc., N.Y.C., 1964-66; asst. treas. internat. div. Mobil Internat., 1966-68; treas. Mobil Europe Inc., London, 1968-70; treas. N. Am. div., N.Y.C., 1970-72, dep. treas., 1972-73; corp. treas. Mobil Oil Corp., 1974-95; treas. Mobil Corp., 1976-95; mem. adv. bd. Chem. Bank, 1978-95, dir. Pioneer Natural Resources, Inc., Irving, Tex., Oil Investment Corp. Ltd., Hamilton, Bermuda. Served to 1st lt. USAF, 1956-59. Mem. Am. Petroleum Inst., Fin. Execs. Inst. (chmn. 1986-87). Democrat.

GARDNER, RICHARD KENT, retired librarian, educator, consultant; b. New Bedford, Mass., Dec. 7, 1928; s. Francis and Millicent Annetta (Kent) G. A.B. cum laude, Middlebury Coll., Vt., 1950; Dipl. Litt., U. Paris, 1954; M.S. in Library Sci., Western Res. U., 1955; Ph.D., Case Western Res. U., 1968. Asst. librarian Case Inst. Tech., 1955-57; library adviser Mich. State U. adv. group pub. adminstrn. to govt. South Vietnam, 1957-58; librarian, assoc. prof. Marietta Coll., Ohio, 1959-63; founding editor Choice: Books for Coll. Libraries, Middletown, Conn., 1963-66, editor, 1972-77; lectr., then. assoc. prof. Case Western Res. U. Sch. Library Sci., 1966-69; prof. agrege Ecole de Bibliotheconomie, U. Montreal, 1969-70, prof. titulaire, 1970-72, 82-93, dir., 1970-72, 82-87; prof. Grad. Sch. Library and Info. Sci. UCLA, 1977-82; ret., 1993; internat. libr. edn. cons., 1966—. Author: Cataloging and Classification of Books, with the Vietnamese Decimal Classification, 1958, rev. edit., 1966, Opening Day Collection, 1965, rev. edit., 1974, Education for Librarianship in France: An Historical Survey, 1968, Library Collections: Their Origin, Selection, and Development, 1981 (Blackwell award 1982), Education of Library and Information Professionals: Present and Future Prospects, 1987; also articles. Mem. Forest Press com. Lake Placid Ednl. Found., 1972-87; trustee Russell Library, Middletown, 1975-77. Served with AUS, 1951-53. Mem. ALA, Ohio Library Assn. (exec. bd. 1962-63), Can. Library Assn., Assn. Coll. and Research Libraries, Music Library Assn., Ohio Coll. Assn. (v.p. librarians sect. 1962-63, pres. 1963), Corp. des Bibliothecaires professionsals du Que. (adminstrv. council 1970-72), Tudor Singers Montreal (v.p. 1970-72), Assn. internat. des ecoles des scis. de l'information. Home: 13610 Shaker Blvd Apt 403 Cleveland OH 44120-1551

GARDNER, RICHARD NEWTON, diplomat, lawyer, educator; b. N.Y.C., July 9, 1927; s. Samuel I. and Ethel (Elias) G.; m. Danielle Luzzatto, June 10, 1956; children: Nina Jessica, Anthony Laurence. AB magna cum laude, Harvard U., 1948; JD, Yale U., 1951; PhD, Oxford U., 1954. Bar: N.Y. 1952. Corr. UP, 1946-47, AP, 1948; teaching fellow internat. legal studies Harvard Law Sch., 1953-54; with Coudert Bros., N.Y.C., 1954-57; assoc. prof. law Columbia U., 1957-60, prof., 1960-61, 65-66, Henry L. Moses prof. law and internat. orgn., 1967-77, 81—; of counsel Morgan, Lewis & Bockius, 1997—; U.S. amb. to Italy Am. Embassy, Rome, Italy, 1977-81; U.S. amb. to Spain Am. Embassy, Madrid, 1993-97; dep. asst. sec. state internat. orgns. Dept. State, 1961-65; vis. prof. U. Istanbul, 1958, U. Rome, 1967-68; dep. U.S. rep. UN Com. on Peaceful Uses of Outer Space, 1962-65; U.S. alt. del. 19th UN Gen. Assembly; sr. adviser U.S. del. to 20th and 21st UN Gen. Assemblies; rapporteur UN Com. Experts on Econ. Restructuring, 1975; mem. Pres.'s Commn. on Internat. Trade and Investment Policy, 1970-71, U.S. Adv. Com. on Law of Sea, 1971-76; cons. to sec.-gen. UN Conf. on Human Environment, 1972, UN Conf. Environment and Devel., 1992; mem. pres.'s adv. com. Trade Policy and Negotiations, 1998—. Author: Sterling-Dollar Diplomacy, 1956, New Directions in U.S. Foreign Economic Policy, 1959, In Pursuit of World Order, 1964, Blueprint for Peace, 1966, (with Max F. Millikan) The Global Partnership: International Agencies and Economic Development, 1968; note editor: Yale Law Jour, 1950-51. Bd. dirs. Freedom House, Am. Ditchley Found., Salzburg Seminar. Served with AUS, 1945-46. Recipient Detur prize for disting. scholarship Harvard U., 1948, Arthur S. Flemming award, 1963; Harvard Club scholar, 1944, Rhodes scholar, 1951-53. Mem. ABA, UN Assn. (dir.), Assn. Bar City N.Y., Council Fgn. Relations, Am. Acad. Arts and Scis., Am. Philosophical Soc., Phi Beta Kappa, Order of Coif, Century Assn, Met. Club. Clubs: Century Assn. (N.Y.C.); Met. (Washington). Office: Columbia U Sch Law 435 W 116th St New York NY 10027-7297

GARDNER, RICKI, retail store official, minister; b. Scott AFB, Ill., Nov. 6, 1957; s. V. Joseph and Lula Mae (Calmese) G.; m. Durlene Reed, Nov. 11, 1995; children: Lisa D., Robert D., Uneka L., Iona S. Student, So. Bible Inst., Dallas, 1994-98, North Lake Coll., Irving, Tex., 1996—. Press opeator USA Today, Nashville, 1984-90, DFW Suburban News, Arlington, Tex., 1993-95, 97-98, Willamette Industries, Irving, 1995-96; motor coach operator Kerrville Bus Co., Grand Prairie, Tex., 1990-93; 1st asst. mgr. Casual Male Big & Tall, Arlington, 1998—; pastor The Ch. at Grand Prairie, 1994—. Vol. Just Say No Kids Club, Dalworth Cmty., Grand Prairie, 1994—. Recipient Golden Rule award J.C. Penney, 1997, Vol. of Yr. award Heritage Place Nursing Home, Grand Prairie, 1997. Mem. Phi Theta Kappa. Baptist. Avocations: reading, writing, cooking, biking. Home: 930 Hoke Smith Dr Dallas TX 75224-3327

GARDNER, ROBERT CHARLES, systems analyst, administrator; b. Charlotte, N.C., June 11, 1961; s. Gary Kent and Betty Joyce (Sells) G.; m. Ginger Adair Lawing, Feb. 23, 1985; children: Robert Cameron, Sarah Ashley. Student, Western Carolina U., 1979-83. Systems support analyst Miller Svcs., Charlotte, N.C., 1983-85; program mgr. Computer Task Group, Charlotte, 1986-87; installation support analyst Systems Assocs., Inc., Charlotte, 1985-86, programmer, analyst, 1987; systems analyst Day Data Systems subs. E.I. DuPont, Charlotte, 1987-90, systems specialist, 1990-91; project leader Tultex Corp., Martinsville, Va., 1991-92; cons. Am. Systems Profls., Charlotte, 1992-93; systems adminstr. 3 HBO & Co. (formerly First Data Corp.), Charlotte, 1993-96; systems engr. First Union Nat. Bank, Charlotte, 1996—. Cub scout leader Pack 38 1995—; v.p. Oakdale Elementary PTA 1996-97. Mem. Optimists (little league baseball coach 1986), Pi Lambda Phi. Democrat. Methodist. Avocations: computers, music, movies. Home: 3508 Kelly Rd Charlotte NC 28216-5731

GARDNER, ROBERT MEADE, retired building contractor; b. Portsmouth, Ohio, Aug. 12, 1927; s. David Edward and Mary Petrea (Gableman) G.; m. Ruth Sieker, Aug. 8, 1952; children: Leslie, Robert Jr., Stephen, Lorianne. BA, Ohio Wesleyan U., 1951. Engr. J.A. Jones, Charlotte, N.C., 1944; v.p. D.E. Gardner Co., Columbus, Ohio, 1951-55; pres. The Gardner Co., Columbus, Ohio, 1955-92, chmn., 1993-96; ret., 1996; Dir. Builders Exchange, Columbus, 1959-60; officer Young Pres.' Orgn. Cen. Ohio, 1969-79. Mem. athletic bd. Ohio Wesleyan U., Del., 1965-96, alumni bd., 1969-96; mem. Columbus Bldg. Code Commn., 1974, World Pres. Orgn., Columbus, 1980—, chmn., 1995-96; officer Upper Arlington (Ohio) Booster Assn., 1974; pres. Vision Ctr. Ctrl. Ohio, Columbus, 1981, Ohio Valley Tennis Assn., 1977-78; bd. dirs. Jazz Arts Group, Columbus, 1989-95, First Cmty. Village, 1988-98. Named to Athletic Hall of Fame Ohio Wesleyan U.; recipient Disting. award Phi Gamma Delta, Medick award, Vision Ctr. Cen. Ohio, Gillespie award Ohio Valley Tennis Assn. Mem. World Pres. Orgn. (chpt. chmn. 1996), Scioto Country Club (bd. dirs.), Athletic Club, Racquet Club, Players Club. Home: 4500 Dublin Rd Columbus OH 43221-5006

GARDNER, ROBERTA JOAN, library director; b. N.Y.C., Apr. 12, 1932; d. Philip R. and Rae (Spiegel) Beller; m. Edgar Talmus, Apr. 19, 1951 (div.); children: Evie Talmus, Laura Talmus. BA in Econs., Queens Coll., Flushing, N.Y., 1962; MLS, Pratt Inst., 1964. Dir. libr. svcs. Bus. Internat., Inc., 1965-70; mgr. bus. libr. Dun & Bradstreet Corp., 1970-78, mgr. info. svcs., 1978-80, dir. info. svcs., 1980-81; dir. commn./info. svcs. Moran, Stahl & Boyer, Inc., 1981-82; dir. info. svcs. Bernard Hodes Advt., 1983-84; cons. Pub. Rels. Soc. of Am., 1984—; mgr. records ctr. Real Estate dept. Met. Trans. Authority, 1986; libr. dir. Parade Publs., Inc., 1987—; cons. World Trade Inst. Libr. Author: (with others) Information Management, 1984; contbr. articles to profl. jours. Mem. Spl. Librs. Assn. Avocations: theater, reading, crossword puzzles, gardening. Office: Parade Publs Inc 711 3rd Ave New York NY 10017-4014

GARDNER, ROBIN PIERCE, engineering educator; b. Charlotte, N.C., Aug. 17, 1934; s. Robin Brem and Margaret (Pierce) G.; m. Linda Jean Gardner, Oct. 21, 1976. B.Ch.E., N.C. State U., 1956, M.S., 1958; Ph.D., Pa. State U., 1961. Scientist Oak Ridge Inst. Nuclear Studies, 1961-63; research engr., asst. dir. measurement and controls lab. Research Triangle Inst., Research Triangle Park, N.C., 1963-67; research prof. nuclear engring. and chem. engring., dir. Center Engring. Applications of Radioisotopes, N.C. State U., 1967—; cons. Oak Ridge Inst. Nuclear Studies, Research Triangle Inst., Oak Ridge Nat. Lab., Internat. Atomic Energy Agy., NASA, AEC, TVA, Alcoa. Author: (with Ralph L. Ely, Jr.), Radioisotope Measurement Applications in Engineering, 1967; regional editor Applied Radiation and Isotopes, Jour. Fine Particle Soc.; contbr. articles to sci. jours. Served to 1st lt. AUS, 1956. Recipient Alcoa Found. Disting. Rsch. award N.C. State U. Sch. Engring., 1986, Alumni Disting. Grad. Professorship award, 1996, R.J. Reynolds award for excellence in tchg. and rsch., 1998; Centennial fellow Coll. Earth and Mineral Scis., Pa. State U., 1996. Fellow Am. Nuclear Soc. (Radiation Industry award isotopes and radiation div. 1984), Am. Inst. Chem. Engrs., Sigma Xi, Phi Kappa Phi, Phi Lambda Upsilon. Home: 3005 Randolph Dr Raleigh NC 27609-6941 Office: NC State U Ctr Engring Appications of Radioisotope Dept Nuclear Engring Raleigh NC 27695-7909

GARDNER, SANDRA LEE, nurse, outreach consultant; b. Louisville, Dec. 1, 1946; d. Jane Marie (Schwab) Gardner. Nursing diploma, Sts. Mary and Elizabeth Hosp., Louisville, 1967; BSN magna cum laude, Spalding Coll., 1973; MS, U. Colo., 1975, Pediatric Nurse Practitioner, 1978. RN. Premature coordinator Meth. Evang. Hosp., Louisville, 1967-71; charge nurse Children's Hosp., Louisville, 1971-73; staff/charge nurse Children's Hosp., Denver, 1973-74, perinatal outreach coord., 1974-76; asst. prof. U. Colo. Sch. Nursing, 1976-79; co-founder, vice chmn. bd. dirs. Denver Birth Ctr., 1977-79; dir., cons. Profl. Outreach Consultation, Aurora, Colo., 1980—; founding mem. Colo. Perinatal Car Council, Denver, 1975—; founding dir. Neonatal Nursing Edn. Found., Aurora, 1982—. Co-editor: Handbook of Neonatal Intensive Care, 1985, 89, Legal Aspects of Maternal-Child Nursing Practice, 1997; contbr. articles to profl. jours. Foster parent educator Dept. Social Svcs., 1976-78; in pub. edn. KVOD Radio/Channel 2, Denver, 1978; nursing supr. 9 Health Fair, Denver, 1980. Recipient Gerald L. Hencemann award March of Dimes, Denver, 1978. Mem. ANA (Book of Yr. 1986, 89), Nat. Neonatal Nurses Assn. Democrat. Avocations: downhill skiing, hiking, biking, gardening, reading, travel. Home: 12095 E Kentucky Ave Aurora CO 80012-3233

GARDNER, SHERYL PAIGE, gynecologist; b. Bremerton, Wash., Jan. 24, 1945; d. Edwin Gerald and Dorothy Elizabeth (Herman) G.; m. James Alva Beat, June 20, 1986. BA in Biology, U. Oreg., 1967, MD cum laude, 1971. Diplomate Am. Bd. Ob-Gyn. Intern L.A. County Harbor Gen. Hosp., Torrance, Calif., 1971-72, resident in ob-gyn., 1972-75; physician Group Health Assn., Washington, 1975-87; pvt. practice Mililani, Hawaii, 1987—; med. staff sec. Wahiawa (Hawaii) Gen. Hosp., 1994-95. Mem. Am. Coll. Ob-Gyn., Am. Soc. Colposcopy and Cervical Pathology, Hawaii Med. Assn., N.Am. Menopause Soc., Sigma Kappa, Alpha Omega Alpha. Democrat. Avocation: supporter numerous environ., peace and social concern groups. Office: 95-1249 Meheula Pkwy Ste B10A Mililani HI 96789-1763

GARDNER, STEPHEN DAVID, lawyer, law educator; b. Newark, N.J., Dec. 3, 1939; s. Henry and Florence (Temeles) G.; m. Mary Francis Voce, Sept. 19, 1973; children: Benjamin Voce-Gardner, Daniel Voce-Gardner. BA, U. Fla., 1961, LLB, 1964; LLM in Taxation, NYU, 1965. Bar: Fla. 1964, N.Y. 1967, U.S. Supreme Ct. 1980. Assoc. Maguire Voorhis & Wells, Orlando, Fla., 1965-66; assoc. prof. law NYU Sch. Law, N.Y.C., 1966-68, adj. prof. law, 1969—; assoc. Hughes Hubbard & Reed, N.Y.C., 1968-71; ptnr. Kronish Lieb Weiner & Hellman, N.Y.C., 1971—, mng. ptnr., 1980—; dir. Safra Nat. Bank, N.Y.C., 1987—, David Schwartz Found., N.Y.C., 1980—. Contbr. articles and revs. to profl. jours. Sgt., USAR, 1969-72. Mem. N.Y. State Bar Assn., Fla. Bar, Assn. Bar of City of New York, Tax Club of N.Y., Order of Coif. Jewish. Avocations: skiing, swimming, gardening. Office: Kronish Lieb Weiner & Hellman 1114 Ave of Americas New York NY 10036

GARDNER, SUSANNE, women's basketball coach. BS in Phys. Edn., U. Ga., 1986. Asst. coach U. Ga., 1986-88; head coach women's basketball Anderson (S.C.) Coll., 1988-92; asst. coach San Diego State U., 1992-96; head coach women's basketball Austin Peay State U., Clarksville, Tenn., 1996—. Office: Austin Peay State U Women's Athletics Dept PO Box 4515 Clarksville TN 37044*

GARDNER, THOMAS EARLE, investment banker, managment/financial consultant; b. Greenwich, Conn., Apr. 4, 1938; s. Edward Theodore and Mary Elizabeth (Johnson) G.; m. Elizabeth Pennock Candee, Nov. 4, 1968 (div. 1982); m. Leslie Adams Henshaw, Sept. 7, 1984; children: Geoffrey Haines, Justin Chandler. BA, Williams Coll., Williamstown, Mass., 1961; MBA, NYU, 1971. Asst. brand mgr. Pitts. Nat. Bank, 1961-65; v.p., sales mgr. Morgan Guaranty Trust Co., N.Y.C., 1966-79; sr. v.p., treas. R.I. Hosp. Trust Nat. Bank, Providence, 1979-91; dir. mgmt. info., treas. Bank of Boston, 1991-92; with Gov.'s Office and dept. econ. devel. State of R.I., 1992-93; fin. and mgmt. cons. LJT Assocs., Providence, 1993—; CFO, treas., bd. dirs. Access Solutions Internat. Inc., 1994—; bd. dirs. CDS, Inc. Team Works, Inc., Mossberg Ind., Inc.; curriculum com. New Eng. Sch. Banking, 1985-90; chmn. DEPCO Performance Rev. Com., 1992—, Providence Arts and Entertainment Dist. Working Group, 1992-94, Rethinking Govt. Task Force, 1993, Providence Lighting Commn., 1993—. Bd. dirs., pres. Genesis Ctr., South Providence, 1988-94; bd. dirs., pres. Keep Providence Beautiful, 1988-94; trustee R.I. Coun. on Econ. Edn., 1985-90; mem. Leadership R.I., 1982-89, Providence Preservation Soc., 1985—; interim exec. dir. Depositors Econ. Protection Corp., 1991; mem. Gov.'s Jobs Task Force, 1992, State Commn. to Study State Debt, 1992-93, Mayor's Salary Rev. Commn., 1992—, R.I. Commodores, 1994—. Mem. Providence C. of C. Avocations: tennis, theatre. Home: 93 Power St Providence RI 02906-1013 Office: 731 Hospital Trust Bldg Providence RI 02903

GARDNER, THOMAS NEVILLE, communications educator; b. New Orleans, July 7, 1946; s. Edward Neville and Margaret Agnes (Guess) G.; m. Karen Levine, Mar. 12, 1994; m. Jennifer N. Johnston, Dec. 22, 1979 (div. Aug. 1990); children: Sarah Rose Johnston-Gardner, Koby Leor Gardner-Levine. BA in Sociology, U. Va., 1971; MA in Journalism, U. Ga., 1981; MPA, Harvard U., 1985. Chmn. So. Student Organizing Com. Nashville, 1967-69; rsch. dir. Va. Rsch. Inst., Charlottesville, 1971-73; media specialist Atlanta Jr. Coll., 1975-77; teaching asst. journalism U. Ga., Athens, 1977-79; reporter, columnist Montgomery (Ala.) Advertiser, 1980-83; pub. rels. dir. Ala. State Employees Assn., Montgomery, 1983-84; dir. commn. Union Concerned Scientists, Cambridge, Mass., 1985-87; pub. affairs officer Harvard U. Div. Sch., Cambridge, 1987-88; sr. editor Harvard Inst. Internat. Devel., Cambridge, 1988-92; pres., comm./editorial cons. Thomas N. Gardner & Assocs., Cambridge and Amherst, Mass., 1992—; teaching asst. comm. dept. U. Mass., Amherst, 1993-96; mng. dir. Media Edn. Found. Author: Rah's Hidden Treasure, 1992; Contbr.: We Won't Go, 1967; mng. editor: Reforming Economic Systems in Developing Countries, 1991. Bd. dirs. Cultural Environment Movement. Recipient 1st Prize Photography So. Regional Coun., Atlanta, 1978, Govt. Reporting award Ala. State Employees Assn., Montgomery, 1982. Mem. Soc. Profl. Journalists, Nat. Comm. Assn., Internat. Comm. Assn., Assn. for Edn. in Journalism and Mass Comm. Office: Media Edn Found 26 Center St Northampton MA 01060-3027

GARDNER, WARNER WINSLOW, lawyer; b. Richmond, Ind., Sept. 25, 1909; s. Frank Karl and Camilla (Winslow) G.; m. Henrietta Gertrude Tucker, Sept. 10, 1940 (dec. Mar. 19, 1989); children: Hannah Winslow, William Tucker, Richard Randolph, Frances Winslow; m. Josephine P. McGowan, Oct. 28, 1989. A.B., Swarthmore Coll., 1930; M.A., Rutgers U., 1931; LL.B., Columbia U., 1934. Law clk. Justice Stone, U.S. Supreme Ct., 1934-35; atty. and spl. asst. to atty. gen. Office Solicitor Gen., Dept. Justice, 1935-41; solicitor U.S. Dept. Labor, 1941-42; solicitor U.S. Dept. Interior, 1942-46, asst. sec., 1946-47; mem. firm Shea & Gardner, Washington, from 1947; dir. Natomas Co., 1971-76; spl. counsel Fed. Maritime Bd., 1957; chmn. informal action com. Adminstrv. Conf. U.S., 1968-76; life trustee Bermuda Biol. Sta., 1991—. Author: Building and Loan Liquidity, 1931, Taxation of Government Bondholders and Employees, 1938; Contbr. articles to mags. Served with AUS, 1943-45. Decorated Legion of Merit; Croix de Guerre. Mem. Phi Beta Kappa. Mem. Soc. of Friends. Clubs: Metropolitan, Cosmos.

GARDNER, WILFORD ROBERT, physicist, educator; b. Logan, Utah, Oct. 19, 1925; s. Robert and Nellie (Barker) G.; m. Marjorie Louise Cole, June 9, 1949; children: Patricia, Robert, Caroline. BS, Utah State U., 1949; MS, Iowa State U., 1951, PhD, 1953. Physicist U.S. Salinity Lab., Riverside, Calif., 1953-66; prof. U. Wis., Madison, 1966-80; physicist, prof., head dept. soil and water sci. U. Ariz., Tucson, 1980-87; dean coll. natural resources U. Calif., Berkeley, 1987-94; dean emeritus, 1994—; adj. prof. Utah State U., 1995—. Author: Soil Physics, 1972. Served with U.S. Army, 1943-46. NSF sr. fellow, 1959; Fulbright fellow, 1971-72. Fellow AAAS, Am. Soc. Agronomy; mem. Internat. Soil Sci. Soc. (pres. physics commn. 1968-74), Soil Sci. Soc. Am. (pres. 1990, Rsch. award 1962), Nat. Acad. Scis.

GARDNER, WILLIAM EARL, university dean; b. Hopkins, Minn., Oct. 11, 1928; s. William Henry and Ida (Swenson) G.; m. Crystal K. Meriwether, July 5, 1990; children by previous marriage: Mary Gardner Fenwick, Bret, Anne Gardner Smith, Eric. B.S., U. Minn., 1950, M.A., 1959, Ph.D., 1961. Tchr. pub. schs. Balaton, Rockford, New Ulm, Minn., 1950-54; instr. Univ. High Sch., U. Minn., Mpls., 1954-61; prof. edn. U. Minn., 1961—; assoc. dean U. Minn. (Coll. Edn.), 1970-76, dean, 1976-91, dean emeritus, 1991—; dir. Minn. Curriculum Lab., 1965-67; vis. prof. U. York, Eng., 1967-68; Mem. Bd. Edn., St. Louis Park, Minn., 1971-77; mem. Tchr. Standards and Certification Commn., 1973-80; mem. Nat. Council Accreditation of Tchr. Edn., 1979-85; chmn. Minn. Council Econ. Edn., 1985-87; trustee Joint Council Econ. Edn., 1985—. Author: (with others) Education and Social Crisis, 1967, Social Studies in Secondary Schools, 1970, Selected Case Studies in Am. History, 1971, The Education of Tchrs., 1982. Mem. Nat. Coun. Social Studies, Am. Ednl. Rsch. Assn., Am. Assn. Colls. for Tchr. Edn. (bd. dirs. 1984-87, pres. 1987-88), Assn. Supervision and Curriculum Devel., Luth. Human Rels. Assn., Phi Delta Kappa. Lutheran. Office: U Minn Coll Edn 136 B Burton Hall 178 Pillsbury Dr SE Minneapolis MN 55455-0296

GARDNER, WILLIAM MICHAEL, state official; b. Manchester, N.H., Oct. 26, 1948; s. William George and Mildred Irene (Claus) G.; m. Kathleen Gordon, May 21, 1978; children: William Gordon, Kathleen Meghan. BA, U. N.H., 1970; diploma, London Sch. Econs., 1972; ME, U. N.C., Greensboro, 1973; MPA, Harvard U., 1985. Mem. N.H. Ho. of Reps., Concord, 1973-76; sec. state State of N.H., Concord, 1976—; chmn. N.H. Mcpl. Records Bd., 1978—. Editor: Towns Against Tyranny: Hills Borough County New Hampshire During the American Revolution 1775-83, 1976, New Hampshire: The State That Made Us a Nation, 1989. Mem. exec. com. Hillsborough County, N.H., 1973-74; chmn. Manchester Del., 1974-75; trustee Belanger-Gardner Found., Bishop's U., Can., 1985—. Democrat. Roman Catholic. Office: Office Sec. State State House Rm. 204 Concord NH 03301-3222*

GARDOCKI, CHRISTOPHER, football player; b. Stone Mountain, Ga., Feb. 7, 1970; m. Sally Gardocki. Student, Clemson U. Punter Chgo. Bears, 1991-94, Indpls. Colts, 1995-98, Cleve. Browns, 1998—; co-creator game NFL Trivia Blitz. Named to Pro Bowl, 1996. Office: Cleve Browns 1085 W 3rd St Cleveland OH 44114 also: PO Box 535000 Indianapolis IN 46253-5000*

GARDOM, GARDE BASIL, lieutenant governor of British Columbia; b. Banff, Alta., Can., July 17, 1924; s. Basil and Gabrielle Gwladys (Bell) G.; m. Theresa Helen Eileen Mackenzie, Feb. 11, 1956; children: Kim Gardom Allen, Karen Gardom MacDonald, Edward, Brione Gardom MacDonald, Brita Gardom McLaughlin. BA, LLB, U. B.C., Vancouver, 1949. Bar: called to bar 1949. With Campbell, Brazier & Co., 1949; sr. partner Gardom & Co., Vancouver, 1960-75; apptd. Queen's Counsel, 1975; mem. B.C. Legis. Assembly for Vancouver-Point Grey, B.C., 1966-87; atty. gen. B.C., 1975-79, min. intergovtl. rels., 1979-86; policy cons. Office of Premier, 1986-87; agt. gen. for B.C. London, 1987-92; mem. Premier's Econ. Adv. Coun., 1988-91; apptd. lt.-gov. B.C., 1995—; dir. Crown Life Ins. Co., 1993-95. Named to B.C. Sports Hall of Fame, 1995; named Freeman of City of London, 1992. Mem. Can. Bar Assn., B.C. Law Soc., Vancouver Lawn Tennis and Badminton Club, Union Club of B.C., Royal Overseas Club, Phi Delta Theta. Anglican. Office: Govt House, 1401 Rockland Ave, Victoria, BC Canada V8S 1V9

GARDUNIO, JOSEPH, landscaping company executive; b. Chgo., Feb. 12, 1955; m. Marta Salas; children: Joey, Ricky, Alex, Selena. Pres. Unico Landscaping Inc., 1991—. Office: Unico Landscaping Inc 5119 S Hoyne Ave Chicago IL 60609-5513

GARELICK, MARTIN, retired transportation executive; b. Rochester, N.Y., May 18, 1924; s. Samuel and Esther (Gerber) G.; m. Betty J. Mann, Jan. 18, 1951. B.S.C.E., Purdue U., 1947. With Milw. Rd. R.R., 1947-78; asst. v.p. mktg. devel. and planning Milw. Rd. R.R., Chgo., 1973-76; v.p. ops. Milw. Rd. R.R., 1976-78; exec. v.p., chief operating officer AMTRAK, Washington, 1978-80; v.p. Wyer, Dick & Co., Chgo., 1980-82; v.p., gen. mgr. N.J. Transit Rail Ops., Newark, 1982-84; dir. Kyle Rys., Inc., Scottsdale, Ariz., 1979-97; ret., 1997. Served with U.S. Army, 1943-46. Mem. Am. Soc. Traffic and Logistics, Am. Assn. R.R. Supts., Tau Epsilon Phi. Jewish. Home: 20876 Del Luna Dr Boca Raton FL 33433-1788

GARELICK, MELVIN STEWART, engineering educator, aerospace engineer; b. N.Y.C., Feb. 7, 1945; s. Martin Israel and Elizabeth Garelick; m. Jacqueline Gail Lipnick, Dec. 24, 1970; children: Rachel, Joanna, Adam. BS in Aero. and Astro., MIT, 1966, MS in Aero. and Astro., 1967, BSEE, 1970; PhD in Mech. Engring., Yale U., 1988. Registered profl. engr., Conn. Mech. engr. Sci. Energy Systems, Inc., Waltham, Mass., 1973-76; aero. engr. Grumman Aerospace Corp., Bethpage, N.Y., 1977-82; sr. mech. engr. Perkin-Elmer Corp., Danbury, Conn., 1982-85; asst. prof. mech. engring. Worcester (Mass.) Poly. Inst., 1988-90; asst. prof. engring. U.S. Merchant Marine Acad., Kings Point, N.Y., 1990-93; assoc. prof. mech. engring. BEI Sch. Engring. Fairfield (Conn.) U., 1996—; lectr. in engring. tech. Ctrl. Conn. State U., New Britain, 1999. Contbr. articles to Jour. Am. Helicopter Soc., Compters in Edn. Jour. Recipient James Means Meml. prize MIT, 1966. Mem. Am. Soc. Engring. Edn. (Merl K. Miller award 1994, 96, 98), Tau Beta Pi, Sigma Xi. Democrat. Jewish. Achievements include research in computational fluid mechanics; aerodynamic design of wing and canard X29 forward-swept-wing technology demonstrator aircraft. Home and Office: 52 Fawn Meadow Dr Trumbull CT 06611-1646

GARELL, PAUL CHARLES, family practice physician; b. Williamsport, Pa., July 18, 1930; s. Paul C. and Della Mary (Deime) G.; m. Teresa Ann Sullivan, Aug. 7, 1954; children: Ann, Della, Paula, P. Charles. BS in Biology, Villanova U., 1952; MD, Hahnemann U., 1956. Intern Williamsport Hosp., 1956-57; resident in aviation medicine USN Hosp., Pensacola, Fla., 1957-58; flight surgeon USN, Norfolk, Va., 1958-60; pvt. practice Beacon, N.Y., 1960-98; founder Park Med. Group, Beacon, 1970; dir. M.V.P. Health Plan, Poughkeepsie, N.Y., 1986-96. Lt. M.C., USN, 1957-60. Fellow Am.

Acad. Family Physicians (chartr); mem. N.Y. State Acad. Family Physicians, Dutchess County Med. Soc. (pres. 1977-78). Avocations: tennis, skiing.

GAREN, ALAN, biophysics professor; b. Bklyn., May 26, 1926; m. 1959; five children. BS, U. Colo., 1945, PhD in Biophysics, 1953. Chemist Oak Ridge Nat. Lab., 1946-48; fellow Nat. Found Infantile Paralysis, Cold Spring Harbor, N.Y., 1951-55; rsch. assoc. Purdue U., Lafayette, Ind., 1955-57; sr. rsch. assoc. Biol. dept. MIT, Cambridge, Mass., 1957-60; from assoc. prof. to prof. Biol. dept. U. Penn., Phila., 1960-63; prof. Molecular Biophysics and Biochemistry Yale U., New Haven, CT, 1963—; prof. Genetics Yale U., 1970—; Guggenheim fellow, 1970. Recipient Waksman Medal in Microbiology, 1962. Mem. Fellow AAAS; Nat. Acad. Scis. Office: Dept Molecular Biophysics and Biochemistry Yale U Kline Biology Tower New Haven CT 06511

GAREY, DONALD LEE, pipeline and oil company executive; b. Ft. Worth, Sept. 9, 1931; s. Leo James and Jessie (McNatt) G.; m. Elizabeth Patricia Martin, Aug. 1, 1953; children: Deborah Anne, Elizabeth Laird. BS in Geol. Engring., Tex. A&M U., 1953. Registered profl. engr., Tex. Reservoir geologist Gulf Oil Corp., 1953-54, sr. geologist, 1956-65; v.p., mng. dir. Indsl. Devel. Corp. Lea County, Hobbs, N.Mex., 1965-72, dir., 1972-86, pres., 1978-86; v.p., dir. Minerals, Inc., Hobbs, N.Mex., 1966-72; pres., dir. Minerals, Inc., Hobbs, 1972-86, CEO, 1978-82; mng. dir. Hobbs Indsl. Found. Corp., 1965-72, dir., 1965-76; v.p. Llano, Inc., 1972-74, exec. v.p., COO, 1974-75, pres., 1975-86, CEO, also dir., 1978-82; pres., CEO Pollution Control, Inc., 1969-81; pres. NMESCO Fuels, Inc., 1982-86; chmn., pres., CEO Estacado, Inc., 1986—, Natgas Inc., 1987—; pres. Llano Co2, Inc., 1984-86; cons. geologist, geol. engr., Hobbs, 1965-72. Chmn. Hobbs Manpower Devel. Tng. Adv. Com., 1965-72; mem. Hobbs Adv. Com. for Mental Health, 1965-67; chmn. N.Mex. Mapping Adv. Com., 1968-69; mem. Hobbs adv. bd. Salvation Army, 1967-78, chmn., 1970-72; mem. exec. bd. Conquistador coun. Boy Scouts Am., Hobbs, 1965-75; vice chmn. N.Mex. Gov's Com. for Econ. Devel., 1968-70; bd. regents Coll. Southwest, 1982-85. Capt. USAF, 1954-56. Mem. AIPG, AAPG, SPE of AIME. Home: 315 E Alto Dr Hobbs NM 88240-3905 Office: Broadmoor Tower PO Box 5587 Hobbs NM 88241-5587

GAREY, PATRICIA MARTIN, artist; b. State College, Miss., Nov. 11, 1932; d. Verey G. Martin and Eva Myrtle Jones; m. Donald L. Garey, Aug. 1, 1953; children: Deborah Anne Garey Furst, Elizabeth Laird Garey Spurlock. BS in Costume Design, Tex. Women's U., 1953; MFA, Tex. Tech. U., 1973; postgrad. in art history, Two-Dimensional Studio Art, 1970-73. Prodn. mgr. Cox Advt. Agy., Roswell, N.M., 1958-63; art instr. Coll. of Southwest, Hobbs, N.M., 1967-69, 72-73; artist-in-residence N. Mex. Arts Commn., Santa Fe and Hobbs, 1974-76; studio artist Hobbs, 1976—; prof. art/painting and drawing N.Mex. Jr. Coll., 1997—; instr. Cloudcroft (N.Mex.) Artists Sch., 1991, prof. drawing, painting N.Mex. Jr. Coll., prof. art hist. Coll. of Southwest. One-woman shows include N.Mex. Jr. Coll., Hobbs, 1969, Coll. of SW, 1974, 79, Sangre de Cristo Arts Ctr., Pueblo, 1979, U. Tex. of Permian Basin, Odessa, 1980, N.Mex. Jr. Coll.; represented at Beverly Gordon Gallery, Dallas, Sylvia Ullman Am. Crafts, Cleve., Design Today, Lubbock Tex., El-Dor Galleries Old-Town, Albuquerque, Galeria de la Paloma, Santa Fe; work exhibited at Roswell Mus. Art, Southeastern N.Mex. Small Painting Exhibit (2d pl., 1966), Llano Estacado Art Exhbn. 1967 (Hon. Mention Oil Painting), 68 (2d pl. Graphics), 69 (Hon. Mention Graphics, 2d pl. Sculpture, 2d pl. Acrylics), 75 (1st pl. Ceramics), 76 (1st pl. Drawing, 2d pl. Painting), Americas Gallery, Taos, 1974, Blair Gallery, Santa Fe, 1974, Mus. Fine Arts, Santa Fe, 1976, Tex. Tech. U., 1977, Little Rock Art Ctr., Ark., 1978, Hills Gallery, Santa Fe, 1979, Dallas Mus. Fine Art, 1986, 87, 88, 90, Beaux Arts Ball Art Auction, 1990, Okla. City Mus. Art, Little Rock Art Ctr., El Paso (Tex.) Sun Carnival, Govs. Gallery, State Capitol, Santa Fe, 1997; represented in collections Beverly Gordon Gallery, Dallas, Tex. Tech. U., The Round House/State Capitol, Santa Fe, Villa Maria Ctr. for the Arts, Perugia, Italy; docent Meadows Mus. of Art So. Meth. U., Dallas, 1990. Bd. dirs. The Bridge Breast Ctr., Dallas, 1992—, S.W. Symphony, Hobbs, 1987-99. Recipient Best of Show award L.E.A.A. Regional Show, Hobbs, N.Mex., 1996, 98. Mem. Delta Phi Delta, Chi Omega. Democrat. Methodist. Avocations: swimming (mem. Sr. Olympics Swim Team 1997), southern cooking, skiing, classical music, book collecting. Studio: 315 E Alto Dr Hobbs NM 88240-3905 also: Piney Woods Cloudcroft NM 88350

GARFIELD, ERNEST, bank consultant; b. Colorado River, Ariz., July 14, 1932; s. Emil and Carmen (Ybarra) G.; m. Betty Ann Redden, Apr. 18, 1953; children: Laural, Jeffery Alan. BS, U. Ariz., 1975; B of Internat. Mgmt., Am. Grad. Sch., Phoenix, 1975, M of Internat. Mgmt., 1976. Owner Garfield Ins. Agy., Tucson, 1962-70; senator State of Ariz., Phoenix, 1967-68, dep. treas., 1970-71, treas., 1971-74; commr. Ariz. Corp. Commn., Phoenix, 1974-79; chmn. United Bancorp Systems, Inc., Phoenix, 1979—, Interstate Bank Developers, Inc., Scottsdale, 1994—; chmn. The White House Conf. on Energy, Com. on Energy Policy of Nat. Assn. Regulatory Utility Commn.; pres. Western Conf. Pub. Svc. Commns.; mem. Ad Hoc Com. on Regulatory Reform, Electric and Nuclear Energy Com. Mem. Ariz. Kidney Found., Multiple Sclerosis Soc., Rep. Senatorial Inner Circle, 1989; mem. Pres. Bush Task Force, 1989; mem. adv. bd. St. Joseph's Hosp., Phoenix; mem. establishment com. Pima County Jr. Coll., Tucson; mem. orgn. com. Pima County Halfway House, Tucson; chmn. Ariz. Gov. Commn. on Rape Prevention, 1988, Nat. Commn. on Rape Prevention, 1990—; commr. Ariz. Gov. Commn. on Violence Against Women, 1993—. With U.S. Army, 1952-55. Recipient Outstanding Young Men Ariz. award, Press Club award; named to U.S. Army. Hall of Fame, 1999. Mem. Ariz.-Mexican C. of C., Thunderbird Internat. Banking Inst. (mem. adv. coun. 1990—). Republican. Roman Catholic. Avocations: graphology. Home and Office: 8442 N 72nd Pl Scottsdale AZ 85258-2762

GARFIELD, GERALD, lawyer; b. Detroit, Jan. 9, 1946; s. Benjamin Robert and Merle (Rosenberg) G.; m. Diana Feldman, Mar. 4, 1977; children: Jeremy, Stephanie, Jameson. BA with honors, U. Mich., 1968, JD cum laude, 1971. Bar: Conn. 1971, U.S. Dist. Ct. Conn. 1971. Assoc. Day, Berry & Howard, Hartford, Conn., 1971-77, ptnr., 1978—; lawyers com. Nuclear Energy Inst. Dir. Hartford Stage Co., 1980-87. Mem. Internat. Bar Assn, Fed. Energy Bar Assn., Conn. Bar Assn. (pub. utility law sect., 1972—), Assn. of the Bar N.Y.C. (energy sect. 1988—). Avocations: skiing, golf. Office: Day Berry & Howard CityPlace I 185 Asylum St Hartford CT 06103-3499

GARFIELD, JOAN BARBARA, statistics educator; b. Milw., May 4, 1950; d. Sol. L. and Amy L. (Nusbaum) G.; m. Michael G. Luxenberg, Aug. 17, 1980; children: Harlan Ross and Rebecca Ellen (twins). Student, U. Chgo., 1968; BS, U. Wis., 1972; MA, U. Minn., 1978, PhD, 1981. Assoc. prof. ednl. psychology Coll. Edn., U. Minn., Mpls., 1995—, coord. rsch. and evaluation The Gen. Coll., 1984-87. Mem. Am. Ednl. Rsch. Assn., Nat. Coun. Tchrs. of Math., Internat. Assn. for Statis. Edn. (v.p. 1997—), Am. Statis. Assn., Internat. Study Group on Learning Probability and Stats. (sec. 1987-95). Jewish. Office: U Minn Dept Edn Psychology 332 Burton Hall Minneapolis MN 55455

GARFIELD, LESLIE JEROME, real estate executive; b. N.Y.C., Mar. 23, 1932; s. Jack and Anne (Weinert) G.; m. Johanna Rosengarten, Sept. 28, 1960; children: Clare Louisa, Jed Herbert, Cory Alexander. BA, U. Wis., Madison, 1953; MA, Harvard U., 1956; MBA, Columbia U., 1958. V.p. Pease & Elliman, Inc., N.Y.C., 1965-68, William A. White & Sons, Inc., N.Y.C., 1968-78; pres. Leslie J. Garfield & Co., Inc., N.Y.C., 1978—; bd. dirs. Internat. Print Ctr. Chmn. bd. dirs. N.Y. Youth Symphony, 1986, pres. bd. dirs., 1975-86; bd. dirs. Carnegie Hill Neighbors, N.Y.C., 1985—; coun. mem. Elvehjem Mus. Art; mem. com. on prints and illustrated books Mus. Modern Art. Mem. Real Estate Bd. N.Y. (chmn. sales brokers com. 1985-86), The Drawing Soc. (bd. dirs.), Century Assn., Nat. Arts Club (coun. mem.), Grolier Club (mem. coun.). Avocation: print collecting. Office: 654 Madison Ave New York NY 10021-8404

GARFIELD, NANCY ELLEN, marketing and advertising professional; b. Cin., Sept. 18, 1954; d. M. Robert and Pegge (Gerber) G. BA in Econs., Rollins Coll., 1976; MBA, Xavier U., 1980. Mktg. svcs. specialist Am. Standard, Inc., Cin., 1977-81; mktg. specialist F.H. Lawson Co., Cin., 1982-83; dir. mktg. Talsol Corp./Mar-Hyde subs. RPM Inc., Cin., 1983-88; pvt. practice Cin., 1988—. Mgmt. advisor Cin. Jr. Achievement, 1978-81; bd. dirs. Cin. sect. mem. Nat. Coun. Jewish Women, 1992-96, v.p. cmty. svc. 1993-95, pres. 1995-96; mem. Cin. Civic Confedn., 1991-95; mem. recruitment com. Big Bros./Big Sisters Assn. Cin., 1992-94; mem. employers choice adv. com. Jewish Vocat. Svc., 1997—; mem. home instrn. program for preschschoolers adv. com. YWCA, 1995—; mem. pub. policy com. Cin. Mayor's Commn. on Children, 1995—. Mem. Cin. Indsl. Advertisers, Chi Omega.

GARFIELD, ROBERT EDWARD, newspaper columnist; b. Phila., June 20, 1955; s. Samuel M. Garfield and Nancy G. Rowen; m. Carla Patricia Cain, Dec. 16, 1977; children—Kathryn Sarah, Allison Patricia. B.A., Pa. State U., 1977. Reporter Reading Times, Pa., 1977-81; reporter Wilmington News-Jour., Del., 1981-82; columnist USA Today, Washington, 1982-85, Crain News Service and Advt. Age, Washington, 1985—; corr. Nat. Public Radio, 1986—. Host Ad Age Reports program Fin. News Network, 1989-91; polit. advt. analyst CBS This Morning, 1992; contbg. writer Washington Post Mag., 1985-97; corr. Here and Now, Sta. WETA-TV, 1995; contbg. editor Civilization Mag., 1996; contbg. columnist U.S.A. Today, 1995—; contbr. CNBC "Power Lunch", 1996—, Adam Smith's Money Game, 1998; author: Waking Up Screaming from the American Dream, 1997. Recipient Keystone award Pa. Newspaper Pubs. Assn., 1981, Best of Gannett award Gannett Co. Inc., 1982, journalism award Saatchi & Saatchi/Compton Advt., 1984, 85, award Am. Soc. Bus. Press Editors, 1994, Neal award Am. Bus. Press, 1996. Mem. Nat. Press Club. Jewish.

GARFIN, LOUIS, actuary; b. Mason City, Iowa, June 7, 1917; s. Sam and Etta (Larner) G.; m. Clarice Fagen, Apr. 11, 1943; children: Eugene Arthur, Erica. Student, Mason City Jr. Coll., 1934-36; B.A., State U. Iowa, 1938, M.S., 1939, Ph.D., 1942. Instr. USAAF, Scott Field, Ill., 1942-43; instr. math. Ill. Inst. Tech., Chgo., 1943, U. Minn., 1943-44; actuary Oreg. Ins. Dept., Salem, 1946-52; asso. actuary Pacific Mut. Life Ins. Co., Los Angeles, 1952-62; actuary Pacific Mut. Life Ins. Co., 1962-64, v.p., chief actuary, 1964-82, cons. actuary, 1982-90; ret., 1990. Bd. dirs. Calif. Health Decisions, 1989-95, chairperson, 1993-94, Laguna Beach Cmty. Clinic, 1989-93; treas. Laguna Canyon Found., 1990-99. Fellow Soc. Actuaries; mem. Am. Acad. Actuaries (v.p. 1976-78), Internat. Congress Actuaries (dir. 1977-80), Actuarial Club Pacific States (pres. 1967-68), Los Angeles Actuarial Club (pres. 1959-60), Am. Math. Soc., Phi Beta Kappa, Sigma Xi. Home: 4013 Arcadia Way Oceanside CA 92056

GARFINKEL, ALAN, Spanish language and education educator; b. Chgo., Sept. 6, 1941; s. Bernard D. and Tillie (Schaffner) G.; m. Sonya Pickus, July 10, 1965; children: Eli Louis, Noah Baruch. BA, U. Ill., 1961, MA, 1963; PhD, Ohio State U., 1969. Tchr. Spanish Waukegan (Ill.) Twp. H.S., 1964-65; asst. prof. Okla. State U., Stillwater, 1969-72; asst. prof. Purdue U., West Lafayette, Ind., 1972-74, assoc. prof., 1974-93, prof., 1993—; cons. Cath. U. of Chile, Santiago, 1976; vis. scholar U. Queensland, Brisbane, Australia, 1993; cons. various publishers and sch. dists., 1972—. Co-author: Modismos al Momento, 1978, Trabajo y Vida, 1983, Explorando en la Casa de los Monstruos, 1997; contbr. articles to profl. jours. Bd. dirs. Congregation Sons Abraham, Lafayette, 1986-93; committeeman Dem. Party, West Lafayette, 1993; co-chair steering com. Profl. Devel. Schs. Consortium, Purdue U.; pres. gov. bd. Purdue U. Hillel Found., 1997—. Recipient Sr. Lectr. award Fulbright Commn., 1978, Acad. Specialist award U.S. State Dept., 1985, Tchr. Ctr. award U.S. Dept. Edn., 1978-81. Mem. MLA, Am. Coun. Teaching Fgn. Langs. (nat. textbook com. 1992), Ind. Fgn. Langs. Tchr.'s Assn. (pres. 1993-95), Lafayette Daybreak Rotary Club (Rotarian of the Yr.) 1997-98, Phi Delta Kappa (del., chpt. pres. 1975). Jewish. Avocation: philatelist. Home: 2229 Carberry Dr West Lafayette IN 47906-1943 Office: Purdue U FLL-SC West Lafayette IN 47907-1359

GARFINKEL, BARRY HERBERT, lawyer; b. Bklyn., June 19, 1928; s. Abraham and Shirley (Siegel) G.; m. Gloria Lorenz, Feb. 16, 1969; children—David, James, Paul. BSS, CCNY, 1950; LLB, Yale U., 1955. Bar: N.Y. State 1955, U.S. Supreme Ct. 1959. Law clk. to Hon. Edward Weinfeld U.S. Dist. Ct., N.Y.C., 1955-56; assoc. Skadden, Arps, Slate, Meagher & Flom, N.Y.C., 1956-61; ptnr. Skadden, Arps, Slate, Meagher & Flom, 1961—; trustee, chmn. Practising Law Inst., Law Ctr. Found. of N.Y. U. Sch. Law Aperture Fedn., program com. 2d. Cir. Jud. Conf. Mng. editor: Yale Law Jour. Bd. dirs., former dir. Jewish Mus., Legal Aid Soc.; dir. Aperture Found.; trustee N.Y. Community Trust; pres. coun. Mus. City of N.Y.; chmn. lawyers' div., spl. gifts campaign United Jewish Appeal/Fedn. Jewish Philanthropies, 1979-81; mem. print com. Whitney Mus., Com. on Rsch. Libraries N.Y. Pub. Lib. Recipient Torch of Learning award Am. Friends of Hebrew U., 1983, Brandeis Distingish. Community Svc. award Brandeis U., 1985. Fellow Am. Coll. Trial Lawyers, Am. Bar Found.; mem. ABA, Am. Arbitration Assn., Assn. of Bar of City of N.Y. (exec. com., judiciary com., past chmn. fed. cts. com.), N.Y. State Bar Assn., Am. Law Inst. Club: Yale (N.Y.C.). Home: 211 Central Park W New York NY 10024-6020 Office: Skadden Arps Slate Meagher & Flom 919 3rd Ave New York NY 10022-3902

GARFINKEL, HARMON MARK, specialty chemicals company executive; b. Bklyn., May 20, 1933; s. Samuel and Elsie (Schwartz) G.; m. Lorraine Plawsky, Mar. 4, 1956; children—Elyse, Michelle. B.A., Bklyn. Coll., 1957; Ph.D., Iowa State U., 1960; postgrad. program for mgmt. devel., Harvard U. Bus. Sch., 1973. Dir. bio-organic tech. Corning Inc., N.Y., 1973-74, dir. applied chemistry and biology, 1974-75, dir. biomed. and chem. tech., 1975-78, dir. research, 1978-85; v.p. R&D Engelhard Corp., Edison, N.J., 1985-95, cons., 1995—; instr. math. Elmira Coll., 1964. Patents and publs. in field. Mem. AAAS, Am. Chem. Soc., Am. Phys. Soc., Am. Inst. Chemists, Am. Ceramics Soc. Republican. Jewish. Home: 3836 Outlook Ct Jupiter FL 33477-1309

GARFINKEL, HERBERT, university official; b. N.Y.C., June 16, 1920; s. Julius Louis and Gertrude (Goldstone) G.; m. Evelyn Epstein, Sept. 3, 1940; children—Laura, Paul. M.A., U. Chgo., 1950, Ph.D., 1956. Instr. polit. sci. Ill. Inst. Tech., 1948-51; research asst. Nat. Opinion Research Ctr., U. Chgo., 1950-51; instr. Mich. State U., 1951-53; asst. prof. Dartmouth, 1953-59; faculty Mich. State U., East Lansing, 1959—; prof. polit. sci. Mich. State U., 1964-73; dean James Madison Coll., 1966-73; provost, vice chancellor acad. affairs U. Nebr., Omaha, 1973-78, interim chancellor, 1977-78; v.p. acad. affairs and prof. polit. sci. U. Louisville, 1978-85, v.p. emeritus, prof. emeritus, 1985—; NATO prof. Inst. Social Studies, The Hague, Netherlands, 1965-66. Author: When Negroes March, 1959, 2d edit., 1969, (co-author) The Democratic Republic, 1966, 2d edit., 1970, The Constitution and The Legislature, 1961; contbr. articles to profl. jours. Served as officer U.S. Mcht. Marine, 1943-45. Ctr. for Advanced Study Behavioral Scis. fellow, 1958-59; research fellow Social Sci. Research Council, 1960-61. Mem. Am. Polit. Sci. Assn. Home: 4204 N Timber Cir Peoria IL 61614-7864 Office: U Louisville Dept of Political Sci Louisville KY 40292

GARFINKEL, JANE E., lawyer; b. N.Y.C., Dec. 2, 1952; d. Albert E. and Rita H. (Halpern) G.; m. Louis F. Solimine, May 20, 1979. BA, Wheaton Coll., 1974; MA, U. Mich., 1975, JD, 1979. Bar: Ohio 1980. Assoc. Smith & Schnacke, Cin., 1980-88, ptnr., 1988-89; ptnr. Thompson, Hine & Flory, Cin., 1989—. Office: Thompson Hine & Flory 312 Walnut St Ste 1400 Cincinnati OH 45202-4089

GARFINKEL, LAWRENCE SAUL, academic administrator, educator, television producer; b. N.Y.C., Mar. 9, 1932; s. Benjamin and Rose (Rochkind) G.; m. Adrienne Rederer, June 26, 1960; children: Andrew, Rodger, Craig. BS in Art Edn., NYU, 1953, MA in Higher Edn., 1955, postgrad. in Edn., 1975. Tchr., supr. art, prin. high schs. West Hempstead Pub. Schs., N.Y., 1954-56, dir. related arts, 1957-69, dir. cmty. rels., 1961-71; prof. edn. adminstrn. and comm., dir. instrnl. comm. program Hofstra U., Hempstead, N.Y., 1969-76; dir. gifted programs Sachem Pub. Schs., Lake Ronkonkoma, N.Y., 1978-79; dir. ednl. comm. Coll. Dentistry, Kriser Dental Ctr., NYU, 1979-91, ret.; adj. prof. dept. speech Baruch Coll., CUNY, 1980-82, Adelphi U., C.W. Post-L.I. Univ., 1991—, Stern Coll.-Yeshiva U., St. Johns U., Temple U.; adj. assoc. prof. Nassau C.C.; cons. bd. regents N.Y. State Edn. Dept., Ctr. Urban Edn., N.Y.C. Editor: Restorative Dentistry, 1985; illustrator: Classroom Television, 1970; illustrator N.Y. Times, John Huston Prodns., Century Theatres, Nat. Audio Visual Assn., and numerous publs.; editl. cartoonist Merrick Life; asst. prodr. WPIX-TV; pub. Garson Assocs.; contbr. articles to profl. jours. Coord. youth edn. Mothers Against Drunk Driving, Long Island Area, 1997-99; bd. dirs. Hist. Soc. Merricks, 1983—, Higher Edn. Assn. TV, 1972; v.p. Health Equities, N.Y.C.; oral historian Bi Centennial Commn., 1975. Recipient Grad. Arch award medal NYU, numerous awards Nat. Com. Sch. Pub. Rels.; grad. fellow NYU. Mem. N.Y. Acad. Scis., L.I. Art Tchrs. Assn. (pres. 1967-68), Nat. Com. Art Edn. (co-pres. 1967). Avocations: illustrating, lecturing on communications theory, arts, visual literacy, teaching. Home and Office: Garson Assocs 172 Babylon Tpke Merrick NY 11566-4407

GARFINKEL, LEE, advertising agency executive; married; 2 children. BA, CUNY. From copywriter to exec. v.p., exec. creative dir. Levine, Huntley, Schmidt & Beaver; exec. v.p., sr. creative dir., also dir. BBDO; creative officer, chmn. Lowe & Ptnrs./SMS, N.Y.C., 1992—; stand-up comedian and musician. Named 1986 East Coast All-Star Team as Best TV Copywriter, Adweek, Creative Dir. of Yr. on 1994 Nat. Creative All-Star Team; selected ann. Forty Under Forty feature Crain's New York Bus.; named one of top three creative dirs. as well as number one copywriter in U.S., Winners mag., 1989; inducted in Am. advt. Fedn. Hall of achievement. Mem. One Club for Art and Copy (bd. dirs., pres. 1992-95). Avocations: song writing, collecting guitars, animated art, cars. Office: Lowe & Ptnrs/SMS 1114 Ave of Americas New York NY 10036-7703*

GARFINKEL, NEIL B., lawyer; b. New Hyde Park, N.Y., Jan. 29, 1964; s. Elliot Z. and Diana (Fein) G.; m. Shari Chaitin, Aug. 14, 1988; children: Alyssa Hope, Joshua Phillip. BA summa cum laude, SUNY, Albany, 1986; JD, Cornell U., 1989. Bar: N.Y. 1990. Assoc. Proskauer, Rose, Goetz & Mendelsohn, N.Y.C., 1989-91, Bank & Bank, Garden City, N.Y., 1992-94; pntr. Abrams, Garfinkel & Rosen, LLP, N.Y.C., 1994—. Mem. N.Y. State Bar Assn., Phi Beta Kappa. Office: Abrams Garfinkel & Rosen LLP 370 Lexington Ave Rm 802 New York NY 10017-6503 also: 12301 Wilshire Blvd Ste 402 Los Angeles CA 90025

GARFINKEL, PATRICIA GAIL, speech writer, policy analyst, poet; b. N.Y.C., Feb. 15, 1938; d. Wynn E. Walker and Rose Davis; divorced; children: Jon A. Garfinkel, Jef Adam Garfinkel. BA, NYU, 1959; studied poetry with Poet Henry Taylor, Va., 1972-75. Speech writer U.S. Ho. of Reps. Com. on Sci., Washington, 1976-94; speechwriter Nat. Sci. Found., Arlington, Va., 1995—. Author (books of poetry): Ram's Horn, 1980, From the Red Eye of Jupiter, 1990 (award). Poetry posted in pub. places, N.Y.C., including 2000 buses. Avocations: sketching, painting. E-mail: pgarfink@nsf.gov. Home: 900 N Stuart St 1001 Arlington VA 22203

GARG, AJAY, systems administrator; b. Ghaziabad, India, Aug. 8, 1964; s. Kailash Chandra Gupta and Sushila Mittal Devi; m. Anju Tandon Garg, Mar. 13, 1994; 1 child, Vandana. BSc, Delhi U., 1986, MSc, 1988; Diploma in Sys. Mgmt., NIIT, New Delhi, 1989. Statis. analyst Dte of N.M.E.P., Delhi, India, 1989-90; programmer Parle Biscuits Ltd., Delhi, 1990-93; sys. exec. Parle Biscuits Ltd., $, 1993-94, asst. sys. mgr., 1995—. Avocations: soft music, sketching, problem solving. Home: 223 Swastik Kunj Sector 13, 110085 Delhi India Office: Parle Biscuits Ltd, Delhi-Rohtak Rd, 124507 Bahadurgarh India

GARG, DEVENDRA, financial executive; b. Mathura, India, Feb. 14, 1948; came to U.S., 1972; s. Lalta Prasad and Sushila (Elhence) G.; m. Manju Gupta, May 8, 1973; children: Sumeet, Preeti. BSc, U. Allahabad, India, 1967; BE, ME, Indian Inst. Sci., Bangalore, 1970, 72; MBA, Rensselaer Poly. Inst., Troy, N.Y., 1977. Product analyst Comten/Univac, Hartford, Conn., 1973-77; audit specialist, then mgr. region audit Xerox Corp., Rochester, N.Y., 1977-85; mgr. cost devel. and control, strategic fin. analysis Xerox Corp., Webster, N.Y., 1985-87, mgr. planning and analysis Reprographics Bus. Unit, 1987-89, mgr. bus. analysis, 1989-90, mgr. fin. planning and systems devel., 1990-92, contr. worldwide mfg., 1992-95; v.p. fin. ops. U.S. customer ops. Xerox Corp., Rochester, 1995-96, v.p. fin prodn. sys., 1997—; adj. faculty St. John Fisher Coll., Rochester, 1988-91. Mem. budget steering com. Rochester Sch. Bd., 1989-91; treas. Sch. Indian Culture, Rochester, 1990-91; bd. dirs. United Way of Rochester, 1994—. Avocations: travel, reading, geopolitical structures. Home: 7 Roxbury Ln Pittsford NY 14534-4202 Office: Xerox Corp 290 Woodcliff Dr Fairport NY 14450-4212

GARG, DEVENDRA PRAKASH, mechanical engineer, educator; b. Roorkee, India, Mar. 22, 1934; came to U.S., 1965; s. Chandra Gopal and Godawari (Devi) G.; m. Prabha Govil, Nov. 19, 1961; children: Nisha, Seema. BSc, Agra (India) U., 1954; BSME, U. Roorkee, 1957; MS, U. Wis., Madison, 1960; PhD, NYU, 1969. Lectr. mech. engring. U. Roorkee, 1957-62, reader, 1962-65, vis. prof., 1978; instr. NYU, 1965-69; asst. prof. MIT, Cambridge, 1969-71, assoc. prof., 1971-72, chmn. engring. projects lab., 1971-72, lectr., 1972-75, vis. prof., 1976-80; prof. Duke U., Durham, N.C., 1972—, dir. undergrad. studies dept. mech. engring. and materials sci., 1977-86; vis. prof. dept. automatic control Georgian Tech. U., Tbilisi, USSR, 1988; program dir. dynamic sys. and control program civil and mech. sys. divsn. NSF, Washington, 1992-98; chmn. strategic planning and evaluation com. Directorate for Engring., 1994-95; invited fellow Japan Sci. and Tech. Agy., Mech. Engring. Lab., Tsukuba Sci. City, Japan, 1997. Author: An Introduction to the Theory and Use of the Analog Computer, 1963, A Textbook of Descriptive Geometry, 1964; assoc. editor Jour. Dynamic Systems, Measurement, and Control, 1971-73, Jour. Interdisciplinary Modeling and Simulation, 1978-80; assoc. editor Internat. Jour. of Knowledge-Based Intelligent Engring. Systems, 1997—, edit. adv. bd. Internat. Jour. of Intelligent Control and Systems, 1995—. Tech. Coop. Mission Merit scholar U. Wis., 1960; recipient Founder's Day award NYU, 1969, Fulbright Sr. scholar award, 1987-88, cert. of commendation Acoustical Soc. Am., 1983; U.S. dept. Transp. faculty fellow, 1980-81, NASA/ASEE faculty fellow, 1986-87, U.S. Army faculty fellow, 1988; sr. fellow Japan Soc. Promotion Sci., Tokyo Inst. tech., 1996, Cert. of Appreciation NASA, 1987, U.S. Dept. of Transp., 1981. Fellow ASME (reviewer, co-guest editor spl. issues on ground transp. 1974, socioecon. and ecol. sys. 1976, sec. dynamic sys. and control divsn. 1980-83, vice chmn. 1984-85, chmn. divsn. 1985-86, cert. of appreciation tech. and society divsn. 1986-87, chmn. adv. panel on DSCD 1987-88, 89-98, chmn. honors com. 1987-88, mem. nat. nominating com. 1989-94, mem. sys. and design group operating bd. 1989—, vice chmn. 1994-95, mem. publ. com. bd. on comm. 1995—, Dedicated Svc. award 1996, Leadership award 1998). Home: 2815 Dekalb St Durham NC 27705-5601 Office: Duke U Sch Engring PO Box 90300 Durham NC 27708-0300

GARG, PREM K., civil engineer; b. Raman Mandi, Punjab, India, May 14, 1944; s. Chanan R. and Parsini D. G.; m. Sunita Gupta, May 5, 1973; children: Sherry S., Salil. BS in Civil Engring., Punjab U., 1967; MS in Civil Engring., U. Cin., 1974. Registered profl. engr., Ohio. Engr. City Cin., 1974-79, sr. engr., 1979-84, supervising engr., 1984-90, city stormwater engr., 1990-92, acting supt. sanitation, 1992-93, dept. dir. pub. works, 1993, city engr., 1993—; mem. adv. bd. Coll. Civil and Environ. Engring., U. Cin., 1997-98. Treas. Hindu Soc. Greater Cin., 1992, 93; vol. Clean Sweep-Reading Rd., Cin., 1994, United Way, Cin., 1996. Mem. Am. Pub. Works Assn. (mem. exec. coun. water resource inst. 1991-95), Archs. and Profl. Engrs. in City Svc., Am. Pub. Works Assn., Water Environment Fedn., Engrs. and Scientists Cin. (pres. 1995-96). Avocations: running, reading spiritual material, fine foods. Office: City Cin 801 Plum St Ste 405 Cincinnati OH 45202

GARG, VIJAY KUMAR, telecommunications engineer; b. Jahangirabad, India, July 7, 1938; came to U.S., 1965; s. Reoti S. and Prem V. (Mittal) G.; m. Pushpa Bansal, May 11, 1961; children: Nina Taneja, Meena Dorr, Ravi K. Garg. BS, Banaras U., Varanasi, India, 1960; MS, U. Calif., Berkeley, 1966; PhD, Ill. Inst. Tech., 1973. Registered profl. structral engr., Ill., profl. engr., Ill. Asst. prof. engring. U. Jodhpur, India, 1960-65; structural engr. Chgo. Bridge, Oakbrook, Ill., 1967-69; devel. engr. GMC, Lagrange, Ill., 1969-76; mgr. dynamic rsch. AAR, Chgo., 1976-84; assoc. prof. engring. U. Maine, Orono, 1984-85; dist. mem. tech. staff Bell Labs Lucent Techs., Naperville, Ill., 1985—, Motorola Inc., Arlington Heights, Ill., 1997; vis. prof. elec. and comm. engring. U. Ill., Urbana, 1996-97; adj. prof. engring. Ill. Inst. Tech., Chgo., 1976-84. Author: Wireless and Personal Communications System, 1996, Applications of CDMA in Wireless Communications, 1997, Dynamics of Railway Vehicle System, 1984, Advanced Dynamics, 1984, Principles and Applications of GSM, 1999. Recipient NSF travel grants India, 1984, China, 1985. Fellow ASME, ASCE; mem. IEEE (sr.).

Democrat. Hindu. Avocations: gardening, travel, reading, music. Home: 146 Somerset Rd Hinsdale IL 60521-5429 Office: Lucent Tech Inc Bell Labs 263 Shuman Blvd Naperville IL 60563-1443

GARGARO, JOHN TIMOTHY, financial executive; b. Detroit, Apr. 20, 1954. BS in Acctg., U. Detroit, 1976; MBA, Mich. State U., 1984. CPA Mich. Acct. Peat, Marwick, Mitchell, Detroit, 1974-79; sr. internal auditor Lear Siegler, Inc., Troy, Mich., 1979-81; mgr. corp. audit Allied Signal, Southfield, Mich., 1981-85, Washington, 1981-85; mgr. fin. analysis Bendix Wire/Allied Signal, Farmington Hills, Mich., 1985-86; dir. planning Pulte Home Corp., Bloomfield Hills, Mich., 1986-89; chief fin. officer, treas. Ring Screw Works, Madison Heights, Mich., 1989-93; dir. fin., audit Lear Corp., Southfield, Mich., 1993-95; v.p. European fin. Lear Corp., Frankfurt, Germany, 1995-97; v.p. fin. Chrysler divsn. Lear Corp., Rochester Hills, Mich., 1998; v.p. fin. Ford divsn. Lear Corp., Allen Park, Mich., 1999—. Mem. AICPA, Mich. Assn. CPAs, U. Detroit Alumni Assn., Mich. State U. Alumni Club, Mfg. Alliance. Office: Lear Corp 21557 Telegraph Rd Southfield MI 48034-4248

GARGIULO, ANDREA W., lawyer; b. Hartford, Conn., Apr. 26, 1946; d. Charles M. and Irma S. (Rubin) Weiner; m. Richard A. Gargiulo, Nov. 26, 1975; 1 child, John K. BA, Smith Coll., 1968; JD cum laude, Suffolk U., 1972. Bar: Mass. 1972, U.S. Dist. Ct. Mass. 1975, U.S. Ct. Appeals (11th cir.) 1981, U.S. Supreme Ct. 1983. Asst. dist. atty. Middlesex County, Mass., 1972-75; chmn. Boston Fin. Commn., 1975-77; counsel Gargiulo, Rudnick, & Gargiulo, Boston, 1976—; chmn. Boston Licensing Bd., 1977-89; lectr. Northeastern U. Coll. Criminal Justice, Boston, 1978, 80; bd. dirs. Arbella Mut. Ins. Co.; host (TV show) Women Today, 1994-96. Mem. Mass. Ethics Commn., 1985-88; mem. bd. overseers Children's Hosp., Boston, 1983—; chmn. Mass. Bd. Overseers, 1996. Mem. Bay Club, Beacon Hill Garden Club, Harvard Mus. Assn., Wianno Yacht Club, Univ. Club. Democrat. Avocation: sailing, acting. Home: 13 W Cedar St Boston MA 02108-1211 Office: Gargiulo Rudnick & Gargiulo 66 Long Wharf Boston MA 02110-3605

GARIBALDI, LOUIS E., aquarium administrator. Curator New Eng. Aquarium, 1971-83; with Steinhart Aquarium; curator of fishes Marine World, 1968-69; curator Nat. Fisheries Ctr. & Aquarium, Washington, 1969-71; assoc. dir. N.Y. Aquarium, Bklyn., 1983-88, dir., v.p. aquatic sci., 1988—; v.p. N.Y. Zoological Soc./Wildlife Conservation Soc., 1993—. Recipient Edward H. Bean Meml. award Am. Assn. Zoological Parks & Aquariums, 1992. Office: Aquarium for Wildlife Conservation Boardwalk & W 8th St Brooklyn NY 11224*

GARIBALDI, MARIE LOUISE, state supreme court justice; b. Jersey City, Nov. 26, 1934; d. Louis J. and Marie (Serventi) G. BA, Conn. Coll., 1956; LLB, Columbia U., 1959; LLM in Tax. Law, NYU, 1963. Atty. Office of Regional Counsel, IRS, N.Y.C., 1960-66; assoc. McCarter & English, Newark, 1966-69; ptnr. Riker, Danzig, Scherer, Hyland & Pernutti, Newark, 1969-82; assoc. justice N.J. Supreme Court, Newark, 1982—. Contbr. articles to profl. jours. Trustee St. Peter's Coll.; co-chmn. Thomas Kean's campaign for Gov. of N.J., 1981, mem. transition team, 1981; mem. Gov. Byrne's Commn. on Dept. of Commerce, 1981. Recipient Disting. Alumni award NYU Law Alumni of N.J., 1982; recipient Disting. Alumni award Columbia U., 1982. Fellow Am. Bar Found.; mem. N.J. Bar Assn. (pres. 1982), Columbia U. Sch. Law Alumni Assn. (bd. dirs.). Roman Catholic. Home: 34 Kingswood Rd Weehawken NJ 07087-6930

GARINGER, LOUIS DANIEL, religion educator; b. Johnson City, Tenn.; s. Merrion X. and Hilda (Gasteiger) G.; m. Joanne Mazna, June 21, 1958. A.B., U. Tenn., 1947, J.D., 1949; M.A. in Govt, Harvard, 1957. Staff writer Christian Sci. Monitor Youth Forums, Boston, 1949-51; teaching fellow, tutor govt. Harvard, 1955-58; assoc. dir. Salzburg Seminar in Am. Studies, 1958-60; editorial writer Christian Sci. Monitor, 1965-67, religious affairs editor, 1967-71; research, 1971-72; asso. prof. polit. sci. and religion Principia Coll., Elsah, Ill., 1973-86; dir. Found. Bibl. Research, Charlestown, N.H., 1987-88; vis. scholar Boston U. Sch. Theology, 1980, Grad. Theol. Union, Berkeley, Calif. Contbr. articles to profl. jours. Served with AUS, 1951-53. Recipient Religious Pub. Relations Council merit award, 1969; William E. Leidt award for religious reporting, 1970. Mem. Scarabbean, Pi Kappa Phi, Phi Kappa Phi, Phi Eta Sigma, Sigma Delta Pi, Phi Alpha Eta. Home: 105 Spaulding Hill Rd West Chesterfield NH 03466-3120 *Unless religion means a deep and heartfelt love for God and man expressed in very concrete and practical ways, unless it cuts to the very core of our being and radically changes our lives, it is worth little or nothing.*

GARISON, LYNN LASSITER, real estate executive; b. El Dorado, Ark., Dec. 19, 1954; d. Robert Weaver and Iris Amy (Horton) Lassiter. Student, Randolph-Macon Woman's Coll., 1973-76; BS, Tex. A&M U., 1978. Lic. real estate broker, Tex. From broker assoc. to regional mgr. J. B. Goodwin, Realtors, Residential, Inc., Austin, Tex., 1979-82; comml. broker assoc. Christon Co., Realtors, Inc., Dallas, 1983-87; v.p. Dallas Mkt. Ctr., Dallas, 1987-89; regional v.p. Tenenbaum and Assocs., Inc., Dallas, 1989-92; pres. Artemis Co., Dallas, 1992—; bd. dirs. Consumer Credit Counseling Svc. Bd. dirs. Dallas Coun. World Affairs; mem. Mayor's Task Force on Child Abuse, Highland Pk. Presbyn. Ch. Mem. DAR, Daus. of the Republic of Tex., Nat. Assn. Corp. Real Estate, Cert. Comml. Investment Mem., Urban Land Inst., Rotary Internat. (bd. dirs. Park Cities club, v.p., pres.). Avocations: fly fishing, collecting antique silver. Home: PO Box 12681 Dallas TX 75225-0681

GARLAND, CARL WESLEY, chemist, educator; b. Bangor, Maine, Oct. 1, 1929; s. Cecil G. and Blandena Couillard (Wadell) G.; m. Joan A. Donaghy, July 30, 1955; children: Leslie J., Andrew E. B.S., U. Rochester, 1950; Ph.D., U. Calif.-Berkeley, 1953. Instr. chemistry U. Calif.-Berkeley, 1953; faculty MIT, 1953—, assoc. prof. chemistry, 1959-68, prof. chemistry, 1968-98; prof. emeritus, 1998—; vis. prof. U. Calif., San Diego, 1972, U. Rome, 1974, Cath. U. Leuven, Belgium, 1977, Ben Gurion U., Israel, 1980, U. Paris, 1981, 82, U. Bordeaux, France, 1990; chmn. Gordon Rsch. Conf. Orientational Disorder in Crystals, 1984. Author: (with D.P. Shoemaker, J.W. Nibler) Experiments in Physical Chemistry, 6th edit., 1996; editor: Optics and Spectroscopy, 1960-81, Liquid Crystals, 1991-95; contbr. numerous articles to profl. jours. A.P. Sloan fellow, 1954-60; Guggenheim fellow, 1963. Fellow Am. Acad. Arts and Sci.; mem. Am. Phys. Soc. Home: 4 Edward St Belmont MA 02478-2343 Office: MIT Rm 6-237 Cambridge MA 02139-4307

GARLAND, CEDRIC FRANK, epidemiologist, educator; b. La Jolla, Calif., Nov. 10, 1946; s. Cedric and Eva (Caldwell) Garagliano. BA, U. So. Calif., 1967; MPH, UCLA, 1970, DPH, 1974. Asst. prof. Johns Hopkins U., Balt., 1974-81; prof. U. Calif. Sch. Medicine, La Jolla, 1981—. Contbr. chpts. to books, articles to profl. jours. Chmn. info. resources Physicians for Social Responsibility, San Diego, 1982—. Recipient Aristotle award for acad. excellence UCLA, 1974; Golden Apple award for Teaching Excellence Johns Hopkins U., 1980; Environ. Health Coalition Disting. Service award, 1984; NIH Research Career award, 1982. Fellow Am. Coll. Epidemiology; mem. Am. Coll. Epidemiol., Soc. Epidemiol. Research, Sierra Club (chmn. Save Our Shore 1982—, Disting. Achievement award 1984). Roman Catholic. *Dr. Cedric Garland, working with Dr. Frank Garland and Dr. Edward Gorham, played a role in establishing the association between deficiency of vitamin D and calcium, and risk of intestinal, breast and ovarian cancer. This group also played a role in establishing the ultraviolet A energy, that is an important factor in the etiology of melanoma humans* Office: Dept Family & Preventive Medicine U Calif Dept 0631C 9500 Gilman Dr La Jolla CA 92093-5003

GARLAND, G(ARFIELD) GARRETT, sales executive, golf professional; b. Lakewood, Ohio, Dec. 17, 1946; s. Garfield George and Lois Marie (Calavan) G.; m. Debra Ann Threlkel; children, Brandon Palmer, Blake Hamilton. BA, U. Colo., 1974. Broker Marcus & Millichap, Newport Beach, Calif., 1982-84; v.p. Pacific Coast Fed., Encino, Calif., 1984-85; dir. of acquisitions Prudential Investment Fund, L.A., 1985-86; v.p. A.S.A.I., L.A. and Tokyo, 1986-89; exec. dir. sales Lojack Corp., L.A., 1989—; pres. Collegiate Scholarship Svcs. of Am., 1991-92; cons. Centinela Hosp. Fitness Inst. Mem. Pres.'s Coun. on Competitiveness, 1992, Childhelp USA. Capt. U.S. Army, 1967-71. Mem. VFW, PGA of Am., L.I.F.E. Found., Am. Legion, World Affairs Coun., Internat. Platform Assn., U.S. Ski Team, Natural Historic Preservation Trust. Avocations: golf, reading. Home: 17638 Raymer St Northridge CA 91325 Office: Lojack Corp 9911 W Pico Blvd Ste 1000 Los Angeles CA 90035-2700

GARLAND, HARRY THOMAS, research administrator; b. Detroit, Jan. 18, 1947; s. Harry George and Rose (Bonn) G.; m. Roberta Joy Siciliano; children: Eva, Harry, Brad, Ken. BA, Kalamazoo Coll., 1968; PhD, Stanford U., 1972. Lectr. Stanford (Calif.) U., 1972-73, asst. dept. chmn., 1973-76; pres. Cromemco, Inc., Mountain View, Calif., 1976-89; v.p. Canon Rsch. Ctr., Palo Alto, Calif., 1990—; trustee Kalamazoo (Mich.) Coll., 1986—; pres. bd. Industry Initiatives for Sci. and Math Edn., 1994—. Author: Introduction to Microprocessor System Design, 1979; co-author: Understanding IC Operational Amplifiers, 1971, Understanding CMOS Integrated Circuits, 1975; contbr. articles to profl. jours.; patentee in field. Recipient NIH traineeship, Disting. Alumni award Kalamazoo Coll., 1986. Office: Canon Rsch Ctr 4009 Miranda Ave Palo Alto CA 94304-1218

GARLAND, JAMES C., college president; b. Columbia, Mo., Aug. 11, 1942. BA in Physics, Princeton U., 1964; D in Solid State Physics, Cornell U., 1969; postgrad., Cambridge U., 1969-70. Asst. prof. physics Ohio State U., 1970-75, assoc. prof. physics, 1975-80, prof., 1980-96, chairperson dept. of physics; pres. Miami U., Oxford, Ohio, 1996—; acting vice pres. for rsch. and grad. studies Ohio State U., dir. materials rsch. lab., 1986-90; pres., bd. dirs. Ohio State U. Rsch. Found., 1982-83. Contbr. articles to profl. jours. Recipient numerous rsch. grants; postdoctoral fellowship NSF. Fellow Am. Phys. Soc. Office: Miami U Oxford OH 45056

GARLAND, JAMES H., bishop; b. Wilmington, Ohio, Dec. 13, 1931. Attended, Wilmington (Ohio) Coll.; B.A. Edn., Ohio State U., 1953; M.A. Philosophy, Mt. St. Mary's Sem., Cin., 1960; M.S. Soc. Work, Cath. U., Washington, 1965. Ordained priest Aug. 15, 1959; appointed to the Episcopacy, July 25, 1984. Titular bishop of Garriana; aux. bishop Archdiocese of Cincinnati, 1984-92; bishop Diocese of Marquette, 1992—; chmn. U.S. Catholic Conf. Comm. for the Campaign for Human Dev.; mem. admin. comm. & bd. U.S. Catholic Conf./Nat. Conf. of Catholic Bishops. Address: Pastoral Office 300 Rock St PO Box 550 Marquette MI 49855-0550*

GARLAND, JAMES WILSON, JR., retired physics educator; b. Washington, Aug. 1, 1933; s. James Wilson and May M. (Midgett) G.; m. Katherine Elizabeth Landgraf, Dec. 27, 1958; children—Caroline Elizabeth, Margaret Lee. Student, Oberlin Coll., 1954; MS, U. Chgo., 1958, PhD, 1963. Acting asst. prof. U. Calif., Berkeley, 1963-66; asst. prof. U. Calif., 1966-67; assoc. prof. physics U. Ill., Chgo., 1967-69; prof. U. Ill., 1969-94; retired, 1994; vis. prof. Cambridge U., Eng., 1965; cons. Argonne Nat. Lab., Westinghouse, Gould, Standard Oil. Contbr. articles to profl. jours. Vol. mentoring program Wise Men and Women. With U.S. Army, 1954-56. Sloan Found. fellow, 1964-66. Democrat. Presbyterian. Home: 2889 Tramway Pl NE Albuquerque NM 87122-2277

GARLAND, LINDA M., nursing case manager; b. New Orleans, Sept. 14, 1949; d. Richard Paul Coman and Lula June Tinker; children: Michelle Selvy, Nichole Rene. ADN with honors, Memphis State U., 1977; BSN cum laude, Maryville Coll., 1989. RN, Tenn. Tax examiner IRS, 1968-74; nurse clinician Bapt. Meml. Hosp., Memphis, 1977-83, postpartum unit supr., 1983-93; nursing case mgr. Third Party Claims Mgmt., 1994-97, St. Francis Hosp., Memphis, 1997—. Recipient award of merit Nat. Deans List, 1989. Mem. NAFE, Tenn. Nurses Assn. (One of Top 100 Nurses in Shelby County 1990), Golden Key Nat. Honor Soc., Alpha Lambda Delta. Home: 3787 Eddington Cv Memphis TN 38125-2108

GARLAND, MERRICK BRIAN, federal judge; b. Chgo., Nov. 13, 1952; s. Cyril and Shirley Garland. AB summa cum laude, Harvard U., 1974, JD magna cum laude, 1977. Bar: D.C. 1979, U.S. Dist. Ct. D.C. 1980, U.S. Ct. Appeals (D.C. and 9th cirs.) 1980, U.S. Ct. Appeals (4th cir.) 1983, U.S. Supreme Ct. 1983. Law clk. to judge U.S. Ct. Appeals (2d cir.), N.Y.C., 1977-78; law clk. to justice U.S. Supreme Ct., Washington, 1978-79; spl. asst. to U.S. atty. gen. Dept. Justice, Washington, 1979-81; from assoc. to ptnr. Arnold & Porter, Washington, 1981-89; asst. U.S. atty. Dept. Justice, Washington, 1989-92; ptnr. Arnold & Porter, Washington, 1992-93; dep. asst. atty. gen., criminal divsn. Dept. Justice, Washington, 1993-94, prin. assoc. dep. atty. gen., 1994-97; circuit judge U.S. Ct. Appeals, Washington, 1997—; assoc. ind. counsel, 1987-88; lectr. on law Harvard U. Law Sch., 1985-86. Author: Antitrust and State Action Yale Law Jour., 1983, Deregulation and Jud. Rev., Harvard Law Rev., 1985. Mem. Phi Beta Kappa. Office: US Courthouse 333 Constitution Ave NW Washington DC 20001-2866

GARLAND, RICHARD ROGER, lawyer; b. Princeton, Ill., Aug. 20, 1958; s. Louis Roger and Irene Marie (Tonozzi) G. BA in Polit. Sci. summa cum laude, U. S. Fla., 1979; JD with honors, U. Fla., 1982. Bar: Fla. 1982, U.S. Dist. Ct. (mid. dist.) Fla. 1983, U.S. Ct. Appeals (11th cir.) 1987, U.S. Supreme Ct. 1988, U.S. Ct. Appeals (fed. cir.) 1995; Fla. Bar cert. in appellate practice, 1995. Instr., supr. appellate advocacy U. Fla., Gainesville, 1981-82; assoc. Dickinson, O'Riorden, Gibbons, Quale, Shields & Carlton, Venice, Fla., 1983-85, Sarasota, Fla., 1986-90; ptnr., sr. atty. Dickinson & Gibbons, Sarasota, Fla., 1991—. Pres. parish coun. San Pedro Cath. Ch., North Port, Fla., 1986-92; mem. Sarasota County Libr. Adv. Bd., 1999-2001. Mem. ABA, Fla. Bar Assn., Sarasota County Bar Assn. (editor newsletter 1991-93, bd. dirs. 1994-96, treas. 1996-97, sec. 1997-98, v.p. 1998-99), Judge John M. Scheb Am. Inn of Ct. (treas., master), U. South Fla. Alumni Assn., Phi Kappa Phi, Pi Sigma Alpha. Democrat. Roman Catholic. Office: Dickinson & Gibbons PA 1750 Ringling Blvd Sarasota FL 34236-6836

GARLAND, ROBERT SANDFORD JOHN, classical studies educator; b. London, Sept. 25, 1947; came to U.S., 1985; s. Sandford John and Ena Gladys (Shuter) G.; m. Anita Johnson Jan. 8, 1993; 1 child, Richard. BA, Manchester U., 1969; MA, McMaster U., 1973; PhD, Univ. Coll., London, 1981. Lectr. Reading U., Berkshire, Eng., 1980-81, Keele U., North Staffs, Eng., 1981-84, London U., 1984-85; jr. fellow Ctr. for Hellenic Studies, Washington, 1985-86; from vis. asst. prof. to assoc. prof. Colgate U., Hamilton, N.Y., 1986-91, Roy D. and Margaret B. prof. classics, 1991—. Author: The Greek Way of Death, 1985, The Piraeus, 1987, The Greek Way of Life, 1990, Introducing New Gods, 1992, Religion and the Greeks, 1994, The Eye of the Beholder, 1995, Daily Life of the Ancient Greeks, 1998. Fulbright scholar Ctr. Hellenic Studies, 1985-86. Mem. Joint Assn. Classical Tchrs. (London) (exec. bd. dirs. 1984-85). Anglican. Avocations: acting, directing, sculpting, listening to opera, playing squash. Home: 91 Eaton St Hamilton NY 13346-9701 Office: Colgate U Oak Dr Hamilton NY 13346

GARLAND, SIMON GREVILLE, service technician; b. Palmerston North, New Zealand, June 20, 1960; came to US., 1989; s. Guy Owen and Helen Constance (Free) G.; m. Laurie Smith, Nov. 26, 1989. B Commerce in Agrl. Valuation Mgmt., Lincoln (New Zealand) U., 1984. Registered valuer Inst. Valuers, New Zealand. Valuer Valuation New Zealand, Gisborne, 1985-86, Keri Keri, 1987-88; sailmaker Spinnaker Shop, Palo Alto, Calif., 1989-90, Windwing Designs, Berkeley, Calif., 1990; rigger Bay Riggers, Sausalito, Calif., 1990-92; technician North Tech. Sys., San Francisco, 1992-94, Eastman Tech. Sys., Buffalo, 1995—. Avocations: yacht racing, windsurfing, travel, skiing, reading. Home: 1115 Sutter St San Diego CA 92103-2823 Office: Eastman Tech Sys 779 Washington St Buffalo NY 14203-1308

GARLAND, SYLVIA DILLOF, lawyer; b. N.Y.C., June 4, 1919; d. Morris and Frieda (Gassner) Dillof; m. Albert Garland, May 4, 1942; children: Margaret Garland Clunie, Paul B. BA, Bklyn. Coll., 1939; JD cum laude, N.Y. Law Sch., 1960. Bar: N.Y. 1960, U.S. Ct. Appeals (2d cir.) 1965, U.S. Ct. Claims 1965, U.S. Supreme Ct. 1967, U.S. Customs Ct. 1972, U.S. Ct. Appeals (5th cir.), 1979. Assoc. Borden, Skidell, Fleck and Steindler, Jamaica, N.Y., 1960-61, Fields, Zimmerman, Skodnick & Segall, Jamaica, 1961-65, Marshall, Brater, Greene, Allison & Tucker, N.Y.C., 1965-68; law sec. to N.Y. Supreme Ct. justice Suffolk County, 1968-70; ptnr. Hofheimer, Gartlir & Gross, N.Y.C., 1970—; asst. adj. prof. N.Y. Law Sch., 1974-79; mem. com. on character and fitness N.Y. State Supreme Ct., 1st Jud. Dept., 1985—, vice chmn., 1991—Judge Charles W. Froessel award N.Y. Law Sch., 1997. Author: Workman's Compensation, 1957, Labor Law, 1959, Wills, 1962; contbg. author: Guardians and Custodians, 1970; editor-in-chief Law Rev. Jour., N.Y. Law Forum, 1959-60 (svc. award 1960); contbr. articles to mag. Trustee N.Y. Law Sch., 1979-90, trustee emeritus, 1991—; pres. Oakland chpt. B'nai Brith, Bayside, N.Y., 1955-57. Recipient Disting. Alumnus award N.Y. Law Sch., 1978, Judge Charles W. Foressel award N.Y. Law Sch., 1997. Mem. ABA (litigation sect.), N.Y. State Bar Assn., Queen's County Bar Assn. (sec. civil practice 1960-79), N.Y. Law Sch. Alumni Assn. (pres. 1976-77), N.Y. Law Forum Alumni Assn. (pres. 1963-65). Jewish. Home: 425 E 58th St New York NY 10022-2300

GARLAND, WILLIAM JAMES, engineering physics educator; b. St. John's, Nfld., Can., July 26, 1948. B in Engring. Physics, McMaster U., Hamilton, Ont., Can., 1970, M in Engring. Physics, 1971, PhD in Chem. Engring., 1975. Registered profl. engr., Ont. Design engr. Ont. Hydro, Toronto, Can., 1975-79; design specialist Atomic Energy of Can. Ltd., Mississauga, Ont., 1979-83; assoc. prof. McMaster U., 1983-97, chmn. dept. engring. physics, 1988-94, prof., 1997—; dir. McMaster Nuclear Reactor, 1994-95; cons. System Analytics, Burlington, Ont., 1982—. Mem. Am. Nuclear Soc., Can. Nuclear Soc., Assn. Profl. Engrs. Ont. Office: McMaster U Dept Engring Physics, 1280 Main St W, Hamilton, ON Canada L8S 4L7

GARLATHY, FRANK BRYAN, minister; b. Johnstown, Pa., May 6, 1946; s. Frank and Helen Rebecca (Casriel) G.; m. Mary Kay Campbell, July 27, 1968; children: Joshua, Elizabeth. BA in Philosophy cum laude, Otterbein Coll., 1967; MDiv, United Theol. Sem., Dayton, Ohio, 1970; D Ministry, Grad. Theol. Found., Notre Dame, Ind., 1988. Ordained to ministry United Meth. Ch., 1970. Pastor Christy Park United Meth. Ch., McKeesport, Pa., 1970-71, Fayette City (Pa.) United Meth. Ch., 1972-79, Riverview United Meth. Ch., Beaver Falls, Pa., 1979-83; assoc. dir. McKeesport Neighborhood Ministry, 1971-72, Trinity United Meth. Ch., Indiana, Pa., 1983-91; First United Meth. Ch., Erie, Pa., 1991-95; pastor First United Meth. Ch., Vandergrift, Pa., 1995-99, Rochester, Pa., 1999—; chaplain Beaver County Jail, Beaver, Ind., 1981-83, Ind. Borough Police Dept., 1990-91; mission amb. Western Pa. Conf., Pitts., 1985-86; pres. Ind. Area Coun. Chs., 1985-87, United Campus Ministry, Ind., 1990-91. Composer, performer (record album) Sweet Release, 1978, Spirit, 1991. Mem. Belle Vernon (Pa.) Area Sch. Bd., 1977-79. Mem. Am. Acad. Religion, Bibl. Archaeology Soc., Quiz and Quill. Home: 345 Jefferson St Rochester PA 14074-2003 Office: 341 Jefferson St Rochester PA 15074 *Our lives are a series of choices based upon the words "open" and "closed." We can extend an open hand or a closed fist. We can cultivate an open mind or a closed rationality. God gives us many choices.*

GARLING, CAROL ELIZABETH, real estate executive and developer; b. Detroit, Sept. 23, 1939; d. Elmer Daniel and Elizabeth Aldene (Kish) Champagne; m. Fred C. Garling, Mar. 7, 1963 (dec. Nov. 1972). BA, U. Detroit, 1960, degree in criminology, 1972. Lic. real estate broker. Land developer, builder Garling Bldg. Co., Dearborn, 1962-73; specialist indsl. security Cen. Security, Inc. and Garling Security Services, Dearborn, 1973-79; owner, realtor, broker Carol Garling Realty, Inc., Dearborn, 1976-80; broker, realtor Embassy Realty, Inc., Ft. Lauderdale, Fla., 1981—; land developer Garling Bldg. and Devel., Raleigh, N.C., 1986-98; exec. Garling Realty, Scottsdale, Ariz., 1992—. Mem. Ft. Lauderdale Bd. Realtors, Scottsdale, Ariz. Bd Realtors, Plum Hollow Colf Club (Southfield Mich., life mem.). Avocations: fishing, golf, boating. Home: 7750 N Via De La Sombre Scottsdale AZ 85258-3210

GARLOFF, SAMUEL JOHN, psychiatrist; b. Erie, Pa., Nov. 14, 1947. BS, Mansfield (Pa.) State Coll., 1969; MS, Johns Hopkins U., 1974; DO, Phila. Coll. Osteo. Medicine, 1978. Flexible intern Walter Reed Army Med. Ctr., Washington, 1978-79; resident in psychiatry Dwight David Eisenhower Army Med. Ctr., Ft. Gordon, Ga., 1981-84; officer in charge USA Health Care Clinic, Rock Island, Ill., 1980-81; divsn. psychiatrist Ft. Hood, Tex., 1984-86; pvt. practice, Pottsville, Pa., 1986-93; med. dir. counseling ctr. Good Samaritan Regional Med. Ctr., Pottsville, 1988-96, asst. med. dir., 1988-91, med. dir., 1991-94, v.p. med. affairs, 1994-97; med. dir. regional devel. Behavioral Health Ctrs., Pottsville, 1998—; clin. cons. III Corps Drug and Alcohol Program, Ft. Hood, Tex., 1984-86; psychiat. cons. Turning Point, Pottsville, Pa., 1986-88, med. dir., 1988-91; psychiat. cons. Luzerne County MH/MR, Hazleton, Pa., 1987-88, Operation Plus Adolescent Partial Hospitalization Program, Pottsville, 1987-95; instr. to physician asst. students Rock Island Arsenal, Rock Island, Ill., 1979-80, Ft. Hood, 1985; lectr., psychiat. nursing students, Ft. Gordon, Ga., 1982-84, family practice medicine residents, Ft. Hood, 1983-84, emergency medicine residents, Ft. Hood, 1984-85; presenter in field. Chmn. spl. gifts com. St. Joseph Ctr. for Spl. Learning, Pottsville, 1989; bd. dirs. Good Samaritan Found., Pottsville, 1989-95, sec. 1993-95; bd. dirs. Schuylkill Unit Am. Cancer Soc., 1990-91, St. Joseph's Ctr. Spl. Learning Devel. Bd., 1990-93, Mansfield Univ. Found., 1991—, AIDSNET, 1991-92; chairperson physician divsn. Schuykill United Way, Pottsville, 1994—; active Nat. Coalition Physicians Against Family Violence. Maj. U.S. Army Med. Corps, 1978-86. Recipient Achievement award for cmty. outreach/edn. Hosp. Assn. Pa., 1993. Fellow Am. Coll. Med. Quality (bd. cert., treas. Pa. chpt. 1993-95, sec. Pa. chpt. 1995-97, v.p. Pa. chpt. 1997—, feature writer 1996—, Disting. fellow 1996), Am. Acad. Pain Mgmt. (bd. cert.); mem. Am. Osteo. Assn., Am. Coll. Neuropsychiatrists, Am. Osteo. Acad. Addictionology, Assn. Mil. Osteo. Physicians and Surgeons, Internat. Assn. Med. Specialists, Pa. Osteo. Med. Assn. (vice chmn. dist. 11 1997—, trustee 1998—), Schuylkill County Osteo. Med. Soc. Home: 1759 Tall Oaks Rd Orwigsburg PA 17961-9543 Office: Good Samaritan Med Mall PO Box 254 Orwigsburg PA 17961-0254

GARLOUGH, WILLIAM GLENN, marketing executive; b. Syracuse, N.Y., Mar. 27, 1924; s. Henry James and Gladys (Killam) G.; m. Charlotte M. Tanzer, June 15, 1947; children: Jennifer, William, Robert. BEE, Clarkson U., 1949. With Knowlton Bros., Watertown, N.Y., 1949-67, mgr. mfg. svcs., 1966-67; v.p. planning, equipment systems divsn. Vare Corp., Englewood Cliffs, N.J., 1967-69; mgr. mktg. Valley Mould divsn. Microdot Inc., Hubbard, Ohio, 1969-70; dir. corp. devel. Microdot Inc., Greenwich, Conn., 1970-73, v.p. corp. devel., 1973-76, v.p. adminstrn., 1976-77, v.p. corp. devel., 1977-78; v.p. corp. devel. Am. Bldg. Maintenance Industries, San Francisco, 1979-83; pres. The Change Agts., Inc., Walnut Creek, Calif., 1983—; bd. dirs. My Chef Inc.; mem. citizens adv. com. to Watertown Bd. Edn., 1957. Bd. dirs. Watertown Cmty. Chest, 1958-61; ruling elder Presbyn. Ch. With USMCR, 1942-46. Mem. Am. Mgmt. Assn., Inst. Mgmt. Cons. (cert.), Bldg. Svc. Contractors Assn., Internat. Sanitary Supply Assn., Mensa, Am. Mktg. Assn., TAPPI, Assn. Corp. Growth (pres. San Francisco chpt. 1984-85, v.p. chpts. west 1985-88), Lincoln League (pres. 1958), Marine's Meml. Club, Am. Contract Bridge League (life master), Clarkson Alumni Assn. (Watertown sect. pres. 1955), No. N.Y. Contract Club (pres. 1959), No. N.Y. Transp. Club, Tau Beta Pi. Office: The Change Agts Inc 2557 Via Verde Walnut Creek CA 94598-3451

GARMAN, DALE S., JR., sculptor; b. Montgomery, Ala., July 15, 1945; s. Dale Sweigart and Marion Tripp (Champion) G.; m. Barbara Ann Rose, July 13, 1969 (div. Aug. 1992).; 1 child, Michael Garman; m. Sharon Quinn, July 3, 1999. BA, Wittenberg U., Springfield, Ohio, 1966; MDiv, Luth. Theol. Sem., Gettysburg, Pa., 1970; postgrad., Huntsville (Tex.) State U., 1983-87. Pastor Hope-Redeemer Luth. Chs., Erie/Harborcreek, Pa., 1970-75; piano tuner/technician The Woodlands, Tex., 1975-88; artist-in-residence, sculptor John Cooper Sch., The Woodlands, 1988-99, chmn. art dept., 1998-99. Artist/commn. bronze sculptures: Smokedance, 1989-90, oak and aluminum sculpture: The Vigil, 1997; solo exhbn. at Tex. A&M U., 1998; other exhbns. include The John Cooper Sch. 1989—; gallery affiliations include: Discovery Art-Houston, 1984, U.S. Olympic Festival, 1994, New Trends Gallery, Santa Fe, N.Mex., 1985-86, Galleria Del Mar, Manalaplan, Fla., 1986, Herbert Orvis Gallery, West Palm Beach, Fla., 1986, High Art with Houston Symphony, 1988, Lampros Gallery, Woodlands, 1991—, Seraphim Gallery, Englewood, N.J., 1992-93, Montgomery Coll., Conroe, Tex., 1996, Dunn/Mehler Gallery, Half Moon Bay, Calif., 1997—. Founder, chair The Woodlands Harvest Festival, 1980, The Woodlands Chamber Music Series, 1981-83. Avocations: reading, travel, music. Home and Studio: 184 Echo Valley Rd Prunedale CA 93907

GARMAN, JON KENT, anesthesiologist; b. Reading, Pa., Nov. 27, 1939; s. Roy S. and E. Marie (Buffington) G.; m. Judith C. Encelewski, June 19, 1965; children: Ingrid E., Gregory S., Kimberly A., Karen D. AB, Duke U., 1961; MD, Temple U., 1965; MS in Mgmt., Stanford U., 1983. Cert. physician exec. Certifying Commn. Med. Mgmt., 1998. Intern U. Va. Hosp.,

Charlottesville, 1965-66; resident anesthesiologist U. Pa., Phila., 1969-71, rsch. fellow, 1971-72; clin. prof. anesthesia Stanford (Calif.) U. Sch. Medicine; clin. prof.; acad. practice; capt. med. corps USNR, 1963-93; sr. assoc. examiner Am. Bd. Anesthesiology, N.C., 1982—; pres., chief of staff Sequoia Hosp. Med. Staff, Redwood City, Calif., 1994-95; hon. bd. dirs. Sequoia Hosp. Found., Redwood City, Calif., 1994—; bd. dirs. San Mateo County Med. Assn., 1994-97, Calif. Med. Polit. Action com., San Francisco, 1995-96. Fellow Am. Coll. Cardiology; mem. Am. Coll. Physician Execs. Home: 27742 Stirrup Way Los Altos CA 94022-1813

GARMEL, MARION BESS SIMON, journalist; b. El Paso, Tex., Oct. 15, 1936; d. Marcus and Frieda (Alfman) Simon; m. Raymond Louis Garmel, Nov. 28, 1965 (dec. Feb. 1986); 1 child, Cynthia Rogers; 1 stepchild, Christine Blum. Student, U. Tex., El Paso, 1954-55; BJ, U. Tex., Austin, 1958. Exec. sec. Nat. Student Assn., Phila., 1958-59, pub. rels. dir., 1960-61; sec. World Assembly Youth, Paris, Brussels, 1959-60; dictationist Wall Street Jour., Washington, 1961; libr., staff writer Nat. Observer, Silver Spring, Md., 1961-70; art critic Indpls. News, 1971-91, editor Free Time sect., 1975-91, critic radio and TV, 1991-95; theater critic Indpls. Star and News, 1995—; television critic Indpls. News, 1995—. Mem. Nat. Fedn. Press Women (1st Place Critics award 1974), Hadassah Women's Zionist Orgn. Am. (life), Women's Press Club Ind. (1st Place Critics award 1995). Jewish. Avocation: tennis. Home: 226 E 45th St Indianapolis IN 46205-1712 Office: Indpls Star and News 307 N Pennsylvania St Indianapolis IN 46204-1811

GARMENDIA, FRANCISCO, bishop; b. Lozcano, Spain, Nov. 6, 1924; came to U.S., 1964, naturalized.; Ordained priest Roman Cath. Ch., 1947. Ordained titular bishop Limisa and aux. bishop. N.Y.C., 1977—; Episcopal vicar of the South Bronx N.Y. Archdiocese, Bronx.

GARMENT, ROBERT JAMES, clergyman; b. Hanover, Pa., May 2, 1951; s. Stanley J. and Mary Elizabeth (Maire) G.; m. Mary Evelyn Kunze, Aug. 17, 1974; children: Sarah, Emily, Robert J. Jr., Laura. Student, Stetson U., 1969-70; BA in Social Sci., U. Ctrl. Fla., 1973; MDiv, Louisville Presbyn. Sem., 1976; postgrad., Ref. Sem., Orlando, Fla. Ordained to ministry Presbyn. Ch. U.S., 1976, Evang. Presbyn. Ch., 1985. Pastor Westover Hills Presbyn. Ch., Charlotte, N.C., 1976-78, Dutton Meml. Presbyn. Ch., Ft. Pierce, Fla., 1978-85; founding pastor, sr. pastor Trinity Evang. Presbyn. Ch., Ft. Pierce, 1985—; vis. prof. Ctrl. Bible Inst., Ft. Pierce; stated clk. Presbytery of Fla. Evang. Presbyn. Ch.; advisor Women's Aglow Fellowship, Presbyn. Charismatic Communion; Fla. bd. dirs. Presbyn. and Ref. Renewal Ministries; spiritual dir., speaker Via de Cristo (Cursillo) retreats; spiritual dir., speaker Kairos prison ministries; conf. speaker Luth.'s men's retreat. Pres. Citizens Against Pornography, St. Lucie County Right to Life; chmn. bd. Crisis Pregnancy Svcs. Treasure Coast; mem. Fla. Coalition for Clean Cable, Coalition for Religious Freedom, Christian Coalition; coord. evangelism outreach Am. for Jesus Crusade, Fla.; former mem. ch. zoning reform com. St. Lucie County Commn.; past pres. Fla. Right to Life; former mem. bd. dirs. One Nation Under God; former mem. Freedom Coun.; speaker at banquets and civic clubs; also others. Mem. St. Lucie County Ministerial Assn. (past pres.). Republican. Avocations: singing, computers, mountain hiking. Office: Trinity Evang Presbyn Ch 5150 Oleander Ave Fort Pierce FL 34982-4028*

GARMER, WILLIAM ROBERT, lawyer; b. Balt., May 8, 1946; s. William M. and Grace (DeLane) G.; 1 child, Lindsey DeLane; m. Kimberly Nichols. BA, U. Ky., 1968, JD, 1975. Bar: Ky. 1975, U.S. Dist. Ct. (ea. dist.) Ky. 1977, U.S. Ct. Appeals (6th cir.) 1980, U.S. Supreme Ct. 1979. Law clk. to chief judge U.S. Dist. Ct. (ea. dist.) Ky., Lexington, 1975-76; assoc. prof. law litigation skills U. Ky. Law Sch., Lexington, 1981—; ptnr. Savage, Garmer & Elliott, P.S.C., Lexington, 1984—. Casenote editor St. Mary's Law Jour., 1975; contbr. articles to profl. jours. Elder Presbyn. Ch. With USAF, 1969-73. Fellow Am. Coll. Trial Lawyers; mem. ABA, ATLA, (bd. govs., chair coun. state pres.), Ky. Bar Assn. (com. on specialization and cert. 1982—, litigation com. 1989—), Fayette County Bar Assn., Ky. Acad. Trial Attys. (bd. govs. 1984-89, treas. 1990, sec. 1991, v.p. 1992, pres. 1994, named Trail Lawyer of Yr. 1998), Phi Delta Phi (named One of Best Lawyers in Am. 1989-99). Democrat. Office: Savage Garmer & Elliot PSC 141 N Broadway St Lexington KY 40507-1230

GARMIRE, ELSA MEINTS, electrical engineering educator, consultant; b. Buffalo, Nov. 9, 1939; d. Ralph E. and Nelle (Gubser) Meints; m. Gordon P. Garmire, June 11, 1961 (div. 1975); children: Lisa, Marla; m. Robert Heathcote Russell, Feb. 4, 1979. AB in Physics, Harvard U., 1961; PhD in Physics, MIT, 1965. Rsch. scientist NASA Electronics Rsch. Ctr., Cambridge, Mass., 1965-66; rsch. fellow Calif. Inst. Tech., Pasadena, 1966-73; sr. rsch. scientist U. So. Calif. Ctr. for Laser Studies, L.A., 1974-78, prof. elec. engring. and physics, 1981-95, assoc. dir. Ctr. for Laser Studies, 1978-83, dir., 1984-95, William Hogue prof. of engring., 1992-95; dean Thayer Sch. Engring. Dartmouth Coll., Hanover, N.H., 1995-97, prof. engring., 1997—; vis. fellow Standard Telecommunication Labs., Eng., 1973-74; cons. Aerospace Corp., L.A., 1975-91, sci. adv. bd. Air Force, Washington, 1985-89, TRW, L.A., 1988-89, McDonnell Douglas, St. Louis, 1990-93; mem. com. Nat. Medal Sci., 1996—. Contbr. over 200 sci. papers and articles to profl. publs.; patentee in field. Recipient Soroptimist Achievement award Soroptimist Club L.A., 1970, K.C. Black Award N.E. Electronics Rsch. and Engring. Meeting, 1972, Soc. Women Engrs. Achievement award 1994, U. So. Calif. Rschr. award, 1994; named Mademoiselle Women of Yr. Mademoiselle Mag., 1970. Fellow IEEE (bd. dirs. 1985-89), Optical Soc. Am. (bd. dirs. 1983-86, pres. 1992, 93), Am. Phys. Soc. (bd. dirs. 1994-97), Am. Acad. Arts and Scis., NAE (life), Soc. Women Engrs. (life, Achievement award 1994). Democrat. Avocations: music, gardening. Office: Dartmouth Coll Thayer Sch of Engring Hanover NH 03755-8000

GARN, EDWIN JACOB (JAKE GARN), former senator; b. Richfield, Utah, Oct. 12, 1932; s. Jacob Edwin and Fern (Christensen) G.; m. Hazel Rhae Thompson, Feb. 2, 1957 (dec. 1976); children: Jacob Wayne, Susan Rhae, Ellen Marie, Jeffrey Paul; m. Kathleen Brewerton, Apr. 8, 1977; children: Matthew Spencer, Christopher Brook, Jennifer Kathleen. B.S., U. Utah, 1955. City commr. Salt Lake City, 1968-72, mayor, 1972-74; U.S. Senator from Utah, 1974-93; vice chmn. Huntsman Corp., Salt Lake City, 1993—; bd. dirs. Dean Witter InterCapital, N.Y.C., Franklin Covey, Salt Lake City. Served to lt. USNR, 1956-60; brig. gen. Utah Air N.G., 1963-79; payload specialist, space shuttle mission 51D, 1985. Recipient Tom McCoy award Utah League Cities and Towns, 1972, Wright Bros. Meml. trophy, 1992. Mem. Utah League Cities and Towns (pres. 1971-72, dir. 1968—), Nat. League Cities (1st v.p. 1973-74, hon. pres. 1975), Sigma Chi. Mem. LDS Ch. Office: Huntsman Chem Corp 500 Huntsman Way Salt Lake City UT 84108-1235*

GARN, STANLEY MARION, physical anthropologist, educator; b. New London, Conn., Oct. 27, 1922; s. Harry and Sadie Edith (Cohen) G.; m. Priscilla Crozier, Apr. 8, 1950; children: Barbara, William David. AB, Harvard U., 1942, AM, 1947, PhD, 1948. Rsch. assoc. chem. engring. Chem. Warfare Svc. Devel. Lab. MIT, 1942-44; tech. editor Polaroid Co., 1944-46; cons. applied anthropology, 1946-47; rsch. fellow cardiology Mass. Gen. Hosp., Boston, 1946-52; instr. anthropology Harvard U., 1948-52; anthropologist Forsyth Dental Infirmary, Boston, 1947-52; dir. Forsyth face size project Army Chem. Corps, 1950-52; chmn. dept. growth and genetics Fels Rsch. Inst., Yellow Springs, Ohio, 1952-68; fellow Ctr. Human Growth and Devel. U. Mich., Ann Arbor, also prof. nutrition and anthropology, 1968-92, prof. emeritus, 1993—; Raymond Pearl lectr. Human Biol. Coun., 1992—; E.B.D. Neuhauser lectr. Soc. Pediatric Radiology, 1981. Author: Human Races, 1970, Gain and Loss of Cortical Bone, 1970; also numerous articles; editorial bds. numerous jours. Recipient Disting. Svc. award U. Mich., Charles Darwin Lifetime Achievement award Am. Assn. Phys. Anthropologists, 1994. Fellow AAAS, Am. Acad. Pediatrics (hon. assoc.), Am. Anthropol. Assn., Am. Acad. Arts and Scis., Human Biology Coun., Am. Soc. Clin. Nutrition, Am. Soc. Nutrition Scis.; mem. NAS, Am. Assn. Phys. Anthropologists, Internat. Assn. Dental Rsch., Internat. Orgn. Study Human Devel., Am. Soc. Naturalists, Internat. Assn. Human Biologists (coun.). Home: 2410 Londonderry Rd Ann Arbor MI 48104-4016 Office: U Mich Ctr Human Growth & Devel 300 N Ingalls St Ann Arbor MI 48109-2007

GARNER, ALBERT HEADDEN, investment banker; b. Memphis, Dec. 17, 1955; s. Jesse B. Jr. and Noella (Headden) G.; m. Wanatha Porter, July 2, 1977; children: Cyrus Dalton, Shelby Harris, Pleasant Noel. BS in Engring., Princeton U., 1977. Assoc. Devel. and Resources Corp., N.Y.C., 1977-79; assoc. Lazard Freres & Co., N.Y.C., 1979-83, v.p., 1984-88; gen. ptnr. Lazard Freres & Co. LLC, N.Y.C., 1989-95, mng. dir., 1995—. Dir. Prospect Park Alliance. Home: 1510 Albemarle Rd Brooklyn NY 11226-4506 Office: Lazard Freres & Co LLC 30 Rockefeller Plz Fl 59 New York NY 10112-5900

GARNER, ALTO LUTHER, retired education educator; b. Dothan, Ala., Dec. 10, 1916; s. Albert Early and Martha (DeBardeleben) G.; m. Katie Mae Sanders, Oct. 5, 1945 (div. 1980); 1 son, Robert Edward Lee. Student, Howard Coll., 1940-43; AB, U. Ala., 1944; postgrad., So. Bapt. Theol. Sem., 1944-45, U. Tex., Austin, 1947; MA, NYU, 1947; EdD, U. Ky., 1954. Ordained to ministry Bapt. Ch., 1942; pastor and/or interim pastor various Bapt. Chs. Ala., Ky., Tex., 1942-94; instr. history and polit. sci. Georgetown Coll., 1947-49, asst. prof., 1949-53; asso. prof. edn. Howard Coll., 1953-54; prof. edn. Samford U., Birmingham, Ala., 1954-81; chmn. div. tchr. edn., head dept. edn. and psychology Samford U., 1964-66; prof. Samford U. (Sch. Edn.), 1980-88, Disting. prof. edn., 1981, dean, 1966-80, dean emeritus, 1982—, disting. prof. emeritus, 1997—; Ala. regional ednl. cons. State Farm Ins. Cos., 1955-73. Served with AUS, 1941. Named hon. lt. a.d.c. Ala. Militia, 1972, hon. adm. Ala. Navy, 1978. Mem. Kappa Phi Kappa, Kappa Delta Pi, Phi Alpha Theta, Phi Kappa Phi. Home: 102 N Bell St Dothan AL 36303-4308

GARNER, CARLENE ANN, fundraising consultant; b. Dec. 17, 1945; d. Carl A. and Ruth E. (Mathison) Timblin; m. Adelbert L. Garner, Feb. 17, 1964; children: Bruce A., Brent A. BA, U. Puget Sound, 1983. Adminstrv. dir. Balletacoma, 1984-87; exec. dir. Tacoma Symphony, 1987-95; prin. New Horizon Cons., Tacoma, 1995-98; co-owner Stewardship Ministries for Congl. Growth, 1998—; cons. Wash. PAVE, Tacoma, 1983-84. Treas. Coalition for the Devel. of the Arts, 1992-94; pres. Wilson High Sch. PTA, Tacoma, 1983-85; chmn. Tacoma Sch. Vol. Adv. Bd., 1985-87; pres. Emmanuel Luth. Ch., Tacoma, 1984-86, chmn. future steering com., 1987-93; sec.-treas. Tacoma-Narrows Conf., 1987-98; vice chmn. Tacoma Luth. Home, 1996-98; pub. mem. Wash. Sta te Bd. Pharmacy, 1993-98. Mem. N.W. Devel. Officers Assn. (chair Tacoma/Pierce County com. 1994-96), Jr. Women's Club Tacoma (pres. 1975-76, pres. Peninsula dist. 1984-86), Gen. Fedn. Women's Club-Wash. State (treas. 1988-90, 3d v.p. 1990-92, 2d v.p. 1992-94, 1st v.p. 1994-96, pres. 1996-98, Clubwoman of Yr. 1977, Outstanding FREE chmn. Gen. Fedn. 1982), Commencement Bay Woman's Club (pres. 1990-92), Gen. Fedn. of Women's Club (bd. dirs., chair nat. conv. 1995, state pres. 1996-98, chair cmty. improvement program 1998—). Lutheran. Home: 1115 N Cheyenne St Tacoma WA 98406-3624 Office: New Horizon Cons 1115 N Cheyenne St Tacoma WA 98406-3624

GARNER, CAROL LYNN, executive; b. Shelby, Ohio, Feb. 2, 1949; d. Robert Q. and Evelyn F. G.; m. Otho S. Eyster, May 25, 1989. Exec. dir. Big Bros./Big Sisters, Mt. Vernon, Ohio, 1979-86, Columbus (Ohio) Coun. World Affairs, 1986—; mem. adv. bd. Inernat. Programs CIBER, Columbus, 1995—; advisor Internat. Action Com., Columbus, 1992-94. Bd. dirs. Big Bros./Big Sisters, Columbus, 1988—. Mem. Rotary (pres. 1997-98, asst. gov. 1998—). Office: Columbus Coun World Affairs 2 Nationwide Plz #705 Columbus OH 43215

GARNER, CHARLES WILLIAM, educational administration educator, consultant; b. Pine Grove Mills, Pa., Apr. 18, 1939; s. Adam Krumrine and Blanche Ella (Gearhart) G.; m. Karyl J. Packer, Sept. 8, 1962; children: Ronald Adam, Juliet Paige. Student, U.S. Navy Electronics Airborne Sonar Sch., 1959; BS in Bus. Edn., Pa. State U., 1965, MEd in Higher Edn. Adminstrn., 1968, EdD in Vocat. Indsl. Edn., 1974. Cert. govt. fin. mgr. Adminstrv. asst. dept. psychology Pa. State U., 1965-75; asst. prof., site adminstr. March AFB, Calif. for So. Ill. U., 1975-77; asst. prof., coordinator Ft. Knox Ctr.- U. Louisville, 1977-78; assoc. prof., acting vice dean Rutgers U., Camden, N.J., 1978-79; assoc. prof. urban edn., chmn. dept. edn. Univ. Coll. Rutgers U., New Brunswick, N.J., 1978-81, assoc. prof. vocat. tech. edn. Grad. Sch. Edn., 1981—, chmn. dept. vocat. tech. edn., 1982-85, assoc. prof. edn. adminstrn., 1985—, exec. dir. Vocat. Edn. Resource Ctr., 1983-88, dir. continuing edn., 1987-89, program chair edn. adminstrn., 1990-96; cons. CWG Assocs., Plumsteadville, Pa., 1989—; pres. Penn State Auto Repair, Inc., Williamsport, Pa., 1997—; mem. adv. com. 15th Air Force Noncommd. Officer Leadership Sch., Strategic Air Force Command, 1976-77; mem. N.J. state leadership team Leadership Tng. Inst.-Vocat. and Spl. Edn., 1980-81; mem. adv. council Vocat. Tng. Project, Eastern European Coalition Am., Perth Amboy, N.J., 1981-82; cons. IEEE. Author: Accounting and Budgeting in Public and Nonprofit Organizations: A Manager's Guide, 1991, Financial Management of School Districts in New Jersey: For School Leaders, 1996; contbr. articles to profl. jours.; co-editor: Occupational Edn. Forum, 1979-85; editl. reader Jour. Indsl. Tchr. Edn., 1981; producer, host talk show pilot for pub. TV, 1979; producer, host: TV tape series Rutgers U.: Current Issues in Vocat. Edn., 1979; editor edn. sect. Pub. Budgeting and Financial Management, 1995. With USN, 1959-62. Bd. dirs., treas. Cerebral Palsy League of Union County, N.J., 1996-99. Grantee N.J. Dept. Edn. Div. Vocat. Edn., 1978-88; grantee HEW, 1979-80. Mem. AAUP, DAV (life), Am. Assn. Higher Edn., Am. Edn. Rsch. Assn., Am. Edn. Fin. Assn., Am. Vocat. Assn. (editl. bd. Jour. Gen. and Related Instrn. 1982, trade and industry rsch. com. 1985-87), Assn. Govt. Accts., N.J. Assn. Vocat. Edn., Acad. Mgmt., Spl. Needs Pers. (exec. coun. 1980-81, pres. 1981-82), Non-Commnd. Officers Assn. (life), Elks (exalted ruler 1972-73), Phi Delta Kappa, Omicron Tau Theta, Epsilon Pi Tau (trustee 1983-88). Home: PO Box 456 Mc Elhattan PA 17748-0456 Office: Rutgers U Dept Ednl Theory Admin New Brunswick NJ 08903 *Our influence in life is determined by the good deeds we do rather than by the emotions that we feel.*

GARNER, DORIS TRAGANZA, educator; b. Phila., Oct. 13, 1934; d. Charles Thomas and Elizabeth Marie (Blatteau) Traganza; m. Joseph Anthony DeMatteo, Apr. 12, 1958 (dec. Aug. 1968); children: Maria Louise, Carol Ann, Nicholas Joseph, Elizabeth Joan, Charles Traganza, Ann Seton; m. Doyle Daniel Garner, July 11, 1970 (div. Feb. 1989); 1 child: Jean Estelle. BA in Psychology cum laude, U. Pa., 1955; postgrad., Temple U., 1955-59; MS in Ednl. Adminstrn., SUNY, Albany, 1978, EdD in Ednl. Adminstrn. and Higher Edn., 1983. Cert. tchr., N.Y. Elem. tchr. Phila. Sch. Dist., 1955-59; asst. to assoc. dean grad. studies SUNY, Albany, 1977-78, asst. to asst. v.p. acad. affairs, 1979; curriculum rsch. assoc. John Jay Coll., CUNY, N.Y.C., 1979; asst. in higher edn. doctoral office N.Y. State Edn. Dept., Albany, 1979-84, coord. program rev. master's programs, 1985-87, assoc. in higher edn. coll./univ. evaluation, 1987-89, asst. to dep. commr. higher edn. and professions, 1989-95, divsn. dir. coll./univ. evaluation, 1995-96; staff dir. N.Y. State Regents Task Force on Tchg. N.Y. State Edn. Dept., 1996-98, supr. acad. program rev., 1998—; invited participant Inaugural Portfolio Conf. , Annenberg Inst. for Sch. Reform, Boston, 1998; chair session on state policy Am. Assn. Colls. for Tchr. Edn., New Orleans, 1988; plenary session panelist on tchg. reform Edn. Conf. of Empire State Reports, 1998; presenter at confs. in field. Editor: History of Regents College, 1998. Mem. Shaker H.S. Theater Support, Latham, N.Y., 1988-89; pianist at non-profit functions, Albany, N.Y., 1992-94; cmty. theater actor Stagecrafters, Phila., 1951. Avocations: grandchildren and children, reading on social and political issues, piano, plays, concerts, nature. Home: 27 Henkes Ln Latham NY 12110-5013 Office: NY State Edn Dept Ed Bldg Fifth Fl Mezzanine Albany NY 12234

GARNER, EDWIN BRUCE, government official; b. Atlanta, July 28, 1949; s. Edwin Floyd and Janie Mae (Glass) G. BS in Biology, Emory U., 1971. Claims rep. Social Security Adminstrn., Rome, Ga., 1973-76; ops. supr. Social Security Adminstrn., Savannah, Ga., 1976-78; assistance programs specialist Social Security Adminstrn., Atlanta, 1978-81, field svcs. specialist, 1981-98; lead social ins. program specialist Tel Opers., 1998—. Mem. Nat. Episcopal AIDS Coalition, 1989—, mem. Nat. AIDS Cons. Planning Com., 1989, 91, 92, bd. dirs. Nat. Episcopal AIDS Coalition, 1998—, mem. standing commn. on AIDS, Episcopal Ch., 1998—; nat. pres. Integrity, Inc., 1990-94, past nat. pres., 1994-96; mem. Standing Commn. on Human Affairs of Episcopal Ch. U.S., 1991-97, vice chair, 1995-97; founding mem. Episcopal Diocese Atlanta, Commn. on AIDS, 1986—, treas., 1986-91, chair, 1992—; alt. del. Gen. Conv. Episcopal Ch., 1994, 1st alt. del. Diocese of Atlanta, 1997, 2000; convener Integrity Atlanta, 1995-96; lay eucharistic min. Episcopal Ch., 1967—; verger All Saints Parish, 1992-96, head verger, 1996—; mem. Task Force on AIDS, State of Ga.; mem. Ryan White HIV Planning Coun., chair Ryan White HIV Planning Coun., 1997—, Met. Atlanta; mem. State of Ga. HIV Prevention Planning Coun., parliamentarian; bd. mem. Jerusalem House, 1991-95, sec., 1993-95; bd. mem. The Names Project Atlanta chpt., 1988-95, chair, 1993-94, 89-91; spkr. AIDS and Substance Abuse Spkrs. Bur., 1991-95, AID Atlanta Spkrs. Bur., 1984; mem. AID Atlanta Gay Cmty. Outreach Com., 1992—; quilt display coord. Names Project Nat. Found., 1989—; cons. Social Security Adminstrn. Regional Task Force on AIDS, 1988—; bd. mem. AID Atlanta Inc., 1984-90, pres., 1986-88, bd. treas., 1985-86, bd. sec., 1985. Mem. Atlanta Area Alumni Assn. (past pres.), Beta Theta Pi (v.p.,ritualist, steward 1967—). Avocations: collecting Asian antiques, collecting CD's, yard work, volunteer activities. Home: PO Box 1151 Atlanta GA 30301-1151 Office: Social Security Adminstrn 61 Forsyth St NW Ste 22T64 Atlanta GA 30303-2219

GARNER, GIROLAMA THOMASINA, retired educational administrator, educator; b. Muskegon, Mich., Sept. 15, 1923; d. John and Martha Ann (Thomas) Funaro; student Muskegon Jr. Coll., 1941; B.A., Western Mich. U., 1944, M.A. in Counseling and Guidance, 1958; Ed.D., U. Ariz., 1973; m. Charles Donald Garner, Sept. 16, 1944 (dec.); 1 dau., Linda Jeannette Garner Blake. Elem. tchr., Muskegon and Tucson, 1947-77; counselor Erickson Elem. Sch., Tucson, 1978-79; prin. Hudlow Elem. Sch., Tucson, 1979-87, adj. prof. U. Ariz., 1973-98, Tuscon Pima Community Coll., 1981-93, Prescott Coll., 1986-93; mem. Ariz. Com. Tchr. Evaluation and Cert., 1976-78; del. NEA convs. Active ARC, Crippled Children's Soc., UNESCO, U.S.-China People's Friendship Assn., DAV Aux., Rincon Renegades; bd. dirs. Hudlow Community Sch., 1973-76. Recipient Apple award for teaching excellence Pima Community Coll., 1982. Mem. Nat. Assn. Sci. Tchrs., Tucson Edn. Assn., Ariz. Edn. Assn., NEA, Assn. Supervision and Curriculum Devel., AAUW, Tucson Adminstrs., Pima County Retired Tchrs., Delta Kappa Gamma, Kappa Rho Sigma, Kappa Delta Pi. Democrat. Christian Scientist. Home: 6922 E Baker St Tucson AZ 85710-2230

GARNER, HARVEY LOUIS, computer scientist, consultant, electrical engineering educator; b. Lake, Colo., Dec. 23, 1926; s. Homa and Violet (Thuelin) G.; m. Yvonne Lillian King, Aug. 7, 1949; children-Susan Ann, Harvey Thomas. B.S., U. Denver, 1949, M.S., 1951; Ph.D., U. Mich., 1958. Engr. with devel. MIDAC and MIDSAC computers U. Mich., 1951-55, instr. elec. engring., 1955-58, asst. prof., 1958-60, assoc. prof., 1960-63, prof., 1963-70; dir. Information Systems Lab., 1960-64; dir. Systems Engring. Lab., 1964-66, acting chmn. dept. communications scis., 1965-67, prof. computer and communications scis., 1967-70; prof. elec. engring. Moore Sch. Elec. Engring., 1970-86, dir., 1970-76; dir. Microelectronics and Computer Tech. Corp., Austin, 1984-88; cons. in system design and computer arithmetic, 1988—; gen. chmn. 1st Nat. Computer Conf. and Exhbn., N.Y.C., 1973; gen. chmn. Islands Applications Conf., Tokyo, Japan, 1972. Contbr. articles to profl. jours. Served with USNR, 1945-46. Fellow IEEE; mem. Assn. Computing Machinery (apptd. nat. lectr. 1965), AAAS, Am. Assn. Artificial Intelligence, Sigma Xi, Eta Kappa Nu, Sigma Pi Sigma. Home and Office: 7400 Rockberry Cv Austin TX 78750-7920

GARNER, J. WAYNE, state agency administrator; married; 3 children. Mem. Ga. State Senate, 1980-93, chmn. corrections com., 1982-91, majority leader, pres. pro tem, 1991-93; mem. Ga. State Bd. Pardons and Paroles, 1993-95, chmn., 1994-95; commr. Dept. of Corrections, State of Ga., 1995—. Trustee West Ga. Coll.; bd. dirs. Camp Sunshine; hon. mem. bd. dirs. CURE at Emory Hosp., Atlanta. Named to Ga. Trend's 100 Most Powerful and Influential List. Office: State of Ga Dept of Corrections 2 ML King Jr Dr Ste 866 Atlanta GA 30334

GARNER, JAMES (JAMES SCOTT BUMGARNER), actor; b. Norman, Okla., Apr. 7, 1928; m. Lois Clarke, Aug. 17, 1956; children: Kimberly, Gretta, Scott. Student, N.Y. Berghof Sch., U. Okla. Motion picture debut in Toward the Unknown; films include Sayonara, 1957, Shoot-out at Medicine Bend, 1957, Darby's Rangers, 1958, Up Periscope, 1959, Cash McCall, 1960, The Children's Hour, 1962, The Great Escape, 1963, The Americanization of Emily, 1964, 36 Hours, 1964, The Thrill of It All, Move Over Darling, The Art of Love, 1965, A Man Could Get Killed, 1966, Duel at Diablo, 1966, Mister Buddwing, 1966, Grand Prix (co-producer), 1966, Hour of the Gun, 1967, How Sweet It Is, 1968, Marlowe, 1969, Support Your Local Sheriff, 1971, Support Your Local Gunfighter, 1971, Skin Game, 1971, They Only Kill Their Masters, 1972, One Little Indian, 1973, HEALTH, 1979, The Fan, 1980, Victor/Victoria, 1982, Tank, 1984, Murphy's Romance, 1985, Sunset, 1987, Fire in the Sky, 1993, Maverick, 1994, My Fellow Americans, 1996, Wild Bill: Hollywood Maverick, Twilight, 1998; TV appearances include: Maverick, 1957-60, Nichols, 1971-72, Rockford Files (Emmy award, 1977), 1974-80, Man of the People, 1991, (miniseries) Space, 1985, Streets of Laredo, 1995 Century of Country, 1999; TV film appearances include: The Long Summer of George Adams, 1982, Heartsounds, 1984, Promise (also producer, Emmy award 1986), 1986, My Name Is Bill W. (also producer), 1989, Decoration Day, 1990, Breathing Lessons, 1994 (Emmy nomination, Lead Actor - Special, 1994); TV movie The Rockford Files: I Still Love LA, 1994, The Rockford Files: The Crime and Punishment, 1996, The Rockford Files: The Friends and Foul Play, 1996, The Rockford Files: If the Frame Fits, 1996, The Rockford Files: Godfather Knows Best, 1996, The Rockford Files: A Blessing in Disguise, 1996, Dead Silence, 1997; cable TV movie Barbarians at the Gate, 1993 (Emmy nomination, Lead Actor - Miniseries, 1993, Golden Globe Award, Best Actor in a mini-series or movie made for television, 1994). Joined U.S. Mcht. Marine; served with U.S. Army, Korea. Decorated Purple Heart; recipient Clio award for Polaroid commls., 1978. *

GARNER, JAY MONTGOMERY, career officer; b. Arcadia, Fla., Apr. 15, 1938; s. James Harley and Consuello Adelaide (Pooser) G.; m. Mary Connie Kreigh, Dec 30, 1958; 1 child, Lori Lee Gibson. BA, Fla. State U., 1962; MA, Shippensburg U., 1983; attended, Air Defense Artillery Sch., Marine Corps. Command and Staff Coll., US Army War Coll., US Army Air Defense Sch., Ft. Bliss, Tex., 1962, Defense Lang. Inst., SW br., Ft. Bliss, 1966-67, Air Defense Artillery Officer Advanced Course, US Army Air Defense Sch., Ft. Bliss, 1969, Vietnam Tng. Ctr. Fgn. Svc. Inst., Dept. State, Washington, 1970-71, Marine Corps. Command and Staff Coll., Quantico, Va., 1974-75, US Army War Coll. Carlisle Barracks, Pa., 1982-83. With Fla. Nat. Guard; enlisted USMC; commd. 2d lt. US Army, 1962, advanced through grades to lt. gen., 1994, asst. platoon leader to platoon leader to exec. officer, Battery C, 3d Missile Battalion, 7th Artillery, US Army Europe, 1962-64, inactive Army Nat. Guard, 1964-65; ops. officer 53d Artillery Brigade US Army, Maxwell AFB, Ala., 1965-66; asst. subsector advisor, later dep. dist. sr. advisor adv. team 38, military assistance command US Army, Vietnam, 1967-68; comdr. Battery B, 5th Battalion, 7th Artillery, US Army Air Defense Commd. US Army, Franklin Lakes, N.J., 1968; chief, programs br., logistics divsn., office milit. assistance, US Army Southern Commd. US Army, Ft. Amador, Canal Zone, 1969-70; dist. sr. advisor, adv. team 36, military assistance commd. US Army, Vietnam, 1971-72; S-3, then plans, tng. officer, reserve component study, later S-3, 1st Battalion, 3d Air Defense Artillery, 101st Airborne Divsn. (Airmobile) US Army, Ft. Campbell, Ky., 1972-74; staff officer, firepower divsn., requirements directorate, later asst. exec. officer, office dept. chief staff ops. US Army, Washington, 1975-78; comdr. 1st Basic Combat Tng. Battalion, tng. and doctrine command US Army, 1978-79, comdr. 2d Battalion, 59th Air Defense Artillery, 1st Armored Division, US Army Europe, 1979-81, comdr. 108th Air Defense Artillery Brigade, 32d Army Air Defense Command, US Army Europe, 1984-86; dir. force requirements (combat support systems) office of dep. chief of staff ops. and plans US Army, Washington, 1986-88; dep. commdg. gen. US Army Air Defense Artillery Ctr., asst. commandant US Army Air Defense Artillery Sch. US Army, Ft. Bliss, 1988-90; dep. commdg. gen. V Corps. US Army Europe, 7th Army US Army, 1990-91; commdg. gen. joint task force BRAVO US Army, Northern Iraq, 1991; dep. commdg. gen. V Corp. US Army Europe, 7th Army US Army, 1991; asst. dep. chief staff ops. and plans force devel, Office of Dep. Chief of Staff Ops. and Plans US Army, Washington, 1992-94; commdg. gen. U.S. Army Space and Strategic Def. Command, 1994-96; asst. vice chief of staff U.S. Army, 1996-97; ret., 1997; pres. Sy Tech. Inc. Decorated DSM with oak leaf cluster, Def. Superior Svc. Medal with oak leaf cluster, Legion of Merit with 4 oak leaf clusters, Bronze Star, Air medal, Meritorious Svc. Medal, Joint Svc. Commendation Medal, Army Commendation Medal, Combat Infantryman Badge, Parachutist Badge, Army Staff Identification Badge. Democrat. Episcopalian. Avocations: health, fitness. Office: SY Tech Inc Ste 1000 1745 Jefferson Davis Hwy Arlington VA 22202-3402*

GARNER, JEFFREY L., accountant; b. Orange, Calif., Mar. 1, 1955; s. Gordon Abner and Jane Holmes (Milne) G.; m. Wanda Jean White, Dec. 16, 1979; children: Heather, Amanda, Jeremy, Laura, Kaitlyn. BBA summa cum laude, Loyola Marymount U., L.A., 1977; postgrad., Calif. State U., Long Beach, 1977-83. Sr. computer operator to cost acct. Aerospace divsn. Armco Steel-Oilfield Equip., Los Nietos, Calif., 1974-85; mgmt. acctg. mgr. Thermos Co., Batesville, Miss., 1985-87; plant cost mgr. Consol. Aluminum Corp., Jackson, Tenn., 1988-89; plant acctg. mgr. Procter & Gamble, Cin., 1990-95, sr. acct. MRP II project, 1996-98; acctg. and systems cons., 1999—. Soccer coach Parks and Recreation, Jackson, Tenn., 1992-93; forum leader Girl Scouts U.S., Jackson, 1988-93; mem. Jackson Archael. Soc., 1996-99, Calvary Singles, Jackson, 1995-99, Singles Vision, Westchester, Ohio, 1997-98; treas. PTO, 1992-93; vol. Jackson Food Band and Disaster Relief, 1998-99. Mem. Inst. Mgmt. Accts. (cert.), Am. Prodn. and Inventory Control Soc. (cert.). Republican. Baptist. Avocations: hiking, amateur naturalist, herpetology, woodworking, stamp and coin collecting. Address: PO Box 10034 Jackson TN 38301

GARNER, JIM D., state legislator, lawyer; b. Coffeyville, Kans., June 14, 1963; s. Wayne W. and Carol L. Garner. AA with honors, Coffeyville C.C., 1983; BA in History with distinction, U. Kans., 1985, JD, 1988. Bar: Kans. 1988. Jud. clk. for Dale E. Saffels U.S. Dist. Judge, Kans., 1988-90; atty. Hall, Levy, Lively, DeVore, Belot and Bell, Coffeyville, 1990-92; pvt. practice Coffeyville, 1992—; mem. Kans. Ho. of Reps., 1991—; minority leader Kans. House of Reps., 1999—; mem. assembly on fed. issues Nat. Conf. ofState Legislatures; mem. Program for Emerging Polit. Leaders, Darden Sch. of Bus., U. Va., 1994, Bowhay Inst. for Legis. Leadership Devel., Coun. of State Govts., U. Wis., 1995. Active cmty. co-chair, City of Coffeyville's Youth Focus Task Force, 1998; adv. com. Youth and Bus. Tng. Program; bd. dirs. Hospice Care Inc., Coffeyville, 1993-97, Pioneer chpt. ARC; mem. task force Coffeyville C.C. Honors Program; leadership Coffeyville Class of 1995. Mem. Kans. Bar Assn., Order of Coif, Phi Alpha Theta, Phi Kappa Phi, Coffeyville Lions Club. Home: 601 E 12th St Coffeyville KS 67337-6615 Office: PO Box 538 121 W 8th St Coffeyville KS 67337-5805

GARNER, JUNE BROWN, journalist; b. Detroit, July 19, 1923; d. Simpson and Vela (Wilkerson) Malone; m. Warren C. Garner, June 28, 1961; 1 dau., Sylvia G. Mustonen. Student, Wayne State U., 1941. Columnist, classified advt. mgr. Mich. Chronicle, Detroit, 1945-74; columnist Detroit News, 1974-87, Mich. Chronicle, 1990-92; CFO Warren Garner Realty, Southfield, Mich., 1992-96; reading tchr. North Tazewell (Va.) Elem. Sch., 1996—. Author: June Brown's Guide to Let's Read, 1981. Founder The Let's Read Summer Sch., 1980—. Recipient Best Column awards Detroit Press Club, 1971, 72, Nat. Newspaper Pubs. Assn., 1968, 69, Sch. Bell award Mich. Edn., Assn., 1989. Methodist. Home: 107 Vernon Ave Tazewell VA 24651-1432

GARNER, KAREN BURNETTE, artist, administrative assistant; b. Duluth, Ga., Jan. 29, 1957; d. Ronnie Alfred and Kathryn Burnette; m. Larry Garner, June 15, 1974; children: James, Lara. Student, Dekalb Coll., Workshop Adventures. Artist Dacula, Ga., 1983—; artist-in-residence Gwinnett County Pub. Schs., Snellville, Ga., 1995; tchr. Gwinnett County Gifted Program, Lawrenceville; pub. spkr. Studio ELMS, Buford, Ga. One-woman shows include Unique Selections, 1997; exhibited in group shows; featured artist GNET/TV, Lawrenceville, 1998, Creative Loafing Mag., 1998. Pres. PTA, Duluth, Ga., 1995; mem. Gwinnett Coun. for Arts. Recipient Purchase award Ga. Transplant Soc., 1997, Purchase award Gwinnett Coun. for Arts, 1987. Mem. Ga. Watercolor Soc. Avocations: gardening, music, public speaking. E-mail: kgarner@compuserve.com. FAX: 770-232-3296. Home: 2804 Armada Ln Dacula GA 30019 Office: Duluth Mid Sch 3057 Main St Duluth GA 30019

GARNER, MARY MARTIN, lawyer; b. Little Rock; d. Jared Owen and Mary Augusta (Conery) Martin; m. Meryl Everett Garner, Aug. 24, 1943 (dec.). JD, George Washington U., 1942. Bar: D.C. 1942, U.S. Supreme Ct. 1973. Atty. Office of Gen. Counsel, Div. Natural Resources, USDA, Washington, 1944-72, dep. dir., 1972-74; sole practice, Washington, 1975—; legal counsel Nat. Assn. Soil Conservation Dists., Washington, 1975—; mem. adv. task force on pollution in Great Lakes, U.S.-Can. Joint Commn., Windsor, Ont., Can., 1976-79; bd. dirs. Inter-Am. Bar Found., Washington, 1976—, Fed. Bar Bldg. Corp., 1983—. Pres. Wash. Club Preservation Fund, 1991—. Recipient Citation for Outstanding Contbn. to Advancement of Human Rights, Capital Area div. UN Assn. of U.S., Washington, 1983, Nat. Assn. Conservation Dists. Disting. Service award, 1972. Mem. ABA (vice chmn. com. on agr., adminstrv. law sect. 1979-81), Fed. Bar Assn. (chmn. internat. law sect. 1981-82, Outstanding Leadership award 1982), Internat. Bar Assn. (mem. governing council 1976-91), Washington Fgn. Law Soc., Inter-Am. Bar Assn. (asst. sec. 1978-85, mem. governing council 1985—), Bar Assn. D.C. (chmn. Inter-Am. relations com. 1976-77, Superior Service award 1977), Zonta Internat. Found. (bd. dirs. 1988-93), Women's Bar Assn. of D.C. (pres. 1957-58), Phi Alpha Delta, Soil Conservation Soc. Am. Democrat. Roman Catholic. Clubs: Nat. Lawyers (bd. govs.), The Washington Club Preservation Fund (dir.). Contbr. articles to profl. jours., chpt. to books, papers.

GARNER, PAUL TRANTHAM, data services administrator; b. Cameron, Tex., May 25, 1951; s. W.H. and Dorothy L. (Gohmert) G.; m. Tatyana Tokareva; children: Paul Christopher, Gregory Trantham. BBA, U. Tex., 1973; MS in Bus. Adminstrn., U. No. Colo., 1980. Cert. systems profl. Engr. Tex. Instruments, Inc., Austin, 1980; mgr. performance audit divsn. State of Tex. Auditor's Office, Austin, 1980-95; dir. data svcs. Tex. Workers Compensation Commn., Austin, 1995-98; info. tech. cons. Audit Force, Inc., Dallas, 1998—; mem. faculty Austin C.C., 1982; seminar lectr. in field. Mem. Bergstrom-Austin Community Coun. Capt. U.S. Army, 1973-80. U.S. Army ednl. scholar, 1969. Mem. Assn. for Systems Mgmt. (pres.), Am. Evaluation Assn., Legis. Prog. Evaluation Soc., Tex. Assn. State Sys. for Computing and Comms. (treas.), Austin Endowment Soc. (bd. dirs.), Austin Bus. Club., Rotary. Avocations: numismatics, scuba diving. Home: 1517 Merritt Dr Flower Mound TX 75028 Office: Audit Force Inc 500 N Akard St Ste 3201 Dallas TX 75201

GARNER, PHIL, professional baseball manager; b. Jefferson City, Tenn., Apr. 30, 1949; m. Carol; children: Eric, Bethany, Ty. BS, U. Tenn., Knoxville, 1973. Profl. baseball player Oakland Athletics, 1973-76, Pitts. Pirates, 1977-81, Houston Astros, 1981-87, L.A. Dodgers, 1987, San Francisco Giants, 1988; coach Houston Astros, 1989-91; mgr. Milw. Brewers, 1991—. Named to All-Star team, 1976, 80, 81. Office: Milw Brewers County Stadium PO Box 3099 Milwaukee WI 53201-3099*

GARNER, ROBERT EDWARD LEE, lawyer; b. Bowling Green, Ky., Sept. 26, 1946; s. Alto Luther and Katie Mae (Sanders) G.; m. Suzanne Marie Searles, Aug. 22, 1981; children: Jessica Marie, Abigail Lee. B.A., U. Ala.-Tuscaloosa, 1968; J.D., Harvard U., 1971. Bar: Ga. 1971, Ala. 1982, S.C. 1992, U.S. Dist. Ct. (no. dist.) Ga. 1974, U.S. Ct. Appeals (5th cir.) 1974, U.S. Ct. Appeals (11th cir.) 1981, U.S. Ct. Appeals (4th cir.) 1991. Assoc., Gambrell, Russell & Forbes, Atlanta, 1972-76, ptnr., 1976-80; ptnr. Haskell, Slaughter & Young and predecessor firms, Birmingham, Ala., 1981-88, mng. ptnr., 1986-87, of counsel, 1988-90; gen. counsel and sec. Builders Transport, Inc., 1988-90; ptnr. Nelson, Mullins, Riley & Scarborough, Atlanta and Columbia, S.C., 1991-96; mem. Haskell Slaughter & Young, L.L.C., Birmingham, Ala., 1996—. Served to 1st lt. JAGC, USAF, 1971-72. Mem. ABA (com. on fed. reg. of securities, subcom. on reporting companies under the 1934 act, mem. task force on disclosure of forward looking info.), Ga. Bar Assn., Ala. State Bar, Birmingham Bar Assn., U. Ala. Alumni Assn., Harvard U. Alumni Assn., Am. Soc. Corporate Secs., Inc. (mem. securities law com.), Phi Alpha Theta, Pi Sigma Alpha. Republican. Home: 913 Water Willow Ct Birmingham AL 35244-1477 Office: Haskell Slaughter & Young LLC 1200 Am South/Harbert Plaza 1901 6th Ave N Birmingham AL 35203-2618

GARNER, ROBERT F., bishop; b. Jersey City, Apr. 27, 1920. Student, Seton Hall U., Immaculate Conception Sem., N.J. Ordained priest Roman Cath. Ch., 1946. Ordained titular bishop Blera and aux. bishop Newark, 1976—. Office: Chancery Office 31 Mulberry St Newark NJ 07102-5202*

GARNER, TED, artist; b. Seattle, Feb. 10, 1957; s. James C. and Beatrice (Medicine) G.; m. Suzanne Martin, Sept. 27, 1986. BFA, Kans. City Art Inst., 1982. Artist, 1974—; v.p. Warrior Women, Wakpala, S.D., 1996—; lectr. Iowa State U., Ames, 1982, DePauw U., Greencastle, Ind., 1997, Smithsonian Instn., Washington, 1993; vis. artist, lectr. Oberlin, 1992. One-man shows include C.N. Gorman Mus., U. Calif.-Davis, 1978, The Grayson Gallery, Chgo., 1983, Jan Cicero Gallery, Chgo., 1994, 98, Sacred Circle Gallery Am. Indian Art, Seattle, 1997; sculpture commn. Field Mus. Natural History, Chgo., 1991, City of Chgo., 1996. Recipient Martin and Doris Rosen award Appalachian State U., 1992, Purchase award Eiteljorg Mus. Western Art, 1996. Avocation: electric and double bassist. Home: 1538 W Cortez St Chicago IL 60622-3955 Office: Ted Garner Artist 1544 N Sedgwick St Chicago IL 60610-1223

GARNER, THOMAS EMORY, JR., health insurance executive; b. Dublin, Ga., Apr. 4, 1945; s. Thomas Emory and Virginia (Register) G.; m. Betty Cook, June 18, 1967 (div. Feb., 1996); children: Kelly, Neil; m. Debra Stallworth, Sept. 5, 1997. BBA, Ga. So. U., 1967; M in Health Adminstrn., Ga. State U., 1970. Adminstrv. resident Rush Presbyn. St. Luke's Med. Ctr., Chgo., 1969-70; assoc. exec. dir. Grady Meml. Hosp., Atlanta, 1970-82; exec. dir. R.T. Jones Hosp., Canton, Ga., 1982-86; COO HMO Ga. (Blue Cross), Atlanta, 1986-93; pres., CEO PCA Health Plan of Ga., Atlanta, 1993-96, Master Health Plan, Atlanta, 1996-97; CEO Prime Living, Inc., Roswell, Ga., 1997—; bd. dirs. Prime Living, Inc., Atlanta, Master Health Plan, Inc., Atlanta; guest lectr. Inst. Health Adminstrn., Ga. State U., 1985—. Republican. Methodist. Avocations: boating, golf, skeet shooting. Office: Prime Living Inc 3500 Piedmont Rd Ste 211 Atlanta GA 30305-3899*

GARNER, WENDELL RICHARD, psychology educator; b. Buffalo, Jan. 21, 1921; s. Richard Charles and Lena Belle (Cole) G.; m. Barbara Chipman Ward, Feb. 18, 1944; children: Deborah Ann, Peter Ward, Elinor. A.B., Franklin and Marshall Coll., 1942, D.Sc., 1979; A.M., Harvard U., 1943, Ph.D., 1946; A.M. (hon.), Yale U., 1967; D.H.L., Johns Hopkins U., 1983. Teaching fellow Harvard U., 1942-43, research assoc., 1943-46; instr. Johns Hopkins U., 1946; asst. prof. Johns Hopkins, 1947-51; assoc. prof. Johns Hopkins U., 1951-55, prof., 1955-67; dir. Psychol. Lab. Inst. Coop. Research, 1949-55, chmn. dept. psychology, 1954-64; James Rowland Angell prof. psychology Yale U., 1967-89, prof. emeritus, 1989—, dir. social scis., 1972-73, 81-88, chmn. dept. psychology, 1974-77; dean Yale U. (Grad. Sch.), 1978-79; Paul M. Fitts Meml. lectr. U. Mich., 1973. Author: Uncertainty and Structure as Psychological Concepts, 1962, Processing of Information and Structure, 1974; editor: Ability Testing, 1982. Recipient alumni citation and award Franklin and Marshall Coll., 1975, Wilbur Cross medal Yale U., 1980, Gold medal Am. Psychology Found., 1999. Fellow AAAS (v.p. psychology 1967), Am. Psychol. Assn. (Disting. Sci. Contbn. award 1964, pres. div. exptl. psychology 1974), Am. Psychol. Soc. (William James fellow 1989), Acoustical Soc. Am.; mem. NAS, AAUP, Soc. Exptl. Psychologists (chmn. 1959, 75, Warren medal 1976), Md. Psychol. Assn. (pres. 1961-62), Ea. Psychol. Assn., Sigma Xi. Office: Yale U Psychology Dept New Haven CT 06520-8205

GARNES, RONALD VINCENT, marketing executive, finance broker, consultant; b. Washington, Mar. 7, 1947; s. Ernest W. Love and Vauda Hall Love G.; student U. Dayton, 1965-68, U. Md., 1975. Adminstrv. mgr. Western Union Electronic Mail, Inc., McLean, Va., 1976; dir. mktg. Communications Cons., Inc., Silver Spring, Md., 1977; ptnr. CAC, Washington, 1977; account mgr. PRC Computer Ctr., Inc., McLean, Va., 1978-79, sr. account mgr., 1979—; mktg. exec. Dun and Bradstreet Corp.; prin., CEO, RVG Assocs., Ltd., McLean, 1990—. Cons. Mem. Fairfax County Rep. Com. Mem. Nat. Coun. Tech. Svc. Industries, Nat. Assn. Market Developers, Am. Entrepreneurs Assn., Internat. Assn. Bus. and Fin. Cons., Mortgage Bankers Assn. Am., Internat. Assn. Entrepreneurs Am., Greater Washington Bd. Trade, Fairfax County C. of C., Lincoln Club, U.S. Senatorial Club. Roman Catholic. Office: 7918 Jones Branch Dr Ste 600 Mc Lean VA 22102-3307

GARNETT, KATRINA A., information technology executive; b. Brisbane, Australia, Oct. 17, 1961. BS, SUNY; MBA, Webster U., Geneva, Switzerland. CEO, pres. Cross Worlds Software, Burlingame, Calif., 1996—. Office: Cross Worlds Software Ste 800 577 Airport Blvd Burlingame CA 94010-2024

GARNETT, LINDA KOPEC, nurse, researcher; b. Springfield, Mass.; d. Frank J. and Anna (Paul) Kopec; m. Thomas R. Garnett, Oct. 6, 1990. BSN cum laude, Fitchburg (Mass.) State Coll., 1983; MS in Health Svcs. Adminstrn., Ctrl. Mich. U., 1996. RN, Va. Nurse intern Med. Coll. Va. Hosps., Richmond, 1983, nurse clinician in neurosci. ICU, 1984-86; terr. mgr., patient care specialist Kinetic Concepts Therapeutic Svcs., Richmond, 1986-89; rsch. coord. dept. neurology Med. Coll. Va./Va. Commonwealth U., Richmond, 1989—. Mem. Sigma Theta Tau.

GARNETT, STANLEY IREDALE, II, lawyer, utility company executive; b. Petersburg, Va., Aug. 11, 1943; s. Stanley Arthur and Edith (Keirstead) G.; children: Matthew S.A., Andrew F.W. BA, Colby Coll., 1965; MBA, U. Pa., 1967; JD, NYU, 1973. Bar: N.Y. 1974. Sr. fin. analyst Standard Oil Co. of N.J., N.Y.C., 1967-70; assoc. Milbank, Tweed, Hadley & McCloy, N.Y.C., 1973-81; v.p.-legal and regulatory Allegheny Power Sys., Inc., N.Y.C., 1981-90, v.p. fin., 1990-94, sr. v.p. fin., 1994-95; sr. advisor Putnam, Hayes & Bartlett, 1996-97, 98—; exec. v.p. Fla. Progress Corp., St. Petersburg, 1997-98; bd. dirs. Bay Corp Holdings, Inc. Vice chmn. Episcopal Ch. Bldg. Fund; trustee, sec. I(CB Internat. Ctr. for Disabled. Joseph P. Wharton scholar, 1965-67. Mem. ABA, N.Y. State Bar Assn. Republican. Episcopalian. Home: PO Box 67390 Saint Pete Beach FL 33736

GARNETT, SUSAN ELLEN, special education educator; b. Charleston, W.Va., Dec. 22, 1955; d. Carroll Leon and Minta Jane (Duffield) Ash; m. Robert David Garnett, Aug. 5, 1978. BA, Alderson-Broaddus Coll., 1978; postgrad., W.Va. Grad. Coll., 1996. Spl. edn. tchr. Rand Elem. Sch., Charleston, 1978-94, mem. sch. improvement coun., 1991—, vice-chair faculty senate, 1992-93, screening referral agt., 1988-94; resource tchr. Bridgeview Elem. Sch., South Charleston, W.Va., 1994-97; tchr. mild/moderate mentally impaired Bridgeview Elem. Sch., South Charleston, 1997—, past mem., 1996-98; screening referral agt. Bridgewater Ctr. Elem. Sch., South Charleston, 1994—. Mem. Am. Bapt. Ch., Charleston, 1990-91. Mem. PTO. Home: 5240 Rocky Fork Rd Cross Lanes WV 25313-2207 Office: Bridgeview Elem Ctr 5100 Ohio St South Charleston WV 25309-1126

GARNETT, WILLIAM, photographer; b. Chgo., 1916. Student, Art Center Sch. of Los Angeles, 1937-38. Free-lance advt. and mag. photographer, including aerial photography, 1938—; prof. design U. Calif.-Berkeley, 1968-84; fellow Ctr. for Advanced Visual Studies, MIT, 1967; appeared on TV programs The Pursuit of Happiness, NBC, 1976, From Here to There, CBS, 1980, Evening Mag, CBS, 1981; illustrator, collaborator: The American Aesthetic (Nathanial Owings), 1968; author, photographer: The Extraordinary Landscape, 1982, William Garnett Aerial Photographs, 1994. Exhibited in one-man shows including George Eastman House, Rochester, N.Y., 1955, numerous group shows in U.S. and abroad including Mus. Modern Art, N.Y.C., Met. Mus. Art, San Francisco Mus. Art, White House, 1979, Smithsonian Instn. Air and Space Mus. of Aerial Photography, Washington, 1979, also at several world fairs; represented in permanent collections George Eastman House, Mus. Modern Art, Smithsonian Instn., Polaroid Collection, Cambridge, Mass., Met. Mus. Art, N.Y.C., Gilman Paper Co., N.Y.C.; works include: photo mural for Wrigley Stadium, Los Angeles, 1938, two essays on beauty of America as seen from the air for Life Mag., 1965, numerous mag. articles. Recipient award Am. Soc. Mag. Photographers, 1983. Home: 1286 Congress Valley Rd Napa CA 94558-5310

GARNICK, JERRY JACK, periodontist, educator; b. Bklyn., Dec. 31, 1932; s. Harry and Dora (Borenstein) G.; m. Bernice Alpert, June 30, 1957; children: Nettie Noma Albrecht, Murray Richard, Ilene Lenore Goldman. MS, U. Mich., 1959, DDS, 1957. Diplomate Am. Bd. Periodontology. Assoc. prof., dept. periodontics U. Conn., 1971-74, acting head dept. periodontics, 1973-74; assoc. prof. Med. Coll. Ga., Augusta, 1974-77, prof. periodontics, 1977-98, dir. grad. studies, 1974-91, prof. grad. studies, 1980-98, acting chair dept. periodontics, 1987-91, chair, 1991-98, prof. emeritus, 1998—; assoc. head clin. periodontology Eastman Dental Ctr., Rochester, N.Y., 1966-71, assoc. in periodontics, 1964-66, rsch. assoc., 1961-64. Contbr. articles to profl. jours. Chmn. B'nai B'rith, Rochester, N.Y., 1965, Walton Way Temple, 1981-85; pres. AYS Synagogue, Augusta, 1997-98. Fellow Am. Coll. Dentistry; mem. Am. Acad. Periodontology, Internat. Assn. Dental Rsch., Am. Assn. Dental Schs., Conn. State Dental Assn., Ga. Dental Assn., So. Acad. Periodontology. Avocations: tennis, walking.

GARNISS, JOAN BREWSTER, musician, educator; b. Bangor, Maine, Aug. 10, 1940; d. William Ayer Brewster and Constance Miriam (Witham) Page; adopted d. Woodrow Evans Page; m. Howard Freeman Garniss, Aug. 26, 1962; children: Gretchen, Jonathan. MusB, Boston U., 1962, MusM, 1991. cert. music tchr., Music Tchrs. Nat. Assn. Pvt. practice Dover-Foxcroft, Maine, 1954-58, Hingham, Mass., 1963-65, Waltham, Mass, 1974—. Mem. LWV (v.p. 1979-83, pres. 1983-85, sec. 1997—, outstanding mem. award, 1995); co-founder Waltham Band Parents, 1979-82, Waltham Music Festival, 1994-97; pres. Friends Waltham Public Library, 1980-83 (bd. dirs. 1980-89, 1995—); trustee Waltham Public Libr., 1986— (co-chmn. fundraising com., 1995-96); dir. children's choir, All Saints Ch., 1963-66; vol. Boston Public Schs., 1969-73; mem. City Coun. Citizens Com. Transp., Waltham, 1977. Cultural Affairs Commn. grantee, 1988-89. Mem. UUA/MA Northeast Dist. (Human Rels. chmn. 1967-70), Music Tchrs. Nat. Assn.(rep. East Divsn. Cmty. Outreach, 1995-97,) Ind. Music Tchrs. Forum oversight com., 1997-99, Mass. Music Tchrs. Assn. (v.p. 1987-91, pres.-elect 1991-93, pres. 1993-97, immediate past pres. 1997-99), New England Piano Tchrs. Assn. (co-chmn. junior recitals com. 1982-88, student master class 1988-90), Duo Con Anima 1989—, Mass. Libr. Trustees Assn., Mu Phi Epsilon, Pi Kappa Lambda. Avocations: needlework, travel, reading, grandchildren.

GAROFALO, DONALD R., window manufacturing executive. CEO Anderson Corp., Bayport, Minn. Office: Anderson Corp 100 4th Ave N Bayport MN 55003-1096

GAROFALO, JANEANE, actress, comedienne; b. Newton, N.J., Sept. 28, 1964. BA in History and Am. Studies, Providence Coll. TV appearances include The Ben Stiller Show, 1992-93, The Larry Sanders Show, 1992-97, Saturday Night Live, 1994-95, Comedy Product, 1995, emcee, prodr., (movies) Late for Dinner, 1991, Armistead Maupin's Tales of the City, 1993, Reality Bites, 1994, Bye Bye Love, 1995, Cold Blooded, 1995, The Truth about Cats and Dogs, 1996, HBO 1 Hour Special, 1997; appearances include (films) The Cable Guy, 1996, Larger Than Life, 1996, Sweethearts, 1997, Touch, 1997, Romy and Michele's High School Reunion, 1997, Cop Land, 1997, Clay Pidgeons, 1997, The Matchmaker, 1997, Permanent Midnight, 1998, Dog Park, 1998, Half Baked, 1998, Thick as Thieves, 1999, Steal This Movie, 1999, The Minus Man, 1999, Dogma, 1999, Can't Stop Dancing, 1999, 200 Cigarettes, 1999, Mystery Men, 1999. Office: care Messina Baker Entertainment 955 Carrillo Dr Ste 100 Los Angeles CA 90048-5400 also: UTA Inc 9560 Wilshire Blvd Fl 5 Beverly Hills CA 90212-2401*

GARON, PHILIP STEPHEN, lawyer; b. Duluth, Minn., Nov. 11, 1947; s. Lawrence and Helen (Cohen) G.; m. Phyllis Sue Ansel, Mar. 22, 1970; children: Edward B., Sara B. BA summa cum laude, U. Minn., 1969, JD summa cum laude, 1972. Bar: Minn. 1972, D.C. 1973, U.S. Dist. Ct. Minn. 1974. Assoc. Covington & Burling, Washington, 1972-74; assoc. Faegre & Benson, Mpls., 1974-79, ptnr., 1980—; mem. mgmt. com. Faegre & Benson, 1992—. Co-author: Minnesota Corporation Law & Practice, 1996. Bd. dirs. Herzl Camp, Webster, Wis., 1985-91, Beth El Synagogue, Mpls., 1989—, v.p., 1993-96. Mem. Minn. Bar Assn. (pres. exec. coun. bus. law sect. 1996-97). Avocations: tennis, reading, bridge. Office: Faegre & Benson 2200 Norwest Ctr 90 S 7th St Ste 2200 Minneapolis MN 55402-3901

GARON, RICHARD JOSEPH, JR., chief of staff, political worker; b. Bronxville, N.Y., Sept. 9, 1948; s. Richard Joseph Sr. and Jeane Helen (Schlemmer) G.; m. Karen Barclay, Jan. 15, 1972; children: Cynthia Beth, Timothy Michael. BA, Hartwick Coll., 1972; MA, NYU, 1975, PhD, 1983. Legis. asst. U.S. rep. Benjamin A. Gilman, Washington, 1977-79, adminstrv. asst. U.S. rep., 1985-89; staff cons. House Com. on Fgn. Affairs, Washington, 1983-85; staff asst. House Com. on Post Office & Civil Svc., Washington, 1979-83, dep. minority staff dir., 1989-92; Rep. chief of staff House Com. on Fgn. Affairs, Washington, 1993-95; chief of staff House Com. on Internat. Rels., Washington, 1995—. NYU scholar, 1976-77. Republican. Episcopalian. Home: 11526 Gunner Ct Woodbridge VA 22192-5745

GARON, ROSS ANDEN, investment banker; b. N.Y.C., June 17, 1971. AB, Harvard Coll., 1993. With D.E. Shaw & Co., N.Y.C., 1993-94; assoc. dir. D.E. Shaw Securities Internat., London, 1994-95; gen. rep. Tokyo Rep. Office D.E. Shaw Securities Japan, Tokyo, 1995-97; global bus. mgr. Commerzbank AG Global Equities, Frankfurt, Germany, 1998-99; mng. dir. Comerzbank Capital Mkts. Corp., N.Y.C., 1999—. Democrat. Home: 178 E 80th St Apt 8E New York NY 10021 Office: Commerzbank Capital Mkts Corp 1251 Ave of the Americas New York NY 10020

GARONZIK, SARA ELLEN, stage director; b. Phila., Jan. 12, 1951; d. Milton and Bernice (Kohn) G. BA in Spanish cum laude, Temple U., 1972. Producing artistic dir. The Phila. Theatre Co., 1982—. Bd. dirs. Arts and Bus. Coun. Greater Phila., Artreach, Phila. Theatre Co. Recipient prize Sigma Delta Pi, 1972, award of Honor, Alumnae Assn. Girls H.S., 1997. Office: Phila Theatre Co 1811 Chestnut St Philadelphia PA 19103-3721

GARPOW, JAMES EDWARD, financial executive; b. Detroit, July 30, 1944; s. Roy Joseph and Jeanne Beechner (Brader) G.; BBA, U. Mich., 1968; m. Elizabeth Marie Conte, Aug. 30, 1969; children—Barbara Jean, Susan Marie. CPA, Mich. Audit mgr. Ernst & Young, Detroit, 1966-73; mgr. corp. acctg. Fed. Mogul Corp., Detroit, 1973-79; corp. contr. LOF Plastics, Inc., Detroit, 1979-80; treas., chief fin. officer KMS Industries, Inc., Ann Arbor, Mich., 1980-83; asst. sec., corp. contr. Simpson Industries, Inc., Mich., 1983—, treas., 1995—. Mem. AICPA, Mich. Assn. CPAs, Fin. Execs. Inst., Beta Alpha Psi, Alpha Kappa Psi. Office: Simpson Industries Inc 47603 Halyard Dr Plymouth MI 48170-2429

GARR, CARL ROBERT, manufacturing company executive; b. Olean, N.Y., Apr. 4, 1927; s. Frederick H.J. and Mary Magdalene (Zimmerman) G.; m. Arlene Crawford, Dec. 20, 1947; children: Christine Garr Weber, Anne Garr Shields, Elizabeth Garr Reese. B.S. in Physics, Kent State U., 1950; M.S. in Physics, Case Inst. Tech., 1953, Ph.D. in Metall. Engring, 1957. Supr. engring. Bettis plant Westinghouse Co., 1956-58; supt. tech. services, nuclear fuel ops. Olin Mathieson Chem. Corp., 1958-62; dir. engring. and research Albuquerque div. ACF Industries Inc., N.Y.C., 1962-68, v.p. research and devel., 1968-70; v.p. ACF Industries, Inc., N.Y.C., 1976-82; pres., chief exec. officer Polymer Corp. subs. ACF Industries, Inc., Reading, Pa., 1970-76, 1984-86, chmn., 1987—; pres., chief exec. officer Empire Steel Castings, Inc., Reading, 1982-84; v.p. Chesebrough-Pond's Inc., 1984-86; chief exec. officer, chmn. bd. Bank of Pa., Reading, 1988-92; vice-chmn. Dauphin Deposit Corp., 1988-92. Served with USN, 1944-46. Mem. Am. Soc. Metals, Sigma Xi. Club: Berkshire Country (Reading), The Boulders Club (Carefree, Ariz.). Home: 2017 Meadow Gln Wyomissing PA 19610-2719

GARR, DANIEL FRANK, restaurateur; b. Chgo., Sept. 4, 1950; s. Daniel Jacob and Sophie Evelen (Kurranty) G.; m. Dawn Marie Ciciora, May 7, 1983. AA, No. Ill. U., 1970; cert. recording engr., Inst. Audio Research, 1974. V.p. Garbaczewski Corp., Chgo., 1979-89, pres., 1989—; treas., chief exec. officer Gemtech Packaging Inc., Chgo., 1990—; pres. Fantasy Food Corp., Chgo., 1985-93; v.p. Dynamic Design Products, 1990; pres. Proline Tools, Md., 1998—. Bd. dirs. Am. Cancer Soc., 1993. Republican. Roman Catholic. Avocations: music, racquetball, photography. Home: 13713 Cavecreek Ct Lockport IL 60441-8653 Office: Chesdan Restaurant 4465 S Archer Ave Chicago IL 60632-2845

GARR, TERI (ANN), actress; b. Lakewood, Ohio, 1952; m. John O'Neil, Nov. 1993; 1 adopted child, Molly. Began career as dancer performing with San Francisco Ballet at age 13; in original road show co. of West Side Story; stage appearences include One Crack Out, 1978, Broadway, 1978, Ladyhouse Blues, 1979, Night of 100 Stars II, 1985; appeared in films including Viva Las Vegas, Head, 1968, Maryjane, 1968, Moonshine War, 1970, The Conversation, 1974, Young Frankenstein, 1974, Won Ton Ton, The Dog Who Saved Hollywood, 1976, Oh God!, 1977, Close Encounters of the Third Kind, 1977, Mr. Mike's Mondo Video, 1979, The Black Stallion, 1979, Honky Tonk Freeway, 1981, The Escape Artist, 1982, Tootsie, 1982, One From the Heart, 1982, The Sting II, 1983, The Black Stallion Returns, 1983, Mr. Mom, 1983, Firstborn, 1984, After Hours, 1985, Miracles, 1987, Out Cold, 1988, Let It Ride, 1989, Short Time, 1990, Waiting for the Light, 1990, Mom and Dad Save the World, 1992, Ready to Wear, 1994, Dumb and Dumber, 1994, Michael, 1996, A Simple Wish, 1997, Changing Habits, The Definite Maybe, 1997; TV movies include Doctor Franken, 1980, Prime Suspect, 1982, The Winter of Our Discontent, 1983, To Catch a King, 1984, Intimate Strangers, 1986, Fresno, 1986, Pack of Lies, 1987, Teri Garr in FlapJack Floozie, 1988, Drive, She Said (Trying Times), 1987, Mother Goose Rock n Rhyme, Stranger in the Family, 1991, Deliver Them From Evil: The Taking of Alta View, 1992, Fugitive Nights: Danger in the Desert, 1993, Ronnie and Julie, 1996; regular on TV series The Sonny and Cher Comedy Review, 1974, Good and Evil, 1991, Good Advice, 1994, Duckman, 1994, The Women of the House, 1995, Double Jeopardy, 1996, Nightscream, 1997, Murder Live!!, 1997; other TV appearances include Law and Order, 1976, Fresno, Late Night with David Letterman, The Frog Prince, Tales from the Crypt, Friends, 1997—. Office: William Morris Agy 151 S El Camino Dr Beverly Hills CA 90212-2775*

GARRA, RAYMOND HAMILTON, II, marketing executive; b. Chgo., Apr. 2, 1934; s. Raymond Hamilton and Dorothy (Gardner) G.; student Duke, 1951-53; BA, U. Calif. at Los Angeles, 1956; m. Sandra Beatrice Pheasant, Dec. 27, 1962 (div. May, 1970); children: Terese Helene, Raymond Hamilton III. Gen. mgr. fine paper div. Noland Paper Co., Inc., Buena Park, Calif., 1959-67; v.p. sales Western Lithograph Co., Inc., Los Angeles, 1967-71; pres. Los Angeles Lithograph Co., 1971-73; pres. World Sports Mktg., Inc., also Miss Calif. Teen-ager, Inc., 1974-79; pres. Westaire Properties, Inc., Westaire Travel and Tours, 1975-93; pres. Teragar Mktg., 1994—; pres. Gamra Graphics, Inc., 1998—. Mem. Republican State Central Com., 1966-67; exec. bd. U. Calif., Irvine Sports Assocs.; founder Internat. Divers Festivals, 1979, West Coast Challenge Cup Yacht Regatta, 1983; participant Nat. Sr. Olympics (swimming), 1995, 97. Served with USCGR, 1956-59; lt. comdr. Res. Flotilla Comdr., USCG Aux., 1990. Recipient Sports Family of Year award, 1975. Mem. Nat. Coronado 25 Assn. (pres. 1969-70; Yachtsman of Year award 1971), Buena Park C. of C. (sec. 1967), Mensa (founder Orange County Soc. 1964), Balboa Bay, Bahia Corinthian Yacht, Shriner (pres. El Bandito Shrine Club 1992), Pacific Golf and Country Club, Phi Kappa Psi (pres. Orange County Alumni Assn. 1994—). Home: 3 Sea Island Dr Newport Beach CA 92660-5100

GARRATT, REGINALD GEORGE, electronics executive; b. Birmingham, Eng., Sept. 25, 1929; came to the U.S., 1974; s. Wallace Thomas and Beatrice Maud (Round) G.; m. Gwendoline Jean Parry (dec. 1986); children: Mark, Jonathan, Sean; m. Gail Elizabeth Mansfield, July 1, 1989. Degree in mech. engring., Aston U., 1951. Dir. mktg. Honeywell (UK) Ltd., London, 1965-70; mng. dir. Honeywell (South Africa) Ltd., Johannesburg, 1970-74; gen. mktg. mgr. components divsn. Honeywell, Freeport, Ill., 1974-77; v.p. mktg. Knowles Electronics, Inc., Itasca, Ill., 1977-89, pres., COO, 1989-91, pres., CEO, 1991-97, chmn., CEO, 1997—. Bd. dirs. Hear Now, Denver, 1993—, Hearing Industries Assn., Washington, 1983—, Better Hearing Inst., Washington, 1981-90. Avocations: squash, tennis, bridge, golf, antiques. Home: 138 Circle Ridge Dr Burr Ridge IL 60521-8379 Office: Knowles Electronics Inc 1151 Maplewood Dr Itasca IL 60143-2071*

GARRELICK, JOEL MARC, acoustical scientist, consultant; b. N.Y.C., May 20, 1941; s. Samuel J. Garrelick and Phyllis Weidenbaum; m. Renee Brosell, Dec. 23, 1963; chilren: Kevin, Jenine, Daniel. BCE, CCNY, 1963, ME, 1965; PhD, CUNY, 1969. Lectr. CCNY, 1968-69; scientist Cambridge (Mass.) Acoustical Assocs., 1969-75, corp. scientist, 1976—, gen. mgr., 1998—. Contbr. articles to profl. jours. Fellow Acoustical Soc. Am.; mem. ASME. Office: CAA Inc 84 Sherman St Cambridge MA 02140-3261

GARREN, LISA ANN, veterinarian; b. Lima, Pa., Mar. 27, 1964; d. William and Vivian Charlene (MacDonald) Moore; m. Charles Harold Garren Jr., Aug. 30, 1996; children: Nicole Marie, Katelyn Hope. Diploma, Camillus Mercy Hosp., 1984; BS, U. Tenn., 1993, DVM, 1996. LPN, Fitzgerald Mercy Hosp., Lansdowne, Pa., 1984-86, St. Luke's Hosp., Bethlehem, Pa., 1987-90, U. Tenn. Hosp., Knoxville, 1990-92; veterinarian Garren Equine Vet. Svc., Knoxville, 1996-98, Garren Equine Vet. Svcs., Seymour, Tenn., 1998—, Parkway Animal Hosp., Sevierville, Tenn., 1996-98, Stonegate Animal Hosp., Dandridge, Tenn., 1998—. 4-H leader Sevier County (Tenn.) Extension., 1997—; chair com. Seymour United Meth. Ch., 1997. Mem. AVMA, Am. Assn. Equine Practitioners. Republican. Avocations: needlework, showing Western Pleasure, reading, camping. Home and Office: 1036 Stanton Rd Seymour TN 37865

GARRETSON, DONALD EVERETT, retired manufacturing company executive; b. Elizabeth, N.J., Nov. 22, 1921; s. James W. and Helen (Crane) G.; m. Adele F. Anderson, Sept. 17, 1949; children—James Robert, Katherine Crane, Donald Everett, Peter Andrew, Andrea Drew. A.B. in Commerce, Washington and Lee U., 1943; M.B.A., Harvard U., 1947; student, Northwestern U., 1942, 48; Ph.D. (hon.), Macalester Coll., 1985. With Arthur Andersen & Co. (C.P.A.'s), Chgo., 1947-50; with Minn. Mining & Mfg. Co., St. Paul, 1950-88; asst. treas. Minn. Mining & Mfg. Co., 1963-67, treas., 1967-77, v.p., 1972-77, v.p. fin., chief fin. officer, 1977-82; corp. v.p., pres. 3M Found., 1982-85; cons. 3M Community Svc. Program, 1985-88; bd. dirs. Delta Dental Plan Minn.; past mem. acctg. coun. of Conf. Bd. and Machinery and Allied Products Inst.; past chmn. Internat. Auditors of Midwest. Dir., past pres. Liberty Plaza Corp., St. Paul; past dir. First Mchts. State Bank, St. Paul; past chmn. bd. trustees Macalester Coll., St. Paul, now hon. trustee; past bd. dirs. Minn. Orchestral Assn.; bd. dirs. St. Paul Chamber Orch.; past pres., chmn. fund drive, lifetime dir. various coms., past regional chmn. St. Paul United Way; nat. bd. dirs. Jr. Achievement; past chmn. Jr. Achievement of Upper Midwest; chmn., past pres. Minn. Landmarks, Inc.; dir. Mairs and Power Growth and Balanced Funds., 1994—; cons. J&B Wholesale, Inc.; dir., past chmn. Minn. Pvt. Coll. Fund; hon. trustee Minn. Ind. Sch. Fund; mem. endowment investment com. Sci. Mus. Minn.; past chmn. bd., dir. Presbyn. Homes of Minn., 1989—. Served to lt. USNR, 1943-46. Presbyterian (elder). Clubs: Lilydale Tennis, Pool and Yacht. Home: 1146 Ivy Hill Dr Saint Paul MN 55118-1829

GARRETSON, HENRY DAVID, neurosurgeon; b. Woodbury, N.J., June 8, 1929; s. O.K. and Mary Marjorie (Davis) G.; m. Marianna Schantz, July 4, 1964; children: John, Steven. B.S., U. Ariz., 1950; M.D., Harvard U., 1954; Ph.D., McGill U., 1968. Diplomate: Am. Bd. Neurol. Surgery (mem. 1981-87, vice chmn. 1985-86, chmn. 1986-87. Surg. intern Royal Victoria Hosp., Montreal, 1954-55; resident Montreal Neurol. Inst., 1959-63; asst. prof. neurosurgery McGill U., Montreal, 1966-71; prof. U. Louisville, 1971-98, chmn. divsn. neurol. surgery, 1971-93; chmn. dept. neurol. surgery, 1993-97; assoc. dean clin. affairs Sch. Medicine U. Louisville, 1975-79, dir. neuroscis. programs Sch. Medicine, 1979-82; individual practice medicine, specializing in neurosurgery, Montreal, 1963-71; with Grantham & Garretson, Louisville, 1971-90, Neurosurgery Inst. Ky., 1990—; mem. staff Humana Hosp. U., Norton Children's, VA, Suburban Ky. Bapt. Hosps., all Louisville; staff Inst. Phys. Medicine and Rehab. Contbr. numerous articles, abstracts, editorials, presentations in field. Served with USNR, 1955-58. Fellow ACS; mem. AAAS, AMA, Am. Assn. Neurol. Surgeons (bd. dirs. 1983-85, sec. 1985-86, pres. elect 1986-87, pres. 1987-88), Am. Acad. Neurol. Surgery (pres. 1991-92), Congress Neurol. Surgeons, Ky. Neurosurg. Soc., Ky. Surg. Soc., Louisville Surg. Soc., Ky. Med. Assn., Soc. Neurol. Surgeons, Soc. U. Neurosurgeons (pres. 1983-84), So. Neurosurg. Soc. (pres. 1986-87), Jefferson County Med. Soc., Phi Beta Kappa, Phi Kappa Phi, Sigma Xi. Home: 517 Tiffany Ln Louisville KY 40207-1438 Office: Neurosurg Inst Ky Ste 1105 210 E Gray St Louisville KY 40202-3907

GARRETSON, OWEN LOREN, mechanical and chemical engineer; b. Salem, Iowa, Feb. 24, 1912; s. Sumner Dilts and Florence (White) G.; m. Erma Mary Smith, Jan. 23, 1932; children: John Albert, Owen Don, Susan Marie, Leon Todd. Student, Iowa Wesleyan Coll., 1930-32; BSME, Iowa State U., 1937. Registered profl. engr., Okla., N.Mex., Iowa, Mo. Engr. Bailey Meter Co., Cleve., 1937, St. Louis, 1937-38; engr., dist. mgr. Phillips Petroleum Co., Bartlesville, Okla., 1938-39, Amarillo, Tex., 1939-40; engr., dist. mgr. Phillips Petroleum Co., Detroit, 1940-41, wholesale mgr. liquefied petroleum gas sales divsn., 1941-42; mgr. product supply and transp. divsn. Phillips Petroleum Co., Bartlesville, 1942-44, mgr. engring. devel. divsn., 1944-46, mgr. spl. products engring. devel. divsn., 1946-47; pres. Gen. Tank & Steel Corp., Roswell, N.Mex., United Farm Chem. Co.; pres., dir. Garretson Equipment Co., Mt. Pleasant, Iowa; v.p., dir. Valley Industries, Inc., Mt. Pleasant; pres., dir. Garretson Carburetion of Tex., Inc., Lubbock; v.p., dir. Sacra Gas Co. Roswell, 1957-58; exec. v.p., dir. Arrow Gas Co. & Affiliated Corps., Roswell, N.Mex., Tex., Utah, 1958-60; asst. to pres. Nat. Propane Corp., Hyde Park, N.Y.; pres., chmn. bd. Plateau, Inc. Oil Refining, Farmington, N.Mex., 1960-82, also bd. dirs.; chmn. bd. S.W. Motels, Inc., Farmington; organizing dir. Farmington Nat. Bank, 1964; cons. Suburban Propane Gas Corp. Whippany, N.J. Contbr. articles to profl. jours.; 44 patents issued in several fields; inventor WWII aircraft engine power boost sys., 1942. Mem., past pres. Farmington Indsl. Devel. Svc., N.Mex. Liquefied Petroleum Gas Commn., 1955-76, chmn., 1956-58; mem. Iowa Gov.'s Trade Commn. to No. Europe, 1970, Iowa Trade Mission to Europe, 1979; mem. com. natural gas/liquefied natural gas Internat. Petroleum Expn. and Congress, 1970-71; mem. Nat. Coun. Crime and Delinquency. Recipient Merit award Iowa Wesleyan Coll. Alunmi Assn., 1968, Profl. Achievement Engring. citation Iowa State U., 1986. Mem. ASME, NSPE, Nat. Liquefied Petroleum Gas Assn. (bd. dirs., Disting. Svc. award 1979), Am. Petroleum Inst., Nat. Petroleum Refiner's Assn. (bd. dirs., pres.), Ind. Refiners Assn. Am., Agrl. Ammonia Inst. Memphis (bd. dirs.), N.Mex. Liquefied Petroleum Gas. Assn. (pres., bd. dirs.), Ind. Petroleum Assn. Am., N.Mex. Acad. Sci., Am. Soc. Agrl. Engrs., Am. Soc. Automotive Engrs., N.Mex. Amigos., Am. Inst. Chem. Engrs., Newcomen Soc. N.Am., Soc. Indsl. Archeology, Ancient Gassers (sec., pres.), 25 Yr. Club Petroleum Industry, Masons, Rotary, Phi Delta Theta, Tau Beta Pi. Home: 500 E La Plata St Farmington NM 87401-6940 Office: PO Box 108 Farmington NM 87499-0108

GARRETSON, PETER P., historian, educator; b. N.Y.C., May 8, 1947; s. Albert Henry and Agnes Ernst (Phillips) G.; m. Rufina Alamo. BA, Haverford Coll., 1969; PhD, U. London, 1974. Lectr. U. Khartoum, Sudan, 1974-78; asst. prof. Bklyn. Coll., 1978-79, Swarthmore (Pa.) Coll., 1980-81; assoc. prof. Fla. State U., Tallahassee, 1981—, assoc. v.p. internat. program, 1987-94; mem. adv. bd. Florica, Tallahassee, 1987-94, Fla./France Linkage Inst., Tallahassee, 1988-94, Fla. West Africa Linkage Inst., Tallahassee, 1990-94; bd. dirs. Badlissy Ctr., Tallahasse. Author: A History of Addis Ababa, 1998; contbr. articles to profl. jours. Recipient Palms Academique, Govt. France, 1993. Mem. African Studies Assn., Middle East Studies Assn., Sudan Studies Assn. (treas. 1983-85). Episcopalian. Avocations: reading, jogging. Home: 1130 Lothian Dr Tallahassee FL 32312-2836 Office: Dept History Fla State U Tallahassee FL 32312

GARRETSON, STEVEN MICHAEL, PC support manager; b. L.A., Nov. 2, 1950; s. Fredrick Harmon and Mildred (Mason) G.; m. Candice Kay Clouse, Sept. 23, 1972; children: Joshua Steven, Amanda Jeanine. BA, U. Calif., Irvine, 1972, tchr. credential, 1974; postgrad., U. Calif., Santa Barbara, 1973; MA, U. San Francisco, 1980. Cert. tchr., adminstr., Calif. Tchr. Irvine Unified Sch. Dist., 1974—; energy conservation cons. Irvine Unified Sch. Dist., 1981-85, grant writer, 1983—, archtl. design cons., 1975—, mentor tchr., 1984-86; presenter state social studies conf., 1980. Mem. Irvine Tchrs. Assn. (grievance chmn. 1980-82, treas., 1977-78, v.p., 1978-79, contract negotiator, 1976-84, 89-93, benefits mgmt. bd. 1990—, pres. 1993-97, technology support 1997—), Phi Delta Kappa. Roman Catholic. Avocations: volleyball, woodworking, computers, antique cars. Office: Irvine Unified Sch Dist 5050 Barranca Pkwy Irvine CA 92604-4698

GARRETT, BRAD, actor, comedian; b. Apr. 14, 1960. Actor in films including: Eight Men Out, 1988, Suicide Kings, 1997, George B, 1998, Postal Worker, 1998, Woody Allen Fall Project, 1998-99; TV series include: The Transformers, 1986, First Impressions, 1988, Eck! the Cat, 1992, Biker Mice From Mars, 1993, 2 Stupid Dogs, 1993, Pursuit of Happiness, 1995, Project G.e.e.K.e.R., 1996, Everybody Loves Raymond, 1996—, Toonsylvania, 1998, Hollywood Squares; voice in Jetsons: The Movie, 1990, 2 Stupid Dogs, 1993, Hollyrock-a-Bye Baby, 1993, Spy Hard, 1996, Superman: The Last Son of Krypton, 1996, Mighty Ducks the Movie: The Face-Off, 1997, Fallout, 1997, Bug's Life, 1998, Batman/Superman Movie, 1998; TV guest appearances include: Seinfeld, 1990, Superman, 1996, Roseanne, 1988, The King of Queens, 1998, Problem Child, 1993, Batman: The Animated Series, 1992. Office: Metropolitan Talent Agy 4526 Wilshire Blvd Los Angeles CA 90010*

GARRETT, C. LYNN, researcher, business consultant; b. Corpus Christi, Tex., Aug. 6, 1962; d. Billie Doyle and Ruth L. (Conklin) Grundy; m. James Glass, Aug. 18, 1979; children: Joshua Curran, Leah Michelle. BA in Psychology, Calif. State U., San Bernardino, 1992, MS in Indsl./Orgnl. Psychology, 1994. Orgnl. cons. Bethesda (Md.) Tri-Star Navy Hosp. Family Treatment Program, 1995-96, Betty Ford Ctr., Rancho Mirage, Calif., 1996-97; staff adminstr. GTE Telephone Ops., Irving, Tex., 1995-96, staff mgr. bus. market segmentation, 1996-97, staff mgr. market scis. dept., 1997—; CEO, owner, founder Garrett Evaluation and Measurement Corp., 1997—. Co-author, editor customer opinion report; author: Developing a Measure of Co-Dependent Behavioral Intentions, 1994. Mem. APA (assoc.). Avocations: family activities, reading, biking, boating, water skiing. Fax: (972) 291-1147. Office: 604 Trees Dr Cedar Hill TX 75104-5081 also: GTE Corp 700 Hidden Ridge HQW02C22 Irvine TX 75038

GARRETT, CHARLES GEOFFREY BLYTHE, physicist; b. Ashford, Kent, Eng., Sept. 15, 1925; came to U.S., 1950, naturalized, 1989; s. Charles Alfred Blythe and Laura Mary (Lotinga) G. B.A. in Natural Scis., Trinity Coll., Cambridge U., Eng., 1946; M.A. in Natural Scis., Ph.D. in Physics, Cambridge U., 1950. Instr. physics Harvard U., 1950-52; mem. tech. staff Bell Labs., Murray Hill, N.J., 1952-54; supr. Bell Labs., 1955-56, dept. head, 1960-69; dir. AT&T Bell Labs., Murray Hill-Morristown, N.J., 1969-87; chmn. Gordon Conf. on non-linear optics, 1964. Author: Magnetic Cooling, 1954, Gas Lasers, 1963; contbr. articles to profl. jours.; patentee in field. Named knight of Sovereign Order St. John of Jerusalem (Orthodox). Fellow Am. Phys. Soc., IEEE; mem. Guild of Carillonneurs in N.Am. Episcopalian. Avocations: piano, harpsichord, carillon, restoring 18th century houses and older Rolls-Royce cars. Home: 7 Fithian Ln East Hampton NY 11937-2605

GARRETT, CHERYL GAY, secondary education educator, writer; b. Plainview, Tex., Nov. 20, 1949; d. Jack Charles and Veda Fay (Ramsower) G.; m. Bradley I. Robertson, Dec. 19, 1973 (div. July 1980); m. Douglas L. Shriner, June 20, 1992; children: Chloe Shriner, Jack Shriner. BA in History, English, Tex. Christian U., 1972, MA in Comparative Studies, 1978; PhD in Secondary Edn., Composition, North Tex. U., 1985. Cert. secondary tchr., ESL tchr., Tex. Tchr. Ft. Worth Schs., 1972-75; prof. Tarrant County Jr. Coll., Ft. Worth, 1975-85; tchr. Gatewood Pvt. SCh., Ft. Worth, 1975-85, Ft. Worth Sch., 1978-79; mem. applied learning cert. New Stds. and Applied Learning, Ft. Worth, 1972-85, 90—, new stds. field tests, 1995—. Contbr. articles to mags. Mem. Nat. Abortion Rights League, Ft. Worth, Sisters Cities, Zoo Friends; docent Ft. Worth Zoo, 1985-90, Mus.Sci. and History, Ft. Worth, 1987-88. Recipient Silver medal in women's rifle Nat. Competition, 1972. Mem. NEA, Nat. Coun. English Tchrs. (local pres. 1978-80), Tex. State Tchrs., Ft. Worth Classroom Tchrs. Avocations: archeology, mystery writer, travelling.

GARRETT, CHRISTOPHER ARTHUR, secondary education educator; b. San Diego, Dec. 21, 1961; s. Louis Allen and Carmen (Barbara) G. B Music Edn., Bowling Green (Ohio) State U., 1984; MusM, Western Mich. U., Kalamazoo, 1992. Dir. bands Eastwood High Sch., Wood County, Ohio, 1984-87; grad. teaching asst. Western Mich. U., Kalamazoo, 1987-89; fine arts coord., music dir. Hackett Cath. Cen. High Sch., Kalamazoo, 1987-92; band dir. Vicksburg (Mich.) High Sch., 1992-98; instr. music Glen Oaks C.C., Centreville, Mich., 1998—; mem. adj. faculty Lake Michigan Coll., 1992-95, musician Battle Creek (Mich.) Symphony, 1987-89; horn instr. Rapid City Express Drum and Bugle Corps, Grand Rapids, Mich., 1989-91; music dir. St. Augustine's Cathedral, Kalamazoo, 1989—; participant in Courage to Teach Program, 1996-98. Musician, Kalamazoo Civic Theatre. Recipient Significant Educator award Kalamazoo Excellence in Edn. Assn., 1990. Mem. Phi Mu Alpha Sinfonia. Avocations: reading, camping, soccer. Home: 408 S Main St Vicksburg MI 49097-1317

GARRETT, DELORIS BRINK (DEE), school psychologist, psychology educator; b. Terre Haute, Ind., Mar. 29, 1939; d. William Frederick and Bernice M. (Piper) Brink; m. David A. Garrett, July 12, 1958. BS magna cum laude, Ind. State U., 1958, MA, 1962; postgrad., Butler U., Ind. U. Lic. sch. psychologist, lic. speech pathologist, lic. pvt. practice sch. psychologist, Ind.; cert. clin. social worker, Ind. Speech pathologist Americana Nursing Home, Indpls., 1968-72; speech pathologist Indpls. Pub. Schs., 1958-86, sch. psychologist, 1986—; adj. prof. psychology Ind. U.-Purdue U., Indpls., 1994—. Life trustee Indpls. Mus. Art, 1986—; bd. dirs. Herron Sch. Art and Gallery, Indpls., 1975—, Ind. Rep. Theatre, Indpls., 1977-90, Ptnrs. in Housing, Indpls., 1990—; mem. adv. bd. Dance Kaleidoscope Indpls., 1995—; v.p., mem. women's com. Ind. State Symphony Soc., 1963-75; pres., bd. dirs. Contemporary Art Soc., 1965—; pres. Christamore Aid Soc., Indpls., 1974-75; mem. bd. childhood mental health com. Mental Health Assn., 1994—; v.p. jr. group, designer cultural calendar for Indpls., Ind. Symphony Soc., 1969. Recipient TRACE (To Reward Advancement of Cultural Enhancement) vol. award City of Indpls., 1981. Mem. NASP, Am. Speech and Hearing Assn., Ind. Assn. Sch. Psychologists (pres. 1997-98, Outstanding Speech Pathologist 1971, Outstanding Sch. Psychologist 1993). Lutheran. Avocations: collecting contemporary art, travel, skin diving, reading. Home: 7943 Clearwater Pkwy Indianapolis IN 46240-4902

GARRETT, DON JAMES, philosophy educator; b. Salt Lake City, June 5, 1953; s. James Raymond and Bula (Fisher) G.; m. Frances Clark, Aug. 8, 1975; children: Matthew, Christopher. BA, U. Utah, 1974; PhD, Yale U., 1979. Asst. prof. Harvard U., Cambridge, Mass., 1979-82; asst. prof. U. Utah, Salt Lake City, 1982-85, assoc. prof., 1985-95, prof., 1995-99, chair dept. philosophy, 1996-99; Kenan Disting. Tchg. prof. U. N.C., Chapel Hill, 1999—; vis. assoc. prof. Johns Hopkins U., Balt., 1988. Author: Cognition and Commitment in Hume's Philosophy, 1997; editor: The Cambridge Companion to Spinoza, 1996, (jour.) Hume Studies, 1994—. Office: Univ NC Chapel Hill Caldwell Hall CB # 3125 Chapel Hill NC 27599-3125

GARRETT, DUANE DAVID, hospitality executive; b. N.Y.C., Mar. 28, 1952; s. Gloria Lynne (Magliana) G.; m. Chahla Zarinzad, Nov. 10, 1977 (div. Feb. 1987). BBA, SUNY, Albany, 1989; postgrad., West Coast U. Gen. mgr. Reise Orgn., N.Y.C., 1974-77, Burger King Corp., L.A., 1977-83; staff acct. Baar Accountancy Corp., Encino, Calif., 1983-85; comptroller The Playboy Club of Hollywood, L.A., 1985-86, The Mayfair Hotel, L.A., 1986-87; administr. employees stock purchase plan Litton Industries, Inc., Beverly Hills, Calif., 1987-90; fin. mgr. Armored Transport Inc., Pasadena, Calif., 1990—; cons. No. Star Prodn. Co., Beverly Hills, 1985-89, Video Butler Enterprises, Van Nuys, Calif., 1984-86; cons., auditor Bank of Am., L.A., 1987; adv. bd. Restaurant Bus. Mag., L.A., 1985-89. Fund raiser Rep. Party, Calif., 1986-88; publicity chmn. Calif. State Women's Ctr., Northridge, 1985. Mem. NAFE (site coord. 1988-89), Internat. Student Orgn. Republican. Episcopalian. Avocations: computers, collecting rare books. Home: 15353 Weddington St #C102 Van Nuys CA 91411 Office: Armored Transport Inc 3452 E Foothill Blvd 360 N Crescent Dr Pasadena CA 91107

GARRETT, DWAYNE EVERETT, veterinary clinic executive. Office: Wentzville Veterinary 602 E Pearce Blvd Wentzville MO 63385-1538*

GARRETT, FRANKLIN MILLER, historian; b. Milw., Sept. 25, 1906; s. Clarence Robert and Ada (Kirkwood) G.; m. Frances F. Finney, 1978; children by previous marriage: Patricia A. Garrett, Franklin Miller Garrett Jr. LLB, Woodrow Wilson Coll. Law, 1941; PhD, Oglethorpe U., 1970, Ga. State U., 1998. Br. mgr. Western Union Telegraph Co., Atlanta, 1934-38; salesman Ward Wight & Co., Atlanta, 1939-40; mem. exec. staff pub. relations, historian Coca-Cola Co., Atlanta, 1940-68; chmn. Fulton County (Ga.) Civil Service Bd., 1955-72; ofcl. historian City of Atlanta, 1973—, Fulton County, 1975—. Author: Atlanta and Environs I-III, 1954, rev. edit., 1969; Yesterday's Atlanta, a picture history, 1974. Bd. dirs. Children's Center Met. Atlanta, 1958-70. Served with AUS, 1942-45. Named a City Shaper, Atlanta mag., 1976; recipient Meritorious Pub. Service medal Nat. Assn. Secs. of State, 1985, Shining Light award for Svc. as Atlanta's Historian, 1993; mainline diesel locomotive Ga. R.R. named in his honor, 1980. Mem. Nat. Ry., Va., Ga., Atlanta Hist. Soc. (chmn. bd. trustees 1967-68, dir. 1968-74, historian 1974—, trustee 1932—), DeKalb County hist. socs., Newcomen Soc. N.Am., Atlanta Art Assn., Atlanta Civil War Round Table, Grand Jurors Assn. Fulton County, Ga. Geneal. Soc., Rotary, Commerce Club, Piedmont Driving Club. Presbyterian. Home: Apt 1106 3747 Peachtree Rd NE Atlanta GA 30319-1364 Office: 130 W Paces Ferry Rd NW Atlanta GA 30305-1380

GARRETT, GEORGE PALMER, JR., creative writing and English language educator, writer; b. Orlando, Fla., June 11, 1929; s. George Palmer and Rosalie (Toomer) G.; m. Susan Parrish Jackson, June 14, 1952; children: William, George, Rosalie. Grad., Hill Sch., 1947; A.B., Princeton U., 1952, M.A., 1956, Ph.D., 1985; DLitt (hon.), U. South, 1995. Asst. prof. English Wesleyan U.; writer-in-residence, resident fellow in creative writing Princeton U., 1964-65; former assoc. prof. U. Va.; prof. English Hollins Coll. Va., 1967-71; prof. U. S.C., Columbia, 1971-73, Princeton U., 1974-78, U. Mich., 1979-80, 83-84; Hoyns prof. creative writing U. Va., Charlottesville, 1984—; prof. Bennington Coll., 1980; Coal Royalty chair U. Ala., 1994. Author The Reverend Ghost: Poems (Poets of Today IV), 1957, King of the Mountain, 1958, The Sleeping Gypsy and Other Poems, 1958, The Finished Man, 1959, Which Ones Are the Enemy, 1961; (poems) Abraham's Knife, 1961, In the Briar Patch, 1961; (plays) Sir Slob and the Princess, 1962, Cold Ground Was My Bed Last Night, 1964; (screenplays) The Young Lovers, 1964, The Playground, 1965, Do, Lord, Remember Me, 1965, For a Bitter Season, 1967, A Wreath for Garibaldi, 1969, Death of the Fox, 1971, The Magic Striptease, 1973, Welcome to the Medicine Show, Postcards/Flashcards/Snapshots, 1978, To Recollect a Cloud of Ghosts: Christmas in England 1602-03, 1979, Luck's Shining Child: Poems, 1981, The Succession: A Novel of Elizabeth and James, 1983, The Collected Poems of George Garrett, 1984, James Jones, 1984, An Evening Performance: New and Selected Short Stories, 1985, Poison Pen, 1986, Understanding Mary Lee Settle, 1988, Entered from the Sun, 1990, The Sorrows of Fat City, 1992, Whistling in the Dark, 1992, My Silk Purse and Yours, 1992, The Old Army Game, 1994, The King of Babylon Shall Not Come Against You, 1996, Days of Our Lives Lie in Fragments, 1998, Bad Man Blues, 1998; editor The Girl in the Black Raincoat, 1966, The Sounder Few, 1971, Film Scripts I-IV, 1971, Craft So Hard to Learn, 1973, The Writer's Voice, 1973, Intro V, 1974, Intro 6: Life As We Know It, 1974, Intro 7: All of Us and None of You, 1975, Botteghe Obscure Reader, 1975, Intro 8: The Liar's Craft, 1977, Intro 9: Close to Home, 1978, Eric Clapton's Lover, 1990, The Wedding Cake in the Middle of the Road, 1992, Elvis in Oz, 1992, That's What I Like (About the South), 1993. Served in occupation of Trieste, Austria and Germany. Recipient Rome prize Am. Acad. Arts and Letters, 1958-59, Sewanee Rev. fellow poetry, 1958-59, Am. Acad. and Inst. of Letters award, 1985, T.S. Eliot award Ingersoll Found., 1990, Penn/Malamud award, 1990, Hollins Coll. medal, 1992, U. Va. Pres.'s Report award, 1992; named Cultural Laureate of Va., 1986; Ford Found. grantee in drama, 1960, Nat. Found Arts grantee, 1966, Guggenheim fellow, 1974. Fellow Am. Acad. in Rome; mem. MLA, Author's League, Writers Guild Am. East, Poetry Soc. Am., PEN, Fellowship So. Writers (vice chancellor 1988, chancellor 1993-97). Democrat. Episcopalian. Home: 1845 Wayside Pl Charlottesville VA 22903-1630 Office: Univ Va Dept English Charlottesville VA 22903

GARRETT, GLORIA SUSAN, social services professional; b. Tampa, Fla., Nov. 30, 1951; d. Howard Leon and Marie Leonora (Garcia) G.; m. Michael Thomas McClain, May 16, 1973; children: Molly Kathleen Garrett McClain, Andrew Michael Garrett McClain. Student, Agnes Scott Coll., 1969-71, U. South Fla., 1971-72; BA, Ga. State U., 1977, MEd, 1979. Sr. caseworker DeKalb County Dept. Family and Children Services, Decatur, Ga., 1979-80, 82-84, prin. caseworker, 1980-82, 84-85, casework supr., 1985-86, sr. casework supr., 1986-91; disability adjudicator Ga. Disability Adjudication Sect., Decatur, 1991-93, sr. disability adjudicator, 1993-94, case cons., 1994-96, disability adjudication casework supr., 1996—. Mem. Nat. Assn. Disability Examiners, Ga. Assn. Disability Examiners. Office: Disability Adjudication PO Box 1187 Decatur GA 30031-1187

GARRETT, JAMES JOSEPH, lawyer, partner; b. L.A., Dec. 17, 1939; s. Joseph Robert and Catherine Agnes (Cavanaugh) G.; m. Mary Isabel McNeil, June 22, 1963 (div.); children: Sean, Drew, Craig; m. Maria Pamela Rivera, July 26, 1980; children: Joshua, Matthew. AB, Stanford U., 1961; JD, Harvard U., 1964. Bar: Calif. 1965. Atty. Morrison & Foerster, San Francisco, 1966—. Author: Antitrust Compliance, 1978; gen. editor and contbg. author: World Antitrust Law and Practice, 1995; author chpt.: A Guide to Foreign Investment in the United States, 1992. Capt. U.S. Army, 1964-66. Mem. ABA, Calif. Bar Assn. Roman Catholic. Avocations: collecting historical newspapers, running, fly fishing, backpacking. Office: Morrison & Foerster Ste 450 101 Ygnacio Valley Rd Walnut Creek CA 94596-4094

GARRETT, JAMES LEO, JR., theology educator; b. Waco, Tex., Nov. 25, 1925; s. James Leo and Grace Hasseltine (Jenkins) G.; m. Myrta ann Latimer, Aug. 31, 1948; children: James Leo III, Robert Thomas, Paul Latimer. BA, Baylor U., 1945; BD, Southwestern Bapt. Theol. Sem., 1948, ThD, 1954; ThM, Princetoon Theol. Sem., 1949; PhD, Harvard U., 1966; postgrad., Oxford U., 1968-69, St. John's U., 1977, Trinity Evang. Div. Sch., 1989. Ordained to ministry Baptist Ch., 1945. Pastor Bapt. chs. in Tex., 1946-48, 50-51; sucessively instr., asst. prof., assoc. prof., prof. theology, disting. prof. emeritus Southwestern Bapt. Theol. Sem., Ft. Worth, 1949-59, 79—, assoc. dean for PhD degree, 1981-84; prof. Christian theology So. Bapt. Theol. Sem., Louisville, 1959-73; dir. J.M. Dawson Studies in Ch.-State, prof. religion Baylor U., Waco, Tex., 1973-79, Simon M. and Ethel Bunn prof. Ch.-State Studies, 1975-79; interim pastor Bapt. chs. in Tex., D.C., Ind. and Ky.; guest prof. Hong Kong Bapt. Theol. Sem., 1988; coord. 1st Conf. on Concept of Believers' Ch., 1967; chmn. study commn. on coop. Christianity, Bapt. World Alliance, 1968-75; sec. Study Commn. on Human Rights, 1980-85; co-chmn. Study and Rsch. Divsn., 1995-99; theol. lectr. Wake Forest, N.C., Torreon, Mex., Cali., Colombia, Recife, Brazil, Montefideo, Uruguay, Oradea, Romania, Dallas, Yalta and Odessa, Ukraine. Author: The Nature of the Church According to the Radical Continental Reformation, 1957, Baptist Church Discipline, 1962, Evangelism for Discipleship, 1964, Baptists and Roman Catholicism, 1965, Reinhold Niebuhr on Roman Catholiticism, 1972, Living Stones: The Centennial History of Broadway Baptist Church, Fort worth, Texas, 1882-1982, 2 vols., 1984-85, Systematic Theology Vol. 1, 1990, Vol. 2, 1995; co-author: Are You Southern Baptists "Evangelicals"?, 1983; co-editor: The Teacher's Yoke: Studies in Memory of Henry Trantham, 1964; editor: The Concept of the Believers' Church, 1970, Baptist Relations with Other Christians, 1974, Calvin and the Reformed Tradition, 1980, We Baptists, 1999; editor Southwestern Jour. Theology, 1958-59, Jour. of Ch. and State, 1973-79. Mem. Am. Soc. Ch. History, Am. Acad. Religion, So. Bapt. Hist. Soc., Conf. on Faith and History. Home: 5525 Full Moon Dr Fort Worth TX 76132-2309 Office: PO Box 22117 Fort Worth TX 76122

GARRETT, JAMES LOWELL, contractor; b. Stillwater, Okla., Dec. 29, 1946; s. Calvin L. Garrett and Jetta L. (Hubbel) Newberry; m. Deborah F. Files, Sept. 3, 1987; 1 child, Kristina D. BS in Indsl. Engring. and Mgmt., Okla. State U., 1969. Pres. Garrett Devel., Oklahoma City, 1970-80, T.A.O. Inc. Gen. Contractor (merged with Garrett Devel.), Tulsa, 1981—. Mem. Investments and Constrn. Mgmt., Tulsa C. of C. Office: T A O Inc Gen Contractor 8218 E 121st St S Bixby OK 74008-2700

GARRETT, JANE NUCKOLS, editor, priest; b. Dover, Del., July 16, 1935; d. David Elwood and Edna Earle (Davidson) Nuckols; m. Wendell Douglas Garrett, June 22, 1957 (div. 1973). BA, U. Del., 1957; LittD (hon.), Middlebury Coll., 1997. Acquisitions dept. Boston Athenaeum Libr., Boston, 1957-58, asst. to dir., 1959-68; editor N.Y. Hist. Soc., N.Y.C., 1966-67; editor, asst. Alfred A. Knopf, Inc., N.Y.C., 1967-73, editor, 1974-96, sr. editor, 1996—; book rev. editor New England Quar., Boston, 1959-66. Co-compiler: The Arts in Early Am. History, 1965; contbr. articles to profl. jours. Pub. developer Adult Lit. Orgn. of Rhodesia, Salisbury, 1973-74; adv. coun. Inst. Early Am. History-Culture, Williamsburg, Va., 1988-91. Episcopal. Home: 206 Fairway Vlg Leeds MA 01053-9706 Office: 201 E 50th St New York NY 10022-7703

GARRETT, JOHN R., communication executive; b. Evanston, Ill., Jan. 14, 1939; m. Cheryl C. Garrett, Sept. 15, 1992; children: Timothy, Wendy. BA, Antioch Coll., Yellow Springs, Ohio, 1961; PhD, Union Grad. Sch., 1975. Dir. market devel. Copyright Clearance Ctr., Danvers, Mass., 1988-91; dir. info. resources Corp. for Nat. Rsch. Initiatives, Reston, Va., 1991-95; CEO Cybervillages, Andover, Mass., 1995-96; v.p. bus. devel. Planet Direct, Andover, 1996-99; dir. internet bus. Cross Country Group, Medford, Mass., 1999—; co-chair task force on digital preservation Rsch. Librs. Group, Berkeley, Calif., 1994-95. Editor: Preserving Digital Information, 1996; contbr. articles to profl. jours. Avocations: family and friends, tennis, travel. Home: 4 Beacon Heights Ln Marblehead MA 01945-1578 Office: Cross Country Group 226 Mystic Ave Medford MA 02155

GARRETT, JOSEPH EDWARD, aerospace engineer; b. Hendersonville, N.C., Mar. 4, 1943; s. Kenneth Pace and Anna Lou (Lytle) G.; m. Aurelia Jane Pryor, Aug. 7, 1971. BS in Aerospace Engring., N.C. State U., 1966; MS in Aerospace Engring., Ga. Inst. Tech., 1978. Registered profl. engr., Ga. Basic and fatigue loads assoc. aircraft engr. LASC-Ga. (formerly Lockheed-Ga.), Marietta, 1966-67, basic and fatigue loads structures engr., 1967-75, fatigue and fracture mechanics sr. structures engr., 1975-80, company planning, 1980-82, fracture mechanics structures engr., 1982-91, advanced structures sr. engr., 1991-96; fatigue and fracture mechanics sr. structures engr., 1996—. Loaned exec. United Way, Atlanta, 1984, Cobb County chmn. for Individual Gifts, Marietta, 1985, chmn. Cobb County Adv. Com., Marietta, 1987-88, bd. dirs., Atlanta, 1987-88. Assoc. fellow AIAA (dir. Regional II 1990-96), Mem. of Yr. Atlanta sect. 1986, Booster of Yr. 1988, 92, 94, 95); mem. Inst. Cert. Mgrs. Lockheed Ga. Mgmt. Assn. (v.p. mem. achievement 1988-89, v.p. adminstrn. 1989-90, Booster of Month 1980, 1st Cert. Mgr. of Yr. 1989). Republican. Baptist. Avocations: landscaping, woodworking. Home: 2291 Goodrum Ln Marietta GA 30066-5200 Office: LASC-Ga Dept 73-25 Zone 0160 86 S Cobb Dr Marietta GA 30063-1000

GARRETT, KATHERINE ANN, interior designer; b. Macon, Ga., Sept. 20, 1970; d. Billy Francis and Nancy (Knighton) G. BS in Family Consumer Sci., Ga. So. U., 1994. Former interior designer Homeworks, Macon; pvt. practice interior designer. Mem. Am. Soc. Interior Designers, Golden Key, Phi Upsilon Omicron, Gamma Beta Phi. Avocations: swimming, walking, cross-stitch, sewing. Home: 1035 S Pine Knoll Dr Macon GA 31204-1110

GARRETT, LAURIE, science correspondent; b. L.A., Sept. 8, 1951; d. Banning and Lou Ann (Pierose) G. Grad. with honors, U. Calif., 1975, postgrad. With KPFA, Berkeley, Calif., Calif. Dept. Food and Agr.; freelance journalist So. Europe, E. Africa, 1979; freelance reporter, 1980-88; sci. corr. Newsday, N.Y.C., 1988—; vis. fellow Harvard Sch. Pub. Health, 1992-93. Author: The Coming Plague: Newly Emerging Diseases in a World Out of Balance, 1994; contbr. articles to periodicals including Omni, Washington Post, L.A. Times, Foreign Affairs, others; TV appearances include Dateline, McNeil/Lehrer Newshour, Nightline, others; contbr. reports including Science Story (George Foster Peabody Broadcasting award 1977), Hard Rain: Pests, Pesticides, and People (Edwin Howard Armstrong Broadcast award 1978), The VDT Controversy (Nat. Press Club award Best Consumer Journalism 1982), Why Children Die in Africa (Media Alliance Meritorious Achievement award in Radio 1983, World Hunger Media award First Prize 1987), AIDS in Africa (J.C. Penney/Mo. Journalism Cert. Merit, award of Excellence Nat. Assn. Black Journalists Second Place, 1989), Breast Cancer (Best Beat Reporter Deadline Club N.Y. 1993, First Place N.Y. State AP Writing Contest Press Club L.I., Soc. Silurians 1994), AIDS in India (Bob Considine award Overseas Press Club Am. 1995), Ebola Virus Outbreak in Zaire (Pulitzer prize in Explanatory Journalism, 1996). Office: Newsday 235 Pinelawn Rd Melville NY 11747-4250 also: care Charlotte Sheedy 65 Bleecker St New York NY 10012-2420*

GARRETT, LELAND EARL, nephrologist, educator; b. Spartanburg, S.C., Jan. 8, 1949; s. Leland Earl and Mary Lillian (Butler) G.; m. Sarah Anne Pryor, Aug. 13, 1970 (div. 1978); 1 child, Katherine; m. Nancy Jean Swenson, May 3, 1980; children: Christopher, Jennifer. BS, N.C. State U., 1971; MD, Med. U. S.C., 1976. Commd. 2d lt. USAF, 1971, advanced through grades to lt. col., 1985, ret., 1991; intern Wilford Hall, USAF Med. Ctr., 1976-77; resident USAF Med. Ctr., 1977-79; fellowship Duke U. Med. Ctr., 1979-81; pvt. practice Wake Nephrology Assocs., Raleigh, N.C., 1991—; clin. prof. medicine U. N.C., Chapel Hill, 1998—. Contbr. articles to profl. jours. Bd. dirs. South Tex. Organ Bank, San Antonio, 1984-86, Urban Ministries, 1997—; data chair, bd. dirs. Southeastern Kidney Coun., Raleigh, 1993-97, 98—; med. adv. chmn. N.C. affiliate Nat. Kidney Found., Charlotte, 1994—; med. dir. Open Door Clinic/Urban Ministries, Raleigh, 1996-98. Named Physician of Yr. N.C. affiliate Nat. Kidney Found., 1995. Fellow ACP, Am. Soc. Nephrology, Internat. Soc. Nephrology. Lutheran. Avocation: medical informatics. Office: Wake Nephrology Assocs 3604 Bush St Raleigh NC 27609-7511

GARRETT, LINDA SILVERSTEIN, financial planner; b. Pitts., May 14, 1949; d. Maurice J. and Mary H. (Reagan) Silverstein; m. Mark B. Garrett, Apr. 1, 1978 (div. Aug. 1987). BS in Social Work, W.Va. U., 1972. CFP, Fla.; registered rep. N.Y. Stock Exch., Nat. Assn. Securities Dealers. Group worker, dir. Miami Jewish Home & Hosp. for the Aged, 1976-80, registered rep., 1980-84; rsch. asst. Prescott, Ball & Turben, North Miami, Fla., 1980-84; acct. exec. Prudential Securities, Ft. Lauderdale, Fla., 1984-88; v.p. Morgan Keegan, Ft. Lauderdale, 1988-89; fin. cons. Merrill Lynch, Ft. Lauderdale, 1989-94; v.p. Dean Witter, Plantation, Fla., 1994—. Instr., lectr. Assn. Women CPA, Ft. Lauderdale, 1985; cons. Jr. Achievement, Broward County, Fla., 1993; counselor Switchboard Miami, 1976-80; active Archdiocese Miami Planned Giving Coun. 1988-90, lectr. 1988-89; mem. exec. com. profl. adv. coun. Found. Jewish Philanthropies, 1995—, Gwen Cherry chpt. Women's Political Caucus, 1995—; trustee Broward Jewish Cmty. Found. Mem. Internat. Assn. Fin. Planners, Nat. Coun. Aging. Democrat. Jewish. Avocations: scuba diving, swimming, reading, sky diving. Home: 544 NE 17th Way Fort Lauderdale FL 33301-1352 Office: Dean Witter Reynolds Cornerstone 1 1200 S Pine Island Rd # Rp Plantation FL 33324-4413

GARRETT, MARILYN RUTH, nurse; b. Columbia, Mo., Mar. 28, 1957; d. Charles Filmore and Mable Ruth (Rice) Pasley; m. Donald Burce Garrett, June 9, 1983 (div. Mar. 1994); children: Patrick Bryan, Christopher Ryan. ADN, Cen. Meth. Coll., 1985. Cert. psychiat. and mental health nurse. Staff nurse Fulton (Mo.) State Hosp., 1985, clin. nursing supr., 1989-91, overall nursing supr., 1991-92, nurse educator, nursing edn. and staff devel., 1992-94, psychosocial rehab. tng. specialist, 1994—; instr. CPR, 1987—; aggressive mgmt. tng. instr., 1990-96, non-violent crisis prevention instr., 1998—, instr., trainer, 1998—; chair nurse recruitment and retention com., Mo., 1991-93; mem. planning com. Annual Forensic Conf., 1998—; team cons. Nurse Practice/Policy and Procedure. Mem. vol. task force team Callaway County unit Am. Cancer Soc.; mem. panel Smoking Cessation Group for County Health Svcs., 1993; vol. CPR instr. Callaway County and Fulton Pub. Schs., 1997, Dept. of Transp., 1997-98; case mgmt. Role Recovery Workshop, 1997-98; mem. program devel. team Intermed. Care Ward, 1995-96. Named Employee of the Month State of Mo., Dept. Mental Health, 1991. Home: 1015 Bluff St Fulton MO 65251-2320 Office: Fulton State Hosp 600 E 5th St Fulton MO 65251-1798

GARRETT, NAOMI MILLS, foreign language educator, retired; b. Columbia, S.C., Aug. 24, 1906; d. Casper George and Anna Maria (Threewitts) G. AB, Benedict Coll., 1927; MA, Atlanta U., 1937; PhD, Columbia U., 1954; postgrad., U. Paris, 1958; LLD, Denison U., 1979; DHL, W.Va. State Coll., 1981. Instr. fgn. langs. Pub. Sch. Systems, Kittrell Coll., N.C., S.C., 1927-42; mem. U.S. English Project, Haiti, 1942-44; prof. fgn. lang. dept., dept. chair W.Va. State Coll., Institute, 1947-72; Disting. prof. R.I. Coll., 1971; univ. prof. Denison U., Granville, Ohio, 1972-74, adj. prof., 1975-79; guest lectr. U.S. Cultural Svcs., French W. Africa, 1958, U. of Lille, France, 1959, Cath. U. of Strasbourg, France, 1959; mem. African Studies Group, UCLA, 1968, 69, others; cons. in field. Contbg. editor: Handbook of Latin American Studies, 1959-92, Ency. Poetry and Poetics, 1965; contbr. articles to profl. jours. Bd. dirs. Kanawha Pastoral Counseling Ctr. Rosenwald fellow N.Y., 1944-45, Columbia U. fellow, N.Y., 1946-47, Ford fellow, N.Y., 1951-52, Fulbright fellow, Paris, 1958-59; recipient Martin Luther King award for edn. State of W.Va., 1988, Disting. West Virginian award Gov. Gaston Caperton, 1992, W.Va. Women's Commn. Celebrate Women award, 1997, others. Mem. MLA, AAUW (bd. dirs.), Am. Assn. Tchrs. of French, Nat. Assn. Fgn. Student Affairs, Coll. Lang. Assn., African Lit. Assn., Internat. Coun. on Edn. for Tchg., Am. Coun. on Tchg. of Fgn. Langs., Friendship Force (bd. dirs. W.Va.), Humanities Found. of W.Va. (bd. dirs.). Home: PO Box 111 Institute WV 25112-0111

GARRETT, PAUL EDGAR, insurance executive, writer, poet; b. Timpas, Colo., Nov. 18, 1909; s. Charles Calvin and Ida Pauline (Guire) G.; m. Vera Griggs, Sept. 21, 1927 (dec. 1941); children: Donald (dec.), Gerald (dec.); m. Muriel Gladys Goodroad, Mar. 10, 1945 (dec. Aug. 1983); m. Ornetta Gardner, Oct. 27, 1984. BS in Biol. Scis., U. Wyo., 1935; CLU, Am. Coll., 1978. Pub. sch. adminstrn. Wyo., Alaska, 1932-36; dist. mgr. Ohio Nat. Life, Laramie, Wyo., 1936-37; gen. agt. Ohio Nat. Life, Billings, Mont., 1937-50; mem., chmn. field adv. bd. Ohio Nat. Life, Spokane, 1946-66, gen. agt. for Mont., Idaho and Wash., 1950-66; mem., chmn. Ins. Examining Bd., Olympia, Wash., 1962-70. Author: (poems) Song of the North, 1936, Down By The Sea, 1994; author hunting and fishing stories, short stories, historical stories. Lt. USN, 1942-46, PTO. Mem. Wash. State Life Underwriters, Elks, Ret. Officers Assn., Sigma Chi. Avocations: short story writing. Home: 1518 E Cambridge Ln Spokane WA 99203-3933 also: 119 Viscount Ln Lake Havasu City AZ 86403-5141

GARRETT, REGINALD HOOKER, biology educator, researcher; b. Roanoke, Va., Sept. 24, 1939; s. William Walker and Lelia Elizabeth (Blankenship) G.; m. Linda Joan Harrison, Mar. 15, 1958 (div.); children: Jeffrey David, Randal Harrison, Robert Martin; m. Catherine Leigh Touchton, June 12, 1989 (div.). BS, Johns Hopkins U., 1964, PhD, 1968. Asst. prof. biology U. Va., 1968-73, assoc. prof., 1973-82, prof., 1982—; sci. cons. Author textbooks; contbr. articles to profl. jours. NIH fellow, 1964-68; Fulbright Hays fellow, 1975-76; Thomas Jefferson vis. fellow, 1983; grantee NIH, NSF. Mem. Am. Soc. Biochemistry and Molecular Biology, Am. Soc. Microbiology, Am. Soc. Plant Physiology, Soc. Gen. Physiology, Sigma Xi, Phi Lambda Upsilon, Phi Sigma. Office: U Va Dept Biology Gilmer Hall Charlottesville VA 22903

GARRETT, RICHARD G., lawyer; b. N.Y.C., Oct. 16, 1948. BA magna cum laude, Emory U., 1970, JD, 1973. Bar: Ga. 1973, Fla 1979; U.S. Dist. Ct. (no. dist.) Ga. 1973, (so. dist.) Fla. 1979, U.S. Dist. Ct. (so. dist. trial bar) Fla. 1979; U.S. Ct. Appeals (5th cir.) 1974; U.S. Ct. Appeals (9th. cir., 11 cir.) 1981; U.S. Supreme Ct. 1981. Program dir., instr. rsch., writing and advocacy Emory U., Sch. of Law, 1972-73; chmn. litigation dept., exec. com. bd. dirs. Greenberg, Traurig, Miami, Fla. Editor: Emory Law Journal, 1972-73. Recipient 1st place and Best Brief award Region V Nat. Moot Ct. Competition, 1972. Mem. ABA, The Fla. Bar Assn., State Bar Ga., Omicron Delta Kappa, Order of the Barristers. Office: Greenberg Traurig 1221 Brickell Ave Miami FL 33131-3224*

GARRETT, ROBERT, financial advisory executive; b. Morristown, N.J., Feb. 27, 1937; s. Harrison and Grace Dodge (Rea) G.; m. Jacqueline E. Marlas, July 10, 1965; children: Robert Jr., Johnson. AB, Princeton U., 1959; MBA, Harvard U., 1965. V.p. Smith, Barney & Co., N.Y.C., 1965-69, Robert Garrett & Sons, N.Y.C. and Balt., 1969-71; 1st v.p. Smith, Barney, Harris Upham & Co., N.Y.C., 1972-78; sr. v.p. Smith, Barney Real Estate Corp., N.Y.C., 1978-84; exec. v.p. Security Capital Corp., N.Y.C., 1978-85; pres. Robert Garrett & Sons Inc., N.Y.C., 1986—; pres. AdMedia Ptnrs. Inc., 1990—; bd. dirs. Mickelberry Corp., Penn Virginia Corp.; chmn. bd. dirs. S.E. Pub. Ventures Inc. Trustee Near East Found., Cleveland H. Dodge Found., Abell Found., N.Y. Bot. Garden, Adirondack Mus. With AUS, 1959-63. Mem. Univ. Club of N.Y., Nantucket Yacht Club, Piping Rock Club (L.I.), River Club of N.Y., Knickerbocker Club of N.Y. Republican. Episcopalian. Home: 800 Park Ave New York NY 10021-2760 Office: 444 Madison Ave New York NY 10022-6903

GARRETT, ROBERTA KAMPSCHULTE, nurse; b. Amityville, N.Y., Aug. 15, 1947; d. Robert Henry and Gertrude Ann (Schweitzer) Kampschulte; m. Paul R. Garrett Jr., Nov. 26, 1977; children: Samantha Kristine, Kelly Nicole. BS, U. Fla., 1969. RN, Fla.; cert. in oncology nursing. Staff nurse Valley Hosp., Ridgewood, N.J., 1969-70; asst. head nurse Broward Gen. Hosp., Ft. Lauderdale, Fla., 1970-71; CCU nurse Grady Meml. Hosp., Atlanta, 1972-77; nurse to pvt. physician Orlando, Fla., 1977-94; case mgmt. Fla. Healthcare Sys., Orlando, 1996—. Republican. Lutheran. Avocation: jogging.

GARRETT, SANDY LANGLEY, school system administrator; b. Muskogee, Okla., Feb. 8, 1943; 1 child, Charles Langley (Chuck). BS in Elem. Edn., Northeastern U., Tahlequah, Okla., 1968, MS in Counseling, 1980; grad. John F. Kennedy Sch. Govt., Harvard U., 1989. Lic. tchr., adminstr., supt. std., Okla. Tchr. Hillsdale Schs., Muskogee, Okla., 1968-80, coord. gifted program, 1980-82; coord. gifted and talented State Dept. Edn., Oklahoma City, 1982-85, dir. rural edn., 1985-87, exec. dir. ednl. svcs., 1987-88, state supt. pub. instn., 1991-95; sec. edn. Gov.'s Office, Oklahoma City, 1988—; state supt. pub. instrn. State Dept. Edn., Oklahoma City, 1991—; chair State Bd. Edn., Oklahoma City, 1991—, State Vo-Tech. Edn., Oklahoma City, 1991—; bd. dirs. So. Regional Edn. Bd.; regent Okla. Colls., 1991—; mem. Nat. Coll. Bd. Equality Project; chair. Okla. Lit. Initiatives Commn.; mem. So. Regional Ednl. Bd. Co-author: (curriculum guide) Gifted Galaxy; mem. editorial bd. Rural and Small Schs.; contbr. articles to profl. jours. Co-chair Dem. Party, Muskogee, 1978; del. Dem. Nat. Conv., N.Y.C., 1980, 82; mem. Leadership Okla., 1990. Recipient Cecil Yarbrough award, 1989, Claude Dyer Legis. award, 1989. Mem. Muskogee County Ednl. Assn., Delta Kappa Gamma, Phi Delta Kappa, Delta Kappa Gamma. Methodist. Avocations: tennis, swimming, computer programming, travel, politics. Home: Apt 2410 11300 N Pennsylvania Ave Oklahoma City OK 73120-7781 Office: State Dept Edn 2500 N Lincoln Blvd Oklahoma City OK 73105-4503*

GARRETT, STEVEN LURIE, physicist; b. L.A., Apr. 3, 1949; s. Fred Ellis and Vivian Dorothy (Lurie) G.; m. Gloria Kalisher, Nov. 26, 1975. BS in Physics, UCLA, 1970, MS in Physics, 1972, PhD in Physics, 1977. Asst. prof. Naval Postgrad. Sch., Monterey, Calif., 1981-85, assoc. prof., 1985-88, prof., 1988-95; United Techs. prof. of Acoustics Pa. State Univ., State College, Pa., 1995—; Rosen prof. Technion, Haifa, Israel, 1985; vis. staff Los Alamos (N.Mex.) Nat. Labs., 1981—; cons. in field, Monterey, Calif., 1982—. Contbr. articles to profl. jours.; patentee in field. Fellow Miller Inst. Basic Research in Sci., 1978-81. Fellow Acoustical Soc. Am. (Hunt fellow 1978, Silver Medal in Phys. Acoustics and Engring.Acoustics, 1993); mem. ASME, Am. Phys. Soc., Am. Soc. Engring. Edn., Sigma Xi. Home: PO Box 10271 State College PA 16805-0271 Office: Grad Program in Acoustics PO Box 30 State College PA 16804-0030

GARRETT, THEODORE LOUIS, lawyer; b. New Britain, Conn., Sept. 4, 1943; s. Louis and Sylvia (Greenberg) G.; m. Bonnie Garrett, Nov. 27, 1968; children—Brandon, Natalie. B.A., Yale U., 1965; J.D., Columbia U., 1968. Bar: N.Y. 1968, D.C. 1971, U.S. Supreme Ct. 1973. Law clk. to Judge J. Joseph Smith U.S. Ct. Appeals for 2d Circuit, 1968-69; spl. asst. to asst. atty. gen. William H. Rehnquist Dept. Justice, Washington, 1969-70; law clk. to Chief Justice Warren E. Burger U.S. Supreme Ct., 1970-71; assoc. Covington & Burling, Washington, 1971-76, ptnr., 1976—. Editor, prin. author: Corporate Counsel Environmental Law Guide, 1993; co-author: Clean Air Act Desk Book, 1991; contbg. author: A Practical Guide to Environmental Law, 1987, Liability for Hazardous Waste Sites Under CERCLA, 1988, Practice Under the New Federal Sentencing Guidelines, 3d edit., 1993, Environmental Dispute Handbook, 1991, Environmental Litigation, 1991; editor, contbg. author: The Environmental Law Manual, 1992, RCRA Policy Documents, 1993, RCRA Practice Manual, 1994; contbr. articles to profl. jours. Named One of 100 Influential Lawyers in Nat. Law Jour., 1994. Mem. ABA (chair-elect and exec. com. of sect. environ., energy and resources, exec. bd. Environ. Lawyer, adv. bd. ABA Jour., editorial bd. In Brief, mem. task force on superfund reform), D.C. Bar Assn. (steering com. of environment, energy and natural resources sect., 1991-97, chair coun. on sects, 94-95). Home: 6604 Broxburn Dr Bethesda MD 20817-4710 Office: Covington & Burling 1201 Pennsylvania Ave NW PO Box 7566 Washington DC 20044-7566

GARRETT, THOMAS W., career officer; b. Jan. 2, 1947. Commd. officer U.S. Army, advanced through grades to maj. gen., commdg. gen. Total Army Pers. Command, 1997—. Office: US Total Army Pers Command 200 Stovall St Alexandria VA 22332-0400

GARRETT, WILBUR (BILL), magazine editor; b. Kansas City, Mo., Sept. 4, 1930; s. Clay Dean and Cecil Zora (Melton) G.; m. Lucille Hall, Dec. 26, 1950; children: Michael Dean, Kenneth Lewis. BJ, U. Mo., 1954; LittD (hon.), U. Miami. With Nat. Geog. mag., 1954-90, editor, 1980-90; faculty photojournalism workshop U. Mo., 1963, 64, 69, 70, 73, 74, 75, 77, 78, 79, 80, 94; editor Cosmos Jour., 1995-98; designer photog. exhbn. U.S. Pavilion, N.Y. World's Fair, 1965; designer-producer Nat. Geog. Soc. exhbns. 23d, 24th, 25th Picture of Year Competition; mem. XIX Olympiad Cultural Com.; bd. dirs. Congentrix Energy, Inc., Nat. Geographic Soc., 1980-90, rsch. and exploration com., 1981-90; bd. advisors Corbis Prodns., Inc. Ptnrs. for Livable Cmtys.; bd. govs. The Nature Conservancy, 1988-98, Am. Land Conservancy; bd. dirs. Heritage USA; trustee W. Eugene Smith Meml. Fund.; founder, pres. La Ruta Maya Conservation Found., 1990. With USNR, 1946-52. Decorated Order of the Quetzal (Guatemala). Recipient Newhouse citation U. Syracuse, 1963, Rotondi award, Italy, 1998, Mag. Photographer of Year award, 1968, Disting. Service in Journalism award U. Mo., 1978, Nat. mag. awards for excellence, 1984, 89, 90, 91; leadership medal UN Environ. Programme, Chevron Environ. award 1990, La Pluma Plata Pres. of Mex., 1990. Mem. Cosmos Club (Washington). Home & Office: 209 Seneca Rd Great Falls VA 22066-1108

GARRETT, WILLIAM L., federal judge; b. 1922. LLB, U. Calif., Hastings, 1946. With Landram, Silveira, Garrett & Gaul, 1950-86; U.S. commr. ea. dist. U.S. Dist. Ct. Calif., 1950-70, magistrate judge ea. dist., 1970-86, apptd. part-time magistrate judge no. dist., 1988. Fax: (408) 373-7699. Address: PO Box 1390 Monterey CA 93942-1390

GARRIDO, AUGIE, university athletic coach. Head coach Calif. State Fullerton Titans, 1973-87, 1991-96, U. Ill., 1987-91, U. Texas, Austin, 1996—. Named 4th Winningnest active divsn. IA coach, 1103 victories. Champions NCAA divsn. IA, 1979, 84. Office: U Tex Austin Intercollegiate Athletics 2400 Inner Campus Dr Austin TX 78712

GARRIGA, MARK, state government administrator; m. stephanie Strickland; 1 child, Alexandra. BS in Fin., Miss. State U., 1981; JD, U. Miss., 1985. Ptnr. Allen, Cobb and Hood, Gulfport, Miss., 1985-94; chief of staff Gov. of Miss., Jackson, 1994—. Del. Rep. Nat. Conv., Houston, 1992; mem. nat. bd. dirs. Initiative and Referendum Inst., Washington. Fellow Miss. Bar Found. Office: PO Box 139 Jackson MS 39205

GARRIGAN, RICHARD THOMAS, finance educator, consultant, editor; b. Cleve., Mar. 4, 1938; s. Walter John and Priscilla Marie (Hill) G.; m. Kristine Ottesen, Dec. 26, 1962; 1 child, Matthew Osborne. BS summa cum laude, Ohio State U., 1961, MA, 1963; MS, U. Wis., 1966, PhD, 1973. Asst. prof. fin. U. Wis., Whitewater, 1974-76, assoc. prof., 1976-77; v.p. rsch. Real Estate Rsch. Corp., Chgo., 1975-76; presdl. exch. exec. Fed. Home Loan Bank Bd., Washington, 1977-78; assoc. prof. DePaul U., Chgo., 1978-83, prof., 1983—; mem. Midwestern regional adv. bd. Fed. Nat. Mortgage Assn., 1993-96; mem. adv. bd. Bell Fed. Bank, Chgo., 1996-98; bd. dirs. Fed. Home Loan Bank Chgo., 1983-86. Co-editor: The Handbook of Mortgage Banking, 1985, Real Estate Investment Trusts, Structure, Analysis and Strategy, 1998; editor Dow Jones-Irwin Series in Real Estate, 1987-90; contbr. articles to profl. jours. Served with U.S. Army, 1955-58. Alfred P. Sloan scholar, 1959-61; recipient Excellence award Haskins and Sells, 1960, Achievement award Pres.'s of U.S. Commn. on Exec. Exchange, 1978; fellow Mershon Nat. Security, Ohio State U., 1961-62, urban studies Ford Found., 1964-65, bus. Ford Found., 1965-66. Mem. Am. Real Estate Soc., Am. Real Estate and Urban Econs. Assn., Bldg. Owners and Mgrs. Assn. of Chgo. (adv. bd. 1994-98), Sphinx, Univ. Club Chgo., Lambda Alpha Internat. (Ely chpt. sec. 1984, v.p. 1985, pres. 1986), Beta Gamma Sigma, Phi Kappa Phi,

Phi Eta Sigma. Home: 920 Romona Rd Wilmette IL 60091-1222 Office: DePaul U Fin Dept 1 E Jackson Blvd Chicago IL 60604-2201

GARRIGLE, WILLIAM ALOYSIUS, lawyer; b. Camden, N.J., Aug. 6, 1941; s. John Michael and Catherine Agnes (Ebeling) G.; m. Jeannette R. Regan, Aug. 15, 1965 (div.); children: Maeve Regan, Emily Way; m. Rosalind Chadwick, Feb. 17, 1984; 1 child, Susan Chadwick. BS, LaSalle U., 1963; LLB, Boston Coll., 1966. Bar: N.J. 1966, U.S. Dist. Ct. N.J., U.S. Ct. Appeals (3rd cir.) 1973, U.S. Supreme Ct., 1973; cert. civil trial atty., N.J.; cert. civil trial adv., Nat. Bd. Trial Advocacy; diplomate Am. Bd. Profl. Liability Attys. Assoc. Taylor, Bischoff, Neutze & Williams, Camden, 1966-67, Moss & Powell, Camden, 1967-70; ptnr. Garrigle Palm & Thomasson, Cherry Hill, N.J., 1970—. With USAR, 1959-67. Mem. ABA, N.J. State Bar Assn., Burlington County Bar Assn., Camden County Bar Assn., Internat. Assn. Def. Counsel, Def. Rsch. Inst., N.J. Def. Assn., Am. Bd. Trial Advs. (diplomate), Fedn. of Ins. and Corp. Counsel, Trial Attys. N.J., Camden County Inn of Ct. (master of the bench, chmn. 1989-96, treas. 1996—), Tavistock Country Club. Home: 223 E Main St Moorestown NJ 08057-2905 Office: Garrigle Palm & Thomasson 1415 Route 70 E Cherry Hill NJ 08034-2210

GARRIGUS, UPSON STANLEY, animal science and international agriculture educator; b. Willimantic, Conn., July 2, 1917; s. Harry Lucien and Bertha May (Patterson) B.; m. Olive Tyler, July 2, 1942; children—Beth Ellen, Mark Tyler. B.S. with high honors, U. Conn., 1940; M.S., U. Ill., 1942, Ph.D., 1948; cert., Washington and Lee U., 1943, Sorbonne, 1944. Asst. U. Conn., Storrs, 1936-40; grad. asst. U. Ill., Urbana-Champaign, 1940-42, 46-48; asst. prof., then assoc. prof. U. Ill., 1948-55, prof., 1955—, head Sheep div., 1949-64, head Runinant div., 1964-70, prof. animal sci., internat. agr., assoc. head dept. animal sci., 1972-87, prof. emeritus, 1987—; mem. Am. Dehydrator's Rsch. Coun., 1958-70; mem. Nutrient Requirements of Sheep Com., NRC, 1953-75, Nonprotein Nitrogen Utilization Com., NRC, 1970-76; cons. Midwest Univs., Consortium Internat. Activities Higher Edn., Indonesia, 1980, AID, Thailand, 1981, U. New Eng., Australia, Higher Edn. Indonesia, 1989. Contbr. numerous articles to profl. jours. Active Comty. United Ch. of Christ; bd. dirs. Univ. YMCA, Champaign, Ill., 1956-62, 64-70; chmn. Baily Scholarships, 1972-76. Lt. maj. U.S. Army, 1942-46. Decorated Bronze Star. Recipient Nat. Block and Bridle Merit trophy, 1940; Am. Assoc. Advancement of Sci. Fell., 1957; Service award Eastern States Exposition, 1959; Disting. Service award YMCA, 1970, 77; Animal Sci. Teaching and Counseling award U. Ill., 1980; Nat. Feed Ingredients Assn. travel fellow, 1971; outstanding alumni award Coll. Agriculture & Natural Resources U. Conn., 1996. Fellow AAAS, Am. Soc. Animal Sci. (Jean Claude Bouffault Meml. award in internat. animal agriculture 1994); mem. Soc. Exptl. Biology and Medicine, Am. Inst. Nutrition, Am. Inst. Biol. Sci., Coun. Agr. Sci. and Tech., Am. Registry Profl. Animal Scientists, Sigma Xi, Phi Kappa Phi, Phi Sigma, Gamma Sigma Delta. Home: 811 W William St Champaign IL 61820-5832 Office: 186 Animal Scis Lab 1207 W Gregory Dr Urbana IL 61801-3838

GARRIOTT, LOIS JEAN, clinical social worker, educator; b. Avon Park, Fla., Mar. 22, 1944; d. John Arnold and Katherine Faith (Morton) G.; m. Bertram Paul Martin, Mar. 9, 1963 (div. Dec. 1978); children: Heidi, Ivy, Kurt, Aaron. AA, Macomb County Community Coll., Warren, Mich., 1969; BA in Psychology, U. Mich., Dearborn, 1974; MSW in Group Work, Wayne State U., 1978. Family therapist Cath. Social Svcs., Port Huron, Mich., 1978-79; specialist St. Clair County Community Mental Health, Algonac and Marine City, Mich., 1979-80; clinician St. Clair County Community Mental Health, Algonac and Marine City, 1980-85, clin. supr., 1985-88; clinician Ctr. for Personal Growth, Port Huron, Mich., 1986—; pvt. practice Roseville, Mich., 1988—; adj. lectr. Wayne State U., Detroit, 1987-89, mem. faculty, 1990—. Mem. Acad. Cert. Social Workers (diplomate). Avocations: crocheting, cake decorating, acting in murder mysterys. Office: Wayne State U Thompson Home Rm 418 Detroit MI 48202

GARRIOTT, OWEN KAY, astronaut, scientist; b. Enid, Okla., Nov. 22, 1930; m. Evelyn Long; children by previous marriage: Randall O., Robert K., Richard A., Linda S. BSEE, U. Okla., 1953; MS, Stanford U., 1957, PhD, 1960, DSc (hon.), Phillips U., Enid, 1973. NSF fellow Cambridge (Eng.) U., Radio Research Sta., Slough, Eng., 1960-61; asst. and assoc. prof. elec. engring. Stanford U., 1961-65; astronaut, scientist Johnson Space Ctr. NASA, Houston, 1965-86; sci. pilot Skylab-3 NASA, 1973, dep. dir. Sci. and Applications Directorate, 1974-76, dir. Sci. and Applications Directorate, 1976, asst. dir. for space and life scis., 77-78, mission specialist on first Spacelab flight, 1983, project scientist Space Sta. Program, 1984-86; v.p. Space Programs Teledyne Brown Engring., Huntsville, Ala., 1988-93; co-founder, dir. Immutherapeutics, Inc., Huntsville, 1993—. Served with USN, 1953-56. Recipient Disting. Svc. medal NASA, 1973, Gold medal City of Chgo., 1974, Robert J. Collier trophy, 1974, V.M. Komarov diploma Fedn. Aeronautique Internationale, 1974, Robert H. Goddard Meml. trophy, 1975; inducted into Okla. Hall of Fame, 1980, U.S. Astronaut Hall of Fame, 1997. Fellow Am. Astronautical Soc., AIAA (assoc.); mem. Am. Geophys. Union, IEEE, Internat. Sci. Radio Union, Assn. Space Explorers (dir.), Internat. Acad. Astronautics, Astronaut Scholarship found. (dir.), Sigma Xi, Tau Beta Pi.

GARRISH, THEODORE JOHN, lawyer; b. Detroit, Jan. 6, 1943; s. Theodore and Adella Beatrice (Kimball) G.; m. Joy Ann Ziegler, Aug. 4, 1967 (div. 1979); children: Theodore John, Amelia Sutter. A.B., U. Mich., 1964; J.D. cum laude, Wayne State U., 1968. Bar: Mich. 1969, D.C. 1972. Trial atty. U.S. Dept. Justice, Washington, 1969-72; pub. opinion analyst Com. for Reelection of Pres., Washington, 1972; chief advt. substantiation FTC, Washington, 1973-74; asst. spl. counsel to Pres. Washington, 1974; asst. to sec. U.S. Dept. Interior, Washington, 1976, legis. counsel, 1981-82; gen. counsel Consumer Product Safety Commn., Washington, 1976-78; ptnr. Deane, Snowdon, Shutler, Garrish & Gherardi, Washington, 1978-81; gen. counsel Dept. Energy, Washington, 1983-85, asst. sec., 1985-89; fed. inspector Alaska Natural Gas Transp. System, 1986-89; Wash. counsel The Flanagan Group, 1989-91; pres. Brewery Mgmt. Co., 1989-94; pres. Kent Island Investment Co., 1989-91, chmn., 1991-94; mng. ptnr. Wild Gooose Brewery, 1989-91, dir., 1994-98; mem. U.S. Adminstrv. Conf., Washington, 1976-78, 83-85, President's Commn. on Catastrophic Nuclear Accidents, 1988-90; sr. v.p. Am. Nuclear Energy Coun., 1991-94; v.p. Nuclear Energy Inst., 1994—; instr. George Washington U., 1995-98. Del. Mich. Rep. Conv., 1966; asst. to group dir. Presdl. Inaugural Com., 1973, dep. exec. dir., 1981; mem. adv. com. on human concerns Rep. Nat. Com., 1979; adv. Nat. Policy Forum, 1994—; dir. Nat. Energy Resources Orgn., 1987—. Mem. FBA, Mich. Bar Assn., D.C. Bar Assn., Alpha Delta Phi. Congregationalist. Home: 103 Chesapeake Ave Annapolis MD 21403-3305 Office: 1776 I St NW Ste 4D Washington DC 20006-3700

GARRISON, ALTHEA, government official; b. Hahira, Ga., Oct. 7, 1940; d. Charles and Lenora Mae (Davis) G. AS, Newbury Jr. Coll., 1978; BS, Suffolk U., 1982; cert. in social studies, Harvard U., 1986; MS, Lesley Coll., 1984. Counselor, supr. Charlotte House Dorchester (Mass.), 1977-77; with EDP dept., sr. assessor Mass. Dept. Revenue, Boston, 1979-81; sr. examiner Office State Compt., Boston, 1982-90; human resource mgr. Office of State Comptr. Commonwealth of Mass., 1991—; state rep. gen. ct. 5th suffolk Rep. Dist., Mass., 1992-95; bd. dirs. Uphams Corner Health Ctr., Dorchester, 1983—, v.p., 1987—, Disting. Svc. award, 1991. Charter mem. adv. bd. Christian Record Braille, Lincoln, Neb., 1983; alumna coun. Lesley Coll. Grad. Sch., Cambridge, Mass., 1986-88; active Nat. Rep. Congl. Com., 1988—, Rep. Presdl. Task Force, 1989—, Met. Area Planning Coun., 1994; charter founder Ronald Reagan Rep. Ctr., Washington, 1989; nominee City Coun. Dorchester, 1989, State Rep. Rep. Primary, 1990; town com. woman Ward 13, Boston, 1992, commn. vice-chair, treas. city com., 1994-96; exec. com. Met. Area Planning Coun., 1995-98; apptd. Notary Pub., 1994—, Justice of Peace, 1997; mem. Irish Immigration Ctr., 1996-98; coord. Toys for Tots, Office State Comptr., 1997. Recipient Senator's citation Commonwealth Mass., 1982, Merit medal Rep. Task force, 1989, Appreciation cert. Mass. Rep. Party, Outstanding Vol. award Suffolk U., 1991, Achievement cert. Conf. New Legislators, 1993, Rep. Leadership award, 1993-94, Book award Dearborn Middle Sch., 1994, Legis. Yr. award Gtr. Boston Labor Coun. AFL-CIO, 1994, Excellent Svc. award Holborn, Gannett, Gaston, Otisfield Betterment Assn., 1995, Cmty. Svc. Honor award Winthrop St. Crime Assn., 1996, Benefactor Cert. Mayo Found., 1998; hon. fellow John F. Kennedy Libr., 1987-90; named one of 100 Women Making History North Shore Women's Coalition, Rep. Presdl. Legion of Merit Honor Roll, 1993; cert. of appreciation USMC Res.; Cmty. Svc. Honor award Winthrop Street Crime Assn., 1996. Mem. Am. Mgmt. Assn., Nat. Assn. Govt. Employees (negotiator, organizer 1979-81), Suffolk U. Gen. Alumni Assn. (bd. dirs. 1986-89), Heritage Found., Nat. Found. Cancer Rsch. (hon., citation 1991), DAV Comdrs. Roman Catholic. Avocations: walking, music, reading, research. Home: 18 Jerome St Apt 2 Dorchester MA 02125-2021

GARRISON, ARLENE ALLEN, engineering executive, engineering educator. BA in Liberal Arts, U. Tenn., 1975, PhD in Analytical Chemistry, 1981, BS in Elec. Engring., 1988. Instr. analytical chemistry, grad. rsch. asst. U. Tenn., Knoxville, 1975-81, postdoctoral rsch. assoc., 1981, sr. electonic design engr. dept. chemistry, 1985-89, rsch. asst. prof. dept. chemistry, 1989—; dir. measurement and control engring. ctr. Coll. Engring. U. Tenn., Knoxville; licensing exec. UTRC, 1998—; mem. Nat. Rsch. Coun. bd. of assessment for Nat. Inst. Standards & Tech., Panel for Chem. Sci. and Tech., 1996—; U. Tenn. Knoxville, Chemistry Dept. Alumni Steering Com., 1994-99; participant in NATO Advanced Study Inst. on Analytical Applications of Fourier transform infrared to Molecular and Biolog. Systems, Florence, Italy, 1980; organizer insl. spectroscopy symposium at 14th Internat. Conf. on Raman Spectroscopy, Hong Kong; co-chair Soc. Photo-Optical Instrumentation Engrs. conf. on optical methods for chem. process control, 1994; mem. sci. bd. Iternat. Forum Process Analytical Chemistry, 1993—. Contbr. over 29 articles to profl. jours.; presenter at regional, nat. and internat. sci. confs. Chair bd. trustees Fountain City United Meth. Ch., 1991-94; sec. Wesley Found. Bd., 1992-93; bd. dirs. Appalachian Sci. Fair, 1993-99, WATTec, 1994-96, Discovery Ctr., 1995-98; mem. Pub. Bldg. Authority, 1995-2000. Recipient Chancellors Citation for extraordinay comty. svc., 1993. Mem. Soc. for Applied Spectroscopy (Meggars award 1982), Soc. of Photo Instrumentation Engrs., Coblentz Soc. (bd. mgrs. 1989-92, pres. 1997-98), Am. Chem. Soc. (sec. East Tenn. sect. 1988-90, chair-elect 1991, chair 1992, steering com. divsns. chem. edn. and analytical chemistry, chair Williams Wright award com. 1991, 92). Phi Beta Kappa, Phi Kappa Phi, Alpha Lambda Delta. Office: U Tenn Coll Engring Measurement & Control Engring Ctr 102 Estabrook Hall Knoxville TN 37996-2350

GARRISON, BETTY BERNHARDT, retired mathematics educator; b. Danbury, Ohio, July 1, 1932; d. Philip Arthur and Reva Esther (Meter) Bernhardt; m. Robert Edward Kvarda, Sept. 28, 1957 (div. 1964); m. John Dresser Garrison, Jan. 17, 1968; 1 child, John Christopher. BA, BS, Bowling Green State U., 1954; MA, Ohio State U., 1956; PhD, Oreg. State U., 1962. Teaching asst. Ohio State U., Columbus, 1954-56; instr. Ohio U., Athens, 1956-57, San Diego State Coll., 1957-59; teaching asst. Oreg. State U., Corvallis, 1959-62; asst. prof. San Diego State U., 1962-66, assoc. prof., 1966-69, prof., 1969-96. Reviewer of articles and books, 1966-98; contbr. articles to profl. jours. NSF fellow, 1960-61, 61-62. Home: 5607 Yerba Anita Dr San Diego CA 92115-1027

GARRISON, DAVID LEE, language educator; b. May 10, 1945. BA, Wesleyan U., 1968; MA, Cath. U. Am., 1972; PhD, Johns Hopkins U., 1975. Prof. Ind. U., Bloomington, Ind., 1975-76, Wash. Coll., Chestertown, Md., 1977, U. Kans., Lawrence, Kans., 1978-79, Wright State U., Dayton, Ohio, 1979—. E-mail: david.garrison@wright.edu. Office: Dept Modern Languages Wrtigh State Univ Dayton OH 45419-3544

GARRISON, ELIZABETH JANE, artist; b. Elmira, N.Y., Feb. 11, 1952. BFA, Ringling Sch. Art and Design, 1973; postgrad., Mansfield U., 1976-78; MS, Fla. State U., 1980. Exhibits include Mus. Contemporary Art, The Netherlands, Mus. Fine Arts, St. Petersburg, Fla., Renwick Gallery, The Smithsonian Inst., Washington, and others; represented in permanent collections Yale U. Art Gallery, New Haven, Conn., Kunstgewerbe Mus., Berlin, Honolulu Acad. Arts. Nat. Endowment Arts fellows, 1981, 88; Saltonstall Found. grantee, 1996. Home: 317 Elm St Ithaca NY 14850-5463

GARRISON, EVA HEIM, school counselor; b. Dettingen, Bavaria, Germany, Sept. 23, 1940; came to U.S., 1964; d. Josef Fridrich and Barbara Fridericke (Vogt) Heim; m. Floyd Garrison, Sept. 15, 1962; children: Cindy Elizabeth, Michele Maria. AA, Solano C.C., 1973; BA in Spl. Edn., Cen. Wash. U., 1983; MEd in Counseling, City U., Bellevue, Wash., 1994. Cert. sch. counselor, tchr. 2d and 3d yr. high sch. German. Police officer Vallejo (Calif.) Police Dept., 1970-77; interim sch. instr. Ctrl. Kitsap Sch. Dist., Silverdale, Wash., 1983-84, interim sch. coord., 1984-87, instr. h.s. German, 1987-88, substance abuse coord., 1992-93; coord. in-sch. suspension program Camden County H.S., St. Mays, Ga., 1988-89; sch. counselor, tchr. 2d and 3d yr. German Olympic H.S., Silverdale, 1995—. Mem. Substance Abuse Adv. Bd., Kitsap County, Wash., 1989-92, At-Risk Task Force, Kitsap County, 1985-87; chair Cen. Kitsap Comty. Coalition, Silverdale, 1989-93; comty. vol. Recipient Gov.'s award in substance abuse prevention, 1992. Mem. Wash. State Sch. Counselors Assn., Wash. Mental Health Counselors Assn. Avocations: swimming, biking, gardening, traveling, hiking, walking. Home: 4709 Chico Way NW Bremerton WA 98312-1219

GARRISON, GEORGE HARTRANFT HALEY, curator; b. Norfolk, Va., Aug. 6, 1938; s. George Hartranft Haley and Ione (Taylor) G.; m. Hannelore Emmy Lydia Buckel, June 6, 1968; 1 child, Ione Gerhild. BA in History, Va. Mil. Inst., 1961; translators cert., U. Heidelberg. Comnd. 2d lt. U.S. Army, 1961, advanced through grades to capt., 1967; trust mgr. pvt. estate Nags Head, N.C., 1976-79; curator of scripophily, dir. rsch. and sales Antique Stocks & Bonds Co., Williamsburg, Va., 1979—. Author: (workbook) Insider's Guide to Antique Securities, 1987; contbr. articles to internat. newspapers and jours. Pres., sr. curator, trustee Soc. for Preservation Am. Bus. History. Recipient Disting. Svc. award as ofcl. Scripophilist, State of Va., 1981; named Entrepreneur on the Go, Entrepreneur Mag., 1991. Mem. Internat. Bond and Share Soc. (Dynamic Leadership award). Avocations: collecting, researching and marketing of important financial history 1700-1900's. Home and Office: Antique Stocks & Bonds Drawer JH Williamsburg VA 23187-3632

GARRISON, GEORGE WALKER, JR., mechanical and industrial engineering educator; b. Statesville, N.C., May 21, 1939; s. George Walker and Gladys Mary (Bell) G.; BSME, N.C. State U., 1961, MS, 1963; PhD, 1966; MBA, Vanderbilt U., 1980; m. Nancy Carole Mayfield, June 10, 1961; children: Jennifer Renee, George W. Rsch. and tchg. asst. N.C. State U., 1964-66; rsch. engr. Sverdrup/ARO, Inc., Arnold Air Force Sta., Tenn., 1966-70, sr. lead engr., 1970-75, sect. supr., 1975-78, br. mgr., 1978-80, dir. energy systems Sverdrup Tech. Inc., Tullahoma, Tenn., 1980-81; prof. mech. engring. U. Tenn., Tullahoma, 1981—, chmn. engring. mgmt. program, 1994—; tech. dir. Ctr. for Advanced Space Propulsion, 1987-89, dir., 1989—; exec. dir. Ctr. Space Transp. and Applied Rsch. John W. Harrelson Scholarship award, 1957; NDEA fellow, 1961; named Outstanding Profl. of Yr., 1987. Fellow ASME; mem. AIAA, Nat. Mgmt. Assn. (pres. 1991-92, Silver Knight Mgmt. award 1992), Sigma Xi. Mem. Christian Ch. (Disciples of Christ) (elder, chmn. bd. 1984-87). Contbr. articles to sci., tech. jours. Home: 567 Waters Edge Dr Estill Spgs TN 37330-1606 Office: U Tenn Space Inst Tullahoma TN 37388

GARRISON, GUY GRADY, librarian, educator; b. Akron, Ohio, Dec. 17, 1927; s. Grady and Emma (Dodson) G.; m. Joanne Ruth Sergeant, Mar. 22, 1964; 1 dau., Anne Olivia. BA, Baldwin-Wallace Coll., 1950; MS, Columbia U., 1954; PhD, U. Ill., 1960. Mem. staff Oak Park (Ill.) Pub. Library, 1954-58; head reader services Kansas City (Mo.) Pub. Library, 1960-62; prof., dir. library research center Grad. Sch. Library Sci., U. Ill., 1962-68; prof., dean Coll. Info. Studies, Drexel U., 1968-87, Alice B. Kroeger prof., 1987-91, dean emeritus, prof. emeritus, 1992—. Contbr. articles to profl. jours. Served with AUS, 1950-52. Mem. ALA, Assn. for Library and Info. Sci. Edn., Beta Phi Mu. Home: 731 Limehouse Rd Wayne PA 19087-2856

GARRISON, HOWARD H., public relations executive; b. Detroit, Apr. 2, 1949; s. Morris H. and Catherine S. G.; m. Ellen Greenberg, Apr. 12, 1986; children: Rachel, David. BA, U. Mich., 1970; MS, U. Wis., 1971, PhD, 1976. Asst. prof. Va. Commonwealth U., Richmond, 1976-79; social sci. analyst U.S. Civil rights Commn., Washington, 1979-81; statistician U.S. GAO, Washington, 1981-83; project dir. Inst. Medicine, Washington, 1983-86; group mgr. Aspen Systems Corp., Rockville, Md., 1986-93; dir. office pub. affairs Fed. Am. Socs. Exptl. Biology, Bethesda, Md., 1993—; evaluator Westinghouse Scis. Talent Search, Washington, 1985-93. Author: Career Achievements, 1986, Levels of Mathematics Achievement, 1991. Rsch. grantee Spenser Found., Chgo., 1977. Mem. Am. Sociological Assn., Soc. Applied Sociology (pres. 1990-94). Jewish. Avocation: handball. Office: FASEB 9650 Rockville Pike Bethesda MD 20814

GARRISON, JEAN ANNE, social science educator; b. Santa Rosa, Calif., Feb. 28, 1968; d. Elliott Gell and Ruth Bush Garrison. MA, U. S.C., 1992, PhD, 1996; BA, U. Wyo., 1996. Asst. prof. social sci. Boston U. Coll. Gen. Studies, 1996—. Author: Games Advisors Play: Foreign Policy in the Nixon and Carter Administrations, 1999. Mem. Internat. Studies Assn., Internat. Soc. Polit. Psychology, Am. Polit. Sci. Assn. Avocations: reading, biking. E-mail: jgarriso@bu-edu. Home: Apt 14 530 Washington St Brighton MA 02135

GARRISON, JOHN RAYMOND, organization executive; b. Bridgeton, N.J., Jan. 30, 1938; s. Raymond Wilson and Clara Ella (Moore) G.; m. Sally Anne Woodruff, Sept. 10, 1960; children: Glenn Thomas Wilson, Matthew Moore. AB, Harvard U., 1960; MPA (scholastic award), NYU, 1964. Adminstrv. asst. N.Y. State Banking Dept., 1962-63; planner N.J. Dept. Econ. Devel. and Conservation, 1963-64; sr. planner N.Y. State Office Regional Devel., 1964-66; mem. staff Gov. N.Y. State Exec. Chamber, 1966-71; program sec. Office of Lt. Gov., N.Y. State, 1971-73; dep. commr. adminstrn. N.Y. State Health Dept., 1973-75; exec. v.p. Hosp. Assn. N.Y. State, 1975-78; chief exec. officer Nat. Easter Seal Soc., 1978-90, Am. Lung Assn., N.Y.C., 1990—. Mem. exec. com. Internat. Union Against TB and Lung Disease, 1996—. Mem. Harvard Club (N.Y.C.). Office: Am Lung Assn 1740 Broadway New York NY 10019-4315

GARRISON, LARRY RICHARD, accounting educator; b. Kansas City, Mo., Jan. 10, 1951; s. Robert Milton and Virginia Claire (Huntington) G.; m. Sheila Caroline Murry, Aug. 10, 1973. BBA, Cen. Mo. State U., 1973; MS in Acctg., U. Mo., 1982; PhD, U. Nebr., 1986. CPA, Mo. Mgr. Garrison & Co., CPAs, Kansas City, 1973-79; controller G.F. & F. Enterprises, Kansas City, 1979-82; instr. U. Nebr., Lincoln, 1983-86; prof. U. Mo., Kansas City, 1986—; exec. dir. Tax Policy Rsch. Project. Contbr. articles to profl. jours. Recipient Disting. Teaching award U. Nebr., 1984-85. Mem. Am. Inst. CPA's, Am. Taxation Assn., Mo. Soc. CPA's (Outstanding Educator of Yr. award 1999), Am. Acctg. Assn., Beta Alpha Psi, Beta Gamma Sigma. Office: U Mo 5100 Rockhill Rd Kansas City MO 64110-2446

GARRISON, P. GREGORY, diversified financial services company executive. Chmn. entertainment, media and comm. Price Waterhouse L.L.P.-U.S., L.A. Office: Price Waterhouse LLP US 400 S Hope St Ste 2300 Los Angeles CA 90071-2889*

GARRISON, PAUL CORNELL, retired office products company executive; b. Marietta, Ohio, June 18, 1935; s. William John and Alice Ray (Wilson) G.; m. Carole Virginia Whinery, July 3, 1960; children: Kristin, Holly, Craig, Kelee. Student, Ohio State U., 1953, Marietta Coll., 1958. V.p. Garrison Brewer Co., Marietta, 1955-64, pres., 1965-93; dir. of design Garrison Brewer Co. Div. of Stationers, Inc., 1992-93; asst. v.p. Barry R. Ankney, Inc., Mariette and Akron, Ohio, 1996—; v.p. Innerspace Interiors, Inc., Marietta, 1980-88. Pres. Eve, Marietta, 1982-85, YMCA, 1974-76; chmn. Marietta Com., 1986, United Way Campaign, 1986. With U.S. Army, 1957-61. Republican. Presbyterian.

GARRISON, PITSER HARDEMAN, lawyer, mayor emeritus; b. Lufkin, Tex., Mar. 7, 1912; s. Homer and Mattie (Milam) G.; m. Berneice Jones, Dec. 3, 1936 (dec. Apr. 1992); m. Reba Brent, Sept. 29, 1993. Student Lon Morris Jr. Coll., 1929-30, student Stephen F. Austin State U., 1930-32; LL.B., U. Tex., 1935. Bar: Tex. 1935; U.S. Dist. Ct. (ea. dist.) Tex. 1936, U.S. Dist. Ct. (so. dist.) Tex. 1938, U.S. Ct. Appeals (5th cir.) 1939. Ptnr. Garrison, Renfrow, Zeleskey, Cornelius & Rogers, Lufkin, 1935-52, sr. ptnr., 1952-68; chmn., gen. counsel Lufkin Nat. Bank, 1968-81; sole practice, Lufkin, 1981—. Mayor City of Lufkin, 1970-88, mayor emeritus, 1988—; past bd. dirs., past pres. Angelina and Neches River Authority, Lufkin; past pres. Deep East Tex. Council of Govts., Jasper; past bd. dirs., past chmn. Angelina County Tax Appraisal Dist., Lufkin; bd. dirs. Meml. Hosp., Lufkin, 1975-91. Served to maj. U.S. Army, 1942-46. Recipient Disting. Alumnus award Lon Morris Jr. Coll., 1974; Disting. Alumnus award Stephen F. Austin State U., 1976; named East Texan of the Month, East Tex. C. of C., 1966, East Texan of the Yr., East Tex. C. of C., 1981, East Texan of Yr., Deep East Tex. Council of Govts., 1980. Fellow Am. Coll. Trial Lawyers, Tex. Bar Found. (charter); mem. Angelina County Bar Assn. (past pres.), Tex. Bar Assn., ABA, Phi Delta Phi. Democrat. Methodist. Lodges: Rotary (past pres.), Masons, Shriners. Home: 1302 Tom Temple Dr Apt 302 Lufkin TX 75904-5552 Office: PO Box 150537 515 S 1st St Lufkin TX 75901-3867

GARRISON, RICHARD NEIL, artist; b. Ft. Bidwell, Calif., Nov. 26, 1912; s. John Henry and Vera Calista (Bell) G.; m. Ruth Geraldine George, Mar. 1, 1932 (div. Jul. 1968); m. Jeanne Trimble, Oct. 12, 1968. Student, Visalia (Calif.) Jr. Coll., 1930-32. Dir. Art League of Manatee Co., Bradentoa, Fla., 1964-70. Author book of poetry, 1996, 95, 97. Mem. Art League of Manatee County, Longboat Key Art Ctr. Republican. Home: 260 47th St W Bradenton FL 34209-2830

GARRISON, ROBERT FREDERICK, astronomer, educator; b. Aurora, Ill., May 9, 1936; s. Robert W. and Dorothy I. (Rydquist) G.; m. Ada V. Mighell, June 7, 1957 (div. 1980); children—Forest L., Alexandra, David C. B.A. in Math., Earlham Coll., 1960; Postgrad., U. Wis., 1961-62; Ph.D. in Astronomy and Astrophysics, U. Chgo., 1966. Research assoc. Mt. Wilson and Palomar Obs., Pasadena, Calif., 1966-68; asst. prof. U. Toronto, Ont., Can., 1968-74; assoc. prof. U. Toronto, Ont., 1974-78, prof. astronomy, 1978—, assoc. dir. D. Dunlap Obs.; dir. U. Toronto So. Obs., Chile, 1970-98. Editor: The MK Process and Stellar Classification, 1984; co-editor: The MK Process at Fifty Years: A Powerful Tool for Astrophysical Insight, 1994; contbr. articles to profl. jours. Bd. dirs. Bruce Trail Assn., 1975-76. Served with USMC, 1954-56. Mem. Can. Astron. Soc., Am. Astron. Soc., Astron. Soc. of Pacific, Am. Assn. Variable Star Observers, Royal Astron. Soc. Can. (v.p. 1996—), Internat. Astron. Union (pres. com. 45 on stellar classifications 1985-88), Royal Canadian Inst. (v.p. 1991-93, pres. 1993-94), U. Chgo. Club of Can. (v.p. schs. 1982-88, pres. 1988-90). Office: David Dunlap Obs, 123 Hillsview Dr, Richmond Hill, ON Canada L4C 1T3

GARRISON, SUSAN KAY, lawyer; b. Renton, Wash., Sept. 6, 1952; d. Walter Raymond and Rose Faye (Wilson) G.; m. William W. Mayer Jr., Aug. 4, 1973 (div. July 1988); 1 child, Jonathan William Mayer; m. Michael J.J. Campbell, Oct. 22, 1993; 2 stepchildren: Michael Sean and Andrew Jack Campbell. BA in Sociology cum laude, Gettysburg Coll., 1974; JD, Villanova U., 1980, LLM in Taxation, 1988. Assoc. Dechert Price and Rhoads, Phila., 1980-83, Surrick and Gollatz, Media, Pa., 1983-86; pvt. practice Media, 1986—; exec. trustee Garrison Family Found., Media, 1990—; pres., bd. mem. Nat. Abortion Rights Action League Pa., Phila., 1986-94. Mem. com. Middletown Twp. (Pa.) Open Space Commn., 1984-86; bd. dirs. Clara Bell Duvall Edn. Fund, Phila., 1987-90, NARAL-Pa. Found.,1994—; nat. coord. Nat. Evang. Women's Caucus, Chgo., 1990-91; commr. Delaware County Women's Commn., Media, 1989-92; pres. Friends of Delaware County Women's Commn., Media, 1990-96; trustee Media-Providence Friends Sch., 1988—; dir. The Ctr. Found., 1995—; chair Reps. Choice Pa., 1995—; mem. Delaware County Planning Commn., 1997—; mem. adv. bd. Women's Assn. Women's Alternatives, Inc., 1997—; commr. Pa. Commn. for Women, 1998—; bd. dirs. Pa. Ct. Apptd. Spl. Advocates Assn., 1998—. Mem. ABA, Nat. Assn. Women and Law, Nat. Women History Network, Nat. Assn. Commn. for Women (bd. dirs. 1998—), Delaware County Estate Planning Coun., Pa. Bar Assn., Delco Bar Assn. Republican. Office: 220 N Jackson St Media PA 19063-2807

GARRISON, TRUITT B., architect; b. Lubbock, Tex., Apr. 6, 1936; s. Miles Elisha and Iva J. (Greenway) G.; m. Joyce Ann Ward, June 27, 1959; children: Todd Michael, Craig Mitchell. BArch, Tex. Tech U., 1962; postgrad., Grad. Sch. Design Exec. Program, Harvard U., 1971. Registered architect, 42 states. With Welton Becket & Assocs., Houston, 1962-63; sr.

v.p. Caudill Rowlett Scott, Houston, 1963—, also dir.; sr. v.p., dir. ops. Internat. Group CRS Sirrine, 1963-97, cons., 1997—; bd. dirs. Global Group; exec. v.p., gen. mgr. archtl. svcs. divsn. CRSS Architects, Inc., 1988, pres., 1990, exec. v.p., 1992-94; exec. v.p. CRSS Inc. Peace Shield Divsn., 1994-96, cons., 1997-99; mem. bd. Houston Architecture Found., 1992-96. Bd. dirs. St. Lukes Meth. Ch., 1970-71, Epernay Homeowners Assn., 1977-86, pres. bd., 1978; bd. dirs. Decordova Bend Estates Homeowners Assn., Happy Hill Farm Acad., sec. bd., 1999—; mem. fin. com. Celebrate Arch., 1994, 95, 96, 98. With U.S. Army, 1958-59. Named Officer of Yr. Caudill Rowlett Scott, 1980. Fellow AIA; mem. Tex. Soc. Architects, Nat. Council Archtl. Registration Bds., Dobe Country Club (bd. dirs., pres. 1999—). Home and Office: 4917 Rio Vista Dr Granbury TX 76049-5172

GARRISON, WALTER R., corporate executive; b. St. Louis, July 7, 1926; s. Walter Raymond and Esther Elizabeth (Kohlhepp) G.; m. Rose Faye Wilson, Aug. 10, 1946 (dec.); children: Bruce, Susan Garrison, Mark, Pamela Garrison Phelan, C. Jeffrey; m. Jayne Bacon, Apr. 15, 1973; stepchildren: James (dec.), Jack. B.S.A.E., U. Kans., 1948, M.S.A.E., 1950; DBA (hon.), Spring Garden Coll., 1986. Registered profl. engr., Pa., N.J., Fla., Ill. Structural engr. Boeing Airplane Co., Seattle, 1950-53, cons. engr., 1953-56; staff engr. CDI Corp. and predecessor Comprehensive Designers, Inc., Phila., 1956-58, v.p., 1958-61, pres., chmn. bd., 1961—; dir., chmn. bd.; mem. World Affairs Coun., Phila., 1983, World Pres.' Orgn., 1985. Chmn. bd. trustees Pa. Inst. Tech., Media, 1953—; mem. Upper Providence Twp. Environ. Adv. Coun., 1977-82, Pa. Bd. Pvt. Schs., 1965-71; mem. adv. bd. Sol C. Snider Entrepreneurial Ctr. Wharton Sch., U. Pa., 1987—. Recipient Disting. Engring. Svcs. award, U. Kans., 1990, Good Scout award Boy Scouts Am., 1995, Legend CEO of the Year award, 1996, 1st recipient of World Affairs Coun. Annual Atlas award, 1998. Mem. ASME (industry adv. bd. 1987—), NSPE, Phila. Pres. Orgn. (past chmn., bd. dirs.), Young Pres.' Orgn., Tau Beta Pi, Sigma Tau, Union League Club. Republican. Presbyterian. Home: 238 Sycamore Mills Rd Rose Tree PA 19063-2028 Office: CDI Corp 800 Manchester Ave Fl 3D Media PA 19063-4036

GARRISON, WILLIAM LLOYD, cemetery executive; b. Ridgway, Pa., Dec. 26, 1939; s. Lloyd and Mary Rebecca (Morrow) G.; m. Mary Jo Florio, May 30, 1964; children: David, Mark. BA in Psychology, Ohio Wesleyan U., 1962; postgrad., Garrett Theol. Sem., 1962-63, U. Pa., 1963-64; MSW, Fla. State U., 1967; MS in Mgmt., Case Western Res. U., 1976. Caseworker Mpls. Ct. Chgo., 1963-64, United Cerebral Palsy Assn., Phila., 1964-65; psychiat. social worker Bellefaire, Shaker Heights, Ohio, 1967-74; dir. pers. and tng. Ctr. Human Services, Cleve., 1974-81, dir. resource devel., 1981-83; exec. dir. Cleve. Soc. for the Blind, 1983-85, Cleve. Eye Bank, 1983-85; exec. v.p. Lake View Cemetery Assn., Cleve., 1985-87, pres., CEO, 1987—; v.p. Lake View Cemetery Found., Cleve., 1988—; adj. prof. Sch. Applied Social Sci., Case Western Res. U., 1974-80; v.p. E.A. Mabry Inc., Akron, Ohio, 1970—; chmn. agri-bus. adv. com. Cleve. Pub. Schs., 1990—, bus. adv. directorate, 1991-97. Dist. cub scout chmn. Boy Scouts Am., 1979-81, dist. chmn., 1981-84, scoutmaster, 1983-87, mem. exec. bd., 1981—, asst. coun. commr., 1984-87, v.p. Boy Scouting, 1987-89, scoutmaster to world jamboree in Australia, 1988, coun. commr., 1989-92, cubmaster, 1997—, area v.p., 1992-95, area pres., 1995-97, region exec. com., 1995-97, nom. com. 1997—; mem. nat. coun., 1989—; area chmn. 19th World Jamboree, Chile, 1997-98, nat. cub scout leader tng. chmn., 1998—, nat. cub scout leader tng. chmn., 1998—; mem. pers. com. Lake Erie coun. Girl Scouts U.S., 1982-89; mem. Big Bros., Cleve., 1968-73; pres. Mayfield Heights Homeowners Assn., 1974-84, Cuyahoga County Reach Out Counseling Svcs., trustee, 1977-95, pres., 1991-95; bd. dirs. Garfield Meml. United Meth. Ch., 1979-81, vice chair pastor/parish rels.com., 1999—; mem. del. assembly United Way Svcs. of Cleve., 1987-95; trustee Alta House Comty. Ctr., 1994—, Ctr. for Families and Children, 1995—; co-founder, v.p. East Cleveland Park Commn., 1998—. Recipient Dist. award Merit Boy Scouts Am., 1980, Silver Beaver award, 1984, Silver Antelope award, 1994; Menninger Found fellow. Mem. NASW, Acad. Cert. Social Workers, Soc. Human Resource Mgmt., Pers. Accreditation Inst., Internat. Cemetery and Funeral Assn. (cert. cemetary exec. 1997, membership com. 1993—, strategic planning com. 1994-96, hist. cemetery adv. com., 1994—), Ohio Assn. Cemetery Supts. and Ofcls. (exec. bd. 1992-97, v.p. 1993, pres.-elect 1994, pres. 1995-96), Greater Cleve. Cemetery Assn. (pres. 1987-90), Nat. Eagle Scout Assn., Greater Cleve. Pers. Coun., Social Agys. Employee Union (pres. 1970-73), Greater Cleve. Growth Assn., St. Luke's Hosp. Assn., Cleve. U. Cir. Inc., Am. Field Svc., Cleve. Playhouse Club, Rotary (trustee Cleve. club 1993-96, v.p. 1996, pres.-elect 1996-97, pres. 1997-98, del. 88th Rotary Internat. conv. Glasgow, Scotland, 89th Indpls.), Cleve. Rotary Found. (trustee 1997—), Hist. Cemetery Alliance (co-founder), Univ. Club, Delta Tau Delta, Phi Mu Alpha. Office: Lake View Cemetery Assn 12316 Euclid Ave Cleveland OH 44106-4313

GARRISON, WILLIAM LOUIS, civil engineering educator; b. Nashville, Apr. 20, 1924; s. Sidney Clarence and Sara (Elisabeth) McMurry; s. Marcia Fordyce Stanley, Aug. 31, 1938; children: Sara, Ann, Helen, Deborah, James, Jane, John. BS, Peabody Coll., 1946, MS, 1947; PhD, Northwestern U., 1950. From asst. prof. to prof. dept. geography U. Wash., Seattle, 1950-60; prof. dept. geography, civil engring. Northwestern U., Evanston, Ill., 1960-67, dir. transp. ctr., 1965-67; dir. ctr. for urban studies U. Ill., Chgo., 1967-69; Weidlein Prof. Environ. Engring. U. Pitts., 1969-73; dir. Inst. for Transp. Studies U. Calif., Berkeley, 1973-81, prof. civil engring., 1981—; cons. U.S. Bur. Pub. Rds., Washington, 1960-68; bd. govs. Regional Sci. Research Inst., Phila., 1964—; adv. com. on econs. NSF, Washington, 1958-63; panel on values of social sci. research Nat. Sci. Bd., Washington, 1963-64. Author: Geographical Impact of Highway Improvements, 1960; author, editor Jour. Transp. Tech., 1985; editor: Quantitative Geography, 1969; articles in field. Served to capt. USAF, 1943-46. Mem. Transp. Research Bd. (chmn. 1972-73, Roy C. Crum award 1973), Regional Sci. Assn. (pres. 1960), ASCE, Assn. Am. Geographers (Outstanding research award 1958), AAAS. Home: 10 Rancho Diablo Dr Lafayette CA 94549-2722 Office: U Calif Dept Civil Engring Berkeley CA 94720

GARRISON-FINDERUP, IVADELLE DALTON, writer; b. San Pedro, Calif., Oct. 4, 1915; d. William Douglas and Olive May (Covington) Dalton; m. Fred Marion Garrison, Aug. 8, 1932 (dec. Nov. 1984); children: Douglas Lee, Vernon Russell, Nancy Jane; m. Elmer Pedersen Finderup, Apr. 8, 1994. BA, Calif. State U., Fresno, 1964; postgrad., U. Oreg., 1965, U. San Francisco, 1968. Cert. secondary tchr., Calif. Tchr. Tranquillity (Calif.) H.S., 1964-78, West Hills Coll., Coalinga, Calif., 1970-74; lectr. in field. Author: Roots and Branches of Our Garrison Family Tree, 1988, Roots and Branches of Our Dalton Family Tree, 1989, The History of James' Fresno Ranch, 1990, 3d edit., 1993, There is a Peacock on the Roof, 1993; (with Vernon R.) William Douglas Dalton, a Biography, 1995, Sam (The Cat That Thought He Was a Boy), 1997, Amanda and Her Feathered Friends, 1997, Freddy Goes on a Trailer Outing, 1998, David Learns to Count, 1998. Mem. DAR (sec. 1987-89, regent 1989-91, regent Fresno chpt. 1989-91), Archaeology Inst. Am., Frazier Clan N.Am., Fresno City and County Hist. Soc. (life), Fresno Archaeology Soc. (sec.), Children of the Am. Revolution (sr. pres. 1991-97), Westerners Internat., Fresno Gem and Mineral Soc., Thora # 11 Dannebrog, Friends of the Libr. (Fresno), Chaffee Zoolog. Gardens of Fresno, Archaeological Inst. Am. (San Joaquin Valley chpt., charter mem.), Fresno County Archaeological Soc. Republican. Lutheran. Avocations: quilting, faceting. Office: Garrison Libr 3427 Circle Ct E Fresno CA 93703-2403

GARRISON-JACKSON, ZINA, retired tennis player; b. Houston, Nov. 16, 1963; m. Willard Jackson. mem. U.S. Olympic tennis team, 1988 (Bronze Medal in Singles and Gold Medal in Doubles - with Pam Shriver). Winner tournaments including Wimbledon Jr. Singles, 1981, U.S. Open Jr. Singles, 1981, U.S. Open Doubles Title (with Mary Joe Fernandez), 1993, Can. Doubles, 1986, 87, Birmingham, 1990; finalist Wimbledon, 1990. Office: c/o USTA 70 W Red Oak Ln White Plains NY 10604-3602 Office: c/o Advantage International 1751 Pinnacle Dr Ste 1500 Mc Lean VA 22102-3833*

GARRISS, PHYLLIS WEYER, music educator, performer; b. Hastings, Nebr., Dec. 25, 1923; d. Frank Elmer and Mabelle Claire (Carey) Weyer; m. William Philip Garriss, Aug. 28, 1954; children: Daniel, Meredith, Margaret. AB, MusB, Hastings Coll., 1945; MusM, U. Rochester, 1948. Instr. DePauw U., Greencastle, Ind., 1948-51; assoc. prof. music Meredith Coll., Raleigh, N.C., 1951-94, assoc. prof. emerita, part-time prof., 1994—; instr. Cannon Music Camp, Appalachian State U., Boone, N.C., 1973-98; vis. instr. Ball State U., Muncie, summers 1951, 53; dir. Lamar Stringfield Chamber Music Camp, Meredith Coll., 1980—; bd. dirs. Raleigh Symphony Orch., Raleigh Chamber Music Guild; mem. various symphonic groups as violinist, including Roanoke Symphony, Raleigh Civic Symphony, Duke U. Symphony, Tri-City Chamber Orch., Raleigh Symphony Orch., Capital Chamber Music Ensemble. Mem. Raleigh Civic Coun., 1958-60; bd. dirs. Raleigh Comty. Mus. Sch., 1993-97, N.C. Fedn. Music Clubs, 1988-96; mem. PEO. Recipient Medal of Arts, City of Raleigh Arts Commn., 1987. Mem. Am. String Tchrs. Assn. (corr. sec. 1950-54, Disting. Svc. award 1979), Music Tchrs. Nat. Assn., Music Educators Nat. Conf., Local 500 Musicians Assn. (bd. dirs. 1980—), Raleigh Music Club (pres. 1958-60, 93-95), Pi Kappa Lambda, Mu Phi Epsilon. Democrat. Presbyterian. Avocations: cooking, traveling. Home: 3400 Merriman Ave Raleigh NC 27607-7004 Office: Meredith Coll 3800 Hillsborough St Raleigh NC 27607-5237

GARRITY, JAMES, JR., federal judge. Bar: N.Y. Bankruptcy judge for so. dist. N.Y., U.S. Bankruptcy Ct., N.Y.C., 1991—. Office: US Bankruptcy Ct US Custom House 6th Fl One Bowling Green New York NY 10004-1408

GARRITY, RODMAN FOX, psychologist, educator; b. Los Angeles, June 10, 1922; s. Lawrence Hitchcock and Margery Fox (Pugh) G.; m. Juanita Daphne Mullan, Mar. 5, 1948; children—Diana Daphne, Ronald Fox. Student, Los Angeles City Coll., 1946-47; B.A., Calif. State U., Los Angeles, 1950; M.A., So. Meth. U., Dallas, 1955; Ed.D., U. So. Calif., 1963. Tchr. elem. sch. Palmdale (Calif.) Sch. Dist., 1952-54; psychologist, prin. Redondo Beach (Calif.) City Schs., 1954-60; asst. dir. ednl. placement lectr., ednl. adviser U. So. Calif., 1960-62; asso. prof., coordinator credentials programs Calif. State Poly. U., Pomona, 1962-66; chmn. social sci. dept. Calif. State Poly. U., 1966-68, dir. tchr. preparation center, 1968-71, coordinator grad. program, 1971-73, prof. tchr. preparation center, 1968—, coordinator spl. edn. programs, 1979—; cons. psychologist, lectr. in field. Pres. Redondo Beach Coordinating Council, 1958-60; mem. univ. rep. Calif. Faculty Assns., 1974-76. Served with Engr. Combat Bn. AUS, 1942-45. Mem. Prins. Assn. Redondo Beach (chmn. 1958-60), Nat. Congress Parents and Tchrs. (hon. life), Am. Psychol. Assn., Calif. Tchrs. Assn. Democrat. Office: Calif State U Dept Special Edn Pomona CA 91768 *Empathetic reaching out to others transcends the obvious importance of achievement and intellectual ability. This has been a basic guide for my endeavors in the helping professions.*

GARRITY, VINCENT FRANCIS, JR., lawyer; b. Phila., July 26, 1937; s. Vincent Francis and Anne (Glenn) G.; m. Maryellen O'Brien, May 8, 1965; children: Vincent III, Ellen, Christopher, Elisa. AB cum laude, Coll. of Holy Cross, Worcester, Mass., 1959; LLB, Harvard U., 1962. Bar: Pa. 1963, U.S. Dist. Ct. (ea. dist.) Pa. 1963. Assoc. Duane, Morris & Heckscher, Phila., 1963-70, ptnr., 1970—, co-chmn. bus. law dept., 1981-94; mem. firm mgmt. com. Duane, Morris & Heckscher, 1983-98; dir. profl. standards Duane, Morris & Heckscher, Phila., 1994-96; Presenter numerous seminars, courses; panelist bar assns. and insts. Contbr. numerous articles to profl. jours. With USAR, 1962-68. Fellow Am. Bar Found.; mem. ABA (com. on corp laws bus. law sect. 1983-89, participant in preparation Model Bus. Corp. Act, vice chmn. com. on negotiated acquistitions, 1991-95, chmn. 1995-98), Pa. Bar Assn. (chmn. sect. corp. banking and bus. law 1981-83, vice chmn. Title 15 task force on 1988 Pa. Bus. Corp. Law 1983—, Spl. Achievement award 1982), Am. Law Inst., Merion Golf Club (Ardmore, Pa.); Union League Phila. Roman Catholic. Home: 118 Derwen Rd Bala Cynwyd PA 19004-2710

GARRITY, WENDELL ARTHUR, JR., federal judge; b. Worcester, Mass., June 20, 1920; s. W. Arthur and Mary B. (Kennedy) G.; m. Barbara A. Mullins, May 24, 1952; children: W. Arthur III, Charles A., Anne M. Singleton, Jean M. Garrity Kennedy. A.B., Holy Cross Coll., 1941; LL.B., Harvard U., 1946; LLD (hon.), Coll. of Holy Cross, 1976, U. Mass., 1978, Northeastern U. Law. Sch., 1986; JD (hon.), New Eng. Law Sch., 1978; HLD (hon.), Simmons Coll., 1982, Worcester State Coll., 1986. Bar: Mass. 1946, U.S. Dist. Ct. Mass. 1948, U.S. Supreme Ct. 1954. Law clk. to presiding justice U.S. Dist. Ct. Mass., 1946-47, asst. U.S. atty., 1948-50, U.S. atty., 1961-66, judge, 1966-85, sr. judge, 1985—; ptnr. Maguire, Roche & Leen, 1950-61; lectr. in field. Contbr. articles to profl. jours. Treas. Dem. Party, Wellesley, 1952-55; town coord. Kennedy Congl. Campaigns, 1952-60; coord. Wis. hdqrs. Kennedy Presdl. Campaign, 1960. Sgt. U.S. Army ETO. Recipient Rabb Human Rels. award Am. Jewish Community, 1979, Roger Baldwin award Mass. CLU Found., 1986, Meml. award 16th Ann. Martin Luther Breakfast, 1986. Mem. ABA. Mass. Bar Assn., Boston Bar Assn. (v.p. 1965-66), Harvard Club, Knights of Malta, Wellesley Club. Democrat. Roman Catholic. Avocation: swimming, cycling. Office: US Dist Ct Ste 4120 1 Courthouse Way Ste 4120 Boston MA 02110

GARROP, BARBARA ANN, elementary education educator; b. Chgo., Sept. 2, 1941; d. Marshall and Esther (Barbakoff) Stickles; widowed; children: Alana Beth, Stacy Lynn. AA with honors, Wright Jr. Coll., Chgo., 1961; BA with honors, Roosevelt U., 1963; MS with honors, Calif. State U., Hayward, 1982. Cert. elem. tchr., reading specialist, Calif. Tchr. Von Humboldt Sch., Chgo., 1963-64, Haugan Sch., Chgo., 1964-67; primary grades reading specialist Mt. Diablo Sch. Dist., Concord, Calif., 1979-80, Mills Elem. Sch., Benicia, Calif., 1980-87, Mary Farmar Sch., Benicia, 1987—; mentor tchr. Benicia Unified Sch. Dist., Benicia, 1989, 92, 96—; inst. tchr. leader Calif. Lit. Project, 1991-93; instr. Chapman U. Acad. Ctr., Fairfield, Calif., spring, 1992; mem. reading delegation to China citizen amb. program People to People Internat., 1993, Russia & Czech citizen amb. program, 1998. Author phonic manual, 1982; featured in article Woman's Day mag., 1982; contbr. reading program to Excellence In Educational Programs Throughout Solano County, 1994-97; contbg. author Celebrating The National Reading Initiative, 1988. Bd. dirs. Sisterhood of Congregation B'nai Shalom, Walnut Creek, Calif., 1987-88. Named Benicia Tchr. of Yr., 1998, 99; grantee Reading Is Fundamental, 1979-80, Golden Bell award Calif. Sch. Bd. Assn., 1997. Mem. NEA, AAUW, Internat. Reading Assn., Calif. Reading Assn. (Achievement award 1984), Constra Costa Reading Assn., Calif. Tchrs. Assn., Pi Lambda Theta. Jewish. Lodge: B'nai Brith Women (v.p. Columbus, Ohio 1971-72, pres. Walnut Creek 1973-74). Avocations: singing, theater, reading, drawing, painting. Office: Mary Farmar Sch 901 Military W Benicia CA 94510-2598

GARROT, PATRICIA MARY, secondary education educator; b. Cassville, Wis., Apr. 9, 1938; d. Christopher Hubert and Frances Majella (Wiest) Esser; m. George Maurice Garrot, Oct. 29, 1977. BA, Alverno Coll., 1959; MEd, Marquette U., 1969. Cert. tchr., Wis. Tchr. grade 4 Our Lady of Sorrows, Milw., 1959-60, tchr. grade 6, 1960-62; math. and sci. tchr. Pius XI High Sch., Milw., 1962-76; math. tchr. Cath. Meml. High Sch., Waukesha, Wis., 1976—. NSF grantee Marquette U., 1963, 64, Clarke Coll., 1971. Mem. Wis. Math. Coun. (Cert. of Appreciation 1984), Nat. Coun. Tchrs. Math. Roman Catholic. Office: Cath Meml High Sch 601 E College Ave Waukesha WI 53186-5538

GARROTT, FRANCES CAROLYN, architectural technician; b. Bowling Green, Ky., Mar. 10, 1932; d. Irby Reid and Carrie Mae (Stahl) Cameron; m. Leslie Othello Garrott, Oct. 12, 1951 (dec. Feb. 1978); children: Dennis Leslie, Alan Reid; adopted children: Carolyn Maria, Karen Roxana; m. Raymond William Scerbo, May 31, 1978 (div. Oct. 1990). Student Fla. State U., 1951, St. Petersburg Jr. Coll., 1962-74; grad. Pinellas Vocat. Tech. Inst., 1975. With Sears, Roebuck and Co., Rapid City, S.D., 1951-52, St. Petersburg, Fla., 1961-62; bookkeeper Ohio Nat. Bank, Columbus, 1953-54, Sunbeam Bakery, Lakeland, Fla., 1955-56; with Christies Toy Sales, Pennsauken, N.J., 1958-60; exec. sec. Gulf Coast Automotive Warehouse, Inc., Tampa, Fla., 1970-73, office mgr., 1975-78; sec., treas., chief pilot, co-owner Tech. Devel. Corp., St. Petersburg, Fla., 1970-78; freelance archtl. draftsman and designer, archtl. cons., constrn. materials estimator, 1975—, Fla. state judge Vocat. Indsl. Clubs of Am. Skills Olympics, 1986. Nat. Assn. Women in Constrn. scholar, 1974. Mem. Nat. Assn. Women in Constrn., Alpha Chi Omega. Democrat. Home and Office: 8156 Timberidge Loop W Lakeland FL 33809-2357

GARROW, DAVID JEFFRIES, historian, author; b. New Bedford, Mass., May 11, 1953; s. Walter and Barbara Mae (Fassett) G.; m. Susan Foster Newcomer, Dec. 18, 1984. BA, Wesleyan U., Middletown, Conn., 1975; MA, Duke U., 1978, PhD, 1981. Instr. polit. sci. Duke U., Durham, N.C., 1978-79; vis. mem. Sch. Social Sci., Inst. Advanced Study, Princeton, N.J., 1979-80; asst. prof. polit. sci. U. N.C., Chapel Hill, 1980-84; assoc. prof. polit. sci. City Coll. N.Y., CUNY Grad. Ctr., 1984-87, prof., 1987-91; vis. fellow Joint Ctr. Polit. Studies, Washington, 1984; sr. advisor Eyes on the Prize: Am.'s Civil Rights Yrs., PBS TV documentary broadcast, 1985-90; bd. dirs. Martin Luther King Jr. Papers Project, King Ctr., Atlanta, 1985—; fellow 20th Century Fund, 1991-93; James Pinckney Harrison vis. prof. history Coll. William and Mary, 1994-95; disting. historian in residence Am. U., 1995-96, disting. Presidential prof., Emory U., 1997—. Author: Protest at Selma: Martin Luther King and the Voting Rights Act of 1965, 1978 (Chastain award 1979), The FBI and Martin Luther King, Jr.: From "Solo" to Memphis, 1981, Bearing the Cross: Martin Luther King, Jr. and the Southern Christian Leadership Conference, 1986 (Pulitzer Prize for Biography 1987, Robert F. Kennedy book award 1987), Liberty and Sexuality: The Right to Privacy and the Making of Roe v. Wade, 1994; editor: The Montgomery Bus Boycott and the Women Who Started It: The Memoir of JoAnn Gibson Robinson, 1987; co-editor: The Eyes on the Prize Civil Rights Reader, 1987, 91; contbr. articles to publs. and profl. jours. Recipient NEH grant, 1984-85, Ford Found. grant, 1979-80, Lyndon B. Johnson Found. grant, 1979-80, Eisenhower World Affairs Inst. grant, 1985-86. Phi Beta Kappa. Democrat. Avocations: bicycling, hiking. Home and Office: Emory U Law Sch Atlanta GA 30322-2770

GARROW, TIMOTHY ALAN, nutrition science educator; b. South Bend, Ind., July 14, 1960; s. Stanley Harrison and Melba Marie (Welsh) G.; m. Linda Sue Collins, May 19, 1990; children: Nathaniel Alan, Sarah Grace. BS in Nutrition Sci., U. Calif., Davis, 1986, MS in Nutrition, 1988; PhD in Comparative Biochemistry, U. Calif., Berkeley, 1992. Assoc. prof. U. Ill., Urbana, 1994—. Contbr. articles to profl. jours. Recipient 1st award NIH, 1996. Mem. Am. Soc. Nutritional Scis. Office: U Ill 905 S Goodwin Ave Urbana IL 61801-3816

GARRUTO, JOHN ANTHONY, cosmetics executive; b. Johnson City, N.Y., June 18, 1952; children: James, Christopher, Catherine, Gabrielle. BS in Chemistry, SUNY, Binghamton, 1974; AAS in Bus. Adminstrn., Broome Coll., 1976. Rsch. chemist Lander Co. Inc., Binghamton, 1974-77; rsch. dir. Lander Co. Inc., St. Louis, 1977-79, Olde Worlde Products, High Point, N.C., 1979-81; v.p. rsch. and devel. LaCosta Products Internat., Carlsbad, Calif., 1981-89; chief ops. officer Randall Products Internat., Carlsbad, 1989-91; pres. Dermasearch Internat., 1991-92; chief tech. officer Innovative Bioscis. Corp., Oceanside, Calif., 1992-95; v.p. rsch. Garden Botanika, Oceanside, Calif., 1995—; cons. Trans-Atlantic Mktg., Binghamton, 1975-78; instr. cosmetic sci UCLA, 1991—, UCLA Ext.; lectr. to cosmetic industry. Patentee in field. Mem. AAS, Soc. Cosmetic Chemists (newsletter editor 1980-81, publicity chmn. 1984—, edn. chmn. 1987, employment chmn. 1994—, sec. beauty industry west, chmn. elect 1999—), Inst. for Food Technologists, Pacific Tech. Exch., Fedn. Am. Scientists, N.Y. Acad. Scis. Office: Garden Botanika # 115 4168 Avenida De La Plata Oceanside CA 92056-6031

GARRUTO, RALPH MICHAEL, research anthropologist, educator, biologist; b. Binghamton, N.Y., Nov. 20, 1943; s. Ralph Anthony and Josephine Janet (DiMartino) G.; children: Jessi ca Anne, Jason Michael, John Ralph. BS, Pa. State U., 1966, MA, 1969, PhD, 1973. Postdoctoral fellow NIH, Bethesda, Md., 1972-73, staff, then sr. staff fellow, 1973-78, supervisory rsch. biologist, 1978—; adj. prof. med. genetics Coll. Medicine U. South Ala., Mobile, 1982—; adj. sr. scientist biol. anthropology Pa. State U., University Park, 1985—; rsch. prof. anthropology neuroscis. SUNY, Binghamton, N.Y., 1997—; participant anthropol. and biomed. fieldwork, Asia, Pacific Islands, L.Am., 1969—; mem., NIH rep. U.S. Nat. Com. U.S. Man and the Biosphere Program, 1993-95; founding mem. bd. trustees Nat. Mus. Health and Medicine Found., Washington, 1989-91; exec. sec. Commn. on Aging and the Aged, Zagreb, Yugoslavia, 1985-89; cons. WHO, 1987; chair selection com. Paul T. Baker Disting. lectr. in human biology and anthropology Pa. State U., 1986-98. Co-editor: Biological Anthropology and Aging: Perspectives on Human Variation over the Lifespan, 1994, Dermatoglyphics: Science in Transition, 1991; contbr. articles on neurodegenerative disorders, neurosci. and aging to profl. jours.; patentee bil. agts. Recipient Commendation for Rsch., Guam Legislature, 1987, Spl. Achievement award, 1990, Merit award NIH, 1991, Dir.'s award, 1993; Wenner-Gren Found. leadership grantee, 1986, grantee, 1993-95; Alumni fellow Pa. State U., 1987. Fellow Am. Coll. Epidemiology, Am. Dermatoglyphics Assn. (sec.-treas. 1981-82, pres. 1987-89, disting. achievement award 1995), Human Biology Assn. (pres./pres.-elect 1993-96, exec. com. 1991-93), Internat. Genetic Epidemiology Soc. (founding fellow), NAS, Third World Acad. Scis. (assoc.); mem. Soc. for Neurosci., World Fedn. Neurology (rsch. com. on neurepidemiology). Avocations: fishing, camping, gardening, field trialing.

GARRY, JAMES B., historian, storyteller, researcher, writer; b. Taylor, Tex., Apr. 28, 1947; s. Mahon Barker and Grace (Dellinger) G. BS, U. Mich., 1970, MS, 1975. Part-time wilderness guide, naturalist Triangle X Ranch, Moose, Wyo., 1969-75; community organizer, media cons., tchr. Hobart St. Project, Detroit, 1974-75; media specialist, lobbyist Powder River Basin Resource Coun., Sheridan, Wyo., 1975-76; pvt. practice media and polit. cons. Big Horn, Wyo., 1976-78; video and film artist-in-residence Wyo. Coun. on the Arts/Sheridan Coll., Sheridan, 1978-80; mem. staff Great Plains Lore and Natural History, Big Horn, 1980—; storyteller part-time Buffalo Bill Hist. Ctr., Cody, Wyo., 1980—; tchr. Yellowstone (Wyo.) Inst., summers 1986—; tour study leader, rsch. collaborator Smithsonian Instn., Washington, part-time 1984—. Co-author: Writing About Wildlife, 1974; author, editor: Buck: Stories by Lloyd Buck Bender, 1984, This Ol' Drought Ain't Broke Us Yet But We're All Bent Pretty Bad, 1992, The First Liar Never Has a Chance: Curly, Jack and Bill (and Other Characters of the Hills, Brush and Plains), 1994; storyteller in field. 2d lt. U.S. Army, 1970. Recipient Spl. Heritage award Old West Trail Found., 1983; named one of Individual Humanist of Yr., Wyo. Coun. for Humanities, 1986. Democrat. Roman Catholic. Home: PO Box 805 Gillette WY 82717-0805 Office: Great Plains Lore & Natural History PO Box 805 Gillette WY 82717-0805

GARRY, JOHN THOMAS, II, lawyer; b. Albany, N.Y., Dec. 12, 1923; s. Joseph A. II and Jean Theresa (Cramond) G.; m. Mary Regina Hoffman (dec.); children: John, Michael, Regina, Maureen, Suzanne, Patricia; m. Claire Bogne Guy, 1989. Student, Cornell U., 1942-43; BA, St. Bernadine of Siena Coll., 1949; LLB, JD, Union U., 1952. Bar: N.Y. 1952, U.S. Supreme Ct. 1952. Asst. corp. counsel City of Albany, 1953-55, asst. dist. atty., 1955-58, dist. atty., 1958-68; sr. ptnr. Garry & Cahill, Albany, 1968—. Exec. chmn. Dem. Cen. Com., Albany, Albany Big Bros./Big Sisters Am., 1971; trustee Siena Coll., Loudonville, N.Y., 1987-97; mem. Empire State Art Commn., 1990-95, N.Y. State Plz. Art Commn. Served with USAAF, 1943. Decorated Air medal. Mem. ABA, N.Y. State Bar Assn. (character com. admission), Albany County Bar Assn., Am. Judicature Soc., Internat. Narcotic Enforcement Officers Assn., N.Y. State Dist. Attys. Assn. (v.p. 1967), St. Bernadine of Siena Coll. Alumni Assn. (pres. 1964, trustee 1989-97), Am. Legion, VFW, KC (Grand Knight 1956). Club: Wolfert's Roost Country. Lodges: K.C. (past grand knight), Elks.

GARRY, WILLIAM JAMES, magazine editor; b. San Francisco, May 8, 1944; s. William James Garry and Nancy Jean (Gaillard) Chadwick. B.A., Dartmouth Coll., 1966; M.F.A., Columbia U., 1969. Mng. editor True mag., N.Y.C., 1971-72; exec. editor Epicure mag., N.Y.C., 1972-74; mng. editor spl. pubs. House Beautiful mag., N.Y.C., 1975-77; editor Free Enterprise mag., N.Y.C., 1977-79; mng. editor Bon Appetit mag., L.A., 1980-85, editor-in-chief, 1985—. Mem. Am. Soc. Mag. Editors, Soc. Profl. Journalists. Office: Bon Appetit 6300 Wilshire Blvd Los Angeles CA 90048-5204*

GARSCADDEN, ALAN, physicist; b. Glasgow, Scotland, June 10, 1937; came to U.S., 1962; s. Andrew and Sarah Florence (Black) G.; m. Avril Margaret Thompson Garscadden, Jan. 24, 1962; children: A. Graeme, A.K. Neil, A.K. Gael, A.E. Hilary. BS (hon.), Queens U., Belfast, Ireland, 1958; PhD in Physics, 1962. Rsch. physicist Aerospace Rsch. Labs, Wright-Patterson AFB, 1962-73; lab. dir., 1973-75; rsch. physicist Aero Propulsion and Power Divsn., 1975-91; chief scientist Aero Propulsion Directorate, 1991-94, Wright Lab., 1995-97; chief scientist Propulsion Directorate/Air Force Rsch. Lab., Wright-Patterson AFB, 1997—, Edwards AFB, Calif.,

1997—; adj. prof. physics Air Force Inst. Tech., Wright Patterson AFB, 1969—; bd. dirs. Von Karman Inst., Brussels; trusteeOhio Aerospace Inst., 1996-98; bd. dirs. Von Karman Inst., 1998—. Contbr. articles to profl. jours. Commr. Planning Commn., Village of Yellow Springs, 1985-96. Fellow IEEE, Am. Phys. Soc.; mem. AIAA (Disting. Svc. medal 1998). Avocation: history of colonial science. Office: AFRL/PR Air Force Rsch lab 1950 5th St Wright Patterson AFB OH 45433-7251

GARSH, THOMAS BURTON, publisher; b. New Rochelle, N.Y., Dec. 12, 1931; s. Harry and Matilda (Smith) G.; m. Beatrice J. Schmidt; children: Carol Jean, Thomas Burton, Janice Lynn. B.S., U. Md., 1955. Edn. rep. McGraw Hill Book Co., N.Y.C., 1959-68; mktg. mgr. D.C. Heath & Co., Boston, 1969-71; dir. mktg. Economy Co., Oklahoma City, 1971-72; sr. v.p. Macmillan Pub. Co., N.Y.C., 1972-78; pres. Am. Book Co., N.Y.C., 1978-81; founder, pres., dir. Am. Ednl. Computer, Inc., Palo Alto, Calif., 1981-86; founder, chmn., chief exec. officer OmnyEd Corp., Palo Alto, 1987-91; pres. Silver Burdett & Ginn divsn. of Simon and Schuster, 1991-92; dir. Fifty Plus Fitness Assn., Palo Alto, Calif. Publ. Homes and Land of Santa Clara, 1998—. Mem. county council Boy Scouts Am., 1963-65; mem. ch. council on Interracial Affairs, 1966-68, pres., 1967; vice-chmn. Madison County Democratic Party, 1967. Mem. Assn. Am. Pubs., Profl. Bookman's Assn., Omicron Delta Kappa, Sigma Alpha Epsilon. Club: Cazenovia Country (founder). Home: 401 Old Spanish Trl Portola Valley CA 94028

GARSON, ARNOLD HUGH, newspaper publisher; b. Lincoln, Nebr., May 29, 1941; s. Sam B. and Celia (Stine) G.; m. Marilyn Grace Baird, Aug. 15, 1964; children: Scott Arnold, Christopher Baird, Gillian Grace, Megan Jane. BA, U. Nebr., 1964; MS, UCLA, 1965. Reporter Omaha World-Herald, 1965-69; reporter Des Moines Tribune, 1969-72, city editor, 1972-75; reporter Des Moines Register, 1975-83, mng. editor, 1983-88; editor San Bernardino (Calif.) County Sun, 1988-96; pub., pres. Sioux Falls (S.D.) Argus Leader, 1996—. Recipient Pub. Svc. Reporting award Am. Polit. Sci. Assn., 1969, Profl. Journalism award U. Nebr. at Omaha, 1969, John Hancock award for excellence in bus. and fin. journalism, 1979, Mng. Editors Sweepstakes award Iowa AP, 1976, Calif.-Nev. AP award for column writing, 1995. Mem. Am. Soc. Newspaper Editors, Soc. Profl. Journalists, v.p. S.D. Newspaper Assn. Jewish. Home: 5 S Riverview Hts Sioux Falls SD 57105-0252 Office: Sioux Falls Argus Leader PO Box 5034 Sioux Falls SD 57117-5034

GARSTANG, ROY HENRY, astrophysicist, educator; b. Southport, Eng., Sept. 18, 1925; came to U.S., 1964; s. Percy Brocklehurst and Eunice (Gledhill) G.; m. Ann Clemence Hawk, Aug. 11, 1959; children—Jennifer Katherine, Susan Veronica. B.A., U. Cambridge, 1946, M.A., 1950, Ph.D., 1954, Sc.D., 1983. Research assoc. U. Chgo., 1951-52; lectr. astronomy U. Coll., London, 1952-60; reader astronomy U. London, 1960-64, asst. dir. Obs., 1959-64; prof. astrophysics U. Colo., Boulder, 1964-94, chair faculty assembly, 1988-89, prof. emeritus, 1994—; chmn. Joint Inst. for Lab. Astrophysics, 1966-67; cons. Nat. Bur. Standards, 1964-73; v.p. commn. 14 Internat. Astron. Union, 1970-73, pres., 1973-76; Erskine vis. fellow U. Canterbury, N.Z., 1971; vis. prof. U. Calif., Santa Cruz, 1971. Editor: Observatory, 1953-60; Contbr. numerous articles to tech. jours. Recipient Excellence in Svc. award U. Colo., 1990. Fellow Am. Phys. Soc., AAAS, Optical Soc. Am., Brit. Inst. Physics, Royal Astron. Soc.; mem. Am. Astron. Soc., Royal Soc. Scis. Liege (Belgium). Achievements include rsch. on atomic physics and astrophys. applications; calculation of atomic transition probabilities, atomic spectra in very high magnetic fields and magnetic white dwarf stars; modelling of light pollution. Home: 830 8th St Boulder CO 80302-7409 Office: U Colo JILA Boulder CO 80309-0440 *It is a privilege to help others to learn about the wonderful universe in which we live.*

GART, HERBERT STEVEN, communications executive, producer; b. Phila., June 11, 1937; s. Jack and Celia (Strauss) G.; m. Lillian Allen Jay, Aug. 12, 1969; 1 child, Heather Joy. Student, Temple U., 1955-59. Pres. BSM Prodns., Inc., N.Y.C., 1965-70, Herbert S. Gart Mgmt., Inc., N.Y.C., 1963-84, Whitfeld Music, Inc., N.Y.C., 1965-90; Touchstone Music Inc., 1965—; pres. The Rainbow Collection, Ltd., N.Y.C., 1971—. Personal mgr.: (1963—) Bill Cosby, Buffy Sainte-Marie, Jose Feliciano, Jesse Colin Young, The Youngbloods (Gold Record award Rec. Industry Assn. Am. and RCA Records 1968), Don McLean (5 Platinum Record awards Rec. Industry Assn. Am. and United Artists 1972), Andy Breckman (3 Emmy awards 1982, 85), Peter Tork (The Monkees), Ed Begley Jr. (several Emmy nominations), Jack Bruce (Cream), Felix Pappalardi (Mountain), Tim Hauser (Manhattan Transfer), Tommy West, The Persuasions, Headsoup, Roger Davidson, Roxy Dawn, Ashley Cleveland; record producer: (1965—) Janis Ian (Gold Record award Rec. Industry Assn. Am. and Columbia Records 1975, 2 Grammy awards Nat. Acad. Rec. Arts and Scis. 1975), Dick Feller, Roy Buchanan, Charlie Daniels, Mississippi John Hurt, Felix Pappalardi, Headsoup, Roger Davidson. Office: The Rainbow Collection Ltd PO Box 300 Solebury PA 18963-0301

GART, MURRAY JOSEPH, journalist; b. Boston, Nov. 9, 1924; s. John and Frieda (Fisher) G.; m. Jeanne Brooks, Feb. 26, 1950; children: Mitchell Brooks, Marcia Anne. B.A. in Econs, Northeastern U., 1949, LHD (hon.), 1970. Reporter Honolulu Star-Bull., 1949-50; editor Weekly Ind. Record, Cape May County, N.J., 1950-51; reporter, city editor Wichita Beacon, 1951-53; reporter, news editor Wichita Eagle, 1953-55; bur. chief Time-Life mag. News Svc., Toronto, Can., 1955-57, Boston, 1957-59; chief Midwest corr. Time mag., 1959-61; bur. chief Time mag., Chgo., 1961-64, London, 1964-66; asst. mng. editor Fortune mag., N.Y.C., 1966-69; chief of corrs. Time-Life News Svc., 1969-78; asst. mng. editor Time mag., 1972-78; editor The Washington Star, 1978-81; sr. editor Time Inc., 1981-82; assoc. Johns Hopkins Fgn. Policy Inst., Washington, 1982-84; cons. Time, Inc., 1982-89; dir. Mid. East Inst., 1988—, Am. Near Ea. Refugee Aid, 1993—, Geopolitics of Energy, 1985-94. Editor: Cosmos Jour., 1992-95. Served with AUS, 1943-46. Mem. Coun. on Fgn. Rels., Cosmos Club, Northeasetern U. Corp. Home: 2126 Connecticut Ave NW Washington DC 20008-1729

GARTEN, DAVID BURTON, lawyer; b. Iowa City, Mar. 23, 1952; s. William B. and Linda (Laird) G.; m. Anita Wallner, Mar. 12, 1983. BA summa cum laude, honors in Econs., Yale U., 1974, JD, 1977. Law clk. to Hon. Anthony M. Kennedy U.S. Ct. Appeals (9th cir.), Sacramento, 1977-78; assoc. Kirkland & Ellis, Chgo., 1979-84, ptnr., 1984-90; v.p., gen. counsel NL Industries Inc., Houston, 1990—. Mem. Phi Beta Kappa. Avocations: skiing, hunting, golf. Office: NL Industries Inc 16825 Northchase Dr Ste 1200 Houston TX 77060-6012

GARTENBERG, SEYMOUR LEE, retired recording company executive; b. N.Y.C., May 27, 1931; s. Morris and Anna (Banner) G.; m. Anna Stassi, Feb. 18, 1956 (dec. Feb. 3, 1998); children: Leslie, Karen, Mark; m. Phyllis H. Hecker, Mar. 14, 1999. BBA cum laude, CCNY, 1952, LHD (hon.), 1996. Asst. contr. Finlay Straus, Inc., N.Y.C., 1950-56; contr. Tappin's Inc., Newark, 1956; sr. v.p. Columbia House divsn. CBS, N.Y.C., 1956-65; v.p. fin. Columbia Records divsn. CBS, N.Y.C., 1965-67; exec. v.p. Columbia House div. CBS, N.Y.C., 1967-73; pres. CBS Toys Div., Cranbury, N.J., 1973-78; v.p. CBS/Columbia Group, N.Y.C., 1978—; sr. group v.p. CBS Records Group, 1979-87; exec. v.p. CBS Records Inc., 1987-91; ret., 1991; dir. C-Phone Corp., Wilmington, N.C. Mem. Inst. of Mgmt. Accts., Am. Mgmt. Assn., Mill Island Civic Assn., Am. Arbitration Assn. (panel mem.).

GARTENHAUS, SOLOMON, physicist; b. Kassel, Germany, Jan. 3, 1929; came to U.S., 1937, naturalized, 1943; s. Leopolt and Hanna (Brandler) G.; m. Johanna Lore Weisz, Aug. 30, 1953; children: Michael M., Kevin M. B.S., U. Pa., 1951; M.S., U. Ill., 1953, Ph.D., 1955. Instr. Stanford U., 1955-58; faculty physics Purdue U., Lafayette, Ind., 1958—; prof. Purdue U., 1963—; asst. dean Grad. Sch., 1972-77, sec. of faculties, 1980—; disting. vis. prof. USAF Acad., Colo., 1977-78; dir. Purdue-Ind. Studienprogram, U. Hamburg, W. Ger., 1979-80; cons. Lockheed, summers 1958-60; officer, dir. Advanced Research Corp., 1961-65. Author: Elements of Plasma Physics, 1964, Physics-Basic Principles, 1975; contbr. articles to profl. jours. Fellow Am. Phys. Soc.; mem. N.Y. Acad. Scis., Am. Assn. Physics Tchrs., Phi Beta Kappa, Sigma Xi. Home: 2102 S 9th St Lafayette IN 47905-2132 Office: Purdue U Dept Physics Lafayette IN 47907

GARTH, BRYANT GEOFFREY, law educator, foundation executive; b. San Diego, Dec. 9, 1949; s. William and Patricia (Feild) G.; children: Heather, Andrew, Daniela. BA magna cum laude, Yale U., 1972; JD, Stanford U., 1975; PhD, European U. Inst., Florence, Italy, 1979. Bar: Calif. 1975, Ind. 1988. Law clk. to judge U.S. Dist. Ct. (no. dist.) Calif., San Francisco, 1978-79; asst. prof. Ind. U., Bloomington, 1979-82, assoc. prof., 1982-85, prof., 1985-92, dean Law Sch., 1986-90; dir. Am. Bar Found., Chgo., 1990—; cons. Ont. Law Reform Commn., 1984-85, 94, World Bank Argentina Project, 1993-94, World Bank Peru Project, 1996; vis. assoc. prof. U. Mich., Ann Arbor, 1983-84; bd. dirs. Internat. Human Rights Law Inst.; mem. bd. visitors Stanford U. Law Sch., 1993—. Author: Neighborhood Law Firms for the Poor, 1980; co-editor: Access to Justice: A World Survey, 1978, Access to Justice: Emerging Issues and Perspectives, 1979, Dealing in Virtue, 1996; contbr. articles to profl. jours. V.p. H.G. & K.F. Montgomery Found. Rsch. grantee NSF, 1982, 91, 92, 95, Nat. Inst. Dispute Resolution, 1985, Ind. Supreme Ct., 1989, Italian Coun. Rsch., 1989, Keck, 1995, MacArthur, 1997. Mem. Am. Law Inst. (exec. com.), Law and Soc. Assn., Internat. Assn. Procedural Law. Democrat. Office: Am Bar Found 750 N Lake Shore Dr Chicago IL 60611-4403

GARTH, LEONARD I., federal judge; b. Bklyn., Apr. 7, 1921; s. Frank A. and Anne F. (Jacobs) Goldstein; m. Sarah Miriam Kaufman, Sept. 6, 1942; 1 child, Tobie Gail Garth Meisel. BA, Columbia U., 1942; postgrad., Nat. Inst. Pub. Affairs, 1942-43; LLB, Harvard U., 1952. Bar: N.J. 1952. Mem. firm Cole, Berman & Garth (and predecessors), Paterson, N.J., 1952-70; judge U.S. Dist. Ct. for Dist. N.J., Newark, 1970-73; U.S. cir. judge Ct. Appeals for 3d Cir., 1973—; lectr. Inst. Continuing Legal Edn.; lectr., coadj. mem. faculty Rutgers U. Law Sch., 1978-98, Seton Hall Law Sch., 1980-95; mem. N.J. Bd. Bar Examiners, 1964-68; mem. com. on revision gen. and admiralty rules Fed. Dist. Ct. N.J.; former mem. com. on fin. disclosure Jud. Conf. U.S.; adv. bd. Fed. Cts. Study Com. Adv. bd. Law and Soc. Major of Ramapo Coll.; Served as 1st lt. AUS, 1943-46. Mem. ABA (N.J. fellows, appellate judges conf.), Fed. Bar Assn., Passaic County (N.J.) Bar Assn. (pres. 1967-68), Am. Law Inst. Office: ML King Jr Fed Bldg/Court 50 Walnut St Rm 5040 Newark NJ 07102-3506 also: 20613 US Courthouse Philadelphia PA 19106

GARTHOFF, RAYMOND LEONARD, diplomat, diplomatic historian; b. Cairo, Mar. 26, 1929; parents Am. citizens; s. Arnold Alexander and Margaret Louise (Frank) G.; m. Vera Alexandrovna Vasilieva, Sept. 16, 1950; 1 child, Alexander Raymond. AB, Princeton U., 1948; MA, Yale U., 1949, PhD, 1951. Rsch. staff RAND Corp., Washington, 1950-57; estimates officer CIA, Washington, 1957-61; with U.S. Dept. of State, Washington, 1961-79, ambassador, 1977-79; sr. fellow Brookings Instn., Washington, 1980-94. Author: Detente and Confrontation, 1985, rev. edit., 1994, Deterrence and Revolution in Soviet Military Doctrine, 1990, The Great Transition, 1994, Reflections on the Cuban Missile Crisis, 1987, rev. edit. 1989, 11 other books; editor, co-author 75 books; contbr. over 100 articles to profl. jours. Recipient Arthur S. Flemming award Jaycees, 1965, Superior Honor award Dept. of State, 1965, Disting. Honor award, 1972. Mem. Coun. Fgn. Rels., Am. Assn. for Advancement of Slavic Studies, Soc. for Historians of Am. Fgn. Rels., Internat. Inst. for Strategic Studies, Acad. Polit. Sci., Assn. Diplomatic Studies. Home: 2128 Bancroft Pl NW Washington DC 20008-4020

GARTHWAITE, GENE RALPH, historian, educator; b. Mt. Hope, Wis., July 15, 1933; s. Ralph Albert and Merle I. (Quarne) G.; div.; children: R. Andrew, Alexander, Martin. BA, St. Olaf Coll., 1955; postgrad., U Chgo., 1958-59; PhD, U. Calif., 1969; MA, Dartmouth Coll., 1987. From instr. to prof. history Dartmouth Coll., Hanover, N.H., 1968-98, chair Asian studies, 1980-92, chair history dept., 1992-96; Jane & Raphael Bernstein prof. in Asian studies Dartmouth Coll., Hanover, 1998—. Author: Khans and Shahs, 1983; contbr. articles to profl. jours. Capt. USAF, 1955-58. Grantee Social Sci. Rsch. Coun., NEH, 1979-80, 91-93. Mem. Middle East Studies Assn. (dir. 1968—), Soc. Iranian Studies (exec. sec. 1969—), Phi Beta Kappa. Democrat. Episcopalian. Avocation: gardening. Office: Dartmouth Coll Dept History Hanover NH 03755

GARTLAN, PHILIP M., secondary school director. Asst. dir. Midland Mid. Sch., N. Branch, N.J., exec. dir., 1994—. Recipient Elem. Sch. Recognition award U.S. Dept. of Edn., 1989-90. Office: The Midland Sch PO Box 5026 North Branch NJ 08876-1301*

GARTLAND, JOHN JOSEPH, physician, writer; b. Phila., Nov. 16, 1918; s. John Joseph and Jane Madelyn (Lafferty) G.; m. Madelyn T. Duffy, Jan. 5, 1944; children: Lynn, Barbara, John Jr., Patricia, Mary Ellen. AB, Princeton U., 1941; MD, Jefferson Med. Coll., 1944. Diplomate Am. Bd. of Orthopaedic Surgery. Chief orthopaedic surgery Meth. Hosp., Phila., 1960-68, Lankenau Hosp., Phila., 1968-70; James Edward prof., chmn. dept. of orthopaedic surgery Jefferson Med. Coll., Thomas Jefferson U., Phila., 1970-85, dir. office departmental rev. Jefferson Med. Coll., 1986-89, univ. med. editor, 1990—. Author: Fundamentals of Orthopaedics, 1965, 4th edit., 1986, Medical Writing and Communicating, 1993; contbr. numerous articles to profl. jours. Trustee Thomas Jefferson U., 1996—. Served to capt. U.S. Army, 1945-47. NIH grantee, 1971-74. Fellow Am. Acad. Orthopaedic Surgeons (pres. 1979-80), Am. Orthopaedic Assn.; mem. Coun. Med. Splty. Socs. (pres. elect 1987, pres. 1988), Overbrook Golf Club (Bryn Mawr, Pa.), Alpha Omega Alpha, Sigma Xi. Democrat. Roman Catholic. Avocations: tennis, writing. Office: Thomas Jefferson U 615 Scott Bldg 1020 Walnut St Philadelphia PA 19107-5585

GARTLAND, WILLIAM JOSEPH, JR., research institute administrator; b. N.Y.C., Apr. 15, 1941; s. William Joseph and Mary (Klik) G.; m. Margaret Louise Wenstadt, June 20, 1981. BS, Holy Cross Coll., 1962; MA, Princeton U., 1964, PhD, 1967. Asst. rsch. scientist NYU Med. Ctr., N.Y.C., 1967-69; postgrad. rsch. biologist U. Calif., San Diego, 1969-70; grants assoc. div. rsch. grants NIH, Bethesda, Md., 1970-71; program adminstr. genetics program Nat. Inst. Gen. Med. Scis., 1971-76; exec. sec. Recombinant DNA Adv. Com., 1975-88; dir. Office Recombinant DNA Activities, 1976-88; U.S. rep. European Sci. Found. Liaison Com. on Recombinant DNA Rsch., 1976-81; NIH rep. Recombinant DNA Com. of USDA, 1978-88; asst. dir. for preclin. scis. AIDS program Nat. Inst. Allergy and Infectious Diseases, NIH, Bethesda, Md., 1988-89; chief resources and ctrs. br. AIDS div. Nat. Inst. Allergy and Infectious Diseases, NIH, Bethesda, Md., 1989—; mem. exec. recombinant DNA com. NIH, 1976-88; U.S. head U.S.-Japan Coop. Program for Recombinant DNA Rsch., 1982-88; U.S. head AIDS panel U.S.-Japan Coop. Med. Sci. Program, 1988—; mem. faculty CSC exec. seminar program and advanced study program Brookings Instn. Co-author articles in field. Recipient Dirs. award NIH, 1978, spl. recognition award USPHS, 1988. Mem. AAAS, Am. Soc. Human Genetics, Am. Soc. Microbiology. Clubs: Sierra, Washington Ski. Home: 12300 Morning Light Ter Gaithersburg MD 20878-2090 Office: Natcher Bldg Rm 4AN-38E 45 Center Dr MSC 6402 Bethesda MD 20892-6402

GARTMAN, MAX DILLON, language educator; b. Mobile, Ala., May 3, 1938; s. Noah Christopher and Edna Olga (Schwartzauer) G.; m. Marcia Ann Hubbard, Aug. 31, 1962; children: Noel Don, Polly Antoinette, Paul Dillon. AB in French and History, Samford U., Birmingham, Ala., 1960; MA in French, U. Ala., Tuscaloosa, 1962, PhD in Romance Langs., 1974; cert., U. Nice, France, 1985. NDEA fellow U. Ala., Tuscaloosa, 1960-65; prof. Romance langs. Samford U., 1965-82, head dept. fgn. langs., 1975-82; chmn. dept. fgn. langs., prof. romance langs. U. North Ala., Florence, 1982—; pres. Internat. Edn. Travel, Florence, 1982—. Editor SU Faculty Forum Ann., 1967-72; performer rec. The Holy City, 1976. Chmn. Ala. Assn. Fgn. Lang. Tchrs., 1973-74, So. Conf. Lang. Tchg., 1976; bd. dirs. Ala. Humanities Found., 1992-96. Mem. Ala. Assn. Tchrs. of French (chairperson 1995-97), Ala. Consortium for Fgn. Langs. (chairperson 1995-97), Rotary (sec. Oxmoor club 1981-82, music dir. 1982—). Baptist. Avocations: tennis, music, European travel. Home: 122 Lambeth St Florence AL 35633-1550 Office: U North Ala Box 5074 Florence AL 35632-0001

GARTNER, ALAN P., university official, author; b. N.Y.C., Apr. 4, 1935; s. Harold J. and Mary T.; children: Jonathan, Rachel, Daniel. B.A., Antioch Coll., 1956; M.A., Harvard U., 1960; Ph.D., Union Grad. Sch., 1973. Cmty. rels. dir. Congress of Racial Equality, 1965-66; exec. dir. Econ. Opportunity Coun. of Suffolk County, 1966-68; dir. New Careers Tng. Lab., N.Y.C., 1968-81; prof. Queens Coll., 1972-76; prof. Grad. Sch., CUNY, 1976-81, 83—, dir. Ctr. for Advanced Study in Edn. Grad. Sch., 1978-81, dir. Office of Sponsored Rsch., 1983-92, dean Rsch. and Univ. Progs., 1992-98; exec. dir. divsn. spl. edn. N.Y.C. Pub. Schs., 1981-83; exec. dir. N.Y.C. Districting Commn., 1990-92; pub. Social Policy mag., N.Y.C., 1971-93; exec. dir. task force on N.Y.C. Comty. Sch. Bd. Governance, 1998. Author: Paraprofessionals and Their Performance, 1971, The Preparation of Human Services Professionals, 1976; co-author: Children Teach Children, 1971, The Service Society and Consumer Vanguard, 1974, Self Help in the Human Services, 1977, Help: A Working Guide to Self-Help Groups, 1979, Supporting Families With a Child With Disabilities, 1991, Inclusion and School Reform, 1997; co-editor: After Deschooling, What?, 1973, Public Service Employment, 1973, What Nixon is Doing to Us, 1973, The New Assault on Equality, 1974, What Reagan is Doing to Us, 1982, The Self-Help Revolution, 1985, Beyond Reagan, 1985, Images of the Disabled/Disabling Images, 1987, Caring for America's Children, 1989, Beyond Separate Education, 1989. Bd. dirs. N.Y. Civil Liberties Union, 1973—; bd. dirs. Antioch Coll., 1974-75; treas. Congress Racial Equality, N.Y.C., 1962-64, chairperson, Boston, 1960-64. Ford Found. fellow, 1956-58; Florina Lasker fellow, 1961-62; Poynter fellow, 1976. Office: CUNY Grad Sch and Univ Ctr 33 W 42nd St New York NY 10036-8099

GARTNER, DANIEL LEE, computer information executive; b. Newark, Ohio, Jan. 24, 1945; s. Harold Jerome and Hazel Marie (Wright) G.; m. Holly L. Hanbaum, July 31, 1993; 1 child, Sarah Marie. Student, Ohio State U., 1967-74; BA, Park Coll., 1978; MS, USAF Inst. Tech., 1982. Computer programmer USAF, Newark AFB, 1974-78, computer systems analyst, 1978-82, chief info. ctr., 1981-82, chief customer support div., 1988-92, chief office staff support, 1992-95; adj. prof. logistics and computers Park Coll., Newark, 1986-91; cons. pvt. sector, Newark, 1983—. Designer 1st broadband local area network, 1st info. ctr. Air Force Logistics Command. Adv. Boy Scouts Am., Newark AFB, 1984-86; active Big Bros. and Big Sister, Newark AFB, 1986; bd. dirs. Newark YMCA, Licking County Planning Commn.; 1st chmn. Licking Park Dist., 1990-91. Mem. Newark C. of C. (mem. leadership tomorrow 1986). Avocation: computers. Home: 1500 Londondale Pkwy Newark OH 43055-1696 Office: DSDC-MMO Columbus OH 43213-1152

GARTNER, HAROLD HENRY, III, lawyer; b. L.A., June 23, 1948; s. Harold Henry Jr. and Frances Mildred (Evans) G.; m. Denise Helene Young, June 7, 1975; children: Patrick Christopher, Matthew Alexander. Student, Pasadena City Coll., 1966-67, George Williams Coll., 1967-68, Calif. State U., Los Angeles, 1969; JD cum laude, Loyola U., Los Angeles, 1972. Bar: Calif. 1972, U.S. Dist. Ct. (cen. dist.) Calif. 1973, U.S. Ct. Appeals (9th cir.) 1973. Assoc. Hitt, Murray & Caffray, Long Beach, Calif., 1972; dep. city atty. City of L.A., 1972-73; assoc. Patterson, Ritner & Lockwood, L.A., 1973-79; mng. ptnr. all offices Patterson, Ritner, Lockwood, Gartner & Jurich, L.A., Ventura, Bakersfield, and San Bernardino, Calif., 1991—; instr. law Ventura Coll., 1981. Recipient Am. Jurisprudence award Trusts and Equity, 1971. Mem. ABA, Calif. Bar Assn., Ventura County Bar Assn., Nat. Assn. Def. Counsel, Assn. So. Calif. Def. Counsel, Ventura County Trial Lawyers Assn., Direct Relief Internat. (bd. trustees). Republican. Club: Pacific Corinthian Yacht. Avocations: sailing, scuba diving, skiing. Home: 6900 Via Alba Camarillo CA 93012-8279 Office: Patterson Ritner Lockwood Gartner & Jurich 260 Maple Ct Ste 231 Ventura CA 93003-3570

GARTNER, JOSEPH CHARLES, business systems administrator; b. Detroit, Feb. 3, 1945; s. Joseph Owen and Frances Alice (Harrington) G.; m. Marilyn Jean Kern, June 26, 1971; children: Stephanie, Jonathan, Jamie Lynn. Student, U. Mich., 1963-66; BSE, Marquette U., 1968; MBA, U. Rochester, 1979. Cert. systems profl. Constrn. engr. B.A.S.F., Wyandotte, Mich., 1966-67; systems engr. IBM Corp., Milw., 1968-70; mgr mgmt. info. systems Borg Warner Corp., Toledo, Ohio, 1970-73; dir. info. systems Donnelly Corp., Holland, Mich., 1973-75; mgr. fin. systems Bausch & Lomb, Rochester, N.Y., 1975-82, mgr. EDP audit, 1982-85; mgr. bus. systems Wegmans Food Markets Inc., Rochester, 1985-97; group mgr. bus. sys. The Penn Traffic Co., Syracuse, N.Y., 1997—. Trustee Fairport (N.Y.) Pub. Libr., 1992—. Mem. Assn. for Systems Mgmt. (internat. dir. 1984-87, Disting. Svc. award 1988), KC (grand knight 1985-87), Genesee Valley Dist. PTA (legis. chmn. 1985—). Home: 3139 Fox Rd Syracuse NY 13215 Office: The Penn Traffic Co PO Box 4737 1200 State Fair Blvd Syracuse NY 13221-4737

GARTNER, LAWRENCE MITCHEL, pediatrician, medical college educator; b. Bklyn., Apr. 24, 1933; s. Samuel and Bertha (Brimberg) G.; m. Carol Sue Blicker, Aug. 12, 1956; children— Alex David, Madeline Hallie. AB, Columbia U., 1954; MD, Johns Hopkins U., 1958. Intern pediatrics Johns Hopkins Hosp., 1958-59; resident pediatrics Albert Einstein Coll. Medicine, 1959-60, chief resident, 1960-61, instr. pediatrics, 1962-64, asst. prof., 1964-69, assoc. prof., 1969-74, prof., 1974-80, dir. div. neonatology, 1967-80, dir. div. pediatric hepatology, 1967-80; dir. clin. research unit Rose F. Kennedy Ctr., 1972-80; attending physician Hosp. of Albert Einstein Coll. Medicine, 1967-80; prof. dept. pediatrics U. Chgo. Pritzker Sch. Medicine, 1980-98, prof. dept. obstetrics and gynecology, 1995-98, prof. emeritus pediatrics and obstetrics and gynecology, 1998—; chmn. dept. pediatrics, med. dir. Wyler Children's Hosp., U. Chgo. Med. Ctr., 1980-93; chmn. Physician's Breastfeeding Network of Ill., 1993-98. Contbr. articles to med. jours. and textbooks. Pediatrician-of-the-Yr. award Ill. chpt. Am. Acad. Pediatrics, 1995; recipient award NIH, 1967-74; Appleton Century Crofts prize, 1956; Mosby book award, 1958. Mem. AAAS, Am. Pediatric Soc. (chmn. coun. 1989-90), Soc. Pediatric Rsch., Perinatal Rsch. Soc., Am. Assn. Study Liver Disease, Chgo. Pediatric Soc. (editor 1990—, treas. 1992-93, sec. 1993-94, v.p. 1994-95, pres. 1995-96), Am. Acad. Pediatrics (chair breastfeeding workgroup 1994—), N.Am. Soc. Pediatric Gastroenterology (pres. 1974-75), The Milk Club (chmn. 1994-96), Acad. Breastfeeding Medicine (founding bd. dirs. 1994-95, editor newsletter 1995—, v.p. 1997-98, pres., 1998—), LaLeche League Internat., Phi Beta Kappa, Alpha Omega Alpha.

GARTNER, MICHAEL GAY, editor, television executive; b. Des Moines, Oct. 25, 1938; s. Carl David and Mary Marguerite (Gay) G.; m. Barbara Jeanne McCoy, May 25, 1968; children: Melissa, Christopher (dec.), Michael. BA, Carleton Coll., 1960; JD, NYU, 1969; LittD (hon.), Simpson Coll., 1984; LLD (hon.), James Madison U., 1989; LittD (hon.), Grand View Coll., 1990, Iowa Wesleyan Coll., 1997. Bar: N.Y., Iowa. With Wall St. Jour., N.Y.C., 1960-74, page one editor, 1970-74; exec. editor Des Moines Register and Tribune, 1974-76, editor, 1976-82, editorial chmn., 1982-85, v.p., 1975-76, exec. v.p., 1977, pres., chief operating officer, 1978-85; editor Courier-Jour. and Louisville Times, 1986-87; gen. news exec. Gannett Co., 1987-88; pres. NBC News, 1988-93; editor, co-owner Ames (Iowa) Daily Tribune, 1986—; dir., co-owner McCoy Broadcasting Co. Syndicated Columnist on lang., 1978—; columnist USA Today, 1993-98. Trustee Freedom Forum First Amendment Ctr. at Vanderbilt U.; commentator Iowa Pub. Radio and Voice of Am.; hon. trustee Simpson Coll.; mem. Pulitzer Prize Bd., 1982-92, chmn., 1991-92. Recipient Pulitzer prize for editorial writing, 1997. Mem. ABA, Iowa Bar Assn., Assn. Bar City N.Y., Am. Soc. Newspaper Editors (pres. 1986-87), Wakonda Club, Garden of Gods Club. Home: 5315 Waterbury Rd Des Moines IA 50312-1923 also: 366 W 11th St New York NY 10014-6225 Office: 317 5th St Ames IA 50010-6101

GARTNER, MURRAY, lawyer; b. N.Y.C., Sept. 23, 1922; s. Leo and Celia G.; m. Anne Ellis Thompson, June 9, 1961; children: Marion Moreau, Thomas Murray. AB, NYU, 1942; LLB, Harvard U., 1945. Bar: N.Y. 1946, Calif. 1948. Law clk. to assoc. justice Robert H. Jackson U.S. Supreme Ct., Washington, 1945-47; assoc. Pillsbury, Madison & Sutro, San Francisco, 1947-51; lectr. law Hastings Coll. Law, San Francisco, 1948; asst. to gen. counsel U.S. rep. in Paris, Econ. Coop. Adminstrn. Mut. Security Adminstrn., 1951-53; assoc. Roosevelt, Freidin & Littauer, N.Y.C., 1953-59; ptnr. Poletti, Freidin, Prashker & Gartner (and predecessors), N.Y.C., 1959-85, Proskauer Rose, LLP, N.Y.C., 1985—. Trustee Children's Aid Soc. Office: Proskauer Rose LLP 1585 Broadway New York NY 10036-8200

GARTON, ROBERT DEAN, state senator; b. Chariton, Iowa, Aug. 18, 1933; s. Jesse Glenn and Ruth Irene (Wright) G.; m. Barbara Hicks, June 17, 1955; children: Bradford, Brenda. BS, Iowa State U., 1955; MS, Cornell U., 1959. Pers. rep. Cummins Engine Co., Columbus, Ind., 1959-61; owner Garton Assocs. Mgmt. Cons., Columbus, 1961-96; exec. asst. to pres. in charge of profl. devel. Ivy Tech. State Coll., Columbus, 1996—; mem. Ind. Senate, Indpls., 1970—, minority caucus chmn., 1976-78, majority caucus chmn., 1978-80, pres. pro tempore, 1980—; bd. dirs. Rural Water System, Columbus. Mem. exec. com. Nat. Conf. State Legislatures, 1989-92; chmn. Mid-West Conf. State Legislatures, Coun. State Govts., 1984-85, mem. gov. bd., 1985—; bd. dirs. Monroe Guaranty Ins. Co.; chmn. Ind. Civil Rights Commn., 1969-70; mem. exec. com. Nat. Fedn. Young Reps., 1966; trustee Franklin Coll. With USMCR, 1955-57. Named Hon. Citizen Iowa, 1962, Tenn., 1977; winner internat. speech contest Toastmasters, 1962; recipient Disting. Svc. award Jr. C. of C. Columbus, 1968, Guardian Small Bus. award Nat. Fedn. for Ind. Bus., 1990, 93, 94, Lee Atwater Leadership award Nat. Rep. Legislator Assn., 1991, United Sr. Action Legis. Leadership award, 1994, Outstanding Govt. Leader award Apt. Assn. Ind., 1998, Outstanding Pub. Svc. award Podiatric Assn., 1993; named One of 5 Outstanding Young Men in Ind., 1968, Man of Yr., Ind. Rep. Mayor's Assn., 1991, Small Bus. Champion Ind. Small Bus. Coun., 1997. Mem. Rotary, Beta Theta Pi. Office: Ivy Tech State Coll PO Box 1111 Columbus IN 47202-1111

GARTON, THOMAS WILLIAM, lawyer; b. Ft. Dodge, Iowa, Jan. 19, 1947; s. H. Boyd and Ruth A. (Porter) G.; m. Marcia K. Hoover, June 21, 1969; children: Geoffrey, Matthew. BA, Carleton Coll., 1969; JD magna cum laude, U. Minn., 1974. Assoc. Fredrikson & Byron, PA, Mpls., 1974-80, shareholder, 1980—; adj. prof. William Mitchell Coll. Law, St. Paul, Minn., 1977-80, U. Minn. Law Sch., Mpls., 1980; bd. dirs. Eden Programs; presenter continuing legal edn. seminars on tax, mergers and acuqisitons, and bus. planning, 1977—. With U.S. Army, 1969-71. Mem. ABA (tax sect.), Minn. Bar Assn. (dir. tax coun. 1987-89). Office: Fredrikson & Byron PA 1100 International Ctr 900 2nd Ave S Minneapolis MN 55402-3314

GARTZ, PAUL EBNER, systems engineer; b. Chgo., July 17, 1946; s. Friedrich Samuel and Lillian Louise (Koroschetz) G. BSEE, Ill. Inst. Tech., 1969; MSEE, Stanford U., 1970. Engring. co-op Western Electric, Chgo., 1965-69; mem. tech. staff Bell Telephone Labs., Whippany, N.J., 1969-74; sales mgr. Evelyn Wood Reading Dynamics, N.Y.C., 1975-78; owner Gartz Design, Montclair, N.J., 1976-79; mktg. rep. United Computing Systems, Seattle, 1979; assoc. tech. fellow Boeing, Seattle, 1980—; bd. dirs. Walla Walla (Wash.) Coll. of Engring.; chmn. bd., pres. SDF, Inc., L.A.; educator Seattle U., 1987—, Walla Walla Coll., 1989, U. Wash., 1992—. Contbr. articles to profl. publs. Recipient Nat. Hist. Preservation award Nat. Hist. Preservation Soc., N.J., 1980. Mem. AIAA (mem. Digital Avionics Tech. com.), IEEE (sr. mem., bd. govs. Aerospace Electronic Sys. Soc., disting. lectr. to India 1997, Harry Rowe Mimno award 1987, chmn. 17th Digital Avionics Systems Conf. 1998), Sys. Devel. Forum (bd. dirs. 1987-95), Internat. Coun. Sys. Engring. (tech. bd. dirs.). Achievements include advances in systems engring., scis., methods and tools on aerospace and computing software systems; rsch. in state-of-the-art application of general systems theory to man-made systems, human engring. and mgmt. orgnl. structures, bus. analysis. Home: 9912 Arrowsmith Ave S Seattle WA 98118-5907 Office: The Boeing Co MS 6X-LC PO Box 3707 Seattle WA 98124-2207

GARTZKE, DANA G., legislative administrator; b. Siloam Springs, Ark., Sept. 4, 1956. BS, U. South Fla., 1979; MBA, Fla. Inst. Tech., 1982. Chief of staff to Rep. Dave Weldon, U.S. Ho. of Reps., Washington, 1995—. Office: US Ho of Reps 332 CHOB Washington DC 20515

GARVAN, STEPHEN BOND, artist manager; b. Hartford, Conn., Mar. 29, 1952; s. Joseph Bond Garvan and Catherine (Wheeler) Jones; m. Frances Jurga, Sept. 6, 1979 (div. 1984); m. Priscilla Lombard Lewis, 1994. BA, Clark U., 1974, postgrad., 1975; postgrad., Stanford U., 1998. Agt. Supreme Artists, N.Y.C., 1974-75, It's a Hit Prodns., Acton, Mass., 1975-79; artist mgr., chief exec. officer Bullet Mgmt., N.Y.C. and Harvard (Mass.), 1979-91, Boulder, Colo., 1991; artist mgr., CEO, Garvan Mktg. and Garvan Mgmt., Niwot, Colo., 1997—. Exec. producer records: Are You Afraid of Falling, Estes Boys, 1978, Save the Whales, Allen Estes Band, 1981, others. Treas., then chmn. Harvard Dem. Town Com., 1979-85; treas. 53 W. 87th St Coop. Corp., 1986-92, 97-99; bd. dirs. Swallow Hill Music Assn., 1994—, pres., 1998-99. Mem. NARAS, NEA, County Music Assn., Earth Comm. Office, Assn. Am. Pubs. (chair telemktg. com. 1986-88), Rocky Mountain Book Pubs. Assn. (bd. dirs. 1992-94), Young Dems., Warner Free Lectr. Series (bd. 1978-84, treas. 1979-84). Avocations: reading, tennis, travel, collecting books, music. Fax: 303-652-3610. Home and Office: 7919 Fairfax Ct Niwot CO 80503-7626

GARVENS, ELLEN JO, art educator, artist; b. Omro, Wis., Aug. 15, 1955; d. Leonard Kenneth and Eugenia Mary (Wetter) G.; m. James Patrick Phalen, Oct. 18, 1988; 1 child, Cole Garvens Phalen. BS in Art, U. Wis., 1979; MA, U. N. Mex., 1982, MFA, 1987. Asst. prof. of art Oberlin (Ohio) Coll., 1990-94, U. Wash., Seattle, 1994—. Artist: one person shows include: Jayne H. Baum Gallery, N.Y.C., 1986, 89, 93, Wooster (Ohio) Mus. of Art, U. R.I., Kingston. Recipient Wis. Women in Arts award Madison, 1978, Fullbright Hays scholarship Internat. Comm. Agy., Washington, 1979-80; grantee, NEA, Washington, 1986, HC Powers grant, Oberlin Coll., 1991, Royalty Rsch. Fund grant, U. Wash., 1996. Home: 19518 67th Ave NE Seattle WA 98155-3447 Office: U Wash Sch of Art PO Box 353440 Seattle WA 98195-3440

GARVER, FREDERICK MERRILL, industrial engineering executive; b. Indpls., Mar. 25, 1945; s. Clyde Louis and Elizabeth Kemp (Finch) G.; m. Ruth Sikkema, Nov. 8, 1969. BS, Western Mich. U., 1967; postgrad., Grand Valley State U., 1976-77; MS, Western Mich. U., 1990. Cert. mfg. engr. Methods analyst Boeing Co., Seattle, 1968-69; indsl. engr. Wolverine World Wide, Inc., Rockford, Mich., 1969-72; mgr. indsl. engring. Leigh Products Inc., Cooperville, Mich., 1972-77; dir. indsl. engring. Integrated Metal Techs., Spring Lake, Mich., 1977-79; mgr. mfg. engring. Haworth Inc., Holland, Mich., 1979-88, Hart & Cooley, Inc., Holland, 1988-92; mfg. engr. Trumark Inc., Lansing, Mich., 1992-94; sr. adv. process engr. Walker Mfg. Inc., Grass Lake, Mich., 1994-97; sr. mfg. engr. Pridgeon and Clay Inc., Grand Rapids, Mich., 1997—. Mem. Inst. Indsl. Engrs. (sr.), Soc. Mfg. Engrs. (sr., ad hoc govt. relations com.), Chem. Coaters Assn., Assn. Bus. Advocating Tariff Equity, Assn. Finishing Processes, Jaycees (treas. Ithaca, Mich. chpt. 1971-72). Republican. Avocations: computers, skiing, tennis. Home: 9466 Tannis Rd Clarksville MI 48815-9727 Office: Pridgeon and Clay Inc 50 Cottage Grove SW Grand Rapids MI 49507-1685

GARVER, JAMES AMOS, municipal official; b. Tylertown, Miss., Dec. 4, 1937; s. Harold Ray and Alyce Delores (Walters) G.; m. Nancy Jo Crowl, May 3, 1959; children: Dale Lee, Delores Elizabeth, Brian Keith. Student, Kans. State Coll., 1955-56, U. Md., 1957-58, Kings Coll., Cambridge, Eng., 1958, U. Ark., 1959-60, Drury Coll., 1961-62, Kans. U., 1962-63. Certified econ. developer Am. Econ. Devel. Council. Various positions Dun & Bradstreet, Inc., Kansas City, Mo., 1960-66, Mid-Am., Inc., Parsons, Kans., 1966-70; v.p. Com. of 100, Charleston, W.Va., 1970-72; exec. v. p. Bus. & Indsl. Devel. Corp., Charleston, W. Va., 1972-77; prin. Jamon Realty, Charleston, 1977-78; dep. dir. Gov.'s Office Econ. Devel., Charleston, 1977-79; sales and mktg. dir. Md. Economic Growth Assn., Balt., 1979-82; pres., CEO Broward Econ. Devel. Bd., Ft. Lauderdale, Fla., 1982-91; pres. Browards Com. of 100 Inc., Ft. Lauderdale, 1986-91, Broward Econ. Devel. Coun., Inc., Ft. Lauderdale, 1991-98, Broward Alliance, Ft. Lauderdale, 1998—; assoc. cons. Vismor, McGill & Bell, Columbia, S.C., 1969-79; assoc. Walter W. Harper & Assocs., Greensboro, N.C., 1969-79; prin. Assoc. Cons., Charleston, 1969-79. Chmn. legis. com. Fla. Econ. Devel. Coun., 1984-85, bd. dirs., 1986-89, pres., 1987, mem. exec. com., 1987-89; mem. svc. resolution Broward Sch. Bd., 1988; mem. bd. advisors Cleve. Clinic Fla., 1989—; bd. dirs. Jr. Achievement South Fla., 1982-93, Ronald McDonald Children Charities/South Fla., 1990-93. With USAF, 1956-60. Named Econ. Devel. Profl. of Yr. State of Fla., 1986. Fellow Am. Econ. Devel. Coun. (bd. dirs. 1973-77, 89—, vice chair so. region 1991-93, exec. com. 1992—, vice chair sects. 1993-95, 2d vice chair 1995-96, 1st vice chair 1996-97, chair elect 1997-98, chair 1998—, Pres.' award 1977, Dist. Svc. award 1992); mem. So. Indsl. Devel. Coun. (pres. 1988-89, hon. life), Am. C. of C. Execs., Nat. Assn. Indsl. and Office Parks, Profl. Assocs., Indsl. Devel. Rsch. Coun., Internat. Assn. Corp. Real Estate (treas. assoc. com. 1990-94), Ft. Lauderdale Bd. Realtors (Outstandinf Svc. award 1987), Tower Club (bd. govs. 1988). Presbyterian. Home: 1880 NE 65th St Fort Lauderdale FL 33308-1053 Office: Broward Alliance 3505 E 2d St Ste 400 Fort Lauderdale FL 33301-2276

GARVER, ROBERT VERNON, research physicist; b. Mpls., June 2, 1932; s. Walter Burdette and Daveda Margaret (Hansen) G.; m. Shirley Marie Phillips, June 15, 1957; children: Debra, Douglas, Daniel, Mary, Jennifer. B.S., U. Md., 1956; M.E.A., George Washington U., 1968. Physicist Harry Diamond Labs., Washington, 1956-69; supervisory physicist Harry Diamond Labs., Adelphi, Md., 1969-89; program mgr. Army High Power Microwave Hardening Tech., 1982-89; cons. Weinschel Engring., Gaithersburg, Md., 1970-75; chmn. electromagnetic effects subcom. DoD VHSIC Qualification Com., 1981-89; pvt. cons., 1989-95; sr. engr. Xeta Internat. Corp., Crystal City, Va., 1990-95. Author: Microwave Diode Control Devices, 1976; inventor Microwave Diode Switch; patentee in field. Elder Presbyn. Ch., Germantown, Md., 1975. Served with U.S. Army, 1953-54. Fellow IEEE (editor Jour. Solid State Circuits 1969-73, mem. nat. adminstrv. com. porfl. group on microwave theory and techniques); mem. Sigma Pi. Republican. Lodge: Toastmasters. Home and Office: 2393 Bear Den Rd Frederick MD 21701-9328

GARVER, THOMAS HASKELL, curator, art consultant, writer; b. Duluth, Minn., Jan. 23, 1934; s. Harvie Adair and Margaret Hope (Foght) G.; m. Natasha Nicholson, Apr. 13, 1974. BA, Haverford Coll., 1956; MA, U. Minn., 1965. Asst. to dir. Krannert Art Mus., U. Ill., Urbana, 1960-62; asst. dir. fine arts dept. Seattle World's Fair, 1962, Rose Art Mus., Brandeis U., Waltham, Mass., 1962-68; dir. Newport Harbor Art Mus. (now Orange County Mus. Art), Calif., 1968-72, 77-80; curator exhbns. Fine Arts Mus. of San Francisco, 1972-77; dir. Madison (Wis.) Art Ctr., 1980-87; asst. prof. Calif. State U., 1970-71, 79-80; curator art collection Rayovac Corp., Madison, 1985—. Author: Twelve Photographers of the American Social Landscape, 1967, Just Before the War: Urban American from 1935-41, 1968, The Paintings of George Tooker, 1985, rev. edit., 1992, The Last Steam Railroad in America: Photographs by O. Winston Link, 1995; exhbn. catalogues including Robert Rauschenberg, 1969, Tom Wesselmann, 1971, Reginald Marsh, 1972, Joseph Raffael, Paintings From the California Years, 1977, George Herms, 1978, 83, Nathan Oliveira, 1984, George Tooker, Paintings, 1983-87, 88, Mind and Beast: Contemporary Artists and the Animal Kingdom, 1992, Flora: Contemporary Artists and the World of Flowers, 1995, Trains that Passed in the Night: The Railroad Photographs of O. Winston Link, 1998, WATER: Contemporary Artists Who Use Water as a Theme in Their Art, Gibbes Mus. of Art, Charleston, S.C., 1999. Trustee U.S.S. Mass. Meml. Commn., Fall River, 1965-68; trustee South Coast Repertory Co., Costa Mesa, Calif., 1970-72; trustee Wis. Citizens for Arts, 1985-87; mem. Newport Beach Art Commn., 1978-79; mem. steering com. Archives Am. Art, San Francisco, 1977-80; mem. Madison Com. for Arts, 1984-87. Mem. Western Assn. Art Mus. (pres. 1970-71, trustee 1970-73), Art Mus. Assn. Am. (pres. 1979-82, trustee 1979-85). Office: PO Box 3493 Madison WI 53704-0493

GARVEY, BRIAN THOMAS, educator in English, university administrator; b. Neptune, N.J., Sept. 10, 1950; s. Thomas James Garvey and Bereda Dimpna Healey; m. Janice Carol Stapley, July 26, 1997; children: Edward, Victoria. BA, Sacred Heart U., 1972; PhD, U. Bradford, Eng., 1985. Adj. prof. Brookdale C.C., Lincroft, N.J., 1986-87; mem. faculty The New Sch., N.Y.C., 1986-88; adj. prof. Monmouth Coll., West Long Branch, N.J., 1986-87; instr. Monmouth Coll., West Long Branch, 1987-88, asst. prof., 1988-92, hons. dir., assoc. prof., 1992—, chair dept. interdisciplinary studies (founder), 1995—; editl. referee Jour. Utopian Studies, Greenville, N.C., 1992—; mem. adv. bd. Brookdale C.C. Hons., Lincroft, N.J., 1997—. Contbr. articles to profl. jours. mem. Inst. Dem. Leadership, West Long Branch, N.J., 1990-91, Concerned Citizens, Fair Haven, 1998-99; mem. exec. bd. Two Rivers Theater Co., Red Bank, N.J., 1999. Named Keynote Spkr. Johns Hopkins Inst. for Acad. Advancement of Youth, 1998; grantee: Aarmaut Found., 1997-99, Jane Freed Gift-Honors Program, 1992—. Mem. MLA, Assn. Sci., Tech. and Soc., Soc. for Utopian Studies, Assn. for Integrative Studies, Amnesty Internat., Nat. Hons. Coun. Avocations: photography, biking, hiking, swimming. Home: 61 De Normandie Ave Fair Haven NJ 07704 Office: Monmouth U 400 Cedar Ave West Long Branch NJ 07264

GARVEY, DORIS BURMESTER, environmental administrator; b. N.Y.C., Oct. 3, 1936; d. William Henry and Florence Elizabeth (Sauerteig) Burmester; m. Gerald Thomas John Garvey, June 6, 1959; children: Deirdre Anne, Gerald Thomas John Jr., Victoria Elizabeth. BA with honors, Wilson Coll., 1958; MA with honors, Yale U., 1959. Rsch. assoc. Princeton U., N.J., 1967-76; environ. scientist Argonne (Ill.) Nat. Lab., 1976-84; staff mem. Los Alamos (N.Mex.) Nat. Lab., 1984-86, regulatory compliance officer, 1986-89, sect. leader environ. protection group, 1989-92, dep. group leader, environ. protection group, 1992-94, leader sitewide Environ. Impact Statement project, 1994—, leader land transfer project, 1998—. Contbr. articles to profl. jours. Bd. dirs. N.Mex. Repertory Theater, Santa Fe, 1987-88; mem. Environ. Improvement Bd., Glen Ellyn, Ill., 1980-82. Mem. AAUW, N.Mex. Hazardous Waste Soc., Women in Sci., Gov.'s Task Force Emergency Response, Nat. Assn. Environ. Profls., Phi Beta Kappa. Democratic. Roman Catholic. Avocations: backpacking, cross-country skiing, gourmet cooking. Home: 368 Calle Loma Norte Santa Fe NM 87501-1278 Office: Los Alamos Nat Lab PO Box 1663 Los Alamos NM 87544-0600

GARVEY, EUGENE FRANCIS, state legislator; b. South Kingston, R.I., Nov. 12, 1933; m. Mary Jane Murphy, Apr. 18, 1959; children: David, Jonathon, Peter, Carolyn. BS, Northeastern U., 1960. Mem. R.I. Ho. of Reps., 1992—; ins. broker Wheelock Ins. Agy., Wakefield, R.I., 1993—, ret., 1993—. Mem. Ind. Ins. Agt. Assn., Profl. Ins. Agt. Assn., Assn. for Retarded Citizens (pres. South County chpt.). Democrat. Address: 614 Green Hill Beach Rd Wakefield RI 02879-6216*

GARVEY, JANE, federal aviation administrator. BA, Mount Saint Mary Coll.; MA, Mount Holyoke Coll.; fellowship program for pub. leaders, Harvard U. Assoc. commr. Mass. Dept. Pub. Works, Boston, commr., 1988-91; dir. Logan Internat. Airport, Boston, 1991-93; dep. adminstr. Fed. Hwy. Adminstrn. U.S. Dept. Transp., Washington, 1993-97; acting adminstr. Fed. Hwy. Adminstrn. U.S. Dept. Transp., 1997; apptd. 14th adminstr. FAA U.S. Dept. Transp., Washington, 1997—. Office: FAA US Dept Transp 800 Independence Ave SW Washington DC 20591-0001

GARVEY, JOANNE MARIE, lawyer; b. Oakland, Calif., Apr. 23, 1935; d. James M. and Marian A. (Dean) G. AB with honors, U. Calif., Berkeley, 1956, MA, 1957, JD, 1961. Bar: Calif. bar 1962. Assoc. firm Cavaletto, Webster, Mullen & McCaughey, Santa Barbara, Calif., 1961-63, Jordan, Keeler & Seligman, San Francisco, 1963-67; ptnr. Jordan, Keeler & Seligman, 1968-88, Heller, Ehrman, White & McAuliffe, 1988—; bd. dirs. Mexican-Am. Legal Def. and Ednl. Fund; chmn. Law in a Free Soc., Continuing Edn. of Bar; mem. bd. councillors U. So. Calif. Law Center. Recipient Paul Veazy award YMCA, 1973, Internat. Women's Yr. award Queen's Bench, 1975, honors Advs. for Women, 1978, CRLA award, Boalt Hall Citation award, 1998. Fellow Am. Bar Found.; mem. ABA (gov., state del., chmn. SCLAID, chmn. delivery of legal svcs.), Calif. State Bar (v.p., gov., tax sect., del., Jud Klein award, Joanne Garvey award), San Francisco Bar Assn. (pres., pres. Barristers), Am. Law Inst., Calif. Women Lawyers (founder), Order of Coif, Phi Beta Kappa. Democrat. Roman Catholic. Home: 16 Kensington Ct Kensington CA 94707-1010 Office: 333 Bush St San Francisco CA 94104-2806

GARVEY, JOHN CHARLES, violist, conductor, retired music educator; b. Canonsburg, Pa., Mar. 17, 1921; s. Frank Sherwood and Esther (Gegenheimer) G.; m. Evelyn Ficarra, Mar. 13, 1947; children: Deborah, Frank, Deirdre. Student, Temple U., 1940-43. Prof. music Sch. Music, U. Ill., Urbana, 1948-91. Violinist, violist Jan. Savitt and Jerry Wald Jazz orchs., 1943-45; prin. violist Columbus Philharm. Orch., 1945-48, Aspen Festival Orch., 1964; condr. NIRTV Chamber Orch., Iran, 1973; founder, dir. Jazz Band, 1959, Chamber Orch., 1964, Russian Folk Orch., 1974; violist Walden Quartet, 1948-69, State Dept. Jazz Tours, 1968-69; condr. Harry Partch Ensemble, 1959-63 (Wihner Nat. Coll. Jazz Band champaionships 1967-69, Russian Ctr. grantee for study balalaika in Moscow 1970, 72, Ctr. for Advanced Studies grantee for study ethnic music 1972-73, recipient Ill. Gov.'s award in arts 1980); dir. U. Ill. Jazz Band tour of USSR, 1990; guest condr. Belarus State Jazz Band, Minsk, 1992; condr. New Ill. Jazz Band, 1995-96. Balinese Gamelan study grantee K.O.K.A.R., Bali, 1979, 87; grantee for study of Catalan Sardana music, Barcelona, 1986. Mem. Am. Fedn. Musicians (Local 196), Soc. for Ethno-musicology, Internat. Assn. Jazz Educators, Balalaika and Domra Assn. Am. Home: 1739 Westhaven Dr Champaign IL 61820-7051 Office: Nomad Imports 119 W Church St Champaign IL 61820-3510

GARVEY, JOHN LEO, lawyer, educator; b. Covington, Ky., Mar. 22, 1927; s. Charles Francis and Anna Garvey; m. Virginia Ann Hinzman, Sept. 13, 1952; children: John Gerard, Lawrence Charles. BA, Xavier U., Cin., 1945, LLD (hon.), 1978; LLB, Catholic U. Am., 1948; SJD, U. Mich., 1967. Bar: Ky. 1948. Pvt. practice Erlanger, 1948-51; instr. law Cath. U., Washington, 1951-57, asst. prof., 1957-61, assoc. prof., 1961-65, prof., 1965—, dean Law Sch., 1977-79. Contbr. to Probate Court Practice in the District of Columbia, 1960, 62, 65, 67, 70, 72, 75, 77; mem. editorial adv. com. jour. Legal Edn, 1976-79. Mem. Am. Law Inst., ABA (real property, probate and trust law sect.), Ky. Bar Assn., Am. Coll. Probate Counsel. Home: # 811 3310 N Leisure World Blvd Silver Spring MD 20906-5666 Office: Cath U 4th and Michigan Ave NE Washington DC 20064

GARVEY, MICHAEL STEVEN, veterinarian, educator; b. Chgo., Dec. 5, 1950; s. Charles Anthony and Jane O. G. BS in Vet. Medicine, U. Ill., 1972, DVM, 1974; cert. internship, The Animal Med. Ctr., N.Y.C., 1976, cert. med. residency, 1978; cert. advanced mgmt. program, Wharton Sch., U. Pa., 1992. Diplomate Am. Coll. Vet. Internal Medicine, Am. Coll Vet. Emergency and Critical Care. Staff veterinarian Bevlab Vet. Hosp., Blue Island, Ill., 1974-75; intern in medicine and surgery The Animal Med. Ctr., N.Y.C., 1975-76, resident in medicine, 1976-78; staff internist Bevlab Vet. Hosp., Blue Island, 1978-81; dir. medicine The Animal Med. Ctr., N.Y.C., 1981-83, chmn. dept. medicine, 1983-97, vice-chief of staff, 1993—; dir. The Elmer and Mamdouha Bobst Hosp., 1995—, chmn. dept. emergency medicine and critical care, 1997—; cons. Office of Animal Care, U. Chgo. Sch. Medicine, 1979—, Nat. Bd. Vet. Examiners, Schaumburg, Ill., 1981—, Mercy Coll. Animal Health Tech., Dobbs Ferry, N.Y., 1984—, Reader's Digest and Good Housekeeping mags., N.Y.C., 1984—, Pfizer Animal Health, Westchester, Pa., 1994—; tech. cons. Sesame St., N.Y.C., adv. bd. Profl. Examination Svc., N.Y.C., 1981—, vice chmn., 1991—; vet. adv. panel Alpo Pet Foods, Inc., Allentown, Pa., 1981-95; vet. adv. panel Friskies Pet Care, 1995-96; adj. prof. vet. medicine Tex. A&M U., 1986—; faculty assoc. U. Maine Animal Health Tech., Orono, 1976-78; chmn. vet. adv. panel Schering Plough Inc., Madison, N.J., 1993—; mem. cmty. adv. bd. N.Y. Hosp./Cornell U. Med. Sch., 1995—; chmn. emergency room oversight com. N.Y. Presbyn. Hosp. Cornell Campus, 1998—. Author: Animal Medical Center Hospital Formulary, 1990, 96, (with others) Keeping Your Dog Healthy, 1985, Canine Emergencies, 1985, Symptoms of Illness in Dogs, 1985, Infectious and Contagious Diseases in Dogs, 1985, Feline Emergencies, 1985, Sysmtoms of Illness in Cats, 1985, Infectious and Contagious Diseases in Cats, 1985, Feeding the Sick Cat, 1989; editor: Canine Allergic Inhalant Dermatitis, 1982; cons. editor Small Animal Medicine, 1990; editorial review bd. Jour. of Am. Animal Hosp. Assn., 1985-93, Jour. Vet. Emergency Critical Care, 1992—; contbr. articles to profl. jours. Bd. dirs. Blue Island Cmty. Theatre, 1974-75, 78-80, treas., 1984-94, pres., 1985—; treas. 440 E 62d St Owners' Corp., N.Y.C.; mem. cmty. adv. bd. N.Y. Hosp./Cornell U. Med. Sch., 1995—; mem. N.Y.C. Office Emergency Mgmt. Task Force Biol. Terrorism, 1997—. Recipient Disting. Leadership award Am. Biog. Inst., 1993, 96. Mem. AVMA (del. 1990-91), Am. Animal Hosp. Assn. (Friskie's award for excellence in feline medicine 1993), Am. Assn. Vet. Clinicians (exec. bd. 1986—, pres. 1988-89, President's Gavel award 1989, Faculty Achievement award 1993), Am. Coll. Vet. Emergency Critical Care (v.p. 1993-95), Am. Coll. Vet. Internal Medicine (pres. internal medicine splty. 1994—), Acad. Vet. Cardiology, N.Y. State Vet. Med. Soc. (Outstanding vet. award 1995), Soc. Gastroenterology Soc., Vet. Med. Assn. N.Y.C. (Outstanding Svc. award 1984, Outstanding Vet. award 1995), Vet. Endoscopy Soc., Soc. Internat. Vet. Symposia (bd. dirs. 1990—, pres. 1992-94), Vet. Intern and Resident Matching Program (co-chmn. 1986—). Republican. Roman Catholic. Avocations: golf, swimming, snorkeling, personal computers. Home: 440 E 62nd St Apt 2B New York NY 10021-8341 Office: The Animal Med Ctr 510 E 62nd St New York NY 10021-8302

GARVEY, RICHARD ANTHONY, lawyer; b. N.Y.C., Jan. 10, 1950; s. James Joseph Garvey and Janet Mary (Mooney) Rowse. AB, Boston Coll., 1972; JD, Harvard U., 1975. Bar: N.Y. 1976. Assoc. Simpson Thacher & Bartlett, N.Y.C., 1975-82, ptnr., 1982-93, 97—. Mem. ABA, N.Y. State Bar Assn., Assn. Bar City N.Y., Phi Beta Kappa. Home: 330 E 38th St Apt 44N New York NY 10016-2783 Office: Simpson Thacher & Bartlett 425 Lexington Ave New York NY 10017-3903

GARVEY, RICHARD CONRAD, journalist; b. Northampton, Mass., May 23, 1923; s. Michael Edward and Lucy Lillian (Bradford) G.; m. Anne Elizabeth Vanasse, May 18, 1957 (dec. Jan. 1988); children: Philip, John, Mary, Margaret; m. Allison McCrillis Lockwood, Dec. 29, 1990. Student, U. Mass., 1941-43, LHD (hon.), 1974; D of Humanics (hon.), Springfield Coll., 1982; LLD (hon.), Our Lady of Elms Coll., 1982. Reporter Daily Hampshire Gazette, Northampton, 1943-44; reporter Springfield (Mass.) Daily News, 1944-50, asst. mng. editor, 1950-66, editor, 1966-87; assoc. pub. Springfield Union-News, Sunday Rep., 1987—. Author: Oliver Smith, Esq., 1948, (with others) The Northampton Book, 1954, St. Mary's of Haydenville, 1968, History of Springfield College, 1985; contbr. articles to World Book Ency., 1977—. Trustee Forbes Libr., Northampton, 1952-57; chmn. bd. dirs. Springfield Coll., 1979-81, Mercy Hosp., Springfield, 1980-82. Decorated Knight-Comdr. of Holy Sepulchre; recipient Grenville Clark award World Federalists, 1962, Humanitarian award NCCJ, 1989. Mem. Rotary (pres. 1984-85, Paul Harris award 1985). Roman Catholic. Home: 19 Washington Ave Northampton MA 01060-2822 Office: Union-News and Sunday Rep 1860 Main St Springfield MA 01103-1073

GARVEY, SHEILA HICKEY, theater educator; b. Erie, Pa., Dec. 23, 1949; d. Robert Francis and Mary Virginia (Sullivan) H.; children: Sean Timothy, Darragh Burgess. BS, Emerson Coll., 1971; MA, Northwestern U., 1973; PhD, NYU, 1984; grad., The Circle in the Square, N.Y.C., 1975. Preceptor NYU, N.Y.C., 1978-80; sabbatical replacement Rutgers U., Camden, N.J., 1980-81; asst. prof. Dickinson Coll., Carlisle, Pa., 1981-88; full prof. So. Conn. State U., New Haven, 1988—. Contbr. articles to profl. jours. Scholar JFK Ctr. Performing Arts, Am. Coll. Theatre Festival, 1993; rsch. grantee So. Conn. State U., 1988, 89, 90, 92, 94, 98, faculty devel. grantee, 1988, 89, 90, 92, 94, 97, rsch. grantee Dickinson Coll., 1987, 88; Dana fellow Dickinson Coll., 1987. Bd. dirs. New Eng. Theatre Conf. (coll. divsn. 1992-95, chairperson coll. and univ. com. 1991-95); mem. Eugene O'Neill Soc. (bd. dirs. 1999), Conn. Critics' Cir. Roman Catholic. Home: 273 Knob Hill Dr Hamden CT 06518-2737 Office: So Conn State U 501 Crescent St New Haven CT 06515-1330

GARVICK, KENNETH RYAN, broadcast engineer, announcer, educator; b. Akron, Ohio, Apr. 11, 1945; s. Kenneth Rodger and Dorothy Lillian (Lincks) G. Diploma, DeVry Inst. Tech., Chgo., 1966, Cleve. Inst., 1970, 81. Cert. electronic technician. Electronic repairman RCA Consumer Electronics, Indpls., 1966-70; compilation technician Howard W. Sams & Co., Indpls., 1970-73; broadcast engr. Sta. WIBC/WNAP Fairbanks Broadcasting, Indpls., 1973; announcer, engr. Stas. WHYT-AM, WNON-FM, 1974-76; transmitter engr. Sta. WISH-TV, Indpls., 1976-79; electronics instr. Arsenal Tech. High Sch., Indpls., 1979-82; announcer, engr. Stas. WSVL AM/FM, 1979-81; instr. various schs., Ohio, 1987—; announcer, engr. Sta. WMAN-AM, 1994-95. Author: Gerberich Descendants from York, PA, 1987; contbr. articles to profl. jours. With Signal Corps U.S. Army, 1966-72, Vietnam. Mem. Soc. Broadcast Engrs., Arsenal Tech., Radio Club (sec. 1979-82). Republican. Avocations: film history, amateur radio, bicycling. Address: PO Box 88 Shauck OH 43349-0088

GARVIN, ANDREW PAUL, information company executive, author, consultant; b. N.Y.C., July 24, 1945; s. Gene G. and Nora (Sheldon) London; m. 2d Linda Gail Bernstein, Oct. 1, 1983; children: Kira, Jeffrey. B.A., Yale U., 1967; M.S., Columbia U., 1968. Corr. Newsweek mag., N.Y.C., 1967-68; v.p. Four Elements, Inc., N.Y.C., 1968-69; co-founder, pres. FIND SVP, Inc., N.Y.C., 1970—, Info. Clearing House, Inc., N.Y.C., 1970—; bd. dirs. Esquire Comm., Inc. Author: How to Win With Information, 1983, The Art of Being Well Informed, 1996. Chmn. Nat. Info. Conf. and Expn., Washington, 1979. Mem. Info. Industry Assn. (dir. 1979-82 Product of Yr. award 1974), Assn. Info. Mgrs. (dir. 1978-82), Am. Mktg. Assn., Am. Mgmt.

Assn., Spl. Libraries Assn., St. Elmo Soc. (treas. 1974-81), Young Pres.' Orgn. Home: 315 E 72nd St New York NY 10021-4625 Office: FIND SVP 625 Avenue Of The Americas New York NY 10011-2095

GARVIN, FLORENCE WARD, management consultant; b. Ft. Sam Houston, Tex., Oct. 6, 1928; d. Edward Joseph and Florence Emily (Bock) Ward; m. Sheldon R. Rappaport, Mar. 2, 1950 (div. July 1969); children: Bruce Ward, Lisa Lynn; m. Stefan J. Garvin, Oct. 3, 1981. BA, Our Lady of Lake U., San Antonio, 1949; postgrad., Trinity U., San Antonio, 1949-50. Co-founder, asst. to pres. Pathway Sch., Norristown, Pa., 1961-68; adminstrv. dir. Neurosurg. Clinic for Children, Media, Pa., 1968-70; v.p. for devel. Vanguard Schs., Haverford, Pa., 1970-72; asst. to pres. Elwyn (Pa.) Inst., 1972-75; pvt. practice Media, 1976-78; cons. employee rels. dept. E.I. DuPont de Nemours & Co., Inc., Wilmington, Del., 1978-85; sr. bus. assoc. internat. dept. E.I. DuPont de Nemours & Co., Inc., Wilmington, 1985-89, mgr. bus. rels. devel., 1989-90, mgr. internat. human resources devel. human resources dept., 1990-94; ; pres. bd. dirs. AIDS Task Force/Phila. Community Health Alternatives, 1994-96; bd. dirs. Pacific Rim Bus. Coun., 1994-96, Nationalities Svc. Ctr., 1996-98, Green Cir. Program, 1996-98; bd. dirs. East Side Charter Sch., Wilmington, Del., 1996-98; mem. Phila. Com. AmFar, 1996-98; dir. spl. projects Gabriella and Paul Rosenbaum Found., 1997—. Pres. bd. dirs. Montgomery County Mental Health Clinics, 1965-68; bd. dirs. Phila. United Fund, 1969-72; bd. mgrs., sec. Garrett-Williamson Found., 1973-85; bd. dirs. Mary Campbell Ctr., Wilmington, 1978-81; trustee Wilmington Coll., 1981—, Curtis Inst. Music, 1985-92; mem. devel. com. Mercy Haverford Hosp., 1994-95; mem. policy coun. Del. County Head Start, 1994-96; pres. bd. dirs. AIDS Task Force/Phila. Cmty. Health Alternatives, 1994-96; bd. dirs. Pacific Rim Bus. Coun., 1994-96, Nationalities Svc. Ctr., 1996-98, Green Cir. Program, 1996-98; bd. dirs. East Side Charter Sch., Wilmington, Del., 1996-98, Delaware County AIDS Network, 1998—, Moore Eye Found., 1998—; mem. Phila. Com. AmFar, 1996-98. Home: 2 Yarmouth Ln Media PA 19063-4327

GARVIN, PAUL JOSEPH, JR., toxicologist; b. Toledo, Nov. 16, 1928; s. Paul Joseph and Laura Mary (Blanchet) G.; m. Priscilla Ann Haines, Aug. 23, 1952; children: Peter, Thomas, Paul III, Peggy, Priscilla, Polly. BA, St. John's U., 1950; MS, U. Minn., 1958. Rsch. assoc. Sterling-Winthrop Rsch. Inst., Renssaeler, N.Y., 1954-58; sr. rsch. pharmacologist Baxter-Travenol Inc., Morton Grove, Ill., 1958-72, mgr. safety evaluation, 1972-77; dir. toxicology Amoco Corp., Chgo., 1977-88, sr. health sci. advisor, 1988-92; toxicology cons. pvt. practice, Mt. Prospect, Ill., 1992—; mem. adv. com. ctr. risk analysis Harvard U. Sch. Pub. Health, Boston, 1991-92; sci. adv. panel hazardous substance mgmt. rsch. ctr. U. Medicine and Dentistry, Newark, 1988-91, adv. panel ctr. alternatives to animal testing Johns Hopkins U. Sch. Hygiene and Pub. Health, Balt., 1990-92, scientific adv. com. CIIT, Research Triangle Park, N.C., 1986-88. Contbr. over 50 articles to profl. jours. Chmn. Mt. Prospect Bd. Health, 1960-70. Mem. AAAS, Am. Indsl. Hygiene Assn., Am. Soc. Pharmacology & Exptl. Therapeutics, N.Y. Acad. Sci., European Soc. Toxicology, Soc. Toxicology. Home and Office: 309 N Wille St Mount Prospect IL 60056-2454

GARVIN, WILFORD L., sales and marketing manager. BA, U. Man., Winnipeg, Can., 1975. Sales and mktg. mgr. Hydroseal Valve Co., Kilgore, Tex., 1993—. Treas. East Tex. Treatment Ctr., Kilgore, 1993-95, v.p., 1996-97, pres., 1997—. Mem. Valve Mfrs. Assn. (vice-chmn. pressure relief valve com. 1994-98, chmn., 1998— comm. com., 1994—, editl. rev. bd., 1998—, Kilgore C. of C. (leadership chair, bd. dirs. 1994—). Avocations: family, foreign travel. Home: PO Box 2191 Kilgore TX 75663-2191 Office: Hydroseal Valve Co Inc PO Box 2191 Kilgore TX 75663-2191

GARWIN, RICHARD LAWRENCE, physicist; b. Cleve., Apr. 19, 1928; married; 3 children. BS, Case Western U., 1947, DSc (hon.), 1966; MS, U. Chgo., 1948, PhD, 1949. Instr. to asst. prof. physics U. Chgo., 1949-52; physicist T.J. Watson Ctr. IBM, Yorktown Heights, N.Y., 1952-65, dir. applied rsch., 1965-66, lab. dir., 1966-67, fellow, 1967-93; fellow emeritus, 1993—; cons. Los Alamos (N.Mex.) Sci. Lab., 1950-93, Sandia Nat. Lab., 1994—; mem. com. Pres.'s Sci. Adv. Com., 1962-65, 69-72, cons., 1958-62; adj. prof. physics Columbia U., 1957—; prof. pub. policy Harvard U., Cambridge, 1979-81, vis. prof. applied physics, 1974. Recipient Ettore Majorana-Erice Sci. for Peace award Ettore Majorana Ctr., 1991, R.V. Jones Intelligence award U.S. Govt. Fgn. Intelligence Cmty., 1996, Enrico Fermi award, 1997. Fellow Am. Phys. Soc.; mem. NAS, NAE, Inst. of Medicine, Am. Philos. Soc., Am. Acad. Arts and Scis. Office: IBM T J Watson Rsch Ctr PO Box 218 Yorktown Heights NY 10598-0218

GARWOOD, JOHN DELVERT, former college administrator; b. Carroll, Nebr., Mar. 20, 1915; s. Harvey and Forrest (Hill) G.; m. Kathleen Marie Schnoor, Aug. 6, 1943; children: Jan Dierks, Shelley Hill. A.B., Wayne (Nebr.) State Coll., 1936; Ph.M., U. Wis., 1940; postgrad., U. La., 1940-41, U. So. Calif., 1947; Ph.D. in Econs, U. Colo., 1951. Supt. schs. Lindsay, Nebr., 1936-38; teaching fellow U. La., 1940-41, U. Colo., 1949-51; instr. Morningside Coll., Sioux City, 1941- 42; prof. econs. Ft. Hays (Kans.) State U., 1947- 49, 51-62, dean faculty, 1962-79, v.p. for acad. affairs, 1979-80. Author: Back to the Basics, 1978. Mem. exec. com. Kans. Council Econ. Edn., 1961—; pres. Smoky Hill Pub. TV Corp., 1977-79, Danforth assoc., 1957—. Served with AUS, 1942-46. Recipient Disting. Service award Ft. Hays State U., 1982. Mem. NEA, Kans. Tchrs. Assn. (pres. 1969-70), Am. Econ. Assn., Phi Kappa Phi, Sigma Phi Sigma, Pi Gamma Mu, Phi Delta Kappa, Lambda Delta Lambda, Kappa Mu Epsilon. Lutheran. Home: 1231 Leisure World Mesa AZ 85206-3090

GARWOOD, ROBERT ASHLEY, JR., network communications analyst; b. Cordele, Ga., Sept. 11, 1955; s. Robert Ashley Sr. and Mary Ann (Meng) G.; m. Christine Allison Haire, Aug. 31, 1981. BA, LaGrange Coll., 1978. Rep. sales Met. Life Ins. Co., Atlanta, 1978-79; assoc. ptnr. Stephen D. Jones & Assocs., Roswell, Ga., 1979-80; supr. Six Flags Over Ga., Atlanta, 1979-86; asst. mgr. Wolf Camera, Kennesaw, Ga., 1986; asst. mgr. data base Days Inn Corp., Atlanta, 1986-92; comm. analyst The Emory Clinic, Atlanta, 1992-97; owner So. Visions-Comm. Cons., Norcross, Ga., 1997—. Pastor United Meth. Ch., West Ga., 1975-79. Mem. Pi Tau Chi. Democrat. Avocations: writing, sports, philosophy. Home and Office: 3276 Harmon Ridge Ct Buford GA 30519

GARWOOD, VICTOR PAUL, retired speech communication educator; b. Detroit, Sept. 13, 1917; s. Paul J. and Helen (Garwood) Schultz; m. Dorothy Anne Olson, Mar. 13, 1942; children: Don Paul, Martha Hill Garwood Steelmon. BA, U. Mich., 1939, MS, 1948, PhD, 1952. Teaching fellow, head exam. div. Speech-Hearing Clinic, U. Mich., 1946-50; instr., asst. prof., assoc. prof., prof. dept. speech U. So. Calif., Los Angeles, 1950-67, prof., chmn. grad. program in communication disorders, 1967-71; on leave as sr. ednl. audiologist Los Angeles Unified Sch. Dist., 1972-76; prof. speech communication, speech sci. and tech., and otolaryngology, 1964-87, prof. emeritus, 1988—; cons. audiology Childrens Hosp., Los Angeles; cons. audiology and speech pathology Medi-Cal Benefits div. Dept. Health Services, State of Calif., 1970-87, com. on employees with disabilities, 1979-86; mem. profl. adv. com. on speech and hearing Welfare Planning Coun., L.A., 1966-68; mem. hearing aid dispensers examining com. Bd. Mem. Quality Assurance State Calif., 1971-79, chmn., 1977-79; mem. adv. bd. Hope for Hearing Rsch. Found. UCLA; reviewer register SERS U.S. Dept. Edn., 1993; mem. Health and Long Term Care Commn., Area Agy. and Aging Adv. Coun., L.A. County, 1995—; co-chair 16th Internat. Conf. on Retirement in Colls. & Univs., 1998. Contbr. articles to profl. jours. Postdoctoral fellow NIH, 1957-58; Spl. Research fellow NIH, 1960-63. Fellow Am. Speech and Hearing Assn. (life), Calif. Acad. of Audiology, Am. Acad. of Audiology; life mem. Am. Psychol. Assn., Western Psychol. Assn., Psychonomic Soc., Acoustical Soc. Am., Acad. Rehab. Audiology, Calif. Speech and Hearing Assn. (trustee Found. 1989-91, Honors award 1983), Calif. Speech Pathologists and Audiologists in Pvt. Practice (appreciation award 1987), So. Calif. Communication Group (bd. dirs. 1986-88); mem. AAUP (chmn. comm. 1996—), Retired Faculty Assn. U. So. Calif. (historian 1988-90, pres. 1990-92, treas. 1993-95, Emeriti coun., spkr. 1990—), Sigma Xi. Home: 1240 Chautauqua Blvd Pacific Palisades CA 90272-2603

GARWOOD, WILLIAM LOCKHART, federal judge; b. Houston, Tex., Oct. 29, 1931; s. Wilmer St. John and Ellen Burdine (Clayton) G.; m. Merle Castlyn Haffler, Aug. 12, 1955; children: William Lockhart, Mary Elliott. BA, Princeton U., 1952; LLB with honors, U. Tex., 1955. Bar: Tex. 1955, U.S. Supreme Ct. 1959. Law clk. to judge U.S. Ct. Appeals (5th cir.), 1955-56; mem. Graves, Dougherty, Hearon, Moody & Garwood (and predecessor firms), Austin, Tex., 1959-79, 81; justice Supreme Ct. Tex., Austin, 1979-80; judge U.S. Ct. Appeals (5th cir.), 1981-97, sr. judge, 1999-; dir. Anderson, Clayton & Co., 1976-79, 81, exec. com., 1977-79, 81; mem. adv. com. on appellate rules U.S. Cts., 1994—, chair 1997—. Pres. Child and Family Service of Austin, 1970-71, St. Andrew's Episcopal Sch., Austin, 1972; bd. dirs. Community Council Austin and Travis County, 1968-72, Human Opportunities Corp. Austin and Travis County, 1966-70, Mental Health and Mental Retardation Ctr. Austin and Travis County, 1966-69, United Fund Austin and Travis County, 1971-73; mem. adv. bd. Salvation Army, Austin, 1972—. Served with U.S. Army, 1956-59. Fellow Tex. Bar Found. (life); mem. Tex. Law Rev. Assn. (pres. 1990-91, dir. 1986-96), Am. Law Inst. (life), Am. Judicature Soc., Order of Coif, Chancellors, Phi Delta Phi. Episcopalian. Office: US Ct Appeals Homer Thornberry Jud Bldg 903 San Jacinto Blvd Austin TX 78701-2450

GARY, JAMES FREDERICK, business and energy advising company executive; b. Chgo., Dec. 28, 1920; s. Rex Inglis and Mary Naomi (Roller) G.; m. Helen Elizabeth Gellert, Sept. 3, 1947; children: David Frederick, John William, James Scott, Mary Anne. BS, Haverford (Pa.) Coll., 1942. With Wash. Energy Co. and predecessors, Seattle, 1947-67; v.p. Wash. Energy Co., 1956-67; pres., CEO Pacific Resources Inc., Honolulu, 1967-79, chmn., CEO, 1979-84, chmn., 1985, chmn. emeritus, 1986—, internat. bus. and energy advisor, 1987—; bd. dirs. Dole Food Co., Inc., Kennedy Assocs., Inc., Seattle; chmn. bd. dirs. Inter Island Petroleum, Inc.; bd. dirs. Episcopal Homes Hawaii, The Salk Inst. Coun., La Jolla; adv. bd. Harris-Manchester Coll. U. Oxford (Eng.), 1997—. Mem. Pacific Coast Gas Assn., 1965-75, pres., 1974-75; pres. Chief Seattle coun. Boy Scouts Am., 1966-67, Aloha coun., 1973-74, mem. nat. coun., 1964—, v.p. Western region, 1978-85, pres., 1985-91, also bd. dirs.; chmn. Aloha United Way, 1978, pres., 1979-80, chmn., 1980; mem. bd. regents U. Hawaii, 1981-89; trustee Hawaii Loa Coll., 1968-85, Linfield Coll., McMinnville, Oreg., 1983-89; mem. bd. mgrs. Haverford Coll., 1983-92; bd. dirs. Rsch. Corp. of U. Hawaii, 1971-77, chmn., 1974-77, Hawaii Ednl. Coun.; bd. dirs., officer, trustee Oahu Devel. Conf., Hawaii Employers Coun., Friends of East-West Ctr., Honolulu Symphony Soc., East-West Ctr. Internat. Found.; chmn. Hawaii Comty. Found., 1987-92, mem. bd. govs., 1987-94; mem. bd. regents Chaminade U., 1991-93. Capt. AUS, 1942-46. Recipient Pres.' trophy Pacific Gas Assn., 1960, Disting. Eagle award Boy Scouts Am., 1972, Silver Beaver award, 1966, Silver Antelope award, 1976, Silver Buffalo award, 1988. Mem. Am. Gas Assn. (bd. dirs. 1970-74), Nat. LP-Gas Assn. (bd. dirs. 1967-70), Am. Petroleum Inst., Inst. Gas Tech. (trustee 1975-86), Hawaii Econ. Coun., Nat. Petroleum Coun., Hawaii Dist. Export Coun., Japan-Hawaii Econ. Coun., U.S Nat. Com. for Pacific Econ. Cooperation, Pacific Basin Econ. Coun. (chmn. U.S. com. 1985-86), Japan-Am. Soc. Honolulu, Ctr. for Strategic and Internat. Studies-Pacific Forum, Honolulu Commn. on Fgn. Rels., Hawaii C. of C. (chmn. 1979). Episcopalian. Clubs: Pacific Union (San Francisco); Oahu Country, Waialae Country, Outrigger Canoe, Pacific, Plaza (Honolulu); Seattle Tennis, Wash. Athletic Rainier (Seattle). Office: 130 Merchant St Ste 1080 Honolulu HI 96813-4426

GARY, NANCY ELIZABETH, nephrologist, academic administrator; b. N.Y.C., Mar. 4, 1937; d. Walter Joseph and Charlotte Elizabeth (Sayer) G. BS, Springfield (Mass.) Coll., 1958; MD, Med. Coll. Pa., 1962. Diplomate Am. Bd. Internal Medicine, Am. Bd. Nephrology. Resident Nassau County Med. Ctr., East Meadow, N.Y., 1962-64; resident St. Vincent's Hosp. and Med. Ctr., N.Y.C., 1964-65, chief renal sect., 1967-74; fellow in nephrology Georgetown U. Med. Ctr., Washington, 1965-67; instr. medicine NYU Sch. Medicine, N.Y.C., 1968-74; asst. prof. U. Medicine and Dentistry of N.J.-Rutgers Med. Sch., Piscataway, 1974-76, assoc. prof., 1976-81, prof., 1981-88, assoc. dean, 1981-87, exec. assoc. dean, 1987-88; dean Albany (N.Y.) Med. Coll., 1988-90; sr. med. adv. to adminstr. health care financing HHS, Washington, 1990-91; clin. prof. medicine George Washington U. Sch. Medicine, 1991—; prof. medicine Uniformed Svcs. U. Health Scis., Bethesda, Md., 1992—; exec. v.p., dean Sch. Medicine Uniformed Svcs. U. Health Scis., 1992-95; dean emeritus, 1996; clin. prof. Howard U. Coll. Medicine, Washington, 1992-95; pres., CEO Ednl. Commn. Fgn. Med. Grads., Phila., 1995—; dean emeritus, 1996. Contbr. chpts. to books, articles to profl. jours. Robert Wood Johnson Health Policy fellow NAS Inst. Medicine, 1987-88; recipient Joseph F. Boyle, M.D. award for Disting. Pub. Svc., Am. Soc. Internal Medicine, 1992. Mem. ACP (Master), AMA, Nat. Kidney Found., Alpha Omega Alpha. Office: Ednl Commn Fgn Med Graduates 3624 Market St 4th Fl Philadelphia PA 19104-2685*

GARY, RICHARD DAVID, lawyer; b. Richmond, Va., Apr. 25, 1949; s. Morton Nathan and Blanche (Rudy) G.; m. Linda Levene, Aug. 6, 1972; children: Brent Ryan, Lauren Renee. AB in Econs., U. N.C., 1971; JD, U. Va., 1974. Bar: Va. 1974. From assoc. to ptnr. Hunton & Williams, Richmond, 1974—; guest lectr. law Coll. William and Mary, Williamsburg, 1983-90. Pres. Beth Sholom Home Cen. Va., Richmond, 1989-91; chmn. Beth Sholom Home Va., 1991-92. Recipient Disting. Svc. award Beth Sholom Home Cen. Va., 1984. Mem. ABA (pub. utilities sect. council mem.), Va. State Bar (chmn. adminstrn. law sect. 1982-83), Va. Bar Assn., Richmond Bar Assn., Fed. Energy Bar Assn. Avocation: sports. Home: 1518 Helmsdale Dr Richmond VA 23233-4722 Office: Hunton & Williams Riverfront Plz East Twr PO Box 1535 Richmond VA 23218-1535

GARYPIE, RUDOLPH RENWICK, library director; b. Massapequa, N.Y., May 21, 1932; s. Rudolph Seigfried and Muriel Anderson Garypie; m. Barbara Mathilda Phillips, July 13, 1963; children: Robert, Catherine. BA, Hamilton Coll., 1954; MLS, U. Mich., 1956. Cert. Libr. of Mich. Profl. asst. Wayne (Mich.) Libr., 1956-62; libr. dir. Ingham County Libr., Mason, Mich., 1962-67, Sioux City (Iowa) Pub. Libr., 1967-69, Genesee Dist. Libr., Flint, Mich., 1969-76, Oxford (Mich.) Pub. Libr., 1976-84, Garfield County Libr., New Castle, Colo., 1984-90, Marshall (Mich.) Dist. Libr., 1990—; judge Am. Film Festival, N.Y.C., 1961-62. Organizer regional libr. coop. sys. Capital Libr. Coop., Lansing, Mich., 1965, Siouxland Libr. Coop., Sioux City, 1968, Marshall Dist. Libr., 1995; founder, pres. Garfield County Literacy, Glenwood Springs, Colo., 1984-90; pres., treas. Calhoun County Literacy, Battle Creek, Mich., 1992—. Mem. ALA (life), Pub. Libr. Assn., Mich. Libr. Assn., Detroit Suburban Librs. Roundtable, Rotary Club (Paul Harris fellow 1998). Unitarian Universalist. Avocation: family camping. E-mail: eholzwar@monroe.lib.mi.us. Home: 411 W Michigan Ave Marshall MI 49068 Office: Marshall Dist Libr 124 W Green St Marshall MI 49068

GARZA, ELIZEO, director solid waste management, Tucson; b. Chgo., July 21, 1951. BA, U. Tex., 1972; MEd, Antioch U., 1976. Asst. dir. neighborhood ctr. City of Tucson, 1974-79, planner, dep. asst. dir., 1979-93, dir. solid waste mgmt., 1993—. Mem. Solid Waste Assn. N. Am. Office: City Tucson Office Solid Waste Mgmt PO Box 27210 Tucson AZ 85726-7210*

GARZA, EMILIO M(ILLER), federal judge; b. San Antonio, Tex., Aug. 1, 1947; s. Antonio Peña and Dionisia (Miller) G. BA, U. Notre Dame, 1969, MA, 1970; JD, U. Tex., 1976. Assoc. Clemens, Spencer, Welmaker & Finck, San Antonio, 1976-82; ptnr. Clemens, Spencer, Welmaker & Finck, San Antonio, Tex., 1982-87; dist. judge 225th Dist. Ct., Bexar County, San Antonio, 1987-88; U.S. dist. judge U.S. Dist. Ct. (we. dist.) Tex., San Antonio, 1988-91; U.S. cir. judge U.S. Ct. Appeals (5th cir.), San Antonio, 1991—. Bd. dirs. Symphony Soc. San Antonio, 1987-89; mem. Century Club San Antonio, 1987-88; adv. coun. U. Tex. San Antonio Coll. Fine Arts and Humanities, 1992-98; adv. bd. Phoenix Inst., 1992—; bd. advisors Hispanic Law Jour. U. Tex. at Austin Sch. Law, 1992-96; adv. com. Notre Dame Law Sch., 1998. Capt. USMCR, 1970-79, active duty, 1970-73. Mem. State Bar Tex., San Antonio Bar Assn. Office: 8200 I-10 W Ste 501 San Antonio TX 78230

GARZA, FERNANDO RAUL, small business owner; b. June 28, 1949. BA, Tex. A&I U., 1971. Dir. corp. affairs U.S. Dept. Labor, Dallas, 1978-82; owner, mgr. Nick's Billiards, McAllen, Tex., 1983-87, Doc's Billiards, Pharr, Tex., 1987—.

GARZA, FIDENCIO C., JR., federal judge; b. 1932. AA, Edinburgh Jr. Coll., 1951; BA, Tex. A&I U., 1955; JD, South Tex. Coll. Law, 1961. Pvt. practice, 1962-84; judge Brook County, 1971-78; magistrate judge U.S. Dist. Ct. (so. dist.) Tex., Brownsville, 1981—. Office: US Dist Ct So Dist Tex 333 Fed Bldg 500 E 10th St Brownsville TX 78520

GARZA, JAIME RUPERTO, plastic/reconstructive surgeon; b. San Antonio, Tex., Jan. 15, 1954. BA, Tulane U., New Orleans, 1976; DDS, La. State U., 1983, MD, 1987. Chief of plastic surgery U. Tex. Health Sci. Ctr., San Antonio, 1994—. Office: Divsn Plas Surgery 7703 Floyd Curl Dr San Antonio TX 78284-6200

GARZA, OSCAR, newspaper editor. Daily calendar editor-arts L.A. Times, Calif. Office: Los Angeles Times Times Mirror Sq Los Angeles CA 90053

GARZA, REYNALDO G., federal judge; b. Brownsville, Tex., July 7, 1915; s. Ygnacio and Zoila (Guerra) G.; m. Bertha Champion, June 9, 1943; children: Reynaldo G., David C., Ygnacio Daniel, Bertha Victoria, Monica Bernadette. BA, LLB, U. Tex.; LLD (hon.), U. St. Edwards, Austin, Tex., 1965. Bar: Tex. 1939. Sole practice, 1939-42, 46-50; ptnr. Sharpe, Cunningham & Garza, 1950-60, Cunningham, Garza & Yznaga, 1960-61; judge U.S. Dist. Ct. Tex., Brownsville, from 1961, chief judge, 1974-79; senior judge U.S. Ct. Appeals (5th cir.), 1979—. Treas. Cameron County Child Welfare Bd., 1950-52; mem. Tex. Good Neighbor Commn., 1957-61; commr. City of Brownsville, 1947-49; trustee Brownsville Ind. Sch. Dist., 1941-42. Served with USAAF, 1942-45. Recipient Pro Ecclesia et Pontifice medal Pope Pius XII, 1952; decorated knight Order St. Gregory the Great, Pius XII, 1954. Mem. Cameron County Bar Assn., State Bar Tex. Office: US Ct Appeals PO Box 1129 Brownsville TX 78522-1129*

GARZI, JOHN JOSEPH, maintenance engineer; b. Mt. Vernon, N.Y., Oct. 1, 1942; s. John and Alberta (Galbina) G.; m. Dorothy Loretta Fleissner, July 10, 1961 (div. Feb. 1975); children: John Michael, Katherine Jane; m. Carol Isabella Castelli, Nov. 30, 1991. Grad. high sch., Mt. Vernon, N.Y. Stock rm. foreman , material cutter Precision Circuits, Inc., New Rochelle, N.Y., 1965-66; ship painter USCG Yard, Curtis Bay, Md., 1966-67; salesman Coca-Cola Bottling Co., Balt., 1967-80; owner Kemo-Sabe Trading, Severna Park, Md., 1978-86; ceramic tile installer The Tile Shop, Guilford, Conn., 1987-91; maintenance engr. Richmond County Savs. Bank, S.I., N.Y., 1992—. Motion picture movie extra Quiz Show, City Hall, Eddie. Candidate Rep. County Councilman, Anne Arundel County, Md., 1982. With USCG, 1960-65. Mem. Disabled Am. Vets. (life). Republican. Roman Catholic. Avocations: jewelry making, home improvement. Home: 158 Armstrong Ave Staten Island NY 10308-3103 Office: Richmond County Savs Bank 4523 Amboy Rd Staten Island NY 10312-4198

GARZIA, SAMUEL ANGELO, lawyer; b. Highland Park, Mich., July 7, 1920; s. Angelo and Josephine G.; m. Josephine Lupo, June 6, 1946; children: Samuel Angelo, Sandra Jo, Frank. J.D., Wayne State U., Detroit, 1943. Bar: Mich. 1943. Asst. friend of ct. Wayne County, Mich., 1946-48; practice law Detroit, 1948-97; sr. ptnr. Vandeveer Garzia, 1960-97. Served with AUS, 1943-45, ETO. Decorated Bronze Star; Croix de Guerre Luxembourg). Mem. ABA, Mich. Bar Assn., Detroit Bar Assn. (dir. 1976-83), Oakland Bar Assn., Assn. Def. Counsel Mich. (1st pres. 1966-67), Internat. Assn. Ins. Counsel, Am. Coll. Trial Lawyers, Am. Legion (judge advocate Mich. 1958). Roman Catholic. Home: 5229 Greenbriar Ct West Bloomfield MI 48323-2322 Office: 333 W Fort St Detroit MI 48226-3115

GARZIONE, JOHN EDWARD, physical therapist; b. Newburgh, N.Y., Jan. 3, 1950; s. John Edward and Della Elizabeth (Gentila) G.; m. Anita Louise Hirschman, Sept. 21, 1974; children: Adriana, Katrina. AAS, Orange County C.C., Middletown, N.Y., 1970; BS, Ithaca Coll., 1973. Mem. staff phys. therapy Chenango Meml. Hosp., Norwich, N.Y., 1973-74; sr. phys. therapist N.Y. State Vets. Home, Oxford, N.Y., 1974-86; CEO Chenango Therapeutics, Norwich, 1975—; lic. examiner N.Y. State, 1976-86; cons. phys. therapy Broome Devel. Ctr., Binghamton, N.Y., 1985—, Upstate Home for Children, Milford, N.Y., 1986-88, Hospice Chenango County, Norwich, 1991—; adj. instr. Czenovia Coll., 1982-87, Ithaca Coll., 1993-94; clin. instr. EMPI Corp., 1996—; cons. BlueCross/Blue Shield, Utica, 1998; presenter in field. Contbr. articles to profl. jours. Mem. Am. Phys. Therapy Assn. (sec. pain mgmt. spl. interest group), Am. Coll. Sports Medicine, Am. Acad. Pain Mgmt. (clin. assoc., Continuing Edn. Excellence award 1996), N.Y. Acad. Scis., Lions (v.p. 1990). Home: PO Box 451 Sherburne NY 13460-0451 Office: Chenango Therapeutics Country Club Rd Norwich NY 13815-1613

GASBARRO, PASCO, JR., lawyer; b. Providence, Apr. 3, 1944; s. Pasco and Helen (Casali) G.; m. Mary Alyce McNamara, May 30, 1967; children: Pasco, John A., Christopher E. AB, Brown U., Providence, 1966; JD, Boston U., 1969. Bar: R.I. 1969, U.S. Dist. Ct. R.I. 1971, Mass. 1972, U.S. Dist. Ct. Mass. 1974. Law clk. R.I. Supreme Ct., Providence, 1969-70; atty. R.I. Legal Svcs., Providence, 1970-71, New Eng. Elec., Westborough, Mass., 1971-76; counsel Narragansett Elec. Co., Providence, 1976-79; asst. gen. counsel New Eng. Elec., Westborough, 1979-83; ptnr. Hinckley, Allen & Snyder, Providence and Boston, 1983—; del. White House Conf. on Small Bus., 1995. Chmn. adv. coun. R.I. Small Bus. Devel. Ctr. Mem. ABA, R.I. Bar Assn., Brown Club of R.I. Office: Hinckley Allen & Snyder 1500 Fleet Ctr Providence RI 02903-2319

GASCH, OLIVER, judge; b. 1906. AB, Princeton U., 1928; LLB, George Washington U., 1932. Ast. corp. counsel, 1937-53, prin. U.S. atty., 1953-56; U.S. atty. D.C., 1956-61; ptnr. Craighill, Aiello, Gasch & Craighill, 1961-65; dist. judge U.S. Dist. Ct., Washington, 1965—. With U.S. Army, 1942-46, PTO. Fellow Am. Bar Found., Am. Coll. of Trial Lawyers, mem. ABA, Bar Assn D.C. (pres. 1964-65), Fed. Bar Assn. (chmn. com. of gen. counsel 1960-61), Fed. Bar Assn., Am. Law Inst. (life), Barristers D.C. (pres. 1963). Office: US Dist Ct US Courthouse 3d & Constitution Ave NW Washington DC 20001

GASCHEL-CLARK, REBECCA MONA, special education educator; b. Hudson, N.Y., Sept. 10, 1972; d. Michael Anthony and Ellen Michele (Wright) Gaschel; m. Eric Clark, Nov. 8, 1997. BS in Spl. Edn., Early Childhood Edn., U. Hartford, 1994, MEd, 1997. Cert. spl. edn. tchr., Conn., pre-kindergarten-12. Spl. edn. educator Regional Sch. Dist. #1, Falls Village, Conn., 1994—; mem. consultation team Salisbury Ctrl. Sch., Lakeville, Conn., 1996—. Lector Ch. of the Resurrection, Germantown, N.Y., 1989—. Named tchr. of elem. sch. Exemplary Program, Conn. Assn. of Schs., 1996. Mem. Phi Delta Kappa, Alpha Chi, Kappa Delta Pi. Democrat. Roman Catholic. Avocations: water skiing, opera, cooking, camping. Office: Regional Sch Dist # 1 246 Warren Tpke Falls Village CT 06031-1600

GASH, LAUREN BETH, lawyer, state legislator; b. Summit, N.J., June 11, 1960; d. Ira Arnold and Sondra Regina (Stetin) G.; m. Gregg Allen Garmisa, June 12, 1983; children: Sarah, Benjamin. BA in Psychology, Clark U., 1982; JD, Georgetown U., 1987. Bar: Ill. 1989. Projects dir. U.S. Senator Alan Dixon, Washington, 1981-83; statewide constituency coord., dir. Women for Simon, U.S. Senator Paul Simon, Chgo., 1990; aide State Rep. Grace Mary Stern, Highland Park, Ill.; atty. Prairie State Legal Svcs., Waukegan, Ill.; mem. Ill. State Ho. of Reps., chair judiciary-criminal com. Mem. women's health adv. bd. Highland Park Hosp., southeast adv. bd Coll. Lake County, JUF govt. agencies divsn. campaign cabinet, 1999, chair, Highland Park 2000 com., human needs subcom. Women in Law as 2d Career grantee; recipient Disting. Svc. award Ill. Com. for Honest Govt., 1996, Best Legis. Record Voting award Ind. Voters Ill., 1996; named Legis. of Yr. Alliance for the Mentally Ill, 1997. Mem. Ill. State Bar Assn. (mem. com. cmty. involvement), Formerly Employed Mothers at the Leading Edge (cofounder North Shore chpt.), Chgo. Women in Govt. Rels., Women Employed, Ravinia PTA (bd. dirs., polit. action chair), Com. for Interdist. Cooperation, North Shore Synagogue Beth El (social action com.) LWV (bd. dirs. Highland Park chpt., bd. dirs. Lake County chpt.). Avocations: flute, French, Spanish. Office: 108 Wilmot Rd Ste 210 Deerfield IL 60015-5131 also: 2052-L Stratton Bldg Springfield IL 62706

GASICH, WELKO ELTON, retired aerospace executive, management consultant; b. Cupertino, Calif., Mar. 28, 1922; s. Elija J. and Catherine (Paviso) G.; m. Patricia Ann Gudgel, Dec. 28, 1973; 1 child, Mark David. A.B. cum laude in Mech. Engring. (Bacon scholar), Stanford U., 1943, M.S. in Mech. Engring., 1947, cert. in fin. and econs. (Sloan exec. fellow), 1967; Aero. Engr., Calif. Inst. Tech., 1948. Aerodynamicist Douglas Aircraft Co., 1943-44, supr. aeroelastics, 1947-51; chief aero design Rand Corp., 1951-53; chief preliminary design aircraft div. Northrop Corp., Los Angeles, 1953-56; dir. advanced systems Northrop Corp., 1956-61, v.p., asst. gen. mgr. tech., 1961-66, corp. v.p., gen. mgr. Northrop Ventura div., 1967-71, corp. v.p., gen. mgr. aircraft div., 1971-76, corp. v.p., group exec. aircraft group, 1976-79, sr. v.p. advanced projects, 1979-85, exec. v.p. programs, 1985-88, ret., 1988; aerospace cons., Encino, Calif., 1988—. Author: 40 Years of Ferrari V-12 Engines, 1990; patentee in field. Chmn. adv. council Stanford Sch. Engring., 1981-83; past mem. adv. council Stanford Grad. Sch. Bus.; chmn. United Way, 1964; chmn. Scout-O-Rama, Los Angeles council Boy Scouts Am., 1964; chmn. explorer scout exec. com., 1963-64. Served to lt. USN, 1944-46. Fellow AIAA, Soc. Automotive Engrs.; mem. NAE, Navy League, Stanford Grad. Sch. Bus. Alumni Assn. (pres. 1971), Conquistadores del Cielo Club, Bel Air Country Club. Republican. Office: 3517 Caribeth Dr Encino CA 91436-4103

GASIORKIEWICZ, EUGENE ANTHONY, lawyer; b. Milw., Jan. 7, 1950; s. Eugene Constantine and Loretta Ann (Kasprzak) G.; m. Jana Jamieson, Jan. 12, 1980; children: Suzanne A., Alexei E. AB, Regis Coll., 1971; JD, U. Miss., 1974. Bar: Wis. 1974, U.S. Supreme Ct. 1986. Law clk. to presiding justice Miss. Supreme Ct., Jackson, 1974-75; assoc. Schoone, McManus & Hanson S.C., Racine, Wis., 1975-79; ptnr. Hanson & Gasiorkiewicz S.C., Racine, Wis., 1979-90; pres., shareholder Hanson, Gasiorkiewicz & Weber, S.C., Racine, 1990-96, Hanson & Gasiorkiewicz, S.C., Racine, 1997—; lectr. labor law U. Wis., Racine, 1975-76, worker's comp., State Bar Wis., 1984-86, med. malpractice, Wis. Acad. Trial Lawyers, 1986. Mcpl. judge Village of Wind Point, Wis., 1983-85; moot ct. instr., The Prairie Sch., Racine, 1986-87. Mem. State Bar Wis., Assn. Trial Lawyers Am., Am. Arbitration Assn., Wis. Acad. Trial Lawyers, Nat. Bd. Trial Advocacy (cert. civil trial advocate). Roman Catholic. Avocation: tennis. Home: 3929 S Brook Rd Franksville WI 53126-9303 Office: Hanson & Gasiorkiewicz SC 2932 Northwestern Ave Racine WI 53404-2249

GASKELL, IVAN GEORGE ALEXANDER DE WEND, art museum curator; b. Weston-super-Mare, Somerset, U.K., Feb. 26, 1955; came to U.S., 1991.; s. William George Keith de Wend and Johanna Catharina (van Leeuwen) G.; m. Jane Susan Whitehead, May 9, 1981; 1 child, Alexander Leo Ralph de Wend. Attended, Worcester Coll., Oxford, 1973-76, Courtauld Inst. Art, London, 1976-80; MA in Modern History, Oxford U.; MA in History of Western Art, London U.; PhD in History of Art, Cambridge U. Rsch. fellow, acad. curatorial asst. Warburg Inst. London U., 1980-83; fellow Wolfson Coll. Cambridge U., 1983-91, mem. faculty architecture, history of art, 1983-91; sr. lectr. fine arts Harvard U., Cambridge, Mass., 1991—, head dept. paintings and sculpture Fogg Art Mus., 1991—, Margaret S. Winthrop curator of paintings, 1991—; presenter papers at numerous internat. confs., 1978—; chair seminars in field; lectr. Royal Acad., Nat. Gallery, London, Courtauld Inst. Art, 1982—. Author: The Thyssen-Bornemisza Collection: Dutch and Flemish Painting, 1990; co-editor: The Language of Art History, 1991, Landscape, Natural Beauty and the Arts, 1993, Explanation and Value in the Arts, 1993, Nietzsche, Philosophy and The Arts, 1998, Vermeer Studies, 1998; joint gen. editor: Cambridge Studies in Philosophy and the Arts, 1988—; contbr. articles, revs. to profl. jours. Mem. Coll. Art Assn., Am. Soc. for Aesthetics. Avocations: sight-seeing. Office: Harvard U Fogg Art Mus 32 Quincy St Cambridge MA 02138-3845

GASKEY-SPEAR, NANCY JANE, nurse anesthetist; b. California, Pa.; d. Frank and Rose Gaskey; m. Robert L. Spear (dec. Jan. 1988). RN, Mercy Hosp., Pitts., 1960, Nurse Anesthetist, 1963; BS in Nursing Edn., California (Pa.) U., 1970; MEd in Curriculum and Supervision, U. Pitts., 1975, PhD in Edn. Comm. and Tech., 1983. Cert. nurse anesthetist; RN, Pa. Staff nurse Mercy Hosp., Pitts., 1960-61, staff nurse anesthetist 1963-70; dir. Sch. Nurse Anesthesia Western Pa. Hosp., Pitts., 1970-86; staff nurse anesthetist Western Pa. Anesthesia Assocs. Ltd., Western Pa. Hosp., Pitts., 1987—; on-site visitor Coun. on Accreditation Nurse Anesthesia Ednl. Programs, Schs., 1981-86; ednl. cons. Nursing Expo, Pitts., 1982; mem. Allegheny County Bd. Health, Pitts., 1976-85; instr. workshops, seminars, various orgns. Prodr. slide/cassette: Radial Artery Cannulation, Western Pa. Hosp. Sch. Anesthesia Recruitment, Instrns. for Assembling the Gould Transducer Pressure Monitoring Sys., Brachial Plexus Blocks: Interscalene Technique, Evolution of Inhalation Anesthesia; prodn. coord. videotapes Close-Ups in Anesthesia; contbr. articles to profl. jours.; mem. editl. bd. Current Revs. for Nurse Anesthetists; profl. corr. Antique Collector, Salem, Ohio, Bee Pub. Co., Newtowne, Conn. Recipient Cmty. Citation of Merit Allegheny County Bd. Commrs., 1985. Mem. Am. Assn. Nurse Anestetists (edn. com. 1973-74, rsch. in action recognition award 1985), Pitts. Bibliophiles, Mid-Atlantic Assn. Nurse Anesthetists (sec.-treas. 1970-71, chmn. elect 1971-72, chmn. 1972-73, chmn. program com. 1973-74), Southwestern Pa. Soc. Nurse Anesthetists (pres. 1972-73), Pa. Assn. Nurse Anesthetists (trustee 1972-74, pub. rels. com. 1972-74, safety com. 1974-75, pres.-elect 1975-76, pres. 1976-77, editor Pennsylvania Tidings 1976-77, founder, chmn. spl. com. Assembly Sch. Faculty), Hosp. Coun. Western Pa. (anesthesia circuits project com. 1982-83). Avocations: antiques, art. Home: 552 N Neville St Pittsburgh PA 15213-2855 Office: Western Pa Hosp Liberty Ave Pittsburgh PA 15224

GASKILL, HERBERT LEO, accountant, engineer; b. Seattle, July 1, 1923; s. Leo Dell and Vesta Rathbone (Dahlen) G.; m. Margaret Helen Jenkins, Mar. 1, 1944 (div.); children—Margaret V., Herbert Leo; m. Opal Jordan, June 13, 1992; 1 child, Ann. B.S. and M.S. in Chem. Engring., U. Wash., 1949, M.B.A., 1976. C.P.A., Wash. Asst. prof. dental materials, exec. officer dept. dental materials Sch. Dentistry, U. Wash., 1950-56; ops. analyst The Boeing Co., Seattle, 1958-71, mktg. cons. govt. programs, 1972-74; pvt. practice acctg., Seattle, 1976-80; hazardous waste mgr. Boeing Co., Seattle, 1980-86, project mgr. Western Processing Remediation, 1986-95, ret. 1995. Active Seattle Art Mus., Pacific Northwest Aviation Hist. Found. Served to lt. (j.g.) USNR, 1941-46. TAPPI fellow, 1956; U. Wash. Engring. Expt. Sta. fellow, 1957. Mem. Wash. Soc. C.P.A.s. Contbr. articles to profl. jours. Home: 1236 NE 92nd St Seattle WA 98115-3135

GASKIN, FELICIA, biochemist, educator; b. Carlisle, Pa., Jan. 17, 1943; d. Joseph A. and Wanda J. (Rakowski) G.; m. Shu Man Fu, Nov. 29, 1969; children: Kai-Ming, Kai-Mei. AB in Chemistry, Dickinson Coll., Carlisle, Pa., 1965; MA in Organic Chemistry, Bryn Mawr Coll., 1967; PhD in Biochemistry, U. Calif., San Francisco, 1969. Postdoctoral fellow Stanford U., Palo Alto, Calif., 1969-71; rsch. assoc. Rockefeller U., N.Y.C., 1971-72, Columbia U., N.Y.C., 1972-74; asst. prof., then assoc. prof. Albert Einstein Coll. Medicine, N.Y.C., 1974-82; prof. Sch. Medicine U. Okla., Oklahoma City, 1982-88, U. Va., Charlottesville, 1988—; mem. Okla. Med. Rsch. Found., 1982-88. Contbr. articles to profl. jours. Recipient rsch. career devel. award NIH, 1975-80; Nat. Inst. Neurol. Diseases and Stroke spl. fellow, 1972-74. Mem. AAAS, Am. Soc. Biochemistry and Molecular Biology, Am. Soc. for Cell Biology, Soc. Neurosci. Office: U Va Sch Med Charlottesville VA 22908

GASKINS, LINDA CAROL, educator; b. Memphis, Aug. 3, 1963; d. Frank Rogers and Colleen (Coffey) Brewer; m. Jeffrey Thomas Gaskins, May 25, 1991; children: Frank Everett, Casey William, Joseph Earl. BS in Edn., U. Tenn. at Martin, 1985, MS in Edn., 1989. Cert. tchr., Tenn. Math. and reading tutor Dyslexia Found. of Memphis, 1982-88, math. supr., 1987-88, 91; tchr. 5th grade Briarcrest Ridgeway Elem. Sch., Memphis, 1985-88; tchr. 6th grade math. and sci. Shelby County Schs., Memphis, 1990-91; grad. asst. U. Tenn., Martin, 1988-89; tchr. 4th grade nongraded classroom St. Benedict at Auburndale, Cordova, Tenn., 1991-93; instr. workshop facilitator reading, writing, listening State. Tech. Inst. at Memphis, 1993—; curriculum devel. for Work Keys Tng. Workshops, Memphis, also Greenwood, Miss., 1996—; speaker in field. Contbr. poetry to Old Hickory Rev., 1990, Tranquil Rains of Summer/Anthology of the Nat. Libr. of Poetry, 1998; author ednl. articles. Vol. coord. West Tenn. Spl. Olympics, Martin, 1984, 85, 86; organizer alumni readers bur. Briarcrest Christian Sch., Memphis, 1995-96. Mem. ASCD, Internat. Dyslexia Assn. (charter West Tenn. chpt., sec. 1988-91), Dyslexia Found. Memphis, Nat. Coun. Tchrs. English, Quill and Scroll, Phi Delta Kappa. Republican. Christian. Avocations: singing, cooking, writing, gardening, fishing. Home: 871 Wood Cade Cv Cordova TN 38018-6469 Office: State Tech Inst Dept Devel Studies 5983 Macon Cv Dept Devel Memphis TN 38134-7642

GASKINS, WILLIAM DARRELL, ophthalmologist; b. Columbia, S.C., June 7, 1951; s. William and Virginia G. Herron; m. Cynthia Gaile Harper, Sept. 7, 1973; children: William Darrell Jr., Craig E., Trenton F. BS in Pharmacy, U. S.C., 1973; MD, Med. U. S.C., 1977. Diplomate Am. Bd. Ophthalmology. Intern in gen. surgery Med. U. S.C., Charleston, 1977-78; resident in ophthalmology U. Miss. Med. Ctr., Jackson, 1981-84; pvt. practice, Naples, Fla., 1984—. Capt. M.C., USAF, 1978-81. Paul Harris fellow Rotary Internat., 1986. Fellow ACS, Am. Acad. Ophthalmology; mem. AMA, Fla. Soc. Ophthalmology, Collier County Med. Soc. Presbyterian. Avocations: hunting, fishing. Office: 2335 9th St N Ste 304 Naples FL 34103-4457

GASKINS-CLARK, PATRICIA RENAE, dietitian; b. Ft. Sill, Okla., July 24, 1959; d. Jay Frank and Iwana (Robinson) Gaskins; m. Gene Martin Clark, June 6, 1986; children: Taylor Renae, Kyle Gene. BS, Cameron U., 1982; MS, Cen. State U., 1986. Cert. home econ.; registered dietitian. Nutrition specialist William E. Davis & Sons, Inc., Oklahoma City, 1985-87; dietitian intern Okla. Teaching Hosps., Oklahoma City, 1987; clin. dietitian Grady Meml. Hosp., Chickasha, Okla., 1987-89; chief clin. dietitian Presbyn. Hosp., Oklahoma City, 1989-90; mgr. nutrition svcs. Norman (Okla.) Regional Hosp., 1990—. Mem. Am. Dietetic Assn., Cameron U. Alumni Assn., Oklahoma City Dist. Dietetic Assn., Okla. Dietetic Assn., Cen. State U. Alumni Assn., Phi Upsilon Omicron. Republican. Baptist. Avocations: reading, jazzercise, weight lifting. Office: Norman Regional Hosp 901 N Porter Ave Norman OK 73071-6482

GASNER, WALTER GILBERT, retired dermatologist; b. N.Y.C., May 6, 1912; s. Charles and Gussie Gasner; m. Shirley M. Friedman, Dec. 31, 1937; children: Douglas, Jane, John, Mary. MD, Med. Coll. S.C., 1936. Diplomate in dermatology and syhilology. Assoc. prof. Albert Einstein Med. Sch., Bronx, N.Y., 1955-75; chief of dermatology Grasslands Hosp., Westchester County, N.Y., 1955-75. Contbr. articles to med. jours. Lt. col. USAF, 1936-64. Fellow ACP. Avocations: skiing, fishing. Home: Harbor Pond Farm Block Island RI 02807-0391

GASPAR, ANNA LOUISE, retired elementary school teacher, consultant; b. Chgo., May 12, 1935; d. Miklos and Klotild (Weiss) G. *Father, Miklos Gaspar, born in Kaba, Hungary in 1885, was a member of the Hungarian Art Institute and exhibited at the Gallery of Arts and National Salon of Budapest. Was a war painter during World War I for the Hungarian Government and the Imperial and Royal Press. He came to the US in 1921 and was recognized as a mural painter of historical subjects and as an ecclesiastical artist. He died in 1946. Photographs, original letters and prizes are on file at the Smithsonian Institutions Archives of American Art in the Huntington Library in San Marino, California. Mother, Klotild (Weiss), born in Subotica, Hungary in 1900, lived in Chicago from 1932-57. She edited and typed masters theses and doctoral dissertations for college and university graduate students.* BS in Edn., Northwestern U., 1957. Cert. elem. tchr., Calif. Tchr. 6th grade Pacific Palisades Elem. Sch., L.A., 1957-58; tchr. 1st grade Eastman Street Elem. Sch., L.A., 1959, Glassell Park, L.A., 1959-62, Stoner Ave. Elem. Sch., L.A., 1962-67; 2nd-4th grade tchr. Brentwood Elem. Sch., L.A., 1967-78; tchr. 4th and 5th grades Brockton Avenue Elem. Sch., L.A., 1978-90; vol., established Swakopmund Tchrs. Resource Ctr., Peace Corps, Namibia, 1991-93; tchr. English, Atlantic Sr. Primary Sch., Swakopmund, Namibia, 1992; career info. cons. Peace Corps., 1991—; substitute tchr. Hebrew Acad./Pre-Primary, Las Vegas, 1994—. Mem. Hadassah, Bet Knesset Bamidbar, and numerous other cmty. clubs. Mem. Internat. Platform Assn., Calif. Ret. Tchrs. Assn., Northwestern U. Alumni Assn., Peace Corps, So. Nev. Peace Corps Assn. Democrat. Jewish. Avocations: world travel, playing piano, art, collecting costume dolls, folk music. Home: 2700 Hope Forest Dr Las Vegas NV 89134-7322

GASPARRO, FRANK, sculptor; b. Phila., Aug. 26, 1909; s. Bernard and Rosa G.; m. Julia Florence Johnston, Nov. 11, 1939; 1 dau., Christina Julia. Ed., Phila. Indsl. Arts, Pa. Acad. Fine Arts. With U.S. Mint, Phila., 1942—; asst. chief engraver-sculptor U.S. Mint, 1962-65, chief-sculptor engraver, 1965-81; instr. sculpture Fleisher Art Meml., Phila., Pa. Acad. Fine Arts, 1981. Designer: Am. coinage including Lincoln Meml. cent reverse, 1959, John F. Kennedy half-dollar reverse, 1964, Eisenhower dollar, 1972, Susan B. Anthony dollar, 1979, Phila. Medal of Honor, 1955; FAO medals Lillian Carter and Shirley Temple Black; Presdl. medals Congl. Medal of Honor; George Washington bicentennial medal; Statue of Liberty Commemorative Medal series, 1986; fgn. coinage including Guatemala, 1943, Philippine Islands, 1967, Panama, 1971, 75, $2500 proof gold coin (reverse design Isabella and Columbus) The Bahamas, 1987, Pearl Harbor 50th Anniversary medal, 1941-91, 1991, Am. Numismatic Assn. 100th Anniversary medal, 1981-91, 1991; Olympic U.S. five dollar gold coin obverse and reverse, 1995. Recipient Order of Merit Italian Republic, 1973, United Vets. Am. Disting. Citizens award of Phila., 1975, Outstanding Achievement award Da Vinci Art Alliance, 1967, Commemorative Medal George Washington 250th Ann., 1982, Pres.'s Day Celebration Medal Washington and Lincoln, 1983, Baseball Hall of Fame 50th Ann. medal, 1989, K.K. Mikveh Israel Synagogue medal, 1990, Pearl Harbor Commemorative medal 1941-91, 1991, World War II Victory Anniversary Commemorative medal, 1945-95. Fellow Pa. Acad. Fine Arts (Percy Owens award 1979). Home: 216 Westwood Park Dr Upper Darby PA 19083-4422 *Every day is a challenge to me: to plan, to approach my problems and to solve them. In my art work the ultimate goal is for its appreciation and enjoyment. As I look forward to the next project, I always feel that the great ones are looking over my shoulder to see the results. The challenge to me is what makes my day worthwhile.*

GASPARRO, MADELINE, banker; b. Jersey City, Oct. 5, 1928; d. Donato and Anna (D'Urso) D'Achille; m. Dominick J. Gasparro, Apr. 30, 1949; children: Dorothy, Joseph, Donato, Frank. Grad. high sch., Jersey City. Salesperson credit dept. and employee sales J.C. Penney, Parlin, N.J.; head teller Amboy Madison Nat. Bank, Old Bridge, N.J., bank mgr., br. mgr., 1983-97; ret., 1997. Chpt. chmn. South Amboy Hosp., mem. fin. com.; eucharist minister St. Bernadette Ch. of Parlin. Mem. NAFE, Nat. Assn. Bank Women (past hostess), Fin. Women Internat. (chmn. membership Raritan Bay group 1990-91, v.p. 1991-92, pres. 1992-93), Altar Rosary Soc. (past pres.). Address: 17 Parkway Pl Parlin NJ 08859-1905

GASPER, GEORGE, JR., mathematics educator; b. Hamtramck, Mich., Oct. 10, 1939; s. George Gregory and Anastasia Gasper; m. Brigitta Gasper, July 1, 1967; children: Karen, Kenneth. BS, Mich. Technol. U., 1962; MA, Wayne State U., 1964, PhD, 1967. Predoctoral traineeship NASA, 1966-67; vis. lectr. U. Wis., Madison, 1967-68; postdoctoral fellow U. Toronto, Ont., Can., 1968-69, vis. asst. prof., 1969-70; asst. prof. math. Northwestern U., Evanston, Ill., 1970-73, assoc. prof., 1973-77, prof., 1977—. Co-author: Basic Hypergeometric Series, 1990; assoc. editor Jour. Math. Analysis and Applications, 1985-95, The Ramanujan Jour., 1995—. Fellow Alfred P. Sloan Found., 1973-75. Mem. Am. Math. Soc., Soc. Indsl. and Applied Math. (assoc. editor Jour. Math. Analysis 1984-85, vice chair activity group on orthogonal polynomials and spl. functions 1993-95). Office: Northwestern U Dept Math Lunt Bldg Evanston IL 60208

GASPER, JO ANN, consulting firm executive; b. Providence, Sept. 25, 1946; d. Joseph Siegleman and Jeanne Van Matre Shoaf; m. Louis Clement Gasper, Sept. 21, 1974; children: Stephen Gregory, Jeanne Marie, Monica Elizabeth, Michelle Bernadette (dec.), Phyllis Anastasia, Clare Genevieve. B.A., U. Dallas, 1967, M.B.A., 1969. Adminstrv. asst. U. Dallas, 1964-68; asst. dir. adminstrn. Britian Convalescent Ctr., Irving, Tex., 1964-68; pres. Medicare Ctrs., Inc., Dallas, 1968-69; bus. mgr., treas. U. Plano, Tex., 1969-72; ins. agt. John Hancock Ins. Co., Dallas, 1972-73; systems analyst Tex. Instrument, Richardson, 1973-75; pvt. practice acctg., bus. cons. McLean, Va., 1976-81; editor, pub. Congl. News for Women and the Family, McLean, Va., 1978-81, Register Report, McLean, Va., 1980-81; dep. asst. sec. for social services policy HHS, Washington, 1981-85; exec. dir. White House Conf. on Agys., HHS, Washington, 1982-85; dep. asst. sec. for population affairs HHS, Washington, 1985-87; policy advisor to under sec. U.S. Dept. Edn., Washington, 1987-88, cons.; pres. Franklin Pk. Assocs., 1989—; exec. dir. Nat. Assn. for Abstinence Edn., 1989-94; mgr. TSR, 1995-98. Co-chmn. St. John's Refugee Resettlement Commn., Va., 1977; bd. dirs., treas. Coun. Inter-Am. Security, Washington, 1978-80; active Fairfax County Citizens Coalition for Quality Child Care, Va., 1979-80; del. White House Conf. on Families, Va., 1979-80; mem. U.S. adv. Inter-Am. Commn. on Women, OAS, 1982-85; U.S. del. XVI Pan Am. Child Congress, Washington, 1984; mem. nat. family policy adv. bd. Reagan-Bush Campaign, 1980. Recipient Eagle Forum award, 1979, Wanderer Found. award, 1980, Bronze medal HHS, 1982; named Outstanding Conservative Woman, Conservative Digest, 1980, 81. Mem. Exec. Women in Gov. (treas. 1985, sec. 1986). Roman Catholic.

GASPER, RUTH EILEEN, real estate executive; b. Valparaiso, Ind., July 16, 1934; d. Reuben John and Effie (Wesner) Tenpas; m. Ralph L. Gasper, May 25, 1957. Student, Purdue U., 1952-56; BA, Govs. State U., 1982. Analyst computer sys. Leo Burnett Advt., Chgo., 1958-69; nat. adminstr. registrars Sports Car Club Am., Denver, 1977-79; pres. Ainslie Inc., Chgo., 1982—; mem. North River Commn. Housing Com., Chgo., 1982-83, fin. com. Mayor's Task Force on Homelessness City of Chgo. Area coord. Concerned Action party, Lansing, Ill., 1977; chief race registrar Ind. N.W. Region Sports Car Club Am., 1969-80; co-founder, Single Rm. Operators Assn., 1987-98. Mem. Condo. Assn. (sec. Fantasy Island II). Avocations: sports car racing, classical music.

GASPERINI, ELIZABETH CARMELA (LISA GASPERINI), marketing professional, graphic designer; b. Newark, Sept. 26, 1961; d. Enrico Caesar and Wanda Claudia (Stanziale) G. BFA, Caldwell (N.J.) Coll., 1983. Advt. specialist J.C. Penney Corp., Wayne, N.J., 1982-83; asst. prodn. mgr. Internat. Postal Mktg. Corp., Montville, N.J., 1983-84; art dir. Healy, Dixcy & Forbes, W. Caldwell, N.J., 1984-86; sr. mktg. specialist Am. Varityper Corp., E. Hanover, N.J., 1986-88; product promotion mgr. Brother Internat. Corp., Somerset, N.J., 1988-90; mktg. specialist Ishida USA Inc., Lincoln Park, N.J., 1990-92; mktg. promotions mgr. Nat. Electronic Info. Corp., Secaucus, N.J., 1992-95; self-employed mktg. cons. Towaco, N.J., 1995-96; mgr. mktg. svcs. AmeriHeath Ins. Co. N.J., Iselin, N.J., 1996—; telemktg. specialist Sears, Roebuck & Co., Fairfield, N.J., 1984-96; owner, cons. Gasperini Graphics, Towaco, N.J., 1984—; art cons. Italico Pubs., Livingston, N.J., 1982—. Mem. N.J. Art Assn., N.J. Italian-Am. Assn. (cons. 1982—). Republican. Roman Catholic. Avocations: photographer, painter, pianist, crafts designer, unique and antique jewelry collector. Home: 10 Willard Ln Towaco NJ 07082-1517

GASPERONI, EMIL, SR., realtor, developer; b. Hillsville, Pa., Nov. 13, 1926; s. Attico and Rose Mary (Sarnicola) G.; m. Ellen Jean Lias, May 28, 1955; children: Samuel Dale, Emil Attico, Jean Ellen. Diploma real estate U. Pitts., 1957. Owner, pres. Gasperoni Real Estate, New Castle, Pa., 1956-63, Ft. Lauderdale, Fla., 1965-86, Gasperoni Internat. Group, Longwood, Fla., 1986—; founder, chmn. bd. Fill-R-Up Auto Wash Systems Inc., Ft. Lauderdale, 1967-72. Served with U.S. Army, 1945-46, ETO. Mem. Nat. Inst. Real Estate Brokers, Fla. Assn. Mortgage Brokers, Sweetwater Country Club (Longwood, Fla.), Lake Toxaway (N.C.) Country Club. Home: 92 Cold Mountain Rd Lake Toxaway NC 28747-9630 Address: 931 Wekiva Springs Rd Longwood FL 32779-2501

GASQUE, (ALLARD) HARRISON, disc jockey, volunteer; b. Richmond, Va., Oct. 10, 1958; s. Thomas Nelson and Susan (Folline) G.; m. Diane Cynthia Phillips, Nov. 14, 1992; 1 child, Folline Elaine. Grad., Columbia Sch. Broadcasting, Washington, 1982; BA, U. S.C., 1984; student, Midlands Tech. Coll., 1996—. Announcer, disc jockey Sta. WKDK-AM, Newberry, S.C., 1981-82, Sta. WEEL-AM, Washington, 1983-85; announcer Sta. WWGO-FM, Columbia, 1986-87, Sta. WNOK-AM, Columbia, 1987-88, Sta. WODE-AM, Columbia, 1989-90, Sta. WYYS-FM, Columbia, 1991, Sta. WSCQ-FM, Columbia, 1991-94, Sta. WCOS-FM, Columbia, 1994—; v.p. transp. Palmetto Optical Supply, 1986—. Extra in movie Chattahoochie. Vol. Lexington-Richland Alcohol and Drug Abuse Coun., 1996—; pres. human svcs. club Midlands Tech. Coll., 1996—. Recipient Presdl. Order of Merit award, 1991. Mem. S.C. Assn. Alcoholism and Drug Abuse Counselors, SCV, Robert Burns Soc., SAR, Mil. Order of Stars and Bars (lt. comdr. Maxey Gregg chpt.), S.C. Rep. Party, John Birch Soc., 1st Tuesday Rep. Club (bd. dirs. 1999—), Phi Kappa Psi, Alpha Epsilon Rho. Avocations: singing, coin, stamp and record collecting, tennis, basketball, football. E-mail: gasque@compuzone.net. Home: 3728 Linbrook Dr Columbia SC 29204-4438

GASQUE, LAUREL, educator; b. Chgo., July 17, 1942; d. Ingeman and Doris Klatt Sandfor; m. W. Ward Gasque, Aug. 25, 1961; 1 child, Catherine Michelle. BA, UCLA, 1964; MEd, Ea. Coll., 1994. Tutor, lectr. Regent Coll., Vancouver, B.C., Can., 1970-79, dir. alumni svcs., 1982-87; assoc. dir. Lookout Gallery, Vancouver, B.C., Can., 1989-90; coord. faculty Inter-Varsity Christian Fellow, Toronto, Ont., Can., 1995—; adj. prof. New Coll. Berkeley (Calif.), 1979-82, Ea. Coll., St. Davids, Pa., 1990-95, Sem., Tyndale, Toronto, Ont., Can., 1996—; bd. dirs. New Coll. Berkeley; cons. in field. Contbr. articles to profl. jours. Mem. Am. Acad. Religion, Christians in Visual Arts, Coll. Art Assn. Independent. Avocations: languages, walking, classical music. Home: PO Box 936 Stanwood WA 98292 Office: Inter-Varsity Christian, 64 Prince Andrew Pl, Toronto, ON Canada M36 2H4

GASQUE, THOMAS JAMES, English educator; b. Florence, S.C., Sept. 6, 1937; s. Thomas Jefferson and Margaret Olive (Reaves) G.; m. Alice Marie Tealey, May 31, 1969; 1 child, Susanna Rachel. AB, Wofford Coll., 1959; MA, Emory U., 1962; PhD, U. Tenn., 1970. Instr. Clemson (S.C.) U., 1961-62, Columbia (S.C.) Coll., 1962-63; tchg. asst. U. Tenn., Knoxville, 1963-68; asst. prof. U. S.D., Vermillion, 1968-72, assoc. prof., 1972-88, prof., 1988—, chmn. dept. English, 1971-76. Editor: Anthology of Humanities Essays, 1997; contbr. articles to profl. jours. Lt. Infantry, 1960. Fulbright Rsch. and Tchg. grantee German Fulbright Commn., Oldenburg, Germany, 1988-89. Mem. MLA, Am. Name Soc. (bd. advisors 1986-88, v.p. 1999—, editor Names: A Journal of Onomastics 1988-92), New Chaucer Soc. Home: 119 N Yale St Vermillion SD 57069-2720 Office: Univ SD English Dept 414 E Clark St Vermillion SD 57069-2390

GASS, ARTHUR EDWARD, JR., chemist; b. Dallas, July 23, 1931; s. Arthur E. and Alice Elizabeth (Fooshee) G.; m. Gloria Jean Carter, Apr. 18, 1954; children: Kathleen, Mark E., Laura, Amy, Andrew C., Susan G. BS in Biology, So. Meth. U., 1953; MS in Biology, Trinity U., 1965. Registered med. technologist. Civilian rsch. chemist USAF Sch. Aerospace Medicine, San Antonio, 1959-75; sr. indsl. hygienist OSHA, U.S. Dept. Labor, Washington, 1975-89; mgr. health and safety Gassco Petroleum Corp., Seguin, Tex., 1989-95; instr. biology grad. sch. Trinity U., San Antonio, 1963-66. Author monograph on health hazards and prevention of cancer in rubber industry; contbr. 20 articles to tech. sci. jours. Presbyn. elder, 1976—; dir. San Antonio Cmty. Chs., 1995-98. Grantee USAF, Dept. Def., 1968-69, 71-72; recipient Rsch. Chemist Outstanding Civilian award USAF, 1967, Spl. Achievement awards U.S. Dept. Labor, 1977, 79, 87. Mem. Am. Chem. Soc., Am. Indsl. Hygiene Assn., Am. Conf. Govt. Indsl. Hygienists, Sigma Xi. Achievements include establishment of passive gut transport of chloride; development of federal field sanitation health standard; publication that promotes or protects health of 600,000 migrant workers on a yearly basis.

GASS, GERTRUDE ZEMON, psychologist, researcher; b. Detroit; d. David Solomon and Mary (Goldman) Zemon; m. H. Harvey Gass, June 19, 1938; children: Susan, Roger. BA, U. Mich., 1937, MSW, 1943, PhD, 1957. Lic. clin. psychologist, Mich. Mem. faculty Merrill-Palmer Inst., Detroit, 1958-69, lectr., 1967; mem. faculty Advanced Behavioral Sci. Ctr., Grosse Pointe, Mich., 1969-72; pvt. practice clin. psychology Birmingham, Mich., 1972—; adj. prof. psychology U. Detroit, 1969-75; cons. Continuum Ctr. Oakland U., Rochester, Mich., 1961-77, Traveler's Aid, Detroit, 1959-75; pres. Shapero Sch. Nursing, Detroit, 1967-72, cons. 1958-78; psychol. cons. Physician's Ins. Co. of Mich., 1988—, mgt. Mich. Bell Telephone, 1979-82. Mem. Adv. Com Sch. Needs, 1954-56; trustee Sinai Hosp. Detroit, 1972—; bd. dirs. Tribute Fund United Community Services, 1955-67. Fellow Am. Assn. Marriage-Family, Am. Orthopsychiatric Assn. (v.p. 1975-76), Mich. Psychol. Assn.; mem. Am. Psychol. Assn., Psychologists Task Force (v.p. 1977-84), Mich. Inter-Profl. Assn. (pres. 1976-78), Mich. Assn. Marriage Counselors (1979-80, pres. 1979-80), Mental Health Adv. Svc., Blue Cross and Blue Shield of Mich., Phi Kappa Phi, Pi Lambda Theta. Office: 30200 Telegraph Rd Bingham Farms MI 48025-4502

GASS, MANUS M., accountant, business executive; b. Montreal, Que., Can., June 28, 1928; came to U.S., 1948, naturalized, 1953; s. Maurice and Bertha (Silverberg) G.; m. Estella L. Gass; children: Thomas Evan, Winifred Caitlyn. Student, McGill U., 1945-48; B.B.A. cum laude, CCNY, 1953. CPA, N.Y. Pres., dir. Buitoni Foods Corp., South Hackensack, N.J., 1966-86; chief exec. officer Stavola Constrn. Inc., Tinton Falls, N.J., 1989—; dir. Buitoni Perugina Inc., N.Y.C., Perugina Chocolates & Confections Inc., Little Ferry, N.J.; acct. Am. Jewish Tercentenary Com., 1953-54. Chmn. River Edge-Oradell United Jewish Appeal, 1964-65, 67-76; mem. Shade Tree Commn., River Edge, 1987—; bd. govs. Hackensack Med. Center. Mem. Am. Inst. C.P.A.s, N.Y. State Soc. C.P.A.s, Fin. Execs. Inst. Home: 184 Woodland Ave River Edge NJ 07661

GASS, SAUL IRVING, educator; b. Chelsea, Mass., Feb. 28, 1926; s. Louis and Bertha Gass; m. Gertrude Gass, June 30, 1946; children: Ronald S., Joyce A. BS in Edn., Boston U., 1949, MA in Math., 1949; PhD in Engrng. Sci., U. Calif., Berkeley, 1965. Applied sci. rep. IBM, Washington, 1955-58; dir. ops. rsch. CEIR, Inc., Arlington, Va., 1959; mgr. project mercury IBM Fed. Systems, Gaithersburg, Md., 1960-63; mgr. civil programs IBM Fed. Systems, Gaithersburg, 1965-69; sr. v.p. World Systems Lab., Bethesda, Md., 1969-70; v.p. Mathematica, Inc., Bethesda, 1970-75; prof. U. Md., College Park, 1975—; cons. Nat. Inst. Std. and Tech., Gaithersburg, 1976—. Author: Linear Programming, 1958, Illustrated Guide to Linear Programming, 1970, Decision Making, Models and Algorithms, 1985; editor: Encyclopedia of Operations Research and Management Science, 1996. With U.S. Army, 1944-46. Fulbright scholar Fulbright Commn., 1995-96; recipient Steinhart Meml. award Ctr. of Naval Analysis, 1996, Kimball award Ops. Rsch. Soc. of Am., 1991. Mem. Assn. for Computing Machinery (coun. mem. 1960-62), Inst. for Ops. Rsch. and the Mgmt. Scis. (Expository Writing award 1997), Math. Assn. of Am., Soc. for Indsl. and Applied Math., Math. Programming Soc. Office: U Md College Park MD 20742

GASS, WILLIAM H., author, educator; b. Fargo, N.D., July 30, 1924; s. William Bernard and Claire (Sorensen) G.; m. Mary Patricia O'Kelly, 1952 (div.); children: Richard, Robert, Susan; m. Mary Alice Henderson, 1969; children: Elizabeth, Catherine. AB, Kenyon Coll., 1947, LHD (hon.), 1973, 85; PhD, Cornell U., 1953. Instr. philosophy Coll. of Wooster, Ohio, 1950-54; asst. prof. Purdue U., Lafayette, 1954-60, assoc. prof., 1960-66, prof. philosophy, 1966-69; prof. philosophy Washington U., St. Louis, 1969-79, David May Disting. Univ. prof. in humanities, 1979-99; dir. Internat. Writers Center, 1990—; vis. lectr. U. Ill., 1958-59; mem. Rockefeller Commn. on Humanities, 1978-80; mem. literature panel Nat. Endowment for the Arts, 1979-82. Author: Omensetter's Luck, 1966, In the Heart of the Heart of the Country, 1968, Willie Masters' Lonesome Wife, 1968, Fiction and the Figures of Life, 1970, On Being Blue, 1974, The World Within the Word, 1978, The Habitations of the Word: Essays, 1984, The Tunnel, 1995, Finding a Form, 1996, Cartesian Sonata, 1998, Reading Rilke, 1999; contbr. to periodicals including N.Y. Rev. of Books, N.Y. Times Book Rev., New Republic, TriQuar., Salmagundi, others. Office: Washington U Campus Box 1071 7425 Forsyth Blvd Saint Louis MO 63105-2161

GASSEL, PHILIP MICHAEL, lawyer; b. Chgo., June 5, 1947; s. Arnold and Claire (Segal) G.; m. Mollyann Pollak, Aug. 29, 1971; children: Miriam, Harry, Naomi. BS, Northwestern U., 1968; JD, Columbia U., 1972. Bar: N.Y. 1973, U.S. Dist. Ct. (ea. and so. dists.) N.Y. 1974, U.S. Ct. Appeal (2nd cir.) 1975, U.S. Supreme Ct. 1976. Sr. atty. N.Y.C. Dept. Consumer Affairs, 1972-74, Legal Svcs. for the Elderly, N.Y.C., 1974-79; assoc. Epstein Becker Borsody & Green P.C., N.Y.C., 1979-84; ptnr. Epstein Becker & Green P.C., N.Y.C., 1984—. Trustee Lincoln Square Synagogue, N.Y.C., 1978—. Mem. Am. Health Lawyers Assn., Assn. of Bar of City of N.Y. Office: Epstein Becker & Green PC 250 Park Ave New York NY 10177

GASSER, WILBERT (WARNER), JR., retired banker; b. Marquette, Mich., Apr. 5, 1923; s. Wilbert Warner and Mildred (Carpenter) G.; m. Mary C. Kratz, Dec. 6, 1952; 1 child, Wilbert Warner III. Student, Purdue U., 1941-42; BS in Bus., Ind. U., 1948. With Gary (Ind.) Nat. Bank (name changed later to Gainer Bank), 1948-92, v.p., 1953-63, chmn. bd., 1964-92, ret. Pres. Gary YMCA, 1960-62; treas. Gary Urban League, 1960-65, N.W. Ind. Heart Assn., 1961-64; bd. dirs., treas. Meth. Hosp., Gary. With USAAF, 1943-46. Mem. Gary C. of C. (v.p. 1961), Kiwanis (treas. Gary club 1963—). Presbyterian. Home: 149 Shore Dr Portage IN 46368-1015

GASSERE, EUGENE ARTHUR, lawyer, business executive; b. Beaumont, Tex., Oct. 20, 1930; s. Victor Eugene and Althea June (Haight) G.; m. Mary Alice Engelhard, Aug. 4, 1956; children—Paul, John, Anne. B.S., U. Wis., 1952, J.D., 1956; postgrad., Oxford U., 1956-57. Bar: Wis. bar 1956. Asst. counsel Wurlitzer Co., Chgo., 1958-61, Campbell Soup Co., Camden, N.J., 1961-65; asst. to pres. Thilmany Pulp & Paper Co., Kaukauna, Wis., 1966-68; with Skyline Corp., Elkhart, Ind., 1968-92, v.p., gen. counsel, asst. sec., 1973-92, ret., 1992—. Pres., bd. dirs. Elkhart Urban League, 1972-73, Elkhart Symphony, 1975-76, Elkhart Concert Club, 1976-77. Served with U.S. Army, 1952-54. Mem. Wis. Bar Assn., Phi Mu Alpha. Home: PO Box 165 Mindoro WI 54644-0165 Office: Skyline Corp 2520 Bypass Rd Elkhart IN 46514-1584

GASSERT, RICHARD ADAM, engineering company executive; b. Pinewald, N.J., Sept. 17, 1945; s. John A. and Grace E. Gassert; m. Moira M. Gassert, Sept. 15, 1971; children: Carla M., Deborah C., Lisa A. AS, SUNY; student, U. Va., 1963-65, Brevard Coll., LaSalle Coll. Materials mgr. Catalytic Inc., Phila., 1965-67, planning engr., 1967-74, project controls mgmt., 1976-87; planning supr. Chemico Cryogenics System Co., London, 1974-76; mgr. project controls/adminstrn. D&Z Internat., Inc., Phila., 1987-93, v.p. fin. and adminstrn., 1994-96, sr. v.p. project svcs., 1996-98; pres. GRASP Cons., Medford, N.J., 1998—. Contbr. articles to profl. jours. Recipient Silver Snoopy award NASA, 1968. Mem. Am. Assn. Cost Engrs., Constrn. Industry Inst. (bd. advisors).

GAST, ROBERT GALE, agriculture educator, experiment station administrator; b. Philadelphia, Mo., July 28, 1931; s. Fred W. and Lolabel (McPike) G.; m. Mary Lou Parrish, June 6, 1954; children: Regina Rae, Roger Eugene, Kimberly Kay. B.S., U. Mo., 1953, M.S., 1956, Ph.D., 1959. Asst. prof., assoc. prof. U. Tenn. AEC Agr. Research Lab., Oak Ridge, 1959-70; prof. soil sci. U. Minn., St. Paul, 1970-77; head dept. agronomy U. Nebr., Lincoln, 1977-83; dir. Agr. Expt. Sta., Mich. State U., East Lansing, 1983-95; chair Nat. Agrl. Biotech. Coun., 1993-94; acting v.p., v.p. for Rsch. and Graduate Studies Mich. State U., 1995-97. Editor: Jour. Environ. Quality, 1975-77. Served to 1st lt. USAF, 1953-55, Korea. Recipient Alumni award U. Mo., 1980. Fellow AAAS, Am. Soc. Agronomy (pres. 1987), Soil Sci. Soc. Am. (pres. 1982); mem. Clay Minerals Soc., AAAS, Agriculture Rsch. Inst. (pres. 1996), Sigma Xi. Presbyterian. Home: 3805 Viceroy Dr Okemos MI 48864-3844

GASTEYER, CARLIN EVANS, museum administrator, museum studies educator; b. Jackson, Mich., Mar. 30, 1917; d. Frank Howard and Marian (Spencer) Evans; student Barnard Coll., 1934-35; B.A., CUNY, 1983; m. Harry A. Gasteyer, Jan. 8, 1944; 1 dau., Nancy Catherine. Clk., First Nat. City Bank, 1939-42; statistician Bell Telephone Labs., 1942-45; dir. asst. S.I. Mus., 1956-61; bus. mgr. Mus. of the City of N.Y., 1961-63; mus. adminstr., 1963-66; asst. dir. Monmouth (N.J.) Mus., 1966-67, Mus. of City of N.Y., 1967-70; vice dir. adminstrn. Bklyn. Mus., 1970-74; dir. planning Snug Harbor Cultural Center, S.I., N.Y., 1975-79; cable TV Cons., 1980—; adj. lectr. mus. studies Coll. S.I. CUNY, 1985-94, asst. higher edn. officer, 1995, ret. 1995. Active Girl Scouts. Co-founder, pres. Jr. Mus. Guild, S.I. Mus., 1956-58. Mem. N.Y.C. Local Sch. Bd. 54, 1960-61. Mem. Am. Assn. Mus., Mus. Council of N.Y.C. Home: 50 Fort Pl Staten Island NY 10301-2415

GASTIL, RUSSELL GORDON, geologist, educator; b. San Diego, June 25, 1928; s. Russell Chester and Frances (Duncan) G.; m. Emily Janet Manly, Sept. 13, 1958; children—Garth Manly, Mary Margaret, George Christopher, John Webster. A.B, U. Calif. at Berkeley, 1950, Ph.D., 1954. With Shell Oil Co., 1954, Canadian Javelin Co., 1956-58; lectr. U. Calif. at Los Angeles, 1958-59; faculty San Diego State U., 1959—, prof. geology, 1965—, chmn. dept., 1969-72. Publisher: We Can Save San Diego, 1975; Contbr. papers to profl. lit. Democratic candidate U.S. Ho. of Reps., 1976; mem. Calif. Dem. Central Com., 1977-78; coordinator 41st Congl. dist. Common Cause, 1977; pres. Grossmont-Mt. Helix Improvement Assn., 1978-80; mem. San Diego County Air Pollution Hearing Bd., 1977-80. Fellow Geol. Soc. Am. (vice chmn. Cordilleran sect. 1967, gen. chmn. ann. meeting San Diego 1991); mem. AAAS, Soc. Econ. Mineralogists and Paleontologists, Am. Geophys. Union. Home: 9435 Alto Dr La Mesa CA 91941-4226 Office: San Diego State U Dept Geol Scis San Diego CA 92182

GASTON, CITO, former professional baseball manager; b. San Antonio, Mar. 17, 1944; m. Denise Gaston; children: Adrian, Carly, Shawn, Rochell. Grad. high sch., Corpus Christi, Tex., 1962. Player Atlanta Braves, 1967, 75-78, minor league coach, 1981; player San Diego Padres, 1969-74, Pitts. Pirates, 1978; hitting instr. Toronto (Can.) Blue Jays, 1982-89, mgr., 1989-97; mgr. Am. League All Star Team, 1994; exec. dir. Playdium, Mississauga, Can. Named to All-Star team, 1970. Office: Playdium, 99 Rathburn Rd W, Mississauga, ON Canada L5B 2C1*

GASTON, MARGARET ANNE, retired business educator; b. Regina, Sask., Can., Aug. 28, 1930; Came to U.S., 1948.; d. William Julius and Mary Josephine (Collins) Grogan; m. Robert F. Gaston, 1955 (dec. Mar. 1970); 1 child, Robert. BA in Bus. Edn., Cen. Wash. U., 1959; MEd, Western Wash. U., 1972; postgrad., Boston U., 1984. Cert. tchr. K-12, cert. vocat. tchr., Wash. Bus. educator Manson (Wash.) Sch. Dist., 1956-59; instr. K-12 Eastmont Sch. Dist., East Wenatchee, Wash., 1959-63; instr. Shoreline Community Coll., Seattle, 1969-70; instr., chmn. dept. bus. Skagit Valley Coll. Whidbey Campus, Oak Harbor, Wash., 1970-90; part-time instr. bus. edn. Wenatchee Valley Coll., 1959-65. Contbr. articles to profl. jours. Fellow Western Wash. U., Bellingham, 1968-69. Mem. AAUW, NEA, Wash. Edn. Assn., Bus. and Profl. Women, Delta Pi Epsilon, Beta Sigma Phi. Home: 118 S 12th St Mount Vernon WA 98274-4036

GASTON, MARILYN HUGHES, health facility administrator; b. Cin.; 2 children, Amy Marie, Damon Allen. AB in Zoology, Miami U., Oxford, Ohio, 1960; MD, U. Cin., 1964. Diplomate Am. Bd. Pediat. Intern Phila. Gen. Hosp., 1964-65; resident in pediat. Childrens Hosp. Med. Ctr., Cin., 1965-67, asst. dir. out-patient dept., 1967-68; asst. dir. out-patient dept. Convalescent Hosp. for Children, Cin., 1968-69; med. dir. Lincoln Heights (Ohio) Health Ctr., 1969-72; dir. Sickle Cell screening clinic Cin. Health Dept., 1972-76; med. expert Nat. Heart, Lung & Blood Inst./NIH, Bethesda, 1976-79; commd. 2d lt. USPHS, 1979-89; dir. divsn. medicine Bur. Health Professions, Rockville, Md., 1989-90; dir. Bur. Primary Health Care, Rockville, Md., 1990—; instr. pediat. U. Cin. Coll. Medicine, 1967-68, asst. clin. prof. divsn. cmty. pediat., 1968-70, asst. prof. pediat., 1970-76, assoc. prof. pediat., 1976-77; asst. clin. prof. pediat. Cin. Tech. Coll., 1974-76, Howard U. Coll. Medicine, 1978-91, Uniformed Svcs. U. the Health Scis., 1987—; attending pediatrician Childrens Hosp. Med. Ctr., 1969-76, attending pediatrician and clinician, 1969-76, dir. med. staff, 1969-76; attending pediatrician Bethesda Hosp., 1974-76; pediatrician Hosp. Albert Schweitzer, Deschapelles, Haiti, 1967; presenter, lectr. and spkr. in field. Author: A Bibliography: Comprehensive Sickle Cell Centers, 1977, (with C.L. Calhoun) 2d edit., 1981, Management and Therapy of Sickle Cell Disease, 1984, 88; (with others) Newborn Screening for Sickle Cell Disease and Other Hemoglobinopathies, 1989; contbr. articles to profl. jours. Med. advisor Sickle Cell Awareness Group, 1971-77, State Crippled Childrens Svcs., 1975-77; advisor Cin. Health Dept., 1971-76; co-chair Nat. Sickle Cell Dirs., 1974; chair black commd. officers retention subcom. USPHS, 1989—; bd. trustees Child Health assn., 1974-77; bd. dirs. U. Cin. Found., 1989—, George Washington U. Life Scis., 1993—, U. Md. Ctr. for Minority Rsch. External Adv. Bd., 1993—. Recipient Phyllis Wheatley award State of Ohio, 1975, Appreciation award Jack & Jill, Inc., 1975, Hildrus A. Poindexter award Pub. Health Svcs., 1990, Excellence award Pitts. Sickle Cell Soc., 1980, State of Ohio Govs. award, 1987, Disting. Alumnae award U. Cin., 1989, Pub. Health award D.C. Health Care for the Homeless Project, Inc.; named one of Outstanding Young Women in Am., 1973, Outstanding Black Women in Cin., 1974, Woman of Yr. in Medicine, Harriet Tubman Black Womens Dem., 1976, Woman of Yr., Cmty. Health Found., Fla., 1993; named to Temple Bible Coll. Hall of Fame, 1976, Ohio Womens Hall of Fame, 1990. Mem. AAAS, APHA, Am. Acad. Pediat., Nat. Assn. Med. Minority Educators, Nat. Med. Assn. (Lifing Legend award), Am. Soc. Hematology, Am. Pediat. Soc., Am. Med. Womens Assn., N.Y. Acad. Scis., Sigma Delta Epsilon, Alpha Kappa Alpha. Office: Bur of Primary Health Cre 4350 E West Hwy Fl 11 Bethesda MD 20814-4410*

GASTON, MICHAEL, library director. BA, U. Ala., 1976; MLS, U. Oreg., 1977. Dir. New Office for Vol. Action, Tuscaloosa, Ala., 1974-75; libr. Land County Adult Corrections, Eugene, Oreg., 1976-78; city libr. City of Florence, Oreg., 1978-85; dir. Siuslaw Libr. Dist., Florence, 1985-97; county libr. dir. Deschutes County, Bend, Oreg., 1997-99; dir. Deschutes Pub. Libr. Dist., Bend, 1999—; v.p. CoastNet, 1996-97; pres. Sch. of Librarianship U. Oreg., 1977. Editor OLA Quar., 1995. Exec. bd. mem. Pledge Campaign for Performing Arts Ctr., 1993. Named Florence Kiwanian of Yr. 1996. Mem. ALA, Oreg. Libr. Assn. (pres. 1989-90), Kiwanis Club (pres. 1985-86). Avocations: folk music, travel. E-mail: michaelgaston@deschutes.org. Office: Deschutes Pub Libr Dist 537 NW Wall St E Bend OR 97701

GASTON, PAUL E., professional basketball team executive; m. Dana Halsey; children: John and Peter (twins), Sarah. BA, Brown U., MA. Staff in fin. advertising and pub. rels. London; pres Brookwood Investments, N.Y.C.; chmn. of the bd. Boston Celtics Ltd., 1992—. Office: Celtics Ltd Partnership 151 Merrimac St Boston MA 02114-4714*

GASTON, PAUL LEE, academic administrator, English educator; b. Hattiesburg, Miss., Aug. 23, 1943; s. Paul Lee and Ruth (Gooch) G.; m. Eileen Margaret Higgins, June 29, 1968; children: Elizabeth, Tyler Lee. BA, S.E. La. U., 1965; MA, U. Va., 1966, PhD, 1970. Prof. English, So. Ill. U., Edwardsville, 1969-88, assoc. v.p., 1984-88; dean Coll. Arts and Scis. U. Tenn., Chattanooga, 1988-93; provost, exec. v.p. No. Ky. U., Highland Heights, 1993-99; provost Kent (Ohio) State U., 1999—; bd. dirs. Ky. Sci. and Tech. Coun. Author: W.D. Snodgrass, 1978, Concordance Conrad, Arrow of Gold, 1980; contbr. articles to profl. jours. Active in Episc. diocese of Lexington, 1990—. Fellow Soc. for Values in Higher Edn.; mem. Assn. Am. Colls. and Univs. (bd. dirs.), Covington (Ky.) Rotary, Phi Beta Kappa. Democrat. Avocations: softball, hiking, calligraphy. Home: 67 Covert Pl Fort Thomas KY 41075-1075

GASTON, RANDALL WALLACE, police chief; b. Lake Charles, La., Mar. 18, 1944; s. Wallace Howard and Mary Jean (Hubbs) G.; m. Linda Lou Lockwood; children: Debora Gaston Ricks, Aaron, Bryan, Allison. BS, Long Beach State Coll., 1971; MPA with honors, U. So. Calif., 1974; grad., FBI Nat. Acad., 1982. Police officer Anaheim (Calif.) Police Dept., 1965-69, police sgt., 1969-73, police lt., 1973-83, police capt., 1983-94, police chief, 1994—; instr. Orange County (Calif.) C.C.s, 1971-94. Mem. Internat. Police Chiefs Assn., Calif. Police Chiefs Assn., Orange County Police Chiefs Assn., FBI Nat. Acad. Assocs., Kiwanis Club of Greater Anaheim (bd. dirs. 1990-95), Phi Kappa Phi. Avocations: gardening, bicycling. Office: Anaheim Police Dept 425 S Harbor Blvd Anaheim CA 92805-3773

GATANAS, HARRY D., career officer; b. Bklyn., Mar. 21, 1947. Commd. officer U.S. Army, advanced through grades to brig. gen.; commdg. officer White Sands Missile Range U.S. Army, Whites Sands, N.Mex., 1998—. Office: US Army White Sands Missile Range White Sands NM 88002

GATCH, CHARLES EDWARD, JR., academic administrator; b. St. George, S.C., Feb. 26, 1939; m. Dolores Bull, Aug. 13, 1961; children: Michael and Jerald (twins), Victoria. BSEd, U. S.C., 1962; MMEd, La. State U., 1964; EdD in Adminstrn., U. S.C., 1991. Cert. supt., elem. prin., secondary prin., instrumental music tchr. Band dir. Westdale Elem. Sch., Baton Rouge, 1962-64; asst. prof. music edn. Campbell U., Buies Creek, N.C., 1964-70; grad. asst. La. State U., 1970-72; band dir. Episcopal High Sch., Baton Rouge, 1970-72; asst. prof. music edn. U. S.C., Columbia, 1972-74; prin. Pelion (S.C.) High Sch., 1974-77; tchr., band dir. part-time Oak Grove Elem. Sch., Lexington, S.C., 1977-78; tchr., choral dir. part-time Gilbert (S.C.) High Sch., 1977-78; prin. Lexington Mid. Sch., 1978-93; intern S.C. State Dept. of Edn., 1993-94; coord. student svcs. Lexington Sch. Dist. I, 1995—; part-time adminstrv. asst. dist. office Lexington County Sch. Dist. I, 1977-78, coord. tech. prep and at risk programs, 1994-96, coord. student svcs., 1996—; presenter Nat. NAESP Conv., 1987, SCASSP Conf., 1990; mem. prin. evaluation adv. com. S.C. State Dept. Edn. Com., 1984-87, trainer for new prins., 1985—; mem. adv. com. NTE Successor Project, 1989; mem. panel conf. on Preventing Teen Pregnancies and Enhancing Human Sexuality, 1985; mem. supt. internship program S.C. Dept. Edn. Leadership Acad., 1986; presenter U. Pa. Ethnography in Edn. rsch. Forum, 1987, Summer Leadershp Inst., Myrtle Beach, S.C., 1987, Leadership Acad., 1986, trained as an assessor, 1986. Site visitor Nat. Blue Ribbon Schs. Award, 1993; mem., adult choir dir. Lexington United Meth. Ch., 19 yrs., former mem. adminstrn. bd., former Sunday sch. tchr. grades 9-12 and adult Sunday sch., former youth choir dir.; dir. Columbia Youth Orch., 1978-83; prin. trombonist S.C. Philharm. Orch., 1983-84; participant Lexington musical revues Lexington County Arts Assn.; musical conductor Annie, 1989; musical dir. Lexington Musical Revue, 1973; dir. Lexington Bicentennial Chorus, 1976; judge state music competition Richland Sch. Dist. 2, 1985. Recipient Outstanding Contributions award S.C. ASCD, 1991, Nat. Disting. Prin. award S.C., 1987; named one of Outstanding Young Men of Yr., Jaycees, 1968. Mem. S.C. Mid. Sch. Assn. (pres. 1985-86, pres.-elect 1984-85, program com. 1981-82, 85, 86, presenter S.C. Leadership Acad. Workshop, prin. evaluation adv. com., SCASA rep. exec. com. for S.C. Alliance for Arts Edn.), S.C. Assn. Elem. and Mid. Sch. Prins. (presenter conf. for new prins. and asst. prins., program com. 1983 for Spring 1984 conf., Palmetto's finest com. 1983-84, judge 1985, 86, 90, program com. for workshop asst. prins. 1983, chmn. fin. com. 1986-87, entertainment com. for S.E. prins. conf. 1990, program participant discussion of EIA 1984), S.C. Assn. Mid. Level Prins. (chmn. winter conf. 1993, pres.-elect 1992-93, pres. 1993—, rep. SCASA legis. com.), PTA (life), Lexington Lions Club (2d v.p. 1985-86, 1st v.p. 1986-87, pres. 1987-88, zone chmn. 1988-89, 89-90, program chmn. Ladies Night 1985, chmn. Candy Day Sale 1984), Rotary Club Lexington. Avocations: jogging, golf, fishing, dance band leader, swing set jazz dance band. Home: 129 Foxglen Cir Lexington SC 29072-9199 Office: Lexington Sch Dist I PO Box 1869 Lexington SC 29071-1869*

GATCH, MILTON MCCORMICK, JR., library administrator, clergyman, educator; b. Cin., Nov. 22, 1932; s. Milton McCormick and Mary (Curry) G.; m. Ione Georganna White, Aug. 25, 1956; children: Ione Waite, Lucinda McCormick, George Crosby White. AB, Haverford Coll., 1953; student, U. Cin. Sch. Law, 1953-55; BD, Episc. Theol. Sch., Cambridge, Mass., 1960; MA, Yale U., 1961, PhD, 1963. Ordained priest Episc. Ch., 1961. Chaplain Wooster Sch., Danbury, Conn., 1963-64; chaplain, chair humanities dept. Shimer Coll., Mt. Carroll, Ill., 1964-67; assoc. prof. English No. Ill. U., DeKalb, 1967-68; prof. English U. Mo., Columbia, 1968-78, chair dept., 1971-74; prof. ch. history Union Theol. Sem., N.Y.C., 1978-98, acad. dean and provost, 1978-89, dir. Burke Libr., 1990-98; mem. coun. Coll. of Preachers, 1992-98; vis. fellow Emmanuel Coll., Cambridge, 1991; Bonhöffer vis. scholar Humboldt U., Berlin, 1998; fellow Pierpont Morgan Libr. Author: Death: Meaning and Mortality in Christian Thought and Contemporary Culture, 1969, Loyalties and Traditions: Man and His World in Old English Literature, 1971, Preaching and Theology in Anglo-Saxon England, 1977, So Precious a Foundation: The Library of Leander van Ess, 1996; contbr. numerous articles on antiquarian, medieval subjects. With U.S. Army, 1955-57. NEH sr. fellow, 1974-75. Fellow Soc. of Antiquaries London, Medieval Acad. Am. (del. to Am. Coun. Learned Socs. 1981-93); mem. ALA, Internat. Soc. Anglo-Saxonists (founding, mem. adv. bd. 1980-85), Am. Coun. Learned Socs. (bd. dirs. 1992-93), Early English Text Soc., Bibliog. Soc., Bibliog. Soc. Am., Am. Printing History Assn. (trustee 1995—), Century Assn., Grolier Club. Democrat. Avocations: book collecting, gardening, running. E-mail: mgatch@uts.columbia.edu.

GATELY, MARK DONOHUE, lawyer; b. Balt., Jan. 6, 1952; s. Bernard Patrick and Margret (Donahue) G.; m. Rosemary Connolly, Dec. 27, 1986; children: Maeve Donohue, Harry John Connolly, Fiona Anne McCourt. BA, U. Md., 1974, JD, 1977. Bar: Md. 1977, U.S. Dist. Ct. Md. 1978, U.S. Ct. Appeals (4th cir.) 1978, U.S. Ct. Appeals (D.C. cir.) 1981, D.C. 1982, U.S. Supreme Ct. 1994, U.S. Ct. Appeals (3d cir.) 1988, U.S. Dist. Ct. (D.C. cir.) 1991, U.S. Ct. Appeals (7th cir.) 1993. Law clk. to Hon. C. Stanley Blair U.S. Dist. Ct. Md., Balt., 1977-78; asst. atty. gen. Office Md. Atty. Gen., Balt., 1980-81; assoc. Miles & Stockbridge, Balt., 1978-84, ptnr., 1984—, chair litigation dept., 1992—. Fellow Internat. Acad. Trial Lawyers; mem. Order of the Coif. Office: Miles & Stockbridge 10 Light St Ste 1100 Baltimore MD 21202-1487

GATES, BARBARA T., English literature educator; b. Sheboygan, Wis., Aug. 4, 1936; d. Robert F. and Martha (Baker) Timm; children: Robert David, Thomas Edward. BA, Northwestern U., 1958; MA, U. Del., 1961; PhD, Bryn Mawr Coll., 1971. Lectr. in English, Widener Coll., Chester, Pa., 1965-67; asst. prof. English, U. Del., Newark, 1971-76, assoc. prof. English, 1976-88, prof. English, 1988-94; Alumni Disting. prof. English and women's studies U. Del., 1994—; exch. prof. Monash U., Melbourne, Australia, 1983, 90; vis. prof. U. Calif., Davis, 1986; cons. in excellence in tchg. and disting. acad. svc. Dept. Edn., Commonwealth of Pa.; lectr. in field. Mem. editl. adv. bd. Nineteenth-Century Studies, Australasian Victorian Studies Ann.; contbr. articles to profl. jours. Recipient Lindback award for excellence in tchg., 1974, E. Arthur Trabant award U. Del., 1992; named CASE Prof. of Yr., 1995; Danforth fellow, 1967-71, Danforth assoc., 1973—; grantee Am. Philos. Soc. 1976, DIMER, 1977, ACLS, 1979, NEH, 1981, 89, others. Mem. MLA, N.E. MLA, AAUP, Wordsworth-Coleridge Assn., Dickens Soc., Bronte Soc., Soc. for Values in Higher Edn., N.E. Victorian Studies Assn., Australasian Victorian Studies Assn., Nineteenth-century Studies Assn. Office: U Del Dept English Newark DE 19716

GATES, BRUCE CLARK, chemical engineer, educator; b. Richmond, Calif., July 5, 1940; s. George Laurence and Frances Genevieve (Wilson) G.; m. Jutta M. Reichert, July 17, 1967; children: Robert Clark, Andrea Margarete. BS, U. Calif., Berkeley, 1961; PhD in Chem. Engring., U. Wash., 1966. Rsch. engr. Chevron Rsch. Co., Richmond, Calif., 1967-69; from asst. prof. to assoc. prof. U. Del., Newark, 1969-77, prof. chem. engring., 1977-85, H. Rodney Sharp prof., 1985-92, assoc. dir. Ctr. Catalytic Sci. & Tech., 1977-81, dir. Catalytic Ctr. Sci. & Tech., 1981-88; prof. chem. engring. U. Calif., Davis, 1992—. Author: Catalytic Chemistry, 1992; co-author: Chemistry of Catalytic Processes, 1979; co-editor: Metal Clusters in Catalysis, 1986, Surface Organometallic Chemistry, 1988, Advances in Catalysis, 1996—. Fulbright Rsch. grantee Inst. Phys. Chemistry U. Munich, 1966-67, 75-76, 83-84, 90-91; recipient Sr. Rsch. award Humboldt Found., U. Munich, 1998, Sr. Humboldt Found. fellow Inst. Phys. Chemistry, U. Munich, 1998-99. Mem. AIChE (Alpha Chi Sigma award 1989, William H. Walker award 1995), Am. Chem. Soc. (Del. sect. award 1985, Petroleum Chemistry award 1993), Catalysis Soc. N.Am. (bd. dirs. 1997—). Achievements include research in catalysis, surface chemistry and reaction kinetics, chemical reaction engineering, petroleum and petrochemical proccesses, catalysis by solid acids, zeolites, soluble and supported transition-metal complexes and clusters, catalytic hydroprocessing. Office: U Calif Dept Chem Engring & Materials Sci Davis CA 95616

GATES, CHARLES CASSIUS, rubber company executive; b. Morrison, Colo., May 27, 1921; s. Charles Cassius and Hazel LaDora (Rhoads) G.; m. June Scowcroft Swaner, Nov. 26, 1943; children: Diane, John Swaner. Student, MIT, 1939-41; BS, Stanford U., 1943; DEng (hon.), Mich. Tech. U., 1975, Colo. Sch. of Mines, 1985. With Copolymer Corp., Baton Rouge, 1943-46; with Gates Rubber Co., Denver, 1946-96, v.p., 1951-58, exec. v.p., 1958-61, chmn. bd., 1961-96, CEO; chmn. bd. The Gates Corp., Denver, 1982-96, CEO, 1982-96, also bd. dirs.; pres. The Gates Corp., 1994-96; chmn. Cody Co., Denver, 1996—, Gates Capital Mgmt., LLC, Denver, 1996—; bd. trustees Gates Found. Trustee Denver Mus. Natural History, Calif. Inst. Tech., Pasadena, Denver Art Mus. Found., Graland Country Day Sch. Found. Recipient Cmty. Leadership and Svc. award Nat. Jewish Hosp., 1974; Mgmt. Man of Year award Nat. Mgmt. Assn., 1965; named March of Dimes Citizen of the West, 1987; inductee Colo. Bus. Hall of Fame, 1998. Mem. Conf. Bd. (dir.), Conquistadores del Cielo, Denver Country Club, Outrigger Canoe Club, Waialae Country Club, Boone and Crockett Club, Club Ltd., Old Baldy Club, Country Club of Colo., Roundup Riders of Rockies, Shikar-Safari Internat., Augusta Nat. Golf Club, Castle Pines Golf Club, The Wigwam Club. Office: Cody Co Ste 680 3773 Cherry Creek North Dr Denver CO 80209-3816

GATES, CHARLES W., SR., city official; b. Dayton, Ohio, Jan. 14, 1943; s. Theodore and Nellie M. (Black) G.; m. Nina J. Wright, Sept. 27, 1969;

children: Charles W. Jr., Stephanie L. BSBA, U. Dayton, 1965. Acct. NCR Corp., Dayton, 1966-68, asst. sect. head mktg. and acctg., 1968-70; asst. contr. Montgomery County Community Action Agy., Dayton, 1970; airport compt. City of Dayton, 1970-75, supt. airport adminstrn., 1975-89; dir. aviation fin. and adminstrn. City of Austin, Tex., 1989—. Sec. West Area YMCA, Dayton, 1979-89; bd. dirs. Dayton Area YMCA, 1985-89, Austin Area Urban League, 1992—. Recipient nat. achiever's award Airport Minority Adv. Coun., 1991, Outstanding Black in Govt. award BOSS, 1991. Mem. Am. Assn. Airport Execs., Airport Operators Coun. Internat. (econ. com. 1974—). Home: 8108 Forest Mesa Dr Austin TX 78759-8714 Office: Austin Dept Aviation 3600 Manor Rd Austin TX 78723-5801*

GATES, DONNA MARIE, special education educator; b. Milton, Fla., Dec. 14, 1961; d. Lawrence C. and Theresa M. (Bechard) Bonneau; m. David J. Gates, June 25, 1994; 1 child, Matthew. BS in Edn., Fitchburg State Coll., 1983; MEd, Wheelock Coll., 1997. Head counselor, counselor WAARC-Camp Joy, Worcester, Mass., 1977-81; house staff Cape Cod Summer Vacation Program, Hyannis, Mass., 1982; case mgr. NCM Friends of Retarded Coop. Apt. Program, Fitchburg, Mass., 1983; head tchr. May Inst., Chatham, Mass., 1983-85; tchr. Asabet Valley Collaborative Elem. Spl. Needs Program, Marlborough, Mass., 1985-88; primary resource tchr. Town of Auburn (Mass.), 1988—; tchr. Project Challenge Assabet Valley Collaborative, 1993. Mem. Mass. Tchrs. Assn., Nat. Assn. Edn. Young Children, Alpha Delta Kappa. Avocations: camping, hiking.

GATES, HENRY LOUIS, JR., English language educator; b. Keyser, W.Va., Sept. 16, 1950; s. Henry-Louis and Pauline Augusta (Coleman) G.; m. Sharon Lynn Adams, Sept. 1, 1979; children: Maude Augusta Adams, Elizabeth Helen-Claire. BA summa cum laude, Yale U., 1973; MA in English Lang. and Lit., U. Cambridge, Eng., 1974, PhD in English Lang. and Lit., 1979; hon. degrees, Darmouth Coll., 1989, U. W.Va., 1990, U. Rochester, 1990, U. W.Va., 1990, U. New Hampshire, 1991, Manhattan C.C., 1992, Bryant Coll., 1992, George Washington U., 1993, Williams Coll., 1993, U. Mass., Boston, 1993, Bates Coll., 1995, Maaclester Coll., 1995, Emory U., 1995, Colby Coll., 1995, Purchase Coll., 1995, Bard Coll., 1995, Bethany Coll., 1995, N.Y.U., Sch. Visual Arts, 1996, Haverford Coll., 1996, Nazareth Coll., 1996, U. Palacky, Czech Republic, 1996. Lectr. English and Afro-Am. studies Yale U., New Haven, 1976-79, asst. prof., 1979-84, assoc. prof., 1984-85; prof. English, comparative lit. and Africana studies, Cornell U., Ithaca, N.Y., 1985-88, W.E.B. DuBois prof. lit., 1988-90; John Spencer Bassett prof. English and Lit., Duke U., 1990-91; W.E.B. Du Bois prof. humanities, prof. English Harvard U., 1991—, chair Dept. of Afro-Am. Studies, 1991—, dir. W.E.B. Du Bois Inst., 1991—; pres. Afro-Am. Acad., 1984—. Author: Figures in Black, 1987, Signifying Monkey, 1988, Loose Canons, 1992, Colored People: A Memoir, 1994, (with Cornel West) The Future of the Race, 1996; editor: Black is the Color of the cosmos: Charles T. Davis's Essays on Black Literature and Culture, 1942-81, 1982, Our Nig, 1983, The Slave's Narrative, 1985, Black Literature and Literary Theory, 1985, Race, Writing, and Difference, 1986, The Classic Slave Narratives, 1987, The Souls of Black Folk, 1989, Reading Black, Reading Feminist, 1990, Bearing Witness, 1991; series editor: Oxford-Schomburg Library of 19th Century Black Women, 1988; co-editor: Encarta Africana Encyclopedia, 1999; co-editor, mem. editorial bd. Transition, 1991—; mem. editorial bd. Black Am. Lit. Forum, 1981-86, Am. Quar., 1981, Studies in Am. Fiction, 1981, Proteus, 1984—, Diacritics, 1985—, Publs. of MLA, 1987, Critical Inquiry, 1987, Cultural Critique A/B. Recipient MacArthur prize MacArthur Found., 1981—, Faculty prize Yale Afro-Am. Cultural Ctr., 1984, Am. Book award, 1989, Anisfield-Wolfe Book award, 1989, Zora Neale Hurston prize, 1986, George Polk award for social commentary, 1993, Lillian Smith Book award, Chgo. Tribune Heartland award, W. Virginian of Yr. award, 1994. Mem. Am. Acad. Arts and Scis., African Lit. Assn., Am. Studies Assn., MLA, Assn. for Study of Afro-Am. Life and History, Coll. Lang. Assn., PEN, Caribbean Studies Assn., Coun. on Fgn. Rels., Lincoln Ctr. Theater (bd. dirs.), Century Club, Elizabethan Club, Phi Beta Kappa. Episcopalian. Avocations: jazz, pocket billiards. Office: Harvard U Dept Afro-Am Studies Barker Ctr 12 Quincy St Cambridge MA 02138-3804

GATES, HERBERT STELWYN, retired obstetrician-gynecologist; b. Washington, Aug. 19, 1933; s. Herbert Stelwyn Sr. and Pearl Wiltshire Gates; m. Diane Dickson, June 23, 1956; children: Herbert S. III, Susan Gates Taylor, Robert Paul. AB, Duke U., 1954; MD, George Washington U., 1958. Diplomate Am. Bd. Ob-Gyn. Pvt. practice obstetics-gynecology McLean and Norfolk, Va., 1964-81; prof. ob-gyn. Oral Roberts U., Tulsa, 1981-86, prof., chmn. ob-gyn., 1988-89; assoc. prof. ob-gyn. U. Md., Balt., 1987-88; prof. ob-gyn. East Carolina, Greenville, N.C., 1989-95; assoc. chief of staff Overton Brooks VA Hosp., Shreveport, La., 1995-98; ret., 1998; chief of staff DePaul Hosp., Norfolk, 1978-79; cons. in ob-gyn. King Fahd Nat. Guard Hosp., Rihadh, Saudi Arabia, 1995. Lt. comdr. USPHS, 1962-64. Recipient Colposcopy Recognition award Am. Soc. for Colposcopy and Cervical Pathology, 1992, award of merit Am. Soc. for Colposcopy and Cervical Pathology, 1996. Fellow Am. Coll. Ob-Gyn.; mem. AMA (Physicians Recognition award 1996), Am. Mensa Ltd., Masons. Avocations: amateur radio, flying, action and practical pistol competition. E-mail: hgates@mail.clis.com. Home: 7016 Ocean Dr Emerald Isle NC 28594

GATES, JAMES DAVID, retired association executive, consultant; b. East Cleveland, Ohio, July 9, 1927; s. James Adelbert and Margaretta (Voigt) G.; m. Carol Marie Schreiber, June 9, 1956; children: David, Keith, Robert. AB, Hiram (Ohio) Coll., 1951; MA, Columbia, 1956; EdD, George Washington U., 1975. Tchr. Maple Heights (Ohio) City Schs., 1951-61; profl. asst. Nat. Council Tchrs. Math., Reston, Va., 1961-63; exec. sec. Nat. Council Tchrs. Math., 1963-76, exec. dir., 1976-95; mem. faculty U. Va., 1963-66, George Washington U., 1966-75; assoc. dir. Math. Scis. Edn. Bd., Ctr. for Sci., Math., and Engring. Edn., Nat. Rsch. Coun. Served with AUS, 1945-46. Fellow AAAS; mem. NEA, Nat. Coun. Tchrs. Math., Math. Assn., Am., Rotary. Home: 11303 Fieldstone Ln Reston VA 20191-3905

GATES, JEFF, writer; b. Chgo., Mar. 4, 1946; s. James Edward and Harriet Reed G.; m. Jeffrey Jr., Erin Christine, Michael Taylor. BA, U. Va., 1968; JD, U. Calif., San Francisco, 1975. Bar: Calif. Counsel Hewitt Assocs., Chgo., 1978-80, U.S. Sentate Com. Fin., Washington, 1980-87; of counsel Finley, Kumble, Washington, 1987-88; counsel Kelso & Co., N.Y.C., 1988-90; ptnr. Powell, Goldstein, Frazer & Murphy, Washington, 1990-92; pres. The Gates Group, Atlanta, 1992—, Shared Capitalism Inst., Atlanta, 1998—. Author: the Ownership Solution, 1998. 1st lt. U.S. Army, 1968-70. Home: # 284 1266 West Paces Ferry Rd Atlanta GA 30327

GATES, LAURA JEAN CUMMINGS, journalist; b. Mpls., Oct. 18, 1975; d. Donn Paul and Tanya Laverne (Saracoff) Cummings; m. William David Gates, July 13, 1996. BA in Journalism, Ball State U., 1996. Editl. intern Kokomo (Ind.) Tribune, 1995; gen. assignment reporter The Muncie (Ind.) Star, 1995-96; bus./govt./edn. reporter The Daily Ledger, Noblesville, Ind., 1997-99; freelance writer, Indpls., 1996—. Mem. Soc. Profl. Journalists. Avocations: photography, scuba diving.

GATES, LISA, private chef, caterer; b. Washington, July 11, 1955; d. Chester Robert and Peggy Jean (Dalton) Gates; m. Sergio Vivoli, Nov. 3, 1978 (div. Nov. 1984); m. Mitchell Cohen, Sept. 21, 1987 (div. Febr. 1995). AA, Fleming Coll., Florence, Italy, 1974. Dir. The Am. Sch. in Switzerland, Lugano, 1974-80; counter person Bar Gelateria Vivoli, Florence, 1978-80; costumer, choreographer, scene designer English Theatre of Florence, 1978; tchr. Dance Sch. Theatre, Florence, 1978-81; sec., treas. Vivoli Da Firenze, Inc., L.A., 1981-82; event coord. Calif. Catering Co., Beverly Hills, Calif., 1983; chef, sales rep. St. Germain To Go, West Hollywood, Calif., 1984; chef, cons. Posh Affair Catering Co., L.A., 1984-87; owner, chef, party planner Lisa Gates-Vivoli Catering, L.A., 1985—; catering mgr. Maple Drive Restaurant, Beverly Hills, 1990-91; pvt. chef, 1991—. Mem. Mus. Contemporary Art, L.A., L.A. County Mus. Art, L.A. Music Ctr. Unified Fund. Recipient Outstanding Achievement in Art award Bank of Am., Miraleste, Calif., 1972. Mem. Am. Inst. Wine and Food, Roundtable for Women in Foodsvc., Women Chefs and Restaurateurs. Democrat. Avocation: dance, dining, music. Home and Office: 1227 N Orange Grove Ave West Hollywood CA 90046-5311

GATES, MAHLON EUGENE, applied research executive, former government official, former army officer; b. Tyrone, Pa., Aug. 21, 1919; s. Samuel Clayton and Elsie (Nieweg) G.; m. Esther Boone Campbell, July 4, 1972; children by previous marriage: Pamela Townley, Lawrence Alan. B.S., U.S. Mil. Acad., 1942; M.S., U. Ill., 1948; postgrad., Command and Gen. Staff Coll., 1957, Army War Coll., 1962, Harvard U., 1965. Commd. 2d lt. U.S. Army, 1942, advanced through grades to brig. gen., 1966; area engr. Iran, Gulf Dist., 1960-61; chief, engr. br., officer Personnel Directorate, Dept. Army, 1963-64; gen. staff Dept. Army, 1964-66; comdg. gen. Cam Ranh Bay, Vietnam, 1966-67; dir. constrn. Vietnam, 1967; dir. research, devel. and engring. Army Materiel Command, Washington, 1971; ret., 1972; mgr. Nev. ops. office AEC now Dept. Energy, Las Vegas, 1972-82; sr. v.p. S.W. Rsch. Inst., San Antonio, 1982-89, ret., 1989; leader U.S. sci. tesm to N.W. Territories during recovery ops. for crashed nuclear-powered Russian satellite, 1978. Past pres. Boulder Dam Area council Boy Scouts Am.; past chmn. adv. bd. Clark County Community Coll. Decorated D.S.M., Legion of Merit, Bronze Star, Air medal; Army Distinguished Service Order 1st class Govt. Vietnam; Meritorious Service award; named Meritorious Exec. ERDA. Home: 1 Towers Park Ln Apt 2011 San Antonio TX 78209-6439 *Cherish the past; do not worship it.*

GATES, MARSHALL DEMOTTE, JR., chemistry educator; b. Boyne City, Mich., Sept. 25, 1915; s. Marshall DeMotte and Virginia (Orton) G.; m. Martha Louise Meyer, Sept. 9, 1941; children—Christopher David, Catharine Louise, Marshall DeMotte III, Virginia Alice. B.S., Rice Inst., 1936, M.S., 1938; Ph.D., Harvard, 1941; D.Sc. (hon.), MacMurray Coll., 1963. Asst. prof. chemistry Bryn Mawr Coll., 1941-43; vis. prof. Harvard, 1946; assoc. prof., 1947-49, Max Tishler lectr., 1953; tech. aid NDRC, 1943-46; lectr. chemistry U. Rochester, 1949-52, part-time prof., 1952-60, prof., 1960-68, Charles Frederick Houghton prof. chemistry, 1968-81, prof. emeritus, 1981—; Welch Found. lectr., 1960; adv. bd. Chem. Abstracts Services, 1974-76; vis. prof. Dartmouth Coll., 1982, 84, 85, 86; charter fellow Coll. Problems Drug Dependence, 1992—. Mem. com. on drug addiction and narcotics, div. med. scis. NRC, 1956-70, also com. on organic nomenclature div. of chemistry; mem. Pres.'s Com. on Nat. Medal of Sci., 1968-70. Recipient Edward Peck Curtis award for excellence in undergrad. teaching, 1967; Armed Services cert. of appreciation, 1946; Disting. Alumnus award Rice U., 1986. Fellow Am. Acad. Arts and Scis., N.Y. Acad. Scis.; mem. Am. Chem. Soc. (editor Jour. 1963-69), Nat. Acad. Scis. Achievements include first synthesis of morphine, 1952. Office: U Rochester Chemistry Dept Rochester NY 14627

GATES, MARTINA MARIE, food products company executive; b. Mpls., Mar. 19, 1957; d. John Thomas and Colette Clara (Luetmer) G. BSBA in Mktg. Mgmt. cum laude, Coll. St. Thomas, 1984, MBA in Mktg., 1987. Tchrs. asst. Mpls. Area Vocat. Tech. Inst., Mpls., 1978-79; sec., regional sales mgr. Internat. Multifoods, Mpls., 1979, sec. bakery mix, mktg. mgr., 1979-80, sec., v.p. sales and new bus. devel., 1980, customer svc. rep. regional accounts, 1980-81, customer svc. rep. nat. accounts, 1981-82, credit coordinator indsl. foods div., 1982-85, asst. credit mgr. consumer foods div., 1985, advt./sales promotion mgr. indsl. foods div., 1985-86, asst. credit mgr. fast food and restaurant div., 1986-87, dir. devel. USA and Can. franchise area, 1987-89; dir. franchise devel. FIRSTAFF, Inc., Mpls., 1989-90; dir. adminstrn. Robert Half Internat., Inc., Mpls., 1990-94; dir. client svcs. The NPD Group, Inc., Chgo., 1994—. Vol. seamstress Guthrie Theater Costume Shop, Mpls., 1975—; alumni mem. New Coll. Student Adv. Council St. Thomas, St. Paul, 1984—; vol. Mpls. Aquatennial, 1987. Mem. Omicron Delta Epsilon. Avocations: golf, fine arts, needlework, tennis, skiing.

GATES, MILO SEDGWICK, retired construction company executive; b. Omaha, Apr. 25, 1923; s. Milo Talmage and Virginia (Offutt) G.; m. Anne Phleger, Oct. 14, 1950 (dec. Apr. 1987); children: Elena Motlow, Susan Gates, Virginia Lewis, Anne Symington, Milo T.; m. Robin Templeton Quist, June 18, 1988; stepchildren: Robert L. Quist, Catherine Quist, Sarah Mazzocco. Student, Calif. Inst. Tech., 1943-44; B.S., Stanford U., 1944, MBA, 1948. With Swinerton & Walberg Co., San Francisco, 1955—, pres., 1976—, chmn., 1988-96; ret. Bd. dirs., trustee Children's Hosp. San Francisco; trustee Grace Cathedral, San Francisco; bd. dirs. Calif. Acad. Scis. Lt. (j.g.), USNR, 1944-46. Mem. Pacific-Union Club, Bohemian Club. Republican. Home: 7 Vineyard Hill Rd Woodside CA 94062-2531

GATES, MIMI GARDNER, museum administrator. Dir. Seattle Art Mus., Wash. Office: Seattle Art Museum PO Box 22000 Seattle WA 98122-9700*

GATES, RICHARD DANIEL, retired manufacturing company executive; b. Trenton, Mo., Mar. 27, 1942; s. Daniel G. and Effie White (Johnson) G.; m. Jean Gates, Jan. 26, 1966; 1 child, Daniel Wright. B.S., U. Mo., 1964; M.C.S., Rollins Coll., Winter Park, Fla., 1968; postgrad., Harvard U., 1976. Mgmt. assoc. Western Electric Co., N.Y.C., 1964-66; bus. mgmt. adminstr. Martin Marietta Aerospace Co., Orlando, Fla., 1966-68; chief indsl. engring. Martin Marietta Aerospace Co., 1968-69; fin. analyst Martin Marietta Co., N.Y.C., 1969-70; sr. acct. Martin Marietta Co., 1970-71; controller Dragon Cement Co., div. Martin Marietta Co., 1971-72, N.E. div. Martin Marietta Aggregates Co., 1972-73; asst. controller, then asst. treas. Rubbermaid, Inc., Wooster, Ohio, 1973-79; treas. Rubbermaid Inc., 1979-80, v.p., treas., 1980-91, sr. v.p., bus. deve., investor rels. and corp. communications, 1991-98; ret., 1998; pres. The Rubbermaid Found., Wooster. Mem. Wooster City Fin. Task Force, All Am. City Com.; chmn. Wooster Growth Assn.; active local Cub Scouts.; adviser Art Center, chmn. maj. indsl. capital campaign Boy Scouts Camp; trustee, chmn. Wayne Ctr. Arts; mem. parents' com. St. Paul's Sch., Wesleyan U. Mem. Nat. Assn. Corporate Treas., Main St. Wooster Inc. (bd. trustees), Beta Gamma Sigma, Omicron Delta Kappa. Clubs: Harvard Bus. Sch, Wooster Country (bd. dirs.). Home: Apt 5317 6110 W Pleasant Ridge Rd Arlington TX 76016-4307

GATES, STEPHEN FRYE, lawyer, business executive; b. Clearwater, Fla., May 20, 1946; s. Orris Allison and Olga Betty (Frye) G.; m. Laura Daignault, June 10, 1972. BA in Econs., Yale U., 1968; JD, Harvard U., 1972, MBA, 1972. Bar: Fla. 1972, Mass. 1973, Ill. 1977, Colo. 1986. Assoc. Choate Hall & Stewart, Boston, 1973-77; atty. Amoco Corp., Chgo., 1977-82; gen. atty. Amoco Corp., 1982-86; regional atty. Amoco Prodn. Co., Denver, 1987-88; asst. treas. Amoco Corp., Chgo., 1988-91, assoc. gen. counsel, corp. sec., 1991-92; v.p. Amoco Chem. Co., 1993-95; v.p., gen. counsel Amoco Corp., Chgo., 1995-98; exec. v.p., group chief of staff BP Amoco p.l.v., London, 1998—; bd. dirs. Nat. Legal Ctr. Pub. Interest, Wash., 1999—. Nat. trustee Newberry Libr., Chgo., 1998—; bd. dirs. Chgo. Sister Cities Internat. Program, Inc., Friends of Prentice Hosp.; mem. adv. coun. Chgo. Schweitzer Urban Fellows Program, 1996—; mem. adv. bd. Chgo. Vol. Legal Svcs., Found., 1996-98; mem. Chgo. Crime Commn., 1997-98. Knox fellow, 1972-73. Mem. ABA, Am. Soc. Corp. Secs., Univ. Club, Mid-Am. Club, Yale Club. Office: BP Amoco plc, 1 Finsbury Circus, London EC2M 7BA, England

GATES, SUSAN INEZ, magazine publisher; b. San Francisco, Jan. 14, 1956; d. Milo Sedgwick and Anne (Phelger) G. BA in English/French magna cum laude, U. Colo., 1978; MS in Journalism, Columbia U., 1983. With GEO Mag., N.Y.C., 1978-79, New York mag., N.Y.C., 1981-82; dir. Ladd Assocs., N.Y.C., 1983-85, McNamee Cons., N.Y.C., 1986-88; founding pub. BUZZ mag., L.A., 1989-97; co-chmn. Mind Over Media, Sherman Oaks, Calif., 1997—. Contbg. writer San Francisco Chronicle and Examiner Book Rev., 1983-86. So. Calif. adv. bd. Natural Resources Def. Coun., L.A., 1989—. Mem. Advt. Club of L.A. (bd. dirs. 1995—), Phi Beta Kappa.

GATES, THEODORE ALLAN, JR., database administrator; b. Washington, May 24, 1933; s. Theodore Allan and Margaret (Camp) G.;m. Anne Bissell, Sept. 8, 1955; children: Virginia Anne, Nancy Bissell, Theodore Allan III (dec.), Margaret Kenyon. Student, U. Md., 1951-53, 56-57, 68-69. Mem. staff Arthur D. Little Sys., Burlington, Mass., 1976-77, Corp. Tech. Planning, Portsmouth, N.H., 1977-78; project mgr. Honeywell Info. Sys., Phoenix, 1978-81; tech. mgr. Honeywell Info. Sys., Seattle, 1981-83; mgr. data and software engring. ISC Sys. Corp., Spokane, Wash., 1983-90; project mgr. Boeing Computer Svcs., Richland, Wash., 1990-96, The Boeing Co., Bellevue, Wash., 1996—. With U.S. Army, 1953-56, Korea. Recipient Superior Performance award Census Bur., 1958. Mem. Air Force Assn., U.S. Naval Inst., Smithsonian Assocs., Internat. Oracle Users Group, Mus. of Flight, Commodores Club (Boston), Masons, Shriners. Lutheran. Avocations: photography, sailing, music. Home: 3208 168th Pl SE Bellevue WA 98008-5730 Office: The Boeing Co M/S 7W-43 PO Box 3707 Seattle WA 98124-2207

GATES, THOMAS EDWARD, civil engineer, waste management administrator; b. Tachikawa AFB, Japan, June 25, 1953; came to U.S., 1954; s. Harold Charles and Masako (Endo) G. BS, Kans. State U., 1979, MS, 1981; postgrad., Seattle U., 1998—. Registered profl. engr., Wash., Kans., Alaska. Advt. salesman Junction City (Kans.) Daily Union, 1972-74; co-op student Burns & McDonnell, Kansas City, Mo., 1975-76; state insp. Riley County Pub. Works, Manhattan, Kans., 1977-78, field supr., 1978, cons., 1979; grad. rsch. asst. Kans. State U., Manhattan, 1979-81; engr. Battelle Pacific N.W. Labs., Richland, Wash., 1981-83, rsch. engr., 1983-85; sr. rsch. engr. Battelle Pacific N.W. Labs., Richland, 1985-86; mgr. waste package projects BWIP, 1986-88, acting mgr. support projects, 1988; mgr. for def. programs Westinghouse Hanford Co., Richland, 1988-89, staff mgr. engring. and devel. divs., 1990, mgr. tech. assessment and application, 1990-91, mgr. tech. demonstration program ops., 1991-94; mgr. Sonalysts, Inc., Kennewick, Wash., 1994-97, PLG, Inc., Richland, 1997-98; cons. Elec. Power Rsch. Inst., Washington, Atomic Energy of Can., Ltd. Rsch. Co., Ottawa, Can.; lead judge Wash. State Sci. Talent Search, Richland, 1985-90; chmn. Wash. State Solid Waste Adv. Com., 1996-98. Contbr. 7 articles to profl. jours., 14 tech. reports; session works, obtaining accelerated data on concrete degradation, 1981, concrete durability and degradation processes, 1986, Wash. state air transp. com., 1993-94. Councilman City of Richland, 1988-93, mayor, 1990; mem. Phys. Planning Com., Richland, 1982-87, chmn., 1984-87; instr. Christian catechism doctrine Christ The King Ch., Richland, 1981-82; bd. dirs. Salvation Army Adv. Coun., Richland, 1987-89, chmn., 1988-89; vice chmn., program chmn. Benton-Franklin Cmty. Action Com., Pasco, Wash., 1988-89, bd. dirs., 1992-93; mem. bd. March of Dimes, Junction City, Kans., 1976-80, Walk-A-Thon, 1973-80, campaign chmn., 1978-79, chmn. bd., 1979-80; chmn. dept. campaign United Way, Richland, 1984; bd. dirs. Assn. Wash. Cities, 1990-93, mem. resolution com., 1989-91, mem. legis. com., 1989-92, mem. energy adv. com., 1990-93, mem. local govt. adv. com., 1990-93, mem. mcpl. rsch. coun., 1991-93; mem. Benton County Solid Waste Adv. Com., 1990-98, chmn., 1990-98; mem. hazardous materials mgmt. tech. adv. com. Columbia Basin Coll., 1990-95, chmn., 1991-95. Mem. ASCE (tech. coun. on computer practices pub. com. 1986-96), Am. Concrete Inst. (tech. com. on computers 1983—, com. on radioactive and hazardous waste mgmt. 1983—, com. on student activities 1984—, com. on concrete nuclear structures subcoms. 1 and 4 1996—, Harry F. Thomson scholar 1980), Kiwanis Club of Richland (disting. pres. 1995-96), KC (Sir Knight of Yr. 1992). Roman Catholic. Avocations: gardening, woodworking, reading. Home: 2302 151st St E Tacoma WA 98445-3421 Office: Seattle U Sch Law 950 Broadway Tacoma WA 98402-4470

GATES, WALTER EDWARD, small business owner; b. Glens Falls, N.Y., Aug. 15, 1946; s. William B. and Dawn K. (Preston) G.; m. Toni A. Naren, June 26, 1945; children: Lindsey Erin, Ryan Walter. BS, SUNY, Albany, 1968; EdM, Boston U., 1972; MBA, Harvard U., 1974. Asst. mgr. Wilson Sporting Goods Inc., River Grove, Ill., 1974-76; mgr. Wilson Sporting Goods Inc., River Grove, 1976-79; dir. Pizza Hut Inc., Wichita, Kans., 1979; sr. dir. Pizza Hut Inc., Wichita, 1979-80, v.p., 1980-82, sr. v.p., 1982-85; exec. v.p. Rent-A-Ctr. Inc., Wichita, 1985-86, pres., chief operating officer, 1986-87, pres., chief exec. officer, chief operating officer, 1987-92; pres., CEO THORN Americas, 1991, chmn., CEO, 1992-96; CEO Gates Enterprises, Wichita, 1996—; pres., CEO Gates Enterprises, 1985—. Bd. dirs. Wichita Symphony, 1984-87, Wichita Children's Theater, 1984-87; active Wichita Music Theatre, 1987—, Boy Scouts of Am., 1989—. Mem. Wichita C. of C. Avocations: skiing, water skiing, golf. Office: Bldg 2100-3 8100 E 22nd St N Ste 2100-3 Wichita KS 67226-2330*

GATES, WILLIAM HENRY, III, software company executive; b. Seattle, Wash, Oct. 28, 1955; s. William H. and Mary M. (Maxwell) G.; m. Melinda French, January 1, 1994. Grad. high sch., Seattle, 1973; student, Harvard U., 1975. With MITS, from 1975; founder, chmn. bd. Microsoft Corp., Redmond, Wash., 1976—, now also chief exec. officer. Author: The Future, 1994, The Road Ahead, 1996. Recipient Howard Vollum award, Reed Coll., Portland, Oreg., 1984, Nat. medal Tech. U.S. Dept. Commerce Tech. Adminstrn., 1992; named CEO of Yr., Chief Executive mag., 1994. Office: Microsoft Corp 1 Microsoft Way Redmond WA 98052-8300

GATEWOOD, BARBARA J., medical legal consultant, lawyer; b. Akron, Ohio, June 4, 1954; d. Nicholas and Olive (Jones) Rusyn; m. Paul D. Gatewood, Aug. 7, 1987; children: Elizabeth Anne, Joseph Paul. RN, Akron City Hosp., 1975; BA, U. Akron, 1985, JD, 1988. RN, Ohio; bar: Ohio 1989. Asst. head nurse/surg. nurse Akron City Hosp.; staff nurse Canton (Ohio) Aultman Hosp.; med. legal cons. Akron. Mem. ABA, Am. Soc. Law and Medicine, Ohio Bar Assn., Cleve. Bar Assn., Akron Bar Assn., Akron City Hosp. Sch. Nursing Alumni Assn., Summit County Med. Soc. Aux., U. Akron Sch. Law Alumni Assn., Soc. of Law and Medicine, Phi Alpha Delta.

GATEWOOD, JUDITH ANNE, roofing company administrator; b. Wichita, Kans., May 28, 1944; d. Alec Hunter and Mary Louise (Grecian) Stratton; m. Charles Eugene Gatewood, Jan. 26, 1962; children: Lori Lynn Gatewood Murphy, Charles Hunter Gatewood. Cert. bus. communication, Topeka High Sch., 1983, cert. micro-computer ops., 1986; cert., Kaw Area Tech. Sch., 1999. Clk. typist State of Kans., Topeka, 1964; exec. sec. H.M. Goodman and Co., Topeka, 1965-71; payroll supr. Hwy. Oil, Inc., Topeka, 1971-95; co-owner, corp. sect.-treas. Gatewood Roofing, Inc., Topeka, 1983—; office mgr. HouseMasters LLC, Remodeling Co., 1995—. Commr. Mayor's Commn. Status of Women, Topeka, 1987-93, elected chair, 1990-91; Fortune 100 mem. Everywoman's Resource Ctr., 1993-97; deacon Westminster Presbyn. Ch., 1993. Recipient cert. appreciation Washburn Rural H.S., 1999. Mem. NAFE (charter), Am. Bus. Women's Assn. (pres. Panache chpt. 1985-86, echo chpt. 1984-85, sec.-treas. Topeka area coun. 1987-88, v.p. exec. chpt. 1988-90, Woman of Yr. Echo chpt. 1984, Exec. chpt. 1990, 96, sec. Exec. chpt. 1996-97, Star in Your Crown award Nat. Hdqrs. 1985, chmn. bull. receiving West Ctrl. Spring Conf. 1986, pres. area coun. 1990-91, elected gen. chair West Ctrl. Spring Conf. of 1994, pres. Exec. chpt. 1989-90, 97-98, nat. v.p. dist. III 1994-95, Amb. 1998—), Pi Tau Omega. Democrat. Presbyterian. Avocations: collecting demitasse cups, plates. Home and Office: 3829 SE 23rd Ter Topeka KS 66605-1804

GATEWOOD, ROBERT PAYNE, financial planning executive; b. Nebr., Mar. 4, 1923; s. Robert Harvey and Bess (Payne) G.; m. Marilyn Wengert, June 6, 1946; children: Robert, Lottie, Traber, Cy, Marilyn, Bess, John, Anthony, Judemarie, Anne, Tressa, Joseph, Ruth. BS, U.S. Naval Acad., 1946; postgrad. La. State U., 1974. CLU. Estate planner J.D. Marsh & Assocs., 1950-56; pres. estate planning Fin. Corp. Am., 1956-61; pres. Robert P. Gatewood & Co., specialists in tax and estate planning, 1961—; internat. lectr.; mem. sales execs. adv. bd. Inst. Ins. Mktg., La. State U., 1970-79. Contbr. articles to profl. jours. Bd. dirs. Planned Giving Coun. Palm Beach. Served with USN, 1946-50. Recipient Bernard L. Wilner Meml. award. Mem. D.C. Assn. Life Underwriters (pres. 1965-66), Assn. Advanced Life Underwriting, Million Dollar Round Table, Am. Soc. CLUs & Chartered Fin. Cons. (pres. 1975-76), Washington D.C. Estate Planning Coun., East Coast Estate Planning Coun., Fla. Assn. CLUs and ChFCs, Palm Beach Assn. Life Underwriters, 25 Million Dollar Internat. Forum (founder), Knights of Malta. Republican. Roman Catholic. Home: 1171 N Ocean Blvd Delray Beach FL 33483-7273

GATEWOOD, WILLARD BADGETT, JR., historian; b. Pelham, N.C., Feb. 23, 1931; s. Willard Badgett and Bessie Lee (Pryor) G.; m. Mary Lu Brown, Aug. 9, 1958; children: Willard Badgett III, Elizabeth Ellis. BA, Duke U., 1953, MA, 1954, PhD, 1957. Asst. prof. history East Tenn. State U., 1957-58, East Carolina U., 1958-60; assoc. prof. N.C. Wesleyan Coll., 1960-64; prof. U. Ga., 1964-70; Alumni Disting. prof. history U. Ark., 1970-98, ret., 1998, provost and chancellor, 1984-85. Author: Theodore Roosevelt and the Art of Controversy, 1970, Smoked Yankees, 1971, Black Americans and the White Man's Burden, 1975, Slave and Freeman, 1979, Free Men of Color, 1982, Aristocrats of Color, 1990, Arkansas Delta, 1993; mem. bd. editors Ga. Rev., 1968-70, Jour. Negro History, 1972-74, Ark. Hist. Quar., 1992-94. Bd. dirs. Winthrop Rockefeller Found., 1990-96. Recipient Parks Excellence in Teaching award Phi Alpha Theta, 1970, Michael Rsch. award, 1967; Outstanding Teaching award Omicron Delta Kappa, 1979, rsch. award

U. Ark. Alumni Assn., 1980, Gingles award Ark. Hist. Assn., 1982, Chancellor's medal, 1994, Ledbetter prize, 1994; Truman Libr. fellow, 1963; Acad. Arts and Scis. grantee, 1962. Mem. So. Hist. Assn. (pres. 1986-87), Ark. Hist. Assn., Orgn. Am. Historians, Assn. Study Afro-Am. Life and History, Phi Beta Kappa. Presbyterian. Office: U Ark Old Main # 416 Fayetteville AR 72701

GATHERS, EMERY GEORGE, computer science educator; b. Meadville, Pa., Oct. 10, 1942; s. George Edward and Martha Elizabeth (McCaughty) G.; m. Judith Ann Harbison, Aug. 5, 1967; children: Ann D., Adam E. BS in Math., Edinboro U. Pa., 1964; MA in Math., Bowling Green State U., 1967; Ed.S. in Higher Edn., Okla. State U., 1975, ED.D. in Higher Edn., 1982. Math. tchr. Toms River (N.J.) H.S., 1964-65; grad. asst. Bowling Green (Ohio) State U., 1965-66; tchr. Fostoria (Ohio) Jr. H.S., 1967; prof. math., computer sci. U. Tenn, Martin, 1967—; grad. asst. Okla. State U., Stillwater, 1977-78; mem. faculty senate U. Tenn. 1990-93, 95—, grad. coun., 1995—, acad. student advisor, 1985—, promotion and tenure com., 1990—. Contbr. articles to UTM Math. Placement Exam, Spl. Interest Group on Computer Sci. Edn. Bull. Tchr. Sunday sch. First Bapt. Ch., Martin, Tn., 1990—, treas., 1993—. Recipient Meritorious award Phi Kappa Phi, 1988, Outstanding Tchg. award U. Tenn alumni, 1989; Faculty Devel. grantee U. Tenn, 1984, 95, 96, 97. Mem. Assn. Computing Machinery, Sigma Xi (treas. 1984—), IEEE, Masonic Order, Lions Club. Democratic. Achievements include development of student retention model for higher education. Home: 112 Clark St Martin TN 38237-2904 Office: U Tenn Dept Math and Computer Sci Martin TN 38238

GATHRIGHT, HOWARD T., lawyer; b. Phila., May 3, 1935; s. Howard W. and Rose (McGurk) G.; m. Natalie Acquaviva, June 22, 1963 (div. May 1991); children: Donna Marie, Gary Thomas. BA, U. Pa., 1957; JD, Temple U., 1963. Bar: Pa. 1964, U.S. Dist. Ct. Pa. 1964, U.S. Supreme Ct. 1968. Ptnr. Pratt, Gathright & Brett, P.C., Doylestown, Pa., 1964—; with Gathright & Leonard, Doylestown, Pa., 1990—; asst. dist. atty. of Bucks County, Pa., 1966-69; solicitor Doylestown Twp., Pa., 1970-75, New Hope Sewage Project of Bucks County Water and Sewer Authority, 1971-76; bd. dirs. Bean, Mason & Eyer, Doylestown. Bd. dirs. Am. Lung Assn., 1970—; pres. Bucks County Estate Planning Coun., 1972; active Bucks County Emergency Health Coun., Inc., 1977-79; apptd. by court to Bucks County Spl. Trial Ct. Nominating Commn., 1987. Served in U.S. Army, 1957, USAR, 1958-63. Mem. ABA, Phila. Bar Assn., Pa. Bar Assn., Bucks County Bar Assn. (pres. 1986-87), Assn. Trial Lawyers Am., Pa. Trial Lawyers Assn., Cen. Bucks C. of C. (pres. 1975, chmn. bd. dirs. 1976, Man of Yr. 1975). Democrat. Roman Catholic. Avocations: sports, tennis. Fax: 215-230-7736. E-mail: gathrightg@aol.com. Office: PO Box 310 Doylestown PA 18901-4220

GATHRIGHT, JOHN BYRON, JR., colon and rectal surgeon, educator; b. Oxford, Miss., Sept. 29, 1933; s. J. Byron Sr. and Connie (Love) G.; m. Barbara Cooper, Sept. 19, 1959; children: John Byron III, Lin, John Miles, Peter C. BS, U. Miss., 1955; MD, Northwestern U., 1957. Diplomate Am. Bd. Colon and Rectal Surgery (pres. 1989-90). Intern Charity Hosp., New Orleans, 1957-58, resident in gen. surgery, 1958-62; fellow in colon & rectal surgery Alton Ochsner Med. Found., New Orleans, 1962-63; mem. staff So. Bapt. Hosp., New Orleans, 1963-69; mem. staff Ochsner Found. Hosp., New Orleans, 1969-97, chmn. colon and rectal surgery dept.; clin. prof. surgery Tulane U., New Orleans, 1991—; vis. surgeon So. La. Med. Ctr., Houma, 1977-97; trustee, exec. com., bd. dirs. Alton Ochsner Med. Found., 1980-97. Assoc. editor Diseases of the Colon and Rectum, 1977-93, Perspectives in Colon and Rectal Surgery, 1987-97, Colon and Rectal Surgery Outlook, 1987-97; mem. bd. editors Current Concepts in Gastroenterology, 1980-89. Fellow ACS (grad. edn. com. 1981-89, Am. Soc. Colon and Rectal Surgeons (pres. 1989-90), Soc. Coloproctology of Eng. and Ireland (hon.), Internat. Soc. Univ. Colon and Rectal Surgeons (sec. 1990—), Mex. Soc. Colon and Rectal Surgeons (hon.). Republican. Presbyterian. Avocations: boating, photography. *

GATI, TOBY T., international advisor; b. Bklyn., July 27, 1946; m. Charles Gati; 2 children; 3 stepchildren. BA, Pa. State U., 1967; MA in Russian Lit., Columbia U., 1970, M in Internat. Affairs, 1972. Rsch. asst, project dir., dep. v.p., v.p., sr. v.p. UN Assn. of the U.S.A., 1972-93; spl. asst. to the pres. for nat. security affairs Nat. Security Coun., sr. dir. for Russia, Ukraine and Eurasian States, 1993; asst. sec. for intelligence and rsch. Dept. State, Washington, 1993-97; sr. internat. advisor Akin Gump Strauss Hauer & Feld LLP, Washington, 1997—; cons. ABC World Tonight, 1986, Ford Found., 1987-89, BDM Internat., 1989; mem. Coun. on Fgn Rels., Internat. Inst. for Strategic Studies. Home: 5137 Macomb St NW Washington DC 20016-2611 Office: Akin Gump Strauss Hauer & Feld LLP Ste 400 1333 New Hampshire Ave NW Washington DC 20036-1564

GATI, WILLIAM EUGENE, architect, designer and planner; b. Apr. 10, 1959; s. John and Edith Gati. Student, The Juilliard Sch. of Music, 1965-77; BS in Architecture, CCNY, 1980, BArch cum laude, 1982; MS in Urban Planning, CUNY, 1985. Registered architect, N.Y., N.J. Freelance designer N.Y.C., 1978-83; designer Urban Living, Inc., N.Y.C., 1983-84, Robert L. Henry, Architect, N.Y.C., 1984-86, Glass & Assocs., N.Y.C., 1986-87; prin. architect William E. Gati, RA, AIA, N.Y.C., 1987—; prin. Architecture Studio, N.Y.C., 1991—; reporter Home Editor Resident Publs., 1995—; prof. architecture N.Y. Inst. Tech., Old Westbury, 1985-89; instr. religious architecture Cooper Union, N.Y.C., 1989; instr. architecture St. John's U., N.Y.C., 1995—; curator Fundamentals of Architecture, N.Y. Inst. Tech., 1987; lectr. in field. Archtl. designs include offices for Here's Life, N.Y.C., alterations to Calvary Bapt. Ch., N.Y.C., El Eden Ch., Bklyn., Living Word Christian Ctr., N.Y.C., All Saints Ch., Queens, N.Y.C., Dr. Aviles Med. Ctr., Queens, Tampellini Residence, Queens, expansion for Flushing Christian Sch., Queens, N.Y., Faith Assembly Ch., Queens, P.S. 68 annex, Queens, Perkovich Residence, Queens, Kaufman Residence, L.I., Cardinal Residence, Mas, Lindas Natural Kitchen, Queens, Resurrection Ch., Bklyn., Dr. Peter Chin's Med. Offices, Queens, Dr. Peter Murowski's Med. Offices, Queens; author: Solar Energy Techniques, 1979 (AIA Recognition 1979), Frank L. Wright, 1981, Theory of Modern Architecture, 1981, Boston Pub. Space, 1985, Vacant Lots, Architectural League N.Y.C., 1987; contbg. illustrator Jonathan Friedman Creations in Space, Fundamentals of Architecture. Chmn. religious architecture com., organized series: Places for Worship, N.Y.C. 1990; planning bd. Kew Gardens. Mem. AIA, Mcpl. Art Soc. (assoc.), Archtl. League (assoc.), CCNY Alumni Assn. (v.p. 1983-92), N.Y. Arts Group, Christian Architects Fellowship (pres.). Avocations: photography, chess, concert pianist, fine artist.

GATIPON, BETTY BECKER, medical educator, consultant; b. New Orleans, Sept. 8, 1931; d. Elmore Paul and Theresa Caroline (Sendker) Becker; m. William B. Gatipon, Nov. 22, 1952 (dec. 1986); children: Suzanne, Ann Gatipon Sved, Lynn Gatipon Pashley. BS magna cum laude, Ursuline Coll., New Orleans, 1952; MEd, La. State U., 1975, PhD, 1983. Tchr. Diocese of Baton Rouge, 1960-74, edn. cons. to sch. bd., 1974-78; dir. Right to Read program Capital Area Consortium/Washington Parish Sch. Bd., Franklington, La., 1978-80; dir. basic skills edn. Capital Area Consortium/Ascension Parish Sch. Bd., Donaldsonville, La., 1980-82; instr. Coll. Edn. La. State U., Baton Rouge, 1982-84; evaluation cons. La. Dept. Edn., Baton Rouge, 1984-85; dir. basic skills edn. Capital Area Basic Skills/East Feliciana Parish Sch. Bd., Clinton, La., 1985-86; program coord. La. Bd. Elem. and Secondary Edn., New Orleans, 1987-89; dir. divsn. of med. edn., dept. family medicine Sch. Medicine La. State U. Med. Ctr., New Orleans, 1989—; evaluator East Feliciana Parish Schs., 1982-86; presenter math. methods workshops Ascension Parish Schs., 1980-84. Author curriculum materials, conf. papers; contbr. articles to edn. jours. Curatorial asst. La. State Mus., New Orleans, 1987—; soprano St. Louis Cathedral Concert Choir, New Orleans, 1988—; chmn. Symphony Store, New Orleans Symphony, 1990—; lector St. Angela Merici Ch. Mem. Am. Ednl. Rsch. Assn., Assn. Am. Med. Colls., Midsouth Ednl. Rsch. Assn., La. Ednl. Rsch. Assn., Soc. Tchrs. Family Medicine, New Orleans Film and Video Buffs, Phi Kappa Phi, Phi Delta Kappa. Roman Catholic. Avocations: music, aerobic walking, classic movies. Home: 105 10th St New Orleans LA 70124-1258 Office: LA State U Med Ctr Sch Medicine 1542 Tulane Ave New Orleans LA 70112-2825

GATJE, ROBERT FREDERICK, architect; b. Bklyn., Nov. 27, 1927; s. Frederick Christopher and Erna Henrietta (Kelting) G.; m. Barbara Mansfield Wright, Oct. 20, 1956 (div. Aug. 1981); children: Alexandra Lord, Marianna Gatje Perrier, Margot Gatje Small. B.Arch., Cornell U., 1951; Fulbright scholar, Archtl. Assn. Sch. Architecture, London, 1951-52. Architect Gatje, Papachristou Smith (formerly Marcel Breuer Assocs.), N.Y.C., 1953-56, assoc., 1956-87, ptnr., 1965-87, dir. Paris office, 1964-66; ptnr. Richard Meier and Ptnrs., N.Y.C., 1987-95. Architect: Broward County Main Library, 1980; co-architect: IBM France Research Center, 1962, Ski Town, Flaine, France, 1969, IBM Mfg. Center, Boca Raton, Fla., 1969, Armstrong Rubber Co. Hdqrs, New Haven, 1969, Baldegg (Switzerland) Convent, 1972, Mundipharma GmbH Hdqrs, Limburg, Ger., 1975. Trustee Deep Springs Coll., Calif., 1974-82, N.Y. Hall of Sci., 1985-96, N.Y. Found. for Arch., 1994-96; pres. Telluride Assn., 1953-55; bd. dirs. Franklin and Eleanor Roosevelt Inst. With C.E., AUS, 1946-47. Telluride scholar, 1947-51; Skidmore, Owings and Merrill scholar, 1950-51; recipient Clifton Beckwith Brown medal Cornell U. Coll. Architecture, 1951, Charles Goodwin Sands medal, 1951. Fellow AIA (pres. N.Y. chpt. 1975-76, Sch. medal 1951);l mem. Ordre des Architectes Francais, Century Assn., Am. Arbitration Assn. Democrat. Home: 1040 5th Ave Apt 6A New York NY 10028-0137

GATLIN, FRED, agricultural program administrator, former state legislator; b. Colby, Kans., Sept. 19, 1948; s. Wayne Issac and Darlene (Grant) G.; m. Karen Sue Downing, Aug. 12, 1981; 1 child, Hannah. BS, Kans. State U., 1970. Farmer Atwood, Kans., 1970-91; owner, mgr. Seed House, Inc., Atwood, 1983—; mem. Kans. Ho. of Reps., Topeka, 1986-97; program mgr. agrl. commodities assurance program Kans. Dept. Agr., Topeka, 1997—; mem. agr. com. Kans. Ho. of Reps., 1990-94, mem. comml. and fin. instns. com., 1986-88, mem. pub. health and welfare com., 1986-88, energy and natural resources com., 1988-94, appropriations com., 1988-96; mem. joint com. on health care for the 90's Kans. Legislature, 1990-94, healthcare oversight com., 1994; mem. Strategic Planning Telecom. Kans., 1994-95. Mem. Atwood City Coun., 1997. Mem. Kans. Sheep Assn. (pres. 1976), Kans. Crop Improvement, Kans. Seed Dealers, Rotary (pres. 1989-90). Republican. Home: 2809 SW Plass Ave Topeka KS 66611-1629 Office: Kans Dept Agr Agrl Commodities Assistance 901 S Kansas Ave Fl 7 Topeka KS 66612-2216

GATLIN, KAREN CHRISTENSEN, English language educator; b. Iowa City, Iowa, Feb. 18, 1943; d. Carl Archibald and Esther Agnes (Bradley) Christensen; m. John Charles Gatlin, Apr. 4, 1964 (div. Sept. 1976); children: Britt Jonene, Shawna Lynne. BS in Secondary Edn., N.E. Mo. State U., 1964; MA in Multicultural Edn., U. N.Mex., 1989. Cert. secondary English tchr., reading K-12, French. Tchr. 8th grade English Ernie Pyle Jr. H.S., Albuquerque, 1964-69; tchr. 7th grade English Truman Mid. Sch., Albuquerque, 1974-81; tchr. 6th/7th grade English and 8th grade French Madison Mid. Sch., Albuquerque, 1981-87; clin. supr. student tchg. U. N.Mex., Albuquerque, 1987-89; French instr. U. N.Mex. Continuing Edn., Albuquerque, 1988-93; tchr. English Sandia H.S., Albuquerque, 1989-96; mem. profl. stds. com. A.F.T.-APS, Albuquerque, 1989-90; mem. restructuring com. APS-Sandia H.S., Albuquerque, 1989-90; participant United World Coll. Restructuring Symposium, Las Vegas, 1990; tour leader, counselor E.F. Inst. for Cultural Exch., France, Gt. Britain and Germany, 1985, 90, 95, 96; guest spkr. multi-cultural tchr. edn. Auburn U., Montgomery, Ala., 1989. Mem. LWV, Albuquerque Tchrs. Fedn., Delta Kappa Gamma, Phi Delta Kappa, Kappa Delta Pi (v.p. 1964). Avocations: travel, art, writing. Home: 1038 Claudine St NE Albuquerque NM 87112-5602

GATLIN, MICHAEL GERARD, lawyer, educator; b. Kittery, Maine, May 9, 1956; s. James Patrick and Florence (Lesperance) G.; m. Judith E. Ziman, Nov. 7, 1987; children: Vanessa Marie, Alexandra Elizabeth. BA, Framingham State Coll., 1978; JD, New Eng. Sch. Law, 1982. Bar: Mass. 1982, U.S. Dist. Ct. Mass. 1983, U.S. Ct. Appeals (1st cir.) 1983. Mem. adj. faculty dept. law Dean Jr. Coll., Franklin, Mass., 1986-92; ptnr. Gaynor & Gatlin, Framingham, Mass., 1988—. Bd. dirs., pres. Wayside Cmty. Programs, Inc., Framingham, 1978—; bd. dirs. South Middlesex Consumer Assistance Office-Metrowest, Inc., Framingham; mem. Framingham Planning Bd., 1992-93; chmn. Metrowest AIDS Consortium, 1993—. Recipient citation Mass. Ho. of Reps., 1984. Mem. Mass. Bar Assn., South Middlesex Bar Assn. (pres. 1991-92). Democrat. Home: 727 Salem End Rd Framingham MA 01702-5542 Office: Gaynor & Gatlin 14 Vernon St Ste 108 Framingham MA 01701-4733

GATONS, ANNA-MARIE KILMADE, government official; b. Albany, N.Y., Oct. 21, 1946; d. Daniel Joseph Jr. and Tomasina (Fallone) Kilmade; m. Robert A. McCarthy, Sept. 3, 1967 (div. Apr. 1990); children: Daniel Kilmade McCarthy, Kevin Michael McCarthy; m. Paul K. Gatons, July 28, 1991. BA, Coll. of St. Rose, 1970. Staff support positions HUD, Washington, 1976-79, mgmt. analyst, 1979-81, staff budget analyst, 1981-83, chief of the budget and legislation coord. br., 1983-91, dir. exec. secretariat for HUD cabinet sec., 1992-95; dir. exec. secretariat for atty. gen. Dept. of Justice Hdqs., Washington, 1995—. Mem. U.S. Holocaust Meml. Mus., St. Rose Alumni Assn., Nat. Italian-Am. Found. Roman Catholic. Avocations: reading, needlework, decorating. Home: 7705 Huntsman Blvd Springfield VA 22153-3912 Office: Dept Justice Executive Secretariat #4545 950 Pennsylvania Ave NW Washington DC 20530-0001

GATOS, HARRY CONSTANTINE, engineering educator; b. Greece, Dec. 27, 1921; came to U.S., 1946, naturalized, 1955; s. Constantine B. and Paraskevi (Merintzos) G.; m. Dawn Spiropoulos, July 15, 1950 (div. 1980); children: Pamela Dawn, Niki Ann, Constantine Harry; m. Ronna M. Galipeau, Apr. 10, 1988. Diploma in chemistry, U. Athens, Greece, 1945; MA in Chemistry, Ind. U., 1948; PhD, MIT, 1950; DSc, Ind. U., 1983. Instr. U. Athens, 1943-46; mem. research staff MIT, 1948-52; from sect. leader to div. head solid state div. Lincoln Lab., 1955-64; prof. materials sci. and elec. engring. MIT, Cambridge, 1962-90, prof. emeritus, 1990—; research engr. E.I. duPont de Nemours & Co., Inc., 1952-55; Cons. to industry, govt., 1962—. Editor-in-chief Surface Sci.; contbr. 350 articles to profl. jours. Trustee Longy Sch. Music, Cambridge, Mass. Decorated golden cross Order of Merit Poland; recipient medal for exceptional sci. achievement NASA, 1974; Solid State Sci. and Tech. award Electrochem. Soc., 1975, Acheson medal Electrochem. Soc., 1982, Harry C. Gatos Disting. Lecture and Prize, 1991, Gallium Arsenide award, 1992, Welker Gold medal, 1992. Fellow AAAS; mem. Electrochem. Soc. (hon. mem., pres. 1967-68), Materials Research Soc. (pres. 1972-75), Am. Phys. Soc., Am. Inst. Metall. Engrs., Nat. Acad. Engring., Am. Acad. Arts and Scis., Acad. Athens (corr.), Cambridge Soc. for Early Music (trustee). Home: 83 Cambridge Pkwy Unit W301 Cambridge MA 02142-1241 Office: MIT Dept. of Materials S&E Cambridge MA 02139

GATTA, MARY LIZABETH, sociologist; b. Red Bank, N.J., July 12, 1972; d. John Anthony and Maria (Grilli) G. BA in Social Scis., Providence Coll., 1994; MA in Sociology, Rutgers U., 1996, postgrad., 1996—. Rschr. polit. sci. dept. Brookdale Coll., Lincroft, N.J., 1992-93; instr. sociology Rutgers U., New Brunswick, N.J., 1974-97, rsch. asst., 1997—; presenter in field. Mem. Am. Sociol. Assn. (assoc. editor sociology of emotions subsect. newsletter 1997—). Avocations: art history, reading. Home: 27 Horicon Ave Oceanport NJ 07757-1708 Office: Rutgers U Sociology Dept Lucy Stone Hall New Brunswick NJ 08903

GATTI, DANIEL JON, lawyer; b. Racine, Wis., Apr. 22, 1946; s. Daniel John and Rosemary J. (Moore) G.; divorced; children: Danny, DiAndra. BS, Western Oreg. State U., 1968; JD, Willamette U., 1973. Bar: Oreg. 1973, U.S. Dist. Ct. Oreg. 1973, U.S. Ct. Appeals (9th cir.) 1974, U.S. Ct. Appeals (2d cir.) 1985, U.S. Supreme Ct. 1979; cert. trial specialist. Tchr. Lake Oswego (Oreg.) High Sch., 1970; specialist in edn. law Oreg. Dept. Edn., Salem, 1973-75; pres., atty., ptnr. Gatti & Gatti, P.C., Salem, 1975—. Co-author: The Teacher and The Law, 1972, Encyclopedic Dictionary of School Law, 1975, New Encyclopedic Dictionary of School Law, 1983, The Educator's Encyclopedia of School Law, 1990, (fiction) White Knuckle, 1999. V.p., trustee Western States Chiropractic Coll., Portland, Oreg., 1976-94. Mem. ATLA, Ariz. Bar Assn., Oreg. Bar Assn., Am. Bd. Trial Advocacy (cert. as trial specialist 1987), Am. Adjudicature Soc., Illahe Club. Home: 3601 Augusta National Dr S Salem OR 97302-9715 Office: Gatti Gatti Maier & Assocs 1761 Liberty St SE Salem OR 97302-5158

GATTI, JIM, editor; b. Detroit, July 4, 1943; m. Carol A. Gatti; children: Theresa, Julie, Thomas, John. BA in English, Wayne State U., 1966. News editor Detroit News, city editor, asst. mng. editor, dep. mng. editor; editor Honolulu Advertiser, 1995—. With U.S. Army, 1966-68. Recipient Silver Gavel, ABA, Robert F. Kennedy Pub. Svc. award. Office: Honolulu Advertiser 605 Kapiolana Blvd Honolulu HI 96813

GATTING, CARLENE J., lawyer; b. Hartford, Conn., Apr. 12, 1955; d. Charles W. and Jean A. (Murkowicz) G. BS, U. Conn., 1977; JD, Rutgers U., 1983. Counsel Skadden, Arps, Slate, Meagher & Flom, N.Y.C., 1987—. Mem. ABA. Office: Skadden Arps Slate Meagher & Flom 919 3rd Ave New York NY 10022-3902

GATTO, JOHN TAYLOR, educational consultant, writer; b. Monongahela, Pa., Dec. 15, 1935; s. Andrew Michael Mario and Frances Virginia (Zimmer) G.; m. Janet MacAdam, Dec. 29, 1961; children: Briseis Lucrezia, Raven Taylor. *The Gatto children are the result of five major streams of immigration: The McManus family, which came from Ireland in the 1840s and 1850s; the Zimmers and Hoffmans who came from Germany in the 1860s and 1870s; the Gattos and Calabros who came from Italy around 1905; and the McAdams and Browns of Scotland who came in the 1930s. One great grandmother, however, Isabella Waddington, came from England in 1885.* BA, Columbia U., 1959; MA, Hunter Coll., 1971; postgrad., Cornell U., 1954, 55, 86, U. Pitts., 1956, Yeshiva U., 1963, Calif. State U., 1984, Lehman Coll., 1987, Reed Coll., 1990. Cert. secondary tchr., N.Y. Copywriter Ted Bates Advt., N.Y.C., 1960-61; screenwriter Lotus Prodns., N.Y.C., 1961-62; instr. in English N.Y.C. Bd. Edn., 1962-71; lectr. Queens Coll., N.Y.C., 1971-76; dir. The Lab Sch., N.Y.C., 1976—; pres. Oxford Ednl. Cons., Oxford, N.Y., 1991—; songwriter (ASCAP listed), N.Y.C., 1967-72; ednl. cons. Bd. Higher Edn., N.Y.C., 1971-76; script cons. Marvel Comics, DC Comics, N.Y.C., 1972-73; sr. staff designer Huckleberry Designs, N.Y.C., 1976—; pres. Lava MT Records. *John Taylor Gatto is in partnership with Roland Legiardi-Laura, Director of the Nyoriquan Poet's CafÒ in Manhattan to produce a three-part documentary film about the history of American schooling and the heavy corporate involvement in it for over a century. He is also developing a 128 acre property near Oxford, New York, as a retreat and library for school reform groups, and is working on abook, The Guerrilla Curriculum: How to Get an Education in Spite of School.* Author: One Flew Over the Cuckoo's Nest: A Critical Study, 1975, Howard Phillips Lovecraft: A Critical Study, 1976, The Adventures of Snider, the CIA Spider, 1979, Are You My Father? An Odyssey Across the Barren Land of Adoption and Homelessness, 1990, Dumbing Us Down: The Hidden Curriculum of Compulsory Schooling, 1991, The Exhausted School, 1992, The Empty Child: A Teachers Essay on Modern Schooling, 1999; contbr. articles to jours. and newspapers; composer Ballads of Sorrow and Sadness, 1968, Iphigenia in Aulis, 1969; recordings include Richard Nixon's Checkers Speech, 1976, Two Attacks on the Media, 1977, The Rats in the Walls, 1978, The Haunter of the Dark, 1979. Founder The I.S. 44 Market, sch. fundraiser, N.Y.C.; dist. leader N.Y. Conservative Party, 1973—, state Committeeman, 1978—; candidate N.Y. State Senate, Albany, 1986, 88, 90; candidate for pres. Manhattan Borough, N.Y.C., 1989; mem. adv. bd. TV-Free Am., 1995—; sec. edn. Libertarian Party Shadow Cabinet, 1993—. Recipient Pres.'s Vol. Action award, 1984, Citizen of the Week award Assn. for a Better N.Y., 1986, 1st prize Nat. Writing Contest Geraldine Dodge Found. and Tchrs. Coll., Columbia U., 1990, Spectrum Medal World Soc. Achievement of Human Potential, 1993, Alexis de Tocqueville award, 1998; named N.Y.C. Tchr. of Yr., Coun. Chief State Sch. Officers and Nat. Assn. Secondary Sch. Prins., 1989, N.Y. State Senate Resolution, 1990, N.Y. Alliance for Pub. Edn., 1991; named N.Y. State Tchr. of Yr., N.Y. State Edn. Dept., 1991; NEH grantee, 1983, 86, 90; N.Y. Tchr. Consortium grantee, 1984; Coun. for Basic Edn. Ind. Study fellow, 1984; Lehman Coll. fellow, 1987; Mario Salvadori fellow Inst. for the Built Environment, CUNY, 1989, Snowbird fellow Met. Life Ins. Co., 1990; commendations from Pres. Ford, Pres. Carter, Pres. Reagan, N.Y. Gov. Cuomo, N.Y. Mayors Koch and Dinkins. Fellow Scholars Cir., Chenango Upland Pistol Club (pres. 1975-90), Marshall Chess Club, Audubon Soc., U.S. Mycol. Soc., Scottish Heritage Assn., Working Press of the Nation. Roman Catholic. Avocations: pistol-hunting, mycology, chess, ancient religions, graphoanalysis. Home: 725 McDonough Rd Oxford NY 13830-9802 Office: The Odysseus Group Inc 235 W 76th St New York NY 10023-8210

GATTO, JOSEPH DANIEL, investment banker; b. Italy, Feb. 25, 1956; came to U.S., 1956; s. Philip and Gilda Gatto; m. Susan Elizabeth Rehm, May 9, 1987; children: Philip, Catherine, Peter, Elizabeth. AB magna cum laude, Princeton U., 1978; JD cum laude, U. Pa., 1984, MBA, 1984. Bar: N.Y. 1985. Assoc. Goldman, Sachs & Co., N.Y.C., 1984-87, v.p., 1987-90, group head strategic devel., 1990-94, gen. ptnr., 1994—; mem. adv. bd. Wharton Dirs. Inst.; lectr. World Econ. Forum. Editor-in-chief Jour. Corp. Law and Securities Regulation, 1984. Mem. Maritime Ctr. Mem. World Wildlife Fund, Aubudon Soc., Wharton Club, Young Press.'s Orgn. Roman Catholic. Avocations: golf, skiing, cooking. Office: Goldman Sachs & Co 85 Broad St New York NY 10004-2456

GATTO, KATHERINE GYÉKÉNYESI, modern languages and literatures educator; b. Braunau, Austria, Nov. 27, 1945; came to U.S., 1951; d. György László and Katalin (Korcsmár) Gyékényesi; m. Gregory Francis Gatto, Aug. 10, 1968; children: Gregory, Georgina, Peter, Stephen. AB magna cum laude, John Carroll U., 1967; MA, Case Western Res. U., 1971, PhD, 1975. Asst. prof. modern langs. and lits. John Carroll U., Cleve., 1975-80, assoc. prof., 1980-92, prof., 1992—, chmn. dept. classical and modern langs. and cultures, 1990-97. Author: Treasury of Hungarian Love, Poems, Quotations and Proverbs, 1996; co-author: Manual Terapéutico para el Adulto con Dificultades del Habla y Lenguaje, 1985, Of Kings and Poets: Cancionero Poetry of the Trastámara Courts, 1992, The Lapidary of King Alfonso X, The Learned, 1997. NDEA fellow Case Western Res. U., 1967-70, George E. Grauel faculty rsch. fellow, 1981-82, 1995-96; Fulbright-Hayes rsch. scholar, Madrid, 1972-73; grantee NEH, 1987, 90. Mem. MLA (exec. bd. Hungarian lit. discussion group 1982-88, 99—), Am. Assn. for Tchrs. Spanish and Portuguese, Am. Hungarian Educators Assn. (pres. 1992-94), Am. Assn. for Advancement Slavic Studies, Acad. Hungarian Scientists, Writers and Artists Abroad, Ohio Fgn. Lang. Assn., Fulbright Assn. (bd. dirs. N.E. Ohio chpt. 1994-99, v.p., program chmn. 1996-98). Avocations: opera, folklore, travel, theater. Office: John Carroll U Dept Classical-Modern Langs & Cultures University Heights OH 44118

GATTO, LOUIS CONSTANTINE, educational authority executive; b. Chgo., July 4, 1927; s. Louis S. and Marie (Bacigalupo) G.; m. Kathleen M. Paquette, July 7, 1951 (dec.); children: Christine Gatto Glasgow, Beth Gatto Roberts, Mark, Gregory, Janine Gatto Bass, Sandra Gatto Minniear; m. Marilyn R. Bennett, Feb. 9, 1991. Student, Amherst Coll., 1945-46; BA, St. Mary's Coll., Minn., 1950; postgrad., U. Minn., 1950-51; MA, DePaul U., 1956; PhD, Loyola U., Chgo., 1965; LittD (hon.), Marian Coll., Indpls., 1989; LHD (hon.), Martin U., Indpls., 1996. Speech asst. St. Mary's Coll., 1949-50; staff artist TV Times, Mpls., 1950-51; chmn. dept. English Zion-Benton H.S., Ill., 1951-56; tchr. New Trier H.S., Winnetka, Ill., 1956-57; instr. English St. Josephs Coll., Rensselaer, Ind., 1957-58, asst. prof., 1958-63, assoc. prof. Medieval and Renaissance lit., 1963-66, prof., 1966-71, asst. acad. dean, dir. summer session, 1967, acad. dean, 1968, v.p. acad. affairs, 1969-71; pres., prof. English Marian Coll., Indpls., 1971-89; dir. spl. projects, cons. svc. Independent Colls. of Ind., 1989—; amb. Independent Colls. Ind. Found., 1989—; dir. Ind. Compact, 1989—, West Point liaison officer, 1990—, dir. Operation Expanded Horizons, 1992—; mem. Ind. N.W. Consortium Pvt. and Pub. Instns., 1968-71; selection com. Ind. Fulbright Found., 1968-70; mem. community adv. council Indpls. Pub. Schs., 1976-77; mem. policy adv. council parent/child devel. project Bank Street Coll. Edn., 1976-79; mem. Hist. Landmarks Found. Ind., 1973-89; mem. long range devel. plan adv. com. Ind. Vocat. Tech. Coll., 1985-86; mem. adv. com. Alcohol Safety Action Project, 1972-75; mem. exec. com., adv. bd. Ctr. for Econ. Edn., Ind. U.-Purdue U., Indpls., 1978-89; mem. exec. com. Ind. Conf. on Higher Edn., 1973-75, 78-81, 87-89, pres., 1979-80; chmn. council of presidents Consortium for Urban Edn., 1974-75, pres., 1975-89; dir. spl. projects Ind. Conf. of Higher Edn., 1992-94, exec. sec., 1994—. Contbr. articles to profl. jours. Bd. dirs. Greater Indpls. Progress Com., ARC, Hosp. Audiences, Indpls., 1974-76, Ind. Higher Edn. Telecomm. Sys., 1987-95; bd. dirs. Hamilton County ARC, 1998—, vice chair, 1999—; bd. dirs., sec. Cath. Social Svcs., 1978-80; vice chmn. Ind. Health Careers, Inc., 1978-81, chmn.-elect, 1981-82, chmn., 1982-83; bd. dirs., treas. Associated Colls.

Ind., 1976-78, v.p., 1984-86; bd. dirs. Ind. Colls. and Univs. of Ind., chmn., 1979-80, 86-88; mem. Benjamin Harrison Meml. Commn., 1987-91; mem. adv. bd. Sta. WYFI; mem. gov.'s commn. for Hoosier Celebration, 1988; Ind. lobbyist for Ind. Higher Edn., 1989-90; chmn. Ind. Ameritech. Partnership Awards Program, 1990-95; asst. dir. Ind. Ednl. Facilities Auth., 1991-93, exec. dir., 1994—; with Army War Coll., 1974; mem. Senator's Lugar's Merit Selection com. for West Point; adv.com. 21st century scholars program State Student Assistance Commn., 1998—. Served with AUS, 1945-46, Ill. NG, 1946-50. ACE fellow in acad. adminstrn., 1966-67; recipient Sagamor of the Wabash award State of Ind., 1980, 89, Outstanding Svc. award Ind. Health Careers, 1983, Circle award Ind. Coalition of Blacks in Higher Edn., 1986, Outstanding Contbns. award Army Career and Alumni Assn., 1994. Mem. Ind. Conf. on Higher Edn. (Dedicated Svc. award 1994), Heslar Naval Armory Club (life), Alpha Phi Omega. Home: 24 Apple Tree Cir Fishers IN 46038-1110

GATZA, LOUISE RUTH, freelance medical writer, small business owner; b. St. Charles, Va., Feb. 17, 1939; children: Roxann Allana, Diane Lynn. A in Gen. Studies, Triton Jr. Coll., River Grove, Ill., 1993; Cert. with hons. in Med. Transcription, Coll. DuPage, Glen Ellyn, Ill., 1993. Owner, mgr. Fashionette Beauty Salon, Ill., 1973-74. Contbr. articles Ill. Newsletter of Assn. Med. Transcription, 1994; creator of Med. Reference Text, 1995 (pseudonym Lou Parker); freelance writer. Sunday Sch. tchr. Westchester (Ill.) Bible Ch., 1993-97, numerous ch. positions. Avocations: aerobics, songwriting, piano, gardening, reading. Home: 613 Coventry Way Noblesville IN 46060-9027

GAUBERT, LLOYD FRANCIS, shipboard and industrial cable distribution executive; b. Thibodaux, La., Jan. 6, 1921; s. Camille J. and Leonise (Henry) G.; children: Lloyd Francis, Leonise, Bruce, Blane, Gwen, Greg. Student Southwestern La. Inst., 1939-41, U.So. Calif., 1941-42, Tex. Christian U., 1946-47. Tool engr. Consol.-Vultee Aircraft Corp., San Diego, 1941-45; tool project engr. Fort Worth plant Convair, 1946-47; founder, owner, pres. L.F. Gaubert & Co., Inc., New Orleans, 1947—; pres. Michoud Indsl. Complex, Inc., Marine Indsl. Cable Corp., Carmel Devel. Corp.; dir. First Nat. Bank Commerce, New Orleans; pres. Holiday Inn Thibodaux. Chmn. regional planning commn. New Orleans Mayor's Coordinating Com. for NASA, 1961-63, chmn. mfrs. com., 1961-63; bd. dirs. Better Bus. Bur., New Orleans, Met. New Orleans Safety Coun., New Orleans Pub. Belt R.R., New Orleans Port Com., New Orleans Traffic and Transp. Bur., USCG Acad., New Orleans Opera House Assn., Christian Bros., New Orleans; trustee Sta. WYES-TV, New Orleans; exec. com. Sugar Bowl Football; founder, chmn. Greatest Bands in Dixie; pres. Holiday Inn of Thibodaux; dir., USCG Acad.; state pres. navy league adv. coun. Loyola U., New Orleans. Served with USAAF, 1942-45. Recipient St. Louis medallion Archdiocese of New Orleans, 1990; named Man of the Yr., Christian Bros.' Sch., 1989. Mem. Am. Soc. Tooling and Mfg. Engrs. (pres. 1948-49), Soc. Naval Architects and Marine Engrs., Am. Soc. Naval Engrs., La. Engring. Soc., Navy League (past pres. New Orleans coun., nat. dir., state pres. La.), New Orleans Petroleum Club, Sugar Bowl (exec. com.), Am. Legion, Plimsoll Club, Bd. of Trade Club, Internat. House, Optimists (pres. 1957-58, lt. gov. 1959-60), K.C., Ancient Order Hibernians in Am. Republican. Roman Catholic. Home: 5668 Bancroft Dr New Orleans LA 70122-1306 Office: LF Gaubert & Co Inc 700 S Broad St New Orleans LA 70119-7417

GAUBERT, RONALD JOSEPH, gas and oil industry executive, management consultant; b. Lafayette, Ind., Dec. 1, 1946; s. Harold E. and Cecile (Mouton) G.; m. Linda Bock; children: Ellen, Brad. BS, U. So. La., Lafayette, 1973. Controller Lafayette Drug Co., 1973-76; treas. Mar-Low Corp., Lafayette, 1976-78; pres. Ron J. Gaubert & Assoc., Lafayette, 1978—, Lanscor Devel. Corp., Lafayette, 1978—, Energy R&D Corp., 1994—; chmn. Venture Capital Forum, Lafayette. Pres. adv. bd. Cathedral Carmel Parents Booster Assn., Lafayette, 1985-86, mem. sch. bd., 1985-86, pres. Parish Council, Holy Cross Ch.; fin. chmn. St. Thomas More H.S., 1997-99. Served with U.S. Army, 1966-69. Mem. Nat. Assn. Realtors, Am. Assn. Petroleum Inds., La. Assn. Ind. Producers and Royalty Owners, La. Realtors Assn., Lafayette C. of C. (bd. dirs.), Petroleum Club (bd. dirs.), Krewe of Gabriel. Republican. Roman Catholic. Office: PO Box 53152 Lafayette LA 70505-3152

GAUCH, EUGENE WILLIAM, JR., former air force officer; b. Newark, Dec. 6, 1922; s. Eugene William and Wilhelmina Katrina (Beiswenger) G.; m. Beryl Merle Walker, Jan. 15, 1947; children: Kathryn A. (Mrs. Jerry T. Stansfield), Tracey L. Student, Syracuse U.; grad., Nat. War Coll., 1969. Enlisted as pvt. USAAF, 1942; advanced through grades to brig. gen. USAF, 1972; assigned Okinawa, World War II and Korean War; tng. and standardization officer SAC, Offutt AFB, Neb., 1955-59; ops. staff officer 72 Bombardment Wing, Ramey AFB, P.R., 1959-63; asst. exec. sec. to air staff bd. Office Vice Chief Staff Air Force, Washington, 1963-67; asst. chief staff, exec. to comdr. 7th Air Force, Vietnam, 1967-68; faculty Nat. War Coll., 1969; exec. to comdr. Hdqrs. Tactical Air Command, Langley AFB, Va., 1969-70; chief staff Hdqrs. Tactical Air Command, 1970-72; comdr. 834th Air Div., Little Rock AFB, 1972-74; dir. automated mobility requirements DSC/Plans and Ops., Hdqrs. USAF, Washington, 1974-76; dir. Florida Race Pilots Assn., Inc., Port Orange. Decorated Legion of Merit with 3 oak leaf clusters, D.F.C., Air medal with 4 oak leaf clusters, Air Force Commendation medal. Home: 628 Owl Way Sarasota FL 34236-1928

GAUCHER, DONALD HOLMAN, public opinion research company executive; b. Port Arthur, Tex., Aug. 2, 1931; s. Leon Phillip and Hattie Lu (Holman) G.; m. Jane Peel Heyck, June 15, 1957; children: Susan Heyck, Beverly Jane. *Great-grandfather Reverend John Haynie established the family roots in Texas. He was the first Chaplain of the first Congress of the Republic of Texas and of the first Texas State Legislature. Great-great-grandfather and great-grandfather served in the Confederate States army as Captain and Sergeant, respectively. Wife Jane graduated from the Kinkaid School in Houston in 1953 and served on the Alumni Board of Directors (1995-98). She graduated cum laude from Brown University in 1957 and is past-president of the Houston Brown Club. She served on the Houston Junior League Board of Directors and Sustaining Board. She is manager of bridal registry at Bering's in Houston.* BA, The Rice Inst., Houston, 1953, BSChemE, 1954; grad., Sch. of Reactor Tech., Oak Ridge, Tenn., 1955; JD, U. Houston, 1962. With Humble Oil and Refining Co., Houston, 1957-64, Std. Oil (N.J.), N.Y.C., 1964-68, Exxon Co. USA, Houston, 1968-91; pres. Gaucher Rsch. Assoc., Houston, 1991—; mem. pub. opinion task force Am. Petroleum Inst., Washington, 1986-91, Chem. Mfrs. Assn., Washington, 1991-96; cons. Exxon Chem. Co., Houston, 1991-97. Pres. Mus. So. History, Sugar Land, Tex., 1997—. Mem. Am. Nuc. Soc., Am. Inst. Mining, Metall. and Petroleum Engrs., Am. Assn. Pub. Opinion Rsch., Tex. Bar Assn., Kiwanis, Sons of Confederate Vets. (past comdr. Albert Sidney Johnston Camp), Mil. Order of Stars and Bars (past comdr.), Sons of the Republic of Tex., Terry's Tex. Rangers Assn. Avocations: tennis, bird photography. Home: 1905 B Potomac Houston TX 77057

GAUCHER, JANE HEYCK, retail executive; b. Houston, Feb. 11, 1936; d. Theodore Richard and Gertrude Paine (Daly) Heyck; m. Donald Holman Gaucher, June 15, 1957; children: Susan Heyck, Beverly Jane. AB cum laude, Brown U., Providence, 1957. Mgr. Bride and Groom Registry Berings, Houston, 1990—; pres. Antique Study Group, Houston, 1974-75. Mem. bd. Jr. League Houston, 1963, mem. sustaining bd., 1990-93; mem. Kinkaid Sch. Alumni Bd., Houston, 1995-98. Avocations: tennis, running, swimming, mai jonge, bridge. Home: 1905B Potomac Dr Houston TX 77057-2921

GAUCHER, KIM ELIZABETH, artist, art director; b. Bklyn., July 17, 1960; d. Clifford Prior Marvin and Lilliane M. Gaucher; m. Steven Scot Srebrenick, Sept. 6, 1998; 1 child, Dylan Kent Srebrenick. AA in Fine Arts, Miami Dade C.C., 1982; BFA, Parsons Sch. of Design, N.Y.C., 1986; postgrad. studies in computer graphics, Sch. Visual Arts, N.Y.C., 1991; postgrad. studies in painting, drawing, Pratt Inst., N.Y.C., 1993; studies painting, drawing, sculpture, Art Students League, N.Y.C., 1995. Graphic urban designer, model maker Downtown Devel. Authority, N.Y.C., 1982-84; graphic artist Simplicity Pattern Co., Inc., N.Y.C., 1984-85; graphic designer, draftsperson CEO, Inc., N.Y.C.; exhibit designer ECOFA, Inc., Long Island, N.Y., 1986-87; graphic artist, design asst. Rolling Stone Mag., N.Y.C., 1987-90; graphic artist and design asst. Sony Music Entertainment, Inc Creative Svcs., N.Y.C., 1991-97; assoc. art dir. PACE Comm., Greensboro, N.C., 1998—; free lance desgner KEG Designs, N.Y., Miami, 1983-98. Exhbns. at Mary Wolfson Art Gallery, Miami, 1984, Arnold & Sheila Aronson Gallery, N.Y., Sculpture, 1986; several paintings in private collections, 1984—. Mem. NOW at Pro-Choice Rally, 1995, 96. Recipient Creativity award for Album Design, Art Direction Mag., 1995. Mem. NAFE. Avocations: knitting, hiking, swimming, roller blading, bike riding. Office: Pace Comm 1301 Carolina St Greensboro NC 27400

GAUDIERI, ALEXANDER V. J., museum director; b. 1940; separated; 1 child. BA, Ohio State U., 1962; diploma, Sorbonne U. Paris, 1962; postgrad., Colgate U., 1963; MBA in Internat. Fin., Am. Grad. Sch. Internat. Commerce, 1965; MA, NYU, 1976. Internat. banking officer Marine Midland Bank, N.Y.C., 1965-71; with Sotheby Parke Bernet, 1972—; dir. Telfair Acad. Arts and Scis., Savannah, Ga., 1977-83; dir. Montreal (Can.) Mus. Fine Arts, 1983-87; adj. prof. mus. studies program Grad. Sch. Arts and Scis., NYU; dir. Samuel F.B. Morse hist. site Locust Grove, Poughkeepsie, N.Y., 1995-96; pres. Hirschfeld Realty, N.Y.C., 1997—. Bd. dirs. Young Concert Artists, N.Y.C., Marietta/Cobb Museum of Art; mem. bd. sponsors Attingham Park Program, Eng. Barton Kyle Yount scholar. Mem. Assn. Art Mus. Dirs., Am. Assn. Mus. (accreditation commn.), Brit. Nat. Trust, Soc. Archtl. Historians. Office: 30 Atlanta St Marietta GA 30060

GAUDIERI, MILLICENT HALL, association executive; b. East Liverpool, Ohio, Jan. 26, 1941; d. John Thompson and Sara (Pollock) Hall; m. Alexander V.J. Gaudiere, June 10, 1967; 1 son, Alexandre Barclay Everson. A.A., Centenary Coll., Hackettstown, N.J., 1961; postgrad., U. Pitts., 1962. Polit. researcher U.S. embassy, Paris, 1964-65; asst. to pres. RTV Internat., Inc., N.Y.C., 1966-71; exec. dir. Assn. Art Mus. Dirs., N.Y.C., 1973—. Bd. dirs. Ga. Pub. Radio, Savannah, 1978-79. Mem. N.Y. Jr. League (dir. 1973-75 Vol. of Yr. award), Am. Assn. Mus. Republican. Presbyterian. Office: Assn of Art Mus Dirs 41 E 65th St New York NY 10021-6508*

GAUDREAU, JULES OSCAR, JR., insurance and financial services company executive; b. Springfield, Mass., Dec. 27, 1961; s. Jules O. Sr. and Joyce Anne (Fontaine) G.; m. Celine A. Thompson, Apr. 6, 1984; children: Jules, Chelsea, Elise. BA in Econs., Am. Internat. Coll., 1983. Cert. ins. counselor, lic. ins. advisor. Prin. The Gaudreau Group, Inc., Wilbraham, Mass., 1984—. Councilor City of Chicopee, Mass., 1982-84; mem. Hampden County Estate Planning Coun. Mem. Nat. Assn. Profl. Ins. Agts., Mass. Assn. Life Underwriters (pres.), Profl. Ind. Ins. Agts. Mass. (dir.), Springfield Assn. Life Underwriters (past pres.), Springfield C. of C., K.C., Rotary Club of Wilbraham. Avocations: golf, boating, fishing. Home: 14 Apple Hill Rd Wilbraham MA 01095-2614 Office: The Gaudreau Group Inc 2031 Boston Rd Wilbraham MA 01095-1103

GAUDREAU, RUSSELL A., JR., lawyer, educator; b. Weymouth, Mass., Feb. 25, 1943; s. Russell A. and Jean (Sandwen) G.; m. Elizabeth Flanagan, Dec. 26, 1966; children: Russell A. III, Seth F. BA, U. Mass., Amherst, 1965; JD cum laude, Suffolk U., 1968; LLM in Taxation, NYU, 1969. Law clk. to Hon. Harold R. Tyler, Jr., U.S. Dist Ct. (so. dist.) N.Y., 1969-70; assoc. Ropes & Gray, Boston, 1970-79; mng. ptnr. Ropes & Gray, Washington, 1990-94; ptnr. Ropes & Gray, Boston, 1979—; adj. prof. law Bentley Coll., 1978-80; adj. prof. law Boston U. Law Sch., 1980—; adj. prof. law Georgetown U. Law Ctr., 1991—; frequent spkr. in field. Editor-in-Chief Suffolk U. Law Rev. Bd dirs. BBB, Parents' and Children's Svcs., Handel and Haydn Soc. Mem. ABA (tax sect., com. employee benefits), New Eng. Benefits Coun. (dir.), D.C. Bar Assn., D.C. ERISA and Tax Discussion Groups. Office: Ropes & Gray One International Pl Boston MA 02110

GAUDRY, ROGER, chemist, university official; b. Quebec, Que., Can., 1913. B.A., Laval U., 1933, B.Sc. in Chemistry, 1937, D.Sc. in Organic Chemistry, 1940; postgrad. (Rhodes scholar), Oxford U., Eng., 1937-39. Faculty medicine Laval U., Quebec, 1940-54; asst. dir. research labs. Ayerst, McKenna Harrison Ltd., Montreal, Que., 1954-57; dir. Ayerst, McKenna Harrison Ltd., 1957-65, v.p., 1963-65; bd. govs., mem. exec. com. U. Montreal, 1961-65, rector, 1965-75; pres. Jules and Paul-Emile Lèger Found., 1983-95, hon. pres., 1995—; chmn. Network for Neural Regeneration and Functional Recovery, 1990-94, hon. chmn., 1994—. Contbr. sci. papers to profl. lit. Mem. coun. UN U., 1974-80, chmn., 1974-76. Decorated companion Order Can., 1968, grand officer Order of québec, 1992; recipient World Award Edn. World Cultural Coun., 1996. Fellow Royal Sco. Can., Chem. Inst. Can. (pres. 1955-56), Sci. Coun. Can. (vice chmn. 1966-72, chmn. 1972-75), Assn. Univs. and Colls. Can. (pres. 1969-71), Académie du Monde Latin Paris, Corp. Profl. Chemists Québec (life), Assn. Univs. Partiellement ou Entièrement de Langue Française (v.p. 1973-75), Internat. Assn. Univs. (pres. 1975-80), Conf. Rectors and Prins. Que. Univs. (pres. 1970-72). Office: Univ Montreal, Pavillon 2910 Bur 6 CP 6128, Montreal, PQ Canada H3C 3J7

GAUDUIN, MARIE-CLAIRE ELISABETH, microbiologist, immunologist, pilot; b. Freiburg, Germany, July 16, 1960; d. Alphonse and Elisabeth Marguerite (Nemeth) G.; m. Frederick Robert Vogel, Apr. 9, 1988 (div. Mar. 22, 1994); 1 child, Elizabeth Marie Vogel. BS in Med. Biology, Ecole Superieure de Biologie-Biochimie, Paris, 1982; MS in Immunology magna cum laude, Ecole Pratique Hautes Etudes Sorbonne, Paris, 1989; MS in Basic Med. Scis., NYU, 1993, PhD in Basic Med. Scis., 1996. Med. technologist in bacteriology and virology Inst. Sexually Transmitted Diseases, Paris, 1982-83; med. technologist in cytology, hematology, and parasitology Plouvier-Rondeau Lab., Montfermeil, France, 1983-84; rsch. technician dept. mycology Pasteur Inst., Paris, 1984-86; rsch. assoc. immunotoxicology dept. environ. medicine NYU, Tuxedo, 1989-90; asst. rsch. The Aaron Diamond Aids Rsch. Ctr. City of N.Y., 1992-96; postdoctorate rsch. fellow in medicine in immunology Harvard Med. Sch.-New England Regional Primate Rsch. Ctr., Boston, 1996-99, instr. medicine divsn. immunology, 1999—; study dir. rsch. projects United Biomed, Inc., N.Y.C., 1995-96; speaker in field. Contbr. articles to profl. jours. Recipient Student Intern award Pediat. AIDS Found., 1992-95, Scholar award, 1998, 1999. Mem. AAAS, Am. Soc. Microbiology, Assn. Women in Scis., Internat. Orgn. Women Pilots, Aircraft Owners and Pilots Assn. (pilot project mentor), N.Y. Acad. Scis. Roman Catholic. Avocations: private pilot, scuba diving, sky diving, piano, traveling in Europe and Africa. Home: 29 Hickory Rd Wellesley MA 02482 Office: Harvard Med Sch-New England Regional Primate Rsch Ctr PO Box 9102 One Pine Hill Dr Southborough MA 01772-9102

GAUDY, EDWARD, landscape architect, consultant; b. Buenos Aires, Dec. 27, 1927; came to U.S., 1957; s. Fernando and Elena (Duval) G.; m. Celia Nora Valls. Grad. in Landscape Arch., U. Buenos Aires, 1952. Lic. landscape arch., N.Y., Mass., Conn., N.J., Pa., Coun. Landscape Archtl. Registration Bds. Jr. landscape arch. Clarke & Rapuano, L.A.'s, N.Y.C., 1958-63; assoc. landscape arch. Zion & Breen, L.A.'s, N.Y.C., 1963-70; prin. Edward Gaudy, Environ. Design, South Nyack, N.Y., 1970-79; ptnr. Gaudy-Hadley Assocs., Nyack, 1979-89; prin. E.G.A. Site and Land Planning, Nyack, 1989—; cons. cmty. devel. Nyack Village. Designer waterfront projects: Haverstraw Marina, Clermont Condos Marina, Nyack, N.Y.; contbr. articles to profl. jours. Mem. Planning Bd., South Nyack, 1974. Mem. Am. Soc. Landscape Archs. (N.Y. chpt. v.p. 1972-73), Rotary Internat. (sr., Paul Harris fellow 1978). Avocations: sailing, swimming, oil painting. Office: EGA Site and Land Planning 42 Main St Nyack NY 10960-3204

GAUEN, PATRICK EMIL, newspaper correspondent; b. St. Louis, July 15, 1950; s. Louis Otto and Wilma Ellen (Rogers) G.; m. Patti Lynn Seib, Dec. 8, 1972 (div. 1992); children: Bethany, Heather; m. Karen Earhart, July 11, 1992; 1 stepchild, Christopher Stephenson. Student, So. Ill. U., 1968-70. Reporter, photographer Collinsville (Ill.) Herald, 1969-72, news editor, 1972-78; reporter St. Louis Globe-Democrat, 1978-84, mng. editor, 1984-85; reporter Ill. affairs St. Louis Post-Dispatch, 1985-89, polit. corr., 1989—; faculty univ. coll. Washington U., St. Louis, 1991—. Recipient Outstanding Med. News Series award Ill. State Med. Soc., 1970, Best Feature Story award Suburban Newspapers Am., 1971, Best News Story award Suburban Newspapers Am., 1973, Best Spot News Story award UPI Editors Ill., 1972, Best Pub. Svc. Reporting award Ill. Press Assn., 1974, Best Feature Story award, 1975, Bar-News Media award Bar Assn. Met. St. Louis, 1987, Bob Hardy award Southern Ill. Chiefs of Police and Southwestern Law Enforcement, 1996, Terry Hughes award St. Louis chpt. Newspaper Guild, 1996, Liberty Bell award Madison County Bar Assn., 1999. Mem. Mid-Am. Press Inst. (bd. dirs. 1985—), Press Club Met. St. Louis (bd. dirs. 1985—), Sigma Delta Chi (bd. dirs. St. Louis chpt. 1985—, chpt. pres. 1985-86, 86-87). Avocations: reading; photography. Home: 30 Meadowlark Ln Highland IL 62249-3000 Office: St Louis Post Dispatch 120 N Main St Edwardsville IL 62025-1902

GAUER, WILLIAM KEITH, accountant; b. Ft. Worth, Tex., Aug. 8, 1962; s. Robert James and Betty Sue (Burns) G.; m. Jennifer Sue Easterly, May 23, 1998. BS, Angelo State U., San Angelo, Tex., 1993. CPA, Tex. Ptnr., mgr. Golden Corral Corp., Jacksonville, Tex., 1981-85; ptnr. Louana Seafood, Houston, 1985-88; mgr. Cracker Barrell, Marion, Ill., 1989-90; staff Answer Angelo, San Angelo, 1991-93; cons. Schwartz Spilker & Co., Houston, 1993-98; sr. assoc. BDO Seidman, LLP, Houston, 1998—; editl. advisor Atlantic Infos. Publs., Washington, 1995-96. Treas., Memorial Dr. Bapt. Ch., Houston, 1997-99. Mem. Am. Inst. Pub. Acctg., Tex. Soc. CPAs. Baptist. Avocations: scuba, scale models, cycling, golf. Home: 10774 Briar Forest Dr # Dt Houston TX 77042-2321 Office: BDO Seidman LLP 1200 Smith St Ste 3060 Houston TX 77002-4401

GAUFF, LISA, broadcast journalist; b. Seattle; d. Joseph F. and Patricia A. (Lee) G. BA in Comm., U. Wash., 1987; MA in Journalism & Pub. Affairs, Am. U., 1988. Pub. info. asst. King County Coun., Seattle, 1985-86; reporter Sta. KUOW-FM, Seattle, 1985-86; news anchor Sta. KCMU-FM, Seattle, 1986-87; TV field prodr. Group W/Newsfeed Network, Washington, 1988-89; anchor, reporter Capitol TV, Washington, 1989-90, Newschannel 8, Washington, 1991-93; prodr., writer Sta. WJLA-TV, Washington, 1990-91; weekend anchor Sta. WHTM-TV, Harrisburg, Pa., 1993-94; morning anchor Sta. WJW-TV, Cleve., 1994-97; traffic anchor Sta. KNX-AM, L.A., 1998—; freelance reporter KABC-TV, UPN-TV, Fox TV, Sunworld, Satellite News, Media Gen., NPR Radio, 1988-89; ind. video prodr., 1989-91. Host, editor TV documentary Coming to Terms, 1993. Bd. dirs. NE Ohio AAU Baseball Com., 1995-96; moderator Ohio Acad. Decathalon, Cleve., 1995, 96; vol. United Way, Cleve., 1995, 96; honorary chair Women's Ctr. Greater Cleve., 1995; celebrity spokesperson Cleve. Christian Home for Children, 1995. Recipient John Merriman award Writer's Guild Am., 1988, Appreciation cert. United Negro Coll. Fund, 1995, 96; named One of 20 Top Women in Media, Washington D.C. Tchrs. Assn., 1993. Mem. NATAS, AFTRA. Avocations: art history, skiing, quiz shows. Office: Sta KNX-AM 6121 W Sunset Blvd Los Angeles CA 90028-6423

GAUGER, MICHELE ROBERTA, photographer, studio administrator, corporate executive; b. Elkhorn, Wis., Feb. 28, 1949; d. Robert F. and Christiane J. (Guiffaut) Marszalek; m. Richard C. Gauger, May 3, 1969 (div.). Student U. Wis., Superior, 1967-69, U. Wis., Whitewater, 1978-80, Winona Sch. Profl. Photography-Chgo., 1984-91; Degree in Photographic Craftsmenship, Profl. Photographers of Am., 1990, MA in Photography, 1994. Wedding photographer Fossum Studio, Elkhorn, 1973-78; owner Photography by Michele, Whitewater, 1978-81; pres., photographer, mgr., Michele Inc. of Wis., Whitewater, 1981—, Foxes Reg., 1987; speaker Wedding Photographers Internat. Conv., Las Vegas, Nev., 1987, 89, 97, Nashville, 1988, 93, Tenn. Profl. Photographers Assn., Nashville, 1987, Twin Cities Profl. Photographers, Mpls., 1987; lectr. Supra Color Seminar, Mpls., 1987, 89, San Francisco Profl. Photographers Assn., 1988, Monterey Profl. Photographers Assn., Nev. Profl. Photographers Assn., 1989, Mich. Profl. Photographers Assn., 1989, 94, Wis. Profl. Photographers Assn., 1993, 94, N.J. Profl. Photographers Assn., 1995, Nat. Conv. Profl. Photographers Assn., Las Vegas, 1997, New Orleans, 1998. Contbr. articles to profl. jours.; works exhibited Chinese Nat. Gallery, Beijing, 1987, 88, 89, 91, 94, 95, 96, Mem. Nat. Arbor Found, Nebr., 1984—. Recipient 1st place Wedding Photography award Internat. Wedding Photography, 1983, 84, 87, 88 (two awards), 89, 91, 96, 2nd place award, 1985, 96, Grand award, 1988; named to Wis. Ct. Honor, 1991, 96. Mem. Profl. Photographers Am. (Nat. Loan Collectional 1984, Epcot Exhibit 1996), Exhibited Chinese Nat. Gallery, Beijing, China (2d place award 1988, Bronze medal 1989, Bill Stockwell Lifetime Achievement award 1995), Wis. Profl. Photographer Assn., Wedding Photographer Internat., Winona Sch. Profl. Photography Alumni Assn., North Am. Hunters Assn., Whitewater C. of C. Republican. Roman Catholic. Avocations: world travel, big game hunting, horseback riding, cooking. Home and Office: Michele Inc N7240 Sand Pyramid Rd Whitewater WI 53190-4479

GAUGER, RANDY JAY, minister; b. Pekin, Ill., June 24, 1947; s. Wallace Earl and Opal Ellen (Berchtold) G.; m. Mary Beth Kane, Mar. 10, 1967; children: Cathy Lynn Gauger Loeppky, Christy Renee. BA, Judson Coll., 1969; MDiv, Bethel Theol. Sem., St. Paul, 1973; DMin, No. Bapt. Sem., 1996. Ordained to ministry, Am. Bapt. Chs., 1974. Pastor Delavan (Ill.) Bapt. Ch., 1973-80; sr. pastor 1st Bapt. Ch., ElDorado, Kans., 1980-87, Topeka, 1987-96; sr. pastor 1st Bapt. Ch. of Champaign at Savoy, Ill., 1996—; bd. dirs. cen. region Am. Bapt. Chs., Topeka, 1984-87, chmn. dept. evangelism, 1985-87, chmn. task force on regional mission statement, 1990-91, chmn. Facing Our Future campaign, 1990-95; bd. dirs. Judson Coll.; condr. workshops and preaching missions; host, phone person Your Question Please, Sta. WIBW-TV, 1989-94; trustee Ctrl. Bapt. Theol. Sem., Kansas City, Kans., 1995—. Trustee Ottawa (Kans.) U., 1990-96; v.p. Am. Bapt. Ch., 1996-97. Named Best Min., Topeka Metro News, 1990. Mem. Mins. Coun. Am. Bapt. Chs., Am. Bapt. Men U.S.A. (pastor, counselor 1991-93). Republican. Office: 1st Bapt Ch 1602 S Prospect Ave Savoy IL 61874-9546 *I have chosen to live my life under the Lordship of Jesus Christ, who gives meaning, purpose and direction to my life. This relationship has not only brought profound satisfaction but has given me a reference point for life and helped make sense out of a sometimes confusing world.**

GAUGHAN, DENNIS CHARLES, lawyer; b. Buffalo, July 3, 1955; s. Charles Joseph Gaughan and Mary Lynn Rucker; m. Mary Rose DeBergalis, Sept. 22, 1989; children: Charles Joseph, Dennis Charles Jr., Joseph Rocco. BA, Syracuse U., 1978; JD, N.Y. Law Sch., 1982. Bar: N.Y. 1984, U.S. Dist. Ct. (we. dist.) N.Y. 1984, U.S. Ct. Appeals (2d cir.) 1984, U.S. Supreme Ct. 1988. Counsel Erie County Dept. Social Svcs., Buffalo, 1984-89; pvt. practice, Hamburg, N.Y., 1989—; asst. town atty. Town of Hamburg, 1995—; prosecutor Village of Blasdell, N.Y. Chmn. Hamburg Rep. Ctrl. Com. 1988-90. Served with USAR, 1983-89. Mem. Nat. Assn. Criminal Lawyers, N.Y. Trial Lawyers Assn., Erie County Bar Assn., KC, Am. Legion, Am. Vets. Roman Catholic. Home: 5516 Pebble Beach Dr Hamburg NY 14075-5860 Office: 6161 S Park Ave Hamburg NY 14075-3837

GAUGHAN, EUGENE FRANCIS, accountant; b. Paterson, N.J., Aug. 31, 1945; s. Eugene Francis and Ruth Mae (Webster) G.; m. Arlene Barber, July 8, 1972 (dec. May 1981); m. Margaret Duffy, Jan. 2, 1983. AB, Coll. Holy Cross, 1967; MBA, Rutgers U., 1968; postgrad., Duke U., 1989; MME, Insead, France, 1990. CPA, N.Y., N.J., Conn. Staff acct., Price Waterhouse, LLP, 1968-70, sr. acct., 1970-72, mgr., The Hague, Netherlands, 1972-75, mgr., N.Y.C., 1975-78, sr. mgr., 1978-79, ptnr., 1979-98; ptnr. PricewaterhouseCoopers, 1998—, World Firm Coun. Ptnrs., 1987-90; mem. supr. bd. Price Waterhouse Eastern Europe, 1991-97; adv. assoc. Rutgers Grad. Sch. Mgmt. Trustee Lenox Hill Hosp., N.Y.C., 1981—. Mem. AICPA, N.Y. State Soc. CPAs (bd. dirs. 1986-89), Am. Acctg. Assn., The Netherlands-Am. Found. (bd. dirs.), Healthcare Trustees of N.Y., The Netherlands C. of C. in U.S. Clubs: N.Y. Athletic, Boca Raton Resort and Club. Lodges: K.C., Elks. Roman Catholic. Home: 164 E 72nd St New York NY 10021-4363 also: 33 Niamogue Ln PO Box 1675 Quogue NY 11959-1675 Office: PricewaterhouseCoopers LLP 1301 Avenue of the Americas New York NY 10019 also: 914 Jeffery St PO Box 1017 Boca Raton FL 33429-1017

GAUGHAN, PATRICIA ANNE, judge; b. Cleve., Oct. 21, 1953; d. John James and Alma Marie (Friedmann) G.; m. Roger Andrew Andrachik, Apr. 24, 1987; children: Brett Gaughan, Kathryn Gaughan. BA, St. Mary's Coll., 1975; JD, U. Notre Dame, 1978. Bar: Ohio 1978, Ind. 1978. Asst. county pros. Cuyahoga County Pros. Office, Cleve., 1978-83, 84-87; asst. U.S. atty. U.S. Atty.'s Office, Cleve., 1983-84; assoc. Reid, Johnson, Downes, Andrachik & Webster, Cleve., 1984-87; judge Common Pleas Ct. Cuyahoga County, Cleve., 1987-96, exec. com., 1993-96; judge U.S. Dist. Ct. (no. dist.) Ohio, Eastern divsn., 1996—; adj. prof. trial advocacy Cleve. Marshall Coll. of Law, 1983-87; mem. rules adv. com. Supreme Ct. of Ohio, Columbus, 1991-97; mem. paralegal studies adv. bd. Notre Dame Coll., Cleve., 1991—.

Bd. dirs. Nat. Conf. Met. Cts., 1993—, Newburgh House of Hope, Cleve., 1994-96, Conflict Resolution Ctr., Cleve., 1995-98; mem. children's trust fund bd. Cuyahoga County Commrs., Cleve., 1984-92. Mem. Ohio State Bar Assn., Ohio Jud. Conf. Assn., Cleve. Bar Assn. (trustee 1994-97), Cuyahoga County Bar Assn., Cuyahoga Women's Polit. Caucus, Common Pleas Ct. Judges Assn., Citizens League, Harold H. Burton Inn of Ct. (master of the bench), Kappa Gamma Pi. Office: US Dist Ct 201 Superior Ave E Ste 202 Cleveland OH 44114-1201

GAUGLER, ROBERT WALTER, retired career military officer; b. Paterson, N.J., Aug. 12, 1940; s. Roland Crosby and Frances Mabel (Martin) G.; m. Catherine Rosine Lindenmeyer, Sept. 4, 1965; children: David, Melinda, Matthew. BA, Hope Coll., 1963; MS, Pa. State U., 1966; PhD, Georgetown U., 1973. Rsch. biochemist Nat. Naval Dental Ctr., Bethesda, Md., 1970-76, Naval Dental Rsch. Inst., Great Lakes, Ill., 1976-80; rsch. adminstr. Uniformed Svcs. U., Bethesda, Md., 1980-83; spl. asst.for rsch. U.S. Navy Bur. Medicine & Surgery, Washington, 1983-87; dep. cmdr. Naval Med. Rsch. & Devel. Command, Bethesda, 1987-93; scientific adminstr. Naval Med. Rsch. Inst., Bethesda, 1993-96; ret. USN, 1996; rsch. program mgr. Geo-Centers Inc., 1996—. Capt. USN, 1966—. *

GAUKEL, ERICH JOHN, magazine editor; b. Sioux City, Aug. 11, 1970; s. Dennis Eugene and Carolyn Jean (McNeill) G.; m. Ramona Anne Kosbau, Aug. 19, 1995; children: Geneva, Hanne. BA, U. Iowa, 1993. Staff writer The Des Moines Register, 1994-95; mgmt. prodn. assocs. Songline/Tone Field Prodns., Berkeley, Calif., 1995-96; editor FFA New Horizons Mag., Carol Stream, Ill., 1996—; exec. sponsor Nat. FFA Orgn., Alexandria, Va., 1996—. Prodn. asst.: (CD recording) If Four Was One, 1996 (Grammy nominee 1997), T.J. Mem. Am. Agrl. Editors. Assn., Nat. Agri-Mltg. Assn. (Best of NAMA Nat. award for best co./assn. publ. 1997), Internat. Fedn. of Agrl. Journalists. Avocations: music, Architecture, baseball, raising twings, photography. Office: FFA New Horizons 191 S Gary Ave Carol Stream IL 60188-2095

GAULIN, JEAN, gas distribution company executive; b. Montreal, July 9, 1942; s. Paul and Berthe (Lariviere) G.; m. Andrée LeBoeuf; children: Marie-Claude, Philippe, Mathieu. Student, St.-Jean Royal Mil. Coll.; chem. Engr. and B.A.Sc., Ecole Polytechnique Montreal U., 1967. Dir. Que. Refinery of Canadian Ultramar Ltd., 1976-79; v.p. Golden Eagle Can., Montreal, 1977-79; v.p. supply and refining Ultramar Can. Inc., Toronto, 1979-80, pres., 1985-89; pres. Nouveler Inc., Montreal, 1980-82; pres., COO Gaz Métropolitain, Inc., Montreal, 1982-85; CEO Ultramar PLC/Am. Ultramar, Ltd., 1989-92; chmn. bd., CEO Ultramar Corp., Greenwich, Conn., 1992-96; vice chmn., pres., COO Ultramar Diamond Shamrock, 1996, corp. vice chmn., pres., COO, 1997-99, CEO, 1999—; bd. dirs. Scepter Resources Ltd, Ultramar PLC London, Quebec Telephone, Ultramar Can., Inc. Bd. dirs. Internat. Centre for Research and Studies in Mgmt., Montreal, 1982—; bd. dirs. Foundation de l'Universite du Quebec a Montreal, 1982—, Institut de Cardiologie de Montreal, 1983—; pres. Telethon for Quebec Soc. for Disabled Children, 1986. Served with Canadian Navy, 1958-62. Mem. Canadian Gas Assn. (dir. 1982—), Am. Gas Assn., Ordre des Ingénieurs du Que. Club: St. Denis. Office: Ultramar Diamond Shamrock Inc PO Box 696000 San Antonio TX 78269-6000*

GAULIN, LYNN, experiential education educator; b. Chgo., Nov. 26, 1937. BA, U. R.I., 1979, MA in Adult Edn., 1991; MSW, Boston Coll., Newton, Mass., 1981. Lic. social worker, Mass. Planner King Philip Elder Svcs., Foxboro, Mass., 1981-84; field coord. U. R.I., Kingston, 1984—, acting dir., 1995-96, instr. human sci. and svcs., 1988-98, acting dir. Office Internship and Field Experience, 1995-96; dir. svc. learning and UYA internship program Feinstein Ctr., 1997—; dir. Feinstein Ctr. for Svc. Learning/UYA Internship Program, 1997. Chmn. North Attleboro (Mass.) Dem. Town Treas. Com., 1990-96; mem., chmn. sch. com. North Attleboro Pub. Schs., 1981-91; mem. North Attleboro Bd. Selectmen, 1991-94; mem. edn. com., chmn. leadership com. Commn. on Women, Providence, 1989-97; mem. liaison adv. com. Washington (D.C.) Ctr., 1997—. Mem. Acad. Cert. Social Workers, Assn. Profl. and Acad. Women, New Eng. Orgn. Human Svc. Edn. (bd. dirs., membership chairwoman 1994—), Nat. Soc. Exptl. Edn. (chair internship spl. interest group 1997—), Phi Beta Kappa, Phi Kappa Phi (pres. U. R.I. chpt. 1994-95). Democrat. Avocation: travel. Home: PO Box 664 605 Broadway North Attleboro MA 02760-1167 Office: U RI Taft Hall Kingston RI 02881

GAULT, JANICE ANN, ophthalmologist, educator; b. Hammond, Ind., Sept. 3, 1965; d. William Wallace and Waltraud Anna (Konhäuser) G. BS, Duke U., 1987, MD, 1991. Diplomate Am. Bd. Ophthalmology. Intern in internal medicine Santa Barbara (Calif.) Cottage Hosp., 1991-92; resident in ophthalmology Wills Eye Hosp., Phila., 1992-95, clin. instr., 1995—. Contbr. articles to med. jours. Mem. AMA, ACS, Am. Acad. Ophthalmology, World Affairs Coun., Jr. League Phila., Duke Club Phila. (pres., treas. 1992—), Phi Beta Kappa, Alpha Omega Alpha. Avocations: tennis, scuba diving, photography, wine, travel. Office: Wills Eye Hosp 900 Walnut St Ste 1 Philadelphia PA 19107-5599

GAULT, JEANNIE FARMER, gerontological nurse, nursing home administrator; b. Norfolk, Va., May 26, 1944; d. Harrison Wesley and Frances Ailene (Neece) Farmer; m. Edward Dean Gault, Oct. 23, 1965; children: Greg, Jeff. Diploma in nursing, Burge-Protestant Hosp., Springfield, Mo., 1966. RN, Okla., Mo.; cert. gerontol. nurse.; lic. nursing home adminstr. Office nurse Mark M. Tendai, M.D., Springfield; RN supr. Aurora (Mo.) Nursing Ctr.; staff nurse Thomas (Okla.) Hosp.; nursing dir. McMahonúTomlinson Nursing Ctr., Lawton, Okla.; com. mem. Great Plains Vocat.-Tech. Health Occupation. Mem. Mo. State Student Nurses Assn. (first v.p. 1965), Nurses for Nurses (pres. 1987-88). Home: PO Box 363 Elgin OK 73538-0363

GAULT, ROBERT MELLOR, lawyer; b. Pitts., Sept. 3, 1945; s. James Edward and Laura (Mellor) G.; m. Mary Joan Donnelly, Sept. 18, 1983; children: Sarah, Laura, Matthew. BA, Williams Coll., 1968; JD, U. Mich., 1971. Bar: Wash. 1972, U.S. Dist. Ct. (we. dist.) Wash. 1972, U.S. Ct. Appeals (9th cir.) 1972, Mass. 1973, U.S. Dist. Ct. Mass. 1974, U.S. Ct. Appeals (1st cir.) 1974, U.S. Supreme Ct. 1977, U.S. Ct. Appeals (D.C. cir.) 1983, U.S. Ct. Appeals (7th cir.) 1984. Law clk. U.S. Dist. Ct. (we. dist.) Wash., Seattle, 1971-73; assoc. Mintz, Levin, Cohn, Ferris, Glovsky, and Popeo, P.C., Boston, 1973-78, mem., 1978—, chmn. employment, labor, benefits, and immigration dept.; former mem. adv. bd. Law Firm Resources Project. Former bd. dirs. Greater Boston Legal Svcs., 1982-95. Avocations: swimming, biking, fishing. Office: Mintz Levin Cohn Ferris Glovsky & Popeo PC 1 Financial Ctr Fl 39 Boston MA 02111-2657

GAULTNEY, JOHN ORTON, life insurance agent, consultant; b. Pulaski, Tenn., Nov. 7, 1915; s. Bert Hood and Grace (Orton) G.; m. Elizabethine Mullette, Mar. 30, 1941; children: Elizabethine G. McClure, John Mullette, Walker Orton, Harlow Denny. Student, Am. Inst. Banking, 1936; diploma, Life Ins. Agy. Mgmt. Assn., 1948, Little Rock Jr. Coll., 1950; Mgmt. C.L.U. diploma, 1952; grad. sales mgmt. and mktg., Rutgers U., 1957. CLU. With N.Y. Life Ins. Co., 1935—; regional v.p. N.Y. Life Ins. Co., Atlanta, 1956-64; v.p. N.Y. Life Ins. Co., N.Y.C., 1964-67; v.p. in charge group sales N.Y. Life Ins. Co., 1967-68, v.p. mktg., 1969-80, agt., 1980—; life ins. cons., 1981—; v.p. N.Y. Life Variable Contracts Corp., 1969-80; hon. dir. Bank of Frankewing (Tenn.), 1984—. Elder Presbyn. Ch., 1952; chmn. Downtown YMCA, Atlanta, 1963-65; mem. Bd. Zoning Appeals, Bronxville, N.Y., 1970-80; mem. Nashville YMCA, 1981—; mem. pub. rels. com. Nat. Coun. YMCAs, 1965-80; mem. internat. world svc. com. YMCA, 1968-80; chmn. Vanderbilt YMCA, N.Y.C., 1974-76, bd. dirs., 1966-76; bd. dirs. Memphis YMCA, 1939-40, Little Rock YMCA, 1941-55, Atlanta YMCA, 1959-65, Greater N.Y. YMCA, 1975-80; dir. Internat. Assn. Y's Men's Club, 1936-42. Capt. inf. AUS, 1942-45, MTO. Decorated Silver Star, Bronze Star with 3 clusters, Purple Heart with 2 clusters.; recipient Devereux C. Josephs award N.Y. Life Ins. Co., 1954, Cross of Mil. Svc. United Daughters of the Confederacy, 1973; named Ark. traveler, 1955; hon. citizen Tenn., 1956; Tenn. ambassador, 1981-87; Ky. col., 1963. Mem. Am. Soc. CLUs, Tenn. Soc. CLUs, Ark. Soc. CLUs (pres. 1950-51), Nat. Assn. Life Underwriters, Heritage Found., Carnton Assn. (bd. dirs. 1981-90, pres. 1987-88), N.Y. So. Soc. (trustee 1965-80), Williamson County Hist. Soc. (pres. 1983-85), Brentwood Hist. Trust, Giles County Hist. Soc., 361st Inf. Assn. World War II (pres. 1967-70), Mass. Soc. of the Cin., SAR (N.Y. state dir. 1970-80), Soc. Colonial Wars, Descendants of Colonial Clergy, Tenn. Sons of Revolution, Assn. Preservation Tenn. Antiquities (trustee 1984-93), Tenn. Soc. in N.Y. (pres. 1971-74, trustee 1980-85), Newcomen Soc. in Am., English Speaking Union, Capital City Club (Atlanta), Nashville City Club, Victory Svcs. Club (London), Sojourners, Heroes of '76 (comdr. 1993-94), Sovereign Mil. Order of the Temple of Jerusalem, Rotary, Masons, York Rite, Scottish Rite, Shriners. Home: 6109 Johnson Chapel Rd Brentwood TN 37027-5720 Office: NY Life Ins Co 17 Nationsbank Plz Nashville TN 37219-1606

GAUNCE, MICHAEL PAUL, insurance company executive; b. Paris, Ky., Oct. 17, 1949; s. Paul D. and Mary E. (Gardner) G.; m. Annette Beauchamp. BA, U. Ky., 1971. Cert. Life Underwriters Tng. Coun. Agt., mgr. Equitable Life of N.Y., Lexington, Ky., 1972-74; agt., regional mgr. Assn. Ins. Marketers, Inc., Indpls., Cin., South Bend, Ind., 1974-77; pres., chmn. Ins. Corp. Am., Indpls., 1977—; chmn. bd. Argent Ins. Corp., Indpls., Alternative Healthcare Marketers, Inc., Indpls.; dir., past chmn. Brokers Ins. Corp., Indpls.; dir. Brokers Ins. Corp. Tenn., Nashville, Brokers Ins. Agy., Atlanta; dir., Brokers Ins. Corp., Ky., Agy. Mgmt. Corp., Indpls.; cons. adv. bd. Blue Cross/Blue Shield, Indpls., 1982-89; mem. adv. bd. Acordia, Inc., Indpls., 1996-98. Active Rep. Nat. Com. Mem. Ind. Assn. Employee Benefit cons. (pres. 1984-88), Elks, Greenwood C. of C., Franklin C. of C., Seymour C. of C. Republican. Avocations: fishing, swimming, reading, investments, travel. Office: Ins Corp Am 5140 Commerce Cir Indianapolis IN 46237-9744

GAUNT, JANET LOIS, arbitrator, mediator; b. Lawrence, Mass., Aug. 23, 1947; d. Donald Walter and Lois (Neuhart) Bacon; m. Frank Peyton Gaunt, Dec. 21, 1969; children: Cory C., Andrew D. BA, Oberlin Coll., 1969; JD, Wash. U., St. Louis, 1974. Bar: Wash. 1974, U.S. Dist. Ct. (we. dist.) Wash. 1974, U.S. Ct. Appeals (9th cir.) 1978. Assoc. Davis, Wright, Todd, Riese & Jones, Seattle, 1974-80; arbitrator/mediator Seattle, 1981—; ldir. Seattle King County Labor Law Sect., 1976-77; mem. Pacific Coast Labor Law Planning Com., 1977-83; com. vice chmn. Wash. State Task Force on Gender and Justice on the Cts., 1987-89; chmn. Wash. Pub. Employment Rels. Commn., Olympia, 1989-96. Author, editor: Alternative Dispute Resolution, 1989; author: Public Sector Labor Mediation and Arbitration, Arbitration and Mediation in Washington, 2d edit., 1995. Pres. State Bd. of Wash. Women Lawyers, 1986. Mem. Nat. Acad. Arbitrators (dir. rsch. and edn. found. 1991-96, bd. govs. 1998—), Am. Arbitration Assn., Wash. State Bar Assn., Mediation Rsch. Edn. Project (cert. mediator), Wash. Women Lawyers.

GAUNTLETT, DAVID ALLAN, lawyer; b. Long Beach, Calif., May 16, 1954; s. Allan Leonard Gauntlett and Nelly (Brown) Mayne. BA in History magna cum laude, U. Calif., Irvine, 1976; JD, U. Calif., Berkeley, 1979. Bar: Calif. 1980, U.S. Dist. Ct. (cen. dist.) Calif. 1980, U.S. Dist. Ct. (ea., no. and so. dists.) Calif. 1982, U.S. Ct. Appeals (9th cir.) 1987, U.S. Ct. Appeals (4th cir.) 1993, U.S. Supreme Ct. 1994. Assoc. Paul, Hastings, Janofsky & Walker, L.A., 1979-81, Vitti, Miles & Robinson, Newport Beach, Calif., 1981-83, Burkley, Moore, Greenberg & Lyman, Torrance, Calif., 1983-86; ptnr. Callahan & Gauntlett, Irvine, Calif., 1986-95, Gauntlett & Assocs., Irvine, 1995—. Prodn. mgr. U. Calif. Law Rev., 1978-79. Calif. state scholar. Mem. ABA (chmn. emeritus intellectual property com. torts and ins. practice sect. 1995-96, mem. emerging issues com. 1995—, chmn. com. on ins. intellectual property sect. 1995—, vice chmn. ins. coverage com. litigation sect. 1995-96), Orange County Bar Assn., Calif. State Bar, Am. Bar Assn., Assn. Bus. Trial Lawyers. Republican. Episcopalian. Avocations: bicycling, art collection, cooking, sailing, tennis. Office: Gauntlett & Assocs 18400 Von Karman Ave Ste 300 Irvine CA 92612-1514

GAUQUIER, ANTHONY VICTOR, special education counselor; b. Rockland, Mass., Feb. 9, 1951; s. George Joseph and Mary Grace (Horrigan) G.; m. Beverly Marie Thomas, Sept. 5, 1975; children: Lydie, Kimberly, Edmund, Jason, Joshua, David. BA in History and Edn., Bridgewater State U., 1973. Bldg. maintenance staff Vets. Hosp., Brockton, Mass., 1974-77; hwy. laborer Hwy. Dept., Bridgewater, Mass., 1977-78; tchr. history and psychology Hanover (Mass.) H.S., 1978-79; spl. edn. counselor St. Colletta's Inc., Hanover, 1978—; part time freelance pub., 1980—, freelance ins. broker, 1984—; chair Rockland Spl. Edn. Parent Adv. Coun., 1992-93, scholarship chmn., 1993-97. Pub.: Pilgrim Recipes, 1980-97. State senate candidate Rep. Party, Plymouth Dist., 1990, 92, state rep. candidate, 1996; town com. chairperson Town of Rockland, 1992—; conv. del. Rep. Conv., Springfield, Mass., 1994; mem.-at-large Mass. Rep. Party, Boston, 1990-97, Rep. Nat. Com., 1990-97, Plymouth County Club, 1990-97, Lions Club, 1995-97, Gun Owners Action League, 1995, 97; coach Rockland Youth Soccer, 1992. Recipient Best Govt. award Pioneer Inst., Boston, 1994. Roman Catholic. Avocations: reading, gardening, hunting, fishing, bicycling. Home: 335 Spring St Rockland MA 02370-2636 Office: North River Collaborative Spring St Rockland MA 02370

GAUS, CLIFTON R., healthcare executive. MHA, U. Mich.; ScD, Johns Hopkins U. Mem. faculty Johns Hopkins U. Sch. Pub. Health, Balt., Georgetown U. Med. Sch., Washington; assoc. adminstr. policy, planning and rsch. Health Care Financing Adminstrn.; former adminstr. Agy Health Care Policy and Rsch. HHS; sr. v.p. for R & D, Kaiser Permanente, Oakland, Calif.; co-founder, past. pres., bd. dirs. Assn. Health Svcs. Rsch. Office: Kaiser Permanente 1 Kaiser Plz Ste 2600 Oakland CA 94612-3600

GAUS, DAVID SHEERIN, publisher; b. Indpls., Aug. 4, 1943; s. Arthur Richard and Laura Sheerin Gaus. BA in Zoology, U. Chgo., 1964; MA in Biology, Northwestern U., 1965. Chmn., CEO D.S. Gaus Corp., Indpls., 1983—. Pub., writer (newsletter) Sci-Notes, 1981—. Vol. Peace Corps, 1965-67. Avocations: physical fitness, walking, cooking. Home: 566 1/2 N Keystone Ave Indianapolis IN 46201-2040 Office: DS Gaus Corp 566 1/2 N Keystone Ave Indianapolis IN 46201-2040

GAUSE, CHARLES MARVIN, artist; b. Yakima, Wash., June 20, 1955; s. Paul E. and Margaret J. (Lutz) G.; m. Joyce F. Hayes, Oct. 9, 1976; children: Jonathan, Christel, Charlene. Author: Alaskan Art of Charles Gause, 1991, 2d edit., 1996; one-man shows include Fine Arts Gallery, 1982, 86,; represented in permanent collections Arco, Cominico Corp. and Sea-Land Corp. Ofcl. fundraising print artist Iditarod Trail Com., Anchorage, 1988-97; ofcl. artist Anchorage Fur Rendezvous, 1991-94. Recipient first lady's vol. award State of Alaska, 1991. Avocations: archery, handball, golf.

GAUSE, VAL HOLLIS, middle school educator; b. Atlanta, Feb. 19, 1949; s. Rufus Hollis and Beulah Eda (Hunt) G.; m. Amanda Kay Fuller, Dec. 28, 1974. BA, Lee U., 1971. Cert. secondary educator in journalism and English, Tex. Tchr. Windham Sch. Sys., Huntsville, Tex., 1975-81; news dir. KFRD Radio, Rosenberg, Tex., 1982-85; anchor Columbia Cable TV, Rosenberg, Tex., 1983-85; stringer UPI, 1982-85, Tex. State Network, Dallas, 1982-85, KIKK Radio, Houston, 1985; tchr. Fort Bend Ind. Sch. Dist., Sugar Land, Tex., 1985—; news dir., anchor for 1st radio/cable TV simulcast in USA, 1983; originated broadcast journalism in mid. sch. in Fort Bend Ind. Sch. Dist., 1993. Author of syndicated newspaper column of Before and AFterthoughts, 1984-91; inventor: (ednl. tool) Gause Grammar Wheel, 1993; author: (textbook) A Beginner's Guide to Media Communications, 1997. Dem. Party nominee County Cmmr., Fort Bend County, 1988. Named Outstanding Young Men of Am., U.S. Jaycees, 1983, United Way honoree, 1984, State of Tex. honoree Disting. Vol. Svc., 1984. Mem. Tex. Classroom Tchrs. Assn., Reporters and Mid. Sch. Suprs. (founder, pres. 1997—). Avocations: chess, fishing, hunting. Home: 8606 Grand Knolls Dr Houston TX 77083-5505

GAUSTAD, EDWIN SCOTT, historian; b. Rowley, Iowa, Nov. 14, 1923; s. Sverre and Norma (McEachron) G.; m. Helen Virginia Morgan, Dec. 19, 1946; children—Susan, Glen Scott, Peggy Lynn. B.A., Baylor U., 1947; M.A., Brown U., 1948, Ph.D., 1951. Instr. Brown U., 1951-52, Am. Council Learned Socs. scholar in residence, 1952-53; dean Shorter Coll., 1953-57; prof. humanities U. Redlands, 1957-65; assoc. prof. history U. Calif., Riverside, 1965-67; prof. U. Calif., 1968-89, prof. emeritus, 1989; prof. Princeton Theological Seminary, Princeton, N.J., 1991-92, Auburn U., 1993; vis. prof. Baylor U., 1976, U. Calif., Santa Barbara, 1986, U. Richmond, 1987. Author: The Great Awakening in New England, 1957, Historical Atlas of Religion in America, 3d edit., 1999, Religious History of America, revised edit., 1990, Dissent in American Religion, 1973, Baptist Piety: The Last Will and Testimony of Obadiah Holmes, 1978, George Berkeley in America, 1979, Faith of Our Fathers, 1987, Liberty of Conscience: Roger Williams in America, 1991, Revival, Revolution, and Religion in Early Virginia, 1994, Sworn on the Altar of God: A Religious Biography of Thomas Jefferson, 1996, Church and State in America, 1998, Memoirs of the Spirit, 1999. Served to 1st lt. USAAC, 1943-45. Decorated Air medal; Am. Council Learned Socs. grantee, 1952-53, 72-73; Am. Philos. Soc. grantee, 1972-73. Mem. Am. Soc. Ch. History (pres.), Orgn. Am. Historians, Phi Beta Kappa. Democrat. Baptist. Home: 599 Vista De La Ciudad Santa Fe NM 87501-6300 Home: PO Box 882 Gualala CA 95445-0882

GAUSTAD, RICHARD DALE, financier; b. Anchorage, Alaska, Oct. 22, 1952; s. Sidney O. and Beulah (Pierce) G.; m. Lynell Dory, May 7, 1982; children: Kelsey, Eric. MusB, Utah State U., 1974; Diploma, LDS Inst. of Religion, Logan, Utah, 1975; postgrad. in law, Newport U. Sch. of Law, 1992—. Pres. Advt. Specialists, Logan, Utah, 1975-77, Cache Card, Logan, Utah, 1976-77, Northridge Enterprises, Inc., Logan, Utah, 1977-81, Nova's Gen. Store, Salt Lake City, 1981-82; chmn. Handicapped Distbrs., Inc., Mesa, Ariz., 1990-91; pres. Phase III Mktg. Corp., Mesa, Ariz., 1982-91, Infocom Capital Corp., Gilbert, Ariz., 1992—, Western Systems, Inc., Carson City, Nev., 1989—; dir. Western Systems, Inc., Gilbert, 1989-92; pres. Factor's Clearing House, Gilbert, 1992, Infocom Capital Corp., Gilbert, 1992, Handicapped Warehouse, Inc.; ind. rep. Island Funding Ltd.; pvt. bus. cons.; pres. Skytech Direct, Inct., FCH, Inc., mktg. dir., bus. fin. cons., Capital Svc. Grp., LLC, 1999. Author: Financial Report Series, Vol. 1, 1990, Vol. II, 1992. Mem. Gilbert C. of C. LDS. Avocations: guitar, piano, drums, tennis, martial arts. Home: 1733 W 12600 S Riverton UT 84065-7043 also: Factors Clearing House 425 E Guadalupe Rd Ste 103 Gilbert AZ 85234-4636

GAUT, NORMAN EUGENE, software firm executive; b. Gilman, Colo., Sept. 20, 1937; s. Marvin Joseph and Margaret Elmo (Carl) G.; m. Madeleine Suzanne Dupuy, Aug. 29, 1964; children: Christopher Carl, Eric Kerwin, Jeffrey Gareth. BA in Physics, UCLA, 1959; MS in Meteorology, MIT, 1964, PhD in Meteorology, 1967; postgrad., Harvard U., 1976. V.p. Environ. Research and Tech., Inc., Concord, Mass., 1968-77, pres., 1977-85; pres., CEO, PictureTel Inc., Peabody, Mass., 1986-98; CEO, Continuity Solutions, Inc., San Francisco, 1998-99, chmn., 1999—, also bd. dirs.; bd. dirs. PictureTel Corp., Teloquent, Inc., EmPower, Inc.; trustee Boston U.; mem. MIT Corp. Served with USAF, 1959-62. NASA grantee, 1963-67. Mem. Sigma Xi, Phi Beta Kappa. Office: Continuity Solutions Inc 524 2d St San Francisco CA 94107

GAUTHIER, MARY ELIZABETH, librarian, researcher, secondary education educator; b. Tudor, Alta., Can., May 17, 1917; d. Harold Bertram and Mary Evelyn (Foley) Bliss; m. Louis Lyons Gauthier, May 31, 1947 (dec. 1976). PhB, Northwestern U., 1970; MA in Edn., Lewis U., 1976; EdD, Pacific States U., London, 1979. Clk. LaGrange (Ill.) Pub. Libr., 1956-57; package libr. AMA, Chgo., 1958-60; staff libr. Duff, Anderson & Clark, Chgo., 1960-63; libr./tchr. Fremont Sch. Dist. 79, Mundelein, Ill., 1970-75; substitute tchr. Valleyview Sch. Dist. 365-U, Romeoville, Ill., 1978-89; dormitory dir./tchr. Project Upward Bound, Romeoville, Ill., 1984-94, enrichment studies, 1991-94; ind. researcher South Bend, Ind., 1990-94; instr. Joliet (Ill.) Jr. Coll., 1986-89; cons. Wash. High Sch.; bd. of advisors Ivy Tech. Coll., Southbend, 1993. Author: Some Basic Principles of New Scientific Attitudes in Education, 1980, Communication: Roots of Tradition, 1986; contbr. monograph and articles to profl. jours. Active Manor Pk. Community Assn., Ottawa, Can., 1953. With RCAF, 1943-45. Recipient Gold medal Internat. Symposium on the Mgmt. of Stress, Monte Carlo, 1979; grantee Ill. State Bd. Edn., 1985, Ind. U. South Bend, 1992. Mem. AAAS, N.Y. Acad. Scis.

GAUTHIER, SERGE GASTON, neurologist; b. Montreal, Que., Can., Sept. 18, 1950; s. Gaston and Suzanne (Tremblay) G.; m. Louise Gauthier; children: Eric, Judith. BA, Coll. Ste-Marie, 1969; MD, U. Montreal, 1973; neurology, McGill U., 1977. Fellow Med. Rsch. Coun. Can., 1976-78; staff Montreal Neurol. Hosp. and Inst., 1978-86; dir. McGill Ctr. for Studies in Aging, Verdun, Que., 1987-97. Contbr. articles on treatment of Alzheimer's disease to med. jours. Office: McGill U Ctr Studies in Aging, McGill U Ctr Aging Studies, 6825 Blvd La Salle, Verdun, PQ Canada H4H 1R3

GAUTIER, DICK, actor, writer; b. Los Angeles, Oct. 30, 1937; s. Aldoma Napoloeon and Marie Antionette Gautier; children: Christine, Rand, Denise. Student pub. schs., Los Angeles. Comedian, hungry i, San Francisco; appeared in N.Y.C. supper clubs including Blue Angel, Bonsoir, Coconut Grove; starred on Broadway as Conrad Birdie in Bye Bye Birdie, 1960-62 (Tony award and Most Promising Actor nominee); appeared in motion pictures including Billy Jack Goes to Washington, Divorce, American Style, Ensign Pulver, Manchu Eagle, Fun with Dick and Jane; played Hymie in series Get Smart; starred in TV series Mr. Terrific, CBS, It's Your Bet, NBC, Can You Top This?, Here We Go Again, ABC; starred as Robin Hood in TV series When Things Were Rotten, ABC, 1975; author: The Art of Caricature, 1985, The Creative Cartoonist, 1988, The Career Cartoonist, 1992, Actors as Artists, 1992, Drawing and Cartooning 1001 Faces, A Child's Garden of Weirdness, 3 books art instrn., 1992, Musicians as Artists, 1994; (screenplay) Uncle Sam; contbg. writer to numerous TV situation comedies; composer numerous songs. Active in Thalians Charity. Served with Spl. Services br. USN. Mem. Actors Equity Assn., AFTRA, Screen Actors Guild, ASCAP, Am. Guild Variety Artists. Office: 11333 Moorpark St Studio City CA 91602-2618

GAUVEY, RALPH EDWARD, JR., writer, poet; b. Columbus, Ohio, Oct. 24, 1947; s. Ralph Edward and Frances Jean (Horswell) G. BA, Union Inst., Cin., 1972. Contbg. author Little Mag., 1973, Zen Poems, 1983, A Selection of Poems, 1987, Love in Enlightenment, 1997. Buddhist. Home: 128 Blackstone St Apt 6 Woonsocket RI 02895-3028

GAUVEY, SUSAN K., judge; b. Van Wert, Ohio, Mar. 1, 1948; d. Richard David and Asta Walburga (Frericks) G.; m. David E. Kern, May 10, 1975; children: Megan E. Gauvey-Kern, Kathryn A. Gauvey-Kern, Elizabeth H. Gauvey-Kern. Student, Georgetown U., 1968-69; BA cum laude Polit. Sci., Rosary Coll, River Forest, Ill., 1970; JD, Northwestern U., 1973; postgrad. Mental Hygiene, Johns Hopkins U., 1976-77. Bar: Wash. 1974, Md. 1975. Law clerk to fed. dist. ct. judge We. Dist. Ct., Seattle, Wash., 1973-74; staff atty. Mental Health Law Project Legal Aid Bur., Balt., 1975-77; chief Mental Health Law Project, 1977-79; asst. atty. gen. Dept. Health and Mental Hygiene Office of Atty. Gen., Balt., 1979-81, asst. atty. gen. Civil Divsn., 1981-86, prin. counsel trial litigation, 1984-86; with litigation divsn. Venable, Baetjer and Howard L.L.P., Balt., 1986-96; magistrate judge U.S. Dist. Ct. for Md., Balt., 1996—. Contbr. articles to profl. jours. Chair bd. dirs. Marian House for Women. Mem. Md. Inst. Continuing Profl. Edn. Lawyers (instr.), Md. State Bar Assn., Women's Bar Assn., Balt. City Bar Assn., Wranglers Law Club. Democrat. Episcopalian. Avocations: jogging, music. Office: US Courthouse 101 W Lombard St Baltimore MD 21201-2626

GAUVIN, CHARLES F., professional society administrator. AB magna cum laude, Brown U., 1978; JD, U. Pa., 1985. Legis. coord. R.I. Statewide Planning Program, Providence, 1980-82; tchg. asst. Brown U., Providence, 1982; summer assoc. litigation/labor depts. Goodwin Proctor & Hoar, Boaston, 1984; assoc. Pierce, Atwood, Scribner, Allen, Smith & Lancaster, Portland, Maine, 1985-86, Beveridge & Diamond, P.C., Washington, 1986-91; pres., CEO, mem. bd. trustees Trout Unltd., Arlington, Va., 1991—. Editor U. Pa. Law Rev.; contbr. articles to profl. jours. Avocations: fly fishing, hunting, gardening, art, literature. Office: Trout Unlimited 1500 Wilson Blvd Ste 310 Arlington VA 22209-2427*

GAUWITZ, DONNA FAYE, nursing educator; b. Ottawa, Ill., Nov. 20, 1955; d. DeWitt F. and Grace V. (Siegert) Eckerman; m. William J. Gauwitz Jr., Oct. 15, 1977. Diploma, St. Francis Hosp. Sch. Nursing, Peoria, Ill., 1976; BS, Bradley U., Peoria, 1980; MS, Northwestern U., 1988; student, Barry U., 1996—. Instr. nursing Ill. Wesleyan U., Bloomington, Ill. Cen. Coll., Peoria; founder, dir. eating disorders clinic St. Francis Med. Ctr., Peoria; instr. nursing Meth. Med. Ctr. Sch. Nursing, Peoria, 1988-95; asst. prof. Broward C.C., 1998—; item writer for nat. licensure exam. for RNs,

Monterey, Calif., 1992, San Francisco, 1993, Princeton, N.J., 1993, 94, 99. Contbr. articles to profl. jours. Mem. Sigma Theta Tau. Home: 2992 SW 174th Ave Miramar FL 33029-5551

GAVALÁS, ALEXANDER BEARY, artist; b. Limerick, Ireland, Jan. 6, 1945; came to U.S., 1946; s. Emmanuel Zenon and Mary (Beary) G. Diploma, Sch. Art & Design, N.Y.C., 1963; student Guilmant Organ Sch., 1970, Kerpel Sch. Dental Tech., 1972; BA, Coll. New Rochelle, 1995. Cert. 20th Century Hudson River Artist. One man shows at Krasl Art Ctr., St. Joseph Mich., 1980, The Tweed Mus. Art, U. Minn., Duluth, 1980, Fine Arts Center of Clinton, Ill., 1980, Western Ill. U. Library Gallery, Macomb, 1981, Ft. Wayne Mus. Art, Ind., 1982, Mary Crest Coll., Eberdt Art Gallery, Davenport, Iowa, 1982, Arnot Art Mus., Elmira, N.Y., 1982, Queens Coll. Art Ctr., Flushing, N.Y., 1983; exhibited in group shows Taft Hotel, N.Y.C., 1964, J. Walter Thompson Art Gallery, N.Y.C., 1964, Hudson River Mus., Yonkers, N.Y., 1974-75, Far Gallery, N.Y.C., 1976-79, Eric Galleires, N.Y.C., 1981-82, Served as Art Juror for NYC Scholastic Art Awds., Scholastic, Inc., NYC, 1999. Contbr. articles to profl. jours. Juror N.Y.C. Scholastic Art award, 1999. Honorable mention Congl. record 88th congress for cultural contbr. to Life or Nation, 1964, award for work on spl. file Smithsonian Inst. from Harry Rand. Address: 65 Horton St Malverne NY 11565-1512

GAVALAS, GEORGE R., chemical engineering educator; b. Athens, Greece, Oct. 7, 1936; s. Lazaros R. and Belouso A. (Matha) G. BS, Nat. Tech. U., 1958; MS, U. Minn., 1962, PhD, 1964. Asst. prof. chem. engring. Calif. Inst. Tech., 1964-67, asso. prof., 1967-75, prof., 1975—; cons. in field. Author: Nonlinear Differential Equations of Chemically Reacting Systems, 1968, Coal Pyrolysis, 1983; contbr. articles to profl. jours. Mem. AIChE (Tech. award 1968, Wilhelm award 1983), Am. Chem. Soc., N.Am. Membrane Soc. Home: 767 S Orange Blvd # 3 Pasadena CA 91105-1779 Office: Calif Inst Tech Caltech 210-41 1201 E California Blvd Pasadena CA 91125-0001

GAVALER, JUDITH ANN STOHR VAN THIEL, bio-epidemiologist; b. Pitts., Aug. 5; d. Frank Howell and Nancy Helen (Hoovler) Stohr; m. John Raymond Gavaler, Nov. 17, 1962 (div. Apr. 1974); children: Joan Susan, Christopher Paul; m. David Hoffman Van Thiel, May 13, 1978 (div. July 1997). BS, Hood Coll., 1961; PhD, U. Pitts., 1986. Jr. engr. Westinghouse Rsch., Pitts., 1961-63; rsch. asst. U. Pitts. Sch. Medicine, 1974-78, rsch. assoc., 1978-86, asst. prof., 1986-88, assoc. prof., 1988-92, prof., 1993; asst. prof. dept. epidemiology U. Pitts. Grad. Sch. Pub. Health, 1988-93; mem., head women's health Okla. Med. Rsch. Found., Okla. City, 1993—; sr. scientist women's rsch. Okla. Transplantation Inst., Bapt. Med. Ctr. Okla., chief women's rsch., 1994-96, chief statis. and database svcs., 1994-96; mem. Inst. Medicine Conf. Com., 1991; adj. prof. biostats. and epidemiology U. Okla. Health Sci. Ctr., 1994—; mem. rsch. rev. com. biochem. physiol. medicine NIAAA, 1993-96; mem. rsch. rev. com. NIH, ALTX-4, 1996—. Mem. editl. bd. Alcoholism, Clinical and Experimental Research jour., 1989-94 (assoc. editor 1994-98), Digestive Diseases and Scis. jour., 1990-94; contbr. articles to profl. jours. Active LWV, Pitts., 1965-93, Oklahoma City, 1993—; mem. Oklahoma City Art Mus. Assocs., 1995—. Grantee Nat. Inst. Alcohol Abuse and Alcoholism, 1985—; recipient Young Investigator award Rsch. Soc. Alcoholism, 1990. Fellow Am. Coll. Nutrition; mem. Internat. Assn. Study of the Liver, Rsch. Soc. on Alcoholism (Young Investigator award 1990), Internat. Soc. Biomed. Rsch. on Alcoholism, Am. Assn. for Study of Liver Diseases, Am. Gastroenterol. Assn. Democrat. Achievements include research on beneficial effects of moderate alcoholic beverage consumption in normal postmenopausal women of all ethnic/racial backgrounds, presence of plant estrogens (phyto estrogens) in alcoholic beverages, hormonal status of women with end stage liver disease, deleterious effects of ethanol on reproductive parameters in both male and female experimental animals, endocrinopathy of end-stage liver disease in women, effects of liver transplantation on quality of life and hormonal status of women, variability in hormonal responds to estrogen replacement therapy and the role of moderate alcohol consumption as an effect modulator. Home: 1816 Huntington Ave Oklahoma City OK 73116-5524 Office: Okla Med Rsch. Found 825 NE 13th St Oklahoma City OK 73104-5005

GAVENCAK, JOHN RICHARD, pediatrician, allergist; b. Bklyn, June 21, 1949; m. Madeline Gavncak Aug. 12, 1972. BA, NYU, 1970; MD, N.Y. Med. Coll., Valhalla, 1974. Diplomate Am. Bd. Pediatrics, Am. Bd. Allergy and Immunology. Resident in pediats. Met. Hosp., N.Y.C., 1974-76, fellow in allergy and immunology, 1976-78; pvt. practice allergist East Rockaway, N.Y., 1976—. Fellow Am. Coll. Pediatrics, Am. Coll. Allergy and Immunology.; mem. N.Y. Allergy Soc., Long Island Allergy Soc. Avocations: fishing, gardening, boating. Office: John R. Gavencak MD 53-42 Francis Lewis Blvd Bayside NY 11364

GAVENDA, J(OHN) DAVID, physicist; b. Temple, Tex., Mar. 25, 1933; s. Edward and Rose Katherine (Machalek) G.; m. Janie Louise Yeoman, Dec. 22, 1952; children—Victor Joseph, Philip Martin. Student, U. Chgo., 1950-51; B.S., U. Tex., Austin, 1954, M.A., 1956; Ph.D., Brown U., 1959. Asst. prof. physics U. Tex., Austin, 1959-62; assoc. prof. U. Tex., 1962-65, assoc. prof. physics and edn., 1965-67, prof., 1967-99, prof. emeritus, 1999—. Contbr. artices on physics of metals and electromagnetic wave propagation to profl. jours. Sr. rsch. fellow Inst. Study of Metals, U. Chgo., 1963, NATO sr. fellow in sci. U. Oslo, 1969. Fellow Am. Phys. Soc., Tex. Acad. Sci.; mem. AAUP, AAAS, IEEE, Am. Assn. Physics Tchrs. (Robert N. Little award 1988, Disting. Svc. citation 1997), Phi Beta Kappa, Sigma Xi. Democrat. Baptist. Home: RR 3 Box 204D Leander TX 78641-6101 Office: Univ Tex Dept Physics Austin TX 78712

GAVIN, AUSTIN, retired lawyer; b. Phila., Feb. 6, 1909; m. Helen A. Blaisdell; 1 child, Susan. AB, Ursinus Coll., 1930, LLD (hon.), 1974; LLB, U. Pa., 1933; LLD (hon.), Lehigh U., 1991. Bar: Pa. 1933. Jr. counsel Pa. Dept. Revenue, 1934-35; law clk. to justice Pa. Supreme Ct., 1935-36; with Pa. Power & Light Co., Allentown, 1936-74; gen. counsel Pa. Power & Light Co., 1958-60, v.p., gen. counsel, 1960-65, v.p. mgmt. services, 1965-69, exec. v.p., 1969-74; exec. cons. Lehigh U., 1974-88; Chmn. Lehigh County Charter Study Comm., 1974-76. Bd. dirs. Minsi Trails coun. Boy Scouts Am., pres., 1966-71. 1st sgt. AUS, WWII. Decorated Silver Star, Purple Heart. Mem. Am. Pa., Lehigh County bar assns., Am. Arbitration Assn. (nat. panel arbitrators). Home: 6285 Sweetwood Dr Macungie PA 18062-9145

GAVIN, DELANE MICHAEL, television writer, producer, director; b. Pierre, S.D., Oct. 6, 1935; s. Daniel Everett and Evelyn Agnes (Michaelson) G.; m. Paula Ethel Handelman, Feb. 22, 1969. BA in Journalism, San Francisco State U., 1962; MA in Journalism, UCLA, 1971; MBA in Organizational Behavior, U. So. Calif., 1982. With San Francisco Examiner, 1961-62; corr. AP, San Francisco, Reno and Las Vegas, Nev., 1962-64; reporter Las Vegas Rev.-Jour. Sun, 1964-65; editor suburban sect. Los Angeles Times, 1965-66; writer, producer news Sta. KNXT-TV, Hollywood, Calif., 1966-68; writer, reporter, dir., producer news Sta. KNBC-TV, Burbank, Calif., 1968-76; documentary writer, producer, dir. NBC-News, N.Y.C., 1976-78; med. producer KABC-TV, Hollywood, 1978—; instr. journalism U. So. Calif., 1978-90; sr. lectr. Calif. State U., Northridge, 1994-95. Served with USNR, 1955-57. Recipient Christopher award for directing Sta. NBC News TV The Christophers, 1973, for producing, 1976, Golden Mike award Radio and TV Assn., 1968, 69, 70, 72, 74, 75. Mem. Acad. TV Arts and Scis. (bd. govs. 1976-80, 82-86, 88-92, Emmy award 1968, 69, 70, 72, 73, 74), Dirs. Guild Am., Writers Guild Am., AFTRA, Nat. Assn. Broadcast Employees and Technicians, Wire Service Guild, Am. Newspaper Guild, Sigma Delta Chi. Home: 12508 Sarah St Studio City CA 91604-1112 Office: 4151 Prospect Ave Los Angeles CA 90027-4524

GAVIN, JAMES JOHN, JR., diversified company executive; b. Phila., July 18, 1922; s. James John and Mary E (Ludlow) G.; m. Zita C. Kabeschat, Aug. 23, 1952; children—William, James, Kevin, Steven, Peter. B.S. in Econs, U. Pa., 1949. Sr. acct. Peat, Marwick, Mitchell & Co., Phila., 1949-53; chief acct. Indian Head Mills, Inc. (name changed to Indian Head Inc.), N.Y.C., 1953, asst. treas., 1953-56, contr., 1956-61, treas., v.p., 1961-66, v.p. fin., 1966-68; v.p. fin., contr. Borg-Warner Corp., Chgo., 1968-75, sr. v.p. fin., 1975-85, vice-chmn., 1985-87. Served with USNR, 1943-46. Mem. Delta Sigma Pi, Beta Alpha Psi, Beta Gamma Sigma. Home: 161 Thorntree Ln Winnetka IL 60093-3731

GAVIN, JAMES RAPHAEL, III, biochemist; b. Oviedo, Fla., Nov. 23, 1945; m. Annie Ruth Jackson, June 19, 1971; children: Hakkim, Lamar. BS in Chemistry, Livingstone Coll., Salisbury, N.C., 1966; PhD in Biochemistry, Emory U., 1970; MD, Duke U., 1975. Diplomate Am. Bd. Internal Medicine, Nat. Bd. Med. Examiners. With USPHS, 1971—; staff assoc. diabetes br. NIH, Bethesda, Md., 1971-73; intern dept. pathology Duke U., Durham, N.C., 1975-76; intern dept. internal medicine Barnes Hosp., St. Louis, 1976-77, resident dpet. internal medicine, 1977-78, asst. physician, 1978-85, assoc. physician, 1985-87; prof. medicine, chief diabetes sect. U. Okla. Health Scis. Ctr., Oklahoma City, 1988-89, William K. Warren prof. diabetes studies, 1989-91; sr. scientific officer Howard Hughes Med. Inst., Chevy Chase, Md., 1991—; asst. prof. medicine Washington U., St. Louis, 1978-85, dir. RIA core lab., diabetes, rsch., tng. ctr., 1978-87, assoc. prof., 1985-87; George H. Howard, Jr. lectr. Meharry Med. Coll., 1988; Dr. Martin L. King, Jr. lectr. Washington U., 1988; Zollicofer vis. prof. U. N.C., 1990, Ralph Landes lectr., 1996; George H. Hamwi Meml. lectr. Ohio State Coll., 1991; Marty Alpern lectr. Henry Ford Hosp., 1991; Edward Hook Disting. lectr. U. Va., Charlottesville, 1994; Roerig Diabetes vis. prof. U. Hawaii Med. Ctr., Honolulu, 1995; mem. med. sci. adv. com. Juvenile Diabetes Found. Internat., 1981; mem. adv. com. minority med. faculty devel. program Robert Wood Johnson Found., 1983-93, nat. program dir., 1992—, sr. program cons., 1987—, nat. program dir. minority med. edn. program, 1987-93, ; bd. trustees, 1996—; mem. adv. com. ctr. drugs biologics FDA, 1986-90; mem. Nat. Diabetes Adv. Bd., 1988-92; spl. reviewer endocrinology study sect. NIDDK, 1989-91, chmn. study sect. initiative diabetes minorities, 1991, chmn. study sect. intervention minotities diabetes, 1993, chmn. spl. rev. group prevention type 2 diabetes, 1994, chmn. investigator's working group diabetes minorities, 1995, mem. data monitoring bd. diabetes prevention program, 1995—; mem. com. increasing minority participation in health professions Inst. Medicine, Washington, 1992-94; mem. bd. overseers urban inst. Liberty Med. Ctr., Balt., 1993; mem. adv. coun. Miles Inst. Health Care Comm., 1994—; chmn. diabetes adv. bd. Bayer Pharm., Inc., 1995—; mem. steering com. Nat. Diabetes Edn. Program, 1995—; various vis. prof. Author: (chpt.) Immunopharmacology, 1977, Introduction to Endocrine Investigation: Techniques and Concepts, 1987, Key Issues in Minority Education: Research Directions and Practical Implications, 1989; co-author: (chpt.) Advances in Human Growth Hormone Rsch., 1973; mem. editl. bd. Am. Jour. Physiology, 1982-88, Am. Jour. Med. Sci., 1989-94, Acad. Medicine, 1994—; contbr. articles to Endocrinology, Sci., Biochemistry Biophysics Rsch. Comm., Nature New Biology, Jour. Biol. Chem., Jour. Clin. Endocrinology Metabolism, Pharmacology Rev., Israel Jour. Med. Sci., Jour. Pediat., Jour. Exptl. Medicine, Metabolism, Archives Internal Medicine, Jour. Applied Physiology, Obstetrics Gynecology, Diabetes, Am. Jour. Physiology, Am. Jour. Medicine, Nephron, Diabetes Edn., Bone, Am. Jour. Nursing, Diabetologia, Brain Rsch., Acta Diobetol, Preventive Medicine, Internat. Jour. Obesity, Diabetes Forecast, Am. Clin. Climatol. Assn., Patient Care. Founder, bd. dirs. Alpha Edn. Found. Bd., St. Louis, 1988—; mem. Okla. State Student Loan Authority, 1989-90; bd. trustees Okla. Sch. Sci. Math. Found., 1991—. Elk's scholar, 1962; recipient traineeship award NSF, 1966-70, Spl. Achiever award St. Louis Sentinel Newspaper, 1982, Disting. Alumnus award Nat. Assn. Opportunity Higher Edn., 1987, Excellence award Okla. Alliance Affirmative Action, 1988, Caniel Hale Williams award Chgo. Med. Assn., 1993, E.E. Just award Am. Soc. Cell Biology, 1995—; USPHS Predoc. fellow, 1970, Hastings Inst. Ethics Life Scis. fellow, 1971-75, Washington U. Sch. Medicine fellow, 1978-79; named Outstanding African Am. in Medicine, Aetna, 1993. aem. Am. Assn. Physicians, Am. Diabetes Assn. (mem. rsch. com. St. Louis affiliate 1982-84, chmn. patient edn. com. 1982-86, v.p. 1985-86, mem. nat. com. scientific programs 1986-89, vice-chmn. 1987-88, chmn. 1988-89, pres.-elect Okla. affiliate 1989-90, pres. 1990-91, mem. nat. com. budget fin. 1989-91, nat. v.p. 1991-92, pres.-elect 1992-93, pres. 1993-94, immediate past pres. 1994-95, bd. dirs. rsch. found. 1994-95, chmn. workgroup reclassification diabetes 1995—, Outstanding Clinician 1990, Banting medal 1994), Am. Fedn. Clin. Rsch., Am. Soc. Acad. Black Surgeons, Am. Soc. Clin. Investigation, Assn. Acad. Minority Physicians, Ctrl. Soc. Clin. Rsch., Assn. Am. Physicians, So. Soc. Clin. Rsch., Endocrine Soc., Am. Clin. Climatol. Assn., Inst. Medicine, Sigma Xi, Alpha Omega Alpha, Beta Kappa Chi, Alpha Phi Alpha (life, William Alexander Cmty. Leadership award 1982), Omicron Delta Kappa, Sigma Pi Phi. Office: Howard Hughes Med Inst 4000 Jones Bridge Rd Chevy Chase MD 20815-6789*

GAVIN, ROBERT MICHAEL, JR., college president; b. Coatesville, Pa., Aug. 16, 1940; s. Robert Michael and Helen Regina (Finnegan) G.; m. Charlotte Marie Dugan, June 2, 1962; children—Anne, Patricia, Robert, Charles, Sean. B.A., St. John's U., Collegeville, Minn., 1962; Ph.D., Iowa State U., 1966; DSc (hon.), Haverford Coll., 1986, St. John's U., 1996. Mem. faculty Haverford (Pa.) Coll., 1966-84, prof. chemistry, 1975-84, dir. computing, 1979-80, provost, dean faculty, 1980-84, interim pres., 1996-97; pres. Macalester Coll., St. Paul, 1984-96, Cran Brook Ednl. Cmty., Bloomfield Hills, Mich.; bd. dirs. Fortis Funds Rsch. Corp. Author papers in field. Pres. Haverford Twp. Sch. Bd., 1975. Recipient Dreyfus Tchr.-Scholar award, 1973; NSF fellow, 1969-70. Democrat. Roman Catholic. Office: Cran Brook Ednl Cmty 380 Loan Pine Rd PO Box 801 Bloomfield Hills MI 48303-0801

GAVIN, SARA, public relations executive. Degree in History and Polit. Sci., Coll. St. Catherine, St Paul, Minn. Investor rels. programs Doremus & Co.; v.p. Hill and Knowlton/Twin Cities, Dorn Swenson Meyer, 1985-86; exec. v.p. Mona Meyer McGrath, 1986-93; pres. Mona Meyer McGrath & Gavin (Shandwick), Minn., 1993-95; mgr. dir. Shandwick Internat., 1995—. Bd. dirs. Minn. Women's Economic Round Table; trustee Coll. of St. Catherine, Minn. Pub. Radio. Recipient various awards PRSA, IABC. Mem. PRSA, Recognized Phi Beta Kappa. Office: Shandwick Ste 500 8400 Normandale Lake Blvd Minneapolis MN 55437-3889*

GAVIN, THOMAS MICHAEL, retired English educator, writer; b. Feb. 1, 1941. BA in English, U. Toledo, 1969, MA in English, 1972. Lectr. in English Delta Coll. U. Ctr., Mich., 1972-75; asst. prof. English Middlebury (Vt.) Coll., 1975-80; prof. English U. Rochester, N.Y., 1980-97, emeritus prof. English, 1997—. Author: (novels) Kingkill, 1977, The Last Film of Emile Vice, 1986, Breathing Water, 1994. Home: PO Box 155 East Middlebury VT 05740

GAVIRIA TRUJILLO, CESAR, international organization administrator, former president of Colombia, economist; b. Pereira, Colombia, Mar. 31, 1947; m. Ana Milena Muñoz Gómez; children: Simón, María Paz. BA, economics, U. de Los Andes, Bogota; JD (hon.), U. Libre de Colombia, 1990. Chief of planning Dept. of Risaralda, 1969; mem. council Pereira, 1970-74; asst. to chief Nat. Planning Dept., 1971-72; dir. Transformadores T.P.L., SA, 1972-73; mem. Ho. of Reps., 1974-90; mayor Pereira, 1975-76; dep. min. of devel. Republic of Colombia, Bogota, 1978-79; pres., third commn. Ho. of Reps., 1980-81, pres., 1983-84; adj. dir. Liberal Party, 1986; min. of fin. and pub. credit Republic of Colombia, Bogota, 1986-87, min. of interior, 1987-89, pres., 1990-94; sec. gen. Orgn. Am. States, 1994—. La Intervención del Estado en la Economia, Aspectos Políticos del Plan de Integración Nacional, Deuda Pública Latinoamericana; columnist El Tiempo. Office: OAS Office of Secretary General 17th St and Constitution Ave NW Washington DC 20006*

GAVRAS, KONSTANINOS See COSTA-GAVRAS

GAVRITY, JOHN DECKER, insurance company executive; b. S.I., N.Y., Oct. 26, 1940; s. John S. and Eleanor R. (Decker) G.; m. Camille Appello, April 16, 1998; children: John, Joseph. BS, Wagner Coll., 1963. From staff to assoc. actuary U.S. Life, N.Y.C., 1963-74; from actuary to exec. v.p., fin. actuary USLIFE Corp., N.Y.C., 1975-97, exec. v.p., chief actuary, 1997-98, ret., 1998. Fellow Soc. Actuaries; mem. Am. Acad. Actuaries. Republican. Roman Catholic. Home: 688 New Dorp Ln Staten Island NY 10306-4933

GAW, JAMES RICHARD, corporate manager; b. Bklyn., Sept. 2, 1943; s. James A. and Catharine (Clough) G.; m. Lorraine Osenbruk, July 21, 1973; children: Sean James, Joshua Timothy, Desiree Ann. BA, L.I. U., 1965; MA, St. John's U., 1967. Cert. Health Cons. Underwriter Royal-Globe Ins. Co., N.Y.C., 1969-70; rep. Blue Cross/Greater N.Y., N.Y.C., 1970-75; mktg. specialist Community Health Plan, Albany, N.Y., 1975-78; dir., mktg. support Blue Cross/Northeastern N.Y., Albany, 1978-82, sr. advisor to pres., 1982-84; dir. program svcs. Empire Blue Cross/Shield, N.Y.C., 1984-89, dir. records mgmt., 1989-90; dir. adminstrn., 1990—; N.Y. state project dir. Blue Cross Assn., Chgo., 1979-83; preceptor Union U., Schenectady, N.Y., 1980-82. V.p. Cath. Charities, Albany, 1983-88; gov. Adirondack Mountain Club, Inc., Glen Falls, N.Y., 1980-83; mem. Nat. Com. on Alcohol & Drugs, Chgo., Washington, 1980-82; pres. Schoharie Family & Community Svcs., Cobleskill, N.Y., 1976-78; coord. Health Info. Sharing Project, Albany, 1979-81. With USMC, 1967-69, Vietnam. Recipient Svc. Award Recognition Schoharie Family and Cmty. Svcs., 1988, Energy Conservation awrd Silverlight/Am. Energy Care, 1994; grantee Nat. Inst. Drug Abuse, 1981-83. Mem. Internat. Facilities Mgmt. Assn., Assn. Records Mgmt. and Administr., Bldg. Owners & Mgrs. Assn., Am. Inst. Arch. (affiliate). Roman Catholic. Avocations:hiking, camping, photography, furniture design, bagpiping. Office: Empire Blue Cross/Shield PO Box 11800 Albany NY 12211-0800

GAW, ROBERT STEVEN, lawyer, state representative; b. Moberly, Mo., July 7, 1957; s. William Robert and Julia Marie (Bentley) G.; m. Fannie Beth Bowdish, Aug. 18, 1990. BS in Physics summa cum laude, N.E. Mo. State U., 1978; JD, U. Mo., 1981. Bar: Mo. 1981. Atty. State of Mo., Jefferson City, 1982-84, James Wheeler, Keytesville, Mo., 1984, City of Moberly, Mo., 1985-92, Schirmer & Gaw, Moberly, 1984-94, Schirmer, Suter & Gaw, 1994—; elected spkr. Mo. House of Reps., 1996. State rep. Dist. 22, Mo., 1993—; chmn. Dem. Ctrl. Com., Randolph County, Mo., 1984-89; bd. dirs. Am. Diabetes Assn., Randolph County, 1990—; mem. com. Huntsville (Mo.) Horse Show, 1980's—, Mo. Children's Svcs. Commn., KIDS COUNT adv. com., Mo. Bar Commn. Children & the Law. Recipient award Am. Cancer Soc., 1993, award United Way; nominee Truman scholarship N.E. Mo. State U., 1977, Charles Dick Medal of Merit Nat. Guard Assn. of the U.S., 1995, Geyer award for pub. svc. to higher edn. U. Mo. Alumni Assn. and U. Mo.-Columbia; named Alumni of Yr., Truman State U., 1996. Mem. Mo. Bar Assn., Randolph County Bar Assn. (pres. 1984—), Moberly Area C. of C. (bd. dirs. 1991—), Moberly Rotary Club. Methodist. Avocations: singing, hunting, saddlebred horses. Office: Mo Ho of Reps State Capitol Building Jefferson City MO 65101-1556*

GAWEHN-FRISBY, DOROTHY JEANNE, freelance technical writer; b. Omaha, Jan. 20, 1931; d. Robert Floyd and Margaret Marie (Sitzman) Sealock; m. Kenneth Emil Gawehn, Apr. 17, 1951 (div. Jan. 1985); children: Marilyn Gawehn Jeffries, Kenneth M., Eric M., Celeste Gawehn-Yates; m. Charles Frisby, Mar. 17, 1990. Grad. high sch., Omaha. Systems technician Nat. Welding Co., Richmond, Calif., 1962-63; lead data entry operator United Grocers Co., Fresno, Calif., 1964-68, data processing mgr., 1968-72, computer operator shift supr., Oakland, Calif., 1972-76, documentation specialist, 1976-82; mgr. adminstrv. systems Baddour, Inc., Memphis, 1983-89; with Fed. Express Corp., 1989-91; sr. tech. writer Autozone, Memphis, 1991-95; freelance writer; contract tech. writer with Ctrl. Technical Svcs. Reader for the blind Sta. WTTL, Memphis, 1983-89; vol. worker Crisis and Suicide Intervention, Memphis, 1985-89, Docent for Ramesses exhibit, 1987. Recipient Key to Memphis. Mem. Internat. Tng. Communication (club pres. 1989-90, 96—, Communicator of Yr. award, Dixie region 1988-89, coun. 4 exec. bd. 1992-93), Data Processing Mgmt. Assn (Performance award 1973, Yosemite chpt.), Mensa (chmn. 1989-90, 96, 97). Republican. Roman Catholic. Avocations: backpacking, reading, writing, travel, hiking. Home and Office: 6644 Elkgate Memphis TN 38141-1205

GAWEL, MAUREEN SALTZER, newspaper executive; b. Winchester, Mass., Mar. 21, 1959; d. William Charles Saltzer and Janet Ann Child; m. O. Lee Brotherton, June 27, 1981 (div. 1984); m. Robert Chester Gawel, Oct. 14, 1995; 1 child, Lauren Roberta. BS in Journalism summa cum laude, Boston U., 1981; postgrad., Northeastern U., Boston, 1984, U. Calif., Riverside, 1994. Freelance corr. Concord (N.H.) Monitor, 1981-82; advt. sales rep. N.H. Times, Concord, 1981-82, circulation mgr., 1982-83; circulation and promotion mgr. Century Publs. Inc., Winchester, Mass., 1983-84, asst. gen. mgr., 1984-85; ad dir., ops. mgr. Provincetown (Mass.) Adv., 1985-86; gen. mgr. Healdsburg (Calif.) Tribune, Lesher Comm., 1986-87, Valley Times, Lesher Comm., Pleasanton, Calif., 1987-90; corp. oper. bd. dirs. Lesher Comm. Inc., Walnut Creek, Calif.; pub., v.p. Victor Valley Daily Press and Barstow Desert Dispatch divsn. Freedom Comm., Victorville, Calif., 1990-96; pub. Ft. Pierce (Fla.) and Port St. Lucie Tribune divsn., Freedom Comm., 1996—. Bd. dirs. United Way St. Lucie County, Boys and Girls Club, Leadership St. Lucie, Cottage and Camp Assn., Am. Heart Assn., Manatee Observation and Edn. Ctr., Exch. Club Castle. Recipient Woman of Achievement award Bus. and Profl. Women, San Orco, 1991, Golden Nike award, 1991, 94, Hall of Fame-Bus. award for State of Calif., 1992, Humanitarian award Desert Comtys., United Way, 1991, Outstanding Exec. Achievement award U. Calif. Riverside, 1994-95; named Citizen of Yr., Boy Scouts Am. Serrano Dist., 1994. Mem. Newspaper Assn. Am., Fla. Press Assn., So. Newspaper Pubs. Assn., St. Lucie County C. of C. (bd. dirs.), Rotary. Democrat. Avocations: skiing, scuba diving, reading, oenology, sailing. Home: 8413 Belfry Pl Port Saint Lucie FL 34986-3020 Office: The Tribune 600 Edwards Rd Fort Pierce FL 34982-6230

GAWF, JOHN LEE, foreign service officer; b. Salida, Colo., July 22, 1922; s. John and Gertrude (Bondurant) G.; m. Elizabeth Laflin, Dec. 31, 1950; children: Mary Anne, Katherine, Matilda, Anthony, Margaret, John Alan. B.S., U.S. Naval Acad., 1945; M.S., George Washington U., 1969, Instr. U. Colo., 1947-48; elec. engr. Bechtel Corp., San Francisco, 1948-50, TVA, Knoxville, Tenn., 1950-52; vice consul Fgn. Service, State Dept., Guadalajara, Mexico, 1954-56; policy info. officer Washington, 1956-57; internat. relations officer, 1957; officer-in-charge El Salvadoran affairs, 1958-59, Honduran affairs, 1958-60; consul Genoa, Italy, 1960-63; 1st sec. Am. Embassy, Caracas, Venezuela, 1963-65; 1st sec. Am. Embassy Ottawa, Ont., Can., 1965-68; detailed to Nat. War Coll., Washington, 1968-69, congl. relations officer, 1969-70; internat. relations officer Naples, Italy, 1970-74; consul gen. Belize City, Belize, 1974-78; counselor Am. Embassy, Rome, 1978-82; minister counselor Am. Embassy, 1981-83; detailed to Stanford U. Ctr. for Internat. Security and Arms Control, 1983-84; detailed to Armed Forces Staff Coll., 1984-87, cons. in field, 1987—. Served to lt. comdr. USNR, 1945-47, 52-54. Home: 13100 Riverside Dr Lake Oswego OR 97034-2431

GAWLIKOWSKI, VLADIMIR C., organization executive; b. Gary, Ind., May 8, 1967; s. David Adam and Joni Ann (Nyberg) G.; m. Dawn Marie Moskowitz, Apr. 26, 1996; children: Steffan Daveed, Corydon Mykeal. BA, Jersey City State Coll., 1991; MS, Ea. Ky. U., 1993. Dir. Raritan Valley YMCA, East Brunswick, N.J., 1996—; dir. youth sports YMCA of USA, Holiday Hills, N.Y., 1994, dir. strength tng., Springfield, Mass., 1994, dir. camp, Langhorne, Pa., 1997. Democrat. Roman Catholic. Avocations: theatre, music, swimming, tennis, golf. Office: Raritan Valley YMCA 206 Durhams Corner Rd East Brunswick NJ 08816

GAWTHROP, DAPHNE WOOD, performing company executive; b. Houston, July 22, 1940. Dir. programs and devel. Houston Mus. Natural Sci., 1987-89; dir. Inst. Mus. Svcs., Washington, 1989-91; dir. spl. projects Houston Grand Opera, 1991-92; dep. chmn. (pub. partnership) Nat. Endowment for the Arts, Washington, 1991-92; interim dir. Fotofest Ctr. for Photography, Houston, 1992; exec. dir. Sacramento Ballet, 1994—. Mem. Pres. Com. Arts and Humanities, Arts in Embassies coun. U.S. Dept. of State; adv. Arts Indemnity Program U.S. Info. Agy.; trustee Houston Ballet, Mus. of Fine Arts, Houston, Contemporary Arts Mus., Alley Theater. Recipient Nat. Devel. award Am. Assn. Museums; citation of Highest Achievement Nat. Endowment Arts. Office: Sacramento Ballet 1631 K St Sacramento CA 95814-4019*

GAWTHROP, ROBERT SMITH, III, federal judge; b. 1942. BA, Amherst Coll., 1964; JD, Dickinson Sch. Law, 1970. Law clk. to Ho. Lee F. Swope Harrisburg, Pa., 1969-70; mem. firm Gawthrop & Greenwood, West Chester, Pa., 1970-78; asst. dist. atty. Office Dist. Atty., West Chester, 1971-78, Wayne County, Pa., 1976-77; judge Ct. Common Pleas, Chester County, 1978-88; dist. judge U.S. Dist. Ct. (ea. dist.) Pa., 1988—; adj. prof. trial advocacy Dickinson Sch. Law, Carlisle, Pa., 1981-82. Contbr. articles to profl. jours. Mem. Berks Grand Opera. 1st lt. Artillery OCS, 1965-67. Mem. ABA, Am. Judicature Soc., Federalist Soc. Law & Pub. Policy Studies, Pa. Bar Assn., Fed. Judges Assn., Fed. Bar Assn., The Savoy Co., The Ardensingers, Gilbert and Sullivan Players, Chester County Gilbert and

Sullivan Soc., Orpheus Club, Quarry Club, Appalachian Mountain Club, Delta Kappa Epsilon, Phi Mu Alpha. Office: US Dist Ct 7613 US Courthouse 601 Market St Philadelphia PA 19106-1713*

GAY, ALEDA SUSAN, mathematician, educator; b. Frederick, Okla., Oct. 25, 1951; d. Paul W. and Evelyn (Tefertiller) G. BS, Okla. State U., 1973, MS, 1975, EdD, 1990. Cert. tchr., Okla. Tchr. math. Stillwater (Okla.) Pub. Schs., 1973-83; math. specialist Okla. Dept. Edn., Oklahoma City, 1983-89, computer cons., 1984-89; instr. Okla. State U., Stillwater, 1988-90; asst. prof. math. edn. U. Kans., Lawrence, 1991-97, assoc. prof. math. edn., 1997—; cons. math. textbook Houghton Mifflin, 1985-86; presenter panelist at profl. confs.; presenter workshops. Co-author: Principal Resources in Secondary Mathematics, 1985; developer high sch. algebra curriculum syllabus; contbr. articles to profl. jours. Mem. Assn. State Suprs. Math. (sec. 1988-90), Okla. Coun. Tchrs. Math. (v.p. 1982-84, rep. to Nat. Coun. Tchrs. Math. 1985-90, Outstanding Svc. award 1990), Math. Assn. Am., Nat. Coun. Suprs. Math., Kans. Assn. Tchr. Math. (v.p. colls. 1993-95), Assn. Math. Tchr. Educators (bd. dirs. 1995-97, sec. 1997-98, pres. 1999—), Phi Delta Kappa. Avocations: reading, needlework. Office: U Kans Dept Tchg & Leadership 202 Bailey Hall Dept Tchg& Lawrence KS 66045-2340

GAY, CARL LLOYD, lawyer; b. Seattle, Nov. 11, 1950; s. James and Elizabeth Anne (Rogers) G.; m. Robin Ann Winston, Aug. 23, 1975; children: Patrick, Joel, Alexander, Samuel, Nora. Student, U. of Puget Sound, 1969-70; BS in Forestry cum laude, Wash. State U., 1974; JD, Willamette U., 1979. Bar: Wash. 1979, U.S. Dist. Ct. (we. dist.) Wash. 1979. With Taylor & Taylor, 1979-82, Taylor, Taylor & Gay, 1982-85; prin. Greenaway & Gay, Port Angeles, Wash., 1985-91, Greenaway, Gay & Tassie, Port Angeles, 1991-96, Greenaway, Gay & Angier, Port Angeles, 1996—; judge pro tem Clallam County, Port Angeles, 1981-85; commr. superior Ct., 1985-91; judge Juvenile Ct., 1985-87; instr. Guardian Ad Litem Program, Port Angeles, 1985—, Peoples Law Sch., 1989—. Bd. dirs. Cmty. Concert Assn., Port Angeles, 1982-85, 94—, pres., 1984-85, 88-89, 99—; bd. dirs. Am. Heart Assn., 1987—, Clallam County YMCA, 1988—, exec. com., 1995—; mem. adv. bd. Salvation Army, Port Angeles, 1982—; subdivsn. chmn., bd. dirs. United Way Clallam County, 1987—; bd. dirs., pres. Friends of Libr., Port Angeles, 1983-91; trustee Fisher Cove, 1988—; advisor youth in govt. program YMCA, 1986—; advisor United Meth. Youth Coun., 1987—, trustee, 1989—; chmn. long-range planning com. Port Angeles Sch. Dist. Mem. ABA (real property, probate and trust and gen. practice sects.), ATLA, Wash. Bar Assn. (real property, probate, elder law and trust sects.), Clallam County Bar Assn. (pres. 1995), Nat. Coun. Juvenile and Family Ct. Judges, Superior Ct. Judges Assn. (com.), Wash. State Trial Lawyers Assn., Kiwanis (local bd. dirs. 1982-84, pres. 1986-87, Kiwanian of Yr. 1983-84), Elks. Lutheran. Avocations: backpacking, cross country skiing, raquetball, sailing. Home: 3220 Mcdougal St Port Angeles WA 98362-6738 Office: Greenaway Gay & Angier 829 E 8th St Ste A Port Angeles WA 98362-6418

GAY, DAVID BRAXTON, stockbroker; b. Louisburg, N.C., Aug. 29, 1957; s. Braxton and Doris (Richards) G.; m. Mary Angela Swider, May 24, 1980; children: Ryan A., Justin D. BA, U. N.C., Charlotte, 1979. Computer operator Texasgulf, Inc., Raleigh, N.C., 1979-80; customer svc. rep. Texasgulf Chems. Co., Raleigh, 1980-84; sr. sales rep. U.S. Sprint Comms., Charlotte, 1984-85, account rep., 1985-86, maj. account rep., 1986-88; maj. account exec. Telecom U.S.A., Charlotte, 1988-90; stock broker J.C. Bradford & Co., Charlotte, 1990-94, investment v.p., 1994-96, investment ltd. ptnr., 1996—, br. mgr., 1997-98; trainee adv. coun. J.C. Bradford & Co., 1992, leadership coun., 1991, 92, 96, 97, 98. Author: (monthly articles) The Bus. Jour., 1991-93. Bd. dirs. U. N.C.-Charlotte Athletic Found.; mem. devel. adv. coun. U. N.C.-Charlotte. Mem. U. N.C. Alumni Assn. (bd. govs. 1989-93), Lambda Chi Alpha (alumni adviser 1988-92), Beta Upsilon Alumni Corp. (bd. dirs. 1988-94). Democrat. Presbyterian. Avocations: tennis, reading, pool, basketball. Office: J C Bradford & Co 6337 Morrison Blvd Charlotte NC 28211

GAY, DAVID EARL, chemicals executive, chemist; b. Decatur, Ind., Nov. 10, 1944; s. Robert Earl and Miriam Evelyn (Haley) G.; m. Peggy Ann Sheets, Sept. 2, 1966 (div. Oct. 1981); children: Jeffery David, Christopher David; m. Lou Ann Gluesenkamp, Apr. 22, 1989; 1 child, Robert William. BS, Ball State U., 1967. Process engr. Delco Remy Div., GMC, Anderson, Ind., 1970-76, sr. chemist, 1976-89; sr. exptl. chemist Delphi Automotive Sys., Indpls., 1989—; mgr. advanced powder metal divsn. Delphi Automotive Sys.; analytical liaison GM, Delco Remy, Anderson, 1978-89; chmn. Local Hazardous Material Com., Indpls., 1986—; hygiene officer M.G. Corp., Indpls., 1989—. Patentee (14) in field; contbr. articles to profl. jours. Vol. St. John's Hosp., Anderson, 1987-90; pres. Social Health Ctrl. Ind., Indpls., 1990-96; Sunday Sch. supt. 1993-94, deacon 1998—. Recipient Paper of Yr. award Metal Powder Internat. Fedn., 1995, Delphi Innovation Hall Fame award 1996, EIRN ,1996, Boss Kettering award, 1998. Mem. Am. Chem. Soc., Am. Soc. Metals, Metal Powders Indsl. Fedn. (dir.), Am. Stds. Testing Materials, Sigma Xi. Presbyterian. Avocations: cooking, reading, volleyball, history, tennis. Home: 9062 S 760 W Pendleton IN 46064-9795 Office: Delphi Automotive Sys 7601 E 88th Pl Indianapolis IN 46256-1260

GAY, ELISABETH FEITLER, actress; b. Vienna, Dec. 16, 1916; d. Paul and Loni (Rosenbaum) Feitler; m. Joseph Gay (dec.); children: Cathy, Paul, Jill. BA, Sarah Lawrence Coll., 1974, MFA, 1977; PhD, NYU, 1986. Head of acting co. Sara Lawrence Players, Bronxville, N.Y., 1974-79; artist in residence Westchester Schs., 1974-79; acting tchr. U. Bridgeport, Conn., 1977-79; drama therapist, acting tchr. Bellevue Hosp., N.Y.C., 1984-86; acting tchr. Sarah Lawrence Coll., 1986. Author short stories. Brownie leader Stephenson Sch., New Rochelle, 1951-53; actress Guidance Ctr., New Rochelle, 1950. Mem. AFTRA, Actors Equity, Assn. Sr. Profls. at Eckerd Coll., Kappa Delta Pi. Democrat. Jewish. Avocations: play directing, theatre, movies, gardening, reading. Home: 65 Seaview Ave New Rochelle NY 10801-5329

GAY, E(MIL) LAURENCE, lawyer; b. Bridgeport, Conn., Aug. 10, 1923; s. Emil D. and Helen L. (Mihalich) G.; m. Harriet A. Ripley, Aug. 2, 1952; children: Noel L., Peter C., Marguerite S., Georgette A. BS, Yale U., 1947; JD magna cum laude, Harvard U., 1949. Bar: N.Y. 1950, Conn. 1960, Calif. 1981, Hawaii 1988. Assoc. Root, Ballantine, Harlan, Bushby & Palmer, N.Y.C., 1949-51; mem. legal staff U.S. High Commr. for Germany, Bad Godesberg, 1951-52; law sec., presiding justice appellate div. 1st dept. N.Y. Supreme Ct., N.Y.C., 1953-54; assoc. Debevoise, Plimpton & McLean, N.Y.C., 1954-58; v.p., sec.-treas., gen. counsel Hewitt-Robins, Inc., Stamford, Conn., 1958-65; pres. Litton Gt. Lakes Corp., N.Y.C., 1965-67; sr. v.p. finance AMFAC, Inc., Honolulu, 1967-73; vice chmn. AMFAC, Inc., 1974-78; fin. cons. Burlingame, Calif., 1979-82; of counsel Pettit & Martin, San Francisco, 1982-88, Goodsill, Anderson, Quinn & Stifel, Honolulu, 1988—. Editor Harvard Law Rev., 1948-49. Pres. Honolulu Symphony Soc., 1974-78; trustee Loyola Marymount U., 1977-80, San Francisco Chamber Soloists, 1981-86, Honolulu Chamber Music Series, 1988—; officer, dir. numerous arts and ednl. orgns. 2d lt. AUS, 1943-46. Mem. ABA, State Bar of Hawaii, Pacific Club (Honolulu), Nat. Assn. of Securities Dealers, Am. Arbitration Assn. (mem. arbitration panels), Phi Beta Kappa. Republican. Roman Catholic. Avocations: music, arts. Home: 1159 Maunawili Rd Kailua HI 96734-4641 Office: Goodsill Anderson Quinn & Stifel PO Box 3196 Honolulu HI 96801-3196

GAY, MARILYN FANELLI MARTIN, television producer, talk show hostess; b. San Francisco, July 16, 1925; d. Louis and Gertrude (Dondero) Fanelli; m. William Thomas Martin, Jan. 11, 1953 (div. 1956); m. Mel Raymond Gay, May 3, 1963. Student U. Calif., Berkeley, 1943-46, U. Oreg., 1946; prodr./dir. Young Set Playhouse, Radio KRE, Berkeley, 1944-45; prodr., hostess, writer; (TV) In God We Trust, Protestant Ch. Fedn., 1954-55, A Woman's World, Las Vegas, 1956; (radio) Party with the Stars, KBIG, L.A., 1958; writer Passing Parade Films ABC-TV Network, 1958, Tel. Time; asst. editor Gen. Practice mag., L.A., 1961; prodr., hostess, writer The Marilyn Gay Show, Group W Cable, Valley Cable, Cox Cable, Century Cable, King Cable, Cablevision, Simmons Cable, Century Cable, Verdugo Hills TV, King Cable, Jones Intercable, Am. Cable, Copley Colony Cable, Time Warner, 1982—. Nat. dir. spl. features, coord. radio and TV, Invest in America Nationwide Campaign, 1957. Contbg. by-lined feature writer Los Angeles Times, 1957. Recipient Outstanding Good Citizen award DAR, 1943, Commemorative medal of Honor Hallmark, 1985; named to Hall of Fame of personalities of Am., 1985. Mem. Writers Guild Am.-West (founding mem.), Internat. Platform Assn., U. Calif. Alumni Assn., Alpha Delta Pi. Mem. Ch. of Religious Science. Address: 1990 Ginger St Apt 101 Oxnard CA 93030-9022

GAY, MATHEW FRANK, secondary education educator; b. Youngstown, Ohio, July 22, 1972; s. Gilbert Frank and Judith Irene (Seaton) G. BA, Shippensburg U., 1995. Tchr. English, Frederick County Pub. Schs., Frederick, Md., 1995-98, Cumberland Valley Sch. Dist., Mechanicsburg, PA., 1998—; migrant edn. tchr. Lincoln Intermediate Unit, Chambersburg, Pa., 1995—. Mem. Nat. Coun. Tchrs. English. Home: 305 E King St Apt 3 Shippensburg PA 17257

GAY, PAMELA DIANE, dance critic, historian; b. Dayton, Ohio, Dec. 1, 1945; d. Richard Lewis and Patricia Rose (Jacques) G. BA, U. Calif., Berkeley, 1977; MA, Hunter Coll., 1989; PhD in French, La. State U., 1998. Interpreter Arts Am., Washington, 1985-86; vis. scholar in dance history U. Calgary, Alta., Alberta, 1980; lectr. Franche-Comté, Besancon, France, 1992-93; instr. La. State U., Baton Rouge, La., 1995—; dir. Arts Seminars Internat., San Francisco, 1982-85; adv. Lagniappe Studies Unlimited, La. State U., 1993-99; liaison La. State U. in Paris, 1993. Author: International Dictionary of Ballet, 1994; author: (jour.) Pensée Libre, 1998; contbg. editor The Phoenix, Dance Scope, Les Saisons de la Danse. Active Baton Rouge chpt. Nat. Alliance Mentally Ill, 1998. Mem. Eighteenth Century Soc., Modern Lang. Assn., Rousseau Assn. Anglican. E-mail: pdgaywhite@aol.com. Home: 134 Maximilian St Baton Rouge LA 70802

GAY, PETER, history educator, author; b. Berlin, Germany, June 20, 1923; came to U.S., 1941, naturalized, 1946; s. Morris Peter and Helga (Kohnke) G.; m. Ruth Slotkin, May 30, 1959; stepchildren: Sarah Khedouri, Sophie Glazer Cohen, Elizabeth Glazer. BA, U. Denver, 1946; MA, Columbia U., 1947, PhD, 1951; LHD (hon.), U. Denver, 1970, U. Md., 1979, Hebrew Union Coll., Cin., 1983, Clark U., 1985, Suffolk U., Boston, 1987, Tufts U., 1988. Faculty Columbia U., N.Y.C., 1947-69, prof. history, 1962-69, William R. Shepherd prof. history, 1967-69; prof. comparative European intellectual history Yale U., New Haven, 1969—, Durfee prof. history, 1970-84, Sterling prof., 1984-93, Sterling prof. emeritus, 1993—; dir. Ctr. for Scholars and Writers N.Y. Pub. Libr., 1997—; dir. Ctr. Scholars and Writers N.Y. Pub. Libr. Author: The Dilemma of Democratic Socialism: Eduard Bernstein's Challenge to Marx, 1952, Voltaire's Politics: The Poet as Realist, 1959, The Party of Humanity: Essays in the French Enlightenment, 1964, A Loss of Mastery: Puritan Historians in Colonial America, 1966, The Enlightenment: An Interpretation, vol. I, The Rise of Modern Paganism, 1966 (Nat. Book award 1967), (Melcher Book award 1967), Weimar Culture: The Outsider as Insider, 1968 (Ralph Waldo Emerson award Phi Beta Kappa 1969), The Enlightenment, vol. II, The Science of Freedom, 1969, The Bridge of Criticism: Dialogues on the Enlightenment, 1970, (with R.K. Webb) Modern Europe, 1973, Style in History, 1974, Art and Act, 1976, Freud, Jews, and Other Germans, 1978, Education of the Senses, 1984, Freud for Historians, 1985, The Tender Passion, 1986, A Godless Jew: Freud, Atheism, and the Making of Psychoanalysis, 1987, Freud: A Life for Our Time, 1988, A Freud Reader, 1989, Reading Freud: Explorations and Entertainments, 1990, The Cultivation of Hatred, 1993, The Naked Heart, 1995, Pleasure Wars, 1998, My German Question: Growing Up in Nazi Berlin, 1998. Fellow Am. Coun. Learned Soc., 1959-60, Ctr. Advanced Study Behavioral Scis., 1963-64; Guggenheim fellow, 1967-68, 77-78; Overseas fellow Churchill Coll., Cambridge, 1970-71; Rockefeller Found. fellow, 1979-80; Wissenschaftskolleg zu Berlin, 1984; recipient First Amsterdam prize in Hist. Sci., 1991. Mem. Am. Philos. Soc., Am. Inst. Arts and Letters (gold medal in history 1996), Phi Beta Kappa. Home: 105 Blue Trl Hamden CT 06518-1618

GAY, ROBERT DERRIL, public agency director; b. Savannah, Ga., June 23, 1939; s. Roscoe Degomar and Mollie Ann (Jones) G. B.A., Oglethorpe U., 1962; M.A., Emory U., 1966, Ph.D., 1984. Dep. dir. Div. Mental Health and Mental Retardation Ga. Dept. Human Resources, Atlanta, 1975-77; asst. commr. Ga. Dept. Human Resources, 1977-78, dir. Div. Mental Health and Mental Retardation, 1978-81; dep. dir. DeKalb County Health Dept., Decatur, Ga., 1981-94; dir. DeKalb Community Mental Health, Mental Retardation and Substance Abuse Svc. Bd., Decatur, 1994—; vis. instr. Oglethorpe U., 1966, 67, 85-94, Emory U. Sch. Nursing, 1970; mem. Ga. Gov.'s Coun. on Devel. Disabilities, 1978-81, Ga. Gov.'s Coun. on Mental Health and Mental Retardation, 1978-81, DeKalb County Coun. on Devel. Disabilities, 1981—. Bd. dirs. St. Joseph's Mercy Care Svcs., 1994—. Mem. Am. Sociol. Assn. So. Sociol. Soc., Ga. Sociol. Assn., Ga. Pub. Health Assn., Nat. Assn. State Mental Health Program Dirs. (bd. dirs. 1986-92, pres. 1990-91), Atlanta Mercy Mobile Health Program (bd. dirs. 1987-94, chair 1991-94). Home: 2295 Dunwoody Xing Apt I Atlanta GA 30338-7332 Office: DeKalb Community Svc Bd PO Box 1648 Decatur GA 30031-1648

GAY, SARAH ELIZABETH, lawyer; b. Cambridge, Mass., May 24, 1950; d. Frank Smith and Jane (Spencer) Fussner; m. Kirk D. Gay; 1 child, John Russell. BA, Harvard/Radcliffe, 1972; JD, U. Oreg., 1975. Bar: Alaska 1976, U.S. Dist. Ct. Alaska 1976, U.S. Ct. Appeals (9th cir.) 1976, U.S. Supreme Ct. 1980. Assoc. Ely, Guess & Rudd, Anchorage, 1975-77; asst. atty. gen., natural resources sect. State of Alaska, Anchorage, 1977-88; asst. atty. gen., oil spill sect., 1989-91; sect. supr. natural resources sect. State of Alaska, Anchorage, 1991-93; corp. counsel Alaska Safari, Inc., Anchorage, 1993—; pvt. practice Anchorage, 1993—; workshop leader U. Oreg. Law Sch., Eugene, 1989; chmn. Anchorage (Alaska) Mcpl. Airports Adv. Com., 1990-93. Mng. bd. editor U. Oreg. Law Rev., Eugene, 1975. Mem. Citizens' Adv. Bd., Land Conservation & Devel. Bd., Salem, Oreg., 1975. Mem. Alaska Bar Assn. Law Examiners, Phi Delta Phi. Avocations: commercial pilot, sport fish lodge operator. Address: Valhalla Lodge Nondalton AK 99640

GAY, SUSAN MATTHEWS, publishing professional; b. Atlanta, Dec. 14, 1954; d. Brinton Bizzelle, Jr. and Evelyn (Ward) G.; m. Jonathan P. Andrews, Dec. 14, 1991; children: Katherine Rose Andrews, Paul Brinton Andrews. BS, Presbyn. Coll., 1976; MA, Emory U., 1980. Continuing edn. coord. Emory U. Sch. of Medicine, Atlanta, 1976-79; editor Ctrs. for Disease Control, Atlanta, 1979; editor, sr. editor Butterworth Pubs., Inc., Boston, 1979-82; sr. editor to exec. editor Grune & Stratton, Inc., N.Y.C., 1982-85; exec. editor J.B. Lippincott, Inc., Phila., 1986-88; exec. editor to editor-in-chief Mosby, Inc., Phila., 1988-95; v.p., pub. Williams and Wilkins (Waverly, Inc.), Balt. and Phila., 1995-99; pres., CEO InfoBrand Pub. Inc., Phila., 1999—; spkr. Thomas Jefferson Med. Coll., Phila., 1997, others. Co-author: (book) Clinical Methods Learning System, 1979. Sec. Presbyn. Coll. Alumni Assn., Clinton, S.C., 1980-81; bd. dirs. New Gulph Children's Ctr., Villanova, Pa., 1996-98, Found. for Architecture, Phila., 1989-91. Mem. Am. Med. Writers Assn. (bd. dirs., chmn. audiovisual sect. 1978-85), Am. Med. Publishers Assn. (pres.-elect). Avocations: hist. architecture, design, gourmet cooking.

GAY, TITO (VIRGINIA LEWIS GRAY FINDLAY), artist, educator; b. St. Louis, Sept. 22, 1932; d. George William and Eugenea (Smith) Gay; m. Alexander George Findlay, Feb. 10, 1967 (div. 1969); 1 child, David Alexander. BA, Smith Coll., 1954; BFA, Washington U., St. Louis, 1958; MS, U. Wis., 1959. Cert. tchr., Mo. Art tchr. Mary Inst., St. Louis, 1972-76; asst. prof. art Fontbonne Coll., St. Louis, 1975-77; contract tchr. St. Louis Art Mus., 1975—. Portrait artist; commd. by Washington U., Mo. Hist. Soc., St. Louis U., Lambert Internat. Airport, Sunnen Corp., Mo. Bot. Garden, others. Recipient Julius Hallgarten award Nat. Acad. Fine Arts, 1965, 66. Mem. St. Louis Artists Guild (Disting. Mem.), Knickerbocker Artists. Episcopalian.

GAY, WILLIAM ARTHUR, JR., thoracic surgeon, educator; b. Richmond, Va., Jan. 16, 1936; s. William Arthur and Marion Harriette (Taylor) G.; m. Frances Louise Adkins, Dec. 17, 1960; children—William Taylor, Mason Arthur. BA, Va. Mil. Inst., 1957; MD, Duke U., 1961. Diplomate Am. Bd. Surgery (bd. dirs. 1989-95), Am. Bd. Thoracic Surgery (bd. dirs. 1988-97). Intern Duke U. Med. Ctr., Durham, N.C., 1961-63, resident in surgery, 1965-71; asst. prof. surgery Cornell U. Med. Coll., N.Y.C., 1971-74, assoc., prof., 1974-78, prof., 1978-84; cardiothoracic surgeon-in-chief N.Y. Hosp., 1976-84; prof., chmn. dept. surgery U. Utah Sch. Medicine, 1984-92; v.p. for health scis. U. Utah, 1990-91; chmn. Am. Bd. Thoracic Surgery, 1995-97; thoracic surgeon Barnes Hosp., St. Louis; prof. surgery Sch. Medicine Washington U., St. Louis. Contbr. articles to profl. jours. Served with USPHS, 1963-65. Recipient Career Scientist award Irma T. Hirschl Charitable Trust, 1972. Mem. ACS, Soc. Vascular Surgery, Soc. Thoracic Surgery, Am. Assn. Thoracic Surgery (treas. 1989-94), Am. Surg. Assn., Soc. Univ. Surgeons (treas. 1977-80). Office: 1 Barnes Hospital Plz Saint Louis MO 63110-1036

GAY, WILLIAM INGALLS, veterinarian, health science administrator; b. Sussex, N.J., Jan. 25, 1926; s. William David and Dorothy Julia (Ingalls) G.; m. Millicent Ruth Chapman, June 10, 1948. DVM, Cornell U., 1950; grad., Fed. Exec. Inst., 1972. Diplomate Am. Coll. Lab. Animal Medicine. Pvt. practice vet. medicine Richmond Hill, N.Y., 1950-52; chief animal hosp. sect. lab. aids br. div. research services NIH, Bethesda, Md., 1954-63; asst. chief lab. aids br. div. research services NIH, 1962-63, asst. chief animal resources br. div. research facilities and resources, 1964-65; program dir. comparative medicine Nat. Inst. Gen. Med. Scis., NIH, 1966-67, program adminstr. radiology and physiology tng. programs, 1966, chief research grants br., 1967-70, acting assoc. dir., 1970; assoc. dir. extramural programs Nat. Inst. Allergy and Infectious Diseases, NIH, 1970-80, dir. animal resources program, div. research resources, 1981-88; cons. ROW Svcs., Rockville, Md., 1989-98; pvt. practice Bethesda, Md., 1999—; mem. com. on primates Inst. Lab. Animal Resources, NRC, 1961-63, chmn. subcom. on cat standards, 1963-64, mem. standards com., 1965-66; program chmn. Internat. Symposium on Lab. Animals, 1969. Author numerous papers on expt. surgery and lab. animal research.; editor: Methods of Animal Experimentation, 7 vols. Mem. sci. adv. bd. Mark L. Morris Found., 1966-71, trustee, 1971-84; mem. grants adv. council The Seeing Eye, 1971-74. Served as lt. Vet. Corps, AUS, Walter Reed, 1952-54. Recipient Superior Service cert. HEW, 1975, NIH Dir's. award, 1983, Superior Service award USPHS, 1987. Mem. AVMA (sec.-treas. D.C. chpt. 1957-58, v.p. 1962, pres. 1963), AAAS, Am. Assn. Lab. Animal Sci. (dir. 1961-69, program chmn. 1962-64, exec. bd. 1963, 66, nat. pres. 1968, chmn. awards com. 1969, Griffin award 1971, pres. Washington br. 1962), NIH Alumni Assn. (bd. dirs. 1994, v.p. 1995-98), Phi Zeta, Cosmos Club.

GAYLE, GIBSON, JR., lawyer; b. Waco, Tex., Oct. 15, 1926; s. Gibson and Elsie (Little) G.; m. Martha Jane Wood, May 29, 1948; children: Sally Ann, Alice, Gibson III, Jane, Philip. AB, LLB, Baylor U., 1950; D Human Medicine (hon.), Baylor Coll. Medicine, 1991. Bar: Tex. 1950. Since practiced in Houston; sr. ptnr., chmn. exec. com. Fulbright & Jaworski., 1979-92; adj. prof. U. Tex. Law Sch.; instr. U. Houston Law Sch., 1951-55; bd. dirs. Daniel Industries Inc. Bd. editors: Am. Bar Assn. Jour, 1967-72. Trustee M.D. Anderson Found.; bd. govs. Harris County Ctr. for Retarded, 1956-76; Tex. Med. Ctr. Inc., Leon Jaworski Found.; bd. dirs., pres. Am. Bar Endowment, 1970-80; chmn. Baylor Coll. Medicine, 1982-91, trustee, 1977—. 2d lt. F.A. AUS, 1945-47. Fellow Am. Bar Found. (dir. 1978-79), Tex. Bar Found. (chmn. 1968-69); mem. ABA (chmn. jr. bar conf. 1959-60, ho. of dels. 1960-62, 63—, sec. 1963-67), Houston Bar Assn., State Bar Tex. (dir. 1966-69, pres. 1976-77), Houston C. of C. (dir. 1979-87). Home: 11727 Broken Bough Cir Houston TX 77024-5115 Office: Fulbright & Jaworski LLP 1301 Mckinney St Ste 5100 Houston TX 77010-3031

GAYLE, HELENE D., federal agency administrator, pediatrician; b. Buffalo. BS in Psychology cum laude, Columbia U., 1976; MD, U. Pa., 1981; MPH, John Hopkins U., 1981. Diplomate Am. Bd. Pediats. Intern then resident in pediats. Children's Hosp. Nat. Med. Ctr., Washington, 1981-84; epidemic intelligence svc. officer br. epidemiology divsn. nutrition Ctr. Health Promotion and Edn., 1984-86; preventive medicine resident divsn. evaluation and rsch. office internat. health program Ctrs. Disease Control Ga. State Dept. Health, 1986-87; med. epidemiologist pediats. and family studies sect., AIDS program Ctrs. Disease Control, 1987-89, acting spl. asst. minority HIV policy coordination office dep. dir. (HIV), 1988-89, asst. chief sci., 1989-90; chief internat. activity divsn. HIV/AIDS Ctrs. Disease Control, Atlanta, 1990-92; assoc. dir. Ctrs. Disease Control, Washington, 1994-96; agy. AIDS coord., chief divsn. HIV-AIDS Agy. Intl. Devel., Washington, 1992-94; dir. Nat. Ctr. HIV, Sexually Transmitted Diseases and Tb Prevention HHS, Washington, 1996—; lectr. Sch. Medicine Morehouse U., 1987-92; lectr. masters in pub. health program Emory U., Atlanta, 1989, 90; clin. asst. prof. cmty. medicine, 1996—; cons. WHO, others; bd. dirs. Gorgas Meml. Inst. Tropical and Preventive Medicine, Inc., Internat. Ctr. Rsch. in Women. Contbr. articles to profl. jours. Capt. USPHS. Merit scholar Henry J. Kaiser Family Found., 1981; recipient Henrietta and Jacob Lowenburg prize, 1981, Model Excellence award Colgate-Palmolive Co., 1992. Mem. AAS, AMA, APHA, Am. Coll. Epidemiology, Internat. AIDS Soc., Soc. Against AIDS in Africa. Office: Nat Ctr HIV STD and TB Prevention MSE-07 Bldg 11 Corporate Square Blvd Atlanta GA 30333

GAYLE, MARGOT, preservationist, writer; b. Kansas City, Mo., May 14, 1908; d. David Bunn and Edith Mildred (Cheatham) McCoy; widowed; children: Carol, Gretchen Gayle Ellsworth. BA, U. Mich., 1930; MS, Emory U., 1933. Dir. Civil Def. Vol. Office, Washington, 1941-45; script writer CBS, N.Y.C., 1945-48; dir. pub. rels. N.Y.C. Dept. Commerce and Pub. Events, 1953-56; dep. dir. pub. info. N.Y.C. Planning Commn., 1956-58; columnist N.Y. Daily News, N.Y.C., 1976-92; mem. N.Y. Art Commn., N.Y.C., 1981-84. Author: Cast Iron Architecture in New York: A Photographic Survey, 1974; co-author: Metal in America's Historic Buildings, 1980, The Art Commission and the Municipal Art Society Guide to Manhattan's Outdoor Sculpture, 1988; (with Carol Gayle) Cast-Iron Architecture in America: The Significance of James Bogardus, 1998; contbr. articles to profl. jours., introductions to books. Co-founder Victorian Soc. Am., N.Y.C., 1966; Dem. state committeewoman, dist. leader, Manhattan, 1953-61. Recipient Nat. Trust for Hist. Preservation award, 1980, Doris Freedman award City of N.Y., 1986, Henry-Russell Hitchcock award Victorian Soc. in Am., 1989, Lucy Moses award Landmarks Conservancy, 1990, George Lewis award AIA, 1993, Robert Ponte award Am. Planning Assn., 1994, Preservation award Met. Hist. Structures Assn., 1995, Assoc. of the Art Commn., 1995. Mem. Friends of Cast Iron Architecture (founder, pres.), Mcpl. Art Soc. N.Y. (Jacqueline Kennedy Onassis medal for preservation of the Soho cast iron hist. dist. 1997), Victorian Soc. Am. (met. chpt. Lifetime Achievement award 1997, Book award 1999), Fine Arts Fedn. N.Y., Women's City Club, Soc. Indsl. Archaeology (Gen. Tools Lifetime Achievement award 1997), N.Y. Hist. Soc., Preesrvation League N.Y. State (Lifetime Achievement award 1999).

GAYLES, JOSEPH NATHAN, JR., administrator, fund raising consultant; b. Birmingham, Ala.; s. Joseph Nathan Webster and Ernestine Williams G.; children: Jonathan, Monica. A.B. summa cum laude, Dillard U., 1958, LL.D. (hon.), 1983; Ph.D., Brown U., 1963; postgrad., Oreg. State U., 1962-63, U. Uppsala, Sweden, 1965; various exec., mgmt. programs, various exec. and mgmt. programs, 1976-78, 80, 82. Asst. prof. chemistry Oreg. State U., 1962-63; Woodrow Wilson teaching asso., asst. prof. chemistry Morehouse Coll., 1963-66, assoc. prof. chemistry, 1969-71, program dir. med. edn. project, 1971-75; program dir. Sch. Medicine, 1975-77, prof., 1971-77; pres. Talladega (Ala.) Coll., 1977-83; v.p., research prof. medicine Morehouse Sch. Medicine, Atlanta, 1983-97; chmn., CEO Jon-Mon and Assocs., Inc., Fund Raising Cons., 1983—; cons. v.p. Clark Atlanta U., 1996-98; staff scientist, project dir. IBM Research Lab., San Jose, Calif., 1966-69. Contbr. articles to profl. jours. Bd. dirs. Woodrow Wilson Nat. Fellowship Found., 1978-98, Rotary Internat., 1991—, Found. Ctr. Bd., 1994-96; bd. overseers Sch. Medicine, Morehouse Coll., 1977-81; bd. dirs. Donoho Sch., Anniston, Ala., 1979-83, Camp Cosby, YMCA, 1978-80, Met. Atlanta Coun. on Alcohol and Drug Abuse, 1972-74, Coun. for Internat. Exchange Scholars, 1979-83; exec. bd. North Ctrl. Ga. Health Sys. Agy., 1975-77; mem. Indsl. Devel. Com., Talladega, 1979-83; mem. exec. bd. Choccolocco coun. Boy Scouts Am., 1980-83; mem. Gov.'s Commn. on Future of Ala. in Yr. 2000, 1982-83; trustee Morehouse Coll., 1976-77, Talladega Coll., 1977-83, Morehouse Med. Coll., 1981-83; mem. nat. adv. coun. divsn. rsch. resources NIH, 1980-85; pres. Ala. Ctr. for Higher Edn., 1980-83; bd. visitors MIT, 1981-88. Woodrow Wilson fellow, 1958-59; Dreyfus Found. Tchr.-scholar, 1972; recipient Tchr. of Yr. award Morehouse Coll., 1976; Alumnus of Yr. award Dillard U., 1977; Presdl. Leadership award Morehouse Sch. Medicine, 1986. Mem. Am. Phys. Soc., Am. Chem. Soc., Am. Assn. Polit. and Social Scientists, Nat. Assn. Equal Opportunity in Higher Edn. (bd. dirs. 1979-82), Sigma Xi, Phi Beta Kappa, Alpha Phi Alpha. Office: Jon Mon Assoc Inc 1515 Austin Rd SW Atlanta GA 30331-2205

GAYLIN, NED L., psychology educator; b. Cleve., May 2, 1935; s. Harry C. and Fay I. G.; m. Rita Atran, June 30, 1957; children: Hilarie C., Ann E., Jed J., Daniel S. BA, U. Chgo., 1956, MA, 1961, PhD, 1965. Counselor Bellefaire Children's Home, Cleve., 1953, Sonja Shankman Orthogenic Sch., Chgo., 1954-56; group worker, supr. Jewish Community Ctrs. Chgo., 1957-60; grad. rsch. asst. Com. Human Devel., U. Chgo., 1959-60; intern Inst. Juvenile Rsch., Chgo., 1960-61, staff psychologist, 1965-68; intern Counseling and Psychotherapy Rsch. Ctr., U. Chgo., 1961-63; grad. teaching asst. dept. psychology U. Chgo., 1961-63; psychol. cons. State Ill., Rockford, 1961-64; psychotherapist, cons. Counseling and Psychotherapy Rsch. Ctr., U. Chgo., 1963-65, psychol. cons., lectr., 1965; lectr. dept. social sci. S.E. Jr. Coll., Chgo., 1965-66; psychol. cons. Peace Corps, No. Ill. U., DeKalb, 1966-68; chief psychologist S.W. Suburban Mental Health Assn., LaGrange, Ill., 1966-68; psychol. cons. Virginia Frank Child Devel. Ctr., Chgo., 1966-68; child clin. rsch. psychologist NIMH, Bethesda, Md., 1968-70; lectr., cons. Washington Sch. Psychiatry, 1968-72; chmn. dept. family and community devel. Coll. Human Ecology U. Md., College Park, 1970-77, prof., dir. family therapy tng. Coll. Health and Human Performance, 1977—; mem. rsch. com. Md. Community Coordinated Child Care, 1970-75. Contbr. articles in field to profl. jours. USPHS grantee, 1961-63; U. Chgo. fellow and scholar, 1954-56, 58-60; State Ill. edn. and tng. grantee, 1963-65. Mem. APA, Nat. Coun. on Family Rels., Am. Assn. Marriage and Family Therapy, Groves Conf. on the Family, Assn. for Devel. of Person-Centered Approach, Sigma Xi. Home: 4617 Norwood Dr Chevy Chase MD 20815-5348 Office: Univ Md 1204 Marie Mount Hall # D College Park MD 20742-7515

GAYLIN, WILLARD, physician, educator; b. Cleve., Feb. 23, 1925; s. Harry C. and Fay (Baumgard) G.; m. Betty Schofer, June 15, 1947; children: Joan Deborah, Ellen Andrea. A.B., Harvard U., 1947; M.D., Western Res. U., 1951. Lic. psychiatrist, N.Y. Intern Cleve. City Hosp., 1951-52; resident psychiatry Bronx VA Hosp., 1952-54; faculty Columbia Psychoanalytic Sch., 1956—, clin. prof. psychiatry, 1972—; adj. prof. psychiatry Union Theol. Sem.; adj. prof. psychiatry and law Columbia Sch. Law, 1970; founder The Hastings Ctr., Briarcliff Manor, N.Y., 1970—, chmn. bd., 1970-96; vis. prof. Harvard U. Med. Sch., 1978. Author: The Meaning of Despair, 1968, In The Service of Their Country: War Resisters in Prison, 1970, Partial Justice: A Study of Bias in Sentencing, 1974, Caring, 1976, (with others) Doing Good: The Limits of Benevolence, 1978, Feelings: Our Vital Signs, 1979, The Killing of Bonnie Garland: A Question of Justice, 1982, The Rage Within: Anger in Modern Life, 1984, Rediscovering Love, 1986, Adam and Eve and Pinnocchio, 1990, The Male Ego, 1992, The Perversion of Autonomy, 1996; contbr. articles to profl. jours. Bd. dirs. Helsinki Watch., Nat. Bd. Planned Parenthood. Served with USNR, 1943-45. Recipient George E. Daniels medal of Merit for contbns. to psychoanalytic medicine, 1973; Elizabeth Cutter Morrow lectr. Smith Coll., 1970; Chubb fellow Yale U., 1972. Fellow Am. Psychiat. Assn.; mem. Inst. Medicine of NAS, Am. Psychoanalytic Assn., N.Y. Psychiat. Soc. Office: 4th Fl 20 E 63rd St New York NY 10021-7252*

GAYLIS, NORMAN BRIAN, internist, rheumatologist, educator; b. Johannesburg, South Africa, May 31, 1950; came to the U.S., 1976; s. Bernard Gaylis and Jesse Gaylis Berelowitz; children: Brett-Ari, Jarrod Michael. MB, BChir, U. Witwatersrand, Johannesburg, 1973. Diplomate Am. Bd. Internal Medicine. Intern Mt. Sinai Med. Ctr., Miami, Fla., 1976; resident Mt. Sinai Med. Ctr., Miami, 1977-78, chief resident in medicine, 1978-79; clin. rsch. fellow U. Miami, 1979-81; practice medicine specializing in rheumatology and internal medicine North Miami, Fla., 1981—; mem. staff Parkway Med. Ctr., North Miami Gen. Hosp., North Shore Hosp., Biscayne Med. Ctr.; clin. assoc. prof. U. Miami, 1982—; host health talk show sta. WINZ, Miami. Editor: Problems in Rheumatology, 19981, 82 (award Arthritis and Rheumatology Assn.). Bd. dirs., adviser Lupus Found. South Fla., 1981-83; bd. dirs., mem. coun. edn. Arthritis Found. South Fla., 1982-83. Mem. ACP, AMA, Am. Rheumatism Assn. (S.E. 1st prize for case presentation 1981), South African Med. Assn., Brit. Med. Assn. Jewish. Home: 21376 Marina Cove Cir # 16C Aventura FL 33180-4002 Office: 160 NW 170th St Miami FL 33169-5521

GAYLOR, BARBARA GAIL DAVIS, geriatric nurse; b. Tampa, Fla., Sept. 26, 1956; d. Roscoe and Audrey Iris (Knowles) Davis; m. Frank Hogan Gaylor, Apr. 12, 1980; children: Cassandra Michelle, Jennifer Lynn, Catherine Ann. AA, St. Petersburg Jr. Coll., 1976, AS, 1978. RN, Fla.; cert. gerontol. nurse, ANCC. Nurse Bay Pines VA Hosp., St. Petersburg, Fla., 1995—. Leader, co-leader Girl Scouts Am., Va., Fla., 1992-98. Republican. Lutheran. Avocations: sailing, swimming, camping.

GAYLOR, DONALD HUGHES, surgeon, educator; b. Bklyn., Apr. 17, 1926; s. Norman Hunter and Frances (Hughes) G.; m. Joan Winifred Power, Apr. 3, 1948; children: David, Christopher, Steven, Susan, Timothy. AB, U. Rochester, 1946, MD, 1949. Diplomate Am. Bd. Surgery, Am. Bd. Thoracic Surgery. Commd. lt. (j.g.) USN, 1949, advanced through grades to capt. M.C., 1966; intern U.S. Naval Hosp., Phila., 1949-50; student flight surgeon Sch. Aviation Medicine, Pensacola, Fla., 1950-51; flight surgeon U.S. Naval Sta., Trinidad, B.W.I., 1951-53; resident gen. surgery U.S. Naval Hosp., St. Albans, N.Y., 1953-57; postgrad. fellow surgery Royal Victoria Hosp., McGill U., Montreal, Can., 1957; resident thoracic surgery U.S. Naval Hosp., St. Albans, N.Y., 1957-59; resident cardiovascular surgery St. Francis Hosp., Roslyn, N.Y., 1958; staff thoracic surgeon U.S. Naval Hosp., Portsmouth, Va., 1959-64; surgeon U.S.S. Enterprise, 1964; staff thoracic surgeon U.S. Naval Hosp., Nat. Naval Med. Ctr., Bethesda, Md., 1964-65, chief thoracic and cardiovascular surgery, 1965-68; chief surgery, exec. officer U.S.S. Repose, 1968-69; exec. officer Naval Med. Sch., Bethesda, Md., 1969-72; ret., 1972; clin. assoc. surgery U. Pa. Sch. Medicine, 1976-90; prof. clin. surgery Hahnemann U. Sch. Medicine, 1986-96; chief surgery Allentown (Pa.) Hosp., 1972-90, Sacred Heart Hosp., 1973-76, Lehigh Valley Hosp. Ctr., 1974-90. Contbr. articles to profl. jours. Fellow ACS; mem. AMA, Am. Thoracic Soc., Am. Trauma Soc. (pres. Pa. divsn. 1979-83, treas. 1985-91), Soc. Thoracic Surgeons (founding), Pa. Assn. for Thoracic Surgery, Assn. Mil. Surgeons U.S., Am. Trauma Soc. (founding mem.). Roman Catholic. Home and Office: 3761 Devonshire Rd Allentown PA 18103-9628

GAYLOR, JAMES LEROY, biomedical research director; b. Waterloo, Iowa, Oct. 1, 1934; s. David P. and Lena (Livingston) G.; m. Marilyn Louise Gibson, Mar. 25, 1956; children—Douglas, Ann, Robert, Kenneth. BS, Iowa State U., 1956; MS, U. Wis., 1958, PhD, 1960. From asst. prof. to prof. biochemistry Cornell U., Ithaca, N.Y., 1960-77, chmn. biochemistry, molecular and cell biology sect., 1970-76; prof., chmn. dept. biochemistry U. Mo., Columbia, 1977-80; assoc. dir. life scis. rsch. E.I. duPont Cen. Rsch., Wilmington, Del., 1981-83, dir. health sci. rsch., 1984-85; dir. biol. rsch. E.I. duPont Pharms., Wilmington, Del., 1986-87; corp. dir. sci. and technology Johnson & Johnson, New Brunswick, N.J., 1987-97; adj. prof. biochemistry Emory U. Sch. Medicine, 1997—; vis. prof. U. Ill., summer, 1964-65; sabbatical leave U. Oreg. Sch. Medicine, 1966-67, U. Osaka, Japan, 1973-74; vis. lectr. La Molina, Peru, summer 1962; nutrition cons. Pew Found., Phila., 1986-92; mem. bd. sci. counselors div. cancer prevention Nat. Cancer Inst., NIH, Bethesda, Md., 1987-91. Contbr. over 150 rsch. articles to profl. jours.; mem. editl. bd.: Jour. Biol. Chemistry, 1970-76, Biochimica Biophysica Acta, 1971-81, Jour. of Lipid Rsch., 1972-87, assoc. editor, 1983-87. NIH fellow, 1958-60, Spl. fellow, 1966-67, Guggenheim fellow, 1973-74. Mem. AAAS, Am. Chem. Soc., Am. Soc. Biochemistry and Molecular Biology, Am. Soc. for Nutritional Scis., Am. Heart Assn., Am. Assn. Pharm. Scientists, N.Y. Acad. Scis. Achievements include patents for specific synthetic inhibitors of cholesterol synthesis; research on biosynthesis of cholesterol and other membrane-bound enzymes. E-mail: jgaylor@emory.edu. Office: Emory U Sch Medicine Biochemistry Dept 4127 Rollins Rsch Ctr 1510 Clifton Rd NE Atlanta GA 30322-4218

GAYLORD, EDWARD LEWIS, publishing company executive; b. Denver, May 28, 1919; s. Edward King and Inez (Kinney) G.; m. Thelma Feragen, Aug. 30, 1950; children: Christine Elizabeth, Mary Inez, Edward King II, Thelma Louise. A.B., Stanford U., 1941; LL.D., Oklahoma City U., Okla. Christian Coll., Pepperdine U., 1984. Chmn. Okla. Pub. Co., Oklahoma City; also bd. dirs. Okla. Pub. Co.; editor, pub. Daily Oklahoman, Sunday Oklahoman; pres. Sun Resources, Inc., Greenland (Colo.) Ranch, OPUBCO Resources, Inc., OPUBCO Devel. Co.; chmn./pub. Gaylord Entertainment, Nashville; chmn. Opryland U.S.A., Inc., Nashville, chmn. bd. Gayno, Inc., Colorado Springs; ptnr. Cimarron Coal Co., Denver; chmn., bd. dirs. Broadmoor Hotel, Colorado Springs. Chmn., trustee Okla. Industries Authority; hon. chmn. bd. govs. Okla. Christian Coll.; bd. dirs. Okla. State Fair, pres., 1961-71; past chmn. bd. dirs. Nat. Cowboy Hall of Fame and Western Heritage Ctr.; past chmn. Okla. Med. Rsch. Found.; past trustee Casady Sch., Oklahoma City U. Served with AUS, 1942-46. Recipient Brotherhood award NCCJ, 1961, Humanitarian award NCCJ, 1971, Disting. Svc. award U. Okla., 1981, Golden Plate award Am. Acad. Achievement, 1985, Pathmaker of Oklahoma County award Oklahoma City/County Hist. Soc., 1996, Pres.'s award for 50 Yrs. of Svc., 4-H and Future Farmers Am., 1996, Disting. Citizen award Last Frontier Coun. Boy Scouts Am., 1996, Adam Smith award Hillsdale Coll. and Shavano Inst., 1996; named to Okla. Hall of Fame, 1974, Okla. Journalism Hall of Fame, 1994; first recipient Spirit of Am. award U.S. Olympic Com., 1984. Mem. Oklahoma City C. of C. (dir., past pres.), So. Newspaper Pubs. Assn. (past pres.). Congregationalist. Home: 1506 Dorchester Dr Oklahoma City OK 73120-1203 Office: The Daily Oklahoman 9000 Broadway Ext Oklahoma City OK 73114-3799

GAYLORD, NORMAN GRANT, chemical and polymer consultant; b. Bklyn., Feb. 16, 1923; s. Irving M. and Tillie (Horowitz) G.; m. Marilyn Einhorn, June 24, 1945; children—Lori Gaylord Wright, Kathy Gaylord Fleegler, Richard, Cory Gaylord-Ross. B.S., CCNY, 1943; M.S., Poly. Inst. Bklyn., 1949, Ph.D., 1950. Chemist Elko Chem. Works, Pittstown, N.J., 1943-44; chemist Pa. Salt Mfg. Co., Pittstown, 1945, Merck & Co., Rahway, N.J., 1946-48; research chemist E.I. duPont de Nemours & Co., Buffalo, 1950-54; group leader Interchem. Corp., N.Y.C., 1955-56, asst. dept. dir., 1957-59; v.p. Western Petrochem. Corp., Newark, 1959-61; pres. Gaylord Research Inst., New Providence, N.J., 1961-87, Gaylord Assocs., New Providence, 1987—; fellow Research Inst. for Scientists Emeriti, Drew U., Madison, N.J., 1987—; adj. prof. polymer chemistry Canisius Coll., Buffalo, 1951-54, Poly. Inst. Bklyn., 1955-62, U. Lowell, Mass., 1981—. Author: Reduction with Complex Metal Hydrides, 1956, Linear and Stereoregular Addition Polymers, 1959, Polyalkylene Sulfides and Other Polythioethers, 1962, Polyalkylene Oxides and Other Polyethers, 1963; mem. editorial adv. bd. Jour. Macromolecular Sci.-Chemistry, 1968—, Macromolecular Syntheses, 1963—, Jour. Polymer Sci., 1959-80, Jour. Applied Polymer Sci., 1959-74, Ency. of Polymer Sci. and Tech., 1964-72, Soc. Plastics Engrs. Transactions, 1963-64, Polymer Engring. and Sci., 1965-66, Revs. in Macromolecular Chemistry, 1968-73, Macromolecular Reports, 1991; contbr. numerous articles to profl. publs.; patentee in field. Recipient Honor Scroll, N.J. Inst. Chemists, 1984, Founders' award Am. Acad. Optometry, 1985. Fellow Soc. Plastics Engrs.; mem. TAPPI, Am. Chem. Soc., Soc. Plastics Engrs., Sigma Xi. Home and Office: 28 Newcomb Dr New Providence NJ 07974-1729

GAYLORD, SANFORD FRED, physician; b. Cleve., May 18, 1923; s. Samuel Goldberg and Eva Neidus; m. Sarah Leslie Hoffmann, Jan. 1, 1944; children—Scott, Randy, Gregg, Shelley, Wendy, Judd, Brett, Glenn; m. Sondra Hill, Mar. 29, 1980. Student, John Carroll U., 1945-47; M.D., Chgo. Sch. Medicine, 1951, Chgo. Sch. Medicine, 1951. Intern Ill. Central Hosp., Chgo., 1951-52; resident Dearborn VA Hosp., 1952-53, Mt. Sinai Hosp., Cleve., 1953-54; practice medicine specializing in internal medicine and gastroenterology Youngstown, Ohio, 1954—; chief of medicine, chief gastroenterology St. Elizabeth Med. Center, Youngstown; assoc. prof. medicine, acad. coun. Northeastern Ohio U. Coll. Medicine, cons. gastroenterology, 1976—. Former piano student of Boris Goldovsky, 1st place winner piano Nat. Solo Contest, 1939, 40, 41; pioneered Vitamin B12 therapy in treatment of multiple sclerosis, tetracycline flourescence therapy in stomach cancers. Vice pres. Youngstown Symphony Soc., 1965-70; trustee Mahoning County Med. Soc. Found. Served with USAAF, 1943-45, ETO. Decorated D.F.C. with 3 oak leaf clusters, Air medal with 3 battle stars, ETO ribbon. Fellow ACP, Am. Coll. Gastroenterology; mem. AMA (med. sch. sect. representing tching faculty Northeastern U. Coll. Medicine, del. coun. on med. edn., del. med. sch. sect.), Am. Soc. Internal Medicine, Am. Soc. Gastrointestinal Endoscopy, Northeastern Ohio Soc. Gastrointestinal Endoscopy (v.p.), Ohio State Med. Soc., Mahoning County Med. Soc., Ohio Soc. Internal Medicine, Flying Physicians Assn., Aircraft Owners and Pilots Assn. Home and Office: 5670 Lamplighter Dr Girard OH 44420-1628

GAYNOR, JOSEPH, chemical engineer, technical-management consultant; b. N.Y.C., Nov. 15, 1925; s. Morris and Rebecca (Schnapper) G.; m. Elaine Bauer, Aug. 19, 1951; children: Barbara Lynne, Martin Scott, Paul David, Andrew Douglas. B in Chem. Engring., Poly. Inst., 1950; MS, Case Western Res. U., 1952, PhD, 1955. Rsch. asst. Case Inst., Cleve., 1952-55; with Gen. Engring. Labs. GE, Schenectady, N.Y., 1955-66, mgr. R & D sect., 1962-66; group v.p. rsch. Bell & Howell Co., 1966-72; mgr. comml. devel. group, mem. pres.' office Horizons Rsch., Inc., Cleve., 1972-73; pres. Innovative Tech. Assocs., Ventura, Calif., 1973—; mem. nat. materials adv. bd. com. NAS; chmn. conf. com. 2d internat. conf. on bus. graphics, 1979, program chmn. 1st internat. congress on advances in non-impact printing techs., 1981, mem. adv. com. 2d internat. congress on advances in non-impact printing techs., 1984, chmn. publs. com. 3rd internat. congress on advances in non-impact printing techs., 1986, chmn. internat. conf. on hard copy media, materials and processes, 1990. Editor: Electronic Imaging, 1991, Procs. Advances in Non-Impact Printing Technologies, Vol. I, 1983, Vol. II, 1988, 3 spl. issues Jour. Imaging Tech., Proc. Hard Copy Materials Media and Processes Internat. Conf., 1990; patentee in field. Served with U.S. Army, 1944-46. Fellow AAAS, AIChE, Imaging Sci. and Tech. Soc. (sr., gen. chmn. 2nd internat. conf. on electrophotography 1973, chmn. bus. graphics tech. sect. 1976—, chmn. edn. com. L.A. chpt. 1978—), Am. Soc. Photobiology, Sigma Xi, Tau Beta Pi, Phi Lambda Upsilon, Alpha Chi Sigma. Home: 108 La Brea St Oxnard CA 93035-3928 Office: Innovative Tech Assocs 3639 Harbor Blvd Ste 203E Ventura CA 93001-4255

GAZIANO, MARY J., lawyer, educator; b. Rockford, Ill., Mar. 14, 1957; d. Seraphino Joseph and Rose Mary G. JD, U. Fla. Assoc. Remencues & Assocs., Ltd., Rockford, 1982-89; pvt. practice Rockford, 1989—; adj. faculty Harper C.C., Palatine, Ill., 1990—; dir. Ducks Unltd., 1990—, AmCon Mortgage Co., Rockford, 1996-98. Chmn., Winnebego County Rep. Party, 1992—. Mem. Winnebego County Bar Assn., Winnebego County Women's Bar Assn. (pres. 1990, sec.-treas. 1988-90), Quota Club Rockford (sec. 1994-96). Roman Catholic. Avocation: singing. E-mail: mtgaziano@aol.com. Office: Mary J Gaziano 1 Court Pl Ste 200 Rockford IL 61101

GAZZANIGA, ANTONETTE J., secondary school educator; b. Lawrence, Mass., Feb. 6, 1945; d. Anthony George and Lena (LaSpina) Calderone; m. Angelo L. Gazzaniga Jr., Aug. 6, 1966 (dec. Feb. 1993); 1 child, David. BA, Merrimack Coll., 1966; MEd, Mass. State Coll., North Adams, 1972; adminstrn. cert., Fordham U., 1990. Cert. tchr., supr., Mass., N.Y., N.J. English and applied art instr., supr. McCann Tech. Sch., North Adams, Mass., 1969-79; English instr., chair dept. J.S. Burke H.S., Goshen, N.Y., 1979-85; English instr. Goshen H.S., 1985—; adj. instr. humanities Marist Coll., Poughkeepsie, N.Y., 1993—; cons. to corp. execs. on Am. culture and idiom Minolta Advanced Tech., Inc., Goshen, 1994—; presenter in field. Mem. ASCD, N.Y. State Tchrs. Assn., Nat. Coun. Tchrs. English, Goshen Tchrs. Assn., Delta Kappa Gamma (sec. 1995—). Roman Catholic. Avocations: needlework, gardening, computer. Home: 36 Pine Hill Rd Highland Mills NY 10930

GAZZARA, BEN, actor; b. N.Y.C., Aug. 28, 1930; s. Antonio and Angelina (Cusumano) G.; m. Louise Erickson, 1952 (div. 1956); m. Janice Rule, 1 child, Elizabeth; m. Elke Stuckmann; 1 adopted child, Danja. Student, CCNY, 1947-48, Erwin Piscator Dramatic Workshop of New Sch. for Social Research, 1948-49; mem., Actors Studio, from 1951. Actor: stage appearances include Jezebel's Husband, 1952, End As a Man, 1953, Cat on a Hot Tin Roof, 1955, Hatful of Rain, 1955, The Night Circus, 1959, Epitaph for George Dillon, 1959, Two for the Seesaw, 1960, Strange Interlude, 1963, Traveller Without Luggage, 1964, Hughie/Duet, 1974, Who's Afraid of Virginia Woolfe, 1975, Shimada, 1992, Chinese Coffee, 1994; motion pictures include The Strange One, 1957, Anatomy of Murder, 1959, Joy of Laughter, 1960, The Passionate Thief, 1960, The Young Doctors, 1961, Convicts Four, 1961, A Rage to Live, 1964, Husbands, 1969, Al Capone, 1974, High Velocity, 1976, Killing of a Chinese Bookie, 1976, Voyage of the Damned, 1976, Opening Night, 1977, Bloodline, 1978, Saint Jack, 1978, Inchon, 1979, They All Laughed, 1980, Tales of Ordinary Madness, 1981, The Girl from Trieste, 1985, The Cammorista, 1985, A Lovely Scandal, 1986, Quicker than the Eye, 1987, Roadhouse, 1989, And Quiet Flows the Don, 1992, Nefertiti, 1992, People across the Way, 1993, Els de Devart, 1993, Swallows Never Die in Jerusalem, 1994, Farmer and Chase, 1994, Shadow Conspiracy, 1995, Stag, 1996, The Spanish Prisoner, 1996, Buffalo 66, 1997, The Great Lebowski, 1997, Too Tired to Die, 1997, Illuminata, 1997, Happiness, 1998, Buffalo 66, 1998, Undertaker's Paradise, 1999; TV series Arrest and Trial, 1963-64, Run for Your Life, 1965-68 (4 Emmy Nominations), Police Story, 1987; appeared: TV dramas including Playhouse 90, DuPont Show of the Month (Recipient Drama Critics award for role in End As a Man 1953, Theatre World award 1953, 3 nominations Antoinette Perry award, 4 Emmy nominations), An Early Frost, 1985, A Letter to Three Wives, 1985, Downpayment on Murder, 1987, People Like Us, 1990, Lies Before Kisses, 1991, Blindsided, 1993, Fatal Vows: The Alexandra O'Hara Story, 1994, Parallel Lives, 1994, Strangers, 1995, Valentine's Day, 1998, Angelo Nero (miniseries), 1998, Tesoro di Damasco (miniseries), 1998, Tre Stelle (miniseries), 1999; author, director, actor Beyond the Ocean, 1990; Ladykiller, 1996; Vicious Circle, 1997. Office: care J Julien 1501 Broadway New York NY 10036-5601*

GAZZAWAY, KENNETH M., information systems consultant, educator; b. Pt. Arthur, Tex., Aug. 1, 1977; s. Gary Lee and Paula Kathleen (Yates) Dowling. AA in Elec. Engring., Lamar U., 1993; diploma in letters, U. North Tex., 1995. Sys. lab. mgr. U. North Tex., Denton, 1993-95; cloakroom page U.S. Ho. of Reps., Washington, 1994-95; LAN mgr. Internat. Student Exch. Program, Washington, 1995-96; instr. advanced math. Emerson Prep. Sch., Washington, 1996-97; info. sys. cons. Integrated Sys., Inc., Washington, 1996—; intergovtl. orgns. educator Georgetown U., Washington, 1996—; com. chair student life adv. bd. U. North Tex., Denton, 1994-95; confs. coord. Georgetown Internat. Rels. Assn., Washington, 1996-97. Pres. local chpt. UN Assn., Denton, 1994. Rsch. fellow Inst. for Study of Diplomacy, 1996-97. Republican. Avocations: traveling, Middle East politics, Arabic and Western European languages. Home: 101 E 21st St # W-0522 Austin TX 78705-5695

GEAKE, RAYMOND ROBERT, state senator; b. Detroit, Oct. 26, 1936; s. Harry Nevill and Phyllis Rae (Fox) G.; m. Carol Lynne Rens, June 9, 1962; children: Roger Rens, Tamara Lynne, William Rens. BS in Spl. Edn., U. Mich., 1958, MA in Guidance and Counseling, 1959, PhD in Edn. and Psychology, 1963. Coord. child devel. rsch. Edison Inst., Dearborn, Mich., 1962-66; dir. psychology dept. Plymouth (Mich.) State Home and Tng. Sch., Mich. Dept. Mental Health, 1966-69; pvt. practice ednl. psychology Northville, Mich., 1969-72; mem. Mich. Ho. of Reps., 1973-76, Mich. Senate, 1977—; adj. asst. prof. edn./psychology dept. Madonna Coll., Livonia, Mich., 1984-86. Co-author: Visual Tracking, A Self-instruction Workbook for Perceptual Skills in Reading, 1962. Trustee-at-large Schoolcraft C.C., 1969-72, chmn. bd. trustees, 1971-72; vice chmn. nat. adv. com. on mental health and illness of elderly HEW, 1976-77; vice chmn. human svcs. com., assembly fed. issues Nat. Conf. State Legislatures, 1994-95. Recipient Recognition award Found. for Improvement of Justice, 1993. Fellow Mich. Psychol. Assn.; mem. NEA (life), APA, Mich. Soc. Geneal. Rsch., Rotary. Republican. Office: Mich Senate PO Box 30036 Lansing MI 48909-7536*

GEALT, ADELHEID MARIA, museum director; b. Munich, May 29, 1946; came to U.S., 1950; d. Gustav Konrad and Ella Sophie (Daeschlein) Medicus; m. Barry Allen Gealt, Mar. 15, 1969. BA, Ohio State U., 1968; MA, Ind. U., 1973, PhD, 1979. Registrar Ind. U. Art Mus., Bloomington, 1972-76, curator Western art, 1976—, acting/interim dir., 1987-89, dir., 1989—; adj. assoc. prof. H.R. Hope Sch. Fine Arts, Ind. U., Bloomington, 1985-89, assoc. scholar, 1986, assoc. prof., 1989—; mem. nat. adv. coun. Valparaiso U. Art Mus; commn. Ind. Arts Commn., 1997—; commr. Indiana Arts Commn., 1997—. Author: Looking at Art, 1983, Domenico Tiepolo The Punchinello Drawings, 1986; co-author: Art of the Western World, 1989, Painting of the Golden Age: A Biographical Dictionary of Seventeenth-Century European Painters, 1993, Domeinco Tiepolo: Master Draftsman, 1996, Giandomenico Teipolo, Disegni dal mondo, 1996; contbg. author Critic's Choice, 1999. Grantee Nat. Endowment for Arts, 1982, 83, Am. Philos. Soc., 1985, NEH, 1985. Mem. Assn. Art Mus. Dirs. Office: Ind U Art Mus 7th St Bloomington IN 47405-3024

GEAR, CHARLES WILLIAM, computer scientist; b. London, Feb. 1, 1935; came to U.S., 1962, naturalized, 1977; s. Charles James and Margaret (Dumbleton) G.; m. Sharon Sue Smith, Jan. 25, 1958 (div. Oct. 1970); children—Kathlyn Jo, Christopher William Gilpin; m. Ann Lee Morgan, Nov. 19, 1976. BA, Cambridge U., 1956, MA, 1960; MS, U. Ill., Urbana, 1957, PhD, 1960; D (hon.), Royal Inst. Tech., Stockholm, 1987. Engr. IBM, Hursley, Eng., 1960-62; prof. dept. computer sci. U. Ill., Urbana, 1962-90, head dept., 1985-90; v.p. NEC Rsch. Inst., Princeton, N.J., 1990-92, pres., 1992—; vis. prof. Stanford U., Calif., 1969-70, Yale U., New Haven, 1976. Author: Computer Organization and Programming, 1969, 74, 80, 85, Numerical Initial Value Problems, 1971, Introduction to Computer Science, 1973, Introduction to Computers, Programming and Applications, 1978; Pascal Programming, 1983; Computer Applications and Algorithms, 1986. Recipient Fulbright award, 1956, Forsythe award Spl. Interest Group for Numerical Analysis, 1979, Alumni Honor award Engring. Coll., U. Ill., 1992. Fellow AAAS, IEEE, Am. Acad. Arts and Scis., Assn. Computing Machinery (coun. 1976-78); mem. Nat. Acad. Engring., Soc. Indsl. and Applied Math. (coun. 1980-85, pres. 1987-88). Office: NEC Rsch Inst 4 Independence Way Princeton NJ 08540-6685

GEARAN, MARK D., federal agency administrator; m. Mary Herlihy; children: Madeleine, Kathleen. BA cum laude, Harvard U., 1978; JD, Georgetown U., 1991. Press sec. Robert F. Drinan, Mass., 1978; reporter Fitchburg (Mass.) Sentinel, 1978-79; press sec., chief of staff Rep. Berkley Bedell, Iowa, 1980-83; dir. Mass. Office Fed. Rels. Gov. Michael Dukakis, 1983-87, 88-89; hdqs. press. sec. Dukakis for Pres. Campaign, 1987-88; exec. dir. Dem. Gov. Assn., 1989-92; sr. advisor Clinton for Pres. Campaign, 1992-93; dep. dir. Presdl. Transition Team, Washington, 1992-93; asst. to President U.S., dir. comm. White House, Washington, 1993-95; dir. The Peace Corps, Washington, 1995—. Office: Peace Corps Office of the Director 1111 20th St NW Washington DC 20526

GEAREN, JOHN JOSEPH, lawyer; b. Wareham, Mass., Sept. 1, 1943. BA, U. Notre Dame, 1965; MA (Rhodes Scholar), Oxford U., 1967; JD, Yale U., 1970. Bar: Ill. 1972. Ptnr. Mayer, Brown & Platt, Chgo., 1970—. Democrat. Roman Catholic. Home: 408 Linden Ave Oak Park IL 60302-1661 Office: Mayer Brown & Platt 190 S La Salle St Ste 3100 Chicago IL 60603-3441*

GEARON, JOHN MICHAEL, professional basketball team executive; b. Englewood, N.J., May 6, 1934; s. C.P. and Elizabeth (Asbury) G.; m. Patricia Smith, Jan. 1, 1960 (div.); children: Tierney, Michael, Tim; m. Mary F. Davis, Mar. 4, 1989. Chmn. bd. dirs., former gov. Atlanta Hawks Profl. Basketball, 1983—; owner Gearon & Co., Atlanta, 1983—; bd. dirs. Turner Broadcasting Systems Inc. Office: Atlanta Hawks One CNN Ctr South Tower Ste 405 Atlanta GA 30303*

GEARY, AMY JO, librarian; b. Salem, Ohio, Apr. 24, 1968; d. John Edgar and Pauline Sue Baker; m. Darryl Earl Geary, Mar. 19, 1994. BA, Youngstown State U., 1990; MLS, Kent State U., 1992. Children's libr. Huron (Ohio) Pub. Libr., 1993-95; libr. asst. Columbiana (Ohio) Pub. Libr., 1989-93, young adult libr., 1996—. Mem. Ohio Libr. Coun. Avocations: reading, bird watching. Office: Columbiana Pub Libr 332 N Middle St Columbiana OH 44408

GEARY, DANIEL PATRICK, postal service worker; b. St. Louis, May 2, 1963; s. John James and Kathleen Mary (Hogan) G. ASBA, Lewis and Clark C.C., Godfrey, Ill., 1983; B Liberal Studies, St. Louis U., 1990. Laborer U.S. Postal Svc., St. Louis, 1991—. Roman Catholic. Avocations: reading, television, radio. Home: 913 Alpine Ridge Dr Ballwin MO 63021-7627 Office: US Postal Svc 1720 Market St Saint Louis MO 63155-0001

GEARY, DAVID LESLIE, communications executive, educator, consultant; b. Connellsville, Pa., Sept. 30, 1947; s. Harry and Edith Marie (Halterman) G. BA, Otterbein Coll., 1969; MSJ, W.Va. U., 1971; DLitt (hon.), Fairfax U., 1998; postgrad., U. Denver, 1974-75; diploma, Def. Info. Sch., 1971, exec. communications curriculum, U. Okla., 1978, Def. Dept. Sr. Pub. Affairs Officers Course, 1984, Fgn. Svc. Inst., U.S. Dept. State, 1984, Nat. Def. U., 1986; postgrad., U. Sarasota, 1992-95, U. N.Mex., 1998, U. San Jose, 1998—; D Lit. (hon.), Fairfax U., 1998. Admissions counselor Otterbein Coll., 1968-69; instr. English, staff counselor Office of Student Edni. Svcs. W.Va. U., Morgantown, 1969-71; dir. info. Luke AFB, Ariz., 1971-72; course dir. English and comm. U.S. Air Force Acad., Colo., 1972-76; dir. pub. affairs Loring AFB, Maine, 1976-79; spl. asst. pub. affairs Seymour Johnson AFB, N.C., 1980; dir. pub. affairs USAF Engring. and Svcs., Tyndall AFB, Fla., 1980-84, UN and US Air Forces, Korea, 1984-85; asst. prof., asst. dept. chmn., mem. coun. of assoc. and asst. deans U. Ala., 1985-88; dir., nat. cmty. rels. dir., acting dir. pub. affairs USAFR, 1988-92; prin. Leadership Comm. Counsel, 1992-95; comm. program mgr., dir. pub. affairs U.S. Dept. Energy, Albuquerque, 1995—; adj. prof. pub. rels. Ga. State U., Atlanta, 1993-95; guest lectr. U. Maine, 1976-79, USAF Inst. Tech., 1981-82, Fla. State U., 1982-83, U. Md., 1984-85, U.So. Calif., 1984-85, Seoul (Korea) Nat. U., 1985, U. Ala., 1988, Ga. State U., 1991, U. Ga., 1991, U. N.Mex., 1997—; profl. advisor Pub. Rels. Student Soc. Am. Contbr. articles to profl. jours.; mem. bd. profls. Pub. Rels. Rev.: A Jour. of Rsch. and Comment, 1996—; mem. editl. bd. Jour. of Employee Comm. Mgmt., 1996—. Decorated 4 U.S. Meritorious Svc. medals, 2 Air Force Commendation medals, Air Force Achievement medal, Armed Forces Res. medal, Humanitarian Svc. medal, 2 Nat. Def. Svc. medals, Pres.'s Extraordinary Svc. award Otterbein Coll., 1969, Hon. Citizen of Ariz. award, 1971, Mayor's Community Svc. medallion, Songtan, Korea, 1985, Nat. Disting. Svc. medal Arnold Air Soc., 1986, Nat. citation Angel Flight, 1986, George Washington Honor medal from Freedom's Found., 1988, Outstanding Faculty Advisor award U. Ala. Student Govt. Assn., 1988, Exemplary Svc. award Nat. Com. for Employer Support of Guard and Res., 1991, U.S. Dept. Energy Quality award, 1995, U.S. Dept. Energy Spl. Orgnl. Achievement Recognition, 1995, 96, 97, 98; Readers Digest Found. grantee, 1970. Mem. NATAS, VFW, Assn. for Edn. in Journalism and Mass Commn., Internat. Comm. Assn., Pub. Rels. Soc. Am. (profl. advisor U.N.Mex.), Internat. Assn. Bus. Communicators (bd. dirs. N.Mex. chpt. 1998—), SAR, Am. Legion, N.Mex. Pub. Affairs Roundtable (founding), Air Force Pub. Affairs Alumni Assn. Republican. Episcopalian. Office: Office Pub Affairs US Dept Energy PO Box 5400 Albuquerque NM 87185-5400

GEARY, MARIE JOSEPHINE, art association administrator; b. Boston, Dec. 1, 1933; d. Vincent and Maryanne (DeAngelo) Bianco; m. John Francis Geary, Oct. 11, 1959; 1 child, John Francis Jr. Grad., Medford H.S., 1951. Registrar grad./postgrad. div. Tufts U. Sch. Dental Medicine, Boston, 1951-60; reporter, arts editor Chelmsford (Mass.) Newsweekly, 1970-82; owner, mgr. Village Sq. Art Gallery, Chelmsford, 1976-80; founder, owner A Way With Words, Chelmsford, 1980—; founder, dir. Eastcoast Quilters Alliance, Westford, Mass., 1988—; mktg. cons. Westford Regency Inn, 1991. Contbr. articles to profl. mags. Pub. rels. dir. New England Quilt Mus., Lowell, 1986-88; founder, pres. Chelmsford Art Soc., 1970-75; founder, bd. dirs. Chelmsford Cultural Coun., 1980-84; founder, dir. pub. rels. Chelmsford Crafters, Inc., 1976-80; publicity dir. Chelmsford Town 4th of July Celebration, 1971-74; founder Women in Bus. Conf., 1994. Mem. Am. Quilting Soc., Chelmsford Quilters (pres. 1985-89), New England Quilters Guild (Compass editor 1985-88), Chelmsford Book Discussion Soc., Quilters Connection (Quiltations editor 1992-93, v.p. 1994-95, pres. 1995-96), Middlesex Women's Network, Women in Bus. (formed 1993, coord. 1st conf. 1994), Enterprising Women. Republican. Roman Catholic. Avocations: art, antiques, reading, economics, marketing trends. Home: 38 Amble Rd Chelmsford MA 01824-1968 Office: Eastcoast Quilters Alliance PO Box 711 Westford MA 01886-0021

GEARY, PAMELA BLALACK, community health and medical/surgical nurse; b. Shelby County, Tenn., Oct. 27, 1961; d. Walker Ernest Jr. and Pauline Eliose (Holbrook) Blalack; m. Carl Dewayne Geary, Oct. 17, 1981; children: Michelle Dawn, Micheal Dewayne. Diploma, Meth. Hosp. Sch. Nursing, Memphis, 1984. RN, Tenn. Supplemental nurse Meth. Home Care, Memphis, staff home health nurse; staff nurse Meth. Hosp.-North, Memphis, Bapt. Meml. Hosp.-Tipton, Covington, Tenn. Named one of Celebrate Nursing Top 100, 1996.

GEARY, PATRICK JOSEPH, naval security administrator; b. Milw., Mar. 6, 1957; s. David Patrick and Mary Ann (Delavan) G. BS, Va. Commonwealth U., 1984; MA, U. Richmond, 1987. Tech. publs. writer Dept. Def. Security Inst., Richmond, Va., 1987-88; ops. security officer David Taylor Naval Rsch. Ctr., Bethesda, Md., 1988-91, Space and Naval Warfare Sys. Command, Arlington, Va., 1991-92; divsn. head office of security Naval Sea Sys. Command, Arlington, 1992—. Pres. Ybor City Jaycees, Tampa, Fla., 1979, Reno Jaycees, 1980-81; regional/dist. dir. Nev. Jaycees, Reno, 1981-83; co-campaign mgr. state assembly Rep. Party of Nev., Reno, 1982; senator Jaycees Internat., Coral Gables, Fla., 1983, life mem.; active West End Jaycees Richmond, 1983—. Decorated superior civilian svc. medal Dept. Navy, 1995; recipient Charles Kulp meml. award U.S. Jaycees, 1981, Nat. Interagy. award for individual achievment in ops., 1998; Albright grad. fellow U. Richmond, 1985. Mem. NRA, KC, Nat. Def. Indsl. Assn. (life), Ops. Security Profls. Soc. (charter, nat. bd. dirs. 1995—), Nat. Assn. Parliamentarians, Am. Inst. Parliamentarians, Nat. Mil. Intelligence Assn. (life), Pi Sigma Alpha, Alpha Phi Sigma. Roman Catholic. Avocations: water skiing, basketball, football, parliamentary procedure, pistol shooting. Home: 816 Cresthill Rd Fredericksburg VA 22405-1614

GEARY, ROBERT FRANCIS, JR., English educator; b. Boston, May 4, 1944; s. Robert Francis and Anne Theresa (Glynn) G.; m. Anna Rose Perrone, Dec. 18, 1971; children: Teresa, Maria. BA, Boston Coll., 1966; MA in English, U. Va., 1967, PhD in English, 1971. From asst. prof. to prof. English James Madison U., Harrisonburg, Va., 1971-85; prof. James Madison U., Harrisonburg, 1985—, head dept., 1981-90. Author: The Supernatural in Gothic Fiction, 1992; contbg. editor Lord Ruthven Lit. Bulletin, 1995—. Grantee James Madison U., 1991, 92, 94. Mem. Internat. Assn. Fantastic in Arts (divsn. head sci. fiction 1996-97), S. Atlantic MLA, Phi Beta Kappa. Avocations: detective and horror fiction. Home: 1440 Crawford Ave Harrisonburg VA 22801-2905 Office: Dept English James Madison U Harrisonburg VA 22807

GEBAIDE, STEPHEN ELLIOT, mathematics and computer science educator; b. Bklyn., N.Y., Oct. 28, 1946; s. David and Ruth (Kaplan) G. BS, Bklyn. Coll., 1968; MS, Pratt Inst., 1975. Tchr. math., computer sci., coach math/computer teams Robert H. Goddard Jr. High Sch., Ozone Park, N.Y., 1968—, mentor tchr.; adj. asst. prof. computer info. systems Fiorello H. LaGuardia C.C., Long Island City, N.Y., 1984—; math. team coach and advisor, computer team coach and advisor, mentor tchr., math. curriculum devel., computer sci. curriculum devel. Robert H. Goddard Jr. High Sch., Ozone Park; microcomputer instr. for sch. dist. pers. Cmty. Sch. Dist. 27, Ozone Park. Recipient 1st place team award N.Y.C. Interscholastic Math. League, 1981, NSPE, 1988. Mem. United Fedn. Tchrs., Assn. Computer Educators, Assn. Tchrs. Math. N.Y.C., Nat. Coun. Tchrs. Math., Assn. Math. Tchrs. N.Y. State, Mensa. Jewish. Avocations: computers, logical puzzles, physical fitness, volleyball. Home: 67-15 Dartmouth St Forest Hills NY 11375-4024 Office: Robert H Goddard Jr HS 138-30 Lafayette St Ozone Park NY 11417-2730

GEBALLE, RONALD, physicist, university dean; b. Redding, Calif., Feb. 7, 1918; s. Oscar and Alice (Glaser) G.; m. Marjorie Louise Cohn, Oct. 31, 1940; children—Margaret Gilbert, Thomas R., Leslie A., Daniel T., Robert O., Jonathan L., Emily R., Anthony J. B.S., U. Calif. at Berkeley, 1938, M.S., 1940, Ph.D., 1943. Teaching asst. physics U. Calif., Berkeley, 1938-42, physicist radiation lab., 1943; physicist Applied Physics Lab. U. Wash., Seattle, 1943-46, mem. faculty, 1946—, prof., 1959-86, prof. emeritus, 1986—, chmn. dept. physics, 1957-73, assoc. dean Coll. Arts and Scis., 1973-75, acting dean, 1975-76, vice provost for research, also dean of grad. sch., 1976-81, dean emeritus, 1981—; Guest scientist Lab. for Atomic and Molecular Physics, Amsterdam, 1964-65; cons. NSF, Army Research Office; mem. research adv. com. electro-physics NASA, 1962-64; Mem. com. atomic and nuclear physics Nat. Acad. Scis., 1970-72; mem. Nat. Acad. Scis.-NRC evaluation panels for Nat. Bur. Standards panel on Inst. for Basic Standards, 1973-75, chmn. panel on lab. astrophysics, 1973-75; mem. Nat. Acad. Scis.-NRC exec. com. for evaluation panels for Nat. Bur. Standards, 1975-78; also adv. bd. to Office Phys. Scis., Assembly Math. and Phys. Scis., 1975-77; sec. Internat. Conf. on Physics of Electronic and Atomic Collisions, 1967-77; mem. adv. com. grants Research Corp., 1967-73; mem. Commn. on Coll. Physics, 1966-71; mem.-at-large U.S. Nat. Com. for Internat. Union of Pure and Applied Physics, 1974-76; Solomon Katz disting. lectr. humanities, 1978; mem. Grad. Record Exams. Bd., 1978-79. Mem. citizens com. edn. Wash. State Legislature, 1960; trustee Pacific Sci. Center, 1977—. Fellow Am. Phys. Soc. (chmn. div. electron and atomic physics 1968), AAAS (chmn. section B 1988—); mem. AAUP, Am. Assn. Physics Tchrs. (pres. 1969-70, Distinguished Service citation 1973), Fedn. Am. Scientists, ACLU, Pacific N.W. Assn. Coll. Physics (chmn. bd. dirs. 1965-70), Am. Inst. Physics (governing bd., exec. com. 1968-71), Assn. Grad. Schs. (sec.-treas. 1977-80, v.p. 1980-81, pres. 1981-82), Phi Beta Kappa, Sigma Xi. Home: 4201 NE 92nd St Seattle WA 98115-3834*

GEBAUER, AUGUST WILLIAM, editor; b. Little Rock, Apr. 7, 1940; s. August William and Mary Elizabeth (Lee) G. AB, Hendrix Coll., 1962; MA, Tulane U., 1964, PhD, 1975; MLS, George Peabody U., 1978. Instr. English U. New Orleans, 1965-69; instr. English, libr. Memphis State U., 1969-74, 76-79; tech. writer Williams-Fenix & Scisson, New Orleans, 1979-81, OAO Corp., New Orleans, 1981-84, Walk, Haydel & Assocs., New Orleans, 1984-85; tech. editor Systematic Mgmt. Svcs., New Orleans, 1985-89, Tucker & Assocs., New Orleans, 1990-97, Critique, Inc., New Orleans, 1997-98; English instr. Delgado C.C., New Orleans, 1997—. Mem. ALA, MLA, Sierra Club, Wilderness Soc. Home: 838 Lowerline St Apt 14 New Orleans LA 70118-5161 Office: Delgado CC Dept Comms 501 City Park Ave New Orleans LA 70119-4324

GEBAUER, RÜDIGER, publishing company executive; b. Heidelberg, Germany, Sept. 8, 1951. MA, U. Heidelberg. Rsch. fellow IBM, 1985-87; math. editor, editl. dir., then v.p. Springer-Verlag N.Y. Inc. subs. Springer-Verlag GmbH, N.Y.C., 1987-95, pres., CEO, 1995—. Office: Springer-Verlag NY Inc 175 5th Ave Ste 910 New York NY 10010-7858*

GEBB, SHELDON ALEXANDER, lawyer; b. Long Beach, Calif., Jan. 12, 1935. AB, U. Calif., Berkeley, 1957; LLB, U. Calif., 1963. Bar: Calif. 1964. Mng. ptnr. Baker & Hostetler, L.A., Long Beach and Beverly Hills, Silicon Valley, Calif. Chmn. bd. trustees Southwestern U. Sch. Law, 1985-91. Mem. ABA, State Bar Calif., Maritime Law Assn. U.S. Office: Baker & Hostetler 600 Wilshire Blvd Los Angeles CA 90017-3212*

GEBBIA, ROBERT JAMES, tax executive; b. New Castle, Pa., Nov. 29, 1947; s. Joseph A. and Helen M. (Staransky) G.; m. Eileen A. Zuk, Oct. 2, 1971; children: Jamie, Christopher, Maria. BS, Youngstown State U., 1969; MBA, Canisius Coll., 1979. CPA, Va. Tax law specialist IRS, Washington, 1972-74; IRS agt. IRS, Detroit and Buffalo, 1974-77; tax supr. Peat, Marwick, Mitchell, Buffalo, 1977-79; tax mgr. Coopers & Lybrand, Pitts., 1979-81; tax dir. UNC Resources, Falls Church, Va., 1981-85; sr. tax mgr. Occidental Petroleum, Tulsa, 1985-88; dir. taxes Carpenter Tech., Reading, Pa., 1988—; evening instr. Albright Coll., Reading, 1989—; treas. Carpenter Tech. Fed. Pac, Carpenter Tech. Pa. Pac. Treas. Carpenter Tech. Pa./Fed. PAC. With U.S. Army, 1970-71, Vietnam. Decorated Bronze Star, Army Commendation medals (2). Mem. Mfrs. Alliance for Productivity and Innovation, Pa. Chamber of Bus. and Industry, Tax Execs. Inst., Nat. Assn. Corp. Treasurers, Berks County C. of C. Roman Catholic. Avocation: tennis. Home: 217 Logan Ave Reading PA 19610-2655 Office: Carpenter Tech PO Box 14662 101 Bern St Reading PA 19601-1203

GEBBIE, KRISTINE MOORE, health science educator, health official; b. Sioux City, Iowa, June 26, 1943; d. Thomas Carson and Gladys Irene (Stewart) Moore; m. Lester N. Wright; children: Anna, Sharon, Eric. BSN, St. Olaf Coll., 1965; MSN, UCLA, 1968; DPH, U. Mich., 1995. Project dir. USPHS Tng. Grant, St. Louis, 1972-77; coord. nursing St. Louis U., 1974-76, asst. dir. nursing, 1976-78, clin. prof., 1977-78; adminstr. Oreg. Health Div., Portland, 1978-89; sec. Wash. State Dept. Health, Olympia, 1989-93; coord. Nat. AIDS Policy, Washington, 1993-94; assoc. prof. Sch. Nursing Columbia U., 1994—; assoc. prof. Oreg. Health Scis. U. Portland, 1980—; chair U.S. dept. energy secretarial panel on Evaluation of Epidemiologic Rsch. Activities, 1989-90; mem. Presdl. Commn. on Human Imunodeficiency Virus Epidemic, 1987-88. Author: (with Deloughery and Neuman) Consultation and Community Orgn., 1971, (with Deloughery) Political Dynamics: Impact on Nurses, 1975, (with Scheer) Creative Teaching in Clinical Nursing, 1976. Bd. dirs. Luth. Family Svcs. Oreg. and S.W. Wash., 1979-84, Oreg. Psychoanalytic Found., 1983-87. Recipient Disting. Alumna award St. Olaf Coll., 1979; Disting. scholar Am. Nurses Found., 1989. Fellow Am. Acad. Nursing; mem. Assn. State and Territorial Health Ofcls. (pres. 1984-85, exec. com. 1980-87, McCormick award 1988), Am. Pub. Health Assn. (exec. bd.), Inst. Medicine, N.Am. Nursing Diagnosis Assn. (treas. 1983-87), Am. Soc. Pub. Adminstrn. (adminstrn. award II 1983). Office: Columbia U Sch Nursing 630 W 168th St New York NY 10032-3702

GEBELEIN, RICHARD STEPHEN, judge, former state attorney general; b. Upper Darby, Pa., June 8, 1946; s. Walter C. and Margaret E. (Stratton) G.; m. Anna Grace Thomason.; children: R. Zachary, Lauren E. V., Alexandra D. B.S. in Math., U. Pitts., 1967; J.D., Villanova U., 1970. Bar: Pa. 1971, Del. 1971, U.S. Supreme Ct. 1975. Justice of peace Kennett Twp., Pa., 1967-70; dep. atty. gen. State of Del., 1971-74, state solicitor, 1974-75, chief dep. public defender, 1975-76; ptnr. firm Wilson & Whittington, Wilmington, Del., 1976-79; atty. gen. State of Del., Wilmington, 1979-83; assoc. judge Del. Superior Ct., 1984—; adj. prof. Del. Law Sch., Widener Coll.; instr. U. Del.; mem. Del. Gov.'s Sentencing Reform Commn.; chmn. Sentencing Accountability Commn. State of Del., 1989—. Republican. Roman Catholic. Home: One Rock Manor Ave Wilmington DE 19803

GEBERTH, FRANCES WHITE, painter; b. Mt. Vernon, N.Y., May 9, 1925; d. Milo J. and Frances Bame White; m. William J. Geberth, June 27, 1948; children: Elizabeth, Deborah. Student, Parsons Sch. Design, 1946-48. Pub.'s asst. Moore-Robbins Pub., N.Y.C., 1943-45; display advt. Macy Newspapers, White Plains, N.Y., 1945-46; propr. Summer Gallery, Harwich Port, Mass., 1985-87, Fo'cas'le House Gallery, Harwich Port, Mass., 1987—. Illustrator: A Quest for Good Eating, 1994, To Always Persevere, 1995. Chair Arts Lottery Coun., Harwich, 1984-90; mem. Archtl. Adv. Bd., Harwich, 1990-94. Mem. Guild Harwich Artists (bd. dirs., pub. rels. 1996—), Harwich Hist. Soc. (museum chair 1996-98, pres. 1999—), Questers Chpt. 950 (treas. 1996-99), Gen. Soc. Mayflower Descendants, Costume Soc. Am. Avocation: antique costume identification and preservation. Home: 35 Wendys Way Harwich MA 02645-2507 Office: Fo'cas'le House Gallery 35 Wendys Way Harwich MA 02645-2507

GEBHARD, BOB, professional baseball team executive. Gen. mgr. Colorado Rockies. Office: Colo Rockies 2001 Blake St Denver CO 80205-2008

GEBHARD, DIANE KAY, county administrator, political advisor; b. Indpls., Aug. 9, 1947; d. John Allen and Ruth Ethel (Bolin) Wortman; children: Christine Cummings, David McNeely II; m. Gary O. Gebhard, Sept. 16, 1994. Grad. h.s., Indpls. Dep. clk. Johnson County Clk.'s Office, Franklin, Ind., 1976-84; adminstrv. asst. Ind. State Senate, Indpls., 1984-88, Ind. Ho. of Reps., Indpls., 1988-95; Perry County adminstr. County Commrs., Tell City, Ind., 1995—. Campaign cons. State rep. Dennis Heeke, Majority Caucus Chmn., Ind. Ho. of Reps., Jasper, Ind., 1994, State Rep. Larry Lutz, Evansville, Ind., 1996, State Rep. Dennie Oxley; bd. dirs. So. Ind. Rural Devel., 1997. Named Ky. Col., Gov. Ky., 1992. Mem. Am. Legion Aux., Indpls. Press Club, Women of the Moose. Democrat. Avocations: reading, campaigning, gardening, flying, golf. Office: Perry County Commrs 2219 Payne St Tell City IN 47586-2832

GEBHART, CARL GRANT, security broker; b. Santa Monica, Calif., Jan. 24, 1926; s. Carl V. and Hazel (Grant) G.; m. Margaret Mary del Bondio, Nov. 29, 1952 (dec. Feb. 1989); children: Elizabeth G. Gebhart-Hardin, Peggy G. McFarland, Julia Ann Seamon. *Carl's daughter Betsy Gebhart graduated with a BA in 1977 from the University of California, Santa Barbara. His daughter Peggy McFarland graduated with a BA in 1979 from University of California, Santa Barbara and earned a MA in 1981 from Cornell University. She is also a former executive with the U.S. Army, civilian branch. His daughter Julie Seamon graduated with a BA in 1981 from University of California, Irvine and earned a MA in 1991 from UCLA. She is a CPA with Coopers Lybrand in Cincinnati, Ohio. Carl has nine grandchildren: Alexander, Andrew, and Abigail Gebhart-Hardin, Kate, Joshua, and Kelly McFarland, and Gwen, Courtney, and Meredith Seamon.* B.A. in Journalism, U. So. Calif., 1947; M.B.A. in Fin, Harvard U., 1949. Registered rep. Mitchum, Jones & Templeton, Inc., Los Angeles, 1949-56; gen. partner Mitchum, Jones & Templeton, Inc., 1956-62, sr. v.p., sec., dir., 1962-73; v.p. investments Paine Webber, Los Angeles, 1973—; financial reporter radio sta. KABC, Los Angeles, 1968-73. Mem. L.A. Soc. Fin. Analysts (v.p. 1959), Spring St. Forum (pres. 1962), Petroleum Club (L.A.), Univ. Club L.A., Univ. Assocs. U. So. Calif. (life), Tennis Patrons Santa Monica (life), Beach Club (Santa Monica), Phi Beta Kappa, Phi Kappa Phi, Phi Eta Sigma, Chi Phi, Sigma Delta Chi. Republican. Presbyterian. Home: 749 Amalfi Dr Pacific Palisades CA 90272-4509 Office: 777 S Figueroa St Los Angeles CA 90017-5800

GECHT, MARTIN LOUIS, physician, bank executive; b. Chgo., July 12, 1920; s. Max and Sarah (Rolnick) G.; m. Francey Ann Heytow; children: Lauren Paula Gecht Kramer, Susan Ellen Gecht Rieser, Robert David. B.A., U. So. Calif., 1941; M.D., U. Health Sci./Chgo. Med. Sch., 1945. Intern Brookdale Med. Center, N.Y.C., 1944-45; resident in dermatology Cook County Hosp., 1955-58; gen. practice medicine, 1946-59, practice medicine specializing in dermatology, 1959-99; organized Allport Med. Group, 1948, now pres.; chmn. bd. Albany Bank & Trust Co. N.A., 1976—. Trustee, mem. exec., fin. coms., chmn. audit com. Finch U. Health Sci./Chgo. Med. Sch.; participant numerous activities Jewish Fedn. Chgo.; Chgo. Com. Weizmann Inst. Sci., internat. bd. dirs.; mem. adv. com. on prints and drawings Art Inst. Chgo.; bd. dirs. Lyric Opera of Chgo. Recipient Disting. Service award Anti-Defamation League, B'nai B'rith, 1975, 83. Mem. Am. Bankers Assn., Ill. Bankers Assn., AMA, Ill. Med. Soc., Chgo. Med. Soc. Councilors, Am. Acad. Dermatology (life), Soc. Indsl. Medicine and Surgery. Jewish. Clubs: Metropolitan, Standard, High Ridge (Palm Beach, Fla.). Home: 1110 N Lake Shore Dr Apt 37 Chicago IL 60611-1054 Office: Albany Bank & Trust Co NA 3400 W Lawrence Ave Chicago IL 60625-5188

GECHTOFF, SONIA, artist; b. Phila., Sept. 25, 1926; d. Leonid and Etya (Freedman) G.; children: Susannah Kelly, Miles Kelly. BFA, Phila. Mus. Sch. Art, 1950. Instr. painting, drawing Calif. Sch. Fine Art, 1957-58; adj. asst. prof. art NYU, 1966-70; lectr. Queens Coll., N.Y.C., 1970-74; assoc. prof. U. N.Mex., 1974-75; artist-in-residence Skidmore Coll., summers 1988, 89, 90, Adelphi U., N.Y., 1991, 93; vis. artist Chgo. Art Inst., 1989. One-woman shows include DeYoung Mus., San Francisco, 1957, Ferus Gallery, L.A., 19157, 59, Poindexter Gallery, N.Y.C., 1959, 60, Cortella Gallery, N.Y.C., 1976, 78, Gruenebaum Gallery, N.Y.C., 1979, 80, 82, 83, 85, 87, Witkin Gallery, N.Y.C., 1984, 89, Kraushaar Gallery, N.Y.C., 1990, 92, 95, Fine Arts Gallery, San Francisco, 1991, Adelphi U., 1993, Skidmore Coll., N.Y., 1995, Harrison Mus. Art, Utah, 1996; group shows include Guggeneim Mus., N.Y.C., 1954, San Francisco Mus. Art, 1953-58, Brussels World's Fair, 1958, 1st Paris Biennale, 1959, Whitney Mus., N.Y.C., 1959, 60, Sao Paulo Biennale, 1961, Nat. Gallery Am. Art Smithsonian Instn., 1976, Mus. Modern Art, N.Y.C., 1977, Aldrich Mus. Contemporary Art, Ridgefield, Conn., 1981, Bennington Coll., Vt., 1985, Weatherspoon Gallery, Greensboro, 1987, Gruenebaum Gallery, 1987, The Butler Inst. of Am. Art: 56th Nat. Mid-Yr. Exhbn., Youngstown, Ohio, 1992, Santa Cruz (Calif.) Mus., 1993, Laguna Art Mus., Laguna Beach, Calif., 1996, San Francisco Mus. Modern Art, 1996; represented in permanent collections, San Francisco Mus. Modern Art, Guggenheim Mus., Mus. Modern Art, Met. Mus., N.Y.C., Balt. Mus. Art, Harrison Mus. Art at Utah State U., Worcester (Mass.) Art Mus., Laguna (Calif.) Art Mus.; also pvt. and corp. collections. Ford Found. fellow Tamarind Inst., L.A., 1963; recipient Purchase awards San Francisco Mus. Art, 1955-59; grantee Esther and Adolph Gottlieb Found., 1987, Mid. Atlantic NEA, 1988, Pollock-Krasner Found., 1994, Richard Florsheim Art Fund, 1994. Mem. Nat. Acad. Design. *I have, since my early twenties, always thought of myself as a painter. As the mother of two children (now adults), I was able to work on my paintings and to develop my art continuously. My life is my work.*

GECK, FRANCIS JOSEPH, furniture designer, educator, author; b. Detroit, Dec. 20, 1900; s. Jacob C. and Anna Mary (Angermeyer) G.; m. Evelyn Marie Sturdyvin, July 22, 1937 (dec.). Diploma, N.Y. Sch. Fine and Applied Art, 1924; MFA in Interior Design, Syracuse U., 1946. Instr. N.Y. Sch. Fine & Applied Art, Paris, 1924-27; interior architect and designer William Wright Co., Detroit, 1927-30; interior architect, consultant T. Eaton Co., Toronto, 1930; prof. interior design U. Colo., Boulder, 1930-69; prof. emeritus; dir. exhibits Boulder Hist. Soc., 1944-58; curator of exhibits U. Colo., 1947-57; dir. exhibits Pioneer Mus., Boulder, Colo., 1958-79; design cons. Mullins Plastics, 1969-71. Author: French Interiors and Furniture: Gothic through Louis XVI, 9 vols., 1982-96; designer 17 pvt. offices in Fisher Bldg. Recipient Honorable Mention award Fla. Internat. Art Exhbn., Lakeland, 1952, Grumbaker Award of Merit, 1952, Gold Award Winner Am. Artists Profl. League, 1953, Silver medal Accademia Internazionale di Letters-Arti-Scienze, 1970, Cert. of Merit Benedictine Art award, 1971. Home: 18360 Martin Rd Roseville MI 48066-4805

GECKLE, GEORGE LEO, III, English language educator; b. Danbury, Conn., Dec. 2, 1939; s. George Leo and Dorothy Marion (Hill) G.; m. Justine Virginia Carroll, Aug. 19, 1961; children: George, Richard. AB, Middlebury Coll., 1961; MA, U. Va., 1962, PhD, 1965. Asst. prof. English U. Wis., Madison, 1965-68; asst. prof. English U. S.C., Columbia, 1968-70, assoc. prof. English, 1970-74; prof. English U S.C., Columbia, 1974—; dir. honors program U. S.C., Columbia, 1970-73, dir. English grad. studies, 1974-76, 77-78, chmn. English dept., 1978-87. Author: John Marston's Drama, 1980, Tamburlaine and Edward II: Text and Performance, 1988; editor: Twentieth Century Interpretations of Measure for Measure, 1970. Fulbright grantee sr. prof. category U. Bamberg, Fed. Republic Germany, 1984-85; recipient 1st Jo Ann Boydston Essay prize Assn. for Documentary Editing, 1995. Mem. MLA, South Atlantic MLA, Shakespeare Assn. Am., Southeastern Renaissance Conf. (pres. 1985-86). Home: 5925 Timle Ln Columbia SC 29206-1629 Office: U South Carolina Dept English Humanities Bldg Columbia SC 29208

GECKLE, ROBERT ALAN, manufacturing company executive; b. Newtown, Conn., July 12, 1944; s. George Leo and Dorothy Marion (Hill) G.; m. Katherine Bernarda Landry, July 22, 1967; children: Sarah Nicole, Robert Alan Jr. BA in Econs., Middlebury Coll., 1967; MBA in Mktg., U. Pa., 1969. Sales mgr. Branson Cleaning Equipment Co., Stamford, Conn., 1969-71; product mgr. Branson Cleaning Equipment Co., Shelton, Conn., 1971-73, dir. mktg., 1973-75, gen. mgr., 1975-78, pres., 1978-86; pres. Branson Ultrasonics Corp., Danbury, Conn., 1987-94; pres., CEO Scan-Code, Inc., Rocky Hill, Conn., 1994-97; pres. Fluid and Power Systems Group, Textron, Providence, 1997—. Contbr. articles on ultrasonics to profl. jours.; patentee in field. Bd. dirs. Danbury Health Systems, 1988—; mem. Pres.'s Club, 1988—; bd. dirs. German Studies Orgn., Western Conn. Coll., 1987—. Mem. Conn. Bus. Industry Assn. (bd. dirs. 1991, exec. com., 1992), Ridgewood Country Club, Danbury C. of C. Republican. Roman Catholic. Avocations: golf, gardening. Office: Textron 40 Westminster St Ste 2 Providence RI 02903

GECKLER, RICHARD DELPH, metal products company executive; b. Toledo, Nov. 4, 1918; s. Maurice T. and Edith (Payne) G.; m. Elaine Mary Campbell, June 27, 1965; children: Elaine Demian, Sharon Jean (Mrs. Alex Bellehumeur); 1 dau. by previous marriage, Carole Faye (Mrs. Gene Hendrix). A.B., DePauw U., 1939. Chem. engr. Standard Oil Co., Ind., 1939-45; with Aerojet-Gen. Corp., Calif., 1945-68, v.p., mgr. solid rocket plant, Sacramento, 1956-63, corp. v.p., El Monte, 1963-68; chmn. bd., chief exec. Aerojet Delft Corp., 1968-69; exec. v.p. Anellux Systems Corp., El Segundo, Calif., 1970-71; pres. Marquardt Co., 1972-73, Geckler Industries, Inc., 1972—, Pitter Metal Products, Inc., 1972-89, J.L. Mallard Co., 1972-89; asst. dir. strategic weapons Office Sec. Def., 1964-66. Recipient Meritorious Pub. Service citation Navy Dept., 1961. Fellow Am. Inst. Aeros. and Astronautics; mem. Am. Chem. Soc., Am. Math. Soc., Am. Assn. of Artificial Intelligence, The Athenaeum, Phi Beta Kappa. Home: 7450 Olivetas Ave # 7542A La Jolla CA 92037-4902

GEDDES, JANE, professional golfer; b. Huntington, N.Y., Feb. 5, 1960; d. Gerard George and Helen Evelyn (Zielinski) G. Student, Fla. State U., 1978-82. Profl. golfer, 1983—. Winner U.S. Women's Open, 1986, Boston 5 Classic, 1987, Jamie Farr Toledo Classic, 1987, GNA-Glendale (Calif.) Fedn. Classic, 1987, Women's Kemper Open, 1987, LPGA Championship, 1987, Women's Brit. Open, 1989, Jamaica Classic, 1991, Atlantic City Classic, 1991, Oldsmobile Classic, 1993, Chgo. Sun-Times Classic, 1994; named Most Improved Golfer, Golf Digest, 1986. Roman Catholic. Avocations: piano, music, sports. *

GEDDES, LANELLE EVELYN, nurse, physiologist; b. Houston, Sept. 15, 1935; d. Carl Otto and Evelyn Bertha (Frank) Nerger; B.S.N., U. Houston, 1957, Ph.D. (fellow), 1970; m. Leslie Alexander Geddes, Aug. 3, 1962. Staff nurse Houston Ind. Sch. Dist., 1957-62; instr. to asst. prof. physiology Baylor U. Coll. Medicine, 1972-75; asst. prof. nursing Tex. Women's U., 1972-75; prof., head Sch. Nursing, Purdue U., 1975-91. Recipient teaching awards. Mem. Am. Nurses Assn., Nat. League Nursing, Am. Assn. Critical-Care Nurses, AAAS, N.Y. Acad. Scis., Phi Kappa Phi, Sigma Theta Tau, Iota Sigma Pi. Lutheran. Contbr. articles sci. jours., chpts. in books. Office: Purdue Univ West Sch Nursing Lafayette IN 47907

GEDDES, LESLIE ALEXANDER, bioengineer, physiologist, educator; b. Scotland, May 24, 1921; s. Alexander and Helen (Humphrey) G.; m. Irene P. Bloomer; 1 child, James Alexander; m. La Nelle E. Nerger, Aug. 3, 1962. BEE, MEngring., ScD (hon.), McGill U.; PhD in Physiology, Baylor U. Med. Coll. Demonstrator in elec. engring. McGill U., 1945, research asst. dept. neurology, 1945-52; cons. elec. engring. to various indsl. firms Que., Can.; biophysicist dept. physiology Baylor Med. Coll., Houston; asst. prof. physiology Baylor Med. Coll., 1956-61, assoc. prof., 1961-65, prof., 1965-74; dir. Lab. of Biophysics, Tex. Inst. Rehab. and Research, Houston, 1961-65; prof. physiology Coll. Vet. Medicine, Tex. A. and M. U., College Station, 1965-74, prof. biomed. engring., 1969-74; Showalter Disting. prof. bioengring. and elec. engring. Purdue U., West Lafayette, Ind., 1974-91, Showalter Disting. prof. emeritus, 1991—; cons. NASA Manned Spacecraft Center, Houston, 1962-64, USAF, Sch. Aerospace Medicine, Brooks AFB, 1958-65. Author: 22 books; cons. editor: Med. and Biol. Engring., 1969—, Med. Research Engring., 1964-74, Med. Electronics and Data, 1969—; mem. editorial bd.; Jour. Electrocardiology, 1968—, med. instr., 1974—; contbr. over 700 articles to bioengring. Served with Canaidan Army OTC. Fellow NSPE, Nat. Acad. Forensic Engrs., AAAS, IEEE (Leadership award, Edison medal, World of Difference award), Am. Coll. Cardiology, Australasian Coll. Physicists in Biology and Medicine, Am. Inst. for Med. and Biol. Engring., Royal Soc. Medicine, NAE, Tex. Soc. Profl. Engrs., Biomed. Engring. Soc., Am. Inst. Biol. Scis., Assn. for Advancement Med. Instrumentation (Leadership award), Am. Physiol. Soc., Nat. Acad. Forensic Engrs. (sr.), Sigma Xi, Tau Beta Pi, Phi Zeta. Home: 400 N River Rd Apt 1724 West Lafayette IN 47906-3158 Office: Purdue U POTR Bldg West Lafayette IN 47907-1296

GEDDES, ROBERT, architect, educator; b. Phila., Dec. 7, 1923; s. Louis J. and Kay (Malmed) G.; m. Evelyn Basse, June 15, 1947; children: David, Ann. Student, Yale U., 1941-46; M.Arch., Harvard U., 1950; LHD, N.J. Inst. Tech., 1998. Sr. ptnr. Geddes-Brecher Qualls Cunningham (architects), Phila., 1954-89, Princeton, 1965-89; pvt. practice Robert Geddes, Arch., Princeton and N.Y.C., 1990—; prof. architecture and civic design U. Pa., 1951-65; prof. architecture, dean Sch. Architecture Princeton U., 1965-82, William Kenan prof., 1968-89; Henry Luce prof. architecture, urbanism and history NYU, 1989-98; univ. lectr. U. London, 1972-98; dir. Manville Corp., Butler Mfg. Co.; chmn. adv. bd. design Redevel. Authority Phila., 1959-66; bd. dirs. Citizens Council City Planning, Phila., 1961-63, Urban America, Inc.; cons. Regional Plan Assn., N.Y.; advisor on architecture and urban design, U.S. Delegation to UN, Habitat II Conf., Istanbul, 1996. Contbr. articles on architecture to Ency. Brit., 1974-79; editor Principles and Precedents, Process Architecture jour., 1985; prin. works include Moore Sch. Elec. Engring, U. Pa., 1958, Police Hdqrs, Phila., 1962, resident halls U. Del., 1966, U. Pa., 1967, housing projects, Westchester, Pa., also, Phila. and, Trenton, 1966-77, U. Pa. Med. Sch. and Hosp., 1978-84, dining hall and acad. bldg., libr. common room for astronomy, 1996, Inst. for Advanced Study, Princeton, 1971, humanities and social scis. bldg., So. Ill. U., Carbondale, 1968-74, Stockton State Coll, 1971-75, Corning (N.Y.) Downtown Renewal, 1975; master plan and design Liberty State Park, N.J., 1975-77; master plan Miami Downtown Govt. Center, 1978-84; Lab. bldgs., Mobil Corp., 1981, J. B. Speed Art Mus., Louisville, 1983; Muhlenberg Coll. Library, 1986, Center City plan, Phila., 1985-87, Hosp. U. Pa., 1987, Pub. Safety Bldg., White Plains, N.Y., 1985—, Franklin Inst., Phila., 1987-90, Stern Sch. Bus. NYU, 1987-93, Alexanderpolder urban design, Rotterdam, 1993; xco-dir. Crosstown 116 Upper Manhattan HUD U. Partnership, 1997; editor: Cities in Our Future, 1997. Fellow, N.Y. Inst. for the Humanities, 1989—, Appleton Traveling fellow Harvard U., 1950-51; recipient 6 Design awards Progressive Architecture, First Design award, 1958; 2d prize Nat. Opera House, Sydney, Australia, 1958; first prize Internat. Town Planning Competition for Expansion of Vienna, Austria, 1971, award for Excellence in Archtl. Edn. ACSA-AIA, 1984. Fellow for design AIA (dir. edn. research project 1965-67, pres. N.Y. chpt. 1997, Nat. First Honor award 1960, 77, Archtl. Firm award 1979, Gold medals Phila. chpt., Silver medals Pa. Soc., medals N.J. Soc., pres. N.Y. chpt. 1997); mem. Harvard Grad. Sch. Design Alumni Assn. (past pres.). Clubs: Century Assn.

GEDDIE, THOMAS EDWIN, retired small business owner; b. Athens, Tex., Oct. 7, 1930; s. Nolen Dawson and Fannie (Troublefield) G.; BS in Agr., Okla. State U., 1951; postgrad. Tex. A&M U., 1951; m. Minnie Maxine Smith, Feb. 18, 1968; children: Susan, Tommy, Sherry. Owner, operator Thomas E. Geddie Assocs., Athens, 1955-96, ret. 1996; active as pvt. investor. Served with U.S. Army, 1952-54. Republican. Presbyterian. Mem. Masons (32 deg.). Home: 901 Clifford St Athens TX 75751-2959 Office: 314 N Faulk St Athens TX 75751-2030

GEDDIE, TOM, business communications consultant; b. Terrell, Tex., Mar. 30, 1946; s. T.D. and Lucille (Matthews) G. Student, U. Tex., Arlington, 1965-73. Editor UPI, Dallas, 1967-69, 71-74; asst. city editor Dallas Times Herald, 1975-79; editor ORYX (formerly Sun Gas Co.), Dallas, 1979, 81; assoc. editor Dallas Downtown News, 1981-84, Soc. Petroleum Engrs., Richardson, Tex., 1984, Parkland Meml. Hosp., Dallas, 1985-89; cons. internal comm. Ctrl. and S. W. Corp., Dallas, 1990-93; prin. Tom Geddie Comm., Dallas, 1993—. Contbr. articles to profl. jours. With U.S. Army, 1970-71. Recipient numerous awards in comm., mktg., news and editorial writing, 1980—. Mem. Internat. Assn. Bus. Communicators (exec. bd. 1997—, pres. Dallas chpt. 1994-95). Avocations: Texan music, N.Mex. pottery, movies, books, poetry. Home and Office: 8404 Forest Ln Apt 1401 Dallas TX 75243-4030

GEDDY, VERNON MEREDITH, JR., lawyer; b. Norfolk, Va., Apr. 12, 1926; s. Vernon Meredith and Carrie Cole (Lane) G.; m. Marie Lewis Sibley, Dec. 22, 1949; children: Anne Lewis Geddy Cross, Vernon M. Geddy III. A.B. cum laude, Princeton U., 1949; LL.B., U. Va., 1952. Bar: Va. Ptnr. Geddy & Harris (and predecessor firms), Williamsburg, Va., 1952-80; ptnr. McGuire, Woods, Battle & Boothe (and predecessor firms), Williamsburg, Va., 1980-91; Geddy, Harris & Geddy, 1991—; former dir. United Va. Bankshares, Nat. Ctr. for State Cts. Mem. Williamsburg City Coun., Va., 1968-80; trustee Colonial Williamsburg Found., 1981-95, Va. Hist. Soc., Richmond, 1981-88, 94—, Va. Mus. Fine Arts, 1982-91; bd. dirs. Williamsburg Cmty. Hosp., 1969-85, WHRO, Pub. Telecoms. for Hampton Roads, Jamestown-Yorktown Found. Sgt. USAAF, 1944-46, PTO. Named to Raven Soc. Fellow Am. Bar Found. (award 1976); mem. ABA, Va. Bar Assn. (pres. 1972-73), Va. State Bar, Williamsburg Bar Assn. (pres. 1975-93), Omicron Delta Kappa, Commonwealth Club. Episcopalian. Home: PO Box 379 Williamsburg VA 23187-0379 Office: Geddy Harris & Geddy PO Box 379 516A S Henry St Williamsburg VA 23185-4151

GEDEBOU, MESSELE, microbiologist, educator; b. Addis Ababa, Ethiopia, Feb. 12, 1941; arrived in Saudi Arabia, 1996; s. Gedebou Woldeyes and Elfyilaku Semunegus; m. Fantaye Alemayehu, Nov. 27, 1967; children: Tewodros M., Mikyas M. BSc in Biology and Chemistry, U. Coll. Addis Ababa, 1961; MA in Microbiology, UCLA, 1965; PhD in Epidemiologic Sci., U. Mich., 1972. Lectr. faculty of medicine Addis Ababa U., 1965-68, from asst. prof. to assoc. prof. to prof., 1972-88; prof. Sch. Medicine U. Zimbabwe, Harare, 1988-89; rschr. Cedars-Sinai Med. Ctr., L.A., 1989-96; prof. Coll. Medicine King Saud U., Abha, Saudi Arabia, 1996—; chmn. dept. med. microbiology faculty of medicine Addis Ababa U., 1974-77, 85-88, dean faculty of medicine, 1977-80; head of bacteriology lab. Addis Ababa Sewerage Authority, 1978-88. Mem. editl. bd. Ethiopian Med. Jour., 1975-86, assoc. editor, 1980-86; contbr. articles to profl. jours. Recipient Gold Mercury Internat. Ad Personam award, 1984; WHO fellow U. Mich., 1968-72, U. Nairobi, Kenya, 1974; WHO exch. tchr. in health scis. U. Ibadan, Nigeria, 1979. Mem. Am. Soc. Microbiology. Avocations: walking, jogging, table tennis, music, movies. Tel-fax: (966) 7-2293492. E-mail: messele@ksu.edu.sa. Office: King Saud U Abha br, Coll Medicine PO Box 641, Abha Saudi Arabia

GEDEON, LUCINDA HEYEL, museum director; b. Port Chester, N.Y., Oct. 13, 1947; d. Philip H. and Isabel (Oldham) H.; m. Francis A. Sprout, Feb. 8, 1987. BA, Calif. State U., Long Beach, 1978; MA, UCLA, 1981, PhD, 1990. Asst. curator Grunwald Ctr. UCLA, 1978-81, asst. dir. Grunwald Ctr., 1981-83, acting dir. Grunwald Ctr., 1983-85; chief curator Ariz. State U. Art Museum, Tempe, 1985-91; dir. Neuberger Mus. SUNY, Purchase, 1991—. Author: (exhbn. catalogues) Tamarind: Los Angeles to Albuquerque, 1985, Fiber Concepts, 1989 (book) The Art of Leonard Lehrer, 1986; gen. editor: Melvin Edwards Sculpture: A Thirty Year Retrospective, 1993, Shared Beginnings Separate Passages: A Retrospective of the Work of Carol Anthony and Elaine Anthony, 1996, June Wayne; A Retrospective, 1997, Elizabeth Catlett Sculpture: A Fifty-Year Retrospective; contbr. articles to profl. jours. Chairperson Tempe Mcpl. Arts Commn., 1989-90; bd. dirs. Balboa Art Conservation Ctr., San Diego, 1986-91, Arttable, N.Y., 1995—, Westchester Arts Coun., 1998—. Edward A. Dickson History of Art fellow UCLA, 1984, Afro-Am. Studies fellow, 1984. Mem. Am. Assn. Mus., Assn. Art Mus. Dirs. Office: Neuberger Mus Art SUNY at Purchase 735 Anderson Hill Rd Purchase NY 10577-1445

GEDER, LASZLO, neurologist, educator; b. Debrecen, Hungary, Aug. 11, 1932; came to U.S., 1974, naturalized, 1982; s. Joseph and Irene (Kardoss) G.; M.D., U. Debrecen, 1956, Ph.D., 1969; m. Julianna Toth, Sept. 22, 1956; children—Judith, Martha, Laszlo. Assoc. prof. dept. microbiology Med. Sch., U. Debrecen, Hungary, 1956-72; research assoc. Children's Hosp., Cin., 1964-65; Welcome research fellow dept. virology Med. Sch., U. Birmingham, Eng., 1970-71; acting head dept. microbiology, Ahmadu Bello U., Zaria, Nigeria, 1972-74; assoc. prof. dept. microbiology Coll. of Medicine, Pa. State U., Hershey, 1974-80; physician in neurology, dept. medicine Milton S. Hershey Med. Center, 1980-85, assoc. prof. neurology dept. medicine, 1985—; dir. adult rehab. U. Hosp. Rehab. Ctr., 1988—; mem. Nat. Prostatic Cancer Project. Mem. Am. Soc. Microbiology, Am. Acad. Neurology, AAAS, N.Y. Acad. Scis., Sigma Xi. Presbyterian. Contbr. numerous articles on viral oncology and neurorehab. to profl. jours. Home: 3360 Colebrook Rd Elizabethtown PA 17022-9075 Office: Pa State U Milton S Hershey Med Ctr Div Neurology Hershey PA 17033

GEE, CHUCK YIM, dean; b. San Francisco, Aug. 28, 1933; s. Don Yow Elsie (Lee) G. AA, City Coll. of San Francisco, 1953; BSBA, U. Denver, 1957; MA, Mich. State U., 1958; PhD (hon.), China Acad. Chin. Cultural U., 1972; D of Pub. Svc. (hon.), U. Denver, 1991. Assoc. dir. Sch. of Hotel and Restaurant Adminstn. U. Denver, 1958-68; cons. East West Ctr., Honolulu, 1968-74; assoc. dean and prof. Sch. of Travel Industry Mgmt. U. Hawaii, 1968-75, dean and prof. Sch. Travel Industry Mgmt., 1976—, dean Travel Industry Mgmt. Sch., 1998—; interim dean Coll. Bus. Adminstrn., U. Hawaii, 1998—; vis. prof. Sch Bus. and Commerce, Oreg. State U., 1975; hon. prof. Nankai U., Tianjin, China, 1987—, Shanghai Inst. Tourism, 1994—, Dept. Tourism Huaqiao U., Xiamen, China, 1995—; cons. Internat. Sci. and Tech. Inst., Washington, 1986—; trustee Pacific Asia Travel Assn. Found., San Francisco; chmn. Govs. Tourism Tng. Coun., Honolulu, 1989-92, chmn., 1992-96, chmn. industry coun. PATA, 1994-96, PATA Human Resource Devel. Coun., 1996—; mem. State Workforce Devel. Coun., 1997—; mem. Pacific Asia Travel Assn. Human Resource Devel. Coun, 1996—; acad. Inst. Cert. Travel Agts., Wellesley, Mass., 1989—; mem. Coun. on Hotel, Restaurant and Edn., Honolulu Commn. on Fgn. Rels., Pacific Asian Affairs Coun.; sr. acad. adv. China Tourism Assn. Cons., Inc., 1993—; adv. World Tourism Orgn. Internat. Tourism Edn. and Tng. Ctr., 1991—; external examiner sch. accountancy and bus. Nanyang Tech. U., Singapore, 1996-98; mem. bd. advisors Cyberspace Entrepreneurs, Hawaii Dept. Edn., 1997—. Author: Resort Development and Management, 1988, 2d edit.; co-author: The Travel Industry, 1988, 3d edit., 1997, Professional Travel Agency Management, 1990, International Hotels: Development and Management, 1994; editor: International Tourism: A Global Perspective, 1997; mem. adv. bd. Asian Hotelier mag., 1997—. bd. dirs. Hawaii Visitors Bur., 1993-95, Kaukini Med. Ctr., Honolulu, 1986-95, KMC, 1996—, Travel and Tourism Adv. Bd., U.S. Dept. Commerce, Washington, 1982-90, Pacific Rim Found., Honolulu, 1987—; vice-chmn. Tourism Policy Adv. Coun., Dept. Bus. and Econ. Devel., Honolulu, 1978-92; chmn. Kaukini Geriatric Care, Inc., bd. dirs., 1992-95; trustee Pata Found., 1984-95, Kuakini Health System, 1988—; consulting com. Beijing Inst. Tourism, 1992—; v.p. Hawaii Vision 2020, 1992-93; mem. Mayor's Task Force on Waikiki Master Plan, 1992-93; mem. workforce devel. coun. Hawaii Dept. of Labor and Indsl. Rels., 1996—; bd. dirs. Cyberspace Enterprises, Hawaii Dept. Edn., 1997—. With U.S. Army, 1953-55. Recipient NOAH award Acad. Tourism Orgns., 1987, Gov.'s Proclamation honors State of Hawaii, 1998; named State Mgr. of Yr., State of Hawaii, 1995. Fellow Internat. Acad. Hospitality Rsch.; mem. Pacific Asia Travel Assn. (bd. dirs. 1993-96, 99—, chmn. industry coun. 1994-96, Grand award for individual edn. 1991, Life award 1990, Presdl. award 1986), Travel Industry Am. (Travel Industry Hall of Leaders award 1988), China Tourism Assn. (award of excellence in tourism edn. 1992, Gov.'s Proclamation award 1998), C. of C. of Hawaii, Soc. for Advancement of Food Svc. Rsch., Chaine des Rotisseurs. Office: U Hawaii Sch Travel Industry Mgmt 2560 Campus Rd Honolulu HI 96822-2217

GEE, ELWOOD GORDON, university administrator; b. Vernal, Utah, Feb. 2, 1944; s. Elwood A. and Vera (Showalter) G.; m. Elizabeth Dutson, Aug. 26, 1968 (dec. Dec. 1991); 1 dau., Rebekah. B.A., U. Utah, 1968; J.D., Columbia U., 1971, Ed.D., 1972. Asst. dean U. Utah, Salt Lake City, 1973-74; jud. fellow U.S. Supreme Ct., Washington, 1974-75; assoc. dean Brigham Young U., Provo, Utah, 1975-79; dean W.Va. U., Morgantown, 1979-81, pres., 1981-85; pres. U. Colo., 1985-90, Ohio State U., Columbus, 1990-97, Brown U., Providence, R.I., 1998—. Author: Education Law and Public Schools, 1978, Law and Public Education, 1980, Violence, Values and Justice in American Education, 1982, Fair Employment Practice, 1982. W.K. Kellogg fellow, 1971-72; Mellon fellow, 1977-78. Mem. ABA, Adminstrv. Conf. U.S., Phi Delta Kappa, Phi Kappa Phi. Mem. LDS Ch. Home: 1 Prospect St # 1860 Providence RI 02912-9100 Office: Brown U PO Box 1860 Providence RI 02912-1860*

GEE, GAVIN M., state government official. Dir. dept. finance State of Idaho, Boise. Office: 700 W State St Fl 2 Boise ID 83702-5822*

GEE, GREGORY WILLIAMS, lawyer; b. Toronto, Ont., Can., Dec. 31, 1948; s. Arthur Melbourn and Margaret Zillah (Williams) G.; m. Valerie Jean Fizzell, Sept. 23, 1977; children: Carolyn Elaine, Lisa Jean, Brian Gregory. B.A., U. Toronto, 1970; LL.B., Osgoode Hall Law Sch., Toronto, 1973. Bar: Ont. 1975. Of counsel Blake, Cassels & Graydon, Toronto, 1975-78; gen. counsel, dir. corp. affairs, sec. Am. Motors (Can.), Inc., Brampton, Ont., 1978-88; v.p., gen. counsel, sec. Sun Life Assurance Co. of Can., Toronto, Ont., 1988-94, sr. v.p., gen. counsel, sec., 1994-98, exec. v.p., 1998-99, vice-chmn., 1999—; instr. bus. law U. Toronto, 1981-87; bd. dirs. various Sun Life cos. Mem. ABA, Can. Corp. Counsel Assn. (bd. dirs. 1987-95, pres. 1993-95), Am. Corp. Counsel Assn., Internat. Bar Assn., Assn Life Ins. Counsel, Can. Life Health Assn. (chmn. legal sect. 1993-94), Can. Bar Assn. (chmn. Ont. corp. counsel sect. 1983-85). Avocations: photography, music. Home: 2548 Mississauga Rd, Mississauga, ON Canada L5H 2L5 Office: Sun Life Assurance Co Can, 150 King St W Ste 600, Toronto, ON Canada M5H 1J9

GEE, IRENE, food products executive, school administrator; b. N.Y.C., Aug. 17, 1950; d. Jimmy Set and Lin Fung (Ng) G.; m. Oct. 17, 1981. BA, Hunter Coll., 1971; MS in Family and Consumer Studies, Lehman Coll., 1974, MS in Guidance and Counseling, 1978; MS in Adminstrn. and Supervision, Coll. New Rochelle. Cert. secondary prin. Tchr. Olinville Jr. H.S., Bronx, N.Y., 1971-75, Lehman Coll., Bronx, 1975-77, Harry Eiseman Jr. H.S., Bklyn., 1978-80; asst. prin. adminstrn. A. Philip Randolph Campus H.S., 1994—; food stylist, recipe developer Ladies Home Jour., 1977-78; food stylist, recipe developer Woman's Day Mag., 1979—, home economist, 1980—; owner, operator Irene's Catering, 1984—; food coordinator Evander Childs High Sch.; food cons. Corn Products Corp., 1978—; food stylist Nabisco, 1978, also Perdue Co.; reciper writer, judge natural food contets Scholastic Mag.; judge nat. contests Choices mag.; developer recipe booklets various cos. including Progresso and Fla. Mushrooms; cons. food cos. and publs.; comml. model Mauna Loa Macadamia Nuts, Lewis & Neale; recipe developer Lipton Co. Food exhibitor Avant Grade Foods; bd. dirs. Found. for Excellent Schs.; bd. dirs. Consortium Ednl. Excellence through Partnerships; presenter nat. confs. var. issues. Contbr. articles to Forecast mag., Choices mag., and Woman's World mag. Mem. ACA, Nat. Assn. Secondary Suprs. and Prins., Nat. Assn. Secondary Sch. Prins. (Asst. Prin. of Yr. 1996), Am. Home Econs. Assn., Home Economists in Bus., N.Y.C. Adminstrv. Women in Edn., Consortium Ednl. Excellence Through Partnerships (bd. dirs.), H.S. Asst. Prins. Assn. (mem. exec. bd.), Omicron Nu.

GEE, ROBERT LEROY, agriculturist, dairy farmer; b. Oakport Twp., Moorhead, Minn., May 25, 1926; s. Milton William and Hertha Elizabeth (Paschke) G.; m. Mae Valentine Erickson, June 18, 1953. B.S. in Agronomy, N.D. State U., 1951, postgrad., 1955; postgrad., Colo. A&M U., 1954. Farm labor controller Minn. Extension Service, Clay County, 1944-45, county 4-H agt., 1951-57; rural mail carrier U.S. Postal Service, Moorhead, Minn., 1946-47; breeder registered shorthorn cattle and registered southdown sheep Moorhead, Minn., 1950-63; owner, operator Gee Dairy Farm (Oak Grove Farm), Moorhead, Minn., 1957—; asst. prof. status U. Minn., 1951-57; bd. dirs. Red River Valley Fair, West Fargo, N.D., 1960-86, Minn. Dairy Promotion Bd., St. Paul, 1968-69; bd. dirs. Red River Valley Devel. Assn., Crookston, Minn., 1973—, v.p., 1992—; bd. dirs. Red River Milk Producers Pool, Minn., N.D., 1963-78, treas., 1968-78; bd. dirs. Cass Clay Creamery Inc., Fargo, N.D., 1969-96, chmn. bd., 1982-85, 92-95, v.p., 1990-91; bd. dirs. U.S. Meat Animal Rsch. Ctr., Clay Ctr., Nebr., 1970; mem. Nat. Dairy Promotion Bd., Washington, 1984-88. Treas. Oakport Twp., 1974-82, supr., 1986—, v.p., 1987—; mem. Clay County Planning and Zoning Commn., 1991, vice chmn., 1992-96, chmn., 1996—; mem. Clay County Bd. Adjustment, 1995, chmn., 1996—. With USN, 1945-46. Recipient Grand Champion Farm Flock award Man. Expn., 1960, Clay County's Outstanding Agriculturist award, 1996; named Clay County King Agassiz, Red River Valley Winter Shows, 1966, Grand Champion forage exhibit Red River Valley Winter Shows, 1979, 82; co-recipient Clay County Dairy Farm Family of Yr. award Red River Valley Dairymen's Assn., 1979. Mem. Minn. Milk Producers Assn. (bd. dirs. 1977-88, 93-97, sec. 1972-78, treas. 1977-87), Minn. Assn. Coops. (bd. dirs. 1984-96), State Coop. Assn. (dairy council 1975-96), Am. Farm Bur. Fedn., Nat. Farmers Union, Kragnes Farmers Elevator Assn., Red River Valley Livestock Assn., Am. Shorthorn Breeders Assn., Am. Southdown Breeders Assn., Holstein-Friesian Assn. Am. Republican. Mem. United Ch. of Christ. Club: Agassiz (v.p. 1979-81, pres. 1981-82) (Moorhead). Avocations: hunting; fishing; skiing. Home and Office: RR 1 Box 118 Moorhead MN 56560-9729

GEE, ROBERT W., energy administrator; m. Pauline Wong. BA in Govt. with honors, U. Tex., JD. Gen. atty. Tenneco Oil Co.; of counsel Akin, Gump, Strauss, Hauer & Feld; mem. Pub. Utility Commn. Tex., 1991-97, chmn., 1991-95; asst. sec. policy and internat. affairs Dept. of Energy, Washington, 1997—; atty. advisor Interstate Commerce Commn.; supervisory trial atty. Fed. Energy Regulatory Commn.; mem. Harvard Electricity Policy Group, Kennedy Sch. Govt.; mem. adv. coun. Ctr. for Pub. Utilities of N.Mex. State U.; bd. advisors Tex. Ctr. for Pub. Policy Dispute Resolution, U. Tex. Sch. Law; mem. Dallas regional panel Pres.'s Commn. on White House Fellowships. Trustee St. Edward's U., Austin. Mem. Am. Leadership Forum (sr.), Nat. Assn. Regulatory Utility Commrs. (com. on electricity, ad hoc com. elec. industry restructuring), Tex. Bar Found. Office: Dept of Energy Policy and Internat Affairs 1000 Independence Ave SW Washington DC 20585-0002

GEEKER, NICHOLAS PETER, lawyer, judge; b. Pensacola, Fla., Dec. 15, 1944. B.A. in English, La. Poly. Inst., 1966; J.D., Fla. State U., 1969. Bar: Fla. 1969, U.S. Dist. Ct. 1970, US. Supreme Ct., 1980. Assoc. firm Merritt & Jackson, Pensacola, 1969; law clk. U.S. Dist. Judge D.L. Middlebrooks, Tallahassee, 1970-73; asst. state atty. Fla. 1st Jud. Circuit, 1973; asst. U.S. atty. No. Dist. Fla., 1973-76, U.S. atty., 1976-82; sole practice Pensacola, Fla., 1982-85; circuit judge Fla. 1st Jud. Circuit, 1985—; mem. Fed.-State Joint Com. on Law Enforcement. Mem. Fla. Bar Assn., Fla. Trial Lawyers Assn. (editor Newsletter 1975), Phi Delta Phi. Office: 190 Government St Pensacola FL 32501-5773

GEENTIENS, GASTON PETRUS, JR., former construction management consultant company executive; b. Garfield, N.J., Apr. 6, 1935; s. Gaston Petrus and Margaret (Piros).G.; m. Barbara Ann Chamberlin, Oct. 14, 1960; children: Mercedes Frith, Faith Piros. BSCE, The Citadel, 1956. Registered profl. engr., 15 states. Plant engr. Western Elec. Co., Inc., Kearny, N.J., 1956-58, owner's rep., N.Y.C., 1960-64; v.p. Gentyne Motors, Inc., Passaic, N.J., 1958-60; project engr. Ethyl Corp., Baton Rouge, La., 1964-65; mgr. Timothy McCarthy Constrn. Co., Atlanta, 1965; asst. to v.p. A.R. Abrams, Inc. and Columbia Engring., Inc., Atlanta, 1965-66; supr. engring. and constrn. Litton Industries, N.Y.C., 1966-71; pres. G.P. Geentiens Jr., Inc., Charleston, S.C., 1971-82; gen. ptnr. Engineered Enterprises Co., Charleston, 1973-76; dir. Cayman Broadcasting Assos., Cayman Islands, B.W.I., 1977-82. Mem. Ramapo (N.Y.) Republican Com., 1961-64. Served to 1st lt. C.E., AUS, 1956-58. Mem. ASCE, Tau Beta Pi. Home: 1219 Pembrooke Dr Charleston SC 29407-7748

GEER, DENNIS F., insurance executive; b. Clarinda, Iowa; m. Bonnie Geer. BBA, U. Iowa, 1966. Exec. positions Depts. Commerce, Housing and Urban Devel., Labor and Treas.; v.p. divsn. adminstrn. and corp. rels. Resolution Trust Corp.; dep. to chmn. and COO Fed. Deposit Ins. Corp., Washington, 1994—. With U.S. Army, 1967-69. Office: Fed Deposit Ins Corp Office of CFO 550 17th St NW Washington DC 20429

GEER, JAMES HAMILTON, JR., counselor, consultant; b. Spartanburg, S.C., Nov. 2, 1948; s. James Hamilton and Josephine Carraway (Sessions) G. BA with honors, U. N.C., 1971; MBA, U. Ga., 1977; JD, U. S.C., 1980. Bar: Fla. 1981, S.C. 1981, U.S. Dist. Ct. S.C. 1981, U.S. Ct. Appeals (4th, 5th, 11th and fed. cirs.) 1982, U.S. Tax Ct. 1982, U.S. Ct. Claims 1983, U.S. Ct. Internat. Trade 1983, U.S. Supreme Ct. 1984. Retail mgr. WT Grants, N.Y.C., 1972-73; ops. mgr. Bank Am., Charlotte, N.C., 1974-76; software developer Legal Software Systems, Athens, Ga., 1976-96; pvt. practice Geer Free Legal Clinic, Columbia, S.C., 1981-87, Dunedin, Fla., 1987-92, Landrum, S.C., 1992-98; fund mgr. Geer Global Fund, Tryon, N.C., 1992—. Author: The Geer Genealogy, 1987, World Family Tree, 1992, Legal Net/Law Web, 1996. Exec. committeeman Rep. Party, Columbia, 1978-87; mem. Friendship Coun., Tryon, N.C., 1992—, Harvest Moon Folk Soc., Greenville, S.C., 1992—, Tryon Fine Arts Ctr., Tryon, 1992—. Honors Rsch. grant NSF, 1970; fellowship U. Ga., 1976. Mem. Soc. of the Cin., Magna Charta Sureties, Mayflower Soc., Charlemagne Soc., Hoods Tex. Brigade Assn. Soc. of Friends. Avocations: genealogy, theatre, folk music and dance, internet. Fax: (561) 258-0791. E-mail: jhgeerjr@hotmail.com, jhgeerjr@justicemail.com.

GEER, JOHN FARR, retired religious organization administrator; b. N.Y.C., Oct. 15, 1930; s. William Montague and Edith Jaffray (Farr) G.; m. Carolyn Boston, June 25, 1954; children: Jennifer, Evelyn, John Farr. BA, Princeton U., 1952; LLB, Columbia U., 1957. Bar: N.Y. State 1957. Asso. firm Sullivan & Cromwell, N.Y.C., 1957-65, Whitman & Ransom (and predecessor firms), N.Y.C., 1965-67; ptnr. Whitman & Ransom (and predecessor firms), 1967-73; v.p., gen. counsel, sec. Am. Standard Inc., N.Y.C., 1973-89, ret., 1989; sr. v.p., gen. counsel, sec. The Church Pension Fund, N.Y.C., 1991-97. Trustee Protestant Episcopal Soc. for Promoting Religion and Learning in State N.Y., 1960-82, treas., 1968-82; trustee Gen. Theol. Sem., 1980-95, vice chmn. bd. trustees, 1986-95; mem. Corp. for Relief Widows and Children of Protestant Episcopal Clergymen in State of N.Y., 1960—, treas., 1967-98. 1st lt. F.A. AUS, 1952-54, Korea. Mem. Phi Delta Phi. Episcopalian. Club: Princeton (N.Y.C.). Home: 151 Central Park W New York NY 10023-1514

GEER, RONALD LAMAR, mechanical engineering consultant, retired oil company executive; b. West Palm Beach, Fla., Sept. 2, 1926; s. Marion Wood and Bertha (Lightfoot) G.; m. Geneva Yvonne Chappell, Dec. 24, 1951; children—Ronald Lamar, Mark Randall. B.M.E., Ga. Inst. Tech., 1951. With Shell Oil Co., 1951—; sr. staff mech. engr., head office Shell Oil Co., Houston, 1969-71; cons. mech. engr. Shell Oil Co., 1971-86; mem. various govt., univ. adv. coms. Contbr. articles on petroleum drilling and prodn. to profl. jours. Recipient Robert Earll McConnell award Am. Inst. Mech. Engrs., 1995. Mem. Nat. Acad. Engring., NRC (marine bd.), Nat. Security Indsl. Assn. (petroleum panel, research and engring. adv. com.), ASME (hon.), Marine Tech. Soc., Am. Petroleum Inst., Model-A Ford Club Am., Classic T-Bird Club Internat., Thistle Class Assn., Pi Tau Sigma. Republican. Patentee petroleum drilling and prodn. equipment; mem. Shell Oil Co. team recognized in Offshore Tech. Conf. Disting. Achievement award to co., 1971, for individuals, 1984. Home: 14723 Oak Bend Dr Houston TX 77079-6418 also: 135 Sky Valley Way Sky Valley GA 30537

GEERDES, JAMES D(IVINE), chemical company executive; b. Davenport, N.D., Apr. 13, 1924; s. William A. and Martha (Buchholz) G.; 1 child from first marriage, Andrew B.; 1 child from second marriage, Margaret; m. Monika Rose Smith-Gutowski, May 3, 1988. B.S., N.D. State U., 1949, M.S., 1950; Ph.D., U. Minn., 1953. Instr. biochemistry U. Minn., 1950-53; research chemist E.I. duPont de Nemours & Co., Inc., Richmond, Va. and Seaford, Del., 1954-58; group supr. E.I. duPont de Nemours & Co., Inc., 1958-60, tech. supr., 1960-62, research asso., 1962-64; dir. research Entoleter, Inc., Hamden, Conn., 1964-65; exec. v.p. Entoleter, Inc., 1965-66, pres., 1966-67; asst. to v.p. fibers div. Allied Chem. Corp., N.Y.C., 1967; asst. to pres. Allied Chem. Corp., 1967-68, exec. v.p., 1968, pres., 1968-71; pres., dir. Alrac Corp., Stamford, Conn., 1971-73, Geerdes Industries, Richmond, Va., 1971—; pres. Geerdes Internat., Inc., Richmond, Va., 1981—; pres. Geerdes Internat. Assocs., Inc., Manasses, Va., 1993—. Contbg. editor jour. Fiber Producer, Fiber World, Internat. Fiber Jour.; contbr. articles to profl. jours. advisor bd. dirs. Richmond Children's Museum. Served to 1st lt. C.E. AUS, 1943-46. Mem. Textile Inst., Del. Acad. Sci., Am. Chem. Soc., AAAS, Textile Research Inst., Fiber Soc., Sigma Xi, Phi Kappa Phi, Gamma Sigma Delta, Gamma Alpha. Patentee in field. Home: 10109 Windstream Dr Columbia MD 21044-2530 Office: Geerdes Internat 9326 Main St Manassas VA 20110-5115 Office: 12719 Lake Wilderness Ln Spotsylvania VA 22553-8122

GEERTZ, CLIFFORD JAMES, anthropology educator; b. San Francisco, Aug. 23, 1926; s. Clifford James and Lois (Brieger) G.; m. Hildred Storey, Oct. 30, 1948 (div. 1981); children: Erika, Benjamin; m. Karen Blu, 1987. A.B., Antioch Coll., 1950; Ph.D., Harvard U., 1956, LL.D. (hon.), 1974; L.H.D. (hon.), No. Mich. U., 1975, U. Chgo., 1979, Bates Coll., 1980, Knox Coll., 1982, Brandeis U., 1984, Swarthmore Coll., 1984, New Sch. for Social Research, Yale U., 1987, Williams Coll., 1991, Princeton U., 1995, Cambridge (Eng.) U., 1997; stud., Georgetown Univ., 1998. From asst. prof. to prof. dept. anthropology U. Chgo., 1960-70; prof. dept. social sci. Inst. for Advanced Study, Princeton, N.J., 1970—; Harold F. Linder prof. social sci. Inst. for Advanced Study, 1982—; Eastman prof. Oxford U., 1978-79. Author: The Religion of Java, 1960, Peddlers and Princes, 1963, The Social History of an Indonesian Town, 1965, Islam Observed, 1968, The Interpretation of Cultures, 1973, (with H. Geertz) Kinship in Bali, 1975, (with L. Rosen and H. Geertz) Meaning and Order in Moroccan Society, 1979, Negara: The Theatre State in Nineteenth-Century Bali, 1980, Local Knowledge, 1983, Works and Lives, 1988, After the Fact, 1995, Welt in Stücken, 1996. Served with USNR, 1943-45. Nat. Acad. Scis. fellow, 1973—; recipient Asian Cultural prize, 1992. Fellow AAAS, Am. Philos. Soc., Am. Acad. Arts and Scis., Brit. Acad. (corr.); mem. Am. Anthrop. Assn., Assn. for Asian Studies, Middle East Studies Assn. Office: Inst for Advanced Study Princeton NJ 08540

GEERTZ, HILDRED STOREY, anthropology educator; b. N.Y.C., Feb. 12, 1927; d. Walter Rendell and Helen (Anderson) Storey; m. Clifford Geertz, 1948 (div. 1979); children: Erika, Benjamin. BA, Antioch Coll., Yellow Springs, Ohio, 1948; PhD, Radcliffe Coll., 1956. Lectr. U. Chgo., 1963-68; from assoc. prof. to prof. anthropology Princeton (N.J.) U., 1970-98; retired, 1998; chmn. dept. anthropology Princeton U., 1972-77, 86, 88-89. Author: The Javanese Family, 1961, Kinship in Bali, 1974, Images of Power: Balinese Paintings Made for Gregory Bateson and Margaret Mead, 1994, (with Lawrence Rosen) Meaning and Order in Moroccan Society, 1979; editor: State and Society in Bali, 1992. Office: Princeton Univ Dept Anthropology Princeton NJ 08544

GEESEMAN, ROBERT GEORGE, lawyer; b. Shreveport, La., Oct. 23, 1944; s. George Robert and Cora (Hamilton) Glasgow; m. Rosemary Monahan, Aug. 19, 1967; 1 child, Regan Glasgow. B.A., Yale U., 1966; J.D., U. Mich., 1969. Bar: Pa. 1969, U.S. Dist. Ct. (we. dist.) Pa. 1969, U.S. Supreme Ct., 1973, U.S. Tax Ct. 1979. Assoc. Blaxter, O'Neill, Houston & Nash, Pitts., 1969-75; ptnr. Lynch, Lynch, Carr & Kabala, Pitts., 1975-81, Lynch, Kabala & Geeseman, Pitts., 1981, Kabala & Geeseman, Pitts., 1981—; lectr. on tax law and employee benefits; legal adv. bd. Small Bus. Council Am. Mem. ABA (mem. profl. service corps. com. sect. on taxation, chmn. profl. corp. com. sect. econs.; bd. editors Withdrawal Retirement and Disputes, What You and Your Firm Should Know), Pa. Bar Assn., Allegheny County Bar Assn., Pitts. Inst. Legal Medicine, Phi Delta Phi. ClubsL Rosslyn Farms Country, Rivers, Chartiers Country; Mory's (New Haven, Conn.); John's Island Country (Vero Beach, FLa.). Office: Kabala & Geeseman 200 1st Ave Pittsburgh PA 15222-1575

GEFFE, KENT LYNDON, lawyer, educator; b. Charles City, Iowa, Jan. 29, 1957; s. Herbert Frederick and Clarice Ona (Wood) G.; m. Susan Kay Leise, Aug. 12, 1978 (div. July 1986) 1 child, Jeremiah Kevin; m. Barbara Ann Cox, July 3, 1987; 1 child, Anastasia Catherine. BA, Cornell Coll., Mt. Vernon, Iowa, 1975; JD, U. Iowa, 1981. Bar: Iowa 1981, U.S. Dist. Ct. (no. and so. dists.) Iowa 1982. Intern U.S. Congressman, Washington, 1978, Prisoner Assistance Clinic, Iowa City, 1980-81; jud. magistrate State of Iowa, Marshalltown, 1983-87; city atty. City of Melbourne, Iowa, 1982—; ptnr. Welp & Geffe, Marshalltown, 1981—; adj. faculty Marshalltown C.C., 1981—; adv. bd. consumer credit counseling svcs. Northea. Iowa, Inc., 1998—. Bd. dirs. Runaway and Youth Svcs. Ctr., Marshalltown, 1985-86, Mid-Iowa Workshops, Inc., Marshalltown, 1985-91; mem. adv. coun. Iowa Valley Continuing Edn., Marshalltown, 1992; state legal counsel Iowa Jaycees, 1982-85; grad. Iowa Valley Leadership, Marshalltown, 1990; mem. Mid-Iowa coun. Boy Scouts Am., Des Moines, 1990-95. Named one of Outstanding Young Men of Am., 1984, 85. Mem. Iowa State Bar Assn., Iowa Jaycees, Marshalltown Jaycees (pres. 1985-86), Kiwanis, Nebr.-Iowa Kiwanis Found. (life), Phi Beta Kappa. Avocations: sailing, carpentry, reading. Office: Welp & Geffe Law Offices 110 W Southridge Rd PO Box 555 Marshalltown IA 50158-0555

GEFFE, PHILIP REINHOLD, electrical engineer, consultant; b. Napa, Calif., Oct. 22, 1920; s. Eugene Carl and Mary Rebecca (Woliston) G.; m. Barbara Ann Wean; children: Bethann, Philip, Timur. Student, Calif. Inst. Tech., 1947-49. Chief filter engr. Triad Transformer Corp., Venice, Calif., 1952-56; dir. engring. Hycor, Inc., Sylmar, Calif., 1957-60; sr. staff engr. Axel Electronics Inc., Jamaica, N.Y., 1962-65; fellow engr. Westinghouse Electric Corp., Balt., 1965-74; staff engr. Lynch Communication Systems, Inc., Reno, 1974-80, Scientific-Atlanta, Inc., Atlanta, 1980-85, K&L Microwave, Inc., Salisbury, Md., 1985-87; ind. cons., 1988—; sr. engr. PULSE divsn. Technitrol, San Diego, 1997—. Author: Simplified Modern Filter Design, 1963; contbr. articles to profl. jours.; patentee in field. Master U.S. Chess Fedn. New Windsor, N.Y., 1968. Fellow IEEE; mem. AAAS. Address: 9952 Kika Ct Apt 5211 San Diego CA 92129-5012

GEFFEN, BETTY ADA, theatrical personal manager; b. Lachine, Que., Can., May 12, 1911; came to U.S., 1942, naturalized, 1945; d. Joseph and Minnie (Illievitz) Gottheil; student public schs., Montreal, Que.; m. Jacob N. Geffen, Dec. 23, 1944; 1 child, JoAnn Merle. Sec., Saul Cohen/Trustee in Bankruptcy, Montreal, 1926-28, Maxwell Cummings Real Estate, 1928-30, Monroe Abbey, Atty., 1930-31; with Tic-Toc, Stanley Grill and Chez Maurice, Montreal, 1931-41; sec. H.L. Green, N.Y.C., 1941-44; pvt. theatrical personal mgr., casting cons., N.Y.C., 1950—; v.p., sec. Mor-Lite Corp., 1994—; cons. Consab Assocs. Corp., N.Y.C., 1977-95. Trustee Israel Cancer Rsch. Fund., 1977-95; vol. Floating Hosp. Mem. NATAS, Women of the Motion Picture Industry, Motion Picture Pioneers (life), Internat. Platform Assn., The Nat. Mus. Women in the Arts (charter). Democrat. Clubs: Variety Women N.Y. (v.p. 1977-81, pres. 1982-86, chmn. bd. 1986-88), Brandeis U. Home and Office: 17 W 71st St Apt 7A New York NY 10023-4142

GEFFEN, DAVID, recording company executive, producer; b. Bklyn., Feb. 21, 1943; s. Abraham and Batya (Volovskaya) Geffen. U of Texas, Austin, Brooklyn Coll. of CUNY. Agt. with William Morris, N.Y.C., 1964-68; agt. with Ashley Famous, 1968; exec. V.P. and agent Creative Management Associates, 1969; founder (with Laura Nyro) and pres. Tuna Fish publishing co.; pres. Asylum Records, 1970-73, Geffen-Roberts, Inc., 1970-71, Elektra-Asylum Records, 1973-76; founder and pres. Geffen Records, L.A., 1980—; vice-pres. Warner Bros. Pictures, 1975; chmn. Geffen Records, L.A.; head Geffen Film Co.; vice-chmn. Warner Brothers Pictures, 1974; exec. asst. to chmn. Warner Communications, 1977; co-founder Dreamworks SKG, Universal City, 1995—; mem. music faculty Yale U., 1978; apptd. Regent U. Calif., Gov. Calif., 1980-87. Producer films including After Hours, Lost in America, Personal Best, 1982, Risky Business, 1983, Little Shop of Horrors, 1986, Social Security, 1986, Beetlejuice, 1988, Men Don't Leave, 1990, Interview with the Vampire, 1994; co-producer Master Harold...and the Boys, 1982, Cats, 1982, Good, 1982, Dreamgirls, 1983, Madam Butterfly, 1988 (9 Tony award, Best Play); musical Miss Saigon. Bd. dirs. Los Angeles County Art Mus. Avocations: collector modern art. Office: Dreamworks SKG 100 Universal City Plz Bldg 477 Universal City CA 91608-1002*

GEFKE, HENRY JEROME, lawyer; b. Milw., Aug. 4, 1930; s. Jerome Henry and Frances (Daley) G.; m. Caroline Ann Lawrence, June 25, 1955 (div. Jan. 1968); children: Brian Lawrence, David Jerome; m. Mary Clare Nuss, Aug. 28, 1976; children: Lynn Marie, James Scott. B.S., Marquette U., 1952, LL.B., 1954; postgrad., Ohio State U., 1955-56. Bar: Wis. 1954, Tax Ct. U.S 1969; C.P.A., Wis. Accountant-auditor John G. Conley & Co. (C.P.A.s), Milw., 1956-59; with J.I. Case Co., Racine, Wis., 1959-68; corp. sec., asst. gen. counsel J.I. Case Co., 1965-68; assoc. Maier & Mulcahy, S.C., Milw., 1968-69; prin. Mulcahy, Gefke & Wherry, S.C., Milw., 1969-73; individual practice law Milw., 1973—; corp. officer, dir. various bus. corps. Pres., bd. dirs. Big Bros., Greater Racine, 1965-67; trustee Racine County Instns., 1960-63; bd. dirs., sec., legal counsel Racine Transitional Care, Inc., 1973-76; bd. dirs., legal counsel Our Home Found., Milw., 1979-82; bd. dirs. Racine county Mental Health Assn., 1963-67, Alliance for Mentally Ill Milw. County, 1986-88; bd. dirs., sec., legal counsel Glendale Econ. Devel. Corp., 1996—; bd. dirs. Glendale Bus. Coun., 1996-97, treas., bd. dirs. Glendale Assn. of Commerce, Inc., 1997—. Mem. Wis. Bar Assn., Milw. Bar Assn., Wis. Inst. CPA's, Delta Sigma Pi, Delta Theta Phi. Home: 5521 N Lydell Ave Glendale WI 53217-5042 Office: 400 W Silver Spring Dr Milwaukee WI 53217-5091

GEHA, ALEXANDER SALIM, cardiothoracic surgeon, educator; b. Beirut, June 18, 1936; came to U.S., 1963; s. Salim M. and Alice I. (Hayek) G.; m. Diane L. Redalen, Nov. 25, 1967; children—Samia, Rula, Nada. BS in Biology, Am. U. Beirut, 1955, MD, 1959; MS in Surgery and Physiology, U. Minn.-Rochester, 1967; MS (privatum), Yale U., 1978. Asst. prof. U. Vt., Burlington, 1967-69; asst. prof. Washington U., St. Louis, 1969-73, assoc. prof., 1973-75; assoc. prof. Yale U., New Haven, 1975-78, prof., chief cardiothoracic surgery, 1978-86; prof., chief cardiothoracic surgery Case Western Res. U. and U. Hosp. of Cleve., 1986-98; Jay L. Ankeney prof. cardiothoracic surgery Case W. Reserve U., 1994-98; pres. Univ. Cardiothoracic Surgeons, Inc., Cleve., 1986—; prof., chief cardiothoracic surgery U. Ill., Chgo., 1998—; cons. VA Hosp., West Haven, Conn., 1975-86, VA Hosp., Cleve., 1986-98, Westside VA Hosp., Chgo., 1998—, Cleve. Met. Health Med. Ctr., 1986-98, Mt. Sinai Med. Ctr., Cleve., 1990-98, Waterbury Hosp., 1976-86, Sharon Hosp., 1981-86; mem. study sect. Nat. Heart Lung and Blood Inst., 1981-85. Editor: Glenn's Thoracic and Cardio-vascular Surgery, 4th edit. 1983, 5th edit. 1991, 6th edit. 1995; editor Basic Surgery, 1984. Bd. dirs. New Haven Heart Assn., 1981-85. Mem. AMA, Assn. Clin. Cardiac Surgery (chmn. membership com. 1978-80, sec.-treas. 1980-83, pres. 1988), Am. Heart Assn. (bd. dirs. 1981-85. councils on basic sci., cardiovascular surgery), Am. Coll. Chest Physicians (steering com. 1980-84), Am. Assn. Thoracic Surgery, Am. Coll. Cardiology, ACS (chmn. coordinating com. on edn. in thoracic surgery, chmn. 1992-95), Am. Lung Assn., Am. Physiol. Soc., Am. Surg. Assn., Assn. Acad. Surgery, Central Surg. Assn., European Assn. Cardiothoracic Surgery, Internat. Soc. Heart and Lung Transplantation, Internat. Soc. Cardiovascular Surgery, Lebanese Order Physicians, New Eng. Surg. Soc., Pan Am. Med. Assn., Halsted Soc., Soc. Thoracic Surgeons (govt. rels. com., manpower com., program com., edn. and resources com.), Soc. for Vascular Surgery, Soc. Univ. Surgeons, also others. Home: 854 W Fullerton Ave Chicago IL 60614 Office: ILL Chgo Ste 417 CSB (M/C 958) 840 S Wood St Chicago IL 60612-7321

GEHAN, MARK WILLIAM, lawyer; b. St. Paul, Dec. 19, 1946; s. Mark William and Jean Elizabeth (McGee) G.; m. Lucy Lyman Harrison, Aug. 25, 1971; children: Hark Harrison, Alice McGee. BA, U. Notre Dame, 1968; JD, U. Minn., 1971. Asst. county atty. Ramsey County Atty.'s Office, St. Paul, 1972-76; prosecutor, Met. Area Dist. Urban County Attys. Bd., St. Paul, 1976-77; ptnr. Collins Buckley Sauntry & Haugh, St. Paul, 1978—; bd. dirs. Minn. State Bd. Pub. Def., St. Paul, 1982-90. Pres. St. Paul Charter Commn., 1986-94. Mem. Minn. State Bar Assn. (sec. 1995-96, treas. 1996-97), Ramsey County Bar Assn. (pres. 1990-91). Avocations: scuba diving, tennis, guitar. Office: Collins Buckley Sauntry & Haugh First Nat Bank Bldg 332 Minnesota St Ste W1100 Saint Paul MN 55101-1379*

GEHM, DAVID EUGENE, construction and environmental management executive; b. St. Louis, Nov. 15, 1952; s. John Francis and Rosemary Helen (Krupp) G. Cert. civil engring. tech., St. Louis Community Coll. Florissant Valley, 1973. Quality control inspector Fla. Testing and Engr., Ft. Lauderdale, 1973-76; surveyor Wunderlich Co., Union, Mo., 1976-77; quality control inspector The Binkley Co., Warrenton, Mo., 1977-78, Daniel International., Fulton, Mo., 1978-79; project mgr. Booker Assocs., Inc., St. Louis, 1979-86; pres. GEHM Corp., Boonville, Mo., 1986—. Mem. Nat. Inst. Cert. Engring. Techs., Inst. Cert. Engr. Techs., Tau Alpha Pi, Sons of the Am. Legion. Avocations: hunting, fishing. Home: PO Box 265 Boonville MO 65233-0265 Office: 1480 W Ashley Rd Boonville MO 65233-2141

GEHM, DENISE CHARLENE, ballerina, arts administrator; b. Miami, Fla., Dec. 14, 1951; d. Charles William and Verna Mae (Wiley) Gehm; m. Gary Edward MacDougal, June 15, 1992. BA cum laude, NYU, 1994; MA, Columbia U., 1998; studied ballet with, George Milenoff, Thomas Armour, 1998. Soloist ballerina Harkness Ballet Co., N.Y.C., 1970-71, Nat. Ballet Washington, 1971-73; prin. ballerina Chgo. Ballet, 1974, Ballet de Caracas, Venezuela, 1975; featured ballerina Joffrey Ballet, N.Y.C., 1976-91. Appeared in Broadway plays West Side Story, 1979, Phantom of the Opera, 1988; with Rudolf Nureyev in Nijinsky's L'Apres-Midi d'Un Faune, 1979; prin. dancer Homage to Diaghilev, Broadway and State Theatre N.Y., 1979; featured roles include Joffrey's Nutcracker, Arpino's Suite St.-Saens, Cranko's Taming of the Shrew, Ashton's Midsummer Night's Dream, Robbin's N.Y. Export Opus Jazz; performed in numerous maj. cities, theatres and festivals including Champs Elysees in Paris, Herod Atticus Odeon, Athens, An der Vien, Vienna, and Spoleto (Italy)/U.S.A. festivals; featured in numerous TV commls. and print. Recipient Founders Day award NYU, 1994, Disting. Alumni award NYU Gallatin Sch., 1998; Harkness House for Ballet and Arts scholar, 1969. Episcopalian.

GEHO, WALTER BLAIR, biomedical research executive; b. Wheeling, W.Va., May 18, 1939; s. Blair Roy and Susan (Yonko) G.; m. Marjorie Cooper, Aug. 25, 1962; children: Hans, Alison, Robert, David, Daniel. BS, Bethany Coll., 1960; PhD in Pharmacology, Western Res. U., 1964, MD, 1966. Instr. pharmacology Sch. of Medicine Western Res. U., Cleve., 1966-67; pres., CEO SDG Inc., Cleve., 1993—; staff researcher Procter & Gamble Co., Cin., 1968-74, head pharmacology rsch. sect., 1974-81; v.p., dir. rsch. Tech. Unltd., Inc., Wooster, Ohio, 1981-89, pres., 1989-93; chief sci. officer, dir. AMDG, Inc., Cleve., N.J., 1997—. Contbr. articles to Phamacology of Disphosphates, Clin. Pharmacology of Didronel, Genetics of Myositis Ossificans. Recipient 2 Ohio Innovator awards Edison Fund Ohio, 1987, Innovation award Enterprise Devel. Inst., 1995. Mem. AMA, Am. Chem. Soc. Achievements include patents in pharmaceuticals; contributions to development of osteoscan and didronel, and targeted drug delivery systems, commercialization of liposome inventions into consumer and pharmaceutical products. Office: SDG Inc 1350 Euclid Ave Ste 200 Cleveland OH 44115-1815

GEHRIG, EDWARD HARRY, electrical engineer, consultant; b. Portland, Oreg., Oct. 31, 1925; s. Henry Oscar and Selma Victoria (Charf) G.; m. May 20, 1950; children: Cynth Ann, Nanette Lou, Timothy Alexander. BA in Physics, Reed Coll., 1948; BSEE, Stanford U., 1949; MSEE, Oreg. State U., 1951. Registered profl. engr., Oreg. Physicist AEC, 1950-52; head system planning Bonneville Power Adminstrn., Portland, 1963-72, chief transmission design, 1972-76, chief R & D, 1976-81; ind. cons. Lake Oswego, Oreg., 1982—; participant Electric Power Rsch. Inst. and GE Project UHV; designer, distbr. for Lindal Cedar Homes, Seattle, 1987—. Patentee in field; contbr. articles to profl. jours. Chmn. Lake Grove Zoning Bd., Lake Oswego, Oreg., 1962-64; elder First Presbyn. Ch., Portland; coach basketball, soccer, Lake Grove. Sgt. U.S. Army, 1944-46, ETO. Recipient Meritorious Svc. award Dept. of Interior, 1979. Fellow IEEE. Democrat. Avocations: woodcraft, golf. Home: 6631 SW Ebb Ave Lincoln City OR 97367-1037

GEHRING, DAVID AUSTIN, physician, administrator, cardiologist; b. Bryn Mawr, Pa., Dec. 6, 1930; s. Harry Rittenhouse and Anne Gardiner (Bozarth) G.; m. Joan Helen Lotz, June 7, 1953 (div. Aug. 1982); children: David, Paul, Peter, Sue, Barbara, Eric; m. Victoria Marie Damiano, Sept. 2, 1982; children: Theresa, Judy Lynne, Michael Austin. BA magna cum laude, U. Pitts., 1952, MD, 1956. Diplomate Am. Bd. Internal Medicine; cert. geriatric medicine. Commd. USN, 1956, advanced through grades to lt. comdr.; intern, then resident in internal medicine U.S. Naval Hosp. USN, Phila., 1956-60, mem. staff internal medicine U.S. Naval Hosp., 1960-61; chief internal medicine heart sta. U.S. Naval Hosp. USN, Annapolis, Md., 1961-63; resigned USN, 1963; cardiologist K.G.E. Med. Group, Woodbury, N.J., 1963-82; cardiologist, pres. Hobbs Cardiology, P.A., Hobbs, N.Mex., 1982-86; med. dir. Polk (Pa.) Ctr., 1986-91; physician, chief grade VA Med. Ctr., Coatesville, Pa., 1991-97, assoc. chief of staff for ambulatory care, 1993-96, chief med. svc., 1995-96, chief primary care and chief of staff, 1995-96, chief of staff, 1995-96, cardiologist, 1996-97; assoc. med. dir. for correctional med. svcs. South Jersey, 1997-98; site med. dir. South Woodstate Prison, 1997-98; clin. dir. Del. Hosp. Chronically Ill, 1998—; clin. dir. long term care pub. health divsn. State of Del., 1998-99; clin. dir. Del. Hosp. for Cronically Ill, Symrna, 1998-99; testing cardiologist Anthropometrics United Med. Group, Cherry Hill, N.J., 1974-82; clin. asst. prof. medicine Temple U. Hosp., Phila., 1975-82; adj. asst. prof. medicine Jefferson Meml. Coll., Phila., 1981-82; chief cardiac rehab. unit Lea Regional Hosp., Hobbs, 1982-86; chief med. svcs. 829th Sta. Hosp. USAR, Lubbock, Tex., 1984-86; cons. cardiology Oil City, Pa., 1986-91; staff Franklin (Pa.) Regional Med. Ctr., 1986-90, Oil City Area Health Ctr., 1986-91; teaching staff St. Joseph Hosp., Lancaster, Pa., 1991-97; clin. preceptor U. Pa. Sch. Nursing, 1993-96; cons. Southeastern Vets. Ctr., Spring City, Pa., 1997-98, Providence Med. Ctr., Media, Pa., 1997-98, others; assoc. med. dir. Correctional Med. Svcs. for South Jersey, 1997-98; mem. adult protective svcs. adv. coun. State of Del., 1998-99; chair pharmacy and therapeutics com. Dept. of Health and Social Svcs., State of Del., 1998-99; cons. in field. Author: EKG Workbook, 1972, EKG Workbook I, 1978; contbr. articles to profl. jours. Project dir. 23 Greater Del. Valley Reg. Med. Prog., Pa., 1971-75; mem. ACLS Inst. and affiliated faculty Pa. Heart Assn., 1986-98, bd. dirs. N.W. chpt. 1988-90, Inst. Christianna Hosp., Del., 1998-99; bd. dirs. adv. com., chmn. personnel com. med. health, rehab., drugs and alcohol Venango County, Franklin, Pa., 1986-90, pres., 1988-89; mem. Health Care Adv. Com. to Congressman William F. Clinger, Jr., 23d Dist., Pa., 1989-91; lector St. Joseph Ch., Oil City, 1987-91, eucharistic min.. 1990-92; eucharistic min. St. Joseph Ch., Swedesboro, N.J., 1992-93, Sacred Heart Ch., Mt. Ephraim, N.J., 1994-99, lector, 1998-99. Lt. col. USAR, 1983-90. Recipient Outstanding Svc. award Am. Cancer Soc. N.J., 1967, Benjamin Berkowitz award N.J. Heart Assn., 1975, Nat. Def. Svc. medal, 1975, USAR Components Achievement medal, 1988, Letter of Commendation USAR, 1988, 90, Pres.'s medal of Merit, Rep. Task Force, 1984Letter of Commendation Sec. of Vets. Affairs, 1994; Cert. of Appreciation, Sec. of State N.Mex., 1982, Venango County Commrs., 1987, 88, 89, 90, Polk Ctr. award of Merit, 1991, Spl. Contbn. award and Mgr. of Yr. award VAMC Coatesville, 1996. Fellow ACP (life, Recognition awards 1967-70), Am. Coll. Cardiology, Am. Coll. Chest Physicians, Coll. Physicians of Phila., Am. Coll. Clin. Pharmacology; mem. AMA, Am. Geriatrics Soc., St. Jude Soc., Holy Name Soc., Assn. Miraculous Medal (promoter 1987—), Venango County Med. Soc. (pres. 1989-91), Assn. Mil. Surgeons, Am. Coll. Physician Execs., Am. Legion. Democrat. Roman Catholic. Avocations: stamp collecting, reading, walking, swimming, opera. Home: 10742 Henry Ct Naples FL 34109 Office: 865 W Red Bank Ave Woodbury NJ 08096-4095

GEHRING, DONALD D., education educator; b. Trenton, N.J., Oct. 9, 1937; s. Philip F. and Elsie E. (Jackson) G.; m. Bettie Groover, Aug. 6, 1960; children: Lisa Seger, David. BS, Ga. Inst. Tech., 1960; MEd, Emory U., 1966; EdD, U. Ga., 1971. Asst. to dean men Emory U., Atlanta, 1962-66; dir. housing West Ga. Coll., Carrollton, 1966-69; dean student devel. Mars Hill (N.C.) Coll., 1971-78; prof. higher edn. U. Louisville, 1978-91; prof. Bowling Green State U., 1991—; tchr. People's Republic China, El Salvador. Editor Coll. Student Affairs Jour.; contbr. numerous articles to profl. jours. Founder Assn. Student Jud. Affairs. Lt. USN, 1960-62. Recipient S. Earl Thompson award Assn. Coll. and Univ. Housing Officers, Outstanding Tchr. Sch. Edn. award. Mem. Nat. Assn. Student Pers. Adminstrn. (Outstanding Contbr. to Lit. or Rsch. award, Excellence as Grad. Faculty Mem. award), Am. Coll. Pers. Assn. (sr. scholar), Assn. Student Jud. Affairs (Disting. Svc. award), Am. Assn. for Higher Edn., So. Assn. for Coll. Student Affairs (past pres., Melvene Hardee and H. Howard Davis awards). Office: Bowling Green State U Rm 330 Edn Bldg Bowling Green OH 43403

GEHRING, FREDERICK WILLIAM, mathematician, educator; b. Ann Arbor, Mich., Aug. 7, 1925; s. Carl E. and Hester McNeal (Reed) G.; m. Lois Caroline Bigger, Aug. 29, 1953; children: Kalle Burgess, Peter Motz. BSE in Elec. Engring., U. Mich., 1946, MA in Math, 1949; PhD (Fulbright fellow) in Math, Cambridge U., Eng., 1952, ScD, 1976; PhD (hon.), U. Helsinki, Finland, 1977, U. Jyväskylä, Finland, 1990, Norwegian U. Sci. & Technology, 1997. Benjamin Peirce instr. Harvard U., Cambridge, Mass., 1952-55; instr. math. U. Mich., Ann Arbor, 1955-56, asst. prof., 1956-59, assoc. prof., 1959-62, prof., 1962-96, T.H. Hildebrandt prof. math., 1984-96, prof. emeritus, 1996; chmn. dept. math. U. Mich., 1973-75, 77-84, disting. univ. prof., 1987—; hon. prof. Hunan U., Changsha, People's Republic of China, 1987; vis. prof. Harvard U., 1964-65, Stanford U., 1964, U. Minn., 1971, Inst. Mittag-Leffler, Sweden, 1972, Mittag-Leffler, Sweden, 1990; Lars Onsager prof. Norwegian Tech. Hochschule, Norway, 1995; chair program in Geo Function Theory, Math. Scis. Rsch. Inst., Berkeley, 1986. Editor Duke Math. Jour., 1963-80, D. Van Nostrand Pub. Co., 1963-69, North Holland Pub. Co., 1970—, Springer-Verlag, 1974—; editl. bd. Procs. Am. Math. Soc., 1962-65, Ind. U. Math. Jour., 1967-75, Math. Revs., 1969-75, Bull. Am. Math. Soc., 1979-85, Complex Variables, 1981—, Mich. Math. Jour., 1989, Annales Academiae Scientiarum Fennicae, 1996, Conformal Geometry and Dynamics, 1997—; contbr. numerous articles on rsch. in pure math. to sci. jours. With USNR, 1943-46. Decorated Comdr. Finnish White Rose, 1986; NSF fellow, 1959-60; Fulbright fellow, 1958-59; Guggenheim fellow, 1958-59; Sci. Research Council sr. fellow, 1981; Humboldt fellow, 1981, 88; Finnish Acad. fellow U. Helsinki, 1989. Mem. NAS, Am. Acad. Arts and Scis., Assn. Women in Math., Math. Assn. Am., Am. Math. Soc. (coun. 1980-83, trustee 1983-93, mem. editl. bd. 1997-98), Inst. for Math. and Its Applications (gov. 1981-84), Swiss Math. Soc., Finnish Math. Soc., London Math. Soc., European Math. Soc., Finnish Acad. Sci., German Math. soc., Royal Norwegian Soc. Scis. and Letters. Home: 2139 Melrose Ave Ann Arbor MI 48104-4067*

GEHRING, PERRY JAMES, toxicologist, chemical company executive; b. Yankton, S.D., Mar. 15, 1936; s. Rinold Lou and Bertha (Reiger) G.; m. Barbara Tennis, Aug. 8, 1959; children: Daniel, Matthew, Elizabeth, Heidi. B.S., D.V.M., U. Minn., 1960, Ph.D. in Pharmacology, 1965. Research asso. Iowa State U., 1960-61; with Dow Chem. Co., Midland, Mich., 1965-68, 70-89; dir. toxicology Dow Chem. Co., 1974-78, dir. health and environ. scis., 1978-81, v.p. agrl. chems. research and devel., dir. health and environ. sci., 1981-89; v.p. R & D Dow Agro Scis., Indpls., 1989-98; asso. prof. pharmacology Mich. State U., 1968-70, adj. prof., 1970-92; adj. prof. toxicology Ind. U., 1996—; trustee Nutrition Found., 1981; chmn. sci. adv. panel Chem. Industry Inst. Toxicology, 1976-80; mem. safe drinking water subcom. organic contaminants Nat. Acad. Scis., 1975-76, mem. nat. center toxicol. research rev. com., 1976-77; participant internat. meetings. Asso. editor: Toxicology and Applied Pharmacology Jour., 1977-80; mem. editorial bds. profl. jours.; contbr. articles to profl. publs. Recipient Founders award Chem. Industry Inst. Toxicology, 1983; inducted into U. Minn. Athletic Hall of Fame, 1993; NIH fellow, 1961-65. Mem. Soc. Toxicology (pres. 1980-81, coun. 1975-77, Frank R. Blood award 1979, Merit award 1983), Internat. Union Toxicology (v.p. 1983-86, dir. 1981-83, pres. 1986-90), Am. Soc. Pharmacology and Exptl. Therapeutics, Am. Crop Protection Assn. (chmn. sci. regulatory oversight coun. 1989-93). Presbyterian (trustee 1983-86). Home: 3928 Kitty Hawk Ct Carmel IN 46033-4801

GEHRING, RONALD KENT, lawyer; b. Ft. Wayne, Ind., Feb. 5, 1941; s. Ronald G. and Beverly M. (Failor) G.; m. Teresa L. Eyer, June 18, 1966; children—Gregory D., Douglas K., Suzanne C. AB, Ind. U., 1963, JD, 1967. Bar: Ind. 1967, U.S. Dist. Ct. (no. dist.) Ind. 1967, U.S. Dist. Ct. (so. dist.) Ind. 1967, U.S. Ct. Appeals (7th cir.) 1975. Assoc., Peters, McHie, Enslen & Hand, Hammond, Ind., 1967-70; ptnr. Tourkow, Danehy, Crell, Hood & Gehring, Ft. Wayne, 1971-79, Grossman, Boeglin & Gehring and predecessor, Ft. Wayne, 1980-84; pvt. practice, Ft. Wayne, 1984—; panelist Ind. Collection Law Seminar, 1982-83; bd dir. Concordia Cemetery Assn., 1982-83, Luth. Assn. Broadcasting, Inc.; atty. Ind. Dist. Luthern Church. Mem. ABA, Ind. Trial Lawyers, Comml. Law League, Ind. Bar Assn., Allen County Bar Assn., Phi Delta Phi. Office: 202 W Berry St Ste 321 Fort Wayne IN 46802-2242

GEHRING, WALTER JAKOB, biology and genetics educator; b. Zurich, Switzerland, Mar. 20, 1939; s. Jakob and Marcelle (Rebmann) G.; m. Elisabeth Lott, Jan. 31, 1964; children: Stephan, Thomas. Diploma in Zoology, U. Zurich, 1963, PhD, 1965. Rsch. assoc. U. Zurich, 1963-67; postdoctoral fellow Yale U., New Haven, Conn., 1967-69, assoc. prof., 1969-72; prof. U. Basel, Switzerland, 1972—. Assoc. editor Development, Jour. Exptl. Zoology, Mechanisms of Devel., Trends in Genetics, Devel., Growth & Differentiation. Recipient Otto Nägeli prize Zurich, 1982, Warren Triennial Harvard Med. Sch., Cambridge, Mass., 1986, Dr. Albert Wander prize City of Bern, Switzerland, 1986, Charles Léopold Mayer prize Inst. of France, Paris, 1986, Louis Jeantet prize for medicine City of Geneva, 1987, Prix d'Honneur, Moet Hennessy Louis Vuitton, 1993, Newcomb Cleve. prize AAAS, 1994-1995, Otto Warburg-medaille, 1996, Paul Wintrebert prize U. Pierre and Marie Curie, 1996, March of Dimes prize Devel. Biology, 1997. Mem. European Molecular Biology Orgn., European Devel. Biology Orgn., AAAS, NAS, Deutsche Akademie der Naturforscher Leopoldina, Academia Europaea, Genetics Soc. Am., Internat. Soc. for Developmental Biology, Swiss Soc. for Cell Biology, Molecular Biology and Genetics, Am. Soc. for Developmental Biology, Human Genome orgn., Royal Soc. London (fgn.), Acad. Scis. (fgn.), Sigma Xi. Avocations: birdwatching, photography. Home: Hochfeldstrasse 32, CH-4106 Therwil Switzerland Office: U Basel Biozentrum, Klingelbergstrasse 70, CH-4056 Basel Switzerland

GEHRINGER, RICHARD GEORGE, publishing executive; b. Newark, Oct. 31, 1949; s. George John and Constance Mary (Volz) G.; m. Phyllis Jean Salerno, Nov. 13, 1977; children: Alexandra Rane, Skyler George. BS, U. S.C., 1972; MBA, St. John's U., Jamaica, N.Y., 1976. Cert. cash mgr. Mgmt. trainee Avdel Corp., Teterboro, N.J., 1972-74; purchasing analyst Resistoflex Corp., Roseland, N.J., 1974-76; staff acct. McGraw-Hill Pub. Co., Hightstown, N.J., 1976-78; fin. analyst corp. real estate McGraw-Hill, Inc., N.Y.C., 1978-79; bus. mgr., corp. real estate McGraw-Hill Inc., N.Y.C., 1979-80; asst. contr. McGraw-Hill Book Co., N.Y.C., 1980-81; contr. Oxford U. Press Inc., Fair Lawn, N.J., 1981-86; v.p., CFO Oxford U. Press Inc., N.Y.C., 1986-95, sr. v.p., chief fin. officer, 1995—; fin. advisor Pi Kappa Alpha, Columbia U., N.Y.C., 1988-89; bd. dirs. Fin. Execs. Inst., Dickens Pen & Inc. Mem. Fin. Execs. Inst., Nat. Assn. Accts., Treasury Mgmt. Assn., Bldg. Owners' and Mgrs.' Assn. of Greater N.Y., N.C. Citizens for Bus. and Industry, Raleigh C. of C. Republican. Roman Catholic. Home: 120 Overleigh Rd Bernardsville NJ 07924-1510 Office: Oxford U Press Inc 198 Madison Ave New York NY 10016-4341

GEHRY, FRANK OWEN, architect; b. Toronto, Ont., Can., Feb. 28, 1929; came to U.S., 1947; s. Irving and Thelma (Caplan) G.; children: Leslie, Brina; m. Berta Aguilera, Sept. 11, 1975; children: Alejandro, Samuel. B. in Architecture, U. So. Calif., 1954; postgrad., Harvard U., 1956-57. Registered profl. architect, Calif. Designer Victor Gruen Assocs., L.A., 1953-54, planning, design and project dir., 1958-61; project designer, planner Pereira & Luckman, L.A., 1957-58; prin. Frank O. Gehry & Assocs., Santa Monica, Calif., 1962—. Architect Loyola Law Sch., L.A., 1978-92, Temporary Contemporary Mus., L.A., 1983, Calif. Aerospace Mus., L.A., 1984, Frances Goldwyn Regional Br. Libr., Hollywood, Calif., 1986, U.C.I. Info. and Computer Sci./Engring. Rsch. Lab. and Engring. Ctr., Irvine, Calif., 1986-88, Vitra Internat. Mfg. Facility and Design Mus., Weil am Rhein, Germany, 1989, Chiat/Day Hdqs., Venice, Calif., 1991, Am. Ctr., Paris, 1994, Advanced Tech. Labs. Bldg., Iowa City, 1992, U. Toledo Ctr. for Visual Arts, 1992, Walt Disney Concert Hall, L.A., Frederick R. Weisman Art Mus., Mpls., 1993, Vitra Internat. Hdqs., Basel, Switzerland, 1994, Disney Ice, Anaheim, Calif., 1995, EMR Communication and Tech. Ctr., Bad Oeynhausen, Germany, 1995, Team Disneyland Adminstrn. Bldg., Anaheim, 1996, Nationale-Nederlanden Bldg., Prague, Czech Republic, 1996, Guggenheim Mus., Bilbao, Spain, 1997. Trustee Hereditary Disease Found., Santa Monica, Calif., 1970—. Recipient Arnold W. Brunner Meml. prize in architecture, 1983, Eliot Noyes Design chair Harvard U., 1983, Charlotte Davenport Professorship in architecture Yale U., 1982, 85, 87-89, Pritzker Architecture prize, 1989, Wolf prize in art, 1992, Praemium Imperiale, 1992, Dorothy and Lilian Gish award, 1994, Nat. Medal of Arts, 1998. Office: Frank O Gehry & Assocs 1520B Cloverfield Blvd Santa Monica CA 90404-3502

GEHRZ, ROBERT GUSTAVE, retired railroad executive; b. Milw., July 9, 1915; s. Gustave Gerhardt and Paula (Frey) G.; m. Mary Gilbert Laubscher, Feb. 12, 1944; children: Robert Douglas, Richard Campbell, William Rolfe, Elizabeth Hart, Thomas Frank, James Charles. B.A., U. Wis., 1938, LL.B., 1941. Bar: Wis. 1941, Minn. 1951. Legal editor West Pub. Co., St. Paul, 1947-52; atty. Soo Line R.R. Co., Mpls., 1952-57; gen. atty. Soo Line R.R. Co., 1957-59, gen. solicitor, 1959-79, v.p., gen. counsel, 1979-80, ret., 1980. Served with USNR, 1942-46. Mem. State Bar Assn. Wis., Minn. Bar Assn., Ramsey County Bar Assn., Mpls. Athletic Club. Home: 2251 Princeton Ave Saint Paul MN 55105-1159

GEIB, VIOLET M., elementary education educator. Tchr. Sporting Hill Elem. Sch., Manheim, Pa. Named Pa. State Tchr. of Yr., 1993. Office: Sporting Hill Elem Sch 65 S Colebrook Rd Manheim PA 17545-1901

GEIDUSCHEK, E(RNEST) PETER, biophysics and molecular biology educator; b. Vienna, Austria, Apr. 11, 1928; came to U.S., 1945, naturalized, 1946; s. Sigmund and Frieda (Tauber) G.; m. Joyce Barbara Brous; 2 children. B.A., Columbia U., 1948; A.M., Harvard U., 1950, Ph.D., 1952. Instr. chemistry Yale U., New Haven, 1952-53, 55-57; asst. prof. chemistry U. Mich., Ann Arbor, 1957-59; asst. prof. biophysics U. Chgo., 1959-62, assoc. prof., 1962-64, prof., 1964-70; prof. biology U. Calif., San Diego, 1970-94, rsch. prof., 1994—, chmn. dept., 1981-83, 94; cons. USPHS, 1963-69, NIH, 1991-94, 98—. Editl. bd. Biophys. Jour., 1967-69, Ann. Revs. Biophysics and Bioengring., 1971-74, Virology, 1972—, Sci., 1977-84, Seminars in Virology, 1990—, Ency. Virology, 1990—. Served with U.S. Army, 1953-55. Recipient rsch. award Am. Postgrad. Med. Assn., 1962, USPHS, 1962, Order of Merit of Italian Republic; Guggenheim fellow, 1964-65. Fellow AAAS, Am. Acad. Microbiology; mem. NAS, Am. Acad. Arts and Scis., Am. Soc. Biochemistry and Molecular Biology (pub. affairs com. 1988-90), Am. Soc. Microbiology, Am. Soc. Virology (coun. 1985-87). Office: U Calif Dept Biology Ctr Molecular Genetics La Jolla CA 92093

GEIER, PHILIP HENRY, JR., advertising executive; b. Pontiac, Mich., Feb. 22, 1935; s. Philip Henry and Jane (Gillen) G.; m. Faith Power, children: Hope Geier Smith, Johanna Geier. B.A., Colgate U., 1957; M.S., Columbia U., 1958. With McCann-Erickson, Inc., Cleve., 1958-60, N.Y.C., 1960-68; chmn. McCann-Erickson Internat. U.K. Co., London, 1969-73; exec. v.p. McCann-Erickson Europe, 1973-75; vice chmn. internat. ops. McCann Worldwide, London, 1973-75; vice chmn. internat. Interpublic Group of Cos., Inc., N.Y.C., 1975-77; pres., chief operating officer Interpublic Group of Cos., Inc., 1977-80, chmn., chief exec. officer, 1980—, pres., 1985—; bd. dirs. Woolworth Corp., Fiduciary Trust Corp. Dir. Sch. of Am. Ballet, Internat. Tennis Hall of Fame; bd. overseers Meml. Sloan-Kettering Cancer Ctr., Columbia U. Bus. Sch.; trustee Whitney Mus. of Am. Art; trustee MU of Delta Kappa Epsilon Found. Clubs: Doubles (N.Y.C.); River (N.Y.C.); Sloane (London); Hurlingham (London). Office: Interpublic Group Cos Inc Ste 383 1271 Avenue Of The Americas Fl 44 New York NY 10020-1459*

GEIER, PHILIP OTTO, III, college president; b. Cin., 1948; s. Philip O. Jr. and Susanne (Ernst) G.; m. Amy Yeager, Dec. 27, 1975; children: Katherine, Elizabeth, Christopher. BA in Am. Civilization with honors, Williams Coll., 1970; attended, U. Paris, 1973; MA in History, Syracuse U., 1975, PhD in Am. Studies and History, 1980. Instr. history and Am. studies Dickinson Coll., Carlisle, Pa., 1976-77; Fulbright lectr. U. Paris-Sorbonne, 1977-78; interim exec. dir. French-Am. Found., N.Y.C., 1978-79; assoc. dir. Am. Farm Sch., Thessaloniki, Greece, 1979-82; v.p. external affairs World Learning, Brattleboro, Vt., 1982-93; pres., dir. Armand Hammer United World Coll., Montezuma, N.Mex., 1993—; bd. dirs. Fulbright Assn. and Fulbright Prize Com., Washington, Pine Manor Coll., Am. Found. Realty; chair social Svcs. and Internat. Exch. Commn. 2d U.S.-USSR Emerging Leaders Summit, Moscow and Sochi, 1990, del. to 1st Commn., Phila., 1988; mem. Coun. Fgn. Rels. Bd. dirs. Pacific Coun. on Internat. Policy, L.A. 2d lt. Supply Corps, USN, 1970-72, Vietnam. Fulbright award Fed. Republic of Germany, 1988. Avocations: internat. rels. Office: United World Coll PO Box 248 Montezuma NM 87731-0248

GEIGER, ALEXANDER, lawyer; b. Kosice, Czechoslovakia, May 21, 1950; came to U.S., 1965; s. Emil and Alice (Brickmann) G.; m. Helene R. Mortar, May 28, 1972; children: Theodore, Aviva. AB, Princeton U., 1972; JD, Cornell U., 1975. Bar: N.Y. 1976, U.S. Dist. Ct. (we. dist.) N.Y. 1976, U.S. Supreme Ct. 1980, U.S. Ct. Appeals (2d cir.) 1985, U.S. Tax Ct. 1986. Assoc. Nixon, Hargrave, Devans & Doyle, Rochester, N.Y., 1975-82; sr. ptnr. Geiger & Rothenberg, Rochester, 1982—; adj. asst. prof. St. John Fisher Coll., Rochester, 1977-78. Mem. N.Y. State Bar Assn., Monroe County Bar Assn., Assn. Trial Lawyers Am., Rochester Inns of Ct. (master). Jewish. Home: 194 Edgemoor Rd Rochester NY 14618-1230 Office: Geiger & Rothenberg 45 Exchange Blvd Ste 800 Rochester NY 14614-2093

GEIGER, H. JACK, medical educator; b. Nov. 11, 1925; m. Nicole Schupf. Student, U. Wis., 1943, U. Chgo., 1947-50; MD, Case Western Res. U., 1958; M in Sci. Hygiene, Harvard U., 1960; ScD (hon.), SUNY, Purchase, 1992. Intern Boston City Hosp. Harvard U., 1958-59, asst. resident in medicine, 1962-63, sr. resident in medine, 1963-64, clin. asst. in medicine, 1964-65; postdoctoral rsch. fellow social sci. and medicine Harvard U., 1959-61, instr. preventive medicine, 1961-62; asst. prof. pub. health, 1964-65; assoc. prof. Tufts U. Sch. Medicine, 1965-66; prof., 1966-71, chmn. dept. cmty. health and social medicine, 1969-71; dir. health ctrs. Columbia Point, Boston, Mound Bayou, Miss., 1965-71; project co-dir. SUNY, Stonybrook, 1971-73, prof., chmn. dept. cmty. medicine, 1971-77; Henry J. Kaiser sr. fellow Stanford U., 1983-84; Arthur C. Logan prof. chmn. cmty. health/social medicine CUNY Med. Sch., 1978-87; prof. emeritus, 1987—; vis. prof. medicine Harvard U., 1972-73. Mem. editorial Bd. Am. Jour Pub. Health; contbr. numerous articles to profl. jours. Recipient Disting. Svc. award Miss. Assn. Community Health for Poor, 1973, Nat. Health Achievement award in cmty. health Blue Cross and Blue Shield Assns. N.Am., 1979, Disting. Pub. Svc. award Nat. Assn. Cmty. Health Ctrs., 1981, Mass. League Community Health Ctrs., 1986, Robert H. Felix Disting. Svc. award St. Louis U. Sch. Medicine, 1986, Founders award Miss. Delta Health Ctr., 1990, Disting. Alumnus award of merit Harvard U. Sch. Pub. Health, 1992. Fellow AAAS (Inst. Medicine Mission to South Africa 1989, organizer conf. on health care for post-apartheid South Africa 1990), APHA (1st Ann. Excellence award 1972), Scientists Inst. Pub. Info.; mem. Inst. Medicine NAS (sr.), Am. Coll. Preventive Medicine, Internat. Edidemiol. Assn., Assn. Tchrs. Preventive Medicine, Assn. Behavioral Scis. and Med. Edn., Assn. Health Svcs. Rsch., Physicians for Human Rights (founding mem., pres., expert med. cons. to UN Human Rights Ctr. to Yugoslavia 1992, leader human rights missions to Yugoslavia 1993, Iraq and Kurdistan 1991, West Bank and Gaza Strip 1988, 90, and numerous others), Com. on Health in South Africa (nat. pres.), Physicians for Social Responsibility (founding mem.), Soc. Advancement of Ambulatory Care, Soc. Health and Human Value, Herman Biggs Soc. Office: CCNY Sch Medicine New York NY 10031

GEIGER, JAMES NORMAN, lawyer; b. Mansfield, Ohio, Apr. 5, 1932; s. Ernest R. and Margaret L. (Bauman) G.; m. Paula Hunt, May 11, 1957; children: Nancy G., John W. Student Wabash Coll., Crawfordsville, Ind., 1950-51; BA, Ohio Wesleyan U., 1954; JD, Emory U., 1962, LLD, 1970. Bar: Ga. 1961, U.. Dist. Ct. (mid. dist.) Ga. 1966, U.S. Ct. Appeals (5th and 11th cirs.) 1980, U.S. Dist. Ct. (so. dist.) Ga. 1983. Ptnr. Henderson, Kaley, Geiger and Thurmond, Marietta, Ga., 1962-64, Nunn, Geiger and Hunt, Perry, Ga., 1964-72, Geiger & Geiger, P.C. and predecessors, 1972—. Trustee Westfield (Ga.) Schs., 1970-74; mem. civilian adv. bd. Warner Robins AFB, 1976; chmn. coun. ministries Perry United Meth. Ch., 1970-71, mem. adminstrv. bd., 1968—. Capt. USAF, 1954-57. Mem. ABA, Ga. Bar Assn., Houston County Bar Assn., South Ga. C. of C. (bd. dirs.) Perry C. of C. (pres. 1976, 90), Perry Kiwanis (pres. 1968, Man of Yr. 1968), Perry Club Coun. (pres. 1967), Phi Delta Phi, Pi Sigma Alpha. Methodist. Home: 1910 Northside Rd Perry GA 31069-2223 Office: Geiger & Geiger 1007 Jernigan St Perry GA 31069-3325

GEIGER, LOREN DENNIS, classical musician; b. Buffalo, Jan. 23, 1946; s. Carroll Chester and Edith Lucile (Swedenborg) G.; m. Elaine Louise Sivers, Aug. 21, 1976; children: Rebecca, Sarah, Diana. MusB, U. Rochester, 1968, MusM, 1970. Cert. educator, N.Y. Band dir. Orchard Pk. (N.Y.) Cen. Schs., 1969—; orch. libr. Clarence (N.Y.) Orch., 1996—, Orchard Park (N.Y.) Symphony, 1998—; tubist Niagara Falls (N.Y.) Philharm., 1970-73, Orchard Park Symphony, 1973—, Amherst Symphony, Snyder, N.Y., 1974—, Clarence Summer Orch., 1974—; condr. 20th Century Band, Buffalo, 1984-91. Editor: Boombah Herald, 1973-98; arranger numerous mus. selections. Committeeman Orch. Park Symphony Music, 1976-84, 94—; active Music Educators Nat. Conf. Mem. Am. Fedn. Musicians, N.Y. State Sch. Music Assn., Circus Windjammers Unltd. (charter), Tubists Universal Brotherhood Assn., Internat. Mil. Music Soc. (charter), Pi Kappa Lambda. Avocations: photography, composition. Home: 15 Park Blvd Lancaster NY 14086-2510 Office: Orchard Park Cen Sch 60 S Lincoln Ave Orchard Park NY 14127-2664

GEIGER, MARK WATSON, management educator; b. Grand Forks, N.D., Aug. 22, 1949; s. Louis George and Helen Marjorie (Watson) G.; children: Harley, Uintah, Klaus. BA, Carleton Coll., 1971; MBA, U. Pa., 1975. CPA, N.Y. Bldg. contractor Spiral Remodeling, Phila., 1976-78; EDP project mgr. Ariz. State Govt., Phoenix, 1978-81; mgr. internal audit Gulf & Western Industries, N.Y.C., 1981-85; v.p. spl. projects Kidder, Peabody & Co., Inc., N.Y.C., 1986-90; v.p., chief adminstrv. officer Analytical Bio-Chemistry Labs., Inc., Columbia, Mo., 1990-92; ind. mgmt. cons. Columbia, 1992-94; asst. prof. fin. William Woods U., Fulton, Mo., 1994—. Rsch. grantee William Woods U., 1994, Mo. State Hist. Soc., 1997. Mem. AICPA, Mensa, SAR, Mo. Hist. Soc. Avocations: creative writing, long-distance swimming, target shooting, horseback riding. Home: PO Box 95 Fulton MO 65251-0095

GEIGER, TERRY, state legislator. BA in Pub. Svc., Alma Coll. Rep. Mich. State Dist. 87, 1995—. Address: 351 Capitol Bldg Lansing MI 48909-7514*

GEIMAN, J. ROBERT, lawyer; b. Evanston, Ill., Mar. 5, 1931; s. Louis H. and Nancy O'Connell-Crowe G.; m. Ann L. Fitzgerald, July 29, 1972; children: J. Robert, William Patrick, Timothy Michael. BS, Northwestern U., 1953; JD, Notre Dame U., 1956. Bar: Ill. 1956, U.S. Ct. Appeals (7th cir.) 1956, U.S. Supreme Ct. 1969. Assoc. Eckert, Peterson & Lowry, Chgo., 1956-64; ptnr. Peterson, Lowry, Rall, Barber & Ross, Chgo., 1964-70; ptnr. Peterson & Ross, Chgo., 1970-96, of counsel, 1996—; mem. com. on civil jury instructions Ill. Supreme Ct., 1979-81. Case editor Notre Dame Law Rev., 1956. Bd. advisors Cath. Charities of Archdiocese of Chgo., 1973-96. Fellow Internat. Acad. Trial Lawyers, Am. Coll. Trial Lawyers, Ill. Bar Found.; mem. ABA (aviation com., tort and ins. practice sect. 1980-90), Ill. Bar Assn. (sec. 1969-70, sec. bd. govs. 1969-71), Chgo. Bar Assn. (aviation law com. 1970-73), Bar Assn. of 7th Fed. Ct. (meetings com. 1968-70, vice chmn. membership com. 1973-75), Soc. Trial Lawyers, Cath. Lawyers Guild of Chgo. (bd. advisors 1973-96), Law Club Chgo., Chgo. Athletic Assn. (pres. 1973). Republican. Home: 900 SW Bay Point Cir Palm City FL 34990-1758 Office: Peterson & Ross 200 E Randolph St Ste 7300 Chicago IL 60601-7012

GEIS, BERNARD, book publisher; b. Chgo., Aug. 30, 1909; s. Harry M. and Bessie (Gesas) G.; m. Darlene Stern, Mar. 28, 1940; children: Peter, Stephen. BA, Northwestern U., 1931. Newspaper reporter, contbr. mags., 1931-33; editor Apparel Arts mag., 1933-38; asst. editor Esquire mag., 1938-45; editor Coronet mag., 1939-45; war corr., ETO for Coronet and Esquire mags., 1942-43; editor-in-chief Grosset & Dunlap Pub. Co., 1945-53, v.p., 1949-53; editor Prentice-Hall Pub. Co., 1954-57; pres. Bernard Geis Assocs., N.Y.C., 1958—. Chmn. pubs. group N.Y.C. Salvation Army ann. appeal, 1960-66; bd. dirs. council N.Y. Heart Assn.; bd. dirs. Ams. for Democratic Action, mem. exec. com., 1965—.

GEIS, DUANE VIRGIL, retired investment banker; b. Okeene, Okla., Apr. 16, 1923; s. Harry H. and Margareth (Tieman) G.; m. Lois Blakey, Mar. 11, 1944; children—Duane Gregory, Paul Geoffrey. B.A., Okla. State U., 1947. Accounting machine salesman IBM Corp., 1948-54; with Rotan Mosle Dallas Union, Inc., Houston, 1954-59; partner Rotan Mosle Dallas Union, Inc., 1959-66, 1st sr. v.p., 1966-70, also bd. dirs.; ptnr., officer Paine, Webber, Jackson & Curtis, 1970—. Dir. emeritus Star of Hope Mission; past trustee annuity bd. So. Bapt. Conv. Mem. Houston C. of C. (life), Phi Kappa Phi, Phi Eta Sigma (pres. 1942-43), Beta Alpha Psi (pres. 1946-47), Kappa Sigma, Blue Key (v.p., 1946-47). Republican. Baptist. Clubs: Houston Country (Houston). Home: 522 Shadywood Rd Houston TX 77057-1438 Office: 4544 Post Oak Place Dr Ste 140 Houston TX 77027-3104

GEIS, JEROME ARTHUR, lawyer, legal educator; b. Shakopee, Minn., May 28, 1946; s. Arthur Adam and Emma Mary (Boegemann) G.; m. Beth Marie Bruger, Aug. 11, 1979; children: Jennifer, Jason, Joan, Janice. BA in History, Govt. magna cum laude, St. John's U., Collegeville, Minn., 1968; JD cum laude, U. Notre Dame, 1973; LLM in Taxation, NYU, 1975. Bar: Minn. 1973, U.S. Dist. Ct. Minn. 1973, U.S. Tax Ct. 1973, U.S. Ct. Appeals (8th cir.) 1973. Law clk. to presiding justice Minn. Supreme Ct., St. Paul, 1973-74; assoc. Dudley & Smith, St. Paul, 1975-76; assoc. Briggs & Morgan P.A., St. Paul, 1976-79, chief tax dept., 1983-95; prof. tax law William Mitchell Coll. of Law, St. Paul, 1976—. Columnist Minn. Law Jour., 1986-89, Bench & Bar, 1990—; editorial cons.: Sales and Use Tax Alert; reviewer Summary Reporter: Finance and Commerce, Minnesota State Bar Assn.; corr. State Tax Notes. Bd. dirs. Western Townhouse Assn., West St. Paul, 1979, St. Matthews Cath. Ch., West St. Paul, 1981; adv. bd. Minn. Inst. of Legal Edn., 1984—. Served to specialist 4th class U.S. Army, 1969-71. Fellow Am. Coll. Tax Counsel; mem. ABA, Am. Law Inst., Tax Inst. Am. (chmn. sales and use tax commn. 1988-90), Nat. Tax Assn., Am. Judicature Soc., Minn. Bar Assn. (bd. dirs. tax coun. sect. 1984-93, chmn. 1990-91), Ramsey County Bar Assn., Minn. Taxpayers Assn. (bd. dirs. 1988—), Inst. Property Taxation, Supreme Ct. Hist. Soc., Nat. Assn. of State Bar Tax Sections (exec. com. 1993—), Minn. Club (bd. dirs. 1997—), KC, Kiwanis (bd. dirs. 1997—). Home: 1116 Dodd Rd Saint Paul MN 55118-1821 Office: Briggs & Morgan PA 2200 1st St N Saint Paul MN 55109-3210

GEIS, JOHN P., military career officer; b. Jonesboro, Ark., Jan. 31, 1947. Commd. officer U.S. Army, advanced through grades to brig. gen.; brig. gen., commanding gen. U.S. Army Armament Rsch., Devel. and Engring. Ctr., Dover, N.J., 1998—. Office: US Army Armament Rsch Devel & Engring Ctr Picatinny Arsenal Dover NJ 07806-5000

GEIS, TARJA PELTO, educational coordinator, consultant, counselor, teacher, professor; b. Pietarsaari, Finland, Mar. 31, 1945; m. John J. Geis, June 18, 1966; children: Jeffrey, Steven. BS in Edn. and Art, Towson State U., Balt., 1967, MEd in Elem. Edn., 1970; EdD in Edn., Nova U., Ft. Lauderdale, 1986. Tchr. Balt. County, Balt., Md., 1967-70, Prince George's County, Bowie, Md., 1970-73; tchr. Dade County, Miami, Fla., 1979-84, ednl. specialist fed. programs, 1984-85, tchr., chairperson, 1985-89; co-originator, saturn coord. Gilbert L. Porter Elem., Miami, Fla., 1990-96; counselor Kendale Lakes, Miami, 1995—, advanced acads. eductator, 1997—; adj. prof. Barry U., 1996—. Editor: Chapter I Connection newsletter, 1984, Leo-T Times newsletter, 1987, Phi Delta Kappa newsletter, 1987. Validator NAEYC, Dade Reading Coun.; chair Restructuring Pub. Edn. Internat. Conf., Miami, 1990; mem. Lindgren Lakeowner Assn., Miami, 1991—; svc. Feeding the Needy, Miami, 1990—. Named Tchr. of Yr. South Area Dade County Pub. Schs., 1987, Fla. Master Tchr. Dept. Edn. Fla., 1988; grantee Found. for Excellence, 1986, 88, 89, 91; P.D.K. Travel scholarship, 1997-98. Mem. Phi Delta Kappa (pres. U. Miami chpt. 1991-92, Svc. Key award 1994). Avocations: art and design, writing, parapsychology. Home: 12764 SW 112th Ter Miami FL 33186-4721

GEISEL, CAMERON MEADE, JR., investment professional; b. Harrisburg, Pa., Oct. 7, 1937; s. Cameron Meade and Dorothy Mae G.; m. Martha L. Frohring, Sept. 3, 1977 (dec.); children: Melissa Ellen, Gregory Stuart, Andrew Frohring, Martha Bliss; m. Saskia Hessler, Sept. 8, 1991. BA, Bucknell U., Lewisburg, Pa., 1960; grad. Sch. Credit and Fin. Mgmt., Harvard U., 1970; Advanced Mgmt Program, Harvard Bus. Sch., 1985. With Phila. Nat. Bank, 1961-86, asst. v.p., then v.p., 1965-77, sr. v.p., 1977-86; bd. dirs. Hessler Properties, Inc. Trustee The Shipley Sch., Lankenau Hosp. Found., Fox Chase Cancer Ctr., Cardigan Mountain Sch. Corp.; chmn. adv. bd. mgrs. Morris Arboretum. 2d lt. inf. U.S. Army, 1960-61. Mem. U.S. Coun. Internat. Bus. (trustee, exec. com.), Merion Golf Club, Merion Cricket Club, Phila. Club, Racquet Club (Phila.), Royal Ashdown Forest Golf Cloub, Royal and Ancient Golf Club of St. Andrews, Honourable Co. of Edinburgh Golfers, Loblolly Pines Golf Club. Republican. Episcopalian. Home: 1411 Youngsford Rd Gladwyne PA 19035-1232

GEISEL, HAROLD WALTER, diplomat; b. Chgo., May 11, 1947; s. Gustav and Stefi Geisel; m. Susan L. Gordon, Oct. 2, 1983; children: Jacqueline Julie, Katherine Louise. BA in History, Johns Hopkins U., 1968; MBA, U. Va., 1970. Commd. fgn. service officer Dept. State, 1970; adminstrv. officer Dept. State, Washington, 1973-75; 1st sec. Am. embassy, Bern, Switzerland, 1975-78, Bamako, Mali, 1978-80; adminstrv. officer Dept. State, Washington, 1980-82; consul gen. U.S. consulate gen., Durban, South Africa, 1982-85; mem. NATO Def. Coll., Rome, 1985-86; adminstrv. counsellor Am. embassy, Rome, 1986-88; adminstrv. minister-counsellor Am. embassy, Bonn, 1988-92; adminstrv. minister-counselor Am. Embassy, Moscow, 1992-93; exec. asst. to under-sec. Dept. State, Washington, 1993-94, deputy inspector gen., 1994-95; dep. asst. sec. for info. mgmt. U.S. State Dept., Washington, 1995-96; amb. to Mauritius, Seychelles, and Comoros U.S. State Dept., 1996—. Jewish. Office: US State Dept Port Louis Washington DC 20521-2450

GEISEL, HENRY JULES, lawyer; b. Cin., Oct. 3, 1947; s. Albert and Else Geisel; m. Ellyn Anne Levy, Sept. 1, 1975; children: Noah L., Gideon L. BS in Econs., U. Pa., 1969; JD, U. Cin., 1972. Bar: Colo. 1972, U.S. Dist. Ct. Colo. 1972. Dep. dist. atty. 20th Jud. Dist., Boulder, Colo., 1973-74, 10th Jud. Dist., Pueblo, Colo., 1974-76; assoc. John R. Naylor, Pueblo, 1976-82, Naylor & Geisel P.C., Pueblo, 1982—. Pres. Temple Emanuel, Pueblo, 1981-82, 85-88; bd. dirs. Pueblo Youth Svcs. Bur., 1978-93, sec., 1989-93; bd. dirs. Pueblo Intensive Phonics Literacy Ctr., Inc., 1989-96, Parkview Hosp. Found., Pueblo, 1986-93, chmn., 1988. Mem. ABA, Colo. Bar Assn., Pueblo County Bar Assn., Colo. Trial Lawyers Assn. Avocations: tennis, bicycling, web-surfing, travel. Office: Naylor & Geisel PC 1123 N Elizabeth St Pueblo CO 81003-2233

GEISEL, MARTIN SIMON, college dean, educator; b. Grand Rapids, Mich., Nov. 27, 1941; s. Bernard and Jeanette (Rozema) G.; m. Susan Amendola, Sept. 28, 1963 (div. 1974); children: Sandra L., Matthew B.; m. Kathy E. Bell, Jul. 25, 1987. BS in Mgmt. Sci., Case Inst. Tech., 1963; MBA in Bus. Econs., U. Chgo., 1965, PhD in Bus. Econs., 1970. Process engr. E.I. DuPont de Nemours, East Chicago, Ind., 1963-65; asst. then assoc. prof. Carnegie-Mellon U., Pitts., 1968-75; assoc. prof. grad. sch. mgmt. U. Rochester, N.Y., 1975-79, assoc. dean for acad. affairs, 1979-85; dean sch.

mgmt. U. Tex. at Dallas, Richardson, 1985-87; dean, prof. Owen grad. sch. mgmt. Vanderbilt U., Nashville, 1987—; bd. dirs. Nashville Bank Commerce. Contbr. articles to profl. jours. Bd. dirs. Nat. Coalition for Advanced Mfg., Washington, 1990-93, Jr. Achievement Mid. Tenn., 1991-95; mem. bd. visitors Edwin L. Cox Sch. Bus. So. Meth. U., Dallas, 1988-90; mem. migratory waterfowl adv. com. State of N.Y., 1984-85; bd. dirs. Am. Assembly Collegiate Sch. Bus., St. Louis, 1987-88, 94-97, Grad. Mgmt. Admissions Coun., McLean, Va., 1998—; mem. Leadership Nashville. Mem. Soc. Internat. Bus. Fellows, Univ. Club, Rotary, Beta Gamma Sigma (bd. govs. 1990-94). Avocations: fishing, hunting. Home: 453 Beech Creek Rd N Brentwood TN 37027-3406 Office: Vanderbilt U Dean Owen Grad Sch Mgmt 401 21st Ave N Nashville TN 37203

GEISELHART, LORENE ANNETTA, English language educator; b. Rake, Iowa, June 28, 1929; d. Charles Tobias and Altha May (Mills) Knutson; m. James Willis Geiselhart, June 1, 1947 (div. 1971); children: Nancy Joyce, Larry Paul, Richard Ray, Kathleen Ann. Cert., Luther Coll., 1949; BA, U. No. Iowa, 1965, MA, 1989; postgrad., U. Iowa, 1990—. Pub. sch. tchr. Postville, Iowa, 1947-48; adminstrv. asst. to county supt. schs. Decorah, Iowa, 1948-49; pub. sch. tchr. Galesville and Trempealeau, Wis., 1949-51, Iowa Braille and Sight-Saving Sch., Vinton, 1959-70, South Winneshiek Community Sch., Ossian, Iowa, 1970-94; instr. English to univ. students Nanchong Inst. Edn., Sichuan, China, 1995-96; student tchr. supr. Luth. Coll., Decorah, 1971-94; instr. English to univ. students Inst. Edn., Nanchong, Sichuan Province, China, 1995-96. Sec. Calmar (Iowa) Improvement Assn., 1987-92; active Calmar Luth. Ch. Coun., 1975-80, 89-91, mem. choir, 1975-80, pres. Ch. Circle, 1975-77, 88-92. Mem. AAUW (pres. 1969-70, 96—, sec. 1990-92), NEA, Iowa Reading Coun., Iowa State Edn. Assn., NE Iowa Rosemaling Assn. (sec. 1991-94), Delta Kappa Gamma (pres. Beta Eta chpt. 1978-81, state fellowship com. 1982-84, grantee 1988). Democrat. Avocations: rosemaling, golf, bridge, rug hooking, reading.

GEISENDORFER, JAMES VERNON, author; b. Brewster, Mass., Apr. 22, 1929; s. Victor H. and Anne B. (Johnson) G.; m. Esther Lillian Walker, Sept. 23, 1949; children: Jane, Karen, Lois. Student, Augustana Coll., 1950-51, Augsburg Coll., 1951-54, Orthodox Luth. Sem., 1954-55; BA, U. Minn., 1960; LLD, Burton Coll. and Sem., 1961. Grain buyer Pillsbury Mills, Inc., Worthington, Minn., 1947-48, hatchery acct., 1949-50; night supr. Strutwear, Inc., Mpls., 1951-52; dispatcher Strutwear, Inc., Chgo. and Northwestern Ry, 1953-54; office mgr. Froedtert Malt Corp., Mpls., 1955-56, Nat. Automotive Parts Assn., 1957-60; sr. creative writer Brown & Bigelow, St. Paul, 1960-72; religious rschr., writer, 1972—; rsch. cons. Inst. for the Study of Am. Religion; mem. panel of reference Chelston Bible Coll., New Milton, Eng. Author: (with J. Gordon Melton) A Directory of Religious Bodies in the United States, 1977, Religion in America, 1983, Religion USA, 1989; mem. editl. bd. Biog. Dictionary of American Cult and Sect Leaders; contbr. articles to books and periodicals; cons. editor Directory of Religious Organizations in the United States, 1977. Recipient Amicus Poloniae medal Polish Ministry of Culture and Edn., 1969. Mem. AAAS, Am. Acad. Religion, Philos. Soc. Eng., Acad. Ind. Scholars, Wis. Evang. Luth. Synod Hist. Inst., Augustana His. Soc., Royal Anthropological Inst., Ea. Territorial Hist. Soc. (charter), Medieval Acad. Am., Renaissance Soc. Am., George Elliot Fellowship, Wis. Acad. Scis., Arts and Letters, N.Y. Acad. Scis., Aristotelian Soc., Hegel Soc. Am., Sixteenth Century Studies Conf., Am. Cath. Philosophical Assn., Internat. Soc. for Comparative Study of Civilizations, Collingswood Soc., Internat. Assn. Greek Philosophy, Boethius Soc., Brit. Soc. Philosophy Religion, Inst. Interdisciplinary Rsch. Lutheran. Address: 1001 Shawano Ave Green Bay WI 54303-3020

GEISER, ELIZABETH ABLE, publishing company executive; b. Phillipsburg, N.J., Apr. 28, 1925; d. George W. and Margaret I. (Ross) G. AB magna cum laude, Hood Coll., 1947. Promotion mgr. coll. dept. Macmillan Co., N.Y.C., 1947-54; promotion mgr. R.R. Bowker, N.Y.C., 1954-60; sales mgr. R.R. Bowker, 1960-67, dir. mktg., 1967-70, v.p., 1970-73, sr. v.p., 1973-75, sr. v.p., pub. book divsn.; adj. prof., dir. U. Denver Pub. Inst., 1976—; sr. v.p. Gale Rsch. Co., 1976-91, cons., 1991—; cons. Excerpta Medica, Elsevier, 1976-82; lectr. pub. procedures Radcliffe Coll., 1966-75; lectr. schs. libr. sci. U. Wash., U. So. Calif.; panel mem. TV series Living Library, 1970. Editor: The Business of Book Publishing, 1985; contbr. Manual of Bookselling, 1969. Trustee Hood Coll., 1993—. Inducted into Publishing Hall of Fame, 1988. Mem. Assn. Am. Pubs. (exec. coun. prof. and scholarly pub. divsn. 1989-91, adv. coun. Frankfurt book fair 1971, sch. and libr. promotion and mktg. com. 1972-76, bd. dirs. 1982-85), ALA (pres. exhibits roundtable 1968-70, bd. dirs. exhibits roundtable 1968). Presbyterian. Home: 24 Forest Dr Springfield NJ 07081-1124 Office: Pub Inst D-114 2075 S University Blvd Denver CO 80210-6765

GEISER, THOMAS CHRISTOPHER, lawyer; b. Bern, Switzerland, Aug. 13, 1950; came to U.S., 1952; s. Henry Abraham and Pia Margaret (Tschudin) G.; m. Catherine Barlow Yeakle, Oct. 20, 1973 (div. Mar. 1983); m. Donna Lea Schweers, Jan. 3, 1987; 1 child, Kelsey Schweers. BA, U. Redlands, Calif., 1972; JD, U. Calif., San Francisco, 1977. Bar: Calif. 1978. Atty. Internat. Bur. Fiscal Documentation, Amsterdam, The Netherlands, 1977-78; assoc., ptnr. Hanson, Bridgett, Marcus, Vlahos & Stromberg, San Francisco, 1979-85; ptnr. Epstein, Becker, Stromberg & Green, San Francisco, 1985-90, Brobeck, Phleger & Harrison, San Francisco, 1990-93; sr. v.p., gen. counsel, sec. WellPoint Health Networks Inc., Woodland Hills, Calif., 1993-96, exec. v.p., gen. counsel, sec., 1996—. Mem. Nat. Health Lawyers Assn., Calif. Soc. Health Care Attys., Order of Coif. Office: WellPoint Health Networks Inc 120 S Via Merida Thousand Oaks CA 91362

GEISER, WILLIAM FRANCIS, education educator; b. N.Y.C., Feb. 23, 1944; s. Joseph Francis and Catherine Rose Geiser; m. Joanne Bortz, Oct. 4, 1969; children: Kirsten, Eric. BA, CUNY, 1971, MS, 1973; EdD, St. John's U., N.Y., 1998. Cert. tchr. math., social studies, common brs., N.Y. Facilities asst. engring. N.Y. Tel., N.Y.C., 1969-71; tchr. Baldwin (N.Y.) Pub. Schs., 1971-73, North Rockland Schs., Garnerville, N.Y., 1973-99; asst. prof. Mt. St. Mary Coll., Newburgh, N.Y., 1999—. Pres. Cornwall (N.Y.) Cmty. Theater, 1983; mem. zoning bd. appeals Village of Cornwall on Hudson, N.Y., 1992—. With U.S. Army, 1962-65. Mem. ASCD, Am. Ednl. Rsch. Assn., Nat. Coun. Math. Tchrs., N.Y. State Math. Tchrs., Phi Delta Kappa. Avocations: cross country skiing, hiking, acting. Home: 20 Washington St Cornwall On Hudson NY 12520-1606 Office: Mt St Mary Coll Powell Ave Newburgh NY 12550-1238

GEISERT, WAYNE FREDERICK, educational consultant, retired administrator; b. Elmo, Kans., Dec. 20, 1921; s. Frederick Jacob and Martha E. (Lauer) G.; m. Ellen Maurine Gish, July 2, 1944; children: Gregory Wayne, Bradley Kent, Todd Wilfred. AB, McPherson Coll., Kans., 1944; PhD in Econs, Northwestern U., 1951; LLD (hon.), Manchester Coll., 1987; HHD (hon.), James Madison U., 1992; LHD (hon.), Bridgewater Coll., 1994, McPherson Coll., 1994. Instr. Hamilton (Kans.) High Sch., 1946-48; part-time instr. Kendall Coll., Evanston, Ill., 1948-50; grad. asst. Northwestern U., 1950-51; from assoc. prof. to prof. and head dept. econs. and bus. Manchester Coll., North Manchester, Ind., 1951-57; dean coll. McPherson Coll., 1957-64; pres. Bridgewater (Va.) Coll., 1964-94, pres. emeritus, 1994—; chmn. bd. First Va. Bank/Planters, Bridgewater, 1988-94; vice chmn. bd. First Va. Bank of the Shenandoah Valley, 1994-95; cons. in ednl. field; pres. Assn. Va. Colls., 1970-71; exec. com. Church-related Colls. and Univs. in the South, 1973-74. Bd. dirs. Univ. Center in Va., 1964-78; pres. Council Ind. Colls. in Va., 1984-85; bd. dirs. Shenandoah Valley Ednl. TV, chmn. bd., 1979-84; bd. dirs. Va. Found. Ind. Colls., v.p., 1974-76, pres., 1976-78; moderator Ch. of Brethren, 1973-74, chmn. rev. and evaluation com., 1975-77, mem. gen. bd., 1977-82, vice chmn., 1977-78, chmn. gen. services commn., 1979-82, chmn. pension bd., 1979-82; chmn. United Way campaign, 1979-80; ednl. del. Dalian U. Fgn. Langs., Peoples Republic China, 1985, 90, 94. Served with USNR, 1944-46, PTO. Recipient Alumni Citation of Merit, McPherson Coll., 1974, Profl. Educator of Yr. award James Madison U., 1983; Geisert Hall named in his honor by Bridgewater Coll., 1990; named Meritorious Alumnus, Chapman (Kans.) H.S., 1994. Mem. Am. Econ. Assn., Harrisonburg-Rockingham County C. of C. (bd. dirs. 1977-82, pres. 1980-81), Rotary, Omicron Delta Kappa, Pi Kappa Delta, Alpha Psi Omega, Lambda Soc. Home: 1492 Cumberland Dr Harrisonburg VA 22801-8608 Office: Bridgewater Coll Office of the Pres Emeritus Bridgewater VA 22812

GEISINGER, JANICE ALLAIN, accountant; b. Iroquois County, Ill., June 21, 1927; d. Carl Oliver and Constance Kathryn (Risser) Irps Allain; m. Robert Bond Geisinger, Oct. 17, 1947 (div. 1976); children: Jacque K., Holly D., Terry Joe. AA, Blackburn U., Carlinville, Ill., 1947. Lab. technician Mich. Health Lab., East Lansing, 1947-48; with Southwestern Bell Telephone, Tulsa, 1948-49; bookkeeper Geisinger Ent., Dallas, 1951-69; salesman Earl Page Real Estate, Irving, Tex., 1969-71; food purchaser Town & Country vending, Dallas, 1971-75; bookkeeper/sec. Belco C & I Wiring Inc., Irving, 1976-85; leasing bookkeeper Copiers Etc., Inc., Dallas, 1985-89; bookkeeper Kennedy Elec. Inc., Mesquite, Tex., 1989; ret., 1990; cons. Ross Mech., Irving, 1989—; asst. bookkeeper Metroplex Dental Group (now Dr. Julian M. Chong), 1990—. Crew leader Census Bur., Dallas, 1990. Mem. Am. Contract Bridge Assn. Avocations: flying, gardening, knitting, rug making. Home: 1216 E Grauwyler Rd Irving TX 75061-5031

GEISINGER, KURT FRANCIS, university administrator, psychometrician; b. Danville, Pa., Jan. 11, 1951; s. Karl William and Florence Eva (Graber) G.; m. Janet Frances Carlson, Sept. 22, 1984. AB with honors, Davidson Coll., 1972; MS, U. Ga., 1974; PhD, Pa. State U., 1977. Instr. Pa. State U., University Park, 1975-76; dir., rsch. svcs. Bartell Assocs., State College, Pa., 1976-77; asst. prof. to prof. and chmn. dept. psychology Fordham U., Bronx, N.Y., 1977-92; prof. psychology, dean of arts and scis. SUNY, Oswego, 1992-97; acad. v.p., prof. psychology LeMoyne Coll., 1997—; mem. tech. adv. com. on Grad. Record Exam., Ednl. Testing Svc., Princeton, N.J., 1995—, vis. rsch. assoc., 1976; cons. expert witness N.Y.C. Depts. Law and Pers., 1981-92, Fox and Fox Counsellors at Law, N.Y.C., 1986—; cons. Assessment Alternatives, Florham Park, N.J., 1987—; co-chair Joint Com. on Testing Practices, 1993-97. Cons. editor Psychol. Assessment, Ednl. Rsch. Quar. Fellow APA (com. on psychol. testing and assessment 1998—), Am. Psychol. Soc.; mem. Am. Ednl. Rsch. Assn., Nat. Coun. on Measurement in Edn., Northeastern Ednl. Rsch. Assn. (newsletter editor 1988-91, pres. 1986-89, bd. dirs. 1984-86), Phi Kappa Phi (Fordham U. chpt. pres. 1984-86), Psi Chi, Sigma Xi, Alpha Sigma Mu. Democrat. Lutheran. Avocations: swimming, softball, golf, computer activities. Home: 2 Mayflower Cir Oswego NY 13126-4163 Office: Acad Vice Pres LeMoyne Coll Syracuse NY 13214-1399

GEISLER, NATHAN DAVID, financial consultant; b. Kokand, Russia, Jan. 22, 1946; s. Leon and Esther (Korn) G.; B.A., Ohio State U., 1968; J.D., U. Toledo, 1970; m. Susan D. Starsky, 1982; 1 child, Jonathan Starsky Geisler. Asst. v.p. Merrill Lynch Pierce Fenner & Smith, Toledo, 1973-89, v.p., 1989—. Capt. USAF, 1971-73; lt. col. Ohio Air N.G. Mem. Air Force Assn., Ohio Air N.G. Assn., Ohio State Alumni Assn., U. Toledo Alumni Assn., The Temple Shomer Emunim, Sylvania, Ohio (pres.), Phi Alpha Delta. Home: 2600 Forestvale Rd Toledo OH 43615-2251 Office: 333 N Summit St Toledo OH 43604-2617

GEISLER, SHERRY LYNN, magistrate; b. Durango, Colo., Aug. 18, 1956; d. George Walter and Evelyn Ruth (MacLean) Geisler; m. Harvey Lee Slade, June 6, 1981 (div. Aug. 11, 1993); 1 child, Sherry (Rachel) Orona. Grad. H.S., Springerville, Ariz., 1974; student, Northland Pioneer Coll., Springerville, Ariz., 1986-90, Res. Police Acad., 1986. Clk. Round Valley Justice Ct., Springerville, 1981-84; chief clk. Round Valley Justice Ct., 1984-88, office mgr., judge pro tem, 1988-93, justice of the peace, 1993—; city magistrate City of Springerville and Eagar, Ariz., 1993—; mentor judge Ariz. Supreme Ct., 1994—; edn. chair Ariz. Justice Ct. Assn, 1994-96. Mem. Nat. Judges Assn., Am. Judges Assn., Ariz. Cts. Assn., State of Ariz. Justice of the Peace Assn. (pres.). Ariz. Magistrates Assn. Democrat. Avocations: crafts, gardening, travel, scuba diving. Home: PO Box 1202 Springerville AZ 85938-1202 Office: Round Valley Justice Ct PO Box 1356 Springerville AZ 85938-1356

GEISMAR, RICHARD LEE, communications executive; b. Paterson, N.J., Aug. 22, 1927; s. Sylvan and Marjorie (Leeser) G.; m. Patricia Willard, Nov. 27, 1954; children: John, Elisabeth, Nancy. B in Mgmt. Engring., Rensselaer Poly. Inst., 1949; MBA, Harvard, 1951. With DuMont TV Network, 1951-55; Metromedia, Inc. (and predecessors), N.Y.C., 1955-69; also bd. dirs. Metromedia, Inc. (and predecessors); pres., dir. Reeves Telecom Corp., 1969-70; comm. cons. BGW Assocs., Inc., 1970-84; chmn. Broad St. Comm. Corp., 1971-84; pres. Broad St. Ventures, 1984-98; chmn. Broad St. TV, 1989-96. Bd. dirs., treas. Greenwich chpt. ARC, mem. state svc. coun, 1992-96. Served with USNR, 1945-46. Mem. Riverside Yacht Club, Sigma Xi. Republican. Congregationalist. Home: 37 Tower Rd Riverside CT 06878-2514 Office: Broad St Communications LLC 37 Tower Rd Riverside CT 06878-2514

GEISMAR, THOMAS H., graphic designer; b. Glen Ridge, N.J., July 16, 1931; s. Arthur D. and Adeline (Caro) G.; m. Joan Hyams, Nov. 9, 1958; children: Peter, Kathryn, Pamela. BA, Brown U., 1953; MFA, Yale U., 1955; DFA (hon.), Corcoran Sch. of Art, Washington, 1995. Founder Brownjohn, Chermayeff & Geismar, N.Y.C., 1957; founder Chermayeff & Geismar Assos., N.Y.C., 1960; prin. Chermayeff & Geismar Assos., 1960-90; pres. Chermayeff & Geismar Inc., 1991—; prin. Cambridge Seven Assocs. (Architects), 1963-99; founder, partner MetaForm, Inc., N.Y.C., 1980-90; lectr. Chmn. com. signs and symbols Dept. Transp.; mem. council Yale U. Mem. Pres. coun. Carnegie Mellon U., Pitts. Served with U.S. Army, 1955-57. Recipient 1st Internat. Design award, Osaka, Japan, 1983, 1st Presdl. Design award Pres. Reagan, 1985, Yale Arts award, 1985; named to Hall of Fame, N.Y. Art Dirs.' Club, 1998. Mem. Am. Inst. Graphic Arts (Gold medal 1979), Alliance Graphique Internationale, Phi Beta Kappa. Office: Chermayeff & Geismar Inc 15 E 26th St Fl 12 New York NY 10010-1505

GEISSBUHLER, STEPHAN, graphic designer; b. Zofingen, Kanton Aargau, Switzerland, Oct. 21, 1942; came to U.S., 1967; s. Theodor and Ruth (Schneider) G.; m. Elissa Beth Feuerman, June 26, 1983; children by previous marriage: Marc Phillip, Christopher Luke; children: Alexander Charles, Benjamin Adam. M.A., Sch. Design Basel, 1964. Designer J.R. Geigy A.G., Basel, Switzerland, 1964-67; assoc. prof., dept. chmn. Phila. Coll. Art, 1967-73; design cons. Murphy-Levy-Wurman Architects, Phila., 1968-71; designer/assoc. Anspach-Grossman-Portugal, Inc., N.Y.C., 1973-75; assoc. ptnr. Chermayeff & Geismar, Inc., N.Y.C., 1975-79, ptnr., 1979—; mem. Faculty for Improvement of Fed. Graphics, Washington, 1976—; vis. lectr. in field. Served with Swiss Army, 1962-67. Recipient nat. prize for applied art Fed. Govt. Switzerland, 1966, 67, Gold medal N.Y. Art Dirs. Club, 1984; recipient others. Mem. Am. Inst. Graphic Arts (v.p., dir. 1980-83, pres. N.Y. chpt. 1984-86), Am. Ctr. for Design, Group for Environ. Edn., Alliance Graphique Internat. (pres. U.S. membership 1993—), N.Y. Art Dirs. Club. Methodist. Office: Chermayeff & Geismar Inc 15 E 26th St Fl 12 New York NY 10010-1505

GEISSER, PETER JAMES, artist, educator for hearing impaired; b. Providence, Oct. 19, 1945; s. John H. and Helen L. (Callaghan) G.; m. Maura Jane McNamara, May 14, 1972; 1 child, Mary Alicia. BS in Edn., Tufts U., 1969, MFA, 1971; diploma, Sch. Mus. Fine Arts, Boston, 1970, grad. cert., 1971; DFA (hon.), RISD, 1997. Cert. tchr., R.I. Art instr. Mus. Fine Arts, Boston, 1967-73; painting instr. Belvoir Terr. Fine Arts Camp, Lenox, Mass., 1969; art instr. H.S. Scholarship Program, Boston, 1969-70; art coord. Boston Sch. for Deaf, Randolph, Mass., 1970-73; art dir. R.I. Sch. for Deaf, Providence, 1973—; summer lectr. in Rome, Am. Leadership Study Groups, Clarke U., Worcester, Mass., 1971-72; art instr. RISD Continuing Edn., Providence, 1987—; dir. Cir. of Clay project Very Spl. Arts R.I., Pawtucket, 1992-96; spl. needs adv. bd. Mus. Fine Arts, Boston, 1979—; tchr. adv. bd. R.I. Com. on Humanities, 1984—, RISD, Providence, 1989—, Nat. Gallery of Art, Washington, 1991-92; mem. bd. dirs. Perishable Theatre, Providence, 1994-96. Group exhbns. include Cohen Art Ctr., Tufts U., Medford, Mass., 1971, Warwick (R.I.) Mus., 1988, R.I. Sch. Design, 1989, R.I. Tchrs. Assn., 1992, 93, 94, R.I. Art Edn. Assn. 2nd prize, 1996; Circle of Clay ceramic murals Hasbro Children;s Hosp.; commd. stained glass installations include St. Joseph's Rectory/Regina Caeli, Providence, Hasbro Children's Hosp., Providence, St. Mark's Ch., Cranston, R.I., Notre Dame Coll., Manchester, N.H., Roger Williams Park Mus., Providence, Trinity Ch., Concord, Mass., St. Michael's Ch., Providence, Cathedral Sts. Peter and Paul, Providence, other churches, pvt. collections. Named 50th Anniversary scholar Nat. Gallery of Art, Washington, 1991; recipient R.I. State of Arts award R.I. Coun. on Arts, 1992, Humanitarian award Bus. Vols. for Arts/R.I., 1994, 1st prize NAEA Electronic Gallery '97, New Orleans. Mem. Nat. Art Educators Assn., R.I. Art Edn. Assn (exec. bd. 1995—, pres.-elect 1997, pres. 1999), R.I. Forum for Humanities. Home: 19 Philmont Ave Cranston RI 02910-5814 Office: RI Sch for Deaf Corliss Park Providence RI 02903

GEISSINGER, FREDERICK WALLACE, investment banking executive; b. Huntingdon, Pa., Oct. 3, 1945; s. Harry Lloyd and Elizabeth Gertrude (Munkelt) G.; m. Anne Beth Lawrenz, Feb. 14, 1970; children: Amy Elizabeth, Jacqueline Marie. AB, Dartmouth Coll., 1967; MBA, U. Chgo., 1969. Lic. in securities and real estate, N.Y.C. Corp. banking officer Chase Manhattan Bank, N.Y.C., 1969-74, dir. corp. planning, 1974-76; asst. gen. mgr. Chase Manhattan Bank, Tokyo, 1976-80; chief staff Western Hemisphere Chase Manhattan Bank, N.Y.C., 1980-83, budget dir., 1983-86, sr. v.p. real estate, 1986-90; exec. v.p. Daiwa Securities Am. Inc., N.Y.C., 1990-92; prin. Geissinger and Assocs., N.Y.C., 1993; CEO Am. Gen. Land Devel. Inc., Houston, 1994-95, Am. Gen. Mortgage and Land Devel. Inc., 1995; chmn., CEO Am. Gen. Finance, Evansville., Ind., 1995—. Trustee Pelham (N.Y.) Bd. Edn., 1983-86. Mem. Urban Land Inst. (coun. 1986—), Real Estate Bd. N.Y., Pelham Country club (bd. govs. 1987-92, pres. 1990-92). Republican. Presbyterian. Avocations: skiing, golf, tennis, coaching girls soccer, classical music. *None of us is much better than any other. Success comes to those who try their best always. What gives life its value, you can find and lose, but never possess.*

GEIST, JILL MARIE, medical writer; b. Oak Park, Ill., Nov. 11, 1959; d. Raymond and Julia Weiner; children: Samantha Rae, Jacob Lee. Line worker Zenith Microcircuits, Elk Grove, Ill., 1978, inspector, 1978, prodn. screen specialist, 1978-79, group leader screen print, 1979-80, process control inspector, 1980-81, engring. technician, 1981-83; engring. specialist Abbott Labs., Abbott Park, Ill., 1983-89, process devel. engr., 1989-93; new product coord. Abbott Labs., Abbott Park, Ill., 1993-95, med. writer, 1995—. Patentee in field. Pres., co-founder Abbott Parent Network, Abbott Park, Ill., 1989-91, pres. emeritus, 1992. Office: Abbott Labs D-7B4AP6A-2 100 Abbott Park Rd Rm 2 Abbott Park IL 60064-3502

GEIST, KATHE STERNBACH, art history, cinema and English educator, writer; b. Lansing, Mich., Mar. 6, 1948; d. Robert John and Margaret Antoinette Geist; m. Steven Sternbach, Feb. 14, 1991. BA, U. Mich., 1970, PhD, 1981. Prof. Ill. State U., Normal, 1983-88, Koryo Coll., Nagoya, Japan, 1991-93, Bentley Coll., Waltham, Mass., 1993-97; panel chair Soc. for Cinema Studies, New Orleans, 1986, Coll. Art Assn., Houston, 1988; editor Asian Cinema Studies Soc., 1986-88; consumer advocate. Author: Cinema of Wim Wenders, 1988; contbr. chpts. to books and articles to profl. jours. Exec. bd. Friends of the Muddy River, 1997—; chair Open Studios, Brookline Arts Coun., 1997—.

GEISTFELD, RONALD ELWOOD, retired dental educator; b. St. James, Minn., Nov. 9, 1933; s. Victor E. and Viola (Becker) G.; m. Lois N. Tolzman Wilkens, June 15, 1955 (div. June 1974); m. Annette L. Swenson, Jan. 14, 1977; children: Shari, Mark, Steven, Ann, Leah, Erik. AA, Bethany Jr. Coll., 1952; BS, U. Minn., 1954, DDS, 1957. Pvt. practice dentistry Northfield, Minn., 1959-72; clin. asst. prof. dentistry U. Minn. Sch. Dentistry, Mpls., 1969-72, assoc. prof., 1972-82, chmn. dept. operative dentistry, 1978-87, prof., 1982-97, prof. emeritus, 1997; dir. quality programs Pentegra Dental Group, Inc., 1998—; dental cons. Hennepin County Med. Ctr., Mpls., 1975-96, VA Hosp., Mpls., 1977-96, VA Hosp., St. Cloud, Minn., 1978-96, Human Performance and Informatics Inst., Atama, Japan, 1990-95, K-9 Dental Sys. Quidnunc Australia Pty. Ltd., 1994-95, Metro Dental Group, Mpls., 1995—, The Dentists Ins. Co., 1995-99, VGM Expert Systems, 1996-98, Met. Life Ins. Co., 1996—, Pentegra Ltd., 1997—; mem. resource faculty for Bush faculty devel. program on excellence and diversity in teaching U. Minn., 1993-94; bd. dirs. Pentegra Dental Group Inc. Pres. PTA, Northfield, 1965, Arts Guild, Northfield, 1968; bd. dirs., chairperson Rice County Health and Sanitation Bd., Faribault, Minn., 1966-74; bd. dirs. Northfield Bd. Edn., 1969-74; pres. Roseville Luth. Ch., 1987-88. Capt. U.S. Army, 1957-59. Am. Coll. Dentists fellow, 1972; recipient Prof. of Yr. award Century Club, 1996-97. Mem. Am. Dental Assn. (chairperson operative dentistry sect. 1979-80, curriculum cons. 1981-88, grants and spl. projects request evaluator 1988-92, Am. fund for Dental Health, edit. review bd. JADA 1992-96), Minn. Dental Assn. (ethics com. 1969-76, chairperson sci. and ann. sessions com. 1984-86, spkr. house del. 1992-96, del. to ADA 1992-96, bd. dirs. 1992-96), Mpls. Dist. Dental Soc. (program chairperson 1978-79, peer rev. com. 1988-92, bd. dirs. 1979-80, 87-89, MDA del. 1989-92), Minn. Acad. Restorative Dentistry (pres. 1979-80), Minn. Acad. Gnathological Rsch. (pres. 1986-87), Am. Assn. Dental Schs. (chairperson operative dentistry sect. 1984-85, edit. rev. bd. 1984-88), Acad. Operative Dentistry (exec. council 1978-81, rsch. com. 1987-89), Am. Acad. Gold Foil Operators, Northfield C. of C. (treas. and chairperson 1968-70), Delta Sigma Delta, Omicron Kappa Upsilon (Theta chpt.). Lodge: Rotary (pres. Northfield 1972-73). Home: 13964 N Willow Bend Dr Tucson AZ 85737-5829

GEITGEY, DORIS ARLENE, retired nursing educator, dean; b. Monroe, Mich., Nov. 3, 1920; d. Harry and Nellie Love (Richardson) C. B.A., U. Toledo, 1942; diploma, Los Angeles County Gen. Hosp., 1948; M.S., Immaculate Heart Coll., 1951; Ed.D., UCLA, 1966. Asst. prof. nursing San Diego State Coll., 1957-62; specialist nursing edn. UCLA, 1962-66; assoc. prof. U. Wash. Sch. Nursing, 1966-73, assoc. dean, 1970-75, prof., 1973-75; prof., dean U. Kans. Sch. Nursing, 1975-88, prof. emerita, 1988—; cons. teaching and curr. design ADN Programs, Western U.S. and Can., 1960-75. Author: The Art and Science of Nursing, 1954, 59, A Handbook for Head Nurses, 1961; contbr. articles to profl. jours. Helene Fuld Health Trust Fund grantee. Fellow Am. Acad. Nursing (past).

GEITHNER, PAUL HERMAN, JR., banker; b. Phila., June 7, 1930; s. Paul Herman and Henriette Antonine (Schuck) G.; m. Irmgard Hagedorn, Sept. 6, 1956; children: Christina, Amy, Paul. BA cum laude, Amherst Coll., 1952; MBA with distinction, U. Pa., 1957. Sec.-treas. Ellicott Machine Co., Balt., 1964-68; successively v.p., sr. v.p., exec. asst to the chmn., First Va. Banks, Inc., Falls Church, 1968-85, pres., chief adminstrv. officer, 1985-95, also bd. dirs., vice chmn., 1986-95; pres. First Va. Life Ins. Co., 1974-96. Bd. dirs. Fairfax (Va.) Symphony Orch., 1988—, pres., 1991-92; bd. dirs. Va. Coll. Fund, 1987-91; trustee Va. Banker Sch. Bank Mgmt., 1988-92, Bridgewater Coll., 1989—; dir. Ellicott Machine Corp., 1996—. Lt. USNR, 1952-55. Mem. Va. Bankers Assn. (pres. 1992-93). Home: 5406 Colchester Meadow Ln Fairfax VA 22030-5444 Office: 1st Va Banks Inc 6400 Arlington Blvd Falls Church VA 22042-2336

GEJDENSON, SAM, congressman; b. Eschwege, Fed. Republic of Germany, May 20, 1948; children: Mia, Ari. AS, Mitchell Coll., 1968; BA, U. Conn., 1970. Mem. Conn. Ho. of Reps., 1974-78; coal broker, 1978-79; legis. liaison Conn. Office Policy and Mgmt., Hartford, 1979-80; mem. 97th to 106th Congresses from 2d Conn. dist., 1981—. Office: US Ho of Reps 2304 Rayburn Bldg Washington DC 20515-0702*

GEKAS, GEORGE WILLIAM, congressman; b. Harrisburg, Pa., Apr. 14, 1930; m. Evangeline Charas, 1971. B.A., Dickinson Coll., 1952, J.D., 1958. Bar: Pa. 1959. Asst. dist. atty. Dauphin County, Pa., 1960-66; mem. Pa. Ho. of Reps. from 103d dist., Harrisburg, 1966-74, Pa. Senate from 15th dist., Harrisburg, 1977-82, 98th-106th Congresses from 17th Pa. dist., 1983—; mem. judiciary com., chmn. house judiciary subcom. comml. and adminstrv. law. Office: US Ho of Reps 2410 Rayburn Bldg Washington DC 20515-3817

GELARDI, ROBERT CHARLES, trade association executive, consultant; b. Bklyn., Aug. 25, 1940; s. Charles Anthony and Ann Frances (Perrella) G.; m. Cecile Hilary Hyland, Dec. 5, 1970; children: Michael, Diane. Student, MIT, 1958-59; BA with honors and distinction, Wesleyan U., 1962; MA, George Washington U., 1965. Nat. dir. recruitment selection and assignment Job Corps, Washington, 1965-68; sec., treas., dir. adminstrn. Nat. Alliance of Businessmen, Washington, 1968-69; sec., treas. CFO Econ. and Manpower Corp., N.Y.C., 1969-71; exec. asst. to chmn. and pres. Bendix Corp., Southfield, Mich., 1971-73; dir. corp. devel. Bendix Home Systems, Atlanta, 1973, v.p., gen. mgr. sales and mktg., 1974-76; exec. dir. Calorie Control Coun., Atlanta, 1976-94, exec. v.p., 1994-95, pres., 1995—; exec. dir. Infant Formula Coun., Atlanta, 1976-96, pres., 1996—; exec. dir. Healthcare Conv. and Exhibitors, Atlanta, 1986—; exec. v.p. The Kellen Co., Atlanta, 1976-91, pres., 1991—, chmn., pres., 1996—; pres. HQ Svcs., Inc., Atlanta, 1992, chmn., CEO, 1996—. Co-editor: Alternative Sweeteners, 1986; contbr. articles to profl. jours. Recipient Spl. Svc. award U.S. Treasury Dept., Assn. Internat. Students in Econs. Mgmt. Trainership award Lyle & Scott, Ltd. Mem. Am. Soc. Assn. Execs., Internat. Assn. of Assn. Mgmt. Cos. (bd. dirs., v.p.), Aberdeen Cmty. Assn. (treas.). Avocations: reading, travel, tennis. Home: 415 Dogwood Trail Marietta GA 30067-4643 Office: The Kellen Co Ste G500 5775 Peachtree Dunwoody Rd NE Atlanta GA 30342-1542*

GELATT, CHARLES DANIEL, manufacturing company executive; b. La Crosse, Wis., Jan. 4, 1918; s. Philo Madison and Clara (Johnson) G.; m. Jane Leicht, Mar. 6, 1942 (div. 1972); children: Sarah Jane Gelatt Gephart, Charles D., Philip Madison; m. Paula Jo Evans, Aug. 22, 1973 (div. 1978); m. Sue Anne Jimieson, Dec. 11, 1983. BA, MA, U. Wis., 1939. V.p. Gelatt Corp., La Crosse, 1940-52, pres., 1952-95; chmn., 1995—; pres. No. Engraving Corp., Sparta, Wis., 1958-67, chmn., 1967-96, chmn. emeritus, 1996—. Trustee Northwestern Mut. Life Ins. Co., Milw., 1960-88, mem. exec. com., 1961-77; chmn. North Ctrl. Trust Co., La. Crosse, 1989-93; mem. bd. regents U. Wis., 1947-74, pres. bd. regents, 1955-57, v.p., 1964-68, pres., 1968-69; mem. Wis. Coordinating Com. for Higher Edn., 1955-59, 64-69, chmn., 1956; chmn. Assn. Governing Bds. Univs. and Colls., Washington, 1971-72; trustee Carroll Coll., Waukesha, Wis., 1971-79, Viterbo Coll., La. Crosse, 1972—; trustee Gundersen Found., La Crosse, 1973-95. Mem. Phi Beta Kappa. Home: 1326 Cass St La Crosse WI 54601-4854 Office: PO Box 1087 La Crosse WI 54602-1087

GELB, ARTHUR, science association executive, electrical and systems engineer; b. N.Y.C., Sept. 20, 1937; m. Linda Lewis; children: Ronald, Caren, Laurie. BEE, CUNY, 1958; MS in Applied Math., Harvard U., 1959; ScD in Systems Engring., MIT, 1961. Engr. Aviation Gas Turbine div. Westinghouse Electric Corp., Kansas City, Mo., 1956, Am. Dist. Telegraph Co., N.Y.C., 1957-58, Draper Lab., Cambridge, Mass., 1959; dept. mgr. Dynamics Research Corp., Stoneham, Mass., 1961-66; pres., chief exec. officer TASC (The Analytic Sciences Corp.), Reading, Mass., 1966-93, chmn., 1993-94, sr. chmn., 1994; pres. Four Sigma Corp., Woburn, Mass., 1995—; chmn. adv. bd. Ctr. for Tech., Policy and Indsl. Devel., MIT, 1987; mem. MIT Corp., 1996—; mem. Lincoln Lab. Adv. Bd. Co-author: Multiple-Input Describing Fns., 1968, Applied Optimal Estimation, 1974; contbr. articles to profl. jours. Bd. dirs. Massport, Boston, 1977-85; bd. regents Higher Edn., Mass., 1989-90; mem. Higher Edn. Coord. Coun., Mass., 1990-95. Named Outstanding Young Engr. CUNY, 1969. Fellow AIAA, IEEE (bd. editors Control Systems Mag. 1981-91); mem. Mensa. Avocations: music, tennis, golf, microcomputing, math. Office: Four Sigma Corp 61 Holton St Woburn MA 01801-5263

GELB, ARTHUR, newspaper editor; b. N.Y.C., Feb. 3, 1924; s. Daniel and Fanny G.; m. Barbara Stone, June 2, 1946; children: Michael, Peter. BA, NYU, 1946; DHL (hon.), CCNY, 1997. Mem. N.Y. Times, 1944—; reporter, 1947-58; asst. drama critic N.Y. Times, 1958-61, chief cultural corr., 1961-63, culture and met. editor, 1967-76, dep. mng. editor, 1976-86, mng. editor, 1986-89; pres. The N.Y. Times Co. Found., 1990—, N.Y. Times Neediest Cases Fund. Author: (with Barbara Gelb) O'Neill, 1962, (with Dr. Salvatore Cutolo) Bellevue Is My Home, 1956, (with A.M. Rosenthal) One More Victim, 1967; editor: The Pope's Journey to the United States, 1965, The Night the Lights Went Out, 1965, Sophisticated Traveler series, 1986-88, Great Lives of the Twentieth Century, 1989. Trustee Ind. Journalists Found.; mem. adv. bd. NYU Ireland House, Nat. Arts Journalism Fellowship Program, Columbia Journalism Rev., Earth Times; chmn. adv. bd. N.Y. City 100; co-chmn. J. Anthony Lukas Prize Project. Decorated comdr. Order Arts and Letters (France); recipient Pipe Night award Players Club, 1989, Eugene O'Neill Soc. medal, 1995, Eugene O'Neill Found. award, 1996, Leadership award Arthur Ashe Athletic Assn., 1996, Award Cath. Interracial Coun., 1996, NYU Alumni Achievement award, 1997. Mem. Century Club. Office: NY Times Co Found Inc 229 W 43rd St New York NY 10036-3959

GELB, BRUCE STUART, city commissioner, consultant; b. N.Y.C., Feb. 24, 1927; s. Lawrence M. and Joan Friedman (Hewett) G.; m. Lueza Denise Thirkield, June 6, 1953; children: John T., Joan H., Richard E., M. Constance. BA, Yale U., 1950; MBA, Harvard U., 1953. With Clairol Inc., 1950-51, 1959-61, v.p. mktg., 1961-65, exec. v.p., pres., 1965-76; brand mgr. Procter & Gamble, 1953-57; brand mgr. Bristol-Myers Co., N.Y.C., 1957-77, sr. v.p., 1977-85, exec. v. p., 1981-84, pres. consumer products group, 1985-89; dir., vice-chmn. Bristol-Myers Squibb, 1985-88, sr. cons.; dir. USIA, Washington, 1989-91; amb. to Belgium Brussels, 1991-93; N.Y.C. commr. UN Consular Corps and Internat. Bus., N.Y.C., 1994-97. sr. cons. Bristol Myers, 1997. Hon. life trustee Choate Rosemary Hall Sch.; mem. Pres.'s Arts and Humanities Com., 1989-91; trustee John F. Kennedy Ctr. for Performing Arts, 1989-91, Howard U., 1987-89. Office: 150 E 52nd St Fl 12 New York NY 10022-6017

GELB, HAROLD SEYMOUR, industrial company executive, investor; b. N.Y.C., Apr. 26, 1920; s. Daniel and Fanny (Gelb) G.; m. Sylvia M. Miller, Sept. 24, 1942; children: Richard, Alan. BBA, CCNY, 1941. CPA, N.Y. With S.D. Leidesdorf & Co. (CPAs), N.Y.C., 1943-78; mng. partner S.D. Leidesdorf & Co. (CPAs), 1969-78; sr. ptnr. Ernst & Young, N.Y.C., 1978-82; chmn. United Indsl. Corp., N.Y.C., 1995; past vice chmn. Citizens Budget Commn., N.Y.C., now trustee emeritus; past chmn. N.Y. State Bd. Pub. Accountancy; mem. bd. arbitrators Am. Arbitration Assn. Pres. Bronx-Lebanon Hosp. Ctr., 1977; bd. dirs., v.p. S.D. Leidesdorf Found., 1969-80; trustee Accts. Found., 1973-80, Adelphi U., 1997—; bd. overseers Albert Einstein Med. Coll., 1977-79; bd. dirs., sec. Benjamin Cardozo Law Sch., 1977-89; mem. Gov.'s Task Force, Bus. Alliance with Edn., Mayor's Com. on Tax Regulatory Issues, 1981-82. Recipient Disting. Cmty. Svc. award Brandeis U., 1978. Mem. AICPA (coun. 1970-76), N.Y. State Soc. CPAs (past v.p., bd. dirs.), Metropolis Country Club (White Plains), Town Club (Scarsdale), Econ. Club (N.Y.). Home: 181 Fox Meadow Rd Scarsdale NY 10583-2334 Office: 570 Lexington Ave New York NY 10022-6837 also: 570 Lexington Ave New York NY 10022-6837

GELB, JOSEPH DONALD, lawyer; b. Wilkes-Barre, Pa., Dec. 13, 1923; s. Edward and Esther (Fierman) G. m. Anne Mirman, July 3, 1955; children: Adam, Roger. Student, Pa. State Coll., 1943; BS, U. Scranton, 1950; LLB, George Washington U., 1952. Bar: D.C. 1954, Md. 1963, U.S. Supreme Ct. 1972. Adjudicator War Claims Commn., 1952-54; pvt. practice Washington and Md., 1954-69; ptnr. Gelb & Pitsenberger, Washington, 1969-74; prin. Joseph D. Gelb Chartered, Washington, 1974-80, Gelb, Abelson & Siegel, P.C., Washington, 1980-82, Gelb & Siegel, P.C., Washington, 1982-85, Joseph D. Gelb, Chartered, Washington, 1985-93, Gelb & Gelb, P.C., Washington, 1994—. Served with USAAF, 1943-46. Mem. Md. Bar Assn., D.C. Bar Assn., Bethesda Country Club, B'nai B'rith, Masons. Home: 9620 Annlee Ter Bethesda MD 20817-1410 also: 525 N Ocean Blvd Pompano Beach FL 33062-4640 Office: Gelb & Gelb PC 1120 Connecticut Ave NW Washington DC 20036-3902

GELB, JUDITH ANNE, lawyer; b. N.Y.C., Apr. 5, 1935; d. Joseph and Sarah (Stein) G.; m. Howard S. Vogel, June 30, 1962; 1 child, Michael S. B.A., Bklyn. Coll., 1955; J.D., Columbia U., 1958. Bar: N.Y. 1959, U.S. Dist. Ct. (so. dist. and ea. dist.) N.Y. 1960, U.S. Ct. Appeals (2d cir.) 1960, U.S. Ct. Mil. Appeals 1962. Asst. to editor N.Y. Law Jour., N.Y.C., 1958-59; confidential asst. to U.S. atty. ea. dist. N.Y., Bklyn., 1959-61; assoc. Whitman & Ransom, N.Y.C., 1961-70, ptnr., 1971-93; ptnr. Whitman Breed Abbott & Morgan LLP, N.Y.C., 1993—. Mem. ABA (individual rights sect., real property & trust law sect.), Fed. Bar Counsel, N.Y. State Bar Assn. (trusts and estates com.), N.Y. State Dist. Attys. Assn., Assn. of Bar of City of N.Y., Columbia Law Sch. Alumni Assn. (bd. dirs.), Girls, Inc. (resources com.), Princeton Club. Home: 169 E 69th St New York NY 10021-5163 Office: Whitman Breed Abbott & Morgan LLP 200 Park Ave New York NY 10166-0005

GELB, LESLIE HOWARD, organization president, lecturer; b. New Rochelle, N.Y., Mar. 4, 1937; s. Max and Dorothy (Klein) G.; m. Judith Cohen, Aug. 2, 1959; children: Adam, Caroline, Alison. AB magna cum laude in Govt. and cum laude in Philosophy, Tufts U., 1959; MA, Harvard U., 1961, PhD, 1964. Teaching fellow govt. and social scis., non-resident tutor Winthrop House, Harvard U., 1962-64, asso. def. studies program, 1963-64; asst. prof. govt. Wesleyan U., Middletown, Conn., 1964-65; exec. asst. to U.S. Senator Jacob K. Javits, 1966-67; dep. dir. policy planning staff Dept. Def., Washington, 1967-68, dir., 1968, acting dep. asst. sec. def. for policy planning and arms control staff, 1968-69; dir. sec. def. Vietnam task force, 1967-68; sr. fellow Brookings Instn., Washington, 1969-73; corr. N.Y. Times, Washington, 1973-77; dir. bur. politico-mil. affairs Dept. State, Washington, 1977-79; sr. assoc. Carnegie Endowment for Internat. Peace, 1979-81; chmn. Carnegie Endowment Panel on Future U.S. Security and Arms Control, 1980-81; nat. security corr. N.Y. Times, 1981-86, dep. editorial page editor, op-editorial page editor, 1986-90, fgn. affairs columnist, 1991-93; pres. Coun. Fgn. Rels., 1993—; bd. dirs. certain funds advised by Salomon Bros. Asset Mgmt.; bd. dirs. certain registered investment cos. advised by subs. of CIBC Oppenheimer Corp.; mem. The Trilateral Commn. Author: The Irony of Vietnam: The System Worked, 1979, Anglo-American Relations, 1945-49, 1988; co-author: Our Own Worst Enemy: The Unmaking of American Foreign Policy, 1984; contbr. numerous articles to mags.; sr. cons. and producer "The Crisis Game," 1983 (Emmy, DuPont, Hood awards); sr. editor postwar history of U.S. "45/85," 1985. Trustee Tufts U., Carnegie Endowment for Internat. Peace; mem. adv. bd. Sch. Internat. and Pub. Affairs, Columbia U. Recipient Woodrow Wilson award, 1980, Page One award in explanatory journalism, 1985, Nat. Father of Yr. award U.S. Nat. Com. on Fathers and Mothers of Yr. Awards, 1993; mem. N.Y. Times Pulitzer Prize Winning Team, 1985. Fellow Am. Acad. Arts and Scis.; mem. Internat. Inst. Strategic Studies, Council on Fgn. Relations. Home: 150 E 69th St New York NY 10021-5704 Office: Coun on Fgn Rels 58 E 68th St New York NY 10021-5939

GELBAND, CRAIG HARRIS, physiologist, pharmacologist; b. San Clemente, Calif., Aug. 30, 1963; s. Henry and Ellen Brooke (Charin) G.; m. Susan Judith Cataldo, June 2, 1991; children: Jessica Ellen, Hannah Lauren. BS, Duke U., 1985; PhD, U. Miami, Fla., 1990. Predoctoral fellow U. Miami, 1985-90; postdoctoral fellow U. Nev., Reno, 1990-93, rsch. asst. prof., 1993-94; asst. prof. physiology U. Fla., Gainesville, 1994—, asst. prof. pharmacology, 1995—. Mem. editl. bd. Circulation Rsch., 1995—, Am. Jour. Physiology-Heart and Circulatory, 1998—. Recipient 1st Prize award Ea. Student Rsch. Forum, 1989, Young Investigator Rsch. award Summer Conf. Smooth Muscle, 1991, finalist Young Investigator award cardiopulmonary and critical care Am. Heart Assn., Goldblatt award in cardiovascular sci. Am. Heart Assn. Coun. for Hypertension, 1999; Nat. Kidney Found. grantee, 1994-95, NIH F.I.R.S.T. Award grantee, 1996—; NIH predoctoral fellow, 1985-90, Lucille P. Markey Found. fellow, 1988-90, NIH postdoctoral fellow, 1991-94; Tobacco Rsch. Coun. scholar, 1996—. Mem. Am. Physiol. Soc. (Rsch. Career Enhancement award, Shin Chun Wang Young Investigator award 1999), Am. Heart Assn. (Initial Investigatorship 1995-96, grant-in-aid 1997—, Harry Goldblatt award 1999), Biophys. Soc., Soc. for Neurosci. Democrat. Jewish. Office: U Fla Dept Physiology PO Box 100274 Gainesville FL 32610-0274

GELBAND, HENRY, pediatric cardiologist; b. Austria, Aug. 31, 1936; came to U.S., 1941, naturalized, 1951; s. Herman and Charlotte (Rubin) G.; m. Ellen Brooke Charin, Aug. 26, 1962; children—Craig Harris, Mark Evan, Todd David. B.A., Washington (Pa.) and Jefferson Coll., 1958; M.D., Jefferson Med. Coll., Phila., 1962. Intern Beth Israel Hosp., Newark, 1962-63; resident in pediatrics Mt. Sinai Hosp., N.Y.C., 1965-67; fellow in pediatric cardiology Columbia U. Coll. Phys. and Surg., 1967-69, spl. research fellow in pharmacology, 1969-71; mem. faculty U. Miami (Fla.) Med. Sch., 1971—, prof. pediatrics, vice chmn. clin. affairs, 1976—, prof. pharmacology, 1977—; prin. investigator NIH grants, 1976—; vice chair dept. pediatrics U. Miami (Fla.) Med. Sch., 1995—; Vice pres. Ronald McDonald House, South Fla., Miami, 1978—. Co-author: Infant and Child, 1977; contbr. articles to med. jours. Served as officer M.C. USNR, 1963-65. Mem. Am. Physiol. Soc., Soc. Pediatric Research, Am. Soc. Pharmacology and Exptl. Therapeutics, Internat. Study Group Research Cardiac Metabolism, Am. Acad. Pediatrics, Am. Heart Assn., Am. Coll. Cardiology, Internat. Coll. Pediatrics, Am. Coll. Chest Physicians, Fla. Assn. Pediatric Cardiology. Democrat. Jewish. Home: 181 Crandon Blvd Apt 406 Key Biscayne FL 33149-1549 Office: U Miami Med Sch PO Box 16820 Miami FL 33101-6820

GELBARD, ALENE H., demographer, policy analyst; b. Seattle, June 17, 1945; d. William Edmund and Terttu (Eastman) Hanola; m. Robert S. Gelbard, July 27, 1968; 1 child, Alexandra. BA, U. Wash., 1967; PhD, Johns Hopkins U., 1979. Program evaluator Family Planning Orgn. of The Philippines, Manila, 1969-70; rchr. Archdiocese Pôrto Alegre (Brazil), 1971-72; cons. UNESCO, Paris, 1978-79; policy analyst Orgn. for Econ. Cooperation and Devel., Paris, 1980-82; policy analyst/project mgr. Westinghouse Corp., Columbia, Md., 1983-87; sr. policy advisor USAID, Washington, 1988; dir. internat. programs Population Reference Bur., Washington, 1991—; cons. Devel. Assocs., Santo Domingo, Dominican Republic, 1989, Coordination Program for child Survival, La Paz, Bolivia, 1989-91, Rsch. Triangle Inst., 1990-91. Mem. Population Assn. Am., Women's Fgn. Policy Group. Office: Population Reference Bur 1875 Connecticut Ave NW Ste 520 Washington DC 20009-5738

GELBARD, ROBERT SIDNEY, ambassador; b. N.Y.C., Mar. 6, 1944; s. Charles and Ruth (Fisher) G.; m. Alene Marie Hanola, July 27, 1968; 1 child, Alexandra Pauline. AB, Colby Coll., 1964; MPA, Harvard U., 1979; JD (hon.), Villanova U., 1998. Vol. Peace Corps, Bolivia, 1964-66; joined Fgn. Svc., Dept. State, 1967; staff asst. sr. seminar in Fgn. Policy, Fgn. Svc. Fgn. Svcs., Dept. State, 1967-68; assoc. dir. Peace Corps, The Philippines, 1968-70; vice consul U.S. Consulate, Porto Alegre, Brazil, 1970-71, prin. officer, 1971-72; internat. economist Office Devel. Fin., Bur. Econ. and Bus. Affairs, Washington, 1973-75, Office Regional Polit. Econ. Affairs, Bur. European Can. Affairs, Dept. State, Washington, 1976-78; first sec. Am. Embassy, Paris, 1978-82; dep. dir. Office Western European Affairs, Bur. European and Can. Affairs, Washington, 1982-84; dir. Office So. African Affairs, Bur. African Affairs, Washington, 1984-85; dep. asst. sec. Bur. Inter-Am. Affairs, Dept. State, Washington, 1985-88; amb. to Bolivia La Paz, 1988-91; prin. dep. asst. sec. Bur. Inter-Am. Affairs, Dept. State, 1991-93; asst. sec. of state Internat. Narcotics and Law Enforcement Affairs, Washington, 1993-97; special rep. of pres. and sec. state for implementation of Dayton Peace Accords, 1997—. Mem. internat. adv. coun. Mus. Am. Folk Art, N.Y.C., 1989. Mem. Am. Fgn. Svc. Assn. Office: Dept of State Washington DC 20520

GELBART, LARRY, writer, producer; b. Chgo., Feb. 25, 1928; s. Harry and Frieda (Sturner) G.; m. Pat Marshall, Nov. 25, 1956; children: Gary, Paul, Adam, Becky. LittD (hon.), Union Coll., Schnectady, N.Y., 1986; LHD (hon.), Hofstra U., 1999. Writer: for radio series The Eddie Cantor Show, 1946, Maxwell House Coffee Time with Danny Thomas, 1946, Duffy's Tavern, 1946, Command Performance, 1946-47, Jack Carson, 1947-48, The Jack Paar Show, 1949, The Joan Davis Show, 1949, The Bob Hope Show, 1949-52; for ballet, Peter and the Wolf, 1992; for theatre My L.A., 1950, The Conquering Hero, 1960, A Funny Thing Happened on the Way to the Forum, 1962 (Tony award with Burt Shevelove best musical play 1963), Sly Fox, 1976, One, Two, Three, Four, Five, 1988, City of Angels, 1989 (Drama Desk award best book of musical 1989, Tony award best musical, best book of musical 1990, Best New Musical citation N.Y. Drama Critics Circle 1990, Outer Critics Circle award outstanding Broadway musical, contbn. to comedy award 1990, Edgar Allan Poe award best mystery play 1990), Mastergate, 1989 (Outer Critics Circle award contbn. to comedy 1990), (co-author) Jerome Robbins' Broadway, 1989; for films The Notorious Landlady, 1962, The Thrill of It All, 1963, (also co-producer) The Wrong Box, 1966, Not With My Wife You Don't, 1966, The Chastity Belt, 1968, A Fine Pair, 1969, Oh, God, 1977 (Acad. award nomination best screenplay material from another medium 1977, Edgar Allan Poe award, Mystery Writers Am. award, Writers Guild award), Movie, Movie, 1978 (Writers Guild award, Christopher award), Neighbors, 1981, Tootsie, 1982 (Acad. Award nomination best screenplay written directly for screen 1982, L.A. Film Critics award, N.Y. Film Critics award, Nat. Soc. Film Critics award), (also exec. producer) Blame It on Rio, 1984; writer, prodr., co-prodr. TV shows M*A*S*H, 1972-76 (Emmy award nomination outstanding writing comedy 1972, 75, Writers Guild Am. award 1972, 74, Emmy award outstanding comedy series 1973, Emmy award nominations outstanding comedy series 1974, 75, George Foster Peabody award 1975, Humanitas award), Roll Out!, 1973-74, Karen, 1975, United States, 1980, AfterM*A*S*H, 1983-84 (Emmy award nomination outstanding directing comedy series 1983); TV adaptation Mastergate, 1992; writer, exec. prodr. HBO film Barbarians at the Gate, 1993 (Outstanding Made-for-TV-Movie Emmy award, Best Made-for-TV-Motion Picture award The Am. TV Awards, Program of Yr., The TV Critics Assn., Cable Ace award, Writing in a Movie or Miniseries), Weapons of Mass Distraction, 1997; Best Teleplay Awd., PEN Ctr. USA West, writer TV shows The All-Star Revue, 1950-53, The Red Buttons Show, 1952-55, Honestly, Celeste!, 1954, The Patrice Munsel Show, 1954-62, Caesar's Hour, 1955-57 (Emmy award nominations best comedy writing 1955, 56, 57), The Pat Boone Chevy Showroom, 1957-60, The Danny Kaye Show, 1963 (Emmy award nomination outstanding writing comedy or variety show 1963), The Marty Feldman Comedy Machine, 1972: author: Laughing Matters, 1998. Served with AUS, 1945-46. Recipient Emmy award nomination best writing comedy-variety, variety, or music for Barbra Streisand...and Other Musical Instruments, 1973, Lee Strasberg Lifetime Achievement in Arts and Scis. award, 1990. Mem. Dramatists Guild, Writers Guild Am. (award 1972, 74), ASCAP, Writers Guild Gt. Britain, Dirs. Guild Am. Address: 807 N Alpine Dr Beverly Hills CA 90210-2901

GELBEIN, JAY JOEL, accountant; b. Bklyn., Sept. 11, 1949; s. Leo and Sara (Eskolsky) G. B.S., Bklyn. Coll., 1972; M.S. with distinction, L.I. U., 1978; m. Marilyn Stern, Dec. 8, 1974; children—Moshe, Avi, Danielle. Cert. fin. planner. Appellate conferee IRS, N.Y.C., 1971-79; tech. mgr. Am. Inst. C.P.A.s, N.Y.C., 1979-81; pvt. practice acctg. and tax cons., Staten Island, N.Y., 1979—; prof. bus. Kingsborough Community Coll., Bklyn., 1981—; nat. tax lectr. C.P.A., N.Y. Mem. Am. Inst. C.P.A.s, N.Y. State Soc. C.P.A.s (mem. profl. service corp. com.), Inst. Cert. Fin. Planners. Author: Tax-wise Investing for High Income Taxpayers, 1992, 2d. edit., 1993; contbr. to The Practical Accountant, 1991; co-author: Accounting Demonstration Problems Workbook. Home and Office: 13 President St Staten Island NY 10314-4119

GELBER, DON JEFFREY, lawyer; b. L.A., Mar. 10, 1940; s. Oscar and Betty Sheila (Chernitsky) G.; m. Jessica Jeasun Song, May 15, 1967; children: Victoria, Jonathan, Rebecca, Robert. Student UCLA, 1957-58, Reed Coll., 1958-59; AB, Stanford U., 1961, JD, 1963. Bar: Calif. 1964, Hawaii 1964, U.S. Dist. Ct. (cen. and no. dists. Calif.) 1964, U.S. Dist. Ct. Hawaii 1964, U.S. Ct. Appeals (9th cir.) 1964, U.S. Supreme Ct. 1991. Assoc. Greenstein, Yamane & Cowan, Honolulu, 1964-67; reporter Penal Law Revision Project, Hawaii Jud. Council, Honolulu, 1967-69; assoc. H. William Burgess, Honolulu, 1969-72; ptnr. Burgess & Gelber, Honolulu, 1972-73; prin. Law Offices of Don Jeffrey Gelber, Honolulu, 1974-77; pres. Gelber & Wagner, Honolulu, 1978-83, Gelber & Gelber, Honolulu, 1984-89, Gelber, Gelber, Ingersoll, Klevansky & Faris, Honolulu, 1990—; legal counsel Hawaii State Senate Judiciary Com., 1965; adminstrv. asst. to majority floor leader Hawaii State Senate, 1966, legal csl. Edn. Com., 1967, 68; majority counsel Hawaii Ho. of Reps., 1974; spl. counsel Hawaii State Senate, 1983. Contbr. articles to legal publs. Mem. State Bar Calif., ABA (sect. bus. law), Am. Bankruptcy Inst., Hawaii State Bar Assn. (sect. bankruptcy law, bd. dirs. 1991-93, pres. 1993). Clubs: Pacific, Plaza (Honolulu). Office: Gelber Gelber Ingersoll Klevansky & Faris 745 Fort Street Mall Ste 1400 Honolulu HI 96813-3877

GELBER, LOUISE C(ARP), lawyer; m. Milton Gelber (dec.); children: Jack, Bruce, Julie McCoy. BA, JD, U. Calif., 1944. Bar: Calif. 1945, U.S. Dist. Ct. (so. dist.) Calif. 1945, U.S. Supreme Ct. 1965. Pvt. practice; commr. Calif. Bd. Examiners for Nursing Home Adminstrs.; adminstr. Calif. Dept. Consumer Affairs; speaker local drug rehab. hosp.; mem. Vis. Nurses Bd.; commr. Calif. Adv. Cost Control to State Govt.; mem. temporary judge panel L.A. County; settlement officer dispute resolution svc. Pasadena Superior Ct. Mem. editorial staff U. Calif. Law Rev. Calif. nominee for State Assembly, 1992; judge pro tem Rio Hondo Mcpl. Ct.; pro bono Bd. Legal Aid; v.p. local PTA; mem., invocator Arcadia Coord. Coun.; bd. dirs. Foothill Apt. Assn., People-For People; active ARC, Community Chest, United Way, Boy Scouts Am., Girl Scouts U.S. Mem. ABA, Calif. Bar Assn., Foothill Bar Assn., L.A. County Bar ASsn., Pomona Valley Bar Assn., Citrus Bar Assn., Arcadia C. of C. (legis. com.), So. Calif. Women Lawyers (treas.), Pasadena C. of C., Bus. and Profl. Women Lawyers (past state legis. chmn., state legis. adv.), Order of Eastern Star, LWV, Sierra. Home and Office: 1225 Rancho Rd Arcadia CA 91006-2241

GELBKE, CLAUS-KONRAD, nuclear physics educator; b. Celle, Germany, May 31, 1947; came to the U.S., 1976; s. Heinz and Gertraud Gelbke; m. Brigitte Zabeschek, Apr. 6, 1973; children: Susanne, Martin. Diploma für physik, U. Heidelberg, Germany, 1970, doctor rerum naturalium, 1973. Wissenschaftlicher asst. Max-Planck-Inst für Kernphysik, Heidelberg, 1973-76; physicist Lawrence Berkeley (Calif.) Lab., 1976-77; assoc. prof. physics Mich. State U., East Lansing, 1977-81, prof. physics, 1981-87, assoc. dir. nuclear sci. Nat. Superconducting Cyclotron Lab., 1987-90, disting. prof., 1990—, dir. Nat. Superconducting Cyclotron Lab., 1992—; summer visitor Brookhaven Nat. Lab., Upton, N.Y., 1974, U. Washington, Seattle, 1975. Alfred P. Sloan fellow, 1979-83; Scholarship Studienstiftung des Deutschen Volkes, 1971-72; Humboldt Rsch. award U.S. Scis. Fellow Am. Physical Soc. Office: Mich State U Cyclotron Lab S Shaw Ln East Lansing MI 48824

GELBOIN, HARRY VICTOR, biochemistry educator, researcher; b. Chgo., Dec. 21, 1929; s. Herman and Eva (Jurkowsky) G.; m. Marlena Maisels, Apr. 1, 1962; children: Michele Ida, Lisa Rebecca, Sharon Anna, Tamara Rachel. BA in Chemistry, U. Ill., 1951; MS in Chemistry and Oncology, U. Wis., 1956, PhD in Chemistry and Oncology, 1958; PhD (hon.), U. Inonu, Molaty, Turkey. Devel. chemist U.S. Rubber Co., Chgo., 1952-54; rsch. asst. McArdle Meml. Lab. for Cancer Rsch., U. Wis., 1954-58; biochemist lab. cellular pharmacology NIMH, 1958-60, biochemist lab. clin. sci., 1960-61; supervisory biochemist chemistry sect., diagnostic rsch. br. Nat. Cancer Inst., 1962-64, head chemistry sect., carcinogenesis studies br., 1964-66, chief lab. molecular carcinogenesis, div. cancer etiology, 1966—; adj. prof. Georgetown U., 1974-78; vis. prof. Hebrew U., Jerusalem, 1985-86; Keynote speaker Carcinogenesis, Gordon Res. Conf., 1965; Franz Bielschowsky Meml. lectr., Dunedin, New Zealand, 1966; Smith Kline French hon. lectr. U. Fla., 1974, U. Mich., 1976; hon. lectr. Israel Cancer Soc. and U. Tel Aviv, Israel, 1983; Keynote lectr. Internat. Conf. Carcinogenesis, Alghero, Italy, 1986; Nakasone hon. lectr. Japan Found. Promotion Sci., Tokyo, Osako, 1989; keynote speaker U.S. organizer and co-chmn. Princess Takamatsu Cancer Symposium, Tokyo, 1990; plenary lectr. Glinos Found., Athens, 1996; mem. bd. dirs. Internat. Soc. Polycyclic Aromatic Com.; also speaker numerous domestic lectures and in 25 foreign countries. Editor 8 profl. books; assoc. editor Cancer Rsch., 1968-79, 83-87, mem. editl. adv. bd., 1965-67; assoc. editor Biochem. Toxicology, 1984—; mem. editl. bd. Chemico-Biol. Interactions, 1969-75, Archives Biochemistry and Biophysics, 1969-76, Life Scis., 1976, Environ. Health Scis., 1976-78; contbr. and co-contbr. over 420 sci. papers to med. publs.; editor/co-editor 10 books, 3 patents. Recipient Superior Svc. award NIH, 1970, Claude Bernard award U. Montreal, 1970, New Horizons award Radiol. Soc. N.Am., 1970, Merit awards Sr. Sci. Svc. NIH, 1983, 85, EEO award NIH, 1989. Mem. AAAS, Am. Assn. for Cancer Rsch., Am. Cancer Soc. (adv. com. on carcinogenesis, mem. coun. 1975—), Am. Soc. Biol. Chemists, Am. Soc. for Pharmacology and Exptl. Therapeutics, Internat. Soc. for Preventive Oncology, Internat. Soc. for Study Xenobiotics. Achievements include rsch. on molecular mechanism chem. carcinogenesis, enzyme regulation, genetics of metabolism and activation of drugs and environ. agts., toxicology of xenobiotics, biochem. individuality in carcinogenesis and drug metabolism enzymatic (P450) basis for drug activation and toxicity. Office: Nat Insts Health Bethesda MD 20014

GELDER, JOHN WILLIAM, lawyer; b. Buffalo, Aug. 7, 1933; s. Ray Horace and Grace Catherine (Kelly) G.; m. Martha J. Kindleberger, June 12, 1953; William R., Mark S., Cathryn J. Gelder Brooks, Carolyn G. Gelder Bird. B.B.A., U. Mich., 1956, J.D. with distinction, 1959. Bar: Mich. 1960, D.C. 1981, U.S. Supreme Ct. 1982. Assoc. Miller, Canfield, Paddock and Stone, P.L.C., Detroit, 1959-68, mng. ptnr., 1975-81, 90-93, ptnr., 1968-93, prin., 1994—; bd. dirs. Tecumseh Products Co., 1989—. Asst. editor Mich. Law Rev., 1958, 59. Trustee, officer Herrick Found., Detroit, 1989—. Mem. State Bar Mich. (coun. mem. bus. law sect. 1984-90), Order of Coif, Bloomfield Hills Country Club. Home: 30865 River Crossing St Bingham Farms MI 48025 Office: Miller Canfield Paddock & Stone PLC 1400 N Woodward Ave Ste 100 Bloomfield Hills MI 48304-2855

GELEHRTER, THOMAS DAVID, medical and genetics educator, physician; b. Liberec, Czechoslovakia, Mar. 11, 1936; married 1959; 2 children. BA, Oberlin Coll., 1957; MA, U. Oxford, Eng., 1959; MD, Harvard U., 1963. Intern, then asst. resident in internal medicine Mass. Gen. Hosp., Boston, 1963-65; rsch. assoc. in molecular biology NIAMD NIH, Bethesda, Md., 1965-69; fellow in med. genetics U. Wash., 1969-70; asst. prof. human genetics, internal medicine and pediatrics Sch. Medicine Yale U., 1970-73, assoc. prof., 1973-74; assoc. prof. U. Mich., Ann Arbor, 1974-76; prof. internal medicine and human genetics U. Mich., 1976-87, dir. div. med. genetics, 1977-87, chmn. dept. human genetics, prof. human genetics and internal medicine, 1987—; Josiah Macy, Jr. Found. faculty scholar and vis. scientist Imperial Cancer Rsch. Fund Labs., London, 1979-80; vis. fellow Inst. Molecular Medicine; Keeley vis. fellow Wadham Coll., U. Oxford, Wellcome Rsch. Travel grantee, 1995. Mem. editl. bd. Jour. Biol. Chemistry, 1995—. Trustee Oberlin Coll., 1970-75. Rhodes scholar, 1957-59. Fellow AAAS, Am. Coll. Med. Genetics; mem. Am. Soc. Human Genetics (bd. dirs. 1994-96), Am. Soc. Clin. Investigation, Am. Soc. Biochemistry and Molecular Biology, Assn. Am. Physicians. Office: U Mich Med Sch Dept Human Genetics Box 0618 1301 Catherine St Ann Arbor MI 48109-0618

GELFAND, ANDREW, software developer, consultant; b. N.Y.C., Jan. 7, 1947; s. Alex and Shirley (Press) G.; m. Lynne Gelfand; 1 child, Christoph Eli. BA, SUNY, Stony Brook, 1969; MFA, Rochester Inst. Tech., 1974; MS summa cum laude, N.Y. Inst. Tech., 1991. Cert. limited broker rep. Nat. Assn. Securities Dealers. Applications mgr. Scitex Am. Corp., Bedford, Mass., 1982-84; sr. product mgr. Eastman Kodak/Atex Inc., Burlington, Mass., 1984-86; mktg. mgr. Xyvision Inc., Wakefield, Mass., 1986-88; mgr. curriculum devel. Linotype Hell Co., Hauppauge, N.Y., 1988-93; dir. electronic performance support sys. Mellon Bank/Dreyfus Corp., N.Y.C., 1993-95; pres. Stillwater Media, LLC, Northport, N.Y., 1995—; chmn. vocat. tng. subcom. Assn. Graphic Arts, 1992-93. Mem. working com. The Edn. Network, N.Y. chpt., 1990; gen. mgr. Ctr. for the Study of Zen Martial Arts, Newburyport, Mass., 1979; regional support team Werner Erhard & Assocs., N.Y. chpt., 1989; bd. trustees, membership chmn. Newburyport Arts Coun., 1979. Recipient Devel. grant City Redevel. Office, 1979, Ct. of honor N.Y. State Craftsmen Fair, 1976, Outstanding Achievement award Rochester Craftsmen Guild, 1975, graphic design award 55th Ann. Graphic Arts Exhbn., N.Y.C., 1997. Mem. ASTD (mem. nat. exec. com. profl. practice area 1993-95), Nat. Soc. Performance and Instrn., Soc. Applied Learning Tech. (instrnl. design excellence award 1992). Avocations: textile arts, folk guitar, zen sword, multi-media development. Home: 368 Half Hollow Rd Dix Hills NY 11746-5866 Office: Stillwater Media LLC PO Box 789 Northport NY 11768-0789

GELFAND, ISRAEL MOSEEVICH, mathematician, biologist; b. Ukraine, Russia, Sept. 2, 1913; came to U.S., 1990; m. Tanya Alexeevskaya, 1979; children: Sergey, Vladimir, Tanya. DSc, Moscow State U., 1935; doctoral degree (hon.), U. Oxford, Eng. Hon. prof. Oxford U., 1973, Harvard U., 1976, Paris VI-VII, U. Pa., 1990; disting. vis. prof. dept. math. Rutgers U., New Brunswick, N.J., 1990—, prof. emeritus, 1999; chair depts. math. and biology Ctr. for Math., Sci., and Computer Edn., Inst. Discrete Math. and Computer Sci., Rutgers U.; originator Gelfand Outreach Program, 1992. Fellow MacArthur Found., 1994; recipient Wolfe prize Wolfe Found., 1978, Achievements Math and Physics Wigner medal, 1979, Kyoto prize Inamory Found., 1989. Mem. Nat. Acad. Sci., Acad. Sci., Royal Soc. Sweden, Royal Soc. (Eng.), Japan Acad. Sci., Acad. Sci. (Paris). Achievements include development of theory of commutative normed rings; research on various mathematical theories and applications; research in fields of biology and medicine, including development of general principles of organization of control in complex multi-cell systems. Office: Rutgers U Hill Ctr/Busch Campus 110 Frelinghuysen Rd Piscataway NJ 08854-8019*

GELFAND, JANELLE ANN, music critic; b. Oakland, Calif., Jan. 24, 1951; d. David E. and Ruth J. (Ainsworth) Magnuson; m. Michael J. Gelfand, Mar. 24, 1973; children: Rebecca, Karin. BA, Stanford U., 1973; MusM, U. Cin., 1976, PhD, 1999. Rotating instr. U. Cin. Coll. Conservatory Music, 1991-92; classical music critic The Cin. Enquirer, 1993—. Author: (tchr. guides) Cincinnati Symphony Orchestra Children's Concerts, 1986-89; editor Music Rsch. Forum, 1993-94; contbr. articles to profl. jours. Bd. dirs. Friends of Women's Studies, U. Cin., 1997. Recipient Corbett award for grad. rsch. Ohio Fedn. Music Clubs, 1996; named Wyoming Citizen of Yr., City of Wyoming, Ohio, 1993. Mem. Music Critics Assn. N.Am., Soc. Profl. Journalists, Ohio Newspaper Woman's Assn. Office: The Cincinnati Enquirer Cincinnati OH 45202

GELFAND, JEFFREY ALAN, physician, educator; b. N.Y.C., Sept. 13, 1946; s. Michael R. and Doris (Eichmann) G.; m. Janet Vullemier, Aug. 31, 1969; children: Jennifer, Lauren, Melissa. BS, U. Pa., 1967; MD, Tufts U., 1971. Bd. cert. internal medicine, 1976, infectious diseases, 1980, allergy and immunology, 1981. Intern Johns Hopkins Hosp., Balt., 1971-72, resident, 1972-73, chief resident, 1976-77; rsch. fellow NIH, Bethesda, Md., 1973-76; asst. prof. Tufts Univ. Sch. Medicine, Boston, 1977-82, assoc. prof., 1982-90, prof., 1991—; vice chmn. dept. medicine New Eng. Med. Ctr., Boston, 1991, acting chmn., 1994-95, chmn. dept. medicine, physician-in-chief, 1995-98, dr. v.p. rsch. & technology, 1998—; dir. rsch. Tufts U. Sch. Medicine, Boston, 1998—; dean rsch. Tufts U. Sch. Medicine, Boston, 1998—. Contbr. articles to profl. jours. Lt. commdr. USPHS, 1973-76. Office: New Eng Med Ctr 750 Washington St # 480 Boston MA 02111-1526*

GELFAND, LAWRENCE EMERSON, historian, educator; b. Cleve., June 20, 1926; s. Maurice Hirsch and Rachel S. (Shapiro) G.; m. Miriam J. Ifland, June 14, 1953; children: Julia M., Daniel B., Ronald S. BA, Western Res. U., 1949, MA, 1950; PhD, U. Wash., 1958. Asst. prof. history U. Hawaii, 1956-58; acting asst. prof. history U. Wash., 1958-59; asst. prof. history U. Wyo., 1959-62; asst. prof. history U. Iowa, Iowa City, 1962-64, asso. prof., 1964-66, prof., 1966-94, chmn. history dept., 1989-92; prof. emeritus, 1994—; vis. prof. U. Oreg., summer 1966, U. Mont., summer 1970, U. Wash., 1974; Mary Ball Washington prof. Am. History, Univ. Coll., Dublin, Ireland, 1987-88. Author: The Inquiry: American Preparations for Peace 1917-1919, 1963; contbg. editor: The Treaty of Versailles: A Reassessment after 75 Years, 1999; editor: A Diplomat Looks Back (Memoirs of Lewis Einstein), 1968; Essays on the History of American Foreign Relations, 1972; Herbert Hoover: The Great War and Its Aftermath 1914-1923, 1979. Bd. curators State Hist. Soc. Iowa, 1970-72; mem. adv. bd. Nat. Archives for Region VI, 1968-74; chmn. Ctr. for Study Recent History of U.S., Iowa City, 1981-91; mem. rsch. and book prize com. Hoover Presdl. Libr., 1996—. Served with AUS, 1944-46. Decorated Purple Heart; Am. Council Learned Socs. grantee in Korean studies, summer 1951; Rockefeller Found. grantee, 1964-65. Mem. Am. Hist. Assn., Orgn. Am. Historians, Soc. for Historians of Am. Fgn. Relations (v.p. 1981, pres. 1982). Home: 1437 Oakcrest St Iowa City IA 52246-1622

GELFAND, MORRIS ARTHUR, librarian, publisher; b. Bayonne, N.J., June 1, 1908; s. Joseph Samuel and Sadie (Schneider) G.; m. Beatrice Margaret Traube, Feb. 1, 1948; children: James Munn, Lisa Jay. B.S., NYU, 1933, M.A., 1939, Ph.D., 1960; B.S. in Library Service, Columbia U., 1934. Supr. res. reading room Washington Sq. Library, NYU, 1931-37; library asst. Queens Coll. Library, Flushing, N.Y., 1937-41; asst. librarian Queens Coll. Library, 1941-42, librarian, 1946-59, prof. librarian, 1959-70; chmn. dept. library sci. Queens Coll., 1970-76; founder, propr. The Stone House Press, 1978—; pres. Godwin-Ternbach Mus., 1981-85; Fulbright lectr., cons. U. Rangoon, Burma, 1958-59; mem. visitation coms., commn. instns. higher edn. Middle States Assn. Colls. and Secondary Schs., 1949-69, 74-77; cons. AID, Venezuela, 1970; UNESCO libr. expert, Thailand, 1962; vis. prof., libr. cons. U. Delhi, India, 1966; libr. cons. Ford Found., Brazil, 1964, 66, 67, 69; UNESCO cons. Hacettepe (Turkey) U., 1976; pres. Roslyn (N.Y.) chpt. Am. Field Svc., 1964-65; trustee Coun. on Rsch. in Bibliography, Inc., Bryant Libr., Roslyn, Nassau Libr. Sys., N.Y. Met. Reference and Rsch. Libr. Agy., pres. bd. trustees, 1973-79; chmn. chancellor's task force on libraries CUNY, 1979-81. Author: University Libraries for Developing Countries, 1968; editor: N.Y. Library Club Bull., 1940-41, 51-52; contbr. to library publs. Served with U.S. Army, 1942; 2d lt. to maj., A.C. 1942-45; statis. officer, adj. ETO; library officer U.S. Army Forces, 1945-46, Pacific. Mem. AAUP (pres. Queens Coll. 1952-53), ALA (rep. to UN Orgn. 1962-65), Am. Printing History Assn. (pres. 1982-84), Typophiles (pres. 1990-95, pres. emeritus 1996—), Assn. Coll. and Ref. Librs. (chmn. program com., coll. sec. 1949-50), Bibliog. Soc. Am., N.Y. Libr. Club (pres. 1947-48), Steering Com. on Libr. Cooperation in Met. N.Y. (sec. 1949), Sigma Soc. of NYU (pres. 1928), Archons of Colophon Club (N.Y.C.), Grolier Club (N.Y.C.), Century Assn. (N.Y.C.), Rowfant Club (Cleve., hon.), Phi Delta Kappa, Alpha Lambda Phi. Home: 139 E 63rd St # 11D New York NY 10021-7405

GELFAND, NEAL, oil company executive; b. Bronx, N.Y., Nov. 8, 1944; s. Daniel and Faye (Frank) G.; m. Jane Auerbach, Sept. 11, 1982; children: Alexandra, Laura. B.S. in Psychology, CCNY, 1965; M.S. in Indsl. Psychology, Western Mich. U., 1967; Ph.D. in Organizational Psychology, U. Houston, 1972. Ptnr. Hay Assocs., N.Y.C., 1972-80; sr. v.p. human resources Amerada Hess Corp., N.Y.C., 1980—. Mem. APA, N.Y. Acad. Scis. Office: Amerada Hess Corp 1185 Ave Of The Americas New York NY 10036-2601

GELFER, JEFFREY IAN, early childhood education educator; b. Bklyn., June 18, 1952; s. George Ralph and Ruth (Seltzer) G.; m. Peggy Gardner Perkins, Dec. 7, 1980; children: Sacha, Daniel. BA, Wilmington Coll., 1974; MS, U. Oreg., 1975; PhD, Fla. State U., 1981. Reading and learning disability specialist Columbia County Schs., Westport, Oreg., 1975-77; kindergarten tchr. Creative Presch., Tallahassee, 1978-79; asst. prof. SUNY, Fredonia, 1985-87; dir. Easter Seal Soc. of S.W. Fla., Sarasota, 1987-89; assoc. prof. Univ. Nev., Las Vegas, 1989—; vis. asst. prof. U. S. Fla., Tampa, 1981-85; cons. Clark County Sch. Dist., Las Vegas, 1991, Sarasota County Sch. Dist., 1984-85, Fla. State U., Tallahassee, 1979; presenter/participant workshops in field. Contbr. articles to profl. jours. Grantee Health Rehab. Svcs. of State of Fla., 1987, 88, Sarasota County Sch. Dist., 1988, Frank Stanley Beveridge Foun., 1989, Univ. Nev. Las Vegas, 1991. Mem. Assn. Childhood Edn. Internat. (mem. rev. com. 1991—), Nat. Assn. Edn. Young Children, ASCD, Coun. Exceptional Children, Nat. Coalition Campus Child Care, Am. Evaluation Assn., Phi Delta Kappa. Avocations: mountain climbing, piano, film making, jogging, golf. Home: 401 Donner Pass Dr Henderson NV 89014-3401 Office: Univ Nev Las Vegas 4505 S Maryland Pky Las Vegas NV 89154-9900

GELFMAN, ROBERT WILLIAM, lawyer; b. N.Y.C., Jan. 22, 1932; s. Irving and Lillian (Meltzer) G.; m. Phyllis Trustman, Dec. 18, 1955; children: Lisa Jane (Mrs. Gary S. Matthews), Peter Trustman. B.S., U. Pa., 1953; LL.B., Harvard U., 1956. Bar: N.Y. 1956, Mass. 1956. Ptnr. Battle Fowler LLP, N.Y.C.; dir. Graycor, Inc.; trustee Independence Savs. Bank; adj. prof. Columbia U. Grad. Sch. Bus. Adminstrn.; past chmn. bd. dirs. Arrow Lock Corp. Former trustee, v.p. Jewish Bd. Guardians; past chmn. bd. Hawthorne Cedar Knolls Sch., past pres. bd. edn. Served to capt. USAF, 1957-60. Mem. Am. Law Inst., Am. Arbitration Assn., ABA, Assn. of Bar of City of N.Y., N.Y. County Lawyers Assn. Jewish. Clubs: Harvard (N.Y.C.); Metropolis Country (White Plains, N.Y.). Home: 18 West Ln Greenwich CT 06831-2632 Office: Battle Fowler LLP 75 E 55th St New York NY 10022-3205

GELHAUS, ROBERT JOSEPH, lawyer, publisher; b. Missoula, Mont., Oct. 17, 1941; s. Francis Joseph and Bonnie Una (Mundhenk) G. A.B. magna cum laude, Harvard Coll., 1963; LL.B., Stanford U., 1968. Bar: Calif. 1970, U.S. Dist. Ct., U.S. Ct. Appeals 1970. Assoc. firm Howard, Prim, Rice, Nemerovski, Canady & Pollak, San Francisco, 1970-74; sole practice, San Francisco, 1974—; editor in chief Harcourt Brace Jovanovich Legal & Profl. Publs., Inc., 1974-78; pres. Robert J. Gelhaus, A Profl. Corp., 1978—; instr. econs. U. Wash., 1964-65; instr. law Stanford Law Sch., 1968-69; cons. FCC, 1968-69; asst. Calif. Law Revision Commn., 1967-68. Mem. Calif. Bar Assn., Omicron Delta Epsilon, Order Coif. Club: Harvard of San Francisco. Author: (with James C. Oldham) Summary of Labor Law, 11th edit., 1972. Home: 1756 Broadway San Francisco CA 94109-2458

GELINAS, MARC ADRIEN, healthcare administrator; b. Springfield, Mass., Aug. 25, 1947; s. Marcel Joseph and Jeanette G.; m. Mary Lillian Smith, Mar. 3, 1984; 1 child, Alexander Joseph Marcel. BS in Zoology, U. Mass., 1969; Cert. in Phys. Therapy, Duke U. Med. Ctr., 1970; MHA, Duke U., 1978; D (hon.) Hamburgerology, McDonald's Hamburger U., Oak Brook, Il., 1988. Acting dir. patient svcs. div. U. Mass. Health Ctr., Amherst, 1975-76, mgr. clin. support svcs., 1976; adminstr. Health Care Systems, Inc., Durham, N.C., 1978; dir. gen. support svcs. Burlington County Meml. Hosp., Mt. Holly, N.J., 1978-80; v.p. facilities and program devel. Nexus Healthcare Corp., Mt. Holly, 1980-82; adminstr. Burlington Geriatric Ctrs., Inc., Mt. Holly, 1982-84; regional v.p. northeast Vol. Hosps. of Am., Inc., Irving, Tex., 1984-86, v.p. bus. devel., 1986-88; pres., owner LSG Bus. Devel. Group, Colleyville, Tex., 1988-93; v.p. strategic devel. Harris Meth. Health System, Ft. Worth, 1993-95; v.p. product mgmt. Harris Meth. Health Plan, Arlington, Tex., 1995-97; pres. Bus. Directions, Inc., Southlake, Tex., 1997—. Mem. Planning and Zoning Commn., Colleyville, 1987-89; com. mem. Woodland Hills Homeowners Assn., Colleyville, 1986-87; scoutmaster Boy Scouts Am., 1995—, cubmaster pack 575, 1996-97; pres. Parent Tchr. Club, St. Vincent's Sch., 1995-97. 1st lt. U.S. Army, 1970-71; capt. USAR, 1971-76. Fellow Am. Coll. Healthcare Execs.; mem. Am. Hosp. Assn. Democrat. Episcopalian. Avocation: sailing. Office: Business Directions Inc 1710 Egret Ln Southlake TX 76092-5800

GELLER, BRUCE, music publisher, composer; b. Long Beach, Calif., Mar. 13, 1968. Grad. in electronic music composition, U. Calif., Irvine, 1991. Multi-instrumentalist freelance musician, Orange, Calif., 1986-90; prodr., rec. artist AKIBA, Corona, Calif., 1990-97; founder, artist and repertory developer AKIBA Music, Hoffman Estates, Ill., 1990—; freelance artist developer, Orange. Rec. artist Symbiosis, 1995. Active in entertainment and tech. support Cypress (Calif.) Parks Dist., 1995-95; active in entertainment support Corona Parks and Recreation Dept., 1990-93, Am. Diabetes Assn., Irvine, 1995, Am. Recovery Ctr. Charitable Found., Azuza, Calif., 1996. Mem. BMI, Performance Rights Soc. Avocations: composing comtemporary instrumental music, cooking, performing music, software programming. E-mail: akiba@writeme.com. Office: AKIBA Music PO Box 95536 Hoffman Estates IL 60195

GELLER, BUNNY ZELDA, poet, writer, publisher, sculptor, artist; b. N.Y.C., May 21, 1926; d. Herman and Shirley (Shoenfeld) Juster; m. Lester Roy Geller; children: Judy Lynn, Robert Douglas, Sheryl Sue, Wayne Mitchell. Student, UCLA, 1944-46, Fla. Internat. U., 1989-97. invited artist Pegasus Internat. Corp., N.J., 1981-85, Internat. Art Expo., N.Y., 1982-83; invited guest artist Broward County Main Lib., Ft. Lauderdale, Fla., 1988; pres. BZG Enterprises. Author: Bunny Geller Original Poetry, 1995, Destiny, 1995, Choices, 1996, The Monkey and the Parakeet (A Poetic Tale for Children), 1997, Kaleidoscope, 1997, Impressions, 1999, (non-fiction) Bunny Geller Original Sculpture, 1985; one woman shows include Bowery Savings Bank, N.Y.C., 1978, Lynn Kottler Galleries, N.Y.C, 1978, Hollywood (Fla.) Art Mus., 1978-79; group exhbns. include All Broward Exhibit 78, Ft. Lauderdale, Fla., 1978, Old Westbury Hebrew Congregation, Westbury, N.Y., 1978, De Ligny Galleries, Ft. Lauderdale, Fla., 1979, 1983-84, Internat. Treas. Fine Art, Plainview, N.Y., 1978, 79, 80, 81, Artists Equity Assn. Hollywood (Fla.) Art Mus., 1979, Limited Edition Galleries, Bal Harbour, Fla., 1979, Temple Beth-El, Boca Raton, Fla., 1979, Expo 79, Pompano, Fla., 1979, Hilda Rindom Galleries, Hallendale, Fla, 1980, Jockey Club Art Gallery, Miami, 1980, 81, 83, 84, Gallery SO-HO 7, Ltd., Great Neck, N.Y., 1979-80, Exhibition of Fine Art Nassau Mus. of Fine Art Assn., 1985, Gallery at Turnberry, Turnberry Isle, Fla., 1980-81, Galleria Martin, Palm Beach, Fla., 1981, Contextual Fine Arts, Ft. Lauderdale, Fla., 1980-81, Art and Culture Ctr. of Hollywood (Fla.), 1981, Miami Convention Ctr., 1981, Anita Gordon Gallery, Inc., North Miami Beach, 1981, Collier Art Internat., Ltd., Westbury, N.Y., 1981, Tavistock Country Club, Haddonfield, N.J., 1982, Internat. Art Expo, N.Y.C., 1982, 83, Ohio All Arabian Show and Buckeye Sweepstakes, Columbus, 1982, West Elec. Co., Hopewell, N.J., 1982, Devon (Pa.) Arabian Horse Show, 1982, Bondstreet Art Gallery, Pitts., 1982, Blumka II Gallery, N.Y.C., 1982, Korby Gallery, Cedar Grove, N.J., 1982, Washington Internat. Horse Show, Gaithersburg, Md., 1982, Pegasus Internat. Corp., Pennington, N.J., 1981, 82, 83, 84, 85, Patricia Judith Art Gallery, Boca Raton, Fla., 1983-84, Panache Gallery, Ft. Lauderdale, Fla., 1983, The Nelson Rockefeller Collection, Inc., N.Y.C., 1983, Shorr Goodwin Gallery, N.Y.C., 1983, Carrier Found. Auxiliary, Belle Meade, N.J., 1983, First Annual Internat. Wildlife Exposition, Atlantic City, N.J., 1983, Amann Gallery, Inc., Palm Beach, Fla., 1984-85, Robert's One-of-a-Kind, Bal Harbour, Fla., 1984, Hallandale (Fla.) Pub. Lib., 1984-85, Galleria Camhi, Bar Harbor Is., Fla., 1984-85, Tatem Galleries, Ft. Lauderdale, Fla., 1984-85, Westbury (N.Y.) Meml. Lib., 1984, Trenton Country Club, 1984, Designers' Showcase 1985 Cashelmara, Glen Cove, N.Y., 1985, UN Conf., Nairobi, 1985, Hallandale Cultural Ctr., Fla., 1998, others; sculptures on permanent exhbt.; featured in (book) Artists/USA, 1979-80, The Am. Album, Nat. Mus. Women Arts permanent collection, Washington, 1985, Art Expo N.Y. catalogue, 1982, 83, 92, Limited Collectors Edition, 1982, Town and Country mag., 1982, Gold Coast Life mag., 1983, Art in America mag., 1983-84, Sunstorm Arts Mag., 1984; represented in permanent collection Kushi Found.; Wrote words, music to song One World, 1989. Pres. Sisterhood Westbury Hebrew Congregation, Westbury, N.Y., 1967-69; judge Fine Art and Craft Show, Ft. Lauderdale, Fla., 1979-81; art adv. coun. Westbury Meml. Libr., 1990-94. Recipient 1st prize Carrier Found. Aux. 2d Ann. Arts Festival, 1983; named to Internat. Poetry Hall Fame, 1996. Mem. Nat. Mus. Women in the Arts (assoc.), Nat. Libr. Poetry (Editor's Choice award 1995, published in Best Poems of the 90s 1996), Internat. Soc. Poets (disting. mem. 1995, Poet of Merit 1995, semi-finalist symposium 1995, inducted into Internat. Poetry Hall of Fame 1996). Avocations: tennis, all sports, cultural events, national events, art shows. Home: 400 Diplomat Pkwy Apt 711 Hallandale FL 33009-3732

GELLER, ERIC P., lawyer, cinema company executive; b. 1947. BA, Washington U., 1969; JD, Harvard U., 1972. Bar: Mass. 1972. Assoc. Goodwin, Procter & Hoare, 1972-79; v.p., assoc. gen. counsel Gen. Cinema Corp., Chestnut Hill, Mass., 1979-92, sr. v.p., gen. counsel, sec., 1992—. Office: Gen Cinema Theatres Inc 27 Boylston St Chestnut Hill MA 02467-1700*

GELLER, ESTHER (BAILEY GELLER), artist; b. Boston, Oct. 26, 1921; d. Harry and Fannie (Geller) G.; m. Harold Shapero, Sept. 21, 1945; 1 child, Hannah. Diploma, Sch. Boston Mus. Fine Arts, 1943. Tchr. Boston Mus. Sch., 1943, Boris Mirski Sch., 1945-49; art cons. Leonard Morse Hosp., Natick, Mass. One-woman shows at Boris Mirski Art Gallery, Boston, 1945-46, 49, 52, 61, Addison Gallery Am. Art, Children's Art Centre, Andover, Mass., 1953-55, Mayo Gallery, Provincetown, Mass., 1958, Marion (Mass.) Art Centre, 1966, St. Mark's Sch., Southboro, Mass., 1969, Decenter Gallery, Copenhagen, 1969, Regis Coll., Weston, Mass., 1970, Am. Acad. Gallery, Rome, 1971, Newton (Mass.) Libr., 1973, Newton Art Centre, 1978, Artworks of Wayne, Providence, 1979, Stonehill Coll., Easton, Mass., 1986; exhibited in group shows at San Francisco Mus., Va. Mus. Art, Chgo. Art Inst., Worcester Art Mus., U. Ill., Smith Coll., Inst. Contemporary Art, DeCordova Mus., USIA traveling show, USIS circulating exhbn., Far East, Boston Mus., Regis Coll., 1984, Danforth Mus. Art, 1995, Boston Ctr. for Arts, 1997, Firehouse Artists Show, Natiek, 1998, Univ. Place, Cambridge, 1999. Cabot fellow, 1949; Studios Am. Acad. fellow, 1949-50, 70-71, 75; MacDowell Colony-Yaddo fellow, 1945, 67, 69. Mem. Boston Visual Arts Union, Arts Wayland Assn. Home: 9 Russell Cir Natick MA 01760-1223 Studio: 5 Summer St Natick MA 01760-4511

GELLER, JANICE GRACE, nurse; b. Auburn, Ga., Feb. 25, 1938; d. Erby Ralph and Jewell Grace (Maughon) Clack; m. Joseph Jerome Geller, Dec. 23, 1973; 1 child, Elizabeth Joanne. Student, LaGrange Coll., 1955-57; BS in Nursing, Emory U., 1960; MS, Rutgers U., 1962. Nat. cert. group psychotherapist; cert. clin. nurse specialist. Psychiat. staff nurse dept. psychiatry Emory U., Atlanta, 1960; nurse educator Ill. State Psychiat. Inst., Chgo., 1961; clin. specialist in mental retardation nursing Northville, Mich., 1962; faculty Coll. Nursing Rutgers U., Newark, 1962-63, faculty Advanced Program in Psychiat. Nursing, 1964-66; faculty Coll. Nursing U. Mich., Ann Arbor, 1963-64; faculty, Teheran (Iran) Coll. for Women, 1967-69; clin. specialist psychiat. nursing Roosevelt Hosp., N.Y.C., 1969-70; faculty, guest lectr. Columbia U., N.Y.C., 1969-70; supr. Dept. Psychiat. Nursing Mt. Sinai Hosp., N.Y.C., 1970-72; pvt. practice psychotherapy N.Y.C., 1972-77, Ridgewood, N.J., 1977-96; faculty, curriculum coord. in psychiat. nursing William Alanson White Inst. Psychiatry, Psychoanalysis and Psychology, N.Y.C., 1974-84; mem. U.S. del. of Community and Mental Health Nurses to People's Republic of China, 1983. Contbr. articles to profl. jours.; editorial bd. Perspectives in Psychiat. Care, 1971-74, 78-84; author: (with Anita Marie Werner) Instruments for Study of Nurse-Patient Interaction, 1964. Mem. Bergen County Rep. Com., 1989. Recipient 10th Anniversary award Outstanding Clin. Specialist in psychiat.-mental health nursing in N.J., Soc. Cert. Clin. Specialists, 1982; Fed. Govt. grantee as career tchr. in psychiat. nursing, Rutgers U., 1962-63; cert. psychiat. nurse and clin. specialist, N.J., N.Y. Mem. AAAS, ANA (various certs.), N.C. Nurses Assn., Soc. Cert. Clin. Specialists in Psychiat. Nursing (chmn.), Coun. Specialists in Psychiat./Mental Health Nursing, Am. Group Psychotherapy Assn. (cert. group psychotherapist), Am. Assn. Mental Deficiency, World Fedn. Mental Health, Sigma Theta Tau. Address: 307 Chatterson Dr Raleigh NC 27615-3137

GELLER, JEFFREY LAWRENCE, financier; b. N.Y.C., Sept. 23, 1953; s. Jerome Charles Geller and Harriet (Rogers) Blum; m. Karina Musheli, Nov. 22, 1990. BA, Columbia U., 1975, MBA, 1979. Sr. fin. analyst W.R. Grace & Co., N.Y.C., 1979-83, asst. to the pres., 1983; v.p. Bank of Am., N.Y.C., 1984-86; exec. v.p. Union Holdings, Inc., N.Y.C., 1986-91; pres., CEO Geller Ptnrs., Inc., N.Y.C., 1991—, also bd. dirs.; pres. Std. Capital Holdings L.L.C., N.Y.C., 1996—; v.p. Idle Wild Foods, Inc., Liberal, Kans., 1986-91, ZG Holding Corp., N.Y.C., 1986-91, also bd. dirs., Acorn Internat. Ltd., N.Y.C., 1993-94, pres. 1995-96; bd. dirs. Deran Holding Co., Inc., Nicola Corp., Soprigest Corp. Fin. Ltd., The Silverstone Corp. Co-author: President's Private Sector Survey on Cost Control, 1983. Mem. com. Am. Cancer Soc., N.Y.C., 1982-86, Friends of Lenox Hosp., N.Y.C., 1985—, Children's Village, Dobbs Ferry, N.Y., 1985-87, Save Venice, Inc., N.Y.C., 1987—. Mem. Columbia Club, Rockefeller Club, Le Club. Avocations: tennis, riding, skiing. Home: 829 Park Ave New York NY 10021-2846 Office: Std Capital Holdings LLC 12th Flr 430 Park Ave Fl 12 New York NY 10022-3505

GELLER, KENNETH STEVEN, lawyer; b. N.Y.C., Sept. 22, 1947; s. Edward and Sylvia R. (Tannenbaum) G.; m. Judith B. Ratner, Sept. 9, 1990; children: Eric Jonathan, Lisa Beth. BA magna cum laude, CCNY, 1968; JD magna cum laude, Harvard U., 1971. Bar: N.Y. 1972, D.C. 1986, U.S. Dist. Ct. (so. and ea. dists.) N.Y. 1972, U.S. Dist. Ct. D.C. 1991, U.S. Ct. Appeals (2d cir.) 1972, U.S. Ct. Appeals (D.C. cir.) 1974, U.S. Supreme Ct. 1975, U.S. Ct. Appeals (10th cir.) 1976, U.S. Ct. Appeals (6th cir.) 1987, U.S. Ct. Appeals (4th cir.) 1987, U.S. Ct. Appeals (9th cir.) 1988, U.S. Ct. Appeals (5th and 11th cirs.) 1990, U.S. Ct. Appeals (3rd, 7th cirs.) 1991, U.S. Ct. Appeals (Armed Forces) 1995, U.S. Ct. Appeals (8th cir.) 1996. Law clk. U.S. Ct. Appeals (2d cir.) 1971-72; assoc. Nickerson, Kramer, Lowenstein, Nessen & Kamin, N.Y.C., 1972-73; asst. spl. prosecutor Watergate Spl. Prosecution Force, Washington, 1973-75; asst. to solicitor gen. Dept. Justice, Washington, 1975-79, dep. solicitor gen., 1979-86; ptnr. Mayer, Brown & Platt, Washington, 1986—, mng. ptnr., 1995—; mem. adv. bd. State and Local Legal Ctrs, 1986-92; mem. adv. com. on rules U.S. Ct. Appeals for Armed Forces, 1994—. Co-author: (Stern, Gressman, Shapiro & Geller) Supreme Court Practice 7th edit. 1993; contbr. articles to profl. jours. Mem. vis. com. Harvard U. Law Sch.; bd. trustees, chmn. publs. com. Supreme Ct. Hist. Soc. Recipient Younger Fed. Lawyer award Fed. Bar Assn., 1981; Presdl. Disting. Exec. award, 1983. Office: Mayer Brown & Platt 1909 K St NW Washington DC 20006-1101

GELLER, LISA MICHELE, copy editor; b. Freeport, N.Y., June 4, 1957; d. Richard and Annette Theresa (DeGrace) Green; married. BA in Psychology, Adelphi U., 1980. Pers. recruiter, adminstrv. asst. Lloyd Personnel Cons., Great Neck, N.Y., 1979-82; sec./advt. coord. Biomed. Information Systems, Inc., N.Y.C., 1982-83; editorial asst. Scholastic, Inc., N.Y.C., 1983-85; editorial prodn. asst. McGraw-Hill, Inc., N.Y.C., 1985-87; jr. copywriter, proofreader Siebel/Mohr, Inc., N.Y.C., 1987-88; proofreader/copyeditor AC&R Advt., Inc., N.Y.C., 1988-90; copy editor Doubleday Book & Music Clubs, Garden City, N.Y., 1990-91; copy editor, jr. copywriter Lintas: Mktg. Communications, Inc., N.Y.C., 1991-93; proofreader Bates USA, N.Y.C., 1993-94; proofreading supr. Atlantic Records, N.Y.C., 1994-96; freelance copyeditor, proofreader Harman Consumer Group, Woodbury, N.Y., 1996-98. Copyeditor: Bruce Springsteen: The Boss, 1985. Democrat. Jewish. Avocations: tennis, reading, travel, museums, movies.

GELLER, MARGARET JOAN, astrophysicist, educator; b. Ithaca, N.Y., Dec. 8, 1947; d. Seymour and Sarah Geller. AB, U. Calif.-Berkeley, 1970; MA, Princeton U., 1972, PhD, 1975; DScHC Conn. Coll., 1995, DSHC, Gustavus Adolphus Coll., 1997. Rsch. fellow Center for Astrophysics, Cambridge, Mass., 1974-78; rsch. assoc. Harvard Coll. Obs., Cambridge, 1978-80; sr. vis. fellow Inst. of Astronomy, Cambridge, Eng., 1978-82; asst. prof. Harvard U., 1980-83; prof. astronomy Harvard U., 1988—; astrophysicist Smithsonian Astrophys. Obs., Cambridge, 1983—; Goodspeed-Richardo lectr. U. Pa., 1992; Brickwedde disting. lectr. JHU, 1993, Hogg lectr. Royal Astro. Soc. Can., 1993, Bethe lectr. Cornell U., 1996; Hilldale lectr. U. Wis., 1999; orator Harvard U., 1995. Contbr. articles to profl. jours., sci. films. Bd. reviewing editors Sci., 1991—. NSF fellow, 1970-73, MacArthur Found. fellow, 1990-95; recipient Newcomb-Cleve. prize, 1989-90, Klopsteg award Am. Assn. Physics Tchrs., 1996, Libr. Lion, N.Y. Pub. Libr., 1997. Fellow APS, AAAS, Internat. Astron. Union; mem. NAS, Am. Acad. Art and Scis., Am. Astron. Soc. (councillor), Assoc. Univs. Rsch. in Astronomy (dir-at-large), Phi Beta Kappa (senator 1998—). Office: Harvard/Smithsonian Ctr for Astrophysics 60 Garden St Cambridge MA 02138-1516

GELLER, NORMAN HARVEY, music arranger, conductor; b. Pitts., Dec. 30, 1934; s. Jack and Rose (Block) G. Student, John Carroll U., 1953-55, Cleve. Conservatory Music, 1952-53. Music dir., pianist RCA Records, N.Y.C. and Los Angeles; arranger, condr., orchestrator NBC-TV, N.Y.C.; music dir. The Great Radio City Spectacular, Las Vegas, 1995—. Music dir., arranger numerous performers including Lena Horne, 1990-93, Vic Damone 1977-96, Diahann Carroll, 1985-96, Ed Ames, 1967-73, Ed McMahon, 1976-77, John Gary, 1968-69, Phil Ford and Mimi Hines, 1972-77, Joe Williams, 1973, Ethel Merman, 1964, Peter Nero, 1965-66, Paul Lynde, 1976-77, Monty Hall, 1976, Ray Bolger, 1962-63, Kay Armen, 1963-68, Allen and Rossi, Dick Haymes, 1971-72, Rip Taylor, 1972, Susan Anton, 1995—; music dir. Playboy Clubs, 1961-62, Thunderbird Hotel, 1973, Sands Hotel, 1981-82, (TV series) The New Original Amateur Hour, 1992-93. Mem. Nat. Acad. Rec. Arts and Scis. Club: Friars (N.Y.C.).

GELLER, ROBERT JAMES, advertising agency executive; b. N.Y.C., May 5, 1937; s. Jerome and Pearl (Klein) G.; m. Lois Dee Fromkin, June 9, 1968; children: Richard Evan, Stephen Laurence. BS CCNY, 1958. Account exec. Furman, Feiner & Co., N.Y.C., 1958-62; media supr. Interpublic Group of Cos., N.Y.C., 1962-64; asst. media dir. Foote, Cone & Belding, N.Y.C., 1964-69; pres. Adforce Inc., N.Y.C., 1970-92; pres. Robert J. Geller & Assocs., Inc., N.Y.C., 1993—. Contbr. numerous articles to profl. jours. Mem. Assn. Nat. Advertisers (mem. mgmt. policy com. 1980-92, corp. membership com. 1990-92), Am. Advt. Fedn. (bd. dirs. 1988—, mem. corp. membership com. 1989—, plans rev. com. 1990—, asst. sec. 1992—), Advt. Club N.Y.C. Republican. Home: 155 E 76th St New York NY 10021-2810 also: Ocean Rd Bridgehampton NY 11932 Office: Robert J Geller & Assocs Inc 122 E 42nd St Rm 1017 New York NY 10168-1017

GELLER, RONALD GENE, health administrator; b. Peoria, Ill., Jan. 15, 1943; s. Harold H. and Rose G.; m. Lois S. Geller, Sept. 5, 1971; children—Andrea, Steven, Lauren. B.S. in Zoology, U. Wis., 1964, Ph.D. in Physiology, 1969. Spl. research fellow Nat. Heart Inst. NIH, Bethesda, Md., 1969-71, sr. staff fellow Nat. Heart, Lung and Blood Inst., 1971-72, grants assoc., 1972-73, asst. chief, chief hypertension and kidney diseases br. Nat. Heart, Lung and Blood Inst., 1973-78, assoc. dir. extramural and collaborative programs Nat. Eye Inst., 1978-86, acting dir. div. program analysis Office Program Planning and Eval., 1986, dir. div. program analysis, 1987-89, dir. div. extramural affairs Nat. Heart, Lung and Blood Inst., 1989-99; dir. Office of Extramural Programs, Office of Dir., NIH, 1999—; instr. Found. for Advanced Edn. in Sci.; USPHS trainee, 1966-67. Contbr. articles to profl. jours. Wis. Heart Assn. fellow, 1967-69. Mem. Am. Heart Assn. (mem. med. adv. bd. coun. for high blood pressure rsch.), Am. Physiol. Soc. Home: 14960 Dufief Dr North Potomac MD 20878-2593 Office: NIH Rockledge Bldg 2 Rm 6182 Bethesda MD 20892-7911

GELLER, SEYMOUR, retired educator, researcher; b. N.Y.C., Mar. 28, 1921; m. Sarah Levine, Aug. 23, 1942; children: Margaret J., Susan C. BA, Cornell U., 1941, PhD, 1949. Rsch. chemist E.I. du Pont de Nemours Co., Waynesboro, Va., 1950-52; mem. tech. staff Bell Telephone Labs., Murray Hill, N.J., 1952-64; group leader Rockwell Internat. Sci. Ctr., Thousand Oaks, Calif., 1964-71; prof. dept. elec. and computer engring. U. Colo., Boulder, 1971-90, prof. emeritus, 1990—, faculty fellow, 1977-78, 85-86, Croft Rsch. prof. Coll. Engring. and Applied Sci., fall 1980, rsch. lectr., 1985; lectr. Enrico Fermi Internat. Sch. Physics, Varenna on Lake Como, Italy, 1977. Contbr. over 200 papers to profl. publs.; two papers on garnets Citation Classics; holder 7 patents on ferrimagnetic garnets. 1st lt. U.S. Army, 1943-46, PTO. Recipient Creativity award NSF, 1983; duPont postdoctoral fellow Cornell U., 1949-50. Fellow IEEE, Am. Phys. Soc., Mineral. Soc. Am.; mem. Sigma Xi, Phi Kappa Phi. Jewish. Substantial number of discoveries in work on ferrimagnetic garnets; discovery and prediction of superconductivity in non-transition metal compounds with sodium chloride and related type structure; determination of crystal structures of substantial number double-salt halogenide solid electrolytes and structural features which account for conductivity in highly conducting ionic solids. Avocation: Am. Indian artifacts.

GELLER, STEPHEN ARTHUR, pathologist, educator; b. Bklyn., Apr. 26, 1939; s. Sam John and Alice (Podber) G.; m. Kate Eleanor DeJong, June 24, 1962; children: David Phillip, Jennifer Lee. BA, Bklyn. Coll., 1959; MD, Howard U., 1964. Diplomate Am. Bd. Pathology, Nat. Bd. Med. Examiners. Intern Lenox Hill Hosp., N.Y.C., 1964-65; resident in pathology Mt. Sinai Hosp., N.Y.C., 1965-69; chief lab. Naval Hosp., Beaufort, S.C., 1969-71; asst. prof. pathology Mt. Sinai Med. Ctr., N.Y.C., 1971-75, assoc. prof., 1975-78, prof., 1978-84; chmn. dept. pathology Cedars-Sinai Med. Ctr., L.A., 1984—; prof. pathology UCLA, 1984—. Co-author: Histopathology, 1989; contbr. articles to profl. jours. Recipient Excellence in Teaching award CUNY, 1974. Fellow Coll. Am. Pathologists, Am. Soc. Clin. Pathologists; mem. Am. Assn. Study of Liver Diseases, Hans Popper Hepatopathology Soc., Calif. Soc. Pathologists (sec. 1989-91, v.p. 1991-93, pres. 1994-96), L.A. Soc. Pathologists (v.p. 1989-91, pres. 1992), N.Y. Pathol. Soc., Alpha Omega Alpha. Democrat. Jewish. Avocations: music, writing fiction. Office: Cedars-Sinai Med Ctr 8700 Beverly Blvd Los Angeles CA 90048-1865

GELLERT, EDWARD BRADFORD, advertising agency executive; b. Meadowbrook, Pa., Sept. 8, 1924; s. N. Henry and Edna Louise (Smith) G.; m. Audrey Marie Bethilde Freese, Dec. 18, 1948; children: Audrey M.F. Gellert Taylor, E. Bradford III, Christina M.H.E. BA, Yale U., 1945, PBK, 1946-48; student Law, NYU, 1950-51, Advt. studies, 1950-51; French, Berlitz Sch., 1967; student, Inst. Fin., N.Y.C., 1972; student creative writing course, U. Conn., real estate broker's lic., 1971. From trainee to new product mgr. Vick Chem. Co., N.Y.C., 1948-55; account exec. Compton Advt., N.Y.C., 1956=60; v.p., acct supr. Young and Rubican Advt. Agy., N.Y.C., 1960-67; pres. Gellert & Jackson Acquisitons and Mergers, N.Y.C., 1969-74; sales and mktg. dir. The Gellert Co., Boise, Idaho, 1975-79; pres., owner CIPRA Advt., Boise, 1979—; bd. dirs. Healthwise, Boise, Idaho, 1993—. Author, illustrator, publisher: You're Not Too Old to Win at Tennis, 1984 (1988 selected by U.S. Dept. Info. 1 of 200 Sports Books for exhibit in 100 internat. cities). 2d lt. Army Air Corps, 1943-45. Harvard Club award, 1941; Bronze award Am. Legion, 1939. Mem. Boise C. of C., Nat. Fedn. Ind. Bus., Nat. Eagle Scout Assn. (life), U.S. Tennis Assn. (life), Yale Club N.Y.C., Boise Racquet and Swim Club. Republican. Episcopalian. Avocations: tennis, creative writing, art, yard work. Home and Office: Cipra Advt 314 E Curling Dr Boise ID 83702

GELLERT, EDWARD BRADFORD, III, architect, consultant; b. Norwalk, Conn., Aug. 19, 1954; s. Edward Bradford and Audrey Marie (Freese) G.; m. Juliet Pendleton Kostritsky, Dec. 21, 1980. B.A., Yale U., 1976; M.Arch., Columbia U., 1979; cert. Real Estate Inst., NYU, 1983, Nat. Council Archtl. Registration Bds. Registered architect, N.Y. Research asst. Regional Plan Assn., N.Y.C., 1977-78; architect Urban Devel. Authority, Colombo, Sri Lanka, 1979-80, Mullen Palandrani, N.Y.C., 1980-81, Cossutta & Assocs., N.Y.C., 1981-83; project architect Smotrich & Platt, N.Y.C., 1983-84, Teare Herman Gibans, Inc., Cleve., 1984-85, Dalton, Dalton, Newport/URS, Cleve., 1985—. Prin. works include Keuffner residence, Darien, Conn., 1982-83. Contbg. author: Cousteau Almanac of the Environment, 1981. Columbia U. Grad. Sch. Architecture and Planning William Kinne Fellows fellow, 1979; recipient 2d prize for fiction Atlantic Monthly, 1972. Mem. AIA (energy com. hist. preservation com.), Nat. Trust for Hist. Preservation. Democrat. Episcopalian. Club: Yale (N.Y.C.). Home: 3330 Maynard Rd Cleveland OH 44122-3436 Office: URS/Dalton 3605 Warrensville Center Rd Shaker Heights OH 44122

GELLERT, GEORGE GEZA, food importing company executive; b. N.Y.C., Apr. 15, 1938; s. Imre and Martha (Tessler) G.; m. Barbara Rubin, July 21, 1963; children—Andrew, Amy, Thomas. B.S., Cornell U., 1960, M.B.A., 1962, LL.B., 1963. Bar: N.Y. State bar 1963. Atty. SEC, Washington, 1963-64; v.p., exec. v.p., pres. Atalanta Corp., N.Y.C., 1966—; chmn. bd. Atalanta Corp., 1978—; chmn. U.S.-Rumanian Econ. Council; bd. dirs. Am. Importers Meat Products Group:. Trustee Cornell U., 1995—, mem. Cornell U. Council. Served to 1st lt. Office Staff Judge AUS, 1964-66. Decorated Army Commendation medal. Mem. Am. Importers Assn. (dir., exec. com. meat product group), Am. Assn. Exporters and Importers (bd. dirs.), Met. Pres.'s Orgn. Home: 625 Briarwood Ct Oradell NJ 07649-1207 Office: Atalanta Corp Atalanta Pla Elizabeth NJ 07206

GELLERT, MARTIN FRANK, biochemist; b. Prague, Czechoslovakia, June 5, 1929; s. Oswald Rudolf and Grete (Petschek) G.; m. Leslie Morgan, 1955 (dec. 1971); m. Barbara Smith, Oct. 4, 1974. A.B., Harvard U., 1950; Ph.D., Columbia U., 1956. Asst. prof. Dartmouth Med. Sch., N.H., 1958-59; research chemist NIMH, NIH, Bethesda, Md., 1959-62, NIAMD, NIH, Bethesda, Md., 1962-69; chief sect. on metabolic enzymes, Lab. Molecular Biology Nat. Inst. Diabetes, Digestive and Kidney Diseases, NIH, Bethesda, Md., 1969—. Mem. editorial bds. Jour. Biol. Chemistry, 1976-81, Jour. Molecular Biology, 1979-84, Ann. Rev. Biochemistry, 1990, Biochemistry, 1991—, Nucleic Acids Rsch., 1992—. Recipient Richard Lounsbery award Nat. Acad. Sci., 1985. Fellow Am. Acad. Arts and Scis.; mem. AAAS, Am. Soc. Biochemistry and Molecular Biology (pres. 1993-94), Nat. Acad. Sci. Office: NIH Inst Diabetes Digestive and Kidney Diseases Lab Molecular Biology Bethesda MD 20892

GELLERT, MICHAEL ERWIN, investment banker; b. Prague, Czechoslovakia, June 15, 1931; s. Oswald Rudolf and Grete (Petschek) G.; m. Mary Crombie, Jan. 11, 1969; children: John Matthew, Catherine Ann. BA, Harvard U., 1953; MBA, U. Pa., 1955. Exec. dir. Drexel Burnham Lambert and predecessor cos., N.Y.C., 1958-89; gen. ptnr. Windcrest Ptnrs., N.Y.C., 1967—; bd. dirs. Bristol Capital Ltd., Brit., V.i., Devon Corp., Oklahoma City, Humana Inc., Louisville, Premier Parks Inc., Oklahoma City, Smith Barney Worldwide Funds Inc., N.Y.C., Syncsort Inc., Woodcliff Lake, N.J., NAD Electronics, Copenhagen, SCF Corp., N.Y.C.; mem. Putnam Trust adv. bd. to Bank of N.Y.; bd. dirs. Seacor Smit, Inc., N.Y.C. Chmn. bd. trustees Caramoor Ctr. for Mus. and Arts, Katonah, N.Y.; vice chmn. bd. trustees, chmn. devel. com. New Sch. for Social Rsch., N.Y.C.; trustee Carnegie Instn. Washington, Greenwich (Conn.) Hosp. With U.S. Army, 1955-57. Mem. Burning Tree Country Club (Greenwich, Conn.), Harvard Club (N.Y.C.), Penn Club (N.Y.C.), The Field Club (Greenwich). Office: Windcrest Ptnrs 122 E 42nd St New York NY 10168-0002

GELLES, RICHARD JAMES, sociology and psychology educator; b. Newton, Mass., July 7, 1946; s. Sidney S. and Clara (Goldberg) G.; m. Judy S. Isacoff, July 4, 1971; children: Jason Charles, David Philip. AB, Bates Coll., 1968; MA, U. Rochester, 1971; PhD, U. N.H., 1973. Asst. prof. sociology U. R.I., Kingston, 1973-76, assoc. prof., 1976-81, prof., 1982-98, dean Coll. Arts and Scis., 1984-90; Joanne and Raymond Welsh chair child welfare/family violence Sch. of Social Work, U. Pa., 1998—; cons. Children's Hosp. Med. Ctr., Boston, 1973—; lectr. Harvard Med. Sch., Boston, 1979-88, 95—; rsch. dir. Louis Harris and Assocs., N.Y.C., 1981-82, cons., 1982-86; cons. Sage Pubs., Newbury Park, Calif., 1986—. Author: (books) The Violent Home, 1974, Family Violence, 1979; co-author: Behind Closed Doors: Violence in the American Family, 1980, Intimate Violence, 1988, The Book of David, 1996. Mem. Am. Sociol. Assn. (chair family sect. 1985-86, recipient Disting. Contributions to Teaching award Sect. on Undergrad. Edn. 1979), Nat. Council Family Relations (chair rsch. and theory sect. 1989-91, v.p. publs. 1996-98). Jewish. Avocations: tennis, golf. Office: Sch of Social Work U Pa 3701 Locust Walk Philadelphia PA 19104-6214

GELLHORN, ALFRED, physician, educator; b. St. Louis, June 4, 1913; s. George and Edna (Fischel) G.; m. Olga Frederick, Aug. 4, 1939; children—Martha, Anne, Christina, Maria, Edna. Student, Amherst Coll., 1930-32, DSc (hon.), 1969; MD, Washington U., St. Louis, 1937; DSc (hon.), CCNY, 1979, SUNY, 1984, Albany Med. Coll., 1986, U. Pa., 1992. Diplomate Am. Bd. Internal Medicine. Gen. surg. tng. Barnes Hosp., St. Louis, 1937-39; gynecology trainee Passavant Meml. Hosp., Chgo., 1939-40; fellow Carnegie Instn. of Washington, Balt., 1940-43; instr., later asst. prof. physiology Coll. Physicians and Surgeons, Columbia U., N.Y.C., 1943-45, asst., then assoc. prof. pharmacology, 1945-48, assoc. prof. clin. cancer research dept. medicine, 1948-52, assoc. prof. medicine, 1952-58, prof. medicine, 1958-68; prof. medicine and pharmacology, dean Sch. Medicine, also dir. Med. Ctr. U. Pa., Phila., 1968-73; dir. Ctr. Biomed. Edn., City Coll., v.p. for health affairs CUNY, 1974-79, emeritus, 1979—; dir. med. affairs N.Y. State Dept. Health, Albany, 1983-96; rsch. dir., cons. diamond fund fell. prgm. Aaron Diamond Post Doctoral Rsch. Fell. Prgm., 1996—; sr. cons. Commonwealth Fund, N.Y., 1979-80, Aaron Diamond Found., 1987—; vis. prof. Harvard Sch. Pub. Health, 1980-83; physician Francis Delafield Hosp., N.Y.C., 1949-52, chief med. service, 1952-68; vis. prof. medicine Albert Einstein Med. Sch.; dir. Inst. Cancer Research, Columbia; bd. regents Nat. Library Medicine. Mem. ACP, Coll. Physicians Phila., Soc. for Clin. Investigation, Assn. Am. Physicians, N.Y. County Med. Soc., Am. Assn. Cancer Research (pres. 1962-63), Am. Soc. Pharm. and Exptl. Therapeutics, Inst. Medicine, Am. Soc. Biol. Chemistry. Office: 11 W 81st St New York NY 10024-6021

GELLHORN, ERNEST ALBERT EUGENE, lawyer; b. Oak Park, Ill., Mar. 30, 1935; s. Ernst and Hilde Betty (Obermeier) G.; m. Jaquelin Ann Silker, Feb. 1, 1958; children: Thomas Ernest, Ann Lois. BA cum laude, U. Minn., 1956, LLB magna cum laude, 1962. Bar: Ohio 1962, Va. 1975, Ariz. 1976, D.C. 1986, Calif. 1990. Assoc. Jones, Day, Reavis & Pogue, Cleve., Washington, L.A., 1962-66; prof. law Duke U. Law Sch., 1966-70, U. Va. Law Sch., 1970-75; dean Coll. Law, Ariz. State U., Tempe, 1975-78, Law Sch., U. Wash., Seattle, 1978-79; T. Munford Boyd prof. U. Va. Law Sch., Charlottesville, 1979-82; dean, Galen J. Roush prof. Case Western Res. U. Sch. Law, Cleve., 1982-86; ptnr. Jones, Day, Reavis & Pogue, L.A., Washington, 1986-94; George Mason U. Found. Prof. Law, 1995—; sr. counsel Commn. CIA Activities Within U.S., 1975. Co-author: Antitrust Law and Economics, 4th edit., 1994, Administrative Law and Process, 4th edit., 1997, The Administrative Process, 4th edit., 1993. Lt. USNR, 1956-59. Mem. ABA, Ariz. Bar Assn., Va. Bar Assn., Ohio Bar Assn., D.C. Bar Assn., Calif. Bar Assn., Phi Beta Kappa, Order of Coif. Home: 2907 Normanstone Ln NW Washington DC 20008-2725

GELLIN, GERALD ALAN, dermatologist; b. Bklyn., May 24, 1934; m. Lucille E. Gellin. AB, U. Pa., 1954; MD, NYU, 1958. Diplomate Am. Bd. Dermatology. Chief sect. dermatology VA Hosp., Bklyn., 1964-67; clin. prof. U. Calif. Med. Ctr., San Francisco, 1969—; chief dermatology divsn. VA Hosp., Bklyn., 1963-67, San Francisco Gen. Hosp., 1969-73, Calif. Pacific Med. Ctr., 1986—. Contbr. articles to profl. jours. With USPHS, 1967-69. Fellow ACP. Office: 3838 California St San Francisco CA 94118-1522

GELLIS, SYDNEY SAUL, physician; b. Claremont, N.H., Mar. 6, 1914; s. Morris Aaron and Minnie (Bernstein) G.; m. Matilda Lichter, March 6, 1939; children: Beth Louise Gellis Crocker, Stephen E. AB magna cum laude, Harvard U., 1934; MD, Harvard Med. Sch., 1938. Diplomate Am. Acad. Pediatrics. Resident in pediatrics Yale-New Haven Hosp., 1938-39, Children's Hosp., Cin., 1939-41; chief resident in pediatrics Johns Hopkins Hosp., Balt., 1941-42; captain armed forces epidemiol. bd. M.C., epidemiology bd. U.S. Army, ETO, 1942-46; asst. prof. pediatrics Harvard Med. Sch., Boston, 1946-55; chief outpatient and emergency Children's Hosp., Boston, 1946-53; prof., chmn. pediatrics Boston U. Med. Sch., 1955-65, dean, 1963-65; pediatrician-in-chief Boston City Hosp., 1955-65; prof., chmn. dept. pediatrics Tufts U. Med. Sch., Boston, 1965-83; prof. pediatrics New Eng. Med. Ctr., Boston, 1965—, pediatrician-in-chief, 1965-83. Editor: Yearbook of Pediatrics, 1952-85, Pediatric Notes, 1977—; contbr. articles to profl. jours. Fellow Am. Acad. Pediatrics (Jacobi award 1978, lifetime Med. Edn. award, 1993); mem. Am. Pediatric Soc. (John Howland medal award 1994), Pediatric Rsch. Soc. (sec.-treas. 1946-52, pres. 1972); corr. mem. Acad. Pediatrics (France), New Zealand Pediatric Soc. Home: 77 Alderwood Rd Newton MA 02459-1226 Office: Tufts-New England Med Ctr 750 Washington St Boston MA 02111-1526

GELLMAN, GLORIA GAE SEEBURGER SCHICK, marketing professional; b. La Grange, Ill., Oct. 5, 1947; d. Robert Fred and Gloria Virginia (McQuiston) Seeburger; m. Peter Slate Schick, Sept. 25, 1978 (dec. 1980); 2 children; m. Irwin Frederick, Gellman, Sept. 9, 1989; 3 children. BA magna cum laude, Purdue U., 1969; student, Lee Strasberg Actors Studio; postgrad., UCLA, U. Calif.-Irvine. Mem. mktg. staff Seemac, Inc. (formerly R.F. Seeburger Co.); v.p. V.I.P. Properties, Inc., Newport Beach, Calif.; pres. Glamglo Prodns.; host radio show Orange County Art Bytes, Sneak Previews from the Orange County Performing Arts Ctr. Profl. actress, singer, artist, writer; television and radio talk show hostess, Indpls., late 1960s; performer radio and television commls., 1960s—. Mem. Orange County Philharm. Soc., bd. dirs. women's com.; mem. Orange County Master Chorale, Orange County Performing Arts Ctr., v.p., treas. Crescendo chpt. OCPAC Ctr. Stars, 1st v.p. membership; bd. dirs. Newport Harbor (Calif.) Art Mus., v.p. membership, mem. acquisition coun.; bd. dirs., mem. founders soc. Opera Pacific, mem. exec. com. bd. dirs.; patron Big Bros./Big Sisters Starlight Found.; mem. Visionaries Newport Harbor Mus., Designing Women of Art Inst. Soc. Calif.; pres. Opera Pacific Guild Alliance; immediate past pres. Spyglass Hill Philharm. Com.; v.p. Pacific Symphony Orch. League, chair endowment sect., spl. events chair; bd. dirs. Pacific Symphony Orch.; mem. Calif. State Libr. Found. Bd., U. Calif. Irvine Found. Bd., mem. devel. com., honors com., pub. affairs and advocacy com.; mem. social scis. dean's adv. coun. U. Calif., Irvine; chmn. adv. coun. Cold War Studies Ctr., Chapman U.; chmn. numerous small and large fundraisers; mem. com. Red Cross; bd. dirs. Pacific Symphony Orch.; mem. Fashionables of Chapman U. Recipient Lauds and Laurels award U. Calif., Irvine, 1994, Gellman Courtyard Sculpture honoring contbn. to Sch. of Humanities, U. Calif., Irvine. Mem. AAUW, AFTRA, SAG, Internat. Platform Assn., Actors Equity, U. Calif.-Irvine Chancellor's Club, U. Calif.-Irvine Humanities Assocs. (founder, pres., bd. dirs.), Mensa, Orange County Mental Health Assn., Balboa Bay Club, U. Club, Club 39, Islanders, Covergirls, Pacific Symphony Supper Club (founder), Alpha Lambda Delta, Delta Rho Kappa. Republican. Home: PO Box 1993 Newport Beach CA 92659-0993

GELLMAN, ISAIAH, environmental consultant; b. Akron, Ohio, Feb. 19, 1928; s. Meyer and Pearl (Milker) F.; m. Lola Malkis, Dec. 27, 1947; children: Paula, Judith. B in Chem. Engring., CCNY, 1947; MS, Rutgers U., 1950, PhD, 1952. Rsch. assoc. Rutgers U., 1948-52; process engr. Abbott Labs., 1952-56; with Nat. Coun. Paper Industry for Air and Stream Improvement Inc., N.Y.C., 1956—, tech. dir., 1969-77, exec. v.p., 1977-87, pres., 1987-95; environ. cons. Gellman Assocs., N.Y.C., 1995—; lectr. Johns Hopkins U., 1961-65. NIH fellow, 1948-52. Fellow TAPPI; mem. Sigma Xi.

GELLMAN, YALE H., lawyer; b. Yonkers, N.Y., Sept. 16, 1934; s. Abraham and Ray (Goldstein) G.; m. Estelle Sheila Klittnick, Aug. 23, 1964; children: Douglas Zane, Russell Marc, Beth Margot. BA, NYU, 1954; JD, Harvard U., 1957. Bar: N.Y. 1958, Fla. 1978, D.C. 1980. Assoc. Hall, Casey, Dickler, Howley & Brady, Inst. for Bus. Planning, N.Y.C., 1958-61, Marshall, Bratter, Greene, Allison & Tucker, N.Y.C., 1961-62, Dreyer & Traub, N.Y.C., 1962-65; assoc. Proskauer, Rose, Goetz & Mendelsohn, N.Y.C., 1965-71, ptnr., 1971-93; lectr. Practicing Law Inst. Mem. ABA, Internat. Bar Assn. (vice chmn. real property com. 1989-92), N.Y. State Bar Assn. (lectr.), Assn. of Bar of City of N.Y., Nassau County Bar Assn. Home: 131 Schenck Ave Great Neck NY 11021-3818 Office: 98 Cuttermill Rd Great Neck NY 11021-3006*

GELL-MANN, MURRAY, theoretical physicist, educator; b. N.Y.C., Sept. 15, 1929; s. Arthur and Pauline (Reichstein) Gell-M.; m. J. Margaret Dow, Apr. 19, 1955 (dec. 1981); children: Elizabeth, Nicholas; m. Marcia Southwick, June 20, 1992; 1 stepson, Nicholas Levis. BS, Yale U., 1948; PhD, Mass. Inst. Tech., 1951; ScD (hon.), Yale U., 1959, U. Chgo., 1967, U. Ill., 1968, Wesleyan U., 1968, U. Turin, Italy, 1969, U. Utah, 1970, Columbia U., 1977, Cambridge U., 1980; D (hon.), Oxford (Eng.) U., 1992. Mem. Inst. for Advanced Study, 1951, 55, 67-68; instr. U. Chgo., 1952-53, asst. prof., 1953-54, assoc. prof., 1954; assoc. prof. Calif. Inst. Tech., Pasadena, 1955-56; prof. Calif. Inst. Tech., 1956-67, R.A. Millikan prof. physics, 1967-93, R.A. Millikan prof. emeritus, 1993—; 1993—; disting. fellow Santa Fe Inst., 1993—, co-chmn. sci. bd.; vis. prof. MIT, spring 1963, CERN, Geneva, 1971-72, 79-80; mem. Pres.'s Sci. Adv. Com., 1969-72, Pres.'s Adv. Com. on Sci. and Tech., 1994—; mem. sci. and grants com., Leakey Found., 1977-80; chmn. bd. trustees Aspen Ctr. for Physics, 1973-79; founding trustee Santa Fe Inst., 1982, chmn. bd. trustees, 1982-85, co-chmn. sci. bd. 1985—. Author: (with Y. Ne'eman) Eightfold Way. Citizen regent Smithsonian Instn., 1974-88; bd. dirs. J.D. and C.T. MacArthur Found., 1979—. NSF post doctoral fellow, vis. prof. Coll. de France and U. Paris, 1959-60; recipient Dannie Heineman prize Am. Phys. Soc., 1959; E.O. Lawrence Meml. award AEC, 1966; Overseas fellow Churchill Coll., Cambridge, Eng., 1966; Franklin medal, 1967; Carty medal Nat. Acad. Scis., 1968; Research Corp. award, 1969; named to UN Environ. Program Roll of Honor for Environ. Achievement, 1988; Nobel prize in physics, 1969. Fellow Am. Phys. Soc.; mem. NAS, Royal Soc. (fgn.), Am. Acad. Arts and Scis. (v.p., chmn. Western ctr. 1970-76), Council on Fgn. Relations, French Phys. Soc. (hon.). Clubs: Cosmos (Washington); Century Assn., Explorers (N.Y.C.); Athenaeum (Pasadena). Address: Santa Fe Institute 1399 Hyde Park Rd Santa Fe NM 87501-8943*

GELMAN, ANDREW RICHARD, lawyer; b. Chgo., June 20, 1946; s. Sidney S. and Beverly (Burg) G.; m. Amy Herfort, Sept. 1, 1985; children: Stephen S., Adam P., Elizabeth F. BA, U. Pa., 1967; JD, U. Va., 1970. Bar: Va. 1970, Ill. 1971. Assoc. Roan & Grossman Law Firm, Chgo., 1971-74; assoc. McBride, Baker & Coles Law Firm, Chgo., 1974-77, ptnr., 1978—; mem. com. on character and fitness of Ill. Supreme Ct., Chgo., 1979-95. Bd. dirs. Scholarship and Guidance Assn., Chgo., 1979—, Inst. for Edn. and Rsch. of Children's Meml. Hosp., Chgo., 1991—, vice-chair, 1998—; chmn. Med. Rsch. Inst. Coun., 1983-86, 91-92; trustee Michael Reese Hosp. and Med. Ctr., Chgo., 1987-91. Recipient Weigle award Chgo. Bar Found., 1980. Mem. ABA (pub. understanding about the law com. 1987-91, chair probate and estate planning com. gen. practice sect. 1994-97, commn. on mental and phys. disability law 1995-97), Chgo. Bar Assn. (past chmn. divsn. probate practice com., bd. mgrs. 1978-80, chmn. young lawyers sect. 1976-77), Chgo. Estate Planning Coun. Office: McBride Baker & Coles 500 W Madison St Fl 40 Chicago IL 60661-2511

GELMAN, ELAINE EDITH, nurse; b. Bklyn., Feb. 16, 1927; d. Michael Levi and Shirley (Drezner) Rodkinson; m. David Graham Gelman, Apr. 6, 1952; children: Eric, Andrew, Amy. BS, CUNY, Queens, 1946; RN, NYU, 1948. Cert. PNP. Mem. oper. rm. staff, supr. Queens Gen. Hosp., Bellevue, Beth-El Hosp., N.Y.C., 1948-61; mem. labor and delivery rm. staff, supr. Georgetown Hosp., Washington, 1962-66; pub. health nurse N.Y.C. Dept. Pub. Health, 1966-72; PNP Roosevelt Hosp., N.Y.C., 1972-82; pvt. practice, N.Y.C., 1982-95; exec. dir. N.Y. State Coalition Nurse Practitioners, Inc., Albany, 1996-98; editor, mem. adv. bd. Patient Care for Nurse Practitioners, 1998—; mem. N.Y. State Bd. Nursing, 1990-96. Editor adv. bd. Patient Care for the Nurse Practitioner, 1998—. Mem. County Dem. Com., N.Y.C., 1984-99. Named Nurse of Distinction N.Y. State Legis., 1991; recipient Spl. Presdl. award N.Y. State Coalition of Nurse Practitioners, 1991. Fellow Nat. Assn. PNPs (legis. chmn. 1986-88, cert. of recognition 1986, 87), Coalition of Nurse Practitioners, Inc. (pres. 1984-85, 87-88). Jewish. Avocation: needlework. Home: 229 W 78th St New York NY 10024-6604

GELMAN, JON LEONARD, lawyer; b. Paterson, N.J., Mar. 14, 1946; s. Carl and Gussie (Weiss) G.; m. Nancy R. Sugarman, Oct. 2, 1971; children: Michael A., Jason L. BA, Rutgers U., 1967; JD, John Marshall Law Sch., 1971. Bar: N.J. 1971, U.S. Dist. Ct. N.J. 1971, U.S. Tax Ct. 1973, U.S. Ct. Appeals (D.C. cir.) 1973, U.S. Supreme Ct. 1974, U.S. Ct. Appeals (3d cir.) 1980, N.Y. 1985. Pvt. practice Wayne, N.J., 1979—. Author: Workers' Compensation Law, 1999; contbg. columnist N.J. Law Jour.; contbr. articles to profl. jours. Mem. ATLA, Nat. Orgn. Social Security Claimants Rep.,

Asbestos Litigation Group, Trial Attys. N.J., D.C. Bar Assn., N.J. Bar Assn. (workers' compensation sect.), Passaic County Bar Assn., Workplace Litig. Group (trustee). E-mail: jon@gelmans.com. Office: 1455 Valley Rd 3rd Flr PO Box 934 Wayne NJ 07474-0934

GELMAN, LARRY, actor, director; b. Bklyn., Nov. 3, 1930; s. Frank and Dorothy (Slepakoff) G. Student, CCNY, 1954-55. Appeared on numerous TV shows, 1965—, including The Odd Couple, Bob Newhart Show, Maude, Mary Tyler Moore Show, Eight Is Enough, Kojak, Raid on Entebbe, Triangle Factory Fire, Barney Miller, Simon and Simon, Night Court, Amazing Stories, Hill St. Blues, Remington Steele, Our House, Cagney and Lacey, Scarecrow and Mrs. King, Grand Slam, Jake and the Fat Man, In the Heat of the Night, Doogie Howser, M.D., Thunder Alley, On Our Own, Kirk, Weird Science, Home Improvement, Touched By An Angel; appeared in feature films Funny Girl, Super Dad, O'Hara's Wife, Dreamscape, Double Exposure, Mr. Saturday Night; short subject live action film A Different Approach (nominated for Motion Picture Acad. award 1979); now on worldwide tour as Einstein: The Man Behind the Genius. Pres. Nat. Jewish Theater So. Calif. With USMC, 1951-53. Nominated Acad. TV Arts and Scis. award for outstanding single performance by a supporting actor in a comedy or drama series 1977-78. Mem. SAG, AFTRA, Am. Guild Variety Artists, Actors Equity Assn., Acad. Motion Picture Arts and Scis., Acad. TV Arts and Scis. Jewish.

GELMANN, EDWARD PAUL, oncologist, educator; b. N.Y.C., May 31, 1950; m. Connie Sommers; children: Lauren R., Elyssa R., Emily B. BS magna cum laude, Yale U., 1972; MD, Stanford U., 1976. Diplomate Nat. Bd. Med. Examiners, Am. Bd. Internal Medicine. Intern then resident U. Chgo. Hosps., 1976-78; med. staff fellow Nat. Cancer Inst., Bethesda, Md., 1979-83, sr. investigator, 1983-88; adj. assoc. prof. microbiology Georgetown U., Washington, 1986-88, prof. medicine and cell biology, 1988—, chief med. oncology divsn., 1988-93, chief hematology/oncology divsn., 1993-95, vice chair Dept. Medicine, 1997—; dir. urologic oncology program Lombardi Cancer Rsch. Ctr., 1990-93, dir. prostate cancer program, 1993—. Mem. editorial bd. jour. Blood, 1985-90; ad hoc reviewer jours.; contbr. 140 articles to profl. jours. Sr. surgeon USPHS, 1978-88. Grantee Nat. Cancer Inst., 1990—. Fellow ACP; mem. AAAS, Am. Soc. Clin. Investigation, Am. Assn. Cancer Rsch., Am. Soc. Clin. Oncology. Office: Georgetown U 3800 Reservoir Rd NW Washington DC 20007-2196

GELOTTE, BOB GUNNAR, musician; b. Quincy, Mass., Dec. 26, 1950; s. Oscar Ragnar and Elvie Teresa (Holmgren) G. BS, Coll. of William and Mary, 1972. Recording musician various record labels, music pubs., producers and artists, Nashville, 1974-82; producer/composer various TV and radio comml. jingle cos. and music pubs., Nashville, 1976-80; pub. Big Gun Music, Nashville, 1979—; mgr. Studio Prodns., Inc., Nashville, 1983-93. Recording musician with various artists including: Lynn Anderson, Chet Atkins, Ronnie Milsap, Hank Snow, Marty Robbins, Dave Loggins, Perry Como, Johnny Cash, George Strait; assoc. producer various TV and films, 1983-93. Mem. AFTRA, ASCAP, Am. Fedn. Musicians, Phi Beta Kappa.

GELPI, ALBERT JOSEPH, English educator, literary critic; b. New Orleans, July 19, 1931; s. Albert Joseph and Alice Marie (Delaup) G.; m. Barbara Charlesworth, June 14, 1965; children: Christopher Francis Cecil, Adrienne Catherine Ardelle. A.B., Loyola U., New Orleans, 1951; M.A., Tulane U., 1956; Ph.D., Harvard U., 1962. Asst. prof. Harvard U., 1962-68; asso. prof. Stanford U., 1968-74, prof. Am. lit., 1974—, Wm. Robertson Coe prof. Am. lit., 1978—, chmn. Am. studies program, 1980-83, 94—, asso. dean grad. study and research, 1980-85, chmn. English dept., 1985-88. Author: Emily Dickinson: The Mind of the Poet, 1965, The Tenth Muse: The Psyche of the American Poet, 1975, A Coherent Splendor: The American Poetic Renaissance 1910-1950, 1987; editor: The Poet in America: 1650 to the Present, 1974, (with Barbara Charlesworth Gelpi) Adrienne Rich's Poetry, 1975, Wallace Stevens: The Poetics of Modernism, 1985, (with Barbara Charlesworth Gelp) Adrienne Rich's Poetry and Prose, 1993, Denise Levertov: Selected Criticism, 1993, The Blood of the Poet: Selected Poems of William Everson, 1994; editor Cambridge Studies in American Literature and Culture, 1981-91, Living in Time: The Poetry of C. Day Lewis, 1998. Served with U.S. Army, 1951-53. Guggenheim fellow, 1977-78. Mem. MLA, Am. Lit. Assn. Democrat. Roman Catholic. Home: 870 Tolman Dr Palo Alto CA 94305-1026 Office: Stanford U Dept English Stanford CA 94305

GELPI, ARMAND PHILIPPE, internist; b. Denver, Aug. 27, 1925. BS, U. Calif., Berkeley, 1946; MD, U. Calif., San Francisco, 1949. Diplomate Am. Bd. Internal Medicine. Intern Santa Clara Valley Med. Ctr., San Jose, Calif., 1949-50; asst. resident U. Calif. Med. Ctr., San Francisco, 1952-53, San Francisco Gen. Hosp., 1953-54; chief resident Santa Clara Valley Med. Ctr., 1954-55; staff physician VA Med. Ctr., Fresno, Calif., 1955-58; fellow hematology/oncology VA Med. Ctr., San Francisco, 1957-58; pvt. practice San Leandro, Calif., 1958-59; chief medicine Arabian Am. Oil Co., Dhahran, Saudi Arabia, 1959-68; trainee, immunology Stanford U., Palo Alto, Calif., 1967-68; med. dir. Charles E. Drew Health Ctr., East Palo Alto, Calif., 1968-70; assoc. med. dir. student health Stanford U., 1970-78, 79-81; physician specialist Stanford U. Med. Ctr., 1978-79, 81-83; staff physician NASA/Ames Rsch. Ctr., Mountain View, Calif., 1983-97; prof. emeritus Stanford U., 1987—; attending physician Chaboya Clinic, San Jose, 1983-86, Dept. Veterans Affairs, Palo Alto, 1986-94. Vol. Sonoma Valley Sch. Dist., 1994—. Lt. med. corps USN, 1950-52.

GELTMAN, EDWARD MARK, cardiologist, educator; b. Oceanport, N.J., Feb. 22, 1946; s. Irving Robert and Goldie (Bazoll) G.; m. Nancy Milner, Aug. 24, 1968; 1 child, Joshua, Aaron. BS, MIT, 1967; MD, NYU, 1971. Diplomate Am. Bd. Internal Medicine, Am. Bd. Cardiovasc. Diseaes. Intern in internal medicine Bellevue Hosp., N.Y.C., 1971-72, resident in internal medicine, 1972-74; fellow in clin. cardiology Washington U., Barnes Hosp., St. Louis, 1976-78, instr. medicine, 1978-79, asst. prof., 1979-84, assoc. prof., 1984-92, prof., 1992—, dir. heart failure and transplant program, 1994—; steering com. mem., chmn. ancillary studies, publs. com. SAVE Study (Bristol-Myers Squibb), Princeton, N.J., 1987-92; steering com. mem. MACH-1 Study, Roche, 1995-98. Reviewer of 16 med. jours.; contbr. over 97 articles to profl. jours. and books to chpts. Pres. St. Louis chpt. Am. Heart Assn., 1987-88, also bd. dirs., pres. Mo. affiliate, 1992-94, bd. dirs, exec com. coun. on clin cardiology 1990-92. Maj. M.C., USAF, 1974-76. Fellow ACP, Am. Coll. Cardiology (regional councilor Mo. chpt. 1993-98. Avocations: photography, golf, rowing. Home: 15 Crosswinds Dr Olivette MO 63132-4303 Office: Washington Univ Sch of Medicine Campus Box 8086 660 S Euclid Ave Saint Louis MO 63110-1010

GELTZER, SHEILA SIMON, public relations executive; b. N.Y.C.; d. Sidney E. and Bertie (Rome) Simon; m. Howard E. Geltzer, Sept. 10, 1967; children: Jeremy Niles, Gabriel Lewis. BA, Queens Coll., 1961. With Philip Lesly Co., N.Y.C., 1962-63, Benjamin Co., N.Y.C., 1963-68; ptnr. Simon and Geltzer, Inc., N.Y.C., 1968-74, Ries and Geltzer, N.Y.C., 1974-79; pres. Geltzer and Co., Inc., N.Y.C., 1979—. Mem. Pub. Relations Soc. Am. (counselors acad.), Women in Communications, Women in Pub. Relations, Nat. Council of Women. Office: Geltzer & Co Inc 1301 Avenue Of The Americas New York NY 10019-6022

GELZER, DAVID GEORG, English educator, missionary; b. Vevey, Vaud, Switzerland, Oct. 7, 1919; came to U.S., 1937; s. Heinrich Gelzer and Charlotte Elisabeth Lüdecke; m. Elisabeth Genilla Bennett, June 12, 1949; children: Charlotte, Rebekah, Miriam, Christian, Stuart. BA, U. Dubuque, 1941, B. in Div., 1943; PhD, Yale U., 1952; D. Humane Letters (hon.), Wilson Coll., Chambsburg, Pa., 1972; D. Div. (hon.), Tainan (Taiwan) Theol. Sem., 1994. Ordained to ministry Presbyn. Ch., 1943. Prof. religion, German Albertson Coll., Caldwell, Idaho, 1946-50, Coll. Evangélique Libamba, Makak, Cameroon, 1952-61; prof. history, English Faculté Théologie Protestante, Yaoundé, Cameroon, 1960-75, dean, 1960-69; prof. theology, ch. history Tainan Theol. Sem., 1975-84; lectr., ecumenics Yale Div. Sch., New Haven, Conn., 1982; lectr. ecumenics McCormick Theol. Sem., Chgo., 1984; prof. theology, ecumenics Talua Ministry Training Ctr., Luganville, Vanuatu, 1985-88; acting prin. Talua Ministry Training Ctr., Luganville, 1985-87. Canterbury Cleric (pres. 1992-95, sec. 1995—), Phila., governing bd. Stony Point, N.Y.; election judge Swarthmore (Pa.) We. Dist., 1994—; treas., bd. dirs. Swarthmore Sr. Citizen Assoc., Swarthmore, 1997—. Recipient Alumnus Distinction award U. Dubuque, 1949. Internat. Assn. Mission Studies. Democrat. Presbyn. Avocations: classical music, reading, swimming. Home and Office: 912 Harvard Ave Swarthmore PA 19081-2208

GEMELL, NICHOLAS I., retired radiologist; b. Kaunas, Lithuania, 1921; s. Nicholas Simon Gemelitzki; m. Karen Elinor Moroni, Sept. 3, 1964; children: Julie Helene, Kathryn Lynn. MD, U. Munich, 1950. Diplomate Am. Bd. Radiology. Intern St. Francis Hosp., Poughkeepsie, N.Y., 1951-52; resident in radiology Mt. Sinai Hosp., Chgo., 1954-55, Ohio State U. Hosp., Columbus, 1956-57; asst. chief, dept. radiology Michael Reese Hosp. and Med. Ctr., Chgo., 1958-63, consulting radiologist, 1965-74; consulting radiologist, med. dept. Amoco Oil Company, 1975-77; consulting forensic radiologist Med. Examiner's Office, County of Cook and City of Chgo., 1975-77; radiologist Sherman Hosp., Elgin, Ill., 1978-89; mem. Health Planning Agy. Task force, Kane, Lake and McHenry counties, Ill., 1975-77; chief staff McHenry (Ill.) Hosp., 1975-77, chief radiology, 1964-77. Mem. AMA, Am. Coll. Radiology, Radiolog. Soc. N.Am.

GEMERY, HENRY ALBERT, economics educator; b. Shelton, Conn., Sept. 5, 1930; s. John and Mary (Benco) G.; m. Pamela Joyce Malcolm, Aug. 30, 1958; childen: John Malcolm, Pamela Ann. B.S., So. Conn. State Coll., 1952; M.B.A., Harvard U., 1958; Ph.D., U. Pa., 1967; M.A. hon., Colby Coll., 1977. Asst. dir. admissions Colby Coll., Waterville, Maine, 1958-61, from instr. to Pugh Family prof. econs., 1961—; assoc. Charles Warren Ctr., Harvard U., 1989-90. Contbg. author, co-editor: The Uncommon Market, 1979, Science Technology and Environment, 1994; author: monograph Emigration from the British Isles, 1980, European Emigration to North America, 1984. Served to 1st lt., C.E. U.S. Army, 1953-56. NDEA fellow U. Pa., 1963-65; NIH postdoctoral fellow U. Pa., 1968-69; Charles Warren fellow Harvard U., 1982-83. Mem. Am. Econs. Assn., Cliometric Soc., Econ. History Assn., Internat. Union for Sci. Study of Population. Home: 1185 Pond Rd Sidney ME 04330-2015 Office: Colby Coll Mayflower Hill Waterville ME 04901

GEMIGNANI, JOSEPH ADOLPH, lawyer; b. Hancock, Mich., Apr. 17, 1932; s. Baldo A. and Yolanda M.; m. Barbara A. Thomson, Sept. 5, 1953; children: Joseph, Jon. BSME, Mich. Technological U., 1953; JD, U. Mich., 1958. Bar: Wis. 1959, Mich. 1960, U.S. Dist. Ct. (ea. and we. dists.) Wis., U.S. Ct. Appeals (7th cir.), U.S. Ct. Appeals (fed. cir.). In-house counsel McGraw Edison Co., Milw., 1958-60; ptnr. Michael, Best & Friedrich, Milw., 1960—. 1st lt. USAF, 1953-55. Home: 616 E Day Ave Milwaukee WI 53217-4841 Office: Michael Best & Friedrich 100 E Wisconsin Ave Ste 3300 Milwaukee WI 53202-4108

GEMIGNANI, MICHAEL CAESAR, clergyman, retired educator; b. Balt., Feb. 23, 1938; s. Hugo J. and Dorothy G.; m. Carol A. Federico, June 30, 1962 (dec.); children: Stephen, Susan; m. Nilda B. Keller, May 18, 1985. B.A., U. Rochester, 1962; M.S., U. Notre Dame, 1964, Ph.D., 1965; J.D., Ind. U., 1980. Bar: Ind. 1980, U.S. Dist. Ct. Ind. 1980, Maine 1987, U.S. Dist. Ct. Maine 1987, Tex. 1990; ordained to ministry Episcopal Ch., 1973. Asst. prof. math. SUNY, Buffalo, 1965-68; assoc. prof. Smith Coll., 1968-72; prof., chmn. dept. math. scis. Ind. U.-Purdue U., Indpls., 1972-81; dean Coll. Scis. and Humanities Ball State U., Muncie, Ind., 1981-86; dean Coll. Arts and Scis. U. Maine, Orono, 1986-88; sr. v.p., provost U. Houston-Clear Lake, 1988-91, prof. math. and computer sci., 1991-92; rector St. Paul's Episcopal Ch., Freeport, Tex., 1991—; vicar St. Francis Episcopal Ch., Zionsville, Ind., 1974-79; pres. Met. Indpls. Campus Ministry, 1975-76, bd. dirs., 1974-81; mem. adv. bd. Ind. Office Campus Ministry, 1973-86, pres., 1983-85; chair divsn. spiritual formation Episcopal Diocese of Tex., 1997—. Author: books including Elementary Topology, 1967, 2d rev. edit., 1972, Introductory Real Analysis, 1970, Law and the Computer, 1981, Computer Law, 1985, Legal Guide for EDP Managers, 1989; composer; rsch., publs. in math. Mem. ABA, AAAS, Am. Math. Soc. (chmn. N.E. sect. 1970-71, chmn. Ind. sect. 1975-76), Scribes, Sigma Xi, Kappa Sigma.

GEMMA, PETER BENEDICT, JR., political, public relations and fund raising consultant; b. Providence, Sept. 13, 1950; s. Peter B. and Jane M. (St. Amand) G.; m. Fran Griffin, Oct. 3, 1981 (div. Oct. 1986); children: Peter B. Gemma III; m. Jodi Moody, Oct. 13, 1989; children: Adrienne Grace, Allyson Hope. Student, Roger Williams Coll., 1968-70, Providence Coll., 1975-76. Employment cons. Bus. Careers, Inc., Providence, R.I., 1970-71; sales mgr. C.E. Ryder Corp., Bristol, R.I., 1972-74; mayoral campaign mgr. Vincent A. Cianci, Providence, R.I., 1974; mayoral aide City of Providence, Providence, R.I., 1975-77; campaign cons. various clients, N.J./Maine, 1978; exec. dir. Nat. Pro-Life P.A.C., Falls Church, Va., 1979-88; pres. Associated Direct Mktg. Svcs., Inc., Arlington, Va., 1979-88; ind. pub. rels./fund raising counsel Arlington, Va., 1989—; writer editorials USA Today, 1985—. Contbr. articles and commentaries to profl. jours. Mem. Providence Rep. City Com., 1974-77; chmn. R.I. 10th Senatorial Com., 1975-77; mem. exec. com. R.I. Young Reps., 1974-76; treas. Friends Roger Williams Park, 1974-76; del. Va. Rep. Conv., 1981, 83, 85, 86, 91, 93, 94, 95, 96, 97; mem. Fairfax County Rep. Com., 1983-85, Arlington (Va.) Rep. Com., 1990-98, mem. exec. com., 1992-93, vice chair 1998; mem. cmty. health svcs. bd. Arlington County Bd. Suprs., 1991-93; bd. dirs., chmn. Arlington County chpt. ARC, 1994-95; bd. dirs. Falls Church (Va.) Players, 1982-83. Recipient commendation for leadership Commonwealth of Ky., 1985, hon. Ky. col., 1991; George Washington honors medal Freedoms Found. at Valley Forge, 1989. Mem. Nat. Soc. Fund Raising Execs. (pub. rels. com. Greater Washington chpt. 1989-90, bd. dirs. 1992-95, 99—, newsletter editor 1992-94, 98—, Abel Hanson award 1993). Avocation: travel. Office: 1474 N Point Village Ctr Reston VA 20194-1568

GEMMETT, ROBERT JAMES, university dean, English language educator; b. Schenectady, Mar. 11, 1936; s. A James and Dorothy M. (MacFarlane) G.; m. Kendra B. Baxter, Jan 24, 1964; children: Stephen, Scott, David, Kerry. BA cum laude, Siena Coll., 1959; MA, U. Mass., 1962; PhD, Syracuse U., 1967. Instr. Clarkson U., N.Y., 1964-65; assoc. prof. English SUNY, Brockport, 1965-70, prof., 1970-92, 97—, chmn. dept., 1975-79, dean humanities, 1979-82, dean letters and scis., 1982-92; prof. English, provost, v.p. for acad. affairs SUNY, Buffalo, 1992-97. Author: Poets and Men of Letters, 1975, William Beckford, 1977; editor: Biographical Memoirs of Extraordinary Painters, 1969, Dreams, Waking Thoughts and Incidents, 1971, The Consummate Collector, 1999. 2d lt. U.S. Army, 1959. Recipient Chancellor's Excellence in Teaching award SUNY, 1975; fellow, rsch. grantee SUNY, 1967-69, 84-85. Mem. Am. Assn. for Higher Edn., Assn. Am. State Colls. and Univs. Office: SUNY Dept English Brockport NY 14220

GEN, MARTIN, corporate executive; b. Feb. 14, 1926; s. Max and Gussie (Bluestone) G.; m. Sara Tobin; children: Gilda Gen Paul, Sam Gen. Student, Syracuse U., 1946-50; BA, Pace U., 1950; MBA, LLB. Lic. pvt. detective. V.p., treas. Merlin, Inc., North Bergen, N.J., 1950-73; pres. Washmasters, Inc., North Bergen, 1950-73; pres., exec. dir., CEO Expert Investigation and Protective Industries, Inc., Kenilworth, N.J., 1974—; pres. InterGlobal Trading, Kenilworth, N.J.; pres., exec. dir. EIP, Inc., Kenilworth, N.J., 1973-74; pres. Expert Investigation. Bd. dirs. Jewish Nat. Fund, Teaneck, N.J., 1986—, YMHA, Union, N.J., 1970, Fedn. Union County, N.J., 1970, Jewish Ednl. Ctr., Elizabeth, N.J., 1960. Served with USN, 1943-46, ETO, PTO. Named Man of Yr., YMHA, Bnai Brith. Mem. Am. Soc. Indsl. Security, Club 100. Home and Office: PO Box 195 Kenilworth NJ 07033-0195

GENARO, DONALD MICHAEL, industrial designer; b. Hoboken, N.J., Feb. 22, 1932; s. Gustav G. and Margaret (DeMave) G.; m. Margaret Hermes, June 23, 1956; children: Susan, Karen. BID, Pratt Inst., 1957. Archtl. designer F.W. Fisher-Architects, N.J. and N.Y., 1951-52; indsl. designer Henry Dreyfuss Assocs., N.Y.C., 1957-63, assoc., 1963-68, ptnr., 1968-82, sr. ptnr., 1982-94; ret., 1994; cons. AT&T, Bell Labs., John Deere, Polaroid, and various others; lectr. on design, 1962—. Designer of Trimline Phone; holder over 200 patents; contbr. numerous articles to profl. jours. Trustee, chmn., bd. dirs. Pascack Valley Hosp.; bd. dirs. Well Care Group, Inc. Represented in permanent collection at Mus. of Modern Art and Cooper-Hewitt (Smithsonian) Museum; recipient Contemporary Achievement award Pratt Inst., 1970, Best Product Design 1983 Time Mag., several design awards from Indsl. Designers Soc. of Am. and Indsl. Design Mag.; named one of 25 Best Designed Products Fortune Mag., 1977. Mem. Indsl. Designers Soc. Am. Office: Henry Dreyfuss Assocs 114 W 26th St New York NY 10001-6812

GENBERG, IRA, lawyer; b. Newark, July 27, 1947; s. Jack and Ann (Lerman) G.; m. Rosemary Lawlor, Jan. 15, 1981; children: Jack Michael, Anne Rebecca. AB magna cum laude, Rutgers U., 1969; JD, U. Pa., 1972. Bar: Ga. 1972, D.C. 1978. Assoc. Haas, Holland, Levison & Gibert, Atlanta, 1972-75; ptnr. Stokes, Shapiro, Fussell & Genberg, Atlanta, 1975-87; ptnr., head litigation sect. Smith, Gambrell & Russell LLP, Atlanta, 1987—; spkr. Seminar on Constrn. Litigation, Atlanta, 1985, Seminar on Constrn. Law, Atlanta, 1986; co-chmn. Seminar on Trying A Complex Constrn. Case, 1994. Contbr. articles to Constrn. Bus. Review Mag. Mem. ABA, Ga. Bar Assn., Atlanta Bar Assn., D.C. Bar Assn. Office: Smith Gambrell & Russell LLP 1230 Peachtree St NE Atlanta GA 30309-3592

GENCO, ROBERT JOSEPH, scientist, immunologist, periodontist, educator; b. Silver Creek, N.Y., Oct. 31, 1938; s. Joseph A. and Santa (Barone) G.; m. Sandra Clarke, Sept. 14, 1957; children: Deborah Genco Powell, Robert M., Julie Clarke Alford. DDS cum laude, SUNY, 1963; PhD, U. Pa., 1967. Asst. prof. dept. oral biology Sch. Dental Medicine SUNY, Buffalo, 1967-69, assoc. prof., 1969-72, prof., 1972—, chmn. dept. oral biology, 1977—, Disting. Univ. Prof., 1990—. Editor Jour. Periodontology, 1988—. Recipient Gold medal ADA, 1991. Fellow AAAS (chmn. dental sect. 1980); mem. Am. Assn. Dental Researchers (pres. 1985), Inst. Medicine, Internat. Assn. Dental Researchers (pres. 1991-92), Am. Acad. Periodontology, Am. Assn. Immunology. Avocations: music, sports. Office: SUNY at Buffalo Periodontal Disease Rsch Ctr Foster Hall Buffalo NY 14214*

GENDELL, GERALD STANLEIGH, retired public affairs executive; b. Stamford, Conn., June 14, 1929; s. Irving and Henrietta (Lund) G.; m. s. Marion F. Belvin, July 28, 1952; children: Carin Gaye, Danna Joyce, Adrian Leigh, Jeffrey Lund, David Blake, Marc Steven, Bradley Howard. BS, NYU, 1949. With Procter & Gamble Co., Cin., 1954-91, dir. community affairs and contbns., 1976-80, mgr. external affairs div., 1980, mgr. pub. affairs div., 1981—, also pres., trustee Procter & Gamble Fund. Trustee Glen Manor Home, 1978-80, Queen City Housing Corp., Cin., 1981-89, Cin. Local Initiative Support Corp., The Spire Found., Jewish Fedn. So. Ariz.; vice chmn. bd. trustees Jewish Hosp. of Cin.; bd. dirs., trustee Nat. Coun. on Econ. Edn., 1985-91; mem. met. adv. coun. U. Cin.; mem. adv. coun. George Mason U. Sch. Law, 1988-91; mem. Cin. Mayor's Com. on Econ. Devel.; chmn. Found. for Pub. Affairs; mem. bd. overseers Hebrew Union Coll.; pres. Jewish Cmty. Found. of So. Ariz. 1st lt. U.S. Army, 1950-53. Mem. Pub. Affairs Coun. Am. (bd. dirs. 1981-91, chmn. 1988-89), Greater Cin. C. of C. (vice chmn., mem. exec. com. 1981-87), Conf. Bd., Bankers Club (bd. govs. 1988-93).

GENDELMAN, HOWARD ELIOT, biomedical researcher, physician; b. Phila., Mar. 18, 1954; s. Seymour and Soffia (Raphael) G.; m. Bonnie Rae Bloch, June 15, 1980; children: Lesley, Sierra, Adam. BS, Muhlenberg Coll., 1975; MD, Pa. State U., 1979. Rsch. assoc. Pa. State U., Hershey, 1978-79; resident in internal medicine Montefiore Hosp. Ctr. Albert Einstein Coll. Medicine, Bronx, N.Y., 1979-82; clin. and rsch. fellow depts. neurology and medicine Johns Hopkins U. Med. Sch., Balt., 1982-85, asst. prof. divsn. infectious diseases, 1985-89; staff physician in infectious diseases Walter Reed Army Inst. Rsch., Washington, 1987-93; spl. expert sect. biochem. virology Lab. Molecular Microbiology/NIH, Bethesda, Md., 1985-87; prin scientist Henry M. Jacksoun Found. Advance. Mil. Med. Uniformed Svcs. Univ. Health Sci. Ctr., 1988-92, rsch. assoc., prof. dept. pathology, 1990-92; chief lab. viral pathogenesis U. Nebr. Med. Ctr., Omaha, Nebr., 1993-97; David T. Purtilo Disting. prof. pathology and microbiology U. Nebr. Med. Ctr., 1997—; dir. Ctr. for Neurovirology and Neurodegenerative Disorders, Omaha, Nebr., 1997—; lectr. dept. infectious diseases The Johns Hopkins U. Sch. Pub. Health, Balt., 1985-92; cons. Glax Wellcome, Research Triangle Park, N.C., 1987, Schering-Plough, Kenilworth, N.J., Applied Biotechs., Beltsville, Md., 1990, Viragen, 1990, others. Editl. reviewer Jour. Histochemistry and Cytochemistry, Jour. Virology, Am. Jour. Pathology, Jour. Clin. Investigation, New Eng. Jour. Medicine, Jour. Neuroimmunology, AIDS, Jour. Immunology, Gastroenterology, Lab. Investigation, Jour. Infectious Disease, Revs. of Infectious Disease Sci.; sect. editor Jour. Leukocyte Biology; assoc. editor Jour. Neurovirology; mem. editl bd. JAMA; contbr. articles to New Eng. Jour. Medicine, Sci., Jour. Immunology, Jour. Virology, Jour. Exptl. Medicine, others. Lt. col. USAR, 1984-97. Grantee NIH, Amfar; Carter Wallace fellow, 1987-93. Mem. ACP, AMA, Am. Soc. Virology, Am. Soc. Microbiology, Reticuloendothelial Soc. Achievements include discovery of the role that glial (microglia and astroglial) cells play in the neurodegenerative and neuroregenerative mechanisms of Alzheimer's Disease and HIV dementia. Home: 125 S 127th St Omaha NE 68154 Office: Univ Nebr Med Ctr 600 S 42nd St Omaha NE 68198-1002

GENDRE, MICHAEL, philosophy educator; b. Casablanca, Morocco, Oct. 12, 1954; s. Jacques and Simone (Taffard) G. MA in Philosophy, U. Provence, France, 1978, Stanford U., 1982; PhD in Philosophy, Boston Coll., 1996. Instr. Boston Coll., 1987-94; asst. prof. Al Akhawayn U., Morocco, 1997-99. Translator: Heidegger and the Project of Fundamental Ontology, 1991, Poetics, Speculation and Judgement, The Work of Art from Kant to Phenomenology, 1993, Heidegger From Metaphysics to Thought, 1994, Nietzsche and Metaphysics, 1996, The Shadow of that Thought, Heidegger and the Question of Politics, 1996. Rotary scholar, 1980-81, Fulbright scholar, 1979-80, scholar Goethe Inst., 1996. Mem. Am. Philosophy Assn.

GENDREAU, BERNICE MARIE, retired women's health nurse; b. Danforth, Maine, Oct. 11, 1934; d. Henry Augustus Harding and Leah Orale (Gould) Crossman; m. Scott Andrew Dunn, Oct. 19, 1957 (dec. 1986); children: Audrey M. Nutter, E. Lee Dunn Shirland, Janet L. Dunn Doucette, John E. II; m. Leo Maurice Gendreau, Jan. 25, 1997; stepchildren: Kathy Gallimore, Leo Gendreau II, Gail Gendreau, Roland Gendreau. Diploma in nursing, Ea. Maine Med. Ctr., Bangor, 1975. RN, Maine. Psychiat. aide to LPN, RN State of Maine, Bangor, 1953-76; aide, charge aide, charge LPN, med. nurse to supr. ob/gyn Ea. Maine Med. Ctr., 1976-95, ret., 1995. Vol. March of Dimes; organist, pianist, choir dir., Sunday Sch. tchr., Faith Bible Ch., Olarnon, Maine, 1957-82. Mem. ANA, AWHONN (cert.), Maine State Nurses Assn., Nat. Assn. ACOG. Democrat. Baptist. Avocations: needlework, reading, continuing education.

GENDRON, GEORGE, magazine editor. Editor-in-chief Inc. mag., Boston, 1983—. Office: Inc 38 Commercial Wharf Boston MA 02110-3801*

GENDRON, MARY, company executive; b. Wis., Jan. 6, 1954. BA, U. Wis., 1976. Pres. Middleton & Gendron, N.Y.C., 1989—. Mem. Pub. Rels. Soc. Am. Office: Middleton & Gendron 130 E 59th St New York NY 10022

GENDRON, MICHÈLE MARGUERITE MADELEINE, librarian; b. Paris, Mar. 15, 1947; came to U.S., 1950; d. Gerard Joachim and Denise Marie Louise (Le Morvan) G. BA, Orlinda Pierce Coll. for Women, Athens, Greece, 1969; MS, U. Ill., 1971. Libr. Free Libr. Phila., 1971-75, head, Kingsessing Br., 1975-76, head, Ramonita G. de Rodriguez Br., 1976-91, curator spl. collections ctrl. children's dept., 1991-92, head, lit. dept., 1992—; cons. devel. Hist. Children's Lit. Collection Montgomery County-Norristown (Pa.) Pub. Libr., 1993-94; organizing mem. Pa. Libr. Assn.'s 1st Conf. Svcs. to Youth, Harrisburg, Pa., 1987-89, Women's Network's 1st Conf. on P.R. Woman in Phila., 1981. Author: (bibliographies) Booklist, 1983; contbr. bibliographies Destination World, 1979, Stories to Share, 1985. Trustee Legal Svcs. Fund Dist. Coun. 47 of Am. Fedn. State, County and Mcpl. Employees, 1985-95, mem. exec. bd. Local 2186, 1996—. Recipient Charles Scribner award Scribner Pub., 1976, Nat. Security Forum, Air War Coll., 1985. Mem. ALA (Assn. Libr. Svcs. Children, Mildred Batchelder award selection com. 1979-81, 85-87, internat. rels. com. 1981-85, chair 1984-85, libr. instrn. round table 1991-93), Pub. Libr. Assn. (mktg. to pub. librs. 1991—, svcs. to multicultural populations 1991, sec. exec. com. mktg. pub. libr. svcs. sect. 1995-96), Alliance Francaise de Phila., Beta Phi Mu. Roman Catholic. Office: Free Libr of Phila Lit Dept 1901 Vine St Philadelphia PA 19103-1116

GENDRON, ODORE JOSEPH, retired bishop; b. Manchester, N.H., Sept. 13, 1921; s. Francis and Valida (Rouleau) G. Student, St. Charles Borromeo Sem., Can., 1936-42, U. Ottawa, 1942-47. Ordained priest Roman Catholic Ch., 1947; assoc. pastor Angel Guardian Ch., Berlin, N.H., 1947-52, Sacred Heart Ch., Lebanon, N.H., 1952-60, St. Louis Ch., Nashua, N.H., 1960-65; pastor Our Lady of Lourdes Ch., Pittsfield, N.H., 1965-67, St. Augustine Ch., Manchester, N.H., 1967-71; monsignor, 1970, episcopal vicar for religious, 1972-74, episcopal vicar for clergy, 1974—; consecrated bishop of Manchester, 1975-90; ret., 1991. Office: 153 Ash St PO Box 310 Manchester NH 03105-0310*

GENDZIER, STEPHEN J., foreign language educator; b. N.Y.C., July 14, 1930; s. Louis and Sally (Koenig) G.; m. Irene Sophie Dominique Henriette Lefel, Mar. 30, 1958 (div. Apr. 1970); 1 child, Alexander A.; m. Rhea Mendoza Diamond, Aug. 5, 1973; children: Christopher Evan, Joshua Diamond. BA, Oberlin Coll., 1952; MA, Columbia U., 1953, PhD, 1959; cert., U. Paris, 1985. Instr. Columbia U., N.Y.C., 1956-60; asst. prof. MIT, Cambridge, 1960; asst. prof. fgn. langs. Brandeis U., Waltham, Mass., 1962-66, assoc. prof., 1966—, chmn. dept. Romance and comparative lit., 1977-81, 97—. Author, editor: Denis Diderot: The Encyclopaedia, 1967, rev., edit., 1969; contbr. nuermous articles, revs. and transls. to various publs. Henry Alfred Todd fellow Columbia U., 1953; Fulbright grantee, Paris, 1954-56. Democrat. Jewish. Avocations: collecting wine and antiques, gardening, tennis, travel. E-mail: gendzier@bimah.cc.brandeis.edu. Home: 36 Hayes Ave Lexington MA 02420-2063 Office: Brandeis U Mailstop 024 Waltham MA 02254-9110

GENDZWILL, JOYCE ANNETTE, retired health officer; b. Milw., Aug. 8, 1927; d. Felix Vincent and Antoinette Marie (Borske) G.; m. Lauren E. Trombley, June 13, 1952 (div. Jan. 1960); children: Regan Eve Trombley Kovacich, Eugene Vincent, Paul Quentin. BS, U. Mich., 1949, MD, 1952, MPH, 1961. Cert. pub. mgr., Ala. Internship USPHS, Detroit, Cleve., 1952-53; dir. extern edn. Beyer Meml. Hosp., Ypsilanti, Mich., 1953-54; resident in radiology St. Luke's Hosp., Denver, 1954-55; health officer Dickinson-Iron Dist. Health Dept., Stambaugh, Mich., 1959-76; dir. bur. local health svc. Ala. Dept. Pub. Health, Montgomery, Ala., 1976-81; asst. state health officer Ala. Dept. Pub. Health, Montgomery, 1981-91; ret., 1991. Mem. AMA, So. Med. Assn., Mensa, Phi Beta Kappa, Delta Omega, Phi Kappa Phi. Home: 6580 Thorman Rd Pt Charlotte FL 33981-5579

GENEL, MYRON, pediatrician, educator; b. York, Pa., Jan. 6, 1936; s. Victor and Florence (Mowitz) G.; m. Phyllis Norma Berkman, Aug. 25, 1968; children: Elizabeth, Jennifer, Abby. Grad., Moravian Coll., 1957; MD, U. Pa., 1961; MA (hon.), Yale U., 1983; DSc (hon.), Moravian Coll., 1995. Diplomate Am. Bd. Pediat. Intern Mt. Sinai Hosp., N.Y.C., 1961-62; resident in pediat. Children's Hosp. Phila., 1962-64; trainee pediat. endocrinology Johns Hopkins Hosp., Balt., 1966-67; instr. pediat. U. Pa. Sch. Medicine, 1967-69, assoc. in pediat., 1969-71; trainee in genetics, inherited metabolic diseases Children's Hosp. Phila., 1967-69, assoc. physician, 1969-71; attending physician Yale-New Haven Hosp., 1971—; faculty Yale U. Sch. Medicine, New Haven, 1971—, dir. pediat. endocrinology, 1971-85, program dir. Children's Clin. Rsch. Ctr., 1971-86, prof., 1981—, assoc. dean, 1985—, dir. Office Govt. and Cmty. Affairs, 1985—; genetic adv. bd. State of Conn., 1979-82, 94—; cons. subcom. investigations, oversight com. sci. and tech. U.S. Ho. of Reps., 1982-84; mem. adv. bd. New Eng. Congenital Hypothyroidism Collaborative; cons. Hosp. St. Raphael, Milford Hosp., Norwalk Hosp., Stamford Hosp., Danbury Hosp.; chmn. transplant adv. com. Office of Commr., Conn. Dept. Income Maintenance, 1984-92; health policy fellowship bd. Inst. Medicine, 1989-95; bd. dirs. Rsch. America!. Contbr. articles to profl. jours. Capt. U.S. Army, 1964-66. Robert Wood Johnson Health Policy fellow Inst. Medicine NAS, Washington, 1982-83; recipient ann. award Conn. Campaign Against Cooley's Anemia, 1979, Ann. Comenius Alumni award Moravian Coll., 1990, Abraham Jacobi Meml. award Am. Acad. Pediat. and AMA, 1999. Fellow AAAS; mem. APHA, AMA (med. schs. sec. 1985—, alt. del. governing coun., med. schs. sec. 1995-98, del. 1998—, coun. on sci. affairs, 1994—, Task force on fin. grad. med edn. 1995), Am. Acad. Pediatrics (task force organ transplants, coun. on govt. affairs), Am. Assn. Clin. Endocrinologists, Am. Coll. Nutrition, Am. Coll. Preventive Medicine, Am. Diabetes Assn. (co-recipient Jonathan May award 1979), Am. Fedn. Med. Rsch., Am. Pediatric Soc., Am. Soc. Bone and Mineral Rsch. Assn. Am. Med. Colls. (mem. adminstrv. bd. coun. acad. socs. 1987-92, chmn.-elect coun. acad. socs., 1989-91, mem. exec. coun. 1989-92, mem. advisory panel on rsch. 1999—), Assn. Health Svcs. Rsch., New Haven County Med. Assn. (bd. govs. 1990—), Assn. Program Dirs. (pres.-elect 1980-81, pres. 1981-82), Nat. Assn. Biomed. Rsch. (bd. dirs. 1990-93, exec. com. 1991-93), Conn. Endocrine Soc., Conn. United for Rsch. Excellence (chmn. steering com. 1989-90, pres. 1990-93, chmn. bd. dirs. 1993-94), Endocrine Soc. rsch. initiative com., 1995-99), Soc. Pediat. Rsch., Conn. Acad. Sci. and Engring., N.Y. Acad. Medicine, N.Y. Acad. Scis., Sigma Xi. Jewish. Home: 30 Richard Sweet Dr Woodbridge CT 06525-1126 Office: PO Box 3333 New Haven CT 06510-0333

GENERAS, GEORGE PAUL, JR., finance educator, lawyer; b. Erie, Pa., Dec. 24, 1943; s. George Paul and Helen Sophie (Chesney) G.; m. Darlene Ann Hosey, Nov. 8, 1980; 1 child, George Paul III. BS, U. Scranton, 1966, MBA, 1968; JD, U. Conn., 1991. Bar: Conn., CPA, Conn., N.Y. Sr. acct. Arthur Andersen & Co., N.Y.C., 1968-74; controller JOC Oil Ltd., Bermuda and Holland, 1974-78; asst. prof., chair U. Hartford, Conn., 1979-85; dir. MBA U. Hartford, Paris, 1985-86; asst. prof., chair U. Hartford, Conn., 1986-94; assoc. dean, 1994-95; lawyer Hartford, Conn., 1995—; of counsel Rome McGuigan; chair Ednl. Adv. Commn. State Bd. Acct., Hartford, Conn., 1983-89, 92-94; bd. mem. Community Acctg. Aid and Svcs., Hartford, Conn., 1991-94. Co-author: Collaboration Between Higher Education and Big Six Accounting Firms, 1991. Bd. dirs. No. Conn. chpt. Leukemia Soc., 1992-97, treas., 1994-97. Mem. AICPA, Conn. Soc. CPAs, Am. Acctg. Assn., ABA, Conn. Bar Assn. Roman Catholic. Home: 9 Old Barge Rd Simsbury CT 06070-1741 Office: Univ Hartford 200 Bloomfield Ave Hartford CT 06117-1599

GENESI, SUSAN PETROVICH, educator; b. Philipsburg, Pa., Mar. 24, 1957; d. Richard and Margaret (Ohs) P.; 1 child, Lindsay Margaret. BS in Elem. Edn., Pa. State U., 1981, cert. ednl. adminstrn., 1998. Cert. elem. tchr., Pa.; cert. kindergarten tchr., Pa. Tchr. Philipsburg-Osceola Area Sch. Dist., Pa., 1981—; commr. Pa. Profl. Stds. and Practices Commn., Harrisburg, Pa., 1995—; mem. content validation panel for early adolescence English Nat. Bd. for Profl. Tchg. Stds., Atlanta, 1997; workshop presenter on topics of coop. learning; presenter Keystone State Reading Assn., Hershey, Pa., 1995, 96; coop. tchr. Pa. State U., State College, 1994—; mem. various coms. throughout the sch. dist. Contbr. articles to profl. jours. Mem. Philipsburg Bicentennial Com., 1996-97; organizer Philipsburg Elem. Philipsburg Days, 1994. Mem. ASCD, NEA, Pa. State Edn. Assn., Philipsburg-Osceola Area Edn. Assn. (com. 1981—), Phi Delta Kappa. Republican. Presbyterian. Avocations: traveling and shopping with daughter, computer technology, exploring new trends in education and technology, relaxing at the beach. E-mail: sxg23@psu.edu. Office: Philipsburg Elem Sch Ninth and Laurel Sts Philipsburg PA 16866

GENEST, JACQUES, physician, researcher, administrator; b. Montreal, Que., Can., May 29, 1919; s. Rosario and Annette (Girouard) G.; m. Estelle Deschamps, Oct. 3, 1953; children: Paul, Suzanne, Jacques, Marie, Helene. BA, Coll. Jean de Brebeuf, Montreal, 1937; MD, U. Montreal, 1942; LLD (hon.), Queen's U., 1966, U. Toronto, Can., 1970; DSc (hon.), Laval (Can.) U., 1973, Sherbrooke U., 1974, Meml. U. Nfld., 1978, McGill (Can.) U., 1979, U. Ottawa, 1980, St. Francis Xavier U., 1983, SUNY, Buffalo, 1984, Rockefeller U., 1986, Concordia U., Montreal, 1986, Chinese Acad. Med. Scis., 1987, U. Montpelier, France, 1989. Summer student Harvard Med. Sch., Boston, 1938, 39; resident medicine and pathology Hôtel-Dieu Hosp., Montreal, 1942-45, cons. physician specializing in nephrology and hypertension,, 1952-91; rsch. fellow Johns Hopkins Hosp., Balt., 1945-48, Harvard Sch. Chemistry, Boston, 1948, Rockefeller Hosp. Med. Research, N.Y.C., 1948-51; prof. medicine U. Montreal, 1965-96; prof. exptl. medicine McGill U., Montreal, 1960-98; dir. Clin. Research Inst. Montreal, 1965-84, adviser, 1984-94; bd. dirs. Merck & Co., Rahway, N.J., Montreal Trust. Editor: (with Erich Koiw) Hypertension, 1972, (with Erich Koiw and Otto Kuchel) Hypertension: Physiopathology and Treatment, 1977, 83, (with Marc Cantin, Otto Kuchel, Pavel Hamet) 2d edit., 1983. Decorated companion Order of Can., grand officer Ordre Nat. du Que.; recipient award Gairdner Found., 1963, Archambault medal Can. Assn. for Advancement Sci., 1965, Marie-Victorin Sci. prize Govt. of Que., 1977, Royal Bank award, 1980, Isaac Walton Killam award, 1986, Armand Frappier prize Govt. of Que., 1996; named to Can. Med. Hall of Fame, 1994. Master ACP; fellow Royal Coll. Physicians and Surgeons Can. (James H. Graham award of merit 1993), Royal Soc. Can. (Flavelle medal and award 1968); mem. Assn. Am. Physicians, Am. Clin. and Climatol. Assn., Am. Heart Assn. (Srouffer prize 1969), Peripatetic Club. Roman Catholic. Home: 5955 Wilderton Ave PH-L6, Montreal, PQ Canada H3S 2V1 Office: Inst de Recherches Cliniques, 110 Pine Ave W, Montreal, PQ Canada H2W 1R7

GENETSKI, ROBERT JAMES, economist; b. N.Y.C., Dec. 26, 1942; s. Alex and Helen Genetski. BS, Ea. Ill. U., 1964; MA, NYU, 1968, PhD, 1972. Tchr. English St. Procopius Acad., Lisle, Ill., 1965-66; research analyst Nat. Econ. Research Assn., N.Y.C., 1967-68; lectr. econs. NYU, N.Y.C., 1969-70; econ. analyst Morgan Guaranty Trust Co., N.Y.C., 1969-71; sr. v.p., economist Harris Trust & Savs. Bank, Chgo., 1971-88; pres. Stotler Econs., Chgo., 1988-90; sr. v.p., chief economist The Chgo. Corp., 1990-91; pres. Robert Genetski & Assocs., 1991—; sr. mng. dir. Chgo. Capital, 1995—; lectr. econs. NYU, 1969-70, U. Chgo., 1973; vis. prof. Wheaton (Ill.) Coll., 1986; mem. census adv. com. U.S. Dept. Commerce, 1983-86; bd. dirs. Fin. Security Corp., Suburban Fed. Savs. Bank. Author: (with Beryl Sprinkel) Winning with Money, 1977, Taking the Voodoo out of Economics, 1986, 88, A Nation of Millionaires, 1997. Chmn. ednl. com. Sch. Bd. Dist. 25, West Chicago, Ill., 1973-79; bd. dirs. Ctrl. DuPage Health Svcs., 1988-94. Mem. Am. Statis. Assn., Am. Econ. Assn. (fin. com. 1983—), Nat. Assn. Bus. Economists (editor Newsletter 1978), Western Econ. Assn., Am. Bankers Assn. (econ. adv. com. 1980-83), U.S. C. of C. (econ. adv. com. 1985—). Office: Chgo Capital 200 W Madison St Ste 2000 Chicago IL 60606-3415

GENETTI, ALBERT J., JR., army officer; b. Ancon, Panama Canal Zone, Mar. 6, 1941. BS, U.S. Mil. Acad., 1963; MS in Civil Engring., U. Ill., 1968. Commd. 2d lt. U.S. Army, 1963, advanced through grades to maj. gen., numerous positions with U.S. Army C.E., 1963—, dep. dir. civil works for Upper Miss. Basin, 1993; dep. chief engrs., dep. comdr. U.S. Army C.E., 1996—; instr., asst. prof. math. U.S. Mil. Acad., West Point, N.Y. Decorate Legion of Merit medal, Bronze Star medal (2), others. Office: Office of Chief of Engrs 20 Massachusetts Ave NW Washington DC 20314-1000

GENGE, WILLIAM HARRISON, advertising executive, writer; b. Warren, Pa., May 7, 1923; s. Valleau Francis and Beatrice (Badger) G.; m. Beverly Ann Milway, June 23, 1945 (dec. May 1991); children: Deborah Ann, William Dean. B.A., U. Pitts., 1948; grad., Internat. Mktg. Inst., Harvard U., 1967. Writer Bull. Index, Pitts., 1947-48; editor Gulf Oil Corp., 1948-53; with Ketchum Communications, Inc., 1953—, sr. v.p., 1965-68, exec. v.p., 1968-70, pres., 1970-79, chmn., 1979-93, also dir.; pres. Civique, Inc., Pitts., 1993—; nat. vice-chmn. The Children's Health, Edn. and Fitness Found. Bd. dirs. Pitts. Symphony, Chatham Coll., Pitts. Youth Symphony, Exec. Svc. Corps, U. Pitts.; chmn. bd. visitors U. Pitts. Press, U. Pitts. Grad Sch. Bus., Pitts. Opera Theatre, City Theatre. 1st lt. USAAF, 1942-46; prisoner of war, 1944-45. Decorated Purple Heart. Mem. Pitts. Golf Club, Univ. Club, Fox Chapel Golf Club, Duquesne Club, Rolling Rock Club, Pelican Marsh Golf Club, Phi Gamma Delta. Republican. Presbyterian (elder). Avocations: tennis, sailing, golf, reading, writing. Home: 5045 5th Ave Pittsburgh PA 15232-2130 *Whatever degree of achievement I've attained is due to unflagging optimism, perseverance and effort, a Christian outlook and at least 50% of the time, and recognition that no man can do it alone. You need friends and supporters all along the way.*

GENGOR, VIRGINIA ANDERSON, financial planning executive, educator; b. Lyons, N.Y., May 2, 1927; d. Axel Jennings and Marie Margaret (Mack) Anderson; m. Peter Gengor, Mar. 2, 1952 (dec.); children: Peter Randall, Daniel Neal, Susan Leigh. *Virginia Anderson Gengor grew up in Guatemala where her parents were missionaries. As a result, she is fluent in Spanish. She is active in many bi-national civic and government groups in the border area with Mexico* AB, Wheaton Coll., 1949; MA, U. No. Colo., Greeley, 1975, 77. Chief hosp. intake service County of San Diego, 1966-77, chief Kearny Mesa Dist. Office, 1977-79, chief Dependent Children of Ct., 1979-81, chief child protection services, 1981-82; registered rep. Am. Pacific Securities, San Diego, 1982-85; registered tax preparer State of Calif., 1982—, registered rep. (prin.) Sentra Securities, 1985—; assoc. Pollock & Assocs., San Diego, 1985-86; pres. Gengor Fin. Advisors, 1986—; cons. instr. Nat. Ctr. for Fin. Edn., San Diego, 1986-88; instr. San Diego Community Coll., 1985-88. Mem. allocations panel United Way, San Diego, 1976-79, children's circle Child Abuse Prevention Found., 1989—; chmn. com. Child Abuse Coordinating Council, San Diego, 1979-83; pres. Friends of Casa de la Esperanza, San Diego, 1980-85, bd. dirs., 1980—; 1st v.p. The Big Sister League, San Diego, 1985-86, pres., 1987-89. Mem. NAFE, Inst. Cert. Fin. Planners, Internat. Assn. Fin. Planning, Inland Soc. Tax Cons., AAUW (bd. dirs.), Nat. Assn. Securities Dealers (registered prin.), Nat. Ctr. Fin. Edn., Am. Bus. Women's Assn., Navy League, Freedoms Found. Valley Forge, Internat. Platform Assn. Presbyterian. Avocations: community service, travel, reading. Home: 6462 Spear St San Diego CA 92120-2929 Office: Gengor Fin Advisors 4950 Waring Rd Ste 7 San Diego CA 92120-2700

GENIA, JAMES MICHAEL, lawyer; b. Chgo., Sept. 16, 1964; s. Anthony Leo and Anne Louise (Hawley) G. BA, Augsburg Coll., 1987; JD, William Mitchell Coll. Law, 1990. Bar: Minn. 1990, U.S. Dist. Ct. Minn. 1992, U.S. Ct. Appeals (8th cir.) 1994, U.S. Supreme Ct. 1999. Judicial law clk. State Minn., Duluth, 1990-92; dep. solicitor gen. Mille Lacs Band of Ojibwe Indians, Onamia, Minn., 1992-93, solicitor gen., 1993-99; solicitor gen. Lockridge Grindal Nauen, Mpls., 1999—; bd. dirs. Woodlands Nat. Bank, Onamia, 1996—, chmn., 1997—; vice-chmn. bd. dirs. Anishinabe O.I.C., Onamia, 1992—; bd. dirs. Johnson Inst. Found., 1998—; lectr. Am. Indian sovereignty and treaty rights various univs., cntinuing edn. seminars, civic groups, 1992—; adj. prof. St. Cloud State U., 1999—. Actor Mille Lacs Cmty. Theater, Onamia, 1996—. Bd. dirs. Johnson Inst. Found., 1998—. Mem. ABA, Am. Trial Lawyers Assn., Minn. Am. Indian Bar Assn., Minn. State Bar Assn., William Mitchell Coll. Law Alumni Assn. (bd. dirs. 1996—). Avocations: softball, golf, jogging, reading, acting. Office: Lockridge Grindal Nauen Ste 2200 100 Washington Ave S Minneapolis MN 55401

GENIA, VICKY, psychologist; b. N.Y.C., June 6, 1950; d. Vincent and Victoria (Bondzio) Auletta; m. Howard D. Genia Jr., Feb. 26, 1971 (div. Nov. 1984); 1 child, Howard D. III; m. Billy G. Witt, Jan. 11, 1985. BA in Math., Buffalo State Coll., 1971; MA in Psychology, U. No. Colo., 1981, D of Counseling Psychology, 1989. Lic. psychologist Md., Washington. Psychologist Ctr. Psychol. and Learning Svcs. Am. U., Washington, 1990—; adj. prof. dept. psychology Am. U., 1995-96. Author: Counseling and Psychotherapy of Religious Clients, 1995; contbr. articles to profl. jours. With U.S. Army, 1974-76. Mem. Am. Psychol. Assn., Soc. Scientific Study Religion, Religious Rsch. Assn. Home: 1945 1/2 Calvert St NW Washington DC 20009-1501 Office: Am U 4400 Massachusetts Ave NW Washington DC 20016-8003

GENIESSE, ROBERT JOHN, lawyer; b. Appleton, Wis., Sept. 16, 1929; s. Arthur John and Rhoda (Miller) G.; m. Jane Elizabeth Fletcher, June 10, 1961; children: Julia Forrest, Thomas Guy. BA magna cum laude, Williams Coll., 1951; LLB cum laude, Harvard U., 1957. Bar: N.Y. 1958, D.C. 1982. Assoc. Debevoise and Plimpton, N.Y.C., 1957-61, 64-66, ptnr., 1966-94; asst. U.S. atty. So. Dist. N.Y., 1962-63, chief appellate atty., 1963-64. Editor Harvard Law Rev., 1955-57. Bd. dirs. Legal Action Ctr., N.Y., 1973-78, Environ. Def. Fund, 1974-82; trustee Williams Coll., 1974-87; trustee World Monuments Fund, 1993—, sec., gen. counsel, 1995—; trustee Nat. Bldg. Mus., 1994—; trustee Sterling and Francine Clark Art Inst., Williamstown, Mass., 1974—, pres., 1987-98. 1st lt. Inf. U.S. Army, 1952-54. Mem. N.Y. State Bar Assn., D.C. Bar ASsn., Soc. Alumni of Williams Coll. (pres. 1973-74), Phi Beta Kappa. Home: PO Box 516 Boca Grande FL 33921-0516 Office: Devevoise & Plimpton 555 13th St NW Ste 1100E Washington DC 20004-1163

GENINI, RONALD WALTER, history educator, historian; b. Oakland, Calif., Dec. 5, 1946; s. William Angelo and Irma Lea (Gays) G.; m. Roberta Mae Tucker, Dec. 20, 1969; children: Thomas, Justin, Nicholas. BA, U. San Francisco, 1968, MA, 1969. Cert. secondary edn. tchr., Calif.; adminstrv. svcs. credential. Tchr. Ctrl. Unified Sch. Dist., Fresno, Calif., 1970—; judge State History Day, Sacramento, 1986-94; mem. U.S. history exam. devel. team Golden State, San Diego, 1989-93; securer placement of state-registered landmarks. Author: Romualdo Pacheco, 1985, Darn Right It's Butch, 1994, Theda Bara, 1996; contbr. articles to profl. jours. Bd. dirs. Fresno Area 6 Neighborhood Coun., 1973-74, Fresno City and County Hist. Soc., 1975-78, St. Anthony's sch. bd., Fresno, 1980-84. Named one of Outstanding Young Educators Am., Fresno Jaycees, 1978; recipient recognition for Tchr. Cares award Calif. State Assembly and Fresno City Coun., 1996. Mem. Calif. Hist. Soc. Democrat. Avocations: writing history 19th century Calif. and early Hollywood, motion picture scriptwriter. Home: 1486 W Menlo Ave Fresno CA 93711-1305 Office: Ctrl HS 3535 N Cornelia Ave Fresno CA 93722-7020 also: Cinema Talent Agency 2609 W Wyoming Ave Apt A Burbank CA 91505-1950

GENKIN, BARRY HOWARD, lawyer; b. Phila., Aug. 8, 1949; s. Paul and Pearl (Rosenfeld) G.; m. Marian Block, Aug. 15, 1975; children: Matthew Todd, Kimberly Beth. BS cum laude, Pa. State U., 1971; JD cum laude, U. Balt., 1974; LLM in Taxation, Georgetown U., 1977. Bar: Pa. 1975, Wash. 1977, N.Y. 1995. Spl. counsel div. corp. fin. SEC, Washington, 1975-78; ptnr. Blank Rome Comisky & McCauly LLP, Phila., 1979-93, co-chmn. corp. dept., dist. com., mgmt. com., chmn. budget com.; bd. dirs. Smeal Bus. Sch., Pa. State U.; lectr. various orgns. Contbr. U. Balt. Law Rev., 1991—; lectr. various orgns. Mem. ABA, Pa. Bar Assn., Savs. Insts., Pa. Savs. League, N.J. Savs. League, Meadowlands Country Club, Heuisler Honor Soc., Omicron Delta Kappa. Home: 544 Howe Rd Merion Station PA 19066-1129 Office: Blank Rome Comisky & McCauley LLP One Logan Sq Philadelphia PA 19103

GENKINS, GABRIEL, physician; b. Berlin, Mar. 20, 1928; came to U.S., 1940, naturalized, 1945; s. Arkady and Tamara (Schlesinger) G.; children: Karen Lee Genkins Fairbank, Steven M., Amy E. B.S., NYU, 1949, M.D., 1952. Diplomate Am. Bd. Internal Medicine, Diplomate Am. Bd. Cardiology. Intern, resident Mt. Sinai Hosp., N.Y.C., 1952-57; practice medicine specializing in cardiology N.Y.C.; clin. prof. medicine Mt. Sinai Med. Ctr., N.Y.C., 1973—, chief myasthenia gravis clinic and rsch. labs., 1972—; attending physician in cardiology Mt. Sinai Hosp., N.Y.C., 1973—; v.p. bd. dirs. Myasthenia Gravis Found., 1973—, mem. nat. med. adv. bd., 1956—. Contbr. articles to profl. jours., chpts. to books. Served with airborne inf., U.S. Army, 1945-46. Democrat. Office: 30 E 60th St New York NY 10022-1008

GENN, NANCY, artist; b. San Francisco; d. Morley P. and Ruth W. Thompson; m. Vernon Chathburton Genn; children: Cynthia, Sarah, Peter. Student, San Francisco Art Inst., U. Calif., Berkeley. lectr. on art and papermaking Am. Ctrs. in Osaka, Japan, Nagoya, Japan, Kyoto, Japan, 1979-80; guest lectr. various univs. and art mus. in U.S., 1975—; vis. artist Am. Acad. in Rome, 1989, 94. One woman shows of sculpture, paintings include, De Young Mus., San Francisco, 1955, 63, Gumps Gallery, San Francisco, 1955, 57, 59, San Francisco Mus. Art, 1961, U. Calif., Santa Cruz, 1966-68, Richmond (Calif.) Art Center, 1970, Oakland (Calif.) Mus., 1971, Linda/Farris Gallery, Seattle, 1974, 76, 78, 81, Los Angeles Inst. Contemporary Art, 1976, Susan Caldwell Gallery, N.Y.C., 1976, 77, 79, 81, Nina Freudenheim Gallery, Buffalo, 1977, 81, Annely Juda Fine Art, London, 1978, Inoue Gallery, Tokyo, 1980, Toni Birckhead Gallery, Cin., 1982, Kala Inst. Gallery, Berkeley, Calif., 1983, Ivory/Kimpton Gallery, San Francisco, 1984, 86, Eve Mannes Gallery, Atlanta, 1985, Richard Iri Gallery, L.A., 1990, Harcourts Modern and Contemporary Art, San Francisco, 1991, 93, 96, Am. Assn. Advancement of Sci., Washington, 1994, Anne Reed Gallery, Ketchum, Id., 1995, Michael PeTronko Gallery, N.Y., 1997, Mills Coll. Art Mus., Oakland, Calif., 1999, Takada Gallery, San Francisco, 1999; group exhbns. include San Francisco Mus. Art, 1971, Aldrich Mus., Ridgefield, Conn., 1972-73, Santa Barbara (Calif.) Mus., 1974, 75, Oakland (Calif.) Mus. Art, 1975, Susan Caldwell, Inc., N.Y.C., 1974, 75, Mus. Modern Art, N.Y.C., 1976, traveling exhbn. Arts Coun. Gt. Britain, 1983-84, Inst. Contemporary Arts, Boston, 1977, J.J.Brookings Gallery, San Francisco, 1997, Portland (Oreg.) Art Mus., 1997—; represented in permanent collections Mus. Modern Art, N.Y.C., Albright-Knox Art Gallery, Buffalo, Libr. of Congress, Washington, Nat. Mus. for Am. Art, Washington, L.A. County Mus. Art, Art Mus. U. Calif., Berkeley, McCrory Corp., N.Y.C., Mus. Art, Auckland, N.Z., Aldrich Mus., Ridgefield, Conn., (collection) Bklyn. Mus., (collection) U. Tex., El Paso, Internat. Ctr. Aesthetic Rsch., Torino, Italy, Cin. Art Mus., San Francisco Mus. Modern Art, Oakland Art Mus., L.A. County Mus., City of San Francisco Hall of Justice, Harris Bank, Chgo., Chase Manhattan Bank, N.Y.C., Modern Art Gallery of Ascoli Piceno, Italy, Mills Coll. Art Mus., Oakland, Calif., Mills Coll. of Art, Oakland, Calif., various mfg. cos., also numerous pvt. collections; commd. works include, Bronze lectern and 5 bronze sculptures for chancel table, 1st Unitarian Ch., Berkeley, Calif., 1961, 64, bronze fountain, Cowell Coll., U. Calif., Santa Cruz, bronze menorah, Temple Beth Am, Los Altos Hills, Calif., 1981, 17, murals and 2 bronze fountain sculptures, Sterling Vineyards, Calistoga, Calif., 1972, 73, fountain sculpture, Expo 1974, Spokane, Wash; vis. artist Am. Acad., Rome, 1989. U.S./Japan Creative Arts fellow, 1978-79; recipient Ellen Branston award, 1952; Phelan award De Young Mus., 1963; honor award HUD, 1968. Home: 1515 La Loma Ave Berkeley CA 94708-2033

GENNARO, ANTONIO L., biology educator; b. Raton, N.Mex., Mar. 18, 1934; s. Paul and Mary Lou (Gasperetti) G.; m. Virginia Marie Sullivan, May 15, 1955 (div. 1979); children: Theresa Ann, Carrie Marie, Janelle Elizabeth; m. Marjorie Lou Cox, Sept. 27, 1980. BS, N.Mex. State U., 1957; MS, U. N.Mex., 1961, PhD, 1965. Tchr. biology Las Cruces H.S., N.Mex., 1957-58; asst. prof. biology St. John's U., Collegeville, Minn., 1964-65; prof. biology Eastern N.Mex. U., Portales, 1965—. Contbr. articles to profl. jours. Bd. trustees N.Mex. Mus. of Natural History, 1996—. Served to capt. U.S. Army, 1958-59; mem. Res., 1959-66. Recipient Presdl. Faculty award Eastern N.Mex. U., 1970, Pres.'s Faculty award for excellence in rsch., 1988, Spirit of Ea. award, 1995; Outstanding Sci. award N.Mex. Acad. Sci., 1975. Mem. Southwestern Naturalists (treas. 1974-78), Am. Soc. Mammalogists, Herpetologists League, Sigma Xi, Phi Kappa Phi (pres. 1970-74). Roman Catholic.

GENNARO, RICHARD FRANCIS, JR., chiropractor; b. Bronx, N.Y., Oct. 27, 1962; s. Richard Francis Sr. and Adelina Cecilia (Hughes) G.; m. Kimberly Perry Elwell, Dec. 30, 1989. BS, U.S. Mil. Acad., 1984; D of Chiropractic, N.Y. Chiropractic Coll., 1994. Cert. sports and fitness chiropractor. Prin. Gennaro Family and Sports Chiropractic, Poughkeepsie, N.Y., 1995—; adj. prof. Marist Coll., Poughkeepsie, 1997—; cons. Scientific Stretch Ltd., Halifax, Can., 1995—; offcl. pro divsn. Internat. Fedn. of Body Builders, 1998—. bd. dirs. YMCA, Poughkeepsie. Mem. Internat. Chiropractics Assn. (bd. dirs. coun. on fitness and sports health sci. 1994—, chmn. sports coun. com. on exercise and fitness 1997—, editl. adv. bd. jour. 1997—), Bus. Network Internat. (Poughkeepsie chpt. pres. 1996), Pleasant Valley C. of C. (bd. dirs. 1996), LaGrange Lions Club (quest coord. 1997), West Point Soc. of N.Y., Abner Doubleday Soc. (bd. dirs. 1991), N.Y. State Chiropractors Assn. Roman Catholic. Home: RR 2 Box 290 Pleasant Valley NY 12569-9631 Office: Gennaro Family/Sports Chiropractic 232 Freedom Plains Rd Poughkeepsie NY 12603-6324

GENNETT, TIMOTHY, academic administrator; b. Richmond, Ind., July 25, 1951; s. Henry and Barbara Milda (Collignon) G.; m. Sharon Gail Cox, Mar. 5, 1976. BS in Chemistry, Purdue U., 1973, MS in Indsl. Adminstrn., 1974, MSEd, 1984. Lic. amateur radio operator. Sales engr. Gulf Oil Corp., San Antonio, 1975-77; asst. mgr. residence halls Purdue U., West Lafayette, Ind., 1977-82, mgr. residence halls, 1982-90, asst. dir. residence halls, 1990-95, dir. facilities housing and food svcs., 1995—; dir. Gennett Graphics, Lafayette, Ind., 1992—; presenter Assn. Coll. and Univ. Housing Officers, 1994, 96. Contbr. articles to profl. jours. Sec. disaster svcs. com. ARC, Tippecanoe County, Ind., 1995-97. Named Vol. of Yr. Disaster Svsc. ARC, 1996. Mem. Assn. Higher Edn. Cable TV Adminstrs., Tippecanoe Amateur Radio Assn. (sec. 1995—97), Soc. Cable TV Engrs. Office: Purdue U 105 Smalley Ctr West Lafayette IN 47906-4205

GENOVA, DIANE MELISANO, lawyer; b. Yonkers, N.Y., Aug. 8, 1948; d. Joseph Louis and Ines (Fiumana) Melisano; m. Joseph Steven Genova, Jan. 15, 1983; children: Anthony Robert, Matthew Edward. AB, Barnard Coll., 1970; postgrad. Harvard U., 1970-71; J.D., Columbia U., 1975. Assoc., Milbank, Tweed, Hadley & McCloy, N.Y.C., 1975-80, Tung, Drabkin & Boynton, N.Y.C., 1980-81; v.p., asst. resident counsel Morgan Guaranty Trust Co. N.Y., N.Y.C., 1981-90, managing dir., assoc. gen. counsel, 1990—. Harlan Fiske Stone scholar, 1972-75. Mem. Assn. of Bar of City of N.Y., N.Y. State Bar Assn. Roman Catholic. Office: J P Morgan & Co Inc 60 Wall St New York NY 10005-2888

GENOVA, JOSEPH STEVEN, lawyer; b. Red Bank, N.J., Nov. 12, 1952; s. M. Leonard and Margaret (Coons) G.; m. Janet Scott, May 18, 1974 (div. Dec. 1980) ; m. Diane Melisano Genova, Jan. 15, 1983; children: Anthony Robert, Matthew Edward. BA, Dartmouth Coll., 1974; JD, Yale U., 1977. Bar: N.Y. 1978, U.S. Dist. Ct. (no., so. and ea. dists.) N.Y., Calif. 1993. Assoc. Milbank, Tweed, Hadley & McCloy, N.Y.C., 1977-85, ptnr., 1986—; ct. appointed arbitrator U.S. Dist. Ct. (ea. dist.) N.Y., 1986—; mediator U.S. Dist. Ct. (so. dist.) N.Y., 1992—. Bd. dirs. Legal Aid Soc., N.Y.C., 1995—; N.Y. Lawyers Pub. Interest, 1997—; apptd. N.Y. Chief Judge Pro Bono Review Com. (1990-94), Legal Svcs. Project., 1997—. Fellow Am. Bar Found., N.Y. Bar Found.; mem. ABA (Pro Bono Pub. award 1992, William Reece Smith award 1996, ABA Commn. on Iolta 1996—), Assn. Bar City N.Y. (com. on housing and urban devel. 1982-85, com. on judiciary 1988-91, vice chmn. 1990-91, frequent interim mem., com. pro bono legal svcs., 1993—), N.Y. State Bar Assn. (com. on legal aid 1980—), chmn. 1986-91, co-chmn. pres.'s com. on access to justice 1990—, mem. task force on law guardian sys. 1989—, mem. special com. future profession, 1998—), Fed. Bar Coun. (com. on 2d cir. cts. 1988-98, com. pub. svc. responsibility 1991—, chmn. 1994—, trustee 1998—). Roman Catholic. Avocations: fishing, skiing. Office: Milbank Tweed Hadley & McCloy 1 Chase Manhattan Plz Fl 47 New York NY 10005-1413

GENOVESE, FRANCIS CHARLES (FRANK GENOVESE), economist, consultant, editor, writer; b. Toronto, Ont., Can., Feb. 16, 1921; came to U.S., 1946, naturalized, 1960; s. Francis A. and Florence M. (Ferguson) G.; m. Candace E. Moorhouse, June 17, 1944; children: Margaret, Steven, Jeremy, Michael. BA, U. Toronto, 1942, MA, 1946; PhD, U. Wis., 1953. Mem. faculty Babson Coll., Babson Park, Mass., 1955—, dean Grad. Sch., 1962-73, prof. econs., 1962-87, prof. emeritus, 1987—; pres. Pleiad Corp., 1974-76; advisor Ctrl. Bank Jordan, 1975; vis. prof. NYU, 1960-62; vis. faculty Brown U. Grad. Sch. Banking, 1962-64, Wellesley Coll., 1962; pres. Am. Jour. Econs. & Sociology, Inc., 1997-99. Editor: Lombard Street; editor in chief Am. Jour. Econs. and Sociology, 1989-97; dir. Babson-Bernays Competition, 1976; contbr. articles to profl. jours., newspapers. Mem. Dem. Town Com., 1978—; mem. Nelson Small Bus. Task Force; bd. dirs. Mass. Higher Edn. Loan Corp., 1978-81, Schalkenbach Found., 1983-99; corp. mem. Mass. Goodwill Industries, 1973-86. With Can. Army, 1944-45. Fellow U. Wis., 1946-47. Mem. Am. Econ. Assn., Am. Fin. Assn., Can. Econ. Assn., Harvard Faculty Club. Unitarian. Fax: (781) 239-6465. E-mail: genovese@babson.edu. Home: 18 Massasoit Rd Wellesley MA 02481-2411 Office: Babson Coll Dept Econs Babson Park MA 02481-0310

GENOVESE, LAWRENCE MATTHEW, secondary education educator; b. N.Y.C., Jan. 1, 1949; s. Robert Pascuale Sisto and Jean Laura (Lundari) G.; m. Laura Gail Vukich, Aug. 9, 1975; 1 child, Lawrence Matthew II. BS, Queens Coll., 1971, MS, 1973; profl. diploma, St. John's U., Jamaica, N.Y., 1976. Cert. elem. speech and English tchr., sch. adminstr., supr., sch. dist. adminstr., N.Y. Cluster tchr. Mark Twain Middle Sch., Yonkers, N.Y., 1971-72; elem. tchr. N.Y.C. Pub. Schs., 1972-75; English, lang. arts tchr. Burr's Ln. Jr. High Sch., Dix Hills, N.Y., 1975—; lang. arts tchr. Half Hollow Hills High Sch., Dix Hills, N.Y., Candlewood Middle Sch, Dix Hills, N.Y., 1975—; supr. Summer Youth Employment Program, N.Y.C., 1971—. Author: No One Would Play With Peppe, 1970, We Are Children of the Zuni, 1972, How to Teach the Recorder, 1974. Recipient Humanitarian award Half Hollow Hills Parent Tchrs. Students Assn., 1979, Dr. Jenkins award, 1990. Mem. L.I. Bd. Realtors, Masons, Phi Delta Kappa. Avocations: piano, gardening, theater, opera, real estate.

GENOVESE, PHILIP WILLIAM, civil engineer; b. New Haven, Jan. 22, 1917; s. Anthony and Angelina (Ingianni) G.; m. Restituta Adelaide Buononcore, Jan. 25, 1947; children: A. Felicity Bruns, Philip A.V. BE, Yale U., 1938; MBA, U. New Haven, 1979. Registered profl. engr., Conn., N.Y.; lic. land surveyor, Conn. Field engr. Clarence M. Blair, Inc., New Haven, 1939-40, Bridgeport (Conn.) Hydraulic Co., 1940-41; design engr., ptnr. Argraves & Mort, New Haven, 1946-49; ptnr. Newman E. Argraves & Assocs., New Haven, 1949-54; pres. Philip W. Genovese & Assocs., Inc., Woodbridge, Conn., 1955-95; joint venture ptnr. Buckley Bridge over Conn. River, Barstow and Mulligan; joint venture ptnr. Genovese and Cahn-New Haven Devel. Program; ptnr. World Wide Cons., Saigon, Vietnam; cons. and design engr.; bd. dirs. Conn. Nat. Bank, New Haven; adv. bd. 1st Bank. Chmn. Sch. Bldg. Com.; conservation commr.; asst. project mgr. Underground Fuel Storage Nat. Historic Civil Engring. Landmark, Pearl Habor, Hawaii, 1994. Lt. comdr. Civil Engring. Corps. USNR, 1941-46. Mem. ASCE (life), NSPE (bd. dirs. 1951-63), Conn. Soc. Profl. Engrs. (past pres., Outstanding Svc. award, Engr. of Yr. award) Conn. Engrs. in Pvt. Practice (pres. 1983-85), Bd. Supervision of Dams, Am. Arbitration Assn. (panelist), C. of C. (chmn. energy and environ. com.), Farms Country Club (Wallingford, Conn.), Yale Club New Haven.

GENOWAYS, HUGH HOWARD, systematic biologist, educator; b. Scottsbluff, Nebr., Dec. 24, 1940; s. Theodore Thompson and Sarah Louise (Beales) G.; m. Joyce Elaine Cox, July 28, 1963; children: Margaret Louise, Theodore Howard. AB, Hastings Coll., 1963; postgrad. U. Western Australia, 1964; PhD, U. Kans., 1971. Curator The Mus., Tex. Tech U., Lubbock, 1972-76, lectr. Mus. Sci. Program, 1974-76; curator Carnegie Mus. Natural History, Pitts., 1976-86; dir. U. Nebr. State Mus., Lincoln, 1986-94; chair mus. studies program U. Nebr., 1989-95, 97—, prof. state mus., 1986—, prof. biol. scis., 1987—, prof. mus. studies, 1990—, prof. natural resource scis., 1997—. Author, editor: Mammalian Biology in South America, 1982; Natural History of the Dog, 1984; Contributions in Vertebrate Paleontology, 1984; Species of Special Concern in Pennsylvania, 1985; Current Mammalogy, 1987, 90; Biology of the Heteromyidae, 1993, Storage of Natural History Collections: A Preventive Conservation Approach, 1996, Contributions in Mammalogy: A Memorial Volume Honoring Dr. J. Knox Jones, Jr., 1996. Packmaster, Allegheny Trails coun. Boy Scouts Am., 1981-83, asst. scoutmaster, 1983-86. Grantee, Fulbright, 1964, NSF, 1977-86, R.K. Mellon Found., 1981-86, Smithsonian Fgn. Currency Program, 1983-84, Inst. Mus. Svcs., 1989-96. Mem. Am. Soc. Mammalogists (pres. 1984-86, C. Hart Merriam award 1987, editor Spl. Pubs. 1995-96, historian 1997—), Internat. Theriological Congress (steering com. 1985—), Southwestern Assn. Naturalists (pres. 1984-85), Am. Assn. Museums, Nebr. Mus. Assn. (pres. 1990-92, 1st Hugh H. Genoways Achievement award 1994, sec. 1997—), Assn. Systematics Collections (bd. dirs. 1993-94), Nat. Inst. for Conservation Cultural Property (bd. dirs. 1993-94), Soc. Conservation Biology, Sociedad Argentina para Estudio Mamíferos, Lincoln Attractions and Mus. Assn. (chair 1987-94), Soc. Systematic Biologists, Rotary (bd. dirs. Lincoln N.E. club, 1990-92). Office: U Nebr-Lincoln State Mus W436 Nebraska Hall Lincoln NE 68588-0514

GENRICH, JUDITH ANN, real estate executive; b. Milw., Mar. 10, 1949; d. Einar and Eleanor Svea (Russell) Barnes; divorced; children: Krista Svea, Erik Leif. BA, Gustavus Adolphus Coll., 1970; grad., Wis. Sch. Real Estate, Milw., 1979; postgrad., Carroll Coll., 1980, U. Wis., 1978-80, 92. Tchr. Oak Grove Mid. Sch., Bloomington, Minn., 1970-71, Mukwonago (Wis.) H.S., 1971-72; sales mgr. Lincoln Park Homes, West Allis, Wis., 1972-73, v.p., 1973-74, pres., 1974-97; pres. Lincoln Park Homes, Palm Coast, Fla., 1997—; chmn. Mfrd. Housing Subdivision Sec., Madison, 1978-80; sec. Southeastern Wis. Housing, Milw., 1981-82, treas., 1982-84. Bd. dirs. Waukesha YMCA, 1985-87, v.p. 1987-89; bd. dirs. YMCA Heritage Found., 1994-97; bd. dirs. Waukesha County United Way, 1984-87; coun. pres. Stetson U., 1996—; mem. alumni bd. Gustavus Adulphus Coll., St. Peter, Minn., 1974-80; trustee The Cooper Inst., Naples, Fla., 1987-93, mem. adv. bd., 1993—. Recipient Dedicated Svc. award Wis. Mfrd. Housing, 1975-84, 88, Vol. of Yr. award Univ. Lake Sch., 1995. Mem. Wis. Mfrd. Housing Assn. (bd. dirs. 1975-80), Ind. Bus. Assn. Wis. (trustee U. Lake 1991-96), Merrill Hills Country Club (chair golf 1991), Milw. Women's Dist. Golf Assn. (bd. dirs. 1993, v.p. 1994, pres. 1995-96), Vasa Lodge, Eagle Creek Country Club, Hammock Dunes Country Club. Republican. Lutheran. Avocations: golf, photography. Home: 840 S Collier Blvd Apt 305 Marco Island FL 34145-6129

GENRICH, MARK L., newspaper editorial writer, columnist; b. Buffalo, Aug. 28, 1943; m. Allison Forbes, 1967; children: Audrey, Liza, Colby. BA, Bucknell U., 1966. Editl. writer Palladium-Item, Richmond, Ind., 1970; writing exec. Bruce Eberle & Assocs., Inc., Vienna, Va., 1975-77; dep. editor editl. pgs. Phoenix Gazette, 1977-96; editl. writer, columnist The Ariz. Republic, Phoenix, 1996-98; dir. Warne Ctr. Goldwater Inst., Phoenix, 1998—; participant U.S. Army War Coll., Carlisle, Pa., U.S. Naval War Coll., Newport, R.I.; participant arms control, disarmament programs including Space & Arms talks, Geneva; chmn. New Tech. Com., Journalism in Edn. Com.; mem. various coms. Created, hosted cable TV program focus on polit. figures; regional editor The Masthead. Grantee European Cmty. Visitor Programme, 1993; recipient highest honors editl. writing, newspaper design Ariz., Western Region; highest honor Maricopa County Bar Assn.; Stanford U. media fellow, 1985. Mem. Nat. Conf. Editl. Writers (bd. dirs., included vol. Editl. Excellence), First Amendment Cong. (bd. dirs.), Soc. Profl. Journalists/Sigma Delta Chi, ABA (com. prisons, sentencing). Avocations: coaching competitive soccer, tennis, photography, riding. Home: 130 W Pine Valley Dr Phoenix AZ 85023 Office: The Goldwater Inst 201 N Central Ave Phoenix AZ 85004

GENRICH, WILLARD ADOLPH, lawyer; b. Buffalo, Feb. 19, 1915; s. John E. and Emma P. (Luescher) G.; m. Eleanor M. Merrill, Mar. 15, 1941; children: Willa Genrich Long, Ellen Genrich Rusling, Willard A., Jeffrey M. LLB, U. Buffalo, 1938; LHD, Medaille Coll., 1973, N.Y. Med. Coll., 1981, Hofstra U., 1985, SUNY, 1986; LLD, Canisius Coll., 1975, L.I. U., 1979, Hobart Coll., 1981, Fordham U., 1984, N.Y. Inst. Tech., 1979; D in Comml. Sci., Niagara U., 1980; D in Civil Law, Mercy Coll., 1981; D in Chiropractic Sci., N.Y. Chiropractic Coll., 1983; LLD, D'Youville Coll., 1987. Bar: N.Y. 1939. Spl. agt. FBI, 1942-46; pvt. practice Amherst, N.Y., 1946—; pres. Genrich Builders, Inc., Buffalo, 1966—; owner, operator 2 hotels; dir. real estate corps.; bd. dirs. N.Y. State Higher Edn. Assistance Corp., 1962-73; bd. regents U. State N.Y., 1973-95, vice chancellor bd. regents, 1977-79, chancellor, 1980-85, chancellor emeritus, 1986—; del. N.Y. State Constl. Conv., 1967. Past trustee N.E. br. YMCA; trustee First Presbyn. Ch. Recipient Pres.'s award Daemen Coll., 1975; Disting. Citizen's award DeVeaux Sch., 1975; Disting. Alumni award U. Buffalo Law Sch., 1978; Disting. Alumni award Alumni Assn. SUNY-Buffalo, 1980; Disting. Citizen's Achievement award Canisius Coll. Bd. Regents, 1980; Citation of Appreciation, Commn. of Ind. Colls. and U. Western N.Y. Consortium of Higher Edn., 1978; Pres.'s award Hilbert Coll., 1983; John Jay award Commn. Ind. Colls. and Univs., 1984; Svc. award Daemen Coll., 1984, Bernard E. Hughes Recognition award N.Y. State Assn. Health, Phys. Edn. Recreation and Dance, 1986; Disting. Svc. award N.Y. State 4201 Schs. Assn., 1986, Merit award N.Y. State Assn. of Two Yr. Colls., 1986; 1st Disting. Alumnus award Benett High Sch., 1990; Friend of Children award N.Y. Assn. Sch. Psychologists, 1991; Community Svc. award AmherstGOP, 1991. Hon.life membership award, N.Y. State, Parent Tchr. Assn.,1993, Daemen Coll. Pres. award, 1994, Park Sch. award, Disting. Edn. Svc., award 1995, Home Economic Tchr. Assn. Corning award, hon. mem. of bd. of visitors of Batavia School for the Blind, hon. mem. Amherst So. Rotary Club. Mem. ABA, N.Y. State Bar Assn., Erie County Bar Assn., Am. Judicature Soc., N.Y. Hon. State PTA (life), Rotary. Home: 66 Getzville Rd Buffalo NY 14226-3514 Office: 4287 Main St Snyder NY 14226-3504

GENS, RALPH SAMUEL, electrical engineering consultant; b. Berlin, Germany, Nov. 25, 1924; s. Alexander and Renata Gens; m. Ida L. Mattson; children: Marilyn R., David A. BS in Elec. Engring., Oreg. State U., 1949. Registered profl. engr., Oreg. Engr. Bonneville Power Adminstrn., Portland, Oreg., 1949-80, chief, system engr., 1966-74, mgr. planning, research and devel., 1974-77, chief engr., asst. adminstr. for engring and constrn., 1977-80; cons. Portland, 1980—; advisor NSF, 1971-76; mem. adv. com. Project UHV, 1968-79; mem. Electricity Commn. of Papua, New Guinea, 1981-88; chmn. energy rsch. adv. bd. U.S. Dept. Energy, 1984-85, mem., 1985-89; chmn. planning coordination com. of Western Systems Coordinating Coun., 1975-76. Contbr. articles to profl. jours.; patentee in field. Served as sgt. U.S. Army, 1943-46, PTO. Recipient Disting. Service award Dept. Interior, 1978. Fellow IEEE (chmn. surge protective devices com. 1971, chmn. Portland sect. 1968, William M. Harbishaw award 1984, Centennial medal 1984); mem. NAE, Internat. Conf. Large High Voltage Electric Systems (U.S. v.p. 1979-80, chmn. study com. system analysis and technique 1986-92, Atwood award 1990, Internat. honorary mem., 1992), Electric Power Rsch. Inst. (rsch. adv. com. 1977-80), Tau Beta Pi, Sigma Tau, Eta Kappa Nu, Pi Mu Epsilon.

GENSHEIMER, ELIZABETH LUCILLE, software specialist; b. Louisville, Jan. 25, 1955; d. Theodore Rudolph and Florence Virginia (Nieder) G. BS in Computer Sci., U. Louisville, 1976, postgrad., 1977-78; postgrad., U. Tex., Dallas, 1993—. Weapons analyst CIA, Washington, 1975-76; engr. software Tex. Instruments, Dallas, 1978-81, No. Telecom, Inc., Richardson, Tex., 1981-83; mem. sci. staff Bell No. Rsch., Richardson, 1983-88, magnet mgr. univ. interrels. program U. Southwestern La., 1986-88, mgr. product test Meridian Data Network Sys., 1988-89; mgr. devel. software test Convex Computer Corp., Richardson, Tex., 1989-93; software cons. Ft. Worth Tech. Cons., 1993-95; software devel. and verification Compaq Computer (Tandem Telecom), 1995—; cons. webpage design Telereality/faire.net, 1996—. Mem. APA, Soc. Computers in Psychology, Nature Conservancy, Nat. Geog. Soc., North Tex. Water Garden Soc. (bd. membership 1997—), Whale Watch Soc., Piaget Soc. Avocations: cycling, hiking, photography, Renaissance faires, tennis. Home: PO Box 796005 Dallas TX 75379-6005

GENSLER, GARY, federal agency administrator; b. Balt.; m. Francesca Danieli; children: Anna, Lee, Isabel. BS in Econs., U. Pa., 1978, MBA, 1979. With mergers and acquistion dept. The Goldman Sachs Group, L.P., 1979-84, supr. advisor media cos., 1984-88, ptnr., 1988, with fixed income divsn., with ops. tech. and fin. divsn., 1994, co-head fin., 1995—; asst. sec. treasury for fin. markets Dept. Treasury, Washington, 1997—. Nat. trustee Balt. Mus. Art. Office: Dept Treasury 15th and Pennsylvania Ave Washington DC 20220

GENT, ALAN NEVILLE, physicist, educator; b. Leicester, Eng., Nov. 11, 1927; came to U.S., 1961, naturalized, 1972; s. Harry Neville and Gladys (Hoyle) G.; m. Jean Margaret Wolstenholme, Sept. 1, 1949; children: Martin Paul Neville, Patrick Michael, Andrew John; m. Ginger Lee, Sept. 4, 1997. B.S., U. London, Eng., 1946, B.S. in Physics, 1949, Ph.D. in Sci, 1955; DHC, U. Haute-Alsace, France, 1997; DSc (hon.), De Montfort U., Eng., 1998. Lab. asst. John Bull Rubber Co., Leicester, Eng., 1944-45; research physicist Brit. (now Malaysian) Rubber Producers' Research Assn., 1949-61; prof. polymer physics U. Akron, Ohio, 1961-88; Dr. Harold A. Morton prof. polymer physics and polymer engring. U. Akron, 1988-94; prof. emeritus, 1994—; dean grad. studies and research U. Akron, 1978-86; vis. prof. dept. materials Queen Mary Coll., U. London, 1969-70; vis. prof. dept. chem. engring. McGill U., 1983; Hill vis. prof. U. Minn., 1985; cons. Goodyear Tire & Rubber Co., 1963—, Gen. Motors, 1973-87. Contbr. articles to profl. publs. Served with Brit. Army, 1947-49. Recipient Mobay award, Cellular Plastics divsn. Soc. of Plastics Industry, 1963, Colwyn medal Plastics and Rubber Inst. Gt. Brit., 1978, Adhesives award Com. F-11, ASTM, 1979, Internat. Rsch. award Soc. Plastics Engrs., 1980, Whitby award Rubber Chem. divsn. Am. Chem. Soc., 1987, Pub. Svc. medal NASA, 1988, Charles Goodyear medal Rubber Chem. divsn. Am. Chem. Soc., 1990; installed Ohio Sci. Tech. and Industry Hall of Fame, 1993. Mem. NAE, Soc. of Rheology (pres. 1981-83, Bingham medal 1975), Adhesion Soc. (pres. 1978-80, 3M award 1987, Pres.'s award 1997), Am. Phys. Soc. (chmn. divsn. high polymer physics 1977-78, High Polymer Physics prize 1996). Democrat. Office: U Akron Inst Polymer Science Akron OH 44325-3909

GENTER, JOHN ROBERT, grocery industry executive; b. Huntsville, Ala., Oct. 16, 1957; s. John C. and Madge (McDaniel) G.; m. Margaret F. MacNaughton, Sept. 5, 1981; children: John Thomas, Lois Katharine. BS in Mktg. and Bus., U. Ala., 1980. Sales rep. food div. Procter & Gamble, Cin. and Jacksonville (Fla.), 1980-81, dist. field rep., 1981; unit mgr. Procter & Gamble, Cin., Tampa (Fla.), 1982-84; div. trade devel. mgr., regional mgr. Frito-Lay, Inc., Dallas, Tampa, 1984-85; field mktg. mgr. vintage div. E&J Gallo Winery, Modesto (Calif.), Tampa, 1985, state mgr., 1986, div. mgr., 1986-91, region mgr. chain div., 1992-95; dir. mktg. Purity Wholesale Grocers, Boca Raton, Fla., 1995-96; bus. mgr. Acosta Sales Co., Tampa, 1996-97; divsn. mgr. Sutter Home Winery, Tampa, 1998-99, gen. sales mgr. South,, 1999—; trainer sales mgmt., 1999—; trainer Sales Mgmt. Tng. Sch. Procter & Gamble, Cin., 1982-83, Sales Devel. Program Frito-Lay, Dallas, 1984-85. Author: (with others) E&J Gallo Field Marketing Manual, 1986. Mem. vestry St. John's Ch., Tampa, 1985—, active Father's Ministry, chmn. Every Mem.; youth soccer, baseball and basketball coach YMCA; trustee Patrons of St. John's Sch. Recipient Coach of Yr. award Tampa Tribune. Mem. U. Ala. Alumni Assn., Soc. de Vinum Honoratus, Beta Gamma Sigma. Republican. Episcopalian. Home and Office: 559 Ladrone Ave Tampa FL 33606-4036 Office: Sutter Home Winery 559 Ladrone Ave Tampa FL 33606

GENTILCORE, JOHN C., school principal. Prin. Mt. Sinai (N.Y.) Union Free Sch Dist.

GENTILE, ANTHONY, coal company executive; b. Aquila, Italy, Nov. 1, 1920; s. Gregorio and Antonietta (Duronio) G.; m. Nina Angela DiScipio, Mar. 4, 1943; children: Robert Henry, Anita Marie, Rita Ann, Thomas Gregory. Student Youngstown Coll., 1939-42; LHD (hon.), U. of Steubenville, 1977, DHL (hon.), 1988. Co-owner Pike Inn-Restaurant, Bloomingdale, Ohio, 1946-52; asst. to owner Huberta Coal Co., Steubenville, Ohio, 1952-55; gen. mgr. Half Moon Coal Co., Weirton, W.Va., 1955-57; gen. mgr. Ohio River Collieries Co., Columbus, 1957-59, pres., 1959—; pres. Lafferty Coal Mining Co., Eastern Ohio Coal Co., 1959—; v.p. Big Mountain Coals, Inc., Prenter, W.Va., 1962—, chmn. bd., 1962—; pres. Bither Mining Co. W.Va.; v.p. N & G Constrn., Bannock Land Co.; chmn., pres. Bannock Coal Co., Lafferty, Ohio, 1985-88, chmn., 1988—; chmn. bd. dirs. Mining and Reclamation Council Am., Washington; bd. dirs. Union Bank, Steubenville. Mem. 1st Ohio Trade Commn. to Europe, 1965; mem. adv. bd. St. John Med. Ctr., Steubenville; mem. bd. trustees Coll. Steubenville, Ohio Valley Hosp., past chmn., Steubenville. Served to 1st lt AUS, 1942-45, capt. Res. ret. Decorated Purple Heart, Silver Star; recipient Citizen of Yr. award Wintersville C. of C., 1976, Conservation award for Ohio River Collieries from Gov. Ohio, 1977, Humanitarian award Jeffersonian Lodge, Jefferson County, Ohio, 1979. Mem. Am. Mining Congress (mem. adv. council coal div. 1965). Home: 4 Normandy Dr Steubenville OH 43953-3800 Office: Ohio River Collieries Co PO Box 128 Bannock OH 43972-0128

GENTILE, JOSEPH F., lawyer, educator; b. San Pedro, Calif., Jan. 15, 1934; s. Ernest B. and Icy Otie (Martin) G.; m. Kathleen McMahon, Aug. 11, 1976; children—Kim Yvonne, Kevin James, Kelly Michele, Kristien Elyse, Kerri Nicole. B.A. cum laude, San Jose State U., 1955; J.D., U. La Verne, 1966; cert. in indsl. rels., UCLA, 1959; teaching credential, Calif. C.C., 1972; M.Pub. Adminstrn., U. So. Calif., 1976. Bar: Calif. 1967, U.S. Supreme Ct. 1972. Mem. indsl. relations staff Kaiser Steel Corp., Fontana Works, 1957-62; labor relations counsel Calif. Trucking Assn., Burlingame, Calif., 1964-68; acting dir. indsl. relations, labor relations counsel McDonnell Douglas Corp., Santa Monica, Calif., 1968-70; sr. partner Nelson, Kirshman, Goldstein, Gentile & Rexon, Los Angeles, 1970-76; individual practice, 1976—; Evening instr. bus. econs., indsl. relations U. Calif., 1969-94; evening instr. personnel and indsl. relations San Bernardino Valley Coll., 1969-72; evening instr. transp. Mt. San Antonio Coll., 1972-74; lectr. labor law Loyola U., 1973-74; lectr. Grad. Sch. Pub. Adminstrn., U. So. Calif., 1975-80; adj. prof. law Pepperdine U., 1981—; chmn. Employee Relations Commn., Los Angeles County, 1979—; mem. arbitration panel Fed. Mediation and Conciliation Service, Calif. Counciliation Service. Contbr. articles to profl. jours. Served with AUS, 1955-57. Mem. ABA, Calif. Bar Assn., Los Angeles County Bar Assn. (past chmn. exec. com. labor law sect.), Am. Arbitration Assn. (chmn. regional adv. coun., arbitration panel, nat. bd. dirs. 1985-91), Phi Sigma Alpha, Phi Alpha Delta. Office: PO Box 491117 Los Angeles CA 90049-9117

GENTILE, ROBERT DALE, optometrist, consultant; b. Pottsville, Pa., Oct. 24, 1946; s. Joseph and Evelyn Marie (Warfield) Gentile; m. Patricia Diane Fernsler, June 20, 1969; 1 child, Heather Ly Luxon. BA in Sci., Pa. State U., 1968; BS in Optometry, Pa. Coll. of Optometry, Phila., 1974, OD, 1977; MA in Human Resources, Webster U., 1985. Bd. cert. Am. Acad. Optometry. Advanced through ranks to lt. col. AUS, 1968-94; chief optometry 9th Gen. Dispensary, Aschaffenburg, Germany, 1977-80; optometrist Brook Army Med. Ctr., Ft. Sam Houston, Tex., 1980-82; chief eye sect., medicine and surgery divsn. Acad. Health Scis., Ft. Sam Houston, 1982-84; chief optometry Dunham Army Health Clinic, Carlisle Barracks, Pa., 1984-88, Med. Dept. Activity, Berlin, 1988-91, 121st Evacuation Hosp., Seoul, Republic of Korea, 1991-93; optometry cons. 18th Med. Command, Seoul, 1991-93; chief optometry Raymond W. Bliss Army Cmty. Hosp., Ft. Huachuca, Ariz., 1993-94; optometrist Naval Hosp., Camp Pendleton, Calif., 1994-96; cons. New Vision Internat., Escondido, Calif., 1996—; adj. prof. U. Houston Coll. Optometry, 1980-84, Pa. Coll. Optometry, 1980-84, New England Coll. Optometry, Boston, 1980-84. Decorated Legion of Merit, Meritorious Svc. medal with 3 Oak Leaf Clusters, Army Commendation medal with 4 Oak Leaf Clusters. Fellow Am. Acad. Optometry; mem. Am. Optometric Assn., Armed Forces Optometric Assn., Calif. Optometric Assn., Berlin Internat. Med. Soc., 38th Parallel Med. Soc., Silver Caduceus Soc. of Korea. Avocations: golf, gymnastics, table tennis, nutrition, exercise. Home and Office: 2241 Canyon View Gln Escondido CA 92026-5020

GENTINE, LEE MICHAEL, marketing professional; b. Plymouth, Wis., Feb. 18, 1952; s. Leonard ALvin and Dolores Ann (Becker) G.; m. Debra Ann Suemnicht, Dec. 29, 1973; children: Amanda, Joshua, Jonathan. BBA, U. Notre Dame, 1974; MBA, DePaul U., 1977. Acct. Hurdman & Cranston, Chgo., 1974-75; sales rep. Sargento Cheese Inc., Plymouth, 1975-78, mktg. mgr., 1978-81, sr. v.p. mktg., 1981-84, exec. v.p. mktg., 1984-89, pres. consumer products divsn., 1989-97; mem. adv. bd. Kaytee Products Inc., Chilton, Wis., 1994-98; mng. ptnr. Dairyland Investors Group, L.L.P., 1997—; bd. dirs. Sargento Foods Inc. Bd. dirs. Plymouth Softball Assn., 1980-95; pres. Plymouth Indsl. Devel. Corp., 1981-85, Parish Coun., 1989-90; chmn. Plymouth Advancement Com., pres., 1992-96; mem. adv. bd. St. Nicholas Hosp., 1998—. Named One of 100 Best and Brightest Advt. Execs., Advt. Age, 1986. Mem. Am. Mktg. Assn., Sheboygan County C. of C. (bd. dirs. 1987-89), Beta Gamma Sigma. Roman Catholic. Avocations: softball, golf, home rehabilitation. Office: Dairyland Investors Group LLP 601 Eastern Ave Plymouth WI 53073-1913

GENTLE, KENNETH WILLIAM, physicist; b. Oak Park, Ill., Oct. 27, 1940; s. William and Cathryn Mary (Spence) G. B.S., MIT, 1962, Ph.D., 1966. Asst. prof. dept. physics U. Tex., Austin, 1966-69, assoc. prof., 1970-75, prof. physics, 1976—, chair dept. physics, 1997—. Sloan fellow, 1973-75. Fellow Am. Phys. Soc. Home: 212 Buckeye Trl Austin TX 78746-4420 Office: Univ Tex Dept Physics Austin TX 78712

GENTNER, PAUL LEFOE, architect, consultant; b. Seattle, Feb. 24, 1944; s. Edward George and Opal Eloise (Davis) G.; m. Glenda Frank Hoy, May 25, 1975; 1 stepchild, Robert Michael Hurd. AA in Architecture, Anne Arundel C.C., Arnold, Md., 1970; BS in Engring., Century U., 1984. Registered arch., Md., Tex. Project rep. RTKL Assocs., Inc., Balt., 1970-73; staff architect James R. Grieves Assocs., Balt., 1973-77; sr. engr. Morrison-Knudsen (MKSAC), Columbia, Md., 1977-79; staff engr. Morrison-Knudsen (MKSAC), Saudi Arabia, 1979-81; planning mgr. Morrison-Knudsen Internat. Inc., Barranquilla, Colombia, S.Am., 1981-86; staff architect RTKL Assocs., Inc., Balt., 1986-92; specifications writer Sverdrup Cpr., Arlington, Va., 1992-93; mgr. specifications Daniel, Mann, Johnson, & Mendenhall, Balt., 1993-95, Arlington, Va., 1995-96; cons. Marriott Internat., Washington, 1996-98; with arch. and constrn. design mgmt. Marriott Internat. Corp., Washington, 1998—. With USNR, 1965-68, Vietnam; Persian Gulf, 1990-91. Mem. AIA, Constrn. Specifications Inst. (cert. constrn. specifier, bd. dirs. Balt. chpt. 1991-92, 1st v.p. 1993-94, pres. 1994-95), Soc. Am. Mil. Engrs., Bricklayers (local # 1). Home: 2028 Park Ave Baltimore MD 21217-4816 Office: Marriott Internat Dept 70-101-01 Marriott Dr Washington DC 20058

GENTRY, ALBERTA ELIZABETH, elementary education educator; b. Richter, Kans., Feb. 18, 1925; d. John Charles and Dessie Lorena (Duvall) Briles; m. Kenneth Neil Gentry, June 1, 1947; children: Michal Neil, Alan Dale, Elisa Ann. BE, Emporia (Kans.) Tchrs. Coll., 1975. Cert. tchr., Kans. Tchr. Chippewa Rural Sch., Ottawa, Kans., 1943-44; prin., tchr. Pomona (Kans.) Grade Sch., 1944-47, tchr., 1960-61; tchr. Silverlake Rural Sch., Pomona, 1947-48, Hawkins Rural Sch., Ottawa, 1948-49, Davy Rural Sch., Ottawa, 1950-53, Eugene Field Sch., Ottawa, 1953-54, Centropolis Grade Sch., Ottawa, 1964; tchr. Appanoose Elem. Sch., Pomona, 1964-90, ret., 1990; trainer student tchr., 1985-86. Author: Proven Ideas for Classroom Teachers, 1988. Project leader, supporter 4-H, Franklin County, Kans., 1963-67; den mother Boy Scouts Am., Ottawa, 1955-66; dir. Bible sch., tchr. Trinity Meth. Ch., Ottawa, 1955-70, supt., 1955-66, mem. choir, 1947—. Named to Kans. Tchrs. Hall of Fame, 1991. Mem. NEA, Kans. Tchrs. Assn., Kans. Edn. Assn., Alpha Delta Kappa (sec. 1988-90). Republican. Methodist. Avocations: bird watching, arts and crafts, family genealogy, flower gardening, music. Home: PO Box 2 Pomona KS 66076-0002

GENTRY, ALVIN, professional basketball coach; m. Suzanne Gentry; children: Ryan Marcus, Alexis. BA in Mgmt., Appalachian State U. Asst. coach U. Colo., Baylor U., U. Kans., 1985-88, San Antonio Spurs, L.A. Clippers; asst. coach Miami Heat, interim head coach, 1995; asst. coach Detroit Pistons, 1995-97, interim head coach, 1997-98, head coach, 1998—. Office: Detroit Pistons Two Championship Dr Auburn Hills MI 48326*

GENTRY, BERN LEON, SR., minority consulting company executive; b. Goldsboro, N.C., Sept. 9, 1941; s. Theodore Alfonso and Ruth Ester (Taylor) G.; m. Jane A. Price, Nov. 11, 1965; children: Michelle Lorraine, Bern Leon. Student, Rutgers U., 1959-61, Temple U., 1961-63, Cornell U., 1966-67, U. Okla., 1971. Tax acct. IRS, Phila., 1965-66; collection mgr., credit mgr., appliance store mgr., soft goods mdse. mgr. Sears, Roebuck & Co., Phila., 1966-71; program mgr., dir. nat. urban affairs U.S. Jr. C. of C., 1971-73, cons., 1973—; pres. Together, Inc., Tulsa, 1973—. Contbr. articles to profl. jours. Mem. nat. adv. bd. Boys Clubs Am., 1971—; mem. nat. Black alliance for grad. level edn. U. Mich.; past pres., bd. dirs. Tulsa Econ. Opportunity Task Force; pres. Community Service Agy.; bd. dirs. Jr. Achievement. Recipient award of accomplishment Sears Staff Sch., 1967; award of appreciation Black Peoples Unity Movement Econ. Devel. Corp., 1971; George Washington Honor medal Freedoms Found., 1974, 76; Keys to cities of Roanoke, Va.; Keys to cities of Baton Rouge, La.; Keys to cities of New Orleans; named Outstanding Young Man Camden, 1970; Outstanding Chpt. Pres. N.J. Jaycees; Outstanding Jaycee. Mem. Nat. Urban League, NAACP, Am. Mgmt. Assn., Nat. Assn. Human Rights Workers, Assn. Black Found. Execs., Nat. Assn. Pub. Relations Execs., Nat. Civil Service League, Nat. Assn. Community Devel., Nat. Assn. Vol. Services Coordinator, Camden Jaycees (pres. 1970-71), Tulsa Met. C. of C. Office: Together Inc PO Box 52528 3739 S Peoria Ave Tulsa OK 74105-3264

GENTRY, DAVID RAYMOND, engineer; b. Easley, S.C., Sept. 26, 1933; s. Thomas Herbert and Rosalie (Howard) G.; m. Mary Lynn White, June 5, 1955; children: David R. Jr., Mary Diane Gentry Windsor. BS, Clemson Coll., 1955; MS, Inst. Textile Tech., Charlottesville, Va., 1957; PhD, Clemson U., 1972. Rsch. engr. WestPoint (Ga.) Mfg. Co., 1957-60; asst. prof. Clemson (S.C.) U., 1960-67; mgr. testing and evaluation Phillips Fibers Corp., Greenville, S.C., 1967-73; assoc. prof. Ga. Inst. Tech., Atlanta, 1973-78; sr. devel. engr. Amoco Fabrics & Fibers Co., Atlanta, 1978-80, mgr. fibers devel., 1980-84, dir. fibers devel., 1985-90, rsch. assoc., 1990-92, sr. rsch. assoc., 1992—. fellow NSF, 1966, Sirrine Found., 1965-67, Inst. Textile Tech., 1955-57. Mem. ASTM (sec. com. D-13 textiles 1974-80), Am. Assn. Textile Technologists (sec. Piedmont chpt. 1963-65), The Fiber Soc., The Textile Inst. (assoc.), Phi Psi (sec., pres. Iota chpt. 1953-55, faculty adviser 1961-65), Phi Kappa Phi. Home: 3456 Embry Cir Atlanta GA 30341-5612 Office: Amoco Fabrics and Fibers Co 260 The Bluffs Atlanta GA 30336-1143

GENTRY, DON KENNETH, academic dean; b. Crawfordsville, Ind., Mar. 1, 1939; m. Carol A. Kern; children: Alynn, Alan, Andrew. BS in Animal Sci. & Agr. Edn., Purdue U., 1962, MS in Secondary Edn. & Ednl. Adminstrn., 1967; EdD in Ednl. Adminstrn., Ind. U., 1979; D (hon.), Vincennes U., 1983. Instr. in vocat. agr. North Montgomery Community Schs., Linden, Ind., 1962-67; state supr. agrl. edn. Ind. State Dept. Pub. Instruction, 1967-69, chief program planning, rsch. & evaluation div. vocat. edn., 1969, asst. dir. div. vocat. edn., 1969-70, dir. div. vocat. edn., 1970-71, exec. officer, state dir. vocat. edn., 1971-83; dir. Purdue Statewide Tech. Program Purdue U., West Lafayette, Ind., 1983-87, prof. indsl. tech., 1984—, asst. dean sch. tech., 1985-86, assoc. dean sch. tech., 1986-87, dean sch. tech., 1987—; univ. rep. to Nat. Engring. Tech. Coun., 1989—. Contbr. articles to profl. jours.; over 20 papers & presentations in field. Bd. dirs. Ind. Corp. for Sci. & Tech., 1982-83. Recipient Outstanding Svc. award Ind. Distbv. Edn. Clubs Am., 1972, Disting. Hoosier award Gov. Edgar D. Whitcomb, 1972, Hon. Future Homemaker award Future Homemakers Am., 1973, Outstanding Hoosier award Gov. Otis R. Bowen, 1975, Sagamore of Wabash award, 1980, Outstanding Svc. awards Ind. Vocat. Assn., 1973, Nat. Office Edn. Assn., 1975, Nat. Vocat. Edn. Spl. Needs Assn., 1980, Ind. Employment & Tng. Assn., 1982, Outstanding Leadership award Ind. Vocat. Adminstrs. Assn., 1983, Appreciation award U.S. Dept. Def., 1991. Mem. Am. Soc. for Engring. Edn. (engring. tech. div.), Am. Vocat. Assn. (life mem.), Engring. Tech. Leadership Inst., Engring. Tech. Coun., Nat. Consortium for Four Year Degree Engring. Tech. Schs., Indiana Health Careers, Inc. (membership chmn. 1980-83), Nat. Assn. State Dirs. Vocat. Edn. (bd. dirs., sec. 1979, pres. 1980, past pres. 1981), Nat. Consortium for Vocat. Edn. Leadership (devel.-charter pres. 1980, bd. dirs. 1979-82), Office Edn. Assn. (hon. life mem.), John Purdue Club, Ceres, Alpha Zeta, Alpha Tau Alpha, Tau Alpha Phi. Office: Purdue U Sch Tech West Lafayette IN 47907

GENTRY, DONALD WILLIAM, mine engineering executive; b. St. Louis, Jan. 18, 1943; s. William Henry and Roberta Elizabeth (Bardelmeier) G.; m. Sheila Carol Schuepbach, Aug. 21, 1965; children: Tara Cassandre, Chad Ryan. B.S.E., U. Ill., 1965; M.S., U. Nev., 1967; Ph.D., U. Ariz., 1972. Asst. prof. mining engring. Colo. Sch. Mines, Golden, 1972-74, assoc. prof., 1974-77, asst. to dean faculty, assoc. prof., 1977-78, asst. to dean faculty, 1978-79, prof. mining engring., 1978-83, dean undergrad. studies, 1983-84, dean engring. and undergrad. studies, 1990-95, head dept. mining engring., 1995-98, prof. mining-engring., 1998—; pres., CEO PolyMet Mining Corp., Golden, 1998—, also bd. dirs. Contbr. articles to profl. jours. Mem. Nat. Acad. Engring., Soc. Mining Engrs. of AIME (pres. 1993), AIME (dir. Colo. sect. 1982-83, Krumb lectr. 1987, pres. 1996, Krumb lectr. 1987, Mineral Industry Edn. award 1991, Daniel C. Jackling award 1998), Nat. Acad. Engring. (elected 1996), Sigma Tau, Sigma Gamma Epsilon. Republican. Lutheran. Home: 6590 Ridgeview Dr Morrison CO 80465-2700 Office: PolyMet Mining Corp 13949 W Colfax Ave Ste 205 Golden CO 80401-3209

GENTRY, FRANCIS G., German language educator; b. June 8, 1942; s. Louise M. (Casey) Denehy; m. Edda Schrader, Oct. 27, 1972. BS in German and English cum laude, Boston Coll., 1963; MA in German, Ind. U., 1966, PhD in German, 1973. Instr. SUNY, Albany, 1969-74, asst. prof., 1974-75; asst. prof. U. Wis., Madison, 1975-80, assoc. prof., 1980-84, prof., 1984-91; prof. Pa. State U., Univ. Park, 1991—; guest prof. Universität Freiburg, 1984; asst. to chair dept. German, U. Wis., Madison, 1980-84, chair, 1988-91, chair medieval studies program, 1986-89; head dept. German, Pa. State U., 1991-97; co-dir. Max Kade Inst. Forgerman-Am. Rsch.; served on numerous coms. U.Wis., Madison, Pa. State U.; councillor Medieval Assn. of the Midwest, 1980-82, v.p., 82-83, pres., 83-84; chair various sects. Internat. Cong. on Medieval Studies, 1977—; mem. USA Fellowship Selection Com. (Freiburg), 1984-85, Fulbright Selection Com. (Freiburg), 1985, commn. for selection of summer stipend awards NEH, Washington, 1988, exec. com. German-Am. Inst. (Freiburg), 1984-85; lectr. in field. Author: Triuwe and Vriunt in the Nibelungenlied, 1975, Bibliographie zur frühmittelhochdeutschen Dichtung, 1992, (with James K. Walter) German Epic Poetry, 1995, (with Christopher Kleinhenz) Medieval Studies in North America: Past, Present, Future, 1982, (with others) Monatshefte, 1982, Medieval Tales, 1983, Festschrift for Frank Banta, 1988, Deutsche Literatur: Eine Sozialgeschichte, 1988, Gottfried von Strasburg, 1988, Studies in Medievalism, 1991; mem. edit. bd. Monatshefte, 1975-92, editl. cons. 1992—, book rev. editor, 1975-91; mem. edit. bd. Allegorica, 1976-86; German editor Studies in Medievalism, 1986-91; mem. nat. adv. bd. dirs. The German Quarterly, 1991-94; assoc. editor: Medieval Germany: An Encyclopedia, 1992—; co-editor: The Nibelungenlied: An Encyclopedia, 1993—; reviewer various profl. jours., including Monatshefte, German Studies, German Studies Rev., German Quarterly, Germanistik, Modern Lang. Jour., Speculum, Choice; contbr. articles to profl. jours. Organizer Jr. Year in Freiburg 25th Anniversary Celebration, 1985; bd. dirs. Madison-Freiburg Sister City Assn., 1987-91, v.p., 1988-89, pres., 1989-91; adv. bd. dirs. Wis.-Hessen Ptnr. State Coun., 1990-91. Recipient Campion Disting. Alumnus award Boston Coll., 1977; Ind. U.-Kiel Universität Exch. fellow, 1964; fellow Inst. for Rsch. in the Humanities, 1977; Alexander von Humboldt-Stiftung fellow, 1978, 1982; Vilas Assoc. fellow U. Wis., Madison, 1986-88. Mem. Am. Assn. Tchrs. of German, Medieval Acad. Am. (chmn. local arrangements for ann. meeting 1989), Internat. Arthurian Soc., Internat. Courtly Lit. Soc., Internat. Mediävisten-Verband, Oswald-von-Wolkenstein-Gesellschaft, Wolfram-von-Eschenbach-Gesellschaft, Alexander Von Humboldt Assn. Am. (pres. Pa. chpt. 1997—), Delta Phi Alpha (pres. Beta chpt. 1968), Alpha Sigma Nu, Alpha and Omega. Avocations: hiking, travel.

GENTRY, JAMES WALTER, chemical engineer, educator; b. Hobart, Okla., Nov. 27, 1939; s. J. Bryan and Juanita F. (Davis) Gentry. BSChemE, Okla. State U., 1961; MSChemE, U. Birmingham, U.K., 1963; PhDChemE, U. Tex., 1969. Asst. prof. U. Md., Coll. Pk., 1969-72; assoc. prof. U. Md., 1972-78, prof., 1978—; ofcl. rep. GAeF at founding meeting Aerosol Soc. U.K.; cons. Bur. Comml. Fisheries, Asphalt Inst., 1975, Fraunhofer Gesellschaft, 1977, Health and Safety Exec., London, others; vis. scientist Institut fur Aerobiologie, Schmallenberg, West Germany, 1976-77, 1979, 1977-85, Kernforschung Zentrum, Karlsruhe, West Germany, 1986, Forschungszentrum fur Umwelt und Gesundheit, Frankfurt, 1993. Mem. edit. bd. Jour. Aerosol Rsch., 1982-86; contbr. numerous chpts. to books and articles to profl. jours. Fulbright fellow, 1961-62; grantee NSF, 1970-71, 77-78, 78-79, 80-84, Am. Standard Corp., 1972, EPA, 1979-81, 3M Corp., 1985, others. Fellow AIChE, Washington Acad. Sci. (Engring. Scis. award 1983); mem. Am. Chem. Soc., Gesellschaft fur Aerobiologie, Fine Particle Soc., N.Y. Acad. Scis., Phi Kappa Phi, Phi Lambda Upsilon, Omega Chi Epsilon, Pi Mu Epsilon (Alexander von Humboldt Sr. Scientist award 1993, Internat. Aerosol fellow 1996). Achievements include research in aerosol science and serosol mechanics with particular emphasis on non-spherical particles and electrical charging. Office: U Md Dept Chem Engring College Park MD 20742-2111

GENTRY, JAMES WILLIAM, retired state official; b. Danville, Ill., Aug. 14, 1926; s. Carl Lloyd and Leone (Isham) G.; A.B., Fresno State Coll., 1948; M.J., U. Calif., Berkeley, 1956; m. Dorothie Shirley Hechtlinger, Mar. 18, 1967; 1 stepdau., Susan Mushkin. Field rep. Congressman B.W. Gearhart, Fresno, Calif., 1948, Assemblyman Wm. W. Hansen, Fresno, 1950, sec., 1953-56; exec. asst. Calif. Pharm. Assn., Los Angeles, 1956-69, editor, pub. Calif. Pharmacy Jour., 1956-69; pub. relations dir. PAID Prescriptions, 1963-64; dir. pub. info. comprehensive Health Planning Council, Los Angeles County, 1969; asst. adminstr., dir. pub. info. So. Calif. Comprehensive Health Planning Council, 1969-71, acting adminstr., 1971-72; exec. sec., 1972-73, Calif. Adv. Health Council, 1973-85, fed. cons., 1986-88; Calif. Health Care Commn., 1973-75; acting public info. officer Calif. Office Statewide Health Planning and Devel., 1978-79; interim dir. , 1983; mem. L.A. Civil Svc. Police Interview Bd., 1967-72; asst. sgt.-at-arms Calif. State Assembly, 1950; exec. sec. Calif. Assembly Interim Com. on Livestock and Dairies, 1954-56; mem. adv. bd. Am. Security Council; mem. Calif. Health Planning Law Revision Commn.; former mem. Calif. Bldg. Safety Bd. Mem. Fresno County Republican Central Com., 1950; charter mem. Rep. Presdl. Task Force. Served to col. AUS, 1949-50, 50-53; Korea. Decorated Legion of Merit, Bronze Star medal, Commendation Ribbon with metal pendant ; recipient pub. awards Western Soc. Bus. Publns. Assn., 1964-67. Mem. Am. Assn. Comprehensive Health Planning, Pub. Relations Soc. Am., Ret. Officers Assn. (life), Allied Drug Travelers So. Calif., L.A. Press Club, Mil. Police Assn., Res. Officers Assn. (life), Assn. U.S. Army, U.S. Senatorial Club, The Victory Svcs. Club of London, Pi Gamma Mu, Phi Alpha Delta. Sigma Delta Chi. Editor: Better Health, 1963-67; Orientation Conf. Comprehensive Health Planning, 1969; Commentary, 1969-71. Editorial adv. Pharm. Svcs. for Nursing Homes: A Procedural Manual, 1966. Editor: Program and Funding, 1972; Substance Abuse, 1972. Home: 1603 Patriots Colony Dr Williamsburg VA 23188-1341

GENTRY, JERRY L., manufacturing executive; b. Tulsa, Mar. 19, 1935; s. Lloyd Walker and Beulah Pearl (Powers) G.; m. Susan Leigh Moors, July 14, 1991. Student, U. Okla., 1953-56; BA, U. Tulsa, 1963. Owner Gentry Group, Dallas, 1979-85; pres. Contract Wall Sys., Inc., Dallas, 1981—, Custom Installation Products & Svcs., Inc., Dallas, 1998—; co-developer pvc extrusion for constrn. acoustical walls; developer framing sys. for attaching fabric to ceiling tiles; co-owner nat. distbn. for French ceiling sys. for Barrisol; developer installation sys. for the peace Sheild Project, Saudi Arabia, 1991-95. Republican. Avocations: wine tasting, travel. Office: 2741 Satsuma # 106 Dallas TX 75229

GENTRY, MARSHALL BRUCE, English educator; b. Little Rock, July 28, 1953; s. Robert Bruce and Daisy Belle (Stockwell) G.; m. Alice Ruth Friman, Sept. 24, 1989. BA in English and Journalism with high honors, U. Ark., 1975; MA in English, U. Chgo., 1976; PhD in English, U. Tex., 1984. Instr., teaching asst. U. Tex., Austin, 1976-82; vis. asst. instr. English Tex. A&M U., College Station, 1983-84, vis. asst. prof., 1984-85; asst. prof. U. Indpls., 1985-91, assoc. prof., 1991-98, prof., 1998—. Author: Flannery O'Connor's Religion of the Grotesque, 1986; co-editor: Conversations with Raymond Carver, 1990, The Practice and Theory of Ethics, 1996; contbr. articles to profl. jours. Mem. AAUP (chpt. pres. 1989-91), MLA, Midwest MLA, South Cen. MLA, South Atlantic MLA, Soc. Study So. Lit., Soc. Study Midwestern Lit., Ind. Coll. English Assn. (co-pres. 1989-90), Flannery O'Connor Soc., Writer's Ctr. Ind., Phi Beta Kappa, Phi Kappa Phi. Office: U Indpls Dept English 1400 E Hanna Ave Indianapolis IN 46227-3697

GENTRY, PAMELA, ; m. Newton Gentry III; 2 children. Grad., U. Detroit Mercy. Journalist Tenn.; writer, editor, prodr. TV news W*USA-TV, Washington; dep. dir. Office Pub. Liaison, Health Care Financing Adminstr., 1993-95, acting assoc. adminstr. external affairs, 1995-97, dir. Office Comm. and Ops. Support,, 1997—; mem. welfare reform steering com. and balance budget amendment steering com. Children's Health Ins. Program; chair Presdl. Initiative on Historically BLack Coll. and Univs., Health Care Financing Adminstrn., rep. deptl. minority initiatives coordinating com.; dir. several nat. pub. affairs campaigns; spkr. tng. seminars on media rels. and pub. affairs. Developer Health Care Financing Adminstr. newsletter Healthwatch and homepage on world-wide web. Recipient Exceptional Media Merit award Nat. Women's Polit. Caucus. FAX: 202-401-2708. Office: Health Care Financing Adminstrn 200 Independence Ave SW Washington DC 20201-0004

GENTRY, RICKY GLYN, accountant; b. Cookeville, Tenn., Dec. 13, 1958; s. Glyn Austin and Joyce (Whiteaker) G.; m. Lisa Gay Stringer, Sept. 7, 1964; children: McKenzie Eden, Madison Eve. BSBA in Acctg., Tenn. Tech. U., 1980, MBA, 1994. CPA, Tenn. Acct. Totherow, Haile & Welch CPA's, McMinnville, Tenn., 1980-86, Davis, White & Assocs. CPA's, Murfreesboro, Tenn., 1986-87; comptr. 1st Am. Bank, Cookeville, 1987-90; cost acct. Nielsen Mfg., Gainesboro, Tenn., 1990—. Deacon Stevens Street Bapt. Ch., Cookeville, 1990—. Avocations: tennis, softball. Home: 1420 Hillsdale Dr Cookeville TN 38506-4213

GENTRY, ROBERT VANCE, physicist, researcher, writer; b. Chattanooga, July 9, 1933; s. Vance Ault and Sara Frances (Northington) G.; m. Patricia Ann Gentry, Jan. 20, 1953; children: Patricia Lynn, Michael Vance, David Wayne. B.S. in Physics, U. Fla., 1955, M.S., 1956; D.Sc. (hon.), Columbia Union Coll., Takoma Park, Md., 1977. Nuclear engr. Gen. Dynamics Co., Ft. Worth, 1956-58; sr. engr. Martin Co., Orlando, Fla., 1958-59; instr. math. U. Fla., Gainesville, 1959-61, Walla Walla (Wash.) Coll., 1961-62; instr. physics Ga. Inst. Tech., 1962-64; research physicist Archeol. Research Found., Atlanta, 1965-66; mem. faculty Columbia Union Coll., 1966-84, assoc. prof. physics, 1977-84; cons. physicist, 1984-86; research physicist Earth Sci. Assocs., Knoxville, Tenn., 1986—; guest scientist chemistry div. Oak Ridge Nat. Lab., 1969-82, 89; hon. asst. res. prof. physics U. Tenn.-Knoxville, 1982-83. Author: Creation's Tiny Mystery, 1986, 2d edit., 1988, 3d edit., 1992; chief rschr. (video) Fingerprints of Creation (Telly award 1993), The Young Age of the Earth, 1994; contbr. articles to profl. jours. Fellow NSF, 1962, grantee, 1971-77; grantee NASA, 1970-72. Mem. AAAS, Am. Phys. Soc., Am. Geophys. Union, N.Y. Acad. Scis., Sigma Xi (assoc.). Seventh-day Adventist. Achievements include discovery of polonium radioactive halos in granites, a new model of the universe to explain the Hubble redshift relation and the 2.7K Cosmic Blackbody Radiation without the use of spacetime expansion. Home: 6321 Cate Rd Powell TN 37849-4952 *To recognize that success in any field is not the result of chance or destiny but instead the reward of faithfully developing those talents endowed by the Creator provides the highest possible incentive for achieving that station in life for which each individual is uniquely fitted.*

GENTRY, VICKI PAULETTE, museum director; b. Bessemer, Ala., June 2, 1952; d. Gerald Vance and Marjorie Jean (Bush) George; children: Alissa Hubbard, Rebecca Hubbard. Office worker Mining Corp. of the South, Vance, Ala., 1978-79; artist, sign painter Bob's Sign Shop, Midfield, Ala., 1979-80; dir. Iron & Steel Mus. of Ala., McCalla, 1980—; program completion Office of Mus Programs, Smithsonian, Washington, 1987. Artist (book) Tannehill Crafts, 1982. Events Planner Ala. Reunion State of Ala., Montgomery, 1989. Recipient Top 20 Events in the South East award SE Tourism Soc., Atlanta, 1986-87, 88, 91, Head Start Vol. award, 1994. Mem. Ala. Preservation Alliance, Soc. Indsl. Archaeology, Nat. Trust for Hist. Preservation, Birmingham Area Mus. Assn., Am. Assn. State and Local History (program completion 1980), Am. Assn. Mus., Ala. Mus. Assn. (sec.-treas. 1983-85, Meritorious Svc. award 1983), Ala. State Employees Assn. (pres. Tannehill chpt. 1993-95). Democrat. Baptist. Avocations: pen, ink drawings, painting. Home: 16920 Brooke Dr Mc Calla AL 35111 Office: Tannehill Historical State Park 12632 Confederate Pkwy Mc Calla AL 35111

GENUARDI, CHARLES A., retail executive. CEO Genuardi Super Markets. Office: Genuardi Supermarkets 805 E Germantown Pike Ste 112 Norristown PA 19401-2497*

GENUIT, DAVID WALTER, podiatrist; b. Stockton, Calif., May 12, 1949; s. Walter Morales and Betty Alice (Behney) G. BS in Biology, U. Calif., Davis, 1971; BS in Med. Sci., Calif. Coll. Podiatric Medicine, 1973, D in Podiatric Medicine, 1975. Diplomat Am. Bd. Podiatric Surgery, Nat. Bd. Podiatry Examiners, Am. Acad. Pain Mgmt., Am. Bd. Forensic Examiners; cert. therapist; registered hypnotherapist; cert. hypnotherapist. Practice medicine specializing in podiatry Bremerton, Wash., 1975—; pres., chief exec. officer The Nemesis Corp.; pvt. practice hypnotherapy Bremerton, 1990—; clin. instr. Edmonds (Wash.) Community Coll., 1979-84, Bremerton Naval Hosp., 1981—, Olympic Coll., Bremerton, 1987—. Contbr. articles to profl. jours. Med. Explorer Search and Rescue, Bremerton, 1981—; mem. Nat. Assn. for Search and Rescue, 1980—. Fellow Am. Acad. Podiatric Sports Medicine; mem. Am. Podiatric Med. Assn., Wash. State Podiatric Med. Assn. Office: 1935 Wheaton Way Bremerton WA 98310-4343

GENUNG, NORMAN BERNARD, computer consultant; b. Dayton, Ohio, June 6, 1951; s. Paul Kenneth and Mary Elizabeth (Rose) G.; m. Sharon Rose Lynch, June 9, 1973; children: Jeffrey, Sarah. BS in Psychology, Mich. State U., 1973; MS in Ops. Mgmt., U. Ark., 1977. Chief plans br. Western Space and Missile Ctr., Lompoc, Calif., 1980-84; chief engring. div. Fgn. Tech. Div., Fairborn, Ohio, 1984-87; chief ops. div. 5S Satellite Control Sq. Spokane, Wash., 1987-88; owner Genung Assocs., Spokane, 1989-95. Lt. col. USAF, 1973-95. Avocations: jogging, horseback riding, golf.

GENUNG, SHARON ROSE, pediatrician; b. Williamsport, Pa., Oct. 6, 1951; d. Joseph Patrick and Jeanette (Mossendew) Lynch; m. Norman Bernard Genung, June 9, 1973; children: Jeffrey, Sarah. BS in Microbiology cum laude, Mich. State U., 1973; MS in Clin. Microbiology, U. Ark., 1979, MD, 1984. Lic. physician, Wash., Ark. Clin. resident in pediatrics Wright State U./Children's Med. Ctr., Dayton, Ohio, 1987; dir. pediatrics USAF Hosp. Fairchild, Spokane, Wash., 1987-88, dir. med. svcs., 1988-91; pvt. practice in pediats. Kapstaffer, Maixner & Genung, Spokane, 1991—; instr. in pediatric advanced life support, neonatal resuscitation. Contbr. articles to profl. jours. Maj. USAF M.C., 1980-91. Fellow Am. Acad. Pediatrics; mem. So. Med. Assn., Wash. State Soc. Pediatrics, Spokane Med. Soc., Spokane Pediatric Soc., Spokane Women's Assn. Physicians, Alpha Omega Alpha. Avocations: horseback riding, hiking, dance. Office: Kapstaffer Maixner & Genung 105 W 8th Ave Ste 318 Spokane WA 99204-2318

GENZ, MICHAEL ANDREW, lawyer; b. N.Y.C., Jan. 24, 1947; s. Leonard Francis and Martha Virginia (Tidwell) G.; m. Patricia Ann Hayes, July 8, 1972; children: Andrew, Daniel. BS in Fgn. Svc., Georgetown U., 1969; MA in Tchg., Yale U., 1970; JD, Cath. U., 1980. Police officer New Haven Police Dept., 1971-73; program analyst Nat. Planning Assn., Washington, 1974-76; staff atty. Client Centered Legal Svcs. S.W. Va., Inc., Castlewood, 1980-83; chief atty. So. Md. office Legal Aid Bur., Inc., Hughesville, 1983-95; program officer Legal Svcs. Corp., Washington, 1995-98, dir. office of program performance, 1999—; atty. mem. Md. Trial Ct. Jud. Selection Com. Dist. 12, Charles County, Md., 1986-95; mem. bd. govs. ACLU of Md., Balt., 1986-91. Contbr. articles to profl. jours. Bd. mem. Campaign for Human Devel., Washington, 1986-91; pres. Charles County Human Svcs. Coun., La Plata, Md., 1987-88. Mem. ABA, Va. State Bar Assn., Md. State Bar Assn., Charles County Bar Assn. Home: 7706 Spring Oak Dr La Plata MD 20646-3984 Office: Legal Svcs Corp 750 1st St NE Washington DC 20002-4241

GEOFFREY, IQBAL (MOHAMMED JAWAID IQBAL JAFREE), artist, lawyer; b. Chiniot, Pakistan, Jan. 1, 1939; s. Syed Iqbal Hussain and Shahzadi Mumtazjehan Shah; m. Regina Wai-ling Cheng, 1967 (div. 1978); children: Syed Hussain Haider, Shahzadi Zohra Elinoi Cheng-Jafree; m. Ceyyeda Ferzawna Nuccwe, Mar. 3, 1988. BA with distinction, Govt. Coll., Lahore, 1957; LLB summa cum laude, Punjab U., Lahore, 1959; trained under Chief Justice of Pakistan, Malik Mohammed Akram, 1959-60; LLM with honors, Harvard U., 1966; A.I.C.E.A., London, 1961, A.M.B.I.M., 1969; PhD, Read U., 1970; also LLD; MA with highest honors, Sangamon State U., Springfield, 1973; cert. in postgrad. bus. adminstrn., Bradford U., 1976. Bar: Pakistan 1959, U.S. Supreme Ct. 1975, Pakistan Supreme Ct., 1996. Ptnr., chair firm Geoffrey & Khitran (internat. lawyers), 1960—; gen. counsel Pakistan Inst. Human Rights, 1960—; human rights officer UN, 1966-67; chief acct. Brit. Lion Films, London, 1968-69; asst. atty. gen. State of Ill., 1972-73; gen. counsel The Shahzadi Mumtaz Jehan Trust, 1972—; chief acct. Embassy of Kuwait, London, 1974-75; disting. vis. prof., mem. bd. govs. Hunerkada Coll. of Art, Islamabad, 1991—; drafted Art. 164 of the Pakistan Law of Evidence, Establishment of Office of Ombudsman Order, Pakistan, 1983; spl. advisor to the Pres. of Pakistan, 1980-84; examiner Pub. Internat. Law Punjab U., 1969-70; prof. St. Mary's Coll., 1967-68, CWS U., 1970-71, Cleve. State U., 1971-72; disting. vis. prof. Hunerkada Coll. Art, Lahore Law Coll. and Silver Jubilee U. prof. Read U. Law Ctr.; lectr., art critic, conceptual art, urban affairs and aesthetics. Author: Qose-Qizah, 1957, Justice is the Absence of Dictatorial Prerogative, 1965, Human Rights in Pakistan, Harvard 1966, A Critical Study of Moral Dilemmas, Iconographical Confusions and Complicated Politics of XX Century Art Harvard U., 1967, The Concept of Human Rights in Islam (foreword by Richard R. Baxter), 1980 Art Embodies Cerebral Legerdemain of Accelerated Communal Soul; co-author: ABA: BLI Recognition and Enforcement of Money Judgments, 1994, International Agency and Distribution Law, 1996; editor: Law Rev., 1958-59; grad. editor: Harvard Art Rev., 1965-66; one-man shows include Hyde Park, London, 1960-62, Alfred Brod Galleries, 1962, New Vision Centre, 1963, Drian Gallery, 1965, London, Ward-Nasse, Boston, Hull (Eng.) U., Birmingham (Eng.) U., Queens U., Arts Council No. Ireland, Los Angeles Mcpl. Art Gallery, Pakistan Arts Council, Lahore, Grand Central Moderns, N.Y.C., Henri Gallery, Washington, St. Mary's Coll., Ind., Franklin Coll., Miami Mus. Modern Art, Herbert Johnson Art Mus. Cornell U., Everson Art Mus., Syracuse, N.Y., Indus Gallery, Karachi, 1988, Hayward Gallery, London, 1989-90, The Embassy of France, Islamabad, 1992, Victoria Miro Gallery, 1992-93, Royal Coll. Art, 1993, The Lavatory, NI, 1993—, The Southall Graveyards, Middlesex, 1993—, The Highbury Cemetery, London, 1994—, Nat. Art Gallery, Pakistan, 1994, H.W. Janson Gallery Modern Art, 1994, Lahore Art Gallery, 1993, 95, 98-99, Shakir Ali Mus. Art, Lahore, 1996, Golden Jubilee, Sua Sponte Artfest, Tate Gallery, 1999, Nat. Gallery, London, 1998—; Durriya Kazi/AN Gallery, Karachi, 1998—, Sadiq Pub. Sch., 1999, Croweaters Gallery, Lahore,

1999—; group shows include bicentennials, Paris, Sao Paolo, Brazil, N.Y.C., Montreal, Tokyo World Fairs, Ljubljana, Yugoslavia, Arts Council Gt. Britain touring exhibits, Hayward Gallery, London; represented in permanent collections Herbert Johnson Mus. Cornell U., Philips Collection, Washington, Boston Mus. Fine Arts, Pasadena Mus. Art, Arts Council Gt. Britain, Tate Gallery, London, Eng., Brit. Mus., London, Chase Manhattan Bank, N.Y.C., Boston Safe Deposit and Trust Co., St. James's Palace, U. Mass., Smith Coll., Lord Baden-Powell House, London, also pvt. collections. Recipient Paris Biennial award, 1965, pub. radio tribute by Pakistan Pres., Sir Ayub Khan, 1964, Sir Philip Hendy and Lord Goodman Bursary award Arts Coun. Gt. Britain, 1968, Disting. Comty. Svc. award L.A.W., 1970, Outstanding Citizenship award Citizenship Coun. Met. Chgo., 1979, Sir Herbert Read medal, 1992, State of Wash. Cen. Wash. State U. award for creativity, 1970; Aug. 14 designated Syed Iqbal Jafree Day by Gov. Thompson, Ill., 1977, Iqbal Geoffrey Day-Jan. 20 Gov. Edgar, Ill., 1992; Huntington Hartford II and John D. Rockefeller III fellow, 1962-65, Queen Elizabeth II fellow Bradford U. Mgmt. Ctr., 1975-76, Fay B. Kent fellow Alpha Chi Omega, 1963, 65. Fellow Royal Soc. Arts, London, 1961. An artist empowers your dreams, endeavoring to quash the otherness while ameliorating virtual gaps that segregate ideas. Easier said than done! Inevitabe that any catalyst distresses status quo. Dissent is the ascent of art. Art is always an inquisition of truth. It is neo-wisdom along new mores. Very simply, art is the chip on the shoulder of the bridge between now and zen. An artist implements what you did not expect from art. The bottom line (take it for a ride) remains that only art can make a difference. Else knowthing. Home: 416 S Warson Rd Saint Louis MO 63124-1212 Office: Geoffrey & Khitran, Iqbal Geoffrey Sq, Lahore 54000, Pakistan

GEOFFROY, CHARLES HENRY, retired business executive; b. Longford, Ireland, Sept. 24, 1926; came to U.S., 1927, naturalized, 1945; s. Francis Louis and Kathleen Elizabeth (Fetherston) G.; m. Alida Baird McClenahan, Apr. 24, 1954; children: Evan Lloyd, Mark Lee, Douglas Baird. BA, Haverford Coll., 1949; postgrad., U. Pa., 1950. With GM Ins. Corp., Phila., 1950-51; mgr. rsch. dept. Ward Wheelock Co., Phila., 1951-54; assoc. rsch. dir., account exec. Lennen & Newell, Inc., N.Y.C., 1954-59; account exec. Young & Rubicam, Inc., N.Y.C., 1959-64; v.p. Young & Rubicam, Inc., L.A., 1965-67; pres., mng. dir. Young & Rubicam, Ltd., Toronto, Ont., Can., 1968-74; pres., dir. J.K. Gill Co. Ltd., Portland, Oreg., 1974-80; pres., chief operating officer Grantree Corp., Portland, 1980-83; pres. Rathcline Corp., Portland, 1984-86; chmn. Wide Travel Internat., Portland, 1986-94; ret. Wide Travel Internat., 1994. With AUS, 1945-46. Fellow Inst. Can. Advt.; mem. Portland Execs. Assn., Waverley Country Club, Arlington Club, Huguenot Soc. Great Britain and Ireland, Rotary.

GEOFFROY, GREGORY L., academic administrator; b. Honolulu, July 8, 1946; s. Glenn Gaylord and Lucille Lavaughn (Lewis) G.; m. Kathleen Carothers, Apr. 17, 1971; children: Susan, Janet, David, Michael. BS in Chemistry, U. Louisville, 1968; PhD in Chemistry, Calif. Inst. Tech., 1974. Asst. prof. dept. chemistry Pa. State U., University Park, 1974-78, assoc. prof. dept. chemistry, 1978-82, prof. dept. chemistry, 1982-88, head dept. chemistry, 1988-89, dean Eberly Coll. Sci., 1989-97; provost, sr. v.p. acad. affairs U. Md., 1997; bd. dirs. Assn. Advancement Res. Astro., Washington; cons. Union Carbide Corp., South Charleston, W.Va., 1984-95, ARCO Chem., Newtown Square, Pa., 1988-92. Author: Organometallic Photochemistry, 1979; contbr. articles to profl. jours. Recipient Tchr.-Scholar award Camille & Henry Dreyfus Found., 1978, fellowship John Simon Guggenheim Found., 1982. Fellow AAAS; mem. Am. Chem. Soc. (chair inorganic chemistry divsn. 1990). Avocations: mountain biking, skiing. Office: U Md Main Adminstrn Bldg Rm 1119 College Park MD 20742

GEOGA, DOUGLAS GERARD, real estate development company executive, lawyer; b. Detroit, Aug. 13, 1955; s. Christ and Virginia M. (Juras) G. AB, Harvard U., 1977, JD, 1980. Bar: Mich. 1980., Ill. 1984. Assoc. Miller, Canfield, Paddock and Stone, Detroit, 1980-83; devel. counsel Hyatt Devel. Corp., Chgo., 1983-85, gen. counsel, 1985-86, v.p., gen. counsel, 1986-88, sr. v.p., 1988-89, exec. v.p., 1989—. Bd. dirs. United Way of LaGrange (Ill.). Mem. ABA, Urban Land Inst. (assoc.). Democrat. Roman Catholic. Office: Hyatt Devel Corp 200 W Madison St Chicago IL 60606-3414

GEOGHAN, JOSEPH EDWARD, lawyer, chemical company executive; b. N.Y.C., May 26, 1937; s. Joseph Edward and Margaret Anne (Degnan) G.; m. Kathleen Mary Normile, July 15, 1961; children: Margaret, Johanna, Mary, Joseph Edward III, Daniel. BBA, St. John's U., Jamaica, N.Y., 1959; JD, Fordham U., 1964. Bar: N.Y., 1964. Staff asst., various positions law dept. Union Carbide Corp., N.Y.C., 1957-71, area atty., 1971-73, chief internat. counsel, 1973-76, sr. group counsel, 1976-80; asst. gen. counsel Union Carbide Corp., N.Y.C., Danbury, Conn., 1980-85; dep. gen. counsel Union Carbide Corp., Danbury, 1985-87, v.p., gen. counsel, 1987—, sec., 1990—, also bd. dirs. Mem. ABA, N.Y. State Bar Assn., Assn. Bar City N.Y., Corp. Bar Assn. Westchester and Fairfield (bd. dirs., pres. 1996), Assn. Gen. Counsel, Univ. Club (N.Y.C.). Roman Catholic. Avocations: reading, deep sea fishing, golf. Office: Union Carbide Corp 39 Old Ridgebury Rd Danbury CT 06810-5108*

GEOGHEGAN, PATRICIA, lawyer; b. Bayonne, N.J., Sept. 9, 1947; d. Frank and Rita (Mihok) G. BA, Mich. State U., 1969; MA, Yale U., 1972, JD, 1974; LLM, NYU, 1982. Bar: N.Y. 1975. Assoc. Cravath, Swaine & Moore, N.Y.C., 1974-82, ptnr., 1982—. Mem. ABA, N.Y. State Bar Assn., Assn. of Bar of City of N.Y. Office: Cravath Swaine & Moore 825 8th Ave Fl 38 New York NY 10019-7475

GEOGHEGAN, WILLIAM DAVIDSON, religion educator, minister; b. Wilmington, Del., July 16, 1922; s. Presley Downs and Mildred Alphaeus (Davidson) G.; m. Sarah Elizabeth Phelps, Oct. 5, 1946; children: Grace, Andrew, Emily, William Davidson II. BA, Yale U., 1943; postgrad., Harvard U., 1943-44; MDiv, Drew U., 1945; PhD, Columbia U., 1951. Ordained to ministry United Meth. Ch. as deacon, 1947, as elder, 1948. Pastor United Meth. Ch., Christiana, Del., 1947-50; chaplain, asst. prof. religion U. Rochester, N.Y., 1950-54; asst. prof. religion Bowdoin Coll., Brunswick, Maine, 1954-62, assoc. prof., 1962-66, prof., 1966-90, prof. emeritus, 1991—, chmn. dept. religion, 1954-79, 81-85, spring 1988; vis. scholar Columbia U. and Union Theol. Sem., 1964-65; founder, chair Bowdoin Coll. Jung Seminar, 1980—. Author: Platonism in Recent Religious Thought, 1958. Recipient Alumni award Bowdoin Coll. Alumni Assn., 1981. Mem. AAUP, Am. Acad. Religion, Hegel Soc. Am., Internat. Soc. for Neoplatonic Studies, Soc. Christian Philosophers, Town and Coll. Club, Phi Beta Kappa, Zeta Psi. Address: Bowdoin Coll 8400 College Sta Brunswick ME 04011-8484 also (summer): PO Box 336 10 Burroughs Ln Wolfeboro NH 03894-4917

GEO-KARIS, ADELINE JAY, state legislator; b. Tegeas, Greece, Mar. 29, 1918; student Northwestern U.; LLB, DePaul U. Bar: Ill. Founder Adeline J. Geo-Karis and Assocs., Zion, Ill.; former mcpl., legis. atty. Mundelein, Ill., Vernon Hills, Ill., Libertyville (Ill.) Twp., Long Grove (Ill.) Sch. Dist.; justice of peace; former asst. state's atty.; mem. Ill. Ho. of Reps., 1973-79; mem. Ill. Senate, 1979—, asst. majority leader, 1992—; mayor, City of Zion, Ill. Served to lt. comdr. USNR., Res. ret. Recipient Americanism medal DAR; named Woman of Yr. Daughters of Penelope, Outstanding Legislator Ill. Fedn. Ind. Colls. and Univs., 1975-78, Legis. award Ill. Assn. Park Dists., 1976. Sponsor Guilty but Mentally Ill Law. Greek Orthodox. Office: Ill State Senate State Capitol Springfield IL 62706*

GEORGAKAKOS, KONSTANTINE PETER, research hydrologist; b. Athens, Greece, Sept. 12, 1954; came to U.S., 1977; MS, MIT, 1980, ScD, 1982. Postdoctoral rschr. NOAA-Nat. Rsch. Coun., Silver Spring, Md., 1982-85, rsch. hydrologist Office Hydrology, 1985; asst. prof. CEE U. Iowa, Iowa City, 1986-89, assoc. prof., 1989-94; dir., sr. rsch. hydrologist Hydrologic Rsch. Ctr., San Diego, 1994—; full rsch. hydrologist IV Inst. Oceanography U. Calif., San Diego, 1994—; cons. Food & Agriculture Orgn. UN, Rome, 1995—; sci. rev. panelist Nat. Oceanography Atmosphere Adminstrn., Silver Spring, 1996; reviewer NSF, NOAA, NASA, Washington, 1986—. Editor Jour. Applied Meteorology, 1995, Jour. Hydrology, 1996; contbr. articles to profl. jours. Coach Little League Soccer Club Del Mar, San Diego, 1994—. Rsch. associateship Nat. Rsch. Coun., Washington, 1982; recipient Presdl. Young Investigator award NSF, Washington, 1987. Mem. ASCE (assoc. editor 1996—), Am. Geophys. Union (chair hydrology 1991-93), Am. Meteor. Soc. (chair hydrology sect. 1991-93, elected expert on the WMO Commn. Hydrology Working Group on Applications). Achievements include development of flash flood prediction system used nationally by U.S. Nat. Weather Svc., elucidated dynamics and scaling of rainfall and soil water, role of soil water in development of future land surface hydrologic response; performed integrated impact assessments of climate variability and temperature change. Office: Hydrologic Rsch Ctr 12780 High Bluff Dr Ste 250 San Diego CA 92130-2069

GEORGAKAS, DAN, writer, educator; b. Mar. 1, 1938; s. Xenophon and Sophia (Pousoukas) G. BA in Am. History, Wayne State U., 1959; MA in Labor History, U. Mich., 1961. Tchr. English and social studies Detroit Pub. Schs., 1959-64; tchr. history Overseas Sch. Rome, 1965; tchr. N.J. Coun. on Arts, 1972-78; instr. English and history LaGuardia C.C., CUNY, 1972-81; instr. Van Arsdale Sch. Labor Studies, Empire Coll., SUNY, 1979-94; instr. Queens Coll., CUNY, 1988—; instr. Am. history dept. continuing edn. NYU, N.Y.C., 1991—; guest lectr. Wayne State U., U. Mich., Mich. State U., Antioch Coll., Rutgers U., U. Calif., Berkeley, York U., U. Chgo., Harvard U., Fordham U., numerous others, 1965—; speaker profl. confs.; instr. labor and film course Cornell U., N.Y.C. Ctr., 1992; script cons. labor history project Sta. WGBH, TV, 1976; curator Greek Ethnographic Film Festival, N.Y.C., 1983, N.Y. Soc. for Ethical Clubure, 1987-88; media cons. Am. Left project Tamiment Libr., NYU, 1983; exec. dir. Smyrna Press, 1964—; others. Author: Ombre Rosse, 1968, The Broken Hoop, 1973, Red Shadows, 1973, (with Marvin Surkin) Detroit: I Do Mind Dying, 1975, 2d edit., 1998, The Methuselah Factors, 1981, paperback edit., 1996, Spanish lang. edit., 1997, (with others) In Focus: A Guide to Using Films, 1980; co-editor various books, 1983—, including The Cineaste Interviews, 1983, Solidarity Forever: An Oral History of the IWW, 1985, Encyclopedia of the American Left, 1990, New Directions in Greek American Studies, 1991, The Immigrant Left, 1996; mem. editorial bd. Cineaste, 1970—, Jour. Hellenic Diaspora, 1975-82; contbg. editor, columnist The Greek Am., 1987—. Judge Helen Z. Papanikolas Found., 1990-93. Recipient ann. excellence in scholarship award Empire State Coll., 1986; Fulbright scholar, Greece, 1963; rsch. grantee in urban studies Rabinowitz Found., 1975, grantee N.Y. Coun. for Humanities, 1991; rsch. fellow Queens Coll. Modern Greek Studies and Byzantine Ctr., 1987. Mem. Nat. Writers Union, Am. Labor Coun., Historians Am. Communism, United Univ. Profls., Labor Educators Local 189. Home: 200 Park Ave S Apt 1601 New York NY 10003-1503

GEORGAKIS, CHRISTOS, chemical engineer educator, consultant, researcher; b. Patra, Greece, Aug. 13, 1947; came to U.S., 1970; s. Theofilaktos and Penelope (Rompoti) G.; m. Konstantina Hinou, July 12, 1970; children: Alexander, Natalie. Chem. engring. diploma, Nat. Tech. U., Athens, Greece, 1970; MSChemE, U. Ill., 1972; PhDChemE, U. Minn., 1975. Cert. chem. engr., Greece. Asst. prof. MIT, Cambridge, 1975-79, assoc. prof., 1979-83, Du Pont prof., 1975-76, Edgerton prof., 1977-79; prof. U. Thessaloniki, Greece, 1979-83; assoc. prof. chem. engring. Lehigh U., Bethlehem, Pa., 1983-87, prof., 1987—, dir. Process Modeling & Control Rsch. Ctr., 1985—; vis. prof. Delft (Th Netherlands) Univ. Tech., 1993-96. Recipient Best Paper award Am. Control Conf., 1998; Dreyfus Found. tchr.-scholar, 1979-83. Mem. AIChE (chmn. process control area 10b 1990-92, vice chmn. 1988-90, dir. CAST divsn. 1994-97). Achievements include elucidation of interaction between process modeling and process control with several applications in different types of continuous and batch reactors; development of overall approach to the optimization and control of chemical processes based on approximate models called tendency models; research on the use of thermodynamic variables in the systematic understanding of process dynamics; nonlinear model predictive control; statistical process control of continuous processes, on-line estimation of unmeasured process variables. Office: Lehigh U PMC Rsch Ctr Iacocca Hall 111 Research Dr Bethlehem PA 18015-4732

GEORGALAS, ROBERT NICHOLAS, English language educator; b. N.Y.C., Nov. 11, 1951; s. Nicholas and Dora (Patisso) G.; m. JoAnne Louise Pepe, Sept. 5, 1981. BA, Lehman Coll., 1972; MA, CCNY, 1974; MFA, Columbia Coll., Chgo., 1997. Mktg. coord. Am. Express Co., N.Y.C., 1978-79; media supr. Wunderman Ricotta & Kline, N.Y.C., 1979-82, Needham Harper & Steers, N.Y.C., 1982-84; v.p., media dir. J. Walter Thompson Direct, N.Y.C., 1984-88, Leo Burnett USA, Chgo., 1988-91; prof. English Coll. of DuPage, Glen Ellyn, Ill., 1991—; adj. assoc. prof. English Marymount Manhattan Coll., N.Y.C., 1979-88; voting judge Echo Awards, N.Y.C., 1987. Contbr. fiction to mags. Recipient Gold Effie award Am. Mktg. Assn., 1983, 91. Mem. NEA, MLA, Nat. Coun. Tchrs. English. Avocations: writing, swimming, traveling, theater, cinema. Home: 360 E Randolph St Chicago IL 60601-7330 Office: Coll of DuPage 425 22nd St Glen Ellyn IL 60137-6784

GEORGANAS, NICOLAS D., electrical engineering educator; b. Athens, Greece, June 15, 1943; s. Demetrios N. and Athanasia (Kotsovou) G.; m. Jacynthe Savard, June 17, 1972; children: Nikita, Emmanuel. Diploma in Engring., Nat. Tech. U. Athens, 1966; PhD summa cum laude, U. Ottawa, Ont., Can., 1970. Registered profl. engr., Ont. Lectr., elec. engring. U. Ottawa, 1970-71, asst. prof., 1971-76, assoc. prof., 1976-80, prof., 1980—, chmn., 1981-84, dean engring., 1986-93; vis. prof. IBM, LaGaude, France, 1977-78, INRIA/Bull-Transac, Paris, 1984-85, Bell-No. Rsch., Ottawa, 1993-94, CRC, Ottawa, 1997. Author: Queueing Networks—Exact Computational Algorithms: A Unified Theory by Decomposition and Aggregation, 1989; contbr. over 80 articles to profl. jours., more than 140 conf. articles. Fellow IEEE, Can. Acad. Engring., Royal Soc. Can., Engring. Inst. Home: 1915 Montereau Ave, Gloucester, ON Canada Office: U Ottawa Faculty Engring, SITE 161 Pasteur St, Ottawa, ON Canada K1N 6N5

GEORGE, ALEXANDER ANDREW, lawyer; b. Missoula, Mont., Apr. 26, 1938; s. Andrew Miltiadin and Eleni (Efstathiou) G.; m. Penelope Mitchell, Sept. 29, 1968; children: Andrew A., Stephen A. BBA honors, U. Mont., 1960, JD, 1962; postgrad., John Marshall U., 1964-66. Bar: Mont. 1962, U.S. Ct. Mil. Appeals 1964, U.S. Tax Ct. 1970. Sole practice Missoula, 1966—; mem. adv. com. U. Mont. Tax Inst., 1973-76; adj. lectr. U. Montana Law Sch. Corp. Taxation. Pres. Missoula Civic Symphony, 1973; nat. dir. Assn. Urban and Cmty. Symphony Orch., 1974, Mont. Eye Endowment Found.; pres. Greek Orthodox Ch., 1978, 91. Served to capt. JAG U.S. Army, 1962-66. Recipient Jaycee Disting. Svc. award, 1973. Mem. State Bar Mont. (pres. 1981), Western Mont. Bar Assn. (pres. 1971, lifetime achievement award 1998), Mont. Law Found. (treas. 1986-92), Mont. Soc. CPA, Phi Delta Phi, Alpha Kappa Psi, Sigma Nu (alumni trustee 1966-71), Rotary (pres. 1972, state chmn. found. 1977, membership com. chmn. 1978), Ahepa (pres. 1967, state gov. 1968). Home: 4 Greenbrier Ct Missoula MT 59802-3342 Office: 210 N Higgins Ave Ste 234 Missoula MT 59802-4497

GEORGE, ALEXANDER LAWRENCE, political scientist, educator; b. Chgo., May 31, 1920; s. John and Mary (Sargis) G.; m. Juliette Lombard, Apr. 20, 1948; children: Lee Lawrence, Mary Lombard. AM, U. Chgo., 1941, PhD, 1958; DHL (hon.), U. San Diego, 1987; PhD (hon.), U. Lund, Sweden, 1994. Rsch. analyst OSS, 1944-45; dep. chief rsch. br. Info. Control divsn. Office Mil. Govt. for Germany, 1945-48; specialist study of decision-making and internat. rels. RAND Corp., Santa Monica, Calif., 1948-68; head dept. social sci. RAND Corp., Santa Monica, 1961-63; prof. polit. sci. and internat. rels. Stanford (Calif.) U., 1968—; lectr. U. Chgo., 1950, Am. U., 1952-56; chmn. com. on Conflict Resolution NRC/NAS, 1995—. Author: (with Juliette L. George) Woodrow Wilson and Colonel House: A Personality Study, 1956, Propaganda Analysis, 1959, The Chinese Communist Army in Action, 1967; (with others) The Limits of Coercive Diplomacy, 1971; (with Richard Smoke) Deterrence in American Foreign Policy: Theory and Practice, 1974 (Bancroft prize for Deterrence in Am. Fgn. Policy 1975), Towards A More Soundly Based Foreign Policy: Making Better Use of Information, 1976, Presidential Decisionmaking in Foreign Policy, 1980, Managing U.S.-Soviet Rivalry, 1983; (with Gordon Craig) Force and Statecraft, 1983, 3rd edit., 1995; editor: (with others) U.S.-Soviet Security Cooperation: Achievements, Failures, Lessons, 1988, Avoiding War: Problems of Crisis Management, 1991, Forceful Persuasion, 1992, Bridging the Gap: Theory and Practice of Foreign Policy, 1993; (with William E. Simons) The Limits of Coercive Diplomacy, 2d. edit., 1994; (with Juliette L. George) Presidential Personality and Performance, 1998. Mem. Carnegie Commn. on Preventing Deadly Conflict, 1993-97. Fellow Ctr. Advanced Study Behavioral Scis., 1956-57, 76-77, NIMH, 1972-73, MacArthur Prize, 1983-88, Disting. fellow U. S. Inst. Peace, 1990-91, 91-92; Founds. Fund for Rsch. in Psychiatry grantee, 1960, NSF rsch. grantee, 1971-73, 75-77; recipient award for behavioral rsch. relevant to prevention of nuclear war NAS, 1997, Johan Skytte prize in polit. sci., Uppsala U., Swden, 1998. Mem. Am. Acad. Arts and Scis., Coun. on Fgn. Rels., Am. Polit. Sci. Assn., Internat. Studies Assn. (pres. 1973-74), Phi Beta Kappa. Home: 944 Lathrop Pl Stanford CA 94305-1060

GEORGE, ALFRED L., JR., medical educator, researcher; b. Batavia, N.Y., June 14, 1956. BA in Chemistry, Coll. of Wooster, Ohio, 1978; MD, U. Rochester, 1982. Diplomate Am. Bd. Internal Medicine, Am. Bd. Nephrology. Intern and resident in internal medicine Vanderbilt U. Hosps., Nashville, 1982-86; chief resident in medicine St. Thomas Hosp., Nashville, 1985-86; instr. medicine Vanderbilt U. Sch. Medicine, Nashville, 1985-86, asst. prof. dept. medicine nephrology and pharmacology, 1992-95; assoc. prof. medicine and pharmacology Vanderbilt U., Nashville, 1995—; postdoctoral fellow in clin. nephrology renal-elctrolyte sectl dept. medicine Hosp. of U. Pa., Phila., 1986-87; rsch. fellow dept. medicine and dept. biochemistry and biophysics U. Pa., Phila., 1988-91, rsch. assoc. dept. medicine and Inst. Neurol. Scis., 1991-92; vis. postdoctoral fellow Inst. Suisse de Recherches Experimentales sur le Cancer, Lausanne, Switzerland, 1987-88. Mem. editl. bd. Am. Jour. Physiology, 1996—; jour. reviewer Neuron, Nature Genetics, Jour. Membrane Biology, Jour. Biol. Chemistry, Kidney Internat., Jour. Physiology. Mem. AAAS, Am. Soc. Nephrology, Am. Heart Assn. (mem. coun. on kidney disease, established investigator award 1996), Biophys. Soc. Office: Vanderbilt U Med Ctr Nephrology Divsn S-3223 MCN 21st and Garland Aves Nashville TN 37232*

GEORGE, ALLEN VAN, manufacturing company executive; b. West Liberty, Ky., Feb. 11, 1961; s. Jerry Vance and Joan Daisy (Stoney) G.; m. Anna Marie Rayburn, Sept. 4, 1981; children: Robert, Samuel, Maxwell, Eileen, Kara. BS in Chem. Engring., U. Cin., 1984; MS in Materials Sci., Duke U., 1987. Process engr. United Technologies, West Carrollton, Tex., 1984-85; sr. engr. GE Semicondr., Research Triangle Park, N.C., 1985-87; lead engr. Harris Corp., Melbourne, Fla., 1987-89; engring. mgr. Crysteco, Wilmington, Ohio, 1989-92; quality mgr. Lucas Sumitomo Brakes, Inc., Lebanon, Ohio, 1992-97; v.p. mfg., v.p. ops. Marathon Monitors, Inc., Cin., 1997—. Cubmaster Boy Scouts Am., Cin., 1991-97. Mem. IEEE, ASM, Am. Soc. Quality Control. Republican. Roman Catholic. Avocations: tennis, golf, tae kwon do/martial arts. Home: 5821 Charteroak Dr Cincinnati OH 45236-2015 Office: Marathon Monitors Inc 3100 E Kemper Rd Cincinnati OH 45241-1517

GEORGE, ANNA, book designer, artist; b. Oceanside, N.Y., July 12, 1951; d. Walter Palchik and Helen Pashkewich; m. John Post, June 1, 1975 (div. Nov. 1981); m. Herbert W. George, Sept. 11, 1988. BFA cum laude, Syracuse U., 1973. Art tchr. Braintree (Mass.) Pub. Schs., 1973-74; pasteup, layout artist Sports Eye Inc. Newspapers, Great Neck, N.Y., 1975; art dir. Patriot Profile Newspaper, Dedham, Mass., 1975-76; book designer Little, Brown & Co., Boston, 1976-80; owner freelance book design bus. Boston, 1980-86, Chgo., 1986-92, Beverly Shores, Ind., 1992—. Catologue designer Cultural Ctr., Chgo., 1990, Muskegan (Mich.) Mus. Art, 1992, 98, Blank Ctr. Arts, Michigan City, Ind., 1999. Bd. dirs. Assn. Beverly Shores of Residents, 1993-98, installation and design fine art exhbns. in Beverly Shores Depot Gallery, 1998-99. Recipient Excellence in Book Design award New England Bookbuilders, 1982, Cert. Merit, Bookbuilders West, 1989, 91, 92, 93, Cert. Merit for printing and design, Arcata Graphics Book Group, 1991, Cert. Excellence, Bookbuilders West, 1996, 97, 98, Excellence in Book Design award Bookbuilders Boston, 1997. Mem. Phi Kappa Phi (hon.), Phi Lambda Theta (hon.). Russian Orthodox. Avocations: painting, gardening, Tai Chi.

GEORGE, AUBREY WESTMORELAND, director Spokane public library; b. Marshall, Tex., May 20, 1950. BA, Stephen F. Austin U., 1972, MA in Polit. Sci., 1974; MLS, N. Tex. State U., 1975. Asst. dir. Corpus Christi (Tex.) Pub. Libr., 1975-91; mgr. pub. svc. Spokane (Wash.) Pub. Libr., 1991-96, dep. dir., 1996, dir., 1996—. Mem. Am. Libr. Assn., Wash. Libr. Assn. Office: Spokane Pub Libr 906 W Main Ave Spokane WA 99201-0976*

GEORGE, BEAUFORD JAMES, JR., lawyer, educator; b. Kansas City, Mo., Oct. 16, 1925; s. Beauford James and Elizabeth (Pope) G.; m. Grace Isabella Loucks, June 17, 1950; children—Paul, Andrew, Nancy. BA, U. Mich., 1949, JD with honors, 1951; MDiv, N.Y. Theol. Sem., 1993. Asst. prof. law U. Mich., Ann Arbor, 1952-55; asso. prof. U. Mich., 1955-58, prof., 1958-68; lectr. law Kyoto U., 1956-57; lectr. fgn. law Tokyo U., 1962-63; asso. dir. Practicing Law Inst., N.Y.C., 1968-71; adj. prof. law N.Y. U., 1968-71; prof. law, dir. Center for Adminstrn. Justice, Wayne State U., Detroit, 1971-77; pres. Southwestern Legal Found., Richardson, Tex., 1977-79; vis. prof. law Baylor U., 1979-80; prof. N.Y. Law Sch., N.Y.C., 1980-93, prof. law emeritus, 1993—; lectr. fgn. law Tokyo U., 1987. Editor-in-chief: Am. Jour. of Comparative Law, 1966-68. Mem. Gov. Mich. Commn. on Criminal Justice, 1966-68, 71-77; mem. Mich. Corrections Commn., 1976-77; pastor Bernardsville (N.J.) United Meth. Ch., 1993-96, Westside Paterson United Meth. Ch., 1996-97, Frenchtown and Finesville United Meth. Ch., 1997—. Mem. Am. Law Inst., Am. Bar Assn., State Bar Mich., State Bar Tex., Internat. Penal Law Assn. (past pres. Am. chpt.), Order of Coif, Japan Order of the Sacred Treasure with Gold Rays (decorated 1996). Office: NY Law Sch 57 Worth St New York NY 10013-2960

GEORGE, BOYD LEE, consumer products company executive; b. 1942. BBA, U. Notre Dame, 1963; LLB, U. Va., 1966. With Merchants Distbrs., Inc., 1969-72, v.p., 1972-76, pres., COO, 1976-83, chmn. bd., 1983—; chmn., CEO Alex Lee, Hickory, N.C., 1992—. Capt. USMC, 1966-69. Office: Alex Lee 120 4th St SW Hickory NC 28602-2947 also: Merchants Distributors Inc PO Box 800 Hickory NC 28603-0800*

GEORGE, CAROLE SCHROEDER, computer company executive; b. Bloomington, Ind., Mar. 20, 1943; d. Melburne Evert and Neva Mae (Bechtel) Gibson; m. Richard D. White, Aug. 31, 1962 (div. 1972); 1 child, Kenneth Donald; m. Charles R. Schroeder, Apr. 7, 1973 (div. 1983); m. Thomas H. George III, May 4, 1991. BS in Pharmacy, Wayne State U., 1972; postgrad., Va. Commonwealth U., 1980-83. Registered pharmacist, Mich. Va. Staff pharmacist St. Joseph Hosp., Pontiac, Mich., 1972-73; dir. pharmacy St. Mary Hosp., Livonia, Mich., 1974-76; resident Detroit Receiving Hosp., 1977-78; clin. faculty pharmacy Med. Coll. of Va., Richmond, 1978-83; dir. pharmacy ops. Med. Coll. Va. Hosps., Richmond, 1978-83; mktg. mgr. TDS Healthcare Systems Corp., Atlanta, 1983-86; sr. cons. Gerber Alley, Norcross, Ga., 1986; dir. product mgmt. Baxter Healthcare Systems, Reston, Va., 1986-89; sr. v.p. Integrated Systems Tech. Inc., Reston, 1989-96; prin. Intelligent Bus. Consulting, Reston, 1996—; v.p. Horizon Data Corp., Reston, 1996-97. Mem. Healthcare Info. and Mgmt. Systems Soc., Am. Soc. Hosp. Pharmacists, Nat. Assn. for Healthcare Quality, Rho Chi. Avocations: sailing, golf.

GEORGE, DAVID BRUCE, hotel executive; b. Wichita, Kans., Feb. 28, 1944; s. Harold R. and Helen V. (Gray) G.; m. Leslie A. Blake, Aug. 14, 1965 (div. Nov. 1980); children: David Blake, Alison Ann; m. Helen Angela Linn, Sept. 2, 1988; stepchildren: Andrew Ferguson, Ian Ferguson. BSBA, Kans. State U., 1966. With Target Stores, Inc., 1966-74; personnel mgr. Target Stores, Inc., Houston, 1969-71; ops. mgr. Target Stores, Inc., Clinton, Iowa, 1971-74; pres., chief operating officer Local Loan Co., Wichita, 1974-81; gen. mgr. Residence Inn Co., Tulsa, 1981-85; v.p. ops. TMH Hotels, Inc., Wichita, 1985—; bd. dirs., chmn. Local Loan Co., Wichita; gen. ptnr. DG Properties, L.P., Wichita, 1986—; mem. com. for operating stds. and procedures Residence Inn by Marriott, Bethesda, Md., 1988—. Co-chmn. United Way, Clinton, 1973. Mem. Nat. Pawnbrokers Assn., Tulsa Hotel and Motel Assn. (v.p. 1983), Jaycees (pres. Clinton chpt. 1974, Outstanding Pres. 1974), Optimists (v.p. Wichita chpt. 1977), Phi Delta Theta. Republican. Methodist. Home: 133 N Fountain St Wichita KS 67208-3831 Office: TMH Hotels Inc 250 N Water St Ste 325 Wichita KS 67202-1218

GEORGE, DAVID WEBSTER, architect; b. Tulsa, Dec. 26, 1922; s. Calvin Webster and Ollie (McReynolds) G.; m. Xena Ruth Gill, Nov. 25, 1950; 1 dau., Molly Evelyn; m. Elizabeth Howard, Dec. 30, 1984. Student U. Okla., 1940-43, 46, 47-48; B.Arch., N.C. State U., 1949. Assoc., Frank Lloyd Wright, Taliesin Assoc. Architects, Scottsdale, Ariz., 1947-48; assoc. Harwell

Hamilton Harris, Ft. Worth, Tex., 1954-56; founding ptnr. The Architects Partnership, and predecessor firm, Dallas, 1959—. Bd. dirs. Dallas Theater Ctr. Served to capt. AUS, 1942-46, 51-52. Fellow AIA; mem. Tex. Soc. Architects, Nat. Council Archtl. Registration Bds. Methodist. Club: Horseshoe Bay Country. Home and Office: 2980 Burney Ln Southlake TX 76092-2704

GEORGE, DEINABO DABIBI, writer, computer specialist, educator; b. Boston, Jan. 31, 1970; s. Orlando and Carol (Gibbons) G.; m. Michelle Ann Catherine Young, May 24, 1994 (div. Feb., 1998). Student, Tuskegee U., 1988, Bronx Cmty. Coll., 1989-90; BA in Black Studies, CCNY, 1993. Cashier, stock clerk Barnes and Nobles Bookstore, N.Y.C., 1989-90; office asst. fin. aid office CCNY, N.Y.C., 1991-92; substitute tchr. Bd. Edn., Bklyn., 1994; computer instr. Boys of Yesteryear, Inc., N.Y.C., 1994; tchr. phys. edn. Intermediate Sch. 306, Bronx, 1994—; pres., owner Black Odyssey Enterprises, Inc., Bronx, 1995; adj. prof. Marymoutn Manhattan Coll., 1997—. Author: (literary anthology) Death Standard, 1993. Mem. Black Alumni Assn. City Coll., Alumni Assn. City Coll. Avocations: working out, collecting comic books and related memorabilia, creating ideas for new stories, computer technology. Home and Office: Black Odyssey Enterprises Inc 1992 Morris Ave Bronx NY 10453-4829

GEORGE, DEVERAL D., editor, journalist, advertising consultant; b. Dallas, Nov. 23, 1939; s. Jack Weldon and Lleen Lelia (Hume) G. Student, U. Tex., 1958-61; B.A., North Tex. State U., 1964; P.B.A., U. Houston, 1974. Copywriter advt. agys. Houston, Dallas, 1964-70; free lance journalist, 1970-73, 75-76; copy and creative dir. Schey Advt., Houston, 1973, Bruce Advt., Houston, 1973-75; editor-in-chief, v.p. Bus. and Energy Internat., Houston, 1976-80; editor Ultra mag., 1980-81; freelance journalist Houston, 1981-83, 84-85; editor Saudi Bus. Mag.; cons. Saudi Research and Mktg. Inc., Houston, Washington, and Jeddah, Saudi Arabia, 1983-84; writer, advt. cons. Dale Carnegie & Assocs., Garden City (N.Y.) and Houston, 1985-90; mng. editor internat. Offshore Mag., Houston, 1991-97; editor Schlumberger Oilfield Rev., 1997-98; editor Oil and Gas Online, Vertical Net, Horsham, Pa., 1998—, Houston, 1998—. Author: Cathedrals of Mexico, and Other Poems, 1963, The Erratic Pilgramage, 1973, The Whole World Cookbook, 1976, The Offshore Atlas, 1995; screenplays: The Monument, 1980, Armageddon, 1981; television series Treasure Hunt, 1984; editor: Worldwide Directory of Petroleum Ministries and National Oil Companies, 1995; mem. editl. bd. Xi'an Petroleum Inst., China. Del., Democratic Conv., 1972; mem. Houston Outdoor Group. Mem. ACLU, Am. Assn. Petroleum Geologists, Soc. Exploration Geophysicists, Geophys. Soc. Houston, Soc. Internat. Devel., N.Am. Congress on Latin Am., Amnesty Internat., Internat. Platform Assn., Ctr. for Study of Dem. Instns., Asia Soc., World Expeditionary Assn., Soc. Profl. Journalists-Sigma Delta Chi, Houston Press Club. Club: Houston Press. Home: 8310 Braesdale Ln Houston TX 77071-1228 Office: Box 711030 Houston TX 77271-1030

GEORGE, DONALD RICHARD, retired principal; b. Coffeyville, Kans., Oct. 1, 1926; s. Murl C. and Georgia M. (Leib) G.; m. Zepha Lowry, June 5, 1949; children: Donna L. Kellison, David L., Mary M. Tribby. BS in Edn., Pitts. State U., 1960; MS in Edn., Emporia State U., 1965. Tchr., asst. prin. Hugoton (Kans.) Elem. Sch., 1954-75; prin. Nelson Elem. Sch., Haysville, Kans., 1975-80; prin. W.D. Munson Primary Sch., Mulvane, Kans., 1980-93, ret., 1993. IDEA Kettering Found. fellow, 1978-83. Mem. Nat. Assn. Elem. Sch. Prins., Kans. Assn. Elem. Sch. Prins., United Sch. Adminstrs. Kans., Lions, Phi Delta Kappa. Mem. Ch. of God. Avocations: farming, golf, woodworking. Home: 713 Tristan Dr Mulvane KS 67110-1212

GEORGE, DONALD WARNER, online columnist and editor, freelance writer; b. Middlebury, Conn., June 24, 1953; s. Lloyd Foster and Vivian (Minor) G.; m. Kuniko Ninomiya, Apr. 24, 1982; children: Jennifer Ayako, Jeremy Naoki. BA, Princeton U., 1975; MA, Hollins (Va.) Coll., 1977. Tchg. fellow Athens (Greece) Coll., 1975-76, Internat. Christian U., Tokyo, 1977-79; TV talk show host Japan Broadcasting Corp., Tokyo, 1977-79; freelance writer, 1980-81; travel writer San Francisco Examiner, 1981-82, sr. editor Calif. Living mag., 1982-85, sr. editor Image mag., 1985-87, travel editor, 1987-95; cyber columnist, Global Network Navigator American Online, Berkeley, Calif., 1995-96; editor Salon Wanderlust Online Travel Mag., 1997—. Recipient gold award Pacific Asia Travel Assn., 1987-94). Mem. Soc. Am. Travel Writers (Lowell Thomas award 1987-94). Office: Wanderlust Salon Internet Inc 706 Mission St Fl 2D San Francisco CA 94103-3113

GEORGE, EDDIE, professional football player; b. Sept. 24, 1973. Student, Fork Union Mil. Acad. Running back Tenn. Oilers, 1996—. Recipient Heisman Trophy; named NFL Rookie of Yr., 1996, first alternate to Pro Bowl; placed third AFC rushign and in total yards from scrimmage. Office: Bapt Sports Park 7640 Highway 70 S Nashville TN 37221-1758*

GEORGE, EMERY EDWARD, foreign language and studies educator; b. Budapest, Hungary, May 8, 1933; came to U.S., 1946, naturalized, 1954; AB, U. Mich., 1955, MA, 1959; postgrad., Fed. Rep. Germany, 1961-62; PhD, U. Mich., 1964. Instr. U. Ill., Champaign-Urbana, 1964-65; asst. prof. German U. Ill., 1965-66, U. Mich., Ann Arbor, 1966-69; assoc. prof. U. Mich., 1969-75, prof., 1975-88, prof. emeritus, 1988—, faculty program in comparative lit., 1969—, faculty program Center for Russian and East European Studies, 1975—. Author: Hölderlin's Ars Poetica, 1973, Mountainwild: Poems, 1974, Black Jesus, 1974, A Gift of Nerve: Poems, 1966-77, 1978, Kate's Death, 1980, The Poetry of Miklós Radnóti: A Comparative Study, 1986, The Boy and the Monarch, 1987, Voiceprints, 1987; (essay) The Allegory of Spandau, 1990 (Kenyon Rev. 2d ann. nonfiction award 1991), Hölderlin and the Golden Chain of Homer, 1992, Blackbird: Poems on the World and Work of Franz Kafka, 1993, Valse Triste: Songs and Ballads, 1997; editor: Friedrich Hölderlin: An Early Modern, 1972, (with L.T. Frank) Husbanding the Golden Grain, 1973, Contemporary East European Poetry: An Anthology, 1983, expanded, 1993, (with D. E. Sattler) Friedrich Hölderlin, Homburger Folioheft (Frankfurter Hölderlin-Ausgabe, Supplement III), 1986, 93; also transls.; contbr. poetry, non-fiction prose, transls., articles, revs. to scholarly jours., lit. publs.; founding editor Mich. Germanic Studies; assoc. editor Russian Lit. Triquar.; mem. editl. bd. advisors Germano-Slavica, 1973-77; editl. bd. Mich. Monographs in the Humanities, 1979—, (yearbook) Cross Currents, 1986—. Served with M.I. U.S. Army, 1957-58. Recipient Avery and Jule Hopwood award in poetry U. Mich., 1960; Ottendorfer Meml. fellow, 1961; Am. Council Learned Socs. Publs. award, 1964; Rackham Publ. award U. Mich., 1973, 80; Hungarian PEN Research and Travel grant, 1979; IREX Exchange fellow to Hungary, 1981, Deutsche Forschungsgemeinschaft research and travel grantee, 1986. Fellow Internat. Acad. Poets; mem. MLA, Hölderlin-Gesellschaft, Poetry Soc. Am., Shelley Soc. N.Y., Hungarian Writers' Assn. Home: 16 Buckingham Ave Trenton NJ 08618-3312 *Listen carefully to language, to words; to try to write each day. Make no separation between writing and scholarship, between old and new literature. Monitor the eternal present. Try to achieve newness, a sense of experiment from within.*

GEORGE, ERNEST THORNTON, III, financial consultant; b. Charleston, S.C., Dec. 29, 1950; s. Ernest Thornton and Betty (Long) T.; m. Frances Thomson, Sept. 30, 1977; children: Ernest Thornton IV, Andrew Neal, Katherine Frances. Student, U. Miss., 1969-71; BS in Mktg., Miss. State U., 1973. CFP; CLU; registered investment advisor. Ins. cons. for Hall of Fame Mut. of N.Y., 1974—; product cons. mgr. Mfrs. Life Ins. Co., 1981—; prin. N.Y. Stock Exch., 1977—; rep., br. mgr. Raymond James Fin. Svcs., Starkville, Miss., 1989—; owner, prin. Investment Mgmt. Group Inc., Starkville, 1982—, Wealth Mgmt. Group, Inc.; founding mem. bd. dirs. First Citizens Nat. Bank of Starkville; guest lectr. Miss. State U.; Dalbar rated adv. Mem. editorial bd. Life and Health Ins. Sales; contbr. articles to profl. jours. Bd. dirs. exec. bd. Pushmataha area coun. Boy Scouts Am., Republican party; past pres. Men of Ch., Presbyn. Ch., chmn. bd. deacons, elder, men's Sunday Sch. tchr.; bd. dirs. Oktibbeha County Libr., past pres.; bd. dirs. Oktibbeha Devel. Coun., Starkville Acad.; mem. stds. com. Miss. Pub. Libr.; bd. dirs. Miss. chpt. Nat. Com. on Planned Giving. Mem. Nat. Assn. Christian Fin. Advisors, Nat. Assn. Life Underwriters (nat. committeeman nat. mtg.), Nat. Assn. Securities Dealers, East Miss. Life Underwriters Assn. (past pres.), Soc. Fin. Svcs. Profls. (bd. dirs. Miss. chpt.), Miss. Estate Planning Coun., Inst. for Investment Mgmt. Cons., Internat. Assn. for Fin. Planning (bd. dirs. Miss. chpt.), Million Dollar Round Table (life, qualifying), Ct. Round Table, Oktibbeha County C. of C. (exec. bd.), Rotary (bd. dirs. Starkville, Paul Harris fellow), Sigma Chi, Pi Sigma Epsilon. Home: 1672 Valley Hill Cir Starkville MS 39759-9748 Office: Raymond James Fin Svcs 102 S Jackson St PO Box 963 Starkville MS 39760-0963

GEORGE, FRANCIS CARDINAL, archbishop; b. Chgo., Jan. 16, 1937. Ordained priest Roman Cath. Ch., 1963. Provincial ctrl. region Oblates of Mary Immaculate, 1973-74, vicar gen., 1974-86; bishop Diocese of Yakima, Wash., 1990-96; archbishop Archdiocese of Portland, Oreg., 1996-97, Archdiocese of Chgo., 1997—; chancellor Cath. Ch. Extension Soc., U. St. Mary of the Lake, 1997; mem. Congregation Divine Worship and the Discipline of the Sacraments, Congregation Insts. Consecrated Life and Socs. of Apostolic Life, and Pontifical Coun. "Cor Unum", 1998, Congregation Evangelization of Peoples. Mem. Coll. Cardinals. Office: Archdiocese of Chicago Pastoral Ctr PO Box 1979 Chicago IL 60690-1979

GEORGE, FRANK WADE, small business owner, antiquarian book dealer; b. Austin, Tex., Aug. 22, 1918; s. Frank Wade and Rosa Scott (Slaughter) W.; m. Marjorie Ann Miller, Dec. 27, 1948 (div. Jan. 1955); children: Frank Wade III, Gregory Scott, Barbara Lee; m. Martha Jeanne Wagner, Feb. 8, 1964 (dec. 1996); m. Wenona Thoma, 1996. Student, Tex. Sch. Fine Arts, 1936-41, Mexico City Coll., 1947; BJ, U. Tex., 1948. Office mgr. Tex. Sch. Fine Arts, 1936-41; mgr. Austin Symphony Orch., 1946-48, Erie (Pa.) Philharmonic Orch., 1948-49, Birmingham (Ala.) Symphony Orch., 1949-50; asst. cashier First Nat. Bank Birmingham, 1950-80; mgr. Ala. Pops Orch., Birmingham, 1955-62, Town and Gown Theatre, Birmingham, 1962-65; pres. Birmingham Opera Co., 1973-75; owner Books! By George, Birmingham, 1981—; co-founder Margo George Fashion Prodns., 1951, Hanna Antiques, 1981. Treas. Greater Birmingham Arts Alliance, 1971-75, Birmingham Opera Guild, 1971-74, So. Regional Opera, 1981-84; trustee Birmingham Symphony Assn., 1973-75; chmn. artist hospitality Arts Hall of Fame, Birmingham, 1974; judge nat. coun. auditions Met. Opera Assn., 1981; docent Birmingham Mus. Art, 1980-82. Mem. Gideons Internat. (pres. 1980-83), Allegro Mus. Club (v.p. 1993-94), Ala. Symphonic Assn. (dir. speakers bur. 1995). Avocations: lay preaching, public speaking, reading, writing, travel. Home: 1851 Rockwood Rd Birmingham AL 35216-1425 Office: Books! By George 2424 7th Ave S Birmingham AL 35233-3318

GEORGE, GERALD WILLIAM, author, administrator; b. Caldwell, Kans., Aug. 4, 1938; s. Chester Dale and Mildred M. (Jolitz) G.; m. Patricia Rae Woolsey, Sept. 23, 1961 (div. 1989); children: Brian William, Roxane Elizabeth; m. Carol Maryan Bell, Sept. 18, 1993. BA, U. Wichita, 1960; MA, Yale U., 1962. Instr. Bethany Coll., Lindsborg, Kans., 1962; reporter Salina (Kans.) Jour., 1962-64; staff writer The Nat. Observer, Washington, 1964-67; editorial assoc. Woodrow Wilson Nat. Fellowship Found., Princeton, N.J., 1967-68; spl. asst. to chmn. NEH, Washington, 1969-70; free-lance writer Washington, The Netherlands, 1971-73; mng. editor book series Am. Assn. State and Local History, Nashville, 1973-78, dir., 1978-87; free-lance writer, cons. to hist. orgns. Arlington, Va., 1987-90; exec. dir. Nat. Hist. Publs. and Records Commn., 1990-94; program devel. officer Coun. on Libr. Resources, Washington, 1995; exec. dir. Nat. Hist. Publs. and Records Commn., Washington, 1995-97; dir. policy and commns. Nat. Archives and Records Adminstrn., College Park, Md., 1997—. Author: Visiting History, Arguments Over Museums and Historic Sites, 1990, Imitations of Indonesia and Other Poems, 1997; co-author: Starting Right: A Basic Guide to Museum Planning, 1986; mng. editor: The States and the Nation; mem. editl. bd.: Ency. of the Am. West; contbr. articles to profl. jours. and mags. Recipient Woodrow Wilson fellow, 1960-61. Mem. Am. Assn. State and Local History, Am. Assn. Mus. (coun. 1978-87), Nat. Trust Hist. Preservation, Soc. Am. Archivists, Hist. Soc. of Washington, Kans. State Hist. Soc., Scenic Am. Office: Nat Archives 8601 Adelphi Rd College Park MD 20740-6001

GEORGE, JAMES, retired diplomat, foundation executive; b. Toronto, Ont., Can., Sept. 14, 1918; s. Ruggles Kerr and Helen (Heaton) G.; m. Caroline Parfitt, Nov. 7, 1942; children: Daniel, Graham, Caroline Randolph Dolphi. Degree, Upper Can. Coll., 1936, U. Grenoble, France, 1938; BA, U. Toronto, 1940. Lt. comdr. Royal Can. Naval Vol. Res., 1940-45; head Can. Naval Hist. Overseas, London, 1943-45; with Dept. External Affairs, Athens, Greece, 1945-48; dep. permanent rep. UN Dept. External Affairs, N.Y.C., 1951-55; disarmament com. Dept. External Affairs, N.Y.C. and Geneva, Switzerland; minister, dep. rep. NATO Dept. External Affairs, Paris, 1957-60; high commr. to Ceylon (Sri Lanka) Dept. External Affairs, 1960-64; head European divsn. Dept. External Affairs, Ottawa, Ont., Can., 1964-66; minister Can. Embassy, Paris, 1966-67; high commr. to India, amb. to Nepal, 1967-72, amb. to Iran, Kuwait, Oman, Bahrain, UAE, Qatar, 1972-77; co-founder, pres. Threshold Found., London, 1977-82; sec.-treas. Threshold Found., N.Y.C., 1982-84; pres. Sadat Peace Found., N.Y.C., 1984-92. Author: Asking for the Earth: Waking Up to the Spiritual/Ecological Crisis, 1995. hmn. Harmonic Arts Soc., Cath. St. John the Divine, N.Y.C., 1984-92; founding mem. Rainforest Action Network, San Francisco, 1987; chmn. Asian NGO Conf. Tropical Forests, New Delhi, 1987; leader mission to Kuwait and Gulf to assess post-war environ. damage Friends of the Earth Internat., 1991. Rhodes scholar, 1940. Mem. State of the World Forum (internat. adv. coun.), Gurdjieff Found., Soc. Traditional Studies, Asian Arts Soc. Avocations: skiing, sailing. Home: 360 Bloor St E Apt 1105, Toronto, ON Canada M4W 3M3 Office: 80 Schofield St City Island NY 10464

GEORGE, JAMES EDWARD, accountant; b. Mt. George, Ark., May 22, 1943; s. Opal W. Sr. and Mildred M. (Dacus) G.; m. Corliss Ann Johnson, Sept. 3, 1965; children: J. Mark, Ty C., Ryan E. BA in Acctg., U. Ark., Little Rock, 1967; MS in Logistics, Air Force Inst. Tech., 1979; grad., Air Command and Staff Coll. of USAF, 1987, USAF Air War Coll., 1992. CPA, Ark. Commd. 2d lt. USAF, 1967, advanced through grades to capt.; commdr. Field Tng. Detachment, Mt. Clemens, Mich., Kadena AFB, Japan and Kunsan AFB, Korea, 1967-73; supr. maintenance Field Maintenance Squadron, Craig AFB, Ala., 1973-75; flightline br. chief Royal AFB, Bentwater, Eng., 1976-77; officer in charge quality control Tactical Fighter Wing, Royal AFB, Bentwater, 1977-78; left active duty USAFR, 1978, advanced through grades to lt. col., 1988, ret., 1994; pub. utility auditor Ark. Pub. Svc. Commn., Little Rock, 1979-98; exec. dir. Ark. State Bd. Pub. Accountancy, Little Rock, 1998—; lectr. pub. utility income taxes and depreciation 12th and 13th ann. ea. utility rate seminar Nat. Assn. Regulatory Utility Commrs., 1984, 85; adj. faculty U. Ark., Fayetteville. Bd. dirs. North Little Rock 1st Ch. of Nazarene, 1989-94, 98—. Mem. AICPA (mem. info. retrieval com. 1987-90), Ark. Soc. CPA's (pres. Ctrl. Ark. chpt. 1992-93, 95-96, chmn. membership com. 1991-93, bd. dirs. 1994-97, mem. exec. com. 1996-97, chmn. public rels. com. 1997—, Outstanding Ark. CPA in Industry and Bus. award 1995), Toastmasters (pres. Uptown chpt. 1985, Able Toastmaster award 1988), Officers Club (bd. dirs. Kadena AFB 1971-72). Home: PO Box 95232 North Little Rock AR 72190-5232

GEORGE, JAMES NOEL, hematologist-oncologist, educator; b. Columbus, Ohio, Sept. 23, 1938. BA, MD, Ohio State U., 1962. Diplomate Am. Bd. Internal Medicine, subspecialty in hematology; lic. Okla. Bd. Med. Licensure and Supervision, Tex. State Bd. Med. Examiners, Ohio State Med. Bd. Intern, resident dept. medicine Vanderbilt U. Sch. Medicine, Nashville, 1962-63, 66-67; resident in medicine, hematology fellow, chief resident med. Strong Meml. Hosp., U. Rochester (N.Y.) Sch. Medicine, 1967-70; rsch. hematologist Walter Reed Army Inst. Rsch., Washington, 1963-66; from asst. prof. to assoc. prof. dept. med. divsn. hematol. U. Tex. Health Sci. Ctr., San Antonio, 1970-81, prof. dept. medicine divsn. hematology, 1981-89; rsch. assoc. Theodor Kocher Inst., Berne, Switzerland, 1975-76; prof. dept. medicine, chief hematology-oncology sect. U. Okla. Health Sci. Ctr., Oklahoma City, 1990—; staff physician Okla. Blood Inst., Oklahoma City, 1994—; vis. prof. dept. physiol. chemistry U. Wis., Madison, 1987-88; prof. associe U. Paris VII, Hopital Lariboisiere, Paris, 1988-89; mem. transfusion com. Bexar County Hosp., 1970-87; chmn. hematology peer rev. panel NASA Life Scis. Space Flight Experiment Program, 1978; mem. NIH Hematology Study Sect. I, 1986-94; mem. adv. bd. Gladstone Found. Labs. for Cardiovasc. Rsch., U. Calif., San Francisco, 1991; bd. trustees Gorgas Sci. Found., Inc., Brownsville, Tex., 1992—. Mem. editl. bd. Blood, 1985-90. Mem. oncology task force Midwest City Regional Hosp., 1995—. Capt. M.C., U.S. Army, 1963-66. Recipient 1st Ann. Lyndon B. Johnson award Tex. affiliate Am. Heart Assn., 1976. Fellow ACP; mem. Am. Fedn. for Clin. Rsch., Am. Heart Assn. (thrombosis coun.), Am. Soc. Clin. Investigation, Am. Soc. Hematology (com. on ednl. affairs and tng. 1986-89, sci. subcom. on platelets 1986-89, chmn. subcom. on platelets 1995, com. on publs. 1991—, chmn. edn. program on platelets 1993, 94, 96, ad hoc com. on practice guidelines 1994—, nominating com. 1995), Cen. Soc. Clin. Rsch., So. Soc. for Clin. Investigation, Alpha Omega Alpha (councilor Tex. Epsilon chpt. 1978-81). Office: U of Okla Health Scis Ctr Dept Medicine Hemat-Onc Sec PO Box 26901 Oklahoma City OK 73190*

GEORGE, JEAN CRAIGHEAD, author, illustrator; b. Washington, July 2, 1919; d. Frank Cooper and Carolyn (Johnson) Craighead; m. John L. George, Jan. 28, 1944 (div. Jan. 1964); children: Twig George Pittenger, John Craighead, Thomas Lothar. BA, Pa. State U., 1941. Reporter Washington Post, 1943-44; artist Pageant mag., 1945; reporter United Features, 1945-46; roving editor Reader's Digest, 1966-80; continuing edn. tchr. Chappaqua, N.Y., 1960-68. Author, illustrator: My Side of the Mountain, 1959, Summer of the Falcon, 1962, Gull Number 737, 1964, The Thirteen Moons, 1967-69, Coyote in Manhattan, 1968, River Rats, Inc., 1968, Who Really Killed Cock Robin, 1972, Julie of the Wolves, 1972, American Walk Book, 1978, Cry of the Crow, 1980, Journey Inward, 1982, The Talking Earth, 1983, One Day in the Alpine Tundra, 1984, How to Talk to Your Animals, 1985, One Day in the Prairie, 1986, Water Sky, 1987, (mus.) One Day in the Woods, 1988, The Shark Beneath the Reef, 1989, On the Far Side of the Mountain, 1990, One Day in the Tropical Rain Forest, 1990, The Missing 'Gator of Gumbo Limbo, 1992, The Fire Bug Connection, 1993, The First Thanksgiving, 1993, Dear Rebecca, Winter Is Here, 1993, Animals Who Have Won Our Hearts, 1994, Julie, 1994, To Climb a Waterfall, 1995, Acorn Pancakes & Dandelion Salad, 1995, There's an Owl in the Shower, 1995, Everglades, 1995, The Case of the Missing Cutthroat Trout, 1996, The Tarantula in My Purse, 1996, Look to the North, A Wolf Pup Diary, 1997, Julie's Wolf Pack, 1997, Arctic Son, 1997, Rhino Romp, 1998, Giraffe Trouble, 1998, Dear Katie, the Volcano Is a Girl, 1998, Survival Filmstrips, 1984, (film) My Side of the Mountain, 1965, Nature Filmstrips, 1978-80, One Day in the Woods Musical for Children (music by Chris Kubie), 1997, Giraffe Trouble, 1998, Rhino Romp, 1998, Elephant Walk, 1998, Gorilla Gang, 1999, Morning, Noon and Night, 1999, Frightful's Mountain, 1999, Snow Bear, 1999. Recipient Aurianne award, 1957, Newbery Honor Book award, 1961, medal, 1973, Hans Christian Andersen Honor List award, 1964, Pa. State Woman of Yr. award, 1968, World Book award, 1971, Kerlan award, 1982, U. So. Miss. award, 1986, Washington Irving award, 1991, 92, Knickerbocker award, 1991, Washington Post Children's Book Guild award, 1998, Empire State award, 1998. Address: 20 William St Chappaqua NY 10514-3114

GEORGE, JOEY RUSSELL, lawyer; b. Bklyn., Oct. 8, 1963; s. Jonas and Celeste Dorothy (Russell) G. BA, Howard U., 1985; JD, Harvard U., 1988. Bar: N.Y. 1989, Conn. 1989, U.S. Dist. Ct. (so. and ea. dists.) N.Y. 1989, U.S. Supreme Ct. 1992. Asst. prosecutor Queens County Dist. Atty., Kew Gardens, N.Y., 1988-90; asst. gen. counsel Exec. Office of the Pres., Office Mgmt. and Budget, Washington, 1990-91; assoc. dir. for policy The White House, Washington, 1991-93; pvt. practice, 1993-95; chief staff, chief counsel com. govt. reform subcom. on govt. mgmt., info. and tech. U.S. Ho. Reps., Washington, 1995—. Trustee Howard U., Washington, 1984-85; big brother Big Bros. Am. Cambridge, Mass., 1986—; bd. advisers City Harvest, 1993-95. Mem. ABA (vice chmn. govt. ops. com., adminstrv. law sect. 1997—), Ripon Soc. (pres. Harvard chpt. 1986-87, nat. v.p. 1987-88, bd. dirs. ednl. fund 1989-97, pres. ednl. fund 1993-97), Harvard Club, Phi Beta Kappa, Pi Sigma Alpha, Phi Alpha Theta. Republican. Home: 13129 225th St Laurelton NY 11413-1722 Office: US Ho Reps US Capitol Washington DC 20515

GEORGE, JOHN ANTHONY, health corporation executive; b. New Kensington, Pa., July 11, 1948; s. Moses and Veronica (Raymond) G.; m. Leah Diane Vota, Oct. 30, 1971 (div. 1992); children: Jessica, Cara, John, Ethan. BS, Duquesne U., Pitts., 1970; MBA, U. Pitts., 1973; MS in Taxation, Robert Morris Coll., Pitts. CFP. Asst. adminstr. mental health and mental retardation program Western Psychiat. Inst. and Clinic, Pitts., 1971-72; adminstrv. dir. Latrobe (Pa.) Area Hosp., 1973-76; asst. dir. Presbyn. U. Hosp., Pitts., 1976-80; owner, prin. George-Anstey Food Distributing Corp., Pitts., 1978-81; mgmt. cons. Arthur Young & Co., Pitts., 1980-82; exec. dir. Ea. Allegheny County Health Corp., 1982-85; pres. Alpha Health Network, 1985-88; pres., bd. dirs. Intergroup Svc. Corp., 1988—; mng. ptnr. Med. Benefit Svc., 1991—; bd. mgrs. Health Coalition Ptnrs.; lectr. in field. Contbr. articles to profl. jours. Bd. dirs. Southwestern Pa. chpt. ARC. Mem. Am. Coll. Health Care Execs., Assn. Managed Healthcare Orgns. (adv. bd. dirs., regional bd. dirs., editl. bd. Jour. of AAPPO), Assn. Healthcare Providers and Purchasers (bd. dirs., pres.). Roman Catholic. Home: 5121 Ellsworth Ave Pittsburgh PA 15232-2115 Office: 401 Shady Ave Apt D101 Pittsburgh PA 15206-4460

GEORGE, JOYCE JACKSON, judge emeritus, lawyer; b. Akron, Ohio, May 4, 1936; d. Ray and Verna (Popadich) Jackson; children: Michael Eliot, Michelle René. BA, U. Akron, 1962, JD, 1966; postgrad., Nat. Jud. Coll., Reno, 1976, NYU, 1983. Bar: Ohio 1966, U.S. Dist. Ct. (no. dist.) Ohio 1966, U.S. Ct. Appeals (6th cir.) 1968, U.S. Supreme Ct. 1968. Tchr. Akron Bd. Edn., 1962-66; asst. dir. law City of Akron, 1966-69, pub. utilities advisor, 1969-70, asst. dir. law, 1970-73; pvt. practice Akron, 1973-76; referee Akron Mcpl. Ct., 1975, judge, 1976-83; judge 9th dist. Ct. Appeals, Akron, 1983-89, Peninsula, Ohio, 1989; U.S. atty. No. Dist., Ohio, 1989-93; v.p. adminstrn. Telxon Corp., Akron, 1993-96; pres. Ind. Bus. Info. Svcs., Inc., Akron, 1996—; tchr., lectr. Ohio Jud. Coll., Nat. Jud. Coll.; cons. in field. Author: Judicial Opinion Writing Handbook, 1981, 3d edit., 1993, Referee's Report Writing Handbook, 1992; contbr. articles to profl. publs. Recipient Outstanding Woman of Yr. award Akron Bus. and Profl. Women's Club, 1982; Alumni Honor award U. Akron, 1983, Alumni award U. Akron Sch. Law, 1991; Dept. Treasury award, 1992; named Woman of Yr. in politics and govt. Summit County, Ohio, 1983. Mem. ABA, Ohio Bar Assn., Ohio Trial Lawyers Assn., Akron Bar Assn.

GEORGE, KATHRYN ELAINE, economist, financial writer; b. Glen Ridge, N.J., Sept. 25, 1952; d. Ray Randall and Vivian Viola (Brog) G. BS in Indsl. Engring., Cornell U., 1973; M of Systems Engring., U. Pa., 1975; MBA, Harvard U., 1978. Civil engr. N.J. Bur. Solid Waste Mgmt., Trenton, 1973-75; energy cons. Gaithersburg, Md., 1978-79; staff asst., Europe Texaco Inc., White Plains, N.Y., 1979, asst. mgr., alternate energy, 1980-82; project mgr. Catalyst Energy Devel. Corp., N.Y.C., 1982-85; floor trader N.Y. Futures Exch., N.Y.C., 1985-87; cons. N.Y.C., 1987-89; fin. analyst Synergics, Inc., Annapolis, Md., 1990-91; sr. economist Princeton Econ. Rsch., Inc., Rockville, Md., 1992—; ind. mktg. cons., 1998—; contbg. writer Securities Traders' Monthly, N.Y.C., 1989-92; ind. market cons. Contbr. articles to fin. mags. Recipient 2d prize Fine Arts scholarship N.J. State Fedn. Women's Clubs, 1970, N.J. State Clear Air and Water scholar, 1970-73. Mem. Soc. Profl. Journalists, Huguenot Soc. Am., Women's Nat. Rep. Club, DAR. Congregationalist. Avocations: sketching, tennis, travel, gardening. Home: 16625 Alden Ave Gaithersburg MD 20877-1503 Office: Princeton Econ Rsch Inc 1700 Rockville Pike Rockville MD 20852-1631

GEORGE, KATIE, lawyer; b. Chillicothe, Ohio, Sept. 4, 1953; d. Harry Paul and Tina Lillian George; m. Nov. 25, 1972 (div. Nov. 1983); 1 child, Alison; m. Timothy John Nusser, June 30, 1985. BBA, U. Toledo, 1983, JD, 1986, MBA, 1989. Bar: Ohio 1987, U.S. Dist. Ct. (no. dist.) Ohio 1993, Fla. 1994. Law clk. Allotta, Singer & Farley, Co., LPA, Toledo, 1985-86; mgmt. specialist Dept. Pub. Utilities City of Toledo, 1987-91, acting commr. Dept. Health, 1992-93, acting mgr. Dept. Pub. Safety, 1991-94; pvt. practice Toledo, 1987-96, Pensacola, Fla., 1996—; asst. dist. legal counsel State of Fla., 1996-97, chief legal counsel, 1997—; part-time instr. U. Toledo, 1987-88, U. West Fla., 1997. Bd. dirs. Toledo BlockWatch, 1993, Ohio Pub. Employers Labor Rels. Assn., 1991-92; mem. Missing and Exploited Children Comprehensive Action Program, 1997-99. Mem. Fla. Bar Assn., Escambia Santa Rosa Bar Assn. Avocations: photography, scuba diving. Office: Ste 601 160 Governmental Ctr Pensacola FL 32501

GEORGE, LINDA OLSEN, mathematics educator, writer; b. Terre Haute, Ind., Aug. 25, 1940; d. Paul Hugo and Velma Agnes (Bennie) Olsen; m. Robert Glen George, Aug. 30, 1964; children: Daniel George, David George. BS magna cum laude, Ind. State U., 1961, MS, 1963; EdD, Ind. U., 1970. Instr. Ind. State U., Terre Haute, 1962-66; lectr. Ind. U., Bloomington, 1966-68, asst. prof., 1970-71, adj. faculty, 1972—; ednl. writer Terre Haute, 1972—; vis. faculty Ind. U.-Purdue U., Indpls., 1971; assoc. faculty Ind. U., South Bend, 1972; pres. REM Assocs., Inc., 1992—. Author: Helping Children Learn Mathematics, 1976, 2d edit., 1985, Mathematics in the Elementary School, 1976, Helping Teachers Learn Mathematics, 1985; contbr. articles to profl. publs. Mem. Nat. Coun. Tchrs. Math., Delta Theta Tau, Kappa Delta Pi, Omega Alpha Delta, Pi Lambda Theta. Avocations: travel, needlework. Home: 12555 E Kyle Ave Rosedale IN 47874-9333

GEORGE, LINDA SHUMAKER, writer, educator; b. Lenoir, N.C., Sept. 24, 1949; d. Thomas Craig and Mary Poole Shumaker; m. Richard George, Feb. 14, 1986; 1 child, Alexander Thomas Oscar. BA, NYU, 1971; MA, Harvard U., 1975, PhD, 1980. V.p. internat. divsn. Mfrs. Hanover Trust Co., N.Y.C., 1981-87; adj. asst. prof. dept. history Drew U., Madison, N.J., 1989-91; vis. scholar Hagop Kevkorian Ctr. for Near Ea. Studies NYU, 1992-93; lectr. in Mid. Ea. langs. and civilizations Columbia U., N.Y.C., 1992-94; freelance writer, 1992—. Author: The Golden Age of Islam, 1998; editor Far Brook Bull., Short Hills, N.J., 1995—. Charles McGann scholar NYU, 1967-68; fellow Ctr. for Arabic Study Abroad, Cairo, 1973-74; Radcliffe grantee for grad. women Harvard U., 1980, summer seminar for coll. tchrs. grantee NEH, 1991. Mem. The Authors Guild, Am. Rsch. Ctr. in Egypt (fellow 1977-78), Mid. East Studies Assn., Soc. Children's Book Writers and Illustrators. Avocations: opera, ice hockey.

GEORGE, LLOYD D., federal judge; b. Montpelier, Idaho, Feb. 22, 1930; s. William Ross and Myrtle (Nield) G.; m. LaPrele Badouin, Aug. 6, 1956; children: Douglas Ralph, Michele, Cherie Suzanne, Stephen Lloyd. BS, Brigham Young U., 1955; JD, U. Calif., Berkeley, 1961. Ptnr. Albright, George, Johnson & Steffen, 1969-71, George, Steffen & Simmons, 1971-74; judge U.S. Bankruptcy Ct. (Nev. dist.), 1974-84, U.S. Dist. Ct. Nev., 1984—, chief judge, sr. judge, 1997—; justice of peace Clark County, Nev., 1962-69. Served with USAF, 1955-58. Office: US Dist Ct Foley Fed Bldg Rm 316 300 Las Vegas Blvd S Fl 3 Las Vegas NV 89101-5833

GEORGE, LYNDA DAY, actress; b. San Marcos, Tex., 1946; m. Christopher George, May 15, 1970; 1 child by previous marriage, Nicky. Formerly model, motion picture actress; TV series include Silent Force, 1970-71, Mission Impossible, 1971-73; numerous other TV appearances including Wonder Woman, 1976, Blacke's Magic, 1986, Mission: Impossible, 1989; TV films She Cried Murder, 1973, Panic on the 5:22, 1974, The Trial of Chaplain Jensen, 1975, The Barbary Coast, 1975, Death Among Friends, 1975, Twin Detectives, 1976, Mayday at 40,000 Feet, 1976, Once An Eagle, 1977, It Happened At Lakewood Manor, 1977, Cruise into Terror, 1978, Casino, 1980, Quick & Quick, 1981; motion pictures include The Gentle Rain, 1966; TV miniseries include Rich Man, Poor Man, 1976, Roots, 1977; films include Young Warriors, 1983, Mortuary, 1984, The Legend of Forrest Tucker, 1997. Mem. LDS Ch. Office: The Irv Schecter Co 9300 Wilshire Blvd Ste 400 Beverly Hills CA 90212-3210*

GEORGE, MELVIN DOUGLAS, retired university president; b. Washington, Feb. 13, 1936; s. Douglas Elmer and Catherine Evelyn (McNelly) G.; m. Meta Jane Barghusen, Aug. 17, 1958; children—Elizabeth Anne, Margaret Susan. B.A., Northwestern U., 1956; Ph.D., Princeton U., 1959. From asst. to assoc. prof. math. U. Mo., Columbia, 1960-67, prof., assoc. dean, 1967-70, v.p. acad. affairs, 1975-85; dean Coll. Arts and Scis. U. Nebr., Lincoln, 1970-75; pres. St. Olaf Coll., Northfield, Minn., 1985-94, pres. emeritus, 1994—; v.p. instnl. rels. U. Minn., Mpls., 1994-96; prof. math. emeritus U. Mo., Columbia, 1996—, interim pres., 1996-97; pres. emeritus U. Mo., 1997—. Contbr. articles to profl. jours. Recipient Robert W. Martin award for Acad. Freedom, Mo. conf. AAUP, 1985. Mem. Am. Math. Soc., Math. Assn. Am. Lutheran. Avocations: music; swimming. Home: 1509 W Rollins Rd Columbia MO 65203-2378

GEORGE, NICHOLAS, criminal defense lawyer, entrepreneur; b. Seattle, July 11, 1952; s. Harry and Mary (Courounes) G.; children: Harry Nicholas, James Michael. BA in Polit. Sci. cum laude, Whitman Coll., 1974; MBA in Mktg. and Corp. Planning, U. Chgo., 1979; JD, U. Puget Sound, 1989. Bar: Wash. 1991, U.S. Dist. Ct. (we. dist.) Wash. 1991, U.S. Ct. Appeals (9th cir.) 1991, U.S. Tax Ct. 1992, U.S. Dist. Ct. (ea. dist.) Wash. 1994, U.S. Supreme Ct. 1994. Fin. cons. Pacific Western Investment Co., Lynnwood, Wash., 1975-77; planning dir. Clinton Capital Ventures, Seattle, 1979-81; corp. planning mgr. Tacoma Boatbldg., 1981-83; pres. MegaProf Investors, Bellevue, Wash., 1983-89; practice trial-settlement law bus., Seattle, 1989—; free-lance coll. counselor, Seattle, 1980—. Author: Legitimacy in Government: Ideal, Goal, or Myth? 1974. Bd. auditor St. Demetrios Greek Orthodox Ch., Seattle, 1982-83; bd. dirs. Hellenic Golfers Assn., Seattle, 1981-83. Mem. ABA, Assn. Trial Lawyers Am., Wash. State Bar Assn., Wash. Assn. Criminal Def. Lawyers, Wash. State Trial Lawyers Assn., Fed. Bar Assn., Nat. Assn. Criminal Def. Lawyers, Tacoma-Pierce County Bar Assn., Seattle-King County Bar Assn., Wash. Defender Assn., Wash. State Hist. Soc., Am. Inst. Archeol., Phi Alpha Delta. Greek Orthodox. Avocations: weightlifting, travel, family history, football coaching, writing. Home: 5007 80th St SW Lakewood WA 98499-4077 Office: 1201 Pacific Ave Ste 1502 Tacoma WA 98402-4322

GEORGE, ORLANDO JOHN, JR., state representative, college administrator; b. Wilmington, Del, Dec. 14, 1945; s. Orlando John and Lena (Ficca) G.; m. Linda Mary Krystopolski, July 29, 1967; children: Melanie Lynn, Leana Marie, Natalie Rae, Olivia Julene. BA in Math., U. Del., MEd, EdD. Math. instr. Del. Tech. and C.C., Wilmington, 1969-75, chmn. math. dept., 1975-79, asst. to campus dir., 1979-82, dean instrn., 1982-83, asst. campus dir., 1983-89, v.p. campus dir., 1989-95, pres., 1995—; mem. Del. Ho. of Reps., chmn. fin. com., 1974-80, minority leader, 1980-82, 84-95, speaker, 1982-84; city councilman, chmn. edn. com., sch. tax commr., 1972-74. Bd. pres. Cmty.'s in Schs.; mem. Del. Bus. Roundtable, Bus. Pub. Edn. Coun., Pvt. Industry Coun.; mem. adv. bd. The Mary Campbell Ctr.; bd. dirs. C.C.'s for Internat. Devel., Inc. Recipient Com. 39 Good Govt. award, 1979; named U.S. Jaycees Outstanding Man of Yr., 1981, Disting. Legis. Service award Del. State Bar Assn., 1983, Disting. Alumni award U. Del., 1985, Superior Ct. Amicus Curiae award, 1995, N.E. Alliance of Min.'s Graybeal Ct. of Hon., 1997, Alexis I. DuPont award for govt. svc., 1998; named Coll. Pres. of Yr. Alpha Beta Gamma, 1998. Mem. Del. State C. of C. (bd. dirs.), Del. Coun. Pres.'s, Del. Sci. Alliance (mem. adv. bd.), Del. Math Coalition (co-chair hon. bd.). Home: 4401 Whittier Rd Wilmington DE 19802-1231

GEORGE, PATRICIA BYRNE, artist; b. Cheyenne, Wyo.; d. Vincent Patrick and Margaret Mae (Adams) Byrne; m. Edward Palmer George, Jr.; children: Stacy Elizabeth George O'Reilly, Kristie Anne. BA, UCLA. Artist (mag. covers) Art Passion mag., June, 1999, Mus. of Sapporo Catalogue, June 1997, Calif. Living, Dec. 1994, Huntington Harbour, July 1994, Family Living, June 1993, Manhattan Arts, Sept. 1993; exhibited in group shows at Hellenic Inst., Athens, 1990, Matrix Gallery, San Francisco, 1991, 92, Neville Gallery, Toronto, Ont., Can., 1991, 92, Chapelle de la Sorbonne, Paris, 1992, Panopoulos Gallery, Athens, 1993, Internat. Artists, Tokyo, 1994, Fine Art Collection, Sausalito, Calif., 1994, Mark Alan Gallery, Laguna Beach, Calif., 1995, Gail Roff Fine Art Gallery, Newport Beach, Calif., 1995, 96, Galerie Klimintiris, Montreal, Que., Can., 1996, Sapporo (Japan) Mus., 1997, Hidden Dreams Gall., Calif., 1998, Coast Gall., Calif., 1998; represented in numerous pvt., mus. and corp. collections, including Internat. Trade Ctr., Hilton Hotels, Newport Coast Resort, Disney Corp., others. Recipient Laureate award Mayor of Paris, 1990, Spl. award of jury Musee d'art Moderne, France, 1993; Cover Contest winner Manhattan Arts, 1993, Grand Cordon of the Templars, Japan, 1997. Office: European Expressions 4141 Ball Rd # 221 Cypress CA 90630-3400

GEORGE, PETER JAMES, economist, educator; b. Toronto, Sept. 12, 1941; s. Ralph Langlois and Kathleen May (Larder) G.; m. Gwendolyn Jean Scharf, Oct. 19, 1962 (dec. Mar. 1997); children—Michael James, Katherine Jane; m. Allison Mary Barrett, July 31, 1998. BA with honors, U. Toronto, 1962, MA, 1963, PhD, 1967; DU (hon.), U. Ottawa, 1995. Lectr. McMaster U., 1965-67, asst. prof., 1967-71, assoc. prof., 1971-80, prof. econs., 1980—, assoc. dean grad. studies, 1974-79, dean social scis., 1980-89, pres., vice chancellor, 1995—; spl. lectr. U. Toronto, 1967; vis. lectr. U. Cambridge, 1974; economist Govt. of Ont., 1963; project mgr. Tanzania Tourist Corp., 1970-71; pres. Coun. Ont. Univs., Toronto, 1991-95; hon. prof. Beijing U. Sci. and Tech., 1998. Author: Government Subsidies and the Construction of the Canadian Pacific Railway, 1981, The Emergence of Industrial America: Strategic Factors in American Economic Growth Since 1870, 1982; Appointed to Ont. Coun. on Univ. Affairs, 1987-91. recipient, commemorative medal 125th Aniv. Confederation of Canada, 1993. Mem. Can. Econs. Assn., Can. Hist. Assn., Am. Econ. Assn., Econ. History Assn., Econ. History Soc. Office: McMaster U Office Pres GH-238, 1280 Main St W, Hamilton, ON Canada L8S 4L8

GEORGE, RICHARD NEILL, lawyer; b. Watertown, N.Y., Apr. 6, 1933; s. Wendell Dow and Frances Laura (Small) G.; m. Patricia Harman Jackson, June 21, 1958; children—Frances Harman, Richard Neill, Mary Elizabeth. A.B., Yale U., 1955; J.D., Cornell U., 1962. Bar: N.Y. 1962. Assoc. Nixon, Hargrave, Devans & Doyle, Rochester, N.Y., 1962-70, ptnr., 1970—. Committeeman, Brighton Town Republican Com., Rochester, 1966-78; ruling elder Twelve Corners Presbyn. Ch., Rochester, 1977-79, 84-87; mem. permanent jud. commn. Presbytery of Genesee Valley, 1988-94, also moderator. Capt. USAF, 1956-59. Mem. ABA, N.Y. State Bar Assn., Monroe County Bar Assn., Fed. Energy Bar Assn., Exeter Alumni Assn. of Rochester (pres. 1970—). Republican. Clubs: Country of Rochester, Yale of N.Y.C., Amelia Island. Avocations: golf; reading. Home: 90 Oak Ln Rochester NY 14610-3135 Office: Nixon Hargrave Devans & Doyle PO Box 1051 Clinton Sq Rochester NY 14604-1729

GEORGE, ROBERT PETER, educator, lawyer; b. Morgantown, W.Va., July 10, 1955; s. Joseph Michael and Catherine Victoria (Sellaro) G.; m. Cindy Schrom, Dec. 11, 1982; children: David, Rachel. BA, Swarthmore Coll., 1977; MTS, JD, Harvard U., 1981; PhD, Oxford U., 1986. Bar: Pa. 1987, N.J. 1987, U.S. Dist. Ct. N.J. 1987, U.S. Ct. Appeals (4th cir.) 1991, U.S. Supreme Ct. 1990. Lectr. New Coll. Oxford U., Eng., 1982-85, vis. fellow, 1988; from asst. prof. to assoc. prof. Princeton (N.J.) U., 1986-99, McCormick prof. jurisprudence, 1999—; of counsel Robinson & McElwee, Charleston, W.Va., 1990—; dir. Mellon Law Seminar, Princeton U., 1986-88, faculty parliamentarian, 1987—; chmn. vis. examiners Swarthmore (Pa.) Coll., 1988, 92; mem. acad. adv. bd. Judiciary Leadership Devel. Coun., 1990—; presdl. apt. U.S. Commn. Civil Rights, 1993-98; Royden B. Davis vis. prof. Georgetown U., 1994; bd. govs. Ave Maria Law Sch., Ann Arbor, Mich.; internat. adv. bd. Ctr. for the Study of Constitutionalism, U. London; adv. bd. mem. Program in Medicine and Human Rights, U. Minn., Of the People Found.; bd. dirs. Inst. for Am. Values. Author: Making Men Moral: Civil Liberties and Public Morality, 1993, In Defense of Natural Law, 1999; editor: Natural Law Theory, 1992, The Autonomy of Law: Essays on Legal Positivism, 1996, Natural Law, Liberalism and Morality, 1996, Natural Law and Moral Inquiry: Ethics, Metaphysics and Politics in the Work of Germain Grisez, 1998; mem. editl. bd. Am. Jour. Jurisprudence, 1990—; mem. editl. adv. bd. First Things, 1996—; series editor New Forum Books of Princeton U. Press, 1996—; mem. bd. cons. editors Academic Questions, 1997—; contbr. articles to profl. jours. Chmn. Federalist Soc. Religious Liberties Practice Group. U.S. Supreme Ct. Jud. fellow, 1989, Frank Knox fellow Harvard U., 1981; Howard Found. grant, 1988; recipient Justice Tom C. Clark award, 1990, ABA Silver Gavel award, 1991, Paul Bator award Federalist Soc., 1994, Outstanding Prof. award Templeton Found., 1997, Cardinal Wright award Fellowship of Cath. Schs., 1999, David W. Peck medal for eminence in law Wabash Coll., 1999. Mem. Nat. Assn. Scholars (bd. dirs. 1996—), Am. Pub. Philosophy Inst. (bd. dirs.), Philosophy Edn. Soc. (bd. dirs.), Johnson and Chesterton Club, Cosmos Club, Phi Beta Kappa. Avocations: fishing, literature, bluegrass banjo, guitar, folk music. Home: 371 Prospect Ave Princeton NJ 08540-4078 Office: Princeton U 244 Corwin Hall Princeton NJ 08544

GEORGE, RONALD BAYLIS, physician, educator; b. Nov. 17, 1932. MD, Tulane U., 1958. Diplomate in internal medicine and pulmonary diseases Am. Bd. Internal Medicine. Intern Charity Hosp. La., New Orleans, 1958-59, resident, 1962-64; resident Tulane Med. Svc., New Orleans, 1959-60; assoc. prof. medicine Tulane U. Sch. Medicine, New Orleans, 1969-72; assoc. prof. medicine La. State U. Sch. Medicine, Shreveport, 1972-74, prof. medicine, 1974—, chief pulmonary sect., 1972-92, acting chmn. dept. medicine, 1991-92, chmn. dept. medicine, 1992—; chief med. svc. VA Med. Ctr., Shreveport, 1978-82. Capt. USAF, 1960-62. Recipient H.M. Cotton Faculty Excellence award La. State U., Shreveport, 1987, Owls Club award Tulane U., 1968. Fellow ACP, Am. Coll. Chest Physicians (pres. 1993-94); mem. Am. Thoracic Soc., Am. Soc. for Clin. Investigation, Am. Assn. for Respiratory Care, Shreveport Med. Soc., Alpha Omega Alpha. Office: La State U Med Sch Dept Medicine PO Box 33932 Shreveport LA 71130-3932*

GEORGE, RONALD M., state supreme court chief justice; b. L.A., Mar. 11, 1940. AB, Princeton U., 1961; JD, Stanford U., 1964. Bar: Calif. 1965. Dep. atty. gen. Calif. Dept. Justice, 1965-72; judge L.A. Mcpl. Ct., L.A. County, 1972-77; judge Superior Ct. Calif., L.A. County, 1977-87, supervising judge criminal divsn., 1983-84; assoc. justice 2d dist., divsn. 4 Calif. Ct. Appeal, L.A., 1987-91; assoc. justice Calif. Supreme Ct., San Francisco, 1991-96, chief justice, 1996—. Mem. Calif. Judges Assn. (pres. 1982-83). Avocations: hiking, skiing, running. Office: Calif Supreme Court 350 McAllister St 5th fl San Francisco CA 94102-3600

GEORGE, ROY KENNETH, minister; b. Haskell, Tex., Sept. 23, 1934; s. Roy F. and Jimalee (Scott) G.; m. Patsy Sue Brasher, May 14, 1955; children: Janis Sue, Cheryl Anne. Ordained to ministry Assemblies of God Ch., 1959. Evangelist U.S., Africa, Europe, Asia, 1954-63; pastor Highland Assembly of God Ch., Bakersfield, Calif., 1964-65, 1st Assembly of God Ch., Carlsbad, N.Mex., 1966-67, Sem. South Ch., Ft. Worth, 1968-73, Christian Ctr., Ashland, Oreg., 1973-74, 1st Family Ch., Albuquerque, 1974-93; broadcaster religious radio and TV programs, including Moments with the Master, Sta. KKIM, Albuquerque, 1975-85; state exec. presbyter Assemblies of God N.Mex., 1976—; asst. dist. supt. Assemblies of God, 1981-93, dist. supt. N.Mex. dist., 1993—, mem. Gen. Presbytery, 1981—; mem. exec. bd. Am. Indian Coll. of the Assemblies of God, Phoenix, Ariz., 1993—. Contbr. articles to profl. jours. Bd. regents Southwestern Assemblies of God U. at Waxahachie, Tex., 1981—. Mem. Albuquerque Ministerial Assn., Greater Albuquerque Pentecostal Fellowship (pres. 1975-76), Rogue Valley Nat. Assn. Evangels. (v.p. 1974-75), Civitains (chaplain 1969-73), Kiwanis (pres. Albuquerque club 1982-83, lt. gov. S.W. dist. 1985-86). Office: Assemblies of God NMex Dist 6640 Caminito Coors NW Albuquerque NM 87120-3119 *The only way to win in the Game of Life, is to overcome evil with good. To conquer evil by being bad is folly. The Game plan that wins, is when you return Good for Evil.*

GEORGE, SHARON A., nurse educator, nurse practitioner; b. Boston, Nov. 14, 1942; d. William and Rachael (Tocio) Luther; m. Paul F. George, Oct. 24, 1964; children: Michelle, Justin. Diploma, Lawrence Meml. Hosp., Medford, Mass., 1963; BSN, Northeastern U., Boston, 1978; MS, U. Mass., Lowell, 1983; postgrad., U. Mass., 1999—. Cert. adult nurse practitioner, ANA. Instr. advanced med./surg. nursing Lawrence Meml. Hosp.; grad. faculty primary care nurse practitioner program Boston U.; coord. family/community health nurse practitioner program U. Mass., Lowell; adult nurse practitioner Salem (Mass.) Hosp., Harvard Community Health Plan; dir., lectr. Nurse Practitioner Cert. Rev. Course, Bedford, Mass., 1992—; speaker in field. Mem. ANA, Mass. Nurses Assn. (past mem. cabinet nursing edn.), Sigma Theta Tau.

GEORGE, STEPHEN CARL, reinsurance executive, educator, consultant; b. Miami, Fla., July 11, 1959; s. Joseph P. and Beatrice P. George; 3 children. BS in MIS, Fla. State U., 1983; MBA in Health Adminstrn., U. Miami, 1986. Provider rels. spec. Travelers Health Network, Phila., 1987-89; prin. Tyler & Co., Atlanta, 1989-93; risk mgmt. cons. John Alden - Provider Group, Miami, 1994; pres. Provider Risk, Inc., Miami, 1995—; spkr. U. Miami, 1995-97; adj. prof. Nova U. Southeastern, 1996—; speaker in field. Contbr. articles to profl. jours. Vol. Habitat for Humanity, Miami, Fla., 1995—. A.A. Green scholar. Mem. Am. Coll. of Health Care Execs. (regents adv. coun. 1995-97), Toastmasters Internat. (CTM), South Fla. Exec. Forum, Alpha Kappa Psi. Avocations: family, water sports. Office: Provider Risk Inc 9761 SW 123rd St Ste 1000 Miami FL 33176-4929

GEORGE, SUSAN E. GOULD, health facility administrator; b. Bedford, Pa., Sept. 21, 1952; d. Robert Neil and Joan Louise (Robertson) Gould; m. Scott O. George, Aug. 17, 1974; children: Seth, Seleste. BSN cum laude, U. Pitts., 1974; MPH in Health Policy and Mgmt., U. South Fla., 1997. RN, Fla.; nat. cert. in nursing adminstrn. advanced, ANA. Staff nurse med./surg. unit Bedford (Pa.) County Meml. Hosp., 1974; staff nurse surg. unit Gainesville (Fla.) Hosp., 1974-75; staff nurse neurol.-med. unit James A. Haley Vets. Hosp., Tampa, Fla., 1975-76, staff nurse surg. ICU, 1976-78, staff nurse post anesthesia care unit, 1978-82, head nurse operating room, 1982-83, coord. operative svcs., 1983-92, asst. chief nursing svc., ICU/operative svcs., 1992—; cons. Health Care Auditors; nat. cons. for implementation of automated med. record for surg. svcs.; lectr. in field. Developer surg. computer package. Mem. Assn. Operating Room Nurses (exec. bd. Tampa Bay chpt. 1988-91, bd. dirs. 1991-93), U. Pitts. Alumni Assn., Sigma Theta Tau.

GEORGE, THOMAS, artist; b. N.Y.C., July 1, 1918; s. Rube and Irma (Seeman) Goldberg; m. Lavergne Burton, July 16, 1951; children: John R., Geoffrey T. B.A., Dartmouth Coll., 1940. One-man shows include Feragil Gallery, N.Y.C., 1951, 53, Korman Gallery, N.Y.C., 1954, Dartmouth Coll., 1965, Contemporaries Gallery, N.Y.C., 1956, Bridgestone Mus., Tokyo, 1957, Betty Parsons Gallery, N.Y.C., 1959, 63, 65, 66, 68, 70, 72, 74, 76, 78, 81, Reid Gallery, London, 1962, 64, Del. Mus., 1971, 76, Henie-Onstad Art Mus., Oslo, 1971, Princeton U. Art Mus., 1975, Dartmouth Coll., 1979, 90, Nat. Gallery, Oslo, 1980, Maxwell Davidson Gallery, N.Y.C., 1983, 85, 88, 90, Riis Gallery, Oslo, 1982, 84, 86, 88, 90, Hood Art Mus., Dartmouth Coll,1990, Snyder Fine Art, N.Y.C., 1991, Snyder Fine Art, N.Y.C., 1991, 93, 96, Julian Hartnoll Gallery, London, 1993; retrospective exhbn. N.J. State Mus., 1987; group exhbns. include Met. Mus. Art, N.Y.C., Am. Fedn. Arts, Mus. Modern Art, N.Y.C., Whitney Mus. Ann., N.Y.C., Carnegie Internat., Pitts., Pa. Acad., Japan Internat Biennial Art, Tokyo, White House, Lausanne (Switzerland) Mus.; represented in permanent collections Whitney Mus., Mus. Modern Art, N.Y.C., Bklyn. Mus., Tate Gallery, London, Nat. Coll. Fine Arts at Smithsonian Instn., Washington, Chase Manhattan Coll., N.Y.C., Library of Congress, Bridgestone Mus., Hood Art Mus., Dartmouth Coll., Lausanne Mus. Art, Mus. Fine Arts, Houston, U. Calif. Art Mus., Berkeley, Santa Barbara Mus. Fine Arts, Okla. Art Ctr., U. Calif. Mus., Santa Clara, Yale U. Art Gallery, Flint (Mich.) Inst., N.J. State Mus., Rose Art Mus., Brandeis U., Heine-Onstad Art Mus., San Francisco Mus. Art, Del. Art Mus., Nat. Gallery, Oslo, Princeton Art Mus., Inst. Advanced Study, Princeton, many corp. collections; vis. painter, Edward MacDowell Colony, 1956, vis. artist, U. Tex., 1978, artist-in-residence, Dartmouth Coll., 1979 (Recipient purchase prize Bklyn. Mus. 1955, Ford Found. 1961, Whitney Mus. Ann. Art. Painting 1962, N.J. State Mus. 1971, Purchase prize N.J. State Mus. 1971, Olympic games Poster/Print Commn. 1974). Served with USNR, 1942-45. Recipient Presdl. medal Dartmouth Coll., 1991; Princeton Arts Council award, 1992; Rockefeller Found. grantee, 1957. Address: 20 Greenhouse Dr Princeton NJ 08540-4801 *A good artist must work hard all his life. He must know his craft and, most important of all, he must feel deeply about something in life.*

GEORGE, THOMAS FREDERICK, chemistry educator; b. Phila., Mar. 18, 1947; s. Emmanuel John and Veronica Mather (Hansel) G.; m. Barbara Carol Harbach, Apr. 25, 1970. BA in Chemistry and Math., Gettysburg (Pa.) Coll., 1967; MS in Chemistry, Yale U., 1968, PhD, 1970. Rsch. assoc. MIT, 1970; postdoctoral fellow U. Calif., Berkeley, 1971; mem. faculty U. Rochester, N.Y., 1972-85; prof. chemistry U. Rochester, 1977-85; dean Faculty Natural Sci. and Math., prof. chemistry and physics SUNY-Buffalo, 1985-91; provost, acad. v.p., prof. chemistry and physics Wash. State U., Pullman, 1991-96; chancellor, prof. chemistry and physics U. Wis., Stevens Point, 1996—; Disting. vis. lectr. dept. chemistry U. Tex., Austin, 1978; lectr. NATO Advanced Study Inst., Cambridge, Eng., 1979; Disting. speaker dept. chemistry U. Utah, 1980; Disting. lectr. Air Force Weapons Lab., Kirtland AFB, N.Mex., 1980; mem. com. recommendations U.S. Army Basic Sci. Research, 1978-81; lectr. NATO Summer Sch. on Interfaces under Photon Irradiation, Maratea, Italy, 1986; organizer NSF workshop on theoretical aspects of laser radiation and its interaction with atomic and molecular systems Rochester, N.Y., 1977; vice chmn. 6th Internat. Conf. Molecular Energy Transfer, Rodez, France, 1979; chmn. Gordon Rsch. Conf. Molecular Energy Transfer, Wolfeboro, N.H., 1981; adj. rsch. prof. physics Korea U., Seoul, 1994-99; Dow lectr. polymer sci. U. Detroit Mercy, 1996; mem. program com. Internat. Conf. on Lasers, San Francisco, 1981-83, ACS Symposium on Recent Advances in Surface Sci., Rochester sect., 1982, Internat. Laser Sci. Conf., Dallas, 1985, external rev. com. for chemistry Gettysburg Coll., 1984, awards com. ACS Procter and Gamble student prizes in chemistry, 1982-83, Free-electron Laser peer rev. panel Am. Inst. Biol. Sci. Med., alt., bd. trustees alt. Calspan-UB Rsch. Ctr., 1989-91; organiser APS Symposium on Laser-Induced Molecular Excitation/Photofragmentation, N.Y., 1987; co-organizer ACS Symposium on Phys. Chemistry High-Temp. Supercondrs., L.A., 1988; co-organizer MRS Symposium on High-Temperature Superconductors, Alfred, N.Y., 1988; chmn. SPIE Symposium on Photochemistry in Thin Films, L.A., 1989; mem. internat. program adv. com. Internat. Sch. Lasers and Applications, Sayanogorsk, East Siberia, USSR, 1989; lectr. on chemistry at cutting edge Smithsonian Instn./Am. Chem. Soc., Washington, 1990; Musselman lectr. Gettysburg Coll., 1999; mem. internat. adv. com. Xth Vavilov Conf. Nonlinear Optics, Novosibirsk, USSR, 1990; Am. coord. NSF Info. Exchange Seminar for U.S.-Japan Program of Cooperation in Photoconversion and Photosynthesis, Honolulu, 1990; mem. program com. Optical Soc. Am. Topical Meeting on Radiative Processes and Dephasing in Semiconductors, Coeur d'Alene, Idaho, 1998; mem. sci. com. Sixth Brijuni Internat. Conf. on Interdisciplinary Topics in Physics and Chemistry, Brijuni Isles, Croatia, 1998; mem. exec. bd. N.Y. State Inst. on Superconductivity, 1990-91; mem. ONT/ASEE rev. panel for Engring. Edn. postdoctoral fellowship program, 1990; mem. rev panel rsch. experiences for undergrads of sci. and tech. rsch. ctrs., NSF, 1989, mem. rev. panel grad. res. traineeships NSF, 1992; cons., lectr. in field. Co-author: (textbook) Notes in Classical and Quantum Physics, 1990, Fundamentals in Chemical Physics, 1998; also over 550 papers in field; mem. editl. bd. Molecular Physics, 1984-90, Jour. Cluster Sci., 1989-97; mem. adv. bd. Jour. Phys. Chemistry, 1980-84; mem. adv. editl. bd. Chem. Physics Letters, 1979-81, Chem. Materials, 1989; mem. editl. bd. Jour. Quantum Nonlinear Phenomena (Soviet jour), 1991-96, Nova Jour. Theoretical Physics, 1996-97, Internat. Jour. of Theoretical Physics, Group Theory and Nonlinear Optics, 1998—; editor-at-large Marcel Dekker, 1989; editor: Photochemistry in Thin Films, 1989; co-editor: Chemistry of High-Temperature Superconductors, Vol. I, 1987, vol. II, 1988, ACS Symposium Series, Internat. Jour. Theoret. Physics, Group Theory and Nonlinear Optics, 1999—, Computational Studies of New Materials, 1999; feature editor Jour. of Optical Soc. of Am., Spectrochimica Acta, Optical Engring. Tchr., scholar Camille and Henry Dreyfus Found., 1975-85; bd. mgrs. Buffalo Mus. Sci., 1986-92; mem. exec. bd. N.Y. State Inst. on Superconductivity, 1990-91; mem. canvassing com. ACS; mem. external rev. com. for chemistry Gettysburg Coll., 1984; mem. NEASC site visit team Boston U., ten-yr. accreditation, 1989; bd. dirs. Wash. State Inst. for Pub. Policy, 1991-96; trustee Wash. State U. Found., 1991-96; bd. dirs. Wash. Tech. Ctr., 1992-96; mem. exec. com. Northwest Acad. Forum, 1992-96, chmn. 1994-95; mem. rev. panel Grad. Rsch. Traineeships, NSF, 1992, mem. rev. panel for sci. and tech. ctr. proposals, 1998, rev. panel for preproposals for sci. and tech. ctrs., 1998; mem. Project 435 Dist. Leadership Coun., Wis. Assn. Biomed. Rsch. and Edn./Research America!, 1997; mem. Commn. on the Future of Gettysburg Coll., 1997-98; bd. dirs. Portage County Bus. Coun., 1998—, Stevens Point Area YMCA, 1998—, United Way Portage County, Wis., 1997—, chmn. 1999 campaign, Tech. Alliance State Wash., 1996, U. Wis.-Stevens Point Found., 1996—, Paper Sci. Found., 1996—; bd. trustees/dirs. (alt.) Assoc. Western Univs., 1993-96; bd. dirs. alt. Joint Ctr. Higher Edn., Spokane, 1996; mem steering com. Ctr. for Advanced Tech. in Healthcare Instruments and Devices, 1988-90; with Midwestern Higher Edn. Commn., 1999—; exploring chair Mushkodany Dist. Wis. Samoset Coun. Boy Scouts Am., 1998. Sloan fellow, 1976-80, postdoctoral fellow, 1990, Guggenheim fellow, 1983-84; recipient Disting. Alumni award Gettysburg Coll., 1987. Fellow AAAS, Soc. Photo-Optical Instrumentation Engrs., Am. Phys. Soc., N.Y. Acad. Scis., Inst. Superconductivity (steering com. 1987-91); mem. Am. Chem. Soc. (exec. com. phys. div. 1979-82, 85-89, 94-97, vice chmn. 1985-86, chmn.-elect 1986-87, chmn. 1987-88), Am. Assn. State Colls. and Univs. (acad. affairs subcom. on sci. edn. rsch. and tng.), Wis. Assn. for Biomed. Rsch. and Edn., European Phys. Soc., Am. Assn. of State Colls. and Univs. (coun. of state reps. 1998—), Royal Soc. Chemistry (Marlow medal and prize 1979), Phi Beta Kappa, Sigma Xi (exec. com. U. Rochester 1984-85). Democrat. Lutheran. Office: U Wis Office of Chancellor 213 Old Main Stevens Point WI 54481-3897

GEORGE, VANCE, conductor; b. Bremen, Ind., Sept. 30, 1933. BA in Music Edn., Goshen Coll., Ind., 1955; Grad., Bhatkande Sch. Music and Dance, India, 1959; student, Goethe Inst., Germany, 1961; MusM in Conducting, Ind. Univ., 1963, Mus D in Conducting, 1965; Mus D (hon.), Kent State U., 1998. Chorus master Opera Theater, Ind. Univ., Bloomington, Ind., 1963-65; dir. Women's Chorus, Ind. Univ., Bloomington, Ind., 1963-65; dir. choral activities Univ. Wis., Madison, 1965-71; instr. Choral Inst., Am. Choral Found., Madison, 1967, 69; dir. choral activities Kent State Univ., Ohio, 1971-82; assoc. chorus conductor Cleveland Orch. Chorus, Cleveland Orch. Chamber Chorus, Ohio, 1977-83; prof. conducting Festival of the Rockies, Whitefish, Mont., 1987; conductor Phoenix Bach Soc., Ariz., 1988-90; dir. San Francisco Symphony Chorus, Calif., 1983—; bd. dirs. Choris Am.; former chmn. Cleve. Orch. Chorus, Sch. of the Cleve. Orch.; guest chorus dir. Kent State Univ. Chorus, Canton Symphony Orch., 1976-77, 80-81; vis. assoc. prof. Univ. Calif., Berkeley, 1983, 85, 87, 88. Condr. San Francisco Symphony, San Francisco Symphony Chorus, oratorio, seasonal concerts, pops, Asian Youth Orch., Asian Youth Chorus, Ein Deutsches Requiem (Grammy award Best Choral Performance 1995); studies in U.S., Europe, Canada, India. Recipient Grammy award for Best Choral Performance, 1992; nominee Grammy award Mahler Symphony #2, 1994. Mem. IFCM, ACDA, Pi Kappa Lambda. E-mail: vygeorg@aol.com. Office: San Francisco Symphony Chorus 201 Van Ness Ave Ste 107 San Francisco CA 94102-4585

GEORGE, W. PEYTON, lawyer; b. Ada, Okla., Oct. 2, 1936; s. William Peyton and Jodie (Kite) G.; m. Nancy Whorton, Aug. 14, 1966; 1 child, Richard Peyton. BS, U. Ctrl. Okla., 1961; grad., FBI Acad., 1962; JD, Am. U., 1969; postgrad., Army War Coll., 1981. Bar: Va. 1969, D.C. 1970, Okla. 1986. Oil field worker Okla. and Tex., 1954-59; officer Oklahoma City Police Dept., 1959-62; agt. FBI, Va., N.J., D.C., 1962-69; congl. liaison for sec. Agr. USDA, Washington, 1969-73; ptnr. W. Peyton George, P.C., Washington, 1973-81, Miles & Stockbridge, Washington, 1981-90, Lathrop & Gage, L.C., Washington, 1990—. Col. USAR, 1957-91. Decorated Legion of Merit, Meritorious Svc. medal with oak leaf cluster. Mem. City Club, Masons (32 deg.), Shriner. Republican. Home: 1601 Chapel Hill Dr Alexandria VA 22304-1601 Office: Lathrop & Gage LC 1200 G St NW Ste 800 Washington DC 20005-3814*

GEORGE, WALTER EUGENE, JR., architect; b. Wichita Falls, Tex., Oct. 28, 1922; s. Walter Eugene and Mamie Alta (Evans) G.; m. Mary Carolyn Hollers Jutson, May 20, 1980. B.Arch., U. Tex., 1949; M.Arch., Harvard, 1950. Designer Wiltshire and Fisher (architects), Dallas, 1950-51; partner Pendley, George and Bowman (architects and engrs.), Austin, 1952-57; asst., then asso. prof. architecture U. Tex., 1956-62; prof. architecture, chmn. dept. U. Kans., 1962-67; dean Coll. Architecture, U. Houston, 1967-69; practice of architecture Austin, 1969-71, 74—; resident architect Colonial Williamsburg, Va., 1971-73; sr. lectr. engring. U. Tex., Austin, 1975-96; San Antonio Conservation Soc. prof. architecture U. Tex., San Antonio, 1997—. Served as pilot USAAF, 1943-46, ETO. Decorated Air medal with oak leaf cluster, Purple Heart; recipient Mont San Michele and Chartres award AIA, 1949; 2d award 1st ann. Southwestern furniture competition Dallas Mus. Fine Arts; award for teaching excellence U. Tex., 1960. Mem. Archaeol. Inst. Am., Soc. Archtl. Historians, Tau Sigma Delta. Episcopalian. Office: PO Box 4426 Austin TX 78765-4426

GEORGE, WILLIAM DOUGLAS, JR., retired consumer products company executive; b. Chgo., Nov. 21, 1932; s. William D. and Kathryn (McWhinney) G.; m. Elinor A. Elsing, June 20, 1964; children: David W., Douglas E., Stephen J. B.A., Depauw U., 1954; M.B.A., Harvard U., 1959. With Gen. Mills, Mpls., 1959-70; dir. corp. devel. Brown Group, Inc., St. Louis, 1970-74, v.p., 1974-81; exec. v.p. S.C. Johnson & Son, Inc., Racine, Wis., 1981-89, pres., COO worldwide consumer products, 1990-92; pres., CEO SC Johnson and Son, 1993-97, ret., 1997; bd. dirs. Arvin Inds., Inc., Ralcorp Holdings, Inc. Bd. dirs. St. Luke's Meml. Hosp., Inc., Racine, 1988-91; trustee Carthage Coll. With U.S. Army, 1955-57.

GEORGE, WILLIAM WALLACE, manufacturing company executive; b. Muskegon, Mich., Sept. 14, 1942; s. Wallace Edwin and Kathryn Jean (Dinkeloo) G.; m. Ann Tonnlier Pilgram, Sept. 6, 1969; children: Jeffrey, Jonathan. BS in Indsl. Engring. with honors, Ga. Inst. Tech., 1964; MBA with high distinction, Harvard U., 1966. Asst. to asst. sec. Dept. Def., Washington, 1966-68; spl. civilian asst. to sec. Navy, Washington, 1968-69; with Litton Industries, 1969-78; dir. long-range planning Litton Industries, Cleve., 1969-70; v.p. Litton Industries, 1976—; with Litton Microwave Cooking Products, 1970-78; v.p. Litton Microwave Cooking Products, Mpls., 1970-71; exec. v.p. Litton Microwave Cooking Products, 1971-73, pres., 1973-78; v.p. corp. devel. Honeywell, Mpls., 1978-80, exec. v.p., 1983-87; pres. Honeywell Europe (S.A.), 1980-82, Indsl. Automation, 1987, Space and Aviation Systems, Mpls., 1988-89; pres., chief oper. officer Medtronic Inc., Mpls., 1989-91, pres., CEO, 1989-96, chmn., 1996—; bd. dirs. Dayton-Hudson, Imation. Bd. dirs. Minn. Symphony Orch., 1976-80, United Way, 1976-79, 96—, nat. chmn., Belgium, 1982-83, campaign chair, 1997; bd. dirs., pres., treas. Guthrie Theater, 1977-84; vice-chmn. United Theol. Sem., 1977-80, Abbott-Northwestern Hosp., 1984—, vice-chair, 1989-91, chair, 1991-93, Health Span, 1989-94; trustee Macalaster Coll., 1987-93, Allin Health Sys., 1994—, vice-chair, 1997—, Mlps. Inst. Arts, 1993—,chmn. Minn. Thunder Pro Soccer, 1994—. Recipient Meritorious Civilian Service Award Sec. Navy, 1969. Mem. Sigma Chi (Internat. Balfour award 1964, trustee 1971-77, Disting. Alumni award Harvard U., 1997). Episcopalian. Clubs: Minneapolis, Minikahda. Home: 2284 W Lake Of The Isles Pky Minneapolis MN 55405-2434 Office: Medtronic Inc 7000 Central Ave NE Minneapolis MN 55432-3576*

GEORGE-LEPKOWSKI, SUE ANN, echocardiographic technologist; b. Altoona, Pa., Sept. 17, 1948; d. Charles Frederick and E. Anita (Haller) G.; m. Walter Lepkowski. AS, BS in Agronomy, Pa. State U., 1968, 70, MEd in Agronomy, Biol. Scis., Edn., 1972; PhD, Columbia & Columbia Pacific U., 1980; DS, Columbia Pacific U., 1981. Internship echocardiology West Pa. Hosp., Pitts., 1979-80; echocardiography tech. Bronson Meth. Hosp., Kalamazoo, 1981-82; echocardiographic technologist Nalle Clinic, Charlotte, 1983-85; tech. dir. Carolina Cardiology, Asheville, N.C., 1985-86; chief echocardiographic technologist Candler Gen. Hosp., Savannah, Ga., 1986-88; echocardiography, clin. specialist, technical spl. edn. specialist, chief technologist Self Meml. Hosp., Greenwood, S.C., 1988-97; clin. specialist, educator, echocardiographic technologist Anderson Area Med. Ctr., Anmed, 1997—; sr. technologist Anderson Area Med. Ctr., 1997—; journalist; cons., rschr., lectr. in field. Author: My Readheaded Angel, 1999, On Duty, 1999; contbr. over 90 articles to profl. jours.; co-author: Clinical 2-D Echocardiography. Past mem. choir, Carolina Mountain Brass, Gospell Quartet; percussionist Images; past edn. chmn. Greenwood Lupus Group, past pres.; former edn. chmn. S.C. Lupus Found.; team leader Fibromyalgia Syndrome; vol. in veterinary ultrasound; mission work in pediat. echo. Recipient ACP award, Berkeley-Whittinger award for rsch. and acad. excellence, various citations. Mem. Am. Soc. Ultrasonic Tech. Specialists, Am. Inst. Ultrasonic Medicine (sr.), Soc. Diagnostic Med. Sonographers, Am. Registry Diagnostic Med. Sonographers (registered diagnostic cardiac sonographer adult &pediatric echo.), Altoona/Pa. State U. Alumni Assn., Columbia Pacific U. Alumni Assn., Altoona H.S. Alumni Assn., IPTAY, S.C. Ultrasound Soc., N.C. Ultrasound Soc., Am. Soc. Echocardiography, Pa. State Carolina Club, USGA, PGA, LPGA, Soc. Pediatric Echocardiography, Phi Epsilon Phi. Mem. Dutch Reformed Ch. Avocations: music, hiking, aerobics, animals, golf. Home: 113 Green Forest Dr Anderson SC 29625-4903

GEORGES, MAURICE OSTROW, retired lawyer; b. Portland, Oreg., Nov. 6, 1921; s. Thomas T. and Daisy P. (Ostrow) G.; m. Evelyn Stella Scher, Nov. 25, 1948; children: Andra R., Emily A. Georges Gottfried, Daniel O. AB, Reed Coll., 1947; LLB, Columbia U., 1950. Bar: Calif. 1951, Oreg. 1951. Assoc. in law U. Calif., Berkeley, 1950-51; assoc. King, Miller, Anderson, Nash & Yerke, Portland, 1951-56; ptnr. Miller, Nash, Wiener, Hager & Carlsen (and predecessors), Portland, 1956-92, of counsel, 1992-97. Contbr. articles to legal jours. Trustee Reed Coll., Portland, 1966-82; dir. Portland Opera Assn., 1983-89; v.p., dir. Contemporary Crafts Assn., 1969-72, Cmty. Music Ctr., Portland, 1974-76, Oreg. Humanities Coun., 1994-97. Staff sgt. AUS, 1942-46, ETO. Mem. ABA, Oreg. Bar Assn. (chmn. tax sect. 1960-61), Tualatin Country Club (pres. 1964-66), Astoria Golf and Country. Office: Miller Nash Wiener Hager et al 111 SW 5th Ave Ste 3500 Portland OR 97204-3699

GEORGES, PAUL GORDON, artist; b. Portland, Oreg., June 15, 1923; s. Thomas Theseus and Daisy G.; m. Lisette Blumenfeld, Jan. 23, 1950; children: Paulette, Yvette. Student, U. Oreg., Fernand Leger U., Paris. Hans Hoffman prof. fine arts Brandeis U., Waltham, Mass., from 1977; now prof. emeritus Brandeis U.; founding mem., chmn. bd. Artist Choice Mus.; represented by Salander-O'Reilly Gallery, N.Y.C.; vis. artist U. Pa., Phila., Queens Coll., Bklyn., Boston U., Yale U., Dartmouth U. One-man shows include Reed Coll., 1948, 56, 01, Tibor De Nagy Gallery, 1955, 57, Zabriskie Gallery, N.Y.C., 1959, Great Jones Gallery, 1960, 61, Allan Frumkin Gallery, N.Y.C.; 1962, 63, 64, 66, 68, Fischbach, N.Y.C., 1974, 76, Rose Art Mus., Brandeis U., 1981, Zolla Lieberman Gallery, Chgo., 1982, More Gallery, Pa., 1983, 91, Anne Plumb Gallery, N.Y.C., 1984, 86, 88, 91, Vered Gallery, East Hampton, N.Y., 1989, 91, 96, Greenville (N.C.) Mus., 1989, Salander-O'Reilly Gallery, N.Y.C., 1992, 94, 96, 98, Galerie Darthea Speyer, Paris, 1995, Sordoni Art Gallery, Wilkes U., Wilkes-Barre, Pa., 1995; group shows at PS i Mus., L.I. City, 1991, Am. Acad., 1999; represented in pub. collections, including Whitney Mus., Va. Mus. Fine Arts, Frances and Sydney Lewis Collection, Corcoran Art Collection, Hirshorn Mus., Mus. of Modern Art, Heckscher Mus., Portland Art Mus., Guildhall Mus., others. Recipient Hallmark award, Carol Beck Gold medal, award Longview Found., Hassam Purchase award, Am. Acad., 1990, Arthur and Esther Gottlieb Found., 1992, Pollock/Krasner award, 1993, Bernard Altman prize Nat. Acad., 1981, Andrew Carnegie prize, 1982; grantee CAPS. Mem. NAD, Am. Acad. Inst. Arts Letters (art award 1986), Nat. Acad. (Ranger Purchase award 1986). Office: care Salander-O'Reilly Galleries 20 E 79th St New York NY 10021-0106

GEORGES, PETER JOHN, lawyer; b. Wilmington, Del., Sept. 8, 1940; s. John Peter and Olga Demetrius (Kazitoris) G. BS in Chemistry, U. Del., 1962; JD, John Marshall Law Sch., 1970; LLM in Patent and Trade Regulations, George Washington U., 1973. Bar: Ill. 1970, U.S. Ct. Appeals (fed. cir.) 1972, D.C. 1973, U.S. Supreme Ct. 1973, Del. 1977. Chemist engring. labs Bell & Howell Co., Chgo., 1966; patent coordinator Armour & Co., Chgo., 1967; patent agt., atty. UOP Inc., Chgo., 1968-71; Washington counsel UOP Inc., Arlington, Va., 1972-77; ptnr. Kile, Gholz, Bernstein & Georges, Arlington, 1977-78; assoc., then ptnr. Law Office Sidney W. Russell, Arlington, 1978-83; mng. officer Breneman & Georges (and predecessor law firms), Alexandria, 1983—; founding ptnr. Lenastri Properties and Joanastri Properties, Alexandria, Va. Served to 1st lt. USMC, 1963-65, Vietnam. Mem. ABA, Ill. Bar Assn., D.C. Bar Assn., Del. Bar Assn., Fed. Cir. Bar Assn., Assn. Trial Lawyers Am., Am. Intellectual Property Law Assn., Am. Hellenic Lawyers Soc. Home: 1637 13th St NW Washington DC 20009-4302 Office: Breneman & Georges 3150 Commonwealth Ave Alexandria VA 22305-2712

GEORGES, ROBERT AUGUSTUS, emeritus professor, researcher, writer; b. Sewickley, Pa., May 1, 1933; s. John Thomas and Pauline Pantzis G.; m. Mary Virginia Ruth, Aug. 11, 1956; 1 child, Jonathan Gregory. BS, Ind. U. of Pa., 1954; MA, U. Pa., 1961; PhD, Indiana U., 1964. Tchr. Bound Brook (N.J.) High Sch., 1954-56, Southern Regional High Sch., Manahawkin, N.J., 1958-60; asst. prof. U. Kans., Lawrence, 1963-66; asst. prof. UCLA, 1966-70, assoc. prof., 1970-76, prof., 1976-94; prof. emeritus, 1994—; vice chmn. Folklore and Mythology Program UCLA, 1966-82, chmn. 1983-86. Author: Greek-American Folk Beliefs and Narratives, 1980; co-author: People Studying People: The Human Element in Fieldwork, 1980, American and Canadian Immigrant and Ethnic Folkore: An Annotated Bibliography; co-author: Folkloristics: An Introduction, 1996; editor: Studies on Mythology, 1968; translator: Two Studies on Modern Greek, Folklore by Stilpon P. Kyriakides, 1968; contbr. numerous articles to folklore periodicals. With U.S. Army, 1956-58. NDEA fellow, 1962-63, Guggenheim fellow, 1969-70. Fellow Am. Folklore Soc.; mem. Calif. Folklore Soc. Home: 906 Fiske St Pacific Palisades CA 90272-3841

GEORGESCO, VICTOR, printing company executive; b. Bucharest, Romania, Mar. 17, 1948; came to U.S., 1978; s. Paul D. and Maria C. (Bender) G. B.S., Poly. U., Bucharest, 1968. Overseas br. mgr. Metal Import Export, Bucharest, 1968-77; asst. mgr. Otto Botner GMBH, Duesseldorf, W. Ger., 1977-78; purchasing agt. Trico Industries, Torrance, Calif., 1978-86; exec. v.p. ops. Beverly Ctr. Printing Co., Los Angeles, 1986—. Mem. Purchasing Mgmt. Assn. (Los Angeles chpt.). Office: 8104 W 3rd St Los Angeles CA 90048-4309

GEORGESCU, PETER ANDREW, advertising executive; b. Bucharest, Romania, Mar. 9, 1939; came to U.S., 1954, naturalized, 1954; s. V.C. Rica and Lygia (Bocu) G.; m. Barbara Anne Armstrong, Aug. 21, 1965; 1 son, Peter Andrew. A.B. cum laude, Princeton U., 1961; M.B.A., Stanford U., 1963. With Young & Rubicam, Inc., N.Y.C., 1963—; dir. mktg. Young & Rubicam, Inc., 1977-79; exec. v.p. Cen. Region Young & Rubicam, Inc., Chgo., dir., 1979-82; pres. Young & Rubicam Internat., N.Y.C., 1982-86, Young & Rubicam Advt., N.Y.C., 1986—; pres., CEO Young & Rubicam Inc., 1994—; now CEO, chmn bd of dirs. Young & Rubicam Inc; bd. dirs. Briggs & Stratton, Inc. Mem. Coun. on Fgn. Rels., Am. Assn. Advt. Agencies (bd. dirs.), Internat. Advt. Assn., Inc. (bd. dirs.), Links Club, River Club, Racquet Club, Casino Club, Brooks Club. Office: Young & Rubicam Inc 285 Madison Ave New York NY 10017-6486

GEORGHIOU, MICHAEL, construction and development executive; b. Cyprus, Nov. 14, 1932; s. George and Ourania (Haralambous) G.; m. Helen P. Modenos, Aug. 15, 1961; 1 child, Christina. BS in Acctg. and Fin., London U., 1952. Comptroller, treas. James W. Elwell & Co., Inc., N.Y.C., 1968-83; exec. v.p., treas. Theodore & Theodore Assocs., Inc., N.Y.C., 1984-93; bd. dirs. Theodore & Theodore Assocs., Inc., (pres 68-70), Broadway Corp., 1993—, Transteck Svc. Network, Inc. Trustee St. Demetrios Greek Orthodox Ch., N.Y.C., 1969—; v.p. Am. Cyprus Congress, N.Y.C., 1984—. Recipient Humanitarian award Greek Orthodox Archdiocese, 1975, Govt. of Cyprus, 1975. Home: 76-44 170th St Flushing NY 11366-1344

GEORGIADE, NICHOLAS GEORGE, plastic and oral surgeon, educator; b. Lowell, Mass., Dec. 25, 1918; s. George Nicholas and Stephanie (Englisch) G.; m. Ruth Katherine Sauer, Sept. 21, 1942; children—Gregory Stephen, Robert Charles, Nancy Jeanne. Student, Fordham U., 1937-40; DDS, Columbia U., 1944; MD, BS in Medicine, Duke U., 1950. Diplomate: Am. Bd. Plastic Surgery (vice chmn. 1974-75), Am. Bd. Oral Surgery. Intern Kings County Hosp., N.Y.C., 1944; intern surgery Med. Center, Duke U., Durham, N.C., 1949-50; resident gen. surgery, plastic maxillofacial recon. surgery Med. Center, Duke U., 1950-54; mem. faculty Med. Center, Duke U. (Sch. Medicine), 1953—, assoc. prof. plastic, maxillofacial, oral surgery, 1957-61, prof., 1961—; prof. div. plastic, maxillofacial and oral surgery; mem. staff Duke Hosp., 1981—, chmn. div. plastic, maxillofacial and reconstructive surgery. Co-author: Textbook of Plastic and Reconstructive Surgery, 1964, Textbook on Burns, 1965; editor: Plastic and Maxillofacial Trauma Symposium, 1969, Aesthetic Breast Surgery, 1983, Cleft Lip-Palate Symposium, 1973, Reconstructive Breast Surgery, 1976, Reconstructive Surgery Following Mastectomy, 1979; co-editor: Pediatric Plastic Surgery, 1983, Essentials of Plastic Maxillofacial and Reconstructive Surgery, 1987, Textbook of Plastic, Maxillofacial and Reconstructive Surgery, 1987, 2nd edit., 1992, Aesthetic Surgery of the Breast, 1990; internat. editor: Cleft Palate Jour, 1970-79, assoc., editor Jour. Internat. Soc. Aesthetic Plastic Surgery; contbr. numerous articles to profl. jours. Served with AUS, 1944-46. Recipient Disting. Alumnus award Duke U. Sch. Medicine. Fellow A.C.S. (chmn. plastic and maxillofacial adv. com. 1972-73), So. Surg. Assn.; mem. Am. Soc. Maxillofacial Surgeons (pres. 1962-63), AMA (vice chmn. sect. plastic and maxillofacial surgery), Am. Assn. Plastic Surgeons (v.p., nat. sec., pres. 1977-78), Am. Soc. Plastic and Reconstructive Surgeons (exec. com., chmn. postgrad. edn. com. Ednl. Found.), Am. Soc. Plastic Surgeons (recipient jr. rsch. award 1955, 1st prize sr. rsch. paper 1972, Dieffenbach Outstanding Contributions in Plastic Surgery award 1992), Soc. Head and Neck Surgeons, Plastic Surgery Rsch. Coun., Internat. Surg. Soc., Internat. Soc. Aesthetic Surgery (sec. N.Am. 1979—, internat. sec.-gen. 1984-90), So. Surg. Assn., Am. Burn Assn., Tissue Culture Assn., Sigma Xi, Alpha Omega Alpha. Patentee in field. Home: 2523 Wrightwood Ave Durham NC 27705-5829 Office: Duke U Med Ctr PO Box 3098 Durham NC 27710-3098

GEORGIADES, ARISTOTLE, artist, educator; b. Pitts., May 10, 1955; s. Alexander Martin and Maria (Grazziani) G.; m. Gail Simpson, Jan. 16, 1988. BFA, U. Mich., 1981; MFA, Art Inst. Chgo., 1984. Prof. art sculpture Western Wash. U., Bellingham, 1992—; ptnr. Actual Size Artworks, Bellingham, 1994—. One-man shows Abel Joseph Gallery, Chgo., 1990, 91, Univ. Galleries, Normal, Ill., 1992, Space Gallery, Chgo., 1994, Anderson-Glover Fine Arts, Kirkland, Wash., 1996, Port Angeles (Wash.) Fine Arts Ctr., 1998; group shows include Chgo. Pub. libr., 1984, Ill. Art Galleru, Chgo., 1985, Randolph St. Gallery, Chgo., 1986, N.A.M.E. Gallery, Chgo., 1987, Space One Eleven, Birmingham, Ala., 1988, Perkinson Gallery, Decatur, Ill., 1989, Rosenfield Gallery, Chgo., 1990, Hyde Park Art Ctr., Chgo., 1992, 93, Ctr. On Contemporary Art, Seattle, 1994, San Francisco Art Fair, 1995, Anderson-Glover Fine Arts, 1996, Chgo. Ineternat. Art Expo, 1997, others; represented in permanent collections Mr. & Mrs. Katz, Seattle, Warren Weisberg, Chgo., John Hechenger Sr., The Kohler Co., Wis., Ill. State U., Robert Wislow/U.S. Equities Corp., William Leiberman, Oskar Friedl, Bette Hill & Bruce Sagan, Barry Blinderman, Mike Lash, Dann & Brenda Nardi, Frances Waddock, Sam Marts, Lucy & Dirk Herrman, Mike Dunbar, Mary O'Shaughnessy. Bd. dirs. Bellingham Arts Commn., 1997—; mem. Allied Arts, Bellingham, 1994—. Recipient Excellence in Teaching award Western Wash. U., 1998; Artists Trust grantee, Was. State Arts Commn., 1998. Mem. Internat. Sculpture Soc.

GEORGIADES, WILLIAM DEN HARTOG, educational administrator; b. Chgo., May 30, 1925; s. George and Alice (Den Hartog) G.; m. Ruth Taylor Long, Oct. 29, 1983; children from previous marriage: Sheldon Franklin, Beverly Jo; stepchld, Samantha Taylor Long. AB, Upland Coll., 1946; MA, Claremont Grad. Sch., 1949; EdD, UCLA, 1956. Tchr. Whittier (Calif.) High Sch., 1947-49; teaching asst. UCLA, 1950-51; dean Upland Coll., 1951-53; chmn. dept. English Whittier High Sch., 1953-56; prof. edn., chmn. dept. curriculum and instrn. U. So. Calif., 1956-79, asso. dean edn. program devel., 1977—; dean Coll. Edn., U. Houston, 1979-94; exec. dir. Rsch. Collaborative/Office Internat. Edn., 1994-98; vis. prof. Amsterdam, The Netherlands, 1994—; Fulbright lectr. Cyprus and Greece, 1962; vis. lectr. in U.S., Eng., Vietnam, Malaysia, The Netherlands, Iraq, Pakistan, India, Iran, Japan, Saudi Arabia, Indonesia, Kenya, Costa Rica, Mexico and the Dominican Republic, Guatemala, Columbia, South Africa, Venezuela; assoc. dir. Danforth Found./Nat. Assn. Secondary Sch.; dir. World Bank Malaysia Project, 1993-98; with Prins. model sch. project, 1968-75; cons. in field. Author: Models for Individualized Instruction, 1974, New Schools for a New Age, 1977, How Good Is Your School? Program Evaluation for Secondary Schools, 1978, How to Change Your School, 1978, Take Five: A Methodology for the Humane School, 1979, (with others) A Leaders Guide to School Restructuring, 1992; editor bulls.; contbr. to research and edn. jours. Pres. La Cresta PTA, 1966, Sr. Danforth asso., 1962. Named One of 70 Leaders in Edn. in U.S., Assn. Tchr. Educators, 1990. Mem. AAUP, Assn. Higher Edn., Assn. Supervision and Curriculum Devel. (bd. dirs.), Nat. Soc. Study Edn., World Curriculum Council, Doctoral Alumni Assn. (Disting. Leadership award 1982), Phi Delta Kappa (Research award 1978). Presbyn. (elder 1959—). Home: 19119 Match Play Dr Atascocita TX 77346-6148 Office: U Houston Coll Edn Houston TX 77204 *I believe that education is the greatest tool humans have yet discovered to bring about the betterment of humankind everywhere. If the peace dreams of the centuries are ever to become a reality, it will be necessary for those of us who live in this century to commit ourselves as never before to the education of our young.*

GEORGIEV, GOSHKO ATANASOV, agrometeorologist, researcher; b. Sofia, Bulgaria, May 29, 1959; came to U.S., 1996; s. Atanas Dimitrov and Maria Georgieva (Nenova) G.; m. Raynichka Tonuva Toncheva Georgieva, Nov. 4, 1984; 1 child, Maria Goshkova Georgieva. MS, Hydrometeorlogical Inst., Odessa, Ukraine, 1983; PhD, Hydromet Ctr. of Russia, Moscow, 1990. Grad. asst. Nat. Inst. Meteorology and Hydrology, Sofia, Bulgaria, 1983-86; vis. scientist Hydromet Ctr. Russia, Moscow, 1986-90; asst. prof. NIMH-BAS, Sofia, Bulgaria, 1990-96, head agromet forecasting, 1995-96; post doc assoc. U. Ga. Coll. Agr. and Environ. Sci., Griffin, Ga., 1996—; cons. ACT-Sofia Ltd., Bulgaria, 1992-95; cons., developer Hardware Design Ltd., 1995-96, Pyramid Computers Inc., 1997—. Contbr. articles to profl. jours. Mem. Bulgarian Physics Assn. Avocations: soccer, tennis, software. Office: U Ga 1109 Experiment St Griffin GA 30223-1731

GEORGIJE, DJOKIC, bishop; b. Bijeljina, Bosnia, Yugoslavia, May 6, 1949; arrived in Can., 1984; s. Krsto and Krunija (Arsenovic) D. BA in Theology, Faculty of Theology, Yugoslavia, 1981. Ordained priest Serbian Orthodox Ch., 1971. Parish priest, spiritual advisor Monastery Tavna, Bosna, 1971-82; parish priest St. Peter and Paul Serbian Orthodox Ch., Darby, Eng., 1982-84; bishop, pres. Serbian Orthodox Diocese Can., Toronto, 1984—; pres. Diocesan Eccles. Ct. Can., 1984—, Diocesan Exec. Bd. Can., 1984—; v.p. Cen. Ch. Coun., Serbian Orthodox Ch. in U.S.A. and Can., 1984—; mem. Holy Assembly Bishops, Belgrade, Yugoslavia, 1984—. Author Istocnik jour., 1987—. Mem. Can. Coun. Chs. Home and Office: Serbian Orthodox Diocese, 7470 McNiven Rd RR # 3, Campbellville, ON Canada L0P 1B0*

GEORGINE, ROBERT ANTHONY, union executive; b. Chgo., July 18, 1932; s. Silvio and Rose (Hogue) G.; m. Mary Rita Greener; children: Robert A., Georgine, Rosemarie, Mary Beth. Student, U. Ill., DePaul U. Asst. bus. mgr. Lathing Found., Chgo., 1962-64; internat. rep. Wood, Wire and Metal Lathers Internat. Union, 1964-65, asst. to gen. pres., 1965-70, pres., 1970-71; sec.-treas. Bldg. and Constrn. Trades Dept., AFL-CIO, Washington, 1971-74, pres., 1974—; pres., CEO, chmn. Union Labor Life Ins. Co., 1990—; v.p., exec. coun. AFL-CIO, 1965—; bd. dirs. Am. Nuclear Energy Coun., Am. Productivity Ctr., Mut. Life Ins. Co. Washington, Nat. Corp. for Housing Partnerships, Nat. Housing Conf., Union Labor Life Ins. Co., Fed. Res. Bank Richmond, 1982-88, chmn., 1988, Nat. Coordinating Com. for Multiemployer Plans, 1974—; mem. U.S. Congress-Joint Econ. Commn. Adv. Com., 1983—, Pres.'s Com. on Employment of Handicapped, 1974—, presdl. mission to Poland, 1989—; Presdl. Drug Adv. Coun., 1989; co-chmn. Nat. Citizens Coalition for Windfall Profits Tax, 1979-80; mem. Pres.'s Adv. Commn. on Consumer Quality and Protectionin the Health Care Industry, 1997—. Bd. dirs. Conservation Found., 1978—; mem. nat. labor adv. Coun. March of Dimes, 1981—; mem. adv. com. Harvard-MIT Joint Com. Urban Studies, 1978—; bd. dirs. Seabee Meml. Scholarship Assn., 1976—. With U.S. Army, 1955-57. Recipient numerous awards and honors including Brotherhood award NCCJ, 1976, 90, Man of Yr. award Joint Civic Com. Italian Ams. in Chgo., 1977, Nat. Labor-Mgmt. Achievement award Citizen's Asthma Research Inst. Hosp., 1979. Mem. Gas Rsch. Inst. Nat. Planning Assn. (long range land use planning com. 1978—, adv. coun. 1976—). Office: AFL-CIO Dept Bldg & Constrn Trades 1155 15th St NW Fl 4 Washington DC 20005-2706*

GEORGIOU, RUTH SCHWAB, retired social worker; b. Milford, Del., June 9, 1922; d. Lafayette and Ola (Moody) Burlingame; m. Matheos Georgiou, July 16, 1960 (dec. Sept. 1984); children: Eleni Georgiou Strawn, Diana Maria, Theodora Evtychia. BA in Liberal Arts with honors, U. Mich., 1943; MS in Social Adminstrn., U. Pitts., 1945. Cert. social worker, N.Y. Child welfare officer Unitarian Svc. Com., Germany, 1947-48; dir. Camp Bluebird Jewish Bd. of Guardians, N.Y.C., 1949; asst. dir. Girls Club of Bklyn. Bklyn. Hebrew Orphan Asylum, 1949-52; asst. dir. Suburban Agy., Hempstead, N.Y., 1954-57; co-dir. Suburban Homemaking & Maternity Agy., Hempstead, 1957-61; med. social worker Glen Oaks (N.Y.) Nursing Home, 1967-68; sr. care worker N.Y. Dept. Health-Social Svcs. Dept., Mineola, 1968-69; social work supr. Tampa (Fla.) Lighthouse for the Blind, 1976-78; med. social worker Global Home Health Svcs., Pinellas and Pasco, Fla., 1979-89; ret., 1989; social work cons. Spanish Gardens Nursing Home, Dunedin, Fla., 1980-82, St. Mark's Village, Palm Harbor, Fla., 1982-83; mem. adv. bd. Med. Pers. Pool, New Port Richey, 1986-98. Author: (manual) Homemaker's Manual, 1956. Co-chmn. sr. care of Planned Approach to Community Health, New Port Richey, 1988-89; pres. Community Svc. Coun. West Pasco, New Port Richey, 1985-86, bd. dirs., 1985-91. Recipient cert. of appreciation Cmty. Svc. Coun. West Pasco, 1986, 91. Mem. NASW (membership chmn. Pasco subunit Fla. chpt. 1991—, chmn. membership Tampa Bay unit 1992-97, Social Worker of Yr. award 1991, Ret. Social Worker of Yr. award 97), Acad. Cert. Social Workers. Avocations: Bible studies. Home: 300 S Walton Ave Apt 53 Tarpon Springs FL 34689-6011

GEORGIS, WILLIAM THEODORE, architect; b. Chgo., May 14, 1958; s. Ted W. and Mitzie T. (Chronos) G. BA, Stanford U., 1980; MArch, Princeton U., 1983. Registered architect N.Y. Architect Venturi Rauch Scott Brown, Phila., 1983; assoc. Robert A.M. Stern Architects, N.Y.C., 1983-92; architect pvt. practice, N.Y.C., 1992—. Mem. AIA. Office: 41 5th Ave New York NY 10003-4319

GEORGITIS, JOHN, allergist, educator; b. Columbus, Ohio, June 19, 1950; s. William James and Mary Helen (Wyman) G.; m. Marilyn Howard; children: Nancy Lynn, Kathryn Mary, Matthew Walter. BA, Bowdoin Coll., Brunswick, Maine, 1972; MD, U. Vt., 1976. Diplomate Am. Bd. Pediatrics, Am. Bd. Allergy and Immunology. Resident in pediatrics James Whitcomb Riley Hosp., Indpls., 1976-78, pulmonology fellow, 1978-79; allergy fellow SUNY, Buffalo, 1979-81, rsch. asst. prof., 1981-84; assoc. prof. Bowman Gray Sch. Medicine, Winston-Salem, N.C., 1984-94, prof., 1994—; dir. allergy and immunology tng. program Bowman Gray Sch. of Medicine, Winston-Salem, 1987—. Office: Wake Forest U Sch Medicine Med Ctr Blvd Winston Salem NC 27157

GEORGIUS, JOHN R., bank executive; b. 1944. BBA, Ga. State U., 1967. With 1st Union Nat. Bank N.C., Charlotte, 1975—, chmn., CEO, 1988-93; pres. 1st Union Corp., Charlotte, 1993-95, vice chmn., 1996—, pres., 1998—, mem. corp. mgmt. com., also bd. dirs. Office: 1st Union Corp 1 First Union Ctr 301 S College St Charlotte NC 28288-6000*

GEPFERT, ALAN HARRY, management consultant, business educator, author; b. Cleve., Sept. 24, 1930; s. Joseph Harry and Freda Natalia (Schleicher) G.; m. Mary Caroline Austin, Aug. 26, 1959; 1 child: Grace Mary Cooper. BS in Engring. Adminstrn., Case Western Res. U., 1953, MS in Ops. Rsch., 1953, postgrad., 1953-56. Instr. Case Western Res. U., Cleve., 1953-58; mem. ops. rsch. cons. Case Western Res. U., 1953-58; dir. statis. rsch. Chgo. and North Western Rlwy., 1958-62; cons. McKinsey & Co., Inc., N.Y.C., 1962-70; exec. Mobil Oil, N.Y.C., 1970-86; prin. Strategic Systems Solutions, New London, N.H., 1986—; instr. Colby-Sawyer Coll., New London, 1992-97, N.H. Tech. Coll., 1992-97. Author (with others) The Arts of Top Management, 1971, Turnaround Management, 1972, Strategic Planning For MIS, 1977; cons. editor Modern Railroads mag., 1959-70; contbr. articles to profl. jours. Trustee 1st Bapt. Ch., White Plains, N.Y., 1969-70; deacon 1st Bapt. Ch., New London, N.H., 1999— dir. Pegasus Therapeutic Riding, Darien, Conn., 1985-88, Masonic Charity Found., Wallingford, Conn., 1989-93, New London Hosp., 1990-92. Mem. Inst. for Ops. Rsch. and Mgmt. Scis. (acad. practitioner com. 1989-91, chmn. edn. com. 1992-97, vice chmn. coll. on info. sys. 1981-82, chmn. fin. com. 1964-65), Masons (32 deg., dist. edn. officer Grand Lodge of N.H. 1998—), Shriners (sec. 1994-96), Sigma Xi, Tau Beta Pi. Republican. Avocations: stone sculpting, mineralogy, paleontology, geology, piano. Office: Strategic Systems Solutions 40 Little Sunapee Rd New London NH 03257-4519

GEPHARDT, RICHARD ANDREW, congressman; b. St. Louis, Jan. 31, 1941; s. Louis Andrew and Loreen Estelle (Cassell) G.; m. Jane Ann Byrnes, Aug. 13, 1966; children: Matthew, Christine, Katherine. B.S., Northwestern U., 1962; J.D., U. Mich., 1965. Bar: Mo. 1965. Ptnr. Thompson & Mitchell, St. Louis, 1965-76; alderman 14th ward City of St. Louis, 1971-76; mem. 96th-106th Congresses from 3d Mo. dist., 1979—; Dem. leader, mem. house dem. policy com., minority leader. Dem. committeeman 14th ward, St. Louis, 1968-71; pres. Children's Hematology Rsch. Assn., St. Louis Children's Hosp., 1973-76; candidate for Dem. nomination for Pres. of U.S., 1987-88. Mem. Mo. Bar Assn., St. Louis Bar Assn., Am. Legion, Young Lawyer's Soc. (chmn. 1972-73). Club: Mid-Town (St. Louis). Lodge: Kiwanis. Office: US Ho of Reps 1226 Longworth HOB Washington DC 20515-2503 also: Office of Dem Leader H-204 The Capitol Washington DC 20515-6502*

GER, SHAW-SHYONG, accountant; b. Kaohsiung, Taiwan, Nov. 19, 1959; s. Jing-Ru and Jui-Mei (Lee) G. BA in econs., Nat. Taiwan U., Taipei, 1981; MBA, Ariz. State U., 1986, M in acctg., 1989. CPA, Ariz.; CMA, CFM, Novell MCNE, Microsoft MCP. Rsch. asst. Ariz. State U., Tempe, 1988-89; contr. CLH Internat., Inc., Tempe, 1989—. Recipient All Am. Scholar award U.S. Achievement Acad., 1989. Mem. Assn. MBA Exec., Nat. Geog. Soc., Inst. Cert. Mgmt. Accts., Beta Gamma Sigma. Address: PO Box 601 Tempe AZ 85280-0601

GERACE, DIANE, journalist; b. Phila., Mar. 28, 1963; d. Rudolph and Rosemarie (Boccelli) G. BA in Journalism, Temple U., 1985. Sports writer N.E. Times, Phila., 1981-87, sports editor, 1987—. Recipient Sports Writing award Phila. Press Assn., 1987, 89, 90, 91, 92, 94, 95, Sports Writing award Pa. Newspapers Pubs. Assn., 1995. Mem. Phila. Sports Writers Assn. Roman Catholic. Avocations: ice hockey goalie, reading, traveling, listening to music, golf. Office: Pro Media Pub 2512 Metropolitan Dr Trevose PA 19053-6796

GERACE, ROBERT F., secondary school principal. Prin. Alcott Mid. Sch., Wolcott, Conn. Recipient Blue Ribbon Sch. award U.S. Dept. Edn., 1990-91. Office: Alcott Mid Sch 1490 Woodtick Rd Wolcott CT 06716-1538

GERACI, DAMIANO, architect; b. Locati, Palermo, Italy, May 20, 1970; came to U.S., 1973; s. Giuseppe and Rosetta (Cascio) G. BArch, Pratt Inst., 1993. Arch. Swanke Hayden Connell Archs., N.Y.C., The Switzer Group, N.Y.C., Giovanni Ptnr. Assocs., New Hyde Park, N.Y., DPM Arch. P.C., N.Y.C.; pvt. practice Bklyn. Libertarian. Home: # 2C 97-01 Shore Rd Brooklyn NY 11209 Office: Swanke Hayden Connell Archs 295 Lafayette St New York NY 10012-2701

GERAGHTY, JOHN VINCENT, public relations consultant; b. Seattle, Feb. 23, 1934; s. John V. and Gladys I (Johnson) G.; children: Marcella Maile, Sheila Leek, Brigid Krause, Nora Lipton. BA in Comm., U. Wash., 1956; MPA (hon.), Ea. Washington U., 1994. Reporter Spokane (Wash.) Daily Chronicle, 1959-62; sec. to mayor/coun. City of Spokane, 1962-64; county commr. Spokane (Wash.) County, 1964-71; vp. guest rels. EXPO '74 Corp., Spokane, 1971-74; publisher, owner The Falls Newspaper, Spokane, 1974-76; v.p. Haworth & Anderson, Inc., Spokane, 1976-83; owner, pres. Jack Geraghty & Assocs., Spokane, 1983—; prin. Alliance Pacific, Inc., Spokane, 1985—; mayor City of Spokane, 1994-98; bd. dirs., past pres. Future Spokane, 1983-89; cons. Citizens League of Greater Spokane. Bd. dirs. and past pres., Spokane Comty. Mental Health Ctr., 1980-95; mem. and past chmn. bd. trustees Ea. Wash. U., Cheney, Wash., 1985-97; mem. and vice chair Spokane Centennial Projects Com., 1988. Mem. Pub. Rels Soc. Am. (pres. Spokane chpt. 1983), Spokane Pub. Rels. Coun. (past pres.), Spokane Club, Beta Theta Pi. Democrat. Roman Catholic. Avocations: golf, sailing, cooking. Home: PO Box 251 Spokane WA 99210-0251 Office: Jack Geraghty and Assoc 621 W Mallon Ave Spokane WA 99201-2163

GERAGHTY, PATRICK JAMES, organ transplant coordinator; b. Evanston, Ill., June 23, 1971; s. Martin Patrick and Maureen (Ganey) G.; m. Diana Lee Stanton, June 17, 1995; 1 child, Mary Katherine. BS, George Washington U., 1993. Nationally registered emergency med. technician-paramedic, cert. procurement transplant coord. Paramedic/firefighter Bethesda (Md.)/Chevy Chase Rescue Squad, 1991—, sgt., ALS svcs. coord., 1994-96; organ recovery coord. Washington Regional Transplant Consortium, Falls Church, Va., 1993-96; transplant coord. Lifenet Transplant Svcs., Richmond, Va., 1996—. Rep. EMS Com., Montgomery County, Md., 1993-96. Office: Lifenet 3001 Hungary Spring Rd Ste F Richmond VA 23228-2428

GERALD, BARRY, radiology educator, neuroradiologist; b. Greenville, Miss., Feb. 10, 1934; s. Louis Elmo and Eula (Mitchell) G.; m. Marjorie Brown, Aug. 6, 1955; children: Lucy Gerald Cook, Lee, Paul. Student, U. Miss., Oxford, 1951-54; MD, U. Miss., Jackson, 1958. Diplomate Am. Bd. Radiology. Intern Hermann Hosp., Houston, 1958-59, resident in radiology, 1959-62; fellow in pediatric radiology Children's Hosp. Med. Ctr., Cin., 1962-64; mem. faculty dept. radiology U. Ark., Little Rock, 1964-65, 67-69; dir. radiology dept. Children's Hosp. Med. Ctr., Oakland, Calif., 1965-66; mem. faculty dept. radiology U. Tenn. Coll. Medicine, Memphis, 1969—, prof., chmn. dept., 1979-95; fellow in neuroradiology Tufts-New Eng. Med. Ctr., Boston, 1971-72; dir. radiology dept. Le Bonheur Children's Hosp., Memphis, 1983-88, 91—; acting dir. radiology dept. St. Jude Children's Rsch. Hosp., Memphis, 1985-87; trainee Nat. Cancer Inst., 1960-62. Contbr. articles to med. jours., chpts. to books. Fellow Am. Coll. Radiology; mem. Am. Soc. Neuroradiology, Soc. for Pediatric Radiology, Radiol. Soc. N.Am. (councillor 1980-85), Am. Roentgen Ray Soc., Southeastern Neuroradiologic Soc. (founder, pres. 1977-78), So. Radiologic Conf. (pres. 1975-76). Avocations: tennis, American history. Home: 694 Clanlo Dr Memphis TN 38104-5067 Office: U Tenn Dept Radiology 800 Madison Ave Memphis TN 38103-3400

GERALD, MICHAEL CHARLES, pharmacy educator, college dean; b. N.Y.C., Nov. 20, 1939; s. Tobias Gerson and Ruby Rose (Weinstock) G.; m. Gloria Elaine Gruber, Jan. 31, 1965; children—Marc Jonathan, Melissa Suzanne. B.S. in Pharmacy, Fordham U., 1961; Ph.D., Ind. U., 1968. Registered pharmacist, N.Y. Postdoctoral fellow USPHS, U. Chgo., 1968-69; asst. prof. Coll. Pharmacy Ohio State U., Columbus, 1969-74, assoc. prof., 1974-80, prof., 1980-93, prof. and assoc. dean., 1984-93; dean, prof. Sch. Pharmacy U. Conn., Storrs, 1993—; cons. WHO, Geneva, 1983-84; mem. adv. panel U.S. Pharmacopeia Com. Revision, Washington, 1980-85. Author: Pharmacology: An Introduction to Drugs, 2d edit. 1981, Nursing Pharmacology and Therapeutics, 2d edit. 1988, The Poisonous Pen of Agatha Christie, 1993; (co-author) The Nurse's Guide to Drug Therapy: Drug Profiles for Patient Care, 1984, Editor: Instruction in Pharmacology: New Approaches and New Faces, 1979. Mem. FDA Drug Abuse Adv. Com., 1993—. Served to 1st lt. USAF, 1963-65. USPHS fellow Ind. U., 1965-68; Gustavus A. Pfeiffer Meml. Research fellow Am. Found. Pharm. Edn., 1983-84. Fellow Acad. Pharm. Scis. (sect. sec. 1975-77, sect. v.p. 1978-79). (sect. sec. 1975-77, sect. v.p. 1978-79); mem. Am. Assn. Colls. of Pharmacy (bd. dirs. 1980-82), Am. Soc. Pharmacology and Exptl. Therapeutics, N.Y. Acad. Scis., Soc. Neurosciences. Avocations: photography, reading, music, walking, cycling.

GERALDSON, RAYMOND I., lawyer; b. Racine, Wis., Oct. 7, 1911; s. Gerald and Christina (Johnson) G.; m. Evelyn A. Thorpe, Aug. 5, 1939; children: Raymond I. Jr., Mary G. Nelson, Martha G. Driscoll. BA, U. Wis., 1933, JD, 1935; LLM (Grad. fellow), Columbia U., 1936; LLD (hon.), Am. U., 1983; LHD (hon.), Kendall Coll., 1984. Bar: Wis. 1935, Ill. 1945, U.S. Supreme Ct. 1965, D.C. 1972. Practiced in Racine, 1937-45, Chgo., 1945—; partner firm Seyfarth, Shaw, Fairweather & Geraldson, Chgo.; bd. dirs. various profit and non-profit corps. Mem. Midwest Pension Conf., 1958-80, chmn., 1965-66; del. No. Ill. Conf., United Methodist Ch., 1961-75; trustee Am. U., 1963—, mem. exec. com., 1965-76, chmn. bd. trustees, 1970-76; bd. govs. Am. Nat. Red Cross, 1972-78, mem. exec. com., 1975-78, vice chmn., 1976-78, chmn. nat. planned giving com., 1978-82, mem. nat. fin. devel. com., 1981-85, chmn. subcom. on United Way relationships, 1981-85; del. to Internat. Conf. of Red Cross, Geneva, 1986; lectr. at seminar on Internat. Humanitarian Law, Honolulu, 1983, organizer, lectr., Beijing, China, 1987; bd. dirs. ARC of Greater Chgo., 1963—; bd. dirs., sec. YMCA, Racine, 1943-45, Curtis P. Kendall Found., Evanston, Ill., 1950-71; bd. dirs. Protestant Found. Greater Chgo., 1976-88; trustee Kendall Coll., Evanston, 1947—, chmn. bd. trustees, 1952-68; trustee Chgo. Home Missionary and Ch. Extension Soc., 1949-65 , pres., 1957-61; trustee Met. Crusade of Mercy, Chgo., 1971-81; legal advisor Peace Mission to Soviet Union, Auspices Bd. of World Peace Meth. Ch., 1958; trustee Found. for Evangelism, Lake Junaluska, N.C., 1996—. Recipient The Harriman award ARC, 1987. Mem. ABA, Ill. Bar Assn., Chgo. Bar Assn., D.C. Bar Assn., Wis. Bar Assn., Am. Judicature Soc. (dir. 1978-82, investment com. 1978-82, chmn. 1979-82), Geneva Lake Assn. (bd. dirs. 1980—, v.p. 1992-94, pres. 1994—), Order of Coif, Phi Beta Kappa, Phi Kappa Phi. Republican. Methodist (steward, trustee, chmn. various commns. and com., chmn. adminstrv. bd. 1970-72). Club: Union League (Chgo.). Home: 1410 Sheridan Rd Wilmette IL 60091-1895 also: N1963 Birches Dr Lake Geneva WI 53147-4120 Office: Seyfarth Shaw Fairweather & Geraldson 55 E Monroe St Ste 4200 Chicago IL 60603-5863

GERALDSON, RAYMOND I., JR., lawyer; b. Racine, Wis., Oct. 19, 1940; s. Raymond I. Sr. and Evelyn (Thorpe) G.; m. Melinda Paine, June 13, 1964; children: Amy, Raymond I. III. BA, DePauw U., 1962; JD, Northwestern U., 1965. Bar: Ill. 1965, D.C. 1966, U.S. Dist. Ct. (no. dist.) Ill. 1967. Ptnr. Pattishall, McAuliffe, Newbury, Hilliard & Geraldson, Washington, 1965-67, Chgo., 1967—; adj. prof. John Marshall Law Sch. 1978—; lectr. in field. Contbr. articles on trademark law to profl. jours. Trustee Kendall Coll., 1985—, chmn., 1990—. Mem. ABA, Ill. State Bar Assn. (coun. sect. intellectual property law 1978-82, chmn. 1980-81), Chgo. Bar Assn., 7th Crct. Intellectual Property Law Assn. Chgo. (bd. dirs. 1984-86, 92-93, pres. 1991-92), Internat. Trademark Assn. (bd. dirs. 1985-87), Am. Intellectual Property Law Assn., Lawyers for Creative Arts (hons. coun. 1994—, bd. dirs. 1974-94, pres. 1976-78), Legal Club Chgo., Law Club Chgo., Econ. Club Chgo., Sunset Ridge Country Club, Union League Club of Chgo., Sigma Chi. Office: Pattishall McAuliffe Newbury Hilliard & Geraldson 311 S Wacker Dr Ste 5000 Chicago IL 60606-6622

GERARD, GARY, neurologist; b. N.Y.C., Apr. 16, 1949; s. Victor and Sylvia G.; m. Pauline Judd; 1 child, Michael. BA, NYU, 1971; MD, Hahnemann U., 1975. Diplomate Am. Bd. Neurology and Psychiatry. Intern medicine Brookdale Med. Ctr., Bklyn., N.Y., 1975-76; resident in diagnostic radiology Mt. Sinai Med. Ctr., N.Y.C., 1976-78; resident in neurology L.I. Jewish Med. Ctr., New Hyde Park, N.Y., 1978-81; chief of neurology Winthrop U. Hosp., Mineola, N.Y., 1984-89; assoc. prof. neurology and radiology, dir. cerebrovascular lab. Med. Coll. Ohio, Toledo, 1990-94, vice chmn. neurology, 1991-94; med. dir. Neurology Ctr. Ohio, Toledo, 1994—, dir., 1994-96. Contbr. chpts. to books; guest editor jour. Seminars in Neurology, 1986. Bd. dirs. Ohio Rsch. Ctr., Toledo, 1994-97. Recipient Robert J. Tidrick award Med. Coll. Ohio, 1991. Fellow Am. Heart Assn. (stroke coun.); mem. Am. Acad. Neurology (neuroimaging com. 1985-90), Am. Pain Soc., Am. Acad. Pain Mgmt., Am. Assn. Study of Headache, Am. Soc. Neurorehab., Nat. Headache Found., Am. Soc. Neuroimaging (bd. dirs. 1984-90).

GERARD, JAMES WILSON, book distributor; b. Chgo., May 16, 1935; s. Ralph Waldo and Margaret (Wilson) G.; student U. Vt., 1955, Roosevelt U., 1955-59. Ptnr. UNIPUB, N.Y.C., 1962-77; pres. Brookfield Pub. Co., Vt., 1977-87, Ashgate Pub. Co., Brookfield, 1987—, bd. dirs. Renouf Pub. Co., Ltd., Am. Red Cross, Reech, Gifford Med. Ctr., Brookfield Hist. Soc., Vt. Pub. Rsch. Interest Group; also U.S. divs. of Avebury Pub. Co., Scolar Press, Dartmouth Pub. Co., The Inst. of Materials. Mem. Brookfield Hist. Soc., Assn. Scholarly Pub. Instn. Democrat. Club: Les Ambassadeurs. Home: 333 E 34th St New York NY 10016-4977 Office: Ashgate Pub Co Old Post Rd Brookfield VT 05036-9700

GERARD, JULES BERNARD, law educator; b. St. Louis, May 20, 1929; s. John Baptist and Faith Vera (Clinton) G.; m. Camilla Roma Smith, Aug. 8, 1953; children—Lisa, Karen Julia. Student, Iowa State Coll., 1947-49; A.B., Washington U., St. Louis, 1957, J.D., 1958. Bar: N.Y. 1959, U.S. Supreme Ct. 1979. Assoc. Donovan, Leisure, Newton & Irvine, N.Y.C., 1958-60; asst. prof. law U. Mo., Columbia, 1960-62; asst. prof., assoc. prof. law Washington U., 1962-67, prof., 1967-99, prof. emeritus, 1999—; dir. Ctr. for Jud. Studies; mem. adv. bd. Washington Legal Found., 1984—. Author: Local Regulation of Adult Businesses, 1992, Proposed Washington D.C. Amendment, 1979, (with others) Sum and Substance Constitutional Law, 1976, (with others) Federal Land Use Law, 1986; editor: 100 Years of 14th Amendment, 1973; editor-in-chief Washington U. Law Quar., 1958; contbr. articles to profl. jours., chpts. to books. Mem. Mo. Adv. com. U.S. Commn. on Civil Rights, 1987-92. Served to 1st lt. USAF, 1950-54. Mem. ABA. Republican. Avocations: collecting scrimshaw and antique photographica, photography. Home: 1564 Yarmouth Point Dr Chesterfield MO 63017-5639 Office: Washington U Campus Box 1120 Saint Louis MO 63130-4899

GERARD, ROY DUPUY, oil company executive, retired; b. New Orleans, Sept. 14, 1931; s. Lester Charles and Helene (Dupuy) G.; m. Minnie Harper, May 17, 1958; children: Roy Dupuy Jr., Nannette Gerard Helmcamp, Carl, Denise. BSChemE, La. State U., 1953, MSChemE, 1958. Registered profl. engr., La. Chemist, technologist various plants Shell Chem. Co., Houston, La., N.Y., Calif., 1958-69; dept. head Shell Devel. Co., Emeryville, Calif., 1969-71; dir. indsl. chems. and petrochems. Shell Devel. Co., Houston, 1973-75, mgr. chem. R & D, 1975-77, gen. mgr. Westhollow rsch., 1982-90; pres. Saudi Petrochem. Co., Al Jubail, Saudi Arabia, 1980-82; mgr. logistics econs., supply and econs. and mktg. Shell Oil Co., Houston, 1971-73, gen. mgr. engring. products, 1977-80, v.p. health, safety and environ., 1990-92, ret., 1992; pvt. investor, stocks, bonds, etc., 1992—; mem., vice chmn. coun. environ. affairs Conf. Bd., 1991—; mem., chmn. chem. engring. vis. com. U. Tex., Austin, 1985-87; mem. chem. engring. vis. com. La. State U., Baton Rouge, 1987-90, mem. dean's adv. com., 1990—; mem. chem. engring. vis. com. Tex. A&M U., College Station, 1989, U. Tenn., Knoxville, 1989;. 1st lt. C.E., U.S. Army, 1954-56. Mem. AICE, Coun. for Chem. Rsch. (chmn. 1991—), Am. Indsl. Health Coun. (bd. dirs., exec. com. 1990—), Am. Petroleum Inst. (health and environ. gen. com. 1990—), Raveneaux Country Club (Spring, Tex.). Republican. Roman Catholic. Avocations: fishing, golf, woodworking.

GERARD, WHITNEY IAN, lawyer; b. N.Y.C., Oct. 31, 1934; s. Harold Todd and Beatrice Roma (Meyer) G.; m. Marion Lehane, Apr. 1, 1966; children: Ian Alexandre, Stefan Meredith. AB, Princeton U., 1956; JD, Harvard U., 1963. Bar: N.Y. 1964. Wine exporter Alexis Lichine et Cie, Bordeaux, France, 1956-58; wine cons. S.S. Pierce Co., Boston, 1960-75; assoc., then ptnr. Alexander and Green, N.Y.C., 1963-84; ptnr., chmn. internat. practice comm. Chadbourne and Parke LLP, N.Y.C., 1984—; bd. dirs. U. Cape Town Fund, Inc., N.Y.C., Dreyfus Liquid Assets, Inc., The Dreyfus Fund, Inc., Dreyfus Worldwide Dollar Money Market Fund, Inc., Dreyfus Asset Allocation Fund, Inc., Dreyfus Lifetime Portfolios, Inc., Dreyfus Short Intermediate Mcpl. Bond Fund, Dreyfus Short Intermediate Govt. Fund. and other Dreyfus funds. 1st lt. USAF, 1958-60. Mem. ABA, N.Y. State Bar Assn., Internat. Bar Assn., Univ. Club, Ancient Order of Beefeaters (Chief Warder 1965-90). Democrat. Avocations: classical music, ballet, theater, mountain hiking, literature. Home: 940 Park Ave New York NY 10028-0311 also: 102 W Center Rd West Stockbridge MA 01266-9378 Office: Chadbourne & Parke LLP 30 Rockefeller Plz New York NY 10112-0002

GERARDI, JOAN LOIS, art educator; b. Bronx, Feb. 19, 1947; d. Louis and Joan (Collica) Gnocchi; m. Daniel William Gerardi, June 26, 1971; children: Dawn, Danielle. BA, Lehman Coll., 1969, MA, 1974. Art tchr. P.S. 108, Bronx, N.Y., 1969-73, 4th grad tchr., 1973-74; art tchr. Our Lady of Assumption Sch., Bronx, 1986—. Home: 3283 Polo Pl Bronx NY 10465-1309

GERARD-SHARP, MONICA FLEUR, communications executive; b. London, Oct. 4, 1951; came to U.S., 1975; d. John Hugh Gerard-Sharp and Doreen May (Kearney) Dewhurst; m. Ali Edward Wambold, Nov. 21, 1981; children: Marina, Daniela, Dominica. BA in Philosophy and Lit. with honors, U. Warwick, Eng., 1973; MBA in Fin., Mktg. and Internat. Bus., Columbia U., 1980. Editor Inst. Chem. Engrs., London, 1973-74; sub-editor TV Times Ltd., London, 1974-75; press officer, editor UN, N.Y.C., 1975-78; bus. mgr. Time-Life Video, N.Y.C., 1980-81; mgr. fin. analysis Time-Life Films, N.Y.C., 1981; v.p. T.V.I.S., N.Y.C., 1982-83; dir. strategy and devel. video group Time Inc., N.Y.C., 1984-85, asst. treas., officer, 1985-87; pub. Travel Today mags. Fairchild Pubs. subs. Capital Cities/ABC, N.Y.C., 1987-88; dir. video programming Fairchild Pubs., Capital Cities/ABC, N.Y.C., 1988-89; pub. Entrée and Home Fashions Mag., N.Y.C., 1988-90; pres. Monali Inc., N.Y.C., 1991—; cons. UN Bus. Council, N.Y.C., 1979; bd. rep. U.S.A. Network, N.Y.C., 1983-85. Editor: Everyone's United Nations, 1977; contbg. editor Asia Pacific Forum, 1976-77; contbr. articles to profl. jours. and mags., 1973-78. Treas. Help the Aged, Eng.; pres. bd. Am. Friends of Royal Ct. Theatre. Bronfman fellow, 1979-80. Mem. Nat. Acad. Cable Programming, Am. Film Inst., Beta Gamma Sigma. Roman Catholic. Avocations: antiques, photography, wildlife. Home: Deer Park Sunset Hill Rd Pleasant Valley NY 12569 Office: Monali Inc 26 E 80th St New York NY 10021-0110

GERATHY, E. CARROLL, former insurance executive, real estate developer; b. Long Island City, N.Y., June 25, 1915; s. Joseph Hewson and Emma E. (Donady) G.; m. Julia F. Gill, Sept. 7, 1942; children: Nancy, John; m. Joyce K. Baker, Dec. 31, 1972; children: Stephen Baker, Nancy Baker; m. Betty Ann Durkin, Jan. 27, 1984. M.B.A., U. Chgo., 1962. C.L.U. With McKesson & Robbins, Inc., 1933-48; with Prudential Ins. Co. Am., 1948-78, sr. v.p., 1964-78; project dir. Hilton Hawaiian Village, Hilton Hotels Corp., 1979-81, Third Newark Gateway Urban Renewal Assn., 1981-91. Mem. N.J. C. of C., Canoe Brook Country Club (N.J.). Home: 42 Knob Hill Dr Summit NJ 07901-3051

GERATY, LAWRENCE THOMAS, academic administrator, archaeologist; b. St. Helena, Calif., Apr. 21, 1940; s. Thomas Sinclair and Hazel Mae (McVicker) G.; m. Gillian Anne Keough, Aug. 5, 1962; children: Brent, Julie. BA, Pacific Union Coll., 1962; MA, Andrews U., 1963, BD, 1965; PhD, Harvard U., 1972. Pastor 7th Day Adventist Ch., Calif., 1962-66; instr. old testament Andrews U., Berrien Springs, Mich., 1966-72, asst. prof. archaeology and history, 1972-76, assoc. prof. archaeology and history, 1976-80, prof., 1980-85; curator S.H. Horn Archaeol. Mus., Berrien Springs, Mich., 1976-85; dir. Inst. Archaeology Andrews U., Berrien Springs, 1981-85; pres. Atlantic Union Coll., Lancaster, Mass., 1985-93, La Sierra U., Riverside, Calif., 1993—; project dir. Excavation of Tell Hesban, Jordan, 1973-76, Madaba Plains Project, Jordan, 1984—; v.p. Am. Ctr. of Oriental Rsch., Amman, 1985—. Editor, contbr. articles to profl. jours. Bd. dirs. Thayer Symphony Orch., Lancaster, Mass., 1985-93; mem. Edn. Forum of Clinton, Mass., 1990-93. Fulbright fellow, 1970-71, Robert H. Pfeiffer fellow, 1970-71; grantee Ford Found., 1969-70, Ctr. Field Rsch., 1976, NEH, 1979. Mem. Soc. Bibl. Literature (pres. 1988-90), Archeol. Inst. Am., Clinton C. of C. (bd. dirs. 1985-92), Riverside C. of C. (bd. dirs. 1996—), Raincross Club, Employers Group (bd. dirs. 1996—). Seventh-Day Adventist. Office: La Sierra Univ Office of Pres 4700 Pierce St Riverside CA 92505-3332*

GERBEHY, CHRISTINE PETRIC, medical/surgical and mental health nurse; b. Jersey City, Mar. 21, 1952; d. Miro and Eileen M. (Schmidt) Petric; m. Steven John Gerbehy; children: Rachel Lauren, Emily Rose. AAS, Bergen Community Coll., Paramus, N.J., 1978; BSN with honors, Felician Coll., Lodi, N.J., 1988. With med. and surg. dept. Bergen Pine County Hosp., Paramus, 1978-88, staff nurse, psychiatry, 1988-98; staff nurse, psychiatry Bergen Regional Med. Ctr., Paramus, 1998—. Mem. ANA, Sigma Theta Tau (Mu Theta chpt.).

GERBER, ALBERT B., lawyer, former legal association executive; b. Phila., July 10, 1913; s. Jacob and Jennie (Suffrin) G.; m. Rhona C. Posner, Nov. 22, 1939; children—Jack J., Gail, Lynne. BS in Edn., U. Pa., 1934, JD, 1937, LLM, 1941; MA in Govt., George Washington U., Washington, 1940. Bar: Pa. 1938. Chief opinion unit Dept. Agr., Washington, 1938-42; ptnr. Gerber & Gafand, Phila., 1946-72; adminstrv. dir. 1st Amendment Lawyers Assn., Phila., 1970-87; pres. Assn. for Research, Inc., Phila., 1972-84; of counsel Galfand, Berger Lurie & March, Phila., 1984-94; counsel United Nat. Ins. Co., Phila., 1972—. Author: Bashful Billionaire, 1967, The Lawyer, 1972, Book of Sex Lists, 1981, Miracles on Park Avenue, 1985; also numerous articles; editor Tax Sense, 1980-83, Internat. Intelligence, 1981-84. Democratic committeeman, Phila., 1950-60, Montgomery County, Pa., 1979-81. Served to sgt. inf. U.S. Army, 1942-45, PTO. Recipient Best Novel award Pa. Assn. Writers, 1980. Mem. ABA, Phila. Bar Assn., Order of Coif. Jewish. Avocations: handball; tennis; volleyball. Office: United Nat Ins Co 3 Bala Plz Ste 300 Bala Cynwyd PA 19004-3481

GERBER, CHARLES M., sales and marketing executive; b. Buffalo, Oct. 6, 1949; s. William W. and Patricia (Dillon) G.; m. Sheila Kierman Gerber, Mar. 35, 1974 (div. Dec. 25, 1989); children: Jill, Corey K.; m. Leslie Brooks, Apr. 6, 1996. MBA, Queens Coll., Charlotte, N.C., 1995. Inst. estate sales Tompkins & Fink, Buffalo, 1972-74; sales rep. Nat. Gypsum Co., Buffalo and Rochester, N.Y., 1974-77; asst. dist. sales mgr. Nat. Gypsum Co., Chgo., 1977-80; product mgr. mktg. Nat. Gypsum Co., Charlotte, N.C., 1980-84; dir. sales devel. Nat. Gypsum Co., Charlotte, 1984-85; dist. sales mgr. Nat. Gypsum Co., L.A., 1985-90; dir. nat. accounts Nat. Gypsum Co., Charlotte, 1990—. Cpl. USMC, 1969-71. Avocations: travel, golf, athletics. Office: Nat Gypsum Co 2001 Rexford Rd Charlotte NC 28211-3415

GERBER, DOUGLAS EARL, classics educator; b. North Bay, Ont., Can., Sept. 14, 1933; s. Earl Jacob and Bertha (Cox) G.; m. Joan Isobel Warner,

Nov. 22, 1986; 1 dau., Allison S. B.A., U. Western Ont. (Can.), London, 1955, M.A., 1956; Ph.D., U. Toronto, 1959. Lectr. Greek U. Toronto, 1958-59; mem. faculty dept. classics U. Western Ont., London, 1959-99; assoc. prof. U. Western Ont., 1964-69, prof., 1969-99, chmn. dept., 1969-97, vice provost for acad. affairs, 1984-86, W.S. Fox chair of classics. Author: A Bibliography of Pindar, 1513-1966, 1969, Euterpe: An Anthology of Early Greek Lyric, Elegiac and Iambic Poetry, 1970, Emendations in Pindar, 1513-1972, 1976, Pindar's Olympian One: A Commentary, 1982, Lexicon in Bacchylidem, 1984; editor Greek Poetry and Philosophy; Studies in Honor of Leonard Woodbury, 1984, A Companion to the Greek Lyric Poets, 1997. Mem. Classical Assn. Canada (treas. 1960-62, pres. 1988-90), Am. Philol. Assn. (editor trans. 1974-82), Classical Assn. Middle West and South, Classical Assn. (Gt. Britain). Home: 2 Grosvenor St, London, ON Canada N6A 1Y4 Office: U Western Ont, Dept Classics, London, ON Canada N6A 3K7

GERBER, EDWARD F., lawyer, educator; b. Houston, Oct. 10, 1932; s. Edward F. and Lucille (Beaver) G.; m. Eileen Healy, Sept. 1, 1956; children: Gretchen, Eric, Nils. BS, Syracuse U., 1957, LLB, 1960, JD, 1968. Bar: N.Y. 1960, U.S. Dist. Ct. (no. dist.) N.Y. 1960. Pvt. practice law, Syracuse, N.Y., 1960-64; first asst. dist. atty. Onondaga County, Syracuse, N.Y., 1964-67; spl. prosecutor Onondaga County, 1976; pvt. practice law, Syracuse, 1977—; lectr. Coll. of Law Syracuse U., 1968—; counsel Onondaga County Sheriff, 1978-94, N.Y. State Police Benevolent Assn., 1983—, N.Y. State Police Investigators Assn.; faculty Criminal Law Services Syracuse U. Trial Practice Sessions. Bd. dirs. Onondaga County Young Rep. Club, 1964-66. With USN, 1951-54. Named one of Best Lawyers in Am., 1989. Fellow Am. Coll. Trial Lawyers; mem. ATLA, N.Y. State Bar Assn. (lectr.), Upstate Trial Lawyers Assn. (pres. 1978-79), Onondaga County Bar Assn. (dir. 1969-71), Onondaga Bar Found. (pres. 1983). Home: 21 Drumlins Ter Syracuse NY 13224-2217 Office: 224 Harrison St Ste 500 Syracuse NY 13202-3060

GERBER, EUGENE J., bishop; b. Kingman, Kans., Apr. 30, 1931; s. Cornelius John and Lena Marie (Tiesmeyer) G. B.A., St. Thomas Sem., Denver; B.S., Wichita State U.; B.S.Th., Catholic U. Am.; S.T.L., Angelicum, Rome. Ordained priest Roman Catholic Ch., 1959; asst. chancellor Wichita Diocese, 1963, sec. to bishop, 1964, vice chancellor, 1967, mem. diocesan bd. adminstrn., 1973, diocesan cons., 1973, chancellor, 1975; chaplain, mem. governing bd. Holy Family Center for Mentally Retarded; bd. dirs. Cursillo; bishop of Dodge City, Kans., 1976-82, Diocese of Wichita, 1982—. Office: 307 E Central Ave Wichita KS 67202-1055 also: Diocese of Wichita Chancery Office 424 N Broadway St Wichita KS 67202-2310*

GERBER, GWENDOLYN LORETTA, psychologist, educator; b. Calgary, Alta., Can.; came to U.S., 1958; d. Ernest and Alma (Tesky) G. AB, UCLA, 1961, MA, 1964, PhD, 1967; cert. in psychoanalysis, NYU, 1970. Lic. psychologist, N.Y. Clin. psychologist Hillside Hosp., Glen Oaks, N.Y., 1970-73; asst. prof. psychology John Jay Coll. of Criminal Justice CUNY, N.Y.C., 1973-77, assoc. prof. psychology, 1977-90, prof., 1991—; pvt. practice in psychotherapy N.Y.C., 1970—. Contbr. chpts. to books and numerous articles to profl. jours. USPHS fellow, 1962-63, 66-67, NIMH fellow, 1967-69; CUNY grantee, 1989-92, 45 Found. grantee, 1991-96. Fellow APA (bd. dirs. divsn. 39 1997-99, sect. III 1988-92, 94-95, sec., mem. exec. coun. divsn. 39 sect. VI 1991-99, divsn. 35, liaison to divsn. 39, 1989-98, mem. N.Y. State Psychol. Assn. (pres. acad. divsn. 1989-90, coun. rep. 1991-96, William Wundt award 1993, disting. svc. award 1996), N.Y. Acad. Scis.; mem. Phi Beta Kappa, Chi Delta Pi. Office: John Jay Coll CUNY 445 W 59th St New York NY 10019-1104

GERBER, JACK, artist; b. Phila., May 19, 1927; s. Benjamin Samuel and Jean (Ginzberg) G. Student, Pa. Acad. Fine Arts, Phila., 1949-53. curator Phila. Water Color Club; juror Sketch Club Phila., 1987, 90, Artists' Equity, 1985, Perkins Ctr. for the Arts, 1984, others. One-person shows include Roger LaPelle Gallery, Phila., 1983, 84, Pavilion Galleries, Mt. Holly, N.J., 1990, Congregation Beth Orr, 1995, Plastic Club, Phila., 1995, Library of the Swedenborg Acad., Pa., 1996, The Hill Sch., Pottstown, 1997; exhibited in group shows at Pa. Acad. Fine Arts, Phila. Mus. Art, The Library of Congress, Rutgers Nat. Drawing Show, Nat. Acad. Design, 1988, 90, others. Recipient numerous prizes at art shows; Phila. Bd. Edn. scholar; Branywine Workshop fellow, 1983. Mem. Am. Color Print Soc. (First prize 1996), Phila. Watercolor Club, Phila. Sketch Club, Plastic Club (Gold medal 1997), The Woodmere Mus. (Harry A. Harris award 1997), Phila. Mus. Art. Democrat. Home and Studio: 540 W Chew Ave Philadelphia PA 19120-2229

GERBER, JOEL, federal judge; b. Chgo., July 16, 1940; s. Peter H. and Marcia L. (Weber) G.; m. Judith R. Smilgoff, Aug. 18, 1963; children—Jay Lawrence, Jeffrey Mark, Jon Victor. B.S.B.A., Roosevelt U., Chgo., 1962; J.D., DePaul U., Chgo., 1965; LL.M., Boston U., 1968. Bar: Ill. 1965, Ga. 1974, Tenn. 1978. Trial atty. IRS, Boston, 1965-72; staff asst. to regional counsel IRS, Atlanta, 1972-76; dist. counsel IRS, Nashville, 1976-80; dep. chief counsel IRS, Washington, 1980-83, acting chief counsel, 1983-84; judge U.S. Tax Ct., Washington, 1984—; gen. counsel ATF Credit Union, Boston, 1968-70; lectr. Vanderbilt U. Sch. Law, Nashville, 1976-80; lectr. U. Miami Grad. Law Sch., 1986-90. Recipient awards U.S. Treasury Dept., 1979, 81, 82; Presdl. Meritorious Exec. Rank award, 1983. Mem. ABA (chmn. spl. com. for lawyers in govt. 1986-90). Office: US Tax Ct 400 2nd St NW Rm 432 Washington DC 20217-0002

GERBER, JOHN CHRISTIAN, English language educator; b. New Waterford, Ohio, Jan. 31, 1908; s. Christian G. and Leonora (Hauptmann) G.; m. Margaret E. Wilbourn, Sept. 3, 1941; children: Barbara Page Barrett, Ann Wilbourn Gerber Sakaguchi. A.B., U. Pitts., 1929, M.A., 1932; Ph.D., U. Chgo., 1941; D.Letters (hon.), Morningside Coll., 1979. Instr. English U. Pitts., 1931-36; instr. English U. Chgo., 1938-42, pre-meteorology, 1942-44; asst. prof. English U. Iowa, 1944-47, asso. prof., 1947-49, prof., 1949-76, Carpenter prof. emeritus, 1976—, chmn. dept. English, 1961-76, dir. Sch. Letters, 1967-76, coordinator fine arts, 1984-86; prof. English State U. N.Y. at Albany, 1976-84, chmn. dept., 1976-81, acad. Laureate, 1984; vis. asso. prof. English U. So. Calif., summer 1949; vis. prof. U. N.Mex., summers 1952, 57, Trinity Coll., summers 1960, 63, U. Calif. at Berkeley, 1960-61, U. Colo., summer 1965, U. Philippines, 1969, Am. U. at Cairo, 1970, Korean univs., summers; 1972, 1984 Chinese univs., summer 1979; cons. English U.S. Office Edn., 1964-65. Author: (with Walter Blair) Factual Prose, 1945, Literature, 1948, Writers Resource Book, 1953, (with Fleece and Wylder) Toward Better Writing, 1958, (with Arnold and Ehninger) Repertory, 1960, Twentieth Century Interpretations of the Scarlet Letter, 1968, Studies in Huckleberry Finn, 1971; Mark Twain, 1988; (with Brown, Kaufmann and Lindberg) Pictorial History of the University of Iowa, 1988; Marvelous Model-T!, 1991, The First Hundred Years of the Teaching of English at the University of Iowa, 1995; also chpts. in Toward General Education, 1948; editorial bd.: Coll. English, 1947-48, 65-71, Am. Quar, 1963-68; editorial adviser: Philol. Quar, 1951-57; editorial adv. bd.: Resources for American Literary Study, 1971-92; chmn. editorial bd.: Windhover Press, 1968-72; mem. editorial bd.: U. Iowa Press, 1963-67; chmn. editorial bd.: Iowa-California Edit. of the Works of Mark Twain, 1965-83; hist. editor: Tom Sawyer vol., 1980; editor: Teaching Coll. English, 1965, Scott-Foresman Key Edits; contbr. articles to profl. jours.; author intros. several books. Recipient Disting. Service award Iowa Council Tchrs. English, 1972, Academic Laureate for disting. and sustained service SUNY Albany, 1984, Resolution of Commendation N.Y. Legis., 1984, Citation, State of N.Y. Gov. Cuomo, 1984. Mem. Nat. Council Tchrs. English (Hatfield award 1964, Exec. Com. award 1974, trustee of research found. 1962-65, pres. 1955, Disting. Lectr. award 1966), Conf. Coll. Composition and Communication (chmn. 1950, Founders award 1976), Modern Lang. Assn. (chmn. Am. lit. sect. 1969, mem. exec. council 1972-75, mem. nominating com. 1981-83), Midwest Modern Lang. Assn. (pres. 1966), N.E. Modern Lang. Assn., Assn. Depts. English (chmn. 1964, Disting. Svc. award 1984), Mark Twain Cir., Phi Beta Kappa. Address: 359 Magowan Ave Iowa City IA 52246-3515

GERBER, LAWRENCE, lawyer; b. Chgo., Oct. 2, 1940. BBA, Loyola U. Chgo., 1962; JD, Northwestern U., 1965. Bar: Ill. 1965; CPA Ill. Ptnr. McDermott, Will & Emery, Chgo., mng. ptnr., 1991—. Author: Hospital Restructuring: Why, When and How, 1983. Mem. Am. Acad. Hosp. Attys., Ill. Assn. Hosp. Attys. Office: McDermott Will & Emery 227 W Monroe St Ste 3100 Chicago IL 60606-5096

GERBER, LUCILLE D., elementary education educator; b. Adrian, Mich., Nov. 22, 1952; d. William C. and V. Lucille (Wilson) Brooks; m. Gerald F. Gerber, Aug. 3, 1985. BS, Ea. Mich. U., 1976, cert. in continuing edn., 1981, 87—. Tchr. 3d grade Ypsilanti (Mich.) Pub. Schs., 1977-78; tchr. 1st grade Adams Elem. Sch. Ypsilanti (Mich.) Pub. Schs., 1978—. Contbr. poetry to various publs. Mem. NEA, Mich. Edn. Assn. Address: 615 N Mansfield St Ypsilanti MI 48197-2028 Office: Ypsilanti Pub Schs 1885 Packard Rd Ypsilanti MI 48197-1846

GERBER, MERRILL JOAN, writing educator; b. Bklyn., Mar. 15, 1938; s. William M. and Jessie Sorblum G.; m. Joseph Spiro, June 23, 1960; children: Becky ann, Joanna Emily, Sisanna Willa. BA in English, U. Fla., 1959; MA, Brandeis U., 1980. Lectr. creative writing Pasadena (Calif.) City Coll., 1980-89, Calif. Inst. Tech., Pasadena, 1989—. Author: King of the World, 1989 (Pushcart Press Editors' Book award 1989), The Kingdom of Brooklyn, 1992 (Ribalow award Hadassah Mag. 1993), Old Mother, Little Cat, 1995, Anna in Chains, 1998. Recipient O'Henry prize, 1986; Wallace Stegner Fiction fellow, 1962. Office: Calif Inst Tech Humanities Dept 228-77 Pasadena CA 91125

GERBER, MITCHEL, political scientist, educator; b. N.Y.C., Dec. 29, 1951; s. Stanley and Jeanette (Slossman) G.; m. Barbara Shanetzky, May 24, 1974; 1 child, Yale. BA cum laude, Bklyn. Coll., 1973; MA, Columbia U., 1975; PhD, NYU, 1982. Asst. prof. dept. polit. sci. Ill. State U., 1985-87, Hofstra U., 1987-89; asst. prof. polit. sci. S.E. Mo. State U., Cape Girardeau, 1989-93, assoc. prof. polit. sci., 1993-97, prof. polit. sci., 1998—; vis. prof. Imperial Coll., London, spring 1996; tchg. asst. dept. politics, NYU, 1979-80; faculty cons., reader Coll. Bd. Advanced Placement, Clemson U., 1993; co-dir. conf. on ethics and pub. svc. S.E. Mo. State U., 1991. Reviewer Polit. Rsch. Quar.; contbr. articles to profl. jours. Mem. Nat. Social Sci. Assn. (bd. govs., cons. jour. editor), Am. Polit. Sci. Assn. (Found. of Polit. Theory, Found. of Computers and Multimedia), Acad. Polit. Sci., So. Polit. Sci. Assn., Midwest Polit. Sci. Assn., Northeastern Polit. Sci. Assn., Soc. for Study of Greek Polit. Thought, N.Am. Conf. on British Studies, Assn. for Integrative Studies, Mo. Polit. Sci. Assn. Jewish. Avocations: antiquarian books, political memorabilia, Cincinnati Reds baseball. Home: 2019 Kevin Dr Cape Girardeau MO 63701-1819 Office: Southeast Mo State U Dept Polit Sci Cape Girardeau MO 63701

GERBER, MURRAY A., molding manufacturing company executive. BSME, MIT, 1956; MBA, U. New Haven, 1979, D of Bus (hon.), 1997. Founder, pres. Prototype & Plastic Mold Co. Inc., Middletown, Conn.; chmn. 1982 Conn. Conf. on Small Bus.; mem. conn. delegation to White House Conf. on Small Bus., 1980, chmn. continuing group; mem. Conn. Small Bus. Adv. Commn.; small bus. advisor to Vice-pres. George Bush; guest lectr. various schs. and assns.; bd. dirs. Va. Industries, Rocky Hill, Conn. Mem. indsl. tech. plastics adv. com. Cen. Conn. State U.; chmn. meriden-Middlesex Pvt. Industry Coun., conn. Pub. Expenditure Coun.; bd. govs U. New Haven, mem. exec. com., vice chmn., 1993-98, exec. vice chmn., 1998—. Mem. Conn. Tooling and Machining Assn. (bd. dirs.), smaller Bus. Assn. New Eng. (bd. dirs.), Middlesex County C. of C. (bd. dirs.), Conn. Bus. and Industry Assn. 1995 vice chmn. 1988—, chmn. 1989—), Nat. Tooling and Machining Assn. (nat. polit. action com.), Nat. Assn. Mfrs. (bd. dirs. 1995—, chmn. tax and budget com., exec. com. mem.). Avocations: wine making, golf, bridge, photographer. Office: Prototype & Plastic Mold Co 35 Industrial Park Pl Middletown CT 06457-1501

GERBER, PHILLIP, advertising executive; b. 1963. Formerly with Edward H. Weiss & Co., Chgo.; mng. ptnr., media ops. dir. Euro Rscg Tathaw, Chgo., 1983—. Office: Euro Rscg Tatham 980 N Michigan Ave Chicago IL 60611-4501*

GERBER, ROBERT EVAN, lawyer; b. N.Y.C., Feb. 12, 1947; s. Milton M. and Miriam (Simon) G.; m. Jane Flanagan, Nov. 10, 1996. BS with high honors, Rutgers U., 1967; JD magna cum laude, Columbia U., 1970. Bar: N.Y. 1971, U.S. Dist. Ct. (so. and ea. dists.) N.Y. 1972, U.S. Ct. Appeals (2d cir.) 1973, U.S. Ct. Appeals (9th cir.) 1974, U.S. Ct. Appeals (10th cir.) 1975, U.S. Ct. Appeals (11th cir.) 1983, U.S. Supreme Ct. 1983, U.S. Ct. Appeals (5th cir.) 1987, U.S. Ct. Appeals (6th cir.) 1989, U.S. Ct. Appeals (3d cir.) 1997. Assoc. Fried, Frank, Harris, Shriver & Jacobson, N.Y.C., 1970-71, 72-78, ptnr., 1978—. Served to 1st lt. USAF, 1971-72. James Kent scholar, 1970, Harlan Fiske Stone scholar, 1969. Mem. ABA, Assn. Bar City N.Y. (sec. spl. com. on energy 1974-79), Fed. Bar Coun., Am. Bankruptcy Inst., Tau Beta Pi. Home: 13 Colt Rd Summit NJ 07901-3002 Office: Fried Frank Harris Shriver & Jacobson 1 New York Plz Fl 22 New York NY 10004-1980

GERBER, ROGER ALAN, lawyer, business consultant; b. Bklyn., Jan. 27, 1939; s. Edward and Anne (Rothstein) G.; m. Jane E. Satlow, Sept. 20, 1964; children: Dina Huebner, Deborah Tor, Tamar Gerber. B.A. magna cum laude (Rufus Choate scholar), Dartmouth Coll., 1959; J.D., Harvard U., 1962. Bar: N.Y. 1963. Real estate atty. ABC, Inc., 1965-68; assoc. Kaye, Scholer, Fierman, Hays & Handler, other law firms, 1968-75; v.p., gen. counsel ISS Internat. Service System, Inc., N.Y.C., 1975-83; v.p., sec., gen. counsel Meyers Parking System, Inc., N.Y.C., 1975-89, sr. exec. v.p., chief oper. officer, 1989-95, also bd. dirs., 1981-91; pres. Meyers Realty Co., N.Y.C., 1982-95; abritrator Am. Arbitration Assn., 1973—; bd. dirs. Nat. Parking Assn., 1991-92; mem. adv. bd. Mid. East Forum, 1995—; bd. dirs. Jewish Inst. for Nat. Security Affairs, 1995—. Treas. Scarsdale (N.Y.) Democratic Com., 1977-83; v.p., exec. com. Bd. Jewish Edn., Greater N.Y., 1977—; bd. trustees PEF-Israel Endowment Fund, 1997—; bd. dirs. Conf. Jewish Social Studies, 1975-93, Jewish Conciliation Bd., N.Y.; class agt. Dartmouth Coll. Mem. N.Y. State Bar Assn., Phi Beta Kappa. Club: Harvard (N.Y.C.). Home: 26 Sage Ter Scarsdale NY 10583-2045

GERBER, RUDOLPH JOSEPH, judge, educator; b. St. Louis, Oct. 25, 1938; s. Rudolph Vogt and Isable Helen (Bauer) G.; children: Jennifer, Kristin, Joseph. MA in Comparative Lit., Columbia U., N.Y.C., 1964; PhD with grand distinction, U. Louvain, Belgium, 1966; JD, Notre Dame U., 1971; LLM, U. Va., 1986; Anglo-Am. law cert., Cambridge (Eng.) U., 1992, Oxford (Eng.) U., 1994. Bar: Ariz. 1972, Calif. 1987. Asst. prof. philosophy St. Louis U., 1966-67, U. Notre Dame, Ind., 1967-71; legal counsel bd. suprs. County of Maricopa, Phoenix, 1972-74, pub. defender, 1972-76, atty., 1976-79, judge superior ct., 1979—, assoc. chief presiding judge, 1985-88; judge Ariz. Ct. Appeals, Phoenix, 1988—; prof. Western Internat. U., 1983—; legal editor Kennikat Press, N.Y.C., 1985-88; del. Nat. Conf. State Cts.; mem. faculty Nat. Jud. Coll. Author: Contemporary Punishment, 1972, Contemporary Issues in Criminal Justice, 1976, Criminal Law of Arizona, 1979, 2d edit., 1993, The Insanity Defense, 1984, Lawyers, Courts and Corrections, 1989, The Grand Canyon Railroad, 1990, 2d edit., 1994, Cruel and Usual, 1999; contbr. articles to profl. jours. mem. editl. bd. Am. Jour. Jurisprudence. Minority counsel Ariz. Senate, Phoenix, 1977-78. Fulbright fellow, Belgium, 1964-66. Mem. Ariz. Bar Assn., Calif. Bar Assn. Democrat. Roman Catholic. Avocations: swimming, hiking, skiing, gardening, tennis. Home: 15807 N 15th Way Phoenix AZ 85022 Office: Ariz Ct Appeals State Capital Phoenix AZ 85007

GERBER, SANDRA ELAINE, neonatal nurse practitioner; b. St. Paul, Aug. 16, 1954; d. Warren and Elaine G. Diploma, Fairview Hosp. Sch. Nursing, Mpls., 1976; BS in Profl. Arts, St. Joseph's Coll., North Windom, Maine, 1987. Cert. pediatric nurse practitioner; cert. neonatal nurse practitioner. Staff nurse Riverview Meml. Hosp., St. Paul, 1976-79; staff nurse ob-gyn. and nursery Bethesda Luth. Med. Ctr., St. Paul, 1979-84, asst. head nurse nursery, ob-gyn. and pediatrics depts., 1984-88; neonatal nurse practitioner Health East, St. Paul, 1989—. Mem. NAACOG, Nat. Assn. Pediatric Nurse Assocs. and Practitioners, Nat. Assn. Neonatal Nursing, Minn. Plains Orgn., Gt. Plains Orgn., Sigma Theta Tau. Office: Health East 1575 Beam Ave Maplewood MN 55109-1126

GERBER, SEYMOUR, retired publishing company executive; b. Chgo., Feb. 19, 1920; s. Hyman and Fannie (Walton) G.; m. Rose Kaminker, Dec. 25, 1941; children: Ila Barrie Gerber Richter, Avis Hope Gerber Jones, Larry Alan. Grad., U. Ill. Pres. Graphic Advt., Inc., Miami, Fla., 1953-69, Graphic Arts Inc., Miami, 1953-69; chmn., CEO Halsey Pub. Co., North Miami, Fla., 1969-95. Capt. Ordnance Corps, AUS, 1941-45. Recipient awards from various assns. Clubs: Art Dirs. Miami (pres.); St. Andrews Country (Boca Raton, Fla.); La Costa Country (Carlsbad, Calif.). *If in the space of my lifetime, I can as a communicator, contribute to an understanding among all people for a peaceful coexistence and eliminate at least a modicum of bigotry, my efforts will have been worthwhile.*

GERBER, WILLIAM NORMAN, motion picture executive; b. Las Vegas, Nev., Apr. 30, 1957; s. Roy Herbert and Constance Doris Gerber. West coast dir. Nemporer Records, Los Angeles, 1978-79; exec. v.p. Lookout Mgmt., Los Angeles, 1979-84; prin. owner Gerber/Rodkin Co., Los Angeles, 1985-86; v.p. theatrical prodn. divsn. Warner Bros., Inc., Burbank, 1986-98; co-pres. worldwide theatrical prodn. Warner Bros., Inc., Burbank, Calif., 1998; prodr. Gerber Pictures, 1998. Fax: 310 385-5881. Office: Gerber Pictures 9465 Wilshire Blvd Beverly Hills CA 90212*

GERBERDING, MILES CARSTON, lawyer; b. Decatur, Ind., Oct. 25, 1930; s. Arnold H. and Luella E. (Lapp) G.; m. Ruth H. Hostrup, Aug. 20, 1955 (dec. Mar. 1992); children: Karla M. Smith, Greta E. Cowart, Kent E., Brian K.; m. Joan W. Fackler, Jan. 2, 1993; stepchildren: Stephen W. Fackler, Deborah E. Holbrook. BS, Ind. U., 1954, JD, 1956. Bar: Ind. 1956, U.S. Dist. Ct. (so. and no. dists.) Ind. 1956, Mich. 1981. Ptnr. Nieter & Smith, Ft. Wayne, Ind., 1956-58, Barrett, Barrett & McNagny, Ft. Wayne, 1958-85; ptnr. Barnes & Thornburg, Ft. Wayne, 1985-97, of counsel, 1998—; of counsel Barnes & Thornburg, Frankfort, Mich., 1998—, Running, Wise, Ford & Phillips; lectr., writer Ind. Continuing Legal Ednl. Forum. Contbr. articles to profl. jours. Pres. Luth. Assn. Elem. Edn., 1968-69; vice chmn., mem. Ind. Supreme Ct. Commn. on Continuing Legal Edn., sec.; bd. dirs. Big Bros., Ft. Wayne, Jr. Achievement, Ft. Wayne, United Way Allen County; pres. Concordia Ednl. Found., Greater Ft. Wayne C. of C. Found., Martin Fischer Meml. Found.; chmn. bd. visitors Ind. U. Sch. Law, Bloomington, 1984-85, mem. 1979-94; vice chmn. United Way of Allen County Campaign, 1990-92, chmn., 1992-93, dir., 1992—; trustee Boys and Girls Club Ft. Wayne; sec. Willoughby Rotary Found., 1999. With USMC, 1950-52. Decorated UN medal, Korean Svc. medal with star; recipient Christus Magister award Luth. Edn. Assn., 1971; named Grad. of Yr., Concordia Alumni Assn., 1993. Fellow Am. Bar Found., Am. Coll. Trust and Estate Counsel, Am. Coll. Tax Counsel, Ind. Bar Found.; mem. ABA (rep. Nat. Conf. Lawyers and CPAs 1980-86), nominating com., ho. dels. credentials com., Ind. del. 1985-94, chmn. ho. dels. mem. com., standing com. on bar svc., coordinating com. on outreach, med. profl. liability com., com. on pub. understanding about law, vice-chmn. com. on state and local bars-sr. lawyers divsn., marital deduction com. taxation sect.), Ind. Bar Assn. (pres. 1979-80, del. ABA 1979-94), State Bar Mich. (coun. Sr. Lawyers 1998—), Allen County Bar Assn. (dir. coun.), Lawyer-Pilot Bar Assn., Allen County Bar Found. (former bd. dirs., sec.), TerraLex (former co-vice chmn. N.Am., dir. 1993-96), Am. Judicature Soc., Ind. Continuing Legal Edn. Forum (pres. 1978-79), Ind. Bar Found. (dir.), Nat. Conf. Bar Pres. (exec. coun. 1983-86), Arcadia Lions Club (bd. dirs.), Rotary Club, Am. Legion, Korean War Vets. Assn., VFW. Republican. Lutheran. Home: 17726 N Ridgewood PO Box 6 Arcadia MI 49613-0006 Office: PO Box 272 Frankfort MI 49635-0272

GERBERDING, WILLIAM PASSAVANT, retired university president; b. Fargo, N.D., Sept. 9, 1929; s. William Passavant and Esther Elizabeth Ann (Habighorst) G.; m. Ruth Alice Albrecht, Mar. 25, 1952; children: David Michael, Steven Henry, Elizabeth Ann, John Martin. B.A., Macalester Coll., 1951; M.A., U. Chgo., 1956, Ph.D., 1959. Congl. fellow Am. Polit. Sci. Assn., Washington, 1958-59; instr. Colgate U., Hamilton, N.Y., 1959-60; research asst. Senator E.J. McCarthy, Washington, 1960-61; staff Rep. Frank Thompson, Jr., Washington, 1961; faculty UCLA, 1961-72, prof., chmn. dept. polit. sci., 1970-72; dean faculty, v.p. for acad. affairs Occidental Coll., Los Angeles, 1972-75; exec. vice chancellor UCLA, 1975-77; chancellor U. Ill., Urbana-Champaign, 1978-79; pres. U. Wash., Seattle, 1979-95; bd. dirs. Wash. Mut. Bank, Safeco Corp., Seattle; cons. Dept. Def., 1962, Calif. Assembly, 1965. Author: United States Foreign Policy: Perspectives and Analysis, 1966; co-editor, contbg. author: The Radical Left: The Abuse of Discontent, 1970. Trustee Macalester Coll., 1980-83, 96—. With USN, 1951-55. Recipient Distinguished Teaching award U. Calif., Los Angeles, 1966; Ford Found. grantee, 1967-68. Office: Univ Wash Box 351380 Seattle WA 98195-1380

GERBERG, JUDITH LEVINE, human resource company executive; b. N.Y.C., Mar. 21, 1940; d. Murray Joseph and Pearl (Berens) Levine; m. Mort Gerberg, Feb. 1, 1969; 1 child, Lilia Anya Berens. BA in Comparative Lit., Columbia U., 1963, postgrad. in organizational devel., 1989; MA in Psychology and Art, NYU, 1970. Registered art therapist; cert. clin. mental health counselor; nat. cert. counselor. Program dir. Women's Selling Game, N.Y.C., 1979-84; mem. faculty Parsons Sch. Design, N.Y.C., 1979-85; pres. Judith Gerberg Assocs., N.Y.C., 1984—; orgnl. devel. mgmt., leadership devel., valuing diversity, team bldg., comm. skills, stress mgmt.; founder Powerhouse, 1st outplacement for creative profls.; mem. N.Y. steering com. Women's Study in Religion Program Harvard Div. Sch. Co-author: The New York Women's Directory, 1973; contbr. articles and book revs. to various publs. Chmn. pub. rels. Profl. Women's Caucus, 1972; facilitator N.Y.C. Contr.'s Women's Econ. Task Force, 1994-95; mem. Harvard Divinity Sch.: Women in Religion Leadership Conf. N.Y. State scholar. Mem. Am. Art Therapy Assn. (life, bd. dirs. 1980-84), N.Y. Art Therapy Assn. (founding v.p. 1975), The Forum at Stephen Wise (co-chmn. 1986-87), Fin. Women's Assn., Women's Venture Fund. Fax: 212-315-2324. E-mail: jlgerberg@aol.com. Home: 35 W 82nd St New York NY 10024-5607 Office: 250 W 57th St Ste 1019 New York NY 10107-1019

GERBERICH, WILLIAM WARREN, engineering educator; b. Wooster, Ohio, Dec. 30, 1935; s. Harold Robert and Clarissa Thelma (Ross) G.; m. Susan Elizabeth Goodwin, Aug. 15, 1959; children—Bradley Kent, Brian Keith, Beth Clarice. BS in Engring. Adminstrn, Case Inst. Tech., 1957; MS in Indsl. Engring, Syracuse U., 1959; PhD in Materials Sci. and Engring, U. Calif., Berkeley, 1971. Registered profl. engr. Calif. Research engr. Jet Propulsion Lab., Calif. Inst. Tech., Pasadena, Calif., 1959-61; research scientist Aeronutronic, Newport Beach, Calif., 1961-64; engring. research specialist Aerojet Gen., Sacramento, 1964-67; lectr. U. Calif., Berkeley, 1967-71; dir. materials sci. U. Minn., Mpls., 1972—; assoc. prof., dept. chem. engring. and materials sci. U. Minn., 1971-75, prof., 1975—, assoc. head dept., 1980—; cons. material rev. bd. Argonne Nat. Labs., steel, med. products and aerospace cos.; chmn. bd. Inst. Mechanics and Materials U. Calif., San Diego, 1994—. Chmn. bd. Acta Metallurgica publs., 1986-89; co-editor 6 books; contbr. articles to tech. jours. Recipient Teleen English prize Case Inst. Tech., 1959, William Spraragen award Welding Jour., 1968, Outstanding Paper award Acta Met. Jour., 1994. Fellow Am. Soc. Metals; mem. AIME, Materials Rsch. Soc., Sigma Xi, Tau Beta Pi, Pi Delta Epsilon, Phi Delta Theta. Home: 21035 Radisson Inn Rd Christmas Lk Shorewood MN 55331 Office: U Minn Chem Engring Materials Minneapolis MN 55455

GERBIE, ALBERT BERNARD, obstetrician, gynecologist, educator; b. Toledo, Nov. 20, 1927; s. Louis and Fay (Green) G.; m. Barbara Hirsch, June 29, 1952; children: Gail Diane, Stephen Ralph. MD, George Washington U., 1951. Intern Michael Reese Hosp., Chgo., 1951-52; preceptorship in Ob-Gyn under Drs. R.A. Reis, J.L. Baer, E.J. DeCosta, Chgo., 1952-55; practice medicine specializing in Ob-Gyn Chgo., 1955—; mem. faculty Northwestern U. Med. Sch., Chgo., 1952—; prof. Ob-Gyn Northwestern U. Med. Sch., 1972—, dir. continuing grad. edn., 1975—; mem. staff Northwestern Meml. Hosp., 1955—; chief divsn. ob-gyn. Children's Meml. Hosp.; v.p., dir. Am. Bd. Ob-Gyn, 1976—, chmn. 1988—, pres. 1990, historian, 1998; chmn. liaison com. for ob-gyn., 1989. Author textbooks; assoc. editor Surgery, Gynecology, and Obstetrics, Am. Jour. Ob-Gyn.; editor ACOG Current Jour. Rev.; contbr. chpts. to books, articles to profl. jours. Served with U.S. Army, 1946-47. Mem. ACS (bd. govs.), ACOG (chmn. learning resources commn.), AMA, Am. Gynecol. Soc., Am. Assn. Obstetricians and Gynecologists, Am. Gynecol. and Obstet. Soc., Am. Coll. Sports Medicine, Ctrl. Assn. Ob-Gyn, Soc. Human Genetics, Southwestern Ob-Gyn. Soc., Chgo. Gynecol. Assn. (pres. 1977-78). Office: 707 N Fairbanks Ct Ste 500 Chicago IL 60611-4814

GERBIE, S. RALPH, real estate executive, property investor; b. Chicago, Ill., Sept. 13, 1959; s. Albert Bernard and Barbara (Hirsch) G.; m. Jody Lynn Newman, Nov. 30, 1986; children: David, Danielle, Kevin. BA Econs., U. Colorado, Boulder, 1981; MBA, U. Michigan, Ann Arbor, 1984. Lic. real estate broker (various states). Dir. rsch. and fin. svcs. Equis Corp., Chicago, 1984-86, v.p. natl. accts., sr. v.p., 1990—; chmn., founder HomeSpace Properties, LLC, Oak Park, Ill., 1988—; bd. mem. Gottlieb Meml. Hosp., Melrose Park, Ill., 1997; cons. The Art Inst. of Chicago, 1992—, Watson Wyatt Worldwide, ITT Corp., The Prudential Ins. Co., AT&T Corp., others. Author several articles. Chmn. Zoning Bd. of Appeals, Oak Park, Ill., 1996-01; mem. Oak Park Regional Housing Ctr., The Frank Lloyd Wright Conservancy. Recipient Historic Preservation award Village of Oak Park, Pryor Entrepreneurial award U. Mich., GM Case Competition award. Mem. Nat. Trust Historic Preservation, Internat. Devel. Rsch. Coun., Bldg. Owners and Mgrs. Assn., Omicron Delta Epsilon. Office: Equis Corp 161 N Clark St Ste 2700 Chicago IL 60601-3241

GERBINO, JOHN, advertising executive; b. N.Y.C., Mar. 28, 1941; s. John and Pauline (Valenti) G.; m. JoAnna LoPresti, Jan. 20, 1962 (div.); 1 son, John Paul; m. E. Randall McConahy, Aug. 14, 1976; 1 son, Christopher Laughlin. Student, N.Y. Community Coll., 1959; student design, Sch. Visual Arts, 1963-66. Designer Lashe and Driscoll Studio, N.Y.C., 1959-61, Dell Pub. Co., N.Y.C., 1961-64; asst. art dir. Harper's Bazaar mag., 1964-66; art dir. New York mag. and Book Week mag. of World Jour. Tribune Co., 1966-67; asst. to editorial dir. Condé Nast Publs., 1967-69; art dir., designer U.S. Mag.; art dir. Essence Mag., 1969, New Woman Mag., 1969-72; formed John Nicholas Gerbino Advt., Inc., Ft. Lauderdale, Fla., 1973—; v.p. graphics EDSA, Ft. Lauderdale, 1998—; bd. govs. Nova U. Sch. Oceanography, Nat. Safety Coun., Broward chpt. Designed, illustrated: 1st edit. Nixon Poems; freelance book jacket designer 1st edit. Mem. N.Y. N.G., 1966-70. Home: 901 SE 11th St Deerfield Beach FL 33441-7016 Office: EDSA 1512 E Broward Blvd Ste 110 Fort Lauderdale FL 33301-2126*

GERBINO, PHILIP PAUL, university president, consultant; b. Jersey City, N.J., Mar. 11, 1947; s. Anthony Milton and Marie Patricia (Ribaudo) G.; m. Michele Cynthia Pierson, Aug. 6, 1982; children: Ryan; wards: Kevin Howard, Stephan Howard. BS, Phila. Col. Pharmacy and Sci., 1969, D in Pharmacy, 1970. Registered pharmacist, N.J., Penn., N.Y. Prof. Phila. Col. Pharmacy and Sci., 1975-95, dir. pharmacy edn., 1983-87, exec. dir. geriatric inst., 1987-92, v.p. profl. progs., 1990-92, v.p. acad. affairs, 1992-94, dean sch. pharmacy, 1993-94, pres., 1995—; cons. pharmaceutical industry, 1980. Contbr. articles to profl. jours. Dep. mayor West Windsor Twp., Princeton, N.J., 1979; twp. com., West Windsor Twp., 1979-81; bd. health, West Windsor Twp., 1975-79; dist. chmn. BSA, Phila., 1995-98. Civilian cons. to USAF, 1994-95. Recipient George Archambault award Am. Soc. Cons. Pharmacists, Washington, 1986. Mem. Acad. Pharmacy Practice (pres. 1990-91), Am. Soc. Cons. Pharmacists, Am. Pharmacists Assn., Col. Physicians Phila., Union League Phila. Republican. Roman Catholic. Avocations: golf, travel, classics, theater. Office: U of the Sciences in Philadelphia 600 S 43rd St Philadelphia PA 19104-4418

GERBNER, GEORGE, communications educator, university dean emeritus; b. Budapest, Hungary, Aug. 8, 1919; came to U.S., 1939, naturalized, 1944; s. Arpad and Margaret (Muranyi) G.; m. Ilona Kutas, Oct. 8, 1946; children: John C., Thomas J. Student, U. Budapest, 1937-38, UCLA, 1940-41; BA, U. Calif.-Berkeley, 1943; MS, U. So. Calif., 1951, PhD, 1955; LHD (hon.), LaSalle Coll., Phila., 1980, Emerson Coll., 1989, Worcester State Coll., 1992. Reporter, asst. fin. editor The Chronicle, San Francisco, 1942-43; engaged in free-lance publicity, 1947-48; instr. Pasadena (Calif.) Jr. Coll., 1948-51, El Camino Coll., Los Angeles, 1951-56; asst. prof., then asso. prof. U. Ill., Urbana, 1956-64; prof. communications Annenberg Sch. Communications, U. Pa., 1964—, dean, 1964-89, dean emeritus, 1989—; Bell Atlantic Prof. of Telecomms. Temple U., Phila.; founder, dir. Cultural Indicators Project, 1968—; founder, pres. Cultural Environment Movement, 1993—; vis. prof. Temple U., Phila., 1997—, U. Budapest, 1993, Salesian U., Rome, 1992; Disting. vis. prof. Am. U., Washington, 1995, 96; vis. lectr. U. Athens, 1996, Am. U., 1995-96, Temple U., 1997. Author numerous articles and books in field.; editor Jour. of Communication, 1974-91; chmn. editorial bd. Internat. Ency. of Communications. 1st lt. inf., AUS, 1943-46, ETO. Decorated Bronze Star; grantee U.S. Office Edn., 1959, NSF, 1962, 80, 83, NIMH, 1958, 71-82, Internat. Sociol. Assn., 1963, UNESCO, 1963, 83, 85, Nat. Commn. Causes and Prevention Violence, 1969, Surgeon Gen.'s Sci. Adv. Com., 1970, White House Office Telecomm. Policy, 1977, U.S. Adminstrn. on Aging, 1978, AMA, 1979, Com. on Religious Rsch., 1983, Nat. Inst. Drug Abuse, 1985-86, W. Alton Jones Found., 1987-88, Hoso Bunka (Japan) Found., 1990-91, U.S. Commn. on Civil Rights, 1991, Nat. Cable TV Assn., 1992, SAG, AFTRA, 1992-93, Turner Broadcasting Sys., 1993, AARP, 1994, Ark. Trust, 1994, Ctr. for Substance Abuse Prevention, 1994, Robert Wood Johnson Found., 1995-97, Sloan Found., 1997; recipient Excellence in Media award Internat. TV Assn., 1992. Fellow Internat. Communication Assn.; mem. Am. Sociol. Assn., Internat. Assn. Mass Communication Research (hon. life), Assn. Edn. Journalism (Paul J. Deutschman award for excellence in rsch. 1996). Home: 234 Golfview Rd Ardmore PA 19003-1002 *Here's to the success of our hopeless endeavor.*

GERBRACHT, ROBERT THOMAS (BOB GERBRACHT), painter, educator; b. Erie, Pa., June 23, 1924; s. Earl John and Lula Mary (Chapman) G.; m. Delia Marie Paz, Nov. 27, 1952; children: Mark, Elizabeth, Catherine. BFA, Yale U., 1951; MFA, U. So. Calif., 1952. Cert. tchr., Calif. Art tchr. William S. Hart Jr. and Sr. High Sch., Newhall, Calif., 1954-56; stained glass artist Cummings Studios, San Francisco, 1956-58; art tchr. McKinley Jr. High Sch., Redwood City, Calif., 1958-60, Castro Jr. High Sch., San Jose, Calif., 1960-79; portrait artist, tchr. San Jose, San Francisco, 1979—; instr. art Coll. of Notre Dame, Belmont, Calif., 1955-60, San Jose City Coll., 1967-71, Notre Dame Novitiate, Saratoga, 1976-79, U. Calif., Santa Cruz, 1980-81; art cons. Moreland Sch. Dist., Campbell, Calif., 1979-80; instr. nationwide workshops, Calif., Colo., Fla., Kans., Mass., Nebr., N.Mex., N.Y., Oreg., S.C., Vt., Wash., Wis., Mex., 1980—. Exhibited in Charles and Emma Frye Mus. Fine Art, Seattle, Rosicrucia Mus., San Jose, Calif., San Jose Mus. of Art, Denver Art Mus., Erie Mus. Art, Triton Mus. of Art, Santa Clara, Calif., Israel, Austria, China; represented in permanent collection Triton Mus. Art, Santa Clara, Calif.; portraits include Marie Gallo, Mrs. Bruce Jenner, Austin Warburton, Rev. Jack La Rocca, Rev. Cecil Williams; subject of articles in Today's Art and Graphics, Art and Antique Collector, Am. Artist, U.S. ART; work reproduced and included in Best of Pastel, Best of Oil Painting, 1996, Postal Highlights, 1996, Portrait Inspirations, The Best of Portrait Painting, 1997, Best of Pastel 2, 1998. Cpl. U.S. Army, 1943-46. Recipient Am. Artist Achievement award Tchr. of Pastels, 1993. Mem. Pastel Soc. Am. (master pastellist), Pastel Soc. West Coast (advisor, Best of Show 1988), Soc. Western Artists (trustee 1989-97, Best of Show 1982, 85, 90, Best Portrait award 1984, Best of Show Nat. Open Exhbn. 1999), Oil Painters Am. Home: 1301 Blue Oak Ct Pinole CA 94564-2145

GERDE, CARLYLE NOYES (CY GERDE), lawyer; b. Long Beach, Calif., Oct. 22, 1946; m. Priscilla A. Murphy, July 4, 1976. BA in Am. Studies, Purdue U., 1967; JD, Ind. U., 1970. Bar: Ind. 1971, U.S. Supreme Ct. 1976, U.S. Tax Ct. 1980. Ptnr. Hanna & Gerde, Lafayette, Ind., 1972-86; registered lobbyist Ind. Twp. Assn., 1975-86; spl. counsel Nat. Assn. Towns and Twps., Washington, 1976-86; adj. prof. indsl. engring. Purdue U., 1972-96; participant White House Conf. Rural Policy, 1978, White House Conf. on Block Grants, 1981, White House Conf. on Liability Ins., 1986; mem. Ind. Gen. Assembly Study Commn. Bd. of govs. Tippecanoe County Hist. Assn., Lafayette, 1976—, Ams. for Nuclear Energy, Washington (co-founder, v.p. 1977—); pres. Battle Ground (Ind.) Hist. Corp., 1986; del. State of Ind. GOP Conventions. Mem. Ind. State Bar Assn., Tippecanoe County Bar Assn., Assn. Trial Lawyers Am., Nat. Assn. Town and Twp. Attys. (co-founder, v.p. 1985-88), Am. Agrl. Lawyers Assn., Lafayette Country Club, Skyline Club, Columbia Club. Office: Hanna & Gerde PO Box 1098 Lafayette IN 47902-1098

GERDEMANN, JAMES WESSEL, plant pathologist, educator; b. Warrenton, Mo., Nov. 13, 1921; s. Carl Edward and Cora Wilhelmina (Wessel) G.; m. Janice Mae Olbrich, July 2, 1949; children—Stephen, Dale, Glenn. B.A., U. Mo., 1945, M.A., 1946; Ph.D., U. Calif., Berkeley, 1948. Teaching asst. U. Mo., Columbia, 1945-46; research asst. U. Calif., Berkeley, 1946-48; prof. plant pathology U. Ill., Urbana, 1948-81; prof. emeritus U. Ill., 1981—. Author: Taxonomy of the Endogonaceae, 1974; condr. research in field; contbr. writings to publs. Recipient Ruth Allen award, 1977, Funk award, 1977, excellence in undergrad. teaching award U. Ill., 1976. Fellow Am. Phytopathol. Soc.; mem. Am. Mycol. Soc. Home: PO Box 391 Yachats OR 97498-0391

GERDES, MICHELLE ANN, designer; b. Trenton, N.J., Sept. 23, 1961; d. Paul and Kathryn (Sinchock) Kaniuka; m. Christopher John Gerdes, Apr. 5, 1986; children: Andrew Paul, Alexander Robert. BA magna cum laude, Kean Coll. N.J., 1983. Asst. art dir. Medecommunications (div. Med. Econs. Co.), Oradell, N.J., 1983-84; sr. designer mag. Med. Econs. Co., Oradell, 1984-85, asst. art dir. mag., 1985-86; asst. art dir. Butterfly Originals, Mt. Laurel, N.J., 1986-87; design coord. J.B. Lippincott Co., Phila., 1987-88; asst. art dir. TV Guide, Radnor, Pa., 1988-91; freelance art dir. Sewell, N.J., 1991-92; advt. designer Current Science, Phila., 1992-95; freelance art director, designer Norristown, Pa., 1995-96; asst. art dir. Lapidary Jour. Primedia, Inc., Devon, Pa., 1996—. Recipient Cert. of Excellence award Art Dirs. Club of N.J., 1986, Merit award, 1987. Roman Catholic. Avocations: travel, photography, crafts, exercise training. Home and Office: 2816 Breckenridge Blvd Norristown PA 19403-1200

GERDES, NEIL WAYNE, library director; b. Moline, Ill., Oct. 19, 1943; s. John Edward and Della Marie (Ferguson) G. AB, U. Ill., 1965; BD, Harvard U., 1968; MA, Columbia U., 1971; MA in Libr. Sci., U. Chgo., 1975; DMin, U. St. Mary of the Lake, 1994. Ordained to ministry Unitarian Universalist Assn., 1975. Copy chief Little, Brown, 1968-69; instr. Tuskegee Inst., 1969-71; libr. asst. Augustana Coll., 1972-73; editl. asst. Library Quar., 1973-74; libr., prof. Meadville Theol. Sch., Chgo., 1973—; libr. program dir. Chgo. Cluster Theol. Schs., 1977-80; dir. Hammond Libr., 1980—; prof. Chgo. Theol Sem., 1980—. Mem. exec. bd. Sem. Coop. Bookstore, Chgo., 1982—, Ctr. for Religion and Psychotherapy, Chgo., 1984-97, Ind. Voters of Ill., 1986-89, Hyde Park-Kenwood Cmty. Orgn., Chgo., 1988-89; pres. Hyde Park-Kenwood Interfaith Coun., 1986-90; chair libr. coun. Assn. Chgo. Theol. Sch., 1984-88, 96-98; trustee Civitas Dei Found., 1994—. Mem. ALA, Am. Theol. Library Assn., Chgo. Area Theol. Library Assn., Unitarian Universalist Mins. Assn. (sec., treas. nat. body 1990-94), Assn. Liberal Religious Scholars (sec., treas. 1975—), Phi Beta Kappa. Office: Chgo Theol Sem Hammond Libr 5757 S University Ave Chicago IL 60637-1507

GERDES, RALPH DONALD, fire safety consultant; b. Cin., Aug. 11, 1951; s. Paul Donald and Jo Ann Dorothy (Meyer) G. BArch, Ill. Inst. Tech., 1975. Registered architect, Ill. Architect Schiller & Frank, Wheeling, Ill., 1976; sr. assoc. Rolf Jensen & Assocs., Inc., Chgo., 1976-84; pres. Ralph Gerdes & Assocs., Inc., Indpls., 1984-88, chmn., 1988—; gen. mgr. Ralph Gerdes Cons., LLC; lectr. Purdue U., Ind. U., Ill. Inst. Tech., Butler U., Ball State U.; bd. dirs. Ind. Fire Svcs. Inst. Co-author: Planning and Designing the Office Environment, 1981. Recipient Joel Polsky prize Am. Soc. Interior Designers, 1983. Mem. ASHRAE, AIA (bldg. performance and regulations com. liaison to Nat. Fire Protection Agy., liaison to Internat. Code Coun.), Soc. Fire Protection Engring. (assoc., exec. com. Ind. chpt. 1992—, pres. 1995-96), Nat. Fire Protection Assn. (tech. coms.), Bldg. Ofcls. and Code Adminstrs., Internat. Conf. Bldg. Ofcls., Ind. Fire Safety Assn. (bd. dirs. 1986-92, 94-95, pres. 1989-91), Archs. and Engrs. Bldg. Ofcls. (bd. dirs. 1994—, Ind. code devel. com.), Maple Creek Country Club. Roman Catholic. Home: 556 Lockerbie Cir N Indianapolis IN 46202-3600 Office: 127 E Michigan St Ste 400 Indianapolis IN 46204-1518

GERDINE, LEIGH, retired academic administrator; b. Sheyenne, N.D., June 22, 1917; s. O. E. and Margaret E. (Mattson) G.; m. Alice Strauch Meyer, Nov. 21, 1961. AB, U. N.D., 1938, MusD (hon.), 1989; MusB (Rhodes scholar), Oxford (Eng.) U., 1941, postgrad., 1946-48; PhD, U. Iowa, 1941; HHD (hon.), Washington U., St. Louis, 1979; LHD (hon.), Tarkio Coll., 1984, Webster U., 1990; HHD (hon.), U. N.D., 1990. Asst. prof. music Miss. State Coll. for Women, Columbus, 1941-42; assoc. prof., exec. sec. dept. music Miami (Ohio) U., 1948-50; prof., chmn. dept. music Washington U., St. Louis, 1950-70; pres. Webster U., St. Louis, 1970-90, pres. emeritus, 1990—; chmn. bd. dirs. Block Partnership, Inc., 1968-70; program annotator St. Louis Symphony Orch., 1950-66, acting mgr., 1965-67; trustee Gateway Found., 1993—. Translator: Phrasing and Articulation (by Hermann Keller), 1965, The Well-Tempered Clavier (by Hermann Keller), 1976, New Music with Thirty-One Notes (by Adriaan Fokker), 1975; pub. orchestrations Brahms sonatas, realizations of Handel violin sonatas, Bach flute sonatas; original works: Violin Concerto, 1996, (opera) Serafina, 1998. Bd. dirs. St. Louis Symphony Soc., Opera Theatre St. Louis; chmn. emeritus bd. Sheldon Arts Found. With USAAF, 1942-46, ETO. Decorated Bronze Star medal, Croix de Guerre France, Nat. Medal of Arts, 1989; recipient St. Louis award, 1989, Right Arm of St. Louis award Regional Commerce and Growth Assn., 1989; hon. fellow Lincoln Coll., Oxford U., 1991. Home: 801 S Skinker Blvd Apt 14B Saint Louis MO 63105-3265 Office: Ste 211 7750 Clayton Rd Saint Louis MO 63117-1353

GERDTS, WILLIAM HENRY, art history educator; b. Jersey City, N.J., Jan. 18, 1929; s. William Henry and Suzanne (Zanowick) G.; m. Elaine Evans, Apr. 4, 1953 (div. 1962); 1 child, Jeffrey Evans Dee; m. Abigail Booth, July 23, 1976. BA, Amherst Coll., 1949; MA, Harvard U., 1950, PhD, 1966; LHD (hon.), Amherst Coll., 1992; DFA (hon.), Syracuse U., 1996. Resident dir. Hist. Myers House, curator Norfolk (Va.) Mus., 1953-54; curator paintings and sculpture Newark (N.J.) Mus., 1954-66; prof. art history U. Md., College Park, 1966-69; v.p. Coe Kerr Gallery, N.Y.C., 1969-71; prof. art history CUNY, 1971-99, prof. emeritus, 1999—, acting exec. officer art history PhD program, 1977-79, exec. officer, 1979-85; vis. lectr. Johns Hopkins U., Balt., 1969-71; adj. prof. Rutgers U., New Brunswick, N.J., 1975, Washington U., St. Louis, 1977; mem. adv. bd. Archives Am. Art, Smithsonian Instn., N.Y.C., 1981—. Author: American Still-Life Painting, 1971, American Neo-Classic Sculpture: The Marble Resurrection, 1973, The Great American Nude: A History in Art, 1974, A Man of Genius: The Art of Washington Allston, 1979, Masters of the Humble Truth: Masterpieces of American Still Life, 1801-1930, 1981, American Impressionism, 1984, The Art of Henry Inman, 1987; (with James L. Yarnall) The National Museum of American Art's Index to American Art Exhibition Catalogues From the Beginning through the 1876 Centennial Year, 6 vols., 1986, Art Across America: Regional Painting in America through 1920, 3 vols., 1990, numerous others. Summer rsch. grantee U. Md., 1968, Mellon Found., 1974; Guggenheim Found. fellow, 1980, Am. Philos. Soc. fellow, 1980. Office: CUNY Grad Ctr 33 W 42nd St New York NY 10036-8099

GERE, JAMES MONROE, civil engineering educator; b. Syracuse, N.Y., June 14, 1925; s. William S. and Carol (Hixson) G.; m. Janice M. Platt, June 1, 1946; children—Susan M., William P., David S. B.S., Rensselaer Poly. Inst., 1949, M.S., 1951; Ph.D., Stanford, 1954. Registered profl. engr., Calif., N.Y. Instr. Rensselaer Poly. Inst., 1949-51; faculty Stanford, 1954—; prof. civil engring., 1962—; assoc. dean Sch. Engring., 1960-67, exec. head dept. civil engring., 1967-72; cons. and lectr. in field, 1954—. Author 7 textbooks in field, also tech. papers. Served with USAAF, 1943-46, ETO. Fellow ASCE; mem. Am. Soc. Engring. Edn., Earthquake Engring. Research Inst., Sigma Xi, Tau Beta Pi. Home: 932 Valdez Pl Stanford CA 94305-1076

GERE, RICHARD, actor; b. Phila., Aug. 31, 1949; m. Cindy Crawford, 1991 (div.). Attended, U. Mass. Played trumpet, piano, guitar and bass and composed music with various musical groups. acting appearances with Provincetown Playhouse in Great God Brown, Camino Real, Rosencrantz and Guildenstern are Dead; off-Broadway prodn. Killer's Head, Richard Farina: Long Time Coming and Long Time Gone, Back Bog Beast Bait; in Broadway prodn. Taming of the Shrew; London and Broadway prodns. Midsummer Night's Dream; Broadway prodns. Habeas Corpus, Bent; on Broadway Soon, Grease; appeared in and composed music for Volpone at Seattle Repertory Theatre; film debut in Report to the Commissioner, 1975; other films include Baby Blue Marine, 1976, Looking for Mr. Goodbar, 1977, Days of Heaven, 1978, Blood Brothers, 1978, Yanks, 1979, American Gigolo, 1980, An Officer and a Gentleman, 1982, Breathless, 1983, Beyond the Limit, 1983, The Cotton Club, 1984, King David, 1985, Power, 1986, No Mercy, 1986, Miles from Home, 1988, Internal Affairs, 1990, Pretty Woman, 1990, Rhapsody in August, 1991, Final Analysis, (also exec. prodr.) 1992, Sommersby, 1993, Mr. Jones, 1993, Intersection, 1994, First Knight, 1995, Primal Fear, 1996, Untitled, 1995, The Jackal, 1997, Red Corner, 1997, An Alan Smithee Film: Burn Hollywood Burn, 1998, Autumn in New York, 1999, Runaway Bride, 1999; TV movie Strike Force, 1975, And the Band Played On, HBO, 1993 (Emmy nomination, Supporting Actor - Special, 1994), AFI's 100 Years...100 Movies, 1998; author: Pilgrim Photo Collection, 1998; exec. prodr. (films) Final Analysis, 1992, Mr. Jones, 1993, Sommersby, 1993; TV guest appearance Kojak, 1973. *

GEREIGHTY, ANDREA SAUNDERS, polling company executive, poet; b. New Orleans, July 20, 1938; d. Andrew Jackson and Jeanne Teresa (Martin) Saunders; m. Dennis Anthony Gereighty Jr., May 19, 1959 (wid.); children: Deni Ann, David Dennis, Peggy T. Cert., Exeter Coll., Oxford, Eng., 1972; BA, U. New Orleans, 1974, MA in English with distinction, 1978. Cotton analyst Anderson-Clayton, Metairie, La., 1956; records retrieval profl. Shell Oil Co., New Orleans, 1956-60; census coord. St. Vincent De Paul Ch., New Orleans, 1960-65; bldg. funds dir. St. Francis Xavier Ch., Metairie, 1965-70; tchr. spl. edn. Deckbar Elem. Sch., Jefferson, La., 1966-70; tchr. secondary edn. Chalmette (La.) H.S., 1971-72; assoc. prof. English dept. U. New Orleans, 1972-73; tchr. secondary edn. Berlin-Am. H.S., 1980-81; owner, founder, CEO New Orleans Field Svcs. Assocs., 1974—; guest speaker Delgado Coll., New Orleans, 1989; guest presenter Rabouin Vo-Tech., New Orleans, 1980; lectr., guest presenter poetry at New Sarpy Sch., 1994, 95; guest presenter St. Mark's Episcopal Ch., Latter Libr., N.O. Pub. Libr., others. Author: Asking Q's, 1980, (poetry books) Illusions and Other Realities, 1974, Restless for Cool Weather, 1990, Season of the Crane, 1994; publ., editor Desire Street, 1997, 98; contbr. to poetry mags. Recipient Coda award Poets and Writers, 1983, Poetry award of honor Nat. League Am. Pen Women, 1973, Deep South Writers, 1984, 88, 90, 92, 94, 2d place award Nuyarikin Poet's Cafe, N.Y.C., Ellipsis Poetry prize, 1983, 85, 87, 90. Mem. Am. Mktg. Assn., Mktg. Rsch. Assn., Nat. Geneal. Soc., Jefferson Geneal. Soc., New Orleans Poetry Forum (dir. 1990—), New Orleans Track Club. Democrat. Roman Catholic. Avocations: writing poetry, jogging, genealogy, dogs, camping. Home: 257 Bonnabel Blvd Metairie LA 70005-3738 Office: New Orleans Field Svcs Rear Office Ste 257 Bonnabel Blvd Metairie LA 70005-3738

GEREN, GERALD S., lawyer; b. Chgo., Nov. 10, 1939; s. Ben and Sara (Block) G.; m. Phyllis Freeman, Feb. 11, 1962; children: Suzanne, Gregory, Bradley. BSMetE, Ill. Inst. Tech., 1961; JD, DePaul U., 1966. Bar: Ill. Supreme Ct. 1966, U.S. Ct. Customs and Patent Appeals 1967, U.S. Patent and Trademark Office 1967, U.S. Dist Ct. (no. dist.) Ill. 1969, U.S. Supreme Ct. 1972, U.S. Ct. Appeals (7th cir.) 1972, U.S. Ct. Appeals (fed. cir.) 1982. Engr. Internat. Harvester, Chgo., 1961-64; atty. Corning Glass Works, Corning, N.Y., 1966-69, Silverman & Cass, Chgo., 1969-70, Siegal & Geren, Chgo., 1970-71, Epton, Mullin & Druth, Chgo., 1971-84; ptnr. Hill, Steadman & Simpson, Chgo., 1984-94, Gerald S. Geren Ltd., Chgo., 1994-96, Lee, Mann, Smith, McWilliams, Sweeney & Ohlson, 1997—. Contbr. articles to Indsl. Rsch. and Devel., Design News mags. Pres. Chgo. High Tech. Assn., 1981-86, v.p., 1986-87; mem. strategic planning com. Econ. Devel. Commn., Chgo., 1986-91; mem. Ill. Ctr. for Indsl. Tech., 1984-90, Ill. Mfg. Tech. Network, Chgo., 1986-91; mem. pres.' coun., rsch. coun., alumni bd. Ill. Inst. Tech., 1991—, The Leukemia Soc. Am. (Ill. chpt. bd. mem. 1988-90). Mem. ABA, Ill. State Bar Assn., Chgo. Bar Assn., Patent Law Assn. Chgo., Am. Intellectual Property Law Assn., Execs. Club, Chgo. Econ. Club, Comml. Club Chgo. (small bus. com. 1985—), Met. Club Chgo. Office: Lee Mann Smith McWilliams Sweeney & Ohlson 209 S La Salle St Ste 410 Chicago IL 60604-1203

GEREN, PETE (PRESTON GEREN), former congressman; b. Ft. Worth, Jan. 29, 1952; m. Beckie Ray; 3 children. Student, Ga. Inst. tech.; BA, U. Tex., 1974, JD, 1978. Atty. pvt. practice, 1978-83; exec. asst. Sen. Lloyd Bentsen, 1983-85; mem. 101st-104th Congresses from Tex. 12th dist., Washington, 1989-96; sr. v.p. Pub. Strategies, Inc., Ft. Worth, 1997-98, atty., 1999—. Office: 500 Throckmorton St Ste 1400 Fort Worth TX 76102-3712

GERETY, PETER LEO, archbishop; b. Shelton, Conn., July 19, 1912; s. Peter Leo and Charlotte (Daly) G. Student, St. Thomas Sem., Bloomfield, Conn., 1934, Seminaire St. Sulpice, Paris, France, 1939. Ordained priest Roman Catholic Ch., 1939; asst. pastor New Haven, 1939-42; dir. Blessed Martin de Porres Interracial Center, 1942-56; pastor New Haven, 1956-66; coadjutor bishop Portland, Maine, 1966—; apostolic administr. Portland, 1967—, bishop, 1969-74; archbishop of Newark, 1974-86; archbishop emeritus, 1986—. Address: St John Vianney Residence 60 Home Ave Rutherford NJ 07070-1760

GERETY, ROBERT JOHN, microbiologist, pharmaceutical company executive, pediatrician, vaccinologist; b. Jersey City, Oct. 16, 1939; s. James Leo and Helen (Beck) G.; m. Joan Imelda Grant, Feb. 3, 1967; children: Andrew, Kathleen, Nancy. BA with spl. honors, Rutgers U., 1962; MA, Stanford U., 1966, PhD, 1971; MD, George Washington U., 1970. Diplomate Nat. Bd. Med. Examiners. Rsch. assoc. dept. med. microbiology Stanford (Calif.) U. Med. Sch., 1969-70; intern in pediatrics Stanford U. Hosp., 1970-71, resident, 1974-75; staff assoc. Lab. Viral Immunology, NIH, Bethesda, Md., 1971-72; staff assoc. Bur. Biologics, FDA, Bethesda, 1972-73, dir. hepatitis br., 1973-84, assoc. dir. medicine and sci., chief infectious diseases br., 1984-85; exec. dir. virus & cell biology Merck Rsch. Labs., West Point, Pa., 1985-89, chief clin. evaluation of vaccines and antiviral drugs, 1985-89; v.p. devel. ops. Biogen, Inc., Cambridge, Mass., 1989-93; v.p. pharm. ops. Immulogic Pharm. Corp., Waltham, Mass., 1993-94, CEO, pres. and dir., 1994-96; v.p. devel. and regulatory affairs ORAVAX, Cambridge, Mass., 1997-99; exec. v.p. corp. devel. Cell Gate Inc., Sunnyvale, Calif., 1999—; adj. prof. medicine Jefferson Med. Sch., Phila., 1985; Plenary lectr. Internat. Symposium on Viral Hepatitis and Liver Disease, London, 1987; mem. U.S. Army Med. R&D Adv. Bd., 1987; mem. AIDS subcom. Nat. Inst. Allergy and Infectious Diseases, 1988; mem. Nat. Vaccine Adv. Com., 1990-92, sci. bd. Oravax, Cambridge, Mass., 1991-94, numerous others; participant confs., symposia and workshops. Editor: Non-A, Non-B Hepatitis, 1981, Hepatitis A, 1984, Hepatitis B, 1985; mem. editl. bd. Biols., 1990-94; contbr. over 200 articles to sci. jours. Med. dir. USPHS, 1970-85. Recipient commendation medal USPHS, 1975, Outstanding Svc. medal, 1982, Disting. Svc. medal, 1985; Patriotic Svc. award U.S. Dept. Treasury, 1983; Henry Rutgers fellow USPHS, 1961-62, fellow NIH, 1962-65, Calif. Tb and Health Assn., 1964-67, U.S. Health Professions scholar and microbiology fellow, 1966-70. Fellow Infectious Disease Soc. Am.; mem. AMA, Am. Soc. for Microbiology, Am. Acad. Pediatrics, Am. Assn. Immunologists, William Beaumont Soc., Henry Rutgers Soc., Internat. assn. for Biol. Standards, Internat. Soc. Interferon Rsch. Achievements include development and/or approval of vaccines against Hepatitis A and Hepatitis B, pediatric vaccines including Hemophilus Influenza B and pneumococcal infections, and Biogen's beta interferon product to treat multiple sclerosis (Avonex); patents for Inactivation of Non-A, Non-B Hepatitis Agent; Hepatitis B Immune Globulin used to Inactivate Hepatitis B Virus in Injectable Biological Products; Detection of Non-A, Non-B Hepatitis Associated Antigen; Heat Treatment of a Non-A, Non-B Hepatitis Agent to Prepare a Vaccine; Hepatitis B Core Antigen Vaccine; Hepatitis B Core Antigen Vaccine Made by Recombinant DNA; Purified Antigen from Non-A, Non-B Hepatitis Causing Factor: Screening Test for Reverse Transcriptase Containing Virus. Home: 103 Livingston Rd Wellesley MA 02482-7308

GERETY, TOM, college administrator, educator; b. N.Y.C., July 22, 1946; m. Adelia Moore, Oct. 7, 1972; children: Finn, Carrick, Amias, Rowan. BA, Yale U., 1969, MPhil, 1974, JD, 1976, PhD, 1976; LLD (hon.), Williams Coll., 1995. Tchr. Peru project Joint Ctr. Urban Studies Harvard-MIT, Lima, 1966-67; bilingual tchr. Boston Pub. Schs., 1970-71; assoc. lectr. philosophy, master's asst. Morse Coll. Yale U., New Haven, 1972-74; asst. prof., fellow Ctr. Profl. Ethics Chgo. Kent Coll. Law, Ill. Inst. Tech., 1976-78; prof. law U. Pitts., 1978-86; dean, Nippert prof. Coll. Law U. Cin., 1986-89; pres., prof. philosophy Trinity Coll., Hartford, Conn., 1989-94; pres. Amherst (Mass.) Coll., 1994—; vis. asst. prof. Ind. U. Sch. Law, Bloomington, 1977-78; vis. prof. constl. law and jurisprudence Stanford U. Sch. Law, 1983-84; occasional appellate litigation in constl. law ACLU, 1981—; nominator MacArthur Found., 1985-86; mem. com. on profl. practices and ethics Assn. Am. Law Schs., 1988-89; chair New Eng. Small Coll. Athletic Conf., 1991-92, 1998-99; chair bd. dirs. Consortium on Financing Higher Edn., 1993—, pres., 1993-95; testimony before the Senate Judiciary Com., Subcom. on Constitution on various proposed amendments. Law corr. KDKA-TV, Pitts., 1980-83; writer, cons., on-air corr., fundraiser Visions of the Constitution, Nat. Endowment for Humanities TV series in constl. law, 1985-88; host A Conn. Town Meeting, Conn. Pub. TV series, 1993-94; commentaries in various media Washington Post, Boston Globe, Chgo. Tribune, Christian Sci. Monitor, L.A. Times, MacNeil Lehrer Report, Nat. Pub. Radio; contgr. articles to profl jours. Bd. mem., chair administrv. com., exec. com. mem. Internat. Rescue Com., 1989—; chair City of Hartford Ethics Task Force, 1990-91; bd. mem. Conn. State Bd. Edn., 1992-94. Kent fellow Danforth Found., 1972-76; fellow Soc. for Profl. and Legal

Philosophy, 1980—;, Woodrow Wilson fellow, 1983. Office: Amherst Coll PO Box 2208 103 Converse Hall Amherst MA 01002-5000

GERGIANNAKIS, ANTHONY EMMANUEL See ANTHONY, METROPOLITAN, OF SOUROZH

GERGIS, SAMIR DANIAL, anesthesiologist, educator; b. Beni-Suef, Egypt, Sept. 24, 1933; came to U.S., 1968; s. Danial and Hekmat (Assaad) G.; m. Dorothy K. Auen, June 16, 1973 (div. 1983); 1 child, Michael. M.B., Ch. B., Cairo U., 1954, D.A., 1957, D.M., 1958, M.D. in Anesthesia (Ph.D.), 1962; D.A., U. Copenhagen, 1963. Intern Cairo U. Hosp., 1955-56, resident, 1957-59; instr. dept. anesthesia U. Iowa Coll. Medicine, Iowa City, 1968-69, asst. prof., 1969-72, assoc. prof., 1972-76, prof., 1976—. Fellow Am. Coll. Anesthesiology; mem. AAAS, Am. Soc. Anesthesiologists, Internat. Anesthesia Rsch. Soc., N.Y. Acad. Scis., Am. Soc. Pharmacology and Exptl. Therapeutics, Soc. Exptl. Biology and Medicine, Nat. Soc. Med. Rsch., Soc. for Neurosurgery, Anesthesia and Neurologic Supportive Care Assn., Assn. Anesthesia Clin. Dirs., Am. Soc. Clin. Pharmacology, Assn. Univ. Anesthesiologists. Coptic Orthodox Christian. Home: 1019 Sunset St Iowa City IA 52246-4938 Office: U Iowa Dept Anesthesia Coll Medicine Iowa City IA 52242

GERHARD, HARRY E., JR., counter trader, management and trade consultant; b. Phila., Aug. 7, 1925; s. Harry E. and Frances Jane (Edwards) G.; children: Susan Jillson, John, Barbara Thomas. Student, Muhlenberg Coll., 1943-44; AB, George Washington U., 1968, MA, 1969. Commd. ensign USN, 1943, advanced through grades to rear adm., 1971, exptl. test pilot, 1955-57; ret., 1976; exec. v.p., COO Costa Line Cargo Svcs., Inc., N.Y.C., 1976-80; gen. mgr. Olayan Transp. Group, Dammam, Saudi Arabia, 1980-82; pres., owner Domestic & Overseas Countertrade & Cons. Svcs., Ltd., Washington, Pa., N.Y., 1983—; arbitrator AAA & AAA Asia/Pacific Ctr., B.C. Internat., Comml. Arbitration Ctr., FDIC, Miami Maritime Arbitration Coun., Mcpl. Securities Rulemaking Bd., Nat. Assn. Securities Dealers, N.Y. Stock Exch., Soc. Maritime Arbitrators. Active Boy Scouts Am. Decorated Silver Star, D.F.C. (2), Meritorious Svc. medal (2), Air medals (16), Navy Commendation medal with combat v (2). Fellow The Chartered Inst. of Arbitrators, Am. Coll. Forensic Examiners, Chartered Inst. Arbitrators; mem. Am. Arbitration Assn., Nat. Forensic Ctr., Assn. Naval Aviation, Air Force Assn., Am. Def. Preparedness Assn., Internat. Soc. Air Safety Investigators, Inter-Pacific Bar Assn., Maritime Law Assn. U.S., Navy League U.S., Nat. Aero. Assn., Ret. Officers Assn., Order of Daedalians, Tailhook Assn., Cousteau Soc., Fleet Res. Assn., Maritime and Aviation Cons., Mil. Order World Wars, Nat. War Coll. Alumni Assn., Soc. Maritime Arbitrators, Soc. Marine Cons., Soc. Naval Architects and Marine Engrs., Am. Soc. Naval Engrs., Soc. Profl. in Dispute Resolution, U.S. Def. Com., Am. Security Coun., Internat. Platform Assn., Greater Pitts. C. of C., Smaller Mfrs. Coun., Wings Club, N.Y. Yacht Club, Army Navy Club, Masons, Shriners. Republican. Address: 320 Fort Duquesne Blvd Ste 20F Pittsburgh PA 15222-1133

GERHARD, LEE CLARENCE, geologist, educator; b. Albion, N.Y., May 30, 1937; s. Carl Clarence and Helen Mary (Lahmer) G.; m. Darcy LaFollette, July 22, 1964; 1 dau., Tracy Leigh. B.S., Syracuse U., 1958; M.S., U. Kans., 1961, Ph.D., 1964. Exploration geologist, region stratigrapher Sinclair Oil & Gas Co., Midland, Tex. and Roswell, N.Mex., 1964-66; asst. prof. geology U. So. Colo., Pueblo, 1966-69, assoc. prof., 1969-72; assoc. prof., asst. dir. West Indies Lab. Fairleigh Dickinson U., Rutherford, N.J., 1972-75; asst. geologist State of N.D., Grand Forks, 1975-77, geologist, 1977-81; prof., chmn. dept. geology U. N.D., Grand Forks, 1977-81; mgr. Rocky Mountain div. Supron Energy Corp., Denver, 1981-82; owner, pres. Gerhard & Assocs., Englewood, Colo., 1982-87; prof. petroleum geology Colo. Sch. Mines, Denver, 1982—, Getty prof., 1984-87; state geologist, dir. geol. survey State of Kans., Lawrence, 1987—; founder, co-dir. Energy Rsch. Ctr., U. Kans., 1990-94; presdl. appointee Nat. Adv. Com. on Oceans and Atmosphere, 1984-87. Contbr. articles to profl. jours. Served to 1st lt. U.S. Army, 1958-60. Danforth fellow, 1970-72. Fellow Geol. Soc. Am.; mem. Am. Assn. Petroleum Geologists (hon. mem., Disting. Svc. award 1989, Journalism award 1996, pres. divsn. environ. geosci. 1994-95, hon. mem. divsn. environtl. geoscis. 1998), Am. Inst. Profl. Geologists, Rocky Mountain Assn. Geologists, Colo. Sci. Soc., Kans. Geol. Soc. (hon.), Sigma Xi, Sigma Gamma Epsilon. Home: 1628 Alvamar Dr Lawrence KS 66047-1714 Office: Kans Geol Survey 1930 Constant Ave Lawrence KS 66047-3724

GERHARDT, HEINZ ADOLF AUGUST, aircraft design engineer; b. Biedenkopf, Hessen, Germany, Jan. 31, 1934; came to U.S., 1962; s. Heinrich Ludwig and Emilie Henriette (Schuechler) G.; m. Heide Hanne Waltraud von Ryschkowsky, Sept. 3, 1962; children: Heinrich, Friederike, Helmar. MS in Mech. Engring., Tech. U. Darmstadt, Germany, 1961. Engr. Heinkel AG, Munich, 1962; from engr. to mgr. advanced aerodesign Northrop Corp., Hawthorne, Calif., 1962-91; prin. engr. Northrop Corp., Hawthorne, 1991-99; ret., 1999. Patentee in field. Recipient Otto Lilienthal prize Wissenschaftliche Gesellschaft fuer Luftfahrt, 1954, Aerodynamic award Am. Inst. of Aeronautics and Astronautics, 1994. Mem. AIAA (assoc. fellow, Aerodynamics award 1994), Soc. Automotive Engrs., Deutsche Gesellschaft fuer Luft und Raumfahrt. Avocations: flying, sailplanes, swimming, hiking.

GERHARDT, JON STUART, mechanical engineer, engineering educator; b. Springfield, Ohio, June 5, 1943; s. Robert William and Mary Josephine (Jones) G.; m. Claudia Jay Sadler, Feb. 7, 1970; children: Kirsten Lea, Benjamin Luke. BSME, U. Cin., 1966, MSME, 1968, PhD, 1971; MBA, Kent (Ohio) State U., 1997. Registered profl. engr., Ohio. Asst. prof. U. N.C., Charlotte, 1971-73; project engr. Duff-Norton, Charlotte, 1973; sr. devel. engr. Gen. Tire and Rubber Co., Akron, Ohio, 1973-77, group leader, 1977-79, mgr. tech. staff devel., 1979-84, mgr. product engring., rsch. ctr. adminstrn., 1984-87, dir. rsch., Gen. Tire, Inc., 1987-92, dir. rsch. and tire testing, 1992-95, v.p. tech. dir., Stds. Testing Labs., Massilion, Ohio, 1995—; instr. U. Akron, 1976—. Mem. ASME (bd. dirs. 1981-85), Akron Rubber Group, Soc. Automotive Engrs., Sigma Xi.

GERHARDT, LESTER A., engineering educator, dean; b. Bronx, N.Y., Jan. 28, 1940; s. David and Mary g.; m. Karen Rita Zimmerman, Sept. 2, 1961; children: Brian, Douglas. BEE, CUNY, 1961; MSEE, SUNY, Buffalo, 1964, PhD, 1969. Engr., asst. dir rsch. Bell Aerospace, Buffalo, 1961-70; assoc. prof. Rensselaer Polytechnic Inst., Troy, N.Y., 1961-74, prof., 1974—, chmn. elect., computer and systems engring. dept., 1975-86, dir. CIM Program, 1986-91, assoc. dean engring., 1991—; acting dir. Ctr. for the Mfg. Productivity, 1991-92, founding dir., 1979-80, dir. Ctr. for indsl. Innovation, 1993—; nat. del. NATO, 1980—, chair Rsch. Collaborative Grants Programme; mem. AFSB com. on Robotics and Artificial Intelligence, 1986-89, mem. com. Tactical Communications Nat. Acad. Scis.; mem. adv. bd. N.Y. Gov. Carey's Panel on Telecommunications, NSF, chair. adv. bd.; active internat. cons. to industry, the gov't, and other Universities. Recipient Inventor of Yr. award N.Y. State Intellectual Property Law Assn., 1997. Fellow IEEE; mem. ASEE (chmn. engring. rsch. coun. 1996—, bd. dirs. 1996—). Avocations: sailing, photography, tennis. Office: Rensselaer Poly Inst Deans Office Sch Engring JEC 3002 Troy NY 12180

GERHARDT, PHILIPP, microbiologist, educator; b. Milw., Dec. 30, 1921; s. Philipp W. and Agnes (Daigh) G.; m. Vera Mary Armstrong, Feb. 24, 1945; children: Ellen Daigh, Stephen Philipp, Doris Mary. Ph.B. with honors, U. Wis., 1943, M.S., 1947, Ph.D., 1949. Diplomate: Am. Bd. Med. Microbiology. Faculty microbiology Oreg. State U., 1949-51, Med. Sch., U. Mich., Ann Arbor, 1953-65; prof., chmn. dept. microbiology and pub. health Colls. Natural Sci., Human Medicine, Osteo. Medicine, Vet. Medicine and Agr. Expt. Sta. Mich. State U., East Lansing, 1965-75, prof., assoc. dean for research and grad. study Coll. Osteo. Medicine, 1975-87, prof. dept. microbiology and pub. health, 1987-91, prof. emeritus, 1992—; adj. sr. sci. Mich. Biotech. Inst., 1985—; dir. Ribi Immuno Chem Research Inc., 1985—; cons. various univs. and corps. Editor in chief: Manual of Methods for General Bacteriology, 1981, Methods for General and Molecular Bacteriology, 1993. Served with AUS, 1943-46, 51-52. Wis. Alumni Rsch. Found. fellow, 1946-47; NIH rsch. fellow, 1947-49; recipient Disting. Faculty award Mich. State U., 1982, Pasteur award Ill. Soc. Microbiology, 1993. Fellow AAAS, Am. Acad. Microbiology (charter, bd. govs. 1970-76); mem. Am. Soc. Microbiology (hon., sec. 1961-67, v.p. 1973-74, pres. 1974-75, coun. and coun. policy com. 1961-67, 74-76), Brit. Soc. Gen. Microbiology, Internat. Union Microbiol. Socs. (v.p. 1978-82, pres. 1982-86, exec. bd. 1978-90), Internat. Coun. Sci. Unions (steering com. internat. bioscis. network 1985-91, pres. com. biotech. 1987-89), Polish Med. Soc. (hon.), Phi Beta Kappa, Sigma Xi. Achievements include rsch. and publs. on microbial endospores, permeability, fermentations. Home: 529 Woodland Dr East Lansing MI 48823-3273 Office: Mich State Univ Dept Microbiol East Lansing MI 48824

GERHART, DOROTHY EVELYN, insurance executive, real estate professional; b. Monett, Mo., Apr. 20, 1932; d. Manford Thomas and Norma Grace (Barrett) Ethridge; m. Robert H. Gerhart, Apr. 11, 1952 (div. Dec. 1969); children: Sandra Gerhart Kreamer, Richard A., Diane Gerhart Lacey. Grad. high sch., Tucson; student, U. Ariz., 1950-53. Lic. real estate broker. Owner, pres. Gerhart Ins., Inc., Tucson, 1967-70, 89—; agt. Mahoney-O'Donnell Agy., Tucson, 1970-73, Gerhart & Mendelsoh Ins., Tucson, 1973-78; agt., mgr. personal lines dept. Tucson Realty and Trust, 1978-83; ins. agt. San Xavier Ins. Agy., Tucson, 1985-89; pres. Gerhart Ins., Inc., Tucson, 1989-93, Koty-Leavitt Ins., Inc. (formerly Gerhart Ins., Inc.), Tuscon, 1993—, Gerhart Realty, Inc., Tuscon, 1993—. Vol. Palo Verde Psychiat. Hosp. Mem. Nat. Fedn. Ind. Bus., Ind. Ins. Agts. Tucson (bd. dirs. 1973, 74, v.p. 1975, pres. 1976, First Woman Pres.), Fed. Home Life Ins. Co. (Pres.'s Club award 1986), Nat. Fedn. Small Bus., Altrusa Club of Tucson (bd. dirs. 1984, membership chmn. 1985, fund raising chmn. 1986). Republican. Avocations: arts, crafts, antiques. Address: PO Box 13421 Tucson AZ 85732-3421 Office: Gerhart Realty Inc 6339 E Speedway Blvd Ste 200 Tucson AZ 85710-1147

GERHART, EUGENE CLIFTON, lawyer; b. Bklyn., Apr. 7, 1912; s. Herman Eugene and Mary Elizabeth (Hamilton) G.; m. Mary Richardson Schreiber, Mar. 30, 1939; children: Catherine Gerhart Landon, Virginia Gerhart Mason. AB, Princeton U., 1934; LLB, Harvard U., 1937. Bar: N.J. 1938, N.Y. 1945. Practiced in Newark, 1938-43, Binghamton, N.Y., 1946—; counsel firm Coughlin & Gerhart, Binghamton; sec. to Judge Manley O. Hudson, Secretariat/League of Nations, Geneva, 1934; lectr. bus. law U. Newark, 1942-43, Triple Cities Coll., 1946-48, Harpur Coll., Endicott, N.Y., 1953-55; lectr. indsl. and labor relations Cornell U., Ithaca, N.Y., 1946; dir., gen. counsel Columbian Mut. Life Ins. Co., 1949-83, acting pres., 1969-70, chmn. bd., 1970-82; mem. coun. SUNY, Cortland, 1967-77, chmn., 1971-77; mem. Select Task Force on Ct. Reorgn. N.Y. State Senate; mem. jud. nominating com. 3d Jud. Dept., State of N.Y.; mem. N.Y. Unified Ct. Sys. Judicial Records Disposition and Archives Devel. Com. Author: American Liberty and Natural Law, America's Advocate: Robert H. Jackson, Robert H. Jackson: Lawyer's Judge, Arthur T. Vanderbilt: The Compleat Counsellor, Quote It!, Quote It II, The Lawyer's Treasury, Quote It Completely!, 1998, World Reference Guide to more than 5500 Memorable Quotations from Law and Literature, 1998; spl. contbg. author: Law Office Econs. and Mgmt, 1962—; mem. editl. bd. Quar. Report of Conf. on Personal Fin. Law, 1965; contbr. articles to legal, other publs. Chmn. Harpur Forum SUNY, Binghamton, 1983-84. Lt. USNR, 1943-46. Fellow Am. Bar Found., Am. Coll. Probate Counsel; mem. ABA (editor Jour. 1946-67, Ross Essay award 1946), Internat. Assn. Ins. Counsel, Assn. Life Ins. Counsel, Am. Judicature Soc., Am. Law Inst., N.Y. State Bar Assn. (editor-in-chief jour. 1961—, Disting. Svc. award 1998), Assn. Bar City N.Y., Broome County Bar Assn. (pres. 1961-62, Lifetime Achievement award 1995), Selden Soc., Broome County Princeton Alumni Assn., Harvard Law Sch. Assn. Upstate N.Y. (pres. 1955-57), Scribes (pres., dir. 1966-67), St. Andrew's Soc. Republican. Clubs: Rotary (pres. 1969-70), Cosmos, Oteyokwa Lake (pres. 1971-73), Nassau, Harvard of N.Y, Princeton of N.Y. Home: 34 W End Ave Binghamton NY 13905-4026 Office: One Marine Midland Pla Binghamton NY 13902

GERHART, GLENNA LEE, pharmacist; b. Houston, June 11, 1954; d. Henry Edwin and Gloria Mae (Mrnustik) G. BS in Pharmacy, U. Houston, 1977. Registered pharmacist, Tex. Staff pharmacist Meml. City Med. Ctr., Houston, 1977-84; asst. dir. pharmacy Meml. Hosp.-Meml. City Med. Ctr., Houston, 1984-98; pharmacy supr. Meml. Hermann-Meml. City Hosp. Pharmacy, Houston, 1998—. Mem. Am. Pharm. Assn., Am. Soc. Hosp. Pharmacists, Tex. Pharm. Assn., Tex. Soc. Health-System Pharmacists, Houston-Galveston Area Soc. Hosp. Pharmacists, Plumeria Soc. Am., U. Houston Alumni Orgn. (life), Houston Cat Club, Nat. Cougar Club, Slavonic Benevolent Order of Tex., Greentrails Ladies Club, Kappa Epsilon. Republican. Methodist. Avocations: reading, orchid collecting, gardening, running, raising cats. Home: 19811 Cardiff Park Ln Houston TX 77094-3031 Office: Memorial Hospital-Memorial City Med. Ctr. 920 Frostwood Dr Houston TX 77024-2312

GERHART, JAMES BASIL, physics educator; b. Pasadena, Calif., Dec. 15, 1928; s. Ray and Marion (van Deusen) G.; m. Genevra Joy Thomesen, June 21, 1958; children: James Edward, Sara Elizabeth. B.S., Calif. Inst. Tech., 1950; M.A., Princeton, 1952, Ph.D., 1954. Instr. physics Princeton, 1954-56; asst. prof. physics U. Wash., Seattle, 1956-61; asso. prof. U. Wash., 1961-65, prof., 1965-98, prof. emeritus, 1998—; exec. officer Pacific Northwest Assn. for Coll. Physics, 1972-94, bd. dirs., 1965-99, chmn., 1970-72; governing bd. Am. Inst. Physics, 1973-76, 78-81. Recipient Disting. Teaching award U. Wash. Regents and Alumni Assn., 1982, Ann. Gerhart lectr., 1997. Fellow Am. Phys. Soc, AAAS; mem. Am. Assn. Physics Tchrs. (sec. 1971-77, v.p. 1977, pres.-elect 1978, pres. 1979, Millikan medal 1985). Home: 2134 E Interlaken Blvd Seattle WA 98112-3433

GERHART, PETER MILTON, law educator; b. Milw., July 4, 1945; s. Howard Leon and Ann (Baker) G.; m. Virginia Ann Herold, Feb. 9, 1969 (div. Oct. 1980); 1 child, Matthew; m. Ann Tarbutton, Apr. 9, 1983; children: Mary Elizabeth, Margaret Ann, Grace Kendall. BA, Northwestern U., 1967; JD, Columbia U., 1971. Bar: N.Y. 1971, U.S. Dist. Ct. (so. dist.) N.Y. 1973. Assoc. Weil, Gotshal & Manges, N.Y.C., 1971-75; prof. law Ohio State U., Columbus, 1975—, assoc. dean, 1983-86; dean Case Western Res. U., Cleve., 1986-96, prof., 1996—; cons. Pres.'s Commn. Antitrust, Washington, 1978-79, Adminstrv. Conf., Washington, 1976-77. Contbr. articles to profl. jours. Mem. ABA (cons. com. to study FTC 1969). Democrat. Presbyterian. Avocations: piano, jogging. Home: 14400 Shaker Blvd Cleveland OH 44120-1611 Office: Case Western Res U Sch Law 11075 East Blvd Cleveland OH 44106-5409*

GERHART, PHILIP MARK, engineering educator; b. Kokomo, Ind., Aug. 5, 1946. BS in Mech. Engring., Rose-Hulman Inst. Tech., 1968; MS, U. Ill., 1969, PhD, 1971. Registered profl. engr. Ohio, Ind. Asst. prof. mech. engring. U. Akron (Ohio), 1971-76, assoc. prof., 1976-82, prof., 1982-84; dept. chair U. Evansville, Ind., 1984-95; dean coll. engring. and computer sci. U. Evansville, 1995—; summer faculty fellow NASA Lewis Rsch. Ctr., Cleve., 1972, 73, aerospace engr., summer 1974; engr. NED performance tech. Babcock & Wilcox Co., Barberton, Ohio, summers 1978, 79; co-devel., instr. tng. program for performance engrs. Ohio Edison Co., Akron, summer 1981-84; cons. Goodyear Aerospace Co., Buffalo Forge Co., Elec. Power Rsch. Inst., Bristol-Meyers USPNG, George Koch Sons Inc., Mohler Techs. Inc.; presenter papers in field. Author: (with R.J. Gross) Fundamentals of Fluid Mechanics, 1985, (with R.J. Gross and J.I. Hochstein) 2d edit., 1992; contbr. articles to profl. jours. Asst. scoutmaster, scoutmaster, troop com. chmn., scouting coord., unit commr., Boy Scouts Am., 1968—; deacon, Bible sch. supt., chmn. bldg. com., elder Northwest Ave. Ch. of Christ, Tallmadge, Ohio, 1973-84; chmn. corp., elder Cullen Ave. Christian Ch., Evansville, 1985-92. Recipient Outstanding Tchr. award Bd. Higher Edn. United Meth. Ch., 1994, 25 Yr. Vet. Cert. from Boy Scouts Am. Mem. ASME (Dedicated Svc. award 1986, Performance Test Codes Gold medal 1993, Student Sect. Outstanding Tchr. 1983, 84, performance test code 11 on fans 1975—, vice chair 1989—, performance test code 4.1 steam generators 1981—, bd. performance test codes 1990—, instr. profl. devel. course 1991—), Am. Soc. Engring. Edn., Lambda Chi Alpha, Tau Beta Pi, Pi Tau Sigma (founding advisor U Evansville chpt.), Sigma Xi, Phi Kappa Pi, Phi Beta Chi. Office: Coll Engring & Computer Sci Univ of Evansville 1800 Lincoln Ave Evansville IN 47722*

GERICKE, PAUL WILLIAM, minister, educator; b. St. Louis, Apr. 8, 1924; s. Orville Herman and Irma Rose (Reinhart) G.; m. Jean Fisher, Feb. 18, 1953; 1 child, Michael Paul. BSEE, Washington U., St. Louis, 1949; BD, So. Bapt. Theol. Sem., 1960; ThD, New Orleans Bapt. Theol. Sem., 1964; MA, U. New Orleans, 1972. Ordained to ministry So. Bapt. Conv., 1952. Instr. electronics USAF, 1949; calibration engr. Emerson Electric Co., St. Louis, 1950; asst. pastor Calvary Bapt. Ch., St. Louis, 1951-53, Forest Ave. Bapt. Ch., Kansas City, Mo., 1954; pastor First Bapt. Ch., Marceline, Mo., 1955-56, New Hope Bapt. Ch., St. Louis, 1957, Summit Park Bapt. Ch., Louisville, 1959-60, Logtown (Miss.) Bapt. Ch., 1960-64; asst. prof., dir. libr. svcs. New Orleans Bapt. Theol. Sem., 1965-73, assoc. prof., dir. libr., 1973-91, assoc. prof. comms., dir. Comm. Ctr., 1991-92, dir. rsch. and planning, 1992-93, prof. comms. N. Ga. Campus, 1993, acad. counselor, prof. comms. emeritus, 1993-96; dir. of libr., prof. communications, emeritus, 1996—; mgr. Sta. WSBN-FM, New Orleans, 1979-85, chmn., 1985-92; bd. dirs. religious access channel REACH, New Orleans, 1985-93. Author: The Preaching of Robert G. Lee, 1967, The Ministers Filing System, 1971, Sermon Building, 1973, Crucial Experiences in the Life of D.L. Moody, 1978, Pastor's Library, 1986, Great Preachers of the Church, 1996. Served with AC USNR, 1942-46. Mem. Am. Radio Relay League, Theta Xi. Republican. Avocation: amateur radio. Home: 2727 Sycamore Wood Ln Lawrenceville GA 30044-7402 Office: New Orleans Bapt Theol Sem N Ga Campus 862 Columbia Dr Decatur GA 30030-4159 *My life has been completely changed by a personal encounter with Jesus Christ in 1951. Through faith in Him as Savior and Lord, I received a new life, a new sense of values, a new purpose in life, and a new hope both for this life and the life to come. My purpose now is to seek first the kingdom of God and all the other things I need will be given unto me.*

GERICKE, SHANE WILLIAM, writer; b. Joliet, Ill., May 23, 1956; s. Lee and Almarimor (Moore) G.; m. Jerrle Miller, June 3, 1979. BS, No. Ill. U., 1978; grad., Citizen Police Acad., Naperville, Ill., 1996. Journalist Herald, Mokena, Ill., 1973-74, No. Star, DeKalb, Ill., 1974-78, Moline (Ill.) Daily Dispatch, 1978-81, Joliet Herald-News, 1981-82, Chgo. Sun-Times, 1982—; novelist Naperville, Ill., 1994—. Author: Crusade, 1998, Dead Center, 1998. Bd. dirs. Congregation Beth Shalom, Naperville, Ill., 1990-94. Mem. Chgo. Newspaper Guild (chmn. 1993-94, vice chmn. 1990-93, Stick O'Type awards 1983-93), Citizen Police Acad. Alumni. Avocations: pistolry, cigars, travel, Judaica.

GERINGER, JAMES E., governor; b. Wheatland, Wyo., Apr. 24, 1944; m. Sherri Geringer; children: Jen, Val, Rob, Meri, Beckie. BS in Mechanical Engring., Kans. State U., 1967. Commd. officer USAF; with contract administration Mo. Basin Power Project's Laramie River Sta., 1977-79; elected mem. Wyo. Legislature, 1982; farm owner, 1987—; Governor State of Wyoming, 1994—; participant in various space devel. programs, Calif., devel. variety Air Force and NASA space boosters including launches of reconnaissance satellites, the NASA Viking Mars lander, an upper stage booster for the space shuttle and the Global Positioning Satellite System; chief of computer programming at a ground receiving station for early warning satellites. Mem. Nat. Fedn. Ind. Bus., Am. Legion, Farm Bur., Farmer's Union, Rotary, Lions, Ducks Unlimited, Pheasants Forever, C. of C. Lutheran. Office: Office of the Gov State Capitol Bldg 124 200 W 24th St Cheyenne WY 82002-0010

GERJUOY, EDWARD, physicist, lawyer; b. Bklyn., May 19, 1918; s. Abraham and Clara (Hirsch) G.; m. Clark Jacqueline Reid, Aug. 26, 1940; children: Neil, David Leif. B.S. cum laude, CCNY, 1937; M.A., U. Calif., Berkeley, 1940, Ph.D., 1942; J.D. magna cum laude, U. Pitts., 1977. Bar: Calif. 1977, Pa. 1978. Asso. dir. sonar analysis group Div. War Research, Columbia, 1942-46; mem. faculty U. So. Calif., Los Angeles, 1946-51; vis. asso. prof. N.Y. U., 1951-52; mem. faculty U. Pitts., 1952-58, 64-82, prof. physics, 1964-82, prof. emeritus, 1982—; mem. Pa. Environ. Hearing Bd., 1982-86, cons. hearing examiner, 1987-89; of counsel Rose, Schmidt, Hasley & DiSalle, Pitts., 1987—; mem. rsch. staff Gen. Atomic div. Gen. Dynamics Corp., San Diego, 1958-62; dir. plasma and space applied physics RCA Labs., Princeton, N.J., 1962-64; cons. Westinghouse Rsch. Labs., 1952-58; mem. adv. com. health physics div. Oak Ridge Nat. Labs., 1967-71, chmn. com., 1971-74; assoc. Tucker Arensberg Very & Ferguson, Pitts., 1978-80; vis. fellow Joint Inst. Lab. Physics, U. Colo., Boulder, 1970; vis. sci. USSR Acad. Sci. Lebedev Inst., Moscow, 1972; hearing examiner Pa. Environ. Hearing Bd., 1980-81; vis. scholar Stanford Math. Dept., 1987; cons. EPA, 1977-81,; cons. atty. Reed, Smith, Shaw & McClay, Pitts., 1993—. Author: (with A. Yaspan) Reverberation, in series The Physics of Sound in the Sea, 1968; editor: Physics Text Series, 1960-62, Jour. Comments on Atomic and Molecular Physics, 1971-74, Jurimetrics Jour. of Law Sci. and Tech., 1980-87; contbr. chpts. and numerous articles to tech. and legal lit. Bd. dirs. Pitts. ACLU, 1975-80, 92-95, vice-chmn., chair-elect Am. Phys. Soc. Forum on Physics and Soc., 1994-97. Fellow AAAS, Am. Phys. Soc. (mem. panel on pub. affairs 1976-79, 94-96, chmn. 1981), Inst. Physics, Phys. Soc. (Eng.); mem. ABA (chmn. phys. scis. com., sect. sci. and tech. 1976-77, mem. coun. sci. and tech. 1977-80, 84, 87-91), Phi Beta Kappa, Sigma Xi, Order of Coif. Achievements include first predictions of interference in Zeeman Effect allowing magnetic dipole and electric quadrupole transitions, and (with others) of beats between photons of different frequencies; first derivation of transition rates in many-particle collisions from a purely time-independent formalism; first development (with others) of routine procedure for constructing variational estimates of very wide class of quantities. Home and Office: 400 Richland Ln Pittsburgh PA 15208-2732 *I have tried to avoid overspecialization, while not letting myself descend into dilettantism. I believe I have succeeded in these endeavors. The last phase of my career, embarking on a law degree at age 56, earning the degree and passing the bar at 59, and then being employed full time as a judge in environmental disputes, probably is an extreme example of career restlessness. I am not sorry to have strayed from a straight line career path, and it has kept me feeling young in my so-called golden years. Nevertheless—and this is more a comment about the present world than about me—I do not believe I would advise young men today to be guided by me.*

GERKEN, WALTER BLAND, insurance company executive; b. N.Y.C., Aug. 14, 1922; s. Walter Adam and Virginia (Bl) G.; m. Darlene Stolt, Sept. 6, 1952; children: Walter C., Ellen M., Beth L., Daniel J., Andrew P., David A. BA, Wesleyan U., 1948; MPA, Maxwell Sch. Citizenship and Pub. Affairs, Syracuse, 1958. Supr. budget and adminstrv. analysis Wis., Madison, 1950-54; mgr. investments Northwestern Mut. Life Ins. Co., Milw., 1954-67; v.p. finance Pacific Mut. Life Ins. Co., L.A., 1967-69, exec. v.p., 1969-72, pres., 1972-75, chmn. bd., 1975-87; chmn. exec. com. Pacific Mut. Life Ins. Co., Los Angeles, 1987-95, also dir.; sr. advisor Boston Consulting Group; chmn. PIMCO Advisors, L.P.; bd. dirs. Mullin Cons., Inc. Bd. dirs. Keck Found., Hoag Meml. Presbyn. Hosp.; trustee emeritus Occidental Coll. L.A., Wesleyan U., Middletown, Conn.; bd. dirs. Nature Conservancy Calif., Exec. Svc. Corp.; mem. Calif. Citizens Budget Com., Calif. Commn. Campaign Fin. Reform, Calif. Commn. on Higher Edn.; chair Exec. Svc. Corps. So. Calif.; v.p. Orange County Cmty. Found.; mem. adv. bd. The Maxwell Sch. Citizenship and Pub. Affairs, Syracuse U. Decorated D.F.C., Air medal. Mem. Calif. Club, Dairymen's Country Club (Boulder Junction, Wis.), Balboa Bay Club (Newport Beach, Calif., former bd. dirs.), Automobilce Club So. Calif. (bd. dirs.), Calif. Ind. Coll. Network (co-chair), Pauma Valley Country Club, Edison Internat., Times Mirror Co. Office: Pimco Advisors LP 800 Newport Center Dr Newport Beach CA 92660-6309

GERLACH, DANIEL J., budget and tax policy analyst; b. Columbus, Ohio, June 20, 1967; s. Thomas J. and Mary M. Gerlach; m. Marguerite Woodward, Nov. 24, 1990; 1 child, Laura. BA, U. Notre Dame, 1989; MPA, Syracuse U., 1990. Prin. budget analyst N.Y. State Assembly, Albany, 1991-94; dir. N.C. State U., Raleigh, 1995—, N.C. Budget and Tax Ctr., Raleigh, 1995—. Adv. pub. policy bd. United Way of N.C., Raleigh, 1997—; fin. chair, bd. dirs. Cath. Social Ministries, Raleigh, 1998-99; treas. Fairfax Hills Swim and Tennis Club, Raleigh, 1998-99. Mem. ASPA, Phi Beta Kappa. Home: 5616 Alpine Dr Raleigh NC 27609 Office: NC Budget & Tax Ctr PO Box 28068 Raleigh NC 27611

GERLACH, DOUGLAS ELDON, financial writer internet developer; b. Columbus, Ohio, May 19, 1963; s. Eldon Chloral and Judith Ann (Benadum) G.; 1 child. BA, Bennington (Vt.) Coll., 1985. Sr. editor, co-creator website Nat. Assn. of Investors Corp., 1995—; pres., CEO, webmaster Investorama.com, N.Y.C., 1995—; internet bus. analyst First Albany Corp., N.Y.C., 1997-98; sr. editor Armchair Millionaire. com, New York, NY, 1998—. Author: Investor's Web Guide, 1997, Complete Idiot's Guide to Online Investing, 1998; contbr. articles to mags. Recipient Disting. Svc. award Investment Edn. Inst., 1996. Mem. Nat. Writers Union, Computer

Press Assn., Pioneer On-Line Investment Club (pres. 1994—), Blue Chip Posse (pres., treas. 1993—), Am. Assn. of Individual Investors (life), Nat. Assn. of Investor Corp. Computer Group (bd. dirs. 1995—), Mensa. Office: iVillage Inc 170 5th Ave New York NY 10010

GERLACH, FRANKLIN THEODORE, lawyer; b. Portsmouth, Ohio, Apr. 11, 1935; s. Albert T. and Nora Alice (Hayes), G.; m. Cynthia Ann Koehler, Aug. 1, 1958; children—Valarie, Philipp. B.B.A., U. Cin., 1958; M.P.A., Syracuse U., 1959; J.D., U. Cin., 1961. Bar: Ohio 1961, U.S. Dist. Ct. (so. dist.) Ohio 1969, U.S. Supreme Ct. 1971. Dir. Purchasing, Planning and Renewal, City of Portsmouth, 1961-62, city mgr., 1962-66, mayor, 1990-98; asst. dir. Ohio U., Portsmouth, 1966-68; sole practice, Portsmouth, 1968—; solicitor Village New Boston, Ohio, 1968-70; trustee Ohio Acad. Trial Lawyers, Columbus, Ohio, 1984-85. Recipient Outstanding Young Man of Ohio award (1 of 5) Portsmouth Jaycees, 1968, Ohio Jaycees, 1969. Mem. Portsmouth Bar and Law Libr. Assn. (pres. 1986). Democrat. Avocation: antiques. Home: 1221 20th St Portsmouth OH 45662-2924 Office: 814 7th St Portsmouth OH 45662-4128

GERLACH, FREDERICK HERMAN, international business consultant; b. Milw., Aug. 9, 1938; s. Arthur John and Margaret Mary (Williamson) G.; m. Ana L. de la Cuesta. BA, U. Wis., 1961; MIA, Columbia U., 1963, PhD, 1968. Fgn. svc. officer Dept. of State, Washington, 1966-87; internat. bus. cons. Frankfurt, Germany, 1988-96, Milw., 1997—; dir. fin. svcs. cons. firm, 1993—, Ea. Publ. Ltd., 1996—. Co-author, editor (book series) Aspects of the Market Economy; contbr. articles to profl. jours., chpts. to books. Recipient Superior Honor award State Dept., 1979, 87; Fulbright-Hays Rsch. fellow, 1965-66. Mem. Middle East Inst., Am. Fgn. Svc. Assn., Diplomatic and Consular Officers Ret., Milw. World Trade Assn., Global Bus. Profls. Wis., U. Wis.-Milw. Inst. World Affairs. United Ch. of Christ. Avocations: wind-surfing, biking, choral singing. Home: 3248 S New York Ave Milwaukee WI 53207-3040 Office: 207 E Buffalo St Ste 553 Milwaukee WI 53202-5775

GERLACH, G. DONALD, lawyer; b. Toledo, July 13, 1933; s. Werner George and Marian (Peiter) G.; m. Betty Lou Smith, Dec. 19, 1959 (dec.); children: Lisa A., Gregory D., Jeffrey S.; m. Diane Bonfigli, July 30, 1983; stepchildren: Kevin, Michael Chase. BA, MS, Princeton U., 1955; LLB, Harvard U., 1960. Bar: Pa. 1961. Assoc. Reed Smith Shaw & McClay, Pitts., 1960-66, ptnr., 1967—, mng. ptnr., 1983-92; bd. dirs. Mine Safety Appliances Co.; vice-chmn. Keystone Fin. Corp., 1991-97; mem. Allegheny Conf., 1990-93; fin. com. U. Pitts. Med. Ctr. Trustee Shadyside Hosp., 1983-87; bd. dirs. United Way of Allegheny County, 1985-93, Allegheny Trails coun. Boy Scouts. Am., 1989-93. Fellow Am. Coll. Trust and Estate Counsel; mem. ABA (real property, probate and trust sect., adv. com. on decedent's estates 1978—), Pa. Bar Assn. (chmn. real property, probate and trust sect. 1977-78), Allegheny County Bar Assn., Duquesne Club (bd. dirs. 1986-89), Harvard-Yale-Princeton Club (pres. 1981-82), Fox Chapel Golf Club, Dunkirk Yacht Club, Law Club, Teutonia Mannerchor. Republican. Lutheran. Office: Reed Smith Shaw & McClay 435 6th Ave Ste 2 Pittsburgh PA 15219-1886

GERLACH, JEANNE ELAINE, English language educator; b. Charleston, W.Va., Oct. 20, 1946; d. Lafayette and Edith Lorraine (Robinson) Marcum; m. Roger Thomas Gerlach Sr., Dec. 30, 1966; children: Roger Thomas Jr., Kristen Elaine. BS, W.Va. State Coll., Institute, 1974; MA, W.Va. State Coll., 1979; EdD, W.Va. U., 1985, U. North Tex., 1992. Lang. arts tchr. Ohio County Schs., Wheeling, W.Va., 1974-79; English instr. West Liberty (W.Va.) State Coll., 1979-82; continuing edn. instr. Seattle Pacific U., 1982-85; asst. prof. English W.Va. U., Morgantown, 1985-86, Tarrant County Jr. Coll., Ft. Worth, 1986-88; dir. Communications Unlimited, Dallas, Pitts., 1986—; assoc. prof. English edn. W.Va. U., Morgantown, 1989-97, spl. asst. to the provost, 1994-97, dir. ctr. women's studies, 1993-94; dean sch. of edn. U. Tex., Arlington, 1997—; cons. to bus. and corps., 1986—; co-dir. advanced writing project W.Va. U., Morgantown, 1989, lang. arts camps, 1988, 89, 90, young writers inst. Editor: English Internat.; contbr. articles to profl. jours. Mem. LWV, W.Va., DAR, Young Republicans, W.Va. Faculty Devel. grantee W.Va. U., 1989; recipient 1st. place Creative Writing award W.Va. Women's Clubs, 1976. Mem. AAUW, AAUP, Nat. Coun. Tchrs. English (chair women's com. 1986—, chair nominating com. 1988-89, Outstanding Tchr. in Coll. of Human Resources and Edn. award W.Va. U. 1992, Rewey Belle Inglis award 1992), Am. Ednl. Rsch. Assn., W.Va. U. Alumni Assn. (sec. 1990, pres.), Nat. Women's Studies Assn., Nat. Soc. Daus. Am. Revolution. Republican. Methodist. Avocations: tennis, golf, writing poetry, photography, doll collecting.

GERLACH, LUTHER PAUL, anthropologist; b. Oct. 25, 1930; married; 3 children. B.A., U. Minn., 1952; PhD, U. London, 1960. Vis. lectr. anthropology U. Minn., 1961-71, assoc. prof., 1965-71, prof., 1971—, adj. prof. Hubert Humphrey Inst. Pub. Affairs, 1983—; asst. prof. anthropology and sociology Lafayette Coll., 1961-63; vis. assoc. Calif. Inst Tech., 1971-72; sr. cons. Aspen Inst. Humanistic Studies, 1972-73; vis. fellow Sci. Ctr., West Berlin; cons. and Oak Ridge Nat. Lab., Tenn., summer and fall 1986. Author: (with Virginia H. Hine) People, Power, Change: Movements of Social Transformation, 1970, Lifeway Leap: The Dynamics of Change in America, 1973; rschr., contbr. articles on societal dimensions of global environ. change and ecosys. mgmt. to profl. and popular jours., chpts. to books; prodr. films and filmstrips including Zanj-Africa, 1970, People Eco-Action, 1970, Systemic Thinking, 1973, Grassroots Energy, 1978, TV series Lifeway Leap, Energy, Resource Use and System Change. Served with AUS, 1952-54. Fulbright jr. fellow, 1958-60, Bush fellow, 1983-84; grantee N.W. Area Found., 1967-80, Rockefeller Found., 1969-70, Office of Water Resources Rsch., 1969-72, 75-78, Solar Energy Rsch. Inst., 1978-79, Legis. Commn. on Minn. Resources, Blandin Found., 1988-89, NOAA Minn. sea grant, 1991-94, Weyerhauser Family Found., Inc., 1991-92, USDA Forest Svc., 1993-94, 95-96, NSF-EPA, 1996—. Fellow Am. Anthropol. Assn., Soc. Applied Anthropology.

GERLICK, HELEN J., tax practitioner, accountant; b. Denver, Dec. 11, 1931; d. JAmes Jeffries and Margaret (Fitzwater) Farrell; m. Jerald James Gerlick, Aug. 25, 1950; children: Michael James, Daniel Lee, Kenneth Dwayne. Grad., Barnes Bus. Sch., 1950, H&R Block Sch., 1974. CPA, Cert. Tax Preparer. Acctg. clerk Colo. Teamsters, Denver, 1956; ins. div. NSLI, Denver, 1956-58; assoc. St. Lukes Acctg., Denver, 1958; acctg. office mgr. Mundix Control Systems, Denver, 1964-83; tax preparer H & R Block, Denver, 1977-79; acct., tax preparer Gerlick's Tax Svc., Wheat Ridge, Colo., 1979—. Mem. NAFE, Am. Bus. Women's Assn. (named Women of Yr. 1977, 81, 94), Nat. Assn. Tax Practitioners, Nat. Pub. Accts. Assn., Pub. Accts. Soc. of Colo. Democrat. Lutheran. Avocations: teaching at senior center, painting, collecting and making porcelain dolls. Home and Office: 4601 Robb St Wheat Ridge CO 80033-2536

GERLING, STEPHEN P., federal judge; b. 1942. BA, Niagara U., 1964; JD, St. John's U., 1967. Bar: N.Y. 1969. Assoc. Kehoe, Murnane, Garramone, Utica, N.Y., 1969-73; ptnr. Schwartz, Blaney & Gerling, Utica, 1973-76; pvt. practice, Utica, 1976-85; chief bankruptcy judge for no. dist. N.Y., U.S. Bankruptcy Ct., Utica, 1985—; instr. Mohawk Valley C.C., 1970-75, Utica Coll. of Syracuse U., 1980-85; asst. county atty. Oneida County, 1973-80; spl. counsel Town of Whitestown, N.Y., 1980-85; asst. counsel to spkr. N.Y. State Assembly, Albany, 1980. Chmn. Whitestown Zoning Bd. Appeals, 1982-85. Capt. Mil. Police, U.S. Army, 1967-69, Vietnam. Decorated Bronze Star; named Citizen of Yr., Whitestown post Am. Legion, 1984. Mem. N.Y. State Bar Assn. (bus. and backing com.), Oneida County Bar Assn. (CLE com.), Legal Aid Soc. Oneida County. Office: US Bankruptcy Ct 220 US Courthouse 10 Broad St Utica NY 13501-1233

GERLITS, FRANCIS JOSEPH, lawyer; b. Chgo., Mar. 29, 1931; s. John T. and May (Cameron) G.; m. Suzanne Long, June 20, 1953; children: Kathleen, Karen, Mary Cameron, Francis Jr. Ph.B., U. Notre Dame, 1953; J.D., U. Chgo., 1958. Bar: Ill. 1958. Ptnr. Kirkland & Ellis, Chgo., 1964-95; of counsel Internat. Harvester Co. (now Navistar Internat. Corp.), Chgo., 1985-90. Mem. ABA, Order of Coif. Clubs: Tavern (Chgo.), Chicago (Chgo.). Office: Kirkland & Ellis 200 E Randolph St Fl 54 Chicago IL 60601-6636

GERLITZ, CURTIS NEAL, business executive; b. Jan. 26, 1944; s. Gustav Albert and Elna G.; m. Audrey Jean D'Almaine, Oct. 6, 1973. BSBA, U. Minn., 1966; MBA, No. Ill. U., 1990. Purchasing agt. I. S. Berlin Press, Chgo., 1973-75; asst. purchasing agt. Daubert Chem. Co., Oak Brook, Ill., 1975-78; purchasing mgr. IBG Internat., Wheeling, Ill., 1978-86; dir. purchasing Advance Process Supply Co., Chgo., 1986-91; pres. Selectech, Mount Prospect, Ill., 1991—. Decorated Purple Heart. Mem. Nat. Assn. Purchasing Mgmt., Purchasing Assn. Chgo., Mfrs. Agts. Nat. Assn., United Assn. Mgrs. Reps. (mem. nat. bd. advisors 1994-96), Beta Gamma Sigma, Sigma Iota Epsilon. Home: 404 S Helena Ave Mount Prospect IL 60056-2854 Office: Selectech Internat Inc 800 W Central Rd Mount Prospect IL 60056-2382

GERMAIN, CLAIRE MADELEINE, law librarian, educator; b. Chaumont, France, Sept. 22, 1951; d. Pierre and Jeanne (Despujols) G.; m. Stuart M. Basefsky, Aug. 16, 1976; 1 child, Nicolas. Licence-es. lettres, U. Paris, 1971, LLB, 1974; M in Comparative Law, La. State U., 1975; M in Law Librarianship, U. Denver, 1977. Reference librarian Duke U. Law Library, Durham, N.C., 1977-80, head reference librarian, 1982-84, asst. librarian, sr. lectr. comparative law, 1984-89, assoc. dir., sr. lectr. comparative law, 1989-93; Edward Cornell law libr., prof. law Cornell U., Ithaca, N.Y., 1993—; research fellow Max Planck Inst., Hamburg, Federal Republic of Germany, 1980. Author: Germain's Transnational Law Research: A Guide to Attorneys, 1991, (with Szladits) Guide to Foreign Legal Materials, French, 2d edit., 1985; contbr. and editor articles to profl. jours. Mem. Am. Assn. Law Librs. (chair fgn. law sect. 1985-86), ABA, Am. Assn. Law Schs. (chair libr. and tech. com.). Catholic. Office: Cornell Law Libr Myron Taylor Hall Ithaca NY 14853

GERMAN, EDWARD CECIL, lawyer; b. Phila., Dec. 28, 1921; s. Samuel Edward and Reba (Trimble) G.; m. Jane Harlos, Sept. 2, 1950; 1 child, Jeffrey Neal. JD, Temple U., 1950. Bar: Pa. 1951. Ptnr. LaBrum & Doak, Phila., 1953-80, German, Gallagher & Murtagh, Phila., 1980—; cons., lectr. to law schools including Harvard U., U. Pa., Syracuse U., others; bd. dirs., mem. products liability, def. research coms. Def. Research Inst., Def. Research Regional Library Inst.; instr. Practicing Law Inst. Contbr. chpts. to books, articles to profl. jours. Dist. dir. United Fund Campaign, 1960; solicitor-counsel Civic Assns. Delaware County, 1955-60; sec. Haven Beach Assn., 1962-63, v.p., 1963-64; trustee Pop Warner's Little Scholars, 1968—; sec., treas. Henryville Conservation Club. Served with USAAF, 1942-46, with USAF, 1950-51. Mem. ABA (chmn. trial techniques com. 1969, mem. profl. and officers and dirs. liability law com. ins. sect. 1974—, pvt. antitrust litigation com. litigation sect. 1974—, subcom. miscellaneous malpractice re accts., bankers, etc. 1976—), Pa. Bar Assn. (com. unauthorized practice 1976—), Phila. Bar Assn. (mem. Pa. rules of civil procedure com. 1963-71, unauthorized practice law com. 1965—, common pleas ct. com. 1964-71, com. antitrust laws corp. sect., mem. Federal bench-bar conf.), Am. Law Firm Assn. (chmn. bd. 1985-86), Fedn. Ins. Counsel (bd. govs. 1960-62, v.p. 1962-63, sec.-treas. 1963-65, exec. v.p. 1965-66, pres. 1966-67, chmn. bd. 1967-68), Maritime Law Assn., U.S. Am. Legion, 40 and 8, Internat. Assn. Ins. Counsel (def. research com., profl. liability and malpractice com.), Internat. Assn. Humble Humbugs, Pa. C. of C., Phila. Def. Counsel Assn., Scribes, Phi Delta Phi. Lodges: Masons, Shriners. Clubs: Union League, Down Town, Maxwell Meml. Football, Union League (Phila.), Beach Haven (N.J.) Yacht, Little Egg Harbor Yacht, Urban (pres. 1987-88) (Phila.), Little Mill Country, Belleplain Farms Shooting Preserve. Home: 129 The Mews Haddonfield NJ 08033-1344 Office: German Gallagher & Murtagh 200 S Broad St Philadelphia PA 19102-3803

GERMAN, JOHN GEORGE, retired transportation consultant; b. Devils Lake, N.D., Sept. 22, 1921; s. George and Dorothy Florence (Stenson) G.; m. Mary Alice Chambers, Sept. 15, 1973; 1 child, John R. B.S.M.E., Case Sch. Applied Sci., Cleve., 1943. With Gt. No. Ry. Co., 1943-61; with Mo. Pacific R.R. Co., St. Louis, 1961-83, chief mech. officer, 1961-66, asst. v.p. engring., 1966-75, v.p. engring., 1975-83; pres. John German Ry. Engring. Cons. Ltd., 1983-94; ret. Fellow ASME; mem. Internat. Heavy Haul Assn. (exec. dir., sec., treas. 1983-94). Republican. Lodges: Masons; Shriners; Scottish Rite. Home: 19 Holloway Dr Lake Saint Louis MO 63367-1357

GERMAN, JUNE RESNICK, lawyer; b. N.Y.C., Feb. 24, 1946; d. Irving and Stella (Weintraub) Resnick; m. Harold Jacob German, May 31, 1974; children: Beth Melissa, Heather Alice, Bret. BA, U. Pa., 1965; JD, NYU, 1968. Bar: N.Y. 1968, U.S. Dist. Ct. (ea. and so. dists.) N.Y. 1974, U.S. Ct. Appeals (2d cir.) 1973, U.S. Supreme Ct. 1973. Atty., sr. atty., supervising atty. Mental Health Info. Svc., N.Y.C., 1968-77; atty./advisor Course in Human Behavior Mems. of N.Y. State Judiciary, Nassau and Suffolk County, 1980; pvt. practice, Huntington, N.Y., 1985—. *June Resnick German brought several test cases which guaranteed rights to mentally disabled persons in the civil and criminal justice system, including a landmark case which established that, in New York State, civil involuntary patients have (a) a right to treatment, (b) a right to be treated in a facility that is least restrictive of their liberty, and (c) a right not to be transferred to a correctional facility. She has written several articles pertaining to the rights of the mentally disabled and has prepared amicus curiae briefs to the United States Supreme Court in the fields of mental health and environmental law.* Contbg. author: Bioethics and Human Rights, 1978, Mental Illness, Due Process and the Acquitted Defendant, 1979; contbr. chpts. to books, articles to profl. jours. Chmn. Citizen's Ad Hoc Com. Constrn. of the Dix Hills Water Adminstrn. Bldg., Huntington, N.Y., 1985-90; mem. Citizens Adv. Com. for Dix Hills Water Dist., Huntington, 1992—; dir. House Beautiful Assn. at Dix Hills, 1986—; dir. Citizens for a Livable Environment and Recycling, Huntington, 1989-93; mem. Suffolk County (N.Y.) Dem. Com., 1986—; mem. Deer Park Avenue Task Force, Town of Huntington, 1997-98; mem. Dix Hills Revitalization Com., 1999—. Mem. Suffolk County Bar Assn. Jewish. Avocations: tennis, hiking, travel. Office: 150 Main St Huntington NY 11743-6908

GERMAN, LYNNE CUMMINGS, music educator; b. Columbus, Ohio, Feb. 25, 1958; d. W. Dean and Naomi Faye (Cook) Cummings; m. Kenneth W. German, July 31, 1982; children: Madelaine Anne, Eliza Lynne, Brooke Nicole, Iris Noel. BS in Music Edn., Bob Jones U., 1980, MA in Piano, 1982. Dir. Southside Christian Sch. Flute Choir, Greenville, S.C., 1981-82; founder, owner, tchr. German Piano Studio, Mt. Crawford, Va., 1983—; tchr. James Madison U., Harrisonburg, Va., 1989-94; dir. Harrisonburg Flute Choir, 1994-95, Grace Covenant Ch. Vocal Choir and Brass Choir, Harrisonburg, 1995—; spkr. in field. Contbr. articles to profl. jours. Mem. Nat. Guild Piano Tchrs., Music Tchrs. Nat. Assn., Va. Music Tchrs. Assn. (western Va. chpt. music theory chmn. 1995—), Harrisonburg Piano Tchrs. Forum. Avocations: composing, arranging music, writing, hiking, bicycling. Home and Office: 5006 Cross Keys Rd Mount Crawford VA 22841-9522

GERMAN, RANDALL MICHAEL, materials engineering educator, consultant; b. Bainbridge, Md., Nov. 12, 1946; s. Eugene Knox and Helen (Schrufer) G.; m. Carol Jean Hosmer, Dec. 21, 1968; children: Eric, Garth. BS in Materials Sci., San Jose State U., 1968; MS in Metall. Engring., Ohio State U., 1971; PhD in Materials Sci., U. Calif., Davis, 1975; cert. mgmt. devel., Hartford Grad. Ctr., 1979. Materials scientist Batteille Columbus Labs., Columbus, Ohio, 1968-69; tech. staff Sandia Nat. Lab., Livermore, Calif., 1969-77; dir. R&D Mott Metall. Corp., Farmington, Conn., 1977-78; dir. rsch. J.M. Ney Co., Bloomfield, Conn., 1978-80; Hunt prof. Rensselaer Poly. Inst., Troy, N.Y., 1980-91; Brush chair prof. materials Pa. State U., University Park, 1991—; founder Six Cos., Inc., Troy, 1989—, Xform; dir. PIM Symposium, 1990—. Author: Powder Metallurgy Science, 1984, 2d edit., 1994, Liquid Phase Sintering, 1985, Powder Packing Characteristics, 1989, Injection Molding, 1990, Sintering Theory and Practice, 1996, Injection Molding of Metals and Ceramics, 1997, Powder Metallurgy of Iron and Steel, 1998; contbr. numerous articles to profl. jours.; patentee in field. Named Hon. Prof. N.E. U. Tech., 1985, Disting. Alumni U. Calif., 1990, Penn State Engring. Soc. Outstanding and Premiere Rschr. award, 1995. Fellow ASM Internat. (chmn. Geissler award 1983), Am. Powder Metallurgy (spkr., organizer, bd. dirs.); mem. Minerals, Metals, Materials Soc. (chmn. 1983-85), Am. Ceramic Soc., Materials Rsch. Soc., Alpha Sigma Mu (hon.). Avocation: bicycling. Home: 1145 Outer Dr State College PA 16801-8240

GERMAN, RONALD STEPHEN, health care facility administrator; b. Jersey City, May 26, 1946; s. Steve and Eleanor (Gruttke) G.; m. Diana Lynn Jones, Dec. 3, 1972 (div. 1983); m. Cheryl Dunbar Gardner, Apr. 26, 1985; children: Scott James Gardner, Brian Dunbar Gardner. BSBA cum laude, U. Tenn., 1974; MBA summa cum laude, Bristol U., 1991. With Bankers Trust Co., N.Y.C., 1969-70; dir. employee tng. and devel. personnel dept. U. Tenn., Knoxville, 1975-78; mgr. East Tenn. Orthopaedic Ctr., Knoxville, 1978-97; sr. med. practice cons. State Vol. Mut. Ins. Co., Brentwood, Tenn., 1997—; bd. dirs. Knoxville Acad. Medicine Med-Staff Placement Inc. Mem. First United Meth. Ch., Knoxville, 1987—. Served with USAF, 1965-69. Mem. Med. Group Assn. (pres. 1982), Am. Coll. Med. Practice Execs. (cert.), Knoxville Med. Group Mgrs. Assn. (pres. 1992), Tenn. Valley Pers. Assn. (treas. 1987-88, sec. 1989), Knoxville Rotary (Paul Harris fellow). Republican. Home: 420 Dixieview Rd Knoxville TN 37922-2609 Office: State Vol Mut Ins Co 101 Westpark Dr Ste 300 Brentwood TN 37027-5031

GERMAN, WILLIAM, newspaper editor; b. N.Y.C., Jan. 4, 1919; s. Sam and Celia (Norack) G.; m. Gertrude Pasenkoff, Oct. 12, 1940; children: David, Ellen, Stephen. B.A., Bklyn. Coll., 1939; M.S., Columbia U., 1940; Nieman fellow, Harvard U., 1950. Reporter, asst. fgn., news, mng., exec. editor, editor San Francisco Chronicle, 1940—; editor Chronicle Fgn. Service, 1960-77; mng. editor KQED, Newspaper of the Air, 1968; lectr. U. Calif., Berkeley, 1946-47, 68-70. Editor: San Francisco Chronicle Reader, 1962. Bd. trustees World Affairs Coun. Served with AUS, 1943-45. Mem. AP Mng. Editors Assn., Am. Soc. Newspaper Editors, Commonwealth Club of Calif. (pres. 1995). Home: 150 Lovell Ave Mill Valley CA 94941-1883 Office: San Francisco Chronicle 901 Mission St San Francisco CA 94103-2905

GERMANN, RICHARD PAUL, pharmaceutical company chemist, executive; b. Ithaca, N.Y., Apr. 3, 1918; s. Frank E.E. and Martha Minna Marie (Knechtel) G.; m. Malinda Jane Plietz, Dec. 11, 1942; 1 child, Cheranne Lee. Student, U. N.Mex., 1938-39; BA, U. Colo., 1939, postgrad., 1940-41; postgrad., Western Res. U., 1941-43, Brown U., 1954. Chief analytical chemist Taylor Refining Co., Corpus Christi, 1943-44; rsch. devel. chemist Calco Chem. divsn. Am. Cyanamid Co., 1944-52; devel. chemist charge pilot plant Alrose Chem. Co. divsn. Geigy Chem. Corp., 1952-55; new product devel. chemist, rsch. divsn. W.R. Grace & Co., Clarksville, Md., 1955-60; chief chemist soap-cosmetic divsn. G.H. Packwood Mfg. Co., St. Louis, 1960-61; coord., promoter chem. product devel. Abbott Labs., North Chicago, Ill., 1961-71; internat. chem. cons. to mgmt., 1971-73; pres. Germann Internat. Ltd., 1973-82, Ramtek Internat. Ltd., 1973—; real estate broker, 1972-90; cons. major Japanese chem. cos., 1971-85; cons. dept. chemistry Bowling Green (Ohio) State U., 1988. Author: The Technical Man of the Sea of Change, 1965, Decontamination of Plant Wastes--An Overview, 1969, Science's Ultimate Challenge--The Re-evaluation of Ancient Occult Knowledge, 1978, Science and Innovation, 1993; patentee in U.S. and fgn. countries on sulfonamides, vitamins, detergent-softeners and biocides. Rep. Am. Inst. Chemists to Joint Com. on Employment Practices, 1969-72; vestryman St. Paul's Episc. Ch., Norwalk, Ohio, 1978-81, chmn. adminstrn. and long-range planning commn., 1980-81, The Ch. of Light; trustee Svcs. for the Aging, Inc., 1982-94, treas., 1992-93, pres., 1994; mem. nutritional coun. Ohio Dist. Five Area Agy. on Aging, 1983-84; sr. adv. Ohio Assn. Ctrs. for Sr. Citizens, Inc., 1982-90; bd. dirs. Christie Lane Industries, 1981—, chmn., 1988-94; mem. com. Huron County Disaster Svcs. Agy., 1987-89, sec. Fellow AAAS, Am. Inst. Chemists (chmn. com. employment rels. 1969-72), Chem. Soc. (London); mem. Am. Chem. Soc. (councilor 1971-73, chmn. membership com. chem. mktg. and econs. div. 1966-68, chmn. program com. 1968-69, del. at large for local sects. 1970-71, chmn. 1972-73, chmn. Chgo. program com. 1966-67, chmn. Chgo. endowment com. 1967-68, dir. Chgo. sect. 1968-72, chmn. awards com. 1972-73, sec. chem. mktg. and econs. group Chgo. sect. 1964-66, chmn. 1967-68), Am. Numastic, Internat. Sci. Found., Sci. Rsch. Soc. Am., Comml. Chem. Devel. Assn. (chmn. program com. Chgo. conv. 1966, mem. fin. com. 1966-67, ad hoc com. of Comml. Chem. Devel. Assn. and Chem. Market Rsch. Assn. 1968-69, co-chmn. pub. rels. Denver conv. 1968, chmn. membership com. 1969-70, mem. directory com. 1967-68, employment com. 1969-70), Nat. Security Indsl. Assn. (com. rep. ocean sci. tech. com., maintenance adv. com., tng. ad. com. 1962-70), Midwest Planning Assn., Am. Assn. Textile Chemists and Colorists, Am. Pharm. Assn., Midwest Chem. Mktg. Assn., Am. Mgmt. Assn., N.Y. Acad. Scis., Internat. Platform Assn., Am. Meteorol. Soc., Water Pollution Control Fedn., Lake County Bd. Realtors, World Future Soc., Midwest Planning Assn., Am. Fedn. Astrologers, Washington Astrological Assn. (v.p. 1959-60), Ancient Astronaut Soc., Am. Philatelic Soc., Am. Numismatic Assn., Am. Rose Soc., AARP (pres. Huron county Firelands chpt. #4110 1986-88, chmn. legis. com. 1988-90, active project vote, pres. 1997-98, bd. dirs. 1998—), Friends Norwalk Pub. Libr. (sec. 1997-98, pres. 1998—), Chemists Club (N.Y.C.,Chgo.), Torch Club, Toastmasters, Lions (sec. Allview, Md. 1956-57), Kiwanis, Masons, (32nd degree, Knights Templar, Rotary, Gamma Delta (pres. Cleve. chapt. 1941-42), Sigma Xi, Alpha Chi Sigma (chmn. profl. activities com. 1968-70, pres. Chgo. chpt. 1968-70). Adventures through many rebirths both here on this earth and on earths in many ddistant galaxies far out in the universe as God allows us to increase our knowledge of the real reason for our existence. Home and Office: 6 Vinewood St Norwalk OH 44857-1919 *Total knowledge, whether it be in business, science, history, or religion, is a mirage. That which we believe to be true today will be subject to continuous modification throughout all eternity as understanding of the universe continues to expand. This belief has made my life an adventure in which I have attempted to find the many "reasons why" which determine the way we think and live. It is obvious that all the fields in question are interrelated in many ways. History shows that dogma in any discipline or a lack of knowledge of the past has always inhibited or prevented man's spiritual, scientific or material growth. The incorrect beliefs thus perpetuated become the cross we bear that prevents us in no small part from living our lives to the fullest during our short stay here on earth. Since I believe that there is a hidden reason for everything that happens during our lifetime, logic tells me that in the eons to come each soul will continue its adventures through many rebirths both*

GERMANN, STEVEN JAMES, museum director; b. Dayton, Ohio, Sept. 4, 1947; s. James Howard and Doris Olive (Smith) G.; m. Elizabeth Haifley, Oct. 13, 1979; children: Alison Haifley, Andrew Ryan. BA in History, Wright State U., 1969, MA in History, 1973, cert. Mus. Adminstrn., 1977. Dir. edn. svcs. Montgomery County Hist. Soc., Dayton, Ohio, 1976-82; mus. adminstr. Mont. Hist. Soc., Helena, 1982-89; dir. Alfred P. Sloan Mus., Flint, Mich., 1989—; exec. v.p. Midwest Mus. Conf., St. Louis, 1992—. Bd. dirs. Flint Area Conv. and Visitors Bureau, 1992—. Mem. Am. Assn. Mus. (mem. mus. accreditation vis. com. 1989—), Midwest Mus. Assn., Genesee County Hist. Soc. (bd. dirs.), Flint Rotary, Phi Alpha Theta (hon. Rho Sigma chpt.). Home: 1701 Lincoln Dr Flint MI 48503-4715 Office: Sloan Museum 1221 E Kearsley St Flint MI 48503-1988

GERMANO, MARY CATHERINE, writer; b. Washington, D.C., Dec. 16, 1949; d. Robert F. and Mary C. (Lahatte) Pierozak; m. Donald J. Germano, May 26, 1973; children: David, Peter, Michael, Mary. BS, St. Bonaventure U., 1972; MLS, Rutgers U., 1975. Libr. Lincoln 1st Bank, Rochester, N.Y., 1975-81, Gates-Chili (N.Y.) Sch. Dist., 1981—; pvt. practice Fairport, N.Y., 1988—. Author: Silent Witness, 1993. Mem. special edn. com. Fairport (N.Y.) Sch. Dist., 1992-95, regional trauma oversight com. Strong Meml. Hosp. Trauma Ctr., Rochester, N.Y., 1994—; bd. dirs. Perinton Vol. Ambulance Corps., Fairport, 1996-98. Mem. Mystery Writers Am., Am. Trauma Soc., Sisters in Crime. Avocations: reading, listening to people, gardening, karate, Aiki Jujitsu. Home: 48 South Ave Fairport NY 14450-2454 Office: 48 South Ave Fairport NY 14450-2454

GERMANO, WILLIAM PAUL, publisher; b. Yonkers, N.Y., Oct. 10, 1950; s. William Peter and Edna Mary (Gilmore) G.; m. Diane Grace Gibbons, July 21, 1973; 1 child, Christian. BA in English, Columbia U., 1972; PhD in English, Ind. U., 1981. Editor Columbia U. Press, N.Y.C., 1980-83, editor in chief, 1983-85; v.p., editorial dir. Routledge, Chapman and Hall Inc., N.Y.C., 1986-92; v.p., editorial dir. Routledge, Inc., N.Y.C., 1992-96, v.p., dir. pub. humanities, 1996—. Mem. MLA, The English Inst., Am. Acad. of Religion, Am. Anthropol. Assn. Home: 33 Riverside Dr New York NY 10023-8012 Office: Routledge Inc 29 W 35th St New York NY 10001-2299

GERMANOTTA, JEFFREY STEVEN, investment banker; b. Milw., June 30, 1958; s. Louis Robert and Marily Jean (Robinson) G.; 1 child, Daniel Scott. BBA, U. Wis., Milw., 1980; MBA, Marquette U., 1989. Credit analyst First Wis. Nat. Bank, Milw., 1981, comml. loan officer, 1982-83, comml. banking asst. v.p., 1984-85; corp. banking group asst. v.p. Bank One, Milw. N.A., Milw., 1985-86; corp. planner Banc One Wis. Corp., Milw., 1986-87; v.p. corp. fin. Bank One Milw., N.A., 1987-94, v.p. and mgr. capital markets divsn., 1994—; sr. v.p. equity rsch. Robert W. Baird & Co. Inc., 1994—.

GERMANOWSKI, JANET, women's health and medical surgical nurse, educator, researcher; b. Augusta, Ga., Oct. 29, 1943; d. Leonard and Marion (Davis) Volkin; m. Peter J. Germanowski, Dec. 28, 1970; children: Peter, Lauren. BSN, U. Pitts., 1965, MSN, 1990, CCRC, 1999. Rsch. assoc. HealthAmerica, Pitts.; project coord. Aminoguanidine Drug Trial, U. Pitts.; project nurse cholesterol lowering intervention program U. Pitts.; head nurse, office mgr. dept. ob-gyn. Magee Women's Hosp., Pitts., 1971-86; acting clin. instr. U. Pitts. Sch. Nursing, 1989, grad. student asst., 1987-90; project nurse cholesterol lowering intervention program U. Pitts., 1990-94; project coord. Aminoguanidine Drug Trial, U. Pitts., 1994-95; rsch. assoc. HealthAmerica, Pitts., 1995-97; head nurse, office mgr. dept. ob-gyn. Magee Women's Hosp., Pitts.; grad. student asst. U. Pitts. Sch. Nursing; sr. clin. rsch. coord. nTouch Rsch., Pitts., 1997—. Contbr. articles to profl. jours. Mem. ANA, NAACOG, Pa. Nurses Assn., Sigma Theta Tau. Home and Office: 54 Ridgecrest Dr Pittsburgh PA 15235-4548

GERMANY, DANIEL MONROE, aerospace engineer; b. Lake Village, Ark., Sept. 14, 1937; s. Jones Harry and Sara (Farrar) G.; m. Edie Germany; children: Cheryl Germany, Danel Germany, Dianne Germany, Randall Robertson, Rick Robertson, Vaughn Loiuse. B.S.M.E., Miss. State U., 1959. Aerospace systems engr. NASA Marshall Space Flight Center, Huntsville, Ala., 1960-78; tech. exec. asst. to asso. adminstr. of shuttle transp. systems NASA Hdqrs., Washington, 1978-79; dir. orbiter programs NASA Hdqrs., 1979-81; asst. mgr. Orbiter Project Office Johnson Space Ctr., Houston, 1982, mgr. Flight Equipment Project Office, 1983-85; dep. mgr. Space Sta. Project Office Johnson Space Ctr., 1985-86, dep. mgr. Orbiter and GFE Projects Office, 1987-90, mgr. Orbiter and GFE Projects Office, 1990-95; ind. aerospace cons., 1995-97; program dir. Allied Signal Aerospace, Houston, 1997—. Republican.

GERMANY, JOHN FREDRICK, lawyer; b. Daviston, Ala., Jan. 16, 1923; s. Thomas Brooks and Aldora Toles (Finley) G.; m. Mary Ellen Cook, June 15, 1951; children: Sue Ellen Germany Lucas, John Jr., Jan Fielder Germany Gruetzmacher, Lindsey Brooks Robbins. BA, U. Fla., 1943; JD, Harvard U., 1950; LLD (hon.), Stetson U., 1974. Bar: Fla. 1950, U.S. Dist. Ct. (mid. dist.) Fla., 1951, D.C., 1981. Assoc. Fowler, White, Gillen, Yancey & Humkey, Tampa, Fla., 1950-52; ptnr. Coles, Himes & Germany, Tampa, 1952-59; judge 13th Jud. Cir., Tampa, 1959-66; ptnr. Knight, Jones, Whitaker & Germany, Tampa, 1966-68, Holland & Knight, Tampa, 1968—; asst. county atty. Hillsborough County, Tampa, 1955-59; legal asst. to gov. State of Fla., 1955-57. Served to 1st lt. U.S. Army, ETO, PTO. Fellow ABA (state chmn.); mem. Atty.'s Liability Assurance Soc. Ltd. (bd. dirs.). Democrat. Episcopalian. Clubs: Univ. (pres. 1964-65), Tampa (pres. 1983-85) (Tampa). Lodge: Ye Mystic Krewe of Gasparilla King. Avocations: reading, travelling, walking. Office: Holland & Knight PO Box 1288 Tampa FL 33601-1288*

GERNER, DEBORAH JEANNE, political scientist, educator; b. San Jose, Calif.; d. Henry and Dorothy (Love) G. BA, Earlham Coll., 1977; MA, Northwestern U., 1979, PhD, 1982. Asst. prof. U. Iowa, Iowa City, 1982-84, Hamilton Coll., Clinton, N.Y., 1983-86, Northwestern U., Evanston, Ill., 1985-88; from asst. prof. to assoc. prof. U. Kans., Lawrence, 1988—. Author: One Land, Two Peoples: The Conflict Over Palestine, 1991, 2d edit., 1994; series editor: New Millenium Books. Fulbright scholar, 1996; grantee NSF, 1991-93, 94-96. Mem. Am. Polit. Sci. Assn., Assn. Arab-Am. Univ. Grads., Internat. Soc. Polit. Psychology, Internat. Studies Assn., Middle East Studies Assn. N.Am., Midwest Polit. Sci. Assn., Women's Caucus for Polit. Sci. Office: U Kans 504 Blake Hall Lawrence KS 66044-7508

GERNER, EDWARD WILLIAM, medical educator; b. N.Y.C., Nov. 8, 1940; s. David and Anne (Robbins) G.; m. Judith E. Delbaum, June 5, 1983; 1 child, Danielle. BA magna cum laude, Clark U., 1961; MD, NYU, 1965. Diplomate Am. Bd. Ophthalmology, Am. Bd. Neurology. Intern Presbyn. U. Pitts. Hosp., 1965-66; resident Hosp. U. Pa., Phila., 1967-69; instr. dept. neurology U. Pa. Sch. Medicine, Phila., 1967-69, instr. dept. ophthalmology, 1972-74; attending neurologist Tulane U. Sch. Medicine, New Orleans, 1969-71; asst. surgeon Wills Eye Hosp., Phila., 1981-88, assoc. surgeon, 1988—; asst. prof. dept. neurology T. Jefferson U. Sch. Medicine, Phila., 1978-88, asst. prof. dept. ophthalmology, 1982-88, assoc. prof., 1988—; bd. dirs. Pa. Physicians Healthcare Plan, Harrisburg. Contbr. chpts. to books and articles to profl. jours. Lt. comdr. USPHS, 1969-72. N.Y. State Regent scholar N.Y. State Bd. Regents, 1957-61; Jones fellow Mayo Clinic, Rochester, Minn., 1965. Fellow Am. Acad. Ophthalmology, Am. Acad. Neurology; mem. Royal Soc. Medicine (affiliate), Phi Beta Kappa. Avocations: photography, gardening. Office: 834 Chestnut St # (T-130) Philadelphia PA 19107-5127

GERNERT, ERIC VINCENT, telecommunications analyst; b. Pitts., Sept. 7, 1961; s. William and Marie Francis (Sochacki) G. BS, U. Pitts., 1983, MS in Telecomm., 1989. Programmer, analyst U. Pitts., 1983-85; data analyst Opus Corp., Germantown, Md., 1985-87; field engr. AT&T, Bala-Cynwyd, Pa., 1989-90; sys. cons. AT&T, Pitts., 1990-91, facilities adminstr., 1991-97, tech. staff mem., 1998—. Divsn. chmn. Allegheny County Transit Coun., Pitts., 1994-1995, 1997. Mem. IEEE, Pa. R.R. Mus. Assn., U. Pitts. Alumni Assn., Iota Beta Kappa Alumni Assn. (exec. dir. 1994-98). Democrat. Roman Catholic. Avocations: public transit advocate, collegiate and professional sports, music, photography. Home: 6370 Pleasant St Library PA 15129-9715 Office: AT&T Corp 635 Grant St Pittsburgh PA 15219-4404

GERNERT, JEFFREY JARED, psychologist; b. Takoma Park, Md., Dec. 15, 1961; s. Earl Clifford and Darlene (Grant) G. BA, U. Pa., 1987; MPhil, George Washington U., 1993, PhD, 1995. Lic. psychologist, D.C., Md. Psychology intern St. Elizabeth's Hosp., Washington, 1993-94, postdoctoral fellow, 1994-96; clin. psychologist Comprehensive Geriatric Svcs., Towson, Md., 1996—. Contbr. articles to profl. jours. Mem. APA. Home: 1623 R St NW Washington DC 20009-6420

GERNON, GEORGE OWEN, JR., civil engineer; b. New Orleans, Dec. 15, 1950; s. George Owen and Loretta Cecile (Conners) G.; m. Vilma Velozo de Souza, June 11, 1974; children: Marco Antonio, Adrianna Elizabeth. BS, U. Southwestern La., 1972. Registered profl. engr., La. Field engr. Oceanic Contractors SE Asia, Brazil and Trinidad, 1972-74; structural engr. J. Ray McDermott, New Orleans, 1974-75; sr. design engr. Santa Fe Engrng. Svcs., Orange, Calif., 1975-77; sr. project engr. Santa Fe Engrng. and Constrn. Co., Houma, La., 1978-79, project mgr., 1979-87; asst. ops. mgr. Pipelines Unltd. Svcs., Houma, La., 1987-88, ops. mgr., 1989-90; sr. ops. engr. McDermott Inc., Morgan City, La., 1990-93, sr. project mgr., 1993-96; sr. project mgr. J. Ray McDermott SA, Houston, 1996-97, divsn. mgr., 1997-98, gen. mgr., 1998—. Mem. NSPE, Project Mgmt. Inst., Am. Welding Soc., La. Engrng. Soc., Mensa. Republican. Roman Catholic. Home: 2810 Mission Hills Ct Katy TX 77450-8694 Office: J Ray McDermott Inc 801 N Eldridge Pkwy Houston TX 77079-2701

GERO, ANTHONY GEORGE, securities and commodities trader; b. London, May 31, 1936; came to U.S., 1947; s. Stephen Gero and Ilona (Braun) Von Rieger; m. Joan Selinger, Nov. 20, 1969 (div. 1980); m. Gale Gendason, Feb. 14, 1989; 1 child, Danielle Joy. BS, NYU, 1959; cert., Investment Bankers Inst. U. Pa., 1965. Reporter USIS Chilean Eartquake Relief/Am. Embassy, 1959-60; ptnr. Goodbody & Co., 1960-64, Charles Plohn & Co., N.Y.C., 1964-67; v.p., dir. Internat. First Hanover Corp., N.Y.C., 1967-69; v.p. Drexel Burnham & Co., N.Y.C., 1971-80; 1st v.p. Prudential Securities, N.Y.C., 1981—; mem. U.S. Dept. Commerce, NDER, 1989—; bd. dirs. Commodity Clearing Corp. Author: Precious Metals, 1985. Dir., treas. children's fund Commodities Exch. Ctr., N.Y.C., 1980—; chmn. NYMEX Charitable Trust, N.Y.C., 1990—. Recipient Cert., Holocaust Meml., 1991. Mem. N.Y. Produce Exch., N.Y. Merc. Exch. (bd. dirs., treas. N.Y.C. chpt. 1974—), Commodity Exch. Inc. (bd. dirs. 1995), N.Y. Coffee, Sugar and Cocoa Exch., N.Y. Cotton Exch. (bd. dirs. 1995), Commodity Fl. Brokers and Traders Assn. (chmn. 1990—), Investment Brokers Assn., Westchester County Policy Revolver Age, Westchester County Sheriff's Assn., N.Y. Police Res. Assn., Securities Industry Assn. (swaps and derivatives commn.). Republican. Avocations: photography, amateur radio, chess. Home: 180 E End Ave New York NY 10128-7763 Office: Prudential Securities 1 Liberty Plz New York NY 10006-1404

GERONEMUS, DIANN FOX, social work consultant; b. Chgo., July 4, 1947; d. Herbert J. and Edith (Robbins) Fox; BA with high honors, Mich. State U., 1969; MSW, U. Ill., 1971; 1 dau., Heather Eileen. Diplomate Am. Bd. Clin. Social Work; lic. clin. social worker, marriage and family therapist, Fla.; cert. case mgr.; bd. cert. diplomate clin. social work. Social worker neurology, neurosurgery and medicine Hosp. of Albert Einstein Coll. Medicine, 1971-74; prin. social worker ob-gyn and newborn infant service Rush-Presbyn.-St. Luke's Med. Center, Chgo., 1974-75; social worker neurology, adminstr. Multiple Sclerosis Treatment Center, St. Barnabas Hosp., Bronx, N.Y., 1975-77, socio-med. researcher (Nat. Multiple Sclerosis Soc. grantee), dept. neurology and psychiatry, 1977-79, dir. social service, 1979-80; field work instr. Fordham U. Grad. Sch. Social Service, 1979-80; preceptor, social work program Fla. Atlantic U., Fla. Internat. U.; mem. edn. com., med. adv. bd., program cons. Nat. Multiple Sclerosis Soc., 1980-83, area service cons., 1983-86 ; pvt. practice psychotherapy; social work cons.; cons. in gerontology, rehab. and supervision, 1980—. Mem. Ombudsman Coun., 1992-94, vice chmn. 1993-94. Mem. NASW, Acad. Cert. Social Workers, Registry Clin. Social Workers, Am. Orthopsychiat. Assn. Jewish. Contbr. articles to profl. jours. Home: 833 NW 81st Way Fort Lauderdale FL 33324-1216

GEROU, PHILLIP HOWARD, architect; b. Natick, Mass., July 20, 1951; s. James Francis and Enid (Meymaris) G.; m. Cheri Rodgers, Nov. 24, 1979; children: Gregory Bedford, Sara Christine. BArch, U. Nebr., 1974, MArch, 1975. Architect Colo., 1975-77; project mgr. Henningson, Durham, Richardson, Denver, 1978-82; dir. architecture Daniel Mann Johnson Mendenhall, Denver, 1982-85; v.p., dir. comml. design Downing Leach Architects, Boulder, 1985-86; prin., designer, owner Gerou & Assocs. Ltd., Evergreen, Colo., 1986—; design cons. Kilimanjaro Children's Hosp., Tanzania, 1988-91, World Alpine Ski Championships, Vail, Colo., 1988. Pres. Colo. Soc. of Architects Ednl. Fund., Denver, 1986; del. State Rep. Assembly, Denver, 1986; trustee Rockland Community Ch., Denver, 1986-89. Recipient Citation award Nat. Assn. of Remodeling Industry, 1991, 96, Design Excellence Wood, Inc., 1990, Citation award, 1990. Fellow AIA (pres. Colo. chpt. 1986, bd. dirs. 1981-87, nat. dir. 1991-94, v.p. 1995, dir. Nat. Ethics Coun. 1997—, chmn., 1998—, conf. chair Western Mtn. region design conf. 1990, Spl. Recognition award 1990), Nat. Coun. Archl. Adminstrn. Bds. (examiner 1985). Republican. Mem. United Ch. of Christ. Avocations: skiing, travel, architectural design. *

GERRARD, JOHN M., state supreme court justice; b. Schuyler, Nebr., Nov. 2, 1953. BS, Nebr. Wesleyan U., 1976; MPA, U. Ariz., 1977; JD, U. of Pacific, 1981. Pvt. practice Norfolk, 1981-95; city atty. City of Battle Creek, Nebr., 1982-95; justice Nebr. Supreme Ct., Lincoln, 1995—. Office: Nebr Supreme Ct 2214 State Capitol Lincoln NE 68509-8910*

GERRATANA, THERESA B., state legislator; b. New Britain, Conn., Oct. 7, 1949; d. Steven Jr. and Mary Ann (Luppino) Bielinski; m. Frank J. Gerratana, 1977; children: Frank L., Gregory J. BS, Ctrl. Conn. State U., 1975. Justice of peace New Britain, 1985-93; mem. ethics commn. City of New Britain, 1990-93; mem. Dist. 23 Conn. Ho. of Reps., 1993—. Pres. Jr. League of Greater New Britain, 1990-92. Mem. LWV (pres. 1986-88). Address: 674 Lincoln St New Britain CT 06052-1833 Office: Conn Ho of Reps State Capitol Hartford CT 06106

GERRATT, BRADLEY SCOTT, presidential library director; b. Norwood, Mass., Apr. 21, 1953; s. Irving and Lucille (Levine) G.; m. Susan Lathrop Powers, Oct. 11, 1981; children: Nathan Powers, Aaron Powers. BA, Clark U., 1975; MA, MBA, U. Chgo., 1979. Gov.'s fellow Ill. Dept. Pub. Aid, Springfield, summer 1978; budget analyst Mass. Dept. Social Svcs., Boston, 1979-81, adminstrv. svcs. mgr., 1981-84; CFO City of Boston, Neighborhood Devel. and Employment Agy., 1984-85; dir. adminstrn. and fin. Pub. Facilities Dept. City of Boston, 1985-88; dep. dir. John F. Kennedy Libr., Boston, 1988-94, dir., 1994—. Office: John F Kennedy Libr Columbia Point Boston MA 02125*

GERRAUGHTY, DAVID R., newspaper editor. Nat. news editor Houston Chronicle, 1989—. Office: Houston Chronicle 801 Texas St Houston TX 77002-2996*

GERRETSEN, GILBERT WYNAND (GIL GERRETSEN), marketing consultant, coach; b. Rotterdam, The Netherlands, May 8, 1955; arrived in Can., 1957, Can. citizen, 1960; arrived in U.S., 1980, naturalized, 1983; s. Everhardus Hubertus and Johanna (Boers) G.; m. Susan Boggs, June 27, 1980. B of Commerce, U. Calgary, Alberta, Canada, 1976. Group ins. adminstr., asst. supr. group acctg. Great-West Life Assurance, Winnipeg, Canada, 1978-80; supr. policyholder svc. Founders Life Ins., Tampa, Fla., 1980-81; cons. specialist group ins. William M. Mercer, Inc., Tampa, Fla., 1981-82; exec. dir. Junior Achievement, Greenville, S.C., 1982-85; pres. Jr. Achievement So. Ariz., Tucson, 1985-88; sr. dir. devel. Junior Achievement, Seattle, 1988-90; sr. dir. mktg. Washington Special Olympics, Seattle, 1990-92; chief mktg. officer ALM Internat., Greenville, 1992-94; pres. ListenUp Mktg., Inc., Greenville, 1994—; founder, chmn. BizTrek Internat., Greenville, 1997—. Pub. (newsletter) BizTrek Mktg. Minute. Bd. dirs. Jr. Achievement, 1995-99, Greenville Humane Soc., 1996-97, S.C. Soc. for Prevention of Cruelty to Animals, 1996-97, Child Evangelism Fellowship, 1996, C. of C. Small Bus. Coun., 1996-99, Clemson U. Small Bus. Devel. Coun., 1996-99, Greenville Chamber Edn. Com., 1996-99, CEO Roundtable, 1995-99, Downtown Greenville Christian Businessmen's Com.; bd. dirs. Greenville Work Tng. Ctr., chmn., 1997-99. Avocations: Biblical studies, model railroading, oil painting. Office: 710 E McBee Ave Greenville SC 29601

GERRING, CLIFTON, III, corporate executive; b. Clarksdale, Miss., Oct. 6, 1952; s. Clifton and Ollie Rose (Brown) G.; m. Karen Blue, Apr. 20, 1974 (div. July 12, 1976); 1 child, Clifton IV. BS in Gen. Edn. and History, Northwestern U., 1976. Gen. mgr. Signature Fin. Mktg., Evanston, Ill., 1976-82; cons. Kestnbaum & Co., Chgo., 1982-83; sr. v.p., CIO Bronner Slosberg Humphrey, Boston, 1983-95; pres. Am. Market Connection, Boston, 1985—. Chmn. bd. dirs. Bus. Vols. for the Arts, Boston, 1992—; chmn. bd. dirs. Roxbury Outreach Shakespeare Experience, Boston, 1992—; bd. overseers Computer Mus., Boston, 1993—. Mem. Assn. Computing Machinery (bd. dirs. 1995—), Data Processing Mgmt. Assn., Black Data Processing Assocs., Direct Mktg., List Coun., Info. Tech. Coun. Home: 10 Lothrop Ave Milton MA 02186-1408

GERRISH, BRIAN ALBERT, theologian, educator; b. London, Aug. 14, 1931; s. Albert and Doris (King) G.; children from previous marriage: Carolyn, Paul; m. Dawn Ann De Vries, Aug. 3, 1990; 1 child, Heather. B.A., Queens' Coll., Cambridge, Eng., 1952, M.A., 1956; cert., Westminister Coll., Cambridge, 1955; S.T.M., Union Theol. Sem., N.Y.C., 1956; Ph.D., Columbia U., 1958; D.D. (hon.), U. St. Andrews, Scotland, 1984. Ordained to ministry Presbyn. Ch., 1957. Asst. pastor West End Presbyn. Ch., N.Y.C., 1956-58; tutor philosophy of religion Union Theol. Sem., N.Y.C., 1957-58; instr. ch. history McCormick Theol. Sem., Chgo., 1958-59; asst. prof. McCormick Theol. Sem., 1959-63, asso. prof., 1963-65; asso. prof. hist. theology U. Chgo., 1965-68, prof., 1968-85, John Nuveen prof., 1985-96, John Nuveen prof. emeritus, 1996—; disting. Svc. prof. theology Union Theol. Sem., Va., 1996—; Cunningham lectr. U. Edinburgh, Scotland, 1990. Author: Grace and Reason: A Study in the Theology of Luther, 1962 (Japanese transl. 1974), reprinted, 1979, Tradition and the Modern World: Reformed Theology in the Nineteenth Century, 1978, The Old Protestantism and the New: Essays on the Reformation Heritage, 1982, A Prince of the Church: Schleiermacher and the Beginnings of Modern Theology, 1984, Korean transl., 1988, Grace and Gratitude: The Eucharistic Theology of John Calvin, 1993, Continuing the Reformation: Essays on Modern Religious Thought, 1993; editor: The Faith of Christendom: A Source Book of Creeds and Confessions, 1963, Reformers in Profile, 1967, Reformatio Perennis: Essays on Calvin and the Reformation in Honor of Ford Lewis Battles, 1981; co-editor: Jour. Religion, 1972-85; contbr. articles to profl. jours. Am. Assn. Theol. Schs. faculty fellow, 1961; Guggenheim fellow, 1970; Nat. Endowment Humanities fellow, 1980. Fellow Am. Acad. of Arts and Scis.; mem. Am. Acad. Religion, Am. Soc. Church History (pres. 1979), Ernst-Troeltsch-Gesellschaft, Am. Theol. Soc. (Midwest divsn. pres. 1973-74). Home: 9142 Sycamore Hill Pl Mechanicsville VA 23116-5806 Office: Union Theol Seminary 3401 Brook Rd Richmond VA 23227-4514

GERRITSEN, HENDRIK JURJEN, physics educator, researcher; b. The Hague, The Netherlands, Jan. 19, 1927; came to U.S., 1957; s. Hendrik Pieter and Augusta (Koopmans) G.; m. Lida Buitelaar, June 13, 1955 (div. 1968); children: Robert, Steven, Albert, Leon; m. Heide Robertson Hoppe, Dec. 28, 1978. A.B. in Physics and Chemistry, U. Leiden, 1948; Ph.D. in Physics, 1955. Scientist RCA Labs., Zurich, Switzerland, 1955-57, Princeton, N.J., 1957-67; lectr. electrophysics Chalmers U., Sweden, 1961-62; prof. physics Brown U., Providence, 1967-97, prof. emeritus, prof. rsch., 1997—; prof. physics U. Utrecht, Netherlands, 1974, U. Karlsruhe, W. Germany, 1981-82; cons. Polaroid Corp., Cambridge, Mass., 1968-70; prin. investigator U.S. Bur. Mines, Brewster, Pa., 1970-76, Honeywell, Mpls., 1980-87, NSF, Dept. Energy and AERG., 1968-98; cons. Krieger Corp., Providence, 1986-89; dir. Ladd Observatory, Providence, 1985-89. Contbr. sci. articles to profl. jours., 1968—; patentee. Vis. IREX scholar, Baltic Republics. Fulbright grantee Rostock, Germany, 1995, 96. Mem. Fedn. Am. Scientists, Union of Concerned Scientists, Profl. Photographers Soc. Am. (hon.), Am. Optical Soc., Celestial Observers (hon.), Sigma Xi. Office: Brown U Physics Dept Hope/George St Providence RI 02912

GERRITY, DANIEL WALLACE, real estate developer; b. Albany, N.Y., Nov. 21, 1948; s. Joseph Warren and Phyllis Van Buren (Richard) G.; m. Maria Farley, May 30, 1970; children: Jeanne, Vera, Samuel. BA, U. Va., 1970; JD, Boston U., 1973; MS, Columbia U., 1977. Bar: Mass. 1973, N.Y. 1978. Atty. U.S. Dept. of HUD, Boston, 1973-75; real estate developer, pres. DWG Devel. Inc., N.Y.C., 1978-91, Boston, 1991—; sec.-treas. Salisbury Chevrolet, Inc., Scotia, N.Y., 1991—; pres. Marriner & Co., Boston, 1987—; dir. Saratoga Raceway, 1987—. Pres. Greenhope Housing, N.Y.C., 1986-91; bd. dirs. Community Svc. Soc., N.Y.C., 1990-91; trustee, treas. Preservation League of N.Y. State, Albany, 1980-88. Recipient Cmty. Svc. award Pres. of the U.S., 1984, Young Lion award Sons of Italy, 1979; Equitable Life fellow, 1976-77. Office: 3 Center Plz Fl 4 Boston MA 02108-2003

GERRITY, J(AMES) FRANK, II, building materials company executive; b. Newton, Mass., Dec. 3, 1918; s. Joe Warren and Margaret (McKee) G.; m. Ruth Mathes, Jan. 30, 1943; children: Margot Gerrity Finley, James F. III, Peter, Ruth Gerrity Timme, Betsey Gerrity Lamson. AB, Harvard U., 1939, MBA, 1943. Salesman Gerrity Co., Boston, 1946-49, pres., 1949-79, chmn., 1979—; pres. Gerrity Co., Newton, Mass., 1994—. Trustee York Health Found.; treas. Mass. Eye and Ear Infirmary, Boston, 1980—; chmn. bd. dirs. Jackson Lab., Bar Harbor, Maine, 1975-79; pres. York Hosp., Maine, 1980—; trustee Episcopal Diocese Boston, 1978-82, Dumaine's Trust, York Hist. Landmarks; vestryman Ch. of the Redeemer; hon. consul Iceland, 1969—. Lt. (sr. grade) USNR, 1943-46. Mem. The Country Club (Brookline, Mass.), Harvard U. Club (Boston). Republican. Home: 59 Cramond Rd Chestnut Hill MA 02467-2830 Office: Gerrity Co 90 Oak St Newton MA 02464-1439*

GERRITY, THOMAS P., dean; b. Savannah, Ga., July 13, 1941; s. Thomas Patrick and Margaret Ellen (Briscol) G.; m. Anna Rita Zablocki, Sept. 22, 1984. BSEE, MIT, 1963, MSEE, 1964, PhD, 1970; Masters (hon.), U. Pa., 1991. Mem. faculty Sloan Sch. Mgmt. MIT, Cambridge, Mass., 1968-72; chmn., CEO Index Group, Inc. (formerly Index Systems, Inc.), Cambridge, 1969-89; pres. CSC Consulting, Cambridge, 1989-90; dean Wharton Sch. U. Pa., Phila., 1990—; bd. dirs. Fannie Mae, Washington, Sun Co., Inc., Phila., 1990—, Reliance Group Holdings, N.Y.C., 1993—, CVS Corp., Woonsocket, R.I., 1995—; exec. com. Tech. Leaders, Phila., 1991—, IKON Office Solutions, Malvern, Pa., 1998—, Knight-Ridder Inc., Miami, 1998—. Rhodes scholar Oxford U., 1964-65. Episcopalian. Office: U Pa Wharton Sch 3620 Locust Walk Philadelphia PA 19104-6302*

GERRODETTE, CHARLES EVERETT, real estate company executive, consultant; b. Alderwood Manor, Wash., June 18, 1934; s. Honoré Everett and Marjorie Violet (Stapley) G.; m. Laurine Carol Manley, Mar. 16, 1956 (div. 1977); children: Stephen Everett, Suzanne Gerrodette Prince; m. Diane Marie Drumm, Dec. 6, 1984. BA in Bus. Adminstrn., U. Wash., 1956, postgrad., 1959; postgrad., NYU, 1956-57. Credit analyst and corr. comml. credit dept. Chase Manhattan Bank, N.Y.C., 1956-57; reviewing appraiser Prudential Ins. Co. Am., Seattle, 1959-67; v.p., sr. loan officer real estate group Seattle 1st Nat. Bank, 1967-90; pres., CEO, Portal Pacific Co., Inc., Seattle, 1990—; real estate advisor, fin. cons. Charles E. Gerrodette, MAI, Seattle, 1990—; instr. appraising Shoreline C.C., Seattle, 1974-76. Contbg. author: Prentice Hall Ency. of Real Estate Appraising, 3d edit., 1978. Mem. blue ribbon com. for planning Shoreline Sch. Dist., Seattle, 1974-75. With U.S. Army, 1957-59. Mem. Am. Arbitration Assn. (panel of arbitrators), Appraisal Inst. (MAI designation 1972, officer, bd. dirs. Wash.-B.C. chpt. 1980-89, pres. 1984, nat. fin. and adminstrn. com. 1982-87, nat. governing counselor 1987-89, nat. fin. com. 1990-96), Mortgage Bankers Assn. (income property com.), Columbia Tower Club, Lambda Alpha, N.W. Grad. Assn. Theta Delta Chi (trustee 1960-70, past pres.). Episcopalian. Avocations: travel, investing, architectural appreciation, photography. Office: 2125 1st Ave Ste 1204 Seattle WA 98121-2118

GERROIR, RICHARD ERNEST, retired computer industry executive; b. Cambridge, Mass., June 27, 1936; s. Ernest E. and Alice M. (Carbonneau) G.; m. Susan M. Gunther, June 26, 1965; children: Russell, Danielle, Heather. BS, Boston Coll., 1958. Sales rep. Gramar Mfg., Wakefield, Mass., 1962-64; mfg. supr. Honeywell Computers, Brighton, Mass., 1964-69, dept. mgr., 1969-75, planning analyst, 1975-79; program mgr. Honeywell Computers, Billerica, Mass., 1979-91; ret., 1991. Part-time clk. Coun. on Aging, Maynard, Mass., 1996—; Youth Hockey coach, Maynard, 1972-80, pres. Soccer Assn., 1974-86, pres. Maynard Cmty. Chest, 1977—, coach and umpire Little League, 1972-76; mem. Maynard Sch. Com., 1980-86, chmn., 1982-83; moderator Town Meeting, 1987—, mem., Dem. Town Com., Maynard, 1975—, chmn., 1996—; eucharistic min. St. Bridget's Ch., 1987—. Lt. comdr., USNR, 1959-80. Democrat. Roman Catholic. Home: 23 Durant Ave Maynard MA 01754-1034

GERRY, DEBRA PRUE, psychotherapist, recording artist, writer; b. Oct. 9, 1951; d. C.O. and Sarah E. Rawl; m. Norman Bernard Gerry, Apr. 10, 1981 (div. 1998); 1 child, Gisele Psyche Victoria. BS, Ga. So. U., 1972; MEd, Armstrong State U., 1974; PhD, U. Ga., 1989. Cert. Ariz. Bd. Behavioral Health Examiners. Spl. edn. tchr. Chatham County Bd. Edn., Savannah, Ga., 1972-74; edn. and learning disabilities resource educator Duval County Bd. Edn., Jacksonville, Fla., 1974-77; ednl. resource counselor spl. programs adminstr. Broward County Bd. Edn., Ft. Lauderdale, Fla., 1977-81; pvt. practice Scottsdale, Ariz., 1990—. Contbr. author coll. textbooks; contbr. articles to profl. jours.; prodr. musical album Welcome to this World. Vol., fundraiser, psychol. cons., group leader Valley AIDS Orgns., Phoenix, 1990-96; fundraiser Hosp. Health Edn. Programs, Scottsdale, 1992-93; mem. com. for women's issues Plz. Club, Phoenix, 1992-93; pres. Laissez Les Bon Temps Rouler, Wrigley Club, Phoenix, 1993-96; mem. bd. Sojourner' Ctr., 1996, exec. bd., 1997-98, v.p., 1999; exec. bd. Breast Found., Inc., Phoenix, 1997-98; appointee Ariz. Supreme Ct., Foster Care Rev. Bd., Phoenix, 1996—. Recipient Rudy award Shanti Orgn., 1991. Mem. APA, NOW, ACA, Internat. Soc. Poets (disting., Poet of Merit award 1996), Nat. Assn. Women Bus. Owners, Assn. for Multicultural Coun., Assn. for Specialists in Group Work, Mensa, Phi Delta Kappa, Kappa Delta Epsilon, Sigma Omega Phi, Kappa Delta Pi. Avocations: ballroom dancing, playing musical instruments, singing, travel, air sports.

GERRY, JOSEPH JOHN, bishop; b. Millinocket, Maine, Sept. 12, 1928; s. Bernard Eugene and Blanche Agnes (McManemon) G. AB summa cum laude, St. Anselm's Coll., Manchester, N.H., 1950; postgrad., St. Anselm's Sem., 1954; MA, U. Toronto, 1955; PhD, Fordham U., 1959; LLD,

Benedictine Coll., 1986, St. Anselm Coll., 1986; DD, St. Joseph's Coll., Windham, Maine, 1990. Joined Order of St. Benedict, Roman Catholic Ch., 1948 ordained priest: Roman Catholic Ch., 1954. Asst. dean studies St. Anselm's Coll., 1958-59, dean studies, 1971-72; chancellor St. Anselm's Coll., N.H., 1972-86; consecrated bishop, 1986; auxiliary bishop Manchester, N.H., 1986-89; bishop Portland, Maine, 1989—. Home: 199 Western Promenade Portland ME 04102-3514 Office: 510 Ocean Ave Portland ME 04103-4936

GERRY, MARTIN HUGHES, IV, federal agency administrator, lawyer; b. San Francisco, Jan. 3, 1943; s. Martin Hughes III and Emily (Kuhl) G.; m. Robin Lucile MacAskill, Sept. 9, 1963 (div. June 1971); 1 child, Carol Elizabeth; m. Beatrice Ann Borowski, Apr. 28, 1984; children: Emily Irena, David Edward. BA, Stanford U., 1964, JD, 1967. Bar: N.Y. 1967, D.C. 1977, U.S. Dist. Ct. D.C. 1979, U.S. Supreme Ct. 1985. Assoc. Nixon, Mudge, Rose, Guthrie, Alexander & Mitchell, N.Y.C., 1967-69; exec. asst. to dir. Office for Civil Rights, HEW, Washington, 1969-70; asst. to sec. HEW, Washington, 1970-74; dir. Office for Civil Rights, HEW, Washington, 1975-77; pres. Policy Ctr. for Children and Youth, Bethesda, Md., 1978-89; asst. sec. for planning and evaluation HHS, Washington, 1990-93; exec. dir. The Austin (Tex.) Project, 1993-95; rsch. prof., dir. Ctr. for Study of Family and Cmty. Policy U. Kans., 1995—; mem. adv. bd. on welfare indicators U.S. Dept. HHS, 1996-98; spl. counsel Wednesday Group, U.S. Ho. of Reps., Washington, 1977-89, vice chair Commn. on Spl. Needs of Children, 1982-83; vice chair Nat. Legal Ctr. for Medically Dependent, Indpls., 1986-90; sr. cons. Orgn. for Econ. Cooperation and Devel., Paris, 1986-90; vis. rsch. scholar U. Md., 1988-89; vis. scholar Stanford U., 1989-90; dir. Nat. Tech. Assistance Ctr. on Welfare Reform, 1997—. Contbr. numerous articles on social policy, edn., pub. financing, and civil rights related subjects to profl. jours. Mem. disability adv. coun. Social Security Adminstrn., HHS, Washington, 1986-88; edn. expert Superior Ct. D.C., Washington, 1986-90; sr. policy advisor Bush-Quayle '88. Oscar Cushing Law fellow Stanford U., 1965. Mem. Fed. Bar Assn. Republican. Episcopalian. Avocations: sailing, hiking. Office: U Kans 1059 Dole Ctr Lawrence KS 66045

GERS, HARVEY, marketing professional; b. St. Louis, May 27, 1947; s. Bernard S. and Jean (Brody) G.; m. Susan Lynn Kozloff, June 6, 1971; children: Andrew S., Jeffrey B. BA, Washington U., St. Louis, 1969, MBA, 1971. Engring. asst. Brasch Mfg. Co., St. Louis, 1966-70; mgmt. trainee Fed. Res. Bank St. Louis, 1971-72; sr. site selection analyst May Dept. Stores Co., St. Louis, 1972-76; sr. mktg. analyst Am. Investment Co., Clayton, Mo., 1976-79; sr. fin. analyst ITT Comml. Fin. Corp., Clayton, 1979-93, mgr. mktg. rsch., 1994-97; dir. mktg. planning and analysis Deutsche Fin. Svcs., St. Louis, 1998—, Y2K program mgr., bus. group, 1998—; pres. Computer Support Corp., St. Louis 1985; cons. Sr. Mgmt. Svcs., St. Louis 1986-88. Co-developer automated comml. bankruptcy prediction sys., 1986, physician referral sys., 1987, expert credit sys., 1988, preliminary design of bankruptcy predictor using neural networks, 1992. Mem. Mo. Real Estate Brokers Assn. (former), Mystery Club. Avocations: computers, tennis, walking, fishing, bicycling. Home: 14945 Manor Ridge Dr Chesterfield MO 63017-7712 Office: Deutsche Fin Svcs 655 Maryville Centre Dr Saint Louis MO 63141-5815

GERSBACHER, EVA ELIZABETH, special education administrator; b. Carbondale, Ill., Dec. 31, 1949; d. Willard Marion and Eva (Oxford) G. BA, Hope Coll., 1970; postgrad., Grand Valley State Coll., 1971-73; MA, S.E. Mo. State U., 1974; postgrad., So. Ill. U., 1975-78. Cert. adminstr., tchr. learning disabilities, educable mentally impaired, severe mentally impaired, behavior disordered, physically handicapped, presch., elem. Tchr. Fairport (Mich.) Elem. Sch., summer 1970; support tchr. Day Sch. for Emotionally Disturbed, Carbondale, Ill., 1970-71, West Ottawa Sch. Dist., Holland, Mich., 1971-72, Ottawa Intermediate Sch. Dist., Grand Haven, Mich., 1972-73; diagnostic tchr. Tri-County Spl. Edn., Murphysboro, Ill., 1974-76; grad. asst. So. Ill. U., Carbondale, 1974-76, instr., 1976-78; coord. So. Ill. Ednl. Svcs. Ctr., Marion, Ill., 1978-82; prin. Tri-County Edn. Ctr., Anna, Ill., 1982-85; program adminstr. Tri-County Spl. Edn., Murphysboro, Ill., 1985—; cons. Head Start, So. Ill., 1975-77, So. Ill. Ednl. Svc. Ctr., 1976-77, Southwestern Ill. Regional Spl. Edn., 1977. Pres., treas., sec. Developmental Disabilities Protective Svc. Bd., Anna, Ill. Spl. edn. fellow Ill. Office Edn., So. Ill. U., 1976. Mem. Assn. Persons with Severe Handicaps, Assn. Citizens with Learning Disabilities, Assn. Behavior Analysis, Am. Assn. Mental Deficiency, Ill. Assn. Persons with Severe Handicaps (mem. governing bd. 1980-82), Coun. Exceptional Children (pres. 1990-93), Ill. Adminstrs. Spl. Edn., Ill. Women Adminstrs., Kappa Delta Pi, Phi Kappa Phi. Avocations: gardening, reading. Home: 1507 W Taylor Dr Carbondale IL 62901-2221 Office: Tri County Spl Edn 1725 Shomaker Dr Murphysboro IL 62966-2507

GERSEMEHL, WILLIAM TERRY, information systems manager; b. Columbus, Ohio, Oct. 27, 1947; s. William Emil and Jo Ann Leticia (Mohr) G.; m. Ruth Ann Marti, Aug. 22, 1970 (div. July 17, 1987); children: Nathan, Sara, Leah; m. Nen Marie Morton, June 20, 1995; children: Alex, Michael. BA, St. Olaf Coll., 1971; postgrad., U. Dallas, 1989, U. St. Thomas, 1991. Mgr. systems and programming Locke Supply, Oklahoma City, 1975-80; cons. Advance Systems, Oklahoma City, 1980-90; info. systems mgr. Benson-Quinn Co., Mpls., 1990—; pres. Unisys Midwest Bus. Users Group, Mpls., 1993-94. Mem. Profl. Ski Instrs. of Am. Avocations: snow skiing, golf. Office: Benson-Quinn Co 301 4th Ave S Ste 1075 Minneapolis MN 55415-1449

GERSHENGORN, MARVIN CARL, physician, scientist, educator; b. N.Y.C.. M.D., NYU, 1971. Diplomate Am. Bd. Internal Medicine. Intern Strong Meml. Hosp., Rochester, N.Y., 1971-72, asst. resident in medicine, 1972-73; asst. prof. medicine NYU Sch. Med., 1976-80, assoc. prof., 1980-83; prof. medicine Cornell U. Med Coll., N.Y.C., 1983—; Abby Rockefeller Mauze disting. prof. Weill Med. Coll. Cornell U. Office: Cornell Univ Weill Med Coll 1300 York Ave New York NY 10021-4896

GERSHENSON, HARRY, lawyer; b. St. Louis, July 8, 1902; m. Dorothy Rose Lupfer; children—Harry, Dorothy (Mrs. Ralph Clock). LL.B., Benton Coll. Law, 1924. Bar: Mo. bar 1923. Practiced in St. Louis, 1923—; sr. ptnr. firm Gershenson & Gershenson; lectr. law St. Louis U., 1948-57. Mem. adv. bd. Salvation Army. Fellow Am. Coll. Probate Counsel (v.p. life bd. regents, pres. 1965-66); mem. Fed. Bar Assn. (life), Am. Bar Found. (life), Mo. Bar Found. (pres. 1965-70, bd. dirs. 1970—), ABA (ho. of dels. 1948-66, bd. govs. 1962-64, com. on profl. ethics, past chmn. Lawyers' Title Guaranty Fund and Lawyer' Referral Fund), Bar Assn. St. Louis (pres. 1946-47, past mem. exec. com.), Scribes Law Writers Assn. (past pres.), Practising Law Inst. (past bd. dirs.), Mo. State Bar (pres. 1957-58, bd. govs., Pres.'s Distinguished Service award 1966, Spurgeon Smithson award 1984), Am. Judicature Soc. (past bd. dirs.), Assn. Trial Lawyers Am., Phi Alpha Delta. Clubs: Mason (St. Louis) (33 deg., grand orator, grand lodge 1963-64), Mo. Athletic (St. Louis), Lawyers (St. Louis); Clayton. Home: 542 Warder Ave Saint Louis MO 63130-3926 Office: 7733 Forsyth Blvd Saint Louis MO 63105-1817 *To strive mightily for worthwhile endeavors for my fellowman and myself.*

GERSHMAN, CARL SAMUEL, foundation administrator; b. N.Y.C., July 20, 1943; s. Joseph Saul and Josephine (Cohen) G.; m. Laurie Pfeffer, Jan. 25, 1970; children: Sarah, Joseph, Jacob. BA, Yale U., 1965; MEd, Harvard U., 1968. Researcher Anti-Defamation League of B'nai B'rith, N.Y.C., 1968; dir. rsch. A. Philip Randolph Inst., N.Y.C., 1969-71; exec. dir. Youth Inst. for Peace in the Mid. East, N.Y.C., 1971-74, Social Dems., U.S.A., N.Y.C., 1974-80; sr. rsch. fellow Freedom House, N.Y.C., 1980-81; sr. counselor U.S. Mission to the U.N., N.Y.C., 1981-84; pres. Nat. Endowment for Democracy, Washington, 1984—. Author: Foreign Policy of American Labor, 1975; editor: Israel, the Arabs and the Middle East, 1972; mem. editorial bd. Washington Quarterly, 1988—, Society Mag., 1989—; contbr. articles to popular mags. and jours. Avocations: reading, jogging, travel. Office: Nat Endowment for Democracy 1101 15th St NW Ste 700 Washington DC 20005-5000*

GERSHMAN, JOHN JEREMY, research analyst, consultant; b. Bklyn., Nov. 28, 1964; s. Lewis Charles and Barbara Breen G. BA, Colgate U., 1987; MA, U. Calif., Berkeley, 1988. Mng. dir. Berkeley, 1988-90; policy dir. Oakland, Calif., 1991-95; rsch. fellow Cambridge, Mass., 1995—; rsch. assoc. Boston, 1995—. Co-editor: Dying For Growth, 1999, Trading Freedom, 1999. Mem. Internat. Studies Assn., Assn. Asian Studies, Am. Polit. Sci. Assn.

GERSHON, BERNARD, broadcast executive. V.p. ABC Radio News, N.Y.C. Office: ABC Radio News 125 W End Ave New York NY 10023-6390*

GERSHON, ELAINE A., medical and surgical nurse, nursing administrator; b. Ft. Worth, Sept. 23, 1963; d. Jim Joseph and Rose Margaret (Anello) Bezdek; m. J. Robert Gershon Jr., Sept. 9, 1989. AAS in Nursing, Cooke County Coll., Gainesville, Tex., 1985. RN, Tex.; cert. CPR, intravenous therapy. Nurse med.-surg. outpatient unit Denton (Tex.) Regional Med. Ctr., 1989-91; nurse Denton Home Health Care, 1991-92; DON DON Kern Manor, Pilot Point, Tex., 1992—. Office: 1100 Dallas Dr Ste 106 Denton TX 76205

GERSHON, NINA, federal judge; b. Chgo., Oct. 16, 1940; d. David and Marie Gershon; m. Bernard J. Fried, May 15, 1983. BA, Cornell U., 1962; LLB, Yale U., 1965; postgrad., London Sch. Econs., 1965-66. Former magistrate judge U.S. Dist. Ct. (so. dist.) N.Y., N.Y.C.; U.S. dist. judge Eastern Dist. N.Y., Bklyn., 1996—. Fulbright scholar. Office: US Courthouse 225 Cadman Plz E Brooklyn NY 11201-1818*

GERSHON, WILLIAM I., copywriter, voiceover actor, communications executive; b. Chgo., Apr. 12, 1934; s. Irving and Ruth (Gershbein) G.; m. Matilda (Marion) K. May, June 29, 1957. Grad., Wright Jr. Coll., Chgo., 1954; BA in Speech and English, Roosevelt U., 1956. Classical music dir., announcer Sta. WNIB-FM, Chgo., 1955-57; writer H. Epstein Advt., Chgo., 1956-59; asst. to copy chief Walgreen Co., Deerfield, Ill., 1959-61; advt. mgr. Lyon & Healy, Inc., Chgo., 1961-63; writer/account mgr. Garfield-Linn & Co., Chgo., 1963-78, v.p., 1978-82; sr. writer Abelson-Taylor, Inc., Chgo., 1983-84; owner Bill Gershon Mktg. Communications, Skokie, Ill., 1982—. Creator name Expocenter for Chgo.'s Apparel Ctr. Expn. Hall; voiceover actor American Heritage Voices From the Front (The Civil War, World War I), children's book narrations, sales tng. and employee tng. modules, radio and TV commls. Mem. Independent Writers of Chgo. Avocations: reading, photography, language study, short-wave radio. Office: Bill Gershon Mktg Comm 9828 Crawford Ave Skokie IL 60076-1107

GERSKE, JANET FAY, lawyer; b. Chgo., Nov. 14, 1950; d. Bernard G. Gerske and L. Fay (Knight) Capron; m. James P. Chapman, Dec. 5, 1982. BS, Northwestern U., 1971; JD, U. Mich., 1978. Bar: Ill. 1978, U.S. Dist. Ct. (no. dist.) Ill. 1978. Pvt. practice, Chgo., 1978-80, 84—; assoc. Jerome H. Torshen Ltd., Chgo., 1980-84. Chpt. chmn. Ind. Voters Ill./Ind. Precinct Orgn., Chgo., 1982-84; co-chmn. Ill. Women's Agenda Com., 1985-88, fin. officer, 1987-88; dir. Chgo. Abused Women Coalition, 1986-90, sec., treas., 1988-90. Mem. Women's Bar Assn. Ill. (co-chmn. rights of women com. 1985-86, dir. 1988-90), Chgo. Bar Assn. (co-chmn. legal status of women com. young lawyers sect.), Nat. Orgn. Social Security Claimants' Rep. Democrat. Home: 850 W Oakdale Ave Chicago IL 60657-5122 Office: 203 N La Salle St Chicago IL 60601-1210

GERSON, ELLIOT FRANCIS, healthcare executive; b. New Haven, July 15, 1952; s. Louis Lieb and Elizabeth (Shanley) G.; children: Emily, Hilary, Alexander, Marissa, Jillian; m. Amy Shapiro, May 23, 1993. AB summa cum laude, Harvard Coll., 1974; BA with first class honors, Oxford U. (Eng.), 1976, MA, 1981; JD, Yale U., 1979. Bar: Conn. 1981, D.C. 1982, U.S. Dist. Ct. Conn. 1982, U.S. Ct. Appeals (D.C. cir.) 1982, U.S. Supreme Ct. 1985. Law clk. to judge U.S. Ct. Appeals, Washington, 1979; staff asst. to sec. Dept. Def., The Pentagon, Washington, 1979-80; law clk. to Justice Stewart, U.S. Supreme Ct., Washington, 1980-81; assoc. Verner, Liipfert, Bernhard & McPherson, Washington, Hartford, Conn., 1981-83; dep. atty. gen. State of Conn., Hartford, 1983-86; v.p. Travelers Corp., Hartford, Conn., 1986-90, sr. v.p., 1990-93; pres. Travelers Ins. Co., 1993-95; exec. v.p. MetraHealth Cos., Inc, 1995-96, United Healthcare, 1996; pres. ETC, Inc., 1996—, CEO, 1997—; dir. Bazelon Ctr. Menta Health Law, 1997—. Editor: Conn. Law Tribune, 1986-88. Mem. Sec. State's Adv. Com. Internat. Law, Washington, 1984-86; mem. Gov's. Commn. Design Environ. Policy for Conn., 1969; dir. Eastern Conn. Develop. Coun. Inc., 1981-86, Hartford Stage Co., 1985-95, pres., 1990-93, Hartford Ballet, 1986-88, Greater Hartford Arts Council, 1986-90, 94-95; mem. Conn. Humanities Council, 1987-90; dir. Conn. Civil Liberties Union, 1987-89, Conn. Women's Ednl. and Legal Fund, 1987-91; staff mem. commn. Critical Choices Ams., 1973-74; mem. Council Fgn. Relations Inc., N.Y.C., 1981-86, Yale Law Sch. Com. Pub. Interest Law, New Haven, 1983-85; elector Wadsworth Atheneum, Hartford, 1983-93; sec. Conn. Rhodes Scholar Selection Com., 1982-94; asst. Am. sec. Rhodes Scholarship Trust, 1976-79, Am. sec., Eng., 1998—; treas. Am. South African Scholarship Assn., Inc., 1986-94; trustee Conn. Pub. Broadcasting, 1988-92, Conn. Hist. Soc., 1993-95, The Shakespeare Theatre, Washington, 1996—; trustee Hartford Courant Fedn., 1988-95, pres., 1992-94. Rhodes scholar 1974. Recipient Sec. Def. Meritorious Civilian Service Medal 1980. Mem. Conn. Bar Assn. (long range planning com. 1984-87), Phi Beta Kappa. Democrat. Clubs: Spee (pres. 1973-74) (Cambridge, Mass.), Cosmos (Washington), River Bend (Great Falls, Va.). Home: 480 River Bend Rd Great Falls VA 22066-4016 Office: PO Box 7490 Mc Lean VA 22106*

GERSON, GARY STANFORD, rabbi; b. Ypsilanti, Mich., June 17, 1945; s. Bernard and Ruth Edith (Levin) G.; m. Carol Roberts, Oct. 12, 1969; children: Jordana, Jessica. BA magna cum laude, Western Mich. U., 1967; MA in Religion, Temple U., 1976; grad., Reconstructionist Rabbinical Coll., 1976; MA in Psychology, Temple U., 1977; Dr. Ministry, Chgo. Theol. Seminary, 1984. Ordained rabbi, 1976. Rsch. fellow U. Pa., 1969, teaching asst., 1972; teaching asst. Temple U., Phila., 1974-75; rabbi Temple Brith Achim, King of Prussia, Pa., 1974-78; asst. rabbi Temple Beth Israel, Chgo., 1978-79; rabbi Oak Park (Ill.) Temple B'nai Abraham Zion, 1979—; psychologist Benjamin Rush Ctr. for Mental Health and Mental Retardation Svcs., Phila., 1977-78. Contbr. articles to profl. jours. Mem. adv. bd. Ctr. for Jewish-Christian Studies, Chgo., 1985—, Nat. Abortion rights Action League, Ill., 1985—, Ctr. for Ch.-State Studies, Chgo., 1986—, Comty. Response, 1989—; chmn. Religious Coalition for Abortion Rights policy coun., 1984-88; active Justice Campaign, 1985; bd. dirs. ACLU, Ill., 1999—; bd. dirs. Jewish Fedn. Met. Chgo., 1995-96; exec. bd. Anti-Defamation League. Fulbright grantee, 1967, Hebrew U. fellow, 1969-70, Dropsie U. fellow, 1970-71. Mem. Chgo. Assn. Reform Rabbis (v.p. 1987-91, pres. 1991-93), Cen. Conf. Am. Rabbis (exec. bd. 1991-93), Chgo. Bd. Rabbis (exec. com. 1983—), Union Am. Hebrew Congregations (exec. com. Gt. Lakes region 1991-93), Olin-Sang-Ruby Union Inst. (bd. govs. 1990, chmn. rabbinic adv. com.), United Jewish Appeal (rabbinic cabinet 1980—), Oak Park-River Forest Comty. of Congregations (v.p. 1994-96, pres. 1996-98), Fulbright Assn., Omicron Delta Kappa. Avocations: hiking, travel, classical and folk music. Office: Oak Park Temple Bnai Abraham Zion 1235 N Harlem Ave Oak Park IL 60302-1397

GERSON, IRWIN CONRAD, advertising executive; b. N.Y.C., Mar. 18, 1930; s. Leon and Charlotte (Steinhause) G.; m. Lenore Greenblatt, Nov. 29, 1953; children: Jill Beth, Matthew Ted. B.S., Fordham U., 1953; M.B.A., N.Y. U., 1959; D of Humane Letters, Albany Coll. Pharmacy, 1992. Ter. mgr. Wyeth Labs. div. Am. Home Products, 1956-58; account exec., supr. William Douglas McAdams, Inc., N.Y.C., 1958-66; v.p. William Douglas McAdams, Inc., 1966-68, sr. v.p., 1969-70, exec. v.p., 1971-74, pres., 1974-86, chmn. bd., 1987-96; chmn. bd. Lowe McAdams Healthcare, N.Y.C., 1996-98, chmn. emeritus, 1999—; instr. sales mgmt. Columbia Coll. Pharm. Scis., 1967-77; bd. dirs. ANDRX Corp., Cytoclonal Pharms. Inc. Editorial adv. bd.: U.S. Jour. Drug and Alcohol Dependence, 1977-83. Trustee, bd. dirs. Chemotherapy Found., 1971-86; bd. dirs. Nutritional Rsch. Found., 1977-85, Am. Found. for Pharm. Edn., 1996—, Conn. Grand Opera, 1983-93, Stamford Chamber Orch., 1985-93; mem. coun. overseers Arnold and Marie Schwartz Coll. Pharmacy and Health Scis., L.I. U., 1986-90, chmn., 1990—; bd. trustees Bus. Publs. Audit of Circulation, 1988-95, vice chmn., 1992-93, chmn., 1993-94; bd. trustees L.I. U., 1989—; trustee Albany Coll. Pharmacy, Union U., 1993-97. With AUS, 1954-56. Mem. Am. Assn. Advt. Agys. (bd. govs. N.Y. coun. 1991-95, ea. region 1995-98), Pharm. Advt. Coun. (bd. dirs. 1974-84, treas. 1976-77, v.p. 1979-81), Alpha Zeta Omega. Home: 132 W Village Way Jupiter FL 33458-7820 also: Sky Farm Rd Copake NY 12516 Office: Lowe McAdams Healthcare 1740 Broadway New York NY 10019-4315

GERSON, KATHLEEN, sociology educator; b. Montgomery, Ala., Aug. 6, 1947; d. Myron Gerson and Rose (Baum) Blum; m. John Hull Mollenkopf, Nov. 27, 1981; 1 child: Emily. BA, Stanford U., 1969; MA, U. Calif., Berkeley, 1974, PhD, 1981. Asst. prof. NYU, 1980-87; vis. scholar Russell Sage Found., N.Y.C., 1987-88; from assoc. prof. to prof. sociology NYU, 1988-95, prof. sociology, 1995—; mem. Sloan Found. Network on Work Redesign & Work-Family Issues, N.Y.C., 1995-97; vis. scholar Ctr. for the Life Course, Bremen, Germany, 1995. Author: Hard Choices, 1985, No Man's Land, 1993; co-author: Networks and Places, 1977; contbr. articles to profl. jours. Grantee NSF, 1989. Mem. Am. Sociol. Assn., Eastern Sociol. Soc., Soc. for the Study of Social Problems, Sociologists for Women in Society. Democrat. Office: NYU Dept Sociology 269 Mercer St Fl 4 New York NY 10003-6633

GERSON, MARTIN LYONS, secondary school educator; b. Morristown, Tenn., Sept. 12, 1961; s. Allan Jerome and Bernice (Misner) G. BS, Purdue U., 1984; MA for Tchrs., Ga. State U., 1986, cert. ednl. specialist, 1994. Cert. secondary math. tchr., Ga. Tchr. math. Cross Keys High Sch., Atlanta, 1984-97; tchr. S. Gwinnett High Sch., Snellville, Ga., 1997—; instr. math. Ga. State U., Atlanta, 1988-90, Dekalb Coll., Atlanta, 1990—. Named Tchr. of Month math. students Cross Keys High Sch., 1989, HERO Club, Cross Keys High Sch., 1990, Tchr. of Yr. faculty Cross Keys High Sch., 1990, West Dekalb Rotary Club, Atlanta, 1991. Mem. Nat. Coun. Tchrs. Math., Ga. Coun. Tchrs. Math., B'nai B'rith. Jewish. Avocations: bowling, collecting bobbleheads, hats and crystal figures. Home: 1196 Mandalay Ct Lilburn GA 30047 Office: South Gwinnett High Sch 2288 E Main St Snellville GA 30078

GERSON, RALPH JOSEPH, corporate executive; b. Detroit, Nov. 30, 1949; s. Byron Hayden and Dorothy Mary (Davidson) G.; m. Erica Ann Ward, May 20, 1979. BA, Yale U., 1971; MSc, London Sch. Econs., 1972; JD, U. Mich., 1975. Bar: Mich. 1975, D.C. 1976, U.S. Dist. Ct. D.C. 1976, U.S. Ct. Appeals (D.C. cir.) 1976. Counsel Dem. Nat. Com., Washington, 1975-77; spl. asst. U.S. Spl. Trade Rep., Washington, 1978-79; counselor to spl. Middle East negotiator Office of Pres., Washington, 1979-80; ptnr. Akin, Gump, Strauss, Hauer and Feld, Washington, 1981-83, 85-87; dir. Mich. Dept. Commerce, Lansing, 1983-84; exec. v.p. Guardian Industries Corp., Auburn Hills, Mich., 1988-93, also bd. dirs., 1988—; pres., CEO Guardian Internat. Corp., 1993—; chmn. bd. OIS Optical Imaging Sys., Auburn Hills, 1993—. Bd. dirs. Pistons-Palace Found., U.S. Spain Coun.; chmn. Hungarian-U.S. Bus. Coun.; trustee Henry Ford Mus., Detroit Symphony Orch. Hall, and Henry Ford Hosp., Citizens Rsch. Coun.; mem. U.S. Adv. Com. for Trade Policy and Negotiations. Mem. ABA, D.C. Bar Assn., Mich. Bar Assn., Coun. Fgn. Rels., Young Pres. Orgn., U.S. C. of C., Royal Automobile Club, Franklin Hills Country Club, Bloomfield Open Hunt Club, Yale Club of NYC. Office: Guardian Industries Corp 2300 Harmon Rd Auburn Hills MI 48326-1714

GERSON, ROBERT ELISHA, periodical editor-in-chief; b. White Plains, N.Y., Apr. 18, 1933; s. Jack Herman and Eva (Sharlach) G.; m. Sandra Nathalie Solomon, Aug. 17, 1958 (dec.); 1 child, Philip Bennett; m. Barbara E. Shapiro Cercone, Oct. 25, 1998. BS, NYU, 1958. Editor Hartsdale (N.Y.) News, 1958-60; press sec. Rep. Robert Barry, Yonkers, N.Y., 1960-61; mktg. coord. Electronic Industries Assn. Japan, N.Y.C., 1961-68; mng. editor Television Digest, N.Y.C., 1968-85; founding editor, editor-in-chief TWICE (This Week in Consumer Electronics), N.Y.C., 1985—. Dir. Art Levis Found., Washington, Electronics/Appliance divsn. Anti-Defamation League, N.Y.C. Cpl. U.S. Army, 1954-56. Named S. David Feir Humanitarian award Anti-Defamation League, 1992. Jewish. Avocations: hiking, travel, reading, gardening. Home: 36 Birch Way Tarrytown NY 10591-4602 Office: TWICE Magazine 245 W 17th St New York NY 10011-5300

GERSON, ROBERT WALTHALL, judge, retired lawyer; b. Macon, Ga., Aug. 6, 1935; s. John Oscar and Margaret Rose (Walthall) G.; m. Naomi Brooks, Apr. 25, 1964; children: Kimberly Brooks, Allison Lee. AB in Law, Emory U., 1959, JD, 1960. Bar: Ga. 1960. Atty. State of Ga., Atlanta, 1960-65, Ryder Truck Lines, Jacksonville, Fla., 1965-67; ptnr. Troutman, Sanders, Lockerman & Ashmore, Atlanta, 1968-91; adminstrv. law judge State Bd. Workers Compensation, Atlanta, 1992—; instr. pub. speaking Ga. State U., 1977-78. Contbr. articles to profl. jours. Bd. dirs. North Arts Ctr. Mem. ABA, Ga. Bar Assn. (chmn. adminstrv. law sect. 1979), Atlanta Bar Assn., Macon Bar Assn. (bench and bar com. 1998-99), Atlanta Phoenix Soc., Atlanta Lawyers Club, City Club of Macon, Sigma Phi Epsilon. Episcopalian. Avocations: teaching, tennis. Home: 718 Allison Park Macon GA 31210-1518 Office: Bd of Workers' Compensation Ste 235 3312 Northside Dr Bldg D Macon GA 31210-2500

GERSON, STUART MICHAEL, lawyer; b. N.Y.C., Jan. 16, 1944; s. James and Ethel (Cherney) G.; m. Pamela Somers, July 28, 1979; children: James Barker, Somers Elizabeth, Lindsey Dakota. BA in Polit. Sci., Pa. State U., 1964; JD, Georgetown U., 1967. Bar: D.C. 1968, U.S. Supreme Ct. 1974, U.S. Ct. Appeals (DC cir.) 1972, U.S. Ct. Appeals (5th cir.) 1972, 81, U.S. Ct. Appeals (9th cir.) 1978, U.S. Ct. Appeals (2d cir.) 1979, U.S. Ct. Appeals (11th cir.) 1981, U.S. Ct. Appeals (6th cir.) 1982, U.S. Ct. Appeals (4th cir.) 1984, U.S. Ct. Appeals (3d cir.) 1985, U.S. Ct. Appeals (8th cir.) 1986, U.S. Ct. Appeals (1st, 7th, 10th, fed. cirs.) 1989. Asst. U.S. atty. City of Washington, 1972-75; assoc., then ptnr. Reed Smith Shaw & McClay, Washington, 1975-80; pvt. practice; ptnr. in charge litigation Epstein, Becker & Green, Washington, N.Y.C., 1980-89; adj. prof. of law Georgetown U., 1991; asst. atty. gen. in charge civil div. U.S. Dept. Justice, Washington, 1989-93; acting Atty. Gen. U.S., 1993; atty. and head of litigation Epstein, Becker & Green, P.C., Washington and N.Y.C.; bd. dirs. CHANGE-All Souls Housing Corp., Washington. Contbr. articles to profl. jours. Gen. counsel Nat. Rep. Senatorial Com., Washington, 1985-86; sr. advisor presdl. campaign George Bush, 1988; leader transition team Office Pres. Elect, 1988. Capt. USAF, 1967-72. Decorated Meritorious Svc. Medal. Mem. ABA, D.C. Bar Assn. (steering com. litigation 1985-93), The Barristers (pres.), Nat. Health Lawyers Assn., Am. Inns of Ct., Metro. Club, Lawyers Club. Unitarian. Avocations: competitive running, national track and field official, sailing, reading history. Office: Epstein Becker & Green PC 1227 25th St NW Washington DC 20037-1156 also: 250 Park Ave New York NY 10177-0001

GERSONI-EDELMAN, DIANE CLAIRE, author, editor; b. Bklyn., Apr. 16, 1947; d. James Arthur and Edna Bernice (Krinski) Gersoni; B.A. cum laude, Vassar Coll., 1967; m. James Neil Edelman, Oct. 5, 1975; children—Michael Lawrence, Sara Anne. Asst. editor, then asso. editor Sch. Library Jour. Book Rev., 1968-72; free lance writer, 1972-74, 77—; writer, editor Scholastic Mags., Inc., N.Y.C., 1974-77; author: Sexism and Youth, 1974; Work-Wise: Learning About the World of Work from Books, 1980; cons., speaker in field. Club: Vassar (N.Y.C.). Contbr. articles, book revs. to anthologies, newspapers, mags. Home: care Edelman 301 E 78th St New York NY 10021-1322

GERSONY, WELTON MARK, physician, pediatric cardiologist, educator; b. Syracuse, N.Y., Nov. 19, 1931; s. Irving and Ann (Cohen) G.; m. Susan; children: Neal, Anne, Richard, Deborah. AB, Syracuse U., 1954; MD, SUNY, Syracuse, 1958. Diplomate Am. Bd. Pediatrics, Sub Bd. Pediatric Cardiology. Intern Cleve. Met. Gen. Hosp., 1958-59, resident in pediatrics, 1959-61; resident in pediatrics Babies and Childrens Hosp., Cleve., 1959-61; fellow in cardiology Harvard U., 1963-65; asst. prof. pediatrics U. Tex., Dallas, 1965-68; asst. prof. pediatrics Columbia U., 1968-71, assoc. prof., 1971-74, prof., 1974—; adj. prof. Cornell U., 1998—; dir. div. pediatric cardiology Columbia-Presbyn. Med. Ctr., N.Y. Hosp.; vis. dir. pediatric cardiology Gt. Ormond St. Hosp. Sick Children, London, 1984-85; organizer 2d World Congress Pediatric Cardiology, N.Y.C., 1985; chmn. steering com. World Congress Pediatric Cardiology and Cardiac Surgery, 1989-97; mem. Sub.-bd. Pediatric Cardiology, 1976-83, chmn., 1981-83, com. ofcl. examiners, 1983-90; cons. in drug evaluation AMA, 1985—; cons. Extramural Affairs div. Nat. Heart Lung and Blood Inst., 1988—; James Overall vis. prof. pediatrics Vanderbilt U., 1991; lectr. Brit. Heart Found., 1991, Toby Keenan Meml. Symposium U. Md., 1994; Gladys Fashena lectr. Southwestern Med. Ctr. Dallas, 1994; Jerome D. Solomon Meml. lectr. Nat. Ctr. Advanced Med. Edn., Chgo., 1994, 98; mem. adv. bd. Congress of Pediat. Cardiology Internat., 1998—. Author: Nelson's Textbook of Pediatrics, 1983, 3d edit., 1991; mem. editl. bd. Pediatric Cardiology, 1978-90, Jour. of Pediatrics, 1986-93, Jour. Am. Coll. Cardiology, 1990-94, Cardiology in the Young, 1990—, Progress in Pediatric Cardiology, 1991—; editl. bd. Circulation, 1993-96, cons. editor, 1996—; internat. adv. bd. Japanese Circulation Jour., 1996—; contbr. revs. to profl. jours., chpts. to books. Prin. investigator NIH grants; mem. internat. com., bd. dirs. Internat. Cardiology Found., 1993—; mem. program com. Internat. Kawasaki Disease Chmn. Cardiology Symposium, 1989, 92, 95. Capt. M.C., U.S. Army, 1961-63. Falkner fellow U. Sydney, Australia, 1983. Fellow Am. Coll. Cardiology, Am. Acad. Pediatrics; mem. AMA (accreditation coun. for grad. med. edn. 1994—), Soc. Pediatric Rsch., Am. Pediatric Soc., Am. Heart Assn. (pres. coun. cardiovascular disease in the young 1988-90, T. Duckett Jones lectr. 1998), Am. Fedn. Clin. Rsch., Harvey Soc., Assn. European Paediatric Cardiologists (corr.), Internat. Soc. for Adult Congenital Heart Disease, Am. Contract Bridge League (life master). Rsch. on cardiovascular disease in infants and children, natural history of congenital heart disease in children; patent ductus arteriosus in premature infants; persistence of the fetal circulation. Office: Columbia U 630 W 168th St New York NY 10032-3795

GERST, JERALD ROBERT, physician; b. Burlington, Iowa, Jan. 11, 1947; s. Robert Clarence and LaVera Evelyn; m. Carole Karin Delany, June 27, 1970; children: Robert Severin, Jocelyn Colleen, Jeremy Michael. AB, Harvard Coll., 1969; MD, U. Calif., Davis, 1973; MPH, U. Calif., Berkeley, 1973. Diplomate Am. Bd. Internal Medicine, Am. Bd. Preventive Medicine, Am. Bd. Emergency Medicine. Intern then resident USPHS Hosp., San Francisco, 1973-76; staff physician USCG TRACEN, Alameda, Calif., 1976-77; emergency physician Emanuel Hosp., Turlock, Calif., 1977-88, Petaluma (Calif.) Valley Hosp., 1984-86; occupl. physician N. Bay Corp. Health Svcs., Santa Rosa and Petaluma, 1986-87; med. dir., owner Redwood Occupl. Medicine Assocs., Santa Rosa and Petaluma, Calif., 1988-96; occupl. physician Work Care N. Coast Health Ctrs., Santa Rosa and Petaluma, 1996—; cons. paramedic and MICN continuing edn. Emergency Med. Svcs. Agy., Modesto, Calif., 1982-84; instr., course dir. ACLS Emanuel Hosp., Turlock, Calif., 1980-86. Founding dir. Twin Hills--Apple Blossom Ednl. Found., Sebastopol, Calif., 1986-89; mem. El Molino H.S. Site Coun., Forestville, Calif., 1997-98, mem. Bus. Roundtable, Forestville, 1997—; mem. Environ. Def. Fund, Nature Conservancy. LCDR USPHS/USCG, 1973-77. Nat. scholar Harvard U., 1968; U. Calif. Regents scholar, 1969. Fellow Am. Coll. Occupl. and Environ. Medicine; mem. ACP, Sierra Club, Phi Beta Kappa. Avocations: photography, hiking, white-water rafting. Office: Work Care 1287 Fulton Rd Santa Rosa CA 95401

GERST, PAUL HOWARD, physician; b. Sept. 24, 1927; s. David and Hilde (Werbel) G.; m. Elizabeth Carlsen, Aug. 3, 1957; children—Steven R., Jeffrey C., Andrew L. A.B., Columbia U., 1948, M.D., 1952. Diplomate: Am. Bd. Surgery, Am. Bd. Thoracic Surgery. Intern Columbia Presbyn. Med. Center, N.Y.C., 1952-53; resident Columbia Presbyn. Med. Center, 1956-62, mem. staff, 1962—; instr. physiology U. Pa., 1955-56; practice medicine specializing in surgery N.Y.C., 1962—; asst. clin. prof. surgery Columbia U., 1964-72; prof. surgery Albert Einstein Coll. Medicine, 1972—; dir. surgery Bronx-Lebanon Hosp. Center, N.Y.C., 1964—. Contbr. articles to profl. jours. Served to 1st lt. U.S. Army, 1953-55. USPHS postdoctoral fellow, 1955-56; Recipient Research Career Devel. award, 1964-65. Fellow A.C.S.; mem. Am. Physiol. Soc., N.Y. Soc. for Thoracic Surgery, N.Y. Surg. Soc., N.Y. Soc. for Cardiovascular Surgery, Am. Heart Assn. Home: 141 Tekening Dr Tenafly NJ 07670-1218 Office: Bronx Lebanon Hosp Ctr 1650 Grand Concourse Bronx NY 10457-7606

GERST, STEVEN RICHARD, healthcare director, physician; b. N.Y.C., Oct. 20, 1958; s. Paul Howard and Elizabeth (Carlsen) G.; m. Isabelle Sylvie Meier, Apr. 21, 1987 (div.); 1 child, Chantal Elizabeth. BA, Columbia U., 1981, MD, 1986, MPH, 1987; MBA, Emory U., 1996. Lic. ins. broker, N.C. Med. affairs coord. Sun Health Care Plans, Charlotte, N.C., 1987-88, cons., 1988-90; asst. v.p., dir. Preferred Provider Orgns. Crawford & Co., Atlanta, 1994, Preferred Provider Arrangements Crawford & Co., Atlanta, 1990-94; v.p. Imaginative Devices Inc., Atlanta, 1993-94, Columbia/HCA Healthcare Corp., Nashville, Tenn., 1994-95; pres., CEO Health Advantage Network, Orlando and Atlanta, Fla., 1994—, Woodland Hills, Calif., 1994-95; sr. cons. Coopers & Lybrand, Atlanta, 1995—; interim pres. PCA Health Plans Ga. (HMO), Atlanta, 1996—; pres. SRG Cons., Inc., 1997—; interviewer Columbia Coll., N.C., 1987; adj. prof. Emory U., 1996—; pres. SRG Cons., Inc.; v.p. Adli Audio, Inc.; interim dir. Medicare & Choices HMO program of Grady Ikallu Systems, Inc.; bd. dirs. Internet Gamtuy Inc.; dir. network devel. Grady Health Systems Inc., 1999—. Editor-in-chief: Handbook Coll. Physicians and Surgeons (Alumni award), 1983, Columbian (Robert Shellow Gerdy award), 1981. Vol. Presbyn. Hosp., N.Y.C., 1979-81, St. Lukes Hosp., N.Y.C., 1978-79. Mem. AMA, Am. Acad. Med. Dirs., Am. Coll. Med. Staff Affairs, Am. Coll. Physician Execs., Am. Coll. Health Care Execs., Am. Assn. Physician-Hosp. Orgns., Am. Assn. Preferred Provider Orgns., Andover Alumni Soc. N.Y. (dir. 1986-87), Alliance Francaise (v.p. Charlotte, N.C. chpt. 1987-88). Avocations: bicycling, tennis, golf, dance, gardening. Home: 5450 Glenridge Dr NE Apt 372 Atlanta GA 30342-4921 Office: 1155 Peachtree Rd NE Atlanta GA 30309-7629

GERSTEIN, DAVID BROWN, hardware manufacturing company executive, professional basketball team executive; b. N.Y.C., Jan. 30, 1936; s. Frank and May G.; m. Jane Ellen Bender, May 4, 1963; children: Mark, James. Student, Columbia U., 1951-54, postgrad., 1954-58; B.S., Seton Hall U., 1959. With Thermwell Products Co., Paterson, N.J., 1958—; sales mgr. Thermwell Products Co., 1965-68, v.p., 1968-74, pres., 1974—; prin. owner N. J. Nets NBA franchise, 1978—; v.p. Lever Mfg. Co., Paterson; pres. Woodlowe Realty, Paterson, Wait Assocs., Paterson, Dim Assocs., Mahwah, N.J. Chmn. adv. council energy and conservation State of N.J.; co-chmn. athletic program Seton Hall U. Office: NJ Nets Meadowlands Arena East Rutherford NJ 07073

GERSTEN, RUSSELL MONROE, educational foundation administrator; b. May 10, 1947. BA in Phys. Sci., Brandeis U., 1967; PhD in Spl. Edn., U. Oreg., 1978. Music critic, freelance writer Rolling Stone, Boston, Phoenix, N.Y.C., 1970-81; prof. Coll. Edn. U. Oreg., Eugene, 1991—; pres. Eugene Rsch. Inst., 1990-91, 92-97; pres. divsn. for rsch. Coun. Exceptional Children, 1997-98. E-mail: rgersten@oregon.uoregon.edu. Office: Eugene Rsch Inst 132 E Broadway Ste 747 Eugene OR 97401

GERSTENBERGER, DONNA LORINE, humanities educator; b. Wichita Falls, Tex., Dec. 26, 1929; d. Donald Fayette and Mabel G. AB, Whitman Coll., 1951; MA, U. Okla., 1952, PhD, 1958. Asst. prof. English U. Colo., Boulder, 1958-60; prof. U. Wash., 1960-96, prof. emeritus, 1996—, chmn. undergrad. studies, 1971-74, assoc. dean Coll. Arts and Scis., dir. Coll. Honors and Office Undergrad. Studies, 1974-76, chmn. dept. English, 1976-83, vice chmn. faculty senate, 1984-85, chmn. faculty senate, 1985-86; cons. in field; bd. dirs. Am. Lit. Classics; mem. grants-in-aid com. Am. Coun. Learned Socs.; chmn. region VII, Mellon Fellowships in Humanities, 1982-92; mem. adv. com. Grad. Record Exams, 1990-93, Coun. Internat. Exch. of Scholars, 1992-95. Author: J.M. Synge, 1964, 2d edition, 1988, The American Novel: A Checklist of Twentieth Century Criticism, vols. I and II, 1970, Directory of Periodicals, 1974, The Complex Configuration: Modern Verse Drama, 1973, Iris Murdoch, 1974, Richard Hugo, 1983; editor: Microcosm, 1969, Swallow Series in Bibliography, 1974—; assoc. editor: Abstracts of English Studies, 1958-68; founder, editor jour. Seattle Rev., 1983-96. Bd. dirs. N.W. Chamber Orch., Seattle, 1975-78, Wash. Friends Humanities, 1991—; trustee Wash. Commn. Humanities, 1985-91, pres., 1988-90; mem. vis. com. Lehigh U., 1987-92; pres. Am. Commn. for Irish Studies/West, 1989-91. Grantee Am. Council Learned Socs., 1962, 88, Am. Philos. Soc., 1963. Mem. MLA, Am. Com. Irish Studies. Office: U Wash Box 354330 Dept English Seattle WA 98195-4330

GERSTER, J. ALEC, communications executive. From media dir. to exec. v.p., worldwide media and programming svcs. dir. Grey, N.Y.C., 1981—; exec. v.p. Grey; dir. Audit Bur. Circulations. Mem. Internat. TV and Radio Soc., 4As (past chmn. media policy com.). Office: Grey Advt Inc 777 3rd Ave New York NY 10017-1401*

GERSTING, JUDITH LEE, computer science educator, researcher; b. Springfield, Vt., Aug. 20, 1940; d. Harold H. and Dorothy V. (Kinney) MacKenzie; m. John M. Gersting, Jr., Aug. 17, 1962; children: Adam, Jason. BS, Stetson U., 1962; MA, Ariz. State U., 1964, PhD, 1969. Assoc. prof. computer sci. U. Ctrl. Fla., Orlando, 1980-81; asst. prof. computer sci. Ind. U.-Purdue U., Indpls., 1970-73, assoc. prof., 1974-79, prof., 1981-93; prof. computer sci. U. Hawaii, Hilo, 1994—; staff scientist Indpls. Ctr. for Advanced Rsch., 1982-84. Author: Mathematical Structures for Computer Science, 1999, Visual Basic Programming, 1996; contbr. articles to computer sci. jours. Mem. Assn. for Computing Machinery, IEEE Computer Soc. Avocations: youth soccer, reading. Office: U Hawaii 200 W Kawili St Hilo HI 96720-4075

GERSTMAN, GEORGE HENRY, lawyer; b. N.Y.C., July 25, 1939; m. Rozanne Millman, Dec. 24, 1960; childrn: Heidi Ann, Gary Daniel. BSEE, U. Ill., 1960; JD with honors, George Washington U., 1963. Bar: Ill. 1964, U.S. Dist. Ct. (no. dist.) Ill. 1964, U.S. Patent Office 1964, U.S. Supreme Ct. 1971, U.S. Ct. Appeals (7th cir.) 1971, U.S. Ct. Appeals (2d cir.) 1980, U.S. Ct. Appeals (Fed. cir.) 1982. Patent examiner U.S. Patent Office, Washington, 1960-63; assoc. Dressler, Goldsmith et al, Chgo., 1963-70; ptnr. Lettvin & Gerstman, Chgo., 1970-75, Gerstman, Ellis & McMillin, Ltd., Chgo., 1976—. Asst. patent editor George Washington Law Rev., 1962-63. Govt. appeal agt. Selective Svc. System, Evanston, Ill., 1967-73; mem. Northbrook (Ill.) Bd. Zoning Appeals, 1971-90. Mem. ABA, Chgo. Bar Assn., Am. Intellectual Property Law Assn., Patent Law Assn. Chgo., Fed. Cir. Bar Assn., Order of Coif, Standard Club (Chgo.), Monroe Club. Avocations: tennis, art, boating. Home: 219 Sheridan Rd Kenilworth IL 60043-1216 Office: Gerstman Ellis & McMillin Ltd 2 N La Salle St Chicago IL 60602-3702

GERSTMAYR, JOHN WOLFGANG, lawyer; b. Lauingen-Donau, Germany, Mar. 3, 1949; s. Bernhard and Augusta (Merkle) G.; m. Pamela Ann Meyer, July 17, 1971; children: Amanda, Emily, Julie. BS, Rensselaer Poly. Inst., 1971, MS, 1972; JD magna cum laude, U. Pa., 1975. Assoc. Ropes & Gray, Boston, 1975-84, ptnr., 1984—. Chmn. adv. com. Town of Wellesley, Mass., 1986-87, mem. personnel bd., 1994—. Mem. ABA, Boston Bar Assn., The Wellesley Club (dir. 1993-95, pres. 1995-96), Handel & Haydn Soc. (bd. overseers 1994—), Miramichi Salmon Assn. Inc. (bd. dirs. 1998—). Republican. Episcopal. Avocations: gardening, piano, hunting, fishing. Home: 131 Glen Rd Wellesley MA 02481-1515 Office: Ropes & Gray One International Pl Boston MA 02110

GERSTNER, LOUIS VINCENT, JR., diversified company executive; b. Mineola, N.Y., Mar. 1, 1942; s. Louis Vincent and Marjorie (Rutan) G.; m. Elizabeth Robins Link, Nov. 30, 1968; children: Louis, Elizabeth. BA in Engring., Dartmouth Coll., 1963; MBA, Harvard U., 1965; DBA (hon.), Boston Coll., 1994; LLD (hon.), Wake Forest U., 1997, Brown U., 1997. Dir. McKinsey & Co., N.Y.C., 1965-78; exec. v.p. Am. Express Co., N.Y.C., 1978-81; vice-chmn. bd. Am. Express Co., 1981-83, chmn. exec. com., 1983-85, pres., 1985-89, chmn., CEO travel related svcs., 1985-89; chmn., CEO RJR Nabisco Inc., N.Y.C., 1989-93; chmn. bd., CEO IBM, Armonk, NY, 1993—, also dir.; mem. Pres.'s Nat. Security Telecom. Adv. Com., 1994-97, Adv. Com. for Trade Policy and Negotiations, 1995—. Co-author: Reinventing Education: Entrepreneurship in America's Public School, 1994. Bd. dirs. Meml. Sloan Kettering Hosp., 1978-89, 98—, United Negro Coll. Fund, 1987-91, Lincoln Ctr. for Performing Arts, 1984—, Am.-China Soc., 1987—, N.Y. Times, AT&T, Caterpillar; trustee Joint Coun. on Econ. Edn., 1975-87, chmn. 1983-85; active Bus. Roundtable, 1991-98, The Bus. Coun., 1992; vice-chmn., bd. dirs. New Am. Schs. Devel. Corp., 1991-98; adv. bd. Ctr. for Strategic and Internat. Studies, 1987—; trustee N.Y. Pub. Libr., 1991-96; bd. regents Smithsonian Instn., 1996—. Recipient Cleveland E. Dodge Medal for disting. svc. to edn. Tchrs. Coll., Columbia U., Disting. Svc. to Sci. and Edn. award Am. Mus. Natural History. Mem. Coun. Fgn. Rels., N.Y. Cit Partnership, Japan Soc. (bd. dirs. 1992-97). Office: IBM Corp New Orchard Rd Armonk NY 10504-1709

GERSTNER, MARY JANE, nurse; b. Rochester, N.Y., June 27, 1953; d. Thomas J. and Jane E. Gerstner. Diploma, St. Joseph's Hosp. Health Ctr. Sch. Nursing, 1974; BSN, Nazareth Coll., 1982. RN, N.Y. Staff nurse operating rm. U. Rochester Med. Ctr./Strong Meml. Hosp., 1974-79, staff nurse ob.-gyn. unit, 1981-83, 84-86; staff nurse operating rm. St. Mary's Hosp., Rochester, 1983-84; staff nurse oper. rm. Genesee Hosp., Rochester, 1985-95; nurse 1st asst. Genesee Valley Plastic Surgery, Canandaigua, N.Y., 1995; staff nurse oper rm. U. of Rochester (N.Y.) Med. Ctr., 1996—. Mem. ARC. Mem. Assn. Oper. Rm. Nurses, Sigma Theta Tau.

GERSTNER, ROBERT WILLIAM, structural engineering educator, consultant; b. Chgo., Nov. 10, 1934; s. Robert Berty and Martha (Tuchelt) G.; m. Elizabeth Willard, Feb. 8, 1958; children: Charles Willard, William Mark. B.S., Northwestern U., 1956, M.S., 1957, Ph.D., 1960. Registered structural and profl. engr., Ill. Instr. Northwestern U., Evanston, Ill., 1957-59; research fellow Northwestern U., 1959-60; asst. prof. U. Ill., Chgo., 1960-63; assoc. prof. U. Ill., 1963-69, prof. structural engring., architecture, 1969-92, prof. emeritus, 1992—; structural engr. cons., 1959—; mem. State of Ill. Structural Engring. Bd., 1992-94. Contbr. articles to profl. jours. Pres. Riverside Improvement Assn., 1973-77, 79-82. Mem. AAUP, ACLU, ASCE, Am. Soc. Engring. Edn., Structural Engrs. Assn. Ill. (bd. dirs. 1986-89, 92-94, sec. 1989-91, pres. 1991-92). Home: 2628 W Agatite Ave Chicago IL 60625-3011

GERT, BERNARD, philosopher, educator; b. Cin., Oct. 16, 1934; s. Max and Celia (Yarnovsky) G.; m. Esther Libbye Rosenstein, Aug. 3, 1958; children: Heather Joy, Joshua Noah. BA, U. Cin., 1956; PhD, Cornell U., 1962. Instr. philosophy Dartmouth Coll., Hanover, N.H., 1959-62, asst. prof. philosophy, 1962-66, assoc. prof., 1966-70, prof., 1970—, chmn. dept. philosophy, 1971-74, 79-81, 1998—, Stone prof. intellectual and moral philosophy, 1981-92, 98—, Eunice and Julian Cohen prof. ethics and human values, 1992-98; vis. assoc. prof. philosophy Johns Hopkins U., Balt., 1967-68; vis. prof. philosophy Edinburgh U., fall 1974, Hebrew U. Jerusalem, 1985-86, Nacional U. de la Plata and U. Buenos Aires, Argentina, fall 1995; adj. prof. psychiatry Dartmouth Med. Sch., 1976—. Author: The Moral Rules: A New Rational Foundation for Morality, 1970, 1973, 1975, German edit. 1983, Morality: A New Justification of the Moral Rules, 1988, Morality: Its Nature and Justification, 1998; co-author: Philosophy in Medicine: Conceptual and Ethical Issues in Medicine and Psychiatry, 1982, Japanese edit. 1984; first author: Morality and the New Genetics: A Guide for Students and Health Care Providers, 1996, Bioethics: A Return to Fundamentals, 1997; editor: Hobbes' Man and Citizen, 1972, reprinted with revisions, 1991; contbr. chpts. to books, articles to profl. jours. NEH fellow, 1969-70, Hastings Ctr. fellow; recipient NSF-NEH Sustained Devel. award, 1980-84, Fulbright lectureship, Israel, 1985-86, Argentina, fall 1995; prin. investigator NIH, 1990-93. Mem. Am. Philos. Assn., Am. Soc. Polit. and Legal Philosophy. Avocations: squash, poker. Home: 8 Bridgman Rd Hanover NH 03755-1302 Office: Dartmouth Coll Dept Philosophy Hanover NH 03755

GERTENBACH, ROBERT FREDERICK, medical research organization executive, accountant, lawyer; b. N.Y.C., Feb. 26, 1923; s. Charles and Margaret (Klag) G.; m. Arlene Turney (div. 1968); m. Carol Jean Roberts, Aug. 20, 1977; children: Stephen, Gail. BBA, CCNY, 1947; JD, Fordham U., 1952. Bar: N.Y. 1952; CPA, N.J., N.Y. Acct. Orens, Reiner, Weissbarth, N.Y.C., 1947-50, Price Waterhouse & Co., N.Y.C., 1950; asst. gen. counsel Thomas J. Lipton Inc., Englewood Cliffs, N.J., 1950-68; asst. to pres. Eastwood-Nealley Inc., Belleville, N.J., 1968-69; sr. product mgr. CPC Internat., Englewood Cliffs, 1970-73; v.p. Council of Better Bus. Burs., Inc., N.Y.C., 1973-80; pres. Council for Tobacco Research-U.S.A., Inc., N.Y.C., 1984-92, ret., 1992. Served to 1st lt. USAAF, 1943-45, PTO. Mem. ABA. Avocations: reading, walking.

GERTH, DONALD ROGERS, university president; b. Chgo., Dec. 4, 1928; s. George C. and Madeleine (Canavan) G.; m. Beverly J. Hollman, Oct. 15, 1955; children: Annette, Deborah. BA, U. Chgo., 1947, AM, 1951, PhD, 1963. Field rep. S.E. Asia World Univ. Svc., 1950; asst. to pres. Shimer Coll., 1951; Admissions counselor U. Chgo., 1956-58; assoc. dean students, admissions and records, mem. dept. polit. sci. San Francisco St. U., San Francisco, 1958-63; assoc. dean instnl. relations and student affairs Calif. State Univ., 1963-64; chmn. commn. on extended edn. Calif. State Univs. and Colls., 1977-82; dean of students Calif. State U., Chico, 1964-68, prof. polit. sci., 1964-76, assoc. v.p. for acad. affairs, dir. internat. programs, 1969-70, v.p. acad. affairs, 1970-76; co-dir. Danforth Found. Research Project, 1968-69; coordinator Inst. Local Govt. and Public Service, 1968-70; pres., prof. polit. sci. and public adminstrn. Calif. State U., Dominguez Hills, 1976-84; pres., prof. govt. and adminstrn. Calif. State U., Sacramento, 1984—; past chair Accrediting Commn. for Sr. Colls. and Univs. of Western Coll. Assn.; chmn. admissions coun. Calif. State U.; bd. dirs. Ombudsman Found., L.A., 1968-71; com. continuing edn. Calif. Coordinating Coun. for Higher Edn., 1963-64; lectr. U. Philippines, 1953-54, Claremont Grad. Sch. and Univ. Ctr., 1965-69; chair Sacramento World Trade Ctr.; chmn. Calif. State U. Inst. Co-author: The Learning Society, 1969; author, editor: An Invisible Giant, 1971; contbg. editor Education for the Public Service, 1970, Papers on the Ombudsman in Higher Education, 1979. Mem. pers. commn. Chico Unified Sch. Dist., 1969-76, chmn., 1971-74; adv. com. on justice pgorams Butte Coll., 1970-76; mem. Varsity Scouting Coun., 1980-84; chmn. United Way campaign Calif. State Univs., L.A. County, 1981-82; bd. dirs. Sacramento Area United Way, campaign chmn., 1991-92, exec. com., 1991-96, vice chmn., 1992-94, chmn.-elect, 1994-95, chmn., 1995-96; mem. bd. dirs. South Bay Hosp. Found., 1979-82; mem. The Cultural Commn., L.A., 1981-84; mem. com. govtl. rels. Am. Coun. Edn. Capt. USAF, 1952-56. Mem. Internat. Assn. Univ. Pres. (pres. 1996-99), Am. Polit. Sci. Assn., Am. Soc. Pub. Adminstrn., Soc. Coll. and Univ. Planning, Western Govtl. Rsch. Assn., World Affairs Coun. No. Calif., Assn. Pub. Adminstrn. Edn. (chmn. 1973-74), Western Polit. Sci. Assn., Am. Assn. State Colls. and Univs. (bd. dirs.), Calif. State C. of C. (edn. com.), Assn. Governing Bds. of Univs. and Colls., Calif. State U. Inst. (chmn. bd. dirs.), UN Ednl., Sci. and Cultural Orgn. (mem. adv. com.), UN Univ. Coun., World Trade Ctr. Sacramento, (chmn.), Sacramento Club (bd. dirs.), Comstock Club. Democrat. Episcopalian. Avocations: tennis, skiing, reading. Home: 417 Websters Ct Roseville CA 95747-8339 Office: Calif State U 6000 J St # 206 Sacramento CA 95819-6022

GERTJEJANSEN, DOYLE, artist, educator; b. Tracy, Minn., Sept. 1, 1948. BA, Mankato State U., 1969; MFA, U. Minn., 1971. Instr. fine arts U. New Orleans, 1971-75, grad. coun., 1986—, prof. fine arts, 1988—, chmn. dept. fine arts, 1995—; panelist Instns. and the Artist, Optima Studio, New Orleans, 1982; visual arts com. New Orleans Contemporary Arts Ctr., 1983-86; dir. Sculpture Front, U. New Orleans, 1984-86, project dir. for traveling exhbn. So. Folk Images, Univ. Senate, 1984, permanent art collection com., 1984-87; task force on pub. sculpture Downtown Devel. Dist. and Arts Coun. New Orleans, 1985; mem. downtown pub. art com. Arts Coun. New Orleans, 1986, percent for art com., 1987-89, bd. dirs., 1988-89; bd. dirs. New Orleans Contemporary Arts Ctr., 1996—. One-man shows include Augusta Coll. Fine Arts Gallery, Sioux Falls, S.D., 1968, Coffman Gallery, U. Minn., Mpls., 1971, U. No. Ala., Florence, 1975, La. Crafts Coun., New Orleans, 1980, Arthur Roger Gallery, New Orleans, 1983, 85, New Orleans Ctr. for the Performing Arts, 1984, Susan Abeline Gallery, Zurich, Switzerland, 1986, Galerie Simonne Stern Ltd., Atlanta, 1989, 96, Conkling Gallery, Mankato (Minn.) State U., 1989; group exhbns. include Galerie Simonne Stern, New Orleans, 1994, New Orleans Ctr. for Contemporary Art, 1995, La. Arts and Sci. Ctr., Baton Rouge, 1995, New Gallery, Houston, 1995, Fine Arts Gallery U. New Orleans, 1995, Contemporary Arts Ctr., New Orleans, 1995, Positive Space Gallery, New Orleans, 1996, Delfina Studio Trust, London, 1996, Southeastern Ctr. for Contemporary Art, Winston-Salem, N.C., 1997, numerous others; represented in pub. and corp. collections at Adams & Reese, New Orleans, Ariz. State U., Ark. Art Ctr., Atlantic Richfield, Corp. Realty, New Orleans, Emeril's Restaurant, New Orleans, Hotel Intercontinental, New Orleans, Houston Effler Advt. Co., Boston, Joseph Canizaro Interests, New Orleans, Middleberg, Riddle & Gianna Attys., New Orleans, New Orleans Mus. Art, Pan Am. Life, New Orleans, Premier Bank, Baton Rouge, Scudder, Stevens and Clark, Boston, State St. Rsch. and Mgmt. Co., Boston, TJM Corp., New Orleans, Westminster, Corp., New Orleans, and other pvt. collections. Office: c/o Galerie Simonne Stern 518 Julia St New Orleans LA 70130*

GERTLER, MENARD M., physician, educator; b. Saskatoon, Sask., Can., May 21, 1919; came to U.S., 1947, naturalized, 1953; s. Frank and Clara (Handelman) G.; m. Anna Paull, Sept. 4, 1943; children—Barbara Lynn, Stephanie Jocelyn, Jonathan Paull. BA, U. Sask., 1940; MD, McGill U., 1943, MS, 1946; DSc, NYU, 1960. Intern Royal Victoria Hosp., Montreal, Que., Can., 1943-44; resident Mass. Gen. Hosp., Boston, 1947-50; also research fellow in medicine Mass. Gen. Hosp., Harvard Med. Sch., 1947-50; dir. cardiology Francis Delafield div. Columbia Presbyn. Med. Ctr., N.Y.C., 1950-54; spl. research fellow NIH, NYU Dept. Biochemistry, 1954-56; prof. Sch. Medicine, dir. cardiovascular research Rusk Inst. NYU Med. Ctr., 1958-71; sr. med. examiner FAA, 1975; dir. Washington Fed. Savs. & Loan Assn., 1972-83; adj. prof. medicine McGill U., 1996—; clin. prof. medicine N.Y. Hosp.-Cornell Med. Ctr., attending physician; med. dir. Sinclair Oil Corp., 1958-68; internat. cons. cardiovascular diseases, social and rehab. svcs. HEW, Washington, 1968-92; clin. prof. medicine N.Y. Hosp.-Cornell Med. Ctr., N.Y.C., 1998—. Author: Coronary Heart Disease in Young Adults, 1954, Coronary Heart Disease, 1974; Contbr. articles to profl. jours. Pres. Friends of McGill U.; mem. dean's com. McGill U. Med. Sch. With M.C., Royal Can. Army, 1940-43. Recipient Founders Day award NYU, 1959, medal of honor McGill U., 1993, award of merit McGill U., 1993. Mem. Gallatin Assocs. NYU, Cosmos Club (Washington), Harvard Club (Boston), Univ. Club. Home: 1000 Park Ave Apt 2C New York NY 10028-0934 Office: 317 E 34th St Rm 902 New York NY 10016-4974

GERTLER, STEPHANIE JOCELYN, journalist; b. N.Y.C.; d. Menard M. and Anna Paull Gertler; m. Mark B. Schiffer, Sept. 19, 1981; children: David, Elyena, Benjamin. BA, NYU, 1974. Office mgr. Newsweek mag., Miami, Fla., 1975-77; sr. prodn. editor Grune & Strathon, N.Y.C., 1978-81; art/lifestyles editor Greenwich (Conn.) News, 1995-97, Greenwich Post, 1997—; sr. writer Greenwich Mag., 1997—, Westport (Conn.), 1998—. Co-author: Ballet, Tap and All That Jazz, 1997; feature writer, contbr. weekly column to the Hour, Norwalk, Conn., 1996—, Wilton Villager, 1997—; contbr. to Spotlight Mag. Recipient 2d pl. award for feature article Soc. Profl. Journalists, 1995, 1st pl. award for gen. column Soc. Profl. Journalists, 1997. Avocations: dance, exercise. E-mail: SGert1211@aol.com. Office: 23 Grand park Ave Scarsdale NY 10583

GERTNER, NANCY, federal judge, educator; b. May 22, 1946; d. Morris and Sadie Gertner; m. John C. Reinstein, Apr. 27, 1985; 3 children. BA cum laude with honors, Columbia U., 1967; MA, JD, Yale U., 1971; degree (hon.), New England Sch. Law, 1979, Suffolk U., 1997. Bar: Mass., U.S. Dist. Ct., U.S. Ct. Appeals (1st and 3rd cirs.), U.S. Supreme Ct. Law clerk to Hon. Luther M. Swygert U.S. Ct. Appeals (7th cir.), Chgo., 1971-72; ptnr. Silverglate, Gertner, Fine & Good, 1973-90, Dwyer, Collora & Gertner, 1990-94; judge U.S. Dist. Ct. Mass., Boston, 1994—; instr. Sch. Law Boston U., 1972-86, 87-90, 94-95; vis. prof. Law Sch. Harvard U., 1985-86, Yale Law Sch., 1997—; instr. Boston Coll. Law Sch., 1995-98; mem. civic justice adv. com. to U.S. Dist. Ct., 1991; mem. adv. com. U.S. Ct. Appeals (1st cir.), 1991-92. Co-author: The Law of Juries; contbr. articles to legal jours. Bd. dirs. Women's Rights Com. Recipient Mass. Choice award, 1987, Black Educator's Alliance award Profl. Svc. to Edn., 1983, New England Hadassah award, 1992, Abigail Adams award Mass. Women's Polit. Caucus Edn. Fund., 1994; voted Best Fed. Judge in Mass., 1999. Mem. ATLA (basic trial advocacy course com., vice chair 1985-86), Mass. Acad. Trial Lawyers, Mass. Civil Liberties Union (bd. dirs., Abraham T. Alper award for Excellence in Civil Liberties, 1980), Boston Bar Assn. (lawyers com. for civil rights under law, steering com. 1979—), Women Judges Hon. Assn. Fax: 617-204-5821. E-mail: honorablenancyúgertner@mad.uscourts.gov. Office: US Dist Ct 1 Courthouse Way Boston MA 02210-3002

GERTRUDE, KATY See WILHELM, KATE

GERTZ, DAVID LEE, homebuilding company executive; b. Denver, July 30, 1950; s. Ben Harry and Clara (Cohen) G.; m. Bonnie Lee Schulein, June 2, 1973; children: Joshua, Eva. BS, U. Colo., 1972; MBA, U. Colo., Denver, 1993. Real estate broker Crown Realty, Denver, 1972-73; pres. Sunshine Plumbing Co., Lakewood, Colo., 1974-76, Sunshine Diversified, Inc., Lakewood, 1976—, Sunshine Master Builders, Ltd., Lakewood, 1990—; sec.-treas. Wight Lateral Ditch Co., Lakewood, 1987-91. *David Gertz is founder* *and president of Sunshine Master Builders Ltd., a 22 years old company listed in the Denver Business Journal as the 22nd largest homebuilding company in the Denver Metro area. Sunshine has built over 400 custom homes, an office building and a 50,000 sq. ft. commercial project. It employs 20 full time people, and engages over 150 trade contractor companies. Currently, it's building over 60 homes valued at over 25 million dollars. David earned an MBA at the University of Colorado at Denver in 1993, and serves on the board of the Denver Home Building Association and chairman of the 1999 Parade of Homes.* Builder of custom and semi-custom homes. Cub master Boy Scouts Am., Lakewood, 1989-91, asst. scout master, 1991-94; co-chair bldg. com. Hebrew Ednl. Alliance, bd. dirs., Denver, 1991-94; mem. Anti-Defamation League, Denver, 1989—; chmn. Parade of Homes com., 1999. Scholar, Evans Scholars, U. Colo., 1968-72. Mem. Home Builders Assn. of Denver (bd. dirs., legis. com.), Colo. Assn. Home Builders (alt. dir.). Avocations: skiing, golf, softball. Office: Sunshine Master Builders 8125 W Belleview Ave Littleton CO 80123-1203

GERTZ, ELMER, lawyer, author, educator; b. Chgo., Sept. 14, 1906; s. Morris and Grace (Grossman) G.; m. Ceretta Samuels, Aug. 16, 1931 (dec.); children: Theodore, Margery Ann Hechtman; m. Mamie L. Friedman, June 21, 1959 (dec.); 1 child, Jack M. Friedman. Ph.B., U. Chgo., 1928, J.D., 1930; LLD (hon.), John Marshall Law Sch., 1999, Lincoln Coll., 1999. Bar: Ill. 1930. Formerly assoc. firm McInerney, Epstein & Arvey, Chgo.; sole practice Chgo.; asst. to masters in chancery Jacob M. Arvey, Samuel B. Epstein, 1930-43; atty. for Nathan Leopold in successful parole procs., 1957-58; atty. various censorship litigations including Tropic of Cancer, 1962-64, atty. for Jack Ruby in setting aside death sentence, other capital cases; counsel commn. to investigate disorders in Chgo. during, spring, summer 1968; prof. John Marshall Law Sch., 1970—; mem. mission to USSR, Commn. Soviet Jewry, 1981; successful plaintiff in landmark libel case Gertz vs. Robert Welch, Inc., 1969-83; adj. prof. John Marshall Law Sch. Author: (with A.I. Tobin) Frank Harris: A Study in Black and White, 1931, The People vs. The Chicago Tribune, 1942, (play) Mrs. Bixby Gets a Letter, 1942, Joe Medill's War, 1946, American Ghettos, 1946, A Handful of Clients, 1965, Moment of Madness: The People vs. Jack Ruby, 1968, foreword Tropic of Cancer On Trial, 1968, For the First Hours of Tomorrow, 1971, To Life, 1974 (Friends of Lit. award), rev. and enlarged edit. 1990, Henry Miller: Years of Trial and Triumph: The Letters of Henry Miller and Elmer Gertz, 1978, German edit., 1980, Odyssey of a Barbarian, 1979, (with Joseph Pisciotte) Charter for a New Age, 1983, (with Edward Gilbreth) Quest for a Consitution: A Man Who Wouldn't Quit, 1985, Gertz v. Robert Welch, Inc.-The Story of a Landmark Libel Case, 1992, Henry Miller and Elmer Gertz Selected Letters 1964-1975, 1997, Remembering Mamie, 1998, others; editor: Short Stories of Frank Harris, 1975; contbr. to Henry Miller and the Critics, 1963, Mass Media and the Law, 1969; author articles in various periodicals and encys. Dir. pub. rels. Ill. Police Assn., 1934; mem. exec. com. Ill. Com. Equal Job Opportunity ; mem. nat., Chgo. adv. bd. commn. on law and social action Am. Jewish Congress; chmn. soldier vote com. Profl. and Bus. People, 1944; mem. law and order com. Chgo. Commn. on Human Rels., 1945; v.p. Ill. Freedom to Read Com.; chmn. Vets. Housing Com., 1945-47; mem. Mayor's Housing Com., 1946-48, legal chmn., 1946-47; mem. Chgo. Com. on Housing Action, 1947-49; adv. com. Chief Justice Mcpl. Ct. Chgo., 1950-51; pres. Greater Chgo. coun. Am. Jewish Congress, 1959-63; elected del. 6th Ill. Constl. Conv., 1969-70; chmn. conv. Bill of Rights com., 1969-70; bd. dirs. Jackson Park Hosp.; pres. Blind Svc. Assn., 1988-92; trustee Belefaire; nat. bd. trustees City of Hope; mem. Auditorium Theatre Coun. Recipient Golden Key award City of Hope, 1966; award Ill. div. A.C.L.U., 1963, 74; award U. Chgo. Alumni Assn., 1959; State of Israel Prime Minister's medal, 1972; selected for Chicagoland honor roll Chgo. Council Against Discrimination, 1946, 47, Hadassah, 1975, Educator of Year award, 1975, Disting. Svc. award Kagan Home for the Blind, Bill of Rights Bicentennial award IVI-IPO, Constl. Rights Found. Bill of Right in Action award, Jackson Pk. Hosp., Chgo. Bar Assn., Auditorium Theatre Coun. award, 1997; Elmer Gertz Day in Ill. proclaimed in his honor by Gov. Edgar, Elmer Gertz Day in Chgo. proclaimed by Mayor Richard M. Daley and City Coun., numerous other awards. Mem. Pub. Housing Assn. (founder, counsel, pres. 1943-49), Civil War Round Table (founder, exec. com., pres., hon. life), Adult Edn. Council Chgo. (sec., pres.), Shaw Soc. (founder, pres., exhibit chmn. Shaw Centennial 1956, Darrow Centennial 1957), ABA, Fed. Bar Assn., Chgo. Bar Assn. (chmn. legal edn. com. 1970-71,chmn. civil rights com. 1978-79), Ill. State Bar Assn. (sr. counsellor, chmn. civil rights com. 1979-80), Bar Assn. 7th Circuit, Am. Judicature Soc., Decalogue Soc. Lawyers (mgr., pres., editor Jour.), First Amendment Lawyers Assn. (pres. 1978-79, chmn. 1979-80), Soc. Midland Authors (award 1969, sec. 1976), Authors Guild, Appellate Lawyers Assn. Ill. Clubs: Chicago Literary (v.p. 1968-69, 1978-79, pres. 1979-80), Cliff Dwellers, Caxton Club. Home: 2960 N Lake Shore Dr Apt 1402 Chicago IL 60657-5654 Office: 315 S Plymouth Ct Chicago IL 60604-3969 *Now that I have passed the magical age of 90, I look upon it as the beginning of a new youthfulness, rather than second childhood or senility. I am challenged by new ideas and new tasks.*

GERTZ, THEODORE GERSON, lawyer; b. Chgo., Sept. 8, 1936; s. Elmer and Ceretta (Samuels) G.; m. Suzanne C., June 19, 1960; children: Craig M., Candace C., Scott W. BA, U. Chgo., 1958; JD, Northwestern U., 1962. Bar: Ill. 1962, U.S. Dist. Ct. (no. dist.) Ill. 1962. Assoc. Marks, Marks & Kaplan, Chgo., 1962-64; assoc. Lowitz, Vihons & Stone, Chgo., 1964-66, ptnr., 1966-71; ptnr. Pretzel & Stouffer, Chgo., 1971-94, Shefsky, Froelich, Chgo., 1995—; gen. counsel Hull House Assn., Chgo., 1977—, Blind Svc. Assn., Chgo., 1987—, Citizens Against Suburban Sprawl, Mettawa, Ill., 1995—, Am. Student Dental Assn., Chgo., 1977—. Author: A Guide to Estate Planning, Illinois Advance Estate Planning. Dir., treas. Mettawa Open Lands, 1987—; former trustee Village of Mettawa, 1994—. Pub. Interest Law Initiative, Chgo. With U.S. Army, 1962-64. Fellow Ill. Bar Found., Ill. Bar Assn., Chgo. Bar Assn., Law Club. Democrat. Jewish. Avocations: reading, nature, working out, dancing, traveling. Home: 950 Benson Ln Libertyville IL 60048-2406 Office: Shefsky and Froelich 444 N Michigan Ave Ste 2600B Chicago IL 60611-3998

GERTZMAN, STEPHEN F., lawyer; b. Cin., Aug. 18, 1946. BSBA with high honors, U. Fla., 1968, MA, 1970, JD with high honors, 1972. Bar: Fla. 1972, Ga. 1973. Mem. Sutherland, Asbill & Brennan, Atlanta; nat. dir., fed. tax acctg. Ernst & Young LLp, Washington, 1998—; adj. prof. law Sch. Law Emory U., 1973-93; trustee Ga. Tax Conf., 1984-98; trustee So. Fed. Tax Inst., 1990—. Author: Federal Tax Accounting, 1988, 2nd edit., 1992; exec. editor Fla. Law Review, 1971-72. Mem. ABA (chmn. tax acctg. problems com. taxation sect. 1980-82), Order of Coif, Phi Kappa Phi, Beta Gamma Sigma. Office: Ernst & Young LLP 1225 Connecticut Ave NW Washington DC 20036-2604

GERVAIS, SISTER GENEROSE, hospital consultant; b. Currie, Minn., Sept. 18, 1919; d. Philip Frederick and Elizabeth Eleanor (Sandgathe) G. B.S., Stout State U., Menomonie, Wis., 1945; M.Hosp. Adminstrn., U. Minn., 1954. Joined Sisters of St. Francis, Roman Catholic Ch., 1938; adminstrv. dietitian St. Marys Hosp., Rochester, Minn., 1948-50; adminstrv. asst. St. Marys Hosp., 1951-52, asst. adminstr., 1954-63, assoc. adminstr., 1963-71, hosp. adminstr., 1971-81, exec. dir., 1981-85, bd. trustees, 1968-86; hosp. cons., 1985-90; cons. dietitian Mercy Hosp., Portsmouth, Ohio, 1950-51; bd. dirs. 1st Nat. Bank, Rochester, 1974-78, Fed. Res. Bank Mpls., 1978-86, St. Francis Med. Ctr., LaCrosse, Wis., 1979-87, S.E. Minn. Health Systems Agy., 1978-83, S.E. Minn. Health Coun., 1983-87, Unity Home Health Svcs., Inc., LaCrosse, 1994-95; v.p., sec. Family Health Ctr. LaCrosse, Inc., 1985-91, pres., 1991-93; mem. residency adv. bd. St. Francis-Mayo Family Practice, 1993-95; mem. v.p., bd. dirs. Caledonia Health Care Ctr., 1986-90; bd. dirs. Franciscan Health System, LaCrosse, 1987-94, mem., treas., bd. dirs. St. Franciscan Community Program,s 1985-94. Bd. dirs. United Way of Olmstead County, 1968-73, Sr. Citizens Svcs. Inc., Rochester, Minn., 1988-94, Diocese of Winona Found., 1991—, Madonna Towers, Rochester, 1987—, chair, 1991-97, Olmstead County Hist. Soc., 1994-97, Regina Med. Ctr., Hastings, Minn., 1996—; pres. Poverello Found., Rochester, 1983; bd. adv. Winona State U. Rochester Ctr., 1985-93; mem. fin. coun. Diocese of Winona, 1986-91; mem. Franciscan Skemp Healthcare Cmty. Bd., LaCrosse, 1995—. Decorated Lady of Equestrian Order of Holy Sepulchre, 1989; recipient Alumni Disting. Service award U. Wis.-Stout, 1978, Teresa of Avila award Coll. of St. Teresa, 1980, Outstanding Achievement award Rochester chpt. U. Minn. Alumni Assn., 1981, Women of Achievement in Area of Bus. award YWCA, 1985, Pro Ecclesiae et Pontifice medal, 1985, Service to Mankind award Sertoma 700 Club, 1987, Mayor's Medal of Honor City of Rochester, 1990, The Athena award, 1994; named Boss of Yr., Rochester Jaycees, 1980, named in her honor Sister Generose Gervais Bldg. St. Marys Hosp., 1991. Mem. Cath. Health Assn. U.S. (trustee 1979, vice chair 1981-82, chair 1982-83, speaker membership assembly 1983-84), Am. Coll. Hosp. Adminstrs., Am. Hosp. Assn., Minn. Hosp. Assn., Minn. Conf. Cath. Health Facilities (past dir.), Rochester Area C. of C. Republican. Address: 1216 2nd St SW Rochester MN 55902-1906

GERVAIS, MICHEL, academic administrator; b. Levis, Que., Can., May 27, 1944; s. Paul and Ghislaine (Gosselin) G. BA, Coll. Levis, 1962; LTh, U. Laval, Can., 1966, LPh, 1968; DTh, Pontifical U. of St. Thomas Aquinas, Rome, 1973; D Civil Law (hon.), Bishop U., 1993; DDiv (hon.), McGill U., 1993; LLD (hon.), U. Man., 1994; D (hon.), U. Montreal, 1996. Mem. faculty theology, now prof. U. Laval, also rector, 1987-97; chmn. Quebec Commn. on Univ. Programs, 1998—. Office: U Laval, Cite Universitaire, Quebec, PQ Canada G1K 7P4

GERVAIS, PAUL NELSON, foundation administrator, psychotherapist, public relations executive; b. Augusta, Maine, June 28, 1947; s. Adrien and Phyllis (Sullivan) G. B in Bible and Doctrine/Ministerial Studies, Berean Coll., 1975; M, U. Maine, 1987; M in Marriage and Family Therapy, Coll. Clin. Family Sci., 1988; cert. in Constl. Law, U. Maine, 1969; Dr., N.Am. Biblical Sem., Buffalo, 1987; M. in Marriage and Family, San Antonio Theol. Sem., 1988; PhD in Psychology, San Antonio Theol. Sem., St. Paul, 1989; PhD in Marriage and Family Therapy, Minn. Grad. Sch., 1990. Cert. behavioral analyst, clin. supr.; registered clin. therapist; lic. marriage and family therapist, Tex.; lic. marriage and family therapist, clin. profl. counselor, profl. counselor, pastoral counselor, Maine. Reporter No. New Eng. div. News dept. NBC Radio div., N.Y.C., 1966-70; dir. pub. relations Kennebec Valley Med. Ctr., Augusta, 1970-73, Penobscot Bay Med. Ctr., Rockport, Maine, 1973-74; pres., chmn. bd. dirs. Ministry of Miracles Evangelistic Assn., Maine, 1975—; news dir. Maine Broadcasting System, Augusta, 1966-70; advisor, assoc. dir. pub. rels. state VA svcs., Maine, 1969-70; family counselor Gracelawn Meml. Pk., Auburn, Maine, assoc. dir., 1987; pres., CEO Motivational Resources. Pioneered one of first radio and TV health edn. programs from which proceeded other nat. and internat. programs in field; mental health columnist Maine Sunday Paper. Active Rep. Nat. Com., Washington, 1987, Dole for Pres. exploratory Com., 1987—, also adv. com., 1987, steering com. Campaign Am., 1987-88; mem. Presdl. Task Force, Washington, 1989, Rep. Senatorial Inner Circle, 1989—, U.S. Senatorial Club, Washington, 1989-90, Nat. Rep. Senatorial Com., Washington, 1990; CEO Gracelawn Meml. Park, Auburn, Maine, 1988—; spl. advisor, dep. Kennebec County Sheriff's Office, also dep. sheriff. Recipient vice-presdl. Citation Office of U.S. V.P. Hubert Humphrey, 1968, Malcolm T. MacEachern Citation Am. Health Congress, 1973; cert. in pub. rels. Chgo. chpt. Am. Hosp. Assn.; Presdl. Medal of Merit Pres. George Bush, 1989. Fellow Profl. Assn. Christian Counselors and Therapists; mem. AACD, Am. Acad. Family Therapists (exec. dir.), Acad. for Eating Disorders, Nat. Assn. Anorexia Nervosa and Associated Disorders, Publicity Club Boston (disting. bell ringer award 1974), Nat. Christian Counselors Assn. (mem. licensing bd., chmn. legal com.), Am. Mental Health Counselors Assn., Maine Network Associated Profl. Practitioners, Maine Assn. for Counseling and Devel., Mensa. Baptist. Home and Office: Am Acad Profl Family Therapists 16 Julianne Ln Augusta ME 04330-6251

GERVASON, ROBERT J, advertising executive. Exec. v.p., exec. media dir. Campbell Ewald Advertising, Warren, Mich. Office: Campbell Ewald Advt 30400 Van Dyke Ave Warren MI 48093-2368*

GERVER, JOSEPH LEONIDE, mathematics educator; b. N.Y.C., Sept. 30, 1949; s. Israel and Joan Sara (Menkin) G.; m. April Lynn Kihlstrom, Aug. 24, 1974; children: Daniel, Rachel. BA, Columbia U., 1970; PhD, U. Calif., Berkeley, 1975. Asst. prof. U. Hawaii, Honolulu, 1976-79, U. Ga., Athens, 1979-81; assoc. prof. Rutgers U., Camden, N.J., 1981—. Bd. dirs. Alice Rich Northrop Camp, Mt. Washington, Mass., 1996—. NSF NATO Postdoctiral fellow, Paris, 1975-76. Mem. AAUP, Am. Math. Soc. Office: Rutgers U Camden NJ 08102

GERVITS, LEONID, art educator, artist; b. Odessa, Ukraine, USSR, Apr. 12, 1946; came to U.S., 1991; s. Vladimir Mikhailovich Gervits and Polina Abramovna Gurevich; m. Irina Tatarinova; 1 child, Mikhail. BFA, Art Coll., Odessa, 1966; MFA in Painting and Drawing, Nat. Acad. Art Repin Inst., Russia, 1973. Asst. then assoc. prof. Nat. Acad. Art Repin Inst., St. Petersburg, Russia, 1975-91; instr. painting and drawing N.Y. Acad. Art, N.Y.C., 1992—; instr. painting Art Student's League, N.Y.C., 1998—; vis. prof. Korean Nat. U. Art, Seoul, Korea, 1998; leader workshops Akademie der Bildende Künste, Stuttgart, Germany, 1989, Seattle Acad. Realist Art, 1995, 99. Art dir. Internat. Pushkin Soc. Mag. Arzamas, 1998-99.

GERWICK, BEN CLIFFORD, JR., construction engineer, educator; b. Berkeley, Calif., Feb. 22, 1919; s. Ben Clifford and Bernice (Coultrap) G.; m. Martelle Louise Beverly, July 28, 1941 (dec. Jan. 1995); children: Beverly (Mrs. Robert A. Brian), Virginia (Mrs. Roy Wallace), Ben Clifford III, William; m. Ellen Chaney Lynch, May 18, 1996. B.S., U. Calif., 1940. With Ben C. Gerwick, Inc., San Francisco, 1946—, pres. Ben C. Gerwick, Inc., 1952-88, chmn., 1988—; exec. v.p. Santa Fe-Pomeroy, Inc., 1968-71; prof. civil engring. U. Calif., Berkeley, 1971-89; prof. emeritus U. Calif., 1989—; sponsoring mgr. Richmond-San Rafael bridge substructure, 1953-56, San Mateo-Hayward bridge, 1964-66; lectr. constrn. engring. Stanford U., 1962-68; cons. major bridge and marine constrn. projects; cons. engr. for ocean structures and overwater bridges, also offshore structures in U.S., North Sea, Arctic Ocean, Japan, Australia, Indonesia, Arabian Gulf, Hong Kong, Europe, Can., S.E. Asia, S.Am.; mem. U.S. Arctic Rsch. Commn., 1990-95. Author: Russian-English Dictionary of Prestressed Concrete and Concrete Construction, 1966, Construction of Prestressed Concrete Structures, 1971, 2d edit., 1996, Construction and Engineering Marketing for Major Project Services, 1981, Construction of Offshore Structures, 1986; contbr. articles to profl. jours. Chmn. Marine Bd., Nat. Rsch. Coun., 1978-80. Served with USN, 1940-46; comdr. Res. ret. Recipient Golden Beaver, Beavers Constrn. Soc., 1974, Mörsch medal Deutsche Beton Verein, Weisbaden, Germany, 1978, Blakely Smith ocean engring. medal Soc. Naval Architects and Marine Engrs., 1981, Lockheed Ocean Engring. award Marine Tech. Soc., 1982, U. Calif. Berkeley Citation, 1989. Fellow ASCE (hon. mem., Karp award 1976, G. Brooks Earnest award 1980, Peurifoy award 1989, Pres.'s award 1989), Am. Concrete Ins. (hon. mem., dir. 1960, Turner award 1974, Corbetta award 1981, Franklin Inst. Brown award 1984, Offshore Tech. Rsch. Ctr. honors award 1992), Deep Founds. Inst. (Disting. Svc. award 1996); mem. NAE, Fédn. Internat. de la Precontrainte (pres. 1974-78, now hon. pres., Freyssinet medal 1982), Prestressed Concrete Inst. (pres. 1957-58, hon.). Congregationalist. Clubs: Bohemian (San Francisco); Claremont Country (Oakland), World Trade Club (San Francisco). Home: 5727 Country Club Dr Oakland CA 94618-1717 Office: Ben C Gerwick Inc 601 Montgomery St Ste 400 San Francisco CA 94111-2607

GERWICK-BRODEUR, MADELINE CAROL, marketing and timing professional; b. Kearney, Neb., Aug. 29, 1951; d. Vern Frank and Marian Leila (Bliss) Gerwick; m. David Louis Brodeur; 1 child, Maria Louise. Student, U. Wis., 1970-72, U. Louisville, 1974-75; BA in Econs. magna cum laude, U. N.H., 1979; postgrad., Internat. Trade Inst., Seattle. Cert. profl. cycles cons., 1995; cert. bus. astrologer. Indsl. sales rep. United Radio Supply Inc., Seattle, 1980-81; mfrs. rep. Ray Over Sales Inc., Seattle, 1981-82; sales engr. Tektronix, Inc., Kent, Wash., 1982-83; mktg. mgr. Zepher Industries, Inc., Burien, Wash., 1983-85, Microscan Systems Inc., Tukwila, Wash., 1986.; market devel. URS Electronics, Inc., Portland, 1986-88; sr. product specialist Fluke Corp., 1989-95; owner Astro Cycles Cons. L.L.C., Seattle, 1995—; bd. dirs., sec. Starfish Enterprises Inc., Tacoma, 1984-87; com. chmn. Northcon, Seattle and Portland, 1984-86, 88, 90; speaker to Wash. Women's Employment and Edn., Tacoma, 1983—. *Since not all days are created equal, Madeline Gerwick-Brodeur offers good timing for new business ventures, product introductions, new team starts or major events, to get them off to a good start and assure the best possible outcomes. Her 15 years of business experience, 20 years of cycle and timing experience, plus astrological certification, uniquely qualifies her for this work. Her Good Timing Guide provides daily cycles for all types of business activities and includes quarterly newsletters with trends and special opportunity days.* Writer daily column for Zodiac Zone, 1995-96, Online Noetic Network; pub. The Good Timing Guide; co-author The Complete Idiot's Guide To Astrology, 1997, Pocket Idiot's Guide to Horoscopes, 1998. Bd. dirs. Kepler Coll. of Astrol. Arts and Scis. Recipient Jack E. Chase award for Outstanding Svc. and Contbr. Northcon Founder's Orgn., 1988. Mem. Electronic Mfrs. Assn. (sec. 1982, sec.-treas. 1988, v.p. 1989), Inst. Noetic Scis., Internat. Soc. for Astrol. Rsch., Wash. State Astrol. Assn. (bd. dirs. 1996-98), Phi Kappa Phi. Avocations: writing, healing arts, metaphysics. E-mail: mgb@astro-cycles.com. Office: Astro Cycles PO Box 27065 Seattle WA 98125-1465

GERWIN, BRENDA ISEN, research biochemist; b. Boston, May 2, 1939; d. Maurice Joshua and Jeannette (Hershon) Isen; m. Robert David Gerwin, Dec. 18, 1960; children: David, Daniel, Joel. BA, Radcliffe Coll., 1960; PhD, U. Chgo., 1964. Instr. biochemistry Rockefeller U., N.Y.C., 1964-66, Case-Western Res. U., Cleve., 1966-69; biochemist molecular anatomy program Oak Ridge Nat. Lab., Rockville, Md., 1969-71; sr. staff fellow Nat. Cancer Inst. NIH, Bethesda, Md., 1971-73, chemist Lab. of Tumor Virus Genetics, Nat. Cancer Inst., 1973-81, chemist Lab. of Molecular Oncology, Nat. Cancer Inst., 1981-83, rsch. chemist Lab. Human Carcinogenesis, Nat. Cancer Inst., 1983—; treas. Internat. Mesothelioma Interest Group. Contbr. articles to profl. jours. Mem. AAAS, Am. Soc. Biochemistry and Molecular Biology, Am. Soc. Microbiology, Sigma Xi. Jewish. Avocations: backpacking, handcrafts, study and teaching of Jewish culture. Office: Nat Cancer Inst Bldg 37 Room 2C08 Bethesda MD 20892

GERZSO, GUNTHER, painter, graphic artist; b. Mexico City, June 17, 1915. Exhbns. include FIAC Art Contemporain, Grand Palais, Paris, 1978, Inst. Fine Arts, Mex., 1980, El Arbol Fla., 1981-82, Mus du Petit Palais, 1982, Mary-Ann Martin Fine Arts, N.Y.C., 1984, Galeria de Arte Mex., 1990, others. Guggenheim fellow, 1973; recipient Nat Prize Fine Arts, Mex., 1978. Office: Mary-Anne Martin/Fine Art 23 E 73rd St New York NY 10021*

GESCHKE, CHARLES M., computer scientist, computer company executive; b. Cleve., Sept. 11, 1939; married, 1964; 3 children. AB, Xavier U., 1962, MS, 1963; PhD in Computer Sci., Carnegie-Mellon U., 1972. Instr. math. John Carroll U., 1963-68; rsch. scientist computer sci. Palo Alto Rsch. Ctr., Xerox Corp., 1972-80, mgr. Imaging Sci. Lab., 1980-87; pres., chmn. bd. Adopbe Sys. Inc., Mountain View, Calif., 1987—. Mem. NAE, Assn. Computer Math., Math. Assn. Am. Achievements include research in programming languages; machine design for efficient emulation of higher level languages; computer imaging and graphics. Office: Adobe Systems Inc 345 Park Ave San Jose CA 95110-2704*

GESEK, THADDEUS, artist; b. Salem, Mass., Mar. 14, 1925; s. Frank Stefan and Antonina (Lech) G.; m. Mary Elizabeth Meeker, Aug. 9, 1962; children: Mary Elizabeth, Thaddeus Stefan. BS in Edn., Tufts U., 1951; MFA in Theatre, Yale U., 1959. Art dir. Windsor Mt. Sch., Lenox, Mass., 1951-55; prof. Vassar Coll., Poughkeepsie, N.Y., 1959—, chair, 1986-95. One-woman shows include Mus. Fine Arts, Boston, 1959, 63, Three Arts Gallery, Poughkeepsie, 1964, 66, 68, Vassar Coll., Poughkeepsie, 1967, Colo. State U. Mus., 1975, Linocln Ctr. Performing Arts Gallery, 1977, Vassar Coll. Ctr. Gallery, 1978, 98, Mt. Gulian Soc., Beacon, N.Y., 1979, Kosciuszko Found., N.Y.C., 1985, others; patentee in field. Bd. dirs. Bardavon Opera Ho., Poughkeepsie, 1995—. With ESMCR, 1943-45. Zelosky grantee, 1969. Mem. United Scenic Artist Am. Roman Catholic. Avocation: golf, travel. Home: 3 Vassar Lake Dr Poughkeepsie NY 12603

GESELOWITZ, DAVID BERYL, bioengineering educator; b. Phila., May 18, 1930; s. Sidney W. and Fannie (Charny) G.; m. Lola Wood, June 21, 1953; children: Daniel, Michael, Ari. B.S. in E.E, U. Pa., 1951, M.S. in E.E, 1954, Ph.D., 1958. Asst. prof., asso. prof. U. Pa., Phila., 1951-71; prof., head biomed. engring. Pa. State U., University Park, 1971-88, prof. medicine, 1982—, Alumni disting. prof. biomed. engring., 1985-98, prof. emeritus, 1998—; cons. to med. dir. Provident Mut. Life Ins. Co., Phila., 1959-71; vis. assoc. prof. elec. engring. MIT, Cambridge, 1965-66; vis. prof. biomed. engring. Duke U., Durham, N.C., 1978-79; vis. prof. medicine U. Okla., Oklahoma City, 1987-88; vis. prof. math. and stats. U. N.Mex., Albuquerque, 1994. Editor: (with C. V. Nelson) Theoretical Basis of Electrocardiography, 1976, IEEE Transactions on Biomed. Engring, 1967-72; mem. editorial bd.: Jour. Electrocardiology, 1974—, CRC Critical Revs., 1979-88; contbr. articles to various publs. Chmn. com. electrocardiography Am. Heart Assn., 1976-81. J.S. Guggenheim fellow, 1978-79. Fellow Am. Coll. Cardiology, IEEE (Career Achievement award 1985); mem. NAE, AAAS, ISE (founding), Am. Inst. Engring. Medicine and Biology (founding), Biomed. Engring. Soc., Am. Assn. Physics Tchrs. Office: Pa State Univ University Park PA 16802

GESELOWITZ, MICHAEL NORMAN, anthropology educator; b. Phila., Mar. 27, 1957; s. David Beryl and Lola Rita (Wood) G. B.S. in E.E., MIT, 1978, B.S. in Humanities and Sci., 1980; M.A. in Anthropology, Harvard U., 1982, PhD in Anthropology, 1987. Electronics engr. Naval Surface Weapons Ctr., Silver Spring, Md., 1976-78; teaching asst. MIT, Cambridge, 1979-80; teaching fellow Harvard U., Cambridge, 1980—, rep. student faculty com. dept. anthropology, 1981-82, dir. x-ray facility Peabody Mus., 1982-86, archeol. collections mgr., 1987-89; lectr. MIT, 1989-93; vis. asst. prof. Yale U., 1993—. Contbr. articles to profl. jours. Recipient Certs. Distinction in Teaching, Harvard U., 1983, 84. Mem. Archeol. Inst. Am., Assn. Field Archaeology, Soc. Am. Archaeology, Sigma Xi. Jewish. Office: Yale U Dept Anthropology PO Box 208277 New Haven CT 06520-8277

GESKIN, ERNEST S(AMUEL), science administrator, consultant; b. Dnepropetrovsk, Ukraine, USSR, June 4, 1935; came to U.S., 1977; s. Samuel A. and Rosa M. (Raskin) G.; m. Doris M. Osherenko, June 12, 1964; 1 child, Ellen. M in MetE, Inst. Mettalurgy, Dnepropetrovsk, 1957; PhD in ME, Inst. Steel and Alloys, Moscow, 1967. Engr. Inst. Automation, Dnepropetrovsk, 1957-67, mgr. lab., 1967-74; assoc. rsch. prof. George Washington U., Washington, 1977-78; assoc. prof. Clarkson Coll. Tech., Potsdam, N.Y., 1979-80; rsch. scientist, lab. mgr. Revere Rsch. Inc., Edison, N.J., 1981-83; dir. waterjet cutting lab. Revere Rsch. Inc., Edison, 1986—; spl. lectr. N.J. Inst. Tech., Newark, 1984-85, assoc. prof., 1986-90, prof. 1991—. Author/co-author over 90 papers and presentations; editor various symposia (Cert. Recognition 1984, 89), 22 U.S. and USSR patents, 1969—. Mem. Internat. Soc. Waterjet Tech., Waterjet Tech. Assn., Sigma Xi. Avocations: swimming, gardening. Office: NJ Inst Tech 323 King Blvd Newark NJ 07102-1982

GESLER, ALAN EDWARD, lawyer; b. Milw., Aug. 25, 1945; s. Paul and Caroline Gesler; m. Judith A. Joy, May 6, 1967; children: Amy, Molly, Joshua. BS cum laude, U. Wis., Milw., 1967; JD, U. Wis., Madison, 1970. Bar: Wis. 1970, U.S. Dist. Ct. (ea. dist.) Wis. 1971, U.S. Supreme Ct. 1974. Mem. Warshafsky, Rotter, Tarnoff, Gesler, Reinhardt & Bloch, S.C., Milw., 1970-94; of counsel Slattery & Hausman, Ltd., Waukesha, Wis., 1994—. Assoc. editor Litigation News, 1978-80. Vice chmn. County Task Force on Mental Retardation, Milw., 1974; active health adv. subcom. Milw. County Suprs., 1975. Fellow Internat. Acad. Trial Lawyers; mem. ABA, Wis. Bar Assn., Assn. Trial Lawyers Am. (bd. govs. 1985-88), Wis. Acad. Trial Lawyers (bd. govs. 1979—, pres. 1983), Am. Bd. Trial Advs. (pres. Wis. chpt. 1991, nat. bd. rep. 1992-95). E-mail: agesler@execpc.com. Office: Slattery & Hausman Ltd N240 W1221 Pewaukee Rd Waukesha WI 53187

GESSAMAN, DONALD EUGENE, consultant, former government executive; b. Dayton, Ohio, Nov. 11, 1939; s. Stanley Loran and Alma Elizabeth (Tevis) G.; m. Jane Alexander Giles, Oct. 16, 1965; 1 child, William Arthur. BS in Indsl. Mgmt., U. Cin., 1964; MS in Indsl. Engring., Stanford U., 1972. Exec. trainee Office of Sec. of Def., Washington, 1966; with nat security divsn., dep. divsn. chief Office Mgmt. and Budget, Exec. Office of Pres., Washington, 1967-90, dep. assoc. dir., 1990-95; cons. EOP Group, Inc., Washington, 1995—. Office: EOP Group Inc 819 Seventh St NW Washington DC 20001

GESSAMAN, MARGARET PALMER, mathematics educator, college dean; b. Florence, Ariz., Oct. 7, 1934; d. William Lee Sr. and Lillian Maude (Henkle) Palmer; m. Paul Hayden Gessaman, June 11, 1965. BS, Mont.

State Coll., 1956, MS, 1965, PhD, 1966. Statistician Fatstock Mktg. Corp., London, 1957-59; ops. researcher Richard, Thomas and Baldwin, Ebbw Vale, South Wales, 1959-60; market researcher Nestle Co., Inc., London, 1960-61; instr. Mont. State U., 1966-67; asst. prof. math. Ithaca Coll., 1967-70; asst. prof., assoc. prof., prof. math. U. Nebr., Omaha, 1970—, chmn. dept. math., computer sci., 1973-80, 98—, dean grad. studies rsch., 1980-93; cons. grad. and rsch. activities, Coll. Bd., Chgo., 1981-88, Ednl. Testing Svc., Princeton, N.J., 1976-80, various govt. units, univs.; panelist NSF, Washington. Contbr. articles to profl. jours. Program chair Nebr. Commn. United Ministries in Higher Edn., Lincoln, 1976-81, 88-90. Mem. Coun. Grad. Schs. (bd. dirs.), Inst. Math. Stats., Am. Statis. Assn., Grad. Women in Sci.(nat. treas. 1994-95), Fulbright Assn., Mid-Am. State Univs. Assn. (chair 1988-89), Midwestern Assn. Grad. Schs. (chair-elect, chair, past chair 1986-89). Methodist. Avocations: travel, Mayan history, cat lore. Office: Univ Nebr 60th Dodge St Omaha NE 68182

GESSOW, ALFRED, aerospace engineer, educator; b. Jersey City, Oct. 13, 1922; s. Morris Samuel and Emma (Levovsky) G.; m. Elaine E. Silverman, Nov. 23, 1947; children: Laura Gessow Goldman, Lisa Gessow Michelson, Miles Jory, Andrew Jody. BCE, CCNY, 1943; M of Aero. Engring., NYU, 1944. Scientist aero. rsch. Nat. Adv. Com. for Aeros. Langley (Va.) Rsch. Ctr., 1944-59; chief fluid physics rsch. NASA, Washington, 1959-66, asst. dir. research div., 1966-70, dir. aerodynamics, 1970-79; chmn. dept. aerospace engring. U. Md., College Park, 1980-88, prof. aerospace engring., 1980-93, prof. emeritus, 1993—; dir. emeritus, Alfred Gessow Ctr. for Rotorcraft Edn. and Rsch., 1982-93; lectr. U. Va., Va. Poly. Inst. and State U.; adj. prof. NYU, N.Y.C., Cath. U. Am., Washington; vis. prof. Korean Inst. Advanced Sci., Seoul; cons. NATO, U.S. Army, Inst. for Def. Analyses; chmn. aerospace divsn. adv. coun. Pa. State U.; mem. NAS/NRC Bd. Army Sci. and Tech., 1982-86, Army Sci. Bd., 1986-91. Sr. author: Aerodynamics of the Helicopter, 8th printing, 1985; contbr. articles to encys. and profl. jours. Recipient medal for exceptional svc. NASA, 1974, award for excellence in Grad. Aviation Edn. from the Fed. Aviation Adminstrn., 1991. Fellow AIAA, Am. Helicopter Soc. (hon., Nikolsky hon. lectureship award 1985, Alexander Klemin award 1996). Jewish. Achievements include use of analytical and flight rsch. to advance the capability to understand and predict rotorcraft performance and handling qualities characteristics; provision of the first computer programs to predict helicopter performance; worldwide recognition as author of a classic text on helicopter theory in continuous use for the past forty-five years as the primary means to educate engineers with helicopter design and prodn. Home: 7308 Durbin Ter Bethesda MD 20817-6127 Office: Univ Maryland Dept Aerospace Engring College Park MD 20742 *The human psychology is such as to require and respond to an awards system that is made up of many factors—challenge, variety, peer recognition and economic benefits. The young generally place more importance on the first two, while the last two are more significant in later years. The chances of achieving such rewards are enhanced by starting early to develop expertise in a specialty area, to be interested and knowledgeable in one or more allied areas, and to take on challenging tasks that are not required but are self motivated. If these steps are followed, success and satisfaction will follow.*

GEST, HOWARD, microbiologist, educator; b. London, Oct. 15, 1921; m. Janet Olin, Sept. 8, 1941 (dec. 1994); children: Theodore Olin, Michael Henry, Donald Evan; m. Virginia Davies Ollis, Jan. 6, 1998. B.A. in Bacteriology, UCLA, 1942; postgrad. in biology (Univ. fellow), Vanderbilt U., 1942; Ph.D. in Microbiology (Am. Cancer Soc. fellow), Washington U., St. Louis, 1949. Rsch. asst. Metall. Lab. (Manhattan Project) U. Chgo., 1943; from jr. to assoc. chemist Clinton Labs. (Manhattan Project), Oak Ridge, 1943-46; Instr. microbiology Western Res. U. Sch. Medicine, 1949-51, asst. prof. microbiology, 1951-53, asso. prof., 1953-59; USPHS spl. research fellow in biology Calif. Inst. Tech., 1956-57; prof. Henry Shaw Sch. Botany, Washington U., 1959-64, dept. zoology, 1964-66; prof. Ind. U., Bloomington, 1966-78, disting. prof. microbiology, 1978—, disting. prof. emeritus microbiology, 1987—, adj. prof. history and philosophy of sci., 1983—, chmn. dept. microbiology, 1966-70, disting. faculty rsch. lectr., 1987; NSF sr. postdoctoral fellow Nat. Inst. Med. Rsch., London, 1965-66; Guggenheim fellow Imperial Coll., London, U. Stockholm, U. Tokyo; vis. prof. dept. biophysics and biochemistry U. Tokyo and Japan Soc. Promotion Sci., 1970; mem. study sect. bacteriology and mycology NIH, 1966-68, chmn. study sect. microbial chemistry, 1968-69, mem. study sect. microbial physiology and genetics, 1988-90; mem. com. microbiol. problems of man in extended space flight Nat. Acad. Scis.-NRC, 1967-69. Guggenheim fellow Imperial Coll., London, UCLA, 1979-80. Fellow AAAS; mem. Am. Soc. Microbiology (hon.). Office: Ind U Dept Biology Bloomington IN 47405

GEST, HOWARD DAVID, lawyer; b. Bergenfield, N.J., Jan. 24, 1952; m. Lucy Acevedo; 1 child, Aaron. AB in Econs., U. Calif., Berkeley, 1974; JD, Hastings Coll., 1977. Bar: Calif. 1977. Staff atty. U.S. Ct. Appeals (9th cir.), San Francisco, 1977-78; asst. U.S. atty. Cen. Dist. Calif., L.A., 1978-83; ptnr. Sidley & Austin, L.A., 1983—. Office: Sidley & Austin 555 W 5th St Los Angeles CA 90013-1010

GEST, KATHRYN WATERS, public affairs professional; b. Boston, Mar. 20, 1947; d. Mendal and Anna Waters; m. Theodore O. Gest, May 28, 1972; 1 child, David Mendal. B.S., Northwestern U., 1969; M.S., Columbia U., 1970. Reporter The Patriot-Ledger, Quincy, Mass., 1968; writer Europe desk Voice of Am., Washington, 1969; reporter St. Louis Globe-Democrat, 1970-77; reporter Congl. Quar., Washington, 1977-78, news editor, 1978-80, asst. mng. editor, 1980-83, mng. editor, 1983-87; St. Louis corr. Time Mag., 1975-77, The Christian Sci. Monitor, 1976-77; press sec. to Sen. William S. Cohen, Washington, 1987-96; chmn., U.S. del. Internat. Labor Orgn. Tripartite Meeting on Conditions of Employment and Work of Journalists, Geneva, 1990; sr. v.p., dir. internat. issues Powell Tate, 1996—; election observer Nat. Dem. Inst., Albania, 1996. Recipient award for investigative reporting Inland Daily Press Assn., 1975. Mem. Soc. Profl. Journalists, Women's Fgn. Policy Group, Internat. Women's Media Fund, Nat. Press Club. Office: Powell Tate 700 13th St NW Ste 1000 Washington DC 20005-5926

GESTON, MARK SYMINGTON, lawyer; b. Atlantic City, N.J., June 20, 1946; s. John Charles and Mary Tobiatha (Simmington) G.; m. Gayle Francis Howard, June 12, 1971 (div. Aug. 1972); m. Marijke Havinga, Aug. 14, 1976; children: Camille LaCroix, Robert L. LaCroix, Emily S. Geston. AB in History, Kenyon Coll., 1968; JD, NYU, 1971. Bar: Idaho, U.S. Ct. Appeals (9th cir.). AB in History with high honors Eberle & Berlin, Boise, Idaho, 1971—. Author: Lords of the Starship, 1967, Out of the Mouth of the Dragon, 1969, The Day Star, 1972, The Seige of Wonder, 1975, Mirror to the Sky, 1992, The Stronghold If, 1973; contbr. stories to Amazing Stories, Fantasy and Sci. Fiction. Recipient prize for achievement in lit., Kenyon Coll., 1968; named Root-Tilden fellow NYU, 1968-71. Mem. Idaho State Bar Assn., Phi Beta Kappa. Avocation: writing. Office: Eberle & Berlin PO Box 1368 Boise ID 83701-1368

GETCHELL, CHARLES WILLARD, JR., lawyer, publisher; b. Los Angeles, May 29, 1929; s. Charles Willard and Katharine (Fitch) G.; m. Angela Winthrop, Sept. 16, 1961; children—Katharine Chisholm, Emily Erskine, Sarah Fields. A.B., Stanford U., 1951, J.D., 1954. Bar: Calif. 1955, Mass. 1979, U.S. Dist. Ct. (no. dist.) Calif. 1960, Mass. 1983, U.S. Ct. Appeals, 9th cir. 1960, U.S. Supreme Ct., 1985. Atty., Air Materiel Force, Chateauroux, France, 1958-59; asst. U.S. atty. No. Dist. Calif., San Francisco, 1960-61; asst. mgr. Citibank, N.Y.C., Brussels, Belgium, 1961-68; v.p. Wood Struthers & Winthrop, N.Y.C., Brussels, 1969-77; ptnr. Gray, Wendell, Chalmers & Dahlen Boston, 1981-87; pres., dir. Yorkham Timber Co., Inc., 1986—; bd. dirs. Sabre Trust (UK); chmn. Sabre Europe (Belgium); sec. Sabre Found., 1995—; sr. fellow Salzburg Seminar, 1997—. pub. The Ipswich Press, Mass., 1980—. Transl.: European Monetary Unity: For Whose Benefit? (Pascal Salin), 1980. Contbr. occasional essays, verse in N.Y. Times, Boston Globe, Beverly Times. Mem. steering com. Bilderberg Meetings, The Hague, 1980-85; bd. dirs. Salzburg Seminar, 1985-89, trustee Shore Country Day Sch., 1978-84. Served to lt. (j.g.), USNR, 1955-58. Mem. Belgian Am. Ednl. Found., Mass. Hist. Soc., Tavern Club. Republican. Office: Ipswich Press PO Box 291 Ipswich MA 01938-0291

GETCHELL, SYLVIA FITTS, librarian; b. Dover, N.H., July 3, 1925; d. Perley Irving and Marguerite Elizabeth (Marden) F.; m. L. Forbes Getchell, July 17, 1948; children: Ann Marden, Faith Perley, Edward Fitts, William Forbes. BA in History magna cum laude, U. N.H., 1947; BS in Libr. Sci., Simmons Coll., 1948. Profl. cataloger Libr. Columbia U., N.Y.C., 1948-51, U. N.H., Durham, 1951-52; sch. libr. Newmarket (N.H.) Pub. Schs., 1970-85; curator Stone Sch. Mus., Newmarket, 1966—. Author: Marden Family Genealogy, 1974, Tide Turns on the Lamprey: History of Newmarket, N.H., 1984, Fitts Families: A Genealogy, 1989. Bd. govs. Am. Ind. Mus., Exeter, N.H., 1992—; bd. dirs. Newmarket Hist. Soc., 1966—, past pres.; bd.dirs. Piscataqua Pioneers, Portsmouth, N.H., 1969—, past pres.; 18th century reenactor 1st Newmarket Colonial Militia, 1973—; former chair ann. fund drive local chpt. ARC; past collector, Sun. sch. tchr. Newmarket Cmty. Ch.; former treas. Aux. of N.H. Dental Soc.; mem. N.H. Hist. Soc. Mem. DAR (mem. and past sec. attic commn. N.H. chpt. 1994—), New Eng. Hist. Geneal. Soc., Newmarket Women's Club (past treas.), Huguenot Soc. N.H. Republican. Avocations: genealogy, oil painting, needlework, travel. Home: 51 N Main St Newmarket NH 03857-1216

GETER, RODNEY KEITH, plastic surgeon; b. Baton Rouge, La., Nov. 13, 1946; s. Argless William and Jewel Alma (Rudolph) G. BA in Chemistry with honors, U. Mo., 1975, MD, 1979. Resident in gen. surgery U. Mo., Columbia, 1979-83, fellow in microvascular surgery, 1983-84, resident in plastic surgery, 1984-86; pvt. practice Springfield (Mo.) Clinic, 1986—; chmn. dept. surgery St. John's Regional Health Ctr., Springfield, 1992-94, chmn. two hosp. coms., 1994-97; v.p. med. staff St. John's Hosp., 1996-97. Contbr. articles to profl. jours. Pres. Springfield Music Found., 1989—; leader troop 210 Boy Scouts Am., Springfield, 1995-98. Sgt. U.S. Army, 1968-71, Vietnam. Mem. Am. Soc. Plastic and Reconstructive Surgeons, Greene County Med. Soc., Mo. State Med. Assn., Phi Beta Kappa, Phi Lambda Upsilon. Avocations: playing keyboard in band, fishing, backpacking. Office: Springfield Clinic 3231 S National Ave Springfield MO 65807-7396

GETIS, ARTHUR, geography educator; b. Phila., July 6, 1934; s. Samuel J. and Sophie Getis; m. Judith M. Marckwardt, July 23, 1961; children: Hilary Hope Tarazi, Victoria Lynn, Anne Patterson Tibbetts. BS, Pa. State U., 1956, MS, 1958; PhD, U. Wash., 1961. Asst. instr. geography U. Wash., 1960-61; asst. prof. Mich. State U., 1961-63; faculty Rutgers U., New Brunswick, N.J., 1963-77; prof. geography Rutgers U., 1969-77, dir. grad. programs in geography, 1970-73, chmn. New Brunswick geography dept., 1971-73; prof. geography U. Ill., Urbana-Champaign, 1977-90; prof. geography San Diego State U., 1990—, doctoral program coord., 1990-92, Stephen/Mary Birch Found. Endowed Chair of Geog. Studies, 1992—, Albert W. Johnson Univ. Rsch. Lectureship, 1995; head dept. U. Ill., 1977-83, dir. Sch. Social Scis., 1983-84; centennial fellow Pa. State U., 1996; A. Robinson lectr. Ohio State U., 1999; vis. lectr. Bristol U., Eng., 1966-67, UCLA, summers 1968, 74, U. B.C., 1969; vis. prof. Princeton U., 1971-74; vis. disting. prof. San Diego State U., 1989; mem. Regional Sci. Research Group, Harvard U., 1970; panelist NSF, 1981-83. Author: (with B. Boots) Models of Spatial Processes, 1978, Point Pattern Analysis, 1988, (with J. Getis and J.D. Fellmann) Geography, 1981, Human Geography, 6th edit., 1999, Introduction to Geography, 6th edit., 1998, (edited with J. Getis) The United States and Canada, 1995, The Tyranny of Data, 1996, (edited with M.M. Fischer) Recent Developments in Spatial Analysis, 1997; editor Jour. Geographical Systems, 1992—; contbg. editor, assoc. editor: Jour. Geography, 1972-74; mem. editl. bd. Nat. Geog. Rsch., 1984-90, Rsch. and Exploration, 1991-95, Geog. Analysis, 1991—; contbr. articles to profl. jours. Mem. Urbana Zoning Bd. Appeals, 1980-84; co-pres. Univ. High Sch. Parent-Faculty Orgn., 1982-83; bd. dirs. Univ. Consortium for Geog. Info. Scis., 1997—. Rutgers U. faculty fellow, 1970; East-West Center sr. fellow, 1974; NSF grantee, 1983-85, 1992-94; recipient Walter Isard award N.Am. Regional Sci. Coun., 1997. Mem. Assn. Am. Geographers (grantee 1964-65, vis. scientist 1970-72, chair math. models and quantitative methods splty. group 1991-92), Western Regional Sci. Assn. (bd. dirs. 1992-97, pres. 1998—), Regional Sci. Assn. (pres. N.E. sect. 1973-74, bd. dirs. 1998—), Internat. Inst. Brit. Geographers, Internat. Geog. Union (sec. commn. math. models 1988-96), Sigma Xi. Home: 5135 Jumilla St San Diego CA 92124-1503 Office: San Diego State U Dept Geography San Diego CA 92182

GETLIN, JOSH, reporter; b. N.Y.C., 1950. BS in History, U. Calif. - Santa Cruz, 1971; MA in Journalism, U. Columbia, 1972. Press sec./speechwriter San Francisco Mayor George Moscone (D), 1975-78, San Francisco Mayor Dianne Feinstein, 1979; staff writer, San Fernando Valley Edit. L.A. Times, 1979-80, staff writer, 1980-83, staff writer Orange County edit., 1983-89, N.Y. bur. staff writer, 1989—. Office: Los Angeles Times Times Mirror Square Los Angeles CA 90053*

GETMAN, JULIUS GERSON, law educator, lawyer; b. 1931. J.D., Harvard U., 1958, LL.M., 1963. Bar: D.C. 1959, Ind. 1970. Atty. NLRB, Washington, 1959-61; from asst. prof. to prof. law Ind. U., Bloomington, 1963-75; prof. Stanford U., Calif., 1975-77; William K. Townsend prof. law Yale U., New Haven, 1977-86; Earl E. Sheffield regent chair in law, assoc. dean U. Tex., Austin, 1986-89; cons. legal edn. Ford Found.; vis. prof. Benares Hindu U., 1967-68, Indian Law Inst., 1967-68; chief negotiator Conn. State Police, 1978—; spl. inst. for labor and mgmt. groups, arbitrator, 1963—; mem. editorial com. and exec. com. Labor Law Group; gen. counsel AAUP, 1980-82; regents chair Earl E. Sheffield U. Tex., Austin, 1986. Author: (with Steve Goldberg and Jeanne B. Herman) Union Representative Elections: Law and Reality, 1976, Labor Relations: Law, Practice and Policy; editor: (with John Blackbourn) Employment Discrimination Casebook, 1979, (with. B. Pogrobin) Labor Relations Law, 1987, In the Company of Scholars, 1992, The Betrayal of Local 14, 1998. Mem. Am. Assn. Univ. Profs. (pres. 1986-88). Office: U Tex Sch of Law 727 E 26th St Austin TX 78705-3224

GETMAN, WILLARD ETHERIDGE, lawyer, mediator; b. Cin., Jan. 31, 1949; s. Frank Newton and Dorothy Dill (Etheridge) G. BA, U. N.C., 1971; JD, Stetson U., 1974. Bar: Fla. 1974, N.Y. 1985, U.S. Dist. Ct. (so. dist.) Fla. 1975, U.S. Dist. Ct. (mid. dist.) Fla. 1996, U.S. Supreme Ct. 1997; County Ct. cert. mediator. Assoc., Law Offices John M. Callaway, Lake Worth, Fla., 1974-75; sole practice, West Palm Beach, Fla., 1976-80, Boynton Beach, Fla., 1980-93, Jacksonville, Fla., 1993—. mem./agt. Attys' Title Ins. Fund, Inc., Fla., Atty's. Real Property Coun. NE Fla., Inc. Mem. ABA, N.Y. State Bar Assn., Assn. Trial Lawyers Am., Fla. Bar (trust law com. 1975-76, summary rules com. 1980-84, probate and guardianship rules com. 1981-82), Jacksonville Bar Assn., Estate Planning Coun. N.E. Fla., Cedar Lake Club (Clayville, N.Y.), Trailside Lions, Elks, Moose, Masons, Shriners, Delta Theta Phi. Republican. Presbyterian. Home and Office: 567 Lazy Meadow Dr E Jacksonville FL 32225-3428 also: 38 Morgan St PO Box 477 Ilion NY 13357-0477

GETNICK, NEIL VICTOR, lawyer; b. Bklyn., Oct. 28, 1953; s. Irving Murray and Zita (Ellman) G.; m. Margaret Joan Finerty, May 21, 1978. BA in Govt. magna cum laude, Cornell U., 1975, JD, 1978. Bar: N.Y. 1979, U.S. Dist. Ct. (so. and ea. dists.) N.Y. 1983. Asst. dist. atty. trial div. N.Y. County, N.Y.C., 1978-81, asst. dist. atty. frauds bur., 1981-82; ptnr. Getnick & Getnick, N.Y., 1983—; mem. Criminal Justice Act panel U.S. Dist. Ct. for So. Dist. N.Y., N.Y.C., 1984-89. Editor-in-chief: Civil Prosecution News, 1994-96. Recipient Pub. Citizenship award N.Y. Pub. Interest Rsch. Group, 1977. Mem. ABA (litigation and criminal law sects.), N.Y. State Bar Assn. (exec. com. comml. and fed. litigation sect., chair com. on civil prosecution), Assn. of Bar of City of N.Y., N.Y. County Lawyers Assn., Internat. Assn. Ind. Pvt. Sector Inspectors Gen. (pres. 1994—), Internat. Assn. of Ind. Pvt. Sector Inspectors Gen. (pres. 1994—). Office: Getnick & Getnick Rockefeller Ctr 630 5th Ave Fl 27 New York NY 10111-0100

GETS, LISPBETH ELLA, educational administrator; b. Jhelum, Pakistan, Mar. 18, 1931; came to U.S., 1952, naturalized, 1955; d. Henry Ellis and Constance Selina (Bodell) Glenn; m. Terence Mathew Gets, Jan. 19, 1952; children: Erik Charles, Alison Beth, Hugh Malcolm, Adrienne Lea. AA, Santa Fe Community Coll., 1973-74; BA with high honors U. Fla., 1976, postgrad., 1977-89, MS, ednl. specialist cert., 1989. Cert. adminstr., supr., Fla. Editorial asst. John Trundell Pub., London, 1950-52; exec. secretarial positions, various cos., Chgo., Ft. Smith, Ark. and Jamestown, N.Y., 1952-58; tchr. spl. edn. Buchholz High Sch., Gainesville, Fla., 1976-81; asst. prin. Sidney Lanier Sch., Gainesville, 1981-83, 1987—; prin. Monarch Ctr. for Exceptional Students, Gainesville, 1983-87 . Named Tchr. of Yr. Gatorland chpt. Coun. for Exceptional Children, 1981. Mem. Council Exceptional Children (chpt. pres. 1983—), Fla. Assn. Exceptional Sch. Adminstrs. (state chmn. 1988-90), Phi Delta Kappa. Democrat. Episcopalian. Home: 4601 NW 13th Ave Gainesville FL 32605-4534 Office: 312 NW 16th Ave Gainesville FL 32601-4205

GETTELFINGER, GERALD ANDREW, bishop; b. Oct. 20, 1935. Ordained priest Roman Cath. Ch., 1962, ordained bishop, 1989. Bishop Diocese of Evansville, Ind., 1989—. Home: 3980 Woodcastle Dr Evansville IN 47711-2776 Office: Cath Ctr PO Box 4169 Evansville IN 47724-0169*

GETTELMAN, ROBIN CLAIRE, media specialist; b. Milw., Jan. 6, 1952; d. Robert Otto and Virginia Mae (Proffit) G.; m. Ted Bayard Johnson, Sept. 25, 1976 (div. Jan. 1985). BS in Secondary Edn., U. Wis., 1974; MA in Librarianship, U. Denver, 1975. Dir. instructional material ctr. Cripple Creek (Colo.)-Victor Sch. Dist., 1975-81; dir. Franklin Ferguson Meml. Libr., Cripple Creek, 1975-81; dir. instructional materials ctr. D.C. Everest Jr. High Sch., Schofield, Wis., 1981—; dist. media coord. D.C. Everest Area Schs., Schofield, 1988—; reviewer Sch. Evaluation Consortium, Madison, Wis., 1986, Marshfield, Wis., 1987, reviewer, coord., Ashland, Wis., 1989; chair media com. D.C. Everest Area Schs., Schofield, 1988—; mem. Wis. Dept. Pub. Instrn. Task Force, 1998. Recipient Svc. award of the Yr., Franklin Ferguson Meml. Libr., 1981. Mem. Wis. Sch. Libr. Media Assn. (chair profl. devel. com. 1983, chair 1984, 85 confs. exec. bd. 1985), Wis. Ednl. Media Assn., Wausau Area Jaycees (community dir. 1986-87, chair cancer ski-a-thon 1987, chair 4th of July concessions 1989, Project Chmn. of the Month 1987), Sierra Club, Friends of Libr. Methodist. Avocations: skiing, physical fitness, walking, photography, travel. E-mail: rgettelman@dce.k12.wi.us. Home: 2405 Petunia Rd Wausau WI 54401-9351 Office: DC Everest Jr High Sch 1000 Machmueller St Schofield WI 54476-3811

GETTIG, MARTIN WINTHROP, retired mechanical engineer; b. South Bend, Ind., Nov. 8, 1939; s. Joseph H. and Esther (Scheppele) G.; m. Nancy Caroline Buchannan, June 25, 1960 (dec. 1965). Student, Pa. State U., 1957-60, 89—. Process engr. Gettig Tech. Inc., Spring Mills, Pa., 1960-88. Inventor ultralight non-solid state miniature ignition systems for model aircraft employing small two cycle spark ignition engines. Staff sgt. Pa. N.G., 1961-67. Mem. NRA, Model Engine Collectors Assn., Soc. Antique Modelers and Model Airplanes, Acad. Model Awronautics, Univ. Club Pa. State U., Delta Phi. Republican. Lutheran. Home: PO Box 85 Boalsburg PA 16827-0085

GETTING, IVAN ALEXANDER, physicist, former aerospace company executive; b. N.Y.C., Jan. 18, 1912; s. Milan and Harriet (Almasy) G.; m. Dorothea Louise Gracy, Oct. 2, 1937 (dec. Sept. 1976); children: Nancy Louise Secker, Ivan Craig, Peter Alexander; m. Helen Avery, Jan. 9, 1977. SB, MIT, 1933; DPhil, Oxford U., 1935; DSc (hon.), Northeastern U., 1954, U. So. Calif., 1986. Jr. fellow Harvard U., Cambridge, Mass., 1935-40; mem. staff, head div. 8 radiation lab. MIT, Cambridge, 1940-45, assoc. prof. elec. engring., 1945-46, prof., 1946-50; asst. for devel. planning, dep. chief of staff USAF, Washington, 1950-51; v.p. engring and research Raytheon Corp., Waltham, Mass., 1951-60; pres., chief exec. officer The Aerospace Corp., El Segundo, Calif., 1960-77; cons. USAF, USN, U.S. Army, NRC, Dept. Def., others, 1945—. Contbr. articles to profl. jours.; patentee in field. Dir. Los Angeles World Affairs Council, 1961—. Fellow AIAA (hon.), IEEE (pres. 1978), Am. Inst. Physics, Am. Acad. Arts and Scis.; mem. Nat. Acad. Engring., L.A. Yacht Club, Cosmos Club.

GETTINGER, STEPHEN H., journalist; b. L.A., Nov. 3, 1948; s. Leonard A. Gettinger and Barbara B. Hubbard; m. Mary C. Hamill, Aug. 7, 1985. BA, Pomona Coll., 1970; MS, Columbia U., 1975. Supr. VISTA, Auburn, Ala., 1972-74; assoc. editor Police Mag., N.Y.C., 1976-83, Corrections Mag., N.Y.C., 1976-83; sr. editor Congl. Quarterly, Washington, 1984-95. Author: Sentenced to Die, 1979. Home: 19 Overhill Rd Catonsvill MD 21228 Office: Congl Quarterly 1414 22nd St NW Washington DC 20037

GETTLEMAN, ROBERT WILLIAM, judge; b. Atlantic City, May 5, 1943; s. Charles Edward and Beulah (Oppenheim) G.; m. Joyce Reinitz, Dec. 23, 1964; children: Lynn Katheryn, Jeffrey Alan. BSBA cum laude, Boston U., 1965; JD cum laude, Northwestern U., 1968. Bar: Ill. 1968, U.S. Dist. Ct. (no. dist.) Ill. 1968, U.S. Ct. Appeals (7th cir.) 1968, U.S. Dist. Ct. (ea. dist.) Wis. 1972, U.S. Supreme Ct. 1973. Law clk. to presiding justice U.S. Ct. Appeals, Chgo., 1968-70; assoc. D'Ancoma & Pflaum, Chgo., 1970-74, ptnr., 1974-94; judge U.S. Dist. Ct., Ill., 1994—; bd. dirs. John Howard Assn., Chgo., 1973-94, pres., 1978-81, chmn. legal and policy coms.; commr., chmn. devel. disabilities and individual rights coms. Gov.'s Commn. to Revise Mental Health Code of Ill., 1973-77; chmn. steering com. Chgo. Project on Residential Alternatives, 1984-85; mem. Cook County State's Atty.'s Profl. Adv. Com., 1984—; treas. Ill. Guardianship and Advocacy Commn., 1984, vice chmn., 1985, chmn., 1986; bd. dirs., chmn. legal com. Pact, Inc., 1985—; mem. mcpl. officers election bd. Village of Lyons, Ill., 1985. Contbr. articles to law revs. Bd. dirs. Ill. div. ACLU, 1973-78. Recipient August W. Christmann award Mayor of Chgo., 1994. Fellow Am. Bar Found.; mem. ABA, Ill. Bar Assn., Chgo. Bar Assn., 7th Fed. Cir. Bar Assn., Chgo. Council Lawyers. Office: US Dist Ct 1788 Dirksen Bldg 219 S Dearborn St Fl 17 Chicago IL 60604-1702*

GETTLER, BENJAMIN, lawyer, manufacturing company executive; b. Louisville, Ky., Sept. 16, 1925; s. Herbert and Gertrude (Cohen) G.; m. Deliaan Angel, Mar. 1972; children: Jorian, Thomas, Gail, John, Benjamin. BA in Econs. with high honors, U. Cin., 1945; JD (Frankfurter scholar), Harvard U., 1948. Bar: Ohio 1949, U.S. Supreme Ct. 1955. Ptnr. Brown & Gettler, Cin., 1951-73, Gettler, Katz & Buckley, Cin., 1973-87, Gettler & Buckley, 1987—; chmn. bd. Am. Controlled Industries Inc., Cin., 1973-86; chmn. bd. dirs., pres. Colorpac Inc., Franklin, Ohio, 1973-86; chmn. bd., pres. Vulcan Internat. Corp., Wilmington, Del., 1988—, Vulcan Corp., Clarksville, Tenn., 1988—; chmn. exec. com. Valley Industries, Inc., Cin., 1973-86; vice chmn. bd. Cin. Southern R.R., 1987-91; chmn. bd. Trusthouse, Inc., Cin., 1987—; chmn. bd. dirs. ACI Internat., Inc., Cin., 1990—; spl. counsel U. Cin., 1975-77, trustee, 1994—, vice chmn. bd., 1999—; bd. dirs. PNC Bank, Ohio, 1988-96. Chmn. bd. Jewish Inst. Nat. Security Affairs, 1994-98, chmn. policy com., 1998—; chmn. Cin. Bonds for Israel, 1969; chmn. Nat. Israel Commn., Nat. Jewish Cmty. Rels. Adv. Coun., 1981-82; mem. Ohio, Ky. and Ind. Mass Transit Policy Com., 1970-75; pres. Cin. Jewish Cmty. Rels. Coun., 1978-80; trustee Jewish Hosp. Cin., 1978-92, chmn., 1991-92; trustee U. Cin., 1994—; chmn. Midwest Hosp. Sys., Inc., 1987-90, 92-93; pres. Jewish Found. Cin., 1995—; trustee Health Alliance Greater Cin., 1995-96; chmn. Cin. Coalition for Reagan, 1980; co-chmn. Hamilton County Reagan Bush Campaign Ohio, 1984; chmn. Rep. Fin. Com., Hamilton County, 1991-92; mem. Hamilton County Rep. Policy Com., 1990—. Capt. U.S. Army, 1955-56. Mem. ABA, Cin. Bar Assn., Shoe Last Mfrs. Assn. (pres. 1984-85), Footwear Industries Am. (bd. dirs. 1989—), Phi Beta Kappa, Omicron Delta Kappa. Clubs: Coldstream Country, Harvard. Office: Vulcan Corp 30 Garfield Pl Suite 1040 Cincinnati OH 45202-4322

GETTS, NINO, studio owner; b. White Plains, N.Y., Nov. 12, 1944; s. William and Mary L. (Riccardi) G.; m. Karen Larish, Feb. 6, 1976 (div. June 1984). Student, SUNY Purchase, 1992-95. V.p. Chess Media Unlimited, Inc., Mamaroneck, N.Y., 1995—. Composer numerous musical compositions. Avocations: winemaking, stamp collecting, coin collecting. Home: 7 Lincoln Pl Ossining NY 10562-5212

GETTY, ESTELLE, actress; b. N.Y.C., July 25, 1923; m. Arthur Gettleman, Dec. 21, 1947; children: Barry, Carl. Student, New Sch. for Social Rsch., Herbert Berghof Studios; studied with Gerald Russak. Appeared in numerous stage prodns. on and off Broadway including Death of a Salesman, The Glass Menagerie, All My Sons, 6 Rms Rv Vu, Blithe Spirit, Arsenic and Old Lace, I Don't Know Why I'm Screaming, Widows and Children, Torch Song Trilogy, 1981-83; film appearances include The Chosen, 1982, Tootsie, 1983, Mask, 1984, Protocol, 1984, Mannequin, 1987, Stop or My Mom Will Shoot, 1991, Fortune Hunters, 1999, Stuart Little (voice), 1999; TV appearances include (series) The Golden Girls, 1987-92, (Emmy award as outstanding supporting actress in a comedy series 1988, Golden Globe award for best actress in a comedy, Am. Comedy award for best supporting actress in a series 1990), Golden Palace, 1992-93, Empty Nest, 1993-95; (TV movies) No Man's Land, 1984, Victims for Victims: The Teresa Saldana Story, 1984, Copacabana, 1985; author: If I Knew Then What I Know Now...So What?, 1988. Office: Innovative Artists Talent and Literary Agency 1999 Ave Of Stars Ste 2850 Los Angeles CA 90067-4612 Office: Green/Siegel & Associates 100 Universal City Plz # 507-3D Universal Cty CA 91608-1002*

GETTYS, THOMAS WIGINGTON, medical researcher. BS in Biology, Lander Coll., 1978; PhD in Nutrition, Clemson U., 1984. Grad. rsch. asst. animal sci. dept. Coll. Agriculture Clemson (S.C.) U., 1979-84; rsch. assoc. Howard Hughes Med. Inst., Dept. Molecular Physiology and Biophysics Vanderbilt U. Sch. of Medicine, Nashville, 1985-87; rsch. assoc. divsn. gastroenterology, dept. medicine Duke U. Med. Ctr., Durham, N.C., 1987-90, rsch. asst. prof. divsn. gastroenterology, dept. medicine, 1990—, rsch. asst. prof. dept. cell biology, 1992-93; assoc. prof. medicine Med. U. S.C., Charleston, 1993—, assoc. prof. biochemistry and molecular biology, 1995—. Contbr. articles to profl. jours., chpts. to books. Predoctoral rsch. fellow Clemson U., 1981-82; NIH grantee, 1990, 94, 96, 98; recipient Rsch. award Am. Diabetes Assn., 1996. Mem. Am. Soc. Biochemistry and Molecular Biology, Sigma Xi. Office: Med U SC 916 Clin Sci Bldg 171 Ashley Ave Charleston SC 29425-0001

GETZ, ERNEST JOHN, lawyer; b. Toronto, Ont., Can., Apr. 14, 1918; came to U.S., 1925; s. Lewis and Florence (Bell) Gietz; m. Dorothy Miller, Aug. 30, 1948; children: Christopher, Susan, Timothy. BA, U. Rochester, 1940; MBA, Harvard U., 1942; JD, U. Mich., 1947. Bar: Mich. 1947, U.S. Tax Ct. 1948, Ct. Fed. Claims 1955, U.S. Supreme Ct. 1964; CPA, Mich. With prodn. control dept. Divine Bros. Co., Utica, N.Y., 1942-43; mgr. Yerges Mfg. Co., Fremont, Ohio, 1943-44; pub. acct. Wideman Madden & Co., Toledo, 1944-45, Seidman & Seidman, Grand Rapids, Mich., 1947-50; ptnr. Dickinson Wright PLLC, Detroit, 1950—; lectr. on taxation topics Inst. Continuing Legal Edn. Co-editor: Michigan Tax Practice and Procedure, 1979, 2d edit., 1983; contbr. articles to profl. jours. Mem. Pleasant Ridge (Mich.) City Coun. 1958-70; Dem. precinct del., Oakland County, Mich., 1966-68; pres. bd. dirs. Downtown YMCA, Detroit, 1976-78; pres. Grand Circus Park Devel. Assn. and Found., Detroit, 1979-89; trustee Henry M. Seldon Charitable Trust, 1979—, pres., 1982—; mem. YMCA of Met. Detroit Investment Supervisory Com., 1985—; trustee YMCA Found. Met. Detroit, 1985-93, YWCA of Metro Detroit, 1993-96, Ctrl. United Meth. Ch., 1998—; mem. adv. coun. Salvation Army Bagley Corps, Detroit, 1998—. Named Pleasant Ridger of Yr., Pleasant Ridge Found., 1970, Downtown Detroit Amb., Cen. Bus. Dist. Assn., 1981, Layperson of Yr., Detroit Downtown YMCA, 1977. Mem. AICPA, State Bar Mich. (chmn. taxation sect. 1977-78), Detroit Bar Assn., Mich. Assn. CPA's. Avocations: mountain climbing, trekking, travel, handball. Home: 19 Oakland Park Blvd Pleasant Ridge MI 48069-1110 Office: Dickinson Wright PLLC 500 Woodward Ave Ste 4000 Detroit MI 48226-3416

GETZ, HERBERT A., lawyer. BA, Ill. Wesleyan U., 1977; JD, Harvard U., 1980. Bar: Ill. 1980. Assoc. Bell, Boyd & Lloyd, Chgo., 1980-83; gen. counsel Waste Mgmt. Ptnrs., Inc. (now Waste Mgmt., Inc.), Oak Brook, Ill., 1983-85; asst. gen. counsel Waste Mgmt., Inc., Oak Brook, 1985-88; sec., asst. gen. counsel WMX Techs., Inc., Oak Brook, 1988-92, sr. v.p., gen. counsel, sec., 1992—. Office: WMX Techs Inc 3003 Butterfield Rd Oak Brook IL 60523-1107*

GETZ, JAMES EDWARD, legal association administrator; b. Shelbyville, Ill., June 8, 1950; s. William Forrest and Betty Jean (Mitchell) G.; m. Rita Genevieve Boyd, June 16, 1973; children: Christopher Brandon, Sarah Lynne. BS in Edn., Eastern Ill. U., 1972, MA, 1974. Grad. asst. Political Sci. Dept. Eastern Ill. U., Charleston, 1972-73; tchr. Plano (Ill.) Community Schs., 1973-74; conservation police officer Ill. Dept. Natural Resources, Office Law Enforcement, Springfield, Ill., 1974-77; region IV Ops. supr. Ill. Dept. Natural Resources, Office Law Enforcement, Springfield; region IV comdr. Ill. Dept. Conservation Div. Law Enforcement, Springfield, 1980-82; deputy chief Ill. Dept. Natural Resource, Office Law Enforcement, 1982-86; region II comdr. Ill. Dept. Natural Resource, Office Law Enforcement, Springfield, 1986-90; Lake Mich. enforcement ops. comdr. Ill. Dept. Natural Resources divsn. Law Enforcement, Springfield, 1990—; boating law adminstr. State Ill., 1984-86; chmn. several coms. Nat. Assn. State Boating Law Adminstrs.; mem Nat. Boating Safety Adv. Coun. U.S. Coast Guard; pres. Conservation Police Lodge #146, Fraternal Order Police, 1993-96. Author: Illinois Public Act 84-515, 1985; Illinois Public Act 85-147, 1987. Mem. Nat. Marine Mfr. Assn. Boat Cert. Com., Gt. Lakes Fisheries Commn. Law Enforcement Com. (vice chmn. 1986-90, chmn. 1990-92), Am. Boat & Yacht Coun. (bd. dirs. 1992-99). Avocations: boating, history, genealogy. Home: 1709 N Orleans St Mc Henry IL 60050-3885 Office: Ill Dept Natural Resources 701 N Point Dr Winthrop Harbor IL 60096-1371

GETZ, LOWELL VERNON, financial advisor; b Schenectady, Feb. 28, 1932; s. Leon and Harriet Esther (Friedman) G.; BS in Econs., U. Pa., 1953; MBA, Harvard U., 1955; m. Judith Ruth Schwartz, Oct. 14, 1956; children: Marshall, Andrew. Treas., R. Dixon Speas Assos., Inc., Manhasset, N.Y., 1969-72, Coverdale & Colpitts, Inc., N.Y.C., 1972-74; fin. mgr. Bovay Engrs., Inc., Houston, 1974-79; sec., treas. Rice Center, Houston, 1979-82; guest lectr. U. Houston, 1980-81, Harvard Grad. Sch. Design, 1985—; Univ. of Wisconsin, Madison, 1998; overseas instr. Hong Kong Mgmt. Assn., 1986—, Advanced Mgmt. Inst. for Architecture & Engring., 1993-96; cons. in fin. mgmt. to architects, engring. firms., 1980—; overseas instr. Tongji U., Shanghai, People's Republic of China, 1990, Shanghai Mcpl. Constrn. Commn., 1992, Assn. Consulting Engrs., London, 1995 and 1998; condr. seminars in field. Served as lt. USNR, 1955-58. Mem. Profl. Svcs. Mgmt. Assn. (pres. 1988, treas. 1981-82, bd. dirs. 1979-88, 86-88), Tex. Soc. CPAs (chmn. mgmt. adv. svcs. com. Houston chpt. 1982-83), Am. Inst. CPAs (mem. various mgmt. adv. svcs. subcoms. 1981-87, cert. of Ednl. Achievement in Bus. Valuation), Am. Soc. Appraisers (sr.), Inst. Mgmt. Cons. (cert.). Author: Financial Management and Project Control for Consulting Engineers, 1983; Financial Management for the Design Professional, 1984, Business Management in the Smaller Design Firm, 1986, Managing Ownership Transition in Design Firms, 1987, Mergers, Acquisitions, and Sales, 1987; co-author: Ownership Transition, Options and Strategies, 1996; contbg. editor: Valuation Survey of Design Firms, 1991-97, Insider's Guide to Cashing in on your Equity in an A/E/P or Environmental Consulting Firm, 1993, Financial Management for Design Firms, 1997, (with others) Architect's Handbook of Professional Practice, 1993; contbr. articles to profl. publs. Home: PO Box 19159 Houston TX 77224-9159 Office: 820 Gessner Rd Ste 265 Houston TX 77024-4258

GETZ, MARY E., medical/surgical nurse; b. North Towanda, Pa., July 16, 1947; d. Leo T. and Ruth (Goodrich) Squires: m. Robert R. Getz, Dec. 23, 1971; children: Jesse T., Megan K. Diploma, Jefferson Hosp., Phila., 1968. RN, Pa.; cert. ACLS, med./surg. nurse. Staff nurse Meml. Hosp. Inc., Towanda, Pa., 1968—. Mem. ANA, Pa. State Nurses Assn., Jefferson Nurses Alumni Assn., Acad. of Med.-Surg. Nurses, Ethic com. Home: RR 2 Box 2368 Dushore PA 18614-9301

GETZ, ROBERT LEE, newspaper columnist; b. Francesville, Ind., Oct. 1, 1943; s. Benjamin Jacob and Helen Juanita (Thomas) G.; m. Lisa Gale Schneller, Sept. 11, 1972 (div. June 1988); children: Chase H., Page L., Tracy M.; m. Jeannie McCoy, Mar. 17, 1994. Student, Andrews U., 1962. Reporter Logansport (Ind.) Pharos-Tribune, 1964; sports editor Rochester (Ind.) Sentinel, 1965; sports writer, columnist Bloomington (Ind.) Herald-Telephone, 1967-70; sports editor Boca Raton (Fla.) News, 1972-74, columnist, feature writer, 1973-74; columnist Wichita (Kans.) Eagle, 1975—. Author: A Bookful of Bob Getz, 1992. With U.S. Army, 1965-67. Avocations: tennis, basketball. Office: Wichita Eagle 825 E Douglas Ave Wichita KS 67202-3594

GETZ, WAYNE MARCUS, biomathematician, researcher, educator; b. Johannesburg, Republic of South Africa, Apr. 26, 1950; came to U.S., 1979; m. Jennifer Bryna Gonski, Feb. 15, 1972; children: Stacey Lynn, Trevor Russell. BSc with honors, U. Witwatersrand, South Africa, 1972, PhD, 1976; DSc, U. Cape Town, South Africa, 1995. Rsch. scientist Coun. for Sci. and Indsl. Rsch., Pretoria, South Africa, 1974-79; biomathematician U. Calif., Berkeley, 1979—, prof. entomology, 1987-93, prof. environ. scis., 1993—, chair divsn. insect biology, 1996—, Berkeley chancellor's prof., 1998—; cons. Nat. Marine Fisheries Svc., 1980-89. Author: (with R. Haight) Population Harvesting: Demographic Models of Fish, Forest, and Animal Resources, 1989; editor Oxford U. Press book series Biol. Resource Mgmt., 1983-97; assoc. editor jour. Natural Resources Modeling; mem. editl. bd. Ecol. Applications, 1994-96, Annales Zoologica Fennici; contbr. articles to profl. jours. Rsch. grantee NSF, Whitehall Found., Alfred P. Sloan Found., Def. Advanced Rsch. Programs Adminstrn.; Alexander von Humboldt U.S. Sr. Scientist awardee, 1993. Fellow AAAS; mem. Internat. Soc. for Neuroethology, Soc. Am. Naturalist, Internat. Soc. for Ecol. Modelling, Internat. Neurol. Network Soc., Ecology Soc. Am., Resource Modelling Assn. (pres. 1995-96, bd. dirs. 1992-98), Soc. for Math. Biology. Office: Univ Calif Dep Env Sci Policy and Mgmt Berkeley CA 94720-3112

GEUSIC, JOSEPH EDWARD, physicist; b. Nesquehoning, Pa., Nov. 21, 1931; s. Joseph John and Mary Martha (Kosch) G.; m. Irene Jean Hosak, July 18, 1953; children: Patricia, Mark, Michael, Mary Ellen, Robert, Joseph. BS in Physics, Lehigh U., 1953; MS in Physics, Ohio State U., 1955, PhD in Physics, 1958. Rsch. assoc. physics dept. Ohio State U., Columbus, 1955-58; mem. tech. staff AT&T Bell Labs., Murray Hill, N.J., 1958-62, supr. solid state maser group, 1962-66, head solid state optical device dept., 1966-70, head magnetics dept., 1970-84, head semiconductor laser dept., 1984-94; pres. Geusic Info. Svcs., Inc., 1996—; adj. fellow Micron Tech. Advanced Rsch. Inst. Recipient R.W. Wood prize Optical Soc. Am., 1993, Clinton J. Davisson Patent award trophy AT&T, 1993. Fellow IEEE (Quantum Electronics award 1992); mem. Am. Inst. Physics, Sigma Xi. Achievements include first report of paramagnetic spectra of Cr^{3+} in Ruby; invention and devel. of Nd/YAG laser, barium sodium niobate nonlinear optical material; first demonstation of continuous operating optical parametric oscillator; devel. of semiconductor lasers for terrestrial and undersea lightwave communication systems, magnetic bubble materials and devices; over 62 publs. and 30 patents in field. Home: 261 Lorraine Dr Berkeley Heights NJ 07922-2341

GEVERS, MARCIA BONITA, lawyer, lecturer, mediator, consultant; b. Mpls., Oct. 11, 1946; d. Sam and Bessie (Gottlieb) Fleisher; m. Michael A. Gevers, Sept. 13, 1970; children: Sarah Nichole, David Seth. BA, Nat. Coll. Edn., 1968; MA, Northea. Ill. U., 1973; JD, DePaul U., 1980. Bar: Ill. 1980, U.S. Dist. Ct. (no. dist.) Ill. 1980, U.S. Supreme Ct. 1985. Tchr. The Harris Sch., Chgo. Bd. Edn., N. Suburban Spl. Edn. Dist., Highland Park, Ill., 1968-73; legis. asst., campaign mgr. Ill. State Rep., Dolton, 1974-79; sole practice Park Forest, Dolton, Ill., 1980-83; ptnr. Getty and Gevers, Dolton, 1983-87; pvt. practice Marica B. Gevers & Assocs., Flossmoor, Ill., 1987—; adj. prof. Gov.'s State U., University Park, 1986-87. Contbr. articles to profl. jours.; producer, host cable TV show, The Law and You, 1982-83. Bd. dirs. Park Forest Zoning Bd. Appeals, Fair Housing Rev. Bd., Housing Bd. Appeals, EEO Rev. Bd., 1975-88; pres. bd. dirs. South Suburban Cmty. Hebrew Day Sch., Olympia Fields, Ill., 1982-86; bd. dirs. Congregation Beth Sholom Ch., Park Forest, 1980-82, Congregation Beth Sholom Ch., Park Forest, 1980-82, Anita M. Stone Jewish Cmty. Ctr., 1996—; pres. Ill. Women's Polit. Caucus; mem. steering com. Nat. Women's Polit. Caucus, Washington; pres., founder Metro South Women's Polit. Caucus, Chgo. suburbs; alt. del. Dem. Nat. Conv., N.Y.C., 1980. Mem. ABA (family law sect.,juvenile, stepfamilies and pub. rels. coms.), Ill. State Bar Assn., Chgo. Bar Assn. (matrimonial law com., Guardian Ad Litem subcom.), Am. Arbitration Assn. (arbitrator), Lodges: Hadassah, B'nai B'rith Women. Office: Marcia B Gevers & Assocs 19710 Governors Hwy Flossmoor IL 60422-2040

GEWARTOWSKI, JAMES WALTER, electrical engineer; b. Chgo., Nov. 10, 1930; s. Joseph Walter and Irene Dorothy (Dziekanowski) G.; m. Marion Ruth Wakeman, June 23, 1956; children: Marion, Diane, Patricia, John, Karen. B.S. in Elec. Engring., Ill. Inst. Tech., 1952; S.M., MIT, 1953; Ph.D., Stanford U., 1958. Research asst. Stanford Electronics Lab., Calif., 1954-57; supr. microwave research AT&T Bell Labs., Inc, Murray Hill, N.J., 1957-71; supr. high bit rate optical data link group AT&T Bell Labs., Inc, Allentown, Pa., 1971-88; supr. SL optical relay/receiver group AT&T Bell Labs., Inc, Breinigsville, Pa., 1988-89, ret. Co-author: Principles of Electron Tubes, 1965, Fundamentals of Electron Tubes, 1969; contbg. author: Microwave Semiconductor Devices and Their Circuit Applications, 1969; contbr. articles to profl. jours. Fellow IEEE (Browder J. Thompson Meml. prize 1960); mem. Sigma Xi, Tau Beta Pi, Eta Kappa Nu, Serra Internat. Republican. Roman Catholic. Home: 2908 Edgemont Dr Allentown PA 18103-5410

GEWEKE, JOHN FREDERICK, economics educator; b. Washington, May 11, 1948; s. Robert William and Winnifred Lois (Quies) G.; m. Lynne Marie Osborn, Aug. 22, 1970; children: Andrew Robert, Alan Reid. BS, Mich. State U., 1970; PhD, U. Minn., 1975. Asst. prof. U. Wis., Madison, 1975-79, assoc. prof., 1979-82, prof., 1982-83; prof. Duke U., Durham, N.C., 1983-86, William R. Kenan Jr. prof., 1986-90, dir. Inst. Stats. and Decision Scis., 1987-90; prof. U. Minn., Mpls., 1990—. Editor Jour. Bus. and Econs. Stats., 1989-92; co-editor Jour. Applied Econometrics, 1993—; assoc. editor Econometrica, 1984-88, 95—. Rsch. fellow Sloan Found., N.Y.C., 1982. Fellow Econometric Soc., Am. Statis. Assn.; mem. Am. Econ. Assn., Internat. soc. for Bayesian Analysis (pres. 1999). Office: U Minn Dept Econs Minneapolis MN 55455

GEWERTZ, BRUCE LABE, surgeon, educator; b. Phila., Aug. 27, 1949; s. Milton and Shirley (Charen) G.; children: Samantha, Barton, Alexis; m. Diane Weiss, Aug. 31, 1997. BS, Pa. State U., State Coll., 1968; MD, Jefferson Med. Coll., Phila., 1972. Diplomate Am. Bd. Surgery. Surg. resident U. Mich., Ann Arbor, 1972-77; asst. prof. U. Tex., Dallas, 1977-81; assoc. prof. U. Chgo., 1981-87, prof. surgery, 1988—, faculty dean med. edn., 1989-92, Dallas Phemister prof., chmn. dept. surgery, 1992—; teaching scholar Am. Heart Assn., Dallas, 1980-83; pres. Assn. Surg. Edn., 1983-84. Author: Atlas of Vascular Surgery, 1989; editor Jour. Surg. Rsch., 1987—; patentee removable vascular filter. Recipient Jobst award Coller Surg. Soc., 1975, Coller award Mich. chpt. Am. Coll. Surgeons, 1975. Mem. Soc. Vascular Surgery, Midwestern Vascular Soc. (pres. 1994-95), Soc. Clin. Surgery, Soc. Univ. Surgeons, Chgo. Surg. Soc. (treas. 1989-92), Am. Surg. Assn., Point O'Woods Club (Benton Harbor, Mich.). Office: U Chgo MC 5029 5841 S Maryland Ave Chicago IL 60637-1463

GEWIRTZ, JEFFREY BRIAN, lawyer; b. Baldwin Harbor, N.Y., Feb. 26, 1969; s. Arnold David and Clara (Lisogurski) G. BA, Tufts U., 1991; JD, Bklyn. Law Sch., 1994. Bar: N.J. 1994, U.S. Dist. Ct. N.J. 1994, N.Y. 1995, U.S. Dist. Ct. (so. and ea. dists.) N.Y. 1995. Assoc. Dunnington Bartholow & Miller,LLP, N.Y.C., 1994-96; atty. WTA TOUR, Stamford, Conn., 1996-98; pro bono gen. counsel Eastern Tennis Assn., Inc., 1997—; gen. counsel Ladies Profl. Golf Assn., Daytona Beach, Fla., 1998—; adj. prof. sports law N.Y. Law Sch., N.Y.C., 1996-98; adj. asst. prof. sports law Bklyn. Law Sch., 1998. Contbr. articles on sports law to profl. jours. Bklyn. Law Sch. Admissions Merit scholar, 1991-94. Mem. ABA (forum on entertainment and sports industries 1992—), Nat. Sports Law Inst., Soc. for Study of Legal Aspects of Sport and Phys. Activity, N.Y. State Bar Assn. (chair profl. sports com. 1995—), Assn. of Bar of City of N.Y. (com. sports law 1995—). Office: LPGA 100 International Golf Dr Daytona Beach FL 32124-1092

GEWIRTZ, LEONARD BENJAMIN, rabbi; b. N.Y.C., Jan. 25, 1918; s. Henry and Leah Peshe (Greenberg) G.; m. Gladys Sarah Kerstein, Nov. 21, 1948; children: Isaac Meir, Joseph Jacob. BS cum laude, CCNY, 1941; grad., Hebrew Theol. Coll., 1945; postgrad., Dropsie Coll., 1952. Ordained rabbi, 1945. Supply rabbi Beth Shalom Congregation, Danville, Ill., 1943-45; rabbi Congregation Oir Chodosh, Chgo., 1945-47, Congregation Adas Kodesh Shel Emeth, Wilmington, Del., 1947-88; rabbi emeritus, 1988—; dir. campus activities Hillel U. Del., Newark, 1960-63; instr. Gratz Hebrew High Sch., Wilmington, 1971-83; founder, speaker WDEL weekly radio program Rabbi Speaks, 1950—. Author: Authentic Jew and His Judaism, 1961, Authentic Jewish Living, 1977, Jewish Spirituality: Hope and Redemption, 1985, A Jewish Voice, 1998; contbr. articles religious jours. Pres. Del. Citizens Conf. Social Work, Wilmington, 1954-56; bd. govs. Del. Mental Health Assn., 1967-71, Jewish Community Ctr. Recipient Heritage award Israel Bonds, 1992, Reunification award, 1992; Sanctuary of Synagogue Rabbi Leonard B. Gewirtz named in his honor, 1994, Mezuza award for Cmty. Svc. State of Israel Bonds, 1997. Mem. ACLU, Pacem En Terris, Rabbinic Assn. Del. (pres. 1967-69, 75-77, 80-82), Rabbinical Coun. Am. (chmn. social actions 1966-68, exec. com. 1960-64), Phila. Bd. Rabbis (40 Yr. Continuous Svc. award 1984), Jewish Fedn. (bd. govs.), B'nai Brith (cert. honor). Home: 406 Hawthorne Dr Wilmington DE 19802-1242 Office: Adas Kodesh Shel Emeth Synagogue Washington Blvd & Torah Way Wilmington DE 19802

GEWIRTZ-FRIEDMAN, GERRY, editor; b. N.Y.C., Dec. 22, 1920; d. Max and Minnie (Weiss) G.; m. Eugene W. Friedman, Nov. 11, 1945; children: John Henry, Robert James. BA, Vassar Coll., 1941. Editor Package Store Mgmt., 1942-44, Jewelry Mag., 1945-53; freelance editor promotion dept. McCall's Mag., Esquire, 1953-56; free-lance fashion and gifts editor Jewelers Circular Keystone, N.Y.C., 1955-71; editor, pub. The Fashionables, 1971-74, The Forecast, 1974—, Nat. Jeweler, Ann. Fashion Guide, 1976-80; editor, assoc. pub. Exec. Jeweler, 1980-83; editor The Fashion Source (formerly Internat. Fashion Index), N.Y.C., 1984—; free-lance editor and mktg. specialist, 1995—; ptnr. Gary Gewirtz-Editl. and Mktg.; free-lance editl. wrtier, 1995—. Corr. Internat. Mktg. News. Mem. exec. com. Inner City Council of Cardinal Cooke, N.Y.; chairperson women's task force United Jewish Appeal Fedn.; former bd. govs. Israel Bonds; former trustee Israel Cancer Research Fund, Central Synagogue; bd. dirs. Double Image Theater; former pres. women's aux. Brandeis U. Honored guest Am. Jewish Com., 1978; Israel Cancer Research Fund, 1978-81; recipient Disting. Community Service award Brandeis U., 1987; named to Jewellry Hall Fame, 1988. Mem. N.Y. Fashion Group, Nat. Home Fashions League (former pres.), Women's Jewelry Assn. (pres. 1983-87, named editor who has contbd. most to jewelry industry 1984, free lance editor). Home: 45 Sutton Pl S New York NY 10022-2444

GEX, WALTER JOSEPH, III, federal judge; b. Bay St. Louis, Miss., Mar. 20, 1939. BA, U. Miss., LLB, 1963. Bar: Miss. 1963. With Satterfield, Shell, Williams & Buford, Jackson, Miss., 1963-72, ptnr., 1966-72; ptnr. Gex, Gex & Phillips, Bay St. Louis, Miss., 1972-86; judge U.S. Dist. Ct. (so. dist.) Miss., Biloxi, 1986—. Fellow Miss. State Bar Found.; mem. Fed. Bar Assn., Miss. State Bar Assn.. Republican. Roman Catholic. Office: US Dist Ct 725 Washington Loop Rm 238 Biloxi MS 39530-2267*

GEYER, DENNIS LYNN, university administrator and registrar; b. Bay City, Mich., Feb. 17, 1950; s. Walter R. and Bettie Jane (Powers) G.; m. Karen Sue Bickel, Sept. 5, 1970; children: Sarah Denise, Zachary Dennis. Student, Northwestern Luth. Coll., 1967-68; BA, Mich. State U., 1971, MA, 1976. Tchr., coach Aurora (Colo.) Jr. High Sch., 1972-74; asst. to the registrar Lansing (Mich.) C.C., 1974-77; counselor Adams County Sch. Dist. # 14, Commerce City, Colo., 1977-78; registrar, asst. dir. student svcs. U. Colo. Health Sci. Ctr., Denver, 1978-88; univ. registrar, NCAA compliance officer, instnl. rsch. rep. Humboldt State U., Arcata, Calif., 1988-98; dir. admissions and records Humboldt State U., Arcata, 1996-98; univ. registrar SUNY, Stony Brook, 1998—. Co-author: A Guidebook for Student Services, 1977. Mem. Jaycees, Bay City, 1971-73; mem. Luth. Ch. of Arcata, pres., 1993-96, chair edn. com., 1990-93, mem. campus ministry bd., 1993-98, co-chair pastoral search com., 1996-97; mem. Messiah Evang. Ch., Lord of Life Luth. Ch., sec., 1983-87, pres., 1987-88; mem. Promise Keepers, 1994-98; active Messiah Luth. Ch. Mem. Am. Assn. Collegiate Registrars and Admissions Officers, Nat. Collegiate Athletic Assn. (instn. compliance officer 1990-98), Calif. Assn. Instl. Rsch., SUNY Registrar's Assn. Avocation: traveling. Home: 79 Quaker Path Stony Brook NY 11790 Office: SUNY PO Box 584 Stony Brook NY 11790-0584

GEYER, GEORGIE ANNE, syndicated columnist, educator, author, biographer, TV commentator; b. Chgo., Apr. 2, 1935; d. Robert George and Georgie Hazel (Gervens) G. BS, Northwestern U., 1956, LHD (hon.), 1993; postgrad., U. Vienna, Austria, 1956-57; LittD (hon.), Lake Forest Coll., 1980, Coll. Mt. St. Joseph, 1986, Notre Dame, 1986, Wilson Coll., 1987, Linfield Coll., 1987, St. Mary-of-the-Woods Coll., 1989, U. Indpls., 1991, Colby-Sawyer Coll., 1992, Franklin Coll., 1992, Cabrini Coll., 1994; LHD (hon.), Chgo. State U., 1984, U. S.C., 1991, Rockhurst (Jesuit) Coll., Kansas City, 1992, Spring Hill Coll., 1993, Lebanon Valley Coll., 1994, Hofstra U., 1995, Loyola U., Chgo., 1996, Westminster Coll., 1996, Govs. State U., 1997. Reporter Southtown Economist, Chgo., 1958; soc. reporter Chgo. Daily News, 1959-60, gen. assignment reporter, 1960-64, corr. Lat. Am., Ctrl. Am., Soviet Union, Middle East, Europe, 1964-75, roving fgn. corr. and columnist, 1967-75; syndicated columnist Los Angeles Times Syndicate, 1975-80, Universal Press Syndicate, 1981—; Lyle M. Spencer prof. journalism Syracuse U., 1977; regular news commentator PBS' Washington Week in Review; questioner on Presdl. debate, Oct., 1984; steering com. Aspen Inst. Latin Am. Governance Project, 1981-82; commentator on the BBC; regular panelist Voice of America; sent by Internat. Communication Agy. on 3 worldwide speaking tours on Am. journalism: Nigeria, Zambia, Tanzania and Somalia, 1979, Philippines and Indonesia, 1981, Iceland, Norway, Belgium and Portugal, 1982; rep. Fulbright scholar program 40th anniversary, New Zealand, 1987; commencement speaker various colls., univs. including U. S.Carolina, Rockhurst Coll., St. Mary's Notre Dame; sr. fellow Annenburg Washington, 1992-93; columnist on fgn. policy, internat. affairs The Chgo. Tribune, The Wash. Times, Universal de Caracas, The Dallas Morning News, Diario las Americas, The Denver Post, others; speaker, lectr. in field. Author: The New Latins, 1970, The New 100 Years War, 1972, The Young Russians, 1976; (autobiography) Buying the Night Flight, (Weintal prize citation Sch. Fgn. Svc. Georgetown U. 1984, Chgo. Found. for Lit. award 1984), 1983, reissued, 1996, Guerilla Prince, The Untold Story of Fidel Castro, 1991, Waiting for Winter to End, An Extraordinary Journey Through South Central Asia, 1994, Americans No More: The Death of Citizenship, 1996; subjects of interviews include Prince Sihanouk of Cambodia, Yassar Arafat, Anwar Sadat, King Hussein of Jordan, Pres. Khaddafy of Libya, the Ayatollah Khomeini, Sultan Qaboos of Oman, Pres. Juan Peron of Argentina, Pres. Siad Barre of Somalia, Prime Minister Mauno Koivisto of Finland, Anastasio Somoza, Jerzy Urban, Janusz Onyszkiewicz, Prime Minister Edward Seaga of Jamaica, Pres. Ronald Reagan, Pres. George Bush, others; discovered and had first interview with second most-wanted Nazi, Walter Rauff in Tierra del Fuego, Chile, 1966; found Dominican pres. Juan Bosch in hiding in P.R. during Dominican revolution, 1965; held by Palestinians as Israeli spy, 1973; imprisoned in Angola for writing about revolutionary government, 1976; contbr. chpts. to books, articles numerous pubs. Active Orgn. for S.W. Community Chgo., 1960-64; trustee Am. U., Washington, 1981-86; Coun. Fgn. Rels. Recipient 1st prize Am. Newspaper Guild, 1962; 2d prize Ill. Press Editors Assn., 1962; award for best writing on Latin Am. Overseas Press Club, 1966; Merit award Northwestern U., 1968; Nat. Headliner award Theta Sigma Phi, 1968; Maria Moors Cabot award Columbia U., 1970; Hannah Solomon award Nat. Council Jewish Women, 1973; Ill. Spl. Events Commn. Woman's award, 1975; Northwestern U. Alumni award, 1991; Fulbright scholar U. Vienna, 1956-57; Woodrow Wilson fellow Rollins Coll., Winter Park, Fla., 1982; Presdl. Citation award Am. Univ., 1985; Disting. fellow Mortar Bd. Nat. Sr. Honor Soc., Am. U., 1982; Sr. fellow Annenberg Washington Program, Washington, 1982-83; fellow Soc. Prof. Journalists, 1992. Mem. Soc. Profl. Journalists, Women in Comm., Inst. Internat. Edn. (bd. dirs.), Midland Authors, Internat. Inst. Strategic Studies, Internat. Soc. Polit. Psychology, Women's Inst. for Freedom of Press, Washington Inst., Chgo. Coun. Fgn. Rels. (bd. dirs.), Gridiron Club, Cosmos Club (1st women out-of-town mem.), Travern Club (1st woman mem.), Cliff Dwellers Club (hon.). Home Fax: (202) 333-3198. Office Fax: (816) 932-6658. Home and Office: The Plaza 800 25th St NW Washington DC 20037-2207 *I have never compromised seriously on any ethical or moral principle, and I truly believe that the women of my generation can bring a new and cleansing element to American public life. Whatever I have accomplished I could not have done without profoundly analyzing myself: but I also find that in professional life the old injunction to "Know Thyself" reaches women more than men. It has been a constant struggle, often with little personal approval or backing, which I feel also adds to a woman's inner strength.*

GEYER, HAROLD CARL, artist, writer; b. Cold Spring, N.Y., Aug. 16, 1905; s. Harold Carl and Mary Brindsmaid (de Camp) G.; m. Ina Helen Doane, July 29, 1943. B.A., Yale U., 1926, B.F.A., 1930. Exhibited one-man shows, Aux Arcades, Troyes, France, 1984, group shows, Library of Congress, Soc. Am. Etchers, NAD, N.Y.C.; represented permanent collections, Library of Congress, Bibliotheque, Paris; (featured etchings) Ombres Et Lumieres de Troyes, 1989; author, artist: All Men Have Loved Thee, 1941, The Long Way Home, 1949. Recipient 3d Purchase prize Library of

Congress, 1945. Mem. NAD, Soc. Am. Graphic Artists. Home: RR 1 Chilmark MA 02535-9801

GEYER, SIDNA PRIEST, business education educator; b. Anderson, Ind., Dec. 9, 1943; d. James Dale and Lavada Belle (Lantz) Priest; m. James Eugene Geyer, Aug. 29, 1965; children: Jonathan Andrew, Susan Leigh. BS in Edn., Ball State U., 1969; MS in Edn., U. Wis., Oshkosh, 1975; EdS, U. Wis., Stout, 1980. Cert. secondary tchr., post-secondary tchr., Wis.; lic. supr., coord., counselor, Wis. Tchr. 6th grade St. Mary's Sch., Charlotte, Mich., 1966-67; tchr. bus. edn. Oak Hill High Sch., Converse, Ind., 1969-70, Stockbridge (Wis.) High Sch., 1970-72; tchr. bus., counselor Fox Valley Tech. Coll., Appleton, Wis., 1972-83, assoc. dean bus. edn., 1983-87; tchr. bus., English, computer sci. Baraboo (Wis.) Sr. High. Sch., 1988-90; dir. continuing edn. and performing arts U. Wis. Ctr. Baraboo-Sauk County, 1990-95; mgr. edn. outreach program U. Wis., LaCrosse, 1995-96; assoc. dean bus. occ. Blackhawk Tech. Coll., Janesville, Wis., 1996-98; mgr. customer svc., asst. dir. Conf. Ct., U. Wis., Milw., 1998—; evaluator bus. edn. U. Wis., Stout, 1981, N.E. Wis. Tech. Coll., Green Bay, 1985; mem. bus. adv. com. Brillion (Wis.) High Sch., 1983-87; mem. state-wide task force on develop curriculum for a sex equity course VTAE staff, 1983. Bd. dirs. Baraboo Literacy Coun., 1990-93; mem. bd. Baraboo Cmty. Scholarship Corp., 1993-94; mem. aux. bd. St. Clare Hosp., 1991-95. Mem. ASTD, AAUW (bd. dirs. 1971-95), Wis. Vocat. Assn. (mem. awards com.), Wis East Ctrl. Assn. Vocat. Edn. (treas. 1984), Women in Mgmt. (mem. edn. com.), Notth Ctrl. Assn. (bus. edn. evaluator 1984, 87—), Wis. Assn. Adult and Cntinuing Edn. (bd. dirs. 1993-94), Nat. U. Continuing Edn. Assn., Wis. Vocat. Assn. Methodist. Avocations: reading, playing bridge. Home: 7390 S Delaine Dr Oak Creek WI 53154-2405 Office: U Wis Milw Outreach/ Continuing Edn Ext 161 W Wisconsin Ave Ste 6000 Milwaukee WI 53203-2602

GEYER, THOMAS POWICK, newspaper publisher; b. Phila., Dec. 13, 1946; s. John Alvin and Jean (Powick) G. BA, St. John's Coll., 1969. Reporter The Mercury, Pottstown, Pa., 1969-73; editor Internat. Data Corp., Waltham, Mass., 1974, The Eagle-Times, Claremont, N.H., 1975; editor, pub. The Daily Freeman, Kingston, N.Y., 1976-81; pres. Ingersoll Pubs. Co., Princeton, N.J., 1982-86; pub. New Haven Register, 1986-91, The Daily Record, Parsippany, N.J., 1991-98. Bd. govs. St. John's Coll., Annapolis, Md., 1991—; chmn. First Night, Morristown, N.J., 1993. Fellow Berkeley Coll. Yale, 1988—. Home: 7 Budd St Morristown NJ 07960-5075

GEYMAN, JOHN PAYNE, physician, educator; b. Santa Barbara, Calif., Feb. 9, 1931; s. Milton John and Betsy (Payne) G.; m. Eugenia Clark Deichler, June 9, 1956; children: John Matthew, James Caleb, William Sabin. A.B. in Geology, Princeton U., 1952; M.D., U. Calif., San Francisco, 1960. Diplomate: Am. Bd. Family Practice. Intern L.A. County Gen. Hosp., 1960-61; resident in gen. practice Sonoma County Hosp., Santa Rosa, Calif., 1961-63; pvt. practice specializing in family practice Mt. Shasta, Calif., 1963-69; dir. family practice residency program Community Hosp. Sonoma County, Santa Rosa, 1969-71; assoc. prof. family practice, chmn. div. family practice U. Utah, 1971-72; prof., vice chmn. dept. family practice U. Calif., Davis, 1972-77; prof., chmn. dept. family medicine U. Wash., 1977-90, prof. family medicine, 1990-93; prof. family medicine emeritus, 1993—. Author: The Modern Family Doctor and Changing Medical Practice, 1971, Family Practice: Foundation of Changing Health Care, 1980, 2d edit., 1985; editor: Content of Family Practice, 1976, Family Practice in the Medical School, 1977, Research in Family Practice, 1978, Preventive Medicine in Family Practice, 1979, Profile of the Residency Trained Family Physician in the U.S. 1970-79, Funding of Patient Care, Education and Research in Family Practice, 1981, The Content of Family Practice: Current Status and Future Trends, 1982, Archives of Family Practice, 1980, 81, 82; founding editor Jour. Family Practice, 1973-90; editor Jour. Am. Bd. Family Practice, 1990—; co-editor: Behavioral Science in Family Practice, 1980, Evidence-Based Clinical Practice: Concepts and Approaches, 1999; editor: Family Practice: An International Perspective in Developed Countries, 1983. Served to lt. (j.g.) USN, 1952-55, PTO. Recipient Gold-headed Cane award U. Calif. Sch. Medicine, 1960, Alumnus of Yr., 1998. Mem. Am. Acad. Family Physicians, Soc. Tchrs. Family Medicine, Inst. Medicine of Nat. Acad. Scis. Unitarian. Home: 4909C Hannah Rd Friday Harbor WA 98250-9422 Office: Univ Wash Sch Medicine Dept Family Medicine PO Box 354696 Seattle WA 98195-4795

GEZURIAN, DOROTHY ELLEN, accounting executive; b. N.Y.C., May 7, 1956; d. John and Surpug Susan (Sarkisian) G. BBA in Acctg., Econs. summa cum laude, CUNY, 1976. Sr. auditor Ernst & Ernst, N.Y.C., 1977-79; spl. asst. to v.p. fin. Olivetti Corp., N.Y.C., 1977-79; mgr. corp., bus. planning Olivetti Corp., Tarrytown, N.Y., 1979-82; treas., CFO The Ctr. for Humanities, Inc., Mt. Kisco, N.Y., 1982-85; contr., CFO 235 Main St. Assocs., affiliated cos., White Plains, N.Y., 1985-87; v.p. fin., CFO Mid-Atlantic Med. Svcs., Ft. Lee, N.J., 1987-90; contr. Med. Edn. Programs Ltd., Wilton Conn., Conn., 1991-93; v.p. fin., CFO Med. Edn. Programs, Ltd., Wilton, Conn., 1994—. Recipient N.Y. Soc. of CPA's award, 1976. Mem. Nat. Assn. Female Execs. Republican. Home: 10 Clearview Ave Danbury CT 06811-3333

GFELLER, DONNA KVINGE, clinical psychologist; b. Chgo., Jan. 15, 1959; d. Milton Melvin and Doris Ann (Chapman) Kvinge; m. Jeffrey Donald Gfeller, Aug. 2, 1986. BS in Biol. Scis., Ill. State U., 1980, MS in Clin. Psychology, 1984; PhD in Clin. Psychology, Ohio U., 1987. Lic. psychologist. Staff psychologist Cardinal Glennon Children's Hosp., St. Louis, 1986-87, sr. psychologist, 1988-89, dir. dept. psychology, 1990—. Mem. APA (divsn. clin. psychology, clin. child psychology), Soc. Pediatric Psychology, World Wildlife Fund. Avocations: travel, horseback riding. Office: Cardinal Glennon Children's Hosp 1465 S Grand Blvd Saint Louis MO 63104-1003

GHALI, ANWAR YOUSSEF, psychiatrist, educator; b. Cairo, May 30, 1944; came to U.S., 1974, naturalized, 1980; s. Youssef and Insaf Wahba (Soliman) G.; m. Violette Fouad Saleh, May 23, 1968; 1 child, Susie. MD, Cairo U., 1966, DPM, 1970, DM, 1971. Diplomate Am. Bd. Psychiatry and Neurology; cert. adminstrv. psychiatry. Registrar in psychiatry Woodilee Hosp., Glasgow, Scotland, 1973-74; resident in psychiatry N.J. Med. Sch., Newark, 1974-77, instr., 1977-78, clin. asst. prof., 1978-79, asst. prof., 1979-83, clin. assoc. prof., 1983—; chief Outpatient Dept.-Community Mental Health Ctr., N.J. Med. Sch., Newark, 1978-86; dir. Emergency Psychiat. Svcs. Univ. Hosp., U. Medicine and Dentistry of N.J., Newark, 1986-87; med. dir. Profl. Counsel Ctr., Westfield, N.J., 1984-87; med. chief ambulatory psychiat. svcs. Elizabeth (N.J.) Gen. Hosp., 1987-89; dir. psychiat. tng. VA Med. Ctr., East Orange, N.J., 1989—, asst. chief psychiatry, 1990-91, assoc. chief psychiatry, 1991—. Contbr. articles to profl. jours. Recipient Exceptional Merit award Coll. Medicine & Dentistry, Newark, 1981. Mem. AMA, Christian Med. Soc., Am. Psychiat. Assn., N.J. Psychiat. Assn., N.Y. Acad. Scis. Republican. Presbyterian. Home: 22 Benvenue Ave West Orange NJ 07052-3202

GHALY, EVONE SHEHATA, pharmaceutics and industrial pharmacy educator; b. Cairo; d. Shehata Ghaly Shenouda and Amalia Elias Tadros; m. Nagdy Roshdy Mehany; children: Maichel Nagdy Roshdy, Mary Nagdy Roshdy. B in Pharm. Scis., Assiut U., Egypt, 1970; M in Pharm. Sci., Cairo U., 1979, PhD of Pharmaceutics, 1984; postdoctoral fellow, Phila. Coll. Pharm., 1986-88. Specialist and pharmacist in R&D Arab Drug Co., Cairo, 1970-75, sr. pharmacist in R&D, mgr. rsch. devel., 1975-86; assoc. rschr. Phila. Coll. Pharm., 1988-89; vis. prof., asst. prof. Sch. Pharmacy U. P.R., San Juan, 1989-92, assoc. prof., 1992-97, prof., 1997—; cons. Smith Kline & Beecham, Inc., P.R., 1990—, Eli Lilly found., P.R., 1993—, Merck Sharp and Dohme Inc., P.R., 1994; instr., lectr. FDA, 1991, Warmer Lambert Inc., P.R., 1993-94, Ciba Geigy Inc., P.R., 1995. Contbr. articles to profl. jours. Grantee Colorcon Pharm. Inc., 1993-94, Baker Norton Pharm. Inc., 1993, INDUNIV Rsch. Ctr., 1990-92, 92-93, IBM, NIH-BRSG, 1991-92, Knoll AG Co., 1983, others. Mem. AAAS, Fed. Internat. Pharmaceutics, Am. Assn. Pharm. Scientists, Am. Pharm. Assn., Am. Assn. Coll. Pharmacy, Controlled Release and Bioactive Material, Sigma Xi, Rho Chi. Avocations: chess, piano, photography, sports, travel. Home: Condominio Puerta Sol 2000 San Juan PR 00926 Office: Univ PR Sch Pharmacy PO Box 5067 San Juan PR 00936-5067

GHANDHI, SORAB KHUSHRO, electrical engineering educator; b. Allahabad, India, Jan. 1, 1928; came to U.S., 1947, naturalized, 1960; s. Khushro S. and Dina (Amroliwalla) G.; m. Cecilia M. Ghandhi; children: Khushro, Rustom, Behram. B.Sc. in Elec. and Mech. Engring, Benares (India) Hindu U., 1947; M.S., U. Ill., 1948, Ph.D., 1951. Mem. electronics lab. Gen. Electric Co., 1951-60; mgr. electronic components and functions lab., research div. Philco Corp., 1960-63; prof. elec. engring. Rensselaer Poly. Inst., Troy, N.Y., 1963—, chmn. electrophysics and electronic engring. div., 1968-75, prof. electrophysics, elec., computer and systems engring. dept., 1975-92, active emeritus prof., 1992—; cons. to industry, 1963—. Co-author: (with R.F. Shea editor) Principles of Transistor Circuits, 1953, Transistor Circuit Engineering, 1957, Amplifier Handbook, 1966; author: The Theory and Practice of Microelectronics, 1968, Semiconductor Power Devices, 1977, VLSI Fabrication Principles: Silicon and Gallium Arsenide, 1983, 2d edit., 1994; editor Solid State Electronics, 1993-98. J.N. Tata fellow, 1947-51. Fellow IEEE; mem. Electrochem. Soc., Am. Standards Assn., Sigma Xi, Eta Kappa Nu, Pi Mu Epsilon, Phi Kappa Pi. Address: 2716 Cita Ave Escondido CA 92029-5816

GHANE, KAMRAN, computer engineer. BSEE, Sharif U. Tech., Tehran, 1986; MSEE, UCLA, 1994. Sr. engr. Siemens-Nixdorf, Microsoft Co., Redmond, Wash., 1992; sr. cons. Neda Comm., Bellevue, Wash., 1994-97, Intermec, Everet, Wash., 1997; sr. engr. Mariposa Tech., Petaluma, Calif., 1997—. Contbr. articles to profl. jours. Mem. IEEE, Assn. Computing Machines. Office: Mariposa Tech 1736 Corp Cir Petaluma CA 94954

GHARIB, SUSIE, television newscaster; b. N.Y.C., Nov. 27, 1950; d. Ali and Homa (Razzaghmanesh) G.; m. Fereydoun Nazem, Jan. 20, 1973; children: Alexander, Taraneh. BA magna cum laude, Case Western Res. U., 1972; M in Internat. Affairs, Columbia U., 1974. Reporter Cleve. Plain Dealer, 1972-73; assoc. editor Fortune Mag., N.Y.C., 1974-83; anchor, reporter Bus. Times/ESPN, N.Y.C., 1983-85; bus. reporter ABC News, N.Y.C., 1986-87; anchor Fin. News Network, N.Y.C., 1989-90, CNBC Network, Ft. Lee, N.J., 1993-98, Nightly Bus. Report, N.Y.C., 1998—; moderator/host Xerox Corp., Stanford, Conn., 1989-95, KPMG Peat Marwick, N.Y.C., 1992-95; cons. Adam Smith's Money World/PBS, N.Y.C., 1987. Bd. dirs. First Fortis, Inc., 1991—, Ice Theatre of N.Y., 1988-90. Mem. N.Y. Fin. Writers Assn., Overseas Press Club, Phi Beta Kappa, Sigma Delta Chi. Democrat. Avocations: figure skating, tennis. Home: 44 E 73rd St New York NY 10021-4173

GHAUSI, MOHAMMED SHUAIB, electrical engineering educator, university dean; b. Kabul, Afghanistan, Feb. 16, 1930; came to U.S., 1951, naturalized, 1963; s. Mohammed Omar and Homaira G.; m. Marilyn Buchwold, June 12, 1961; children: Nadjya, Simine. B.S. summa cum laude, U. Calif., Berkeley, 1956, M.S., 1957, Ph.D., 1960. Prof. elec. engring. NYU, 1960-72; head elec. scis. sect. NSF, Washington, 1972-74; prof., chmn. elec. engring. dept. Wayne State U., Detroit, 1974-77; John F. Dodge prof. Oakland U., Rochester, Mich., 1978-83; dean Sch. Engring. and Computer Sci., Oakland U., 1978-83; dean Coll. Engring., U. Calif., Davis, 1983-96, interim vice chancellor rsch., vice provost, dean grad., 1996-97; mem. adv. panel NSF, 1989. Author: Principles and Design of Linear Active Circuits, 1965, Introduction to Distributed-Parameter Networks, 1968, Electronic Circuits, 1971, Modern Filter Design: Active RC and Switched Capacitor, 1981, Electronic Devices and Circuits: Discrete and Integrated, 1985, Design of Analog Filters, 1990, also numerous articles.; cons. editor Van Nostrand Rinehold Pub. Co., 1968-71. Mem. disting. alumni rev. panel Elec. Engring. and Computer Sci. programs U. Calif., Berkeley, 1973; mem. external bd. visitors U. Pa., 1974. Recipient Outstanding Alumnus award in Elec. Engring. and Computer Sci., U. Calif., 1998. Fellow IEEE (chmn. edn. medal com. 1990-92, Centennial medal, Alexander von Humboldt prize, circuits and systems soc. edn. award); mem. Circuits and System Soc. (v.p. 1970-72, pres. 1976), N.Y. Acad. Scis., Engring. Soc. Detroit, Sigma Xi, Phi Beta Kappa, Tau Beta Pi, Eta Kappa Nu. Office: Office of Dean U Calif Coll Engring Davis CA 95616

GHEBREHIWET, BERHANE, immunologist, educator; b. Asmara, Eritrea, Sept. 28, 1946. D.V.M., Sch. Vet. Medicine, Warsaw, Poland, 1971; MVSc, Ecole Nationale Vétérinaire D'Alfort, France, 1973; DSc, U. Paris VII, 1974. Rsch. assoc. dept. molecular immunology Scripps Clinic and Rsch. Found., La Jolla, Calif., 1974-79; asst. prof. medicine SUNY, Stony Brook, 1979-85, asst. prof. pathology, 1983-85, assoc. prof. medicine and pathology, 1985-92, prof. medicine and pathology, 1992—; vis. scientist Green Coll., U. Oxford, 1991-92, 95; mem. immunology, virology, pathology study sect. NIH, 1992-96. Contbr. articles to profl. jours. Fogarty Internat. sr. fellow MRC immunochemistry unit U. Oxford, Eng., 1991-92, Burroughs Wellcome Rsch. fellow, 1995. Mem. Am. Assn. Immunology, Am. Fedn. Clin. Rsch., N.Y. Acad. Sci., Am. Chem. Soc., Am. Assn. Vet. Immunology, Clin. Immunology Soc., Soc. Leukocyte Biology, The Planetary Soc., Sigma Xi. Coptic Orthodox. Office: SUNY Stony Brook HSC T-16 Rm 040 New York NY 11794-8161

GHENT, PEER, management consultant; b. Washington, Sept. 13, 1939; s. Pierre Mowell Ghent and Helen V. (Mork) Dyer; m. Sonya Renate Schmid, Oct. 12, 1962 (div. 1975); children: Carol R. Ghent-Singley, Erika Lynn, Peer Jr., Valerie. BCE, Cornell U., 1961; MBA, Harvard U., 1966. Registered civil engr. and land surveyor, La. Sr. ops. research analyst Office Sec. Def., Washington, 1966-69; pres. Plaskolite Inc., Columbus, Ohio, 1969-71; cons. U.S. Price Commn., Washington, 1971-72; dir. corp. devel. Buckeye Internat., Columbus, 1972-74; pres. Peterson Baby Products, North Hollywood, Calif., 1974-78; v.p., chief fin. officer Oakleaf Corp., Chatsworth, Calif., 1980-81; v.p. CMB Investment Counselors, Los Angeles, 1983-85, Stars to Go Inc., Los Angeles, 1986-88; prin. Peer Ghent & Assocs., Van Nuys, Calif., 1989—; sr. cons. Mgmt. Action Programs, Inc., Sherman Oaks, Calif., 1993-96; lectr. Grad. Sch. Mgmt. UCLA, 1979-88. Author: (with others) Computer Graphics: A Revolution in Design, 1966. Served to capt. U.S. Army, 1961-63. Democrat. Episcopalian. Avocations: private aviation, photography. Home: 13422 Oxnard St Valley Glen CA 91401-4041 Office: 13422 Oxnard St Valley Glen CA 91401-4041

GHERLEIN, GERALD LEE, lawyer, diversified manufacturing company executive; b. Warren, Ohio, Feb. 16, 1938; s. Jacob A. and Ruth (Matthews) G.; m. Joycelyn Hardin, June 18, 1960; children: David, Christy. Student, Ohio Wesleyan U., 1956-58; B.S. in Bus. Adminstrn, Ohio State U., 1960; J.D., U. Mich., 1963. Bar: Ohio 1963. Assoc. Taft Stettinius & Hollister, Cin., 1963-66; corp. atty. Eaton Corp., Cleve., 1966-68; European legal counsel Eaton Corp., Zug, Switzerland, 1968-71; asst. sec., asso. counsel Eaton Corp., Cleve., 1971-76, v.p., gen. counsel, 1976-91, exec. v.p., gen. counsel, 1991—. Pres. Citizens League Greater Cleve., 1979-81; trustee Cleve. Ballet, 1983-88, vice chmn. 1985-87; trustee WVIZ Pub. Television, 1990—, Armada Funds, 1997—. Mem. ABA, Greater Cleve. Bar Assn. (pres. 1989, trustee), Ohio Bar Assn., Am. Soc. Corp. Secs. (pres. Ohio regional group 1977), Pepper Pike Country Club. Clubs: Union, Tavern, Mayfield Country. Home: 3679 Greenwood Dr Cleveland OH 44124-5502 Office: Eaton Corp 1111 Superior Ave E Cleveland OH 44114-2584

GHERTY, JOHN E., food products and agricultural products company executive; b. 1944; married. BBA, U. Wis., 1965, JD, 1968, MA, 1970. Lawyer corp. law dept. Land O' Lakes Inc., Arden Hills, Minn., 1970-79, asst. to pres., 1979-81, group v.p., 1981-89, pres., CEO, 1989—; bd. dirs. Recovery Engring., Mpls.; bd. dirs., mem. exec. com. CF Industries, Long Grove, Ill. Bd. dirs. Grad. Inst. Coop. Leadership. Mem. Nat. Coun. Farmer Coops. (bd. dirs.), Minn. Bus. Partnership (bd. dirs.), Nat. 4-H Found. (bd. dirs.). Office: Land O'Lakes PO Box 64101 Saint Paul MN 55164-0101 Office: 4001 Lexington Ave N Saint Paul MN 55126-2934

GHETTI, BERNARDINO FRANCESCO, neuropathologist, neurobiology researcher; b. Pisa, Italy, Mar. 28, 1941; s. Getulio and Iris (Mugnetti) G.; m. Caterina Genovese, Oct. 8, 1966; children—Chiara, Simone. M.D. cum laude, U. Pisa, 1966, specialist in mental and nervous diseases, 1969. Lic. physician, Italy; cert. Edn. Council for Fgn. Med. Grads.; diplomate Am. Bd. Pathology. Postdoctoral fellow U. Pisa, 1966-70; research fellow in neuropathology Albert Einstein Coll. Medicine, Bronx, N.Y., 1970-73, resident, clin. fellow in pathology, 1973-75, resident in neuropathology, 1975-76; asst. prof. pathology Ind. U., Indpls., 1976-77, asst. prof. pathology and psychiatry, 1977-78, assoc. prof. pathology and psychiatry, 1978-83, prof. pathology, psychiatry, assoc. dir. program in med. neurobiology, 1983—, assoc. dir. div. neuropathology, 1989-93, prof. pathology, psychiatry, med. and molecular genetics, 1991-97, dir. div. neuropathology, 1993—, Disting. prof. pathology and lab. medicine, psychiatry, med. and molecular genetics, neurology, 1997—; mem. Nat. Inst. Neurol. Disorders and Stroke rev. com. NIH, 1985-89; mem. NIH Reviewers Res., 1989-93. Contbr. articles and abstracts to profl. jours. Mem. Internat. Soc. Neuropathology, Am. Assn. Neuropathologists (pres. 1996-97), Soc. Neurosci., Assn. Research in Nervous and Mental Diseases, Internat. Brain Research Orgn., Am. Soc. Cell Biology, Italian Soc. Psychiatry, Italian Soc. Neurology, Sigma Xi. Roman Catholic. Home: 1124 Frederick Dr S Indianapolis IN 46260-3421 Office: Ind U 635 Barnhill Dr Rm 138 Indianapolis IN 46202-5126

GHEZ, ANDREA MIA, astronomy and physics educator; b. N.Y.C., June 16, 1965; d. Gilbert and Susanne (Gayton) G.; m. Tom La Tourette, May 1, 1993. BS, MIT, 1987; MS, Calif. Inst. Tech., 1989, PhD, 1993. Hubble postdoctoral fellow U. Ariz., Tucson, 1992-93; vis. rsch. scholar Inst. Astronomy, Cambridge, England, 1994; asst. prof. physics and astronomy UCLA, 1994-97, assoc. prof. physics and astronomy, 1997—. Recipient Young Investigator award NSF, 1994, Fullam Dudley award, 1995; fellow Pacific Telesis, 1991, Sloan fellow, 1996, Packard fellow, 1996, Pierce prize, 1998, Maria Goeppert-Meyer award, Am. Phys. Soc., 1999. Mem. Am. Astron. Soc., AAUW (Anne Jump Cannon award 1994), Phi Beta Kappa. Achievements include discovery of formation of young low mass stars in multiple star systems, production of the first diffraction-limited image with the keck 10-m telescope (the largest telescope in the world), and measurement of stellar motions which indicate the presence of a supermassive black hole at the center of our own galaxy. Home: 8641 Kirkwood Dr Los Angeles CA 90046 Office: UCLA Dept Astronomy 405 Hilgard Ave Los Angeles CA 90095-9000

GHIARDI, JAMES DOMENIC, lawyer, educator; b. Gwinn, Mich., Nov. 10, 1918; s. John B. and Margaret M. (Trosello) G.; m. Phyllis A. Lindmeier, Sept. 5, 1945; children—Catherine, Jeanne, Mary. PhB, Marquette U., 1940, LLB, 1942, JD, 1968. Bar: Wis. bar 1942. Prof. law Marquette U. Law Sch., Milw., 1946-89; prof. law emeritus Marquette U. Law Sch., 1990—; research dir. Def. Research Inst., Milw., 1962-72; of counsel firm Kluwin, Dunphy, Hankin & McNulty, Milw., 1972-87. Author: Personal Injury Damages, Wisconsin, 1964, Punitive Damages, Vol. I, 1981, Vol. II, 1985; contbr. articles to profl. jours. Served to capt. Med. Adminstrv. Br. U.S. Army, 1942-45. Recipient award for teaching excellence Marquette U. Faculty, 1971, Edward A. Uhrig Found., 1971, Alumni of Yr. award Marquette U. Law Sch., 1971, Charles L. Goldberg award for outstanding pub. svc. Wis. Law Found., 1986, Charles C. Pinckney award for legal scholarship and svc. to the legal profession N.Y. Def. Bar Assn., 1986. Fellow Am. Bar Found.; mem. ABA (mom. ho. of dels. 1967-80, Disting. Prof. Torts and Ins. Law award Torts and Ins. Practice sect. 1989), Milw. Bar Assn. (Lifetime Achievement award 1993), State Bar Wis. (gov., mem. exec. com. 1962-72, pres. 1970-71), Am. Law Ins., Wis. Bar Found., Am. Legion. Office: Sensenbrenner Hill Marquette U Law Sch PO Box 1881 Milwaukee WI 53201-1881

GHIGLIA, OSCAR ALBERTO, classical guitarist; b. Livorno, Italy, Aug. 13, 1938; s. Paulo and Giuliana (Folena) G.; m. A-M Boulet d'Hauteserre, Dec. 1, 1966 (div. Apr. 1991); 1 child, Thalia Emmanuelle. Grad. with honors, Conservatory Santa Cecilia, Rome, 1962. Instr. Aspen (Colo.) Music Festival, summers 1969-86; instr. summers Academia Musicale Chigiana, Siena, Italy, 1976—, Banff (Can.) Music Festival, 1978-87; artist-in-residence Hartt Sch. Music, 1981-87, Basel Music Acad., 1983—. European debut: Two World Festival, Spoleto, Italy, 1961; concert tours in N.Am., 1966—; performer with: Juilliard String Quartet, Tokyo String Quartet, Emerson Quartet, Cleve. Quartet, Victoria de Los Angeles, Jean-Pierre Rampal; records includeL Oscar Ghiglia Plays Scarlatti and Other Baroque Masters; author: (transcription) Bach's 3d Lute Suite, 1976, Bach's Suite in E Major, 1979. Recipient grant to study with Segovia, 1958-63, with Jacques Chailley Paris, 1963-64; unanimous winner Internat. guitar competition ORTF Paris, 1963. Home: Helfenberg Strasse 14, CH 4059 Basel Switzerland Office: c/o Anne Marie Ghiglia 3705 N Chadam Ln Apt 2A Muncie IN 47304-5298

GHIL, MICHAEL, atmospheric scientist, geophysicist; b. Budapest, Hungary, June 10, 1944; s. Louis and Ilona V. (Dobo) Cernat; m. Michèle J. Denizot, July 8, 1982; children: Emmanuel A., Mirella J. BSc cum laude, Technion-Israel Inst. Tech., Haifa, Israel, 1966, MSc in Mech. Engring., 1971; MS, NYU, 1973, PhD in Math., 1975. Rsch. asst. to instr. Technion-Israel Inst. Tech., Haifa, 1966-71; rsch. assoc. NASA Goddard Inst. Space Studies, N.Y.C., 1975-76; rsch. asst. prof. math. Courant Inst. Math. Scis., N.Y.C., 1976-79, rsch. assoc. prof. atmos. sci., 1979-82, rsch. prof., 1982-86; prof. atmos. sci. and geophysics UCLA, 1985—; chmn. dept. atmospheric scis., UCLA, 1988-92; dir. Climate Dynamics Ctr., UCLA, 1986-92, Inst. Geophys. Planet Phys. UCLA, 1992—; disting. vis. sci. Jet Propulsion Lab, Calif. Inst. Tech./NASA, Pasadena, Calif., 1988—; Condorcet chair Ecole Normale Supérieure, Paris, 1995; Elf-Aquitaine/CNRS chair Acad. Scis., Paris, 1996, Collège de France, Paris, 1997. Author: Topics in GFD: Atmospheric Dynamics, Dynamo Theory and Climate Dynamics, 1987; editor: Turbulence and Predictability in Geophysical Fluid Dynamics and Climate Dynamics, 1985, Dynamic Meteorology: Data Assimilation Methods, 1981, Natural Climate Variability on Decade-to-Century Time Scales, 1995, Data Assimilation in Meteorology and Oceanography: Theory and Practice, 1997. Mem. adv. bd. Calif. Space Inst., San Diego, 1986-90; chmn. sci. adv. coun. Climate Sys. Modeling Program, Boulder, Colo., 1988-00; bd. dirs. New Sun Found. Geneva, 1994—, bd. govs. Weizmann Inst. Sci. Rehovot, Israel, 1995—. Fellow Am. Meteorol. Soc. (profl. com. 1989-92), Am. Geophys. Union, mem. Nat. Rsch. Coun. (climate rsch. com. 1989-98), Soc. for Indsl. and Applied Math., Acad. Europaea (fgn.), Sigma Xi. Democrat. Jewish. Avocations: hiking, climbing, squash, skiing, swimming, arts, literature, music, languages. Office: UCLA Inst Geophys Planet Phys 405 Hilgard Ave Los Angeles CA 90095-9000

GHILARDUCCI, TERESA, economist, educator; b. Roseville, Calif., July 22, 1957; d. Harry Enrico and Marion (Phillips) G.; m. William Andrew O'Rourke, July 9, 1986; 1 child, Joseph Ghilarducci O'Rourke. BA, U. Calif., Berkeley, 1978, PhD, 1984. Rsch. asst. Inst. Indsl. Rels., Berkeley, 1982-84; prof. econs. U. Notre Dame, Ind., 1984—; adv. bd. Pension Benefit Guaranty Corp., Washington, 1995—; cons. Pension Edn. Rsch. and Tech. Asst. Project, Rome, 1996—. Author: Labor's Capital: The Economics and Politics of Private Pensions, 1992, Portable Pensions for Casual Labor Markets, 1995. Trustee Ind. Pub. Employees Retirement Fund, Indpls., 1997—. Mem. Am. Econs. Assn. Democrat. Roman Catholic. Avocations: reading, running, biking. Office: Dept Econs U Notre Dame Notre Dame IN 46556

GHISELIN, BREWSTER, author, English language educator emeritus; b. Webster Groves, Mo., June 13, 1903; s. Horace and Eleanor (Weeks) G.; m. Olive F. Franks, June 7, 1929; children: Jon Brewster, Michael Tenant. A.B., UCLA, 1927; M.A., U. Calif.-Berkeley, 1928, student, 1931-33; student, Oxford U., Eng., 1928-29. Asst. in English U. Calif., Berkeley, 1931-33; instr. English U. Utah, 1929-31, 34-38, lectr., 1938-39, asst. prof., 1939-46, assoc. prof., 1946-50, prof., 1950-71, prof. emeritus, 1971, Distinguished Research prof., 1967-68; dir. Writers' Conf., 1947-66; poetry editor Rocky Mt. Rev., 1937-46; assoc. editor Western Rev., 1946-49; lectr. creativity, cons. Inst. Personality Assessment and Research, U. Calif., Berkeley, 1957-58; editorial adv. bd. Concerning Poetry, 1968—. Author: Against the Circle, 1946, The Creative Process, 1952, new paperback edit., 1985, 95, The Nets, 1955, Writing, 1959, Country of the Minotaur, 1970, (with others) The Form Discovered: Essays on the Achievement of Andrew Lytle, 1973, Light, 1978, Windrose: Poems, 1929-1979, 1980, (with others) Contemporary Authors, 1989; (poems) Flame, 1991. Bd. advisors Silver Mountain Found. Ford Found. fellow, 1952-53; recipient award Nat. Inst. Arts and Letters, 1970; Blumenthal-Leviton-Blonder prize Poetry mag., 1973; Levinson prize, 1978; William Carlos Williams award Poetry Soc. Am., 1981; Gov.'s award for arts Utah Arts Council, 1982; LHD hc, U of Utah, 1994. Mem. MLA, Utah Acad. Scis., Arts and Letters (Charles Redd award), Phi Beta Kappa, Phi Kappa Phi. Home (winter): 1115 Jefferson Way Laguna Beach CA 92651-3022 also (summer): 1747 Princeton Ave Salt Lake City UT 84108-1810 *To be human is to be a user of the basic resources of society, those* *modes and forms of vision and action that by determining the character and quality of men's experience shape everything men do and are.*

GHORAYEB, FAY ELIZABETH, nurse educator, secondary education educator; b. Sydney, Australia, 1936; d. Claude Ernest and Doris Venezia (Shannon) Seabrook; m. Ibrahim Anis Ghorayeb, July 20; children: Anthony, Mark. RN, Royal Prince Alfred Hosp., Sydney, 1959; Postgrad. Diploma, St. Luke's Hosp., N.Y.C., 1961; BA, Rutgers U., 1992. Jr. sister and sr. sister Royal Prince Alfred Hosp., Sydney, 1959-60; vis. nurse Vis. Nurse Assn., N.Y.C., 1960-61; pub. health instr. Beirut Coll. for Women, Lebanon, 1967-71, instr. sport and pub. health, 1974-75; coord. Women's Wellness Ctr. U. Medicine and Dentistry N.J., New Brunswick, 1991-98. Mem. Theatre Guild, Naples Comty. Hosp. Aux. Mem. Douglass Alumni Club, PEO, Naples Women's Club (bd. dirs.), Internat. Club. Mem. Ch. England. Avocations: travel, walking, swimming, reading, family. Home: 137 2d Ave N Naples FL 34102

GHOSH, BHASKAR KUMAR, statistics educator, researcher; b. Dibrugarh, India, Feb. 10, 1936; came to U.S., 1961; s. Saroj Kumar and Usha Rani (Bose) G.; m. Hedwig Graf, 1960; children: Monica, Anita, Rebecca. BSc, Calcutta U., 1955; PhD, London U., 1959. Statistician Atomic Power Constrn., London, 1959-60; asst. prof. U. London, 1960-61; asst. prof. Lehigh U., Bethlehem, Pa., 1961-63, assoc. prof., 1963-68, prof., 1968—; vis. prof. MIT, Cambridge, Mass., 1968, Va. Tech., Blacksburg, 1978-80, U. Munster, Germany, 1986-87. Author: Sequential Tests of Statistical Hypotheses, 1970; editor: Handbook of Sequential Analysis, 1991; editor: Sequential Analysis, 1982-95. Recipient U.S. Sr. Rsch. Scientist award Alexander von Humboldt Found., 1986-87, 92. Fellow Royal Statis. Soc., Inst. Math. Statistics. Home: 1440 E University Ave Bethlehem PA 18015-4718 Office: Lehigh U Dept Math 14 E Packer Ave Bethlehem PA 18015-3175

GHOSH, SOUMITRA KUMAR, electrical engineer; b. Calcutta, Bengal, India, Aug. 15, 1959; came to U.S., 1991; s. Kali P. and Suparna (Mitra) G.; m. Sumona Dutt, June 30, 1989; 1 child, Semanti. B in Engring. with hons., Jadavpur U., Calcutta, 1981; M in Engring., So. Ill.U., Edwardsville, 1993. Registered profl. engr., Ill. Asst. engr. Brown Boveri Co., Baroda, India, 1981-83, Engrs. India Ltd., New Delhi, 1983-85; sr. engr. Al Jizzi Electricals, Muscat, Oman, 1985-91, Magnum Techs., Belleville, Ill., 1993-94; sys. engr. Sverdrup Facilities, St. Louis, Mo., 1994—; standard advisor Inst. Soc. Am., Raleigh, N.C., 1993—; examiner Nat. Coun., Clemson, S.C., 1996—. Contbr. articles to IEEE Jour., IEEE Mag. Nat. Merit scholar Govt. India, 1976. Mem. IEEE. Avocations: journalism, soccer, teaching, internet. Home: 219-4A Enchanted Ct Manchester MO 63021 Office: Sverdrup Facilities 400 S 4th St Saint Louis MO 63102-1807

GHOSHAL, NANI GOPAL, veterinary anatomist, educator; b. Dacca, India, Dec. 1, 1934; came to U.S., 1963; s. Priya Kanta and Kiron Bala (Thakurata) G.; m. Chhanda Banerjee, Jan. 24, 1971; 1 child, Nupur. G.V.Sc., B.V.C., India, 1955; DTVM, U. Edinburgh, 1961; Dr. med. vet., Tieraertzliche Hochschule Hannover, Fed. Republic Germany, 1962; PhD, Iowa State U., 1966. Vet. asst. surgeon West Bengal State Govt., India, 1955-56; instr. Bengal Vet. Coll., U. Calcutta, 1955-56; research asst. M.P. Govt. Coll. Vet. Sci. and Animal Husbandry, Mhow, India, 1956-59; research officer ICAR, India, 1963; instr. Iowa State U., Ames, 1963-66, asst. prof., 1967-70, assoc. prof., 1970-74, prof. vet. gross anatomy, 1974—; chmn. Internat. Vet. Medicine Com., 1967-79; cons. Morocco-Minn. project U. Minn. Internat. Agrl. Programs, AID, 1983-88; adj. prof. Inst. Agronomique et Veterinaire, Hassan II, Rabat, Morocco, 1984-88. Co-author, editor: Getty's Anatomy of Domestic Animals, 5th edit., 1975; author: (with Tankred Koch, Peter Popesko) Venous Drainage of Domestic Animals, 1981; contbr. chpts. to books, articles to profl. jours. Recipient German Acad. Exchange Service award Govt. Fed. Republic of Germany, Bonn, 1961-62, Norden Disting. Tchr. award, 1978, Dr. William O. Reece award for outstanding advising Coll. of Vet. Medicine, 1997; various scholarships and grants. Fellow Royal Zool. Soc. Scotland (life); mem. World Assn. Vet. Anatomists, Am. Assn. Vet. Anatomists, AAAS, Am. Assn. Anatomists, Pan Am. Assn. Anatomy, N.Y. Acad. Scis., Iowa Vet. Med. Assn., Sigma Xi, Phi Zeta, Gamma Sigma Delta, Phi Kappa Phi. Home: 1310 Glendale Ave Ames IA 50010-5526 Office: Iowa State U Coll Vet Medicine 2086 Dept Biomed Scis Ames IA 50011

GHRIST, JOHN RUSSELL, computer technician; b. Hammond, Ind., Feb. 6, 1949; s. Glenn H. and Marjorie (Fancher) G.; divorced; children: Timothy, Thomas, Peter, James, Bonnie. BS, Ind. U., 1997. Lic. radiotelephone operator, amateur radio. Religious music host WYCA, Hammond, Ind., 1967-71; news reporter WJOB, Hammond, 1971-73; music show host WFLM, Crown Point, Ind., 1979-85, WTAS, Beecher, Ill., 1982-86; radio traffic reporter WLTH, Gary, Ind., 1985-88, Shadow Traffic Network (WLS/WMAQ), Chgo., 1985-87; computer technician Ill. Dept. Transp., Schaumburg, 1985-97; music show host WFXW, Geneva, Ill., 1985-89; program host WEPS-FM Elgin H.S., Ill., 1997; Host of "Elgin Hour", WEPS-FM, 1997, Jazz Casual. Author: (books) Valley Voices, 1997, Jct. 20: The Story of Udina, 1996, Radioville, The Town That Never Was, 1996, Billy Sunday - The Dundee Prophet, 1995, Plato Center Memories, 1998. Community activist, Elgin, 1996—. Recipient award "Ill. Reaches Out", State of Ill., Springfield, 1994, Ind. Bell Pioneers Com. Svc. award Bell Telephone Co., Crown Point, 1987, Com. Svc. award USDA Soil Conservation, Crown Point, 1979, others; inducted into Elgin Hist. Soc. Heritage Hall of Fame, 1997, Elgin Sch. Cmty. Svc. award, 1998, Mayor's Heritage Commn. award, 1998. Mem. Valley AM Radio Assn., Udina Hist. Soc. Nazarene. Avocations: softball player, collector of old records, astronomer, historian, writer. Office: Ill Dept Transp 201 Center Ct Schaumburg IL 60196-3169

GHYMN, ESTHER MIKYUNG, English educator, writer; b. Seoul; d. Yong Shik and Kyung hee (Park) Kim; m. Kyung-Il Ed Ghymn; children: Jennifer, Eugene. MA, U. Hawaii; MAT, U. Pitts.; PhD, U. Nev., Reno, 1990. Lectr. English, U. Nev., Reno, 1993—, ESL coord., 1996—, mem. ethnic studies bd., 1998—. Author: The Shapes and Styles of Asian American Prose Fiction, 1990, Images of Asian American Women Writers, 1995; editor APANN News. Bd. dirs. Asian Americans N. Nev., 1992-95, Multicultural Office, Truckee Meadows C.C., Reno, 1994-96, mem. steering com. Access to Success, 1996; mem. affirmative action adv. bd. U. Nev., Reno, 1998, ethnic studies bd., 1997—, women's studies bd., 1998—; series editor Peter Lang Pub. Mem. Phi Beta Delta (sec.). Avocations: teaching, writing, reading, travel.

GIACALONE, FRANK THOMAS, energy and environmental company executive; b. Alexandria, Va., Aug. 4, 1951; s. Benedict and Frances Lillian (Scibilia) G.; m. Barbara A. Dye, July 21, 1989. BSMechE, Widener U., 1973, postgrad., 1977-85. Registered profl. engr., N.Y. Installation engr. GE Internat. Installations, Schenectady, N.Y., 1973-75; application engr. Gen. Electric, Schenectady, N.Y., 1977-79, sr. sales specialist, 1979-81, mgr. mktg., 1981-83, project devel. mgr., 1983-86; project engr. Potomac Electric Power Co., Washington, 1975-77; mgr. cogeneration market devel. Tenneco Gas Mktg. Co., Houston, 1986-88; dir. bus. devel. Falcon Seaboard Oil Co., Houston, 1988-89, Hadson Devel. Corp., Fairfax, Va., 1989-90; sr. v.p. JWP Energy and Environ. Purchase, N.Y., 1990-92; dir. bus. devel. CRSS Capital, Inc., Houston, 1992-95; sr. v.p. CHI Power, Inc., Houston, 1995-96; sr. v.p., chief devel. officer CHI Energy, Inc., Houston, 1996-99; ptnr. Syntec Partnership, LLC, 1999—. Co-author: Cogeneration and Natural Gas, 1989; contbr. articles to profl. jours. Mem. Rep. Nat. Com. Pres. Club, Washington, 1978—, Niskayuna (N.Y.) Zoning Bd., 1985; chmn. Town Resources Adv. Com., Niskayuna, 1979; head coach Pop Warner Football-Jr. Midgets, Niskayuna, 1980. Mem. ASME, NRA, Tex. Rifle Assn., Gulf Coast Cogeneration Assn. Avocations: bicycling, trophy sport hunting, gun collecting, antique car restoration. E-mail: bjack711@aol.com. Home: 6711 Apple Valley Ln Houston TX 77069-2444

GIACCO, ALEXANDER FORTUNATUS, chemical industry executive; b. San Giovanni di Gerace, Italy, Aug. 24, 1919; naturalized in 1927; s. Salvatore J. and Maria Concetta (de Maria) G.; m. Edith Brown, Feb. 16, 1946; children: Alexander Fortunatus Jr., Richard John, Mary P. Giacco Walsh, Elizabeth B. Giacco Brown, Marissa A. Giacco Rath. BSChemE, Va. Poly. Inst., 1942; postgrad. in mgmt., Harvard Grad. Sch. Bus., 1965. With Hercules Inc., Wilmington, Del., 1942-87, gen. mgr. polymers dept., 1968-73, dir., 1970-87, gen. mgr. operating dept. (Hercules Europe), 1973, v.p. parent co., 1974-76, mem. exec. com., 1974-87, exec. v.p., 1976-77, pres., CEO, chmn. exec. com., 1977-87, chmn. bd. dirs., 1980-87; chmn. bd. dirs. HIMONT Inc., Wilmington, Del., 1983-91, CEO, 1987-91; dep. chmn. Montedison SpA, Milan, 1988-89; mng. dir. Axess Corp., 1991—; bd. dirs. China Trust Bank, N.Y.C., 1988-97, Erbamont, N.V., 1983-91, Feruzzi Finanziaria, Milan, Italy, 1988-91. Trustee, bd. dirs., mem. exec. com. Med. Ctr. of Del., 1975-88; trustee, bd. visitors Va. Poly. Inst. and State U., 1980-87, rector, 1984-87; chmn. bd. dirs. Grand Opera House, Wilmington, 1980-94; exec. com. Pres. Pvt. Sector Survey, Grace Commn., Washington, 1982-86; mem. U.S. Com. on New Initiatives in East-West Cooperation, 1976-86, Adv. Coun. on Japan-U.S. Econ. Rels., 1982-88; dep. chmn. Propulsion Com. for Guided Missiles and JATO, 1960; bd. dirs. Jr. Achievement Internat., 1995—; mem. Jr. Achievement of Del., 1976-84, pres., chmn., 1971-78, hon. chmn., 1979-84; dir. Palm Beach Civic Assn. Decorated commendatore Order of Merit (Italy); recipient Disting. Achievement award Va. Poly. Inst. and State U., 1989, Honor award Comml. Devel. Assn., 1987; named One of Ten Outstanding Chief Exec. Officers Fin. World, 1980, 87, Best Chief Exec. Officer in Chem. Industry Fin. World, 1984, Outstanding Chief Exec. Officer in the Chem. Industry Wall Street Transcript, 1983, 84, 85, 87, Excellence in Mgmt. award Administrv. Mgmt. Soc. (Del. chpt.), 1986, Ann. Indsl. award Nat. Italian Am. Found., 1980 named to Del. Bus. Leaders Hall of Fame by Jr. Achievement of Del. and Hagley Mus. and Libr., 1992. Mem. Nat. Acad. Engring., Am. Assn. Sovereign Mil. Order of Malta, Wilmington Club, Wilmington Country Club, Vicmead Hunt Club, Everglades Club, Palm Beach Civic Assn.(dir.). Office: Axess Corp 100 Interchange Blvd Newark DE 19711-3549

GIACCONI, RICCARDO, astrophysicist, educator; b. Genoa, Italy, Oct. 6, 1931; came to U.S., 1956, naturalized, 1967; s. Antonio and Elsa (Canni) G.; m. Mirella Manaira, Feb. 15, 1957; children: Guia Giacconi Trutter, Anna Lee, Marc A. Ph.D., U. Milan, Italy, 1954; Sc.D. (hon.), U. Chgo., 1983; laurea ad honorem in astronomy, U. Padua, 1984; laurea honoris causa in astronomy, Warsaw U., 1996. Asst. prof. physics U. Milan, 1954-56; research assoc. Ind. U., 1956-58, Princeton U., 1958-59; exec. v.p., dir. Am. Sci. & Engring. Co., Cambridge, Mass., 1959-73; prof. astronomy Harvard U.; also assoc. dir. high energy astrophysics divsn. Center Astrophysics, Smithsonian Astrophys. Obs./Harvard Coll. Obs., Cambridge, 1973-81; dir. Space Telescope Sci. Inst., Balt., 1981-92; prof. astrophysics Johns Hopkins U., 1981-99, rsch. prof., 1999—; prof. astrophysics U. Milan, Germany, 1991-99; dir.-gen. European Soc. Obs., Garching, Germany, 1993-99; pres. Assoc. Univs., Inc., Washington, 1999—; Richtmyer meml. lectr. Am. Assn. Physics Tchrs., 1975; mem. space sci. adv. com. NASA, 1978-79, mem. adv. com. innovation study, 1979—; mem. NASA Astrophysics Council; mem. adv. com. innovation study astronomy adv. com., 1979—; mem. high energy astronomy survey panel Nat. Acad. Scis., 1979-80, mem. Space Sci. Bd., 1980-84, 89—; mem. adv. com. Max-Planck Inst. für Physik und Astrophysik; chmn. bd. dirs. Instituto Guido Donegani, Gruppo Montedison, 1987-89; mem. vis. com. to div. of phys. scis. U. Chgo., U. Padua; chmn. ISC E-1 (galactic and extragalactic astrophysics) Com. on Space Rsch. (COSPAR), 1982-93. Co-editor: X-ray Astronomy, 1974, The X-Ray Universe, 1985; author numerous articles and papers in field; inventor x-ray telescope, discovered x-ray stars. Decorated Targhe d'Oro della Regione Puglia; Fulbright fellow, 1956-58; recipient Röntgen prize astrophysics Physikalish-Medizinische Gesellschaft, Wurzburg, Germany, 1971; Exceptional Sci. Achievement medal NASA, 1971, 80; Disting. Public Service award, 1972; Space Sci. award AIAA, 1976; Elliott Cresson medal Franklin Inst., 1980; Gold medal Royal Astron. Soc., 1982; A. Cressy Morrison award N.Y. Acad. Sci., 1982; Bruce medal; Heinneman award, Wolf Prize in Physics, 1987; Russell lectr. Mem. Am. Astron. Soc. (Helen B. Warner award 1966, chmn. hign energy astrophysics dept. 1976-77, councilor 1979-82, NASA Disting. Pub. Svc. award 1992, Henry Norris Russel lectr. 1981, Darwin lectr. Royal Soc. 1993), Italian Phys. Soc. (Como prize 1967), AAAS, Internat. Astron. Union (nat. Acad. Scis. rep. 1979-82), Nat. Acad. Scis., Am. Acad. Arts and Scis., Md. Acad. Sci. (sci. coun. 1982—), Accademia Nazionale dei Lincei (fgn.), Royal Astron. Soc., Am. Phys. Soc. Club: Cosmos (Washington). Office: Associated Univs Inc 1400 16th St NW # 730 Washington DC 20036

GIACOLETTO, LAWRENCE JOSEPH, electronics engineering educator, researcher, consultant; b. Clinton, Ind., Nov. 14, 1916; s. Pete and Antonia (Savio) G.; m. Maxine Lorraine Dicks, May 31, 1941; 1 child, Carol Giacoletto. BSEE, Rose-Hulman Inst. Tech., 1938; MS in Physics, State U. Iowa, 1939; PhDEE, U. Mich., 1952. Rsch. engr. RCA Labs., Princeton, N.J., 1946-56; rsch. mgr. sci. lab. Ford Motor Co., Dearborn, Mich., 1956-61; prof. elec. engring. Mich. State U., East Lansing, 1961-87, prof. emeritus, 1987—; owner CoRes Inst., Okemos, Mich., 1965—. Author: Differential Amplifiers, 1970; editor: Electronics Designers' Handbook, 1977; patentee in field. Lt. col. USAR, 1941-87. Fellow IEEE (bd. dirs. 1964-65), AAAS (del. 1977-79), University Club (Lansing, Mich.), Sigma Xi. Republican. Roman Catholic. Home: 4465 Wausau Rd Okemos MI 48864-2741 Office: CoRes Inst PO Box 109 Okemos MI 48805-0109

GIACOPONELLO, JOSEPH A., hotel executive. Dir. ops. The Leading Hotels of the World, Ltd., N.Y.C., 1972-74, v.p., 1974-76, pres., CEO, 1976—, also bd. dirs.; chmn. Hotel Representative, Inc., 1998—, exec. com. of consortium, 1998—; bd. dirs. The Algonquin Hotel and Baccarat, Inc., N.Y.C., Westin Hotels and Resorts, Prima Reservations, Inc., Adluxe Advt. Inc., SureCheck, Inc., DataLEAD Comms., Inc. Recipient Personality of Yr. award, 1984. Office: Hotel Representatives Inc 747 Third Ave New York NY 10017-2803

GIAEVER, IVAR, physicist; b. Bergen, Norway, Apr. 5, 1929; came to U.S., 1957, naturalized, 1963; s. John A. and Gudrun (Skaarud) G.; m. Inger Skramstad, Nov. 8, 1952; children: John, Anne Kari, Guri, Trine. Siv. Ing., Norwegian Inst. Tech., Trondheim, 1952; Ph.D., Rensselaer Poly. Inst., 1964. Patent examiner Norwegian Patent Office, Oslo, 1953-54; mech. engr. Can. Gen. Electric Co., Peterborough, Ont., 1954-56; applied mathematician Gen. Electric Co., Schenectady, 1956-58, physicist Research and Devel. Ctr., 1958-88; Inst. prof. Rensselaer Poly. Inst., Troy, N.Y., 1988—; also prof. U. Oslo, 1988—. Served with Norwegian Army, 1952-53. Recipient Nobel Prize for Physics, 1973; Guggenheim fellow, 1970. Fellow Am. Phys. Soc. (Oliver E. Buckley prize 1965); mem. IEEE, Norwegian Profl. Engrs., Nat. Acad. Sci., Nat. Acad. Engring. (V.K. Zworykin award 1974), Am. Acad. Arts and Scis., Norwegian Acad. Sci., Norwegian Acad. Tech. Office: Rensselaer Poly Ins Physics Dept 110 8th St Troy NY 12180-3522

GIAIMO, KATHRYN ANN, performing arts company executive; b. Milw., Jan. 20, 1961; d. Samuel Patrick and Marilyn Eunice G. BA, U. Minn., 1983; MA, NYU, 1989. Adminstrv. dir. Thalia Spanish Theatre, Sunnyside, N.Y., 1989—; steering com. Coalition to Develop Young Theatre Audiences, N.Y.C., 1992; panelist Queens (N.Y.) Coun. Arts, 1992-93, Nancy Quinn Fund for Alliance of Resident Theatres, N.Y., 1994 and N.Y.C. Dept. of Cultural Affairs, 1997; performer Theater for a Greater Peace, Flying Bridge Prodns., 1993-97. Vol. Increase the Peace Vol. Corps., N.Y.C., 1992-93. Mem. Kiwanis (sec. Sunnyside chpt. 1993-95). Avocation: improvisational acting. Office: Thalia Spanish Theatre PO Box 4368 41-17 Greenpoint Ave Sunnyside NY 11104

GIALLO, VITO, antiques dealer; b. Mt. Vernon, N.Y., June 10, 1930; s. Vito and Vera (Verbasco) G. Diploma, Franklin Sch. Profl. Arts, N.Y.C., 1952. Artist advt. agy., N.Y.C., 1952-58; asst. artist to Jack Wolfgang Beck, N.Y.C., 1956-58; gallery dir. Loft Gallery (i.e. Jack Wolfgang Beck Studio), N.Y.C., 1956-58; art asst. to Andy Warhol, N.Y.C., 1958-59; antiques dealer N.Y.C., 1960—. Home: 222 E 83rd St New York NY 10028-2801

GIALLORENZI, THOMAS GAETANO, optical engineer; b. N.Y.C., Feb. 28, 1943; s. Amedeo and Eleanor (Spica) G.; m. Margaret Mary Marrin, Sept. 6, 1966; children: Thomas R., Kathy. BS in Engring. Physics, Cornell U., 1965, MS in Engring. Physics, 1966, PhD, 1969. Tech. staff Gen. Tel. & Electronics Lab., Bayside, N.Y., 1969-70; sect. head, optical techniques br. Naval Rsch. Lab., Washington, 1970-76, head optical techniques br., 1976-79, supt. optical scis. divsn., 1979—; lectr. in field and at profl. soc. confs. Editor Jour. Lightwave Tech., 1983-88; contbr. over 80 articles to profl. jours.; over 30 patents in field. Mem. adv. bd. U. Va., 1986-92. Recipient Applied Sci. award Rsch. Soc. Am., 1973, Meritorious Civilian Svc. award USN, 1978, Conrad award USN, 1985, Disting. Exec. Rank award Pres. of U.S., 1990, 98, Meritorious Exec. Rank award Pres. of U.S., 1984, Disting. Civilian Svc. award Dept. Def., 1987. Fellow IEEE (assoc. editor Procs. 1990-95, Lightwave Comms. 1989-92, Harry Diamond award 1986, John Tyndell award 1990), IEEE Laser and ElectroOptics Soc. (pres. 1996), Optical Soc. Am. (editor Jour. Lightwave Tech. 1983-89, assoc. editor Applied Optics 1991-94); mem. Nat. Acad. Engring., U.S. Naval League (Albert Michelson award 1995, USN Rodger Easton award Office of Naval Rsch. 1998). Home: 8704 Side Saddle Rd Springfield VA 22152-2731 Office: Naval Rsch Lab Optical Scis Divsn Washington DC 20375-5000

GIAM, CHOO-SENG, marine science educator; b. Singapore, Apr. 2, 1931; came to U.S., 1964, naturalized, 1970; s. Chong-Hing and Eng-Keow (Tan) G.; m. Mun-Yung Ng, Feb. 25, 1956; children: Benny Y.B., Patrick Y.Y., Michael Y.K. M.Sc., U. Sask, 1961, Ph.D., 1963. Research chemist Imperial Oil, Sarnia, Can., 1963-64; postdoctoral fellow Pa. State U., State College, 1964-65; research assoc. U. Calif.-Irvine, 1965-66; asst. prof. Tex. A&M U., College Station, 1966-70, assoc. prof., 1970-72, prof. dept. chemistry, 1972-81, prof. chemistry/oceanography, chmn. organic div. chemistry, 1972-82; dean Coll. Sci., prof. chemistry and geol. scis. U. Tex., El Paso, 1981-82; prof. chemistry U. Pitts., 1983-87; prof. marine sci., dir. Coastal Zone Lab. Tex. A&M U., Galveston, 1987—; adj. prof. dept. preventive medicine and community health U. Tex. Med. Br. Contbr. articles to profl. jours.; patentee in field. Mem. Am. Chem. Soc., Can. Chem. Soc., Royal Inst. Chemistry, N.Y. Acad. Scis., Sigma Xi, Phi Lambda Upsilon. Home: 9 Quintana Pl Galveston TX 77554-8300 Office: Tex A&M U 5007 Avenue U Galveston TX 77551-5926

GIAMBALVO, VINCENT, training and career development executive; b. Bklyn., Nov. 10, 1942; s. Frank and Anna (Pepey) G.; m. Rose Marie Esposito, Sept. 8, 1968; 1 child, Gina Marie. BA, Hunter Coll., 1966; MA, Northeastern U., 1970, PhD, 1973. Rsch. assoc. Northeastern U., Boston, 1972; asst. prof. behavioral sci. SUNY, N.Y.C., 1973-77; tng. specialist ADP Network Svcs., Ann Arbor, Mich., 1978-80; mgr. human resource devel. ADT Security Systems, Parsippany, N.J., 1981-88; dir. tng. and devel. Duro-Test Corp., Fairfield, N.J., 1989-93, dir. human resources, 1993-97, human resource cons., 1997-98; v.p. tng. and career devel. Great Atlantic and Pacific Tea Co., Montvale, N.J., 1998—; instr. Am. Soc. Tng. and Devel. cert. program Kean Coll., 1982-85; nat. and internat. sales and mktg. cons. Biofeedtrac Inc., Bklyn., 1984-92. Contbr. articles on edn. and vision sci. to profl. jours. With USNR, 1964-71. NDEA Title IV fellow, 1968-71. Mem. ASTD (sec. Ann Arbor chpt. 1978-79, pres. 1980, leadership devel. coord. North N.J. chpt. 1989-90, pres.-elect 1991, pres. 1992), Am. Mgmt. Assn. Democrat. Roman Catholic. E-mail: Giambalv@aptea.com. Fax: (201) 930-8144. Home: 21 Eldor Ave New City NY 10956-1433 Office: 2 Paragon Dr Montvale NJ 07645

GIAMBASTIANI, EDMUND P., JR., military officer, federal agency administrator; b. Canastota, N.Y.. Grad. with leadership distinction, US Naval Acad., 1970. Commd. ensign USN, 1970, advanced through grades to rear admiral, various assignments including weapons officer, USS Puffer, 1971-75, enlisted program mgr., staff Navy Recruiting Command Hdqrs., 1975-78, flag aide to dep. comdr., 1975-78, engr. officer, USS Francis Scott Key, 1978-82, comdr. Submarine NR-1, 1982-85, mem. staff of Asst. Chief Naval Ops. for undersea warfare, 1985-86, spl. asst. to dep. dir. for intelligence, CIA, comdr. USS Richard B. Russell, 1987-90, fellow Chief Naval Ops. Strategic Studies Group, 1991, comdr. Submarine Devel. Squadron 12, 1991-93, jt. task group comdr., spl. warfare exercise; dir. strategy and concepts Naval Doctrine Command USN, Norfolk, Va.; currently dir. submarine warfare divsn. USN, Washington, 1996-98; comdr. Submarine Force, U.S. Atlantic Fleet USN, Norfolk, Va., 1998—. Decorated legion of merit with one gold star, disting. svc. medal with two gold stars. Office: Comdr Submarine Force US Atlantic Fleet 7958 Blandy Rd Norfolk VA 23551-2492*

GIAMBRA, JOEL ANTHONY, city comptroller; m. Michelle Giambra; children: Gabriella, Nicholas, Dominic. Student, Bryant & Stratton Bus. Inst., 1973; AAS in Bus. Adminstrn., Erie C.C., 1978. Legis. asst. Erie County Legis., Buffalo, 1975-76, cmty. aide, mem. citizens adv. com., 1976; sgt.-at-arms Buffalo Common Coun., 1976-77; dir. field ops. western N.Y. Carter/Mondale Re-Election Com., Buffalo, 1980; monitor/evaluator Divsn. Employment & Tng., Buffalo, 1982-90; comptroller City of Buffalo, 1990—. Bd. dirs. Buffalo Fine Arts Acad.; mem. Loaned Exec. Club, United Way Buffalo & Erie County. Recipient Bus. First 40 under 40 award, 1995, Erie C.C. Found. Disting. Alumni award, Be-A-Friend Big Brother/Big Sister Program Dir.'s award, Disting. Svc. to Preservation award Landmark Soc. Niagara Frontier, 1984; Appreciation award Preservation Coalition Erie County, 1984. Mem. NCCJ, N.Y. State Fin. Officers Assn. (bd. govs. 1992), West Side Bus. & Taxpayers' Assn. (Man of Yr. 1984), Forest Dist. Civic Assn., Jr. C. of C., Kiwanis Club Buffalo, Leadership Buffalo (adv. bd.), Romulus Club. Office: Office of Comptroller 1225 City Hall 65 Niagara Sq Buffalo NY 14202-3331*

GIAMPIETRO, WAYNE BRUCE, lawyer; b. Chgo., Jan. 20, 1942; s. Joseph Anthony and Jeannette Marie (Zeller) G.; B.A., Purdue U., 1963; J.D., Northwestern U., 1966; m. Mary E. Fordeck, June 15, 1963; children—Joseph, Anthony, Marcus. Bar: Ill. 1966, U.S. Dist. (no. dist.) Ill. 1966, U.S. Tax Ct. 1977, U.S. Ct. Appeals (7th cir.) 1967, U.S. Supreme Ct. 1971. Assoc. Elmer Gertz, Chgo., 1966-73; mem. firm Gertz & Giampietro, Chgo., 1974-75; sole practice, 1975-76; ptnr. Poltrock & Giampietro, 1976-87, ptnr. Witwer, Burlage, Poltrock and Giampietro, 1987-94, Witwer, Poltrock & Giampietro, 1995—. Former cons. atty. Looking Glass div. Traveler's Aid Soc. Contbr. articles to profl. jours. Pres. Chgo. 47th Ward Young Republicans, 1968. Bd. dirs. Ravenswood Conservation Commn. Mem. Ill. Bar Assn. (chmn. sect. on Individual Rights and Responsibilities, 1986-87, 2d pl. Lincoln award 1975), Chgo. Bar Assn., Ill. Bar Assn., First Amendment Lawyers Assn. (sec. 1982, treas. 1983, pres. 1986, nat. chmn. 1987), Chgo. Coun. of Lawyers (mem. ethics com. 1992—), Order of Coif, Phi Alpha Delta. Lutheran. Avocation: stamp collecting. Home: 23 Windsor Dr Lincolnshire IL 60069-3410 Office: Witwer Poltrock & Giampietro 125 S Wacker Dr Ste 2700 Chicago IL 60606-4402

GIANAKOS, PATRICIA ANN, social services supervisor; b. Warren, Ohio, Oct. 14, 1948; d. Jimmie Lambros and Julie (Mougianis) G. BA in Pre-Profl. Social Work, Kent State U., 1970; MSSA (Master of Sci. in Social Administration), Case Western Res. U., 1998. Lic. social worker, diplomate, Amer. Psychotherapy Assn. Aid for aged workers Trumbull County Human Svcs. Dept., Warren, 1970-71, social svc. worker, 1971-88, adult svcs. worker, 1988—, excellence com., 1991, 93, contbg. editor County Line newsletter, 1991-98, mem. awards com., 1991-93, chmn. awards com., 1993-98; mem. Trumbull County Task Force on Wellness in Later Yrs., Warren, 1991-92. Vol. St. Demetrios Festival, Warren, 1979—; mem. Dem. Nat. Com., Warren, 1992—, Ladies Philoptochos Soc., Warren, 1979—; co-founder, adviser Sr. Citizens Orgn. St. Demetrios Ch., Warren, 1979—. Mem. ACA, NASW, Am. Bus. Women's Assn., Assn. for Adult Devel. and Aging, Nat. Com. for Prevention of Elder Abuse, Tri-County Social Workers Assn., Sr. Svcs. Network, Early Intervention County Collaborative Grp.; Mentoring Mom's Oversight Com. Greek Orthodox. Avocations: reading, crafts, decorating, movies. Home: 1786 Dodge Dr NW Warren OH 44485-1823 Office: Trumbull Cou Human Svcs 150 S Park Ave Warren OH 44481-1018

GIANCOTTI, FILIPPO GIUSTO, cell and molecular biologist; b. Rome, Mar. 25, 1958. MD, U. Torino, Italy, 1981, PhD, 1987. Diplomate Italian Bd. Hematology/Oncology. Intern and resident dept. hematology U. Torino Sch. Medicine, 1979-83; sr. rsch. fellow La Jolla (Calif.) Cancer Rsch. Found., 1987-91; asst. prof. Sch. Medicine, NYU, 1991-96, assoc. prof., 1996; assoc. prof. Sch. Medicine Cornell U., N.Y.C., 1996—; assoc. mem. Sloan-Kettering Inst. Meml. Sloan-Kettering Cancer Ctr., 1996—; cons. NIH, 1994—. Contbr. articles to profl. jours. including Cell, European Molecular Biology Orgn. Jour., Jour. of Cell Biology, Molecular Biology of The Cell. Sr. postdoctoral fellow European Molecular Biology Orgn., 1987-89; postdoctoral fellow European Orgn. for Rsch. and Treatment Cancer and Nat. Cancer Inst., 1987-89, Am. Cancer Soc., 1989-90, Arthritis Found., 1990-93; Whitehead Presdl. fellow, 1992-93; recipient Lucille P. Markey Charitable Trust award, 1992-96, Established Investigatorship award Am.

Heart Assn., 1996—. Mem. AAAS, ASCB. Achievements include patents on novel fibronectin receptor, reduction of cell tumorigenicty using the fibronectin receptor, a single-chain integrin. Office: Cellular Biochemistry/ Biophysics Program Box 216/1275 York Ave Meml Sloan-Kettering Cancer New York NY 10021

GIANGUZZI, JOSEPH CUSTODE, sculptor; b. N.Y.C., Mar. 4, 1941; s. Lorenzo and Vincenza Gianguzzi. Group shows include Burr Galleries, N.Y.C., Sagittarius Gallery, N.Y.C., Salmagundi Club Galleries, N.Y.C., The Barn Gallery, Hartford, Conn., 1979; solo show Queensborough C.C., 1977; commns. from Thomas P.F. Hoving, La Guardia C.C., Bklyn. Coll., CUNY. Mem. Burr Artists. Home: 724 W Las Olas Blvd Fort Lauderdale FL 33312-7145

GIANINI, PAUL C., JR., college university. BA, Yankton Coll.; M in Edn., U. Nebr.; D in Coll. Adminstn., U. Fla. Pres. Spoon River Coll., Canton, Ill., Valencia C.C. Bd. dirs. Ctrl. Fla. YMCA, Orlando Sci. Ctr., SunTrust Adminstrv. Bd.; regional bd. Ctrl. Fla. Jobs and Edn. Partnership. Mem. Am. Assn. of C.C. (chair joint commn. on fed. rels.), Assn. of C.C. Trustees, Am. Coun. on Edn. (commn. govtl. rels). Office: Valencia Cmty Coll PO Box 3028 Orlando FL 32802

GIANINO, JOHN JOSEPH, former insurance executive; b. Waltham, Mass., Aug. 3, 1935; s. Salvatore and Elizabeth Louise (Chapin) G.; m. Elaine Margaret Barry, Sept. 1, 1956; children: John J., Jr., Paul Barry. A.B. in Math., Providence Coll., 1957; exec. program in bus. Columbia U., 1978. Various actuarial positions John Hancock Mut. Life Ins. Co., Boston, 1957-72, 2d v.p., 1972-77, v.p., 1977-94; ret., 1994. Alumni chmn. St. John's Prep. Sch., Danvers, Mass., 1979-80. Fellow Acad. Actuaries, Soc. Actuaries; Roman Catholic. Club: Boston Actuaries (pres. 1974-75). Home: 2 Westway Lynnfield MA 01940-2126*

GIANITSOS, ANESTIS NICHOLAS, surgeon; b. Chios, Greece, Aug. 31, 1961; came to U.S., 1966; s. Dimitrios and Soultani (Zannikos) G.; m. Laurie S. Hallmark, 1 child, Alexia Soultani. BA summa cum laude, Boston U., 1983, MD, 1987. Physician U. Wis. Hosp., Madison, 1987-92; pres. Tricorp Informational Svcs., Williams Bay, Wis., 1989-93; staff urologist Riverview Clinic, Janesville, Wis., 1992-98; pres. Geneva Mktg. Sys., Lake Geneva, Wis., 1996—; med. dir. Men's Health Ctr. Mercy Health Sys., So. Wis., No. Ill., 1998—; staff urologist Mercy Health Sys., Janesville, 1998—; cons. Rural Wis. Hosp. Coop., Sauk City, 1989-93; staff urology Mercy Health Sys., Janesville, 1998—; med. dir. So. Wis. chpt. US TOO, 1993—. Contbr. articles to profl. jours. Commonwealth scholar, Augustus Howe Buck scholar. Fellow Internat. Coll. Surgeons; mem. Am. Assn. Clin. Urologists, Am. Urologic Assn., Wis. Med. Soc. Republican. Greek Orthodox. Avocations: photography, travel, baseball, investing, rare wine. Home: 1237 Geneva National Ave W Lake Geneva WI 53147-5009 Office: Mercy Men's Health Ctr Men's Health Ctr 1000 Mineral Point Ave Janesville WI 53545-2982

GIANNAMORE, DAVID MICHAEL, electronics engineer; b. Steubenville, Ohio, May 25, 1956; s. Robert Anthony and Marjorie Irene (Smith) G.; m. Tracy Lynn Rayburn, Apr. 3, 1982; children: Cynthia Marie, Robert Joseph. AAS in Electronic Engring., Jefferson County Tech. Inst., 1977. Video tech. Sta. WSTV-TV, Steubenville, 1977; svc. tech. TCI of Ohio, Steubenville, 1978-80; cable splicer Gen. Telephone Ohio, Cadiz, 1980-81; customer svc. rep. Ohio Power Co., Steubenville, 1981-84; svc. engr. Warner Amex, Columbus, Ohio, 1985-86; tng. instr. Liebert Global Svcs., Worthington, Ohio, 1986-90, tng. instr., supr., 1990-93, project mgr., 1993-95, quality mgr., 1995—. Mem. Am. Soc. for Quality (cert. quality mgr.), Assn. for Svc. Mgmt. Internat. Avocations: family activities, camping, karate, sports, music. Office: Liebert Global Svcs 250 E Wilson Bridge Rd Ste 100 Worthington OH 43085-2323

GIANNAROS, DEMETRIOS SPIROS, economist, educator, politician; b. Karlovasi, Samos, Greece, Oct. 4, 1949; came to U.S., 1964; s. Spiridon Demetrios and Irene (Kiriakou) G.; m. Elizabeth Sampson, June 5, 1977; children: Edward, Spiros Jason. BA in Econs., U. Mass., 1972; MA in Econ. Devel., Boston U., 1976, MAPE in Polit. Econ., 1977, PhD in Econs., 1981. Mgr. Samos Imex Corp., Boston, 1974-77; asst. prof. econs. Suffolk U., Boston, 1977-79; prof. U. Hartford, West Hartford, Conn., 1980—, dir. internat. programs, 1993-94; dir. exec. MPA program U. Hartford, West Hartford, 1986-88, assoc. to sr. v.p., dir. internat. studies, 1988-91; mem. Bd. Edn., Farmington, Conn., 1993-95; dir. U.S. Consortium for Mgmt. Edn. in Ctrl. and Ea. Europe, 1993-98; vice chmn. fin. com. Conn. Gen. Assembly, 1995-98; state rep. Conn., 1995—; chmn. energy & tech. com., 1999—; mem. Conn. Internat. Trade Coun., 1995-96; spl. asst. to pres. George Washington U., Washington, 1988-89; cons. to pub. and pvt. orgns., 1977—. Bd. dirs. Coll. Southea. Europe, 1992-97. NSF grantee, 1983-84, U. Hartford Coffin grantee, 1983-8, Mellon Found. grantee, 1991-92; Am. Coun. on Edn. fellow, 1988-89. Fellow Am. Coun. on Edn. (mem. exec. bd. coun.); mem. Am. Hellenic Ednl. and Progressive Assn., Am. Econ. Assn., Internat. Econ. Assn., N.E. Bus. and Econs. Assn. (pres. 1990-92, bd. dirs. 1989-95), Exchange Club, Helicon Soc. (pres., bd. dirs. 1975-78), Hellenic Soc., Paideia, World Affairs Coun., World Hellenic Interparliamentary Union (v.p.). Greek Orthodox. Avocations: travel, water sports, museums, political activities, nature. Home: 56 Basswood Rd Farmington CT 06032-1142 Office: U Hartford Econs Dept 200 Bloomfield Ave Hartford CT 06117-1545

GIANNELLA, SUSANNE R., maternal/women's health nurse, medical/ surgical nurse; b. Passaic, N.J., July 24, 1941; d. Anthony and Susan (De Gondea) De Salvo; m. Alfred Giannella, June 30, 1962; children: Donald, Marisa, Annmarie, Alfred Jr., John. Student, Seton Hall U., 1962; AAS in Nursing, Passaic County Community Coll., Paterson, N.J., 1982. RN, N.J.; cert. childbirth educator; cert. inpatient obstetric nurse. Tchr. asst. Hawthorne (N.J.) Bd. Edn.; clin. shift coord. labor and delivery Valley Hosp., Ridgewood, N.J., labor and delivery/maternal health nurse. Contbr. articles to nursing jours. Mem. ANA, NAACOG, Nat. Assn. Childbirth Edn. Specialists.

GIANNETTI, LOUIS DANIEL, film educator, film critic; b. Natick, Mass., Apr. 1, 1937; s. John and Vincenza (Zappitelli) G.; m. Justine Ann Gallagher, Sept. 7, 1963 (div. 1980); children: Christina, Francesca. B.A., Boston U., 1959; M.A., U. Iowa, 1961, Ph.D., 1967. Asst. prof. English Emory U., Atlanta, 1966-70; prof. English and film Case Western Res. U., Cleve., 1970—. Author: Understanding Movies, 1972, rev. 8th edit., 1999, Godard and Others, 1975, Masters of the American Cinema, 1981, (with S. Eyman) Flashback, 1986, 3d rev. edit., 1996. Democrat. Office: Case Western Res U Dept English Euclid Ave Cleveland OH 44106-2706

GIANNETTI, THOMAS LEONARD, lawyer; b. Stamford, Conn., June 7, 1947; s. Thomas and Lucille Giannetti; m. Charlene Canape, Jan. 12, 1974; children: Joseph, Theresa. BS, Yale U., 1968; MSEE, Carnegie-Mellon U., 1970; JD, George Washington U., 1976. Bar: N.Y. 1977, U.S. Dist. Ct. (so. and ea. dists. N.Y.) 1978, U.S. Ct. Appeals (fed. cir.) 1984, U.S. Dist. Ct. (no. dist.) Calif. 1993, U.S. Supreme Ct. 1996, U.S. Patent and Trademark Office 1975. Engr. Westinghouse Electric Corp., Pitts. and Phila., 1968-73; assoc. Fish & Neave, N.Y.C., 1976-86, ptnr., 1986—. Mem. ABA, Am. Intellectual Property Law Assn. N.Y. Intellectual Property Law Assn., Assn. of Bar of City of N.Y., Fed. Cir. Bar Assn., Yale Club (N.Y.C.). Home: 1158 5th Ave New York NY 10029-6917 Office: Fish & Neave 1251 Avenue Of The Americas New York NY 10020-1104

GIANNI, GASTON L., JR., federal agency administrator; b. Steubenville, Ohio, Aug. 12, 1942; m. Sue Gianni; three children. BS in Acctg., Franciscan U. Steubenville, 1964; postgrad., Pa. State U., Harvard U. Various positions to sr. exec. Gen. Acctg. Office; inspector gen. Fed. Deposit Ins. Corp., 1996—; mem., chair audit com. Pres. Coun. on Integrity and Efficiency. With D.C. Nat. Guard, 1964-70. Mem. Inst. Mgmt. Accts., Assn. Govt. Accts., Inst. Internal Auditors. Office: Fed Deposit Ins Co Office Inspector Gen 801 17th St NW Washington DC 20434

GIANNINI, VALERIO LOUIS, investment banker; b. N.Y.C., Feb. 7, 1938; s. Gabriel M. and Luisa M. (Casazza) G.; m. Linda Martin, Oct. 6, 1979; children: Martin Louis, Alexander Elliot, Charles Gabriel. BSE, Princeton U., 1959. With Kidder Peabody & Co., N.Y.C., 1961-64; sr. cons. IIT Research Inst., Chgo., 1964-66; sec. Giannini-Voltex, L.A., 1966-68; pres. V.L. Giannini & Co., L.A., 1968-76; chmn. Namco Chems., Inc., 1975; dir. White House ops., Washington, 1977-78; dep. spl. asst. to Pres. for adminstrn. White House, 1979-80; dep. asst. sec. Dept. Commerce, Washington, 1980-81; prin. Cumberland Investment Group, N.Y.C., 1981-87; pres. Numex Corp., 1986-87; CEO, Geneva Bus. Network, Inc., Irvine, Calif., 1987-90; founder Eurosearch Ptnrs., Newport Beach, Calif., 1990; prin. Newcap Ptnrs., 1995; bd. dirs. Meridian Health, Inc., Aqua Ventures 2000, Dudek & Assocs., iMet Technologies, Inc. Lt. USNR, 1959-61. Mem. N.Y. Yacht Club, Newport Harbor Yacht Club. Home: 131 Via Genoa Newport Beach CA 92663-4636

GIANNINY, OMER ALLAN, JR., retired humanities educator; b. Charlottesville, Va., Dec. 5, 1925; s. Omer Allen and Frances Belle (Bussenger) G.; m. Jean Claire Post, July 31, 1948; children: Donald Hagen, James Emory, Peter Arnold, Robert Matthew, Gary Lee. BME, U. Va., Charlottesville, 1947; MEd, U. Va., 1958, EdD, 1967; postgrad., Rutgers U., 1947-48. Registered profl. engr., Va. Refinery engr. Esso Std. Oil Co., Linden, N.J., 1947-51; rsch. engr. U. Va., Charlottesville, 1953-56, asst. prof. Sch. Engring., 1955-65, 67-71, lectr., 1965-67, assoc. prof. humanities Sch. Engring., 1971-82, prof. humanities Sch. Engring., 1982-93, chmn., 1979-80, 90-93, prof. emeritus, 1993—; ednl. cons. Newport News Shipbuilding, Va., 1962, Inst. Textile Tech., Charlottesville, 1984—. Co-author: Thomas Jefferson's Rotunda Restored, 1981. Served to lt. USNR, 1944-46, 51-53. Mem. Am. Soc. Engring. Edn. (dir. 1980-82), Soc. History Tech. (group chmn. 1983-85), The Raven Soc., Phi Beta Kappa, Tau Beta Pi, Phi Delta Kappa. United Methodist. Home: 1711 King Mountain Rd Charlottesville VA 22901-3047

GIANNOTTA, STEVEN LOUIS, neurosurgery educator; b. Detroit, Apr. 4, 1947; s. Louis D. and Betty Jane (Root) G.; m. Sharon Danielak, June 13, 1970; children: Brent, Nicole, Robyn. Student, U. Detroit, 1965-68; MD, U. Mich., 1972. Diplomate Am. Bd. Neurol. Surgeons. Surg. intern U. Mich., Ann Arbor, 1972-73, neurosurg. resident, 1973-78; asst. prof. neurosurgery UCLA, 1978-80; asst. prof. neurosurgery U. So. Calif., Sch. Medicine, L.A., 1980-83, assoc. prof. neurosurgery, 1983-89, prof. neurosurgery, 1989—; sec. Congress Neurol. Surgeons, Washington, 1986-89, v.p., 1993; pres. L.A. (Calif.) Soc. Clin. Neuroscis., 1992-93; bd. dirs. Am. Bd. Neurol. Surgery, 1995—. Fellow ACS, Am. Heart Assn. (stroke coun., rsch. grantee 1980, 84), So. Calif. Neurol. Soc. (pres. 1993-94), sec., Amer. Bd. of Neurological Surg. Democrat. Roman Catholic. Avocations: golf, skiing, sports cars. Office: Dept Neurosurgery Box 239 1200 N State St Los Angeles CA 90033-1029

GIANNULLI, MOSSIMO, designer, apparel business executive. Owner, chmn. bd. Mossimo Inc., Irvine, Calif. Office: Mossimo Inc 2450 White Rd 2nd Fl Irvine CA 92614-6250

GIANTURCO, DELIO E., management consultant; b. Washington, Sept. 28, 1940; s. Elio and Valentine (McGillycuddy) G.; m. Mary Elizabeth Jordan, Jan. 31, 1961; children: Lisa, Grace, Mark. B.S. in Fgn. Trade, Georgetown U., 1963; M.A., George Washington U., 1967. Staff asst. to Robert J. Corbett of Pa. U.S. Ho. of Reps., Washington, 1960-62, legis. asst. to Robert L.F. Sikes of Fla., 1962-63; dep. v.p. project devel., dep. sr. v.p. guarantees and ins., sr. v.p. guarantees, ins. and exporter credits, exec. v.p., vice chmn., 1st v.p. Export-Import Bank, Washington, 1963-77, treas., comptr., 1963-77; pres. First Washington Assocs., 1978—; dir. Fgn. Credit Ins. Assn., N.Y.C., 1971-76; adj. prof. George Mason U., 1995—. Recipient Arthur Fleming award, 1974, William Jump award for exemplary achievement pub. adminstrn., 1971; named One of Ten Outstanding Young Men in Govt., 1974. Office: First Washington Assocs 1501 Lee Hwy Ste 302 Arlington VA 22209-1147

GIANTURCO, PAOLA, management consulting company executive; b. July 22, 1939; d. Cesare and Verna Bertha (Daily) G.; m. David Sanderson Hill, Mar. 12, 1988; 1 child from previous marriage, Scott Sangster. BA, Stanford U., 1961; postgrad., U. So. Calif., 1971. Dir. pub. rels. Joseph Magnin, San Francisco, 1961-67; dir. pub. rels., acct. exec. Hall & Levine Advtsg. Agy., L.A., 1968-73, v.p., acct. supr., 1973-76, sr. v.p., 1977-82; v.p. Dancer Fitzgerald Sample, 1982-87; exec. v.p., mgmt. supr. Saatchi and Saatchi, 1988-91; pres. The Gianturco Co., Mill Valley, Calif., 1991—; co-developer, instr. exec. insts. on women and leadership Stanford U., 1994, 95; bd. dirs. Inca Floats Adventure Travel. Past bd. dirs. The Country Schs.; bd. dirs. Above the Line Homeless Teen Shelter. Mem. Women in Comms., Assn. of Women in Devel., Stanford Inst. Women (past bd. dirs.), Stanford Inst. Rsch. Women and Gender, Corp. Assocs. Bd. Home and Office: 30 Cecily Ln Mill Valley CA 94941-3300

GIARGIARI, MICHELLE, retail executive, artist; b. Framingham, Mass., Apr. 5, 1950; d. Armando Louis Giargiari and Evelyn Agnes Irwin. BA, Salem State Coll., 1998. Exec. dir. Swedenborg Bookstore, Boston, 1974—. Curator Visual Art Gallery, Boston. Sec. Mass. New Ch. Union, Boston. Avocations: media artist, oil painting, writing, counseling. E-mail: Visuartz. Office: Swedenborg Bookstore/Visual Art Gallery 79 Newbury St Boston MA 02115

GIA-RUSSO, A(NTHONY) PAUL, retired minister, lawyer; b. Petrella Tifernina, Italy, Jan. 25, 1910; s. Vincenzo and Anita (Amorosa) G-R.; m. Eleanor L Bauer, Feb. 12, 1938; children: Don Paul, Mark Henry. AB in Citizenship and Pub. Affairs, Syracuse U., 1932, JD, 1936; MA, U. Chgo., 1939; MDiv, Chgo. Theol. Sem., 1940. Ordained to ministry United Ch. of Christ, 1940. Min. Congl. Ch., Oak Lawn, Ill., 1938-42, Pilgrim Congl. Ch., Milw., 1942-56; tchr. comparative religion, philosophy of religion U. Wis., Milw., 1958-65; min. Congl.-United Ch. of Christ, Brown Deer, Wis., 1969-80, ret., 1980. Speaker in field. Lilly Endowment grantee. Mem. Delta Sigma Rho. Home: 2340 Memorial Dr Brookfield WI 53045-4324 *The fundamental forces of history are rarely comprehended or controlled. We can never return to Eden and we will never reach Utopia. There are great prices to be paid for being civilized.*

GIAVARAS, FAITH E., minister; b. Lowell, Mass., Dec. 13, 1948; d. Stavros and Mary (Kirkiles) G.; children: Dimitri, Alexis. BA in Edn. and Child Psychology, U. Mass., 1966; MA in Urban Edn. and Health, Boston State Coll., 1976; MA in Counseling Psychology, Ga. Sch. Profl. Psychology, 1996; postgrad., The Union Inst. Founding mother, inter-faith min., feminist Inter-Denominational Ch., Atlanta, 1993—. Office: MarketInk 5072 Lavista Rd Tucker GA 30084-3500

GIAVIS, THEODORE DEMETRIOS, commercial illustrator, artist; b. Lowell, Mass., Feb. 24, 1920; s. Demetrios Harry and Nicoletta (Karas) G.; m. Theano Theofanus, May 11, 1958; 1 child, Andrew. BFA, Mass. Coll. Art, Boston, 1942; postgrad., Franklin Inst. Photography, 1950-51. Freelance comml. advt. artist Boston, 1946-47; staff artist Sunday mag. sect. Boston Post, 1947-53, art dir. Sunday mag., 1953-54; comml. advt. artist Rahl Studios, N.Y.C., 1955-75; freelance comml. advt. artist Westport, Conn., 1975-85, fine artist, 1985—. Staff sgt. USAF, Guam, 1943-46. Recipient 1st place New Canaan (Conn.) Arts Show, 1971, 72, 23d New Eng. Show at Silvermine (Conn.). Mem. Milford Fine Arts Coun. (Anya Maganus award 1991). Greek Orthodox. Avocations: tennis, bowling. Home and Studio: 2220 Pinnacle Cir S Palm Harbor FL 34684-1761

GIBALA, RONALD, metallurgical engineering educator; b. New Castle, Pa., Oct. 3, 1938; s. Steve Anthony and June Rose (Frank) G.; m. Janice Claire Grichor; children: Maryellen, Janice, David, Kristine. B.S., Carnegie Inst. Tech., 1960; M.S., U. Ill., 1962, Ph.D., 1964. Engring. technician Crane Co., New Castle, Pa., 1956-59; engr. U.S. Steel Research Labs., Monroeville, Pa., 1960; research asst. U. Ill., Urbana, 1960-64; asst. prof. metallurgy Case Western Res. U., Cleve., 1964-69; assoc. prof. Case Western Res. U., 1969-76, prof. metallurgy and materials sci. and macromolecular sci., 1976-84, co-dir. materials research lab., 1981-84; dir. metallurgy program NSF, 1982-83; prof., chmn. dept. materials sci. and engring. U. Mich., Ann Arbor, 1984-94, Francis E. Van Vlack Prof. Materials Sci. and Engring., 1998—. Contbr. articles to profl. jours.; editor: Hydrogen Embrittlement and Stress Corrosion Cracking, 1984. Pres. Woodhaven Hills Homeowners Assn., 1989-91. Recipient Alfred Noble prize ASCE, 1969, NASA Materials Sci. Divsn. Paper award, 1992; named Outstanding Young Mem. Cleve. chpt. Am. Soc. Metals, 1971; Tech. Achievement award Cleve. Tech. Socs. Council, 1972; vis. research fellow C.E.N.G. Labs., Grenoble, 1973-74; Matthias fellow Los Alamos Nat. Lab., 1991-92, Disting. Merit award U. Ill., 1998; vis. scientist Sandia Nat. Labs., 1998-99. Mem. TMS/AIME (dir. 1981-87), Am. Soc. Metals (chpt. chmn. 1975-76, Life Mem. award 1998), AAAS, Materials Research Soc. (councillor 1995-97, v.p. 1998, pres. 1999), Am. Ceramic Soc., Sigma Xi, Tau Beta Pi, Alpha Sigma Mu. Democrat. Club: Suburban Ski (pres. 1981-82). Home: 1543 Stonehaven St Ann Arbor MI 48104-4149 Office: U Mich Dept Materials Sci Engring Ann Arbor MI 48109-2136

GIBALDI, JOSEPH, publishing executive; b. Bklyn., Aug. 20, 1942; s. Ignatius G. and Angela Peritore; m. Anita, Aug. 15, 1962; children: Laura G. Pise, Joseph M. BA in English, CCNY, 1965, MA in English, 1967; PhD in Comparative Lit., NYU, 1973. Tchr. English Bklyn. Tech. H.S., 1965-70; instr. English Bklyn. Coll., 1970-73; asst. prof. comparative lit. U. Ga., 1973-76; dir. book acquisitions Modern Lang. Assn., N.Y.C., 1976—; adj. prof. humanities New Sch. U., N.Y.C., 1985—, NYU, 1994—. Author: MLA Handbook for Writers of Research Papers, 1977, 5th edit., 1999, MLA Style Manual, 1985, 2d edit., 1998, Introduction to Scholarship, 1981, 2d edit., 1992, Interrelations of Literature, 1982, others; contbr. articles to profl. jours. NYU fellow, 1972, Duke U. fellow, 1976. Mem. Am. Comparative Lit. Assn., Modern Lang. Assn. Avocation: opera. E-mail: joseph.gibaldi@mla.org. Office: Modern Lang Assn 10 Astor Pl New York NY 10003

GIBALDI, MILO, dean; b. N.Y.C., Dec. 17, 1938; s. Ignatius and Angela G.; m. Florence D'Amato, Dec. 26, 1960; 1 child, Ann Elizabeth. BS, Coll. Pharmacy, Columbia U., 1960, PhD, 1963. Asst. prof. pharmacy Columbia U., N.Y.C., 1963-66; asst. prof. pharmaceutics SUNY, Buffalo, 1966-67, assoc. prof., 1967-70, prof., 1970-78, chmn. dept., 1970-78; prof. pharmaceutics U. Wash., Seattle, 1978—; dean U. Wash. Sch. Pharmacy, Seattle, 1978-95, dean emeritus, 1995—; cons. Bur. Drugs, FDA, 1970-72, VA, Washington, 1971-72; vis. prof. U. Rochester, 1972-74; program dir. clin. pharmacokinetics and biopharmaceutics NIH, 1973-78, pharmacology study sect., 1976-80; sci. adv. bd. G.D. Searle & Co., 1978—. Author: (with Donald Perrier) Pharmacokinetics, 1976; contbr. articles to profl. jours. Fellow Acad. Pharm. Scis., AAAS; mem. Am. Chem. Soc., Am. Pharm. Assn., Acad. Soc. Clin. Pharmacology, Am. Soc. Pharmacology and Exptl. Therapeutics, N.Y. Acad. Scis., Am. Assn. Colls. Pharmacy, Nat. Acad. Scis. (mem. Inst. Medicine 1986), Health Scis. U. Wash. (assoc. v.p. 1983), Sigma Xi, Rho Chi. Office: U Wash Sch Pharmacy Dept Pharmaceutics Box 357610 Seattle WA 98195-7610*

GIBANS, JAMES DAVID, architect; b. Akron, Ohio, Feb. 10, 1930; s. Myer Jacob and Sylva (Hirsch) G.; m. Nina Freedlander, July 16, 1955; children: David Myer, Jonathan Samuel, Amy, Elisabeth. BA, Yale U., 1951, BArch, 1954, MArch, 1954. Architect George K. Raad & Assocs. et al, San Francisco, 1958-63; project architect Ward and Schneider, Cleve., 1964-68; sr. assoc. William A. Gould and Assocs., Cleve., 1968-74, Don M. Hisaka and Assoc., Cleve., 1974-76; pvt. practice architecture Cleve., 1976-81; v.p. Teare Herman & Gibans, Inc., Cleve., 1981-89; v.p., treas. Herman Galvin Gibans, Inc., Cleve., 1989-91, HGG, Inc., Cleve., 1991-94, Herman Gibans Fodor, Inc., 1994—; faculty Edn. for Aesthetic Awareness Cleve. State U., 1977-79. Trustee, mem. exec. com., 1st v.p. Cleve. Chamber Music Soc., 1970-78; mem. adv. bd. Environ. Resource Ctr., Cleve. Pub. Libr., 1973-76; mem. design rev. com. Shaker Square Hist. Dist., 1991-93; mem. Cleve. Landmarks Commn., 1993—; bd. dirs. Cleve. Soc. Contemporary Art, 1985-86, Friends of Shaker Square, 1994-96, Shaker Square Area Devel. Corp., 1996—, v.p., 1996-97, treas., 1997-99. With U.S. Army, 1955-57. Fulbright grantee, 1954-55. Mem. AIA (sec. Cleve. chpt. 1972-74, bd. dirs. 1984-86, treas. 1989, v.p. 1990, pres. 1991), Architects Soc. Ohio (trustee 1975-76, bd. dirs. 1985-88), Cleve. City Club, Fulbright Assn. (bd. dirs. N.E. Ohio chpt. 1995—, treas. 1998—), N.E. Ohio Jazz Soc. (bd. dirs. 1991-96, v.p. 1993-95, pres. 1995-96). Democrat. Jewish. Avocations: music, art, jogging, cross-country skiing. Home: 13800 Shaker Blvd Cleveland OH 44120-1584 Office: Herman Gibans Fodor Inc 1304 W 6th St Cleveland OH 44113-1304

GIBARA, SAMIR S. G., manufacturing executive. Pres., CEO, chmn. Goodyear Tire & Rubber Co., Akron, Ohio. Office: Goodyear Tire & Rubber Co 1144 E Market St Akron OH 44316-0002*

GIBB, BARRY, vocalist, songwriter; b. Douglas, Isle of Man, England, Sept. 1, 1946; s. Hugh and Barbara G.; m. Linda Gray; children: Stephen, Ashley, Travis, Michael. Performed in: (with bros. Robin and Maurice) amateur shows The Blue Cats, Manchester, Eng., 1950's; formed: (with bros.) The Bee Gees, 1958, disbanded, 1969, reunited, 1971; appeared in (with bros.) local clubs, Brisbane, Australia; released: (with bros.) 1st single record Three Kisses of Love, Australia, 1963; appeared on (with bros.) weekly TV show, Australia, 1960's; returned to Eng., 1967, signed with NEMS Enterprises; made: (with bros.) 1st U.S. TV appearance on Am. Bandstand, 1967; former rec. group for Robert Stigwood Orgn., from 1973; composer: (with bros.) music and lyrics for film Saturday Night Fever, 1977; title song of film Grease, 1978; appeared in: film Sergeant Pepper's Lonely Hearts Club Band, 1978; albums include Bee Gees First, 1967, Horizontal, 1968, Idea, 1968, Rare, Precious and Beautiful, Volume I, 1968, Odessa, 1969, Best of the Bee Gees, 1969, Rare, Precious and Beautiful, Volume II, 1970, Cucumber Castle, 1970, Two Years On, 1971, Trafalgar, 1971, To Whom It May Concern, 1972, Life in a Tin Can, 1973, Best of Bee Gees, Volume II, 1973, Mr. Natural, 1974, Main Course, 1976, Children of the World, 1976, Bee Gees Gold Volume I, 1976, Odessa, 1976, Here At Last...Bee Gees...Live, 1977, Saturday Night Fever, 1977, Sergeant Pepper's Lonely Hearts Club Band, 1978, Spirits Having Flown, 1978, Bee Gees Greatest Hits, 1979, Living Eyes, 1979, Now Voyager (solo), 1984, E.S.P., 1987, Idea, 1987, Main Course, 1988, Children of the World, 1989, Here...At Last...Live, 1990, High Civilization, 1991, Size Isn't Everything, 1993; wrote, sang, co-produced album for, Barbra Streisand, Guilty (Named Composer of Yr.), Kenny Rogers, Eyes That See In the Dark, Dionne Warwick, Heartbreaker, Diana Ross, Eaten Alive. Recipient Top Talent award Radio Adelaide KA, Australia, 1965; named Pop Stars of Yr., Holland, 1967; recipient Grammy award, 1971, 78, 81; citation of achievement BMI, 1971, 75, 76, 77; Record of Yr. award Stereo Rev., 1973; Trendsetter award Billboard, 1977; Best Movie Soundtrack award Italian Record Reviewers, 1978; Ampex Golden Reel award; numerous RIAA Gold and Platinum albums and singles, numerous gold and platinum albums and singles from various locations, including Can., South Africa, Germany, Belgium, Holland, Australia, N.Z., France, Hong Kong; Hon. Citizens of Man. (Can.) City of Winnipeg, 1975; Hon. Citizens State of Fla., 1978; recipient Nat. 2UE award Australia, 1966, Golden Lion award Radio Luxemburg, 1967, Carl-Allan award Eng., 1967, Valentine award Eng., 1968, Ivor Novello award, 1968-69, 76-77, 77-78, John Stephen Fashion award, 1969; inducted Rock and Roll Hall Fame, 1997. Office: care Polygram Group Dist Worldwide Plaza 825 8th Ave New York NY 10019-7416*

GIBB, ROBIN, vocalist, songwriter; b. Douglas, Isle of Man, Eng., Dec. 22, 1949; s. Hugh and Barbara G.; m. Dwina Murphy, July 31, 1986; 1 child, Robin John; children from previous marriage: Spencer, Melissa. Performed in: (with bros. Barry and Maurice as group) amateur shows The Blue Cats, Manchester, in 1950's; formed: (with bros.) The Bee Gees, 1958; disbanded (with bros.), 1969, reunited (with bros.), 1971; appeared in (with bros.) local clubs, Brisbane, Australia; released: (with bros.) 1st single record Three Kisses of Love, Australia, 1963; appeared on (with bros.) own weekly TV show, Australia, in 1960's; returned to (with bros.), Eng., 1967, signed with (with bros.), NEMS Enterprises; made: (with bros.) 1st U.S. TV appearance on Am. Bandstand, 1967; rec. group for, Robert Stigwood Orgn.; composer (with bros.); music and lyrics for film Saturday Night Fever, 1977 (40 million copies sold/biggest selling soundtrack); appeared in: movie Sgt Pepper's Lonely Hearts Club Band, 1978; albums include Bee Gees First, 1967, Horizontal, 1968, Idea, 1968, Rare, Precious and Beautiful, Volume I, 1968, Odessa, 1970, Best of the Bee Gees, 1969, Rare, Precious and Beautiful, Volumes I, II, III, 1970, Two Years On, 1972, Trafalser, To Whom It May Concern, 1973, Life In A Tin Can, 1974, Best of Bee Gees, Volumes I, II, 1973, Mr. Natural, 1974, Main Course, 1976, Children of the World, 1976, Bee Gees Gold Volume I, 1976, Odessa, 1976, Here At Last...Bee Gees...Live, 1977, Saturday Night Fever (Biggest Selling Soundtrack of All

Time), 1977, Sgt Pepper's Lonely Hearts Club Band, 1978, Spirits Having Flown, 1978, Bee Gees Greatest Hits, 1979, (solo) Robins Reign, Secret Agent, 1983, E.S.P., 1989 (Platinum album), High Civilization, 1991, Size Isn't Everything, 1994, (solo) How Old Are You?, Walls Have Eyes, Children Of The World, 1976, Living Eyes, 1982, Secret Agent (solo), 1986, One, 1989, The Very Best of The Bee Gees, 1990, Tales from The Brothers Gibb-A History in Song 1967-90, 1990, High Civilization, 1991, Size Isn't Everything, 1993, Still Waters, 1997; writer songs (with bros.) Guilty, Heartbreaker, Islands in the Stream, and numerous others; charity performances include UNICEF, UN Show, 1978, N.Y. Police Athletic League, Madison Sq. Garden, 1979, Free Nelson Mandela Concert, Wembly Stadium, Eng., 1990, Hurricane Relief, Joe Robbie Stadium, Miami, 1992. Recipient Ivor Novello awards, 1968-69, 76-77, 77-78, Six (6) Grammy awards, numerous Gold and Platinum albums and singles RIAA, numerous gold and platinum albums and singles worldwide; inducted into Songwriters Hall of Fame, 1994, Rock 'n Roll Hall of Fame, 1997; Internat. Artists award at Am. Music Awards, outstanding contribution to British Music at The Brit Awards, London, Lifetime Achievement award at World Music Awards, 1998-99. Office: Middle Ear 1801 Bay Rd Miami FL 33139-1415

GIBBARD, JUDITH R., library director; b. N.Y.C., Jan. 27, 1945; d. Charles J. and Esther (Polonsky) Popovits; m. Bruce Gregory Gibbard, June 19, 1966. AB in Edn., U. Mich., 1966, AM in English, 1968; MLS, Syracuse U., 1978. Cert. pub. libr., cert. secondary English/French tchr. Slide cataloger history of art dept. U. Mich., Ann Arbor, 1969-70; tchr. Assn. des Habitants de la Ville de Meyrin, Switzerland, 1970-71; cataloger Cornell U. Olin Libr., Ithaca, N.Y., 1972-78; head cataloging sect. Suffolk Coop. Libr. System, Bellport, N.Y., 1979-81; cataloging svcs. div. chief Suffolk Coop. Libr. System, Bellport, 1981-82; head tech. svc./automation Patchogue (N.Y.)-Medford Libr., 1983-89, asst. dir., 1989-90, dir., 1991—. Coord. Community Youth Com., Patchogue, 1992. Mem. Pub. Libr. Assn. (chair cataloging needs com. 1989-90), N.Y. Libr. Assn., Suffolk County Libr. Assn. (mem.-at-large 1988-89). Avocations: skiing, running, backpacking. Office: Patchogue-Medford Libr 54 E Main St Patchogue NY 11772-3131

GIBBES, WILLIAM HOLMAN, lawyer; b. Hartsville, S.C., Feb. 25, 1930; s. Ernest Lawrence and Nancy (Watson) G.; m. Frances Hagood, May 1, 1954; children: Richard H., William H. Jr., Lynn. BS, U. S.C., 1952, LLB, 1953. Bar: S.C. 1953, U.S. Ct. Mil. Appeals 1954, U.S. Dist. Ct. S.C. 1956, U.S. Supreme Ct. 1959, U.S. Ct. Appeals (4th cir.) 1965. Asst. atty. gen. Columbia, S.C., 1957-62; ptnr. Berry & Gibbes, Columbia, 1962-68, Berry, Lightsey, Gibbes, Columbia, 1968-72; mem. Gibbes Law Firm, P.A., Columbia, 1972—; house of dels. S.C. Bar, 1994-96; chief judge U.S. Army Legal Svcs. Agy., 1980-83. Author: Control of Highway Access - Its Prospects and Problems, Legal Dimensions of Community Health Planning, 1969, Manual for Fee Appraisors, 1960; contbr. articles to S.C. Law Review, Law Rev. Digest, 1960. Chmn. bd. dirs. U. S.C. YMCA, 1956-60. Brig. gen. JAGC, USAR 1980-83. Recipient Legion of Merit, U.S. Army, 1983. Mem. ABA (mil. laws com. 1984-90, meml. com.), S.C. Bar Assn. (exec. com. 1961-62), Am. Bd. Trial Advocates (sec.-treas. 1994-95, pres-elect 1995-96, pres. 1996-97), Judge Advs. Assn. (pres. 1982-83), Richland County Bar Assn., S.C. Credit Ins. Assn. (gen. counsel 1963-94), Tarantella Club, Caprician Club, Summit Club, Forest Lake Country Club, Kiawah Island Club, Kappa Sigma Kappa, Omicron Delta Kappa. Episcopalian. Home: 287 Windward Point Rd Columbia SC 29212-8417 Office: PO Box 8265 Columbia SC 29202

GIBBINS, BOB, lawyer; b. Seminole, Okla., Feb. 27, 1936; s. Robert Lee and La-Ceile Rene (Shackelford) G.; m. Suzanne K. Gibbins (div. Oct. 1975); children: Bob Jr., Steven, Jenny Durbin, Kyndall Krebs; m. Pam Reed, Feb. 26, 1982. BBA, U. Tex., 1958, LLB, 1961. Bar: Tex. 1961, U.S. Dist. Ct. (no. dist.) Tex. 1961, U.S. Ct. Appeals (5th cir.) 1971, U.S. Supreme Ct. 1974, Colo. 1991; diplomate Am. Bd. Trial Advs., Am. Bd. Profl. Liability Attys. Assoc. Morehead, Sharpe, Tisdale & Gibbins, Plainview, Tex., 1961-71; ptnr. Gibbins & Spivey, Austin, Tex., 1971-76; pvt. practice, Austin, 1976-78; sr. ptnr. Gibbins, Wash and Bratton, Austin, 1978-79, Gibbins, Burrow, Wash & Bratton, Austin, 1979-81, Gibbins, Burrow & Bratton, Austin, 1981-86, Gibbins & Bratton, Austin, 1986-89, Gibbins, Winckler & Bayer, Austin, 1989-91, Gibbins, Winckler & Harvey, Austin, 1991-97; pvt. practice law Austin, 1997—. Co-author: Texas Practical Guide: Personal Injury, 1988, Products Liability Litigation: Trial Strategy, 1988. Recipient War Horse award So. Trial Lawyers Assn., 1991, Faculty Svc. award, Univ. Tex. Sch. of Law, 1992; Bob Gibbins endowed presdl. scholarship named in his honor U. Tex. Sch. of Law, Austin, 1991. Fellow Internat. Acad. Trial Lawyers (bd. dirs. 1993-97), Internat. Soc. Barristers, State Bar Tex., Coll. of the State Bar Tex.; mem. Assn. Trial Lawyers Am. (pres. 1991-92, Lifetime Achievement award 1998, Champion of Justice award 1999), Nat. Bd. Trial Advocacy (civil trial adv.), Am. Bd. Trial Advocates (pres. Austin chpt. 1981), Trial Lawyers for Pub. Justice (bd. dir.s 1993), Tex. Trial Lawyers Assn. (dir. emeritus). Office: 500 W 13th St Austin TX 78701-1827

GIBBONS, CONNIE SUE, art association administrator; b. Phoenix, July 13, 1955; d. Richard Thomas Harmon and Loretta Jean (Harmon) Lipe; m. Hugh James Gibbons, Oct. 26, 1987; 1 child from previous marriage, Tracy Lynn Hudson. BA magna cum laude, Drury Coll., 1984; MFA, Tex. Tech. U., 1987. Instr. photography Drury Coll., Springfield, Mo., 1982-84; asst. dir. Fine Arts Ctr. City of Lubbock, Tex., 1984-88; dir. Fine Arts Ctr. City of Lubbock, 1988-95, dir. cultural arts, 1995-98; project mgr. Rennovation Hist. Depot, planning visual arts, music hist., Lubbock, 1999—. Curator (exhbn./catalogue) Visual Vanguards, 1992-97, Pieces, Parts & Passion: The Quilted Medium, 1996, (exhbn., symposium, catalogue) Las Mujeres Hablan, 1993; curator, project mgr. (permanent exhbn.) Buddy Holly--The Influence. Visual arts panelist Tex. Commn. on the Arts, Austin, 1994-95; visual arts co-chair Lubbock Arts Festival, 1994. Named Outstanding Alumni, Tex. Tech. U. Art Dept., Lubbock, 1992. Mem. Am. Assn. Mus., Ams. for the Arts, Tex. Assn. Mus. Office: Lubbock Fine Arts Ctr 2600 Avenue P Lubbock TX 79405-1418

GIBBONS, DORIA DESAIX, gastroenterology nurse; b. Mobile, Ala., Sept. 30, 1960; d. Elliott Graham and Betty Henrietta (Weil) G. BS in Psychology and Counseling, U. Montevallo, Ala., 1982; BSN, Vanderbilt U., 1985. RN, Tenn. Staff nurse Centennial Med. Ctr., Nashville, 1985-89; nursing supr. Nashville Gastroenterology Cons., 1989—. Mem. Soc. Gastroenterology Nurses and Assocs., Inc.

GIBBONS, EDWARD FRANCIS, psychobiologist; b. Bronx, N.Y., Dec. 25, 1949; s. Edward Francis and Mary Theresa (Westervelt) G. BS, SUNY, Stony Brook, 1977, PhD, 1986. Dir. ctr. for sci. and tech. Briarcliffe Coll., Woodbury, N.Y., 1992-96; asst. prof. liberal arts dept. Briarcliffe Coll., Patchogue, N.Y., 1993—. Series editor: SUNY Press Series on Endangered Species, 1986-95, Naturalistic Environments in Capitivity for Animal Behavior Research, 1994, Conservation of Endangered Species in Captivity: An Interdisciplinary Approach, 1995; contbr. articles to profl. jours. Sgt. USAF, 1970-74. Grantee Inst. Mus. Svcs., 1988-90, N.Y. State Dept. Edn., 1993-95. Mem. AAAS, Animal Behavior Soc., Soc. Behavioral Medicine, L.I. Soc. Women in Sci. and Tech. (bd. dirs., founder), Soc. for Conservation Biology, Soc. History of Tech., Sigma Xi. Roman Catholic. E-mail: edgibbons@aol.com. Home: 33 Warren St Brentwood NY 11717-1531 Office: Briarcliffe Coll 10 Lake St Patchogue NY 11772-2506

GIBBONS, ERIN, secondary education educator; b. Savannah, Ga., Mar. 27, 1965; d. John and Marjorie Gibbons. BA, U. Fla., 1989, MEd, 1990. Cert. English tchr. K-12, Fla. Tchr. Miami Ctrl. H.S., 1991—. Mem. Nat. Coun. Tchrs. English, Fla. Coun. Tchrs. English, Internat. Reading Assn.

GIBBONS, GREGORY DENNIS, minister; b. Saginaw, Mich., May 23, 1953; s. Everett Durward and Doris Lorraine (Miller) G.; m. Susan Rae Schulz, Jan. 17, 1982; children: Stephanie Grace, Michael Everett, Naomi Susan, Matthew Gregory, Christopher Donald. BA, Northwestern Coll., Watertown, Wis., 1975; MDiv, Wis. Luth. Sem., 1979. Ordained to ministry Luth. Ch., 1979. Pastor Cross of Glory Luth. Ch., Baton Rouge, 1979-81, Good Shepherd Luth. Ch., West Bend, Wis., 1981-85, Mt. Zion Luth. Ch., Kenosha, Wis., 1985-94, Lola Park Luth. Ch., Redford, Mich., 1994—; mem. S.E. Wis. Bd. of Evangelism, Milw., 1989-93, mem. nominating com., 1990, chmn. So. Pastoral Conf., Kenosha, 1990—; dir., vice chmn. Shoreland Luth. High Sch., 1988-94; bd. regents Huron Valley Luth. H.S., 1995-98. Republican. Home: 29522 Oakview St Livonia MI 48154-4464 Office: Lola Park Luth Ch 14750 Kinloch Redford MI 48239-3118 *The only thing that's truly important in life is sharing Jesus Christ as our crucified and risen Savior. That makes a difference, not only for this life but for all eternity.*

GIBBONS, JAMES ARTHUR, congressman; b. Reno, Dec. 16, 1944; s. Leonard A. and Matilda (Hancock) G.; m. T. Dawn Sanders-Snelling, June 21, 1986; children: Christopher, Jennifer, James A. Jr. BS in Geology, U. Nev., Reno, 1967, MS in Mining Geology, 1973; JD, Southwestern U., 1979. Bar: Nev. 1982, U.S. Dist. Ct. Nev. 1982. Hydrologist U.S. Fed. Water Master, Reno, 1963-67; geologist Union Carbide Co., Reno, 1972-75; comml. pilot Western Airlines, Inc., L.A., 1979-88; pilot Delta Airlines, Salt Lake City, 1988—; sr. land mgr., atty. Homestake Mining Co., Reno, 1980-82; pvt. practice Reno, 1982—; mem. 105th Congress from Nev. 2nd Dist., 1997—; environ. atty. Alaskan Wilderness Soc., Anchorage, 1982-83; mem. Congressional Com. on Nat. Security, 1997—, Resources, 1997—, Intelligence, 1998—. Contbr. articles to profl. pubs. Mem. Nev. Coun. on Econ. Edn., 1986; mem. Nev. State Assembly, 1988—. Lt. col. Nev. Air Nat. Guard, Persian Gulf, 1990-91; with USAF, 1967-72. Decorated DFC. Mem. Assn. Trial Lawyers of Am., Nev. Trial Lawyers Assn., Rocky Mt. Mineral Law Found., Comml Law League Am., Am. Inst. Mining Engrs., Nev. Landman's Assn. (chmn. 1981-82, cons. atty. 1982-83). Republican. Avocation: flying. Office: US Ho Reps 100 Cannon Washington DC 20515-2802

GIBBONS, JAMES FRANKLIN, electrical engineering educator; b. Leavenworth, Kans., Sept. 19, 1931; s. Clifford Hugh and Mary Jewel (Petty) G.; m. Mary Lynn Krywick; children—Robert, Sally, Laura. B.S., Northwestern U., 1953; Ph.D., Stanford U., 1956. Prof. elec. engring. Stanford U., Calif., 1956-84, 96—, Reid Weaver Dennis prof. elec. engring., 1983-84, 96—, dean Sch. Engring., 1984-96; Frederick Emmons Terman prof. engring. Stanford U., 1984-96; bd. dirs. Centigram, Cisco Systems, Raychem Corp., Menlo Park, Calif., Lockheed Martin, Bethesda, Md., El Paso (Tex.) Energy; founder, chmn. Sera Learning Techs.; cons. Shockley Transistor Corp., 1957-63, Fairchild Semiconductor, 1964-71, Avantek, Inc., 1964-91; chmn. grad. fellowship panel NSF, 1967-70; mem. Newman com. HEW Task Force on Higher Edn., 1969-74; mem. ednl. tech. panel Pres. Sci. Adv. Com., 1971-73; Fulbright guest lectr. European univs.; vis. prof. nuclear physics dept. Oxford U., 1970-71; vis. prof. U. Tokyo, 1971; cons. electronics br. Atomic Energy Research Establishment, 1971; mem. sci. team for exchanges on ion implanation and beam processing U.S. Nat. Acad. Scis., 1971, 76, 77, 79, 81. Author: (with J. G. Linvill) Transistors and Active Circuits, 1961, (with P. E. Gray, D. DeWitt and A. R. Boothroyd) SEEC Vol. 2: Physical Electronics and Models of Transistors, 1964, Semiconductor Electronics, 1966; editor: Fundamentals of Electronic Science, 1970-78; contbr. articles to profl. jours.; inventor tutored video instruction technique. Recipient Western Electric Fund award Am. Soc. Engring. Edn., 1971, award for Outstanding Achievement, No. Calif. Solar Energy Assn., 1975, Founder's prize Tex. Instruments, 1983, Outstanding Alumni award Northwestern U., 1985, Rappaport award IEEE Electron Devices Soc., 1990, Univ. Rsch. award Semicondr. Industry Assn., 1996, Medal of Achievement award Am. Electronics Assn., 1966; NSF and NAS fellow, 1953-56; Fulbright fellow Cambridge (Eng.) U., 1956-57; NSF postdoctoral fellow, 1963-64; inducted Santa Clara County Bus. Hall of Fame, 1997, Silicon Valley Engring. Hall of Fame, 1997. Fellow IEEE (Jack A. Morton award 1980, Edn. medal 1985, Solid State Sci. and Tech. award Electrochem. Soc. 1989); mem. Nat. Acad. Engring., Nat. Acad. Sci., Swedish Acad. Engring. Scis., Norwegian Acad. Tech. Scis., Am. Acad. Arts and Scis., Sigma Xi, Tau Beta Pi (award for outstanding undergrad. engring. teaching 1976), Eta Kappa Nu. Home: 320 Tennyson Ave Palo Alto CA 94301-3835 Office: Elec Engring Dept CISX-201X Paul G Allen Bldg Stanford CA 94305-4075

GIBBONS, JANET M., home health services admininstrator; b. Windber, Pa., Sept. 3, 1952; d. John and Irene (Zugrovich) Sesack; m. Donald Harry Creveling, Nov. 3, 1973 (div. 1987); children: Megan, Colin; m. Merle Dayton Gibbons, Oct. 4, 1992; 1 child, Michael. RN, Sacred Heart Sch. Nursing, Allentown, Pa. RN, Pa. Operating rm. nurse Sacred Heart Hosp., Allentown, 1973-88; supervisor Leader Manor Care Home., Bethlehem, Pa., 1988-90; contracted charge nurse Skilled Nursing Inc., Flourtown, Pa., 1988-92; dialysis nurse Good Samaritan, Johnstown, Pa., 1992-93; home health nurse Windber (Pa.) Hosp., 1993-94; clin. supervisor 1st Am. Home Care, Everett, Pa., 1994-96; dir. profl. svcs. IHS Home Care, Everett, 1996—. Office: IHS Home Care RR 1 Box 78B Everett PA 15537-9511

GIBBONS, JOHN HOWARD (JACK GIBBONS), government official, physicist; b. Harrisonburg, Va., Jan. 15, 1929; s. Howard K. and Jessie Diana (Conrad) G.; m. Mary Ann Hobart, May 21, 1955; children: Virginia Neil, Diana Conrad, Mary Marshall. BS in Math. and Chemistry, Randolph-Macon Coll., 1949, ScD (hon.), 1977; PhD in Physics, Duke U., 1954; PhD in Humane Letters and Sci. (hon.), Ill. Inst. Tech., 1994; PhD in Sci. (hon.), Mt. Sinai Med. Sch., 1995; ScD (hon.), U. Delaware, 1996, Duke U., 1997, U. Md., 1997. Physicist and group leader nuclear geophysics Oak Ridge Nat. Lab., 1954-69, dir. environ. program, 1969-73; dir. Energy Conservation Office, Fed. Energy Adminstrn., Washington, 1973-74; prof. physics, dir. Energy, Environ. and Resources Center, U. Tenn., Knoxville, 1974-79; dir. Office of Tech. Assessment, U.S. Congress, 1979-92; asst. to Pres. for sci. and tech. Exec. Office of the Pres., Washington, 1993-98; dir. of sci. and tech. policy Exec. Office of Pres., Washington, 1993-98; Karl T. Compton lectr. MIT, 1998-99; sr. fellow NAE, 1999—; mem. sr. adv. panel Energy Modeling Forum, 1980-92; mem. steering com. Symposium Series on Tech. and Soc., NAE, 1984-92; mem. energy rsch. adv. bd. U.S. Dept. Energy, 1978-79; bd. dirs. Resources for the Future, 1983-92; mem. energy and resources com. Aspen Inst., 1979—; mem. adv. com. Stanford U. Sch. Engring., 1984-87, Electric Power Rsch. Inst., 1986-92; mem. Carnegie Corp. Sci., Tech. and Govt. Task Force on Long Term Goals and Priorities, 1990-92; bd. dirs. Quantum Energy Techs. Corp., Dynamac Corp., Gibbons Surg. Corp.; mem. com. advisors Nat. Renewable Energy Lab., 1998—. Author: This Gifted Age: Science and Technology at the Millenium, 1997; contbr. articles to profl. jours. Chmn. bd. assocs. Randolph-Macon Coll., Ashland, Va., 1980-83, trustee, 1977-79; bd. dirs. World Resources Inst., 1998—. Decorated comdr. Ordre des Palmes Academiques (France), officer's cross Order of Merit (Germany); recipient Disting. Svc. award Fed. Energy Adminstrn., 1974, Pub. Svc. award Fedn. Am. Scientists, 1990, Disting. Alumni award James Madison U., 1993, Life Achievement in Sci. award Commonwealth of Va., 1995, First Seymour Cray High Performance Computing Industry Recognition award, 1997, Disting. Svc. medal NASA, 1998. Fellow AAAS (bd. dirs. 1988-90, Philip Hauge Abelson prize 1993), Assn. for Women in Sci., Am. Phys. Soc. (Leo Szilard award for physics in pub. interest 1991), NSF (Disting. Pub. Svc. award 1998), Am. Assn. Engring. Socs. (chmn.'s award 1998); mem. NAE (Arthur Bueche award 1998), Coun. Fgn. Rels., N.Y. Acad. Scis. (bd. govs. 1998—, trustee 1998—), Cosmos Club (pres.-elect), Sigma Xi (pres. 1999—), Phi Beta Kappa, Pi Gamma Mu, Omicron Delta Kappa, Pi Mu Epsilon, Sigma Pi Sigma, Sigma Xi (John P. McGovern Sci. and Soc. award and medal 1997). Episcopalian. Home: PO Box 497 The Plains VA 20198-0497 *My formal training in physics, backed by a liberal arts education, enabled me to drink deeply from the sweet spring of basic research for many years. When I took leave from disciplinary research and became immersed in analysis of socio-technical issues, it was a most discomforting step. But having taken it, the new challenges were not only enlivening, but also surprisingly susceptible to the problem-solving approaches I had learned in science. The lessons: (1)Training in physics is an effective instrument to learn how to solve many kinds of problems; (2)A change in professional direction about every decade or so is a great tonic; (3)Attacking issues from fresh perspectives is a natural ingredient of creativity.*

GIBBONS, JOHN MARTIN, JR., physician, educator; b. N.Y.C., Feb. 25, 1933; s. John Martin and Mary Frances (Darr) G.; m. Mary Therese Peyser, Dec. 26, 1955; chidlren: Catherine Way, Mary Sloan, John M. III, Fredericka Kerr, Myles. AB, Holy Cross Coll., 1954; MD, Georgetown U., 1958. Diplomate Am. Bd. Ob-Gyn., Am. Bd. Maternal and Fetal Medicine. Intern and resident ob-gyn Saint Vincent's Hosp., N.Y.C., 1958-63; from asst. to assoc. prof. ob-gyn. U. Conn., Farmington, 1970-78, prof. ob-gyn., 1978—; chief dept. ob-gyn. Fordham Hosp., N.Y.C., 1968-70; dir. dept. ob-gyn. Saint Francis Hosp. and Med. Ctr., Hartford, Conn., 1970-93, sr. v.p. for med. affairs, 1993-99. Mem. Capital Area Health Consortium Bd., 1978—; mem. exec. com. Combined Hosps. Fund, 1978-82, Mt. Sinai Hosp. Bd., 1990-95; mem. Bristol Hosp. Bd.; mem. Hartford Ballet Bd., 1978-83, hon. mem., 1983-95, v.p., 1993-95, pres., 1995-97; mem. Med. Delivery Sys., Inc., 1985-88, Greater Hartford Arts Coun., 1988-92, 95-97; corporator Wadsworth Atheneum, 1987-97; overseer Bushnell Meml. Hall, 1990—. Capt. USAR, 1961-68. Fellow ACOG (dist. treas. 1987-91, dist. vice chmn. 1991-94, nat. fin. com. 1992—, dist. chmn. 1994-97, nat. treas. 1997—), ACS, Soc. Perinatal Obstetricians, Obstet. Soc. Boston; mem. Conn. State Med. Soc. (sec. ob-gyn., vice chmn. 1979-82, chmn. 1982-85), Hartford Med. Soc., Hartford Club, Hartford Golf Club, Harvard Club of N.Y.C., Lotos Club (N.Y.C.). Office: Saint Francis Hosp Med Ctr 114 Woodland St Hartford CT 06105-1200

GIBBONS, JULIA SMITH, federal judge; b. Pulaski, Tenn., Dec. 23, 1950; d. John Floyd and Julia Jackson (Abernathy) Smith; m. William Lockhart Gibbons, Aug. 11, 1973; children: Rebecca Carey, William Lockhart Jr. B.A., Vanderbilt U., 1972; J.D., U. Va., 1975. Bar: Tenn. 1975. Law clk. to judge U.S. Ct. Appeals, 1975-76; assoc. Farris, Hancock, Gilman, Branan, Lanier & Hellen, Memphis, 1976-79; legal advisor Gov. Lamar Alexander, Nashville, 1979-81; judge 15th Jud. Cir., Memphis, 1981-83; judge U.S. Dist. Ct. (we. dist.) Tenn., Memphis, 1983-94, chief judge, 1994—. Fellow Am. Bar Found., Tenn. Bar Found.; mem. Tenn. Bar Assn., Memphis Bar Assn., Order of Coif, Phi Beta Kappa. Presbyterian. Office: US Dist Ct 1157 Federal Bldg 167 N Main St Memphis TN 38103-1816

GIBBONS, MARTHA BLECHAR, psychotherapist, educator, consultant; b. Santa Fe, Aug. 9, 1950; d. Theodore Joseph and Margaret Estelle (Harvey) Blechar; m. Myles David Gibbons, June 18, 1977; 1 child, Adam David. BSN, San Jose (Calif.) State U., 1973; MS in Maternal-Child Nursing, Med. Coll. of Va., 1977, PNP, 1978; PhD in Human Devel., U. Md., 1990. PNP Pa. Hosp., Phila.; clin. nurse specialist pediatric urology dept. Children's Hosp. of Phila.; cmty. health nurse Frankfurt (Germany) Mil. Cmty.; psychiat. liaison nurse Tex. Children's Hosp., Houston; pediatric oncology nurse practitioner M. D. Anderson Hosp. and Tumor Inst., Houston; clin. nurse specialist pediatric oncology dept. NIH, Bethesda, Md.; pvt. practice psychotherapy and cons. Chevy Chase, Md.; pediat. psychiat. liaison NIH; dir. pediat. nurse practitioner program sch. nursing U. Md.; assoc. dir. children's program St. Francis Ctr., Washington. Editor (newsletter) Children's Hospice Internat. Fellow Nat. Assn. Pediatric Nurse Assocs. and Practitioners (bd. dirs. Chesapeake chpt., pres.); mem. ANA, Assn. Death Edn. & Counseling, Md. Nurses Assn., D.C. Nurses Assn., Assn. Pediatric Oncology Nurses, Assn. for Care Children's Health, Sigma Theta Tau. Home: 6669 Barnaby St NW Washington DC 20015-2331 Office: 5135 Macarthur Blvd NW Washington DC 20016-3315 also: 4500 N Park Ave Ste 801N Chevy Chase MD 20815-7239

GIBBONS, MARY PEYSER, civic volunteer; b. N.Y.C., Dec. 15, 1936; d. Frederick Maurice and Catherine Mary (McKelvey) Peyser; m. John Martin Gibbons, Dec. 26, 1955; children: Catherine Way, Mary Sloan, John, Fredericka Kerr, Myles. Trustee Wadsworth Atheneum, 1978—, Hartford Art Sch., 1985-95; regent U. Hartford, 1988-95—; bd. dirs. Hartford Ballet, 1981-95, Conn. Valley Girl Scouts, 1994-95, U.S. Found. World Fedn., Friends of Museums, 1990—; vol. Com. Art Mus., U.S. and Can., 1982-91; pres. Am. Assn. Mus. Vols., 1983-91, adv. bd. mem., 1991—; corporator St. Francis Hosp., 1990—, Hartford Ballet, 1995—. Mem. Hartford Golf Club, Town and County Club. Office: Sefton & Sheil Ltd 1130 Prospect Ave Hartford CT 06105-1124

GIBBONS, MICHAEL LAWRENCE, software engineer; b. New Haven, Conn., May 15, 1969; s. Robert Joseph and Kathryn Antoinette (Sheldon) G.; m. Mary Juanita Dewhirst, Apr. 15, 1992. Student, Villanova U., 1986-88; AS, Ohlone Coll., Fremont, Calif., 1990-92; BS in Computer Sci. Engring., U. Tex., Arlington, 1994. Systems engr. Tandy Corp., Phila., 1986-87; systems engring. mgr. Tandy Corp., Orange, Conn., 1988; systems engr. Grid Systems, Stamford, Conn., 1989; mktg. mgr. Grid Systems, Fremont, Calif., 1990-92, Fort Worth, 1992-93; instr. U. Tex., Arlington, 1994; software engr. Digital Print, Inc., Ft. Worth, 1995-96; systems engr. Telxon Corp., Dallas, 1996-98; dir. info. systems The Great Train Store Ptnrs., L.P., Dallas, 1998-99, chief info. officer, 1999—. Mem. Aircraft Owners and Pilots Assn., Alpha Gamma Sigma. Home: 1814 Hunters Ridge Dr Grapevine TX 76051-7923

GIBBONS, MILES J., JR., foundation administrator; b. Scranton, Pa., June 25, 1935; s. Miles J. and Claire (Kennedy) G.; m. Carole Forker; children: Miles D., Elisabeth D. BA, Dickinson Coll., Carlisle, Pa., 1957; JD, Georgetown U., 1964; postgrad., Harvard U., 1996. Cost acct. U.S. Steel, Johnstown, Pa., 1957-60; acct. RCA Svc. Co., Alexandria, Va., 1961-64; atty. Keating, Waterval and Johnson, Falls Church, Va., 1964-65; staff atty. AMP Inc., Harrisburg, Pa., 1965-68; counsel to minority leader Ho. of Reps. Commonwealth of Pa., Harrisburg, 1968-70; assoc. atty. Morgan, Lewis and Bockius, Harrisburg, 1968-71, ptnr., 1971-81, of counsel, 1981-84; exec. dir. The Helen F. Whitaker Fund, Mechanicsburg, Pa., 1984—, The Franklin H. and Ruth L. Wells Found., Machanicsburg, 1983—; pres. The Whitaker Found., Rosslyn, Va. and Mechanicsburg, Pa., 1981—. Mem. sch. bd. Northern York County Sch. Dist., Dillsburg, Pa., 1984-88; chair problem solving com. United Way of Capital Region, Harrisburg, 1990-91; bd. dirs. United Way of Pa., 1994-95; bd. dirs. South Ctrl. Pa. Housing Devel. Found., Harrisburg, 1990-95, mem. exec. com., 1991-95; bd. dirs. Coun. for Pub. Edn., Harrisburg, 1989-92, The Fredricksen Found., Mechanicsburg, Pa., 1990—; mem. adv. bd. Milton S. Hershey Med. Sch., 1992-98; vol. Big Bros./Big Sisters, Harrisburg, 1990-95; co-chair Found. Exec. Rountable, Harrisburg, 1989—; bd. dirs. Capital Campaign Review Com., Harrisburg, 1989—, chair, 1992—. Mem. Rotary Club Harrisburg (pres. 1988-89, Community Svc. award 1990). Office: The Whitaker Found 1700 N Moore St Ste 2200 Arlington VA 22209-1923

GIBBONS, PATRICK CHANDLER, physicist, educator; b. Washington, Dec. 18, 1943; s. Myles Francis and Margaret Mack (Chandler) G.; m. Jane Elizabeth Forsell, Aug. 17, 1968; children: Elizabeth Jane, Jonathan Myles, Jane Chandler, Katherine Forsell. BS, Georgetown U., 1965; PhD, Harvard U., 1971. Physics instr. Princeton (N.J.) U., 1971-73, asst. prof. physics, 1973-76; asst. prof. physics Washington U., St. Louis, 1976-79, assoc. prof. physics, 1979-89, prof. physics, 1989—. Contbr. articles to Philos. mag., Jour. Non-Crystal Solids. Trustee Univ. Hills Subdiv., University City, Mo., 1984-87. Mem. Am. Phys. Soc., Univ. City Swim Club (pres. 1988-90, 94-95), Sigma Xi, Phi Beta Kappa. Office: Washington U PO Box 1105 Saint Louis MO 63188-1105

GIBBONS, REX VINCENT, geologist; b. Lumsden, Nfld., Can., Feb. 12, 1946; s. Clayton Manuel and Nita Mildred (Vincent) G.; m. Marjorie Stagg, May 20, 1966; children: Kim, Emily, Vince. BA in Edn., BSc, Meml. U. of Nfld., 1967, MSc in Geology, 1969; PhD in Geology, Calif. Inst. Tech., 1974. Registered profl. geologist, Nfld. Rsch. scientist NASA/Johnson Space Ctr., Houston, 1974-76; sr. geologist Nfld. Dept. Mines & Energy, St. John's, 1976-89; mem. Ho. of Assembly, St. John's West, Nfld., 1989-97, minister of mines and energy, 1989-94, 96-97, minister of natural resources, 1994-96; exec. v.p., sr. geosci. cons. Jacques Whitford Environment Ltd., Nfld. Geoscis. Ltd., St. John's, 1997—; bd. dirs. Newfoundland Power, Donner Minerals Ltd., St. John's Bd. Trade, Newfoundland Ocean Industries Assn. Contbr. numerous articles to profl. jours.; assoc. editor Geosci. Canada, 1980-85. Mem. Avalon Consol. Sch. Bd., St. John's, 1982-89, chmn., 1986-89; bd. mgmt. St. James United Ch., 1983-87; bd. regents Meml. U. of Nfld., 1978-81. Nat. Rsch. Coun. Can. grad. bursary, 1968-69; Nfld. Govt. grad. fellow, 1967-68, Centenary scholar, 1966-67. Mem. Can. Inst. Mining, Metallurgy & Petroleum (councilor, nat. v.p. 1982-87), Assn. Profl. Engrs. and Geoscientists of Nfld. Liberal Party. United Ch. Avocations: fly fishing, curling, canoeing, hunting, genealogy. E-mail: rex@road.nf.net. Home: 34 Spratt Pl, Saint John's, NF Canada A1E 4M2 Office: Jacques Whitford Environ, 607 Torbay Rd, St Johns, NF Canada A1A 4Y6

GIBBONS, ROBERT EBBERT, university official; b. Sharon, Pa., Nov. 15, 1940; s. Thomas Michael and Mary Jane (Ebbert) G.; m. Patricia Arlene Fox, Aug. 18, 1962; children: Patrick, Timothy, Roberta, Aaron. B.S., John Carroll U., 1962; M.A., Bowling Green State U., 1963, Ph.D., 1967. Pres. Viterbo Coll., La Crosse, Wis., 1980-91; asst. prof. English Our Lady of the Lake U., San Antonio, 1969-72, chmn. English dept., 1972-74, dir. humanities div., 1974-77, exec. asst. to pres., 1977-80, exec. v.p., 1991—. Bd. dirs.

Wis. Found. of Ind. Colls., Milw., 1980-91, pres., 1987-88; mem. USCC Com. on Cert. and Accreditation, 1988-94, vice chair, 1991-93. Mem. Nat. Assn. Ind. Colls. and Univs., Assn. Cath. Colls. and Univs., Soc. for Coll. and Univ. Planning, Phi Kappa Phi. Roman Catholic. Home: 3518 Hunters Gate St San Antonio TX 78230-2820 Office: Our Lady of the Lake U 411 SW 24th St San Antonio TX 78207-4666

GIBBONS, ROBERT PHILIP, management consultant; m. Mary Jane M. Jamieson, June 12, 1965; children: Laura Ann, Robert John. BSME, Stevens Inst. Tech., 1955; MS in Indsl. Mgmt., Purdue U., 1959. Ptnr., Touche Ross Co., N.Y.C., 1959-74; v.p., gen. mgr. Carborundum Co., Niagara Falls, N.Y., 1975-78; ptnr. Main Hurdman, N.Y.C., 1978-84, Zolfo, Cooper & Co., 1984-86, ptnr. Gibbons, Quintero & Co., N.Y.C., 1986-90, Gibbons & Co., 1990—; apptd. trustee U.S. Trustee and U.S. Bankruptcy Ct.; bd. dirs., chmn. audit com., compensation com. Weldotron Corp., 1974-91. Contbr. sect. to Am. Mgmt. Assn. Management Handbook, 1970. With U.S. Army, 1956-58. Mem. Am. Prodn. and Inventory Control Soc. (cert.), Inst. Mgmt. Cons. (cert.), Am. Bankruptcy Inst., Turnaround Mgmt. Assn. Office: Gibbons & Company 46 Knoll Rd Tenafly NJ 07670-1050

GIBBONS, SAM MELVILLE (SAM GIBBONS), business executive, former congressman; b. Tampa, Fla., Jan. 20, 1920; s. Gunby and Jessie Kirk (Cralle) G.; m. Martha Hanley, Sept. 14, 1946; children: Clifford, Mark, Timothy. JD, U. Fla., 1947. Bar: Fla. 1947. Mem. Fla. Ho. of Reps., 1952-58, Fla. Senate, 1958-62, 88th-104th Congresses from 7th (now 11th) Fla. dist., 1962-96; ranking minority mem. ways and means com., mem. joint taxation com.; chmn. Gibbons and Co., Washington, 1996—. Founder, 1st pres. U.S. Fla. Found., 1958. Served to maj. AUS, 1941-45, ETO. Decorated Bronze Star; named Outstanding Young Man Tampa Jr. C. of C., 1954; recipient President's award Tampa C. of C., 1955. Mem. Tampa Bar Assn. (dir.), Hillsborough Bar Assn. (dir.), Greater Tampa C. of C. (dir.). Democrat. Presbyterian (deacon). Office: Gibbons and Co 1455 Pennsylvania Ave NW Washington DC 20004-1008*

GIBBONS, WILLIAM JOHN, lawyer; b. Chgo., Jan. 22, 1947; s. Edward and Lottie (Gasiorek) G.; m. Marcia Guthridge, Dec. 31, 1976; children: Maximilian Clay, Bartholomew David, Ariel Katherine. BA, Northwestern U., 1968, JD, 1972. Bar: Ill. 1972, U.S. Dist. Ct. (no. dist.) Ill. 1972, U.S. Ct. Appeals (9th cir.) 1980, U.S. Supreme Ct. 1982, U.S. Ct. Appeals (7th cir.) 1984. Assoc. Kirkland and Ellis, Chgo., 1972-76; ptnr. Hedlund, Hunter and Lynch, Chgo., 1976-82; ptnr. Latham and Watkins, Chgo., 1982—, mng. ptnr. Chgo. office, 1995—. Bd. dirs. Pegasus Players, Chgo. Served with USAR, 1968-74. Mem. ABA, Chgo. Bar Assn. (chairperson class action com. 1994-95), Chgo. Coun. Lawyers, Seventh Cir. Bar Assn. Met. Club, Riverpark Club (Chgo.). Home: 4900 S Kimbark Ave Chicago IL 60615-2922 Office: Latham & Watkins Sears Tower Ste 5800 Chicago IL 60606-6306

GIBBONS, WILLIAM PATRICK, coach; b. Worcester, Mass., Mar. 20, 1959; m. Lisa Gibbons; children: William Robert, Robert Charles. BS, Clark U., Worcester, 1981, MS, 1983. Asst. boys' coach Doherty H.S., 1979-80; asst. men's coach Clark U., 1980-81; asst. men's coach Holy Cross Coll., Worcester, Mass., 1981-85, head women's basketball coach, 1985—; mem. NCAA Women's Basketball East Regional Adv. Com., 1992—, Kodak All-Am. Selection Com., 1991—; mem. CNN/USA Today Coaches Poll, 1990—; chmn. Greater Media CAble H.S. Scholar Athlete award; dir. Holy Cross Girls Basketball Camp; commr. Holy Cross Boys' Basketball Camp. Religious edn. vol. Holy Rosary Ch. Patriot League Coach of Yr., 1990-91. Mem. Women's Basketball Coaches Assn., Worcester Area Basketball Assn., Young Men's Bus. Assn. Worcester. Office: Coll Holy Cross Womens Athletic Dept College St Worcester MA 01610

GIBBONS, WILLIAM REGINALD, JR., poet, novelist, translator, editor; b. Houston, Jan. 7, 1947; s. William Reginald and Elizabeth (Lubowski) G.; m. Virginia Margaret Harris, June 8, 1968 (div. July 1982); m. Cornelia Maude Spelman, Aug. 18, 1983. AB, Princeton U., 1969; MA, Stanford U., 1971, PhD, 1974. Instr. Spanish Rutgers U., Brunswick, N.J., 1975-76; lectr. creative writing Princeton U., 1976-80, Columbia U., N.Y.C., 1980-81; prof. English Northwestern U., Evanston, Ill., 1981—, editor TriQuarterly, 1981-97; prof. MFA Program for Writers Warren Wilson Coll., 1989—. Author: Roofs Voices Roads, 1979 (Quar. Rev. prize), The Ruined Motel, 1981, Saints, 1986, Maybe It Was So, 1991, Five Pears or Peaches, 1991, William Goyen: A Study of the Short Fiction, 1991, Sweetbitter, 1994, Sparrow: New and Selected Poems, 1997, Homage to Longshot O'Leary, 1999; translator: Selected Poems of Luis Cernuda, 1978, Guillén on Guillén, 1979; editor: The Poet's Work, 1979, (with G. Graff) Criticism in the University, 1985, The Writer in Our World, 1986, Fiction of the Eighties, 1990, Thomas McGrath: Life and the Poem, 1991. Woodrow Wilson fellow Stanford U., 1969-70; Fulbright fellow Spain, 1971-72; Guggenheim fellow, 1983-84; NEA fellow, 1984; Ill. Arts Coun. fellow, 1988; recipient Translation prize Denver Quar., 1977, Short Story award Tex. Inst. Letters, 1986, Carl Sandburg award, 1992, Anisfield-Wolf Book award, 1995, Jesse Jones award Tex. Inst. Letters, 1995, Ill. Arts Coun. Lit. awards, 1996, 97, Balcones Poetry prize, 1998. Mem. PEN Am. Ctr., Poetry Soc. Am. (John Masefield Meml. award 1991), Associated Writing Programs (bd. dirs. 1984-87), The Guild Complex (bd. dirs. 1989—). Office: Northwestern U Dept English Univ Hall 215 Evanston IL 60208-0801

GIBBS, ANTONY (TONY), film editor. Editor: (films) The Loneliness of the Long Distance Runner, 1962, A Taste of Honey, 1962, Tom Jones, 1963, The Luck of Ginger Coffey, 1964, The Knack...And How to Get It, 1965, The Loved One, 1965, Petulia, 1968, Performance, 1970, Walkabout, 1971, (with Robert Lawrence) Fiddler on the Roof, 1971, Jesus Christ Superstar, 1973, Rollerball, 1975, The Sailor Who Fell from Grace with the Sea, 1976, A Bridge Too Far, 1977, (with Graeme Clifford) F.I.S.T., 1978, Yesterday's Hero, 1979, (with George Trirogoff) Butch and Sundance: The Early Days, 1979, (with Anne V. Coates and Stanley Warnow) Ragtime, 1981, The Dogs of War, 1981, Bad Boys, 1983, Dune, 1984, Agnes of God, 1985, Tai-Pan, 1986, Russkies, 1987, Stealing Home, 1988, (with Lou Lombardo) In Country, 1989, The Runner, 1990, The Taking of Beverly Hills, 1992, The Man Without a Face, 1993, Don Juan DeMarco, 1995, Ronin, 1998, (TV movies) Devlin, 1992, A Case for Life, 1996, Crime of the Century, 1996, George Wallace, 1997. Office: 15691 Royal Ridge Rd Sherman Oaks CA 91403-4208

GIBBS, ARLAND LAVERNE, retired real estate agent; b. New Lyme, Ohio, July 24, 1916; s. Myrl DeForest and Freda Amber (Ritter) G.; m. Winifred Imogene Willard, Apr. 13, 1941; children: Marjorie Ann Gibbs Flock, Suzanne Elizabeth Gibbs Wludyga. Student, Youngstown State U., 1985. Owner, operator Gibbs Bakery Delivery Svcs., Ashtabula County, Ohio, 1937-40; grinder Lake City Malleable, Ashtabula, Ohio, 1943; sales agt. Town & Village Ins. Svc. Inc. of Columbus, Ohio, 1940-81; owner, operator retail flea market "I Saw It Here", Jefferson, Ohio, 1981-96; realtor Joan Curtis Realty, Ashtabula, 1992-96; founder Gibbs Ins. Svc., Andover, Ohio, 1940—. Pres. Jefferson Music Boosters, 1961, Ashtabula County Hist. Soc., 1982-84. Sgt. armored inf. U.S. Army, 1941-43. Named Citizen of Yr., Jefferson Area C. of C., 1983. Mem. SAR (pres. Northeastern Ohio chpt. 1996), DAV (life), Am. Legion (life), Masons (master 1950-80, high priest, 32 degree mem. Valley of Cleve. chpt.), Order Ea. Star (50 yr. membership award 1991), Lions Club. Republican. Methodist. Avocations: collecting stamps, small household antiques, historian. Home: 206 S Chestnut St Jefferson OH 44047-1315

GIBBS, BRIAN J., behavioral scientist, business educator; b. Vancouver, BC, Canada, July 28, 1959; came to the U.S., 1985; s. Richard H. and Jean E. G. BSc in Biopsychology, U. B.C., 1982, MA in Psychology, 1985; PhD in Behavioral Sci. and Mktg., U. Chgo., 1992. Rschr. Psychophysics Lab., Vancouver, B.C., 1980-82, Attention Lab., Vancouver, B.C., 1982-85; researcher Decision Rsch. Lab., Chgo., 1985-90; asst. prof. mktg. and behavioral sci. Grad. Sch. Bus. Stanford (Calif.) U., 1990-98; assoc. prof. mgmt. Owen Grad. Sch. Mgmt. Vanderbilt U., Nashville, 1998—; bd. dirs. (hon.) Round Table Group, Inc.; presenter rsch. seminars in field in U.S. and abroad. Contbr. articles to profl. jours. Fellow Natural Scis. and Engring. Rsch. Coun. Can., Social Scis. and Humanities Rsch. Coun. Can., Am. Mktg. Assn. doctoral consortium fellow. Mem. Am. Mktg. Assn., Am. Psychological Soc., Assn. Consumer Rsch., Inst. for Ops. Rsch. and Mgmt. Sci., Soc. for Consumer Psychology, Soc. Judgement and Decision Making. Avocations: martial arts, photography, snorkeling, hiking, film. Office: Vanderbilt U Owen Grad Sch Mgmt 401 21st Ave S Nashville TN 37203

GIBBS, DAVID GEORGE, retired food processing company executive; b. Vancouver, B.C., Can., May 5, 1925; s. Albert Edward and Florence (Bedford) G.; m. Lenore Joyce De Geer, Oct. 7, 1949; 1 dau., Susan Caroline. Grad. high sch.; M.B.A., Simon Fraser U., 1975. C.P.A., Can. Audit clk. Price Waterhouse (chartered accountants), 1943-46; with Kelly Douglas Co. Ltd., Vancouver, 1946-89; controller Kelly Douglas Co. Ltd., 1965-89, v.p., 1975-89; elected bd. dirs., elected pres. Western Lettuce Now Inc., 1996. Treas. Burrard Yacht Club, Coalition to Eliminate Abuse of Srs., D.K.G.D. Enterprises Ltd. Named Ky. col., 1968. Mem. Fin. Execs. Inst. Clubs: Capilano Lions (charter pres. 1977), Masons. Home: 956 Belgrave St, North Vancouver, BC Canada V7R 1Z2

GIBBS, DENIS LAUREL, radiologist; b. Wayne, Mich., Mar. 6, 1945; s. Laurel Pierce and Alwyn Marie (Larson) G.; m. Paula Kay Lynn, Sept. 6, 1974 (div. Aug. 1988); children: Jeremy Paul, Matthew Ryan, Kevin Christopher, Denis Patrick; m. Kathleen Marie DeLaFuente, July 9, 1989; 1 child, Andrew Zachery. BS, Andrews U., Berrien Springs, Mich., 1967, postgrad., 1967-69; DO, Kansas City Coll. Osteopathic Medicine, 1974. Bd. cert. radiology, bd. cert. nuclear medicine Am. Osteo. Coll. Radiology. Intern, radiology resident Doctors' Hosps., Columbus, Ohio, 1974-78, staff radiologist, 1978; chmn. dept. radiology Rocky Mountain Hosp., Denver, 1978-88, vice chief of staff, 1982, chief of staff, 1983, 84; chmn. dept. radiology Colo. Plain Med. Ctr. Regional Trauma Ctr., Ft. Morgan, 1988—, vice chief of staff, 1992; med.-legal cons., Colo., Calif., Fla., 1979—; consulting radiologist East Morgan Hosp., Luth. Health Sys., Brush, colo., 1988—; CEO IRS Radiology Cons., P.C., Ft. Morgan, 1988—. Med. reviewer Post Grad. Medicine. Acad. booster Fort Morgan H.S./Morgan C.C. Mem. Am. Osteopathic Assn., Am. Osteopathic Coll. Radiology, Nat. Assn. Seventh-Day Adventist Osteopaths, Colo. Med. Soc., Colo. Osteopathic Soc., Ft. Morgan Med. Soc., Colo. Radiology Soc. Republican. Avocations: snorkeling, skin diving, racquetball, sports car enthusiast and owner. Home: PO Box 1243 Fort Morgan CO 80701-1243 Office: IRS Radiology Cons PC 1000 Lincoln St Fort Morgan CO 80701-3210

GIBBS, FREDERICK WINFIELD, lawyer, communications company executive; b. Buffalo, Mar. 22, 1932; s. Walter L. M. and Elizabeth Mari (Georgi) G.; m. Josephine Janice Jarvis, Dec. 20, 1954; children: Michael, Mathew, Robyn. BA cum laude, Alfred U., 1954; JD with Tax honors, Rutgers U., 1989. Bar: Pa. 1989, N.J. 1989, U.S. Dist. Ct. N.J. 1989. With N.Y. Tel. Co., 1954-65, ITT, 1965-86; mng. dir. ITT Standard Electrica, S.A., 1971-75; chief exec. officer ITT Standard Electrica, Brazil, 1975-77; exec. dir. ops. ITT Communications Ops. Group ITT Communications Ops. Group, 1977; corp. v.p. ITT, 1977-80; pres. U.S. Tel. and Tel. Corp., 1977-79, exec. dir., sr. group exec., 1980-86; dir. System 12, ITT, 1979-80; exec. v.p. ITT, 1980-86, ITT Telecommunications Corp., 1983-86; pvt. practice law Pemberton, N.J., 1989-95; founding ptnr. Gibbs & Gregory Attys. at Law, Pemberton, 1995—; cons. ITT, 1986-89, The World Bank/IFC, 1989—; pres. Mulberry Hill Enterprises, 1989—; bd. dirs. CMC Ind. Trustee Alfred U., 1981—, Whitesbog Found., 1996—; mem. planning bd. Barnegat Light, N.J.; elected Borough Coun., Barnegat Light, 1992, re-elected, 1995, 98. Named Hon. Citizen of Rio de Janeiro, 1973; inducted to Alfred Univ. Athletic Hall of Fame, 1993. Mem. ABA, N.J. Bar Assn., Pa. Bar Assn., Burlington County Bar Assn., Barnegat Light Taxpayers Assn. (v.p. 1989-90, pres. 1990-92), Rotary Internat. (bd. dirs. Pemberton club 1996-97, v.p. 1997-98, pres. 1999-00, Pemberton Rotarian of Yr. 1996-97). Home: 12 E 17th Street Rd Barnegat Light NJ 08006

GIBBS, JAMES ALANSON, geologist; b. Wichita Falls, Tex., June 18, 1935; s. James Ford and Clovis (Robinson) G.; m. Judith Walker, June 18, 1966; children: Ford W., John A. BS, U. Okla., 1957, MS, 1962. Cert. profl. geologist. Geologist Calif. Co., New Orleans, 1961-63, Lafayette, La., 1963-64; cons. geologist, oil producer, Dallas, 1964—; chmn. Five States Energy Co., 1984—. Author: Finding Work as a Petroleum Geologist: Hints to the Jobseeker, 1984. Trustee Inst. for Study Earth and Man, So. Meth. U. Lt. USNR, 1957-59. Recipient Regents award U. Okla., 1996. Mem. AAAS, Am. Geol. Inst. (trustee, William B. Heroy Disting. Svc. award 1994), Geol. Soc. Am., Dallas Geol. Soc. (pres. 1975-76, hon. mem. 1986), Am. Assn. Petroleum Geologists (sec. 1983-85, pres. 1990-91, Disting. Svc. award 1987, hon. mem. 1995), Am. Inst. Profl. Geol., Ind. Petroleum Assn. Am., Nat. Petroleum Coun., Tex. Ind. Producers and Royalty Owners Assn., Houston Geol. Soc., West Tex. Geol. Soc., Soc. Ind. Profl. Earth Scientists (past chmn. Dallas chpt., hon. mem. 1999), Petroleum Engrs. Club, Dallas Country Club, Dallas Petroleum Club, Explorers Club, Sigma Xi, Sigma Gamma Epsilon, Phi Delta Theta. Republican. Methodist. Home: 3514 Caruth Blvd Dallas TX 75225-5001 Office: 4925 Greenville Ave Ste 1220 Dallas TX 75206-4020

GIBBS, JAMIE, landscape architect, interior designer; b. D, Aug. 24; s. Irvin Lee and Glenna Lillian (Reid) G. BS in Landscape Architecture, BSA, MSA, Purdue U., 1977; MA in Historic Preservation, Columbia U., 1981. Cert. landscape architect; registered interior designer. Prin. designer Ind. Dept. Natural Resources, Indpls., 1977-78, Stoeppelwerth and Assocs., Indpls., 1978-79; dir. Bronx (N.Y.) Frontier Devel. Corp., 1979-81; owner, prin. Jamie Gibbs and Assocs., N.Y.C., 1979—; instr. Parsons Sch. Design, 1994—. Author: Landscape It Yourself, 1988, (booklet) All About Roses, 1990; mem. editl. bd. Window Fashions, 1994—, Fine Furniture Internat. 1995-98; contbr. articles to popular mags., profl. jours.; major projects include residential and resort design in U.S., P.R., St. Maarten, Moscow, Rio de Janeiro, Jamaica, Hilton Head, N.C. Bd. dirs. Coalition to Save City and Suburban Homes, N.Y.C., CityLore, N.Y.C., Civitas, 1992—, N.Y. Coun. on Alcoholism, 1997—; bd. dirs., assocs. com. Fedn. Protestant Welfare Agys., N.Y.C., 1987—, Grosvenor Neighborhood House, N.Y.C., 1990-97; adv. bd. N.Y. Found. for Sr. Citizens, N.Y.C., 1988-97, Counseling in Schs., Inc., N.Y.C., 1982-92, Hudson River Park Alliance, 1998—. Recipient various certs. of appreciation; Design scholar Columbia U., 1980. Mem. Am. Soc. Landscape Designers, Am. Soc. Interior Designers, Assn. Profl. Landscape Designers, Allied Bd. Trade., Internat. Furniture and Design Assn. Republican. Episcopalian. Avocation: collecting 18th and 19th high style furniture and decorative objects. Fax: 212-369-6332. Office: Jamie Gibbs and Assocs 340 E 93rd St New York NY 10128-5547

GIBBS, JOE JACKSON, former professional football coach, broadcaster, professional sports team executive; b. Mocksville, N.C., Nov. 25, 1940. BS, San Diego State U., 1964, MS, 1966. Asst. coach San Diego State U., 1966, Fla. State U., 1967-68, U. So. Calif., 1969-70, U. Ark., 1971-72, St. Louis Cardinals, NFL, 1973-77, Tampa Bay Buccaneers, 1978, San Diego Chargers, 1979-80; head coach Washington Redskins, 1981-93; sports commentator NBC, 1994—; team owner NHRA Top Fuel, Pro Stock with Funny Car, 1994—, NASCAR, 1994—; announcer NBC; race car owner. Coached Washington Redskins to Super Bowl Championship, 1982, 88, 91. Address: Joe Gibbs Racing 9900 Twin Lakes Pkwy Charlotte NC 28269-7652*

GIBBS, JORDAN SMITH, music educator, artist; b. Kinston, N.C., Sept. 11, 1936; d. Ernest Simpson Smith and Nell Brown (Johnson) Griffin; m. Gerald Goodwin Gibbs Jr., July 7, 1956; children: Anne, Stephen. Student, Duke U., 1954-56, George Washington U., 1974-77; Cert. in Piano, Conservatoire Royal de Musique, Mons, Belgium, 1980; BA in Music, Old Dominion U., 1984. Pvt. piano tchr. Cornwall-on-Hudson, N.Y., 1960-61; ch. organist TUSLOG Interdenominational Chapel, Ankara, Turkey, 1962-63; pvt. piano tchr. Mons, Belgium, 1978-79; piano tchr. Friends Sch., Virginia Beach, Va., 1984-86; pvt. piano tchr. Virginia Beach, 1993—; & Duke U. Libr. Assocs., 1989-92. Sec. bd. ARC, West Point, N.Y., 1959-60, hosp. vol., Ft. Sill, Okla., 1961, Ft. hood, Tex., 1969-70, Carlisle, Pa., 1970-71, vol. controller office, Norfolk, Va., 1987-88; asst. leader Girl Scout Mt. Vernon Scout Dist., Alexandria, Va., 1972-73; vol. Meals on Wheels Mt. Vernon Presbyn. Ch., Alexandria, 1972-73, Art League of Alexandria, 1972-73; vol. radiology clinic Internat. Red Cross, Mons, Belgium, 1978-80; sec.-treas. Shape Cycling Club, 1978-79; active docent Chrysler Mus., Norfolk, Va., 1992-99, bd. dirs. glass assocs., 1997-99; mem. worship com., fellowship com., flower guild First Presbyn. Ch., Virginia Beach, Va.; mem. Colonial Williamsburg (Va.) Found. Assocs., Libr. Assocs. Flower Guild, 1997-99; publicity chmn. SHAPE Art Assn., Mons, Belgium, 1978-79, Popular Choice Art Exhibit, SHAPE Hdqs., 1979; piano soloist Rachmaninoff Anniversary Celebration, Georgetown, Washington, 1974. Recipient Radiology Svc. award Red Cross, 1978-80. Mem. Met. Mus. Art, Va. Mus. FineArts, Phillips Collection, The Walters Art Gallery, Ctr. Contemporary Art, Muscarelle Mus. Art, Va. Hist. Soc., Nat. Trust, Nat. Mus. Women in the Arts, Am. Liszt Soc., Inc., Hermitage Found. Aux., Norfolk Soc. of Arts, Linkhorn Park Garden Club (editor yearbook 1992-94, sec. 1994-96, 1st v.p. 1996-98, rec. sec. 1998—, Ann. Flower Arrangements award 1999), Southwood Garden Club (rec. sec. 1971-72, 1st v.p. 1972-73), SACLANT Officers Wives Club (bd. dirs. 1982), Zeta Tau Alpha Alumnae (v.p. 1984-86, Sigma Alpha Iota (bd. dirs. 1980-84, Sword of Honor 1982, Grad. SAI Scholastic award 1984, SAI alumnae treas. 1990-99, treas. 1990-98, Stephen ministry program 1999—). Avocations: golf, tennis, skiing, needlepoint. Home: 160 Pinewood Rd Virginia Beach VA 23451-3958

GIBBS, JUNE NESBITT, state senator; b. Newton, Mass., June 13, 1922; d. Samuel Frederick and Lulu (Glazier) Nesbitt; m. Donald T. Gibbs, Dec. 8, 1945; 1 child, Elizabeth. BA in Math., Wellesley Coll., 1943; MA in Math., Boston U., 1947; postgrad. computer sci., U. R.I., 1981-84. Mem. from R.I. Rep. Nat. Com., 1969-80, sec., 1977-80; mem. R.I. State Senate, 1985—; mem. def. adv. com. Women in Svcs., 1970-72, vice chmn., 1972. Mem. Middletown Town Coun., 1974-80, 82-84, pres., 1978-80. Lt. (J.G.) USNR, 1943-46. Avocation: windsurfing. Home: 163 Riverview Ave Middletown RI 02842-5324 Office: Senate Minority Office State House Providence RI 02903 *To help restore faith in our government every elected official must constantly seek to do all he can for the people he serves and continually guard against doing anything which is self-serving or takes personal advantage of his office in any way.*

GIBBS, LAWRENCE B., lawyer; b. Hutchinson, Kans., Aug. 31, 1938; married; 2 children. BA, Yale U., 1960; JD, U. Tex., 1963. Assoc., then ptnr. Branscomb, Gary, Thomasson & Hall, Corpus Christi, Tex., 1963-72; dep. chief counsel IRS, Washington, 1972-73, acting chief counsel, 1973, asst. commr., 1973-75; ptnr. Johnson and Swanson, Dallas, 1976-86; commr. IRS, Washington, 1986-89; ptnr. Johnson & Gibbs, Washington and Dallas, 1989-94; mem. Miller & Chevalier, Washington, 1994—. Bd. advisors Taxation Mergers and Acquisitions; trustee Southwestern Legal Found., So. Fed. Tax Inst., Am. Tax Policy Inst.; mem. adv. coun. NYU Tax Inst. Mem. ABA (vice chmn. adminstrn. sect. taxation 1991-92), FBA, State Bar Tex. (chmn. taxation sect. 1978-86), D.C. Bar Assn., Am. Law Inst., Communities Found. Tex. Advv. Bd., Am. Coll. Trust and Estate Counsel (bd. regents 1990-96). E-mail: lgibbs@milchev.com. Office: Miller & Chevalier 655 15th St NW Ste 900 Washington DC 20005-5799

GIBBS, MARLA (MARGARET GIBBS), actress; b. Chgo., June 14, 1931; d. Douglas Bradley and Ophelia Birdie (Kemp) G.; children: Angela Elayne, Jordan Joseph, Dorian Demetrius. Student, Cortez Peters Bus. Sch., Chgo., 1950-52. Receptionist Service Bindery, Chgo., 1951-56; Addressograph machine operator Kelly Girls, 1956; switchboard operator Gotham Hotel, Chgo., 1957; info. operator Dept. Street Rwys., Chgo., 1957; travel cons. United Airlines, Detroit, 1963-74; v.p. Hormar, Inc., Los Angeles, 1978—; pres. Marla Gibbs Enterprises, Los Angeles, 1978—; restaurant owner Marla's Memory Lanes. Actress: (TV series) The Jeffersons (Florence the maid), 1974-85, Checking In, 1981, Pryor's Place, 1984-85, 227, 1985-90; rotating host The Late Show (Fox). TV miniseries include The Moneychangers, 1976, The Fire Next Time, 1993, (TV movies) The Missing Are Deadly, 1975, Menu for Murder, 1990, Lily in Winter, 1994; film appearances include Sweet Jesus, Preacher Man, 1973, Black Belt Jones, 1974, Up Against The Wall, 1991, The Meteor Man, 1993, Border to Border, 1998, Foolish, 1999, Lost & Found, 1999, The Visit, 2000. Recipient Image award NAACP, 1979-83, Appreciation award Los Angeles Sch. Dist., 1978, Nat. Acad. TV Arts and Scis. awards, 1976, Miss Black Culture Pageant awards, 1977, United Negro Coll. Fund awards, 1977, Nat. Com. Household Employment awards, 1978, Women Involved awards, 1979, Paul Robeson Players awards, 1980, Watts Reportory Co. awards, 1980, Calif. State Assembly awards, 1980, Community Service award Crenshaw High Sch., 1980; nominated Emmy awards, 1981-85. Mem. Sci. of Mind Ch. Office: Hormar Inc 7085 Hollywood Blvd Ste 731 Los Angeles CA 90028-6007 *I thought I knew how to love but forgot to include myself. I learned my lesson and took my first real step in faith.**

GIBBS, MARTIN, biologist, educator; b. Philadelphia, Penn., Nov. 11, 1922; s. Samuel and Rose (Sugarman) G.; m. Svanhild Karen Kvale, Oct. 11, 1950; children: Janet Helene, Laura Jean, Steven Joseph, Michael Seland, Robert Kvale. BS, Phila. Coll. Pharmacy, 1943; PhD, U. Ill., 1947. Scientist Brookhaven Nat. Lab., 1947-56; prof. biochemistry Cornell U., 1957-64; Abraham S. and Gertrude Berg prof. biology, chmn. dept. Brandeis U., Waltham, Mass., 1965-93; cons. NSF, 1961-64, 69-72, NIH, 1966-69; mem. corp. Marine Biol. Lab., Woods Hole, Mass., 1970, RESA lectr., 1969; NATO cons. fellowship bd., 1968-70; mem. Coun. Internat. Exch. of Scholars, 1976-82; chmn. adv. com. selection Fulbright Scholars for Eastern Europe; adj. prof. Bot. Inst., U. Munster, Fed. Republic of Germany, 1978, 80, 87; adj. prof. dept. botany U. Calif., Riverside, 1979-89. Author: Structure and Function of Chloroplasts, Crop Productivity-Research Imperative, Revisited, Hungarian-USA Binational Symposium on Photosynthesis; editor in chief Plant Physiology, 1963-92; assoc. editor: Physiologie Vegetale, 1966-76, Ann. Rev. Plant Physiology, 1966-71. Recipient Charles Reid Barnes award, 1984, Adolph E. Gude award, 1993, Martin Gibbs medal, 1993, U. Ill. Achievement award, 1996; Alexander von Humboldt fellow, 1987. Mem. NAS, AAUP, Am. Soc. Plant Physiologists (Barnes, Gude, Gibbs medal), Russian Soc. Plant Physiologists (hon. life mem.), Am. Acad. Arts and Scis., Am. Soc. Biochem. Molec. Biology, Can. Soc. Plant Physiologists (hon. life mem.), Acad. Scis. France. Home: 32 Slocum Rd Lexington MA 02421-5622

GIBBS, MARY BRAMLETT, banker; b. Corona, Calif., Sept. 18, 1953; d. Kenneth Frank and Kathy Lee (Hill) Harris; m. Charles Merrill Gibbs, 1987; 1 child, Meryl Elisabeth. Student U. Md., 1974-77, Southwestern Grad. Sch. Banking. Br. mgr. Peoples Nat. Bank of Md., Suitland, 1972-77; with Post Oak Bank, Houston, 1977-82, asst. v.p. ops. mgmt., 1980-82; v.p. loan ops. First City Nat. Bank Houston, 1982-89; sr. v.p. First Interstate Bank Tex., 1989-96; mgr. market devel. & pub. rels. Bank One, Houston, 1996—. Bd. dirs., life mem. Big Sisters-Big Bros. of Houston; mediator Neighborhood Justice Ctr., 1981; mem. Christ Ch. Cath.; bd. dirs. Ctrl. Houston, United Cerebral Palsy; pres. bd. dirs. Houston Women's Bus. Coun. Named Outstanding Young Houstonian, 1985, Woman on the Move, 1987; recipient Disting. Leadership award Nat. Assn. Cmty. Leadership, 1990, Regional SBA Women in Bus. Adv. award, 1999. Contbr. articles to profl. jours. Office: Bank One 910 Travis St # 4 Houston TX 77002-5800

GIBBS, OSCAR KEITH, physician assistant; b. N.Y.C., July 29, 1962; s. Keith Tam Gibbs and Judith Ellen (Burch) Rhodes; m. Tonya Marie Rush, Apr. 14, 1984; children: Ellsworth, Ellen. BS, U. Nebr., 1994, MS, 1997; grad., USAF Squadron Officer Sch., 1999. Cert. in primary care and surgery Nat. Commn. Cert. Physician Assts. Commd. airman basic USAF, 1980, advanced through grades to capt., 1998; staff physician asst. 42d MDOS, Maxwell AFB, Ala., 1994-98; sr. physician asst. Columbia Regional Med. Ctr., Montgomery, Ala., 1995-98, 86th ATH, Ramstein AFB, Germany, 1998—; sr. physician asst. 86th MDOS, Ramstein AFB, Germany, 1999—, chief primary care mgmt. team, 1999—; supr. Physician Asst. Phase II course, USAF, 1994-97; aeromed. physician asst., 42d MDOS, 1997. Vol. coord. ARC, Maxwell AFB, 1997. Capt., USAF, 1998—. Fellow Soc. Air Force Physician Assts.; mem. Am. Acad. Physician Assts., Co. Grade Officers Coun. Home: PSC 2 Box 7221 APO AE 09012-7219

GIBBS, PATRICIA HELLMAN, physician; b. Boston, Oct. 22, 1958; d. Frederick Warren and Patricia Christina (Sander) H.; m. Richard D. Gibbs, Dec. 22, 1984; children: Ruth, Samuel, Matthew, Kate, Frank. BA summa cum laude, Williams Coll., 1982; MD, Yale U., 1987. Diplomate Am. Bd. Family Practice. Intern, resident in family practice U. Wash., Seattle, 1987-90; ptnr. Tricia Gibbs, MD and Richard Gibbs, MD, San Francisco, 1990-95; co-founder, med. dir. San Francisco Free Clinic, 1993—; supervising physician San Francisco Ballet, 1990-95. Co-author: Medical and Orthopedic Issues of Active and Athletic Women-Skiing, 1993, Spine Care-Dance, 1993. Women's scholar Williams Coll., 1982, Class of '25 Athlete scholar, 1982; named Family Physician of Yr., Calif. Acad. Family Physicians, 1998. Mem. AMA, Am. Acad. Family Physicians, Phi Beta Kappa, Sigma Xi. Avocations: distance running, ski racing, computers. Office: San Francisco Free Clinic 132 Clement St San Francisco CA 94118-2420

GIBBS, ROBERT T. (TOM), sculptor, consultant; b. Dubuque, Iowa, Sept. 17, 1942; s. Robert Francis and Norma Margaret (Kieffer) G.; m. Dorothy Christena Burbach, June 8, 1968; 1 child, Jennifer Marie. BA in Art, Loras Coll., Dubuque, 1964; MA in Sculpture, U. Iowa, 1969, MFA in Sculpture, 1970. Instr. art Clarke Coll., Dubuque, 1968-69; asst. prof. art Ariz. State U., Tempe, 1970-72; supr. sculpture installations Hemmeter Devel. Corp., Kauai, Hawaii, 1988; mem. creative artists' planning project Iowa Arts Coun., Des Moines, 1988, mem. visual arts adv. panel, 1985-86. Sculpture comms. at Tween Mus., Duluth, Minn., 1989, Molly Rose Gallery, Garden, Fla., 1993, U. Dubuque, 1992, Morningside Coll., 1992, U. Ctrl. Ark., 1994, U. No. Iowa, 1995, Pier Walk, Chgo., 1998. Witness Congl. Hearing, Reauthorization of NEA, U.S. Congress, Washington, 1980. Grantee Iowa Arts Coun., 1977; recipient honorable mention Nat. Vietnam War Meml. Design Co., Washington, 1981, Gov.'s award for svc. to arts Gov. Iowa, Des Moines, 1989. Mem. Nat. Sculpture Soc. Avocation: computers. Home and Office: 1333 Kaufmann Ave Dubuque IA 52001-3162

GIBBS, RONALD STEVEN, obstetrician-gynecologist; b. Phila., Mar. 31, 1943. MD, U. Pa., 1969. Intern Hartford (Conn.) Hosp., 1969-70; resident ob.-gyn. U. Pa. Hosp., Phila., 1970-74; fellow maternal-fetal medicine U. Tex. Health Ctr., San Antonio, 1976-78; obstetrician-gynecologist Univ. Hosp. U. Colo., Denver, 1989—; prof., chmn. dept. ob.-gyn. U. Colo., Denver, 1989—. Dir., treas, Am. Bd. of Obstetric and Gyn, Residency Review Com. Mem. ACOG, AMA, Am. Gynecologic and Obstetric Soc. (sec.), Infectious Disease Soc. Am., Infectious Disease Soc. Ob/Gyn, Soc. Gynecologic Investigation, Soc. Perinatal Obstetric (bd. dirs.). Office: U Colo Health Sci Ctr 4200 E 9th Ave # Denver CO 80220-3706

GIBBS, SARAH PREBLE, biologist, educator; b. Boston, May 25, 1930; d. Winthrop Harold and Edith Dorothea (Hill) Bowker; m. Robert H. Gibbs, June 9, 1951 (div. 1962); 1 dau., Elizabeth Dorothea; m. Ronald J. Poole, Feb. 2, 1963 (div. 1980); 1 son, Christopher Harold. A.B., Cornell U., 1952, M.S., 1954; Ph.D., Harvard U., 1962. Research assoc. Inst. Animal Genetics Edinburgh U., 1963-65; asst. prof. botany McGill U., Montreal, Que., Can., 1966-69, assoc. prof. biology, 1969-74, prof., 1974-98, McDonald prof. bot., 1998, Macdonald emeritus prof., 1999—. Recipient Darbaker prize Bot. Soc. Am., 1975; NSF fellow, 1958-61; NIH fellow, 1961-63. Fellow AAAS, Royal Soc. Can.; mem. Can. Soc. Cellular and Molecular Biology (pres. 1972-73), Am. Soc. Cell Biology, Phycol. Soc. Am., Can. Assn. Univ. Tchrs., Phi Beta Kappa, Sigma Xi, Phi Kappa Phi. Home: 70 Henley Ave, Montreal, PQ Canada H3P 1V3 Office: McGill U Dept Biology, 1205 Avenue Docteur Penfield, Montreal, PQ Canada H3A 1B1

GIBBS, WILLIAM HAROLD, finance company executive; b. Evanston, Ill., Apr. 10, 1950; s. Harold William and Margaret Rose (Heidbreder) G. BS, Ariz. State U., 1973; MBA, U. Ill., 1975. CPA. Mgr. Price Waterhouse, Phoenix, 1975-82; chief fin. officer Apollo Group Inc., Phoenix, 1983-87; pres. U. Phoenix, 1987-98; sr. v.p. Apollo Group, Inc., Phoenix, 1998—. Office: Apollo Group Inc 4615 E Elwood St Phoenix AZ 85040-1958

GIBBY-SMITH, BARBARA, psychologist, nurse; b. Woodburn, Oreg., Dec. 13, 1938; d. Chester Clifton and Marvel Elizabeth (Hill) Gibby; m. Roy Milton Smith, June 2, 1957 (div. June 1990); children: Thomas Clifton, Jeffery Shawn, Mark Anderson. ADN, Chemeketa C.C., Salem, Oreg., 1972; BS, SUNY, Albany, 1980; MS, Western Oreg. State Coll., 1982; D of Psychology, Pacific U., Forest Grove, Oreg., 1993. Diplomate Am. Bd. Profl. Disability Cons., Am. Bd. Specialist, Am. Bd. Forensics Medicine; cert. addiction examiner. Adminstr. Birch St. Manor, Dallas, Oreg., 1973-81; disability determination specialist State of Oreg. Workers' Compensation Dept., Salem, 1983-85; counselor Women's Crisis Ctr., Salem, 1986-88; rehab. counselor Employer Rehab. Svcs., Portland, Oreg., 1985-87; therapist, counselor Pacific U., Hillsboro, Oreg., 1988-89, Forest Grove, 1989-91; intern in psychology Portland State U., 1991-92, Kaiser-Permanente, Salem, 1991-92; resident in psychology Tillamook (Oreg.) Counseling Ctr., 1993-95; hosp. privileges psychology and medicine Quality Healthcare, 1996—; pvt. practice psychologist; group therapy counselor Women's Crisis Ctr., Dallas, 1982-83; eating disorders group therapy facilitator, Salem, 1986-88; nat. register Doctoral Addiction Examiner. Active Women's Coalition Orgn., Salem, 1988—. Mem. APA (clin. neuropsychology divsn. 40), Am. Coll. Forensic Examiners (diplomate), Nat. Bd. Addiction Examiners (diplomate), Oreg. Psychol. Assn., Prescribing Psychologist Assn. (diplomate), Internat. Soc. Police Surgeons, Inc. Democrat. Avocations: golf, bicycling, traveling, geneology. Office: Mountain View Counseling Ctr 1911 Mountain View Ln Ste 500 Forest Grove OR 97116-2248

GIBERT, CHARLENE WEST, gifted education educator; b. Ft. Worth; m. Wayne Gibert, 1975; 1 child, Christine. MusB, Tex. Tech U., 1964; MEd, U. Houston, 1978, EdD, 1991. Cert. tchr., profl. counselor, Tex. Elem. tchr. music Lubbock (Tex.) Ind. Sch. Dist., 1965-68; jr. high sch. tchr. lang. arts Clear Creek Ind. Sch. Dist., Houston, 1968-79, tchr. gifted and talented edn. Spring Br. Ind. Sch. Dist., 1981—; cons. gifted and talented field. Editor, contbr: Biographical Dictionary of Gifted Education, 1988; also articles. Mem. First Presbyn. Ch., Houston. Mem. Nat. Assn. for Gifted Children, Tex. Assn. for Gifted and Talented, T. Avocations: music, travel. Home: 1926 Abby Aldrich Ln Katy TX 77449-2817

GIBIAN, GEORGE, Russian and comparative literature educator; b. Prague, Czech Republic, Jan. 29, 1924; came to U.S., 1940, naturalized, 1944; s. Richard and Vera (Sindelarova) G.; m. J. Catherine Annis, Sept. 2, 1950 (div. Aug. 1967); children: Peter, Mark, Stephen, Gregory, Lauren Mackenzie. AB, U. Pitts., 1943; MA, Johns Hopkins U., 1947; PhD, Harvard U., 1951. Instr. to assoc. prof. Smith Coll., 1951-59; asst. prof. Amherst Coll., 1952-54; asso. prof. Russian lit. U. Calif., Berkeley, 1959-60; Goldwin Smith prof. Russian and comparative lit. Cornell U., Ithaca, N.Y., 1961—; chmn. dept. Russian lit. Cornell U., 1962-73, 78-82, 90, chmn. Soviet Studies com., 1981-82, 90; sr. assoc. Columbia U. Russian Inst., 1969; exec. sec. Masaryk Publs. Trust, 1978-90; chmn. bd. overseers com. to visit Ukrainian Rsch. Inst., Harvard U. Author: Tolstoy and Shakespeare, 1957, Interval of Freedom: Soviet Literature During the Thaw, 1960, Russia's Lost Literature of the Absurd, 1971; editor: (critical editions) Dead Souls, 1985, Crime and Punishment, 1989, Anna Karenina, 1995, War and Peace, 1995, Portable 19th Century Russian Reader, 1993, Jana Cerna, Kafka's Milena, 1993; co-editor: Russian Modernism: Culture and the Avant-Garde, 1976, The Man with the Black Coat, 1997; translator, co-editor: The Poetry of Jaroslav Seifert, 1998; contbr. articles to profl. jours. Served with inf. AUS, 1943-46. Decorated Bronze Star medal with V; Guggenheim fellow, 1959-60; Fulbright research fellow U. Paris, 1960; NEH sr. fellow, 1974; Internat. Research Exchanges Bd. grantee to visit USSR and Czechoslovakia, 1965-66; Rockefeller Found. scholar, 1985. Mem. Am. Assn. Tchrs. Slavic and East European Langs., Am. Assn. for Advancement of Slavic Studies, Assn. Lit. Scholars and Critics. Home: 311 Roat St Ithaca NY 14850-2739 Office: Cornell U Dept Russian Lit Ithaca NY 14853-3201

GIBLETT, ELOISE ROSALIE, hematology educator; b. Tacoma, Wash., Jan. 17, 1921; d. William Richard and Rose (Godfrey) G. B.S., U. Wash., 1942, M.S., 1947, M.D. with honors, 1951. Mem. faculty U. Wash. Sch. Medicine, 1957—, research prof., 1967-87, emeritus research prof., 1987—; asso. dir., head immunogenetics Puget Sound Blood Center, 1955-79, exec. dir., 1979-87, emeritus exec. dir., 1987—; former mem. several research coms. NIH. Author: Genetic Markers in Human Blood, 1969; editorial bd. numerous jours. including Blood, Am. Jour. Human Genetics, Transfusion, Vox Sanguinis; Contbr. over 200 articles to profl. jours. Recipient fellowships, grants, Emily Cooley, Karl Landsteiner, Philip Levine and Alexander Wiener immunohematology awards, distinguished alumna award U. Wash. Sch. Med., 1987. Fellow AAAS; Mem. Nat. Acad. Scis., Am. Soc. Human Genetics (pres. 1973), Am. Soc. Hematology, Am. Assn. Immunologists, Brit. Soc. Immunology, Internat. Soc. Hematologists, Am. Fedn. Clin. Research, Western Assn. Physicians, Assn. Am. Physicians, Sigma Xi, Alpha Omega Alpha. Home: 6533 53rd Ave NE Seattle WA 98115-7748 Office: Puget Sound Blood Ctr 921 Terry Ave Seattle WA 98104-1256

GIBLETT, PHYLIS LEE WALZ, middle school educator; b. Denver, July 17, 1945; d. Henry and Leah (Pabst) Walz; B.S.B.A. (Estelle Hunter scholar 1963, Denver Classroom Tchr.'s scholar 1963, Outstanding Bus. Edn. Student scholar 1967), U. Denver, 1967, MBA, 1969; m. Thomas Giblett, May 31, 1975; children: Leann Ruth, Douglas Henry, John Peter. Tchr. bus. Aurora (Colo.) South Middle Sch., info. specialist, 1996—; tchr. Aurora Pub. Schs., 1967-80, 82-86, 88-96, on leave, 1980-82, 86-88, chmn. bus. dept., 1972-79; evening tchr. S.E. Met. Bd. Coop Services, 1967-68, post secondary/adult classes Aurora Pub. Schs., 1972-75, C.C. Denver, North Campus, 1973, Aurora Pub. Schs. Adult Edn., 1983-84; mem. Aurora Pub. Sch. System, mem. tech. com. 1991—, dist. tech. trainer, 1992—, Program Cadre mem., 1995-97, tech. cadre facilitator, 1996—, steering com. shared decision making, 1990-96, zero tolerance com., 1992-94, facilitator Mentor com., 1991-92, exploratory tchr. facilitator, 1992-96; mem. dist. tech. com. South Middle Sch., Aurora Dist. Tech. Com., 1975-79; adviser chpt. Future Bus. Leaders Am., 1976-78; mem. Colo. Curriculum Specialist Com., 1976-77. Treas. Aurora Coun. PTA, 1987-89, Century Elem. Sch. PTA, 1988-89, reflections chmn., 1987-89, 90-93; mem. PTA. Named Miss Future Bus. Tchr., Phi Beta Lambda of Colo., 1965. Mem. Nat., Mountain-Plains (participant leadership conf. 1977), Colo. Bus. Edn. Assns. (pres. 1976-77), Colo. Educators for/About Bus., Am., Colo. vocat. assns., NEA, Colo., Aurora edn. assns., Delta Pi Epsilon (pres.-elect Eta chpt. 1978, pres. 1980-81). Republican. Lutheran.

GIBLIN, JAMES CROSS, author, editor; b. Cleve., July 8, 1933; s. Edward Kelley and Anna Belle (Cross) G. BA, Case Western Res. U., 1954; MA, Columbia U., 1955. Asst. editor Criterion Books, N.Y.C., 1959-62; editor Lothrop, Lee & Shepard Co., N.Y.C., 1962-67; editor in chief Clarion Books, N.Y.C., 1967-79, pub., 1979-89, contbg. editor, 1989—. Author: The Scarecrow Book, 1980, The Skyscraper Book, 1981, Chimney Sweeps: Yesterday and Today, 1982 (Am. Book award 1983, Golden Kite award 1983), Fireworks, Picnics and Flags: The Story of the Fourth of July Symbols, 1983, Walls: Defenses Throughout History, 1984 (Golden Kite award 1985), The Truth About Santa Claus, 1985 (Boston Globe-Horn Book Nonfiction Honor Book award 1986), Milk: The Fight for Purity, 1986, From Hand to Mouth, 1987, Let There Be Light: A Book About Windows, 1988 (Golden Kite award 1989), Writing Books for Young People, 1990, The Riddle of the Rosetta Stone: Key to Ancient Egypt, 1990, The Truth About Unicorns, 1991, Edith Wilson: The Woman Who Ran the United States, 1992, George Washington: A Picture Book Biography, 1992, Be Seated: A Book About Chairs, 1993, Thomas Jefferson: A Picture Book Biography, 1994, When Plague Strikes: The Black Death, Smallpox, AIDs, 1995, The Dwarf, the Giant and the Unicorn: A Tale of King Arthur, 1996, Charles A. Lindbergh: A Human Hero, 1997 (Orbis Pictus Honor Book award 1998), The Mystery of the Mammoth Bones, and How it Was Solved, 1999; also numerous articles and short stories. Mem. Authors Guild, Soc. Children's Book Writers and Illustrators (bd. dirs.). Avocations: traveling, museum exhibits, movies, plays, walking. Home: 200 E 24th St Apt 1606 New York NY 10010-3919 *Having written books for both children and adults, I find the juvenile field more stimulating and exciting because of the responsibility the children's writer has to his or her impressionable young readers. If the writer gives them solid, truthful, imaginatively treated books, he or she is contributing in a very real sense to their education and development.*

GIBLIN, PATRICK DAVID, retired banker; b. St. Louis, July 24, 1932; s. Patrick Joseph and Ann Jane (Gill) G.; children: Mary Clare, Christopher, Gregory. BBA, Manhattan Coll., 1954; MBA, St. John's U., Jamaica, N.Y., 1965. Staff auditor KPMG Peat Marwick, N.Y.C., 1956-59; chief plant acct. div. Am. Machine & Foundry, Bklyn., 1959-63; with CBS, N.Y.C., 1963-73; controller electronic video rec. div. CBS, 1968-73, dir. corp. acctg., 1967-68; vice chmn., chief fin. officer CRESTAR Fin. Corp., Richmond, 1973-95; ret., 1995. Served with U.S. Army, 1954-56. Mem. Delta Mu Delta. Roman Catholic. Home: 3 Silver Bluff Way Savannah GA 31411-2510

GIBLIN, THOMAS PATRICK, labor union administrator; b. East Orange, N.J., Jan. 15, 1947; s. John Joseph and Theresa Elizabeth (Moran) G.; m. Mary Katherine Hughes, June 20, 1970; children: Thomas P. Jr., Noreen M., Edward M., Patrick F., Anne T. BA, Seton Hall U., 1969. Pres. Internat. Union of Oper. Engrs. Local 68, West Caldwell, N.J., 1975—; freeholder Essex County, Newark, 1977-78, 82-89, surrogate, 1990-93; now chmn. Dem. Party State of N.J. Candidate from 25th legis. dist. N.J. Assembly, 1973; chmn. Essex County Dem. Com., Newark, 1993—; treas. Essex County Dem. Com., Newark, N.J., 1979-82; alt. del. Dem. Nat. Conv., San Francisco, 1984, Atlanta, 1988, del. Chgo., 1996; commr. N.J. Real Estate Commn., Trenton, 1979-82; lay adv. bd. St. Vincent Acad., 1984—; chmn. bd. trustees St. Barnabas Burn Found., 1989-93, United Way Essex, 1976-82, 89-95; bd. dirs. Essex unit Assn. Retarded Citizens, 1986-96; trustee North Jersey Blood Ctr., 1991—. Named Man of Yr. United Cerebral Palsy, 1980; recipient Cert. of Merit, U.S. Dept. of Labor, 1979, Community Svc. award Frontiers Internat., 1985, Humanitarian award, N.J. Blood Ctr., 1988. Mem. N.J. Ins. Underwriting Assn. (bd. dirs. 1982-90). Democratic. Roman Catholic. Avocations: reading, swimming, traveling. Home: 40 Montague Pl Montclair NJ 07042-2820 Office: State Dem Party 150 W State St Trenton NJ 08608-1105*

GIBNEY, FRANK BRAY, publisher, editor, writer, foundation executive; b. Scranton, Pa., Sept. 21, 1924; s. Joseph James and Edna May (Wetter) G.; m. Harriet Harvey, Dec. 10, 1948 (div. 1957); children: Alex, Margot; m. Harriet C. Suydam, Dec. 14, 1957 (div. 1971); children: Frank, James, Thomas; m. Hiroko Doi, Oct. 5, 1972; children: Elise, Josephine. BA, Yale U., 1945; DLitt (hon.), Kyung Hee U., Seoul, Korea, 1974. Corr., assoc. editor Time mag., N.Y.C., Tokyo and London, 1947-54; sr. editor Newsweek, N.Y.C., 1954-57; staff writer, editorial writer Life mag., N.Y.C., 1957-61; pub., pres. SHOW mag., N.Y.C., 1961-64; pres. Ency. Brit. (Japan), Tokyo, 1965-69; pres. TBS-Brit., Tokyo, 1969-75, vice chmn., 1976—; v.p. Ency. Brit., Inc., Chgo., 1975-79; vice chmn., bd. editors Ency. Brit., Chgo., 1978—; pres. Pacific Basin Inst., Pomona Coll., Claremont, Calif., 1979—; prof. Pomona Coll., 1997—; bd. dirs. U.S. Com. for Pacific Econ. Cooperation, 1988—, v.p., 1993-95; cons. com. on space and aeros. U.S. Ho. of Reps., Washington, 1957-59; vice chmn. Japan-U.S. Friendship Commn., 1984-90, U.S.-Japan Com. Edn. and Cultural Interchange, 1984-90. Author: Five Gentlemen of Japan, 1953, The Frozen Revolution, 1959, (with Peter Deriabin) The Secret World, 1960, The Operators, 1961, The Khrushchev Pattern, 1961, The Reluctant Space Farers, 1965, Japan: The Fragile Super-Power, 1975, rev. edit., 1996, Miracle by Design, 1983, The Pacific Century, 1992, Korea's Quiet Revolution, 1993; co-author: The Battle for Okinawa, 1995; editor: The Penkovskiy Papers, 1965, Senso, 1995, Unlocking The Bureaucrats' Kingdom, 1998. Served to lt. USNR, 1942-46. Decorated Order of the Rising Sun 3d Class Japan, Order of Sacred Treasure 2d Class Japan. Mem. Council on Fgn. Relations, Tokyo Fgn. Corr. Club, Am. C.of C. (Tokyo), Japan-Am. Soc., Japan Soc. Roman Catholic. Clubs: Century Assn., Yale (N.Y.C.); Tokyo; Tavern, The Arts (Chgo.). Home: 1901 E Las Tunas Rd Santa Barbara CA 93103-1745

GIBRAN, KAHLIL, sculptor; b. Boston, Nov. 29, 1922; s. Nicholas and Rose (Gibran) G.; m. Jean English, July 1, 1957; children: Timothy; by previous marriage, Nicole. Student, Boston Mus. Sch., 1940-43. Exhibited widely as painter, 1949-52, life sized steel sculpture, 1953—, one person show bronzes, Cambridge Art Assn., 1977, Cathedral City, Va., 1993; exhbn.: Boston Arts Festival, 1985, Santa Fe, 1993; ann. exhbn. Bologna-Landi Gallery, East Hampton, L.I., N.Y., Denenberg Fine Arts, San Francisco, 1997, Contemporary Sculpture Chesterwood, 1997, St. Botolph Club, 1998, Art of the Spirit Forest Hills Cemetery, 1998; commd. bronze plaque of Kahlil Gibran, Copley Sq., Boston, 1977, Judge Francis Ford, Fed. Ct. House, Boston, 1977, Judge Anthony Julian, Fed. Ct. House, Boston, Elliot Norton medal, Boston, 1983, bronze figure of Kahlil Gibran, Worcester State Coll., 1987, West Canton Street Child, Hayes Pk., Boston, 1992, Processional Cross All Soul's Episcopal Ch., San Diego, 1993, bronze plaque composer Amy Beach, 28 Commonwealth Ave., Boston; inventor Gibran Tripod, Mus. Modern Art collection; sculpture and painting show Copley Soc., 1994; represented in permanent collections Pa. Acad., Tenn. Fine Arts Ctr., Norfolk (Va.) Mus., Chrysler Mus., William Rockhill Gallery, Swope Gallery, Brockton Fine Arts Ctr.; author: Sculpture--Kahlil Gibran, 1970, (with wife Jean Gibran) Introduction to Lazarus and His Beloved, 1973, Kahlil Gibran, His Life and World, 1974, rev. edit., 1991; author: (monograph) Observations on the Reasons for the Cremona Tone, 1993. Pres. Kahlil Gibran Scholarship Fund, Boston, 1974. Recipient George Widener award Pa. Acad., 1958; Guggenheim fellow, 1959-61; award Nat. Inst. Arts and Letters, 1961; Grand prize Boston Arts Festival, 1964; John Gregory award sculpture, 1965; Gold medal Internat. Sacred Art Show, Trieste, Italy, 1966. Address: 160 W Canton St Boston MA 02118-1216

GIBSON, ALTHEA, retired professional tennis player, golfer, state official; b. Silver, S.C., Aug. 25, 1927; d. Daniel and Annie B. (Washington) G.; m. William A. Darben, Oct. 17, 1965; m. Sydney Llewellyn, Apr. 11, 1983. B.S., Fla. A&M Coll., 1953; D. Pub. Service (hon.), Monmouth Coll., 1980; LittD (hon.), U. N.C., Wilmington, 1987; LHD (hon.), Upsala Coll., 1989. Amateur tennis player U.S., Europe, and S.Am., 1941-58; asst. instr. dept. health and phys. edn. Lincoln U., Jefferson City, Mo., 1953-55; made profl. tennis tour with Harlem Globetrotters, 1959; community rels. rep. Ward Baking Co., 1959; joined Ladies Profl. Golf Assn. as profl. golfer, 1963; apptd. to N.Y. State Recreation Council, 1964; staff mem. Essex County Park Commn., Newark, 1970; recreation supr. Essex County Park Commn., 1970-71; dir. tennis programs, profl. Valley View Racquet Club, Northvale, N.J., 1972; tennis pro Morven, 1973—; athletic commr. State of N.J., Trenton, 1975—; recreation mgr. City of East Orange, N.J., 1980; mem. N.J. State Athletic Control Bd., 1986; spl. cons. Gov.'s Coun. Phys. Fitness and Sports, N.J., 1988—; winner world profl. tennis championship, 1960, Wimbledon Women's Singles Championship, 1957, 58, Wimbledon Women's Doubles Championship, 1956-58, U.S. Women's Singles Championship, 1957, 58. Appeared in the movie The Horse Soldiers, 1958; author: I Always Wanted to Be Somebody, 1958. Named Woman Athlete of Yr., AP Poll, 1957-58; named to Lawn Tennis Hall of Fame and Tennis Mus., 1971, Black Athletes Hall of Fame, 1974, S.C. Hall of Fame, 1983, Fla. Sports Hall of Fame, 1984, Sports Hall of Fame of N.J., 1994. Mem. Alpha Kappa Alpha. Office: CTA Patrons Foundation Friends of Althea Gibson 6100 Lake Forrest Dr NW Ste 120 Atlanta GA 30328-3835*

GIBSON, ANNEMARIE, writer, editor; b. Linz, Austria, Oct. 6, 1947; d. Marion Alfred and Maria Anna (Ostermann) Green; m. Stephen Rawlings Gibson, Mar. 2, 1968; children: Stephanie Anne, Timothy Michael. AA, Cecil C.C., 1984; BA, Towson (Md.) State U., 1993. Editl. asst. U.S. Army Environ. Hygiene Agy., Aberdeen Proving Ground, 1979-84; writer, editor U.S. Army Environ. Hygiene Agy., Aberdeen Proving Ground, Md., 1984-90; public affairs specialist U.S. Army Ctr. for Health Promotion and Preventive Medicine, Aberdeen Proving Ground, 1990-95, supervisory tech. writer, editor, 1995—; editl. adv. bd. U.S. Army Ctr. for Health Promotion and Preventive Medicine, Aberdeen Proving Ground, 1990—, spkrs. bur., 1993—, facilitator 1992—, mentor 1996—. Pres. Cecil County Ladies Aux. Md. State Firemen's Assn., Elkton, Md., 1995-98; sec. Ladies Aux. Water Witch Fire Co. Port Deposit, Md., 1985—. Mem. Federally Employed Women (sec. 1991—), U.S. Army Environ. Hygiene Agy. Fax: (410) 436-1039. Office: US Army Ctr Health Promotion/ Preventive Medicine 5158 Black Hawk Rd Aberdeen Proving Ground MD 21010-5403

GIBSON, ARLENE JOY, headmaster. BA, Bryn Mawr Coll., 1965; MA, U. Republic Montevideo, Uruguay, 1966. Dir. middle school Bryn Mawr Sch., Balt., 1981-84; dir. lower sch. Ho Hon Arms Sch., Bethesda, Md., 1984-87; headmistress Kent Place Sch., Summit, N.J., 1987-96; head of sch. Spence Sch., N.Y.C., 1998—. E-mail: agibson@spenceschool.org. Office: Spence Sch 22 E 91st ST New York NY 10128

GIBSON, BARRY JOSEPH, magazine editor; b. Boston, Feb. 6, 1951; s. Joseph Wray and Marjorie Mitchell (Jacobs) G.; m. Jean Harley Reese, Oct. 11, 1980; 1 child, Michael Reese. B.A., U. Miami, 1973. Assoc. editor Salt Water Sportsman, Boston, 1977-81; assoc. boating editor Outdoor Life, N.Y.C., 1981-82; editor Directory for Boats, Accessories and Fishing Tackle, Boston, 1981-83; editor Salt Water Sportsman, Boston, 1981—, v.p., 1981-88; adviser Internat. Commn. for Conservation Atlantic Tuna, Washington, 1986-89; mem. New Eng. Fishery Mgmt. Coun., 1987-96, chmn., 1992; cons. sport fishing industry. Contbr. numerous articles to profl. jours. Charter boat capt., Boothbay Harbor, Maine, 1971—. Recipient Mako Outdoor Writer Yr., Mako Marine Inc., 1982. Mem. Outdoor Writers Assn. Am., New England Outdoor Writers Assn. (excellence in writing award 1982), Northeast Charterboat Capts. Assn. (founding mem. 1988—), Atlantic Sportfishing Assn. (bd. dirs. Natick, Mass. 1988-90). Club: Boothbay Harbor Tuna (pres. 1979). Avocation: sport fishing. Office: Salt Water Sportsman Inc 263 Summer St Boston MA 02210.

GIBSON, BEATRICE ANN, retired systems analyst, artist; b. Canton, Ohio, Feb. 4, 1926; d. Paul Cummins Gibson and Luella Mae (Clements) Gibson Ward. Student, Cleve. Sch. Art, 1941-44, Carnegie Mellon U., 1945-47; BA, U. Chgo., 1951; postgrad., Northwestern U., 1955-57, Oxbow Summer Sch., 1957-59, Sch. Art Inst. Chgo., 1956-60; ind. study, Italy, Greece, Spain, France, England, 1960-61, France, Netherlands, England, 1987; postgrad., EBA Sch. Art, San Francisco, 1988. Procedure analyst U.S. Steel Corp., Chgo., 1955-61; methods analyst Continental Ins. Cos., San Francisco, 1962-64; forms, methods analyst Ins. & Securities Inc., San Francisco, 1964-74; sr. systems analyst Calif. State Automobile Assn., San Francisco, 1974-91; ret., 1991; mem., editor, officer San Francisco Ins. Women's Assn., 1962-68. One-woman exhibits include Diablo Valley Coll., Pleasant Hill, Calif., 1983, EBA Sch. Art, San Francisco, 1991; group exhbns. include Old Town Art Fair, Chgo., 1955, Navy Pier Exhbn., 1956, Laguna Beach (Calif.) Gallery, 1963, San Francisco Civic Ctr. Exhbn., 1964, Hayward (Calif.) Art Show, 1983, EBA Sch. Art, 1988-93. Recipient Recognition award Calif. State Automobile Assn., 1991. Mem. Assn. Systems Mgmt. (emeritus, editor, sec. 1968—, v.p. 1973-74, pres. San Francisco chpt. 1975-76, Disting. Svc. Merit award 1978, Achievement award 1985).

GIBSON, BENJAMIN F., federal judge; b. Safford, Ala., July 13, 1931; s. Eddie and Pearl Ethel (Richardson) G.; m. Lucille Nelson, June 23, 1951; children: Charlotte, Linda, Gerald, Gail, Carol, Laura. B.S., Wayne State U., 1955; J.D. with distinction, Detroit Coll. Law, 1960. Bar: Mich. 1960. Acct. City of Detroit, 1955-56, Detroit Edison Co., 1956-61; asst. atty. gen. Mich., 1961-63; asst. pros. atty. Ingham County, Mich., 1963-64; pvt. practice law Lansing, Mich., from 1964; prof. Thomas Cooley Law Sch., 1979; judge U.S. Dist. Ct. Western Dist. Mich., Grand Rapids, 1979—, chief judge U.S. Dist. Ct., 1991-95, now sr. judge; bd. dirs. Cooley Law Sch.; adj. prof. Cooley Law Sch. Mem. United Way Project Blueprint; met. bd. dirs. YMCA. Mem. Fed. Bar Assn., Mich. State Bar Assn., Grand Rapids State Bar Assn., Black Judges of Mich., Floyd H. Skinner Bar Assn., Fed. Judges Assn., Sigma Pi Phi. Club: Peninsular Club. *

GIBSON, BENJAMIN FRANKLIN, physicist; b. Madisonville, Tex., Sept. 3, 1938; s. Mitchell Osler and Christine (Bennett) G.; m. Margaret Alice Ferguson, July 20, 1968; children: James M., Michael W., Stuart W. BA, Rice U., 1961; PhD, Stanford U., 1966. Postdoctoral fellow Lawrence Livermore (Calif.) Nat. Lab., 1966-68; rsch. assoc. NAS, Nat. Bur. Stds., Gaithersburg, Md., 1968-70, CUNY, Bklyn., 1970-72; group leader, T-5 Los Alamos (N.Mex.) Nat. Lab., 1982-86, staff mem., 1972—; detailee Dept. of Energy Divsn. Nuclear Physics, 1980-81; program adv. com. MIT Bates Electron Accelerator, Boston, 1985-89, 98—; mem. subatomic physics grant selection com. Can. Natural Scis. and Engring. Rsch. Coun., 1994-96, theory rev. panel NSF, 1997, 98. Co-editor: Three-body Force in the Three-Nucleon System, 1986, Procs. of LAMPF Workshop on pi K Physics, 1991, New Vistas in Physics with High-Energy Pion Beams, 1993, Properties and Interactions of Hyperons, 1994, Baryons '95, 1996, 20 Years of Meson Factory Physics: Accomplishments and Prospects, 1997; assoc. editor Phys. Review C, 1988—, mem. editl. bd., 1978-79, 87-88; mem. editl. bd. FEW Body Sys., 1986—; contbr. articles to profl. jours. Recipient Sr. Scientist Rsch. award Alexander von Humboldt Found., 1992; Japan Soc. Promotion of Sci. rsch. fellow Tohoku U., 1984; vis. fellow U. Melbourne, Australia, 1986, Flinders U., Adelaide, Australia, 1987, Murdoch fellow Inst. for Nuclear Theory, U. Wash., Seattle, 1992. Fellow Am. Phys. Soc., Few-Body Sys. Topical Group (vice chmn. 1990-92, chmn. 1992-93, divsn. nuclear physics sec.-treas. 1995—). Achievements include patents in field of epithermal-neutron well logging. Office: T-5 Ms # B283 Los Alamos NM 87545

GIBSON, BRIAN, film director; b. Reading, Eng., Sept. 22, 1944. Dir. (films): Joey, 1975, (TV) Where Adam Stood, 1976, Billion Dollar Bubble, 1976, Dinner at the Sporting Club, 1978, (TV) Blue Remembered Hills, 1980, Poltergeist II: The Other Side, 1986, The Murderers Among Us: The Simon Wiesenthal Story, 1989, (TV) Drug Wars: The Camarena Story, 1990, What's Love Got to Do With It, 1993, (TV) The Josephine Baker Story, 1991, The Juror, 1996, Still Crazy, 1998; writer, dir. Breaking Glass, 1980. Office: Creative Artists Agy 9830 Wilshire Blvd Beverly Hills CA 90212*

GIBSON, CHARLES DEWOLF, broadcast journalist; b. Evanston, Ill., Mar. 9, 1943; s. Burdett and Georgiana (Law) G.; m. Arlene Joy Gibson, July 20, 1968; children: Jessica Law, Katherine Burdett. A.B., Princeton U., 1965. Corr. RKO Radio, Washington, 1966; anchorman Sta.-WLVA-TV, Lynchburg, Va., 1967-69, Sta.-WMAL-TV (now WJLA-TV), Washington, 1970-73; corr. TVN, Inc., Washington, 1974-75; corr. ABC News, Washington, 1975-80, Capitol Hill corr., 1981-87; co-host Good Morning Am. ABC TV, N.Y.C., 1987-98, 99—; co-host 20/20, 1999—. Nat. journalism fellow NEH, U. Mich., 1973-74. Office: Good Morning America 147 Columbus Ave New York NY 10023-5900

GIBSON, CHIP, publishing executive; b. N.Y.C., Sept. 13, 1957. BA, Brown U., 1982. Sales rep. Randon House, N.Y.C., 1982-90, sr. v.p. trade shows and mktg. divsn., 1992-95; v.p., assoc. pub. Crown Pub. Group, N.Y.C., 1990-92, pres., pub., 1995—. Mem. Pub. Lunch Club. Office: Crown Pub Group 201 E 50th St New York NY 10022-7703*

GIBSON, COLVIN DONALD, human resources specialist; b. N.Y.C., Nov. 10, 1945; s. Beatrice White; m. Ann T. Tucker, June 15, 1985; 1 child: Rachel C. BA in History, Va. State Coll., 1968. Various positions Exxon Corp., Tex., La., 1971-88; coord. hdqrs. employee resl. Exxon Corp., Irving, Tex., 1991-97, advisor compensation and exec. programs, 1998—; sect. supr. Exxon U.S.A., Houston, 1984-88, benefits advisor, 1988; sr. cons. Staff Resources and Assocs., Chesapeake, Va., 1988-91; compensation adv., 1998—. Chmn. scouting com. Wheeler Ave. Bapt. Ch., Houston, 1978-86, scoutmaster, asst. scoutmaster; co-chmn. fin. Salvation Army, Irving, 1992—; mem. Irving Cmty. Devel. Corp., former pres. Irving Black Arts Coun. Capt. U.S. Army, 1968-70. Mem. Nat. Soc. Stock Profls., Nat. Alumni Assn. Norfolf State U. (pres. 1983-87, dist. alumnus 1990), Rotary. Baptist. Avocations: travel, tennis, visual and performing arts. Home: 2110 Texas Ash Dr Irving TX 75063-3464

GIBSON, COUNT DILLON, JR., physician, educator; b. Covington, Ga., July 10, 1921; s. Count Dillon and Julia (Thompson) G.; m. Katherine Vislocky, June 10, 1950; children—Gabriella, Thomas, Alexis, George. B.S., Emory U., 1942; M.D., 1944. Diplomate: Am. Bd. Internal Medicine. Intern Columbia-Presbyn. Med. Center, 1944-45, asst. resident medicine, 1947-50, med. resident, 1950-51; asst. prof., asso. prof. medicine Med. Coll. Va., 1951-57; prof. preventive medicine, chmn. dept. Tufts U. Sch. Medicine, Boston, 1958-69; physician-in-chief Home Med. Service; attending physician New Eng. Med. Ctr. Hosps.; gen. dir. Tufts-Columbia Point Health Ctr.; vis. physician Boston City Hosp., to 1969; prof., chmn. dept. family, community and preventive medicine Stanford (Calif.) U., 1969-87, prof. dept. health research and policy, 1988-91, prof. emeritus, 1991—; mem. Calif. Health Manpower Policy Commn., 1977-85; pres. SimulMed, Inc., 1997—. Contbr. articles to profl. jours. Bd. dirs. Hayward (Calif.) Vesper Hosp., 1980-85, Drew Health Found., 1988-90. Capt. M.C., AUS, 1945-47. Mem. A.C.P. Roman Catholic. Office: Stanford U Med Ctr Stanford CA 94305

GIBSON, DAVID ALLEN, civil engineer; b. Neon, Ky., Sept. 5, 1957; s. Hubert and Ramona Blanche (Stallard) G.; m. Alice Marie Clarkston, May 28, 1977; children: Mary Elizabeth, Douglas Lee. BS in Civil Engring., Ohio State U., 1984; MS in Bus. Mgmt., U. LaVerne, 1990. Registered profl. engr., Va., Tenn. Commd. 2d lt. USAF, 1984, advanced through grades to capt., 1988; contract planning engr. 2854 CES/DEEX USAF, Tinker AFB, Oka., 1984-85, chief requirements 2854 CES/DEMR, 1985-86, design civil engr. 2854 CES/DEM-2, 1986-87; lead program engr. 343 CES/DEEP USAF, Eielson AFB, Alaska, 1987-90, chief civil engr. 343 CES/DEEE, 1990-92; program devel. engr. HQ AMC USAF, Scott AFB, Ill., 1992-94; 673 ABG/LS Eareckson AFB, Alaska, 1994-95; civil engr. Thompson & Litton, Inc., Wise, Va., 1995-97; prin. engr. So. Engring. & Consulting, Kingsport, Tenn., 1999—; adj. prof. engring./indsl. tech. Mountain Empire C.C., 1995-97. Mem. NSPE, ASCE, Am. Concrete Inst. Home: 217 E 23rd St N Big Stone Gap VA 24219-3521 Office: Southern Engring and Consulting 3196 E Stone Dr Kingsport TN 37664

GIBSON, DAVID ROGER, optometrist; b. Big Spring, Tex., Nov. 24, 1952; s. Alfred Marion Gibson and Juanita Joan (Nowlin) Haas; m. DeAnna May Myers, Mar. 15, 1975; children: Andrew, Bryan. BS, U. Houston, 1975, OD, 1977. Pvt. practice optometry Plano, Tex., 1977-79; ptnr., optometrist Drs. Armistead, Moure & Gibson, Lubbock, Tex., 1979—. Bd. dirs. South Plains Food Bank, Lubbock; bd. mem. Prevent Blindness, Lubbock, 1997-98. Fellow Am. Acad. Optometry; mem. Am. Optometric Assn., Tex. Optometric Assn., South Plains Optometric Assn. (pres. 1981), Rotary (bd. dirs.). Methodist. Avocations: waterskiing, Boy Scouts. Office: 2132 50th St Lubbock TX 79412-2603

GIBSON, ELEANOR JACK (MRS. JAMES J. GIBSON), retired psychology educator; b. Peoria, Ill., Dec. 7, 1910; d. William A. and Isabel (Grier) Jack; m. James J. Gibson, Sept. 17, 1932; children: James J., Jean Grier. BA, Smith Coll., 1931, MA, 1933, DSc (hon.), 1972; PhD, Yale U., 1938, DSc (hon.), 1996; DSc (hon.), Rutgers U., 1973, Trinity Coll., 1982, Bates Coll., 1985, U. S.C., 1987, Emory U., 1990, Middlebury Coll., 1993; LHD (hon.), SUNY, Albany, 1984, Miami U., 1989. From asst. to asst. prof. Smith Coll., 1931-49; rsch. assoc. psychology Cornell U., Ithaca, N.Y., 1949-66, prof., 1972—; Susan Linn Sage prof. psychology Cornell U., 1972—; fellow Inst. for Advanced Study, Princeton, 1959-60, Inst. for Advanced Study in Behavioral Scis., Stanford, Calif., 1963-64, Inst. for Advanced Study, Ind. U., fall 1990; vis. prof. Mass. Inst. Tech., 1973, Inst. Child Devel., U. Minn., 1980; Disting. vis. prof. U. Calif., Davis, 1978; vis. scientist Salk Inst., La Jolla, Calif., 1979; vis. prof. U. Pa., 1984; Montgomery fellow Dartmouth Coll., 1986; Woodruff vis. prof. psychology Emory U., 1988-90. Author: Principles of Perceptual Learning and Development, 1967 (Century award), (with H. Levin) The Psychology of Reading, 1975, Odyssey in Learning and Perception, 1991. Recipient Wilbur Cross medal Yale U., 1973, medal for disting. svc. Tchrs. Coll. Columbia U., 1983, Nat. Medal Sci., 1992, Lifetime Achievement award Internat. Soc. for Ecol. Psychology; Guggenheim fellow, 1972-73, William James fellow Am. Psychol. Soc., 1989. Fellow AAAS (divsn. chair 1983), Am. Psychol. Assn. (Disting. Scientist award 1968, G. Stanley Hall award 1970, pres. div. 3 1977, Gold medal award 1986); mem. NAS, Eastern Psychol. Assn. (pres. 1968), Soc. Exptl. Psychologists (Howard Crosby Warren medal 1977), Nat. Acad. Edn., Psychonomic Soc., Soc. Rsch. in Child Devel. (Disting. Sci. Contbn. award 1981), Am. Acad. Arts and Scis., Brit. Psychol. Soc. (hon.), N.Y. Acad. Scis. (hon.), Italian Soc. Rsch. in Child Devel. (hon.), Vt. Acad. Sci. and Engring., Phi Beta Kappa, Sigma Xi. Home: 266 Washington Street Ext Middlebury VT 05753-8517

GIBSON, EMMITT E., career officer; b. Feb. 7, 1944. Commd. officer U.S. Army, advanced through grades to maj. gen.; commdg. gen. Aviation and Missile U.S. Army, Redstone Arsenal, Ala., 1997—. Office: US Army Aviation & Missile Redstone Arsenal AL 35898-5000

GIBSON, ERNEST L., III, healthcare consultant; b. Baton Rouge, Oct. 29, 1945; s. Ernest L. Jr. and Ethel (Dunning) G.; m. Susan R. Wilson, Aug. 29, 1970; children: E. Lee, Elizabeth K.. BS in Pharmacy, U. of the Pacific, 1968, PharmD, 1969. Resident hosp. pharmacy U. Tex. Med. Br., Galveston, 1972; assoc. dir. pharmacy U. Calif. Med. Ctr., Sacramento, 1970-78; dir. pharmacy mgmt. Svc. Master Industries, Downers Grove, Ill., 1978-82; exec. v.p. DOSE Sys., 1982-93; pres. HealthCare Solutions Group, Plano, 1992—; lectr. Sacramento Jr. Coll., 1975-78. Stephens min. Custer Rd. United Meth. Ch., Plano, Tex., adminstrv. bd. dirs., 1984-87; bd. dirs. Lupus Found. North Tex., 1996—; pres. Lupus Found., 1998. Mem. Tex. Pharmacy Assn., Dallas County Pharmacy Assn., Calif. Soc. Hosp. Pharmacists, Sacramento Valley Soc. Hosp. Pharmacists (prs. 1975), Jaycees (state chmn. drug abuse campaign 1976), Kiwanis. Republican. Avocations: gourmet cooking, golf, travel, skiing. Home: 4549 Miami Dr Plano TX 75093-5511 Office: Healthcare Solutions Group 4549 Miami Dr Plano TX 75093-5511

GIBSON, ERNEST WILLARD, III, retired state supreme court justice; b. Brattleboro, Vt., Sept. 23, 1927; s. Ernest William and Dorothy Pearl (Switzer) G.; m. Charlotte Elaine Hungerford, Sept. 10, 1960; children: Margaret, Mary, John. BA, Yale U., 1951; LLB, Harvard U., 1956. Bar: Vt. State's atty. Windham County, Vt., 1957-61; mem. Vt. Ho. of Reps., 1961-63, chmn. judiciary com., 1963; chmn. Vt. Pub. Svc. Bd., 1963-72; judge Vt. Superior Ct., 1972-83; assoc. justice Vt. Supreme Ct., 1983-97, ret., 1997. Chancellor Episcopal Diocese Vt., 1977-98. trustee, 1973—, pres. bd. trustees, 1991—, dep. to gen. conv., 1976-94. Served in U.S. Army, 1945-46, 51-53, Vt. Army Nat. Guard, 1956-71. Mem. Vt. Bar Assn. Avocations: bridge, tennis. Home: 11 Baldwin St Montpelier VT 05602-2110

GIBSON, EVERETT KAY, JR., space scientist, geochemist; b. Seagraves, Tex., May 13, 1940; s. Everett Kay and Lillie Gertrude (Ivey) G.; m. Mary Morgan Shott, Oct. 13, 1973; 1 son, Bradford Pierce Gibson. BS, Tex. Tech U., Lubbock, 1963, MS, 1965; PhD, Ariz. State U., 1969. Instr. Tex. Tech U., 1963-65; postdoctoral research assoc. NASA Johnson Space Center, Houston, 1969-70; space scientist, geochemist NASA Johnson Space Center, 1970-91; sr. scientist NASA-Johnson Space Ctr., 1991—; vis. program mgr. NSF, Washington, 1979; mission sci. advisor Apollo 14; test dir. Lunar Receiving Lab. NASA, 1971, prin. investigator Lunar Sample Analysis Program, 1971-90, mem. Lunar Sample Analysis Planning Team,, 1974-77, prin. investigator Planetary Geology Program,, 1978-86, prin. investigator Mars Data Analysis Program,, 1979-84, prin. investigation Exobiology Program,, 1983—; mem. U.S. Antarctic Meteorite Search Team, 1979-80; adj. prof. geology U. Houston, 1975-90; sr. Leverhulme vis. fellow Open U., Milton Keynes, Eng., 1984-85; cons. The Economist (London), BBC, London. Assoc. editor 5th, 6th, 7th, 8th, 9th and 12th Proc. Lunar and Planetary Sci. Conf., 1974-81; assoc. editor: Chondrules and Their Origins, 1983; contbr. articles to sci. jours. Bd. dirs. Clear Creek Basin Authority, Harris County, Tex., 1974-75; col. Confederate Air Force, 1983—, life mem., 1987, aircraft sponsor, 1988, exec. officer, 1990—; exec. bd. Wings Over Houston Air Show, 1990—. Recipient award for lunar sci. team participation NASA Johnson Space Ctr., 1974, cert. of recognition, 1979, Manned Flight Awareness award, 1993, Space award Aviation Week and Space Tech., 1997; recipient Exceptional Sci. Achievement medal NASA, 1997, Disting. Achievement award Ariz. State U., 1980, Silver Magnolia award Confederate Air Force, 1993, Ariz. State U. Hall of Fame award, 1998. Fellow Meteoritical Soc. (sec. 1974-80, councilor 1987-90); mem. Am. Chem. Soc., Internat. Soc. for Study of Origin of Life, AAAS, Am. Geophys. Union, Sigma Xi, Phi Lambda Upsilon. Baptist. Home: 1015 Trowbridge Dr Houston TX 77062-2726 Office: NOW SN2 Planetary Sci Nasa Johnson Space Ctr AHZ 2101 Nasa Rd 1 Houston TX 77058

GIBSON, FLORENCE ANDERSON, talking book company executive, narrator; b. San Francisco, Feb. 7, 1924; m. V.H. Carlos Gibson, Aug. 30, 1947; children: Nancy Derwent, Christopher Carlos, Katherine Wayne Bolland, Diana Corona. Student, Finch Jr. Coll., N.Y.C., 1941-42; BA in Dramatic Lit., U. Calif., Berkeley, 1944; student, Neighborhood Playhouse, N.Y.C., 1944-45. Radio actress San Francisco, 1944, 46, 47; chmn. Washington com. Am. Field Svc., 1958-60, 62-65; founder, chmn. Peruvian Com. Am. Field Svc., Lima, 1960-62; treas., distbn. mgr. Living Garden and Concern 1975 calendars, 1971-75; sec. exec. com Fgn. Student Svc. Coun., 1973-76; narrator Talking Books Libr. of Congress div. for Blind and Physically Handicapped, 1975-96; narrator Recorded Books, Inc., 1979; founder, pres. Audio Book Contractors, Inc., 1982—; narrator numerous unabridged books on cassettes. Actress, appearing in Blithe Spirit, 1945, Ah, Wilderness, 1946, Traffic Ct. TV series, others, 876 books on cassettes. Bd. dirs. Fgn. Student Svc. Coun., Concern, Inc., Rec. for the Blind, Children's Theater of Washington; vol. in occupational therapy Children's Hosp., Washington, 1949-50; vol. lobbyist student exch. program Am. Field Svc. Recipient 3 Parents' Choice awards, 1983, 84, 86; named Best Female Narrator, Book World; selected as A Notable Children's Recording, ALA, 1987, 88, 89. Home: 4626 Garfield St NW Washington DC 20007-1025 Office: Audio Book Contractors Inc PO Box 40115 Washington DC 20016-0115

GIBSON, FLOYD ROBERT, federal judge; b. Prescott, Ariz., Mar. 3, 1910; s. Van Robert and Katheryn Ida G.; m. Gertrude Lee Walker, Apr. 23, 1935; children: Charles R., John M., Catherine L. A.B., U. Mo., 1931, LL.B., 1933. Bar: Mo. 1932. Practiced law Independence, 1933-37, Kansas City, 1937-61; mem. firm Johnson, Lucas, Bush & Gibson (and predecessor), 1954-61; county counselor Jackson County, 1943-44; judge U.S. Dist. Ct. (we. dist.) Mo., 1961-65, chief judge, until 1965; judge U.S. Ct. Appeals (8th cir.), Kansas City, Mo., 1965-79, sr. judge, 1979—, chief judge, 1974-80; former chmn. bd. Mfrs. & Mechanics Bank, Kansas City, Mo., Blue Valley Fed. Savs. & Loan Assn.; mem. Nat. Conf. Commrs. Uniform State Laws, 1957—, Jud. Conf. U.S., 1974-80; chmn. Chief Judges Conf., 1977-78; bd. mgrs. Coun. State Govts., 1960-61; pres. Nat. Legis. Conf., 1960-61. Mem. Mo. Gen. Assembly from 7th Dist., 1940-46; mem. Mo. Senate, 1946-61, majority floor leader, 1952-56, pres. pro tem, 1956-60; del. Nat. Democratic Conv., 1956, 60; Mem. Mo. N.G. Named 2d most valuable mem. Mo. Legislature Globe Democrat, 1958, most valuable, 1960; recipient Faculty-Alumni award U. Mo., 1968; citation of merit Mo. Law Sch. Alumni, 1975; Spurgeon Smithson award Mo. Bar Found., 1978. Fellow ABA (adv. bd. editors Jour., chmn. jud. adminstrn. div. 1979-80, chmn. conf. sect. 1980-81, chmn. appellate judges conf. 1973-74, mem. ho. of dels.); mem. Fed. Bar Assn., Mo. Bar, Kansas City Bar Assn. (Ann. Achievement award 1980), Lawyers Assn. Kansas City (past v.p., Charles Evans Whittaker award 1985), Mo. Law Sch. Found. (life), Mo. Acad. Squires, Order of Coif, Phi Delta Phi, Phi Kappa Psi (Man of Yr. 1974). Democrat. Roman Catholic. Clubs: University, Carriage, Mercury. Office: US Ct Appeals 8th Cir US Courthouse 400 E 9th St Ste 1020 Kansas City MO 64106-1991*

GIBSON, FRANCES, nurse; b. Junction, Tex., Sept. 28, 1936; d. August and Juanita (Corpus-Garcia) Rehwoldt; m. Richard Gibson, July 4, 1954 (dec. July 25, 1962); children; Kenneth, René, Allison. AA, East Los Angeles Coll. Lic. vocat. nurse, Calif.; RN, Calif.; cert. oper. rm. technician, Calif.; cert. adult edn. tchr.; paralegal. Instr., profl. expert East Los Angeles Coll., Monterey Park, Calif., 1971-74; hostess talk show (in Spanish) Sta. KMEX-TV, L.A., 1970-76; tchr. adult edn. Garvey Sch. Bd., Rosemead, Calif., 1976-77; case mgr. AIDS Healthcare Found., L.A., 1991-93; clin. nurse Los Angeles County/U. So. Calif. Med. Ctr., 1981-89, AIDS clinician, 1993; vol. nurse Lung Assn., L.A., 1970-76; ARC, L.A., 1969—; instr. health classes ARC, also instr. Spanish to ARC pers., mgr. info. booths at health fairs and convs., provider first aid at various gatherings, immunization clinics, chmn. adv. bd., 1971-72, bd. dirs., 1972-75, 79-82; med. editor, legal asst. Ivie & McNeill, L.A., 1986—. Author: Spanish for English-Speaking Personnel, 1972. Recipient Spotlight award ARC, 1972, Clara Barton award ARC, 1976, Associate Womens Students award East L.A. Coll., 1969; named one of Ten Prettiest Chicanas in East Los Angeles, East L.A. Merchants, 1970. Mem. Nat. Assn. Chicano Nurses, Nursing Edn. Associates, AFL-CIO, ACLU, Alpha Gamma Sigma. Democrat. Baptist. Avocations: gardening, crafts. Home: 2241 Charlotte Ave Rosemead CA 91770-3624

GIBSON, JAMES ELLIOTT, architect; b. McMinnville, Oreg., Aug. 14, 1922; s. James H. and Julia Etta (Cummins) G.; m. Clara June Bosson, Dec. 19, 1948 (dec. Sept. 1967); children: Graeme E.B., Randolph U., James B.P.; m. Suzan Bailliere Brand Brown, Jan. 1, 1980 (dec. June 1998); children: John W. Brown, Natalie T. Brown, Frank D. Brown, Susannah Brown Kavanaugh. BS in Music, U. Oreg., 1944; BArch, U. Mich., 1950. Registered architect, Mich., Fla., S.C., Ohio; cert. NCARB. Architect Harley, Ellington & Day, Inc., Detroit, 1950-69, James E. Gibson, Architects & Assocs., Inc., Vero Beach, Fla., 1969-83, Gibson & Silkworth, Architects & Assocs., Inc., Vero Beach, 1983-97, Gibson & Assocs., Architects, Inc., Vero Beach, 1997—. Pres. Vero Beach Concert Assn., 1971-79, 81-83, pres. Treasure Coast Opera Assn., Vero Beach, 1979-81; bd. dirs. Atlantic Classical Orch., Vero Beach, 1992—, pres., 1998—; bd. dirs., mem. adv. bd. Riverside Theatre, Vero Beach; mem. adv. bd. Ctr. for the Arts, Vero Beach. Staff sgt. U.S. Army, 1942-46, ETO. Recipient Bus. in the Arts award, 1986, Aurora Grand award Assoc. Gen. Contractors, 1985. Mem. AIA, John's Island Club (Vero Beach), Riomar Bay Yacht Club (Vero Beach), Carolina Yacht Club (Charleston, S.C.). Avocations: musical performance, antiques collecting, sculpture, historical preservation. Office: Gibson & Assocs Architects 606 Azalea Ln Vero Beach FL 32963-1832

GIBSON, JAMES JOHN, electronics engineer, consultant; b. St. Albans, Eng., Mar. 12, 1923; came to U.S., 1956, naturalized, 1964; s. Paul Erik Waern and Helga Irene (Cöster) G.; m. Eva Berit Bäck, Sept. 21, 1957; children: John David, James Alexander, Sally Ann. BSEE, Royal Inst. Tech., Stockholm, 1947; MSEE, Chalmers Inst. Tech., Gothenburg, 1971, D.Eng. (hon.), 1985. Registered profl. engr., N.J. Engr. Swedish Air Force, 1945-46; rsch. engr. Rsch. Inst. Nat Def., Stockholm, 1947-52; with RCA Labs., Princeton, N.J., 1952-54, 56-87, Am. Scandinavian Found. trainee, 1952-54, mem. tech. staff David Sarnoff Rsch. Ctr., 1956-69, fellow tech. staff, 1969-87; leader transistor cirs. rsch. group Royal Inst. Tech., Stockholm, 1954-56; cons. electronics engr. Signal Systems Rsch., Princeton, 1987—; vis. prof. elec. engring. dept. Rutgers U., New Brunswick, N.J., 1978-91; working group chmn. adv. coms. on cable TV and TV noise measurements FCC, mem. FCC adv. com. on Advanced TV Svc., nat. quadraphonic radio com.; lectr. Royal Inst. Tech.; tchr. communica tions La Salle Coll., Phila. Contbr. numerous papers to profl. jours.; inventor 32 patents. Recipient David Sarnoff award for multichannel TV sound RCA, 1985, also 6 tech. achievement awards, contbr. to Emmy award received by co., 1985. Fellow IEEE, Audio Engring. Soc.; mem. IEEE Consumer Electronics Soc. (adminstrv. com. 1986-89), Soc. Motion Picture and TV Engrs., AAAS, NSPE, Sigma Xi. Avocations: piano, literature, music, tennis. Office: Signal Systems Rsch 47 Castle Howard Ct Princeton NJ 08540-4025

GIBSON, JANNETTE POE, educator, consultant; b. Lubbock, Tex., Oct. 29, 1948; d. Hugh Miller and Norma Grace (Harrison) Poe; m. William Carroll Gibson, June 30, 1967; children: Darin L., Arminda L. Gibson Peery, Victoria L. Gibson Dixon. BS, East Tex. State U., 1971, MEd, 1981; postgrad., Tex. A&M U., Commerce, 1992—. Tchr. Como (Tex.)-Pickton Ind. Sch. Dist., 1971-77; tchr., cons. Diocese of Dallas, Diocese of Tyler, Tex., 1982-87; tchr., supr. Hyder Migrant Ctr., Dateland, Ariz., 1987-88; tchr., adult ESL edn. dir. Ariz. Western U., Hyder Campus, 1988-89; tchr. Sulphur Springs (Tex.) Ind. Sch. Dist., 1989-98; cons., presenter Multicultural/Migrant Edn., 1987—; edn. diagnostician Sulphur Springs ISD Spl. Edn. Dept., 1998—; cons. ESL edn. and early childhood edn. and child devel. U.S. Dept. Edn., 1988-89; profl. adv. com. Sulphur Springs Ind. Sch. Dist., 1990, 92, 96; doctoral adv. bd. East Tex. State U., 1993-96; regional adv. com. migrant edn. Region V111 Svc., 1994-97, advisor Tex. Edn. Agy. assessments of ESL/LEP children, 1997-98; cons. for devel. of culture and lang. bias-free assessments to sch. dists. in Tex.; presenter in fields of migrant edn. and ESL. Mem. AAUW, NEA, Tex. State Tchrs. Assn., TAMU Doctoral Students Assn., TESOL, Classroom Tchrs. Assn. Tex., Tex. Ednl. Diagnosticians Assn., N.E. Tex. Assn. Ednl. Diagnosticians, Mensa, Alpha Chi, Phi Beta Kappa, Kappa Delta Pi. Democrat. Methodist. Avocations: reading, gardening. Home: 1707 Houston St Sulphur Springs TX 75482-2319 Office: 613 Connally St Sulphur Springs TX 75482-2401

GIBSON, JERRY LEIGH, oil company executive; b. El Dorado, Ark., Jan. 24, 1930; s. Oscar Edward and Ruth (Coleman) G.; m. Alma Gail Peoples, Apr. 11, 1953; children: Sallie Gail, Gregory Leigh. BBA with honors, U. North Tex., 1951; MBA, So. Meth. U., 1956. With Mobil Oil U.S.A., 1952-59, 60-62, asst. to asst. comptr., 1961-62; mgmt. cons. KPMG Peat Marwick Co. CPAs, 1959; with Exxon Corp., 1962-66, asst. contr., 1965-66; v.p., sec., treas. Riviana Foods Inc., Houston, 1966-69; pres., treas., chief exec. officer Intermedco Inc., Houston, 1969-73; pres., chief exec. officer Automated Fin. Svcs., Houston, 1973-75; v.p. fin. A-Z Internat. Tool Co., Houston, 1975-80; pres., chief exec. officer, owner JHJ Drilling Co., Houston, 1980-85; pres., chief exec. officer Kellywood Corp., Houston, 1986—; tchr. acctg. So. Meth. U., 1956-57. With USAF, 1950-52. Home and Office: 14223 Kellywood Ln Houston TX 77079-7432

GIBSON, JOHN, news anchor, correspondent. B film sch., UCLA. Reporter Hollywood Reporter, L.A., 1969-72, various locations, Calif., 1974-77; bur. chief, anchor Weekend Mag., Sta. KCRA-TV, San Francisco, 1979-89; anchor, corr. In Am., 1989-92; corr. NBC News, Burbank, Calif., 1992-94; West Coast corr. NBC News Channel, 1994; anchor News Chat and InterNight MSNBC, N.Y.C. Office: c/o MSNBC 1 MSNBC Plz Secaucus NJ 07094*

GIBSON, JOHN C., state legislator; b. Atlantic City, N.J., Mar. 30, 1934. BS, Villanova U. Engr. Cape May County, N.J.; assembly mem. dist. 1 N.J. State Assembly. Mem. Sea Isle Italian Am. Club. E-mail: asm.jcgibson@worldnet.att.net. Address: 14 Route 50 Ste A Ocean View NJ 08230-1106

GIBSON, JOHN ROBERT, federal judge; b. Springfield, Mo., Dec. 20, 1925; s. Harry B. and Edna (Kerr) G.; m. Mary Elizabeth Vaughn, Sept. 20, 1952 (dec. Aug. 1985); children: Jeanne, John Robert; m. Diane Allen Larrison, Oct. 1, 1986; stepchildren: Holly, Catherine. AB, U. Mo., 1949, JD, 1952. Bar: Mo. 1952. Assoc. Morrison, Hecker, Curtis, Kuder & Parrish, Kansas City, Mo., 1952-58, ptnr., 1958-81; judge U.S. Dist. Ct. (we. dist.) Mo., 1981-82; judge U.S. Ct. Appeals (8th cir.), Kansas City, 1982-94, sr. judge, 1994—; mem. Mo. Press-Bar Commn., 1979-81; mem. com. on adminstrn. of magistrate sys. Jud. Conf. U.S., 1987-91, mem. security and facilities com., 1995—. Vice chmn. Jackson County Charter Transition Com., 1971-72; mem. Jackson County Charter Commn., 1970; v.p. Police Commrs. Bd., Kansas City, 1973-77. Served with AUS, 1944-46. Recipient Citation of Merit award U. Mo. at Columbia Sch. of Law, 1994. Fellow Am. Bar Found.; mem. ABA, Mo. State Bar (gov. 1972-79, pres. 1977-78; Pres.' award 1974, Smithson award 1984), Kansas City Bar Assn. (pres. 1970-71), Lawyers Assn. Kansas City (Charles Evan Whittaker award 1980), Fed. Judges Assn. (bd. dirs. 1991-97), Phi Beta Kappa, Omicron Delta Kappa. Presbyterian. Office: US Ct Appeals 8th Cir 400 E 9th St Rm 10-40 Kansas City MO 64106-2605

GIBSON, JOSEPH WHITTON, JR., retired chemical company executive; b. Norristown, Pa., Feb. 24, 1922; s. Joseph Whitton and Nellie (Dear) G.; m. Norma Jean Stewart, Sept. 21, 1946; children: Joseph Whitton, Winn S. Gobeil, Philip B. BS, Worcester Poly. Inst., 1944; postgrad., Princeton U., 1944, MIT, 1945. With E. I. duPont de Nemours & Co., Wilmington, Del., 1946-91; sr. research engr. E. I. duPont de Nemours & Co., 1961-79, sr. tech. specialist printing systems, imaging systems, 1979-91; mem. pantyhose sizing com. Nat. Assn. Hosiery Mfrs., 1969-71. Contbr. articles to profl. jours. Treas. Mayfield Civic Assn.; v.p. Brandywine Babe Ruth; treas. Shellcrest Swim Club; IRS VITA vol., 1995—. Served to lt. USNR, 1944-46. Recipient Joseph W. Gibson Jr. award tech. excellence established duPont, 1992, Internat. Man of Yr. award Internat. Biog. Centre, Cambridge, Eng., Dateline Recognition award Chem. Heritage Found., Phila. Mem. Am. Assn. Textile Chemists and Colorists (mem. history and archives com. 1994—, Olney medal 1979), Am. Chem. Soc., Fiber Soc. (hon.), Internat. Platform Assn., Planetary Soc., Sigma Xi, Tau Beta Pi. Republican. Episcopalian. Inventor thermosol dyeing, sparkle hosiery, synthetic leather, fish swimway, printing plates. Home: 1215 Hillside Blvd Wilmington DE 19803-4211

GIBSON, MARGARET FERGUSON, poet, educator; b. Phila., Feb. 17, 1944; d. John Spears and Mattie Leigh (Doyle) Ferguson; m. Ross Shackelford Gibson Jr., Aug. 27, 1966 (div. 1971); m. David W. McKain, Dec. 27, 1975; stepchildren: Joshua, Megan. BA, Hollins Coll., 1966; MA, U. Va., 1967. Instr. Madison Coll., Va., 1967-68, Va. Commonwealth U., 1968-70; asst. prof. George Mason U., Va., 1970-75; vis. prof. U. Conn., 1976-77, lectr., 1977-84; writer in residence Phillips Acad./Andover, Mass., 1984-87; vis. prof., MFA program Va. Commonwealth U., 1988-89, U. Mass., 1991-92; asst. prof. Ea. Conn. State U., 1989-91; vis. prof. U. Conn., 1992—. Author: Signs, 1979, Long Walks in the Afternoon, 1982 (Lamont Selection award 1982), Memories of the Future, 1986 (co-winner Melville Cane award 1986-87), Out in the Open, 1989, The Vigil, 1993 (finalist Nat. Book award in poetry 1993), Earth Elegy, New and Selected Poems, 1997; contbr. poetry to anthologies including Ardis Anthology of New Am. Poetry, Contemporary New Eng. Poetry, Fifty Years of American Poets; contbr. to mags. including Ga. Rev., Prairie Schooner, Minn. Rev., Mich. Quar. Rev. Woodrow Wilson grantee, 1966, Nat. Endowment for Arts grantee, 1985, Individual artist grantee Conn. Commn. on Arts, 1976, 88; Lila Wallace teaching fellow Woodrow Wilson Found., 1994—. Mem. Phi Beta Kappa.

Democrat. Buddhist. Avocations: environment, hiking, gardening. Address: La State U Press 152 Watson Rd Preston CT 06365-8837

GIBSON, MCGUIRE, archaeologist, educator; b. Bushwood, Md., Nov. 6, 1938; s. Thomas Laurie and Essie Mae (Owens) G. BA, Fordham U., 1959; MA, U. Chgo., 1964, PhD, 1968. Asst. prof. anthropology U. Ill.-Chgo., 1968-71; asst. prof. anthropology U. Ariz., Tucson, 1971-72; asst. prof. U. Chgo., 1972-73, assoc. prof., 1973-81, prof., 1981—; ann. prof. Am. Schs. Oriental Rsch., Baghdad, Iraq, 1969-70; dir. Nippur Expdn., Iraq, 1972—; chmn. Coun. Am. Overseas Rsch. Ctrs., 1984-88, treas., 1988-92, mem. exec. com., 1995—. Author: The City and Area of Kish, 1972; author, editor: Excavations at Nippur, 12th Season, 1978, Uch Tepe I, 1981; editor: Irrigation's Impact on Society, 1974, Seals and Sealing in the Ancient Near Est, 1977, The Organization of Power: Aspects of Bureaucracy in the Ancient Near East, 1987, Uch Tepe II, 1990, Nippur III, 1993. Mem. arts com. Union League Civic and Arts Found., Chgo., 1984-86. Grantee Am. Numismatic Soc., 1966, Am. Philos. Soc., 1969, Nat. Geog. Soc., 1978, 89, NSF, 1994, NEH, 1995-98. Fellow Brit. Sch. Archaeology in Iraq, Royal Anthrop. Inst., Deutsche Orient-Gesellschaft; mem. AAAS, Am. Inst. Archaeology, Am. Anthrop. Assn., Am. Inst. for Yemeni Studies (pres. 1978-80, 92-96), Middle East Studies Assn., Am. Assn. Rsch. in Baghdad (pres. 1989—), Sigma Xi (Yememi Arch. Svc. award 1998). Democrat. Club: Quadrangle. Avocations: architectural restoration; study of Oriental rugs. Office: U Chgo Oriental Inst 1155 E 58th St Chicago IL 60637-1540

GIBSON, MEL, actor, director; b. Peekskill, N.Y., Jan. 3, 1956; emigrated to Australia, 1968; s. Hutton and Anne Gibson. Grad., Nat. Inst. Dramatic Art, Sydney, Australia, 1977. Founder Icon Prodns. Works include: (films) Summer City, 1977, Mad Max, 1979, Tim, 1979, Attack Force Z, Gallipoli, 1981, The Road Warrior (Mad Max II), 1982, The Year of Living Dangerously, 1983, The Bounty, 1984, The River, 1984, Mrs. Soffel, 1984, Mad Max Beyond Thunderdome, 1985, Lethal Weapon, 1987, Tequila Sunrise, 1988, Lethal Weapon II, 1988, Bird on a Wire, 1989, Hamlet, 1990, Air America, 1990, Lethal Weapon III, 1992, Forever Young, 1992, Maverick, 1994, Pocahontas, 1995 (voice only), Father's Day, 1997, Conspiracy Theory, 1997, Lethal Weapon 4, 1998, The Million Dollar Hotel, 1999, Payback, 1999; actor, dir.: The Man Without a Face, 1993; actor, dir., prodr.: Braveheart, 1995 (Golden Globe award for best dir. of film 1996, Acad. award for best dir. 1996, Acad. award for best picture of yr. 1996, Outstanding Directorial Achievement in Motion Picture award nominee Dir. Guild Am. 1996, Oscar award for Best Dir.), Ransom, 1996; performed with Nimrod Theatre Co. in plays including Death of a Salesman, Romeo and Juliet, with South Australian Theatre Co., from 1978, appeared in plays including Oedipus, Henry IV, Cedoona; work in TV series includes The Sullivans, The Oracle (Australia). Favorite Movie Actor, People's Choice award, 1997. Roman Catholic. Office: ICONS Productions Producers Bldg # 3 4000 Warner Blvd Rm 17 Burbank CA 91522-0001*

GIBSON, MICHAEL, artist; b. Atlanta, 1962. BFA, U. Ga., 1989. Exhbns. include U. Ga. Main Gallery, Athens, 1988, 89, N.B.H.V. Internat. Hamburg, West Germany, 1989, Athens Ga. Art Space, Atlanta, 1990, Art Space, Atlanta, 1991, Swan Coach House, 1991, Lowe Gallery, Atlanta, 1992, 93, Contemporary Internat. Mus. Art, 1992, Lowe Gallery, L.A., 1993, Chassie Post, N.Y., 1994, 95, Chassie Post Gallery, Atlanta, 1994, 95, Caesarea Gallery, Boca Raton, Fla., 1994, Nexus Contemporary Arts Ctr., 1995, New Mus. Contemporary Art, N.Y.C., 1995, Consult Art, Atlanta, 1997, So. Ctr. Contemporary Art, Winston-Salem, N.C., 1997, Fay Gold Gallery, Atlanta, 1997, Art Walk, Atlanta, 1998, Columbus Mus., 1998, Miss. Mus. Art, 1998, Mobile Mus. Art, 1998, Cummer Mus. Art, 1998; represented in permanent collections N.B.H.V., Hamburg, West Germany, Hunter Mus., Chattanooga, Tenn., Peter Gabriel, London, others; featured numerous publs. and catalogues. Fax: 404/365-8633. Office: care Fay Gold Gallery 247 Buckhead Ave Atlanta GA 30305

GIBSON, PAUL RAYMOND, international trade and investment development executive; b. Cathay, Calif., Apr. 10, 1924; s. Otto and Louella (Vestal) G.; m. Janice Elizabeth Carter, dec. 19, 1952; children: Scott C., Paula S. BS in Internat. Commerce, Georgetown U., 1956. With U.S. Govt. Marshall Plan, Heidelberg, Germany, 1948-52; export mgr. Asia, Philip Morris Co., San Francisco, 1952-54; founder, v.p., gen. mgr. McGregor and Werner Internat. Corp., Washington, 1954-62; v.p., dir. McGregor and Werner Corp., 1955-62; v.p. fin. Parsons & Whittemore, Inc., N.Y.C., 1962-65; founder, pres. Paul R. Gibson & Assocs., Washington, 1965-70; mng. dir. Black Clawson Pacific Co., Sydney, Australia, 1970-72; pres. Envirotech Asia Pacific, Sydney, 1972-75, Envirotech Internat., Menlo Park, Calif., 1975-80; founder, pres. INTERACT, San Francisco, 1980-91; pres. The Manchester Group, Ltd., Washington, 1987-89; pres., mng. assoc. Projects Internat. Assocs., Inc., Washington, 1991-96; pres. Projects Internat., Inc., 1996—, sustainable Project Mgmt. USA, 1994—. Mem. Pacific Basin Econ. Coun., vice chmn. policy and planning U.S. sect., 1976-91, chmn. Vietnam Task Force, 1998—; mem. San Francisco Com. Fgn. Rels., 1980-91; mem. World Affairs Coun., Washington. Served to sgt. USMC, 1941-45. Mem. U.S. C. of C. (chmn. Asia-Pacific coun. Am. C. of C. 1973-74, mem. adv. com. 1975—), Dirs. Cir., Mus. Natural History, Smithsonian Inst., Confrerie des Chevaliers du Tastevin (chevalier, sous commanderie de Washington 1992—), Am. Nat. Club (Sydney). Home: 4951 Gulf Shore Blvd N #204 Naples FL 34103-3465 Office: Projects Internat Inc 1800 K St NW Ste 1018 Washington DC 20006-2202

GIBSON, RALPH H(OLMES), photographer; b. Jan. 16, 1939. Student in photography, U.S. Navy, 1956-60, San Francisco Art Inst., 1960-61; DFA (hon.), U. Md., 1991, Ohio Wesleyan U., 1997. lectr. at numerous schs., museums. Exhibited photography in one-man shows including Madison (Wis.) Arts Ctr., 1975, Hoesch Mus., Duren, W. Ger., 1975, Castelli Graphics, N.Y.C., 1976, 80, 82, 91, Balt. Mus. Art, 1976, Van Reekum Galerji Mus., Apeldoorn, Netherlands, 1977, Swedish Mus. Photography, 1977, Mus. Modern Art, Oxford, Eng., 1977, Photographers Gallery, Melbourne, Australia, 1977, Robert Self Gallery, London, 1978, Mus. Modern Art, Brisbane, Australia, 1978, I.C.A. Mus. Art, Richmond, Va., 1979, Canon Gallery, Geneva, 1979, Grapestake Gallery, San Francisco, 1979, Kunstmuseum, Dusseldorf, Fed. Republic Germany, 1980, Night Gallery, London, 1980, Mus. Folkwang, Essen, Fed. Republic Germany, 1981, Mattingly Baker Gallery, Dallas, 1981, Sprengel Mus., Hanover, W. Ger., 1981, Cantieri Navali, La Giudeca, Venice, Italy, 1981, F.I.A.C., Paris, 1982, Olympus Gallery, London, 1892, Centre Georges Pompidou, Paris, 1982, Shadai Gallery, Tokyo, 1982, Sun Valley Ctr. for the Arts, Idaho, 1983, Seattle Art Mus., 1983, Weston Gallery, Carmel, Calif., 1984, Consejo Argentino de Fotografia, Buenos Aires, Argentina, 1985, Bouwfonds Hovelaken, The Netherlands, 1985, Castelli Uptown, N.Y.C., 1985, Galerie Agathe Gaillard, Paris, 1985, Leo Castelli Gallery, N.Y.C., 1985, 87, Ministry of Culture Hall, Marrakech, Morocco, 1986, Nat. Exhibit Hall, Moabane, Swaziland, 1986, Musee Carnavalet, Paris, 1986, Hellenic Ctr. Photography, Athens, 1987, Mus. Fine Arts, Alexandria, Egypt, 1987, Museo Archivi Alinari, Florence, Italy, 1987, Circulo de Bellas Artes, Madrid, 1987, Internat. Ctr. Photography, N.Y.C., 1987, Villa Medici, Rome, 1987, Mpls. Inst. Arts, 1988, Bibliotheque Nationale, Paris, 1988, Moderna Museet, Fotografiska Museet, Stockholm, 1989, Arts Club Chgo., 1989, Albin O. Kuhn Libr. and Gallery, U. Md., Balt., 1990, Musee Nicephore Niepce, Chalon Sue Soane, France, 1990, Princessehof Mus., Leuwarden, Holland, 1991, Okla. City Art Mus., 1991, Espace Photo Paris Audiovisuel, 1991, Photography House, Prague, 1992, Kunstverein Emmerich, Haus imm Park, 1996—, High Museum of Art, Atlanta, GA., 1997, MMK, Frankfurt, Germany, 1998, Maison Européenne De La Photographie, Paris, 1999; Greenville Cnty. Museum of Art, Greenville, Whitney Museum of American Art- N.Y.C., Ger., 1992, Boca Mus. Art, Boca Raton, Fla., 1993, 94, Butler Mus. Am. Art, Ohio, 1994, Frankfurt Kunstverein, 1996, Internat. Ctr. Photography 5-yr. world wide travelling exhbn., Villa Medici, Rome, 1986—, Mus. Carnavalet, Paris, 1986—, Leo Castelli Gallery, N.Y., Galerie Eric Van de Weghe, Brussels, Expo 1991, ICAC/Weston Gallery, Tokyo, others; exhibited in numerous group shows, including, Mus. Modern Art, N.Y.C., 1978, Hayden Gallery, MIT, Cambridge, 1978, Bologna Art Fair, Italy, 1978, Walker Art Center, Liverpool, Eng., 1978, Cleve. Mus. Art, 1978, Musée Marseilles, 1980, Addison Gallery of Art, Phillips Acad., Andover, Mass., 1981, Mus. Folkwang, Essen, 1981, San Francisco Mus. of Modern Art, 1982, 84, 85, Met. Mus. Art, N.Y.C., 1982, Whitney Mus. Art, N.Y.C., 1983, Houston Ctr. for Photography, 1983, Mus. Art, Phila., 1983, Denver Art Mus., 1984, Nat. Mus. Art, Washington, 1984, Sesnon Gallery, U. Calif.-Santa Cruz, 1984, Mus. of Modern Art, Paris, 1984, Pace-McGill Gallery, N.Y.C., 1985, Barbican Art Gallery, London, 1985, Bronx Mus., N.Y.C., 1985, Kunsterin, Stuttgart, Fed. Republic Germany, 1985, Musee Cantonal, Lausanne, Switzerland, 1985, Lehigh U., Pa., 1985, Gallery Hirondelle, N.Y.C., 1986, Villa Medici, Rome, numerous others; represented in permanent collections, including Nat. Gallery Ottawa, Ont., Can., Whitney Mus. Am. Art, Bibliotheque National de France, Paris, Mus. Modern Art, N.Y.C., Internat. Mus. Photography, George Eastman House, Rochester, N.Y., Fogg Art Mus., Boston, Met. Mus. Art, N.Y.C., Australian Nat. Gallery, Canberra, Nat. Gallery Victoria, Australia, Art Gallery South Australia, Victoria and Albert Mus., London, Mus. Modern Art, Brisbane, Fotografiska Museet, Moderna Museet, Stockholm, Sweden, Musee Reattu, Arles, France, G. Ray Hawkins Gallery, Los Angeles, Mus. Fine Arts, Alexandria, Egypt, Mus. Art, Athens, Greece; author: Apropos de Mary Jane, 1990, Chiaroscuro, 1990; author, illustrator: The Strip, 1966, The Hawk, 1968, The American Civil Liberties Union Calendar, 1969, The Somnambulist, 1970, Deja-vu, 1973, Days at Sea, 1975, Syntax, 1983, Tropism, 1987, Archive-Early Work, 1988; navarin editor: In-Situ, 1988, Les Cahiers des La Photographie, 1988, L'Histoire de France, 1991. Decorated officier Ordre Arts et Lettres (France); recipient Leica medal of excellence award, 1988, grand medal City of Arles, France, 1994; fellowship grantee Nat. Endowment for Arts, 1973, 75, 86-87, creative artists pub. svc. grantee N.Y. State. Coun. Arts, 1977, grantee Eastman Kodak Co., 1989, Murray and Isabella Rayburn Found., 1994; Guggenheim fellow, 1985-86. Address: 331 W Broadway New York NY 10013-2265 *Photography is a way for measuring my perception—I trust my photographs and study them intensely. After working over thirty years, I realize that the years of struggle are over. Now begin the years of struggle.*

GIBSON, RANKIN MACDOUGAL, lawyer; b. Unionville, Mo., Oct. 9, 1916; s. Alexander R. and Murle L. (Fletcher) G.; m. Eloise M. Corns, Sept. 13, 1941; children: Phillip, Barbara. Student, N.E. Mo. State Tchrs. Coll., 1934-36; LL.B., U. Mo., 1939; B.S. in Law, St. Paul Coll. Law, 1948; LL.M., George Washington U., 1950. Bar: Mo. 1939, Ohio 1954, Supreme Ct. U.S 1951. Gen. practice law Unionville, 1939-40; atty. T.H. Mastin & Co., St. Louis, 1940-42, VA, Des Moines, St. Paul, Washington, 1945-51; enforcement and litigation atty. Nat. Wage Stblzn. Bd., 1951; asso. prof. law U. Toledo Coll. Law, 1951-56; mem. firm DiSalle, Green, Haddad & Lynch, Toledo, 1956-59; asst. to gov., Ohio, 1959-61; dir. Ohio Dept. Commerce, 1961-62; mem. Pub. Utilities Commn., Ohio, 1962-63; judge Supreme Ct., Ohio, 1963-65; ptnr. firm Lucas, Prendergast, Albright, Gibson & Newman, Columbus, Ohio, 1965-95, of counsel, 1995—; tchr. adminstrv. law Franklin Sch. Law, 1960; tchr. labor law Franklin Law Sch., Capital U., 1967-95; Mem. Nat. Enforcement Commn. Econ. Stblzn. Agy., 1952-53; chmn. labor law round table council Assn. Am. Law Schs., 1952-53; labor arbitrator panels Am. Arbitration Assn., Fed. Mediation and Conciliation Service, Toledo Labor-Mgmt. Citizens Com., 1952-53; rep. Ohio on interstate Coop. Com.; chmn. Gov. Ohio Com. Pub. Information, 1959-61; mem. Ohio Water Pollution Bd., Civil War Centennial Commn.; mem. Ohio Housing Bd.; Ohio rep. on Interstate Oil Compact Commn. and Nat. Rivers and Harbors Congress, 1961-62; arbitrator Arbitration Forums Inc., 1989—. Contbr. articles to profl. jours. Dem. nominee for rep. Mo. Gen. Assembly, 1940. Served to 2d lt. AUS, 1942-45. Mem. Fed. Bar Assn. (pres. Columbus chpt. 1967-68), Ohio Bar Assn., Columbus Bar Assn. (pres. 1972-73), Indsl. Relations Research Assn. (pres. central Ohio chpt. 1966-68), Nat. Acad. Arbitrators (chmn. region 9 1975—), Am. Judicature Soc., Soc. Profls. in Dispute Resolution. Home: 7355 Feder Rd Galloway OH 43119-8880 Office: 600 S High St Columbus OH 43215-5656

GIBSON, RAYMOND EUGENE, clergyman; b. Shelbyville, Ky., Mar. 10, 1924; s. Wallace and Laura Belle (Lee) G.; m. Susan Cochran, June 29, 1945; children: Cyrus Noel, Mark Scott, Christopher Watt, Laurence Kristin, Jonathan Geoffrey. A.B. in Philosophy and History, Berea Coll., 1944; B.D., Union Theol. Sem., N.Y.C., 1947; Ph.D., Columbia U., 1963. Ordained to ministry Congl. Ch., 1947; adminstrv. asst. Inst. Religious and Social Studies, N.Y.C., 1947-48; pastor in New Lebanon, N.Y., 1948-49, Pittsfield, Mass., 1950-61; pastor in Central Congl. Ch., Providence, 1961-88; prof. religious studies Providence Coll., 1971-87; Mem. com. evangelism and devotional life R.I. Congl. Conf., 1962-65, dir., 1965-76; exec. com. R.I. br. Acad. Religion and Mental Health, 1962; Danforth Found. Kenneth Underwood fellow, 1970-71. Author: God, Man and Time, 1966, The Parables of Jesus and the Apostles Creed, 1988, Ministry Recalled - The Central Years, 1992, Leonard Swain, 1995, Tales from the Pewter Shop, 1999; editor: Conversations with God: The Devotional Journals of Myrtie L. Elmer, 1962; assoc. editor: Minister's Quar., 1958-67. Chmn. R.I. adv. com. U.S. Commn. Civil Rights; mem. mayor's com. to end de facto segregation in Providence pub. schs.; bd. dirs. R.I. Group Health Assn., Inc.; trustee Berea Coll., 1963-85; founder, vice chmn. Corp. for Hamilton House, 1972; founder, mem. exec. com. Hospice Care R.I., 1975-86. Recipient Howard prize for citizenship Berea Acad., 1941, Disting. Svc. award Pittsfield Jr. C. of C., 1959, Stevens Metal award, 1992, Disting. Alumnus award Berea Coll., 1999; named Man of Yr. in Pittsfield Area, 1959, one of four Outstanding Young Men in State of Mass. Jr. C. of C., 1959. Mem. Nat. Acad. Religion and Mental Health, Nat. Geog. Soc. Home: 18 E Washington Rd Hillsboro NH 03244-4005 *Life is inward and outward: personal and public. There is a private search for meaning, love, friendship, for being attuned to nature and at peace within. The outward focus relates to communities, of family, neighborhood, state, nation and world. Our task is to share in every effort possible that enhances the human condition and agenda. The art of living lies in finding a balance between these two worlds, so that each enriches the other.*

GIBSON, REGINALD WALKER, federal judge; b. Lynchburg, Va., July 31, 1927; s. McCoy and Julia Ann (Butler) G.; 1 child, Reginald S. B.S., Va. Union U., 1952; postgrad., Wharton Grad. Sch. Bus. Adminstrn., U. Pa., 1952-53; LL.B., Howard U., 1956. Bar: D.C. 1957, Ill. 1972. Agt. IRS, Washington, 1957-61; trial atty. tax div. U.S. Dept. Justice, Washington, 1961-71; sr. tax atty. Internat. Harvester Co., Chgo., 1971-76, gen. tax atty., 1976-82; judge U.S. Ct. of Fed. Claims, Washington, 1982-95; sr. judge U.S. Ct. Fed. Claims, Washington, 1995—. Mem. bus. adbv. council Chgo. Urban League, 1974-82. Served with AUS, 1946-47. Recipient cert. award U.S. Dept. Justice Atty. Gen., 1969, recipient spl. commendation U.S. Dept. Justice Atty. Gen., 1970, Wall St. Jour. award, 1952, Am. Jurisprudence award, 1956; named Alumni of Yr. Howard U. Sch. Law, 1984. Mem. D.C. Bar Assn., Chgo. Bar Assn., Fed. Bar Assn., Nat. Bar Assn., Claims Ct. Bar Assn., J. Edgar Murdock Am. Inn of Ct. (taxation com.). Baptist. Club: Nat. Lawyers (Washington). Home: 6305 Chaucer View Cir Alexandria VA 22304-3548 Office: US Ct Fed Claims 717 Madison Pl NW Washington DC 20005-1011

GIBSON, REX HILTON, lawyer; b. Galveston, Tex., May 17, 1963. BBA, Southern Meth. U., 1985, JD, 1988. Bar: Tex. 1988, U.S. Tax Ct. 1989, U.S. Ct. Claims 1992. Tax assoc. Exxon Co., U.S.A., Houston, 1988, tax atty., 1988-92, sr. tax atty., 1992; sr. tax atty. Exxon Co., Internat., Florham Park, N.J., 1992-95, Exxon Ventures (CIS) Inc., Houston, 1995—. Mem. ABA (taxation sect., natural resources com. 1995—, environ. taxes com. 1990—), State Bar Tex. (taxation sect., oil, gas & minerals law sect. 1989—), Houston Bar Assn. (taxation sect. 1995—), Houston Livestock Show and Rodeo Assn., Beta Alpha Psi. Avocations: snow skiing, hiking, fishing, golf. Office: Exxon Ventures (CIS) Inc 800 Gessner Rd Ste 990 Houston TX 77024-4257

GIBSON, ROY L., city planner; b. Sarasota, Fla., May 7, 1965; s. Lewis Russell and Carol Ann (St. Louis) G. BS in Agr., U. Fla., 1988, MA in Planning, 1990. City planner city of Sanibel, Fla., 1990—. Mem. Am. Inst. Cert. Planners, Am. Planning Assn. Home: PO Box 461 Sanibel FL 33957-0461 Office: City of Sanibel 800 Dunlop Rd Sanibel FL 33957-4096

GIBSON, SAM THOMPSON, internist, educator; b. Covington, Ga., Jan. 1, 1916; s. Count Dillon and Julia (Thompson) G.; m. Alice Chase, Oct. 31, 1942 (dec. Jan. 1971); children: Lena S., Stephen C. (dec.), Judith Gibson Meador, Lucy Gibson Simpson; m. Madge L. Crouch, Sept. 20, 1986. BS in Chemistry, Ga. Inst. Tech., 1936; MD, Emory U., 1940. Diplomate: Am. Bd. Internal Medicine. Med. house officer Peter Bent Brigham Hosp., Boston, 1940-41, asst. resident medicine, 1946-47, asst. medicine, 1947-49; rsch. fellow medicine Harvard Med. Sch., 1941-42, spl. rsch. assoc., 1943, Milton fellow medicine, 1947-49; assoc. medicine George Washington U. Med. Sch., also George Washington U. Hosp., 1949-63, asst. clin. prof. medicine, 1963—, clin. asst. prof. medicine, Uniformed Svcs., Univ. Health Scis., 1980—; asst. med. dir. ARC Blood Program, 1949-51, assoc. med. dir., 1951-53, assoc. dir., 1953-56, dir., 1956-66; sr. med. officer ARC, 1957-67; asst. dir. div. biologics standards NIH, 1967-72; asst. dir. Bur. of Biologics, FDA, Bethesda, Md., 1972-74; asst. to dir. Bur. Biologics, FDA, Bethesda, Md., 1974-77, dir. div. biologics evaluation, 1977-83; dir. div. biol. product compliance Ctr. for Drugs and Biologics, 1983-85; assoc. dir. sci. and tech. Office of Compliance, Ctr. Drugs and Biologics, FDA, 1985-88; dir. sci. and tech. Office of Health Affairs FDA, Rockville, Md., 1988-89; cons. blood Naval Med. Sch., Nat. Naval Med. Center, Bethesda, 1950-63; mem. med. adv. bd. CARE-Medico, 1962-70, cons., 1970-89; chmn. U.S. com. for tranfusion equipment for med. use Am. Standards Assn., 1954-66, tech. adv. group transfusion equipment for med. use Nat. Commn. Clin. Lab. Standards/Am. Nat. Standards Inst., 1975-89; adviser orgn. blood transfusion services League Red Cross Socs., 1955-66. Contbg. editor: Vox Sanguinis Jour. Blood Transfusion, 1956-65; mem. adv. bd., 1965-76. Served from lt. (j.g.) to comdr., M.C. USNR, 1941-46; capt. Res. ret. Mem. AMA, AAAS, Internat., Am. socs. hematology, Nat. Health Coun. (dir. 1957-60, 61-64), Internat. Soc. Blood Transfusion (regional counselor 1962-66), Am. Fedn. for Med. Rsch., N.Y. Acad. Scis., Delta Tau Delta, Alpha Kappa Kappa, Alpha Chi Sigma, Tau Beta Pi, Phi Kappa Phi, Omicron Delta Kappa, Alpha Omega Alpha. Home: 5801 Rossmore Dr Bethesda MD 20814-2229

GIBSON, SARAH ANN SCOTT, art librarian; b. Harrisburg, Pa., Mar. 2, 1932; d. John Young Scott and Alice Virginia (Cooper) Rowe; m. Walter Samuel Gibson, Dec. 16, 1972. AB in History, Smith Coll., 1953; postgrad., Université de Strasbourg, France, 1953-54, École du Louvre, Paris, 1965-66; MLS, Case Western Reserve U., 1968, MA in Art History, 1972, PhD in Libr. and Info. Sci., 1975. Asst. cataloger Denison U., Granville, Ohio, 1958-69; asst. prof. U. Mich., 1972-73; asst. prof. Case Western Reserve U., 1975-82, asst. dean Sch. Libr. Sci., 1979-82, assoc. prof., 1982-86; exec. officer Matthew A. Baxter Sch. Info. and Libr. Sci., 1984-86; libr. Sterling & Francine Clark Art Inst., Williamstown, Mass., 1987-96; vis. prof. Sch. Info. Studies Syracuse U., 1986. Author: (with Lois Swan Jones) Art Libraries and Information Services: Development, Organization and Management, 1986, (with others) Book Illustration From Six Centuries in the Library of the Sterling & Francine Clark Art Institute Library, 1990; contbr.: Encyclopedia of Comparative Iconography, 1998; assoc. editor RILA Internat. Repertory of Lit. of Art, 1986-87; contbr. articles to profl. jours. Fulbright fellow, 1953-54. Mem. Art Librs. Soc. N.Am., Jr. League Cleve., Princeton Club N.Y.C., Historians Netherlands Art. Home: RR 2 Box 461H Pownal VT 05261-9767

GIBSON, SCOTT RUSSELL, nurse; b. New Castle, Pa., Feb. 5, 1956; s. Earle A. and Barbara (Gormley) G.; m. Michele Moshier, May 10, 1980; children: Kathleen, Andrew, Benjamin. BSN with honors, Indiana U. Pa., 1989; postgrad., Cert. Registered Nurse Anesthetist Sch., Altoona, 1992-94. Cert. transplant technician, U.S. Navy Sch.; cert. emergency nurse. Staff nurse Indiana (Pa.) Hosp., 1989-96; regional faculty BLS program Am. Heart Assn., 1989—; faculty instr. Indiana Vocat. Tech. LPN Sch., 1990-92; with infusion dept. Diamond Drugs, Inc., 1996—. Mem. Am. Heart Assn., 1979, ARC, 1974. With USN, 1979-86. Mem. Emergency Nurses Assn.

GIBSON, THOMAS FENNER, III, public affairs strategist, political cartoonist; b. Indpls., Jan. 23, 1955; s. Thomas Jr. and Lois (Hilkene) G.; m. Kimberly Timmons, Feb. 13, 1988; children: Thomas Fenner, Lucy Kirkwood, William Henry. BA cum laude, Princeton U., 1977; MPA, Harvard U., 1982. Legis. asst. U.S. Sen. Dewey Bartlett, Washington, 1978-79; lobbyist Arnold & Porter Law Firm, Washington, 1979; govt. affairs dir. Brick Inst. Am., Washington, 1979-81; editor, opinion staff USA Today, Washington, 1982-83; assoc. dir. Cabinet Affairs, The White House, Washington, 1983-85; spl. asst. to Pres., dir. pub. affairs The White House, Washington, 1985-87; v.p. Porter/Novelli, Washington, 1988-90; sr. v.p. The Wexler Group, Washington, 1990-96; exec. MCI, Washington, 1996-98; exec. v.p. Mooney Aircraft Corp., 1999—; prin. Kirkwood/Gibson, 1999—. Freelance polit. cartoonist Washington Post, 1977—. Chmn. chapel adv. coun. Princeton U., N.J., 1979-87; mem. Civil Air Patrol, College Park, Md., 1979-80; dir. speech writing Rep. Conv., 1996; sec. Children's Express Found. Mem. Nat. Found. for Caricature and Cartoon Art (founder, chair), Aircraft Owners and Pilots Assn., Ivy Club (Princeton, N.J.), Met. Club (Washington). Republican. Presbyterian. Avocations: aviation, auto restoration, competitive tennis. Home: 4400 Edmunds St NW Washington DC 20007-1117 Office: MCI Corp HQ Rm 733 1701 K St NW Ste 800 Washington DC 20006

GIBSON, THOMAS RICHARD, automobile import company executive; b. Sept. 2, 1942; s. Gilbert G. and Mary Ellen (Wilbraham) G.; m. Sophie Harned, Oct. 14, 1967; children: Matthew B., Katherine A., Caroline Q.; AB, DePauw U., 1964; MBA, Harvard U., 1967. Various sales mgmt. positions, Ford Motor Co., Dearborn, Mich., 1967-80; dir. mktg. ops., Chrysler Corp., Highland Pk., Mich., 1980-81, sr. v.p. sales and mktg., Subaru of Am., Cherry Hill, N.J., 1981-84, exec. v.p. ops., 1984-86, pres., chief operating officer, 1986-92; chmn., CEO Asbury Automotive Group, 1994—. Bd. dirs. Childrens Hosp. Phila., 1986-89, Glassboro (N.J.) State Coll, 1985-89; trustee U.S. Ski Team, 1990-95. Served with USMC, 1964-65. Mem. DePauw U. Alumni Assn. (bd. dirs. 1987, trustee 1992-96). Avocations: tennis, golf, paddle tennis. Office: Asbury Automotive Group 1 Tower Bridge 14th Fl Conshohocken PA 19428*

GIBSON, TOBY ALLEN, systems analyst, poet; b. Fort Sill, Okla., Aug. 28, 1959; s. Jimmy Allen Gibson and Rita Doyce (Durrett) Craig; m. Sherri Lee Campbell, March 7, 1997. BSEE, Tex. Tech. U., 1987. Site engr. St. Marys Hosp., Lubbock, Tex., 1987-90; computer programmer Gen. Dynamics, Sterling Heights, Mich., 1990-93; sys. analyst Chrysler Corp., Auburn Hills, Mich., 1993—. Author, pub.: Inside of Life, 1990; author: The Wayfarer Poems, 1997. Royal ranger comdr. Auburn Hills (Mich.) Christian Ctr., 1993, tchr., 1993—. Home: 4660 Mesa Ct Clarkston MI 48348-2265

GIBSON, WALKER, retired English language educator, poet, writer; b. Jacksonville, Fla., Jan. 19, 1919; s. William Walker Sr. and Helen (Jones) G.; m. Nancy Close, 1942; children: David R., Susan M., William Walker. III, John S. BA, Yale U., 1940; MA, U. Iowa, 1946. Rsch. asst. writers workshop U. Iowa, 1945-46; instr. English Amherst (Mass.) Coll., 1946-48, asst. prof., 1948-54, assoc. prof., 1954-57; assoc. prof., dir. freshman English Washington Square Coll. NYU, N.Y.C., 1957-61, prof., 1961-67; prof. English U. Mass., Amherst, 1967-87, dir. freshman English, 1967-70, dir. rhetoric program, 1970-72, dir. undergrad. studies in English, 1974-76, prof. emeritus, 1984; lectr. Yale Summer Music Sch., 1948-56; dir. NYU Summer Inst. for Secondary Tchrs. English, 1962, NDEA Summer Inst. for Secondary Tchrs. English, NYU, 1965, Summer Seminars for Coll Tchrs, NEH, 1973-75; prof. summer intern teaching program Smith Coll., 1963, 64, 66, 67; vis. prof. Swarthmore Coll., 1965-66; prof. NDEA Summer Inst. at Mass., 1968, Bread Loaf Sch. English, Middlebury Coll., 1976, 77. Author: (verse) The Reckless Spenders, 1954 Come As You Are, 1957, (texts) Seeing and Writing: Fifteen Exercises in Composing Experience, 1959, Tough Sweet & Stuffy, 1966, Persona: A Style Study for Readers and Writers, 1969, (antholgy text) Poems in Progress, 1963; co-author: The Macmillan Handbook of English, 1960, 2nd edit, 1965; contbg. author: Traditions of Inquiry, 1985, The Legacy of Language, 1987, others; editor: Limits of Language, 1962, New Students in Two-Year Colleges, 1979; co-editor: The Play of Language, 1971; prose and verse published in The New Yorker, Story, Atlantic, Harpers, Saturday Review, The Nation, Furioso, Carleton Miscellany, Mass. Review, N.Y. Times Mag., others, reprinted in anthologies and texts; book reviews in N.Y. Times Book Review, Coll. English, Poetry, Nation, others; acad. articles in Victorian Studies, Modern Language Notes, N.Y.U. Law Review, Coll. Composition and Comm., ADE Bulletin, Coll. English, English Jour., The Quarterly Review of Doublespeak, Rhetoric Review, Chronicle of Higher Edn., others; contbns. to TV and film include Sunrise Semester, CBS-TV, full-year course Modern Literature: British and American, 1962-63, semester course Studies in Style, 1966-67, film The Speaking Voice and the Teaching of Composition, 1963, videotapes on dramatic role-playing in student writing, 1971, 84. 1st lt. U.S. Army Air Corps, 1941-45. Ford Found. fellow 1955-56; John Simon Guggenheim Found.

fellow, 1963-64; grantee NEH, 1973-77. Mem. MLA (selection com. for scholar's libr. 1968-71, del. assembly 1976-77, exec. com. divsn. on tchg. of writing 1976-80, chmn. divsn. 1979), Nat. coun. Tchrs. English (commn. on curriculum 1962-65, chmn. coll. sect. 1969-71, pres. elect and pres. coun. 1971-73, pres. 1972-73, com. pub. doublespeak 1972-90, chmn. emeritus assembly 1986-87, Disting. Lectr. award 1969, Disting. Svc. award 1988), CCCC (exec. com. 1966-69), 5 Coll. Learning in Retirement (pres. 1990-91). Avocation: gardening. Home: 300 Market Hill Rd Amherst MA 01002-1243

GIBSON, WILLIAM FORD, author; b. Conway, S.C., Mar. 17, 1948; s. William Ford and Otey (Williams) G.; m. Deborah Thompson, June 1972; children: Graeme Ford, Claire Thompson. BA, U. B.C., 1977. Author: (novels) Neuromancer, 1984 (Hugo award World Sci. Fiction Soc. 1985, Philip K. Dick award Phila. Sci. Fiction Soc. 1985, Nebula award Sci. Fiction Writers Am. 1985, Porgie award West Coast Rev. of Books 1985), Count Zero, 1986, Mona Lisa Overdrive, 1988, (with Bruce Sterling) The Difference Engine, 1990, Virtual Light, 1993; (short story collections) Burning Chrome, 1986; text to accompany performance art by Robert Longo: Dream Jumbo, 1989; story: (film) Johnny Mnemonic, 1995. Office: care Martha Millard Lit Agency 293 Greenwood Ave Florham Park NJ 07932*

GIBSON, WILLIAM LEE, financial consultant; b. Newark, Dec. 1, 1949; S. Joseph Wilton Gibson and Margaret (Reynolds) Gibson Leavens; stepson William Barry Leavens, Jr.; m. Lorraine Wrightson Besch, July 10, 1982. BA in chemistry, Bucknell U., 1972; postgrad., Harvard Bus. Sch., 1977; MBA, NYU, 1987; Sch. of Advanced Fin. Mgmt., 1995. With Bur. Solid Waste Mgmt EPA, Cin., 1970-71; chemist Dow Chem. Co., Midland, Mich., 1972-75; mktg. cons. Westvaco, Charleston, S.C., 1976; sales rep. Diamond Shamrock Co., Cleve., 19777-79; market devel. specialist strategic planing and ventures operation GE, Pittsfield, Mass., 1979-81; mktg. programs mgr. Allied-Signal Corp., Morristown, N.J., 1981-86, mgr. tech. and bus. devel., 1986-91, sr. sales mgr., 1991-93; asst. v.p. Merrill Lynch, Short Hills, N.J., 1994—; Former pres., trustee Hartford Family Found; v.p. Leavens Found.; trustee N.J. Symphony Orchestra. Trustee Jr. Achievement No. N.J. Home: 8 Lone Oak Rd Basking Ridge NJ 07920-1613 Office: 51 John F Kennedy Pky Short Hills NJ 07078-2702

GIBSON, WILLIAM MICHAEL, oceanographer; b. Bethesda, Md., Oct. 13, 1955; s. William Ross and Barbara Elizabeth (Bell) G. BS in Oceanography, George Washington U., 1981; PG in Gemology, Columbia Sch. Gemology, Silver Spring, Md., 1992; FGA in Gemology, Gemol. Assn. Gt. Britain, London, 1993. Cert. scuba diver Profl. Assn. Diving Instrs. (PADI). Oceanographer Nat. Oceanic and Atmospheric Adminstrn., Silver Spring, 1976—. Fellow Gemol. Assn./Gt. Britain; mem. Gemol. Inst. Am. Avocations: scuba diving, martial arts, goldsmithing, skiing. Home: PO Box 2745 Kensington MD 20891-2745 Office: Nat Oceanic/Atmospheric Adm 1305 E West Hwy Rm 6507 Silver Spring MD 20910-3278

GIBSON, WILLIAM SHEPARD, management consultant; b. Bklyn., Jan. 2, 1933; s. William S. and Mary (Keeney) G.; m. Charmaine Wallett, May 26, 1967; children: Susan, Joshua/1 stepdau., Tracy; children by previous marriage: William, Gregory. BS in Acctg., U. Ill., 1954, JD, 1959. Counsel Am. Ins. Assn., Chgo., 1963-69; asst. dir. ins. State of Ill., Chgo., 1969-71; v.p. midwest Am. Ins. Assn., Chgo., 1971-77; v.p., gen. counsel Continental Ins., N.Y.C., 1977-82; v.p. govt. affairs Continental Corp., N.Y.C., 1982-95; dep. supt. N.Y. Ins., N.Y.C., 1995-97; v.p. Peterson Worldwide, N.Y.C., 1997—; chmn. bd. N.J. Auto Ins. Assn., Newark, 1983-89; chmn. Continental PAC, 1981-95; mem. N.Y. Motor Vehicle Indemnity Corp. Bd. dirs. Lower Manhattan Cultural Coun. Served with U.S. Army, 1954-56. Mem. ABA, Ill. State Bar Assn., N.Y. Bar Assn., Internat. Assn. Ins. Counsel, N.Y. Med. Malpractice Ins. Assn. Congregationalist. Home: 80 Warren St Apt 67 New York NY 10007-1039 Office: 450 Lexington Ave New York NY 10017-3911

GIBSON, WILLIAM WILLARD, JR., law educator; b. Amarillo, Tex., Mar. 5, 1932; s. William Willard and Genelle (Works) G.; m. Beth Smyth, July 31, 1953; children—William Willard, Michael Murray, Timothy Thomas, Elizabeth Mills. BA, U. Tex., Austin, 1954, LLB, 1956. Assoc. Gibson, Ochsner, Harlin, Kinney & Morris, Amarillo, Tex., 1956-60, ptnr., 1960-65; assoc. prof. U. Tex.-Austin Sch. Law, 1965-69, prof., 1969-76, Albert Sydney Burleson prof. law, 1976-83, Sylvan Lang prof. law, 1983-98, Sylvan Lang prof. emeritus, 1998—, dir. continuing legal edn., 1981-85, assoc. dean, 1979-86; Austin; provost jud. edn. Supreme Ct. Tex., 1992-93. Author: Teaching Materials on Wills and Estates, 1967; Selected Provisions from Texas Statutes Pertaining to Wills and Estates, 1973; also articles. Vice chancellor Diocese of Tex., Protestant Episcopal Ch. Recipient Leon Green award Tex. Law Rev. Assn. of Ex-Editors, Austin, 1983. Mem. Am. Coll. Real Estate Lawyers. Democrat. Avocations: walking, fishing, hunting. Office: U Tex Sch Law 727 E 26th St Austin TX 78705-3224

GICOLA, PAUL, middle school science educator, administrator; b. Bklyn., Nov. 21, 1950; s. Frank and Ann (Lionti) G.; m. Rosanne Signa, Aug. 3, 1974; children: Sabrina, Elise. BS, Southampton Coll., 1972; MS, L.I. U., 1976, profl. diploma in sch. bus. adminstrn., 1982, profl. diploma in sch. dist. adminstrn., 1983. Tchr. sci. Amityville (N.Y.) Pub. Schs., 1972—, asst. prin. summer sch., 1987, 88, chair sci. dept., 1986-89, dist. dir. sci., 1989-92; advisor Sci. Soc., Amityville Jr. High Sch., 1974-85, mem. mid. states steering com., 1979-81, audio-visual coord., 1986-89; mem. bldg. planning team Amityville H.S., 1990-92, chmn., 1991-92; middle level sci. mentor N.Y. State, 1991-95. Co-author dist. textbooks. Mem. ASCD, Nat. Sci. Tchrs. Assn., Sci. Tchrs. Assn. N.Y. State, N.Y. State United Tchrs., Nat. Sci. Suprs. Assn. (dir. 1996-99), L.I. Inst. Sci. and Tech., Suffolk County Sci. Tchrs. Assn. (exec. bd., v.p. 1991-94, chmn. elect 1995, chmn. 1996-98), Phi Delta Kappa. Avocations: computers, travel. Office: E W Miles Mid Sch Rt 110 Amityville NY 11701-3858

GIDDENS, DON PEYTON, engineering educator, researcher; b. Augusta, Ga., Oct. 24, 1940. BS in Engring., Ga. Inst. Tech., 1963, MS in Aerospace Engring., 1965, PhD, 1967. Assoc. aircraft engr. Lockheed-Ga. Co., Atlanta, 1963; mem. tech. staff Aerospace Corp., San Bernardino, Calif., 1966-67; asst. prof. Ga. Inst. Tech., Atlanta, 1968-70, assoc. prof., 1970-77, prof., 1977-82, Regents prof., 1982-92, dir. Sch. Aerospace Engring., 1988-92; dean engring. Johns Hopkins U., Balt., 1992-97; prof., chmn. dept. biomed. engring. Ga. Inst. Tech./Emory Med. Sch., Atlanta, 1997—; mem. sci. adv. com. Whitaker Found. Contbr. numerous articles to profl. jours. Fellow ASME, Am. Inst. Med. Biol. Engrs.; mem. AAAS, AHA, BMES, Natl. Acad. Engrg., Soc. Sigma Xi (nat. lectr. 1983-87). Avocation: whitewater canoeing. Office: Ga Inst Tech GT/Emory Dept Biomed Engr Atlanta GA 30332-0535*

GIDDENS, PAUL JOSEPH, human resources executive; b. Oil City, Pa.; s. Willard A. and Elizabeth Giddens; m. H. Barbara Giddens, Dec. 23, 1973; children: Linda Anne, Michele Jacqueline, Katherine Ernst. BA in Fin., U. Tex., 1966; MA in Mgmt. Devel., Va. State U., 1978. Dir. mgmt. devel., mgr. human resources Continental Group Inc., Atlanta, Ga., 1978-81; mgr. indsl. rels. Continental Group/Fibre Drume Div., Charlotte, N.C., 1979-80; area mgr. human resources Continental Group/Fibre Drume Div., Atlanta, 1980-81; dir. human resources planning Hanes Group, Sarah Lee Corp., Winston-Salem, N.C., 1981-82; mgr. assoc. rels. M&M/MARS, Hackettstown, N.J., 1982-85; mgr. quality effectiveness GE Aircraft Engines, Cin., 1985-89, mgr. human resources planning, tng. and orgn. devel., 1989-92; sr. dir. orgn. effectiveness Ga.-Pacific Corp., Atlanta, 1992-94, sr. dir. bus. devel., 1994-96; v.p., human resource integration cons. York & Assocs., Mpls., 1996-97; dir. human resources Barnes Group, Inc., Bristol, Conn., 1997-98; v.p. human resources, info. tech. Quanex Corp., Houston, 1998—; commr. Sec. Labor Commn., Washington, 1990-92; pub. speaker various assn., 1986—; lectr. various univs., 1989—. Contbr. articles to profl. jours. Bd. dirs. Cin. Union Bethel United Way Agy., Cin., 1988—, Great Rivers Girl Scout Coun., Cin., 1989—. Capt. U.S. Army, 1967-76. Decorated Silver Star, Purple Heart, U.S. Army, Vietnam, Gold medal of German Army. Mem. Delta Chi (Pres. 1964-66). Avocations: writing, pub. speaking. Office: Quanex Corp 1900 West Loop S Ste 1500 Houston TX 77027-3267

GIDDINGS, CLIFFORD FREDERICK, retired corporate executive; b. East Dorset, Vt., May 28, 1936; s. Frederick Daniel and Natalie (Abbott) G. BA, U. Vt., 1958; MA, U. Wis., 1961; postgrad., Sorbonne U., Paris, 1958, U. Chgo., 1963-65. French master Lake Forest (Ill.) Acad., 1961-63; asst. head reference dept. The Newberry Library, Chgo., 1964-68, assoc. head reference dept., 1972-74; dir. library services Scott, Foresman and Co., Glenview, Ill., 1968-71; asst. mgr. Albert E. Barrett, Inc., Trenton, N.J., 1975-80, exec. v.p., 1980-97; ret. Fulbright scholar U.S. Dept. State, Grenoble, France, 1958-59. Mem. Associated Gen. Contractors of N.J., N.J. Asphalt Pavement Assn., Nat. Asphalt Pavement Assn., Utility and Transp. Contractors Assn. N.J., Fulbright Assn. Episcopalian. Avocations: classical discography, Am. antique furniture, philately. Home: 66 Line Rd West Windsor NJ 08550

GIDDINGS, PAULA JANE, author, educator; b. Yonkers, N.Y., Nov. 16, 1947; d. Curtis Gulliver and Virginia Iola (Stokes) G. BA, Howard U., 1969; DHL (hon.), Bennett Coll., 1990, Wesleyan U., 1995. Prof. Spelman Coll., Atlanta, 1986-87; prof., Laurie N.J. chair women's studies Rutgers U., New Brunswick, N.J., 1989-91; prof. Princeton (N.J.) U., 1992-93, Duke U., Durham, N.C., 1996—; bd. dirs. Author's Guild Found., N.Y.C. Author: (books) When and Where I Enter: The Impact of Black Women on Race and Sex in America, In Search of Sisterhood: Delta Sigma Theta and the Black Sorority Movement. Guggenheim fellow, 1993, Nat. Humanities Ctr. fellow, 1993-95. Mem. Century Club, Delta Sigma Theta (bd. dirs. 1997—).

GIDDINGS, WILLIAM GLENN, community college president; b. Oct. 3, 1945. BS, Iowa State U., 1968, MS, 1974, PhD, 1985. Assoc. dean instructional svcs., adult comty. edn. Iowa Ctrl. C.C., Fort Dodge, 1977-85, dean adult and comty. edn., 1985-92; pres. Ctrl. C.C., Grand Island, Nebr., 1992—; math. instr. Ankeny (Iowa) Comty. Schs. 1968-69, 71-73; vocat. counselor Iowa Vocat. Rehab. Divsn., Fort Dodge, 1973-74; adj. instr. ednl. stats. Drake U., Des Moines, Iowa, 1992, adj. math. instr. Buena Vista Coll., Storm Lake, Iowa, 1981-92, adj. stats. instr. Bellevue (Nebr.) U., 1994; presenter to ednl. confs. and assns. in midwest, 1973-99. Coun. chmn. Christ Luth. Ch., Fort Dodge, Iowa, 1977; active Peace Luth. Ch., Grand Island, Nebr., stewardship com. 1995-96, evangelism com., 1997—; mem. bus. contact group Grand Island Area Econ. Devel. Coun. 1995—, bd. dirs. 1999, adv. bd. Grand Island Area Sch.-to-Work Consortium, exec. bd. 1996—, Grand Island Leadership Tomorrow, 1992-93, Grand Island Edn. 2000 Com., 1994-97, Heartland Vision Strategic Planning Com., 1997—; exec. bd. dirs. Overland Trails Boy Scout Coun. 1995—. Named Internat. Disting. Pres., Fort Dodge Civitan Club 1982, Disting. Svc. award Iowa Assn. Lifelong Learning, Fort Dodge, 1992. Mem. Am. Assn. of Adult and Continuing Edn., Adult and Continuing Edn. Assn. Nebr. (Nebr. Outstanding Adult Educator award 1999), Heartland Assn. of Two-Year Coll. Presidents, Nebr. Coun. of Campus Execs. (vice-chair 1994-95, chair 1995-97), Nat. Coun. for Continuing Edn. and Tng. (Nebr. rep. 1996—), Sunrise Rotary Club, Grand Island (bd. dirs. 1993-95. v.p. 1995-97), Grand Island Area C. of C. (bd. dirs. 1995-99, chair 1999). bgiddings@cccneb.edu. Home: 2311 Viking Ct Grand Island NE 68803-1446 Office: Ctrl Cmty Coll PO Box 4903 Grand Island NE 68802-4903

GIDDINS, GARY MITCHELL, music critic, columnist; b. Bklyn., Mar. 21, 1948; s. Leo and Alice (Gelber) G.; m. Susan Rogers, Apr. 23, 1972 (div. 1979); m. Deborah Halper, May 19, 1985; 1 child, Lea Aviva. BA, Grinnell (Iowa) Coll., 1970, DFA (hon.), 1988. Film reviewer Hollywood (Calif.) Reporter, 1972; contbg. editor Down Beat, 1972-74; jazz columnist Village Voice, N.Y.C., 1973—, film critic, 1989-90; jazz critic N.Y. Mag., N.Y.C., 1975-80; jazz columnist Hifi-Stereo Buyer's Guide, N.Y.C., 1975-78; prodr., disc jockey Sta. WBAI-FM, N.Y.C., 1975-80; freelance writer various publs., 1970—; instr. jazz tradition NYU Continuing Edn. program, 1977-87; instr. writing program Columbia U., 1988—; vis. prof. history of jazz U. Pa., 1982-83; vis. prof. Am. music Rutgers U., 1985; founder, artistic dir. Am. Jazz Orch., 1985-92. Prodr.: 35 concerts, 2 at Kool Jazz Fest, N.Y.C., 1981, concert tribute to Gil Evans, Lincoln Ctr., N.Y.C., 1983, JVC Jazz Festival, 1992; author: Riding on a Blue Note, 1981, (with Carol Friedman) A Moment's Notice, 1983, Rhythm-a-ning, 1985, Celebrating Bird: The Triumph of Charlie Parker, 1986 (Am. Book award 1987, Deems Taylor award ASCAP 1988), Satchmo, 1988, Faces in the Crowd, 1992 (Deems Taylor award ASCAP 1993), Visions of Jazz: The First Century, 1998 (Nat. Book Critics Cir. award 1998); writer, co-dir.: (documentary video) Celebrating Bird: The Triumph of Charlie Parker, 1987 (Am. Video Conf. award 1988); writer, dir. (documentary film) Satchmo, 1989 (Vira award 1990); writer (documentary film) John Hammond, 1990 (Peabody award, Cine award 1991); columist Modern Maturity mag., 1-94—; contbr. to Vanity Fair, 1983, Entertainment Weekly, 1991-93, Fi mag., 1995-99. Recipient Deems Taylor award ASCAP, 1976, 77, 84, Gerald Marks award ASCAP, 1997; Merit award Art Dirs. Club, 1985, Grammy award for liner notes, 1987; Smithsonian Instn. fellow in jazz studies, 1974; Guggenheim fellow, 1986. Jewish. Office: Village Voice 36 Cooper Sq New York NY 10003-7149

GIDDON, DONALD B(ERNARD), psychologist, educator; b. Newark, May 1, 1930; s. William and Ruth (Franklin) G.; m. Phoebe L. Rothman, Aug. 28, 1955; children: David, Kenneth, Joanna, James. *Together with brother James Giddon, A.B. Lehigh, 90', son Kenneth Giddon, A.B.Brown University 81', he returned his grandfather's famous clothing store, Rothman's , to profitability in Union Square, N.Y.C. He was cited as small businessman of the year by Crane's, recently written up in the Wall St. Journal and interviewed for CNN. His sister Joanna, Lafayette U., 1990, is a press manager with NBC in New York.* A.B., Brown U., 1952; M.A., Boston U., 1953; D.M.D., Harvard U., 1959; Ph.D. in Psychology, Brandeis U., 1961. Lectr. psychology Brandeis U., 1954-71, 82-84, lectr. physical edn., 1985-89; prof., chmn. dental ecology Harvard U., 1972-75, vis. prof., 1976-89, lectr., 1989-98, clin. prof., 1999—, lectr. health services adminstrn. Sch. Pub. Health, 1972-75, asst. dean adminstrn. Sch. Dental Medicine, 1973-75; assoc. staff New Eng. Med. Center, 1964-73; assoc. prof., chmn. dept. social dentistry Tufts U., Boston, 1964-67, prof., chmn. dept. social dentistry, 1967-72, asst. dean, 1967-69, assoc. dean, 1969-71; dean NYU Dental Ctr., 1975-78, prof. behavioral sci. and community health, 1976—; prof. psychology Grad. Sch. Arts and Scis., prof. anesthesiology NYU Med. Center, 1976-80; prof. Faculty of Medicine, U. Groningen, The Netherlands, 1980-81; cons. Astra Pharm. Products, Inc., 1960—; cons. dept. medicine and surgery VA, 1966-69, med. rsch. cons., 1988—, Peter Bent Brigham Hosp., 1975-76, Meml. Sloan-Kettering Cancer Ctr., 1976-78; vis. staff physician (surgery) NYU Med. Ctr., 1976—, Brookdale Hosp. Med. Ctr., 1977—, Goldwater Meml. Hosp., 1977-80; cons. psychologist dept. anesthesiology Brigham and Women's Hosp., 1979—; vis. prof. U. Gothenburg, Sweden, 1971, Royal Dental Coll., Aarhus, Denmark, 1972, U. Pa., 1972, McGill Med. U., 1981-83; vis. prof. psychology Mass. Coll. Pharmacy and Allied Health Scis., 1984-89; lectr. Brown U., 1985-89, clin. prof., 1989—; clin. prof. psychology U. Ill., Chgo., 1994—; founding dir. Rsch. Inst., Royal Victoria Hosp., Montreal, Can., 1981-82. Contbr. articles to profl. jours. Bd. dirs. Mass. Health Coun., 1965-70, pres., 1968-69; pres. Hamilton sch. PTA, Newton Lower Falls, Mass., 1963-64; trustee Emerson Coll., 1991—, Berkshire Opera, 1996—; mem. Com. on Univ. Resources, bd. overseers Harvard U., 1991—. Fulbright scholar, 1971. Fellow AAAS, APA, Am. Pub. Health Assn., Am. Coll. Dentists, Internat. Coll. Dentists, Internat. Coll. Psychosomatic Medicine, Royal Soc. Medicine; mem. AAUP, Am. Statis. Assn., Internat. Assn. Study Pain, Am. Psychosomatic Soc., Am. Coll. Sports Medicine, Am. Dental Soc. Anesthesiology (assoc. editor 1965-72, chmn. ethics com. 1979-81), Acad. Behavioral Med. Rsch., Behavioral Sci. in Dental Rsch. (pres. 1976-77), Internat. Assn. Dental Rsch. (pres. Boston sect. 1965-66), Am. Pain Soc. (dir. 1977-79), Soc. Behavioral Med., Soc. Psychophys. Rsch., Soc. Clin. and Experimental Hypnosis, Sigma Xi. Office: 277 Linden St Wellesley MA 02482-5920

GIDEL, ROBERT HUGH, real estate investor; b. Ft. Dodge, Iowa, Sept. 19, 1951; s. Wayne D. and Mary A. (Ziegler) G.; m. Linda Carol Lombardo, Oct. 23, 1976; children: Jill, Allison, Robert. BSBA, U. Fla., 1973. Comml. loan officer Century Bank, St. Petersburg, Fla., 1975-77; asst. v.p. N.Y. Life, Washington, 1977-81; exec. v.p. Heller Real Estate Fin. Co., Chgo., 1981-86; pres., mng. dir., bd dirs. Alex Brown Realty Advisors, Balt., 1986-90; mng. dir., bd. dirs. Alex Brown Kleinwort Benson Realty Advisors, Balt., 1990-93; pres., bd. dirs. Brazos Ptnrs. L.P., Dallas, 1993-98; bd. dirs. Am. Indsl. Properties, Lone Star Opportunity Fund II, Brazos Fund, Lone Star Fund, Am. Indsl. Properties; pres., COO, bd. dirs. ParagonGroup Inc., 1996-97; CEO, bd. dirs. Meridian Realty Trust VIII, 1997-98; pres., bd. dirs. Liberty Ptnrs., 1997—. Contbr. articles to profl. publs. Fellow Homer Hoyt Inst. Mem. Nat. Coun. Real Estate Investment Fiduciaries, Pension Real Estate Assn., Assn. Fgn. Investors in Real Estate, Nat. Assn. Real Estate Investment Trusts, L'Hirondelle Club (Balt.), Bent Tree Country Club (Dallas). Republican. Roman Catholic. Home: 5427 Edgehollow Pl Dallas TX 75287-7506 Office: Liberty Ptnrs 2200 Ross Ave # S4200W Dallas TX 75201-2787

GIDEON, FRANCIS C., JR., military officer. BS in Engring. Scis., USAF Acad., 1966; grad., Squadron Officer Sch., 1970, Indsl. Coll. Armed Forces, 1971; MS in Sys. Mgmt., Air Force Inst. Tech., 1974; grad., Air Command and Staff Coll., 1979, Air War Coll., 1981; exec. devel. program, U. Pitts., 1988; grad., Def. Sys. Mgmt. Coll., 1990. Cert. program mgmt. level II, test and evaluation level III. Commd. 2d lt. USAF, 1966, advanced through grades to maj. gen., 1994; F-4 test pilot 6512th Test Squadron, Edwards AFB, Calif., 1975-76; A-10 test pilot, ops. officer A-10 Joint Test Force, Edwards AFB, 1976-80; chief devel. plans aircraft divsn. Air Force Sys. Command, Andrews AFB, Md., 1981; dep. dir. Devel. Plans Tactical Sys. Directorate, Andrews AFB, 1982-84; chief F-15 projects and test divsn. F-15 Sys. Program Office, Wright-Patterson AFB, Ohio, 1984-85; dir. Fighter Attack Sys. Program Office, Wright-Patterson AFB, 1985-86, Strike Sys. Program Office, Wright-Patterson AFB, 1986-87; comdr. 4950th Test Wing, Wright-Patterson AFB, 1987-88, Fgn. Aerospace Sci. and Tech. Ctr., Wright-Patterson AFB, 1988-92; vice comdr. Sacramento Air Logistics Ctr., McClellan AFB, Calif., 1992-93; dir. of ops. Hdqs. Air Force Materiel Command, Wright-Patterson AFB, 1993-97; chief of safety USAF, comdr. Hdqs. Air Force Safety Ctr., Kirtland AFB, N.Mex., 1997—. Decorated Disting. Svc. medal, Legion of Merit with oak leaf cluster, D.F.C. Office: HQ USAF/SE Ste 240 9700 G Ave SE Kirtland AFB NM 87117-5670

GIDEON, KENNETH WAYNE, lawyer; b. Lubbock, Tex., July 25, 1946; s. Melton Jean and Mary B. (Lanham) G.; m. Carol Almack, June 2, 1968; children—Christopher Lynn, Kevin Almack, Timothy Charles, Emily Susan. BA, Harvard U., 1968; JD, Yale U., 1971. Bar: Tex. 1971, U.S. Tax Ct. 1971, U.S. Ct. Claims 1972, U.S. Supreme Ct. 1981, D.C. 1984. Assoc. Fulbright & Jaworski, Houston, 1971-78, ptnr., 1978-81; ptnr. Fulbright & Jaworski, Washington, 1983-86; chief counsel IRS, Washington, 1981-83; ptnr. Fried, Frank, Harris, Shriver & Jacobson, Washington, 1986-89, 92-93; asst. sec. tax policy Dept. Treasury, Washington, 1989-92; ptnr. Wilmer, Cutler & Pickering, Washington, 1994—. Mem. Spring Valley (Tex.) City Coun., 1978-79. Capt. U.S. Army, 1971-72. Fellow Am. Bar Found., Am. Coll. Tax Counsel (regent 1999—); mem. ABA (vice chair govt. rels. 1995-97, mem. coun. 1987-89, sect. taxation), Am. Law Inst., Orgn. Econ. Cooperation and Devel. (Paris, vice chmn. com. on fiscal affairs 1990-92). E-mail: kgideon@wilmer.com. Fax: 202-663-6363. Office: Wilmer Cutler & Pickering 2445 M St NW Washington DC 20037-1420

GIDEON, RANDALL CLIFTON, architectural firm executive; b. Dallas, June 26, 1952; s. D.N. and Gailya W. (Devenport) Dixon; m. Karen Kay Williams Kothmann; children: Hali, Alden; m. Elizabeth Runyon Gideon, Oct. 2, 1993; 1 stepchild, Chelsea Tabor; 1 child, John Randall. BS in Architecture, U. Tex., 1975. Registered architect, Tex.; cert. interior designer Tex. Intern Elbert R. Spence Assocs., Fort Worth, 1973-77; urban designer, planner City of Arlington, Tex., 1977-79; assoc. Griffay and Brown Architects, Fort Worth, 1979-84; co-founder Pruett Gideon Architects, Inc., Fort Worth, 1984-89; v.p. Kirk Voich Gist Inc., Fort Worth, 1989-91; pres., CEO Gideon Toal, Inc., Fort Worth, 1991—. Bd. dirs. Downtown Fort Worth, Inc., Forum Fort Worth, Urban Strategies of Tarrant County. Mem. AIA (Ft. Worth chpt. Outstanding Young Profl. 1990, Design award 1993), Tex. Soc. Architects (bd. dirs., past pres.), Am. Planning Assn., Ft. Worth C. of C. (bd. dirs.), Alpha Rho Chi. Methodist. Avocations: tennis, reading, travel, painting/drawing. Home: 3916 Monticello Dr Fort Worth TX 76107-1760 Office: KVG Gideon Toal Inc 1401 Henderson St Fort Worth TX 76102-6026*

GIDEON-HAWKE, PAMELA LAWRENCE, fine arts small business owner; b. N.Y.C., Aug. 23, 1945; d. Lawrence Ian Verry and Lily S. (Stein) Gordon; m. Jarrett Redstone, June 27, 1964; 1 child, Justin Craig Hawke. Grad. high sch., Manhattan. Owner Gideon Gallery Ltd., L.A. and Las Vegas, 1975—; prin. Pamela L. Gideon-Hawke Pub. Rels., L.A., 1984—. Pres. San Fernando Valley West Point Parents Club, 1990-93. Named Friend of Design Industry Designers West Mag., 1987, Knighted, Dame of grace, Lady Pamela Gideon-Hawke, by order of St. John, Knights of Malta, 1999. Mem. Am. Soc. Interior Designers (publicist), Internat. Soc. Interior Designers (trade liaison 1986-88), Network Exec. Women in Hosp. (pres. Las Vegas chpt., pres. Las Vegas program, L.A. chair), Internat. Furnishings and Design Assn. (pres.). Avocations: ice-skating, fashion design, writing, cooking, law enforcement. Office: Gideon Gallery Ltd 8121 Lake Hills Dr Las Vegas NV 89128-7089 also: 8748 Melrose Ave Los Angeles CA 90069-5015

GIDLEY, JOHN LYNN, engineering executive; b. Lytle, Tex., Dec. 30, 1924; s. Andrew Jackson and Alice Josephine (Lytle) G.; m. Betty Jane Boggus, Dec. 23, 1950 (dec. July 1955); 1 child, Michael Andrew; m. Virginia Anne Platz, Nov. 7, 1959; children: John Mark, Carol Lynn, Paul William, Brian David, Allyson Anne, Neil Patrick. BSChemE, U. Tex., 1950, MSChemE, 1952, PhDChemE, 1955. Registered profl. petroleum and chem. engr., Tex. Rsch. engr. Humble Prod. Rsch., Houston, 1955-63; advisor Standard Oil of N.J., N.Y.C., 1963-64; rsch. assoc. Exxon Prodn. Rsch. Co., Houston, 1964-68; sr. supervising engr. Humble Oil & Refining Co., Houston, 1968-72, tech. advisor, 1972-81; sr. tech. advisor Exxon Co. USA, Houston, 1981-86; pres. John L. Gidley & Assocs. Inc., Houston, 1986—; vis. prof. dept. petroleum engring. Tex. A&M U., 1993—; disting. lectr. Soc. Petroleum Engrs., 1990. Co-author: Acidizing Fundamentals, 1979; editor in chief: Recent Advances in Hydraulic Fracturing, 1989; patentee in field. 1st lt. USAF, 1943-45. Mem. NAE, Am. Petroleum Inst. (pres. Houston chpt. 1972), Soc. Petroleum Engrs. (Disting. Svc. award 1990, John Franklin Carll award for distinctive contbns. to petroleum engring. 1992), Am. Chem. Soc. Republican. Roman Catholic. Home and Office: John L Gidley & Assocs Inc 5211 Caversham Dr Houston TX 77096-2505

GIDWITZ, GERALD, retired hair care company executive; b. Memphis, 1906; married; 5 children. PhB, U. Chgo., 1927. Co-founder, former chmn. bd. and chmn. exec. com. Helene Curtis Industries, Inc., Chgo.; ret. Trustee Roosevelt U., Auditorium Theatre Coun.; bd. dirs. Chgo. Crime Commn., Jamestown Found. Mem. Ill. Mfg. Assn. (past bd. dirs.).

GIEBEL, MIRIAM CATHERINE, librarian, genealogist; b. Williamsburg, Iowa, Oct. 10, 1934; d. John Timothy and Helen Gertrude (Wright) Donahoe; m. William Herbert Giebel, Sept. 30, 1967; 1 child, Sara Ann Giebel Ward. BS, Marquette U., Milw., 1956; MS in Library Science, Rosary Coll., River Forest, Ill., 1960; Cert. Paralegal, Roosevelt U., Chgo., 1992; Cert. in Family History Rsch., Brigham Young U., Provo, Utah, 1992. Asst. acquisitions dept. Marquette U., Milw., 1956-58; tech. svcs. librarian Chicago Heights (Ill.) Pub. Libr., 1959-63; librarian Little Company of Mary Nursing, Evergreen Park, Ill., 1963-64; asst. librarian hdqrs. ALA, Chgo., 1964-67; extension, reference librarian Chicago Heights (Ill.) Pub. Libr., 1974-99, vol. coord./webmaster, 1999—. Mem. Ill. Fedn. Bus. Profl. Women (state library chair 1994-96), U.S. Daughters of 1812 (Ill. state registrar 1994-97, Ill. state pres. 1997-99, chpt. pres. 1991-97, state pres. (hon., life) nat. chair lineage and geneal. records 1997—, chpt. registrar 1997—), DAR (chpt. registrar 1994—), Ill. Cameo Soc. of DAR (state v.p. 1996-99, state pres. 1999—), Soc. Ind. Pioneers (life). Roman Catholic. Avocations: reading, personal genealogical research, surfing internet.

GIEBISCH, GERHARD HANS, physiology educator; b. Vienna, Austria, Jan. 17, 1927; s. Hans Otto and Valery (Friedlaender) G.; m. Ilse Riebeth, Dec. 10, 1952; children—Christina Marie, Robert Gerhard. MD, U. Vienna, 1951, PhD (hon.), 1996; PhD (hon.), U. Uppsala, Sweden, 1977, U. Bern, Switzerland, 1979, U. Lausanne, Switzerland, 1991. Asst. prof. physiology Cornell U., N.Y.C., 1957-60, assoc. prof., 1960-65, prof. physiology, 1965-68; chmn. dept. physiology Yale U., New Haven, 1968-73, Sterling prof. cellular and molecular physiology, 1970—; mem. coun. Nat. Inst. Diabetes and Digestive and Kidney Disease, NIH, 1989-92. Editor: Biology of Membrane Transport, 1980, Physiol. Reviews, 1985-91; sect. editor Am. Jour. Physiology, 1967-69; contbr. articles to profl. jours. Recipient Homer Smith award N.Y. Heart Assn., 1971, Faculty Scholar award Josia Macy, Jr. Found., 1974, Disting. Svc. award Cornell U. Med. Coll., 1983, Johannes Muller medal German Physiol. Soc., 1980, Alexander von Humboldt award,

1987, Volhard medal German Nephrol. Soc., 1988, Jung-Stiftung for Wissenschaft and Forschung prize, 1990, A.N. Richards award Internat. Soc. Nephrology, 1992, Disting. Svc. award Chairmen of Depts. of Physiology, 1992, Berliner award, 1994. Mem. NAS, Am. Acad. Arts and Scis., Am. Physiol. Soc. (coun. 1988-90, Cannon lectr. 1993), Biophys. Soc., Soc. Gen. Physiologists (coun. 1980-82, pres. 1986-87), Am. Soc. Nephrology (pres. 1971-72, Berliner award 1994), Soc. Clin. Rsch. Home: 5 Carriage Dr Woodbridge CT 06525-1212 Office: Yale Sch Medicine Dept Cellular & Molecular Physiol 333 Cedar St New Haven CT 06510-3289

GIEDT, BRUCE ALAN, paper company executive; b. Fargo, N.D., May 7, 1937; s. Alexander and Alice Mildred (Rognaldson) G.; m. Suzanna Tae Abbott, Apr. 30, 1963; children: Alex, Jeffrey, Marybeth; m. 2d, Gail Ann Platt. BA, U. Wash., 1959; MBA, Harvard U., 1965. From regional sales mgr. to v.p. service products bus. units Crown Zellerbach Corp., San Francisco, 1965—; pres. Champion Paper Distbrs., Inc., Riverside, Calif., 1981-87, Pioneer Packaging, Phoenix, 1987—, Pionin Packaging, Woodale, Ill., 1997—. Author: The Future of Commercial Arbitration, 1965. V.p. exec. com. Keep Riverside AHead, econ. devel. com., bd. dirs.; exec. com. mem. Riverside C. of C., devel. com. Served to Capt. USAF, 1959-63. Evans scholar Western Golf Assn., 1967. Mem. Am. Paper Inst. (past com. chmn.). Republican. Lutheran. Lodge: Elks. Home: 6217 E Yucca St Scottsdale AZ 85254-5448 Office: 730 E University Dr Phoenix AZ 85034-6509

GIEGENGACK, ROBERT, university administrator; b. Nov. 27, 1938; m. Francesca Marshall, May 14, 1967; children: Jonathan, Matthew, Catharine Hae Kyung. BA in Geology, Yale U., 1960, PhD in Geology, 1968; MS in Geology, U. Colo., 1962. Geologist prehist. expdn. to Nubia, Egypt Yale U., 1963-67; acting instr. dept. geology Yale U., New Haven, 1966-67; asst. in rsch. Peabody Mus. Natural History Yale U., 1967-68; asst. prof. geology, landscape arch. and regional planning U. Pa., Phila., 1968-74, assoc. prof., 1974-86, chmn. dept. geology, 1978-85, prof., 1987-92, co-dir. Inst. for Environ. Studies, 1992-98; geologo asesor Ministerio de Minas e Hidrocarburos, Venezuela, 1972, Ministerio de Energia y Minas, 1975-76. Contbr. articles to profl. jours. Bd. trustees The Canterbury Sch., New Milford, Conn., 1980-90, 91-95; bd. dirs. Sea Edn. Assn., Woods Hole, Mass., 1984—, A Better chance, Wallingford-Swarthmore (Pa.) Sch. Dist., 1992-95; adv. bd. dept. geol. scis. U. Colo., 1992—; councilor Yellowstone-Bighorn Rsch. Assn., Red Lodge, Mont., 1985—. Recipient Lindback Award for Disting. Tchg., 1979, Ira Abrams Disting. Tchg. award, 1994. Office: University of Pennsylvania Inst Environ Studies Dept Earth Environ Sci 240 S 33rd St Haden Hall Philadelphia PA 19104-3802*

GIEL, JAMES ARTHUR, JR., steel company executive; b. Pitts., Aug. 29, 1952; s. James and Suan Helen (Barry) G.; m. Sharyl Dawn Unrath, Apr. 22, 1978; children: James Arthur III, Maggie Anne. BA, Westminster Coll., New Wilmington, Pa., 1974; MA in Pers. Administrn. and Indsl. Rels., St. Francis Coll., Loretto, Pa., 1987. Tchr. Shaler Area Schs., Glenshaw, Pa., 1974-77; group ins. underwriter Equitable Life Assurance Soc., N.Y.C., 1977-79; pension clk. Allegheny Ludlum Industries, Inc., Pitts., 1979-86; benefits adminstr. Allegheny Internat., Pitts.; mgr., asst. v.p. employee benefits Union Nat. Corp., Pitts., 1986-89; v.p., dir. employee benefits Integra Fin. Corp., Pitts., 1989-96; mgr. employee benefits Armco Inc., Pitts., 1996—. Dir. Strawberry Way Child Ctr., Pitts., 1985-92; Rep. committeeman Allegheny County, Glenshaw, 1992—; elder Elfinwild Presbyn. Ch., Glenshaw, 1986—, deacon, 1980-86; bd dirs. Shaler Twp.-Shaler Oaks, 1994—; mem. strategic planning com. Shaler Area Sch. Dist., 1994—, sch. bd. dir., 1997— (pres. 1999); mem. com. Allegheny Policy Coun., 1995-96. Mem. Human Resource Info. Specialist Soc., Workers in Employee Benefits, Pitts. Pers. Assn., Pitts. Bus. Group on Health (exec. com. 1997), Human Resources Sys. Profls., Travelers Aid Soc. Pitts. (bd. dirs. 1994—), Westminster Coll. Alumni Assn. (alumni coord. 1988—), Elfinwild Lions (pres. 1984), Shaler Soccer Club (treas. 1993-95, pres. 1995-97, bd. dirs. 1997—, booster 1998, pres. 1998—), Rivers Club. Avocations: coaching soccer and baseball, music, civic activities. Home: 800 Pictwood Dr Glenshaw PA 15116-1522 Office: Armco Inc One Oxford Ctr 1 Oxford Ct Pittsburgh PA 15219-1407

GIELGUD, SIR (ARTHUR) JOHN, actor, director; b. London, Apr. 14, 1904; s. Frank and Kate (Terry-Lewis) G. Student, Hillside Godalming, 1913-18, Westminster Sch., 1918-20, Lady Benson, 1920-21, Royal Acad. Dramatic Art, 1922-23; LLD (hon.), U. St. Andrews, 1950, U. London, 1977; LittD (hon.), Oxford (Eng.) U., 1953. Established repertory theater in London, 1938, Haymarket, 1943-44. Shakespearean roles include Hamlet, 1929, 30, 34, 36, 37, 39, 44, Richard II, 1929, 38, Macbeth, 1929, 42, Mark Antony in Julius Caesar, 1929, Hotspur in Henry IV, 1930, Malvolio in Twelfth Night, 1930, Shylock in The Merchant of Venice, 1938; achieved first London success as Lewis Dodd in The Constant Nymph, 1926, other stage appearances in The Good Companions, 1930, Musical Chairs, 1931, Richard of Bordeaux, 1932, School for Scandal, 1938, Dear Octopus, 1939, The Importance of Being Earnest, 1930, 39-40, 43, Love for Love, Eng. and U.S.A., 1942-44, 47, The Duchess of Malfi, 1944, Crime and Punishment, London, 1946, Medea, U.S.A., 1947-48, The Return of the Prodigal, 1948, Much Ado About Nothing, 1949, 50, 52, 55, N.Y.C. and Boston, 1959, Ages of Man, 1959, 63, Australia and New Zealand, 1963-64, Othello, 1961, as Gaev in Cherry Orchard, Broadway, 1961, Aldwych, London, 1962, as Julian in Tiny Alice, N.Y.C., 1964-65 (Della Austrian medal Drama League of N.Y. 1965), at Stratford-On-Avon Festival in Measure for Measure, Julius Caesar, Much Ado About Nothing, King Lear, 1950, A Winter's Tale, 1951, The Best of Friends, 1988; also toured in King Lear with Stratford-On-Avon Co., London and other locations, 1955; dir., actor in Nude With a Violin, 1956-57, The Tempest, 1957, 58, Joseph Surface in School for Scandal, Broadway, 1963, Ages of Man, Lyceum Theater, N.Y.C., 1963, Australia and New Zealand, 1963-64, Julian in Tiny Alice, Broadway, 1964-65, Hamlet, Broadway, Boston and Can., 1974, The Best of Friends, 1988; dir. plays Lady Windemere's Fan, 1946, The Glass Menagerie starring Helen Hayes, 1948, Medea, 1948, The Heiress, 1949; producer, dir. Berlioz's The Trojans, Covent Garden, 1958, Britten's A Midsummer Nights Dream, Royal Opera House, Covent Garden, London, 1961, Big Fish, Little Fish, Broadway, 1961 (Tony award), Dazzling Prospect, 1961, The School for Scandal, Haymarket Theatre, 1962; film appearances include Diary for Timothy, The Good Companions, 1932, The Secret Agent, 1937, The Prime Minister, 1940, Julius Caesar, 1952, A Day By The Sea (also dir.), 1953, The Cherry Orchard (also dir.), 1954, Richard III, 1955, The Barretts of Wimpole Street, 1957, St. Joan, 1957, Becket, 1964, The Loved One, 1964, Chimes at Midnight, 1966, Mister Sebastian, 1967, The Charge of the Light Brigade, 1968, The Shoes of the Fisherman, 1968, Oh! What a Lovely War, 1968, Julius Caesar, 1970, Lost Horizon, 1972, Eagle in a Cage, 1973, Murder on the Orient Express, 1974, 11 Harrowhouse, 1974, Gold, 1974, Aces High, 1976, Joseph Andrews, 1977, Providence, 1977, Portrait of a Young Man, 1977, Caligula, 1977, The Elephant Man, 1979, The Human Factor, 1979, The Conductor, 1980, Murder by Decree, 1980, The Formula, 1980, Chariots of Fire, 1981, Arthur, 1981, (Academy award for best supporting actor) Sphinx, 1981, Lion of the Desert, 1981, Priest of Love, 1982, Gandhi, 1982, Wagner, 1983, Invitation to the Wedding, 1983, Scandalous, 1983, The Wicked Lady, 1983, Camille, 1984, The Shooting Party, 1985, Plenty, 1985, Leave All Fair, 1985, The Whistle Blower, 1987, Appointment With Death, 1988, Arthur 2, 1988, Getting It Right, Strike It Rich, Prospero's Books, 1991, Shining Through, 1992, Power of One; TV appearances include Probe, 1972, QB VII, 1973, Frankenstein: The True Story, 1973, Les Miserables, 1978, Richard II, 1979, Brideshead Revisited, 1981, Marco Polo, 1982, Inside the Third Reich, 1982, The Hunchback of Notre Dame, 1982, Neck, 1983, The Scarlet and the Black, 1983, The Master of Ballantrae, 1984, The Far Pavillions, 1984, War and Remembrance, 1988, Someday's Dream, Morse, Alleyn Mysteries, Lovejoy, Swansone, Quarmaines Ferms, Scarlett, Hand in Glove, 1994; author: (autobiography) Early Stages, 1938, Stage Directions, 1964, Distinguished Company, 1972, Gielgud: An Actor and His Time, 1980, Backward Glances, 1989. Decorated Knight Order Brit. Empire, Companion of Honor, chevalier Legion of Honor; recipient Antoinette Perry award Ages of Man, 1958, spl. award, 1959, Best Actor award Providence N.Y. Film Critics, 1977, Emmy award for Outstanding Lead Actor in a Miniseries or Special ("Summer's Lease," PBS) Nat. Acad. TV Arts and Scis., 1991; named Brandeis University Companion, 1960. Mem. Shakespeare Reading Soc. (pres. 1958—), Royal Acad. Dramatic Art (pres. 1977-89). Clubs: Garrick, Players (N.Y.C.). Office: care Internat Famous Agy, Oxford House 76 Oxford SE, London W1R 1RB, England

GIEM, ROSS NYE, JR., surgeon; b. Corvallis, Oreg., May 23, 1923; s. Ross Nye and Goldie Marie (Falk) G.; children: John, David, Paul, James, Ross N. III, Matthew John, Julie; student U. Redlands, Walla Walla Coll.; BA, MD, Loma Linda U. Intern, Sacramento Gen. Hosp., 1952-53; resident in ob-gyn, Kern County Gen. Hosp., Bakersfield, Calif., 1956-57, in gen. surgery, 1957-61; practice medicine specializing in gen. surgery, Sullivan, Mo., 1961-70; staff emergency dept. Hollywood Presbyn. Med. Center, 1971-73, Meml. Hosp., Belleville, Ill., 1973-87, St. Elizabeth Hosp., Belleville, Ill., 1973-90; St. Luke Hosp., Pasadena, Calif., 1973-89, Doctors Hosp., Montclair, Calif. 1990-93, Harriman Jones Med. Group, Long Beach, Calif., 1993—; instr. nurses, physicians, paramedics, emergency med. technicians, 1973-91. Served with AUS, 1943-46. Diplomate Am. Bd. Surgery. Fellow ACS, Am. Coll. Emergency Physicians; mem. AMA, Ill. Med. Assn., Pan Am. Med. Assn., Pan Pacific Surg. Assn., Royal Coll. Physicians (Eng.) Home: PO Box 5767 Pasadena CA 91117-0767 also: 834 W Huntington Dr Apt 4 Arcadia CA 91007-6610

GIENAPP, HELEN FISCHER, jewelry company owner; b. Saginaw, Mich., Oct. 9, 1921; d. John Frederick and Dorothea (Schleicher) Fischer; m. Walter Lawrence Gienapp, Oct. 10, 1942; children: Karen Lynne, Roger Alan, David Paul, Marcia Lou, Richard Kevin. Grad. h.s., Saginaw. Adminstrv. asst. Muskegon (Mich.) Devel. Corp., 1961-66; exec. asst. to pres. Greater Detroit C. of C., 1966-80; owner Internat. Jewelry, Ferndale, Mich., 1990—. Pres. Internat. Luth. Women's Missionary League, St. Louis, 1979-83; dir. Hist. Trinity, Inc., Detroit, 1990—, English dist. Luth. Ch.-Mo. Synod, Farmington, 1988-97, Mission Opportunities Short Term Ministries, Ann Arbor, Mich., 1995—; area coord. Am. Bible Soc.; mem. Ferndale Youth Assistance Bd., 1998—. Named Luth. Woman of Yr., Mich. Dist. of Luth. Ch.-Mo. Synod, 1983, Mich. Vol. of Yr., Am. Bible Soc., 1998. Mem. Internat. Assn. Adminstrv. Profls., Valparaiso U. Guild, Women's Econ. Club Detroit. Home: 371 Channing St Ferndale MI 48220-2555

GIENAPP, WILLIAM EUGENE, history educator; b. Denton, Tex., Feb. 27, 1944; s. William Herman and June Beatrice (Wade) G.; m. Erica Lee Kilian, Aug. 24, 1968; children: William Kenneth, Jonathan Eric. BA, U. Calif., Berkeley, 1967, PhD, 1980; MA, Yale U., 1969. Acting. instr. U. Calif., Berkeley, 1979-80; asst. prof. U. Wyo., Laramie, 1980-85, assoc. prof., 1985-89; prof. Harvard U., Cambridge, Mass., 1989—; chmn. Lincoln Prize Jury, 1997, Avery Craven Award Com., 1998; bd. advisors Lincoln Forum, Lincoln Studies Ctr., Knox Coll.; mem. adv. bd. Hist. Soc. Author: Origins of the Republican Party, 1987 (Avery Craven award, 1988); co-author: Nation of Nations, 1990, 2d edit., 1993, 3rd edit., 1997, Why the War Came, 1996, Nation of Nations: Concise Narrataive, 1995, 2d edit., 1998. Mem. So. Hist. Assn., Orgn. Am. Historians, Soc. Hists. Early Republic, Soc. Am. Baseball Rsch. Office: Harvard U Dept History Cambridge MA 02138

GIER, AUDRA MAY CALHOON, environmental chemist; b. Bella Vista, Peru, Aug. 21, 1940; came to U.S., 1944; d. Nathan Moore and Olivia Cleo (Hite) Calhoon; m. Delta Warren Gier, Apr. 4, 1968. BA, Austin Coll., 1962; MS in Chemistry, Kans. State Coll., 1964; MA in History of Sci., U. Wis., 1974; postgrad., York U., Toronto, Can., 1974-79. Food technologist Midwest Rsch. Inst., Kansas City, Mo., 1963-64; chemist Mobay (formerly Chemagro), Kansas City, 1964-67; instr. chemistry St. Andrews Presbyn. Coll., Laurinburg, N.C., 1967-68; chemist Cardinal Chem. Co., Columbia, S.C., 1968; asst. prof. chemistry Lea Coll., Albert Lea, Minn., 1969-72; psychology intern emergency unit Thistletown Regional Centre for Children & Adolescents, Toronto, Ont., Can., 1975-77; assoc. prof. chemistry Cleveland Chiropractic Coll., Kansas City, 1979-84; adj. faculty Pk. Coll., Parkville, Mo., 1982-92; environ. chemist, quality assurance specialist Ecology & Environ., Inc., Overland Park, Kans., 1987-95; pres. Delta and Assocs., Inc., Kansas City, 1988-92; co-founder, v.p. Midwest Sci. Found., Kansas City, 1990-98; mem. adj. faculty Donnelly Coll., 1992-94, dean adminstrn. health scis. program, 1992-97; mentor tng. program Option Inst. and Fellowship, Sheffield, Mass., 1994-99; founding mem. Nutrition Enterprises LLC dba Golden West Health Foods, 1997—. Author: Highlights of Organic Chemistry, 1985; co-editor: (with D.W. Gier) History and Directory of Chemical Education, 1974, Peace is Something Speshl, 1985; co-inventor, co-patentee acetylenic ketones as herbicides. Mem. adv. bd. Kansas City Interfaith Peace Alliance, 1980-95, bd. dirs., 1982-85, pres., 1985-86; bd. dirs. Prairie Star Dist./Unitarian-Universalist Midwest (Upper), 1985-91; co-chair Bragg Symposium on Humanism, Kansas City, 1980-90; chair Social Responsibility Com., Prairie Star Dist. UUA, 1986-91; mem. N.Am. Com. for Humanism and Fellowship of Religious Humanists. Recipient Social Justice award Social Justice Com. Prairie Star Dist, 1985; named Woman of Yr., 1982, Humanist of Yr., 1987, All Souls Unitarian Ch., Kansas City. Mem. NAFE, AAUW, ACLU, DAR, NARAL, Am. Chem. Soc., Am. Soc. for Quality Control (cert. 1990-96), Inst. for Soc. Ethics and Life Scis., Midwest Bioethics Ctr., Planned Parenthood, Habitat for Humanity. Democrat. Avocations: bio-med. ethics, peace & social justice activities, needlepoint, knitting, movies. Home: 421 W 99th St Kansas City MO 64114-3908

GIERAS, JACEK FRANCISZEK, electrical engineering educator, scientist; b. Maleniec, Voivodship Piotrkow Tryb, Poland, Apr. 2, 1947; s. Stanislaw Gieras and Zofia Rychlewska-Gieras; m. Janina Omilianczyk, Sept. 25, 1975; children: Izabella Anna, Karolina Maria, Michael Benjamin. MSEE, Tech. U., Lodz, 1971; PhD, Tech. U., Poznan, Poland, 1975, DSc, 1980. Project engr. Factory of Loudspeakers Tonsil, Wrzesnia, Poland, 1971; lectr. Tech. U. Poznan, 1971-73, sr. lectr., 1973-75, asst. prof., 1975-77; asst. prof. Acad. Technology and Agr., Bydgoszcz, Poland, 1977-81, assoc. prof., dean, 1981-83, assoc. prof., head of dept., 1985-87, prof., 1987—; vis. assoc. prof. Queen's U., Kingston, Ont., Can., 1983-85; prof. U. Cape Town, 1989-98; vis. prof. endowed chair in transp. sys. engring. U. Tokyo, 1996; guest prof. Chungbuk Nat. U., Korea, 1996-97; scientist United Technologies Rsch. Ctr., East Hartford, Conn., 1998—. Author: Special Purpose Electric Machines, 1983, Linear Induction Motors, 1990, Linear Induction Drives, 1994, (with M. Dabrowski) Induction Machines with Solid Rotors, 1977, Handbook of Electric Motors (edited by W.H. Middendorf and R.H. Engelmann), 1995, (with M. Wing) Permanent Magnet Motor Technology: Design and Applications, 1996; contbr. articles to profl. jours. Recipient Silver medal Polish Assn. of Elec. Engring., Poland, 1979; fellow Polish Ministry of Edn., 1976, 81, NSERC of Can., 1983, Italian Ministry of Sci. and Tech. Rsch., 1994, Merit awards U. Cape Town, 1995, 96, 97. Fellow N.Y. Acad. Scis.; mem. IEEE (sr. mem.). Roman Catholic. Avocations: railways, music, overseas travel, home improvement. E-mail: gierasjf@utrc.utc.com. Address: United Tech Rsch Ctr Mail Stop 129-53 411 Silver Ln Hartford CT 06118-1127 also: Univ Cape Town, Dept Elec Engring, Rondebosch 7700, South Africa

GIERBOLINI-ORTIZ, GILBERTO, federal judge; b. 1926. B.A., U. P.R., 1951, LL.B., 1961. Asst. U.S. atty. Commonwealth P.R., 1961-66; judge Superior Ct. Bayamon, P.R., 1966-67, Superior Ct. Caguas, P.R., 1967-69; solicitor P.R., 1969-72, asst. atty. gen. for antitrust, 1970-72; pvt. practice Jose H. Pico, 1973-74, Arias Cestero, Gierbolini & Garcia Soto, 1974-75, Nido, Berrios, Menendez & Gierbolini, 1975-77, Dubon, Gonzalez & Berrios, 1977-80; judge U.S. Dist. Ct. P.R., San Juan, 1980—; chief judge U.S. Dist. Ct. P.R., 1991-93; sr. judge, 1993—; prof. U. P.R., Cath. U. Law Sch. Chmn. State Elections Bd., P.R., 1972. Capt. U.S. Army, 1951-57. Office: BBV Tower 254 Ave Munoz Rivera Fl 12 1200-B Hato Rey San Juan PR 00918-1900

GIERHART, MARY KELBLEY, school psychologist; b. Cleve., Nov. 5, 1957; d. Thomas Walter and Ann Cecile (Ferner) Kelbley; m. Gregory Alan Gierhart, Mar. 27, 1993; children: Margaret Cecile, Matthew Alan. BA, Cleve. State U., 1979; MEd, Bowling Green State U., 1985. Cert. sch. psychologist, Ohio. Primary sorter United Parcel Svc., Middleburg Heights, Ohio, 1977-80; child care worker Sagamore Hills (Ohio) Psychiat. Hosp., 1981-82; activity therapist Northeast Ohio Devel. Ctr., Broadview Heights, 1982-84; intern sch. psychologist Bowling Green (Ohio) City Sch., 1985-86; sch. psychologist Delaware (Ohio) City Schs., 1986—. Vol. ARC, Cleve., 1976-78; coach softball & basketball St. John Bosco Ch. & Incarnate Word Acad., Parma Heights, Ohio, 1975-78. Mem. Nat. Assn. Sch. Psychologists, Ohio Sch. Psychologists Assn., Sch. Psychologists Ctr. Ohio (rsch. com. 1985—, bd. dirs. 1995—). Democrat. Avocations: sports, nature, animals. Home: 823 Lone Tree Dr Powell OH 43065-9253 Office: Delaware City Schs 248 N Washington St Delaware OH 43015-1649

GIERKE, HERMAN FREDRICK, III, federal judge; b. Williston, N.D., Mar. 13, 1943; s. Herman Fredrick Jr. and Mary (Kelly) G.; m. Jeanine Gierke; children: Todd H.F., Scott H.F., Craig H.F., Michelle Lynn. B.A., U. N.D., 1964, J.D., 1966; attended, JAG Sch., U. Va., 1967, 69. Bar: N.D. 1966, U.S. Dist. Ct. N.D., U.S. Supreme Ct. Practice law Watford City, N.D., 1971-83; state's atty. McKenzie County, 1974-82; city atty. City of Watford, 1974-83; justice N.D. Supreme Ct., Bismarck, 1983-91; judge, then assoc. judge U.S. Ct. Appeals for the Armed Forces, Washington, DC, 1991—; adj. prof. George Washington U. Nat. Law Ctr., Cath. U. Am., Columbus Sch. Law. Served as capt. JAGC, U.S. Army, 1967-71. Recipient Outstanding Service award Gov. of N.D., 1984. Fellow Am. Bar Found., Am. Coll. Estate and Trust Counsel; mem. ABA, N.D. Trial Lawyers Assn. (bd. govs. 1977-83), N.D. State Attys. Assn. (pres. 1979-80), N.D. Council Sch. Attys. (charter), NW Jud. Dist. Bar Assn. (pres. 1977-79), State Bar Assn. N.D. (pres. 1982-83), Am. Judicature Soc., Assn. Trial Lawyers Am., Nat. Dist. Attys. Assn., Aircraft Owners and Pilots Assn., Am. Legion (N.D. comdr. 1984, judge adv. state assn., nat. vice comdr. 1985-86, comdr. 1988-89), Blue Key, Phi Delta Phi. Lutheran. Avocations: racquetball; golf; tennis; raising horses. Office: US Ct Appeals for the Armed Forces 450 E St NW Washington DC 20442-0001*

GIERTZ, J. FRED, economics educator; b. Wichita, Kans., Jan. 18, 1943; s. Joe L. and Frieda J. (Hamblin) G.; m. Donna Hyland, Sept. 13, 1969; children: Seth H., Gabrielle H. BA, Wichita U., 1964; MA, Northwestern U., 1966, PhD, 1970. Instr. econs. Miami U., Oxford, Ohio, 1968-70; asst. prof. Miami U., 1970-73, asso. prof., 1973-78, prof., 1978-80; prof. econs. Inst. Govt. and Public Affairs, U. Ill., Urbana, 1980—; acting dir. Inst. Govt. and Pub. Affairs U. Ill., 1993-94; rsch. dir. Ill. Tax Reform Commn., 1982-83; dir. Americtech fellowship program U. Ill., 1987-93; dir. office fiscal and regional devel. studies, 1988—; adviser Transition Team of Ill. Gov. Jim Edgar, 1990-91; trustee State Univs. Retirement System, 1995—; cons. in field. Mem. editorial bd.: Quarterly Rev. Econs. and Bus, 1979-88; contbr. articles in field to profl. jours. Mem. athletic bd. U. Ill., 1998—. Mem. Midwest Econs. Assn. (v.p. 1978-79), Am. Econ. Assn., Ill. Econ. Assn. (pres. 1986-87), Pub. Choice Soc., Nat. Tax Assn., Univ. Club Chgo., Champaign Country Club. Home: 601 Park Lane Dr Champaign IL 61820-7630 Office: U Ill Inst Govt Pub Affairs 1007 W Nevada St Urbana IL 61801-3812

GIES, DAVID THATCHER, language educator; b. Pitts., Aug. 18, 1945. BA, Pa. State U., 1967; MA, U. Pitts., 1970, PhD, 1972. Assoc. prof. Spanish lang. and lit. St. Bonaventure (N.Y.) U., 1970-79; assoc. prof. U. Va., Charlottesville, 1979—, now Commonwealth prof. Spanish, former chmn. Spanish dept.; vis. lectr. U. Birmingham, Eng., 1978. Author: Agustin Duran, 1975, NF Moratin, 1979, Theatre and Politics in 19th Century Spain, 1988, The Theatre in 19th Century Spain, 1994, El Teatro en la Espana del Siglo XIX, 1996; editor: The Cambridge Companion to Modern Spanish Culture, 1999. Office: U Va Dept Spanish Italian & Portuguese Wilson Hall Charlottesville VA 22903

GIES, ROBERT JAY, mechanical engineer; b. Washington, July 27, 1967; s. Edward L. and Beatrice Y. Gies; m. Louisa Manalac, May 15, 1993. BS in Mech. Engring., Old Dominion U., 1990, M in Engring. Mgmt., 1994. Registered engr.-in-tng. Facilities analyst Old Dominion U., Norfolk, Va., 1987-90; assoc. engr. Newport News (Va.) Shipbuilding, 1990-94, engr., 1994-96, sr. engr., 1996, engring. supr., 1996—; instr. design apprenticeship program Newport News Shipbuilding, 1994—, instr. carrier engring., 1995—. Author articles, tech. papers, presentations, manuals and guides. Usher Aldersgate United Meth. Ch., Chesapeake, Va., 1994—; asst. scoutmaster Boy Scouts Am., Chesapeake, 1985—; asst. coach Little League Baseball, Poquoson, Va., 1989, 91-92. Recipient NNS Vol. Cmty. Svc. award, Pres. model of Excellence award. Mem. Old Dominion U. Alumni Assn. (co-v.p. univ. rels. com. 1996-98, bd. dirs. 1995—, v.p. alumni orgns. 1998-99, pres.-elect 1999—), ASME (assoc., chair egg drop com. 1995—, exec. com. 1995-99, program dir. 1997-98, treas., 1998-99, sec. 1999—), Soc. Naval Architects and Marine Engrs. (assoc.), Navy League, Nat. Eagle Scout Assn., Am. Soc. of Naval Engrs., Progressive Club, Omicron Delta Kappa. Republican. Home: 2951 Bruce Station Rd Chesapeake VA 23321 Office: Newport News Shipbldg Dept E54 4101 Washington Ave Newport News VA 23607-2704

GIESE, HEINER, lawyer, real estate investor; b. Passau, Germany, Apr. 16, 1944; came to U.S., 1950, naturalized, 1957; s. Heinz Emil and Wilma Maria (Dunner) G.; m. Barbara Ann Kent, June 28, 1969; children: Anna, Peter. BS in Internat. Affairs, Georgetown U., 1966; JD, U. Wis., 1969. Bar: Wis. 1969, U.S. Dist. Ct. (ea. and we. dists.) Wis. 1969, U.S. Ct. Appeals (7th cir.) 1974, U.S. Supreme Ct. 1974. Law clk. U.S. Dist. Ct., Madison, 1969-70; assoc. Cannon, McLaughlin, Herbon & Staudenmeier, Milw., 1969-74; ptnr. Levin & Giese, Milw., 1974-85, Giese & Weden Law Offices, Milw., 1985—. Bd. dirs. German Fest Milw., 1981-84, legal counsel, 1981—; bd. dirs. German Lang. and Sch. Soc., 1976—, pres., 1982—; bd. dirs. Goethe House, Milw., 1982—, sec., 1997—; Wis. gov.'s rep. Presdl. Commn. for German-Am. Tricentennial, 1983. Recipient Outstanding Young Lawyer award, 1979, Order of Merit, Fed. Republic Germany, 1993. Mem. ABA (young lawyers divsn., regional vice chmn. membership com. 1979-81), Wis. Bar Assn., Milw. Bar Assn. (chmn. lawyer referral svc. 1980-83, 91-93, bd. dirs. 1993-96), Milw. Young Lawyers Assn. (pres. 1978-79), Milw. Apt. Assn., Wis. State Bar (mem. lawyer referral com.). Democrat. Lutheran. Home: 2022 N 72nd St Wauwatosa WI 53213-1828 Office: Giese & Weden 1216 N Prospect Ave Milwaukee WI 53202-3014

GIESE, ROBERT JAMES, minister; b. Eau Claire, Wis., Apr. 7, 1950; s. Walter H. and Doris B. (Kuhn) G.; m. Jo Ann P. Zutz, June 19, 1971; 1 child, Rachel. BS in Zoology, U. Wis., 1972; MDiv, Christ Sem.-Seminex, St. Louis, 1978; D Ministry in Pastoral Care and Counseling, Luth. Sch. Theology, Chgo., 1990. Ordained to ministry Evang. Luth. Ch. Am., 1979. Min. Christian Ministry in Nat. Pks., N.Y.C., 1974-77; chaplain Bear Creek Boys Ranch, Lodi, Calif., 1978-79; pastor Trinity Luth. Ch., Rolling Meadows, Ill., 1979—; exec. cons. Stephen Ministries, St. Louis, 1974-82; sec. Chgo.-Milw. Conf. Evang. Luth. Ch. Am., Chgo., 1983-85, v.p., 1985-86; youth adv. Luth. Social Svcs., Chgo., 1987-88. Contbr. articles to profl. jours. Bd. dirs. The Bridge Youth Svcs., Palatine, Ill., 1983-87; pres., bd. dirs. Racetrack Ministries, Arlington Heights, Ill., 1990—; dean N.W. Conf. Chgo. Metro Synod ELCA, 1992-96; mem. steering com. Rolling Meadows Tomorrow, 1995-99; mem. Rolling Meadows Bd. Ethics, 1997—. Mem. AACC, Assn. of Personality Type. Home: 3203 Meadow Dr Rolling Meadows IL 60008-2728 Office: Trinity Luth Ch 3201 Meadow Dr Rolling Meadows IL 60008-2798 *I believe that the more I am able to know and accept myself for who I am as God knows and accepts me for who I am through Christ, the more I will be enabled to know and accept those with whom I am called to minister.*

GIESECKE, NOEL MARTIN, cardiovascular anesthesiologist; b. San Francisco, Sept. 21, 1959; s. Adolph Hartung Jr. and Veronica Elizabeth (Morel) G.; m. Susan Elizabeth Day, Sept. 15, 1990. BA, U. Tex., 1981, MD, 1985. Diplomate Am. Bd. Anesthesiologists. Med. internship and residency John Sealy Hosp., Galveston, Tex., 1985-89; staff anesthesiologist Citizens' Hosp., De Tar Hosp., Regional Med. Ctr., Victoria, Tex., 1989-91, Tex. Heart Inst., Houston, 1991—; asst. prof. anesthesiology U. Tex. Health Sci. Ctr., Houston, 1996—. Mem. Tex. Soc. Anesthesiologists (del. 1993—). Avocations: scuba diving, model railroading. Home: 3519 Maroneal St Houston TX 77025-1322 Office: Tex Heart Inst Divsn Cardiovasc Anesthslgy PO Box 20345 Houston TX 77225-0345

GIESEN, JOHN WILLIAM, advertising executive; b. St. Paul, Apr. 5, 1928; s. William J. and Salome Anna (Shopnitz) G.; m. Mary Lou Gilbertson, May 20, 1950; children: Cynthia, John, Lee Ann, Gregory, David, Laurie. Student, St. Thomas Coll., 1948-50, U. Minn., 1950-52, St. Paul Sch. Assoc. Arts, 1951-53. Advt. rep. St. Paul Dispatch-Pioneer Press, 1950-54; advt. mgr. Bruce Pub. Co., St. Paul, 1954-56; nat. advt. mgr. Duluth Herald News Tribune, 1956-60; account exec. N.W. Ayer & Son, Inc., Chgo., 1960-64, acct. supr., 1964-66; account exec. Leo Burnett, Inc., Chgo., 1966-68, v.p. account supr., 1968-74; exec. v.p. Barickman Advt., Denver, 1974-77, chmn. exec. com., 1977-82; pres. Doyle Dane Bernbach Advt., Denver, 1982-86; pres. DDB Needham Worldwide, Denver, 1986-88, chmn., 1988-89; pres., chief exec. officer The Advt. Consortium, Inc.,

Denver, 1989-94; pres., CEO The Giesen Group, Inc., Denver, 1994, 1995—. Chmn. Sts. Faith-Hope Charity Elem. Sch. Bd., Winnetka, Ill., 1972-74, Rocky Mountain Council 4 A's, 1985; hon. bd. Colorado Spl. Olympics, 1988. With U.S. Army, 1946-48, res. 1949-60. Mem. Denver Advt. Fedn. (dir. 1980-82, pres.-elect 1987). Republican. Roman Catholic. Lodge: Rotary. Home: 6186 E Princeton Ave Englewood CO 80111-1035 Office: The Giesen Group Inc 1777 S Harrison St Ste 2100 Denver CO 80210-3951

GIESEN, RICHARD ALLYN, business executive; b. Evanston, Ill., Oct. 7, 1929; s. Elmer J. and Ethyl (Lillig) G.; m. Jeannine St. Bernard, Jan. 31, 1953; children: Richard Allyn, Laurie J., Mark S. B.S., Northwestern U., 1951. Research analyst new bus. and research depts. Glore, Forgan & Co., Chgo., 1951-57; asst. to pres. Gen. Dynamics Corp., N.Y.C., 1957-60, asst. treas., 1960-61, asst. v.p. ops. and contracts, 1961-63; fin. cons. IBM Corp., 1963, exec. asst. to sr. v.p., 1964-65; treas. subs. Sci. Research Assocs., Inc., Chgo., 1965-66, v.p. fin. and adminstrn., 1966-67, exec. v.p., chief operating officer, 1967-68, pres., chief exec. officer, 1968-80; pres., chief exec. officer, chmn. exec. com., dir. Field Enterprises, Inc., Chgo., 1980-83; pres. RLM Investments, 1983-93; chmn., pres., CEO Am. Appraisal Assocs., Inc., 1984-93; chmn., CEO Continental Glass & Plastic, Inc., Chgo., 1988—, Continere Corp., 1988—; Bd. dirs. Smurfit Stone Container Corp., GATX, Inc.; bd. trustees Asia House Funds, 1994-98. Mem. bus. adv. coun. Chgo. Urban League, 1968-83; prin. Chgo. United, 1980-83; mem. adv. coun. Technol. Inst., Northwestern U.; mem. pres.'s coun. Nat. Coll. Edn., Evanston, Ill., 1977-86; bd. dirs. Am. Cancer Soc.; mem. adv. coun. J.L. Kellogg Grad. Sch. Mgmt., Northwestern U.; dir. Jr. Achievement Chgo., 1993—; trustee Chgo. Edn. TV Assn., 1975-81. Mem. Chgo. Pres. Orgn., Chief Execs. Orgn., Chgo. Assn. Commerce and Industry (bd. dirs.), Chgo. Coun. Com. Fgn. Rels., Webhannet Golf Club, Chgo. Club, Shoreacres (Lake Bluff, Ill) Club, Milw. Club, Alpha Tau Omega, Beta Gamma Sigma. Clubs: Chicago, Shoreacres (Lake Bluff, Ill.), Milw. Office: Continental Glass & Plastic 841 W Cermak Rd Chicago IL 60608-4582

GIESIGE, MARK RICHARD, county official, auditor; b. Celina, Ohio, Mar. 9, 1959; s. Raymond L. and Patricia Ann (McCarty) G.; m. Jean Marie Zehringer, May 30, 1987; children: Raymond, Claire, David, Quinn. Student, Wright State U., Celina, Ohio, 1978-80. Dir. field svc. group Met. Environ., Celina, 1983-93; county auditor Mercer County, Celina, 1993—. Bd. dirs. ARC, Celina, 1993-96, 4-H, Celina, 1993—; mem. Mercer County Dem. Ctrl. and Exec. Coms., 1993—. Named Family of Yr., KC, Celina, 1997. Mem. Internat. Assn. Assessment Officers (assessment adminstrn. splst.), Ohio Auditors Assn. (legis. com. 1995—, future directions com. chair 1999—), Ohio Govt. Fin. Officers Assn., Ohio Weights and Measures Assn., Ohio Twp. Assn., N.W. Auditors Assn. (pres. 1999—), Eagles. Roman Catholic. Avocations: fishing, carpentry, golf. Office: Mercer County 101 N Main St Celina OH 45822-1743

GIESKES, HANS, information services and publishing executive; married; 3 children. BSBA, Netherlands Inst. Mktg. V.p. sales Elsevier Sci., Amsterdam, The Netherlands, 1979-85; CEO Elsevier Sci. U.K., London, 1985-91, Bonaventura, The Netherlands, 1992-96; pres., CEO LEXIS-NEXIS Group, Miamisburg, Ohio, 1997—; past pub. Elsevier, The Netherlands; past mem. sales, tech. & gen. mgmt. staffs Elsevier Sci.; past vice chmn. legal divsn. LEXIS-NEXIS, Reed Elsevier, vice chmn. European divsn. Avocations: reading non-fiction, modern European history, yachting and yacht racing, golf, cricket. Office: LEXIS-NEXIS 9443 Springboro Pike Miamisburg OH 45342-4425

GIESKIENG, JANICE CAROL, assistant principal; b. Denver, May 24, 1948; d. David Harold and Marjorie Eleanor (Sager) G. BS in Edn., Wis. State U., 1971; MA in Edn., Ariz. State U., 1982, U. Colo., 1987. Tchr. 5th and 6th grade Miami (Ariz.) Area Unified Dist., 1976-80; tchr. 4th grade Aurora (Colo.) Pub. Schs., 1980-81, tchr., 1981-87, libr. media specialist, 1987-92, instructional resource tchr., 1992-93, 96-98, learning coord., 1993-94, libr. media specialist, 1994-96, asst. prin., 1998—; sch. grant writer Aurora Pub. Schs., 1987, 89, 95, 97, 98, co-creator peer mentor program, 1990, vol. coord., 1991—; presenter in field. Mem. quaity adv. coun. Pacific Care, Denver, 1997—; mem. Nat. Trust Historic Preservation, Washington, 1997—, Denver Mus. Natural History, 1993—. Recipient Disting. Tchr. Colo. awards APS, Aurora, 1986. Mem. ASCD, Colo. ASCD, Colo. Assn. Sch. Execs., Internat. Reading Assn., Audubon Soc., Phi Delta Kappa. Avocations: history, travel, theater, symphony, reading, opera. Home: 12973 E Cornell Ave Aurora CO 80014 Office: Vassar Elem Sch 18101 E Vassar Ave Aurora CO 80013

GIESSELMANN, MICHAEL GUENTER, electrical engineer, educator, researcher; b. Basel, Switzerland, Oct. 15, 1956; came to U.S., 1986; s. Guenter Fritz and Hedwig Giesselmann. MSEE, Tech. U. Darmstadt, Fed. Republic Germany, 1981, PhDEE, 1986. Rsch. assoc. Tech. U. Darmstadt, 1981-86; asst. prof. Tex. Tech U., Lubbock, 1986-92, assoc. prof., 1992—, grad. advisor, chair grad. com., 1994—; cons. West Pub., San Francisco, 1988, OCR Diasonics, Salt Lake City, 1990-92, ESP Inc., 1995—; researcher Lawrence Livermore (Calif.) Nat. Lab., 1988-90, Tex. Advanced Tech. program, 1992-94, Ballistic Missile Def. Orgn., 1995—. Contbr. tech. papers and reports to confs., symposia and profl. jours. Charter mem., exec. com. mem. Tex. Tech. U. Tchg. Acad. Recipient Halliburton award Halliburton Edn. Found., 1988, New Faculty award Tex. Tech. U. Ex-Students Assn., 1990, Outstanding Faculty award, 1991, Charles L. Burford Faculty award, 1994, Pres.'s Excellence in Teaching award, 1995. Mem. IEEE (sr., sec. 1990-91, treas. 1992-95), Aircraft Owners and Pilots Assn. Avocations: aviation, pvt. pilot. Office: Tex Tech U Elec Engring Ms # 3102 Lubbock TX 79409

GIESSER, BARBARA SUSAN, neurologist, educator; b. Bronx, N.Y., Jan. 21, 1953; d. David and Evelyn (Cohen) G.; m. Philip D. Kanof, June 17, 1979; children: David, Marisa. BS, U. Miami, 1972; MS, U. Tex., Houston, 1974; MD, U. Tex., San Antonio, 1978. Diplomate Am. Bd. Psychiatry and Neurology. Intern Montefiore Hosp., Bronx, 1978-79; resident Bronx Mcpl. Hosp. Ctr. (Albert Einstein Coll. Medicine), 1979-82; asst. prof. neurology Albert Einstein Coll. Medicine, Bronx, 1983-91; med. dir. Gimbel MS Comprehensive Care Ctr., Teaneck, N.J., 1985-90, Rehab. Inst. of Tucson, 1991-95; assoc. prof. clin. neurology Ariz. Health Scis. Ctr., Tucson, 1993—. Author: Neurology Specialty Board Review, 3d edit., 1986, 4th edit., 1996; contbr. articles to profl. publs. Dean's Tchr. scholar Ariz. Health Scis. Ctr., 1995. Fellow Am. Acad. Neurology; mem. Nat. Multiple Sclerosis Soc. (rsch. grant 1989, 97, mem. profl. adv. com. Desert S.W. chpt. 1994—, bd. dirs. 1994—, counselor Am. Acad. Neurology sect. on Multiple Sclerosis 1997-99, chair client edn. com. 1999—). Office: Ariz Health Scis Ctr 1501 N Campbell Ave Tucson AZ 85724-0001

GIESZL, LOUIS ROGER, mathematician; b. Inglewood, Calif., Sept. 14, 1937; s. Clifford G. and Zelma R. (Thompson) G; m. Geraldine C., Cirigliano, Sept. 22, 1963; children: Louis G., Lisa M. BS in Math., U. Houston, 1958; MA in Math., Rice U., 1965; MS in Computer Sci., U. Md., 1976; MS in Tech. Mgmt., Johns Hopkins U., 1985. Designer large-scale simulations USN Ops. Analysis, 1967-80; cons. computer technology USAF, 1980-81; dir. info. sys. project Logistics Command/USAF, 1981-82; computer cons. Warfare Analysis Lab., Johns Hopkins U. Applied Physics Lab., Laurel, Md., 1982—, computer cons. advanced sys. devel. group, 1982—, expert systems devel., 1983-87, test and evaluation mgmt., 1988-90, instr. software engring., 1988—. Referee, mem. editl. bd. and contbr. articles to profl. jours. and publs.; developer computer software/warfare simulation models. Capt. USAF, 1963-67. Mem. IEEE, Am. Legion. Office: Johns Hopkins U Applied Physics Lab Johns Hopkins Rd Laurel MD 20723

GIFFEN, DANIEL HARRIS, lawyer, educator; b. Zanesville, Ohio, Feb. 11, 1938; s. Harris MacArtor and Anne Louise (Crawford) G.; m. Jane Louise Cayford, Nov. 23, 1963 (div. 1970); children: Sarah Louise, Thomas Harris; m. Linda Eastin, Aug. 19, 1972. AB, Coll. of William and Mary, 1960; MA, U. Pa., 1962, U. Pa., 1967; testamur, U. Exeter, Eng., 1971; JD, Case Western Res. U., 1973. Bar: Ohio 1973. Corp. asst. U. Pa. Lippincott Libr., Phila., 1961-63; assoc. curator La. State Mus., New Orleans, 1963-64; sec. N.H. Hist. Soc., Concord, 1964-69; asst. dir. Syracuse (N.Y.) U. Arents Rsch. Libr., 1969-70; pvt. practice Cleve., 1973—; asst. prof. law Cleve. State U., 1976-79; asst. prof. Kent (Ohio) State U., 1980-98; v.p. Village Press, Inc., Concord, 1980—; editor Walter Drane Co., Cleve., 1974-76; lectr. Monadnock C.C., Peterborough, N.H., 1968-69. Author: Adventures in Vermont, 1969, Adventures in Maine, 1969, New Hampshire Colony, 1970; contbr. articles to profl. jours. Hon. life mem. Pres.'s Coun., Coll. William and Mary, 1980. Recipient Kenyon English Prize scholarship, 1956; fellow Heritage Found., 1959-60, Nat. Trust, 1959-61, 67, 73. Fellow Salture Soc. (Scotland); mem. Ohio Bar Assn., Cleve. Bar Assn., ABA, Am. Soc. Interior Design, Am. Assn. Mus., Am. Assn. State and Local Historians, AAUP, Nat. Trust, Soc. Am. Archivists, Soc. Archtl. Historians, Interior Design Edn. Coun., Masons, Shriners. Episcopalian. Home: 92 College St Hudson OH 44236-2925

GIFFEN, LOIS KEY, artist, psychosynthesis counselor; b. Hollis, Okla., Dec. 18, 1932; d. Andrew Finley and Audra Agnes (Griffith) Key; m. Robert Edward Giffen, June 26, 1954; children: John Andrew, Mark Alexander. BA, U. Chgo., 1951, attended, 1951-54; diploma, Inst. Psychosynthesis, London, 1988. Artist, 1945—; social group worker Neighbourhood Clubs, Oklahoma City, Okla., 1956-59; tchr. Unity of the Keys, Key West, Fla., 1994—; workshop facilitator Fla. Coalition for Peace and Justice, 1990; organizer for tchg. student mediators in elem. schs. Peace Edn. and Awareness Ctr., Santa Barbara, 1992-93. *Lois Giffen has lived and worked as an artist on five continents, and her paintings are collected worldwide. In recent years she has turned her attention to sculpture. Working in clay, stone, bronze and steel she creates an atmosphere of calm, serenity and well-being. She enjoys commissions for specific rooms, walls, gardens or churches. Her work is included in collections in Australia, Austria, Cyprus, Great Britain, East and West Malaysia, Malta, Sweden and the United States.* Editor The London Bridge Mag., 1981-84, The CCL Cookbook, 1986; one-woman shows include Gippsland Regional Art Ctr., Sale, Victoria, Australia, 1973, Anjuian Angkatan Pelakis Semalaysia, Kuala Lumpur, 1976, Am. Consulate-USIS, Benghazi, Libya, 1962. V.p., mem. bd. dirs. Internat. Women's Club, Benghazi, Libya, 1960-65; mem. bd. dirs. Gippsland Regional Art Ctr., Sale, Victoria, Australia, 1971-73; com. chmn., mem. bd. dirs. Am. Women's Club, London, 1981-88; mem. bd. dirs. Commonwealth Countries League, London, 1982-88, Welcome to London Internat. Club, London, 1983-88; mem. Univ. Women's Club, London, 1985-88; adv. bd. Monroe Coun. of the Arts, Inc. Mem. Assn. for Transpersonal Psychology, Assn. for the Advancement of Psychosynthesis, Bus. and Profl. Women's Club, Fla. Keys Art Guild, Lower Keys Artists Network, Marathon Sailing Club. Democrat. Mem. Unity Ch. Avocations: sailing, swimming, reading, astrology, gardening. Home: 1600 79th St Ocean Marathon FL 33050-3148

GIFFIN, GLENN ORLANDO, II, music critic, writer, newspaper editor; b. Denver, Feb. 27, 1943; s. Glenn Orlando and E. Louise (Mosler) G. B.Mus., U. Colo., 1965; M.A. in Librarianship, U. Denver, 1967. Scriptwriter, broadcaster radio Sta. KRNW-FM, Boulder, 1965-67; asst. music critic San Francisco Chronicle, 1968; asst. music librarian Norlin libraries U. Colo., 1968-70; music critic, staff writer Denver Post, 1970-73, music editor, 1973-88, book page editor, music critic, 1988-98, editor Colo. Living, Writing/Entertainment, 1998—; host Soundings, Sta. KOA Radio 1985-86; curator Carson-Brierly Dance Library U. Denver, 1986—. Rockefeller Found. fellow, 1966-68; Corbett Found. fellow, 1969; Nat. Endowment for Arts grantee Dance Criticism Inst., Conn. Coll., summer 1971; named Outstanding Alumnus U. Colo., 1985. Mem. Music Library Assn., Am. Musicol. Soc., Dance Critics Assn., Music Critics Assn., Sigma Delta Chi. Office: Denver Post PO Box 1709 1560 Broadway Denver CO 80201-1709*

GIFFIN, GORDON D., ambassador, lawyer; b. Springfield, Mass.; m. Patti Alfred; 1 child, Kelley. BA, Duke U., 1971; JD, Emory U., 1974. Bar: Ga. 1974, Washington. Assoc. Hansell and Post, Atlanta, 19; dir. legis. affairs, chief counsel to Senator Sam Nunn, U.S. Ho. of Reps., Washington; sr. ptnr. Long, Aldridge & Norman, Atlanta and Washington, until 1997; amb. to Can., Am. Embassy, Ottawa, Ont., 1997—; former adj. prof. law Emory U. Sch. Law, Atlanta; bd. dirs. Overseas Pvt. Investment Corp., 1993-97. Treas. Senator Sam Nunn Campaign Com., 20 yrs.; with Senator Nunn and Gov. Clinton founder Dem. Leadership Coun., 1984, mem. bd., 1984-96; mem. com. to host Dem. Nat. Conv., Atlanta, 1988, chmn. site selection com., Chgo., 1996, gen. counsel, 1992, 96; presdl. elector, Ga., 1992, 96; chmn. Ga. Clinton primary campaign, 1992, Clinton-Gore Gen. Election Campaign, 1992; dep. dir. pers. White House Transition Team, 1992; sr. advisor on south, also chmn. Clinton-Gore effort in Ga., Clinton Reelection Campaign, 1996; active Atlanta Olympic Games Com., 1996; former mem. bd. dirs. Ga. C. of C., Trees Atlanta Found., Atlanta Hist. Soc., Atlanta Ballet. Named One of 100 Most Influential Georgians, Ga. Trend mag., 3 times. Office: Dept State Am Ambassador to Canada Washington DC 20521-5480*

GIFFIN, MARGARET ETHEL (PEGGY GIFFIN), management consultant; b. Cleve., Aug. 27, 1949; d. Arch Kenneth and Jeanne (Eggleton) G.; m. Robert Alan Wyman, Aug. 20, 1988; 1 child, Samantha Jean. BA in Psychology, U. Pacific, Stockton, Calif., 1971; MA in Psychology, Calif. State U., Long Beach, 1973; PhD in Quantitative Psychology, U. So. Calif., 1984. Psychometrician Auto Club So. Calif., L.A., 1973-74; cons. Psychol. Svcs., Inc., Glendale, Calif., 1975-76; mgr. Psychol. Svcs., Inc., Glendale, 1977-78, dir., 1979-94; rschr. Social Sci. Rsch. Inst., U. So. Calif., L.A., 1981; dir. Giffin Consulting Svcs., L.A., 1994—; instr. Calif. State U., Long Beach, 1989-90; mem. tech. adv. com. on testing Calif. Fair Employment and Housing Commn., 1974-80, mem. steering com., 1978-80. *Dr. Giffin had provided human resources consulting to a wide range of clients in both the public and private sectors. This consulting has covered the areas of job analysis, employee selection and promotion systems, performance appraisal systems, job analysis, test validation, training, surveys, and affirmative action. She has also consulted in the entertainment industry on the issue of valuation of intellectual property. She has consulted with attorneys in over fifty court cases, and has testified in California State Court and in Federal Court in jury and court trials.* Mem. APA, Soc. Indsl. Organizational Psychology, Pers. Testing Coun. So. Calif. (pres. 1980, exec. dir. 1982, 88, bd. dirs. 1980-92). Home and Office: 260 S Highland Ave Los Angeles CA 90036-3027

GIFFIN, MARY ELIZABETH, psychiatrist, educator; b. Rochester, Minn., Mar. 30, 1919; d. Herbert Ziegler and Mary Elizabeth (Nace) G. BA, Smith Coll., Northampton, Mass., 1939; MD, Johns Hopkins, 1943; MS, U. Minn., 1948. Diplomate Am. Bd. Psychiatry and Neurology. Cons. in neurology and psychiatry Mayo Clinic, Rochester, 1949-58; med. dir. Josselyn Clinic, Northfield, Ill., 1958-89; pvt. practice psychiatry Northfield, 1989—; mem. faculty Inst. for Psychoanalysis, Chgo., 1963-89. Contbr. numerous articles to profl. jour. Mem. Ill. Psychiat. Soc., Am. Acad. Child Psychiatry. Republican. Mem. Am. Bapt. Ch. Avocation: creative writing. Home: 1190 Hamptondale Ave Winnetka IL 60093-1812 Office: 1 Northfield Plz Ste 300 Northfield IL 60093-1214 *Settle into the immediate as if it were the infinite which indeed it is.*

GIFFIN, SANDRA LEE, nursing administrator; b. Tacoma, July 16, 1957; d. Clayton Eugene and Carol Lee (Fisher) Peterson; m. Herbert Kent Giffin, May 6, 1989. Diploma, Tacoma Gen. Hosp. Sch. Nursing, 1978; BSN magna cum laude, Pacific Luth. U., 1980; MS, Oreg. Health Scis. U., 1994. Cert. in nursing adminstrn. Staff nurse Mary Bridge Children's Hosp., 1978-81, evening nurse supr., infection control nurse, 1981-83, asst. med./surg. nurse mgr., 1983-84; med./surg. nurse mgr. Mary Bridge Children's Hosp., Tacoma, 1984-89; dept. dir. Oreg. Poison Ctr. Oreg. Health Scis. U., Portland, 1989—, instr., Sch. Nursing, 1994—, dept. dir. nurse cons. program, 1995—; presenter in field. Author/presenter abstracts in field. Sec. Rocky Butte Neighborhood Assn., 1996; sec. bd. dirs. Make A Wish Found. Oreg., 1989-96; active Oreg. Safe Kids Coalition, Oreg. Interagy. Hazardous Comm. Coun., Oreg. Sch. Health Edn. Coalition. Grantee Agy. for Toxic Substances and Disease Registry/Am. Assn. Poison Control Ctrs., 1992, Oreg. State Health Divsn., 1993-94. Mem. Am. Acad. Ambulatory Care Nursing, Am. Assn. Poison Control Ctrs., N.W. Orgn. Nursing Execs. Avocations: skiing, reading, bicycling, travel, cooking. Office: Oreg Poison Ctr 3181 SW Sam Jackson Park Rd Portland OR 97201-3011

GIFFIN, WALTER CHARLES, retired industrial engineer, educator, consultant; b. Walhonding, Ohio, Apr. 22, 1936; s. Charles Maurice and Florence Ruth (Davis) G.; m. Beverly Ann Neff, Sept. 1, 1956; children—Steven, Rebecca. B. Indsl. Engring., Ohio State U., 1960, M.S., 1960, Ph.D., 1964. Registered profl. engr., Ohio. Research engr. Gen. Motors Research Labs., Warren, Mich., 1960-61; research assoc. systems research group Ohio State U., Columbus, 1961-62, instr. indsl. and systems engring., 1962-64, asst. prof., 1964-68, assoc. prof., 1968-71, prof., 1971-87, prof. emeritus, 1987—; prof. engring. U. So. Colo., Pueblo, 1987-92; ret., 1992—; cons. in field. Author: Introduction to Operations Engineering, 1971; Transform Techniques for Probability Modeling, 1975; Queueing: Basic Theory and Applications, 1978. NASA Research grantee, 1978-83. Club: Exptl. Aircraft Assn. (Oshkosh, Wis. and Pueblo, Colo.). Home: 419 Fairway Dr Pueblo CO 81007

GIFFORD, CHARLES KILVERT, banker; b. Providence, Nov. 8, 1942; s. Clarence H. and Priscilla (Kilvert) G.; m. Anne Dewing, Oct. 3, 1964; children—Ramsay, Charles, John, Jessica. B.A., Princeton U., 1964. With Chase Manhattan Bank, N.Y.C., 1964-66; with BankBoston, 1966—, loan officer, 1967, asst. v.p., 1970, v.p., 1973, first v.p., 1978, sr. v.p., 1979, exec. v.p., 1981; vice-chmn. BankBoston and First Nat. Bank of Boston, 1987, pres., 1989, chmn., CEO, 1995—; group exec. Corp. Banking Group, 1984; dir. Mass. Mut. Life Ins. Co., Boston Edison Co. Trustee New Eng. Aquarium, Boston, 1982, Dana Farber Cancer Ctr., Boston, 1982, Sta. WGBH, Make-A-Wish Found., Northeastern U., Junior Achievement; bd. dirs. Boston Pvt. Ind. Coun., Assn. Res. City Bankers; chmn. success by 6 leadership coun. United Way, mem. exec. com.; chmn. Boston Plan for Excellence in Pub. Schs. Mem. Greater Boston C. of C. (chmn.). Office: BankBoston Corp 100 Federal St Fl 8 Boston MA 02110-1802*

GIFFORD, DONALD ARTHUR, lawyer; b. Derry, N.H., Nov. 21, 1945; s. George Donald and Bertha Margaret (Gibbs) G.; m. Sandra Louise Robaldo, July 25, 1964; children: Adriana, Roy, Stacy. BA, U. South Fla., 1967; JD with high honors, Fla. State U., 1970. Bar: Fla. 1970, U.S. Dist. Ct. (mid. dist.) Fla. 1970, U.S. Dist. Ct. (no. dist.) Fla. 1981, U.S. Dist. Ct. (so. dist.) Fla. 1982, U.S. Ct. Appeals (5th cir.) 1975, U.S. Ct. Appeals (11th cir.) 1981. U.S. Supreme Ct. 1980. Assoc. Raymond, Wilson, Karl, Conway & Barr, Daytona Beach, Fla., 1972; law clk. U.S. Dist. Ct. (mid. dist.) Fla., Tampa, 1972-73; with Shackelford, Farrior, Stallings & Evans, P.A., Tampa, 1973—. Chair divsn. allocations United Way Greater Tampa, 1987-94, treas., 1991-93, pres., 1994-96; mem., trustee U.S. Fla. Found., 1986—, New Coll. Found., 1990-93. Fellow ABA (ho. of dels 1991-92), Am. Judicature Soc., Am. Bar Found.; mem. Fed. Bar Assn., Fla. Bar (bd. govs. 1989-95, mem. exec. com. 1993-94, chair legis. com. 1993-94, legis. com. 1995-98, mem. bd. legal specialization and edn.), Fla. Bar Found. (bd. dirs. 1996—, chair AOJ com.), Hillsborough County Bar Assn. (bd. dirs. 1981-90, pres. 1988-89), U. South Fla. Nat. Alumni Assn. (pres. 1976, bd. dirs. 1970-92, Outstanding Alumnus 1976, Outstanding Svc. award 1996), Fla. State U. Coll. Law Alumni Assn. (bd. dirs. 1982-96, pres. 1987-88), Greater Tampa C. of C. (gen. counsel, mem. exec. com., bd. govs.), Fla. State U. Alumni Assn. (bd. dirs. 1987—, chmn. 1992-94), F.L.A. Inc. (bd. dirs. 1995-98), Outback Bowl (mem. team rels. com. 1986-95), Tiger Bay Club (bd. dirs. 1988-92). Office: Shackleford Farrior Stallings & Evans PA PO Box 3324 Tampa FL 33601-3324

GIFFORD, DONALD GEORGE, academic dean; b. Medina, Ohio, July 26, 1952; s. George W. and Ruth Ann (Reed) G.; m. Nancy Ray Aten, Mar. 24, 1973; children: Rebecca, Caroline. BA, Wooster Coll., 1973; JD, Harvard U., 1976. Bar: Ohio 1976, Fla. 1984. Assoc. Gallagher, Sharp, Fulton, Norman & Mollison, Cleve., 1976-77; ptnr. Noble & Gifford, Millersburg, Ohio, 1977-79; asst. prof. law U. Toledo, 1979-82, assoc. prof. law, 1982-84; prof. U. Fla., Gainsville, 1984-89; assoc. dir. academic task force for rev. ins. and tort systems Fla. Gov.'s Office, Gainsville, 1986-88; dean, prof. law W.Va. U., Morgantown, 1989-92; bd. dirs. 1st Nat. Bank Morgantown, 1990-92; dean, prof. law U. Md., Balt., 1992—. Contbr. articles to profl. jours.; author 2 books. Chmn. Gov.'s Lead Paint Poisoning Commn., Md., 1992-94; vice chair Md. Alt. Dispute Resolution Task Force, 1997—. Mem. Ohio Bar Assn., The Fla. Bar. Office: U Maryland Sch Law 500 W Baltimore St Baltimore MD 21201-1701

GIFFORD, ERNEST MILTON, biologist, educator; b. Riverside, Calif., Jan. 17, 1920; s. Ernest Milton and Mildred Wade (Campbell) G.; m. Jean Duncan, July 15, 1942; 1 child, Jeanette. A.B., U. Calif., Berkeley, 1942, Ph.D., 1950; grad., U.S. Army Command and Gen. Staff Sch., 1965. Asst. prof. botany, asst. botanist expt. sta. U. Calif.-Davis, 1950-56, assoc. prof. botany, assoc. botanist, 1957-61, prof. botany, botanist, 1962-87, prof. emeritus, 1988—, chmn. dept. botany and agrl. botany, 1963-67, 74-78. Author: (with A. S. Foster) Morphology and Evolution of Vascular Plants, 3d edit., 1989, (with T. L. Rost) Mechanisms and control of Cell Division, 1977; editor in chief Am. Jour. Botany, 1975-79; advisor to editor Ency. Brit.; contbr. articles on anatomy, ultrastructure and morphogenesis of higher plants to profl. jours. Served to maj. U.S. Army, 1942-46; ETO; to col. USAR, 1946-73. Decorated Bronze Star medal; named disting. contbr. Ency. Brit., 1964; NRC fellow Harvard U., 1956; Fulbright research scholar, France, 1966; John Simon Guggenheim Found. fellow, France, 1966; NATO sr. postdoctoral fellow, France, 1974; recipient Acad. Senate Disting. Teaching award U. Calif.-Davis, 1986. Mem. Bot. Soc. Am. (v.p. 1981, pres. 1982, merit award 1981), Internat. Soc. Plant Morphologists (v.p. 1980-84), Am. Inst. Biol. Scis., Sigma Xi. Office: U Calif Divsn of Biol Scis Sect of Plant Biology Davis CA 95616-8536

GIFFORD, FRANK NEWTON, sportscaster, commentator, former professional football player; b. Santa Monica, Calif., Aug. 16, 1930; s. Weldon Wayne and Lola (Hawkins) G.; children: Jeffery, Kyle, Victoria; m. Astrid Naess, Mar. 1978 (div. 1986); m. Kathie Lee, 1986; 2 children: Cody Newton, Cassidy Erin. Student, Bakersfield Jr. Coll., 1948-49; B.A., U. So. Calif., 1952. Mem. N.Y. Giants (profl. football team), 1952-65; sports reporter CBS Radio, N.Y.C., 1957-59; Nat. Football League pre-game show host CBS-TV Network, N.Y.C., 1959-62; sports reporter WCBS-TV, N.Y.C., 1962-71; reporter ABC Radio Info., N.Y.C., 1971-77; sports corr. ABC TV Network, N.Y.C., 1971—; corr. Eyewitness News, N.Y.C., 1971—; announcer ABC Monday Night Football, 1971-86, commentator, 1986-98, program show host, 1998; host The Superstars Series.; dir. sports writers and broadcasters Spl. Olympics, 1972-75. Author: Frank Gifford's NFL-AFL Football Guide, 1968, rev. edits., 1969, 70, Frank Gifford's Football Guide Book, 1966, (with Charles Mangel) Gifford on Courage, 1976, (with Harry Waters, Jr.) Gifford: The Whole Ten Yards, 1993. Bd. dirs. Nat. Soc. for Multiple Sclerosis, 1973-78; co-founder Cody House, Cassidy's Place, Children's Healthcare Facilities, N.Y. Named Collegiate All-Am., 1952, NFL MVP, 1956, Sportsman of Yr., Cath. Youth Orgn., 1964; elected to Nat. Football Found. Hall of Fame, 1976, Pro Football Hall of Fame, 1977, U. So. Calif. Athletic Hall of Fame, 1994; recipient Gil Hodges Meml. sports award Cath. Med. Center, 1976, Adam award Men's Fashion Assn. Am., 1976, Emmy award for outstanding sports personality, 1977, Christopher award, 1984, Founder's award Multiple Sclerosis Soc., N.Y., 1984, others. *

GIFFORD, FRANKLIN ANDREW, JR., meteorologist; b. Union City, N.J., May 7, 1922; s. F.A. and Hazel (Sheehan) G.; m. Eleanor Mary Frith, Aug. 7, 1943; children: Michael J., Robert K. BS, NYU, 1947; MS, Pa. State U., 1954, PhD, 1955. Area chief meteorologist Northwest Airlines, N.Y.C., 1945-50; rsch. meteorologist U.S. Weather Bur. (NOAA), Washington, 1950-55; dir. Atmospheric Turbulence Diffusion Lab. NOAA, Oak Ridge, Tenn., 1955-80; cons. Los Alamos Nat. Lab., 1980—, U.S. NRC Adv. Com. on Reactor Safety, Washington, 1958-82; cons. Internat. Atomic Energy Agy., Vienna, 1966-82; mem. U.S.-USSR Bilateral Working Group on Air Pollution, 1974-75. Author: Meteorology and Atomic Energy, 1968; contbr. over 140 articles to profl. jours. Capt. USAF, 1943-45, ETO. Recipient Gold medal U.S. Dept. Commerce, 1963. Fellow AAAS, Am. Meteorol. Soc. (Contbn. to Applied Meteorology award 1990). Home: 109 Gorgas Ln Oak Ridge TN 37830-5417

GIFFORD, GERALD FREDERIC, education educator; b. Chanute, Kans., Oct. 24, 1939; s. Gerald Leo and Marion Lou (Browne) G.; m. Cinda Jean Lowman, June 26, 1982. Student, Kans. U., 1957-60; BS in Range Mgmt., Utah State U., 1962, MS in Watershed Mgmt., 1964, PhD in Watershed Sci., 1968. Asst. prof. watershed sci. Utah State U., Logan, 1967-72, assoc. prof., 1972-80, prof., 1980-84, chmn. watershed sci. unit, 1967-84, dir. Inst. Land Reclamation, 1982-84; head range, wildlife and forestry U. Nev., Reno, 1984-92, chmn. environ. and resource sci. dept., 1992-94; exchange scientist NSF, Canberra, Australia, 1974; cons. Smithsonian Inst., Nat. Park Service, Office of Tech. Assessment, Tex. Tech U., U. Minn., Bur. Land Mgmt. AMAX Coal Co., Nat. Commn. Water Quality, 1967—. Author: Rangeland Hydrology, 1981; assoc. editor Arid Soil Rsch. and Rehab., 1985-90, Jour. of Range Mgmt., 1982-87, 91-95; contbr. papers to profl. pubs. Named Tchr. of Yr., U. Nev. Coll. Agr., 1996. Mem. Am. Water Resources Assn., Soil and Water Conservation Soc. Avocations: racquetball, antiques, garage sales. Home: 3880 Squaw Valley Cir Reno NV 89509-5663 Office: U Nev Environ and Resource Scis 1000 Valley Rd Reno NV 89512-2815

GIFFORD, HEIDI, editor, writer; b. New Haven, Jan. 28, 1961; d. Prosser and Dee Dee (O'Sullivan) Gifford; m. George Melas, July 15, 1995; 1 child, Luke. BA in English Lit., Yale U., 1983; MPA in Internat. Econs., Columbia U., 1991. Editl. asst. Yale U. Press, New Haven, 1985; asst. to the dir. Gov.'s Office of Fed. Rels., Boston, 1987-89; asst. dir. internat. trade and econs. Coun. on Fgn. Rels., N.Y.C., 1991-94; elections analyst Nightly News with Tom Brokaw/NBC News, N.Y.C., 1995-96; writer and editor Comms. Devel., N.Y.C., 1997—; assoc. USIA Fgn. Press Ctr., N.Y.C., 1990-91. Mem. Inst. of World Affairs. Episcopalian. Avocations: crew, marathon running.

GIFFORD, JOHN IRVING, retired agricultural equipment company executive; b. Lockport, N.Y., July 23, 1930; s. John Jacob and Carrie (McAdam) G.; m. Sara Jane Bauer, Jan. 28, 1955; children: John Hutchins, James Scott. BS, Purdue U., 1952, MS, 1956. Sales trainee Am. Nat. Foods, Inc., L.A., 1956; economist Deere & Co., Moline, Ill., 1956-65; pers. adminstr. Deere & Co., Moline, 1965-70, mgr. data svcs., 1970-96; stats. cons. to cos. and trade assns., 1996—; mem. USDA Agrl. Census adv. com., 1997—. Bd. dirs., Rock Island (Ill.) sect. Easter Seal Found., 1981-87; v.p. coun., St. John Luth. Ch., Rock Island, 1981-82; pres., Rock Island Little League, 1981-82; v.p. Babe Ruth Baseball, Rock Island, 1983. 1st lt. U.S. Army, 1952-54, Korea. Recipient Leadership recognition Equipment Mfrs. Inst. Mem. Nat. Assn. Bus. Econs., Equipment Mfrs. Assn., Farm and Indsl. Equipment Inst., Constrn. Industry Mfrs. Assn., Outdoor Power Equipment Inst., Engine Mfrs. Assn., Internat. Farm Tractor Com., Internat. Harvesting Equipment Com. (chmn. statistics com. 1994-95). Avocations: reading, golf.

GIFFORD, NELSON SAGE, financial company executive; b. Newton, Mass., May 3, 1930; s. Gordon Babcock and Hariette Rose (Dooley) G.; m. Elizabeth B. Brow, Nov. 12, 1955; children: Susan Helen, Ian Christopher, Diane Brow. AB, Tufts Coll., 1952; HHD (hon.), U. Mass., 1989; PhD (hon.), Tufts U., 1996. With Dennison Mfg. Co., Framingham, Mass., 1954-90, mem. acctg. staff, 1954-63, controller, 1964-65, gen. mgr., 1965-67, v.p., 1967-72, pres., 1972-86, chmn., 1986-90; vice chmn. Avery Dennison Corp., Boston, 1990-91; prin. Fleetwing Capital, Boston, 1992—; bd. dirs. Reed & Barton, John Hancock Mut. Life Ins. Co., Boston, BEC Energy, Boston, J.M. Huber Corp., Edison, N.J., Nypro Inc., Clinton, Mass.; mng. dir. Ptnr.'s Fund, Boston. Past bd. dirs. New Eng. Colls. Fund; corp. mem. Newton Wellesley Hosp., Mass. Gen. Hosp.; past chmn. Wellesley Pers. Bd.; past trustee Woods Hole Oceanographic Inst., Mass., 1984-90; chmn. bd. trustees Tufts U., 1986-95. Lt. comdr. USNR, 1952-60. Mem. Silvanus Packard Soc., Mass. Bus. Roundtable (bd. dirs., vice chmn. 1982-88), Assoc. Industries Mass. (bd. dirs. 1976-86), Kittansett Club, Brae Burn Country Club, Beverly Yacht Club, Soc. Tufts Followes. Home: 14 Windsor Rd Wellesley MA 02481-6134 Office: Fleetwing Capital 75 Federal St Boston MA 02110-1913

GIFFORD, PORTER WILLIAM, retired construction materials manufacturing company executive; b. Dallas, Dec. 14, 1918; s. Porter William and Evelyn Victoria (Bonorden) G.; m. Elizabeth Butte, Jan. 19, 1946 (dec.); children: Porter William III, Sharon Elizabeth, Geoffrey Butte; m. Kay Williams Manley, Mar. 22, 1997. BSME, Cornell U., 1941. With Gifford-Hill & Co., Inc., Dallas, 1941-86; pres. Gifford-Hill & Co., Inc., 1958-69, chmn. bd. dirs., 1969-71; pres. Qdot Corp., Dallas, 1974-78, Aerological Rsch. Systems, Inc., Dallas, 1991—. Trustee Found. Econ. Edn., Internat. Linguistics Ctr., Dallas, Future of Freedom Found., Fairfax, Va. Maj. USAAC, 1941-46. Decorated Bronze Star. Mem. Tau Beta Pi, Delta Kappa Epsilon. Home: 9106 Esplanade Dr Dallas TX 75220-7800 Office: 5207 Mckinney Ave Ste 12 Dallas TX 75205-3355

GIFFORD, PROSSER, library administrator; b. N.Y.C., May 16, 1929; ż; s. John Archer and Barbara (Prosser) G.; m. Shirley Mireille O'Sullivan, June 26, 1954; children: Barbara, Paula, Heidi. B.A., Yale U., 1951, Ph.D., 1964; B.A., Oxford (Eng.) U., 1953, M.A., 1958; LL.B., Harvard U., 1956; M.A., Amherst Coll., 1969, L.H.D., 1980; LL.D., Doshisha U., Kyoto, Japan, 1979. Bar: D.C. 1956. Asst. to pres. Swarthmore Coll., 1956-58; asst. prof. history Yale, 1964-66; dir. 5 yr. B.A. program, 1965-66; dean faculty Amherst Coll., 1967-79, assoc. prof. history, 1967-69, prof. history, 1969-79; dep. dir. Woodrow Wilson Internat. Ctr. for Scholars, Washington, 1975-76, 80-87, acting dir., 1987-88; dir. scholarly programs Libr. Congress, 1990—; chmn. Merton Coll. Charitable Corp., 1991—. Co-editor, contbr.: Britian and Germany in Aftica, 1967, France and Britain in Africa, 1971, Transfer of Power in Africa, 1982, Decolonization and African Independence, 1988, Creating French Culture, 1995. Trustee, Hotchkiss Sch., 1971-81, Concord Acad., 1972-78; chmn. bd. trustees Woods Hole Marine Biol. Lab., 1978-90. Rhodes scholar, 1951-53; Fgn. Area fellow No. Rhodesia, 1963-64. Mem. Assn. Yale Alumni (gov. 1972-77), Woods Hole Oceanographic Inst. (mem. corp.), Internat. House of Japan, India Internat. Ctr., Century Club, Cosmos Club, Elizabethan Club, Woods Hole Golf and Tennis Club, Quisset Yacht Club. Home: 540 N St SW Apt 903S Washington DC 20024-4512 also: 59 Penzance Rd Woods Hole MA 02543-1043

GIFFORD, RAY WALLACE, JR., physician, educator; b. Westerville, Ohio, Aug. 13, 1923; s. Ray Wallace and Alma Marie (Wagoner) G.; m. Frances Anne Moore, Jan. 13, 1973; 1 son, George; children by previous marriage: Peggy, Cynthia, Susan. BS, Otterbein Coll., 1944, ScD (hon.), 1986; M.D., Ohio State U., 1947; M.Sc., U. Minn., 1952. Diplomate: Am. Bd. Internal Medicine. Intern Colo. Gen. Hosp., Denver, 1947-48; resident in internal medicine Mayo Clinic, Rochester, Minn., 1949-52; practice medicine specializing in hypertension and nephrology; asst. prof. medicine, cons. sect. medicine Mayo Clinic, Mayo Found., Rochester, 1953-61; staff mem. dept. hypertension and nephrology Cleve. Clinic Found., 1961-67, head dept. hypertension and nephrology, 1967-85, sr. physician dept. hypertension and nephrology, 1986-93, acting chmn. dept. hypertension and nephrology, 1991-92, cons. dept. hypertension and nephrology, 1994—, bd. govs., 1973-78, vice chmn., 1977-78, vice chmn. div. medicine, 1978-93, chmn. regional health affairs, 1986-93, 94-98; prof. internal medicine Ohio State U. Coll. Medicine, Columbus, Ohio, 1993—; asst. attending physician U.S. Congress, 1954-56; chmn. hypertension task force Intersoc. Commn. on Heart Disease Resources, 1979-81; mem. nat. high blood pressure coordinating com. Nat. Heart, Lung and Blood Inst., 1978—; mem. 2d, 3d, 4th, 6th and chmn. 5th joint nat. coms. on detection, evaluation and treatment of high blood pressure, 1979-80, 83-84, 87-88, 91-92, 96-97; mem. Congl. Commn. on Drug Approval Process, 1981-82; mem. adv. com. to dir. NIH, 1982-86; mem. Joint Commn. on Accreditation of Healthcare Orgns., 1989-90; mem. Forum on Drug Devel., Inst. Medicine, 1990-94. Author: (with William Manger) Pheochromocytoma, 1977, 96; contbr. numerous papers to med. jours.; editl. bd. Stroke Jour., 1971-74, Am. Jour. Cardiology, 1973-78, Geriatrics, 1974—, Hypertension Rsch., 1994—, Jour. Cardiovascular Risk, 1994-98, Jour. Geriatric Cardiology, 1994-98. Mem. Rochester City Coun., 1960-61, Rep. precinct committeeman, Cleveland Heights, Ohio, 1966-70. Lt. comdr. M.C., USNR, 1954-56. Recipient Alumni Achievement award Ohio State U., 1962, Alumni Medalist award, 1989; Disting. Sci. Achievement award Otterbein Coll., 1970, Spl. Achievement award, 1992; individual achievement award high blood pressure edn. programs Nat. Heart, Lung and Blood Inst., 1989, Bristol Myers lifetime achievement award Am. Heart Assn., 1992; spl. achievement award Cleve. Clinic Alumni Assn., 1994; Ray W. Gifford, Jr. endowed chair in hypertension established at Cleve. Clinic, 1994; named to Cleve. Med. Hall of Fame, 1997. Fellow ACP (master), Am. Coll. Cardiology (bd. trustees 1969-70, gov. Ohio chpt. 1970-73), Am. Coll. Chest Physicians (chmn. com. on hypertension 1970-72, Simon Rodbard Meml. award 1982); mem. AMA (coun. on sci. affairs 1976-85, vice chmn. 1981-83, chmn. 1983-85, trustee 1986-90), Am. Heart Assn. (bd. dirs. 1969-72, chmn. stroke coun. 1970-72), Am. Soc. Clin. Pharmacology and Therapeutics (pres. 1976-77, Oscar B. Hunter Meml. award in Therapeutics 1979, Henry W. Elliott award Disting. Svc. 1995), Ctrl. Soc. Clin. Rsch., Internat. Soc. Hypertension, Interstate Postgrad. Med. Assn. (pres. 1976-77), Interam. Soc. Hypertension, Coun. on Geriatric Cardiology (bd. dirs. 1989-92), Ohio State U. Alumni Assn. (bd. dirs. 1990-95). Methodist. Home: 15222 E Cactus Dr Fountain Hills AZ 85268

GIFFORD, STEVEN, architect. BS in Architecture, U. Va.; MArch, Columbia U. Registered arch., N.Y. Arch. Bond Ryder Assocs., N.Y.C.; ptnr. Davis Brody Bond, LLP, Archs. and Planners, N.Y.C., 1984—. Prin. works include Natural Sci. Bldg. SUNY, Old Westbury, Ctr. for Indsl. Innovation, Rensselaer Poly. Inst., Troy, N.Y., Hampton Housing, N.Y.C., Harlem Gateway Housing, N.Y.C., Tech. and Innovation Ctr., Hallmark, Inc., Kansas City, Mo., 1986, Carnegie Pk., N.Y.C., 1986, Ctr. for Chem. Rsch., Columbia U., N.Y.C., 1989, Natural Sci. Complex, SUNY, Buffalo, 1994, Coll. Vet. Medicine, Cornell U., Ithaca, N.Y., 1994, Econ. Devel. Corp., N.Y.C. Biosci. Ctr., 1994, Audubon Bus. and Tech. Ctr., Columbia U., 1995, Md. Biotech. Ctr., Md. Biotech. Inst., 1996. Mem. AIA. Office: Davis Brody Bond LLP 315 Hudson St New York NY 10013-1009*

GIFFORD, THOMAS EUGENE, writer; b. Dubuque, Iowa, May 16, 1937; s. Eugene Albert and Mabel Jane (Maxwell) G.; m. Kari Sandven (div.); children: Thomas Eaton, Rachel Claire; m. Camille D'Ambrose (div.). BA, Harvard Coll., 1959. Coll. text traveller Houghton Mifflin Co., Mpls., 1960-69; editor Twin Citian Mag., Mpls., 1969-70; dir. pub. rels. & advt. Guthrie Theatre, Mpls., 1970-71; pres. Deja Vu Advt., Mpls., 1971-72; columnist SunSuburban Newspapers, Bloomington, Minn., 1972-74; editor-at-large Sun Newspapers, Bloomington, 1972-75; novelist, 1974—; writer-in-residence Univ. Dubuque, 1994—; columnist Dubuque Telegraph Herald, 1997—; bd. dirs. Wahlert Libr. Loras Coll., Dubuque, 1997—; vis. prof. Loras Coll., 1999. Author: The Wind Chill Factor, The Cavanaugh Quest (Cert. of Merit award Mystery Writers Am. 1976), The Man From Lisbon, The Glendower Legacy, Hollywood Gothic, The Assassini, Praetorian, The First Sacrifice, Saints Rest. Recipient Putnam award, 1974; Harvard Nat. scholar, 1955. Mem. Dubuque Hist. Soc., Dubuque Mus. Art, Harvard Club. Dem. Methodist. Home: 945 Indian Rdg Dubuque IA 52003-8505

GIFFORD, WILLIAM C., lawyer; b. Aurora, Ill., Sept. 18, 1941. A.B., Dartmouth Coll., 1963; LL.B., Harvard U., 1966. Bar: Ill. 1966, D.C. 1968, N.Y. 1976. Ptnr. Ivins Phillips & Barker, Washington, 1967-74; assoc. prof. Cornell Law Sch., 1974-78; counsel and ptnr. Wilmer, Cutler & Pickering, 1978-83; ptnr. Davis Polk & Wardwell, 1983-98, sr. counsel, 1998—. Author: International Tax Planning, 1974, 2d edit., 1979; (with E.A. Owens) International Aspects of U.S. Taxation, 1982. Office: Davis Polk & Wardwell 450 Lexington Ave New York NY 10017-3911

GIGLI, IRMA, physician, educator, academic administrator; b. Cordoba, Argentina, Dec. 22, 1931; d. Irineo and Esperanza Francisca (Pons de Gigli) G.; m. Hans J. Muller-Eberhard, June 29, 1985. B.A., Liceo Nacional Manuel Belgrano, Cordoba, 1950; M.D., Universidad Nacional de Cordoba, 1957. Intern Cook County Hosp., Chgo., 1957-58; resident in dermatology Cook County Hosp., 1958-60; fellow in dermatology NYU, 1960-61; mem. faculty Harvard Med. Sch., 1967-75, asso. prof. dermatology, 1972-75; chief dermatology service Peter Bent Brigham Hosp., Robert B. Brigham Hosp., 1971-75; prof. dermatology and exptl. medicine N.Y. U. Med. Center, N.Y.C., 1976-82; mem. Irvington Houst Inst. N.Y. U. Med. Center, mem. faculty N.Y. Grad. Sch. Med. Scis., dir. Asthma and Allergic Disease Center for Immunodermatology Studies, 1980-91; prof. medicine, chief div. dermatology U. Calif.-San Diego, 1983-95; prof. medicine and dermatology, vice chair medicine for sci. U. Tex. Health Sci. Ctr., Houston, 1995—; assoc. dir. Inst. Molecular Medicine for Prevention Human Diseases U. Tex., Houston, 1998—, Walter and Mary Mischer prof. molecular medicine, 1998—; dir. Rsch. Ctr. Immunology and Autoimmune Diseases, 1995—; mem. Nat. Inst. of Allergy and Infectious Diseases Coun., 1978-79; bd. sci. counselors, 1997—; chmn. study sect. Allergy and Immunology Inst., NIH, 1978-83; Guggenheim Found. Western Hemisphere and Phillippines Com. of Selection; adv. bd. NIH Fogarty Internat. Ctr., 1984-97. Contbr. articles to profl. jours. Recipient Stephen Rothman Meml. award Soc. for Investigative Dermatology, 1996, rsch. award Am. Cancer Soc., 1970-72, NIH, 1972-76; Guggenheim Found., grantee, 1974-75. Mem. Am. Soc. Clin. Investigation, Am. Assn. Immunologists, Am. Acad. Dermatology, Soc. Investigative Dermatology, Am. Acad. Allergy, Assn. Am. Physicians, Am. Dermatol. Assn., Soc. for Investigative Dermatology (pres. 1990-91), Inst. Medicine/NAS, PEN Latin Am. Fellows Program in Biomed. Scis. (nat. adv. com. 1998—). Office: U Tex Health Sci Ctr Inst Molecular Medicine 2121 W Holcombe Blvd Houston TX 77030-3303

GIGLIO, STEVEN RENE, lawyer; b. Denver, Feb. 13, 1952; s. Dominic Mark and Ruth (Strain) G.; m. Susan Dale Carver, Feb. 12, 1987. BA in Russian Studies, La. State U., 1973, JD, 1976. Bar: La. 1976, U.S. Dist. Ct. (ea., mid. and we. dists.) La. 1979, U.S. Ct. Claims 1990, U.S. Ct. Appeals (5th cir.) 1979, U.S. Supreme Ct. 1981. Pvt. practice Baton Rouge, 1976-79, 93—; asst. gen. counsel La. Dept. Health, Baton Rouge, 1979-87; ptnr. Olds & Giglio, Baton Rouge, 1987-88, Kleinpeter, Schwatzberg & Stevens, Baton Rouge, 1988-93. Patentee in field. Mem. La. Bar Assn. Roman Catholic. Office: 2900 Westfork Dr Ste 200 Baton Rouge LA 70827-0004

GIGLIO, WILLIAM VITO, secondary education educator; b. Elizabeth, N.J., Oct. 23, 1946; s. Vito William and Ann (Tobac) G.; m. Carol Lynn Faulkner, July 4, 1970; children: W. Scott, Robert M. BSBA, Seton Hall U., 1968, MA in Secondary Bus. Edn., 1970; prins. and suprs. certs., Montclair State U., 1978. Bus. edn. tchr., coach Middlesex (N.J.) H.S., 1968-72, Mt. Olive H.S., Mt. Olive Township, 1972-74, Ridge H.S., Basking Ridge, N.J., 1974—; chmn. cmty. rels. com. Strategic Planning for Twp. Sch. Bd., Basking Ridge, 1996-97. Baseball coach Am. Legion, Somerset-Hunterdon County, 1991-96; mem. Bernards Twp. Youth Sports Coun.; coach Ctrl. Jersey Baseball League, 1997. Named Somerset County Baseball Coach of Yr., Newark Star-Ledger, 1995. Mem. NEA, N.J. State Interscholastic Atletic Assn., Baseball Coaches Assn., N.J. Edn. Assn., Somerset County Edn. Assn., Bernards Twp. Edn. Assn., Babe Ruth Baseball, Bernards Twp. Youth Sports Coun., N.J. Scholastic Coaches Assn. Roman Catholic. Home: 70 Harrison Brook Dr Basking Ridge NJ 07920-2415 Office: South Finley Ave Basking Ridge NJ 07920

GIGNAC, JAMES E., municipal fire chief, consultant; b. Detroit, Feb. 21, 1942; s. Wilfred Arthur and Lucille (Lamb) G.; m. Nancy Jean Fitzgerald, Jan. 22, 1970 (div. Sept. 1982); m. Margarete Elizabeth Reed, Nov. 2, 1985; children: Daniel Luis, Khrysten Leigh. AS, Madonna Coll., 1974, BS, 1978; M in Bus., U. Beverly Hills, 1982. Cert. constrn. insp., fire insp., safety profl. Ind. contractor Stuttgart, Germany, 1963; firefighter Twp. Plymouth, Mich., 1964-70, fire chief, 1970-78; fire svc. exec. State of Mich., Lansing, 1978-90; safety specialist USNG, Lansing, 1979-97; fire chief Village Pk. Forest, Ill., 1990-92; bldg. commnr. Village Glenwood, Ill., 1992-94; fire chief City Wis. Rapids, 1994—; owner Jim's Painting and Constrn., Plymouth, Mich., 1964-70; bd. dirs. Metro Detroit/Wayne County Emergency Med. Svcs., 1970-78, State Firefighters Meml., Wis. Rapids, 1994—; owner, cons. JAMAR Safety & Bldg. Insp., Wisconsin Rapids, 1990—. Author: Fire Service, 1989; co-author: Emergency Medical Services Wayne County, 1977. Pres. Enlisted Club, Camp Grayling, Mich., 1981-85, Wood County Fire Chiefs, Wis. Rapids, 1996—. Named Firefighter of Yr. VFW, Plymouth, 1971; recipient multiple commendation medals U.S. Army. Mem. Wis. State Fire Chiefs (tng. com. 1995—), North Ctrl. Fire Chiefs, Constrn. Insps., Internat. Assn. Fire Chiefs, Nat. Fire Protection Assn., Kiwanis Club, Optimists Club. Avocations: hunting, gardening, writing, fishing. Home: 900 2nd Ave S Wisconsin Rapids WI 54495-4124

GIGOT, PAUL ANTHONY, newspaper columnist; b. San Antonio, 1955. AB in Govt., Dartmouth Coll., 1977. Editl. asst. Nat. Rev., 1978-79; reporter, editor Far Ea. Econ. Rev., 1979-80; reporter Wall St. Jour., 1980-82, Asia corr., 1982-84, editor editl. page Asian edit., 1984-86; columnist Potomac Watch, mem. editl. bd. Wall St. Jour., N.Y.C., 1987—. mem. editl. bd., columnist Potomac Watch. White Ho. fellow, 1986-87. Office: Wall St Jour 1025 Connecticut Ave NW Ste 800 Washington DC 20036-5419

GIKAS, PAUL WILLIAM, medical educator; b. Lansing, Mich., July 23, 1928; s. John and Minnie (Neumann) G.; m. Lois Suzanne Haglund, Dec. 27, 1952; children—Sandra Jane, Sarah Elizabeth, Paula Suzanne. A.B., U. Mich., 1950, M.D., 1954. Diplomate: Am. Bd. Pathology. Chief lab. service VA Hosp., Ann Arbor, Mich., 1960-68; mem. faculty U. Mich. Med. Sch., Ann Arbor, 1959—; assoc. prof. pathology U. Mich. Med. Sch., 1966-69, prof., 1969-95, prof. emeritus, 1995—, faculty rep. to Big Ten Intercollegiate Conf., Nat. Collegiate Athletic Assn., 1982-88, asst. dean for admissions, 1990-97; cons. Armed Forces Inst. Pathology, 1966-74. Author: The Accident Problem, 1976, Uropathology, 1976, Forensic Aspects of the Highway Crash, 1983; co-editor: The Prevention of Highway Injury, 1967. Mem. adv. com. traffic safety HEW, 1966-68; mem. Gov. Mich. Spl. Commn. Traffic Safety Mich., 1964; chmn. bd. dirs. Pub. Citizen, Inc., 1971—; co-trustee Center Study Responsive Law, Washington, 1969-71. Served to capt. M.C. AUS, 1956-58. Recipient Auto Safety award Med. Tribune, 1966-67, Distinguished Service award U. Mich., 1965, Disting. Svc. award U. Mich. Med. Ctr. Alumni Soc., 1998. Fellow Coll. Am. Pathologists, U.S. and Can. Acad. Pathology, Alpha Omega Alpha, Nu Sigma Nu. Lutheran. Rsch. with preservation of blood for transfusion by freezing and rsch. in pathogenesis of injury in highway crashes. Home: 1900 Mershon Dr Ann Arbor MI 48103-5939

GIL, GUILLERMO, prosecutor. U.S. atty. Dept. Justice, Hato Rey, P.R., 1993—. Office: US Attys Office Fed Bldg Rm 452 Carlos E Chardon Ave Hato Rey San Juan PR 00918*

GILB, CORINNE LATHROP, history educator; b. Lethbridge, Alta., Can., Feb. 19, 1925; d. Glen Hutchison and Vera (Passey) Lathrop; m. Tyrell Thompson Gilb, Aug. 19, 1945; children: Lesley Gilb Taplin, Tyra. BA, U. Wash., 1946; MA, U. Calif., Berkeley, 1951, law student, 1950-53; PhD, Harvard U., 1957. History lectr. Mills Coll., Oakland, 1957-61; prof. humanities San Francisco State U., 1964-68; rsch. assoc. U. Calif., Berkeley, 1953-68; prof. history Wayne State U., Detroit, 1968-94, co-dir. Liberal Arts Urban Studies program, 1976-86; dir. planning City of Detroit, 1979-85; pres. Atherton Press, 1997—; spl. cons. Calif. Legislature, 1963, 64; vis. scholar Hoover Instn., Stanford U., fall 1993; UN Nongovtl. Orgn. rep. Internat. Orgn. for Unification of Terminological Neologisms, 1995—. Author: Conformity of State to Federal Income Tax, 1964, Hidden Hierarchies, 1966, numerous chpts. in books; vol. writer Silicon Valley Global Trading Ctr., 1995-96, Silicon Valley Def./Space Consortium, 1996-97; contbr. articles to profl. jours. Guggenheim fellow, 1957; grantee Social Sci. Rsch. Coun. Mem. Internat. Soc. Comparative Study of Civilizations (five terms exec. coun., 1st v.p. 1995-98), No. Calif. World Affairs Coun., various acad. assns. Presbyterian.

GILBANE, JEAN ANN (MRS. THOMAS F. GILBANE), construction company executive; b. Providence, Aug. 22, 1923; d. Vincent Thaddeus and Edna (Leary) Murphy; m. Thomas F. Gilbane, Sept. 12, 1946; children: Thomas, Robert, Richard, Jean, John, James. Student, Elmhurst Acad., 1941, Coll. New Rochelle, 1945. Sec. Gilbane Bldg. Co., Providence, 1950-81, treas., 1982—; mem. bd. B.T. Equipment Co. Active Women's R.I. Hosp. Guild; mem. corp. Emma Bradley Hosp., Butler Hosp.; former trustee Coll. New Rochelle; bd. dirs. Women's Resource Ctr. South County; bd. dirs. So. County Hosp. Decorated Lady Holy Sepulcher. Roman Catholic. Clubs: Dunes, Point Judith Country (bd. govs. 1985-88); Beach (Palm Beach); University, Wannamoisett. Home: 80 Don Ave Rumford RI 02916-2305 Office: Gilbane Bldg Co 7 Jackson Walkway Providence RI 02903-3694 also: 400 S Ocean Blvd Apt 402 N Palm Beach FL 33480-4469*

GILBANE, WILLIAM JAMES, construction executive; b. Providence, June 16, 1947; s. William James and Catherine Louise (Midgely) G.; m. Nancy Ann Brennan, Apr. 16, 1975; chidlren: William James III, Brennan Patricia, Catherine Louise, Matthew Reynolds, Ted Albert. BA, Brown U., 1970. Pres. BT Equipment Co., Providence, 1970-95; v.p. Gilbane Bldg. Co., Providence, 1995—, also bd. dirs. Mem. R.I. Country Club, Point Judith Country Club, Barrington Yacht Club. Roman Catholic. Fax: (401) 456-5454. E-mail: wgilbane@gilbaneco.com. Home: 140 Adams Point Rd Barrington RI 02806-5045 Office: Gilbane Bldg Co 7 Jackson Walkway Providence RI 02903-3694

GILBERG, KENNETH ROY, lawyer; b. Phila., Feb. 2, 1951; s. Leonard David and Roslyn (Tennis) G.; m. Nanci Jane Schwartz, Sept. 7, 1974. BA, Lebanon Valley Coll., 1973; JD, Widener U., 1976. Bar: Pa. 1976. Assoc. Pechner, Dorfman et. al., Phila., 1976-84, ptnr., 1984-87; ptnr. Myerson & Kuhn, Phila., 1988-89; prin. Kenneth R. Gilberg and Assocs., Bala Cynwyd, Pa., 1989-90; ptnr. Mesirov Gelman Jaffe Cramer & Jamieson LLP, Phila., 1990—. Contbr. articles to profl. jours. Past pres. Golden Slipper Camp. Recipient Meritorious Achievement award Pa. Sports Hall of Fame, 1974; named Most Valuable Player Mid-Atlantic Conf., 1973. Mem. Phi Alpha Delta (charter). Republican. Avocations: lacrosse, racquetball, photography, golf, tennis. Office: Mesirov Gelman Jaffe Cramer & Jamieson 1735 Market St Ste 3901 Philadelphia PA 19103-7598

GILBERG, MARGOT D., secondary school Spanish educator. Tchr. Spanish St. Catherine Acad., Bronx, N.Y.; chair dept. fgn. langs. St. Catherine Acad., Bronx. Mem. Am. Coun. Tchrs. of Fgn. Langs., Am. Assn. Tchrs. Spanish and Portugese, N.Y. State Assn. Tchrs. Fgn. Langs.

GILBERT, ALLAN ARTHUR, manufacturing executive; b. Chgo., Jan. 7, 1925; s. Allan T. and Elizabeth (Boyce) G.; m. Gwendolyn M. Moore, June 24, 1950; children: Debora D. and Elizabeth (twins), Allan M. Buyer Carson Pirie Scott & Co., Chgo., 1949-55; v.p. George Fry & Assocs., Chgo., 1956-65; v.p. mktg. Chamberlain Mfg. Corp., Elmhurst, Ill., 1966-68; v.p. Lester B. Knight & Assocs., Chgo., 1968-75; v.p. manpower devel. Emerson Electric Co., St. Louis, 1975-90, cons., 1990—; asst. prof. Roosevelt U., 1951-52. Mem. Gov.'s Adv. Council, Ill., 1969-70; fund raiser Ill. Republicans., 1966-67. Lt. (j.g.) USNR, 1944-46. Mem. Soc. Colonial Wars (dep. gov. Mo.), Glen View Club, Old Warson Club, Univ. Club, Princeton Club, Harvard Bus. Club. Office: Emerson Electric Co PO Box 4100 Saint Louis MO 63136-8506

GILBERT, ARMIDA JENNINGS, American literature educator; b. Sumter, S.C., July 10, 1953; d. Joseph Gatliff and Katherine Armida (Jennings) G. BS, U. S.C., 1976, MA, 1986, PhD, 1989. Vis. asst. prof. U. S.C., Columbia, 1989-90; asst. prof. Kent (Ohio) State U., 1990-97, Auburn (Ala.) U., 1998—. Asst. editor Bibliography of U.S. Literature, 1989, Contemporary Authors, 1986-87; editl. asst. Studies in the American Renaissance, 1985-89; contbr. articles to profl. jours. Advisor U. S.C. Alliance for Peace, 1988-90; interviewee for film women's studies U. S.C., 1989; reader Kent State U. Press, Longman Press, Prose Studies, others. Travel to Collections grant Nat. Endowment for the Humanities, 1992. Mem. MLA, Ralph Waldo Emerson Soc. (adv. bd. 1996—, founding mem.), Philolog. Assn. of the Carolinas (organizer spl. sessions 1991-95), Sigma Tau Delta (advisor 1993-94). Office: Dept English Auburn Univ Auburn AL 36849-5203

GILBERT, ARTHUR CHARLES, aerospace engineer, consulting engineer; b. N.Y.C., Sept. 23, 1926; s. Phillip Saul and Annie Gilbert; children: Pamela Stephanie Gilbert Remis, Randi Ilene Gilbert Cutler. B Aero. Engring., NYU, 1946, M Aero. Engring., 1947, ScD in Engring., 1956. Registered profl. engr., N.Y., Mich., D.C. Rsch. engr., sr. exec. aerospace manufacturer various orgns., 1947-67; v.p., mng. ptnr. Systems Technology Lab., Inc., 1968-70; mem. sci. staff divsn. sci. and tech. CIA, 1968-70; founder, bd. dirs. Auto-Train Corp., 1969-79; chief scientist Chief Naval Ops. Exec. Panel, 1970-75; v.p., dir. engring. R & D Data Solutions Corp., 1975-77; v.p. Unified Industries, 1977-78; with OAO Corp., 1978-81; pres. Arthur C. Gilbert, SCD, PE, Boston, 1981—; consulting engr. in field; USN-asst. sec. Nav R&D, Washington, 1987-88; vis. pro. Mem. Spitfire Soc. U.K., Cosmos Club Washington. Achievements include 2 patents for high speed machinery, helicopter propulsion systems; contributing to numerous articles and books on structures, acoustics, vibration and photo-elasticity. Home and Office: Arthur C Gilbert SCD PE 330 Beacon St Apt B23 Boston MA 02116-1106

GILBERT, BEN WILLIAM, retired newspaper editor; b. N.Y.C., Feb. 10, 1918; s. Harry and Tessie (Wertheimer) Goldberg; m. Maurine Coffee, Mar. 11, 1941 (dec.); children: Ian R. Gilbert, Amy G. Mann. B of Social Sci., CCNY, 1937; MA in Journalism, U. Mo., 1939. Reporter St. Louis (Mo.) Star Times, 1940-41; reporter Washington Post, Washington, 1941-45, city editor, day mng. editor, assoc. editor, 1945-70; on-air editor newsroom Sta.

WETA-TV, Washington, 1970-71; gen. asst. to mayor Washington City Govt., 1972, planning dir., 1972-78; cons. various orgns., Washington, 1979-84; mem. Nat. Capital Planning Commn., Washington, 1973-78. Author, editor: Ten Blocks From White House, 1968, Lifting the Veil From the 'Secret City': The Washington Post and the Racial Revolution, 1993. Mem. ethics com. Group Health Wash., Tacoma, 1985—, Landmarks Presdl. Commn., 1985—, chair, 1986-91; bd. dirs. Pennsylvania Ave. Devel. Corp., Washington, 1974-78; steering com. Tacoma Cultural Plan, 1992-93; mem. Pub. Art working Group, Tacoma, 1993—; mem. adv. group on comprehensive plans Pierce County Citizens, 1993-94; mem. Group Health Med. Ctr. Coun., Tacom, 1985-86, 99—. Recipient TV Emmy award D.C. TV Assn., 1970, State Historic Preservation award Wash. State Office Hist. Preservation, 1995, Disting. Citizen award Tacoma Mcpl. League, 1995. Mem. Am. Inst. Cert. Planners, City Club Tacoma (vol. editor newsletter, rsch. reports, bd. dirs.), City Club Tacoma (bd. dirs. 1986—), Phi Beta Kappa, Kappa Tau Alpha. Democrat. Avocations: photography, public affairs, reading, writing. Fax: 253-272-2416. E-mail: bengilbert@worldnet.att.net. Home and Office: 421 N 6th St Tacoma WA 98403-3211

GILBERT, BLAINE LOUIS, lawyer; b. Phila., Aug. 26, 1940; s. Arthur I. and Marcia R. (Kaufman) G.; m. Sondra Gilbert; children: Beth M., Kimberly J. AA, Balt. Jr. Coll., 1961; postgrad., Am. U., 1962; JD, U. Balt., 1965. Bar: Md. 1966, U.S. Dist. Ct. Md. 1968, U.S. Supreme Ct. 1974. Exec. asst. ins. commr. State of Md., Balt., 1965-66; assoc. Polovoy & Polovoy, Balt., 1966-72; ptnr. Angeletti & Gilbert, Balt., 1972-79, Gilbert & Levin, Balt., 1979-92, Blaine L. Gilbert and Assocs. P.A., Balt., 1993—. Mem. ABA, Balt. Bar Assn., Am. Immigration Lawyers Assn., Am. Judicature Soc., Md. Trial Lawyers Assn. Avocations: music, screenwriting. Home: 2B Dorsett Hills Ct Owings Mills MD 21117-1131 Office: Blaine L Gilbert & Assocs PA Lower Level 200 E Lexington St Baltimore MD 21202-3530

GILBERT, BRADLEY, professional tennis coach, former professional tennis player, former Olympic athlete; b. Oakland, Calif., Aug. 9, 1961; m. Kim Gilbert; 2 children: Zachary, Julian Elizabeth. Student, Foothills Jr. Coll., Pepperdine. Ranked 9th in U.S. Tennis Assn., 1993; coach Andre Agassi, 1994—; played in over 35 USTA tour events. Recipient Bronze medal Olympics, Seoul, 1988. Winner 20 profl. singles titles. Office: USTA 70 W Red Oak Ln White Plains NY 10604-3602*

GILBERT, CHARLES RICHARD ALSOP, physician, medical educator; b. Phila., May 26, 1916; s. Chauncey McLean and Frances Marguerite (Young) G.; m. Helene Scher, Dec. 24, 1973; children: Anita Ivonne, Charles Richard Alsop Jr. M.D., U. Va., 1944. Bar: Am. Bd. Abdominal Surgeons; diplomate: Am. Bd. Obstetrics and Gynecology. Rotating intern N.Y.C. Hosp., 1944-45, asst. resident in internal medicine, 1945-46; resident in surgery Nix Hosp., San Antonio, 1946; resident in gen. surgery, chief female abdominal surgery Ryder Meml. Hosp., Hunacao, P.R., 1952-55; house staff gynecology Johns Hopkins Hosp., Balt., 1948-49; asst. resident in obstetrics U. Md., 1949, chief resident in obstetrics, 1949-50, asst. resident in gynecology, 1950-51, chief resident in gynecology, 1951-52, assoc. in gynecology, instr. gynecol. pathology, 1952; asst. clin. prof. obstetrics and gynecology U. P.R., 1952-55; asst. clin. prof. obstetrics and gynecology George Washington U., 1972-74, assoc. clin. prof. obstetrics and gynecology, 1974-93; clin. prof. ob/gyn. George Washington U., Washington, 1994—; chief gynecology Doctors Hosp., 1973—; sr. attending in obstetrics and gynecology Washington Hosp. Center; instr. internal medicine Randolph Sch. Aviation, San Antonio, 1946; cons. U.S. Air Force in obstetrics, gynecology, female urology, 1952-54. Author: Childbirth-The Modern Guide to Expectant Mothers, 1960, Better Health for Women, 1964, Abdominal Pelvic Surgery, 1969; co-editor, editor: Symposiumon Abdominal Pelvic Surgery, 1966; contbr. articles to profl. jours.; Mem. editorial staff: Jour. Abdominal Surgery, 1964-74. Served with M.C. USAF, as chief internal medicine, 1946-48, Selfridge AFB, Mt. Clemens, Mich. Fellow ACS (founding fellow), Am. Coll. Obstetrics and Gynecology, Am. Soc. Abdominal Surgeons (teaching faculty 1964-74, mem. exec. com. 1964-74, v.p. 1969-70, pres. 1971-72), Internat. Coll. Surgeons (U.S. sect., regent, exec. com. 1981—, chmn. bd. regents 1983-84, sec. 1982-83, membership chmn. 1983, 2d pres.-elect 1985, pres.-elect 1986, pres. 1987-88, coordinator diplomatic relations 1985—, spl. advisor to pres. 1989-90, mem. internat. bd. govs. 1990, sec. N.Am. fedn. 1991-92, Regent of Yr. award 1981, emeritus 1992, bd. trustees 1993, 96-98, hon. fellow 1995); mem. Pan Am. Med. Assn., Med. Soc. D.C., AMA, Med. and Surgery Soc. Johns Hopkins Hosp., Douglass Obstet. and Gynecol. Soc., Nat. Rifle Assn., African Safari Club Washington (v.p. 1974-77, pres. 1977), Am. Outdoors Council (dir.), Hunting Hall of Fame Found. (dir. 1978), Jefferson Soc. Club: Boone and Crockett. Club: Boone and Crockett. Developer first audiovisual med. corr. teaching courses for continuing med. edn., 1973. Home: 705 E Franklin Ave Silver Spring MD 20901-4707 Office: 2025 I St NW Washington DC 20006-1902

GILBERT, CREIGHTON EDDY, art historian; b. Durham, N.C., June 6, 1924; s. Allan H. and Katharine (Everett) G. BA, NYU, 1942, PhD, 1955; DHL (hon.), Adelphi U., 1990, U. Louisville, 1997. Assoc. prof. Brandeis U., 1961-65, Sidney and Ellen Wien prof. history of art, 1965-69; prof. Queens Coll. City U. N.Y., 1969-77; Jacob Gould Schurman prof. art history Cornell U., 1977-81; prof. Yale U., 1981—; Fulbright sr. lectr. U. Rome, 1951-52; fellow Netherlands Inst. for Advanced Study, 1972-73; vis. prof. U. Leiden, 1974-75; Zacks Found. vis. prof. Hebrew U. Jerusalem, 1985. Author: Change in Piero della Francesca, 1968, History of Renaissance Art, 1972, The Works of Girolamo Savoldo, 1986, Poets Seeing Artists' Work: Instances from the Italian Renaissance, 1991, Michelangelo On and Off the Sistine Ceiling, 1994, Piero della Francesca et Giorgione: Problèmes d'Interpretation, 1994, Caravaggio and His Two Cardinals, 1995; editor: Italian Art 1400-1500, Sources and Documents, 1979, enlarged Italian edit., 1988; editor-in-chief: The Art Bull, 1980-85; series editor: Renaissance Art Texts, 1995—; translator: Complete Poems and Selected Letters of Michelangelo, 1963, 3d edit., 1979. Recipient Mather award Coll. Art Assn., 1964. Fellow Am. Acad. Arts and Scis., Ateneo Veneto (fgn.). Office: Yale U Dept Art History 56 High St New Haven CT 06510-2306*

GILBERT, DANIEL LEE, physiologist; b. Bklyn., July 2, 1925; s. Louis and Blanche (Lutz) G.; m. Claire Gilbert, July 26, 1964; 1 child, Raymond Louis. A.B., Drew U., 1948; M.S., State U. Iowa, 1950; Ph.D., U. Rochester, 1955. Instr. U. Rochester, 1955-56; instr. Albany Med. Coll., 1956-59, asst. prof. physiology, 1959-60; asst. prof. Jefferson Med. Coll., 1960-62, assoc. prof., 1962-63; research physiologist Nat. Inst. Neurol. Disorders and Stroke, NIH, Bethesda, Md., 1962—; head sect. cellular biophysics Nat. Inst. Neurol. and Communicative Diseases and Stroke, NIH, 1963-71, head, unit on reactive oxygen species, biophysics sect., clin. neurosci. br., 1992-94, head. unit on reactive oxygen species, biophysics sect., basic neurosci. program, 1994-97, head unit on reactive oxygen species basic neurosci. program, 1997—; Rebeca Gerschman lectr. Internat. Cell Rsch. Orgn.-UNESCO internat. symposium, Buenos Aires, 1994; Bowditch lectr. Am. Physiol. Soc., 1964, pres. history group, 1995-98; cons. George Washington U., 1965-70, Inst. Venezolane de Investigaciones Cientificas, Caracas, Venezuela, 1969; organizer profl. symposia. Contbr. articles to profl. publs.; editor: Oxygen and Living Processes, 1981; co-editor: Squid as Experimental Animals, 1990, Neurobiology of Nitric Oxide and .Hydroxyl Radicals, 1994, Reactive Oxygen Species in Biological Systems, 1999. Served with U.S. Army, 1943-45. Decorated Purple Heart. Fellow AAAS, Oxygen Soc. (councilor 1987-89, Lifetime Achievement award 1998); mem. Am. Chem. Soc., Am. Physiol. Soc., Am. Soc. Pharm. and Exptl. Therapeutics, Biophys. Soc., Corp. Marine Biol. Lab., Internat. Soc. Study Origin of Life, Soc. Exptl. Biology and Medicine, Soc. Neurosci., Soc. Gen. Physiology, Washington Soc. for History of Medicine (v.p. 1988-89, pres. 1989-90), Oxygen Club Greater Washington (pres. 1987-88, sec. 1998—, Spl. award 1995, honoree Reactive Oxygen Species Symposium 1998), Sigma Xi (pres. Jefferson Med. Coll. Club 1961-62). Home: 10324 Dickens Ave Bethesda MD 20814-2137 Office: BNP Nat Inst Neurol Disorders and Strokes NIH Bldg 36 Rm 5A-25 Bethesda MD 20892-4156

GILBERT, DAVID ERWIN, retired academic administrator, physicist; b. Fresno, Calif., June 23, 1939; s. Erwin Azel and Hester (Almond) G.; m. Carolyn Faye Parker, June 24, 1960; children: Ronald David, Joan Elaine. AB, U. Calif.-Berkeley, 1962; MA, U. Oreg., 1964, PhD, 1968. Prof. physics Eastern Oreg. U., La Grande, 1968-98, dean. acad. affairs, 1977-83, pres., 1983-98; pres. emeritus; vis. rschr. Obs. Paris, 1975-82; commr. N.W. Assn. Schs. and Colls., 1982-88. Contbr. articles on physics to profl. jours. V.p. Ea. Oreg. Regional Arts Coun., 1979-80; vice chair, bd. dirs. Oreg. Ed-Net, 1989-97, Oreg. Pub. Broadcasting Found., 1991-93; mem. Oreg. Task Force Superconducting Super Collider, 1987, Oreg. Pub. Broadcasting Commn., 1991—, Oreg. Bd. Forestry, 1991—, chair, 1996—; mem. Gov.'s Transition Team, 1990, Oreg. visibility adv. com. Dept. Environ. Quality, 1990-91; bd. dirs. Blue Mountains Natural Resources Inst., 1990-98, N.E. Oreg. Area Health Edn. Ctr., Gov.'s Telecomms. Forum Coun., 1996-97. Grantee NATO; grantee Research Corp. U.S.A., U.S. Govt., pvt. founds. Mem. Am. Assn. Colls. and Univs. (bd. dirs. 1995-97, chmn. com. econ. and cmty. devel. 1990-92), Am. Assn. Physics Tchrs. (pres. Oreg. chpt. 1973-74), Pacific N.W. Assn. Coll. Physics (bd. dirs. 1970-74), Sigma Xi, Sigma Pi Sigma, Phi Kappa Phi. Democrat. Home: PO Box 36 Joseph OR 97846-0036

GILBERT, DEBBIE ROSE, entrepreneur; b. Indpls., Jan. 18, 1961; d. James Taylor and Rosemary (Robinson) G. BA, Ind. U., 1984; diploma in computer literacy, St. Augustine Coll., Chgo., 1995. Stud. typing asst. Shortridge High School/Indpls. Pub. Schs., 1978-79; substitute tchr. Indpls. Pub. Schs., 1985-89, Washington Twp. Schs., Indpls., 1992; CHA housewatcher, clothes distbr. The Inner Voice, Inc., Chgo., 1994-95; vol. Lakefront Single Room Occupancy Employment Program, Chgo., 1997—. mem. registrar O.N.E./Bd. Election Commrs., Chgo., 1996—; mem. People for the Am. Way, Chgo., 1995-96; mem. Access Living, Chgo., 1996—, bd. mem. Sch. Commissioners, 1985-89, mem. Southern Poverty Law Ctr., Tchg. Tolerance, Militia Task Force, Klanwatch Org., Montgomery, 1998—. Mem. ACLU, NOW, AAUW, NAACP, The Natl. Mus. of Women in the Arts Org., OWL (The Older Women's League), The Voice of Midlife & Older Women, Wash. D.C., Mental Health Consumer Edn. Consortium, Inc. Democrat. Baptist. Avocations: modeling, singing, race walking, bingo, reading. Home: 5012 N Winthrop Ave Apt 224 Chicago IL 60640-3124 Office: Ste 632/808 4753 N Broadway St Chicago IL 60640-4992

GILBERT, DONALD ROY, lawyer; b. Phila., June 6, 1946. BA, Stanford U., 1968; JD, U. Calif., 1971. Bar: Calif. 1972, Ariz. 1972. Ptnr., dir. Fennemore Craig, Phoenix, 1972—. Mem. ABA, State Bar Ariz., State Bar Calif., Maricopa County Bar Assn. Office: Fennemore Craig 3003 N Central Ste 2600 Phoenix AZ 85012-2913

GILBERT, EDITH HARMON, medical, surgical and occupational health nurse; b. Fla., May 4, 1917; d. Edwin and Blanche Pansy (Howe) Harmon; m. Chas. J. Gilbert, July 27, 1952; 1 child, Karen LaReau Hale. Diploma, S.I. Hosp. Sch. Nursing, 1940; student, Wagner Coll., S.I., 1940. Head nurse Charter Internat. Oil, Houston, A.O. Smith Pipe Mill, Houston, Reed Roller Bit Co., Houston; ret., 1981. Mem. ANA, Tex. Nursing Assn., Occupl. Health Nurses, Occupl. Nurses Assn. Home: 905 Phyllis Ln Groesbeck TX 76642-2021

GILBERT, ELMER GRANT, aerospace engineering educator, control theorist; b. Joliet, Ill., Mar. 29, 1930; s. Harry A. and Florence A. (Otterstrom) G.; m. Lois M. Verbrugge, Dec. 27, 1973. BSEE, U. Mich., 1952, MSEE, 1953, PhD in Instrumentation Engring., 1956. Instr. U. Mich., Ann Arbor, 1954-56, asst. prof., 1957-59, assoc. prof., 1959-63, prof. aerospace engring., 1963—; founder, dir., cons. Applied Dynamics Inc., Ann Arbor, 1957-69. Patentee computer devices, 1968-74. Fellow IEEE (Control Engring. Field award 1994), AAAS; mem. Nat. Acad. Engring., Soc. Indsl. and Applied Math. Office: U Mich Dept Aerospace Engring Ann Arbor MI 48109-2140

GILBERT, FRED D., JR., college official; m. Cynthia Gilbert; children: Fred, Christina. BA, Dillard U., 1970; MA, Loyola U., New Orleans, 1972; PhD, Iowa State U., 1978. V.p. cmty. outreach Des Moines Area C.C., Ankeny, Iowa, 1997—; adminstrv. asst. Loyola U., New Orleans, 1971-73; exec. asst. spl. svcs. Xavier U., New Orleans, 1973-75; rsch. asst. Coll. Edn., Iowa State U., Ames, 1975-76, asst. dir. rsch. inst. for studies in edn., 1977-86, asst. dean Col. of Edn., 1984-86; exec. dean Urban Campus, Des Moines Area C.C., Ankeny, Iowa, 1987-90, v.p. R&D fed. affairs, affirmative action officer, 1990-97; bd. dirs. Nat. Coun. R & D, Washington, Children and Families of Iowa, Des Moines, Iowa Comprehensive Manpower Svcs., Des Moines, Family Enrichment Ctr., Des Moines. V.P. Comm. Outreach, 1997—. Office: Des Moines Area Cmty Col 2006 S Ankeny Blvd Ankeny IA 50021-8995

GILBERT, FREDERICK E., development planner, Africanist, consultant; b. Mpls., May 28, 1939; s. Eugene Lester and Anne Cecelia (Omlie) G.; m. Jane Arey, June 30, 1962; children: Erik O., Christopher A., Peter A. BA, U. Minn., 1961; MALD, Tufts U., 1963, PhD, 1976. Desk officer for Niger, Upper Volta, Cote d'Ivoire, Dahomey and Togo U.S. AID, Washington, 1974-76; asst. dir. U.S. AID, Yaounde, Cameroon, 1976-80; chief Africa econ. policy and analysis U.S. AID, Washington, 1980-81, dir. Sahel and West Africa, 1981-83; prin. officer U.S. AID, Dar es Salaam, Tanzania, 1983-86; dep. mission dir. U.S. AID, Khartoum, Sudan, 1986-88; mission dir. U.S. AID, Khartoum, 1988-90; regional dir. U.S. AID, Abidjan, Cote d'Ivoire, 1990-93; ind. cons. Falls Church, Va., 1994-97; dir. Famine Early Warning Sys., 1998—. Mem. ACLU, Am. Fgn. Svc. Assn., Amnesty Internat., Sierra Club, World Resources Inst. (policy consultative group on natural resources mgmt.). Episcopalian. Avocations: skiing, tennis.

GILBERT, GLEN STUART, marketing executive; b. Hewlett, N.Y., Nov. 13, 1952; s. Marvin Marshal Gilbert and Elaine Roberta Caplan; m. Wendy Seiden, July 3, 1980 (div. Sept. 1985); 1 child, Rebecca; m. Beth Wolchock, Apr. 24, 1994; 1 child, Samantha. BA, Hamilton Coll., 1974. Acct. exec. Young & Rubicam, N.Y.C., 1974-80; dir. advt. Am. Express, N.Y.C., 1980-85; sr. v.p., acct. dir. BBDO, N.Y.C., 1985-96; v.p. advt. and social responsibility GTE, Irving, Tex., 1996—. Office: GTE PO Box 152257 Irving TX 75015-2257*

GILBERT, GLENN GORDON, linguistics educator; b. Montgomery, Ala., Sept. 17, 1936; s. William H. and Margaret (Christensen) G.; m. Erika Wrede, Aug. 8, 1964 (div. Nov. 1993); children: Alexander Martin, Christa Selene; m. Sharon Wright Pape, July 23, 1994. AB in German Lang. and Lit., U. Chgo., 1957; postgrad., U. Frankfurt, Fed. Republic Germany, 1957-59; Diplôme de la Langue Française with honors, Sorbonne, U. Paris, 1960; PhD in Linguistics, Harvard U., 1963. Instr. Germanic langs. and lits. U. Tex., Austin, 1963-66, asst. prof. Germanic langs., 1967-70; vis. asst. prof. linguistics Can. Summer Sch. Linguistics, U. Alta., Edmonton, summer 1966; Fulbright lectr. linguistics U. Marburg, Fed. Republic Germany, 1966-67; assoc. prof. So. Ill. U., Carbondale, 1970-74, prof., 1975—, chmn. dept. linguistics, 1987-89, 99—; Fulbright lectr. linguistics U. Mainz, Fed. Republic Germany, 1973-74; Z.W.O. research fellow in creole langs. U. Nijmegen, The Netherlands, 1984-85; active numerous univ. linguistics coms. and councils; bd. dirs., mem. editorial bd., Ill. bus. rep. Papers in Linguistics, 1979-87; pres. Linguistic Research Inc., 1983-87. Founder, editor Journal of Pidgin and Creole Languages, 1985—; author: Linguistic Atlas of Texas German, 1972; editor: (books) Texas Studies in Bilingualism, 1970, The German Language in America, 1971, Pidgin and Creole Languages: Essays in Memory of John E. Reinecke, 1987; co-editor (with Jacob Ornstein) Problems in Applied Educational Sociolinguistics, 1978; editor and translator: Pidgin and Creole Languages: Selected Essays by Hugo Schuchardt, 1980; editor: (book series) Studies in Ethnolinguistics, 1993—; contbr. numerous articles to profl. jours. and chpts. to books in field; also reviews. Translator, interpreter various community orgns. NDEA fellow in Swedish, Harvard U., 1961-63; research grantee U. Tex.-Austin, 1963-70, Nat. Carl Schurz Meml. Fund, 1968, So. Ill. U.-Carbondale, 1970-84, NEH, 1981, Am. Philos. Soc., 1982; numerous invited lectures. Mem. Soc. Caribbean Linguistics, Soc. for Pidgin and Creole Linguistics. Home: 166 Union Grove Rd Carbondale IL 62901-7687 Office: So Ill U Dept Linguistics Carbondale IL 62901

GILBERT, HAMLIN MILLER, JR., publishing executive; b. Bridgport, Conn., Mar. 12, 1940; s. Hamlin Miller and Charlotte E. (Munn) G.; m. Emmy Lou Chatterton, July 20, 1963; children: Bradley, Kim. BA, Cornell U., 1962. Fin. analyst Chem. Bank, N.Y.C., 1963-64; sales rep. Continental Can Co., Teterboro, N.J., 1964-65, Time, Inc., N.Y.C., 1965-70; package goods mgr. Time Mag., 1970-75, travel advt. mgr., 1975-80, divsn. mgr., 1980-83, assoc. N.Y. dir., 1983-85, U.S. dir. spl. sect., 1985-92; N.Y. advt. sales dir. Smithsonian Mag., N.Y.C., 1992-95, dir. bus. devel., 1995-97, mktg. exec. web site, advt. svcs. dir., 1997—. Editor spl. advt. sect., Time-Am. Cup, 1987, Time-Winter Olympic Preview, 1987. V.p. comm. New Canaan H.S. Sports Council, Conn., 1987-89; instr. U.S. Power Squadron, Darien, Conn., 1986—. Mem. Travel Rsch. Assn. (dir. 1979-81), Cornell U. Alumni Assn. (area dir. 1980-95), Woodway Country Club (bd. dirs. 1980-86), Austin Healey Club Am. Republican. Episcopalian. Avocations: sailing, skiing, golf, tennis, gardening, scuba diving (cert.). Home: 133 Buttery Rd New Canaan CT 06840-5205 Office: Smithsonian Mag 420 Lexington Ave New York NY 10170-0002

GILBERT, HAROLD STANLEY, warehousing company executive; b. Ft. Worth, Jan. 22, 1924; s. Sydney Ralph and Reba Samuels (Lever) G.; m. Jeanne Schwarz, Apr. 6, 1950; children: Marsha Gilbert Kirstein, Mark S. (dec. 1994), John L. BA, U. Tex., 1947, MEd., 1949; grad., Air Command and Staff Coll., 1961, Air War Coll., 1970, Indsl. Coll. Armed Forces, 1970. Sci. tchr., coach Houston Ind. Schs., 1949-51; asst. prin., head sci. dept., athletic dir., coach USAF Dependents Sch. System, Germany, 1953-55; v.p. Coastal Bag & Bagging Corp., Houston, 1968-71; exec. v.p., gen. mgr. Coastal Storehouse, Inc., Houston, 1968-88; chmn., CEO Gilbert & Sons Warehouse and Distbn., Houston, 1988—; mem. def. strategy seminar Nat. War Coll., 1973. Parade marshal Bicentennial Armed Forces Week Parade, Houston, 1976; dir. gen. Armed Forces Week, 1977; bd. dirs. Houston Coun. USO, 1977-82, v.p., 1981; mem. St. Luke's Episcopal. Hosp. Aux., 1999; docent Houston Zool. Gardens, 1999. With AUS, 1943-45; USAF, 1951-53; col. USAF ret. Decorated Legion of Merit, Bronze Star, Meritorious Svc. medal, Purple Heart with oak leaf cluster, combat infantry badge; recipient USAFR Disting. Ednl. Achievement award, 1975. Mem. Tex. Warehouse Assn. (charter), Houston Warehouse and Transfer Assn. (pres. 1980, 89-90), Air Force Assn. (life, v.p. chpt. 1977-78, pres. 1978-79, Tex. conv. chmn. 1976), Res. Officers Assn. (life, pres. Eric Ellington chpt. 1974-75, chmn. rules com. 1975, mem. Tex. mil. affairs com. 1975-78), Air War Coll. Alumni Assn. (life), Nat. Fedn. Temple Brotherhoods (dir.), Jewish Chautauqua Soc. (chmn. S.W. region 1964-70), Houston C. of C. (mil. affairs com. 1969—, vice-chmn. Air Force subcom. 1978-79), T Assn. U. Tex., Houston Tex. Ex-Students Assn. (dir. 1991—), Mil. Order World Wars, Nat. Hist. Soc., Houston Livestock Show and Rodeo Assn. (life), Elks (life), Rotary (pres. activities Houston and Harris County clubs 1969-70, club sec. 1981-87, pres. University Area 1999, Paul Harris fellow 1985), Phi Delta Kappa, Sigma Alpha Mu. Home: 476 N Post Oak Ln Houston TX 77024-5911 Office: PO Box 3207 Houston TX 77253-3207

GILBERT, HARRY EPHRAIM, JR., hotel executive; b. Phila., Feb. 1, 1931; s. Harry Ephraim and Anna (Chilton) G.; children: Ronald C., Glen G.; m. Jacqueline J. Newton. BS in Hotel Adminstrn., Pa. State U., 1954. Resident mgr. Benjamin Franklin Hotel, Phila., 1954-71; gen. mgr. Benjamin Franklin Hotel, 1971-77, Cherry Hill Inns, N.J., 1977-78, Holiday Inn-City Line, Phila., 1978-80, Colony Inn, New Haven, 1980-81; sr. oper. analyst, gen. mgr. Aramark Corp., Phila., 1981—; lectr. Hotel Sch., Pa. State U., 1956-58, Drexel U., Phila., 1962-63. Bd. dirs. Saratoga Council Boy Scouts Am., 1983-86; bd. dirs. Saratoga Conv. and Tourism Bur., 1985—; mem. ch. council Luth. Ch., Saratoga Springs. Mem. N.Y. Hotel/Motel Assn., Phila. Hotel and Motor Inn Assn. (sec. 1971-72, v.p. 1973-74, pres. 1975-76), Pa. Hotel Restaurant Soc. (sec.-treas. 1973-74), Pa. Hotel Motor Inn Assn. (dir. 1975-76, treas. 1976-77), N.J. Hotel-Motel Assn. (dir. 1977-78), Hotel-Motel Greeter Internat., Pa. State Hotel Greeters (pres. 1952-54, 74-79), Phila. Press Assn., Pa. State Alumni Club Phila., Hotel Sales Mgrs. Assn., Chestnut St. Assn. (dir. 1971-76), Skal of N. Am. (treas. 1979-80, sec. 1980-86, v.p. 87-88). Clubs: Skal of North Am. (treas. 1979-80, sec. 1980-86, v.p. 1987-88). Home: 152 Fox Chase Dr Delran NJ 08075-2322 Office: Aramark Tower 1101 Market St Philadelphia PA 19107-2934

GILBERT, HEATHER CAMPBELL, manufacturing company executive; b. Mt. Vernon, N.Y., Nov. 20, 1944; d. Ronald Ogston and Mary Lodivia (Campbell) G.; BS in Math. (Nat. Merit scholar), Stanford U., 1967; MS in Computer Sci. (NSF fellow), U. Wis., 1969. With Burroughs Corp., 1969-82, sr. mgmt. systems analyst, Detroit, 1975-77, mgr. mgmt. systems activity, Pasadena, Calif., 1977-82; mgr. software product mgmt. Logical Data Mgmt. Inc., Covina, Calif., 1982-83, dir. mktg., 1983, v.p. bus. devel., 1983-84; v.p. profl. svcs., 1984-85; mgr. software devel. Unisys Corp., Mission Viejo, Calif., 1985—. Founding bd. dirs., treas. Breast Cancer Survivors Non-profit Orgn. Mem. Assn. Computing Machinery, Am. Prodn. and Inventory Control Soc., Breast Cancer Survivors Non-Profit Orgn. (founding bd. dirs., treas.), Stanford U. Alumni Assn. (life), Stanford Profl. Women Los Angeles County (pres. 1982-83), NAFE, Town Hall. Republican. Home: 21113 Calle De Paseo Lake Forest CA 92630-7037 Office: Unisys Corp 25725 Jeronimo Rd Mission Viejo CA 92691-2792

GILBERT, HOWARD N(ORMAN), lawyer; b. Chgo., Aug. 19, 1928; s. Norman Aaron and Fannie (Cohn) G.; m. Jacqueline Glasser, Feb. 16, 1957; children: Norman Abraham, Harlan Wayne, Joel Kenneth, Sharon. PhB, U. Chgo., 1947; JD, Yale U., 1951. Bar: Ill 1951, U.S. Dist. Ct. (no. dist.) Ill. 1955, U.S. Ct. Appeals (7th cir.) 1956. Ptnr. Rusnak, Deutsch & Gilbert, Chgo., 1962-79, Aaron, Schimberg, Hess & Gilbert, Chgo., 1980-84; sr. ptnr. Holleb & Coff, Chgo., 1984—. Bd. dirs. Jewish Fedn. Met. Chgo., 1977-83; pres. Mt. Sinai Hosp. Med. Ctr., Chgo., 1968-69; trustee Chgo. Hosp. Coun., 1979-84; mem. Bd. Jewish Edn., 1972-77. Lt. (j.g.) USN, 1951-55. Mem. ABA, Chgo. Bar Assn., Chgo. Coun. Lawyers, Ill. Soc. Health Lawyers, Standard Club, Bryn Mawr Country Club. Democrat. Jewish. Office: Holleb & Coff 55 E Monroe St Ste 4100 Chicago IL 60603-5896

GILBERT, J. PHIL, federal judge; b. 1949. BS, U. Ill., 1971; JD, Loyola U., Chgo., 1974. Ptnr. Gilbert & Gilbert, Carbondale, Ill., 1974-83, Gilbert, Kimmel, Huffman & Prosser, Carbondale, 1983-88; circuit judge First Jud. Circuit, Ill., 1988-92; fed. judge U.S. Dist. Ct. (so. dist.) Ill., Benton, 1992—, chief judge, 1993—; spl. asst. atty. gen. Pub. Aid Enforcement Divsn., 1974-75; asst. city atty. City of Carbondale, 1975-78; active Nat. Coun. Govt. Ethics Laws, 1988—; mem. Ill. State Bd. Elections, 1982, vice chmn., chmn., 1983-85. Bd. dirs. Friends of Morris Libr., 1988—; active Edn. Coun. 100, 1989—, Boy Scouts Am. Mem. Ill. State Bar, Jackson County Bar Assn., Ill. Judges Assn. (mem. com. jud. retention), Phi Alpha Delta. Office: US Dist Ct 301 W Main St Benton IL 62812-1362

GILBERT, JAMES CAYCE, minister; b. Nashville, Feb. 26, 1925; s. Gettis and Delia Mae (Snyder) G.; m. Freda Mae Mitchell, Sept. 3, 1949; children—Elizabeth, Suzanne, Kathryn, Rosalie. B.A., Bethel Coll., McKenzie, Tenn., 1945, D.D. (hon.), 1976; B.D., Cumberland Presbyn. Theol. Sem., McKenzie, 1947; M.A., Scarritt Coll., Nashville, 1948. Ordained to ministry Cumberland Presbyn. Ch., 1944; asso. pastor West Nashville Cumberland Presbyn. Ch., 1947-48; pastor River Oaks Cumberland Presbyn. Ch., Houston, 1948-55, Trinity Cumberland Presbyn. Ch., Ft. Worth, 1956-64; exec. dir. Cumberland Presbyn. Children's Home, Denton, Tex., 1964-90, dir. devel., 1991-94; moderator gen. assembly Cumberland Presbyn. Ch., 1979-80; stated clk., Red River Presbytery of the Cumberland Presbyn. Ch., 1993—. Mem. Nat. Assn. Homes Children, Southwestern Assn. Children's Home (past pres.), Tex. Assn. Execs. Homes Children (past pres.), Lions, Masons, K.T. Democrat. Home: 3720 W Biddison St Fort Worth TX 76109-2705

GILBERT, JAMES EASTHAM, academic administrator; b. Bridgeport, Conn., July 1, 1929; s. Carl Ludwig and Anna Maude (Eastham) G.; m. Betty Lee Blankenship, Aug. 26, 1953; 1 child, Gregory Eastham. BS in Psychology, U. N.Mex., 1952, MA in Psychology, 1959; PhD in Psychology, Am. U., 1969. Interviewer Va. State Employment Service, Alexandria, 1952-53; tng. officer Nat. Security Agy., Washington, 1953-55; rsch. psychologist Nat. Security Agy., Ft. Meade, Md., 1957-64, Hdqrs., Sec. to Air Staff, USAF, Washington, 1955-57; assoc. dean adminstrn. Northeastern U., Boston, 1964-71; assoc. vice-chancellor Ind. U.-Purdue U., Ft. Wayne, 1971-78; v.p. acad. affairs Pittsburg (Kans.) State U., 1978-86, interim pres., 1983; pres. East Stroudsburg (Pa.) U., 1986-96, pres. emeritus, 1996—; spl. asst. to provost Med. U. S.C., 1996—. NCES fellow, 1998. Mem. Rotary, Sigma Xi, Psi Chi, Phi Kappa Phi, Omicron Delta Kappa. Democrat. Home: 1296 Waterfront Dr Mount Pleasant SC 29464-9493

GILBERT, JAMES FREEMAN, geophysics educator; b. Vincennes, Ind., Aug. 9, 1931; s. James Freeman and Gladys (Paugh) G.; m. Sally Bonney,

June 19, 1959; children: Cynthia, Sarah, James. BS, MIT, 1953, PhD, 1956; D honoris causa, Utrecht U., 1994. Research assoc. MIT, Cambridge, 1956-57; asst. research geophysicist Inst. Geophysics and Planetary Physics at UCLA, 1957, asst. prof. geophysics, 1958-59; sr. research geophysicist Tex. Instruments, Dallas, 1960-61; prof. Inst. Geophysics and Planetary Physics at U. Calif. San Diego, La Jolla, 1961—, assoc. dir., 1976-88; chmn. grad. dept. Scripps Inst. Oceanography, La Jolla, 1988-91; chmn. steering com. San Diego Supercomputer, 1984-86. Contbr. numerous articles to profl. jours. Recipient Arthur L. Day medal Geol. Soc. Am., 1985, Internat. Balzan prize, 1990; Fairchild scholar Calif. Inst. Tech., Pasadena, 1987; fellow NSF, 1956, Guggenheim, 1964-65, 72-73, Overseas fellow Churchill Coll. U. Cambridge, Eng., 1972-73. Fellow AAAS, Am. Geophys. Union (William Bowie med. 1999); Nat. Acad. Scis., European Union Geoscis. (hon.); mem. Seismology Soc. Am., Am. Math. Soc., Royal Astron. Soc. (recipient Gold medal 1981), Acad. Nat. dei Lincei (fgn.), Sigma Xi. Home: 780 Kalamath Dr Del Mar CA 92014-2630 Office: U Calif Inst Geophysics and Planetary Physics 0225 La Jolla CA 92093

GILBERT, JEROME B., consulting environmental engineer. Consulting engr. pvt. practice, Orinda, Calif., 1991—. Gordon Fair award Am. Acad. Environ. Engring., 1993. Mem. Nat. Acad. Engring. Office: 324 Tappan Ter Orinda CA 94563-1343*

GILBERT, JOHN HUMPHREY VICTOR, speech scientist, educator; b. Bath, Somerset, Eng., Mar. 19, 1941; s. Daniel and Nancy (Johns) G.; m. Carolyn; children: Eliot Daniel, Oliver Gaius, Kristen. Grad., U. London; PhD, Purdue U., 1966. Asst. prof. U. B.C., 1966-69, assoc. prof., 1969-74, prof., 1974—, Med. Research Council postdoctoral scholar, 1969-74, head div. audiology and speech sci., dir. Sch. Audiol. Speech Sci., 1980-88, acting dir. Sch. Rehab. Medicine, 1985-88; coord. health scis. Univ. B.C., Vancouver, Can., 1995—; mem. study sect. NIH, 1983; mem. senate U. B.C., 1984-87, 96—, chair senate libr. com. 93-99; chmn. adv. com. B.C. Med. Svcs. Found., 1981—, chmn., pres. com. lectures, 1986-90; mem. health and welfare com. Vancouver Found.; bd. dirs. B.C. Rsch. Found., deputy chair, 1998—; mem. adv. com. Cmty. Care Found., 1994—. Mem. editl. bd. Cambridge U. Press, J. Child Lang. Fulbright scholar Purdue U., 1963-66; David Ross Rsch. fellow, 1965-66, sr. fellow Green Coll., U. B.C., 1996—; recipient Killam Tchg. prize U. B.C., 1995; named Outstanding Alumnus, Purdue U., 1993. Mem. Can. Assn. Audiologists and Speech Lang. Pathologists (pres. 1984-85, chmn. com. on examinations 1986-88, medal for outstanding profl. achievement 1988), Internat. Assn. Child Lang. (exec. coun. 1983-89), Vancouver Club. E-Mail: john.gilbert@ubc.ca. Home: 3350 W 37th Ave, Vancouver, BC Canada V6N 2V6 Office: Univ BC Health Sci Office, Univ BC Office Coord Health, Rm 400 IRC 2194 Health Mall, Vancouver, BC Canada V6T 1Z3

GILBERT, JOHN JOUETT, aquatic ecologist, educator; b. Southampton, N.Y., July 18, 1937; s. Seymour Parker Gilbert and Louise Ross (Todd) Stanley; m. Caroline Spalding Colburn, June 16, 1959; children: John Spalding, Anne Menefee. BA, Williams Coll., 1959; PhD, Yale U., 1963. Asst. prof. Princeton (N.J.) U., 1964-66; asst. prof. dept. biol. scis. Dartmouth Coll., Hanover, N.H., 1966-69, assoc. prof., 1969-74, prof., 1974—. Contbr. numerous articles to profl. jours. Recipient Career Devel. award, 1973-78; NSF, NIH, EPA grantee, 1965—. Fellow AAAS; mem. Ecol. Soc. Am., Am. Soc. Limnology and Oceanography, Internat. Soc. Theoretical and Applied Limnology (nat. rep. 1971-83). Avocation: fly fishing. Office: Dartmouth Coll Dept Biol Scis Hanover NH 03755

GILBERT, JOHN ROBERT, advertising and public relations agency executive; b. Long Beach, Calif., July 17, 1946; s. Walter E. and Marian S. Gilbert; m. Patricia R. Rector, Apr. 20, 1974; 1 child, Kent E. BA, Washington U., St. Louis, 1969. Announcer Starr Broadcasting, Kansas City, Mo., 1971-72; prime time news mgr. Greater Kansas City C. of C., 1972-74; mgr. pub. info. Mo. Pub. Svc. Co., Kansas City, 1974-80; sr. v.p. The Boasberg Co., Kansas City, 1980-90; CEO, Gilbert, Christopher & Assocs., Kansas City, 1990-95; v.p. Bernstein-Rein Advt., Kansas City, 1995—; bd. dirs. Mo. Bank and Trust, Kansas City. Bd. govs. Am. Royal, Kansas City, 1994—. Capt. U.S. Army, 1969-71. Mem. Pub. Rels. Soc. Am., Greater Kansas City C. of C. (small bus. com. 1994—). Avocations: racing sports cars, collecting classic cars. Office: Bernstein-Rein Advt 4600 Madison Ave Kansas City MO 64112-1277

GILBERT, KENNETH G., art educator; b. Spencer, W.Va., Oct. 29, 1942; s. Delmer L. and N. Marie Gilbert. BA, Glenville (W.Va.) State Coll.; MA, Salem/Teikyo U.; postgrad., W.Va. U., U. Ky. Chmn. visual dept. Parkersburg (W.Va.) H.S.; art coord. Wood County Schs., Parkersburg. Author: Mountain Trace Book I, 1980, Book II, 1982, A Blennerhassett Sketchbook, 1995, Parkersburg High School History Book, 1995, Appalachian/Wildfood Cookbook, 1997; one man shows include Parkersburg Art Ctr., Smoot Theatre, Glenville State Coll. Mem. Nat. Art Edn. Assn. Baptist. Home: 2323 Broad St Parkersburg WV 26101-2819

GILBERT, LAURENT F., SR., state agency administrator. Student, Maine Criminal Justice Acad., 1970; AS, U. Maine, 1976; student, FBI Nat. Acad., 1976, New Eng. Law Enforcement Mgmt. Tng. Inst., 1978. With police dept. Lewiston, Maine, 1969-94; chief of police police dept. Lewiston, 1989-94; U.S. marshall Dist. of Maine, 1994—. Mem. Internat. Assn. Chiefs of Police, Fed. Exec. Assn., Maine Chief of Police Assn. Office: 156 Federal St Portland ME 04101

GILBERT, LAWRENCE IRWIN, biologist, educator; b. N.Y.C., Jan. 24, 1929; s. Charles and Matilda (Bronznick) G.; m. Doris Paule Millstein, Oct. 26, 1952; children—Scott David, Daniel Todd, Joanne Robin. BS, L.I. U., 1950; MS, NYU, 1955; PhD, Cornell U., 1958. Mem. faculty Northwestern U., 1958-80, prof. biol. scis., chmn. dept., 1965-70, 78-80; also sec.-treas. div. comparative endocrinology, chmn. div. comparative endocrinology; William Rand Kenan, Jr. prof., chmn. dept. zoology U.N.C., Chapel Hill, 1980-82, chmn. dept. biology, 1982-92, chmn. dept. radio, T.V., motion pictures, 1992-93; assoc. vice chancellor for Academic Affairs, 1993-96, assoc. provost, 1996—; NSF sr. fellow U. Bern, Switzerland, 1964-65; mem. Presdl. Task Force on Pest Mgmt., 1971-72. Editor: Metamorphosis; A Problem in Development Biology, 1968, 2d edit., 1981, 3rd edit., 1996, The Juvenile Hormones, 1976, Comprehensive Insect Physiology, Biochemistry and Pharmacology, 13 vols., 1985, Immunological Techniques in Insect Biology, 1988; mem. editl. bd. Jours. Invertebrate Reprodn., Gen. Comparative Endocrinology; exec. editor Insect Biochemistry and Molecular Biology, 1984—; contbr. articles to profl. jours. Recipient Gregor Mendel Gold medal Czech Acad. Scis., 1993. Fellow AAAS (Lifetime Mentor Achievement award 1996), Am. Acad. Arts and Scis.; mem. Soc. Devel. Biology, Soc. Exptl. Biology, Phi Beta Kappa. Home: 1105 Phils Creek Rd Chapel Hill NC 27516-5447 Office: U NC Office Provost Chapel Hill NC 27599-3000

GILBERT, LEONARD HAROLD, lawyer; b. Hutchinson, Minn., Apr. 3, 1936; s. Sidney and Clara (Franzblau) G.; m. Jean Buchman, Apr. 21, 1963; children—Jonathan Stuart, Suzanne Elaine. BA, Emory U., 1958; LLB, Harvard U., 1961. Bar: Fla. 1961. With Carlton, Fields, Ward, Emmanuel, Smith & Cutler PA, Tampa, Fla., 1961-98, Holland & Knight, LLP, Tampa, Fla., 1998—. Bd. dirs. Gasparilla Sidewalk Art Festival, Tampa, 1970-74, United Way; trustee Tampa Bay Performing Arts Ctr., Lowry Park Zool. Soc., Univ. Cmty. Hosp.; chmn. Art Coun. Tampa, 1973-74; mem. Hillsborough County (Fla.) Bicentennial Commn., 1973-76, Tampa Charter Revision Com., 1975; chmn. bd. fellows U. Tampa, 1986-87, trustee, 1987-98; pres. Tampa Mus. Art, 1986-87. With USCGR, 1961-69. Fellow Am. Bar Found. (chair 1998), Fla. Bar Found. (dir.); mem. ABA (chmn. sect. gen. practice 1979-80, ho. of dels. 1980-90, chmn. creditors' rights com. corps. sect.), Fla. Bar (chmn. sect. corp. banking and bus. law 1970-71, chmn. sect. gen. practice 1972-73, bd. govs. 1975-79, pres. 1980-81), Bar Assn. Hillsborough County (pres. 1974-75), Am. Judicature Soc. (dir.), Am. Law Inst., Am. Coll. Bankruptcy (dir. 1997—), Internat. Bar Assn., Harvard Law Sch. Assn. Fla. (pres. 1986), Am. Coll. Comml. Fin. Lawyers (pres. 1999—), Tampa C. of C. (bd. dirs.), Eleventh Cir. Hist. Soc. (trustee). Club: The Tampa (pres. 1986-87). Lodges: Kiwanis (pres. 1972), Ye Mystic Krewe of Gasparilla. Office: Holland & Knight LLP PO Box 1288 Tampa FL 33601-1288

GILBERT, LINDA ARMS, music educator. BS in Elem. Edn., Middle Tenn. State U., 1972, MA in Tchg., 1979, EdS in Adminstrn. and Supervision, 1991; EdD in Curriculum and Instrn., Tenn. State U., 1997. 8th grade tchr. Ctrl. Middle Sch., 1972-73; 5th-6th grade band tchr. Mitchell-Neilson Elem. Sch., 1987-90; 5th-6th grade band tchr., K-2 music tchr. Reeves-Rogers Elem. Sch., 1988-90; 5th-6th grade band tchr., K-6 music tchr., chorus tchr. Black Fox Elem. Sch., 1990-98; assoc. dir. instrn., staff devel. Murfreesboro City Schs., 1998—; pvt. music tchr., 1970—; presenter in field; guest conductor mass flute choirs Tenn. Flute Festivals. Guest columnist for edn. Daily News Jour. Organist Bethel United Meth. Ch., various coms.; active Murfreesboro City Schs., 1981-87, Rutherford 2000, 1991-95; vol. VA Med. Ctr., guest spkr. civic orgns.; band of blue exec. bd. Middle Tenn. State U.; chairperson edn. com. Am. Cmty. Summit of Rutherford County. Named Tenn. State Tchr. of Yr., 1998, Radio Educator of Week, Sta. WGNS, Outstanding Tchr. Tenn. Gov.'s Sch. of the Arts, 1995; recipient Apple award WSMV TV's Tchr., 1998, Disting. Classroom Tchr. award, 1992; inducted Band of Blue Hall of Fame, 1998. Mem. Nat. Flute Assn., Middle Tenn. Flute Soc., Am. Orff-Schulwork Assn., Tenn. Educators Assn., Music Educators Nat. Conf., Tenn. Elem. Music Educators Assn., Tennesseans for the Arts, Tenn. Bandmasters Assn., Middle Tenn. Sch. Band and Orch. Assn., Middle Tenn. Vocal Assn. (accompanist mass choir 1992), Tenn. Edn. Assn. (human rels com. 1994-96, summer leadership sch. 1994-96, del. to rep. assembly 1992-96), Middle Tenn. Edn. Assn. (pres.), Murfreesboro Edn. Assn. (grivance com. chairperson, exec. bd., profl. adv. com. 1994-96, pres. 1994-96, pres.-elect, other coms.), Phi Kappa Phi, Kappa Delta Pi, Phi Delta Kappa, Delta Omicron, Delta Kappa Gamma. Office: Murfreesboro City Schs 2552 S Church St Murfreesboro TN 37127

GILBERT, MARIE ROGERS, poet; b. Florence, S.C., Jan. 27, 1924; d. Frank Mandeville and Marie Barringer Rogers; m. Richard Austin Gilbert, Apr. 24, 1946; children: Richard Austin Jr., Laurie Gilbert Sanford. BA in Psychology and Theater Arts, Rollins Coll., 1945. Contbr. poetry to anthologies. Driver ARC, Florence Army Air Base, summer 1943-44; bd. visitors St. Andrews Presbyn. Coll., Laurinburg, N.C., 1995-98. Recipient Poet Laureate Sam Ragan Fine Arts award St. Andrews Presbyn. Coll., 1994. Mem. Poetry Soc. N.C. (v.p., 1988-89, pres. 1990-92), Poetry Soc. S.C. (1st pl. for lyric poetry 1987, 90), N.C. Writers Conf., N.C. Writers Network, Colonial Dames of Am. in state of N.C. (sec. 1990-91, v.p. 1992-93), Jr. League. Avocation: poetry readings and seminars. Home: 2 Saint Simons Sq Greensboro NC 27408-3833

GILBERT, NANCY LOUISE, librarian; b. Norfolk, Va., Nov. 3, 1938; d. Oscar Linwood Jr. and Mary Margaret (Nicholls) Gilbert. BA, Greensboro Coll., 1961; MLS, U. North Carolina, 1968. Libr. Va. Beach (Va.) Pub. Libr., 1968, U.S. Army, Worms, Crailsheim and Mannheim, Germany, 1968-74, Pentagon Libr., Washington, 1974-80, U.S. Army Mil. History Inst., Carlisle Barracks, Pa., 1980—. Mem. ALA, Spl. Librs. Assn., Mid-Atlantic Region Archives Conf. Avocations: travel, reading, photography.

GILBERT, NEIL ROBIN, social work educator, author, consultant; b. N.Y.C., Sept. 18, 1940; s. Alan and Ida (Bedzin) G.; m. Barbara Diane Feinstein, June 2, 1963; children: Evan Mallory, Jesse Arthur. BA, Bklyn. Coll., 1963; MSW, U. Pitts., 1965, PhD, 1968. Caseworker Interdepartmental Service Ctr., N.Y.C., 1963; dir. research Mayor's Com. on Human Resources, Pitts., 1967-69; prof. sch. social welfare U. Calif., Berkeley, 1969—, chmn. doctoral program, 1983—, acting dean sch. social welfare, 1986, 95-97, Milton and Gertrude Chernin prof. social welfare and social svcs., 1989—; advisor Jour. Social Policy, 1982—. Author: Clients or Constituents, 1970, Capitalism and the Welfare State, 1983; (with others) Dimensions of Social Welfare Policy, 1974, 2d rev. edit., 1986, Dynamics of Community Planning, 1978, (with Barbara Gilbert) The Enabling State, 1989, Protecting Young Children from Sexual Abuse, 1989, Practical Program Evaluation, 1990, (with Jill Berrick) With the Best of Intentions, 1992, Welfare Justice, 1995; editor Social Welfare Series, 1977-83, Social Worker and Social Welfare Series, 1977—. Trustee Head Royce Sch.; chair bd. dirs. Seneca Ctr. Fellow NIMH, 1966, U.N. Research Inst. for Social Devel., 1975; Fulbright scholar, U.S. Info. Agy, 1981; Fulbright Research fellow, London, 1981, Fulbright Western European scholar, 1987; recipient Medallion of Distinction U. Pitts., 1987. Mem. Nat. Assn. Social Workers, Assn. Pub. Policy Analysis and Mgmt. Avocations: skiing, moutaineering. Office: U Calif Sch Social Welfare Haviland Hall Berkeley CA 94720

GILBERT, PAMELA, federal agency administrator. BA, Tufts U.; JD, NYU. Dir. consumer program U.S. Pub. Interest Rsch. Group, Washington; dir. Pub. Citizens Congress Watch, Washington; legis. counsel Malkin & Ross, Washington; exec. dir. Consumer Product Safety Commn., Bethesda, Md., 1996—. Office: Consumer Product Safety Commn 4330 East West Hwy Bethesda MD 20814

GILBERT, PAMELA KATHERINE, literature educator; b. L.A., Jan. 16, 1964; d. Harvey Carleton and Katherine Gilbert. BA, Calif. State U., Long Beach, 1983, MA, 1988; PhD, U. So. Calif., 1994. Lectr. Calif. State U., Dominguez Hills, 1990-93; asst. prof. U. Wis.-Parkside, Kenosha, 1993-98, U. Fla., Gainesville, 1998—. Author: Disease, Desire and the Body in Victorian Women's Popular Novels, 1997; co-editor: Mary Elizabeth Braddon in Context, 1999; asst. mng. editor: The Writing Instructor, 1990; contbr. articles to profl. jours. Ctr. for Twentieth Century Studies fellow, 1996-97, Va. Middleton fellow U. So. Calif., 1989-90, 91-92. Mem. MLA, Nat. Coun. Tchrs. English, Victorians Inst. Democrat. Office: U Fla Dept English Box 117310 Gainesville FL 32611

GILBERT, PAUL H., engineering executive, consultant; b. Healdsburg, Calif., Apr. 23, 1936; s. Lindley D. and Beatrice G.; m. Elizabeth A. Gilbert, July 13, 1963; children: Christopher, Gregory, Kevin. BSCE, U. Calif., Berkeley, 1959, MSCE, 1960. Registered profl. engr. in 17 states. Project mgr. Calif. State Water Project, Sacramento, 1959-68; officer U.S. Army Corp Engrs., Heidleberg, Germany, 1960-61, capt., 1961-68; project mgr. Parsons Brinckerhoff, N.Y.C., 1969-73; regional mgr./ptnr. Parsons Brinckerhoff, San Francisco, 1973-85; dir. Parsons Brinckerhoff, N.Y.C., 1973-98, chmn. bd., 1990-98; sr. v.p. Parsons Brinckerhoff, 1973—; project dir. supercollider design and constrn. Parsons Brinckerhoff, Dallas, 1990-95; vice chmn. Parsons Brinckerhoff Internat. Inc., 1993—; Laser Interferometer Gravitational-Wave Observatory reviewer NSF, Washington, 1992-99; prin.-in-charge of award winning projects Glenwood Canyon I-70 tunnels, San Francisco Ocean Outfall, Seattle Bus. Tunnel, Hood Canal Floating Bridge and West Seattle High Level and Low Level Swing Bridges, others. Contbr. articles to profl. jours. Trustee Assoc. Univs. Inc. Named disting. engring. alumnus U. Calif., Berkeley, 1998. Fellow ASCE (Rickey medal 1969, Constrn. Mgmt. award 1994, Lincoln Art Welding award 1966); mem. NAE, Project Mgmt. Inst., Soc. Am. Mil. Engrs., Moles, Nat. Acad. of Engring. Republican. Roman Catholic. E-mail: gilbert@pbworld.com. Office: Parsons Brinkerhoff 999 3rd Ave Ste 2200 Seattle WA 98104-4020

GILBERT, PERRY WEBSTER, emeritus educator; b. North Branford, Conn., Dec. 1, 1912; s. Scott Warren and Hester (Weatherwax) G.; m. Claire Rachel Kelly, Sept. 3, 1938; children: Ann (Mrs. Bradley McDonald), David, Stephen, John, Mary, Lois, Christopher, Philip. A.B., Dartmouth, 1934; Ph.D., Cornell U., 1940; L.H.D. (hon.), York Coll. of Pa., 1978. Asst. in zoology Cornell U., 1937-40, instr., 1940-43, asst. prof., 1943-46, assoc. prof., 1946-52, prof., 1952-78, prof. emeritus, 1978—; dir. Mote Marine Lab., 1967-78, dir. emeritus, 1978—; mem. panel biol. and med. scis. Polar Research Com., 1959-63; leader Tahiti-Tikehau Internat. Expdn., 1964; chief scientist Brit. Honduras Expdn. Shark, 1969; research assoc. Lerner Marine Lab., 1964-72. Editor: Sharks and Survival, 1963, Sharks, Skates and Rays, 1967; contbr. numerous articles to sci. jours. Cramer fellow zoology Cornell U., 1936-37; Carnegie fellow embryology Carnegie Inst. Washington, Balt., 1949-50; Guggenheim fellow Lerner Marine Lab., Bimini, Bahamas, 1957; Guggenheim fellow Scripps Instn. Oceanography, 1963. Fellow AAAS, Am. Elasmobranch Soc.; mem. Am. Inst. Biol. Scis., Am. Soc. Zoology, Am. Assn. Anatomy, Inst. Internat. d'Embryologie, Marine Biol. Assn. India, Am. Soc. Icthyology and Herpetology, Am. Soc. Mammalogists, Am. Ornithologists Union, Am. Littoral Soc., Soc. Study Evolution, Animal Behavior Soc., Explorers Club, Sigma Xi. Home: 852 Siesta Dr Sarasota FL 34242-1054 Office: 1600 City Island Rd Sarasota FL 34236-1004 also: Cornell Univ Stimson Hall Ithaca NY 14853 *As a scientist I have learned that there is no substitute for truth, however painful or disappointing it may be. As an administrator I have learned that listening to, and compassion for others fosters their loyalty and desire to do more than is asked of them.*

GILBERT, RICHARD JOSEPH, economics educator; b. N.Y.C., Jan. 14, 1945; s. Michael N. and Esther (Dillon) G.; m. Sandra S. Waknitz, Sept. 7, 1974; children: Alison, David. BEE with honors, Cornell U., 1966, MEE, 1967; MA in Econs., Stanford U., 1976, PhD, 1976. Rsch. assoc. Stanford U., Calif., 1975-76; from assist. prof. to assoc. prof. econs. U. Calif., Berkeley, 1976-83; assoc. prof engring-econ. systems Stanford U., 1982-83; prof. econs. U. Calif., Berkeley, 1983—, dir. energy rsch. inst., 1983-93, prof. bus. adminstrn., 1990—; dep. asst. atty. gen. antitrust divsn. U.S. Dept. Justice, 1993-95; prin. Law & Econ. Cons. Group, Berkeley, 1989—. Contbr. numerous articles to profl. jours.; editor scholarly jours. Adv. U.S. Dept. Energy, Washington, 1983—, World Bank, Washington, 1980—, NSF, Washington, 1985—, Calif. Inst. Energy Efficiency, Berkeley, 1990—. Fulbright scholar Washington, 1989; vis. scholar Cambridge U., 1979, Oxford U., 1979. Mem. Tau Beta Pi, Eta Kappa Nu, Sigma Xi. Office: U Calif Dept Economics Berkeley CA 94720

GILBERT, ROBERT PETTIBONE, retired physician, educator; b. Chgo., Sept. 29, 1917; s. Newell Clark and Charlotte Louise (Pettibone) G.; m. Anne Cribben Heneage, June 5, 1943 (div. 1964); children: Robert P., Diane H., Nancy C., Anne E., m. Brenda Drake, Oct. 2, 1964; children: Jane D., Newell C. BA, Haverford Coll., 1938; MD, Northwestern U., 1942. Diplomate Am. Bd. Internal Medicine. Cardiology fellow Stanford U. Med. Sch., San Francisco, 1947-48; instr. to assoc. prof. of Medicine Northwestern U. Med. Sch., Chgo., 1949-65; rsch. assoc. in Physiology U. Minn., Mpls., 1956-57; dir. edn. and rsch. Evanston (Ill.) Hosp., 1957-65; assoc. dean Jefferson Med. Coll., Phila., 1965-72, assoc. prof., 1965—; clin. prof. of Medicine and dir. student health Thomas Jefferson U., Phila., 1981-90. Contbr. articles to profl jours. Lt. USNR, 1943-46, PTO. Markle scholar Markle Found. and Northwestern U., 1952-57. Fellow Am. Coll. Physicians. Republican. Presbyterian. Avocations: history, sailing, literature. Home: 363 Youngsford Pl Gladwyne PA 19035-1624

GILBERT, ROBERT WOLFE, lawyer; b. N.Y.C., Nov. 12, 1920; s. L. Wolfe and Katherine L. (Oestreicher) Wolfe; m. Beatrice R. Frutman, Dec. 25, 1946; children: Frank Richard, Jack Alfred. BA, UCLA 1941; JD, U. Calif., Berkeley, 1943. Bar: Calif. 1944, U.S. Ct. Appeals. (9th cir.) 1944, U.S. Ct. Appeals. (D.C. cir.) 1976, U.S. Supreme Ct. 1959. Pres. Gilbert & Sackman, P.C. and predecessors, L.A., 1944—; judge pro tem Los Angeles Mcpl. and Superior Ct., Commr. City of L.A. Housing Authority 1953-63; bd. dirs. Calif. Housing Coun. 1955-63; U.S. faculty mem. Moscow Conf. on Law and Econ. Cooperation, 1990. Sr. editor Internat. Labor and Employment Laws, 1997. Mem. Internat. Bar Assn., Interam. Bar Assn. (co-chmn. labor law and social security com.), ABA (co-chmn. internat. labor law com.), Fed. Bar Assn., L.A. Bar Assn. (past chmn. labor law sect.), Am. Judicature Soc., Coll. Labor & Employment Lawyers, Order of Coif, Pi Sigma Alpha. Contbr. articles to profl. jours. Home: 7981 Hollywood Blvd Los Angeles CA 90046-2611 Office: 6100 Wilshire Blvd Ste 700 Los Angeles CA 90048-5114

GILBERT, RONALD RHEA, lawyer; b. Sandusky, Ohio, Dec. 29, 1942; s. Corvin and Mildred (Millikin) G.; m. Jane Johnson, Jan. 24, 1998; children: Elizabeth, Lynne, Lisa. BA, Wittenberg U., 1964; JD, U. Mich., 1967, postgrad., 1967-68; postgrad., Wayne State U., 1973-74. Bar: Mich. 1968, U.S. Dist. Ct. (ea. and we. dists.) Mich. 1968, U.S. Ct. Appeals (6th cir.) 1968, U.S. Ct. Appeals (9th cir.) 1977, U.S. Ct. Appeals (7th cir.) 1984, U.S. Ct. Appeals (3d cir.) 1988, U.S. Ct. Appeals (4th cir.) 1989, U.S. Ct. Appeals (8th cir.) 1990, U.S. Ct. Appeals (10th cir.) 1991, U.S. Ct. Appeals (11th cir.) 1992, U.S. Ct. Appeals (2nd cir.), 1992. Assoc. prosecutor Wayne County, Mich., 1969; assoc. Rouse, Selby, Dickinson, Shaw & Pike, Detroit, 1969-72; ptnr. Charfoos, Christensen, Gilbert & Archer, P.C., Detroit, 1972-84; sole practice, 1984—; instr. Madonna Coll., Detroit, 1977-81; mem. faculty Inst. Continuing Legal Edn., 1977—; speaker symposium on social security law Detroit Coll. Law, 1984; state bar grievance investigator; vol. chmn. Aquatic Injury Safety Found. Co-author: Social Security Disability Claims, 1983; contbr. articles to legal jours. Founder, chmn. Aquatic Injury Safety Group, 1982, chmn., 1982-89; founder, chmn. Found. for Aquatic Injury Prevention, 1988, Found. for Spinal Cord Injury Prevention, 1988; chmn. aquatic safety com. Nat. Safety Coun., 1987; mem. data collection subcom. of Nat. Swimming Safety Com. for Consumer Products Safety Commn.; bd. dirs. Nat. Coordinating Coun. on Spinal Cord Injuries; patron Detroit Art Inst., Detroit Zool. Soc.; mem. Pres.' Club U. Mich.; mem. Detroit Council on World Affairs, 1968-73, Council for Nat. Coop. in Aquatics; mem. combined fed. campaign Nat. Health Agy. Mich.; founder Spinal Cord Injury Traumatic Brain Injury Adv. Com. Mich. Pub. Health Chronic Adv. Com.; co-founder Safe Kids Coalition Southeastern Mich.; mem. Nat. Safe Kids Coalition. Mem. Assn. Trial Lawyers Am., Mich. Trial Lawyers Assn., System Safety Soc., ABA, Mich Bar Assn., Detroit Bar Assn., Am. Arbitration Assn., Am. Judicature Soc., Nat. Spinal Cord Injury Assn. (sec. 1988, bd. dirs., exec. com., chmn. prevention com.), Nat. Head Injury Assn., Mich. Head Injury Assn., Am. Standards and Testing Materials (com. F-24 on water parks and playgrounds, mem. com. F-8), World Water Parks Assn., Nat. Environ. Health Assn., Nat. Pub. Health Assn., Nat. Eagle Scout Assn. (alumni), Blue Key, Pi Kappa Alpha, Pi Sigma Alpha, Pi Delta Epsilon. Clubs: Detroit Athletic, U. Mich. Office: 1310 Ford Bldg Detroit MI 49226

GILBERT, ROSE BENNETT, communications company executive; b. High Point, N.C., July 11, 1938; d. Ellis Howard and Sadie B. (Vernon) Bennett; BA, Mary Washington Coll., 1960; postgrad. George Washington U., 1964-65; children—Scott Randolph, Bennett J. Reporter, Richmond (Va.) News-Leader, 1960-64; editor 1,001 Decorating Ideas Mag., N.Y.C., 1973-75; columnist Chgo. Tribune-Daily News Syndicate, 1975-77; v.p., partner Sweet & Co., N.Y.C., 1978-80; pres. Gilbert/Green Communications, N.Y.C., 1980-90; assoc. editor Country Decorating Mag., N.Y.C. Adult Sch. Maplewood/South Orange (N.J.) Adult Sch., 1975-90; lectr. N.Y. Sch. Interior Design, 1985-88; syndicated columnist Copley News Svc., San Diego, 1988—. Mem. Mary Washington Coll. Alumni Assn. (v.p. 1966-67), Internat. Furnishings and Design Assn. Episcopalian. Author: You-Do-It Book of Early American Decorating, 1978, Decorating Country-Style, 1980, Your Colors at Home, 1985; co-author: Manhattan-Style, 1990, Hampton Style, 1993. Home: 73 Jefferson Ave Maplewood NJ 07040-1228 Office: 175 5th Ave Ste 2396 New York NY 10010-7703

GILBERT, SCOTT, advertising executive. Co-chmn. bd., CEO Team One Advertising, El Segundo, Calif.; pres., CEO Sachi & Sachi, L.A. Office: Sachi & Sachi 3501 Sepulveda Blvd Torrance CA 90505*

GILBERT, SCOTT FREDERICK, biologist, educator, author; b. N.Y.C., Apr. 13, 1949; s. Marvin Marshall and Elaine (Caplan) G.; m. Anne Marie Raunio, Dec. 30, 1971; children: Daniel, Sarah, David. BA, Wesleyan U., 1971; MA, Johns Hopkins U., 1976, PhD, 1976. Postdoctoral assoc. U. Wis., Madison, 1976-78, 1978-80; asst. prof. Swarthmore (Pa.) Coll., 1980-86, assoc. prof., 1986-92; prof., 1992—. Author: Developmental Biology, 1985, 88, 91, 94, 97, Embryology, 1997; zoology editor Jour. Irreproducible Results, 1979-93, Com. de Patronage, Annales Hist. Philosophie Sci.; mem. editl. bd. Am. Jour. Med. Genetics, Jour. Exptl. Zoology; contbr. articles to sci. jours. Recipient Dwight J. Ingle award Perspectives in Biology and Medicine, 1984, medal of François I, Coll. de France, 1996; Guggenheim fellow, 1999. Fellow AAAS; mem. Soc. Devel. Biology, Soc. Integrative Comparative Biology (exec. bd.), Soc. Human Genetics, Hist. Sci. Soc., Internat. Soc. Hist. Phil. Soc. Stud. Biology, Phi Beta Kappa, Sigma Xi. Democrat. Jewish. Home: 224 Cornell Ave Swarthmore PA 19081-1932 Office: Swarthmore Coll Dept Biology 500 College Ave Ste 2 Swarthmore PA 19081-1390

GILBERT, SHARON L., education educator; b. Celina, Ohio, Aug. 27, 1943; d. Wilbur Orvill and Margaret Kathleen (Bottein) Wright; m. Glenn Gordon Gilbert, July 23; children from previous marriage: Kristin Alysia Pape, Marisa Alexia Pape. BS, Miami U., Oxford, Ohio, 1964, MA, 1965; PhD, Ohio State U., 1988. Assoc. prof. edn. So. Ill. U., Carbondale, 1988—; mem. adv. bd. for book series Studies in Ethno-Linguistics. Contbr. chpts. to books, articles to profl. jours. Mem. Assn. Tchr. Educators (chair tech. interest group 1993-96, commn. on inclusion, commn. on tech., comms.

com.), Phi Delta Kappa, Phi Kappa Phi. Avocation: environmental education. Office: So Ill U Dept Curriculum and Instrn Carbondale IL 62901-4610

GILBERT, STEVEN JEFFREY, venture capitalist, screenwriter, lawyer; b. N.Y.C., Apr. 6, 1947; s. Bernard and Ruth (Turner) G.; m. Anita Schneider, Apr. 25, 1987; children: Steven Turner, Anna Christina. BS in Econs., U. Pa., 1967; JD, Harvard U., 1970, MBA, 1972. Bar: Mass. 1970. Assoc. Morgan Stanley and Co., N.Y.C., 1972-76; v.p. Wertheim and Co., N.Y.C., 1976-78; mng. dir. E.F. Hutton, Internat., N.Y.C., 1978-80; pres., chief exec. officer Lion's Gate Films, Inc., Los Angeles, 1980-82; gen. ptnr. Cen. Devel. Ptnrs., N.Y.C., 1982-83; mng. gen. ptnr. Chem. Venture Ptnrs., N.Y.C., 1983-88; mng. dir. Commonwealth Capital Ptnrs., N.Y.C., 1988—; mng. gen. ptnr. Soros Capital, N.Y.C., 1992—; chmn. bd. Gilbert Global Equity Ptnrs., L.L.C., 1997—; bd. dirs., vice chmn. NFO Worldwide, Inc., A.C.X. Pacific, Inc.; bd. dirs. Vertias-DGC, Inc., Uromed, Inc., Sydney Harbour Casino Holdings, Ltd., Veritas, Inc., Terra Nova Ins. Co., Ltd., Bermuda, The Asian Infrastructure Fund, LCC Internat., Inc., OneTel Ltd.; trustee NYU Med. Ctr., Hosp. for Joint Diseases. Screenwriter Chapter XI, 1982. Mem. Writers Guild Am., Young Pres. Orgn., Coun. on Fgn. Rels. Office: Gilbert Global Equity Ptnrs LLC 785 Smith Ridge Rd New Canaan CT 06840-3228 also: NFO Rsch Inc 2 Pickwick Plz Greenwich CT 06830-5530

GILBERT, SUZANNE HARRIS, advertising executive; b. Chgo, Mar. 8, 1948; d. Lawrence W. and Dorothea (Wilde) Harris: children: Kerry, Elizabeth, Gregory. BS, Maquette U.; MBA, U. Chgo., 1985. Fin. analyst Leo Burnett Co., Chgo.; sr. v.p., fin. administrn., sec.-treas. Clinton E. Frank Inc., Chgo., 1975-85; with Campbell-Ewald Co., Detroit, 1985—; grp. sr. v.p. Campbell-Ewald Co., Warren, Mich., exec. v.p., chief fin. and administrv. officer, 1990—; bd. dirs.; bd. dirs. AAAA Ins. Co. Ltd., Bd. dirs. Boys Hope Detroit, Detroit, Mich. Works-Detroit Workforce Devel.; mem. bd. advs. U. Detroit Mercy Coll. of Bus.; bd. advisors acctg. and fin. Oakland Univ. Mem. Am. Assn. Advertising Agys. (fiscal control com.), Econ. Club Detroit, Fin. Execs. Inst. (bd. dirs. Detroit chpt., sec.). Office: Campbell-Ewald 30400 Van Dyke Ave Warren MI 48093-2368

GILBERT, THOMAS STRONG, Internet entrepreneur, venture capitalist. BA, Princeton U., 1966; MBA, Harvard U., 1968. V.p. Merrill, Lynch, Hubbard, N.Y.C.; v.p., mgr. pub. fin. dept. Reynolds Securities, N.Y.C.; v.p. Allen & Co., Inc., N.Y.C.; mng. dir. Loeb Ptnrs., Inc., N.Y.C.; pres., CEO and dir. Gilbert Capital, Inc., N.Y.C.; chmn., pres., founder GeoDomains, Inc. Contbr. letters and articles to profl. jours. Nat. amateur titles in court tennis, squash, tennis. Avocations: tennis, squash, skiing, politics, golf. Office: GeoDomains Inc Fl 3171 666 3rd Ave New York NY 10017-4011

GILBERT, VINCENT NEWTON, publisher; b. Chgo., Dec. 7, 1955; s. Herman Cromwell and Ivy Newton (McAlpine) G.; m. Denise Sharon Rawlings, Aug. 15, 1982; children; Diona Vinise, Vincent Newton II. BA in Polit. Sci., Ind. U., 1978; JD, John Marshall Law Sch., 1983. Dir., Maple Park Strong Ctr., Chgo., 1976; terr. mgr. Carnation Co., Chgo., 1978-81; sales dir. Path Press, Chgo., 1982—; exec. v.p. CDM Transp. Svc., Inc., Chgo., 1984-86; dir. consumer edn. dept. of consumer svcs., Chgo., 1987-88; dist. dir. Office of Congressman Gus Savage, Chgo., 1988—; apptd. to Small Bus. Utility Advocate State of Ill., 1992—. Host bus. TV show Ask the Advocate, 1992—. Speech writer Savage for Alderman campaign, Chgo., 1983; area coord. Savage for Congress campaign, Chgo., 1982, Washington for Mayor campaign, Chgo., 1983; vice chmn. Danny Davis for Mayor campaign, 1991. Mem. Student Bar Assn., Black Am. Law Student Assn. Methodist. Office: James R Thompson Ctr 100 W Randolph St Ste 3-400 Chicago IL 60601-3219

GILBERT, WALTER, molecular biologist, educator; b. Boston, Mar. 21, 1932; s. Richard V. and Emma (Cohen) G.; m. Celia Stone, Dec. 29, 1953; children: John Richard, Kate. AB, Harvard U., 1953, AM, 1954; PhD, Cambridge U., 1957; DSc (hon.), U. Chgo., 1978, Columbia U., 1978, U. Rochester, 1979, Yeshiva U., 1981. NSF postdoctoral fellow Harvard U., Cambridge, Mass., 1957-58, lectr. physics, 1958-59, asst. prof. physics, 1959-64, assoc. prof. biophysics, 1964-68, prof. biochemistry, 1968-72, Am. Cancer Soc. prof. molecular biology, 1972-81, prof. biology, 1985-86, H.H. Timken prof. sci., 1986-87, Carl M. Loeb Univ. prof., 1987—, chair dept. cellular and devel. biology, 1987-93; chmn. sci. bd. Biogen N.V., Dutch Antilles, 1978-83, co-chmn., supervisory bd., 1979-81, chmn. supervisory bd., chief exec. officer, 1981-84; vice chmn., bd. dirs. Myriad Genetics, Inc., 1992—; chmn. of bd. NetGenics, Inc., 1996—; V.D. Mattia lectr. Roche Inst. Molecular Biology, 1976. Recipient U.S. Steel Found. NAS, 1968, Ledlie prize Harvard U., 1969, Warren triennial prize Mass. Gen. Hosp., 1977, Louis and Bert Freedman Found. N.Y. Acad. Scis., 1977, Prix Charles-Leopold Mayer Academie des Scis., Inst. de France, 1977, Nobel prize in chemistry, 1980, New Eng. Entrepreneur of Yr. award, 1991; co-winner Louisa Gross Horwitz prize Columbia U., 1979, Gairdner prize, 1979, Albert Lasker Basic Sci. award, 1979; Guggenheim fellow, 1968-69; hon. fellow Trinity Coll., Cambridge, U.K., 1991. Mem. Am. Phys. Soc., Nat. Acad. Scis., Am. Soc. Biol. Chemists, Am. Acad. Arts and Scis.; fgn. mem. Royal Soc. Office: The Biol Labs 16 Divinity Ave Cambridge MA 02138-2097

GILBERT, WILLIAM MARSHALL, retired biologist, educator; b. Huntington, W.Va., July 19, 1935; s. Frank Albert and Eleanor (Marshall) G.; m. Claire Arlene Bohn, Aug. 25, 1981; 1 child, Chantal Louise. BSc, Ohio State U., 1957, MA, 1959; PhD, U. Calif., Davis, 1975. Instr. biology Contra Costa Coll., San Pablo, Calif., 1973-79; environ. rsch. analyst San Francisco Bay Marine rsch. Ctr., Emeryville, Calif., 1979-85; instr. environ. sci. Chabot Coll., Hayward, Calif., 1990-94; pvt. ornithol. rschr. on behavior of orange-crowned and Wilson's warblers, 1981—; lit. reviewer Am. Ornithol. Union, 1996—. Contbr. articles to profl. jours. Mem. Nature Sounds Soc. (bd. dirs. 1983-98), Sierra Club (Couples sect. leadership chair 1982—). Avocations: camping, hiking, bird watching, sound recording, photography. Home and Office: 4630 Driftwood Ct El Sobrante CA 94803-1806

GILBERT-BARNESS, ENID F., pathologist, pathology and pediatrics educator; b. Sydney, New South Wales, Australia, May 31, 1927; came to U.S., 1952, naturalized, 1975; d. Christian Henry and Mabel (Milne) Fischer; m. James Bryson Gilbert, Aug. 12, 1954; children: Mary M., Elizabeth A., James C. (dec.), Jennifer E., Rebecca D.; m. Lewis Barness, July 5, 1987. MBBS, U. Sydney, 1950, MD, 1983, DSc (hon.), U. Wis., Madison, 1999, MD (hon.) U. Sydney, 1999. Diplomate Am. Bd. Pediat., Am. Bd. Clin. Pathology, Am. Bd. Anat. Pathology, Am. Bd. Pediat. Pathology. Resident Children's Hosp., Boston, Children's Hosp., Phila., Children's Hosp., Washington, Brackenridge Hosp., Austin, Tex.; asst. prof. U. W.Va., 1963-67, assoc. prof., 1967-70; assoc. prof. pathology and pediat. U. Wis., Madison, 1970-71, prof., 1971-93, Disting. Med. Alumni prof., 1986-93, dir. pediat. pathology, 1970-93, dir. surg. pathology, 1975-93, prof. emeritus pathology and pediat., emeritus Med. Alumni Disting. prof., 1993—; prof. pathology and pediat., U. So. Fla., 1993—. Recipient Disting. Tchg. award U. Wis., 1984, Disting. Med. Alumni Tchg. award, 1984. Author: Introduction to Pathology, 1978, Genetic Aspects Developmental Pathology, 1987, Potters Pathology of the Infant and Fetus, 1997; also numerous chpts., articles. NIH grantee, 1978—. Mem. Am. Soc. Clin. Pathology, Soc. Pediat. Pathology (pres. 1986-87), Internat. Acad. Pathology, Internat. Pediat. Pathology Assn. (pres. 1990-92), Teratology Soc., Cardiovascular Soc. S.Am. (hon.), Am. Pediat. Soc., Am. Acad. Pediat., U.S. Can. Acad. Pathology, Arthur Purdy Stout Soc. Surgical Pathology, N.Y. Acad. Sci., Alpha Omega Alpha. Home: 1115 W Virginia Ave Tampa FL 33603-4538 Office: U So Fla Tampa Gen Hosp Tampa FL 33601

GILBERTSON, DAVID, state supreme court justice. Former judge S.D. Cir. Ct. (5th jud. cir.), Pierre; assoc. justice S.D. Supreme Ct., Pierre, 1995—. Office: 500 E Capitol Ave Pierre SD 57501-5070

GILBERTSON, ERIC RAYMOND, academic administrator, lawyer; b. Cleve., Mar. 5, 1945; s. Ewald R. and Esther V. (Johnson) G.; m. Cynthia F. Forrest, Jan. 25, 1974; children: Sara, Seth. BS, Bluffton Coll., 1966; MA in Econs., Ohio U., 1967; JD cum laude, Cleve. State U., 1970; DLitt (hon.) U. Mysore, Karnataka, India, 1993. Bar: Ohio 1970, Vt. 1984, U.S. Dist. Ct. (no. and so. dists.) Ohio 1971, U.S. Supreme Ct. 1981. Instr. econs. Kent State U., Ohio, 1969-70; law clk. Supreme Ct. of Ohio, Columbus, 1970-71; asst. atty. gen. State of Ohio, Columbus, 1971-73; exec. asst. to pres. Ohio State U., Columbus, 1973-79; assoc. Vorys, Sater, Seymore & Pease, Columbus, 1979-81; pres. Johnson State Coll., Vt., 1981-89, Saginaw Valley State U., University Center, Mich., 1989—. Bd. dirs. Bay County Alliance for Schs., Midland County Econ. Growth and Devel. Corp. Contbr. articles to profl. jours. Mem. Am. Coun. on Edn., Am. Assn. State Colls. and Univs. (com. on policies and purposes), Saginaw County C. of C., Torch Club, Saginaw Club, Bay City Country Club. Home: 7371 Glen Eagle Dr Bay City MI 48706-9316 Office: Saginaw Valley State U Office of Pres University Center MI 48710

GILBERTSON, JOEL WARREN, lawyer; b. Valley City, N.D., Nov. 9, 1949; s. Roy W. and Gwen D. (Haugen) G.; m. Jan Erikson, June 11, 1972; children: David, Lisa. BA, Concordia Coll., Moorhead, Minn., 1972; JD, U. N.D., 1975. Bar: N.D. 1976, U.S. Dist. Ct. N.D. 1976. Ptnr. Binek & Gilbertson, Bowman, N.D., 1976; atty. N.D. Supreme Ct., Bismarck, 1976-78; exec. dir. N.D. Bar Assn., Bismarck, 1978-81; ptnr. Pearce & Durick, Bismarck, 1981-97; exec. v.p., gen. counsel Ind. Cmty. Banks of N.D., 1997—. Served with U.S. Army N.G., 1972-78. Mem. N.D. Bar Assn. (bd. govs. 1989-95, pres. 1992-93), N.D. Bar Found. (vice chmn. 1982-84, chmn. bd. dirs. 1986-89), South Cen. Dist. Bar Assn. (pres. 1987-89). Republican. Lutheran. Avocations: piano, softball. Home: 1025 Crescent Ln Bismarck ND 58501-2463 Office: Ind Comty Banks ND PO Box 6128 Bismarck ND 58506-6128

GILBERTSON, STEVEN E(DWARD) SATYAKI, real estate broker, guidance counselor; b. Winona, Minn., Nov. 5, 1951; s. Conrad Orville and Lorraine Kristina (Munson) G.; m. Jayne Ann Rock, June 13, 1992. BA, U. Minn., Morris, 1974; MS, Winona State U., 1982. Math tchr. Winona Pub. Schs., 1974-76, Owatonna (Minn.) Pub. Schs., 1976-77; tie gang laborer Milw. Railroad, Winona, 1978; spl. edn. tchr. Winona Heights Acad., 1978-79; math tchr. Rushford (Minn.) Pub. Schs., 1980-81, Gale Ettrick Trempealeau Sch., Galesville, Wis., 1981-82; salesperson Winona Realty, 1983-86, broker, 1987—; broker S.G. Realty, Winona, 1986-93; tchr. elem. phys. edn. St. Francis Sch., Rochester, Minn., 1993; spl. edn. tchr. Austin Pub. Schs., 1994-96, Racine Unified Sch. Dist., 1996-97; guidance counselor, dept. head Mpls. Pub. Schs., 1997—; mem. edn. com., multiple listing svc. com. Multiple Listing Svc., Winona, 1988-90, 93. Fundraiser YMCA, Winona, 1990; mem. focus group Winona County Chem. Abuse Prevention Task Force, 1991-93; facilitator Course in Miracles Study Group, Winona, 1991-93, Racine, Wis., 1996-97; creator Adult Children Anonymous, Emotions Anonymous (Winona chpt.), 12-Step Groups, 1990. Mem. Minn. Assn. Realtors, Sons of Norway, Westfield Golf Club (men's league champion 1987, 89), Minn. Sch. Counselors Assn., Minn. Fedn. of Tchrs. Avocations: sports and fitness, basketball, tennis, meeting people. Home: 234 15th Ave SE Rochester MN 55904-4731 Office: Sanford Middle Sch 3524 42nd Ave S Minneapolis MN 55406

GILBERTSON, SUSAN, nurse manager; b. Lancaster, Wis., Nov. 8, 1952; d. Clyde Gene and Florence Adele (Haudenshield) Irish; m. Richard Gilbertson, June 1975. RN, Madison Gen. Hosp., Wis., 1974; BS, Coll. St. Francis, Joliet, Ill., 1983; MS, Coll. St. Francis, 1987. Nurse clinician U. Wis. Hosp., Madison; nurse mgr. U. Wis. Vet. Hosp., Madison, Columbus (Wis.) Hosp.; nursing supr. U. Wis. Hosp., Madison. Mem. Assn. Oper. Rm. Nurses, NAON.

GILBERT-STRAWBRIDGE, ANNE WIELAND, journalist; b. Chgo.; d. David and Joy (Arnold) Wiel; m. George Gale Gilbert III (dec.); children: Douglas, Christopher; m. James Murry Strawbridge. BS, Northwestern U. Columnist Chgo. Daily News, 1971-78, United Features Syndicate, 1978-81; reporter NBC-TV Sunday in, Chgo., 1973; guest expert NBC-TV, N.Y.C. Today, 1974—; mem. Newspapers Features Council. Prodr.: WSNS-TV spl. Collectors World, 1971; performer TV programs, KETC-TV, St. Louis, Donahue, 1975, 77; owner syndicated radio spot The Antique Detective; author: Antique Hunters Guide For Freaks and Fanciers, 1974, Collecting the New Antiques, 1975, How to Be an Antiques Detective, 1978, Investing in the Antiques Market, 1980, Collectors Guide to American Illustrator Art, 1991, Design and Memorabilia 40s-50s, 1995, Design and Memorabilia 70s-80s, 1996, Collecting of Quilts (syndicated news column) Antique Detective, 1983-92. Mem. Soc. Illustrators (assoc.), Newspaper Features Coun., Alpha Gamma Delta. Presbyterian. Address: 854 Pruitt Cove Rd Laurel Springs NC 28644-8349

GILBRETH, FRANK BUNKER, JR., retired communications executive, writer; b. Plainfield, N.J., Mar. 17, 1911; s. Frank Bunker and Lillian Evelyn (Moller) G.; m. Elizabeth Cauthen, Sept. 29, 1934 (dec. 1954); 1 child, Betsy; m. Mary Manigault, June 4, 1955; children: Edward, Rebecca Motte. B.A., U. Mich., 1933. Reporter N.Y. Herald Tribune, 1933-34; corr. AP, 1938-42, cable editor, 1945-47; v.p. News and Courier, Evening Post, Charleston, S.C., 1947-83; bd. dirs. Buenos Aires Herald. Author: (with Ernestine Gilbreth Carey) Cheaper by the Dozen, 1949, Belles on Their Toes, 1950, (with John Held, Jr.) Held's Angels, 1952, I'm a Lucky Guy, 1951, Innside Nantucket, 1955, Of Whales and Women, 1957, How to Be a Father, 1958, Loblolly, 1959, He's My Boy, 1962, Time Out for Happiness, 1971. Served to lt. comdr. USNR, 1942-45. Decorated Air medal, Bronze Star. Home: 1844 Maybank Hwy Charleston SC 29412-2108 also: The Shoe Hulbert Ave Nantucket MA 02554

GILBRIDE, JOSEPH J., advertising executive. BS in Acctg., NYU, MBA in FIn. CPA, N.Y. Audit mgr. Ernst & Young; v.p., contr. Backer and Spielvogel; v.p., contr., dir. acquisitions Interpub. Group of Cos.; exec. v.p., CFO Lowe Group, N.Y.C., 1986—. Mem. N.Y. State Soc. CPAs, Inst. CPAs. Avocations: golf, reading. Office: Lowe & Ptnrs/SMS 1114 Ave of the Americas New York NY 10036

GILBRIDE, WILLIAM DONALD, lawyer; b. Detroit, July 31, 1924; s. William Andrew and Kathryne Agnes (Donnelly) G.; m. Helen A. Posselius, May 1, 1954; 1 son, William Donald. LL.B., U. Detroit, 1950. Bar: Mich. 1950, U.S. Ct. Claims 1955, U.S. Ct. Appeals (6th cir.) 1967, U.S. Supreme Ct. 1985. Assoc. firm Fildew, DeGree & Fleming, Detroit, 1951-53; ptnr. Fildew, DeGree & Fleming, 1953-65; ptnr. firm Fildew, Gilbride, Miller & Todd (and predecessor firm), 1973-80, Fildew, Hinks, Gilbride, Miller & Todd, Detroit, 1980-91; pvt. practice law William D. Gilbride, P.C., Detroit, 1992—; mem. State Bd. Law Examiners, 1972-75; spl. counsel State of Mich. Atty. Grievance Commn., 1980; arbitrator Mich. Employees Rels. Commn.; mediator Wayne County Mediation. Pres. Friends of Detroit Pub. Library, 1968-70; pres. bd. trustees Liggett Sch., 1964-66. Served with AUS, 1943-46. Fellow Am. Bar Found., Mich. Bar Found.; mem. Detroit Bar Assn. (pres. 1972-73), Am. Judicature Soc., U. Detroit Sch. Law Alumni Assn. (pres. 1985-86, Outstanding Alumnus award 1991), Inc. Soc. Irish Am. Lawyers (former bd. dirs.), Am. Legion, Detroit Club, Propeller Club of the U.S.-Port of Detroit (bd. govs. 1992—, sec. bd. 1995, v.p. 1996, pres. bd. govs. 1997), Grosse Pointe Club, Yondotega Club, Racquet Club, Blue Key, Alpha Kappa Psi, Delta Theta Phi. Republican. Roman Catholic. *

GILBY, STEVE, metallurgical engineering researcher; b. Dayton, Ohio, Sept. 22, 1939. BS, U. Cin., 1962; PhD in Metall. Engring., Ohio State U., 1966. Rsch. engr. steelmaking Youngstown Steel Co., 1966-76; rsch. engr. Armco Steel Co., 1967-69, sr. rsch. engr., 1969-72, rsch. assoc., 1972-75, mgr. steelmaking rsch., 1975-82, dir. process rsch., 1982-93; mng. dir. Armco Rsch. and Tech., Pitts., 1993-95, v.p. rsch. & tech., 1995—; asst. pres. Armco Rsch. and Tech., Middletown, Ohio, 1996—; chmn. external adv. commn. materials sci. and engring. dept. Ohio State U., 1988—. Mem. Am. Iron and Steel Soc., Am. Soc. Metals Internat. Achievements include research in steelmaking and continuous casting process development. Office: Armco Inc Rsch & Tech 705 Curtis St Middletown OH 45044-5812

GILCHREST, BARBARA ANN, dermatologist; b. Port Chester, N.Y., 1945. MD, Harvard U., 1971. Diplomate Am. Bd. Dermatology, Am. Bd. Internal Medicine. Intern Boston City Hosp., 1971-72, resident internal medicine, 1972-73, resident dermatology, 1973-76; fellow photobiology Harvard U., Boston, 1974-75; chief dermatology U. Hosp., Boston, Boston City Hosp. (now Boston Med. Ctr.); prof., chmn. dermatology Boston U. Sch. Medicine, 1985—. Mem. AAAS, Am. Acad. Dermatology, Assn. Am. Physicians, Am. Soc. for Clin. Investigation, Inst. Medicine, Soc. for Investigative Dermatology. Office: Boston U Sch Medicine Dermatology 609 Albany St # J507 Boston MA 02118-2515

GILCHREST, THORNTON CHARLES, retired association executive; b. Chgo., Sept. 1, 1931; s. Charles Jewett Gilchrest and Patricia (Thornton) Thornton; m. Barbara Dibbern, June 8, 1952; children: Margaret Mary, James Thornton. B.S. in Journalism, U. Ill., 1953. Cert. tchr., Ill. Tchr. pub. high sch. West Chicago, Ill., 1957; exec. dir. Plumbing-Heating-Cooling Info. Bur., Chgo., 1958-64; asst. to pres. A.Y. McDonald Mfg. Co., Dubuque, Iowa, 1964-68; exec. dir. Am. Supply Assn., Chgo., 1968-77, exec. v.p., 1977-82; exec. v.p. Nat. Safety Coun., Chgo., 1982-83, pres., 1983-95; chmn. Internat. Safety Coun., Chgo., 1992-95; pres. Nat. Safety Coun. Found. for Safety and Health, 1986-95. Bd. dirs. Prevent Blindness Am., 1993. With USN, 1953-55. Mem. Am. Soc. Assn. Execs., Chgo. Soc. Assn. Execs. Methodist.

GILCHREST, WAYNE THOMAS, congressman, former high school educator; b. Rahway, N.J., Apr. 15, 1946; s. Arthur and Elizabeth Gilchrest; m. Barbara Rawley; children: Kevin, Joel, Katie. AA in Liberal Arts, Wesley Coll., 1971; BA in History, Del. State Coll., 1973; postgrad., Loyola Coll., Balt., 1984—. Tchr. social studies Warren Hills Jr. High Sch., Washington, N.J., 1973-76; tchr. history St. Alban's City (Vt.) Elem. Sch., 1976-79, Kent County High Sch., Worton, Md., 1979-90; mem. 102nd-106th Congresses from 1st Md. dist., 1991—, mem. resources com., chmn. transp. and infrastructure subcom. on pub. bldgs. and econ. devel. Vol. Nat. Forest Svc., Bitterroot Nat. Forest, Idaho, 1986-87. Sgt. USMC, 1964-68, Vietnam. Decorated Purple Heart, Bronze Star. Mem. Kent Country Tchrs. Assn., VFW, Am. Legion, Mil. Order Purple Heart. Republican. Methodist. Office: US Ho of Reps 2245 Rayburn HOB Washington DC 20515-2001*

GILCHRIST, ANN ROUNDEY, hospice nurse; b. Utica, N.Y., Dec. 21, 1948; d. William Gilchrist and Adele (Cobb) Roundey; divorced; children: Kristie Ann Hughes, Megean Elizabeth Hughes. Student, Cazenovia Coll., 1967-68; LPN, Utica Sch. Practical Nursing, 1972; postgrad., Mohawk Valley C.C., 1972-75; ADN, SUNY, Morrisville, 1976. RN, Nev.; CNOR. Obstetrics and med., surg. staff nurse St. Elizabeth Hosp., Utica, 1972-76; asst. charge nurse CCU and ICU Mohawk Valley Gen. Hosp., Ilion, N.Y., 1976-78; staff nurse operating room Tucson Med. Ctr., 1978-80, El Dorado Hosp., Tucson, 1978-80; staff nurse oper. rm. and post anesthesia care unit Tucson Gen. Hosp., 1980-85; charge nurse oper. rm. Desert Springs Hosp., Las Vegas, 1985-87, staff nurse GI Lab., 1988-90; charge nurse GI Lab, staff nurse operating room Lake Mead Hosp., Las Vegas, 1991-93; supr. operating room Red Rock Surg. Ctr., Las Vegas, 1993-95; staff nurse Endoscopy Lab., Sunrise Flamingo Surg. Ctr., Las Vegas, 1995-97; nurse case mgr. Odyssey Healthcare (hospice), Las Vegas, 1998—. Mem. Am. Orgn. Oper. Room Nurses, Soc. Gastroenterology Assts., Hospice Nurse Orgn., So. Nev. Land Cruisers. Avocations: professional and published doll artist, ceramicist, equestrian. Home: 4552 Scott Ave Las Vegas NV 89102-8107 Office: 4011 McLeod Las Vegas NV 89121

GILCHRIST, ELLEN LOUISE, writer; b. Vicksburg, Miss., Feb. 20, 1935; d. William Garth and Aurora (Alford) G.; children: Marshall Peteet Walker, Jr., Garth Gilchrist Walker, Pierre Gautier Walker. BA in Philosophy, Millsaps Coll., 1967; postgrad., U. Ark., 1976; LittD (hon.), Millsaps Coll., 1987; LHD (hon.), U. So. Ill., 1991. Freelance writer, journalist; commentator, morning edit. of news Nat. Pub. Radio, Washington, 1984, 85. Author: The Land Surveyor's Daughter, 1979, In The Land of Dreamy Dreams, 1981, The Annunciation (Book of Month Club alternate in U.S. and Sweden), 1983, Victory Over Japan (Am. Book award 1984), 1984, Drunk With Love, 1986, Falling Through Space, 1987, The Anna Papers, 1988, Light Can Be Both Wave and Particle, 1989, I Cannot Get You Close Enough, 1990 (Miss. Inst. Arts and Letters award 1990, fiction award Miss. Libr. Assn. 1990), Net of Jewels, 1992, Starcarbon, 1994, Anabasis, A Journey to the Interior, 1994, The Age of Miracles, 1995, Rhoda, A Life in Stories, 1995, The Courts of Love, 1996, Sarah Conley, 1997, Flights of Angels, 1998; (poems) Riding Out the Tropical Depression; contbr. short stories poems to literary publs. Recipient Poetry award U. Ark., 1976, Craft in Poetry award N.Y. Quar., 1978, Fiction award The Prairie Schooner, 1981, Poetry award Miss. Arts Festival, 1968, Saxifrage award, 1983, Fiction award Miss. Acad. Arts and Sci., 1982, 85, Am. Book award Victory Over Japan, 1984, J. William Fulbright prize U. Ark., 1985, Lit. award Miss. Inst. Arts and Letters, 1985, 90, 91; 2 Pushcart prizes, O. Henry Short Story award, 1995; grantee NEA, 1979. Mem. Author's Guild.

GILCHRIST, EUNICE BASS, nursing educator; b. Nashville, N.C., Apr. 2, 1942; d. Bruzer and Caressa (Wiggins) Bass; m. Leonard Wilbert Gilchrist, Aug. 20, 1966; children: LaJune Fountain, Lenise, Lynda. Diploma, Lancaster Gen. Sch. Nursing, Pa., 1964; BSN, Eastern Mennonite Coll., 1974; MS, Va. Commonwealth U., 1982. RN, Va. Charge nurse Dixie Hosp./ Hampton (Va.) Gen. Hosp., 1964-66; staff nurse Hampton VA Med. Ctr., 1966-67, Washington VA Med. Ctr., 1967-72, 75-76; obstetrics instr. Rockingham Meml. Hosp. Sch. Nursing, Harrisonburg, Va., 1974-75; clin. nursing instr. McGuire VA Med. Ctr., Richmond, Va., 1976-86, 87—; acting assoc. chief nursing/edn. McGuire VA Med. Ctr., 1995; founder, dir. Rhema Adult Day Care Ctr., Richmond, 1986-87; founder, coord. Consortium VA Nurse Educators, 1992—; adv. bd., ednl. cons. Blessed Enterprises Comprehensive Med. Svcs., Richmond, 1992—. Recipient Fed. Woman of Yr. award, 1991, Nat. Leadership award, 1992. Avocations: singing, writing. Office: McGuire VA Med Ctr 1201 Broad Rock Blvd Richmond VA 23249-0001

GILCHRIST, GERALD SEYMOUR, pediatric hematologist, oncologist, educator; b. Springs, Transvaal, South Africa, May 25, 1935; came to U.S., 1962; s. David and Anne (Lipschitz) G.; m. Antoinette E. Besset, May 7, 1967; children: Daniel J., Michael A., Lauren D. MB BCh, U. Witwatersrand Med. Sch., Johannesburg, South Africa, 1957; Diploma in Child Health, Royal Coll. Physicians and Surgeons, London, 1961. Diplomate Am. Bd. Pediatrics (chmn. Sub-Bd. Pediatric Hematology-Oncology 1990-92). Intern Johannesburg Gen. Hosp., 1958-59; resident Transvaal Meml. Hosp. for Children and Baragwanath Hosp., Johannesburg, 1959-60; resident in pediatrics Hosp. for Sick Children, London, 1961, Children's Hosp., Cin., 1962-63; fellow pediatrics, hematology/oncology Children's Hosp. of L.A., 1963-65, cons. hematology and blood banking, 1965-71; attending physician Childrens Hosp. L.A., 1968-71; asst. prof. pediatrics U. So. Calif., Los Angeles, 1966-71; assoc. prof. pediatrics Mayo Med. Sch., Rochester, Minn., 1972-78, chmn. dept. pediatrics, 1984-96; cons. pediatric hematology/oncology Mayo Clinic and Found., Rochester, 1971—; prof. pediatrics Mayo Med. Sch., Mayo Clinic and Found., Rochester, Minn., 1978—; Helen C. Levitt prof. Mayo Clinic and Found., Rochester, Minn., 1987—; mem. Commn. on Cancer, ACS, 1982-85; bd. dirs. Hemophilia Ctr., Dept. Maternal and Child Health, Rockville, Md., 1978—; prin. investigator Childrens Cancer Study Group, Nat. Cancer Inst., Bethesda, 1981—. Co-author: You and Leukemia, 1976; contbr. chpts. to books, numerous articles to profl. jours. Med. advisor Northland Childrens Oncology Svcs., Rochester, Minn., 1978-80; bd. dirs. Minn. chpt. Nat. Hemophilia Found. Found., Mpls., 1981-84; chpt sec. Physicians for Social Respinsibility, Rochester, 1982-85; bd. dirs. Nat. Childhood Cancer Found., 1990-97; chair med. and scientific adv. bd. Nat. Children's Cancer Found., 1995-97. Fellow Am. Acad. Pediatrics (chmn. sect. on pediatric hematology-oncology 1988-90, chair coun. on sects. 1999—); mem. Am. Soc. Clin. Oncology, Am. Soc. Hematology, Am. Pediatric Soc., Am. Bd. Pediatrics (bd. dirs. 1990-91, chmn. sub bd. pediatric hematology-oncology 1989-91), Soc. for Pediatric Rsch. (mem. accreditation coun. grad. med. edn. residency rev. com. pediatrics 1997—), Am. Soc. Pediatric Hematology/Oncology (trustee 1996-98). Democrat. Jewish. Avocations: sailing, bicycling, kayaking, scuba diving. Office: Mayo Clinic Dept Pediatrics 200 1st St SW Rochester MN 55905-0002

GILCHRIST, GRACE, television station executive. V.p., gen. mgr. WXYZ-TV, Detroit. Office: Sta WXYZ-TV PO Box 789 20777 W Ten Mile Rd Southfield MI 48037-0789*

GILCHRIST, HENRY, lawyer; b. Austin, Tex., Nov. 6, 1924; s. Gibb and Vesta (Weaver) G.; m. Patricia Ann Lynch, Nov. 24, 1951; children: Thomas Gibb, Terri Lynn. BS in Civil Engring., Tex. A&M U., 1948; LLB, U. Tex., 1950. Bar: Tex. 1950, U.S. Supreme Ct. 1971. Assoc. Douglass & McGuire, Pampa, Tex., 1951-52; ptnr. Jenkens & Gilchrist, Dallas, 1952—; Bd. dirs. Kirby Corp, Houston. Contbr. articles to profl. jours. Bd. dirs. Dallas County Heritage Soc., 1984-87, chmn. bd. trustees, 1978-81, Ctrl. Dallas Assn., exec. com., chmn., 1984-85, Dallas World Salute 1985—, chmn. pres., 1988-90, Theatre Three, 1986-87, Tex. A&M U. Pvt. Enterprise Rsch. Ctr.,

1987—, Dallas Bus. Com. for Arts, exec. com. 1988—; adv. coun. Communities Found. Tex., Inc., Dallas Citizen Coun., mem. cultural arts task force; mem. planning and zoning commn. Town of Highland Park, Tex., 1976-84; mem. exec. com. Dallas Mus. Art Trustee and Audit Com., 1988—, chmn. 1988-91, TACA Inc., v.p. 1986-89; mem. devel. coun. Tex. A&M U. Coll. Liberal Arts; mem. Tex. A&M U. Commn. Visual Arts, 1982—, chmn. 1982-88; mem. exec. bd. So. Meth. U. Sch. Theology, 1992—; founder Park Cities Hist. Soc. With U.S. Army, 1943-46. Mem. ABA, State Bar Tex., Tex. Bar Found. (life), The Southwestern Legal Found. (trustee, exec. planning com., administrv. com., former chmn. rsch. fellows), Dallas Bar Assn. Methodist. Avocations: reading, walking, gardening. Home: 4809 Drexel Dr Dallas TX 75205-3108

GILCHRIST, JAMES A., communication educator. Chmn. dept. comms. Western Mich. U., Kalamazoo. Office: We Mich U Sprau Tower Dept Comms Kalamazoo MI 49008*

GILCHRIST, JAMES BEARDSLEE, banker; b. Cleve., Apr. 1, 1939; s. Hart D. and Alice (Beardslee) G.; m. Lewayne Dorman, Sept. 14, 1963; children: Hart D., Matthew J. AB, Dartmouth Coll., 1961; LLB, Stanford U., 1964; grad. with honors, Pacific Coast Banking Sch., U. Wash., 1970. Bar: Wash. 1964, Colo. 1964. Dep. pros. atty. King County, Wash., 1964-65; with Seattle First Nat. Bank, 1965-93, v.p., 1973-93, trust officer, 1970-77, corp. sec., 1977-82; sec. Seafirst Corp., 1977-82, mgr. instl. trust dept., 1982-85, mgr. personal trust dept., 1985-93; ptnr. Trust Concepts, 1993—; instr. Am. Inst. Banking, Seattle Community Coll., 1976-78. Mem. candidate evaluation team Seattle Mcpl. League, 1976-79, chmn., 1979; mem. adv. com. Mercer Island Sch. Bd., 1979-81; bd. dirs. Mercer Island Schs. Found., 1981-85; mem. Dartmouth Coll. Alumni Coun., 1987-90. Mem. Wash. Bar Assn., Am. Soc. Corp. Secs. (chpt. pres. 1980-81, corp. practices com. 1981-83, dir. 1982-84), Corp. Trustees Assn. of Wash. (chmn. 1989-91), Seattle Estate Planning Coun. (mem. exec. com. 1987-89, chmn. seminar 1975).

GILCHRIST, JOHN MARK, otolaryngologist; b. Dallas, Dec. 10, 1959; s. Ronald Wallace Jr. and Patricia Gene (Wood) G.; m. Melissa Paige LaBoon, Jan. 4, 1986; children: Sarah, Claire, Michael. BS, Wheaton (Ill.) Coll., 1982; MD, U. Okla., Oklahoma City, 1986. Diplomate Am. Bd. Otolaryngology. Intern U. Okla. Med. Ctr., 1986-87, resident otolaryngology, head and neck surgery, 1987-91; mem. staff Mercy Health Ctr., Oklahoma City, 1991—, Bapt. Med. Ctr., Oklahoma City, 1991—, Deaconess Hosp., Oklahoma City, 1991—; head, otolaryngology sect., dept. of surgery Mercy Health Ctr., Oklahoma City, 1995—; pvt. practice Okla. Otolaryngology Assocs., Inc., Oklahoma City, 1991—; pres. Okla. Acad. of Otolaryngology, 1996-97. Mem. com. Young Life, Oklahoma City, 1987-97. Mem. AMA, Am. Acad. Otolaryngology-Head and Neck Surgery, Okla. Med. Assn., Okla. Acad. Otolaryngology (pres. 1996-97). Office: Okla Otolaryngology Assocs 4200 W Memorial Rd Ste 606 Oklahoma City OK 73120-8359

GILCHRIST, RICHARD IRWIN, real estate developer; b. L.A., Mar. 6, 1946; s. Dennis Samuel and Norma Elizabeth (Irwin) G.; m. Nina Newsom, June 21, 1969; children: Katherine Claire, Kimberly Ann, Brian Roy, Bradley Richard. Student, U. Copenhagen, Denmark, 1967; BA, Whittier (Calif.) Coll., 1968; JD, UCLA, 1971. Bar: Calif. 1972, U.S. Supreme Ct. 1972. Assoc. Flint & MacKay, L.A., 1972-74, ptnr., 1974-81; ptnr. Thomas, Shafran, Wasser & Childs, L.A., 1981-83; founding ptnr. Gilchrist & Rutter, Santa Monica, Calif., 1983, of counsel, 1984—; gen. counsel Maguire Thomas Ptnrs., Santa Monica, Calif., 1983-85, ptnr., 1985-88; sr. ptnr. Maguire Thomas Ptnrs., Santa Monica, 1988-95; co-owner Sacramento Kings NBA Team, 1992—; prin. founding ptnr. Common Wealth Ptnrs., L.A., 1995-99, Alexandria, Va., 1999—; pres., CEO Commonwealth Atlantic Properties, Washington, 1997—; instr. bus. law Calif. State U., L.A., 1973-74. Bd. dirs. Weingardt Ctr., 1993—, L.A. Met. YMCAs, 1993—; trustee Whittier Coll., 1996—. Mem. ABA, Calif. Bar Assn., Whittier Coll. Alumni Assn., UCLA Alumni Assn., Arltington (Va.) County C. of C. (bd. dirs. 1998—). Avocations: running, sports, travel. Home: 1517 29th St NW Washington DC 20007-3061 Office: Common Wealth Ptnrs 66 Canal Center Plz 7th Fl Alexandria VA 22314-1594*

GILCHRIST, WILLIAM AARON, architect; b. N.Y.C., Jan. 31, 1956; s. Johnie Aaron and Juanita Marcella (Hunt) G. BS, MIT, 1977, MArch, 1982, MS, 1982; postgrad., Harvard U., 1996. Registered arch., Ga., Ala., Nat. Coun. Archtl. Registration Bds. Project engr. H.J. Russell & Co., Atlanta, 1982-84, project mgr., 1987-88; project dir. H.J. Russell & Co., Birmingham, Ala., 1988-90, br. mgr., 1990-93; dir. planning and engring. City of Birmingham, 1993-97, dir. planning, engring. and permits, 1997—; architect intern Cherry Roberts Sullivan, Atlanta, 1984-87; project dir. Birmingham Civil Rights Inst., 1988-91; mem. vis. com. dept. architecture MIT, Cambridge, 1997—; mem. adv. com. on cmty. devel. Auburn (Ala.) U., 1994—. Contbg. editor articles to Birmingham News, 1997—. Bd. dirs. Discovery 2000 Sci. Mus., Birmingham, 1991-93, Birmingham Festival of Arts, 1993—, Ala. Symphony Found., Birmingham, 1997-99. Recipient James C. Howland award Nat. League of Cities, 1995; Aga Khan fellow MIT-Harvard U., 1981. Mem. AIA (ala. state coun., mem. task group regional urban design asst. team, mem. urban design com. 1997), Am. Planning Assn. (del. 1996), Constrn. Specifications Inst., Kiwanis (program com.). Roman Catholic. Avocations: linguistics, photography, graphic arts, aikido. Office: City of Birmingham 710 20th St N Birmingham AL 35203-2216

GILCHRIST, WILLIAM RISQUE, JR., economist; b. Lexington, Ky., July 16, 1944; s. William Risque and Susan (McLemore) G.; m. Peggy Linder Gardner, Mar. 20, 1968; children: William Risque, Shannon Linder, Heather Susan. B.B.A., U. Miami, 1966, MBQ, 1970; postgrad., Northwestern U., 1973—. Assoc. dir. conf. svcs. divsn. cont. edn. U. Miami, Coral Gables, 1966-71; asst. dir. edn. and tng. Mortgage Bankers Assn. Am., Washington, 1971-73; pres. Ventura Fin. Corp., Ft. Lauderdale, 1973-76, Gilchrist and Assocs., Pompano Beach, Fla., Santiago, Chile and London, 1976—; pres. Intervault, Inc., Ft. Lauderdale and Basel, Switzerland; cons. in field. Author: International Monetary Systems-Alternatives, 1969, Eurodollar Outlook-OPEC and the LDC's, 1978, The Contra Banker, 1999. Recipient Cert. of Achievement Savings and Loan Execs. Seminr, 1971. Mem. Broward County (Fla.) C. of C., NAB, Econ. Soc. South Fla., Mortgage Bankers Assn., Nat. Assn. Pvt. Security Vaults (pres. 1986-92), Senatorial Inner Cir., Kiwanis, Marina Bay, Mutiny. Republican. Episcopalian. Home: 1341 SE 9th Ave Pompano Beach FL 33060-9558

GILDEA, BRIAN MICHAEL, lawyer; b. New Haven, Nov. 1, 1939; s. Thomas Michael and Lillian Frances (Reilly) G.; children: Larysa Albina, Stefan Bohdan. AS, New Haven U., 1964; BA, Providence Coll., 1967; JD, Suffolk U., 1970. Bar: Conn. 1970, U.S. Dist. Ct. Conn. 1971, U.S. Ct. Appeals (2d cir.) 1975, U.S. Ct. Appeals (3d cir.) 1979, U.S. Ct. Appeals (5th cir.) 1984, U.S. Supreme Ct. 1975. Legal adviser City of Boston, 1969-70; assoc. Celentano, Ivey & Gery, New Haven, 1970-73; ptnr. Celentano & Gildea, New Haven, 1973-74; pvt. practice New Haven, 1974—. Bd. dirs. St. Mary's High Sch., New Haven, 1975-77; mem. Bethany (Conn.) Town Charter Commn., 1976; del. U.S./Japan Bilateral Session, 1988, U.S./China Joint Session on Trade and Econ. Law, 1987. With USAF, 1958-62. Recipient Svc. award Providence Coll., New Haven, 1979, Friar award St. Mary's Alumni Assn., 1980. Mem. ABA, Def. Rsch. Inst., Conn. Bar Assn., New Haven County Bar Assn., Am. Lawyers Assn. Democrat. Roman Catholic. Avocations: bicycling, tennis, skiing, photography. Office: 512 Blake St New Haven CT 06515-1287

GILDEN, ROBIN ELISSA, elementary education educator; b. Albany, N.Y., Aug. 1, 1950; d. Avrom Irwin and Virginia (D'Arcangelo) G. BS, Pa. State U., 1972, cert. in teaching, 1977. Cert. elem. tchr., Pa. Tchr. West Allegheny Sch. Dist., Imperial, Pa., 1972—. Fundraiser Mary Rensel Meml. Fund, Pitts., 1992—, Fanconi Anemia, 1996—. Recipient NASA Tchr. in Space Program, 1986. Mem. Pa. Edn. Assn. (bldg. rep. 1984-86, 91-93), Pa. Framework, PTA, Pa. State U. Alumni Assn., ASCD. Avocations: reading, travel, body building, theater. Home: 1256 Pennsbury Blvd Pittsburgh PA 15205-1638 Office: McKee Sch 1501 Oakdale Rd Oakdale PA 15071-3638

GILDENBERG, PHILIP LEON, neurosurgeon; b. Hazleton, Pa., Mar. 15, 1935; s. Samuel and Ida (Kline) G.; m. Patricia O'Neill Franklin; children: Susan, Steven, Ronald, Laura, Alexandra. AB in Zoology with honors (Edward Pendleton scholar 1952-55), U. Pa., 1955; MD, MS in Exptl. Neurology (Pa. Senatorial scholar 1955-59), Temple U., 1959, PhD in Neurophysiology (Nat. Inst. Neurol. Diseases and Blindness 1966-67, spl. fellow 1967, NIH grantee 1966), 1970. Diplomate Am. Bd. Neurol. Surgery. Intern Grace Hosp., Detroit, 1959-60; resident in surgery Temple U. Hosp., 1962, resident in neurosurgery, 1963-67, lectr. neurosurgery Sch. Nursing, 1963-67, lectr. neurosurgery Philippine Nurse Exchange Program, Health Scis. Ctr., 1965-67; research fellow neurophysiology Max Planck Inst. Brain Research, Frankfurt, Fed. Republic of Germany, 1968; staff neurosurgeon Cleve. Clinic Found., 1968-72, head clinician neurosurg. research, 1969-72; prof., chief div. neurosurgery Med. Ctr., U. Ariz., Tucson, 1972-75, Med. Sch., U. Tex., Houston, 1976-82; clin. prof. neurosurgery Med. Sch. U. Tex., Houston, 1982-96, clin. prof. psychiatry and behavioral medicine, 1988-94; co-dir. pain clinic Med. Sch., U. Tex., Houston, 1975-83; chief neurosurg. service Hermann Hosp., Houston, 1975-82, 90-91; clin. prof. neurosurgery Tex. A & M. Med. Sch., College Station, 1992-94; clin. prof. neurosurgery, clin. prof. radiology Baylor Med. Coll., 1994—; adj. asst. prof. Case Western Res. U., Cleve., 1970-72; vis. prof. Temple U. Med. Sch., 1978, 80, 94, Hahnemann Med. Sch., Phila., 1980, U. Fla. Med. Sch., 1981, U. Pa. Med. Sch., 1985, Wayne State Med. Sch., Detroit, 1988, U. Ariz. Med. Sch., 1995; dir. Houston Stereotactic Ctr., Houston; cons. Tucson VA Hosp., 1972-74; mem. numerous nat. med. coms. and study groups. Author numerous articles in field.; Editor: Applied Neurophysiology, Pain and Headache, Stereotactic and Functional Neurosurgery; mem. editorial bds. profl. jours. Bd. dirs. Houston Stereotactic Ctr., 1995—. Recipient Research award U. Ariz. Med. Sch., 1973, Fan Kane Research award, 1974; grantee NIH. Fellow ACS; mem. World Soc. Stereotactic and Functional Surgery (pres. 1993-96), Am. Soc. Stereotactic and Functional Surgery (pres. 1999—), Am. Assn. Neurol. Surgeons, Congress Neurol. Surgeons, Soc. Neurol. Surgeons, Am. Physiol. Soc., Soc. U. Neurosurgeons, Research Soc. Neurol. Surgeons, Soc. Neurosci., Internat. Assn. Study Pain (a founder), Houston Neurol. Soc., Am. Trauma Soc. (a founder), Am. Acad. Neurology (assoc.), Harris County Med. Soc., So. Neurosurg. Soc., Neuroanesthesia Soc., Nat. Pain Found. (bd. dirs. 1987-92), Coun. Biology Editors (bd. dirs. 1989-93), Am. Assn. Pain Medicine. Republican. Jewish. Home and Office: 6624 Fannin St Ste 1620 Houston TX 77030-2328

GILDENHORN, JOSEPH BERNARD, lawyer, businessman, former diplomat; b. Washington, Sept. 17, 1929; s. Oscar and Celia (Koval) G.; m. Alma Lee Gross, June 28, 1953; children: Carol Winer, Michael Saul. BS, U. Md., 1951; LLB, JD, Yale U., 1954. Bar: D.C. 1954, U.S. Ct. Appeals (D.C. cir.) 1954, U.S. Supreme Ct. 1954. Ptnr. Brown, Gildenhorn & Jacobs, 1955—; vice chmn. D.C. Nat. Sovran Bank, Washington, 1979-89; amb. to Switzerland Dept. State, Bern, 1989-93; ptnr. The JBG Cos.; adj. prof. George Washington U., D.C. Bar Assn.; pres. JBG Properties, Inc., 1956-88; chmn. bd. dirs. Franklin Nat. Bank; bd. dirs. The Mills Corp.; D.C. chmn. Gov. George W. Bush Exploratory Com. Mem. editl. bd. Yale Law Jour., 1954. D.C. campaign chmn. Bush-Quayle, 1988; past pres., bd. dirs. Hebrew Home Greater Washington, 1975-77; bd. dirs. Washington Jewish Cmty. Found., Inst. for Study of Diplomacy, Georgetown U., Ctr. for Strategic and Internat. Studies, Internat. Inst. Strategic Studies; joint distbn. com., pres., bd. dirs. United Jewish Appeal Fedn., 1988-89; vice chmn. D.C. Sports Commn., mem. Woodrow Wilson Internat. Ctr. for Scholars. With AUS, 1954-56. Recipient David Ben Gurion award State of Israel, 1977, Hyman Goldman Humanitarian award, 1984, B'nai B'rith Humanitarian award, 1985, Ourisman Cmty. Svc. award, 1987, Ottenstein Cmty. Svc. award, 1991, B'nai B'rith Disting. Alumnus award, 1983, Jewish Inst. for Nat. Security Affairs Leadership award, 1993, U. Md. Disting. Alumnus award, 1996, Leadership award Washington Inst., 1999; named Washingtonian of Yr. Washingtonian mag., 1996, 97. Mem. Order of Coif, Eagles Club, Presdl. Trust. Home: 2030 24th St NW Washington DC 20008-1608 Office: 1250 Connecticut Ave NW Washington DC 20036-2603

GILDER, GEORGE, communications executive, writer; b. N.Y.C., 1939; m. Nini Gilder; four children. Student, Harvard U. Fellow Kennedy Inst. Politics Harvard U.; sr. fellow Discovery Inst.; pres. Gilder Tech. Group; chmn. Lehrman Inst. Econs. Roundtable; program dir. Manhattan Inst. Author: Men and Marriage, 1972, Visible Man, 1978, Wealth and Poverty, 1981, The Spirit of Enterprise, 1986, Microcosm, 1989, Life After Television, 1992; co-author: The Party That Lost its Head; speech writer for Richard Nixon, George Romney, Nelson Rockefeller; founding editor Forbes ASAP; cons. in field; contbr. articles to profl. mags. and jours. Recipient White House award for Entrepreneurial Excellence. Office: Discovery Inst 1402 3rd Ave Ste 400 Seattle WA 98101-2109 also: PO Box 660 Housatonic MA 01236-0660*

GILDER, RICHARD EARL, clinical information system administrator, data analyst; b. Dallas, July 21, 1951; s. Elbert Earl Jr. and Mary Francis G.; m. Mary Ann Meier, Apr. 26, 1975; children: Stephen Earl, David Andrew, Katherine Rose. AS in Nursing, El Centro Coll., Dallas, 1974; BS cum laude in Nursing, Tex. Woman's U., 1996. RN, Tex.; cert. oper. room nurse. Staff nurse emergency dept. Parkland Hosp., Dallas, 1974-81; chem. engring. cons. Kool-X-Co., Dallas, 1981-82, Hon Mining Co., Laguna Hills, Calif., 1981-82; owner, pres. Gilder Co., Dallas, 1983—; staff nurse, clin. nurse III Presbyn. Hosp., Dallas, 1986-97; clin. info. sys. adminstr. dept. clin. outcomes/resource mt. Presbyn. Healthcare Sys., Inc., 1998—; instr. rifle, pistol and shotgun, 1984. Sustaining mem. Rep. Nat. Com., 1980—; asst. scout master Boy Scouts Am., Dallas, 1985—; founder United Nurses Internat.; asst. moderator Microsoft Nursing Network Forum. Mem. AAAS, Assn. Oper. Rm. Nurses (Dallas chpt. rsch. com. chair 1992—), Am. Soc. Ophthalmil Registered Nurses, Tex. Astron. Soc., Golden Key Nat. Honor Soc., Gamma Beta Phi, Sigma Theta Tau. Republican. Achievements include proposal for structure and name for the third elemental form of carbon. Fax: (214) 345-6436. E-mail: gilderr@wpmail.phscare.org. Home and Office: Gilder Co 13318 Mount Castle Dr Dallas TX 75234-5048 Office: Presbyn Healthcare Sys 8440 Walnut Hill Ln Dallas TX 75231-3833

GILDRED, THEODORE EDMONDS, ambassador; b. Mexico City, Oct. 18, 1935; s. Theodore Edmonds Sr. and Maxine Gildred; m. Suzanne Gail Green (div. 1975); children: Theodore Edmonds III, Jennifer Lynne, Edward Ames, John Taylor; m. Stephanie Ann Moscini, 1978 (div. 1992); children: Tory Boughton, Stephen Eckert. BA, Stanford U., 1959; cert., U. Paris Sorbonne, 1960, U. Heidelberg, Fed. Republic of Germany, 1960. Project supr. Investors Marine, Inc., Newport Beach, Calif., 1961; owner, pres., chief exec. officer Costa Pacifica, Inc., Newport Beach, 1961-65; adminstr. Grupo Lindavista, S.A., Mexico City, 1965-68; owner, pres., chief exec. officer, now chmn bd The Lomas Santa Fe Group, Solana Beach, Calif., 1968—; founder, chmn. bd. Torrey Pines Bank, Solana Beach, 1979-86; chmn. bd. Inst. Ams., La Jolla, Calif., 1984-86; U.S. ambassador to Argentina, 1986-89; chmn. bd. The Lomas Santa Fe Group, 1989—; mem. adv. bd. 1st Nat. Bank San Diego, U. Calif. Ctr. for U.S.-Mex. Studies, San Diego; founding co-owner Stars and Stripes Motorsports Ctr., Carlsbad, Calif.; bd. dirs. BankAm. Corp., N.Am. Airlines. Founding chmn. bd. govs. Inst. of Ams.; pres., trustee Gildred Found.; mem. adv. bd. dirs. Scripps Clinic and Rsch. Found., World Affairs Coun. San Diego, Am. Brit. Cowdary Hosp. Found., Mexico City, Salk Inst., San Diego Aerospace Mus., U. Ams. Found., Pubela, Mex.; founding mem., bd. dirs. San Dieguito Boys and Girls Club; bd. dirs. Grad. Sch. Internat. Rels. and Pacific Area Studies U. Calif., San Diego. With U.S. Army, 1955-57, USAFR, 1957-69. Recipient Gold Medal award for leadership Chgo. Tribune, 1959, Golden Boy award San Dieguito Boys' Club of Am., 1972, Friend of Distinction award Mex. and Am. Found., 1981, Master Key award for spirit of goodwill Panama Canal Commn., 1981, Guest of Honor award for Spirit of Goodwill Dist. of Panama, 1981, San Diego Aerospace Mus. award, 1982, Hon. Command Pilot award Ecuadorian Ministry of Def., 1984, Hon. keys Cities of Hermosillo, Mex., Mazatlan, Mex., Mexico City, Guatemala City, Guatemala, San Jose, Costa Rica, Managua, Nicaragua, Panama City, Panama, Colon, Panama, Esmeraldas, Ecuador, Quito, Ecuador; named to Salk Inst. Soc. of Hon. Mems., 1984. Mem. Am. Mgmt. Assn., Young Pres. Orgn., U. Calif.-San Diego Chancellor's Assocs. (award 1983), Stanford U. Alumni Assn. (founder Mexico City), Airplane Owners and Pilots Assn., Internat. Motor Sports Assn., So. Calif. Automobile Assn. (adv. bd.), Sports Car Cllub Am., Sports Car Club Calif., Sports Car Club San Diego, Fairbanks Polo Club, Lomas Santa Fe Country Club (founder, past pres.), Olivos Golf Club (Buenos Aires), Jockey Club (Buenos Aires), Rotary, Sigma Nu. Republican. Presbyterian. Home: 16056 El Camino Real Rancho Santa Fe CA 92067-9999 Office: The Lomas Santa Fe Group 265 Santa Helena Ste 200 Solana Beach CA 92075-1599*

GILDZEN, ALEX, writer; b. Monterey, Calif., Apr. 25, 1943; s. Al and Helen (Kovach) G. BA, Kent (Ohio) State U., 1965, MA, 1966. Intern Gen. Tire & Rubber, Akron, Ohio, 1965; lectr. English Kent State U. Libr., 1967-70, asst. curator, 1970-77, assoc. curator, 1977-84, curator spl. collections, 1984-93; fellow Inst. for Bibliography and Editing, Kent State U., 1986-94; judge poetry contest Kaleidoscope: A Literary/Art Mag. by Persons with Disabilities, Akron, Ohio, 1983-84. Author: The Year Book, 1974, The Avalanche of Time, 1986; co-author: Joseph Chaikin, 1992; co-editor: A Gathering of Poets, 1992. Bd. dirs. Santa Fe Cares. Recipient Ohioana award Ohioana Libr. Assn., Columbus, 1993. Mem. ALA (mem. exhbn. catalog awards com. 1990-92). Avocations: movies. Home: 2328 Brother Abedon Way Santa Fe NM 87505-6926

GILE, GREG L., military career officer; b. Wellington, Kans., Aug. 6, 1946. BBA, Wichita State U., 1968; MBA, Ohio State U.; grad., U.S. Army War Coll., Armed Forces Staff Coll. Commd. officer U.S. Army, 1968, advanced through grades to maj. gen., various command positions including co. comdr., divsn. ops. officer 101st Airborne Divsn., policy planner Orgn. Joint Chiefs of Staff; dir. ops. readiness and mobilization Dept. of the Army; dir. ops. JE U.S. Atlantic Command. Decorated Army Disting. Svc. medal, Def. Superior Svc. medal, Legion of Merit, Bronze Star with oak leaf cluster, Meritorious Svc. medal with oak leaf cluster, Army Commendation medal with V device and four oak leaf clusters. Office: US Atlantic Command Ste 200 1562 Mitscher Ave Norfolk VA 23551-2488

GILES, ALLEN, pianist, composer, music educator; b. Cambridge, Mass., Dec. 26, 1924; s. Allen Lester and Clara Lillian (Collins) G.; m. Marilla Jane Roberts, May 26, 1950 (div. 1970); children: Marilyn, Andrea, Cynthia; m. Anne Watson Diener, Sept. 26, 1970 (div. 1996); 1 child, Katherine Anne. MusB in Piano, Boston U., 1946, MA in Music, 1949; EdD in Music Edn., Columbia U., N.Y.C., 1981. performing pianist, soloist and chamber musician, U.S., Europe, Japan, 1945—; adjudicator for competitions nationwide, 1956—. Pvt. piano tchr. Mass., N.Y., Calif., 1944—; head piano dept., assoc. dir. music dept. SUNY, Buffalo, N.Y., 1952-64; chair, music dept., dir. Inst. of Music Villa Maria Coll., Buffalo, 1964-68; prof. music, chair performing arts Golden West Coll., Huntington Beach, Calif., 1972-93, prof. emeritus, 1993—; exec. dir. South Bay Conservatory, Torrance, Calif., 1997-98; owner, pres. GME Piano Video, 1984—. Author: (books) Beginning Piano-An Adult Approach Vol. 1, 1978, Vol. 2, 1988, Beginning Piano Telecourse Student Study Guide, 1979; Learning To Play The Piano By Television, 1982; course designer, tchr. on camera (video series) Beginning Piano-An Adult Approach, 1978-80; contbr. articles to profl. jours. Recipient Annual Piano Tchr. award Univ. N.Y., Fredonia, 1968; Radio and TV award for Noteworthy Achievement in Serious Music, Sigma Alpha Iota, 1980; named Master Tchr., Univ. Tex., Austin, 1986, Master Tchr. (piano), Music Tchrs. Nat. Assn., 1989. Mem. Music Tchrs. Nat. Assn., Calif. Assn. Profl. Music Tchrs. (v.p. 1990-91), Nat. Piano Found., Music Tchrs. Assn. Calif., Am. Fedn. Musicians. Home: 31217 Marne Dr Rancho Palos Verdes CA 90275-5617 Office: GME Piano Video PO Box 3788 Palos Verdes Peninsula CA 90274-9529

GILES, CONRAD LESLIE, ophthalmic surgeon; b. N.Y.C., July 14, 1934; s. Irving Samuel Giles and Victoria Ampole; m. Marilyn Toby Schwartz, June 20, 1955 (div. 1978); children: Keith Martin, Suzanne Speer, Kevin William, Brian Alan; m. Lynda Fern Schenk, Nov. 26, 1978; stepchildren: Jared Schenk, Jamie Schenk. MD, U. Mich., 1957, MS, 1961. Diplomate Am. Bd. Ophthalmology. Clin. assoc. NIH, Bethesda, Md., 1961-63; clin. asst. prof. Wayne State U. Sch. Medicine, Detroit, 1965-72, clin. assoc. prof. ophthalmology, 1973-89, clin. prof. ophthalmology, 1989—; chief ophthalmologist Children's Hosp. Mich., 1985—. Contbr. articles to med. jours. Active Jewish Welfare Fedn., Detroit, 1981-86, pres. 1986-89; bd. govs. Jewish Agy. for Israel, 1995—, Fellow Am. Acad. Ophthalmology; mem. AMA, USA Fedns. NA (co-pres. 1997-99), Mich. State Ophthal. Soc., Coun. Jewish Fedns. (v.p. 1992-95, treas. 1995-96, pres. 1996-99), United Jewish Appeal (nat. vice chmn. 1992-99), United Jewish Appeal Fedns. North Am. (pres. 1997-99), Mich. Jewish Conf. (pres. 1992-95). Avocations: golf, tennis, skiing. Home: 6300 Westmoor Rd Bloomfield Hills MI 48301-1359 Office: 4400 Town Ctr Southfield MI 48075-1601

GILES, EUGENE, anthropology educator; b. Salt Lake City, June 30, 1933; s. George Eugene and Eleanor (Clark) G.; m. Inga Valborg Wikman, Sept. 9, 1964; children: Eric George, Edward Eugene. AB, Harvard U., 1955, AM, 1960, PhD, 1966; MA, U. Calif., Berkeley, 1956. Diplomate Am. Bd. Forensic Anthropology (bd. dirs. 1996—). Instr. in anthropology U. Ill., Urbana, 1964-66, assoc. prof., 1970-73, prof., 1973—, head dept. anthropology, 1975-80, 82-83, 93-94; asst. prof. Harvard U., Cambridge, Mass., 1966-70; assoc. dean Grad. Coll. U. Ill., 1986-89, assoc. dean Liberal Arts and Scis. Coll., 1995—. Editor: (with J.S. Friedlaender, jr. editor) The Measures of Man: Methodologies in Biological Anthropology, 1976. Served with U.S. Army, 1956-58. NSF postdoctoral fellow, 1967-68; NSF grantee, 1970-72, NIH grantee, 1965-68. Fellow Am. Anthropol. Assn., AAAS, Am. Acad. Forensic Scis.; mem. Am. Assn. Phys. Anthropologists (exec. com. 1973-76, v.p. 1979-80, pres. 1981-83), Human Biology Assn. (exec. com. 1974-77), Phi Beta Kappa, Sigma Xi. Avocations: history of biological anthropology; rsch. in Papua New Guinea and Australia; forensic anthropology. Home: 1106 S Lynn St Champaign IL 61820-6331 Office: U Ill Dept Anthropology 607 S Mathews Ave Urbana IL 61801-3601

GILES, JAMES FRANCIS, financial executive; b. Teaneck, N.J., Aug. 16, 1954; s. James Francis Giles Sr. and Regina Bianca (Renzo) Micera. BA, Fairleigh Dickinson U., 1977, MBA, 1980. Lic. real estate broker, N.J. Bus. mgr. Bradford Securities, Teaneck, 1977-78; self employed translator Emerson, N.J., 1978-82; real estate broker Micera Realty, Oradell, N.J., 1982-89, Nigito Realty, River Edge, N.J., 1989-96; payroll adminstr. Butler Telecom, Montvale, N.J., 1996-97; pension adminstr. Nat. Assocs. Metro, Totowa, N.J., 1997—; adj. prof., lectr. Bergen C.C., Paramus, N.J., 1985—, chmn. real estate adv. com., 1993-95; adj. prof. William Paterson U., Wayne, N.J., 1993—. Roman Catholic.

GILES, JAMES T., federal judge; b. 1943. B.A., Amherst Coll., 1964; LL.B., Yale U., 1967. Mem. Nat. Labor Relations Bd., Phila., 1967-68; assoc. Pepper, Hamilton & Scheetz, 1968-79; judge U.S. Dist. Ct. (ea. dist.) Pa., Phila., 1979—. Mem. Fed. Bar Assn., Phila. Bar Assn. Office: US Dist Ct 8613 US Courthouse Ind Mall W 601 Market St Philadelphia PA 19106-1713*

GILES, MICHAEL COMER, physical education educator, aquatics consultant; b. Huntsville, Ala., Sept. 14, 1946; s. Comer E. and Temple (Harton) G.; m. Bobby Jean Morris, July 27, 1984; children: Mary Temple Giles Stewart, Michel Comer Jr. BS, U. Ala., 1968; MS, U. So. Miss., 1972. Cert. in aquatics, lifeguard instr. trainer, water safety instr., lifeguard, CPR instr., first aid instr. trainer ARC. 0dir. aquatics, swimming coach Tuscaloosa (Ala.) YMCA, 1968-69; dir. aquatics, instr. phys. edn. John C. Calhoun Community Coll., Decatur, Ala., 1969-71, 72-75, varsity tennis coach, 1972-75; grad. asst. dept. athletic adminstrn. and coaching U. So. Miss., Hattiesburg, 1971-72, dir. aquatics, instr., 1975—, varsity swimming coach, 1979-87; tennis coord. Decatur Recreation Dept., 1972-75; mem. nat. aquatics faculty ARC, Washington, 1988—; presenter in field, 1975—; condr. clins. for Spl. Olympic athletes and lifeguard instr. trainers; supr., trainer lifeguards M.C. Johnson Natatatorium and Lake Sebov; cons. on safety and lifeguard personnel to numerous pub. and pvt. pools, Miss.; tech. advisor for films Home Pool Safety and Preventing Water Emergencies, ARC, 1990. Prin. author: Safety Training for Swimming Coaches, 1988; contbg. author: Basic Water Safety Testbook, 1988; editor: Instructor Trainer Manual on Lifeguarding, 1991. Mem. Hattiesburg Arts Coun., 1990—. Mem. AAHPER and Dance, Am. Swim Coaches Assn., Coll. Swim Coaches Assn., Nat. Assn. Underwater Instrs. (cert. asst. scuba diving instr.), Nat. Intramural and Recreational Sports Assn., Miss. Assn. Health, Phys. Edn. and Recreation, U.S. Swimming. Episcopalian. Avocations: tennis, travel. Home: 3012 Magnolia Pl Hattiesburg MS 39402-2430 Office: U So Miss PO Box 5124 Hattiesburg MS 39406-1000

GILES, NORMAN HENRY, educator, geneticist; b. Atlanta, Aug. 6, 1915; s. Norman Henry and Alice (Guerard) G.; m. Dorothy Lunsford, Aug. 26, 1939 (dec. Jan. 1967); children: Annette Guerard, David Lunsford; m. Doris Vos Weaver, Aug. 1, 1969; stepchildren: Gayle Weaver (dec.), Alix Weaver. AB, Emory U., 1937, ScD (hon.), 1980; MA, Harvard U., 1938, PhD, 1940; MA (hon.), Yale U., 1951. Instr. botany Yale U., New Haven, 1941-45, asst. prof., 1945-46, assoc. prof., 1946-51, prof., 1951-61, Eugene Higgins prof. genetics, 1961-72; Fuller E. Callaway prof. genetics U. Ga., 1972-86, emeritus, 1986—; prin. biologist Oak Ridge Nat. Lab., 1947-50; cons. AEC, 1954-64; mem. genetics study sect. NIH, 1960-64, genetics tng. com., 1966-70; ednl. adv. bd. John Simon Guggenheim Meml. Found., 1977-86. Mem. editorial bd. Radiation Research, 1953-58, Am. Naturalist, 1961-64, Devel. Genetics, 1979-86. Bd. dirs. U. Ga. Research Found., 1979-85. Parker fellow Harvard U., 1940-41, Fulbright and Guggenheim fellow Genetics Inst., U. Copenhagen, 1959-60, Guggenheim fellow Australian Nat. U., Canberra, 1966; recipient Bicentennial Silver medallion U. Ga., 1984, Lamar Dodd award for rsch. U. Ga., 1985, Thomas Hunt Morgan medal Genetics Soc. Am., 1988. Fellow Am. Acad. Arts and Scis., AAAS; mem. Nat. Acad. Scis. (chmn. genetics sect. 1976-79), Genetics Soc. Am. (treas. 1954-56, pres. 1970), Bot. Soc. Am., Am. Soc. Naturalists (pres. 1977), Am. Inst. Biol. Scis., Genetics Soc. Japan (hon.), Royal Danish Acad. Scis. and Letters (fgn.), Am. Ornithologists Union, Phi Beta Kappa, Sigma Xi. Home: 289 Hanover Dr Bogart GA 30622-1734 Office: U Ga Dept Genetics Athens GA 30602-7223

GILES, PATRICIA CECELIA PARKER, retired art educator, graphic designer; b. Chgo., Mar. 8, 1925; d. Frederick Louis and Bernice Clara (Kennedy) Parker; m. Lewis Wentworth Giles, June 20, 1946 (div. 1960); children: Alan Julian, Kay Celeste. BS in Fine Arts, U. Ill., Urbana, 1946; postgrad., Howard U., Washington D.C., 1947, U. Mass., Amherst, 1974-75, Washington Sch. Psychology, 1962. Reg. sec. tchr. art Ill., 1972. Sec. tchr. art Randall Jr. High, Washington, D.C., 1947-48; art cons. Elem. Sch., Washington, 1952-53; tchr., chmn. art dept. Theodore Roosevelt H.S., Washington, 1959-60, Boys Sr. H.S., Washington, 1961-63, Carter G. Woodson Jr. H.S., Washington, 1963-72, Howard D. Woodson Sr. H.S., Washington, 1973-85; v.p. D.C. Art Assn., 1964-65; cons. art-math. with humanities Upward Bounders U. Md., College Park, 1966-67; potential supr. of student tchg. in art therapy Planning Program Staff George Washington U., Washington, 1972; visual arts coord. D.C. Congress PTA Cultural Arts, Washington, 1972; artist-in-residence Washington Srs. Wellness Ctr., 1987-88, 97-98, 98—. Painter: (oil painting) Mud and Roots, 1971 (award 1971), Mural: Infinite Joy, 1991 (Golden Dolphins Commendation award 1991), Kenkin, oils, 1992 (award 1992); author: (book of poetry) Mud and Roots, 1976; illustrator: (children's book) Short Fuzzy Hair, 1999. Taught art workshop in cmty. Fort DuPont Civic Assn., Washington, 1960, defining creative art Channel 14 WOOK-TV, Washington, 1963, comparing and interacting with cultures and govts. Am. Forum for Internat. Study, Senegal, Ghana, Ethiopia, Kenya, Tanzania, 1970; peer leader in tennis and yoga Washington Seniors Wellness Ctr., Washington, 1995, 96, 97, 98. Recipient Commendation award Ft. DuPont Civic Assn., Washington, 1960, 1st prize for watercolor Arch.'s Wives Assn., 1962, Gold medal D.C. Sr. Olympics in Tennis, 1993, 95, 96, 97, Silver medal, 1998, Gold medal in Swimming, 1993. Mem. Nat. Conf. of Artists, D.C. Nat. Tennis Assn. (sr., 2d Place Trophy 1990), Golden Dolphins (Outstanding Swimming Trophy 1993), Alpha Kappa Alpha. Democrat. Seventh Day Adventist. Avocations: tennis, swimming, yoga, tai chi, silk screen. Home: 3942 Blaine St NE Washington DC 20019-3333

GILES, PERCY Z., city official; married; 3 children. BS, U. Ark., Pine Bluff, 1974. Asst. store mgr. Walgreens, 1974-79; mgr. family owned grocery store chair, 1977-83; alderman ward 37 Chgo., 1988—; chmn. hist. landmark preservation com., vice-chmn. econ. and capital devel. com., mem. budget and govt. ops., rules and ethics, energy, environ. protection and pub. utilities, fin., housing and real estate coms. Alt. del. Dem. Nat. Conv., San Francisco, 1984; spl. asst. to Jim Blassingame, 75h Congl. Dist., 1987; mem. Cook County Ctrl. Dem. Com.; pres., CEO Westside Bus. Improvement Assn., 1979-85; mem. fin. com., bd. St. Anne's Hosp.; bd. mem., chmn. fin. com. Miles Sq. Health Ctr.; deacon, chmn. bd. trustees New Galilee M.B. Ch.; adv. mem. Austin Devel. Corp.; pres. Orgn. for a Better Austin; bd. mem. Austin YMCA. Recipient Humanitarian Man of Yr. Nat. League Bus. and Career Women, 1987, Henry Austin award Austin Cmty. Coun., Cmty. Trust award Westside Bus. Improvement Assn. Exceptional Leadership Award, Torch award Westside Orgn., Svc. award Westside Cmty. Coun., Achievement award Greater Chgo. Bus. Assn., City's Cmty. Svc. award Garfield Park Cmty. Svc., Cmty. Hero award 29th Ward People's Assembly, Leadership award Dept. Human Svc./West Garfield Cmty Svc. Ctr. Adv. Coun., Appreciaiton award for disting. svc. New World Patriotism Coalition, Outstanding Young Man of Am. award. Mem. N.E. Austin Orgn., Cosmopolitan C. of C. (bd. mem.), Chgo. Assn. Commerce and Industry, Austin Area Jayees, Lions (past pres.). Office: 4934 W Hirsh St Chicago IL 60651 also: 5255 W North Ave Chicago IL 60639-4429*

GILES, ROBERT EDWARD, JR., lawyer; b. Bremerton, Wash., Dec. 17, 1949; s. Robert Edward Sr. and Alice Louise (Morton) G.; m. Barbara Susan Miller, Aug. 21, 1971; children: Steven, William, Thomas, James. BA in Fin., U. Washington, 1971, JD, 1974. Bar: Wash. 1974, U.S. Tax Ct. 1974. From assoc. to fin. ptnr. Perkins Coie, Seattle, 1974-86, mng. ptnr., 1986—. Bd. dirs. Jr. Achievement, Seattle, 1984—; bd. dirs., sec. Wash. Coun. for Econ. Edn., 1981-91; v.p., chief Seattle coun. Boy Scouts Am., 1996—. Capt. U.S. Army, 1974. Mem. ABA, Wash. State Bar Assn., Greater Seattle C. of C. (trustee 1994-97). Avocations: hiking, climbing. Home: 5208 NE 187th St Seattle WA 98155-4346 Office: Perkins Coie 1201 3rd Ave Fl 40 Seattle WA 98101-3000

GILES, ROBERT HARTMANN, journalist, educator; b. Cleve., June 6, 1933; s. Robert Hamilton and Grace (Hartmann) G.; m. Nancy May Morgan, Feb. 6, 1960; children: David Morgan, Megan Elisabeth, Robert Hamilton II. BA, DePauw U., 1955; MS, Columbia U., 1956; D of Journalism (hon.), DePauw U., 1996. Reporter Newport News Daily Press, 1957-58; reporter Akron (Ohio) Beacon Jour., 1958-63, editorial writer, 1963-65, city editor, 1966-68, mng. editor, 1968-69, mng. editor, 1969-73, exec. editor, 1973-76; spl. lectr. Sch. Journalism, U. Kans., 1976-77; exec. editor Gannett Rochester (N.Y.) Newspapers, 1977-81, editor, 1981-86; v.p., exec. editor Detroit News, 1986-89, editor, pub., 1989-97; sr. v.p. The Freedom Forum, 1997—; exec. dir. Media Studies Ctr., 1997—; pres. Media Mgmt. Books Inc. Author: Newsroom Management: A Guide to Theory and Practice. Trustee William Allen White Found., U. Kans., 1978—. With AUS, 1956-58. Nieman fellow Harvard, 1965-66; co-recipient Pulitzer prize for local reporting, 1971, Scripps-Howard 1st Amendment award, 1978. Mem. AP Mng. Editors Assn. (pres. 1988), Am. Soc. Newspaper Editors (bd. dirs., treas. 1994, v.p. 1995, pres. 1996), Soc. Profl. Journalists, Found. Am. Comm. (chmn. 1993-97), Accrediting Coun. for Edn. in Journalism and Mass Comm. (pres. 1992-98), Alpha Tau Omega. Office: Media Studies Ctr 580 Madison Ave 42d Fl New York NY 10022-2505

GILES, WALTER EDMUND, alcohol and drug treatment executive; b. Omaha, Aug. 9, 1934; s. Walter Edmund and Julia Margaret (Shively) G.; m. Ellen M. Garton, June 13, 1953; m. Dona LaVonne Foster, Sept. 29, 1970 (dec. 1990); children: Sue, Stephen, Theresa, Marcy, Kim, Tim, Nadine, Charles; m. Yvonne Marie Fink, Nov. 29, 1991; children: Jessica Nicole Farr, Walter Edmund III, David Michael. BA, U. Nebr., Lincoln, 1972, MA, 1977. Counselor VA Hosp., Lincoln, Nebr., 1969-70; coord. alcohol programs Mcpl. Ct., Lincoln; dir. Orange County Employee Assistance, Santa Ana, Calif., 1977-79; adminstr. Advanced Health Ctr., Newport Beach, Calif., 1979-81; pres. Great West Health Svcs. Inc., Orange, Calif., 1982-86, Pine Ridge Treatment Ctr. Inc., Running Springs, Calif., 1986—. Author (book) The Workbook, 1985, Intervention, 1986; host (radio show) Addictions, 1984. Mem. Nat. Assn. Alcoholism Counselors, Calif. Assn. Alcoholism Counselors.

GILES, WILLIAM ELMER, newspaper editor; b. Somerville, N.J., July 5, 1927; s. Elmer and Mary Jane (Reed) G.; m. Gloria Mastrangelo, June 4, 1949; children: William J., Michael E., Richard H. and Paul L. (twins), Joseph R. A.B. in Government, Columbia U., 1950, M.S. in Journalism, 1951. Reporter Plainfield Courier-News, N.J., 1946-47; copyreader, reporter Wall Street Jour., 1951- 58; mng. editor S.W. edit. Wall Street Jour., Dallas, 1958-61, news editor Washington bur., 1961; an organizer nat. weekly newspaper Nat. Observer, 1961, editor, 1962-71; asst. gen. mgr. Dow Jones & Co., Inc.; pub. Dow Jones & Co., Inc. (Wall Street Jour. and Nat. Observer), 1971-76; dir. mgmt. programs, mem. Dow Jones mgmt. com., 1972-76; disting. editor in residence Baylor U., 1976; exec. editor Detroit News, 1976-77, editor, v.p., 1977-83; editor-in-residence, lectr. Mich. State U., East Lansing, 1983—; Sunday editor Singapore Monitor, 1984-85; v.p. Sandy Corp., Troy, Mich., 1985-87; prof. journalism La. State U., Baton Rouge, 1987-91, dir. Manship Sch. Journalism, 1988-91; prof. So. U., Baton Rouge, 1992-97; mng. editor The Washington Times, 1997—. Mem. Assn. Educators in Journalism and Mass Comm., Soc. Profl. Journalists, Nat. Press Club. Home: 85 Dogwood Trl London KY 40741-7536

GILES, WILLIAM JEFFERSON, III, lawyer; b. Manila, The Philippines, Apr. 10, 1936; came to U.S., 1938; s. William Jefferson and Gardner (Anderson) G.; m. Nancy Gifford Seff, May 9, 1957; children: William Jefferson IV, Gregory Gifford. BS, U. Calif., Berkeley, 1957; postgrad., Golden Gate Coll., 1958-59, Stanford U., 1960; JD, U. S.D., 1961. Bar: Iowa 1961, U.S. Dist. Ct. Iowa 1961, U.S. Ct. Appeals (8th cir.) 1971, U.S. Supreme Ct. 1971, Nebr. 1982, U.S. Ct. Appeals (9th cir.) 1988. Pvt. practice Sioux City, Iowa, 1961—; of counsel Whicher & Whicher, Sioux City, 1966-75, Whicher & Hart, Sioux City, 1975-77; lectr. in field. Contbr. articles to profl. jours. Bd. dirs. Sioux City Mus. and Hist. Soc., 1976-79, Sioux City Cmty. Theatre, 1974-76. Capt. USAR, 1957-68. Recipient Gold Seal award Phi Beta Kappa, 1953. Fellow Am. Acad. Matrimonial Lawyers (chmn. bankruptcy com. 1992—), Internat. Acad. Matrimonial Lawyers; mem. ABA, ATLA, Iowa Bar Assn., Iowa Assn. Trial Lawyers, Comml. Law League Am., Sioux City Country Club, Phi Delta Phi, Phi Phi. Republican. Home: 3827 Country Club Blvd Sioux City IA 51104-1327 Office: 322 Frances Bldg 505 5th St Sioux City IA 51101 also: 3940 Hideaway Acres Crofton NE 68730-0088

GILES-SIMS, JEAN G., sociology educator; b. June 22, 1945. BA, U. N.H., 1973, MA, 1976, PhD, 1979. From asst. prof. to assoc. prof. Tex. Christian U., Ft. Worth, 1979—. Office: Tex Christian U Box 298710 Fort Worth TX 76129

GILFORD, DOROTHY MORROW, statistician, researcher; b. Ottumwa, Iowa, Feb. 19, 1919; d. Frank Bliss and Mabel Irene (Coate) Morrow; m. Leon Gilford, Mar. 31, 1950. BS in Math., U. Wash., 1940, MS in Math., 1942. Statistics lectr. Bryn Mawr (Pa.) Coll., 1944-45; asst. prof. statistics George Washington U., Washington, 1945-48; chief biometrics br. Civil Aeronautics Adminstrn., Washington, 1948-51; dep. dir. divsn. fin. statistics FTC, Washington, 1951-55; head math. stats. br. & logistics br., dir. math. sci. divsn Office Naval Rsch., Washington, 1955-68; asst. commr., dir. Nat. Ctr. Edn. Statistics, U.S. Office Edn., Washington, 1968-74; dir. bd. on human resource studies NRC, Washington, 1975-77, sr. statistician, 1978-87, dir. bd. internat. edn., 1988-94; prin. ptnr. Gilford Assocs., Bethesda, Md., 1994—; tech. adv. group Nat. Edn. Goals Panel, Washington, 1992-94; mem. adv. groups Coun. Chief State Sch. Officers, Washington, 1990-93, Nat. Ctr. for Edn. Statistics, Washington, 1987-98. Editor: Rural America in Passage: Statistics for Policy, 1981, The Aging Population in the Twenty-First Century, 1988, Precollege Science and Mathematics Teachers, 1990, A Collaboraive Agenda for Improving International Comparative Studies in Education, 1993; author: Women and Minority PhD's in the 1970's: A Data Book, 1977, Framework and Principles for International Studies in Education, 1990, Teacher Supply, Demand and Quality, 1992, Measures of Inservice Professional Development, 1996, Myths About U.S. Science and Mathematics Education, 1998. Econ. adv. coun. Montgomery County Govt., Rockville, Md., 1981-94; coord. Montgomery County Hunger Relief Campaign, 1998. Recipient Fed. Women's award U.S. Civil Svc. Commn., 1965. Fellow Am. Statis. Assn. (v.p. 1974-76); mem. Internat. Statistics Inst., Am. Ednl. Rsch. Assn., Comparative Internat. Edn. Soc., Eistophos Sci. Club (corr. sec. 1997-99), Conf. Bd. Math. Socs. (chmn. 1977-79, trustee 1972-75). Coun. Sci. Soc. (pres. 1977-80, exec. bd. dirs. 1978-80, sec.-treas. 1979, com. on sci. edn. 1977-79), Women's Club of Chevy Chase. Avocations: gardening, travel, needlepoint. Office: Gilford Assocs 6602 Rivercrest Ct Bethesda MD 20816-2178

GILFORD, STEVEN ROSS, lawyer; b. Chgo., Dec. 2, 1952; s. Ronald M. and Adele (Miller) G.; m. Anne Christine Johnson, Jan. 2, 1974; children: Sarah Julia, Zachary Michael, Eliza Rebecca. BA, Dartmouth Coll., 1974; JD, Duke U., 1978, M of Pub. Policy Scis., 1978. Bar: Ill. 1978, U.S. Dist. Ct. (no. dist.) Ill. 1978, U.S. Ct. Appeals (7th cir.) 1981, U.S. Ct. Appeals (D.C. cir.) 1984, U.S. Ct. Appeals (5th cir.) 1988, U.S. Dist. Ct. (ea. dist.) Mich. 1995. Assoc. Isham, Lincoln & Beale, Chgo., 1978-85, ptnr., 1985-87; ptnr. Mayer Brown & Platt, Chgo., 1987—. Adminstrv. law editor Duke Law Jour., 1976-77. Bd. dirs. Evanston (Ill.) YMCA, 1982-92, sec., 1985, vice chmn., 1986-92; participating atty. ACLU, 1983—, bd. dirs. Ill., 1991-96, v.p. devel., 1993-96; bd. dirs. Roger Bawldwin Found., 1993-96; elected mem. bd. edn. dist. 202 Evanston Twp. H.S., 1993—, v.p., 1995-96, pres., 1996-98, mem. joint task force on safety, 1995-96; mem. Met. Family Svcs., Evanston Skokie Valley Cmty. Adv. Bd., 1997-98; mem., bd. dirs. Met. Family Svcs., 1998—. Mem. ABA, Ill. Bar Assn., Chgo. Bar Assn. Home: 2728 Harrison St Evanston IL 60201-1216 Office: Mayer Brown & Platt 190 S La Salle St Ste 3100 Chicago IL 60603-3441

GILFOYLE, NATHALIE FLOYD PRESTON, lawyer; b. Lynchburg, Va., May 4, 1949; d. Robert Edmund and Dorothea Henry (Ward) Gilfoyle; m. Christopher Y.W. Ma, Sept. 9, 1978; children: Olivia Otey, Rohan James. B.A., Hollins Coll., Roanoke, Va., 1971; J.D., U. Va., Charlottesville, 1974. Bar: Mass. 1974, D.C. 1977. Staff counsel Rate Setting Commn., Boston, 1974-76; ptnr. Peabody, Lambert & Meyers, Washington, 1976-84; ptnr. McDermott, Will and Emery, 1984-96; dep. gen. counsel APA, 1996—; bd. dirs. Washington Lawyers Com. Civil Rights Under Law, Washington, 1982—. Bd. dirs. ACLU Nat. Capital Area, Washington, 1980-83, St. Columba's Nursery Sch., 1992—, D.C. Bar Atty. Client Arbitration Bd., chmn. Mem. APA, ABA, D.C. Bar Assn., Mass. Bar Assn., Women's Bar Assn. Episcopalian. Office: APA 750 1st St NE Washington DC 20002-4241*

GILFOYLE, TIMOTHY JOSEPH, historian; b. Harrisburg, Pa., Mar. 24, 1956; s. Joseph Daniel Gilfoyle and Mary Dorothy Norton; m. Mary Rose Alexander, Aug. 19, 1990; 1 child, Maria Adele. BA, Columbia U., 1979, MA, 1980, PhD, 1987. Vis. prof. Sarah Lawrence Coll., Bronxville, N.Y., 1987-88, Barnard Coll., N.Y.C., 1988-89; asst. prof. Loyola U., Chgo., 1989-95, assoc. prof., 1995—. Author: (book) City of Eros: New York City, Prostitution, and the Commercialization of Sex, 1790-1920, 1992; assoc. editor: Encyclopedia of New York City, 1985-95, Jour. Urban History, 1995—; bd. editors: Encyclopedia of Chicago History, 1992—; author: (Making History series) Chicago History, 1996—; editor Hist. Studies in Urban Am. series, U. Chgo. Press, 1999—. Bd. dirs., mem. Chgo. Met. History Fair, 1996—. Recipient Allan Nevins prize Soc. Am. Historians, 1988; fellow John Simon Guggenheim Meml. Found., 1998-99, sr. fellow Nat. Mus. Am. History, Smithsonian Instn., 1997, NEH fellow Newberry Libr., 1993-94. Mem. Am. Hist. Assn. (life), Am. Studies Assn. (life), Orgn. of Am. History (life), Urban History Assn. (life). Democrat. Roman Catholic. Avocation: basketball. E-mail: tgiilfoy@orion.it.luc.edu. Home: 718 W Aldine Ave Chicago IL 60657-3412 Office: Loyola U Dept History 6525 N Sheridan Rd Chicago IL 60626-5385

GILGER, PAUL DOUGLASS, architect; b. Mansfield, Ohio, Oct. 13, 1954; s. Richard Douglass and Marilyn Joan (Hawkins) G. BArch, U. Cin., 1978. Registered architect, Ohio. Architect Soulen & Assocs., Mansfield, Ohio, 1976-81, PGS Architecture/Planning, Los Gatos, Calif., 1981-82, Bottomline Systems, Inc., San Francisco, 1983-85; pvt. practice San Francisco Bay Area, 1985-90; set designer Nomad Prodns. Scenic Studios, San Francisco, 1985-87; architect James Gillam, Architect, San Francisco, 1987-90, Hedgpeth Architects, Santa Rosa, Calif., 1990—, Home Planners, Inc., Tucson, 1994—; booking mgr. 1177 Club, San Francisco, 1985-86, City Cabaret, San Francisco, 1986-87; bd. dirs San Francisco Coun. Entertainment, 1987-90; project architect Lucasfilm Movie Studio Indsl. Light and Magic, San Rafael, Calif., 1991. Author: "The Best of Times", the Jerry Herman Musical Revue. Recipient Ohio Cmty. Theatre Assn. award, 1980, Theatrewest Acting award, 1983, 3 Bay Area Critics Cir. award, 1984, 85, 4 Cabaret Gold awards San Francisco Coun. Entertainment, 1985, 86, 3 Hollywood Dramalogue awards, 1985, 5 awards, 1996; San Francisco Focus award, 1985. Avocations: traveling, piano, automobiles. Home: 530 Juilliard Park Dr Santa Rosa CA 95401-6312 Office: Hedgpeth Architects 2321 Bethards Dr Santa Rosa CA 95405-8536

GIL-GOMEZ, ELLEN MARIE, English language educator; b. San Pedro, Calif., Mar. 22, 1967; d. Alvaro and Marilouise (Hexdall) G.-G.; m. Kelly Andrew Alls, June 29, 1991; children: Hannah Solita Alls, Selina Ruth Alls. BA, U. Calif., Santa Barbara, 1990; MA, Calif. State U., Long Beach, 1991; PhD, Wash. State U., 1995. Instr. Wash. State U., Pullman, 1995-96; asst. prof. Russell Sage Coll., Troy, N.Y., 1996—. Contbr. revs. and essays to profl. jours. Vis. minority scholar Coll. Arts and Scis., U. Wis., Eau Claire, spring 1997. Mem. MLA, Nat. Assn. Ethnic Studies, Nat. Women's Studies Assn. (co-founder taskforce feminist mothers and their allies), Assn. for Study of Multiethnic Lit. in the U.S., MLA Gay and Lesbian Caucus. Office: Russell Sage Coll English Dept Troy NY 12180

GILGUN, JANE FRANCES, social work educator; b. Wakefield, R.I., July 30, 1943; d. James Harold and Rosaria Elvera Costanza Gilgun. BA, Cath. U., 1965; licentiate, U. Louvain, Belgium, 1971; MA, U. R.I., 1979, U. Chgo., 1984; PhD, Syracuse U., 1983. Lic. clin. social worker, Minn. Tchr. Vets. Meml. H.S., Warwick, R.I., 1968-69; coord. family planning Providence Health Ctrs., 1969-70; health educator St. Joseph's Hosp., Providence, 1970-71; social worker R.I. Child Welfare Svcs., Providence, 1971-79; grad. asst. Syracuse (N.Y.) U., 1979-83, U. Chgo., 1983-84; prof. social work U. Minn., Mpls., 1984—; cons. in field. Editor: Qualitative Methods in Family Research, 1992, The Methods and Methodologies of Qualitative Family Research, 1996; contbr. articles to profl. publs. Bd. dirs. Project Pathfinder, St. Paul, 1992—. Recipient Silberman award Silberman Found., 1993, 97; rsch. grantee St. Paul Found., 1986-88, Allina Found., 1996-98. Mem. NASW, Soc. for Rsch. in Social Work, Nat. Coun. Family Rels., Internat. Soc. for Prevention of Child Abuse, Am. Profl. Soc. on Abuse of Children, Coun. Social Work Edn. Avocations: equitation, swimming, writing stories for children, gardening, theater. E-mail: jgilgun@che2.che.umn.edu. Office: U Minn Sch Social Work 1404 Gortner Ave Saint Paul MN 55108

GILHAUS, BARBARA JEAN, secondary education home economics educator; b. Hindsboro, Ill., Aug. 30, 1940; d. Garold Wayne and Lois Marie (Gaede) Farthing; m. Robert Lee Gilhaus, Sept. 28, 1963; 1 child, Gregory Lee. BS in Edn., Ea. Ill. U., Charleston, 1962; postgrad., Ill. State U., 1975-85, No. Ill. U., 1978. Tchr. home econs. and consumer edn. Heritage High Sch., Broadlands, Ill., 1962-93; consumer edn. cons. Ill. State Bd. Edn., Springfield, 1976-80; mem. Ill. White House Conf. on Children, 1980; chair, mem., sec. Edn. Svc. Ctr. 13, Rantoul, Ill., 1985-91. Author booklet and consumer edn. articles; participant radio program In the Consumer Interest, 1975. Chair Homer (Ill.) Zoning Bd. Appeals, 1980—; active in voter registration Champaign County, Urbana, Ill., 1980—. Recipient Ednl. Excellence award Ill. State Bd. Edn., 1985, award Ill. Ho. of Reps., 1985, Educator's award Champaign/Ford County, 1989. Mem. NEA, Ill. Edn. Assn. (bd. dirs. 1982-88), Ill. Consumer Edn. Assn. (bd. dirs., sec., treas., Gladys Bahr award 1985), Ill. Vocat. Home Edn. Tchrs. Assn., Heritage Edn. Assn. (all offices). Methodist. Avocations: sewing, attending sports events, cooking. Home: 607 W 4th St Homer IL 61849-1017

GILHOOLY, DAVID JAMES, III, artist; b. Auburn, Calif., Apr. 15, 1943; s. David James and Gladys Catherine (Schulte) G.; m. Camille Margot Chang, Aug. 23, 1983; children: David James, Andrea Elizabeth, Abigail Margaret, Peter Rodney, Hakan Yuatutsu, Kiril Shintora, Sorgan Subetei. BA, U. Calif., Davis, 1965, MA, 1967. tchr. San Jose (Calif.) State Coll., 1967-69, U. Sask. (Can.), Regina, 1969-71, York U., Toronto, Ont., Can., 1971-75, 76-77, U. Calif.-Davis, summer 1971, 75-76, Calif. State U.-Sacramento, summers 1978-79; lectr. in field. One-man shows include San Francisco Museum Art, 1967, M. H. deYoung Meml. Mus., San Francisco, 1968, Matrix Gallery, Wadsworth Athenuem, Hartford, Conn., 1976, Mus. Contemporary Art, Chgo., 1976, Vancouver (B.C., Can.), Art Gallery, 1976, ARCO Ctr. for Visual Arts, Los Angeles, 1977, Mus. Contemporary Craft, N.Y.C., 1977, E.B. Crocker Art Mus., Sacramento, 1980, St. Louis Mus. Art, 1981, Smith-Anderson Gallery, Palo Alto, 1985, San Jose Mus. Art, 1992, Solomon Dubnick Gallery, Sacramento, 1997; group shows include U. Calif.-Berkeley Art Mus., 1967, Inst. Contemporary Art, Boston, 1967, Whitney Mus. Am. Art, N.Y.C., 1970, 74, 81, Musee d'art de la Ville Paris, 1973, Chgo. Art Inst., 1975, San Francisco Mus. Art and Nat. Collection Fine Art, Washington, 1976-77, Stedelijk Mus., Amsterdam, The Netherlands, 1979, Everson Mus. Art, Syracuse, N.Y., 1979, Whitney Mus. Am. Art, N.Y.C., 1981, Palm Springs Desert Art Mus., 1984, Oakland Mus., 1985, Stanford Mus. Art, 1987, Inst. Contemporary Art, Boston, 1994; represented in permanent collections S. Bronfman Collection Can. Art, Montreal, Que., San Francisco Mus. Art, Phila. Mus. Art, Vancouver Art Gallery, Art Gallery Greater Victoria (B.C.), Albright-Knox Art Gallery, Buffalo, San Antonio Mus. Art, Oakland (Calif.) Mus. Art, Stedelijk Mus., Stanford U., Palo Alto, Calif., Australian Nat. Gallery, Canberra, Govt. Can., Calgary, Alta., Whitney Mus. Am. Art, Eugene (Oreg.) Ctr. Performing Arts. Can. Council grantee, 1975, 78. Mem. Royal Can. Acad. Republican. Mem. Ch. of Scientology. Office: 11140 SE Oak Dr Dayton OR 97114-7447

GILHOUSEN, BRENT JAMES, lawyer; b. Anacortes, Wash., Sept. 24, 1946; s. Darrell J. and Jean Sarah (Sabatine) G.; m. Sandra M. King, Aug. 13, 1983; 2 children: Lindsay Elizabeth, Shane Shroeder. BA, Wash. State U., 1968; JD, U. Oreg., 1973. Bar: Wash. 1973, U.S. Dist. Ct. (we. dist.) Wash. 1973, U.S. Ct. Appeals (9th cir.) 1973, U.S. Supreme Ct. 1980, Mo. 1981, U.S. Ct. Appeals (4th cir.) 1986. From atty.-advisor to sr. atty. U.S. EPA, Seattle, 1973-80; from environ. atty. to asst. gen. counsel-environ. Monsanto Co., St. Louis, 1980-97; asst. gen. counsel-environ. Solutia Inc., St. Louis, 1997—; mem. Superfund Settlements Project, Washington, 1988-95; legal com. Chem. Industry Inst. Toxicology, Rsch. Triangle Park, N.C., 1986-99; mem. environ. law adv. com. Nat. Chamber Litigation Ctr., Washington, 1992-97. Mem. editl. bd. Hazardous Waste Strategies Update, 1994—. With USAR, 1968-74. Mem. ABA (sect. natural resources, energy and environ. law, chair corp. counsel com. 1994-96, vice-chair hazardous waste com. 1991—), Chem. Mfrs. Assn. (enforcement subcom. 1995—), Def. Rsch. Inst., Forest Hills Country Club, Am. Legion. Republican. Avocations: skiing, golf, boating. Home: 1 Peakmont Ln Chesterfield MO 63005-6806 Office: Solutia Inc 10300 Olive Blvd Saint Louis MO 63141-7893

GILIBERTI, MICHAEL RICHARD, financial planner; b. Bklyn., July 5, 1949; s. Michael John and Rosemarie (Lucich) G.; m. Rosemary Kathryn Pettina, June 17, 1972; 1 child, Sean Michael. BS in math., Duquesne U., 1971; cert. fin. planner, Coll. for Fin. Planning, 1993. Cert. fin. planner. Agt. Metropolitan Life, Pitts., 1972-74, sales mgr., 1974-78, acct. exec., 1978-92, fin. planner, 1992—. Mem. Nat. Assn. Life Underwriters, Pitts. Assn. of Life Underwriters, Inst. Cert. Fin. Planners, Registry of CFP Licensed Practitioners, Greater Pitts. Soc. Certified Fin. Planners. Home: 92 Phillips Ln Mc Kees Rocks PA 15136-1075 Office: MetLife Securities Inc Ste 610 1 Thorn Run Ctr Coraopolis PA 15108

GILINSKY, STANLEY ELLIS, department store executive; b. Trenton, N.J., Aug. 7, 1918; s. Charles Edgar and Rose (Kohn) G.; m. Gerry Braslove, Nov. 25, 1945; children: Michael, Ellen. B.S., Lehigh U., 1940; LL.B., J.D., U. Pa., 1944. Bar: Pa. 1944. Law sec. Justice Horace Stern Supreme Ct. Pa., Phila., 1944-45; assoc. firm Wolf, Block, Schorr & Solis-Cohen, Phila., 1944-46; asst. budget dir. L. Bamberger & Co., Newark, 1946-50; research, planning dir. Gimbels, Phila., 1950-58; dir. corp. expansion, devel. Gimbel Bros., Inc., N.Y.C., 1958-64; dir. Gimbel Bros., Inc., 1964-68, corp. v.p., sec., 1968-80; also v.p. charge expansion, planning, devel. for Gimbels and Saks Fifth Ave. subs., 1964-76; v.p. Saks & Co., 1968-76; sr. v.p. corp. devel. and real estate Saks Fifth Ave., 1975—; sr. v.p. corp. devel. and real estate Gimbels, 1977-80, sr. v.p. Batus retail div., 1980-83; vice chmn. The Harlan Co., 1985—, dir.; dir. Saks & Co., Saks Retailing Corp.; v.p., dir. Fifth Win Corp. of Saks Fifth Ave., 1997—. Mem. Teaneck (N.J.) Polit. Assembly, 1962—, Teaneck Redevel. Authority, 1970-74. Mem. Am. Mktg. Assn., Phi Beta Kappa, Pi Lambda Phi. Home: 10504 Red Maple Ln Richmond VA 23233-4177 Office: Fifth Win Corp Saks Fifth Ave 12 E 49th St New York NY 10017-1028

GILINSKY, VICTOR, physicist; b. Warsaw, Poland, May 28, 1934; came to U.S., 1941, naturalized, 1948; s. Shlome Faywysh and Luba (Kantorowicz) G.; children—David, Anessa. B.S. in Engring. Physics, Cornell U., 1956; Ph.D. in Physics, Calif. Inst. Tech., 1961. Physicist Rand Corp., Santa Monica, Calif., 1961-71; head dept. phys. sci. Rand Corp., 1973-75; asst. dir. policy and program rev. AEC, Washington, 1971-73; mem. U.S. Nuclear Regulatory Commn., Washington, 1975-84, cons., 1984—. Mem. IEEE, Am. Phys. Soc., Internat. Inst. Strategic Studies, Internat. Conf. on Large Elec. Sys.

GILJE, PAUL ARN, history educator; b. Bklyn., Aug. 3, 1951; s. Arne and Wladja (Trendowski) G.; m. Ann Elisabeth Liebermann, Aug. 10, 1973; children: Erik, Karin. BA, Bklyn. Coll., 1974; MA, Brown U., 1975, PhD, 1980. Asst. prof. history U. Okla., Norman, 1980-86, assoc. prof., 1986-94, prof., 1994—. Author: The Road to Mobocracy, 1987, Rioting in America, 1996; editor: Wages of Independence, 1997; co-editor: Keepers of the Revolution, 1992, New York in the Age of the Constitution, 1992, American Artisans, 1995. Fellow Rockefeller Found., Johns Hopkins U., 1987-88, Ctr. for History of Freedom, Washington U., St. Louis, 1991. Mem. Am. Hist. Assn., Orgn. of Am. Historians, Soc. of Historians of the Early Republic, Inst. of Early Am. History and Culture. Lutheran. Home: 808 Tarkington Dr Norman OK 73026-0868 Office: Dept History Univ Okla Norman OK 73019

GILKEY, GORDON WAVERLY, curator, artist; b. Albany, Oreg., Mar. 10, 1912; s. Leonard Ernest and Edna Isabel (Smith) G.; m. Vivian Malone, Oct. 17, 1938 (dec. Sept. 1995); 1 son, Gordon Spencer. BS, Albany Coll., 1933; MFA, U. Oreg., 1936; ArtsD (hon.), Lewis and Clark Coll., 1957. Mem. art staff Stephens Coll., Mo., 1939-42; prof. art, head dept. Oreg. State U., 1947-64; dean Oreg. State U. (Sch. Humanities and Social Scis.), 1963-73, Oreg. State U. (Coll. Liberal Arts), 1973-77; curator prints and drawings Portland (Oreg.) Art Mus., 1978—; prof. and printmaker-in-resident Pacific N.W. Coll. Art, 1978—; spl. asst. to exec. dir. Portland Art Mus., 1988-94; dir. Internat. Exc. Print Exhibits, 1956-78; U.S. adviser IV Bordighera Biennale, Italy, 1957; chmn. Gov.'s Planning Coun. for Arts and Humanities in, Oreg., 1965-67; mem. Gov.'s Commn. on Fgn. Lang. and Internat. Studies. Ofcl. etcher New York World's Fair, 1939, 1937-39; etcher Nat. Broadcasting Co., Radio City, N.Y.C., 1937-39; artist-author: Etchings: New York World's Fair, 1939; contbr. articles on art; major work in permanent collection, Met. Mus. Art, others. Trustee Oreg. State U. Found.; bd. govs. Pacific N.W. Coll. Art. Col. U.S. Army Air Corps, 1942-47, ret. Decorated Palmes Academiques (France), officer's cross and comdr.'s cross Order of Merit (Fed. Republic Germany), Order Star of Solidarity (Italy), comdr. Order of Merit (Italy), officer Order Acad. Palms (France), officer Legion of Honor (France), Grand Cross Order St. Gregory the Illuminator, comdr. Order Polonia Restituta, chevalier Order of Holy Sepulchre, chevalier mil. and hospitaller Order of St. Lazarus, chevalier mil. and hospitaller Order of Our Lady of Mt. Carmel, chevalier St. Dennis of Zante, knight Grand Cross Order of St. Basil the Great, knight Imperial Order of St. Eugene of Trebizond, Order of the Knights of Sinai, order of Temple of Jerusalem, comdr. Order St. Stephan the Martyr; recipient King Carl XVI Gustaf's Gold Commemorative medal in art Sweden, German Friendship award; Soc. Mayflower Descendants, Aubrey R. Watzek award; named AIA-Carnegie Corp. fellow, summers 1930, 32. Mem. Am. Print Alliance (bd. dirs.), Portland Art Mus. (founder), Soc. Am. Graphic Artists, Calif. Soc. Printmakers, Coll. Art Assn., UN Assn. Oreg. (past pres.), Oreg. Internat. Coun. (bd. dirs.), Print Coun. of Am., N.W. Print Coun. (trustee), NW Coll. Art (bd. govs.), Oreg. St. U. Fdn. (trustee), Phi Kappa Phi, Kappa Pi. Home: 1500 SW 5th Ave Apt 2401 Portland OR 97201-5437 Office: 1219 SW Park Ave Portland OR 97205-2430

GILL, ARDIAN C., actuary, photographer; b. Griswold, Conn., Oct. 9, 1929; s. Lewis A. and Sarah (Geer) G.; m. Jill Freeman, May 29, 1954; children: Tracy, Claudia, John Freeman; m. 2d, Anna Hannon, Sept. 9, 1988. B.A. with honors in Math, U. Conn., 1951. With Travelers Ins. Co., 1951-54; with Mut. Life Ins. Co., N.Y., 1954-77; 2d v.p., actuary Mut. Life Ins. Co., 1965-66, v.p., actuary, 1966-70, sr. v.p., chief actuary, chief fin. officer, 1970-77; mgmt. cons. N.Y.C., 1977-78; v.p., prin., dir. Tillinghast, Nelson & Warren, N.Y.C., 1978-83; chmn. Gill & Roeser, Inc., 1983-92; pres. Gill & Roeser Life Intermediaries, Inc., N.Y.C., 1992—; adj. prof. Coll. Ins., 1992-94; pres. Local Color, Photographer. Trustee Village of Saltaire, 1970-72. Fellow Soc. Actuaries (bd. govs. 1974-76, 82-84, v.p. 1978-80), Can. Inst. Actuaries; mem. Acad. Actuaries (bd. dirs. 1987-90), N.Y. Actuaries Club (pres. 1971-72). Home: 316 W 79th St New York NY 10024-6125 Office: Studio 506 526 W 26th St New York NY 10001-5517

GILL, CLAIR F., military career officer; b. Johnstown, Pa., July 7, 1943; m. Sherry Angello; children: Clair, Heidi, Christopher. Grad., U.S. Mil. Acad., 1965; MS in Civil Engring., U. Calif., Berkeley; postgrad., Harvard U.; grad., Command & Gen. Staff Coll., Army War Coll. Registered profl. engr., D.C. Commd. officer U.S. Army C.E., 1965, advanced through grades to maj. gen., various positions including platoon leader, 1965-71; asst. exec. officer to dean Mil. Acad., 1971-74; dir. facilities engring., dir. engring. and housing U.S. Mil. Cmty. Activity, Ansbach, Germany; exec. officer 16th Engr. Battalion, 1st Armored Divsn. U.S. Army, Germany, 1977-79; comdr. 14th Engr. Battalion U.S. Army, Ft. Ord, Calif.; chief manpower and force programs analysis divsn. Office of the Chief of Staff, Washington; comdr. 7th Engr. Brigade VII Corps U.S. Army, Germany; comdr. Pacific Ocean divsn. U.S. Army C.E., Ft. Shafter, Hawaii; dep. chief staff, engr. U.S. Army Europe and Seventh Army, Heidelberg, Germany; dir. resource mgmt. U.S. Army Forces Command, Ft. McPherson, Ga.; commdg. gen./commandant U.S. Army Engr. Ctr., Ft. Leonard Wood; dep. asst. sec. Army for Budget Office of the Asst. Sec. of the Army. Decorated Legion of Merit with 3 oak leaf clusters, Bronze Star medal with 2 oak leaf clusters, Meritorious Svc. medal, Air medal. Office: Office of the Asst Sec of the Army 109 Army Pentagon Washington DC 20310-0109

GILL, CLARK CYRUS, retired education educator; b. Winona County, Minn., Feb. 19, 1915; s. John H. and Anna (Fluegel) G.; m. Ethel Spaller, Aug. 15, 1952. B.A., Hamline U., 1935; M.A., U. Minn., 1939, Ph.D., 1948. Tchr., high sch. Lake City, Minn., 1935-41, high sch. U. Minn., 1941-42; mem. faculty State Coll., Clarion, Pa., 1948-50; curriculum dir. U.S. Armed Forces Inst., Madison, Wis., 1950-52; coordinator, course writing project U. Wis., Madison, 1952-54; assoc. prof. curriculum U. Tex., Austin, 1954-66; prof. U. Tex., 1966-81, prof. emeritus, 1981—. Author: Education and Social Change in Chile, 1966, Education in a Changing Mexico, 1969, The Educational System of Mexico, 1977, The Educational System of Costa Rica, 1980. Served with U.S. Navy, 1942-46. Fulbright prof. U. San Marcos, Lima, Peru, 1960. Office: U Tex Coll Edn Austin TX 78712*

GILL, DIANE LOUISE, psychology educator, university official; b. Watertown, N.Y., Nov. 7, 1948; d. George R. and Betty J. (Reynolds) G. BS in Edn., SUNY, Cortland, N.Y., 1970; MS, U. Ill., 1974, PhD, 1976. Tchr. Greece Athena High Sch., Rochester, N.Y., 1970-72; asst. prof. U. Waterloo, Ont., Can., 1976-78; asst. prof. U. Iowa, Iowa City, 1979-81, assoc. prof., 1981-86; assoc. prof. sport & exercise psychology U. N.C., Greensboro, 1987-89; prof. U. N.C., Greenboro, 1989—; assoc. dean U. N.C., Greensboro, 1992-97, head dept. exercise and sport sci., 1997—. Author: (book) Psychological Dynamics of Sports, 1986; editor Jour. of Sport and Exercise Psychology, 1985-90; editorial bd. Jour. of Applied Sport Psychology, 1988—; contbr. articles to profl. jours. Fellow AAHPERD (rsch. consortium pres. 1987-89), APA (pres. divsn. 47 exercise and sport 1999—), Am. Psychol. Soc., Assn. for Advancement of Applied Sport Psychology, Am. Acad. Kinesiology and Phys. Edn.; mem. N.Am. Soc. for Psychology of Sport and Phys. Activity (pres. 1988-91). Democrat. Office: U NC Dept Exercise and Sport Sci Greensboro NC 27402-6169

GILL, DONALD GEORGE, education educator; b. O'Fallon, Ill., Dec. 3, 1927; s. Fred Kenneth and Anna (Mayer) G.; m. Betty Jo Brummal, Dec. 28, 1952; children—Donald Bruce, Ann Brummal, Gay Ellen. AB, Ill. Coll., 1951; MEd, U. Ill., 1954, EdD, 1969; LLD, Ill. Coll., 1981. Tchr. Waverly (Ill.) Public Schs., 1950-52; prin., elem. and jr. high schs. Taylorville, Ill., 1952-60; asst. dir., dir. Labs. Schs. Eastern Ill. U., Charleston, 1960-74; also prof. edn.; supt. schs. Volusia County, Deland Daytona Beach, Fla., 1974-80; supt. Ill. Dept. Edn., Springfield, 1980-85; DuPont prof. edn., chmn. div. edn. Stetson U., DeLand, Fla., 1985—; chmn. Ill. Tchr. Cert. Bd., 1980-85; pres. trustees Ill. Tchr. Retirement System, 1980-85; Ill. commr. Edn. Commn. U.S., 1980-85. Contbr. articles to profl. jours. Mem. Charleston (Ill.) Twp. Bd., 1964-74. Served with USN, 1945-46. Mem. Am. Assn. Sch. Adminstrs., Council Chief State Sch. Officers, Fedn. Urban Suburban Sch. Dists. (exec. com.), Phi Delta Kappa, Omicron Delta Kappa. Office: Stetson Univ Chmn Div Edn Deland FL 32720 *From early in my youth onward I have had a deep commitment to the Democratic Ideal based upon the inherent dignity of man under the sovereignty of God.*

GILL, E. ANN, lawyer; b. Elyria, Ohio, Aug. 31, 1951; d. Richard Henry and Laura (Beeler) G.; m. Robert William Hempel, Aug. 4, 1973; children: Richard, Peter, Mary. AB, Barnard Coll., 1972; JD, Columbia U., 1976. Bar: N.Y. 1977, U.S. Supreme Ct. 1982. Assoc. Mudge, Rose, Guthrie & Alexander, N.Y.C., 1976-77; assoc. Dewey Ballantine L.L.P., N.Y.C., 1977-84, ptnr., 1985—. Mem. ABA, N.Y. State Bar Assn., Nat. Assn. Bond Lawyers. E-mail: anngill@deweyballantine.com. Home: 255 W 90th St New York NY 10024-1109 Office: Dewey Ballantine 1301 Ave Of The Americas New York NY 10019-6022

GILL, EVALYN PIERPOINT, writer, editor, publisher; b. Boulder, Colo.; d. Walter Lawrence and Lou Octavia Pierpoint; m. John Glanville Gill; children: Susan Pierpoint, Mary Louise Glanville. Student, Lindenwood Coll.; BA, U. Colo.; postgrad., U. Nebr., U. Alaska; MA, Ctrl. Mich. U., 1968. Lectr. humanities Saginaw Valley State Coll., University Ctr., Mich., 1968-72; mem. English faculty U. N.C., Greensboro, 1973-74; editor Internat. Poetry Rev., Greensboro, 1975-92; pres. TransVerse Press, Greensboro, 1981—. Author: Poetry by French Women, 1930-1980, 1980, Dialogue, 1985, Southeast of Here: Northwest of Now, 1986, Entrances, 1996; editor: O. Henry Festival Stories, 1985, 87, Women of the Piedmont Triad: Poetry and Prose, 1989, Edge of Our World, 1990, A Turn in Time: Piedmont Writers at the Millennium, 1999. Bd. dirs. Eastern Music Festival, Greensboro, 1981—, Greensboro Symphony, 1982—, Greensboro Opera Co., 1982—, Weatherspoon Assn.; chmn. O Henry Festival, 1985, 95. Recipient numerous poetry prizes, Fortner award St. Andrews Coll., 1995, Altrusa Internat. Cmty. Arts award, Greensboro, 1998. Mem. MLA, Amn. Lit. Translators Assn., N.C. Poetry Soc., Phi Beta Kappa. Home: 2900 Turner Grove Dr N Greensboro NC 27455-1977

GILL, GENE, artist; b. Memphis, June 18, 1933; s. Edward Morris and Annie Zelma (Mondy) G. BFA, Chouinard Art Inst., L.A., 1962. One-man shows include Comara Gallery, L.A., 1970, 71, 74, Orlando Gallery, Sherman Oaks, Calif., 1995; exhibited in group shows Esplanade Gallery, Santa Monica, 1969, L.A. Art Assn. Galleries, 1970, R and W. Gallery, Memphis, 1971, Scripts Coll., 1971, San Diego Fine Arts Mus., 1971, Laguna Beach Mus. Art, 1971, 72, 77, Palm Springs Mus. Art, 1973, L.A. County Mus. Art, 1973, Van Straaten Gallery, Chgo., 1974, Mcpl Art Gallery, L.A., 1976; represented in permanent collections L.A. County Mus. Art, Palm Springs Desert Mus. Art, Atlantic Richfield Corp, Northrop Corp., Container Corp. Am., Home Savings, Pattiz Found., Westside Jewish Cmty. Ctr. With USN, 1954-58. Recipient numerous awards at juried art shows. Home: 3895 Valley Lights Dr Pasadena CA 91107-1345

GILL, GEORGE NORMAN, newspaper publishing company executive; b. Indpls., Aug. 11, 1934; s. George E. and Urith (Dailey) G.; m. Kay Baldwin, Dec. 28, 1957; children—Norman A., George B. A.B., Ind. U., 1957. Reporter Richmond (Va.) News Leader, 1957-60; copy editor, reporter, acting Sunday editor, city editor, mng. editor Courier-Jour., Louisville, 1960-74; v.p., gen. mgr. Courier-Jour. and Louisville Times Co., 1974-79, sr. v.p. corp. affairs, 1979-80, pres., chief exec. officer, 1981-86; chief exec. officer affiliates Standard Gravure Corp., WHAS, Inc., 1981-86; pres., pub. Courier-Jour. and Louisville Times Co., 1986-93. Served with USNR, 1954-56. Recipient Picture Editors award Nat. Press Photographers Assn., 1965. Mem. Am. Soc. Newspaper Editors, Assn. Press Mng. Editors, Louisville Com. on Fgn. Relations, Alpha Tau Omega, Sigma Delta Chi. Club: Mason. Home: PO Box 108 Pewee Valley KY 40056-0108

GILL, GEORGE WILHELM, anthropologist; b. Sterling, Kans., June 28, 1941; s. George Laurance and Florence Louise (Jones) G.; BA in Zoology with honors (NSF grantee), U. Kans., 1963, M.Phil. Anthropology (NDEA fellow, NSF dissertation research grantee), 1970, PhD in Anthropology, 1971; m. Pamela Jo Mills, July 26, 1975 (div. 1988); children: George Scott, John Ashton, Jennifer Florence, Bryce Thomas. Mem. faculty U. Wyo., Laramie, 1971—, prof. anthropology, 1985—, chair dept. anthropology, 1993-96; forensic anthropologist law enforcement agys., 1972—; sci. leader Easter Island Anthrop. Expdn., 1981; chmn. Rapa Nui Rendezvous: Internat. Conf. Easter Island Rsch., U. Wyo., 1993. Served to capt. U.S. Army, 1963-67. Recipient J.P. Ellbogen meritorious classroom teaching award, 1983; research grantee U. Wyo., 1972, 78, 82, Nat. Geog. Soc., 1980, Center for Field Research, 1980, Kon-Tiki Mus., Oslo, 1987, 89, 94, 96, World Monuments Fund, 1989. Diplomate Am. Bd. Forensic Anthropology (bd. dirs. 1985-90). Fellow Am. Acad. Forensic Scis. (sec. phys. anthropology sect. 1985-87, chmn. 1987-88); mem. Am. Assn. Phys. Anthropologists, Plains Anthrop. Soc., Wyo. Archael. Soc. Republican. Presbyterian. Author articles, monographs; editor: (with S. Rhine) Skeletal Attribution of Race, 1990. Home: 649 Howe Rd Laramie WY 82070-6885 Office: U Wyo Dept Anthropology Laramie WY 82071

GILL, GERALD LAWSON, librarian; b. Montgomery, Ala., Nov. 13, 1947; s. George Ernest and Marjorie (Hackett) G.; m. Nancy Argroves, Mar. 5, 1977 (div. 1982). AB, U. Ga., 1971; MA, U. Wis., 1973. Cert. profl. libr., Va. Cataloger James Madison U., Harrisonburg, Va., 1974-76, reference libr., 1976-87, bus. reference libr., 1987-99, acting govt. documents libr., 1998-99, instr., 1974-80, asst. prof., 1980-90, assoc. prof., 1990—; lectr., spkr. nat. and regional groups; cons. in field; mem. faculty senate James Madison U., 1975-79, 96-98, sec. curriculum and instrn. com., 1976-78, chair, 1978-79, univ. coun., 1996-98. Mem. editl. bd. James Madison Jour., 1977-80; reviewer Am. Reference Books Ann.; contbr. articles to profl. jours. Mem. libr. adv. com. State Coun. for Higher Edn. in Va., 1986-87; virtual Va. Coord. Mgmt. Bus. com. Mem. ALA (chmn. bus. reference svcs. com. 1984-86, sec. law and polit. sci. sect. 1982-85, chmn. bus. reference svcs. discussion group 1986-87, chmn. bus. reference in acad. librs. com. 1988-91, Gale Rsch. award 1991), AAAS, Am. Mgmt. Assn., Am. Soc. for Info. Sci., Va. Libr. Assn. (coun. 1986-87, parliamentarian 1979, 81), Spl. Librs. Assn. (treas. Va. chpt. 1983-85, pres. 1986-87), Internat. Platform Assn., World Future Soc., Harrisonburg C. of C. Democrat. Roman Catholic. Avocations: art collecting, travel. Home: 1379 Devon Ln Harrisonburg VA 22801-5201 Office: James Madison U Library Harrisonburg VA 22807

GILL, GORDON N., medical educator; b. Dec. 19, 1937. BA in Chemistry/Lit., Vanderbilt U., 1960, MD, 1963. Diplomate Am. Bd. Internal Medicine with subspecialty in endocrinology and metabolism. Intern in internal medicine Vanderbilt U. Hosp., Nashville, 1963-64; resident Yale-New Haven Hosp., 1964-66; fellow postdoctoral fellow metabolism/endocrinology NIH/Yale U., 1966-68; spl. postdoctoral rsch. fellow NIH/U. Calif., San Diego, 1968-69; asst. prof. medicine U. Calif., San Diego, 1969-73, assoc. prof., 1973-78, prof. medicine, 1978—, chief divsn. endocrinology dept. medicine, 1971-83, chief divsn. endocrinology/metabolism, 1983-95, assoc. chair sci. affairs, 1992-95, chmn. faculty basic biomed. scis., 1995—; chmn. endocrinology study sect. NIH, 1979-80, chmn. task force on endocrinology, 1978, dir. tng. grant on exptl. endocrinology and metabolism, 1978—; prin. investigator interdisciplinary program to study macromolecules regulating growth and oncogenesis U. Calif., San Diego, 1988-95; chmn. Gordon Conf. on Hormone Action, 1979, Gordon Conf. on Peptide Growth Factors, 1990; mem. sci. adv. bd. BioCryst, 1990—; sci. and med. adv. bd. chair Whittier Inst., 1991-95; sci. adv. bd. Liver Ctr., U. Calif., San Francisco, 1991-95, Charles E. Culpepper Found., 1992—, Coun. for Tobacco Rsch. USA, 1991-97, ICN Pharms., 1992—; internat. adv. bd. dept. molecular and structural biology U. Grenoble, France, 1993—; S. Richardson Hill vis. prof. U. Ala., Birmingham, 1991; Berlin lectr. Northwestern U. Sch. Medicine, 1994. Editl. bd. Jour. Cyclic Nucleotide and Protein Phosphorylation Rsch., 1974-84, Endocrinology, 1978-82, Am. Jour. Physiology, Cell Physiology, 1981-87, Jour. Biol. Chemistry, 1983-88, Jour. Cellular Biochemistry, 1984-89, Ann. Rev. Medicine, 1986-91, Analytical Biochemistry, 1980-92; editor Molecular and Cellular Endocrinology, 1974-92; cons. editor Jour. Clin. Investigation, 1992-97; sect. editor: Endocrinology, Best and Taylor Physiological Basis of Medical Practice, 11th and 12th edits., Endocrinology and Metabolism, Cecil's Textbook of Medicine, 20th edit. Bd. dirs. Med. Rsch. and Edn. Found., The Agouron Inst., 1985—; mem. biochemistry and endocrinology sci. adv. com. Am. Cancer Soc., 1989-91; adv. com. Markey Charitable Trust, 1990-97; peer rev. com. Am. Heart Assn., 1991-96. Helen Hay Whitney Found. fellow, 1969-73; NIH Rsch. Career Devel. awardee, 1969-73, Merit award. Fellow ACP, Am. Acad. Arts and Scis.; mem. AAAS, Assn. Am. Physicians, Am. Fedn. Clin. Rsch., Am. Soc. Clin. Investigation, Am. Soc. Biol. Chemistry and Molecular Biology, Endocrine Soc., Western Assn. Physicians, Western Soc. for Clin. Investigation, Am. Soc. for Cell Biology, Phi Beta Kappa, Alpha Omega Alpha. Office: Univ of California 9500 Gilman Dr La Jolla CA 92093-5003

GILL, HARDAYAL SINGH, electrical engineer; b. Amritsar, Punjab, India, Aug. 18, 1952; came to U.S., 1974; BSc with honors, Punjabi U., Patiala, 1971, MSc, 1973; PhD, U. Minn., Mpls., 1978. Sr. engr. Nat. Semiconductor, Santa Clara, Calif., 1978-81; mem. tech. staff Hewlett-Packard, Palo Alto, Calif., 1981-83, project leader, 1983-85, project mgr., 1985-90; sr. engr. IBM, San Jose, Calif., 1990-94, sr. tech. staff, 1994-97; IBM Disting. engr., 1997—. Contbr. articles to profl. jours. Fellow IEEE (chmn. Magnetics Soc. 1987-88, chmn. Santa Clara sect. 1992-93, adminstrv. com. Magnetics Soc. 1992-94); mem. Am. Phys. Soc. Achievements include 40 patents on computer storage/memory devices; avocations: tennis, bike riding. Office: IBM Corp MS N17/142 5600 Cottle Rd San Jose CA 95123-3696

GILL, HENRY HERR, photojournalist; b. Detroit, July 21, 1930; s. Henry Herr and Esther (King) G.; m. Mary Jane Brown, Aug. 26, 1957. Student, Vincennes U., 1948, Northwestern U., 1949, Ind. U., 1951, McNeese State U., La., 1952, U. Miami, 1962. Mem. publ. staff U. Miami, 1960; fgn. service photographer, then dir. photography Chgo. Daily News, 1976; dir. photography Chgo. Sun-Times, 1978-83; pres., exec. editor Globalfoto/Roma, 1983-87; pres., film dir. Fotostar Prodns., 1987—; lectr. in field, exhibitor of photographs, 1964—. Co-author: Mississippi Notebook, 1964; photographer: film A War of Many Faces, 1965, The Cocaine Express, 1982. Recipient photo reporting award on Vietnam Nat. Headliners Club, 1967, Overseas Press Club award, 1967, 81, Emmy award for documentary Nat. Acad. TV Arts and Scis., 1965, Best News Picture of Yr. award Inland Press Assn., 1968, 69, Faculty citation Vincennes U., 1979, Baker Meml. Journalism award, 1980; named to Journalism Hall of Fame, 1994. Mem. Internat. Press Club (Chgo.), Headliner Club (Chgo.), Sigma Delta Chi (Disting. Journalism award 1965).

GILL, JO ANNE MARTHA, middle school educator; b. L.A., July 8, 1940; d. James Hurse Wilson and Martha Grace (Hanson) Wilson Horn; m. Richard Martin Gill, Apr. 18, 1959; 1 child, Richard James. BA in Interdisciplinary Studies, Nat. U., San Diego, 1989; MA in Ednl. Adminstrn., Calif. State U., San Bernardino, 1992. Cert. tchr. pre-sch. through adult edn., social sci., adminstrn. Tchr. grades 6 and 7 Palm Springs (Calif.) Unified Sch. Dist., 1989-94, tchr. 8th grade U.S. history, gifted/regular, 1994—; prof. edn. Calif. State U., San Bernardino; cons. Desert Schs. Consortium, Palm Springs, 1993-95, Inland Empire History/Social Studies, Riverside, Calif., 1991-95; adv. bd. Inland Empire Lit. Project, 1994-98; mem. leadership team Inland Area History/Social Sci. Summer Inst., U. Calif., Riverside, 1994-98. Contbr. articles to profl. jours. Mem. Calif. State History Standards and Course Models Commn.; coach mid. sch. demonstration program. Inland Area History/Social Sci. Adv. Acad. fellow, 1991, NEH fellow, 1993, Calif. History/Social Sci. Project/UCLA fellow, 1994; recipient 1st pl. award/tchr. multimedia group presentation Nat. History Day; 1996, 98. Mem. AAUW (home tour guide 1993), Calif. Coun. for the Social Studies (presenter conf. workshop 1993, 95, 96), Calif. Assn. for Gifted (presenter ann. conf. workshop 1994, 96, 98, Calif. Outstanding Middle Sch. Educator Area 9 1997), Inland Empire Coun. for the Social Studies (pres. 1994-96, Outstanding Middle Sch. Educator area 9 local award 1997), Delta Kappa Gamma (scholarship fundraising com. 1993-94, Theta Zeta Chi state pres. 1998—). Democrat. Roman Catholic. Avocations: hiking, fishing, reading, travel, writing. Office: Palm Springs Unified Schs 333 S Farrell Dr Palm Springs CA 92262-7905

GILL, KEITH HUBERT, lawyer; b. Pocatello, Idaho, May 31, 1929; s. Hubert Samuel and Myrtle Frances (Olsen) G.; m. Glenna Jean Lowery, June 16, 1956; children: Suzanne Marie, Gina Michelle. BA, Idaho State U., 1952; MBA, UCLA, 1962; JD, U. So. Calif., 1968. Bar: Calif. 1969, U.S. Dist. Ct. (cen. dist.) Calif. 1969, U.S. Ct. Appeals (9th cir.) 1972, U.S. Supreme Ct. 1973, U.S. Tax Ct. 1974. Assoc. Kadison, Pfaelzer, Woodard, Quinn & Rossi, L.A., 1968-73, ptnr., 1973-80; of counsel Mitchell, Silberberg & Knupp, L.A., 1980-81; prin. Rodi, Pollock, Pettker, Galbraith & Phillips, L.A., 1981-85; sole practice, Woodland Hills, Calif., 1985-87, 89—; ptnr. Pelletier, Supancic & Gill, 1987-89; lectr. UCLA Law Sch. Clin. Program; dir. Sunland Ford, Inc. Judge pro tem L.A. Mcpl. Ct., 1977—. Mem. Los Angeles County Art Mus.; bd. dirs. Las Virgenes Ednl. Fund, Calabasas Park Homeowners Assn. Mem. Calif. Bar Assn., L.A. County Assn., ABA, Calif. Conf. Dels., Phi Alpha Delta. Republican. Mormon. Office: 21550 Oxnard St Ste 300 Woodland Hills CA 91367-7109

GILL, KENNETH DUANE, minister, missiologist; b. Pomona, Calif., Apr. 23, 1946; s. Roy Heflin and Madelyn Ruth (Reed) G.; m. Judith Ann Haggerton, Apr. 25, 1970; children: Matthew Houston, Manola Roberta. BA, Pepperdine Coll., 1969; MA, Fuller Theol. Sem., Pasadena, Calif., 1977; MSLS, U. Ky., 1982; PhD, U. Birmingham, Eng., 1990. Ordained to ministry Ind. Pentecostal Ch., 1977. Assoc. pastor Parkview Christian Ch., Arcadia, Calif., 1976-77, missionary, 1977-84; assoc. pastor Jesus Chapel, El Paso, Tex., 1984-85; theol. libr. Billy Graham Ctr. Libr., Wheaton, Ill., 1985-96; acting dir. Billy Graham Ctr., Wheaton, 1996-98, assoc. dir., 1998—; coord. CINCOMEX, Mexico City, 1979-81. Book rev. editor The Christian Librarian, 1991—. Mem. Am. Soc. Missiology (pub. 1989—), Assn. Christian Librs. (co-chair Commn. on Internat. Libr. Assistance 1989-97), Chgo. Area Theol. Libr. Assn., Internat. Assn. Mission Studies, Soc. for Pentecostal Studies, Acad. for Evangelism in Theol. Edn. Office: Wheaton Coll Billy Graham Ctr Wheaton IL 60187 *It has always intrigued me that those who claim that we lack the capability to measure God's impact on the universe often posit a universe which precludes the possibility of his existence.*

GILL, LYLE BENNETT, lawyer; b. Lincoln, Nebr., May 11, 1916; s. George Orville and Ruth (Bennett) G.; BA, Swarthmore Coll., 1937; LLB, Nebr. Coll. Law, 1940; m. Rita M. Cronin, Aug. 28, 1975; children by previous marriage: George, Valerie, Marguerite. Bar: Nebr. 1940. Practice law, Fremont, 1945-98; city atty. Fremont, 1959-62, 67-94. Vice chmn. ARC, Dodge County, 1953-59; chmn., Dodge County Republican Com., 1945-51. Served with USNR, 1942-45, 1951-52; lt. comdr. (ret.). Mem. ABA, Nebr. Bar Assn., Dodge County Bar Assn. (pres. 1962), VFW, Am. Legion. Episcopalian. Home: PO Box 642 Fremont NE 68026-0642

GILL, MILTON RANDALL, minister; b. Cheverly, Md., Dec. 8, 1950; s. Milton Thomas and Patricia Georgiana (King) G.; m. Carroll Ann Bennett, Nov. 10, 1979; 1 child, Laura Grace. BS, U. Md., 1973; MDiv, Princeton Sem., 1977; DMin, South Fla. Ctr. Theol. Studies, Miami, 1995. Ordained to ministry Presbyn. Ch., 1979. Pastor First Presbyn. Ch., Theresa, N.Y., 1979-84, Weirsdale (Fla.) Presbyn. Ch., 1984-89, First Presbyn. Ch., Boynton Beach, Fla., 1989—; sem. del. Gen. Assembly Presbyn. Ch. (U.S.A.), Balt., 1976; pres. Thousand Island Clergy Assn., Alexandria Bay, N.Y., 1982-83, Boynton Beach Ministerial Assn., 1994-96. Mem. bd. visitors Presbyn. Coll., Clinton, S.C., 1993-96; mem. adv. bd. Hospice of Palm Beach County, 1998-99; mem. Circle of Friends, Habitat for Humanity, Boynton Beach, Fla., 1998-99. Mem Rotary, Kiwanis (pres. Lake Wor. Fla. club 1986-87). Republican. Office: First Presbyn Ch 235 SW 6th Ave Boynton Beach FL 33435-5517 *We are called to give our best to God, because God gave us His best through His Son Jesus Christ.*

GILL, NIA H., state legislator. BA, Upsala Coll.; JD, Rutgers Law Sch. Law clk. McTeer, Walls & Bailey, Greenville, Miss., 1973; legis. aide Sen. Wynona Lipman, N.J., 1973-74; trial atty. N.J. Pub. Defenders Office, Essex & Passaic Counties, N.J., 1976-82; lawyer del. 3d Jud. Conf., 1987—; state legislator N.J. Ho. of Reps.; assembly N.J. State Dist. 27, 1994—, jud. law & pub. safety com. N.J. State Assembly, sr. citizen & social svc. coms., task force on juvenile crime, criminal justice subcom., Dem. task force on crime & corrections; ptnr. Gill & Cohen, P.C., Montclair. Trustee Montclair Pub. Libr., 1978-83, Cmty. Nursing Svc., Montclair, 1986-87; bd. adjustment Montclair Twp., 1985—; bd. dirs. Playwrights Theater N.J., 1993-94, Luna Theater, Montclair. Recipient legal profession award Nat. Coun. Negro Bus. Women, 1985, citizen award Montclair br. NAACP, 1988. Mem. ABA, Assn. Criminal Def. Lawyers N.J. (trustee 1986-89), N.J. State Bar Assn., Garden State Bar Assn., Essex County Bar Assn., Nat. Conf. Black Lawyers, Black Women Lawyers N.J., Assn. Trial Lawyers Am., Isis Literary Guild (pres.). Office: NJ Gen Assembly South Wing State House PO Box O98 Trenton NJ 08625*

GILL, PATRICIA JANE, human resources executive; b. Mt. Vernon, N.Y., Jan. 20, 1950; d. J. Morgan and Magdalina (Manganiello) G. BA in History, St. Mary's Coll., 1971; MA in Counseling, NYU, 1973; MBA in Mktg., Fordham U., 1979; postgrad., Columbia U. Tchr., counselor Mt. Vernon Bd. Edn., 1970-74; tng. mgr. St. Luke's Hosp., N.Y.C, 1974-78; dir. personnel Bernard Hodes Advt., N.Y.C., 1978-80; mgr. mgmt. programs group Devel. Dimensions Internat., Pitts., 1980-82; v.p. Swan Cons., N.Y.C., 1982-83; nat. sales mgr. Reader's Digest, Pleasantville, N.Y., 1983-84; pres. Alexis-Gill, Inc., White Plains, N.Y., 1985; cons. in field. Author: Roleplaying, 1979. Worker Project Hope, New Rochelle, N.Y., 1986—. Mem. Am. Soc. Tng. and Devel. (pres. 1988), Nat. Speakers Assn. Episcopalian. Avocations: reading, hiking, tennis. Office: Alexis-Gill Inc 222 Mamaroneck Ave Ste 207 White Plains NY 10605-1316

GILL, RICHARD LAWRENCE, lawyer; b. Chgo., Jan. 8, 1946; s. Joseph Richard and Dolores Ann (Powers) G.; m. Mary Helen Walker, July 14, 1990; children: Kyla Marie, Matthew Joseph. BA, Coll. of St. Thomas, St. Paul, 1968; JD, U. Minn., 1971. Bar: Minn. 1971, U.S. Dist. Ct. Minn. 1971, U.S. Supreme Ct. 1979, U.S. Ct. Appeals (8th cir.) 1983, U.S. Ct. Appeals (4th cir.) 1990, Ill. 1992. Spl. asst. atty. gen. State of Minn., St. Paul, 1971-73; assoc. Maun, Hazel, Green, Hayes, Simon & Aretz, St. Paul, 1974-77; ptnr. Gill & Brinkman, St. Paul, 1978-84, Robins, Kaplan, Miller & Ciresi, Mpls., 1984—. Vol. Courage Ctr., Golden Valley, Minn., 1981—; youth football coach Maplewood (Minn.) Athletic Assn., 1978-80. Mem. ABA, Minn. Bar Assn., Hennepin County Bar Assn., Ramsey County Bar Assn., Assn. Trial Lawyers Am., Minn. Trial Lawyers Assn., Town and Country Club. Avocations: skiing, tennis, golf. Office: Robins Kaplan Miller & Ciresi 800 Lasalle Ave Ste 2800 Minneapolis MN 55402-2015

GILL, RICHARD THOMAS, opera singer, economic analyst; b. Long Branch, N.J., Nov. 30, 1927; s. Thomas Grant and Myrtle (Sickles) G.; m. Betty Bjornson, Jan. 6, 1950; children—Thomas Grandon, Peter Severin, Geoffrey Karl. A.B., Harvard U., 1948, Ph.D. in Econs, 1956; postgrad., Oxford (Eng.) U., 1948-49. Master, Leverett House, lectr. econs. Harvard U., 1963-71. Author: Economics and the Public Interest, 5th edit., 1991, Our Changing Population, 1992, Posterity Lost, 1997, others; TV commentator Economics USA (Annenberg/CPB project), 1985-92; debuts in N.Y.C. Opera, 1971, Met. Opera, 1973, Houston Grand Opera, 1972, Chgo. Lyric Opera, 1976, N.Y. Philharm., 1977; appeared at Edinburgh Festival, 1976; soloist numerous opera cos. and symphonies in U.S. and abroad. Served with inf. U.S. Army, 1946-47. Henry fellow, 1948-49; recipient Atlantic Monthly First Short Story prize, 1954. Mem. Am. Econs. Assn. *I have been fortunate enough to pursue several careers, sometimes simultaneously: author, economist, social theorist, college administrator, opera singer, and television commentator. In a time of increasing life expectancies, it may be that multiple careers may become the rule rather than the exception.*

GILL, ROBERT TUCKER, lawyer; b. N.Y.C., Nov. 30, 1946; s. Robert M. and Joan (Tucker) G.; m. Margaret Weiss; children: Elisabeth, Margaret. BA, Union U., 1969; JD, Boston Coll., 1973, MA, 1973. Bar: Ga. 1973, Mass. 1973, U.S. Ct. Appeals (1st and 5th cirs.) 1973, U.S. Supreme Ct. 1993. Staff atty. Ga. Indigents Legal Svcs., Savannah, Ga., 1973-74; assoc. Sherwin & Gottlieb, Fall River, Mass., 1974-75; ptnr. Parker, Coulter, Daley & White, Boston, 1975—. Chmn. Weston (Mass.) Transp. Commn., 1984—; mem., chmn. Weston (Mass.) Cable TV Com., 1987-88; trustee Monsignor George V. Kerr Trust, Boston, 1988—. Mem. ABA, Am. Arbitration Assn. (panel of arbitrators), Mass. Bar Assn., Boston Bar Assn., State Bar of Ga., Mass. Trial Lawyers Assn., Wianno Yacht Club. Avocations: sailing, skiing. Office: Peabody & Arnold 50 Rowes Wharf Fl 7 Boston MA 02110-3342

GILL, SHAYNE H., legislative staff member; b. Birmingham, Ala., Apr. 10, 1970. BA, U. Montevallo, 1992. Staff asst. Office of Rep. Spencer T. Bachus III, Washington, 1993-94, legis. asst., 1994-98, legis. dir., 1998—. Office: Office US Rep Spencer T Bachus 442 CHOB Washington DC 20515-0106*

GILL, STEPHEN PASCHALL, physicist, mathematician; b. Balt., Nov. 13, 1938; s. Robert Lee and Charlotte (Olmsted) G.; m. Margaret Ann Gaskins, Dec. 21, 1961; children: Elizabeth Olmsted, Richard Paschall. B.S., MIT, 1960; M.A., Harvard U., 1961, Ph.D., 1964. Cons. hypersonic aerodynamics Raytheon Corp., Bedford, Mass., 1963-64; research physicist Stanford Research Inst., Menlo Park, Calif., 1964-65, head high energy gasdynamics, 1965-68; head high energy gasdynamics Physics Internat. Co., San Leandro, Calif., 1968-70, mgr. shock dynamics dept., 1970-72; founder, pres. Artec Assocs., Inc., Hayward, Calif., 1972-77, chief scientist, 1977-91; founder, pres. Votan Corp., Hayward, Calif., 1979-91, chief scientist, chmn. bd., 1981-85; founder, chief scientist Magnetic Pulse Inc., 1985—. Mem. San Francisco Symphony Assn.; mem. San Francisco Mus. Art. Mem. IEEE, Am. Phys. Soc., Am. Math. Soc., MIT Alumni Assn., Sigma Xi, Delta Kappa Epsilon. Republican. Episcopalian. Clubs: MIT. Home: 32 Flood Cir Atherton CA 94027-2151 Office: 42000 Christy St Fremont CA 94538-3161

GILL, THOMAS JAMES, III, physician, educator; b. Malden, Mass., July 2, 1932; s. Thomas James and Marguerite (Capobianco) G.; m. Faith Libbie Etoll, July 8, 1961; children: Elizabeth Ruth, Thomas James IV, Christopher Gregory. AB summa cum laude, Harvard U., 1953, AM in Chemistry, 1957, MD, 1957. Diplomate Am. Bd. Pathology. Asst. in pathology Peter Bent Brigham Hosp., Boston, 1957-58; intern N.Y. Hosp.-Cornell Med. Center, 1958-59; jr. fellow Soc. Fellows Harvard U., 1959-62; mem. faculty Harvard U. Med Sch., 1962-71, asso. prof. pathology, 1970-71; prof. pathology, chmn. dept. U. Pitts. Med. Sch., 1971-90; pathologist-in-chief Univ. Health Center Pitts., 1971-90, Maud L. Menten prof. exptl. pathology, 1988-96, prof. human genetics, 1988-98, inaugural Maud L. Menten prof. exptl. pathology, 1996-98, prof. emeritus human genetics and exptl. pathology, 1999—; vis. scholar in biology Harvard U., 1999—; cons. to govt. and industry; mem. sci. adv. bd. St. Jude Children's Rsch. Hosp., Memphis, 1969-77, chmn., 1974-76; mem. allergy and immunology rsch. com. Nat. Inst. Allergy and Infectious Diseases, 1973-76; mem. med. rsch. svc. merit rev. bd. in immunology VA, 1976-79, chmn., 1977-79; mem. sci. adv. com. Damon Runyon-Walter Winchell Cancer Fund, 1978-81; mem. com. on animal models and genetic stocks NRC, 1978-86, chmn. com., 1983-86, mem. com. on rabbit genetic resources, 1979-80, mem. coun. Inst. Lab. Animal Resources, 1986-92, mem. com. on preservation of lab. animal resources, 1985-90, com. on transgenic animals, 1991-92; mem. surgery, anesthesiology and trauma study sect. NIH, 1983-84; sci. adv. com. on immunology and immunotherapy Am. Cancer Soc., 1986-88; mem. Armed Forces Epidemiol. Bd., 1966-72; adj. prof. U. Milan, 1990-92; nutrition found. Italy lectr. U. Milan, 1986-97; trustee Am. Bd. Pathology, 1981-92, pres., 1992; mem. Maternal and Child Health com. Nat. Inst. Child Health and Human Devel., 1992-96; chmn., 1995-96; mem. immunology task force Nat. Inst. Allergy and Infectious Diseases. Mem. editorial bd. several sci. and med. jours.; contbr. articles to profl. jours. Bd. dirs. Easter Seal Soc., Allegheny County, 1972-77, Univs. Asso. for Research and Edn. in Pathology, 1979-90. Recipient Lederle med. faculty award, 1962-65, rsch. career devel. award NIH, 1965-71, cert. of appreciation for patriotic civilian svc. Dept. Army, 1973, Spl. Qualification in Pathology: Immunopathology, 1983, Disting. Scientist award in genetics S.W. Found. for Biomed. Rsch., 1986, Charter with medal U. Rijeka, 1990, medal U. Pitts., 1990; named George H. Fetterman lectr. U. Pitts., 1981, George Hoyt Whipple lectr. U. Rochester, N.Y., 1984, Aron E. Szulman lectr. U. Pitts., 1993, Raymond O. Berry Meml. lectr. Tex. A&M U., 1995, Mühlblock lectr. Internat. Coun. for Lab. Scis., 1995, Spiridion Brusina award Croatian Soc. Natural Scis., 1997. Fellow Assn. Pathology Chairmen (pres. 1978); mem. AMA, Am. Assn. Immunologists, Am. Assn. Pathologists, Am. Soc. Molecular Biology and Biochemistry, Am. Soc. Human Genetics, Transplantation Soc. (v.p. 1982-84), Am. Soc. for Immunology of Reprodn. (v.p. 1988-89, Disting. Investigator award 1991, pres. 1995-96), Genetics Soc. Am., Internat. Acad. Pathology, Internat. Soc. Immunology of Reprodn. (pres. 1992-95, hon. pres. 1995—), Alps Adria Soc. for Immunology of Reprodn. (hon. pres. 1994—), Mass. Med. Soc., Harvard Club (Boston), Harvard Varsity Club.

GILL, VINCE, country musician, singer; b. Oklahoma City; m. Janis Gill, 1980; 1 child, Jenny. With Pure Praire League, 1980; appeared on Dire Straits album, On Every Street,1991; performed duets with Reba McEntre, Emmylou Harris, Patty Loveless, Ricky Skaggs; solo albums include The Things That Matter, 1985, The Way Back Home, 1987, The Best of Vince Gill, 1989, When I Call Your Name, 1989, Pocket Full of Gold, 1991, I Never Knew Lonely, 1992, I Still Believe in You, 1992, Let There Be Peace on Earth, 1993, When Love Finds You, 1994, Vince Gill and Friends, 1994, Souvenirs, 1995, High Lonesome Sound, 1996, The Key, 1998; numerous musical videos. Recipient Grammy award for Best Country Performance by a Male, 1990, Grammy nomination, Best Country Vocal Collaboration for "The Heart Wont Lie", 1994), Grammy award for Best Male Country Vocal Performance, 1996, for Best Country Song, 1995, Best Country Vocal Performance, 1994, 95, Best Country Collaboration With Vocals, 1996, Best Male Country Vocal Performance, 1998, others; (2) Country Music Assn. awards, 1991, Instrumentalist of Yr. award The Nashville Network/Music City News, 1991, 3 Gold albums, 7 Platinum albums, numerous Country Music Assn. awards, including Male Vocalist of Yr., 1991-95, Song of Yr., 1992, 93, 96, Entertainer of Yr., 1993, 94, Album of Yr., 1993, Vocal Event of Yr., 1996, Country Single of Yr. award Am. Music Awards, 1994, awards Acad. Country Music, 1984, 92, 93, TNN/Music City News awards, 1991-94, 96, Music City News Songwriters awards, 1990-94, BMI awards, 1987, 91, 92-93, 95-96, Nashville Music awards, 1994-96, Christian Country Music Assn. awards, 1996, Minnie Pearl award, 1993, Harmony award, 1993, Tennesseean of Yr. award, 1994, Outstanding Nashvillian of Yr. award Kiwanis, 1994, Orville H. Gibson Lifetime Achievement award, 1997; Vince Gill Tenn. PGA Jr. Golf Tournament named in his honor, 1997. Office: MCA Records 60 Music Sq E Nashville TN 37203-4325*

GILL, WILLIAM HAYWOOD, insurance broker, consultant; b. Miami, Fla., Dec. 16, 1929; s. Joseph Henry and Mabel (Jenkins) G.; m. Patricia Gwen Irwin, Aug. 3, 1957 (div. Aug. 1976); children: Bill Jr., Gwen Gill Hayes, Joe H. II, Mary; stepchildren: Eugene Major, Julie Major; m. Loretta Sieg Major, Oct. 6, 1979 (dec. 1991); m. Virginia A. Cumming Gill, Aug. 24, 1995. BA, Rice U., 1952; postgrad., U. Iowa, 1952-55, Wharton Sch., 1981. Underwriter U.S. F & G, Dallas, 1957-63; casualty supt. U.S. F & G, Columbia, S.C., 1963-70; casualty mgr. U.S. F & G, Chgo., 1970-72; spl. risk mgr. Fred S. James Agy., Chgo., 1972-75; sr. cons. Wyatt Co., Chgo., 1975-80; ins. mgr. Gerald J. Sullivan and Assocs. of Ill., Chgo., 1980-88; property and casualty/reins. mgr. R.T. Nelson & Assoc. Ltd., Chgo., 1988-98; prin. WH Gill Cons., Anchorage, 1998—; cons. Univ. Risk and Ins. Mgmt. Assn., 1985-87, Am. Hosp. Assn./Health Providers Ins. Co., 1977-80, Nat. Roofing Contractors Assn., 1992—. Contbr. chpts. to: Handbook of Health Care Risk Management, 1986, Integrated Health Care Delivery Systems Manual, 1994; contbr. articles to profl. publs. Pres. Civic Arts Coun. Oak Park, Ill., 1977; commr. pastoral coun. St. Giles Ch., Oak Park, 1991-94; active Chgo. Symphony Orch. Assn., Art Inst. Chgo. Named to Hon. Order of Ky. Cols., 1977. Mem. Am. Hosp. Assn., Am. Soc. for Health Care Risk Mgmt., Nat. Roofing Contractors Assn., Lloyds Broker's Assn., Ill. Surplus Lines Assn., Smithsonian Inst., Chgo. Symphony Orch. Assn., U.S. Golf Assn. Roman Catholic. Avocations: hi fi, art collecting, record collecting, cabinetmaking, golf. Home and office: 320 E Dowling Rd Unit 8 Anchorage AK 99518-1316

GILL, WILLIAM NELSON, chemical engineering educator; b. N.Y.C., Sept. 13, 1928; s. William Nelson and Frances (Murphy) G.; m. Chandlee Stevens, Aug. 13, 1982; children: Alison Louise, Christine Marie, Douglas Max, Max William. BSChemE, Syracuse U., 1951, MA, 1955, PhD, 1960. Field engr. Am. Blower Corp., 1951-55; mem. faculty Syracuse U., 1957-65, assoc. prof., 1963-65; prof. chem. engring., chmn. dept. Clarkson Coll. Tech., 1965-71; provost engring. and applied sci. SUNY, Buffalo, 1971-78, prof. chem. engring., 1982-87; Glenn Murphy Disting. prof. engring. Iowa State U., Ames, 1980-82; Russell Sage disting. prof. chem. engring. Rensselaer Poly. Inst., Troy, N.Y., 1987—; cons. in field. Editor: Chem. Engring. Communications, 1979—; mem. editorial adv. bd. Fuel, Processing Tech.; mem. bd. cons. editors Elsevier Texts in Engring.; editor Chem. Engring. series Elsevier Sci. Pub. Co.; author numerous articles in field. Named Alumnus of Yr., Bklyn. Tech. H.S., 1977; recipient William H. Wiley Disting. Faculty award in recognition of outstanding tchg. and scholarship Rensselaer Poly. Inst., 1994; Fulbright-Hays sr. rsch. scholar Univ. Coll., London, 1977-78, U. Queensland, Australia, 1986-87, Best Paper award Interconnect Scis. & Tech., Techcon 96 Semiconductor Rsch. Corp., 1996, Lecturship award Chem. Eng. Divsn. ASEE, 1992, Best Paper award Interconnect Modeling and Simulation, Techcon 98, Semiconductor Rsch. Corp., 1998. Fellow AIChE; mem. AAAS, AAUP, Am. Chem. Soc., Am. Soc. Engring. Edn. (lectureship award chem. engring. divsn. for fundamental contbns. to chem. engring. theory and practice 1992), N.Y. Acad. Scis., Sigma Xi. Office: Rensselaer Poly Inst Chem Engring Ricketts Troy NY 12180

GILL, WILLIAM ROBERT, soil scientist; b. McDonald, Pa., July 21, 1920; s. William Merle and Mary Della (Leiden) G.; m. Irene Victoria Majorkiewicz, July 10, 1947; children: William Robert, John Philip, David C., Michael J., Elaine N. BS, Pa. State U., 1942; MS, U. Hawaii, 1949; PhD, Cornell U., 1955. Asst. soil scientist Pineapple Rsch. Inst., Honolulu, 1949-50; rsch. soil scientist USDA-ARS, Auburn, Ala., 1955-80, dir., 1971-80; adj. prof. agrl. engring. Auburn U., 1957-88; collaborator Nat. Soil Dynamics Lab. (formerly Nat. Tillage Machinery Lab.), Auburn, 1980—; exch. scientist in Soviet Union, 1970. Author: Soil Dynamics in Tillage and Traction, 1967, History of the National Tillage Machinery Laboratory, 1990, War Crimes Investigations in Japan 1945-48: A Personal Remembrance, 1995; contbr. articles to profl. jours. and tech. confs.; monographs on soil dynamics. Col. AUS ret., 1943-47, 51-52. Recipient recognition award Internat. Soil Dynamics Conf., 1985, 97; named to Officer Candidate Sch. Hall of Fame, 1993. Mem. Am. Soc. Agrl. Engrs. (Peer Recognition award 1985, Disting. Engr. award 1988, John Deere medal 1990), Soil Sci. Soc. Am. Achievements include translation of Russian soil dynamics articles into English, fgn. analysis and technology transfer for internat. audience.

GILLAM, DAVID ALLEN, elementary school educator; b. Colorado Springs, Colo., May 25, 1957; s. Ernest Allen and Dorothy Jane (Maphis) G.; m. Lori D. Sheppard, Aug. 16, 1980; children: Colin Nathaniel, Aspen Nichole. BEd, U. Alaska, 1979; MAT, Alaska Pacific U., 1993. Cert. elem. tchr., Alaska. Tchr. Anchorage Sch. Dist., 1979-93, sci. tchr. expert, 1993-94; tchr. Susitna Elem. Sch., Anchorage, 1994—; instr. sci. methods, evaluation of students Alaska Pacific U., Anchorage, 1991-98; instr. U. Alaska, Anchorage, 1994-95. Creek honcho Anchorage Waterway Coun., 1993-98. NSF Presdl. awardee (state finalist), 1995, 96, 97, 99; Milken Educator awardee Milken Family Found., 1996. Fellow Alaska Sci. Consortium (exec. bd. 1993-96); mem. Nat. Sci. Tchrs. Assn., Alaska Sci. Tchrs. Assn. (pres. 1995-97), Nat. Coun. Tchrs. Math. Avocations: gardening, reading, walking. Office: Susitna Elementary School 7500 Tyone Ct Anchorage AK 99504-3599

GILLAM, LINDA DAWN, cardiologist, researcher; b. Corner Brook, Nfld., Can., Sept. 23, 1952; d. Donald Samuel and Vera (Pieroway) G.; m. Vincent Charles DiCola, Aug. 30, 1985 (div. 1995); children: John William DiCola, Laura Ann DiCola. BS, McGill U., Montreal, Que., Can., 1972; MD, Queen's U., Kingston, Ont., Can., 1976. Diplomate Am. Bd. Internal Medicine, Am. Bd. Cardiovascular Disease. Intern U. Toronto, 1976; resident in medicine St. Michaels Hosp., Toronto, 1977-79; fellow in cardiology U. Toronto, 1979-81, Mass. Gen. Hosp., Boston, 1981-83; instr. in medicine Harvard U. Med. Sch., Boston, 1983-86; clin. asst. prof. medicine U. Conn., Farmington, 1986-95, clin. assoc. prof., 1995—; dir. echocardiography U. Conn. Health Ctr., Farmington, 1986-90, Hartford (Conn.) Hosp., 1990—; spkr. in field. Contbr. articles to profl. jours. Active St. Thomas's Episcopal Ch., New Haven, 1993—. Rsch. grantee Can. Heart Assn. Fellow Am. Coll. Cardiology (gov. 1996—, chpt. pres. 1996—, govt. rels. com. 1997—, mem. steering com. bd. govs., chair task force on comm., mem. awards com., edtl. bd. website), Am. Heart Assn. (task force on guidelines for echocardiography, com. on women in cardiology, ARDMS adult echo exam task force); mem AMA, Conn. State Med. Soc., Am. Bd. Echo (bd. dirs. 1999—), Am. Soc. Echocard iography (legis. and regulatory affairs com. 1993—, bd. dirs. 1995-98, com. on sonographer tng. 1997—). Avocations: ballet, opera, classical music, aerobics, tennis. Office: Hartford Hosp 80 Seymour St Hartford CT 06102-8000

GILLAM, SIR PATRICK, oil company executive; b. London, Apr. 15, 1933; s. Cyril Bryant and Mary Josephine (Davis) G.; m. Diana Echlin, Nov. 23, 1963; children: Jane, Luke. BA in History with honors, London Sch. Econs., 1954. With Fgn. Office, London, 1956-57; with Brit. Petroleum Co. p.l.c., London, 1957-91, v.p. BP (N.Am.) Inc. subs., N.Y., 1971-74, gen. mgr. supply, 1974-78, dir. BP Internat. Ltd., 1978-81, mng. dir., 1981-91; non-exec. dir. Comml. Union, 1991-96; bd. dirs. Standard Chartered p.l.c., 1988-91, dep. chmn., 1991-93, chmn., 1993—; chmn. ICC U.K., 1989-98, Booker Tate Ltd., 1991-93, Asda p.l.c., 1991-96, Royal & Sun Alliance, 1997—; mem. exec. bd. dirs. ICC World Wide, 1991-98. Created knight, 1998. Avocation: gardening. Office: Std Chartered PLC, 1 Aldermanbury Sq, London EC2V 7SB, England

GILLANI, NOOR VELSHI, atmospheric scientist, researcher, educator; b. Arusha, Tanzania, Mar. 8, 1944; came to the U.S., 1963, naturalized, 1976; s. Noormohamed Velshi and Sherbanu (Kassam) G.; children: Michael, Michelle, Nicole. GCE (Ordinary Level Divsn. I), U. Cambridge, 1960; (Advanced Level), U. London, 1963; AB cum laude, Harvard U., 1967; MS in Mech. Engring., Washington U., St. Louis, 1969, DSc, 1974. Rsch. assoc. Washington U., St. Louis, 1975-76, rsch. scientist, 1976-77, asst. prof., 1977-80, assoc. prof., 1981-84, prof. mech. engring., 1984-91, faculty assoc. Ctr. Air Pollution Impact and Trend Analysis, 1979-91, dir. air quality spl. studies data ctr., 1981-88, dir., mech. engring. rsch. computing facility, 1988-90; pres. N.V. Gillani & Assocs., Inc., 1991—; prin. rsch. scientist NASA-UAH Global Hydrology & Climate Ctr., Huntsville, Ala., 1991—; vis. scientist Stockholm U., 1977, Brookhaven Nat. Lab., 1990-91, EPA/RTP, 1992, TVA Environ. Rsch. Ctr., 1994-95; prof. atmospheric sci. N.C. State U., 1993-95; adj. prof. atmospheric sci. U. Ala., Huntsville, 1995—; organizer NATO CCMS 15th internat. tech. meeting on air pollution modeling and its applications, St. Louis, Apr. 1985; mem. Sci. Bd. NATO/CCMS Air Pollution Pilot Study, 1986-94; mem. tech. adv. bds. U.S. EPA, DOE, and others, 1980—; hon. mem. Aga Khan Bd. Edn. for the U.S.A., 1987-90. Author: (with others) EPA Criteria Document for Particulate Matter, 1994-95; editor: Air Pollution Modeling and Its Applications V, vol. 10, 1986; contbr. chpts. to book and articles to profl. jours. Dir., founder Nat. Aga Khan Bd. Edn. Program for Parental Involvement in Children's Edn., USA. Aga Khan scholar and travel grantee, 1961-63, Harvard Coll. scholar, 1963-67; Rsch. grantee EPA, DOE, EPRI, TVA, 1978—; Washington U. Grad. Engring. fellow, 1967-69; rsch. asst. NIH, EPA, 1971-74. Mem. Am. Meteorol. Soc., Am. Chem. Soc., Nat. Assn. for Edn. Young Children, N.Y. Acad. Scis. Achievements include research on superconductivity, bioengring., atmospheric scis. and air pollution. Avocations: religious studies, music, tennis, early childhood education, computers. Office: NASA-UAH Global Hydrology & Climate Ctr 977 Explorer Blvd NW Huntsville AL 35806-2807

GILLARD, STUART THOMAS, film and television director, writer; b. Coronation, Alta., Apr. 28, 1950; s. Hugh A. and Mary (Williamson) G.; m. Marilyn Majerczyk, Nov. 3, 1990; children: Ryan Stuart, Tyler Bailey, Gideon Henry, Noah McGregor. BA, U. Alta., 1970; BFA, U. Wash., 1972. Writer, dir. (film) Teenage Mutant Ninja Turtles III, 1993, A Man Called Sarge, 1990; dir. (film) Rocket Man, 1997, (TV movie pilot) Forbidden Island, 1999, Legacy, 1998, Poltergeist, 1996, Taking Liberty, 1994, SandKings Outer Limits, 1995 (Cable Ace award, Best dir. Best show), dir. (TV movie) Return of the Shaggy Dog, 1988, The Escape, 1995, (TV programs) Bordertown, 1990 (Silver medal N.Y. Film & TV Festival 1990), Road to Avon Lea, 1990, (Genie award for Best Dir. 1990), (mini-series) Peter Benchley's Creature, 1997; actor (film) Why Rock the Boat, 1976 (Genie and ACTRA awards for Best Actor 1976). Mem. ACTRA, AFTRA, SAG, Actors Equity Assn., WRiters Guild Am., Dirs. Guild Am., Acad. Can. Cinema & TV. Office: William Morris 151 S El Camino Dr Beverly Hills CA 90212-2775

GILLE, JOHN PAUL, agricultural extension educator; b. Hazel Green, Wis., Feb. 27, 1960; s. Edmund Joseph and Edith Catherine (Klaas) G.; m. Juliann Aileen Gruhot, May 23, 1987; children: Lydia, Danielle. BS in Agrl. Edn., U. Wis., Platteville, 1981, MS in Edn. and Program Devel., 1982; postgrad., U. S.D., 1987—, S.D. State U., 1987—. Asst. loan supr. FmHA Burnett County, Spooner, Wis., 1983-84; ext. agt. Ag/4-H Yankton (S.D.) County, 1984-87; ext. agt. Gregory County, Burke, S.D., 1987-89, Union County, Elk Point, S.D., 1989—; advisor 6 commodity groups Union County, Elk Point, 1989—. Co-founder Union County Recovery Network, Elk Point, 1994; dir. youth support group Union County, Elk Point, 1989—; founder, dir. Big Friends-Little Friends, Inc. Union County, 1997. Mem. Nat. Assn. County Agrl. Agents (State Pub. Rels. winner 1996-97, State Comm. award 1994, Regional Finalist 4-H programs 1996, Cmty. Svc. Man of Yr. 1999), S.D. County Agrl. Agents Assn., Elk Point Comml. Club, KC. Roman Catholic. Avocations: reading, gardening, boating. Office: PO Box 428 Elk Point SD 57025

GILLECE, JAMES PATRICK, JR., lawyer; b. Annapolis, Md., May 26, 1944; s. James Patrick and Erna Virginia (Barling) G.; m. Jane C. Szczepaniak, Apr. 24, 1971 (div. 1998); children: Jessica K., Jocelyn J., Jillian N., James P. III, Juliette A., John M. Szczepaniak-Gillece; m. Rosa Beza, Feb. 12, 1999. BA, LaSalle U., 1966; JD, U. Notre Dame, 1969. Bar: Md. 1969, U.S. Dist. Ct. Md. 1969, U.S. Ct. Appeals (4th cir.) 1972, U.S. Supreme Ct. 1974, U.S. Ct. Appeals (7th cir.) 1992, U.S. Ct. Appeals (8th and 11th cir.) 1995. Assoc. Piper & Marbury, Balt., 1969-77, ptnr., 1977-92, dir. poverty law program, 1971-72; ptnr. Miles & Stockbridge, Balt., 1992-93; prin. Miles and Stockbridge, Balt., 1994-98; ptnr. McGuire Woods Battle & Boothe, Balt., 1998—; cons. Mercy Hosp. Dietitians Program, Balt., 1986—. Bd. dirs. Balt. City Fair, 1984-88, Legal Aid Soc. Balt., 1984, Family Cirsis Ctr. Baltimore County, Inc., 1992-97, Everyman Theatre, 1995—; mem. law adv. coun. U. Notre Dame, 1983—; mem. Com. to Keep Supreme Bench Judges, Com. for Mayor Kurt Schmoke, 1987, Lawyers Com. for Jerry Brown, 1976; bd. trustees Everyman Theatre, 1996—. Mem. ABA, FBA, Am. Judicature Soc. (bd. dirs. 1988-90), Md. State Bar Assn. (Disting. Svc. award), Balt. Bar Assn., Notre Dame Law Assn. (pres. 1983-99, bd. dirs. 1977—, exec. coun., life mem.), U. Notre Dame Law Adv. Coun., Internat. Childbirth Edn. Assn. (cons. 1987-97). Democrat. Roman Catholic. E-mail: jpgillec@mwbb.com. FAX: 410-659-4484. Home: 3809 Greenway Baltimore MD 21218 Office: McGuire Woods Battle and Boothe 7 Saint Paul St Ste 1000 Baltimore MD 21202-1626

GILLEN, HOWARD WILLIAM, neurologist, medical historian; b. Chgo., Nov. 25, 1923; s. John Howard and Emily Elizabeth (Bayley) G.; m. Corinne V. Neese, July 24, 1948. BS, U. Ill., 1947; MD, U. Ill., Chgo., 1949. Hon. active neurologist New Hanover Regional Med. Ctr., Wilmington, N.C., 1973-93, emeritus neurologist, 1993—; cons. neurologist Cape Fear Meml. Hosp., Wilmington, 1973-93; clin. prof. neurology U. N.C., Chapel Hill, 1973-93, clin. prof. emeritus, 1993—; adj. prof. biol. sci. U. N.C., Wilmington, 1986—; rsch. assoc. I.R.I.S.C., Wilmington, 1989-93, sr. investigator, 1993—. Capt. USNR, ret. Home: 500 Sand Castle Ct Wilmington NC 28404

GILLEN, JAMES ROBERT, lawyer, insurance company executive; b. N.Y.C., Nov. 14, 1937; s. James Matthew and Katharine Isabel (Fritz) G.; m. Rita Marie Wahleithner, June 15, 1963 (div. 1992); children: Jennifer Elaine, Nancy Louise, Paula Anne; m. Edda Lya Pacheco, Dec. 10, 1994. AB magna cum laude, Harvard U., 1959, LLB cum laude, 1965. Bar: N.Y. 1966, N.J. 1975. Assoc. firm White & Case, N.Y.C., 1965-72; v.p., assoc. gen. counsel Prudential Ins. Co. Am., Newark, 1972-77, sr. v.p., assoc. gen. counsel, 1977-80, sr. v.p. pub. affairs, 1980-84, sr. v.p., gen. counsel, 1984-98; mem. bd. trustees Columbia Inst. Investor Project, 1991-97; legal adv. com. New York Stock Exch., 1986-89. Trustee United Way Essex and West Hudson Counties, 1981-90, pres., 1986-88; mem. Mendham Twp. (N.J.)

Bd. Edn., 1981-82; trustee N.J. Shakespeare Festival, 1991-99, Mendham Twp. Libr., 1979-82; dir., chmn. Neurol. Inst. N.J., 1998—. Lt. (j.g.) USN, 1959-62. Mem. ABA, N.J. Bar Assn., Assn. Life Ins. Counsel, Harvard Club (N.Y.C.), Morris Country Golf Club. Home: 72 Washington Valley Rd Morristown NJ 07960-3332

GILLEN, PATRICK BERNARD, flight nurse; b. Toledo, June 6, 1950; s. Aloysius Martin and Edna Marie (Baugh) G.; m. Dolores Almeda Szabo, June 29, 1973; children: Abraham Joseph, Laura Marie, Kurtis Aloysius, Kathy Jean. BS, U. Toledo, 1973; Diploma in Nursing, Toledo Hosp. Sch., 1978; Enterostomal Therapy Nursing, Cleve. Clinic, 1980; MA in Internat. Rels., Webster U., 1997. Cert. enterostomal therapy nurse. Charge nurse med.-surg. Fulton County Health Ctr., Wauseon, Ohio, 1978-79; float nurse Flower Meml. Hosp., Sylvania, Ohio, 1979-80, enterostomal therapy nurse, 1980-88; pres. enterostomal therapy nurse practice Patient Care Assocs., Toledo, 1988-89; home health nurse Adrian (Mich.) Cmty. Health, 1988-89; commd. 1st lt. USAF Nurse Corps, 1989, advanced through grades to maj., 1998; med. surg., asst. charge nurse Keesler (AFB) Med. Ctr., Miss., 1989-91, nursing supr., 1992-93; flight nurse med. dir. 57th Aeromed. Evacuation, Scott AFB, Ill., 1993-94; instr., asst. charge tng. 375th Aeromed. Evacuation, Scott AFB, Ill., 1993—, flight examiner, 1995-97, asst. flight comdr. standards & evaluations, 1996-97; with USAF Med. Ctr., Wright-Patterson AFB, Ohio, 1997—; enterostomal nurse cons. in field. Contbr. articles to profl. jours. and chpt. to book. Con. United Ostomy Assn., 1980-89, Am. Cancer Soc., Fulton and Lucas Counties, Ohio, 1981-89, Toledo Cmty. Hosps. Oncology Program, 1984-86; leader Boy Scouts of Am., Ohio, 1981-87, counselor 1981-94). Named Nurse of Hope, Am. Cancer Soc. Mem. Aerospace Med. Assn., Am. Air Mus. in Britain, Secular Franciscan Order. Roman Catholic. Avocations: reading, running, writing, painting (oils), guitar, camping, modeling planes. Home: 4921 Honeywood Ct Dayton OH 45424-4804

GILLENWATER, JAY YOUNG, urologist, educator; b. Kingsport, Tenn., July 27, 1933; s. Jay King and Ann Marion (Young) G.; m. Shirley Joyce Brockman; children: Linda, Ann, Jay. BS, U. Tenn., 1954, MD, 1957. Diplomate Am. Bd. Urology (pres. 1988). Intern U. Pa. Grad. Hosp., 1958-59, resident, 1959-60, 62-65; asst. prof. U. Va. Med. Sch., Charlottesville, 1965-67, assoc. prof. urology dept., 1967-95; prof., 1995—; mem. coun. Nat. Inst. Diabetes and Digestive and Kidney Diseases, NIH, 1987-93; pres. AUA, 1991-92. Editor: Adult and Pediatric Urology, 1987, 91, 95; editor Urology Yearbook, 1978-94; assoc. editor Jour.Urology, 1985-93, editor, 1994—. Capt. U.S. Army, 1960-62. Mem. Am. Urol. Assn. (exec. com. 1987—, pres. 1991-92, Hugh Young award, 1989, Mary Scott Hughes edn. award 1985, Ramon Gueteras award 1999), Health Svc. Found. (pres. 1980-91), Am. Bd. Urology (pres. 1988), Am. Found. Urol. Diseases (pres. 1992—). Republican. Methodist. Avocation: gardening. Home: 648 Dry Bridge Rd Charlottesvle VA 22903-7037 Office: U Va Hosps Dept Urology PO Box 422 Charlottesville VA 22902-0422

GILLER, EDWARD BONFOY, retired government official, retired air force officer; b. Jacksonville, Ill., July 8, 1918; s. Edward Bonfoy and Ruth (Davis) G.; m. Mildred Florana Schmidt, July 2, 1943; children—Susan Ann, Carol Elaine, Bruce Carleton, Penny Marie, Paul Benjamin. B.S. in Chem. Engring, U. Ill., 1940, M.S., 1948, Ph.D., 1950. Chem. engr. Sinclair Oil Refining Co., 1940-41; commd. 2d lt. USAAF, 1942; advanced through grades to maj. gen. USAF, 1968; pilot, 1941-46; chief radiation br. (Armed Forces Spl. Weapons Project), Washington, 1950-54; dir. research directorate Air Force Spl. Weapons Center, Albuquerque, 1954-59; spl. asst. to comdr. (Office Aerospace Rsch.), Washington, 1959-64; dir. sci. and tech. Hdqrs. USAF, 1964-67; asst. gen. mgr. for mil. application U.S. AEC, 1967-72; ret. from USAF, 1972; asst. gen. mgr. for nat. security AEC, 1972-75; dep. asst. adminstr. for nat. security U.S. ERDA, 1975-77; rep. of Joint Chiefs of Staff to Comprehensive Test Ban Negotiations, Geneva, Switzerland, 1977-84; sr. scientist Pacific-Sierra Rsch. Corp., Arlington, Va, 1984-92; v.p. Trans Mar Inc., Spokane, Wash., 1992-96; cons. Sandia Nat. Labs., Albuquerque, 1990—; cons. in the field. Decorated Silver Star, D.S.M., Legion of Merit with oak leaf cluster, D.F.C., Air medal with 17 oak leaf clusters, Purple Heart; Croix de Guerre France). Fellow Am. Inst. Chemists; mem. Am. Inst. Chem. Engrs., Sigma Xi, Alpha Tau Omega. Episcopalian. Home: 216 Wapiti Dr Bayfield CO 81122-9243

GILLER, NORMAN MYER, banker, architect, author; b. Jacksonville, Fla., Feb. 14, 1918; s. Morris and Esther (Seltzer) G.; m. Frances Schwartz, June 30, 1946; children: Ira D., Anita Giller Grossman, Brian. Student, Ga. Inst. Tech., 1943-44; BArch, U. Fla., 1945; postgrad. in banking, Bankers Adminstrn. Inst., 1965-66. Chmn. bd. Norman M. Giller and Assocs., Architects, Miami Beach, Fla., 1945—; chmn. bd., pres. Interam. Nat. Bank, Miami Beach, 1964-68; vice chmn. Jefferson Bancorp, Miami Beach, 1968—; pres., vice chmn. Jefferson Nat. Bank, Sunny Isles, Fla., 1968—; bd. dirs. Jefferson Nat. Bank, Miami Beach, Jefferson Nat. Bank of Palm Beach, Boca Raton, Fla., Jefferson Bank of Broward, Hollywood, Fla.; cons. U.S. Dept. State, Washington, 1961-70, Govts. Panama, Nicaragua, Brazil, Colombia, El Salvador, 1961-70. Author: An Adventure in Architecture, 1977, A Century in America, 1986; contbr. articles on architecture to profl. jours. Chmn. Miami Beach Housing Authority, 1970, Fla. State Bd. Architecture, Tallahassee, 1979, Design Rev. Bd. City of Miami Beach, 1985; pres. So. Fla. coun. Boy Scouts Am., 1961-63, Concerned Citizens of N.E. Dade County, Miami Beach, 1970; sec. Nat. Coun. Archtl. Registration Bd., S.E. Atlanta, 1981; mem. Sunny Isles Task Force, Fla., 1982; pres. Mosaic-Jewish Mus. Fla., 1992—, chmn. 1998. Lt. (j.g.) USNR, 1942-46. Named Man of Yr., Gold Coast C. of C., 1973; bridge named in his honor Fla. Legis., Miami Beach, 1983; recipient Man of the Decade award, 1989; named to Hall of Fame, Gold Coast C. of C., 1994. Fellow AIA (pres. South Fla. chpt. 1945—, Silver medal 1979); mem. Fla. Assn. Architecture (bd. dirs. 1945—, Cmty. Svc. award 1982), Am. Bankers Assn., Fla. Bankers Assn. (mem. com. 1965—), Fla. Bankers Holding Co. Assn., Miami Beach C. of C. (Citizen of the Yr. 1995, pres. 1970—). Democrat. Jewish. Lodges: Masons, Shriners. Avocations: photography, writing. Office: 975 Arthur Godfrey Rd # 401 Miami FL 33140-3329

GILLERS, STEPHEN, law educator; b. 1943. BA, Bklyn Coll., 1964; JD, NYU, 1968. Bar: N.Y. 1968. Law clk. to Hon. Gus J. Solomon Oreg., 1968-69; assoc. Paul, Wiess, Rifkind, Wharton & Garrison, N.Y., 1969-71; pvt. practice law N.Y.C., 1973-78; assoc. prof. NYU, N.Y.C., 1978-81, prof. law, 1981—, vice dean, 1999—; mem. deptl. disciplinary com. N.Y. Supreme Ct., 1980-83; bd. dirs. CLU, N.Y., 1982—. Editor: Looking at Law School, 1978, 4th edit., 1997, The Rights of Lawyers and Clients, 1979, Regulation of Lawyers: Problems of Law and Ethics, 5th edit., 1998. Exec. dir. SALT, 1975-78, 78-80, bd. govs. Office: NYU Sch Law 40 Washington Sq S New York NY 10012-1099

GILLESPIE, ALASTAIR WILLIAM, former Canadian government official; b. Victoria, B.C., Can., May 1, 1922; s. Erroll Pilkington and Catherine (Oliver) G.; m. Diana Christie-Clark, June 17, 1947; children: Cynthia Gillespie Webb, Ian Alastair. Student, Brentwood Coll., 1941, U. B.C., 1941, McGill U., 1947; M.A. (Rhodes scholar), Oxford U., 1949; M.Comm., U. Toronto, 1958. Pres. Welmet Industries Ltd., Welland, 1962-68; pres. Can. Chromalox Co., Rexdale, 1966-68; v.p., dir. Can. Corp. Mgmt. Co. Ltd., Toronto, 1963-68; dir. Richardson, Bond & Wright, Ltd., Owen Sound, 1963-68, Internat. Equipment Co. Ltd., Montreal, 1963-68, Cashway Lumber Co. Ltd., 1963-68, Mechanics for Electronics Ltd., Cambridge, Mass., 1964-68; v.p. ops., dir. W.J. Gage Ltd., Toronto, 1949-70; M.P., Etobicoke, 1968-79, vice chmn. finance, trade and econ. affairs com., 1968-70, Parliamentary sec. to pres. of treasury bd., 1970-71, minister of state for sci. and tech., 1971-72, minister of industry, trade and commerce, 1972-75, minister energy, mines and resources, 1975-79; pres. Scotia Synfuels Ltd.; chmn. Nat. Westminster's Bank of Can., Toronto, 1980-95; chmn. Carling O'Keefe Ltd., 1980-83, also bd. dirs.; bd. dirs.; bd. dirs. Rochman's Internat., 1980-83; pres. Alastair Gillespie & Assoc. Ltd., Toronto, 1980—; chmn. Scotia Coal Synfuels Project, 1980-85, Point Tupper Terminals Co., 1992-93; dir. Creemore Springs Brewery Ltd. Bd. govs. Lyndhurst Hosp., Toronto; bd. dirs. Gage Rsch. Inst., Toronto, 1981-94; bd. dirs., past pres. Can. Opera Co.; bd. dirs. Scottish Studies Found., 1997—, Can. Opera Found., 1992—, Music Can., 1995—. Lt. Royal Can. Navy, 1941-45. Mem. Can. Paraplegic Assn. (past bd. dirs.), Champlain Soc. (bd. dirs. 1995—), Order of Can. (officer 1998). Clubs: Toronto, Badminton & Racquet, Toronto Golf, Osler Bluff Ski. Office: 175 Heath St W, Toronto, ON Canada M4V 1V1

GILLESPIE, ANITA WRIGHT, nursing administrator; b. S.C., Jan. 3, 1953; d. Ernest L. and Thelma G. Wright; m. Howard Gillespie Jr.; children: Christopher, Howard III. BSN, N.C. A&T State U., 1974. Cert. CPR instr., ACLS cert., cert. neonatal resusitation. Nursing instr. Norfolk (Va.) Community Hosp., 1975-76, staff nurse emergency dept., 1976-79; asst. nurse mgr. emergency dept. Mercy Hosp., Cin., 1979-83; evening dir. Mercy Hosp. Anderson, Cin., 1983-95; staff nurse emergency dept. Bethesda Oak Hosp., Cin., 1995—; staff nurse labor and delivery maternity dept. Mercy Hosp. Anderson, Cin., 1996-98, mgr. women's splty. unit, 1998—; mem. stds. com., employee activities com., med. records com., forms com., chairperson clin. nurse practice com. Mercy Hosp. Mem. ANA, NAFE, AWHONN, Nat. Coun. Negro Women, N.C. A&T Alumni Assn., Alpha Kappa Alpha (mem.-at-large, chair health com.). Avocation: cake decorating. Home: 2290 Lauren Close Cincinnati OH 45244-2668 Office: Mercy Hosp Anderson 7500 State Rd Cincinnati OH 45255-2439

GILLESPIE, BETTY GLOVER, critical care nurse; b. Abbeville, La., Aug. 7, 1939; d. Thomas F. and Idas (Baumgardner) Glover; m. Alfred H. Gillespie, Dec. 9, 1960; children: Kim E. Hammonds, Rick T. Hammonds, Mark W. BSN cum laude, Nicholls State U., 1987; postgrad., La. State U. Med. Ctr. RN, La.; cert. pediatric advanced life support; CCRN, ACLS. Staff nurse, rehab. unit Terrebonne Gen. Med. Ctr., Houma, La., staff nurse, telemetry; staff nurse, ICU Chabert Med. Ctr., Houma, 1989—; adj. facutly, precepetor BSN nursing program Nicholls State U. Mem. AACN (CCRN), Soc. Critical Care Medicine, Sigma Theta Tau. Home: 16 Parkway Cir Houma LA 70364-2812

GILLESPIE, DANIEL CURTIS, SR., retired non-profit company executive, consultant; b. Shamokin, Pa., Sept. 22, 1922; s. John F. and Verna E. (Erdman) G.; m. Juliet Warren Yearns, Oct. 7, 1950; children: Julia W., Daniel Curtis, David R. B.S., Pa. State U., 1943; M.S. in Chem. Engring., U. Mich., 1948. Devel. engr. Tidewater Associated Oil Co., Bayonne, N.J., 1943-44; jr. scientist Manhattan Project, Los Alamos Sci. Lab., 1946; with Dorr-Oliver Inc., Stamford, Conn., 1948-82, v.p. mktg., 1973-75, exec. v.p., 1975-76, pres. and chief exec. officer, 1976-82, also dir.; v.p. bus. devel. Sohio Chems. & Indsl. Products Co., 1982-84; pres., chief exec. officer Metropool, Inc., 1985-87; cons., 1987-92, ret., 1992. Served with U.S. Army, 1944-46. Fellow Am. Inst. Chem. Engrs.; hon. mem. Process Equipment Mfrs. Assn., Southwestern Area Commerce and Industry Assn. Home: 18 Pepper Bush Cir Savannah GA 31411-3009

GILLESPIE, EDWARD MALCOLM, hospital administrator; b. Mpls., Oct. 19, 1935; s. Harold Livingston and Alice May (Thompson) G.; children: Karin, Timothy, Kenneth. BS, U. Minn., 1957, MPA, 1959, MHA, 1962. Engaged in refugee adminstrn. Linz, Austria, 1958-60; asst. adminstr. Luth. Med. Ctr., Denver, 1962-66; asst. gen. sec. Meth. Bd. Health and Welfare Ministries, Evanston, Ill., 1966-69; adminstr. Meth. Hosp., Rochester, Minn., 1969-74; adminstr. Univ. Hosp., Augusta, Ga., 1974-91, pres. Health Advance, 1991-92; bd. dirs. Augusta Area Mental Health, Augusta Speech and Hearing Ctr., St. John's Towers, CSRA Blood Assurance; chmn. hosp. divsn. certification coun. Meth. Health and Welfare. Bd. dirs. local United Way, Boy Scouts Am., Blue Cross Ga., Bankers First; chmn. Augusta Resource Ctr. on Aging, Brandon Wilde. Fellow ACHA; mem. Am. Hosp. Assn., Ga. Hosp. Assn. (chmn.), Rotary Internat. (bd. dirs. Augusta chpt.). Methodist. Home and Office: Health Advance 12 Indian Creek Rd Augusta GA 30909-3749

GILLESPIE, GEORGE JOSEPH, III, lawyer; b. N.Y.C., May 18, 1930; s. George Joseph Jr. and Dorothy Elizabeth (McKenna) G.; m. Eileen Tracy Dealy, July 27, 1955; children: Gail Gillespie Garcia, John D., Myles D., Eileen G. Fahey. A.B. magna cum laude, Georgetown U., 1952; LL.B. magna cum laude, Harvard U., 1955. Bar: N.Y. 1957. Assoc. Cravath, Swaine & Moore, N.Y.C., 1956-62; ptnr. Cravath, Swaine & Moore, 1963—; bd. dirs. Washington Post Co., White Mountains Holdings Inc. Trustee, treas., John M. Olin Found.; pres., trustee Pinkerton Found., Arthur Ross Found., William S. Paley Found., ; bd. dirs., sec. Mus. TV and Radio; trustee Mt. Sinai/NYU Med. Ctr., chmn. bd. dirs. Madison Square Boys and Girls Club; bd. dirs., chmn. emeritus Nat. Multiple Sclerosis Soc. Frederick Sheldon traveling fellow Harvard U., 1955-56. Century Assn., Winged Foot Golf Club, Prouts Neck Country Club, Falmouth Country Club, Double Eagle Club, Am. Yacht Club, Portland Country Club. Republican. Roman Catholic. Office: Cravath Swaine & Moore Worldwide Pla 825 8th Ave Fl 38 New York NY 10019-7475

GILLESPIE, GERALD ERNEST PAUL, comparative literature educator, writer; b. Cleve., July 12, 1933; s. Francis and Nora Veronica (Quinn) G.; m. Adrienne Amalia Galante, Sept. 5, 1959. AB, Harvard U., 1956; postgrad., U. Tübingen, Germany, 1956-57; MA, Ohio State U., 1958, PhD, 1961; postgrad., U. Munich, 1960-61. Asst. prof. U. So. Calif., L.A., 1961-65; assoc. prof., then prof. SUNY, Binghamton, 1965-74; vis. prof. U. Pa., Phila., 1969, NYU, 1970; prof. Stanford (Calif.) U., 1974—; vis. prof. U. Minn., Mpls., 1978, Peking U., Beijing, 1985, U. East Anglia, Norwich, Eng., 1988, U. Munich, 1993. Author: German Baroque Poetry, 1971, Evolution of the European Novel, 1987, Garden and Labyrinth of Time, 1988; author, editor: Herkommen und Erneuerung, 1976, Studien zum Werk D.C. von Lohenstein, 1983, German Theater Before 1750, 1992, Romantic Drama, 1994, Narrative Ironies, 1997, Mallarmé in the Twentieth Century, 1998; translator, editor: Night Watches, 1972, Puss-in-Boots, 1974, Bohemian Lights, 1976; editor: Littérature Comparée, Littérature Mondiale, 1991, Visions in History, 1995, Powers of Narration, 1995; mem. editl. bd. Comparative Lit., 1977—, Internationales Archiv, 1975—, Utrecht Studies in Comparative Lit., 1987—, Recherche Littéraire, 1991—, Literary Imagination, 1998—; co-editor German Life and Letters, 1987—. Andrew Mellon Found. fellow, 1966-67; John S. Guggenheim Found. fellow, 1967-68; NEH sr. fellow, 1973-74; vis. fellow Clare Hall, Cambridge U., Eng., 1979. Mem. MLA (mem. exec. com. comparative studies in romanticism and the 19th century 1982-87, mem. nat. program com. 1985-88, mem. exec. com. classical studies and modern lit. 1986-91), Internat. Comparative Lit. Assn. (sec. 1979-85, mem. editl. bd. bull. 1979-85, v.p. 1985-88, pres. 1994-97), Berliner Wissenschaftliche Gesellschaft (corr.), Am. Comparative Lit. Assn., Brit. Comparative Lit. Assn., Renaissance Soc. Am., Assn. of Literary Scholars and Critics, Calif. Assn. Scholars (coun. 1998—).

GILLESPIE, HELEN DAVYS, marketing/industry consultant, analyst, author; b. San Jose, Calif., Nov. 23, 1954; d. Robert Bruce and Helen Davys (Street) G.; m. Nigel George Haden, May 1, 1982 (div. June 1986). BA in English with honors, Calif. State U., Chico, 1976; postgrad. in English, U. Sheffield, Eng., 1976-77, Calif. State U., Chico, 1977-78. Cert. bus. communicator. Bus. analyst Dun & Bradstreet, San Jose, 1978-80; personal asst. Times Computer Svcs., London, 1980; adminstr. Exec. Aviation, Palo Alto, Calif., 1981; sr. writer/editor Tymnet/McDonnell Douglas, San Jose, 1982-86; mgr. sales support Pactel Spectrum Svcs., Walnut Creek, Calif., 1987; mgr. product communications Varian Assocs., Inc., Sunnyvale, Calif., 1987-90; mgr. mktg. communications Allergan Humphrey, San Leandro, Calif., 1990-91; owner Write Away Comm., San Jose, Calif., 1987—, Isographics Internat., 1994—; mgr. bus. comms. Lockheed Martin Advanced Tech. Ctr., Palo Alto, Calif., 1997—; editor, pub. LIMS/Letter, 1994—, LIMSource web site, 1996—. Mem. Mus. Modern Art, San Jose. Recipient LIMS award LIMS Inst., 1999. Mem. Bus. Mktg. Assn., Airline Owners and Pilots Assn., Writers Connection, Art Inst. Chgo., Mus. Soc. San Francisco, Commonwealth Club, Am. Soc. Quality Control. Avocations: lap swimming, windsurfing, English riding/dressage, flying, bicycling, snow and water skiing.

GILLESPIE, J. MARTIN, sales and distribution company executive; b. Detroit, Sept. 27, 1949; s. John Martin and Shirley Ann (Rees) G.; BBA, Xavier U., 1971; MBA, U. Mich., 1973; m. Jeannette Downes, Sept. 27, 1975; children: Heather, Tara. Account exec. Foote Cone & Belding, Chgo., 1973-76; account supr., 1976-77; mktg. mgr. Hansen Corp., Walled Lake, Mich., 1977-80, gen. mgr., 1980-82; chmn., chief exec. officer Hansen Mktg. Services, Inc., Walled Lake, 1982—. Recipient Merit award Nat. Alliance Businessmen, 1973. Mem. Assn. MBA Execs., Am. Mgmt. Assn., Nat. Acad. TV Arts and Scis., Nat. Assn. Credit Mgmt., Nat. Bldg. Materials Distbn. Assn. (chmn. govt. rels. com.), Alpha Kappa Psi. Home: 3792 W Pemberton Rd Bloomfield Hills MI 48302-1445 Office: Hansen Mktg Svcs Inc PO Box 638 1000 Decker Rd Walled Lake MI 48390-3218

GILLESPIE, JACQUELYN RANDALL, psychologist; b. Paris, France, Oct. 10, 1927; came to U.S., 1932; d. John Roberts and Hazel Maurine (Hammel) Hunter; m. Thomas Gilbert Gillespie, Apr. 27, 1947 (dec. May 1995); children: Thomas Randall, Catherine Claire Gillespie Laroche. AB, Calif. State U., Long Beach, 1959; MS, Calif. State U., Fullerton, 1965; PhD, Calif. Grad. Inst., L.A., 1977. Lic. psychologist, psychoanalytic psychotherapist, Calif. Guidance cons. Lowell Sch. Dist., Whittier, Calif., 1963-69; psychologist Fullerton (Calif.) High Sch., 1969-82; pvt. practice Orange, Calif., 1976-90; assoc. prof. Calif. Grad. Inst., L.A., 1978-90. Author: Projective Use of Mother-and-Child Drawings, 1994; co-author: (reading test) Diagnostic Analysis of Reading Errors, 1981; contbr. articles to profl. jours. Grantee State of Calif., 1979; rsch. award Calif. Assn. Sch. Psychologists, 1972. Mem. APA (assoc.), Calif. Assn. Lic. Ednl. Psychologists (pres. 1983). Episcopalian. Home: 421 Meadowlark Ln # A Naples FL 34105-2459

GILLESPIE, JAMES DAVIS, lawyer; b. Elkin, N.C., Apr. 30, 1955; s. John Banner and Jerry Sue (Swaim) G.; m. Tommie Lee Johnson, Aug. 13, 1977 (div. Dec. 1995); 1 child, John Foster; m. Regina Lee Robinson, July 11, 1998. BA, U. N.C., 1977; JD, Samford U., 1980. Bar: N.C. 1980, U.S. Dist. Ct. (mid. dist.) 1982, U.S. Dist. Ct. (we. dist.) N.C. 1983, U.S. Ct. Appeals (4th cir.) 1984. Ptnr. Neaves & Gillespie, Elkin, 1980—; mem. Surry-Yadkin Mental Health Authority, Mt. Aiy, N.C., 1981-91, vice chmn., 1987-89, chmn. 1990-91. Bd. editors: Cumberland Law Rev., 1978-80. Commr. Town of Jonesville, N.C., 1983-85, mayor, 1985-93; mem. exec. com. N.W. Piedmont Coun. Govts., 1987, sec., 1988-89, chmn., 1990-91; active Surry-Yadkin Mental Health, Mental Retardation and Substance Abuse Authority, 1981-91, vice chmn., 1987-89, chmn., 1990-91; bd. dirs. Foothills Art Coun., 1987-90. Mem. ABA, Assn. Trial Lawyers Am., N.C. Bar Assn., N.C. Trial Lawyers Assn., Surry and Yadkin Counties Bar Assn., Elkin Jaycees (bd. dirs. 1981-83, v.p. 1983-84), N.C. Acad. Trial Lawyers, Greater Elkin-Jonesville C. of C. (charter, bd. dirs. 1987-90), Phi Alpha Delta, Soc. Curia Honoris. Democrat. Methodist. Avocations: tennis, basketball, reading. Home: 371 Wagoner St Jonesville NC 28642-2658 Office: Neaves & Gillespie 124 W Main St Ste A Elkin NC 28621-3433

GILLESPIE, JOHN FAGAN, mining executive; b. Cleve., Aug. 16, 1936; s. James Patrick and Mary Isabelle (Fagan) G.; m. Rita Kirsch, 1956 (div.); children: John Joseph, Richard Anthony, Rita Therese, Margaret Mary, Veronica Gail; student John Carroll U., 1955-58, U. Tulsa, 1970-71; m. Dorothy May LaForest, July 6, 1962 (div. 1994); 1 son, Kelly Joseph. With Great Lakes Dredge and Dock Co., Cleve., 1955-63, project supt., 1962-63; owner, operator Tri-Angle Bldg. and Wrecking Co., Bay City, Mich., 1963-65; with Martin Marietta Corp., 1965-71; with Aetna Portland Cement Co., Bay City, 1965-69, prodn. supt., 1968-69; maintenance supt. Dewey Rocky Mountain Cement Co., Tulsa, 1969-71; plant mgr. Kellstone Inc., Kelley's Island, Ohio, 1971-73; plant mgr. Lyon Sand and Gravel Co., Wixom, Mich., 1973-75; area mgr. J. P. Burroughs & Son, Inc., Aggregate div. subs. Blount, Inc., Montgomery, Ala., 1975, asst. to pres., 1975-76, mgr. ops., 1976-78, gen. mgr., 1978-81; pres., chief exec. officer, chmn. bd. Tilcon N.Y. Inc., Haverstraw, N.Y., 1981—; pres., chief exec. officer Tilcon Quarries New York Inc., 1981-91; pres., chief exec. officer JFG and Assocs., Inc., 1990—; ptnr. The Pasta-bilities Cafe, Inc., sec., 1994—; pres. The Pasta Co.; regional dir. Statewide Corp. Strategies Corp., 1995—; Vice-chmn. Mich. Mineral Resources Assn., 1977-81; mem. Small Bus. Conf., State of Mich., 1977-81; mem. Restaurant and Hospitality Assn. Rockland, 1993—; pres., CEO The Pasta Co., 1994—. Bd. visitors Helen Hayes Hosp., 1985—; mem. corp. adv. council Columbia Presbyn. Hosp.; mem. adv. bd. to Dean Columbia Presbyn. Dental Sch., bd. dirs., chmn. Rockland Community Coll., 1985—, bd. dirs., chmn. bd. Rockland Econ. Devel. Corp., NYACK Hosp. Found., 1985—; bd. govs. Good Samaritan Hosp. Mem. Detroit Engring. Soc., Am. Mgmt. Assn., Pvt. Industry Council (bd. dirs. 1985—), Mich. Mineral Resources Assn. (past vice-chmn.), Nat. Sand and Gravel Assn., Nat. Crushed Stone Assn. (chmn. flugas com.), Mich. Sand and Gravel Producers Assn. (chief negotiation, sec.-treas.), Restaurant and Hospitality Assn. of Rockland. Republican. Roman Catholic. Home: 11 Wildwood Rd Katonah NY 10536-1733 Office: 572 Route 303 Blauvelt NY 10913-1941

GILLESPIE, JOHN THOMAS, university administrator; b. Thunder Bay, Ont., Can., Sept. 25, 1928; came to U.S., 1954, naturalized, 1961; s. William and Jeannie (Barr) G. BA, U. B.C., 1948; MA, Columbia U., 1957; PhD, NYU, 1969. High sch. tchr. Powell River, B.C., Can., 1949-53; libr. Roslyn (N.Y.) Pub. Sch. Dist., 1955-63; mem. faculty Palmer Grad. Library Sch., C.W. Post Center, LIU, N.Y., 1963—; prof. Palmer Grad. Library Sch., C.W. Post Center, LIU, 1975-80, dean, 1981-83; acad. v.p. C.W. Post Ctr., LIU, 1983-85; vis. prof. Syracuse (N.Y.) U., SUNY, Albany; cons. in field. Author: Juniorplots, 1966, Introducing Books, 1970, Young Phenomenon, 1971, Creating the School Media Program, 1973, A Model School Media Program, 1973, Paperback Books for Young People, 3d edit., 1987, More Juniorplots, 1977, Best Books for Children, Administering the School Library Media Center, 1983, Elementary School Paperback Collection, 1985, Senior High School Paperback Collection, 1986, Juniorplots 3, 1987, Seniorplots, 1989, Best Books for Junior High Readers, 1991, Best Books for Senior High Readers, 1991, Juniorplots 4, 1993, Middleplots 4, 1994, Best Books for Children, 5th edit., 1994, Guides to Library Collection Development, 1994, The Newbery Companion, 1996, Characters in Young Adult Literature, 1997, Guides to Library Collection Development for Children and Young Adults, 1997, Best Books for Children, 6th edit., 1998. Mem. ALA, N.Y. Libr. Assn., Phi Delta Kappa, Kappa Delta Pi. Home: 360 E 72nd St New York NY 10021-4753

GILLESPIE, LARRY, secondary school principal. Prin. Clay County Jr. High Sch., Clay, W.Va. Recipient Blue Ribbon Sch. award U.S. Dept. Edn., 1990-91. Office: Clay Mid Sch PO Box 489 Clay WV 25043-0489*

GILLESPIE, MARILYN, museum administrator. Dir. Las Vegas Natural History Mus., 1991—; pres. Bd. Mus. and Attractions, Nev., sec. 1997—. Vol. promoting environ. concerns, homelessness issues, spl. edn. Mem. Am. Assn. Mus., Nev. Mus. Assn., Allied Arts Coun., S.W. Marine Educators Assn., Kiwanis Club (bd. dirs. Las Vegas Territory, program dir. Uptown). Office: Las Vegas Natural History Mus 900 Las Vegas Blvd N Las Vegas NV 89101

GILLESPIE, MIKE J., university baseball coach; b. L.A., May 7, 1940; m. Barbara Westcott, June 25, 1986; children: Kelly Kreuter, Mitch, Matt, Tiffany. BS in Phys. Edn., U. So. Calif., 1962, MS in Phys. Edn., 1963. Freshman baseball coach Palos Verdes (Calif.) H.S., 1964; baseball coach Rolling Hills (Calif.) H.S., 1965-70; baseball coach, tchr. English, phys. edn., health edn. Coll. of Canyons, 1970-77; baseball coach, athletic dir. Coll. of Canyons, Valencia, Calif., 1977-86; baseball coach U. So. Calif., L.A., 1987—; mgr. N. Pole Nicks, Alaska Semipro Baseball League, 1983-85. Winner 11 Mt. Valley Conf. championships, 3 state championships (Canyon Cmty. Coll.), 3 PAC-10 titles, 9NCAA Regional Appearances (U. So. Calif.); named Calif. Comty. Coll. Co-coach of Yr. 1981, 83, 86; inducted into Calif. C.C. Baseball Coaches Hall of Fame, 1993. Office: U So Calif Heritage Hall Los Angeles CA 90089-0600

GILLESPIE, PENNY HANNIG, business owner; b. Schenectady, N.Y., June 4, 1954; d. William Armand and Freda (Penney) H.; m. Kenneth Scofield Keyes, Jr., Sept. 2, 1984 (div. Aug. 1992). Student, U. Ariz., 1972-74. Cert. EMT, Ariz., N.Y.; completion in skills tng. for profls. in Hakomi psychotherapy, Oreg. Co-founder Ken Keyes Coll., Coos Bay, Ore., 1982-91; pvt. practice counseling Eugene, Ore., 1991-95; founder, pres. The Wellness Network, Eugene, Oreg., 1994—. Co-author: Gathering Power Through Insight and Love, 1986, Handbook to Higher Consciousness: The Workbook, 1989; editor: How to Enjoy Your Life in Spite of It All, 1980, The Hundredth Monkey, 1982, Your Heart's Desire, 1983, Your Life Is a Gift, 1987, Discovering the Secrets of Happiness, 1988, PlanetHood, 1988, The Power of Unconditional Love, 1990. Bd. dirs. Living Love Ch., 1980-91, sec., v.p.; founding bd. dirs., sec., sec.-treas., v.p. The Vision Foundation, Inc., 1982-91; founding bd. dirs., sec., sec.-treas. Cornucopia, The Living Love Ch. of Ky., 1982-91; vol. Victim Advocate Lane County Dist. Attys.

Victim/Witness Svcs. Program, Oreg., 1993. Recipient peace award Coalition for Justice and Peace, Ariz. State U. and the Inst. Peace Edn., 1989; award as site mgr. for Anne Frank exhibit Jewish Fedn. Lane County, Ore., 1993. Avocations: piano, bicycling. Home: PO Box 41532 Eugene OR 97404-0369

GILLESPIE, ROBERT JAMES, manufacturing company executive; b. Halifax, N.S., Can., July 16, 1942; s. Robert Leo and Pearl G.; m. Carol Ann Caliendo, Nov. 16, 1968; children: Erica Christine, Brooke Caroline, Grant Robert. BSc, St. Mary's U., Can., 1962; BMechE, Tech. U. N.S., 1964; MS in Indsl. Adminstrn., Purdue U., 1965. Group product mgr. indsl. div., then v.p. bus. mgmt. indsl. div. CPC Internat. Inc., 1970-76; pres. Can. Starch, 1976-80; pres. corn products unit CPC Internat. Inc., Englewood Cliffs, N.J., 1980-84; exec. v.p. Best Foods Divsn. CPC Internat. Inc., 1984-88, pres., 1988-95, sr. v.p., 1991-95; exec. v.p. CPC Internat. Inc. (now Bestfoods), 1995—; bd. dirs. Bestfoods, Arkwright Mutual Ins. Co.; chmn. bd. advisors Sarah W. Stedman Ctr. for Nutritional Studies, Duke U.; chmn. internat. affairs com. Grocery Mfrs. Am. Author: Selection of Engineering Materials and Their Use in a Marine Environment, 1966, Merger and Acquisiton Fact Book, 1970. Served with Can. Army, 1960-64. Mem. Grocery Mfrs. Am. (chair internat. afairs com.). Clubs: Montreal Badminton and Squash, St. James (Montreal).

GILLESPIE, ROBERT WAYNE, banker; b. Cleve., Mar. 26, 1944; s. Robert Walton and Eleanore (Parsons) G.; m. Ann L. Wible, June 17, 1967; children: Laura, Gwen. B.A., Ohio Wesleyan U., 1966; M.B.A., Case Western Res. U., 1968; postgrad., Harvard U., 1979. Credit analyst Soc. Nat. Bank, Cleve., 1968-70, v.p., 1970-76, sr. v.p., 1976-79; exec. v.p. Soc. Nat Bank, Cleve., 1979-81; vice-chmn., chief operating officer Soc. Nat. Bank, Cleve., 1981-83, pres., chief operating officer, 1983-85, CEO, 1985—, pres., 1987-94; pres., CEO, Key Corp., Cleve., 1995-96, chmn., 1996—. Trustee Case Western Res. U., Ohio Wesleyan U., Cleve. Mus. Art, Cleve. Initiative for Edn. and Musical Arts, Greater Cleve. Roundtable, Cleve. Tomorrow and North Coast Harbor; bd. dirs. Greater Cleve. Growth Assn. Office: Key Corp 127 Public Sq Cleveland OH 44114-1306*

GILLESPIE, RONALD JAMES, chemistry educator, researcher, writer; b. London, Aug. 21, 1924; arrived in Can., 1958; s. James Andrew and Miriam (Kirk) G.; m. Madge Garner, July 5, 1950; children: Ann, Lynn. BSc, London U., 1945, PhD, 1949, DSc, 1957; LLD (hon.), Concordia U., Montreal, Can., 1988, Dalhousie U., Halifax, Can., 1988; D Honoris causa, U. des Scis. et Techniques du Languedoc, 1991; DSc (hon.), McMaster U., 1993. Asst. lectr. dept. chemistry U. Coll., U. London, 1948-50, lectr., 1950-58; assoc. prof. dept. chemistry McMaster U., Hamilton, Ont., Can., 1958-60, prof., 1960-87, prof. emeritus, 1987—, chmn. dept., 1962-65; vis. prof. U. Manchester (Eng.), 1965-66, U. des Scis. et Techniques du Languedoc, Montpellier, France, 1972-73, U. Geneva, 1976, U. Göttingen, Fed. Republic Germany, 1978, Australian Nat. U., Canberra, 1979, U. Auckland, New Zealand, 1980, Panjab U., Chandigarh, India, 1983; Nyholm lectr. Chem. Soc., London, 1978; Gillespie lectr. U. Coll., London, 1990; Muetterties vis. scholar U. Calif., Berkeley, 1990. Author: Molecular Geometry, 1972, (with others) Chemistry, 1986, 2d edit., 1989, (with I. Hargittai) The VSEPR Model of Molecular Geometry, 1991, (with others) Atoms, Molecules and Reactions: An Introduction to Chemistry, 1994; contbr. over 350 articles to profl. jours. Recipient Can. Centennial medal, 1967, Coll. Chemistry Tchr. award Mfg. Chemists Assn., 1972, Silver Jubilee award, 1977, Excellence in Teaching award McMaster u. Students Union, 1983, Izaak Walter Killam Meml. Prize of Can. Coun. for Pure Sci., 1987; Commonwealth Fund fellow Brown U., 1953-54. Fellow Royal Soc. London, Royal Soc. Can. (Henry Marshall Tory medal 1983), Royal Soc. Chemistry (Harrison Meml. medal 1953), Royal Inst. Chemistry, Chem. Inst. Can. (Noranda award 1966, Union Carbide award 1976, medal 1977); mem. Am. Chem. Soc. (N.E. Region award 1971, Tour Speaker of Yr. award 1971, Disting. Svc. award 1973, fluorine chemistry award 1981). Avocations: sailing, skiing, travel. Office: McMaster U, Dept Chemistry, Hamilton, ON Canada L8S 4M1

GILLESPIE, SAMUEL H., III, lawyer, oil company executive. BA, Middlebury Coll., 1966; JD, Vanderbilt U., 1972. Bar: N.Y. 1973. Assoc. Milbank, Tweed, Hadley & McCloy, 1972-82, counsel, 1982-85; asst. gen. counsel Mobil Corp., Mobil South, 1985-87; asst. gen. counsel M&R divsn. Mobil Corp., 1987-89, asst. gen. counsel Exploration and Producing divsn., 1990-94; v.p., gen. cousnel Mobil Oil Corp., Fairfax, Va., 1994—, now sr. v.p., gen. counsel. Office: Mobil Oil Corp 3225 Gallows Rd Fairfax VA 22037-0002*

GILLESPIE, SHAWN PAUL, military pilot; b. Homestead, Fla., June 4, 1966; s. Vernon Paul and Judith Ann (Moen) G.; m. Deborah Ann Saner, July 7, 1990; 1 child, Collin Vernon Thomas. BA in History, Miami U., Oxford, Ohio, 1988; M in Adminstrv. Sci., George Washington U., 1997. Commd. 2d lt. USAF, 1989, advanced through grades to capt., 1993; C-21A pilot, chief of scheduling 458th Airlift Squadron, Scott AFB, Ill., 1990-93; C-17A initial cadre pilot 17th Airlift Squadron, Charleston AFB, S.C., 1994-95; intern HQ USAF-Pentagon, Washington, 1995-97; C-17A pilot, chief of scheduling 14th Airlift Squadron, Charleston AFB, 1997-98; exec. officer to the wing comdr. 437th Airlift Wing, Charleston AFB, 1999—. Mem. Air Force Assn., Airlift/Tanker Assn., Order of Daedalians. Avocations: golf, tennis, reading. Home: 204 Wickford Ct Summerville SC 29485-5828 Office: 437th Airlift Wing Charleston AFB SC 29404

GILLESPIE, THOMAS STUART, lawyer; b. Montreal, July 18, 1938; s. Alexander Robert and Lois Tully (O'Brien) G.; m. Caroline Pierce Doyle, June 28, 1963; children: Caroline Alexandra, Alexandra Olivia, Vanessa Margaret, Joshua William. BA, McGill U., 1959, BCL, 1963. Assoc., Ogilvy, Renault, Montreal, 1964-72; ptnr. Ogilvy, Renault, 1972-89, sr. ptnr., 1989—; sec., bd. dirs. Guerlain Can. Ltd., Bouverie Investments Ltd., H.H. Brown Shoe Co. Can. Ltd., Charlottetown Trust Co., Volvo Can. Ltd. Bd. dirs. Montreal YMCA Found., Phillips Exeter Acad., Can. Scholarship Fund, Carnegie Instn. Can. Mem. Que. Bar Assn., Can. Bar Assn., Can. Tax Found., Internat. Fiscal Assn. Roman Catholic. Clubs: Mt. Bruno Country, Orleans Fish and Game, University, Tarratine. Home: 48 Aberdeen Ave, Westmount, PQ Canada H3Y 3A4 Office: 1981 McGill College Ave, Montreal, PQ Canada H3A 3C1

GILLESPIE, THOMAS WILLIAM, theological seminary administrator, religion educator; b. L.A., July 18, 1928; s. William A. and Estella (Beers) G.; m. Barbara A. Lugenbill, July 31, 1953; children: Robyn C., William T., Dayle E. BA., George Pepperdine Coll., 1951; B.D., Princeton Theol. Seminary, 1954; Ph.D., Claremont Grad. Sch., 1971; DD (hon.), Grove City Coll., 1984; ThD (hon.), Theol. Acad. Debrecen, Hungary, 1988; DTh (hon.), Karoli Gaspar Reformed U., Budapest, Hungary, 1994; DPhil (hon.), Soong Sil U., Seoul, Korea, 1994; DD (hon.), U. St. Andrews, Scotland, 1996. Ordained to ministry Presbyterian Ch., 1954. Pastor 1st Presbyn. Ch., Garden Grove, Calif., 1954-66, Burlingame, Calif., 1966-83; pres., prof. N.T. Princeton (N.J.) Theol. Sem., 1983—. Author: The First Theologians: A Study in Early Christian Prophecy, 1994. Chmn. bd. trustees Ctr. Theol. Inquiry, 1992—. With USMC, 1946-47. Recipient A.A. Hodge prize in systematic theology Princeton Theol. Sem., 1953; Disting. Alumnus award Claremont Grad. Sch., 1984; Disting. Alumnus award Pepperdine U., 1986. Mem. Soc. Bibl. Lit., Studiorum Novi Testamenti Societas, Rotary Internat. Republican. Home: Springdale 86 Mercer St Princeton NJ 08540-6819 Office: Princeton Theol Sem Office of Pres PO Box 552 Princeton NJ 08542-0552

GILLESPIE, WILLIAM HARRY, forestry executive, geology educator; b. Webster Springs, W.Va., Jan. 8, 1931; s. William Marston and Rosalie Casteel (Frazee) G.; m. Betty Jean Rasnick, Dec. 23, 1950; children: William A., Linda M., Clifton P., Laura L., James D. BS, W.Va. U., 1952, MS, 1954, postgrad., 1956-60. Forest biologist W.Va. Dept. Agriculture, Morgantown, 1956-66; asst. dir. plant pest control W.Va. Dept. Agriculture, Charleston, 1966-67, dir. plant pest control, 1967-69, asst. commr., 1969-80, dep. commr., 1980-85; instr. dept. geology W.Va. U., Morgantown, 1958-74, asst. prof. dept. geology, 1974-77, assoc. prof. dept. geology, 1979-80, prof. geology, 1980—; dir. W.Va. Dept. Forestry, Charleston, 1985-93; cons. forester-geologist, W.Va., 1993—; rsch. paleobotanist U.S. Geol. Survey, Reston, Va., 1974-95. Author: W.Va. Geology, Archaeology & Pedology, 1964, W.Va. Plant Fossils, 1978, Wild Foods of Appalachia, 1986; contbr. articles to profl. jours. Recipient Disting. Achievement in Earth Scis. award Am. Fedn. Mineralogical Socs., 1982, Outstanding Contribution to Forestry award W.Va. Forestry Assn., 1986; Outstanding Svc. award Nat. Assn. State Foresters, 1993, Nat. Assn. State Depts. of Agrl., 1994, W. Va. U. Dept. Geology, 1995; W. Va. Coll. Agrl. & Forestry, 1999; fossil plant genus Gillespieisporites named in honor of by J. A. Clendening, 1969, fossil plant genus Gillespia named in honor of by Erwin and Rothwell, 1989; named to W.Va. Agr. and Forestry Hall of Fame, 1998. Fellow Soc. Am. Foresters; mem. W.Va. Assn. Soil Conservation Suprs. (hon. life mem.), Geol. Soc. Am., Am. Assn. Petroleum Geologists, Botanical Soc. Am., Internat. Assn. Plant Taxonomists, Internat. Assn. Paleobotanists, Soc. Am. Foresters, Lions. Democrat. Avocations: woodworking, fishing, photography. Home and Office: 916 Churchill Cir Charleston WV 25314-1747

GILLET, PAMELA KIPPING, special education educator. EdB in Elem. Edn., Chgo. Tchrs. Coll., 1963; MA in Mental Retardation, Northeastern Ill. U., 1966; PhD in Gen. Spl. Edn./Adminstrn., Walden U., 1976. Cert. elem. edn., early childhood edn., learning disabled, mental retardation, behavior disorders, supt., supr. and dir. spl. edn. 4th grade tchr. Dist. # 83 Mannheim, Frankling Park, Ill., 1963-64; high sch. spl. edn. tchr. Dist. # 207 Maine Township, Park Ridge, Ill., 1964-67, prevocational coord., 1967-69, dept. chmn. spl. edn. dept., 1969-70; dir. EPDA Tchr. Tng. Program Chgo. Consortium Colls. and Univs., Northwest Ednl. Coop., Palatine, Ill., 1970-71; prin. West Suburban Spl. Edn. Ctr., Cicero, Ill., 1971-73; supr. West Suburban Assn. Spl. Edn., Cicero, 1973-75; asst. dir. Northwest Suburban Spl. Edn. Orgn., Palatine, 1975-78; supt. Northwest Suburban Spl. Edn. Orgn., Mt. Prospect, Ill., 1978-96; spl. edn. cons., 1996—; adj. coll. instr. Northeastern Ill. U., Chgo. State U., Corcordia Coll., Barat Coll., Nat. Coll. of Edn., Roosevelt U.; mem. task forces ISBE, 1975-97, cons. career edn. project, 1977-78, mem. spl. edn. demandate study group, 1983-85; cons. Ednl. Testing Svc.; mem. tchr. edn. coun. Northeastern Ill. U., 1981-97, dean's grant program, 1982-97; leader of workshops, 1974—; lectr., cons. in field. Author: Auditory Processes, 1974, Career Education for Children, 1978, Of Work and Worth: Career Education Programming for Exceptional Children and Youth, 1981, Auditory Processes, Revised, 1992; contbr. articles to profl. jours., chpts. to books. Bd. dirs. Found. Exceptional Children, 1996—. Recipient Cmty. Svc. award Am. Legion, 1976, 80, Alumnus of Yr. award Northeastern Ill. U., 1984, Learning Disabilities of Am. Contributors award Coun. Understanding Learning Disabilities, 1992, Those Who Excel award of excellence Ill. State Bd. of Edn., 1994, Outstanding Svc. award Divsn. Mental Retardation adn Devel. Disabilities, 1994; Sleznick award, Coun. of Admin. of Spl. Edn., 1996, Outstanding Contbr. award Coun. Exceptional Children, 1996, Burton Blatt award Divsn. on Metal Retardation and Devel. Disabilities, 1997, Outstanding Spl. Edn. Adminstr. of Yr. award Ill. Adminstrs. of Spl. Edn., 1997, Spl. Edn. Leadership award, 1995. Mem. ASCD, Am. Assn. Sch. Adminstrs., Am. Assn. Mental Deficiency, Am. Assn. Educators of Severely-Profoundly Handicapped, Assn. Children with Learning Disabilities, Coun. Exceptional Children (pres. Ill. chpt. 1975-77, bd. govs. 1977-80, 96—, pres. mental retardation divsn. 1983-85, bd. govs. 1986, exec. com. 1989-92, v.p. internat. 1992-93, pres. elect 1993-94, pres. 1994-95, Meritorious Svc. award Ill. 1983), Ill. Adminstrs. Spl. Edn. (pres. 1994-95). Home and Office: 6958 W Hamilton Dr Niles IL 60714-2235

GILLETT, JAMES WARREN, ecotoxicology educator; b. Kansas City, Kans., Sep. 18, 1933; s. Ira Elijah and Atha Arthela (Morlan) G.; m. Mary Francis (Hebert) Goerz, Aug. 7, 1970; children: Grant Jameson, Iain Michael; m. Mary Alexia Stuart, June 26, 1958 (div. Apr. 1970); children: John Stuart, Peter Warren. BS, U. Kans., 1955; PhD, U. Calif.-Berkeley, 1962. Postdoctoral research chemist U. Calif.-Berkeley, 1962-64; asst. prof. agrl. chemistry Oreg. State U., Corvallis, 1964-69, assoc. prof., 1969-74; research ecologist EPA/Environ Research lab., Corvallis, 1974-81, research environ. scientist, 1981-83; prof. ecotoxicology, dept. natural resources Cornell U., Ithaca, N.Y., 1983—, dir. superfund basic rsch. program, 1992—; dir. Inst. for Comparative and Environ. Toxicology, 1986-92. Editor, pub. Biological Impact of Pesticides in the Environment, 1971; editor: Terrestrial Microcosms, 1979; editor jour. Hazard Assessment, Environ. Toxicology & Chemistry, 1988-93; contbr. articles to profl. jours. Chmn. bd. Oreg. Mus. Sci. and Industry, 1969-71, Community Action Program, 1970-72; sec. Willamette Soccer League, 1970-74; coach Corvallis Womens Soccer Team, 1979-81. Summerfield scholar, 1951-54. Mem. Soc. Environ. Toxicology and Chemistry (bd. dirs. 1984-88), Alpha Kappa Lambda. Club: Toastmasters (pres. 1974). Office: Dept Natural Resources Cornell U Ithaca NY 14853

GILLETT, MARY CAPERTON, military historian; b. Richmond, Va., Apr. 28, 1929; d. Lewis Hopkins and Mary Caperton (Horsley) Renshaw; m. Richard Clark Gillett, June 7, 1949; children: Richard Clark Jr., Glenn Douglas, Mary Caperton, Priscilla Elizabeth, Blakeney Diana. Student, Wellesley Coll., 1946-49; BA, Am. U., 1966, MA, 1971, PhD, 1978. Historian U.S. Navy Dept., Washington, 1966-69, U.S. Dept. Army, Washington, 1972-96. Author: The Army Medical Department, 1775-1818, 1981, The Army Medical Department, 1818-1865, 1988, The Army Medical Department, 1865-1917, 1995; contbr. articles to profl. jours. Mem. Am. Assn. for History of Medicine, Nat. Wildlife Fedn., We. Hist. Assn., The Westerners, The Nature Conservancy, The Wilderness Soc., The Sierra Club, Nat. Audubon Soc. Avocations: backpacking, gardening.

GILLETT, PAULA, humanities educator; b. N.Y.C., July 15, 1934; d. Ira and Sophie (Silvershein) Levy; m. Eric Gillett, June 23, 1956; children: Walter, Nadia, Noel. BA, Bklyn. Coll., 1955; MA, Yale U., 1956; PhD, U. Calif., Berkeley, 1979. Project dir. Grad. Sch. Edn., U. Calif., Berkeley, 1984-89; prof. San Jose (Calif.) State U., 1989—; co-chair Com. on History in the Classroom, 1992-96; vis. scholar Inst. for Rsch. on Women and Gender, Stanford U., 1996-97. Author: Worlds of Art: Painters in Victorian Society, 1990. Project dir. New Faces of Liberty, San Francisco, 1985-89. Summer fellow Am. Coun. Learned Socs., 1994; Mellon fellow Harry Ransom Humanities Rsch. Ctr., U. Tex., Austin, 1996. Mem. Am. Hist. Assn., Phi Beta Kappa. Avocation: choral singing. Office: Humanities Dept San Jose State Univ San Jose CA 95192-0092

GILLETT, WARD ROBERT, urologist; b. Dec. 13, 1955. MD, U. Mich., 1980. Pvt. practice Bay Area Urology Assocs., P.C., Traverse City, Mich. Office: 844 E Front St Traverse City MI 49686-2704

GILLETTE, EDWARD LEROY, radiation oncology educator; b. Coffeyville, Kans., May 21, 1932; s. Harold R. and Laura Belle (McLaughlin) G.; m. Carol J. Peterson, June 2, 1956 (div. Oct. 1981); children: William R., Jeffrey S., Timothy E., Jennifer L.; m. Sharon L. McChesney, Nov. 26, 1988. BS, DVM, Kans. State U., 1956; MS, Colo. State U., 1961, PhD, 1965. From instr. to prof. radiology and radiation biology Colo. State U., Ft. Collins, 1959-72, prof., 1972—, dir. comparative oncology, 1974—, chmn. dept. radiol. health scis., 1989-98, assoc. dean rsch. Coll. Vet. Medicine and Biomed. Sci., 1997-98; adj. clin. prof. dept. radiation oncology UCLA Med. sch., 1998—; adj. prof. dept. radiation oncology Duke U. Med. Coll., Durham, N.C.; bd. dirs. The Children's Hosp. Kempe Rsch. Ctr., Denver, 1984-90; vis. scientist M.D. Anderson Cancer Ctr. U. Tex., 1988. Assoc. editor Radiation Rsch., 1979-82, 86-90; assoc. editor, Internat. Jour. of Radiation Oncology Biology and Physics, 1990-95, mem. editl. bd., 1995—; contbr. articles to profl. jours. Bd. dirs. Colo. State Sci. Fair, 1984-90. 1st lt. U.S. Army, 1956-58. Recipient Outstanding Svc. to the Vet. Profession award Am. Animal Hosp. Assn., 1984, Ralston-Purina rsch. award, 1988, Kans. State U. Alumni Assn. Medallion award, 1999; U. Tex. fellow, 1968-69. Mem. AVMA, Am. Coll. Vet. Radiology (cert., pres. 1973-74), Am. Coll. Vet. Internal Medicine, Oncology (cert.), Am. Cancer Soc. (mem. exec. com. Colo. divsn. 1978-82, bd. dirs. Colo. divsn. 1984-90, pres. Larimer County chpt. 1977-81), Vet. Cancer Soc. (pres. 1982-84), Radiation Rsch. Soc. (councilor 1988-91), Am. Soc. Therapeutic Radiology and Oncology, Am. Assn. Cancer Rsch., Colo. State U. Alumni Assn. (Honor Alumnus award 1985). Republican. Avocation: reading. Office: Colo State U Dept Radiol Health Sci Fort Collins CO 80523

GILLETTE, FRANK C., JR., mechanical engineer; m. Jane Gillette; 3 children. BS in Mech. Engring., U. Fla. Mech. designer Pratt & Whitney, 1962-77, chief of structures, 1977-80, engring. mgr. YF119 program, dir. engring. programs F119 engine projects for Govt. Engines and Space Propulsion, 1980-95, dir. advanced mil. programs, 1995-97, dir.-chief engr. F119/JSF engine programs, 1997-98; mem. adv. bd. U. Fla. Coll. Engring., Fla. State U.-Fla. A&M U. Coll. Engring. Recipient Disting. Svc. award U. Fla. Coll. Engring., Laurels award Aviation Week, 1991. Mem. AIAA (Nat. Engr. of Yr. award 1991), ASME, Soc. Automotive Engrs. (Cliff Garrett Turbomachinery Engring. award 1994). Achievements include design of the RL10 rocket chamber, the turbine section of the J58; management of the overall structural engineering effort of the J52, TF30, F100 rockets and preliminary design; patents in field. Home: 8325 Nashua Dr Palm Bch Gdns FL 33418-6047 Office: Pratt & Whitney Large Mil Engines Mail Stop 713-60 PO Box 109600 West Palm Beach FL 33410-9600

GILLETTE, FRANKIE JACOBS, retired savings and loan executive, social worker, government administrator; b. Norfolk, Va., Apr. 1, 1925; d. Frank Walter and Natalie (Taylor) Jacobs; m. Maxwell Claude Gillette, June 19, 1976. BS, Hampton U., 1946; MSW, Howard U., 1948. Lic. clin. social worker; cert. jr. coll. tchr., life. Youth dir. YWCA, Passaic, N.J., 1948-50; dir. program Ada S. McKinley Community Ctr., Chgo., 1950-53; program dir. Sophie Wright Settlement, Detroit, 1953-64; dir. Concerted Services Project, Pittsburg, Calif., 1964-66, Job Corps Staff Devel., U. Calif., Berkeley, 1966-69; spl. program coordinator U.S. Community Services Adminstrn., San Francisco, 1969-83; pres. G & G Enterprises, San Francisco, 1985—; chmn. bd. dirs. Time Savs. and Loan Assn., San Francisco, 1986-87. Commr. San Francisco Human Rights Commn., 1988-93; bd. dirs. Urban Econ. Devel. Corp., 1980-93, San Francisco Conv. and Visitors Bur.; trustee Fine Arts Mus. of San Francisco, 1993—; chmn. San Francisco-Abidjan Sister City Com., 1990—. Mem. Nat. Assn. Negro Bus. and Profl. Women's Clubs (pres. 1983-87), The Links, Inc., Delta Sigma Theta, Inc. Office: G & G Enterprises 85 Cleary Ct Apt 4 San Francisco CA 94109-6518

GILLETTE, HYDE, retired investment banker; b. Chgo., June 23, 1906; s. Edwin Fraser and Mabel (Hyde) G.; m. Marie Clarke Smith, Sept. 7, 1932; 1 child, Marie Clarke Gerald. Grad., Exeter Acad., 1924; AB cum laude, Princeton U., 1928; MBA with distinction, Harvard U., 1930. With Glore, Forgan & Co., 1930-53, ptnr., 1950-53; dep. asst. and dep. under sec. USAF, 1953-57; asst. postmaster gen., bur. finance U.S. Post Office Dept., Washington, 1957-61; ptnr. Auchincloss Parker & Redpath, 1961-70; regional v.p. Thomson & McKinnon Auchincloss, Inc., Washington, 1970-73; v.p. Thomson McKinnon Securities, 1973-89, Prudential Securities, 1989-91. Exec. bd. Chgo. Area Project, 1936-53, chmn., 1948-53; bd. dirs., v.p. Nat. Capital area council Boy Scouts Am.; regent Nat. Eagle Scout Assn.; dir., vice chmn. budget com. Community Fund of Chgo., 1942; chmn. exec. com. Chgo. Opera Theatre, 1947; adv. bd. Dept. Public Welfare Ill., 1949-53; pres. Barrington Country Day Sch., 1941; v.p. Washington Heart Assn., 1961; bd. dirs. Am. Heart Assn., 1960-63. Served as lt. comdr. USNR, 1943-46. Recipient Exceptional Civilian Svc. award USAF, 1956; Disting. Svc. award U.S. Post Office Dept., 1960; disting. Eagle Scout Nat. award. Mem. Mayflower Descs., Soc. Colonial Wars, English Speaking Union (dir. 1977-86), Barrington Countryside Assn. (pres. 1949-50), Phi Beta Kappa. Episcopalian. Clubs: Barrington Hills Country; Quadrangle (Princeton); Fox River Valley Hunt (Chgo.), Commonwealth (Chgo.); Chevy Chase (Washington), Metropolitan (Washington); India House (N.Y.C.); Beverly Yacht (Marion, Mass.), Kittanset (Marion, Mass.). Home: Fox Hill Village 10 Longwood Dr Apt 404 Westwood MA 02090-1144

GILLETTE, MURIEL DELPHINE, nurse; b. Pasadena, Calif., Nov. 10, 1945; d. Edwin and Jean Helen (Fremont) Gillette; m. Larry Houston Potter, Dec. 31, 1971 (dec. 1979); children: Melissa Darlene Genevieve Potter Stephens, Bryan Scott; m. Robert George Baumann Jr., Aug. 18, 1980; 1 child, Robert George III. Student, Western Coll. for Women, Oxford, Ohio, 1963-65; BSN, UCLA, 1968; M of Nursing, Oreg. Health Scis. U., 1991. Sch. nurse, health tchr. Hawthorne (Calif.) Intermediate Sch., 1969-70; nurse St. John's Hosp., Santa Monica, Calif., 1969-71; camp nurse L.A. Girl Scout Coun., 1969-71; nurse UCLA Med. Ctr., 1967-70; ICU/CCU/pediatrics nurse Mercy Med. Ctr., Roseburg, Oreg., 1971-79; nurse Umpqua Valley Community Hosp., Myrtle Creek, Oreg., 1981-91; camp nurse, health coord. Western Rivers Girl Scout Coun., Roseburg, 1984-90; health edn. dir. City of Myrtle Creek, 1986-91; nurse practitioner Umpqua Nat. Forest, Roseburg and Glide, Oreg., 1991-93; camp nurse, health coord. Oreg. Trail Boy Scout Coun., Roseburg, 1981-91, Western Rivers Girl Scout Coun., Roseburg, 1984-90; cmty. health cons. Roseburg, 1984-98, home health nurse, 1995-98; pub. health nurse State of Alaska, Anchorage, 1998—. Musician quartet, orch., soloist; artist in oils; poet. Bd. dirs. River 'N Dell Day Care Ctr., Myrtle Creek, 1983-85; trustee Augusta Bixler Farms, Inc., Stockton, Calif., 1976—; mem. Douglas County Cancer Screening Com.; vol. ARC, 1982-91. Capt. USAF, 1970-89. Umpqua Valley Hosp. Aux. scholar, 1989; L.A. Watercolor Soc. traveling art collection award, 1963. Mem. UCLA Alumni Assn., Umpqua Valley Hosp. Aux., Oreg. Health Sci. U. Alumni Assn., OES, Delta Zeta. Republican. Presbyterian. Avocations: painting, tennis, music, skiing, raising Arabian horses. Home: PO Box 240041 Anchorage AK 99524-0041

GILLETTE, PAUL CRAWFORD, pediatric cardiologist; b. Winston-Salem, N.C., Dec. 1, 1942; s. Crawford Paul and Eileen Marie (O'Rourke) G.; m. Vicki Lynn Zeigler, 1992; 2 children. B.A. in Chemistry, U.N.C., 1965; M.D., Med. Coll. S.C., 1969. Intern, then resident in pediatrics Baylor U. Coll. Medicine, Houston, 1969-71, fellow in pediatric cardiology and cell biophysics, 1971-74, mem. faculty, 1974-84, assoc. prof. exptl. medicine, 1977-84, prof. pediatrics, 1980-84; prof. pediatrics Med. U. S.C., Charleston, 1984-96, chmn. promotions com., dept. pediatrics, 1989-96; dir. S.C. Children's Heart Ctr., Charleston, 1984-96; med. dir. Cook Children's Cardiology, 1996—, Cook Childrens Cardiac Ctr., Fort Worth, Tex., 1996—; dir. electrophysiology and electrocardiography Tex. Children's Hosp.; co-dir. Palmetto Heart Inst., 1988-96; mem. tng. grant manpower rev. com. Nat. Heart, Lung and Blood Inst., 1989-93, chmn., 1992-93. Co-author: A Guide to Pediatric Cardiac Dysrhythmias, 1980, Pediatric Cardiac Dysrhythmias, 1981, A Practical Guide to Cardiac Pacing, 1986, Pediatric Electrophysiology, Arrythmia and Pacing, 1990, Pediatric Cardiac Pacing, 1995; edtl. bd. Circulation, Am. Heart Jour., Pediatric Cardiology, Jour. Am. Coll. Cardiology; contbr. articles to profl. jours. Mem. sports com., treas. St. Thomas More Sch., Houston; bd. dirs. Toler's Cove Homeowners Assn. Charleston, 1989-94. Nat. Heart, Lung and Blood Inst. grantee; named Disting. Alumni, Medical Univ. S.C., 1991; recipient Rsch. award So. Med. Assn., 1994. Fellow Am. Acad. Pediatrics (exec. com. cardiology sect. 1979, ednl. grantee 1970, Young Investigator award 1975, trustee 1987—, chmn. rsch. rev. com. 1987-88 S.C. chpt.), Am. Coll. Cardiology (trustee 1984-90, learning ctr. com. 1984-88, strategic planning com. 1986-90, long range planning com. 1987-88, chmn. pacemaker com. 1990-95, mem. rsch. com. 1990—); mem. Soc. Pediatric Rsch., So. Soc. Pediatric Rsch., Southeastern Pediatric Cardiology Soc. (pres. 1987), N.Am. Soc. Pacing and Electrophysiology (pres. 1986-87, trustee 1987-90, program com. 1987, Pioneer in Cardiac Pacing and Electrophysiology award 1998), Am. Heart Assn. (chmn. rsch. peer rev. com. S.C. chpt. 1989, chmn. rsch. com. 1990, pres.-elect Ft. Worth chpt. 1998-98, pres. 1998-99), Tex. Pediatric Soc., Harris County Med. Soc., Houston Cardiology Soc., Houston Pediatric Soc., S.C. Med. Soc., Charleston County Med. Soc., S.C. Heart Assn. (researcher of the yr. 1991), Alpha Omega Alpha, Phi Chi. Republican. Roman Catholic. Office: Cook Childrens Cardiac Ctr 901 7th Ave Fort Worth TX 76104-2734

GILLETTE, RICHARD GARETH, neurophysiology educator, researcher; b. Seattle, Feb. 17, 1945; s. Elton George and Hazel I. (Hand) G.; m. Sally A. Reams, Feb. 17, 1978 (div. Nov. 1988); 1 child, Jesse Robert. BS, U. Oreg., 1968; MS, Oreg. Health Sci. U., 1976, PhD, 1993. Rsch. asst. dept. otolaryngology Oreg. Health Sci. U., Portland, 1969-72, grad. rsch. asst., 1973-80; instr. physiology Western State Chiropractic Coll., Portland, 1981-85, asst. prof. physiology, 1985-93, assoc. prof. physiology, 1993-99, prof. physiology, 1999—; lectr. neurosci. sch. optometry Pacific U., Forest Grove, Oreg., 1985-86; grad. rsch. asst. Neurol. Sci. Inst. OHSU, Portland, 1988-93, vis. scientist, 1993—. Contbr. articles to profl. jours. NIH Predoctoral Tng. fellow Oreg. Health Sci. U., 1973-76, Tarter fellow Med. Rsch. Found. Oreg., 1989; NIH grantee, 1990-99. Mem. AAAS, Soc. for Neurosci., Am. Pain Soc., Internat. Assn. for Study of Pain, N.Y. Acad. Scis. Avocations: history studies, vocal music performance. Office: WSCC 2900 NE 132nd Ave Portland OR 97230-3014

GILLETTE, (PHILIP) ROGER, physicist, systems engineer; b. Mt. Vernon, Iowa, May 12, 1917; s. Clinton Edgar and Celia (Rogers) G.; m. Bettelaine Dunbar, April 26, 1947 (dec. Mar. 1986); children: Kenneth Lee, Sandra Jo. B.A., in Physics, Cornell Coll., 1937; B.S. in Engring. Physics, U. Ill., 1938, M.S. in Physics, 1939, Ph.D. in Physics, 1942. Staff mem. Radiation Lab. MIT, Cambridge, Mass., 1942-45; research engr. Sperry Gyroscope Co., Great Neck, N.Y., 1945-48; physicist Hanford Works Gen. Electric Co., Richland, Wash., 1948-50; sr. research physicist SRI Internat. Menlo Park, Calif., 1950-92. retired, SRI Internat., 1992. Co-author: Pulse Generators, 1948. Bd. dirs. West Bay Opera Assn., Palo Alto, Calif., 1959-64, 1977-79, Inst. for Continued Learning, Willamette U., Salem, Oreg., 1996-98. Mem. AAAS, IEEE (sr. life mem.), Am. Phys. Soc. (life), Am. Acad. Religion, Inst. on Religion in an Age of Sci., Sigma Xi, Phi Beta Kappa, Tau Beta Pi, Phi Kappa Phi. Achievements include development of pulse transformer theory, of system design concepts for command, control, communications, and intelligence systems, electronic combat systems, and air combat training systems. Home: 2385 Crestview Dr S Salem OR 97302-5373

GILLETTE, W. MICHAEL, state supreme court justice; b. Seattle, Dec. 29, 1941; s. Elton George and Hazel Irene (Hand) G.; m. Susan Dandy Marmaduke, 1989; children: Kevin, Saima, Ali, Quinton. AB cum laude in German, Polit. Sci., Whitman Coll., 1963; LLB, Harvard U., 1966. Bar: Oreg. 1966, U.S. Dist. Ct. Oreg. 1966, U.S. Ct. Appeals (9th cir.) 1966, Samoa 1969, U.S. Supreme Ct. 1970, U.S. Dist. Ct. Vt. 1973. Assoc. Rives & Rogers, Portland, Oreg., 1966-67; dep. dist. atty. Multnomah County, Portland, 1967-69; asst. atty. gen. Govt. of Am. Samoa, 1969-71, State of Oreg., Salem, 1971-77; judge Oreg. Ct. Appeals, Salem, 1977-86; assoc. justice Oreg. Supreme Ct., Salem, 1986—. Avocation: officiating basketball.

GILLETTE, WILLIAM, historian, educator; b. Bridgeport, Conn., Mar. 2, 1933; s. Samuel William and Lillian (Abeson) G.; m. Elisabeth L. Janes, May 23, 1971; children: Scott Douglas, Wendy Elisabeth. B.S., Georgetown U., 1955; M.A., Columbia U., 1956, postgrad., 1958-59; Ph.D., Princeton U., 1963. Instr. Ohio State U., 1962-64; acting asst. prof. U. Conn., Storrs, 1965-66; asst. prof. Bklyn. Coll. CUNY, 1966-67; asso. prof. Rutgers U., 1967-81, prof., 1981—; Fulbright prof. U. Salzburg (Austria), 1982-83, Japan Women's U. and Tsuda Coll., 1997-98. Author: The Right to Vote: Politics and the Passage of the Fifteenth Amendment, 1969, Retreat From Reconstruction, 1869-1879, 1979, Jersey Blue: Civil War Politics in New Jersey, 1995. Served with AUS, 1956-58. Social Sci. Research Council faculty fellow, 1970; recipient Landry award La. State U. Press, 1979, Chastain award So. Polit. Sci. Assn., 1980, award of merit Am. Assn. for State and Local History, 1996, McCormick award N.J. Hist. Commn., 1997; grantee Am. Philos. Soc., N.J. Hist. Commn. Mem. AAUP, Am. Hist. Assn., N.J. Hist. Soc., Advs. for N.J. History, Western Hist. Assn. Democrat. Unitarian. Home: 43 South Dr East Brunswick NJ 08816-1134 Office: Rutgers U Dept History New Brunswick NJ 08903

GILLEY, JAMES WADE, university president; b. Fries, Va., Aug. 15, 1938; m. Nanna Beverly, 1961; children: Cheryl Rice, Wade Jr. BS in Civil Engring., Va. Polytechnic Inst. and State U., 1961, MS in Civil Engring., 1964, PhD in Civil/Environ. Engring., 1966; postgrad., U. Fla., Harvard U. Design engr. Newport News (Va.) Shipbuilding and Drydock Co., 1961-62; asst. prof. engring./coord. off campus engring. programs Va. Polytechnic Inst., State U., Blacksburg, Va., 1962-66; dean Sch. Sci. and Tech. Bluefield (W.Va.) State Coll., 1966-67, pres., 1975-78; pres. Wytheville and J. Sargeant Reynolds instns. Va. C.C. Sys., 1967-75; sec. edn. State of Va., 1978-82; sr. v.p., prof. syss. engring., prof. higher edn. George Mason U., Fairfax, Va., 1982-91; pres., prof. engring., prof. edn. Marshall Univ., Huntington, W. Va., 1991—. Author: Thinking About American Higher Education: the 1990s and Beyond, The Interactive University: A Source of American Revitalization, Searching for Academic Excellence, Administration of University Athletic Programs: Internal Control and Excellence, Leaning Forward: A Public President Confronts the New Realities; contbr. articles to profl. jours. Active Huntington Mus. Art, W. Va. Jobs Investment Trust, Huntington Area Devel. Coun., 5th Ave. Bapt. Ch., Edn. Commn. of the States, other orgns. Mem. W. Va. Roundtable, Huntington Rotary Club, Huntington C. of C., Guyan Country Club. Office: Marshall Univ Office of Pres 400 Hal Greer Blvd Huntington WV 25755-0003*

GILLEY, MICKEY LEROY, musician; b. Natchez, Miss., Mar. 9, 1936; s. Arthur Philmore and Irene Frances (Lewis) G.; m. Vivian McDonald, Dec. 27, 1962; 1 son, Gregory Brent. Student pub. schs., Ferriday, La. Ptnr. Gilley's Club, Pasadena, Tex., 1971-89; owner Gilley's Theatre, Branson, Mo., 1990—; owenr Gilley's Tex. Cafe, Branson, 1992—, Myrtle Beach, S.C., 1995—. Appeared in night clubs in, Houston, New Orleans, Biloxi, Miss., Mobile, Ala., Lake Charles, La., 1957-59; appeared at, Nesadel Club, Houston, 1960-70. Named Most Promising Male Artist, Acad. Country Music 1974, Most Promising Male Artist, Record World 1974, Top New Country Singles Artist, Billboard 1974, Top New Male Vocalist in Album Category, Record World 1975, Most Promising Male Artist, Music City News 1976, Best Male Vocalist, Entertainer of Year, Acad. Country Music 1976; recipient Star in Walk of Fame on Hollywood Blvd., 1984, over 17 #1 records, Grammy award for Orange Blossom Special Nat. Acad. Rec. Arts and Scis., 1981. Mem. Country Music Assn., Acad. Country Music, AFTRA, Musicians Local 65. Club: Moose. Office: 3737 Lily St Pasadena TX 77505-2927

GILLHAM, JOHN KINSEY, chemical engineering educator; b. London, Aug. 7, 1930; came to U.S., 1959, naturalized, 1968; s. Gerald Albert and Doris (Kinsey) G.; m. Helen Alyce Currier, Sept. 18, 1961; children: Matthew, Jane, Martha. B.A., Cambridge U., 1953, M.A., 1957; Ph.D. in Chemistry, McGill U., Montreal, 1959. Research chemist Am. Cynamid Co., Stamford, Conn., 1958-65; vis. research chemist Princeton U., 1964-65, mem. faculty, 1965—, prof. chem. engring., 1975-98, prof. emeritus, 1998—; cons. to chem. and polymer industries; vis. fellow Japan Soc. Promotion Sci., 1983; vis. scholar Chinese Acad. Scis., 1984; sci. exchange visitor USSR Acad. Scis./Nat. Acad. Scis., 1986. Author papers in field. Recipient 1st prize for best tech. paper Roon Found. Awards Competition of Fedn. Socs. for Coatings Techs., 1983, 89, Outstanding Rev. Paper award Electronics Components Conf. of IEEE, 1985. Mem. Am. Chem. Soc. (Borden award 1978, Doolittle award 1980, Roy W. Tess award 1996), N.Am. Thermal Analysis Soc. (Mettler award 1978), Soc. Plastics Engrs. (Internat. Rsch. award 1988, Best Paper award 1991). Home: 11 Vernon Cir Princeton NJ 08540-5415 Office: Princeton U Dept Chem Engring Princeton NJ 08544

GILLHAM, NICHOLAS WRIGHT, geneticist, educator; b. N.Y.C., May 14, 1932; s. Robert Marty and Elizabeth (Enright) G.; m. Carol Lenore Collins, June 2, 1956. A.B., Harvard, 1954, A.M., 1955, Ph.D. (USPHS fellow), 1962. From instr. to asst. prof. Harvard U., 1963-68; assoc. prof. zoology Duke U., 1968-72, prof., 1973-82, James B. Duke prof. zoology, 1982—, chmn. Dept. Zoology, 1986-89; mem. biochemistry, molecular genetics and cell biology interdisciplinary cluster Pres.'s Biomed. Rsch. Panel, 1975; mem. study sect. in genetics NIH, 1976-80; mem. N.C. Gov.'s Bd. Sci. and Tech., N.C. Gov.'s Task Force on Sci. and Tech., chmn., bd. dirs. Am. Type Culture Collection, 1993-96. Author: (with R. Krueger and J. Coggin) Introduction to Microbiology, 1973, Organelle Heredity, 1978, Organelle Genes and Genomes, 1994; mem. editl. bd. Genetics, 1975-78, Jour. Cell Biology, 1977-79, Intl. Review of Cylology, 1987-97; sr. editor Plasmid, 1977-86. Served to 1st lt. Med. Service Corps USAF, 1955-58. Postdoctoral fellow, 1962-63; Spl. fellow, 1967-68; Research Career Devel. Award grantee, 1972-77; all USPHS); Guggenheim fellow, 1984-85. Mem. Genetics Soc. Am., Sigma Xi. Home: 1211 Woodburn Rd Durham NC 27705-5739 Office: DCMB Group PO Box 91000 Durham NC 27708-1000

GILLIAM, ARLEEN FAIN, labor union administrator, finance executive; b. Huntington, W.Va., Jan. 2, 1949; d. Cicero Henry and Lorraine Almeta (Page) Fain; m. Reginald Earl Gilliam Jr., Dec. 29, 1969. BA, Skidmore Coll., 1970; MBA in Mgmt. Sci., MIT, 1976. Tchr. St. Anne Inst., Albany, N.Y., 1970-72; career counselor Williams Coll., Williamstown, Mass., 1972-74; budget analyst Congl. Budget Office, Washington, 1976-77; exec. asst. to Asst. Sec. of Labor U.S. Dept. of Labor, Washington, 1977-81; asst. dir. Social Security Dept. AFL-CIO, Washington, 1981-84, dir. budget planning and pers. policy, 1984-96, asst. to pres. exec. br. rels., 1996—; trustee pension plan AFL-CIO, Washington, 1988-96. Bd. govs. Sloan Sch., MIT, 1989-95; bd. dirs. Fairfax County (Va.) Pk. Authority Bd., 1991-93. Avocations: playing classical piano, reading fiction, solving cryptograms. Office: AFL-CIO Office of Pres 815 16th St NW 7th Fl Washington DC 20006-4104

GILLIAM, CHARLES LAMB, JR., body therapist; b. Norfolk, Va., Mar. 28, 1950; s. Charles Lamb and Margaret Hodges (Kitchin) G.; m. Alma Ruth Burger, 1981 (div. 1989); m. Rebecca Lee Conrad, Sept. 23, 1989; children: Gabriel Conrad, Raphael Lamb. BS in Kinesiological Sci., U. Md., 1981, MA in Biomechanics, 1984. Lic. massage therapist, Fla.; diplomate in craniosacral therapy; cert. in zero balancing. Pvt. practice body therapy, Shutesbury, Mass., 1978; guest lectr. Potomac Massage Tng. Inst., Washington, 1980-89; instr. aikido Aikido Schs. Ueshiba, Washington, 1981-85, bd. dirs., 1981-84; instr. child aikido Tri-Svc. Ctr. Sch., Chevy Chase, Md., 1985-86; mem. faculty craniosacral therapy Upledger Inst., Palm Beach Gardens, Fla., 1986—; staff therapist Upledger Found. Brain and Spinal Cord Dysfunction Ctr., Palm Beach Gardens, 1989-90; mem. faculty Zero Balancing Assn., Aptos, Calif., 1989—; bd. dirs. Stillpoint Sch. Massage, Hatfield, Mass., 1992-94; developer workshop Hands On First Aid for Parents, 1996. Mem. Am. Massage Therapy Assn., U.S. Assn. for Body Psychotherapy (allied profl.), Internat. Assn. Healthcare Practitioners, Md. Assn. Massage Practitioners (strategist for state licensure 1985-87, pres. 1985-87), N.C. Soc. of Cincinnati, Wendel Aikido Club (Mass.) (instr., 2d degree black belt). Avocations: surfing, hiking, gardening, walking, playing with his children. Home and Office: 31 Pelham Hill Rd Shutesbury MA 01072-9702

GILLIAM, EARL B., federal judge; b. Clovis, N.Mex., Aug. 17, 1931; s. James Earl and Lula Mae G.; m. Rebecca L. Prater; children: Earl Kenneth, Derrick James. B.A., Calif. State U., San Diego, 1953; J.D., Hastings Coll. Law, 1957. Bar: Calif. 1957. Dep. dist. atty. San Diego, 1957-62; judge San Diego Mcpl. Ct., 1963-74, Superior Ct. Calif., San Diego County, 1975-80; judge U.S. Dist. Ct. (so. dist.) Calif., San Diego, 1980-93, sr. judge, 1993—; head Trial Practice Dept. Western State U. Law Sch., San Diego, 1969—. Recipient Trial Judge of Yr. award San Diego County Trial Lawyers Assn., 1981. Office: US Dist Ct 5195 US Cthouse 940 Front St San Diego CA 92101-8994*

GILLIAM, JACKSON EARLE, bishop; b. Heppner, Oreg., June 20, 1920; s. Edwin Earle and Mary (Perry) G.; m. Margaret Kathleen Hindley, Aug. 11, 1943; children—Anne Meredith, Margaret Carol, John Howard; m. MarKatheryn Allender Brooks, Oct. 17, 1988. A.B., Whitman Coll., 1942; B.D., Va. Theol. Sem., 1948, S.T.M., 1949, D.D., 1969. Ordained to ministry Episcopal Ch., 1948; rector in Hermiston, Ore., 1949-53; canon St. Mark's Cathedral, Mpls., 1953-55; rector Ch. Incarnation, Great Falls, Mont., 1955-68; bishop Episcopal Diocese Mont., 1968-86; vicar St. Jude's Episcopal Ch., Hawaiian Oceanview Estates, 1987—; asst. bishop of Hawaii, 1997—; chmn. com. on pastoral devel., chmn. council on ministry, mem. program, budget and fin. com. Episc. Ch., 1978, pres. Province VI. Served to 1st lt. AUS, World War II. Decorated companion Order of Cross of Nails, companion Coventry Cathedral, Eng., 1974. Home: PO Box 6502 Ocean View HI 96737-6502

GILLIAM, JAMES H., JR., lawyer, private investor, consultant; b. Balt., Apr. 21, 1945. BA in English, Morgan State U., 1967; JD, Columbia U., 1970. Bar: Del., N.Y. Assoc. Paul, Weiss, Rifkind, Wharton & Garrison, N.Y.C., 1970-73, Richards, Layton & Finger, Wilmington, Del., 1973-76; cabinet sec. Dept. Cmty. Affairs and Econ. Devel. State of Del., 1977-79; sr. v.p. legal Beneficial Corp., 1982-85, sr. v.p., 1986-89, gen. coun., 1986-89, sec., 1987-92, exec. v.p., 1989-98; also mem. exec. com. bd. dirs. chmn. bd. dirs. Beneficial Corp., 1987-99; chmn., bd. dirs. Beneficial Nat. Bank, 1987-98; bd. dirs. Bell Atlantic Corp., Household Internat.; past mem., bd. dirs. Delmarva Power and Light Company; past trustee, past bd. dirs. Med. Ctr. Del.; trustee Howard Hughes Med. Inst., Nat. Geog. Soc. Former chmn., hon. life trustee Goldey Beacom Coll.; former chmn. bd. visitors Del. State U.; mem. Nat. Guardsmen, Inc.; bd. visitors Columbia Sch. Law; former chmn. Wilmington 2000 Inc.; chmn. Jud. Nominating Commn., Del.; past chmn., bd. dirs. Del. C. of C., former chmn. Wilmington 2000 Inc. Fellow Am. Bar Found.; mem. ABA, NBA, Del. Bar Assn., Del. C. of C. (bd. dirs., past chmn.), Brandywine Country Club, Knickerbocker Club (N.Y.C.), Wilmington Club, Wilmington Country Club, Rehoboth Beach Country Club, Monday Club, Natl. Fuardsmen, Inc., Sigma Pi Phi, Kappa Alpha Psi. Avocations: tennis, golf, water sports. Office: Knickerbocker LLC PO Box 2205 Wilmington DE 19899-2205 Address: Brandywine Plz 105 Foulk Rd Ste 101 Wilmington DE 19803

GILLIAM, JOHN CHARLES, economist, educator; b. Boulder, Colo., Sept. 19, 1927; s. Arthur Woodson and Marguerite (Hubbard) G.; m. Katherine Frances Mihevc, July 16, 1947; children: Bruce, Charles, Carol Ann. B.A., Western State Coll., Colo., 1951; M.Bus.Ed., U. Colo., 1952; Ph.D., State U. Iowa, 1959. Instr. bus. Brush (Colo.) High Sch., 1952-55, State U. Iowa, 1955-57; asst. prof. commerce U. Wyo., 1957-62, asso. prof., 1962; asso. prof. bus. edn. Tex. Tech. U., 1962-66, prof., 1966—; asso. dean Tex. Tech. U. (Coll. Bus. Adminstrn.), 1968-73, prof. econs., 1973—; program specialist Ford Found., Ammam, Jordan, 1966-68, cons. in edn. for bus.; cons. to Govt. Saudi Arabia, World Bank, 1993-94; vis. prof. several uivs., including U. Jordan, 1993; cons. bus. and econs.; vis. prof. Mid. East Tech. U., Ankara, Turkey; acad. cons., 1988-90, Jordan U. Sci. and Tech., Irbid, 1989-90; cons. Govt. Turkey, 1992-94. Contbr. articles to profl. jours. Served with USNR, 1945-47. Fulbright-Hays grantee study tour People's Rep. China, 1988; Fulbright-Hays grantee study tour Egypt, 1990. Mem. Beta Gamma Sigma, Omicron Delta Epsilon, Alpha Kappa Psi, Delta Pi Epsilon, Pi Omega Pi, Phi Beta Delta. Episcopalian. Lodge: Elks. Home: 9311 Utica Dr Lubbock TX 79424-4821

GILLIAM, MARY, travel executive; b. Pampa, Tex., Apr. 18, 1928; d. Roy and Hylda O. (Bertrand) Brown; divorced; 1 child, Terry K. AA, Amarillo (Tex.) Bus. Coll., 1949. Flight attendant Braniff Internat. Airways, Dallas, 1950-53; from reservation agt. to mgr. passenger sales Trans-World Airlines, various locations, 1953-81; exec. v.p. Lakewood (Colo.) Travel, 1981; mgmt. cons. Bank One Travel, Columbus, Ohio, 1981-82; pres. Icaria Travel, Inc., Tucson, Ariz., 1986—, Intensive Trainers Inst., Tucson, 1983-92. Mem. Ariz. Rep. Com., 1978—. Recipient Award of Excellence Trans-World Airlines, N.Y.C., 1972, Pres.' Hall of Fame award, 1973. Mem. Am. Soc. Travel Agts. (Industry Svc. award 1980), Inst. Cert. Travel Agts. Methodist. Avocations: reading, travel, music. Office: Icaria Travel Inc 616 W Rio San Pedro Green Valley AZ 85614-3927

GILLIAM, PAULA HUTTER, transportation company executive; b. N.Y.C.; d. Irving and Edna Phyllis (Manes) Hutter; m. Stanley Spencer Rolnick (div.); children: Jeffry Hutter Gilliam, Pamela Sara Bielory; m. Peter Gilliam, 1981. AA, Centenary Coll., 1961. Pres. Paula Rolnick Sales, N.Y.C., 1970-74; mdse. mgr. Kirby Block Internat., N.Y.C., 1974-78; pres. P.M.G. Internat. Ltd, N.Y.C., 1981—; v.p. Rical Air Express, Inc., N.Y.C., Rical Ocean Forwarding, N.Y.C.; ptnr. The Golden Unicorn Restaurant; mem. adv. bd. for internat. bus. Fashion Inst. Tech., 1991—. Producer (Broadway show) Stardust, 1987; exec. producer (plays) Long Days Journey Into the Night, 1988, Ah Wilderness. V.p. Murray Hill Neighborhood Assn., N.Y.C., 1982—, chmn. block party, 1983-92, bd. dirs and sec. John Murray House Owners Corp., 1995—; bd. advisors 132 E 35th St., N.Y.C., 1984-86; vol. aide June Eisland Coun. Women, Riverdale, N.Y., 1979—; bd. dirs. Theater Off Park, 1983-88, Black Goat Entertainment and Enlightenment, 1994—. Mem. Women in Internat. Trade (bd. dirs. 1991-96), Women's Traffic Club, Met. Traffic Club. Democrat. Avocations: travel, horseback riding, gardening, theatre. Home and Office: 220 Madison Ave New York NY 10016-3892

GILLIAM, TERRY VANCE, film director, actor, illustrator, writer; b. Mpls., Nov. 22, 1940; s. James Hall and Beatrice (Vance) G.; m. Margaret Weston; children: Amy Rainbow, Holly du Bois, Harry Thunder. BA, Occidental Coll., 1962, DFA (hon.), 1988; hon. doctorate, Royal Coll. Art, London. Assoc. editor HELP! mag., 1962-64; free-lance illustrator, 1964-65, advt. copywriter, art dir., 1966-67; TV resident cartoonist We Have Ways of Making You Laugh, 1968; animator Do Not Adjust Your Set, 1968-69, The Marty Feldman Comedy Machine, 1971-72; with Monty Python's Flying Circus, 1969-76. Animator (film) And Now For Something Completely Different; illustrator (book) The Cocktail People, 1966; co-dir., actor (film) Monty Python and the Holy Grail, 1974, The Do It Yourself Animation Film, 1974, The Miracle of Flight, 1974; dir. (film) Jabberwocky, 1976; designer, actor, animator (film) Monty Python's Life of Brian, 1978; co-writer, producer, dir. (film) Time Bandits, 1980; actor, dir. (film) Monty Python Live at the Hollywood Bowl, 1982; dir., actor, animator, co-writer (film) Monty Python's Meaning of Life, 1983; dir., writer (film) Brazil, 1985; dir., co-writer (film) The Adventures of Baron Munchausen, 1988; dir. (film) The Fisher King, 1991, Twelve Monkeys, 1995; co-writer, dir. Fear and Loathing in Las Vegas, 1998; co-author: The Brand New Monty Python Book, 1973, Monty Python and the Holy Grail, 1977, Monty Python Life of Brian, 1979 Monty Python's Big Red Book, Monty Python's Papperbok, 1977, Monty Python's Scrapbook, 1979, Animations of Mortality, 1979, Time Bandits, 1981, Monty Python's The Meaning of Life, 1983, The Adventures of Baron Munchausen, 1989, Not the Screenplay of Fear and Loathing in Las Vegas, 1998; presenter TV series The Last Machine, 1995; exec. prodr. (CD ROM) Monty Python's Complete Waste of Time, 1995.

GILLIATT, NEAL, advertising executive, consultant; b. Plainville, Ind., Dec. 24, 1917; s. Oliver Breden and Katherine Ann (Henderson) G.; m. Mary Rees, Feb. 6, 1943; 1 child, David Rees. BS, Ind. U., 1939; MBA, Northwestern U., 1940; postgrad., Harvard U., 1960. Instr. Ind. U., 1940-42; with food price div. OPA, Chgo., 1942-45; with McCann-Erickson, Inc., Chgo., 1945-55, N.Y.C., 1955-66; exec. v.p. Interpublic Group of Cos., Inc., N.Y.C., 1966-70, vice chmn., 1970-80, chmn. exec. com., 1980-82; pvt. practice N.Y.C., 1982—; bd. dirs. Kubin-Nicholson Corp., Csol. Products, Inc. Bd. dirs. Boys and Girls Clubs Am., N.Y. Philharm. Soc., Religion in Am. Life, Ind. U. Found., Nat. Exec. Svc. Corps, United Cerebral Palsy Found., Blanton-Peale Inst. Recipient Broadcasting and Advt. Industries Human Relations award Am. Jewish Com., 1969; Disting. Alumni Service award Ind. U., 1970. Mem. Links Club, Univ. Club, Econ. Club, Beta Gamma Sigma (award 1963, 80), Sigma Alpha Epsilon. Republican. Congregationalist. Office: 1 Rockefeller Plz Rm 1510 New York NY 10020-2002

GILLICE, SONDRA JUPIN (MRS. GARDNER RUSSELL BROWN), sales and marketing executive; b. Urbana, Ill.; d. Earl Cranston and Laura Lorraine (Rose) Jupin; m. Gardner Russell Brown, Jan. 12, 1980; 1 child, Thomas Alan Gillice. BS, Lindenwood Coll.; MBA, Loyola Coll. Pers. officer N.Y. Citibank, 1968-70, 1st Nat. Bank of Chgo., 1970-72; mgr. human resources Potomac Electric Power Co., Washington, 1973-81; dir. pers. U.S. Synthetic Fuels Corp., Washington, 1981-86, v.p. human resources, Guest Svcs., Inc., 1987-90; v.p. sales and mktg., 1990-93; sr. v.p. govt. rels. Drake Beam Morin, Inc., 1994-1988; pres. RusSon, Inc., 1998—. Mem. bd. govs. Loyola Coll., Nat. Coal Coun., mem. exec. com.; bd. dirs., chmn. KHG Dance Theatre, Nat. Women's Econ. Alliance, Life With Cancer, 1996— . Mem. AAUW (pres. Falls Church br. 1976-78), Edison Electric Inst. (chmn. tng. and mgmt. devel. com.), Soc. for Human Resource Mgmt., Greater Met. Washington Bd. Trade, Soroptimists (pres. Washington chpt. 1979-80), DAR, Army Navy Country Club, Soc. Magna Charta Dames, Edgartown Yacht Club, Georgetown Club. Republican.

GILLICK, BETSY BRINKLEY, financial analyst; b. Richmond, Va., May 11, 1959; d. Martha Lou (Caplinger) B. BBA, James Madison U., 1981, MBA, 1983. Procurement analyst Calculon Corp., Germantown, Md., 1983-85; agt. purchasing, subcontracts ORI/Calculon Corp., Rockville, Md., 1986-87; adminstr. contracts ORI/Calculon Corp., Rockville, 1987-89; sr. contracts adminstr. ARC Profl. Svcs. Group subs. ORI/Calculon Corp, Rockville, 1989-90, sr. fin. analyst, 1990-93; sr. fin. and contracts analyst Otsuka Am. Pharm. Inc., Rockville, 1993-94, fin. and contracts mgr., 1994-96, R & D bus. mgr., 1996-97, prof. edn. and sci. comm. mgr., 1997—. Mem. Nat. Contract Mgmt. Assn. Democrat. Presbyterian. Avocations: volleyball, traveling, gardening. Home: 18420 Cape Jasmine Way Gaithersburg MD 20879-4644 Office: Otsuka Am Pharm Inc 2440 Research Blvd Rockville MD 20850-3238

GILLIE, MICHELLE FRANCOISE, industrial hygienist; b. Phila., Oct. 24, 1956; d. Marino and Marcelle Jeannine (Boyer) Lazarich; m. Alan Deane Gillie, May 22, 1982; children: Patrick Alan, Caroline Elizabeth. BS, Pa. State U., 1977; MS, Drexel U., 1981. Diplomate Am. Bd. Indsl. Hygiene. Clin. chemist Pa. Hosp., Phila., 1976-80; indsl. hygienist Stewart-Todd Assocs., Wayne, Pa., 1981-82, S.W. Occupational Health Svcs., Houston, 1982-84; clin. toxicologist Smith-Kline-Beckman Labs., Houston, 1984-85; sr. indsl. hygienist Am. Analytical Labs., Akron, Ohio, 1985-88; indsl. hygiene cons. AMP Technical Svcs., Cleve., 1988-91; sr. indsl. hygienist Environ. Mgmt., Inc., Anchorage, 1991-92; indsl. hygiene cons. AMP Tech. Svcs., Bakersfield, Calif., 1992-94; health and safety mgr. Brown & Root Environ., Wayne, Pa., 1994—. Mem. Am. Indsl. Hygiene Assn. (pub. rels. com. chair Midnight Sun chpt. 1991-92). Avocations: reading, cross-country skiing. Home: 111 Loudoun Pl Phoenixville PA 19460-2814

GILLIES, DONALD RICHARD, advertising agency and marketing consultant; b. Sioux Falls, S.D., Jan. 14, 1939; s. Donald Franklin and Gladys O. (Gullickson) G.; m. Twyla Elaine Bloomquist, Apr. 7, 1962; children: Dawn, Trent, Tara. BA in Journalism/Advt., U. Minn., 1961. Writer, producer Sta. WCCO-TV, Mpls., 1954-60; mgmt. supr., sr. v.p. Campbell-Mithun Advt., Mpls., 1960-86; pres., chief oper. officer Colle & McVoy Inc., Mpls., 1987-89; prin. Gillies group inc. (Gg), Minnetonka, Minn., 1989—; adj. prof. U. St. Thomas, 1990-97. Mem. exec. com. Guthrie Theater, Mpls., 1979-84, bd. dirs.; mem. ch. coun. Mt. Olivet Ch., Mpls., 1988-94; mem. Minn. adv. rev. bd. BBB, 1996—. With USAR, 1961-69. Mem. Am. Assn. Advt. Agencies (regional gov.), Minn. Advt. Fedn. (bd. dirs. 1973-76). Lutheran. Home and Office: Gillies group inc (Gg) 5942 Fairwood Ln Minnetonka MN 55345-6533

GILLIES, TRENT DONALD, television producer; b. Mpls., June 14, 1965; s. Donald Richard and Twyla Elaine (Bloomquist) G. BS in Journalism, Boston U., 1987. Prodn. asst. 60 Minutes, CBS News, N.Y.C., 1987-90, asst. prodr., 1990-91, assoc. prodr. 60 Minutes, 1991-95; prodr. investigative unit Am. Jour., King World, N.Y.C., 1995-97; prodr. Real Sports with Bryant Gumbel, HBO Sports, 1997-98; prodr. SportsCentury ESPN, 1998—. Lutheran. Avocations: music, skiing. Home: 321 E 43d St Apt 701 New York NY 10017

GILLIGAN, CAROL F., psychologist, writer; b. N.Y.C., Nov. 28, 1936; d. William Edward and Mabel (Caminez) Friedman; m. James Frederick Gilligan, June 12, 1960; children: Jonathan Mark, Timothy David, Christopher James. AB, Swarthmore Coll., 1958, hon. degree, 1985; AM, Radcliffe Coll., 1961; PhD, Harvard U., 1964; hon. degree, Regis Coll., 1983, Haverford Coll., 1987, Wesleyan U., 1992. Instr. U. Chgo., 1965-66; lectr. Harvard U., Cambridge, Mass., 1967-69, rsch. asst., 1969-70, asst. prof., 1970-78, assoc. prof., 1978-86, prof., 1986—; Laurie chair in Women's Studies Rutgers U., New Brunswick, N.J., 1986-87; Pitt Prof. U. Cambridge, Eng., 1992-93; founding mem. Harvard Project on Women's Psychology and the Devel. of Girls, 1987—; co-dir. The Company of Women and Girls, 1991—. Author: In a Different Voice, 1982, Mapping the Moral Domain: A Contribution of Women's Thinking to Psychological Theory and Education, 1988, Making Connections: The Relational Worlds of Adolescent Girls at Emma Willard School, 1990, (with Lyn M. Brown) Meeting at the Crossroads: Women's Psychology and Girls Development, 1992; editor: Women, Girls and Psychotherapy: Reframing Resistance, 1991. Bd. dirs. Ms Initiative in Girls, Facing History & Ourselves. Sr. rsch. fellow Spencer Found., 1984—; Mellon Faculty fellow Bunting Inst.-Radcliffe Coll., 1982-83; recipient Grawemayer award U. Louisville, 1992. Mem. APA, Assn. Women in Psychology. Democrat. Jewish. Avocations: music, piano, modern dance, theatre. Office: Harvard U Dept Humanities 503 Larsen Hall Appian Way Cambridge MA 02138-6502*

GILLIGAN, MARY ANN, law librarian; b. Elizabeth, N.J., June 20, 1956; d. John Francis and Margaret Mary (Boyle) G. BA, Park Coll., 1977; MLS, Rutgers U., 1980. Asst. Time Inc., N.Y.C., 1981-83; law libr. Chubb & Son, Inc., Warren, N.J., 1985, Pennie & Edmonds LLP, N.Y.C., 1985—. Mem. ABA, Am. Assn. Law Librs., Spl. Librs. Assn., Law Libr. Assn. Greater N.Y. (bd. dirs. 1998—). Democrat. Roman Catholic. Avocations: crafts, singing. Office: Pennie & Edmonds LLP 1155 Ave Of The Americas New York NY 10036-2711

GILLIGAN, SANDRA KAYE, private school director; b. Ft. Lewis, Wash., Mar. 22, 1946; d. Jack G. and O. Ruth (Mitchell) Wagoner; m. James J.

Gilligan, June 3, 1972 (div. June 1998); 1 child, J. Shawn Gilligan. BS in Edn., Emporia State U., 1968, MS in Psychology, 1971; postgrad., Drake U., 1976, U. Mo., St. Louis, 1977-79. Tchr. Parklane Elem. Sch., Aurora, Colo., 1968-69, Bonner Springs (Kans.) Elem., 1970; stewardess Frontier Airlines, Denver, 1969; grad. teaching asst. Emporia (Kans.) State U., 1970-71; lead tchr. Western Valley Youth Ranch, Buckeye, Ariz., 1971-74; staff mem. program devel., lead tchr. The New Found., Phoenix, Ariz., 1974; ednl. therapist Orchard Pl., Des Moines, 1974-76; ednl. cons. Spl. Sch. Dist. of St. Louis County, 1976-79; founding dir. The Churchill Sch., St. Louis, 1978—; instr. Webster Coll., Webster Groves, Mo., 1978-80; adj. prof. Maryville Coll., St. Louis, summer 1985; mem. profl. adv. bd. Learning Disabilities Assn., St. Louis Learning Disabilities Assn.; keynote spkr. Miss. Learning Disabilities Assn. Conv., 1991; site visitor blue ribbon schs. program U.S. Dept. Edn., 1992; cert. trainer Human Potential Seminars; presenter in field. Active St. Louis Jr. League. Mem. Learning Disabilities Assn., Internat. Dyslexia Assn. Avocations: gardening, painting. Home: 665 S Skinker Blvd Apt 20F Clayton MO 63105-2357 Office: The Churchill Sch 1035 Price School Ln Saint Louis MO 63124-1596

GILLILAND, MARCIA ANN, nurse clinician, infection control specialist; b. Kansas City, Mo., Sept. 15, 1949; d. Robert Joseph and Mary Agnes (Paup) Caton; m. John Lee Gilliland, Mar. 28, 1974 (dec. Oct. 1983); children: Marcella Lyn, John Patrick, Devon Marie. ADN, Kansas City C.C., 1979; BSN, Webster U., 1990. RN, Kans. Staff nurse U. Kans. Med. Ctr., Kansas City, 1979-84, infection prevention and control coord., 1984—, facilitator HIV/AIDS wellness group, 1991—; community health nurse Cath. Charities, Kansas City, 1980-82; pres., owner Kansas City Total Image, Overland Park, Kans., 1981-83. Active Rep. Precinct Committeewoman, Overland Park, Kans., 1994—; Rep. candidate Overland Park City Coun., Kans., 1995; bd. dirs. Johnson County (Kans.) Rep. party. Mem. Nat. Speakers Assn., Assn. Profls. in Infection Control and Epidemiology (pres. Kansas City chpt., 1993-94), Assn. Nurses in AIDS Care, SERTOMA, GOP Club Johnson County, Kans. (bd. dirs. 1999—). Republican. Avocation: reading. Home: 9430 Riggs St Overland Park KS 66212-1443 Office: U Kans Med Ctr Kans Pub Health Assn 3901 Rainbow Blvd Kansas City KS 66160-0001

GILLILLAND, THOMAS, art gallery director; b. Bladen, Nebr., Feb. 14, 1932; s. Whitney and Virginia (Wegmann) G.; m. Cora Lee Critchfield, Aug. 23, 1956; children: Shaun, Ruth, Virginia. Grad., Wentworth Mil. Acad., 1952; BA, Am. U., 1963, MA, 1967. Dep. dir. congl. liaison AID, Washington, 1969-75; congl. liaison officer USDA, Washington, 1975-76, dir. legis. affairs Animal and Plant Health Inspection Svc., 1976-83; dir. external affairs Fin. Mgmt. Svc. U.S. Dept. Treasury, Washington, 1983-93; owner Art in the Hand Gallery, St. Augustine, Fla., 1994—. Contbr. mag. articles. Mem. Nat. Assn. Govt. Communicators (Blue Pencil award 1986), Soc. for Preservation and Encouragement of Barbershop Quartet Singing in Am., Nat. Press Club. Republican. Presbyterian. Home: 65 Fullerwood Dr Saint Augustine FL 32095-2167

GILLIN, CAROL ANN, middle school educator; b. Phila., July 19, 1942; d. Harry Joseph and Louise Dolores (Hewitt) G. AB in English Lit., Chestnut Hill Coll., 1972; MEd in Reading, Temple U., 1978, postgrad., 1990—. Cert. elem. educator, reading specialist, N.J. Tchr. Phila. and N.J. Parochial Schs., 1962-76; reading specialist Camden (N.J.) Bd. Edn., 1976-80, Corpus Christi Sch., Lansdale, Pa., 1980-82; asst. prof. edn., supr. student tchrs. Rosemont (Pa.) Coll., 1982-86, acting dir. edn., asst. acad. dean, 1985-88; mid. sch. tchr. Phila. Sch. System, 1988—; tchr. cons. Phila. Writing Project; presenter, lectr. in field; mem. rsch. project Taking Stock, Making Change, U. Pa.; instr. Chestnut Hill Coll., 1998—; sr. career tchr. Phila. Sch. Sys; adv. bd. Schuylkill Ctr. Environ. Edn., Phila, 1999—. Bd. dirs. Archbishop Prendergast H.S. Alumnae, Drexel Hill, Pa., 1989-95. Mem. Internat. Reading Assn., Am. Assn. Univ. Adminstrs., Nat. Coun. Tchrs. English. Avocations: reading, needlepoint, walking club, cooking.

GILLIN, MALVIN JAMES, JR., lawyer; b. Norfolk, Va., Apr. 28, 1946; s. Malvin James Gillin and Jacqueline A. (Howell) Kyslowsky; m. Arleen Elizabeth Gillin: children: Christine Lynn, Malvin James III, Craig Dean. BA, U. Hawaii, 1969; JD, U. Denver, 1974. Bar: Hawaii 1975, U.S. Dist. Ct. Hawaii 1975, U.S. Ct. Appeals (9th cir.) 1983, U.S. Supreme Ct. 1983, Colo. 1984. Dep. atty. gen. State of Hawaii, Honolulu, 1975-76; pvt. practice law Honolulu, 1976—. Mem. ATLA, Hawaii Bar Assn., Hawaii Assn. Criminal Def. Lawyers (pres. 1998—), Nat. Assn. Criminal Def. Lawyers. Roman Catholic. Avocations: scuba diving, sailing, marathon running. Office: 733 Bishop St Ste 1290 Honolulu HI 96813-4002

GILLINGHAM, BRYAN REGINALD, music educator; b. Vancouver, B.C., Can., Apr. 12, 1944; s. Reginald Pearce and Ethel Gladys (Collier) G.; m. Helen Campbell, Aug. 11, 1970 (div. 1980); children: Gregory, Sara; m. Susanna Catharine Burton, Oct. 29, 1984; children: Gwendolyn, Miranda, Jeremy. BA, U. B.C., 1966, MusB, 1968; MusM, U. London, 1972; PhD, U. Wash., 1976. Lectr. Mt. Allison U., Sackville, N.B., Can., 1972-73, U. Alta., Edmonton, Can., 1975-76; prof., chmn. Carleton U., Ottawa, Ont., Can., 1976-83; dir. Inst. Medieval Music, Ottawa, 1985—. Author: The Polyphonic Sequences in Codex Wolfenbüttel 677, 1982, Saint-Martial Mehrstimmigkeit, 1984, Medieval Polyphonic Sequences, 1985, Modal Rhythm, 1986, Secular Medieval Latin Song, 1993, A Critical Study of Secular Medieval Latin Song, 1995, The Social Background to Secular Medieval Latin Song, 1998, Chant & Its Peripheries, 1998; editor (with Donald Beecher) Dovehouse early music edits.; contbr. articles and book revs. to profl. jours. Avocations: wine making, squash, cross-country skiing. Office: Carleton U Dept Music, Colonel By Dr, Ottawa, ON Canada K1S 5B6

GILLINGHAM, ROBERT FENTON, federal agency administrator, economist; b. Newark, Nov. 13, 1944; s. Evan Stevenson and Eleanor (Fenton) G.; m. Deborah Lynn Wickham, 1989; children: James Stevenson, Sarah Eleanor. BA, Haverford Coll., 1965; PhD, U. Pa., 1973. Economist Bur. Labor Stats., Washington, 1968-73, chief price rsch. div., 1973-82, dep. assoc. commr., 1982-85; dir. office econ. analysis Dept. Treasury, Washington, 1985-88, dep. asst. sec. for econ. policy, 1988-98; tech. asst. advisor Internat. Monetary Fund, Washington, 1998—. Assoc. editor Jour. Bus. and Econ. Stats., 1982-93; contbr. articles to profl. jours. Mem. Am. Econ. Assn., Am. Statis. Assn., Econometric Soc., Western Econ. Assn. (mem. exec. com. 1995—), Conf. on Income and Wealth. Home: 20448 Tappahannock Pl Sterling VA 20165-4786 Office: Internat Monetary Fund 700 19th St NW Washington DC 20431*

GILLINGHAM, STEPHEN THOMAS, financial planner; b. St. Paul, May 30, 1944; s. Thomas Elmwood and Barbara Alice (Sickles) G.; m. Carolyn Jean Alvey, June 5, 1976; children: Kenneth, Brett. BA, Juniata Coll., 1966; JD, The George Washington U., 1969. Bar: Va. 1971; CFP. Tax specialist Price Waterhouse, Washington, 1969-71; tax law specialist IRS, Washington, 1971-77; sr. tax lawyer Internat. Paper Co., N.Y.C., 1977-83; dir. tax rsch. and planning The Singer Co., Stanford, Conn., 1983-88; tax counsel Am. Cyanamid Co., Wayne, N.J., 1988-95; fin. planner The Thompson Group, Inc., White Plains, N.Y., 1995—; lectr. World Trade Inst., 1980-90. Contbg. editor Tax Lawyer, 1984-88. Trustees coun. Juniata Coll. With U.S. Army, 1970-75. Named one of Outstanding Young Men in Am., Jaycees, 1979. Mem. Va. Bar Assn., N.J. Tax Group (chmn. 1991-95), Tax Execs. Inst., Inst. Cert. Fin. Planners. Avocations: golf, swimming, hiking. Home: 4 Northway Hartsdale NY 10530-2109 Office: The Thompson Group Inc 244 Westchester Ave White Plains NY 10604-2907

GILLIOM, BONNIE LEE, arts educator, consultant; b. Mansfield, Ohio, Mar. 1, 1933; d. Gregor Leonard and Rella Hildegard (Jacobs) Cherp; m. Morris Eugene Gilliom, Dec. 29, 1956; children: Gregor William, Julia Lee. BA, Heidelberg Coll., 1955; MA, Ohio State U., 1961, PhD, 1971; postdoctoral, Tucson Creative Dance Ctr., 1976, Chelsea (Eng.) Sch. of Human Movement, 1978. Cert. tchr., Ohio. TV tchr., writer Stas. WOSU, WVIZ, NIT, KPIX, Columbus, Ohio, Cleve. and San Francisco, 1959-68; lectr. Ohio State U., Columbus, 1971-76, 92-95; dir./developer Meanings, Modes and Moods of Movement Program, Ohio, 1979-82; assoc. dir. Inst. for the Advancement of the Arts Edn. Ohio State U., Columbus, 1982-92; lectr. San Francisco State U., 1962-65; dir./developer 4M program 48 schs., Ohio, W.Va., Utah and Mex., 1973-77; project dir. elem. sec. edn. act Columbus Pub. Schs., 1971-73. Co-author: ITV: Promise into Practice, 1972; author: Basic Movement Education for Children, 1970, Hebrew edit., 1977. Mem. Columbus Coun. on World Affairs, Friends of WOSU; mem. adv. coun. Ohio Dept. Edn., Columbus, 1980-86; bd. dirs. Ohio Very Spl. Arts Network, Columbus, 1980-86; bd. trustees Friends of the Arts of Upper Arlington, Grandparents Living Theatre; mem. Greater Columbus Arts Coun. Christopher Sch. Grantee Ohio Edn. Deans Task Force, 1983, 84, 85, Ohio Arts Council, 1985, 86, 87, 88, 89, 90, 91, 92; recipient 1st Place award Inst. for Instruction by Radio and TV, 1962, Meritorious award, Ohio Assn. of Health, Physical Edn. and Dance, Creativity award Nat. U. Continuing Edn. Assn., 1988. Mem. Am. Alliance Health, Physical Edn., and Recreation; Nat. Dance Assn., Heidelberg Fellow, Kappa Delta Pi, Pi Delta Epsilon, Pi Lambda Theta. Democrat. Avocations: travel, art, music, skiing, snorkeling. Home: 2495 Haverford Rd Columbus OH 43220-4203

GILLIOM, JUDITH CARR, government official; b. Indpls., May 19, 1943; d. Elbert Raymond and Marjorie Lucille (Carr) G. B.A., Northwestern U., 1964; M.A., U. Pa., 1966. Feature writer, asst. women's editor Indpls. News, summers 1961-63; research asst. cultural anthropology Northwestern U., 1963-64, asst. instr. freshman English, 1964; editorial asst. to dir. div. cardiology Phila. Gen. Hosp., 1965-67; asst. to ophthalmologist-in-chief Wills Eye Hosp., Phila., 1967-69; editor, writer Nat. Assn. Hearing and Speech Agencies, Washington, 1969-70; free-lance speech writer White House Conf. Children and Youth, 1969-70; free-lance editor, writer, abstractor, 1971-78; free-lance speechwriter President's Com. Mental Retardation, 1971-78; dir. publs. Nat. Assn. Hearing and Speech Action, Silver Spring, Md., 1972-74; dir. communications Nat. Assn. Hearing and Speech Action, 1975-77; editor Hearing & Speech Action mag., 1969-70, 72-77; program mgr. Interagy. Com. on Handicapped Employees, 1978, dep. exec. sec., 1979-83; mgr. disability program Dept. Def., 1983—; cons. U.S. Archtl. and Transp. Barriers Compliance Bd., 1976-77, Office Ind. Living for Disabled, HUD, 1977-78, Office for Handicapped Individuals, HEW, 1978, Women's com. Pres.'s Com. Employment Handicapped, 1985-86. Mem. Nat. Spinal Cord Injury Assn., 1970-90, editor, pub. conv. jour., 1974-82, bd. dirs. D.C. chpt., 1975-81, 89-90, nat. trustee, 1975-81, nat. bd. dirs., 1978-79; bd. dirs. Nat. Ctr. for a Barrier-Free Environment, 1979-84, v.p., 1980-81, pres., 1981-82; nat. bd. dirs., treas. League Disabled Voters, 1980-85; local bd. dirs. Easter Seal Soc. Disabled Children and Adults, 1985-90; active Montgomery County Commn. on People with Disabilities, 1989-95; mem. Taxicab Svcs. Adv. Com., 1995—. Recipient Geico Pub. Svc. award, 1996, Civilian Career Svc. award Office of Sec. of Def., 1997; Woodrow Wilson fellow, 1965. Mem. Phi Beta Kappa, Delta Delta Delta. Home: 901 Arcola Ave Silver Spring MD 20902-3401 Office: Dept Def The Pentagon Rm 3A272 Washington DC 20301-4000

GILLIOM, MORRIS EUGENE, social studies and global educator; b. Bluffton, Ind., Feb. 10, 1932; s. William Orel and Zella Leota (Gallimore) G.; m. Bonnie Lee Cherp, Dec. 29, 1956; children: Gregor William, Julia Lee. BA, Heidelberg Coll., 1954; MA, Ohio State U., 1958, PhD, 1962. Cert. tchr., Ohio. Tchr. social studies Cleve. Pub. Schs., 1956-59; instr. Ohio State U., Columbus, 1959-62; asst. prof. San Francisco State Coll., 1962-65, U. Chgo., 1965-66; from assoc. prof. to prof. social studies, global edn. Ohio State U., Columbus, 1966-95, prof. emeritus, 1995—, dir. social studies edn. program abroad, 1969-95; cons. TraveLearn, Lakeville, Pa., group leader programs abroad; group leader Smithsonian Instn. Programs to China. Author, sr. editor: Practical Methods for the Social Studies, 1977; author, co-editor: Perspectives of Global Education, 1981; contbr. chpts. to books, articles to profl. publs. Trustee Upper Arlington Friends of the Arts, Heidelberg Coll. Fellows. With U.S. Army, 1954-56. Recipient Disting. Teaching award Ohio State U., 1985. Mem. Nat. Coun. Social Studies (coll. and univ. faculty assembly), Social Sci. Edn. Consortium (bd. dirs. 1986-90), Columbus Coun. World Affairs, Ohio Coun. Social Studies, Torch Club. Democrat. Avocations: photography, travel, skiing, reading. Fax: (614) 451-1763. E-mail: genegilliom@compuserve.com. Home: 2495 Haverford Rd Columbus OH 43220-4203 Office: Ohio State Univ 1945 N High St Columbus OH 43210-1120

GILLIS, CHRISTINE DIEST-LORGION, financial planner, stockbroker; b. San Francisco, Apr. 26, 1928; d. Evert Jan and Christine Helen (Radcliffe) Diest-Lorgion; children: Barbara Gillis Pieper, Suzanne Gillis Seymour (twins). BS, U. Calif., Berkeley, 1948; MS, U. So. Calif., 1968. Cert. fin. planner. Account exec. Winslow, Cohu & Stetson, N.Y.C., 1962-63, Paine Webber, N.Y.C., 1964-65; sr. investment exec. Shearson Hammill, Beverly Hills, Calif., 1966-72; fin. planner, asst. v.p. EF Hutton, L.A., 1972-87; 2nd v.p. Shearson Lehman Hutton, Glendale, Calif., 1988; v.p. investments Dean Witter Reynolds, Glendale, 1988-90; fin. planner, asst. v.p. W. J. Gallagher & Co., Inc., Pasadena, Calif., 1991—. Mem. AAUW (life, trustee ednl. found.), Town Hall of Calif. (life, corp. sec. 1974-75, dir., gov. 1976-80), Women Stockbrokers Assn. (founding pres. N.Y.C. 1963), Women of Wall Street West (pres. 1979-84), Navy League (life; dir.), U. Calif.-Berkeley Alumni Assn. (life), U. So. Calif. Alumni Assn. (life), Town and Gown (life), Pasadena Bond Club. Episcopalian. Home: 1224 S Montezuma Way West Covina CA 91791-3736 Office: W J Gallagher & Co Inc 747 E Green St Pasadena CA 91101-2145

GILLIS, JOHN LAMB, JR., lawyer; b. St. Louis, June 13, 1939. Student, Brown U.; AB, Washington U., 1965; LLB, Stanford U., 1968. Bar: Mo. 1968. Ptnr., chmn. securities dept. Armstrong Teasdale LLP, St. Louis. Address: Armstrong Teasdale LLP 1 Metropolitan Sq Saint Louis MO 63102-2733

GILLIS, JOHN SIMON, psychologist, educator; b. Washington, Mar. 21, 1937; s. Simon John and Rita Veronica (Moran) G.; m. Mary Ann Wesolowski, Aug. 29, 1959; children: Holly Ann, Mark, Scott. B.A., Stanford U., 1959; M.S. (fellow), Cornell U., 1961; Ph.D. (NIMH fellow), U. Colo., 1965. Lectr. dept. psychology Australian Nat. U., Canberra, 1968-70; sr. psychologist Mendocino (Calif.) State Hosp., 1971-72; asso. prof. dept. psychology Tex. Tech U., Lubbock, 1972-76; prof. psychology Oreg. State U., Corvallis, 1976—, chmn. dept. psychology, 1976-84; cons. VA, Ciba-Geigy Pharms., USIA, UN High Commn. for Refugees; commentator Oreg. Ednl. and Pub. Broadcasting System, 1978-79; Fulbright lectr., India, 1982-83, Greece, 1992; vis. prof. U. Karachi, 1984, 86, U. Punjab, Pakistan, 1985, Am. U., Cairo, 1984-86. Contbr. articles to profl. jours. Served with USAF, 1968-72. Ciba-Geigy Pharms. grantee, 1971-82. Mem. Am. Psychol. Assn., Western Psychol. Assn., Oreg. Psychol. Assn. Roman Catholic. Home: 7520 NW Mountain View Dr Corvallis OR 97330-9106 Office: Oreg State U Dept Psychology Corvallis OR 97331 *The real pleasures of life seem to come not from avoiding difficult tasks but rather from involving oneself with them - from working hard on those problems that need attention.*

GILLIS, JOHN WILLIAM, retired geologist, retired provincial government legislator; b. Boston, Oct. 31, 1936; s. Michael and Mary Josephine (McDaniel) G.; m. Joan Wiseman, July 1, 1972; children: John Michael, Amy Elizabeth. BSc, St. Francis Xavier U., 1956; PhD, Pa. State U., 1964. Geologist Energy, Mines & Resources, Ottawa, Ont., Canada, 1962-67; asst. prof. St. Francis Xavier U., Antigonish, N.S., Canada, 1967-70; min. mcpl. affairs, agriculture & mktg., social svcs., edn. Nova Scotia Provincial Govt., Halifax, 1970-78; chmn. Pub. Accts. Com., Halifax, 1987-89; dep. premier Nova Scotia Provincial Govt., 1993-98, min. fin., 1996-98, min. justice, 1993-96. Fellow Geol. Assn. Canada; mem. Geol. Soc. Am., Mining Soc. Nova Scotia. Liberal. Avocations: reading, walking, geology. Home: 7 Sunset Terrace, Antigonish, NS Canada B2G 1K2

GILLIS, JUDY WINGATE, elementary educator; b. Ocilla, Ga., Aug. 4, 1955; d. Amos Leonard and Winnie Lavada (Brown) Wingate; m. Willie Dougal Gillis Jr., June 8, 1979; children: Alisha Melanie, Kayla Dianna, Adrianna Katie Gillis. MCE, Valdosta (Ga.) State U., 1989. Clk. Health Dept., Pearson, Ga., 1977-81; shipping clk. Willacoochee (Ga.) Garment, 1982-84; owner Rewind Video, Willacoochee; tchr. Willacoochee Elem., 1990—. Home: PO Box 141 Willacoochee GA 31650-0141

GILLIS, (STEPHEN) MALCOLM, academic administrator, economics educator; b. Dothan, Ala., Dec. 28, 1940; s. Stephen Malcolm and Eva May (Mac Kinnon) G.; m. Elizabeth Cifers, Aug. 18, 1962; children: Eva Leanora, Heather Elizabeth, Stephen Malcolm. BA, U. Fla., 1962, MA, 1963; PhD, U. Ill., 1968; LLD (hon.), Rocky Mountain Coll., 1992. Asst. prof. econs. Duke U., Durham, N.C., 1967-69; lectr. in econs. Harvard U., Cambridge, Mass., 1969-73, inst. fellow, 1974-84; prof. econs., pub. policy Duke U., 1984-93, dean grad. sch., vice provost acad. affairs, 1986-91, Z. Smith Reynolds Disting. prof. pub. policy, 1990-93; dean of Faculty of Arts and Scis., 1991-93; pres. Rice U., Houston, 1993—, prof. econs., 1993—, Irvin Kenneth Zingler prof. econs., 1998—; mem. com. on energy taxation NRC/NAS, 1979-80; mem. coun. econ. policy Office of Gov., State of Alaska, Juneau, 1982-83; mem. Columbia Univ. Seminar on Southeast Asia in World Affairs, 1982, 83, 84; mem. adv. com. Oak Ridge Nat. Lab., Energy divsn., 1984-87, chair adv. com., 1985-86; mem. acad. adv. bd. Internat. Ctr. for Econ. Growth, 1986—; mem. internat. adv. bd. KPMG Peat Marwick Policy Econs. Group, 1988—; cons. World Bank, Washington, 1969, 75, 83-87, Harvard Inst. Internat. Devel., 1984—, many others; Disting. Fulbright prof. Cath. Univ. Chile, 1989; chair bd. trustees Ctr. for World Environ. and Sustainable Devel., 1990-93; mem. adv. bd. Inst. for Policy Reform, 1990—; mem. so. regional adv. bd. Inst. Internat. Edn., 1993—; bd. dirs. Houston Advanced Rsch. Ctr.; presenter in field throughout world. Author (with others): Fiscal Reform For Colombia, 1971, Taxation and Mining, 1978, Tax and Investment Policies for Hard Minerals, 1980, Economics of Development, 1983; editor: Export Diversification and the New Protectionism, 1981, Public Policy and Misuse of Forest Resources, 1988, The Value-Added Tax in Developing Countries, 1991; mem. editl. bd. Quar. Jour. Econs., 1978-79, co-editor, 1979-81; mem. editl. adv. bd. Tex. Bus. Rev., 1979-83; bd. editors Pakistan Devel. Rev., 1977-80, Pakistan Jour. Applied Econs., 1980-83; mem. editl. bd. Comparative Econ. Studies, 1986-88; referee various jours.; contbr. articles to profl. jours. Adviser Navajo Indian Nation, Ship Rock, N.Mex., 1983-84; trustee Found. for Hosp. Art, 1989, Francisco Marroquin Found., 1989—, Friends of Edn. in Chile, 1989—, United Way of Tex. Gulf Coast; bd. dirs. Am. Forestry Assn., 1989-92, South Main Ctr. Assn., 1993—, Greater Houston Partnership, 1993—, St. Luke's Episc. Hosp., 1994—; mem. Houston regional adv. bd. Tex. Commerce Bank, 1994—; mem. exec. com. Houston Advanced Res. Ctr. Bd., 1994—, Assn. Am. Univs.; vice chair higher edn. sector Houston area U.S. Savs. Bond Campaign, 1994; bd. dirs. Amigos de las Ams., Consortium on Financing Higher Edn., 1994—, Independent Colls. and Univs. of Tex., 1995—; mem. bd. advisors Houston Symphony, 1995; chmn. March of Dimes Gulf Coast Walk Am., 1995; active Houston Philos. Soc., 1993—. Grantee U.S. AID, Washington, 1986-87. Mem. Am. Econ. Assn., Nat. Tax Assn., Assn. Pub. Policy Analysis and Mgmt. Republican. Episcopalian. Office: Rice U Office of Pres PO Box 1892 Houston TX 77251-1892*

GILLIS, MARVIN BOB, investor, consultant; b. Treutlen County, Ga., Apr. 5, 1920; s. Bob Lee and Pearl (Gillis) G.; m. Helen Reed, Dec. 23, 1946; children: Margaret Susan, Marvin Reed, Kenneth Robert. B.S.A., U. Ga., 1940; Ph.D., Cornell U., 1947. Rsch. assoc. Cornell U., 1947-51; sr. rsch. chemist Internat. Minerals and Chem. Corp., from 1947, asst. dir. rsch., 1956-57, dir. rsch., 1957-64, dir. animal health and nutrition, 1964-66, div. v.p., 1966-70, corp. v.p., 1970-72, sr. v.p., 1972-82; pres., dir. IMC Chem. Group, Inc., 1976-78; pres. Animal Products Group, 1978-82, cons. to exec. office, 1982-86; mng. gen. ptnr. Gillis Ltd. Partnership; sec. Agrl. Rsch. Inst., NRC, 1958-59, v.p., 1960-62, 66-67, pres., 1962-63, 68-69, mem. agrl. bd., 1962-67; bd. dirs. Animal Health Inst., 1966-69. Author numerous papers in field; patentee in field. Served to 1st lt. USAAF, 1942-45. Decorated DFC with oak leaf cluster, Air medal with 4 oak leaf clusters. Mem. North Shore Country Club (Glenview, Ill.), Sea Island (Ga.) Club, Blue Key, Sigma Xi, Gamma Alpha, Alpha Zeta, Phi Kappa Phi. Baptist. Home: 2116 Larkdale Dr Glenview IL 60025-4107 also: 103 Cascades Saint Simons Is GA 31522-2463

GILLIS, NELSON SCOTT, financial executive; b. Pitts., May 6, 1953; s. Nelson Williams and Elinor (Miller) G.; m. Vickie Sue Hall, Nov. 22, 1980; children: Michael David, Matthew Daniel, Nathan Alexander, Alexander Joshua, Artyom Jonathan, Kirill. BS in Acctg., Fla. State U., 1975; postgrad. AEA Exec. Inst., Stanford, 1984. CPA, Ga.; cert. fin. planner. Audit sr., Price Waterhouse & Co., Atlanta, 1975-78; sr. acct. Siemens Energy and Automation, Inc., 1978-80; div. contr., Portland, Oreg., 1980-83; v.p. fin. Integrated Circuits Inc., Redmond, Wash., 1983-85; dir. Controls Evaluation and Audit Kaufman & Broad, Inc., Atlanta, 1985-89; v.p., contr. SunAm. Life Ins. Co., Anchor Nat. Life Ins. Co., First Sun Am. Life Ins. Co., L.A., 1989-94, sr. v.p., controller, 1994—; sr. v.p., cont. CalAm. Life Ins. Co., 1995—, SunAm. Nat. Life Ins. Co., 1996—; John Alden Life Ins. Co. N.Y., 1997-98; v.p. SunAm., Inc., 1998—. Bd. dirs., treas. Southern Calif. Ski Edn. Found., 1998—. Master fellow Life . Inst.; mem. AICPA (life ins. and disability plans com., 1991-94, 98—, task force on disclosure of risks and uncertainties in the ins. industry, 1992-95, rels. with actuaries com. 1993-96, ins. plans exec. com. 1995-98, chmn. personal lines ins. com. 1995-98), Inst. CFPs, Ins. Internal Audit Group, Life Office Mgmt. Assn. (fin. controls and reports com. 1987-90), Ga. Soc. CPAs (ins. plans com. 1988-89), Calif. Soc. CPAs (L.A. members in industry, acctg. principles/auditing stds. & ins. industry coms. 1991-94), Ins. Acctg. and Systems Assn., Internat. Assn. for Fin. Planning, Am. Assn. Individual Investors, Fla. State Alumni Assn., Nat. Assn. Securities Dealers (registered prin. 1989-98), Beta Gamma Sigma, Lambda Chi Alpha. Republican. Office: Sun Life Ins Co Am/Century City 1 Sun Am Ctr MS 36-07 Los Angeles CA 90067-6022

GILLISPIE, HAROLD LEON, minister; b. Levant, Kans., May 11, 1933; s. Harold Leon and Agnes Anne (Dryden) G. BA in Bus. Adminstrn., Kans. Wesleyan U., 1955. Youth dir. Cen. YMCA, Des Moines, 1957-61; exec. dir. West Des Moines br. YMCA, 1961-65; exec. dir. Aurora Br. YMCA, Denver, 1965-69; exec. dir. YMCA, McCook, Nebr., 1969-75, Junction City, Kans., 1975-79; owner H & R Block Franchise, Manhattan, Kans., 1979-91; lay pastor Presbyn. Ch., Oak Hill, Kans., 1996—; vice moderator Presbyn. of Northern Kans., 1999—; proofreader text H & R Block, Kansas City, Mo., 1986-92. Bd. dirs. Flint Hills Breadbasket, Manhattan, Kans., 1982-89, treas., 1987; bd. dirs. Big Bros. Big Sisters, Manhattan, 1981-85, pres., 1983-85; pres. Downtown Manhattan, Inc., 1986; bd. dirs. Manhattan Main Street, 1986-89; bd. dirs. Ecumenical Campus Ministry, Kans. State U., 1995-99, chmn., 1996-98. Republican. Presbyterian. Avocations: theology, tennis, baking, working with youth. Home: 710 Bertrand St Manhattan KS 66502-5156

GILLISPIE, STEVEN BRIAN, systems analyst, researcher; b. Seattle, Oct. 19, 1955; s. Edwin B. and Claudia Mae (Cooper) G. BS in Physics with distinction, U. Wash., 1979, BS in Math., 1979, BS in Psychology, 1983, BA in Gen. Studies, 1983, MS in Math., 1998. Software specialist Fla. Computer Graphics, Seattle, 1983-84; data analyst coronary artery surgery study U. Wash., Seattle, 1985-87, sci. programmer dept. radiology, 1987-88, systems analyst dept. radiology, 1988—. Dir. devel. med. imaging software Viewbox, 1992; contbr. articles to profl. jours. Mem. Woodland Park Zool. Soc., Seattle, 1986—; contbg. mem. Nordic Heritage Mus., Seattle, 1991—; patron The High Desert Mus., Bend, Oreg., 1991—. Mem. Soc. for Indsl. and Applied Math., U. Wash. Alumni Assn. (life), So. Oreg. hist. Soc. Office: U Wash Dept Radiology Box 356004 Seattle WA 98195-6004

GILLMAN, ARTHUR EMANUEL, psychiatrist; b. N.Y.C., June 6, 1927; s. Hyman David and Sadie Ruth (Ornstein) G.; m. Barbara E. O'Connell, June 29, 1961 (div. 1980); children: Elizabeth Waite Mazzei, Abigail Tenedorio, Theodore Jones, Sarah Ann. BS, U. Vt., 1947; MD, N.Y. Med. Coll., 1950. Diplomate Am. Bd. Psychiatry and Neurology, Child and Adolescent Psychiatry. Intern State U. Iowa Hosps., Iowa City, 1950-51; asst. resident in neurology Montefiore Hosp., Bronx, N.Y., 1951-52; asst. resident in psychiatry Bellevue Hosp., 1952-53; resident in psychiatry Hillside Hosp., Glen Oaks, N.Y., 1953-54; fellow in child psychiatry Child Guidance Inst., Jewish Bd. Guardians, N.Y.C., 1954-56; clin. fellow in child psychiatry Bronx Mcpl. Hosp. Ctr./Albert Einstein Coll. Medicine, 1955-56; clin. dir. community svcs. Rockland Children's Psychiat. Ctr., Orangeburg, N.Y., 1985-95; chief physician child adolescent svcs. Bronx Lebanon Hosp., 1995—; asst. prof. psychiatry Albert Einstein Coll. Medicine, N.Y.C., 1995—; asst. clin. prof. Columbia U., 1989-95; cons. psychiatrist, dir. evaluative studies, dir. rsch. devel., then dir. rsch. N.Y. Assn. for Blind, 1966-85; dir. curriculum in child psychiatry Montefiore Hosp., 1968-69; vis. lectr. Manhattanville Coll., Purchase, N.Y., 1974-76; dir. psychiat. clinic Jewish Guild for Blind, 1962-66; presenter at profl. confs. Contbr. articles to profl. publs. Fellow Am. Psychiat. Assn. (life), Am. Orthopsychiat. Assn. (life), Am. Acad. Child and Adolescent Psychiatry (life); mem. AMA. also: Bronx Lebanon Hosp Child Adolescent Svcs 406 E 176th St Bronx NY 10457-6004

GILLMAN, JOHANNA, artist; b. May 7, 1923. Student, Bklyn. Coll., 1936-38, Pratt Inst., 1959-61, Queens Coll., 1971-74. Works exhibited at Beth Ha Nassi, Jerusalem, Israel, 1972, Isis Gallery, Port Washington, N.Y., 1983, Wunsch Art Ctr., Glen Cove, N.Y., 1990, Broome St. Gallery-Am. Soc. Contemporary Artists, N.Y.C., 1992, Silver Lining Gallery, Bridgeport, Conn., 1994, Ceres Gallery, N.Y.C., 1996, Contemporary Artists Guild, N.Y.C., 1998, Nat. Jewish Mus., Washington, 1998. E-mail: ggdesigns@aol.com. Home and Office: 65 W 90th St New York NY 10024

GILLMAN, LEONARD, mathematician, educator; b. Cleve., Jan. 8, 1917; s. Joseph Moses and Etta Judith (Cohen) G.; m. Reba Parks Marcus, Dec. 24, 1938; children: Jonathan Webb, Michal Judith. Diploma (fellow in piano 1933-38), Juilliard Grad. Sch. Music, 1938; BS, Columbia U., 1941, MA (Carnegie fellow math. statistics 1942-43), 1945, PhD, 1953. Asst. in math. dept. Columbia U., 1941-42, lectr., 1942-43; ops. analyst Tufts Coll., MIT, 1943-51; from instr. to assoc. prof. math. Purdue U., 1952-60; prof. math., chmn. dept. U. Rochester, 1960-69; prof. math. U. Tex., Austin, 1969-87, prof. emeritus, 1987, chmn. dept., 1969-73; mem. Inst. Advanced Study, Princeton, 1958-60; cons. editor W.W. Norton Co., Inc., 1967-80. Author: (with Meyer Jerison) Rings of Continuous Functions, 1960, 76, You'll Need Math, 1967 (with Robert H. McDowell) Calculus, 1973, 78, Writing Mathematics Well, 1987; mem. editorial bd. Topology and Its Applications, 1971-94. Guggenheim fellow, 1958-59; NSF sr. post-doctoral fellow, 1959-60. Mem. Am. Math. Soc. (assoc. sec. 1969-71, mem. com. to monitor problems in commn. 1972-77), Nat. Coun. Tchrs. Math., Math. Assn. Am. (bd. govs. 1973-95, treas. 1973-86, pres.-elect 1986-87, pres. 1987-89, past pres. 1989-90, Lester R. Ford award for expository writing 1994, Yueh-Gin Gung and Dr. Charles Y. Hu award for disting. svc. to math. 1999). Home and Office: 1606 The High Rd Austin TX 78746-2236

GILLMAN, SARAH ANN, management consultant; b. Nov. 6, 1964. AB, Yale U., 1986; MA, Columbia U., 1993, MBA, 1993. Admissions dir. St. Ann's Sch., Bklyn., 1987-90; mgr. KPMG Peat Marwick, N.Y.C., 1993-97; sr. mgr. MBIA-The Stillwater Higher Edn. Group, Armonk, N.Y., 1997—; asst. dir. Columbia U., N.Y.C., 1996-97. E-mail: sarah.gillman@mbia.com./sarah.gillman@marchiony.com. Home: 9B 17 W 71 St New York NY 10023

GILLMAR, JACK NOTLEY SCUDDER, real estate company executive; b. Honolulu, Oct. 18, 1943; s. Stanley Eric and Ruth Dorothy (Scudder) G.; m. Janet Thebaud, June 12, 1967; children: Emily, Bennett. BA, U. Pa., 1965; MA, Harvard U., 1967, Pacifica Grad. Inst., 1994. Vol. Peace Corps/Micronesia, East Caroline Islands, 1967-70; trustee Scudder Gillmar Estate, Honolulu, 1973—; trustee, sec. Parker Sch. Trust, Kamuela, Hawaii, 1991—. Author: Impact of an In-country Peace Corps Training Program, 1970, Specimens of Hwaiian Kapa, 1979, Beauty as Experience and Transcendence, 1994. Trustee, pres. Friendship Graden Found., Honolulu, 1971—; owner Nanue (Hawaii) Forest Preserve, 1986—. Fulbright grantee, 1990. Mem. Pacific Club. Office: Scudder Gillmar Estate PO Box 2902 Honolulu HI 96802-2902

GILLMING, KENNETH, church administrator. Pres. Bapt. Bible Fellowship, Springfield, Mo. Office: Bapt Bible Fellowship Internat PO Box 191 Springfield MO 65801-0191*

GILLMOR, CHARLES STEWART, history and science educator, researcher; b. Kansas City, Mo., Nov. 6, 1938; s. Charles Stewart and Evelyn (Noland) G.; m. Rogene Marie Godding, Nov. 28, 1964; children: Charles Stewart III, Alison Bogue. BSEE, Stanford U., 1962; MA, Princeton U., 1966, PhD, 1968; postgrad., U. Colo., 1963. Ionospheric physicist Bur. Standards, Antarctica and Boulder, Colo., 1960-62; instr. history Wesleyan U., Middletown, Conn., 1967-68, asst. prof., 1968-72, assoc. prof., 1973-79, prof. history and sci., 1979—, chmn. dept. history, 1986-88, 91-94; cons. Office Sci. Edn., AAAS, 1973-75; adv. com. Council Internat. Exchange of Scholars, 1978-82; cons. NSF, 1983; Hennebach vis. prof. Colo. Sch. Mines, 1996-97, Stanford U., 1998—. Author: Coulomb and the Evolution of Physics and Engineering in 18th Century France, 1971; editor: The History of Geophysics, Vol. 1, 1984, Vol. 2, 1986, Vol. 4, 1990, Vol. 7, 1997; jour. editor: Transactions Am. Geophys. Union, 1983-86; mus. dir. Nutmeg Foxtrot-Jazz Orch., 1990-96; contbr. articles to profl. jours.; recording artist with Leo Records, 1998. Deacon Higganum Congl. Ch., Conn., 1978-96. Mt. Gillmor in Antarctica named in his honor, 1963; Social Sci. Research Council grantee, 1971; NSF research grantee, 1972-74, 75-77, 76-79; sr. Fulbright research scholar Cambridge U., Eng., 1976; NASA History scholar, 1980-81; U.S.-France NSF research fellow, Paris, 1984-85; Joseph J. Malone fellow to Tunisia Nat. Coun. U.S.-Arab Rels., 1989. Fellow Am. Phys. Soc. (sec.-treas. history of physics divsn. 1988-94, exec. com. 1996-98, chair 1997-98); mem. AAAS, Am. Geophys. Union, History of Sci. Soc., Soc. History of Tech. (adv. coun. 1978-82), Sigma Xi. Home: 29 Spencer Rd Higganum CT 06441-4034 Office: Wesleyan Univ Dept History Middletown CT 06459-0002

GILLMOR, HELEN, federal judge; b. 1942. BA, Queen's Coll. of CUNY, 1965; LLB magna cum laude, Boston U., 1968. With Ropes & Gray, Boston, 1968-69, Law Offices of Alexander R. Gillmor, Camden, Maine, 1970, Torkildson, Katz, Jossem, Fonseca, Jaffe, Moore & Hetherington, Honolulu, 1971-72; law clk. to Chief Justice William S. Richardson Hawaii State Supreme Ct., 1972; dep. pub. defender Office of Pub. Defender, Honolulu, 1972-74; dist. ct. judge per diem Family Ct. (1st cir.) Hawaii, 1977-83, Dist. Ct., 1st circuit, 1983-85; pvt. practice Honolulu, 1985-94; district judge U.S. Dist. Ct. Hawaii, 9th circuit, 1994—; counsel El Paso Real Estate Investment Trust, 1969; lectr. U.S. Agy. Internat. Devel., Seoul, South Korea, 1969-70, Univ. Hawaii, 1975. Office: Prince J K Kuhio Fed Bldg Rm C-435 300 Ala Moana Blvd Honolulu HI 96850-0435

GILLMOR, JOHN EDWARD, lawyer; b. Phila., Oct. 26, 1937; s. John Edward and Louise Ann (Porter) G.; m. Allis Dale Brannon, Aug. 17, 1968; children: Sarah, Abigail, Susan, Eleanor, John, Matthew. B.A., Swarthmore Coll., 1959; LL.B., U. Pa., 1962. Bar: N.Y. 1963, Tenn. 1972, Pa. 1980, D.C. 1962. Asso. Dewey Ballantine Bushby Palmer & Wood, 1962-63, 66-71; v.p., corp. counsel Hosp. Affiliates Internat., Nashville, 1971-78; sr. v.p., gen. counsel Hosp. Affiliates Internat., 1978-79; staff v.p., asst. gen. counsel INA Corp., Phila., 1980; sr. v.p., gen. counsel INA Health Care Group, 1981; partner Gillmor, Mills & Gillmor, 1981-83; dir., exec. v.p. Health Am. Corp., 1983-86; ptnr. Gillmor, Anderson & Gillmor, 1986-89, Dearborn & Ewing, 1989-92; ptnr. Boult, Cummings, Conners & Berry, Nashville, 1992—, pres. Bd. trustees Univ. Sch. Nashville; bd. dirs. Nashville Opera Assn. With USMC, 1963-66. Mem. ABA, Assn. of Bar of City of N.Y., Nashville Bar Found., Tenn. Bar Assn., Nashville Bar Assn. Republican. Home: 1700 Graybar Ln Nashville TN 37215-2106 Office: Boult Cummings Conners & Berry 414 Union St Ste 1600 Nashville TN 37219-1744

GILLMOR, KAREN LAKO, state agency administrator, strategic planner; b. Cleve., Jan. 29, 1948; d. William M. and Charlotte (Sheldon) Lako; m. Paul E. Gillmor, Dec. 10, 1983; children: Linda D., Julie E., Paul Michael, Connor W., Adam S. BA cum laude, Mich. State U., 1969; MA, Ohio State U., 1970, PhD, 1981. Asst. to v.p. Ohio State U., Columbus, 1972-77, spl. asst. dean law, 1979-81; asst. to pres. Ind. Cen. U., Indpls., 1977-78; rsch. asst. Burke Mktg. Rsch., Indpls., 1978-79; v.p. pub. affairs Huntington Nat. Bank, Columbus, 1981-82; fin. cons. Ohio Rep. Fin. Com., Columbus, 1982-83; chief mgmt. planning and rsch. Indsl. Commn. Ohio, Columbus, 1983-86; mgr. physician rels. Univ. Hosps., Columbus, 1987-91; cons. U.S. Sec. Labor, Washington, 1990-91; mem. Regional Bd. Rev./Indls. Commn., Ohio, 1991-92; assoc. dir. Ctr. Healthcare Policy and Rsch./Ohio State U., 1991-92; state senator Ohio Gen. Assembly, 1993-97; vice-chair State Employment Rels. Bd., 1997—; legis. liaison Huntington Bancshares, Ohio, Ohio State U., Columbus; trustee Heidelberg Coll., 1999—. Grantee Andrew W. Mellon Found. 1978, Carnegie Corp. 1978; named Outstanding Freshman Ohio Legislator, 1994, Watchdog of the Treasury, 1994, 96; recipient Pres. award Ohio State Chiropractic Assn., 1994, Pub. Svc. award Am. Heart Assn., 1995, Outstanding Nat. Freshman Legislator of Yr., 1995; Ctr. Advancement and Study of Ethics award Capitol U. and Trinity Luth. Seminary, 1996, U.S. Dept. of Army Cert. of Ach., 1997, Friend of Medicine award Ohio State Med. Assn., 1997, Legis. Ach. award Am. Acad. Pediatrics (Ohio chpt. 1997); inducted Hall of Fame, Rocky River H.S., 1998, Spirit of Women award, 1999. Mem. Women in Mainstream, Women's Roundtable, Ohio Fedn. Rep. Women, Am. Assn. Higher Edn., Coun. Advancement and Support Edn., DAR, Phi Delta Kappa. Methodist. Office: 65 E State St Ste 1200 Columbus OH 43215-4209

GILLMOR, PAUL E., congressman, lawyer; b. Tiffin, Ohio, Feb. 1, 1939; s. Paul Marshall and Lucy Jeannette (Fry) G.; m. Karen Lee Lako, Dec. 10, 1983; children: Linda Dianne, Julie Ellen, Paul Michael, Connor Sheldon, Adam William. B.A., Ohio Wesleyan U., Delaware, 1961; J.D., U. Mich, 1964; LL.D. (hon.), Tiffin U., Ohio, 1985. Bar: Ohio, 1965. Mem. Ohio Senate, 1967—, minority leader, 1978-81, 83-85, pres., 1981-83, 85-88; mem. 101st-106th Congresses from 5th Ohio dist., Washington, D.C., 1989—; mem. commerce com. 101st-106th Congresses from 5th Ohio dist.; assoc. firm Tomb and Hering, Tiffin, 1967-88; bd. dirs. Old Fort Banking Co., Ohio. Pres. Ohio Electoral Coll., Columbus, 1984. Served to capt. USAF, 1965-67. Recipient Gov.'s award, Ohio, 1980; Phillips medal of pub. service Ohio U. Coll. Osteopathy, 1981; Exec. Order, Ohio Commodores Assn., 1981; Disting. Citizen award Med. Coll. Ohio, 1982; named Legislator of Yr., Ohio VFW, 1994. Mem. ABA, Ohio State Bar Assn., Nat. Republican Legislators Assn. (named Outstanding Legislator of Yr. 1983). Methodist. Office: US Ho of Reps Office House Mems 1203 Longworth Bldg Washington DC 20515-3505*

GILLMOR, ROGENE GODDING, medical technologist; b. El Dorado, Kans., Jan. 25, 1939; d. Marc Antone and Verda May (Bogue) Godding; m. Charles Stewart Gillmor Jr., Nov. 28, 1964; children: Charles Stewart III, Alison Bogue. AA in Liberal Arts, Cottey Coll., 1958; BA in Biology, Stanford U., 1960; postgrad., Wesleyan U., U. Hartford, Foothills Coll. Rsch. asst. genetics Joshua Lederberg lab. Stanford U., 1960-62; assoc. scientist space biology/medicine Lockheed Missiles & Space Co., Palo Alto, Calif., 1962-64; rsch. asst. biology Princeton (N.J.) U., 1965-66, Wesleyan U., Middletown, Conn., 1967-69; lab. technician immunochemistry Hartford (Conn.) Hosp., 1978-84, instr. immunology clin. lab. edn. program, 1985-89, lab. supr. proteins/immunology dept. pathology and lab. medicine, 1986—; rschr. various labs, France and Switzerland, 1984-85. Contbr. articles to profl. jours. Leader Girl Scouts U.S., 1977-85; trustee, deacon Higganum (Conn.) Congl. Ch., 1980—. Recipient Achievement award Girl Scouts U.S., 1985. Mem. Am. Assn. Clin. Chemistry, Am. Soc. Clin. Pathologists (cert. immunology specialist), Am. Soc. Clin. Lab. Sci., Wesleyan Potters (pres. 1982-84), Haddam, Conn. Hist. Soc. (sec. 1970-72), PEO Sisterhood. Avocations: gardening, music, pottery. Home: 29 Spencer Rd Higganum CT 06441-4034 Office: Hartford Hosp Dept Pathology & Lab Medicine 80 Seymour St Hartford CT 06102-8000

GILLMORE, ROBERT, landscape designer, author, editor, publisher; b. Claremont, N.H., Jan. 21, 1946; s. Vern Winslow and Helen Marion (Tyre) G. BA in Polit. Sci. cum laude, Williams Coll., 1968; postgrad., London Sch. Econs., 1970; MA, U. Va., 1971, PhD, 1979. Editl. writer Daily Eagle, Claremont, 1965-66; reporter, editor The Transcript, North Adams, Mass., 1966; reporter Bennington Banner, Vt., 1967; editor, mem. editl. page staff Washington Post, 1970; instr. politics St. Anselm Coll., Manchester, N.H., 1972-73; editor, writer N.H. Times, Concord, 1973; editor N.H. Law Weekly, Manchester, 1974-79; lectr. constl. law New England Coll., Henniker, N.H., 1975; editor Supreme Ct. Bull., Goffstown, N.H., 1979-87; syndicated columnist Bull. Syndicate, Goffstown, 1983-90; pub., editorial dir. Great Walks guides, 1990—; prin. Robert Gillmore, Landscape Consulting, Contracting & Design, 1990—. Author: Liberalism and the Politics of Plunder: The Conscience of a Neo-Liberal, 1987, Great Walks of Acadia National Park and Mount Desert, 1990, Great Walks of Southern Arizona, 1990, Great Walks of Big Bend National Park, 1991, Great Walks of the Great Smokies, 1992, Great Walks of Yosemite National Park, 1993, Great Walks of Sequoia and Kings Canyon National Parks, 1994, Great Walks of Acadia National Park and Mount Desert Island, 1994, The Woodland Garden, 1996, Great Walks of the Olympic Peninsula, 1999. Mem. N.H. Ho. Reps., 1973-74; del. N.H. Constl. Conv., 1974, vice chmn. com. on form and style; mem. N.H. state adv. com. U.S. Commn. on Civil Rights, 1973-76. With U.S. Army, 1968-70, Vietnam. Office: Great Walks Inc PO Box 410 Goffstown NH 03045-0410

GILLMORE, VICKI LONGENECKER, health care administrator; b. Lancaster, Pa., Mar. 10, 1950; d. Harry Kreider and Doris Louise (Heisey) Longenecker; m. Jack L. Gillmore, Aug. 30, 1986. Diploma, Harrisburg Hosp. Sch. Nursing, 1971; BS, U. Md., 1976, MS, 1977, PhD, 1990. Lic. nursing home adminstr., Pa. Dept. Health. Adminstr. healthcare svcs. Masonic Homes, Elizabethtown, Pa., 1997—; coord. critical care Community Hosp. Lancaster, 1978-79; clin. specialist cardiovascular St. Joseph Hosp., Lancaster, 1979-85, asst. dir. nursing, 1985-91; nursing instr. Millersville (Pa.) U., 1981—; v.p. nursing Community Gen. Osteopathic Hosp., Harrisburg, 1991-94; dir. Keystone Health Plan Ctrl., Camp Hill, Pa., 1994-97. Mem. Pa. Orgn. Nurse Leaders, South Ctrl. Org. of Nurse Leaders, Sigma Theta Tau. Home: 1429 Drager Rd Columbia PA 17512-8701

GILLOM, JENNIFER, professional basketball player; b. June 13, 1964. Basketball player Italian League, Milan, 1987-91, Ancona, 1991-94, Messina, 1995-96; basketball player Athens, Greece, 1996-97, Phoenix Mercury, WNBA, 1997—. Recipient Gold medal Pan Am. Games, 1987, Olympic Games, 1988; named to All WNBA 1st Team, 1988. Office: Phoenix Mercury 201 E Jefferson St Phoenix AZ 85004-2412

GILLOOLY, EDNA RAE See BURSTYN, ELLEN

GILLQUIST, PETER EDWARD, church organization executive; b. Mpls., July 13, 1938; s. William Parker and Louise E. (Blitsch) G.; m. Marilyn Joyce Grinder; children: Wendy, Gregory, Ginger, Terri Beth, Heidi, Peter Jon. BA, U. Minn., 1960; postgrad., Dallas Sem., 1960-61, Wheaton (Ill.) Grad. Sch., 1961-62. Regional dir. Campus Crusade, Chgo., 1960-68; dir. devel., exec. v.p. Found., U. Memphis, 1969-72; sr. editor Thomas Nelson Publs., Nashville, 1975-86; dir. missions Antiochian Orthodox Ch., Santa Barbara, Calif., 1987—; presiding bishop Evang. Orthodox Ch., Santa Barbara, 1979-87; pub. Conciliar Press, Ben Lomond, Calif., 1985—; v.p. Orthodox Christian Mission Ctr., St. Augustine, Fla., 1995—. Author: Becoming Orthodox, 1989, Metropolitan Philip, 1991; editor: Coming Home, 1992, Orthodox Study Bible, 1993. Planning dir. Memphis Mayor's Drug Commn., 1970-72. Mem. Four Freshmen Soc., Order of St. Ignatius, Sigma Alpha Epsilon (nat. chaplain). Office: Antiochian Orthodox Ch Dept Missions-Evangelism 777 Camino Pescadero Santa Barbara CA 93117-4620

GILLUM, PERRY EUGENE, religious organization administrator, minister; b. Allen, Okla., Oct. 16, 1933; s. Perry Jefferson and Ruby Margaret (Borden) G.; m. B. Evelyn Griffin, Dec. 23, 1953; children: J. Scott, Carole Genise Gillum Dotson. B in Ministry (hon.), Tomlinson Coll., 1990. Ordained to ministry Ch. of God of Prophecy, 1964. Evangelist Ch. of God of Prophecy, Calif., 1951-53, youth dir., 1955-59; youth dir. Ch. of God of Prophecy, Tenn., 1959-60; pastor Ch. of God of Prophecy, Ridgedale, Chattanooga, Tenn., 1960-64; internat. youth dir. Ch. of God of Prophecy, Cleveland, Tenn., 1964-66, asst. pub., bus. mgr. White Wing Pub. House, 1966-70; Calif. state overseer Ch. of God of Prophecy, 1970-72, dir. pub. rels., 1972-74, dir. Sunday sch., lit. editor, 1974-77, dir. ministerial aid, 1978-80, ea. Can. nat. overseer, 1980-81, dir. pub. rels., lit. editor Sunday sch. div., 1981-87, dir. pub. rels., 1987-89; pres., dir. pub. rels. Tomlinson Coll., 1989—; adminstrv. asst. to gen. overseer Ch. of God of Prophecy, 1992-96, regional overseer Calif.-Hawaii, 1996-98, gen. presbyter, 1998—. Author: Church of God Deacon, 1970, Youth Aflame, 1970, These Stones Speak, 1974, Public Relations, 1984. Bd. dirs. YMCA, Cleveland, 1973-77, UNited Way, Cleveland, 1983—. Cpl. U.S. Army, 1952-55, Korea. Mem. Cleveland C. of C. (bd. dirs. 1983—). Republican. Office: Ch God Prophecy Internat Office Office of the President PO Box 2910 Cleveland TN 37320-2910

GILMAN, ALAN B., restaurant company executive; b. South Bend, Ind., Sept. 24, 1930; s. Sol M. and Lee R. (Rintzler) G.; m. Phyllis Schrager, Feb. 16, 1951; children: Bruce, Jeffrey, Lynn. A.B. with highest honors (Raymond Charles Stoltz scholar), Ind. U., 1952, M.B.A. (John H. Edwards fellow), 1954. With Lazarus Co. div. Federated Dept. Stores, Inc., Columbus, Ohio, 1954-64; div. mdse. mgr. Lazarus Co. div. Federated Dept. Stores, Inc., 1961-64; with Sanger Harris div., 1965-74, chmn. bd., chief exec. officer, 1970-74, corp. v.p., 1974-80; with Abraham & Straus div., 1975-80, chmn. bd., chief exec. officer, 1978-80; pres. Murjani Internat. Ltd., N.Y.C., 1980-85; pvt. investor, 1985-87; chmn. At Ease of Newport Beach (Calif.) Inc., 1988-91; pres., chief exec. officer Consol. Products Inc., 1992—, Steak 'n Shake Inc. Vice chmn. bd. dirs. Ind. U. Found., nat. chmn. ann. giving, 1983, mem. presdl. search com., 1987-88; chmn. dean's adv. coun. Ind. U. Grad. Sch. Bus., 1976-86; mem. dean's adv. coun. Coll. Arts and Scis., Ind. U., 1989—, pres.'s cabinet, 1995; bd. dirs., pres., mem. exec. com. Greater N.Y. Fund-United Way, 1984-87; bd. dirs., mem. exec. com., chmn. strategic planning com. United Way of N.Y.C., 1982-88; dir. Corp. Comty. Coun., Indpls., Greater Indpls. Progress Com., Kelley Restaurants, Inc. Recipient Humanitarian of Yr. award Juvenile Diabetes Found., 1979, Disting. Alumni Svc. award Ind. U., 1996. Mem. Young Pres. Orgn. 49'er, Ind. U. Acad. Alumni Fellows, World Bus. Council, Phi Beta Kappa Assocs., Phi Alpha Theta, Beta Gamma Sigma (charter mem. dirs. table). Home: 2730 Brigs Bnd Bloomington IN 47401-4402 Office: 500 Century Bldg 36 S Pennsylvania St Indianapolis IN 46204-3634 *Value intellectual curiosity, an open mind, the greater import of tomorrow over yesterday, and recognize rapid change as the definition of opportunity while maintaining a sense of humor and honest humility.*

GILMAN, ALFRED GOODMAN, pharmacologist, educator; b. New Haven, July 1, 1941; s. Alfred and Mabel (Schmidt) G.; m. Kathryn Hedlund, Sept. 21, 1963; children: Amy, Anne, Edward. BS, Yale U., 1962; MD, PhD, Case Western Res. U., 1969; DSc (hon.), U. Chgo., 1991, Case Western Res. U., 1995; DMS, Yale U., 1997. Pharmacology research assoc. NIH, Bethesda, Md., 1969-71; from asst. prof. to assoc. prof. pharmacology U. Va., Charlottesville, 1971-77, prof., 1977-81, dir. med. sci. tng. program, 1979-81; prof. pharmacology, chmn. dept. U. Tex. Southwestern Med. Ctr., Dallas, 1981—, Raymond and Ellen Willie disting. chmn. molecular neuropharmacology, 1987—, regental prof., 1994—; MD Yale U., 1997—; mem. pharmacology study sect. NIH, 1977-81, mem. nat. adv. gen. med. scis. coun., 1992-95; bd. sci. counselors Nat. Heart, Lung & Blood Inst. NIH, 1982-86; sci. adv. com. Am. Cancer Soc., N.Y.C., 1982-86; adv. com. Lucille P. Markey Charitable Trust, Miami, Fla., 1984-96; sci. rev. bd. Howard Hughes Med. Inst., Bethesda, 1986-93; dir. Regeneron Pharmaceutics, 1989—, Eli Lilly and Co., Inc., 1995—; mem. vis. com. Sch. Medicine Case Western Reserve U., 1995—; mem. sci. adv. bd. Huntsman Cancer Inst. U. Utah, 1995—, Ernest Gallo Clinic and Rsch. Ctr. U. Calif., San Francisco, 1996—. Editor: The Pharmacological Basis of Therapeutics, 1975, 80, 85, 90; consulting editor, 1996; contbr. over 225 articles to profl. jours. Recipient Poul Edvard Poulsson award Norwegian Pharmacology Soc., 1982, GairdnerFound. Internat. award, Can., 1984, Albert Lasker Basic Med. Rsch. award, 1989, Passano Sr. award Passano Found., 1990, Waterford Biomedical Sci. award Scripps Clinic and Rsch. Found. 1990, Basic Sci. Rsch. prize Am. Heart Assn., 1990, Steven C. Beering award Ind. U., 1990, City of Medicine award, Durham, N.C., 1991, CIBA-GEIGY Drew award, 1991, Nobel Prize in Physiology or Medicine, 1994, ACP award, 1995, Disting. Alumnus award Case Western Reserve U., 1995, Am. Acad. Achievement award, 1995, Med. Honor award Am. Cancer Soc., 1995. Mem. Am. Soc. Pharmacology & Exptl. Therapeutics (John J. Abel award in pharmacology 1975, Louis S. Goodman and Alfred Gilman award 1990, Torald Sollman award 1997), Am. Soc. Biol. Chemistry, Nat. Acad. Scis. (Richard Lounsbery award 1987), Am. Acad. Arts and Scis., Inst. Medicine of NAS. Office: U Tex Southwestern Med Ctr Dept Pharmacology 5323 Harry Hines Blvd Dallas TX 75235-9041

GILMAN, BENJAMIN ARTHUR, congressman; b. Poughkeepsie, N.Y., Dec. 6, 1922; s. Harry and Esther (Gold) G.; m. Jane Prizant, Oct. 19, 1952 (div. 1978); children: Jonathan, Harrison, Susan, David (dec.), Ellen (dec.); m. Rita Gail Keller Kelhoffer, Nov. 9, 1984 (div. 1996); m. Georgia Nickles Tingus, Jan. 12, 1997. BS, U. Pa., 1946; LLB, N.Y. Law Sch., 1950. Bar: N.Y. 1952. Dep. asst. atty. gen. N.Y. Dept. Law, 1952-54, asst. atty. gen., 1954-55; ptnr. Gilman & Gilman, Middletown, N.Y., 1955-72; counsel N.Y. Assembly's Com. on Local Finance, 1956-64; mem. N.Y. State Assembly, 1967-72, 93d-97th Congresses from 26th N.Y. dist., 1972-82; mem. 98th-106th Congresses from 22d (now 20th) N.Y. dist., 1983—, mem. govt. reform and oversight com., chmn. internat. rels. com.; dep. asst. atty. gen. N.Y. Dept. Law, 1952-54; mem. Rep. Policy Com., 1997—; mem. Presdl. Commn. on World Hunger, 1978-80, Ad-Hoc Com. on Irish Affairs, Republican Task Force on Handicapped and Task Force on Econ. Policy; mem. U.S.-Mex. Consultative Mechanism Subcom. on Narcotics Trafficking; U.S. rep. to 36th session UN Gen. Assembly; chmn. House Task Force on Missing in Action, 1983-85; mem. World Hunger Yr. Bd.; mem. adv. com. N.Y. State Div. Youth's Start Ctr., 1962-67; mem. N.Y. State Southeastern Water Study Com., 1971-73, Lawyers' Com. for Civil Rights Under Law, 1963-75; mem. adv. com. Otisville Fed. Correctional Instn.; v.p., bd. dirs. Orange County Health Assn.; adv. council Lamont-Doherty Geol. Obs., Columbia U., 1979-82. Chmn. bd. dirs. Middletown Little League; bd. dirs. Goldenarea Hosp. Fund; bd. visitors U.S. Mil. Acad., 1973-83; lt. col. CAP. Served with USAAF, 1943-45; to col. USNG. Decorated D.F.C., Air medal. Mem. ABA, D.C. Bar Assn., N.Y. State Bar Assn., Assn. of Bar of City of N.Y., Middletown Bar Assn., Orange County Bar Assn., Assn. Trial Lawyers Am., VFW (past county comdr.), Am. Legion, Masonic War Vets. (lt. comdr.), Jewish War Vets., Forty and Eight, Air Force Assn., Internat. Narcotics Enforcement Officers, N.Y. Law Sch. Alumni (bd. dirs.), N.Y. Soc. in Washington (pres.), Grange, La Société des 40 Hommes et 8 Chevaux. Republican. Jewish. Lodges: Masons, Capitol Hill Shriners (pres.), Elks. Office: US Ho of Reps 2449 Rayburn HOB Washington DC 20515*

GILMAN, JOHN JOSEPH, research scientist; b. St. Paul, Dec. 22, 1925; s. Alexander Falk and Florence Grace (Colby) G.; m. Pauline Marie Harms, June 17, 1950 (div. Dec. 1968); children: Pamela Ann, Gregory George, Cheryl Elizabeth; m. Gretchen Marie Sutter, June 12, 1976; 1 son, Brian Alexander. BS, Ill. Inst. Tech., 1946, MS, 1948; PhD, Columbia, 1952. Research metallurgist Gen. Electric Co., Schenectady, 1952-60; prof. engring. Brown U., Providence, 1960-63; prof. physics and metallurgy U. Ill., Urbana, 1963-68; dir. Materials Research Center Allied Chem. Corp., Morristown, N.J., 1968-78; dir. Corp. Devel. Center, 1978-80; mgr. corp. research Amoco Co. (Ind.), Naperville, Ill., 1980-85; assoc. dir. Lawrence Berkeley Lab./U. Calif., 1985-87; sr. scientist Lawrence Berkeley Lab., Calif., 1987-93; adj. prof. UCLA, 1993—. Author: Micromechanics of Flow in Solids, 1969, Inventivity-The Art and Science of Research Management, 1992; editor: The Art and Science of Growing Crystals, 1963, Fracture of Solids (with D.C. Drucker), 1963, Atomic and Electronic Structures of Metals, 1967, Metallic Glasses, 1973, Energetic Materials, 1993; editl. bd. Jour. Applied Physics, 1969-72; contbg. editor Materials Tech., 1994—; contbr. over 250 papers, articles to tech. jours. Served as ensign USNR, 1943-46. Recipient Mathewson gold medal Am. Inst. Metal Engrs., 1959, Disting. Service award Alumni Assn. Ill. Inst. Tech., 1962, Application to Practice award, 1985. Fellow Am. Phys. Soc., The Materials Soc., Am. Soc. for Metals (Campbell lectr. 1966); mem. Nat. Acad. Engring., Phi Kappa Phi, Tau Beta Pi. Home: 2852 Forrester Dr Los Angeles CA 90064-4662 Office: UCLA 6532 Boelter Hall Los Angeles CA 90095

GILMAN, JOHN RICHARD, JR., business consultant; b. Malden, Mass., July 6, 1925; s. John Richard and Philomene (Gradie) G.; m. Julia Streeter, Feb. 6, 1960; children: Derek, Susan. AB, Harvard, 1945; postgrad. Georgetown U., 1945-46; MSW, NYU, 1983. Diplomate Am. Bd. Clin. Social Work; lic. clin. social work, N.Y., R.I. Dir. publicity John H. Breck, Inc., Springfield, Mass., 1949-53, asst. advt. mgr., 1950-53, dir. new products, 1955-56, tech. dir., 1956-63; dir. new products Acco Labs., Am. Cyanamid Co., Wayne, N.J., 1963; treas., exec. v.p. August Sauter of Am., Inc., N.Y.C., 1964, pres., 1965-79, also CEO; pres. John R. Gilman Inc., N.Y.C., 1980-94; dir. Slee Internat., Inc., N.Y.C., Finex Mining Co., Reno; asso., Fisher Cons. Internat. Inc. N.Y.C., 1980-86, assoc. C.M. Oppenheim & Co. Inc. N.Y.C., 1981-86; cons. Right Assocs., Inc., Providence, 1986-89. Trustee, Sculpture Center, N.Y.C., 1977-90, mem. exhibition com., 1980-82, v.p., 1983-86. Augustus St. Gaudens Meml., N.Y.C., 1982—, 1st v.p., mem. exec. com., chmn. facilities com., 1988-91, pres. 1991-93, mem. St. Gaudens exhibition com., 1994—, mem. fin. com., 1988—, meml. music com., 1997—; budget com. Town of Tiverton (R.I.), 1977-79; mem. Shaw Meml. Centennial Project, 1996-98, Friends Augustus St. Gaudens Meml., 1996—. Served with USNR, 1943-46. Fellow Am. Orthopsychiat. Assn. (diplomate); mem. Internat. Sculpture Soc., Art Students League (life), Art Club Washington D.C., Harvard Club (N.Y.C., Boston), Nat. Arts Club (N.Y.C.). Film maker: Water, 1950; Dear Nancy, 1953; co-pub. Arcadia Press, N.Y.C., 1979—. Home and Office: 39 Las Brisas Way Naples FL 34108-8294 also: 3 Water Edge Belfast ME 04915-6053

GILMAN, KAREN FRENZEL, legal assistant; b. Syracuse, N.Y., Jan. 11, 1947; d. Charles Henry and Cora Adell (Haith) Frenzel; m. Lawrence Sanford Gilman, June 5, 1970 (div. Feb. 9, 1977). AAS in Horticulture, SUNY, Morrisville, 1967; BS, Cornell U., 1969, MS in Floriculture and Ornamental Hort., 1971; attended, Syracuse Univ. Coll., 1983. Cert. legal asst. Floral designer Fortino of Fayetteville (N.Y.), 1965-69, 76-79, 81-84, Fallon's Florist, Raleigh, N.C., 1973-74; salesperson Finley Fine Jewelry, N.Y.C., 1979-80; legal asst. Agway, Inc., Dewitt, N.Y., 1984; legal asst. gen. legal Carrier Corp., Syracuse, N.Y., 1984-91, legal asst. intellectual property, 1992—; mem. adv. bd. legal asst. program Syracuse U. Coll., 1986-90. Contbr. articles to profl. jours. Henry Strong Denison fellow, 1969. Mem. Pi Alpha Xi, Phi Theta Kappa. Avocations: gardening, biking. Office: Carrier Corp PO Box 4800 Carrier Pkwy Syracuse NY 13221

GILMAN, NANCY ELLEN HELGESON, medical and surgical nurse; b. Ill., July 5, 1934; d. Elmer Theodore and Florence Fleda (Powell) Helgeson; m. William O. Gilman, July 20, 1955; children: Anita Leihy, Leeanne Gilman White, Jerilyn Szalonek. Diploma, Copley Meml. Hosp., Aurora, Ill., 1955; BSN, Fla. So. Coll., 1989. Cert. med.-surg. nurse. Staff nurse Cmty. Meml. Hosp., La Grange, Ill., 1958-60, 63-68; staff nurse physician's office, Downers Grove, Ill., 1968-75, office mgr., 1975-80; staff nurse Meml. Hosp. of DuPage County, Elmhurst, Ill., 1980-82; nurse, multi-skilled surg. practitioner Lakeland (Fla.) Regional Med. Ctr., 1982-97, multi-skilled team leader, 1991-94; staff nurse Columbia Health Care Svcs., Greenville, S.C., 1998—. Home: 709 Nine Times Rd Pickens SC 29671-9221

GILMAN, NELSON JAY, library director; b. Los Angeles, Mar. 30, 1938; s. Louis L. and Alice (Cohen) G.; children: Justine C., Seth F. BS, U. So. Calif., 1959, MS, 1960; MLS, U. Calif., Berkeley, 1964. Tchr. math. dept. Pasadena (Calif.) High Sch., 1960-61, Tamalpais High Sch., Mill Valley, Calif., 1962-63; intern library adminstrn. UCLA, 1964-65, asst. to librarian, 1965-66, asst. to biomedical librarian, 1966-67, asst. biomedical librarian, 1967-69; assoc. dir. Pacific Southwest Regional Med. Library Service, UCLA, 1969-71; dir. Los Angeles County/U. So. Calif. Med. Ctr. Libraries, 1974-79; asst. prof. dept. med. edn. U. So. Calif. Sch. Medicine, L.A., 1971-95, asst. prof. dept. pediat., 1995—, dir. Norris Med. Library,, 1971—, dir. Health Scis. Librs.,, 1984—, assoc. dir. devel. and demonstration ctr., 1981—; assoc. dean librs., dir. planning for teaching libr. U. So. Calif., 1989-90; interim dir. Ctrl. Libr. System, 1990-91; cons. HEW, San Francisco, 1973-76, NIH, Washington, 1970-71. Assoc. editor U. So. Calif. Sch. Medicine Info. Systems Research Program, 1984-87; contbr. articles to profl. jours. Served with USAR, 1961-67. Mem. Am. Library Assn., Am. Soc. Info. Sci., Assn. Acad. Health Scis. Library Dirs. (bd. dirs. 1980-83), Med. Library Assn. (bd. dirs. 1977-79), Spl. Library Assn. Democrat. Jewish. Avocation: gardening. Home: 615 22nd St Santa Monica CA 90089-9130 Office: U So Calif Norris Med Library 2003 Zonal Ave Los Angeles CA 90033-1034

GILMAN, RICHARD, drama educator, author; b. N.Y.C., Apr. 30, 1925; s. Jacob and Marion (Wolinsky) G.; 1 son, Nicholas; m. Lynn Nesbit; children: Priscilla, Claire; m. Yasuko Shiojiri. B.A., U. Wis., 1947; L.H.D., Grinnell Coll., 1967. Free-lance writer, 1950-54; assoc. editor Jubilee mag., 1954-57; drama critic, lit. editor Commonweal, 1961-64; assoc. editor, drama critic Newsweek mag., 1964-67; lit. editor New Republic, 1968-70; prof. drama Yale U., 1967-78, 79—; vis. lectr. English, Columbia U., 1964-65, vis. prof., 1980, 84; vis. prof. drama Stanford U., summer 1967, theater arts CCNY, 1978-79, Boston U., 1984-85, Barnard Coll.; McGraw Disting. lectr. Princeton U., 1990; pres. PEN Am. Center, 1981-83, v.p., 1983-86. Author: The Confusion of Realms, 1970, Common and Uncommon Masks, 1971, The Making of Modern Drama, 1974, Decadence, 1979, Faith Sex Mystery: A Memoir, 1987, Checkhov's Plays, 1996; contbg. editor Partisan Rev., 1972—. Served with USMCR, 1943-46. Recipient George Jean Nathan award for drama criticism, 1971; Morton Dauwen Zabel award Am. Acad. and Inst. Arts and Letters, 1979; fellow N.Y. Inst. for Humanities., 1977-80.

GILMAN, RICHARD CARLETON, retired college president; b. Cambridge, Mass., July 28, 1923; s. George Phillips Brooks and Karen Elise (Theller) G.; m. Lucille Young, Aug. 28, 1948 (dec. 1978); children: Marsha, Bradley Morris, Brian Potter, Blair Tucker; m. Sarah Gale, Dec. 28, 1984 (dec. 1986). BA, Dartmouth Coll., 1944; student, New Coll., U. London, Eng., 1947-48; PhD (Bordenm Parker Bowne fellow), Boston U., 1952, LHD, 1969; LLD, Pomona Coll., 1966, U. So. Calif., 1968, Coll. Idaho, 1968; LHD, Chapman Coll., 1984, Occidental Coll., 1988. Teaching fellow religion Dartmouth, 1948; mem. faculty Colby Coll., 1950-56, assoc. prof. philosophy, 1955-56; exec. dir. Nat. Council Religion Higher Edn., New Haven, 1956-60; dean coll., prof. philosophy Carleton Coll., 1960-65; pres. Occidental Coll., L.A., 1965-88, pres. emeritus, 1988—; pres., mng. trustee S.W. Mus., L.A., 1994-95; past mem. bd. dirs. Am. Coun. on Edn., Assn. Am. Colls., Assn. Ind. Calif. Colls. and Univs., Coun. for Fin. Aid to Edn., Coun. on Postsecondary Accreditation, Nat. Coun. Ind. Colls. and Univs., Ind. Coll. Funds Am.; mem. Intergovtl. Adv. Coun. on Edn., 1980-84; mem. president's commn. NCAA, 1984-86; exec. asst., counselor to sec. of edn., 1979-80; mem. Calif. Student Aid Commn., 1988-92. Bd. dirs. Exec. Svc. Corps Co. Calif., S.W. Mus., Wellness Cmty.-Foothills (pres. bd. dirs. 1996-98); past mem. bd. dirs. Calif. Mus. Found., Cape of Good Hope Found.; mem. L.A. World Affairs Coun., Westridge Sch. Fellow Soc. for Values in Higher Edn.; mem. Newcomen Soc., Calif. C. of C. (past bd. dirs.), Calif. Club L.A., Twilight Club (Pasadena), Phi Beta Kappa (bd. dirs. coun. of So. Calif. 1996—). Home: 131 Annandale Rd Pasadena CA 91105-1405

GILMAN, RICHARD H., newspaper publishing executive. Sr. v.p. operations The New York Times, N.Y.C. Office: The NY Times Co 229 W 43rd St New York NY 10036-3959*

GILMAN, RONALD LEE, judge; b. Memphis, Oct. 16, 1942; s. Seymour and Rosalind (Kuzin) G.; m. Betsy Dunn, June 11, 1966; children: Laura M., Sherry I. BS, MIT, 1964; JD cum laude, Harvard U., 1967. Bar: Tenn. 1967, U.S. Supreme Ct. 1971. Mem. Farris, Mathews, Gilman, Branan & Hellen, Memphis, 1967-97; judge U.S. Ct. Appeals (6th cir.), 1997—; judge Tenn. Ct. of Judiciary, 1979-87; lectr. trial advocacy U. Memphis Law Sch., 1980-97. Contbr. articles to profl. jours. Regional chmn. ednl. coun. MIT, 1968-88; bd. dirs. Memphis Jewish Home, 1984-87, Chickasaw coun. Boy Scouts Am., 1993—; mem. Leadership Memphis. Recipient Sam A. Myar Jr. Meml. award for outstanding svc.sts to legal profession and cmty., 1981. Mem. ABA (ho. of dels. 1990-97), Am. Law Inst., Am. Judicature Soc., Am. Coll. Trust and Estate Counsel, Memphis Bar Assn. (pres. 1987), Tenn. Bar Assn. (spkr. ho. of dels. 1985-87, pres. 1990-91), 6th Cir. Jud. Conf. (life), Am. Arbitration Assn. (mem. large, complex case panel 1993-97). Democrat. Jewish. Office: Fed Bldg Ste 1176 167 N Main St Memphis TN 38103-1816

GILMAN, SANDER LAWRENCE, German language educator; b. Buffalo, Feb. 21, 1944; s. William and Rebecca (Helf) G.; m. Marina von Eckardt, Dec. 28, 1969; children: Daniel, Samuel. BA, Tulane U., 1963, PhD, 1968; postgrad., U. Berlin and U. Munich, Ger.; LLD (hon.), U. Toronto, Ont., 1997. Lectr. German St. Mary's Dominican Coll., New Orleans, 1963-64; instr. Dillard U., New Orleans, 1967-68; asst. prof. Case Western Res. U., 1968-69; mem. faculty Cornell U., 1969-94, prof. German, 1976-94, prof. Near Eastern studies, 1984-91, prof. humane studies, 1984-87, Goldwin Smith prof., 1987-94, chmn. dept. German lit., 1974-81, 83-84; fellow dept. psychiatry Cornell U. Med. Coll., 1977-78; prof. history of psychiatry Cornell U., 1978-94; prof. German, history of sci. and psychiatry U. Chgo., 1994—, Henry R. Luce prof. Liberal Arts in Human Biology, 1995—, disting. svc. prof., 1999—; O'Connor prof. Colgate U., 1982-83; Mellon prof. Tulane U., 1988, Old Dominion prof. English, Princeton U., 1988; Northrup Frye prof. of comparative lit. U. Toronto, Ont., Can., 1989; vis. prof. German lit. Free U. Berlin, 1989; vis. hist. scholar Nat. Libr. Medicine, 1991-92; vis. Rudolph prof. Jewish studies Syracuse (N.Y.) U., 1992; vis. prof. U. Witwatersrand, South Africa, 1994, U. Potsdam, 1996, U. Cape Town, 1996, Ctr. for Advanced Studies in the Behavioral Scis., 1996-97, Getty Inst. for Art and the Humanities, 1998. Author, editlr 40 books including Bertolt Brecht's Berlin, 1975, Nietzschean Parody, 1976, The Face of Madness, 1976, Klingers Werke, 1978, On Blackness Without Blacks, 1982, Begegnungen mit Nietzsche, 1981, Wahnsinn, Text Difference and Pathology, 1985, Jewish Self-Hatred, 1986, Oscar Wilde's London, 1987, Conversations with Nietzsche, 1987, Diseases and Representation, 1989, Sexuality: An Illustrated History, 1989, Nietzsche on Rhetoric and Language, 1989, The Jew's Body, 1991, Inscribing the Other, 1991, Rasse, Seuche, Sexualitat, 1992, Freud, Race, Gender, 1993, The Case of Sigmund Freud, 1993, Reading Freud Reading, 1993, Reemerging Jewish Culture in Germany, 1994, Jews in Today's German Culture, 1995, Health and Illness, 1995, Franz Kafka: The Jewish Patient, 1996, L'Aute et Le Moi, 1996, Smart Jews, 1996, Yale Companion to Jewish Writing and Thought in German Culture, 1997, Love and Marriage with Death, 1998, Creating Beauty to Cure the Soul, 1998, Making the Body Beautiful, 1999; also essays; mem. editl. bd. Diacritics, 1971-72, Lessing Yearbook, 1974—, German Quar., 1977-86; assoc. editor Confinia Psychiatrica, 1978-80. Guggenheim fellow, 1972-73, IREX exch. fellow German Democratic Republic, 1976, Soc. for Humanities faculty fellow Cornell U., 1981-82, Nat. Libr. Medicine sr. historian, fellow, 1990-91, Ctr. for the Adv. Study of the Behavioral Scis. fellow, Stanford, 1996-97. Mem. Modern Lang Assn. (pres. 1995), Lessing Soc., Am. Assn. Tchrs. German, Soc. Internat. d'Études Littéraires et Psychiatres, Internat. Assn. Germanists. Democrat. Jewish. Home: 5701 S Dorchester Ave Chicago IL 60637-1726 Office: U Chgo 411 Wieboldt Hall Chicago IL 60637

GILMAN, SHELDON GLENN, lawyer; b. Cleve., July 20, 1943. BBA, Ohio U., 1965; JD, Case Western Res. U., 1967. Bar: Ohio 1967, Ky. 1971, Ind. 1982, Fla. 1984, D.C. 1985, Tenn. 1985, U.S. Supreme Ct., 1987. Mem. staff accts. tax dept. Arthur Andersen & Co., Cleve., 1967-68; assoc. Handmaker, Weber & Meyer, Louisville, 1971-74, ptnr., 1974-83; ptnr. Barnett & Alagia, Louisville, 1984-87; ptnr. Lynch, Cox, Gilman & Mahan, P.S.C., 1987—; gen. counsel Louisville Assn. Life Underwriters, 1977, 78, 90; adj. prof. law U. of Louisville Sch. of Law. Bd. dirs., chmn. Louisville Minority Bus. Resource Ctr., 1975-80; pres. Congregation Adath Jeshurun, 1986-88; bd. dirs., v.p., sec. Louisville Orch., 1982-85; bd. dirs. City of Devondale (Ky.), 1976, United Synagogue of Cons. Judaism, N.Y., 1989—, also pres. Ohio Valley region. With JAGC, AUS, 1968-71. Mem. Ky. Bar Assn. (ethics com. 1982—, ethics hotline com. 1990), Louisville Employee Benefit Council (pres. 1980). Office: Lynch Cox Gilman & Mahan 500 Meidinger Tower Louisville KY 40202-3473

GILMAN, SID, neurologist; b. L.A., Oct. 19, 1932; s. Morris and Sarah Rose (Cooper) G.; m. Carol G. Barbour. B.A., UCLA, 1954; M.D., 1957. Intern UCLA Hosp., 1957-58; resident in neurology Boston City Hosp., 1960-63; from instr. to assoc. in neurology Harvard Med. Sch., 1965-68; from asst. prof. to prof. neurology Columbia U., N.Y.C., 1968-76; H. Houston Merritt prof. neurology, 1976-77; William J. Herdman prof., chair dept. neurology U. Mich., Ann Arbor, 1977—; cons. VA Hosp., Ann Arbor, 1977—; mem. peripheral and ctrl. nervous sys. drugs adv. com. FDA, 1983-85, 86-87, 90-94, chmn., 1996—; adj. attending neurologist Henry Ford Hosp., Detroit; mem. chronic disease adv. com. Mich. Dept. Pub. Health, 1988-94; mem. neurol. sci. rsch. and tng. com. NIH, mem. neurol. disorders program project B com., mem. sci. programs adv. com. Nat. Inst. Neurol. Diseases, Communicative Disorders and Stroke, 1982-84, mem. nat. adv. neurol. disorders and stroke coun., 1994-97; dir. Mich. alzheimer's Disease Rsch. Ctr., 1991—; mem. rsch. adv. coun. United Cerebral Palsy Found.; mem. sci. adv. coun. Nat. Ataxia Found., Nat. Amyotrophic Lateral Sclerosis Found., Inc.; mem. profl. adv. bd. Epilepsy Found. Am.; mem. rsch. adv. com. Nat. Multiple Sclerosis Soc., 1986-90; mem. exec. bd. Nat. Coalition for Rsch., 1989-95, Nat. Found. for Brain Rsch., 1989-95; mem. rsch. adv. com. Dana Alliance. Author: (with J.R. Bloedel and R. Lechtenberg) Disorders of the Cerebellum, 1981, (with S.W. Newman) Manter and Gatz's Essentials of Clinical Neuroanatomy and Neurophysiology, 9th edit., 1996, (with J.C. Mazziotta) Clinical Brain Imaging: Principles and Applications, 1992; sect. editor editl. bd. Exptl. Neurology, Current Opinion in Neurology and Neurosurgery, Neurology, Annals Neurology, Jour. Neuropathology and Exptl. Neurology, Neurobase Arbor Pub. Co.; editor-in-chief Contemporary Neurology Series, 1995—, Neurology Network Commentary, 1996—; contbr. articles to profl. jours. Dir. Mich. Dem. Program, 1994—. With USPHS, 1958-60. Recipient Lucy G. Moses prize Columbia U., 1973, Weinstein Goldenson award United Cerebral Palsy Assn., 1981, UCLA Alumni Profl. Achievement award, 1992, UCLA Med. Alumni Profl. Achievement award, 1992. Fellow AAAS; mem. Am. Neurol. Assn. (hon.; 1st v.p. 1985-86, pres.-elect 1987-88, pres. 1988-89), Mich. Neurol. Assn. (pres. 1987-88), Soc. Clin. Investigation, Am. Physiol. Soc., Am. Assn. Neuropathologists, Soc. Neurosci., Am. Acad. Neurology (vice chmn. geriatric neurology subcom. 1992-94, chmn. 1994-96, chmn. Decade of Brain com. 1990-95), Am. Epilepsy Soc., Assn. Rsch. in Nervous and Mental Disease, Inst. Medicine, Nat. Acad. Scis., Phi Beta Kappa, Alpha Omega Alpha. Home: 3411 Geddes Rd Ann Arbor MI 48105-2518 Office: U Mich Dept Neurology Ann Arbor MI 48109

GILMAN, STEVEN A., management consultant; b. Atlanta, Mar. 28, 1953; s. H. Bernard and Sarah (Levy) G.; m. Veronika Litinski, Jan. 21, 1993. BSBA, U. So. Calif., 1980; MBA, USC, 1982. Sys. cons. Hughes Aircraft Co., L.A., 1980-84; cons. mgr. Info. Builders, L.A., 1985; v.p. Metmor Bank, L.A., 1985-88; cmty. devel. cons. Big Sur, Calif., 1988-90; prin. Satori Trading, Atlanta, 1993-94; mgmt. cons. Satori Trading, San Francisco, 1995—; bd. dirs. Digital Village, Novato, Calif., Multimedia Devel. Group, San Francisco. Author: Pilgrim's Tales, 1994. Avocations: yoga, tai-chi, cooking.

GILMAN, TODD SEACRIST, language educator, musician; b. Cambridge, Mass., Feb. 15, 1965; s. Sidney and Linda Louise (Lamlein) G. BA, U. Mich., 1987; MA, U. Toronto, 1988, PhD, 1994. Artistic dir. Arbor Oak Trio, Toronto, 1988-96; lectr., tutor, writing cons. U. Toronto, 1994-96; lectr. Boston U., Stonehill Coll., 1996-97; vis. fellow Houghton Libr., Harvard U., Cambridge, Mass., 1996-97; lectr. dept. English, Suffolk U., Boston, 1997-99; lectr. lit. sect. MIT, Cambridge, 1998—. Contbr. articles to profl. jours. Bd. dirs. Toronto Early Music Ctr., 1993-95. Fletcher Jones fellow The Huntington Libr., San Marino, Calif., 1995. Mem. MLA, Am. Soc. 18th Century Studies (McMaster fellow 1994), Am. Handel Soc. (rsch. fellow 1998), Soc. Theatre Rsch. (travel grantee 1998), Early Music Am. Democrat. Office: MIT Lit Section Rm 14N-409 Cambridge MA 02139

GILMARTIN, CLARA T., volunteer; b. East Stroudsburg, Pa., Jan. 23, 1922; d. Harry and Clarissa (Snearley) Treible; m. John Gilmartin, Jan. 18, 1945 (dec. Feb. 1956); children: Ronald, Donald; m. William Gilmartin, Mar. 17, 1973 (dec., 1992). BA, Rutgers U., 1961, MA, 1966. Elem. sch. tchr. Union Beach (N.J.) Pub. Sch., 1956-61; lang. arts tchr. Holmdel Village (N.J.) Intermediate Sch., 1961-82. *Mrs. Gilmartin served in the Women's Army Corp. from 1943-45. She was a member, and record secretary, of the Juvenile Conference Committee, and served two terms on the Union Beach Board of Health. For four terms, Clara was president of the Monmouth County Retired Education Association, and the record secretary of the Monmouth County Triad. From 1973-74 she was a Fulbright Exchange Teacher to Bombay, New Zealand.* Chair bd. trustees Grace Meth. Ch., Union Beach, 1997—. Mem. Monmouth County Retired Educators Assn., Am. Legion. Democrat. Home: 122 Dock St Union Beach NJ 07735-2506

GILMARTIN, RAYMOND V., health care products company executive; b. Washington, Mar. 6, 1941; m. Gladys Higham; 3 children. BS in Elect. Engring., Union Coll., 1963; MBA, Harvard U., 1968. Sr. cons. Arthur D. Little Inc., 1968-76; v.p. corp. planning Becton Dickinson & Co., Paramus, N.J., 1976-79, pres. Becton Dickinson divsn., 1979-87, group pres., 1982-83, sr. v.p., 1983-86, exec. v.p., 1986-87; pres. Becton Dickinson & Co., Franklin Lakes, N.J., 1987-94, CEO, 1989-94, also bd. dirs.; chmn., pres., CEO Merck, White House Station, NJ, 1994—; bd. dirs. Pub. Svc. Enterprise Group; dir. Gen. Mills, Inc.; chmn. Inter-faculty initative in Health Policy, adv. bd. Harvard U.; vice chmn. Chmn. Valley Health Systems, Inc., Ridgewood, N.J.; bd. dirs. Ethics Resource Ctr., Project HOPE, Coll. Fund/United Negro Coll. Fund, Pharm. Rsch. and Mfrs. Am., Healthcare Leadership Coun.; vice-chmn. Healthcare Inst. of N.J. bd. dirs., bd. assocs. Harvard Bus. Sch.; mem. Bus. Coun., Bus. Roundtable, Conf. Bd., Com. Econ. Devel.; mem. exec. com. Coun. on Competitiveness; mem. Alliance for Healthcare Reform. Office: Merck & Co I Merck Dr Whitehouse Station NJ 08889-3400

GILMER, GORDON, councilman; b. Feb. 25, 1922; m. Elizabeth; 4 children. Student, U. Notre Dame, 1942-43; BS, Butler U., 1947. Sales engr., mgr. Minn. Mining & Mfg. Co., St. Paul, 1947-90; ward chmn. Pike Twp., Marion County, Ind., 1966; del. to state conv., 1966-80; mem. Marion County Floor Control Bd., 1968-69, Bd. Pub. Works, 1970; city councilman City of Indpls., 1972—. Lt. sr. grade USN, 1942-46, PTO. Mem. Nat League of Cities (assoc. dir.), Ind. Assn. Cities and Towns (former dir.), Pike Twp. Resident's Assn., Washington Twp. Rep. Club, Eagle Creek Rep. Club, Pike Twp. Rep. Club (former pres.), Am. Legion, Masons, Lambda Chi Alpha. Home: 8621 Green Braes South Dr Indianapolis IN 46234-2931 Office: City-County Coun Office 200 E Washington St Ste 241 Indianapolis IN 46204-3310*

GILMER, HARRY WESLEY, publishing executive, educator; b. Bristol, Va., Apr. 11, 1937; s. John Axley and Ella Vernon (Porter) G.; m. Jackie Lynne Herron, Dec. 20, 1958; children: Jennifer Lynne, Kelley Elizabeth. BA, Emory & Henry Coll., 1959; BD, Emory U., 1963, PhD, 1969. Prof., assoc. dean Wesleyan Coll., Macon, Ga., 1966-77; dean of faculty Millsaps Coll., Jackson, Miss., 1977-80; pres. Lambuth U., Jackson, Tenn., 1980-87; dir., gen. editor Scholars Press, Atlanta, 1987—; cons. vis., candidacy coms. 7 instns. So. Assn. Coll. Schs., chmn. Appeals Com., 1986, mem. spl. com. 1986; rev., analysis pub. program profl. soc.; cons., mem. pub. coms. nat. socs. Author: Editors Handbook, 1993, The If-You Form in Israelite Law, 1975; contbr. numerous articles, papers; speaker seminars, schs., socs. Bd. dirs. Nat. Assn. Schs. Colls. United Meth. Ch., 1984-86, chmn. planning, implementation com., 1984-86; exec. com. Tenn. Independent Coll. Fund, 1984-86, chmn. computer com., 1985; exec. com. Tenn. Coun. Private Colls., 1982-85; bd. dirs. Jackson Symphony Assn., 1980-86, Jackson Community Concert Assn., 1980-82, United Way of Jackson, 1981-84, Vol. Macon, 1975-76, Macon Urban Ministry, 1975-77, Macon Community Concert Assn., 1968-70; mem. steering com. Macon Coun. World Affairs, 1967-69; pres. Macon Coun. Expt. Internat. Living, 1971-73; trustee Chgo. Theol. Sem., 1999—. Recipient Purple Bathtub award Lambda Chi Alpha, 1980, Advancement Sexual Equality award Sigma Lambda, 1980; Dempster fellow, O.M. Miller scholar, Nat. Defense fellow Emory Univ., Nat. Meth. scholar Emory and Henry Coll. Mem. Tenn. Coll. Assn. (exec. com. 1981-84, pres. 1983-84), Soc. Scholarly Pub., Am. Acad. Religion, Soc. Biblical Lit., Am. Soc. Assn. Execs., Nat. Ctr. for Non-profit Bds., Rotary Club (West DeKalb bd. dirs. 1990-92, classification com. 1989—), Jackson C. of C. (bd. dirs. 1985-86, leadership Jackson 1980), Omicron Phi Tau, Omicron Delta Kappa, Alpha Epsilon Delta (hon.), Beta Beta Beta (hon.), Alpha Gamma Psi (hon.), Theta Phi (hon.), Sigma Mu (hon.), Blue Key. Avocations: electronics, music, genealogical rsch., internat. travel, photography. Office: Scholars Press 825 Houston Mill Rd NE Atlanta GA 30329-4246

GILMER, ROBERT, mathematics educator; b. Pontotoc, Miss., July 3, 1938; s. Robert William and Lucy Marie (Jernigan) G.; m. Rachel Grace Colson, Aug. 24, 1963; children: David Patrick, Stephen Douglas. Student, Itawamba Jr. Coll., 1955-56; B.S., Miss. State U., 1958; M.S., La. State U., 1960, Ph.D., 1961. Instr., Miss. State U., Starkville, 1958; vis. prof. Miss. State U., 1962; research instr. La. State U., Baton Rouge, 1961-62; vis. lectr. U. Wis., Madison, 1962-63; mem. faculty Fla. State U., Tallahassee, 1963—; prof. math. Fla. State U., 1968—, Robert O. Lawton Disting. prof., 1981—; vis. prof. Latrobe U., Bundoora, Victoria, Australia, 1974, U. Tex., Austin, 1976-77; vis. rsch. prof. U. Conn., Storrs, 1982; visitor Inst. for Advanced Study, 1990; vis. scholar U. N.C., Chapel Hill, 1997. Author: Multiplicative Ideal Theory, 1967, 72, 92, Commutative Semigroup Rings, 1984; also articles; assoc. editor Am. Math. Mo., 1971-73; editorial bd. Jour. Communications in Algebra, 1974-85. Named Barrett Meml. Lectr., U. Tenn., Knoxville, 1994; Office Naval Rsch. fellow, 1962-63; Alfred P. Sloan Found. fellow, 1965-67; NSF grantee, 1965-89; Fulbright sr. scholar to Australia, 1974. Mem. Am. Math. Soc., Math. Assn. Am. (gov. Fla. sect. 1986-89, cert. meritorious svc. 1992). Baptist. Home: 2414 Perez Ave Tallahassee FL 32304-1329

GILMORE, BEVERLY J, retired journalist, gallery owner; b. Monroe, Mich., Mar. 7, 1933; d. James B. and Verna L. (Dahlke) G.; m. Richard J. Loftus (div. 1963); m. Irving B. Pearlman (div. 1974); m. Robert E. Huber (div. 1987); children: Richard G. Loftus, Laidainn M. Gilmore, Nicholas E.D. Gilmore. BA in Journalism, U. Wis., 1954, MA in Journalism, 1959; postgrad., NYU. Assoc. editor Elec. Info. Publs., Madison, Wis., 1954-55; editor Gainesville (Fla.) Sun, 1956-57; editor Office Editl. and Comms. Svcs. U. Wis., Madison, 1957-60; editor Grad. Coll. U. Ill., Champaign, 1962-63; asst. book rev. editor Libr. Jour., N.Y.C.; copy editor, reporter S.I. (N.Y.) Advance, 1971-72; trend editor, syndicated writer Newhouse News Svc., 1972-87; co-owner Glen Arbor (Mich.) City Limits, 1987-94; mgr. Molly Phinny Gallery, Glen Arbor, 1995; mem. nat. nominating com. Coty Fashion Critics awards, Cutty Sark Menswear awards, 1974-86; juror sr. style projects Parsons (N.Y.) Sch. Design, 1975-85; judge features category Pa. Press Women's Ann. Contest, 1982. Co-founder Wis. Studies in Contemporary Lit., 1958; contbr. articles to profl. publs. Trustee Leelanau Hist. Soc., 1992-94; mem. steering com. Women Bus. Owners Leelanau, 1989-94; mem. Hudson River Environ. Group Clearwater, Inc., 1982—; mem. Friends of Crystal River Environ. Group, 1986—; mem. Integrated Liberal Studies alumni com. U. Wis., 1982-84, Daily Cardinal Alumni Assn. U. Wis., 1998—; mem. Mud Ln. Soc. for the Renaissance of Stapleton, 1979-87, co-chmn. 5th ann. house tour, 1981; mem., bd. dirs. Conf. House Assn. N.Y.C. Landmark, chmn., membership drive and benefit Evening with Letitia Baldrige, 1977-87; mem., bd. dirs. Preservation League of Staten Island, 1981-85. Recipient Nat. Fashion Journalism Lulu awards Men's Fashion Assn. Am., 1978-85, Cultured Pearl Assn. Am. and Japan Outstanding Media award, 1985, Outstanding Person of Grand Traverse Area-Traverse City (Mich.) Record-Eagle Picks of 1988. Mem. Fashion Group (N.Y. chpt.), Glen Lake-Sleeping Bear C. of C. (co-founder ann. holiday marketplace 1987), bd. dirs. 1988-90), Theta Sigma Phi, Alpha Chi Omega. Home: PO Box 4713 Santa Rosa Beach FL 32459-4713

GILMORE, CATHERINE RYE, arts administrator; b. Birmingham, Ala., Mar. 7, 1947; d. Thomas Aloyisius and Eva Catherine (Hydinger) Crawford; m. James William Rye, May 25, 1968 (div.); children: James William III, Susan Crawford Rye; m. Victor Alan Gilmore, May 23, 1986. BA in Theatre, Birmingham So. U., 1968; postgrad., U. Ala., Birmingham. Actress profl. cabaret theatre Atlanta and Birmingham, 1970-80; talk show host WBMG-TV, Birmingham, 1980-82; exec. dir. Met. Arts Coun., Birmingham, 1996—; instr. U. Ala., Birmingham, 1979-80. Stage appearances include Peter Pan, 1974, Sweet Charity, 1975, Wit's Other End Cabaret Theatre, 1976-80. Mem. The Women's Network, Birmingham; leadership class Birmingham C. of C., 1989; bd. dirs. Operation New Birmingham, Region 20/20. Recipient Silver Bowl award Festival of Arts, Birmingham, 1989, Obelisk award Arts Cmty., Birmingham, 1978; named one of Top 10 Corporate Women in Birmingham, Birmingham Bus. Jour., 1996. Episcopalian. Office: Metropolitan Arts Council PO Box 370263 Birmingham AL 35237-0263

GILMORE, CLARENCE PERCY, writer, magazine editor; b. Baton Rouge, Feb. 8, 1926; s. Clarence Percy and Clara (Cobb) G.; m. V. Elaine Oliver, 1985; children: Robert Dillard, Patricia Anne. Student, La. State U., 1942-44, 46-48. Reporter various radio, TV stas., 1948-56, free-lance mag. writer, 1956—; sci. editor Metromedia TV, 1967-84; exec. editor Popular Sci. Mag., 1971-80, editor-in-chief, 1980-89; dep. editorial dir. Times Mirror Mags., N.Y.C., 1989-92, ret., 1992; cons. in field. With USNR, 1944-46. Recipient Claude Bernard sci. journalism award Nat. Soc. Med. Rsch., 1969, Albert and Mary Lasker Found. award, 1969, Howard W. Blakeslee award Am. Heart Assn., 1969, Spl. Commendation for med. journalism AMA, 1969, 70, Sci. Writing award for physics and astronomy Am. Inst. Physics, 1970, Sci. Writing award AAAS, 1980. Home: 19725 Creekround Ave Baton Rouge LA 70817-1915

GILMORE, GAIL PEARSALL, consultant, writer; b. Toronto, July 6, 1948; d. Francis Samuel and Burrell Irene (Smith) Pearsall; m. Franklin Lee Gilmore, Jan. 1, 1982. BS in Journalism, U. Fla., 1969; MS, Va. Commonwealth U., 1995. Reporter Ft. Lauderdale (Fla.) News and Sun-Sentinel, 1968-71; sr. pub. affairs specialist U. Fla., Gainesville, 1971-75; asst. v.p. pub. rels. United Va. Bank, Richmond, 1976-83; writer/reporter Richmond News Leader, 1983-84; pub. affairs specialist E.I. DuPont, Newark, Del., 1984-92; mem adj. faculty Va. Commonwealth U. and John Tyler C.C., Richmond, 1992—; counselor IRS/AARP Tax-Aide, 1998—. Prodr./host (TV program) Insight, 1984-89; prodn. asst. WCVE-TV, 1998—. Election ofcl. Chesterfield County, Va., 1994—; vol. Ctrl. Va. Pub. TV, Richmond, 1994-97; docent Va. Mus. Fine Arts, 1998—. Recipient Disting. Svc. award Internat. Assn. Bus. Communicators, 1992, Hall of Fame scholarship Va. Commonwealth U., 1994. Mem. Soc. Profl. Journalists (treas. 1993-94, sec. 1994-95, v.p. 1995-96, pres. 1996-97), Sycamore Woman's Club (corr. sec. 1995-97, treas. 1997-99), Phi Kappa Phi.

GILMORE, HELEN CAROL, computer specialist, executive; b. Trenton, N.J.; d. Louis Alfred and Catherine (Peto) Fennimore; m. Lester Wayne Gilmore, Oct. 18, 1963; 1 child, Matthew Todd. Student, Purdue U., 1977-78, St. Mary-of-the-Woods Coll., 1980-85. Stenographer USAF, McGuire AFB, N.J., 1958-63; investigative recorder USAF, McGuire AFB, 1963-65; assoc. realtor Faherty Real Estate, Bordentown, N.J., 1969-74; asst. terminal mgr. G&G Tank Co., Inc., Columbus, N.J., 1974-76; adminstrv. asst. to assoc. dean Krannert Grad. Sch. Mgmt., Purdue U., West Lafayette, Ind., 1976-78; cons. Secs., Inc., Oak Brook, Ill., 1979; adminstrv. asst. to dir. materials Amphenol N.Am., Bunker Ramo Corp., Broadview, Ill., 1979-80; inventory specialist, product planner Amphenol N.Am., Bunker Ramo Corp., Broadview, 1980-81; system analyst Eastman Kodak Co., Oak Brook, Ill., 1981-85; applications engr. Eastman Kodak Co., Oak Brook, 1985-87; sr. system engr. NBI, Inc., Chgo., 1987, mgr. tech. support, 1988; tng. devel. mgr. Crawford & Assocs., Chgo., 1988-89; regional systems cons. Xyvision Inc., Chgo., 1990-91; owner Image Dynamix, Chgo., 1990—; mgr. nat. programs application engring. Frame Tech. Inc., Oak Brook, Ill., 1991-93; dir. tech. svcs. ArborText Inc., Ann Arbor, Mich., 1993-97; dir. tech. resources and cons. svcs. Adobe Sys., Inc., San Jose, Calif., 1997—. Mem. N.J. Assn. Realtors, Am. Bus. Women's Assn. (chpt. v.p. 1979), Nat. Assn. Female Execs., Soc. Office Automation Profls. (charter), Am. Prodn. and Inventory Control Soc. Office: 345 Park Ave San Jose CA 95051

GILMORE, HORACE WELDON, federal judge; b. Columbus, Ohio, Apr. 4, 1918; s. Charles Thomas and Lucille (Weldon) G.; m. Mary Hays, June 20, 1942; children—Lindsay Gilmore Feinberg. A.B., U. Mich., 1939, J.D., 1942. Bar: Mich. bar 1946. Law clk. U.S. Ct. Appeals, 1946-47; practiced in Detroit, 1947-51; spl. asst. U.S. atty., Detroit, 1951-52; mem. Mich. Bd. Tax Appeals, 1954; dep. atty. gen. State of Mich., 1955-56; circuit judge 3d Jud. Circuit, Detroit, 1956-80; judge U.S. Dist. Ct. (ea. dist.) Mich., 1980—; now sr. judge U.S. Dist. Ct. (ea. dist.) Mich., Detroit; adj. prof. law Wayne State U. Law Sch., 1966-82; lectr. law U. Mich. Law Sch., 1969-90; faculty Nat. Coll. State Judiciary, 1966-83; mem. Mich. Jud. Tenure Commn., 1969-76; chmn. Mich. Com. to Revise Criminal Code, 1965-82, Mich. Com. to Revise Criminal Procedure, 1971-79; trustee Inst. for Ct. Mgmt. Author: Michigan Civil Procedure Before Trial, 2d edit, 1975; contbr. numerous articles to legal jours. Served with USNR, 1942-46. Mem. ABA, State Bar Mich., Am. Judicature Soc., Am. Law Inst., Nat. Conf. State Trial Judges. Office: US Dist Ct 867 US Courthouse 231 W Lafayette Blvd Detroit MI 48226-2702*

GILMORE, JAMES STANLEY, JR., broadcast executive; b. Kalamazoo, June 14, 1926; s. James Stanley and Ruth (McNair) G.; m. Diana Holdenreide Fell, May 21, 1949 (dec.); children: Bethany, Sydney, James III, Elizabeth, Ruth. Student, Culver Mil. Acad., Western Mich. U., Kalamazoo Coll., 1945; Litt.D. (hon.), Nazareth Coll. Owner, chmn. CEO Jim Gilmore Enterprises, Kalamazoo, 1960—; CEO Gilmore Broadcasting Corp.; chmn. Cole/Gilmore; chmn., dir. Continental Corp. Mich.; former asst. sec. dir. Fabri-Kal Plastics Corp., Kalamazoo; pres. Wings Stadium Mgmt. Co.; former dir. First Am. Bank-Mich. N.A., First Am. Bank Corp.; former mem. Pres.' Citizens Adv. Com. on Environ. Quality; former dir. Fed. Home Loan Bank Bd., Indpls.; mem. past chmn. Mich. Water Resources Commn.; past mem. Pres.'s Commn. Health Phys. Edn. Sports; Nat. Assn. Broadcasters' adv. com. to Corp. for Pub. Broadcasting; pres. Kalamazoo County Young Rep. Club, 1947-49; mayor Kalamazoo, 1959-61; past mem. Kalamazoo County Bd. Suprs.; past chmn. exec. com. Kalamazoo County Reps., del. Rep. Nat. Conv. Assoc. bd. dirs.; 1st 4-time Indy 500-mile race with AJ Foyt as driver (Gilmore/Foyt Team). Assoc. bd. dirs. Boys Clubs Am.; bd. dirs., past chmn. Kalamazoo County chpt. A.R.C.; former chmn. bd. trustees Nazareth Coll.; trustee, mem. finance com. Greater Mich. Devel. Found.; mem., chmn. bldg. com. fund dr. Constance Brown Speech and Hearing Center; past trustee Kalamazoo Coll.; mem. adv. group Center Urban Studies and Community Services; trustee past vice chmn. Kalamazoo Nature Center; mem. bldg. and exec. coms. Bronson Hosp., also chmn. ad hoc legis. com.; past trustee, past v.p. Mich. Found. for Arts, Detroit; founding chmn. Kalamazoo City High on Heroes; founder bd. dirs. Martin Luther King Meml. Fund; life dir. Family Service Center Kalamazoo; mem. Mich. bd. dirs. Radio Free Europe, Novi Motorsports Mus.; nat. sponsor Ducks Unltd.; life mem. March Dimes; chmn. spl. reorganizational com. United Fund; mem. fund raising com. Pres. Ford Library/Mus.; mem. Pres.'s Council Phys. Fitness and Sports; mem. Republican Nat. Adv. Bd.; hon. trustee Mich. Alvin Bentley Charitable Found.; trustee emeritus coun. Kalamazoo Found. Served with USAAF, 1943-46. Named Kalamazoo Young Man of 1960, One of Mich.'s 5 Young Men of 1960, hon. citizen of Houston and Indpls.; recipient Ann. Service to Mankind award Sertoma Club, Man of Yr. award Mich. Auto Racing Fan Club, Auto Racing Found. Frat., honors Hoosier Racing Assn., Auto Racing Frat. Found., Inc., Milw. Mem. Kalamazoo County C. of C. (past pres., dir., mem. exec. com., indsl. devel. com.), Mich. C. of C. (law and order com.), NAM, Mich. Acad. Sci., Arts and Letters, Capitol Hill Club, Nat. Captioning Inst. (bd. dirs.), CEO Coun. (bd. dirs.), Park Club (past dir.), Mid-Am. Club, Kalamazoo Country Club, Met. Club. Roman Catholic. Office: Jim Gilmore Enterprises 162 E Michigan Ave Kalamazoo MI 49007-3908

GILMORE, JAMES STUART, III, governor; b. Richmond, Va., Oct. 6, 1949; s. James Stuart, Jr. and Margaret Kandle G. BA, U. Va., 1971, JD, 1977. Atty. Harris, Tuck, Freasier & Johnson, 1977-80, Benedetti, Gilmore, Warthen & Dalton, 1984-87; commonwealth's atty. Henrico County, Va., 1987-93; atty. gen. Commonwealth of Va., 1993-97; pntr. LeClair Ryan, Richmond, Va., 1997; gov. Commonwealth of Va., 1998—; alt. del. Rep. Nat. Conv., 1976; chmn. Henrico County Rep. Com., 1982-85. With U.S. Army, 1971-74. Mem. Nat. Dist. Atty. Assn., Va. Bar Assn., Va. Trial Lawyers Assn., Va. Commonwealt Attys. Assn. Methodist. Office: Office of Gov State Capitol Bldg 3rd Fl Richmond VA 23219*

GILMORE, JENNIFER A.W., computer specialist; b. San Fernando, Trinidad, Jan. 12, 1954; came to U.S., 1972; d. Fitzroy Grant and Zelma (Williams) Oudkerk; m. Frederick R. Gilmore, June 17, 1983. BA, MA, Bklyn. Coll., 1984; BBA, MS, Baruch Coll., 1993; MBA, L.I. U., 1994; postgrad., Walden U., 1994—. COBOL programmer MetLife, N.Y.C., 1972-86; computer specialist IV human resources adminstrn. mgmt. info. sys. City of N.Y., 1990—; adj. prof. N.Y.C. Tech. Coll., 1997—, Kingsborough C.C., 1998—, St. Francis Coll., Bklyn., 1998—, Medgar Evers Coll., 1998—, Borough of Manhattan C.C., 1998—, Touro Coll., 1999, Baruch Coll., 1999—. Home: 47 Mckeever Pl Apt 16J Brooklyn NY 11225-2537 Office: NYC-HRA-MIS 111 8th Ave New York NY 10011-5201

GILMORE, JERRY CARL, lawyer; b. Memphis, Tex., Dec. 29, 1933; s. Hugh Bailey and Gladys Herd (Jones) G.; m. Martha Niendorff, Dec. 1, 1956; children: Daniel, Susan, Charles. B.A., U. Tex., 1955, J.D., 1957. Bar: Tex. 1957. Practice law Dallas, 1957—; pres. North Ctrl. Tex. Coun. Govts., 1974-75, gen. counsel, 1986—, also exec. bd.; chmn. steering com. transp. Nat. League of Cities, 1974; mem. Dallas City Coun., 1971-75. Mem. City of Dallas Transit Bd., 1979-80; former bd. dirs., pres. Suicide Prevention of Dallas; former chmn. bd. trustees Dallas County Mental Health-Mental Retardation Ctr.; trustee Dallas C.C. Dist., 1976-92, chmn. 1981-82, 85-86; trustee Meth. Med. Ctr., Dallas, 1986—, vice chmn., 1990-96, chmn., 1996—; bd. dirs. Meth. Hosp. Dallas, 1996—; ; bd. dirs. home mission bd. So. Bapt. Conv., 1979-85, chmn. 1983-85; active Dallas Area Rapid Transit Bd., 1993-95; bd. trustees Tex. Scottish Rite Hosp. for Children, 1994—. Named Outstanding Young Lawyer, Dallas Jr. Bar Assn., 1971; recipient Outstanding Community Service award Oak Cliff Civitan Club, 1972. Mem. ABA, Dallas Bar Assn., Tex. Bar Assn., High Noon Club of Dallas (pres. 1967-68), Dallas Assembly, Oak Cliff C. of C., Masons, Lions, Delta Theta Phi. Methodist. Home: 19 Turtle Creek Bnd Dallas TX 75204-1635 Office: 1717 Main St Ste 4400 Dallas TX 75201-7357

GILMORE, JUDITH MARIE, physician; b. Houston, Dec. 28, 1942; d. Howard Ray and Mary Gardner (Currier) G.; m. Richard E. Kelley, July 21, 1974 (div. 1981); 1 child, Lisa Kelley. BA, U. Maine, 1965; MA, NYU, 1968; MD, Woman's Med. Coll., 1972. Diplomate Am. Bd. Internal Medicine, Am. Bd. Endocrinology. Resident St. Vincent's Hosp., N.Y.C., 1972-74; fellow in endocrinology St. Raphael's Hosp., New Haven, 1974-75, West Haven VA-Yale Hosp., New Haven, 1975-76; pvt. practice Bridgeport, Conn., 1976-80, Cranston, R.I., 1986—; mem. staff St. Joseph's Hosp., Providence, 1986—; mem. cons. staff Newport (R.I.) Hosp., 1986—; mem. courtesy staff Roger Williams Hosp., Providence, 1994—, R.I. Hosp., Providence, 1995. Lt. comdr. USNR, 1980-86. Mem. ACP, AMA, Am. Assn. Endocrine, Am. Diabetes Assn., R.I. Endocrine Assn. Avocations: hiking, music, art. Office: 725 Reservoir Ave Ste 2 Providence RI 02910-4450

GILMORE, KATHI, state treasurer; b. Dec. 23, 1944; m. Richard Gilmore; children: Suzi, Barb, Jeff, Amy. Mem. N.D. Ho. of Reps. from Dist. 6, 1989-92; treas. State of N.D., 1993—; mem. Bd. Tax Equalization, State Hist. Bd., State Investment Bd., Tchrs. Fund for Retirement Bd., State Canvassing Bd., Bd. of Univ. and Sch. Lands. Mem. Nat. Conf. State Liquor Adminstrs., Nat. Assn. State Treas. (pension com.), Retirement and Investment Office Internal Audit Com., Assn. Securities Profls. (hon. cochair pension fund conf. 1994), Task Forces Orgnl. Planning and Coordinating Com. 1993). Democrat. Presbyterian. Office: State Treasurer 600 E Boulevard Ave Bismarck ND 58505-0600

GILMORE, MAURICE EUGENE, mathematics educator; b. N.Y.C., Jan. 2, 1938; s. Maurice Eugene and Mary Wells (Barnes) G.; m. Julie Anne Rogers, June 20, 1964 (div. 1989); children: Peter Barnes, Christopher Alan, Jessica Lynn; m. Cathi Leslie Sonneborn, Sept. 1, 1991. BA, Georgetown U., 1959; MS, Syracuse U., 1961; PhD, U. Calif., Berkeley, 1967. Instr. Northeastern U., Boston, 1966-68, asst. prof., 1968-72, assoc. prof., 1972-78, prof., 1978—, chmn. math. dept., 1975-88; vis. prof. U. Tecnica Del Estado, Santiago, Chile, 1968, U. of Sussex, Falmer, U.K., 1989. NSF grantee, 1979, 92, 99; CNSF grantee, 1999.. Mem. Math. Assn. Am., Am. Math. Soc., Nat. Coun. Tchrs. Math., Assn. Tchrs. Math. Mass., Am. Statis. Assn. Office: Northeastern U 360 Huntington Ave Boston MA 02115-5000

GILMORE, MIKAL GEORGE, critic, journalist, author; b. Portland, Oreg., Feb. 9, 1951; s. Frank Harry and Bessie (Brown) G.; m. Erin Cowley, Aug. 21, 1982 (div. 1985). Student, Portland State U., 1969-74. Freelance writer Rolling Stone Mag., San Francisco, 1976-77; assoc. editor Rolling Stone Mag., L.A., 1977-80, contbg. editor, 1980-90, sr. writer, 1990—; music critic Los Angeles Herald Examiner, 1982-87; freelance journalist, author Los Angeles and N.Y.C., 1987—; sr. writer Rolling Stone Mag., L.A., 1990-98. Author: Shot in the Heart, 1993 (Nat. Book Critics Circle award for biography 1994). Recipient Deems Taylor award ASCAP, N.Y., 1983, 84. Democrat. Mormon. Avocation: studying popular culture and its place in history. Office: Rolling Stone Mag Att Mikal Gilmore 5700 Wilshire Blvd Ste 555 Los Angeles CA 90036-3630*

GILMORE, PHILIP NATHANAEL, finance educator, accountant; b. Northville, Mich., Mar. 13, 1944; s. Herbert Earl and Ruth Elaine (Shull) G.; m. JoAnn Wilson, Aug. 7, 1965; children: Martha K., David P., Rebecca J., Laurel A. BBA, U. Mich., Dearborn, 1967; MBA, U. Mich., 1968; postgrad., Nova Southeastern U., 1998—. CPA, Va.; CFP; cert. internal auditor Inst. Internal Auditors; cert. mgmt. acct. Inst. Mgmt. Accts.; fin. mgr. Inst. Fin. Mgmt. Dir. acctg. Moody Bible Inst., Chgo., 1973-76, asst. mgr. investments, 1976-79; contr. Old Time Gospel Hour, Lynchburg, Va., 1979-81, dir. estates & trusts, 1981-83; prin. Philip N. Gilmore, CPA, Lynchburg, Va., 1984; from asst. to assoc. prof. Liberty U., Lynchburg, Va., 1985—; acctg. cons., Lynchburg, Va., 1979—. Mem. AICPA, Inst. Cert. Fin. Planners, Inst. Cert. Mgmt. Accts. Baptist. Avocations: music, investing, sports. Home: 202 Colington Dr Lynchburg VA 24502-2506 Office: Liberty U PO Box 20000 Lynchburg VA 24506-8001

GILMORE, ROBERT WITTER, foundation administrator; b. College Corner, Ohio, Sept. 6, 1933; s. Robert Foster and Frances Elizabeth (Witter) G.; m. Sara Louise McIntosh, Dec. 23, 1956; children: Susan Lynne, Robert Riley, Christopher Edwin. EdB, Miami U., Oxford, Ohio, 1955; M in Social Work, Ohio State U., 1957. Exec. dir. United Way, Massillon, Ohio, 1960-64, St. Joseph, Mo., 1964-69, Dayton, Ohio, 1969-78, Cin., 1978-88; ret. United Way, 1988, cons., 1988—. 1st lt. U.S. Army, 1957-60. Named Man Of Yr. Jr. C. of C., St. Joseph, 1967. Mem. Assn. Cert. Profl. Social Workers (cert.), Queen City Club, Rotary, Masons, Sigma Chi. Avocation: golf. Home: 6424 Butler Israel Rd College Corner OH 45003-9797 also: 15653 Carriedale Ln Fort Myers FL 33912-3927

GILMORE, ROBIN HARRIS, nursing administrator; b. Wilmington, N.C., Apr. 23, 1964; d. John Sidney and Emily (Newton) Harris; m. Christopher Alan Gilmore, Feb. 20, 1993. AAN, Southeastern C.C., 1987; student, U. N.C. (Pembroke), 1997—. RN, ACLS, BTLS, MICN. From staff nurse to asst. nurse mgr. ER Columbus County Hosp., Whiteville, N.C., 1993-95; critical care nurse mgr., current CCU and emergency dept. Columbus County Hosp., Whiteville, 1995—. Mem. Emergency Nurses Assn. Republican. Baptist. Avocations: cooking, water skiing, snow skiing. Home: PO Box 1835 Whiteville NC 28472-1835 Office: Columbus County Hosp 500 Jefferson St Whiteville NC 28472-3696

GILMORE, ROGER, college president; b. Phila., Oct. 11, 1932; s. Wheeler and Edith Seal (Thompson) G.; m. Beatrice Reynolds, Sept. 17, 1952 (dec. Sept. 1994); children: Christopher, Jennifer E., Lesley Margaret; m. Elizabeth McOuat Lameyer, Oct. 1, 1995. AB, Dartmouth Coll., 1954; postgrad., U. Chgo. Div. Sch., 1958-63; DFA (hon.), Sch. Art Inst. Chgo., 1993. Social worker N.H. Dept. Pub. Welfare, Woodsville, 1954-55; adminstrv. asst. Furn Corp. Lisbon, N.H., 1955-56; office mgr., asst. to pres. Cole's Mill Inc., Littleton, N.H., 1956-58; acct., office supr. U. Chgo., 1958-61, asst. dir. fin. aid, 1961-63; asst. to dean Sch. Art Inst. Chgo., 1963-65, acting dean, 1965-68, dean, 1968-87, provost, v.p. for acad. affairs, 1987-89; pres. Maine Coll. Art (formerly Portland Sch. Art), 1989—; dir. Commn. Accreditation and Membership Nat. Assn. Schs. of Art and Design, 1975-78, v.p. 1984-87, pres., 1987-90; mem. Joint Commn. on Dance and Theatre Accreditation, 1978-82; bd. dirs. Internat. Coun. Fine Arts Deans, 1986-88; pres., bd. dirs. Ox-Bow Summer Sch. and Artists Colony, 1987-89; treas. Assn. Ind. Colls. Art and Design, 1991-95; mem. exec. com. Maine Higher Edn. Coun., 1991-95. Bd. dirs. Maine Alliance for Arts Edn., 1992-94, Greater Portland Landmarks, 1993—, Stanley Mus., 1993-95, World Affairs Coun., 1993-95. Fellow Nat. Assn. Schs. Art and Design (life); mem. Maine Citizens for Hist. Preservation, Nat. Trust for Hist. Preservation, Advs. for Arts, Nat. Art Edn. Assn., Maine Alliance for Arts Edn. Democrat. Episcopalian. Home: 24 Fairmount St Portland ME 04103-3051 Office: Maine Coll of Art 97 Spring St Portland ME 04101-3933

GILMORE, TIMOTHY JONATHAN, paralegal; b. Orange, Calif., June 24, 1949; s. James and Margaret (Swanson) G.; m. Blanche Jean Panter, Sept. 3, 1984; children: Erin, Sean and Brian (twins). BA, St. Mary's Coll., Moraga, Calif., 1971; grad., Denver Paralegal Inst., 1996. Adminstrv. asst. Gov. Ronald Reagan, Sacramento, Calif., 1971-73; salesman Penn Mutual, Anaheim, Calif., 1973-76; asst. devel. dir. St. Mary's Coll., Moraga, 1976-81; devel. dir. St. Alphonsus Hosp., Boise, Idaho, 1981-83; adminstr. Blaine County Hosp., Hailey, Idaho, 1983-86; exec. dir. Poudre Hosp. Found., Ft. Collins, Colo., 1986-87; nat. recruiting dir. Power Securities Corp., Denver, 1987-89; cons. Horn, Fagan & Lund Exec. Search Cons., Ft. Collins, 1989; v.p. Jackson & Coker Locum Tenens, Inc., Denver, 1990-93; pres. Gilmore and Assocs., Ft. Collins, Colo., 1993-98; paralegal Brownstein, Hyatt, Farber & Strickland, P.C., Denver, 1998—. Republican. Mem. LDS Ch. Avocation: fishing. E-mail: TG1527FC@aol.com. Home and Office: 1527 River Oak Dr Fort Collins CO 80525-5537

GILMORE, VANESSA D., federal judge; b. St. Albans, N.Y., Oct. 26, 1956. BS, Hampton U., 1977; JD, U. Houston, 1981. Bar: Tex. 1982, U.S. Ct. Appeals (5th cir.), U.S. Dist. Ct. (so. dist.) Tex. Fashion buyer Foley's Dept. Store, 1977-79; ptnr. Vickery, Kilbride, Gilmore & Vickery, Houston, 1981-85, 86-94; atty. Sue Schecter & Assocs., Houston, 1985-86; judge U.S. Dist. Ct. (So. dist.) Tex., Houston, 1994—; spkr. ATLA, San Diego, 1990, ABA, Atlanta, 1991, N.Y.C., 1993, Leadership Tex., Austin, 1992, Hampton U. Alumni Assn., Dallas, 1992, Laredo Bus. and Profl. Women's Assn., 1993, XI Ann. Border Gov.'s Conf., Monterrey, Mex., 1993, Gov.'s Bus. Devel. Coun., Ausitn, 1993, Tex. A&M U., 1993, State Bar of Tex., Austin, 1993, Houston Bus. Coun., 1993, Minority Enterprise Devel. Week, Houston, 1993, Holman St. Bapt. Ch., 1994, Greater Houston Women's Found., 1994, The Kinkaid Sch., 1995, So. Meth. U., Dallas, 1996, South Tex. Coll. of Law, 1996, among others. Contbr. articles to profl. jours. Bd. dirs. Houston Ballet, Tex. So. Univ. Found., Neighborhood Recovery Community Redevel. Corp., 1992-95; chair African Am. Art Adv. Assn., Mus. Fine Arts; mem. scv. acad. nominations bd. Rep. Jack Fields, Tex., 1993, 94; active Texans for NAFTA; mem. Tex. Dept. Commerce, 1991-94, chairperson, 1992-94; mem. adv. bd. St. Joseph's Hosp.; mem. Leadership Tex. Named One of Houston's Black Achievers, Human Enrichment of Life Program, 1989; recipient Citizen of the Month award Houston Defender, 1990, YWCA award, 1991, Austin Met. Resource Bus. Ctr. award, 1991, Houston Bus. and Profl. Men's Club award, 1992, Disting. Svc. award Nat. Black MBA Assn., 1994, Cmty. Svc. award Holman St. Bapt. Ch., 1994. Mem. ABA, NAACP (chair chs. and orgns. com. Freedom Fund banquets 1989-93), ATLA, Am. Leadership Forum, Tex. Trial Lawyers Assn., Tex. Lyceum Assn., Houston Bar Assn., Houston Lawyers Assn., U. Houston Law Alumni (bd. dirs. 1993—), W.J. Durham Legal Soc., Links, Inc. (Mo. chpt., chair LEAD substance abuse and teen pregnancy prevention program 1990-91). Office: US Courthouse 515 Rusk Ave Rm 9513 Houston TX 77002-2605

GILMORE, VOIT, travel executive; b. Winston-Salem, N.C., Oct. 13, 1918; s. John Merriman and Helen (Hensel) G.; m. Kathryn Kendrick, Jan. 21, 1945 (div. 1975); children: Kathryn, Geraldine, Susan, Peter, David.; m. Tatiana Dominick, July 4, 1982 (div. 1990); m. Josephine Baldwin, Nov. 23, 1990. BJ, U. N.C., 1939, M in Geography, 1985, PhD in Geography, 1987; grad., Nat. Inst. Pub. Affairs, Washington, 1940. Cert. travel counselor Inst. Cert. Travel Agts. Asst. to div. mgr. Pan Am. Airways, Miami, Fla., 1940-41; personnel mgr. Pan Am. Airways-Africa Ltd., Accra, Gold Coast, 1942-43; pub. relations dir. Pan Am. Airways, San Francisco, 1946-48; pres. Storey Corp. and affiliated cos., 1948-61, 64-83, Four Seasons Travel Service, Inc., 1971-95; dir. U.S. Travel Svc., Washington, 1961-64, So. Nat. Bank of N.C., 1980-95; news corr. to Arctic, 1958, Antarctic, 1958, 60, 61, 63; mem. adv. coun. U.S. Travel and Tourism Adminstrn., 1990-96. Contbr. articles on polar exploration to newspapers, mags. Mem. town coun., mayor, Southern Pines, N.C., 1953-57; mem. N.C. Senate, 1965-69, N.C. Bd. Conservation and Devel., 1957-61; trustee U. N.C., Fayetteville, 1981-87; mem. Gov.'s Adv. Com. on Travel and Tourism, 1982, N.C. Forestry Adv. Com., 1986; candidate for U.S. Congress from 8th Dist. N.C., 1968; bd. dirs. U. N.C. Sch. Journalism Found. (Chapel Hill). Lt. (j.g.) USN, 1943-46, PTO. Recipient European Tourism Golden Helm award, West Berlin, 1986, Parker award Travel Coun. N.C., 1997; elected to Travel Industry Assn. Hall of Leaders, 1988; Eagle Scout Boy Scouts Am. Fellow Royal Geog. Soc. (life), Explorers Club (life); mem. Am. Soc. Travel Agts. (pres. 1988-90), Assn. of Am. Geographers, Am. Forestry Assn. (pres. 1973-75), Soc. Am. Travel Writers, Travel Coun. N.C. (pres. 1969-71), Bohemian Club, Cosmos Club, Country Club N.C., Heidelburg Prince Club. Home and Office: 1600 Morganton Rd D-11 Pinehurst NC 28374-9077

GILMOUR, D(AVID) JAMES, strategic planner, systems analyst; b. Phila., July 10, 1947; s. James William and Florence Elizabeth (Weisbrod) G.; m. Deborah Anne Kaufold, July 2, 1977. BS, Muhlenberg Coll., 1969; MS in Adminstrn., George Washington U., 1974; MBA, Temple U., 1981; MS, U. Pa., 1995, MPhil, 1998. Analyst Nat. Security Agy., Ft. Meade, Md., 1970-74; programmer, analyst Rohm & Haas Co., Phila., 1974-77; staff economist Sun Oil Co., Radnor, Pa., 1977-85; project leader Arco Chem. Corp., Phila., 1985-87; asst. v.p. Corestates Fin. Corp., Phila., 1987-98, cons., 1998—; lead cohort U. Pa., Phila., 1997—. Author: How To Write Term Papers Real Good, 1996, The Corestates/University of Pennsylvania Strategic Planning Model, 1997, The Philadelphia Ethos, 1998; co-inventor semi-automatic pistol. With USN, 1970-74. Mem. NRA, Alpha Tau Omega (exchequer 1965-69, Thomas Arcle Clark award 1969), Am. Econ. Model of Core States Financial Corp., 1994. Republican. Anglican. Home and Office: 130 Spruce St Philadelphia PA 19106-4319

GILMOUR, DAVID PATTON, economic and community planner; b. Albany, N.Y., June 7, 1965; s. Francis Landy Patton and Marjorie (Dorn) G.; m. Elizabeth Ann Duncan, Jan. 7, 1995. BS, Northeastern U., 1989; cert. in pub. health, Harvard U., 1992; M in Cmty. Planning, U. R.I., 1996. Cert. Am. Inst. Cert. Planners. Rsch. asst. dept. environ. health Harvard Sch. Pub. Health, Boston, 1990-92; rsch. asst. dept. African and African Am. affairs U. R.I., Kingston, 1992-94, rsch. asst. coop. ext., 1994; environ. planner Practical Applications Inc., Boston, 1994-96; prin. U. & I. Planning Svcs., Beverly, Mass., 1996—; exec. dir., program mgr. Shirley (Mass.) Village Partnership, Inc., 1997-98; regional planner Nashua (N.H.) Regional Planning Com., 1998—; planning intern Providence Housing Authority, Providence, 1993. Mem. Boston Food Coop., 1988-92; dir. Action, Inc., Gloucester, Mass., 1996; mentor Beverly Youth Collaborative, 1997; participant Washington St. Connections/Boston-AIA, 1997—. Recipient Svc. award Northeastern Student Govt., Boston, 1987; named Exch. Student, Rotary Internat.-N.Y. chpt. to Republic South Africa, 1983. Mem. APHA, Am. Planning Assn. (student rep. R.I. chpt. 1992-94, student rep. N.E. region 1993-94, local exhibits com. 1997—, Cert. of Svc. 1994, R.I. Chpt. Student award 1994), U.S. Cycling Fedn., Profl. Ski Instrs. Am.

GILMOUR, DOUG, professional hockey player; b. Kingston, Ont., Canada, July 25, 1963. With St. Louis Blues, 1983-88, Calgary Flames, 1988-92, Toronto Maple Leafs, 1992-97, N.J. Devils, 1997-98, Chgo. Blackhawks, 1998—. Recipient Red Tilson Trophy, 1982-83, Eddie Powers Mem. Trophy, 1982-83, Frank J. Selke Trophy, 1992-93, 94. Member of 1989 Stanley Cup championship team. Played in NHL All-Star game, 1993. Office: Chgo Blackhawks 1901 W Madison St Chicago IL 60612-2459*

GILMOUR, EDWARD ELLIS, psychiatrist; b. Schenectady, May 6, 1930; s. William Ellis and Adeline (Campbell) G. B.Engring., Yale, 1952, M.A. in Philosophy, 1957; M.D., Boston U., 1961. Intern St. Luke's Hosp., N.Y.C., 1961-62, resident in medicine, 1962-64, resident in psychiatry, 1964-66, child psychiatry, 1966-68, asst. attending, child psychiatry, 1968-80, asso., 1980—; cons. community psychiatry, 1973-75, supr. residents, 1968—; individual practice medicine, specializing in adult, child and adolescent psychiatry and psychoanalysis, N.Y.C., 1968-82, Falmouth, Mass., 1982—; psychoanalytic tng. William Alanson White Inst., N.Y.C., 1969-74; attending psychiatrist Columbia U. Health Service, N.Y.C., 1969-74; staff psychiatrist Ittleson Center Child Research, Riverdale, N.Y., 1976-82; staff Falmouth Hosp., 1982—; mem. provisional staff St. Vincent Hosp., Santa Fe, 1995—; asst. clin. prof. N.Y.U., 1979—. Diplomate Am. Bd. Psychiatry and Neurology with subspltys. in adult and child psychiatry. Fellow Am. Acad. Psychoanalysis Am. Acad. Child Psychiatry; mem. Am. Psychiat. Assn., AMA, Mass. Med. Soc., William Alanson White Psychoanalytic Soc., Soc. Adolescent Psychiatry, Mass. Psychiat. Home: PO Box 10108 Santa Fe NM 87504-6108 Office: 1442 S Saint Francis Dr Ste C Santa Fe NM 87505-4031

GILMOUR, ROBERT ARTHUR, foundation executive, educator; b. L.A., Dec. 13, 1944; s. Leon and Helen (Lawrence) G.; m. Cathryn Anne Fontana, June 23, 1979; 1 child, Cathryn Elizabeth. AB magna cum laude, U. Calif., Davis, 1966; MA, Johns Hopkins U., 1969, PhD, 1972. Lectr. history U. Mich., Ann Arbor, 1970-72; asst. prof. U. Mich., 1972, Northwestern U., Evanston, Ill., 1972-75, Princeton (N.J.) U., 1975-81; rsch. fellow Am. Inst. for Econ. Rsch., Great Barrington, Mass., 1983; sr. assoc. Am. Inst. for Econ. Rsch., 1983-85; dir. rsch. Am. Inst. for Econ. Rsch., Great Barrington, Mass., 1985-91; chmn. faculty Am. Inst. for Econ. Rsch., Great Barrington, 1985-91, pres., CEO, 1991—; faculty assoc. Lincoln Inst. of Land Policy, Cambridge, Mass., 1993-98. Author: The Other Emancipation, 1972, How to Cover the Gaps in Medicare, 1983, 10th edit., 1992, America's Unknown Enemy, 1984, How to Cover the Gaps in Medicare after Catastrophic Coverage, 1989; co-author: (with L. Pratt) Coping with College Costs, 1987, Toward an Ethical Tax Base: Land, Labor, or Capital, 1994; gen. editor monetary conf. series Progress Found., Carona, Switzerland, 1988—. Trustee Berkshire C.C. Found., Pittsfield, Mass., 1982-84; mem. AIER Corp., Great Barrington, 1985—, Fin. Com., Peru, Mass., 1987-90; counsel for charitable activities Progress Found., 1991—, trustee, 1993—; bd. dirs. Robert Schalkenbach Found., N.Y.C., 1993—; mem. adv. bd. Found. for Advancement of Monetary Edn., 1997-99. Mem. AAAS, Am. Econ. Assn., Am. Fin. Assn., Union League Club (N.Y.C.), Worthington (Mass.) Golf Club, Phi Beta Kappa, Phi Kappa Phi. Office: AIER E C Harwood Libr Division St Great Barrington MA 01230-1000

GILMOUR, ROBERT S., political science educator; b. Phila., May 16, 1940; s. Albert A. and Irene L. (Owens) G.; m. Nanette Farmer, Mar. 4, 1960 (div. Nov. 1985); children: Robert S. Jr., James Owen, Kara Lynne; m. Barbara Hinkson Craig, Apr. 25, 1986. BA with high honors, U. Fla., 1962, MA in Polit. Sci., 1963; PhD in Pub. Law and Govt., Columbia U., 1968; postgrad., U. Conn., 1977. Bar: Vt. 1977, D.C. 1987, U.S. Dist. Ct. Vt. 1978, U.S. Tax Ct. 1979, U.S. Supreme Ct. 1985. Asst. prof. polit. sci. Columbia U., N.Y.C., 1967-74; assoc. DeBonis & Wright, Poultney, Vt., 1974-76; assoc. prof. polit. sci. U. Conn., Storrs, 1976-81, prof., 1981—, dir. Inst. Pub. & Urban Affairs, master Pub. Affairs program, 1998—; sr. profl. staff mem. U.S. Senate Govtl. Affairs Com., Washington, 1985-87; adminstrv. asst. to Gov. of Fla., Tallahassee, 1962-63; cons. in field. Author: Policy Making for the National Forests, 1973; co-author: Political Alienation in contemporary America, 1975, Politics, Position and Power, 1986, Who Makes Public Policy?, 1994; asst. mng. editor Jour. of Politics, 1959-62. Mem. Am. Soc. Pub. Adminstrn. (nat. coun. 1984-86, pres. Conn. chpt. 1982-83), N.Eng. Polit. Sci. Assn. (pres. 1987-88, mem. coun. 1985-92), Nat. Acad. Pub. Adminstrn. (assoc.), Am. Polit. Sci. Assn., Cosmos Club. Home: 224 Lake Rd Andover CT 06232-1708 Office: U Conn Inst Pub & Urban Affairs 421 Whitney Rd Storrs Mansfield CT 06269-9019

GILMOUR, WILLIAM, government official; b. Powell River, B.C., Can., Dec. 29, 1942. BS in Forestry, U. B.C. Reform party chief, environ. critic House of Commons, Ottawa, Ont., 1993—. Office: House of Commons, Rm 255 Wellington Bldg, Ottawa, ON Canada K1A 0A6*

GILPIN, DEBORAH J., museum administrator; b. Madison, Wis., Oct. 20, 1960. Exec. dir. Discovery Museums, Acton, Mass., 1994—. Office: Discovery Mus 177 Main St Acton MA 01720-3647*

GILPIN, HENRY EDMUND, III, photographer, educator; b. Cleve., Nov. 10, 1922; s. Henry Edmund Jr. and Eloise (Van Der Veer) G.; m. Doris Myers, June 29, 1946; children: Jean Gilpin-Freeman, James Howard. Student, Ansel Adams Yosemite Workshop. Tchr. Ansel Adams Yosemite Workshop, 1959-82, Monterey (Calif.) Peninsula Coll., 1964—; tchr. Aayosemits Workshop, 1967-73. Photographs included in collections of Amon Carter Mus., Ft. Worth, Walker Mus. Art, Mpls., Nat. Mus. Modern Art, Kyoto, Japan, Art and Sci. Mus., Nashua, N.H., Monterey Peninsula Mus. Art, also univs. Trustee Friends of Photography Ctr., San Francisco, 1969-79, Ctr. for Photographic Art, Carmel, Calif., 1989-93. 1st lt. USAF, 1942-45, ETO. Decorated Air Medal with 5 oak leaf clusters; D.F.C., Croix de Guerre, France, 1946. Home: 1353 Jacks Rd Monterey CA 93940-4910

GILPIN, LARRY VINCENT, retail executive; b. Benton, Ill., Sept. 8, 1943; s. Otis Edgar and Beulah May (Stalcup) G.; m. Daryl Elana Scott, Aug. 21, 1965; children: Valory, Lana, Scott, Lorra. B.S., Western Ky. U., 1965; M.B.A., U. Ky., 1971; postgrad., La. State U. Sr. staff cons. IBM Corp.; mgr. orgn. devel. Unijax, Kaiser Aluminium Co.; dir. personnel planning and employment Target Stores div. Dayton Hudson Corp., Mpls., to, 1981; sr. v.p. personnel Target Stores, 1981-90, exec. v.p. team, guest and cmty. rels., 1990-97; exec. v.p. team, guest and comml. rels. DHC & Target, Mpls., 1997—. Named Human Resource Exec. of Yr., Human Resource Mag., 1990. Office: Target Stores CC27E 22 S 6th St Minneapolis MN 55440-1392

GILPIN, PERI, actress; b. Waco, Tex.. Former student, Dallas Theatre Ctr., U. Tex., Brit.-Am. Acad., London. Appeared in (TV series) Frasier, Designing Women, Cheers, Wings, (TV movies) Fight for Justice: The Nancy Conn Story, 1995, The Secret She Carried, 1996. Office: care NBC 3000 W Alameda Ave Burbank CA 91523-0001*

GILPIN, ROBERT GEORGE, JR., political science educator; b. Burlington, Vt., July 2, 1930; s. Robert George and Beatrice (Sandspra) G.; m. Jean Millis, Aug. 13, 1955; children—Linda, Elizabeth, Robert. BA, U. Vt., 1952; MS, Cornell U., 1954; PhD, U. Calif., Berkeley, 1960. Fellow Harvard U., 1960-61; lectr. Columbia U., 1961-62; faculty Princeton U., 1962—, prof. polit. sci., 1970-98, Eisenhower prof. internat. affairs, 1975-98, prof. emeritus, 1998—; mem. Pres.'s Advisory Group Tech. and the Economy, 1975-76. Author: American Scientists and Nuclear Weapons Policy, 1962, France in the Age of the Scientific State, 1968, U.S. Power and the Multinational Corporation, 1975, War and Change in World Politics, 1981, The Political Economy of International Relations, 1987; co-author, co-editor: Scientists and National Policy Making, 1964. Served with USNR, 1954-57. Congl. fellow, 1959-60, Guggenheim fellow, 1969, Rockefeller fellow, 1967-68, 76-77. Fellow AAAS; mem. Am. Polit. Sci. Assn. (v.p. 1984-85). Home: 134 Moore St Princeton NJ 08540-3359

GILREATH, JERRY HOLLANDSWORTH, community planner; b. Smithville, Tenn., Jan. 19, 1934; s. Homer Freeman and Wallee (Hollandsworth) G.; m. Ellen Johnston, June 15, 1974; 1 child, Kathryn Ann. BS, Mid. Tenn. State Coll., 1956; MS in Planning, U. Tenn., 1972. Editor UPI, Frankfurt, Fed. Republic of Germany, 1959-60; proofreader Jones Composition, Inc., Washington, 1961-62; publ. asst. Am. Geophysical Union, Washington, 1963-65; editorial asst. Library of Congress, Washington, 1965-67, adminstrv. asst., 1968-69; community planner Nat. Capital Planning Commn., Washington, 1972—. Prin. author numerous planning reports, 1976-97. Lead Planner in update of the Federal Employment element of the Comprehensive Plan for the Natl. Capital, 1998-99, appointed mem. D.C. Bd. Zoning Adjustment, 1999. Mem. Am. Planning Assn. Democrat. Club: Little Falls Swimming and Tennis (Bethesda, Md.). Avocations: tennis, swimming, bicycling, reading. Home: 5103 Baltimore Ave Bethesda MD 20816-1605

GILROY, FRANK DANIEL, playwright; b. N.Y.C., Oct. 13, 1925; s. Frank B. and Bettina (Vasti) G.; m. Ruth Dorothy Gaydos, Feb. 13, 1954; children: Anthony, John and Daniel (twins). BA magna cum laude, Dartmouth Coll., 1950; postgrad., Yale Sch. Drama. Became TV writer, 1952; orignated TV series Burkes Law; TV writer, scripts prod. on programs including Playhouse 90, U.S. Steel Hour, Omnibus, Kraft Theatre, Lux Video Theatre, Studio One; writer, dir.: 40 Gibbsville, 1975, The Doorbell Rang, 1977, Money Plays, 1997; author play Who'll Save the Plowboy?, 1957, presented off-Broadway, 1962; completed play The Subject Was Roses, 1962, presented on Broadway, 1964; plays presented on Broadway That Summer-That Fall, 1967, The Only Game in Town, 1968, Last Licks, 1979, Any Given Day, 1993; one-act plays produced off-Broadway The Next Contestant, 1978, Real to Reel, 1987, Match Point, 1990, A Way With Words, 1991, Give the Bishop My Faint Regards, 1992; producer, writer, dir. films Desperate Characters, 1970 (best screenplay award Berlin Film Festival), From Noon Till Three, 1977, The Gig, 1985; producer, writer, dir. film Once in Paris (original screenplay), 1978; writer/dir. film The Luckiest Man in the World, 1989; author: Present Tense, prod. off-Broadway, 1972; author novels Private, 1970, (with Ruth Gilroy) Little Ego, 1970, From Noon till Three, 1973, (non-fiction) I Wake Up Screening-Everything You Need to Know About Making Independent Films Including A Thousand Reasons Not To, 1993; author screenplays (with Russell Rouse) The Fastest Gun Alive, 1956, (with Beirne Lay Jr.) Gallant Hours, 1960, Desperate Characters, 1971, The Subject was Roses, The Only Game in Town, From Noon till Three, Once in Paris. Served with AUS, 1943-46, ETO. Recipient Obie award for best Am. play, 1962; Outer Circle award, 1964; Drama Critics Circle award, 1964; N.Y. Theatre Club award, 1964-65; Antoinette Perry award, 1965; Pulitzer prize for drama, 1965. Mem. Writers Guild Am., Dramatists Guild (pres. 1969-71), Dirs. Guild Am.

GILROY, SUE ANNE, state official; m. Dick Gilroy; children: Emily (dec.), Grant. Grad. cum laude, DePauw U.; MA, Ind. U. Ordained elder Presbyn. Ch. Former profl. assoc. Office of Mayor Lugar; former dir. Parks and Recreation; asst. to pres. Ind. Ctrl. U. (now U. Indpls.); chair Mayor Steve Goldsmith's Transition Team, 1991-92; state dir. for Senator Richard Lugar, Ind., 1990-93; sec. of state State of Ind., 1994—. Cons. in fundraising and bus. adminstrn. Tabernacle Presbyn. Ch.; bd. dirs. St. Vincent Hosp Found., Julian Ctr., Cathedral H.S. Mem. Indpls. Rotary Club. Office: Office of the Sec of State State House Rm 201 Indianapolis IN 46204-2728*

GILROY, TRACY ANNE HUNSAKER, lawyer; b. St. Louis, Aug. 13, 1959; d. Raymond Thomas Hunsaker and Dorothy Jayne (Hickman) Hunsaker Reilly. BA, U. Dayton, 1981; JD, St. Louis U., 1984. Bar: Mo. 1984, Ill. 1985. Atty. Mo. State Hwy. and Transp. Dept., St. Louis, 1984-89; of counsel Draheim & Pranschke, St. Louis, 1989-94; pvt. practice The Gilroy Law Firm, St. Louis, 1994—. Mem. ABA (bar svcs. standing com., reporter The Affiliate, bd. dirs. LPM solo divsn.), Mo. Bar Assn. (chair eminent domain com., legis. com., bd. govs. 1998—), St. Louis Bar Found. (pres. 1998-99), St. Louis Met. Bar Assn. (pres. 1997-98, chair young lawyers sect. 1993, chair legis. com. 1985-87, chair, vice-chair, chair trial sect., chair social com., chair auction com., media com.), Woman Lawyers Assn. (mem.-at-large, chair legis. com. 1984-87, sec. 1987), Lawyers Assn., Assn. Trial Lawyers Am. Avocations: golf, skiing, bicycling, writing, painting. Office: Gilroy Law Firm 1610 Des Peres Rd # 300 Saint Louis MO 63131-1813

GILRUTH, ROBERT ROWE, aerospace consultant; b. Nashwauk, Minn., Oct. 8, 1913; s. Henry Augustus and Frances Marion (Rowe) G.; m. E. Jean Barnhill, Apr. 24, 1937 (dec. 1972); 1 dau., Barbara Jean (Mrs. John Wyatt); m. Georgene Hubbard Evans, July 14, 1973. B.S. in Aero. Engring, U. Minn., 1935, M.S., 1936, D.Sc., 1962; D.Sc., George Washington U., 1962, Ind. Inst. Tech., 1962; D.Eng., Mich. Tech. U., 1963; LL.D., N.Mex. State U., 1970. Flight research engr. Langley Aero. Lab., NACA, Langley Field, Va., 1937-45; chief pilotless aircraft research div. Langley Aero. Lab., NACA, 1945-50, asst. dir., 1950-58; dir. NASA Project Mercury, 1958-61, NASA Manned Spacecraft Ctr., Houston, 1961-72; dir. key personnel devel. NASA Manned Spacecraft Ctr., 1972-73, ret., 1973; cons. to adminstr. NASA, 1974—; dir. Bunker Ramo Corp. Ind. experimenter and cons. hydrofoil craft, 1938-58; advisor on guided missiles, aeros. and structures, high temperature facilities U.S. Dept. Def., 1947-58; mem. com. space systems NASA Space Adv. Council, 1972—; chmn. mgmt. devel. edn. panel NASA, 1972-73; mem. ad hoc com. fire safety aspects of polymeric materials Nat. Materials Adv. Bd., 1973-74. Recipient Outstanding Achievement award U. Minn., 1954, Great Living Am. award U.S. C. of C., 1962, Disting. Fed. Civilian Service award Pres. U.S., 1962, Americanism award CBI Vets. Assn., 1965, Spirit of St. Louis medal, 1965, Internat. Astronautics award Daniel and Florence Guggenheim, 1966, Disting. Service medal NASA, spring 1969, fall 1969, Pub. Service at Large award Rockefeller Found., 1969, ASME medal, 1970, James Watt Internat. medal, 1971, Achievement award Nat. Aviation Club, 1971, Robert J. Collier trophy with Nat Aero. Assn., 1972, Space Transp. award Louis W. Hill, Disting. Service medal NASA, medal of honor N.Y.C., Robert H. Goddard Meml. trophy Nat. Rocket Club, Nat. Air and Space Mus. trophy, 1985; named to Nat. Space Hall of Fame, 1969, Internat. Space Hall of Fame, 1976, Internat. Aerospace Hall of Fame, San Diego, 1992, Nat. Aviation Hall of Fame, Dayton, Ohio, 1994. Mem. Nat. Acad. Engring. (aeros. and space bd. 1974—), Nat. Acad. Scis. Home: 2600 Barracks Rd # 38 Charlottesville VA 22901-2100

GILSINN, DAVID EDMUND, mathematician, researcher; b. Washington, Jan. 25, 1943; s. David Leo and Doris (Dyson) G.; m. Judith Helen Forward, Aug. 6, 1966; 1 child, James David. BS, Georgetown U., 1964, PhD, 1969; MS, Rutgers U., 1966. Mathematician Melpar, Inc., McLean, Va., 1969-70, Nat. Inst. Standards & Tech., Gaithersburg, Md., 1970—. Contbr. articles to profl. jours. Fundraiser, co-chair St. Rose Lima Cath. Ch., Gaithersburg, 1993—. Recipient Bronze medal U.S. Dept. Commerce, Washington, 1994. Mem. ASME, Am. Soc. Precision Engring., Soc. Indsl. & Applied Math. Democrat. Office: Nat Inst Standards & Tech Bldg 223 Rm B102 Gaithersburg MD 20899

GILSON, ARNOLD LESLIE, retired engineering executive; b. Perrysburg, Ohio, Apr. 10, 1931; s. Leslie Clair and Velma Lillian (Hennen) G.; m. Phyllis Mary Seiling, Sept. 15, 1951 (dec. May 1982); children: David, Jeffrey, Luann, Suzanne. BSME, U. Toledo, 1962. Engr. Miller, Tillman & Zamis engrs., Toledo, 1962-67, regional mgr. Phoenix br., 1967-69; owner, mgr. ABS Tech. Svcs., Phoenix, 1969—; ret. Patentee in several fields. With U.S. Army, 1952, Korea. Decorated Bronze Star; Commd. extraordinary minister, 1975.. Mem. Nat. Mil. Intelligence Assn. (charter). Republican. Roman Catholic. Home: 8226 E Meadowbrook Ave Scottsdale AZ 85251-1739 Office: A B S Tech Svcs PO Box 2440 Scottsdale AZ 85252-2440

GILSON, GARY, professional society administrator, journalist; b. Newark, Apr. 4, 1936; s. Seymour Frank and Evelyn Adele (Johnson) G.; m. Edith Marie Roos, June 10, 1965 (div. 1973). AB, Dartmouth Coll., 1957; MS, Columbia U. in Journalism, 1961. Reporter Mpls. Star, 1961-64; reporter, producer WNET TV Pub. TV, N.Y.C., 1964-66; producer, exec. producer WNET TV, N.Y.C., 1971-77; editl. writer WCBS Radio, N.Y.C., 1966; writer, producer WABC-TV News, N.Y.C., 1966-67; producer Pub. Broadcast Lab., N.Y.C., 1968-69; instr. in journalism Columbia U., N.Y.C., 1969-71; news dir. KCET TV, L.A., 1977-80; producer, host KTCH TV, Mpls., 1981-85; producer WCCO-TV, Mpls., 1985-87; exec. dir. Minn. News Coun., Mpls., 1992—; faculty coord. Summer Program in Broadcast Journalism for Minority Groups, N.Y.C., 1968-70. Producer (documentary film) Brighton Beach, 1972, (Emmy award 1973); (documentary video) And a Time to Heal, 1984, Mpls. (Am. Women in Radio TV award 1984). Big brother Jewish Family and Children's Svc., Mpls., 1989—. 1st lt. USMC, 1957-59. Recipient 4 other Emmy awards, N.Y.C., 1973, L.A., 1978. Mem. Rotary Club (bd. dirs. #9 Mpls. 1997—). Jewish. Avocations: tennis, double-crosstic puzzles. Office: Minn News Coun 125 6th St Ste 1122 Minneapolis MN 55402

GILSON, JEROME, lawyer, writer; b. Chgo., Jan. 12, 1931; s. William George and Clara Margaret (Loewe) G.; m. Jamie Marie Chisam, June 19, 1955; children: Thomas, Matthew, Anne. AB, U. Mo., 1952; JD, Northwestern U., 1958. Bar: Ill. 1958, U.S. Dist. Ct. (no. dist.) Ill. 1958, U.S. Ct. Appeals (7th cir.) 1962, U.S. Supreme Ct. 1966, U.S. Ct. Appeals (3d cir.) 1967, U.S. Ct. Appeals (5th cir.) 1968, U.S. Ct. Appeals (fed. cir.) 1982, U.S. Ct. Appeals (11th cir.) 1985, U.S. Ct. Appeals (4th cir.) 1988, U.S. Ct. Appeals (8th cir.) 1994. Assoc. Rooks, Pitts, Fullagar & Poust, Chgo., 1958-63; ptnr. Brinks Hofer Gilson & Lione, Chgo., 1963—; mem. faculty John Marshall Law Sch., Chgo., 1961-63; advisor Am. Law Inst.-Unfair Competition Law Restatement, Phila., 1986-91. Author: Trademark Protection & Practice, 1974—, also supplements; contbr. articles to profl. jours. Served as sgt. U.S. Army, 1952-55. Named as top trademark law practitioner in world Managing Intellectual Property, 1998. Mem. ABA, Am. Law Inst., Internat. Trademark Assn. (reporter trademark rev. com. 1985-88, counsel 1991-94), Intellectual Property Law Assn. Chgo., Am. Intellectual Property Law Assn., Union League, Mich. Shores Club. Avocations: tennis, piano. Office: Brinks Hofer Gilson & Lione 445 N Cityfront Plaza Dr Chicago IL 60611-4316

GILSTER, PETER STUART, lawyer; b. Carbondale, Ill., Dec. 10, 1939; s. John Sprigg and Ruth E. (Robinson) G.; m. Carol Clevenger, June 30, 1968; children: John F., Thomas B. BS, U. Ill., 1962, JD, 1965. Bar: Ill. 1965, Mo. 1968, U.S. Dist. Ct. (ea. dist.) Mo. 1969, U.S. Patent Office 1970, U.S. Ct. Appeals (8th cir.) 1978, U.S. Supreme Ct. 1978, U.S. Ct. Customs and Patent Appeals 1980, U.S. Ct. Appeals (fed. cir.) 1983. Assoc. Koenig, Senniger, Powers & Leavitt, St. Louis, 1967-71, ptnr., 1971-72; patent atty. Monsanto Co., St. Louis, 1972-77; ptnr. Kalish & Glister, St. Louis, 1977-96, Peper, Martin, Jensen, Michael and Hetiage, St. Louis, 1997-98, Blackwell, Sanders, Peper Martin, LLC, St. Louis, 1998-99; head patent sect., chair internat. practice group Kalish & Gilster Intellectual Property Group, St. Louis; ofcr. Greensfelder, Hemker & Gale, P.C. Intellectual Property Grp., 1999—; seminar lectr. U. Mo.-St. Louis, 1976-83. Capt. USAR, 1966-67. Decorated Army Commendation medal. Mem. ABA, IEEE, AAAS, Am. Intellectual Property Law Assn., Ill. Bar Assn., Mo. Bar Assn. (patent, trademark, and copyright com.), Lawyer Pilots Bar Assn., Fed. Cir. Bar Assn., Bar Assn. Met. St. Louis (chmn. patent sect. 1975-76), Assoc. Pilots St. Louis (v.p. 1977-83, bd. dirs. 1975-87), World Affairs Coun. St. Louis, Soc. Hispano-Am. St. Louis (bd. dirs. 1993-96, treas. 1994-96), Media Club St. Louis, Phi Delta Phi.

GILSTRAP, LEAH ANN, media specialist; b. Seneca, S.C., Sept. 12, 1950; d. Raymond Chester and Eunice Hazel (Long) G. BA in History, Furman U., 1976, MEd, 1982; MLS, U. S.C., 1991. Cert. tchr., media specialist, S.C. Tchr. Greenville (S.C.) County Sch. Dist., 1978-92, media specialist, 1992—. Mem. NEA (del. 1991-95), ALA, S.C. Assn. Sch. Librs., S.C. Edn. Assn. (bd. dirs. 1994-96), Greenville County Edn. Assn. (bd. dirs. 1988-98, governance chair 1988-98, v.p. 1996-97, pres. 1997-98), Greenville County Coun. Media Specialists (bd. dirs. 1993-94). Democrat. Baptist. Avocations: travel, reading, ednl. studies. Home: 150 Howell Cir Apt 184 Greenville SC 29615-4915 Office: Bryson Mid Sch 3657 S Industrial Dr Simpsonville SC 29681-3295

GIMBLE, JOHNNY, country musician. Musician (solo) Texas Fiddle Collection, Texas Honky-Tonk Hits, (single John Gimble & Texas album Swing Pioneers) Still Swingin. Recipient Best Country Instrumental Performance Grammy award, 1996. Office: c/o Nancy Fly Agy PO Box 90306 Austin TX 78709-0306*

GIMBOLO, ALEKSEI FRANK CHARLES (CIMBOLO), artist, philosopher, author; b. Portland, Oreg., Mar. 29, 1956; s. Frank Charles and Elisabeth McFarlane Gimbolo; m. Lilli M. Colipapa, Dec. 16, 1985; children: Niko Alexander, Romaneé Alexander. Student, U. Hawaii, 1976-78, Coll. Charleston, 1979-80. Winemaker Chateau LaCaia, Hazel Green, Ala., 1980-87; artist, philosopher Portland, 1987—. Author: Illuminati-Wisdom of the Enlightened Ones, 1995; painting pub.: Encyclopedia of Living Artist, 7th edit., 1992, 8th edit., 1993; featured in Voice of Am.; exhibits include Seattle Art Resource, Perimeter Gallery, Houston, Signature Galleries, Calif., Hotel Vintage Plz., Portland, Oreg. Vice-chmn. Pre-Law Soc., Charleston, S.C., 1979; exec. com. chmn. Young Reps. of Am., Charleston, 1979; fencing coach Portland (Oreg.) State U., 1993. Avocations: fencing, antique collecting, martial arts.

GIMBRONE, MICHAEL ANTHONY, JR., research scientist, pathologist, educator; b. Buffalo, Nov. 16, 1943; married, 1971; 3 children. AB, Cornell U., 1965; MD, Harvard U., 1970. Intern, resident fellow Mass. Gen. Hosp., Boston, 1970-72; staff assoc. Nat. Cancer Inst., Bethesda, Md., 1972-74; resch. assoc. Harvard Med. Sch., Boston, 1974-76, from asst. prof. to assoc. prof., 1979-85, Elsie T. Friedman prof. pathology, 1985—; cons. Nat. Heart, Lung and Blood Inst., NIH, 1976—; established investigator Am. Heart Assn., 1977-82; head Vascular Pathophysiol. Rsch. Lab., 1977-85; dir. vascular rsch. div. Brigham and Women's Hosp., 1985—. Mem. AAAS, Nat. Acad. of Scis., Am. Heart Assn. (Basic Rsch. prize 1993), Am. Soc. Cell Biologists, Tissue Culture Assn., Am. Soc. Hematology, Am. Assn. Pathologists (v.p. 1991-92), Am. Soc. Invest. Pathology (pres. 1992-93), Am. Assn. Physicians, Fedn. Am. Socs. for Exptl. Biology (Exptl. Pathologist award 1982, bd. dirs. 1990-94), N.Am. Vascular Biology Orgn. (founding pres. 1994—). Rsch. in cardiovascular pathophysiology, especially atherosclerosis, thrombosis and inflammation, vascular cell biology. Office: Brigham and Womens Hosp Vascular Rsch Div Dept of Pathology Boston MA 02115

GIMELSTOB, JUSTIN, professional tennis player; b. Livingston, N.J., Jan. 26, 1977. Professional tennis player, 1996—. Office: c/o USTA 70 W Red Oak Ln White Plains NY 10604*

GIMENEZ, LUIS FERNANDO, physician, educator; b. Antofagasta, Chile, Mar. 3, 1952; came to U.S., 1979; s. Luis Sr. and Nelly (Basulto) G.; m. Diane Marie Salazar, Sept. 20, 1957; children: Luis Andres, Pilar Elizabeth, Nicholas Miguel. MD, U. Chile, Valparaiso, 1976. Diplomate Am. Bd. Internal Medicine, Am. Bd. Nephrology. Intern U. Chile Sch. Medicine, Valparaiso, 1975-76; resident U. Concepcion Sch. Medicine, Chile, 1976-77, U. Chile Sch. Medicine, Valparaiso, 1977-79; research fellow in nephrology Johns Hopkins U. Sch. Medicine, Balt., 1979-81; intern Johns Hopkins Hosp., Balt., 1981-82, resident, 1982-84, clin. fellow nephrology div., 1984-85; instr. Johns Hopkins U. Sch. Medicine, Balt., 1985-86, asst. prof. medicine, 1986—; dir. dialysis unit The Good Samaritan Hosp., Balt., 1985—, chief renal div., 1990; mem. med. adv. bd. Am. Kidney Found., Balt., 1987—. Contbr. articles to profl. jours. Recipient Outstanding Civic Svc. award Chilean Med. Assn., Valparaiso, 1974. Mem. Am. Fedn. for Clin. Research., Am. Soc. Nephrology, Am. Coll. Physicians, Internat. Soc. Nephrology, Internat. Soc. Peritoneal Dialysis, Am. Coll. Clin. Pharmacology. Avocation: philatelist. Office: Johns Hopkins Hosp Renal Divsn 1830 Bldg Baltimore MD 21205-2109

GIMMILLARO, BRIAN, university head women's volleyball coach; m. Dania Gimmillaro; children: Stefan, Lauren. BA in Econs., Long Beach State U., 1970. Coach Gahr H.S., Cerritos, Calif., 1978-85, L.B. H.S., Long Beach, Calif., 1985—; bus. mgr. U.S. Women's Volleyball Olympic team, 1982-84. Named Tiger Coll. Coach of Yr. ASICS, 1990, Regional Coach of Yr., 1989, 91, Honoree Long Beach Century Club, 1989, N.W. Region Coach of Yr. 1989, 91, 94, Big West Coach of Yr. 1991, 92, 94. Mem. Calif. Jrs. Volleyball Club (pres., owner). Office: Long Beach State U Women's Athletic Dept 1250 N Bellflower Blvd Long Beach CA 90840-0006*

GIN, HAL GABRIEL, university administrator; b. Oakland, Calif., July 2, 1950. BA, Calif. State U., Hayward, 1973, MPA, 1983; EdD, U. San Francisco, 1995. Program advisor Calif. State U., Hayward, 1974-84, coord. orientation, dir. ednl. support svcs., 1984-86, dir. student life, 1988-93, exec. dir. student devel. svcs., 1993—. Bd. dirs. San Lorenzo (Calif.) Village Homes Assn., 1984-86; mem. San Lorenzo Village Found., 1995—. Mem. Nat. Assn. Student Pers. Adminstrs. (v.p. Region VI 1989-92, conf. com. 1996-97, 98-99, exec. com. 1977—, mem.-at-large 1999—), Lions (cabinet sec./treas., 1985-86, pres. 1979, 98—). Office: Calif State U Student Devel Svcs Hayward CA 94542

GIN, JACKSON, architect; b. Chgo., June 11, 1934; s. Frank Tsue and Jennie Shee (Pang) G.; m. Jayne Ping Kan, Oct. 5, 1963; children: Paul L., Michael F., Daniel. BA, U. Ill., 1958. Designer Milton M. Schwartz, Architects, Chgo., 1958-60; project architect Greenberg & Finfer, Architects, Chgo., 1960-62, Hausner & Macsai, Architects, Chgo., 1962-67; project architect, ptnr. Dubin, Dubin, Black & Moutoussamy, Architects, Chgo., 1967-77; prin., pres. Mann, Gin, Dubin & Frazier, Ltd., Architects-Planners, Chgo., 1977—. Trustee Chinese Christian Union Ch., 1968-70; bd. dirs. Neighborhood Redevel. Assistance, 1972-74; active Euclid-Lake Assn., Mount Prospect, Ill. Mem. AIA, Chinese Am. Civic Fedn., Builders of Chgo. Club. Club: Builders of Chgo. Home: 1332 N Peachtree Ln Mount Prospect IL 60056-1826 Office: Mann Gin Dubin & Frazier Ltd 30 S Michigan Ave Chicago IL 60603-3211

GINAITT, PETER THADDEUS, state legislator; b. Warwick, R.I., Dec. 28, 1960; m. Sharon Ann Snyzyk, Apr. 12, 1986; children: Bradford Thomas, Taylor Anne. BA, U. R.I., 1983; AS, C.C. R.I., 1987, ASN, 1995. Mem. R.I. Ho. of Reps.; firefighter Warwick Fire Dept., 1984—; sec. health edn. and welfare, chmn. joint com. on environment and energy R.I. Ho. of Reps. Mem. Warwick Elks, Nathaniel Greene Masonic Lodge, Oakland Beach Vol. Fire Club, Conservation Law Found. Address: 177 Hope Ave Warwick RI 02889-5145*

GINDILIS, VIKTOR MIRONOVITCH, geneticist, researcher; b. Moscow, July 20, 1937; came to U.S., 1991; s. Miron M. and Vera I. (Matz) G.; m. Natalia E. Broude, Sept. 24, 1965 (div. Sept. 1989); children: Yevgeniy, Tatiana. MD, 2d State Med. Inst., Moscow, 1960; PhD in Cytology, Inst. Gen. Genetics, Moscow, 1967; PhD in Genetics, Inst. Med. Genetics, Moscow, 1979. Diplomate in medicine. Physician, radiologist Regional Hosp., Ulianovsk, Russia, 1960-62; rsch. fellow Inst. Molecular Biology, Moscow, 1965-69; assoc. prof. Inst. of Psychiatry, Moscow, 1969-81, head of lab., 1981-86; head of lab. Brain Rsch. Inst., Moscow, 1986-91; rsch. dir. lab. Reproductive Genetics Inst., Chgo., 1991—; head of expert commn. Med.-Genetic Advice coun. Soviet Union Dept. Pub. Health, Moscow, 1987-91. Author: Functional Anatomy of the Human Genome, 1988, Human Genes Encyclopedia, 1991. Grantee Russian Human Genome Program, 1989-91, Scottish Rite Schizophrenia Rsch. Program, Boston, 1992-94. Mem. N.Y. Acad. Scis., Internat. Soc. Psychiat. Genetis, Internat. Soc. Molecular Evolution, Human Genome Orgn. Achievements include research on human chromosome specific alphoid DNA markers; computerized human genome encyclopedia; research on evolutionary systematics of homeotic genes/proteins; anticipation phenemenon in schizophrenia; basic concept of multivariate genetic analysis. Office: Reproductive Genetics Inst 836 W Wellington Ave Chicago IL 60657-9224

GINDIN, WILLIAM HOWARD, judge; b. Perth Amboy, N.J., Sept. 1, 1931; s. Jac Paul and Belle Ruth (Steinberg) G.; m. Jane Hersh, June 24, 1954; children: Thomas L., Suzanne Hinsdale; m. Emily Shimkin, Dec. 25, 1965; children: Geoffrey A. Drucker, Janine Drucker Gordon. A.B., Brown U., 1953; J.D., Yale U., 1956. Bar: N.J. 1956, U.S. Supreme Ct. 1965, U.S. Ct. Appeals (3d cir.) 1980. Assoc., Gindin & Gindin, Plainfield, N.J., 1956-62, ptnr., Plainfield and Bridgewater, N.J., 1962-82; adminstrv. law judge,

Newark, 1982-85; U.S. bankruptcy judge, Trenton, 1985-90, chief judge, 1990-98; adj. prof. Rutgers Camden Law Sch., 1988-93; lectr. Inst. Continuing Legal Edn., Profl. Edn. Systems, Inc.; bd. govs. Nat. Conf. Bankruptcy Judges (3d cir.), 1989-92, Am. Judicature Soc. Mem. bd. editors N.J. Bar Assn. Jour., 1962-72. Mem. Plainfield (N.J.) Human Relations Commn., 1965-72, chmn., 1968-72; pres. Temple Sholom, Plainfield, 1979-81; regional v.p. Union Am. Hebrew Congregations, 1983-86; trustee Princeton Jewish Ctr.; vice chair Opera Festival of N.J. Fellow Am. Bar Found., Assn. Fed. Bar (adv. bd.), Bankruptcy Inn of Ct. N.J. (pres.); mem. ABA, Plainfield Bar Assn., Union County Bar Assn., Mercer County Bar Assn., N.J. Bar Assn., Am. Judicature Soc., Plainfield Rotary (pres. 1974-75). Home: 30 James Ct Princeton NJ 08540-2633 Office: US Bankruptcy Ct 402 E State St Trenton NJ 08608-1507

GINDROZ, RAYMOND L., architect; b. Aug. 4, 1940; s. Theodore Stevens and Harriet (McBride) G.; m. Marilyn Jane Miltenberger, May 27, 1967; 1 child, Monica Ruth Gindroz Candy. BArch with honors, Carnegie Inst. Tech., 1963, MArch in Urban Design with honors, 1965. Registered architect, Pa., Mich., N.J., Va., N.Y., W.Va. With UDA Archs., Pitts., 1964, prin., 1967-87; mng. prin. UDA Architects, Pitts., 1987—; vis. prof. urban design Grad. Ctr. CUNY, 1988-89; critic, lectr. in urban design Yale U., 1967-88; lectr. N.J. Inst. Tech., 1992, Va. Soc. Archts., 1992, U. Paris, Porte Dauphine, 1994, HUD Program, 1995, NAHB Conf., 1995; cons., spkr. livability and design UCLA, Carnegie-Mellon U., 1976, World Cities Conf., Berlin, 1981, Alcan Lectr. Series, Montreal, 1983, APA Conf., Memphis, 1987, The Netherlands Now as Design, Amsterdam, 1989, San Diego Ptnrs. for Livable Places, 1991, others; urban design cons. City of Norfolk, Va., 1990—. Exhbns. include U. Pitts., 1976, Frick Gallery, Contemporary Art Ctr., Cin., 1977, Yale U., 1980, Cooper Hewitt Mus., N.Y.C., 1983, Peninsula Fine Arts Ctr., Hampton, Va., 1995; author: Papal Porticoes and Methodist Porches, 1987, A Pattern Book for Shadyside, 1986, Working with the American Traditions, 1983; author (with others): Representation and Architecture, Urban Structure, The Growth of Cities; selected urban design and planning projects include Pitts. Wall Street Dist., 1980, Tory Mountain Ski Resort, Harmon, W.Va., 1985, Diggstown Pub. Housing Redesign, Norfolk, Va., 1992, Vision Plan for Bluegrass Tomorrow, Lexington, Ky., 1992, Euro-Disney design guidelines, 1995, numerous others; architecture includes Human Resources Ctr., Pontiac, Mich., Three Parks, Younstown, Ohio, 1972-79, Bellefield Towers, Pitts., 1985, Jewish Cmty. Ctr., Pitts., 1985, Tidewater Cmty. Coll., 1992-94, others. Fulbright fellow, 1965-66, Stewardson traveling fellow in architecture, 1963. Fellow AIA; mem. AAUP, Pa. Soc. Architects, Am. Planning Assn. Office: Gulf Tower 31st Fl 707 Grant St Pittsburgh PA 15219

GINDY, BENJAMIN LEE, insurance company executive; b. Detroit, July 23, 1929; s. Roy E. and Anne M. Gindy; B.S., U. Fla., 1951; m. Judith Youngerman, Dec. 20, 1953; children—Deborah, Daniel, David. Field rep. Penn Mut. Ins. Co., 1957-59; brokerage mgr. Mass. Indemnity Co., Miami, Fla., 1959-68; gen. agt. Guardian Life Ins. Co. Am., Miami, 1968—; pres. Internat. Risk Cons., Inc., Wealthcare, Inc.; mktg. dir., Party Magic, Inc., Archer Impact Mktg.; instr. Life Underwriter Tng. Council, C.L.U. diploma course U. Miami; past columnist Miami Rev.; guest speaker in field. Recipient Nat. Health Ins. award Guardian Life Ins. Co. Am., 1977, 83. C.L.U. Mem. Am. Soc. C.L.U.'s (past pres. Miami chpt., named Man of the Yr., 1987), S. Fla. Inter-Profl. Council (past pres.), Gen. Agts. and Mgrs. Assn. (past pres.), Miami Assn. Life Underwriters (past pres., Man of Yr. 1972). Home: 1018 Aduana Ave Coral Gables FL 33146-3326 Office: Gindy Agy/Guardian Life 7615 SW 62nd Ave Miami FL 33143-4906

GINGELL, ROBERT ARTHUR, lawyer; b. Alexandria, Va., July 23, 1923; s. Reginald Jennings and Elizabeth Regina (Stoddard) G.; m. Grace Noffsinger, Oct. 28, 1950 (div. Dec. 1980); children: Robert Arthur, Gentry N.; m. Marianne B. McConnaughey, Dec. 10, 1980. AB, George Washington U., 1947, JD, 1949. Bar: D.C. 1949, Md. 1949, U.S. Dist. Ct. D.C. 1949, U.S. Ct. Appeals (D.C. cir.) 1949. Assoc., Harry J. Daly, Washington, 1949-50; pvt. practice, Washington and Silver Spring, Md., 1952-60; ptnr. Ritterpusch & Gingell, Rockville and Silver Spring, Md., 1960-80; sr. ptnr. Gingell, Prescott & Jenkins Law Offices, Silver Spring, 1988-89, Gingell & Jenkins Law Offices, Silver Spring, 1989—; pres. Gingell & Jenkins PC, 1995—. With USMCR, 1943-46, 50-52. Fellow Am. Coll. Real Estate Lawyers; mem. Washington, D.C. Estate Planning Coun., Chevy Chase Country Club, Rotary (pres. 1964-65, Paul Harris fellow 1980—). Democrat. Episcopalian. Home: 5220 Parkway Dr Bethesda MD 20815-6620 Office: Gingell & Jenkins P C 11160 Veirs Mill Rd Ste 506 Silver Spring MD 20902-2538

GINGERICH, NAOMI R., emergency room nurse; b. Linwood, Mich., Sept. 18, 1945; d. Leroy and Mary Alice (Driver) G. Diploma in Nursing, Kansas City (Mo.) Gen. Hosp., 1967. RN, Pa., Md., Fla., Mo.; cert. advanced trauma life support. Charge nurse emergency rm. Kansas City (Mo.) Gen. Hosp. and Med. Ctr., 1967-70, oper. rm. nurse, 1971-74; charge nurse emergency rm. Univ. Med. Ctr., Kansas City, Kans., 1970-73; oper. room charge nurse Lancaster (Pa.) Gen. Hosp., 1974-79, charge nurse emergency rm., 1979-88; staff nurse emergency room Preferred Nursing Pool, Balt., 1988-90; with home health care, emergency room Norrell Health Care, Sarasota, Fla., 1990-91; office nurse Landisville Family Practice, 1991-92; on-call night nurse Hospice of Lancaster County, 1992-98, pvt. duty nurse, 1998—. Home: 13254 Mt Zion Rd Versailles MO 65084 Office: Hospice Lancaster County PO Box 4125 Lancaster PA 17604-4125

GINGERICH, OWEN JAY, astronomer, educator; b. Washington, Iowa, Mar. 24, 1930; 3 children. BA, Goshen Coll., 1951; MA, Harvard U., 1953, PhD in Astronomy, 1962. Dir. obs. Am. U., Beirut, 1955-58; from instr. to asst. prof. Am. U., 1955-58; lectr. astronomy Wellesley Coll., 1958-59; astrophysicist Smithsonian Astrophys. Obs., 1961-87, sr. astronomer, 1987—; from lectr. to assoc. prof. astronomy and history of sci. Harvard, 1960-69, prof., 1969—, chmn. history of sci. dept., 1992-93; Sigma Xi nat. lectr., 1971; George Darwin lectr. Royal Astron. Soc., 1971; councilor Am. Astron. Soc., 1973-76; astronomy cons. Harvard Project Physics, 1964-69; dir. ctrl. telegram bur. Internat. Astronomical Union, 1965-67, pres. commn. history astronomy, 1970-76, chmn. U.S. nat. com., 1982-84; adv. com. Ctr. Theology Inquiry, Princeton, 1988-97—; ad. bd. John Templeton Humility Theology Info. Ctr., 1994—. Assoc. editor: Jour. History Astronomy, 1975—; mem. editorial bd. Am. Scholar, 1975-80; dir. Harvard mag., 1978-85, incorporator, 1986—. Overseer Boston Mus. Sci., 1979-96, 98—. Decorated Order of Merit comdr. class People's Republic of Poland, 1981. Mem. AAAS (chmn. sect. L 1974, sect D 1981), Academie Internationale d'Histoire des Sciences, Am. Philos. Soc. (v.p. 1982-85, John F. Lewis prize 1976, councilor 1994—), Am. Astron. Soc. (councilor 1973-76, chmn. hist. astronomy div. 1983-85), Royal Astron. Soc. Can. (hon.), Phi Beta Kappa. Clubs: Examiner. Achievements include rsch. and publs. on model stellar atmospheres (to 1971) and in history of astonomy. Office: Harvard-Smithsonian Ctr For Astrophysics Cambridge MA 02138 *Our most earnest ambitions are in effect unspoken prayers-they define our deepest views on the meaning of life far more precisely than any outward profession of religion or ethics.*

GINGHER, MARIANNE B., English educator; b. Feb. 10, 1947. BA, Salem Coll., 1969; MFA, U. N.C., Greensboro, 1974. Dir. creative writing program U. N.C., Chapel Hill, 1996; asst. prof. English Hollins Coll., Roanoke, Va., 1989-91. Author: (novel) Bobby Rex's Greatest Hit, 1986, (collection of short stories) Teen Angel & Other Stories of Wayward Love, 1988.

GINGISS, BENJAMIN JACK, retired formal clothing stores executive; b. St. Paul, Feb. 27, 1911; s. Samuel and Betty (Illiewitz) G.; m. Rosalie Eisenschiml, Apr. 20, 1940; children: Peter J., Joel D., Randall J. Student, U. Ill., 1929-32, Northwestern U., 1934, Ill. Inst. Tech., 1941. Co-founder Gingiss Bros., Inc., Chgo., 1936; (named later changed to Gingiss Formalwear, Inc.); now ret. chmn. Gingiss Formalwear, Inc., Gingiss Internat., Inc. Chmn. Fedn. for an Open Lakefront, Chgo., 1967; pres. USO of, 1969, 73-74; v.p. Welfare Council Met. Chgo., 1968; commr. Lake Mich. and Adjoining Lands Study, 1969—; mem. Urban Action Commn. YMCA, 1969; city commr. Commn. on Youth Welfare, 1966; chmn. men's clothing div. Combined Jewish Appeal, 1959; bd. dirs. Center Sports Medicine, Goodwill Industries, Lyric Opera Chgo., Union Am. Hebrew Congregations; sr. v.p. bd. dirs. USO, Chgo.; bd. dirs., pres. Ill. Humane Soc.; former trustee Rosary Coll.; bd. assos. DePaul U.; former vice-chmn. pres.'s adv. bd. Mus. Sci. and Industry; mem. nat. bd. Wendy Will Case Cancer Fund. Recipient Phoenix award DePaul U., 1969, Prime Ministers medal State of Israel, 1968, U. Dept. Def. awards, U.S. Air Corps awards, U.S.C.G. awards, U.S. Army awards, 9th Naval Dist. awards, U.S.O. awards, 1977, Better Bus. Bur. Chmn.'s Ann. award, 1985; named Great Lakes Naval Tng. Ctr. Guest of Honor, 1987; named to Sr. Citizens Hall of Fame, City of Chgo., 1991. Mem. Ill. Humane Soc. (Disting. Svc. award 1995), Anti-Cruelty Soc. (bd. govs. 1995), Adler Planetarium (gov. mem.), Tavern Club, Execs. Club (Chgo.), Circumnavigators Club (pres. 1987, 88), Chgo. C. of C. Home: 175 E Delaware Pl Apt 8307 Chicago IL 60611-7748 Office: 175 E Delaware Pl Apt 8306 Chicago IL 60611-7748*

GINGOLD, GEORGE NORMAN, insurance company executive, lawyer; b. N.Y.C., Aug. 2, 1939; s. Josef and Gladys (Anderson) G.; m. Anne Brenda Davis, July 7, 1963; children—Rachel June, David Bruce. A.B. magna cum laude, Harvard U., 1960, J.D., 1963. Bar: Ariz. 1964, Conn. 1968, Mass. 1989. Pvt. practice law Phoenix, 1964-65; atty. SEC, Washington, 1965-67; counsel AEtna Life & Casualty, Hartford, Conn., 1967-94; counsel, corp. sec. AEtna Life Ins. and Annuity Co., Hartford, 1981-94; pvt. practice ins. securities law, 1994—; mem. com. on securities regulation Am. Council of Life Ins., Washington, 1978-94, chmn., 1986-88; instr. Hartford Coll. for Women, 1983-95. Author articles in field. Vice pres., bd. dirs. United Cerebral Palsy Assn., Hartford, 1980-87; vice chmn. West Hartford Human Rights Commn., Conn., 1975-79; pres. West Hartford PTA, 1976-78. Mem. ABA (mem. fed. regulation of securities com. 1978—), Am. Soc. Corp. Secs., Fed. Bar Assn. (pres. Hartford County chpt. 1974-76). Lodge: B'nai B'rith Unity (pres. 1971-72). Avocations: classical music; theatre; chess. Home and Office: 197 King Philip Dr West Hartford CT 06117-1409

GINGOLD, HARLAN BRUCE, lawyer; b. Syracuse, N.Y., Jan. 3, 1946; s. Eli and Sarle (Greenhouse) G.; m. Diane Port, Dec. 20, 1970; children: Alan R., Brian M., Eric R. BA, Syracuse U., 1967, JD, 1970. Bar: N.Y. 1971, U.S. Dist. Ct. (no. dist.) N.Y. 1971, U.S. Supreme Ct. 1977. Assoc. Primo & Marino, Syracuse, 1971-72, Driscoll, Mathews, Gingold and Cass, Syracuse, 1972-73; ptnr. Gingold & Gingold, Syracuse, 1973-85; ptnr., v.p., sec. Macht, Brenizer & Gingold, P.C., Syracuse, 1985—; pub. adv. coun. N.Y.S. Ethics Com., 1998—. Bd. visitors Syracuse U. Coll. Law, 1982-84; bd. dirs. Temple Adath Yeshurun, Syracuse, 1984-90, Am. Diabetes Assn., Syracuse, 1989-96, Hiscock Legal Aid Soc., 1998—; Public Adv. Coun. N.Y. State Ethics Commn., 1998—. Mem. ABA, N.Y. State Bar Assn. (ho. dels. 1994-96, 98—, com. on profl. discipline 1999), N.Y. State Bar Leaders(exec. counsel 1994—), Onondaga County Bar Assn. (bd. dirs. 1990-97, past pres., officer 1990-97). Avocation: golf. Office: Macht Brenizer & Gingold PC State Tower Bldg Lbby Fl Syracuse NY 13202-1798

GINGRAS, JOHN RICHARD, lawyer, consultant; b. Paterson, N.J., May 1, 1949; s. Louis Donah and Carol Gilmore (Doyle) G.; m. Nancy Margaret Conway, Aug. 29, 1970; 2 children. BS, St. Joseph's U., 1971, MBA, 1979; MS in Fin. Svcs., Am. Coll., 1980; JD, Widener U., 1983. Bar: Pa. 1984. Trust acct. Girard Bank, Phila., 1969-71; sales mgr. Equitable Life Assurance Soc., Wayne, Pa., 1971-76; pvt. practice fin. planner Newtown Square, Pa., 1976-80; assoc. Huver & Assocs., Villanova, Pa., 1980-86; pres. Settlement Funding, Inc., Broomall, Pa., 1986-95. Pres. bd. dirs. MNJ Community Svcs. Found., 1976-90; bd. dirs. Jaycees; active Valley Forge coun. Boy Scouts Am. Recipient Silver Beaver award Boy Scouts Am., God and Svc. award; named one of Outstanding Young Pennsylvanian, Pa. Jaycees, 1976. Mem. ABA, ATLA, Pa. Bar Assn., Am. Soc. CLUs/ChFC, SAR, Sigma Phi Epsilon (alumni bd.), Delta Theta Phi. Republican. Presbyterian. Avocations: art collector, antiques, golf, skiing.

GINGRAS, PAUL JOSEPH, real estate management company executive; b. Augusta, Maine, Mar. 10, 1948; s. Adolphe Joseph and Antoinette Marie (Lacombe) G.; m. Azucena Figuera Malaver, Nov. 13, 1976; children: Audrey Elena, Natali Elizabeth. BA Math., U. Maine, 1973; student, Boston Archtl. Ctr., 1974-76. Cert. shopping ctr. mgr. Property mgr. Coppola & Co., Boston, 1975-77; property acquisitions and mgmt. William Crocker Corp., White Plains, N.Y., 1979-82; v.p. Roebling Mgmt. Co. Inc., Paramus, N.J., 1983-86, pres., 1986-91; pres. Parkway Asset Mgmt. Corp., Hackensack, N.J., 1992—. With U.S. Army, 1967-70. Mem. Internat. Coun. Shopping Ctrs., Nat. Math. Honor Soc. Avocations: guitar music, sports. Home: 497 Rutland Ave Teaneck NJ 07666-2925 Office: Parkway Asset Mgmt Corp 235 Moore St Hackensack NJ 07601-7417

GINGRICH, NEWT(ON LEROY), former congressman; b. Harrisburg, Pa., June 17, 1943; s. Robert Bruce and Kathleen (Daugherty) G.; children: Linda Kathleen, Jacqueline Sue; m. Marianne Ginther, Aug. 1981. B.A., Emory U., 1965; M.A., Tulane U., 1968, Ph.D. in European History, 1971. Faculty W. Ga. Coll., Carrollton, 1970-78; asst. prof. history W. Ga. Coll., until 1978; mem. 96th-105th Congresses from 6th Ga. dist. U.S. Ho. of Reps., Washington, 1979-99; speaker U.S. Ho. Reps., 104th Congress, 1995-98, 105th Congress, 1997—; speaker, chmn. emeritus GOPAC; co-founder Conservative Opportunity Soc., congl. mil. caucus, space caucus; mem. joint com. on printing, house adminstrn. com.; co-chmn. Leader's Task Force on Health; adj. prof. Reinhardt Coll., Waleska, Ga., 1994-95. Author: (with Marianne Gingrich) Window of Opportunity, 1984, Renewing American Civilization, 1995, (with William Forschen) 1945, 95, To Renew America, 1995. Named Man of Yr., 1995. Mem. AAAS, Ga. Conservancy. Republican. Baptist. Lodges: Kiwanis, Moose. *

GINIGER, KENNETH SEEMAN, publisher; b. N.Y.C., Feb. 18, 1919; s. Maurice Aaron and Pearl (Triester) G.; m. Carol Virginia Wilkins, Sept. 27, 1952 (dec. Aug. 1985). Student, U. Va., 1935-39, N.Y. Law Sch., 1940-41. Ptnr. Signet Press, 1939-40; assoc. editor Arts and Decoration and The Spur, 1940-41; dir. pub. relations Prentice-Hall, Inc., 1946-49, editor-in-chief trade book div., 1949-52; v.p., gen. mgr. Hawthorn Books div., 1952-61; pres. Hawthorn Books, Inc., N.Y.C., 1961-65, K.S. Giniger Co., Inc., N.Y.C., 1965—, Consol. Book Pubs. div. Processing & Books, Inc., Chgo., 1969-74, Tradewinds Group div. IPC Ltd., Sydney, Australia, 1974-76; lectr. New Sch. Social Research, 1948-49, NYU, 1979-81, adj. asst. prof., 1981-83, adj. assoc. prof., 1983-85. *Among the authors whose books Mr. Giniger has edited and published are Sir Hugh Casson, Allen Dulles, Paul Fussell, Yousuf Karsh, Frances Parkinson Keyes, H.V. Morton, Dr. Norman Vincent Peale, Pope John XXIII, Pope John Paul II, Bishop Fulton J. Sheen, George Simenon, Irving Stone, Major General Sir Kenneth Strong, Sir John Templeton and Lowell Thomas.* Author: The Compact Treasury of Inspiration, 1955 (NCCJ Brotherhood Week citation), America, America, America, 1957, A Treasury of Golden Memories, 1958, What Is Protestantism?, 1965, A Little Treasury of Hope, 1968, A Little Treasury of Comfort, 1968, A Little Treasury of Christmas, 1968, The Sayings of Jesus, 1968, Heroes for Our Times, 1969, The Family Advent Book, 1979, Pope John Paul II: Pilgrim of Faith, 1987, (with Sir John Templeton) Spiritual Evolution, 1998; editor: Internat. Pub. News, 1983-91, European Bookseller Pub. World/Update Newsletter, 1991-92; mem. editorial bd.: RAM Reports, 1977-83, Communications and the Law, 1978-94. Sec. Com. Collective Security, 1952-65; nat. adv. bd. Found. Religious Action, 1956-94; dir. Laymen's Nat. Bible Com., 1957—, pres., 1963-71, chmn., 1987-94, chmn. emeritus, 1994—; adv. bd. Templeton Found., 1992—, Am. Theatre Wing, 1999—. Capt. AUS, 1941-45; asst. to dir. CIA, 1951-52. Decorated chevalier French Legion of Honor. Mem. P.E.N., Garrick Club (London), Authors Club (London) Arts Club (London), Army and Navy Club (Washington), Players Club, Yale Club, Dutch Treat Club, Church Club (N.Y.C.), Phi Delta Phi. Republican. Episcopalian. Home: 1045 Park Ave New York NY 10028-1030 Office: 250 W 57th St New York NY 10107

GINKEL, JOHANNES AUGUSTE VAN, geographer, educator; b. Kota-Radjah, Indonesia, June 22, 1940; arrived in the Netherlands, 1950; s. Gysbert and Anna Sipkje W. (Westra) van G.; m. Anna Maria E. Teepen, Aug. 25, 1965; children: Auke Gysbert Heino, Mapje Ank Marit. MS in Geography and History cum laude, Utrecht (Netherlands) U., 1966, PhD in Social Scis. cum laude, 1979. Prof. geography and history Thomas à Kempis Coll., Arnhem, Netherlands, 1965-68; assoc. prof. geography Utrecht U., 1968-80, full prof. human geography and planning, 1980—, mem. bd. govs., 1985-97, rector magnificus, 1986-97; rector UN U., Tokyo, 1997—; chmn. Netherlands Trilateral Adv. Coun. Sci. Policy, 1991-97; bd. dirs. European Assn. Univs., v.p. 1989-98; mem. coun. UN U., 1992-97, v.p., 1995-97; bd. dirs. Internat. Assn. Univs., 1990-95, v.p., 1995—; mem. European Sci. and Tech. Assembly, 1994-97; mem. adv. group higher edn. UNESCO, 1995—; steering group World Conf. on Higher Edn., Paris, 1998. Author: a.o. Zicht op de Stad, 1977, Die Randstad Holland, 1979, Suburbanisatie en Recente Woonmilieus, 1979, Algemene Sociale Geografie, 1984, Nederland in Delen, 1989, University 2050: the Organization of Creativity and Innovation; editor: Geografisch Tijdschrift, 1970-79. Chmn. Regional Conf. of Municipalities, Utrecht, 1988-93; treas. Netherlands' Univs. Found. for Internat. Cooperation, Nuffic, 1986-97. Decorated Knight Netherlands LIon, 1994. Mem. Found. for Fundamental Rsch. in Geog. and Environ. Scis. (chmn. 1982-91), Netherlands Interdisciplinary Demographic Inst. (chmn. sci. com. 1986-95, chmn., bd. govs. 1996—), Internat. Tng. Ctr. for Aerospace Survey and Earth Scis. (bd. dirs. 1986-94, chmn. 1994-98), Internat. Geog. Union (chmn. Netherlands br. 1988-92), Royal Netherlands Geog. Soc., Netherlands' Inst. for Urban and Regional Planning and Pub. Housing, Rotary, Sports Coun. Municipality (chmn., 1969-73, The Netherlands), Hockey Club Amersfoort (mem. tech. com. 1970-75), Sports Club Kampong (chmn. youth divsn. 1976-82). Avocations: sports, travel. Home: Park Arenberg 63, De Bilt NL3731EP, The Netherlands Office: UN U 5-53-70, Jingumae Shibuya-ku Jingumae, Tokyo 150-8925, Japan

GINN, JOHN CHARLES, journalism educator, former newspaper publisher; b. Longview, Tex., Jan. 1, 1937; s. Paul S. and Bernice Louise (Commer) G.; children: John Paul, Mark Charles, William Stanfield. B.J., U. Mo., 1959; M.B.A., Harvard U., 1972. From reporter, to copy editor, to chief copy desk Charlotte (N.C.) Observer, 1959-62; editor Kingsport (Tenn.) Times-News, 1962-63; city editor Charlotte News, 1963-67; mgr. advt., pub. relations Celanese Corp., 1967-70; dir. corp. devel. Des Moines Register & Tribune, 1972-73; editor, pub. Jackson (Tenn.) Sun, 1973-74; publisher Anderson (S.C.) Ind., 1974-91; v.p. Harte-Hanks Communications, Inc., 1978-91, pres. S.E. region, 1977-91; Knight disting. prof. journalism U. Kans., Lawrence, 1991—; pres., pub. Anderson Ind.-Mail, 1974-91; bd. dirs., mem. exec. com. Anderson Meml. Hosp., 1985-91; mem. Pulitzer Prize jury, 1977-79; adj. prof. Northwestern U., 1985-87; frequent lectr., chmn. S.E. region adv. com. Am. Press Inst. Chmn. Anderson County Civic Ctr. Authority, 1985-91; chmn. fund drive Anderson Cancer Treatment Ctr.; pres. Anderson YMCA, 1975-76; mem. adv. coun. Anderson Coll., 1985, bd. visitors, 1989-91; chmn. bd. Columbia Missourian, U. Mo., 1987-91; mem. adv. coun. Strom Thurmond Inst., Clemson U., 1986-91; mem. adv. bd. Clemson Honors Program, 1989-91; vice chmn. So. Newspaper Pubs. Assn. Found., 1990-91; bd. dirs. U. Ga. Red and Black, 1980-91; mem. pres.'s adv. coun. Winthrop Coll., 1985, bd. visitors, 1989-91, bd. dirs. Friends of the Leids Ctr, Lawrence, Kans., 1992—; pres. Celebration of Cultures, Lawrence, 1994—. With USAFR, 1959-61. Recipient award for best editorial of yr. Tenn. Press Assn., 1964, 73, 74, honor award for disting. svc. in journalism U. Mo., 1990; R.H. Macy retail fellow Harvard U., 1972. Mem. Am. Newspaper Pubs. Assn., Am. Soc. Newspaper Editors, So. Newspaper Pubs. Assn. (bd. dirs.), S.C. Press Assn. (exec. com.), Anderson Area C. of C. (pres. 1977, 85), Sigma Delta Chi, Anderson Outstanding Leader awards 1986-91. Home: 4808 Normandy Park St Lawrence KS 66049-1840

GINN, RICHARD VAN NESS, retired army officer, health care executive; b. Miami, Fla., Mar. 23, 1943; s. Philander Jerome and Alida Loring (Van Ness) G.; m. Angelica Suarez, June 29, 1968; children: Angie Ann, Richard Van Ness. BA, Stetson U., 1965; MHA, Baylor U., 1978; MA, Duke U., 1980; grad. with honors, Army Command/Gen. Staff Coll., 1981, Army War Coll., 1990. Commd. 2d lt. U.S. Army, 1965, advanced through grades to col.; chief force devel. USAMRDC; exec. sec. U.S. Army Med. R&D Adv. Panel, Washington, 1978-80; pers. policy officer Office of Army Surgeon Gen., Washington, 1981-83; spl. asst. chief Med. Svc. Corps, U.S. Army, Washington, 1983-86; dep. comdr. for adminstrn. SHAPE (Belgium) Med. Ctr., 1986-89; insp. gen. 7th Med. Command, Heidelberg, Germany, 1989-91; chief of staff USAMRDC, Ft. Detrick, Md., 1991-92; chief edn. and tng. Office of Army Surgeon Gen., Va., 1992-93; chief Health Svcs. divsn. Office Pers. Mgmt., PERSCOM, Alexandria, Va., 1993-95; ret. U.S. Army, 1995; sr. v.p. ops. Capital Health Svcs., Inc., 1996-97, pres., CEO, 1997—. Author: The History of the U.S. Army Medical Service Corps, 1997; contbr. numerous articles to profl. jours. Recipient Sir Henry Wellcome medal and prize, 1977, George Washington Honor medal Freedoms Found., 1978; named Young Fed. Health Care Adminstrn., Assn. Mil. Surgeons U.S., 1982, Disting. Honor Grad., U.S. Army-Baylor U. Program in Health Care Adminstrn., 1977, Disting. Medm. U.S. Army Med. Dept. Rgt., 1998. Fellow Am. Coll. Healthcare Execs.; mem. Nat. Capital Healthcare Execs. (prizes scholarly competition 1982, 84), Fed. Health Care Execs. Inst. Alumni Assn., Soc. History of Fed. Govt., Soc. 173d Airborne Brigade, Order Mil. Med. Merit, Omicron Delta Kappa (chpt. pres. 1964-65), Sigma Tau Delta, Pi Kappa Phi. E-mail: chsginn@aol.com. Home: 6825 Spring Beauty Ct Springfield VA 22152-3111 Office: Capital Health Svcs Inc 12011 Lee Jackson Hwy Ste 501 Fairfax VA 22033-3310

GINN, ROBERT MARTIN, retired utility company executive; b. Detroit, Jan. 13, 1924; s. Lloyd T. and Edna S. (Martin) G.; m. Barbara R. Force, 1948; children: Anne, Martha, Thomas. BS in Elec. Engring., U. Mich., 1948, MS in Elec. Engring., 1948. With Cleve. Electric Illuminating Co., 1948-89, contr., 1959-62, v.p. gen. svcs., 1963-70, exec. v.p., 1970-77, pres., 1977-83, chief exec. officer, 1979-88, chmn., 1983-89; chmn., CEO Centerior Energy Corp., Toledo Edison Co., 1986-88. Mem. Shaker Heights Bd. Edn., (Ohio), 1968-75, pres., 1973-74; pres. Welfare Fedn. Cleve., 1968-69; chmn. Cleve. Commn. on Higher Edn., 1983-86; trustee John Carroll U., 1983-89, exec.-in-residence, 1989—; trustee Martha Holden Jennings Found., 1983—; chmn. Cleve. Opera, 1986-91. With USAAF, 1943-46. Office: 1127 Euclid Ave Ste 343 Cleveland OH 44115-1650

GINN, RONN, architect, urban planner, general contractor; b. Jacksonville, Fla., Apr. 17, 1933; s. Angus Theodore and Joan Adelaide (Bailey) G.; children: Sharon Lee, John Norman. A.A., U. Fla., 1957, B.Arch., 1960, B.Landscape Architecture, 1961. Lic. bldg. ofcl., Fla. Urban design specialist Model Cities Adminstrn., HUD, Washington, 1967-68; pvt. practice landscape architecture, constrn., urban planning St. Petersburg, Fla., 1968—; pres. ARG Constrn. Corp., 1975-76, ARG Corp., 1977—, Ginn Corp., 1967-70, Atrium Corp., 1965-72; urban design lectr. U. N.Mex., 1967; planning cons. State Dept., 1967-68; design cons. Am. Revolution Bicentennial Commn., 1967-69; vis. design critic Rice U., 1974; mem. Pinellas County (Fla.) Bd. Adjustments and Appeals, 1981-88; mem. Albuquerque Fine Arts Commn., 1965-67, St. Petersburg Design Goals Com., 1971-73; moderator radio program Design in Our Community WPKM, Tampa, Fla., 1971-72; founder, bd. dirs. Pinellas County Red Flag Charrette, 1972-76, Catalyst, St. Petersburg; bd. dirs. Fla. Council Clean Air, Fla. Red Flag Charrette; mem. Pinellas County Planning Council, 1972-73. Supervising architect, urban designer: Roswell (N.Mex.) Ctrl. bus. dist. redesign, 1964, Tucumcari (N.Mex.) ctrl. bus. dist. redesign, 1967, Treasure Island (Fla.) civic ctr. design, 1971; architect, urban designer, prin. Atrium One, Albuquerque, 1965-67; contbg. editor Urban Affairs Symposia, 1965-73; guest columnist St. Petersburg Evening Ind., 1974; important works include Albuquerque ctrl. bus. dist. redesign (nat. AIA award 1966), new town Fla. Ctr. (nat. Am. Soc. Landscape Architects award 1970), Brown residence (AIA merit award 1975), Penguin Restaurant, Treasure Island, Fla., 1973, Cross residence, 1974, Sheridan Gallery, 1974, Madeira Beach C. of C., 1975, Greenpepper Restaurant, 1975, Mixon Bldg., Ruskin, Fla., 1976, Congregation Beth Chai Synagogue, Seminole, Fla., 1979, Villa Dos Santos Master Plan, St. Petersburg Beach, Fla., 1979, Congregation Kol Ami Synagogue, Tampa, 1981, Markham residence, St. Petersburg, 1981, The Moorings, Tierra Verde, Fla., 1981, Ginn Residence, St. Petersburg, 1981, Congregation B'nai Israel Synagogue, Clearwater, Fla., 1981, Suncoast Seabird Sanctuary, St. Petersburg, 1982, Lilly Residence, Treasure Island, Fla., 1983, Anchor Bank Office Bldg., St. Petersburg, 1984, 1600 Pasadena Office Bldg., 1984 (nat. design patent), Lighthouse Harbor Marina, 1984, Tugaloo Environ. Edn. Ctr., 1989, Johnnie Ruth Clarke Health Ctr., 1992, Jakabosi Studio, 1995. Mayoral candidate City of Treasure Island, Fla., 1973; bldg. dir. City of Seminole, 1975-78; mem. Leadership St. Petersburg, 1978-79. Recipient numerous archtl., landscape architecture, urban design awards, Addy awards, 1981, 82; named Spiffs Person of Courage, 1984. Mem. AIA (nat. com. on regional devel. 1969-76, vice chmn., commr. pub. affairs Fla. chpt.), Am. Inst. Planners, Constrn. Specifications Inst., Am. Inst. Landscape Architects, So. Bldg. Code Congress, Fla. Planning and Zoning Assn., Nat. Eagle Scout Assn. (chpt. chmn.). Republican. Presbyterian. Office: Jakabosi-Ginn Arch PO Box 1541 Robbinsville NC 28771-1541

GINN, SAM L., telephone company executive; b. Saint Clair, Ala., Apr. 3, 1937; s. James Harold and Myra Ruby (Smith) G.; m. Meriann Lanford Vance, Feb. 2, 1963; children: Matthew, Michael, Samantha. B.S., Auburn U., 1959; postgrad., Stanford U. Grad. Sch. Bus., 1968. Various positions AT&T, 1960-78; with Pacific Tel. & Tel. Co., 1978—; exec. v.p. network Pacific Tel. & Tel. Co., San Francisco, 1979-81, exec. v.p. services, 1981-82, exec. v.p. network services, 1982, exec. v.p., strategic planning and adminstrn., 1983, vice chmn. bd., strategic planning and adminstrn., 1983-84; vice chmn. bd., group v.p. PacTel Cos. Pacific Telesis Group, San Francisco, 1984-86; pres. Air Touch Commn., San Francisco, 1984-87; vice chmn. bd., pres., chief exec. officer PacTel Corp. Pacific Telesis Group, San Francisco, 1986; pres., chief operating officer Pacific Telesis Group, San Francisco, 1987-88, former chmn., pres., chief exec. officer; chmn. Air Touch Commn., San Francisco, 1993—; now chmn. bd., CEO Air Touch Commn., San Francisco, Calif.; mem. adv. bd. Sloan program Stanford U. Grad. Sch. Bus., 1978-85, mem. internat. adv. council Inst. Internat. Studies; bd. dir. 1st Interstate Bank, Chevron Corp., Safeway, Inc. Trustee Mills Coll., 1982—. Served to capt. U.S. Army, 1959-60. Sloan fellow, 1968. Republican. Clubs: Blackhawk Country (Danville, Calif.); World Trade, Pacific-Union; Rams Hill Country (Borrego Springs, Calif.), Bankers. Office: Air Touch Commn 1 California St San Francisco CA 94111-5401*

GINNS, DAVID RICHARD, county official; b. N.Y.C., Mar. 22, 1966; s. Robert Jay Ginns and Maxine (Lundy) Fisher; m. Lorraine Ann Smith, Aug. 14, 1994. BS in Urban Studies & Adminstrn., U. Cin., 1989; M of Urban & Regional Planning, U. Pitts., 1993. Sr. planner Orange County Planning Dept., Orlando, Fla., 1994-96; tranps. planner Citrus County Planning Divsn., Lecanto, Fla., 1993-94; transp. planner St. Lucie Met. Planning Orgn., Fort Pierce, Fla., 1996—; advisor Fort Pierce Main St./Bus. Recruitment Team, Fort Pierce Enterprise Zone Devel. Agy. Advisor Neighborhood Housing Svcs. of Fort Pierce, 1996—. Democrat. Jewish. Avocations: travel, reading. Office: St Lucie Met Planning Orgn 2300 Virginia Ave Rm 203 Fort Pierce FL 34982-5632

GINOS, JAMES ZISSIS, retired research chemist; b. Hillsboro, Ill., Feb. 1, 1923; s. Zissis and Nicoletta M. (Sakellaris) G.; m. Chrisilla Katsas, June 13, 1947; children: Geoffrey, Milton. BA, Columbia U., 1954; MS in Chem. Engring., Stevens Inst. Tech., 1962; PhD in Organic Chemistry, Stevens Inst. Tech., 1964. Chemist, Colgate Palmolive Co., Jersey City, 1953-57; chief chemist Diamond Shamrock Corp., Newark, 1957-58; project coordinator Nopco Chem. Co., Harrison, N.J., 1959-64; asst. scientist Brookhaven Nat. Labs., Upton, N.Y., 1964-68; research asst. prof. Mt. Sinai Sch. Medicine, N.Y.C., 1968-70; assoc. scientist Brookhaven Nat. Labs., 1970-74, scientist, 1974-75; research assoc. prof. Cornell U. Med. Coll., 1975-92, assoc. rsch. prof. neuroscience, 1989-92; ret., 1992; sr. research assoc. neuro-oncology Lab. Meml. Sloan-Kettering Cancer Center, N.Y.C., 1980-84, assoc. lab. mem., 1984-89, assoc. lab. mem. nuclear medicine cyclotron core, 1989-93. Contbr. articles to profl. jours. Mem. Am. Chem. Soc., AAAS, Harvey Soc., Am. Soc. Pharmacology and Exptl. Therapeutics, N.Y. Acad. Sci., Soc. Nuclear Medicine. Research on synthesis of radiopharmaceuticals labelled with shortlived positron emitting radioisotopes used in positron emission tomography. Patentee in field. Home: 200 Winston Dr Apt 3016 Cliffside Park NJ 07010-3234

GINOSAR, D. ELAINE, elementary education educator; b. Red Lodge, Mont., June 14, 1937; d. Alvin Henry and Dorothy Mary (Roberson) Wedemeyer; children: Nathan B., Daniel M., David M. BA, Calif. State U., Northridge, 1964, MA, 1977. Cert. elem. tchr., reading and learning disabilities. Tchr. Sacramento City Unified Sch. Dist., 1977—; math. leader, 1992-95; owner, operator rental properties. Pres. Davis (Calif.) Flower Arrangers, 1993-96. Host family for U. Calif. Davis to 15 fgn. students from Japan, Thailand, Mexico, South Korea, 1990-95. Named Woman of Yr. Am. Biog. Soc., 1996. Mem. AAUW (edn. equity chair 1993-95, edn. chair 1965-93, readers theater, women's history week 1990, 91, treas. 1993-98, pres. 1990-91, 98—), Calif. Tchrs. Assn. Republican. Presbyterian. Home: 3726 Chiles Rd Davis CA 95616-4346

GINOZA, WILLIAM, retired biophysics educator; b. L.A., Feb. 7, 1914; s. Shinkichi and Kame (Yamashiro) G.; m. Midori Sugita, Oct. 4, 1944 (dec. May 1987); children: Lillian, Donn. BA, U. Calif., Berkeley, 1937, MA, 1939; PhD, UCLA, 1952. Asst. rsch. biochemist dept. botany UCLA, 1952-55, rsch. scientist atomic energy commn., 1956-61; assoc. prof. dept. biophysics Pa. State U., University Park, 1961-67, prof., 1967-79, prof. emeritus, 1979—; invited speaker ednl. instns. and sci. confs., including Internat. Congress Biochemistry, Vienna, 1958, Faraday Soc. meeting on nucleic acids, Birmingham, Eng., 1958; vis. fellow Yale U., New Haven, 1958-60; vis. prof. U. Kyoto, Japan, 1974. Co-author: Methods in Virology, Vol IV, 1968.; contbr. reviews to Ann. Reviews Nuclear Sci., Ann. Reviews Microbiology; contbr. articles to profl. jours. Fellow AAAS; mem. Biophys. Soc., Sigma Xi, Phi Lambda Upsilon. Achievements include illucidation of molecular structure of Tobacco Mosaic Virus and its RNA, mechanisms by which heat or high energy radiations destroy the biological functions of nucleic acids of viruses and bacteria. Home: 962 E McCormick Ave State College PA 16801-6529

GINSBERG, BARRY GAVRILLE, psychologist, consultant, trainer; b. Bklyn., July 25, 1936; s. Elias Ginsberg and Lea Schwartz Epstein; m. Mindi Silverberg, Feb. 22, 1962; children: Joshua, Neil Daniel, Jeremy Marc. BS in Pharmacy, columbia U., 1958; MS in Edn./Clin. Sch. Psychology, CCNY, 1969; PhD in Human Devel. and Family Studies, Pa. State U., 1971. Lic. pharmacist, N.Y., N.J., Calif., Fla.; cert. tchr., N.Y.C.; lic. psychologist, Pa., Mass.; diplomate in family psychology Am. Bd. Profl. Psychology; cert. play therapist/supr., cert. marriage and family therapist; nat. cert. sch. psychologist. Pharmacist, mgr. Ginsberg Pharmacy, Bronx, N.Y., 1958-63; tchr. jr. and sr. h.s. N.Y.C. Bd. Edn., 1963-69; psychologist Bucks County Psychiat. Ctr., Chalfont, Pa., 1971-73; dir. child and family unit Lenape Valley Found., Chalfont, 1973-75, dir. cmty. svcs., 1975-78; psychologist dir. Ginsberg Assocs., Doylestown, Pa., 1978—; cons. and trainer, dir. Ctr. Relationship Enhancement, Doylestown, 1981—; adj. assoc. prof. Temple U., 1975-85; cons. Bucks County Area Coun. Aging, 1988—, Bucks County Children and Youth, Doylestown, 1989—, Bucks County Head Start, Bucks County Assn. Retarded Citizens, Doylestown, 1982—; adj. prof. psychology Phila. Coll. Osteopathic Medicine, 1997; bd. dirs. Am. Bd. Family Psychology, 1997. Author: Relationship Enhancement Family Therapy, 1997; columnist Parenting, 1988-89; co-host Caable TV program Parenting, 1994—. Bd. dirs. Big Bros./Big Sisters of Bucks County, 1972—, Bucks County Drug and Alcohol Commn., 1981-87, Network of Victims Assistance, 1990-95. Recipient Sterling Vol. award Ctrl. Bucks C. of C., 1996, Meritorious award Am. Bd. Profl. Psychology, 1992, Meritorious award Bucks County Drug and Alcohol Commn., 1987. Fellow APA (bd. dirs. divsn. family psychology, Meritorious awards divsn. family psychology 1986, 87, 88, 89), Pa. Psychol. Assn. (bd. dirs., pres. cmty. divsn.), Am. Assn. Marriage and Family Therapists (clin. mem., approved supr.), Ctrl. Bucks C. of C. (v.p., bd. dirs. 1975-89). Avocations: racquetball, folk dancing, Nutcracker Ballet. Office: Ginsberg Assocs 17 W State St Doylestown PA 18901-4225

GINSBERG, BENJAMIN, political science educator; b. Poking, Germany, Apr. 1, 1947; came to U.S., 1949, naturalized 1955; s. Herman and Anna (Wolfstein) G.; m. Sandra Joy Brewer, Dec. 15, 1968; children: Cynthia, Alexander. BA, U. Chgo., 1968, MA, 1970, PhD, 1973. Asst. prof. govt. Cornell U., Ithaca, N.Y., 1972-78, assoc. prof., 1978-83, prof., 1983-91, dir. Survey Rsch. Facility, 1985-86, dir. Inst. Pub. Affairs, 1987-91, dir. Washington program, 1988-91; David Bernstein prof. polit. sci., dir. Ctr. Govt. Studies, Johns Hopkins U., Balt., 1992—, dir. MA in Govt. program, 1993—; cons. N.Y. Times, N.Y.C., 1984-85; Taft Meml. lectr. U. Cin., 1992; Exxon Found. lectr. U. Chgo., 1992. Author: Poliscide, 1976, The Consequences of Consent, 1982, Do Elections Matter?, 1985, The Captive Public, 1986, Freedom and Power in American Government, 1989, Politics by Other Means, 1990, 2d edit., 1998, American Government: Readings and Cases, 1992, The Fatal Embrace, 1993, Democrats Return to Power, 1994, Embattled Democracy, 1995, We the People, 1997, American Electoral Politics: 1968-1998, 1999. Trustees' scholar U. Chgo., 1964-68; NIMH fellow U. Chgo., 1968-72; Jonathan Meigs grantee Cornell U., 1985, U.S. Dept. Justice grantee, 1984, Kellogg Found. grantee, 1987; recipient Oraculum award for excellence in teaching, 1993. Mem. Am. Polit. Sci. Assn. Jewish. Home: 10800 Tara Rd Potomac MD 20854-1340 Office: Johns Hopkins U Mergenthaler Hall Baltimore MD 21218

GINSBERG, BURTON, lawyer; b. Detroit, May 23, 1928; s. Sidney and Anna (Briskman) G.; m. Charlotte Wilks, June 1954 (div. 1959); children: Richard, Diane; m. Felice Ginsberg, Mar. 6, 1961; children: Leslie, Anne Marie. BA, U. Miami, 1948; JD, Stetson U., 1970. Bar: Fla. 1970. Pvt. practice North Miami, Fla., 1985—. Mem. com. mem. Rights of Children; guardian ad litem Broward Pro Bono Program, Ft. Lauderdale, Fla.; vol. Put Something Back, Dade County, Fla. Avocations: tennis, golf. Office: 16499 NE 19th Ave Ste 215 N Miami Beach FL 33162-4105

GINSBERG, CARL HARALSON, lawyer; b. Dallas, May 7, 1970; s. Major Cyrus and Scarlett Levi Ginsberg. BA, Duke U., 1991; JD, U. Tex., 1995. Bar: Tex., N.Y. Student atty. U.S. Atty.'s Office Ea. Divsn. N.Y., Bklyn., 1993, N.H. Pub. Defender, Manchester, 1994; briefing atty. Tex. Ct. Appeals, Austin, 1995-96; assoc. Clark Thomas & Winters, P.C., Austin, 1996-97; ptnr. Ginsberg & Assocs., Dallas, 1997—. Assoc. editor Tex. Internat. Law Jour. Wilbur Matthews Presdl. scholar U. Tex., Austin, 1995. Mem. Tex. State Bar, N.Y. State Bar, Phi Beta Kappa. Jewish. Office: Ginsberg & Assocs Ste 1221 8235 Douglas Ave Dallas TX 75225

GINSBERG, CAROL KERRE, women's health nurse practitioner; b. Washington, Dec. 31, 1941; d. Henry Cordover and Erma (Friedman) Cordover Taub; m. Jerome Maurice Ginsberg, Aug. 9, 1964; children: Andrew, Lynn, Peter. Diploma, Mt. Sinai Hosp., N.Y.C., 1962; BS, L.I. U., 1981; MS, Columbia U., 1984. Cert. nurse practitioner in ob-gyn. Ob-gyn. nurse practitioner and nurse colposcopist Queens L.I. Med. Group, Jamaica, N.Y.; clin. asst. prof. SUNY, Stony Brook. Mem. med. adv. bd. Suffolk County Planned Parenthood. Mem. Am. Coll. Ob-Gyn., Assn. Women's Health, Obstetrics and Neonatal Nursing, Nat. Assn. Nurse Practitioners in Reproductive Health, Am. Soc. for Colposcopy and Cervical Pathology, Assn. Reproductive Health Profls., Fulbright Assn. Home: 1 Kennedy Dr Plainview NY 11803-4017

GINSBERG, DAVID LAWRENCE, architect; b. N.Y.C., Sept. 21, 1932; s. Harry Seaman and Zena (Sagal) G.; m. Emily Boor, Dec. 29, 1969; children: Stuart Samuel, Daniel Paul, Laura Ruth. BArch, Cornell U., 1955. Pntr. charge N.Y. offices Perkins & Will, 1957-78; exec. v.p. Perkins & Will, Chgo., 1978-79; exec. v.p. and chief planning officer Columbia-Presbyn. Health Svcs., Inc., N.Y.C., 1979-92; v.p. Columbia-Presbyn. Health Systems, Inc.; dep. to pres. Presbyn. Hosp., N.Y.C., 1993-95; ptnr. Larsen, Shein, Ginsberg, Magnusson LLP, N.Y.C., 1995—; asst. clin. prof. pub. health Columbia U., N.Y.C., 1979-97; sr. cons. U.S. Global Health Svcs., 1992-94. Mem. Washington U. Parents Coun., St. Louis, 1988-91; mem. Scarsdale Planning Bd., 1980-90; trustee Presbyn. Hosp. Infan.t and Child Care Ctr. Recipient medal N.Y. Soc. Architects, 1955, award N.Y. Soc. for Health Planning, 1993. Fellow AIA (Acad. Architecture for Health, Forum for Healthcare Planning); mem. APHA, Am. Hosp. Assn., Assn. Am. Med. Colls., Soc. Hosp. Planning, Regional Planning Assn., Gargoyle Soc. Office: Larsen Shein Ginsberg Magnusson LLP Architect 170 Varick St New York NY 10013-1221

GINSBERG, DONALD MAURICE, physicist, educator; b. Chgo., Nov. 19, 1933; s. Maurice J. and Zelda Ginsberg; m. Joli D. Lasker, June 10, 1957; children: Mark D., Dana L. BA, U. Chgo., 1952, BS, 1955, MS (NSF fellow), 1956; PhD (NSF fellow), U. Calif. at Berkeley, 1960. Mem. faculty U. Ill., Urbana, 1959-97, prof. physics, 1966-97, prof. emeritus, 1997—; vis. scientist in physics Am. Assn. Physics Tchrs.-Am. Inst. Physics, 1965-71; vis. scientist IBM, 1976; mem. evaluation com. for Nat. High-Field Magnet Lab., NSF, 1977-79, 85, 91; mem. rev. com. for solid state sci. div. Argonne Nat. Lab., 1977-83, chmn., 1980; mem. rev. panel for basic energy scis. div. Dept. Energy, 1981. Editor: Physical Properties of High Temperature Superconductors, Vols. 1, 2, 3, 4, and 5, 1989, 90, 92, 94, 96; contbr. to Ency. Britannica, 1971, 82, 88, 94, 96, Concise Ency. of Magnetic and Superconducting Materials, 1992. Alfred P. Sloan rsch. fellow, 1960-64, NSF fellow, 1966-67; U. Ill. scholar, 1994; recipient Daniel C. Drucker award U. Ill. Engring. Coll., 1992. Fellow Am. Phys. Soc. (winner Oliver E. Buckley Consensed Matter Physics prize 1998); mem. AAAS, Phi Beta Kappa, Sigma Xi. Research and publs. on low temperature physics, superconductivity, cryogenic instrumentation. Home: 2208 Grange Cir Urbana IL 61801-6607 Office: 265 Loomis Lab 1110 W Green St Urbana IL 61801-3003

GINSBERG, ERNEST, lawyer, banker; b. Syracuse, N.Y., Feb. 14, 1931; s. Morris Henry and Mildred Florence (Slive) G.; m. Harriet Gay Scharf, Dec. 20, 1959; children: Alan Justin, Robert Daniel. BA, Syracuse U., 1953, JD, 1955; LLM, Georgetown U., 1963. Bar: N.Y. 1955, U.S. Supreme Ct. 1964. Pvt. practice law Syracuse, 1957-61; mem. staff, office chief counsel IRS, Washington, 1961-63; tax counsel Comptr. of Currency, Washington, 1964-65, assoc. chief counsel, 1965-68; v.p. legal affairs, sec. Republic Nat. Bank N.Y., N.Y.C., 1968-74; sr. v.p. legal affairs, sec. Republic Nat. Bank, N.Y.C., 1975-86, exec. v.p., gen. counsel, sec., 1984-86, vice chmn. bd., gen. counsel, 1986-94, vice chmn. bd., 1990—; sr. v.p., sec. legal affairs Republic N.Y. Corp., N.Y.C., 1974-84, exec. v.p., gen. counsel, sec., 1984-86, vice chmn. bd., gen. counsel, sec., 1984-86, vice chmn. bd., gen. counsel, sec., 1986-94, vice chmn. bd., 1986—, also bd. dirs.; bd. visitors Syracuse U. Coll. Law. Chmn. emeritus Roundabout Theatre Co., N.Y.C. With U.S. Army, 1955-57. Mem. Am. Bankers Assn. (bd. dirs. 1995-97), Am. Bankers Coun. (co-chmn. 1992-94), N.Y. State Bankers Assn. (pres. 1993-94), Bankers Roundtable (bd. dirs. 1995-97), Phi Sigma Delta, Phi Delta Phi. Office: Republic NY Corp 452 5th Ave New York NY 10018-2706

GINSBERG, FRANK CHARLES, advertising executive; b. N.Y.C., Mar. 8, 1944; s. Robert G. and Frances (Ginsberg) Porcelli; m. Joan Barbara Cocoziello; 1 child, Alison. BFA, Boston U., 1965; MFA, NYU, 1968. Art dir. Grey Advt., N.Y.C., 1966-69; exec. art dir. Lowe & Ptnrs. Co., N.Y.C., 1969-71, PGI, N.Y.C., 1971-74; creative dir. Avrett Free & Ginsberg, N.Y.C., 1974-82, sr. exec. v.p., creative dir., 1982-86; pres., creative dir. Avrett, Free & Ginsberg, N.Y.C., 1986-93, CEO, co-chmn., creative dir., 1993—; creative cons. Recruiting Young Tchrs., 1987. Bd. dirs. Advt. Club N.Y., Acting Co., Children's Hearing Inst., 1997; bd. dirs., bd. govs. 4A's Creative A Awards, 1997; hon. judge Andy Awards, 1997, Best of N.Y. Advt., 1997; chmn. ann. fund Riverdale Country Sch., 1983-88. Recipient Clio award, 1974, 79; recipient Bronze Lion Cannes Film Festival, 1978, 24 certs. or merit, 1971-83, 14 Andy awards, 1971-83, Gold medal Internat. TV Awards, 1986, Gold Effie award, 1987; over 30 awards for art dir. Mem. Univ. Club, One Club, Art Dirs. Club (5 Silver One Club awards 1971-83), Skyrink Ice Skating, Inc., St. Louis Racquet Club. Office: Avrett Free & Ginsberg Advt Inc 800 3rd Ave 34th Fl New York NY 10022-7604*

GINSBERG, HARLEY GLEN, pediatrician; b. Manhattan, N.Y., Apr. 14, 1955; s. Morton Norbert and Barbara Lois (Besser) G.; m. Susan A. Boudreaux, Aug. 18, 1985; children: Mason, Jacob. BS, Tulane U., 1977, MD, 1982. Diplomate Am. Bd. Pediatrics, Neonatal Medicine. Neonatologist, dir. intensive care unit Ochsner Clinic, New Orleans, 1987—. Contbr. articles to profl. jours. Tchr. religious sch. Touro Synagogue, New Orleans, 1995, 97; baseball coach Little League Metairie, La., 1995—. Fellow Am. Acad. Pediats.; mem. Greater New Orleans Pediat. Soc., Tulane Med. Alumni Assn., Tulane Pediat. Alumni Assn. Avocations: running, chess, numismatics, gardening. Office: Ochsner Clinic 1514 Jefferson Hwy New Orleans LA 70121-2483

GINSBERG, HAROLD SAMUEL, virologist, educator; b. Daytona Beach, Fla., May 27, 1917; s. Jacob and Anne (Kalb) G.; m. Marion Reibstein, Aug. 4, 1949; children: Benjamin Langer, Peter Robert, Ann Meredith, Jane Elizabeth. AB, Duke U., 1937; MD, Tulane U., 1941, DSc (hon.), 1995, hon. degree, 1996. Resident Mallory Inst. Pathology, Boston, 1941-42; intern, asst. resident Boston City Hosp., 4th Med. Service, 1942-43; resident physician, assoc. Rockefeller Inst., 1946-51; assoc. prof. preventive medicine Western Res. U. Sch. Medicine, 1951-60; prof. microbiology, chmn. dept. U. Pa. Sch. Medicine, 1960-73; prof. microbiology, chmn. dept. Coll. Phys. and Surg. Columbia, 1973-85, prof. microbiology and medicine, dir. section molecular pathogenesis of infection, 1986-97; part time expert scientist NIH, Rockville, Md., 1993—; mem. commn. acute respiratory diseases Armed Forces Epidemiological Bd., 1959-73; cons. NIH, 1959-72, 75—, Army Chem. Corps, 1962-64, NASA, 1969-73, Am. Cancer Soc., 1969-73, mem. coun. on rsch. and pers., 1976-80; v.p. Internat. Com. on Nomenclature of Viruses, 1966-75; mem. space sci. bd., chmn. panel microbiology Nat. Acad. Sci., 1973-74; chmn. microbiology exam. com. Nat. Bd. Med. Examiners, 1974-79; mem. microbiology and infectious disease com. Nat. Inst. Allergy and Infectious Disease, NIH, 1976-81, chmn., 1979-81; co-chmn. Inst. Medicine, NAS Roundtable: AIDS: Modern Approaches Vaccines and Anti-Viral Drugs, 1989-92; mem. U.S. Nat. Com. for Internat. Union of Microbiological Socs. (USNC/IUMS), Nat. Rsch. Coun., 1992—. Contbr. textbooks; co-author: Microbiology, 1967, 4th edit., 1990, Virology, 2d edit., 1988, Vaccines 88-95, Modern Approaches to New Vaccines, Including Prevention of AIDS; mem. editorial bd. Jour. Infectious Diseases, Jour. Immunology, Jour. Exptl. Medicine, Jour. Virology and Bacteriological Revs., Jour. Acquired Immune Deficiency Syndromes; editor: Jour. Virology, 1979-84, Cancer Research, 1978-82. Served to lt. col. M.C. AUS, 1943-46. Decorated Legion of Merit; Fogarty scholar NIH, 1993-94; recipient Disting. Svc. award Coll. Physicians and Surgeons, Columbia U., 1991, Acad. medal N.Y. Acad. Medicine, 1994, Bristol-Myers Squibb award for Disting. Achievement in Infectious Disease Rsch., 1994, Outstanding Alumnus award Tulane Sch. Medicine, 1995. Fellow AAAS; mem. NAS, Inst. Medicine of NAS., Assn. Am. Physicians, Am. Acad. Microbiologists (chmn. bd. govs. 1971-72, bd. govs. 1993-99), Am. Soc. Clin. Investigation (councillor 1958-60), Am. Assn. Immunologists, Am. Soc. Microbiology (chmn. virology div. 1961-62, councillor div. 1977-81), Soc. Exptl. Biology and Medicine, Assn. Med. Sch. Microbiology Chairmen (pres. 1972-73), Harvey Soc. (pres. 1984coun. 1985-88), Cen. Soc. Clin. Research, Am. Soc. Biol. Chemists, Am. Soc. Virology (pres. 1983), Alpha Omega Alpha. Home: 5225 Pooks Hill Rd Apt 1313S Bethesda MD 20814-6724 Office: Nat Inst Allergy and Infectious Diseases LMM Twinbrook II 12441 Parklawn Dr Rockville MD 20852-1742

GINSBERG, HERSH MEIER, rabbi, religious organization executive; b. Vienna, Austria, July 8, 1928; s. Lazar Yonah Ginsberg and Perl Roth; m. Fradel Levy; children: Lazar Yonah, Meshulim, Chana. Dir. Union Orthodox Rabbis of U.S. and Can.; rabbinical ct. judge; dean Rabbi Jacob-Joseph Sch., N.Y.C., 1955-73. Founder Kolel Ohel Elemelech Rabbinical Coll., Jerusalem. Office: Union Orthodox Rabbis US & Can 235 E Broadway New York NY 10002-5600

GINSBERG, LEON HERMAN, social work educator; b. San Antonio, Jan. 15, 1936; s. Sam and Lillian (Gindler) G.; m. Elaine Myrna Kaner, July 29, 1956 (div. 1983); children: Robert, Michael, Meryl Sue.; m. Connie Mooney, June 2, 1983; stepchildren: Claire, Kathleen Mooney. BA, Trinity U., 1957; MSW, Tulane U., 1959; PhD, U. Okla., 1966. Dist. dir. B'nai B'rith Youth Orgn., New Orleans, 1958-61; dir. community activities Jewish Community Council, Tulsa, 1961-63; assoc. prof. Sch. Social Work U. Okla., Norman, 1963-68; prof., dir. Sch. Social Work W.Va. U., Morgantown, 1968-71; prof., dean Sch. Social Work W.Va. U., 1971-77; commr. human services State of W.Va., Charleston, 1977-84; chancellor W.Va. Bd. Regents for Higher Edn., 1984-86; Carolina disting. prof. Coll. Social Work U. S.C., Columbia, 1986—; Fulbright prof. U. Pontificia Bolivariana, Medellin, Colombia, fall 1974; cons. tng. programs Peace Corps, Head Start, Community Action, Bur. Indian Affairs, pub. welfare depts. Okla., Pa., W.Va. Author: Understanding Social Problems, Policies and Programs, 1994, Social Work Practice in Public Welfare, 1983, The Social Work Almanac, 1992, 2d edit., 1995, Conservative Social Policy, 1998, Careers in Social Work, 1998; co-author: Human Services for Older Adults, 1979, 2d edit., 1990; editor: Social Work in Rural Communities, 1976, 3d edit., 1998, Supplement Ency. Social Work, 1990; (book series) Social Issues and Social Problems, 1992—; co-editor: Life-Span Development Psychology, 1975, New Management for Social Workers, 1988, 2d edit., 1995, Understanding Social Problems, Policies, and Programs, 1994, 3d edit., 1999, Information Technologies; cons. editor Social Work, Adminstr. in Social Work, Tchg. in Social Work. Capt. AUS, 1957-58. Recipient Disting. Service award W.Va. Welfare Conf., 1970; named W.Va. Social Worker of Yr., 1978, Outstanding Alumnus, Tulane U. Sch. Social Work, 1989. Mem. NASW (past nat. sec., comm. com. 1995-98, Rhoda G. Sarnat Internat. award 1998), Coun. Social Work Edn., Am. Pub. Welfare Assn. (past pres.), Nat. Ctr. for Social Policy and Practice (past chmn. bd.), Internat. Coun. on Social Welfare (past chmn. to U.S. com.), Child Welfare League Am., B'nai B'rith. Office: U SC Coll Social Work Columbia SC 29208

GINSBERG, MARC C., former diplomat, investment company executive; b. N.Y.C., Oct. 18, 1950; m. Janet Louise Ginsberg; two children. BA, Am. U.; JD, Georgetown U. Legis. asst. to Sen. Edward Kennedy, 1973-76; spl. asst. to under sec. of mgmt. Dept. State, 1977-80; dep. sr. adviser to Pres. for Middle East affairs, 1980-81; atty. Surrey & Morse, D.C., 1981-87, Galland, Kharasch, Morse & Garfinkle, D.C., 1987-93; U.S. amb. to Morocco, 1993-98; pres. Georgetown Global Investments Corp., Washington, 1998—. Mem. ABA, D.C. Bar Assn. Office: Georgetown Global Investments Corp, Ste 525, 1455 Pennsylvania Ave NW, Washington Morocco*

GINSBERG, MARVIN A., architect; b. St. Louis, Feb. 22, 1932; s. Sam and Fannie (Satz) G.; m. Sandra Ruth Cohen, Feb. 14, 1966; 1 child, Aren Jennifer. BArch with honors, Washington U., St. Louis, 1955. Lic. architect, Mo., Ill.; cert. NCAR Bd. Programmer, planner, designer Hellmuth, Yamasaki, Leinweber, St. Louis, 1953-55, Hellmuth, Obata & Kassabaum, St. Louis, 1957-63, Bernard McMahon, St. Louis, 1964-67; prin. Marvin Ginsberg & Assocs., St. Louis, 1967-80, Sorkin Ginsberg & Assocs., St. Louis, 1980-96; dir. design and planning SGA Architects, St. Louis, 1997—. Bd. mem. Planning & Zoning Commn., Ballwin, Mo., 1970-80. Recipient Steedman traveling fellowship Washington U., St. Louis, 1960, excellence in sch. design award Am. Assn. Sch. Adminstrs., San Francisco, 1993. Mem. AIA (com. on design and edn. 1980—), Bldg. Ofcls. and Code Adminstrn. Internat., Nat. Trust Historic Preservation. Jewish. Office: SGA Architects LLC 7386 Pershing Ave Saint Louis MO 63130-4206

GINSBERG, MYRON, computer scientist; b. Brockton, Mass., May 3, 1943; s. Frank and Evelyn Hazel (Spekin) G.; m. Judith Beverly Rosenbaum, Nov. 19, 1989; 1 stepchild, Ellen Joy Schoenfeld. BA in Math., Boston U., 1965; MA in Math., Clark U., 1967; PhD in Computer Sci., U. Iowa, 1972. Instr. dept. computer sci. U. Iowa, Iowa City, 1969-72; from asst. prof. to assoc. prof. computer sci. So. Meth. U., Dallas, 1972-77, 77-79; NASA/ASEE rsch. fellow NASA Langley Rsch. Ctr, Hampton, Va., summer 1979; assoc. sr. rsch. scientist GM Rsch. Labs., Warren, Mich., 1979-81, sr. rsch. scientist, 1981-82, staff rsch. scientist, 1982-92; cons. sys. engr. EDS Advanced Computing Ctr., GM NAO R & D Ctr., Warren, 1992-96, EDS High Performance Computing Group, Troy, Mich., 1996-97; ind. cons. High Performance Computing Rsch. and Edn., Farmington Hills, Mich., 1997—; mathematician U.S. Army Ballistics Rsch. Lab., Aberdeen Proving Ground, MD., summers, 1964-67; data sys. analyst NASA Electronics Rsch. Ctr., Cambridge, Mass., summers, 1968-69; adj. assoc. prof. U. Mich., Ann Arbor, 1990-; mem. adv. bd. Cray Rsch. Fortran, 1991-92; grant rev. panelist NSF, 1992-93, 96-97; GM/EDS rep. to Supercomputing Automotive Applications Partnership, 1992-94; founder and first chmn. of AUTOBENCH Project of U.S. Coun. for Automotive Rsch., 1995-96. Editor: Supercomputers in the Auto Industry, 1985, Automotive Applications of Supercomputers, 1988, High-Speed and Large-Scale Computing: A Panoramic View, 1988, Automotive Applications of Vector/Parallel Computers: State-of-the-Art, 1992; contbr. articles to profl. jours.; mem. editl. bd. Computing Sys. in Engring., 1988-93. Grantee, Mobil Oil Found., 1975, U.S. Army C.E., 1977-78, NSF, 1983-84, 77-79, Alfred P. Sloan Found., 1975-78. Fellow Assn. for Computing Machinery (lectr., bd. dirs. SIGNUM 1976-80 editor-in-chief SIGNUM newsletter 1976-80); mem. IEEE (sr.), Computer Soc. of IEEE (lectr.), ASME (lectr.), Soc. for Indsl. and Applied Math. (lectr., spl. group on supercomputing), Soc. Automotive Engrs. (founder, 1st chmn. com. on high performance computing stds. for automotive mfg. applications 1996-97, lectr., award for excellence in oral presentation 1985, 86, 87, Disting. Spkr. plaque 1988, Forest R. McFarland award 1994), Sigma Xi (lectr.). Avocations: playing alto sax, tenor sax, soprano sax, clarinet and flute; listening to jazz and classical music. Office: High Performance Computing R&E 35764 Congress Rd Ste 100 Farmington MI 48335-1222

GINSBERG, MYRON DAVID, neurologist; b. Denver, Aug. 26, 1939; s. Morris Seymour and Evelyn (Fishman) G.; children: Deborah Mara, Emily Michelle. BA, Wesleyan U., 1961; MD, Harvard U., 1966. Intern, resident Harvard Med. Svc., Boston City Hosp., 1966-68; neurology resident, fellow Mass. Gen. Hosp., Boston, 1968-70, 72-73; staff assoc. Lab. Perinatal

Physiology, NIH, Bethesda, Md., 1970-72; asst. prof., assoc. prof. dept. neurology U. Pa., Phila., 1973-79; assoc. prof. neurology U. Miami (Fla.) Sch. Medicine, 1979-81, prof. neurology, 1981—, dir. cerebral vascular disease rsch. ctr., 1981—, dir. neurotrauma clin. rsch. ctr., 1991-95, Peritz Scheinberg endowed chair of neurology, 1992—; mem. study sect. NIH, Bethesda, 1982-86; nat. rsch. com. Am. Heart Assn., Dallas, 1986-91. Editor: Cerebrovascular Diseases, 16th Princeton Conf., 1989; editor Jour. Blood Flow and Metabolism, 1992-97; contbr. over 200 articles to profl. jours. Lt. comdr. USPHS, 1970-72. Recipient Fulbright scholarship U.S. Govt., 1961-62, Jacob Javits Neuroscience Investigator award NIH, 1985-92. Fellow Am. Acad. Neurology; mem. Am. Neurol. Assn. (membership com. 1990-91), Am. Physiol. Soc., Internat. Soc. Cerebral Blood Flow & Metabolism (dir. 1985-89), Phi Beta Kappa, Alpha Omega Alpha. Office: U Miami Sch Medicine Dept Neurology D4-5 PO Box 016960 Miami FL 33101-6960

GINSBERG, NORMAN ARTHUR, physician; b. Chgo., May 28, 1946; m. Denise Ginsberg; children: Melinda, Sara. BA, So. Ill. U., 1968; postgrad., Ill. Coll. Pharmacy, 1968-69, U. Guadalerjara, 1969-72; MD, Chgo. Med. Sch., 1974. Diplomate Am. Bd. Ob-gyn. Intern Michael Reese Hosp. and Med. Ctr., Chgo., 1974-75, resident in ob-gyn., 1975-79, mem. staff, 1979—; pvt. practice in ob-gyn. Chgo.; mem. staff Northwestern Hosp. and Med. Ctr., 1984—; investigator 1st trimester diagnosis of inheritable diseases WHO. Bd. dirs. Nat. Abortion Rights League Ill. Fellow Am. Coll. Ob-gyn., Am. Soc. Human Genetics, Ctrl. Assn. Ob-gyn.; mem. AMA, Am. Fertility Soc., Chgo. Med. Soc. Achievements include pioneering of chorionic villi sampling in U.S.; first trimester screening for Down's Syndrome; pre-implantation genetis in U.S. Home: 1520 Eastwood Ave Highland Park IL 60035-2729 Office: Assn for Women's Health Care Ltd 30 N Michigan Ave Ste 607 Chicago IL 60602-3402

GINSBERG, PHILLIP CARL, physician; b. Fairbanks, Alaska, June 1, 1954; s. Richard and Sondra (Soble) G.; m. Judith Carson, June 19, 1977; 1 child, Rachel Hope. BS in Biology, Villanova U., 1976; MS, Phila. Coll. Osteopath, 1985, DO, 1980; JD, Temple U., 1995. Diplomate Nat. Bd. Osteopathic Examiners; Am. Bd. Osteopathic Surgeons; cert. urological surgery. Intern Hosp. Phila. Coll. Osteopathic Medicine, Phila., 1980-81; resident Albert Einstein Med. Ctr., Phila., 1981-82; resident in urologic surgery Hosp. Phila. Coll. Osteopathic Medicine, Phila., 1981-85; pvt. practice Phila., 1985—; clin. prof. Phila. Coll. Osteopathic Medicine; med. dir. Urodiagnostics, Inc., Del. Valley Continence Ctr.; chmn. div. of urology Albert Einstein Med. Ctr., 1989, Albert Einstein Med. Ctr.; cons. Nat. Cancer Inst. Contbr. numerous articles to profl. jours. Fellow Am. Coll. Osteo. Surgeons, Am. Coll. Legal Medicine; mem. AMA, ABA, Am. Osteo. Assn., Pa. Osteol. Assn., Pa. Med. Soc., Pa. Urology Assn., Am. Fertility Assn., Am. Urol. Assn., Mid Atlantic Urol. Assn., Phila. Urol. soc., Lambda Omicron Gamma. Home: 118 Righters Mill Rd Narberth PA 19072-1313 Office: Albert Einstein Med Ctr 5401 Old York Rd Ste 500 Philadelphia PA 19141-3032

GINSBERG, ROBERT JASON, thoracic surgeon; b. Toronto, Ont., Can., Mar. 30, 1940; came to U.S., 1990; s. Albert and Harriet (Snitzer) G.; m. Charlotte Ina Berger, May 26, 1963; children: Karyn Beth, Harold Jordan, David Lawrence. MD, U. Toronto, 1963. Cert. in thoracic surgery, Can. Chief thoracic surgery Toronto Western Hosp., 1971-80; chief thoracic oncology Toronto Gen. Hosp., 1980-85; chief surgery Mt. Sinai Hosp., Toronto, 1985-90; chief thoracic surgery Meml. Sloan-Kettering, N.Y.C., 1990—; prof. of surgery U. Toronto, 1985-90, Cornell U., N.Y.C., 1990—, surg. chmn. lung cancer study group, 1980-87, surg. chmn. radiation therapy oncology group, 1995—. Editor: (books) Yearbook of Thoracic Surgery, 1993, 94, 95, 96, 97, Thoracic Surgery, 1995, Esophageal Surgery, 1995; mem. editl. bd. jours. Bd. dirs. U. Calif. San Francisco Cancer Ctr., 1999—; chmn. bd. dirs. ALCASE, 1997—. Fellow Royal Coll. Surgeons Can.; mem. ACS, Soc. Thoracic Surgeons (mem. coun. 1989-92), Am. Assn. Thoracic Surgery, Soc. Clin. Oncology, Soc. Surg. Oncology, Am. Surg. Assn., N.Y. Thoracic Soc. (v.p. 1996), N.Y. Thoracic Surgery Soc. (pres. 1997), Gen. Thoracic Surgery Club (founding mem. 1987). Avocations: culinary arts, golf, tennis, hockey, theater. Office: Meml Sloan-Kettering 1275 York Ave New York NY 10021-6007

GINSBURG, CHARLES DAVID, lawyer; b. N.Y.C., Apr. 20, 1912; s. Nathan and Rae (Lewis) G.; m. Marianne Laïs; children by previous marriage: Jonathan, Susan, Mark. AB, W.Va. U., 1932; LLB, Harvard U., 1935. Bar: W. Va. 1935, U.S. Supreme Ct. 1940, D.C. 1946, U.S. Ct. Appeals (2d, 3rd, 4th, 7th, and Fed. cirs.) 1946, U.S. Claims Ct. 1960, U.S. Tax Ct. 1961. Atty. for public utilities div. and office of gen. counsel SEC, 1935-39; law sec. to Justice William O. Douglas, 1939; asst. to commr. SEC, 1939-40; legal adviser Price Stblzn. Div., Nat. Def. Adv. Com., 1940-41; gen. counsel Office Price Adminstrn. and Civilian Supply, 1941-42, OPA, 1942-43; pvt. practice law Ginsburg, Feldman and Bress, Washington, 1946-98; founding ptnr. Ginsburg, Feldman & Bress, 1946-98; sr. counsel, firm Powell, Goldstein, Frazer & Murphy, LLP, 1998; adminstrv. asst. to Senator M.M. Neely, W.Va., 1950; adj. prof. internat. law Georgetown U. (Grad. Sch. Law), 1959-67; sr. counsel Washington, 1998—; Dep. commr. U.S. del. Austrian Treaty Commn., Vienna, 1947; adviser U.S. del. Council Fgn. Ministers, London, 1947; Mem. Presdl. Emergency Bd. 166 (Airlines), 1966; mem. Pres.'s Commn. on Postal Orgn., 1967; chmn. Presdl. Emergency Bd. 169 (Railroads), 1969; exec. dir. Nat. Adv. Commn. Civil Disorders, 1967. Author: The Future of German Reparations; Contbr. to legal jours. Bd. mem., chmn. exec. com. Nat. Symphony Orch. Assn., 1960-69; bd. govs. Weizmann Inst., 1965 (hon. fellow 1972); mem. vis. com. Harvard-Mass. Inst. Tech. Joint Ctr. on Urban Studies, 1969; trustee St. John's Coll., 1969-76, chmn. bd., 1974-76; overseers com. Kennedy Sch. Govt. Harvard, 1971—; mem. coun. Nat. Harvard Law Sch. Assn., 1972—, gen. counsel Dem. Nat. Com., 1968-70. Served from pvt. to capt. AUS, 1942-46; dep. dir. econs. div. Office Mil. Govt., 1945-46, Germany. Decorated Bronze Star, Legion of Merit; recipient Presdl. Cert. of Merit. Mem. Fed. Bar Assn, Am. Law Inst., Coun. on Fgn. Rels., Met. Club, Army and Navy Club, Phi Beta Kappa. Democrat. Home: 619 S Lee St Alexandria VA 22314-3819 Office: 1001 Pennsylvania Ave NW Washington DC 20004

GINSBURG, DAVID, human genetics educator, researcher; b. Newburgh, N.Y., Aug. 11, 1952; s. Leonard and Ruth Helena Henrietta (Falkson) G.; m. Maureen Rose Kushinsky, June 7, 1981; children: Daniel William, Leah Beth. BA magna cum laude, Yale U., 1974; MD, Duke U., 1977. Diplomate Am. Bd. Internal Medicine, subspecialties in med. oncology and hematology; diplomate Am. Bd. Med. Genetics. Resident in pathology Presbyn. Hosp., San Francisco, 1977-78; intern, resident in internal medicine Peter Bent Brigham Hosp., Boston, 1978-81; fellow tng. program in hematology and med. oncology Brigham and Women's Hosp., Harvard Med. Sch., Boston, 1981-84, instr. medicine, 1984-85; asst. prof. dept. medicine U. Mich., Ann Arbor, 1985-89, assoc. prof. with tenure, 1989-93, assoc. prof. human genetics, 1989-93; asst. investigator Howard Hughes Med. Inst. Howard Hughes Med. Inst., Ann Arbor, 1985-89, assoc. investigator, 1989-93; prof. internal medicine and human genetics, 1993—, dir. divsn. molecular medicine and genetics, dept. medicine, 1993—; investigator Howard Hughes Med. Inst., 1993—. Contbr. numerous articles to profl. jours. Recipient Jerome W. Conn award Dept. Medicine, U. Mich., 1987-88, Frank E. Trobaugh Hematology Young Investigator award Midwest Blood Club, 1988; Med. Scientist Tng. Program scholar Duke U., 1974-77. Mem. ACP, Am. Soc. Human Genetics, Am. Soc. Hematology, Am. Heart Assn. (thrombosis coun.), Assn. Am. Physicians, Am. Soc. for Clin. Investigation, Alpha Omega Alpha. Jewish. Office: Howard Hughes Med Inst 1150 W Medical Center Dr Ann Arbor MI 48109-0726

GINSBURG, DOUGLAS HOWARD, federal judge, educator; b. Chgo., May 25, 1946; s. Maurice and Katherine (Goodmont) G.; m. Claudia De Secundy, May 31, 1968 (div. Sept. 1980); 1 child, Jessica DeSecundy; m. Hallee Perkins Morgan, May 9, 1981; children: Hallee Katherine Morgan, Hannah Maurice Morgan. Diploma, Latin Sch. Chgo., 1963; BS, Cornell U., 1970; JD, U. Chgo., 1973. Bar: Ill. 1973, Mass. 1982, U.S. Supreme Ct. 1984, U.S. Ct. Appeals (9th cir.) 1986. Assoc. Covington & Burling, Washington, 1972; law clk. U.S. Ct. Appeals, Washington, 1973-74, U.S. Supreme Ct., Washington, 1974-75; prof. Harvard U., 1975-83; dep. asst. atty. gen. for regulatory affairs antitrust divsn U.S. Dept. Justice, Washington, 1983-84, asst. atty. gen. antitrust divsn., 1985-86; adminstr. for info. and regulatory affairs Exec. Office Pres., Office Mgmt. and Budget, Washington, 1984-85; judge U.S. Ct. Appeals (D.C. cir.), 1986—; vis. prof. law Columbia U., N.Y.C., 1987-88; lectr. law Harvard U., Cambridge, Mass., 1987-91; disting. prof. law George Mason U., Arlington, Va., 1988—; Charles J. Merriam vis. scholar, sr. lectr. U. Chgo., 1990—. Author: Regulation of Broadcasting: Law and Policy Towards Radio, Television and Cable Communications, 1979, Antitrust, Uncertainty, and Technological Innovation, 1980; co-author: Regulation of the Electronic Mass Media, 1991; editor: (with W. Abernathy) Government, Technology and the Future of the Automobile, 1980; contbr. articles to profl. jours. Mecham scholar U. Chgo. Law Sch., 1970-73; recipient Casper Platt award U. Chgo. Law Sch., 1972. Mem. Am. Econ. Assn., Am. Law and Econs. Assn., Mont Pelerin Soc., Order of Coif, Phi Kappa Phi. Avocations: historic preservation, antiques, fox hunting. Office: US Ct Appeals 333 Constitution Ave NW Washington DC 20001-2866

GINSBURG, GERALD J., lawyer, business executive; b. Poughkeepsie, N.Y., Aug. 29, 1930; s. Abraham and Anna (Murkoff) G.; children: Jason Andrew, Stephanie Carla. B.S., Syracuse U., 1952; J.D., Bklyn. Law Sch., 1958. Bar: N.Y. 1959. Pub. acct., 1954-59; v.p. fin. and ops., dir. Sheffield Watch Corp., N.Y.C., 1959-70; dir. Sheffield Watch Corp., 1967-70; exec. v.p., dir. Kurt Orban Co., Wayne, N.J., 1971-83; pres., dir. Pacific Marine Holdings Corp., 1983-87; pres. J&S Cons., Walnut Creek, CAlif.; dir. Ramapo Fin. Corp., Pilgrim State Bank. Served with USNR, 1952-53. Mem. ABA, N.Y. Bar Assn. Office: PO Box 5314 Walnut Creek CA 94596-1314

GINSBURG, GILBERT J., lawyer, law educator; b. Chgo., Aug. 26, 1936; s. Maurice I. and Sarah (Ginsberg) G.; m. Faith D. Rosenson, June 28, 1959; children: Yale Maurice, David Bennett, Benjamin Lavin, Raphael Natan, Herzl, Melissa. BA, U. Chgo., 1954, JD, 1957. Bar: D.C., Ill., U.S. Claims Ct., U.S. Ct. Appeals (2d cir., Fed. cir., D.C. cir.), U.S. Supreme Ct. Atty., advisor Army Corps. Engrs., Chgo., 1958-59; prof. law Army JAG Sch., Charlottesville, Va., 1959-62; atty. NASA Gen. Counsel Office, Washington, 1962-66; prof. law George Washington U., Washington, 1967-80, dir. govt. contracts, 1973-80; dean Touro Law Sch., N.Y.C., 1980-81; sr. ptnr. Epstein Becker & Green, Washington, 1981-96; adj. prof. George Washington U., 1981—, vis. lectr. govt. contracts, 1981—; speaker in field. Author: Federal Labor Standards, 1997, Employer's Guide to FLSA, 1993, FLSA Handbook, 1986, Pricing of Claims, 1999, Loss of Efficiency and Extended Overhead Claims, 1999, The Service Contract Act, 1999, others; contbr. articles to profl. jours. Pres. Yeshiva of Greater Washington, 1965-73, Young Israel, Washington, 1962-65, 75-80; bd. dirs. Touro Coll., 1971—. Capt. U.S. Army, JAGC, 1959-62. Mem. ABA, Fed. Bar Assn., Order of Coif. Democrat. Jewish. Avocations: swimming, bridge. Office: Ste 800 1250 24th St NW Ste 350 Washington DC 20037

GINSBURG, MARTIN DAVID, lawyer, educator; b. N.Y.C., June 10, 1932; s. Morris and Evelyn (Bayer) G.; m. Ruth Bader, June 23, 1954; children: Jane, James. AB, Cornell U., 1953; JD, Harvard U., 1958; LLD (hon.), Lewis and Clark Coll., 1992, Wheaton Coll., 1997. Bar: N.Y. 1959, D.C. 1980. Practiced in N.Y.C., 1959-79; mem. firm Weil, Gotshal & Manges, N.Y.C., 1963-79; of counsel firm Fried, Frank, Harris, Shriver and Jacobson, Washington, 1980—; Charles Keller Beekman prof. law Columbia U. Law Sch., N.Y.C., 1979-80; prof. law Georgetown U. Law Center, Washington, 1980—; lectr. U. Leiden, The Netherlands, 1982; lectr. Salzburg Seminar Austria, 1984; mem. tax div. adv. group Dept. Justice, 1980-81; mem. adv. group to Commr. Internal Revenue, 1978-80; mem. adv. bd. U. Calif. Securities Regulation Inst., 1973-91; adj. prof. law NYU, 1967-79; vis. prof. law Stanford (Calif.) U., 1978, Harvard U., Cambridge, Mass., 1986, U. Chgo., 1990, NYU, 1993; cons. joint com. on taxation U.S. Congress, 1979-80; chmn. tax adv. bd. Commerce Clearing House, 1982-94; mem. bd. advisors NYU/IRS Continuing Profl. Edn. Program, 1983-88, co-chmn., 1986-88; sub coun. on capital allocation, co-chmn. taxation expert group Competitiveness Policy Coun., 1993-95; chmn. tax adv. bd. Little, Brown, 1994-96; bd. dirs. Millennium Chems., Inc., Chgo. Classical Rec. Found.; lectr. various tax insts. Co-author, editor: Tax Consequences of Investments, 1969; co-author: Mergers, Acquisitions and Leverage Buyouts, 1989; contbr. articles to legal jours. Mem. vis. com. Harvard Law Sch., 1994-98. 1st lt., arty. U.S. Army, 1954-56. Chair in taxation named in his honor, Georgetown U. Law Ctr., 1986; recipient Marshall-Wythe Medallion, Coll. of William and Mary Sch. Law, 1996, Outstanding achievemnt award Tax Soc. of NYU, 1993. Fellow Am. Coll. Tax Counsel, Am. Bar Found.; mem. Am. Law Inst. (cons. Fed. Income Tax Project 1974-93), N.Y. State Bar Assn. (mem. tax sect. exec. com. 1969—, chmn. tax sect. 1975, ho. of dels. 1976-77), Assn. Bar City N.Y. (chmn. com. taxation 1977-79, mem. audit com. 1980-81), ABA (mem. com. corp. taxation, tax sect. 1973—, chmn. com. simplification 1979-81, mem. tax sect. coun. 1984-87). Office: 600 New Jersey Ave NW Washington DC 20001-2022

GINSBURG, MITCHELL PAUL, international economist; b. Miami, June 4, 1968; s. Gilbert Barry and Flori (Eisenstat) G. BA, Johns Hopkins U., 1990; MS, Northwestern U., 1992. Intern, writer USIA, Washington, 1988; intern, rsch. asst. OAS, Washington, 1988-89; mgmt. asst. Resolution Trust Corp., Washington, 1992-95, FDIC, Washington, 1995-97; economist Bur. of Labor Statistics, Washington, 1997-98; internat. economist U.S. Internat. Trade Commn., Washington, 1998—. Vice chair mktg., Johns Hopkins Young Alumni Fund, 1993, 1990 Class Rep. Recipient Tchg. Unit fellowship Am. Univ., Washington, 1993-95, Walter S. Murphy fellowship, Evanston, Ill., 1990-91. Home: 7902 Coriander Dr Apt 302 Gaithersburg MD 20879-5308 Office: US Internat Trade Commn 500 E St SW Washington DC 20436-0002 Address: 7902 Coriander Dr Apt 302 Gaithersburg MD 20879-5308

GINSBURG, NORTON SYDNEY, geography educator; b. Chgo., Aug. 24, 1921; s. Morris and Sarah (Ginsberg) G.; m. Diana Roselle Peterson, Aug. 12, 1973; children: Jeremy, Alexander. B.A., U. Chgo., 1941, M.A., 1947, Ph.D., 1949. Geographer U.S. Army Map Service, 1941-42; prof. geography U. Chgo., 1947-86, chmn. dept., 1978-85, assoc. dean Coll., 1963-66, assoc. dean social scis., 1967-69; dean academic program, sr. fellow Center for Study Democratic Instns., Santa Barbara, 1971-74; dir. Environment and Policy Inst. East-West Ctr., Honolulu, 1986-91; cons. Social Sci. Research Council, Ency. Brit., Ford Found. East-West Center, Nat. Acad. Sci., NRC, SCOPE, UN, UNESCO. Author: Atlas of Economic Development, 1961, The Urban Transition: American and Asian Experiences, 1990; co-author, editor: Pattern of Asia, 1958, Malaya, 1958, Essays on Geography and Economic Development, 1960, China: Urbanization and National Development, 1980, China: The 80s Era, 1984, Geographic Perspectives on the Wealth of Nations, 1986; co-author, editor: The Extended Metropolis in Asia, 1991; co-editor: The Ocean Yearbooks, 1978-96. Served to lt. USNR, 1942-46. Guggenheim fellow, 1983. Mem. Assn. Am. Geographers (pres. 1970-71), Quadrangle Club, Cosmos Club, Phi Beta Kappa, Sigma Xi. Home: 1320 E Madison Park Chicago IL 60615-2917

GINSBURG, RUTH BADER, United States supreme court justice; b. Bklyn., Mar. 15, 1933; d. Nathan and Celia (Amster) Bader; m. Martin David Ginsburg, June 23, 1954; children: Jane Carol, James Steven. AB, Cornell U., 1954; postgrad., Harvard Law Sch., 1956-58; LLB Kent scholar, Columbia Law Sch., 1959; LLD (hon.), Lund (Sweden) U., 1969, Am. U., 1981, Vt. Law Sch., 1984, Georgetown U., 1985, DePaul U., 1985, Bklyn. Law Sch., 1987, Amherst Coll., 1991, Rutgers U., 1991, Lewis and Clark Coll., 1992, Radcliffe Coll., 1994, NYU, 1994, Columbia U., 1994, Smith Coll., 1994, L.I. U., 1994, U. Ill., 1995, Brandeis U., 1996, Wheaton Coll., 1997, Jewish Theol. Sem. of Am., 1997, George Washington U. Law Sch., 1997; DHL (hon.), Hebrew Union Coll., 1988. Bar: N.Y. 1959, D.C. 1975, U.S. Supreme Ct. 1967. Law sec. to judge U.S. Dist. Ct. (so. dist.) N.Y., 1959-61; rsch. assoc. Columbia Law Sch., N.Y.C., 1961-62, assoc. dir. project internat. procedure, 1962-63; asst. prof. Rutgers U. Sch. Law, Newark, 1963-66, assoc. prof., 1966-69, prof., 1969-72; prof. Columbia U. Sch. Law, N.Y.C., 1972-80; U.S. Cir. judge U.S. Ct. Appeals, D.C. Cir., Washington, 1980-93; assoc. justice U.S. Supreme Ct., Washington, 1993—; Phi Beta Kappa vis. scholar, 1973-74; fellow Ctr. for Advanced Study in Behavioral Scis., Stanford, Calif., 1977-78; lectr. Aspen (Colo.) Inst., 1990, Salzburg Seminar, Austria, 1984; gen. counsel ACLU, 1973-80, bd. dirs., 1974-80. Author: (with Anders Bruzelius) Civil Procedure in Sweden, 1965; Swedish Code ofJudicial Procedure, 1968; (with others) Sex-Based Discrimination, 1974, supplement, 1978; contbr. numerous articles to books and jours. Fellow Am. Bar Found.; mem. AAAS, Am. Law Inst. (coun. mem. 1978-93), Coun. Fgn. Rels. Office: US Supreme Ct One First St NE Washington DC 20543*

GINSBURG, SIGMUND G., museum administrator; b. N.Y.C., Oct. 12, 1937; s. Saul and Rose (Rich) G.; m. Judith Ann Jacobson, July 4, 1965; children: Beth Alison, David Grant. BA magna cum laude, Dartmouth Coll., 1959; postgrad., London Sch. Econs., 1959-60; MPA, Harvard U., 1961. Mgmt. intern Office of Sec. of Def., Washington, 1961-62; asst. to pres. Hudson Inst., 1964; asst. mgr. pers. adminstrv. svcs., mgmt. analyst Port Authority of N.Y. and N.J., 1964-66; sr. mgmt. cons. and spl. asst. to dep. mayor Office of the Mayor, City of N.Y., City of N.Y., 1966-67; asst. city adminstr. Office of the Mayor, City of N.Y., 1967-72; v.p. for adminstrn. and planning, treas. Adelphi U., Garden City, N.Y., 1972-78; v.p. for fin., treas. U. Cin., 1978-84, adj. prof. higher edn. adminstrn., bus. adminstrn., 1980-84; v.p. fin. and adminstrn. Barnard Coll., N.Y.C., 1984-94; v.p. bus. devel. Am. Mus. Natural History, N.Y.C., 1994, sr. v.p. fin. and bus. devel., 1995—; adj. assoc. prof Adelphi U., 1972-78; adj. asst. prof., lectr. CUNY, 1966-72; founder, dir. N.Y.C. Urban Fellows Program, 1969-72, adv. bd., 1994—; lectr. profl. mtgs.; cons. in field; mgmt. commentator Sta. WGUC, Cin., 1980; instr. Fordham U., 1985-95, New Sch. Social Rsch., 1986, 91; mem. City Mgrs. Working Rev. Com. Cin. 2000 Plan, 1979-82; citizens adv. com. Wyo. Bd. Edn., 1980; adv. coun. Tchrs. Ins. and Annuity Assn.-Coll. Retirement Equities Fund, 1993-96, chmn., 1994-95; bd. dirs. Greenwich House, 1994-97. Co-author: Managing the Higher Education Enterprise, 1980; author: Management: An Executive Perspective, 1982, Ropes for Management Success: Climb Higher, Faster, 1984; editor: Paving the Way for the 21st Century: The Human Factor in Higher Education Financial Management, 1993, Managing With Passion: Making the Most of Your Job and Your Life, 1996; contbr. chpts. to books; contbr. 125 articles on mgmt. topics to profl. jours. Lt. U.S. Army, 1962-64. Decorated Army Commendation medal; recipient Colby prize in govt. Dartmouth Coll., 1959, Merit award City of N.Y., 1969, Neil O. Hines publ. award Nat. Assn. Coll. and Univ. Bus. Officers, 1992; Daniel Webster nat. scholar Dartmouth Coll., 1955-59; James B. Reynolds fellow Dartmouth Coll., 1959-60, Littauer fellow Harvard U., 1961, Disting. Svc. award N.Y.C. Urban Fellows Program, 1994. Mem. Phi Beta Kappa. Office: Am Mus Natural History Central Park West at 79th New York NY 10024

GINSBURGH, BROOK, association executive; b. Phila., Oct. 4, 1942; d. Harrison Stanford and Florence Virginia (Campbell) G. Diploma in nursing, Chestnut Hill Hosp., 1963. RN, Pa. Pediatric nurse Chestnut Hill Hosp., Phila., 1963-66; pediatric charge nurse Ea. Pa. Psychiatric Inst., Phila., 1967-69, Nazareth Hosp., Phila., 1970-76; adminstrv. asst. Subcontractors Assn. Del. Valley, Ardmore, Pa., 1977-79; exec. dir. Am. Subcontractors Assn. Del. Valley, Ardmore, Pa., 1979—; editor monthly newsletter, pub. ann. directory, 1980—. Mem. NAFE, Am. Soc. Assn. Execs., Pa. C. of C. Avocations: volunteer in nursing home visitation programs, church guitar group. Office: Am Contractors Assn Del Vly PO Box 586 63 W Lancaster Ave Ardmore PA 19003-1413

GINTAUTAS, JONAS, physician, scientist, administrator; b. Justinava, Lithuania, Oct. 3, 1938; came to U.S., 1967; s. Jonas and Elena (Zaveckaité) Sinsinas; m. Kristina Zebrauskaite, June 13, 1970; children: Stasys, Pasaka, Vadas. PhD, Northwestern U., 1976; MD, U. Juarez, Mex., 1984; MBA, Century U., 1996. Assoc. prof. Tex. Tech. U., Lubbock, 1975-77; assoc. prof. and dir. rsch. Tex. Tech. U. Health Scis. Ctr., Lubbock, 1979-82; dir. basic and clin. rsch., prof. neurology The Brookdlae U. Hosp. Med. Ctr., N.Y.C., 1985—; cons. Amtorg Corp., N.Y.C., 1987-94, Ralex Internat. Co., Boston, 1988-91, Arrow Biomed Inc., Metuchen, N.J., 1988—. Editorial cons. Jour. Aphasia Agnosia Apraxia, 1979—; contbr. articles on pharmacology, anesthesia and surgery to profl. jours. Charter mem. Rep. Presdl. Task Force, Washington, 1982—; mem. Nat. Rep. Senatorial Com., Washington, 1984—, U.S. Senatorial Club, Washington, 1984—; nat. campaign advisor Nat. Rep. Senatorial Com., Washington, 1995-96. Recipient Gold medal for rsch. in med. sci. Am. Biog. Inst., medal of honor Rep. Presdl. Task Force, 1982; rsch. grantee various pvt. and govtl. agys. Fellow Internat. Coll. Physicians and Surgeons (hon.); mem. Am. Biog. Inst. (dep. gov. 1987—), U.S. Senatorial Club (preferred). Roman Catholic. Avocations: woodworking, camping, scuba diving, fishing, reading. Home: 84-19 107th St Richmond Hill NY 11418-1140 Office: The Brookdale Univ Hosp Med Ctr Linden And Rockaway Brooklyn NY 11212

GINTER, CAROL(YN) AUGUSTA ROMTVEDT, retired bond underwriter; b. Toledo, Oreg., May 24, 1926; d. Fred and Mary Elizabeth (Whitney) Romtvedt; m. Paul Peter Ginter, June 2, 1951 (dec. Dec. 1995); children: Joan Paula, Teresa Ginter Ward, Philip M., Jeffrey G. Student, U. Oreg., 1945-46. Office and dispatch clk. Oregonian Newspaper, Portland, 1943-45; clk. typist USN Supt. of Ships, Portland, 1945; gen. ins. clk. Fidelity & Deposit Co., Portland, 1946-48; bond clk. Aetna Casualty & Surety Fireman's Fund, Transamerica, Portland, 1956-65; surety bond underwirter Cole, Clark & Cunningham/Rollins, Burdick Hunter, Portland, 1965-79; freelance publicity specialist Waldport, Oreg., 1986—. Pub., coord. family history: Fred Romtvedt, His Life and Loves, 1980. Publicity specialist ARC, 1991—; publicity/sec., lay min. Altar Soc., St. Anthony's Cath. Ch., 1990—. Mem. South County Women's Club (sec. 1984-94, 96, 98), Waldport C. of C. (vol. visitors ctr. 1995—), Lincoln County Hist. Soc., Alsi Hist. Soc. Republican. Avocations: family reunion organization, water exercise, travel, gardening. Home: 1802 NW Canal St Waldport OR 97394-9424

GINTER, VALERIAN ALEXIUS, urban historian, educator; b. Chgo., Nov. 4, 1939; s. Valerian Adalbert and Bernice (Podraza) G.; m. Linda Garner Tadlock, Feb. 24, 1968 (div. 1973). BS in Speech, Northwestern U., 1962; postgrad., L.I.U., 1979-81. Investigator Acme Secret Service Ltd., Chgo., 1960-62; producer, dir. Sta. WAAY-TV, Huntsville, Ala., 1965-68; comml. coordinator CBS TV, N.Y.C., 1968-70; buyer SSC&B Lintas Worldwide, Furman-Roth Inc., SFM Media Corp., N.Y.C., 1970-79; prin. Ginter-Gotham Urban History, N.Y.C., 1981—; adj. lectr. Kingsborough C.C., N.Y., 1990—, LaGuardia C.C., N.Y., 1998—. Author: Manhattan Trivia: The Ultimate Challenge, 1985; contbr. articles to profl. jours., The Ency. N.Y.C., 1995. Cons., lectr. Mcpl. Art Soc., N.Y., 1975—, dir. video tng., St. Bartholomew's Cmty. House, N.Y.C., 1974-77. With U.S. Army, 1962-65. Mem. Theatre Hist. Soc., Victorian Soc. Am., Nat. Trust Historic Preservation, Soc. Archtl. Historians. Roman Catholic. Avocation: jazz accordionist. Home and Office: 50 W 72nd St Ste 312 New York NY 10023-4132

GINZBERG, ELI, economist, emeritus educator, government consultant, author; b. N.Y.C., Apr. 30, 1911; s. Louis and Adele (Katzenstein) G.; m. Ruth Szold, July 14, 1946 (dec. Aug. 1995); children: Abigail, Jeremy, Rachel. Student, U. Heidelberg, U. Grenoble, 1928-29; AB, Columbia U., 1931, AM, 1932, PhD, 1934, LittD, 1982; LittD, Jewish Theol. Sem., 1966; LLD, Loyola U., Chgo., 1969; LHD, Rush U., 1985; DHL, Kirksville Osteo. Sch., 1993; LLD, Phila. Coll. Osteo. Medicine, 1994; DHL, State Coll. of Optometry, N.Y., 1995; DSc, N.Y. Coll. Osteo Medicine, 1996. Dir. rsch. econs. and group behavior Columbia U., N.Y.C., 1939-42, 48-49, faculty, 1935—, A. Barton Hepburn prof. econs. Grad. Sch. Bus., 1967-79, prof. emeritus, spl. lectr. Grad. Sch. Bus., 1979—, dir. conservation human resources project, 1950-90, dir. Eisenhower Ctr. for Conservation Human Resources, 1990—; dir. Revson fellows program on future City of NY, 1979—; adj. prof. health and society Barnard Coll., 1980-88; spl. lectr. health and soc., Sch. Pub., Health, Columbia U., 1989—; hon. faculty mem. Indsl. Coll. Armed Forces, 1957-71; chmn. bd. Manpower Demonstration Research Corp., 1974-82, chmn. bd. emeritus, 1982—; Spl. asst. to chief statistician U.S. War Dept., 1942-44; spl. asst. to dir. hosp. div. U.S. War Dept. (Surgeon Gen.'s Office), 1944, dir. resources analysis div., 1944-46; cons. Dept. Army, 1946-70, Dept. State, 1953, 56, 65-69, Dept. Labor, 1954-82, Dept. Def., 1964-71, Dept. Commerce, 1965-66, 79-80, GAO, 1973-82, Exec. Office Pres., 1942; mem. med. adv. bd. to Sec. War, 1946-48; U.S. rep. 5 power Conf. Reparations for Non-Repatriable Refugees, 1946; dir. N.Y. State Hosp. Study, 1948-49; mem. Com. on Wartime Requirements for Sci. and Specialized Personnel, 1942; med. cons. Hoover Commn., 1952; adviser Commn. Chronic Illness, 1950-53; mem. adv. council NIMH, 1959-63; chmn. com. on studies White House Conf. on Children and Youth, 1960; dir. staff studies Nat. Manpower Council, 1951-61; chmn. Nat. Manpower Adv. Com., 1962-74, Nat. Commn. for Manpower Policy, 1974-79, Nat. Commn.

for Employment Policy, 1979-82; mem. Nat. Adv. Allied Health Council, 1968-72; mem. sci. adv. bd. USAF, 1969-73; chmn. taskforce manpower rsch. Dept. Def., 1970-71; mem. Inst. Medicine, Nat. Acad. Scis., 1972—; mem. Office of Sci. and Engring. personnel adv. com. Nat. Acad. Scis., 1984-91; advisor Internat. Inst. Mgmt. Sci. Ctr., Berlin, 1982-89; mem. ORT Acad. Adv. Council, 1984-91, chmn., 1991-98; mem. Econ. Policy Coun. UN Assn. USA, 1984-87; co-chair adv. com. Job Creation Project Nat. Com. for Full Employment, 1984-86; mem. Mayoral Commn. to Consider Future of Child Health in N.Y.C., 1987-88; mem. med. adv. bd. Hadassah-Hebrew U., 1988-97; bd. dirs. Found. Biomed. Rsch., 1988—; mem. Mayoral Commn. to Rev. Health and Hosps. Corp., 1991-92. Author: The House of Adam Smith, 1934, The Illusion of Economic Stability, 1939, Grass on the Slag Heaps: The Story of the Welsh Miners, 1942, The Unemployed, 1943, The Labor Leader, 1948, A Pattern for Hospital Care, 1949, Agenda for American Jews, 1950; Occupational Choice, 1951, The Uneducated, 1953, Psychiatry and Military Manpower Policy, 1953, What Makes an Executive, 1955, The Negro Potential, 1956, Effecting Change in Large Organizations, 1957, Human Resources, 1958, The Ineffective Soldier, 3 vols., 1959, The Nation's Children, 3 vols., 1960, Planning for Better Hospital Care, 1961, The Optimistic Tradition and American Youth, 1962, The American Worker in the Twentieth Century, 1963, The Troublesome Presence, 1964, Talent and Performance, 1964, The Negro Challenge to the Business Community, 1964, The Pluralistic Economy, 1965, Keeper of the Law: Louis Ginzberg, 1966, Life Styles of Educated Women, 1966, Educated American Women-Self-Portraits, 1966, Manpower Strategy for Developing Countries, 1967, The Middle Class Negro in the White Man's World, 1967, Manpower Strategy for the Metropolis, 1968, Business Leadership and the Negro Crisis, 1968, Men, Money and Medicine, 1969, Urban Health Services-The Case of New York, 1971, Career Guidance, 1971, Manpower for Development, 1971, Manpower Advice for Government, 1972, New York Is Very Much Alive, 1973, Corporate Lib: Women's Challenge to Management; editor, 1973, Federal Manpower in Transition, 1974, The Great Society: Lessons for the Future, 1974, The University Medical Center and the Metropolis, 1974, The Future of the Metropolis, 1974, The Manpower Connection: Education and Work, 1975, Jobs for Americans, 1976, The Human Economy, 1976, Regionalization and Health Policy, 1977, The Limits of Health Reform, 1977, The House of Adam Smith Revisited, 1977, Health Manpower and Health Policy, 1978, Good Jobs, Bad Jobs, No Jobs, 1979, American Jews: The Building of a Voluntary Community (in Hebrew), 1979, Employing the Unemployed, 1980, The School/Work Nexus, 1981, Technology and Employment: Concepts and Clarifications, 1986, Medicine and Society, 1987, Executive Talent, 1988, The Financing of Biomedical Research, 1989, Bridges to Work, 1989, Physicians, Politicians, and the Public, 1989; editor: The Delivery of Health Care: What Lies Ahead, 1982, The Coming Physician Surplus: In Search of a Public Policy, 1983, Home Health Care: Its Role in the Changing Health Services Market, 1983, Beyond Human Scale: The Large Corporation at Risk, 1985, American Medicine: The Power Shift, 1985, The U.S. Health Care System: A Look to the 1990s, 1985, Understanding Human Resources: Perspectives, People, and Policy, 1985, From Health Dollars to Health Services: New York City 1965-85, 1986, From Physician Shortage to Patient Shortage: The Uncertain Future of Medical Practice, 1986, Medicine and Society: Clinical Decisions and Societal Values, 1987, The Skeptical Economist, 1987, Young People at Risk: Is Prevention Possible, 1988, Executive Talent: Developing Tomorrow's Leaders, 1988, The Financing of Biomedical Research, 1989, My Brother's Keeper , 1989, Does Job Training Work: The Clients Speak Out, 1989, The Medical Triangle, 1990, Health Services Research: Key to Health Policy, 1991, The Eye Of Illusion, 1993, The Economics of Medical Education, 1993, The Road to Reform: The Future of Health Care in America, 1994, Medical Gridlock and Health Reform, 1994, The Changing U.S. Labor Market, 1994, The Financing of Medical Schools in an Era of Health Reform, 1995, Tomorrows Hospitals, 1996, Improving Healthcare of the Poor: The New York City Perspective, 1996. Dir. research United Jewish Appeal, 1941; bd. govs. Hebrew U., Jerusalem, 1953-59. Fellow AAAS, Am. Acad. Arts and Scis.; mem. Am. Econ. Assn., Indsl. Rels. Rsch. Assn., AAUP, N.Y. Sci. Policy Assn. of N.Y. Acad. Scis., Soc. Med. Cons. to Armed Forces (asoc.), Allen O. Whipple Surg. Soc., AOA (hon.), Phi Beta Kappa, Beta Gamma Sigma. Home: 845 W End Ave New York NY 10025-8435 Office: Columbia U Eisenhower Ctr 475 Riverside Dr Ste 248 New York NY 10115-0248

GINZBURG, VITALY LAZAREVICH, physicist; b. Moscow, Oct. 4, 1916; s. Lazar and Augusta G.; m. Nina Ginzburg, 1946; 1 child. PhD, Moscow U., 1940. With P.N. Lebedev Phys. Inst. Russian Acad. Scis., 1940—, dir. I.E. Tamm dept. theoretical physics, 1971-88, adv., head theoretical group in P.N. Lebedev Physical Inst., 1988—; prof. Gorky U., 1945-68, Moscow Tech. Inst. Physics, 1968—. Author: Theoretical Physics and Astrophysics, 1979, Waynflete Lectures of Physics, 1983, (with S.I. Syrovatskii) Origin of Cosmic Rays, 1964, Propagation of Electromagnetic Waves in Plasma, 1970, (with V.M. Agranovich and Springer-Verlag) Crystal Optics With Spatial Dispersion and Excitons, 1984, Physics and Astrophysics: A Selection of Key Problems, 1985, (with V.N. Tsytovich and Adam Hilger) Trasition Radiation and Transition Scattering, 1990, On Physics and Astrophysics (in Russian), 1992; Contbr. articles to profl. jours. Decorated Order of Lenin; recipient Manelstam prize, 1947, Lomonosov prize, 1962, USSR State prize, 1953, Lenin prize, 1966, M. Smoluchovskii Medal Polish Physics Soc., 1987, Bardeen prize, 1991, Wolf Found. prize, 1994, 95, Vavilov Gold medal, 1995, Big Lomonosov Gold medal, 1995, UNESCO Gold medal, 1998, Nils Bohr Gold Medal, 1998, Nicholson Medal Am. Phys. Soc., 1998; Indian Acad. Sci. hon fellow, 1977, Indian Nat. Sci. Acad. fgn. fellow, 1981, NAS, 1981. Mem. Acad. Sci. USSR (elected people's dep. mem. of Soviet parliament 1989), Royal Astonomy Soc. London (fgn., Gold Medal 1991), Academia Europaea, Internat. Acad. Astronautics, Roy Astonomy Soc. (assoc.), Royal Danish Acad. Sci. (fgn.), Indian Acad. Sci. (hon. fellow), Indian Nat. Sci. Acad. (fgn. fellow). Fax: (095)-135-85-33. Address: PN Lebedev Phys Inst RAN, Leninsky Prospect 53, 117924 Moscow Russia

GINZEL, ANDREW H., artist; b. Chgo., July 14, 1954; s. Roland F. and Ellen (Laynon) G.; m. Kristin A. Jones, June 14, 1986. Student, SUNY, 1978-81, Bennington Coll., 1972-74. Sculpture faculty Sch. of Visual Arts, N.Y.C., 1986—; artistic cons. Hudson River Park Conservancy, N.Y.C., 1997. Solo shows include: Metronome Union Square South Project, N.Y.C., 1999, TZ'Art, N.Y.C., 1996, Acqario Romano, Rome, 1995, Madison Art Ctr., Wis., 1992-93, Three Rivers Arts Festival, Pitts., 1991, Mpls. Coll. of Art and Design, 1991, Damon Brandt Gallery, N.Y.C., 1990, Kunsthalle, Basel, 1989, others; commns. include: Oculus, MTA, N.Y.C., 1999, Olympic Arts Festival, Atlanta, 1996, Battery Park City, N.Y.C., 1992, Pa. Conv. Ctr., 1994, Oreg. Conv. Ctr., Portland, 1990, Kunsthalle, Basel, Switzerland, 1989; group shows include Contemporary Artists and the Am. Acad. in Rome, 1995, 96, Equitable Gallery, N.Y.C., 1996, Paine Webber Gallery, N.Y.C., 1994, The Drawing Ctr., N.Y.C., 1993-94, numerous others; selected collections include; Bklyn. Mus., Beckton Dickinson and Co., Franklin Lakes, N.J., Bklyn. Mus., Centro per L'Arte Contemporanea Luigi Pecci, Prato, Italy, Hoffmann-La Roche, Inc., Pacific Enterprises, L.A., Progressive Corp., Cleve., The Prudential Life Ins. Co., others. Recipient Visual Arts fellowship Nat. Endowment for the Arts, 1986, 94, awards Pollack-Krasner Found., 1994, Louis Comfort Tiffany Found., 1991, fellowship for Indo-Am. Coun. for Internat. Exch. of Scholars, 1990, numerous others in field. Fellow Am. Acad. in Rome (Rome prize 1994-95). Home: 289 Bleecker St New York NY 10014-4106

GIOCONDA, THOMAS F., career officer. BA in History and Polit. Sci., St. Joseph's U., 1970; grad., Squadron Officer Sch., 1974; MBA, U. Mont., 1975; grad., Air Command and Staff Coll., 1976; M in Ednl. Adminstrn., Seton Hall U., 1979; grad., Air War Coll., 1986. Commd. 2d lt. USAF, 1970, brig. gen., 1997; stationed at Malmstrom AFB Mont., 1970-75; asst. prof. aerospace studies AFROTC detachment 750 St. Joseph's U., Phila., 1975-76, prof. aerospace studies AFROTC detachment 750, 1976-77, detachment comdr., detachment closure officer, 1976-77; adminstrn. officer, asst. prof. aerospace studies N.J. Inst. Tech., Newark, 1977-79; stationed at Vandenberg AFB Calif., 1979-83; mission analyst strategic programs Hdqs. Strategic Air Command, Offutt AFB, Nebr., 1983, congl. liaison br. chief, action officer, 1983-85; congl. affairs and resources planner, dep. chief of staff plans and ops. Hdqs. USAF, the Pentagon, Washington, 1985-89; stationed at Whiteman AFB Mo., 1989-91; dep. legis. asst. to chmn. joint chiefs of staff Pentagon, Washington, 1991-93, legis. asst. to chmn. joint chiefs of staff, 1993-97; prin. dep. asst. sec. mil. application Dept. Energy, Washington, 1997—. Mem. K.C., Air Force Assn. (life mem.), The Retired Officers Assn. (life mem.), Soc. Strategic Air Command (life and charter mem.), Kappa Delta Phi. Office: DOE/DP-2 1000 Independence Ave SW Washington DC 20585-0104

GIOIA, (MICHAEL) DANA, poet, literary critic; b. L.A., Dec. 24, 1950; s. Michael and Dorothy (Ortiz) G.; m. Mary Hiecke, 1980; children: Michael (dec.), Theodore, Michael Frederick. BA, Stanford U., 1973, MBA, 1977; MA, Harvard U., 1975. V.p. mktg. General Foods Corp., White Plains, N.Y., 1977-92; pres., bd. dirs. Story Line Press, 1992—; editor Sequoia mag., 1971-73, poetry editor, 1975-77; literary editor Inquiry mag., 1977-79, poetry editor, 1979-83; mem. bd. dirs. Wesleyan U. Writers Conf., 1985—; commentator BBC Radio, 1992—; co-dir. West Chester Writers Conf., 1995—; music critic San Francisco mag., 1997—; librettist for opera Nosferatu, 1998. Author: (poetry) Daily Horoscope, 1986, The Gods of Winter, 1991, (criticism) Can Poetry Matter? Essays on Poetry an American Culture, 1992; editor: The Ceremony and Other Stories, 1984, Poems from Italy, 1985, New Italian Poets, 1990; co-editor: Literature: An Introduction to Fiction, Poetry and Drama, 1995; translator: Eugenio Montale's Mottetti: Poems of Love, 1990; contbr. to periodicals including New Yorker, Atlantic, Washington Post, Hudson Rev., Poetry. Recipient Frederick Bock prize Poetry, 1986. Mem. Poetry Soc. Am. (v.p. 1992-97). Home: 7190 Faught Rd Santa Rosa CA 95403-7835*

GIOIELLA, RUSSELL MICHAEL, lawyer; b. Camden, N.J., Mar. 10, 1954; s. Michael S. and Mildred (Leonardo) G.; m. Nerissa M. Radell, June 28, 1980; 1 child, Natalya. BA summa cum laude, Cath. U., 1976; JD, NYU, 1979, MA, 1980. Bar: N.Y. 1980, U.S. Dist. Ct. (so. and ea. dists.) N.Y. 1980, U.S. Ct. Appeals (2nd and 3rd cirs.) 1980, U.S. Dist. Ct. (no. dist.) N.Y. 1982, U.S. Supreme Ct. 1984. Assoc. Litman, Kaufman and Asche, N.Y.C., 1979-84; ptnr. Litman, Kaufman, Asche and Lupkin, N.Y.C., 1985, Litman, Asche, Lupkin & Gioiella, N.Y.C., 1986-93, Litman, Asche, Lupkin, Gioiella & Bassin, N.Y.C., 1994-96, Litman, Asche & Gioiella LLP, N.Y.C., 1996—; mem. First Jud. Dept. Assigned Counsel Screening Panel, 1998—. Mem. steering com. N.Y. State Coalition to Abolish the Death Penalty, 1992. Mem. ABA, NACDL, Assn. of Bar of City of N.Y. (mem. com. on product liability 1988-91, mem. criminal cts. com. 1992-94), N.Y. Criminal Bar Assn. (pres. 1997-98), N.Y. State Assn. Criminal Def. Lawyers (treas. 1995-97, v.p. 1999—), Columbia Lawyers, Phi Beta Kappa. Democrat. Avocations: fatherhood, music, biking, wine, Russian literature. Office: Litman Asche & Gioiella 45 Broadway New York NY 10006-3007

GIOIOSO, JOSEPH VINCENT, psychologist; b. Chgo., Mar. 6, 1939; s. Vincent James and Mary (Bonadonna) G.; B.A., DePaul U., 1962, M.A., 1963; Ph.D. summa cum laude, Ill. Inst. Tech., 1971; m. Patricia A. Aksamit, June 30, 1990; children by previous marriage: Joseph, Randy Marie, Danielle; stepchildren: Josephine Anne, Jennifer Marie Cammarata. Psychologist, Sch. Assn. for Spl. Edn. in DuPage County, Wheaton, Ill., 1964-67; pvt. practice as clin. psychologist, Chgo. and Downers Grove, Ill., 1966—; clin. psychologist J.J. McLaughlin, M.D., Profl. Corp., Chgo., 1970-92. Founder dept. psychology Ill. Benedictine Coll., Lisle, 1968, chmn. dept. psychology, prof., dir. testing, 1968-71; cons. psychologist Chicago Ridge (Ill.) Sch. Dist. 127 1/2, 1973-76, Cath. Charities Counseling Service, Chgo., 1963-66, St. Laurence High Sch., Oak Lawn, Ill., 1963-64, Oak Lawn-Hometown Sch. Dist. No. 123, 1967-68, Addison (Ill.) Sch. Dist. 4, 1969-72; vis. prof. psychology Inst. Mgmt., Lisle, 1968-69, George Williams Coll., Downers Grove, 1970-71; chief psychologist Valley View Sch. Dist. 365U, Bolingbrook, Ill., 1971-73; dir. Pub. Program for Exceptional Children, Lisle, 1969-71; mem. Nat. Register Health Service Providers in Psychology, 1975—. Bd. dirs. Ray Graham Assn. for Handicapped, DuPage County, Ill., 1970-73; adv. bd. Care and Counseling Center DuPage County, 1977—; founder Aquinpsy Human Svcs. Ctr., 1987. DePaul U. publ. grantee, 1959-61, Fitzgerald Bros. Found. grantee, 1969-71. Fellow Ctr. for the Study of Great Ideas, Chgo., 1994—; mem. AAAS, Am., Midwestern, Ill. psychol. assns., Soc. Pediatric Psychology, Alpha Phi Delta. Author: Completion Intelligence Test, 1963, Children's Emotional Symptoms Inventory, 1979; contbr. articles to profl. jours. Home and Office: 6900 Main St Downers Grove IL 60516-3454

GIOLITO, CAESAR AUGUSTUS, public relations executive, consultant; b. N.Y.C., Aug. 21, 1930; s. Cesare I Giolito and Aida Francesca Bianco; m. Carolyn Lucille Hughes, Apr. 18, 1959; children: Glenn Augustus, Antoinette. BS in Comm. Arts and Philosophy, Fordham Coll., 1951; postgrad., Georgetown U. Law Sch., 1960. Consular attache U.S. Consulate U.S. Dept. State, Trieste, Italy, 1955-57; free-lance writer, internat. orgns. specialist Libr. of Congress, Washington, 1958-60; pres. Am.-Internat. Pub. Rels., Washington, 1960-70; dir. div. govt. rels. Am. Psychiat. Assn., Washington, 1970-78; dir. pub. affairs Nat. Italian Am. Found., Washington, 1978-79; cons. Office of the Sec. Dept. HEW, Washington, 1979-80; spl. asst. U.S. Dept. Interior, Washington, 1980-81; pres. Capital-Internat. Comms., Washington, 1981—. With U.S. Army, 1951-53. Office: PO Box 5793 Carefree AZ 85377-5793

GIONFRIDDO, MAURICE PAUL, aeronautical engineer, research and development manager; b. Medford, Mass., Feb. 19, 1931; s. Santo and Germaine Camille (Gaillard) G.; m. Joan Marie Powers, Apr. 21, 1956; children: Marianne E., Linda. BS in Aero. Engring., MIT, 1953, MS in Aero. Engring., 1969. Rsch. asst. Aeroelastic and Structures Rsch. Lab., MIT, Cambridge, Mass., 1953-54; aero. rsch. engr. Air Force Cambridge Rsch. Ctr., Bedford, Mass., 1956-57; aero. engr. Army Natick (Mass.) Rsch., Devel. and Engring. Ctr., 1957-94; cons. MPG Cons., Westborough, Mass., 1994—; mem. Nat. Parachute Tech. Coun., 1991—. Class agt. MIT Class of 1953, 1968-78. 1st lt. USAF, 1954-56. Fellow AIAA (assoc., charter, aerodyn. decelerator tech. com. 1964-67, Aerodyn. Decelerator award 1990); mem. Sigma Xi. Roman Catholic. Home and Office: MPG Cons 20 Westminster Way Westborough MA 01581-3410

GIORDANO, ANDREW ANTHONY, retired naval officer; b. Passaic, N.J., May 17, 1932; s. Samuel and Sarah (Pollara) G.; m. Felice Rochman, Mar. 3, 1957; children: Andrew Anthony, II, Dean James, Catherine Lisa. B.B.A. cum laude, CCNY, 1953; M.B.A. with distinction, Harvard U., 1962; student, Naval War Coll., 1965; L.H.D. (hon.), Nat. U., San Diego, 1982. Commd. ensign U.S. Navy, 1953, advanced through grades to rear adm., 1978; supply officer U.S.S. Kitty Hawk, Vietnam, 1968-70; ops. officer Aviation Supply Office, Phila., 1970-72; dir. material div. Office of Chief of Naval Ops., Washington, 1977-81; comdr. Naval Supply Systems Command, Chief Supply Corps, 1981-84; sr. v.p. control and ops. Donaldson's of Mpls. unit Allied Stores, 1984-87; exec. v.p., CFO Lamonts Corp., 1987-93; assoc. prof. acctg. George Washington U., 1966-67, Nat. U., 1970-72; prin. The Giordano Group, Ltd., Arlington, Va., 1993—; bd. dirs. Cherry, Webb & Touraine, Graham-Field, Jos. A. Bank, Inc., Nomos, Inc.; hon. pres. Naval Supply Corps Assn. Treas., trustee Navy Marine Coast Guard Residence Found., 1993-98; pres., COO Graham Field, 1998. Decorated Legion of Merit, D.S.M. Mem. NAS (Naval studies bd. 1996), Army-Navy Country Club (chmn. bd. govs. 1993-96). Roman Catholic. Address: PO Box 31059 Palm Beach Gardens FL 33420

GIORDANO, ANTONIO, medical educator; b. Naples, Italy, Oct. 11, 1962; came to U.S., 1987; s. Giovan Giacomo and Maria Teresa (Sgambati) G.; m. Mina Massaro, July 4, 1992; 1 child, Maria Teresa. MD summa cum laude, U. Naples, 1986; PhD in Pathology summa cum laude, U. Trieste, 1990. Intern U. Naples, 1983-86; postdoctoral fellow N.Y. Med. Coll., 1987-88, Cold Spring Harbor Lab., N.Y.C., 1988-92; fellow Irvington Inst. for Med. Rsch., 1990-92; asst. prof. pathology/biochemistry Temple U., Phila., 1992-94; pres., chmn. bd., founder Sbarro Inst. for Cancer Rsch. and Molecular Medicine, 1993—; asst. prof. pathology Thomas Jefferson U., Phila., 1994-96, assoc. prof., 1996—. Editl. bd. Jour. Cellular Biochemistry, Cellular Physiology, Molecular and Cellular Differentiation, Anticancer Rsch.; contbr. numerous articles to profl. jours. Mem. Società Italiana Tumori, Am. Assn. for Cancer Rsch., N.Y. Acad. of Scis. Achievements include identification of a novel tumor suppressor gene and a development of a new test for lung cancer; patent for tumor suppressor protein pRB2, related gene products, and DNA encoding, patents include novel human cyclin-dependent kinase-like proteins and methods of using the same, human retinoblastoma-related, genomic DNA and methods of detecting mutations therein, lung cancer screening on pRb2 gene expression. Home: 303 Ginger Ln Philadelphia PA 19128-4557 Office: Thomas Jefferson Univ 1020 Locust St Philadelphia PA 19107-6731

GIORDANO, DAVID ALFRED, internist, gastroenterologist; b. South Bend, Ind., Feb. 3, 1930; s. Alfred S. and Alice (Gracy) G.; m. Sally Kay Buchanan, Jan. 30, 1960; children: Steven David, Michael Bruce. BS, Northwestern U., 1951; MD, Ind. U., Indpls., 1955. Diplomate Am. Bd. Internal Medicine. Intern Univ. Hosp., Cleve., 1955-56; resident in internal medicine Ind. U. Med. Ctr., Indpls., 1958-60; instr. medicine Duke U. Med. Ctr., Durham, N.C., 1960-61, Ind. U. Med. Ctr., Indpls., 1961-63; cons. gastroenterology Vets. Hosp., Univ. Hosp., Indpls., 1961-63; pvt. practice Sarasota, Fla., 1963—; active staff Sarasota Meml. Hosp., chief of staff, 1970-71, assoc. staff Drs. Hosp., Sarasota; mem. West Cen. Fla. Profl. Standards Review Orgn., 1976, Sarasota County Local Govt. Study Commn., 1967-69; sec. Sarasota County Comprehensive Health Planning Coun., 1969-70, exec. com., 1969-72; bd. dirs. Blue Shield, 1973-80, chmn. Governmental Affairs Com., 1978-80; rep. of state ins. commr. to Russia, Denmark, Sweden, Eng. and France, 1979. Contbr. articles to profl. jours. Med. advisor Planned Parenthood Assn., 1965-70. Lt. comdr. USN, 1956-58. Fellow Am. Coll. Physicians (rep. Fla. coun. med. specialists 1973—, health and pub. policy com. 1987—, governing bd. 1987— Internist of Yr. Fla. chpt. 1997), Am. Coll. Gastroent.; mem. AMA, Fla. Soc. Internal Medicine (med. adv. coun. 1971-90), Fla. Gastroent. Soc. (pres. 1972), West Coast Acad. Internal Medicine (pres. 1977-78); Sarasota County Med. Soc. (co-chmn. peer review com. 1970-71), Fla. Med. Assn., Am. Soc. Internal Medicine, Fla. Med. Assn., Am. Soc. Gastrointestinal Endoscopy, Am. Gastroent. Assn. Avocations: sailing, tennis, nautical antiques. Home: 6 Lands End Ln Sarasota FL 34242-1148 Office: David A Giordano MD PA 1950 Arlington St Ste 119 Sarasota FL 34239-3508

GIORDANO, DONNA LANGONE, foreign language and ESL educator; b. Boston, Feb. 14, 1948; d. Joseph Anthony and Margaret Mary (Interbartolo) Langone; m. James Michael Giordano, Aug. 24, 1969; children: James, Michael, Christopher. BA in French Tchg., Merrimack Coll., 1969; postgrad., SUNY, Buffalo, 1971, Ecole Normale D'Instituteurs, Versailles, France, 1972, Tufts U., 1992; MEd, Cambridge Coll. Cert. ESL tchr. and French as Second Lang. tchr. Tchr. of French Williamsville (N.Y.) Pub. Schs., 1969-73, St. Francis of Assisi Sch., Medford, Mass., 1980-90; tchr. ESL Emmanuel Coll., Boston, summer 1990, Tufts U., Medford, summer 1990, Medford Pub. Schs., 1990—; asst. resource testing specialist Mass. Dept. Edn., Malden, 1996; program coord. European Study Tour, Scholastic Internat., Buffalo, N.Y., 1972, French Students in Am., Am. Inst. Fgn. Study, Boston, 1990; mentoring coord. City of Medford. Author of poetry. Mem. Brooks Sch. Coun., Medford, 1993-96, Friends of Francis - Feeding Homeless, Medford, 1994—. Mem. Mass. Assn. Bilingual Edn., Mass. Assn. Tchrs. of Students of Other Langs., Haitian Parents Adv. Com., Mass. Tchrs. Assn. Roman Catholic. Avocations: cooking, bldg. dollhouses, gardening. Office: Brooks - Hobbs Magnet Sch 388 High St Medford MA 02155-3609

GIORDANO, JAMES JOSEPH, neuroscientist, aeromedical engineer, educator; b. Staten Island, N.Y., Sept. 22, 1959; s. James and Gloria (Timpone) G. BS, St. Peter's Coll., Jersey City, 1981; MA, Norwich U., 1982; MPhil, CUNY, 1985, MS, PhD cum laude, 1986. Diplomate Am. Acad. Pain Mgmt., Am. Soc. Behavioral Medicine, Am. Bd. Clin. Sexuality. Rsch. asst. Einstein Med. Coll., Bronx, N.Y., 1983-86; rsch. fellow Johns Hopkins U., Balt., 1986-88; asst. prof. neurosci. Drake U., Des Moines, Iowa, 1988-92; dir. pain rsch. Iowa Meth. Hosp., Des Moines, 1990-92; commd. lt. USN, 1992; divsn. officer USN, Pensacola, Fla., 1992-93; dept. head aerospace physiology USN, Cherry Point, N.C., 1993-95; neurology prof. Lamar U., Tex., 1996—; dir. pain program, behavioral medicine S.E. Tex. Rehab. Hosp., 1996—; vis. prof. dept. pathology/psychiatry U. Tex. Med. Br., Galveston, 1996—. Textbook author; contbr. articles to profl. jours. Recipient Presdl. Point of Light award Pres. George Bush, 1991. Fellow Am. Bd. Disability Analysts, Internat. Aerospace Med. Assn., Soc. USN Flight Surgeons, Aeromed. Engring. Soc., Nat. Acad. Neuropsychiatrists. Avocations: commercial pilot, weight lifting, equestrian activities, judo, piano.

GIORDANO, JOHN READ, conductor; b. Dunkirk, N.Y., Dec. 31, 1937; s. John C. and Mildred G.; m. Sept. 3, 1960; children: Anne, Ellen, John. MusB, Tex. Christian U., 1960, MusM, 1962. Mem. music faculty North Tex. State U., 1965-72; mem. faculty, condr. univ. symphony Tex. Christian U., 1972-75; chmn. jury Van Cliburn Internat. Piano Competition, Ft. Worth, 1974—; music dir. Ft. Worth Symphony Orch., 1976—; founder, music dir. Ft. Worth Chamber Orch., 1976—, also condr., 1976—. Appeared as saxophone soloist and with orchs. throughout Europe and U.S., 1965-72; music dir. youth orch. Greater Ft. Worth, 1969-75; guest condr. with various orchs. including Nat. Symphony of Belgium, Nat. Symphony of El Salvador, Amsterdam Philharm., Brazilian Nat. Symphony, Belgian Nat. Radio Orch., Nat. Symphony of Portugal, English Chamber Orch.; composer: Composition for Jazz Ensemble and Symphony Orchestra, 1974; subject of feature film Symphony, 1978. Served with USAR, 1960-68. Recipient Premiere Prix with distinction Royal Conservatory Brussels, 1965; Fulbright scholar Royal Conservatory, Brussels, 1965. Mem. Phi Mu Alpha Sinfonia, Phi Kappa Lambda, Kappa Kappa Psi. Office: Ft Worth Symphony Orch 4401 Trail Lake Dr Fort Worth TX 76109-5297*

GIORDANO, JOSEPH, JR., financial planner, investment consulting firm executive; b. Detroit, July 28, 1953; s. Joseph and Josephine Marie (Delicolli) G. BS in Fin., Bus. Econs., Wayne State U., 1977. Cert. fin. planner, 1986. Sr. cost analyst Nat. Bank Detroit, 1978-81; registered rep. Am. Express Fin. Svcs. Inc., Mpls., 1981-83; dist. mgr. IDS Fin. Svcs. Inc., Mpls., 1983-86; pres. Joseph James Fin. Svcs. Inc., Rochester Hills, Mich., 1986—, Investors Fin. Adv. Inc., Rochester Hills, 1986—; instr. Macomb C.C., Warren, Mich., 1988; cons. various clients, 1988—; host Making Sense of Your Money, Sta. WWCM AM 990-Radio. Mem. Nat. Assn. Security Dealers, Elks. Avocations: music, composing songs, biking, tennis, traveling. Office: Joseph James Fin Svcs Inc 705 Barclay Cir Ste 125 Rochester MI 48307-4575

GIORDANO, LAWRENCE FRANCIS, lawyer; b. Buffalo, Feb. 17, 1953; s. Anthony Jerome and Martha Ann (Taylor) G.; m. Elaine Kristie Thomas, May 29, 1976; children: Bradley Thomas, Evan Taylor. BS with highest honors in Psychology, Denison U., 1975; JD, Georgetown U., 1978. Bar: Tenn. 1978, U.S. Dist. Ct. (ea. dist.) Tenn. 1979, U.S. Ct. Appeals (6th cir.) 1980, U.S. Supreme Ct. 1983. Assoc. Stone & Hinds, P.C., Knoxville, Tenn., 1978-81, ptnr., 1981-88; ptnr. Thomforde & Giordano, P.C., Knoxville, 1988-90, McCampbell & Young, P.C., Knoxville, 1990-91, London, Amburn & Giordano, Knoxville, 1991-92, Susano, Sheppeard & Giordano, Knoxville, 1993-94; spl. counsel Lewis, King, Krieg, Waldrop & Catron, P.C., Knoxville, 1994-97, shareholder, 1997—; spl. judge Knox County Gen. Sessions Ct., 1988—; adminstrv. law judge State of Tenn. Dept. Edn., 1994-96; adj. prof. U. Tenn. Coll. Law, 1993—; instr. Knoxville Police Acad., 1989. Mem. exec. bd. Knoxville Metro Soccer League, 1980-85; mem. community network Knox County Youth Alcohol Hwy. Safety Project, Knoxville, 1987-90. Nat. Merit scholar, 1971-75, Kenneth I. Brown scholar, 1974. Mem. ABA, Tenn. Bar Assn., Knoxville Bar Assn. (bd. govs. 1986-92, treas. 1986-90, sec. 1991-92), Def. Rsch. Inst., Am. Inns of Ct. (master of the bench 1991—, pres. 1994-95), Sertoma (v.p. chpt. 1987-89, pres. 1989-90), Phi Beta Kappa, Omicron Delta Kappa. Democrat. Roman Catholic. Avocations: soccer, gardening, reading, theater. Home: 1822 Nantasket Rd Knoxville TN 37922-5769 Office: Lewis King et al 620 Market St Fl 5 Knoxville TN 37902-2231

GIORDANO, NICHOLAS ANTHONY, stock exchange executive; b. Phila., Mar. 7, 1943; s. Nicola and Aida (Gioioso) G.; m. Joanne M. Pizzuto, Oct. 21, 1967; children: Jeannine, Colette and Nicholas (triplets). BS, LaSalle Coll., 1965. CPA, Pa. Mem. staff Price Waterhouse & Co., Phila., 1965-68; with various brokerage cos. Phila., 1968-71; controller stock exchange and stock clearing corp PBW (later Phila.) Stock Exch., Inc., 1971-72, v.p. ops., 1972-75, sr. v.p., 1975-76, exec. v.p., 1976-81, pres., CEO, 1981-97; interim pres. LaSalle U., 1998—; past bd. dirs. PBW (later Phila.) Stock Exch., Inc.; interim pres. LaSalle U., 1998—; vice chmn., bd. trustees La Salle U.; chmn. bd. dirs. Mt. St. Joseph Acad. Trustee LaSalle U.; bd. dirs. Fotoball USA, Inc., Greater Phila. Urban Affairs Coalition, Ind. Blue Cross, Union League Phila.; trustee, bd. dirs. WT Mutual Fund. Fax: 610-

834-0898. Home: 1755 Governors Way Blue Bell PA 19422-2554 Office: PO Box 984 Blue Bell PA 19422-0984

GIORDANO, PATRICIA J., radiation therapist; b. Phila., Aug. 2, 1945; d. Anthony Michael and Louise (Testa) G. AS, Gwynedd-Mercy Coll., 1977, BS, 1981; MS, Beaver Coll., 1985. Staff radiographer Nazareth Hosp., Phila., 1965-66; staff radiation therapist to asst. dept. head, clin. supr. Temple Univ. Hosp., Phila., 1967-84; from asst. program dir. to program dir., asst. prof. Gwynedd-Mercy Coll., Gwynedd Valley, Pa., 1986—; adv. bd. Franklin Learning Ctr., Phila., 1987-92, Abington Meml. Hosp. Sch. of Radiologic Tech., 1998—. Mem. Am. Soc. Radiol. Techs. (edn. del. region 7 1996-97, edn. del. region 9 1997—), Joint Rev. Com. on Edn. in Radiol. Tech. (site visitor team chair radiation therapy 1986-99, dir., bd. dirs. 1999—), European Soc. Therapeutic Radiologists and Oncologists, Am. Soc. Therapeutic Radiology and Oncology, Pa. Soc. Radiologic Technologists, Phila. Soc. Radiologic Technologists. Avocations: reading, traveling, flower arranging. Office: Gwynedd-Mercy Coll Sumneytown Pike Gwynedd Valley PA 19437

GIORDANO, SONDRA, nursing educator, medical and surgical nurse; m. Ralph Giordano; children: Lori, Daniel. BS, Adelphi U., 1965; MS, Russell Sage Coll., 1981. RN, N.Y. Head nurse Maimonides Hosp. Ctr., Bklyn.; clin. instr. Kings County Hosp. Sch. Nursing, Bklyn.; prof. Dutchess C.C., Poughkeepsie, N.Y. Mem. ANA, N.Y. State Nurses Assn., N.Y. Assn. Two-Year Colls., Sigma Theta Tau. Home: 8 North Rd Tillson NY 12486-1000

GIORGI, PETER BONNARD, educator; b. Nice, France, Dec. 25, 1929; came to the U.S., 1935; s. Leonard A. and Donal (Bonnard) G.; m. Detelina Petrova, July 21, 1962; children: Jean-Pierre André, Giséle Elaine. BS in Secondary Edn., Mansfield State U., 1953; MS in Edn., U. Ariz., 1958; postgrad., Johns Hopkins U., U. So. Calif., U. S.C., U. Houston, U. Md., Pa. State U., Temple U., Laverne Coll. Tchr., coach, counselor East Forest H.S., Marienville, Pa., 1953-55; reading specialist, curriculum cons. Spring Jr. High, Tucson, 1955-59; tchr., reading specialist Stephen Decatur H.S., Sigonella, Sicily, Italy, 1959-60, Bitburg (Germany) H.S., 1960-61; tchr., coach, curriculum cons. Dreux (France) H.S., 1961-65; tchr., counselor, work experience coord. Vicenza (Italy) H.S., 1965-95; cons., instr. U. Ariz., Tucson, 1995—; instr., cons. Lincoln U., Jefferson City, Mo., 1956-58, U. Md., 1960-95, Big Bend U., Army Edn. Ctr., Italy, 1985-95; supr. student tchr. program U. Ariz., 1957-59; instr. Air Force Edn. Ctr., Dreux AFB, France, 1960-65; instr., coord. summer sci. program DePauw U., Vicenza, 1980-85. Author: (handbooks) Reading Improvement Methods, 1958, JHS Social Studies Activities, 1987, (curriculum guides) Work Study Programs, 1972, Heritage Museums, 1986. With USN, 1947-49. Recipient Armed Svcs. award Armed Svcs. Recruiting Command, Europe, 1971, 73, 76, Cmty. Svc. award European Task Force-U.S. Army, Vicenza, 1978; GE fellow U. S.C., Columbia, 1973. Mem. NEA, ASCD, Internat. Reading Assn., Internat. Vocat. Guidance Assn., Nat. Geography Assn., Phi Delta Kappa (v.p. 1961-64). Avocations: media production, model building, scouting, photography, reading. Home: 201 N Jessica Ave Apt 149 Tucson AZ 85710-2142

GIORGIO, MARILYN, social worker; b. Jersey City, N.J., Apr. 13, 1948; d. Joseph and Bridget (Territola) Bator; m. Francis J. Giorgio, Apr. 16, 1972; 1 child, Allyson. BA, Jersey City (N.J.) State Coll., 1969. Social worker Hudson County Divsn. Social Svcs., Jersey City, 1969—. Avocations: travel, camping, hiking, cooking. Office: Hudson Co Div Social Svcs 100 Newkirk St Jersey City NJ 07306-3133

GIORLANDO, JEANNE A., labor and delivery nurse; b. Tooele, Utah, Dec. 13, 1957; d. Joseph Richard and Geraldine Ellen (Daniels) Giorlando; m. Francis J. Paglia, May 17, 1983 (dec. Oct. 7, 1985); 1 child, Karen Paglia-Hayes; m. John J. Hayes, Aug. 25, 1990 (div. Apr. 1999). BSN, Hunter Coll., 1978. RN, N.Y.; cert. nurse oper. rm.; cert. nurse inpatient obs., childbirth educator. Staff nurse med./surg. unit St. Vincents Med. Ctr. N.Y., N.Y.C., 1978-80; staff nurse labor and delivery, post-partum and nursery Bapt. Med. Ctr., Bklyn., 1980-81; staff nurse oper. rm., labor and delivery NYU Downtown Hosp., N.Y.C., 1981—. Mem. Assn. Women's Health, Obstetric and Neonatal Nurses. Democrat. Roman Catholic. Avocations: yoga, meditation. Home: 7631 Amboy Rd Staten Island NY 10307-1418 Office: NYU Downtown Hosp 170 William St New York NY 10038-2668

GIORNO, JOHN, poet; b. N.Y.C., Dec. 4, 1936. BA, Columbia Coll., 1958. Author: Balling Buddha, Grasping at Emptiness, You Got to Burn to Shine; pres. Giorno Poetry Systems, a non-profit found. started in 1965, producing numerous record albums, CDs, cassettes and videopaks of poets working with music and performance including The Best of William Burroughs Box Set, 1998; invented Dial-A-Poem, 1968; originator Spoken Word; performance poetry. Founder AIDS Treatment Project, 1984. Tibetan Nyingma Buddhist. Home: 222 Bowery New York NY 10012-4216

GIOSA, RICHARD PETER, pulmonary medicine physician; b. Bklyn., Apr. 23, 1955; s. Peter Gerard and Virginia Mary (Guarini) G.; m. Med. resident Norwalk (Conn.) Hosp., 1981-84; pulmonary fellow N.Y. Med. Coll., Valhalla, 1984-86; attending physician pulmonary medicine Midstate Med. Ctr. (formerly Vets. Meml. Med. Ctr.), Meriden, Conn., 1986—; bd. dirs. Meriden-Wallingford (Conn.) IPA, 1989—, Physician Adv. Bd. Healthworks, Wallingford, 1988—. Congregationalist. Avocations: running, biking, fitness. Home: 30 Suffield Ct Cheshire CT 06410-1862 Office: 546 S Broad St Meriden CT 06450-6600

GIOSEFFI, (DOROTHY) DANIELA, poet, performer, author, educator, jazz singer; b. Orange, N.J., Feb. 12, 1941; d. Daniel Donato Gioseffi; m. Richard J. Kearney, Sept. 7, 19 65 (div.); 1 child, Thea D.; m. Lionel B. Luttinger, June 6, 1986. BA, Montclair State Coll., 1963; MFA, Cath. U. of Am., 1966. Cons., poet Poets-in-the-Schs., Inc., N.Y.C., 1972-85; freelance writer, lectr. at numerous univs. throughout U.S. and Europe; appeared on Nat. Pub. Radio, CBC, BBC; spkr. on world peace and disarmament, 1979—; keynote spkr. Am. Forum for Global Edn. Nat. Conf., Miami, Fla., 1994, State Coun. of Tchrs. of English Conf., Orlando, Fla., 1995, So. Edn. Found., Internat. Conf., Atlanta, 1997. *Daniela Gioseffi is the author of over 12 books. She is also a translator of Latin American literature and a widely traveled lecturer on creative writing, as well as other issues. She is best known as a poet and multi-media performer of poetry. She has won many awards, including the American Book Award, as well as awards from the National Endowment for the Arts, the New York State Council for the Arts, PEN American Center's Short Fiction award and Outstanding Speaker awards. She is the founder and executive director of Skylands Writers & Artists Association, Inc., a non profit literary organization.* Author: (novel) The Great American Belly, 1977, 4th edit., 1979, (collection of poems) Eggs in the Lake, 1979, Word Wounds and Water Flowers, 1995 (non-fiction) Earth Dancing: Mother Nature's Oldest Rite, 1981, Women on War and Survival: International Voices for the Nuclear Age, 1988 (Am. Book award 1990), On Prejudice: A Global Perpective, 1993—, Dust Disappears: Translations of Carilda Oliver Labra of Latin America, 1995, (fiction) In Bed With the Exotic Enemy, 1997, The Psychic Touch, 1996, (plays) The Golden Daffodil Dwarf, Care of the Body, The Sea Hag in the Cave of Sleep, 1988, (radio play) Fathers and Children, 1988, 98; mem. editl. bd. Voices in Italian Americana, Purdue U., 1990—; short stories include Daffodil Dollars (PEN Short Fiction award 1990), (collection of fiction) In Bed With The Exotic Enemy: Stories and Novella, 1997; contbr. poetry, fiction, and lit. criticism numerous periodicals and anthologies: performer stage presentations of work throughout U.S. and Europe; lyricist and composer; singer many concert series, 1979—; editor-in-chief: Wise Women's Web: Internet Mag. of Lit. and Art (Best of Web award 1998). Pres. Bklyn. Citizens for Sane Nuclear Policy, 1987-89; keynote spkr. IV Feminist Internat. Bookfair, Barcelona, Spain, 1989, Miami Internat. Bookfair, 1990; mem. exec. bd., chmn. media watch com. Writers and Pubs. Alliance for Nuclear Disarmament, 1978-91. Recipient poetry and fiction award Creative Artists' Pub. Svc. Program, N.Y. State Coun. on Arts, 1971; grantee N.Y. State Coun. on Arts, 1972, 77, World Peace award Ploughshares Fund, 1989, Womens' Leadership Devel., Thanks Be to Grandmother Winifred Found., 1996. Mem. PEN Am. Ctr., Acad. Am. Poets, Actors Equity Assn., Nat. Book Critics Cir., Poets' House, Skylands Writers and Artists Assn. (founding pres.). E-mail: daniela@garden.net. Address: PO Box 15 Andover NJ 07821-0015

GIOTTONINI, JAMES B., public works director Stockton, California; b. Stockton, Calif., 1945. BS, Calif. State U., San Jose, 1968; MBA, Calif. State U., Sacramento, 1977. Dir. pub. works Town of Morgan Hill, Calif., 1978-82; city engr. City of Stockton, Calif., 1982-89; acting dir. pub. works City of Stockton, 1989, dir. pub. works, 1989—. Mem. ASCE. Office: City of Stockton Dept Pub Works Rm 317 425 N El Dorado St Stockton CA 95202-1997*

GIOVACCHINI, PETER LOUIS, psychoanalyst; b. N.Y.C., Apr. 12, 1922; s. Alex and Therese (Chicca) G.; m. Louise Post, Sept. 29, 1945; children: Philip, Sandra, Daniel. BS, U. Chgo., 1941, MD, 1944; postgrad., Columbia U., 1939; cert., Chgo. Inst. Psychoanalysis, 1954. Diplomate Am. Bd. Psychiatry and Neurology. Intern Fordham Hosp., N.Y.C., 1944-45; resident U. Chgo. Clinics, 1945-46, resident and research fellow, 1948-50; candidate Chgo. Inst. Psychoanalysis, 1949-54, clin. assoc., 1957—; clin. prof. U. Ill. Coll. Medicine, 1961-92, prof. emeritus, 1992—; chief cons. psychodynamic unit Barclay Hosp., Chgo., 1979-81; cons. Wilmette (Ill.) Family Svc. Ctr. and United Charities, Boyer-Marin Lodge, Marin County, Calif., 1986—, Mario Martin Inst. for Psychotherapy, 1989—, Psychoanalytic Ctr. Calif., L.A., 1990—; vis. prof. Smith Coll., Mass.; tng. and supervising analyst Chgo. Ctr. for Psychoanalytic Studies, 1994—. Author: (with L.B. Boyer) Psychoanalytic Treatment of Schizophrenia and Characterological Disorders, 1967, Psychoanalytic Treatment, 1971, also several books on character structure, primitive mental states, psychopathology and psychoanalytic technique, psychoanalysis; also articles.; Co-editor: Annals of Adolescent Psychiatry, 1972-80. Capt. M.C. AUS, 1946-48. Fellow Am. Psychiat. Assn., Am. Orthopsychiat. Assn. (bd. dirs. 1979-83), Am. Coll. Psychoanalysts; mem. Am. Soc. Adolescent Psychiatry, Chgo. Soc. Adolescent Psychiatry (pres. 1972-73), Internat. Psychoanalytic Soc. (chmn. standing com. on rsch. in psychosis 1994—), Am. Psychoanalytic Assn., Chgo. Psychoanalytic Soc. Home: 270 Locust Rd Winnetka IL 60093-3609 Office: 505 N Lake Shore Dr Chicago IL 60611-3427

GIOVACCHINI, ROBERT PETER, toxicologist, manufacturing executive, retired; b. Fresno, Calif., June 2, 1928; s. Robert and Olga (Mencarini) G.; m. Gertrude Joan Stech, June 18, 1949; children: Mary Joan, Diane Marie, Karen Denise. BS, Creighton U., 1948, MS, 1954; PhD, U. Nebr., 1958; DSc (hon.), U. Nebr. Med. Sch., 1980; cert. in bus. adminstrn., Harvard U., 1969. Instr. U. Nebr. Sch. Medicine, Omaha, 1957-58; assoc. dept. anesthesia Bishop Clarkson Meml. Hosp., Omaha, 1957-58; research histopathologist biol. dept. Gillette Co., Boston, 1958-60, supr. toxicological evaluations med. dept., 1960-62, asst. med. dir., 1962-64, v.p. corp. product integrity, 1974-93, ret., 1994; dir. med. evaluations Gillette Med. Research Inst., Washington, 1964-66, v.p., 1967-70, dir. med. evaluations dept., Rockville, Md., 1970-71, v.p., 1970-71; pres. Gillette Med. Evaluation Labs., Rockville, 1971-74; lectr. histopathology of skin Northwestern U. Sch. Medicine and Dentistry, Evanston, Ill., 1960-64. Recipient Gold medal for outstanding contbns. to art and sci. of cosmetics Soc. Cosmetic Chemists, 1976, Alumni merit award Creighton U., 1981. Fellow Acad. Toxicol. Scis.; mem. Am. Acad. Toxicol. Scis. (past pres.), Am. Coll. Toxicology, Am. Acad. Clin. Toxicology, Am. Acad. Dermatology (life), Soc. Toxicology, Sigma Xi. Home: 2518 Fernwood Dr Vienna VA 22181-4019

GIOVALE, VIRGINIA GORE, medical products ecexutive, civic leader; b. Salt Lake City, Oct. 12, 1943; d. Wilbert Lee and Genevieve (Walton) Gore; m. John Peter Giovale, June 20, 1965; children: Peter, Daniel, Michael, Mark. BS in Math., Westminster Coll., Salt Lake City, 1965. With W.L. Gore & Assocs., Inc., Flagstaff, Ariz., 1976-84; bd. dirs. W.L. Gore & Assocs., Inc., Newark, 1976—. Trustee, Westminster Coll., Salt Lake City, 1977—, chair, 1988—; co-chair Ariz. Community Found., 1995—. Recipient Heritage award Westminster Coll., 1994. Avocations: travel, backpacking, skiing, family fun. Office: WL Gore & Assocs Inc 1505 N 4th St Flagstaff AZ 86004-6102

GIOVANIELLI, DAMON VINCENT, physicist, consulting company executive; b. Teaneck, N.J., May 8, 1943; s. Dominick John and Marie Concetta (Conti) G.; m. Eleanor Ruth Rand, Aug. 18, 1968; children: Kira, Tina. AB, Princeton U., 1965; PhD in Physics, Dartmouth Coll., 1970. Instr. dept. engrng. and applied sci. Yale U., New Haven, 1970-72; with Los Alamos (N.Mex.) Nat. Lab., 1972-93, dep. assoc. dir. fusion rsch. and applications, 1984-85, tech. asst. to assoc. dir. for def. rsch. and applications, 1985-87, leader physics div., 1987-93, program dir. for strategic def. policy, liaison-new programs, 1992-93; ret., 1993; chief scientist Tech. Inst. for Internat. Collaboration, Los Alamos, 1992—; pres. Sumner Assocs., Sante Fe, 1993—; v.p. Sci. Applications Internat. Corp., San Diego, 1993—; chmn. bd. dirs. La Mancha Co., 1997—; bd. dirs. Dendrite, Inc.; J. Robert Oppenheimer Meml. Com. Contbr. articles to sci. jours. Mem. alumni schs. com. Princeton U. Fellow AAAS, mem. AIAA, Am. Phys. Soc. (program com. div. plasma physics 1978-79, chmn. nominating com. 1980, mem. exec. com. 1982-83), Am. Def. Preparedness Assn., Fusion Power Assocs., U.S. Space Found., Sigma Xi. Episcopalian. Home: 12 Loma Del Escolar Los Alamos NM 87544-2524 Office: Sumner Assocs 100 Cienega St Ste D Santa Fe NM 87501-2003

GIOVANNOLI, JOSEPH LOUIS, entrepreneur, lawyer. B of Engrng., Stevens Inst. Tech., 1962; JD, Fordham U., 1967. Bar: N.Y. 1967, N.J. 1971, Fed. Dist. Ct. 1967. Mgmt. sci. engr. corp. acctg. Am. Can. Co., N.Y.C., 1962-64; atty. dept. law Union Carbide Corp., N.Y.C., 1967-71; ptnr. Weir & Giovannoli, South Orange, N.J., 1971-74; of counsel Fischer, Kagan, Ascione and Zaretsky, Clifton, N.J., 1974-84; pres., co-founder Capital Resources Corp., Clifton, 1971-80; entrepreneur Saddle River, N.J., 1980-87; pres., chmn., founder U.S. Technologies, Inc., Paramus, N.J., 1987—; pres., chmn. Price Quote Network, Inc., Saddle River, 1995—. Patentee in field of computerized quotation system and method, and in field of elec. distance measurement. Home: PO Box 326 30 Bayberry Dr Saddle River NJ 07458-2610

GIOVINCO, JOSEPH, nonprofit administrator, writer; b. San Francisco, Oct. 12, 1942; s. Joseph Bivona Giovinco and Jean Andrews; m. Sally Garey, Aug. 31, 1970 (div. Mar. 1982); 1 child, Gina Lorraine. BA, U. Oreg., 1964; MA in History, San Francisco State U., 1968; PhD in History, U. Calif., Berkeley, 1973. Asst. prof. history SUNY, Albany, 1974-76; instr. multicultural studies Sonoma State U., Cotati, Calif., 1976-79; exec. dir. Hist. Mus. Found., Sonoma County, Santa Rosa, Calif., 1977-80; exec. dir. no. Calif. affiliate Am. Diabetes Assn., San Francisco, 1980-81; exec. dir. San Francisco Sch. Vols., 1981-85, Calif. Hist. Soc., San Francisco, 1985-87; dir. Ctr. Advancement & Renewal of Educators, San Francisco, 1988—. Contbr. articles to profl. publs. Fellow, NEH and Harvard U., 1973; recipient scholarship U. Minn. Ctr. for Immigration History, Mpls., 1975; Rockefeller Found. grantee, 1977; recipient Covello prize Italian Am. Hist. Assn., 1976; named Alumnus of Yr., San Francisco State U., 1987. Roman Catholic. Avocations: rose gardening, classical music. Office: Ctr Advancement & Renewal Educators 25550 25th Ave San Francisco CA 94116

GIPPIN, ROBERT MALCOLM, lawyer; b. Cleve., Feb. 3, 1948; s. Morris and Helena (Weil) G.; children : Sarah, Joshua, Rebecca, Alanna; m. Susan Smith. A.B., Dartmouth Coll., 1969; J.D., Harvard U., 1973. Bar: Ohio 1973. Asst. to dir. Ohio Dept. Commerce, Columbus, 1973; exec. sec. Ohio Real Estate Commn., Columbus, 1974-75; prosecutor Municipal Ct., Cuyahoga Falls, Ohio, 1975; ptnr. Buckingham, Doolittle & Burroughs, Akron, Ohio, 1975—. Active exec. com. Summit County Democratic Party, Akron, 1976—, Planned Parenthood; pres. Summit County Council, 1982-84. Mem. Akron Bar Assn., Ohio Bar Assn., Phi Beta Kappa. Jewish. Avocations: reading; tennis; cooking. Home: 737 Merriman Rd Akron OH 44303-1768 Office: Buckingham Doolittle & Burroughs PO Box 1500 Akron OH 44309-1500

GIPS, CHRISTIAAN HENDRIK, medical educator; b. The Hague, The Netherlands, Feb. 18, 1932; s. Pieter and Françoise Hendrika (Van Wort) G.; m. Barbara Frey Meihuizen, Nov. 17, 1957 (dec. Apr. 1987); m. Johanna Barones Van Asbeck, July 8, 1988; children: Ariane Yvonne, Paul Jan, Cornelie Ernestine. MD, Leiden (The Netherlands) U., 1957, Copenhagen U., 1962; PhD cum laude, Groningen U., 1968. Resident, chief resident Odense (Denmark) Herning Hosps., 1959-63; asst., assoc. prof. State U. Groningen, The Netherlands, 1963-79, prof. medicine, 1979-93, prof. emeritus, 1993—; head divsn. hepatology U. Hosp., Groningen, 1980-93; dir. Prof. Gips Internat. Sch. Hepatology & Tropical Med. Groningen U., 1993—; cons. Talma-Huis, Veenwouden, The Netherlands, 1969-97; co-founder, coord. Netherlands Liver Transplant Program, 1977-85. Author: Diagnostic Ammonia Tests, 1968; co-author: Atlas of Liver Disease Mortality, 1994; editor: Progress in Liver Transplantation, 1985; editor Netherlands Jour. Medicine, 1970-81; assoc. editor Jour. Liver, 1985-92, Jour. Alcohol and Drugs (Dutch), 1974-95; mem. steering com. Jour. Hepatology, 1984-90. Co-founder, vice chmn. Dutch Alcohol Found., The Hague, 1975-80; co-founder, sec., chmn. Netherlands Assn. Study Liver, Rotterdam, 1977-83; co-founder, chmn., adviser Netherlands Digestive Diseases Found., Nieuwe Gein, 1981—; co-founder, chmn., adviser Groningen Liver Found., 1985—; mem. Project Mgmt. Group consecutive European Union projects on informatics in liver disease, 1990-98; mem. Cochrane Hepato-Biliary Group, 1995—; coord. multictr. liver cell cancer project Groningen-Indonesia Kanker Hati, Indonesia, 1995-98, Groningen-Indonesia Liver Disease, 1997—. 1st lt. M.C. Royal Netherlands Army, 1957-59. Decorated officer Order of Oranje Nassau. Mem. Internat. Assn. Study of Liver, European Assn. Study of Liver (past pres.), Netherlands Assn. Study of Liver (hon.), Netherlands Assn. Internists (past bd. dirs.), Netherlands Assn. Liver Patients (hon.), Danish Assn. Study of Liver, North Netherlands Golf and Country Club. Avocations: mountain walking, golf. Home: Parallelweg 59, NL-9756 CC Glimmen The Netherlands Office: Oostersingel 69, NL-9713 EZ, Groningen The Netherlands

GIPSON, SHELLEY R., artist, educator; b. Nacogdoches, Tex., Apr. 13, 1973; d. Floyd Oigive and Rhonda Gail Tatom Gipson; m. Michael Terry Adams, Mar. 13, 1998. BFA in Printmaking cum laude, Stephen F. Austin State U., 1994, MA in Computer Art, 1999; MFA in Printmaking, Tex. Christian U., 1997. Student asst. phys. plant dept. Stephen F. Austin State U., Nacogdoches, Tex., 1992-94; student asst. to assoc. dean edn. Stephen F. Austin State U., Nacogdoches, 1995, asst. to dir. gallery, 1997, grad. rsch. asst. Office of Instrnl. Tech., 1997-99; asst. art dept. Tex. Christian U., Ft. Worth, 1995-97, instr. extended edn., 1997; instr. Angelina Coll., Lufkin, Tex., 1997—; guest lectr. art dept. Stephen F. Austin State U., Nacogdoches, 1996, programs asst. image and text II art dept., 1998; guest curator Kinetic Coll., Tyler, Tex., 1998; co-curator Control, Nacogdoches, 1998. One-person shows include Kougeas Gallery, Boston, 1998, Angelina Coll., Lufkin, 1998, Olson Gallery, Minot (N.D.) State U., 1998, Contemporary Arts Ctr., Ft. Worth, 1999. Pres. Art Alliance, Nacogdoches, 1993-94; founding mem. SEVEN, Ft. Worth, 1995-97, Twin Creeks Arts Project, Nacogdoches, 1998-99. Mem. Coll. Art Assn., Contemporary Arts Ctr., So. Graphics Coun., Modern Art Mus. Ft. Worth, Mid-Am. Print Coun., Guild Book Workers (Lone Star chpt.). Avocations: printmaking, ice skating, computer art. E-mail: sgipson@sfasu.edu.

GIRA, CATHERINE RUSSELL, university president; b. Fayette City, Pa., Oct. 30, 1932; d. John Anthony and Mary (Stephen) Russell; m. Joseph Andrew Gira, July 17, 1954 (dec.); children: Cheryl Ann, Thomas Russell. B.S., Calif. State U., 1953; M.Ed., Johns Hopkins U., 1957, M.L.A., 1972; Ph.D., Am. U., 1975. Tchr. Balt. County, Balt., 1953-60, head dept., 1958-60; writing cons. Md. State Dept. Edn., 1960-68; instr. Johns Hopkins U., Balt., 1964-65; from asst. prof. to prof. U. Balt., 1965-81, acting dean, 1981-82, provost, 1982-91; pres. Frostburg (Md.) State U., 1991—. Contbr. articles to profl. jours. Am. U. scholar, 1973-75. Mem. Am. Assn. Univ. Adminstrs. (bd. dirs. 1984-87, pres.-elect 1987, pres. 1988-90), Fedn. State Humanities Couns. (bd. dirs. 1990-94, vice-chair 1993-94), Md. Humanities Coun. (chmn. 1989-90), Md. Assn. Higher Edn. (bd. dirs. 1983-85, pres. 1986-87), Shakespeare Assn. Am., Edgar Allan Poe Soc. (bd. dirs. 1982—). Methodist. Home: 106 Jones Ct Frostburg MD 21532-1415 Office: Frostburg State U Office of Pres Frostburg MD 21532-2302*

GIRALDI, ROBERT NICHOLAS, film director; b. Paterson, N.J., Jan. 17, 1939. B.F.A., Pratt Inst., 1960. Assoc. creative dir. Young & Rubicam, N.Y.C., 1960-71; v.p., head creative dept. Della Femina, Travisano, N.Y.C., 1971-73; ptnr. Ampersand Prodns., N.Y.C., 1973-74, dir.; pres. Giraldi Suarez Prodns., N.Y.C., 1974—; instr. head advt. and design, asst. dir. Sch. Visual Arts, N.Y.C., 1969-73; owner N.Y.C. restaurants, Vong Jo Jo Lipstick Cafe, Patria, Gigino, Jean-Georges; owner London restaurant Vong. Dir.: (play) Laughing on the Outside, 1982, (music videos) Say Say Say, 1983, Love Is a Battlefield, 1984, Hello, 1984, Don't Drive Drunk, 1984, Beat It (Michael Jackson), 1983, World Series (Baseball Hall Fame), (TV special) A Christmas to Remember with Dolly Parton and Kenny Rogers, 1985, (feature film) Hiding Out, 1987; art represented in permanent collection Mus. Modern Art, N.Y.C. Bd. dirs. Catholic Big Bros., N.Y.C., 1982—; in numerous ads against AIDS. Recipient numerous gold awards Art Dirs. Club N.Y., N.Y.C., numerous Andy awards Advt. Club N.Y., N.Y.C., numerous Clio awards, numerous One Show awards Copy Club N.Y., N.Y.C., numerous N.Y. Festival awards, numerous Mobius awards, Gold award Cannes Film Festiva, 1974, 76, 79, 81, 88, 96, AICP MOMA gold award, 1992, 94, London Internat. Film Festival gold award, 1992, Italian Key awards, 1990, numerous other awards for excellence in advt., 1993-96, Herschel Levit Scholarship award Pratt Inst., 1994; named to Dir.'s Hall of Fame, 1991. Mem. Dirs. Guild Am., N.Y. Women in Film (patron). Roman Catholic. Office: Giraldi Suarez Prodns 270 Lafayette St Ste 205 New York NY 10012-3327 also: 329 N Wetherly Dr Beverly Hills CA 90211-1605 *If you do quality you will always do quantity, but it never works the other way around.**

GIRARD, ANDREA EATON, communication executive, consultant; b. N.Y.C., Oct. 16, 1946; d. Samuel Robert and Mimi (Eaton) G. Student, Syracuse U., 1964-66; BA cum laude, Finch Coll., 1968; MA, Columbia U., 1971. Talent coord./prodn. asst. Guber-Ford-Gross Prodns., N.Y., 1968-70; v.p. Charing Cross Press, N.Y.C., 1970-72; assoc. producer, talent dir.TV shows "To Tell the Truth" and "Snap Judment" Goodson Todman Prodns., N.Y.C., 1972-80; programming exec. David Letterman-NBC, N.Y.C., 1980; dir. of talent, producer Daytime/Arts and Entertainment Networks (Hearst/ABC Video Enterprises), N.Y.C., 1981-84; dir. current programming acquisition, sr. producer Lifetime Network (Hearst/ABC/Viacom Entertainment Svcs.), N.Y.C., 1984-86; pres. Girard Communications, N.Y.C., 1986—, dir. med. communications advantage internat., 1990-91; v.p. PRNY, N.Y.C., 1990-92; CEO Panache Communications Inc., N.Y.C., 1992—; judge Emmy awards Internat. Film and TV Festival; speaker pub. rels. coun. sch. of continuing edn. NYU; media cons. to med. industry, 1987—. Producer, writer (documentaries) Cave Dwellers of Crete, 1974, Sponge Divers of Kalymnos, 1979, Gypsies of the Camargue, 1983. Active fund raising bd. Jersey Wildlife Preservation Trust, N.Y.; active hospitality com. United Nations, N.Y., Big Apple Com. for the Benefit of the Image of N.Y. Mem. NATAS, NAFE, N.Y. Women in Film & TV, Nat. Assn. Women Bus. Owners, Internat. Assn. Cooking Profls. Avocations: goldsmith, horseback riding, tennis. E-mail: panacheinc@aol.com. Office: Panache Comms 201 E 77th St Ste 7F New York NY 10021-2082

GIRARD, FRANCOIS, film director; b. Lac St-Jean, Que., Can.. Founder, prin. Zone Prodns., 1988-92, Velvet Camera, 1988-92. Writer, dir. feature films including Cargo, 1990, Thirty Two Short Films About Glenn Gould, 1993 (Best Film prix Genie award, 1993, Best Dir. prix Genie award, 1993, Best photography prix Genie award, 1993, Best Editing prix Genie award, 1993, mention Festival of Festival Toronto, 1993, mention Festival du Film de Vancouver, 1993, Prize Figueira Da Foz Festival de Lisbonne, 1994, Badeira Paulista award Mostra de Sao Paulo, 1994), Peter Gabriel's Secret World, 1994 (Prix du Pub. Festival Internat. du Nouveau Cinéma Mtl., 1994, silver rose for best concert film Montreux Film Festival, 1995, Internat. Grammy award for Music Video long version, 1996); dir. medium-length films including Le Dortoir, 1991 (Internat. Emmy award, Gold FIPA, Gemeau award), Le Jardin des Ombres, 1993, After Othello, 1994, Souvenirs d'Othello, 1994; dir. short films including Das Brunch, 1983, Human Scope, 1984, Le Train, 1985, Monsieur Léon, 1986, Tango Tango, 1986, Montréal Danse, 1988, Mourir, 1988, Suspect No 1, 1989, CCA, 1989, Vie Et Mort De L'Architecte, 1989; co-dir. short films including Distance, 1984; co-writer: Thirty Two Short Films About Glenn Gould; dir. various commls.; dir.: The Red Violin, 1998 (8 Genie awards including best film and best director). Office: Rhombus Media, 489 King St W Ste 102, Toronto, ON Canada M5V 1L3*

GIRARD, NETTABELL, lawyer; b. Pocatello, Idaho, Feb. 24, 1938; d. George and Arranetta (Bell) Girard. Student, Idaho State U., 1957-58; BS, U. Wyo., 1959, JD, 1961. Bar: Wyo. 1961, D.C. 1969, U.S. Supreme Ct. 1969. Practiced in Riverton, 1963-69; atty.-adviser on gen. counsel's staff HUD; assigned Office Interstate Land Sales Registration, Washington, 1969-70; sect. chief interstate land sales Office Gen. Counsel, 1970-73; ptnr. Larson & Larson, Riverton, 1973-85; pvt. practice Riverton, 1985—; guest lectr. at high schs.; condr. seminar on law for layman Riverton br. A.A.U.W., 1965; condr. course on women and law; lectr. equal rights, job discrimination, land use planning. Editor Wyoming Clubwoman, 1966-68; bd. editors Wyo. Law Jour., 1959-61; writer Obiter Dictum column Women Lawyers Jour., Dear Legal Advisor column Solutions for Seniors, 1988-94; featured in Riverton Ranger, 1994; also articles in legal jours. Chmn. fund dr. Wind River chpt. ARC, 1965; chmn. Citizens Com. for Better Hosp. Improvement, 1965; chmn. subcom. on polit. legal rights and responsibilities Gov.'s Commn. on Status Women, 1965-69, mem. adv. com., 1973-93; rep. Nat. Conf. G ovs. Commn., Washington, 1966; local chmn. Law Day, 1966, 67, county chmn. Law Day, 1994, 95, 96, 97; mem. state bd. Wyo. Girl Scouts USA, sec. 1974-89, mem. nat. bd., 1978-81; state vol. adv. Nat. Found., March of Dimes, 1967-69; legal counsel Wyo. Women's Conf., 1977; gov. apptd. State Wyo. Indsl. Siting Coun., 1995—. Recipient Spl. Achievement award HUD, 1972, Disting. Leadership award Girl Scouts U.S.A., 1973, Franklin D. Roosevelt award Wyo. chpt. March of Dimes, 1985, Thanks Badge award Girl Scout Coun., 1987, Women Helping Women award in recognition of effective advancement status of women Riverton Club of Soroptimist Internat., 1990, Spl. award plaque in appreciation and recognition of 27 yrs. of svc. to State of Wyo., Wyo. Commn. for Women, 1964-92, Appreciation award Wyo. Sr. Citizens and Solutions for Srs., 1994, Arts in Action Pierrot award for outstanding musician, 1998. Mem. AAUW (br. pres.), Wyo. Bar Assn., Fremont County Bar Assn. (Spl. Recognition cert. 1997), D.C. Bar Assn., Women's Bar Assn. D.C., Internat. Fedn. Women Lawyers, Am. Judicature Soc., Assn. Trial Lawyers Am., Wyo. Trial Lawyers Assn., Nat. Assn. Women Lawyers (del. Wyo., nat. sec. 1969-70, v.p. 1970-71, pres. 1972-73), Wyo. Fedn. Women's Clubs (state editor, pres.-elect 1968-69, treas. 1974-76), Prog. Women's Club (pres.-elect. 1994-95), Riverton Chautaqua Club (pres. 1965-67), Riverton Civic League (pres. 1987-89), Kappa Delta, Delta Kappa Gamma (state chpt. hon.). Home: PO Box 687 Riverton WY 82501-0687 Office: 513 E Main St Riverton WY 82501-4440 *I believe first and foremost in the freedom of the individual: the right of the individual to be different, to be unique, and to pursue his or her particular heart's desire so long as that pursuit does not endanger the life or freedom of another. Perhaps because as a woman lawyer in predominately a man's profession, I have experienced the bitterness and dissolutionment of discrimination, I have actively worked through the equal rights movement toward the realization of individual freedom for all people. I support equality, not in the sense of "sameness," but in the realization of greater opportunities for individual development and differentiation.*

GIRARD, RENÉ NOEL, author, educator; b. Avignon, France, Dec. 25, 1923; came to U.S., 1947; s. Joseph and Thérèse (Fabre) G.; m. Martha McCullough, June 18, 1951; children: Martin, Daniel, Mary. Archiviste-paléographe, Ecole des chartes, Paris, 1947; PhD, Ind. U., 1950. Tchr. Romance langs. Ind. U., 1947-52, Duke U., 1952-53, Bryn Mawr Coll., 1953-57; faculty Johns Hopkins U., 1957-68, prof. French lit., 1961-68, chmn. dept. Romance langs., 1966-68, James M. Beall prof. French and humanities, 1977-80; disting. faculty prof. arts and letters SUNY, Buffalo, 1971-77; Andrew B. Hammond prof. French and Comparative Lit., Stanford U., 1981-95, courtesy prof. religious studies, 1986-95; mem. Ctr. for Internat. Security and Arms Control, 1990-95, emeritus mem., 1995. Author: Mensonge romantique et vérité romanesque, 1961, 78, Marcel Proust: A Collection of Critical Essays, 1962, 77, Deceit, Desire and the Novel, 1967, 76, La Violence et le Sacré, 1972, English transl., 1977, Critique dans un souterrain, 1976, Des Choses cachées depuis la fondation du monde, 1978, To Double Business Bound, 1978, Le Bouc émissaire, 1982, La Route antique des hommes pervers, 1985, Things Hidden since the Foundation of the World, 1987, Job: the Victim of his People, 1987, Shakespeare: Les feux de l'envie, 1990, A Theater of Envy. William Shakespeare, 1991, Quand ces choses commenceront, 1994, The Girard Reader (ed. James Williams), 1996, Resurrection from the Underground: Feodor Dostoevsky (ed. James Williams), 1997; contbr. articles to profl. jours. Guggenheim fellow, 1960, 67; recipient Prix Médicis Essai, 1990, Premio Nonino, 1998. Mem. Acad. Arts and Scis., French Legion Honor, Acad. Francaise (Grand prix de philosophie 1996). Home: 705 Frenchmans Rd Stanford CA 94305-1004 also: 17 Av la Bourdonnais, 75007 Paris France

GIRARDEAU, MARVIN DENHAM, physics educator; b. Lakewood, Ohio, Oct. 3, 1930; s. Marvin Denham and Maude Irene (Miller) G.; m. Susan Jessica Brown, June 30, 1956; children—Ellen, Catherine, Laura. B.S., Case Inst. Tech., 1952; M.S., U. Ill., 1954; Ph.D., Syracuse U., 1958. NSF postdoctoral fellow Inst. Advanced Study, Princeton, 1958-59; research assoc. Brandeis U., 1959-60; staff mem. Boeing Sci. Research Labs., 1960-61; research assoc. Enrico Fermi Inst. Nuclear Studies, U. Chgo., 1961-63; assoc. prof. physics, research asso. Inst. Theoretical Sci., U. Oreg., Eugene, 1963-67; prof. physics, research assoc. Inst. Theoretical Sci., U. Oreg., 1967—, dir., 1967-69, chmn. dept. physics, 1974-76. Contbr. articles to profl. jours. Recipient Humboldt Sr. U.S. Scientist award, 1984-85. NSF research grantee, 1965-79; ONR research grantee, 1981-87. Fellow Am. Phys. Soc.; mem. AAUP. Rsch. on quantum-mech. many-body problems, statis. mechanics, atomic, molecular and chem. physics, nonlinear dynamics and chaos. Home: 2398 Douglas Dr Eugene OR 97405-1711 Office: U Oreg Dept Physics Eugene OR 97403

GIRARDI, JOSEPH ELLIOTT, baseball player; b. Peoria, Ill., Oct. 14, 1964. BS in Indsl. Engring., Northwestern U., 1986. Baseball player N.Y. Yankees, 1995—. Achievements include member of N.Y. Yankees World Series Champions, 1996. Office: NY Yankees Yankee Stadium E 161st and River Ave Bronx NY 10451*

GIRAUD, RAYMOND DORNER, retired language professional; b. N.Y.C., Aug. 26, 1920; s. Gabriel and Mabel (Dorner) G.; m. Lise Kurzmann, Feb. 1, 1948. B.A., Coll. City N.Y., 1941; M.A., U. Chgo., 1949; Ph.D., Yale, 1954. Instr. English and French Ill. Inst. Tech., 1946-49; instr., then asst. prof. French Yale, 1952-58; mem. faculty Stanford, 1958—, prof. French, 1962—, chmn. dept. French and Italian, 1968-72; prof. emeritus, 1986. Author: The Unheroic Hero, 1957, Flaubert, A Collection of Critical Essays, 1964. Served with AUS, 1942-45. Decorated Chevalier, Ordre des Palmes Académique, 1967; Guggenheim fellow, 1961-62. Home: 2200 Byron St Palo Alto CA 94301-4007 Office: Stanford U Dept French and Italian Stanford CA 94305

GIRDEN, EUGENE LAWRENCE, lawyer; b. N.Y.C., Oct. 17, 1930; s. Jules and Freda (Mannes) G.; m. Charlene Margot Tobin, July 4, 1958; children: Lisa Jan, Steven Scott. B.A., U. Md., 1951, LL.B., 1953. Bar: Md. 1953, N.Y. 1957, U.S. Supreme Ct. 1963, U.S. Ct. Mil. Appeals 1954, U.S. Customs Ct., U.S. Ct. Customs and Patent Appeal 1958. Atty. Barnes, Richardson & Colburn, N.Y.C., 1957-58; ptnr. Coudert Bros., N.Y.C., 1959-82, Patterson Belknap Webb & Tyler, N.Y.C., 1982-90; counsel Kelley Drye & Warren, N.Y.C., 1990-93, Kaye Scholer Fierman Hays & Handler, N.Y.C., 1993-95, Shukat, Arrow, Hafer & Weber, N.Y.C., 1995-98, Pollack & Greene, N.Y.C., 1998—; guest lectr. NYU Law Sch., 1965—, Columbia Law Sch., 1975—, Cornell Law Sch., 1973—, Practicing Law Inst., 1965—; counsel Am. Theatre Wing, 1985—. State v.p. Conn. Young Dems., Hartford, 1959; bd. dirs. Stamford Ctr for Arts, 1990—. Served to lt. USN, 1953-57. Mem. ABA, Copyright Soc. U.S.A. (exec. com. 1967-70, 81-83, 87-94, pres. bd. trustees 1994-96), N.Y. Bar Assn., Assn. of Bar of City of N.Y., Libel Def. Resource Ctr. (chmn. law firm sect. 1987-95), Rockrimmon Country Club (gov. 1978-86, ct. sect. 1978-86). Democrat. Home: Brookdale Dr Stamford CT 06903 Office: Pollack & Greene 757 3d Ave New York NY 10017

GIRGUS, SAM B., English literature educator; b. Dec. 30, 1941; m. Judith Scot-Smith; children: Katya Roberts, Meighan St. John, Jennifer Scot-Smith. BA in American Studies, Syracuse U., 1962; MA in English, State U. Iowa, 1963; PhD in American Studies, U. N.Mex., 1972. Reporter, critic Providence (R.I.) Jour., 1967-69; asst. prof. in Am. studies and English U. Ala., 1972-75, dir., 1973-75; assoc. prof., chmn. dept. Am. studies U. N.Mex., 1975-84, prof. English and Am. studies, 1980-87; prof. English, dir. Am. studies U. Oreg., Eugene, 1987-90; prof. English Vanderbilt U., Nashville, 1990—, dir. Am. studies, 1990-92; chmn. disciplinary adv. com. Fulbright Scholars Awards in Am. Culture, 1989-93; cons. USIA visit at Sofia U., Bulgaria, 1985, Los Andes U., Bogota, Columbia, 1992, Hankuk U., Seoul, Korea, 1993, Aarhus U., Odense U., Denmark, 1995; lectr. in field; Uppsala chair in Am. studies Uppsala U., Sweden, 1996. Author: The Law of the Heart: Individualism and the Modern Self in American Literature, 1979, The New Covenant: Jewish Writers and the American Idea, 1984, Desire and the Political Unconscious in American Literature, 1990, The Films of Woody Allen, 1993, Hollywood Renaissance: The Cinema of Democracy in the Era of Ford, Cooper an Kazan, 1998; editor: The American Self: Myth, Ideology and Popular Culture, 1981, The New Eden: Consensus and Regeneration in America, 1988, The Outsider: Dissent and Alienation in America, 1988; guest editor: Am. Literary Realism 1870-1910, 1977; contbr. articles, revs. to profl. jours. With USN, 1963-67. Rockefeller Humanities fellow, 1980-81; Sr. Fulbright lectr. U. Heidelberg, Germany, 1984. Mem. MLA, Cinema Studies Assn., Am. Studies Assn. Home: 402 Lynwood Blvd Nashville TN 37205-3435 Office: Vanderbilt U Dept English PO Box 1654 Sta B 318 Benson Hall Nashville TN 37235

GIRLING, BETTIE JOYCE MOORE, home health executive; b. Feb. 10, 1930; d. Robert and Florence Irene (Shaw) Moore; m. Robert George William Girling, III, Sept. 2, 1960; children: Robert George William IV, Maria Julia Anastasia, Samuel Marcus Shaw, Katherine Susan Jane. BS in Edn., Daniel Baker Coll., 1952; MSSW, U. Tex., Austin, 1956. Tchr. Clairemont (Tex.) Ind. Sch. Dist., 1952-53; caseworker Tex. Dept. Pub. Welfare, 1953-57; licensing supr. Tex. Dept. Pub. Welfare, Dallas, 1960; caseworker Austin State Sch. for Mentally Retarded, 1957-60; with adoption intake Edna Gladney Home, Ft. Worth, 1961-65; rschr. Child Welfare League Am., N.Y.C., 1966; organizer, exec. dir. Girling Home Care, Austin, 1967-69; asst. dir. agy. programs Girling Health Care, Inc.; ex-v.p., COO multi-state comprehensive health care agy. Tex., La., N.Y., Okla., Tenn., 1967—; owner, operator child care facility, 1973-75; mem. long range planning com. Grad. Sch. Social Work, Bd. U. Tex.-Austin Sch. Nursing; mem. home health services adv. council Tex. Dept. Health; organizer, coord. profl. workshops; mem. adv. bd. U. Tex. Sch. Social Work, Austin, 1996. Recipient Ida Mae Herbert award Tex. Assn. for Home Care, 1994, Disting. Alumni award Daniel Baker Coll. Ex-Students Assn., 1988. Mem. NASW, Tex. Hosp. Assn., Tex. Home Health Agys., Nat. Assn. Home Health Agys., Women Symphony League of Austin, Austin Symphony Orch. Soc. (bd. dirs.), Austin Womens Club, Austin Country Club (co-chair Austin Lyric Austin Ball 1988, 89), Daniel Baker Ex-Students Assn. Tex., Heritage Soc. Austin (bd. dirs./advisors 1998—). Democrat. Methodist. Office: Girling Health Care Inc PO Box 4294 Austin TX 78765-4294

GIRLING, ROBERT GEORGE WILLIAM, III, business owner; b. Eldorado, Ark., July 28, 1929; s. Robert George William Jr. and Mildred Addie (Massey) G.; m. Bettie J. Moore, Sept. 2, 1960. BA, Miss. Coll., 1950; BD, New Orleans Bapt. Theol. Sem., 1954; MS in Social Work, U. Tex., 1961. Pastor Bapt. chs., Miss., 1949-58; tchr. high sch. Miss., 1958-59; dir. social work Lena Pope Childrens Home, Ft. Worth, 1961-62, exec. dir., 1962-66; pres., CEO Girling Health Care, Inc., Austin, Tex., 1967—; dir. social work. Austin State Sch., 1966-69, dir. profl. svcs 1970-71; clin. instr. U. Tex. Sch. Social Work, Austin, 1972-75. Capt. USAFR, 1955-65. Named Lord Chancellor, Knights of the Symphony, 1994; recipient Ida Mae Herbert Meritorious award Tex. Home Health Care. Mem. Acad. Cert. Social Workers, Tex. Assn. Home Health Agys. (treas. 1978-82, pres. 1984-86), Nat. Assn. Home Care (chmn. nominating com. 1978), Rotary (chmn. nominating com. 1976), Austin Country Club, Headliners Club, Austin Club. Baptist. Avocations: fishing, ranching, photography, swimming. Office: Girling Health Care Inc PO Box 4294 Austin TX 78765-4294

GIRMAN, TANYA LYNN, dietitian; b. Bitburg, Germany, Apr. 26, 1968; came to the U.S., 1968; d. John Richard and Patricia Lynn (Cekanski) G. BS, U. Calif., Davis, 1990; MPH, U. Calif., L.A., 1993. Registered dietitian Comn. on Dietetic Registration; cert. nutrition support dietitian. Clin. dietitian and rschr. West L.A. (Calif.) VA Med. Ctr., 1992—; part-time inst. clin. nutrition Santa Monica (Calif.) Coll., 1996, 98; mem. dietetic internship selection com. West L.A. VA Med. Ctr., 1993, mem. dietetic internship adv. com., 1993—, chair nutrition edn. com., 1993-95. Contbg. columnist in field. Mem. Am. Soc. for Parenteral and Enteral Nutrition, Am. Dietetic Assn. (Recognized Young Dietitian of Yr. 1996), Calif. Dietetic Assn., L.A. Dist. Dietetic Assn., Calif. Dietitians in Gen. Clin. Practice (founder, chair exec. bd. 1992-96). Avocations: softball, ballroom and Latin dancing, learning foreign languages, cooking, computers, theatre. Home: 1338 18th St Apt 5 Santa Monica CA 90404-1919 Office: West LA VA Med Ctr 11301 Wilshire Blvd 120G Los Angeles CA 90073-1003

GIROD, ERWIN ERNEST, internist; b. L.A., Oct. 1, 1944; s. Dudley Leonard and Rena Merl (Hudson) G.; m. Jill Louise Johnson, Dec, 16, 1967; children: Jeffrey Johnson, Janette Renee. BA, Calif. State U., L.A., 1966; MD, U. Calif., Irvine, 1970. Diplomate Am. Bd. Internal Medicine. Med. intern L.A. County-U. So. Calif. Med. Ctr., 1970-71, resident in internal medicine, 1971-73; ward med. officer, dir. med. ICU, adminstrv. chief U.S. Naval Hosp., San Diego, 1973-75; dir. ICU Christian Med. Coll., Brown Meml. Hosp., Ludhiana, Punjab, India, 1976-77; asst. prof. medicine Punjab U., 1976-77, Loma Linda (Calif.) U., 1978-80; pvt. practice Pasadena, Calif., 1981-86; internal medicine specialist Hanson Med. Group, Inc., San Gabriel, Calif., 1986—; mem. staff Huntington Meml. Hosp., Pasadena, 1981—, St. Luke Med. Ctr., Pasadena, 1981—; assoc. staff mem. Meth. Hosp. So. Calif., Arcadia, Calif., 1986—; lectr. in field. Contbr. articles to profl. publs. Bd. dirs. Lifewater, Internat., Baldwin Park, Calif., 1984-89; med. advisor Overseas Missionary Fellowship, Orange, Calif., 1988-92. Lt. comdr. USN, 1973-75. Fellow ACP, Am. Biographical Inst., Internat. Biographical Ctr. (life); mem. Calif. Med. Assn., Christian Med.-Dental Soc., Ephebian Soc. L.A., Gideons Internat. (chaplain Pasadena camp 1992-95), World Inst. Achievement (Internat. Cultural Diploma of Honor 1989, World Decoration of Excellence Medallion 1989, Disting. Leadership award 1989), Phi Kappa Phi, Alpha Gamma Omega (Legion of Honor). Republican. Congregational. Avocations: swimming, music, roses. Home: 1195 Coronet Ave Pasadena CA 91107-1729

GIROD, FRANK PAUL, retired surgeon; b. Orenco, Oreg., Aug. 13, 1908; s. Leon and Anna (Gerig)G.; m. Nadine Mae Cooper, Aug. 26, 1939; children: Judith Anne, Janet Carol, Franklin Paul, John Cooper. AB, Willamette U., Salem, Oreg., 1929; MD, U. Colo., 1938. Diplomate Am. Bd. Family Practice. Tchr. physics and chemistry, athletic coach Cortez High Sch., Colo., 1929-34; intern U. Colo., Denver, 1938-39; resident surgeon U.S. Marine Hosp., Balt., 1939-41; pvt. practice specializing in family practice and surgery Lebanon, Oreg., 1946-95; ret., 1995; bd. dirs. Lebanon Hosp., 1960—, pres. med. staff. Trustee, sec. Blue Shield Ops., Oreg., 1950-60; grand marshal Lebanon Strawberry Festival, 1988; mem. bd. Coun. of Govts. Sr. Svcs., 1991, 92-97. Maj. Army Med. Corp, 1942-45. Decorated Bronze Star; recipient Disting. Svc. First Citizen award Lebanon, Oreg., 1989; Frank P. Girod Med. Scholarship named in his honor, 1995. Mem. AMA, Oreg. Med. Assn. (trustee), Am. Acad. Family Practice, Kiwanis (pres. 1947-48). Republican. Methodist. Avocation: travel. Home: 625 E Rose St Lebanon OR 97355-4544

GIRONDA, MARIE GRACE, English language educator; b. Jersey City, Jan. 11, 1951; d. John and Mary Elizabeth (Soranno) Misita; m. Michael Mario Gironda; children: Matthew Michael, Megan Marie. BA, Rutgers U., Newark, 1972; postgrad. in English. Cert. tchr. English, 7-12, N.J. Tchr. Newark Pub. Schs., 1972—; debate coach University H.S., Newark, 1989-96, lit. mag. advisor, 1981-89, 97-98; tchr. cable-TV show Newark Cablevision, 1993—. Eucharistic minister Our Lady of Peace Ch., Fords, N.J., 1990—; mem. OLP Columbiettes, JFK H.S. Band Parents. Recipient N.J. State Gov.'s award for Excellence in Tchg., 1994, Commendation for Cable TV Show, Newark City Coun., 1995. Mem. Nat. Coun. Tchrs. English (contest judge), N.J. Coun. Tchrs. English (contest judge), Rutgers U. Alumni Orgn. Roman Catholic. Avocations: writing poetry, reading, music, computer skills, travel. Home: 108 Isabelle St Metuchen NJ 08840-2804 Office: University High Sch 55 Clinton Pl Newark NJ 07108-1295

GIROTTI, ROBERT BERNARD, medical and surgical nurse; b. New London, Conn., Dec. 10, 1962; s. Alfred E. and Patricia (Turello) G. BS, U. Conn., 1985, MS in Nursing, 1995. RN, Conn.; cert. med.-surg. nurse; cert. CPR. Staff nurse respiratory unit Lawrence Meml. Hosp., New London, 1985-90, staff nurse float pool, 1990—; instr. clin. nursing U. Conn., 1997—. Contbr. articles to nursing newsletters. Mem. Cath. Nurses Assn., Conn. Nurses Assn., U. Conn. Sch. Nursing Alumni Assn. (exec. bd. dirs. 1985—), U. Conn. Alumni Assn. (S.E. chpt. bd. dirs. 1994—), Lawrence Meml. Alumnae Assn., Sigma Theta Tau, Phi Kappa Phi. E-mail: robrncm-s@uconect.net. Home: Apt 1510 600 Meridian St Ext Groton CT 06340

GIROUARD, PEGGY JO FULCHER, ballet educator; b. Corpus Christi, Tex., Oct. 25, 1933; d. J.B. and Zora Alice (Jackson) Fulcher; m. Richard Ernest Girouard, Apr. 16, 1954 (div. Mar. 1963); children: Jo Linne, Richard Ernest; m. James C. Boles, May 4, 1996. BS in Elem. Edn., U. Houston, 1970. Ballet Instr. Emmamae Horn Studio, Houston, 1951-81; owner, dir. Allegro Acad. Dance, Houston, 1981—; artistic dir. Allegro Ballet Houston, 1976—; asst. mgr. Sugar Creek Homes Assn., Sugar Land, Tex., 1979-90; coord. 1st Regional Dance Am. Nat. Festival, Houston, 1997. Choreographer (with Glenda W. Brown) Masquerade Suite, 1983, Sebelius Suite, 1983, Shannan, 1984, Papa Shamus, 1986, Silhouettes, 1987, Aspirations, 1989, Here Come the Clowns, 1990. Mem. Cultural Arts Coun. Houston. Mem. Dance Masters Am. (dir. 1977-80), S.W. Regional Ballet Assn. (chmn. craft of choreography 1983-85, coord. to nat. assn. 1983—, Stream award 1986), Regional Dance Am. (bd. dirs. 1986—, sec. 1996—). Democrat. Home: 9945 Warwana Rd Houston TX 77080-7609

GIROUARD, SHIRLEY ANN, nurse, policy analyst; b. New London, Conn., Jan. 16, 1947; d. Maxime Albert Girouard and Irene Barbara (Arnold) Reid. BA in Sociology, Ea. Conn. State Coll., 1972; MA in Sociology, U. Conn., 1974; MSN, Yale U., 1977; PhD in Policy Analysis, Brandeis U., 1988. Nurse Woodstock (Conn.) Pub. Health Assn., 1968-70; staff nurse Clinton (Conn.) Convalescent Ctr., 1970-72; ins. edn. coord. Middlesex Meml. Hosp., Middletown, Conn., 1973-75; clin. nurse specialist Dartmouth Hitchcock Med. Ctr., Hanover, N.H., 1977-83; staff nurse Dartmouth Hitchcock Med. Ctr., Hanover, 1983-84; legis. cons., lobbyist N.H. Nurses Assn., Concord, 1985-87; program officer Robert Wood Johnson Found., Princeton, N.J., 1987-92; exec. dir. N.C. Ctr. Nursing, 1992-93, Am. Nurse's Assn., 1993-94; health policy and nursing cons. pvt. and pub. sector orgns., Washington, 1994-95; v.p. child health and financing Nat. Assn. Children's Hosps. and Related Instns., Alexandria, Va., 1995—; pvt. practice cons., 1983-87; profl. devel. cons., Lebanon, N.H., 1983-87; health policy and nursing cons. Author: (chpt.) Health Policy and Nurse Services, 1989, 98, others; mem. editorial bd. Clin. Nurses Specialist Jour., 1986—, others; contbr. articles to profl. jours. State rep. N.H. Legislature, Concord, 1982-84; counselor City of Lebanon Coun., 1984-87. Fellow Am. Acad. Nursing; mem. ANA (project dir. 1986), Sigma Theta Tau. Democrat. Office: Nat Assn Childrens Hosps & Related Instns 401 Wythe St Alexandria VA 22314-1926

GIROUARD, TINA, artist, curator; b. De Quincy, La., May 26, 1946. BFA, U. La. Established studio Cecilia, La., Port au Prince, Haiti, 1991—. One-woman shows include Univ. Gallery, Lafayette, La., 1968, 73, 74, 112 Greene St. Gallery, N.Y.C., 1971, 72, 73, 75, Vehicule, Montreal, Can., 1975, Alfred (N.Y.) U. Gallery, 1975, Memphis Acad. Tenn., 1975, Holly Solomon Gallery, N.Y.C., 1976, 78, 80, Alexandra Monet Gallery, Brussels, 1979, Forum Stadtpark Mus., Graz, Austria, 1979, Elmhurst Park Gallery, Lafayette, 1981, De Vleeshal, Middelburg, Holland, 1982, Zeeuws Kuntenaarscentrum, 1982, Arthur Roger Gallery, New Orleans, 1983, Museo Tamayo, Mexico City, 1983, Fabric Workshop, N.Y.C., 1984, World's Fair, New Orleans, 1984, PS 1 Long Island City, N.Y., 1985, Arthur Roger Gallery, New Orleans, 1985, Artists' Alliance, Lafayette, 1986, Contemporary Art Ctr., New Orleans, 1987, Quebec Delegation Gallery, Lafayette, 1987, C.A.C., New Orleans, 1989, Mus. Art, Alexandria, La., 1989, Atlantic Ctr. Arts, 1990, Lafayette Regional Airport, 1990, Contemporary Arts Ctr., New Orleans, 1990; exhibited in group shows at 112 Green St. Gallery, N.Y.C., 1972, Leo Castelli Gallery, N.Y.C., 1974, UCLA Gallery, 1976, Cin. Art Mus., 1978, Mus. Modern Art, Oxford, Eng., 1980, Holly Solomon Gallery, N.Y.C., 1982, Arthur Roger Gallery, New Orleans, 1984, Inst. Contemporary Art, 1987, Contemporary Art Ctr., La., 1990, numerous others; commns. include Contemporary Art Ctr., New Orleans, 1989, Lafayette Regional Airport, 1990; videography includes Maintenance I, 1971, Maintenance II, 1972, Maintenance III, 1973, Maintenance IV, 1975, Six of Hearts, 1976, Maintenance V, 1976, WAWA, 1979, 2 C 3 T S, 1981, others. CAPS grantee; Art Matters, Inc. grantee; Nat. Endowment Arts grantee; La. Div. Arts fellow; Nat. Endowment Arts fellow; Creative Artists Pub. Svc. fellow, 1973; Internat. Comm. Agy. fellow, 1979; Lila Wallace Arts Internat. fellow, 1993; Gottlieb Fatn fellow, 1997. Office: Tine Girouard Art Projects PO Box 64 Cecilia LA 70521

GIROUX, ROBERT, editor, book publisher, author; b. N.J., Apr. 8, 1914; S. Arthur J. and Katharine (Lyons) G.; m. Carmen de Arango, Aug. 30, 1952 (div. 1969). A.B. with honors, Columbia U., 1936. Editor in chief Harcourt Brace & Co., 1948-55; chmn. editl. bd. Farrar, Straus & Giroux Inc., 1955—. Author: The Education of an Editor, 1981, The Book Known as Q: A Consideration of Shakespeare's Sonnets, 1982, A Deed of Death, 1990. Served as lt. comdr. USNR, 1942-45. Recipient Alexander Hamilton medal Columbia U., 1987, Nat. Book Critics Circle award, 1987, Campion award Am. mag., 1988, Elmer Bobst award NYU, 1988; Rockefeller Found. fellow, 1995. Mem. Phi Beta Kappa. Club: Century. Office: 19 Union Sq W New York NY 10003-3304

GIROUX, ROBERT-JEAN-YVON, retired Canadian government official; b. Rockland, Ont., Can., Mar. 1, 1939; s. Leo-Romeo and Cecile-Marie (Brunet) G.; m. Therese A. Briand, Aug. 31, 1963; children—Benoit, Andre, Jean-Pierre. BCom in Econs., U. Ottawa, 1961, M in Social Sci., 1970. Pay research officer Can. Civil Service Commn., 1961-65; asst. research dir. Pub. Service Can., 1965-70; dir. Dept. Regional Econ. Expansion, 1970-73; adminstr. Fitness and Amateur Sport, 1973-75; dir. gen. Pub. Service Commn., 1975-78; adminstr. Surface Transport Adminstrn., 1978-82; dep. minister Nat. Revenue Customs and Excise, Ottawa, Ont., Can., 1982-86; dep. minister pub. works Govt. of Can., Ottawa, 1986-90; pres. Pub. Svc. Comn., Ottawa, 1990-94; sec. Treasury Bd., 1994-95; comptr. gen. Canada, 1994-95; pres. Assn. Univs. and Colls. Can., Ottawa, 1995—; lectr. U. Ottawa, 1964-65; bd. govs. Can. Comprehensive Auditing Found., 1994. Bd. dirs. U. Que., Hull, 1993-95, Ottawa Gen. Hosp., 1996-98, Ottawa Hosp., 1998-99, Pub. Policy Forum; mem. Can. Found. for Innovation, 1997; chmn. Inst. on Governance, 1996; mem. Can. Millenium Scholarship Found., 1998; mem. Edn. Mktg. adv. bd., 1998. Mem. Can. Pub. Pers. Mng. Assn., Nat. Film Bd., Inst. Pub. Adminstrn. Can. (bd. dirs. 1990-94, nat. pres. 1992-93). Avocations: golf, cycling. Home: 438 Cannes, Gatineau, PQ Canada J8T 5M5 Office: Assn Univs and Colls Can, 600-350 Albert, Ottawa, ON Canada K1R 1B1

GIROVICH, MARK JACOB, mechanical engineer; b. Kharkov, Ukraine, U.S.S.R., June 23, 1934; came to U.S., 1978; s. Jacob Mark and Talla Abraham (Gindina) G.; m. Galina Michael Voronina, Nov. 14, 1958; 1 child, Irene. MS in Mech. Engring., Poly. Inst. Kharkov, 1957; BS in Physics, State U. Kharkov, 1965; Phd in Mech. Engring., Poly. Inst. Moscow, 1974. Registered profl. engr., Md. Mech. engr. Diesel Mfg. Plant, Kharkov, 1957-59, head. design bur., 1959-61, mgr. dept. automation of mfg. processes, 1961-78; R&D engr. Koppers Co., Balt., 1978-80; chief mech. engr. Koppers Co. div. Enelco, Balt., 1980-81; mgr. enginrg. Enelco Waste Disposal Group, Balt., 1981-86, mgr. spl. incineration systems, 1986-89; mgr. project devel. & thermal processing Bio-Gro Systems, Annapolis, Md., 1989—; lectr. Johns Hopkins U. environ. engring., 1987—. Contbr. articles to profl. jours.; inventor in field. Bd. dirs. Associated Jewish Charity and Welfare Fund, Placement and Guidence Bur., Balt., 1979-86; v.p. Jewish Union of Russian Immigrants, Balt., 1978-85. Mem. ASME. Avocations: skiing, tennis, chess. Home: 13 Suntop Ct Unit 302 Baltimore MD 21209-1383

GIRST, JACK ALAN, computer graphic artist, writer, illustrator; b. Pontiac, Mich., Apr. 27, 1948; s. Lyman and Marian Jane (McCord) G.; m. Kathie Rae Walter, Dec. 27, 1973; children: David, Beth, Jenny. BS, Sterling Coll., 1970. Social worker Kans. Dept. Social Welfare, Hutchinson, 1970-72; pers. mgr. Hartmann Mfg., Hutchinson, 1972-74; mgr. A&W,

Hutchinson, 1975-77; pvt. practice contractor Hutchinson, 1977-96, pvt. practice graphic artist, 1996—; pub. spkr., 1989—; video prodr., 1998—. Writer, illustrator: Deer Rufus You're a Bull, 1989, Renfro Would Rather Rest, 1989, A Mighty Muddy Lesson, 1989, Every Bunny Needs a Bear Friend, 1989. Youth baseball, soccer, basketball coach YMCA, 1982-84; active in various civic activities. Avocations: reading, computer, hiking, canoeing. Home and Office: 2409 N Waldron St Hutchinson KS 67502-1122

GIRTH, MARJORIE LOUISA, lawyer, educator; b. Trenton, N.J., Apr. 21, 1939; d. Harold Brookman and Marjorie Mathilda (Simonson) G. AB, Mt. Holyoke Coll., 1959; LLB, Harvard U., 1962. Bar: N.J. 1963, U.S. Supreme Ct. 1969, N.Y. 1976. Pvt. practice Trenton, 1963-65; rsch. assoc. Brookings Instn., 1965-70; assoc. prof. law SUNY Law Sch., Buffalo, 1971-79, prof., 1979-91, assoc. dean, 1986-87; dean Ga. State U. Coll. Law, Atlanta, 1992-96, prof., 1992—; vis. prof. U. Va. Law Sch., 1979-80; Southeastern Bankruptcy Law Inst. vis. prof. Emory Law Sch., spring 1991, vis. scholar, 1996; vis. legal educator W.Va. U. Coll. of Law Vis. Com., 1994-95; chancellor's search adv. com. Bd. of Regents, 1993-94. Author: Poor People's Lawyers, 1976, Bankruptcy Options for the Consumer Debtor, 1981, (co-author) Bankruptcy: Problem, Process, Reform, 1971. Bd. dirs. Buffalo and Erie County YWCA, 1972-76, Buffalo Unitarian-Universalist Ch., 1981-84, Feminist Women's Health Ctr., 1993-94, ACLU, Ga., 1995—, Unitarian-Universalist Congregation of Atlanta, 1999—; mem. commn. on peace, justice and human rights Internat. Assn. Religious Freedom, 1976-79; chmn. Erie County Task Force on Status of Women, 1985-87. Mem. ABA (mem. coun. bus. law sect. 1985-89, chmn. consumer bankruptcy com. 1983-86), Assn. Am. Law Schs. (nominations com. 1996), Am. Law Inst., N.Y. State Bar Assn. (mem. exec. com. bus. law sect. 1980-91, chmn. bankruptcy law com. 1980-82, chmn. banking corp. bus. law sect. 1986-87, mem. ho. of dels. 1990-91), Ga. Supreme Ct. (commn. on racial and ethnic bias in ct. sys. 1993-95, commn. on equality 1995—, sec. 1998-99), Ga. Assn. Women Lawyers, Law Sch. Admissions Coun. (audit com. 1995-97, finance and legal affairs com., 1997—), Mt. Holyoke Alumnae Assn. (centennial award 1972). Office: Ga State U Coll Law PO Box 4037 Atlanta GA 30302-4037

GIRTON, MARCY, athletic director; b. Brazil, Ind., Oct. 1, 1958; d. Robert K. and Peggy A. G. BS, Taylor U., Upland, Ind., 1981; MA, Ball State U., Muncie, Ind., 1982; MS, Indiana State U., Terre Haute, Ind., 1983; post-grad., Purdue U., West Lafayette, Ind., 1994—. Coach, chair phys. edn. dept. Trinity Coll., Deerfield, Ill., 1983-86; coach women's basketball & tennis Taylor U., Upland, Ind., 1986-89; coach women's basketball U. So. Colo., Pueblo, Colo., 1989-93; with Purdue alumni assn. Purdue U., West Lafayette, Ind., 1994-96; assoc. dir. athletics Western Carolina U., Cullowhee, N.C., 1996—.

GIRVIGIAN, RAYMOND, architect; b. Detroit, Nov. 27, 1926; s. Manoug and Margaret G.; m. Beverly Rae Bennett, Sept. 23, 1967; 1 son, Michael Raymond. AA, UCLA, 1947; BA with honors, U. Calif., Berkeley, 1950; M.A. in Architecture, U. Calif.-Berkeley, 1951. With Hutchason Architects, L.A., 1952-57; owner, prin. Raymond Girvigian, L.A., 1957-68, South Pasadena, Calif., 1968—; co-founder, advisor L.A. Cultural Heritage Bd., 1961—; vice chmn. Hist. Am. Bldgs. Survey, Nat. Park Svc., Washington, 1966-70; co-founder, mem. Calif. Hist. Resources Commn., 1970-78; co-founder, chmn. governing bd. Calif. Hist. Bldgs. Code, 1976-91, chmn. adminstrv. law, 1992—, chmn. emeritus, 1993—; chmn. Calif. State Capitol Commn., 1985-98, chmn. emeritus, 1998—. *Raymond Girvigian's pioneering work in the Post War II Historic Preservation Movement includes many firsts. He initiated or assisted in creating over a score of California's (and the nation's) earliest laws, codes, and regulations for historical landmarks. He served as a pro-bono preservation official at local, state, and federal levels (e.g., California Landmark Commisssion's first historical architect) and led many preservation campaigns in the public interest. His professional resume includes hundreds of landmark examples. He is currently a consulting historical architect. Girvigian's numerous honors and awards recognize his years of innovative contributions to this field.* Co-editor, producer: film Architecture of Southern California for Los Angeles City Schs, 1965; historical monographs of HABS Landmarks, Los Angeles, 1958-80; historical monographs of Califs. State Capitol, 1974, Pan Pacific Auditorium, 1980, L.A. Meml. Coliseum, 1984, Powell Meml. Libr., UCLA, 1989; designed: city halls for Pico Rivera, 1963, LaPuente, 1966, Rosemead, 1968, Lawndale, 1970 (all Calif.); hist. architect for restoration of Calif. State Capitol, 1975-82, Workman/Temple Hist. Complex, City of Industry, Calif., 1974-81, Robinson Gardens Landmarks, Beverly Hills, Calif., 1983-92, Pasadena (Calif.) Ctrl. Libr., 1982-92, 95—, Mt. Pleasant House Mus., Heritage Sq., L.A., 1972-95. With U.S. Army, 1944-46. Recipient Outstanding Achievement in Architecture award City of Pico Rivera, Calif., 1968, Neasham award Calif. Hist. Soc., 1982, Preservationist of Yr. award Calif. Preservation Found., 1987, L.A. Mayor's award for archtl. preservation, 1987, Gold Crown award for advancement of arts Pasadena Arts Coun., 1990, Golden Palm award Hollywood Heritage, 1990; named Hist. Architect Emeritus, Calif. Legislature, 1998, commendation for state and national career achievemtns hist. preservation, Calif. Legislature, 1998; co-recipient honor award for rehab. Los Altos Apts., Calif. Preservation Found., 1999. Fellow AIA, 1972 (Calif. state preservation chmn. 1970-75, state preservation coord. 1970-89, co-recipient nat. honor award for restoration Calif. State Capitol 1983, co-recipient honor award for restoration Pasadena Cen. Libr., Pasadena chpt. 1988); mem. Soc. Archtl. Historians, Nat. Trust for Historic Preservation, Calif. Preservation Found., Calif. Hist. Soc., Xi Alpha Kappa. Democrat. Episcopalian. Office: PO Box 220 South Pasadena CA 91031-0220 *I believe that we must all serve society in whatever way that we are best able; and if a worthy cause I have undertaken appears to have failed, I should ignore that possibility and press on with even greater determination and vigor to succeed. I would hope by that example to encourage others to join the cause and thereby futher the likelihood of a successful effort for the good of all.*

GIRVIN, EB CARL, biology educator; b. Georgetown, Tex., Dec. 27, 1917; s. Fitzhugh Bryson and Meta (Perlitz) G.; m. Virginia Lessor, Aug. 29, 1944; chilren: John Lessor, Eric Reed, Stacey Virginia. BA, U. Tex., 1940, MA, 1941, PhD, 1948. Prof. biology Millsaps Coll., 1948-53; prof. biology, head dept. Southwestern U., Georgetown, 1953-88; Mem. Tex. Bd. Examiners Basic Sci., 1960-79; Mem. div. coll. work Episcopal Diocese Tex., 1962-65. Contbr. articles to profl. jours. Mem. Georgetown City Coun., 1981-87. Lt. comdr. USNR, 1941-45. Mem. Tex. Acad. Sci. (bd. dirs.), AAAS, Sigma Xi. Home: 1703 E 16th St Georgetown TX 78626-7303

GIRVIN, SHIRLEY EPPINETTE, elementary education educator, journalist; b. Apr. 16, 1947, New Orleans; d. Woodie Trevillion and Thelma Elizabeth (Axline) E.; m. Russell Robertson Girvin, Nov. 30, 1996. AA, East L.A. Coll., 1967; BA, Calif. State U., L.A., 1969, postgrad., 1969-70, U. So. Calif., 1982, Chapman Coll., 1983, Loyola Marymount U., L.A., 1986-87. Elem. tchr. Covina-Valley Unified Sch. Dist., 1970-74, San Gabriel (Calif.) Sch. Dist., 1974-75, Alhambra (Calif.) City Sch. Dist., 1976-78; elem. and program mentor tchr., art, social com. and discipline com. chairperson, grade level and faculty rep., lang. devel. specialist. L.A. City Unified Sch. Dist., 1978—; rewrite editor, staff writer San Gabriel Valley Newspaper Publs., 1975-76; contbr. article to profl. publs. Recipient TAP award Alhambra-San Gabriel dist. Soroptimist Club, 1975; Calif. State PTA scholar, 1981, Jounalism Alumni Assn. scholar East L.A. Coll., 1967, Arthur J. Baum Journalism scholar Calif. State U., 1969. Mem. AAUW (mem. com. internat. rels. 1977-78, chmn., ednl. com. 1978-79), NEA, Calif. Tchrs. Assn., L.A. City Tchrs. Math. Assn., United Tchrs. L.A. (chpt. chairperson 1994-95), Women in Comm., Nat. Press Women, Humane Soc. U.S., Soc. for the Prevention of Cruelty to Animals, Handgun Control Inc., Sigma Delta Chi. Avocations: breeding thoroughbred race horses, gardening, country-western dancing. Home: 7318 W 91st St Los Angeles CA 90045-3429

GIRVIN-QUIRK, SUSAN, nursing administrator; b. Owensboro, Ky., Dec. 9, 1950; d. William Fred and Anna (Tillotson) G.; m. Thomas Michael Quirk; 1 child, Thomas Matthew. BSN, U. Ky.; MSN, Ind. U. Owner Legal Advantage-Med.-Legal Consulting, Indpls. Mem. ANA, Am. Assn. Neurosci. Nurses, Am. Mgmt. Assn., Sigma Theta Tau.

GISCHLAR, KAREN LYNN, elementary education educator; b. Trenton, N.J., Sept. 18, 1964; d. William Peter and Carol Patricia G. BS, Trenton State Coll., 1986, MA, 1993. Cert. early childhood/elem. tchr., N.J.; cert. guidance counselor, N.J. Pre-kindergarten tchr. William Penn Ctr., Morrisville, Pa., 1986-87; kindergarten tchr. Sunnybrae Sch., Yardville, N.J., 1987—. Mem. NEA, N.J. Edn. Assn., Hamilton Twp. Edn. Assn. (rep. 1988-91), Kappa Delta Pi, Chi Sigma Iota.

GISH, ANNABETH, actress; b. Albuquerque, Mar. 13, 1971. Student, Duke U., 1993. Appeared in (film) Desert Bloom, Hiding Out, Mystic Pizza, Shaq, Coupe de Ville, Wyatt Earp, 1994, The Red Coat, Nixon, The Last Supper, 1995, Beautiful Girls, 1996, What Love Sees, 1996, Steel, 1997, What He's Got, 1998, S.L.C. Punk!, 1998, Double Jeopardy, 1998; (TV) (series) Courthouse, 1995, (Movies) Hero in the Family, When He's Not a Stranger, The Last To Go, Lady Against the Odds, Silent Cries, 1993, (cable TV movie) Different, 1998, (mini-series) Scarlett, 1994, Don't Look Back, 1996, True Women, 1997, To Live Again, 1998. Office: care Internat Creative Mgmt 8942 Wilshire Blvd Beverly Hills CA 90211-1934*

GISH, EDWARD RUTLEDGE, surgeon; b. St. Louis, Sept. 5, 1908; s. Edward C. and Bessie (Rutledge) G.; A.B., Westminster Coll., 1930; MD, St. Louis U., 1935, MS, 1939; m. Miriam Schlicker, July 8, 1938; children: Ann Rutledge, Mary Priscilla. Intern, St. Louis U. Hosps., 1935-36; resident in surgery St. Mary's Group Hosps., St. Louis, 1936-39; pvt. practice medicine specializing in surgery, Fulton, Mo., 1946—; former sr. instr. surgery St. Louis U. Med. Sch.; staff mem. Callaway Meml. Hosp., Fulton. Author: Plantagenet Portraits in Stone: Unique XII Century, 1989. Bd. dirs. Mo. Symphony Soc., pres., 1981; med. dir. Callaway County CD. Served from maj. to lt. col., AUS, 1943-46; lt. col. ret. Res. Hon. col. Gov.'s Staff Mo. Fellow ACS; mem. Royal Soc. London (affiliate), Internat. Coll. Surgeons, AMA, Mo. Med. Soc., Callaway County Med. Soc. (nat. bd. dirs.), Red Poll Breeders Assn., Am. Law Enforcement Officers Assn., Delta Tau Delta, Alpha Omega Alpha. Contbr. articles to profl. jours. Co-capt. U.S. team World Masters Cross-Country Ski Assn., 1985. Address: 7 W 10th St Fulton MO 65251-1937

GISH, NORMAN RICHARD, oil industry executive; b. Eckville, Alta., Can., Oct. 13, 1935; s. Robert Bruce and Lillian (Foster) G.; m. Joan Ann Thompson, Sept. 5, 1959; children—David Cole, Carolyn Nancy, Graeme Christopher. B.A., U. Alta., 1957; LL.B., U. B.C., 1960. Asst. trade commr. Fgn. Trade Service of Canadian Govt., Ottawa, 1961-62, Hong Kong, 1962-65; asst. to v.p. and sec. B.C. Forest Products, Ltd., Vancouver, 1965-67; sec. B.C. Forest Products, Ltd., 1967-72, gen. counsel, sec., 1972-74, v.p., 1974-76; chmn. B.C. Energy Commn., 1977-80; v.p. Turbo Resources Ltd., 1980-83, chmn., pres., chief executive officer, 1983-85; pres., CEO North Can. Oils Ltd., 1986-93; mng. dir. Emergo China Ltd & Fracmaster China Ltd, Beijing, China, 1994-96; chmn., dir. Alliance Pipeline, Ltd., Calgary, Canada, 1997—; chmn., dir. ICG Propane Inc., Calgary. Address: 8405-400 Eau Claire Ave SW, Calgary, AB Canada T2P 4X2 Office: Alliance Pipeline Ltd, 400 605-5 Ave SW, Calgary, AB Canada T2P 3H5

GISLASON, ERIC ARNI, chemistry educator; b. Oak Park, Ill., Sept. 9, 1940; s. Raymond Spencer and Jane Ann (Clifford) G.; m. Nancy Brown, Sept. 11, 1962 (dec. June 1994); children: Kristina Elizabeth, John Harrison; m. Sharon McKevitt Fetzer, Apr. 25, 1998. BA summa cum laude, Oberlin Coll., 1962; PhD, Harvard U., 1967. Postdoctoral fellow U. Calif-Berkeley, 1967-69; asst. prof. chemistry U. Ill., Chgo., 1969-73; assoc. prof. U. Ill.-Chgo., 1973-77, prof., 1977—; acting head chemistry dept. U. Ill., Chgo., 1993-94, head chemistry dept., 1994—, interim dean Coll. Liberal Arts and Scis., 1997-98; vis. scientist FOM Inst. Atomic and Molecular Physics, Amsterdam, 1977-78; prof. associé U. Paris South, 1985. Contbr. articles to profl. jours. Recipient Silver Circle Teaching award U. Ill., 1982, Excellence in Teaching award U. Ill., 1990. Mem. Am. Chem. Soc. (vis. assocs. program), Am. Phys. Soc., Coun. for Chem. Rsch., Phi Beta Kappa, Sigma Xi. Congregationalist. Achievements include rsch. in theoretical studies of ion-molecule reactions, collision-induced dissociation, nonadiabatic transitions, molecular energy transfer and isotope effects. Home: 7227 Oak Ave River Forest IL 60305-1935 Office: U Ill-Chgo Chemistry M/C 111 Rm 4500 845 W Taylor St Chicago IL 60607-7056

GISO, FRANK, III, lawyer; b. Haverhill, Mass., Feb. 14, 1949; s. Frank and Clementina Paula (Foresta) G; m. Deborah Jean Kracht, May 5, 1979; children: Christopher Anderson, Benjamin Hilding. BA Econs. magna cum laude, Brown U., 1971; JD magna cum laude, Cornell U., 1975. Bar: Mass. 1975, U.S. Dist. Ct. Mass. 1976, U.S. Ct. Appeals (1st cir.) 1976. Law clerk Mass. Superior Ct., Boston, 1975-76; assoc. Peabody & Brown, Boston, 1976-83, ptnr., 1983-88; ptnr., chmn. real estate dept. Choate, Hall & Stewart, Boston, 1988—; bd. dirs. Melrose (Mass.) Coop. Bank. Vice chmn. Melrose Housing Authority, 1986-98, chmn. 1998—. Mem. Mass. Bar Assn., Boston Bar Assn., Phi Beta Kappa, Order of Coif. Avocations: tennis, basketball. Office: Exchange Pl 53 State St Boston MA 02109-2804

GISONDI, JOHN THEODORE, theater and television design; b. Tucson, Ariz., Apr. 7, 1949. BFA, So. Meth. U., 1975. Credits include (TV) Good Morning America, The Arab World with Bill Moyers, ABC Wide World of Sports, National Geographic Explorer, Mariah Carey Spl., Ghost Writer PBS, Buying a Landslide BBC, A Christmas Carol Live from Fords Theatre, ABC, CBS, NBC; prodr. A Texas State of Mind; designer (stage prodns.), N.Y.C.: Sound & Beauty (Drama Desk award), Fathers Day, Three Sisters, Julius Caesar, Dexter Creed, (regional theatres) Guthrie Theatre, Kennedy Ctr., Fords Theatre, (opera) Opera Metropolitana, Caracas, Venezuela, Va. Opera Co. Mem. United Scenic Artists, Dirs. Guild of Am. Home and Office: 21 Cornelia St New York NY 10014-4121*

GISRIEL-BRADFORD, BARBARA ANN, nurse administrator; b. Balt., Sept. 19, 1941; d. Robert G. and Gertrude C. (Hartman) Lessig; m. Daniel Joseph Bradford, Sr., May 14, 1983; children: Keith Clayton, Karen Marie. AA, Essex Community Coll., Balt., 1974; BSN, Coll. Notre Dame, Balt., 1982. Staff nurse med.-surg. ICU Balt. City Hosps.; staff nurse hemodialysis Balt. (Md.) City Hosps., coord. home hemodialysis program; asst. chief Kidney Disease Program Md., Balt., acting chief; acting asst. dir. spl. programs Dept. Health and Mental Hygiene, State of Md., Balt.; chief Kidney Disease Program of Md.; speaker in field. Mem. Am. Nephrology Nurses' Assn. Office: 201 W Preston St Baltimore MD 21201-2323

GISSEL, L. HENRY, JR., lawyer; b. Houston, Oct. 20, 1936. BA, Rice U., 1958; LLB, So. Meth. U., 1961; postgrad., Georgetown U. Bar: Tex. 1961. Sr. ptnr. Fulbright & Jaworski, Houston. Fellow Am. Coll. Trust and Estate Counsel (pres. 1995-96, regent 1981-87, 91-97, regent emeritus 1997—), Am. Bar Found. (bd. cert. estate planning and probate lab, Tex. bd. legal specialization); mem. ABA (sect. real property probate and trust law, chair 1988-89, Internat. Acad. Estate Trust Law (academician 1986-87), coun. 1981-90, 94-97), Am. Bar Assn. (sect. del. 1994-97), Houston Bar Assn. (chmn. probate trust sect. 1982-83). Office: Fulbright & Jaworski 1301 Mckinney St Ste 5100 Houston TX 77010-3031*

GISSLER, SIGVARD GUNNAR, JR., journalism educator, former newspaper editor; b. Chgo., July 2, 1935; s. Sigvard Gunnar Sr. and Louisa (Anderson) G.; m. Mary Catherine Engman, Oct. 23, 1954; children—Gary, Glenn, Gregory. B.A. in Am. Civilization, Lake Forest Coll., 1956; Student, Northwestern U., 1958-61; LLD (hon.), Lake Forest Coll., 1991. News editor Independent Register, Libertyville, Ill., 1958-59; exec. editor News-Sun, Waukegan, Ill., 1963-67; editorial writer Milw. Jour., 1967-77, editorial page editor, 1977-84, assoc. editor, 1984-85, editor, 1985-93; v.p. Jour. Communications, Milw., 1987-93, also bd. dirs.; sr. v.p. Jour./Sentinel Inc., Milw., 1987-93, also bd. dirs.; vis. prof. dept. comms. Stanford U., 1993; assoc. prof. grad. sch. journalism Columbia U., 1994—, acting assoc. dean, 1997, dir. workshops on journalism, race and ethnicity, 1998—. Recipient disting. svc. citation Lake Forest Coll., 1977, Pub. of Yr. award Wis. Newspaper Assn., 1987, 91, 92; journalism fellow Stanford U., 1976, sr. fellow Freedom Forum Media Studies Ctr. Columbia U., 1993-94. Mem. Am. Soc. Newspaper Editors, Internat. Press Inst., Pulitzer Prize Jury, Soc. of Profl. Journalists (Tchr. of Yr. award 1998), Phi Beta Kappa. Home: 101 W 79th St Apt 6D New York NY 10024-6475

GIST, HOWARD BATTLE, JR., lawyer; b. Alexandria, La., Sept. 17, 1919; s. Howard Battle and Marcie (Luckett) G.; m. Rosemary Flynn, Sept. 30, 1950; children: Howard Battle III, Marcie, Stephanie, Robert C., Ellen K., William M. Student, Washington and Lee U., 1936-38; BA, Tulane U., 1941, LLB, JB, 1943. Bar: La. 1943. Mem. firm Gist, Methvin & Hughes (and predecessors), Alexandria, 1946—; bd. dirs. Security First Nat. Bank, Alexandria, chmn. bd., 1983-93, dir. emeritus, 1993. Fellow Am. Coll. Trial Lawyers; mem. La. State Bar Assn. (pres. 1977-78), Alexandria Bar Assn. (pres. 1967), La. City Attys. Assn. (past pres.), La. Def. Attys. (pres. 1972-73), La. State Law Inst. (mem. coun. 1964—, past v.p.). Office: Gist Methvin & Hughes 803 Johnston St Alexandria LA 71301-7672

GIST, MARILYN ELAINE, organizational behavior and human resource management educator; b. Tuskegee, Ala., May 9, 1950; d. Lewis A. and Grace (Perry) G. BA in Edn., Howard U., 1972; MBA, U. Md., 1982, PhD in Bus. Aminstrn. Organizational Behavior, 1985. Tchr. Montgomery County Pub. Schs., Rockville, Md., 1972-76; mgmt. intern NASA Goddard Space Flight Ctr., Greenbelt, Md., 1976-79; procurement mgr. NASA Goddard Space Flight Ctr., Greenbelt, 1980-81, staff asst. to dir. mgmt. ops., 1983-85; dir. contracts OAO Corp., Greenbelt, 1981-83; prof. organizational behavior U. N.C., Chapel Hill, N.C., 1985-87; Boeing Endowed prof. bus. mgmt. U. Wash., Seattle, 1987—; staff cons. U. Md., Coll. Park, 1979-84, CIA, Langley, Va., 1984-85; adj. prof. human resources Cornell U., 1995-96. Contbr. articles to profl. jours. Recipient Outstanding Student award Alumni Assn. Internat. U. Md., 1985, Alan Nash Outstanding Doctoral Student award U. Md., 1985, Chancellor's Disting. lectr. award U. Calif., Irvine, 1993; U. Md. Academic Research grantee, 1982-85. Mem. Acad Mgmt. (Outstanding Paper award 1987), Am. Psychological Assn., So. Mgmt. Assn. Democrat. Roman Catholic. Avocations: stained glass, photography, guitar. Office: U Wash Sch Bus Box 353200 Seattle WA 98195-3200

GIST, RICHARD D., federal judge; b. 1940. BS, U. Wyo., 1963, JD, 1965. Pvt. practice Casper, Wyo., Lander, Wyo., 1970; judge Lander, 1971—; alt. judge Lander Mcpl. Ct., 1974-79; commr. Wyo. Dist. Ct. 9th Jud. Dist., Fremont County, 1982-92. With U.S. Army, 1966-70. Fax: 307-332-2759. Office: Ste A 150 N 3rd St Lander WY 82520

GIST, WILLIAM CLAUDE, JR., dentist; b. Chattanooga, May 14, 1935; s. William Claude and Dorothy Virginia (Gibbs) G.; widower. *Dr. Gist traces his ancestry in the U.S. to Thomas Ballard of Virginia, before 1650, Reverend Johannes Theodorus Polhemius of New York, 1654 and Christopher Gist of Maryland, 1679. He owns and resides in "Springfield", circa 1790, the boyhood home of President Zachary Taylor, Louisville, Kentucky. Even though the National Landmark home, of Georgian colonial architecture, is a private home, it has been opened to thousands of schoolchildren and historical groups for tours. Elizabeth Gist, DAR, Taylor relative, and Dr. Gist's deceased wife is interred in the Taylor family cemetary with Colonel Richard Taylor, an aid-de-camp to George Washington and Zachary Taylor, 12th President of the U.S.* BSc, U. Tenn., Knoxville, 1958; DMD, U. Louisville, 1967. Diplomate Am. Bd. Forensic Dentistry. Practice dentistry Louisville, 1967—. *Dr. Gist has been active and provided leadership to the historical-geneological community at international, national, state and local levels. In 1996, he formally appeared before The First Chamber in The Hague, The Netherlands, accompanied by U.S. Ambassador Dornbush, thanking the Dutch in behalf of the NSSAR for their financial aid during the American Revolution. He made a similar presentation to the Mayor of Maastricht, The Netherlands.* Chmn. celebrations Bicentennial of Pres. Zachary Taylor's Birth, Louisville, 1984; pres. Louisville Civil War Roundtable, 1990-91. Recipient Presdl. commendation Pres. Ronald Reagan, 1985, DAR medal of honor, 1996, DAR history award, 1985. Mem. ADA, Ky. Dental Assn., Louisville Dental Soc., Nat Soc. SAR (pres. gen. 1995-96, Gold Good Citizenship award 1996, Minuteman award 1990), Continental Soc. Sons of Indian Wars (nat. gov. 1990-92), Nat. Order of the Blue and Gray (comdg. gen. 1996-98), Nat. Gavel Soc., Magna Charta Barons (Somerset chpt.), Order Ams. Armorial Ancestry, Jamestowne Soc., Gen. Soc. Colonial Wars, Colonial Order of Acorn, Nat. Soc. Sons and Daughters of Pilgrims, Gen. Soc. Sons Revolution, Hereditary Order Descendants Loyalists-Patriots, Gen. Soc. War 1812, Aztec Club, Military Order Stars-Bars, Filson Club, Ky. Hist. Soc., Kappa Sigma (asst. dist. Grand Master). Republican. Avocations: history, genealogy, historic preservation. Home: Springfield Zachary Taylor House 5608 Apache Rd Louisville KY 40207 Office: 4229 Bardstown Rd Ste 309 Louisville KY 40218-3241

GITELSON, SUSAN AURELIA, business executive, civic leader; b. N.Y.C.; d. Moses Leo and Miriam Evelyn (Silverman) G. BA, Barnard Coll.; MIA, Columbia Sch. Internat. Affairs; PhD, Columbia U. Trainee Rockefeller Found.; asst. prof. internat. rels. Hebrew U., Jerusalem; rsch. assoc. Columbia U., N.Y.C.; dir. internat. affairs and third world World Jewish Congress, N.Y.C.; pres. Internat. Cons., Inc., N.Y.C., S.J. Internat. Corp., N.Y.C., Magic Touch Icewares Internat. Corp., N.Y.C. Author: Multilateral Aid for National Development and Self-Reliance; editor, author: Israel in the Third World; contbr. articles to profl. jours.; mem. editl. com. Jerusalem Papers on Peace Problems. Mem. nat. adv. coun., sponsor Gitelson Essay awards Ctr. for Study of Presidency, N.Y.C.; sponsor Dr. Susan Aurelia Gitelson Fund for Innovative Programs, Columbia Sch. of Internat. Pub. Affairs; pres. Aurelia Found. Inc.; mem. Columbia U. seminars; mem. bd. overseers A Living Meml. to Holocaust--Mus. Jewish Heritage; sponsor Gitelson Lecture on Human Rights and U.S. Fgn. Policy, Columbia U., Gitelson award for human values in internat. affairs Columbia Sch. Internat. and Pub. Affairs, Gitelson-Meyerowitz Human Rights essay award Columbia Ctr. for Study of Human Rights, Gitelson Seminars on UN, City U. Grad. Ctr.; sponsor Gitelson Peace prize Truman Inst.; sponsor Gitelson Peace Papers and Publs., mem. bd. overseers Truman Inst. Hebrew U. Jerusalem; mem. internat. bd. govs. Hebrew U. Jerusalem; v.p. bd. dirs. Am. Friends of Hebrew U.; trustee Sutton Pl. Synagogue; mem. trustees nat. com. Am. Fgn. Policy; sponsor Gitelson-Meyerovitz Disting. Svc. award, Sutton Place Synagogue. Recipient Outstanding Service award Columbia Sch. Internat. and Public Affairs; Alumni medal for conspicuous service Columbia U. Mem. Columbia Sch. Internat. and Pub. Affairs Alumni Assn. (pres. 1980-84), Soc. Internat. Devel. (pres.), Columbia U. Alumni Fedn. (mem. exec. com., chmn. alumni trustee nominating com.), Nat. Com. on Am. Fgn. Policy, Carnegie Coun. on Ethics and Fgn. Affairs, Fgn. Policy Assn., Am. Friends of Hebrew U., Am. Jewish Com. (mem. internat. rels. commn.), UN Assn. N.Y. (mem. adv. coun.). Home: 303 E 83d St New York NY 10028-4318 Office: 1140 Broadway New York NY 10001-7504

GITLOW, ABRAHAM LEO, retired university dean; b. N.Y.C., Oct. 10, 1918; s. Samuel and Esther (Boolhack) G.; m. Beatrice Alpert, Dec. 12, 1940; children: Allan Michael, Howard Seth. BA, U. Pa., 1939; MA, Columbia U., 1940, PhD, 1947. Substitute instr. Bklyn. Coll., 1946-47; instr. NYU, N.Y.C., 1947-50, asst. prof., 1950-54, assoc. prof., 1954-59, prof. econs., 1959-89, prof. emeritus, 1989—; acting dean NYU Coll. Bus. and Pub. Adminstrn., 1965-66, dean, 1966-85, dean emeritus, 1989—; hon. dir. Bank Leumi Trust Co. N.Y.; pres. bd. edn. Ramapo (N.Y.) Cen. Sch. Dist. 2, 1963-66; pres., sec. Samuel and Esther Gitlow Found., N.Y.C. Author: Economics of the Mt. Hagen Tribes, New Guinea, 1947, Economics, 1962, Labor and Manpower Economics, 1971, Being the Boss: The Importance of Leadership and Power, 1992, NYU's Stern School: A Centennial Retrospective, 1995, Reflections on Higher Education: A Dean's View, 1995; co-editor: General Economics: A Book of Readings, 1963; contbr. articles to profl. jours. Served to 1st lt. USAAF, 1943-46, PTO. Recipient Univ. medal Luigi Bocconi U., 1983. Mem. Am. Arbitration Assn. (mem. nat. panel 1948—), Am. Econ. Assn., Royal Econ. Soc., Indsl. Relations Research Assn. Home and Office: 9 Island Ave Apt T3 Miami Beach FL 33139-1349

GITNER, GERALD L., aviation and investment banking executive; b. Boston, Apr. 10, 1945; s. Samuel and Sylvia (Berkovitz) G.; m. Deanne Gebell, June 24, 1968; children: Daniel Mark, Seth Michael. BA cum laude, Boston U., 1966. Staff v.p. TransWorld Airlines, N.Y.C., 1972-74; sr. v.p. mktg. and planning Tex. Internat. Airlines, Houston, 1974-80; pres., founder People Express Airlines, Newark, 1980-82; chmn. Pan Am. World Svcs. Inc., N.Y.C., 1982-85, exec. v.p., chief fin. officer, 1983-85; vice chmn. Pan Am. World Airways, N.Y.C., 1982-85, Pan Am Corp., 1984-85; pres. Tex. Air Corp., Houston, 1985-86; chief exec. officer, pres. ATASCO USA, Inc., aircraft trading firm, N.Y.C., 1986-89; chmn. Avalon Group, Ltd., N.Y.C., 1990-98; co-chmn. Global Aircraft Leasing Ltd., 1991-98, 1990—; dir. Trans World Airlines, Inc., 1993—; chmn., CEO, 1997—; bd. advisors econs. dept.

Boston U.; dir. ICTS Internat. N.V., 1996—; mem. chancellors coun. U. Mo., St. Louis, 1997—. Trustee, mem. exec. com. Boston U., 1984-96; trustee Rochester (N.Y.) Inst. Tech., 1999—; mem. chancellor's coun. U. Mo., St. Louis. Recipient Disting. Alumni award Boston U., 1982, 84. Mem. World Pres.' Orgn., Sky Club, Cornell Club of N.Y., Phi Alpha Theta. Office: 515 N 6th St Saint Louis MO 63101-1842

GITTELMAN, MARC JEFFREY, manufacturing and financial executive; b. N.Y.C., Nov. 26, 1947; s. Sidney and Trudy (Eidus) G.; m. Nanci V. Geiger, Apr. 9, 1988; 1 child, Brandon Michael. BBA, Hofstra U., 1969; MBA in Fin., Adelphi U., 1972; postgrad., U. Colo., Denver. Credit analyst Security Nat. Bank Long Island, Melville, N.Y., 1969-72; dir. adminstrn. Tiger Leasing Group Inc., Chgo., 1973-78; asst. treas. Storage Tech. Corp., Louisville, Colo., 1979-83; v.p., treas. Holnam Inc. (formerly Ideal Basic Industries), Dundee, Mich., 1984-91; treas. Andrew Corp., Orland Park, Ill., 1992—; bd. dirs. Food Bank of Rockies. Mem. Nat. Assn. Corp. Treas. Republican. Jewish. Office: Andrew Corp 10500 153rd St Orland Park IL 60462-3071

GITTELSON, BERNARD, public relations consultant, author, lecturer; b. N.Y.C., June 13, 1918; s. Sam and Gussie (Lefand) G.; m. Rosalind Weinstein, Mar. 1, 1945; children: Louise Barbara, Steven Henry. B.A., St. John's U., 1939. Cons. on race relations N.Y. State War Council, 1939-41, N.Y. Com. on Industry and Labor Relations, 1941-42; dir. N.Y. State Legis. Com. on Discrimination, 1943-45; asso. coordinator Com. on Community Inter-relations, 1945-46; pres. Roy Bernard Co., Inc., 1946-65; chmn. Roy Bernard Co. Ltd., London, 1955-65; pres. Biorhythm Computers, Inc., Med. News. Service, Formulated Health Products, Fairfield Mktg. Corp., Advanced Health Research Products Inc.; chmn. bd. Time Pattern Research Inst., N.Y.C., U.S. Commemoratives Inc., Bernard Gittelson Cons. Inc.; cons. to govts., corps., instns. Author: Gittelson Biorhythm Code Book, Biorhythm, A Personal Science, How to Make Your Own Luck, Intangible Evidence, Special Stories for Children, Our America, Notre America, Nuestra America, Nossa America; syndicated writer column on biorhythm, 1987—; pub. Med. Hot Line. Mem. Am. Journalists and Authors, Authors Guild. Address: Mote Ranch 6808 Corral Cir Sarasota FL 34243-3858

GITTELSON, GEORGE, physician; b. N.Y.C., Sept. 11, 1920; s. Harry and Frances (Spiro) G.; m. Mildred Greenberg, 1942 (div. 1974); children: Howard, Alan, Gary; m. Shari Saslaw, July 24, 1983. BA, Pa. State Coll., 1941; MD, U. Pa., 1951. Diplomate Am. Bd. Allergy and Immunology. Intern Jackson Meml. Hosp., 1951-52; resident Cook County Grad. Sch. Medicine, 1954; pvt. practice Miami, Fla., 1952—; clin. assoc. prof. Sch. Medicine, U. Miami, 1954-79. Capt. USAF, 1942-46, ETO. Fellow Am. Acad. Allergy and Immunology, Am. Coll. Allergy and Immunology. Avocation: travel. Office: 8970 SW 87th Ct Miami FL 33176-2207

GITTER, ALLAN REINHOLD, lawyer; b. Yonkers, N.Y., Aug. 26, 1936; s. George Reinhold and Katherine (Allan) G.; divorced; children: Alison, Ryne, Kent; m. Sandra Case Gitter, Apr. 2, 1988. BA, Washington & Lee U., 1958; LLB, U. Mich., 1961. Bar: N.C. 1963, U.S. Dist. Ct. (mid., ea. and we. dists.) N.C. 1964, U.S. Ct. Appeals (4th cir.) 1964. From assoc. to ptnr. Womble, Carlyle, Sandridge & Rice, Winston-Salem, N.C., 1969—. Fellow Am. Coll. Trial Lawyers; mem. Am. Bd. Trial Advs. Home: 1067 E Kent Rd Winston Salem NC 27104-1113 Office: Womble Carlyle Sandridge & Rice PO Drawer 84 BB&T Fin Ctr Winston Salem NC 27102-0084

GITTER, MAX, lawyer; b. Samarkand, Uzbekistan, Nov. 17, 1943; came to U.S., 1950; s. Wolf and Paula (Nissenbaum) G.; m. Elisabeth Karla Gesmer, June 22, 1969; children: Emily F., Michael A. AB, Harvard U., 1965; LLB, Yale U., 1968. Bar: N.Y., D.C., U.S. Dist. Ct. (so. and ea. dists.) N.Y., U.S. Ct. Appeals (2d, D.C., 4th and 9th cirs.), U.S. Supreme Ct. Instr. U. Chgo. Law Sch., 1968-69; assoc. Paul, Weiss, Rifkind, Wharton & Garrison, N.Y.C., 1969-76, ptnr., 1976—; vis. lectr. law Yale U., 1986-88; mem. Internat. Steering Com. on Free Trade with Israel; vice chmn., Yivo Inst. for Jewish Rsch. Spl. counsel Mayor of N.Y.C. to Investigate Office of Chief Medical Examiner, 1985. Mem. Fed. Bar Coun., Assn. Bar City of N.Y. (vice chmn. com. on profl. and jud. ethics 1985-86), Am. Law Inst. (spkr., panelist 1985-89), Practicing Law Inst. (spkr., panelist 1983-92), N.Y. State Bar Assn. (exec. com. sect. on comml. and fed. litigation 1994—). Office: Paul Weiss Rifkind Wharton & Garrison Rm 900 1285 Avenue Of The Americas Fl 21 New York NY 10019-6065

GITTERMAN, ALEX, social work educator; b. Kolomea, Poland; came to U.S., 1948; s. Paul and Fay (Hirsch) G.; m. Naomi Janet Pines, Sept. 1963; children: Daniel Paul, Sharon Lynn. B.A., Rutgers U., 1960; M.S.W., Hunter Coll., 1962; Ed.D., Columbia U., 1972. Div. dir. Bronx River Settlement, 1962-65; dir. East Side House Millbrook Ctr., Bronx, 1965-66; mem. faculty Columbia U., N.Y.C., 1966—, prof., 1972—; assoc. dean Columbia U., 1981-85; cons. Manhattan VA, N.Y.C., 1974-80, Family Service of Westchester (White Plains), N.Y., 1978-80, Bur. Child Welfare, 1977-80, Drug Abuse Prevention Program, Archdiocese of N.Y., 1985—, Keio Acad. Author: (with C.B. Germain) The Life Model of Social Work Practice, 1980, (with L. Shulman) Mutual Aid Groups and The Life Cycle, 1986, Handbook of Social Work Practice with Vulnerable Populations, 1991, Mutual Aid Groups, Vulnerable Populations and the Life Cycle, 1994, (with C.B. Germain) The Life Model of Social Work Practice: Advances in Theory and Practice, 1996; contbr. articles to profl. jours. Recipient Hexter award Hunter Coll., 1981. Mem. Am. Orthopsychiat. Assn., Am. Pub. Health Assn., Soc. Hosp. Social Work Dirs., Con. on Social Work Edn., Nat. Assn. Social Workers. Democrat. Jewish. Office: Columbia U Sch Social Work 622 W 113th St # U New York NY 10025-7982

GITTES, RUBEN FOSTER, urological surgeon; b. Mallorca, Spain, Aug. 4, 1934; s. Archie and Cicely Mary (Foster) G.; m. K.S. Zipf, June 10, 1955 (div.); m. Rita R. Drum, Feb. 21, 1976 (div.); m. Vera Gomes, Feb. 9, 1996; children: Julia S., Frederick T., George K., Robert F. Grad., Phillips Acad., Andover, Mass., 1952; AB, Harvard U., 1956, MD, 1960. Intern, then resident in surgery and urology Mass. Gen. Hosp., Boston, 1960-67; asst. prof. UCLA Med. Sch., 1968-69; assoc. prof., then prof., chief urology U. Calif. at San Diego Med. Sch., 1969-75; prof. urol. surgery Harvard U. Med. Sch., chmn. Harvard program urology Longwood area, 1975-87; chmn. dept. surgery Scripps Clinic and Rsch. Found., La Jolla, Calif., 1987-98; mem. study sects., task forces NIH, 1973—. Author, editor publs. in field. Served with USPHS, 1963-65. NIH grantee, 1969—. Mem. AAAS, Endocrine Soc., Soc. Univ. Surgeons, Soc. Univ. Urologists, Am. Assn. Genito-Urinary Surgeons, Clin. Soc. Genito-Urinary Surgeons, A.C.S., Am. Surg. Assn., Am. Urol. Assn., Am. Soc. Transplant Surgeons, Soc. Ancient Numismatics, Phi Beta Kappa, Alpha Omega Alpha. Office: Scripps Clinic & Rsch Found 10666 N Torrey Pines Rd La Jolla CA 92037-1092

GITTINGER, D. WAYNE, lawyer; b. Kellogg, Idaho, Jan. 22, 1933; s. Daniel Reese and Evelyn Caroline (Knudson) G.; 1 child, Marni; m. Anne Elizabeth Nordstrom, Dec. 17, 1984; stepchildren: John Hopen, Susan Dunn. BA, U. Wash., 1955, JD, 1957. Bar: Wash. 1957, U.S. Ct. Appeals (9th cir.) 1957, Tax Ct. of U.S., U.S. Supreme Ct. Teaching assoc. Northwestern U. Law Sch., Chgo., 1957-58; ptnr. Lane Powell Spears Lubersky, Seattle, 1959—; bd. dirs. Nordstrom, Inc. Active U. Wash. Alumni Assn., 1965—. Lt. USCGR, 1958-67. Mem. Vintage Club, Seattle Golf Club, Seattle Yacht Club, 101 Club, Overlake Golf and Country Club (past pres. 1978-79). Republican. Avocations: golf, yachting. Office: Lane Powell Spears Lubersky 1420 5th Ave Ste 4100 Seattle WA 98101-2338

GITTINS, ANTHONY J., anthropologist, theology educator; b. Feb. 16, 1943. MA, U. Edinburgh, Scotland, 1972, PhD, 1977. Lectr., head of dept. Missionary Inst., London, 1980-84; assoc. prof. theol. anthropology Chgo., 1984-90, Bishop F. X. Ford prof. missiology, 1998—. Fellow Royal Anthrop. Inst.; mem. Am. Anthrop. Assn., Cath. Theol. Soc. Am., Am. Soc. Missiology, Assn. Local Anthropologists. E-mail: tgittins@ctu.edu. Office: 4740 N Malden St Chicago IL 60640

GITTIS, HOWARD, holding company executive. Vice chmn. MacAndrews Forbes Holdings, Inc., N.Y.C. Office: MacAndrews Forbes Holdings Inc 35 E 62nd St New York NY 10021-8016*

GITTLEMAN, NEAL, orchestra conductor; b. Ancon, Panama Canal Zone, June 29, 1955; s. Edwin and Rosalyn (Leinwand) G.; m. Lisa Fry, Dec. 21, 1984. BA in Music, Yale U., 1975; postgrad., Manhattan Sch. Music, 1977-81; artist's diploma in orch. conducting, Hartt Sch. Music, Hartford, Conn., 1983. Asst. condr. Oreg. Symphony, Portland, 1983-86; music dir. Marion (Ind.) Philharm., 1987-86; assoc. condr. Syracuse (N.Y.) Symphony, 1986-89; assoc. condr. Milw. Symphony Orch., 1989-95, resident condr., 1995-98; music dir. Dayton (Ohio) Philharm. Orch., 1995—; guest condr. San Francisco Symphony, 1989, Rochester Symphony, 1989, Oreg. Symphony, 1990, San Jose Symphony, 1992, Minn. Orch., 1992, 93, Telemann Chamber Orch., Osaka, Japan, 1994, Shinsei Nihon Symphony, Tokyo, 1994, San Antonio Symphony, 1994, Indls. Symphony, 1994, UNAM Philharm., Mexico City, 1995, Grant Park Orch., Chgo., 1995, Buffalo Symphony, 1995, Chgo. Symphony, 1995, 97, Edmonton (Alta., Can.) Symphony, 1996, Augsburg Symphony, 1997. Recipient 2d prize Ernest Ansermet Internat. Conducting Competition, Geneva, 1984, 3d prize Leopold Stokowski Internat. Conducting Competition, N.Y.C., 1985; Karl Böhm fellow Hartt Sch. Music, 1982. Avocations: golf, squash, t'ai chi ch'uan. Office: Dayton Philharm Orch 125 E 1st St Dayton OH 45402-1214*

GITTLEMAN, SOL, university official, humanities educator; b. Hoboken, N.J., June 5, 1934; s. Frank and Edna (Schlanger) G.; m. Robyn Singer, Sept. 9, 1956; children: Julia, Peter Thomas. BA, Drew U., 1955; MA, Columbia U., 1956; PhD, U. Mich., 1961; LHD (hon.), Hebrew Coll., 1993, Stonehill Coll., 1996. Asst. prof., German Mt. Holyoke Coll., South Hadley, Mass., 1962-64; asst. prof. Tufts U., Medford, Mass., 1964-70, prof. German, 1971—, chmn. dept. German and Russian, 1966-81, McCollester prof. religious studies, 1978—, provost, 1981—; acad. v.p. Tufts U., from 1981, now sr. v.p., Alice and Nathan Gantcher prof. Judaic studies, 1992, disting. univ. prof., 1992; dir. summer seminars NEH. Author: Frank Wedekind, 1969, Sholem Aleichem, 1974, From Shtetl to Suburbia, 1978. Recipient Harbison award Danforth Found., 1970; named Alice and Nathan Gantcher Prof. of Judaic Studies, 1992, Disting. Prof., 1992. Mem. MLA, Am. Assn. Tchrs. Yiddish, Am. Assn. Tchrs. German. Office: Tufts U Office of Provost Ballou Hall Braintree MA 02184

GITTLER, JOSEPH BERTRAM, sociology educator; b. N.Y.C., Sept. 21, 1912; s. Morris and Toby (Rose) G.; m. Lami Shapiro, June 28, 1934 (dec. 1966); 1 child, Josephine; m. Susan Wolters, Sept. 15, 1968. BS, U. Ga., 1934, MA, 1936; PhD, U. Chgo., 1941. From instr. to assoc. prof. sociology U. Ga., 1936-43; research assoc. Va. Planning Bd., 1942-43, U. Chgo., 1944; prof. Iowa State U., 1945-54; prof. sociology, chmn. dept. Ctr. Study Group Relations, U. Rochester, 1954-61; dean faculty, prof. social scis. Queensborough Coll., CUNY, 1961-66; prof. sociology, dean Ferkauf Grad. Sch. Humanities and Social Scis., Yeshiva U., N.Y.C., 1966-78; disting. vis. prof. sociology George Mason U. of State U. Va., Fairfax, 1978-79, disting. vis. prof., 1980-90, dir. Ctr. for Study of Race and Ethnic Relations, 1987-90, emeritus prof. sociology, 1990—; vis. prof. Cardoza Law Sch., 1978-79, Hiroshima (Japan) U., 1979-80; lectr. various univs., U.S., Japan, Spain, Germany, Eng., The Netherlands, France, Italy, Mex., Israel, Finland, Taiwan, Ireland, Austria; cons. in field, 1940—; mem. Rochester cmty. coun. N.Y. State Comm. Against Discrimination, 1955-60; chmn. regional selection com. Woodrow Wilson Fellowship Found., 1955-58; co-chmn. Brotherhood Week edn. com. NCCJ, 1950; coun. fellows Upland Inst., 1965-72; disting. vis. prof. dept. sociology Duke U., 1990-94, Disting. Scholar-in-residence, 1994—; Fulbright scholar, vis. prof. Ben Gurion U., Israel, 1990-91. Author: Social Thought Among the Early Greeks, 1941, Virginia's People, 1944, Social Dynamics, 1952, Your Neighbor Near and Far: A Study of Racial and Ethnic Relations in Rural Iowa, 1955, Review of Sociology, 1957, Understanding Minority Groups, 1964, Ethnic Minorities in the U.S.: Perspectives from the Social Sciences, 1977, Jewish Life in the United States, 1977, Jewish Life in the United States, 1981; co-editor: Internat. Jour. Group Tensions, 1986-94; editor, contbg. author: Ann. Rev. Conflict Knowledge and Conflict Resolution, vol. 1, 1989, vol. 2, 1990, vol. 3, 1991, Research in Human Social Conflict Series, Racial and Ethnic Conflict: Perspectives from the Social Disciplines, 1995; editor in chief: Internat. Encyclopedia of Racial and Ethnic Relations, 1996, Ideas of Concord and Discord in Religion, 1998; contbr. numerous articles to profl. jours. Fulbright scholar, Hiroshima (Japan) U. scholar, 1979-80, Ben Gurion U. scholar, Israel, 1990-91; recipient Walter B. Hill prize philosophy U. Ga., 1934, poetry award, best tchr. award, Disting. Faculty award George Mason U., 1984. Fellow Am. Sociol. Assn., N.Y. Acad. Scis.; mem. PEN, Internat. Sociol. Soc., Inst. Internat. Sociology, So. Sociol. Soc., Assn. for Higher Edn., Am. Assn. Acad. Deans, Phi Beta Kappa, Phi Kappa Phi, Pi Mu Epsilon. Home: 5 Glenmore Dr Durham NC 27707-3923 Office: Duke U PO Box 90088 Durham NC 27708-0088

GITTLER, WENDY, artist, art historian, writer; b. Manhattan, N.Y.; d. Lewis Frederic and Esther (Becker) G. Studied with George Grosz, Art Students League, N.Y., 1958-59; studied with Camillio Egas, N.Y.C., 1960; BS in Art History, Columbia U., 1963; MA in Art History, Hunter Coll., 1967; postgrad., NYU, 1968; MFA, Bklyn. Coll., 1973; postgrad., U. Paris, 1977-78. Lectr. art NYU, N.Y.C., 1966-68; lectr. art history Fairleigh Dickinson U., Teaneck, N.J., 1966-68; lectr., art history Hunter Coll., N.Y.C., 1968-80; lectr. art history Sch. Visual Arts, N.Y.C., 1979-86; lectr. Met. Mus., N.Y.C., 1988-89; lectr. art history Parsons Sch. of Design, N.Y.C., 1989-96; lectr. N.Y. Studio Sch., N.Y.C., 1991—; instr. studio U. Haifa, Israel, 1971; curator First Street Gallery, N.Y.C., 1992; lectr. Brown U., R.I., 1993, South Fla. Art Ctr., 1990, Lowe Art Mus., U. Miami, Fla., 1984; moderator artists panels, bd. dirs. Artists Equity, N.Y.C., 1995-99. One-woman shows include 1st Street Gallery, N.Y.C., 1976, 82, 88, 95, 99, Artists Equity, 1999; exhibited in group shows at Blue Mountain Gallery, N.Y.C., 1995-98, N.Y. Studio Sch., 1996, Savahhan Coll. Art and Design, 1997, Fordham U., 1996, Ashawag Hall, East Hampton, N.Y., 1995, LeHigh U., Bethlehem, Pa., 1984, Gallery of Fine Arts, N.Y.C., 1976, N.Y. City C.C., 1975; contbg. author art jours., exhibit catalogues. Mem. Coll. Art Assn., Fedn. Modern Painters and Sculptors, Channel 13, Artist Equity (bd. dirs.). Avocations: archaeology, philosophy, travel. Home: 780 West End Ave New York NY 10025-5573

GITTMAN, ELIZABETH, educator; b. N.Y.C., Mar. 15, 1945; d. Kallman and Rebecca (Santcroos) G.; m. Aug. 5, 1965 (div. 1977); children: Stephen Loeb, Leslie Gulkis, Sherry Loeb; m. Victor Arnel, Mar. 5, 1981. BS, NYU, 1966; MS, CUNY Queens Coll., 1969; PhD, Hofstra U., 1979, Cert. Advanced Study, 1987. Cert. ednl. adminstr., N.Y. Tchr. N.Y.C. Bd. Edn., Kew Gardens, 1966-68; instr. New Sch. for Social Rsch., N.Y.C., 1980-81; ind. cons., 1981-84; coord. instl. rsch. and evaluation Bd. Coop. Ednl. Svcs. of Nassau County, Westbury, N.Y., 1984-94; assoc. prof. N.Y. Inst. Tech., Old Westbury, 1994-97; cons., 1997-98; dir. instrnl. support svcs. Commack (N.Y.) Pub. Schs., 1998—; adj. prof. L.I. U., Brookville, N.Y., 1987-93. Mem. high risk youth rev. com. Ctr. Substance Abuse Prevention, U.S. Dept. HHS, 1990-95; developer numerous ednl. programs. Recipient NYU Founders Day award, 1966; Hofstra U. Doctoral fellow, 1976. Mem. APA, Am. Ednl. Rsch. Assn., Am. Evaluation Assn., Nat. Coun. Measurement in Edn., Northeastern Ednl. Rsch. Assn. (editor 1993-95, treas. 1996-98, membership com. 1989-90, nominating com. 1991, program co-chair 1993, program com. 1989-92, bd. dirs. 1993-98), ASCD, Kappa Delta Pi, Phi Delta Kappa (rsch. rep. 1990-91, sec. 1991-93, conf. co-chair 1992, v.p. 1993-94, pres. 1995-96, exec. bd. 1990—, nominating com. 1996—, Svc. award 1998). Republican. Jewish. Avocations: computer applications, reading, writing. Office: Commack Pub Schs PO Box 150 Commack NY 11725

GIUDICI, MICHAEL CHARLES, cardiac electrophysiologist; b. Sandwich, Ill., Feb. 13, 1953; s. Richard Carl and Joan Marie (Marciewicz) G.; m. Paula Marie Annechino, July 30, 1977; children: Michael Richard, Gregory Edward. BA in Math. and Chemistry, Carleton Coll., 1975; BS in Medicine, U. S.D., 1978; MD, U. Iowa, 1980. Diplomate Bd. Internal Medicine; bd. cert. in cardiology, cardiac electrophysiology. Intern in medicine U. Iowa Hosps., Iowa City, 1980-81; primary care physician USAF, Va., N.J., 1981-84; resident in medicine Thomas Jefferson U., Phila., 1984-86, fellow in cardiology, 1986-88; fellow in electrophysiology U. Mo. Hosp., Columbia, Mo., 1988-89; dir. electrophysiology Genesis Med. Ctr., Davenport, Iowa, 1989—; cons. in pacing Medtronics, Inc., Mpls., 1991—; mem. spkrs. bur. Medtronics, CPI/Guidant, Pfizer, Knoll, In Control, 1991—. Contbr. articles to profl. jours. V.p. Rejuvenate Davenport, 1992—; dir. Greenway Habitat Project, Davenport, 1992—; co-chair Assumption High, Putman Mus., Friendly House, Cmty. Health Care, Quad City Bot. Ctr.; exec. dir. Davenport City Partnership, 1998—. Capt. USAF, 1981-84. Recipient Nat. Arbor Day Found. award, 1996, Nat. Assn. Conservation Dirs. award, 1994, Iowa Dept. Natural Resources award, 1995, Quad Citian of Yr., Quad City Time, 1996; named Iowa Cmty. Forestry Vol. of Yr., 1999. Fellow ACP, Am. Coll. Cardiology; mem. N.Am. Soc. Pacing and Electrophysiology, Izaak Walton League, Cornbelt Running Club, Quad-City Bicycle Club (sec.-treas. 1966-67). Roman Catholic. Avocations: running, bicycling, conservation work. Office: Cardiovascular Medicine PC 1230 E Rusholme St Ste 305 Davenport IA 52803-2400

GIUFFRA, LAWRENCE JOHN, hospital administrator, medical educator; b. N.Y.C., Oct. 13, 1923; s. Lawrence A. and Eugenia (Rossi) G.; m. Yolanda Girulli, Apr. 12, 1947 (dec.); children: Lawrence, Marie, Barbara. Student, Fordham U., 1940-43; MD, L.I. Coll. Medicine, 1946. Diplomate Am. Bd. Internal Medicine. Pathology fellow Mt. Sinai Hosp., 1950-51; chief med. svcs. U.S. Army Hosp., Ft. Monmouth, 1951-53; pvt. practice, 1953—; clin. instr. medicine L.I. Coll. Medicine and Dentistry, 1962—; chmn. dept. medicine St. Francis Hosp., Jersey City, 1988—. Contbr. articles to med. jours. Capt. U.S. Army, 1951-53. Fellow Am. Coll. Gastroenterology. Home: 175 Highfield Ln Nutley NJ 07110-2415 Office: 2787 Kennedy Blvd Jersey City NJ 07306-5531

GIUFFRE, ANTHONY T., television producer, lighting director; b. N.Y.C., June 8, 1934; s. Frank and Mary (Labisi) G.; children: Frank, Thomas, Susan Chenoweth. Student, NYU. Studio prodn. specialist Westinghouse Broadcasting, Balt., 1958-70; sr. studio supr. Md. Pub. TV, Owings Mills, 1970-95, lighting design and prodn. supr., 1995—; photography instr., condr. lighting seminars throughout Md. area and N.Y.c. Recipient Emmy for lighting direction, 1996. Home: 2605 Carrollton Rd Finksburg MD 21048-1026

GIUFFRÉ, JOHN JOSEPH, lawyer; b. Bklyn., Nov. 30, 1963; s. John B. and Marilyn N. G.; m. Lauren P. Dippel, Sept. 1, 1990; children: John, Paul. BA, Columbia Coll., 1984; JD cum laude, U. Pa., 1987. Bar: N.J. 1987, N.Y. 1988, Conn. 1988, Pa. 1988, U.S. Dist. Ct. (so. and ea. dists.) N.Y. 1989. Assoc. labor and employment law sect. Morgan, Lewis & Bockius, N.Y.C., 1987-88; assoc. McLaughlin & McLaughlin, Bklyn., 1988-93; founding ptnr. Giuffré & Kaplan, PC, Hicksville, N.Y., 1994—. Editor: U. Pa. Jour. Comparative Bus. and Capital Market Law, 1985-86; sr. editor: U. Pa. Jour. Internat. Bus. Law, 1986-87. Vol. lawyer Bklyn. Bar Assn. Vol. Lawyer Project, 1992-93; trustee 1st Presbyn. Ch., Flushing, N.Y., 1991-92, pres. bd. trustees, 1993, elder, 1996—; bd. dirs. Flushing Christian Sch., 1994—. Mem. Nassau County Bar Assn., Phi Beta Kappa. Avocations: reading, studying history, ice hockey. Office: Giuffré & Kaplan PC 28 E Old Country Rd Hicksville NY 11801-4207

GIUFFRIDA, THOMAS S., telecommunications executive; b. Meridian, Conn., Sept. 23, 1949; s. Giulio and Helen (Aresco) G.; m. Janet Jo Murawski, July 29, 1972; children: Francis Joseph, Elena Marie. BA, Wesleyan U., 1971; PhD, MIT, 1978. Mem. tech. staff AT&T, Holmdel, N.J., 1977-82, dist. mgr., 1982-96, tech. leader, 1996-98; CEO JRT Ltd., Manasquan, N.J., 1998—. Contbr. articles to profl. jours. Bell Labs. fellow, 1988, AT&T fellow, 1996. Mem. IEEE (sr.), Sigma Xi, Sigma Pi Siga. Avocation: trumpet. Office: JRT Ltd PO Box 294 Manasquan NJ 08736-0294

GIUFFRIDA, TOM A., publisher; b. Glendale, Calif., Feb. 24, 1946; s. Alfred and Anna (LiPera) G.; m. Judith Lynn Price, Aug. 22, 1970; children: Jeffrey, Gregory, Christopher. BA in Journalism, Calif. State U., Northridge, 1967. Copy editor Santa Barbara (Calif.) News-Press, 1967, 69-70; copywriter to asst. dir., promotion and pub. relations L.A. Times (Times Mirror), 1971-79; from promotion dir. to v.p. and gen. mgr. Atlanta Jour. & Constitution (Cox Enterprises), 1979-85; publisher Palm Beach (Fla.) Post, 1985—. Bd. dirs. Palm Beach County Cmty. Found. Lt. (j.g.) USN, 1967-69. Mem. Am. Newspaper Pubs. Assn., Fla. Press Assn. (pres. 1995-96), Soc. Profl. Journalists, Palm Beach Yacht Club, Govs. Club. *

GIULIANI, RUDOLPH W., mayor, former lawyer; b. N.Y.C., May 28, 1944; m. Donna Hanover; children: Andrew, Caroline. A.B., Manhattan Coll.; J.D. magna cum laude, NYU, 1968. Law clk. U.S. Dist. Ct. Judge, N.Y.C., 1968-70; asst. U.S. atty. So. Dist. N.Y., 1970-73; exec. asst. U.S. atty., chief narcotics sect., and chief spl. prosecutions sect. Dept. Justice, 1973-75, assoc. dep. atty. gen., 1975-77; assoc. atty. gen., 1981-83; U.S. atty. U.S. Dist. Ct. (so. dist.), N.Y., 1983-89; mem. firm Patterson, Belknap, Webb and Tyler, N.Y.C., 1977-81, White & Case, N.Y.C., 1989-90, Anderson Kill Olick & Oshinsky PC, N.Y.C., 1990-93; mayor N.Y.C., 1994—. Rep. candidate for mayor N.Y.C., 1989, 93. Office: City Hall New York NY 10007

GIULIANO, MICHAEL PHILIP, arts journalist, educator; b. Somerville, N.J., Aug. 25, 1957; s. Michael N. and Marle M. (Meszaros) G. BA, Johns Hopkins U., 1978, MA, 1979. Journalist Balt. News Am., 1979-86, WJHU-FM, 1986-88; freelance journalist Balt., 1988—. Contbr. articles to Artnews, Art Papers, New Art Examiner, Balt. Sun, Chgo. Reader, Cin. Enquirer, Am. Theatre, Folio, Hadassah Mag., Variety, Sogetsu. Democrat. Roman Catholic. Home: 2317 N Calvert St Baltimore MD 21218-5202

GIULIANTI, MARA SELENA, mayor, civic worker; b. N.Y.C., June 3, 1944; d. Leon and Bertha (Jablonky) Berman; m. Donald Giulianti, May 29, 1966; children: Stacey Alexander, Michael Alan. BA, Tulane U., 1966. Social worker L.A. County Social Svcs., 1966-68; adminstrv. asst. neurosurg. cons. D. Giulianti, MD, Hollywood, Fla., 1980-83; campaign mgr. City Commr. Suzanne Gunzburger, Hollywood, 1982; mayor City of Hollywood, 1986-90, 92—; vice chmn. Broward Employment and Tng. Adminstrn., 1987-89, 92-94, 96—, chmn., 1989-90, 94-96; mem. exec. bd. Fla. League Cities, Tallahassee, 1986-90, 92-94, bd. dirs., 1990-91, 94—; mem. econ. devel. pol. com. Nat. League Cities, Washington, 1987-90, human devel. policy com., 1992-94, fin., adminstrn. and intergovtl. rels. steering com., 1994—; mem. Broward County Met. Planning Orgn., 1986-90. Contbr. articles to local newspapers. Pres. Women in Distress, Broward County, 1982-83, bd. dirs., 1983-90, trustee, 1994-97; v.p. CHARLEE Family Care Homes, Broward County, 1986-88, bd. dirs., 1988-92; mem. Broward County Commn. on Status Women, 1984-86, Fla. Commn. on Drug and Alcohol Concerns, Tallahassee, 1984-85, Broward County Dem. Exec. Com., 1984-88; pres. Hills Dem. Club, 1991-94; bd. trustees Graves Mus. of Archeol. and Nat. History, Dania, Fla., 1993-97; bd. dirs. Hollywood Econ. Growth Corp., 1994-95, 98-99; chmn. Hollywood Comty. Redevel. Agy., 1992—; v.p. South Broward unit Am. Cancer Soc., 1992-93, bd. dirs., 1993-99. Recipient Hannah G. Solomon award, 1983, Giraffe Stick Your Neck Out award Women's Advocacy - the Majority/Minority, 1986, Leadership award Leadership Hollywood Alumnni, 1987, City of Peace award Israel Bonds, Broward County, 1987, Broward County Woman of Yr., Am. Jewish Congress, 1988, Menorah award Histadrut, 1990; named Woman of Yr. Women in Comms., Inc., 1990; inducted Broward County Women's Hall of Fame, 1996, Juliette Gordon Low award Girl Scouts Broward County, 1997. Mem. Nat. Coun. Jewish Women (nat. bd. dirs. 1985-89), Jewish Fedn. So. Broward (chair community rels. com. 1981-82, bd. dirs. 1982-90), Broward County Med. Aux. (br. pres. 1977-78), Nat. Jewish Community Rels. Adv. Coun. (exec. bd. 1985-87), Rotary. Democrat. Avocations: snorkeling, skiing, travel. Office: PO Box 229045 Hollywood FL 33022-9045

GIUNTA, JOSEPH, conductor, music director; b. Atlantic City, May 8, 1951; m. Cynthia Reid, June 5, 1982. MusB in Theory, Northwestern U., 1973, MusM in Conducting, 1974; DFA (hon.), Simpson Coll., 1986. Condr., music dir. Waterloo/Cedar Falls Symphony and Chamber Orch. of Iowa, 1974-89; music dir. Des Moines Symphony Orch., 1989—; guest condr. numerous symphonies, orchs. including Chgo. Symphony, London Philharm., Philharmonia Orch. of London, Minn. Orch., Indpls. Orch., Phoenix Symphony, Fla. Symphony, Akron (Ohio) Symphony, Syracuse (N.Y.) Symphony, R.I. Philharm. Recipient Helen M. Thompson award; named Outstanding Young Condr. in U.S., 1984. Mem. Phi Mu Alpha, Pi Kappa Lambda. Office: Des Moines Symphony 221 Walnut St Des Moines IA 50309-2101*

GIUST, STEVE, television station executive. Gen. mgr. KWEX-TV, San Antonio. Office: KWEX-TV 411 E Durango Blvd San Antonio TX 78204-1398*

GIUSTI, JOSEPH PAUL, retired; b. Harrisburg, Pa., Mar. 4, 1935; s. Joseph and Ellen C. (Carletti) G.; m. Marie D. Mazza, Jan. 30, 1960; children: Jeannine Carolyn, Lynn Christine, Susan Marie. BA in English Lit., Villanova U., 1957; MBA, Pa. State U., 1959, PhD in Higher Edn. Adminstrn., 1962; DLitt (hon.), St. Vincent Coll., 1976. Instr. dept. commerce and fin. Pa. State U., 1958-60, grad. asst., 1961-62, asst. to v.p., 1963-65, mem. grad. faculty, 1963-79, asso. prof. higher edn., 1965-79; campus dir., chief exec. officer Beaver campus, 1965-79; chancellor univ., prof. higher edn. Ind. U.-Purdue U., Fort Wayne, 1979-85; prof. edn. Ind. U., 1985-87; dir. global human resource devel. edn. programs/scholarships AMP, Inc., 1987-98, cons., 1998—; cons. hemolytic disease study group divsn. blood diseases and resources Nat. Heart, Lung and Blood Inst., NIH, 1975-79; mem. adv. com. Edn. Mgmt. Info. Sys., Commonwealth of Pa., 1971-79; mem. joint adv. coun. Ft. Wayne Med. Edn. Program, 1979-85; mem. exec. com. Ft. Wayne Future, Inc., 1979-85, Ft. Wayne Ednl. Found., 1979-85, Allen County (Ind.) United Way, 1979-80; sec. Beaver Campus Adv. Bd., 1966-79, dir. emeritus, 1979—; mem. Corp. Coun., Ft. Wayne, 1981-85, also bd. dirs. Contbr. articles on fin. mgmt. and ednl. adminstrn. to profl. publs.; contbr. chpts. to books on fin. mgmt. and edn. Bd. dirs. Med. Ctr. Beaver County, Pa., 1966-79, chmn. bd. dirs., 1972-75, dir. emeritus, 1979—; bd. dirs. Parkview Meml. Hosp., 1982-85. Recipient Beaver Campus Disting. Service award, 1974; Trustee award Community Coll. of Beaver County, 1972; Civic Improvement League award, 1972; Benjamin Rush award Med. Soc. of Beaver County, 1976; resolutions in his honor for contbrs. to edn. and health care delivery in state Pa. State Senate and Ho. Reps., 1979; Beaver Campus Community Cultural Ctr.'s 1000 seat amphitheater named in his honor, 1980; lit. collection named in his honor Beaver Campus Library, 1980. Mem. Greater Fort Wayne C. of C. (dir. 1981-85), Ind. U. Ft. Wayne Alumni Assn. (life dir. 1982—), Purdue U. Ft. Wayne Alumni Assn. (life dir. 1982—). Roman Catholic.

GIUSTI, KARIN F., artist, educator. MFA in Sculpture, Yale U. Head sculpture dept. Bklyn. Coll., CUNY, 1995—. Selected exhbns., installations and projects exhibited at U. Mass. Fine Arts Ctr., Hartford, 1993, Sculpture Ctr., N.Y.C., 1993, Roosevelt Island, N.Y.C., 1993, Real Art Ways, Hartford, 1994, La Quinta (Calif.) Open Air Mus., 1994, Bklyn. Coll. CUNY, Bklyn., 1995, Thread Waxing Space, N.Y.C., 1995, Socrates Sculpture Park, Queens, N.Y., 1995, Bklyn. Bridge, 1995, Conn. Commn. on the Arts, 1995, The Lytman Allyn Art Mus., 1995, Statewide Mus. Collaborative, 1995, Conn. Resource Recovery Authority, Hartford, Conn., 1996, Woodson Art Mus., Wis., 1998, Anya von Gosslen Gallery, N.Y.C., 1998, Trans Hudson Gallery, N.Y.C., 1998, St. Mary's Cathedral, Limerick, Ireland, 1998, others; commns. include PECO Energy Co., Phila., Excell Techs., Enfield, Conn., Bank of Boston, Western, Mass., others, pvt. collections. Recipient award for innovation pub. art project Divsn. Capitol Planning and Ops., 1% of the Arts Program, Boston, 1988; named artist in industry resident John Michael Kohler Arts Ctr., 1992, internat. artist's resident Lila Wallace-Reader's Digest, Giverny, France, 1995; grantee Conn. Commn. on the Arts, 1991, NEA, 1991, New. Eng. Found. for the Arts, 1991; Guggenheim fellow, 1997-98. Studio: Ste 1105 82 Wall St New York NY 10012 Office: Bklyn Coll Sculpture Dept 2900 Bedford Ave Brooklyn NY 11210-2289*

GIUSTI, ROBERT GEORGE, artist, educator; b. Nov. 30, 1937; came to U.S., 1939; s. George and Margot (Joachimstahl) G. B.F.A., Cranbrook Acad. Art, 1961. Assoc. art dir. Cunningham & Walsh Agy., N.Y.C., 1961-62; art dir. Random House Inc., N.Y.C., 1962-73; artist N.Y.C., 1973—; tchr., instr. Sch. Visual Arts, N.Y.C., 1976-84; lectr. in field. Recipient Silver medal Soc. Illustrators, 1983, Gold medal Art Dir. Club, N.Y., 1976, Silver award Art Dirs. Club, Inc., 1976, Andy award Advt. Club N.Y., 1976, 79, Silver award Australian Writers and Art Dirs., 1981. Episcopalian. *

GIUSTINO, MARYANNE, public relations executive; b. Chgo., Oct. 3, 1961. BA, Columbia Coll., 1983. Pub. affairs officer Ill. Housing Devel. Authority, Chgo., 1984-87; sr. acct. exec. Edelman Worldwide, Chgo., 1987-89; sr. acct. supr., mgr. media rels. Weiser Walek Group, Chgo., 1990-92; dir. pub. rels. Am. Dietetic Assn., Chgo., 1992-99; v.p. consumer products Edelman Pub Rels. Worldwide, Chgo., 1999—; freelance writer Chgo. Tribune, 1997—. Advance detail specialist Daley for Mayor campaign, Chgo., 1989; Nat. press sec. Draft Cuomo for Pres. campaign, Chgo., 1992. John Fischetti scholar, 1986. Mem. Soc. Profl. Journalists. Roman Catholic. E-mail: maryanneugiustino@edelman.com. Office: Edelman 200 E Randolph 63d Chicago IL 60601

GIVAN, BOYD EUGENE, aircraft company executive. With Boeing Co, Seattle, 1986—, sr. v.p., CFO, 1991—. Office: Boeing Co PO Box 3707 Seattle WA 98124-2207

GIVAN, RICHARD MARTIN, state supreme court justice, retired; b. Indpls., June 7, 1921; s. Clinton Hodell and Glee (Bowen) G.; m. Pauline Marie Haggart, Feb. 28, 1945; children: Madalyn Givan Hesson, Sandra Givan Chenoweth, Patricia Givan Smith, Elizabeth Givan Whipple. LL.B., Ind. U., 1951. Bar: Ind. 1952. Partner firm Bowen, Myers, Northam & Givan, 1960-69; justice Ind. Supreme Ct., 1969-74, chief justice, 1974-87, assoc. justice, 1987-95; ret.; dep. pub. defender Ind., 1952-53; dep. atty. gen., 1953-54; dep. pros. atty. Marion County, 1965-66; ret., 1995; mem. Ind. Ho. Reps., 1967-68. Served to 2d lt. USAAF, 1942-45. Mem. Ind. Bar Assn., Indpls. Bar Assn., Ind. Soc. Chgo., Newcomen Soc. N.Am., Internat. Arabian Horse Assn. (past dir., chmn. ethical practices rev. bd.), Ind. Arabian Horse Club (pres. 1971-72), Lions, Sigma Delta Kappa. Mem. Soc. of Friends. Home: 6690 S County Road 1025 E Indianapolis IN 46231-2495

GIVANT, PHILIP JOACHIM, mathematics educator, real estate investment executive; b. Mannheim, Germany, Dec. 5, 1935; s. Paul and Irmy (Dinse) G.; m. Kathleen Joan Porter, Sept. 3, 1960; children: Philip Paul, Julie Kathleen, Laura Grace. BA in Math., San Francisco State U., 1957, MA in Math., 1960. Prof. math. San Francisco State U., 1958-60, Am. River Coll., Sacramento, 1960—; pres. Grove Enterprises, Sacramento, 1961—; pres. Am. River Coll. Acad. Senate, Sacramento, 1966-69; v.p. Acad. Senate for Calif. Community Colls., 1974-77; mem. State Chancellor's Acad. Calendar Com., Sacramento, 1977-79. Founder, producer Annual Sacramento Blues Music Festival, 1976—; producer Sta. KVMR weekly Blues music program, 1978—, music festivals Folsom Prison, 1979-81, Vacaville Prison, 1985. Pres. Sacramento Blues Festival, Inc., 1985—; mem. Lake Tahoe Keys Homeowners Assn., 1983—, Sea Ranch Homeowners Assn., 1977—. Recipient Spl. Service Commendation, Acad. Senate Calif. Community Colls., 1977, Spl. Human Rights award Human Rights-Fair Housing Commn., Sacramento, 1985, W.C. Handy award for Blues Promoter of Yr. Nat. Blues Found., Memphis, 1987, 1st Critical Achievement award Sacramento Area Mus. Awards Commn., 1992. Mem. Faculty Assn. Calif. Community Colls., Am. Soc. Psychical Research, Nat. Blues Found. (adv. com., W.C. Handy Blues Promoter of Yr. 1987). Avocations: tennis, racquetball, reading, music, boating. Home and Office: 3809 Garfield Ave Carmichael CA 95608-6631

GIVELBER, HARRY MICHAEL, pathologist; b. Cleve., Apr. 3, 1938; s. Myer and Hyla (Kanter) G.; m. Judith Gottlieb, June, 1960 (div. Jan. 1973); children: Rachel Joy, Joshua Mark, David Saul; m. Susan Margaret Hess, Feb. 3, 1973; children: Leah, Aron. AB, Harvard U., 1960, MD, 1964. Diplomate Am. Bd. Pathology. Clin. pathologist, hematologist NIH Clin. Ctr., Bethesda, Md., 1970-73; pathologist Geneva (N.Y.) Gen. Hosp., 1973—. Bd. dirs. Temple Beth El, Geneva, 1977-87, Geneva Free Libr., 1984-93. Fellow Coll. Am. Pathologists, Am. Soc. Clin. Pathology. Avocations: book collector. Office: Geneva Gen Hosp 196 North St Geneva NY 14456-1694

GIVEN, ELLEN MARIE, flutist; b. Darby, Pa., Nov. 1, 1946; d. Harvey Erb and M. Eunice (Cole) Rettew; m. Richard William Given, Dec. 1, 1968; children: Marnie, Jennine. BMus, Phila. Mus. Acad., 1968. Flute and piccolo Atlantic Symphony Orch., Halifax, N.S., Can., 1968-69, Can. Broadcasting Corp. Orch., Halifax, 1968-69, East Carolina U. Summer Theatre, Greenville, N.C., 1970, U.S. Nat. Broadway Tour Pirates of Penzance, 1982-83; instr. of flute Wellesley (Mass.) Schs., 1969-76; pvt. studio Sudbury, Mass., 1972—; instr. flute All Newton Music Sch., 1988—, Brandeis U., 1994-96; flutist, founder, mgr. Trio Desjardins, Sudbury, 1978—; coach, founder Lincoln-Sudbury Regional H.S. Flute Ensemble, 1991—; music dir. Taming of the Shrew, Lincoln-Sudbury Boston Players, 1994; choreographer Anything Goes, 1995. Author: Thoughts of a Whale, 1998; composer (chamber music) A Diabolical Child, Kanashii, 1970, Lament for Brass Trio and Soprano, 1978, Trio for Flute, Violin and Cello, 1986; musical commissions: score to Admirable Crichton, 1988, Ceremonial for Brass for 350th Anniversary of Sudbury, Mass., 1989; flutist, piccolo for John Oliver Chorale, MIT Chamber Orch., Wellesley Choral Soc., Westerly (R.I.) Pops and Chorale, (solo) Old South Ch. Chair, editor, Sudbury Town Report, 1988, 89; mem. corr. sec. Cultural Coun., Sudbury, 1994—. Mem. WGBH, Musicians Union, The Acad. of Am. Poets. Avocations: Sudbury women's soccer, landscape gardening, nature conservancy. Home: 60 Greenhill Rd Sudbury MA 01776-2433 Office: Trio Desjardins 60 Greenhill Rd Sudbury MA 01776-2433

GIVEN, KENNA SIDNEY, surgeon, educator; b. Charleston, W.Va., Nov. 22, 1938; s. Virgil and Chessie Given; m. Charlene K. Given; children: Kari, Patrick, Amy. BA, W.Va. U., 1960; MD, Duke U., 1964. Diplomate Am. Bd. Surgery, Am. Bd. Plastic Surgery (chairperson-elect 1996-97, bd. dirs. 1992—). Intern Ind. U. Med. Ctr., Indpls., 1964-65; resident, then chief resident gen. surgery Grady Meml. Hosp./Emory U. Hosp., Atlanta, 1965-69; asst. resident, then chief resident plastic surgery Duke U. Med. Ctr., Durham, N.C., 1975-77; clin. instr. surgery Emory U., Atlanta, 1972-74; chief surgery Lanier Meml. Hosp., Langdale, Ala., 1974; prof., chief divsn. plastic surgery Med. Coll. Ga., Augusta, 1977—, med. dir. oper. rm., 1989-90; assoc. dir. burn unit Med. Coll. Ga. Hosp.; cons. Augusta Correctional and Med. Instrn.; plastic surgery dir. Children's Med. Svc., 1981—; mem. Residency Rev. Commn. for Plastic Surgery, 1991—, chmn., 1994-96; chair Am. Bd. Plastic Surgery, Inc., 1997-99; chmn. residency rev. com. Accreditation Coun. for Grad. Med. Edn., 1994-96; lectr. in field. Contbr. articles to profl. jours. Pres. Med. Rsch. Found. Ga., 1985-88; trustee Plastic Surgery Edn. Found., 1994-97, pres.-elect, 1997; bd. dirs. Augusta Country Day Sch.; bd. dirs. Augusta Prep. Day Sch., 1988, trustee, 1989-90. Fellow ACS; mem. AMA, Am. Assn. Plastic Surgeons (trustee 1994-97), Assn. Acad. Chmn. in Plastic Surgery (pres. 1996-97, bd. dirs. 1985-88, 93—), Southeastern Plastic and Reconstructive Surgery (chmn. continuing med. edn. com. 1987, bd. dirs. 1992-95), Am. Soc. Plastic and Reconstructive Surgery (bd. dirs. 1988), Am. Assn. Hand Surgery, Am. Cleft Palate Assn., Am. Soc. Aesthetic Plastic Surgeons, Internat. Soc. Clin. Plastic Surgeons, Ga. Plastic Surgery Soc. (pres. 1985), Med. Assn. Ga., Richmond County Med. Soc., Southeastern Surg. Congress., So. Med. Assn., Southeastern Soc. Plastic and Reconstructive Surgeons (pres. 1997), So. Surg. Soc. Baptist. Home: 748 Tripps Ct Augusta GA 30909-1816 Office: Med Coll Ga Divsn Plastic Surgery HB-5049 Augusta GA 30912*

GIVEN, KERRY WADE, plastics industry executive; b. Ravenna, Ohio, Nov. 14, 1948; s. Earl Buren and Phyllis Virginia (Hamrick) G.; m. Charlotte Sue Brannon, Dec. 20, 1969; children: Duke Earl, Sean Bryan. BS, U. Fla., 1973; PhD, U. Minn., 1978. Rsch. chemist B.F. Goodrich, Brecksville, Ohio, 1978-80; from rsch. planning analyst to dir. rsch. planning Amoco Corp., Naperville, Ill., 1980-88; from mgr. sys. devel. to strategic planning Amoco Corp., Chgo., 1988-94; mgr. IT Amoco Chem., Lisle, Ill., 1994-99; dir. IT Cadillac Plastics, Troy, Mich., 1999—. Contbr. articles to profl. jours. Home: 2820 Parkwood Ln Aurora IL 60504-1348 Office: Cadillac Plastics 2855 Coolidge Hwy Troy MI 48084

GIVENS, GEORGE FRANKLIN, lawyer; b. Roanoke, Va., Sept. 18, 1946; s. Irvin Carlile and Alice Daniel (McCallum) G.; m. Mary Ann Barnack, Sept. 14, 1973; children: Gregory Franklin, Meredith McCallum, Andrew Ryan. BA in History, Va. Commonwealth U., 1970; MA in Ednl. Adminstrn., East Carolina U., 1979; JD, N.C. Ctrl. U., 1983. Bar: N.C. 1983, Va. 1984. Tchr., asst. prin., coach Gaston (N.C.) Jr./Sr. H.S. Northampton County Schs., 1970-79; prin. Murfreesboro (N.C.) Mid. Sch. Hertford County Schs., 1979-80; staff atty., sr. staff atty., prin. legis. analyst Gen. Assembly N.C., Raleigh, 1985—; counsel environ. rev. com. Gen. Assembly N.C., 1986—; counsel House Environ. Com., Senate Agr./Environ./Natural Resources Com., 1987—. Episcopalian. Avocation: flying. Home: PO Box 85 Raleigh NC 27602-0085 Office: Gen Assembly NC 545 Legis Office Bldg 300 N Salisbury St Raleigh NC 27603-5925

GIVENS, JANET EATON, writer; b. N.Y.C., July 5, 1932; d. Irving Daniel and Matilda (Schmelzle) E.; m. Richard Ayres Givens, Aug. 24, 1957; children—Susan Ruth, Jane Lucile. B.A., Queens Coll., 1953; M.A., Columbia U., 1955. Lic. tchr., N.Y. Tchr. pub. elem. schs., Silver Spring, Md., 1953-55, Mamaroneck, N.Y., 1955-59; supr. prospective tchrs., part-time lectr. Queens Coll., N.Y.C., 1959-68. Author: The Migrating Birds, 1964; Something Wonderful Happened, 1982; Just Two Wings, 1984; contbg. author: Tensions Our Children Live With, 1959. V.p. PTA, Pub. Sch. 219, Queens, N.Y., 1972-73, del. to United Parents Assn., 1971-72, editor PS 219 News, 1971-73. Home: 14711 68th Rd Flushing NY 11367-1332

GIVENS, JOHN KENNETH, manufacturing executive; b. Highland Park, Mich., Aug. 21, 1940; s. John Hamilton and Marion Florence G.; children: Kevin John, Kirk David; m. Patricia Ann Bowlby, May 23, 1980. BA, Mich. State U., 1963. With Lincoln-Mercury divsn. Ford Motor Co., Cleve., 1963-71; sales promotion mgr. Lincoln-Mercury divsn. Ford Motor Co., Dearborn, 1971-73; dir. sales and mktg. Ford South Africa, 1973-75; car advt. mgr. Ford Div., 1975-77; sr. v.p. Wells. Rich, Greene Advt., Los Angeles, 1977-79; v.p. mktg. Chrysler Corp., Highland Park, Mich., 1979-82; pres. Seal-Dry USA, Inc., Little Rock, 1982-92; chmn. Eastar, Inc. holding co. of Seal-Dry/USA, Inc., 1982-98, Sandusky Ltd., 1992—, Splash, LLC, 1997—, Deckrite, LLC, 1997—. Office: Splash LLC 3912 E Progress St North Little Rock AR 72114-5239 also: Sandusky Ltd 3130 W Monroe St Sandusky OH 44870-1811

GIVENS, PAUL EDWARD, industrial engineer, educator; b. Pwhuska, Okla., Aug. 12, 1934; s. George Edward Givens and Myrtle Elizabeth (Whipkey) Stewart; m. Ann Elizabeth Piper, Oct. 26, 1957; children: Scott Andrew, Mark Edward. BS in Indsl. Engring., Univ. Ark., 1957; MBA, Creighton Univ., 1968; PhD in Engring., Univ. Tex., Arlington, 1974. Sr. field engr. Svc. Pipeline Co., Tulsa, 1957-63; mgr. indls. relations Northern Natural Gas Co., Omaha, 1963-69; personnel mgr. The Western Co. of N.A., Ft. Worth, 1969-72; grad. teaching assoc. Univ. Tex., Arlington, 1972-74, instr., 1974; mgmt. cons. Cooperative Extension Svc. Miss. State Univ., Starkville, 1977-80, assoc. prof., 1974-80; v.p. ops. Stapccotn Cooperative, Greenwood, Miss., 1980-83; assoc. prof. Univ. Mo., Rolla, 1983-87; prof., chmn. indsl. and mgmt. systems engring. dept. Univ. S. Fla., Tampa, 1987—; mgmt. cons. several companies, Tex., 1972-74, Miss., 1976-80, Mo., 1983-87. Author: (with others) Team Effort Advances Missouri, 1985; contbr. papers to profl. jours. TV host PBS series, Miss., 1979; bd. dirs. Mo. Incutech Found., Rolla, 1984-85; tribal mem. Osage Indian nation, Pawhuska, Okla., 1934—; pres. ch. coun. St. Joseph's Cath. Ch., Starkville, 1978; mem. sub-com. Fla. High Tech. Coun., Tampa, 1988—; mem. Boy Scouts Am., Ft. Worth, dist. chmn. 1970-72. Recipient 1st Edward A. Smith Rsch. award, Tulsa, 1985. Fellow Inst. Indsl. Engrs. (dir. mgmt. divsn. 1978-79); mem. KC, Soc. Engring. and Mgmt. Sys. (pres. 1991-92, sr. v.p. profl. devel. 1994-96), Am. Soc. Engring. Mgmt. (charter, bd. dirs. 1981-82), Am. Soc. Engring. Edn. (Bernie Sarchet award contbn. engring. mgmt. 1996), Acad. Mgmt., Packaging Inst., Ark. Acad. Indsl. Engrs. Republican. Avocations: golf, fishing. Home: 11501 Moffatt Pl Tampa FL 33617-2415

GIVENS, PAUL RONALD, former university chancellor; b. Wellsburg, W.Va., Nov. 16, 1923; s. George D. and Anna (Peters) G.; m. Leona Janssen, Dec. 20, 1945; children—Gregg, Stann, Rodney, Deborah. Student, Graceland Coll., 1941-43; B.A., George Peabody Coll., 1948, M.A., 1949; postgrad., U. Iowa, 1949-50; Ph.D., Vanderbilt U., 1953. Instr. Lawrence Coll., Appleton, Wis., 1949-51; counselor Vanderbilt U., Nashville, 1951-53; chmn. psychology dept. Birmingham (Ala.) So. Coll., 1953-60, U. So. Fla., Tampa, 1960-67; dean arts and scis. Ithaca (N.Y.) Coll., 1967-72; v.p. acad. affairs Millikin U., Decatur, Ill., 1972-79; chancellor Pembroke (N.C.) State U., 1979-89. Author: (with others) Human Behavior, 1966. Served with USN, 1943-46. Home: 704 Druid Hills Rd Tampa FL 33617-3810

GIVENS, RANDAL JACK, communications educator; b. Borger, Tex., Mar. 17, 1951; s. Fred Frank and Doris Mae (Bley) G.; m. Carol Marie Griffin, May 21, 1973; children: Mary Leanna, Anna Elizabeth. BA in Speech, Lubbock (Tex.) Christian Coll., 1973; MA in Speech Comm., Tex. Tech. U., 1974; MAR in Counseling Psychology, Harding U., Memphis, 1977, MAR in Missiology, MTh in Philosophy, 1978; diploma in French, IFCAD, Brussels, 1982. Diploma in French, I.F.C.A.D., Brussels, 1982. Missionary (in French) Eglise du Christ, Brussels, 1979-82; dir. Internat. Sch. Conversational English, Brussels, 1982-89; acad. dean Internat. Christian U., Vienna, Austria, 1989-94; chmn. dept. comm., dir. forensics York (Nebr.) Coll., 1994-97, dir. grants and program devel., 1997—; counselor Memphis Mental Health Ctr., 1976-78; group therapy coord. Memphis Rehab. Svc., 1976-78; chief coord. of translating 2 internat. confs., Strasbourg, France, 1983, Metz, France, 1987; lectr. in field; ind. grants cons., 1998—. Author: Induced Feedback, 1974; translator (book): Johnson's Notes, 1989; editor Vienna Views newsletter, 1989-94. Recipient Svc. award Lubbock Christian Schs., 1992; Tex. Tech. U. grantee, 1974, 91. Mem. Nat. Soc. Fundraising Execs., Speech Comm. Assn. Am., Nebr. Speech Comm. Assn. (liaison for univ. affairs 1994), Speech Comm. Assn., Martial Arts Black Belt Assn., L'Association de l'Ordinateur, Am. Assn. Grant Profls. (founding pres. 1998). Republican. Ch. of Christ. Avocations: martial arts, drummer, woodworking, computers. Home: 1315 Blackburn Ave York NE 68467-2011 Office: York College 1125 E 8th St York NE 68467-2699

GIVENS, RICHARD AYRES, lawyer; b. N.Y.C., June 16, 1932; s. Meredith Bruner and Ruth Wheelock (Ayres) G.; m. Janet Eaton, Aug. 24, 1957; children: Susan Ruth, Jane Lucile. AB, Columbia U., 1953; MS in Econs., U. Wis., 1954; LLB, Columbia U., 1959. Bar: N.Y. 1959, U.S. Dist. Ctr. (so. and ea. dists.) N.Y. 1960, U.S. Ct. Appeals (2d cir.) 1962, U.S. Supreme Ct. 1966, U.S. Ct. Claims 1980, U.S. Ct. Appeals (4th cir.) 1981. Assoc. Hughes, Hubbard & Reed, N.Y.C., 1959-61; asst. U.S. atty. So. Dist. N.Y., 1961-71; regional dir. FTC, N.Y.C., 1971-77; counsel Botein, Hays & Sklar, N.Y.C., 1977-89; law clk. to Hon. Vincent L. Broderick U.S. Dist. Ct. (so. dist.) N.Y., White Plains, 1992-95; law sec. to Hon. Jay Gold acting Supreme Ct. Justice N.Y., 1995-96; chmn. program on drafting documents in plain lang., 1981. Author: Manual of Federal Practice, 5th edit., 1998, Advocacy: The Art of Pleading a Cause, 1980, 3d rev. edit., 1992, Legal Strategies for Industrial Innovation (Best Law Book of 1982 award Assn. Am. Pubs.), 1982; Antitrust: An Economic Approach, 1983; contbr. articles to profl. jours. With U.S. Army, 1954-56. Mem. ABA, N.Y. State Bar Assn. (chmn. task force on simplification 1985-89, legis. com., antitrust sect. 1980-83), Assn. of Bar of City of N.Y. Democrat. Unitarian.

GIVHAN, EDGAR GILMORE, physician; b. Montevallo, Ala., Aug. 6, 1935; 7. AB in German Lit., Washington and Lee U., 1956; MD, Washington U., St. Louis, 1960. Diplomate Am. Bd. Internal Medicine. Intern Vanderbilt U., 1960, resident in internal medicine, 1965, instr. in hematology, 1965-66; instr. in hematology Auburn U. Sch. Lab. Tech., 1967-85; co-owner Commercial Garden Design, Montgomery, Ala., 1982—; pres. med. staff Montgomery Bapt. Hosp., 1974-75; cons. physician Ala. Medicaid Program, 1982-86; bd. dirs., cons. Humana Hosp. East Montgomery; med. dir. Humana Ins. Co. Ala.; chmn. bd. Direct Care, 1995—; horticulture lectr. Author: (guide and video) How to Grow Great Southern Gardens, 1992, Flowers for South Alabama Gardens, 1980, Conversations with a Southern Gardener, 1999, (with others) Heritage Gardens, 1992 ; contbr. articles to profl. jours. Chmn. bd. South Montgomery YMCA, 1973; bd. dirs. ARC, Montgomery, 1970-73, med. dir. blood processing ctr., Montgomery, 1973-80; bd. dirs. Montgomery Symphony Orch., Blue Cross and Blue Shield Ala., 1979-85, Montgomery C. of C., 1980-84; bd. vis. for the humanities Auburn U. Capt. USAF, 1962-64. Vanderbilt U. fellow, 1965-66. Fellow ACP; mem. AMA, Ala. Soc. Internal Medicine, Montgomery Soc. Internal Medicine (pres. 1970), Montgomery County Med. Soc. (pres. 1976), Ala. Soc. Clin. Oncology (v.p. 1982), Am. Soc. Hematology, So. Garden History Soc. (pres., bd. dirs.), Phi Beta Kappa. Office: 6912 Winton Blount Blvd Montgomery AL 36117-3555

GIVHAN, ROBERT MARCUS, lawyer; b. Mineral Wells, Tex., May 10, 1959; s. Walter Houston Givhan and Marion Blackwell Callen Stothart; m. Janet Lee Dothard, May 6, 1989; children: Vivian Lee, Charlotte Ann, Virginia Mae. BA, U. Ala., Tuscaloosa, 1981; JD, Cumberland Sch. Law, Birmingham, Ala., 1986. Bar: Ala. 1987, D.C. 1989, U.S. Supreme Ct. 1989, U.S. Ct. Appeals (D.C. and 11th cirs.), U.S. Dist. Ct. (so., mid. and no. dists.) Ala. 1987. Assoc. Perry and Russell, Montgomery, Ala., 1987-88; dep. dist. atty. 15th Jud. Cir. of Ala., Montgomery, 1988-91; dep. atty. gen. Office of Atty. Gen. of Ala., Montgomery, 1991-95; ptnr. Johnston Barton Proctor & Powell LLP, Birmingham, 1995—. Fellow Am. Coll. Pros. Attys.; mem. ABA (vice chmn. antitrust competition and trade regulation com. of adminstrv. law sect. 1994—), Ala. State Bar Assn., Birmingham Bar Assn. (co-chmn. econs. of law practice com. 1998, 99), Am. Health Lawyers Assn. Episcopalian. Avocations: whitewater rafting, hiking, music collecting, book collecting. Home: 427 Cliff Pl Birmingham AL 35209-5201 Office: 2900 AmSouth/Harbert Plz 1901 6th Ave N Birmingham AL 35203-2618

GIZA, DAVID ALAN, lawyer; b. Chgo., May 16, 1958; s. Bruno Frank and Marianne Theresa (Mozdren) G.; m. Karen Ann Van Maldegiam, Nov. 5, 1988. BS, DePaul U., 1981; JD, John Marshall U., 1984. Bar: Ill. 1985, U.S. Dist. Ct. (no. dist.) Ill. 1985. Atty. pvt. practice, Chgo., 1985-86; assoc. Larry Karchmar, Ltd., Chgo., 1986-87, Kovitz, Shifrin & Waitzman, Chgo., 1987; atty. W.W. Grainger, Inc., Skokie, Ill., 1987-91; atty. W.W. Grainger, Inc., Lincolnshire, Ill., 1991—, divsn. atty., 1993-96, sr. atty., 1996-98, asst. gen. counsel, 1998—. Trustee Village of Libertyville, Ill., 1995—; chmn. Camp Lake (Wis.)/Ctr. Lake Rehab. Dist., 1990—. Mem. Am. Trial Lawyers Assn., Am. Corp. Counsel Assn., Ill. State Bar Assn., Chgo. Bar Assn., Lake County Bar Assn. Republican. Roman Catholic. Avocations: politics, water sports, reading, travel, cooking. Fax: 847-913-7584. E-mail: giza.d@grainger.com.. Office: W W Grainger Inc 333 Knightsbridge Pkwy Lincolnshire IL 60069-3639

GJERDSET, KRISTIN ANNE, art educator, artist; b. Milw., Feb. 16, 1968; d. Gerald Harvey and Judith Anne (Knoll) G. BFA, U. Wis., Stevens Point, 1991; MFA, U. Wis., Milw., 1995. Assoc. lectr. art Univ. Wis., Milw., 1995-96; asst. adj. prof. art Wis. Luth. Coll., Milw., 1995—; older adults art instr. Greenfield (Wis.) Recreation Dept., 1995-98; children's art instr. Zool. Soc. Milw. County, 1996—; art instr. Milw. Inst. Art & Design, 1996-98; juror Wis. Regional Scholastic Art Awards, Milw., 1996; exhibitor Biennial Faculty Art Exhbn. Milw. Inst. Art & Design, 1996. Exhibited in group shows at Sea Cliff (N.Y.) Gallery, 1996, Artcentric Valenti Gallery, Milw., 1998, Columbia (Mo.) Coll., 1998, Christians in the Visual Arts Ignite traveling exhbn., 1999—. Recipient Top award First Annual Animal Art Competition, 1995. Lutheran. Avocations: animals, running. Home: 3118 S 56th St Milwaukee WI 53219-4437

GJERTSEN, O. GERARD, lawyer; b. Bklyn., June 24, 1932; s. Ole Gerhard and Hilma (Jorgensen) G.; m. Carol Ann Jurkops, June 2, 1962; children: Gerard, Gary, Krista, Karen. BA, Columbia Coll., 1954; JD, NYU, 1958. Bar: N.Y. 1958, U.S. Dist. Ct. (so. dist.) N.Y. 1960. Ptnr. Thacher Proffitt & Wood, N.Y.C., 1964—. Vice chmn. Tuckahoe (N.Y.) Urban Renewal Agy. With U.S. Army, 1954-55. Mem. ABA, N.Y. State Bar Assn., Assn. of Bar of City of N.Y., Westchester County Bar Assn., White Plains Bar Assn., Scarsdale Golf Club. Avocations: music, sports. Home: 262 Dante Ave Tuckahoe NY 10707-3015 Office: Thacher Proffitt & Wood 11 Martine Ave Fl 8 White Plains NY 10606-1934

GJOSTEIN, NORMAN ARTHUR, materials engineer, consultant, educator; b. Chgo., May 26, 1931; m. 1959; 2 children. BS, Ill. Inst. Tech., 1953, MS, 1954; PhD in Metallurgical Engring., Carnegie-Mellon U., 1958. Rsch. engr. Thmopson-Ramo-Wooldridge, Inc., 1958-60; sr. rsch. scientist Ford Motor Co., 1960-61, prin. rsch. scientist assoc., 1961-64, staff scientist, 1964-69, prin. rsch. scientist, 1969-73, mgr. metallurgy dept., 1973-76, mgr. European rsch. liaison, 1976-78, mgr. rsch. planning, 1978-79, dir. long-range and sys. rsch., 1979-81, dir. Sys. Rsch. Lab., 1981-86, dir. power train and materials, 1986-88, dir. Material Rsch. Lab., 1986-96; cons. materials engring. U. Mich., 1996—, adj. prof. materials engring., 1996—. Fellow ASM Internat. (trustee 1991-93, Shoemaker award 1990, C.S. Barrett Silver medal 1996); mem. NAE, IEEE, The Minerals, Metals and Materials Soc., Engring.

Soc. Detroit (bd. dirs. 1991-93), Sigma Xi. E-mail: ngjostei@msn.com. Address: 544 Claremont St Dearborn MI 48124-1518

GJOVIG, BRUCE QUENTIN, manufacturing consultant, entreprenuer; b. Crosby, N.D., Mar. 24, 1951; s. Ronald Daniel and Agnes (Smedberg) G.; children: Mike Mohn, Todd Chaffee. BA, BS, U. N.D., 1974. Rsch. chemist Man-in-the-Sea Project, Grand Forks, N.D., 1975-76; campaign advisor Elkin for Gov. Com., Bismarck, N.D., 1976; exec. officer Grand Forks Bd. Realtors, 1977-81; devel. officer U. N.D. Found., 1981-84; founder, dir. Ctr. for Innovation, Grand Forks, 1984—; bd. dirs. 1st Seed Capital Co., Grand Forks, SBIR Project West, Phoenix; founder, chmn. N.D. Entrepreneur Hall of Fame, 1985—; founder Rural Tech. Incubator, 1994—, N.D. Angel Capital Network, 1998—. Editor: The Business Plan: Step-by-Step, 1988, The Marketing Plan: Step-by-Step, 1990; author, editor: Boxcar of Peaches: Nash Finch Co., 1990, Pardon Me, Your Manners are Showing!, 1992; contbr. articles to profl. jours. Founder, sponsor 67th Patent & Trademark Depository Libr., 1991—; chair N.D. Mus. Art, U. N.d. Nordic Initiative. Named Friend of Sml. Bus., Fargo C. of C., 1988; named U. N.D. Outstanding Greek Alumnus, 1990, Outstanding Svc. award, U. N.D. Alumni Assn., 1984, Western U.S. SBIR Support Person, 1997, Tibbetts award SBA, 1998, Kauffamn Leadership award 1998, others. Mem. Assn. Univ. Tech. Mgrs., Assn. Univ. Related Rsch. Pks., Univ. Small Bus. Tech. Consortium (state dir. 1986-90), Alumni Inter-Fraternity Coun. (chmn. 1982-86, 90-95, Outstanding Alumnus 1990), Rotary, Delta Tau Delta. Republican. Episcopalian. Avocations: reading, politics, art collector, fund raising, entrepreneur history collector. E-mail: bruce@innovators.net. Home: Condo # 31 2501 26th Ave S Grand Forks ND 58201-6454 Office: Ctr for Innovation PO Box 8372 Rural Tech Ctr Grand Forks ND 58202-8372

GLABE, ELMER FREDERICK, food scientist; b. Chgo., Apr. 3, 1911; s. Fred John and Holdina (Jennrich) G.; m. Marjorie Browne; children: John E., Lynne Glabe Mueller, David H. BS in Chemistry, Ill. Inst. Tech., 1942. Analytical chemist W.E. Long Co., Chgo., 1929-38; research chemist, tech. dir. Stein Hall and Co., Chgo., 1938-45; founder, pres. Food Tech., Inc, Chgo., 1946—, Food Tech. Lab. and Food Tech. Products, Northbrook, Ill. Author numerous tech. papers in food sci.; patentee (110) in field. Recipient Hon. Membership and Outstanding Svc. award Am. Coun. Independent Labs., Victor Marx award Am. Soc. Bakery Engrs., 1991. Mem. Am. Chem. Soc. (50 yr. award), Am. Assn. Cereal Chemists (50 yr. award), Inst. Food Technologists (50 yr. award). Lutheran. Office: 3000 Dundee Rd Ste 204 Northbrook IL 60062-2432

GLACEL, ROBERT ALLAN, military career officer; b. Frankfurt, Germany, Oct. 31, 1947; (parents Am. citizens); m. Barbara Pate; children: Jennifer, Sarah, Ashley. Grad., U.S. Mil. Acad., 1969; M in Civil and Mech. Engrng., MIT, 1977; MBA, Boston U., 1977; grad., Command and Gen. Staff Coll., 1982, Indsl. Coll. Armed Forces, 1990. Commd. 2d lt. U.S. Army, 1969, advanced through grades to brig. gen., 1995; FO, fire dir. officer 3d bn., 319th field arty. U.S. Army, Vietnam, 1970-71; comdr. B battery, 1st Bn., 10th Field Arty., 3rd Inf. Divsn. U.S. Army, Germany, 1971-72; S-2 (Intelligence) Divsn. Arty. U.S. Army, 1972-74; asst. prof. engrng. U.S. Mil. Acad. U.S. Army, W. Point, N.Y., 1977-81; ops. officer, exec. officer 1st Bn., 37th Field Arty. U.S. Army, Ft. Richardson, Alaska, 1982-85; with office Dep. Chief of Staff Pers. Hdqrs., Pentagon U.S. Army, Washington, 1985-87; comdr. 1st Bn., 4th Field Arty., 2d Inf. Divsn. U.S. Army, Republic of Korea, 1987-89; polit. mil. planner J-5 (Plans), the Joint Staff, Pentagon U.S. Army, Washington, 1990-92; divsn. arty. comdr. 7th Inf. Divsn. (Light) U.S. Army, Ft. Ord, Calif., 1992-93; exec. officer to the Under Sec. of the Army, Pentagon U.S. Army, Washington, 1993-95; chief requirements and programs br. Office of Asst. Chief of Staff for Policy in SHAPE, Belgium, 1995-97; comdr. U.S. Army Test and Experimentation Command, Ft. Hood, Tex., 1997—. Decorated Legion of Merit, Bronz Star, Def. Meritorious Svc. medal, Meritorious Svc. medal. Office: US Army Test and Expt Command Fort Hood TX 76544

GLACKIN, WILLIAM CHARLES, arts critic, editor; b. Sacramento, July 10, 1917; s. William Martin and Anita Ivy (Derr) G.; m. Helen Bateman, 1941 (div. 1960); children: Christine, Nancy; m. Sandra May Littlewood, Jan. 27, 1962; 1 child, Brendan. BS, St. Mary's Coll., 1939; postgrad., U. Calif., Berkeley, 1939-41. Tchr. Sacramento City Schs., 1941-43; reporter UPI, Sacramento, 1946-48; critic Sacramento Bee, 1948—, arts editor, 1948-76; dir. criticism workshops Nat. Coll. Theater Festival, Sacramento, 1980's, various theater groups, Sacramento, 1948-62. Author: (musical) Anita, 1955. Sgt. U.S. Army, 1943-46. Nominated Pulitzer prize in criticism, 1980; named Conservator of Am. Arts Am. Conservatory Theater Found., 1984. Mem. Am. Newspaper Guild, Am. Theater Critics Assn., Music Critics Assn. Avocations: golf, tennis. Office: Sacramento Bee 2100 Q St PO Box 95852 Sacramento CA 95852

GLAD, JOAN BOURNE, clinical psychologist, educator; b. Salt Lake City, Apr. 24, 1918; d. E. LeRoy and Ethel G. (Rogers) Bourne; m. Donald D. Glad, Sept. 10, 1938 (dec. 1978); children: Dawn JoAnne Lundquist, Toni Ann Saunders, Sue Ellen Winmill, Roger Bruce. BA, UCLA, 1955; MA, U. Utah, 1960, PhD, 1965. Chief psychologist Utah State Dept. Health, Salt Lake City, 1960-65; founder, dir. adminstr. Child and Family Guidance Clinic, Salt Lake City, 1965-68; dir. parent edn. Children's Hosp., Orange County, 1968-75; founder, adminstr. Family Learning Ctr., Santa-Ana Tustin Cmty. Hosp., Santa Ana, Calif., 1975-77; dir. Glas & Assocs., Tustin, Calif., 1977—; instr. Grad. Sch., Chapman Coll., Orange, Calif., 1970-73; cons. Calif. Assn. Neurologically Handicapped Children, Orange, 1970-77; lectr. self esteem Fullerton (Calif.) Coll., 1980-82; pres. Golden State U., Newport Beach, Calif.; pres. Profl. Corp., Orange, Calif. Author: Reading Unlimited, 1965; editor newsletter Between You and Me, 1998—. Pres. Friends of Tustin (Calif.) Libr.; docent Tustin Hist. Soc. Mem. Assn. Holistic Health (a founder San Diego), Assn. Mormon Counselors and Psychotherapists. Republican. Mem. LDS Ch. Office: Glad & Assocs 409 Orangewood Rd Healdsburg CA 95448

GLADDEN, DEAN ROBERT, arts administrator, educator, consultant; b. Columbus, Ohio, Dec. 27, 1953; s. Cyril Robert and Eileen (Faulkner) G.; m. Jane Frances Telfers, Aug. 27, 1953; children: John Dean, Catherine Eileen. B in Music Edn., Miami U., Oxford, Ohio, 1976; MS in Urban Arts Mgmt., Drexel U., 1978; postgrad., Harvard U., 1998. Exec. dir. Council for Arts of Greater Lima, Ohio, 1977-80, Arts Comm. Greater Toledo, 1980-82; dir. devel. and adminstrn. Great Lakes Theater Festival, Cleve., 1982-86; assoc. mng. dir. The Cleve. Play House, 1986, mng. dir., 1987—; cons. Ohio Arts Coun., Cleve., 1977—, chmn. sponsor/touring panel, 1981-83; adj. assoc. prof. U. Akron, Ohio, 1984-87; mem. adv. com. Mandel Sch. of Non-Profit Mgmt., Case Western Res. U., Cleve. Author booklets on the econs. of arts in Ohio, 1981, 83, 85, 87, 89, 91, 93. Mem. League Resident Theatres (exec. com.), Ohio Citizens for Arts (v.p.), Rotary (pres.). Episcopalian. Avocations: piano, drums. Home: 2687 Rocklyn Rd Cleveland OH 44122-2112 Office: The Cleve Play House 8500 Euclid Ave Cleveland OH 44106-2032

GLADDEN, JAMES WALTER, JR., lawyer; b. Pitts., Feb. 23, 1940; s. James Walter and Cynthia Unice (Hales) G.; m. Patricia T. Kuehn, Aug. 21, 1993; children: James, Thomas, Robert. AB, DePauw U., 1961; JD, Harvard U., 1964. Bar: Ill. 1964, U.S. Sup. Ct. 1978. Ptnr. Mayer, Brown & Platt, Chgo., 1964—. Mem. ABA. Home: 2212 Lincoln St Evanston IL 60201-2202 Office: Mayer Brown & Platt 190 S La Salle St Ste 3100 Chicago IL 60603-3441*

GLADDEN, JOSEPH RHEA, JR., lawyer; b. Atlanta, Oct. 5, 1942; s. Joseph Rhea Sr. and Frances (Baker) G.; m. Sarah Elizabeth Bynum, Aug. 21, 1965; children: Joseph III, Elizabeth. AB, Emory U., 1964; LLB, U. Va., 1967. Bar: Ga. 1968, U.S. Dist. Ct. (no. dist.) Ga. 1968, U.S. Ct. Appeals (5th cir.) 1968, U.S. Ct. Appeals (11th cir.) 1985. Assoc. King & Spalding, Atlanta, 1967-73, ptnr., 1973-85; v.p., sr. staff counsel The Coca-Cola Co., Atlanta, 1985-87, v.p. dep. gen. counsel, 1987-90, v.p., gen. counsel, 1990-91, sr. v.p., gen. counsel, 1991—; bd. dirs. Coca-Cola Enterprises; chmn. bd. dirs. Wesley Woods Ctr. of Emory U., Inc., Coca-Cola Amatil. Chmn. bd. trustees Agnes Scott Coll., Food and Drug Law Inst.; bd. dirs. Atlanta Ballet; trustee Lovett Sch., Acad. Search Cons. Svc. Mem. ABA (com. corp. law gen. counsel), Am Corp. Counsel Assn., Ga. Bar Assn., State Bar Ga., Assn. Gen. Counsel, Atlanta Bar Assn., Commerce Club, Piedmont Driving Club, Rotary. Office: The Coca-Cola Co PO Drawer 1734 Atlanta GA 30301-1734

GLADDEN, ROBERT WILEY, corporate executive; b. Barnesville, Ohio, Dec. 17, 1958; s. William R. Gladden and Clara M. (Sidebottom) Dimitro; m. Jorja Abernethy, Nov. 6, 1959; children: Teri Marie, Scott Robert, Corey William, Sara Sylvia, Bridget Kay. BS, West Liberty State Coll., 1981; MA, Bowling Green (Ohio) State U., 1983. Actuarial rsch. analyst Blue Cross of N.W. Ohio, Toledo, 1983-85; dir., actuarial svcs. Co-Med Inc., Dublin, Ohio, 1985-87; sr. v.p., rsch. and analysis McNerney Heintz, Inc., Barrington, Ill., 1987-93; exec. dir. managed care numerics Luth. Gen. Health System, Park Ridge, Ill., 1993-96; exec. Ernst & Young, LLP, Chgo., 1996—. Mem. editorial bd. Aspen Pub., Inc. Fin. chmn., treas., fin. com. chair First United Meth. Ch., Palatine, Ill.; Cub Scout den leader, cubmaster Boy Scouts Am.; soccer coach Palatine Celtic Soccer. Mem. Assn. of Am. Geographers, Am. Statis. Assn. Avocations: shortwave radio, reading. Office: Ernst & Young LLP Sears Tower 233 S Wacker Dr Chicago IL 60606-6306

GLADDING, NICHOLAS C., lawyer; b. Washington, 1945. BA, Yale U., 1967; JD, Vanderbilt U., 1970. Bar: Conn. 1970, U.S. Dist. Ct. Conn. 1974, U.S. Ct. Appeals (2d cir.) 1975, U.S. Supreme Ct. 1976, Mo. 1986, U.S. Dist. Ct. (ea. dist.) Mo. 1986, U.S. dist. Ct. (we. dist.) Mo. 1988. Assoc. Wiggin & Dana, New Haven, 1974-77; assoc. counsel Olin Corp., 1977-78, group counsel, 1978-82, group counsel, sr. counsel, 1982-86; ptnr. Husch & Eppenberger, St. Louis, 1986-88, Bryan Cave, St. Louis. Lt. (j.g.) USN, 1970-74. Mem. ABA, Bar Assn. Met. St. Louis (chmn. environ. law com. 1990-92), Mo. Bar Assn., Conn. Bar Assn. Office: Bryan Cave One Metropolitan Sq 211 N Broadway Saint Louis MO 63102-2733*

GLADE, WILLIAM PATTON, JR., economics educator; b. Wichita Falls, Tex., July 29, 1929; s. William Patton and Billie (Hatcher) G.; m. Marlene Louise Joseph, July 10, 1954; children: Anita, Genie, Patton, John. BBA, U. Tex., 1950, MA, 1951, PhD, 1955. Instr., asst. prof. econs. U. Md., 1957-60; asst., assoc. prof. U. Wis., Madison, 1960-65, prof. Sch. Bus. and dept. econs., 1966-71; prof. econs. U. Tex., Austin, 1970—; dir. Inst. Latin Am. Studies, Austin, 1971-86; dir., Mexico Ctr., 1997—; sr. program assoc. Smithsonian Instn. Wilson Ctr., 1987-88, acting sec. Latin Am. Program, 1989, sr. scholar Latin Am. Program, 1990—; assoc. dir. USIA, 1989-92; mem. rsch. task force Ctr. for Arts and Culture, 1998—. Author: Las empresas gubernamentales descentralizadas, 1959, The Political Economy of Mexico, 1963, The Latin American Economies, 1969, Marketing in a Developing Economy - The Case of Peru, 1970; co-editor (with Charles A. Reilly) Inquiry at the Grassroots, 1993; contbr., editor Privatization of Public Enterprises in Latin America, 1991; author, editor: Bigger Economies, Smaller Governments: The Role of Privatization in Latin America, 1996. Mem. Latin Am. Studies Assn. (v.p. 1978, pres. 1979), S.W. Coun. Latin Am. Studies Assn. (v.p. 1995, pres. 1996), Assn. for Cultural Econs., Assn. Evolutionary Econs. (bd. dirs. 1995-97), Cosmos Club. Office: U Tex Dept Econs Austin TX 78712 also: U Tex Mexican Ctr ILAS Austin TX 78712

GLADECK, SUSAN ODELL, social worker; b. Honesdale, Pa., Apr. 28; d. Lester Albert and Esther Grace (Fleming) Odell; children: Amy Frances, Esther Lena. BA with honors, Cedar Crest Coll., 1960; M. Social Svc., Bryn Mawr Coll., 1962. Lic. clin. social worker, Va.; cert. piano tchr. Social worker Family Svc. of Phila. and Family Svc. of Del. County, Media, Pa., 1962-63, Lehigh U. Child Devel. Ctr., Bethlehem, Pa., 1966, South Terr. Area Neighborhood Ctr., Bethlehem, Pa., 1969-71, Lehigh County Children's Bur., Allentown, Pa., 1971-73; social worker II Fairfax (Va.) County Dept. Human Devel., 1987-90; sr. social worker adult svcs. Loudoun County Dept. Social Svcs., Leesburg, Va., 1990-94; pvt. practice McLean, 1994—. Organist, choir dir. Chesterbrook Presbyn. Ch., Falls Church, Va., 1995—. Mem. NASW, Acad. Cert. Social Workers, Am. Coll. Musicians, Am. Guild Organists, Music Tchrs. Nat. Assn., Nat. Fedn. Music Tchrs., Va. Fedn. Music Tchrs., No. Va. Music Tchrs. Assn. Avocations: animal humane work. Home and Office: 6516 Fairlawn Dr Mc Lean VA 22101-5235

GLADFELTER, WILBERT EUGENE, physiology educator; b. York, Pa., Apr. 29, 1928; s. Paul John and Marea Bernadette (Miller) G.; m. Ruth Isabelle Ballantyne, Jan. 26, 1952; children: James W., Charles D., Mary A. AB magna cum laude, Gettysburg (Pa.) Coll., 1952; PhD, U. Pa., 1960. NSF fellow U. Pa., Phila., 1956-58, NIH fellow, 1958-59, asst. instr., 1954-56; instr. physiology W.Va. U., Morgantown, 1959-61, asst. prof., 1961-69, assoc. prof., 1969-96, prof. emeritus, 1996—. Contbr. articles to profl. jours. Treas., Monongalia County chpt. W. Va. Heart Assn., 1976-95. With USN, 1946-48. NSF fellow, 1956-58. Mem. Am. Physiol. Soc., Soc. Neurosci., Soc. for Integrative and Comparative Biology, Sigma Xi, Phi Beta Kappa, Beta Beta Beta. Lutheran. Home: 70 Pine Tree Ln Morgantown WV 26508-8130 Office: WVa U Health Sci Ctr Dept Physiology Morgantown WV 26506

GLADHILL, BETHANY, community advocate, historic preservation consultant; b. St. Paul, Aug. 12, 1967; d. Dennis Lee and Mary Lou (Hanafin) Gladhill; m. Christopher W. Yerkes, May 28, 1995. BA in Drama and English magna cum laude, Tufts U., 1989; postgrad., Goucher Coll. Bus. cons. freelance, Taipei, Taiwan, 1989-91; mktg. exec. Theatre de la Jeune Lune, Mpls., 1991-96; in graphic arts and copywriting Black Cat Graphics, St. Paul, 1996—; dir. of ops. Theatre de la Jeune Lune, Mpls., 1998—; mem. adv. bd. Minn. Arts and Edn. Partnership, St. Paul, 1996-97; participant Wilder Leadership Seminar, St. Paul, 1997. Neighborhood devel. chair Summit-Univ. Planning Coun., 1995-97, vice chair, 1995—, election chair, 1995; capt. Ashland-Laurel Block Club, St. Paul, 1993—. MacMillan Pub. scholar, 1989, Greenwood scholar, 1989. Mem. Ramsey Hill Assn., Univ. Club, Summit-Univ. Book Club. Democrat. Avocations: reading, travel. Home: 627 Ashland Ave Saint Paul MN 55104-7116 Office: Theatre de La Jeune Lune 105 N 1st St Minneapolis MN 55401

GLADKI, HANNA ZOFIA, civil engineer, hydraulic mixer specialist; b. Krakow, Poland, Dec. 30, 1933; came to U.S., 1984; d. Stanislaw Wojtanowski and Maria (Ekiert) Wojtanowska; m. Jozef Gladki, July 2, 1955 (dec. 1982); 1 child, Ania. ScD, Tech. U., Warsaw, Poland, 1966; postgrad. degree, Agrl. U., Wroclaw, Poland, 1977. Asst. prof. Agrl. Acad. Krakow, 1966-70, assoc. prof., 1970-81, chair dept., 1973-83, dean of faculty, 1977-81, prof., 1981-85; hydraulic mixer specialist ITT Flygt Corp., Norwalk, Conn., 1985—; presenter at profl. confs. Contbr. articles to profl. publs. Mem. AIChE, N.Am. Mixing Forum, Internat. Assn. Hydraulic Rsch. Roman Catholic. Achievements include expertise in hydraulics, flow velocity, pressure, mixing slurry and viscous fluid in tanks, non-Newtonian fluids and slurry for industry; designing mixers in the process industry and for biological and sludge treatment; development of method for sizing mixers in oxidation ditches with clarifier, and method of determining power dissipation and thrust force in the mixing tank with Free Jet Flow Agitators (FJFA). Home: 79 Melville St Stratford CT 06615-5723 Office: ITT Flygt Corp PO Box 1004 Trumbull CT 06611-0943

GLADNER, MARC STEFAN, lawyer; b. Seattle, July 18, 1952; s. Jules A. and Mildred W. (Weller) G.; m. Susanne Tso (div. Feb. 1981); m. Michele Marie Hardin, Sept. 12, 1981; 1 child, Sara Megan. Student, U. Colo., 1970-73; JD, Southwestern U., 1976. Bar: Ariz. 1976, Navajo Tribal Ct. 1978. Law clk. jud. br. Navajo Nation, Window Rock, Ariz., 1976-77, gen. counsel jud. br., 1977-79; pvt. practice law Phoenix, 1979-83; ptnr. Seplow, Rivkind & Gladner, Phoenix, 1983-86, Crosby & Gladner, P.C., Phoenix, 1986—; adj. instr. Coll. Ganado, Ariz., 1978-79. Democrat. Jewish. Avocation: stamp collecting. Office: Crosby & Gladner PC 1726 E Thomas Rd Phoenix AZ 85016-7604

GLADSTONE, CAROL LYNN, assistant principal; b. N.Y.C., Aug. 14, 1944; d. Albert Ludwig and Jeanne (Eisner) Adler; m. Edward Gladstone, Nov. 20, 1973. BA, Hunter Coll., 1965; MA, CCNY, N.Y.C., 1967; PhD, Columbia Pacific U., 1988, postgrad., 1993-94. Cert. tchr. English, French, sch. dist. adminstr., Ariz., Conn., N.J., N.Y. English/reading tchr. Jr. High Sch. #120, N.Y.C., 1965-66; reading coord. Dewitt Clinton High Sch., Bronx, 1966-74; asst. chair John F. Kennedy High Sch., Bronx, 1974-85; asst. prin. James Monroe High Sch., Bronx, 1985-97, Morris High Sch., 1997-98, Flags H.S., 1998—; prin. PM/Saturday Sch. James Monroe H.S., 1993-94; trainer of adminstrv. staff Bronx. Supt.'s Office, 1992—, Manhattan Supt.'s Office, 1989-90; adj. prof. Coll. of New Rochelle, N.Y., 1988-89, Lehman Coll., Bronx, 1987-88. Contbr. articles to profl. jours.; author: Competence in Cloze, 1989; author series of books: Gladstone Comprehensive Writing Program, 1986-88. Sec. Westchester (N.Y.) Alzheimer's Disease Assn., 1980-87; reporter Pub. Access Cable TV, Westchester, 1982-83. Named Supr. of Yr. Bronx Supt.'s Office, 1990-91, 94-95, Educator of Yr. Assn. Tchrs. N.Y., 1987-88, 90-91, Educator as Writer Mayor of City of N.Y., 1986; N.Y. Inst. for Humanities fellow, 1994. Mem. ASCD (assoc.), N.Y. State English Coun. (Educator of Excellence 1992-93, 95-96, regional dir. 1994-98, v.p. supervision 1998), N.Y. State Reading Assn., Bronx Assn. Prins. of English (chmn. 1990—), N.Y.C. Assn. Asst. Prins. (exec. bd. 1995—), Nat. Bd. for Profl. Teaching Standards, Nat. Coun. Tchrs. English (chancellor's com. new stds. 1997, ESL/ELA new stds., 1997, dist. literacy com., 1997). Avocations: travel, reading, gourmet cooking, computer technology.

GLADSTONE, GEORGE RANDALL, planetary scientist; b. North Vancouver, B.C., Can., May 20, 1956; s. George Wilfrid and Alma (Johnson) G.; m. Aileen LeProtti Corelli, Oct. 2, 1987; children: Eleanor Ann, Elizabeth Anne. BS, U. B.C., Vancouver, 1978; MS, Calif. Inst. Tech., 1980, PhD, 1983. Project scientist Ctr. for Rsch. in Earth and Space Sci., York U., North York, Can., 1982-84; rsch. assoc. Lab. for Atmospheric and Space Physics, U. Colo., Boulder, 1984-87; asst. rsch. physicist Space Scis. Lab., U. Calif., Berkeley, 1987-93; sr. rsch. scientist, then staff scientist S.W. Rsch. Inst., San Antonio, 1993—. Contbr. rsch. articles to sci. jours. Mem. Am. Geophys. Union (assoc. editor Geophys. Rsch. Letters jour. 1994-97), Am. Astron. Soc. (divsn. planetary scis.). Home: 347 Brees Blvd San Antonio TX 78209-4825 Office: Southwest Rsch Inst Dept Space Sciences 6220 Culebra Rd Dept Space San Antonio TX 78238-5100*

GLADSTONE, HERBERT JACK, manufacturing company executive; b. N.Y.C., May 12, 1924; s. Joseph D. and Ella (Shabman) G.; m. Sylvia Rosenberg, Dec. 28, 1946; children: Alan, Linda, Karen. Student, Hamilton Coll., 1944, Harvard U., 1945; BBA, CCNY, 1947. Mem. staff Gershon & Strell, CPAs, N.Y.C., 1947-51; budget dir. F.M.C., N.Y.C., 1951-55; v.p., treas. Condec Corp., Old Greenwich, Conn., 1955-85; treas., chief fin. officer Cober, 1985-92; ret., 1992; prof. acctg. Sacred Heart U.; lectr. MBA program U. Conn.; bd. dirs. Consol. Controls Corp., Hammond Valve Corp. Pres. PTA, 1956-57; asst. scoutmaster Toquam coun. Boy Scouts Am., 1960-63. Served with USAAF, 1943-46. Mem. AICPA, Fin. Execs. Inst. (dir.), N.Y. State Soc. CPAs. Clubs: Roxbury Country (dir.), Roxbury Tennis and Swim (trustee). Home: 284 W Hill Rd Stamford CT 06902-1713

GLADSTONE, RICHARD BENNETT, retired publishing company executive; b. Orwell, N.Y., June 29, 1924; s. Irving Rea and Dorothy Bennett (Shufelt) G.; m. Kathleen L. Dandy, June 12, 1953; children: Sarah Martin, Margaret Ellen, Emily Bennett, William Dandy. A.B., Harvard U., 1948. With Houghton Mifflin Co., Boston, 1948-88, editorial dir., 1973, v.p., dir. ednl. div., 1973-74, sr. v.p., 1974-89, sr. v.p., dir. publishing, 1975-80, exec. v.p., publisher, 1981-86, vice chmn., 1986-88, also bd. dirs. Past mem. adv. com. Ctr. for the Book, Libr. Congress; former dir. Book Industry Study Group; overseer Handel & Haydn Soc. With AUS, 1943-46. Mem. Am. Ednl. Pubs. Inst. (past dir.), Assn. Am. Pubs. (past dir.), St. Botolph Club. Home: 90 Brook St Wellesley MA 02482-6619

GLADSTONE, WILLIAM LOUIS, accountant; b. Bklyn., May 23, 1931; s. Archie C. and Bernice T. (Turk) G.; m. Mildred G. Rosenberg, June 21, 1953; children: Susan, Douglas. BS, Lehigh U., 1951; LLB, Bklyn. Law Sch., 1955; grad., Harvard U. Advanced Mgmt. Program, 1970; LLD (hon.), Lehigh U., 1992. CPA, N.Y. Staff acct. Arthur Young & Co., N.Y.C., from 1951, ptnr., 1963, mng. ptnr., 1981-88, chmn., 1985-89; co-chief exec. Ernst & Young, N.Y.C., 1989-91; pres. Nat. Pastime Corp. dba Pittsfield Mets Baseball Club, 1992—; lectr. acctg. Columbia U., N.Y.C., 1962-64; ptnr. N.Y.C. Partnership, 1989-91; bd. dirs. Nat. Baseball Hall of Fame and Mus., Inc.. Contbr. articles to profl. jours. Mem. Corp. Congress N.Y. Pub. Libr., 1987-91, mem. conf. bd., 1987-93, trustee com. for econ. devel., 1988-94; bd. dirs. N.Y.-Pa. Baseball League, 1992—. Lt. USAF, 1952-53. Mem. AICPA, N.Y. State Soc. CPAs, Lehigh Alumni Assn. (award 1976), Bklyn. Law Sch. Alumni Assn., Fin. Acctg. Found. (trustee 1988-91). Home: 5 Knollwood Dr Larchmont NY 10538-1236 Office: 101 Park Ave Rm 2601 New York NY 10178-2699

GLADSTONE, WILLIAM SHELDON, JR., radiologist; b. Des Moines, Dec. 19, 1923; s. William Sheldon and Wanda (Rees) G.; m. Ruth Alice Jensen, June 19, 1944; children—Denise Ann, William Sheldon, Stephen Rees. B.A., State U. Iowa, 1954, M.D., 1947. Diplomate Am. Bd. Radiology. Intern Hurley Hosp., Flint, Mich., 1947-48; gen. practice medicine Iowa Falls, Iowa, 1948-49; asst. dept. pathology State U. Iowa Coll. Medicine, Iowa City, 1949-50; resident in radiology Univ. Hosp., Iowa City, 1950-51, 53-54; practice medicine specializing in radiology Kalamazoo, 1954—; exec. v.p. Kalamazoo Radiology; clin. asst. prof. radiology Mich. State U. Coll. Human Medicine; chief radiology Bronson Meth. Hosp., Kalamazoo, 1973-75, 77-79. Bd. dirs. Kalamazoo County Tb Soc., 1955-59, Mich. Children's Aid, 1960-62, Am. Cancer Soc., Kalamazoo, 1964-66. Served with AUS, 1943-46; served to capt. USAF, 1951-53. Fellow Am. Coll. Radiology; mem. Kalamazoo Acad. Medicine, AMA, Mich. Radiologic Soc. (pres. W. Mich. sect. 1976), Mich. State Med. Soc., SW Mich. Surg. Soc., Am. Roentgen Ray Soc., Phi Beta Kappa (pres. SW Mich. chpt. 1963). Republican. Episcopalian. Club: Kalamazoo Country. Lodges: Masons, Shriners. Home: 1029 Essex Cir Kalamazoo MI 49008-2349 Office: 524 S Park St Kalamazoo MI 49007-5118

GLADWELL, GRAHAM MAURICE LESLIE, mathematician, civil engineering educator; b. Otford, Kent, Eng., Feb. 21, 1934; emigrated to Can., 1969; s. Basil Maurice Edwin and Doris Alexandra (New) G.; m. Joyce Eugenie Nation, Mar. 29, 1958; children: Graham Hugh, Geoffrey Norman, Malcolm Timothy. B.Sc., U. London, 1954, Ph.D., 1957, D.Sc., 1969. Lectr. U. London, 1956-60, U. W. Indies, Jamaica, 1960-62; sr. lectr. U. Southampton, Eng., 1962-69; prof. dept. civil engrng. U. Waterloo, Ont., Can., 1969—, prof. dept. applied math., 1979—. Author: Matrix Analysis of Vibration, 1965, Contact Problems in the Classical Theory of Elasticity, 1980, Inverse Problems in Vibration, 1986, Inverse Problems in Scattering, 1993, Functional Analysis: Applications to Mechanics and Inverse Problems, 1996; editor: Computer Aided Engineering, 1971, Contact Mechanics and Wear of Rail/Wheel Systems, 1983; series editor Solid mechanics and its Applications, 1989—. Fellow Am. Acad. Mechanics (dir. 1979-82), Inst. Math. and Its Applications, Royal Soc. Arts, Royal Soc. Can. Presbyterian. Office: Dept Civil Engring, Univ Waterloo, Waterloo, ON Canada N2L 3G1

GLADYSZ, JOHN ANDREW, chemistry educator; b. Kalamazoo, Aug. 13, 1952; s. Edward Matthew and Margean Alice (Worst) G.; m. Janet Françoise Blümel, Dec. 28, 1997. BS in Chemistry, U. Mich., 1971; PhD in Chemistry, Stanford (Calif.) U., 1974. Asst. prof. U. Calif., L.A., 1974-82; assoc. prof. U. Utah, Salt Lake City, 1982-85, prof., 1985-98; prof., chair organic chemistry U. Erlangen-Nürnberg, 1998—. Assoc. editor Chem. Revs., 1984—; mem. editorial bd. Organometallics, 1990-92, Bull. de la Société Chemique de France, 1992-97. Alfred P. Sloan Found. fellow, 1980-84; Camile and Henry Dreyfus scholar and grantee, 1980-85; Arthur C. Cope scholar, 1988; recipient U. Utah Disting. Rsch. award, 1992, Humboldt award, 1994. Mem. AAAS, Am. Chem. Soc. (award in organometallic chemistry 1994), The Chem. Soc., German Chem. Soc., Alpha Chi Sigma. Avocations: running, skiing. Fax: 011-49-9131-85-29132. E-mail: gladysz@organik.uni-erlangen.de. Home: Kitzingerstr 13, Erlangen D-91056, Germany Office: Institut für Organische Chemie I, Fredrich Alexander U, Henkestrasse 42 D-91054 Erlangen Germany

GLAESSMANN, DORIS ANN, former county official, consultant; b. Northampton, Pa., Feb. 18, 1940; d. Frank G. and Theresa (Fischl) Zwikl; m. Edward Glaessmann, Sept. 1, 1962; children: Edward Jr., Robert F. Grad. high sch., Northampton, 1958. Sec., bookkkeeper John F. Moore Agy., Inc., Allentown, Pa., 1958-64; ct. clk. Criminal div. Clk. of Cts. Office, Allentown, 1968-69, asst. dep. clk., 1969-76, chief dep. clk., 1976-82; clk. of cts., criminal and civil divsns. Lehigh County, Allentown, 1982-95; cons., 1995—. Den mother, sec. Cub Scout Pack 140, Allentown, Pa., 1973-78; mem., past bd. dirs.; mem. coun. St. Peter's Evang. Luth. Ch., Allentown, 1984-89. Mem. Pa. Prothonotaries and Clks. Assn. (past pres., treas.

1993—), Pa. Elected Women's Assn. (past. sec.-treas. and pres. Lehigh Valley chpt.), Quota Internat. of Allentown (pres. 1997-99). Democrat. Avocations: baking, reading, crocheting, walking. Home: 945 E Lynnwood St Allentown PA 18103-5250

GLANCY, ALFRED ROBINSON, III, public utility company executive; b. Detroit, Mar. 14, 1938; s. Alfred Robinson and Elizabeth A. (Tant) G.; m. Ruth Mary Roby, Sept. 15, 1962; children: Joan C., Alfred R. IV, Douglas Roby, Andrew Roby. BA, Princeton U., 1960; MA, Harvard U., 1962. Vice pres. corp. planning Am. Nat. Gas Service, Detroit, 1976-79; econ. and fin. planning staff Mich. Consol. Gas Co., Detroit, 1962-64, supr. econ. studies and rates, 1965-67, mgr. econ. and fin. planning dept., 1967-68, treas., 1969-72, v.p., treas., 1972-73, v.p. customer and mktg. services, 1976-79, v.p. mktg./dist. ops., 1979-81, sr. v.p. mktg./customer services, 1981-83, sr. v.p. utility ops., 1983-84, chmn., chief exec. officer, 1984-92; chmn., pres., CEO MCN Energy Group Inc., 1989—; bd. dirs., exec. com. UNICO Properties, Inc., Seattle; bd. dirs. Ga., Morton Indsl. Group. Past chmn. Detroit Symphony Orch., Detroit Renaissance Inc., exec. com.; past chmn. Detroit Med. Ctr., New Detroit, Inc.. Mem. Princeton Club Mich., Country Club of Detroit, Detroit Athletic Club. Republican. Office: MCN Energy Group Inc 500 Griswold St Detroit MI 48226-3701

GLANCY, DIANE, English educator; b. Kansas City, Mo., Mar. 18, 1941; d. Lewis and Edith (Wood) Hall; m. Dwane Glancy, May 2, 1964 (div. Mar. 1983); children: David, Jennifer. BA, U. Mo., 1964; MFA, U. Iowa, 1988. Prof. Macalester Coll., St. Paul, Minn. Author: (books) Pushing the Bear, 1996, The Only Piece of Furniture in the House, 1996, Flutie, 1998, Fuller Man, 1999, The Closets of Heaven, 1999; author short stories, essays and poetry. Grantee Blandin Pvt. Coll. Found., 1990, 91, 94, Wallace Faculty Travel grant, Macalester Coll., 1993, Nat. Endowment for the Arts, 1990, Minn. State Arts Bd., 1990, Jerome Travel grant, 1990, 95, Intermedia Arts Minn., 1990, NEH, Chgo., 1990; recipient Frances C. Allen fellowship D'Arcy McNickle Ctr. fo History of Am. Ind., Newberry Libr., Chgo., 1988, Edwin Piper fellowship U. Iowa, 1988, Equal Opportunity fellowship U. Iowa, 1987-88.

GLANCY, WALTER JOHN, lawyer; b. L.A., Mar. 8, 1942; s. Walter Perry and Elva Thomasin (Douglass) G.; m. Jane Whetstone Schroeder, Sept. 30, 1995; children by previous marriage: Jill Marie, Gregory Owens. AB, Princeton U., 1964; BA, Oxford U., Eng., 1966; LLB, Yale U., 1969. Bar: Tex. 1971. Law clk. to assoc. justice Byron R. White U.S. Supreme Ct., 1969-70; staff asst. Nat. Security Council, 1970-71; staff asst. to Peter M. Flanigan, The White House, 1971; assoc. then ptnr. Jackson, Walker, Winstead, Cantwell & Miller, Dallas, 1972-76; ptnr. Hughes & Luce and predecessor, Dallas, 1976-85, Baker & Botts, Dallas, 1985-88, Hughes & Luce, Dallas, 1988-90; pvt. practice law Dallas, 1991-95; cons. Meyer, Hendricks, Victor, Osborn & Maledon, Phoenix, 1991-95; ptnr. Weil, Gotshal & Manges LLP, Dallas, 1995-96; pvt. practice Dallas, 1997—; sr. v.p. Holly Corp., 1998—; adj. lectr. corp. taxation So. Meth. U. Sch. Law, 1988. Note and comment editor Yale Law Jour., 1968-69. Mem. bd. mgmt. Dallas YMCA Urban Svcs., 1975-84; bd. dirs. Dallas Family Guidance Ctr., 1982-96, pres. bd. dirs., 1985-86, Child & Family Guidance Ctrs., Dallas, 1996—; mem. adminstrv. bd. Lovers Ln. United Meth. Ch., Dallas, 1984-86, 88-89; bd. dirs. Dallas Opera, 1984-88, 96-97; trustee Hockaday Sch., Dallas, 1989-95; deacon Park Cities Bapt. Ch., Dallas, 1996—. Nat. Merit scholar, 1960-64; Marshall scholar, 1964-66. Mem. ABA, Dallas Bar Assn. (chmn. legal ethics com. 1980-81), Am. Law Inst., State Bar Tex. (profl. ethics com. 1982—, chmn. tax. sect. 1985-86), Park Cities Rotary Club (dir. 1999—), Order of Coif, Phi Beta Kappa. Republican. Home: 9162 Clearlake Dr Dallas TX 75225-2001 Office: 100 Crescent Ct Ste 1600 Dallas TX 75201

GLANCZ, RONALD ROBERT, lawyer; b. Bay City, Mich., Jan. 29, 1943; s. Alexander and Ella (Josehart) G.; m. Margie Joan Pensler, Dec. 28, 1969. BA in Pre-Legal Studies, U. Mich., 1964, JD cum laude, 1968. Bar: Mich. 1968, U.S. Ct. of Appeals (D.C. cir. ct.) 1969, U.S. Supreme Ct. 1972, D.C. 1974. Atty. civil div. Appellate Sec. U.S. Dept. Justice, Washington, 1968-75, asst. dir. civil div., 1975-79; dir. litigation div. Office of the Compt. of the Currency, Washington, 1979-84; asst. gen. counsel Fed. Deposit Ins. Corp., Washington, 1984-88; ptnr. Venable Baetjer Howard & Civiletti, LLP, Washington, 1991—. Contbr. articles to profl. jours. Mem. ABA (chair subcom. on ins. svcs.), FBA (exec. com. banking law sect.), Order of Coif, The Exchequer Club Washington. Office: Venable Baetjer Howard & Civiletti LLP 1201 New York Ave NW Ste 1000 Washington DC 20005-3917

GLANSTEIN, JOEL CHARLES, lawyer; b. Jersey City, May 16, 1940; s. Harry I. and Katherine G.; m. Eleanor Elovich, July 2, 1966; children: David Michael, Stacey Alison. BA with honors, Lehigh U., 1962; LLB, NYU, 1965, LLM in Labor Law, 1969. Bar: N.Y. 1967, D.C. 1975, U.S. Ct. Appeals (2d cir.) 1970, U.S. Supreme Ct. 1971, U.S. Ct. Appeals (1st cir.) 1972, U.S. Ct. Appeals (3d cir.) 1978, U.S. Ct. Appeals (11th and 9th cirs.) 1981, U.S. Ct. Appeals (5th cir.) 1982, U.S. Ct. Appeals (6th cir.) 1984. Assoc. Pressman & Scribner, N.Y.C., 1968-69; ptnr. Scribner, Glanstein & Klein, N.Y.C., 1970-72, Markowitz & Glanstein, N.Y.C., 1972-79, O'Donnell & Schwartz, N.Y.C., 1980-90; O'Donnell, Schwartz, Glanstein & Rosen, N.Y.C., 1991—; adj. assoc. prof. N.Y. Law Sch., N.Y.C., 1980-95. Mem. ABA (labor and employment law sect., com. on internat. labor law 1976, com. on law of alternative dispute resolution 1976), N.Y. State Bar Assn. (labor and employment law sect., chmn. 1987-88), N.Y. County Lawyers Assn., D.C. Bar Assn., Maritime Law Assn. U.S., Downtown Athletic Club. Office: O'Donnell Schwartz Glanstein & Rosen 305 Madison Ave Rm 1022 New York NY 10165-0100

GLANTON, RICHARD H., lawyer; b. Villa Rica, Ga., Nov. 21, 1946; s. Herbert E. and Norace (Hawkins) G.; m. Scheryl Williams, Aug. 17, 1974; children: Morgan Grace, David Howard. BA, W. Ga. Coll., 1968; JD, U. Va., 1972. Bar: Pa. 1973, Ill. 1977, U.S. Dist. Ct. (ea. dist.) Pa. 1977, U.S. Ct. Appeals (3d cir.) 1987. Assoc. atty. Huie & Harland, Atlanta, 1972-73; spl. asst. to chmn. legal div. EEOC, 1973-74; atty. United Airlines, Elk Grove, Ill., 1974-77; litigation counsel Consol. Rail Corp., Phila., 1977-79; dep. counsel Gov. Richard L. Thornburgh, Harrisburg, Pa., 1979-83; ptnr. Wolf Block Schorr & Cohen, Phila., 1983-86, Reed Smith Shaw & McClay, Phila., 1987—; bd. dirs. Gen. Accident Ins. Co. N.Am., Phila., Phila. Indsl. Devel. Corp., PECO Energy Co., Pa., Phila. Suburban Corp. Co-chmn. George Bush Fin. Com., Pa., 1987-88; pres. Barnes Found., Merion, Pa.; trustee Lincoln (Pa.) U., Allegheny U. Health Scis. Mem. Greater Phila. C. of C. (bd. dirs.), Union League Club. Office: Reed Smith Shaw & McClay 2500 One Liberty Pl Philadelphia PA 19103*

GLANTZ, WENDY NEWMAN, lawyer; b. L.I., N.Y., Dec. 16, 1956; d. Sidney and Sarah (Rudnitsky) Newman; m. Ronald Paul Glantz, Dec. 29, 1983. BS, SUNY, Stonybrook, 1978; JD, Nova Law Ctr., 1982. Bar: Fla., 1983. Assoc. Glazer & Glazer, Hallandale, Fla., 1983-85; ptnr. Pasin & Glantz, Lauderhill, Fla., 1985-86; ptnr. Glantz & Glantz, Lauderhill and Plantation, Fla., 1985-86, Plantation and Miami, Fla., 1986—; seminar leader Marital Strategies, Ft. Lauderdale, 1985—. Editor Pipeline, 1985-86; contbr. articles to profl. mags. Co-chairperson, editor Parents Anonymous, 1986—, mem. adv. bd.; chairperson Bus. Profl. Group of Sunrise Jewish Ctr., 1988—; sponsor Jewish Community Ctr., mem. fund raising com.; mem. South Fla. Symphony, Women of Fine Arts. Mem. ABA (family law sect.), NAFE (pres. S.E. chpt. 1985—), Fla. Bar Assn. (family law sect.), Assn. Trial Lawyers Am., Broward County Bar Assn. (program coord. continuing legal edn. family law sect.), West Broward Bar Assn. (pres. 1989-90), Fla. Assn. Women Lawyers (bd. dirs.), Broward County Women Lawyers Assn. (pres. 1988-90), Nat. Assn. Women Bus. Owners (Broward chpt.), Plantation C. of C. Office: Glantz & Glantz 7951 SW 6th St Ste 200 Fort Lauderdale FL 33324-3223

GLANVILLE, ROBERT EDWARD, lawyer; b. Binghamton, N.Y., Aug. 1, 1950; s. Robert S. and Betty J. (Garlick) G.; m. Susan Anne Kime, Sept. 3, 1970. BA magna cum laude, SUNY, Binghamton, 1972; JD magna cum laude, Cornell U., 1976. Bar: N.Y. 1977, U.S. Dist. Ct. (we. dist.) N.Y. 1978, U.S. Supreme Ct. 1981, U.S. Ct. Appeals (2d cir.) 1985, U.S. Ct. Appeals (D.C. cir.) 1991. Law clk. Appellate Divsn., 4th Dept., Rochester, 1976-78; from assoc. to ptnr. Phillips, Lytle, Hitchcock, et. al., Buffalo, N.Y., 1978-85, 88—; ptnr. Prahl & Glanville, Buffalo, 1986-88. Mem. ABA, N.Y. State Bar Assn., Erie County Bar Assn., Am. Gas Assn. Avocations: whitewater kayaking, sailing, mountaineering, flying. Home: 9385 S Hill Rd Boston NY 14025-9667 Office: Phillips Lytle Hitchcock 3400 Marine Midland Ctr Buffalo NY 14203-2887

GLASAUER, FRANZ ERNST, neurosurgeon; b. Khoau, Czechoslovakia, Feb. 19, 1930; s. Rudolf and Marie (Eckert) G.; m. Elizabeth A. Garofalo. M.D. magna cum laude, U. Heidelberg, Germany, 1955. Diplomate Am. Bd. Neurosurgery. Intern St. Mark's Hosp., Salt Lake City, 1955-56; resident in surgery, neurosurgery New Eng. Med. Ctr., Boston, 1957-61; asst. in neurosurgery Tufts U. Sch. Medicine, Boston, 1960-61; asst. prof. neurosurgery SUNY, Buffalo, 1965-69; assoc. prof. SUNY, 1969-72, prof., 1972-96, prof. emeritus, 1996—, acting chmn. dept. neurosurgery, 1983-85; clin. dir. neurosurgery Erie County Med. Ctr., Buffalo, 1983-97; attending neurosurgeon Buffalo Gen. Hosp.; trustee Found. for Internat. Edn. in Neurol. Surgery Inc., 1981—, 1st vice chmn., 1991-96. Author: (with Louis Bakay) Head Injury, 1980; contbr. articles to med. jours. Served with USNR, 1961-63. Mem. ACS, Congress Neurol. Surgeons, Am. Assn. Neurol. Surgeons, Cervical Spine Rsch. Soc., Found. Internat. Edn. Neurol. Surgery, N.Y. State Neurosurg. Soc. (dir. 1971-73), Internat. Med. Soc. of Paraplegia.

GLASBERG, LAURENCE BRIAN, private investor, business executive; b. N.Y.C., Apr. 28, 1943; s. William and Tillie (Liebowitz) G.; m. Lana Lucille Pollack, Aug. 10, 1963; children: Jeffrey Scott, Glenn David. BBA, CUNY, 1964, MBA, 1968. Mgr. bus. affairs Sta. WCBS-TV, N.Y.C., 1970-72, dir. planning and adminstrn., 1972-74; gen. auditor Eastern ops. CBS Inc., N.Y.C., 1975-76, v.p. fin. and adminstrn., CBS Publs., 1976-82, v.p., gen. auditor, 1982-88; sr. v.p. fin. and adminstrn. N.Am. ops. AEG Corp., 1988-89; pres. Nat. Mgmt. Resources Group Inc., 1990—; mng. dir. Future Resource Systems, Inc., 1994-96, exec. v.p. Future Bus. Centre, Inc., 1995-96; sr. v.p., CFO MacDonald Comms. Corp., 1996-98. Mem. fin. and tax com. Princeton Twsp., N.J., 1991, elected comitteeman, 1992, elected mayor, 1993; bd. dirs. AMAS Mus. Theatre, Inc., 1998—. 1st Lt. inf., U.S. Army, 1964-65. Fin. Execs. Inst. (nat. com. on govt. liaison, local bd. dirs. 1987-88, chpt. sec. 1989-92), Economic Club (N.Y.C.). Avocations: physical fitness, outdoor and environmental activities, reading.

GLASBERG, SCOT BRADLEY, plastic surgeon; b. N.Y.C., June 30, 1964; s. H. Mark and Paula (Drillman) G. BA cum laude, Columbia U., 1986; MD with honors, NYU, 1990. Diplomate Am. Bd. Surgery, Nat. Bd. Med. Examiners. Resident in surgery U. Conn./Hartford Hosp., 1990-95, chief resident, 1995-96; craniofacial rsch. fellow Inst. of reconstructive Plastic Surgery, NYU Med. Ctr., N.Y.C., 1992-93; fellow SUNY Health Sci. Ctr., Bklyn., 1996-98, assoc. program dir., dir. plastic surg. edn., 1998—. Contbr. articles to profl. jours. Mem. young plastic surgeons com. Plastic Surgery Ednl. Found., Am. Soc. Plastic Reconstructive Surgery, 1996-97. N.Y. State Regents scholar, 1982-86. Fellow ACS (assoc.); mem. AMA (del. to resident physician sect. 1990-93, 96-98, plastic surgery caucus 1996-97), Northeastern Soc. Plastic Surgery (resident/fellows award 1997), Med. Soc. State of N.Y. (del. to AMA-RPS 1996-98, Outstanding Svc. award 1990), N.Y. County Med. Soc., N.Y. Reg. Soc. Plastic and Reconstructive Surgeons (winner clin. paper competition 1997). Avocations: tennis, golf, swimming, card collecting. Home: 1775 York Ave Apt 34E New York NY 10128-6922 Office: 1755 York Ave New York NY 10128-6827

GLASCO, KIMBERLY, ballet dancer. Grad., Nat. Ballet Sch. With Nat. Ballet of Can., 1979-83, 84—, 2nd soloist, 1981-82, 84-85, 1st soloist, 1982-83, 85-87, prin. dancer, 1987—; with Am. Ballet Theatre, 1983-84; guest appearances at Australian Spoleto Festival, 1987, World Ballet Festival (Japan), Verona (Italy) Festival. Created roles of Alice in Alice (Glen Tetley), and the Parlormaid in La Ronde (Glen Tetley), Swan Lake, Queen/Black Swan, Sleeping Beauty, Aurora, Valantanes (Killian Etudes), Transfigured Night, Elite Syncopations, Paquita, Merry Widow, Month in the Country (Kenneth MacMillan), Volantaires (Glen Tetley), Cruel World (Sames Hudelka), Don Q (Petipa), Les Sylphide, La Sylphide, Giselle, Romeo & Juliet, Manon (Kenneth MacMillan), 4 Temperaments (Balanchine), Mozartina (Balanchin), Episodes, among others; appeared also in Footnotes, Nutcracker, Desir, Musings, Symphony in C, Giselle, Onegin, Cinderella, Daphnis and Chloe. Recipient Silver medal Moscow Internat. Ballet Competition, 1981. Office: National Ballet of Canada, 470 Queens Quay W, Toronto, ON Canada M5V 3K4

GLASCO, SUE ALICE, retired educator; b. Anna, Ill., Nov. 23, 1933; d. Robert Clyde and Katherine Ann (Rockenmeyer) Martin; m. Gerald Dean Glasco Sr., June 15, 1956; children: Katherine Glasco Cedar, Gerald Dean Jr., Jean Claire Glasco Eiler, Mary Ellen Glasco Taylor. BS in Edn., So. Ill. U., 1955, MS in Speech, 1972. Tchr., debate coach Evergreen Park (Ill.) H.S., 1955-56, Marion (Ill.) H.S., 1964-67; adj. instr. Shawnee Coll., 1972, John A. Logan Coll., 1982-83, 86-93; tchr. Johnston City (Ill.) H.S., 1983-85; county family edn. coord. Rend Lake Coll., Ina, Ill., 1992-98; ret., 1998; adj. instr. Southeastern Ill. Coll., 1992, McKendree Coll., 1993; presenter in field. Author of short stories, poems and articles. Vol. church, Ill., 1953—; vol. for establishing Crab Orchard (Ill.) Pub. Libr., 1972-82; mem. Bedford County, Tenn. Hist. Assn., So. Ill. Geneal. Assn., Williamson County Hist. Assn., Johnson County Hist. Assn., Ill. State Hist. Assn., Bread for the World, Nat. Multiple Sclerosis Soc. Mem. Internat. Platform Assn., So. Ill. Writers Guild (program chair 1991-92, newsletter 1991-94), Ill. Speech and Theater Assn., Ill. Adult and Continuing Edn. Assn., So. Ill. Reading Coun., Ill. Reading Coun., Mulkeytown Hist. Assn. Baptist. Avocation: local history. Home: 18100 New Dennison Rd Marion IL 62959-6238 Office: Family Investment Edn Ctr 406 E Main St Benton IL 62812-2154

GLASCOCK, ROBIN, secondary school educator; b. Cynthiana, Ky., Sept. 2, 1966; d. Albert Foster and Roxie Ann (Jones) Wiglesworth; m. Michael Glenn Glascock, Apr. 4, 1992; 1 child, Mark Tyce. BA, Centre Coll., 1988; MA in Edn., Georgetown Coll., 1996. Dir. in charge of hiring and scheduling Acad. Edge Tutoring Facility, Lexington, Ky., 1988-90; asst. dir. spl. needs children Woodbridge Acad., Lexington, Ky., 1988-90; tchr., speech coach Harrison County Mid. Sch., Cynthiana, Ky., 1990—. Recipient Disting. Performance award Ky. Comm. Assn., 1994. Mem. Ky. H.S. Speech League (bd. dirs. 1990—), Ky. Ednl. Speech and Drama Assn. (bd. dirs. 1990-97), Nat. Coun. Tchrs. English, Ky. Mid. Sch. Assn. Baptist. Avocations: theater, volleyball, walking, reading, coaching speech and forensics. Home: RR 2 Box 87A Cynthiana KY 41031-9506 Office: Harrison County Mid Sch 149 Education Dr Cynthiana KY 41031-1663

GLASEL, DAVID PAUL, lawyer; b. Bklyn., Apr. 24, 1944; s. Harry and Celia Glasel; m. Mercedes Florence Millett, July 6, 1950; children: Maria Florence, Solomon Everard. BA cum laude, Hofstra U., 1966; JD, Cornell U., 1969. Bar: N.Y. Mng. atty. Bklyn. Legal Svcs., 1973-75; health atty. C.A.L.S., N.Y.C., 1972-75; assoc. dir. counsel Nat. Coun. Alcoholism, N.Y.C., 1975-77; dir. comm., counsel N.Y. State Dept. Social Svcs., Albany, 1977-84; ptnr. Sherrin & Glasel, Albany, 1984—. Bd. dirs. Capital City Rescue Mission, Albany, 1998—; supr., coord. various state and fed. election, N.Y.C., 1993—; ch. youth worker Bible Bapt. Ch., Ghent, N.Y., 1997—. 1st lt. U.S. Army, 1969-70. Recipient awards Gov. N.Y., 1977-84. Mem. Nat. Health LAwyres, Internat. Computer Law Soc. Democrat. Avocation: baseball. Office: Sherrin & Glasel 74 N Pearl St Albany NY 12207

GLASER, ARTHUR HENRY, lawyer; b. Jersey City, May 1, 1947; s. Ned C. and Lorraine I. (Neil) G.; m. Waynelia Potter, Mar. 19, 1994; children: Kimberly N., Kevin M., Daniel J. BS, Hampden-Sydney Coll., 1968; JD, U. Va., 1973. Bar: Ga. 1973, U.S. Dist. Ct. (no. and mid. dists.) Ga., U.S. Ct. Appeals (11th cir.). Assoc. Swift, Currie, McGhee & Hiers, Atlanta, 1973-78, ptnr., 1978-83; ptnr. Drew, Eckl & Farnham, Atlanta, 1983-98, Self, Glaser & Davis, LLP, Atlanta, 1999—. Mem. ABA, Ga. Bar Assn., Atlanta Bar Assn. Presbyterian. Home: 1540 Burnt Hickory Rd NW Marietta GA 30064-1308 Office: Self Glaser & Davis LLP Ste 1650 Platinum Twr 400 Interstate N Pky Atlanta GA 30339

GLASER, DAVID, painter, sculptor; b. Bklyn., Sept. 29, 1919; s. Samuel and Jennie (Oiffer) G.; m. Millie Sappol, Feb. 19, 1944; children: Susan, Sherry. Student, N.Y. Sch. Indsl. Art, 1937, N.Y. Sch. Contemporary Art, 1947-48, Bklyn. Mus. Art Sch., 1948-50. Illustrator, cartoonist comic books Popular Mechanics, Electronics Illustrated, Popular Sci., N.Y.C., 1939-42, 46-50; pres., designer, inventor Mosamics Co., Bklyn., 1948-50; art dir., advt. mgr. Univ. Loudspeakers, White Plains, N.Y., 1951-60; owner, mgr., graphic designer Studio Concepts, Wantagh, N.Y., 1957—; artist Civilian Conservation Corps, Adirondacks, 1936; tchr. art Ctr. Island Jewish Sch., Freeport, N.Y., 1959; newspaper artist Bering Breeze, Aleutian Islands, 1945-46; co-founder Northwest Pacific chpt. AVC Adak, 1945. Author: (poetry) My Mother Died Dancing, 1960; contbr. poetry to anthologies; three-man show Heckscher Mus., Huntington, N.Y., 1964; exhibited in group shows Mcpl. Gallery, Jackson, Miss., 1943, Allied Artists of Am., 1957-85, Nat. Art Club, N.Y.C., 1959, Art Directions, 1959, ACA Galleries, 1960, Hofstra U., Adelphi U., Nassau C.C., 1980, L.I. Art Dirs. Exhbn. Firehouse Gallery, 1980, Nassau County Art Mus., 1980, Hempstead Harbor Art Assn., Glen Cove, L.I., 1982, Knickerbocker Artists, Islip Mus., 1983, Wantagh Libr., 1975, Levittown Libr., 1986, Freeport Libr., 1987; illustrator: Planets (Willie Ley); author, creator: American Indian, Crime and Punishment, Superstition and Parapsychology, 1947-50; prodr. bicentennial pictorial chronological map of Entire Am. Revolution, Spirit of '76, 1975; inventor process for mass prodn. ceramic and transparent mosaics, silk screen sys. for printing inside compound curves; creator innovative 2 color graphics method; new age art: developer combining chemically colored copper (sculpture) plastic, resins and reflective integral elements with electronics, 1973—; prodr. crossover filming of painting, sculpture and poetry recitation as ongoing creative product of Bridges of Mind, 1993—. Designer war posters visual aids for U.S. Army, 1942-44; creator comic character Giggy F. Useless, used in basic tng. and theatre dramatizations for Army newspaper, 1943-46. Sgt. AUS, 1942-46. Art Student's League scholar, 1936; recipient grand prize for redesign Levitt Home, 1967, Printing Industries, N.Y., 1973, numerous graphics awards, 1973-84, graphic excellence award Monadnock Mills, 1975, Desi grand award, 1980-82, poetry award Nassau County Fine Arts Mus., 1981, award of excellence IEEE, World Trade Ctr., N.Y.C., 1984, Vets. Soc. Am. Artists, 1984, award of excellence Long Beach Art League, 1989. Mem. Internat. Soc. Poets, Freeport Arts Coun., Allied Artists Am. (pres. 1985-86), Huntington Twp. Art League, DAV, Comic Artist Guild (treas.), Nature Conservancy, various environ. groups. Achievements include development of process for mass-producing mosaics, both traditional and current for architecture as well as home decor; transparent (per-stained glass) and opaque. Avocations: swimming, camping, hiking, mechanics. Home and Office: 33 Downhill Ln Wantagh NY 11793-1817

GLASER, DONALD ARTHUR, physicist; b. Cleveland, Ohio, Sept. 21, 1926; s. William Joseph Glaser. BS, Case Inst. Tech., 1946, ScD, 1959; PhD, Calif. Inst. Tech., 1949. Prof. physics U. Mich., 1949-59; prof. physics U. Calif., Berkeley, 1959—; prof. physics, molecular and cell biology, divsn. neurobiology U. Calif., 1964—. Recipient Henry Russel award U. Mich., 1955, Charles V. Boys prize Phys. Soc., London, 1958, Nobel prize in physics, 1960, Gold Medal award Case Inst. Tech., 1967, Golden Plate award Am. Acad. of Achievement, 1989; NSF fellow, 1961, Guggenheim fellow, 1961-62, fellow Smith-Kettlewell Inst. for Vision Rsch, 1983-84. Fellow AAAS, Fedn. Am. Scientists, The Exploratorium (bd. dirs.), Royal Soc. Sci., Royal Swedish Acad. Sci., Assn. Rsch. Vision and Ophthalmology, Neuroscis. Inst., Am. Physics Soc. (prize 1959); mem. Nat. Acad. Scis., Am. Assn. Artificial Intelligence, N.Y. Acad. Sci., Internat. Acad. Sci., Am. Philos. Soc., Sigma Xi, Tau Kappa Alpha, Theta Tau. Home: 41 Hill Rd Berkeley CA 94708-2131 Office: U Calif Dept Molecular & Cell Biology Univ Calif 337 Stanley Hall Berkeley CA 94720

GLASER, EDWIN VICTOR, rare book dealer; b. N.Y.C., June 7, 1929; s. Simon and Dorothy (Goldwater) G.; m. Janice Briggs, May 1, 1959 (div. 1975); children: Peter, Daniel. BA, U. N.Mex., 1950; MS, Columbia U., 1951. Reporter Providence Jour.-Bulletin, 1951-55; sales mgr. R.E.C. Corp., New Rochelle, N.Y., 1955-69; owner Edwin V. Glaser Rare Books, Sausalito, Calif., 1969—; faculty mem., antiquarian book seminar, U. Denver, 1979—. Contbr. numerous articles to profl. jours. Mem. Antiquarian Booksellers Assn. Am. (pres. 1986-87, gov.). Office: Glaser Rare Books PO Box 1765 Sausalito CA 94966-1765

GLASER, GARY A., bank executive. Grad., Baldwin-Wallace, Case Western Res. U. With Nat. City Corp., 1967-84; pres., CEO Nat. City Bank, Columbus, Ohio, 1984—. Office: Nat City Bank 155 E Broad St Ste Ll Columbus OH 43215-3609*

GLASER, GILBERT HERBERT, neuroscientist, physician, educator; b. N.Y.C., Nov. 10, 1920; s. Burnard Richard and Sidelle (Rogers) G.; m. Morfydd Mai Pugh, Mar. 17, 1946; children: Gareth Evan, Sara Elizabeth. A.B., Columbia, 1940, M.D., 1943, Med. Sc.D., 1951; M.A. (hon.), Yale, 1963. Diplomate: Am. Bd. Psychiatry and Neurology. Intern Mt. Sinai Hosp., N.Y.C., 1943-44; resident neurology N.Y. Neurol. Inst., 1944-46; research asst. to assoc. neurology Columbia Coll. Physicians and Surgeons, 1948-52; research scientist N.Y. Psychiat. Inst., 1948-50; head. sect. neurology Sch. Medicine Yale U., 1952-71, chmn. dept. neurology Sch. Medicine, 1971-86, asst. prof. neurology Sch. Medicine, 1952-55, assoc. prof. Sch. Medicine, 1955-63, prof. neurology Sch. Medicine, 1963-91, prof. neurology emeritus, 1991—; Commonwealth Fund vis. prof. neurology U. London, Eng., 1965-66; cons. West Haven (Conn.) VA Hosp., 1955—; vis. prof. neurology Nat. Hosp., London, 1972, Park Hosp., Oxford, Eng., 1973-86, Hunan Med. Coll., Peoples Republic of China, 1986, U. Niigata, Kyoto, Japan, 1989; Fulbright Disting. prof. neurology Zagreb U., Yugoslavia, 1981; vis. scholar Green Coll. Oxford U., Eng., 1987-88; mem. neurology research adv. com. USPHS, 1956-60, 68-72, spl. cons., 1973, epilepsy adv. com., 1974-77, chmn. basic sci. subcom., 1977-80; mem. neurobiology rev. com. VA, 1975-78, chmn., 1977-78. Author: EEG and Behavior, 1963; Editor: Epilepsia, 1958-76; adv. editor, 1976-86; editor: Recent Advances in Clinical Neurology, 1978, 81, 84, Antiepileptic Drugs: Mechanisms of Action, 1980; mem. editorial bd.: Jour. Nervous and Mental Diseases; Contbr. articles to profl. jours. Capt. M.C. AUS, 1946-48. Recipient Janeway prize Columbia U., 1943, Bicentennial medal award, 1968, Book award Commonwealth Fund, 1975. Fellow Royal Soc. Medicine, ACP; mem. Am. Neurol. Assn. (1st v.p. 1977-78), Am. Acad. Neurology (pres. 1973-75 hon. mem. 1998), Am. Epilepsy Soc. (pres. 1963, Lennox lectr. 1985), Am. Electroencephalographic Soc. (council 1958-61, bd. qualifications), Eastern Assn. Electroencephalographers (pres. 1958), EEG Soc. (Gt. Britain), Assn. Brit. Neurologists, Soc. for Neurosci., Epilepsy Found. Am. (med. adv. bd.), Myasthenia Gravis Foundation (med. adv. bd. chmn. 1964-65), Multiple Sclerosis Soc. (chmn. research programs com. 1973-74, med. adv. bd.). Club: Athenaeum (London). Home: 205 Millbrook Rd North Haven CT 06473-4334 Office: Yale U Sch Medicine 333 Cedar St New Haven CT 06510-3289

GLASER, HOWARD B., lawyer; b. 1958; m. Julia Glaser; children: Sarah, Erica. BA, SUNY, 1980; JD cum laude, Harvard U., 1994. Asst. to dir. polit. action and legislation Dist. Coun. 37 Am. Fedn. State, County and Mcpl. Employees, 1981-82; dep. dir. pub. info. N.Y. State Dept. Taxation and Fin., 1983-86; spl. asst. N.Y. Gov. Mario Cuomo, 1986-91; gen. dep. asst. sec. for cmty. planning and devel. U.S. Dept. Housing and Urban Devel., Washington, 1994-97, dep. gen. counsel for programs and regulation, 1997—. Office: Dept Housing & Urban Devel 451 7th St SW Washington DC 20410-0002*

GLASER, LUIS, biochemistry educator; b. Vienna, Austria, Mar. 30, 1932; came to U.S., 1953, naturalized, 1961; s. Hermann and Gisela (Kohn) G.; m. Ruth Walliser, May 18, 1961; children: Miriam, Nicole. B.A., U. Toronto, Ont., Can., 1953; Ph.D., Washington U., St. Louis, 1956. Asst. prof. biol. chemistry Washington U., 1959-62, asso. prof., 1962-67, prof., 1967-75, chmn. dept. biol. chemistry, 1975-86; dir. Div. Biology and Biomed. Scis., 1980-86; exec. v.p., provost U. Miami, 1986—. Contbr. numerous articles on bacterial and mammalian metabolism to profl. jours.; editor Jour. Biol. Chemistry, 1969-74, 81-86, Jour. Supramolecular Structures, 1979-86, Jour. Cell Biology, 1981-92. Helen Hay Whitney fellow, 1956-59; NIH grantee; NSF grantee. Mem. Am. Soc. Biol. Chemists, Am. Chem. Soc., Am. Soc. Microbiology, Am. Soc. Neurochemists, AAAS. Democrat. Jewish. Office: PO Box 248033 Miami FL 33124-8033

GLASER, MILTON, graphic designer and illustrator; b. N.Y.C., June 26, 1929; s. Eugene and Eleanor (Bergman) G.; m. Shirley Girton, Aug. 13, 1957. Student, Cooper Union Art Sch., 1948-51; DFA with honors, Mpls. Inst. Arts, 1971; postgrad., Moore Coll., Phila., 1975, Phila. Mus. Sch.

Visual Arts, 1979, SUNY, Buffalo, 1987; hon. degree, Queen's Coll., CUNY, d1990; Doctorate (hon.), Royal Coll. Art, London, 1995. Co-founder, pres. Push Pin Studios, N.Y.C., 1954-74; co-founder, pres., chmn. bd., design dir. N.Y. mag., 1968-77; v.p., design dir. Village Voice, N.Y.C., 1975-77; pres. Milton Glaser, Inc., N.Y.C., 1974—; designer Grand Union Supermarkets, 1978-97; art dir. graphics, chmn. art selection com. for restoration Rainbow Room at Rockefeller Ctr., 1987-88, pres., 1990—; bd. dirs. Internat. Design Conf., Aspen, Colo., 1972—, co-chmn., 1973, pres., 1990; mem. total identity program mktg. & advt. Queens Coll. Author: (with others) If Apples Had Teeth, 1960, Milton Glaser: Graphic Design, 1973, (with others) The Underground Gourmet, 1974, The Milton Glaser Poster Book, 1977, Milton Glaser Barcelona, 1989, Giorgio Morandi Milton Glaser, I Manifesti Di; illustrator numerous books; designed observation deck and restaurant graphics for World Trade Ctr. Twin Towers, N.Y.C., 1975; graphic and interior designer Sesame Pl., Bucks County, Pa., 1980; designer restaurants Aurora, N.Y.C., Tratorria dell'Arte, N.Y.C., La Hosteria; graphics and signage Rainbow Room, Rockefeller Ctr., N.Y.C.; designer N.Y. Unearthed Mus., N.Y.C., 1990; logo for Tony Kushner's Tony-award-winning play Angels in America, 1993; designer new Windows on the World Bar and Restaurant at the World Trade Ctr., N.Y.C., 1996, Land's End Direct Merchants; design cons. Stony Brook U., others. Trustee Cooper Union Art Sch., Maine Sch. Visual Arts. Recipient St. Gauden's medal Cooper Union, 1972, gold med. Soc. Illustrators, 1979, Soc. Indsl. Artists and Designers medal 1985, honors award AIA, 1992, Fulbright award for individual achievement Metro Internat., 1992; Fulbright scholar Acad. Fine Arts, Bologna, Italy, 1952-53; hon. fellow Royal Soc. Arts, 1979. Mem. Am. Inst. Graphic Arts (co-chair nat. conf. 1989, Gold medal 1972), Art Dirs. Club (Hall of Fame 1979), Alliance Graphique Internat. (Prix Savignac 1996). Jewish. Office: 207 E 32nd St New York NY 10016-6305

GLASER, PETER EDWARD, mechanical engineer, consultant; b. Zatec, Bohemia, Czechoslovakia, Sept. 5, 1923; came to U.S., 1948, naturalized July, 1954; s. Hugo and Helen (Weiss) G.; m. Eva F. Graf, Oct. 16, 1955; children: David, Steven, Susan. Diploma, Leeds Coll. Tech., Eng., 1943; 1st state exam, Czech Tech H.S., Prague, Czechoslovakia, 1948; MS, Columbia U., N.Y.C., 1951, PhD, 1955. Head design dept. Werner Mgmt. Co., N.Y.C., 1948-53; profl. staff Arthur D. Little, Inc., Cambridge, Mass., 1955-64, sect. mgr., 1973-84, v.p., 1973-94, cons., 1994—; cons. NASA, Washington, 1963-67, mem. adv. coun., 1986; mem. case study task force Lunar Energy Enterpise, 1988-89; mgmt. adv. bd. Ctr. for Space Power, Tex. A&M U. System, 1990-94; sr. adv. bd. mem. Space Studies Inst., 1990—; mem. bd. assessment NIST program NRC, 1993-96; cons. NRC, Washington, 1960-62, panel mem., 1994—, Heritage Found., Washington, 1982-83; adv. panelist Office Tech. Assessment, Washington, 1980-81; mem. Awards Adv. Coun. of Space Found., 1988-96. Editor: The Lunar Surface Layer, 1964, Thermal Imaging Techniques, 1964, Solar Power Satellites-The Emerging Energy Option, 1993, Solar Power Satellites-A Space Energy System for Earth, 2d edit., 1998, Solar Power Systems in Space, Standard Handbook of Powerplant Engineering, 1998; assoc. editor Space Power Jour., 1980-86; editor-in-chief Jour. Solar Energy, 1972-85, mem. editl. bd., 1985-93; mem. editl. bd. Space Policy, Space Power, Jour. Practical Applications in Space, Solar Energy; patentee solar power satellite, 1973. Bd. overseers Combined Jewish Philantropies, Boston, 1984—; voting mem. engring. coun. Columbia U., N.Y.C., 1984; advisor Space Solar Power Rsch. Soc., Japan, 1998—. Recipient Carl F. Kayan medal Columbia U., 1974, Farrington Daniels award Internat. Solar Energy Soc., Australia, 1983; named to U.S. Space Found. Space Tech. Hall of Fame, 1996. Fellow AAAS, AIAA; mem. ASME, Internat. Astron. Fedn. (chmn. space power com. 1984-89), Internat. Acad. Astronautics, Internat. Solar Energy Soc. (pres. 1968-69), Am. Astron. Soc. (bd. dirs. 1977-84), Sunsat Energy Coun. (pres. 1978-94, chmn. 1994—), Nat. Space Soc. (bd. advisors 1990-94, dir. 1994-97, bd. govs. 1997—), United Socs. in Space (regent 1997—), Am. Soc. for Macro-Engring., Cosmos Club (Washington). Jewish. Avocation: archeology of Southern Arabia. Home: 62 Turning Mill Rd Lexington MA 02420-1010 Office: Arthur D Little Inc Acorn Park Cambridge MA 02140-2390

GLASER, ROB, communications company executive. CEO and chmn. Progressive Networks, Seattle; CEO Real Networks, Seattle, 1997—. Office: Real Networks 1111 3rd Ave Fl 29 Seattle WA 98101-3292*

GLASER, ROBERT EDWARD, lawyer; b. Cin., Jan. 12, 1935; s. Delbert Henry and Rita Elizabeth (Arlinghaus) G.; m. Kathleen Eileen Grannen, June 17, 1961; children—Petra M., Timothy X., Mark G., Bridget M., Christopher D., Jenny M., Michael F. BS in Bus. Adminstrn. cum laude, Xavier U., Cin., 1955; LLB, U. Cin., 1960; LLM, U. Chgo., 1962; postgrad., U. Tuebingen, Fed. Republic of Germany, 1961. Bar: Ohio 1960, U.S. Dist. Ct. (no. dist.) Ohio 1963, U.S. Ct. Fed. Claims 1992, U.S. Ct. Internat. Trade 1971, U.S. Tax Ct. 1970, U.S. Ct. Appeals (6th cir.) 1964. Assoc. Arter & Hadden, Cleve., 1963-69, ptnr., 1970—, chmn., 1983-92; arbitrator Cuyahoga County Ct. Common Pleas, Ohio, 1972—, Med. Malpractice Panel, 1985—, Mediator Settlement Week, 1990—; lectr. Cleve. Tax Inst., 1966—, mem. exec. com., 1980-84, chmn., 1982; lectr. Can.-U.S. Law Inst., 1980, Res. Officers Assn., 1970—, Ret. Officers Assn., 1995—; bd. dirs. Stelco Enterprises, Inc. Contbr. articles to legal jours. Sec. Bay View Hosp., 1972-81; trustee Mental Health Rehab. and Rsch., Inc., 1975-86, mem. exec. com., 1977-81, pres., 1979-81; mem. men's com. Cleve. Play Ho., 1965—; mem. joint mental health and corrections com. Fedn. Cmty. Planning, 1978-81; mem. Cleve. Coun. on Fgn. Affairs, 1987—; mem. vis. com. Coll. Law Cleve. State U., 1987-97; mem. Soc. of Benchers, Case Western Res. Univ. Coll. Law, 1988—; trustee Univ. Circle, Inc., 1989-99, mem. exec. com., 1989-99. Col. U.S. Army, ret. Ford Found. grantee, 1960. Fellow Am. Bar Found. (life); mem. Ohio Bar Assn., Nat. Bar Assn., Cleve. Bar Assn. (trustee 1983-87, chmn. bd. of com. grievance and discipline trial com. 1993—, gen. tax com. 1983—, lawyer assistance com. 1999—), Legal Aid Soc. Cleve., Am. Judicature Soc., 8th Jud. Conf. (life), Am. Arbitration Assn. (nat. and internat. panel arbitrators 1969—), Citizens League Greater Cleve., Order of Coif, Union Club, Pentagon Officers Athletic Club, Serra Internat., Cleve. Club (exec. com. 1987-88, 90-91, 93-98, pres. 1994-96), KC. Democrat. Roman Catholic. Home: 22895 Mastick Rd Cleveland OH 44126-3145 Office: Arter & Hadden 1100 Huntington Bldg 925 Euclid Ave Ste 1100 Cleveland OH 44115-1475

GLASER, ROBERT HARVEY, SR., pastor; b. Phila., May 4, 1935; s. Harvey A. and Janet (McKechnie) G.; m. Joan Williams, Nov. 16, 1957 (div. July 1979); children: Linda Hartwell, Diane Lim Myra Ward, Linda Carrano, Robert Sr., Teresa Garcia, David Glaser; m. Virginia Sue Fischer, May 27, 1990. AB, Grove City (Pa.) Coll., 1957; MDiv, Princeton (N.J.) Theol. Sem., 1960. Pastor Smithfield Presbyn. Ch., Amenia, N.Y., 1960-64; organizing pastor Westminster Presbyn. Ch., Warner Robins, Ga., 1964-69; pastor First Presbyn. Ch., Forest Hills, N.Y., 1967-81; mem. ch. redevelopment Prospect Heights Presbyn. Ch., Bklyn., 1981-86; pastor Colcord (W.Va.) and Clear Creek Presbyn. Chs., 1987-89; interim pastor First Presbyn. Ch., Nitro, W.Va., 1989; pastor First Presbyn. Ch., Hinton, W.Va., 1989—; moderator Presbytery of N.Y.C., 1976-77; cmn. Maj. Mission Fund, N.Y.C., 1979-81; bd. sec. Edwin Gould Svcs. for Children, N.Y.C., 1987-89. Mem. Second Chance panel D.A.'s Office, Queens, 1977-81. Named Eagle Scout Boy Scouts Am., 1950. Mem. Lions (treas. 1991—), Omicron Delta Kappa, Pi Gamma Mu. Home: 1519 Fayette St Hinton WV 25951-2018 Office: First Presbyn Ch Third Ave Hinton WV 25951

GLASER, ROBERT JOY, retired physician, foundation executive; b. St. Louis, Sept. 11, 1918; s. Joseph and Regina G.; m. Helen Louise Hofsommer, Apr. 1, 1949; children: Sally Louise, Joseph II, Robert Joy. SB, Harvard U., 1940, MD magna cum laude, 1943; DS (hon.), U. Health Scis.-Chgo. Med. Sch., 1972, Temple U., 1973, U. N.H., 1979, U. Colo., 1979; LHD, Rush Med. Coll., 1973; DS, Mt. Sinai Med. Sch., 1984; DS (hon.), Washington U., 1988, Thomas Jefferson U., 1991. Med. intern Barnes Hosp., St. Louis, 1944, asst. resident physician, 1945-46, resident physician, 1946-47, asst. physician, 1949-57; asst. resident physician Peter Bent Brigham Hosp., Boston, 1944-45; NRC fellow med. scis. Wash. U. Med. Sch., 1947-49, instr. medicine, 1949-50, asst. prof., 1950-56, asst. dean., 1947, 53-55, assoc. prof., 1956-57, assoc. dean, 1955-57; dean, prof. medicine Med. Sch. U. Colo., 1957-63, v.p. for med. affairs, 1959-63; vis. physician Washington U. Med. Service, St. Louis City Hosp., 1950, chief service, 1950-53, cons., 1953-57; attending physician Colo. Gen. Hosp., Denver, 1957-63; prof. social medicine Harvard U., Boston, 1963-65; pres. Affiliated Hosps. Ctr., Inc., 1963-65; v.p. med. affairs, dean Sch. Medicine, prof. medicine Stanford U., 1965-70, acting pres., 1968, cons. prof., 1972-97, prof. emeritus, 1997—; bd. dirs. Henry J. Kaiser Family Found., 1970-83, pres., chief exec. officer, 1972-83; attending physician Columbia-Presbyn. Med. Ctr., N.Y.C., 1971-72, clin. prof. medicine, 1971-72; dir. for med. sci. Lucile P. Markey Charitable Trust, 1984-97, trustee, 1989-97; bd. dirs. Alza Corp., Hanger Orthopedic Group; cons. medicine VA Hosp., Denver, 1957-63, Fitzsimons Army Hosp., Aurora, Colo., 1957-63, Lowry AFB, Denver, 1957-63; mem. nat. adv. council NIMH, 1970-72, Harvard Fund Council, 1953-56, Harvard Med. Alumni Council, 1956-59; assoc. mem. streptococal commn. Armed Forces Epidemiologic Bd., 1958-61; chmn. com. study nat. needs biomed. and behavioral research personnel Nat. Acad. Scis.-NRC, 1974-77; mem. vis. com. Med. Sch. Harvard U., 1968-74, Sch. Pub. Health, 1971-77; bd. visitors Charles Drew Postgrad. Med. Sch., 1972-79; mem. com. on med. affairs Yale U., 1969-82, adv. bd. Sch. Orgn. and Mgmt., 1976-84; vis. com. Tufts Med. Sch., 1974-84. Editor: Pharos, 1962-97, editor emeritus, 1997—; contbr. articles to sci. jours. and chpts. to books. Bd. regents Georgetown U., 1976-78; bd. dirs. Kaiser Found. Hosps., Kaiser Found. Health Plan, 1967-79, Council on Founds., 1974-79, Packard Humanities Inst., 1987—; trustee Commonwealth Fund, 1969-88, v.p., 1970-72; trustee David and Lucille Packard Found., 1984-96, Pacific Sch. Religion, 1972-77, Washington U., St. Louis, 1979-87, 88—, Albert and Mary Lasker Found., 1998—; trustee Palo Alto Med. Found., 1974—, vice chmn., 1991—; mem. Sloan Commn. on Govt. in Higher Edn., 1977-79. Master ACP; fellow AAAS, Am. Acad. Arts and Scis. (exec. bd., v.p. 1972-76), Royal Coll. Physicians of London; mem. Am. Clin. and Climatological Assn. (pres. 1982-83), Am. Fedn. Clin. Research (chmn. midwestern sect. 1954-55), Central Soc. Clin. Research (councillor 1955-58), Am. Soc. Clin. Investigation, Assn. Am. Med. Colls. (asst. sec. 1956-60, chmn. com. edn. and research 1958-63, mem. exec. council 1959-63, 76-79, v.p. 1963-64, chmn. exec. council and assembly 1968-69), Assn. Am. Physicians, Western Assn. Physicians (councillor 1960-63), Am. Soc. Exptl. Pathology, Nat. Inst. Allergy and Infectious Disease (tng. grant com. 1957-60), Inst. Medicine, Nat. Acad. Sci. (mem. exec. com. 1971-73, chmn. membership com. 1970-72, acting pres. 1970-71), Harvard Med. Sch. Alumni (pres. 1993-1994), Harvard Club (N.Y.C.), Century Club, Sigma Xi, Alpha Omega Alpha (bd. dirs. 1963-77). Office: 525 Middlefield Rd Ste 130 Menlo Park CA 94025-3447

GLASER, RONALD, microbiology educator, scientist; b. N.Y.C., Feb. 27, 1939; s. Irving and Pauline G.; m. Janice Kiecolt, Jan. 17, 1980; children: Andrew, Erik. BA, U. Bridgeport, 1962; MS, U. R.I., 1964; PhD, U. Conn., 1968; postgrad., Baylor Coll. Medicine, 1968-69. Asst. prof. microbiology Pa. State U., Hershey, 1970-73, assoc. prof., 1973-77; prof. Pa. State U., 1977-78; prof. chmn. dept. med. microbiology and immunology Coll. Medicine Ohio State U., Columbus, 1978-92; reviewer NIH and NIMH study sects., 1978-92; assoc. dean for rsch. and grad. edn. Ohio State U. Med. Ctr., Columbus, 1992-94, assoc. v.p. health sci. rsch., 1994—. Editor: (with T. Gottleib-Stematsky) Human Herpes Virus Infections: Clinical Aspects, 1982; (with others) Epstein-Barr Virus and Human Disease, 1987; (with J. Jones) Human Herpes Virus Infections, 1994; (with J. Kiecolt-Glaser) Handbook of Human Stress, 1994. NIH fellow, 1968-69; Franco-Am. exchange Program; Fogarty Internat. Center; NIH and INSRM fellow, 1975, 77; Leukemia Soc. Am. scholar, 1974-79. Fellow Acad. Behavioral Medicine Rsch.; mem. AAAS, Am. Soc. Microbiology. Office: Ohio State U 2175 Graves Hall 333 W 10th Columbus OH 43210-1239

GLASER, STEVEN JAY, lawyer; b. Tacoma, Dec. 5, 1957; s. Ernest Stanley and Janice Fern (Stone) G.; 1 child, Jacob Andrew. Student, Oxford (Eng.) U., 1979; BSBA, Georgetown U., 1980; JD, John Marshall Law Sch., 1983. ABar: Ill. 1983, Ariz. 1984, U.S. Dist. Ct. Ariz. 1984, U.S. Ct. Appeals (9th and D.C. cirs.) 1984. Law clk. to judge Maricopa County Superior Ct., Phoenix, 1983-84; asst. atty. gen. State of Ariz., Phoenix, 1984-85; staff atty. Ariz. Corp. Commn., Phoenix, 1985-90; sr. atty. regulatory affairs Tucson Electric Power Co., 1990-92, mgr. legal dept., 1992-94, mgr. contracts and wholesale mktg., 1994, v.p. wholesale/retail pricing and system planning, 1994—; v.p. Energy Svcs., 1996—. Mem. ABA, Ariz. Bar Assn., Ill. Bar Assn., Pima County Bar Assn., So. Ariz. Water Resources Assn. (bd. dirs. 1991-93), Tuscon Parks Found., Georgetown U. Alumni Assn., Phi Delta Phi. Republican. Jewish. Avocations: golf, tennis. Office: Tucson Electric Power Co PO Box 711 220 W 6th St Tucson AZ 85701-1093

GLASER, VERA ROMANS, journalist; b. St. Louis, Apr. 21, 1916; d. Aaron L. and Mollie (Romans); m. Herbert R. Glaser, Apr. 16, 1939; 1 dau., Carol Jane Barriger. Student, Washington U., St. Louis, George Washington U., Am. U., 1937-40. Reporter-writer Nat. Aero. mag., 1943-44; reporter Washington Times Herald, 1944-46; pub. relations specialist Great Lakes-St. Lawrence Assn., 1950-51; promotion specialist, writer Congl. Quar. News Features, 1951-54; writer-commentator radio sta. WGMS, Washington, 1954-55; mem. Washington bur. N.Y. Herald Tribune, 1955-56; press officer U.S. Senator Charles E. Potter, 1956-59; dir. pub. relations, women's div. Rep. Nat. Com., 1959-62; press officer U.S. Senator Kenneth B. Keating, 1962-63; Washington corr. N.Am. Newspaper Alliance, 1963-69, bur. chief, 1965-69; columnist, nat. corr. Knight-Ridder Newspapers, Inc., 1969-81; assoc. editor Washingtonian Mag., 1981-88, contbg. editor, 1988—; columnist Maturity News Svc., 1988-94; mem. Pres.'s Commn. on White House Fellows, 1969, Pres.'s Task Force on Women's Rights and Responsibilities, 1970; judge 1981 Robert Kennedy Journalism Awards. Free-lance writer nat. publs.; radio and TV appearances on Stas. WTOP-TV, ABC, PBS, C-SPAN. Mem. nat. bd. Med. Coll. Pa., 1977-88; bd. dirs. Washington Press Club Found., 1986-88; bd. dirs. Internat. Women's Media Found., 1990-98. Mem. White House Corrs. Assn., Nat. Press Club (bd. govs. 1988, 89), Washington Press Club (pres. 1971-72), Cosmos Club. Unitarian. Home and Office: 4201 Cathedral Ave NW Apt 304E Washington DC 20016-4953

GLASGOW, AGNES JACKIE, social welfare administrator, therapist; b. El Paso, Tex., July 23, 1941; d. Carl Lecota Pace and Henrietta Ford (Cozart) Robertson; m. Morgan Walton, Sept. 20, 1958 (div. 1979); children: Scotty Gene, Carley Earlene Walton DeVore; m. Phillip Sidney Glasgow, Aug. 9, 1986. Lic., Trinidad State Jr. Coll., Colo., 1968; AAS, Met. State Coll., Denver, 1979, BS, 1980; MPA, U. Colo., Denver, 1987. Cert. substance abuse counselor, Colo., Tenn. Pvt. practice Life Counseling Ctr., Denver, Memphis, 1980—; coord. masters program for substance abuse Met. State Coll., Denver, 1980-81; exec. dir. Concord Commons Counseling Ctr., Decatur, Ill., 1981-82; child care specialist Adams Community Mental Health Ctr., Commerce City, Colo., 1982-84; adolescent family counselor Parkside Lodge Colo., Thorhton, Colo., 1984-86; family therapist Charter Lakeside Hosp., Memphis, 1986-87; counselor, coord. Shelby State Community Coll., Memphis, 1987-88; supr. adolescent and young adult program Meth. Outreach, Memphis, 1988-90; sr. mental health specialist dual diagnosis unit Meth. Hosp. Cen., 1990-99, relapse prevention specialist, 1994-99; retired; cons., part-time instr. Shelby State C.C., Memphis. Contbr. articles to profl. jours. Com. mem. Youth Suicide Task Force, Memphis, 1988—. Recipient Vol. of Yr. award United Way, Decatur, Ill., 1982, Cmty. Svc. award scholarship Mental Health Soc., 1983, Outstanding Svc. award, 1989, Disting. Svc. award Sheriff Dept., Memphis, 1988; nominated Diamond award Memphis Mental Health Assn., 1994. Mem. Nat. Orgn. Human Svc. Workers, Nat. Orgn. Substance Abuse Counselors, Am. Assn. Counseling & Devel., Psi Chi (treas. 1979-80). Republican. Methodist. Avocations: reading, stained glass, hunting, fishing, sailing. Office: 10 Thomas 1265 Union Ave Memphis TN 38104-3415 also: 1835 Union Ave Ste 203 Memphis TN 38104-3942

GLASGOW, JESSE EDWARD, newspaper editor; b. Monroe, N.C., Mar. 28, 1923; s. Jesse Edwin and Alma (Brown) G.; m. Beth BonDurant, June 25, 1949; children—Jeffrey David, Charles Christopher. B.S., Wake Forest U., 1948. Reporter Kannapolis (N.C.) Ind., 1947, Durham (N.C.) Sun, 1948, Norfolk Virginian-Pilot, 1949-52; reporter Balt. Sun, 1953-59, financial editor, 1960—. Served with AUS, 1943-45. Democrat. Methodist. Home: 4904 Wilmslow Rd Baltimore MD 21210-2329 Office: Balt Sun Calvert And Centre St Baltimore MD 21278

GLASGOW, NORMAN MILTON, lawyer; b. Washington, Aug. 14, 1922; children—Norman M., Heather Glasgow Harris, Glenn. BS, U. Md., 1943; LLB, JD George Washington U., 1949. Bar: D.C. 1949, U.S. Supreme Ct. 1956, Md. 1960. Assoc. Wilkes, McGarraghy & Artis, Washington, 1949-55; ptnr. Wilkes & Artis, Washington, 1955-82; pres. Wilkes, Artis, Hedrick & Lane, Washington, 1982-86, sr. prin., 1988—. Bd. dirs., gen. counsel Greater Washington Bd. Trade, 1986, 87, 88; mem., chmn. Md. PAC, 1981-93; bd. govs. Washington Bldg. Congress; mem. Citizens Tech. Adv. Com. for Drafting Bldg. Code and Zoning Regulations, Washington, Commrs. Citizens Adv. Com. on Zoning, Washington, Balt. Conv. Ctr. Authority Transp. Revenue Com., Gov's. Salary Commn., Gov's. Special Com. on Vehicle Emissions Inspection Program, Gov.'s Adv. Redistricting Com.; chmn. Govs. Task Force Statewide Bldg. Performance Standards, Md. Stadium Authority, 1993-97, Md. Economic Growth, Resource Protection and Planning Commn., co-chair subcom. for updating state planning and zoning laws, 1993-97; chmn. Md. Econ. Growth Task Force; mem. Gov.'s Western. Md. Econ. Devel. Strategies Task Force, 1998—. Served to 1st lt. U.S. Army, 1942-46, ETO. Recipient Outstanding Alumni award George Washington U., 1985, Outstanding Service award D.C. Real Estate, Greater Washington Bd. Trade, 1978. Mem. Supreme Ct. Bar Assn., D.C. Bar Assn., Md. Bar Assn., Urban Land Inst., Am. Soc. Planning Ofcls., Washington Bldg. Congress, Nat. Assn. Bus. Economists, Nat. Conf. of States on Bldg. Codes and Standards, Lambda Alpha. Avocation: gardening. Home: 9012 Brickyard Rd Potomac MD 20854-1634 Office: Wilkes Artis Hedrick & Lane 1666 K St NW Ste 1100 Washington DC 20006-2897

GLASGOW, WILLIAM JACOB, lawyer, venture capitalist, business executive; b. Portland, Oreg., Sept. 29, 1946; s. Joseph Glasgow and Lena (Friedman) Schiff; m. Renée Vonfeld, Aug. 30, 1969; children: Joshua, Andrew. BS magna cum laude, U. Pa., 1968; JD magna cum laude, Harvard U., 1972. Bar: Oreg. 1972, U.S. Dist. Ct. Oreg. 1972, U.S. Ct. Appeals (9th cir.) 1978. Assoc. Rives, Bonyhadi & Drummond, Portland, 1972-76, ptnr., 1976-79; ptnr. Stoel, Rives, Boley, Fraser & Wyse, Portland, 1979-83; mng. ptnr. Perkins Coie, Portland, 1983-88; sr. v.p., gen. counsel PacifiCorp Fin. Svcs. Inc., Portland, 1988-89, chmn., CEO, 1989-95; sr. v.p. PacifiCorp, Portland, 1992-93, sr. v.p., CFO, 1993-95; pres. PacifiCorp Holdings Inc., Portland, 1992-95; pres., dir. NERCO, Inc., Portland, 1992-93; dir. Pacific-Telecom, Inc., 1992-93; co-chmn. Shaw, Glasgow & Co. LLC, 1995-96; pres., CEO BCN Data Sys. (a Bechtel/CellNet Data Sys. joint venture), Portland, 1996—; now sr. v.p., CFO PacifiCorp, Portland. Pres. bd. trustees Oreg. Mus. Sci. and Industry, Portland, 1981; pres. N.W. Fin. Symposium, Portland, 1985; trustee Oreg. Art Inst., 1990-92, 94—, Oreg. Grad. Inst. Sci. and Tech., 1991—, Discovery Inst., 1992—; pres. Portland Met. Sports Authority, 1992—; v.p. NIKE World Masters Games, 1994—; bd. dirs. Internat. World Masters Games, 1994—. Mem. Oreg. Bar Assn., Portland C. of C. (bd. dirs. 1983), Harvard Law Sch. Alumni Assn. (pres. Oreg. chpt. 1981). Democrat. Home: 3111 SW Talbot Rd Portland OR 97201-1673 Office: PacifiCorp 700 N Multnomah St Ste 1600 Portland OR 97232*

GLASHOW, SHELDON LEE, physicist, educator; b. N.Y.C., Dec. 5, 1932; s. Lewis and Bella (Rubin) G.; m. Joan Glashow; children: Jason David, Jordan, Brian Lewis, Rebecca Lee. AB, Cornell U., 1954; AM, Harvard U., 1955, PhD, 1958; DSc (hon.), Yeshiva U., 1978, U. Marseille, 1982, Adelphi U., 1989, Bar Ilan U., 1989, Gustave Adolphus Coll., 1989. NSF fellow U. Copenhagen, Denmark, 1958-60; rsch. fellow Calif. Inst. Tech., 1960-61; asst. prof. Stanford U., 1961-62; asst. prof., assoc. prof. U. Calif. at Berkeley, 1962-66; mem. faculty Harvard U., 1966—, prof. physics, 1967-84, Higgins prof. physics, 1979—, Mellon prof. scis., 1988—; disting. vis. scientist Boston U., 1984; cons. Brookhaven Nat. Lab., 1966-73, 75—; mem. sci. policy com. CERN, 1979-84; vis. prof. U. Marseille, 1971, MIT, 1974-80, Boston U., 1983; affiliated sr. scientist U. Houston, 1983—; univ. scholar Tex. A&M U., 1983-86. Author: (with Ben Bova) Interactions, 1988, Charm of Physics, 1990, From Alchemy to Quarks, 1994; contbr. articles to profl. jours. and popular mags.; founding editor Quantum mag., 1989—. Pres. Andrei Sakharov Inst., 1980-85, Nat. Com. for Excellence in Edn., 1985-88. Recipient J.R. Oppenheimer Meml. prize, 1977, George Ledlie prize, 1978, Nobel prize in physics, 1979, Castiglione di Sicilia prize, 1983, Erice Sci. for Peace prize, 1991; NSF fellow, 1955-60, Sloan fellow, 1962-66, CERN vis. fellow, 1968. Fellow Am. Phys. Soc., AAAS; mem. Am. Acad. Arts and Scis., Nat. Acad. Scis., Sigma Xi. *

GLASRUD, CLARENCE ARTHUR, English educator; b. Cass County, N.D., Oct. 15, 1911; s. Claus Christian Glasrud and Anna Maren Skrove Haugan; m. Barbara Adams Crawford, June 19, 1948; 1 child, Charles Crawford. BS, Moorhead State Tchrs. Coll., 1933; MA, Harvard U., 1951, PhD, 1953. Tchr. Becker County (Minn.) Dist. 107, 1929-30, Jr. H.S., Pelican Rapids, Minn., 1935-36; tchr. H.S., Lake City, Minn., 1936-40, Mankato, Minn., 1940-42; prof. Moorhead (Minn.) State Tchrs. Coll., 1947-57; prof. Moorhead State Coll., 1957-75, chmn. English dept., 1949-72; prof. Moorhead State U., 1975-77; ret. Editor: The Age of Anxiety, 1960, Hjalmar Hjorth Boyesen, 1963, A Heritage Deferred, 1981, Roy Johnson's Red River Valley, 1982, A Special Relationship, 1983, A Heritage Fulfilled, 1984, L'Heritage Tranquille, 1987, The Moorhead Normal School: A History, 1987, Moorhead State Teachers College: A History, 1989. Pres. Clay County Hist. Soc., Moorhead, 1960-78; rsch. dir. Red River Valley Hist. Soc., Moorhead, 1974-84; alderman City Coun., Moorhead, 1980-84. Tech. sgt. U.S. Army Air Corps, 1942-45, ETO. Named Disting. Alumnus, Moorhead State Coll., 1971, Century Alumnus, Moorhead State U., 1987. Mem. NEA (life), MLA (life), Norwegian Am. Hist. Assn. (life, bd. editors 1964-92), Studies in Am. Fiction (adv. editor 1974—), Rotary, Am. Legion. Avocations: tennis, gardening, travel. Home: 422 Sixth St South Moorhead MN 56560

GLASS, ALASTAIR MALCOLM, physicist, research director; b. Harrogate, Yorkshire, Eng., Aug. 2, 1940; s. Malcolm Alexander and Gwendolyn Glass; m. Jan Blandamer, Sept. 4, 1966; children: Fiona, Angus, Robert, Jessica. BS (spl.), Univ. Coll., London, 1961; PhD, U. B.C., 1964. Rsch. fellow Kings Coll., U. London, 1965-67; mem. tech. staff AT&T Bell Labs., Murray Hill, N.J., 1967-78; supr. AT&T Bell Labs., Holmdel, N.J., 1978-83; head optical device materials research AT&T Bell Labs., Murray Hill, 1983-89, asst. dir. material physics rsch., 1989-91, dir. passive components rsch. lab., 1991-96; dir. photonic components rsch. lab. Lucent Techs., 1996-97; dir. Photonics Rsch. Lab, 1997—; mem. U.S. reps. Internat. adv. Com. on Ferroelectricity, 1976-90, chmn. 1977-81; chmn. optical materials subcom. Conf. on Lasers and Electro-Optics, Balt., 1985, 86, program chmn., 1990, gen. chmn., 1993; mem. electronics working group NASA, 1984-85; Schrieffer com. NASA flight programs; adv. com. on piezoelectricity Office Naval Rsch., 1979-85, on materials rsch., 1985, 87, 89; materials rsch. adv. com. Pa. State U., 1983-89, chmn., 1988; NRC adv. com. basic sci. rsch. Army Rsch. Office, 1980-83; NRC com. on Optical Sci. and Tech., 1995—; NRC com. on Optical Sci. and Engring., 1995—; chmn. com. on process challenges in compound semiconductors Nat. Materials Adv. Bd. Author: Principles and Applications of Ferroelectrics, 1977, Application of Ferroelectric Polymers, 1987; editl. bd. Materials Letters, Ferroelectrics, Jour. Materials Chemistry; contbr. over 150 tech. papers to profl. jours.; holder 30 patents. Fellow IEEE (sr., assoc. editor Transactions on Ultrasonics, Ferroelectrics and Frequency Control, subcom. on ferroelectricity, treas. symposium application of ferroelectrics 1988, chair Lasers and Electroptics Soc. awards com. 1992-94), Optical Soc. Am. (bd. dirs. 1996—); mem. NAE. Avocations: sailing, skiing, tennis. Home: Blackpoint Horseshoe Rumson NJ 07760 Office: Bell Labs, Lucent Tech 700 Mountain Ave Rm 1a-164 New Providence NJ 07974-1208

GLASS, AMY JOCELYN, economist; b. Royal Oak, Mich., Mar. 20, 1966. BA, Williams Coll., 1988; PhD, U. Pa., 1993. Instr. Bryn Mawr (Pa.) Coll., 1992-93; asst. prof. Ohio State U., Columbus, 1993—. Contbr. articles to profl. jours. Mem. Am. Econ. Assn., Can. Econ. Assn., Internat. Econ. & Fin. Soc., Econometric Soc. Office: Ohio State U 1945 N High St Columbus OH 43210-1172

GLASS, ANDREW JAMES, newspaper editor; b. Warsaw, Poland, Nov. 30, 1935; came to U.S., 1941, naturalized, 1948; s. Martin Allan and Wanda (Mosewicka) G.; m. Eleanor Attianese Sorrentino, June 3, 1962; 1 child, Samuel Sorrentino. BA, Yale U., 1957. Fin. reporter N.Y. Herald Tribune, 1959-62, chief congl. corr., 1963-66; mem. nat. staff Washington Post, 1966-68; exec. asst. to U.S. Senator Charles Percy, Washington, 1968-70; sr. editor Nat. Jour., Washington, 1970-74; Washington corr. Cox Newspapers, 1974-77, chief Washington bur. 1977-97, sr. corr. 1997—; syndicated columnist N.Y. Times News Svc., 1980—. Chmn. Corr. Com. Refugee Relief, 1975-78. With U.S. Army, 1958; mem. Res., 1958-64. Mem. Am. Soc. Newspaper

Editors, Gridiron Club, Met. Club of Washington. Office: Cox Newspapers Washington Bur Ste 750 400 N Capitol St NW Washington DC 20001-1536

GLASS, CARSON MCELYEA, lawyer; b. Farmersville, Tex., Oct. 8, 1915; s. Emery Carson and Chassie Victoria (McElyea) G.; m. Miriam Celeste Mollberg, Oct. 8, 1938 (div.); 1 son, Christopher C.; m. Lois Adair Felder, Dec. 29, 1960 (dec. 1973); m. Rhoda Swegles Price, Feb. 2, 1979 (dec. 1989). B.A., U. Tex., 1941, LL.B., 1938. Bar: Tex. 1937. Atty. Justice Dept., 1938-39, Dept. Labor, 1939; spl. atty. antitrust div. Justice Dept., 1939-47; spl. asst. to atty. gen. U.S., 1947-48; ptnr. firm Fischer, Wood, Burney & Glass, Corpus Christi, Tex., 1949-50; mem. firm Clifford & Miller, Washington, 1950-68; ptnr. firm Clifford, Warnke, Glass, McIlwain & Finney, Washington, 1968-77, Clifford, Glass, McIlwain & Finney, Washington, from 1977; ptnr. Clifford & Warnke, to 1980; lectr. econs. U. Corpus Christi, 1948-50. Served to lt. (j.g.) USNR, 1943-46. Mem. ABA, Fed. Bar Assn. (nat. council 1961-69), D.C. Bar, State Bar Tex., White House Hist. Assn. (atty.-advisor 1961—, dir. 1975-76, dir. emeritus 1996—), Sat. Morning Coffee Soc. (Corpus Christi); founding mem. Nat. Lawyers Club, U.S. Supreme Ct. Hist. Soc. Home: 4131 Cobblers Ln Dallas TX 75287-6726

GLASS, CHRISTOPHER KEVIN, physician; b. Oakland, Calif., Aug. 13, 1955; s. William Charles and Arden Barbara (Raysor) G.; m. Renee Fitzmorris; children: Erin Rose, Bryan James, Megan Christine, Sean William. BA Biophysics, U. Calif., Berkeley, 1977; MD, U. Calif. San Diego, 1984, PhD Biology, 1984. Intern dept. medicine Brigham & Women's Hosp., Boston, 1984-85, resident dept. medicine, 1985-86; fellow div. endocrinology U. Calif. San Diego, La Jolla, 1986-89, asst. prof. medicine, 1989-95, assoc. prof. medicine, 1995—; cons. Parke-Davis, Ann Arbor, Mich., 1994-95, Ligand Pharms., San Diego, 1994-95. Contbr. articles to profl. jours. Recipient Wilson S. Stone award M.D. Anderson, Houston, 1989, Lucille P. Markey scholarship, Lucille P. Markey Trust, Miami, 1987. Fellow Am. Heart Assn. (Established Investigator award 1995); mem. Endocrine Soc., Am. Soc. for Clin. Investigation, Fedn. Am. Soc. of Exptl. Biologists. Achievements include the discovery that retinoic acid receptors bind to DNA as hetrodimers; discovery of allosteric interactions betwen retinoic acid and retinoid x receptors, nuclear receptor co-activators and corepressors. Office: U Calif San Diego 9500 Gilman Dr La Jolla CA 92093-5003*

GLASS, DAVID CARTER, psychology educator; b. N.Y.C., Sept. 17, 1930; s. Samuel and Dorothy (Braunstein) G.; m. Kathleen Kehoe, May 15, 1982. AB, NYU, 1952, MA, 1954, PhD, 1959, postdoctoral fellow, 1959-62. Mem. staff social psychologist Russell Sage Found., N.Y.C., 1963-71; assoc. prof. psychology Rockefeller U., N.Y.C., 1966-68; prof. psychology N.Y.U., N.Y.C., 1968-72; chmn., prof. dept. psychology U. Tex., Austin, 1972-75; vis. scholar Russell Sage Found., 1975-76; prof. psychology, dir. Lab. Biobehavior, CUNY Grad. Ctr., N.Y.C., 1976-82; prof. psychology and psychiatry SUNY, Stony Brook, 1982-94, vice provost for research and grad. studies, 1982-86, spl. advisor to provost, 1987-89, vice provost for rsch., 1990-93, prof. emeritus psychology, 1994—; vis. prof. psychology Inst. Health, Rutgers U., New Brunswick, N.J., 1994-96; cons. in field. Author: Behavior Patterns, Stress and Coronary Disease, 1977; co-author: (with J.E. Singer) Urban Stress: Experiments in Noise and Social Stressors, 1972 (AAAS prize 1971); contbr. articles to profl. jours. Fellow Am. Psychol. Assn., AAAS; mem. Am. Psychosomatic Soc., Soc. Psychophysiol. Research, Soc. Exptl. Social Psychology, Acad. Behavioral Medicine Research (pres. 1981-82), Sigma Xi, Phi Kappa Phi. Home: 330 E 33rd St Apt 11J New York NY 10016-9437

GLASS, DAVID D., department store company executive, professional baseball team executive; b. Liberty, Mo., 1935; married. Gen. mgr. Crank Drug Co., 1957-67; v.p. Consumers Markets Inc., 1967-76; exec. v.p. fin. Wal-Mart Stores Inc., Bentonville, Ark., to 1976, vice chmn., CFO, 1976-84, pres., 1984—, COO, 1984-88, CEO, 1988—, also bd. dirs.; CEO, chmn. bd. dirs. Kansas City Royals, 1993—. Office: Wal-Mart Stores Inc 702 SW 8th St Bentonville AR 72716 also: Kansas City Royals PO Box 419969 Kansas City MO 64141-6969*

GLASS, DOROTHEA DANIELS, physiatrist, educator; b. N.Y.C.; d. Maurice B. and Anna S. (Kleegman) Daniels; m. Robert E. Glass, June 23, 1940; children: Anne Glass Roth, Deborah, Catherine Glass Barrett, Eugene. BA, Cornell U., 1940; MD, Woman's Med. Coll. Pa., 1954; postgrad., U. Pa., 1960-61; DMS (hon.), Med. Coll. Pa., 1987. Diplomate: Am. Bd. Phys. Medicine and Rehab. (guest bd. examiner 1978, 89). Intern Albert Einstein Med. Center, Phila., 1954-55, clin. asst. dept. medicine, 1956-59, attending phys. medicine and rehab., 1968-70, chmn. dept. phys. medicine and rehab., sr. attending, 1971-85; chief rehab. medicine VA Med. Ctr., Miami, Fla., 1985-95; clin. prof. dept. orthopaedics and rehab. U. Miami Sch. Medicine, 1985—; Lois Mattox Miller fellow preventive medicine Woman's Med. Coll. Pa., 1955-56, instr. preventive medicine, 1956-59, instr. medicine, 1960-62; resident phys. medicine and rehab. VA Hosp., Phila., 1959-62, chief phys. medicine and rehab., 1966-68, cons., 1968-82; asst. clin. dir. Jefferson Med. Coll. Hosp., Phila., 1963-66, Camden County Stroke Program, Cooper Hosp., Camden, N.J., 1963-66; gen. practice medicine, Phila., 1956-59; asst. med. dir., chief rehab. medicine and rehab. Moss Rehab. Hosp., Phila., 1968-70, med. dir., 1971-82, sr. cons., 1982—; mem. active staff Temple U., Phila., 1968—, asso. prof. rehab. medicine, 1968-73, prof., 1973—, dir. residency tng. rehab. medicine, 1968-82; program dir. Rehab. Research and Tng. Center, 1977-80, chmn. dept. rehab. medicine, 1977-82; staff physician Hosp. Med. Coll. Pa., Phila., 1955-59, vis. asso. prof. neurology, 1973-79, clin. prof., 1977-82, vis. prof., 1982-96; mem. cons. staff Frankford Hosp., Phila., 1968-82, Phila. Geriatric Center, 1975-82; mem. active staff Willowcrest-Bamberger Hosp., Phila., 1980-82; asso. phys. medicine and rehab. U. Pa. Sch. Medicine, Phila., 1962-66; asst. prof. clin. phys. medicine and rehab., 1966-68; asst. clin. dir. dept. phys. medicine and rehab. Jefferson Med. Coll., Phila., 1963-66; cons. Vols. in Medicine Martin Meml. Hosp., Stuart, Fla., 1996—. Contbr. articles to profl. jours. Mem. profl. adv. com. Easter Seal Soc. Crippled Children and Adults Pa., 1975-82; active Goodwill Industries Phila., 1973-82, Cmty. Home Health Svcs. Phila., 1974-82, Ea. Pa. chpt. Arthritis Found., 1968-82. Recipient humanitarian svc. cert. Gov.'s Com. on Employment Handicapped, 1974, Outstanding Alumnae award Commonwealth of Pa. Bd., Hosp. Med. Coll. Pa., 1975, humanitarian award Pa. Easter Seal Soc., 1981, John Eiselie Davis award Am. Kinesiotherapy Assn., 1988, Carl Haven Young svc. award, 1994, Disting. Career award Moss Rehab. Hosp., 1997. Mem. AMA, Am. Acad. Med. Dirs., Am. Acad. Phys. Medicine and Rehab. (disting. clinician award 1995), Am. Assn. Electromyography and Electrodiagnosis (assoc.), Am. Assn. Sex Educators, Counselors and Therapists, Am. Burn Assn., Am. Coll. Angiology, Am. Coll. Utilization Rev., Am. Congress Rehab. Medicine (bd. govs., pres. 1986-87, gold Key award 1989), Am. Heart Assn. (coun. on cerebrovascular disease), Am. Lung Assn. Phila. and Montgomery County (bd. dirs. 1977-79), Am. Med. Women's Assn., Assn. Acad. Physiatrists, Assn. Med. Rehab. Dirs. and Coordinators, Coll. Physicians Phila., Emergency Care Rsch. Inst., Gerontol. Soc., Internat. Assn. Rehab. Facilities, Internat. Rehab. Medicine Assn., Pan Am. Med. Assn., Fla. Med. Assn., Fla. Soc. Phys. Medicine and Rehab. (pres. 1975-77), Pa. Med. Soc. (phys. medicine and rehab. adv. com. 1975-82), Pa. Thoracic Soc., Delaware Valley Hosp. Coun. Forum, Phila. Med. Soc., Phila. PSRO (bd. dirs. 1975-82), Phila. Soc. Phys. Medicine and Rehab. (pres. 1968-69), Laennec Soc. Phila., Royal Soc. Health, Alpha Omega Alpha.

GLASS, FRED STEPHEN, lawyer; b. Asheboro, N.C., Oct. 17, 1940; s. Emmett Frederick and Colene F. (Foust) G.; m. Gloria A. Grant, June 12, 1964; 1 child, Elizabeth Foust; m. Martha G. Daughtry, June 9, 1982. BA, Wake Forest U., 1963, JD, 1966. Bar: N.C. 1966, U.S. Dist Ct. (ea. dist.) N.C. 1966, (mid. dist.) N.C., (we. dist.) N.C.; U.S. Ct. Appeals (4th cir.), U.S. Supreme Ct. Research asst. presiding justice N.C. Supreme Ct., 1966-67; ptnr. Miller, Beck, O'Briant and Glass, Asheboro, N.C., 1971-77; exec. dir. and legal counsel N.C. Democratic Party, 1977-78; dep. commr. N.C. Indsl. Commn., 1978; spl. Congl. asst. 4th Congl. Dist. N.C., 1979; ptnr. Harris, Cheshire, Leager and Southern, Raleigh, N.C., 1979-86; ptnr. Poyner and Spruill, Raleigh, 1987-94; Brooks, Stevens & Pope, P.A., Cary, 1994-98; mng. ptnr. Glass & Vining, LLC, 1998—; prof. law and govt. Asheboro Jr. Coll. Bus., 1973-76. Author: Legal Guide for Reserve Commanding Officers; contbg. editor: N.C. Will Drafting and Probate Practice Handbook, 1983; contbr. articles to profl. jours. Basketball coach and fitness instr. Randolph County YMCA; pub. chmn., United Appeal; bd. dirs., Randolph County Emergency Med. Technician Bd., Capital Bank; mem. adv. bd. Naval War Coll. operations law; active Dem. campaigns, Boy Scouts Am., council commr. for Roundtables, 1980-89, asst. dist. commr. 1979-84, asst. scoutmaster; mem. nat. com. Boy Scouts of Am., council ex. bd., council commr., chancellor, council commrs. coll., 1980-83, Boy Scouts Am. Nat. Com., 1987-90, coun. pres. 1994-96; force judge adv. COMRNCF, 1985-89; v.p. Healthcare Bus. Mgmt., LLC. Rear adm. JAGC, USNR. Disting. Svc. Medal award, 1996. Meritorious Svc. medal with gold star, Meritorious Unit Commendation, Nat. Meritorious Svc. award USNR, 1995, Navy Commendation medal with Gold Star, Nat. Defense Svc. medal with Bronze Star, Seabee Combat Warfare Specialist Cert.; recipient numerous Scouters Tng. award Boy Scouts Am., Disting. Eagle Scout award, 1991, Young Man of Yr. award City Asheboro. Mem. ABA (standing com. on armed forces law), Randolph County Bar Assn. (pres. 1971-74), 19th Jud. Dist. Bar Assn. (pres. 1974-75), N.C. Bar Assn. (chmn. young lawyer sect. Randolph County), Dist. Criminal Law Symposium (chmn. 1976), N.C. Def. Lawyers Assn. (computer in litigation support 1989), N.C. Bar Assn. (computers in law office 1995), N.C. Coun. Entrepreneurial Devel., N.C. Bar Found., Cary C. of C. (bd. dirs.), Rotary, Sovereign Mil. Order Temple Jerusalem, Naval Order U.S. Democrat. Methodist. Fax: 919-233-7151. Home: 113 Whispering Pines Ct Cary NC 27511-4059 Office: PO Box 5894 Cary NC 27512-5894

GLASS, HENRY PETER, industrial designer, interior architect, educator; b. Vienna, Austria, Sept. 24, 1911; came to U.S., 1939; s. Ernst and Berta (Zaitschek) G.; m. Eleanor C. Knopp, Mar. 4, 1937; children: Ann Karin, Peter. Diploma architect, Wiener Tech. Hochschule, Vienna, 1933; M.Arch., Meisterschule Prof. Theiss, Vienna, 1935; Indsl. Design, Sch. Design, Chgo., 1953. Prin. architect Studio H. Glass, Vienna, 1935-38; designer Office Gilbert Rohde, N.Y.C., 1939-40, Morris Sanders, N.Y.C., 1940; head design dept. W.L. Stensgaard Assocs., Chgo., 1941-45; prin. Henry P. Glass, Assocs., Northfield, Ill., 1946—; prof. indsl. design Chgo. Art Inst., 1946-69. Designs include, Swingline, Children's Furniture; patentee in field; author: Design & Consumer, 1981, The Shape of Manmade Things, 1996; one-man show Hochschule Für Angewandte Kunst, Vienna, Austria, 1997. Trustee Bd. of Northfield, 1966-67; pres. Am. Friends of Austria, 1990—. Recipient Ann. award Fine Hardwoods Assn., 1955, 56, Best Booth award Ski Show Expo Ctr., Chgo., 1972, Excellence in Design award Indsl. Design Mag., 1978, Golden Merit award City of Vienna, 1986, Cross of Honor for Arts and Scis., Republic of Austria, 1987, Good Design award Chgo. Atheneum, 1992. Fellow Indsl. Design Soc. Am. (chmn. Chgo. chpt. 1959-60, nat. vice chmn. 1960-62). Roman Catholic. Clubs: Am. Friends of Austria (v.p. 1976, then pres.); Austro Am. Council for the Mid-West (Chgo.) (pres. 1983-84). Home: 245 Dickens Rd Northfield IL 60093-3228 Office: Henry P Glass Assocs PO Box 52 Northfield IL 60093-0052 *A designer's Thoughts: Anything man can perceive with his senses that isn't made by God and which is not a one-time creation by an artist, had it's origin on a drawing board.*

GLASS, HERBERT, music critic, lecturer, editor; b. Frankfurt am Main, Germany, 1934; m. Susanne Pleibel; 1 child, Alexander. BA in English, Brandeis U. Asst. pub. rels. dir. N.Y. Philharm., 1962-65; dir. pub. rels. San Francisco Opera, 1965-67; sr. editor, editor in chief Performing Arts Network, Performing Arts mag., L.A., 1967-90; music reviewer, columnist L.A. Times, 1970-97; cons. Nat. Pub. Radio, 1979-84; editorial supr. Calif. Theatre Ann., 1982-84. Columnist On the Record, L.A. Times Sunday Calendar, 1972-97; contbr. Punch mag., London, San Francisco Chronicle, Gramophone, The Strad, Chamber Music, Opera News, Finnish Music Quar., Nordic Sounds, New Grove Dictionary; annotator L.A. Philharm., Salzburg Festival, RCA Victor Records; broadcaster weekly and monthly programs Sta. KUSC-FM, L.A., 1981-86; editor Olympic Arts Festival mag., 1984, UK/LA Festival mag., 1988; broadcaster, commentator CBC. Music lectr. Orange County Performing Arts Ctr. Mem. Nat. Acad. Rec. Arts and Scis., Chamber Music Am. Home: 3264 Primera Pl Los Angeles CA 90068-1554

GLASS, JEAN ANN, special education services professional; b. Phoenix, Ariz., Mar. 15, 1934; d. James Leslie Giffin and Helen Lucille Griffith; m. Dwaine Charles Glass, Nov. 26, 1952; children: Michael James, Stephen Charles, Daphne Ann, Diona Lynn, Helen Louise, Geoffrey Giffin. *A sample of pioneers in Jean's family genealogy include John Flood arriving in America at Jamestown on the "Swan" in 1610, Margaret, the widow of William Flinch, on the "Supply" in 1620, and Edward Fuller and his son, Samuel, arriving at Plymouth on the "Mayflower" in November 1620. Jean's father, Major James Leslie Giffin, was a lawyer and pioneer flyer in all of the Americas, Hawaii, the Philippine Islands, and WWI and WWII. Her mother, Helen Lucille Griffith Giffin VerBrugghen, was one of the earliest Registered Nurses in Arizona and later a pioneer specialist taking electroencephalograms in Nevada.* Student, U. Nev., 1950-52; AA in Psychology, Mt. San Antonio Coll., 1973, AS in Mental Health, 1974; BA in Behavioral Sci., Calif. Polytechnic U., 1975; MA in Spl. Edn., Calif. State U., L.A., 1979, MA in Psychology, 1983; MS in Devel. Disabilities Programming, U. La Verne, 1981, postgrad., 1981-85; postgrad., Azusa Pacific U., 1989. Instr. devel. disabled Chaffey C.C., Alta Loma, Calif., 1975-79; program dir. sch.-age parenting and infant devel. El Monte (Calif.) Union High Sch. Dist., 1981-95, tchr., 1981—; family life educator Nat. Coun. Family Rels., Mpls., 1988—; therapeutic recreation specialist Nat. Coun. Therapeutic Recreation, Thiells, N.Y., 1975—; rschr., psychiat. technician Frank D. Lanterman State Hosp. & Devel. Ctr., Pomona, Calif., 1981-94. Recipient cert. commendation State of Calif., 1985, City of El Monte, 1993. Mem. DAR, AAUW, Nat. Geneal. Soc., Coun. Exceptional Children, Archaeol. Survey Assn. So. Calif., Inc., Bibl. Archaeology Soc., L.A. World Affairs Coun., El Monte Cmty. Cultural Commn.'s Sister City Assn., Pomona Valley Personal Ancestral File Users Group, San Gabriel/Pomona Valley Alumnae Panhellenic Assn., Calif. Fedn. Chaparral Poets, Internat. Biograph. Ctr. (Order of Internat. Fellowship 1998—), Gamma Phi Beta. Republican. Mem. LDS Ch. Avocations: genealogy, archaeology, history, the arts. Office: El Monte Union H S Dist 3537 Johnson Ave El Monte CA 91731-3290

GLASS, JOHN DEREK See HOOPER, IAN

GLASS, JOHN SHELDON, manufacturing executive; b. Glens Falls, N.Y., Mar. 10, 1936; s. John Wilbur and Josephine Emily (Sheldon) G.; m. Sharon Brackett, June 20, 1987; children by previous marriage: John S., Sarah S. AB, Union Coll., Schenectady, 1958; MS, MIT, 1960. Asst. sec. No. Nigeria Ministry of Econ. Planning, Kaduna, 1960-62; mgr. product devel. Polaroid Corp., Cambridge, Mass., 1962-68; mktg. mgr. Millipore Corp., Bedford, Mass., 1968-76; dir. investor relations Millipore Corp., Bedford, 1976-85; v.p. Millicorp, Bedford, 1985-94; v.p., gen. mgr. BioSearch, 1994—; v.p., chief fin. ofcr. MLI Pharmaceuticals, 1995—; bd. dirs., exec. com. Protein Databases, Inc., Li Med., Inc.; founder, dir. Glyko Biomedical Ltd.; founder BioMarin Pharms., 1998; mem. IRB-Dana Farber Cancer Inst., 1995—; faculty mem. Bentley Coll. Pres., regional gov. Sloan Club MIT, Cambridge, 1980-86; mem. Carroll Wilson award com., 1985-86. Recipient Frank Bailey prize, Union Coll., 1958; Eliphalet Nott scholar, 1958; MIT fellow in Africa, 1960-62. Mem. Nat. Investor Rels. Inst. (bd. dirs. 1978-83), Kaduna Club, Phi Beta Kappa, Kappa Sigma. Avocations: golf, sailing, wild flower photography, skiing, pottery. Home: 48 Main St Boxford MA 01921-2502

GLASS, KENNETH EDWARD, management consultant; b. Ft. Thomas, Ky., Sept. 28, 1940; s. Clarence E. and Lucille (Garrison) G.; m. Nancy Romanek, May 9, 1964; children: Ryan, Lara. ME, U. Cin., 1963, MS, 1965, grad. student, 1967. Registered profl. engr., Ohio. With Allis Chalmers Mfg. Co., Cin. and Eng., 1963-73; v.p. mfg. Fiat Allis Contrn. Machinery, Inc., Chgo., 1973-75; pres. Perkins Diesel Corp., Canton, Ohio, 1975-77; pres., chief exec. officer Massey-Ferguson, Inc., Des Moines, 1978, v.p., gen. mgr. N.Am. ops. Massey Ferguson Ltd., Des Moines, 1978; chmn., pres., chief exec. officer Union Metal Mfg. Co., Canton, Ohio, 1979-85; pres. Glass & Assocs. Inc., 1985—, chmn., 1996—; pres. Stony Point Group, Inc., 1996—, also bd. dirs.; chmn. Utica Corp.; bd. dirs. Thames Water Holdings, Turnaround Mgmt. Assn.; trustee U. Cin. Found. Mem. Young Presidents Orgn., ASME, Soc. Automotive Engrs., Turnaround Mgmt. Assn., Assn. Cert. Turnaround Profls. (bd. dirs., v.p. 1993-94, pres. 1995-96), Am. Bankrupcy Inst., Pi Tau Sigma. Patentee in field.

GLASS, LAUREL ELLEN, gerontologist, developmental biologist, physician, retired educator; b. Selma, Calif., Oct. 1, 1923; d. Sydney L. and Marie (Damron) G. B.A., U. Calif.-Berkeley, 1951; Ph.D., Duke U., 1958; M.D., U. Calif., San Francisco, 1974. Teaching asst. zoology Duke U., 1953-56; rsch. assoc. Pathology Rsch. Lab. Med. Rsch. divsn. VA Hosp., Durham, N.C., 1957-58; instr. dept. anatomy U. Calif. Med. Sch., San Francisco, 1958-61, asst. prof., 1961-66, assoc. prof., 1968-72, prof., 1972-89, prof. emeritus, 1989—, prof. psychiatry, 1984-89, prof. emeritus, 1989—, dir. Ctr. on Deafness, 1984-89, adj. prof. family and community medicine, 1983-89; dir. project on adaptation to adult onset hearing loss Langley Porter Psychiat. Inst., U. Calif. Med. Sch., San Francisco, 1989-92; mem. San Francisco adv. com. Child Health and Disability Prevention Program, 1974-79; mem. exec. com., bd. dirs. Mission Neighborhood Health Ctr., 1974-77; mem. med. adv. com. Coalition for Med. Rights of Women, 1974-87; mem. adv. bd. P.R. Orgn. Women Health Edn. Project, 1976-78; v.p. Developmental Disabilities Programs, Inc., 1976-87. Co-author: Beyond Refuge: Coping with Losses of Vision and Hearing in Later Life, 1989; co-editor: State of the Art: Research Priorities in Deaf-Blindness, 1985, Mental Health Assessment of Deaf Clients: A Manual, 1987, Mental Health Assessment of Deaf Clients: Special Conditions, 1989; contbr. articles to profl. jours. Mem. edn. commn. NAACP, Ocean View-Merced Heights Community Stblzn. and Improvement Project, exec. com. Ocean View-Ingleside Dist. Council, Bay Area Social Planning Council, 1969-73, adv. council Nat. Ctr. for Vision and Aging, 1986-94; bd. dirs. Service Com. on Pub. Edn., 1963-66, Constl. Rights Found., 1965-73, Deaf Counseling, Adv. and Referral Agency (DCARA), 1985-86, Hearing Soc. for the Bay Area, Inc., 1984-86, 93-96; trustee Self-Help for Hard of Hearing People, Inc., 1986-89, Glide Found., 1966-75, Gallaudet U., Washington, 1986-99; bd. govs. Pub. Advs. Inc., 1975-79; mem. San Francisco Bd. Edn., 1967-71, pres., 1969; regent Lone Mountain Coll., 1973-76; pres. United Meth. Congress of the Deaf, 1993-99. Recipient Spl. Friend of Persons with Hearing Loss award, 1993. Mem. Am. Assn. Anatomists, Gerontol. Soc. Am., Am. Soc. on Aging, Self Help for Hard-of-Hearing People, Inc., Assn. Late Deafened Adults, Am. Deafness and Rehab. Assn., Phi Beta Kappa, Sigma Xi. Democrat. Methodist. Home: 1300 NE 16th Ave Apt 1408 Portland OR 97232-4405

GLASS, LAWRENCE, business executive. Sr. v.p., dir. devel. SRA Technologies, Inc., Falls Church, Va.; pres. SRA Life Sci., 1998. Office: SRA Life Scis Inc 8110 Gatehouse Rd Falls Church VA 22042-1210*

GLASS, MILTON LOUIS, retired manufacturing company executive; b. Burlington, Vt., Mar. 7, 1929; s. Joseph and Mary Lena (Smith) G.; m. Renee Peritz, Feb. 5, 1950; children: Jill Sharlene, Mikel Lewis. Grad., Bentley Coll., 1948; BBA with high honors, Northeastern U., 1954, MBA, 1956; postgrad. in program for mgmt. devel., Harvard U., 1962. With Gillette Co., Boston, 1952-93; ret., immediate past v.p. fin. and chief investor rels.; chmn. Blue Cross and Blue Shield Mass., Inc., 1968—, Forsyth Dental Ctr., 1983—; co-founder, co-pres. Jawjoints and Allied Musculo-Skeletal Disorders Found., 1982—; exec.-in-residence, prof. fin. Northeastern U., Boston, 1994—; treas. Elderhostel, 1996—; chmn. Health Policy & Prodecure Inst., 1996—. Chmn. Sch. Com., Mashpee, Mass., 1970-76; officer Exec. Res. Corps, U.S. Govt.; chmn. Internat. Bus. Ctr. of New Eng.; bd. dirs., treas. United Way of Massachusetts Bay; mem. vis. bd. overseers Harvard Med. and Dental Schs., 1994—. With AUS, 1948-51. Named Am.'s Best Chief Fin. Officer in Cosmetics Industry, Insltl Investor, 1986, Best Investor Rels. Contact, 1989, 90, 91, 92. Mem. Nat. Investor Rels. Inst. (bd. dirs. 1990—). Home: 790 Boylston St Boston MA 02199-7928 Office: Forsyth Dental Ctr 140 Fenway Boston MA 02115-3799

GLASS, PHILIP, composer, musician; b. Balt., Jan. 31, 1937; s. Benjamin C. and Ida (Gouline) G.; m. JoAnne Akalaitis (div.); children: Juliet, Zachary; m. Linda Burtyk, 1980 (div.); m. Candy Jernigan (dec. 1991). AB, U. Chgo., 1956; MS in Composition, Julliard Sch. Music, 1964; composition student with, Nadia Boulanger, Paris, 1964-66. Composer in residence Pitts. Pub. Schs., 1962-64; founder, performer Philip Glass Ensemble, 1968—; former taxi cab driver. Various European concert tours, 1968—, U.S. tours, 1972—; founder: (record co.) Chatham Sq. Prodns., N.Y.C., 1972; composer: (opera) Einstein on the Beach, 1975 (with Robert Wilson), The Panther, 1980, Satyagraha, 1980, The Photographer, 1982, The Civil Wars: A Tree is Best Measured When It Is Down, 1983, Akhnaten, 1983, (with Robert Morau) Juniper Tree, 1986, The Making of the Representative for Planet 8, 1987, The Fall of the House of Usher, 1988, 1000 Airplanes on the Roof, 1988, The Voyage, 1992, Orphée, 1993, La Belle et la Bete, 1994; (film music) North Star, 1977, Geometry of a Circle, 1979, Koyaanisqatsi, 1981, Mishima, 1985, Dialogue, 1986, Dead End Kids, 1986, Hamburger Hill, 1987, Powaqqatsi, 1987, The Thin Blue Line, 1988, A Brief History of Time, 1992, Candyman, 1992, Candyman II: Farewell to the Flesh, 1994; (symphonies and orchestral music) Company, 1983, Music from the Civil Wars, 1984, Dance from Akhnaten, 1984, Concerto for violin and orch., 1987, The Light, 1987, The Canyon, 1988, Symphony No. 2, 1994; (chamber and instrumental music) String Quartet, 1966, In Again Out Again, 1967, Pieces in the Shape of a Square, 1967, Strung Out, 1967, Gradus, 1969, How Now, 1968, Two Pages, 1968, Music in Contrary Motion, 1969, Music in Eight Parts, 1969, Music in Fifths, 1969, Music in Similar Motion, 1969, Music with Changing Parts, 1970, Music in Twelve Parts, 1971-74, Another Look at Harmony, 1975, Modern Love Waltz, 1977, Music for a Performance/Reading by C. DeJong: Fourth Series Part II, 1978, Mad Rush: Fourth Series Part III, 1979, Dance No. 2, 1979, Dance No. 4, 1979, Facades, 1981, Glassworks, 1984, Floe, 1983, String Quartet No. 2: Company, 1983, String Quartet No. 3: Mishima, 1985, String Quartet No. 4: Boczak, 1989, Low Symphony, 1993; (vocal and choral music) Knee Play No. 3, 1976, Fourth Series Part I, 1978, Vessels, 1981, Habeve Song, 1982, Hymn to the Sun, 1982, Civil Wars, 1984 (Rome sect.), Three Songs, 1986, Itaipu, 1988, Hydrogen Jukebox, 1990; (incidental music) Play, 1965, Red Horse Animation, 1968, Music for Voices, 1972, The Lost Ones, 1975, The Saint and the Football Player, 1975, Dressed Like an Egg, 1977, Cascando, 1979, Mercier and Camier, 1979, Dead End Kids, 1980, Company, 1983, Pages from Cold Harbor, 1983, Endgame, 1984; (pop albums) Songs from Liquid Days, 1986, (spl. events) Ceremonial Music at 1984 Olympics; collaborators: JoAnne Akalaitis, Robert Wilson, Paul Simon, Allen Ginsberg; author: (with C. DeJong) Satyagraha: M.K. Gandhi in South Africa 1893-1914, 1980, Music by Philip Glass, 1987. Recipient Broadcast Music Industry award, 1960, Lado prize, 1961, Benjamin award, 1961-62, Young Composer's award Ford Found., 1964-66; named Musician of Yr., Musical Am. mag., 1985; composition grantee Fulbright, 1966-67, Found. for Contemporary Performance Arts, 1970-71, Changes, Inc., 1971-72, Nat. Endowment for the Arts, 1974-75, Menil Found., 1974. Mem. ASCAP, SACEM (France). Office: Internat Prodn Assoc 584 Broadway Rm 1008 New York NY 10012-3253*

GLASS, RENÉE, educational health foundation executive; b. Elizabeth, N.J., Jan. 27, 1928; d. Samuel and Helen Peritz m. Milton L. Glass, Feb. 5, 1950; children: Jill S., Mikel L. Student, Tufts U., 1952, Northeastern U., 1954, U. Mass., 1984-85. Bd. dirs. Inst. of Contemporary Art, Boston, 1979-83; pres. Connoisier Network, Boston, 1981; founder, pres. Jaw Joints Found., Boston, 1982—; dir. Goldberg Ctr., Northeastern U., Boston, 1993—, exec.-in-residence, 1994—, mem. wellness com., 1994—; participant, lectr. health forums, NIH, 1982—; bd. dirs. Health Practice and Policy Inst. Author numerous booklets and pamphlets on temporomandibular joint disorders, 1982—; mem. editl. bd. Bus. Ethics Resource. Mem. examining com. Boston Pub. Libr., 1983-84. Mem. Internat. Catacomb Soc. (bd. dirs. 1987-97). Office: Jaw Joints/Musculo-Skeletal Disorders Found Forsyth Inst 140 Fenway Boston MA 02115-3782

GLASS, ROBERT DAVIS, judge; b. Wetumpka, Ala., Nov. 28, 1922; s. Isaiah and M.E. (Davis) G.; m. Doris E. Powell, Dec. 9, 1951; children: Robert Jr., Roberta Diane, Rosalyn Doris. BA, N.C. Cen. U., 1949, JD, 1951, LLD (hon.), 1988; LLD (hon.), U. Bridgeport, 1990. Bar: N.C. 1951, Conn. 1962. Pvt. practice Charlotte, N.C., 1951-53, New Bern, N.C., 1953-60; claims examiner Hartford, Conn., 1961-62; pvt. practice Waterbury, Conn., 1962-66; asst. U.S. atty. U.S. Dist. Ct. Conn., New Haven, 1966-67; judge Conn. Juvenile Ct., 1967-78, Conn. Superior Ct., 1978-84; adminstrv. judge, superior ct. Conn. Jud. Dist., Waterbury, 1984-87; assoc. justice Conn. Supreme Ct., Hartford, 1987-92, judge trial referee, 1992—. Pres. Conn. Fedn. Black Dem. Clubs, 1965-66; former mem. Appeals Bd. Conn. Justice Commn.; bd. dirs. Pearl Street Neighborhood House, Waterbury, 1965-66, pres. 1966; trustee Post Coll., Waterbury, 1986; bd. of visitors Law

Sch. N.C. Cen. U., 1988. Served with U.S. Army, 1943-46. Fellow Am. Bar Found.; mem. ABA, Nat. Bar Assn. (life), Nat. Bar Assn. Jud. Coun., Am. Judicature Soc., Conn. Bar Assn., Waterbury Bar Assn., Omega Psi Phi. Baptist. Lodges: Elks, Masons. Avocation: golf. Office: Conn Superior Ct 300 Grand St Waterbury CT 06702-1900

GLASS, STEPHEN TOLMAN, pediatric neurologist; b. Jan. 30, 1948. AB cum laude, Harvard Coll., 1970; MD, U. Vt., 1974. Diplomate Am. Bd. Psychiatry & Neurology, Am. Bd. Pediatrics. Child neurologist pvt. practice, Seattle, 1980—; clin. assoc. prof. neurology, pediatrics & neurosurgery U. Wash., Seattle, 1988—. Office: Nordstrom Med Tower 1229 Madison Ste 1090 Seattle WA 98104

GLASS, WAYNE, legislative staff member; b. Balt., Sept. 1, 1945. BA in Polit. Sci., Princeton U., 1968; MA, U. Denver, 1977, PhD, 1983; MPA with distinction, U. Colo., 1979. Tchr., athletic dir. Green Fields Sch., Tucson, 1972-75; grad. intern arms transfer divsn. U.S. Arms Control and Disarmament Agy., 1978; presdl. mgmt. intern Office Sec. Def., 1979-81, program analyst, 1981-86; prin. analyst Nat. Security Divsn., Congl. Budget Office, 1986—. Contbr. articles to profl. jours. Bd. dirs. Handicapped Encounter Christ Internat., Wasihngton; chmn. Princeton Alumni Schs. Com. Md.; mentor U. Denver Grad. Sch. Internat. Rels.; instr. ESOL, Jewish Cmty. Ctr., Bethesda, Md.; Sunday sch. tchr. Dumbarton United Meth. Ch., Washington. Lt. USN, 1968-72. USNROTC scholar Princeton U., 1963; univ. fellow U. Denver, 1975-79, Fackt fellow U. Denver, 1979. Mem. Pi Alpha Alpha. E-mail: WayneG@CBO.gov. Fax: 202-226-1960. Office: 703 Hart Senate Office Bldg Washington DC 20510-3102

GLASSBERG, ALAN BURNETT, physician; b. Charleston, S.C., Jan. 23, 1937; s. Joseph and Helen (Bebergal) G.; m. Lissa Marie Rohrberg, June 13, 1979; children: Jordan Joseph, Lauren Marie-Helene, Connor Robert, Alexander Forrest. BS, Coll. Charleston, 1958; MD, Med. U. S.C., 1962. Diplomate Am. Bd. Internal Medicine, Am. Bd. Hematology, Am. Bd. Med. Oncology. Intern U. Pa. Hosp., 1962-63, resident, 1963-69; practice medicine San Francisco, 1969-80; dir. med. oncology U. Calif.- Mt. Zion Med. Ctr., San Francisco, 1980—; clin. prof. medicine U. Calif., San Francisco, 1983—; trustee Am. Cancer Soc., San Francisco, 1980-83, Norcal Cancer Program, Palo Alto, Calif., 1980-85; assoc. dir. Univ. Calif. San Francisco Cancer Ctr. Fellow ACP; mem. AMA, Calif. Med. Assn., Calif. Acad. Medicine, San Francisco Med. Soc., Am. Soc. Hematology, Am. Soc. Clin. Oncology. Office: 2356 Sutter St San Francisco CA 94115-3006

GLASSCOCK, JOYCE H., public information officer. BJ magna cum laude, U. Mo., 1985; postgrad., George Washington U., 1993. Adminstrv. asst. Bailey, Deardourff, Sipple Polit. cons., McLean, Va., 1986; legis. corr. U.S. Senator John C. Danforth of Mo., Washington, 1987; press sec. Danforth for U.S. Senate, St. Louis, 1988; field rep. Dole for Pres., St. Louis, 1988; comms. cons. Eisenhower Centennial Found., Washington, 1989; dir .pub. affairs Econ. Devel. Adminstrn., U.S. Dept. Commerce, Washington, 1989-93; press sec. Congress Dave Hobson of Ohio, Washington, 1993-94; campaign dir. Bill Graves for Gov., Topeka, 1994; chief of staff Kans. Gov. Bill Graves, Topeka, 1994—. Office: Office of the Gov State Capitol 2d Fl Topeka KS 66612-1590

GLASSE, JOHN HOWELL, retired philosophy and theology educator; b. Buffalo, June 1, 1922; s. John Alfred and Jessie Elizabeth (Howell) G.; m. Wanda Lou Howard, June 16, 1950; children: Jeffrey Howell, Paulding Howard. B.A., Williamette U., 1945; B.D., Yale U., 1948, Ph.D., 1961. Ordained to ministry Presbyn. Ch., 1948. Dir. field work Christian Activities Council, Hartford, Conn., 1948-50; exec. dir. Christian Activities Council, 1950-52; dir. Danish program Scandinavian Seminar, Inc., 1952-53; mem. faculty Vassar Coll., Poughkeepsie, N.Y., 1956—, prof. religion, 1969-90, prof. emeritus, 1990—, Frederick Weyerhaeuser chair, 1971-90, chmn. dept. religion, 1965-67, 77-83, 87-90; vis. prof. Harvard Div. Sch., 1970, vis. scholar, 1962, 69; vis. scholar Columbia U., Union Theol. Sem., 1980-81. Contbr. articles to profl. jours. Trustee Scandinavian Seminar, 1950—. Hon. fellow Am. Scandinavian Found., 1952; grantee Am. Philos. Soc., 1964; grantee Am. Council Learned Socs., 1965, 67. Mem. Am. Acad. Religion, Am. Philos. Assn., Metaphys. Soc. Am., Soc. Values in Higher Edn., AAUP. Address: Box 347 Vassar Coll 124 Raymond Ave Poughkeepsie NY 12604-0347

GLASSELL, ALFRED CURRY, JR., investor; b. Cuba Plantation, La., Mar. 31, 1913; s. Alfred Curry and Frances (Lane) G.; m. Clare Attwell; children: Jean Curry, Alfred Curry III. B.A., La. State U., 1934. Investor, 1936—; cons. Glassell Producing Co., 1938—; past bd. dirs. Transco Cos., El Paso Nat. Gas, First City Bancorp. Trustee Houston Mus. Natural Sci., Internat. Oceanographic Found., Houston Mus. Fine Arts, chmn. bd.; former trustee Kinkaid Sch., Tex. Children's Hosp., Smithsonian Nat. Bd. Recipient Marine Sci. ann. award Internat. Oceanographic Found., 1971, Soc. Grand Founders medallion U. Miami, 1984, James Smithson award, 1991. Mem. Am. Geog. Soc., Am. Mus. Natural History, Tex. Angus Assn., Can. Chianini Assn., Houston Horse Show Assn., Tex. Cattle Breeders Assn., Am. Nat. Cattlemen's Assn., Tex. and Southwestern Cattle Raisers Assn., Mil. and Hospitaller Order St. Lazarus of Jerusalem. Clubs: Atlantic Tuna (Providence), Boston (New Orleans), Cabo Blanco Fishing (Peru), Tex. Game Fishing (Dallas), Tex. Corinthian Yacht (Kemah), Bay of Islands Swordfish and Mako Shark (New Zealand), Anglers of N.Y., Houston, Petroleum, Ramada, Bayou, Houston Country, River Oaks Country. Holder record of world's largest fish, former holder numerous world record salt water game fish. Office: 1021 Main St Ste 2300 Houston TX 77002-6606

GLASSER, CHARLES EDWARD, university president; b. Chgo., Apr. 3, 1940; s. Julius J. and Hilda (Goldman) G.; m. Hannah Alex, Mar. 8, 1987; children: Gemma Maria, Julian David. BA in History, Denison U., 1961; MA in Polit. Sci., U. Ill., 1967; JD, John F. Kennedy U., 1970. Bar: Calif. 1970, U.S. Ct. Appeals (9th cir.) 1970. Pvt. practice Hineser, Spellberg & Glasser, Pleasant Hill, Calif., 1971-77; dean Sch. Law John F. Kennedy U., Orinda, Calif., 1977-83, pres., 1990—; v.p., gen. counsel Western Hosp. Corp., Emeryville, Calif., 1983-90. Author: The Quest for Peace, 1986. Mem. Calif. Bar Assn. Office: John F Kennedy U 12 Altarinda Rd Orinda CA 94563-2603

GLASSER, IRA SAUL, civil liberties organization executive; b. Bklyn., Apr. 18, 1938; s. Sidney and Anne (Goldstein) G.; m. Trude Maria Robinson, June 28, 1959; children: David, Andrew, Peter, Sally. BS in Math., Queens Coll., 1959; MA in Math., Ohio State U., 1960. Instr. math. Queens Coll., N.Y.C., 1960-63; lectr. math. Sarah Lawrence Coll., Bronxville, N.Y., 1962-65; assoc. editor Current Mag., N.Y.C., 1962-64, editor, 1964-67; assoc. dir. N.Y. Civil Liberties Union, N.Y.C., 1967-70, exec. dir., 1970-78; exec. dir. ACLU, 1978—; cons. U. Ill.-Champaign-Urbana, 1964-65; dir. Asian Am. Legal Def. and Edn. Fund., N.Y.C., 1974—; dir. Drug Policy Found., Washington, 1991—. Author: Visions of Liberty: The Bill of Rights for All Americans, 1991; co-author: Doing Good: The Limits of Benevolence, 1978; contbr. articles to profl. jours. Chmn. St. Vincents Hosp, N.Y.C., Community Adv. Bd., N.Y.C., 1970-72. Recipient Martin Luther King, Jr. award N.Y. Assn. Black Sch. Suprs., 1971, Gavel award ABA, 1972, Allard K. Lowenstein award Park River Ind. Dem., 1981, Malcolm, Martin, Mandela award Greater Bapt. Trinity Ch., 1993. Avocation: sports.

GLASSER, ISRAEL LEO, federal judge; b. N.Y.C., Apr. 6, 1924; s. David and Sadie (Krupp) G.; m. Grace Gribetz, Aug. 24, 1952; children—Dorothy, David, James, Marjorie. LL.B., Bklyn. Law Sch., 1948; B.A., CUNY, 1976. Bar: N.Y. 1948. Fellow Bklyn. Law Sch., 1948-49, instr., 1950-52, asst. prof. law, 1952-53, assoc. prof., 1953-55, prof., 1955-69, adj. prof., 1969-77, dean, 1977-81; judge U.S. Dist. Ct. N.Y., 1981—; judge N.Y. State Family Ct., N.Y.C., 1969-77. Mem. ABA, Assn. of Bar of City of N.Y. Office: US Dist Ct 225 Cadman Plz E Brooklyn NY 11201-1818

GLASSER, JAMES J., leasing company executive, retired; b. Chgo., June 5, 1934; s. Daniel D. and Sylvia G.; m. Louise D. Rosenthal, Apr. 19, 1964; children: Mary, Emily, Daniel. A.B., Yale U., 1955; J.D., Harvard U., 1958. Bar: Ill. 1958. Asst. states atty. Cook County, Ill., 1958-61; mem. exec. staff GATX Corp., Chgo., 1961-69; pres. GATX Corp., 1974-96, chmn. bd., CEO, 1978-96, chmn. emeritus, 1996—, also dir.; gen. mgr. Infilco Products Co., 1969-70; v.p. GATX Leasing Corp., San Francisco, 1970-71, pres., 1971-74; bd. dirs. B.F. Goodrich Co., Harris Bankcorp, Inc., Harris Trust & Savs. Bank, Mut. Trust Life Ins. Co. Bd. dirs. Lake Forest Hosp., Northwestern Meml. Corp., Voices for Ill. Children; trustee Better Govt. Assn., Chgo. Zool. Soc., U. Chgo. Mem. Chgo. C. of C. (dir.), Chgo. Cen. Area Com. (dir.), Econ. Club of Chgo., Commercial Club, Casino Club, Chgo. Club, Racquet Club, Onwentsia Club (Lake Forest, Ill.), Shoreacres (Lake Bluff, Ill.), Tucson Country Club, Chi Psi. Home: 464 N Mayflower Rd Lake Forest IL 60045-2306 Office: 500 W Monroe St Chicago IL 60661-3630

GLASSER, JOSEPH, manufacturing and marketing executive; b. Phila., May 17, 1925. B.S. in Econs., U. Pa., 1947, M.B.A., 1948, postgrad., 1948-51. With NLRB, 1948-51; internal mgmt. cons., 1954-55; mem. faculty Sch. Bus. Adminstrn., U. Conn., 1955-81, prof. emeritus, 1981—; pres. Eljen Corp., 1971—; arbitrator Fed. Mediation and Conciliation Service, VA, Nat. Mediation Bd., Soc. Security Adminstrn., Am. Arbitration Assn.; fact finder Mass. Bd. Mediation and Arbitration, Ct. Bd. Mediation and Arbitration, N.H. Pub. Employee Labor Relations Bd.; mediator Conn. Bd. Edn.; rev. officer FAA; mem. Nat. Def. Exec. Res.-Fed. Emergency Mgmt. Agy.; speaker seminars, also mgmt. groups in Eng., Austria and Hungary, Am. Mgmt. Assn. Author: Fundamentals of Applied Industrial Management; contbr. articles to profl. jours. Served to lt. col. USAF, ETO. Decorated Air medal with four oak leaf clusters, Air Force commendation medal. Mem. Soc. Profls. in Dispute Resolution, Indsl. Rels. Rsch. Assn., Nat. Assns. Mgmt. Educators (Innovative Mgmt. Edn. award 1976), Nat. Assn. Suggestion Systems (winner internat. papers competition 1975), Res. Officers Assn., Air Force Assn. Office: Eljen Corp 15 Westwood Rd Storrs Mansfield CT 06268-2403

GLASSER, LYNN SCHREIBER, publisher; b. Chgo., Sept. 19, 1943; d. Alexander Paul and Beatrice (Bollard) Schreiber; m. Stephen A. Glasser, Dec. 30, 1965; children: Susan, Laura, Jeffrey, Jennifer. BA, Chatham Coll., 1965. Publs. editor Inst. CLE U. Mich. Law Sch., Ann Arbor, 1966-68; asst. to dir. Practising Law Inst., N.Y.C., 1968-71; v.p., COO Law Jour. Press and Law Jour. Seminars, N.Y.C., 1971-78; exec. v.p., pub. Law & Bus./Harcourt Jovanovich, Inc., N.Y.C., 1978-86; co-pres. Prentice Hall Law & Bus., Englewood Cliffs, N.J., 1986-94; cons. Simon and Schuster, N.Y.C., 1994-95; pres. Glasser Publ. Inc., Little Falls, N.J., 1995—; organizer, originator over 1000 CLE seminars, 1986—; organizer Woman Advt. Conf., N.Y.C., Chgo. and San Francisco, 1993-94; chmn. Woman Bus. Lawyer Conf., N.Y.C. and San Francisco, 1994. Trustee N.J. Chamber Music Soc., Montclair, 1989—, Montclair Art Mus., 1998—; Cmty. Found. of N.J., Morristown, 1995—; co-donor Lynn & Stephen Glasser Scholarship Fund, Colgate U., 1988—, Bloomfield Coll., 1993—. Mem. Rockefeller Ctr. Club (N.Y.C.). Office: 150 Clove Rd Little Falls NJ 07424-2138

GLASSER, PAUL HAROLD, sociologist, educator, university administrator, social worker; b. N.Y.C., Aug. 21, 1929; s. David and Rae (Startz) G.; m. Lois Hannah Naefach, Nov. 25, 1954 (div. June 1993); children: Heather Denys, Frederick Naefach. BS, CCNY, 1949; MS, Columbia U., 1951; PhD, U. N.C., 1961. Chief psychiat. social work sect. Mental Hygiene Clinic, Camp Chaffee Army Hosp., Ark., 1952-53; asst. dir. residence Child Guidance Home, Inc., 1953-55; instr. psychiat. group work, dept. psychiatry Med. Sch. U. Cin., 1953-55; asst. prof. U. Mich., Ann Arbor, 1958-63, assoc. prof., 1963-65, prof. Sch. Social Work, 1965-78; dean Grad. Sch. Social Work U. Tex., Arlington, 1978-88; dean Sch. Social Work Rutgers U., State U. of N.J., New Brunswick, 1988-92, prof. II, 1988—; vis. prof. Paul Baerwald Sch. Social Work, Hebrew U., Jerusalem, spring 1987, City U. Hong Kong, fall 1993, Bar-Ilan Sch. Social Work, spring 1997. Author: Small Groups in Hospital Community, 1967, Families in Crisis, 1970, Social Work Education for Family and Population Planning, 1973, Individual Change Through Small Groups, 1974, 2d edit., 1985, Social Work Roles and Functions in Family and Population Planning, 1974, Child Abuse and Neglect: A Challenge to the Caring Community, 1977, Group Workers at Work: Theory and Practice in the 80's, 1986, The First Helping Interview: Engaging the Client and Building Trust, 1996; sr. editor: Ency. Social work, 1971, LaRicerca Valutative, 1972; editor Jour. Health and Social Behavior, 1970-73, Jour. Social Work, 1965-69, Jour. Marriage and Family Counseling, 1974-82, Social Work with Groups, Hong Kong Jour. Social Work, 1998—, Jour. Social Work & Social Policy in Israel, 1988—. Bd. dirs. Washtenaw County Family Service, 1964-66, 69-70. Served to 1st lt. AUS, 1952-53. Fulbright Hays lectr. Italy, 1971; Fulbright Hays lectr. U. Philippines, 1966-67; Fulbright Hays lectr. Australia, 1973-74. Mem. Nat. Assn. Social Workers (chpt. chmn. 1962-63), Am. Sociol. Soc., Masons. Office: State U of NJ Rutgers U Sch Social Work 536 George St New Brunswick NJ 08901-1167 *The generation and the dispersal of knowledge are the two primary ways in which the academician contributes to the society. He is an agent of change as he studies what is, in order to suggest what might be, and communicates this to his students. My career has been devoted to these principles and to stimulating others to follow them.*

GLASSER, STEPHEN ANDREW, publishing executive, lawyer; b. Memphis, July 27, 1943; s. Melvin A. and Esther (Kron) G.; m. Lynn Schreiber, Dec. 30, 1965; children: Susan, Laura, Jeffrey, Jennifer. BA cum laude, Colgate U., 1965; JD, U. Mich., 1968. Bar: D.C., 1968. Asst. dir. Practising Law Inst., N.Y.C., 1968-71; exec. v.p., exec. editor N.Y. Law Pub. Co., N.Y.C., 1971-77; pres. Law & Bus. Inc. div. Harcourt Brace Jovanovich, N.Y.C., 1977-86, Prentice Hall Law & Bus. div. Simon & Schuster Profl Info Group, Englewood Cliffs, N.J., 1986-94; chmn. Glasser Publs. Inc., Little Falls, N.J., 1995—. Co-founder, editor, publisher Legal Times of Washington, 1978-86. Trustee Bloomfield Coll., chmn. fin. and property com.; trustee The Hospice Inc. Mem. ABA, D.C. Bar Assn., Assn. Bar City N.Y., Phi Beta Kappa, Montclair Golf Club. Home: 86 Highland Ave Montclair NJ 07042-1910 Office: Glasser Publs Inc 150 Clove Rd Ste 14 Little Falls NJ 07424-2149

GLASSER, THEODORE L., journalism educator; b. Dec. 17, 1948. MS, Okla. State U., 1973; PhD, U. Iowa, 1979. Asst. prof. U. Hartford, Conn., 1976-81; assoc. prof. U. Minn., Mpls., 1981-90; prof. Stanford (Calif.) U., 1990—. E-mail: glasser@leland.stanford.edu. FAX: 650-725-2472. Office: Stanford Univ Dept Comm Stanford CA 94305-2050

GLASSER, WOLFGANG GERHARD, wood science and chemical engineering researcher, educator; b. Oct. 9, 1941; came to U.S., 1969; s. Joachim and Charlotte (Syjatz) G.; m. Heidemarie Reinecke, Mar. 18, 1969; children: Christine M., Stephan A. Degree in wood tech., U. Hamburg, Germany, 1966; PhD in Wood Chemistry, U. Hamburg, 1969. Rsch. assoc. U. Wash., Seattle, 1969-70, rsch. asst. prof., 1970-71; asst. prof. Va. Poly. Inst. and State U., Blacksburg, 1972-75, prof. wood chemistry, 1980—, assoc. dean rsch. and grad. studies Coll. Forestry and Wildlife Resources, 1993-98; dir. Pulp and Paper Research Inst., Sao Paulo, Brazil, 1976, Biobased Materials Ctr., 1988-91; vis. prof. U. Grenoble (France), Centre de Recherche sur Macromolecules Vegetales, Grenoble, 1985, Nat. U. Singapore, 1993, Kyoto (Japan) U., 1998; chmn. panel Nat. Acad. Scis., 1974-76. Mem. editl. adv. group Holzforschung, Braunschweig, Germany, 1985—, Cellulose, 1994—, Jour. Wood Sci. (Japan), 1998—; patentee in field; contbr. articles to profl. jours.; book editor. Co-recipient George Olmsted award Am. Paper Inst., 1974; recipient Sci. Achievement award Internat. Union Forest Rsch. Orgns., 1986. Fellow Internat. Acad. Wood Sci.; mem. Am. Chem. Soc. (alt. councilor 1983-85, pub. chmn. 1985-88, chmn.-elect 1989, chmn. 1990, councilor 1991—, program chmn. 1993-96), Soc. Wood Sci. Tech., TAPPI, Bio-Environmentally Degradable Polymer Soc., Sigma Xi, Phi Beta Delta. Lutheran. Office: Va Tech 210 Cheatham Hall Wood Sci/Forest Products Blacksburg VA 24061

GLASSGOLD, ALFRED EMANUEL, physicist, educator; b. Phila., July 20, 1929; s. Solomon S. and Anna (Blaukopf) G.; m. Irene Mihaly, Jan. 25, 1953; children—Judith, Eric. B.A., U. Pa., 1950; Ph.D., Mass. Inst. Tech., 1954. Research and teaching physics Oak Ridge Nat. Lab., 1954-55, U. Minn., 1955-57, U. Calif., 1957-63; prof. physics NYU, N.Y.C., 1963—, head dept., 1969-73. Fellow Am. Phys. Soc., Am. Astron. Soc.; mem. AAAS, Internat. Astron Union, Phi Beta Kappa, Sigma Xi. Rsch. on theoretical physics, astrophysics. Home: 3035 Palisade Ave Bronx NY 10463-1000 Office: 4 Washington Pl New York NY 10003-6603

GLASSGOLD, ISRAEL LEON, construction company executive, engineer, consultant; b. Phila., Oct. 14, 1923; s. Solomon Sidney and Anna (Blaukopf) G.; m. Iris Jacqueline Silverman, Dec. 21, 1952; children: Marc Steven, Lori Beth, Jill Ellen. BSCE, U. Pa., 1944, MSCE, 1948. Registered profl. engr., Pa. Instr. U. Pa., Phila., 1946-48; chief engr. Masonry Resurfacing and Constrn. Co., Balt., 1948—, pres., 1948-94. Contbr. articles to profl. jours. Vice pres. Chizuk Amuno Congregation, Balt., 1984-86, pres., 1986-88; trustee Balt. Hebrew U., 1991-97. Ensign USNR, 1944-45, PTO. Fellow ASCE, Am. Concrete Inst. (pres. Md. chpt., bd. dirs. 1984-87, tech. activities com. 1980-86, Bloem award 1979, Turner award 1987, chpt. activities award 1988); mem. ASTM (hon., chmn. subcom. C09.46, shotcrete), Am. Concrete Inst. Internat. (pres. 1991-92), Engrs. Club, Suburban Club, Tau Beta Pi. Democrat. Jewish. Office: Masonry Resurfacing & Constrn Co 33 Stahl Point Rd Baltimore MD 21226-1747

GLASSHEIM, ELIOT ALAN, program officer; b. N.Y.C., Feb. 10, 1938; s. Raymond S. and Edith (Ruthizer) G.; m. Patricia Sanborn, July 20, 1969 (div. Feb. 1979); children: Eagle, Don; m. Dyan Rey, Feb. 14, 1996. BA, Wesleyan U., 1960; MA, U. N.Mex., 1966, PhD, 1972. Copy boy, book reviewer Wash. Post, 1960-61; editl. proofreader Wall St. Jour., N.Y.C., 1962-64; mgmt. trainee Accessory Fashions, N.Y.C., 1964-66; asst. prof. English Augusta (Ga.) Coll., 1968-70; fellow U. N.D., Grand Forks, 1971-73; state rep. N.D. State Legis., Grand Forks, 1975-76, 93—; grant writer, dir. oral history project of 97 flood N.D. Mus. Art, Grand Forks, 1993—; owner used bookstore Dr. Eliot's Twice Sold Tales, Grand Forks, 1992—; dir. Population/Food Fund, Grand Forks, 1977-79; housing coord., grantswriter N.D. Migrant Coun., Grand Forks, 1979-81. Editor: Population and Food Issues, 1977, 78, Voices from the Flood, 1999; author: (poems) The Restless Giant, 1968. Exec. dir. Quad County Cmty. Action Agy., Grand Forks, 1981-87; field rep., office mgr. US Sen Quentin Burdick, Grand Forks, 1987-92; city councilman Grand Forks City Coun., 1982—; mem. planning com. Grand Forks Planning and Zoning Comm., 1984-96, flood response com., 1997—; founder, dir. Red River Valley Habitat for Humanity, Grand Forks, 1988—; chmn. Dist. 17/18 Dems., Grand Forks, 1980-81; bd. dirs. Prairie Pub. TV, 1997—. Jewish. Home: 619 N 3rd St Grand Forks ND 58203-3203 Office: ND Mus Art PO Box 7305 Grand Forks ND 58202-7305

GLASSICK, CHARLES ETZWEILER, academic foundation administrator; b. Wrightsville, Pa., Apr. 6, 1931; s. Gordon J. and Melva G. (Etzweiler) G.; m. Mary Williams, Feb. 27, 1952; children: Bruce, Judith, Jeffrey, Robert, Jonathan. B.S. with honors, Franklin and Marshall Coll., 1953; M.A., Ph.D., Princeton U., 1957; D.Sc. (hon.), U. Richmond, 1977; L.L.D. (hon.), Dickinson Sch. Law, 1986; LLD, Pepperdine U., 1996, Adrian Coll., 1997; LHD (hon.), Franklin & Marshall Coll., 1997. Research chemist Rohm & Haas Co., Phila., 1957-62; instr. gen. chemistry Temple U., Phila., 1957-62; prof. chemistry Adrian (Mich.) Coll., 1962-68; v.p. Great Lakes Colls. Assn., Ann Arbor, Mich., 1968-69; asso. dean for acad. affairs Albion (Mich.) Coll., 1969-71, v.p. for acad. affairs, 1971-72; pres. Va. Inst. Scientific Research, Richmond, 1972-77; provost, v.p. for acad. affairs U. Richmond, Va., 1972-77; pres. Gettysburg (Pa.) Coll., 1977-89, Woodruff Arts Ctr., Atlanta, 1990-96; sr. scholar Carnegie Found. for Advancement of Tchg., Menlo Park, Calif., 1989-90, acting pres., 1995, interim pres., 1996-97, sr. assoc., 1997—; cons. NEH, 1971-72, NSF, 1963-67, Va. Coun. High Edn., 1972-76; mem. exec. com. Luth. Ednl. Conf. of N.Am., 1983-86; mem. Pres.'s Commn. Nat. Collegiate Athletic Assn., 1988-89; interim pres. Converse Coll., 1998-99. Mem. editorial bd. Liberal Education, 1978-82, Educational Record, 1985-97. Mem. Mental Health and Mental Retardation Task Force Manpower Devel., Richmond, 1975-77; mem. ACE Commn. on Minorities; bd. dirs. Atlanta Area Coun. Boy. Scouts Am., 1993—; bd. dirs. Meth. Conf. Homes for Aging, 1985-89, Hist. Gettysburg/Adams County, 1979-89; Midtown Alliance, 1991-97; mem. exec. com. Atlanta Cultural Olympiad, 1991-96; trustee, vice chmn. Carnegie Found. for Advancement of Teaching, 1991-97, Eisenhower Soc., 1985—, Ga. Found. Ind. Colls., 1992—, Literacy Action, Inc., 1994-97, Found. for Hosp. Art, 1994—; chmn. bd. trustees Regent Am. Archtl. Found., 1997—; bd. curators Ga. Hist. Soc., 1997—; bd. regents Am. Arch. Fedn., 1998—. Mem. AAAS, AAUP, Am. Chem. Soc., N.Y. Acad. Scis., Danforth Assocs., Am. Chem. Soc., Phi Beta Kappa (hon.), Beta Gamma Sigma, Omicron Delta Kappa, Alpha Chi Omega. Methodist. Home: 640 Bluff Oak Ct Roswell GA 30076-5818

GLASSMAN, ALEXANDER HOWARD, psychiatrist, researcher; b. Chgo., Feb. 4, 1934; s. Morris and Mindelle (Sosna) G.; m. B. Judith Cohen, Mar. 28, 1958; children: Steven, Laura Glassman Hercher. BS, U. Ill., Chgo., 1956, MD, 1958. Diplomate Am. Bd. Neurology and Psychiatry. Resident in psychiatry Albert Einstein Med. Coll. Medicine, Yeshiva U., N.Y.C., 1954-62; USPH fellow, 1963-64; asst. prof. psychiatry Albert Einstein Coll. Medicine, Bronx, N.Y., 1964-65; cons. psychopharmacologist Albert Einstein Coll. Medicine, Bronx, 1972-78; dir. residency tng. Letterman Gen. Hosp., San Francisco, 1967-68, chief psychiatry svc., 1968-69; dir. affective diseases N.Y. State Psychiat. Inst., N.Y.C., 1973-78, chief clin. psychopharmacology, 1978—; prof. clin. psychiatry Coll. Physicians and Surgeons, Columbia U., N.Y.C., 1980—; Mem. merit rev. bd. VA, Washington, 1987-90. Editor: Treatment Strategies in Refractory Depression, 1990, also 5 other books; contbr. articles to jours. in field; patentee in field. Lt. col. U.S. Army, 1967-69. Recipient Established Investigator award Nat. Assn. for Rsch. Affective Diseases and Schizophrenia, 1990, N.Y. State Psychiat. Rsch. award, 1994; invited spkr. Nobel Com. Conf. of Depression, Stockholm, 1983; Plenery spkr. German Psychiat. Assn., Fed. Republic Germany, 1990, Plenery spkr. Japanese Neurosci. Soc., Nagoya, 1994. Fellow Am. Coll. Neuropsychopharmacology, Am. Psychiat. Assn. (Lifetime achievement prize 1989); mem. AAAS, Am. Psychopath. Assn. (trustee), N.Y. Acad. Sci. Achievements include patent for clonidine in smoking cessation; first to recognize unique treatment response of delusionally depressed patients, to demonstrate relationship between antidepressant drug treatment outcome and individual differences in drug metabolism, to describe the cardiac antiarrhythmic effects of antidepressant drugs, to describe relationship between depression and cigarette smoking. Office: Columbia U Dept Psychiatry 722 W 168th St # 116 New York NY 10032-2695

GLASSMAN, ARMAND BARRY, physician, pathologist, scientist, educator, administrator; b. Paterson, N.J., Sept. 9, 1938; s. Paul and Rosa (Ackerman) G.; m. Alberta C. Macri, Aug. 30, 1958; children: Armand P., Steven B., Brian A. BA, Rutgers U., N.J., 1960; MD magna cum laude, Georgetown U., Washington, 1964. Diplomate Am. Bd. Pathology, Am. Bd. Nuclear Medicine. Intern Georgetown U. Hosp., Washington, 1964-65; resident Yale-New Haven Hosp., West Haven VA Hosp., 1965-69; asst. prof. pathology, Coll. Medicine U. Fla.; chief radioimmunoassary lab. Gainesville VA Hosp.; practice lab. and nuc. medicine, 1969-71; dir. clin. labs., assoc. prof., prof. pathology, cellular, molecular biology Med. Coll. Ga., Augusta, 1971-76; acting chmn. dept. immunology and microbiology Med. U. S.C., Augusta, 1985-87; cons. physician in nuclear medicine Univ. Hosp., Augusta, 1973-76; med. dir. clin. labs. Med. U. S.C. Hosp., Charleston, 1976-87; attending physician in lab. and nuclear medicine Med. U. S.C., Charleston, 1976-87, assoc. med. dir. Med. U. Hosp. and Clinics, 1982-86; med. dir. clin. labs. Charleston Meml. Hosp., S.C., 1976-87; cons. VA Hosp., Charleston, 1976-87; prof., chmn. dept. lab. medicine Med. U. S.C., 1976-87, med. dir. MT and MLT programs, 1976-87, clin. prof. pathology, lab. medicine, and radiology, 1987—, acting chmn. dept. immunology and microbiology, 1985-87, assoc. dean Coll. Medicine, 1979-85, asst. and assoc. dean Coll. Allied Health Sci., 1984-87, chmn. hosp. exec. com., 1985-86, acting med. dir. Univ. Hosp. and Clinics, 1985-86; sr. v.p. med. affairs, prof. lab. medicine and nuclear medicine Montefiore Med. Ctr. and Albert Einstein Coll. Medicine, Bronx, N.Y., 1987-89; v.p., lab. dir. Nat. Reference Lab., Nashville, 1989-92; cons., 1992-95; clin. prof. dept. pathology Vanderbilt U., Nashville, 1990-92, prof. pathology, 1992-94; dir. Vanderbilt Pathology Lab. Svcs., 1992-94; dir. clinical labs. Vanderbilt U. Med. Ctr., 1993-94, O. Stribling chair, prof., 1994—; head and chair divsn./dept. lab. medicine U. Tex., M.D. Anderson Cancer Ctr., Houston, 1994-96, also med. dir. Med. Tech. & Cytogenic Tech. programs, 1994-96, also dir. sect. cytogenetics, 1994-96, 98—; mem. adv. coun. Trident Tech. Coll., 1976-87; bd. dirs. Fetter Family Health Ctr.; founding dir., bd. dirs. Sealite, Inc., 1987—, chmn. bd. dirs., 1995—; mem. med. adv. com. Nashville Red Cross Blood Ctr., 1991-94, acting med. dir., 1991-92; mem. bd. sci. advisors Nat. Health Labs./Nat. Reference Lab., 1992-94, cons., 1992-95; trustee, bd. dirs. Gulf Coast Cmty. Blood Ctr., 1994—. Editor, co-editor 4 books; contbr. more than 140 refereed articles to profl. jours., 30 chpts. to books. Trustee Coll. Prep. Sch., 1979-84, chmn. bd., 1983-84; trustee, bd. dirs., v.p. Mason Prep. Sch., 1984-87; bd. dirs.

United Way, 1983-87, Am. Cancer Soc., 1984-87; co-founder, bd. dirs. Glassman Family Fund, 1998—. With USMCR, 1956-64. Johnson and Avalon Found. scholar Georgetown U., 1961-64; State scholar Rutgers U., 1956-60. Fellow Coll. Am. Pathologists (numerous coms.), ACP, Assn. Clin. Scientists (Diploma of Honor 1987, pres. 1990-91, exec. com. 1990-95, Clin. Scientist of Yr. 1993, C.P. Brown lectr. 1995), Am. Soc. Clin. Pathology (coun. immunohematology and blood banking 1983-89, coun. grad. med. edn. and rsch. 1998—, Commr.'s award for Commn. Continuing Edn. 1989), Am. Bd. Pathology (transfusion medicine/blood bank test com. 1984-88), Am. Coll. Nuc. Medicine, N.Y. Acad. Medicine; mem. Internat. Acad. Pathology, Am. Assn. Pathologists, Soc. Nuc. Medicine (chmn. edn. com. 1973-77, acad. coun. 1979-92), AMA (Physician's Recognition award, instnl. rep. to sect. on med. schs.), So. Med. Assn., Am. Geriat. Soc. (founding fellow So. divsn.), Am. Soc. Microbiology, Am. Assn. Blood Banks (chmn. cryobiology com. 1974-83, edn. com. 1978-85, sci. program com. 1981-84, autologous transfusion com. 1979-83, bd. dirs. 1984-87, transfusion practices com. 1992-96), Assn. Schs. Allied Health Professions (bd. editors jour. 1979-83), Soc. Cryobiology (treas., bd. dirs. 1978-80), AAAS, N.Y. Acad. Scis., Acad. Clin. Lab. Physicians and Scientists (exec. coun. 1978-85, pres. 1982-83), S.E. Area Blood Bankers (pres. 1979-81, exec. coun. 1980-85), Tenn. Assn. Blood Banks (treas. 1993-94), Am. Coll. Physician Execs., Sigma Xi, Alpha Eta, Alpha Omega Alpha. Avocations: jogging, tennis, community svc. Office: MD Anderson Cancer Ctr Lab Medicine Box 73 1515 Holcombe Blvd Houston TX 77030-4009

GLASSMAN, CAROLINE DUBY, state supreme court justice; b. Baker, Oreg., Sept. 13, 1922; d. Charles Ferdinand and Caroline Marie (Colton) Duby; m. Harry Paul Glassman, May 21, 1953; 1 son, Max Avon. LLB summa cum laude, Williamette U., 1944. Bar: Oreg. 1944, Calif. 1952, Maine 1969. Atty. Title Ins. & Trust Co., Salem, Oreg., 1944-46; assoc. Belli, Ashe, Pinney & Melvin Belli, San Francisco, 1952-58; ptnr. Glassman & Potter, Portland, Maine, 1973-78, Glassman, Beagle & Ridge, Portland, 1978-83; justice Maine Supreme Judicial Ct., Portland, 1983-97; lectr. Sch. Law, U. Maine, 1967-68, 80. Author: Legal Status of Homemakers in State of Maine, 1977. Mem. Am. Law Inst., Oreg. Bar Assn., Calif. Bar Assn., Maine Bar Assn., Maine Trial Law Assn. Roman Catholic. Home: 56 Thomas St Portland ME 04102-3639

GLASSMAN, EDWARD, public relations management creativity consultant; b. N.Y.C., Mar. 18, 1929; s. Jacob S. and Riesa (Bronfman) F.; children: Lyn Judith, Susan Fiona, Ellen Ruth, Marjorie Riesa. AB, NYU, 1949, MS, 1951; PhD, Johns Hopkins U., 1955. Mem. staff City of Hope Med. Ctr., Duarte, Calif., 1959-60; prof., faculty biochemistry dept. med. sch. U. N.C., Chapel Hill, 1960-90, head program for team effectiveness and creativity, 1981-90; prof. emeritus, 1990—; pres. Leadership Cons. Svcs., Inc., Creativity Coll., Chapel Hill, 1990—; mem. grants and rev. study sect. NIMH, 1966-69, U. Calif., Irvine, 1978; vis. fellow Ctr. Creative Leadership, Greensboro, N.C., 1983; vis. scientist Stanford Rsch. Inst., Menlo Park, Calif., 1986; pres. Creativity Coll. divsn. Leadership Consulting Svcs., Inc., Chapel Hill. Author: Molecular Approaches to Neurobiology, 1967, For Presidents Only: Unlocking the Creative Potential of Your Management Team, 1990, Creativity Handbook, 1991, The Creativity Factor: Unlocking the Potential of Your Team, 1991; columnist Creativity at Work, Chapel Hill Newspaper, 1991-92, Triangle Bus. Jour., 1992-95, Chapel Hill Herald, 1992-94, Moore County Citizens News Record, 1994-96; mem. editl. adv. bd. Behavioral Biology, 1971-78, Pharmacology, Biochemistry and Behavior, 1973-88; mem. bd. advisors Neurochem. Rsch., 1975-78; contbr. 95 articles to profl. jours. Pub. rels. specialist Lions Club, 1995—. Adam T. Bruce fellow, 1954-55; Am. Cancer Soc. fellow, 1955-57; NIH fellow, 1958-59; NIH Career Devel. award, 1961-71; Guggenheim fellow, 1968-69. Fellow AAAS, Royal Soc. Edinburgh; mem. Soc. Neurosci. (pres. N.C. chpt. 1974-75), Elisha Mitchell Sci. Soc. (v.p. 1965-66). Home and Office: 679 Cedar Pt Vass NC 28394-8686

GLASSMAN, GEORGE MORTON, dermatologist; b. N.Y.C., Sept. 7, 1935; s. Oscar and Jeanette (Bitterbaum) G.; m. Carol Beth Frankford, July 10, 1960; children: Keith F., Laurie C. BA cum laude, Brown U., 1957; MD, NYU, 1962. Diplomate Nat. Bd. Med. Examiners. Rotating intern Greenwich (Conn.) Hosp., 1962-63; resident in dermatology NYU Med. Ctr., N.Y.C., 1963-66; chief dermatology U.S. Navy, St. Albans, N.Y., 1966-68; pvt. practice White Plains, N.Y., 1968-96; clinical asst. prof. Albert Einstein Coll. Medicine, Bronx, N.Y., 1970-75, N.Y. Med. Coll., Valhalla, N.Y., 1975-87; assoc. attending dermatologist Westchester County Med. Ctr., Valhalla, 1974-87, St. Agnes Hosp., White Plains, 1978-96; attending dermatologist White Plains Hosp., 1977-96. Contbr. articles to profl. jours. Lt. comdr. USN, 1966-68. Mem. Am. Acad. Dermatology (Continuing Med. Edn. award, 1980—), Westchester County Med. Soc., Westchester Acad. Medicine (pres. dermatology sect., 1990-91), N.Y. State Soc. Dermatology, AMA (Physician's Recognition award, 1980—), Soc. for Pediatric Dermatology. Home and Office: 268 Stuart Dr New Rochelle NY 10804-1423

GLASSMAN, GERALD SEYMOUR, metal finishing company executive; b. Hartford, Conn., July 6, 1932; s. Abram and Lena (Rulnick)) G.; m. Edwina Wellins, Dec. 1, 1963; children: Cynthia Anne Heilweil, Barbara Diane, Richard Philip. BS, U. Vt., 1954. Exec. Bland Co., Hartford, Conn., 1954-63, Coleco Industries, Hartford, 1963-75; pres. Stanley Plating Co., Forestville, Conn., 1977-82; chmn. CBR Industries, Plainville, Conn., 1977-82; pres. Plainville Plating Co., 1975-97, chmn., 1998—; pres. Internat. Metal Finishing, Inc., 1986—; mem. regional adv. bd. Bank of Boston Ct., Plainville, 1979-89; mem. adv. bd. 1st Nat. Bank of New Eng., 1991—. Pres. Tunxis C.C. Found., 1978-88; trustee Wheeler Clinic, 1979-89, Plainville YMCA, 1980—; mem. Assocs. U. Hartford. Mem. Nat. Assn. Metal Finishers, Conn. Assn. Metal Finishers (v.p.), Metal Finishers Assn. Conn. (pres.), NAM, Am. Electroplaters Soc., Plainville C. of C., Masons. Jewish. Home: 2 Saddle Xing Avon CT 06001-3911 Office: 21 Forestville Ave Plainville CT 06062-2159

GLASSMAN, HERBERT HASKEL, architect; b. Boston, Mar. 29, 1919; s. Jacob and Jennie Rose (Levine) G.; m. Anne Shirley Resnick, June 20, 1948; children: Elsa Jan, Karin Melvey, Jack Ian. Student, Ga. Inst. Tech., 1937-38, Boston Archtl. Ctr., 1939-41; BArch, MIT, 1943; student in structures, Cath. U. Am., 1942-43, George Washington U., 1942-43. With Perley F. Gilbert Assocs., Inc., Lowell, Mass., 1946—, ptnr. in charge archtl. div., 1949-59, v.p., 1950-59, pres., 1959-84; archtl. prin. Gale Assocs., Inc., Weymouth, Mass., 1984-91; critic in archtl. design devel. Boston Archtl. Center Sch., 1947-59; v.p. Sch. Architecture, Boston Archtl. Center, 1973-77, pres., 1977-80, pres. alumni assn., 1992—, bd. dirs. exec. com., 1991—, mem. numerous coms.; vis. lectr. U. Mass. State Coll., Framingham, 1959-72; co-chair archtl. study tours abroad program Boston Archtl. Ctr., 1980—, chmn. honors and awards, 1984—, permanent sec. Ames scholarship, 1990—. Important works include schs. in East Jaffrey, N.H., Springfield, Vt., Ayer, Mass., Attleboro, Mass., Portsmouth, N.H., Sterling (Mass.) High Sch, Brockton (Mass.) High Sch, Ayer (Mass.) Ednl. Park, Acton (Mass.) Ednl. Park; student Union, high rise dormitory U. Lowell, Temple Isaiah, Lexington, Mass., Little Harbour Sch, Portsmouth, N.Y. Bd. dirs., exec. com. Human Services Corp., Lowell, Mass.; v.p. Temple Isaiah, Lexington, 1966-68, cons. bldg. com., 1993—; bd. dirs., steering com. Soc. for Energy Conservation in Architecture. Served with U.S. Coast and Geodetic Survey, 1942-43; Served with USAAF, 1943-44. Fellow Internat. Inst. Arts and Letters, Kreuzlingen, Switzerland, 1960. Mem. Boston, Mass. State assns. architects, AIA, Nat. Trust Hist. Preservation Soc., Lexington Hist. Soc., Constrn. Specifications Inst., Internat. Inst. Fine Arts and Letters, Soc. Archtl. Historians, Boston Soc. Architects, B'nai B'rith. Home: 19 Hancock St Lexington MA 02420-3443 Office: Boston Archtl Ctr 320 Newbury St Boston MA 02115-2703

GLASSMAN, HOWARD THEODORE, lawyer; b. Phila., Jan. 25, 1934; s. Sol Glassman and Claire (Walker) Smith; m. Eta S. Roseman, Oct. 22, 1961; children: Sharon Mindy, Beth Robin. BS, Pa. State U., 1955; LLB, U. Pa., 1958. Bar: Pa. 1959, Fla. 1987, N.J. 1987, D.C. 1988. Assoc. Dennis, Lichtenstein, Cohen & Dennis, Phila., 1960-64, L.J. Lichtenstein, Phila., 1964-69; ptnr. Wexler, Weisman, Forman & Shapiro, Phila., 1969-84, Blank, Rome, Comisky & McCauley, Phila., 1984—. Contbg. author Bankruptcy Practice Handbook, 1983; contbr. articles to profl. jours. Trustee Nat. Mus. Jewish Am. History, 1994—. Served to cpl. U.S. Army, 1958-60. Mem. ABA, Pa. Bar Assn., Fla. Bar Assn., N.J. Bar Assn., D.C. Bar Assn., Green Valley Country Club (bd. dirs. 1985-90, 96—). Jewish. Avocations: golf, tennis. Home: 940 Lindy Ln Hillgate at Cynwyd Bala Cynwyd PA 19004 Office: Blank Rome Comisky et al One Logan Square Philadelphia PA 19103

GLASSMAN, IRVIN, mechanical and aeronautical engineering educator, consultant; b. Balt., Sept. 19, 1923; s. Abraham and Bessie (Snyder) G.; m. Beverly Wolfe, June 17, 1951; children: Shari Powell, Diane Geinger, Barbara Ann. B.E., Johns Hopkins U., 1943, D.Eng., 1950. Research asst. Manhattan Project, Columbia U., N.Y.C., 1943-46; mem. faculty Princeton U., N.J., 1950—, prof. mech. and aero. engring., 1964—, Robert H. Goddard prof. mech. and aero. engring., 1988—, dir. Ctr. for Energy and Environ. Studies, 1972-79; cons. to industry; vis. prof. U. Naples, Italy, 1966-67, 78-79, Stanford U., 1975; mem. adv. com. United Tech. Rsch. Ctr., Sch. of Engring., Colo. Sch. Mines, NSF. Author: (with R.F. Sawyer) Performance of Chemical Propellants, 1971, Combustion, 1987, 3d edit., 1996; editor Combustion Sci. & Tech. Jour., also 3 books; contbr. articles to tech. jours. Served with U.S. Army, 1944-46. NSF fellow, 1966-67. Fellow AIAA (Propellants and Combustion award 1998); mem. AAUP, Nat. Acad. Engring., Combustion Inst. (Sir Alfred Edgerton Gold medal 1982), Am. Soc. Engring. Edn. (Roe award 1984), Am. Chem. Soc., Tau Beta Pi. Achievements include 3 rocket propellant and burner patents. Home: PO Box 14 Princeton NJ 08542-0014 Office: Princeton U Dept Mech & Aero Engring Princeton NJ 08544

GLASSMAN, JAMES KENNETH, editor, writer, publishing executive; b. Washington, Jan. 1, 1947; s. Stanley G. and Elaine Ruth (Schiff) Garfield; m. Mary Claire Hanby, Aug. 16, 1969; children: Zoe Ann, Kate Julia. BA, Harvard, 1969. Editor, pub. Provincetown (Mass.) Advocate, 1971-72; editor-in-chief, exec. pub. Figaro, New Orleans, 1972-78; exec. editor Washingtonian Mag., 1979-81; pub. New Republic mag., Washington, 1981-84; pres. Atlantic mag., Washington, 1984-86; exec. v.p. U.S. News & World Report, Washington, 1984-86; editor-in-chief Roll Call, Washington, 1987-93; fin. and polit. columnist Washington Post, 1993—; DeWitt Wallace-Reader's Digest fellow in comms. Am. Enterprise Inst., Washington, 1996—; host Capitol Gang Sunday, CNN-TV, 1995-98, Techno Politics, PBS-TV, 1995-99. Office: Am Enterprise Inst 1150 17th St NW Washington DC 20036-4603

GLASSMAN, JEROME MARTIN, clinical pharmacologist, educator; b. Phila., Mar. 2, 1919; s. Martin K. and Dorothea (Largeman) G.; m. Justine Helena Rizinsky, June 15, 1952; children: Martin J., Lorna R., Gary J. AB, U. Pa., 1939, MA, 1942; PhD, Yale U., 1950. Research assoc. lab. applied physiology Yale U., New Haven, 1950-51; head dept. pharmacology Wyeth Labs., Phila., 1951-62; dir. biol. research USVRevlon, Yonkers, N.Y., 1962-69; dir. clin. research and pharmacology Wampole Labs., Stamford, Conn., 1969-75; dir. clin. investigation Wallace Labs., Cranbury, N.J., 1975-88; cons. to pharm. industry, 1988—; adj. assoc. prof. pharmacology N.Y. Med. Coll., 1973-82. Contbr. articles to profl. jours.; patentee in field. Scoutmaster Boy Scouts Am., 1957-62, chmn. troop com., 1976-81. Recipient Citation, U.S. Office Scientific Research and Devel. Fellow AAAS, N.Y. Acad. Scis., Am. Coll. Clin. Pharmacology, Am. Coll. Clin. Pharmacology and Chemotherapy; mem. Biometric Soc., Am. Soc. Pharmacology and Exptl. Therapeutics, Soc. Exptl. Biol. Medicine, Soc. Toxicology, Sigma Xi. Office: PO Box 23 280 Sleepy Hollow Rd Briarcliff Manor NY 10510-0023

GLASSMAN, JON DAVID, business executive; b. N.Y.C., Jan. 8, 1944; s. J. and Dorothy (Witkin) G.; m. Francesca Regina Smoot, Dec. 31, 1986; 1 child, Amanda Louise; 1 stepchild, James Smoot Decherd. B in Fgn. Svc., U. So. Calif., 1965; MA, Columbia U., 1968, cert. Russian Inst., 1968, PhD, 1976. Joined Fgn. Svc. Dept. State, 1968; officer Am. Embassy, Madrid, 1968-70, Moscow, 1971-73, Havana, Cuba, 1977-79, Mexico City, 1979-81; officer Dept. State, Washington, 1974-77, 81-87; charge d'affaires Am. Embassy, Kabul, Afghanistan, 1987-89; dep. asst. for nat. security affairs to V.p. The White House, 1989-90, asst. to V.p. of U.S., 1990-91; amb. to Paraguay Asuncion, 1991-94; dept. state chair Indsl. Coll. of the Armed Forces, Washington, 1994-96; dep. for Balkan mil. stabilization Dept. State, Washington, 1996-97; v.p. internat. bus. devel. electronic sensors & sys. sector Northrop Grumman Corp., Balt., 1998—; mem. bd. Bus. Coun. for Internat. Understanding, 1999—. Author: Arms for the Arabs, 1976. Bd. dirs. Bus. Coun. for Internat. Understanding. Recipient Presdl. Meritorious Svc. award, 1991. Mem. City Tavern Club. Home: 3240 Q St NW Washington DC 20007-3032 Office: Northrop Grumman Corp Elec Sensors & Sys Sector PO Box 1897 Baltimore MD 21203

GLASSMAN, LAWRENCE S., plastic surgeon; b. June 20, 1953. BA, Johns Hopkins U., 1975, MD, 1978. Diplomate Am. Bd. Surgery, Am. Bd. Plastic Surgery. C.A.Q. hand surgeon Columbia Presbyn. Med. Ctr., N.Y.C., 1978-83; plastic surgeon Montefiore Med. Ctr. and Albert Einstein Coll. of Medicine, Bronx, N.Y., 1983-85; prof. plastic surgery Albert Einstein Coll. Medicine, 1985—; plastic surgeon, dir. Inst. Aesthetic and Reconstructive Surgery, Pomona, N.Y., 1985—; plastic surgeon Good Samaritan Hosp., Suffern, N.Y., 1985—, Nyack (N.Y.) Hosp., 1985—, Chilton Meml. Hosp., Pompton Plains, N.J., 1985-89. Contbr. articles to profl. jours. Fellow ACS, N.Y. Acad. Medicine; mem. AMA, Am. Soc. Plastic and Reconstructive Surgery, Am. Assn. Surgery of the Hand, Am. Soc. Aesthetic Plastic Surgery, Med. Soc. Rockland County, Phi Beta Kappa, Alpha Omega Alpha. Office: 978 Route 45 Pomona NY 10970-3521

GLASSMAN, RONALD JAY, public health advocate; b. Passaic, N.J., June 5, 1959; s. Paul and Shirley (Leff) G.; m. Meryl Linda Corsover, Sept. 2, 1990. B, Rutgers U., 1981; M, Columbia U., 1983; PhD, Columbia State Coll., 1998. Fellow pub. health Beth Israel Med. Ctr., Newark, 1983-84, project mgr., 1984-85; v.p. Grotta Ctr., West Orange, N.J., 1985-86; pres., founder R.J. Glassman & Co., Edison, N.J., 1986-97. Author: Domestic Abuse Survivors by Proxt: When Dads Hurt Moms They Hurt Kids, Too; rschr., speaker in field of domestic abuse edn. and prevention. E-mail: glassman@webspan.net. Home and Office: 1501 Fox Trl Mountainside NJ 07092-1303

GLASSMEYER, EDWARD, investment banker; b. Jersey City, Sept. 14, 1915; s. Edward and Claire (Stuckert) G.; m. Elizabeth Fellows, Jan. 5, 1939 (dec. Sept. 1982); children: Elizabeth Glassmeyer Treynor, Edward, Mary Glassmeyer Maloney, Edith Glassmeyer Heilman; m. Martha Moody, June 15, 1985. BA, Princeton U., 1936. Statistician Blyth & Co., Inc., N.Y.C., 1936-47, mgr. syndicate, 1947-50, v.p., 1950-62, sr. v.p., 1962-70; pres. Athens (Greece) Coll., 1970-73; chmn. bd. Inter-Am. Life Ins. Co. (subs. INA), Athens, 1973-76; ptnr. Grubb & Williams, Ltd., Atlanta; adv. coun. dept. classics Princeton U.; lectr. in field. Trustee, v.p., past chmn. exec. com. Beekman Downtown Hosp., N.Y.C.; trustee emeritus Athens Coll., Near East Coll. Assn.; bd. dirs. Riverside Theater, Vero Beach, 1992-95; mem. Alumni Council, Princeton. Served with OSS, AUS, 1945-46, Germany. Named Hon. Alumnus, Cornell Coll., Mt. Vernon, Iowa, 1992, Hon. Trustee, 1998. Mem. Am. Numismatic Soc. (coun. 1983-88), Investment Bankers Assn. Am. (v.p., gov. 1958-60, chmn. N.Y. group 1959-60), Archeol. Inst. Am. (trustee 1966-85), Bond Club (pres. 1966-67), Princeton Club, Links Club (N.Y.C.), Reading Room Club (York Harbor, Maine), Riomar Yacht Club, Royal Yacht Club of Greece, Propellor of U.S. in Greece (pres. 1974-75). Republican. Presbyterian. Home: 4119 Indian River Dr Vero Beach FL 32963-1410

GLASSMOYER, THOMAS PARVIN, lawyer; b. Reading, Pa., Sept. 4, 1915; s. James Arthur and Margaretha (Parvin) G.; m. Frances Helen Thieroff, May 9, 1942; children—Deborah Jane Beck, Nancy Parvin Brittingham, Wendy Jean Barber. AB, Ursinus Coll., 1936, LLB (hon.), 1972; LLB, U. Pa., 1939. Bar: Pa. 1940. Law clk. Common Pleas Ct. 6, Phila., 1939-40; assoc. Murdoch, Paxson, Kalish & Green, Phila., 1940-42; atty. Dept. Justice and Office Price Adminstrn., 1942-43; assoc. Schnader, Harrison, Segal & Lewis, Phila., 1946-50, ptnr., 1950-87, retired ptnr., 1988—, chmn. pension com., 1969-84, chmn. tax dept., 1972-84, chmn. investment com., 1984-86, chmn. bd. trustees of Retirement Trust, 1986-89; sec. The Lawrewnce McFadden Co., Phila., 1992, dir., 1994—; lectr. NYU Inst. Fed. Taxation; adv. bd. U. Pa. Tax Conf., 1968-88. Author: (with Sherwin T. McDowell) Legal Problems in Tax Returns, 1949; editor-in-chief U. Pa. Law Rev., 1938-39. Past pres. Upper Dublin Twp. PTA Council; mem. Zoning Bd. Adjustment Upper Dublin Twp., Montgomery County, Pa., 1957-59, bd. commrs., 1959-71, pres., 1968-69; mem. Upper Dublin Environ. Control Bd., 1972-82; bd. dirs. Ursinus Coll., Collegeville, Pa., 1956—, 1st v.p., 1978-81, pres., 1981-90, chmn. exec. com., 1981-97; bd. dirs. Wissahickon Valley Watershed Assn., 1974-76; trustee Bernard G. Segal Found., Phila., 1969—, Charlotte W. Newcombe Found., Princeton, N.J., 1982—. Served to 1st lt. JAG Dept., AUS, 1943-46. Recipient Eagle Scout award, Boy Scouts Am. Fellow Pa. Bar Found. (life, sec. 1993—); mem. ABA, FBA, Pa. Bar Assn. (ho. of dels. 1982-88, membership com., by-laws com.), Phila. Bar Assn., Judge Advs. Assn., Pa. Folklife Soc. (bd. dirs., sec.), Nat. Assn. Coll. and Univ. Attys., 1939 Code Club, Lawyers Club Phila., Manorlu Club, Mfrs. Golf and Country Club, Union League of Phila., Order of Coif, Order of Arrow. Republican. Lutheran. Avocation: golf, philately. Home: 1648 N Hills Ave Willow Grove PA 19090-4231 Office: Schnader Harrison Segal & Lewis 1600 Market St Ste 3600 Philadelphia PA 19103-7240

GLASSON, LINDA, hospital security and safety official, healthcare consultant; b. Nassawadox, Va., July 2, 1947; d. William Robert and Doris (Savage) G.; m. Charles William Lemon, Jr., Mar. 21, 1969 (div. 1973). Student Eastern Shore Br. U. Va., 1965-67, J. Sargent Reynolds C.C., 1976-80, Old Dominion U., 1981, Va. Wesleyan Coll., 1985. Cert. ambulance emergency med. technician. Clk.-typist G.L. Webster Co., Inc., Cheriton, Va., 1962-70; tchrs. aide Cape Charles High Sch., Va., 1970-72; dir. recreation and infirmary asst. United Meth. Children's Home, Richmond, Va., 1972-73; stockroom mgr. Flair Clothing Store, Richmond, 1973-74; with med. record dept. Richmond Meml. Hosp., 1974-75, asst. utilization rev. coord., 1975-80, hosp. police sgt., 1977-80; dir. safety and security Maryview Hosp., Portsmouth, Va., 1980-97, chmn. hosp. safety com., 1980—, mem. disaster com., 1980—, chmn., 1986—; security mgmt. assoc. Safety & Security Solutions, Richmond, 1997—. Contbg. author tng. manuals; contbr. articles to profl. publs. Instr. first aid and personal safety ARC, 1970-85, multimedia first aid instr., 1983-88, first aid chmn. bd. dirs. Henrico chpt., 1979-80, vol. emergency med. technician ambulance state fair annually 1974—. Mem. Internat. Assn. Hosp. Security (sr., chmn. Region III 1985, v.p., sec. 1985-88, spl. appointee to bd. 1988-89), Am. Soc. Indsl. Security (mem. nat. standing com. healthcare security 1979-84, v.p. 1983-84), Internat. Assn. Healthcare Security & Safety (pres.-elect 1990, pres. 1991-92, past pres. 93—), Internat. Healthcare Security and Safety Found. (pres. 1994-95). Baptist. Avocations: golf, softball, swimming, reading, classical music. Office: Maryview Hosp 3636 High St Portsmouth VA 23707-3270

GLASSON, LLOYD, sculptor, educator; b. Chgo., Jan. 31, 1931; s. Albert and Fay G.; m. Cathleen Naso, May 13, 1968. BFA, Sch. Art Inst. Chgo., 1957, MFA, 1959. Mannequin sculptor, 1959-60; exhibits designer Newark Mus., 1961-62; prof. emeritus U. Hartford, (Conn.), 1964—; co-founder Artists Tenants Assn., 1960—. One-man shows Dorsky Gallery, N.Y.C., 1966, 74, Trinity Coll., Hartford, 1977, Salt Box Gallery, West Hartford, 1985, The Greene Art Gallery, Guilford, Conn., 1997, Sculpture Showcase, Ltd., New Hope, Pa., 1997; represented in permanent collections Wadsworth Atheneum, Hartford, Bushnell Auditorium, Hartford, Ch. of St. Helena, West Hartford, U. N.H., Karen Horney Inst., N.Y.C., Yale U., New Haven, Forma Viva, Kostanjevica, Slovenia; recreated the 2 bronze angels atop Soldiers and Sailors Meml. Arch, Hartford; designer, creator Albert Schweitzer Humanitarian award. Served with U.S. Army, 1952-54. Recipient Gold medal 52d ann. exhbn. Nat. Sculpture Soc., 1985, James E. and Frances W. Bent award for Creativity, 1989. Mem. NAD (Thomas Proctor prize 1985, Gold medal 1986), Sculptors Guild, Nat. Sculpture Soc. Studio: 229 Grand St New York NY 10013-4240

GLATMAN-STEIN, MARCIA, executive search company executive; b. N.Y.C., Feb. 28, 1944; d. Martin and Jean (Bykowsky) Eisenberg; m. Allan Glatman, June 27, 1965 (div. 1979); children: Jill, Kim; m. Seymour Stein, Nov. 22, 1983. BA, Hunter Coll., 1965, MA, 1969. Cert. tchr., N.Y. Tchr. N.Y.C. Bd. Edn., 1965-70; counselor Rockland Community Coll., Suffern, N.Y., 1976-77; acct. mgr. Alexander Ross Assoc., N.Y.C., 1978-80; sr. acct. mgr. Stevenson Group, N.Y.C., 1981-83; v.p. Richards Cons., N.Y.C., 1983-84, E.G. Todd Assocs., N.Y.C., 1984-88; pres. HRD Cons., Inc., Clark, N.J., 1989—. Pub. (newsletter) Trends in Human Resources. Mem. ASTD, Internat. Assn. of Corp. and Profl. Recruiters, Am. Compensation Assn., Human Resource Planning Assn., Soc. for Human Resource Mgmt. Avocations: bicycling, jazzercise, reading, travel. Office: HRD Cons Inc 60 Walnut Ave Clark NJ 07066-1606

GLATSTEIN, DAVID, investment company executive. Pres., CEO Southwest Securities, Dallas. Office: Southwest Securities 1201 Elm St Ste 3500 Dallas TX 75270-2108*

GLATT, MITCHELL STEVEN, consumer products company executive; b. N.Y.C., Sept. 2, 1957; s. Herbert and Gloria (Comita) G.; m. Randy Ginsburg, Oct., 1987. BA, NYU, 1978, MBA, 1980. Agt. trainee Internat. Creative Mgmt., N.Y.C., 1980-81; exec. asst. to chmn. bd. Bozell, Jacobs, Kenyon & Eckhardt, Inc., N.Y.C., 1981-87; chmn. of bd. Magla Products Inc., Chatham, 1987—; pres. GiGi Products, Inc., pres. Am. Med. Acceptance Corp., 1998—. Cons. Statue of Liberty Ellis-Island Found., N.Y.C., 1983-87, Juvenile Diabetes Found., N.Y.C., 1987; adv. bd. NYU Sch. of the Arts; mem. Playwrights Theater N.J. Recipient Commendation Advt. Women of N.Y., N.Y.C., 1986. Mem. Am. Mgmt. Assn., Young Pres. Orgn. Office: Am Med Acceptance Corp 11 E 44th St New York NY 10017

GLATTER, KATHLEEN MARY, medical/surgical nurse; b. Albion, Nebr., June 6, 1959; d. James M. and Mary Catherine (Clinch) McQuillan; m. Mark Andrew Glatter, June 9, 1984; children: Melissa Rae, Jessica Ann, Casey James, Mary Kaitlyn (dec.). BSN, Marymount Coll., 1981. RN, Nebr. Nurse's aide St. John's Hosp., Salina, Kans., 1980, Greeley (Nebr.) Care Home, 1977, 78, 79; med.-surg. nurse Good Samaritan Hosp., Kearney, Nebr., 1981-87; oper. rm. nurse Good Samaritan Hosp., 1988-96, prep. clinic nurse, 1996-98, tumor registry nurse, 1999—. Mem. Assn. Oper. Rm. Nurses. Home: 610 E 36th St Kearney NE 68847-3109

GLATZER, ROBERT ANTHONY, marketing and sales executive; b. N.Y.C., May 19, 1932; s. Harold and Glenna (Beaber) G.; m. Paula Rosenfeld, Dec. 20, 1964; m. Mary Ann Murphy, Dec. 31, 1977; children: Gabriela, Jessica, Nicholas. BA, Haverford Coll., 1954. Br. store dept. mgr. Bloomingdale's, N.Y.C., 1954-56; media buyer Ben Sackheim Advt., N.Y.C., 1956-59; producer TV commls. Ogilvy, Benson & Mather Advt., N.Y.C., 1959-62; dir. broadcast prodn. Carl Ally Advt., N.Y.C., 1962-63; owner Chronicle Prodns., N.Y.C., 1963-73; dir. Folklife Festival, Smithsonian Inst., Washington, 1973, Expo 74 Corp., Spokane, Wash., 1973-74; pres. Robert Glatzer Assocs., Spokane, 1974—; ptnr. Delany/Glatzer Advt., Spokane, 1979-84; dir. sales/mktg. Pinnacle Prodns., Spokane; adj. faculty Ea. Wash. U., 1987—. Bd. dirs. Riverfront Arts Festival, 1977-78; bd. dirs. Comprehensive Health Planning Council, 1975-78, Spokane Quality of Life Council, 1976-82, Allied Arts of Spokane, 1976-80, Art Alliance Wash. State, 1977-81, Spokane chpt. ACLU, 1979-83, Wash. State Folklife Council, 1983—, chair 1998—; commr. Spokane Arts, 1987—; mem. Spokane Community Devel. Bd., 1988—; mem. Shorelines Update Commn., 1988—; mem. Wash. State Small Bus. Improvement Coun., 1994—, chair 1998—. Recipient CINE Golden Eagle award (2). Mem. Dirs. Guild Am. Democrat. Jewish. Author: The New Advertising, 1970; co-scenarist Scorpio and other TV prodns.

GLAUBINGER, LAWRENCE DAVID, manufacturing company executive, consultant; b. Newark, Nov. 26, 1925; s. Samuel I. and Pauline (Sandler) G.; m. Lucienne Lefebvre, Nov. 11, 1967. BS with honors, Ind. U., 1949; MBA, Columbia U., 1977; LLD (hon.) Ind. U., 1993. Adminstrv. asst. to pres. Ronson Inc., Newark, 1949-51; mdse. mgr. United Mchts., N.Y.C., 1951-65; v.p. Marietta Silk Mills (Pa.), 1965-66; pres., CEO Channel Textile Co. Inc., Bradford, Vt., 1966-75; chmn. bd., CEO Stern & Stern Industries, Inc., N.Y.C., 1977—, also bd. dirs.; pres. Lawrence Econ. Cons. Inc., Hallandale, Fla., 1977—; bd. dirs. Leucadia Nat. Corp., Marisa Christina, Inc. Bd. overseers Columbia U. Sch. Bus., chmn. ann. funds campaigns, 1980-82; bd. dirs. Ind. U. Found.; bd. advisers Ind. U. Ctr. Entrepreneurship and Innovation, Ind. U. Bus. Sch. Acad. Alumni Fellows, Ind. U. Distinguished Alumni Svc. Awd.; chmn. Dean's adv. coun. Ind. U. Bus. Sch.; mem. Pres.'s Cabinet Ind. U. Served with USCGR, 1943-46. Mem. Hoosier Hundred, Ind. U. Dean's Assos., Columbia U. Bus. Assocs., Campaign for Columbia (co-chmn. bus. sch.), Am. Arbitration Assn., Princeton Club (N.Y.), Green

Brook Country, Beta Gamma Sigma. Republican. Jewish. Home: 437 Golden Isles Dr Hallandale FL 33009-7582 Office: Stern & Stern Industries Inc 708 3rd Ave New York NY 10017-4201

GLAUNER, ALFRED WILLIAM, lawyer, engineering company executive; b. Newark, June 24, 1936; s. William Freidrick and Mary (Prewein) G.; m. Barbara Joyce Lafferty, Oct. 22, 1960; children: William Elton, Melissa Ann, David Elton. BS in Chem. Engring., Lehigh U., 1959; MBA, Rutgers U., 1967; JD, Seton Hall U., 1972. Bar: N.J. 1972, U.S. Dist. Ct. N.J. 1972, Mass. 1979, U.S. Dist. Ct. Mass. 1979. Plant engr. Nuodex Products Div., Elizabeth, N.J., 1959-62; supr., sect. head Squibb Pharms., New Brunswick, N.J., 1962-68; asst. mgr. engring. svcs. E.R. Squibb & Sons, Inc., New Brunswick, 1968-70; contracts mgr. E.R. Squibb & Sons, Inc., Lawrenceville, N.J., 1970-73; assoc. counsel The Badger Co., Inc., Cambridge, Mass., 1973-74, counsel, 1974-75; counsel Badger Am., Inc., Cambridge, 1975-77, gen. counsel, 1977-80; gen. counsel Badger Engrs., Inc., Cambridge, 1980-82, v.p., 1982-94, gen. counsel, 1982-94, asst. sec., 1982-93, sec., 1993-94; gen. counsel The Badger Co., Cambridge, 1993-94, v.p., sec., 1993-94; asst. gen. counsel, asst. sec. Raytheon Engrs. & Constructors, Inc., Cambridge, 1994-95, asst. sec., 1995—; dir. ethics compliance programs Raytheon Engrs. & Constructors Internat., Inc., 1995—; vis. lectr. dept. chem. engring. Tufts U., Medford, Mass., 1983, 84. With U.S. Army, 1961-68. Mem. ABA, Mass. Bar Assn., Licensing Execs. Soc., Nat. Contractors Assn. (govt. affairs and gen. counsels com.), Ethics Officers Assn. Republican. Episcopalian. Avocations: boating, swimming, fishing. Home: 13 Stacey Cir Windham NH 03087-1644 Office: Raytheon Engrs & Constructors Inc 1 Broadway Cambridge MA 02142-1100

GLAUTHIER, T. J., federal official; b. Durham, N.C., Jan. 3, 1944; s. Theodore and Martha May (Myers) G.; m. Carrie L. Bostrom, June 11, 1966 (div. 1973); children: Jeff, Paul, Tad; m. M. Brigid O'Farrell, July 9, 1977; 1 child, Patrick O. AB, Claremont (Calif.) Men's Coll., 1965; MBA, Harvard Bus. Sch., 1967. Cons. Peat, Marwick, Livingston, L.A., 1967-68; v.p. Applied Computer Tech., L.A., 1968-70; cons. Applied Decision Systems, Cambridge, Mass., 1970-74; v.p. Temple, Barker & Sloane, Inc., Lexington, Mass., 1974-90; head Pub. Policy Practice, 1980-90; head Washington office, 1986-90; dir. energy and climate change World Wildlife Fund, Washington, 1990-93; assoc. dir. nat. resources, energy and sci. U.S. Office Mgmt. and Budget, Washington, 1993-98; dep. sec., COO U.S. Dept. Energy, 1999—; overseer budgets, legis. and policy clearance U.S. Dept. Agr., U.S. Dept. Energy, U.S. Dept. Interior, EPA, NASA, NSF, Smithsonian, Corps of Engrs., Kennedy Ctr., TVA, other sml. agencies. Pres. Lake Barcroft Assn., 1989-94; assoc. Lake Barcroft Watershied Improvement Dist., 1989—; del. Va. State Dem. Conv., 1993, 97. Democrat. Unitarian. Home: 6304 Crosswoods Cir Falls Church VA 22044-1302 Office: Dept Energy 1000 Independence Ave Washington DC 20585

GLAVIN, A. RITA CHANDELLIER (MRS. JAMES HENRY GLAVIN, III), lawyer; b. May 11, 1937; d. Pierre Charles and Helen C. (Fox) Chandellier; m. James H. Glavin, III, June 1, 1963; children: Helene, James, Rita, Henry. AB cum laude, Middlebury Coll., 1958; JD, Union U., 1961. Bar: N.Y. 1961, U.S. Dist. Ct. (no. dist.) N.Y. 1961, U.S. Tax Ct. 1965, U.S. Supreme Ct. 1978. Assoc. Eugene Steiner, Albany, N.Y., 1961-64, Helen Fox Chandellier, Schenectady, 1965-76; mem. Glavin and Glavin, Waterford, Schenectady, 1965-86, 87—; del. 4th Jud. Dist. Nominating Conv., 1966-67; confidential law clk. presiding justices N.Y. State Ct. Claims, 1968-71; surrogate judge Saratoga County, 1986. Mem. editl. bd. Albany Law Rev., 1960-61. Bd. dirs., chmn. fin. com. Schenectady YWCA, 1979-81; mem. Univ. Coun. SUNY, Albany, 1985—; tech. advisor HSA of Northeastern N.Y. Maternity and Pediat. Com., 1976; bd. dirs. Schenectady Jr. League, 1974, 76; assn. coun. mem., coll. trustees SUNY, 1991—, sec., 1996—; del. N.Y. State Jr. League Pub. Affairs Com., 1976; sec. Bellevue Maternity Hosp., Inc., 1966—, bd. dirs. 1966-83, bd. advisors, 1984—; trustee Middlebury Coll., 1978-88, chmn. law com., 1982-88, vice chmn. bd. dirs., 1986-87. Mem. N.Y. State Bar Assn. (mem. ho. of dels. 1987-88, nominating com. 1988-90), Saratoga County Bar Assn. (exec. com. 1981—, v.p. 1985, pres. 1986), Schenectady County Bar Assn., Phi Beta Kappa, Kappa Kappa Gamma. Office: Glavin & Glavin PO Box 40 69 2nd St Waterford NY 12188-2493

GLAVIN, JAMES EDWARD, landscape architect; b. Syracuse, N.Y., Aug. 18, 1923; s. James Edward and Florence Ellen (Nelson) G.; m. Helen Catherine Hartnett, Aug. 24, 1946; children—Kathleen Glavin Kopitsky, Timothy, David, Matthew, Martin, Maureen. B.S. in Landscape Architecture, SUNY Coll. Environ. Sci. and Forestry, Syracuse, 1948. City planner Syracuse Planning Commn., 1948-49; chief land planning dept. Sargent Webster Crenshaw & Folley, Syracuse, 1951-56; partner Hueber Hares Glavin (architects, landscape architects, and engr., and predecessor), Syracuse, 1956-88, James E. Glavin & Assos. (landscape architects), Syracuse, 1956-88, Syracuse Scale Models, 1968-88, Glavin & Van Iderstine Landscape Architects, 1980-88; pvt. cons., 1988—; vis. juror, lectr. State U. Coll. Environ. Sci. and Forestry, 1959, 65, 69, State U. Coll. Agr., Cornell U., 1970—; mem. faculty adv. coun. Sch. Landscape Architecture, N.Y. State U. Coll. Environ. Sci. and Forestry, 1990—; cons. N.Y. State Council Arts, 1971; mem. N.Y. State Bd. Landscape Architects, 1987-91. Contbr. articles to profl. pubs.; contbg.; editor: Empire State Architect, 1957-60. Mem. Citizens Found., Syracuse, 1957-77, St. Thomas More Found, 1965-88; bd. mem. Hiawatha Coun., Boy Scouts of Am., 1980-88, adv. bd., 1988—; bd. mem. Adirondack Archtl. Heritage, 1993—, Clifton-Fine Hosp., 1998—; trustee Clifton Cmty. Libr., 1994. Recipient Design award Am. Assn. Nurserymen, 1969, 71; named Outstanding Alumni, SUNY Coll. Environ. Sci. and Forestry Alumni Assn., 1994. Fellow Am. Soc. Landscape Architects (past co-chmn. pvt. practice com., Design award 1968, 71); mem. ASCE (past v.p. Syracuse chpt.), Sigma Lambda Alpha. Home and Office: PO Box 491 Cranberry Lake NY 12927-0491

GLAVINE, TOM (THOMAS MICHAEL GLAVINE), professional baseball player; b. Concord, Mass., May 25, 1966; m. Carri Dobbins, Nov. 7, 1992. Grad. high sch., Mass. Pitcher Atlanta Braves, 1984—. Recipient Cy Young award Baseball Writers' Assn. Am., 1991, 98, Silver Slugger award, 1991, 95; named Nat. League Pitcher Yr., Sporting News, 1991, named to Nat. League All-Star Team, 1991-93, 96-99. Tied as leader of Nat. League pitching victories, 1991-92. Office: Atlanta Braves Turner Field PO Box 4064 Atlanta GA 30302-4064*

GLAZE, LYNN FERGUSON, development consultant; b. Oakland, Calif., May 24, 1933; d. Kenneth Loveland and Constance May (Pedder) Ferguson; m. Harry Smith Glaze, Jr., July 3, 1957; children: Catherine, Charles Richard. BA, Stanford U., 1955, MA, 1966. Devel. dir. Greenwich Acad., Conn., 1982-84; devel. cons. Del. Learning Ctr., Brandywine Mus., Opera Del., others, 1984—. Pres. Darien-Norwalk YWCA, Conn., 1973-76; sec. Darien Republican Town com., 1974-79; dist. chmn. Darien Rep. Meeting, 1974-76, mem. Rep. Nat. Conv. Platform Com., 1988; vestry St. Luke's Ch., Darien, 1979-82; justice of the peace, Darien, 1981-84; bd. dirs. Ingleside Homes, Inc., 1986-92, Henrietta Johnson Med. Ctr., 1994-97; pres. Del. ProChoice Med. Fund, 1997-99; mem. Gov.'s Small Bus. Coun., 1987, EEOC, New Castle County, 1991-94. Fellow Coro Found.

GLAZE, THOMAS A., state supreme court justice; b. Jan. 14, 1938; s. Phyllis Laser; children: Steve, Mike, Julie, Amy, Ashley. BSBA, U. Ark., 1960, JD, 1964. Exec. dir. Election Research Council Inc., 1964-65; legal advisor, 1965-66; staff atty. Pulaski County Legal Aid, 1966-67, asst. then dep. atty. gen., 1967-70; pvt. practice law, 1970-79; chancellor Ark. Chancery Ct., 6th Jud. Cir., 1979-80; judge Ark. Ct. Appeals, 1981-86; assoc. justice Ark. Supreme Ct., 1987—; co-author Ark. Election Act, 1969, Ark. Consumer Act; lectr. U. Ark. Bd. dirs. Vis. Nurses Corp., Youth Home Inc. Office: Ark Supreme Ct Justice Building 625 Marshall St Little Rock AR 72201-1054*

GLAZEBROOK, JAMES G., federal judge; b. 1955. AB, Middlebury Coll., 1977; JD, Case Western U., 1980. Law clk. hon. John A. Reed Jr. U.S. Dist. Ct. (mid. dist.) Fla., 1980-82, asst. U.S. Atty., 1980-82, magistrate judge, 1996—. Mem. ABA, FBA, Am. Judicature Soc., Orange County Bar Assn. Office: Rm 218 80 N Hughey Ave Orlando FL 32801

GLAZEBROOK, RITA SUSAN, nursing educator; b. St. Paul, Apr. 26, 1948; d. David L. and Beverly Ruth (Penhiter) Beccue; m. Harold L. Glazebrook, Dec. 20, 1986; children: Julie, Robert J., Scott, Robert M., Katherine. Diploma, RN, Abbott Hosp. Sch. Nursing, Mpls., 1970; BS in Nursing, Augsburg Coll., Mpls., 1979; MS in Nursing, U. Minn., 1981, PhD in Edn. Adminstrn., 1987. Staff, asst. head nurse United Hosps., Inc., St. Paul, 1970-78; staff Med. Pers. Pool, St. Paul, 1978-81; assoc. prof., chair dept. St. Olaf Coll., Northfield, Minn., 1981. Contbr. articles to profl. jours. Faculty devel. grant Evan. Luth. Ch. Am. Mem. ANA, Minn. Nurses Assn., Assn. of Women's Health Obstetric and Neonatal Nurses, Sigma Theta Tau. Home: 8941 Jasmine Ln S Cottage Grove MN 55016-3422

GLAZER, BARRY DAVID, lawyer; b. Cleve., Oct. 10, 1948; s. Jacob J. and Constance (Schwartz) G.; m. Deborah Werbner, Sept. 28, 1984. A.B., Miami U., Oxford, Ohio, 1970; J.D., Mich. Law Sch., 1973. Bar: Minn. 1973, U.S. Dist. Ct. Minn. 1973, France Conseil Juridique 1981. Assoc., Dorsey & Whitney, Mpls., 1973-78, ptnr., 1979-80, resident ptnr., Paris, 1980-86, London, 1986-91, mng. ptnr., Brussels, 1991—. Mem. ABA, Internat. Bar Assn., Union Internat. des Avocats. Office: Dorsey & Whitney LLP, Square de Meeus 35, B 1000 Brussels Belgium

GLAZER, DONALD WAYNE, lawyer, business executive, educator; b. Cleve., July 26, 1944; s. Julius and Ethel (Goldstein) G.; m. Donna Serino; children: Elizabeth M., Mollie S. AB summa cum laude, Dartmouth Coll., 1966; JD magna cum laude, Harvard U., 1969; LLM, U. Pa., 1970. Bar: Mass. 1970. Assoc. Ropes & Gray, Boston, 1970-78, ptnr., 1978-92, counsel, 1992-96; ptnr. Am. Bus. Ptnrs. LLC, Boston, 1996-98; pres. Mugar/Glazer Holdings, Inc., Boston, 1992-95; vice chmn. fin. New Eng. TV Corp. and WHDH-TV, Inc., Boston, 1992-93; advisor counsel Goodwin Procter & Hoar, Boston, 1997—; co-founder Provant, Inc., Boston, 1998—; instr. corp. fin. Boston U. Law Sch., 1975; lectr. law Harvard U., Cambridge, Mass., 1978-91. Co-author: Massachusetts Corporation Law and Practice, 1991, Fitzgibbon and Glazer on Legal Opinions, 1992; co-editor First Ann. Inst. on Securities Regulation, 1970; contbr. articles to legal jours. Past chmn., trustee Cowen Slavin Found.; past trustee Santa Fe Neuroscis. Inst.; dir. Newton Girls Soccer League, past co-chmn. intramural com.; past trustee, past treas. Hillel Founds. of Greater Boston Inc.; trustee Program for Young Negotiators. Fellow Salzburg Seminar in Am. Studies, 1975. Mem. ABA (chmn. legal opinions com., co-reporter Legal Opinion Prins., past chmn. subcom. on employee benefits and exec. compensation, fed. securities law com., past co-chmn. task force on sec. 16 devels.), Boston Bar Assn. (past chmn., corp. sec., past chmn. securities law com., past co-chmn. legal opinions com.), Am. Law Inst., Tri-Bar Legal Opinions Com. (co-reporter Third-party Closing Opinions). Jewish. Home: 225 Kenrick St Newton MA 02458-2731

GLAZER, GARY MARK, radiology educator; b. Feb. 13, 1950; m. Diane Glazer; children: Daniel I., David A. AB, U. Mich., 1972; MD, Case Western Res. U., 1976. Intern in internal medicine U. Calif., San Francisco, 1976-77, resident in diagnostic radiology, 1977-80, clin. instr., fellow in diagnostic radiology, 1980-81; asst. prof. radiology, dir. div. body computed tomography U. Mich., Ann Arbor, 1981-84, assoc. prof. radiology, 1984-87, dir. divs. magnet resonance imaging and body computed tomography, 1984-89, assoc. prof. cancer ctr., 1986-87, prof. radiology, prof. cancer ctr., 1987-89; prof., chmn. dept. radiology Stanford (Calif.) Sch. Medicine, 1989—. Cons., assoc. editor, reviewer Radiology; cons., reviewer Jour. Computer Assisted Tomogrphy; cons., chmn., reviewer, mem. editorial bd. Radiographics; contbr. articles to profl. publs. Fellow Am. Cancer Soc., 1980-82, Clarence Heller Found., 1980-81. Mem. Am. Roentgen Ray Soc., Radiology Soc. N.Am., Soc. Magnetic Resonance in Medicine, Fred Jenner Hodges Soc., Soc. Magnetic Resonance Imaging, Alpha Omega Alpha. Office: Stanford Sch Med Dept Radiology Stanford CA 94305*

GLAZER, GERALD SHERWIN, real estate broker; b. Milw., Sept. 26, 1942; s. David and Dorothy (Joseph) G.; m. Mildred Susan Cohen, July 4, 1965; children: Channa Glazer Skier, Laya Glazer Witty, Meir, Chaim. BS, U. Chgo., 1963; MS, Northwestern U., 1965. Instr. in math. U. Wis., Waukesha, 1967-74; regional claims mgr. MGIC Investment Corp., Milw., 1974-78; broker Lake Park Inv. Realty, 1978-80; acct. Astronautics Corp. of Am., 1980-82; instr. Milw. Area Tech. Coll., 1983-84, 1983-85; owner/broker Prime Properties, 1985-92; adminstrv. specialist Dept. of City Devel., City of Milw., 1992-94, Milw. Housing Authority, 1992-94; real estate broker Jarvis Realty Inc., Milw., 1994—. Author: Foreclosed Homes, 1988. Ward committeeman Dem. Party, Milw. County, 1970-72; bd. dirs. Milw. Jewish Coun., 1985—, Sherman Park Cmty. Assn., Milw., 1968-70. Alumni fellow U. Wis., 1966-67; recipient State Merit award State of Wis., 1969. Mem. Milw. Bd. Realtors (mem. issues com. 1997), Jewish Sacred Soc. Milw. (v.p. 1980-82, pres. 1982-85), Am. Jewish Congress. Home: 2944 N 50th St Milwaukee WI 53210-1640 Office: Jarvis Realty Inc 5909 W North Ave Milwaukee WI 53208-1058

GLAZER, GUILFORD, real estate developer; b. Knoxville, Tenn., July 17, 1921; s. Aaron Usher and Ida (Bressoff) G.; children: Emerson, Erika; m. Diane Pregerson, Jan. 29, 1967. Mech. Engr., George Wash. U., 1939; Metallurgy, U. Louisville, 1943. Bd. dirs. The Torrance (Calif.) Co., 1990, Del Amo Fashion Ctr., Torrance, Calif., 1990; owner operator Allegheny Ctr., Pitts; bd. dirs. Rand-UCLA Ctr. Study Soviet Internat. Behavior, L.A. developer various shopping ctrs. and office bldgs. in U.S. Pres. Reagan Libr. Found., Nixon Libr. Foun.; trustee L.A. Holocaust Meml., Jerusalem Found., Stop Cancer, Bell Shelter for Homeless; founder Ford's Theatre, Washington, Am. Friends of the Israel Def. Force; mem. Wilshire Blvd. Temple, L.A.County Mus. Art, Unified Fund Music Ctr. With USN, 1942-45. Recipient Hon. Fellow U. Tel Aviv. Mem. World Affairs Coun., Tamarisk Club, Hillcrest Country Club, Monterey Country Club, Palm Desert Club. Jewish. Avocation: golf. Office: Krasne & Mellon LLP 9440 Santa Monica Blvd Ste 610 Beverly Hills CA 90210-4619

GLAZER, JACK HENRY, lawyer; b. Paterson, N.J., Jan. 14, 1928; s. Samuel and Martha (Merkin) G.; m. Zelda d'Angleterre, 1979. BA, Duke U., 1950; JD, Georgetown U., 1956; postgrad. U. Frankfurt (W.Ger.), 1956-57; S.J.D. U. Calif.-Berkeley, 1977. Bar: D.C. 1957, Calif. 1968. Atty., GAO and NASA, 1958-60; mem. maritime div. UN Internat. Labour Office, Geneva, Switzerland, 1960; spl. legal adv. UN Internat. Telecommunication Union, Geneva, 1960-62; atty. NASA Washington, 1963-66; chief counsel NASA-Ames Research Center, Moffett Field, Calif., 1966-88; gov. Calif. Maritime Acad., 1975-78; asst. prof. Hastings Coll. Law, 1985-87; prof., assoc. dean bus. sch. San Francisco State U., 1988-92. Dir. San Francisco Palace of Fine Arts, 1995. Comdr. Calif. Naval Militia, ret. Capt. JAGC, USNR, ret. Mem. Calif. Bar Assn., D.C. Bar Assn., White's Inn (reader). Contbr. articles on internat. law to profl. jours. Office: White's Inn 37 White St San Francisco CA 94109-2609

GLAZER, MALCOLM, professional sports team executive; b. Rochester, N.Y., Aug. 25, 1928; m. Linda; children: Avram, Kevin, Bryan, Joel, Ed, Darcie. Owner, pres. Tampa Bay (Fla.) Buccaneers, 1995—; pres., CEO First Allied Corp.; chmn. of bd. Zapata Corp., Houston, 1992—; bd. dirs. Specialty Equipment Cos. Active Am. Cancer Soc., Sloan-Kettering Cancer Ctr., United Jewish Appeal, Jewish Guild for the Blind. Office: Tampa Bay Buccaneers One Buccaneer Pl Tampa FL 33607*

GLAZER, MICHAEL, lawyer; b. L.A., Oct. 10, 1940. BS, Stanford U., 1962; MBA, Harvard U., 1964; JD, U. Calif., L.A., 1967. Bar: Calif. 1967, D.C. 1980. Law clk. to hon. Roger J. Traynor Calif. Supreme Ct., 1967-68; commr. L.A. Dept. of Water & Power, 1973-76; chmn. Calif. Water Commn., 1976-78; asst. adminstr. nat. oceanic and atmospheric adminstrn. U.S. Dept. of Commerce, 1978-80; dir. Met. Water Dist. of So. Calif., 1984-91; ptnr. Paul, Hastings, Janofsky & Walker LLP, L.A. Articles editor U. Calif. at L.A. Law Rev., 1966-67. Mem. State Bar Calif. (com. on corps. 1986-87), L.A. County Bar Assn. (chair fed. securities regulation com. 1988-90, chair exec. com. bus. and corp. law sect. 1995-96), Order of the Coif, Phi Beta Kappa. Office: Paul Hastings Janofsky & Walker LLP 555 S Flower St Los Angeles CA 90071-2300

GLAZER, REA HELENE See KIRK, REA HELENE

GLAZER, RICHARD BASIL, university program director; b. Boston, Dec. 20, 1933; s. Edward and Marie (Stearns) G. BS in Biol. Scis., Colo. State U., 1957; MS in Zoology and Forestry, Pa. State U., 1959; postgrad., Cornell U. Assoc. dir. Project Biotech Am. Inst. Biol. Scis., Washington, 1971-73; dir. environ. and energy programs Ulster County C.C., Stone Ridge, N.Y., 1974-81; chair divsn. bus. and human resources Ulster County C.C., Stone Ridge, 1981-86; dean divsn. math., phys. engring., computer sci. techs. Westchester C.C., Valhalla, N.Y., 1986-96; dir. corp. found. and govt. rels. Iona Coll., New Rochelle, N.Y., 1996—; pres. SUNY Coun. 4-Yr. Coll. Bus. Faculty Adminstrs. Bus. Schs. and Colls.; mem. SUNY Chancellor's Articulation Task Force in Bus.; chair mini-course devel. project NSF-Purdue U.; mem. nat. task force 2-yr. coll. biologists; vis. lectr. Am. Inst. Biol. Scis.; mem. commn. higher edn. Mid. States Assn. Schs. and Colls. evaluation team; mem. evaluation team N.Y. State Dept. Edn.; chmn. nat. task force on assoc. degrees in higher edn. in bus.; mem. oversight com. Am. Assn. Environ. Engring. Profs. Author over 100 curriculum materials in field. Chmn. health svcs. coun. United Way, Ulster County, N.Y., 1969-71; supr. Town of Rosendale, N.Y., 1974-80; bd. dirs. Mid-Hudson Valley Tech. Devel. Ctr., Fishkill, N.Y., 1988-96; pres. Rosendale Pub. Libr., 1989-95; dist. chmn. Minnewaska Trail Boy Scouts Am.; chmn. shared med. computer facilities com. Kingston and Benedictine Hosp.; bd. dirs. Am. Lung Assn. Hudson Valley chpt.; chmn. bd. rev. Hudson Valley Health Systems Agy.; firefighter Bloomington Fire Dept.;. Recipient cert. Spl. Recognition, U.S. Congress, 1995, Soc. Mfg. Engrs. award; fellow U.S. Dept. Interior Fish and Wildlife Svc., NSF, Cornell U. Mem. Am. Assn. C.C.s., Phi Sigma Soc. (hon.), Tau Alpha Pi (hon.), Alpha Beta Gamma (hon.). Avocations: fishing, hiking, photography, jogging. Home: 69 Pond View Ln Chappaqua NY 10514-3728

GLAZER, RONALD BARRY, lawyer; b. Phila., Jan. 13, 1943; m. Adele J. Kay, June 12, 1965; children: Jodi M. Glazer, Jennifer G. Shorr. AB cum laude, Dickinson Coll., 1964; LLB cum laude, U. Pa., 1967. Bar: Pa. 1967, Fla. 1975. Sr. ptnr. Wolf, Block, Schorr & Solis-Cohen, Phila., 1987—; lectr. Pa. Bar Inst., Temple U. Law Sch., Phila., 1984-86. Author: Pennsylvania Condominium Law and Practice, 1975, 3d edit., 1995. Mem. ABA, Pa. Bar Assn., Phila. Bar Assn. (chmn. real property law sect. 1987), Internat. Conf. Shopping Ctrs., Am. Coll. Real Estate Lawyers, Cmty. Assns. Inst., Coll. of Lawyers. Office: Wolf Block Schorr 111 S 15th St Ste 1200 Philadelphia PA 19102-2678

GLAZER, TOM (THOMAS ZACARIAH GLAZER), folksinger, writer, composer; b. Phila., Sept. 2, 1914; s. Jacob and Sonia (Schochet) G.; m. Miriam Reed Eisenberg, June 25, 1944 (div.); children: John P.; m. Peter R. Student, CCNY, 1938-41. Rec. artist, 1946—; folksinger. Author: (songbooks) Tom Glazer's Treasury of Songs for Children, 1963, America the Beautiful, 1987, others, ltd. edit. selected poems, 1994; composer: Melody of Love (No. 1 song U.S. 1956), Till We Two Are One, A Worried Man, Skokiaan, On Top of Spaghetti; first artist to record Greensleaves and Twelve Days of Christmas, 1946; composer songs and score for film A Face in the Crowd. Recipient several Peabody awards for radio and TV shows. Mem. ASCAP, AFTRA, Am. Fedn. Musicians, Screen Actors Guild, Songwriters Guild Am. Club: The Coffee House (N.Y.C.). Avocations: tennis, literature, French, science, philosophy. Home and Office: 5500 Wissahickon Ave Apt 403A Philadelphia PA 19144-5638

GLAZIER, LYLE, writer, educator; b. Leverett, Mass., May 8, 1911; s. Harry Lee and Mertie Abby (Briggs) G.; m. Amy Louise Niles July 15, 1939 (dec. Mar. 1987); children: Laura, Susan, Alis. AB, Middlebury Coll., 1933, MA Bread Loaf Sch. of English, 1937; PhD, Harvard U., 1950; postgrad. in word processing, Vt. C.C., 1993-94. Prin. Northfield Mass. Ctr. Graded Sch., 1934-35; housemaster Mt. Hermon Sch. for Boys, Gill, Mass., 1935-37; instr. English, Bates Coll., Lewiston, Maine, 1937-42, Tufts Coll., Somerville, Mass., 1942-44; asst. in Shakespeare, Harvard U., Cambridge, Mass., 1944-45; tchg. fellow Harvard U. and Radcliffe Coll., Cambridge, Mass., 1945-47; asst. prof. English, U. Buffalo, 1947-52, assoc. prof., chmn. Am. studies, 1952-63; prof. English and Am. studies SUNY, Buffalo, 1965-72, prof. emeritus, 1972—; Fulbright chair Am. studies U. Istanbul, 1961-63, Fulbright Lectr. Hacettepe U., Ankara, Turkey, 1968-69, vis. prof., 1970, 71; lectr. U. Madras, India, 1970, 71; cons. thematic studies CUNY, 1973-75; vis. prof. Sana'a U., North Yemen, 1980; vol. adj. prof. So. Vt. Coll., Bennington, 1984-86; USIS vol. expert Am. lit., ndia, 1971; vol. prof. Miles Coll., Birmingham, 1967. Author: (novel) Summer for Joey, 1987, Stills from a Moving Picture, 1974, (poetry) Orchard Park and Istanbul, 1965, You Too, 1969, Voices of the Dead, 1971, The Dervishes, 1971, Two Continents, 1976, Azubah Nye, 1988, Recalls, 1986, Prefatory Lyrics, 1991, Searching for Amy, 1993, (criticism) American Decadence and Rebirth, 1971, Great Day Coming, 1988, Bennington Politics and Schools, 1986, Included in Reflections on a Gift of a Watermelon Pickle and Other Modern Verse (children's poetry anathology selected by children), 1966, 95, Contemporary Authors Autobiography Series, 1996; contbr. poems and articles to profl. and lit. jours.; contbr. to Festschrift for S.M. Pandeya, Banaras Hindu U., 1996. Exec. com. Friends of Bennington Free Libr., 1990-92; mem. sch. bd., vice chmn. Orchard Park (N.Y.) Sch. Dist., 1952-58; mem. Town Charter Commn., Bennington, 1987-89; mem. Gamaliel Painter's Cane Soc., Middlebury Coll., 1990—, mem. founders soc. Founders Soc., 1998—, mem. exec. com. Friends of Libr., Middlebury Coll., 1987-89; mem. Ret. Srs. Vol. Program, 1973—; mem. Bennington County Dem. Com., 1984-87; mem. exec. com. Bennington Area AIDS Project, 1990—; mem. nat. steering com. Clinton/Gore 1996, 1995-98, Gore 2000, 1999—; mem. Bennington Area Art Coun., 1990—; mem. Bennington Area Home Health Assn., 1990—, Bennington Counseling Svc., 1990; mem. Bennington County Chorus, 1973-79, patron, 1980—; mem. Grad. Students Supporting Middlebury Gay Lesbians, 1995; mem. Acad. of Am. Poets, ACLU, Bennington Mus. Found. Libr. of Congress Assocs., S.W. Vt. Regional Cancer Ctr., Rattlesnake Gutter Trust. Fellow Am. Coun. Learned Socs., 1951-52. Mem. MLA, Bennington Robert Frost Soc., Vt. Coun. on Arts, League Vt. Writers, Poets and Writers, Am. Assn. Ret. Persons, Edmund Hayes Soc., North Bennington Artists Soc., Bennington County Humane Soc., Vt. Hist. Soc., Nat. Trust for Hist. Preservation. Avocation: music. Home: RR 3 Bennington VT 05201-9803 *Our social, religious, and political institutions are medieval and inconsistent with our knowledge of the physical and biological universe. Unless we rid ourselves of nationalism, militarism and economic imperialism and the notion of an anthropomorphic universe, we are doomed to self destruction.*

GLAZIER, ROBERT CARL, publishing executive; b. Brandsville, Mo., Mar. 26, 1927; s. Vernie A. and Mildred F. (Beu) G.; m. Harriette Hubbard, June 5, 1949; children: Gregory Kent, Jeffrey Robert. Student, Drury Coll., 1944-46; BA, U. Wichita, 1949. Reporter Springfield (Mo.) Daily News, 1944-46; asst. city editor Wichita Eagle, 1946-49; journalism instr. U. Wichita, 1949-53; dir. pub. relations Springfield (Mo.) Pub. Schs., 1953-59; asso. dir. dept. radio and TV The Methodist Ch., Nashville, 1959-61; gen. mgr. WDCN-TV (Channel 2), Nashville, 1961-65, KETC (Channel 9), St. Louis, 1965-76; also exec. dir. St. Louis Ednl. TV Commn.; pres. So. Ednl. Communications Assn., 1976-80; chmn. bd. Springfield Communications, Inc., Mo., 1980—; bd. dirs. Systematic Savs. & Loan Assn.; pres., bd. dirs. Cox Health Systems. Bd. dirs. Adult Edn. Council Greater St. Louis, 1965-76, United Meth. Communications, 1980-86, Springfield Area Council of Chs., 1980-86, Lester E. Cox Med. Ctrs., 1988—. Served with AUS, 1945-46. Mem. Nat. Sch. Public Relations Assn. (past regional dir.), Nat. Acad. TV Arts and Scis. (gov.), Mo. Instructional TV Council, Ill. Instructional TV Commn., Nat. Assn. Ednl. Broadcasters. Methodist. Club: Rotary Internat. Home: 2305 E Meadow Dr Springfield MO 65804-4536 Office: 520 S Union Ave Springfield MO 65802-2660

GLAZIER, RON, zoological park administrator. Dir. Santa Ana Zoo, Santa Ana, Calif. Office: Santa Ana Zoo 1801 E Chestnut Ave Santa Ana CA 92701-5001

GLEACH, FREDERIC WRIGHT, anthropologist; b. Richmond, Va., June 1, 1960; s. Richard Colton and Judith Ann (Wright) G.; m. Vilma Iris Santiago-Irizarry, Feb. 16, 1947. BS, Va. Commonwealth U., 1984; AM, U. Chgo., 1987, PhD, 1992. Archaeologist Va. Commonwealth U., Richmond, 1982-88; Century fellow U. Chgo., 1986-90; vis. asst. prof. Cornell U., Ithaca, N.Y., 1993-94, 96—; asst. prof. Transylvania U., Lexington, Ky., 1994-95; editorial adv. bd. Algonquian Conf., Winnipeg, 1994—. Author: Powhatan's World and Colonial Virginia: a Confict of Cultures, 1997; mem. editorial bd. Chgo. Anthropology Exchange, 1987-90, Critical Studies in the

History of Anthropology, 1997—; contbr. articles to profl. jours. Philips Fund Rsch. grantee Am. Philosophical Soc., Phila., 1991-92. Mem. Am. Anthropological Assn. (centennial exec. com. 1999—), Am. Soc. Ethnohistory (sec., treas., 1994-98), Soc. Humanistic Anthropology (treas. 1998—), Orgn. Am. Historians, Soc. for Study Indigenous Lang. of Ams.

GLEASON, ABBOTT, history educator; b. Cambridge, Mass., July 21, 1938; s. Sarell Everett and Mary Eleanor (Abbott) G.; m. Sarah Caperton Fischer, June 11, 1966; children—Nicholas Abbott, Margaret Holliday. B.A., Harvard U., 1961, Ph.D., 1969. Asst. prof. history Brown U., Providence, 1969-73; assoc. prof. history Brown U., 1973-78, prof. history, 1978—, Keeney prof. history, 1993—; sec. Kennan Inst. for Advanced Russian Studies, Woodrow Wilson Ctr., Washington, 1980-82, chmn. history, 1989-92; dir. Watson Inst., 1999-00; mem. overseers com. to visit Davis Ctr. for Russian Studies, Harvard U., Cambridge, 1981-85, 91-97. Author: European and Muscovite, 1972, Young Russia, 1980, Totalitarianism, 1995; co-editor: Bolshevik Culture, 1985, Shared Destiny, 1985. Howard Found. fellow, 1973-74; Rockefeller fellow Aspen Inst., 1977; Mellon fellow Harvard U., 1985. Mem. Am. Hist. Assn., Am. Assn. Advancement Slavic Studies (del. to Am. Coun. Learned Socs. 1984-87, bd. dirs. 1991-97, exec. com. 1994-97, pres. 1995). Democrat. Home: 30 John St Providence RI 02906-1043 Office: Brown U Dept History 142 Angell St Providence RI 02912-9040

GLEASON, CAROL ANN, rehabilitation nurse; b. Franklin, N.H., June 17, 1950; d. Adam Victor and Rita T. (Robichaud) Novak; m. William J. Gleason, Aug. 24, 1974; 1 child, Stephen Bryan. Diploma, St. Elizabeth Hosp., Boston, 1971; M in Mgmt., Cambridge Coll., Harvard Square, Mass., 1997—. RN, Mass.; cert. rehab. RN; cert. case mgr.; lic. rehab. counselor. Surg. nurse St. Elizabeth Hosp., Boston, 1971-73; pvt. nurse for chief of otolaryngology Mass. Eye and Ear Infirmary, Boston, 1973-74; pvt. duty nurse Met. Nurses, Inc., Boston, 1975; liaison, mktg. RN Spaulding Rehab. Hosp., Boston, 1975-81; admissions nurse Shaughnessy-Kaplan Rehab. Hosp., Salem, Mass., 1982-86; mktg. assoc. New Medico Head Injury System, Lynn, Mass., 1986-88; asst. regional mgr. New Medico, Lynn, 1988-90; rehab. specialist Cost Containment Mgmt., Braintree, Mass., 1990-91; sr. rehab. cons. N.Am. Health and Rehab. Svcs., Nashua, N.H., 1991; sr. mktg. assoc. Greenery Rehab. Group, Newton, Mass., 1992-94; mgr. clin. bus. devel. Beverly Health & Rehab. Svcs., Inc., 1995-96; ind. cons., 1997—; dir. mktg. and census devel. Mariner Post Acute Network, 1997—; speaker Mass. Passenger Safety Bur., Boston, 1988-91; participant Nurse in Washington Internship, 1991. Contbg. author: The Speciality Practice of Rehabilitation Nursing, A Core Curriculum, 3d edit., 1993; editorial/mktg. cons. Pertinent Legislation Affecting Nurses newsletter, 1991-95; contbr. articles to profl. jours. Cert. vision/hearing tester Mass. Dept. Pub. Health, Boston, 1990-93; bd. dirs. Marblehead (Mass.) Festival of Arts, 1989-91, Jr. Aid Soc. Inc., Marblehead, 1979—; mem. MADD, Boston, 1990—. Recipient Occupant Safety award Mass. Nurses Assn., 1989, She Know's Where She's Going award Girls Inc., 1989. Mem. ANA, Mass. Nurses Assn., Nat. Head Injury Found., Nat. Assn. Rehab. Profls. in the Pvt. Sector (chpt. bd. dirs. 1987-90), Pro-Mass (chpt. bd. dirs. 1990-93), Mass. Coun. Nursing Orgns. (bd. dirs. 1986-96), Assn. Rehab. Nurses (chmn. mktg./pub. rels. 1990-91, health policy 1988-94, vice chmn. health policy 1991-92, chmn. health policy 1992-93, pres. bd. dirs. New Eng. chpt. 1988-89), Ins. Rehab. Nurses New Eng. (bd. dirs., co-pres. 1992-94, advisor 1994—, legis. chair 1990-92, advisor 1994-98), Case Mgmt. Soc. New Eng. (bd. dirs. 1998—), Case Mgmt. Soc. Am. Democrat. Roman Catholic. Avocations: cooking, music, travel.

GLEASON, JAMES EDWARD, JR., mining engineer; b. Oak Park, Ill., June 8, 1954; s. James Edward and Lorraine Louise Gleason; m. Joyce Lynn Jones, June 30, 1978 (dec. June 1985); children: Lorraine Gayle, Michael James; m. Teresa Jo Spencer; children: Charles H. Kitts, Joshua Aaron. BSCE, U. Ill., 1977. Indsl. engr. Consolidation Coal, Bluefield, W.Va., 1977; mine engr. Consolidation Coal, Middlesboro, Ky., 1977-79; sect. foreman Consolidation Coal, Middlesboro, 1979-80, shift foreman, 1980-82; asst. supt. Consolidation Coal, Bluefield, 1982-91; sect. foreman Consolidation Coal, Washington, Pa., 1991—. Mem. Am. Inst. Mining Engrs. Republican. Roman Catholic. Home: 69 Woodside Dr Washington PA 15301

GLEASON, JEAN BERKO, psychology educator; b. Cleve., Dec. 19, 1931; d. Arthur E. and Alice (Gelberger) Berko; m. Andrew Mattei Gleason, Jan. 26, 1959; children: Katherine, Pamela, Cynthia. AB, Radcliffe Coll., 1953, AM, 1955, PhD, 1958. USPHS fellow MIT, 1958-59; research assoc. VA Med. Ctr., Boston, 1961—; vis. asst. prof. psychology Boston U., 1972-73, assoc. prof., 1973-76, prof., 1976—, chairperson dept. psychology, 1985-89, acting chair dept. psychology, 1997, dir. grad program devel. psychology, 1975-78, 82-85, dir. grad. program human devel., 1997—; research assoc. edn. Harvard U., Cambridge, Mass., 1968-70, prin. research assoc. psychiatry, 1970-72; rsch. scholar in residence Inst. Linguistics, Hungarian Acad. Sci., 1981, 83; mem. mental retardation rsch. com. Nat. Inst. Child Health and Human Devel., 1981-85; trustee Ctr. for Applied Linguistics, Washington, 1989-94. Author: The Development of Language, 1983, 4th edit., 1997, You Can Take It With You, 1989, Psycholinguistics, 1993, 2nd edit., 1998; mem. editl. bd. Child Development, 1971-77, Discourse Processes, 1982—, Applied Psycholinguistics, 1982—; assoc. editor: Language, 1997—; contbr. articles to profl. jours. Recipient Editors award Jour. Speech and Hearing Research, 1970. Fellow AAAS, APA; mem. ACLU, Linguistic Soc. Am. (chmn. program com. 1980-81), Acad. Aphasia, Soc. for Rsch. Child Devel., New Eng. Child Lang. Assn., Gypsy Lore Soc. (exec. bd. 1983-87, 92—, pres. 1996—), Internat. assn. for Study of Child Lang. (pres. 1990-93), Radcliffe Grad. Soc. (past pres.), Radcliffe Alumni Assn. (bd. dirs. 1969-72), Phi Beta Kappa (pres. Radcliffe chpt. 1965-68). Home: 110 Larchwood Dr Cambridge MA 02138-4639 Office: Boston U Dept Psychology 64 Cummington St Boston MA 02215-2407

GLEASON, JOHN JAMES, theatrical lighting designer; b. Bklyn., Apr. 10, 1941; s. John James and Sue (Manzolillo) G. B.A., Hunter Coll., 1963. Theatre design cons. Mummer Theatre, Oklahoma City, 1968-71, NTID, Rochester, N.Y., 1968-72, Repertory Theatre of Lincoln Ctr., N.Y.C., 1972; theatre design cons. NYU, 1983, master tchr. design, assoc. chair Tisch Sch. of the Arts, 1972-97. Lighting designer The Great White Hope, 1968, Over Here, 1974, My Fair Lady, 1976, The Royal Family, 1976, Der Rosenkavalier, Dallas Opera, 1982, Black Angel, Off Broadway, 1982, The Survivor, Broadway, 1981, The Philadelphia Story, Lincoln Ctr. Theatre Co., Madame Butterfly, Dallas Opera, The Mikado, N.Y.C. Opera, 1984, Werther, N.Y.C. Opera, 1986, The Magic Flute, N.Y.C. Opera, 1987, Dr. Faustus, N.Y.C. Opera, 1992, Vanessa, Juilliard Opera, 1991, Fennimore & Gerda/Les Memelles de Tiresias, Juilliard Opera, 1992, 93, Puccini's Trittico, Juilliard Opera, 1985, Don Giovanni and Le Nozze di Figaro, Juilliard Opera, 1987, Die Zauberflöte, N.Y.C. Opera, 1987, King John, N.Y. Shakespeare Festival, 1988, Enrico IV, Roundabout Theatre, 1989, Jakob Lenz, N.Y. premiere The Crucible, 1988, L'Amico Fritz, 1989, Am. premiere Rothschild's Violin, 1990, Cimarosa's Le Donne Rivali, 1991, Viaggio A Reims, 1994, Incoronazione de Poppea, 1995, Love of 3 Oranges, 196, Really Rosie, Maurice Sendak Nat. Co., Monsieur Choufleuri, Lincoln Ctr., 1997; author: (screenplays) Overdue, 1985, Needing You, 1985, Final Cut, 1986, Into the Dark, 1989; contbg. editor: (mag.) Lighting Dimensions, Falstaff, 1991. Recipient Annual Theatre Design award Maharam Found., N.Y.C., 1972-73; recipient Drama Critics Circle award Los Angeles, 1975.

GLEASON, JOHN PATRICK, JR., trade association executive; b. N.Y.C., Nov. 11, 1941; s. John Patrick Sr. and Ruth T. (Madigan) G.; m. Judith Peper (dec. 1980); children: John P. III, Megan K.; m. Susan Leigh Collier, Mar. 31, 1984; children: Kevin M., Colin P. BS in Fgn. Service, Georgetown U., 1963; PMD, Harvard Bus. Sch., 1972. Gen. mgr. Pappagallo, Inc., Washington, 1964-67; export project mgr. U.S. Dept. Commerce, Washington, 1967-68; investment banker Blyth, Eastman Dillon, Inc., Washington, 1968-70; with U.S. Dept. Commerce, Washington, 1970-77, chief staff domestic and internat. bus. adminstrn., 1970-77, dep. asst. sec. commerce, 1970-77; pres. Brick Inst. Am., Reston, Va., 1977-86, Portland Cement Assn., Skokie, Ill., 1986—; bd. dirs., chmn. Coun. Masonry Rsch., Reston, 1985—, Masonry Industry Com., Washington, 1984—. Recipient Silver medal U.S. Dept. Commerce, Washington, 1978. Mem. Am. Soc. Assn. Execs., Chgo. Soc. Assn. Execs., River Bend Country Club (Great Falls, Va.), Carlton Club (Washington), Skokie Country Club (Glencoe, Ill.). Republican. Office: Portland Cement Assn 5420 Old Orchard Rd Skokie IL 60077-1053

GLEASON, JOHN THOMAS, consultant software development planner; b. South Amboy, N.J., Jan. 14, 1936; s. John Thomas and Evelyn Patricia Gleason; m. Irene Theresa Wallace, June 8, 1957; children: Maureen Gleason Bryant, John Kevin, Diane. BS in Engring., U.S. Mil. Acad., 1957; M Bus., U. Conn., 1964. Cert. nat. security mgmt. Commd. 2d lt. USAF, 1957, advanced through grades to col., 1982; ret., 1982; ops. rsch. analyst USAF Sys. Command, Andrews AFB, 1969-70; chief aircraft maintenance 459th Airlift Wing, Andrews AFB, 1971-77; chief strategic mobility br. Dept. of Def., Joint Chiefs of Staff, Washington, 1978-82; logistics engr. C3 TRW, Washington, 1983-84; logistics engr. space sys. fed. sys. divsn. IBM, Gaithersburg, Md., 1984-87, new bus. coord., 1987-89, planner airport automation gen. systems divsn., 1989-91; lead planner, image and records Image Plus IBM, Bethesda, Md., 1991-93, project mgr., 1993-95; instr. program mgmt. Strategic Resources Inc., Falls Church, Va., 1996-97, ret., 1997; cons. Integrated Computer Engring., Campbell, Calif., 1998—; FAA comml. pilot Cloud Club II, Hyde Field, Md., 1992-94. Mem. coms. Boy Scouts Am., Ohio, Fla., Md., 1959-61, 64-65, 71-78; pres. Ft. Washington (Md.) Pool Assn., 1991-92; pres. So. Prince Georges' Reps. Club, Prince Georges' County, Md., 1990-92, treas., 1995-97; mem. Rep. Ctrl. Com., Prince George's County, 1997—, 2nd vice-chmn., 1999—; chmn. Tax Reform Initiative by Marylanders, Prince Georges' County, 1982-95; bd. dirs. Md. Taxpayers Assn., 1985—, U.S. Mil. Acad. Class of 57, Washington Group, 1989-95; vol. canoe guide Jug Bay Park, Md., 1997—. Mem. Aircraft Owners and Pilots Assn., Ret. Officers Assn., Nature Conservancy, Md. Res. Officers Assn. (pres. Dept. of Md. 1982-83), Exptl. Aircraft Assn., Mensa, Intertel, Beta Gamma Sigma. Republican. Roman Catholic. Avocations: scuba diving, hiking, travel, flying. Home and Office: 13224 Warburton Dr Fort Washington MD 20744-6545

GLEASON, (JOHN) PHILIP, history educator; b. Wilmington, Ohio, Nov. 30, 1927; s. John and Anne Marie (Bergin) G.; m. Maureen Catherine Lacey; children: Ann, Daniel, Margaret, Philip M. BS in Edn., U. Dayton, 1951; MA, U. Notre Dame, 1955, PhD, 1960; LHD (hon.), Loyola U., 1993; LittD (hon.), Marquette U., 1999. Instr. U. Notre Dame, 1959-61, asst. prof., 1965-66, assoc. prof., 1966-74, prof., 1974-96, emeritus prof., 1996—, chmn. dept. history, 1971-74. Author: The Conservative Reformers, 1968, Keeping the Faith, 1987, Speaking of Diversity, 1992, Contending with Modernity, 1995; assoc. editor Rev. Politics, 1985—; mem. editl. bd. Jour. Am. History, 1980-81. With U.S. Army, 1946-48, PTO. Fellow NEH, 1974-75, 86-87; recipient Marianist award U. Dayton, 1994, Hesburgh award Assn. Cath. Colls. and Univs., 1997. Mem. Am. Hist. Assn., Am. Cath. Hist. Assn. (pres. 1978), Cath. Commn. on Intellectual and Cultural Affairs (nat. chmn. 1986-88), Orgn. Am. Historians, Immigration and Ethnic History Soc. (pres. 1997—), Phi Beta Kappa (pres. Notre Dame chpt. 1987-89). E-mail: ipgleason.2@nd.edu. Office: U Notre Dame Dept History Notre Dame IN 46556

GLEATON, HARRIET E., retired anesthesiologist; b. Altoona, Pa., Aug. 25, 1937; d. Munsey Sinclair and Anna Morgan (Scofield) G. BA, Franklin & Marshall Coll., 1959; MD, Temple U., 1962. Diplomate Am. Bd. Anesthesiology. Intern Mt. Sinai Hosp., N.Y.C., 1962-63; resident in anesthesiology Hosp. U. Pa., 1963-65; fellow Hosp. U. Pa., Phila., 1965-66, instr. anesthesiology, 1966-69; clin. anesthesiologist Michael Reese Hosp., Chgo., 1969-71; assoc. prof. U. Okla., Oklahoma City, 1971-81; clin. anesthesiologist Jane Phillips Episcopal Meml. Med. Ctr., Bartlesville, Okla., 1981-92; ret., 1992. Mem. AMA, Am. Soc. Anesthesiologists, Nature Conservancy, World Wildlife Fedn., Environ Def. Fund, Sierra Club. Avocations: photography, jogging, sewing, reading, computers.

GLEAVES, LEON ROGERS, marketing and sales executive; b. Louisville, May 4, 1939; s. Leon Rogers and Fain Mae (King) G.; m. Hallie Virginia Dumke, Apr. 9, 1966 (dec. Dec. 20, 1990); 1 child, Keith Browning. BS, U. Louisville, 1961, MBA, 1966. Sales mgmt. trainee GM, Louisville, 1965-67; advt. rep. The Christian Sci. Monitor, N.Y.C., 1967-72; mktg. and sales coord. White Lily Foods Co., Knoxville, Tenn., 1972-75; v.p. mktg. and sales Wilkins-Rogers, Inc., Ellicott City, Md., 1975—; spkr. in field. Bd. dirs. Bucknell U. Parents Assn., Lewisburg, Pa., 1992, 93, 94, 95; adv. com. Md. Agrl. Edn. Found., Balt., 1993, 94, 95, 96; mem. Home Econ. Adv. Bd. for Howard County Schs., Columbia, Md., 1993-98, 99, Home Econ. Adv. Bd. for Balt. City Schs., 1994, 95, 96, 97; adv. com. Md. Food Bank, Inc., Balt.; fin. com. So. Assn. State Depts. Agr., 1997; spkr. Future Bus. Leaders Am., 1997, 98, 99. Finalist Md. awd. Intl. Bus. Leadership. Mem. Balt./Washington Grocery Mfrs. Reps., Md. Food Exporters Assn., Am. Mktg. Assn., Home Baking Assn. (dir. 1990-92), So. Assn. State Depts. Agr. (fin. com. 1997). Avocations: tennis, classical and vintage jazz music, English mystery books and movies. Office: Wilkins-Rogers Inc 27 Frederick Rd Ellicott City MD 21043-4709

GLEAZER, EDMUND JOHN, JR., retired education educator; b. Phila., Aug. 24, 1916; s. Edmund John and Jane Hunter (Laurie) G.; m. Charlene A. Allen, Apr. 14, 1940; children: Allen, Sandra Jo, John, Susan. A.A., Graceland Coll., 1936; A.B., U. Cal. at Los Angeles, 1938; Ed.M., Temple U., 1943; Ed.D., Harvard, 1953. Minister Reorganized Ch. of Jesus Christ of Latter Day Saints, Phila., 1938-43; pres. Reorganized Ch. of Jesus Christ of Latter Day Saints (So. Iowa dist.), 1943-46, Graceland Coll., Lamoni, Ia., 1946-57; exec. dir. Am. Assn. Jr. Colls., Washington, 1958-81; vis. prof. George Washington U., Washington, 1981-85; Mem. U.S. Tech. Edn. Del. to, USSR, 1961, 76; edn. survey team AID, Kenya, 1962; chmn. Def. Adv. Com. on Edn. in Armed Forces, 1962; mem. vis. com. Stanford U., Sch. Edn., 1962; mem. Pres.'s Commn. on Fgn. Lang. and Internat. Studies, 1979; v.p. for N. Am., Internat. Council for Adult Edn., 1979; vis. prof. c.c. leadership program U. Tex., 1981—. Author: This is the Community College, 1968, Project Focus: A Forecast Study of Community Colleges, 1974, The Community College: Values, Vision and Vitality, 1980; Editor: American Junior Colleges, 1960, 63, 67, 71. Mem. North Central Jr. Colls. (pres. council 1954), Am. Assn. Jr. Colls. (pres. 1957), Am. Council on Edn. (sec., award for outstanding lifetime contbns. to Am. higher edn. 1980), Phi Delta Kappa. Clubs: Rotary (Washington), Cosmos (Washington). Home: 8208 Woodhaven Blvd Bethesda MD 20817-3176

GLEBA, BETH ANN (BETH ANN COLEMAN), communications executive; b. June 27, 1970. Cert. of desktop pub., Moore Coll. Art, 1992; BA, Albright Coll., 1994. Graphic artist Genex Svcs., Wayne, Pa., 1994-96, comm. and graphics adminstr., 1996—. E-mail: beth.coleman@genexservices.com.

GLECKNER, ROBERT FRANCIS, English language professional, educator; b. Rahway, N.J., Mar. 2, 1925; s. Adam F. and Frieda A. (Froehlich) G.; m. Glenda J. Karr, Feb. 7, 1946; children: Jeffrey M., Susan F. BA, Williams Coll., 1948; PhD, Johns Hopkins U., 1954. Instr. English Johns Hopkins U., 1949-51; editor Research Studies Inst., Maxwell AFB, Ala., 1951-52; instr. English U. Cin., 1952-54, U. Wis., 1954-57; asst., then assoc. prof. Wayne State U., Detroit, 1957-62; prof. English U. Calif. at Riverside, 1962-78, chmn. dept., 1962-66, lectr. extension div., 1962-64, 74, divisional dean humanities, 1968-70; dean Coll. Humanities, 1970-75, faculty research lectr., 1973; prof. English Duke U., Durham, N.C., 1978—; chmn. English dept. Duke U., 1982, dir. grad. studies in English, 1986-88; main spkr. UCLA ext. conf. humanities, Lake Arrowhead, Calif., 1964, U. Calif., Berkeley, 1976; spkr. U. N.C. Continuing Edn. Conf., Asheville, 1982; lectr. Am. Blake Found., 1981, U. Tulsa, U. Tex., U. Wash., U. Calif., Berkeley, U. Pa., U. N.Mex., Memphis State U., U. Md., La. State U., U. Tenn., Skidmore Coll., Siena Coll.; manuscript reader jours., univ. presses; del. Am. Assn. Higher Edn. meeting, 1963, 69, 72; cons. NEH, 1975-77, U.S. Dept. Edn., 1994—. Author: The Piper and the Bard: A Study of William Blake, 1959, Byron and the Ruins of Paradise, 1969, 2d edit. 1980, Blake's Prelude: Poetical Sketches, 1982, Blake and Spenser, 1985; (with Mark Greenberg) Approaches to the Teaching of Blake's "Songs of Innocence and of Experience," 1989; editor: (with G.E. Enscoe) Romanticism: Points of View, 1962, rev. edit. (sole editor), 1970, 75, Selected Writings of William Blake, 1967, rev. edit., 1971, The Complete Poetical Works of Lord Byron, 1975, Critical Essays on Lord Byron, 1991, (with B. Beatty) Byron's Plays: Critical Essays, 1996, Gray Agonistes: Thomas Gray and Masculine Friendship, 1996 (with T. Pfau) The Lessons of Romanticism, 1998; contbr. to A James Joyce Miscellany, 3d Series, 1962, A Blake Bibliography, 1964, Twelve and a Tilly: Essays on the 25th Anniversary of Finnegans Wake, 1966, William Blake: Essays for S. Foster Damon, 1969, A Concordance to the Writings of William Blake, 1967, Earl R. Wasserman Memorial Volume of ELH, 1975, Blake and the Moderns, 1981, (ann.) Romantic Movement Bibliography, 1990—, Rhetorical and Cultural Dissolution in Romanticism, 1996, Speak Silence: Rhetoric and Culture in Blake's "Poetical Sketches", 1996; mem. editl. bd. Wayne State U. Press, 1960-62, Romanticism Past and Present, 1979-88, 19th-Century Contexts, 1989—, The Byron Jour., 1990—, South Atlantic Rev., 1997—; mem. editl. adv. bd. Duke U. Press, 1984-89; assoc. editor Criticism: A Jour. for Lit. and the Arts, 1960-62; adv. bd. 1962-76; adv. editor Blake Studies, 1968-80; mem. adv. bd. Studies in Romanticism, 1977—; contbr. articles to profl. jours., chpts. to books. Mem. adv. bd. dirs. Am. Blake Found., 1970-88. Served to 1st lt. USAAF, 1943-45. Recipient Poetry Soc. Am. award, 1959; Faculty Rsch. Lectr. award U. Calif. at Riverside, 1973, Disting. Scholar award Keats-Shelley Assn. Am., 1991; grantee Carl and Lily Pforzheimer Found., 1969, 85, NEH, 1978, 85, Am. Philos. Soc., 1985-86, Am. Coun. Learned Socs., 1978-79; NEH sr. rsch. fellow, 1980-81, fellow The Huntington Libr., 1987, 90. Mem. Am. Com. Byron Soc. (charter), Keats-Shelley Assn., Wordsworth-Coleridge Assn., Internat. Byron Soc., South Atlantic MLA, Am. Soc. 18th Century Studies, N. Am. Soc. Study of Romanticism, Assn. Lit. Scholars and Critics, Phi Beta Kappa, Beta Theta Pi. Episcopalian. Home: 11312 Hickory Grv Church Rd Raleigh NC 27613-5952 Office: Duke Univ PO Box 90015 Durham NC 27708-0015

GLEDHILL, ROGER CLAYTON, statistician, engineer, mathematician, educator; b. Parkersburg, W.Va., July 14, 1943; s. Arthur Clayton and Frances Marie (Freeman) G.; m. Barbara Louise Baker, June 12, 1965; children: Diane Michelle, David Arthur. BBA, Miami U., Oxford, Ohio, 1965; MA, U. Mass., 1972; MS, PhD, Va. Poly. Inst. and State U., 1976. Assoc. prof. statistics Ea. Mich. U., Ypsilanti, 1976—. Author: Numerical Methods, 1993; contbr. articles to profl. publs. Ford Found. fellow, 1975. Mem. Mensa, Alpha Iota Delta, Phi Kappa Phi, Alpha Pi Mu, Pi Mu Epsilon, Omicron Delta Epsilon, Alpha Kappa Psi, Tau Beta Phi, Beta Gamma Sigma, Tau Kappa Epsilon. Avocations: computers, sailing, photography, travel, astrophysics. Office: Ea Mich Univ Owen Hall Ypsilanti MI 48197

GLEESON, JOHN, judge, educator; b. 1953. BA, Georgetown U., 1975; JD, U. Va., 1980. Bar: N.Y. Law clk. to Hon. Boyce F. Martin Jr. U.S. Cir. Ct., 1980-81; assoc. Cravath, Swaine & Moore, N.Y.C., 1981-85; asst. U.S. atty. for ea. dist. N.Y. Dept. Justice, N.Y.C., 1985-94; judge U.S. Dist. Ct. (ea. dist.) N.Y., Bklyn., 1994—; adj. prof. law Bklyn. Sch. Law, 1990-97, NYU Law Sch., 1995—; vis. prof. law U. Va. Sch. Law, 1994. Office: US Dist Ct 225 Cadman Plz W Brooklyn NY 11201-2741

GLEESON, PAUL FRANCIS, lawyer; b. Bronx, June 20, 1941; s. William Francis and Julia Anne (Dargis) G.; children: Kevin F., Sean W., Brendan J., Colleen J. AB in History, Fordham U., 1963; JD, U. Chgo., 1966. Bar: Ill. 1966, Fed. Trial Bar Ill. 1969, U.S. Ct. Appeals (6th cir.) 1972, U.S. Ct. Appeals (7th cir.) 1973, U.S. Ct. Appeals (8th cir.) 1997. Assoc. Vedder, Price, Kaufman & Kammholz, Chgo., 1966-73, ptnr., 1973—; adj. prof. DePaul U. Sch. of Law, 1991. Co-author (with Day, Green & Cleveland) The Equal Employment Opportunity Compliance Manual, 1978; columnist: (with B. Alper) Gleeson and Alper on Employment Law, Merrill's Illinois Legal Times, 1988-90. Capt. U.S. Army, 1966-68, Vietnam. Decorated Bronze Star; Floyd Russell Mechem scholar, 1963-66. Mem. Chgo. Bar Assn., Ill. Assn. Hosp. Attys., Am. Legion, VFW (post comdr. Northbrook, Ill.), Order of Coif, Phi Beta Kappa. Roman Catholic. Office: Vedder Price Kaufman & Kammholz 222 N La Salle St Ste 2600 Chicago IL 60601-1002

GLEICH, CAROL S., health professions education executive; b. Kewanee, Ill., Jan. 18, 1935; d. Carl and Edna (Krause) Gleich. BA, U. Iowa, 1958, MS, 1967, PhD in Health Sci. Edn., 1972. Cert. clin. chemistry technologist, Nat. Registry Clin. Chemistry. From instr. to asst. prof. pathology U. Iowa Sch. Medicine, Iowa City, 1972-77, edn. specialist divsn. allied health, 1977-88, chief resource devel. sec., 1988-90, health manpower edn. officer, physician manpower and credentialing, chief spl. projects and data analysis br. divsn. medicine, 1991-95, exec. sec. coun. grad. med. edn., 1991-95, dir. area health edn. ctr. nat. program, 1996; dir. area health edn. ctr. nat. program Bur. Health Professions, Health Resources & Svcs. Adminstrn., Rockville, Md., 1977—; allied health cons. to Egypt; chief Area Health Edn. Ctrs.; gov. cons. in internat. health profl. end., Russia, 1996; dir. Geriatric Edn. Ctrs. PHS; adj. assoc. prof. U. Md. Sch. Medicine; meme. Iowa Health Manpower Com., 1976—; cons. U. Wis. System Acad. Affairs, 1976; panelist and participant workshops; presenter an dchief del. internat. congress. Assoc. editor Am. Jour. Med. Tech., 1974-83, Jour. Allied Health, 1982-85; contbr. articles to profl. jours. Mem. Am. Soc. Allied Health Professions, Am. Soc. Clin. Pathologists (assoc., cert. med. technologist, sec. aSCPp Bd. Registry 1975-77), Am. Soc. Clin. Lab. Sci., D.C. Soc. Med. Tech. (Outstanding Med. Technologist of Yr. 1975), Beta Beta Beta (Pub. Health Svc. award 1995), Alpha Mu Tau. Home: 14800 Rocking Spring Dr Rockville MD 20853-3635 Office: Parklawn Bldg Room 9A-05 5600 Fishers Ln Rockville MD 20857-1750

GLEICH, GERALD JOSEPH, immunologist, medical scientist; b. Escanaba, Mich., May 14, 1931; s. Gordon Joseph and Agnes (Ederer) G.; m. Elizabeth Louise Hearn, Aug. 16, 1955 (div. 1976); children: Elizabeth Genevieve, Martin Christopher, Julia Katherine; m. Kristin Marie Leiferman, Sept. 25, 1976; children: Stephen Joseph, David Francis, Caroline Louise, William Gerald. B.A., U. Mich., 1953, M.D., 1956. Diplomate: Am. Bd. Internal Medicine. Intern Phila. Gen. Hosp., 1956-57; resident Jackson Meml. Hosp., Miami, Fla., 1959-61; instr. in medicine and microbiology U. Rochester, N.Y., 1961-65; cons. in medicine, prof. immunology and medicine Mayo Clinic-Med. Sch., Rochester, Minn., 1965—; chmn. dept. immunology Mayo Clinic, Rochester, Minn., 1982-90, George M. Eisenberg prof., 1995—; mem. bd. sci. counselors Nat. Inst. Allergy and Infectious Disease, 1981-83; chmn. subcom. on standardization allergens WHO, Geneva, 1974-75; lectr. Am. Acad. Allergy, 1976, 82; mem., chmn. immunological scis. study sect. NIH, 1984-87; John M. Sheldon Meml. lectr., 1976, 82, 88; Steve Lang Meml. Lectureship, 1980, Stoll-Stunkard lectr. Am. Soc. Parasitologists, 1986, David Talmage Meml. lectureship, 1987, Disting. lectr. Med. Scis. Mayo Clinic, 1988. Contbr. articles on eosinophilic leukocyte to profl. jours. Served to capt. USAF, 1957-59. Recipient Landmark in Allergy award, 1990; grantee Nat. Inst. Allergy and Infectious Disease, 1970—; AAAS fellow for studies of structure, biol. properties and role in pathogenesis of disease of basic proteins present in cytoplasmic granules of eosinophilic leukocytes, 1993. Fellow ACP, Am. Acad. Allergy and Immunology (hon. fellow award 1992), AAAS; mem. Am. Soc. Clin. Investigation, Am. Assn. Immunologists, Assn. Am. Physicians, Phi Beta Kappa, Phi Kappa Phi, Alpha Omega Alpha. Roman Catholic. Home: 799 3rd St SW Rochester MN 55902-2979 Office: Mayo Clinic Mayo Found 200 1st St SW Rochester MN 55905-0002

GLEIJESES, MARIO, holding company executive; b. Italy, Feb. 27, 1955; came to U.S., 1985; s. Luigi Gleijeses and Rosalba Catanoso; m. Betsy L. Miller, Mar. 14, 1992; children: Rosalba, Caterina. Student, U. Naples, 1973-77. Chartering mgr. Itex subs. Italgrani, Zurich, 1977-82; asst. to pres. Italgrani Spa, Naples, Italy, 1982-85; exec. v.p., bd. dirs. Italgrani USA Inc. and Italgrani Elevator Co., St. Louis, 1985-89; v.p., bd. dirs. New Eng. Milling Co., Ayer, Mass., 1987-89; bd. dirs. Green Bay Elevator Co., Burlington, Iowa; v.p., bd. dirs. Mayco Export, Inc., Mpls., 1988-89; pres., bd. dirs. McLean Elevator Co., Benedict, N.D., 1989; founder, pres., bd. dirs. Agricorp Holding Inc., 1989-92; pres., bd. dirs. Granicorp Inc., 1989-92, Granicorp Export, Inc., U.S. Virgin Islands, 1989-92; chmn., CEO, bd. dirs. Granicorp France, S.A., Paris, 1991-92; founder, pres., bd. dirs. Gleijeses, Inc., 1993—; founder, chmn. bd. dirs. Lithoflex Corp., 1994—; pres. Hoky-Contico, LLC, 1995-96.

GLEIMAN, EDWARD JAY, federal agency administrator; b. Balt., Mar. 23, 1942; married; 2 children. BS, Loyola Coll., Balt., 1965; postgrad., Johns Hopkins U., 1965-67; JD, U. Balt., 1971. Rsch. asst. dept. pediatrics rsch. Sinia Hosp., 1965-68; examiner U.S. Patent Office, Washington, 1968-71; dir. field ops Pres.'s Cost of Living Coun. and Price Commn., Washington, 1971-73; mem. staff sec.'s operational planing staff U.S. Dept. HEW,

Washington, 1973-75, dir. fair info. practices office, 1975-77; mem. staff subcom. on govt. info., justice and agr. U.S. Ho. of Reps. Govt. Ops. Com., Washington, 1977-87; chief counsel subcom. fed. svcs. post office & civil svc. U.S. Senate Com. on Govtl. Affairs, Washington, 1987-94; chmn. Postal Rate Commn., Washington, 1994—. Office: Postal Rate Commn Office of Chmn 1333 H St NW Washington DC 20005-4707

GLEIS, LINDA HOOD, physician; b. Louisville, Jan. 28, 1952; d. Edgar Pete Hood and Joan Ray (Brenner) Hulsey; m. Gregory Eric Gleis, Aug. 18, 1973; children: Eric, Matthew, Kevin, Anna. BA cum laude, Bellarmine Coll., 1974; MD, U. Louisville, 1978. Diplomate Am. Bd. Phys. Medicine and Rehab. Lic. physician Ky., Ind. Resident Frazier Rehab. Ctr., Louisville, Ky., 1978-81; chief resident, 1981; med. staff Frazier Rehab. Ctr., Louisville, Ky., 1982—, dir. residency tng., 1985-95; asst. clin. prof. medicine U. Louisville, Louisville, Ky., 1985—; chief phys. medicine and rehab. VA Med. Ctr., Louisville, Ky., 1985—; med. staff VA Med. Ctr., Louisville, 1985—; founding ptnr. Rehab. Assoc.-PSC, Louisville, Ky., 1985—; spkr. in field. mem. U. Louisville Med. Alumni Bd., 1986-91, v.p., 1989-90, pres., 1990-91; mem. bd. overseers Bellarmine Coll, 1989-95; adv. bd. Jefferson County Office for Women, 1990-94; health care task force Louisville C. of C., 1991-92; marriage sponsor Archdiocese of Louisville Holy Spirit Parish Couple to Couple Program, 1991—, Salute to Cath. Alumni Steering Com., 1991-97, chair, 1993-94; dir. JCMS Outreach Program, Inc., 1991-98; trustee Spalding U., 1992-99, vice-chair, 1994-98, chair com. Acad. and Student Affairs, 1995-99, Spalding U./Presentation Acad. Com., 1995-97, Devel. Com., 1994-95; adv. panel The Physicians Inc., 1993-95; bd. dirs. mem.-at-large U. Louisville Alumni Assn., 1993—; mem. Leadership Louisville Class of 1992, hon. chair scholarship campaign, 1994; judge exec. Jefferson County Small Bus. Growth Coun., 1992-93; mem. cabinet Metro United Way, 1992-94; bd. dirs. Louisville Cmty. Found., 1992-99; med. adv. group Home of the Innocents Pediatric Convalescent Ctr., 1993-95; adv. coun. Louisville Forum, 1995—. Recipient 1st Ann. Salute to Cath. Schs. Disting. Alumni award Archdiocese Louisville, 1990, Disting. Alumni Svc. award U. Louisville, 1991, Bellarmine Coll. Outstanding Alumnus of Yr., 1991, Assumption H.S. Outstanding Alumna award, Louisville, 1993, Order of Merit U. Louisville Alumni Assn., 1993, Recognition award Ho. of Reps. Commonwealth Ky., 1998; honored with Tribute to Linda Gleis, M.D. Modern Day Heroine Congl. Record, 1992. Fellow Am. Acad. Phys. Medicine and Rehab.; mem. AMA, Am. Assn. Electrodiagnostic Medicine, Assn. Acad. Physiatrists (sec./program chmn. residency program dirs. coun., v.p. 1994-95, pres. 1995-96, mem. grad. med. edn. com. 1995-97), Ky. Med. Assn. (com. sch. health, phys. edn. and med. aspects of sports 1988-96, physician orgn. study com. 1993-96, com. on domestic violence 1992—), Ky. Acad. Phys. Medicine and Rehab. (sec.-treas. 1988—), Jefferson County Med. Soc. (found. bd. dir. 1990-96, 98—, del. to Ky. Med. Assn. 1993—, treas., 1990-91, 1st woman pres. 1991-92, chmn. bd. dirs. 1992-93, physicians Metro United Way campaign chair 1990-94, bd. dirs. outreach program 1993—, 1st v.p. bd. dirs. 1994-96). Roman Catholic. Avocations: reading, tennis, golf, sailing. Office: Rehab Assoc PSC 220 A Flexner Way Ste 500 Louisville KY 40202-1545

GLEISS, HENRY WESTON, lawyer; b. Detroit, Nov. 22, 1928; s. George Herman and Mary Elizabeth (Weston) G.; m. Joan Bette Christopher, July 23, 1955; children—Kent G., Keith W. B.A., Denison U., 1951; J.D., U. Mich., 1954. Bar: Mich. 1955, U.S. Dist. Ct. (ea. dist.) Mich. 1955, U.S. Dist. Ct. (we. dist.) Mich. 1960, U.S. Ct. Appeals (6th cir.) 1964, U.S. Supreme Ct. 1967. Sole practice, Benton Harbor, Mich., 1957-61; ptnr. Globensky, Gleiss, Bittner & Hyrns, P.C., St. Joseph, 1961—; spl. asst. atty. gen. Mich., 1960—. Officer Jaycees, Mich.; bd. dirs. United Fund. Served with U.S. Army, 1955-57. Mem. ABA, Mich. Bar Assn., Berrien County Bar Assn. (pres. 1974), Assn. Trial Lawyers Am., Twin Cities C. of C. (v.p. 1975). Congregationalist. Clubs: Kiwanis, Moose (Benton Harbor); Economic of S.W. Mich.; Elks (St. Joseph). Home: 2409 Langley Ave Saint Joseph MI 49085-2150 Office: 610 Ship St Saint Joseph MI 49085-1120

GLEISSER, MARCUS DAVID, author, lawyer, journalist; b. Buenos Aires, Argentina, Feb. 14, 1923; s. Ben and Riva (Kogan) G.; m. Helga Marianne Rothschild, Oct. 23, 1955; children: Brian Saul, Julia Lynne Wainblat, Hannah Tanya, Ellyn Ruth Klein. B.A. in Journalism, Case Western Res. U., 1945, M.A. in Econs., 1949; J.D., Cleve. State U., 1958. Bar: Ohio 1958, U.S. Dist. Ct. (no. and ea. dists.) Ohio 1981, U.S. Supreme Ct. 1962. Police reporter Cleve. Press, 1942-44, copy editor, 1944-47; advt. copy writer McDonough-Lewy, Inc., 1947-50; copy editor Cleve. Plain Dealer, 1950-52, gen. assignment reporter, 1952-57, courthouse reporter, 1957-63, real estate editor, 1963-81, fin. writer and investment columnist, 1981—. Author: The World of Cyrus Eaton, 1965, Juries and Justice, 1968; also articles.; editor in chief: Cleve.-Marshall Law Rev., 1956, 57. Trustee Cleve. Coll. Alumni Assn., 1968, Euclid Mayor's Exec. Council, 1973-76, Euclid Charter Commn., 1975-76. Recipient Nat. Bronze medal Am. Newspaper Pubs. Assn., 1944, Nat. Silver Gavel award ABA, 1958, Bronze medal Nat. Legal Aid and Defender Assn., 1963, Loeb award for disting. bus. and fin. writing U. Conn., 1966; cert. of recognition NCCJ, 1967, Silver Medal award consistently outstanding spl. feature columns Nat. Headliners club, 1969, award Ohio Bar Assn., 1957, 58, 59, 60, 61, 62, award pub. svc. Cleve. Newspaper Guild, 1959, award for best column, 1976, award Nat. Assn. Real Estate Editors, 1965, 71, 72, 73, 80, 91, award Nat. Assn. Real Estate Bds., 1966, 67, 68, 69, 70, 71, 73, award Nat. Assn. Home Builders, 1970, 1st prize Nat. Assn. Realtors, 1980, Bus.-Fin. Writing award Press Club Cleve., 1969, Disting. Merit award Cleve. Assn. Real Estate Brokers, 1976, Excellence in Bus. Journalism award Press Club Cleve., 1983, 85, Fin. Writing award Pannell, Kerr & Forster, 1985; runner-up Pulitzer Prize in Journalism for local reporting, 1973; named to N.E. Ohio Apt. Assn. Hall of Fame, 1996. Mem. Am. Newspaper Guild, Soc. Profl. Journalists (Disting. Svc. award Cleve. chpt. 1994), City Club. Club: City (Cleve.). Home: 575 Hemlock Dr Cleveland OH 44132-2119 Office: 1801 Superior Ave E Cleveland OH 44114-2107 *Honest and honorable communication with my fellow man is of the utmost importance . . . to inform, debate, educate, understand, persuade, listen, be open to new thoughts-never to ignore.*

GLEKEL, JEFFREY IVES, lawyer; b. N.Y.C., Apr. 8, 1947; s. Newton and Gertrude (Burr) G.; m. Cynthia R. Leder, June 18, 1988; 1 child, David L. AB, Columbia U., 1969; JD, Yale U., 1972. Bar: N.Y. 1973, U.S. Supreme Ct. 1981, U.S. Ct. Appeals (2d cir.) 1974, U.S. Dist. Ct. (so. dist.) N.Y. 1974. Law clk. to judge U.S. Dist. Ct. (so. dist.) N.Y., 1972-73; asst. U.S. atty. So. Dist. N.Y., 1973-77; law clk. to justice Byron R. White, U.S. Supreme Ct., Washington, 1977-78; ptnr. Skadden, Arps, Slate, Meagher and Flom, N.Y.C., 1980—; Editor, contbr.: Civil Litigation Practice, 1990; Business Crimes, 1982; note and comment editor Yale Law Jour., 1971-72. Contbr. articles to law jours. Mem. Assn. Bar City of N.Y. (chmn. com. fed. legislation 1984-87), ABA. Office: Skadden Arps Slate Meagher & Flom 919 3rd Ave New York NY 10022-3902

GLEKLEN, DONALD MORSE, investment company executive; b. Providence, Oct. 16, 1936; s. Leo and Gertrude (Ketover) G.; m. Carol Ann Platzker, May 24, 1964; children: Jonathan, Adam, Rachel. B.A., Cornell U., 1958; J.D., Columbia U., 1963. Bar: N.Y. 1964. Assoc., Demov & Morris, N.Y.C., 1963-65; corp. counsel C.F. Childs & Co., N.Y.C., 1965-67; U.S. rep. Rea Bros. Ltd., London, 1967-68; exec. v.p. Indsl. Valley Bank, Phila., 1968-84; sr. v.p. MEDIQ, Inc., Pennsauken, N.J., 1984-94; pres. Jocard Fin. Svcs., Inc., 1994; chmn., CEO InteliHealth, Inc., 1996—; pres., CEO The Maine Merchant Bank, 1997-98, vice chair, 1998—; bd. dirs. Home Health Corp. Am., King of Prussia, Pa., New West EyeWorks, Inc., Tempe, Ariz., Nutramax Products, Inc., Gloucester, Mass., Lason Sys. Holdings, Inc., Livonia, Mich., Kinetics Tech. Internat., The Hague, Netherlands, 1982-86. Trustee Pa. Coll. Optometry, Phila., 1979—; chmn. bd., 1991—; trustee Walnut St. Theatre, Phila., 1983-96, Coriell Inst. Med. Rsch., Camden, N.J., 1994-96. Served as lt. (j.g.) USNR, 1958-60. Home: 212 Jeffrey Ln Newtown Square PA 19073-2506 Office: Intelihealth 960C Harvest Dr Blue Bell PA 19422-1900*

GLEN, PAUL MICHAEL, management consultant, educator; b. Chgo., Mar. 10, 1965; s. Marren Jay and Ann (Elcrat) G. BA, Cornell U., 1988; M in Mgmt., Northwestern U., 1991. Cons. SEI Info. Tech., Chgo., 1988-95; regional mgr. SEI Info. Tech., L.A., 1995-99; prin. C2 Consulting, Marina Del Rey, Calif., 1999—. Office: C2 Consulting 17 Northstar St Ste 202 Marina Del Rey CA 90292

GLEN, ROBERT ALLAN, history educator; b. Sioux Falls, S.D., Nov. 5, 1946; s. Clarence Rolland and Virginia Carol (Grieme) G. BA, U. Wash., 1968; MA, U. Calif., Berkeley, 1969; PhD, U. Calif., 1978. Teaching asst. U. Calif., Berkeley, Calif., 1972-74; instr. U. Wis., Parkside, Wis., 1975-77, U. Vermont, 1977-78; asst. prof. history U. New Haven, Conn., 1979-83; assoc. prof., chair dept. history U. New Haven, 1983-87, prof., 1987—, chair dept. history, 1994-96; vis. faculty fellow Yale U., 1981-82. Author: Urban Workers in the Early Industrial Revolution, 1984; contbr. articles to profl. jours. Hist. cons. New Dimension Theatre Co., New Haven, 1979-81; tutor Lit. Vols., New Haven, 1985—. Fellow NEH, 1976, 85. Mem. Am. Hist. Assn., Am. Soc. 18th Century Studies, N.Am. Conf. on Brit. Studies, Hist. Assn., Econ. History Soc., Wesley Hist. Soc. Office: U New Haven 300 Orange Ave West Haven CT 06516-1999

GLENDENING, EVERETT AUSTIN, architect; b. White Plains, N.Y., May 20, 1929; s. Gilbert Leslie and Elsie Jane (Fanjoy) G.; m. Wilhelmina Louise Hanley, Nov. 26, 1949; children: Nancy, James, Thomas, Terry, Susan. B.Arch., U. Cin., 1953; M.Arch., M.I.T., 1954. With Duffy Constrn. Co., Cleve., 1951-55, SIS Architects, Cin., 1956-58, T.J. Moore (architect), Denver, 1959; prof. architecture U. Cin., 1960-67; pvt. practice architecture Cin., 1959—. Prin. works include Queen's Towers, Cin., 1964, Summit Chase, Columbus, Ohio, 1966, Norwood High Sch., Cin., 1972, W.Va. Mus., Moundsville, 1978, Douglass Montessori Sch., Cin., 1979, Christie Lane Workshop, Norwalk, Ohio, 1980, Coll. Law U. Cin., 1981, Elks Lodge, Columbus, Ind., 1981, Geology/Physics Sci. Ctr. U. Cin., 1983, U. Rio Grande Dormitory, 1989, U. Rio Grande Student Ctr., 1994, U. Rio Grande Math-Sci.-Nursing Bldg., 1995, Planetarium, Shawnee State U., 1998. Served as 1st lt. USAF, 1954-56. Fellow AIA (honor awards Ohio chpt. 1966-70, 74, 82, 90, 91, Cin. chpt. 1966-68, 70, 76, Bronze medal 1969, Apple award for arch. 1995, mem. U.S. delegation of architects to People's Republic China and Hong Kong 1990); mem. Architect's Soc. Ohio, Scarab. Methodist. Office: 8050 Montgomery Rd Cincinnati OH 45236-2947 *A consistently positive point of view has perhaps been the single, most important factor in making possible what has been accomplished in my lifetime. I have always felt that anything was possible as long as I was willing to make the effort and, in fact, I can recall telling myself as a new college freshman that "while I may not be the most intelligent man in the class, there was no reason why I should not be the hardest working member of that class."*

GLENDENING, PARRIS NELSON, governor, political science educator; b. Bronx, N.Y., June 11, 1942; m. Frances Anne Hughes, Nov. 21, 1976; 1 child, Raymond Hughes. AA, Broward County Jr. Coll., 1962; BA, Fla. State U., Tallahassee, 1964, MA, 1965, PhD, 1967. Asst. prof. U. Md., College Park, 1967-72, assoc. prof., 1972-94; coun. mem. Hyattsville City Coun., Md., 1973-74, Prince George's County Coun., Upper Marlboro, Md., 1974-82; coun. chmn. Prince George's County Coun., 1980, 81, county exec., 1982-95; gov. State of Md., 1995—; vice chair state of Md.'s Chesapeake Bay Critical Area Commn., 1984-94; vice chair bd. dirs. World Trade Ctr., 1990-97; mem. Bd. of Visitors U. Md.'s Sch. of Pub. Affairs, 1990-97; bd. trustees Ptnrs. for Livable Places, 1990-97. Author: (with Mavis Mann Reeves) Controversies of State and Local Political Systems, 1972, Pragmatic Federalism, 1977, 2nd edit., 1984; contbr. numerous articles to profl. pubs. Del. to Dem. nat. Conv., San Francisco, 1984, Atlanta, 1988, N.Y.C., 1992; bd. govs., steering com. Am.'s Clean Water Found. Recipient numerous awards, including City and State mag., Prince George's County, Prince George's High Sch. Prins. Assn., State Assn. Retarded Citizens, Nat. Bus. League So. Md., Spanish Speaking Communities Md., Inc., Rotary Internat., Md. Assn. Psychol. Svcs., Elizabeth and David Scull award for disting. leadership to Washington met. region Coun. Govts., 1995, Dr. Nathan Davis award The Am. Med. Assn., 1991; Disting. Alumni award Fla. State U. Coll. Social Svcs., 1993, Outstanding Alumni The Am. Assn. of Com. Coll., 1997. Mem. AAUP, AAAS (profl. ethics group 1988—), Nat. Assn. Counties (bd. dirs. 1992—, chair large urban county caucus 1992—), Am. Polit. Sci. Assn., ASPA (profl. ethics com. mem. 1989—, chmn. 1991-92, SIAM mem. 1991—), Nat. Coun. Elected County Execs. (1st v.p. 1989-90, pres. 1991-92), Md. Assn. Counties (pres. 1987-88), Nat. Assn. Counties (bd. dirs. 1992—, vice chmn. intergovtl. rels. policy steering com. 1987-90, chair 1990—, taxation and fin. steering com. 1984-87). Office: Office of the Gov State House Annapolis MD 21401

GLENDENNING, DON MARK, lawyer; b. Dallas, Dec. 24, 1953; s. Don Thomas and Nancy (Malloy) G.; m. Carol Peterson, Dec. 30, 1979. BA, Rice U., 1976; JD, Stanford U., 1979. Bar: Tex. 1979. Assoc. Rain Harrell Emery Young & Doke, Dallas, 1979-85; ptnr. Rain, Harrell, Emery, Young & Doke, Dallas, 1985-87; shareholder Locke Liddell & Sapp (formerly Locke Purnell Rain Harrell, P.C.), Dallas, 1987-98; ptnr. Locke Liddell & Sapp LLP, Dallas, 1999—. Vol. legal counsel, dir. The Nat. Tree Trust; bd. dirs. Dallas Trees and Park Found.; vol. legal counsel Dallas Zool. Soc.; vol. legal counsel Quality Tex. Fedn. Republican. Presbyterian. Office: Locke Liddell & Sapp LLP 2200 Ross Ave Ste 2200 Dallas TX 75201-6776

GLENDENNING, JOHN ARMAND, registered nurse; b. Lebanon, Ind., June 25, 1953; s. James Rexford and Mary Alice (White) G.; m. Diana Jo Beard, Mar. 17, 1972; children: Julie Alane, David Armand. ASN, Ind. U., 1991. Cert. EMT, FNATC, ACLS, PALS, ENPC, CEN, TNCC; cert. emergency nurse; cert. flight RN. Pipefitter, welder Marathon Oil Refinery, Indpls., 1972-88; emergency med. technician Aid Ambulance Svc., Indpls., 1987-91; staff nurse emergency rm. Wishard Hosp., 1989-90; staff nurse emergency medicine, trauma ctr. Meth. Hosp., Indpls., 1991—, flight RN Lifeline Helicopter, 1995—; staff nurse emergency rm. Clinton County Hosp., 1992—; staff nurse emergency dept. Witham Meml. Hosp., Lebanon, Ind., 1998—. Mem. ARC, Emergency Nurses Assn., Nat. Flight Nurses Assn., Ctrl. Ind. Med. Response Team, Emergency Nurses Assn., Sons of Am. Legion, Ulen Country Club, Alpha Sigma Lambda, ALpha Lambda Delta (pres. 1989), Phi Eta Sigma (pres. 1989). Republican. Baptist. Avocations: golf, scuba diving, sailing, hiking, kayaking. Home: 110 Terrace Ct Lebanon IN 46052-1130 Office: Meth Hosp Ind I-65 21st St Indianapolis IN 46206

GLENDON, MARY ANN, law educator; b. 1938. BA, U. Chgo., 1959, JD, 1961, M Comparative Law, 1963. Bar: Ill. 1964, Mass. 1980. Legal intern. EEC, Brussels, Belgium, 1963; assoc. Mayer, Brown & Platt, Chgo., 1963-68; prof. Boston Coll., 1968-86; vis. prof. Harvard U., 1974-75, prof., 1986—; vis. prof. U. Chgo., 1983, 84, 86. Author: Rights Talk, 1991, A Nation Under Lawyers, 1994. Foreign Law fellow U. Libre de Bruxelles, 1962-63, Ford Found. fellow, 1975-76. Mem. Am. Acad. Arts & Scis. Office: Harvard U Law Sch Cambridge MA 02138

GLENISTER, BRIAN FREDERICK, geologist, educator; b. Albany, Western Australia, Sept. 28, 1928; came to U.S., 1959, naturalized, 1967; s. Frederick and Mabel (Frusher) G.; m. Anne Marie Treloar, Feb. 16, 1956; children: Alan Edward, Linda Marie, Kathryn Grace. BSc, U. Western Australia, Perth, 1949; MSc, U. Melbourne, Australia, 1953; PhD, U. Iowa, 1956. Lectr., then sr. lectr. geology U. Western Australia, 1956-59; asst. prof. U. Iowa, Iowa City, 1959-62, assoc. prof., 1962-66, prof., 1966-74, chmn. geology dept., 1968-74, A.K. Miller prof. geology, 1974-97, A.K. Miller prof. geology emeritus, 1997—. Mem. AAAS, Paleontol. Soc. (pres. 1988-89), Geol. Soc. Am., Geol. Soc. Iowa (pres. 1991), Paleontol. Rsch. Inst. Home: 2015 Scales Bend Rd NE North Liberty IA 52317-9331

GLENN, CLETA MAE, lawyer; b. Clinton, Ill., Sept. 24, 1921; d. John and Mattie Sylvester (Anderson) G.; m. Rex Eugene Loggans, Sept. 3, 1948 (div.); 1 child, Susan. BS, U. Ill., 1947; JD, DePaul U. Coll. Law, 1976. Bar: Ill. 1977. Real estate builder, developer, 1959-69; comm. dir. Transp. Rsch. Ctr., Northwestern U., Evanston, Ill., 1969-72; pvt. practice law Chgo., 1977—; lectr. Assn. Trial Lawyers Am., John Marshall Law Sch. Editor: Collective Bargaining and Technological Change in American Transportation, 1979; contbr. articles to profl. publs. With USN, 1943-59. Recipient Real Estate Humanitarian award Kislak Co., Miami, Fla., 1962. Mem. ATLA, ABA, Ill. Bar Assn. (assembly rep., mem. standing com. on traffic, family law sect. coun.), Chgo. Bar Assn., Ill. Trial Lawyers Assn., Lex Leggio, Phi Alpha Delta. Home: 200 E Delaware Pl Chicago IL 60611-1757 Office: 200 W Madison St Ste 2850 Chicago IL 60606-3416

GLENN, CONSTANCE WHITE, art museum director, educator, consultant; b. Topeka, Oct. 4, 1933; d. Henry A. and Madeline (Stewart) White; m. Jack W. Glenn, June 19, 1955; children: Laurie Glenn Buckle, Caroline Glenn Galey, John Christopher. BFA, U. Kans., 1955; grad., U. Mo., 1969; MA, Calif. State U., 1974. Dir. Univ. Art Mus. & Mus. Studies program, from lectr. to prof. Calif. State U., Long Beach, 1973—; art cons. Archtl. Digest, L.A., 1980-89. Author: Jim Dine Drawings, 1984, Roy Lichtenstein: Landscape Sketches, 1986, Wayne Thiebaud: Private Drawings, 1988, Robert Motherwell: The Dedalus Sketches, 1988, James Rosenquist: Time Dust: The Complete Graphics 1962-92, 1993, The Great American Pop Art Store: Multiples of the Sixties, 1997; contbg. author: Encyclopedia Americana, 1995—; contbg. editor: Antiques and Fine Arts, 1991-92. Vice-chair Adv. Com. for Pub. Art, Long Beach, 1990-95; chair So. Calif. adv. bd. Archives Am. Art, L.A., 1980-90; mem. adv. bd. ART/LA, 1986-94, chair, 1992. Recipient Outstanding Contbn. to Profession award Calif. Mus. Photography, 1986. Mem. Am. Assn. Mus., Assn. Art Mus. Dirs., Coll. Art Assn., Art Table, Long Beach Pub. Corp. for the Arts (arts adminstr. of yr. 1989), Kappa Alpha Theta. Office: Univ Art Mus 1250 N Bellflower Blvd Long Beach CA 90840-0006

GLENN, DAVID WRIGHT, mortgage company executive; b. Brigham City, Utah, Nov. 22, 1943; s. Alma Wray and Lois (Wright) G.; m. Cherie Jean Tilleman, June 9, 1967; children: David Wray, Shannon, Chelece, Daniel William, Kellie. BS, Weber State Coll., 1968; MBA, Stanford U., 1971, PhD, 1974. Asst. prof. U. N.C., Chapel Hill, 1973-74; vis. asst. prof. Stanford U., (Calif.), 1974-75; asst. prof. U. Utah, Salt Lake City, 1975-78; vis. asst. prof. Harvard U., 1977; assoc. prof. U. Utah, 1978-83; dir. Fed. Savs. & Loan Ins. Corp., Washington, 1983-84; sr. v.p. planning and acquisitions Calfed, Inc., 1984-87; pres., COO Fed. Home Loan Mortgage Corp., Mc Lean, Va., 1987—. Author numerous articles in bus. and fin. Office: Fed Home Loan Mortgage Corp 8200 Jones Branch Dr Mc Lean VA 22102-3107*

GLENN, FRANCES BONDE, dentist; b. Tampa, Fla., Nov. 29, 1933. Student, U. Fla., 1951-52; DDS, U. Pa., 1956. Resident Children's Hosp., Washington, 1956-57; pvt. practice dentistry Miami, 1957—; vis. lectr. U. Miami, 1959—, Miami Dade Sch. of Dental Hygiene, 1979; cons. D.C. Tng. Ctr. for the Retarded and Handicapped, 1956-57; lectr. Lindsey Hopkins Vocat. Sch., 1981, U.S. and other countries; bd. overseers U. Pa. Sch. Dental Medicine; rschr. Pediat. Dent. Ortho. Contbr. articles to Lady's Home Jour., Parents Mag., Chicago Tribune Newspaper, Med. and Dent. Jour. Active Dade County Welfare and Planning Coun., 1959-61; vol. dentist Cerebral Palsy Clinic, 1959-63; advisor, cons. Crippled Children's Soc., 1976—; dental clinic staff mem. Coral Gables Jr. Women's Club, 1959-61. Recipient Alumni award merit U. Pa. Sch. Dental Medicine, 1984. Fellow Am. Acad. of Pedodontics; mem. Am. Orthodontic Soc. (diplomate of bd., Moore Disting. Svc. award 1994), Fla. Soc. Dentistry for Children, Am. Assn. Women Dentists. Discovered that children of expectant mothers who take sodium fluoride don't get cavities. Office: 7741 SW 62d Ave Miami FL 33143-4908

GLENN, G(EORGE) DALE, principal; b. Dec. 7, 1939; s. George Berry and Nola Marie (Huffman) G.; children: Darin, Shannon, Kevin; m. Teresa Sullivan. BS in Edn., Ind. U., 1962, MS in Edn., 1963, EdS, 1973, EdD, 1975. Tchr. English, coach Speedway H.S., Indpls., 1962-70; basketball coach, asst. prin. Huntingburg H.S., Ind., 1970-72; prin. Huntingburg Mid. Sch., 1972-74, Univ. Mid. Sch., Bloomington, Ind., 1975-83, Batchelor Mid. Sch., Bloomington, 1983-99; adj. prof. Ind. U., Bloomington, 1976—. Author: History of IHSAA, 1976; contbr. articles to ednl. jours. Mem. adv. bd. Ctr. Adolescent Studies. Mem. Nat. Assn. Secondary Sch. Prins., Ind. Assn. Sch. Adminstrs. (mid. level com.), Ind. U. Edn. Alumni Assn. (pres. 1981), Ind. U. Alumni Assn. (exec. coun. 1984-94), Monroe County Adminstrs. Assn., North Cen. Assn. Colls. and Schs. (Ind. state com.), Ind. PBA (mem. adv. com.), Ind. Assn. Sch. Prins. (bd. dirs. 1994-99, Dist. 9 Prin. of Yr. 1993-94, Ind. Mid. Sch. Prin. of Yr. 1998). Methodist. Avocations: traveling, reading, golf, tennis, farming. Office: Batchelor Mid Sch 900 W Gordon Pike Bloomington IN 47403-4500

GLENN, GERALD MARVIN, marketing, engineering and construction executive; b. Greenville, S.C., Aug. 20, 1942; s. Oscar Marvin and Lorene (Ashmore) G.; m. Candice Wilson, Oct. 24, 1986; children: Regina Lynn, Gerald Marvin II, Charles Wilson. BSCE, Clemson U., 1964. With Daniel Constrn. Co., Greenville, S.C., 1964-77; with Fluor Corp., Santa Ana, Calif., 1977-94, sr. v.p. mktg., 1982-85, pres. U.S. ops., 1985-86, exec. v.p., 1986; group pres., dir. Fluor Corp., Irvine, Calif., 1986-94; owner, prin. The Glenn Group LLC, Ridgway, Colo., 1994—, Eagle Glen Ranch LLC, Ridgeway, Colo., 1994—; chmn., pres., CEO Chgo. Bridge & Iron Co. N.V., Plainfield, Ill., 1996—. Dir. Chgo. chpt. Am. Heart Asssn. Mem. TAPPI, AIChE, Am. Petroleum Inst., Chgo. Coun. on Fgn. Rels. (mem. Chgo. com.), Chgo. Soc., Inst. Gas Tech. (trustee), Fairway Pines Golf Club, Olympia Fields Country Club, Petroleum Club, Execs. Club Chgo., Met. Club, Ruth Lake Country Club. Republican. Methodist. Home: 413 W Walnut St Hinsdale IL 60521-3233 Office: Chicago Bridge & Iron Co NV 1501 N Division St Plainfield IL 60544-8984

GLENN, GUY CHARLES, pathologist; b. Parma, Ohio, May 13, 1930; s. Joseph Frank and Helen (Rupple) G.; m. Lucia Ann Howarth, June 13, 1953; children: Kathryn Holly, Carolyn Helen, Cynthia Marie. *Though Dr. Glenn's grandfather was a building contractor and his father worked in advertising, he was motivated to study medicine by his uncle, Paul M. Glenn, MD, who received his medical degree in 1935 at Western Reserve University, gastroenterology fellowship at University Hospital, Pennsylvania, and became senior instructor in medicine at Western Reserve. He enlisted in the Army in 1941 and died at 40 while on active duty. While a medical student at the University of Cincinnati, Dr. Edward Gall, Chair Department of Pathology and a dynamic teacher inspired Dr. Glenn to select a pathology career.* BS, Denison U., 1953; MD, U. Cin., 1957. Diplomate Am. Bd. Pathology, Am. Bd. Radioisotopic Pathology. Intern Walter Reed Army Med. Ctr., Washington, 1957-58; resident in pathology Fitzsimmons Army Med. Ctr., Denver, 1959-63; commd. 2d lt. U.S. Army, 1956; advanced through grades to col., 1977; demonstrator pathology Royal Army Med. Coll., London, 1970-72; chief dept. pathology Fitzsimmons Army Med. Ctr., Denver, 1972-77; past pres. med. staff St. Vincent Hosp., Billings, Mont.; past mem. governing bd. Mont. Health Systems Agy. *As Chief, Department of Pathology, Fitzsimmons Army Medical Center, he oversaw a busy laboratory and had eight residents in pathology training. He has published over 25 professional papers and presented others at medical meetings and seminars. He wrote and assisted writing multiple medical case guidelines and published a chapter on urine chemistry quality control in the Clinical Laboratory Annual, 1983. He was awarded the Army Commendation Medal, The Legion of Merit, The College of Pathologists Presidential Honors Medal and became a Paul Harris Fellow of Rotary International.* Contbr. articles to profl. jours. Fellow Coll. Am. Pathologists (chmn. chemistry resources com., chmn. commn. sci. resources, mem. budget program and rev. com. coun. on quality assurance, chmn. practice guidelines com., outcomes com., bd. govs., chmn. nominating com.), Am. Soc. Clin. Pathology, Soc. Med. Cons. to Armed Forces (legal and legis. com.), Midland Empire Health Assn. (past pres.), Rotary (bd. dirs. local chpt.). Home: 3225 Jack Burke Ln Billings MT 59106-1113

GLENN, HARRY J., legislative administrator; b. Coatesville, Pa., Oct. 25, 1958. BA, Pa. State U., 1980. Chief of staff to Rep. C.W. Bill Young, U.S. Ho. of Reps., Washington, 1995—. Office: US Ho of Reps 2407 RHOB Washington DC 20515

GLENN, JAMES FRANCIS, urologist, educator; b. Lexington, Ky., May 10, 1928; s. Cambridge Francis and Martha (Morrow) G.; m. Gale Brooke Morrison, Dec. 29, 1948; children: Cambridge Francis II, Sara Brooke, Nancy Carrick, James Morrison Woodworth. Student (Yale Regional scholar), Univ. Sch., Lexington, 1946; B.A. in Gen. Sci. (Bausch and Lomb Nat. Sci. scholar), U. Rochester, 1949; MD, Duke U., 1952; DSc, U. Ky., 1998. Diplomate Am. Bd. Urology (mem.), Nat. Bd. Med. Examiners. Intern Peter Bent Brigham Hosp., Boston, 1952-54; asst. resident urology Duke U. Med. Ctr., 1956-58, resident, 1958-59; instr. urology Duke U., 1958-59, prof., chief div. urology, 1963-80; asst. prof. Yale U., 1959-61; assoc. prof. Bowman Gray Sch. Medicine, Wake Forest Coll., 1961-63; practice medicine specializing in urology New Haven, 1959-61, Winston-Salem, N.C., 1961-63, Durham, N.C., 1963-80; prof. surgery, dean Med. Sch., Emory U., 1980-83; pres. Mt. Sinai Med. Ctr., 1983-87; prof. surgery U. Ky. Coll. Medicine, Lexington, 1987—; CEO Markey Cancer Ctr., 1989-93; chief staff Univ. Hosp., Lexington, 1993-95, chmn. dept. surgery, 1996-97; sci. dir. Coun. for Tobacco Rsch. U.S.A., 1987-91, chmn. bd., 1991—. Contbg. author: Renal Neoplasia, 1967, Urodynamics, 1971, Textbook of Surgery, 1972, Plastic and Reconstructive Surgery of The Genital Area, 1973, Current Operative Urology, 1975, Campbell's Urology, 1977; author, editor: Diagnostic Urology, 1964, Ureteral Reflux in Children, 1966, Urologic Surgery, 1969, rev. edit., 1975, 84, 90; contbr. numerous articles to profl. jours. Served to capt. M.C., USAF, 1954-56. Mem. Am. Assn. Genitourinary Surgeons (pres. 1992-93, hon. 1998), Am. Surg. Assn., ACS, AMA (sec. sect. urology 1972-73, chmn. 1975-77), Assn. Am. Med. Colls., Internat. Urol Soc. (v.p. 1985-91, pres. 1991-94), Clin. Soc. Genito-Urinary Surgeons (pres. 1990-91), N.Y. Acad. Medicine, Soc. Pediatric Urology (pres. 1972-73), Soc. Pelvic Surgeons (pres. 1980-81), Soc. Univ. Surgeons, Soc. Univ. Urologists (pres. 1971-72), Royal Coll. Surgeons (hon. fellow 1987), German Urol. Assn. (hon.), Australasian Urologic Soc. (hon.), Brit. Assn. Urologic Surgeons (hon.). Home: Glenninish Farm 101 Idle Hour Dr Lexington KY 40502 Office: Univ Ky Med Ctr Hosp Adminstrn 800 Rose St Lexington KY 40536-0084

GLENN, JEROME T., secondary school principal. Prin. San Lorenzo (Calif.) High Sch., to 1999; dir. secondary edn. San Lorenzo (Calif.) Sch. Dist., 1999—. Recipient Blue Ribbon Sch. award U.S. Dept. Edn., 1990-91. Office: San Lorenzo Dist Ednl Svcs 15510 Usher St San Lorenzo CA 94580-1732*

GLENN, JERRY HOSMER, JR., foreign language educator; b. Little Rock, Sept. 5, 1938; s. Jerry Hosmer and Anne (Matthews) G.; m. Renate Drexl, July 29, 1978. BA, Yale U., 1960; MA, U. Tex., 1962; postgrad., Free U. Berlin, 1962-63; PhD, U. Tex., 1964. Asst. prof. German U. Wis., Milw., 1964-67; asst. prof. German U. Cin., 1967-69, assoc. prof., 1969-72, prof., 1972—, head dept., 1980-83, dir. honors program, 1977-79. Author: Deutsches Schrifttum der Gegenwart (ab 1945), 1971, Paul Celan, 1973, Paul Celan: Eine Bibliographie, 1989, Paul Celan: A Bibliography of English Language Secondary Literature 1955-1996, 1996; (with Jeffrey Todd) Paul Celan: Die zweite Bibliographie, 1998; mng. editor: Lessing Yearbook, 1969-74; editor: (with Uwe Faulhaber and others) Exile and Enlightenment, 1987; (with Joachim Herrmann and Rebecca Rodgers) Alfred Gong, Early Poems, 1987; translator (with Jennifer Kelley) On the Wrong Track, 1993. Mem. Lessing Soc. (sec-treas. 1968-74), Mideast Honors Assn. (exec. sec. 1977-78, pres. 1979-80), Am. Assn. Tchrs. German, Soc. German-Am. Studies (v.p. 1987-89). Republican. Home: 54 Fairway Dr Southgate KY 41071-3025

GLENN, JOE DAVIS, JR., retired civil engineer, consultant; b. Fair Play, S.C., Aug. 12, 1921; s. Joe Davis and Elise Glenn; m. Margaret Glenn, Feb. 21, 1946 (dec. Mar. 1986); children: Joe Davis III, William Harry, Diane Elizabeth, Mary Kathryn; m. Ruth Robinson, Mar. 21, 1987. BSCE, Clemson U., 1942; MSCE, U. Tenn., 1955. Asst. prof. civil engring. Clemson (S.C.) U., 1946-56; structural engr. Tidewater Constrn. Corp., Norfolk, Va., 1956-60; owner, pres. Joe D. Glenn Jr. & Assocs., Norfolk, 1960-76; pres. Glenn-Rollins & Assoc., Inc., Norfolk, 1976-82; pres. Joe D. Glenn & Assocs., Inc., Norfolk, 1982-89, chmn., 1989-91; chmn. Glenn and Sadler Assoc. Inc., Norfolk, 1991-93; retired, 1993. Past elder Coleman Place Presbyn. Ch., Norfolk. Served with C.E. U.S. Army, 1942-46. Decorated Bronze Star. Mem. ASCE (life, Hardy Cross Hall of Fame 1991), NSPE (bd. dirs. 1976-80), Va. Soc. Profl. Engrs. (pres. 1975-76, Engr. of the Yr. 1976), Cons. Engrs. Coun. of Va., Hampton Rds. Engrs. Club (pres. 1974), Soc. Am. Mil. Engrs., Norfolk-Princess Anne Club, Kiwanis (pres. 1963). Home: 4516 Mcgregor Dr Virginia Beach VA 23462-4531

GLENN, JOHN HERSCHEL, JR., former senator; b. Cambridge, Ohio, July 18, 1921; s. John Herschel and Clara (Sproat) G.; m. Anna Margaret Castor, Apr. 1943; children: Carolyn Ann, John David. Student, Muskingum Coll., 1939-42, B.Sc., 1962; naval aviation cadet, U. Iowa, 1942; grad. flight sch., Naval Air Tng. Center, Corpus Christi, Tex., 1943, Navy Test Pilot Tng. Sch., Patuxent River, Md., 1954. Commd. 2d lt. USMC, 1943, assigned 4th Marine Aircraft Wing, Marshall Islands campaign, 1944, assigned 9th Marine Aircraft Wing, 1945-46; with 1st Marine Aircraft Wing, North China Patrol, also Guam, 1947-48; flight instr. advanced flight tng. Corpus Christi, 1949-51; asst. G-2/G-3 Amphibious Warfare Sch., Quantico, Va., 1951; with Marine Fighter Squadron 311, exchange pilot 25th Fighter Interceptor Squadron USAF, Korea, 1953; project officer fighter design br. Navy Bur. Aero. Washington, 1956-58; astronaut Project Mercury, Manned Spacecraft Center NASA, 1959-65; pilot Mercury-Atlas 6, 1st orbital space flight launched from Cape Canaveral, Fla., Feb. 1962; ret. as col., 1965; v.p. corp. devel. and dir. Royal Crown Cola Co., 1966-74; pres. Royal Crown Internat.; U.S. senator from Ohio, 1975-99; mem.-at-large Ohio State Dem. Com., 1999—; mem. Spl. Com. on Aging, Armed Svcs. Com., Senate Dem. Tech. and Comm. Com., Intelligence Com.; ranking minority mem. Govtl. Affairs Com.; vice-chmn. Senate Dem. Policy Com. Co-author: We Seven, 1962; author: P.S., I Listened to Your Heart Beat. Made first supersonic transcontinental flight, July 16, 1957; trustee Muskingum Coll. Decorated D.F.C. (six), Air medal (18); recipient Astronaut medal USMC, Navy unit commendation, Korean Presdl. unit citation, Disting. Merit award Muskingum Coll., Medal of Honor N.Y.C., Congl. Space Medal of Honor, 1978, Centennial awd., Nat. Geographic Soc., 1988, other decorations, awards and hon. degrees. Mem. Soc. Exptl. Test Pilots, Internat. Acad. of Astronautics (hon.). Democrat. Presbyterian. Office: Ohio State U John Glenn Inst 100 Bricker Hall 190 N Oval Mall Columbus OH 43210*

GLENN, JULES, psychiatrist; b. N.Y.C., Oct. 27, 1921; s. Ira and Ethel Glenn; m. Sylvia Grauer, June 16, 1943; children: Russell, Mel, Laura, Janet. BA, Columbia U., N.Y.C., 1942; MD, NYU, 1946; grad., N.Y. Psychoanalytical Inst., N.Y.C., 1957. Diplomate Am. Bd. Psyciatry and Neurology; cert. child and adult psychoanalysis Am. Psychoanalytic Assn. Intern Jewish Hosp. of Bklyn., 1946-47; intern in neurology Bellevue Hosp., N.Y.C., 1947-48; resident in psychiatry USPHS Hosp., Ft. Worth, Tex., 1948-50; clin. prof. psychiatry NYU Med. Ctr., N.Y.C., analyst; tng. and supervising emeritus The Psychoanalytic Inst., NYU Med. Ctr., N.Y.C. Co-author: Learning Disabilities and Psychic Conflict; editor: Child Analysis and Therapy; co-editor: Freud and His Patients, Freud and His Self-Analysis; assoc. editor Jour. of the Am. Psychoanalytic Assn.; asst. editor Psychoanalytic Case Studies; contbr. over 70 articles on twins, twinship fantasies, trauma, masochism, psychoanalytic technique, and creativity to profl. publs. Named Kablenell lectr. N.Y. Psychoanalytic Soc., 1993, Schoenfeld lectr. N.Y. Soc. Adolescent Psychiatry, 1995. Mem. Assn. Child Psychoanalysis (pres. 1984-86, Marianne Kris lectr. 1992), Psychoanalytic Assn. N.Y. (pres. 1987-89, Freud Anniversary lectr. 1990), Long Island Psychoanalytic Soc. (pres. 1967-68). Avocations: travel, tennis, photography.

GLENN, LUCIA HOWARTH, retired mental health services professional; b. Bklyn., Apr. 21, 1930; d. Arthur Orrel and Kathryn (Wilcox) Howarth; m. Guy Charles Glenn, June 13, 1953; children: Kathryn Holly, Carolyn Helen, Cynthia Marie. BS, Denison U., 1952; MS, Eastern Mont. Coll., 1980. Lic. profl. counselor; nat. cert. counselor; CC mental health counselor. Staff therapist Pastoral Counseling Ctr., Billings, Mont., Christian Psychol. Svcs., Billings; pvt. practice psychotherapist Billings, 1984-94; ret., 1996; cons. in field. Contbr. articles to profl. jours. Active mid.-Yellowstone affil. Habitat for Humanity, 1992—; 1st v.p., 1996-97, 2d v.p. St. Andrew Presbyn. Ch., 1997-98, elder, leader Christian Parenting Group, 1997-99. Tng. and Rsch. grantee AACD, 1986-87. Mem. Mont. Mental Health Counselors Assn. (past pres.), Am. Mental Health Counselors Assn. (chair spl. interest network on gender issues 1991-96). Home: 3225 Jack Burke Ln Billings MT 59106-1113

GLENN, PAUL M., federal judge; b. 1945. BA, Fla. State U., 1967; JD, Duke U., 1970. Assoc. Mahoney, Hadlow & Adams, P.A., Jacksonville, Miami, Fla., 1970-81; pres., CEO Mobile Am. Corp. and subsidiaries, Jacksonville, 1981-85; assoc. Bledsoe, Schmidt & Glenn, P.A., Jacksonville, 1985-87; exec. v.p., chief adminstrv. officer The Dependable Ins. Group, Inc. Am. and subsidiaries, Jacksonville, 1987-88; assoc. Dale & Bald, Jacksonville, 1989-93; bankruptcy judge U.S. Bankruptcy Ct. (mid. dist.) Fla., Tampa, 1993—. Mem. ABA, Fla. Bar Assn. Fax: 813-243-5111. Office: Ste 260 4921 Memorial Hwy Tampa FL 33634

GLENN, RICHARD ALAN, adult education educator; b. Dec. 23, 1968. BA in English, Carson Newman Coll., 1990; MA in Govt., U. Tenn., 1995, PhD in Govt., 1995. Prof. Millersville (Pa.) U., 1995—.

GLENN, ROLAND DOUGLAS, chemical engineer; b. Somerville, Mass., Mar. 22, 1912; s. Charles Rathford and Anna Amanda (Card) G.; m. Eleanor Norwood Greene, June 19, 1939; children: Meg Mary Eleanor Glenn-Albiez, Nancy Anne Hansen, Sara Elisabeth Baker, Rolene Douglas Ramsey. BSChemE, MIT, 1933, MSChemE, 1934, postgrad. Registered profl. engr., N.Y., Conn., Va. Prodn. supr. Union Carbide Corp., South Charleston, W.Va.; devel. group leader Union Carbide Corp., South Charleston, plant mgr., 1934-56; div. v.p. Union Carbide Corp., N.Y.C., 1957-68; v.p. Pope, Evans & Robbins, N.Y.C., Alexandria, Va., 1969-71; pres. Combustion Processes, Inc., N.Y.C., 1972-90, Darien, Conn., 1991-93. Editor: (directory) Consulting Services, 1978-88; contbr. numerous reports and papers to profl. jours. Sloan fellow MIT, 1939. Mem. Am. Inst. Chem. Engrs., Am. Chem. Soc., Assn. Cons. Chemists & Chem. Engrs. (dir. 1974-92). Office: 53 Goodwives River Rd Darien CT 06820-5919

GLENN, (THEODORE) SCOTT, actor; b. Pitts., Jan. 26, 1942; s. Theodore Glenn; m. Carol Schwartz, Sept. 10, 1968; 2 daughters, Dakota, Rio. B.A., Coll. William and Mary; student, Actors Studio, N.Y.C., from 1968. Made Broadway debut in The Impossible Years, 1965; other theater performances include Zoo Story, Long Day's Journey Into Night, Actors Studio, 1968, Collision Course, Angelo's Wedding, Circle Repertory Theater, 1985, Burn This, 1988; motion pictures include The Baby Maker, 1970, Angels Hard As They Come, 1971, Hex, 1973, Nashville, 1975, Fighting Mad, 1976, Apocalypse Now, 1979, More American Graffiti, 1979, Urban Cowboy, 1980, Cattle Annie and Little Britches, 1981, The Challenge, 1982, Personal Best, 1982, The Keep, 1983, The Right Stuff, 1983, The River, 1984, The Wild Geese II, 1985, Silverado, 1985, Man on Fire, 1987, Off Limits, 1988, Verne Miller, 1988, Miss Firecracker, 1989, The Hunt for Red October, 1990, Silence of the Lambs, 1991, My Heroes Have Always Been Cowboys, 1991, Backdraft, 1991, The Player, 1992, The Flight of the Dove, 1994, The Spy Within, 1995, Tall Tale, 1995, Reckless, 1995, Edie and Pen, 1996, Courage Under Fire, 1996, Carla's Song, 1996, Absolute Power, 1997, Lesser Prophetes, 1997, Larga Distance, 1998, Firestorm, 1998; appeared in TV films Gargoyles, 1972, As Summers Die, 1986, Intrigue, 1988, The Outside Woman, 1989, Women & Men 2: In Love There Are no Rules, 1991 (HBO), Shadow Hunter, 1993, Extreme Justice, 1993, Slaughter of The Innocents, 1993, Past Tense, 1994, Night of The Running Man, 1995. Served M.C. Office: William Morris Agy c/o Lee Stallman 151 S El Camino Dr Beverly Hills CA 90212-2775*

GLENN, STEVEN CLAUDE, financial executive; b. N.Y.C., Jan. 26, 1947; s. Jack and Lillian (Dankner) Goloshin; m. Penelope Wertz, Aug. 9, 1969 (div. 1982); m. Kathy Mathews, May 23, 1985; children: Darren, Ryan, Chad Mathews, Tara Mathews, Roscoe Goloshin, Jasper. BA, U. Miami, Fla., 1970; postgrad., Am. Coll., 1976, 82, 87, 88; MS in Fin. Svcs., The Am. Coll., MS in Mgmt. CLU; Chartered Fin. Cons. Agt. Occidental Life Ins. Co., Miami, 1970-75; assoc. gen. agt. Conn. Mut. Life Ins. Co., Miami, 1975-78; agy. mgr. Bankers Life Ins. Co., Jacksonville, Fla., 1978-84; v.p. Lincoln Planning Group, Inc., Jacksonville, 1985-88; pres. The Glenn Planning Group, Inc., Orange Park, Fla., 1989-97; divsn. v.p., pvt. client group Paine Webber, Orang Park, 1998—. Contbr. to books: Your Money and Your Life, 1979, ABC's of Investing Your Retirement Funds, 1980; contbr. articles to profl. jours. Bd. dirs. Jacksonville Gen. Agts. and Mgrs. Assn., 1981-84. Mem. Internat. Assn. Fin. Planning, Jacksonville Soc. CLUs and Chartered Fin. Cons. Avocations: water skiing, scuba diving, karate. Home: 319 Scenic Point Dr Orange Park FL 32073-7110 Office: PO Box 755 Orange Park FL 32067-0755

GLENNEN, ROBERT EUGENE, JR., retired university president; b. Omaha, Mar. 31, 1933; s. Robert E. and La Verda (Elledge) G.; m. Mary C. O'Brien, Apr. 17, 1958; children: Maureen, Bobby, Colleen, Billy, Barry, Katie, Molly, Kerry. A.B., U. Portland, 1955, M.Ed., 1957; Ph.D., U. Notre Dame, 1962. Asst. prof. U. Portland, 1956-60; asst. prof., assoc. prof. Eastern Mont. Coll., Billings, 1962-65; assoc. dean U. Notre Dame, South Bend, Ind., 1965-72; dean, v.p. U. Nev.-Las Vegas, 1972-80; pres. Western N.Mex. U., Silver City, 1980-84, Emporia (Kans.) State U., 1984-97; bd. dirs. Emporia Enterprises; cons. HEW, Washington, 1964-84. Author: Guidance: An Orientation, 1966. Contbr. articles to profl. jours. Pres. PTA, South Bend, Ind., 1970-71; bd. trustees Am. Coll. Testing Corp., Iowa City, 1977-80; chmn. Kans. Regents Coun. of Pres., 1986-87, 92-93, 95-96. Recipient award of excellence Nat. Acad. Advising Assn., Disting. Alumnus award U. Portland, 1993, Kans. Master Tchr. award, 1994; named Coach of Yr., Coach and Athletic mag., 1958, Pub. Adminstr. of Yr., 1994, Athletic Hall of Fame, Portland, 1995; Rotary Paul Harris fellow, 1995, Ford Found. fellow, 1961-62. Mem. Kans. C. of C. (bd. dirs.), Emporia C. of C. Regional Devel. Assn. (bd. dirs., Bank IV), Am. Personnel and Guidance Assn., Am. Assn. State Colls. and Univs. (chair pres's. commn. on tchr. edn.), Am. Assn. Higher Edn., Nev. Personnel and Guidance Assn., Assn. Counselor Educators and Suprs., Am. Assn. Counseling and Devel., Nat. Assn. Student Personnel Adminstrs. Republican. Roman Catholic. Avocations: racketball, walking, reading; hiking.

GLENNER, RICHARD ALLEN, dentist, dental historian; b. Chgo., Apr. 14, 1934; s. Robert Joseph and Vivian (Prosk) G.; BS, Roosevelt U., 1955; BS in Dentistry, U. Ill., 1958, DDS, 1959; m. Dorothy Chapman, July 13, 1957; children: Mark Steven, Alison, Scott Jay. Pvt. practice, Chgo., 1962—; cons. on dental history to Smithsonian Instn., ADA, various corps., libraries, univs., museums, dental jours., Dr. Samuel D. Harris Nat. Mus. Dentistry; dental and anthropological rschr. Nat. Park Svc., Nat. Mus. Health and Medicine, 1993—; lectr. in field. Served to capt. AUS, 1960-62. Mem. ADA, Ill. Dental Assn., Chgo. Dental Soc., Assn. Mil. Surgeons U.S., Am. Acad. History of Dentistry (historian 1984, chmn. Smithsonian Instn. adv. group 1987, Hayden-Harris award 1983, columnist Jour. of History of Dentistry 1989—, mem. editl. bd., 1993—, hist. display com. 1993—, pub. com., 1993—, Hayden-Harris award com. 1995-97), Fed. Dentaire Internationale, Lindsay Soc. Great Britain, Ill. State Dental Soc. (history com.), The Pierre Fauchard Acad., Am. Med. Writers Assn., Sci. Instrument Soc., Jewish War Vets. U.S.A, Alpha Omega, The Westerners, The Titanic His. Soc., Titanic Internat. Soc. Author: The Dental Office: A Pictorial History, 1984, How It Evolved: Dentistry's Pursuit for Excellence, 1997; co-author: The American Dentist, 1990, A Visit to the Dentist: Then & Now, 1996; appeared in PBS video Scientific American Frontiers: The Wild West, 1995; cons. editor A Bicentennial Salute to Am. Dentistry, 1976; contbr. articles to profl. jours.; film maker The Dental Office, 1994. Home: 6715 N Lawndale Ave Lincolnwood IL 60645-3711 Office: 3414 W Peterson Ave Chicago IL 60659-3447

GLENNON, CHARLES EDWARD, judge, lawyer; b. Monticello, Ill., Apr. 5, 1942; s. William Edward and Beatrice Jane (Pierson) G.; m. Sylvia Ann McClintock, Aug. 24, 1965 (div. Aug. 1972); children: David, Caroline; m. Victoria Louise Pearre, Oct. 26, 1974; 1 child, Andrew. BA, U. Ill., 1964, JD, 1966. Bar: Ill. 1966, U.S. Supreme Ct. 1974. Assoc. Fellheimer & Fellheimer, Pontiac, Ill., 1968-73; ptnr. Gomien & Glennon Ltd., Dwight, Ill., 1973-75; cir. judge State of Ill., Pontiac, 1976-98; chief judge 11th cir., 1991-95; lectr., author criminal law Ill. Village atty., Dwight, 1973-75; chmn. Salvation Army Adv. Bd., Pontiac, 1976; chmn. criminal law com. Ill. Jud. Conf., 1989-99, del., mem. exec. com., 1993-98; former mem. Regional Youth Planning Commn., Livingston County Commn. on Children and Youth; bd. dirs. Nat. Arts Found., 1998—. With U.S. Army, 1966-68. Fellow Ill. Bar Found.; mem. Livingston County Bar Assn. (pres. 1991-93), Ill. Bar Assn., Ill. Judges Assn., Am. Assn. Juvenile and Family Ct. Judges, Lions, Rotary, Elks. Republican. Episcopalian. Home: 10521 E 1700 North Rd Pontiac IL 61764-3113

GLENNON, HARRISON RANDOLPH, JR., retired shipping company executive; b. Port Gibson, Miss., Nov. 4, 1914; s. Harrison Randolph and May (Redus) G.; m. Dickie Glen Bailey, Oct. 27, 1944; children: Harrison Randolph, Francis Whaley (dec.), Blair Bailey. B.S., U.S. Naval Acad., 1937. Supr. ship repair and operation, engring. dept. Moore-McCormack Lines, Inc., N.Y.C., 1937-41, 46-53; supt. engr. Moore-McCormack Lines, Inc., 1953-57, v.p., head engring. div., 1959-62, exec. v.p. ops., dir., 1962-68; chmn. vessel replacement com. Am. S.S. Lines, 1962-64; pres. Comml. S.S. Co., Inc., 1968-71, Gt. Republics Transport, Inc., 1971—, Zapata Bulk Transport, Inc., 1971-77, Titan Nav., Inc., N.Y.C., from 1977, Sea Mobility, Inc., Norfolk, Va., 1987-93; cons. Seahawk Mgmt., Falcon Shipping Group, Houston, 1991-92; founder Equity Carriers, Inc., 1978; dir. Portsmouth Terminals, Inc.; cons. Falcon Carriers, Inc., 1977-78, Ernst & Ernst, 1978, IHI-George Sharp, Inc., 1978, various maritime affairs; mem. N.Y. Shipping Labor Policy Com., 1962—; v.p., dir. N.Y. Shipping Assn., 1967-69. Served from ensign to comdr. USNR, 1941-46. Mem. Soc. Naval Architects and Marine Engrs. (v.p., mem. exec. com. and coun.), Am. Bur. Shipping (classification and engring. com.), Am. Marine Inst. (tng. and upgrading com.), Am. Inst. Mcht. Shipping (chmn. standard ship com.), Maritime Svc. Com. (sec. 1966-67), Riverside Yacht Club. Episcopalian.

GLENNY, LYMAN ALBERT, retired education educator; b. Trent, S.D., Jan. 26, 1918; s. Walter and Ann (Henning) G.; m. Carolyn Joy Ballou, Dec. 19, 1942 (div. Mar. 1977); children—Terence Alan, Celia Joy, Colleen Marie; m. Helen S. Thompson, June 24, 1978 (dec. Aug. 1986). B.S., U. Minn., 1947; M.A., U. Colo., 1948; Ph.D., State U. Iowa, 1950. Instr. U. Iowa, 1948-50; from asst. prof. to prof. Sacramento State Coll., 1950-62; assoc. dir. Ill. Bd. Higher Edn., 1962-65; exec. dir. Ill. Bd. Higher Edn., Springfield, 1965-69; prof. higher edn. U. Calif., Berkeley, 1969-83, dir. Ctr. for Research and Devel. in Higher Edn., 1969-76; dir. Nebr. Study Adminstrn. Higher Edn., 1960. Author: Autonomy of Public Colleges, 1959, Coordinating Higher Education for the 70's, 1971, State Budgeting for Higher Education: Interagency Conflict and Consensus, 1976, Issues in Higher Education: A Six Nation Analysis, 1980, State Coordination of Higher Education: The Modern Concept, 1985, (with J. R. Kidder) State Tax Support of Higher Education: Revenue Appropriation Trends and Patterns, 1963-73, 1973, (with T. K. Dalglish) Public Universities, State Agencies, and the Law: Constitutional Autonomy in Decline, 1973, (with others) Presidents confront reality: From edifice complex to university without walls, 1975, (with Janet Ruyle) Trends in State Revenue Appropriations for Higher Education, 1968-78, (with F.M. Bowen) Uncertainty in Public Higher Education, 1980, Signals for Change: Stress Indicators, 1980, Quality and Accountability, 1981, also other publs. on state budgeting for higher edn.; editor: Statewide Planning for Post-Secondary Education, 1971; contbr. articles, chpts. to profl. publs.; bd. editors: Western Polit. Quar, 1959-62. Served to capt. U.S. Army, 1941-46, 51-52. Mem. AAUP, Am. Assn. Higher Edn., Am. Soc. Public Adminstrn., Assoc. Inst. Research, State Higher Edn. Exec. Officers Assn. (Oho) (hon.), Western Polit. Sci. Assn. Home: 3123 Lippizaner Ln Walnut Creek CA 94598-4606 Office: U Calif Tolman Hall Berkeley CA 94720

GLENZ, NANCY L., educator; b. Washington, Nov. 24, 1943; d. Charles B. and Helen L. (Kircher) G. BA, Trenton State Coll., 1965; MA, Mich. State U., 1970, PhD, 1972. Cert. vocat. edn. tchr., N.C. Tchr. Glassboro (N.J.) H.S., 1965-66, Moorestown (N.J.) H.S., 1966-70; coach Keene (N.H.) State Coll., 1972-73; tchr. Union Coll., Schenectady, N.Y., 1974; asst. prof. N.C. A&T State U., Greensboro, 1974-95, grad. studies coord., 1990—, assoc. prof., 1995—, interim chairperson, 1998—; bd. dirs. ARC, Greensboro, 1986-92. Author: Handbook for New Teachers of Vocational Education, 1993. Instr./trainer/vol. ARC, Greensboro, 1980—. Mem. Am. Soc. Safety Educators, Internat. Tech. Edn. Assn., Epsilon Pi Tau, Kappa Delta Pi. Avocations: reading, traveling, gardening. E-mail: glenzn@ncat.edu. FAX: 336-334-7577.

GLERUM, SALLY JANE, English educator; b. Findlay, Ohio, Feb. 25, 1969; d. David Lawrence and Rebecca Sue (Little) Inbody; m. Brian Jay Glerum, May 20, 1989; 1 child, Matthew David. BA, Grand Valley State U., 1992, MEd in English, 1998. Cert. tchr., Mich. Substitute tchr. Kent County Independent Sch. Dist., Grand Rapids, Mich., 1992; English tchr.. Shelby (Mich.) Pub. Schs., 1992—; chair lang. arts dept. Shelby H.S., 1994-98, mentor, tchr. English dept., 1997—. Advisor Nat. Honor Soc., Shelby, 1997—. Mem. Nat. Coun. Tchrs. English. Avocations: piano, reading, family, cooking. Home: 1884 S 88th Ave Shelby MI 49455-9779 Office: Shelby HS 641 N State St Shelby MI 49455

GLESK, IVAN, physicist, educator, researcher; b. Martin, Czechoslovakia, Sept. 1, 1957; came to U.S., 1990; s. Pavol and Elena (Orszaghova) G.; m. Helena Gleskova, Aug. 18, 1984; 1 child, Ivan. BA, MS in Physics, Comenius U., Bratislava, Slovak Republic, 1981, PhD in Physics, 1989. Assoc. prof. Comenius U., Bratislava, 1986-95, 1996—; vis. fellow Princeton (N.J.) U., 1990-91, vis. rsch. staff mem., 1991-94, rsch. staff mem., 1994-96, rsch. scientist in physics, 1996—; cons. Princeton Optics, Inc., 1995—; chmn. Slovak Com. for Optics, 1998—; presenter at numerous confs. Contbr. over 100 articles to profl. jours. IREX Bd. fellow, 1990. Mem. Optical Soc. Am., SPIE. Achievements include first demonstration of ultrafast all-optically controlled routing switch capable of Tb/s operation; first demonstration of all-optical address recognition and self-routing in a 250 Gb/s packet-switched network; first demonstration of all-optical demultiplexing of TDM data at 250 Gb/s; first demonstration of 100 Gb/s optical shuffle network; pioneering work in ultra fast all-optical switching; first demonstration of 100 Gb/s optical computer interconnect.

GLESNER FINES, BARBARA, law educator. BPh, Thomas Jefferson Coll., Allendale, Mich., 1980; JD, U. Wis., 1983; LLM, Yale U., 1986. Bar: Mo. Assoc. prof. law U. Mo. Sch. Law, Kansas City, 1987—. Office: U Mo Law Sch 5100 Rockhill Rd Kansas City MO 64110-2446

GLESS, SHARON, actress; b. L.A.; m. Barney Rosenzweig. Student, Gonzaga U. Appeared in TV series Faraday and Company, 1973-74, Marcus Welby, M.D., 1974-75, Switch!, 1975-78, Turnabout, 1979, House Calls, 1981-82; star TV series Cagney and Lacey, 1982-88 (6 Emmy nominations 1982-88, Emmy award 1986, 87, Golden Globe award 1985), The Trials of Rosie O'Neill, 1990-92 (Golden Globe award 1990, Emmy nomination 1991, 92); appeared in TV miniseries The Immigrants, 1978, Centennial, 1978, The Last Convertible, 1979; numerous other guest appearances in TV series; TV movies include All My Darling Daughters, 1972, My Darling Daughters' Anniversary, 1973, Clinic on 18th Street, 1974, Richie Brockelman: The Missing 24 Hours, 1976, The Islander, 1978, Crash, 1978, Kids Who Knew Too Much, 1979, Moviola: The Scarlett O'Hara War, 1980, Revenge of the Stepford Wives, 1980, Hardhat and Legs, 1980, The Miracle of Kathy Miller, 1981, Palms Precinct, 1982, Hobson's Choice, 1983, The Sky's No Limit, 1984, Letting Go, 1985, The Outside Woman, 1989, Honor Thy Mother, 1992, Separated by Murder, 1994, Cagney and Lacey: The Return, 1994, Cagney and Lacey: True Convictions, 1995, Cagney and Lacey: Together Again, 1995; Cagney and Lacey: The View Through the Glass Ceiling, 1995; theatrical debut in Watch on the Rhine, 1989; theater: Misery (London), 1992-93; films include Airport 1975, 1974, The Star Chamber, 1983, The Girl Next Door, 1997, (voice) Ayn Rand: A Sense of Life, 1997. Recipient Genii award Hollywood Women in Radio and TV, Best Actress award Viewers for Quality TV, Milestone award, 1988, SI award, 1991, Crystal Airwaves Media award Coalition for Clean Air, 1987, Gideon Media award, 1992, Disting. Artist award, 1992; named Woman of Yr., Ms mag., NCA Woman of Year, 1987, Entertainer of Yr., 1987. Office: William Morris Agy c/o Cary Berman 151 S El Camino Dr Beverly Hills CA 90212-2775 also: Marion Rosenberg Office 8428 Melrose Pl Ste B Los Angeles CA 90069-5308*

GLESSNER, THOMAS ALLEN, lawyer; b. Portland, Oreg., July 15, 1952; s. Ronald Walter and Marian Edna (Brannan) G.; m. Laura Lynn Braendlein, Aug. 27, 1977; children: Joshua Thomas, SaraLynn Joy, Brannan Timothy, Jefferson Samuel. AA, Highline C.C., Midway, Wash., 1972; BA, U. Wash., 1974, JD, 1977. Bar: Wash. 1977, Va. 1998, U.S. Dist. Ct. (we. dist.) 1977, U.S. Supreme Ct. 1989. Assoc. Holm, Glessner, Mogren & Glessner PS, Renton, Wash., 1977-87; instr. law Highline C.C., Midway, 1984-87; pres., gen. counsel Nat. Inst. Family and Life Advocates, 1987—. Rep. precinct committeeman, Renton, 1984-87; mem. state steering comm., Jack Kemp for Pres., Seattle, 1988; nat. co-chmn. Families for Bush/Quayle '92; bd. dirs., Crisis Pregnancy Ctr., King County, Wash., pres., 1987; pres. Christian Action Coun., 1987-93; mem. Coun. Nat. Policy. Recipient Humanitarian award Human Life of Wash., 1987. Mem. ABA, Wash. State Bar Assn., U.S. Supreme Ct. Bar, King County Bar Assn., Christian Legal

Soc., Kiwanis (local pres. 1983, local bd. dirs. 1982-85), Phi Beta Kappa, Sigma Nu. Presbyterian. Home: 6708 Farmstead Ln Fredericksburg VA 22407-1700

GLETNE, JEFFREY SCOTT, forester; b. Mpls., Dec. 10, 1952; s. John Sanford Gletne and Lillian Helen (Berg) Oxford; m. Michelle R. Evans, Feb. 6, 1998; 1 child, John Steven; stepchildren: Sarah Evans, Emily Evans, Alyssa Evans. BS, U. Calif., Berkeley, 1976. Registered profl. forester, Calif. Logger, forester Wickes Forest Industries, Dinuba, Calif., 1975-82; owner Skyline Logging Inc., Dinuba, 1982-89; forester Sierra Forest Products, Terra Bella, Calif., 1989—; mem. Bakersfield (Calif.) Coll. Agrl. Adv. Bd., 1993—; cons. Integrated Forest Mgmt., Springville, Calif., 1994-95. pres. People for the West, Bakersfield, 1994, v.p. People for the West, Porterville, Calif., 1995-96. Mem. Soc. of Am. Foresters (vice-chair, sec.-treas. 1993-94, chmn. 1994-95), Calif. Lic. Foresters Assn., Eagles Lodge. Republican. Avocations: fishing, hunting, reading, sporting events, hiking. Home: 10480 Road 261 Terra Bella CA 93270-9727 Office: Sierra Forest Products PO Box 10060 Terra Bella CA 93270-0060

GLEUE, LORINE ANNA, elementary education educator; b. Lucas, Kans., Feb. 12, 1926; d. Otto Martin and Bertha Marie (Luker) Becker; m. Fred Christoph Gleue, June 12, 1947; children: David Jean, Steven Randolph, Paul Frederick. Assoc., Cloud County C.C., 1969; BS in Edn., Ft. Hays (Kans.) State Coll., 1971; MS in Elem. Edn., Ft. Hays State U., 1977; reading specialist degree, Kans. State U., 1984. Cert. tchr., Kans. Elem. tchr. Coffey County, Kans., 1944-47; libr. Belleville (Kans.) Pub. Libr., 1960-67, Carnegie Free Pub. Libr., Concordia, Kans., 1967-68; elem. tchr. Chester, Nebr., 1971-72, Washington (Kans.) Unified Sch. Dist. #222, 1972-75; Chpt. I program instr. Washington, Kans., 1975-87; tchr. Republic County Schs., Mankato, and USD #333, Concordia, 1987—; Producer, co-owner Gleue's-On-The-Go Shows, Flying Carpet Story Hours, Lorine's Letter Writing Svc. to Shut-ins and Small Fry, Mother's Mender, Gleue-Gomoll Home-Loomed Rag Rugs; co-owner, developer Acres for Wildlife Resource Ctr., Belleville. Published poet; contbr. articles to profl. jours. Mem. book selection com. Kans. State Reading Cir., Topeka, 1979-81. Recipient Golden Poet award 3rd Ann. Poetry Conv., Las Vegas, Nev., 1987, World of Poetry Golden Poet award, 1988, 89, 90, 91, 92; 3rd place award Poetry Rendezvous, 1991, Best of Fair and Blue Ribbon awards, 1993, Celebrate Literacy award Internat. Reading Assn., 1993. Mem. Kans. Authors Club, Kans. Reading Assn. (mem. thunderbird coun.), Internat. Soc. of Poets, Fort Hays Alumni Assn. (life), Washington Sign Lang. Club (charter). Avocations: reading, travel, originating scripts for 35mm slide presentation.

GLEZOS, MATTHEWS, consumer products and services company executive; b. Montreal, Aug. 27, 1927; s. George and Katerina (Bakalos) G.; m. Sophia Protonotarios, Sept. 23, 1953; children: George, Mary. B. in commerce, McGill U., 1952. Tax assessor taxation div. Govt. of Can., Montreal, 1953-55; tax mgr., treas. Imasco Ltd., Montreal, 1955-78, v.p., treas., 1978-84; pres. Imasco B.V., Amsterdam, 1984-89, ret., 1989. Mem. Royal Montreal Golf Club. Home: 366 Kindersley, Mount Royal, PQ Canada H3R 1R9

GLICK, CYNTHIA SUSAN, lawyer; b. Sturgis, Mich., Aug. 6, 1950; d. Elmer Joseph and Ruth Edna (McCally) G. AB, Ind. U., 1972; JD, Ind. U.-Inpls., 1978. Bar: Ind. 1978, U.S. Dist. Ct. (so. dist.) Ind. 1978, U.S. Dist. Ct. (no. dist.) Ind. 1981. Adminstrv. asst. Gov. Otis R. Bowen, Ind., 1973-76; dep. pros. atty. 35th Jud. Cir., LaGrange County, Ind., 1980-82, pros. atty., 1983-90; pvt. practice, LaGrange, Ind., 1979—. Campaign aide Ind. Rep. State Cen. Com., Indpls., 1972-73. Named Hon. Speaker Ind. Ho. of Reps., 1972, Sagamore of the Wabash, Gov. Ind., 1974. Fellow Ind. Bar Found.; mem. ABA, Ind. State Bar Assn., LaGrange County Bar Assn. (pres. 1983-86), DAR, Bus. and Profl. Women's Club, Order of Ea. Star, Phi Delta Phi, Delta Zeta. Republican. Methodist. Home and Office: 113 W Spring St Lagrange IN 46761-1843

GLICK, DEBORAH J., state legislator; b. N.Y.C.. MBA, Fordham U. Formerly dir. gen. svc. Dept. Housing, Preservation and Devel., N.Y.C.; mem. N.Y. State Assembly, mem. children and families com., govt. employees com., also mem. ops. and social svc. coms., co-chair of ethics and guidance coms., 1998—; mem. environment conservation coms., gov. employment coms., ways and means com. N.Y. State Assembly. Mem. Greenpeace, N.Y. Zool. Soc., Defenders of Wildlife. Office: NY State Assembly Rm 454 LOB Albany NY 12224*

GLICK, EARL A., lawyer; b. Chgo., Feb. 20, 1930; s. Simon and Eva (Cohen) G.; m. Janet Esther Klein, Aug. 22, 1953; children: Michael J., Daniel H., Linda J. Richardson, Steven B. BS, U. Ill., 1951; JD, Northwestern U., 1953. Bar: Ill. 1953, Calif. 1962. Asst. atty. gen. State of Ill., Chgo., 1953-57; ptnr. Gerwin & Glick, Chgo., 1957-61, Gendel, Raskoff, Shapiro & Quittner, L.A., 1962-90, Orrick, Herrington & Sutcliffe, L.A., 1990—; gen. counsel S & S Corp., Beverly Hills, Calif., 1961-62; bd. govs. Fin. Lawyers Conf., L.A., 1965—, pres., 1975-76. Fellow Am. Coll. Comml. Fin. Lawyers; mem. ABA (chair program com. fin. svcs. subcom., 1993-96). Republican. Jewish. Avocations: travel, walking, reading. E-mail: eglick@orrick.com. Home: 5560 Ostin Ave Woodland Hills CA 91367-3976 Office: Orrick Herrington & Sutcliffe 777 S Figueroa St Ste 3200 Los Angeles CA 90017-5855

GLICK, GARLAND WAYNE, retired theological seminary president; b. Bridgewater, Va., Jan. 27, 1921; s. John T. and Effie (Evers) G.; m. Barbara Roller Zigler, Jan. 1, 1943; children—Martha (Mrs. Carl Barlett), John, Mary. B.D., Bethany Bibl. Sem., Chgo., 1946; M.A. in N.T, U. Chgo., 1949, Ph.D. in Ch. History, 1957; LL.D., Bridgewater Coll., 1969. Ordained to ministry Ch. of Brethren, 1942, United Ch. Christ, 1978. Pastor Lombard, Ill., 1945-48; instr., then asst. prof. Bibl. studies Juniata Coll., Huntingdon, Pa., 1948-53; mem. faculty Franklin and Marshall Coll., 1955-65, assoc. prof. religion, 1958-65, prof., 1965, v.p., 1962-65, acting pres., 1962-63, dir. rsch. and long-range planning, 1960, asst. to dean, 1960-61, dean coll., 1961-65; pres. Keuka Coll., Keuka Park, N.Y., 1966-74; dir. Moton Center Ind. Studies, Gloucester, Va., 1975-78; pres. Bangor (Maine) Theol. Sem., 1978-86; vis. prof. Lancaster (Pa.) Theol. Sem., 1958-60, 64; coord. cons. Knox Seminars Ednl. Mgmt., 1963-65; seminar dir. Nat. Cath. Assn. Long-Range Planning Seminars, 1968; bd. dirs. Empire State Found. Ind. Liberal Arts Colls., Fund for Theol. Edn. (pres. 1988-92), Lancaster Guidance Ctr. Author: Maker of Modern Theology: Adolf von Harnack, 1967, Songs for my God, 1998; contbr. to Ency. Brit. Mem. Nat. Assn. Bibl. Instrs., Am. Soc. Ch. History, Lancaster Cliosophic Soc. (pres. 1995-97), Am. Conf. Acad. Deans (treas. 1965-66), Societas Orphea, Pi Gamma Mu, Tau Kappa Alpha. Home: 1834 Ridgeview Ave Lancaster PA 17603-4316 *Clearly, a revolution has taken place in the last generation. The meaning of that revolution is not yet clear. I believe the name of the revolution is "longing" and Augustine's "God and the soul I want to know, nothing more," demarks its direction.*

GLICK, J. LESLIE, biotechnology entrepreneur; b. N.Y.C., Mar. 2, 1940; s. Arthur Harvey and Hilda Lillian (Lichtenfeld) G.; m. Judith Sumiye Mihara; children: Geoffrey Michael, Jessica Michele. AB, Columbia U., 1961, PhD, 1964. Nat. Cancer Inst. postdoctoral fellow Princeton U., 1964-65; sr., then asso. cancer research scientist Roswell Park Meml. Inst., Buffalo, 1965-69; assoc. research prof. physiology, physiology chmn. Roswell Park div. SUNY, Buffalo, 1968-70; from exec. v.p. to chmn. bd. Asso. Biomedic Systems, Inc., Buffalo, 1969-77; pres. Inst. Sci. and Social Accountability, Washington, 1975-79; pres., chief exec. officer Genex Corp., Gaithersburg, Md., 1977-87; chmn., CEO Bionix Corp., Potomac, Md., 1987-93; chmn. HTI Corp., Buffalo, 1972-75; dir. Nat. Assn. Life Sci. Industries, 1975-77; rsch. prof. biology Niagara (N.Y.) U., Canisius Coll., Buffalo, 1968-70; mem. exec. com. SUNY Grad. Sch., Buffalo, 1968-70; vis. lectr. NATO Adv. Study Inst., Brussels, 1970; mem. biotech. tech. adv. com. U.S. Dept. Commerce, 1985-87; adj. prof. tech. mgmt. Grad. Sch. Mgmt. and Tech., U. Md. Univ. Coll., 1988—, mem. adv. panel, 1988—, mem. grad. coun., 1992-94; chmn. bd. Marco Polo Techs., Inc., 1998—; bd. dirs. Advanced Processing & Imaging, Inc. Author: Fundamentals of Human Lymphoid Cell Culture, 1980; also articles; patentee in field; mem. editorial advisors bd. Strategic Direction, 1984-87; mem. adv. coun. High Tech. Mktg. Rev., 1986-87; mem. indsl. adv. bd. Biotech. Process Engring. Ctr., MIT, 1986-87; mem. editorial bd. Accountability in Rsch.: Policies and Quality Assurance, 1989—; editor-in-chief Tech. Mgmt., 1992—. Bd. overseers Simon's Rock of Bard Coll., 1984-85; trustee Nat. Faculty Humanities, Arts and Scis., 1985-87. Mem. Internat. Assn. for Mgmt. Tech., Am. Physiol. Soc., Indsl. Biotech. Assn. (pres. 1981-83, bd. dirs.1981-84), N.Y. Acad. Scis., Sigma Xi.

GLICK, JANE MILLS, biochemistry educator; b. Memphis, Nov. 26, 1943; d. Albert Axtell Jr. and Mary Louise (Baynes) Mills; m. John Harrison Glick, May 25, 1968; children: Katherine Anne, Sarah Stewart. AB, Randolph-Macon Woman's Coll., 1965; PhD, Columbia U., 1971. Postdoctoral trainee NIH, Bethesda, Md., 1971-73; postdoctoral fellow Sch. of Medicine Stanford (Calif.) U., 1973-74; rsch. asst. prof. biochemistry Sch. Dental Medicine U. Pa., Phila., 1974-77; asst. prof. biochemistry Med. Coll. Pa., Phila., 1977-82, assoc. prof. biochemistry, 1982-90, prof. biochemistry, 1990-94; sr. rsch. investigator Inst. Human Gene Therapy, U. Pa. Sch. Medicine, 1994—; mem. metabolism study sect. NIH, 1993-97; adj. assoc. prof. U. Pa. Sch. Medicine, 1996—. Assoc. editor: Jour. Lipid Rsch., 1985-86, mem. editorial bd., 1987-99; contbr. articles to profl. jours. Trustee Episcopal Acad., Merion, Pa., 1989-95, Swarthmore Presbyn. Ch., 1995-97, pres. 1997. Recipient Rsch. Svc. award NIH, 1975-77, Young Investigator award, 1980-83, Teaching award Lindback Found., 1985. Mem. AAAS, AAUP (sec. 1990-92), Arteriosclerosis Coun. Am. Heart Assn. (program com. 1990-93), Am. Soc. for Biochemistry and Molecular Biology, Am. Soc. for Human Genetics, Phi Beta Kappa, Sigma Xi. Presbyterian. Office: U Pa Med Coll Inst Human Gene Therapy 613 BRB II/III 421 Curie Blvd Philadelphia PA 19104

GLICK, JOHN H., oncologist, medical educator; b. N.Y.C., May 9, 1943; s. Arthur W. and Sybil (Goldman) G.; m. Jane Mills, May 25, 1968; children: Katherine, Sarah. AB magna cum laude, Princeton U., 1965; MD, Columbia U., 1969. Diplomate Am. Bd. Med. Oncology, Am. Bd. Internal Medicine (sec. subsplty. com. med. oncology 1976-83, mem. subsplty. bd. med. oncology 1983-87, chmn. 1987-89, cert. examination com. 1986-88, mem. bd. govs. 1987-89). Intern in medicine Presbyn. Hosp., N.Y.C., 1969-70, asst. resident in medicine, 1970-71; commd. surgeon, clin. assoc. medicine br. Nat. Cancer Inst., USPHS, Bethesda, Md., 1971-73; postdoctoral fellow in med. oncology Stanford (Calif.) U., 1973-74; asst. prof. medicine U. Pa., Phila., 1974-79, Ann B. Young asst. prof. cancer rsch., 1974, assoc. prof., 1979-83, prof., 1983—, Madlyn and Leonard Abramson prof. clin. oncology, 1988—; dir. clin. trials U. Pa. Cancer Ctr., Phila., 1977-79, assoc. dir. for clin. rsch., 1980-85, dir. Cancer Ctr., 1985—; mem. numerous acad. coms., dept. medicine coms., hosp. coms., 1974—; pres. Abramson Family Cancer Rsch. Inst., Phila., 1998—, also bd. dirs.; attending physician Hosp. of U. Pa., 1974—, dir. Hematology-Oncology Clinic, 1974-76; cons. Phila. VA Hosp., 1974—; mem. NIH clin. trials rev. com., 1980-83, radiosensitizer/radioprotector working group, radiotherapy devel. br., 1980-85, chmn. consensus devel. panel conf. adjuvant therapy for breast cancer, 1985, all Nat Cancer Inst., NIH; mem. com. accreditation med. oncology tng. progams, 1983—, mem. appeals panel, 1987-94, Accreditation Coun. Grad. Med. Edn.; prin. investigator Ea. Coop. Oncology Group, U. Pa.; pres., dir. Abramson Family Cancer Rsch. Inst., 1987—; dir. Pa. Cancer Ctr. Mem. editl. bd. Am. Jour. Clin. Oncology, 1983-89, Blood, 1983-86, Jour. Clin. Oncology, 1986-88, Jour. Cancer Rsch. and Clin. Oncology, 1987-93; mem. bd. editors Internat. Jour. Radiation Oncology, Biology and Physics; assoc. editor Cancer Rsch., 1984-88; contbr. more than 100 original papers to profl. jours. Recipient Am. Cancer Soc. Faculty Rsch. award, 1982-86; rsch. grantee Nat. Cancer Inst., Ea. Coop. Oncology Group, Am. Cancer Soc., others. Fellow ACP (mem. various splty. coms. 1983-85), Coll. Physicians and Surgeons; mem. Am. Soc. Clin. Oncology (chmn. program com. 1983-84, nominating com. 1983-84, mem. pub. issue com. 1984-85, bd. dirs., pres. 1995-96), Am. Assn. Cancer Edn., Am. Assn. Cancer Rsch., Am. Radium Soc. (mem. exec. com. 1986-87), Am. Soc. Hematology, Am. Fedn. Clin. Rsch., John Morgan Soc. U. Pa., Phi Beta Kappa, Alpha Omega Alpha. Office: U Pa Cancer Ctr 3400 Spruce St Philadelphia PA 19104-4204

GLICK, KAREN LYNNE, college administrator; b. Bucyrus, Ohio, Sept. 2; d. Phillip Dole and Bernice Grace Glick; BSJ, Bowling Green State U., 1967, MA, 1979; children: M. Todd, K. Christine. Editor, Bowling Green (Ohio) State U., 1972-74; account exec. Howard E. Mitchell, Jr., Advt., Findlay, Ohio, 1974-77; asst. to dir. Student Devel. Program, Bowling Green State U., 1977-79; dir. pub. info. Bluffton (Ohio) Coll., 1980-83; asst. to v.p. for instl. advancement Findlay (Ohio) Coll., 1983-85; assoc. dir. devel. Bluffton Coll., 1985-90; assoc. dir. divisional support Miami U., Oxford, Ohio, 1990-93; sr. regional dir. devel. U. Ill. Found., Urbana, 1993—. Anglican. Mem. Fla. Sea Kayaking Assn., Bowling Green U. Press Club (charter 1983). Office: U Ill Found Harker Hall MC-386 1305 W Green St Urbana IL 61801-2945

GLICK, LESLIE ALAN, lawyer; b. N.Y.C., May 22, 1946; s. Leo S. and Sylvia (Hall) G. BS, Cornell U., 1967, JD, 1970. Bar: N.Y. 1971, D.C. 1971, Md. 1974, U.S. Ct. Internat. Trade 1971, U.S. Supreme Ct. 1974. Ptnr. Porter Wright Morris & Arthur, Washington, 1989—. Author: Multilateral Trade Negotiations, 1984, Trading with Saudi Arabia, 1980, Guide to U.S. Customs and Trade Laws, 1991, 2d edit., 1996, Understanding the North American Free Trade Agreement, 1993, 2d edit., 1995. Active Dem. State Cen. com., Md., 1982-84; chmn. adv. com. on Consumer Affairs, Montgomery County, Md., 1982-84. Mem. Fed. Bar Assn. (chmn. internat. law sect. 1986-88). Office: Porter Wright Morris & Arthur 1667 K St NW Ste 1100 Washington DC 20006-1660

GLICK, MARION SHEPHERD, psychology, educator; b. N.Y.C., Sept. 30, 1938; d. Hall Edward and Elizabeth (Whiteside) S.; 1 child, Jonathan. BA, Drew U., 1959; MA, Clark U., 1964, PhD, 1968. Lic. clin. psychologist Bd. Examiners Conn. Clin. psychologist Worcester (Mass.) Youth Guidance Ctr., 1963-64, Waterbury (Conn.) Child Guidance Clinic, 1966-68; prof. So. Conn. State U., New Haven, 1968-95; postdoctoral assoc. Yale U., New Haven, 1977-85, assoc. rsch. scientist, 1985—; consulting clin. psychologist New Haven and Guilford, Conn., 1970-98. Author: (with E. Zigler) A Developmental Approach to Adult Psychopathology, 1986; contbr. chpts. to books and articles to profl. jours. Active Caucus of Conn. Dems., 1967-70, Dem. Town Com., Branford, 1968-70; mem., nat. rep. Women's Polit. Caucus, New Haven, Conn., 1970-72. Presdl. Rsch. fellow So. Conn. State U., New Haven, 1980; program project rsch. grantee NIH, Washington, 1985-95. Mem. APA, AAUP. Avocations: writing, traveling, gardening. Home: 229 Stony Creek Rd Branford CT 06405-3201

GLICK, MILTON DON, chemist, university administrator; b. Memphis, July 30, 1937; s. Lewis S. and Sylvia (Kleinman) G.; m. Peggy M., June 22, 1965; children: David, Sander. AB cum laude, Augustana Coll., 1959; PhD, U. Wis., 1965. Asst. prof. chemistry Wayne State U., Detroit, 1966-70, assoc. prof., 1970-74, prof., 1974-83, chmn. dept., 1978-83; dean arts & scis. U. Mo., Columbia, 1983-88; provost Iowa State U., Ames, 1988-91, interim pres., 1990-91; sr. v.p., provost Ariz. State U., Tempe, 1991—. Contbr. articles to profl. jours. Fellow dept. chemistry Cornell U., Ithaca, N.Y., 1964-66. Office: Ariz State U Office of Provost 2803 Adm 210 Tempe AZ 85287

GLICK, RUTH BURTNICK, author, lecturer; b. Lexington, Ky., Apr. 27, 1942; d. Lester Leon and Beverly (Miller) Burtnick; m. Norman Stanley Glick, June 30, 1963; children: Elissa, Ethan. BA, George Washington U., 1964; MA, U. Md., 1967. lectr. S.W. Writers Conf., Houston, 1984, Nebr. Writers' Guild, Omaha, 1985, Bouchercon, Balt., 1986, Triangle Romance and Fiction Writers' Cong., Raleigh, 1988, Romantic Times Booklovers Conf., San Antonio, 1990, Malice Domestic, Bethesda, 1993, Howard C.C., 1995—. Author: (with Nancy Baggett) Dollhouse Furniture You Can Make, 1977, Dollhouse Lamps and Chandeliers, 1979, Soup's On, 1985, Oat Bran Baking, 1989, Skinny Soups, 1992, 100 Percent Pleasure, 1994 (US Today list of 12 best cookbooks of 1994), Skinny Italian, 1996; (with Eileen Buckholtz, Carolyn Males and Louise Titchener) Love Is Elected, 1982 (named one of best romances 1982), Southern Persuasion, 1983, (with Titchener) In the Arms of Love, 1983 (Romance best seller list), Brian's Captive, 1983 (Romance best seller list), Reluctant Merger, 1983 (Romance best seller list), Summer Wine, 1984, Beginner's Luck, 1984, Mistaken Image, 1985, Hopelessly Devoted, 1985, Summer Stars, 1985, Stolen Passion, 1986, Indiscreet, 1988, (with Baggett and Gloria Kaufer Greene) Don't Tell 'Em It's Good for 'Em, 1984, Eat Your Vegetables!, 1985, (with Buckholtz) End of Illusion, 1984, Space Attack, 1984, Mission of the Secret Spy Squad, 1984, Mindbenders, 1984, Doom Stalker, 1985, Captain Kid and the Pirates, 1985, The Cats of Castle Mountain, 1985, Logical Choice, 1986, Great Expectations, 1987, A Place in Your Heart, 1988, Saber Dance, 1988, Postmark, 1988, Roller Coaster, 1989 (Young Adult Best Seller List), Silver Creek Challenge, 1989, Needlepoint, 1989, Life Line, 1990, Shattered Vows, 1991, Whispers in the Night, 1991, Only Skin Deep, 1992, Trial By Fire, 1992, Hopscotch, 1993, Cradle and All, 1993, What Child is This, 1993, Midnight Kiss, 1994, Tangled Vows, 1994, Till Death Us Do Part, 1995, Prince of Time, 1995, Face to Face, 1996, For Your Eyes Only, 1997, Father and Child, 1997 (Peregrine Connection series) Talons of the Falcon, 1986, Flight of the Raven, 1986, In Search of the Dove, 1986 (Lifetime Achievement award for romantic suspense series 1987), (with Kathryn Jensen) The Big Score, 1989 (Young Adult Best Seller List), Night Stalker, 1989 (Young Adult Best Seller List), (sole author) Dollhouse Kitchen and Dining Room Accessories, 1979, Invasion of the Blue Lights, 1982, More Than Promises, 1985, The Closer We Get, 1989, Make Me a Miracle, 1992, Bayou Moon, 1992, Skinny One Pot Meals, 1994, others; contbr. articles to profl. jours. U. Md. Am. studies fellow, 1964-65; recipient Romantic Times Career Achievement award for Romantic Mystery, 1994; nominee Best Series Romance Book of the Yr. 1993-94 Romantic Times, 1995, nominee Series Storyteller of Yr., 1996. Mem. Author's Guild, Romance Writers Am. (lectr. Detroit, 1984, Atlanta 1985, Dallas 1987, 96, Boston 1989, San Francisco 1990, New Orleans 1991), Washington Romance Writers (bd. dirs.), Sisters in Crime, Novelists Inc., Md. Romance Writers. *

GLICK, STEVEN LAWRENCE, financial consultant; b. Phila., July 22, 1959; s. Herbert S. and Esther P. Glick; m. Mari L.; children: Colin H., Courtney H. BA, Northwestern U., 1982; MBA, Harvard U., 1989. CFA. Rsch. reporter Forbes Mag., Chgo., 1981-82; bond trader 1st Boston Corp., N.Y.C., 1982-87; assoc. Pacific Corp. Group, LaJolla, Calif., 1989-90; v.p., bond trader S.G. Warburg & Co., N.Y.C., 1990-91; ptnr. Greenwich (Conn.) Assocs., 1991—; speaker in field. Mem. Assn. Investment Mgmt. and Rsch. Democrat. Jewish. Avocations: tennis, running, skiing, movies. Home: 393 Riversville Rd Greenwich CT 06831-3230 Office: Greenwich Assocs Office Park 8 Greenwich CT 06831

GLICKENHAUS, MIKE, radio station executive. BA in Mktg./Comm., SUNY, Albany, 1975. Sales rep. Fidelity Union Life Ins. Co., San Diego, 1976-78; account mgr. S.C. Enterprises, Long Beach/San Diego, 1978-80; account exec. Sta. XTRA-FM, XTRA-AM Noble Broadcast Group, San Diego, 1980-83, local sales mgr., 1983-85, gen. sales mgr. Sta. XTRA-FM, 1985-88, v.p./gen. mgr., 1988-91, exec. v.p./gen. mgr. Sta. XTRA-FM, XTRA-AM, KWNK-AM (L.A.), 1991-96; market gen. mgr. Jacor Comm., San Diego, 1996-97, co-market mgr. FM stas., v.p./gen. mgr. FM stas., 1997—; gen. mgr. VETRA-AM, San Diego. Office: VETRA-AM/Jacor Comm 4891 Pacific Hwy San Diego CA 92110-4003*

GLICKMAN, ALBERT SEYMOUR, psychologist, educator; b. Bklyn., Feb. 7, 1923; s. Irving and Molly G.; m. Blanche Buller, June 14, 1945; children: Ralph, Marc, Judith, Debra. B.A. summa cum laude, Ohio State U., 1943, M.A., 1947, Ph.D., 1952. Asst. prof. psychology Ga. Inst. Tech., Atlanta, 1947-52; project dir. Am. Insts. for Research, Newport, R.I., Pitts., 1952-55; dir. psychol. research dept. U.S. Naval Personnel Research Activity, Washington, 1955-62; chief personnel research staff U.S. Dept. Agr., Washington, 1962-67; dir. Inst. for Research in Organizational Behavior; dep. dir. Washington office Am. Insts. for Research, 1967-76; v.p. Advanced Research Resources Orgn., Washington, 1976-78; eminent prof. psychology Old Dominion U., Norfolk, Va., 1979-90; eminent prof. emeritus Old Dominion U., Norfolk, 1991—; pres. Orgn. Research Group of Tidewater, Inc., 1979-91; chmn. bd. Third Quarter: Inst. Retirement Research, 1985-91; vis. prof. Tel Aviv U., 1986, Tulane U., 1994. Cons. editor: Jour. Applied Psychology, 1971-81; co-author: Top Management Development and Succession, 1968, Police-community Action: A Program for Change in Police-community Behavior Patterns, 1973, Changing Schedules of Work: Patterns and Implications, 1974; editor: Changing Composition of the Workforce: Implications for Future Research and Its Applications, 1982. Served to lt. (j.g.) USN, 1943-46. Recipient Louis Brownlow Meml. Fund prize Internat. Pub. Personnel Assn., 1965; recipient author award Tng. and Devel. Jour., Am. Soc. Tng. and Devel., 1967. Fellow Am. Psychol. Soc., Am. Psychol. Assn., Internat. Assn. Applied Psychology, Soc. Indsl. and Organizational Psychology, AAAS; mem. Soc. Psychol. Study Social Issues, Phi Beta Kappa. Jewish. Home: 141 S Ridgeley Rd Norfolk VA 23505-4623 Office: Old Dominion U Dept Psychology Norfolk VA 23529 *Old enough to appreciate tradition. Young enough to facilitate change.*

GLICKMAN, CARL DAVID, banker; b. Cleve., July 29, 1926; s. Jack I. and Dora R. (Rubinowitz) G.; m. Barbara H. Schulman, Oct. 16, 1960; children: Lindsay Dale, David Craig, Robert Todd. Student, U. Minn., 1944, Inst. Fin. Mgmt., Harvard U., 1970. Pres. Glickman Orgn., Cleve., 1953—; chmn. bd., chief exec. officer Computer Research, Inc., Pitts., 1964-67, Am. Steel & Pump Corp., N.Y.C., 1968-71, Shelter Resources Corp., Cleve., 1971-75; pres. Leader Bldg., Inc., Cleve., 1959—, Capital Bancorp., Cleve., 1971-75, Real Property Corp., Cleve., 1975—; spl. ltd. ptnr. Bear Stearns & Co., 1978-85, dir., 1985—; chmn. exec. com. Franklin Corp., N.Y.C., 1986-98, Cook United Inc., Cleve., 1986-87, Capital Nat. Bank Cleve., 1970-75, bd. dirs., 1975-80; chmn. bd. dirs. Univ. Nat. Bank, Chgo., 1968-70; ltd. ptnr. S.B. Lewis & Co., N.Y.C., 1980-89; gen. ptnr. Millbrook Assocs., Chester Union Assocs.; founding gen. ptnr. Park Ctrl. Assocs.; pres., bd. dirs. LGT Industries, Durham, N.C., 1987-95; bd. dirs. Nat. Kinney Corp., Royal Petroleum Properties Corp., ETL, Phila., Andal Corp., Blue Coral Inc., Jerusalem Econ. Corp., Israel, Custodial Trust Co., Alliance Tyre and Rubber Co., Tel Aviv,Tnuport Ltd., Tel Aviv, Indsl. Structures, Inc., Tel Aviv, Lexington Corp. Properties, N.Y.C., Office Max, Inc. Mem. Mayor's Com. Urban Renewal, 1965-67; mem. Mayors Task Force on Higher Edn.; trustee Cleve. Growth Assn., 1972-75; co-chmn. Herzog Loan Fund Cleve. State U.; chmn. Med. Arts Hosp., Houston, 1976—; bd. visitors Case Western Res. Sch. Law; trustee Montefiore Home Aged, Mt. Sinai Hosp.; mem. grievance com. Cleve. Bar Assn., 1982-85; foreman Cuyahoga County Grand Jury, Cleve., 1984-85; trustee Cleve. State U. Served with USAAF, 1944-46. Mem. Am. Bankers Assn., Am. Arbitration Assn. (arbitrator), Phi Sigma Delta, Phi Eta Sigma. Clubs: Beechmont Country, City, Univ. (Cleve.); Standard (Chgo.); Harmonie, Town (N.Y.C.), Palm Beach (Fla.) Yacht. Lodge: Masons. Office: 1140 Leader Bldg Cleveland OH 44114 also: 245 Park Ave New York NY 10167-0002 also: 1 N Breakers Row Palm Beach FL

GLICKMAN, DANIEL ROBERT, federal official; b. Wichita, Kans., Nov. 24, 1944; s. Milton and Gladys Anne (Kopelman) G.; m. Rhoda Joyce Yura, Aug. 21, 1966; children: Jonathan, Amy. B.A., U. Mich., Ann Arbor, 1966; J.D., George Washington U., Washington, 1969. Bar: Kans. 1969, Mich. 1970. Trial atty. SEC, 1969-70; assoc., then ptnr. Sargent, Klenda & Glickman, Wichita, 1971-76; mem. 95th-103rd Congresses from 4th Kans. Dist., 1977-95; mem. agrl. com. 95th-10rd Congresses from 4th Kans. Dist., mem. judiciary, sci., space and tech. coms.; chmn. permanent select com. on intelligence 103d Congress; sec. U.S. Dept. Agriculture, Washington, 1995, now chmn. Mem. Wichita Bd. Edn., 1973-76, pres., 1975-76. Mem. Order of Coif, Phi Delta Phi, Sigma Alpha Mu. Democrat. Jewish. Office: Office of the Secretary USDA Ste 200-A 1400 Independence Ave SW Washington DC 20250-0002

GLICKMAN, EDWARD A., real estate investment executive. BS in Econs., U. Pa., 1978, B Applied Sci. in Bioengring., 1978; MBA, Harvard U., 1981. CCM, Treasury Mgmt. Assn. Investment banker, head new products group Shearson Lehman Bros. Smith Barney; exec. v.p., CFO Presdl. Realty Corp.; v.p., CFO Pa. Real Estate Investment Trust, Phila., 1993—; bd. dirs. Liberty Net, Inc., Apex Site Mgmt., LP; spkr. in field. Mem. City of Phila. Telecomms. Policy Adv. Commn. Mem. Pension Real Estate Assn., Internat. Coun. Shopping Ctrs., Nat. Assn. Real Estate Investment Trusts, Nat. Realty Com. Office: Pa Real Estate Investment Trust 200 S Broad St Ste 300 Philadelphia PA 19102

GLICKMAN, FRANKLIN SHELDON, dermatologist, educator; b. Bklyn., Dec. 14, 1929; s. Arthur Zachary and Hilda (Kurtz) G.; m. Leatrice Sallie Alter, Mar. 29, 1953; children: Todd Scott, Jeff Bret. BA cum laude, Hofstra Coll., 1950; MD, SUNY-Bklyn., 1954; MS in Health Care Mgmt., NYU, 1990. Diplomate: Am. Bd. Dermatology. Intern Flushing (N.Y.) Hosp., 1954-55; resident in dermatology Kings County Hosp., Bklyn., 1957-

58, Bronx VA Hosp., 1958-60; practice medicine specializing in dermatology Bklyn., 1960-94; mem. faculty dermatology dept. SUNY-Bklyn., 1960—, clin. prof., 1982-93, adj. clin. prof., 1993—; dir. med. edn. Wyckoff Heights Med. Ctr., Bklyn., 1990-96, chmn. dept. grad. med. edn., 1992-96. Author: General Dermatology, 1978, Fundamentals of Dermatology: A Study Guide, 1990; contbr. articles to profl. jours. Served to capt. M.C. USAF, 1955-57. Fellow N.Y. Acad. Medicine, ACP; mem. Am. Acad. Dermatology, Bklyn. Dermatol. Soc. (pres. 1970-72), N.Y. State Med. Soc., Kings County Med. Soc., AMA, N.Y. State Soc. Dermatology (pres. 1983-85), Phi Beta Kappa. Home: 6841 Treves Way Boynton Beach FL 33437

GLICKMAN, HARRY, professional basketball team executive; b. Portland, Oreg., May 13, 1924; s. Sam and Bessie (Karp) G.; m. Joanne Carol Matin, Sept. 28, 1958; children: Lynn Carol, Marshall Jordan, Jennifer Ann. B.A., U. Oreg., 1948. Press agt., 1948-52; pres. Oreg. Sports Attractions, 1952—; mgr. Multnomah (Oreg.) Civic Stadium, 1958-59; pres. Portland Hockey Club, 1960-73; former exec. v.p. basketball team Portland Trail Blazers, now pres. emeritus. Trustee B'nai B'rith Jr. Camp, 1965; bd. dirs. U. Oreg. Devel. Fund. Served with AUS, 1943-46. Named to Oreg. Sports Hall of Fame, 1986. Mem. Portland C. of C. (bd. dirs. 1968-72), Sigma Delta Chi, Sigma Alpha Mu. Jewish. Office: Portland Trail Blazers 1 Center Ct Ste 200 Portland OR 97227-2103

GLICKMAN, NORMAN JAY, economist, urban policy analyst; b. Bklyn., July 27, 1942; s. Harry and Beatrice (Frankel) G.; m. Elyse M. Pivnick, May 8, 1983; children: Katy Rose, Madeline Claire. BA, U. Pa., 1963, MA, 1967, PhD, 1969. Prof. urban and regional planning U. Pa., Phila., 1980-82; Hogg prof. urban policy U. Tex., Austin, 1983-89; prof. urban planning Rutgers U., New Brunswick, N.J., 1989, dir. Ctr. for Urban Policy Rsch. State of N.J., 1989—; vis. scholar U.S. HUD, Washington, 1978-79; fellow Netherland Inst. Advanced Studies, Wassenaar, 1981-82; sr. rsch. scholar Internat. Inst. Applied Systems Analysis, Laxenburg, Austria, 1977; appointee N.J. Coun. on Job Opportunities, N.J., 1992—. Co-author: The New Competitors, 1989 (Top 10 Bus. Week 1989). Chmn. Econ. Devel. Commn., Austin, 1985-89. Recipient Lindback award U. Pa., 1976, named Disting. Fulbright Prof., Monterrey (Mex.) Inst. of Tech., 1985; fellow Japan Found., 1976. Mem. EEFMS (charter), Regional Sci. Assn. (v.p. 1988-89), Am. Econ. Assn. Office: Rutgers U Ctr Urban Pol Rsch 33 Livingston Ave Ste 400 New Brunswick NJ 08901-1900

GLICKMAN, RONNIE CARL, state official, lawyer; b. Junction City, Kans., Feb. 6, 1956; s. Lawrie Burton and Ruth Lael (Singer) G. AB, Duke U., 1977; MS in Pub. Adminstrn., Fla. State U., 1980, JD, 1981. Bar: Fla. 1981, U.S. Dist. Ct. (mid. dist.) Fla. 1981. Asst. states atty. Hillsborough County, Tampa, Fla., 1981-84, county commr., 1985-86; rep. Fla. Ho. of Reps., Tallahassee and Tampa, 1986-94; retired, 1994. Speaker sch. enrichment resource Vols. in Edn., Tampa, 1986; active Project Graduation Celebrity Auction, Tampa, 1986, celebrity bowlathon Big Bros./Big Susters, Tampa, 1986, Say No To Drugs Marsh, Tampa, 1986, 94. Recipient Martin Luther King Leadership award Starting Together on Progress, 1986. Mem. Phi Beta Kappa, Order of Coif. Democrat. Jewish. Home: 714 S Orleans Ave Tampa FL 33606-2535

GLICKSMAN, ARVIN S(IGMUND), radiation oncologist; b. Bklyn., Mar. 14, 1924; s. Charles and Myrtle (Fetner) G.; m. Bernice R. Grobstein, Jan. 30, 1956; children: Jonathan, Jane Ellen, Merrylee, Caroline, Jeanette. MB, MD, Chgo. Med. Sch., 1949. Intern Kings County Hosp., Bklyn., 1948-50; AEC postdoctoral research fellow Duke U., 1950-51; postgrad. rsch. fellow Brookhaven Nat. Labs., Upton, N.Y., 1951-52; resident in medicine Meml. Hosp., N.Y.C., 1952-54; clin. asst. physician in medicine Meml. Hosp., 1955-64, asst. attending radiation therapist, 1964-65; rsch. fellow Sloan-Kettering Inst., N.Y.C., 1954-60; assoc. Sloan-Kettering Inst., 1960-65; mem. med. rsch. inst. Michael Reese Hosp., Chgo., 1964-65; assoc. chmn. dept. radiation therapy Michael Reese Hosp., 1965-67; dep. dir. radiotherapy Mount Sinai Hosp., N.Y.C., 1967-73; prof. radiotherapy Mount Sinai Sch. Medicine, 1971-73; dir. radiation oncology R.I. Hosp., Providence, 1973-84, chmn. dept. radiol. medicine and biol. rsch., 1984-89; prof. med. scis. Brown U., 1973-95, prof. emeritus, 1995—; chmn. dept. radiation oncology Roger Williams Med. Ctr., 1989-95; practice medicine specializing in radiation oncology; hon. med. cons. NIH, Royal Marsden Hosp.; mem. cancer clinic, investigation rev. com. Nat. Cancer Inst., 1975-79, mem. radiation oncology com., 1976-86, mem. cancer intervention study sect., 1991-94. Editor: (with others) Computers in Radiotherapy, 1970, 73; contbr.: numerous articles to profl. jours. Mem. exec. com. Am. Cancer Soc., R.I., 1987-96—, pres., 1987-89, nat. bd. dirs., 190-93; chmn. radiotherapy com. Cancer and Leukemia Group B.; dir. Quality Assurance Rev. Ctr., R.I. Cancer Control Bd., 1980-98, chmn. task force info. sys., mem. exec. com.; co-chmn. exec. com. ASSIST Program Nat. Cancer Inst./Am. Cancer Soc., 1991-98; exec. dir. R.I. Cancer Coun., 1999—. Dillon fellow Royal Marsden Hosp., Surrey, Eng., 1961-62; Rsch. Career Devel. awardee NIH, 1962-64; Fulbright sr. scholar, 1986-87; recipient St. George medal Am. Cancer Soc., 1991. Fellow Am. Coll. Radiology; mem. New England Soc. Radiation Oncologists (pres. 1975-76), N.Y. Roentgen Ray Soc. (chmn. sect. therapeutic radiology 1972-73), Am. Soc. Clin. Oncology, Am. Assn. Cancer Edn., Am. Assn. Cancer Rsch., Am. Radium Soc., Am. Soc. Therapeutic Radiologists, Brit. Inst. Radiology. Home: Old Blackstone Rd AKA Brown Terrace Uxbridge MA 01569 Office: Radiation Oncology Svcs Warwick RI 02886

GLICKSMAN, MARTIN EDEN, materials engineering educator; b. N.Y.C., Apr. 4, 1937; s. Nathan Henry and Ruth Elaine (Rosensaft) G.; m. Lucinda Jeanette Mulder, May 7, 1967. B in Metall. Engring., Rensselaer Poly. Inst., 1957, PhD, 1961. Metall. engr. Procter & Gamble Co., Cin., 1957-58; research metallurgist Naval Research Lab., Washington, 1961-75, assoc. supt. materials sci. divsn., 1974-75; chmn. materials engr. dept. Rensselaer Poly. Inst., Troy, N.Y., 1975-86, prof., 1986—; prof. materials engring., chmn. dept. materials engring. Rensselaer Poly. Inst., Troy, N.Y., 1975-86; John Tod Horton prof. materials engring. Rensselaer Poly. Inst., 1986—; Van Horn lectr. Case Western Res. U., 1984; cons. in field. Contbr. in articles to profl. jours. Recipient Pure Sci. Rsch. award Rsch. Soc. of Am., 1968, Arthur Flemming award Washington Jr. C. of C., Space Processing medal AIAA, 1998; Minerals Metals and Materials Soc. fellow AIME, 1994. Fellow AAAS, ASM (M.E. Grossman award 1971); mem. AIME (Bruce Chalmers award 1992), U. Space Rsch. Assn. (chmn. bd. trustees 1986, dir. microgravity divsn. 1986—), Nat. Acad. Engring. Home: 22 Schuyler Hills Rd Albany NY 12211-1445 Office: Rensselaer Poly Inst CII-9111 Troy NY 12180-3590

GLICKSMAN, MAURICE, engineering educator, former dean and provost; b. Toronto, Ont., Can., Oct. 16, 1928; came to U.S., 1949, naturalized, 1961; s. Robert Maxwell and Fanny Bella (Lachowitz) G.; m. Yetta Leich, Dec. 18, 1949; children: Howard David, Roslynn Sue, Marcie Ann. Student, Queen's U., 1946-49; M.Sc., U. Chgo., 1952, Ph.D., 1954; ScD (hon.), Brown U., 1997. Research asso. Inst. Nuclear Studies, U. Chgo., 1954; mem. tech. staff RCA Labs., Princeton, N.J., 1954-61; head Plasma Physics Group RCA Labs., 1961-63; dir. research RCA Research Labs., Tokyo, 1963-67; head Gen. Research Group, Princeton, 1967-69; Univ. prof., prof. engring. Brown U., 1969-94, dean Grad. Sch., 1974-76, dean faculty and acad. affairs, 1976-78, provost, dean faculty, 1978-86, provost, 1986-90, prof. physics, 1990-94, prof. engring. rsch., 1994—; cons. RCA Corp., 1969-77; vis. scientist MIT, 1983-84; chmn. com. materials for radiation detection devices NAS, 1971-74; chmn. vis. com. U. Pa., 1977-83, Vanderbilt U., 1977-81; mem. vis. com. Emory U., 1981—, U. Miami, 1990—, Northwestern U., 1991, U. N.C., Greensboro, 1992; bd. dirs. Ctr. Rsch. Librs., 1981-87, chmn., 1983-84; mem. bd. overseers Fermilab, 1983-99, chmn., 1989-94; trustee OCLC, Dublin, Ohio, 1993—; dir. Manisses Comm. Group, Providence, 1993—; dir. Lifespan Corp., Providence, 1994—. Contbr. research articles to profl. jours. Pres. Jewish Ctr., Princeton, 1962-63; v.p. cultural and ednl. affairs Jewish Cmty. Ctr., Tokyo, 1965-67; mem. Bur. Jewish Edn., R.I., 1974—, v.p., 1975-80; v.p. Jewish Fedn. R.I., 1980-83; trustee Miriam Hosp., 1979-85, 87-98, 06-chmn., 1993-97. Recipient Outstanding Achievement award RCA, 1956, 62. Fellow IEEE, Am. Phys. Soc.; mem. AAAS, Am. Soc. Engring. Edn., N.Y. Acad. Scis., Phi Beta Kappa (pres. R.I. Alpha chpt.), Sigma Xi. Patentee frequency multipliers, field-effect devices, semiconductor devices and circuits. Home: 10 Westwood Ln Barrington RI 02806-2614 Office: Brown U Box D 79 Waterman St Providence RI 02912-9079

GLICKSTEIN, HOWARD ALAN, law educator; b. N.Y.C., Sept. 14, 1929; s. Samuel and Fannie (Greenblat) G. BA magna cum laude, Dartmouth Coll., 1951; LLB, Yale U., 1954; LLM, Georgetown U., 1962. Bar: N.Y. 1954, U.S. Supreme Ct. 1962, D.C. 1980. Assoc. proskauer, Rose, Goetz & Mendelsohn, N.Y.C., 1956-60; staff atty. Civil Rights divsn. Dept. of Justice, 1960-65; gen. counsel U.S. Commn. on Civil Rights, Washington, 1965-68, staff dir., 1968-71; cons. in law, 1971-73; adj. prof., dir. Ctr. for Civil Rights U. Notre Dame, 1973-75; prof., dir. equal employment litigation clinic Howard U. Sch. Law, Washington, 1976-80; dir. Task Force on Civil Rights Reorgn., Exec. Office of Pres., Washington, 1977-78; dean, prof. U. Bridgeport Sch. Law, Conn., 1980-85, Touro Coll. Law, 1986—. Contbr. articles to profl. jours. Bd. dirs. Fund for Modern Cts., Am. Soc. of Writers of Legal Subjects; commr. Suffolk County Human Rights Commn. With U.S. Army, 1954-56. Mem. ABA (former chmn. affirmative action com., sect. legal edn. and admissions to bar), Soc. Am. Law Tchrs. (bd. dirs., former pres.), Assn. Am. Law Schs. (mem. com. acad. freedom and tenure), N.Y. State Bar Assn. Office: Touro Coll Sch Law Coll Law 300 Nassau Rd Huntington NY 11743-4346

GLICKSTEIN, STEVEN, lawyer; b. Bklyn., Jan. 3, 1952; s. Alexander and Esther (Camhi) G. BA, Lehigh U., 1973; JD, Columbia U., 1976. Assoc. Kaye, Scholer, Fierman, Hays & Handler, N.Y.C., 1976-84, ptnr., 1985—. Mem. ABA, D.C. Bar Assn., Fla. Bar Assn., N.Y. State Bar Assn. Home: 1619 3rd Ave Apt 9ae New York NY 10128-3459 Office: Kaye Scholer Fierman 425 Park Ave New York NY 10022-3506

GLICK-WEIL, KATHY, library director; b. Milw., Jan. 11, 1950; d. Irving Robert and Janice Esther (Rosner) Glick; m. Gordon Weil, June 20, 1971; children: Jeffrey, Aaron. BA, Tulane U., 1971; MLS, U. Calif., Berkeley, 1972. Children's libr. Thayer Pub. Libr., Braintree, Mass., 1972-73; reference libr. Stoughton (Mass.) Pub. Libr., 1973-77; br. libr. Brockton (Mass.) Pub. Libr., 1977-78; asst. dir. Medford (Mass.) Pub. Libr., 1978-84; dir. Lincoln (Mass.) Pub. Libr., 1984-93, Newton (Mass.) Free Libr., 1993—. Mem. ALA, Mass. Libr. Assn. Home: 46 Acacia Ave Chestnut Hill MA 02467-1351 Office: Newton Free Library 330 Homer St Newton MA 02459-1429

GLIDDEN, JOHN REDMOND, lawyer; b. Sanford, Maine, July 24, 1936; s. Kenneth Eugene and Kathryn (Gilpatrick) G.; m. Jacqueline R. Scales, Aug. 6, 1964; children—Ian, Claire, Jason. Student, U. Wis., 1954-55; B.S., Coe Coll., 1958; LL.B., U. Iowa, 1961. Bar: Iowa 1961, Ill. 1965. Assoc. firm Williams & Hartzell, Carthage, Ill., 1965-67; ptnr. Hartzell, Glidden, Tucker & Hartzell and predecessor firms, Carthage, 1969—; city atty. City of Carthage, 1969—. Capt., judge advocate USAF, 1961-65. Mem. ABA, Fed. Bar Assn., Ill. Bar Assn., Iowa Bar Assn., Hancock County Bar Assn., Am. Trial Lawyers Assn., Ill. Trial Lawyers Assn. (governing bd. 1973-80), Am. Legion, Carthage Golf Club (bd. dirs. 1967—), Phi Delta Phi, Sigma Nu. Home: PO Box 70 1625 N Highway 94 Carthage IL 62321-3435 Office: PO Box 70 Carthage IL 62321-0070

GLIDDEN, ROBERT BURR, university president, musician, educator; b. Rippey, Iowa, Nov. 29, 1936; s. Burr Harold and Lora Elsie (Groves) G.; m. Rene Colete Siefken, Apr. 26, 1964; children: Melissa, Michele, Briana. BA, U. Iowa, 1958, MA, 1960, PhD, 1966. Tchr. instrumental music Morrison Community High Sch., Ill., 1958-63, Univ. Schs., Iowa City, 1963-66; asst. prof. music Wright State U., Dayton, Ohio, 1966-67, Ind. U., Bloomington, 1967-69; also asst. dir. bands; assoc. prof. music U. Okla., 1969-72; asst. dir. bands, assoc. prof. music U. Okla., Norman; dir. grad. studies in music, exec. dir. Nat. Assn. Schs. Music, Washington, 1972-75; treas. Nat. Assn. Schs. Music, 1977-82, v.p., 1982-85, pres., 1985-88; dean Coll. Musical Arts, Bowling Green State U., Ohio, 1975-79; dean Sch. Music Fla. State U., Tallahassee, 1979-91, provost, v.p. for acad. affairs, 1991-94; pres. Ohio U., Athens, 1994—; cons. higher edn., condr.; chmn. Coun. Specialized Accrediting Agys., 1976-77; chair Am. Coun. Edn. Commn. Leadership and Instnl. Effectiveness, 1998—; chair coun. pres. Mid-Am. Conf., 1997—. Bd. dirs. Council on Postsecondary Accreditation, 1977-84, exec. com., 1979-84, chmn., 1981-83; bd. dirs. Arts, Edn. and Ams., Inc., 1978-81; chmn. advanced placement music com. Coll. Bd., 1977-79; mem. Nat. Council on Arts Task Force on Edn., Tng. and Devel. of Profl. Artists and Arts Educators, 1977-78; mem. adv. council on accreditation Nat. League for Nursing, 1977-81; mem. edn. adv. com. Nat. Endowment for the Arts, 1987, adv. com. for the arts in edn., 1989-90. Mem. Coll. Music Soc. (chmn. govt. rels. com. 1976-78, task force on edn. coll. music tchrs. 1987), So. Assn. Colls. and Schs. (mem. commn. on coll. 1993-94), Assn. Specialized and Profl. Accreditors (bd. dirs. 1994-96), Coun. for Higher Edn. Accreditation (chair bd. dirs. 1996-98), Ohio Sci. and TEch. Coun. (biotech. com.), Ohio Higher Edn. Funding Commn., Ohio Supercomputer Ctr. (governing bd. 1996—), Ohio Aerospace Inst. (exec. com. 1995—, chair 1998—, chair Am. Coun. Edn. Commn. on Leadership and Instl. Effectiveness 1998—), Phi Beta Kappa, Phi Kappa Phi, Omicron Delta Kappa, Mortar Bd., Pi Kappa Lambda (nat. v.p. 1979-81, pres. 1981-85). Episcopalian. Home: 29 Park Pl Athens OH 45701-2989 Office: Ohio Univ Cutler Hall Athens OH 45701-2979

GLIEBERMAN, CARY HIRSCH, film producer, director, writer; b. Chgo., June 4, 1943; s. Elmer Isa and Jean (Gerber) G.; m. Mary Helm, Sept. 24, 1983; 1 child, William Cary. Student, Roosevelt U., Chgo., Calif. State U., L.A. Assoc. editor VIP Mag., HMH Pub. Co., Chgo., 1965-68; fellow Am. Film Inst., Beverly Hills, Calif., 1970-72; prodn. mgr. various film cos. L.A. and Beverly Hills, 1972-91; writer, producer, prodn. mgr., dir. various film cos., L.A. and Beverly Hills, 1976-91; guest lectr. U. Calif. Santa Barbara, Brooks Inst., Santa Barbara, Am. Film Inst. Producer/prodn. mgr. (films) Champions, 1983, Spinal Tap, 1983, Crimewave, 1984, Hot Moves, 1984, Beverly Hills Brats, 1988, Back Street Dreams, 1989, Nobody's Perfect, 1989, Peacemaker, 1990, Alligator II, 1990, Rescue Me, 1991, Vincent Price, 1991, Stickfighter, 1993, Walking to Waldheim, 1994, Red Ribbon Blues, 1995, One More Shot, 1995, The Devil Takes a Holiday, 1996, Search for the Elephant Eye Diamonds, numerous others, (TV series) Air America, Born Free, Mike Hammer, Mowgli-The New Adventures of the Jungle Book, High Tide, Eden, FBI The Untold Stories, Ripleys Believe It Or Not, (videos) Rich Little's Little Scams On Golf, Jan Stephenson's How To Golf, Handgun Safety, Rifle and Shotgun Safety, How To Be A Hollywood Stuntman; writer, dir. (play) Acting Out, 1983. With Ill. Nat. Guard, 1965-67. Decorated Honorable Order of Ky. Cols. Mem. Dirs. Guild Am., Inc., Writers Guild Am. West, Wayne County Detectives Assn. Republican. Avocations: aviation, sailing, scuba diving. Home: 32052 Waterside Ln Westlake Vlg CA 91361-3622

GLIEBERMAN, HERBERT ALLEN, lawyer; b. Chgo., Dec. 6, 1930; s. Elmer and Jean (Gerber) G.; m. Evelyn Eraci; children—Ronald, Gale, Joel. Student, U. Ill., 1947, Roosevelt U., 1948-50; J.D., Chgo. Kent Coll. Law, 1953. Bar: Ill. 1954, D.C. 1987. Pvt. practice Chgo., 1954—; lectr. Chgo. Kent. Coll. Law, Ill. Inst. Continuing Legal Edn. *Mr. Glieberman has practiced Divorce Law for 45 years, is the author of 22 articles, chapters and books on divorce and family law. He has lectured at education seminars on Divorce and Family Law at universities, the American Bar Association, Illinois State Bar Association, North Carolina and Idaho Bar Associations, Continuing Legal Education/Satellite Network, Inc., American Academy of Matrimonial Lawyers, Chicago Bar Assocation, International Law Institute, Washington D.C., Illinois Certified Public Accountants Foundation, Illinois Trial Lawyers Association and Association of Trial Lawyers of America.* Author: Some Syndromes of Love, 1965, Know Your Legal Rights, 1974, Confessions of A Divorce Lawyer, 1975, Closed Marriage, 1978, Four Weekends to an Ideal Marriage, 1981; former host 2 radio shows for NBC Sta. WMAQ: Ask the Lawyer, Law and Controversy. Former trustee Chgo. Kent. Coll. Law; former bd. dirs. Chgo. Coun. on Alcoholism. Mem. Am. Acad. Matrimonial Lawyers (cert. of appreciation 1967), Decologue Soc. Lawyers (cert. of appreciation 1965, 66, 68), Assn. Trial Lawyers Am. (cert. of appreciation 1973), Ill. Trial Lawyers Assn. (cert. of appreciation 1974), ABA, Ill. State Bar Assn., Chgo. Bar Assn. Jewish (bd. dirs., pres. Temple). Home: 180 E Pearson St Chicago IL 60611-2130 Office: 19 S La Salle St Chicago IL 60603-1401

GLIEDMAN, MARVIN L., surgeon, educator; b. N.Y.C., Aug. 3, 1929; m. Natalie Gliedman, 1954; children: Charles H., Joanna. B.A., Syracuse U., 1950; M.D., State U. N.Y., 1954. Asst. instr. surgery State U. N.Y. Downstate Med. Center, Bklyn., 1959-60; asst. prof. State U. N.Y. Downstate Med. Center, 1960-64, asso. prof., 1964-66; prof. Albert Einstein Coll. Medicine, 1967—, chmn. dept. surgery, 1972-91; chmn. dept. surgery Montefiore Hosp. and Med. Center, Bronx, N.Y., 1967-72; Surgeon-in-chief Combined Depts. Surgery, Albert Einstein Coll. of Medicine and Montefiore Hosp. and Med. Center, 1976-91; asst. attending surgeon Kings County Hosp., Bklyn., 1960—. Served to lt. M.C. USNR, 1956-58. Recipient Dudley Meml. medal, 1954, Linder Surg. prize, 1954, Alumni Achievement medallion for disting. service to Am. medicine SUNY, 1984; Markle scholar Acad. Medicine, 1964-69. Mem. Am. Soc. Nephrology, Am. Surg. Assn., N.Y. Acad. Sci., ACS (chpt. pres. 1974, gov. 1974), Internat. Cardiovascular Soc., European Soc. for Exptl. Surgery, Internat. Biliary Assn., Transplantation Soc., Soc. Vascular Surgery, Surgery Alimentary Tract, Soc. Surg. Chairmen, Internat. Soc. Surgery, Am. Gastroenterological Soc., Univ. Surgeons Soc., Acad. Surgery, Halsted Soc., Alpha Omega Alpha. Address: Montefiore Hosp and Med Center 111 E 210th St Bronx NY 10467-2401

GLIEGE, JOHN GERHARDT, lawyer; b. Chgo., Aug. 3, 1948; s. Gerhardt John Gliege and Jane Heidke; children: Gerhardt, Stephanie, Kristine. BA, Ariz. State U., 1969, MPA, 1970, JD, 1974. Bar: Ariz. 1974. Pvt. practice Scottsdale, Ariz., 1974-81, Flagstaff, Ariz., 1981-94, 98—, Sedona, Ariz., 1994-97, Williams, Ariz., 1997-98; prof. paralegal studies No. Ariz. U., Flagstaff, 1981-83, prof. urban planning and cmty. devel., 1984—; prof. paralegal studies Yavapai Cmty. Coll., Prescott, Ariz., 1995-97. Mailing Address: PO Box 1388 Flagstaff AZ 86002-1388

GLIER, INGEBORG JOHANNA, German language and literature educator; b. Dresden, Germany, June 22, 1934; came to U.S., 1972; d. Erich Oskar and Gertrud Johanne (Niese) G. Student, Mt. Holyoke Coll., 1955-56; Dr. phil. (Studienstiftung des deutschen Volkes), U. Munich, Germany, 1958; Dr. phil., Habilitation, 1969; M.A. (hon.), Yale U., 1973. Asst., lectr. U. Munich, 1958-69, universitätsdozentin, 1969-72; vis. prof. Yale U., 1972-73, prof. German, 1973—, chmn. dept., 1979-82; chmn. Medieval Studies Yale U., New Haven, 1986-93, chmn. Women's Studies, 1995-96; sr. faculty fellow Yale U., 1974-75; vis. prof. U. Cologne, Germany, 1970-71, U. Colo., Boulder, spring 1983, U. Tubingen, summer 1984. Author: Struktur und Gestaltungsprinzipien in den Dramen John Websters, 1958, Deutsche Metrik, 1961, Artes amandi, Untersuchung zu Geschichte, Uberlieferung und Typologie der deutschen Minnereden, 1971; contbr. articles, book reviews to profl. jours. Mem. Internationaler Germanisten-Verband, Modern Lang. Assn., Mediaeval Acad. Am., Am. Assn. Tchrs. German, Internat. Courtly Lit. Soc., Wolfram von Eschenbach Gesellschaft. Home: 111 Park St Apt 12T New Haven CT 06511-5421 Office: Yale Univ Dept Germanic Langs PO Box 208210 New Haven CT 06520-8210

GLIJANSKY, ALEX, psychiatrist, psychoanalyst; b. Caracas, Venezuela, Oct. 6, 1948; came to U.S., 1975; s. Natalio and Ghenea (Rechtman) G.; m. Belinda Matyas, Aug. 12, 1973; children: Ghena, Avi. MD, Universidad Cen. de Venezuela, 1971, MS, 1974. Resident in psychiatry Hahnemann U., Phila., 1978; med. dir. Fishtown/Lower Kensington Mental Health Ctr., Phila., 1978-82; assoc. psychiatrist dept. psychiatry Abington (Pa.) Meml. Hosp., 1982—; clin. asst. prof. psychiatry, MCP-Hahnemann Sch. Medicine, Phila., 1978. Fellow Am. Psychiat. Assn.; mem. Pa. Psychiat. Soc., Phila. Psychiat. Soc., Phila. Assn. for Psychoanalysis, Am. Psychoanalytic Assn. Avocation: golf. Office: 8302 York Rd Ste B-5 Elkins Park PA 19027

GLIKSBERG, ALEXANDER DAVID, engineering executive; b. Odessa, Ukraine, Feb. 24, 1936; came to U.S., 1978; s. David L. and Eneta S. Gliksberg; m. Sofia M. Heifetz, Dec. 3, 1959; 1 child, Inna A. MS in Mech. Engring., Odessa Inst. Tech., 1963; MS in Elec. Engring., Moscow Polytech. Inst., Moscow, 1971; postgrad., Harvard U., 1984. Lead program mgr. Rsch. and Design Inst., Odessa, Ukraine, 1967-78; dir. quality and reliability Wang Labs., Inc., Lowell, Mass., 1979-85, dir. mfg. engring., 1985-87, dir. engring., 1987-93; dir. engring. Waters Corp., Milford, Mass., 1993—. Patentee in fields of Automatic Control Systems and Automated Equipment; contbr. articles to profl. jours. Recipient Gold medal Nat. Econ. Exhbn., Moscow, 1975. Avocations: chess, collecting stamps, swimming. Office: Waters Corp 34 Maple St Milford MA 01757-3696

GLIMCHER, ARNOLD B., art gallery executive; b. Duluth, Minn., Mar. 12, 1938; s. Paul and Eva (Fishman) G.; m. Mildred Louise Cooper, Dec. 20, 1959; children: Paul William, Marc Cooper. B.A., Mass. Coll. Art., 1969; postgrad., NYU Sch. Psychology, Boston U. Founder, owner Pace Gallery, Boston, 1961-63; founder, chmn. Pace Wildenstein PW, N.Y.C., 1963—; founder Pace Editions, 1968—. Author: Louise Nevelson, 1972, paperback edit., 1976; (with Paul Vitz) Modern Art and Modern Science: The Parallel Analysis of Vision; contbr. articles to art jours.; prodr.: (films) Gorillas in the Mist, The Good Mother; prodr., dir.: (film) The Mambo Kings; editor, cataloger, text writer for various art vols. selector, installer various mus. exhibits and retrospectives. Fellow Israel Mus. (chmn. devel. com. 1976-77); mem. Am. Acad. Arts and Letters, Officier des Arts and Lettres, Art Dealers Assn. Am. (bd. dirs.). Office: Pace Wildenstein PW 32 E 57th St New York NY 10022-2513*

GLIMCHER, DAVID J., real estate executive. Degree in mktg. and location analysis, Ohio State U., postgrad. V.p. Glimcher Realty Trust, Columbus, Ohio, 1972-87, pres., 1987—; pres. David J. Glimcher Co., Blimcher Co., 1974-93. Mem. NAREIT, Internat. Coun. Shopping Ctrs. Office: Glimcher Realty Trust 88 W. Main St Columbus OH 43215

GLIMCHER, HERBERT, real estate company executive; b. Duluth, Minn.. Founder Glimcher Co., 1959—; chmn., pres., CEO Glimcher Realty Trust, Columbus, Ohio, 1994—. Active United Way, United Jewish Appeal. Mem. Internat. Coun. Shopping Ctrs. Office: Glimcher Realty Trust 20 S 3d St Columbus OH 43215

GLIMCHER, MELVIN JACOB, orthopedic surgeon; b. Brookline, Mass., June 2, 1925; s. Aaron and Clara (Fink) G.; m. Geraldine Lee Bogolub, June 22, 1946; children: Susan Deborah, Laurie Hollis, Nancy Blair. Student, Duke U., 1943-44; B.S. in Mech. Engring. with highest distinction; B.S. in Physics with highest distinction, Purdue U., 1946; M.D. magna cum laude, Harvard, 1950; postgrad., Mass. Inst. Tech., 1956-59. Intern surgery Strong Meml. Hosp., Rochester, N.Y., 1950-51; 3d asst. resident surgery Mass. Gen. Hosp., Boston, 1951-52; 2d asst. resident Mass. Gen. Hosp., 1952-53, asst. resident orthopedic surgery, 1954-55, chief resident, 1956, chief orthopedic service, 1965-71, chmn. dept. orthopedic surgery, 1968-71; asst. resident orthopedic surgery Children's Med. Center, Boston, 1953-54; jr. resident Children's Med. Center, 1955-56; mem. faculty Harvard Med. Sch., 1956—, Edith M. Ashley prof. orpthopedic surgery, 1965-71, Harriet M. Peabody prof., 1971—; also chmn. dept.; orthopedic surgeon-in-chief Children's Hosp. Med. Center, Boston, 1971-81, dir. Lab. for Study of Skeletal Disorders and Rehab., 1980—. Trustee Forsyth Dental Infirmary, New England Sinai Hosp. With USMCR, World War II. Recipient Soma Weiss award Harvard Med. Sch., 1950, Borden Research award, 1950; Kappa Delta award, 1959; Internat. Assn. Dental Research award, 1964; Ralph Pemberton award Am. Rheumatism Soc., 1969; Bristol-Meyers/Zimmer instl. grant for excellence; Disting. Achievement in Orthopaedic Research award Orthopaedic Research Edn. Found.; William Neuman award Am. Soc. Bone and Mineral Rsch., 1996; Physician Achievement award Arthritis Found., 1996. Fellow Am. Acad. Arts and Scis., Am. Acad. Orthopaedic Surgeons (Silver anniversary Kappa Delta prize 1974, Alfred Shands award jointly awarded with Orthop. Rsch. Soc 1997), Am. Orthopedic Assn.; mem. Orthopedic Research Soc. (past pres.), Assn. Bone and Joint Surgeons (Nicholas Andry award 1978), Internat. Soc. for Study Lumbar Spine (Volvo award 1983), Societe Internationale de Chirurgie Orthopedique et de Traumatologie. Office: 300 Longwood Ave Boston MA 02115-5724

GLIMM, JAMES GILBERT, mathematician, educator; b. Peoria, Ill., Mar. 24, 1934; s. William Frederick and Barbara Gilbert (Hooper) G.; m. Adele Strauss, June 30, 1957; 1 dau., Alison. A.B., Columbia U., 1956, A.M., 1957, Ph.D., 1959. From asst. prof. to prof. math. MIT, 1960-69; prof. Courant Inst., NYU, 1969-74; prof. math. Rockefeller U., N.Y.C., 1974-82; prof. Courant Inst., NYU, N.Y.C., 1982-89; disting. prof., chair dept. applied math. and statis. SUNY, Stony Brook, 1989—, dir. Inst. for Math. Modeling, 1989—; dir. Ctr. for Data Intensive Computing Brookhaven Nat. Labs., 1999—. Co-author: Quantum Physics, 1981; Collected Papers, Vols. I and II, 1985; mem. editorial bds. profl. jours.; contbr. articles to sci. publs.

Recipient Dannie Heineman prize in math. physics, 1980; Guggenheim fellow, 1963, 65. Mem. NAS, Internat. Assn. Math. Physicists, Am. Phys. Soc., Am. Math. Soc. (Leroy P. Steele prize 1992), Soc. Indsl. and Applied Math., Math. Assn. Am., Am. Acad. Arts and Scis., Soc. Petroleum Engrs., N.Y. Acad. Scis. (award in phys. and math. scis. 1979). Office: SUNY Dept Applied Math and Stats Math Tower Stony Brook NY 11794-3600

GLINDEMAN, HENRY PETER, JR., real estate developer; b. Coeur d'Alene, Idaho, Sept. 26, 1924; s. Henry Peter and Laura Mae (Buchanan) G.; children: Pamela, Henry Peter III, John. B.S., U.S. Naval Acad., 1945; postgrad., U.S. Naval War Coll., 1959-60. Commd. ensign U.S. Navy, 1945, advanced through grades to rear adm., 1973; exec. officer, comdg. officer Fighter Squadron 154, 1962-63; comdr. Attack Carrier Air Wing 15 Attack Carrier Air Wing 15, 1964-65; tng. officer attack carrier air wing, staff, comdr. U.S. Naval Air Forces, U.S. Pacific Fleet, 1965-66; readiness officer, staff comdr. U.S. First Fleet, 1966-68; comdg. officer U.S.S. Passumpsic, 1968-69; head Attack Carrier Weapons Requirements br. Office Chief Naval Ops., 1970-71, comdg. officer U.S.S. Ranger, 1971-73; chief Fleet Coordinating Group Nakhon Phanom, Thailand, 1973-74; dir. Office Program Appraisal, Office Sec. Navy, 1974-75, comdr. Carrier Group 7, 1975-76, comdr. Carrier Group 3, 1976, comdr. Carrier Group 5, Carrier Strike Force, 7th Fleet, 1976-77, comdr. Naval Safety Center, 1977-78; pres. Mr. Quick Lube Inc., Clearwater, Fla., 1978-81; v.p. Fla. Light and Save Inc., 1981-83; real estate developer, 1983-85; pres. GBS Devel. Inc., Redwood City, Calif., 1985-87; chmn., chief exec. officer Stormy Weather Guard, Inc., Clearwater, Fla., 1988-94; bd. dirs., sec.-treas. Guardian Marine Corp., 1990-91; pres. Fiber Am. Inc., Clearwater, Fla., 1991-96. V.p.. Edgar Allan Poe Jr. High Sch. PTA, Annandale, Va., 1960-61, Annandale Am. Little League, 1961-62; sec. exec. com. Troop 674, Boy Scouts Am., Annandale, 1961-62. Decorated Legion of Merit with 4 gold stars, D.F.C., Air medal with gold star, Navy Commendation medal with Combat V. Mem. U.S. Naval Acad. Alumni Assn., Navy League, Mil. Order World Wars, Assn. Naval Aviation, Internat. Erosion Control Assn., Ret. Officers Assn., The Tailhook Assn. Episcopalian. Club: Golden Gate Breakfast (San Francisco). Home: 3976 Long Leaf Dr Melbourne FL 32940-1464

GLINER, ERAST BORIS, theoretical physicist; b. Kiev, USSR, Feb. 3, 1923; came to U.S., 1980; s. Boris Moses Gliner and Bella Boris (Pauckman) Rubinstein; m. Galina Ilchenko, Dec. 12, 1944; children: Bella, Arkady. MS in Physics, Leningrad U., USSR, 1963; PhD in Physics, Tartu U., Estonia, 1972. Head theoretical dept. Spl. Design Office, Leningrad, 1954-63; sr. scientist A Ioffe Inst. for Physics and Tech. of Soviet Acad. Scis., Leningrad, 1963-80; vis. fellow Joint Inst. Lab. Astrophyiscs U. Colo., Boulder, 1982-83; rsch. assoc. McDonnel Ctr. Space Sci. Washington U., St. Louis, 1983-86; vis. scientist Stanford Linear Acceleration Ctr. Stanford U., Palo Alto, Calif., 1987—; guest nuc. physics divsn. Lawrence Berkeley Lab., 1987. Co-author: Differential Equation of Mathematical Physics (English, Russian, Japanese edits.), 1962-65; contbr. articles to profl. jours. Polit. prisoner USSR, 1945-54. Sgt. field arty. Soviet Army, 1942-44. Decorated Russian Orders Red Star and Patriotic War; recipient rsch. award USSR Govt., 1958-60, USSR Acad. Scis., 1977, 78. Mem. Am. Phys. Soc. Jewish. Achievements include patents in field (USSR); research in solar physics (combined effect of global and upper magnetic fields on solar atmosphere, coronal asymmetry as evidence of solar quadrupole magnetic field) and in Einstein gravitational theory (introduction of vacuumlike state of matter, covaiant energy description in general relativity, foundation of general relativity on the basis of Sakharov's concept of gravity; investigation of non singular black hole geometry). Office: Stanford U SLAC PO Box 4349 Palo Alto CA 94309-4349

GLINES, CARROLL VANE, JR., magazine editor; b. Balt., Dec. 2, 1920; s. Carroll Vane and Elizabeth Marion (Cross) G.; m. Mary Ellen Edwards, Oct. 1, 1943; children: Karen Ann, David Edwards, Valerie Jean. Student, Drexel Inst. Tech., 1938-40, Canal Zone Jr. Coll., 1946-48, U. Munich, 1948; BBA, U. Okla., 1952, MBA, 1954; MA, Am. U., 1969. Commd. 2d lt. USAF, 1942, advanced through grades to col., 1965; military service, 1941-68; mgr. publs. Nat. Bus. Aircraft Assn., Washington, 1968; assoc. editor Armed Forces Mgmt. mag., Washington, 1969-70; editor Air Cargo mag., Washington, 1970-71; editor Air Line Pilot mag., Washington, 1971-85, cons. editor, 1985-86, contbg. editor, 1989—; sr. editor Aviation Space mag., 1982-85; editor Profl. Pilot Mag., Alexandria, Va., 1986-88, sr. contbg. editor, 1988-95; sr. contbg. editor Aviation History mag. (formerly Aviation Heritage mag.), Leesburg, Va., 1990—; mgr. publs. Air Line Pilots Assn., 1971-85, dir. comms., 1983-85; lectr. U. Dayton, U. Alaska, Am. U. Author 31 books; contbr. articles to mags.; gen. editor MacMillan, Air Force Acad. series, 1970-74; editl. cons. Van Nostrand Reinhold, 1980-85; contbg. editor Nation's Bus., 1981-86; mem. adv. bd. Hist. of Aviation Collection, U. Tex., Dallas, 1981-90, 94—, Alaska Aviation Heritage Mus., Anchorage, 1993—; curator Doolittle Libr., U. Tex., Dallas, 1995—. Asst. to v.p. for spl. projects Evergreen Internat. Aviation, 1988-93; active Frontiers of Flight Mus., Dallas. Recipient numerous awards from press assns. Freedoms Found. Mem. Aviation-Space Writers Assn. (Lauren D. Lyman award), Air Force Assn., Air Force Hist. Found., Soc. Aerospace Communicators, Quiet Birdmen, Soc. Profl. Journalists, Order of Daedalians, Army-Navy Club. Home: 1531 San Rafael Dr Dallas TX 75218-4444

GLINK, ILYCE RENÉE, writer, publishing executive; b. Chgo., July 13, 1964. BA, U. Ill., 1986. Owner, pub. Real Estate Matters Syndicate, Glencoe, Ill., 1988—. Author: 100 Questions Every First-Time Home Buyer Should Ask, 1994, 100 Questions Every Home Seller Should Ask, 1995, 10 Steps to Home Ownership, 1997, 100 Questions You Should Ask About Your Personnal Finances, 1999. Mem. Nat. Assn. Real Estate Editors (newsletter writer), Nat. Writers Union, Soc. Profl. Journalists (Chgo.), Headline Club (pres. 1997-99). Avocations: screenwriting, hiking. Office: Real Estate Matters Syndicate P.O. Box 366 Glencoe IL 60022-1510

GLINSKI, HELEN ELIZABETH, operating room nurse; b. Gouverneur, N.Y., Apr. 9, 1944; d. Arthur Andrew and Lillian May (MacKenzie) Turnbull; m. David Lee Joseph Glinski, May 13, 1967; children: David Lee Joseph II, Christopher John. Diploma of Nursing, House of Good Samaritan, Watertown, N.Y., 1965; registered nurse 1st asst., Del. County C.C., 1992; student, St. Joseph's Coll., Maine, 1999—. RN, N.Y., Cert. Nurse Operating Room. Staff nurse operating rm. House of Good Samaritan, Watertown, N.Y., 1965-66; staff nurse operating rm. Cmty. Gen. Hosp., Syracuse, N.Y., 1966-68, acting headnurse operating rm., 1968-69, 70, acting asst. head nurse, inservice instr., 1969-70, 70-71; staff nurse operating rm. E.J. Noble Hosp., Gouverneur, N.Y., 1971-72; head nurse, supr. operating rm. Edward John Noble Hosp., Gouverneur, N.Y., 1972-77; sr. staff nurse operating rm. Mercy Hosp., Watertown, N.Y., 1978-79; staff nurse operating rm. Roswell Pk. Meml. Inst., Buffalo, 1979-85, Buffalo VA Med. Ctr., 1985-95; nurse 1st asst. oper. rm. VA Med. Ctr., West Palm Beach, Fla., 1995-97, established/coordinate preoperative clinic, coordinate surg. risk clinic; nursing facilitator Pre Operative Clinic VA Med. Ctr., West Palm Beach, 1997—; reg. nurse first asst. Urology Svc., 1999—; mem. RN First Asst. Spl. Assembly, 1992—; mem. adv. com. N. Tech. Edn. Ctr., Riviera Beach, Fla. Collector Am. Cancer Assn., Buffalo, 1991, 92, 93. Recipient Performance award Dept. Vet. Affairs, Buffalo, 1988, 91, 93. Mem. Assn. Oper. Rm. Nurses (bd. dirs. 1992-93, 96—, corr. sec. 1986-91, pres.-elect 1993-94, pres. 1994-95, officer western N.Y. chpt.), Fla. Coun. Oper. Rm. Nurses, Fla. Assn. RN First Asst. (treas. 1998—). Episcopalian. Avocations: knitting, motorcycling, computers, sewing, gardening. Home: 737 Mill Valley Pl West Palm Beach FL 33409-7613 Office: 7305 N Military Trl West Palm Beach FL 33410-6415

GLISSON, HENRY T., director; m. Sherry G.; 1 child, Shannon. BSc in psychology, N Ga. Coll., 1966; Med, Pepperdine U. Commd. 2d. lt. U.S. Army, 1966, advanced through grades to lt. gen., 1997—. Decorated Bronze Star with V Device, Bronze Star, Purple Heart, Legion of Merit. Office: Defense Logistics Agency Hdqs 8725 John J Kingman Rd Ste 2533 Fort Belvoir VA 22060-6221

GLISSON, MELISSA ANN, dietitian; b. Arlington, Tex., May 19, 1962; d. Benjamin Louis and Mary Francis Doskocil; m. Fredric Brown Glisson Jr., May 11, 1985; children: Zachary David, Ashley Marie. BS in Food, Nutrition and Dietetics, Tex. Christian U., 1985. Cert. weight loss and stress mgmt. Am. Assn. Lifestyle Counselors. Dietitian Woodridge Convalescent Ctr., Grapevine, Tex., 1985; clin. dietitian Thunderbird Samaritan Hosp., Glendale, Ariz., 1988-89; dietitian III Abilene (Tex.) State Sch., 1992-94; mgr. health and wellness program Doskocil Mfg. Co., Arlington, Tex., 1994-97, chmn. loan approval com. credit union, 1996-97; chmn. loan approval com. Doskocil Mfg. Co. Credit Union, 1996-97. Treas., chmn. fin. com., membership coord. Am. European Dietetic Assn., 1989-92. Mem. Am. Dietetic Assn. (Young Dietitian of Yr. 1992). Avocations: golf, tennis, dance, sports. Home: 310 Taylor St Ida Grove IA 51445-1052

GLITMAN, MAYNARD WAYNE, foreign service officer; b. Chgo., Dec. 8, 1933; s. Ben and Reada (Kutok Klass) G.; m. G. Christine Amundsen, Dec. 22, 1956; children: Russell M., Erik W., Karen C., Matthew M., Rebecca S. B.A. with highest honors, U. Ill., 1955; M.A., Fletcher Sch. Law and Diplomacy, 1956; postgrad., U. Calif., Berkeley, 1965-66. Joined fgn. service Dept. State, 1956, economist, 1956-59; vice consul Nassau, Bahamas, 1959-61; econ. officer Am. Embassy, Ottawa, Ont., Can., 1961-65, Dept. State, 1966-67; mem. U.S. Del. to UN Gen. Assembly, 1967, Nat. Security Council staff, 1968; polit. officer, 1st sec. Am. Embassy, Paris, 1968-73; dir. Office of Internat. Trade, Dept. State, Washington, 1973-74; dep. asst. sec. of state for internat. trade policy Office of Internat. Trade, Dept State, 1974-76, dep. asst. sec. def. for Europe and NATO affairs, 1976-77; dep. U.S. permanent rep. to NATO, Brussels, Belgium, 1977-81; ambassador, dep. chief U.S. del. Intermediate Nuclear Forces Negotiations, ACDA, Geneva, Switzerland, 1981-84; ambassador, U.S. rep. Mut. Balanced Force Reductions Negotiations, Vienna, Austria, 1985; ambassador, chief negotiator Intermediate Nuclear Force Negotiations, Geneva, Switzerland, 1985-88; U.S. ambassador to Belgium, 1988-91; diplomat in residence U. Vt., Burlington, 1991-94; adj. prof. U. Vt., Burlington, 1994—. Served with U.S. Army, 1957. Recipient Outstanding and Disting. Pub. Svc. medals U.S. Dept. Def., 1977, 81, Presdl. Svc. award, 1984, 87, Howard Weil award SUNY, 1988, Joseph C. Wilson award, Rochester, N.Y., 1989, Presdl. Disting. Svc. award, 1989. Mem. Phi Beta Kappa. Home: PO Box 438 Jeffersonville VT 05464-0438 Office: U Vermont Dept Polit Sci PO Box 54110 Burlington VT 05405-4110

GLITZ, DOHN GEORGE, biochemistry educator; b. Buffalo, Sept. 28, 1936; s. Arthur Theodore and Viola Theophila (Raven) G.; m. Beryl Davey, Jan. 29, 1966; 1 child, Rachel. B.S., U. Ill., 1958; M.S., U. Wis., 1960; Ph.D., U. Calif.-Berkeley, 1963. Postdoctoral fellow Virus Research Unit, Cambridge, Eng., 1964-66; postdoctoral fellow Virus Lab., U. Calif.-Berkeley, 1966-67; asst. prof. dept. biol. chemistry UCLA, 1967-71, assoc. prof., 1971-77, prof. dept. biol. chemistry, 1977—, vice chmn. dept. biol. chemistry, 1979—. Contbr. articles to profl. jours. Guggenheim fellow, 1974-75. Mem. Am. Soc. Biochemistry Molecular Biology. Democrat. Unitarian. Home: 1029 Harvard St Santa Monica CA 90403-4707 Office: UCLA Sch Medicine Dept Biol Chemistry Los Angeles CA 90095-1737

GLITZ, DONALD ROBERT, insurance underwriting executive; b. Uniontown, Pa., Sept. 30, 1944; s. Joseph William and Helen (Keblis) G.; m. Frances Antonia Sante, Aug. 24, 1968; children: Kristin, Allison, Derek. BA in Econ., Pa. State U., 1969; MA in Liberal Studies, SUNY, Stonybrook, 1976. CPCU. Underwriter comml. ins. CIGNA, Pitts., 1969-73; sr. underwriter comml. ins. CIGNA, Garden City, N.J., 1973-77, mgr. comml. ins., 1977-79; dir. underwriting N.E. region CIGNA, Radnor, Pa., 1979-81, dir. product mgmt. N.E. region, 1981-82; dir. packages product mgmt. CIGNA, Phila., 1982-87, dir. underwriting western area, 1987-89, dir. underwriting western and cen. area, 1989-90; v.p. CIGNA Internat., Phila., 1990—; ins. instr. Villanova U., 1983-85. V.p. Student Govt. Assn. Pa. State U., Fayette, 1966. Fellow CPCU Soc.; mem. Nittany Lions Club. Avocations: jogging, fishing, skiing, Civil War. Home: 118 Taylors Mill Rd Downingtown PA 19335-1637

GLOBER, GEORGE EDWARD, JR., lawyer; b. Edwards AFB, Calif., Aug. 10, 1944; s. George Edward and Catharine (Crain) G.; m. Deirdre Denman, May 22, 1971; children—Denman, Nancy King. A.B., Cornell U., 1966; J.D., Harvard U., 1969. Bar: Tex. 1969, U.S. Sup. Ct. 1976. tchg. fellow natural scis. Harvard U., 1967-69; assoc., Vinson & Elkins, Houston, 1969-77; dir. Houston Dept. Pub. Service, 1977-78; mem. law dept. Exxon Corp. and Affiliates, 1978—, counsel Exxon Corp., 1995—, asst. gen. counsel Exxon Chem. Co., 1991-94; chief atty. refining, environ. and health Exxon Co. USA, 1988-91; gen. counsel Exxon Prodn. Rsch. Co., 1982-88. With Air N.G., 1969-75. Fellow Houston Bar Assn.; mem. ABA, Am. Intellectual Property Law Assn., Internat. Law Assn., Tex. Bar Assn., Dallas Bar Assn., Assn. Corp. Patent Counsel. Office: Exxon Corp 5959 Las Colinas Blvd Irving TX 75039-2298

GLOBOKE, JOSEPH RAYMOND, accountant; b. Kansas City, Kans., Mar. 9, 1955; s. Anthony Joseph and Loretta Margaret (Bartkoski) G.; m. Debra Ruth Neumann, Nov. 13, 1982; children: Theresa Renee, Michael Richard, William Robert. BSBA, Rockhurst Coll., 1977. CPA, Mo., Kans. Intern Ernst & Whinney, Kansas City, Mo., 1976-77; staff acct. Troupe Kehoe Whiteaker & Kent, Kansas City, 1977-84, mgr., 1984-88; sr. acct. Kennedy & Coe, Salina, Kans., 1988-91; audit supr. Robert Garrison & Assocs., Grandview, Mo., 1991-93; sr. staff acct. Logan & Schmidt, Kansas City, Kans., 1993-96; mgr., 1996—. Bd. dirs., pres. Children's Mus. of Kansas City; mem. Cub Scouts, Boy Scouts. Mem. AICPA, Kans. Soc. of CPA, K.C. Roman Catholic. Avocations: reading, gardening. Home: 15601 Ann Ave Belton MO 64012-1459 Office: Logan Schmidt & Lerner 1300 N 78th St Ste 100 Kansas City KS 66112-2493

GLOCER, THOMAS HENRY, lawyer; b. N.Y.C., Oct. 8, 1959; s. Walter W. and Ursula (Goodman) G.; m. Maarit Hanelle Leso, Aug. 5, 1988. BA, Columbia Coll., 1981; JD, Yale U., 1984. Atty. Davis, Polk & Warswell, N.Y.C., 1985-93; corp. counsel Reuters Am. Inc., N.Y.C., 1993-94; exec. v.p., gen. counsel Reuters Am. Holdings Inc., N.Y.C., 1995-98; pres. Reuters Am. and Reuters Info., N.Y.C., 1998—; dir. TVT Records, N.Y.C., 1985-93. Author compter software. Mem. Coney Island Assn. (founder, ptnr.). Avocations: windsurfing, skiing, running. Office: Reuters Am 40 E 52nd 14th Fl New York NY 10038*

GLOCKMANN, WALTER FRIEDRICH, physicist, consultant; b. Gera, Germany, June 3, 1932; came to U.S., 1987; s. Walther Richard and Dorothee Luise (Woehler) G.; m. Waltraut Frieda Meier, Nov. 10, 1951; children: Harald, Eveline, Dagmar. Degree in physics and math., U. Frankfurt, Germany, 1958; degree in physics, U. Mainz, Germany, 1969. R & D mgr. Heimann GmbH, Wiesbaden, Germany, 1969-78; v.p., gen. mgr. Heimann Systems Co. and Siemens Components, Inc., Iselin, N.J., 1978-91; pres. Argus Security, Inc., Stirling, N.J., 1992—; cons. Capintec, Inc., Ramsey, N.J., 1992-94, Heitronics GmbH, Wiesbaden, 1995—, Vivid Techs., Inc., Woburn, Mass., 1995—. Co-author: Handbuch Technische Temperaturmessung, 1976, Temperaturmessung in der Technik, 1976; contbr. article to tech. jour. Sensors, 1994. Mem. ASTM. Achievements include U.S. and European patents on x-ray scanner for detecting plastic articles, European and German patents on optical smoke detectors, and design and development of infrared sensing systems, temperature sensing, intrusion alarms. Home: 162 Pleasant Plains Rd Stirling NJ 07980-1017 Office: Argus Security, Inc 50 Division Ave Millington NJ 07946-1358

GLOCKNER, PETER G., civil and mechanical engineering educator; b. Moragy, Hungary, Jan. 26, 1929; emigrated to Can., 1949; BSc in Civil Engring., McGill U., Montreal, Que., Can., 1955; MSc in Civil Engring., MIT, 1956; PhD in Civil Engring., U. Mich., 1964. Asst. prof. applied mechanics U. Alta., Can., 1958-60; from asst. prof. to prof. emeritus U. Calgary, Alta., 1960-97, prof. emeritus, 1997—, chmn. dept. mech. engring., 1976-87. Author more than 300 articles on shell theory, stability and non-linear behavior of thin-walled structures, dielectrics and non-linear constitutive theory. Whitney fellow, 1955-56, Ford Found. fellow, 1962-64; recipient CANCAM medal, 1993. Fellow ASCE (Moisseiff award and medal 1983), Can. Soc. Mech. Engring., Engring. Inst. Can. (Gzowski Gold medal 1971), Am. Acad. Mechanics (pres. 1995-96); mem. Can. Soc. Civil Engring., Assn. Profl. Engrs., Geologists and Geophysicists Alta. Home: 2536 Charlebois Dr, Calgary, AB Canada T2L OT6

GLOE, DONNA, nursing administrator; b. Moberly, Mo., Apr. 24, 1951; d. James F. and E. Emogene (Semones) Osborn; m. Lloyd R. Gloe, Feb. 14, 1975; children: Darin Robert, Leslie Renee. BA, U. Mo., 1973; MEd, Lincoln U., Jefferson City, Mo., 1977; diploma, St. John's Sch. Nursing, Springfield, Mo., 1983; BSN, S.W. Bapt. U., 1991; EdD, Nova Southeastern U., 1996. Cert. critical care nurse.; cert. nursing staff devel. and continuing edn. Family therapist Burrell Mental Health Ctr., Springfield; edn. coord., staff nurse surg. ICU St. John's Regional Health Ctr., Springfield, knowledge info. module mgr.; adj. faculty S.W. Bapt. U., 1992. Contbr. articles to profl. jours.; author video. Mem. AACN, Nat. Nursing Staff Devel. Orgn., Mo. Assn. Hosp. Educators, Am. Nursing Credentialing Ctr. (mem. nursing staff devel. and continuing edn.). Home: 335 Big Timber Rd Marshfield MO 65706-9005

GLOECKLER, GEORGE, physics educator. BS in Physics, U. Chgo., 1960, MS in Physics, 1991, PhD, 1965. Disting. univ. prof. dept. physics Inst. Phys. Sci. & Tech. U. Md. Fellow APS, Am. Geophys. Union; mem. NAS.

GLOGOWER, MICHAEL HOWARD, public housing senior functional specialist; b. Louisville, Jan. 6, 1944; s. Louis R. and Elaine R. (Switow) G. Student, Louisville Country Day Sch., 1958-61; BA in Polit. Sci., Kenyon Coll., 1965. Lic. real estate broker, Ky., Fla. Asst. gen. mgr. Mail Photo Svc. Inc., Louisville, 1966-69; pres. Mi-Glo Corp., Louisville, 1969-70; v.p. ops. Cherokee Coal Co. Inc., Louisville, 1970-71; area mgr. Owens/Corning Fiberglas Corp., Toledo, 1971-73; gen. mgr. Redd's Auto Parts Inc., Louisville, 1973-74; dist. mgr. Hackney Corp., Birmingham, Ala., 1974-75; area sales rep. J&W Fence Supply Co. Inc., Indpls., 1975-76; broker, salesman comml./investment divsn. Bass & Weisberg Realtors, Louisville, 1976-79; owner Michael H. Glogower Investment Realtor & Bus. Consulting, 1979—; housing programs specialist office pub. and Indian housing HUD, Washington, 1991-96; sr. functional specialist HUD, Honolulu, 1996-98, Miami, Fla., 1998—; former mem. edn. com. Bd. Realtors, Louisville; former subs. instr. Jefferson C.C., Louisville; former moderator, ace designee, counselor Acad. Network II-Nat. Real Estate Exch. Former pres. bd. dirs. Waterford House Condo Assn., Arlington, Va., 1993-96; bd. dirs. Palace Condominium Assn., Miami, 1999—. Avocations: photography, real estate investment, antique and art collection, design work. Home: 1541 Brickell Ave Apt 3804 Miami FL 33129-1229 Office: US Dept HUD 909 SE First Ave Ste 500 Miami FL 33131 *Living different places, doing different things, I have never ceased to be impressed by the resiliance and humanity of my fellow human beings. We should never sell our fellow man short.*

GLOMAN, DAVID J., artist; b. Bryn Mawr, Pa., 1958. Student, Yale U., 1982, MFA, 1986; BFA, Ind. U., 1983. Tchg. asst. Yale U. Sch. Art, 1985-86, Ind. U., Herron Sch. Art, Indpls., 1988-89, Smith Coll., Northampton, Mass., 1990; lectr. Smith Coll., Northampton, 1995-98; tchg. asst. Amherst (Mass.) Coll., 1992-94, 97-98, instr. ASA Studio Art Program, 1993-97; vis. asst. prof. Hampshire Coll., Amherst, 1994-95. One-man shows include Belleview Gallery, Bloomington, Ind., 1989, Fontbonne Coll., St. Louis, 1991, Northampton Ctr. for the Arts, 1993, Eli Marsh Gallery, Amherst Coll., 1994, Rolly-Michaux Gallery, Boston, 1996; group exhibits include Hudson Walker Gallery, Provincetown, Mass., 1986, East End Gallery, Provincetown, 1987, Provincetown Group Gallery, 1988, Julie Heller Gallery, Provincetown, 1989, 90, Babcock Galleries, N.Y.C., 1991, Hart Gallery, Northampton, Mass., 1992, Northampton Ctr. for the Arts, 1992, 93, Vt. Studio Ctr., Johnson, 1994, The Gallery in Monterey, Mass., 1994, Mead Art Mus., Amherst (Mass.) Coll., 1995, Bowery Gallery, N.Y.C., 1995, Rolly-Michaux Gallery, Boston, 1995, 96, WM Baczak Fine Arts, Northampton, 1997, Hackett-Freedman Gallery, San Francisco, 1997, Pepper Gallery, Boston, 1997. *

GLOSBAND, DANIEL MARTIN, lawyer; b. Salem, Mass., July 3, 1944; s. Leon Glosband and Ruth Pauline (Wentworth) Glosband School; m. Merrily Cotton, Dec. 23, 1967; children: Alexander, Gabriel, Oliver. BA, U. Mass., 1966; JD, Cornell, U., 1969. Bar: Mass. 1969, U.S. Dist. Ct. Mass. 1970, U.S. Ct. Appeals (1st cir.) 1971, U.S. Dist. Ct. Conn. 1971, U.S. Dist. Ct. Vt. 1974, U.S. Supreme Ct. 1982. Assoc., then ptnr. firm Widett & Widett, Boston, 1969-75; ptnr. Goldstein & Manello, Boston, 1976-87, Goodwin, Procter and Hoar, Boston, 1988—; adviser Am. Law Inst. Transnat. Insolvency Project, 1994—. Contbr. numerous articles on bankruptcy to profl. jours. Fellow Am. Coll. Bankruptcy (dir. 1999—), Am. Bar Found., Mass. Bar Found.; mem. Mass. Bar Assn. (chmn. bankruptcy com. 1980-83), Boston Bar Assn. (chmn. bankruptcy com. 1977-80), ABA (sect. on corps., chmn. internat. bankruptcy com. 1990-95), Internat. Bar Assn. (sect. bus. law, vice chmn. insolvency and creditors rights com. 1997—, del. UN Commn. Internat. Trade Law). Democrat. Jewish. Home: 34 Atlantic Ave Swampscott MA 01907-2404 Office: Goodwin Procter & Hoar Exchange Pl Boston MA 02109-2803

GLOSECKI, STEPHEN ORIN, English educator, folklorist; b. Springfield, Ill., Mar. 12, 1952; s. Andy Raymond and Edith Irene (Crossland) G.; m. Karen Anne Reynolds, Aug. 15, 1981; children: Dylan Matthew, Christopher Michael. BA in English and History, Beloit (Wis.) Coll., 1974; MA in English, U. Calif., Davis, 1978, PhD, 1980. Asst. prof. U. Ala., Birmingham, 1982-88, assoc. prof. dept. English, 1988—; Fulbright prof. U. Tromso, Norway, 1991-92; folklore cons. local TV, newspaper and radio, 1985—; folklore cons., prodr. Towers Prodns., Chgo., 1999. Author: Shamanism and Old English Poetry, 1989, (poem in Old English) With Saendendum, 1986 (Caedmon prize); contbg. author: Encyclopedia of Medieval Folklore, 1999, also articles. Recipient E.G. Ingalls award U. Ala. Birmingham, 1991; NEH travel grantee, 1990, Fulbright fellow, 1991-92; U. Ala. Birmingham rsch. grantee, 1994. Mem. MLA, Medieval Acad. Am. Avocations: calligraphy, watercolor, linocut, line drawing. Email: gloseck-i@uab.edu. Office: U Ala Birmingham Dept English Birmingham AL 35294-1260

GLOSS, LAWRENCE ROBERT, fundraising executive; b. Colorado Springs, Colo., Oct. 31, 1948; s. Kenneth Edwin and Clara U. (Haeker) G.; m. Carol Berg, June 4, 1977; children: Alexander Edwin, Carolyn Claire. BA, U. Denver, 1970. Dir. natl. congress on volunteerism and citizenship NCVA, Washington, 1975-76; dir. devel. Vis. Nurses Assn., Washington, 1976-77; devel. cons. Am. Lung Assn., Washington and N.Y.C., 1977-78; exec. dir. Colo. Conservation Fund, Denver, Colo., 1978-79, Rose Med. Ctr., enver, 1985-86; dir. devel. Rose Found., Denver, 1979-86; sr. campaign dir. J. Panas, Young and Ptnrs., San Francisco, 1986-88; pres. Gloss and Co., Denver, 1988—; mem. adv. coun. non-profit mgmt. Metro State Coll., Denver, 1994; cons. Native Am. Rights Fund, Boulder, Colo., Arts at the Sta., Denver, 1994, Up With People, 1995, 96, Emily Griffith Ctr. Found., 1995, 96, Colo. CASA, 1998-99, Women of the West Mus., 1998, Sister Cities-Denver and Kumming, China, 1999. Guest spkr. Tech. Assistance Ctr., Denver, 1992-94; bd. dirs. Alzeimer's and Related Disorders Assn., Denver, 1985-86; bd. dirs. Woman's Sch. Network, Denver, 1984-85, Colo. PTA, Englewood, 1991-92; active Emily Griffith Ctr. Found., 1997, U. Denver, Episcopal Ministries of U. Colo., Boulder, 1996, Colo. Pub. Expenditure Coun., 1998—, Srs. Resource Ctr., 1998—, Am. Humane Assn., 1998—. Mem. NSFRE (Colo. chpt. 1992-94, bd. dirs.), Arapahoe House, Englewood Hist. Soc., Am. Humane Assn., Women of the West Mus. Nat. Assn. of Mus. Exhibitors, Colo. Planning Giving Roundtable, Nat. Com. on Planned Giving, Am. Prospect Rsch. Assn., Am. Humane Assn., Colo. Pub. Expenditure Coun., Assn. of Healthcare Philanthropy (regional XII 1993-94), Assn. Profl. Rschrs. Advancement, Rotary Club of Denver. Lutheran. Avocations: dressage, art, soccer. Home: 11126 E Stagecoach Dr Parker CO 80138-8424 Office: Gloss and Company 2755 S Locust St Ste 113 Denver CO 80222-7131

GLOSSER, HARRY JOHN, JR., lawyer; b. Pottsville, Pa., Jan. 13, 1946; s. Harry Joseph and Anne (Rosenberger) G.; m. Lorraine D. Wanner, Jan. 28, 1995. BS in Acctg., Rider U., 1967; JD, Dickinson Sch. Law, 1970. Bar: Pa. 1970, U.S. Dist. Ct. (ea. dist.) Pa. 1974. Law clk., assoc. Curtin and Heefner, Morrisville, Pa., 1970-71; assoc. Timby & Godwin, Newton, Pa., 1970-74; ptnr. Godwin & Glosser, Newton, 1975; pvt. practice Morrisville, Pa., 1975-81, 85—; ptnr. Donahue & Glosser, Morrisville, 1981-85; solicitor Bristol-Bensalem Human Svcs. Ctr., Bristol Twp., Pa., 1978-87, Morrisville Sch. Dist., 1985-88. Sch. bd. mem. Morrisville Sch. Dist., 1974; pres. Morrisville Sch. Bd. Dirs., 1975-78. Mem. Pa. Bar Assn., Bucks County Bar Assn. Home: 1988 Satter Ct Yardley PA 19067-7218 Office: 331 W Bridge St Morrisville PA 19067-2342

GLOSSER, JEFFREY MARK, lawyer; b. 1936; married; 1 child. BS in Econs. with distinction, U. Pa., 1958; LLB, Harvard U., 1961. Bar: D.C.

1962. Law clk. U.S. Ct. Claims, 1963-64; assoc. Emery & Wood, Washington, 1965-69; ptnr. Jeffrey M. Glosser, P.C., Washington, 1969-86, Whiteford, Taylor & Preston, Washington, 1987-95; instr. CLE courses sponsored by D.C. Bar, 1976-95. Mem. ABA (adminstrv. law sect., various coms.), D.C. Bar Assn. (numerous coms.), Fed. Bar Assn. (U.S. Claims Ct. com.), Fed. Cir. Bar Assn. (rules com. 1985-95).

GLOSSER, WILLIAM LOUIS, lawyer; b. Johnstown, Pa., Aug. 30, 1929; s. Saul I. and Eva (Hurwitz) G.; m. Patricia Freeman, Feb. 5, 1952; children: Alix Paul, Jill P., Jonathan. BS Temple U., 1951; LLB, U. Pa., 1954. Bar: Pa. 1954, Fla. 1956, U.S. Dist. Ct. (we. dist.) Pa. 1956, U.S. Dist. Ct. (so. dist.) Fla. 1957. Assoc. Broad and Cassel, Miami Beach, Fla., 1956-57; sole practice, Coral Gables, Fla., 1957-61, Johnstown, Pa., 1962—; magistrate judge U.S. Dist. Ct. (we. dist.) Pa., 1972-93; corp. sec., dir. Glosser Bros., Inc., Johnstown, 1969-85; of counsel Smorto, Persio, Webb & McGill, Johnstown, 1988—. Bd. dirs. Lee Hosp., Johnstown, Greater Johnstown (Pa.) Cmty. Found., ret.; mem. Johnstown adv. council Pa. Human Relations Commn.; pres. United Jewish Fedn. Johnstown, 1970-75; chmn. fund drive United Way, 1985, pres., 1987-88; bd. dirs. Mt. Aloysius Coll., 1980-84, Cmty. Found. Greater Johnstown, Pa., 1990—. Served with U.S. Army, 1954-56. Mem. Pa. Bar Assn., Fla. Bar Assn., Cambria County Bar Assn., Pa. Bar Assn., Greater Johnstown C. of C. (pres. 1985), Rotary (pres, 1990); B'nai B'rith (pres. lodge 1965-67, 83-84). Jewish. Home: 521 Luzerne St Johnstown PA 15905-2324 Office: Smorto Persio Webb & McGill 430 Main St Johnstown PA 15901-1823

GLOSTEN, LAWRENCE ROBERT, engineering executive; b. 1918. Chmn. Glosten Assocs., 1958-98. Mem NAE. Address: 7751 Hansen Rd NE Bainbridge Island WA 98110-1614

GLOSTER, HUGH MORRIS, retired college president, college association consultant; b. Brownsville, Tenn., May 11, 1911; s. John and Dora (Morris) G.; m. Louise Elizabeth Torrence, June 1, 1935 (div.); children—Alice Louise, Evelyn Elaine; m. Beulah Victoria Harold, Sept. 9, 1957 (dec. July 1985); 1 son, Hugh Morris, Jr.; m. Yvonne Arnold King, June 17, 1989. Student, LeMoyne Coll., 1927-29; B.A., Morehouse Coll., 1931; M.A. (Univ. fellow), Atlanta U., 1933; Ph.D. (Gen. Edn. Bd. fellow), N.Y. U., 1943; hon. doctorate, U. Haiti, 1968, N.Y. U., 1971, Wayne State U., 1976, Washington U., St. Louis, 1977, Morgan State U., 1980, Mercer U., 1981, St. Paul's Coll., 1982, Emory U., 1987, Morehouse Sch. Medicine, Morehouse Coll., 1987, LeMoyne Coll., 1993, Hampton U., 1999. Instr., asso. prof. English LeMoyne Coll., 1933-41; prof. English Morehouse Coll., 1941-43; program dir. USO, Ft. Huachuca, Ariz., 1943-44; asso. regional exec. USO, Atlanta, 1944-46; prof. English, chmn. dept. lang. and lit. Hampton Inst., 1946-63, dir. summer session, 1952-62, dean faculty, 1963-67; pres. Morehouse Coll., Atlanta, 1967-87, pres. emeritus, 1987—; co-dir. Coll. Cons. Network So. Assn. Colls. & Schs., 1987-96, trustee, bd. dirs., 1988—; prof. English Atlanta U., summers 1942, 43; guest prof. English N.Y. U., summers 1949, 62; Fulbright prof. English Hiroshima U., Japan, 1953-55; lectr. Orientation Center Fgn. Grad. Students, Coll. William and Mary, summer 1955; vis. prof. Am. lit. U. Warsaw, Poland, 1961-62; mem. summer faculty U. V.I., 1960, U. Krakow, Poland, 1962, U. Valencia, Spain, 1963. Author: Negro Voices in American Fiction, 1948; Co-editor: The Brown Thrush: An Anthology of Verse by Negro College Students, 1935, My Life-My Country-My World: College Readings for Modern Living, 1952; Contbg. editor: Phylon: The Atlanta U. Review of Race and Culture, 1948-53; adv. editor: Coll. Lang. Assn. Jour, 1957—. Vice chmn. Ga. Postsecondary Edn. Commn.; mem. pres.'s council Am. Forum for Internat. Studies and Inst. European Studies; past v.p., mem. exec. com. Assn. Pvt. Colls. and Univs. in Ga.; mem. exec. com. Coll. Entrance Exam. Bd., 1967-71; mem., chmn. exec. com. Ednl. Testing Service, 1971-75; bd. dirs. United Bd. for Coll. Devel., Com. on Econ. Devel., Inst. European Studies, Martin Luther King Jr. Center for Social Change, So. Christian Leadership Conf.; bd. dirs., trustee United Negro Coll. Fund; trustee Atlanta U., Morehouse Coll., Interdenominational Theol. Ctr., Paul Quinn Coll., LeMoyne-Owen Coll.; founder, trustee Morehouse Sch. Medicine, 1973—. Recipient research grant Alpha Phi Alpha, summer 1940; research grant Carnegie Found., 1950-51; distinguished contbns. award Coll. Lang. Assn., 1958; Centennial medallion Hampton Inst., 1968; Alumnus of Year award LeMoyne Coll., 1967. Mem. Coll. Lang. Assn. (founder, pres. 1937-38, 48-50), Am. Assn. Higher Edn. (exec. com. 1967-69), Am. Assn. U. Adminstrs. (trustee), Fulbright Assn., Inquiry Club, Phi Beta Kappa, Sigma Pi Phi Boule, Alpha Phi Alpha, Golden Key. Home: 3390 Dodson Dr Connector East Point GA 30344-5666

GLOSUP, LORENE See DEAN, DEAREST

GLOTTA, RONALD DELON, lawyer; b. Lajunta, Colo., Mar. 18, 1941; s. John Wallace and Marian (Kisner) G.; m. Sharon S. Glotta, Aug. 27, 1961 (div. Mar. 1986); children: Holly Ann, Jeffrey Delon; m. Marietta Lynn Baba, June 23, 1990 (div. Oct. 1998). BA with honors, U. Kans., 1963; JD, U. Mich., 1966. Bar: Mich. 1966. Atty. Marcus, McCroskey, Libner, Reamon, Williams & Dilley, Muskegon, Mich., 1966-68; ptnr. Philo, Maki, Moore, Pitts, Ravitz, Glotta, Cockrel & Robb, Detroit, 1968-70; prin. Glotta & Adelman, Detroit, 1970-85, Glotta, Rawlings & Skutt, Detroit, 1985-96, Glotta, Skutt & Assts, Detroit, 1996—. Mem. Phi Beta Kappa. Home: 2065 Hyde Park Rd Detroit MI 48207-3885

GLOTZER, MORTIMER M., quality assurance consultant; b. Hartford, Conn., Jan. 14, 1930; s. Isidore and Sara J. (Saxe) G.; m. Arline I. Leichtman, Feb. 12, 1956; children: David L., Helen D. B in Mech. Engring., NYU, 1951. Project liaison engr. Combustion Engring., 1968-69, mgr. quality assurance engring. for nuclear fuel mfg., 1969-87, mgr. quality control, 1987-92, dir. quality assurance, 1992, dir. quality systems, 1992-94, quality sys. lead auditor; quality cons. pvt. practice, West Hartford, Conn., 1994—; sec. ASME/Am. Nat. Standards Inst. N45-2.11, 1972-74. PTA pres. King Philip Elem. Sch., West Hartford, Conn., 1978-79; bd. dirs., pres. brotherhood Temple Beth Israel, West Hartford, 1985-86; mem. West Hartford Regents. Recipient Dist. award of merit Boy Scouts Am., Hartford, 1982, Silver Beaver award Boy Scouts Am., Hartford, 1986, Shofar award Jewish Com. on Scouting, Boy Scouts Am. Republican. Avocations: boy scouts, camping. Home: 906 N Main St West Hartford CT 06117-2028

GLOVER, ALBERT DOWNING, retired veterinarian; b. Newark, Mo., Dec. 4, 1907; s. Albert D. and Mattie O. (Downing) G.; m. Mildred Elva Haselwood; children: Allen, Gary, Janet. BS in Agr., U. Mo., 1932; DVM, Colo. State Coll., 1936. Former chmn. City Coun., Canton, Mo., other civic activities. Mem. Mo. VMA (pres. 1951, legis. commn.), AVMA (v.p. 1952), Mo. Vet. Examining Bd., Am. Legion (past comdr.), Shriners, others. Home: 806 Lewis St Canton MO 63435-1449

GLOVER, ASIA WONG, communications services executive; b. Sandersville, Ga., Dec. 7, 1970; d. Horace Lee and Margaret Gene Kendrick; m. Clary Edward Glover Jr., Mar. 21, 1997. BBA, Valdosta State U., 1993, MPA, 1996. Ctr. facilitator Lowndes Drug and Action Coun., Valdosta, Ga., 1994-95; econ. support case mgr. Dept. Family and Children's Svcs., Quitman, Ga., 1995-96; family independence case mgr. Dept. Family and Children's Svcs., Valdosta, 1996-97 dir. admissions Lowndes County Health Svcs., Valdosta, 1997-98; acct. mgr. West Telesvcs., San Antonio, 1998—. Mem. adult literacy adv. bd. Valdosta Tech. inst., 1995-96; mem. mentor program Dept. Family and Children Svds., Valdosta, 1996-97. Mem. ASPA, Nat. Coalition of 100 Black Women, Order of Ea. Star (sec. 1996—). Baptist. E-mail: awglover@west.com.

GLOVER, CLIFFORD CLARKE, retired construction company executive; b. Newnan, Ga., May 15, 1913; s. Howard Clarke and Fannie Virginia (Jones) G.; m. Louise Liles, Jan. 16, 1937; children: Edmund Cook, Nancy Liles Glover Kennedy, Virginia Johnston Glover Lee, Laura Clarke Glover Thatcher. BCE, U. N.C., 1934. With Batson-Cook Co., West Point, Ga., 1934-94; ret., 1994. Mem. West Point Sch. Bd., 1951-69, chmn., 1964-68; chmn. West Point Planning Bd., 1964-98; trustee LaGrange Coll.; pres. George H. Lanier council Boy Scouts Am., 1977-78, dir. Southeast regional bd., 1987, recipient Silver Antelope award, 1992; bd. dirs. Joint Tech. Ga. Devel. Fund, 1987. Served with USNR, 1945-46. Recipient Silver Beaver award Boy Scouts Am., Silver Antelope award Boy Scouts Am.; Presdl. award George H. Lanier Coun. Boy Scouts Am., Disting. Citizen's award, 1988; Award of Merit Greater Valley C. of C., 1984; Golden Hammer award Profl. Constrn. Estimators Assn. Am., 1988; fellow La Grange Coll. Mem. Assoc. Gen. Contractors (past pres. Ga. br., Skill, Integrity and Responsibility award 1991). Methodist (ofcl. bd.). Clubs: Rotary (Paul Harris fellow); Capital City (Atlanta); Riverside (West Point). Home: PO Box 151 West Point GA 31833-0151 Office: Batson-Cook Co PO Box 151 West Point GA 31833-0151

GLOVER, CRISPIN HELLION, actor; b. N.Y.C., Apr. 20, 1964; s. Bruce Herbert and Betty Lillian Marie (Koerber) G. Stage debut The Sound of Music, L.A., 1977; appeared in My Tutor, 1982, Racing With the Moon, 1983, The Orkly Kid, 1983, Friday 13th-The Final Chapter, 1983, Teachers, 1984, Back To The Future, 1984, At Close Range, 1984, Rivers Edge, 1985, Twister, 1987, Where the Heart Is, 1989, Wild At Heart, 1989, The Doors, 1991, Ferdydurke, 1991, Little Noises, 1992, Rubin and Ed, 1992, Crime and Punishment, 1994, What's Eating Gilbert Grape, 1993, Chasers, 1994, Even Cowgirls Get the Blues, 1994, Dead Man, 1995, The People Vs. Larry Flynt, 1996, Nurse Betty, 1999; (TV film) High School U.S.A., 1983; author, pub.: (books) Rat Catching, 1987, Oak Mot, 1990, Concrete Inspection, 1992, What It Is and How It Is Done, 1995; dir., screenwriter, actor, prodr. What is It?, 1997, 98, 99. *

GLOVER, DANNY, actor; b. Ga., July 22, 1947; m. Asake Bomani; 1 child, Mandisa. Degree in Econs., San Francisco State Univ. Researcher mayor's office San Francisco, 1971-75; mem. Am. Conservatory Theatre's Black Actor Workshop. Actor: (Broadway debut) Master Harold...and the Boys, Lyceum Theatre, 1982 (Theatre World award 1982), (stage prodns.) The Blood Knot, 1982, The Island, Sizwe Banzi is Dead, Macbeth, Suicide in B Flat, Nevis Mountain Dew, Jukebox; (feature films) Escape from Alcatraz, 1979, Chu Chu and the Philly Flash, 1981, Out, 1982, The Stand-In, 1984, Iceman, 1984, Places in the Heart, 1984, Birdy, 1984, Silverado, 1985, Witness, 1985, The Color Purple, 1985, Lethal Weapon, 1987, Bat 21, 1988, Lethal Weapon II, 1989, To Sleep with Anger (also exec. prodr.) 1990, Predator 2, 1990, Flight of the Intruder, 1991, A Rage in Harlem, 1991, Pure Luck, 1991, Grand Canyon, 1992, Lethal Weapon III, 1992, The Saint of Fort Washington (also co-prodr.) 1993, Bopha!, 1993, Maverick, 1994, Angels in the Outfield, 1994, Operation Dumbo Drop, 1995, America's Dream, 1996, The Rainmaker, 1997, Wings Against the Wind, 1998, Beloved, 1998, Lethal Weapon 4, 1998, (voice) Prince of Egypt, 1998, Antz (voice), 1998, The Monster, 1999, Boesman and Lena, 2000; (TV movies) The Face of Rage, 1983, Mandela, 1987, Dead Man Out, 1989; (TV miniseries) Chiefs, 1983, Lonesome Dove, 1989, Queen, 1993; (TV episodes) Hill Street Blues, Lou Grant, Many Mansions, others; host Civil War Journal, 1993. Address: William Morris Agy care Arnold Rifkin 151 S El Camino Dr Beverly Hills CA 90212-2704*

GLOVER, DEBORAH JOYCE, school psychologist, consultant; b. Little Rock, Dec. 19, 1950; d. Virgil Roach and Frances Merle (Schafer) Moncrief; m. William Robert Price, Jr., June 14, 1970 (div. Dec. 1979), 1 child, Robert Geoffrey; m. James Leigh Spencer, Nov. 18, 1981 (div. Sept. 1993); children: Alicia Joyce, Leslie Leigh; m. J. Brian Glover, Jan. 2, 1997. Student, Wesleyan Coll., Macon, Ga., 1968-69; BA in Psychology, Ga. State U., 1972, MEd in Sch. Psychology, 1973; EdD, Nova U., 1989. Lic. psychol. examiner, Ark.; cert. sch. psychologist, Ga., Fla., sch. psychology specialist, Ark.; nat. cert. sch. psychologist. Tchr. phys. edn. Immaculate Heart of Mary Sch., Atlanta, 1972-73; cons. sch. psychology West Ga. Coop. Ednl. Svcs. Agy., Newnan, Ga., 1973-76; dir., specialist in sch. psychology Hollander Learning Ctrs., Vero Beach, Ft. Pierce, Fla., 1976-80; psychol. examiner Psychol. Testing Svc., Pine Bluff, Ark., 1981-84; sch. psychologist North Little Rock (Ark.) Sch. Dist., 1984-94; lectr. alternative assessment methods multi-cultural populations U. Witswatersrand, Johannesburg, South Africa, 1994-95; sch. psychologist Forrest City (Ark.) Sch. Dist., 1996-99; sch. psychology specialist Bentonville, Ark., 1999—; Ark. field coord. Psychol. Corp., 1986-88; lectr. ann. conv. Ark. Assn. for Counseling Guidance and Devel., 1986-89, 93, Ann. Ark. Even Start Presch. Parent Conf., 1994. Vol. cons. devel. program alternative learning strategies for learning disabled students Christ the King Cath. Sch., Little Rock, 1988-94. Grantee Rockfeller Found., 1988-89. Mem. Assn. for Measurement and Evaluation in Guidance (chmn. standards com. 1985-86), Nat. Assn. Sch. Psychologists, Ark. Assn. Sch. Psychologists (pres.-elect 1986-87, pres. 1987-88, exec. bd.), Mortar Bd., Phi Kappa Phi, Psi Chi. Republican. Roman Catholic. Home: 10 Paxton Ln Bella Vista AR 72714 Office: Bentonville Pub Sch 400 NW Second St Bentonville AR 72712

GLOVER, FRED WILLIAM, artificial intelligence and optimization research director, educator; b. Kansas City, Mo., Mar. 8, 1937; s. William Cain and Mary Ruth (Baxter) G.; m. Diane Tatham, June 4, 1988; 1 child, Lauren Glover; children from previous marriage: Dana Reynolds, Paul Glover. BBA, U. Mo., 1960; PhD, Carnegie-Mellon U., 1965. Asst. prof. U. Calif., Berkeley, 1965-66; assoc. prof. U. Tex., Austin, 1966-69; prof. U. Minn., Mpls., 1969-70; John King prof. U. Colo., Boulder, 1970-87, US West chair in sys. sci., 1987-98, Media One chair in sys. sci., 1998—; rsch. dir. Artificial Intelligence Ctr., Boulder, 1984-90; invited disting. lectr. Swiss Fed. Inst. Tech., Lausaunne, 1990—, IMAG Labs., U. Grenoble, France, 1991, U. Canterbury, New Zealand, 1997, U. Paris, 1998, U. Toulouse, France, 1999; vis. Regents Chair in Engring., U. Tex., Austin, 1989; cons. U.S. Congress, 1984, Nat. Bur. Stds., 1986, also over 70 U.S. corps. and govt. agys., 1965—; lectr. NATO, France, Italy, Germany, Denmark, 1970, 78, 80, 82, 89, Inst. Decision Scis., 1984; bd. dirs. Heuristec, Boulder, OPTEK, Boulder, Decision Analysis, Rsch. & Computation, Austin, 1971-83; head, rsch. assoc. Global Optimization Space Contrn. Ctr., Boulder, 1988—; rsch. prin. U. Colo.-U.S. West Joint Rsch. Initiative, 1990—; prin. investigator Air Force Office Sci. Rsch., Office Naval Rsch., 1990—; invited rsch. scholar U. B.C., 1994. Author: Netform Decision Models, 1983 (DIS award 1984), Tabu Search I, 1989, Tabu Search II, 1990, Tabu Search (book and special vols.) 1993, 97, 98, Ghost Image Processes for Neural Networks, 1993, Linkages with Artificial Intelligence, 1990, Network Models in Optimization and Their Application in Practice, 1992, also others; contbr. over 280 articles on math. optimization and artificial intelligence to profl. jours. Participant Host Vis. Exchange, Nat. Acad. Scis., 1981; mem. grants com. Queen Elizabeth II fellowships, Australia and U.S., 1984; mem. U.S. nat. adv. bd. Univ. Rsch. Initiative on Combinatorial Optimization. Recipient Internat. Achievement award Inst. Mgmt. Scis., 1982, Energy Rsch. award Energy Rsch. Inst., 1983, Univ. Disting. Rsch. Lectr. award U. Colo., 1988, Rsch. Excellence prize Ops. Rsch. Soc., 1989, Nat. Best Theoretical/Empirical Rsch. Paper award Decision Scis. Inst., 1993, Computer Sci. Rsch. Excellence award Ops. Rsch. Soc. Am., 1994, Nat. Rsch. Excellence award Comp. Sci. Ops. Rsch. Soc., 1994, John Von Neumann Theory award INFORMS, 1998; named first U.S. West Disting. fellow, 1987. Fellow AAAS, Am. Inst. Decision Scis (lectr. 1984, Outstanding Achievement award 1984), Am. Assn. Collegiate Schs. Bus., ICC Inst.; mem. Alpha Iota Delta. Achievements include design of software systems used throughout the U.S. and abroad. Office: U Colo Coll Bus Box 419 Boulder CO 80309-0419

GLOVER, JERE WALTON, lawyer; b. Brownsville, Tenn., June 20, 1944; s. William Lloyd and Betty Ruth (Shropshire) G.; m. Doris Ann Henderson, Mar. 30, 1968. BS, Memphis State U., 1966, JD, 1969; LLM, George Washington U., 1972. Bar: Tenn. 1969, Md. 1981, D.C. 1970. Trial atty. FTC, Washington, 1968-75; dir. legal div. Consumer Product Safety Commn., Washington, 1975-77; counsel small bus. com. Ho. of Reps., Washington, 1978; dep. chief counsel SBA, Washington, 1981; chief counsel advocacy SBA, 1994—; pvt. practice Washington, 1981-94; pres. Met. Lithotripsy Ctr., Inc., Washington, 1987-94; v.p. Scan Am., Inc., Washington, 1986-94. Mem. Md. Bar Assn., D.C. Bar Assn., Tenn. Bar Assn., Alliance for Affordable Health Care (pres. 1991—), Small Bus. Legis. Coun. (bd. dirs. 1981-87). Democrat. Avocation: sailing. Home: 1005 York Ln Annapolis MD 21403-4222 Office: SBA 409 3d St NW Washington DC 20416

GLOVER, JOHN, actor; b. Kingston, N.Y., Aug. 7, 1944; s. John S. and Cade (Mullins) G. Student, Towson State Coll. Appeared in plays Look Homeward Angel, 1963, A Scent of Flowers, 1969, Subject to Fit, 1971, House of Blue Leaves, 1971, The Great God Brown, 1972, Don Juan, 1972, The Selling of the President, 1972, The Visit, 1973, Chemin de Fer, 1973, Holiday, 1973, Rebel Women, 1976, The Importance of Being Earnest, 1977, Treats, 1977, A Man for All Seasons, 1979, Frankenstein, 1981, Hedda Gabler, 1981, Booth, 1982, The Doctor's Delemma, 1982, A Doll's House, 1982, Whodonnit, 1982-83, Criminal Minds, 1984, Design for Living, 1984, Linda Her and the Fairy Garden, 1984, Digby, 1985, Henceforward, 1991, Love! Valour! Compassion!, 1994 (Tony award Featured Actor in a Play, 1995); films include Shamus, 1972, Annie Hall, 1977, Julia, 1977, Somebody Killed Her Husband, 1978, The Last Embrace, 1979, American Success Company, 1979, Mountain Men, 1980, Melvin and Howard, 1980, Brubaker, 1980, The Incredible Shrinking Woman, 1981, A Little Sex, 1982, The Evil That Men Do, 1984, A Flash of Green, 1985, White Nights, 1985, Willy/Milly, 1985, My Sister's Keeper, 1986, 52 Pick-up, 1986, Masquerade, 1988, A Killing Affair, 1988, Rocket Gibraltar, 1988, The Chocolate War, 1988, Scrooged, 1988, Meet the Hollowheads, 1989, Gremlins 2: The New Batch, 1990, Robocop 2, 1990, Dora Was Dysfunctional, 1993, Ed and His Dead Mother, 1993; TV movies include The Face of Rage, 1983, Ernie Kovacs: Between the Laughter, 1984, An Early Frost, 1985, Moving Target, 1988, Hot Paint, 1988, David, 1988, The Traveling Man, 1989, Twist of Fate, 1989, Breaking Point, 1989, El Diablo, 1990, What Ever Happened to Baby Jane?, 1991, Dead on the Money, 1991, Drug Wars: The Cocaine Cartel, 1992, Majority Rule, 1992, Assault at West Point, 1994, Night of The Running Man, 1995, In the Mouth of Madness, 1995, Schemes, 1995, Batman & Robin, 1997, Love! Valour! Compassion!, 1997; mini-series include Kennedy, 1983, Rage of Angels, 1983, George Washington, 1984, Nutcracker: Money, Madness and Murder, 1987, Grass Roots, 1992; TV series appearances include (voice) The Adventures of Batman and Robin, 1992, South Beach, 1993, (voice) Batman: Gotham Knights, 1997, Dead Man's Gun, 1997. Office: The Gersh Agy care Ken Kaplan 232 N Canon Dr Beverly Hills CA 90210-5302*

GLOVER, JOHN TRAPNELL, real estate executive; b. Newnan, Ga., May 30, 1946; s. Howard Clarke Jr. and Margaret Farmer (Trapnell) G.; m. Sandra Barron, May 27, 1967; children: John Trapnell Jr., Jeffrey Barron. BA with highest honors, Emory U., 1968; JD summa cum laude, U. Ga., 1972; B Civil Law with first class honors, Oxford (Eng.) U., 1973. Assoc. King & Spalding, Atlanta, 1973-78, ptnr., 1979-84; pres. Post Properties, Inc., Atlanta, 1984—; bd. dirs. SunTrust Banks of Ga., Inc., SunTrust Bank, Atlanta. Editor-in-chief Ga. Law Rev., 1971-72. Chmn. Atlanta Symphony Orch., 1994-96; trustee Emory U., Atlanta, 1994—; trustee Lovett Sch., Atlanta, 1990—, chmn., 1997—; trustee Robert W. Woodruff Arts Ctr., Inc., Atlanta, 1992—; bd. councilors Carter Ctr., Atlanta, 1991—. Stipe scholar, 1966-68. Mem. Nat. Realty Com. (vice chmn. 1993-96), Nat. Multi Housing Coun. (bd. dirs. 1990—), Urban Land Inst., Atlanta C. of C. (bd. dirs. 1990-92), Wilderness Soc. (governing coun. 1993-96), Phi Beta Kappa. Avocations: golf, fly fishing, bird hunting. Office: Post Properties Inc 4401 Northside Pkwy NW Ste 800 Atlanta GA 30327-3093

GLOVER, KEVIN, football player; b. Washington, June 17, 1963; m. Cestaine Glover. Student. U. Md. Center Detroit Lions, 1985-98, Seattle Seahawks, 1998—. Named to Pro Bowl, 1996; recipient Ed Block Courage award. Office: Seattle Seahawks 11220 NS 53d St Kirkland WA 98033*

GLOVER, LISA MARIE, research analyst; b. Detroit, Oct. 14, 1963; d. Ronald and Denise (Wellons) G. BS, Tuskegee U., 1986; MS, Morgan State U., 1988. Cert. Microsoft profl. Summer intern IBM, Charlotte, N.C., 1982, GM, Pontiac, Mich., 1983, 84, 85, Turner Constrn., Detroit, 1986; grad. intern State of Md., Dept. Transp., Balt., 1987-88; planner Dept. Transp., Detroit, 1988-90, asst. to dir., 1990-91, mgr. Office of Contract Compliance, 1991-93; transp. engr., cons. M2 Internat., Detroit, 1993-94; owner Trans. Svcs., Inc., 1994-97; bus. analyst Met. Atlanta Rapid Transit Authority, Atlanta, 1998—; rsch. asst., bus. analyst info. tech. Met. Atlanta Rapid transit Authority, 1998—; rsch. analyst, ind. contractor tech. support McDermott Sys., 1999—; rep. Detroit Dept. Transp. SEMCOG, Transp. Adv. Coun., Detroit, 1988-93, Labor Mobility Project Steering Com., Detroit, 1991, asst. venue transportation mgr., Atlanta Comm. for the Olympic games, 1996; ind. contractor, 1997; substitute tchr. math., 1998; spl. events planner Von Creations, Inc., 1998; staff asst. office sta. svcs., Met. Atlanta Rapid Transit Authority, 1998—. Mem. Civic Ctr.-Optimist Club, 1992-94, mem. 14th Congl. Dist. Young Dems., spl. projects com., 1992, young adults com. NAACP, 1989-91; math. tutor Ednl. Guidance and Tutoring Ctrs., Inc., 1996—; mem. nat. nominating bd. Outstanding Young Ams.; mem. Total Praise choir, engring. com. New Birth Missionary Bapt. Ch., Decatur, Ga.; vol. registrar LIFE Inst., New Birth Missionary Bapt. Ch. Mem. NAFE, NAACP, Internat. Olympic Family, Assn. Gen. Contractors Am. (pres. 1985-86), Conf. Minority Transp. Ofcls., Tuskegee Nat. Alumni Assn. (Atlanta chpt.), Morgan State Student Transp. Assn. (sec. 1986-87), Trade Union Leadership Coun. Young Adults, Alpha Kappa Alpha (sponsor teen group 1989-95), Delta Nu Alpha,Sigma Lambda Chi (charter). Democrat. Baptist. Avocations: arts, classical/jazz/gospel music, travel, remodeling projects. E-mail: gloverülisa@excite.com.

GLOVER, NATHANIEL, JR., sheriff; b. Jacksonville, Fla., Mar. 29, 1943. BS, Edward Waters Coll., Jacksonville, 1966; MS, U. North Fla., 1987; grad., FBI Nat. Acad., Quantico, Va.; LLD (hon.), Edward Waters Coll., 1995. With Jacksonville Sheriff's Office, 1966-69, investigator, 1969-74, sgt., 1974-86, leader hostage negotiation team, 1975-86, chief of svcs., 1986-88, dep. dir. police svcs., 1988-91, dir. police svcs., 1991-95, sheriff, 1995—; participant White House Leadership Conf. on Youth, Drug Use and Violence. Recipient Martin Luther King Humanitarian award Jacksonville Jewish Commn., 1996. Office: Jacksonville Sheriff's Office 501 E Bay St Jacksonville FL 32202-2927*

GLOVER, NORMAN JAMES, engineering executive; b. Bklyn., Feb. 6, 1929; s. Norman James and Livia Delfine (Bongiorni) G.; m. Laurice White, 18956 (div. 1963), remarried, 1983; m. Ellen Janet Wilson, 1964 (div. 1980); children: Valerie, Norman James, Susan, John. BS in Engring., Columbia U., 1950, postgrad., 1953-56; postgrad., U. Alaska, 1950, Harvard U., 1968-69, Naval War Coll., 1970, CUNY, 1994-97. Registered profl. engr. N.Y., N.J., Ariz., Maine, Va., Ga., Fla., Ind., Tex., Colo., Mont., Alaska, Mass., Oreg., Md., Ala., Mo., Minn., Ky., Wis., Wash., Mich.; chartered engr. U.K. Engr. Alaska Rd. Commn., 1950-51; engr., supt., v.p. Heydt Constrn. Co., N.Y.C., 1955-60; v.p., mgr. fgn. ops., dir. constrn. Thompson-Starret Co., N.Y.C., 1961-66; pvt. engring. practice N.Y.C., 1961-64; v.p., engr. Viking Devel., Boston, 1966-70; v.p., engr. Sheraton Corp., Boston, 1970-76, exec. v.p. design and devel., 1971-75; v.p., dir. ops. ITT Cmty. Devel. Corp., Palm Coast, Fla., 1976-77; v.p. ITT Land Corp., 1975-77; pres. Ramada Devel. Corp., Phoenix, 1977-79; v.p. Ramada Inns, Inc.; v.p., mng. dir. Beaver Creek Devel. Vail (Colo.) Assocs. Inc., 1979-83; pres., mng. dir. Internat. Cons. and Engrs., P.C., N.Y., 1980—; exec. dir. Aegis Inst., N.Y., 1966—; mem. steering com. performacne concept in bldg. Bldg. Rsch. Inst.-Nat. Acad. Scis.; adj. prof. internat. hotel devel. and mgmt. NYU, 1998. Author papers, tech. reports. Mem. adv. coun. Columbia U. FAculty Engring. and Applied Sci., 1964-90; commr. Beaver Creek Metro Dist., 1980-82; chmn. selection bd. A/E/CM Svcs., N.Y. State Facilities Devel. Corp., 1986-87; chair forum on mitigation of effects of urban terrorism, 1995—, NATO Insens. Munitions Incid. Com., 1996—; chmn. joint working group def. against CB terrorism USDOD, DOE, DOJ, 1999—. Lt. comdr. USCGR, 1951-54. Killough scholar Columbia U., 1950. Fellow Inst. Structural Engrs. (U.K.), Soc. Am. Mil. Engrs., Archtl. Engring. Inst. (bd. govs. 1998—), ASCE (task com. structural applications of plastics 1972-65, pub. works com. urban plan and devel. divsn. com. constrn. stds. 1975-78, chmn. A/E divsn. coms. program mgmt. & facilities planning 1994—, exec. com. AE divsn. 1995-98, bd. govs. arctl. engring. inst. 1998—, assoc. editor jour. 1998—); mem. Boston Soc. Civil Engrs., Mass. Soc. Profl. Engrs., Arctic Inst. N.Am., Am. Soc. Quality Control, ASTM, Constrn. Specifications Inst., Am. Mgmt. Assn., U.S. Naval Inst., U.S. Strategic Inst., Inst. European Def. & Strategic Studies, Assn. Former Intelligence Officers, Bering Sea Patrol Vets., Vail Athletic Club, Univ. Club (Boston), Columbia Club (N.Y.C.), Cavalry Club (Bahrain), Ariz. Athletic Club (Phoenix). Office: 271 Central Park W New York NY 10024-3020

GLOVER, RICHARD BERNARD, foundation administrator; b. Jacksonville, Fla., Apr. 17, 1938; s. Houston Bering Sr. and Angela Marie (Cooper) G.; m. Victoria Raye Wells, Oct. 7, 1960 (div.); children: Victoria Renee, Terceria Robyn Kaye Anderson. BS in Computer Sci., Jones Coll., 1967. Prof. data processing dept. Jones Coll., 1968-73; data processing mgr. Purolator Chem. Corp., 1973-74; lead programmer, data processing mgr. Jon H. Swischer & Sons, 1976-77; data processing mgr. St. Lukes Hosp., 1977-

80; owner First Coast Lawn & Gardening Inc., 1980—, RBG Diversified Svcs., Inc., 1980—. With USMC, 1955-64. Mem. Data Processing Mgrs. Assn., Phi Theta Pi (sec./treas. 1978—), Greek Orgns. Against Drugs, Inc. (sec./treas. 1990—). Home and Office: 2111 Cortez Rd Jacksonville FL 32246-2313*

GLOVER, ROBERT CALDWELL, computer graphics specialist, artist; b. Oakland, Calif., May 6, 1965; s. Robert Caldwell Sr. and Mary Jo Ann (Crane) G.; m. Anne-Marie Kraft, Feb. 6, 1993. BFA, Ohio State U., 1988. Freelance artist Cin., 1988—; graphic designer Std. Publ., Cin., 1998—; mem. web design team Vineyard Cmty. Ch., Springdale, Ohio, 1998, dir. Sch. Creative Arts, 1996—; owner SNEAKS Greeting Cards. Author, illustrator: (book, jour.) Here's What I Think About Stuff, 1994-97, Here's What I Think About Being a Christian, 1994-97, Here's What I Think About Me and My Family, 1994-98; one-man shows include Graillville, Loveland, Ohio, 1998, 99. Mem. Loveland Artist Club. Avocations: gardening, low impact camping, backpacking. E-mail: glover@fuse.net. Office: Glover Arts 731 Bramblewood Dr Loveland OH 45140-6904

GLOVER, SAVION, actor, dancer; b. Newark, 1973. Appeared in Broadway plays including The Tap Dance Kid, Black and Blue (Tony award nominee), Jelly's Last Jam (Jefferson award for supporting role in nat. tour)Bring In Da Noise, Bring In Da Funk, 1995 (tony award, Drama Desk award, Outer Critics Cir. award, Obie awards (2), Fred Astaire awards (2), 1996); appeared in films including Tap, The Wall, Savion Glover's Nu York (exec. prodr., choreographer); TV appearances include Dance in America: Tap!, The Acad. Awards, Black Filmmaker's Hall of Fame, The Kennedy Ctr. Honors, (series regular) Sesame Street; choreographer Washington Soc. for Performing Arts. Recipient Dance Mag.'s Choreographer of Yr. award, 1996, endowment grant for choreography NEA. Office: Alliance Agy 1501 Broadway Ste 404 New York NY 10036-5501

GLOVER, THOMAS T., federal judge. Apptd. chief bankruptcy judge we. dist. U.S. Dist. Ct. Wash., 1985. Fax: (206) 553-0187. Office: 315 Park Place Bldg 1200 6th Ave Seattle WA 98101-3123

GLOVER, WILLIAM HARPER, theater critic; b. N.Y.C., May 6, 1911; s. William Harper and Lily P. (Freir) G.; m. Isobel M. Cole, Oct. 26, 1936 (div. 1973); m. Virginia F. Holden, Aug. 29, 1985. LittB, Rutgers U., 1932. City editor Asbury Park (N.J.) Press, 1935-39; news editor AP newsfeatures, 1941-53, theatre writer, 1953-78; drama critic for AP, 1960-78. Contbr. to periodicals. Served to lt. (j.g.) U.S. Maritime Service, 1943-45. Mem. N.Y. Drama Critics Circle (pres.), New Drama Forum, N.Y. Acad. Scis., Phi Beta Kappa, Sigma Delta Chi. Clubs: The Players (N.Y.C.), Overseas Press (N.Y.C.); N.Y. Press.

GLOVSKY, SUSAN G. L., lawyer; b. Boston, Apr. 16, 1955; d. Leonard B. and Marilyn S. (Shapiro) Loitherstein; m. Steven M. Glovsky, May 25, 1980; 1 child, Lowell Eliott. BS in Chemistry, U. Vt., 1977; JD, Boston U., 1980. Bar: Mass. 1980, Mich. 1980, U.S. Dist. Ct. (ea. dist.) Mich. 1980, U.S. Patent Office 1981, N.Y. 1982, U.S. Dist. Ct. Mass. 1982, U.S. Ct. Appeals (1st cir.) 1982, U.S. Ct. Appeals (fed. cir.) 1991, U.S. Supreme Ct. 1995. Assoc. Levin, Levin, Garvett & Dill, Southfield, Mich., 1980-81, Ladas & Parry, N.Y.C., 1981-82, Dahlen & Gatewood, Boston, 1982-83; ptnr. Dahlen & Glovsky, Boston, 1983-85; pvt. practice Boston and Salem, Mass., 1985-93; of counsel Hamilton, Brook, Smith & Reynolds, Lexington, Mass., 1993-97; prin. Hamilton, Brook, Smith & Reynolds, Lexington, 1998—; adj. prof. Suffolk U. Law Sch. Mem. ABA (litigation sect.), Mass. Bar Assn., Boston Bar Assn., Boston Patent Law Assn. (past pres., chmn. litigation com. 1989—), Am. Arbitration Assn. (panel arbitrators 1985—). Jewish. Avocations: swimming, skiing. Home: 131 Federal St Salem MA 01970-3242 Office: Hamilton Brook Smith & Reynolds 2 Militia Dr Lexington MA 02421-4799

GLOWER, DONALD DUANE, university executive, mechanical engineer; b. Shelby, Ohio, July 29, 1926; s. Raymond W.W. and Irva (Scheerer) G.; m. Betty Stahl, June 18, 1953; children: Donald, Michel, Leilani, Jacob. BS, U.S. Mcht. Marine Acad., 1946, Antioch Coll., 1953; MS, Iowa State U., 1958, PhD, 1960; M of Pub. Svc., U. Rio Grande, 1992. Engring. officer Grace Lines, Inc., San Francisco, 1947-49; research engr. Battelle Meml. Inst., Columbus, Ohio, 1953-54; asst. prof. Coll. Engring., Iowa State U., 1954-58, 60-61; mem. research staff Sandia Corp., Albuquerque, 1961-63; head radiation effects dept. Gen. Motors Corp., Milw., 1963-64; prof., chmn. dept. mech. and nuclear engring. Ohio State U., 1964-76, dean Coll. Engring., 1976-90, v.p. univ. com. and devel., 1990-92; Honourable prof. Xidian U., Xian, China, 1992; bd. dirs. Micrys Inc., Internat. Techne Group Inc., Superconductive Components, Inc., Transp. Rsch. Ctr. of Ohio; mem., vice chmn. Ohio Power Siting Bd., 1990; mem. Internat. Cons. Bd. S.E. U., Nanjing, China, 1991. Author: Graphical Theory and Application, 1957, Basic Drawing and Projection, 1957, Working Drawings and Applied Graphics, 1957, Experimental Reactor Analysis and Radiation Measurements, 1965. Bd. dirs. Indsl. Tech Enterprise Bd. Ohio, 1982-89, Orton Found., 1976-90; trustee U. Rio Grande. Recipient Outstanding Bus. Achievement award U.S. Mcht. Marine Acad., 1961; Outstanding Profl. Achievement award Iowa State U., 1979; spl. citation Ohio Senate and Ho. of Reps., 1985; named Tech. Person of Yr., Columbus Tech. Council, 1986. Fellow Am. Nuclear Soc.; fellow ASME; mem. Am. Soc. Engring. Edn. (Donald E. Marlowe award 1987), Ohio Acad. Sci., Argonne Univs. Assn., Sigma Xi, Tau Beta Pi, Texnikoi.

GLOWER, RAPHAEL, personnel management administrator, program analyst; b. San Salvador, El Salvador, Apr. 13, 1958; s. Stanley and Yolanda (Valencia) G. Cert. handicapped asst., Montgomery Coll., 1984; BA in Philosophy and Bus. Adminstrn., Gallaudet U., 1987. Mgmt. asst. Fed. Bur. Prisons Dept. Justice, Washington, 1986-87; govtl. affairs specialist Nat. Industries for the Severly Handicapped, Vienna, Va., 1987-89; investigator, reviewer Office Pers. Mgmt. and Office Fed. Investigation, Washington, 1989; pers. mgmt. specialist Office Pers. Mgmt., Washington, 1989-91; program analyst Dept. Transp., Washington, 1991—; instr. Am. sign lang., Bethesda, 1988—; gov.'s appointee Md. State Planning Coun. Devel. Disabilities, 1990-91, mem. com. pub. policies; mem. Adv. Com. Employees with Disabilities, 1989-91. Vol. worker with mentally retarded persons various agys. including St. John's Child Devel. Ctr., 1981-88; Stephens minister 4th Presbyn. Ch., Bethesda, 1988-90, moderator Victory Fellowship, 1987-88; mem. Teen Missions Internat., 1978—. Named one of Outstanding Young Men of Am., Jaycees, 1989. Mem. Wings of Eagles Inc. (founder, pres. 1993—), Am. Polit. Sci. and Politics Assn., Am. Soc. Assn. Execs., Alpha Phi Omega. Republican. Avocations: reading and writing philosophy and theology, ch. activities, swimming, jogging. Home: 4300 Saul Rd Kensington MD 20895-3729

GLOWINSKI, ROLAND, mathematics educator; b. Paris, Mar. 9, 1937; s. Nathan and Anna (Cukiernik) G.; m. Angela Rimok, Nov. 3, 1963; children: Anne, Tania. B, Ecole Polytechnique, Paris, 1960; M, Ecole Nationale Supérieure des Télécommunications, Paris, 1963; PhD, U. Paris, 1971. Registered profl. engineer; cert. prof. math. Rsch. engr. Office de Radio et Télévision Françaises, Paris, 1963-68, Institut National de Recherches en Informatique et Automatique, Paris, 1968-70; prof. U. Paris VI, 1970—, chmn. math dept., 1981-85; Disting. prof. U. Houston, 1985—; adj. prof. Rice U., Houston, 1986—; Sherman Fairchild Disting. visitor Calif. Inst. Tech., 1988-89; cons. CNET, Paris, 1968-85, Sci. Rsch. Coun., London, 1978-81; bd. dirs. Electricite de France, Paris, 1990-96, U. Leonardo da Vinci, Paris; dir. Centre Européen de Recherches et de Formation Avancée en Calcul Scientifique, Toulouse, France, 1992-94. Lt. France Signal Corps, 1958-61. Decorated officer Nat. Merit, knight Order of Acad. Palms, knight Order Legion of Honor, France; recipient Cray prize Selected Jury, Paris, 1988, Marcel Dassault prize French Nat. Acad. Scis., 1996, Zienkiewicz Disting. lectureship, 1999, IMA, 1999, others. Mem. Soc. for Indsl. and Applied Math., Am. Math. Soc., French Acad. Scis. (correspondent 1987), Academia Europea (London). Office: U Houston Dept Math 4800 Calhoun Rd Dept Math Houston TX 77004-2610

GLOYD, LAWRENCE EUGENE, diversified manufacturing company executive; b. Milan, Ind., Nov. 5, 1932; s. Oran C. and Ruth (Baylor) G.; m. Delma Lear, Sept. 10, 1955; children: Sheryl, Julia, Susan. BA, Hanover Coll., 1954. Salesman Shapleigh Hardware, St. Louis, 1956-60, W. Bingham Co., Cleve., 1960-61; salesman Amerock Corp., Rockford, Ill., 1961-68, regional sales mgr., 1968-69, dir. consumer products mktg., 1969-71, dir. merchandising, 1971-72, dir. mktg. and sales, 1972-73, v.p. mktg. and sales, 1973-81, exec. v.p., 1981-82, pres., gen. mgr., 1982-86; v.p. Hardware Products Group, Anchor Hocking Corp., Lancaster, Ohio, 1983-86; COO CLARCOR, Rockford, Ill., 1986-88, pres., CEO, 1986-95, chmn. bd., CEO, 1995—, also bd. dirs.; bd. dirs. AMcore Fin. Inc., Rockford, Thomas Industries Inc., Louisville, Woodward Gov. Co., Rockford, Ill.; past. chmn. bd. trustees Rockford Coll.; bd. dirs., past chmn. SwedishAm. Corp. Past chmn. bd. dirs. Coun. of 100; bd. dirs. Ill. Coun. on Econ. Edn.; nat. bd. dirs. Big Bros./Big Sisters. Mem. Am. Hardware Mfrs. Assn., Ill. Mfrs. Assn., Nat. Assn. Mfrs., Hardware Group Assn., Pres. Assn., Masons. Republican. Office: CLARCOR PO Box 7007 2323 S 6th St Rockford IL 61104-7117

GLOYNA, EARNEST FREDERICK, environmental engineer, educator; b. Vernon, Tex., June 30, 1921; s. Herman Ernst and Johanna Bertha (Reithmayer) G.; m. Agnes Mary Lehman, Feb. 17, 1946; children: David Frederick, Lisa Anna. BS in Civil Engring., Tex. Technol. U., 1946; MS in Civil Engring., U. Tex., 1949; Dr. Engring., Johns Hopkins U., 1953. Registered profl. engr.; diplomate environ. engring. Jr. engr. Tex. Hwy. Dept., 1945-46; office engr. Magnolia Petroleum Co., 1946-47; instr. civil engring. U. Tex., Austin, 1947-49, asst. prof., 1949-53, assoc. prof., 1953-59, prof., 1959-70, Joe J. King prof. engring., 1970-82, dir. Environ. Health Engring. Labs., 1954-70, dir. Ctr. for Research in Water Resources, 1963-73, dean Coll. Engring., 1970-87, dir. Bur. Engring. Research, 1970-87, Bettie Margaret Smith chair in environ. engring., 1987—; cons. on water and wastewater treatment and water resources, 1947—; dir. Parker Drilling Co.; cons. numerous industries, WHO, World Bank, U.S. Air Force, U.S. Army, U.S. Senate, fgn. cities and govts; mem., past chmn. sci. adv. bd. EPA; chmn. various coms. NRC, Nat. Acad. Sci., Nat. Acad. Engring.; chmn. Tex. State Bd. Registration Profl. Engrs., 1992-93. Author: Waste Stabilization Ponds, 1971 (also French and Spanish edits), (with Joe O. Ledbetter) Principles of Radiological Health, 1969; Editor: (with W. Wesley Eckenfelder, Jr.) Advances in Water Quality Improvement, 1968, Water Quality Improvement by Physical and Chemical Processes, 1970, (with William S. Butcher) Conflicts in Water Resources Planning, 1972, (with Woodson and Drew) Water Management by Electric Power Industry, 1975, (with Malina and Davis) Ponds as a Wastewater Treatment Alternative, 1976, (with Richard B. McCaskill) Commitment to Excellence, 1990; contbr. numerous articles to profl. jours. Served with Corps Engrs. AUS, 1942-46, ETO, lt. col. Ret. Named Disting. Engr. Grad. Tex. Tech. U., 1971, Disting. Alumnus, 1973, Disting. Engring. Grad. U. Tex., Austin, 1982, Disting. Alumnus, 1992, Disting. Alumnus Johns Hopkins U., 1993; recipient Joe J. King award U. Tex., Austin, 1982; EPA regional environ. educator award, 1977, Nat. Environ. Devel. award, 1983, Sci. award Nat. Wildlife Fedn., 1986, Order of Henri Pittier, Nat. Conservation medal Venezuela, 1983, Gabriel Narutowicz medal, Republic of Poland, 1993. Fellow ASCE (Hon. Mem. award, Meritorious Paper award Tex. sect. 1968, Award of Honor Tex. sect. 1985, Simon W. Freese environ. engr. award 1986); mem. NAE (past councilman), NSPE (past dir., Steinman medal 1970, NSPE award 1994), AIChE, Assn. Environ. Engring. Profls. (past pres.), Am. Soc. for Engring. Edn. (Centennial Medallion award 1993), Am. Water Works Assn. (life, water resources divsn. award 1959), Am. Acad. Environ. Engrs. (diplomate, past pres., Gordon Maskew Fair award 1982), Water Environ. Fedn. (life, past pres., hon. mem., Harrison Prescott Eddy medal 1959, Gordon Maskew Fair award 1982, Arthur Bedell award 1991), Tex. Soc. Profs. Engrs. (pres. 1986, Engr. of Yr. award Travis chpt. 1972, Award of Honor 1985, Engr. of Yr. 1994), Southwestern Soc. Nuclear Medicine (hon.), Nat. Acad. Engring. Mex. (fgn. corr. mem.), Nat. Acad. Scis. Venezuela (fgn. corr.), Soc. Mexicana de Aguas (Jack Huppert award), Sigma Xi, Tau Beta Pi, Chi Epsilon, Phi Kappa Phi, Pi Epsilon Tau (hon.), Omicron Delta Kappa. Clubs: Cosmos (Washington), Headliners, Rotary. Office: U Tex Coll of Engring C E Dept Austin TX 78712

GLUBE, CONSTANCE RACHELLE, Canadian chief justice; b. Ottawa, Ont., Can., Nov. 23, 1931; d. Samuel and Pearl (Slonemsky) Lepofsky; m. Richard Hillard Glube, July 6, 1952 (dec.); children: John B., Erica D. Glube Kolatch, Harry S., B. Joseph. BA, McGill U., Montreal, Can., 1952; LLB, Dalhousie U., Halifax, Can., 1955, LLD (hon.), 1983; LLD (hon.), Mount St. Vincent U., Halifax, Can., 1998. Bar: N.S. 1956, created queen's counsel, 1974. Assoc. Kitz, Matheson, Halifax, 1964-66; ptnr. Fitzgerald & Glube, Halifax, 1966-68; sr. solicitor City of Halifax, 1969-74, city mgr., 1974-77; puisne judge Supreme Ct. of N.S., Halifax, 1977-82; chief justice Supreme Ct., Halifax, 1982-98, Nova Scotia, 1998—, Ct. Appeals, 1998—; vice chair Can. Judges Conf., 1978-82; mem. adv. council Family Mediation Can., 1985—; interim bd. dirs. Nat. Jud. Centre, 1987; bd. dirs. Nat. Jud. Inst., 1998—. Contbr. articles and papers to profl. publs. Co-chair Can. Coun. Christians and Jews; hon. chair N.S. divsn. Can. Mental Health Assn., 1984—; bd. dirs. Halifax Heritage Found., 1984-95. Recipient award of merit City of Halifax, 1977, Frances Fish award, 1997, N.S. Women Lawyers Achievement award. Mem. Can. Bar Assn., Can. Jud. Coun. (exec. com., chmn. edn. com. 1986-88, adminstrn. of justice com. 1992-94, equality com. 1994—, jud. benefits com. 1994—). Jewish. Avocations: swimming, gardening. Home: 5920 Inglewood Dr, Halifax, NS Canada B3H 1B1

GLUCK, ANDREW LEE, vocational economic analyst, counselor, philosopher; b. N.Y.C., Mar. 21, 1944; s. Irving and Rhoda (Ross) G.; m. Denise Bernard, Mar. 18, 1968; children: Aaron, Max, Sarah. BA in Econs. and Philosophy, U. Fla., 1965; MA in Religion and Edn., Columbia U., 1972, MEd in Counseling Psychology, 1977, EdD in Philosophy and Edn., 1997; MS in Mgmt., NYU, 1990. Cert. rehab. counselor. Counselor Tchrs. Coll., Columbia U., N.Y.C., 1971-72; caseworker N.Y.C. Housing and Devel. Adminstrn., 1972-76; psychologist N.Y. State Dept. Mental Health, Wingdale, 1977-78; vocat. rehab. counselor N.Y. State Edn. Dept., Hempstead, 1978-89; coord. vocat. and ednl. programs N.Y. Assn. for New Ams., N.Y.C., 1989-92; vocat. econ. analyst Vocat. Econ. Inc., Louisville, 1993-97, sr. analyst, 1997—; lectr. Bramson ORT Tech. Inst., N.Y.C., 1994—; adj. faculty Berkeley Coll., N.Y.C., 1997—, Empire State Coll., SUNY, N.Y.C., 1998—, Hofstra U., 1999—; presenter in field; adj. prof. Hofstra U., 1998—. Editl. bd. reviewer The Jour.: Counseling and Values; contbr. articles to profl. jours. Mem. ACA, Am. Philos. Assn., Am. Law and Econs. Assn., Nat. Assn. Forensic Econs. Republican. Jewish. Avocations: dogs, horses, traveling, bicycling. Home: 284 Route 27B Hudson NY 12534-3919 Office: Vocat Econs Inc 150 Broadway New York NY 10038-4381

GLUCK, CAROL, history educator; b. Newark, Nov. 12, 1941; d. David E. and Doris S. Newman; m. Peter L. Gluck, May 1, 1966; children: Thomas Edward, William Francis. Student, U. Munich, 1960-61, U. Tokyo, 1972-74; BA, Wellesley Coll., 1962; MA, Columbia U., 1970, PhD, 1977. Asst. prof. Columbia U., N.Y.C., 1975-83, assoc. prof., 1983-86, prof., 1986-88, George Sansom prof. history, 1988—; vis. rsch. assoc. faculty law Tokyo U., 1978-79, 85-86, 92; vis. prof. Harvard U., Cambridge, Mass., 1991, Inst. Social Sci. Tokyo U., 1993, Ecole des Hautes Etudes en Scis. Sociales, Paris, 1995, 98; mem. publs. bd. Columbia U. Press, N.Y.C., 1991-96; co-dir. project on Asia in the core Curriuculm NEH, N.Y.C., 1987—; mem. Am. adv. com. Japan Found., 1986-96, chairperson, 1991-96; disting. lectr. N.E. Area Coun., 1988, Japan Soc. for Promotion of Sci., 1989. Author: Japan's Modern Myths, 1985 (Fairbank prize 1986, Trilling award 1987); co-editor: Showa: The Japan of Hirohito, 1992, Asia in Western and World History, 1997; mem. adv. bd. Jour. Japanese Studies, 1989—; contbr. numerous articles to profl. publs. Mem. com. on rsch. librs. N.Y. Pub. Libr., 1987—, mem. humanities adv. coun., 1996—; mem. Coun. on Fgn. Rels., U.S.-Japan Friendship Commn., 1994—. Woodrow Wilson Found. fellow; Fulbright grantee, 1985-86; Japan Found. grantee; Fgn. Area fellow. Fellow Am. Acad. Arts and Scis.; mem. Am. Hist. Assn. (coun. 1987-90), Assn. Asian Studies (coun. 1981-84, nominating com. 1985-86, v.p. 1995-96, pres. 1996-97, past pres. 1997-98), Japan Soc. (bd. dirs. 1990—), Asia Soc. (trustee 1992—), Phi Beta Kappa. Home: 440 Riverside Dr New York NY 10027-6828 Office: Columbia U East Asian Inst 420 W 118th St New York NY 10027-7213

GLÜCK, LOUISE ELISABETH, poet; b. N.Y.C., Apr. 22, 1943; d. Daniel and Beatrice (Grosby) G.; m. Charles Hertz (div.); 1 child, Noah Benjamin; m. John Dranow, 1977 (div.). Student, Sarah Lawrence Coll., 1962, Columbia U., 1963-65; LLD, Williams Coll., 1993, Skidmore Coll., 1995, Middlebury, 1996. Vis. poet Goddard Coll., U. N.C., U. Va., U. Iowa; Elliston prof. U. Cin., 1978; vis. faculty Columbia U., 1979; faculty M.F.A. program Goddard Coll., also Warren Wilson Coll., Swannanoa, N.C.; Holloway lectr. U. Calif., Berkeley, 1982; vis. prof. U. Calif.-Davis, 1983; Scott prof. poetry Williams Coll., 1983, faculty, 1984—, Preston Parrish 3d century prof., 1997—; Regents prof. poetry UCLA, 1985-88; vis. prof. Harvard U., 1995; Hurst prof. poetry Brandeis U., 1996; delivered Phi Beta Kappa poem harvard U. commencement, 1990; baccalaureate spkr. Williams Coll; Hopwood lectr. U. Mich.; spl. cons. Libr. Congress, 2000. Author: Firstborn, 1968, The House on Marshland, 1975, Descending Figure, 1980, The Triumph of Achilles, 1985, Ararat, 1990, The Wild Iris, 1992 (Pulitzer Prize for poetry 1993), Proofs and Theories (collected essays), 1994, Meadowlands, 1996, Vita Nova, 1999. Grantee Rockefeller Found., Nat. Endowment for Arts, 1969-70, 79-80, 88-89, Guggenheim Found., 1975-76, 87-88, NEA, 1988-89; recipient lit. award Am. Acad. and Inst. Arts and Letters, 1981, award in poetry Nat. Book Critics Cir., 1985, Melville Cane award Poetry Soc. Am., 1986, Sara Teasdale Meml. prize Wellesley Coll., 1986, Bobbitt Natil prize Libr. Congress, 1992, Pulitzer prize 1996, William Carlos Williams award, 1993, PEN/Martha Albrand award Non-Fiction, 1995; named Poet Laureate of Vt., 1994. Fellow Am. Acad. Arts and Scis.; mem. Am. Acad. Arts & Letters, Am. Acad. Vt. Poets (chancellor 1999—), Phi Beta Kappa (hon.).

GLUCKSBERG, SAM, psychology educator; b. Montreal, Que., Can., Feb. 6, 1933; came to U.S., 1945; s. Murray and Sonia (Afrin) G.; children: Matthew, Kenneth, Nadia Glucksberg. BS, CCNY, 1956; PhD, NYU, 1960. Instr. NYU, N.Y.C., 1958-60; chair psychology dept. Princeton (N.J.) U., 1974-80, from instr. to prof., 1963—; cons., Princeton, 1980—. Author: Psychology, 5th edit., 1991; editor Jour. Exptl. Psychology: Gen., 1984-89; author 100 sci. articles and book chpts. Capt. U.S. Army, 1958-63. Fellow APA (pres. div. exptl. psychology 1988-89), AAAS, Soc. Exptl. Psychologists (sec.-treas. 1987-90), Am. Psychol. Soc. Avocations: music, theater, cooking. Home: 29 Bainbridge St Princeton NJ 08540-3901 Office: Princeton U Dept Psychology Princeton NJ 08544-1010

GLUCKSTEIN, FRITZ PAUL, veterinarian, biomedical information specialist; b. Berlin, Jan. 24, 1927; came to U.S., 1948; s. Georg Jakob and Hedwig Emilie (Heinrich) G.; m. Ethel Gold, July 31, 1955 (dec. Nov. 1993); 1 child, Ruth; m. Maran Ostchega, Nov. 29, 1996. BS, U. Minn., 1953, DVM, 1955; MLS, U. Md., 1984. Diplomate Am. Coll. Vet. Preventive Medicine. Vet. meat insp. U.S. Dept. Agr., South St. Paul, Minn., 1955-56; asst. vet. pathologist U.S. Dept. Agr., Ames, Iowa, 1958-59; vet. analyst U.S. Dept. Agr., Washington, 1959-63; chief microbiology br. Sci. Info. Exchange Smithsonian Instn., Washington, 1963-66; coordinator for vet. affairs Nat. Library of Medicine, Bethesda, Md., 1966-93; biomed. info. cons., 1993—; mem. coordinating com. for research animal resources NIH, 1982-93; adv. sci. bd. Gorgas Meml. Inst. Tropical Preventive Medicine, Washington, 1967-70; chmn. continuing edn. com. 1989-90. Author: (annotated bibliography) Laboratory Animal Welfare, 1984-93; contbr. chpts. to books. Served to 1st lt. U.S. Army, 1956-58; commd. officer USPHS, 1966-93. Recipient cert. merit U.S. Dept. Agr., 1962. Fellow Royal Soc. Health (London); mem. AVMA, APHA, Assn. Mil. Surgeons of U.S., Am. Assn. Lab. Animal Sci., Am. Soc. Lab. Animal Practitioners, Med. Libr. Assn., Beta Phi Mu. Avocation: music. Home: 11801 Rockville Pike Apt 812 Rockville MD 20852-2723

GLUCKSTERN, ROBERT LEONARD, physics educator; b. Atlantic City, N.J., July 31, 1924. BEE, CCNY, 1944; PhD, MIT, 1948. Asst. prof. physics Yale U., New Haven, Conn., 1950-57, assoc. prof., 1957-64; prof. physics U. Mass., Amherst, 1964-75; head dept. U. Mass., 1964-69, assoc. provost, 1969-70, provost, vice chancellor for acad. affairs, 1970-75; prof. physics U. Md., College Park, 1975-97, chancellor, 1975-82, sr. rsch. scientist, 1997—; vis. prof. U. Tokyo, Japan, 1969; cons. on theory of high energy particle accelerators Brookhaven Nat. Lab., Fermi Nat. Accelerator Lab., Los Alamos Nat. Lab., Stanford Linear Accelerator Ctr. With USNR, 1944-46. AEC fellow U. Calif., Berkeley, 1948-49, Cornell U., Ithaca, N.Y., 1949-50, Yale fellow, 1961-62. Fellow AAAS, Am. Phys. Soc.; mem. SSC (bd. overseers 1990-93), SURA (trustee 1982-98, chmn. bd. trustees 1994-96, high energy physics adv. panel 1990-93), Fedn. Am. Scientists, Am. Assn. Physics Tchrs. Office: U Md Physics Dept College Park MD 20742

GLUECK, SYLVIA BLUMENFELD, writer; b. Tulsa, Dec. 23, 1925; d. Maurice and Sina (Turk) Blumenfeld; m. Norton Shushan Glueck, June 15, 1947; children: Nancy Eisen, Milton Glueck. BJ, U. Mo., Columbia, 1949. Publicity dir. Sta. WDSU, New Orleans, 1946-47; advt. copywriter Swiftway Direct Mail, New Orleans, 1961; freelance writer and author New Orleans and San Antonio, 1965—. Author book, 1990; contbr. fiction articles to mags. and newspaper features, 1984-85, 90 (Golden Pro award 1986). Mem. AAUW, Women in Communication, Mensa. Home and Office: 309 W Magnolia Ave Apt 1 San Antonio TX 78212-3216

GLUSBAND, STEVEN JOSEPH, lawyer; b. Berlin, Jan. 15, 1947; came to U.S., 1949; s. Morris and Docia (Waitman) G.; m. Roberta Gail Jacobs, Nov. 22, 1981; children: Ilana, Jonathan. BBA, CCNY, 1969; JD, Fordham U., 1973; LLM, NYU, 1978. Bar: N.Y. 1974, U.S. Dist. Ct. (so. dist.) N.Y. 1974, U.S. Ct. Appeals (2nd cir.) 1974. Trial atty. SEC, N.Y.C., 1974-75, spl. trial counsel, 1976-77; assoc. Sage Gray Todd & Sims, N.Y.C., 1977-80, ptnr., 1981-87; ptnr. Carter, Ledyard & Milburn, N.Y.C., 1987—; dir. MER Telemanagement Solutions Ltd. Mem. ABA (com. fed. regulation of securities, securities litigation), Assn. of Bar of N.Y.C. (com. on futures regulation 1986-88). Home: 343 E 30th St New York NY 10016-6417 Office: Carter Ledyard & Milburn 2 Wall St Fl 13 New York NY 10005-2072

GLUSHIEN, MORRIS P., lawyer, arbitrator; b. Bklyn., Oct. 15, 1909; s. Isaac and Minnie (Hoffman) G.; m. Anne Williams, Nov. 18, 1945; children: Minna Taylor, Ruth Wedgwood. A.B. with honors, Cornell U., 1929, J.D. with honors, 1931. Bar: N.Y. 1932, U.S. Supreme Ct. 1940. Pvt. practice Bklyn., 1932-38; mem. faculty Cornell Law Sch., 1938-39, New Sch. for Social Rsch., 1977-78; chief U.S. Supreme Ct. sect., assoc. gen. counsel NLRB, 1939-47; gen. counsel Internat. Ladies Garment Workers Union, AFL-CIO, 1947-72; arbitrator, 1972—, spl. master fed. ct., 1976-78; mem. Nat. Acad. Arbitrators; mem. arbitration panels Am. Arbitration Assn., Fed. Mediation and Conciliation Service, various state and city agys. Editorial bd.: Cornell Law Quar, 1930-31; Contbr. legal periodicals. Bd. dirs. Nat. Legal Aid and Defender Assn., 1954-72. Served with AUS, as cryptanalyst, 1942-45. Mem. ABA (past chmn. labor law sect.), N.Y. State Bar Assn. (labor rels. com.), Assn. of Bar of City of N.Y. (past chmn. com. labor and social security legis.), Indsl. Rels. Rsch. Assn., Practicing Law Inst., Am. Jewish Congress (com. law and social action), Am. Judicature Soc., AFL-CIO (past mem. nat. legis. coun.), Civil Svc. Reform Assn. (exec. com.), N.Y. Com. for Modern Cts. (past v.p., bd. dirs.), Nat. and N.Y. State Against Discrimination in Housing Coms., ACLU (com. free speech and assn.), Ams. for Dem. Action, NYU Conf. on Labor, Curia, Phi Beta Kappa, Phi Kappa Phi. Home: Westwood Plaza, Rm 206 2228 Westwood Blvd Los Angeles CA 90064

GLUSHKO, GAIL MARIE, physician, military officer; b. Griffiss AFB, N.Y., Apr. 22, 1960; d. Wasil and Mary Patricia (Hanchowsky) G.. BA, Miami U., Oxford, Ohio, 1982; MD, Wright State U., 1993. From cashier to asst. mgr. Scarff's Garden Ctr., New Carlisle, Ohio, 1983-85; intelligence rsch. specialist Fgn. Tech. Divsn., Wright Patterson AFB, Ohio, 1985-89; commd. U.S. Army, 1989, advanced through grades to maj.; resident in internal medicine William Beaumont Army Med. Ctr., Ft. Bliss, Tex., 1993-96, army physician; staff internist U.S. Army Aeromed. Ctr., Ft. Rucker, Ala., 1996-99, flight surgeon, 1998-99; fellow in allergy and immunology Walter Reed Army Med. Ctr., Washington, 1999—. Contbr. articles to profl. jours. Mem. ACP, AMA, AAAS, Assn. Mil. Surgeons U.S., So. Med. Assn., N.Y. Acad. Scis., Phi Sigma (treas 1981-82), Phi Rho Sigma. Russian Orthodox. Avocations: running, gardening, auto mechanics, most sports. Office: US Army Aeromed Ctr Dept Internal Medicine Fort Rucker AL 36362

GLUSKER, JENNY PICKWORTH, chemist; b. Birmingham, Eng., June 28, 1931; came to U.S., 1955, naturalized, 1977; d. Frederick Alfred and Jane Wylie (Stocks) P.; m. Donald Leonard Glusker, Dec. 18, 1955; children: Ann, Mark John, Katharine. BA in Chemistry, Oxford U. (Eng.), 1953, MA, 1957, DPhil, 1957, DSc (hon.), Coll. of Wooster, Ohio, 1985. Postdoctoral research fellow Calif. Inst. Tech., Pasadena, 1955-56; research fellow Inst.

Cancer Research, Phila., 1956, research assoc., 1957-67, asst. mem., 1967, assoc. mem., 1967-79, sr. mem., 1979—; adj. prof. U. Pa.; mem. U.S. Nat. Com. for Crystallography, 1974-90, sec.-treas., 1977-79, chmn., 1982-84; mem. internat. adv. bd. Molecular Structures in Biology, 1991; vis. fellow Oriel Coll., Oxford, Eng., 1994-95; vis. prof. Internat. Union Crystallography, Egypt, 1997, Natl. Inst. Health, Biophysics chem., A Study Sect., 1972-76; Biotech. Res. Review Com., 1977-80 (chmn. 1979-80); Metallo biochem. Study Sect., 1983-87, Divn. rsch. Grants Adv. Com., 1989-92, Rsch. Res. COunc., 1995-99, governing bd. mem., Cambridge Structural Database, Cambridge, UK, 1988—, vice chmn., 1998—, Computer Graphics Lab. Adv. Com., U. Calif., San Francisco, 1985—, chmn., 1988—; cons. and lectr. in field. Mem. Am. Assn. Cancer Research, The Chem. Soc., Am. Soc. Biol. Chemists, Biophys. Soc., AAAS, Am. Crystallog. Assn. (pres. 1979, Pub. Svc. award 1991, Fankuchen Meml. award, 1995), Am. Chem. Soc. (Phila. sect award 1978, Garvan medal 1979), Am. Phys. Soc., Sigma Xi. Author: (with K.N. Trueblood) Crystal Structure Analysis: A Primer, 1972, 2d edit., 1985; (with Dodson, Ramaseshan, and Venkatesan) The Collected Works of Dorothy Crowfoot Hodgkin; editor: Structural Crystallography in Chemistry and Biology; Structures of Molecules of Biological Interest, 1981; Crystallography in North America, 1982, Aspects of Crystallography in Molecular Biology, S. Parthasarathy and J.P. Glusker, 1997; Acta Crystallographica sect. D, Biological Crystallography, (with M. Lewis, M. Rossi) Crystal Structure Analysis for Chemists and Biologists, 1994; co-editor: Acta Crystallographica, 1987, Patterson and Pattersons, 1987; mem. editorial bd. Biophys. Jour., 1981-86; mem. editorial adv. bd. Accounts of Chem. Research, 1982-87; mem. internat. adv. bd. Molecular Structures in Biology, 1991; contbr. articles to profl. jours. Home: 1011 Anna Rd Huntingdon Valley PA 19006-8610 Office: Inst Cancer Rsch Philadelphia PA 19111

GLUSMAN, DAVID H., healthcare consultant; s. Jack A. and Miriam P. (Pinkser) G.; m. Janis F. finkel, June 27, 1971; children: Sharon, Brian. BS, Pa. State U., 1971. CPA, Pa. Staff acct. Laventhal & Horwath, Phila., 1971-75; contr. Panelrama, Inc., Ardmore, Pa., 1975-76; mgr. Harry K. Cohen & Co., Phila., 1976-77, Silver & Co., Bala Cynwyd, Pa., 1977-80; ptnr. Shotz, Miller & Glusman, Phila., 1980-97, BDO Siedman, LLP, Phila., 1997—; editl. advisor CPA Health Niche Advisor, San Diego, 1997—, CPA Litigation Advisor, San Diego, 1985-92. Internat. treas. Juvenline Diabetes Found., N.Y.C., 1983-86, internat. v.p., 1986-98, chmn., Phila., 1991-94; trustee Main Line Reform Temple Beth Elohim, Wynnewood, Pa., 1997—. Named Vol. of Yr., Juvenile Diabetes Found., Phila., 1997. Avocations: scuba diving, bike riding, photography. Fax: (215) 636-5799. E-mail: dglusman@bdo.com. Home: 540 Putnam Rd Merion Station PA 19066-1021 Office: BDO Seidman LLP 1700 Market St 29th Fl Philadelphia PA 19103

GLUSMAN, DAVID HOWARD, accountant; b. Phila., July 3, 1949; s. Jack A. and Miriam D. (Pinsker) G.; m. Janis Lynn Finkel; children: Sharon, Brian. BS, Penn State U., 1971. CPA, N.J., Pa. Staff acct. Laventhal & Horvath, Phila., 1971-74; asst. contr. Panelrama Corp., Ardmore, Pa., 1974-75; sr. acct. Harry K. Cohen & Co., Phila., 1975-77; mgr. Silver & Co., 1977-80; owner, ptnr. Miller, Glusman, Footer & Magarick P.C., Phila., 1980-97; ptnr., dir. healthcare adv. svcs. Mid-Atlantic region BDO Seidman, LLP, Phila., 1997—, dir. forensic and litigation support svcs., 1997—. Editorial adv. bd. The Health Niche Advisor, 1987—; contbr. articles to profl. jours. Bd. dirs., dir. Jewish Fedn., Phila., 1989-95; v.p. Juvenile Diabetes Found. Internat., 1986-89, treas., 1983-86, chmn. of bd. Phila. chpt., 1991-95, v.p., 1995—; apptd. to Pa. Diabetes Task Force, 1991-95; expert witness Chester County Pa. Ct., 1993, Fed. Dist. Ct., Phila., 1993. Mem. Am. Inst. CPAs, Pa. Inst. CPAs, Internat. Assn. Fin. Planning, Inst. Bus. Appraisers, Inc. Avocations: skiing, scuba diving, bike riding. Office: BDO Seidman LLP 29th Fl 1700 Market St Philadelphia PA 19103

GLUYS, CHARLES BYRON, retired marketing management consultant; b. Richmond, Ind., Apr. 16, 1928; s. J. Howard and Reba Anna (Macy) G.; children: Gary William, Robert Lee, Marcia Kay, James Duke. BS in Indsl. Econs., Purdue U., 1955. Sales mgr. Carlyle Constrn., Columbus, Ohio, 1958; asst. product mgr. Palmer-Donavin Mfg., Columbus, 1958-61; new product mgr. KCL Corp., Shelbyville, Ind., 1963-64; prin. Gluys & Assocs., Greenfield, Ind., 1964—. Asst. scoutmaster Boy Scouts Am., Greenfield, 1953-54, Columbus, 1958-60, chmn. orgn. and extension com., Columbus, 1960-61; vol. counselor Small Bus. Adminstrn., 1976—. Mem. Am. Mktg. Assn. (bd. dirs. 1970-73), Inventor's Assn. Ind. (1st. v.p. 1986), Entrepreneur's Alliance, Assn. Indsl. Advertisers (treas. 1971-72). Club: Venture of Ind. Lodge: Masons.

GLYNN, CARLIN (CARLIN MASTERSON), actress; b. Cleve., Feb. 19, 1940; d. Guilford Cresse and Lois Carlin (Wilks) G.; m. Peter Masterson, Dec. 29, 1960; children: Carlin Alexandra, Mary Stuart, Peter C.B. Student, Sophie Newcomb Coll., 1957-58. Prof. Columbia U. Grad. Film Sch., N.Y.C.; prof. MFA program Actors Studio at New Sch. for Social Rsch.; creative advisor Sundance Inst. Film Lab. Appeared in N.Y. as Miss Mona in: The Best Little Whorehouse in Tex., 1978-80; in London, 1981; starred in Pal Joey, Goodman Theatre, Chgo., 1988 (Joseph Jefferson award 1988), Cover of Life, Am. Place Theatre, N.Y., 1994, The Young Man from Atlanta, Signature Theatre Co., 1995 (Pulitzer prize for drama 1995), Amazing Grace, 1998, The Chemistry of Change, 1999; films include Three Days of the Condor, 1974, Resurrection, 1978, Continental Divide, 1981, Sixteen Candles, 1984, The Trip to Bountiful, 1985, Blood Red, Night Game, Convicts, 1989, blessing, 1992, Judy Berlin, 1997, Committed, 1999; TV series Mr. President, 1987; dir. short film Love Divided By, 1993. Recipient Theatre World award, 1978, Antoinette Perry award, 1979, best actress award in musical Soc. West End Theatres, Lawrence Olivier award, London, 1981. Mem. SAG, AFTRA, Actor's Studio (former exec. chair bd. dirs.), Actors' Equity Assn. Episcopalian. *

GLYNN, EDWARD, college dean; b. Cleve., Jan. 16, 1941; s. Edward Joseph and Francis (Nantell) G.; married. Diploma in art, Cooper Sch. Art., Cleve., 1968; BFA, Columbus Coll. Art and Design, 1970; MFA, So. Ill. U., 1973. Gallery dir., instr. Cooper Sch. Art, 1973-76, Cleve. State U., 1976-79; head dept. 2-dimensional art Lake Erie Coll., Painesville, Ohio, 1979-84; exec. dir. Western Res. Sch. Art, Madison, Ohio, 1985-88; pres. Md. Coll. Art and Design, Silver Spring, 1989-92, dean acad. affairs, 1992-98; exhbn. specialist Md. Nat. Capital Park and Planning Commn., 1998—. 16 one-man shows, 1973-89. Pres. Arts Coun. Montgomery County; active Corp. Vol. Coun., Montgomery County, Md., 1990—. With USN, 1958-62. Mem. Arts Coun. Montgomery County, Montgomery County C. of C., Silver Spring C. of C.

GLYNN, PETER ALEXANDER RICHARD, hospital administrator; b. Toronto, Ont., Can., Oct. 14, 1944; s. John Richard Lewis and Jessie Mackenzie (Dalziel) G.; m. Arlene Dawne Whalen, Aug. 13, 1966; children: Jennifer Dawne, Jeffrey Alexander. B Engring., Royal Mil. Coll., Kingston, Ont., 1965; MASc, U. Waterloo, Ont., 1967, PhD, 1972. Dir. dept. continuing edn. Province of Saskatchewan, Regina, Can., 1975-80, exec. dir. prescription drug plan, 1980-81; assoc. dep. minister Province of Saskatchewan, Ministry of Health, Regina, Can., 1981-84; asst. dep. minister Can. Health and Welfare, Ottawa, Ont., 1984-91; pres., CEO Kingston Gen. Hosp., Kingston, Ont., 1991—. Capt. Can. Army, 1961-69. Recipient Special Recognition award Can. Cancer Soc., 1991, Alumni Achievement medal U. Waterloo, 1998. Avocations: bicycling, camping, canoeing. Office: Kingston Gen Hosp, 76 Stuart St, Kingston, ON Canada K7L 2V7

GLYNN, ROBERT, lawyer, foundation chairman; b. N.J., Oct. 30, 1929; 1 child., Katherine F.J. Glynn. BA, Harvard U., 1951, LLB, 1956. Staff atty. Internat. Fin. Corp., Washington, D.C., 1961-65; ptnr. Fox, Glynn & Melamed, N.Y., 1968-87, Becker, Glynn, Melamed & Muffly LLP, N.Y., 1987—; chmn. bd. dirs. and dir. gen. Lampadia Found., 1993—. Office: Becker Glynn Melamed & Muffly LLP 299 Park Ave Fl 16 New York NY 10171-0002

GLYNN, ROBERT D., JR., energy-based holding company; b. Orange, N.J., 1942. BSME, Manhattan Coll.; MS in Nuclear Engring., L.I. U.; postgrad., U. Mich., Harvard U. With L.I. Lighting Co.; officer, prin. Woodward Clyde Cons.; with PG&E Corp., San Francisco, 1984—, CEO, pres., 1997, chmn. bd., 1998—; chmn. bd. dirs. Pacific Gas and Electric Co. subs. PG&E Corp.; bd. dirs. URS Corp. Bd. govs. San Francisco Symphony. Office: PG&E Corp Spear Tower Ste 2400 One Market St San Francisco CA 94105

GNAEDINGER, JOHN PHILLIP, structural engineer, consultant; b. Oak Park, Ill., Jan. 11, 1926; s. Robert Joseph and Edna Mary (Metz) G.; m. Elizabeth Williams, Mar. 15, 1956; children: John Phillip Jr., Sarah Gnaedinger Booras. BCE, Cornell U., 1946; MCE, Northwestern U., 1947. Registered profl. engr., Ariz., Calif., Conn., D.C., Georgia, Ill., Ind., Iowa, Kan., Kty., Mich., Minn., Mo., Nev., N.J., N.Y., N.C., N.D., Ohio, S.D., Vt., Va., Washington, Wis.; registered structural engr., Ill. Structural engr. Shaw Metz-Dolio, Chgo., 1946-49; founder, pres. Soil Testing Svcs., Inc., Evanston and Northbrook, Chgo., 1948-91, J.P. Gnaedinger Rsch. Corp., Glenview, Ill., 1991—; chmn. emeritus STS Cons., Ltd., Vernon Hills, Ill., 1991—; lectr. China Coal Mine Design Inst., 1984; arch.-engr., mem. adv. bd. Performance Info. Ctr. Contbr. articles to profl. jours.; patentee in field. Creator Careers for Youth; mediation, arbitration Sys. Resolving Disputes. Recipient Merit award Northwestern U., 1966, Quarter Century award BRAB, 1977, John F. Parmer award Structural Engrs. Assn. Ill., 1978. Fellow ASCE (chmn. std. com. on shore protection systems, std. com. on ind. project peer rev., std. com. on design and analysis nuclear safety-related earth structures, Chgo. Civil Engr. of Yr. award 1979), Assn. Soil and Found. Engrs. (founder, past pres.); mem. NAS (past chmn. bldg. rsch. adv. bd.), ASTM (past sec., hon. mem. D-18), Western Soc. Engrs. (past pres., hon.), Chgo. Assn. Technol. Socs. (past pres.), Ill. Soc. Profl. Engrs., Ill. Engring. Coun., Econ. Club Chgo., Chief Execs. Orgn. Republican. Avocations: tennis, bassoonist, golf. Home: 2020 Chestnut Ave Apt 501 Glenview IL 60025-1651 Office: STS Cons Ltd 750 Corporate Woods Pkwy Vernon Hills IL 60061-3153

GNAT, RAYMOND EARL, librarian; b. Milw., Jan. 15, 1932; s. John and Emily (Syperko) G.; m. Jean Helen Monday, June 19, 1954; children—Cynthia, Barbara, Richard. B.B.A., U. Wis., 1954, postgrad., 1959; M.S., U. Ill., 1958; M.P.A., Ind. U., Indpls., 1981. Page Milw. Pub. Library, 1950-53, jr. librarian, 1954, librarian, 1958-63; circulation asst. U. Ill., 1956-57, serials cataloger, 1957-58; asst. dir. Indpls.-Marion County Pub. Library, 1963-71, dir., 1972-94; Exec. dir. Ind. Nat. Library Week, 1965. Served with AUS, 1954-56. Mem. ALA, Ind. Library Assn. (pres. 1980), Bibliog. Soc. Am. Clubs: Literary, The Portfolio. Home: 8246 Shadow Cir Indianapolis IN 46260-2761

GNEHM, EDWARD W., JR., ambassador; b. Nov. 10, 1944; s. Edward Sr. and Beverly (Thomasson) G.; m. Margaret Scott, June 13, 1970; children: Cheryl Lynn, Edward William III. BA, George Washington U., 1966, MA, 1968; postgrad., Am. U., Cairo, 1966-67. Head U.S. liaison office Dept. of State, Riyadh, Saudia Arabia, 1976-78; dep. chief of mission Am. Embassy Dept. of State, Sanaa, Yemen, 1978-81; dir. jr. officer div. pers. Dept. of State, Washington, 1982-83, dir. secretariat staff, 1983-84, dir. gen. fgn. svc., dir. personnel, 1997—; dep. chief mission Am. Embassy Dept. of State, Amman, Jordan, 1984-87; dep. asst. sec. def. for Near East and South Asia Dept. of Def., 1987-89, dep. asst. sec. state Bur. Near East and South Asian Affairs, 1989-90, U.S. amb. to Kuwait, 1990-94, dep. U.S. Permanent Rep. to UN, 1994-97; dir.-gen. of fgn. service, dir. personnel U.S. Dept. of State, Washington, 1998—. Trustee George Washington U.; mem. 4th Presbyn. Ch., Bethesda, Md. Mem. Omicron Delta Kappa, Sigma Chi. Avocations: history, cycling, stamps. Office: M/DgP Room 6218 Dept of State Washington DC 20520-3505

GNICHTEL, WILLIAM VAN ORDEN, lawyer; b. Summit, N.J., Jan. 11, 1934; s. William Stone and Edith Parrot (Van Orden) G.; m. Emily Hopkins Martenet, July 11, 1959 (dec.); children: William Van Orden Jr., Edwin Martenet; m. Mary B. Gayley, June 7, 1996. BA, Trinity Coll., 1956; LLB, Columbia U., 1959. Bar: N.Y. 1961, Mass. 1997. Ptnr. Whitman & Ransom, N.Y.C., 1968-88; resident ptnr. Whitman & Ransom, Saudi Arabia, 1980-85; ptnr. Chadbourne & Parke, N.Y.C., 1988-92; spl. counsel Law Firm of Salah Al-Hejailan, Riyadh, Saudi Arabia, Saudi Arabia, 1986-95; lectr. in field. Contbr. articles to profl. jours. Mem. ABA, Assn. of Bar of City of N.Y., Union Club, Knickerbocker Club, Somerset Club (Boston), Onteora Club (Tannersville, N.Y.; exec. vp. 1974-75, pres. 1976-77, bd. dirs. 1970-77), Masons, Somerset Club (Boston), Phi Delta Phi. Episcopalian. Address: PO Box 431 Lincoln MA 01773-0431

GNIEWEK, RAYMOND LOUIS, newspaper editor; b. Freeport, N.Y., Sept. 3, 1947; s. Edward George and Jane (Park) G.; m. Noreen Ann Kopenhaver, July 28, 1984; 1 child, Edmond Louis; children by previous marriage: Brett Elizabeth, Jared Michael. BA, NYU, 1969; BS, SUNY, Brockport, 1980. News editor Rochester (N.Y.) Dem. and Chronicle, 1981-82; page one editor USA Today, Arlington, Va., 1982-89, sr. editor, 1989—. Author computer program P.C. News Layout, 1985. With U.S. Army, 1970-73, Vietnam. Decorated Bronze Star. Office: USA Today 1000 Wilson Blvd Ste 600 Arlington VA 22209-3905

GO, MARILYN D., federal judge; b. 1950. BA, Radcliffe Coll., 1973; JD, Harvard U., 1977. Bar: Pa. 1977, N.Y. 1978. Law clk. to Hon. William M. Marutani, Pa. Ct. Common Pleas, Phila., 1977-78; asst. U.S. atty. for ea. dist. N.Y., U.S. Dept. Justice, Bklyn., 1978-82; ptnr. Baden Kramer Huffman Brodsky & Go, N.Y.C., 1982-92; magistrate judge for ea. dist. N.Y., U.S. Magistrate Ct., Bklyn., 1993—. Office: US Magistrate Ct 225 Cadman Plz E Brooklyn NY 11201-1818

GO, ROBERT A., management consultant; b. July 29, 1955; s. Michael and Sabina (Tan) G. BS, U Detriot, 1977; MBA, U. Santa Clara, 1981. Ptnr. Deloitte & Touche (formerly Touche Ross & Co.), Detroit, 1977—; Contbr. articles to profl. jours. Mem. Health Care Fin. Mgt. Assn., Am. Hosp. Assn., Renaissance Club. Office: Deloitte & Touche 600 Renaissance Ctr Fl 10 Detroit MI 48243-1804

GOAD, DANNY HARLAN, industrial engineer; b. July 15, 1961. BS in Mech. Engring., Va. Tech. U., 1989; MBA, Coll. William and Mary, 1993. Engr. Newport News (Va.) Shipbuilding, 1989-96, Hoechst Celanese, Narrows, Va., 1996-98; prodn. supt. Indsl. Mfg., Albany, Ga., 1998—. Address: 539 N Westover Blvd Apt 1821 Albany GA 31707-1993

GOBAR, ALFRED JULIAN, economic consultant, educator; b. Lucerne Valley, Calif., July 12, 1932; s. Julian Smith and Hilda (Millbank) G.; B.A. in Econs., Whittier Coll., 1953, M.A. in History, 1955; postgrad. Claremont Grad. Sch., 1953-54; Ph.D. in Econs., U. So. Calif., 1963; m. Sally Ann Randall, June 17, 1957; children—Wendy Lee, Curtis Julian, Joseph Julian. Asst. pres. Microdot Inc., Pasadena, 1953-57; regional sales mgr. Sutorbilt Corp., L.A., 1957-59; market research assoc. Beckman Instrument Inc., Fullerton, 1959-64; sr. marketing cons. Western Mgmt. Consultants Inc., Phoenix and L.A., 1964-66; ptnr., prin., chmn. bd. Darley/Gobar Assocs., Inc., 1966-73; pres., chmn. bd. Alfred Gobar Assocs., Inc., Placentia, Calif., 1973—; asst. prof. finance U. So. Calif., L.A., 1963-64; assoc. prof. bus. Calif. State U., L.A., 1963-68, 70-79, assoc. prof. Calif. State U.-Fullerton, 1968-69; mktg., fin. adviser 1957—; bd. dirs. Quaker City Bancorp, Inc.; pub. speaker seminars and convs. Contbr. articles to profl. publs. Trustee Whittier Coll., 1992—. tee Whittier Coll., 1992—. Home: 1100 W Valencia Mesa Dr Fullerton CA 92833-2219 Office: 721 W Kimberly Ave Placentia CA 92870-6343 *I try not to be too quick to cast aside the social protocal that has taken centuries to evolve and test in order to define effective behavior.*

GOBEL, JOHN HENRY, lawyer; b. Oak Park, Ill., Oct. 21, 1926; s. Henry Andrew and Mary Ann (Coughlan) G.; m. Carol Zvara, Mar. 8, 1969; children: Kristina, Gregory. B.A. cum laude, DePaul U., 1950, J.D. cum laude, 1952. Bar: Ill. 1951, Md. 1975, Ohio 1976. Various positions law dept. Chgo. and North Western R.R. Co., Chgo., 1952-60, Balt. and Ohio R.R. Co., Balt., 1960-75; asst. gen. counsel Chesapeake and Ohio Ry. Co., Cleve., 1975-77, gen. solicitor, 1977-80, gen. counsel, 1980-82; v.p. govt. relations CSX Corp., Cleve., 1982-86; v.p., regional trial counsel CSX Transp., 1987. Served with U.S. Army, 1945-46. Fellow Internat. Soc. Barristers; mem. ABA (spl. com. on rules 1967-71), Ill. Bar Assn. (chmn. profl. ethics com., mem. assembly 1973-74), Nat. Assn. R.R. Trial Counsel (nat. sec. 1971-75), Soc. Trial Lawyers Ill. (dir. 1968-70), Ohio C. of C. (bd. dirs.), Ohio Pub. Expenditures Council (v.p. 1979-88), Ohio R.R. Assn. (chmn. 1979-87), W.Va. R.R. Assn. (chmn. 1975-87). Clubs: Union League (Chgo.), Law (Chgo.).

GOBELI, VIRGINIA C., national program leader; b. Providence, R.I., July 14, 1942; d. Albert and Claire Estelle (Plante) Ouellette; m. Garrett Frederick Gobeli, Aug. 17, 1974; children: Gayla Elizabeth, Gregory Alfred. BA, Salve Regina U., 1964; MA, U. R.I., 1972; EdD, Boston U., 1989. Dietetic internship N.Y. Hosp. - Cornell Med. Ctr.; adminstrv. dietitian N.Y. Hosp. - Med. Ctr., 1965-67; ext. home economist Cooperative Ext. U. of R.I., Kingston, 1967-69; dairy food publicist Am. Dairy Assn., Springfield, 1969-72; state 4-H leader, home economics Cooperative Ext./U. Mass., Amherst, 1972-73; 4-H youth devel. specialist Cooperative Ext./U. Nev., Reno, 1973-81, Cooperative Ext./U. Nebr., Lindoln, 1983-90; youth devel. cons. Cooperative Ext., U. Mass., 1987; cons. FAO/UN, Rome, 1995; amb. tng. Nat. 4-H Conf., Washington, 1981-84. Contbr. articles to profl. jours. Mem. Fine Arts Bd., U. Nev., Reno, 1978-90, Glucester Hist. Soc., R.I., 1981-83; bd. dirs. Cajir/Consejo Asesor Internat. de la Juventud Rural. Mem. Nat. Assn. Ext. 4-H Agts. (Disting. Svc. award 1978, 25 Yr. Svc. award 1998), Assn. Leadership Educators, Soc. for Internat. Devel., Epsilom Sigma Phi (team award 1986). Avocations: handcrafts, needlecrafts, cooking, travel, reading. Office: Families 4-H Nutrition/USDA Stop 2225 1400 Independence Ave SW Washington DC 20250-0002

GOBER, HERSHEL W., government official; b. Monticello, Ark., Dec. 21, 1936; m. Mary Lou Keener. With USMC, 1956-59; with U.S. Army, 1961, advanced through grades to maj., 1978, ret., 1978; supr., dir. N.W. Alaska Pipeline Corp., 1978-83; instr. Jr. Reserve Officers Tng. Corps., Ark.; dir. Ark. Vets. Child Welfare Svc., Ark. Dept. Vets. Affairs, 1988-93; dep. sec. Dept. Vets. Affairs, Washington, 1993—. Decorated numerous military awards. Mem. Am. Legion (adj.). Office: Dept of Veterans Affairs Office of the Secretary 810 Vermont Ave NW Washington DC 20420-0002*

GOBIE, HENRY MACAULAY, philatelic researcher, retired postal executive; b. Bellows Falls, Vt., May 10, 1911; s. Philip Henry and Susan Viorene (Shaw) G.; m. Wilhelmina McGrath, July 17, 1933; children: Jacqueline A. Gobie Ekholm, Kathryn E. Gobie Vowell. Grad. high sch., Miami, Fla., 1929. Spl. delivery messenger U.S. Postal Svc., Miami, 1929-35, postal clk., 1935-43, various supervisory positions to asst. gen. supt. mails, 1943-66, ret.; stockbroker Goodbody & Co., South Miami, Fla., 1967-70; bd. dirs. Am. Philatelic Soc., State College, Pa., 1981-82; pres. Fla. Fedn. Stamp Clubs, 1986-87. Author: The Speedy, 1976 (Am. Philatelic Soc. Gold medal 1976), U.S. Parcel Post, 1979 (Am. Philatelic Soc. Gold medal, 1979).; contbr. articles to various philatelic pubs. Recipient Luff award for rsch. Am. Philatelic Soc., 1987, also 9 Grand awards, 6 Res. Grand awards for 4 different U.S. stamp collections nat. exhbns. Episcopalian. Home: 463 Las Cruces Winter Haven FL 33884-1704

GOBLE, ALAN KEITH, psychology educator; b. Salisbury, N.C., July 19, 1965; s. Paul C. and Kaye F. (Warren) G.; m. Lisa A. Pratt, July 26, 1986; 1 child, Megan Edana. BA in Psychology, U. N.C., 1987, PhD in Psychology, 1993. Post-doctoral rsch. assoc. Princeton U., 1993-95; asst. prof. psychology Bennett Coll., Greensboro, N.C., 1995—. Contbr. articles to profl. jours. Morrison scholar U. N.C., Chapel Hill, 1983-87; Minority Biomed. Rsch. Support grantee Nat. Inst. of Gen. Med. Svcs./NIH, 1997—. Mem. Am. Psychol. Soc. (charter), Acoustical Soc. Am. (tech. com. mem.), N.C. Acad. Scis., Psychonomic Soc. (assoc.), Sigma Xi. E-mail: goble@bennett1.bennett.edu. Office: Bennett College Box 23 900 E Washington St Greensboro NC 27401-3239

GOBLE, PAUL, author, illustrator, artist; b. Haslemere, Eng., Sept. 27, 1933; s. Robert John and Elizabeth Marian (Brown) G.; m. Janet A. Tiller, June 2, 1978; 1 son, Robert George; children by previous marriage: Richard, Julia. Nat. Diploma in Design with distinction, Central Sch. Art and Design, London, 1959. Vis. lectr. indsl. design Central Sch. Art and Design, London, 1960-68; sr. lectr. indsl. design Ravensbourne Coll. Art and Design, London, 1968-77. Author, illustrator numerous children's books including: Custer's Last Battle, 1969, The Fetterman Fight, 1972, Lone Bull's Horse Raid, 1973, The Friendly Wolf, 1974, The Girl Who Loved Wild Horses, 1978 (Caldecott medal), The Gift of the Sacred Dog, 1980, Star Boy, 1983, Buffalo Woman, 1984, The Great Race, 1985, Death of the Iron Horse, 1987, Her Seven Brothers, 1988, Iktomi and the Boulder, 1988, Beyond the Ridge, 1989, Iktomi and the Berries, 1989, Dream Wolf, 1990, Iktomi and the Ducks, 1990, Iktomi and the Buffalo Skull, 1991, I Sing for the Animals, 1991, Crow Chief, 1992, Love Flute, 1992, The Lost Children, 1993, Iktomi and the Buzzard, 1994, Adopted by the Eagles, 1994, Hau Kola—Hello Friend, 1994, The Return of the Buffaloes, 1996, Remaking the Earth, 1996, The Legend of the White Buffalo Woman, 1998, Iktomi and the Coyote, 1998, Iktomi Loses His Eyes. Fellow Royal Soc. Arts, Soc. Indsl. Artists and Designers. *I have felt the pull of the Native American tradition as long as I can remember, probably since the time my mother read to me stories of Grey Owl and Ernest Thompson Seton. As I grew up in England, I read everything I could lay my hands on about Indians. It was the books concerning the wisdom of Black Elk which finally determined my life's orientation.*

GOBLE, ROBERT THOMAS, planning consultant; b. Newton, N.J., Feb. 6, 1947; s. Harold Kenneth and Elizabeth (Snook) G.; m. Camilla Jane Cordray, June 6, 1968; children: Erin Lee, Carrie Elizabeth. BFA, Ohio U., 1969; M Urban Planning, U. Ill., 1971. Research asst. Bur. Urban and Regional Research, Urbana, Ill., 1970-71; sr. planner Dallas Planning Dept., 1971-72; asst. dir. planning Wilbur Smith & Assocs., Columbia, S.C., 1973-75; prin. Carter Goble Assocs. Inc., Columbia, 1975—, also bd. dirs.; bd. dirs. Columbia Leasing, Inc., CGA Facilities, Inc., St. Johns Devel. Corp., Harbison New Town Fin. Bd.; planner projects in 48 states and 4 countries. Chmn. adv. com. S.C. Outdoor Recreation Planning Council, Columbia, 1977-78, Leadership Columbia Com, 1982-83, chmn. Gov.'s Com. on Jobs and Econ. Devel., Columbia, 1982; chmn. bd. Children's Bur. S.C., Columbia, 1985-86. Mem. Am. Planning Assn., Am. Inst. Cert. Planners, Nat. Acad. Scis. (transportation rsch. bd., chmn. rural transp. com. 1983-88, chmn. sect. G com. 1988-89, group 1 coun. 1989-93, com. on transit mgmt. and performance 1993—, com. intermodal transfer facilities 1998—), Nat. Sheriff's Assn., Am. Jail Assn., Am. Correctional Assn., Nat. Juvenile Detention Assn., Columbia World Affairs Coun., Palmetto Conservation Found. (founding mem., chmn. bd. dirs.). Palmetto Trails (bd. dirs.). Presbyterian. Avocations: scuba diving, sailing, golf, fishing. Office: Carter Goble Assocs 1619 Sumter St Columbia SC 29201-2821

GOCHBERG, THOMAS, real estate investor, financial executive; b. Boston, Jan. 18, 1939; s. Hyman and Lee (Goredetsky) G.; m. Leatrice Eckber, Mar. 28, 1965; children: John, Sarah. AB, Columbia U., 1961. Pres., CEO Smith Barney Real Estate Corp., N.Y.C., 1969-84; dir. Smith Barney, Inc., N.Y.C., 1980-84; pres., CEO Security Capital Corp., N.Y.C., 1978-90, dir., 1978—; chmn. Benjamin Franklin Savs. Assn. 1985-89, dir. 1981-89; chmn. Foster Mortgage Co., 1985-89, dir. 1981-89; pres., sole shareholder TJG Holdings Inc., 1991—; prin. TGM Assocs., L.P., 1991—; pres., dir. TGM Realty Corp. I, II, III, IV, V, VI, VII, X, XX, XXX, 1993—. Trustee Birch Wathan Sch. N.Y.C., 1980-88, South Street Seaport Mus., N.Y.C., 1992—, co-chair waterfront com., 1995-98, co-chair devel. com., exec. com.; trustee, treas. Nat. Maritime Hist. Soc., 1990-92; bd. dirs. Am. Sail Tng. Assn., 1994—, exec. com., chmn. devel. com., 1996-98, vice chair, 1999—; v.p. Rep. County Com. of N.Y., 1985-95; bd. assocs. The Whitehead Inst. Biomed. Rsch., 1995—. With U.S. Army, 1960-63. Mem. Pension Real Estate Assn. (pres. 1982—, chmn. 1984-85), N.Y. Yacht Club (seamanship com. 1995—, membership com. 1998—), Univ. Club (N.Y.C.), Royal Western Yacht Club Eng., Ocean Cruising Club Eng., Cruising Club Am. (treas. N.Y. sta. 1996—). Jewish. Home: 791 Park Ave New York NY 10021-3551 Office: TGM Assocs 650 5th Ave Fl 28 New York NY 10019-6108

GOCHNAUER, ELISA ANNE, marketing executive; b. Bellefonte, Pa., Sept. 4, 1960; d. Theodore Frank and Doris Lee (Smith) Schneider; m. Dean Joe Gochnauer, Apr. 23, 1994; 1 child, Sarah Anne Gochnauer, Dec. 26, 1996. Student, Shippensburg U., 1978-80; BA, Millersville U., 1982. Cert. nursing asst., Pa. Sales svc. coord. Fleur de Lait Foods, Ltd., New Holland, Pa., 1982-87; sales adminstr. Northfield Specialty Foods, Lancaster, Pa., 1987-88; mktg. asst. Charles Chips Corp., Lancaster, 1988-89, dir. mktg. svcs., 1989-93; with inside sales R/W Connection, Lancaster, 1994; mktg.

lessons with Heinrich von Herzogenberg whom she followed to Berlin. She went to England in 1909 and received an honorary D.Mus. from Durham University in 1910, Oxford in 1926 and St. Andrews University in 1928. She was the first woman composer to have an opera performed at Covent Garden with her *The Wreckers* in 1910 and in 1922 she was made a Dame of the British Empire. She was a militant leader of the suffragette movement and imprisoned for two months as a result of this involvement. She composed *March of the women* which became the battle song of the Women's Social and Political Union of which she was an avid supporter and the story is that she conducted fellow suffragettes in this march with a toothbrush from her cell window. She later felt that any neglect of her work was due to prejudice against women. DISCOGRAPHY. PHOTOGRAPH.

Compositions
ORCHESTRA
> Concerto for violin and horn (also as Horn concerto) (London: Curwen, 1927)
> Anthony and Cleopatra, overture (1890)
> March of the women (Curwen, 1911)
> Serenade in D-Major (1890)
> Suite for strings (1891) (Leonard)

CHAMBER
> The dance and chrysilla (fl, hp, tri, tam and strs) (1909)
> Quintet, op. 1 (2 vln, vla and 2 vlc) (Leipzig: Peters 1884)
> Six quartets
> String quartet in E-Minor (Vienna, 1914)
> Piano trio (incomplete) (ca. 1880)
> String trio (1880)
> Trio (vln, hn and pf) (1927)
> Two trios (vln, ob and pf) (Curwen, 1927)
> Two interlinked French folk melodies (from Entente Cordiale) (fl, ob and cl) (OUP, 1929)
> Sonata (vln and pf) (1887)
> Sonata in A-Minor (vlc and pf) (1887)
> Violin sonata in A-Minor (1887)

PIANO
> Prelude and fugue (1887)
> Sonata in D, in 2 mvts
> Suite
> Two sonatas (1887)
> Variations (1887)
> Incomplete pieces

ORGAN
> Chorale prelude on an Irish air (1939)
> Five short chorale preludes, Nos. 1, 3, 4 and 5 (also strs; also solo insts) (1913)

VOCAL
> The song of Love, op. 8, cantata (solos, ch and orch) (1888)
> Hey nonny no (ch and orch) (1910)
> Sleepless dreams (ch and orch) (1926)
> A spring canticle (ch and orch) (1926)
> Three Anacreontic odes (vce and orch) (1909)
> Three moods of the sea (m-S or bar and orch)
> The prison (ch a-cap) (1930)
> Soul's joy (ch a-cap) (1923)
> Three songs of sunrise (ch a-cap) (1911)
> Bonny sweet Robin, variations (fl, ob and pf) (1928)
> Chrysilla (m-S or Bar)
> Wood spirits' song
> Songs

SACRED
> Mass in D-Major (solos, ch and orch) (Novello, 1893)

OPERA
> The Boatswain's Mate (1916)
> Der Wald (1902)
> Entente Cordiale (1923)
> Fantasio (1898)
> Fête galante, a dance-dream (1923)
> The Forest (1901)
> On the Cliffs of Cornwall
> The Wreckers (Strandrecht, original title Les Naufrageurs) (1906, rev 1939)

Publications
> *As Time went-on*. London and New York, 1935.
> *Beecham and Pharaoh*. London, 1935.
> *Female Pipings in Eden*. London, 1934.
> *A Final Burning of Boats*. London and New York, 1928.
> *Impressions That Remained*. 2 vols. London and New York, 1919; Da Capo, 1945.
> *Maurice Baring*. 1937.
> *Streaks of Life*. London and New York, 1921.
> *A Three-legged Tour in Greece*. London, 1927.
> *What Happened Next*. London and New York, 1940.

Bibliography
> Beecham, T. *Dame Ethel Smyth (1858-1944)*. In ML (1958).
> Dale, K. *Dame Ethel Smyth*. In ML (1944).
> Dale, K. *Ethel Smyth and Prentice Work*. In ML (1949).
> *Le donne compositrici*. Musica d'oggi 4 (1922): 14.
> *Famous Women Composers*. Etude April 1917: 237-238.
> Hurd, M. *Dame Ethel M. Smyth*. In MGG 12 (1965).
> St. John, Christopher. *Ethel Smyth: A Biography*. Additional chapters by V. Sackville West; K. Dale. London and New York, 1959.
> Ref. 2, 6, 9, 14, 15, 17, 20, 22, 23, 41, 44, 70, 74, 85, 86, 89, 96, 100, 105, 108, 141, 149, 165, 177, 189, 226, 260, 276, 284, 295, 297, 307, 322, 335, 361, 398, 415, 433, 477, 488, 563, 572, 609, 612, 622, 637, 645, 646, 653

SNEED, Anna (Mrs. Cairn)
19th-century American composer.
Compositions
VOCAL
> Songs incl.:
> Break, break o sea

Ref. 226, 276, 433

SNELL, Lillian Lucinda
American pianist, saxophonist, trombonist and composer. b. Dexter, May 15, 1873. Her teachers include Professor Fowler, Carter, Greenley and Leonard. She was the assistant director of the Dexter orchestra club and organized Snell's band and orchestra.
Compositions
VOCAL
> Songs incl.:
> Just for tonight

Ref. 374

SNELREWAARD-BOUDEWIJNS, Nelly. See LINDEN-VAN SNELREWAARD-BOUDEWIJNS, Nelly van der

---

SNIFFIN, Allison
20th-century American pianist and composer.
Compositions
VOCAL
> Now I lay (with everywhere around) (S and pf) (1985)
> Six significant landscapes (W. Stevens) (S and pf) (1985)

THEATRE
> Lunar Baedeker (singing actor, cl and perc) (1985)

Ref. AMC newsletter 1985

SNIZKOVA-SKRHOVA, Jitka
Czech pianist, professor, writer and composer. b. Prague, September 14, 1924. She studied the piano under Jan Herman, S. Sima and O. Kredba at the Masters' School of the Prague Conservatory in 1948, composition under Alois Haba and privately under K. Hofmeister and F. Spilka. At the philosophical faculty of Charles University she studied musicology, aesthetics and Czechoslovak literature. She appears in concerts and recitals and is particularly interested in Czech music from the 15th to the 17th-centuries. She is a professor at Prague Conservatory. PHOTOGRAPH.
Compositions
ORCHESTRA
> Small sinfonietta (cham orch) (1957)
> Interludes (fl and str orch) (1958)
> Two overtures (cham orch) (1959)

CHAMBER
> Chora (str qrt) (1966)
> String quartet No. 1 (1948)
> String quartet No. 2 (1953)
> String quartet No. 3 (1956)
> Laconic concertino (pf, fl and perc) (1965)
> Satiticon (fl, d-b and pf) (1967)
> Tercet (fl, d-b and pf) (1967)
> Trio (fl, ob and hp) (1955)
> Trio inquietto (fl, ob and bsn) (1962)
> Trio ritmico (vln, vlc and pf) (1961)
> Inquiette (fl and pf) (1966)
> Inventions (fl and ob) (1972)
> Pascua (ob and pf) (1974)
> Suite (fl and hpcd)
> Sonata (vla and pf) (1947, rev 1963)
> Sonata (vlc and pf) (1958)
> Sonatina (fl and pf) (1957)
> Dance compositions (pentatonic) (hp) (1944)
> Epithalamia (fl) (1970)
> Gothic dream, 20 etudes (hp) (1944)
> The mosaics, cycle (hp)

SMITH, Margit

20th-century American composer. b. Germany. She is a resident of the Ivory Coast and the United States and composes music incorporating the use of exotic wind, string and percussion instruments. She composes with Marrie Bremer (q.v.) using both old and modern instruments but their music is firmly rooted in tradition. DISCOGRAPHY.
Compositions
CHAMBER
  Traject I (org, baroque and Peruvian fl)
  Traject II (org, 2 African fl, gemshorn, shakuhachi, b-fl, Nepalese and Thai fl)
  Chroai (chin, hpcd, pf and kayagum)
  Elevensevenseven (kayagum and Renaissance b-fl)
ORGAN
  Maqam
  Mobile
  Ombre
Ref. 563

SMITH, Mary Barber

Canadian composer of English origin. b. 1878. She lived in Edmonton and composed organ pieces and vocal works.
Ref. 133

SMITH, May Florence

19th-century American writer and composer. She composed songs and sacred music.
Publications
  A key to perfect reading or Transposition studies at a glance.
Ref. 276, 347, 433

SMITH, Mrs. Gerrit (Eva Munson)

American lecturer, singer and composer. b. Monkton, VT, July 12, 1843. After school she became the head of the music department of Otoe University, Nebraska City.
Compositions
PIANO
  Home sonata
VOCAL
  Songs incl.:
  Joy (1868)
  Woodland warbling
Ref. 226, 276, 433

SMITH, Nellie von Gerichten

American composer. b. 1875.
Composition
OPERA
  The Twins of Bistritz
Ref. 307

SMITH, Nettie Pierson

19th-century American composer.
Compositions
VOCAL
  Songs incl.:
  'Neath the lilies sleeping
  We meet no more
Ref. 276, 292, 347, 433

SMITH, Rosalie Balmer

19th-century American musician and composer.
Compositions
VIOLIN
  Romanza
  Sonatas
Ref. 276, 347, 433

SMITH, Ruby Mae

American artist, authoress, publisher, teacher and composer. b. Joplin, MO, March 20, 1902. She teaches the piano, the guitar, the organ and singing and leads her vocal quartet 'Ruby Smith and The Rubytones.' She is owner and president of Rubytone Record and Publishing Co., Portland, OR.

Compositions
VOCAL
  That beautiful city
  The bells
  Hard luck blues
  Worth more than gold
  Rise or fall
SACRED
  The Lord will come
  When Jesus shall come
Ref. 39, 646

SMITH, Selma Moidel

American violinist, lawyer and composer. b. Warren, OH, April 3, 1919. She studied the violin and theory at the Hollywood Conservatory from 1930 to 1935 and then studied at the University of California, Los Angeles, the University of Southern California and the Pacific Coast University where she obtained her LI.B. She studied the piano both privately and at UCLA. PHOTOGRAPH.
Compositions
PIANO
  Pieces incl.:
  Bagatelle, op. 111 (1967)
  Barcarole (1956)
  Beguine in A-Minor (1960)
  Beguine in F-Minor (1953)
  Bolero in A-Minor (1959)
  Caravan (1955)
  Dark waltz (1957)
  El argentino (1966)
  Espana antigua (1956)
  The Great Wall of China (1955)
  Melody in D-Minor (1954)
  Mission of the Orient (1957)
  Nocturne, op. 136 (1982)
  Nocturne in A-Minor, op. 132 (1972)
  Nocturne in C-Minor, op. 3 (1953)
  Nocturne in G-Minor (1959)
  Oracion de un torero (1959)
  Prelude in C-Minor (1954)
  Reflections, op. 26 (1955)
  Reverie (1958)
  Tango in A-Minor (1953)
  Tango in B-Minor, op. 6 (1954)
  Tango in C-Minor, op. 20 (1955)
  Tango in D-Minor, op. 4 (1954)
  Tango in F-Minor, op. 124 (1968)
  Tango in G-Minor (1954)
  Waltz in B-Minor (1977)
  Waltz in C-Minor, op. 17 (1954)
  Waltz in G (1958)
  Waltz in G-Minor, op. 68 (1959)
Publications
  The American Composer; Classics West. February, 1972.
Ref. composer, 475

SMITH, Sharon

20th-century Canadian composer.
Compositions
ORCHESTRA
  Raining heart (1980)
CHAMBER
  Buque (cl) (1981)
  Kaya (fl) (1980)
  Piano pieces (1975-1978)
Ref. Assoc. of Canadian Women Composers

SMITH, Zelma

20th-century American composer.
Composition
OPERA
  The Gallant Tailor
Ref. 141

SMYSLOVA, Natalia Nikolayevna. See LEVI, Natalia Nikolayevna

SMYTH, Ethel Mary, Dame

English pianist, conductor, writer and composer. b. London or Kent, April 23, 1858; d. Woking, Surrey, May 8, 1944. She was a pupil of composer, Colonel Ewing and studied for a short while at the Leipzig Conservatory under Carl Reinecke and S. Jadassohn in 1877 where she took private asst. Red Rose Transit Authority, Lancaster, 1995-96, mgr. mktg., 1996-97; mktg. asst. Turkey Hill Dairy, Conestoga, pa., 1997—. Republican. Lutheran. Avocations: pets, gardening, music. Home: 748 Lawrence Blvd Lancaster PA 17601-1418 Office: Turkey Hill Dairy River Rd Conestoga PA 17516

GOCKE, DAVID JOSEPH, immunology educator, physician, medical scientist; b. Fairmont, W.Va., June 10, 1933; s. Charles and Josephine G.; m. Barbara Donohoe, Apr. 12, 1958; children: Christopher, Susan, John, Gregory, Patricia, Robert, Mary Anne, Meghan. Ed., St. Vincent's Coll., Latrobe, Pa., 1954; M.D., U. Pa., 1958. Diplomate Am. Bd. Internal Medicine, Am. Bd. Allergy and Immunology. Intern Columbia-Presbyn. Hosp., N.Y.C., 1958-59; asst. resident Columbia-Presbyn. Hosp., 1959-60, program dir. clin. research center, 1971-73; fellow in microbiology Johns Hopkins Sch. Medicine, Balt., 1960-63; from asst. prof. to assoc. prof. medicine Columbia U. Coll. Physicians and Surgeons, N.Y.C., 1963-73; prof. medicine and microbiology, chief div. immunology and infectious disease Robert Wood Johnson Med. Sch., Rutgers U., New Brunswick, N.J., 1973-77, 78—, dean med. sch., 1977-78; spl. cons. Nat. Research Council on Hepatitis. Co-author: Viral Hepatitis, 1978; contbr. articles on infectious diseases and immunology to profl. jours. Mem. Am. Soc. Clin. Investigation, Infectious Diseases Soc. Am., Am. Assn. Immunologists, Am. Assn. Study of Liver Disease, Am. Fedn. Clin. Research, AAAS, Alpha Omega Alpha. Roman Catholic. Office: Robert Wood Johnson Med Sch CN 19 New Brunswick NJ 08903

GOCKEL, JOHN RAYMOND, construction executive; b. Ft. Madison, Iowa, June 12, 1947; s. Carl R. and Virginia Jeanne (Schultz) G.; m. Joleen E. Gunst, Sept. 9, 1989; children: Rose M. Van Zandt, Chrstina Ann Ellis. BSCE, Iowa State U., 1970. Registered profl. engr., Mich., Minn., Wis. Cost estimator Barton Malow Co., Detroit, 1975-76, project mgr., 1976-82, project adminstr., 1982-83; project exec. Gilbane Bldg. Co., Maplewood, Minn., 1983-84; constrn. mgr., dir. phys. plant Minn. Racetrack, Inc., Shakopee, 1984-85; v.p. Scotland, Inc., Shakopee, 1985-86, Knutson Constr. Co., Mpls., 1987-88, Encompass Inc., Bloomington, Minn., 1988-89; ind. constrn. cons. Bloomington, 1989—; pres. John R. Gockel & Assocs., Inc., 1990—; project mgr. Mpls. Metrodome; constrn. mgr. Canterbury Downs, Mpls.; constrn. cons. to owners and attys.; lectr. various civic profl., acad. groups, Minn. Arbitrator Am. Arbitration Assn., throughout Midwest, 1982. Recipient Honor award Cons. Engrs. Coun., Minn., 1985. Mem. ICBO, Profl. Engrs. in Constrn. (v.p. 1983, pres. 1984, bd. dirs. 1984-93), Minn. Soc. Profl. Engrs. (bd. dirs. 1985-86, Seven Wonders of Engring. award 1982, 85), Iowa State U. Alumni Assn., Tau Beta Pi. Republican. Roman Catholic. Avocations: history, woodworking, fishing. Fax: (612) 888-9814. Home and Office: 11120 Stanley Cir S Minneapolis MN 55437-3315

GOCKLEY, BARBARA JEAN, corporate professional; b. Pitts., July 26, 1951; d. William Ervin and Dorothy Marie (Wolf) Cain; m. William Lee Gockley, Mar. 29, 1975 (div. Aug. 1989); children: Ervin Cain, Marianne Cain, William Cain, Malinda Cain. Student, Indiana U. Pa., 1969-70, Thomas Edison State Coll., 1986-88; BA in Bus. Mgmt. and Mktg. Mgmt., Alvernia Coll., 1993; MBA, Univ. Wis., 1997. Cert. in purchasing mgmt.; cert. prodn. and inventory mgmt. Asst. materials mgr. Redman Mobile Homes, Ephrata, Pa., 1972-75; mgr. inventory control Gym-Kin, Inc., Reading, Pa., 1975-77; supr. prodn./inventory control Wyomissing Converting, Reading, 1979-82; mgr. prodn./inventory control Dorma Door Controls, Inc., Reamstown, Pa., 1982-85, project mgr., 1985-86; materials mgr. Powder Coatings Group-Morton Internat., Reading, 1986-94; dir. purchasing Dexter Corp., Waukegan, Ill., 1994-99; dir. procurement Unisource, Berwyn, Pa., 1999—; dir. programs Congress for Progress Inc., 1984-88, vice chmn., 1988-89, chmn., 1989-90; dir. programs PRMS User Group Internat. Conf., 1991, 92; instr. Berks Campus, Pa. State U., Reading, 1985-86. Dir. Reinholds (Pa.) PTA, 1978-81; bd. dirs. Cocalico Sch. Bd., Denver, Pa., 1985-89. Mem. Am. Prodn. and Inventory Control Soc. (cert. prodn. and inventory mgmt., treas. Schuylkill Valley chpt. 1981-82, pres. 1982-84, dir. membership region IX 1985-86, asst. v.p. 1987, v.p. 1988-89, Internat. Vol. Svc. award 1986), Nat. Assn. Purchasing Mgrs., Assn. Mfg. Excellence. Republican. Presbyterian. Office: Unisource 1100 Cassatt Rd Berwyn PA 19312

GOCKLEY, (RICHARD) DAVID, opera director; b. Phila., July 13, 1943; s. Warren and Elizabeth S. Gockley; m. Adair Lewis; children: Meredith, Lauren, Adam. BA, Brown U., 1965; MBA, Columbia U., 1970; DHL (hon.), U. Houston, 1992; DFA (hon.), Brown U., 1993. Dir. music Newark Acad., 1965-67; dir. drama Buckley Sch., N.Y.C., 1967-69; mgr. box office Santa Fe Opera, 1969-70; bus. mgr. Houston Grand Opera, 1970-71, assoc. dir., 1971-72, gen. dir., 1972—; co-founder Houston Opera Studio, 1977. Prodr. (operas): Nixon in China (Emmy award 1988), Harvey Milk, Florencia en el Amazonas, Porgy and Bess (Tony award, Grammy award 1977), Treemonisha, A Quiet Place, Willie Stark, Resurrection, Carmen. Bd. dirs. Tex. Inst. Arts in Edn.; past pres. OPERA Am.; past chmn. Houston Theater Dist. Recipient Tony award League of N.Y Theaters and Producers, 1977, Dean's award Columbia Bus. Sch., 1982, Music Theater award Nat. Inst. Music Theater, 1985, William Rogers award, Brown U., 1995; named one of Outstanding Men Am., Nat. Jr. C. of C., 1976. Mem. Opera Am. (pres. 1985—). Avocation: tennis. Office: Houston Grand Opera 510 Preston St Ste 500 Houston TX 77002-1504*

GODBEE, GARY RUSSELL, artist; b. Miami, Fla., Jan. 20, 1952; s. Jack O. and Phyllis Godbee; m. Irene C. Burtyk, Sept. 17, 1988; children: Nina, Julia. BFA, Boston U., 1974. Gallery artist First St. Gallery, N.Y.C., 1981-89; rep. artist Cudahy's Gallery, N.Y.C., 1990-92; artist Gary Godbee Fine Arts, Westfield, N.J., 1993—; painting/drawing instr. Acad. Realist Art, Workshop Program, Santa Fe, 1994, 95; painting instr. Montclair (N.J.) Art Mus. Sch., 1993—; artist Gary Godbee Portraits, Westfield, 1990—; illustrator Gary Godbee Illustration, Westfield, 1997—; commd. artist State of N.J., Dept. of Labor, Trenton, 1999—; guest instr. Art Student's League, N.Y.C., 1992-93; guest lectr. DuCret Sch. Arts, Plainfield, N.J., 1993. Recipient Painting fellowship N.J. State Coun. on Arts, 1993, Merit award The Portrait Inst., 1996, Cert. of Merit, Soc. of Illustrators, 1998. FAX: 908-301-1734.

GODBEY, HELEN KAY, city official; b. Ft. Worth, Jan. 18, 1946; d. Paschal Lee and Ester Katherine (Williams) Godbey; children: Tammy Denise Thompson, Shelly Rae Thompson. AAS, Tarrant County Jr. Coll., 1985; B in Career Arts Dallas Bapt. U., 1987; MPA, U. Tex., Arlington, 1991. Cert. mcpl. clk., Tex. peace officer. Ct. clk. City of Ft. Worth, 1966-68; transcriber for ct. reporters, Dallas and Tarrant Counties, 1970-75; sec. City of Euless Police Dept., Tex., 1975-81; city sec. Euless, 1981-89; asst. city mgr., 1989-93; city mgr., Burleson, Tex., 1993—; speaker, instr. law enforcement and mgmt. topics Tex. A&M U., Tarrant County Jr. Coll. Police Acad., 1979-81; speaker IBM, various computer groups, Tex., Calif., 1983—, North Tex. State U. Ctr. for Community Svcs., Denton, 1984, 87—. Recipient Disting. Svc. awards Euless Police Dept., 1976, 79, Linda Keithley award for women in pub. mgmt., 1996. Mem. Internat. Inst. Mcpl. Clks. Advanced Acad. (co-chair 1989-90, com. on technol. devel. 1984-89, constl. revisions), Tex. Mcpl. Clks. Assn. Inc. (trustee officer 1987-88, treas. com. 1989, v.p. 1990), Internat. City Mgmt. Assn., North Tex. City Mgmt. Assn. (pres. 1999), Tex. City Mgmt. Assn. (pub. rels. and membership com., profl. devel. com.), Internat. City Mgmt. Assn. (acad. affairs com. 1992—), Burleson C. of C. (bd. dirs. 1995-97, Athena award 1999)), Kiwanis (v.p. Mid-Cities chpt. 1989-90). Mem. Internat. Inst. Mcpl. Clks. Advanced Acad. (co-chair 1989-90, com. on technol. devel. 1984—, constl. revisions), Tex. Mcpl. Clks. Assn. Inc. (trustee officer 1987—, treas. com. 1989, v.p. 1990), Bus. and Profl. Women Assn., Internat. City Mgmt. Assn., Am. Soc. Pub. Adminstrn., N. Tex. City Mgmt. Assn., Tex. City Mgmt. Assn., N. Tex. City Secs. Assn. (pres. 1986), Kiwanis (v.p. Mid-Cities chpt. 1989-90). Home: 1101 Glen Oak Dr Burleson TX 76028-6269 Office: 141 W Renfro St Burleson TX 76028-4261

GODBEY, LUTHER DAVID, architectural and engineering executive; b. Friend, Nebr., May 28, 1938; s. Luther Dobbs and Ruth (Thomas) G.; m. Priscilla White, Oct. 6, 1963 (div. May 1985); children: Emily, Patrick David. BArch, U. Nebr., 1961. Registered architect, Tex. Archtl. designer Selmer A. Solheim & Assoc., Lincoln, Nebr., 1961-63; architect, prin. Golemon & Rolfe Assoc. Inc., Houston, 1963-88; v.p. CRSS, Houston, 1988-90; dir. Corp. program Henningson Durham & Richardson, Dallas, 1990-92; asst. dir. phys. plant Tex. A&M, College Station, 1992—. Author: 52 Ways to Overcome Tennis Elbow, 1980; prin. works include 5000 Montrose Condos., Houston, 1979, Richmond Commerce Bank Office Bldg., Houston, 1980, One Capitol Sq. Office Bldg., Austin, 1985, Marriott Riverwalk Hotel, San Antonio, 1980, Westin O'Hare Hotel, Chgo., 1985, Wyndham Hotel, San Antonio, 1986, L'Hotel Sofitel, Miami, Fla., 1987, Bell Northern Rsch. Ctr., Ottawa, Can., 1988, Yukon Ltd. R & D Complex, Taejon, Korea, 1990, Godbey Residence, Bryan, Tex., 1995; watercolor exhibits include Jefferson Nat. Exhibition, New Orleans, 1963, Houston Art League Show, 1968, Southwestern Watercolor Soc. Regional Exhibition, Dallas, 1969, Houston Arts Festival, 1969, 72, Watercolor U.S.A., Springfield, Mo., 1970, circuit exhibition, 1970-71, 48th Ann. Regional Jury Exhibition Shreveport (La.) Art Guild, 1970, Southwestern Watercolor Soc. 2d Ann. Jury Exhibition, Houston, 1972. Mem. AIA (Brazos chpt. 1992—, pres. 1999), Tex. Soc. Archs. (honor award 1972), Tex. Assn. Phys. Plant Adminstrs., Bryan Zoning Bd. Adjustment, Briarcrest Country Club, Tex. A&M Faculty Club. Avocations: vocal soloist, lute, tennis, running, backpacking, guitar, violin. Office: Tex A&M Phys Plant MS 1371 College Station TX 77843-1371

GODBOLD, BARBARA LOUISE, secondary education educator; b. Edgewood, Md., Mar. 31, 1942; d. Frederick Shepherd and Louise Anna (Keller) G. BA, Montclair State, 1964, MA, 1967; EdD, Rutgers U., 1983. Tchr. lang. arts, social studies Lake Riviera Intermediate, Brick, N.J., 1964-67; tchr. English, social studies Brick Twp. High Sch., 1967-80, supr. English, 1980-82; tchr. English Brick Meml. High Sch., 1982—; instr. anthropology Ocean County Coll., Toms River, N.J., 1971-78. Mem. Ocean County Hist. Soc., Nat. Coun. for the Social Studies, Nat. Coun. Tchrs. English, N.J. Coun. for the Social Studies, Nat. Edn. Assn., N.J. Edn. Assn., Ocean County Edn. Assn., Brick Edn. Assn., Alpha Delta Kappa (treas. 1986-88), Kappa Delta Pi. Republican. Roman Catholic. Avocations: international travel, philately, archaeology, hiking, theatre. Home: 652 Windsor Rd Brick NJ 08723-6333

GODBOLD, FRANCIS STANLEY, investment banker, real estate executive; b. Charleston, S.C., Mar. 4, 1943; s. Francis Stanley and Ula Leigh (Waddey) G.; m. Lelia Elizabeth Harman, Sept. 24, 1966; children: John A., Laura H. Blair. BS in Indsl. Engring. with honors, Ga. Inst. Tech., 1965; MBA, Harvard U., 1969. V.p. Raymond, James & Assocs., Inc., St. Petersburg, Fla., 1969-74, sr. v.p., 1974-78, exec. v.p., 1978—; pres., bd. dirs. Raymond James Fin., Inc., 1987—; mem. regional firms adv. com. N.Y. Stock Exch., 1990-93. Pres. Baypoint Mid. Sch. Parent Action Com., 1982-83, Bay Vista Parent Action Com., 1979-80; mem. Leadership St. Petersburg, 1974—; mem. Lakewood H.S. Parent Action Com., 1984-90, pres., 1987-88; dir. Ga. Tech. Indsl. and Sys. Engring. Alumni award, 1997, mem. tampa Bay area regional devel. coun., 1995; bd. dirs. Acad. Prep. Capt. AUS, 1965-67. Mem. Securities Industry Assn. (vice chmn. so. dist. 1980, chmn. 1987, treas. 1986, exec. com. 1988-96, nat. dir. 1995-97, regional firms com. 1995—, chmn. regional firms com. 1998, tax policy com. 1995—, nominating com. 1997), Harvard Club of West Coast Fla. (sec.-treas 1971-72, v.p. 1972-73, pres. 1973-74), Harvard Bus. Sch. Club (treas. 1984), Squires Club, Lakewood Country Club, Elk River Club, Tau Beta Pi, Pahi Kappa Phi, Alpha Pi Mu, Phi Delta Theta. Republican. Office: Raymond James Fin Inc 880 Carillon Pkwy Saint Petersburg FL 33716-1100

GODBOLD, JOHN COOPER, federal judge; b. Coy, Ala., Mar. 24, 1920; s. Edwin Condie and Elsie (Williamson) G.; m. Elizabeth Showalter, July 18, 1942; children: Susan, Richard, John C., Cornelia, Sally. BS, Auburn U., 1940; JD, Harvard U., 1948; LLD (hon.), Samford U., 1981, Auburn U., 1988, Stetson U., 1994. Bar: Ala. 1948. With firm Richard T. Rives, Montgomery, 1948-49; ptnr. Godbold & Hobbs and successor firms, 1949-66; cir. judge U.S. Ct. Appeals (5th cir.), 1966-81, chief judge, 1981; chief judge U.S. Ct. Appeals (11th cir.), 1981-86, sr. judge, 1987—; dir. Fed. Jud. Ctr., Washington, 1987-90. Mem. Fed. Jud. Ctr. Bd., 1976-81. With field arty. AUS, 1941-46. Mem. ABA, Fed. Bar Assn., Ala. Bar Assn., Montgomery County Bar Assn., Alpha Tau Omega, Omicron Delta Kappa, Phi Kappa Phi. Episcopalian. Office: US Ct Appeals 11th Circuit PO Box 1589 Montgomery AL 36102-1589

GODDARD, DAVID BENJAMIN, physician assistant, clinical perfusionist; b. Panguitch, Utah, Dec. 6, 1947; s. Edward Pershing and Emma Louise (Stander) G.; m. Ann Braodbent, Dec. 22, 1975; children: Cecilee, Yorke B., Chelsea. BS, Brigham Young U., 1974; B. Health Sci., Duke U., 1976, Physician Assoc. Cert., 1976; cert., Stanford U., 1985; MPA, U. Nebr., 1996. Cert. physician asst.-surgery/primary care Nat. Commn. Cert. Physician Assists. Rsch. asst. Dept. Parasitology Brigham Young U., Provo, Utah, 1974; physician asst. Peace Corps, Kingdom of Tonga, 1976-78, Peace Corps Health Svcs., Washington, 1979, Cardiovascular & Chest Surg. Assocs., Boise, Idaho, 1979-81; physician asst., clin. perfusionist Starr-Wood-Chapman-Ahmad, PC, Portland, Oreg., 1981-85, Cardiovascular Surgery Assocs., Las Vegas, Nev., 1985-88; program dir., clin. perfusion sci. U. Nebr. Med. Ctr., Omaha, 1989-91; pvt. practice cons., 1992—. Co-author: Strategic Plan to Advance Telemedicine in the State of Utah, 1996; contbr. articles to profl. jours. Panel mem. Medicare Adv. Panel, Portland, Oreg., 1985. Grantee USDA/Rural Utilities Svc., 1996. Fellow Am. Assn. Surg. Physician Assts. (dir.-at-large 1987-88, pres. 1989-90), Am. Acad. Physician Assts. (reimbursement subcom. 1984), Assn. Physicians Assts. in Cardiovascular Surgery, Nev. Acad. Physician Assts. (chmn. legis. affairs 1987-88), Nebr. Acad. Physician Assts. (alt. del. 1989, legis. affairs com. 1990-92), Am. Soc. Extra-Corporeal Tech.; mem. N. Am. Transplant Coords. Orgn. (assoc.), Idaho' Acad. Physician Assts. (CME chmn. 1980-81), Oreg. Soc. Physicians Assts. (pres. 1983-84). Mormon. Avocations: bicycling, amateur radio, snow skiing, boating, photography. Home: PO Box 2151 Cedar City UT 84721-2151 Office: Orderville Clinic 425 E State St Orderville UT 84758

GODDARD, JAMES RUSSELL, producer, writer, actor; b. Anaheim, Calif., May 8, 1955; s. Russell Nathaniel and Marilyn (Carson) G.; m. Laurie Lynn Ragsdale, June 5, 1982; children: Aaron Russell, Joshua James, Nathaniel Carson. AA, Cypress Coll., 1976; student, Calif. State U., Fullerton, 1976-77. Prodr., writer Creation Artists, Anaheim, 1976—, R & R Prodns., Chatsworth, Calif., 1990—, Love Letters Live Prodns., 1998—; founder, prodr. Creation Theatrical Co., Anaheim & Riverside, 1976—, Actors Promotional Svcs., Hollywood, Calif., 1989—; stage mgr. Super Bowl Half-Time Show, Encore! Three Tenors, 1993. Author: (screenplays) Son of the Morning, 1988, Wait In Silence, 1990, Final Fade Out, 1993, Jack and Charmian London, 1994; (indsl. film) Recycling Kids, 1990; appeared in 98 TV and film prodns., 1977—; teleplays include The Yellow Kite, 1999, Flawed from Inception, 1999; various positions in over 500 profl. entertainment prodns., 1976—. Leader Boy Scouts Am., Anaheim, 1970-74, asst. scoutmaster, Corona, Calif., 1997—; crisis counselor Melodyland Hotline Ctr., Anaheim, 1976-80; mem. Jack London Found., Glen Ellen, Calif.; mgr. Little League Baseball, various locations. Co-recipient Disneyland Cmty. Svc. award Disneyland, 1976-78; recipient Walter Knott Americanism award Walter Knott Assn. Mem. SAG (mem. ethics com. 1992), Nat. Forensics League, Nat. Thespians Soc. Republican. Avocations: backpacking, archery, trains, writing.

GODDARD, JOHN WESLEY, cable television company executive; b. Aberdeen, Wash., May 4, 1941; s. Fred G. and Winifred (Vaughan) G.; m. Susan Ehrhart, Dec. 29, 1962 (div. Oct. 1978); 1 son, John Wesley Jr.; m. Joan Marie McGiff, Sept. 13, 1980. Grad. Stanford U.; M.BA in Fin., U. Calif.-Berkeley. Asst. mgr. Tele-Vue Systems Inc., Dublin, Calif., 1966, mgr., 1967-69, controller, 1969-74, pres., 1974-78; exec. v.p. Viacom Cable, Pleasanton, Calif., 1978-80, pres., 1980—; dir. Viacom Internat. Inc., N.Y.C., 1983-87; treas. Nat. Cable TV Assn., Washington, 1984, sec., 1985-86, vice chmn., 1987, chmn., 1988, bd. dirs., 1981—. Republican. Episcopalian. Office: Viacom Cable 2166 Rheem Dr Pleasanton CA 94588-2613*

GODDARD, RICHARD N., military officer. BS in Polit. Sci., U. Utah, 1966; MS in Bus. Adminstrn., Cen. Mich. U., 1975; grad., Indsl. Coll. of Armed Forces, 1986; grad. Kennedy Sch. Govt., Harvard U., 1994. Commd. 2d lt. USAF, 1966, advanced through grades to maj. gen., 1998; T-37 instr. pilot 3645th Pilot Tng. Squadron, 47th Flying Tng. Wing, Laughlin AFB, Tex., 1969-73; FB-111 combat crew mem., instr. pilot, flight examiner 715th Bombardment Squadron, Pease AFB, N.H., 1976-79; bomber br. chief, B-1 program monitor air vehicles divsn. Hdqs. Strategic Air Command, Offutt AFB, Nebr., 1979-81; comdr. 509th Avionics Maintenance Squadron, Pease AFB, 1981-84; chief strategic aircraft divsn. Hdqs. USAF, Washington, 1984-85; vice comdr., comdr. 380th Bombardment Wing, Plattsburgh AFB, N.Y., 1986-89; asst. dep. chief staff, dep. dir. Nat. Strategic Target List, Offutt AFB, 1989-91; comdr. 27th Fighter Wing, Cannon AFB, N.Mex., 1992-93; dir. logistics Hdqs. U.S. Air Forces in Europe, Ramstein Air Base, Germany, 1993-95, Hdqs. Air Combat Command, Langley AFB, Va., 1995-97; comdr. Warner Robins Air Logistics Ctr., Robins AFB, Ga., 1997—. Decorated Disting. Svc. medal, Silver Star, Def. Superior Svc. medal, Legion of Merit, D.F.C. Office: WRALC/CC Ste 235 215 Page Rd Robins AFB GA 31098

GODDARD, THELMA TAYLOR, critical care nurse, nursing educator; d. James Oscar and Goldie Pearl (Hawkins) Taylor; m. Kenneth L. Goddard; children: Catherine, Sharon, K. John. ADN, W.Va. No. C.C., Weirton, 1980; BSN, West Liberty State Coll., 1986; MSN, W.Va. U., 1991, postgrad. Staff critical care nurse Weirton (W.Va.) Med. Ctr., Pitts., West Pa., Pitts.; instr. nursing W.Va. No. C.C., W.Va. U., Morgantown; staff critical care nurse Cen. Med. Ctr., Pitts.; nursing instr. Waynesburg (Pa.) Coll., 1991-92, Carlow Coll., Pitts., 1992-94; instr. nursing Allegheny County C.C., Pitts., 1993-94; asst. prof. Wheeling (W.Va.) Jesuit Coll., 1994-97; instr. nursing U. Pitts., 1997-98, Allegheny Gen. Hosp., Pitts., 1987-88; critical care nurse St. Francis Ctrl. Hosp., 1990-94; vis. faculty C.C. Allegheny County, Pitts., 1999. Mem. ANA, AACCN, Sigma Theta Tau, Phi Theta Kappa.

GODDEN, JEAN W., columnist; b. Stamford, Conn., Oct. 1, 1933; d. Maurice Albert and Bernice Elizabeth (Warvel) Hecht; m. Robert W. Godden, Nov. 7, 1952 (dec. Dec. 1985); children: Glenn Scott, Jeffrey Wayne. BA, U. Wash., 1974. News editor Univ. Dist. Herald, Seattle, 1951-53; bookkeeper Omniarts Inc., Seattle, 1963-71; writer editorial page Seattle Post-Intelligencer, Seattle, 1974-80, editorial page editor, 1980-81, bus. editor, 1981-83, city columnist, 1983-91; city columnist Seattle Times, 1991—. Author: The Will to Win, 1980, Hasty Put Ins, 1981. Communicator of the Yr. U. Wash. Sch. of Comm., 1995. Mem. LWV (dir. 1969-71), Wash. Press Assn. (Superior Performance award 1979), Soc. Profl. Journalists, Mortarboard, City Club, Phi Beta Kappa. Office: The Seattle Times PO Box 70 Seattle WA 98111-0070

GODDESS, LYNN BARBARA, commercial real estate broker; b. N.Y.C., Mar. 3, 1942; d. Eugene Daniel and Hazel Cecile (Kinzler) G.; divorced. BS, Columbia U., 1963, postgrad., 1964-66. Coord. John M. Burns Assembly Campaign, N.Y.C., 1963; dir. spl. events, projects Kenneth B. Keating Senatorial Campaign, N.Y.C., 1964; dist. dir. fund raising Muscular Dystrophy Assn. Am. Inc., N.Y.C., 1965-66; exec. acct. fund raising, pub. relations Victor Weingarten Co., N.Y.C., 1966-67, Oram Group (formerly Harold L. Oram Inc.), N.Y.C., 1967-70; dir. devel. City Ctr. Music Drama Inc., N.Y.C., 1970; sales person Whitbread-Nolan, N.Y.C., 1971-73; from asst. v.p. to sr. v.p. Cross and Brown Co., N.Y.C., 1973-1985; sr. dir. Cushman & Wakefield, Inc., N.Y.C., 1985—. Trustee Young Adult Inst. Mem. Nat. Soc. Fund Raisers, Assn. Fund Dirs., Real Estate Bd. N.Y. (named Most Ingenious Broker Yr. 1975), Women's Forum (bd. dirs.). Office: Cushman & Wakefield Inc 51 W 52nd St Fl 11 New York NY 10019-6119

GODDU, ROGER, retail executive; b. Springfield, Mass., June 23, 1950; m. Kate Goddu; 5 children. Student, Adrian Coll., U. Toledo; grad., Harvard Bus. Exec. Program, 1995. Mdse. adminstr. LaSalle and Koch divsn. R.H. Macy & Co., 1970-75; v.p., gen. mdse. mgr. Rikes/Lazarus Dept. Stores, 1975-80; mdse. mgr. Dayton Hudson divsn. Target Stores, 1980-83, v.p. Dayton Hudson divsn., 1983-85, sr. v.p., gen. mdse. mgr. Dayton Hudson divsn., 1985-89; exec. v.p., gen. mdse. mgr. Toys R Us, Paramus, N.J., 1989-95, pres. U.S. merchandising, 1996-97; chmn., CEO Montgomery Ward & Co., Inc., Chgo., 1997—; CEO Montgomery Ward Holding Co., Chgo., 1997—. Dir. Kids in Distressed Situations, Project Pride in Living, Mpls.; founder The Nat. Conf., Bergen County, N.J. Office: Montgomery Ward and Co Inc 3-4 Montgomery Ward Plz Chicago IL 60671-0002*

GODEKE, RAYMOND DWIGHT, insurance company executive, accountant; b. San Diego, Nov. 26, 1947; s. Robert Carroll and Julia Mae (Caeser) G.; m. Norma Dean Rhodes, Oct. 31, 1966(div. 1970); 1 child, Melyssa Dawn; m. Vicki Lorraine Coleman, Feb. 19, 1972; 1 child, Kristin Francine. AA, Fullerton Coll., 1976; BA, Calif. State U.-Fullerton, 1978; MBA, Pepperdine U., 1980. Cert. internal auditor, cert. mgmt. accountant. Acct. Robert Johnston & Assocs., Lynwood, Calif., 1974-75; mem. acctg. staff Denny's, Inc., La Mirada, Calif., 1975-82, div. controller, 1982-87; div. contr. Foster Farms, Livingston, Calif., 1987-90; indsl. healthcare exec. Tri-Care, Irvine, Calif., 1990-92; produce distbn. exec. J.C. Produce, L.A., 1992-94; contr. Zacky Farms, South El Montie, Calif., 1994-98; CFO Word & Brown Ins. Adminstrs. Inc., Orange, Calif., 1998—. Chmn. Arrowhead dist. Boy Scouts Am., 1986. Mem. Nat. Assn. Accts. (bd. dirs. 1982-83), Inst. Internal Auditors (cert. internal auditor), Inst. Mgmt. Accts. (cert. mgmt. acct.), Masons, Scottish Rite, York Rite, Shriners. Republican. Presbyterian. Avocations: golf, reading, trap and target shooting. Office: Word & Brown 721 S Parker St Ste 300 Orange CA 92868-4731

GODENNE, GHISLAINE DUDLEY, physician, psychoanalyst, educator; b. Brussels; came to U.S., 1951; d. Pierre and Olive Dudley (Short) G. B.S., Universite Catholique de Louvain, Belgium, 1948, M.D., 1952. Intern Providence Hosp, Washington, 1951-52; resident in pediatrics, 1952-54; fellow in pediatrics Mayo Clinic, Rochester, Minn., 1954-57; fellow in pediatric research Johns Hopkins U., 1957-58, assoc. prof. mental hygiene, 1966-82, assoc. prof. psychiatry and pediatrics, 1966-82, psychoanalyst, 1972—, prof. psychology, 1973-90, prof. psychiatry, pediatrics, and mental hygiene, 1982—; resident in psychiatry Johns Hopkins Hosp., Balt., 1958-62; chief adolescent psychiat. service Johns Hopkins Hosp., 1964-73, dir. counseling and psychiat. services, 1973-90, dir. health svcs., 1978-88, dir. emeritus, 1990—; mem. staff various hosps. Balt., 1978-88; clin. prof. psychiatry U. Md., Balt., 1986—; cons. psychiatrist Cylburn Children's Home, Balt., 1960-81, Catonsville (Md.) C.C., 1968-75, Good Shepherd Ctr., Balt., 1970-74, Assoc. Cath. Charity, Balt., 1970-77, Jewish Family of Children's Svcs., Balt., 1972-77, Mt. Washington Pediat. Hosp., Balt., 1974-81, Sheppard and Enoch Pratt Hosp., Batl, 1973-80, Loyola Coll., Balt., 1990-92. Mem. editorial bd.: Adolescent Psychiatry, 1978-83, Clinical Update Adolescent Psychiatry, 1982-85; contbr. articles to profl. jours. Bd. dirs. Balt. Girl Scouts Assn., 1958-60, 81-82, Met. Balt. Assn. Mental Health, 1965-69, Florence Crittendon Home, 1966-68; trustee McDonough Sch., 1975-83; pres. bd. Trustees Richmond Fellowship Md., 1975-77. Decorated Knight and Officer Order of Leopold (Belgium 1972-84), recipient Christophe Plantin prize (Belgium), 1989; awarded Nobility Concession with the title of Baroness (Belgium) 1991; recipient Career Teaching award NIMH, 1963-65, Schonfeld award Am. Soc. Adolescent Psychiatry, 1995; grantee Fulbright Found., 1951-52, Parke Davis Co., 1957-58, NIMH, 1961-63. Fellow ACP, Am. Psychiat. Assn. (life), APHA (life), Am. Orthopsychiat. Assn. (life), Am. Soc. Adolescent Psychiatry (life, pres. 1981-82), Am. Coll. Health Assn.; mem. AAUP, Am. Psychoanalytic Soc., Md. Soc. Adolescent Psychiatry (pres. 1968-69), Md. Psychiat. Soc. (past chmn. program com., co-chmn. women's com. 1991-96), Md. State Conf. Social Welfare (past mem. child welfare com.), Am. Soc. Adolescent Medicine (charter), Am. U. and Coll. Counseling Ctr. Dirs., Internat. Soc. Adolescent Psychiatry (v.p. 1989-92, sec.-gen. 1992-95, v.p. 1995—). Home: 15 Edgevale Rd Baltimore MD 21210-2215

GODFREY, ALDEN NEWELL, communications educator; b. Quincy, Mass., Jan. 8, 1924; s. Edgar and Lela Winifred (Smith) G.; m. Ruth Mildred Mix, July 20, 1949 (div. Sept. 1968); children: Craig Alden, Brian Kent; m. Elvena Marie Ulrich, July 20, 1972. BA, Boston U., 1950; MA, U. Minn., 1951; D Divinity, Missionary of New Truth, Chgo., 1971. Info. officer U.S. Dept. of State, Manila, 1951-55; exec. various newspapers, Boston, Wilmington, N.C. and San Diego, 1955-68; exec. dir. United Way of Desert, Palm Springs, Calif., 1968-73, Combined Arts and Edn. Coun., San Diego, 1973-75, Inland Empire Cultural Found., Colton, Calif., 1975-79; v.p. Campaign Mgmt., Ltd., Palm Springs, Calif., 1979-83, pres., 1983-85; adj. prof. Coll. of Desert, Palm Desert, Calif., 1991—. Pres. Alliance of Calif. Arts Couns., San Francisco, 1975-77, San Diego chpt. Pub. Rels. Soc. Am., 1965-66, San Diego Press Club, 1966-67; v.p. Calif. Confedn. of Arts, L.A.,

1978-79; campaign mgr. Maryanov for Mayor, Palm Springs, 1993; chmn. Wilson for Supr., Palm Springs, 1995, 98, Mayor's H.O.S.T. Com., San Diego, 1968; mem. Atty. Gen. Adv. Coun., Sacramento, 1964-68. 1st lt. U.S. Army, 1942-46. Mem. Soc. Profl. Journalists, United Way Exec. Assn., Coll. of Desert Adj. Assn., Kiwanis, Press Club of Desert (treas.). Avocations: golf, travel. Home: 467 N Calle Rolph Palm Springs CA 92262-0708 Office: Coll of the Desert 43-500 Monterey Ave Palm Desert CA 92260

GODFREY, ALINE LUCILLE, music specialist, church organist; b. Providence, R.I., Dec. 4, 1943; d. Bernard Almasse and Rita Linda (Laramee) Brindamour; m. George Ruben Godfrey, Aug. 22, 1981; 1 child, Murray Aaron. BA, Rivier Coll., 1970; cert. of attendance, Am. Conservatory of Music, Fontainebleau, France, 1972; M of Music, U. Notre Dame, 1975. Cert. tchr. profl. all level music, provisional elem.-gen., Tex. Choir dir. Scituate (R.I.) High Sch., 1970-74; tchr. grade 4 McDowell Intermediate Sch., Hondo, Tex., 1974-75; tchr. grade 5 Wilson Elem. Sch., Harlingen, Tex., 1975-76; organist St. Albans Episcopal Ch., Harlingen, 1977-80; music specialist St. Mary's Sch. and Immaculate Conception Sch., Brownsville, Tex., 1977-79; choral accompanist Harlingen H.S., 1979-80; tchr. grade 6 Sam Houston Sch., Harlingen, 1980-81; music dir. St. Alban's Episcopal Sch., Harlingen, 1987-90; choral accompanist Marine Military Acad., Harlingen, 1988-90; tchr. Stuart Place Elem. Sch., Harlingen, 1990-91; music specialist Harlingen Ind. Sch. Dist., 1991—; organist St. James Ch., Manville, R.I., 1972-74, First United Meth. Ch., Mercedes, Tex., 1987-93; pianist, accompanist Cardinal Chorale, Harlingen, 1980-81. Composer: Songs for Tots, 1983; playwright: (musical) Why the Bells Rang, 1988, American Tribute, 1995; arranger, dir. (musicals) Across the U.S.A., 1988, Around the World at Wilson School, 1992; dir. Under the Big Top, 1989, United We Stand, 1991; music dir.: Together, 1995, Christmas in the West, 1995, Every Day is Earth Day, 1996. Vol. Hosts Program, Harlingen, 1981, Riofest, 1983, Dishman Spring Festival, Combes, Tex., 1993, 94, Wilson Spring Fest, 1996; dir. Crockett Sch. dedication, 1993. Mem. Tex. Music Educators Assn., Smithsonian Instn., PEO Sisterhood (pres. 1999), Am. Assn. Ret. Persons. Avocations: travel, reading, sewing, aerobics, swimming. Home: PO Box 875 Combes TX 78535-0875 Office: Wilson Elem Sch Box 240 Primera Rd Harlingen TX 78552

GODFREY, CULLEN MICHAEL, lawyer; b. Ft. Worth, Apr. 8, 1945; s. Cullen Aubrey and Agnes (Eiland) G.; m. Melinda McDonald, Aug. 29, 1970. BA, U. Tex., 1968, JD, 1970. Bar: Tex. 1969, U.S. Dist. Ct. (we. dist.) Tex. 1971, U.S. Ct. appeals (5th cir.) 1979, U.S. Ct. Appeals (11th cir.) 1981. Ptnr. Sloan, Muller & Godfrey, Austin, Tex., 1969-72; staff atty. Hunt Oil Co., Dallas, 1972-74; staff atty. Tesoro Petroleum Corp., San Antonio, 1974-75, sr. atty., 1975-78, asst. gen. counsel, 1978-82; asst. gen. counsel Am. Petrofina, Inc. (now FINA, Inc.), Dallas, 1982-88, gen. counsel, 1988-90, v.p., sec., gen. counsel, 1990-95, sr. v.p., sec., gen. counsel, 1995—; Bd. dirs. Normandy Life Ins. Co., Fina Oil & Chem. Co., Trust pipe Line Co., River Pipeline Co. Author: Legal Aspects of the Purchase and Sale of Oil and Gas Properties, 1992; contbr. articles to profl. jours. Bd. trustees Dallas Mus. Art, 1993-95, 98—, chmn. corp. com., 1993-95; bd. dirs. United Way MEt. Dallas, Inc., 1999—, gen. campaign chmn., 1999; bd. dirs. Dallas County Heritage Soc., 1998—. With Tex. N.G., 1968-74. Recipient Anti-Defamation League Kurispirdence award, 1999. Fellow Tex. Bar Found., Dallas Bar Found.; mem. ABA (chmn. subcom. on fgn. investment reporting, internat. law sect. 1984-87), State Bar Tex. (coun. oil gas and mineral law sect. 1992-95, coun. bus. law sect. 1998—, coll. mem. 1989—, com. on continuing legal edn. 1997—, com. legal aspect arts 1998—), Dallas Bar Assn., Tex. Bd. Legal Specialization (bd. cert. oil, gas. and mineral law), Am. Petroleum Inst. (bd. dirs. 1998—, gen. com. law 1989—, chmn. 1997—, gen. com. comms. 1995-97), Tex. Bus. Law Found. 9bd. dirs. 1990—, chmn. 1995-98), Greater Dallas Crime Commn. (dir. 1991—, chmn. 1997-99), Southwestern Legal Found. (rsch. fellow, adv. bd. internat. oil 7 gas edn. ctr., co-chmn. 44th-45th inst. on oil & gas law and taxation). Office: FINA Inc PO Box 2159 Dallas TX 75221-2159

GODFREY, JOHN MORROW, lawyer, retired Canadian government official; b. Port Credit, Ont., Can., June 28, 1912; s. Justice John Milton and Lily (Connon) G.; m. Mary Buwell Ferguson, Sept. 10, 1940; children: John, Sally Godfrey Forrest, Anne. Student Toronto schs., 1922-29; student, Royal Mil. Coll. Can., 1929-31; LLB, Osgoode Hall Law Sch., 1939. Bar: Ont. 1939. Counsel Fasken Campbell Godfrey, Toronto, Ont., Can., 1945—; mem. Senate of Can., Ottawa, Ont., 1973-87, ret.; chmn. fin. and treas. coms. Liberal Party of Can., Ottawa, 1968-74. Pres. Nat. Ballet of Can., Toronto, 1967-69; founding dir. Can. Opera Co., 1949-53. Served as wing comdr. RCAF, 1940-45. Unitarian. Clubs: Toronto, Toronto Golf; Osler Bluff Ski (Collingwood, Ont.). Office: Toronto Dominion Ctr, Box 20, Toronto, ON Canada M5K 1N6

GODFREY, JOHN MUNRO, economic consultant; b. San Antonio, Mar. 20, 1941; s. George Phillips and Frieda (Allen) G.; m. Nancy Porter, June 4, 1966 (div. 1976); 1 son, John Munro, Jr.; m. Flavel Mcmichael, July 30, 1994. AA, Armstrong State Coll., 1964; BBA, U. Ga., 1964, PhD, 1976. Rsch. officer, sr. fin. economist Fed. Res. Bank, Atlanta, 1969-81; sr. v.p., chief economist Barnett Banks Inc., Jacksonville, 1981-95; prin. Fla. Econ. Assocs., Jacksonville; adj. prof. econs. and fin. Davis Coll. Bus., Jacksonville (Fla.) U., 1995-97; mem. Gov.'s Econ. Adv. Com.; mem. econ. adv. com. Am. Bankers Assn. *Dr. John M. Godfrey has over 30 years experience as a professional business economist and his experience encompasses the business, government and academic sectors. He is a nationally recognized authority and is widely cited on business conditions, financial markets, monetary policy and regional economic conditions. He presently heads his own consulting company, Florida Economic Associates, which provides economic and financial consulting services for a wide range of local and national clients. Godfrey assists a number of not-for-profit organizations in the Jacksonville community.* Author: Monetary Expansion in the Confederacy, 1977. Mem. econ. adv. com. U.S. C. of C.; adv. bd. Mitigation Solutions, Inc.; bd. dirs. Fla. Ballet at Jacksonville, Jacksonville Symphony Orch., Cummer Mus. of Art and Gardens, St. Vincent's (Hosp.) Found.; vestryman St. Marks Episcopal Ch., Jacksonville; trustee, treas. St. Marks Episcopal Ch. Found. Recipient Disting. Alumnus award Terry Coll. of Bus., U. Ga., 1994. Mem. Econ. Roundtable of Jacksonville (pres. 1982-89), Nat. Assn. Bus. Economists (dir.), Am. Econ. Assn., So. Econ. Assn., U. Ga. Coll. Bus. Alumni Assn. (bd. dirs., pres.), Ponte Vedra Club, Fla. Yacht Club, Meninak Club (bd. dirs. Jacksonville chpt.), River Club, Timuquana Country Club. Episcopalian. E-mail: godfreyjon@aol.com. Home: 4652 Ortega Forest Dr Jacksonville FL 32210-5823 Office: Fla Econ Assocs 2905 Corinthian Ave Ste 1 Jacksonville FL 32210-4464

GODFREY, MARGARET ANN, educator; b. Hartford, Conn.; d. William Joseph and Filomena Mary (Sauro) G. BA in Econs., Hunter Coll., 1956, MS in Edn., 1960; P.D. in Ednl. Adminstrn., St. John's U., 1977, EdD, 1984. Tchr. Stamford (Conn.) Pub. Schs., 1956-59, N.Y.C. Pub. Schs., 1960-61; with sales Sutton Assocs., New Rochelle, N.Y., 1959-62; asst. to pres. J.J. Lane Inc., N.Y.C., 1962-64; project dir. John J. Henderson and Assocs., N.Y.C., 1964-65; media dir. Groody Advt., N.Y.C., 1965; media estimator-coord. Grey Advt., N.Y.C., 1966-69; rsch. analyst Family Circle Mag., N.Y.C., 1969-70; tchr., ednl. adminstr. N.Y.C. Pub. Schs., 1971—; field cons., grant reviewer IMPACT II, N.Y.C., 1986—; workshop trainer N.Y.C. Pub. Schs., IMPACT II, N.Y.C., 1986-89; adj. faculty Empire State Coll., Hartsdale, N.Y., 1989-90, Marymount Coll., 1993, St. Francis Coll., 1997-99, Iona Coll., 1999—. Contbr. articles to profl. jours. Pres. Echo Heights Neighborhood Assn., 1993—; former chmn. New Rochelle Environ. Conservation Adv. Commn.; dist. leader New Rochelle rep. Orgn.; founder, pres. New Rochelle Citizens Reform Club, 1999. Mem. ASCD, Nat. Coun. Tchrs. Math., Assn. Tchrs. Math. N.Y.C., Nat. Coun. Suprs. Math., Forum Italian Am. Educators, Coun. Suprs. and Adminstrs., Cath. Alumni Club N.Y. (exec. bd. dirs. 1988-89). Avocations: travel, attending theater, singing in church choir, reading.

GODFREY, PATRICK LEWIS, state government official; b. L.A., Nov. 23, 1942; s. Lew Burl and Lois Jean (Lee) Hodges; m. Margie sue Gray, Oct. 1962 (div. 1963); m. Linda Lee Reed, June 1966 (div. 1978); m. Margery May Southworth, Feb. 18, 1979; children: Tracey, Lee Margaret, John Reed, Patrick Jr. Student, El Camino Coll., Lawndale, Calif., 1960-62, Harbor Coll., San Pedro, Calif., 1963-64, Orange Coast Coll., Costa Mesa, Calif., 1965-66. Cert. med. soc. exec., AMA. Asst. exec. dir. Hawaii Med. Soc., Honolulu, 1966-69; pub. affairs mgr. Nat. Assn. Mfrs., L.A., 1969-75, dir. pub. affairs, 1977-79; regional mgr. Nat. Assn. Mfrs., Tacoma, Wash., 1979-80; assoc. George Young & Assocs., L.A., 1975-76; pres. Target Comm., Federal Way, Wash., 1980-82; sr. staff coord. Wash. State Senate, Olympia, 1982—; cons. in pub. affairs program design and implementation to Fortune 1000 cos., polit. actions coms. include Bus.-Industry Polit. Action Com., AMA Polit. Action Com., Polit. Interest Com., The Dillingham Corp. Polit. Action Com., Calif. Congl. Targeting Com., United for Wash., others. Mgr. former Hawaii Gov. William Quinn senatorial race, 1976, Calif. Congl. Targeting Com., 1974; mem. task force Calif. Roundtable; mem. Rep. Nat. Com., U. So. Calif. Ctr. for Study of Pvt. Enterprise. With USAR, 1963-68. Mem. Am. Assn. Med. Soc. Execs., Nat. Rep. Legislator's assn., L.A. Pub. Affairs Officer's assn., San Francisco Pub. Affairs assn., Future Bus. Leaders of Am. Republican. Avocations: fishing, boating, drumming, travel. Office: Wash State Senate 206 Newhouse Bldg Olympia WA 98504

GODFREY, PAUL, publisher. Chmn. bd. dirs. Fla. Sun Pubs., Bradenton; pres., CEO Sun Media Corp. Office: Sun Media Corp. 333 King St E, Toronto, ON Canada*

GODFREY, PAUL JOSEPH, science foundation director; b. Brockton, Mass., Sept. 29, 1944; s. Joseph and Jeannette Aldora (Paul) G.; m. Laurie Ann Rohde, June 13, 1968; children: Darren, Mollie. BS, Tufts U., 1966; MS, U. Mass., 1970; PhD, Cornell U., 1977. Staff asst. Water Resources Rsch. Ctr. U. Mass., Amherst, 1978-80, dir. Water Resources Rsch. Ctr., 1980—. Editor: Ecological Considerations in Wetland Treatment of Municipal Wastewater, 1985. Recipient Cert. of Recognition Gov. Michael Dukakis, 1983, Silver Trout award Trout Unltd., 1984, Conservation award Gulf Oil, 1985, Searching for Success award Renew Am., 1990, Environ. Programs award Friends of the UN, 1990. Mem. Am. Soc. Limnological Oceanography, Nat. Insts. Water Resources (sec.-treas. 1987-93, treas. 1993—), Soc. for Internat. Limnologists, N.Am. Lake Mgmt. Soc. Office: U Mass Blaisdell House Amherst MA 01003*

GODFREY, PAUL VICTOR, communications company executive; b. Toronto, Ont., Can., Jan. 12, 1939; s. Philip and Bella Bessie (Greenbaum) G.; m. Regina Bowman, Nov. 19, 1967; children—Robin James, Noah Adam, Joshua Jay. B.A.S.C. in Chem. Engring., U. Toronto, 1962. Chem. engr., C.I.L., Toronto, Ont., 1962-69; controller City of North York, Ont., Can., 1969-73; chmn. Municipality of Met. Toronto, 1973-84; pub., chief exec. officer Toronto Sun Newspaper, 1984-91, dir., 1985—; pres., chief oper. officer Toronto Sun Pub. Corp., 1991-92, pres., CEO, 1992-96; pres., CEO Sun Media Corp., 1996—; bd. dirs. Delcan, Astral Comm. Inc., Bowes Pubs. Ltd., SkyDome, The Fin. Post Co., Baycrest Centre; chmn. RioCan Real Estate Investment Trust; chmn. bd. trustees Molson Industry; chmn., bd. govs. Can. Newspaper Assn.; mem. governing coun. U. Toronto. Founder Herbie Fund. Jewish. Avocations: politics, baseball, sports in general. Office: Sun Media Corp, 333 King St E, Toronto, ON Canada M5A 3X5*

GODFREY, RICHARD GEORGE, real estate appraiser; b. Sharon, Pa., Dec. 18, 1927; s. Fay Morris and Elisabeth Marguerite (Stefanak) G.; m. Golda Fay Goss, Oct. 28, 1951; children: Deborah Jayne, Gayle Rogers, Bryan Edward. BA, Ripon Coll., 1949. V.p. 1st Thrift & Loan Assn., Albuquerque, 1959-61; pres. Richard G. Godfrey & Assocs., Inc., Albuquerque, 1961-93, owner, 1993—. Mem. Appraisal Inst. (v.p. 1981-82), Counselors of Real Estate. Baptist. Home: 1700 Columbia Dr SE Albuquerque NM 87106-3311 Office: 523 Louisiana Blvd SE Albuquerque NM 87108-3842

GODFREY, ROBERT DOUGLAS, lawyer; b. Danbury, Conn., Sept. 11, 1948; s. Douglas and Rita (Cardinale) G. BA, Fordham U., 1970; JD, U. Conn., 1985. Bar: Conn. 1985. Com. clk. Conn. Gen. Assembly, Hartford, 1977-78; v.p. pub. affairs Greater Danbury C. of C., 1978-82; law clk. to presiding judge Probate Ct., City of Danbury, 1983; atty. Conn. Bank & Trust Co., Hartford, 1986-90; justice of the peace State of Conn., 1977—; mem. U.S. Internet Coun., 1998. Councilman Common Coun. of Danbury, 1985-89; mem. Charter Rev. Commn., Danbury, 1988; with Conn. Ho. of Reps., 1989—, dep. maj. leader, 1995—; mem. exec. com. Coun. State Govts., 1997-99. With USNR, 1970-77. Recipient reproductive rghts award Conn. Coalition for Choice, 1990, environ. e nergy award Peoples Action for Clean Energy, 1992; named Champion for Children, Conn. Coalition for Children, 1990, Legislator of Yr., Conn. Police Chiefs Assn., 1993; recognized Conn. Coalition Against Gun Violence, 1993, spl. recognition award Danbury Dept. Elderly Svcs., 1995, legis. leadership award Housing Authority Danbury, 1995, legis. svc. award Conn. Med. Assn., 1996, cmty. svc. award Midwestern Conn. Coun. on Alcoholism, 1998. Cath. War Vets. (judge advocate 1978—). Home: 13 Stillman Ave Danbury CT 06810-8007 Office: Conn Ho of Reps Legis Office Bldg Rm 4012 Hartford CT 06106

GODFREY, ROBERT GORDON, physician; b. Wichita, Kans., June 11, 1927; s. Henry Robert and Pearl Madeline (Gaston) G.; m. Margaret Scott Ingling, June 24, 1951; children: Timothy, Katherine, Gwendolyn, Melissa. B.A., U. Wichita, 1952; M.D., U. Kans., 1958. Intern Boston City Hosp., 1958-59; resident in internal medicine Peter Bent Brigham Hosp., Boston, 1959-60, Colo. Gen. Hosp., Denver, 1961-63; asst. in medicine Peter Bent and Robert Brigham Hosp.-Harvard Med. Sch., 1959-61; fellow in rheumatology Robert B. Brigham Hosp., 1960-61, U. Colo., Denver, 1963-64; instr. medicine U. Kans. Med. Ctr., Kansas City, 1964-65; asst. prof. med. U. Kans. Med. Ctr., 1965-95, staff physician, chief arthritis sect., 1965-75; ret., 1995; staff physician, sr. rheumatologist VA Med. Ctr., 1980-84; chief rheumatology sect., assoc. chief med. service ambulatory care Leavenworth VA Med. Ctr., Kans., 1984-88; cons. rheumatology Physicians Associated, Overland Park, Kans., 1988-93; pvt. cons. rheumtology, 1995—. Served with M.C., U.S. Army, 1945-47. Recipient Disting. Service award Kans. Arthritis Found., 1975. Fellow ACP, Am. Coll. Rheumatology (founding fellow original Am. Rheumatism Assn.); mem. Am. Soc. Clin. Rheumatology, Sigma Xi, Alpha Omega Alpha. Republican. Office: U Kans Med Ctr Divsn Allergy Clin Immunol Rheumatol 3901 Rainbow Blvd Kansas City KS 66160-0001

GODFREY, ROBERT R., financial services executive; b. Sweetwater, Tex., May 22, 1947; s. Ross R. and Lillian L. (Bradford) G.; m. Diane M. Kalinowski, June 30, 1972. BBA, Tex. Tech. U., 1969, postgrad. in bus. adminstrn., 1969-71. Underwriter Aetna Life and Casualty Co., Hartford, Conn., 1969-72; tchg. fellow Tex. Tech. U., Lubbock, Tex., 1969-71, Ctrl. Conn. State Coll., New Britain, 1972; asst. mgr. Gulf Ins. Group, Dallas, 1972-76; asst. v.p. Scor Reins. Co., Dallas, 1976-79; pres. Rollins Burdick Hunter Mgmt. Co., N.Y.C., 1979-81; founder, pres., dir. St. Regis Ins. Group/Drum Fin. Corp., N.Y.C., 1981-85; exec. v.p. MBIA, Inc., Armonk, N.Y., 1985-95; chmn., founder N/W Capital, Inc., Stamford, Conn., 1995—; dir. Lebenthal Mut. Funds Group, 1995—, dir. MBIA Ins. Corp., 1987-95; corp. adv. coun. NYU Salomon Ctr., 1990-95. Author: Risk Based Capital Charges for Municipal Bonds, 1990, Higher Bond Yields: The Insured Triple A Advantage, 1993, The Municipal Bond Handbook, 1994. Trustee Citizens Budget Commn. of N.Y., 1990-96; sec. Town Dem. Com. New Canaan. With U.S. Army, 1970. Mem. Union League (mem. pension and endowment coms.). Office: 1177 High Ridge Rd Stamford CT 06905-1211

GODFREY, WILLIAM ASHLEY, ophthalmologist; b. Arkansas City, Ark., May 19, 1938. BA, U. Kans., Lawrence, 1961; MD, U. Kans., Kansas City, 1965. Diplomate Am. Bd. Ophthalmology. Intern Tulane U., New Orleans, 1965-66; resident U. Kans. Sch. Medicine, 1968-71; rsch. fellow U. Calif., San Francisco, 1971-73; asst. prof., then assoc. prof. U. Kans. Sch. Medicine, 1973-84, prof. ophthalmology, 1984—; mem. staff St. Luke's Hosp., Kansas City, Mo., 1973—, Kansas U. Med. Ctr., Kansas City, 1973—; cons. Kansas City Vets Hosp., Mo., 1973-89. Contbr. articles to profl. publs. With USAF, 1966-68. NIH fellow, 1971-73. Fellow ACP, Am. Acad. Ophthalmology (honor ward 1983), Am. Uveitis Soc.; mem. Am. COll. Physicians, AMA, Am. Fedn. Clin. Rsch., Am. Rheumatism Assn., Assn. Rsch. in Vision and Ophthalmology, Am. Math. Soc., Ocular Immunology and Microbiology Soc., Kansas City Soc. Ophthalmology, Kans. Med. Soc., Mo. Ophthalmology Soc., Jackson County Med. Soc., Am. Ophthal. Soc., Wyandotte County Med. Soc., Johnson County Med. Soc., Soc. Head Fellows, Assn. Proctor Fellows, Kans. Ophthal. Soc., Alpha Omega Alpha. Office: Hunkeler Vision Ctr 4321 Washington St Ste 6000 Kansas City MO 64111-5900

GODICH, JOHN PAUL, federal magistrate judge; b. Indpls., Nov. 30, 1944; m. Suzanne Steffen Geringer, Sept. 7, 1974. AB cum laude, Princeton U., 1966; JD, Yale U., 1969. Assoc. Barnes Hickam Pantzer & Boyd (now Barnes & Thornburg), Ind., 1971-73; law clk. U.S. Dist. Ct. (so. dist.) Ind., 1969-71; chief U.S. magistrate judge U.S. Dist. Ct. (so. dist.) Inc., 1973—, chief magistrate judge, 1986; apptd. to Jud. Conf. U.S. com. Adminstrn. U.S. Magistrate Judges, 1987, 90, com. Local Rules so. dist. Ind., 1989—, com. to Implement Civil Justice Reform Act, 1991—; chmn. Fed. Jud. Ctr. advanced seminar for U.S. Magistrate Judges, Warren, Vt., 1991, Orientation seminar Newly Apptd. U.S. Magistrates, 1988. Mem. bd. editors Yale Law Jour., 1967-69. Mem. ABA, FBA, Am. Judicature Soc., Ind. State Bar Assn., Indpls. Bar Assn., Fed. Magistrate Judges Assn., 7th Cir. Bar Assn. (mem. edn. com. 1991—, ad hoc com. on high cost of litigation, 1978-79), Phi Beta Kappa. Office: US Dist Ct Rm 230 US Courthouse 46 E Ohio St Indianapolis IN 46204-1903*

GODILO-GODLEVSKY, EUGENE ALEXANDROVICH, poet; b. Bklyn., July 13, 1956; s. Alexander Evgenievich and Paula (Nipp) G.-G. BA in English, Fordham U., 1979, MA in English, 1991. Author: Poems of Faith and Love, 1992, Five-Beat Poems, 1993, Four-Beat Poems, 1994, Migration of the Soul, 1995. Deacon Mt. Kisco (N.Y.) Presbyn. Ch., 1992-98, also mem. ch. choir. Recipient Golden Poet award World of Poetry, 1989, hon. mention Acad. Am. Poets, 1990, Editor's Choice award Nat. Libr. Poetry, 1994. Avocations: volleyball, swimming. Home: 77 Carpenter Ave Apt 6S Mount Kisco NY 10549-2424

GODINER, DONALD LEONARD, lawyer; b. Bronx, N.Y., Feb. 21, 1933; s. Israel and Edith (Rubenstein) G.; m. Caryl Mignon Nussbaum, Sept. 7, 1958; children: Clifford, Kenneth. AB, NYU, 1953; JD, Columbia U., 1956. Bar: N.Y. 1956, Mo. 1972. Gen. counsel Stromberg-Carlson, Rochester, N.Y., 1965-71; assoc. gen. counsel Gen. Dynamics Corp., St. Louis, 1971-73; v.p., gen. counsel Permaneer Corp., St. Louis, 1973-75; ptnr. Gallop, Johnson, Godiner, Morganstern & Crebs, St. Louis, 1975-80; sr. v.p., gen. counsel, sec. Laclede Gas Co., St. Louis, 1980—. Editor Columbia U. Law Rev., 1955-56. Served with U.S. Army, 1956-58. Mem. ABA, N.Y. State Bar Assn., Met. St. Louis Bar Assn., Assn. of Bar of City of N.Y. Club: Noonday (St. Louis). Home: 157 Trails West Dr Chesterfield MO 63017-2553 Office: Laclede Gas Co 720 Olive St Ste 1200 Saint Louis MO 63101-2389*

GODINEZ, MAGDALENA, cardiology nurse; b. Brownsville, Tex., Dec. 30, 1956; d. Ramon Jr. and Virginia (Flores) Godinez; 1 child, Juan-Ramon. Diploma, Tex. Southmost Coll., 1979, student. LVN. Surg. scrub nurse Brownsville Med. Ctr., 1979-80; pediatric/cardiology nurse physician's office, Brownsville, 1980-84, ophthalmology nurse, 1985-89; cardiology nurse Heart Clinic, Inc., Brownsville, 1989—. Office: Heart Clinic Inc Brownsville TX 78520-8704

GODINEZ FLORES, RAMON, auxiliary bishop; b. Jamay, Jalisco, Mexico, Apr. 18, 1936; s. Ortega J. Cleofas G. and Maria del Refugio (Flores). Lic. in Philosophy, Sem. Guadalajara, (Jalisco, Mexico); theology degree, U. Gregoriana, Rome, postgrad. in canon law. Ordained priest Roman Catholic Ch., 1959, aux. bishop, 1980. Prof., superior Diocesan Sem., Guadalajara; chaplain religious communities, Templo de San Jorge, Vallarta-San Jorge, Guadalajara; pastor Parroco de Nuestra Senora de la Luz, Guadalajara; sec. Archdiocese of Guadalajara, 1972-80, aux. bishop, 1980—; bishop Aguascalientes, Aguascalientes, Mex., 1998; with, Diocese of Aguascalientes, 1998, sec. gen. Conferencia del Episcopado Mexicano, 1991—. Contbr. articles to religious jours. Home: Galeana 105 Norte, Apartado Postal 167, CP 20000 Aguascalientes AGS 07020, Mexico

GODLEWSKI, JAMES BERNARD, elementary school educator, principal, consultant; b. Wilkes-Barre, Pa., Nov. 22, 1952; s. Stanley William and Alberta Theresa (Baloga) G.; m. Theresa Anne Boblick, July 9, 1983; children: Michael James, Matthew Joel, Kristofer John. BA in History, Elem. Edn., Wilkes U., 1975, MS in Elem Edn., 1977; EdD in Elem Edn., Temple U., 1987. Cert. elem. tchr., elem. prin., computer specialist, Pa. Educator Wallenpaupack Area Sch. Dist., Hawley, Pa., 1975—; elem. prin. Wyoming Valley West Sch. Dist., Kingston, Pa., 1975—; sports writer The News Eagle, Hawley, 1975-90; prin. Godlewski Assocs., Wilkes-Barre, 1991—, State Street Elem. Sch., Larksville, Pa., 1993—; adj. faculty Pa. Dept. Edn., Harrisburg; adj. prof. Pa. State U., 1990; owner Godlewski Computer Solutions, 1991—. Co-author: (workbook) Reading to Think, 1989; contbr. articles to profl. jours. Mem. Econ. Devel. Coun. Northeastern Pa., 1987. Mem. NEA, PTA, Internat. Coun. Computers for Educators, Nat. Coun. Social Studies, Assn. for Devel. Computer Based Instructional Systems, Assn. Supervision, Curriculum and Devel., Assn. Tchrs. Computers, Math, and Sci., Nat. Mid. Schs. Assn., Pa. Coun. Tchrs. Math., Northeastern Pa. Assn. Math Tchrs., Pa. State Ednl. Assn., Pa. Assn. Supervision, Curriculum and Devel., Northeastern Pa. Amateur Computer Club, Wallenpaupack Area Ednl. Assn., Twins Found., KC, Temple Owl Club, Phi Delta Kappa. Republican. Roman Catholic. Home: 212 Bowman St Wilkes Barre PA 18702-5405 Office: Wyoming Valley W Sch Dist Maple & Pine Sts Kingston PA 18704

GODLY, GORDON THOMAS, retired chemist, consultant; b. Woodbastwick, Norfolk, Eng., Oct. 20, 1919; came to US, 1960; s. Arthur Percy Turley and Daisy Harriet G.; m. Mary Margaret Midgley, July 2, 1955 (dec. July, 1994); children: Gerda Anne, Martin Arthur Turley, Christopher John. BS, London U., Eng., 1951. Chief chemist Reeves & Sons Ltd., Enfield, Eng., 1959-60; chief chemist, v.p. Reeves USA, Inc., N.Y.C., 1966-77, Stfford-Reeves, Inc., N.Y.C., 1966-77; tech. dir., v.p. Rich Art Color Co., Inc., Lodi, N.J., 1977-90, cons., 1990-92. Patent for stain-free tempera paint. V.p. Ptnrs. in Faith for Affordable Housing, Aberdeen, N.J., 1989—; lay reader Episcopal Ch., N.J., 1965—. Capt. Brit. Army, 1940-45. Decorated 1939-45 Star, Africa star, Italy star, Pacific star British War Office, 1946. Mem. AAAS. Episcopalian. Avocations: computer programming, gardening. Home: 401 Pennington Titusville Rd Titusville NJ 08560-2012

GODMAN, GABRIEL CHARLES, pathology educator; b. Albany, N.Y., Jan. 24, 1921; s. Hyman S. and Bertha R. Godman. AB, NYU, 1941, MD, 1944. House officer medicine Bellevue Hosp., N.Y.C., 1944-45; resident in pathology New Haven Hosp.; asst. in pathology Yale U. Med. Sch., New Haven, 1948-50; fellow in pathology Mt. Sinai Hosp., N.Y.C., 1950-51; mem. faculty Columbia U. Coll. Physicians and Surgeons, N.Y.C., 1952—; prof. pathology Columbia U. Coll. Physicians and Surgeons., N.Y.C., 1969—; assoc. Rockefeller U., 1957-60. Contbr. articles and chpts. to jours. and texts in field. Served to capt. M.C., U.S. Army, 1945-47. Mem. Am. Assn. Pathologists, Am. Soc. Cell Biology, Harvey Soc., Internat. Acad. Pathology, Assn. U. Pathologists. Home: 900 W 190th St New York NY 10040-3633 Office: 630 W 168th St New York NY 10032-3702

GODO, EINAR, computer engineer; b. Aalesund, Möre, Norway, May 31, 1926; came to U.S. 1953; s. Lars and Oline (Blindheim) G.; m. Betty Jane Graba, 1955; children: Kjell Einar, Greta Anne, Erik Lars. BS in Aero. Engring., U. Wash., 1956, BSEE, 1958, MS, 1964. Electronic designer Boeing Aerospace, Seattle, 1959-82; prime investigator Computer Devel., Bellevue, Wash., 1982-98, in computer hardware devel., 1998—. Achievements include patent for bating machine (Norway), Word Recognition System(USA, Can., Japan, Brit., France, Ger.); contributor engineering to most or all programs for putting man/hardware on the moon including lunar orbiter, lunar rover, Saturn 5 booster.

GODOFF, ANN, book editor; b. N.Y.C., July 22, 1949; d. Boris and Marilyn (Rosenstock) G. BFA, NYU, 1972. Sr. editor Simon & Schuster, N.Y.C., 1980-86; editor in chief Atlantic Monthly Press, N.Y.C., 1986-91; exec. editor Random House Inc., N.Y.C., 1991-96, pres., editor-in-chief, 1997—. Office: Random House Inc 201 E 50th St New York NY 10022-7703*

GODOFSKY, LAWRENCE, lawyer; b. Yonkers, N.Y., Mar. 30, 1938; s. Eli and Lily (Deutsch) G.; m. Thea Grace Schimel, June 11, 1961; children: Randee Felicia, Howard Charles. BA, Columbia U., N.Y.C., 1960, LLB, 1965. Bar: N.Y. 1965, Fla. 1974. Asst. counsel Mut. Life Ins. Co. of N.Y., N.Y.C., 1964-73; mem. Swann and Glass and predecessor firm, Miami, Fla.,

1973-74; v.p., gen. counsel Diversified Mortgage Investors (formerly Diversified Advisors, Inc.), Miami, 1974-76; mem. Greenberg, Traurig, Hoffman, Lipoff, Rosen & Quentel P.A., Miami, 1976—. Mem. bd. dirs. Infants in Need, Inc., Miami, 1991—. Mem. ABA, N.Y. State Bar Assn., Fla. Bar Assn., Am. Coll. Real Estate Lawyers, Am. Land Title Assn. (assoc.). Office: Greenberg Traurig Hoffman Lipoff Rosen & Quentel PA 1221 Brickell Ave Miami FL 33131-3224

GODOFSKY, STANLEY, lawyer; b. N.Y.C., May 24, 1928; s. Eli and Lily (Deutsch) G.; m. Elaine Gloria Weiss, Dec. 15, 1951 (dec. Feb. 20, 1994). A.B., Columbia U., 1949, J.D., 1951. Bar: N.Y. 1951, U.S. Supreme Ct. 1961. Assoc. Rogers & Wells, and predecessors, N.Y.C., 1951-64, ptnr., 1965-89; co-adj. lectr. Rutgers Law Sch., 1990-91, adj. prof., 1992-93; adj. prof. Nova U. Law Sch., 1991-93; spl. asst. counsel N.Y. State Crime Commn., 1952. Bd. editors Columbia Law Rev., 1950, bd. revising editors, 1951. Trustee Jewish Community Ctr. White Plains, N.Y., 1983-89; mem. commn. on law and social action Am. Jewish Congress, 1986—. Mem. ABA, Am. Law Inst., N.Y. State Bar Assn., Assn. of Bar of City of N.Y., Internat. Assn. Jewish Lawyers and Jurists (bd. govs. Am. sect. 1990-98, exec. com. and coun. 1999—). Home: 1804 Eleuthera Pt Apt C-1 Coconut Creek FL 33066-2835

GODSCHALK, DAVID ROBINSON, architect, urban development planner, educator; b. Enid, Okla., May 14, 1931; s. Harold J. and Helen Faye (Robinson) G.; m. Lallie Moore Kain, June 27, 1959; 1 child, David Kennedy. B.A., Dartmouth Coll., 1953; B.Arch., U. Fla., 1959; M.Regional Planning, U. N.C., 1964, Ph.D., 1971. Vice pres. Milo Smith Assos., Tampa, Fla., 1959-61; planning dir. City of Gainesville, Fla., 1964-65; asst. prof. Fla. State U., Tallahassee, 1965-67; editor AIP Jour., Chapel Hill, N.C., 1968-71; assoc. prof. U. N.C., Chapel Hill, 1972-77, prof., 1977-94, Stephen Baxter prof. planning, 1994—; chmn. dept. city and regional planning U. N.C., 1978-83; cons. and expert witness in field. Author: (with others) Constitutional Issues of Growth Management, 1979, Land Supply Monitoring, 1986, Planning in America: Learning from Turbulence, 1974, Catastrophic Coastal Storms: Hazard Mitigation and Development Management, 1989, Urban Land Use Planning, 1995, Pulling Together: A Planning and Development Consensus Building Manual, 1994, Cooperating with Nature: Confronting Natural Hazards with Land Use for Planning Sustainable Communities, 1998. Natural Hazard Mitigation: Recasting Disaster Policy and Planning, 1999; editor: (with others) Understanding Growth Management, 1989, The Planner as Dispute Resolver, 1989; editor Am. Inst. Planners Jour., 1968-71; mem. editl. bd. Jour. Planning Edn. and Rsch., 1983-89, 93-97, Jour. Am. Planning Assn., 1983-96, Jour. Archtl. Planning Rsch., 1991—, Australian Planner, 1997—. Mem. Town Coun., Chapel Hill, 1985-89, N.C. Legis. Rsch. Commn. on Statewide Comprehensive Planning, 1991-93. Served with USNR, 1953-56, 61-62; comdr. Res.; ret., 1980. Recipient Disting. Alumnus award Dept. City and Regional Planning, U. N.C., 1996. Fellow AICP; mem. Am. Planning Assn. (bd. govs. 1978-79, Profl. Achievement award 1983, Elected Ofcl. award N.C. chpt. 1990), Am. Soc. Planning Ofcls. (bd. dir. 1974-77), Am. Inst. Cert. Planners (Svc. medal 1971), Assn. of Collegiate Schs. of Planning (co-chair com. nat. urban policy 1992-94). Office: Univ NC Dept City & Regional Planning Chapel Hill NC 27599-3140

GODSEY, JAMES MARK, library director; b. Bloomington, Ind., Nov. 26, 1947; s. George Abraham Godsey and Eva Burns; m. Valerie Sue Maddy, June 21, 1969; children: Christopher Mark, Deacon James. BS, U. Minn., 1970; MLS, Ind. U., 1976. Tchr. English Grand Rapids (Minn.) H.S., 1970-76; libr. dir. Huntington (Ind.) Pub. Libr., 1976-83; dep. dir. Rochester (Minn.) Pub. Libr., 1983-96; libr. dir. Council Bluffs (Iowa) Pub. Libr., 1996—. Dir. G.H. Cachiaras Meml. Libr., Minn. Bible Coll., Rochester, 1990-95. Mem. Rotary Internat.

GODSEY, JAMES PAUL (J.P. GODSEY), security firm executive; b. LaPort, Ind., Nov. 1, 1957; s. Paul James Godsey and Doris Matilda Sandquist; m. Sheila Kay Kilpatrick, Nov. 24, 1984 (div. Feb. 1989); m. Judith G. Jones, Mar. 13, 1999; stepchildren: Jeremy, Jessica. BS, W.Va. Wesleyan Coll., 1979. Lic. life and health annuities, series 7, 65, 31. Mgr. 2001/VIP Enterprises, Myrtle Beach, S.C., 1979-82; campaign mgr. Hinkle for Congress, Buckhannon, W.Va., 1982; mktg./pub. rels. Washington Feds. U.S. Football League, 1982-84; fin. advisor Prudential Securities, Virginia Beach, Va., 1995-97; v.p. investments IJL/Wachovia, Virginia Beach, Va., 1997—. Mem. Dale Carnegie Tng., 1989, Thaila Civic League, 1993—, Citizens Action Coalition, 1996—; chmn. Hampton Rds. Rep. Alliance, Virginia Beach, 1996—; chair fin. Rep. Party Virginia Beach, 1991-98, chmn., 1996—; mem. Big Brothers/Big Sisters, Norfolk, 1988-91. Mem. Earning By Learning Found. (treas. 1993—), W.Va. Wesleyan Alumni Coun. (vice-chmn. 1991-95, fin. dir., bd. dirs.), Internat. Found. Theta Chi. Republican. Avocations: politics, volunteering, running charity food and toy drives, Big Band music, sports and fitness. Fax: 757-425-5907. Home: 2329 Simpkins Ct Virginia Beach VA 23452 Office: Interstate/Johnson Ln The Pavilion Ctr Ste 701 2101 Parks Ave Virginia Beach VA 23451

GODSEY, JOHN DREW, minister, theology educator emeritus; b. Bristol, Tenn., Oct. 10, 1922; s. William Clinton and Mary Lynn (Corns) G.; m. Emalee Caldwell, June 26, 1943 (dec. Oct. 1993); children: Emalee Lynn Godsey Murphy, John Drew Jr., Suzanne Godsey Douglas, Gretchen Godsey Brownley; m. Cozette Hapney Barker, Sept. 23, 1995. B.S., Va. Poly. Inst. and State U., 1947; B.D., Drew U., 1953; D.Theol., U. Basel, Switzerland, 1960. Ordained to ministry United Methodist Ch., 1952. Instr. systematic theology, asst. dean Drew U., Madison, N.J., 1956-59, asst. prof., 1959-64, assoc. prof., 1964-66, prof., 1966-68; prof., assoc. dean Wesley Theol. Sem., Washington, 1968-71, prof. systematic theology, 1971-88; emeritus prof. Wesley Theol. Sem., 1988—; Fulbright scholar U. Goettingen, W. Germany, 1964-65. Author: The Theology of Dietrich Bonhoeffer, 1960, Karl Barth's Table Talk, 1963, Preface to Bonhoeffer, 1965, Introduction and Epilogue to Karl Barth's How I Changed My Mind, 1966, The Promise of H. Richard Niebuhr, 1970; co-editor: Ethical Responsibility: Bonhoeffer's Legacy to the Churches, 1981. Mem. Montgomery County Fair Housing Assn., Md. Served with AUS, 1943-46. Recipient Disting. Svc. Alumni award Drew U. Theol. Sch. Alumni/AE Assn., 1995; Am. Assn. Theol. Schs. faculty fellow, 1964-65. Mem. Am. Acad. Religion, Am. Theol. Soc. (pres. 1985-86), Bibl. Theologians, Internat. Bonhoeffer Soc. (editor newsletter 1989-92), Karl Barth Soc. N. Am., New Haven Theol. Discussion Group, Common Cause, Omicron Delta Kappa, Phi Kappa Phi, Alpha Zeta. Democrat. Home: 8306 Bryant Dr Bethesda MD 20817-3137 Office: Wesley Theol Sem 4500 Massachusetts Ave NW Washington DC 20016-5632 *My goal has been to serve others with integrity, to do every job to the best of my ability, and to respect and further the rights and welfare of my fellow creatures on planet earth. Thus should my life be a testimony to my faith.*

GODSEY, MARTHA SUE, speech-language pathologist; b. Abilene, Tex., Jan. 24, 1956; d. John Holbrook and Stella Mae (Blankenship) Chalmers; children: Bo Kilpatrick, Ryan Smith; married, Dec. 18, 1993; 1 child, J. Jordan Godsey. BSN, Tex. Chritian U., 1979; MA, Abilene Christian U., 1988. RN, Tex. RN Hendrick Med. Ctr., Abilene, 1979-80; speech pathologist Abilene Ind. Sch. Dist., 1989-92, Tri-County Edn. Co-op, 1992-94; pvt. practice, 1994-96; speech therapist Therapy Assocs., Inc., 1996-97, Sundance Rehab. Corp., 1997—, West Tex. Rehab. Ctr., 1998—. Mem. Am. Speech/Lang. and Hearing Assn., Tex. Speech/Lang. and Hearing Assn. Avocation: reading. Home: 1669 Us Highway 180 W Anson TX 79501-3101

GODSEY, R(ALEIGH) KIRBY, university president; b. Birmingham, Ala., Apr. 2, 1936; m. Joan Stockstill; children—Raleigh, Hunter, Erica, Stephanie. BA, Samford U., 1957; BD, New Orleans Baptist Theol. Sem., 1960, ThD, 1962; LHD, 1996; MA, U. Ala., 1967; PhD, Tulane U., 1969; LHD, U. S.C., 1984; LLD, Averett Coll., 1996. Asst. prof. philosophy and religion Judson Coll., Marion, Ala., 1962-67; Danforth assoc. Danforth Found., 1964-67; v.p., dean Averett Coll., Danville, Va., 1969-77; dean Coll. Liberal Arts Mercer U., Macon, Ga., 1977-78, exec. v.p., 1978-79, pres., 1979—; trustee So. Assn. Colls. and Schs.; pres. Ga. Fund Ind. Colls.; chief cons. Comprehensive Instl. Devel. Project; cons. Mgmt. Higher Edn. and Organizational Devel. Problems, Planning and Data Systems for Pvt. Colls., Carnegie Found., Task Force on Acad. Affairs for Council of Ind. Colls.; mem. exec. com. Nat. Workshop on Faculty Devel., Lilly and Kellogg Founds.; lectr. Confs. on Personnel Relations, New Orleans, Chgo., Detroit, Seminars on Philos. Ethics for Med. Students, Tulane U., regional confs. and workshops, Chgo., St. Louis, Atlanta, Kansas City. Author: When We Talk About God...Let's Be Honest; contbr. articles to profl. jours. Speaker at civic clubs and organs. and bus. and profl. groups including Rotary, Kiwanis, Exchange, Civitan, Sertoma. Recipient Citizenship award, Danville, Va., 1971. Mem. Am. Assn. Higher Edn. (chmn. conf. on institutional planning), Am. Philosophical Assn., So. Soc. for Philosophy and Psychology, Macon C. of C. (bd. dirs.), Phi Alpha Theta, Phi Kappa Phi. Baptist. Lodge: Rotary. Office: Mercer Univ Cen Office 1400 Coleman Ave Macon GA 31207-0001

GODSEY, WILLIAM COLE, physician; b. Memphis, Dec. 11, 1933; s. Monroe Dowe and Margaret Pauline (Cole) G.; m. Norma Jean Wilkinson, June 18, 1958; children: William Cole, John Edward, Robert Dowe. B.S., Rhodes Coll., 1955; M.D., U. Tenn., 1958. Diplomate Am. Bd. Psychiatry and Neurology, Am. Bd. Forensic Medicine. Intern John Gaston Hosp., Memphis, 1958-59; resident in psychiatry Gailor Meml. Hosp., Memphis, 1960-63; pvt. practice specializing in psychiatry and neurology Memphis, 1963—; asst. supt. Memphis Mental Health Inst., 1965-74; supt. Ctrl. State Hosp., Nashville, 1974-75; med. dir. Whitehaven Mental Health Ctr., Memphis, 1975-84, St. Joseph Hosp. Life Ctr., 1984-88; pres. Civilian Material Assistance, Memphis, 1988; mem. staff Delta Med. Ctr.; asst. prof. U. Tenn. Coll. Medicine, 1965-74, Coll. Pharmacy, 1972-75; chief of staff Lakeside Hosp., Memphis, 1976-77; songwriter, pub.; pres. Memphis Country Music, Inc. Fellow Am. Psychiat. Assn. (life; past pres. West Tenn. chpt.); mem. NRA, Tenn. Psychiat. Assn. (exec. coun., past pres.), Am. Coll. Forensic Examiners, Moose. Methodist. Office: 5118 Park Ave Ste 323 Memphis TN 38117-5711

GODSHALL, BARBARA MARIE, educational administrator; b. Newark, N.Y., Jan. 5, 1958; d. Edward Franklin and Joan Marie (Moon) Moll; m. Clark J. Godshall, Oct. 26, 1985. AS, Cazenovia Coll., 1978; BS summa cum laude, Keuka Coll., 1989; MS, Nazareth Coll., 1991; CAS in Adminstrn., SUNY, Brockport, 1992; postgrad., U. Buffalo, 1995—. Cert. spl. edn. and elem. tchr., adminstr. Spl. edn. tchr. Lockport (N.Y.) Ctrl. Sch. Dist., 1991-92; spl. edn. tchr. Barker (N.Y.) Ctrl. Sch. Dist., 1992-93, dir. pupil pers. svcs. and spl. programs, 1993-97; dir. pupil pers. svcs. and spl. programs Roy-Hart Ctrl. Sch. Dist., Lockport, 1997—; pres., ednl. cons. elem., secondary and spl. edn.; spl. edn. tchr. Niag-Wheat Cen. Sch. Dist., 1995-97. Bd. dirs. ARC, Lockport, 1990—, Lockport Pub. Libr., 1990—. N.Y. State scholar, 1991. Mem. ASCD, Coun. for Exceptional Children, Phi Delta Kappa. Avocations: traveling, bicycling, reading, crafts, gardening. Home and Office: 5494 Forest Hill Rd Lockport NY 14094-6224

GODSIL, RICHARD WILLIAM, minister; b. Estherville, Iowa, Mar. 8, 1953; s. Richard Lee and Shirley Ann (Diamond) G.; m. Laurel Christine Webster, July 17, 1971; children: Richard II, Joshua, Rebekah. AA, Okaloosa Walton Jr. Coll., 1977; BS, Okla. Christian Coll., 1980; postgrad., Pepperdine U., 1984; MS in Family Devel. & Edn., Friends U., 1997. Ordained to ministry Christian Ch., 1989. Youth min. Ch. of Christ, Derby, Kans., 1981-82; assoc. min. Ch. of Christ, Redlands, Calif., 1982-84; youth min. religious edn. Twin Cities Christian Ch., Oceanside, Calif., 1987-88; assoc. min. Montrose (Colo.) Christian Ch., 1988-94; youth min. 1st Christian Ch., Dodge City, Kans., 1994-96, West Valley Christian Ch., West hills, Calif., 1996—; pres. Colo. Christian Concerts, Montrose, 1990—; tchr. 6th grade bible West Valley Christian Sch., 1997-98; Bible tchr. 9th and 10th grades, 1998-99; assoc. Nat. Inst. Youth Ministry. V.p. Gallerya Youth Ctr., Montrose, 1990; advisor home econs. bd. high sch., Montrose, 1990—; mem. budget task force Montrose United Sch. Dist., 1993, mem. dist. accountability com., 1992-94; mem. assessment testing com. Dodge City United Sch. Dist., 1995, mem. dist. accountability com., 1995. Sgt. USAF, 1971-75. Named Young Min. of Yr. Standard Pub. Co., 1989, Softball Coach of Yr., West Valley Christian H.S., 1998. Mem. Mountain Area Christian Educators (v.p. Montrose chpt. 1989—), Assn. Montrose Chs. (pres. 1990), Montrose Youth Mins. Assn. (pres. 1990-93), Valley Youth Pastors Network (steering com. 1998-99), Nat. Network Youth Mins., Campus Life Club (bd. dirs. 1987 Oceanside). Republican. Home: 7831 Ponce Ave West Hills CA 91304-4629 Office: West Valley Christian Ch 22944 Enadia Way West Hills CA 91307-2206 *Allowing young persons to see themselves as worthwhile beings in a confused world is the goal of my ministry. Letting them see that God loves them unconditionally, as they are now and what they can become. This pursuit keeps me up at night, causes tears to fall and brings joy to my heart. What a way to live for God!.*

GODSOE, PETER COWPERTHWAITE, banker; b. Toronto, May 2, 1938; s. J. Gerald and Margaret (Cowperthwaite) G.; m. Shelagh Cathleen Reburn, Nov. 30, 1963; children: Craig, Cynthia, Eden. BSc, U. Toronto, 1961; MBA, Harvard U., 1966. Chartered acct., Can. Gen. mgr. The Bank of N.S., Toronto, 1971-78, sr. v.p., 1979-80, exec. v.p., 1980-82, vice chmn., dir., 1982-92, pres., COO, vice-chmn., 1982-92, dep. chmn., pres., CEO, 1993-95, chmn. bd., CEO, 1995—, also bd. dirs.; chmn., bd. dirs. The Bank of N.S. Internat. Ltd., 1995—; bd. dirs. BNS Internat. (Hong Kong) Ltd.; chmn. The Bank of N.S. Internat. Ltd., Scotiabank (Ireland) Ltd.; bd. dirs. Alexander & Alexander Svcs., Inc., Reed Stenhouse Cos. Ltd., Empire Co. Ltd., BNS Internat. (Panama) S.A., Bank N.S. Jamaica Ltd., Bank N.S. Trinidad and Tobago Ltd., Bank N.S. Trust Co., Bank N.S. Trust Co. (Bahamas) Ltd., Bank N.S. Trust Co. (Cayman) Ltd., N.S. Corp., Scotiabank Jamaica Trust and Mcht. Bank Ltd., West India Co. Mcht. Bankers Ltd., Bank of N.S. Trust Co. Trinidad and Tobago Ltd., Aon Reed Stenhouse; trustee Scotiabank Pension Plan, Scotia Mortgage Corp.; chancellor U. of Western Ont. Bd. dirs. Can. Coun. of Christians and Jews, Toronto, 1972—, Mt. Sinai Hosp., 1986; past pres. Bd. of Trade, Toronto, 1984-85; mem. adv. com. Western Bus. Sch.; assoc. mem. bd. govs. Dalhousie U.; mem. chancellor's coun. Victoria U.; mem. Mayor's Econ. Partnership Coun. Mem. Can. Bankers Assn. (past chmn.), Jr. Achievement of Met. Toronto and York Region (bd. govs.), Can. Club (past pres. 1982-83). Office: Bank of Nova Scotia, Scotia Plz/44 King St W, Toronto, ON Canada M5H 1H1*

GODSON, ROY SIMON, political scientist, think tank executive; b. Bklyn., Oct. 17, 1942; s. Joseph and Rose (Milner) G.; m. Christine Watson, Aug. 27, 1971. BA with honors, Middlebury Coll., 1964; MA, Columbia U., 1967, PhD, 1972. Instr. Carnegie-Mellon U., Pitts., 1967-69; dir. edn. World Affairs Coun. Pitts., 1967-69; prof. govt. Georgetown U., Washington, 1969—, dir. internat. labor program, 1971-86; with Nat. Strategy Info. Ctr., Washington, 1969—, pres., 1993—, coord. Consortium for Study of Intelligence, 1979—; cons. U.S. agys., 1987—, Pres.'s Fgn. Intelligence Adv. Bd., 1982-89, Nat. Security Coun., 1982-86, USIA, 1981-83. Author: Dirty Tricks or Trump Cards: U.S. Covert Action and Counterintelligence, 1995, Labor in Soviet Global Strategy, 1984, American Labor and European Politics: The AFL as a Transnational Force, 1976; co-author: Dezinformatsia: Active Measures in Soviet Strategy, 1984, The CIA and the American Ethic: An Unfinished Debate, 1985, Eurocommunism: Implications for East and West, 1978; editor: Intellgience Requirements for the 1990s: Collection, Analysis, Counterintelligence, and Covert Action, 1988, Comparing Foreign Intelligence: The US, USSR, UK and the Third World, 1988, Intelligence Requirements for the 1980s 5 vol. ser.; co-editor Trends in Organized Crime, 1995—, Security Studies for the 21st Century, 1998. Avocation: riding toward the light. Office: Georgetown Univ Dept Govt Washington DC 20057-1034

GODT, EARL WAYNE, II, technology education educator; b. Coco Solo, Canal Zone, Panama, Aug. 10, 1953; came to U.S., 1955; s. Earl Wayne and Theresa May (Hymel) G.; m. Pamela Rollefson Terry, Aug. 1, 1987; 1 child, Anne Louise Terry. AS, Kilgore Coll., 1983; BS, U. Tex., Tyler, 1984; MS, Purdue U., 1985; postgrad., Ind. U., 1987-91; PhD, Kensington U., 1993. Tech. writer USMC/Civil Svc., Cherry Point, N.C., 1974-77; mgr. Pizza Hut, N.C., Tex., 1977-81; refinery worker Shore Oil Corp., Kilgore, Tex., 1981; lab. asst. Stewart Blood Ctr., Tyler, Tex., 1982; quality assurance engr. East Tex. Lighthouse for the Blind, Tyler, Tex., 1983-84; grad. teaching asst. Purdue U., West Lafayette, Ind., 1984-85; instr. GMC/Chevrolet-Pontiac-Can., Doralville, Ga., 1986; asst. prof. Ind. State U., Terre Haute, Ind., 1986-93, Western Ill. U., Macomb, 1993-96, Spoon River Coll., Canton, Ill., 1996-98, Heartland C.C., Bloomington, Ill., 1998—; cons. Covered Bridge Spl. Edn. Dist., Terre Haute, 1990; judge Student Contest Robotics Internat., 1989, 94, 95; developer/instr. robotics grades 3-6 Ind. State U. Sch., Terre Haute, 1988—; curriculum evaluator Assn. Ind. Colls. and Schs., Washington, 1989—. Presented robotics tutorial 4th Annual Nat. Robotics and Automation Systems Conf., 1987; contbr. articles profl. jours. Chairperson Unitarian-Universalist congregation, Terre Haute, 1990. Faculty devel. grantee TRW Found., 1989, Higher Edn. Cooperation Act grantee Ill. Bd. Higher Edn., 1996. Mem. Soc. Mfg. Engrs., Robotics Internat. (cert. sr. indsl. technologist, cert. mfg. technologist), Nat. Assn. Indsl. Tech. (dir. region 2 1994-96, chair ann. program com.). Democrat. Avocations: golf, bowling, chess. Home: 1719 W Adams St Macomb IL 61455-1203 Office: Heartland CC Bloomington IL 61701

GODWIN, ANNABELLE PALKES, retired early childhood education educator; b. St. Louis, Dec. 23, 1920; d. Louis Aaron and Sadie (Galperin) Palkes; m. Robert Franklin Godwin, Jr., June 7, 1942 (dec. Aug. 1991); children: Sara, Jo Beth, Robert Franklin III. BS in Edn. and Drama, Washington U., St. Louis, 1945; MA in Early Childhood Edn., UCLA, 1967. Cert. secondary English and drama tchr., Mo.; cert. C.C. child devel. tchr., Calif. Tchr. L.A. Child Devel. Ctrs., 1946-47, Burbank (Calif.) Child Devel. Ctrs., 1947-49, Adventure Sch., Studio City, Calif., 1952-53; dir. nursery sch. Temple Emanuel, Burbank, 1959-67, Temple Beth Hillel, North Hollywood, Calif., 1967-75; prof. child devel. L.A. C.C. Dist., 1968-92, prof. emeritus, 1992—; instr. UCLA Ext., 1968-78. Co-chair prodn. com. Setting Up for Infant Care, 1988; prodr. ednl. film Creative Experiences with Body Movement, 1975, Infant/Toddler Environments: Adult/Child Interaction, 1991. Bd. dirs. Calif. Children's Lobby, 1980-92; bd. dirs., legis. chmn., v.p. L.A. Mayor's Adv. Com. on Childcare, 1976—, chair, 1994-95; pres. exec. bd. Childcare Resource Ctr. San Fernando Valley, Calif., 1990—. Scholarship named in her honor L.A. Mission Coll., 1996, play day named in her honor San Fernando Valley, Calif., 1997. Mem. Assn. for Early Jewish Edn. (charter, past pres., bd. dirs., plaque 1975), So. Calif. Assn. for Edn. Young Children (bd. dirs., v.p. 1965—). Democrat. Avocation: working on behalf of children. Home: 1825 Rosita Ave Burbank CA 91504-2818

GODWIN, GAIL KATHLEEN, author; b. Birmingham, Ala., June 18, 1937; d. Mose Winston and Kathleen (Krahenbuhl) G.; m. Douglas Kennedy, 1960 (div. 1961), m. Ian Marshall, 1965 (div. 1966). Student, Peace Jr. Coll., Raleigh, N.C., 1955-57; B.A. in Journalism, U. N.C., 1959; M.A. in English, U. Iowa, 1968, Ph.D., 1971. News reporter Miami Herald, 1959-60; rep., cons. U.S. Travel Service, London, 1961-65; editorial asst. Saturday Evening Post, 1966; instr. Univ. Iowa, Iowa City, 1967-71; lectr. Iowa Writer's Workshop, 1972-73, Vassar Coll., 1977, Columbia U. Writing Program, 1978, 81. Author: (novels) The Perfectionists, 1970, Glass People, 1972, The Odd Woman, 1974 (Nat. Book award nomination 1974), Violet Clay, 1978 (Am. Book award nomination 1980), A Mother and Two Daughters, 1982 (Am. Book award nomination 1982), The Finishing School, 1985, A Southern Family, 1987, Father Melancholy's Daughter, 1991, The Good Husband, 1994, Evensong, 1999; (short stories) Dream Children, 1976, Mr. Bedford and The Muses, 1983;editor: (with Shannon Ravenel) The Best American Short Stories 1985, 1985; librettist: (with Robert Starer) The Last Lover, 1975, Journals of a Songmaker, 1976, Apollonia, 1979, Anna Margarita's Will, 1981, Remembering Felix, 1987, Gregory The Great, 1996, The Other Voice: A Portrait of Hilda of Whitby in Words and Music, 1998, Magdalene At The Tomb, 1999. Recipient Thomas Wolfe Meml. award Lipinsky Endowment of Western N.C. Hist. Assn., 1988, Janet Kafka award U. Rochester, 1988; fellow Center for Advanced Study, U. Ill., Urbana, 1971-72; Am. specialist USIS, 1976; Nat. Endowment Arts grantee, 1974-75; Guggenheim fellow, 1975-76; recipient award in lit. Am. Acad. and Inst. of Arts and Letters, 1981. Mem. PEN, ASCAP, Authors Guild, Authors League. Home: PO Box 946 Woodstock NY 12498-0946

GODWIN, HAROLD NORMAN, pharmacist, educator; b. Ransom, Kans., Oct. 9, 1941; s. Harold Joseph and Nora Elva (Welch) G.; m. Judy Rae Ricketts, June 9, 1963; children: Paula Lynn, Jennifer Joy. BS in Pharmacy, U. Kans., 1964; MS in Hosp. Pharmacy, Ohio State U., 1966. Lic. pharmacist, Kans., Ohio. Instr. Ohio State U. Coll. Pharmacy, Columbus, 1966-69; asst. dir. pharmacy Ohio State U., Columbus, 1966-69; dir. pharmacy U. Kans. Med. Ctr., Kansas City, 1969—; asst. prof. U. Kans. Sch. Pharmacy, Kansas City, 1969-74, assoc. prof., 1974-80, prof. pharmacy, 1980—, asst. dean pharmacy, 1975-89, assoc. dean pharmacy, 1989—, chmn. pharmacy practice, 1984—. Author: Implementation Guide to IV Admixtures, 1977; (with others) Remington's Pharmaceutical Sciences, 1980, 85, 90, 95; contbr. over 100 articles to profl. jours. Recipient Clifton J. Latiolais award Ohio State U. Residents Alumni, 1986, Disting. Alumni award Ohio State U. Coll. Pharmacy, 1995. Mem. Am. Soc. Hosp. Pharmacists (pres. 1982-83, bd. dirs. 1978-81, Harvey A.K. Whitney award 1991), Am. Pharm. Assn., Kans. Pharmacists Assn. (pres. 1977, Kans. Pharmacist of Yr. 1982), Kans. Soc. Hosp. Pharmacists (Kans. Hosp. Pharmacist of Yr. 1982, Harold N. Godwin award 1984), Greater Kansas City Soc. Hosp. Pharmacists (pres. 1972), Am. Coun. Pharm. Edn. (bd. dirs. 1988—, pres. 1992-96). Republican. Methodist. Avocations: tennis, biking, cooking, wine tasting. Home: 10112 W 98th St Shawnee Mission KS 66212-5238 Office: U Kans Med Ctr Rainbow Blvd At 39th St Kansas City KS 66106-7231

GODWIN, JAMES BECKHAM, retired landscape architect; b. Richmond, Va, Nov. 17, 1918; s. James Bunyan and Carrie (Beckham) G.; m. Rebecca Maude Cade, Feb. 5, 1949. B.S., N.C. State U., 1950. Assoc. R.D. Tillson & Assocs., High Point, N.C., 1950-55; ptnr. Godwin & Bell, Raleigh, N.C., 1955-61; pres. James B. Godwin & Assocs., Inc., Raleigh, N.C., 1961—. Pres., Gov.'s Beautification Com., Raleigh, 1967-69; bd. dirs. Keep N.C. Beautiful, Raleigh, 1971—; bd. visitors Louisburg (n.C.) Coll., 1971-80; chmn. travel com. N.C. Art Soc., Raleigh, 1983-84. Served to capt. U.S. Army, 1941-46, PTO. Fellow Am. Soc. Landscape Architects (trustee 1966-72). Democrat. Methodist. Avocations: reading; history; gardening; travel. Home and Office: 707 Smedes Pl Raleigh NC 27605-1140*

GODWIN, KIMBERLY ANN, federal agency administrator, lawyer; b. Fargo, N.D., July 18, 1960; d. Robert Chandler and Kathryn Marie (Haney) G. BA in Polit. Sci., U. N.H., 1980; MS in Mass Comm., Boston U., 1984, JD, 1984. Bar: D.C. 1984, U.S. Supreme Ct. 1990. Legal intern Army Corps of Engrs., Waltham, Mass., 1983-84; assoc. Booz, Allen & Hamilton, Inc., Bethesda, Md., 1986-88; cons. Dept. State, Washington, 1984-86, asst. dir. comm. interagy. affairs, 1988-92, chief of policy diplomatic telecom. svc., 1992-96, dir. external affairs, 1997—; cons. Elton Assocs., Inc., Arlington, Va., 1984—. Mem. ABA (vice chmn. internat. comm. com. 1989—), Phi Beta Kappa, Pi Sigma Alpha. Avocations: flying, tennis, skiing. Home: 6215 Walhonding Rd Bethesda MD 20816-2138 Office: Dept State IRM/EA Rm 4428 2201 C St NW Washington DC 20520-0001

GODWIN, MARY JO, editor, librarian consultant; b. Tarboro, N.C., Jan. 31, 1949; d. Herman Esthol and Mamie Winifred (Felton) Pittman; m. Charles Benjamin Godwin, May 2, 1970. BA, N.C. Wesleyan Coll., 1971; MLS, East Carolina U., 1973. Cert. libr., N.C. From libr. asst. to asst. dir. Edgecombe County Meml. Library, Tarboro, 1970-76, dir., 1977-85; asst. editor Wilson Library Bull., Bronx, N.Y., 1985-89, editor, 1989-92; dir. govt. sales The Oryx Press, Phoenix, 1993-95, dir. mktg. svc., 1995-96, dir. mktg., sales and promotional svcs., 1996—; mem. White House Conf. on Librs. and Info. Svcs. Task Force; bd. dirs. Libr. Pub. Rels. Coun., 1992-95. Bd. dirs. Friends of Calvert County Pub. Libr., 1994, Osborn Edn. Found., sec., 1997-98; mem. Ariz. Ctr. for the Book. Recipient Robert Downs award for intellectual freedom U. Ill. Grad. Sch. of Libr. Sci., 1992. Mem. ALA (3M/Jr. Mem. Roundtable Profl. Devel. award 1981), N.C. Libr. Assn. (sec. 1981-83), Info. Futures Inst., Ind. Librs. Exchange Roundtable (v.p., pres. elect 1994, pres. 1995-96). Democrat. Episcopalian. Office: The Oryx Press 4041 N Central Ave Ste 700 Phoenix AZ 85012-3397

GODWIN, NAOMI NADINE, editor; b. Redfield, Iowa, Aug. 5, 1942; d. Dwayne Ivan and Emma Vernice Marie (Scott) G. BA, U. Iowa, 1964; MA, Columbia U., N.Y.C., 1972. Writer, copy editor Des Moines Register and Tribune, 1964-67; assoc. editor Travel Agt. Mag., N.Y.C., 1969-72; assoc. editor then sr. editor Travel Weekly, N.Y.C., 1972-92, mng. editor, 1992-96; editor Travel Weekly, Secaucus, N.J., 1996—. Author: Complete Guide to Travel Agency Automation, 1982, 2d rev. edit., 1987; contbr. articles to profl. jours.; speaker in field. Democrat. Mem. Disciples of Christ Ch. Avocations: reading history and biographies, sewing, cooking, traveling, photography. *

GODWIN, PAMELA JUNE, financial services executive; b. Council Bluffs, Iowa, Mar. 29, 1949; d. Fred Norman and Carol Ethel (Hatfield) Humphrey;

m. Wallace Gill Godwin, Dec. 20, 1970; 1 child, Christopher Humphrey. BA in French, Pa. State U., 1970; postgrad., West Chester (Pa.) State U., 1971-74. Tchr. various schs., Phila., 1971-74; various underwriting/tng. positions Colonial Penn Ins. Co., Phila., 1974-77, mgr., 1977-81, dir., 1981-84, v.p., 1984-86; v.p. Colonial Penn Group, Inc., Phila., 1986-87, sr. v.p., 1987-88; sr. v.p. customer mgmt. Nat. Liberty Corp., Valley Forge, Pa., 1988-93; pres., COO, Acad. Ins. Group, Frazer, Pa., 1993-95, Nat. Home Life Assurance Co., Frazer, Pa., 1993-95; pres. Change Ptnrs., Inc., Havertown, Pa., 1995-96, 99—; acting pres. Womens Way, Phila., Pa., 1998-99. Bd. dirs. Wheels, Inc., J.F. Kennedy Vocat. Tech. Sch., Phila., 1987-88; bd. dirs. Gt. Valley Cmty. Edn. Found., 1991-95, past pres.; mem. Westgate Hills Civic Assn., Havertown, 1974—; mem. Wharten Exec. Edn. adv. bd.; mem. Pa. State Great Valley adv. bd. Named to Pa. Honor Roll of Women, 1996. Mem. Ins. Soc. Phila. (bd. dirs. 1988-90), Forum of Exec. Women (pres. 1998—), Soc. Property and Casualty Underwriters (past pres. Phila. chpt. 1987-88), Albert Einstein Healthcare Network (bd. dirs. 1997—), Phi Beta Kappa, Phi Sigma Iota. Democrat. Lutheran. Avocations: skiing, walking, reading. Home: 219 Green Briar Ln Havertown PA 19083-2847

GODWIN, RALPH EDWARD, computer operator; b. Wilmington, Del., Sept. 6, 1952; s. Ralph Winfield and Margaret Suzanne (Phillips) G. Diploma, U.S. Army S.W. Signal Sch., Fort Gordon, Ga., 1971, Armed Forces Air Intelligence, Lowry AFB, Colo., 1977, Control Data Inst., 1979; AAS, Del. Tech. & C.C., 1987. File clk. FBI, Washington, 1973-76, coding clk., 1978-79; data technician Carter/Mondale Presdl. Com., Inc., Washington, 1979-80; computer operator I Beneficial Nat. Bank (USA), Wilmington, Del., 1984-87; page Del. State Senate, Dover, Del., 1991; computer operator I New Castle County, Wilmington, 1988—. *Ralph Godwin is a long-time Democratic Party political activist on the national, state and local level. He started as a Block Captain, and then served as an Election Day Block Captain in his hometown of Newark, Delaware for successful Gubernatorial nominee Sherman W. Tribbitt in 1972. Since 1972, he has worked on 5 Presidential, 2 Senatorial, 5 Congressional, 4 Gubernatorial, 1 Lieutenant Governor, 2 State Insurance Commissioner, 2 Mayoral, and a dozen State Representative and Senate campaigns. Additionally, he made campaign trips for 3 Presidential candidates in 1980, 1984, and 1992 to Presidential Primary States.* Dem. dist. committee person 22nd Del. State Rep. Dist. Dem. Com., Newark, Del., 1983-90; political strategist Dem. Nominee Richard A. DiLiberto, Jr., Del. State Ho. of Reps., 14th State Rep. Dist., Newark, 1992; co-campaign mgr. Dem. Nominee Barbara L. Erskine, Del. State Ho. of Reps., 27th State Rep. Dist., 1994; mem. nat. steering com. Clinton/Gore '96, 1995-96. Airman 1st class USAF, 1976-78. Named Unsung Hero-1994 Polit. Campaign, Del. Dem. Women's Club, 1995. Mem. Smithsonian Assocs., John F. Kennedy Libr. Found. (founding mem. hon. fellows), Nat. Trust for Hist. Preservation, Woodrow Wilson Internat. Ctr. for Scholars, Concord Coalition, Carter Ctr., Colonial Williamsburg Found. (hon. citizen 1993—), Am. Legion (sgt.-at-arms Newark chpt. 1994-97). Democrat. Episcopalian. Avocations: politics, photography, travel, reading. Home: 7 Wedgewood Rd Newark DE 19711-2055

GODWIN, RALPH LEE, JR., real estate executive; b. Raleigh, N.C., July 20, 1954; s. Ralph Lee Sr. and Hilda Faye (Sellars) G. BS in Commerce, U. Va., 1976; MBA, Dartmouth Coll., 1982. Fgn. exchange trader N.C. Nat. Bank, Charlotte, 1976-78; mgr. N.Y. office 1st Nat. Bank Atlanta, N.Y.C., 1979-80; assoc. corp. fin. Goldman Sachs & Co., N.Y.C., 1982-84; assoc. Eastdil Realty, Inc., N.Y.C., 1984-88; dir. Jones Lang Wootton, U.S.A., N.Y.C., 1988-92; mng. dir., head real estate group Gruntal & Co., Inc., N.Y.C., 1993-98; sr. mng. dir., head equity capital markets Landauer Assocs., Inc., N.Y.C., 1998—. Recipient Devel. cert. DARE Inc., Wilmington, 1984, 88. Mem. NAREIT, Real Estate Bd., N.Y., Urban Land Inst., N.C. Soc. N.Y., U. Va. Alumni Assn., Dartmouth Coll. Alumni Assn., N.Y. Athletic Club, Omicron Delta Kappa. Republican. Roman Catholic. Avocations: fishing, bridge, golf, tennis. Office: Landauer Assocs Inc 666 Fifth Ave 25th Fl New York NY 10103

GODWIN, ROBERT ANTHONY, lawyer; b. Phila., Apr. 24, 1938; s. Robert Anthony and Mary (MacElderry) G.; m. Isabel A. Tumelty, Jan. 20, 1941; children: Cara G., Marisa A., Elise D. B.S., Villanova U., 1960, J.D., 1963. Bar: Pa. 1964, U.S. dist. ct. (ea. dist.) Pa. 1964, U.S. Ct. Appeals (3d cir.) 1964, U.S. Supreme Ct. 1981. Vol. defender, Phila., 1964; assoc. Eastburn & Gray, Doylestown, Pa., 1968-70; asst. pub. defender Bucks County (Pa.), 1969-71; sole practice Newtown, 1971-73; ptnr. Timby & Godwin, Newtown, 1973-75; owner Robert A. Godwin & Assocs., Newtown, 1975—. Served with JAG, USMC, 1964-68; col. USMCR, ret. Mem. Pa. Bar Assn., Pa. Trial Lawyers Assn., Bucks County Bar Assn. Club: Rotary. Office: Box 450 110 S State St Newtown PA 18940-3508

GOEBEL, JOHN J., lawyer; b. St. Charles, Mo., Feb. 3, 1930; s. Francis Joseph and Elizabeth (Lawler) G.; m. Margaret Mary Rooney, May 10, 1958; children—Laura, Margaret, John, Matthew. B.S., LL.B., St. Louis U., 1953. Bar: Mo. 1953, U.S. Dist. Ct. (ea. dist.) Mo. 1957. Jr. exec. Constrn. Escrow Service Inc., St. Louis, 1955-56; jr. ptnr. Bryan Cave LLP, St. Louis, 1956-66, ptnr., 1966-98, sr. counsel, 1998—; bd. dirs. Stifel Fin. Corp., St. Louis. Served to 1st lt. USAF, 1953-55. Mem. ABA, St. Louis Bar Assn., Mo. Bar Assn., Bellerive Country Club, Noonday Club (St. Louis, Port Royal, Naples, Fla.). Roman Catholic. Home: 9865 Litzsinger Rd Saint Louis MO 63124-1160 Office: Bryan Cave 1 Metropolitan Sq Ste 3600 Saint Louis MO 63102-2750

GOEBEL, WILLIAM MATHERS, lawyer; b. Jacksonville, Ill., Nov. 5, 1922; s. William George and Elizabeth (Mathers) G.; m. Barbara Leeper, Mar. 10, 1944; children: William Mathers, Helen Elizabeth. A.B., Ill. Coll., 1946; J.D., U. Mich., 1948. Bar: Ill. 1949. Practice in Carmi, 1949-59; partner Conger, Elliott, Goebel & Elliott, 1949-59; asst. gen. counsel Ill. Agrl. Assn. (and affiliated cos.), 1959-64; partner Dunn, Goebel, Ulbrich, Morel & Hundman, 1964-89, of counsel, 1989-96; lectr. dept. ednl. adminstrn. Ill. State U.; instr. Ill. Wesleyan U. Contbr. to: U. Ill. Law Forum, 1962. Mem. Ill. Citizens Com. for Uniform Comml. Code; mem. Ill. Sch. Problems Commn., 1965-69; bd. dirs. Bloomington-Normal Symphony Soc., 1967-73; trustee Brokaw Hosp., Normal, Ill., 1964-69; sec. bd. trustees, mem. exec. com. Ill. Wesleyan U., Bloomington, 1964-94. Served with AUS, World War II. Fellow Am. Bar Found., Ill. Bar Found.; mem. Am. Judicature Soc., ABA, Ill. Bar Assn. (past council chmn. comml. banking and bankruptcy law sect., mem. fed. judiciary appointments com. 1976-80), McLean County Bar Assn. (pres. 1983-84). Democrat. Presbyn. Club: Bloomington Country. Lodge: Rotary. Home: 1311 E Washington St Bloomington IL 61701-4228

GOEDICKE, HANS, archeology educator; b. Vienna, Austria, Aug. 7, 1926; s. Erich and Alice V. (Schuller-Götzburg) G.; m. Lucy McLaughlin, Mar. 1969. Ph.D., U. Vienna, 1949. 22d Egyptian sect. Mus. Fine Arts, Vienna, 1949-51; rsch. assoc. Brown U., 1952-56; with UNESCO, 1956-58, U. Göttingen, 1958-60; faculty Johns Hopkins, Balt., 1960—; prof. dept. Near Eastern studies Johns Hopkins, 1968-93, chmn. dept., 1969-73, 79-84; prof. emeritus Johns Hopkins, Balt., 1993—; field dir. archaeol. expdn. Johns Hopkins, Giza, Egypt, 1972, 74; condr. epigraphic survey Johns Hopkins, Aswan area, 1964, 67; dir. survey Wadi Tumilat, 1977, 78, 81; chmn. symposium on ancient Near East Am. Council Learned Socs., 1973; dir. summer seminar on ancient Egypt Nat. Endowment Humanities, 1977; guest prof. U. Vienna, 1978-79, 85, U. Hamburg, 1987; bd. govs. Am. Research Center in Egypt; adviser Nat. Humanities Center. Author: The Report About the Dispute of a Man with his BA, 1970, Near Eastern Studies in Honor of William Foxwell Albright, 1971, Queen Nofretari, The Documentation of her Tomb, 1970, Reused Blocks from the Pyramid of Amenemhet I at Lisht, 1971, Die Geschichte des Schiffbrüchigen, 1974, The Report of Wenamun, 1975, The Protocol of Neferyt, 1977, Die Darstellung des Horus, 1982, Studies in The Hekanakhte Papers, 1984, Perspectives on The Battle of Kadesh, 1985, Egypt and Early Israel, 1986, The Quarrel of Apophis and Seqenenrec, 1986, Studies in the Instruction of King Amenemhet, 1988, An Old Hieratic Paleography, 1989, Studies About Amenhotep III, 1992, Comments on the Famine Stela, 1994, Studies About Kamose and Ahmose, 1995, Pi(Ankh)y in Egypt, 1998; editor-in-chief: Near Eastern Studies. John Simon Guggenheim fellow, 1966; George A. and Eliza Gardner Howard Found. fellow, 1956-57. Mem. Egypt Exploration Soc., Fondation Egyptologique Reine Elisabeth, Société D'Archeologie Copte. Home: 3959 Cloverhill Rd Baltimore MD 21218-1708

GOEGLEIN, GLORIA J., state legislator; b. Ft. Wayne, Ind., Jan. 13, 1931; d. Alton F. and Nellie I. (Black) Woods; m. Leonard O. Goeglein, Oct. 17, 1954; children: Julia, Chris, Mark. Auditor Allen County, Ind., 1979-86; purchasing dir. City of Ft. Wayne, 1988-90; mem. Ind. Ho. of Reps., Indpls., 1990—; mem. Ways and Means Com., 1993-95, Govtl. Affairs Com., 1991-94, Cities and Town Com., 1991-92, Autism Commn., 1991-94, Local Govt. Fin. Study Commn., 1991-94, Mental Health Commn., 1994—, chair, 1996; mem. Interim Study Com. on State Govt. Mgmt. Issues, 1994, Local Govt. Com., 1995—, chair, 1996; mem. Ind. Adv. Commn. on Intergovernmental Rels., 1995—, Interim Study Com. on State Mgmt. Issues, 1995, Families, Children and Human Affairs Com., 1996-98, Pub. Health Com., 1997—, Health Fin. Commn., 1997—, County Govt. Study Commn., 1997—, Mental Health Practices Study Com., chair, 1996; mem. Interim Study Com. on Procurement Law, 1996. Mem. Allen County Coun., 1974-78, v.p., 1975-78. Home: 9339 Maysville Rd Fort Wayne IN 46815-5820

GOEHNER, DONNA MARIE, retired university dean; b. Chgo., Mar. 9, 1941; d. Robert and Elizabeth (Cseke) Barra; m. George Louis Goehner, Dec. 16, 1961; 1 child, Michelle Renee. BS in English, So. Ill. U., 1963; MSLS, U. Ill., 1966, CAS in L.S., 1974; PhD in Edn., So. Ill. U., 1983. Rsch. assoc. U. Ill., Urbana, 1966-67; high sch. librarian St. Joseph-Ogden Sch. System, St. Joseph, Ill., 1967-68; curriculum lab librarian Western Ill. U., Macomb, 1968-73, periodicals librarian, 1974-76, coordinator for tech. svcs., 1977-78, acquisitions and collection devel. librarian, 1979-86, acting dir. library, 1986, dean library svcs., 1988-97; assoc. Univ. librarian for tech. and adminstrv. svcs. Ill. State U., Normal, 1986-88; ret., 1998. Contbr. articles to profl. jours. Mem. ALA, Assn. Coll. and Rsch. Libraries (chmn. univ. libraries sect. 1988-89), Ill. Assn. Coll. and Rsch. Libraries (pres. 1985-86), Ill. Library Assn. (Acad.Librarian of Yr. 1989). Home: 1001 Wigwam Hollow Rd Macomb IL 61455-1035 Office: Univ Library Western Ill U Macomb IL 61455

GOEHRING, KENNETH, artist; b. Evansville, Wis., Jan. 8, 1919; s. Walter A. and Ruth I. (Rossman) G.; m. Margretta M. MacNicol, Dec. 1, 1945. Student, Cass Tech. Inst., 1933-35, Meinzinger Sch. Applied Art, 1945-46, Colorado Springs Fine Arts Ctr., 1947-50. Works have appeared in over 100 exhibitions in 17 states and 20 museums; 17 one-man shows; exhibitor, Terry Inst., Miami, Symphony Hall, Boston, de Cordova Mus., Fitchburg Mus., Mass., Farnsworth Mus., Maine, Corcoran, Washington, Joslyn Meml. Mus., Nebr., Detroit Inst. Arts, Nebr. Galleries, Stanford U. Galleries, Calif. De Young Mus., San Francisco, Denver Art Mus., Okla. Art Ctr., La Jolla Art Ctr., Calif., others; represented in permanent collections, Sheldon Art Ctr., Lincoln, Nebr., Colorado Springs Fine Arts Ctr., Foothills Gallery, Golden Colo., Canon City Fine Arts Ctr., Colo., Washburn U. Gallery, Wichita, Kans., Swedish Consulate, Washington, El Pomar Found., Colo. Springs, in many pvt. collections throughout U.S. Purchase awards include Colorado Springs Fine Arts Ctr., 1958; Washburn U., 1957; Am. Acad. Design, 1977. Address: 2017 W Platte Ave Colorado Springs CO 80904-3429

GOEHRING, MAUDE COPE, retired business educator; b. Persia, Tenn., Jan. 5, 1915; d. James Lawrence and Bobbie C. (Ross) Cope; m. Harvey John Goehring Jr., Aug. 12, 1950 (dec. Mar. 1992). BS in Edn., Ind. U. of Pa., 1948; MEd, U. Pitts., 1950; student, Lebanon Valley Coll., 1944-45. Tchr. Penn Hills Sr. High Sch., Pitts., 1948-68; tchr. U. Pitts., 1959-60, ret., 1968; vol. chmn. ICU, operating rm. info. desk Margaret R. Pardee Meml. Hosp., Hendersonville, N.C., 1989-95; vol. Carolina Village Health Ctr., 1994—; coord. Henderson County Ct. House Vols., Hendersonville, 1983-89; cons., counselor tax aid program Am. Assn. Ret. Persons, Hendersonville, 1981-96. Neighborhood chmn. Girl Scouts U.S., Butler County Pa., 1976-79; bd. dirs. ARC, Hendersonville, 1986-91; sec.-treas., bd. dirs. Crime Stoppers of Henderson County, 1991-96; nat. bd. dirs. Second Wind Hall of Fame, 1991-95. Mem. AAUW (officer 1975-76), Gideon Internat. Aux. (pres., sec. 1969-70), Delta Pi Epsilon (life, Gamma chpt., pres., sec. 1956-59, nat. del. 1957). Republican. Lutheran. Avocations: gardening, crafts, sewing, reading. Home: 21 Kestrel Ct Hendersonville NC 28792-2838

GOEL, AJAY, molecular biophysicist, researcher; b. Ferozepur, Punjab, India, Aug. 23, 1968; came to U.S., 1996; s. Rajinder Kumar and Urmila (Gupta) G.; m. Shivali Garg, Nov. 25, 1997. BSc in Biophysics with honours, Panjab U., Chandigarh, India, 1988, MSc in Biophysics with honours, 1990, PhD in Biophysics, 1996. Jr. rsch. fellow biophysics dept. Panjab U., 1988-90, scientist Regional Sophisticated Instrummentation Ctr., 1991—, sr. rsch. fellow biophysics dept., 1992-96; rsch. assoc. Dept. molecular physics and biophysics U. Va., Charlottesville, 1996—. Author: Advances in Biological Sciences, 1995; contbr. articles to sci. jours. Recipient Best Rsch. in Cancer Young Investigation award AACR-Pharmacia Upjohn, 1999; nat. merit scholar Indian Ministry Edn., 1988-90, scholar Internat. Fedn. Socs. for Electron Microscopy, 1994. Mem. Microscopy Soc. Am., Soc. Biophysicists India, Electron Microscope Soc. India, Assn. Med. Physicists India, Nutrition Soc. India, Soc. Biol. Chemists India, Am. Assn. Cancer Rsch., Am. Gastroenterology Assn. Avocations: surfing the internet, watching cricket and football, hiking, reading science fiction. Home: 9515 Genesee Ave Apt 104 San Diego CA 92121-2017 Office: UCSD Dept Medicine Divsn Gastroenterology La Jolla CA 92093-0688

GOEL, ASHOK KUMAR, electrical engineering educator; b. Kaithal, Haryana, India, Sept. 4, 1953; came to U.S., 1977; s. Daya Nand and Kamal Goel; m. Sangita Gupta, Feb. 14, 1982; children: Sumeet Kumar, Rachna Shikha. BS with honors, Panjab U., Chandigarh, India, 1972, MS with honors, 1973; MPhil, CUNY, 1982; PhD, Johns Hopkins U., 1987. Asst. prof. Mich. Technol. U., Houghton, 1987-91, assoc. prof., 1991—; mem. summer internat. engring. program Oxford U., 1995; faculty Oreg. Grad. Inst. of Sci. and Tech., 1996. Author: High-Speed VLSI Interconnections, 1994, John Wiley & Sons, Inc.; contbr. numerous papers to profl. jours. Recipient Rsch. Initiation award NSF, 1987; rsch. grantee USAF Office of Sci. Rsch., 1990, GM Rsch. Labs., 1991, NSF, 1993; faculty rsch. grantee Wright-Patterson AFB, 1990, Griffiss AFB, 1991, U.S. Army Missile Command, 1992. Mem. IEEE, Am. Soc. for Engring. Edn., Internat. Soc. Computers and their Applications, Internat. Assn. Math. and Computer Modeling, Sigma Xi. Avocations: swimming, tennis, skiing, traveling. Office: Mich Technol U Dept Elec Engring Houghton MI 49931

GOELA, JITENDRA SINGH, researcher, consultant; b. Delhi, India, Apr. 20, 1951; s. Late Umrao Singh and Sushila Devi (Singal) G.; m. Geeta Gupta, Mar. 4, 1979; children: Naveen, Vikas. B in Tech., Indian Inst. of Tech., Delhi, India, 1972; MS, Brown U., Providence, R.I., 1974, PhD, 1976; MBA, Northeastern U., Boston, 1991. Prin. sci. Phys. Sci., Inc., Andover, Mass., 1976-78; asst. prof., lectr. Indian Inst. of Tech., Kanpur, India, 1978-84; prin. sci. Morton Internat. CVD Inc., Woburn, Mass., 1984—; cons. Phys. Sci. Inc., Andover, Mass., 1979-80, CVD Inc., Woburn, Mass., 1983, Sanders Assoc., Nashua, N.H., 1985-86, Efficient Systems, Inc., Andover, Mass., 1987-89. Editor: Lasers and Applications, 1983; patentee: Preventive Backside Growth in a Vapor Deposition System, 1990; contbr. articles to profl. jours. Recipient Arthur L. Williston medal, Am. Soc. of Mech. Engr., 1978, Young Sci. medal, Indian Nat. Sci. Acad., 1982, Polycrystalline Si Property Data, Air Force, Wright-Patterson, Ohio, 1985, Lightweight Si/SiC LIDAR Mirrors, Nasa Langley Rsh. Ctr., Norfolk, Va., 1987, High Temp SiC Fibers, Nasa Lewis Rsch. Ctr., Cleve., 1987. Mem. Am. Soc. of Mech. Engrs., Am. Phys. Soc., Optical Soc. of Am. (Engring. Excellence award 1991), Soc. of Photo-optical and Instrumentation Engrs., Am. Ceramic Soc. Achievements include patents for fabrication of lightweight ceramic mirrors by means of a chemical vapor deposition process; for method of fabricating lightweight honeycomb type structure; for selective area chemical vapor deposition; for a triangular deposition chamber; for highly polishable, highly thermally conductive SiC; for hard disc drives and read/write heads; for chemical vapor deposition furnace and furnace apparatus; for chemical vapor deposition produced SiC having improved properties. Home: 12 Messinia Dr Andover MA 01810-6027 Office: Rohm and Haas 185 New Boston St Woburn MA 01801-6230

GOELDEN-BOWEN, MICHELLE MARIE, occupational therapist; b. Dallas, Oct. 28, 1966; d. David Louis and Barbara Marie (Michiels) Goelden; m. Richard George Bowen, Feb. 6, 1988. BS in Occupational Therapy, Tex. Woman's U., 1993. Lic. Exec. Coun. Phys. Therapy Occupational Therapy Examiners. Occupational therapist Plano (Tex.) Rehab. Hosp., 1993-94, Comty. Rehab. Ctrs., Dallas, 1993, Sundance Rehab. Corp., Dallas, 1994-96; home health occupational therapist Arcadia Healthcare, Lewisville, Tex., 1994-97; occupational therapist Therapists Unltd., Dallas, 1994-96, Premier Health Staff, Inc., Bedford, Tex., 1996-98, Columbia Med. Ctr. at Lancaster, Tex., 1998—; reviewer new product ideas or therapy materials The Psychol. Corp. Therapy Skill Builders, San Antonio, 1996. Mem. World Fedn. Occupational Therapy, Am. Occupational Therapy Assn., Tex. Occupational Therapy Assn., Golden Key. Avocations: reading, drawing, painting, pets. Fax: 972-230-0516. Home: 4254 Malone Ave The Colony TX 75056-3066 Office: Columbia Med Ctr at Lancaster 2600 W Pleasant Run Rd Lancaster TX 75146-1100

GOELET, ROBERT G., investment executive; b. Sandricourt, France, Sept. 28, 1923; s. Robert Walton and Anne Marie (Guestier) G.; m. Alexandra Gardiner Creel, Sept. 9, 1976. A.B., Harvard U., 1945. Chmn. R.I. Corp.; pres. Goelet Realty Co., Goelet Corp. Trustee Am. Mus. Natural History, 1958—, pres., 1975-88, chmn., 1988-89; trustee Boscobel Restoration Inc., 1976—, French Inst.-Alliance Francaise N.Y., 1951—, pres., 1967-93; trustee N.Y. Zool. Soc., 1951—, pres., 1971-75; trustee Carnegie Instn. of Washington, 1980, Mus. Comparative Zoology, 1980—, N.Y. Geneal. & Biographical Soc., 1998—. Office: 425 Park Ave New York NY 10022

GOELL, JAMES EMANUEL, electronics company executive; b. N.Y.C., Oct. 13, 1939; s. Milton Jacob and Amy (Jacob) G.; m. Tamara Greenberg, Sept. 11, 1960; children: Lisa Sue, Fredric Scott. B in Elec. Engring., Cornell U., 1962, MS, 1963, PhD, 1965. Mem. tech. staff Bell Labs., Holmdel, N.J., 1965-74; v.p., dir. engring., dir. fiber optics lab. Electro-Optical Products div. ITT, Roanoke, Va., 1974-81; pres. Lightwave Technologies, Inc., Van Nuys, Calif., 1981-85; v.p. marketing PCO, Chatsworth, Calif., 1985-91; program mgr. HBT Ericsson Components, L.A., 1991-92; dir. engring. end-user bus. AMP, Harrisburg, Pa., 1992-97; dir. Netconnect Engring. Amp, Harrisburg, Pa., 1997—. V.p. Middletown Twp. (N.J.) Bd. Edn. Fellow IEEE; mem. Optical Soc. Am., Am. Phys. Soc., Sigma Xi, Eta Kappa Nu, Tau Beta Pi, Phi Kappa Phi. Home: 2416 Schefield Cir Harrisburg PA 17112-1082 Office: AMP MS140-37 PO Box 3608 Harrisburg PA 17105-3608

GOELLNER, JACK GORDON, publishing executive; b. Cleve., Aug. 16, 1930; s. Fred William and Ella (Rohde) G.; m. Sarah Frances Williams, Aug. 16, 1952 (div. Sept. 28, 1982); children: Katherine, Ellen, Michael, Kirsten.; m. Barbara B. Lamb, Apr. 14, 1984. B.A., Allegheny Coll., 1952, Litt.D., 1979; M.A., U. Wis., 1953. Reporter Springfield (Ohio) Sun, 1955-57; sr. writer, pub. information Cleve. Electric Illuminating Co., 1957-61; mgr. sales and advt. Johns Hopkins U. Press, Balt., 1961-65; editorial dir. Johns Hopkins U. Press, 1965-73, asso. dir., 1973-74, dir., 1974-95; dir. emeritus, 1996; dir. Am. Univ. Press Services, 1963-66, treas., 1972-74, chmn. bd., 1979-80; dir. York Press; bd. dirs. Johns Hopkins Press Ltd., 1974-88; bd. dirs. Internat. Book Bank; mem. nat. adv. bd. and exec. com. Ctr. for the Book, Libr. of Congress, 1979-85; mem. U.S. Govt. Adv. Com. on Internat. Book and Libr. Programs, 1975-78; head pubs. mission to Ea. Europe, Dept. State, 1977; cons. NEH, 1977-84; bd. dirs. Apres Ltd.; mem. acad. affairs com. Winterthur Mus.; mem. bd. advisers The Papers of Dwight D. Eisenhower. Mem. editorial bd. Scholarly Pub., 1980—, Book Rsch. Quar., 1983-88; mem. adv. bd. Lit. Classics of U.S. 1980-86; contbr. articles to profl. and popular jours. Bd. govs. U. Press of New Eng.; mem. mgmt. bd. MIT Press; mem. adv. bd. Brookings Instn. Press; bd. dirs. Sidran Found., Johns Hopkins Fed. Credit Union, 1994—. Recipient Frank Bradway Rogers Info. Advancement award Med. Libr. Assn., 1991; Am. Coun. Learned Socs. fellow, 1952-53; Danforth fellow, 1952-53. Mem. Assn. Am. Univ. Presses (dir. 1972-74, 78-81, treas. 1972-74, pres. 1979-80), Soc. Scholarly Pub. (dir. 1978—), Assn. Am. Pubs. (mem. exec. council profl. and scholarly pub. div. 1981-85, bd. dirs. 1986-90), Md. Fly Anglers (sec. 1970-72), Trout Unltd., Md. Hist. Soc., Phi Beta Kappa. Democrat. Episcopalian. Clubs: Tudor and Stuart, Hamilton St.

GOELTZ, THOMAS A., lawyer. BA in Econs. summa cum laude, DePauw U., 1969; JD magna cum laude, Mich. U., 1973. Assoc. Riddell, Williams, Ivie, Bullitt & Walkinshaw, Seattle, 1973-75; dep. prosecuting atty. civil divsn. King County Prosecuting Atty.'s Office, Seattle, 1976-79; prin. Cohen, Keegan & Goeltz, Seattle, 1979-86; ptnr. Davis Wright Tremaine, Seattle, 1986—; cons. state and local govt. agencies on environ. land use issues; adv. shoreline mgmt. City of Seattle; part-time lectr. Law Sch. U. Wash., Seattle, 1976-79. Editor Mich. Law Rev. Active Gov. Task Force on Regulatory Reform, 1993-95. Mem. ABA (urban, state & local govt. law sect.), Wash. State Bar Assn. (real property sect., past chair land use and environ. law sect.), Seattle-King County Bar Assn., Am. Coll. Real Estate Lawyers, Nat. Assn. Indsl. and Office Park, ICSC, Order of Coif. Office: Davis Wright Tremaine 2600 Century Sq 1501 4th Ave Seattle WA 98101-1688

GOELZ, PAUL CORNELIUS, university dean; b. Bartelso, Ill., Oct. 7, 1914; s. Peter Paul and Clara (Bross) G. Cert., St. Louis U., 1939; BBA, U. Dayton, 1943, MA, 1946; MBA, Northwestern U., 1951, PhD, 1954. Credit mgr. Adjustable Shoe Co., St. Louis, 1937-39; asst. comptr. Key Refinery Equipment Co., St. Louis, 1939-40; auditor GMAC, St. Louis, 1940-41; instr. Southside High Sch., St. Louis, 1943-46; chmn. dept. mktg. St. Mary's U., San Antonio, 1946-62; dean Sch. Bus. Adminstrn., 1962-77; Myra Stafford Pryor prof. free enterprise, 1978-85, dir. Algur H. Meadows Ctr. Entrepreneurial Studies, 1985—; vis. lectr. staff Army Mgmt. Engring. Tng. Agy., U.S. Dept. Def., Rock Island Arsenal; lectr. Exec. Devel. Insts. in U.S. and Mexico; cons. to bus. and govt. Chmn. spl. series of sessions at Internat. Conf. Am. Inst. Indsl. Engrs., 1963; lectr. univs. in Moscow and Kiev, 1992. Editor: Philosophy of the Market System of Economics, 5 vols., 1979, 81, 83, 87, 90; contbr. articles to profl. publs. Bd. trustees World Affairs Coun. of San Antonio. Recipient awards Freedoms Found. at Valley Forge, 1978, 79, 84, 85, 90, Liberty Bell award Young Lawyers Assn., 1982, Entrepreneur of the Yr. award, 1988; inducted into The Inst. Am. Entrepreneurs. Mem. Acad. Mgmt., Am. Mktg. Assn., Sales and Mktg. Execs. Internat., Am. Inst. Indsl. Engrs., San Antonio C. of C., Nat. Assn. Bus. Economists, Southwestern Assn. Bus. Sch. Deans (pres. 1968-69), Fin. Execs. Inst., Assn. Pvt. Enterprise Edn. (pres. 1982-83), Am. Assembly Collegiate Schs. Bus. (bd. dirs.), Delta Epsilon Sigma, Alpha Sigma Tau, Pi Sigma Epsilon. Home: 1 Camino Santa Maria San Antonio TX 78228-5433

GOELZER, DANIEL LEE, lawyer; b. Milw., Feb. 14, 1947; s. Gerald Howard and Roberta (Hart) G.; m. Angela C. Carcone, Jan. 9, 1988; children: Christina H., Mary E.; 1 child by previous marriage, Michael W. BBA, U. Wis., 1969, JD, 1973; LLM, George Washington U., 1979. Bar: Wis. 1973, U.S. Dist. Ct. (we. dist.) Wis. 1973, U.S. Ct. Appeals (7th cir.) 1974, U.S. Ct. Appeals (2d, 9th and D.C. cirs.) 1975, U.S. Supreme Ct. 1976, D.C. 1979. Auditor, Touche, Ross & Co., Milw., 1969-70; law clk. judge U.S. Ct. Appeals, Chgo., 1973-74; atty. SEC, Washington, 1974-78, exec. asst. to chmn., 1978-83, gen. counsel, 1983-90; ptnr. Baker and McKenzie, Washington, 1990—; adj. prof. law Georgetown U. Law Ctr., Washington, 1986-92. Contbr. articles to law jours. Served with USAR, 1969-75. Mem. ABA, AICPA, Fed. Bar Assn. Republican. Congregationalist. Avocation: amateur radio. Home: 5941 Searl Ter Bethesda MD 20816-2022 Office: Baker & Mckenzie 815 Connecticut Ave NW Washington DC 20006-4004

GOEN, BOB, television show host; b. Dec. 1, 1954. Grad., San Diego State U. DJ Stint Sta. KPRO-FM, Riverside, Calif., 1977-81; achor, reporter, prodr., writer, editor Sta. KESQ-TV, Palm Springs, Calif., 1981-86; game show host Perfect Match, 1986, The Home Shopping Game, Blackout; daytime host Wheel of Fortune, 1989-92; game show host The Hollywood Game, 1992; co-host Entertainment Tonight, 1996—; host Miss Universe, Miss USA, Miss Teen USA, 1993—. •

GOEPP, ROBERT AUGUST, dental educator, oral pathologist; b. Chgo., Nov. 3, 1930; s. Charles August and Ernestine Josephine (Mertz) G.; m. Iraida Pineiro, July 9, 1960; children—Robert C., Heidi M., Myra J. B.S. in Biology, Loyola U.-Chgo., 1954, D.D.S., 1957; M.S. in Pathology, U. Chgo., 1961, Ph.D. in Pathology, 1967. Instr. to assoc. prof. Sch. Medicine, U. Chgo., 1961-75, prof. dentistry and pathology, 1975-96, prof. emeritus, 1996—; med. Med. Radiation Adv. Coun. FDA, 1979-82; mem. Nat. Coun. Radiation Protection, Washington, 1976-94. Contbr. articles to profl. jours. Recipient Career Devel. award USPHS, 1970. Fellow Am. Coll. Dentists,

Internat. Coll. Dentists, Am. Acad. Oral Pathology, Am. Acad. Dental Radiology (pres. 1974), Ill. Soc. Oral Pathologists (pres. 1977-78), Inst. Medicine Chgo., Odontographic Soc. Chgo. (bd. dirs., treas. 1993—); mem. ADA (chmn. coun. dental rsch. 1981-82). Roman Catholic. Avocations: music; piano. Office: U Chgo Zoller Dental Clinic 5841 S Maryland Ave Chicago IL 60637-1463

GOERGEN, JUANA IRIS, Latin American studies educator; b. Mar. 9, 1951. PhD, SUNY, Stony Brook, 1990. Assoc. prof. DePaul U., Chgo., 1992—, dir. Latin Am. and Latino studies, 1997—. Email: jgoergen@wp-post.depaul.edu. Office: 719 N Taylor Ave Oak Park IL 60302

GOERING, CARROLL E., agricultural engineering educator; b. Platte Center, Nebr., June 8, 1934; s. Herman Leopold and Mabel Goering; m. Carol Ann, Oct. 29, 1960. B.S., U. Nebr., 1959; M.S., Iowa State U., 1962, Ph.D., 1965. Registered profl. engr., Mo. Design engr. Internat. Harvester Co., Hinsdale, Ill., 1959-61; research asst. Iowa State U., Ames, 1961-65; asst. prof. agrl. engring. U. Mo., Columbia, 1965-69, assoc. prof., 1969-74, prof., 1974-77; prof. agrl. engring. U. Ill., Urbana, 1977—. Author: (textbooks) Engine and Tractor Power, Engineering Principles of Agricultural Machines; contbr. articles to profl. jours. Served with U.S. Army, 1954-56. Fellow Am. Soc. Agrl. Engrs.; mem. ASTM, Am. Soc. Engring. Edn., Soc. Automotive Engrs. Republican. Methodist. Office: U Ill 360R Agrl Engring Scis Bldg 1304 W Pennsylvania Ave Urbana IL 61801-4726

GOERING, KENNETH JUSTIN, college administrator; b. Sunnyvale, Calif., Dec. 26, 1913; s. George Hans and Elsa (Toepper) G.; m. Marjory Gieseker, Aug. 14, 1936; children—Patricia DeBedout, John D., Kenneth Don. B.S., Mont. State Coll., 1936; M.S., Calif. Inst. Tech., 1939; Ph.D., Iowa State U., 1941. Research chemist Anheuser Busch Co., St. Louis, 1941-42; instr. Iowa State U., 1942-43; research chemist WPB, Lincoln, Nebr., 1943-44; asst. chief chemist Omaha Alcohol Plant, 1944-45; v.p., gen. mgr. Mold Bran Co. and Enzymes, Inc., Eagle Grove, Iowa, 1945-49; mem. faculty Mont. State U., Bozeman, 1949—; prof. biochemistry Mont. State U., 1960—, grad. dean, 1967-75; cons. Kurth Malting Co., Sunburst Biochem. Co., Farm Bur., Idaho Potato Foods, Centennial Foods Inc. Asso. editor: Cereal Chemistry. Recipient Blue and Gold award Mont. State U., 1978, Charles and Nora Wiley Career Research award, 1980. Mem. Am. Chem. Soc., Am. Assn. Cereal Chemists, Sigma Xi (Mont. chpt. award 1961), Phi Kappa Phi. Patentee in field. Home: 8383 Saddle Mountain Rd Bozeman MT 59715-8789

GOERING, SHERRILL ANITA, newspaper editor; b. Emporia, Kans., Nov. 7, 1942; d. Herbert Truman Niles and Anita Gale (Thomas) Niles Beattie; m. Donald Steven Goering, July 3, 1965; children: Katrina Dawn, Crystal Anita. BS, Kans. State U., 1964. With Prairie Drummer, Colby, Kans., 1973-74; with Hugoton Hermes, 1975—, editor, 1985—. Pres. Hugoton Planning Commn., 1993—. Mem. Soc. Profl. Journalists, Hugoton C. of C. (bd. dirs. 1996). Republican. Avocations: music, cooking, scuba diving, piloting. Home: 1207 S Monroe St Hugoton KS 67951-2935 Office: Hugoton Hermes 522 S Main St Hugoton KS 67951-0849

GOERKE, GLENN ALLEN, university administrator; b. Lincoln Park, Mich., May 15, 1931; s. Albert W. Goerke and Cecile P. (Crowl) G.; m. Joyce Leslie Walker, Mar. 3, 1973; children: Lynn, Jill, Kurt. AB, Eastern Mich. U., 1952, MA, 1955; PhD, Mich. State U., 1964; LhD (hon.), Univ. Tech. de Santiago, Domincan Republic, 1995, U. Houston, 1997. Dean univ. svcs. Fla. Internat. U., Miami, 1970-71, assoc. dean faculty, 1971-72, assoc. v.p. acad. affairs, provost North campus, 1972-73; v.p. community affairs Fla. Internat U., Miami, 1973-78; dean coll. continuing edn. U. R.I., 1978-81; chancellor Ind. U. East, Richmond, 1981-86; pres. U. Houston, Victoria, 1986-89; interim chancellor U. Houston Sys., 1989; pres. U. Houston, Clear Lake, 1991-95; pres. U. Houston, 1995-97, pres. emeritus, 1997—; dir. Inst. for Future of Higher Edn./U. Houston, 1997—. Recipient Eastern Mich. U. Disting. Alumni award, 1982. Mem. Nat. Univ. Continuing Edn. Assn. (pres. 1973-74), Am. Assn. Univ. Adminstrs. (bd. dirs. 1991-96), Internat. Assn. Univ. Pres. (bd. dirs., v.p. 1991—), Golden Key, Omicron Delta Kappa, Phi Kappa Phi, Phi Delta Kappa.

GOERLER, RAIMUND ERHARD, archivist; b. Wilhelmshaven, Germany, Oct. 17, 1948; s. Max W. and Gerda M. (Spille) G.; m. Sharon A. Cantor, Aug. 28, 1977; children: Jared, Allison. BA, SUNY, Buffalo, 1970; MA, Case We. Res. U., 1972, PhD, 1975; MLS, Kent State U., 1984. Cert. archivist Acad. Cert. Archivists. Manuscripts splst. We. Res. Hist. Soc., Cleve., 1976-78; u. archivist Ohio State U., Columbus, 1978—; adj. asst. profl Sch. Libr. and Info. Sci. Kent State U., Columbus, Ohio, 1990—. Editor: To the Pole: The Diary and Notebook of Richard E. Byrd, 1925-27, 1998. Mem. Soc. Ohio Archivists (Merit award 1996; editor: (monograph) From History to Pre-History, Archivists Face the Future: Essays in Honor of the 25th Anniversary of the Society of Ohio Archivists 1994). Home: 5603 Boulder Crest St Columbus OH 43235-2512 Office: Ohio State U Archives 2700 Kenny Rd Columbus OH 43210-1046

GOERLICH, SHIRLEY ALICE BOYCE, publisher, educator, consultant; b. Oneonta, N.Y., May 17, 1937; d. John Orlo and Nella Virginia (Bartow) Boyce; m. Robert Frank Goerlich, Aug. 19, 1967; children: Robert John, Daniel Lee. AAS, SUNY, Cobleskill, 1957; BA, Parsons Coll., 1962. Cert. tchr, bus. owner, N.Y. Tchr. Milw. Pub. Schs., 1962-64, Huntington Pub. Schs., Huntington, L.I., N.Y., 1964-67, Fairfax (Va.) County Adult Edn., 1970-76; pvt. practice Greene, N.Y., 1979-83; prin., owner RSG Publishing, Sidney, N.Y., 1984—; Cons. Cemetery Bds. Trustees, Chenango, Del. and Otsego counties. Author: Genealogy: A Practical Research Guide, 1984, At Rest in Unadilla, Otsego Co., N.Y., 1987 (CSG award 1988), Legends & Reality, Stories of Chenango, Delaware, Otsego, 1990, Etched in Stone in Sidney, Delaware County N.Y., 1997, East Guilford Cemetery, 1997, History of Unadilla, 4 vols., 1998, History of West Unadilla, 1999. Historian Town of Unadilla, N.Y., 1989-98; trustee Evergreen Hill Cemetery Assoc., Unadilla, 1996—. Recipient Nat award Nat. Soc. New Eng. Women, 1989, Award for Excellence Ostego County Local History Adv. Com., 1995. Mem. Nat. Soc. DAR (chmn. 1989-91, organizing regent Gen. John Paterson chpt. 1978, Nat. Lineage Rsch. award 1987, 1988, 1989), Conn. Soc. Genealogists, Inc. (Special Outstanding award 1989), N.Y. State Historical Assn. Republican. Presbyterian. Avocations: cooking, painting. Home: 217 County Highway 1 Bainbridge NY 13733-9307 Office: RSG Publishing 217 County Highway 1 Bainbridge NY 13733-9307

GOERTZ, AUGUSTUS FREDERICK, III, artist; b. N.Y.C., Aug. 15, 1948; s. Augustus Frederick and Esther (Meyer) G.; m. Christine Matthai, Sept. 2, 1978. B.F.A. with honors, San Francisco Art Inst. Dir. Art. Time Found., N.Y.C.; cons. Downtown Ventures, N.Y.C. One-man shows include N.Y. Law Sch., 1977, Sarah Rentschler Gallery, 1978-99, U. Brussels, Belgium, 1981, Patricia Correia Gallery, L.A., 1994-99, Somers Gallery, N.Y., The Gallery, N.Y.; exhbns. include San Francisco Art Inst., 1971, Adlrich Mus. Contemporary Art, 1973-78, New Britain (Conn.) Mus., 1974, Soho Ctr. for Visual Artists, N.Y.C., 1975, Art Fiera, Bologna, Italy, 1978, Garke-Bernet Gallery, N.Y.C., 1979, Todd Capp Gallery, N.Y.C., 1986-88, Art in Gen., N.Y.C., 1987, Neo Persona Gallery, N.Y.C., 1991, Robin Rice Gallery, N.Y.C., 1992, Patricia Correia, L.A., 1992-99, Kim Foster Gallery, N.Y.C., 1996-99; represented in permanent collections Aetna Bldg., Harrison, N.Y., Huntington Bank of Ohio Collection, Aldrich Mus. Contemporary Art, Chgo. Art Inst., San Francisco Art Inst., N.Y. Law Sch., Harmonious Arts Found. N.Y., Shearson-Lehman, Chubb, Avatar Brokerage, Seimens Electric, The Port Authority of N.Y. and N.J., Duke Power, Durham, N.C., Sungard Tech, N.Y.C., others. Mem. Orgn. Ind. Artists, San Francisco Art Inst. Alumni Assn., Works Project Assn., Inc., Amnesty Internat. Democrat. Address: 319 Greenwich St # 2 New York NY 10013-3339 also: care Kim Foster Gallery 429 W 20th St Chelsea New York NY 10012-4410 *Every person has a responsibility to evolve away from materialistic environmental destruction, and towards linking intellect, spirit, body, and expanding universe.*

GOERTZEN, IRMA, hospital executive. BSN, U. Wash., 1967, MS, 1968, DS in Pub. Svc., 1998. Pres., CEO Magee-Women Hosp. & Rsch. Inst., 1989—. Office: 300 Halket St Pittsburgh PA 15213

GOES, KATHLEEN ANN, secondary education educator, choral director; b. New Bedford, Mass., Jan. 13, 1951; d. Filento Andrade and Lillian (Cabral) G. BA in Psychology, U. Mass., North Dartmouth, 1976; postgrad., Ctrl. Conn. State U., 1987-98. Cert. K-8 elem. tchr., K-12 music tchr., Mass. Social worker Dept. Social Svcs., Cambridge, Mass., 1980-85; pvt. tchr. voice and piano, New Bedford, 1985-88; tchr. vocal music New Bedford Pub. Sch., 1985-90; tchr. music, choral dir. Fairhaven (Mass.) H.S., 1991—; singer, actress, southeastern New Eng., 1974—; dir. music ministry St. Mary's Ch., South Dartmouth, Mass., 1988—; bd. dirs. , sec. New Bedford Festival Theatre, 1990-97, v.p., 1997—. Dir. musicals Bye, Bye Birdie, Little Shop of Horrors, The Boyfriend, Godspell, Jesus Christ Superstar; performed the mother in Amahl and the Night Visitors; actress, singer in musicals Fiddler on the Roof, Godspell, Phantom. Bd. dirs. New Bedford Symphony Orch., 1994-96. Named Promising Young Artist, Crescendo Club, Boston, 1981; recipient outstanding leadership award Fairhaven Assn. for Music Edn., 1995. Mem. NEA, Am. Choral Dirs. Assn., Nat. Pastoral Musicians Assn., New Eng. Theatre Conf., Drama League, Music Educators Nat. Conf., Mass. Tchrs. Assn., Mass. Music Educators Assn., Whale Hist. League. Roman Catholic. Avocations: cooking, crafts, computers, boating, scenic design. Home: 61 Rockdale Ave New Bedford MA 02740-1075 Office: Fairhaven HS 12 Huttleston Ave Fairhaven MA 02719-3122

GOESTENKORS, GAIL, head basketball coach; b. Waterford, Mich., Feb. 26, 1963; m. Mark Simons. BA, Saginaw Valley State U., 1985. Grad. asst. Iowa State U., 1985-86; asst. coach basketball Purdue U., West Lafayette, Ind., 1986-92; head basketball coach Duke U., Durham, N.C., 1992—; coach U.S. Jones Cup Team, taiwan; head coach Festival Trials, 1991, 95; coach 1994 ACC All-Star Team, Latvia, Lithuania. Named ACC Coach of the Yr., 1995-96. Office: Duke University Cameron Indoor Stadium PO Box 90555 Durham NC 27708-0555*

GOETSCH, JOHN HUBERT, consultant and retired utility company executive; b. Merrill, Wis., Apr. 28, 1933; s. John Albert and Ada (Natzke) G.; m. Joyce A. Wilke, June 16, 1956; children: Jody A. Goetsch Beauvais, Jacklyn L., John C., James W. BS in Commerce magna cum laude, U. Notre Dame, 1955; MBA, Ind. U., 1956. Jr. analyst Wis. Electric Power Co., Milw., 1958-62, sr. specialist, 1962-63, adminstrv. asst., 1963-67, asst. sec., 1967-79, sec., 1979-88, v.p., sec., 1988-93; asst. sec. Wis. Natural Gas Co., Milw., 1969-79, sec., 1979-93; asst. sec. Badger Svc. Co., Milw., 1975-79, sec., 1979-95; asst. sec. Wis. Mich. Investment Corp., Milw., 1978-79, sec., 1979-95; sec. Wis. Energy Corp., Milw., 1981-93, v.p., sec., 1994-95; sec. Wispark, Wisvest, Witech Corps., Milw., 1984-95; v.p., sec. Wis. Energy Corp., Milw., 1994-95. 1st Lt. USAF, 1956-58. Mem. Am. Soc. Corp. Secs. (pres., v.p., sec., treas. Milw. chpt. 1981-85, nat. dir. 1989-95, nat. chmn. 1993-94). Avocations: spectator sports, fishing, swimming. Home: 2301 W Brantwood Ave Milwaukee WI 53209-3331

GOETSCHEL, ROY HARTZELL, JR., mathematician, researcher; b. Oak Park, Ill., Apr. 19, 1930; s. Roy Hartzell and Elizabeth Wilhelmina Johanna (Gaude) G.; m. Jane Peterson, June 6, 1971. BS, Northwestern U., 1954; MS, DePaul U., 1958; PhD, U. Wis., 1966. Asst. prof. math. Sonoma State U. of Calif., Rohnert Park, Calif., 1966-69; prof. math. U. Idaho, Moscow, Idaho, 1969-97; prof. emeritus math. U. Idaho, Moscow, 1997—. Author: Advanced Calculus, 1981; contbr. articles to Fuzzy Sets and Systems. Mem. N.Y. Acad. Scis. Achievements include introduction and development of concept of fuzzy darts and fuzzy dart representations of fuzzy numbers; introduction of the topic of fuzzy hypergraphs including methodology and applications (especially Hebbian structures) to the literature through papers published in Fuzzy Sets and Systems; conceptualization and development of the basis of a fuzzy matroid theory. Avocation: music (vocal and instrumental). Home: 1721 Atsirk St Moscow ID 83843-9302

GOETTEL, GERARD LOUIS, federal judge; b. N.Y.C., Aug. 5, 1928; s. Louis and Agnes Beatrice (White) G.; m. Elinor Praeger, June 4, 1951; children: Sheryl, Glenn, James. Student, The Citadel, 1946-48; B.A., Duke U., 1950; J.D. (Harlan Fiske Stone scholar), Columbia U., 1955. Bar: N.Y. 1955. Asst. U.S. atty. So. Dist. N.Y., N.Y.C., 1955-58; dep. chief atty. gen.'s spl. group on organized crime Dept. Justice, N.Y.C., 1958-59; asso. firm Lowenstein, Pitcher, Hotchkiss, Amann & Parr, N.Y.C., 1959-62; counsel N.Y. Life Ins. Co., N.Y.C., 1962-68; with Natanson & Reich, N.Y.C., 1968-69; asso. gen. counsel Overmyer Co., N.Y.C., 1969-71; asst. counsel N.Y. Ct. on the Judiciary, 1971; U.S. magistrate U.S. Dist. Ct., So. Dist. N.Y., 1971-76, U.S. dist. judge, 1976—; now sr. judge; adj. prof. law Fordham U. Law Sch., 1978-87, Pace U. Law Sch., 1988-91; mem. com. on criminal justice act Jud. Conf. U.S., 1981-87, mem. cir. com. on pretrial phase of civil litigation, chmn. dist. coms. on discovery and criminal justice act 1982-85. Mem. council Fresh Air Fund, N.Y.C., 1961-64; bd. dirs. Community Action Program, Yonkers, N.Y., 1964-66. Served to lt. (j.g.) USCG, 1951-53. Club: Greenwoods Country (Winsted, Conn.). Office: 14 Cottage Pl Waterbury CT 06702-1904

GOETZ, CECELIA HELEN, lawyer, retired judge; b. N.Y.C.; d. Isador and Sylvia (Cohen) G.; children: Matthew I. Spiegel, Robert Spiegel. BA cum laude, NYU, 1940, LLB, 1940, LLM in Taxation, 1957. Bar: N.Y. 1940, U.S. Dist. Ct. (so. and ea. dists.) N.Y. 1951, Fla. 1954, U.S. Ct. Appeals (2d cir.) 1958, U.S. Ct. Appeals (1st cir.) 1952, U.S. Ct. Appeals (9th cir.) 1967. Atty. claims div. (now civil div.) Dept. Justice, Washington, 1943-46; assoc. counsel Office Chief of Counsel for War Crimes, Nuremberg, Ger., 1946-48; ptnr. Goetz & Goetz, N.Y.C., 1949-51; asst. chief counsel Office Price Stblzn., Washington, 1951-52; spl. asst. to atty. gen., tax div., Dept. Justice, Washington, 1952-53; assoc. Weisman, Celler, Allan, Spett & Sheinberg, N.Y.C., 1953-58, Kaye, Scholer, Fierman, Hays & Handler, N.Y.C., 1958-64; ptnr. Herzfeld & Rubin, N.Y.C., 1964-78; judge U.S. Bankruptcy Ct., Eastern Dist. N.Y., Bklyn., 1978-93; of counsel Herzfeld & Rubin, P.C., N.Y.C., 1994-95. Mem. Assn. Bar City N.Y., N.Y. State Bar Assn., ABA, N.Y. County Lawyers Assn., NYU Law Rev. Alumni Assn., N.Y. Women's Bar Assn., Women's Bar Assn State N.Y. Nat. Conf. Bankruptcy Judges, Nat. Assn. Women Judges, Assn. Women Judges State N.Y., Women's City Club N.Y. Office: 3400 N Ocean Dr West Palm Beach FL 33404-3220*

GOETZ, CLARENCE EDWARD, retired judge, retired chief magistrate judge; b. Balt., Feb. 4, 1932. AA, U. Balt., 1961, LLB, 1964. Bar: Md. 1964. Assoc. Hackney & Yourtee, Anne Arundel County, Md., 1965-66; asst. U.S. atty. for Md., 1966-70; U.S. magistrate judge for Md. Balt., 1970-97; asst. prof. U. Balt., 1975, Towson State Coll., 1976; cons., arbitrator, mediator. Mem. Fed. Magistrate Judges Assn. Office: Clarence Goetz Inc 400 E Pratt St Ste 800 Baltimore MD 21202-3122*

GOETZ, KENNETH LEE, cardiovascular physiologist, research consultant; b. Java, S.D., Jan. 7, 1932; m. Shirley Anne Caldwell, July 14, 1962; children: Gregory Earl, Anne Katherine. PhD, U. Wis., 1963; MD, U. Kans., 1967. Instr., asst. prof. dept. physiology U. Kans. Med. Ctr., Kansas City, 1963-69; med. intern St. Luke's Hosp., Kansas City, 1969, head, div. of exptl. medicine, 1970-91, dir. rsch., 1980-91; adj. prof. dept. physiology U. Kans. Med. Ctr., 1976-92; vis. prof. U. Kuopio, Finland, 1985, 91, U. Munich, 1992; vis. scientist German Inst. Aerospace Medicine, Cologne, 1993-94. Recipient Alexander von Humboldt award, 1992. Fellow Am. Phys. Soc. (circulation sect.); mem. Am. Physiol. Soc., Alexander von Humboldt Assn. of Am. Achievements include research in Neurohumoral control of body fluid balance; influence of vasoctive peptides on hemodynamics; Vasopressin, atriopeptin, renal natriuretic peptide, endothelin; reflex control of the circulation. Home: 4856 Black Swan Dr Shawnee Mission KS 66216-1237

GOETZ, MAURICE HAROLD, lawyer; b. N.Y.C., Mar. 29, 1924; s. Morton M. and Elsie (Klein) G.; m. Pearl Goldberg, Sept. 12, 1948; children: Susan Goetz Zwirn, Janet L., Jill K. B Social Scis. in Econs. and History, CCNY, 1947; JD, Harvard U., 1950. Bar: N.Y. 1951. Assoc. Bandler Haas & Kass, N.Y.C., 1951-57; ptnr. Bandler Kass & Goetz, N.Y.C., 1957-66, Friedlander, Gaines, Ruttenberg & Goetz, N.Y.C., 1966-74; ptnr. Rosenman & Colin, N.Y.C., 1974-92, of counsel, 1992—; lectr. on labor law. Contbr. articles to Nat. Law Jour., Fed. Publs., Inc., others. Office: Rosenman & Colin 575 Madison Ave New York NY 10022-2585

GOETZ, PETER, safety board director; m. Kate (Kelley); 2 children. Mng. dir. Nat. Transp. Safety Bd., Washington, D.C., 1995—. Fax: 202-314-6060. Office: Nat Transp Safety Bd 490 E L Enfant Plaza SW Washington DC 20594

GOETZ, ROGER MELVIN, minister; b. Chgo., May 17, 1940; s. Charles Albert and Sidonia Helene (Heck) G.; m. Betty Jean Bokelheide, Nov. 22, 1969; 1 child, Anne Katharine. BS in Chemistry, Iowa State U., Ames, 1962, BS in Math., 1967; MDiv, Concordia Theol. Sem., 1967; STM, Luth. Theol. Sem., 1972. Ordained minister Luth. Ch., 1968. Asst. pastor, dir. music Gethsemane Luth. Ch., St. Paul, 1968-80; assoc. pastor, minister of music St. John's Luth. Ch., Topeka, 1980—; instr. Walther Luth. Jr. H.S., St. Paul, 1968-80; archivist Kans. Dist. Luth. Ch.-Mo. Synod, Topeka, 1985-89, chmn. worship com., 1985-94; organ recitalist various Luth. chs., 1970—. Author: The Descendants of Johann Georg Götz, 1976, Double Cousins by the Dozens, 1982; editor: A Century of Grace: Centennial History of the Kansas District, 1888-1988, 1988; composer work for double mixed chorus. Bd. edn. Topeka Luth. Sch., 1996—; Rep. precinct committeeman Ward II/ Precinct 3, Topeka, 1996-98. Mem. Am. Guild Organists (chpt. pres. 1983-84, chpt. chaplain 1994—), Phi Mu Alpha, Alpha Chi Sigma. Office: St Johns Luth Ch 901 SW Fillmore St Topeka KS 66604 *In my life I have found that the less I try to control things and people and rather leave things in the hands of my loving God, the more God brings gifts and joy into my life.*

GOETZ, WILLIAM G., state legislator; b. Hazen, N.D., Jan. 6, 1944; s. Otto E. and Elfrieda (Knoop) G.; m. Marion R. Schock, 1970; children: Marcia, Paul, Mark. AA, Bismarck Jr. Coll., 1964; BA, Minot State Coll., 1966; MA, U. N.D., 1967. Asst. mgr. Medora divsn. Gold Seal Co., 1963-70; dean sch. bus. and adminstrn. Dickinson State U., 1967; state rep. dist. 37, 1975-90, state senator, 1990—; chmn. Rep. Ho. Caucus; asst. majority leader, vice chmn. fin. and tax. com. N.D. Ho. Reps., 1975-90; asst. minority leader; mem. appropriations com., asst. majority leader N.D. State Senate, 1990—. Chmn. dist. 37 Rep. com., 1976—, mem. exec. com.; appointed by pres. to Nat. Coun. for Edn. Rsch. and Improvement. Recipient Pub. Svc. award N.D. Lignite Coun. Mem. Greater N.D. Assn. (formerly bd. dirs., Educator of Yr.), Nat. Conf. State Legislators. Republican. Home: 251 Allen St Dickinson ND 58601-4042*

GOETZEL, CLAUS GUENTER, metallurgical engineer; b. Berlin, July 14, 1913; came to U.S., 1936; s. Walter and Else (Baum) G.; m. Lilo Kallmann, Nov. 19, 1938; children: Rodney G., Vivian L. Holley. Dipl.-Ing., Technische Hochschule, Berlin, 1935; PhD, Columbia U., 1939. Registered profl. engr., Calif. Research chemist, lab. head Hardy Metall. Co., 1936-39; tech. dir., works mgr. Am. Electro Metal Corp., 1939-47; v.p., dir. research Sintercast Corp. Am., 1947-57; adj. prof. NYU, N.Y.C., 1945-57, sr. research scientist, 1957-60; cons. scientist Lockheed Missiles & Space Co., Sunnyvale, Calif., 1960-78; cons. metall. engring. Portola Valley, Calif., 1978—; lectr., vis. scholar Stanford (Calif.) U., 1961-88; vis. prof. Tech. Univ. Karlsruhe, Germany, 1978-80. Author: Treatise on Powder Metallurgy, 5 vols., 1949-63; co-author: (with Lilo Goetzel) Dictionary of Materials and Process Engineering, vol. 1 English-German, 1995, vol. 2, German-English, 1997; inventor or co-inventor of over 40 U.S. patents; contbr. over 50 articles to profl. jours. and handbooks. Recipient Alexander von Humboldt Sr. U.S. Scientist award, Fed. Republic Germany, 1978. Fellow AIAA (assoc.), Am. Soc. Materials Internat.; mem. AIME (life), Am. Powder Metallurgy Inst. (sr.), Materials Sci. Club N.Y. (life, past pres.), Inst. Materials (life, London).

GOETZMAN, BRUCE EDGAR, architecture educator; b. Rochester, June 6, 1931; s. Benjamin Byron and Illa Flowers G.; m. Jane Grady McRae,June 25, 1955; children: Adam Brit, Ben Evan. BArch, Carnegie Mellow U., 1954; MS in Architecture, Columbia U., 1956; M Community Planning, U. Cin., 1965; postgrad., U. London, 1968. Asst. prof. Univ. Cin., 1956-66; prin. Bruce Goetzman & Assocs., Cin., 1965-77; acting chmn. grad. div. Univ. Cin., 1966-67, assoc. prof., 1967-99; prof. emeritus, 1999; ptnr. Goetzman & Follmer Architects, Cin., 1977-85; prin. Bruce Goetzman, Restoration Architect, 1985--. Trustee Miami Purchase Assn. Hist. Preservation, Cin., 1972-91, Ohio Hist. Sites Preservation Adv. Bd., 1980-92; trustee Ohio Hist. Soc., 1986-96, pres., 1995-96; pres. Ohio Preservation Alliance, 1986-88; trustee Cin. Preservation Assn., 1993—. Mem. AIA, Architects Soc. Ohio, Assn. Preservation Tech., Cin. Assn. Democrat. Home: 187 Greendale Ave Cincinnati OH 45220-1223

GOEWEY, GORDON IRA, university administrator; b. Troy, N.Y., June 25, 1924; s. Ira A. and Flossie (Warger) G.; m. Marie Matteson Huening, May 30, 1968; children by previous marriage—Lynne Dee, Todd Ira. B.Mus., Boston U., 1948, Mus.A.D., 1969; M.A. in Teaching, Harvard, 1953. Mem. faculty SUNY Coll. Arts and Sci., Geneseo, 1949-72; prof. music SUNY Coll. Arts and Sci., 1963-72, chmn. dept., 1952-69, dean grad. studies, 1969-72, dir. summer session, 1969-72, chmn. faculty, 1963-64; v.p. acad. affairs Trenton (N.J.) State Coll., 1972-78, provost, 1978-84; Mem. State Negotiating Team, 1973-75; mem. N.J. Licensure and Approval Adv. Bd., 1975-82, chmn., 1975-79; chmn. State Acad. Vice Presidents, 1975-77, 82-83; bd. dirs. N.J. Edn. Consortium, 1975-78; resource asso. Am. Assn. State Colls. and Univs. Author: (with John Kucaba) Understanding Musical Form, 1962; author: (with others) Managing the Academic Enterprise, 1988. Bd. dirs., v.p. George Washington council Boy Scouts Am., 1978-82, Emil Maestre Music Assn.; bd. dirs., v.p. 1985—; bd. dirs., adminstrv. v.p. Ancient City Arts Alliance, 1985-87; chmn. regional rev. panel Harry S. Truman Scholarship Found., Washington, 1976—. Served with AUS, 1943-44. Mem. Music Educators Nat. Conf., N.J. Jazz Soc., Faculty Assn. SUNY (exec. com. 1964-67), Am. Assn. for Higher Edn., Am. Assn. Univ. Adminstrs. (bd. dirs. 1976-82), Am. Coll. Pers. Assn. (N.E. regional dir. 1976-82), Torch of Trenton (bd. dirs. 1977-84), Rotary (dir. Trenton 1976-79, v.p. Trenton 1983), Lions (pres. 1987, sec. St. Augustine chpt. 1986, Sun Center chpt. 1993-96), Phi Mu Alpha.

GOFF, CHRISTOPHER WALLICK, pediatrician; b. Phila., Jan. 24, 1948; s. Donald Heiserman and Jean Christman Wallick G.; m. Holly Lynn Housner, Aug. 1970; children: Heather Elizabeth, Rebecca Ann, Abigail Christine. BA in Psychology, Yale U., 1970; MD, U. Pa., 1974. Diplomate Am. Bd. Pediatrics, Pediatric Endocrinology, Nat. Bd. Med. Examiners. Intern, then resident in pediatrics Yale-New Haven (Conn.) Hosp., 1974-76, chief resident in pediatrics, 1977; pvt. practice specializing in pediatrics Wildwood Pediatrics, Essex, Conn., 1977—; alternate dir. Health Town of Essex, 1980-81, dir. Health, 1981—; co-dir. Child Diagnostic Assocs., Essex, 1983—; assoc. staff Yale-New Haven Hosp., 1977-80, attending staff, 1980—; clin. instr. Pediatrics Yale U. Sch. Med., 1977-79, clin. asst. prof., 1979-97, clin. assoc. prof., 1997—; bd. dirs. Wildwood Med. Ctr. Assn., 1986-89, treas. 1988—; co-med. adviser Mt. St. John Sch., Deep River, Conn., 1977—, Oxford Acad., Westbrook, Conn., 1990-95; acting med. adviser Essex Elem. Sch., 1981—; med. adviser Old Saybrook Sch. sys., 1992-97. Reviewer Clinical Pediatrics; clin. reactor Contemporary Pediatrics; contbr. articles to prof. jours. Chmn. prof. adv. com. Visiting Nurses Lower Valley, 1980—; devel. bd. Tri-Town Youth Svc. Bur., 1987-88; mem. Sexual Abuse Prevention Task Force, 1987-95, Tri-Town Substance Abuse Task Force, 1988-95, Westbrook Sexual Abuse Prevention Task Force, 1988-93, Shoreline Child Protection Team, 1988-93, Tri-Town Sexual Abuse Response Team, 1990-91; vestryman St. John's Episcopal Ch., Essex., 1978-79, sr. warden, 1979-83, coord. Youth Ministry program, 1986-90, treas. 1994-96; lector 1989-96; pres. Marlins Parents Club, 1989-91; bd. dirs. Lower Valley Cmty. Health Svcs., 1979-80, Essex Ambulance Assn., 1985-89, Cougar Aquatic Team, 1992-96, v.p. 1992-93, treas. 1993-94. Recipient Joel Gordon Miller award, 1974. Fellow Am. Acad. Pediatrics; mem. AMA, N. Am. Soc. Pediatric and Adolescent Gynecology, New England Soc. Clin. Hypnosis, Conn. State Med. Soc. (malpractice claims rev. bd., 1981-84), New Haven County Med. Soc., Lawson Wilkins Pediatric Endocrine Soc. Republican. Avocations: sailing, skiing, ballroom dancing, stamp collecting, golf. Office: Wildwood Pediatrics and Adol Med 1 Wildwood Medical Ctr Essex CT 06426-1190

GOFF, HARRY RUSSELL, retired manufacturing company executive; b. San Francisco, May 24, 1915; s. Harry Roy and Ethel S. (Ludwigsen) G.; m. Kathleen K. Kloster, Feb. 10, 1940; children: Kathi, Karen, Betsi. BA, Stanford U., 1937; MBA, Harvard U., 1939 . With Nat. Lead Co., San Francisco, 1939-41; ptnr. James D. Dole & Assocs., San Francisco, 1946-60; pres. James Dole Corp., San Francisco, 1955-79; chmn. bd., Pacific Sci. Co.,

Newport Beach, Calif., 1978-90, dir. emeritus, 1990-91; adv. coun. Stanford U. Libr. Assn., 1979—; mem. Nat. Pub. Adv. Com. on Regional Econs. Devel., 1974-76; trustee Am. Schs. Oriental Rsch., 1978-82, Calif. Hist. Soc., 1993—. Lt. comdr. with USNR, 1941-46. Mem. Calif. Hist. Soc. (trustee), Inst. Food Technologists, Bohemian Club, Univ. Club (San Francisco), Los Altos Golf and Country Club, Roxbourghe Club Calif., Book Club Calif. (past pres.). Republican. Home: 868 Southampton Dr Palo Alto CA 94303-3439

GOFF, JANE E., secondary school educator; b. Denver, Nov. 12, 1949; d. Donald F. and Susanna L. (Commerford) Gallion; m. Harry M. Goff, June 12, 1982. BA, Colo. State U., 1971; student, U. Colo. Cert. modern lang. tchr., Colo. Tchr. French Jefferson County Pub. Schs., Golden, Colo., chmn. dept.; mem. North Ctrl. Accreditation Teams; adminstr. Alternative Compensation/Student Outcomes Task Forces; project dir. Tchr. Performance Pay Pilot. Hon. chmn. West Chamber Good News Breakfast; design group West Chamber Links for Learning; mem. Jefferson County Sch. Anchor Group, Jefferson County Sch. Fin. Task Force/Jefferson Found. Crystal Ball Com., Leadership Jefferson County Steering Com. Mem. NEA, Am. Assn. Tchrs. French, Colo. Edn. Assn. (long-range planning com.), Jefferson County Edn. Assn. (bd. dirs., by-laws chair, bldg. rep., sec. 1990-94, v.p. 1994-98, pres. 1998—, budget com./negotiations team), Jefferson County Coun. PTA (bd. dirs. 1990—), Colo. Children's Code Recodification (subcom. 1995, Colo. legis. liaison 1998—), Phi Delta Kappa.

GOFF, JOHN, state agency administrator; b. Greenwood, S.C., 1938; m. Tanya Goff; children: John, Claire. BS, Clemson Coll., 1961; MEd, U. S.C., 1968; EdD, Auburn U., 1972. Cert. permanent supt., Ohio. Tchr. secondary math., coach Laurens (S.C.) H.S., 1961-64, Camden (S.C.) H.S., 1964-66; asst. prin. Camden Jr. H.S., 1966-69, prin., 1969-70; grad. asst. Auburn (Ala.) U., 1970-72; exec. asst. Am. Assn. Sch. Adminstrs., Nat. Acad. Sch. Execs., Washington, 1972-73; asst. supt. Vandalia (Ohio)-Butler City Schs., 1973-75, supt., 1975-81; supt. Kettering (Ohio) City Schs., 1981-89; asst. supt. Ohio Dept. Edn., Columbus, 1989-92, dep. supt. pub. instrn., interim supt. pub. instrn., 1992-95, supt. pub. instrn., 1995—. Mem. PTA Vandalia-Butler and Kettering; mem. planning com. Good Samaritan Hosp., 1978-81; mem. Vandalia Crime and Juvenile Delinquency Com., 1977-78, Vandalia Comty. Devel. Commn., 1975-76; mem. bd. fin. Shiloh Congl. Ch., Dayton, Ohio, 1976-78; co-chair edn. divsn. United Way Campaign, 1987, chair edn. divsn., 1988. 2d lt. U.S. Army, 1961; capt. USAR, 1961-70. Named Ednl. Adminstr. of Yr., Ednl. Office Pers. Ohio, 1985, Educator of Yr., Dist. IV PTA, 1979; athletic scholar Clemson Coll. Mem. Am. Assn. Sch. Adminstrs. (adv. coun. 1984-87), Nat. Acad. Sch. Execs. (strategic planning com. 1989), Buckeye Assn. Sch. Adminstrs. (ad hoc com. distbn. state funds 1978-79, legis. com. 1978-81, chair profl. devel. com. 1981-83, pres.-elect 1983-84, pres. 1984-85, Exemplary Ednl. Leadership award 1987, Disting. Svc. award 1993, Ohio Supt. of Yr. 1988), Ohio Sch. Bds. Assn., Sertoma Club Camden (sec., v.p., pres. 1966-69), Phi Delta Kappa. Office: State Dept of Edn 65 S Front St Rm 810 Columbus OH 43215-4183

GOFF, KENNETH WADE, electrical engineer; b. Salem, W.Va., June 14, 1928; s. Wetzel and Alma (Beeghley) G.; m. Hazel Lucille Sullivan, July 1, 1950; children—Jerry Kenneth, Deborah Lucille, Brian Lee. B.S., W.Va. U., 1950; M.S., M.I.T., 1952, Sc.D., 1954. Cons. engr. Bolt Beranek & Newman, Inc., Cambridge, Mass., 1954-56; project mgr. Gruen Precision Labs., Cin., 1956-57; mgr. systems analysis Leeds & Northrup Co., North Wales, Pa., 1957-69; mgr. systems devel. Leeds & Northrup Co., 1969-84, corp. scientist, 1984-85; v.p. advanced tech. Performance Controls, Inc., Horsham, Pa., 1986-98, also dir.; v.p. advanced tech. MTS Automation-Performance Controls, Horsham, Pa., 1998—; dir. Eastern Coll.; vis. lectr. Franklin Inst., 1962, 63. Contbr. articles to profl. jours. M.I.T. acoustical materials fellow, 1954. Fellow Instrument Soc. Am., IEEE; mem. Acad. Disting. Alumni of W.Va. U. Elec. and Computer Engring. Dept., Sigma Xi, Tau Beta Pi, Eta Kappa Nu. Baptist. Patentee in field. Home: 1815 Cathedral Rd Huntingdon Valley PA 19006-5003 Office: Performance Controls Inc 433 Caredean Dr Horsham PA 19044-1321

GOFF, LEROY R. (ROB), III, career officer; b. Pelham, Ga., Feb. 20, 1946. Commd. officer U.S. Army, advanced through grades to maj. gen.; dep. chief staff for tng. U.S. Army Tng. and Doctrine Command, Ft. Monroe, Va., 1996—. Office: US Army Tng & Doctrine Fort Monroe VA 23651

GOFF, LILA JOHNSON, historical society administrator; b. Redwood Falls, Minn., Jan. 10, 1944; d. Byron Willard and Camilla (Henry) Johnson; m. Robert Eugene Goff, Apr. 24, 1974; children: Emily Lee, Matthew Byron. BA in History, U. Minn., 1965, MA in History, 1995. Chief Oral History Office Minn. Hist. Soc., St. Paul, 1967-69, head Audio Visual Library, 1969-76, asst. dir. for library and mus. collections, 1976-85, asst. dir. for library and archives, 1985—. Dep. coord. Minn. State Hist. Records Adv. Bd. Mem. Oral History Assn. (pres. 1989-90), Oral History Assn. Minn. (pres. 1985-87), Orgn. Am. Historians, Nat. Assn. Govt. Archivists and Records Adminstrs. (bd. dirs. 1992-94), Coun. State Hist. Records Coords. (chair 1994-95), Rsch. Librs. Group (bd. dirs. 1996—). Home: 1151 Orange Ave E Saint Paul MN 55106-2076 Office: Minn Hist Soc Libr and Archives Div 345 Kellogg Blvd W Saint Paul MN 55102-1906

GOFF, MICHAEL HARPER, retired lawyer; b. Hartford, Conn., Aug. 4, 1927; s. Charles Weer and Fern (Harper) G.; m. Katharine Lyman Bliss, Feb. 11, 1949 (div.); children—Carlin Weer, Peter Lyman; m. Patricia Darilyn King, Apr. 20, 1984. Student, Loomis Sch., Conn., 1942-45, Bethany Coll., 1945, Trinity Coll., Conn., 1949; B.A., Swarthmore Coll., 1950; LL.B., Columbia U., 1953. Bar: N.Y. 1953. Assoc. Debevoise & Plimpton, 1953-60, ptnr., 1961-91; asst. to dir. Legis. Drafting Rsch. fund, 1951-53; lectr. Banking Law Inst., 1966; cons. Atty. Gen. State of N.Y., 1977; spl. cons. Temp. Commn. to Study Orgnl. Structure City N.Y., 1953-54. Served with USNR, 1945-46; to 2d lt. F.A., AUS, 1946-48. Harlan Fiske Stone Scholar, Columbia U., 1951-52; Robert Noxon Toppan prize, Columbia U., 1952; E. B. Convers Prize, Columbia U., 1953. Mem. ABA (sect. on bus. law, com. devels. in bus. financing, sect. on sr. lawyers), N.Y. State Bar Assn., Assn. Bar City N.Y., Met. Club (N.Y.C.), Can. Club (N.Y.C.), Moorings Club (Fla.), Phi Delta Phi, Kappa Sigma. Democrat. Episcopalian. Home: 151 Anchor Dr Vero Beach FL 32963-2957*

GOFF, R. GAREY, architect; b. Nashville, Feb. 2, 1943; s. R. C. and Martha Ann (Garey) G.; m. Diana R. Richardson; children: Gina Leigh, Susan Kimberly. Student, Vanderbilt U., 1961-65; BArch, U. Fla., 1968. Intern architect Earl Swensson Assocs., Nashville, 1968-70; project architect Sverdrup & Parcel, Nashville, 1970-73; project architect Gresham, Smith and Ptnrs., Nashville, 1973-76, dir. of architecture, 1976-81, prin., assoc., 1981-83; prin., assoc. Gresham, Smith and Ptnrs., Charleston, S.C., 1983-84; prin. Goff Assocs., Charleston, 1984-89, NBBJ/Goff-D'Antonio, Charleston, 1989-91, Goff-D'Antonio Assocs., Charleston, 1991—. Mem. Trident 100, Charleston. Recipient Bell System awards Southeastern Bell, 1970, Spl. Recognition awards Prestressed Concrete Inst., Chgo., 1987, 88, Design award Gen. Svcs. Adminstrn., Dept. of Transp., Washington, 1990. Mem. Rotary Internat. Republican. Episcopalian. Avocations: golfing, traveling, boating. Office: Goff-D'Antonio Assocs 180 Meeting St Charleston SC 29401-3154*

GOFF, ROBERT BURNSIDE, retired food company executive; b. Arcadia, La., Aug. 8, 1924; s. Carl and Ruth (Capers) G.; m. Mary Jane Ellis, June 14, 1947; children—Gayle M., Robert B. B.S., Rice U., 1947. Engr. Tex. Pipe Line Co., Tulsa, 1947-48; v.p., dir. Comet Rice Mills, Inc., Houston, 1948-58; sr. v.p., dir. Riviana Foods, Inc., Houston, 1958-75; pres., dir. Food Corp. Internat., Houston, 1975-86. Trustee Found. for Retarded, 1982-90. Served to lt. (j.g.) USNR, 1942-46. Mem. Rice U. Alumni Assn. (exec. bd. 1985-88), River Oaks Country Club. Presbyterian. Home: 2710 Essex Ter Houston TX 77027-5212

GOFF, ROBERT EDWARD, health plan executive; b. Worcester, Mass., Nov. 19, 1952; s. Julius Lewis and Doris (Katz) G.; m. Jinny Sue Yaver, June 30, 1985; 1 child, Blake Adam. BBA with honors, Northeastern U., Boston, 1976; MBA with honors, Babson Coll., 1978; cert., Cornell U., 1981. Adminstrv. dir. Adirondack PSRO Inc., Glens Falls, N.Y., 1977-80; v.p. No. Met. Hosp. Assn., Newburgh, N.Y., 1980-83, Good Samaritan Hosp., Suffern, N.Y., 1983-85; exec. dir., chief exec. dir. WellCare N.Y., Inc., Newburgh, 1985-97; pres. Wellcare Leasing Corp., Newburgh, N.Y., 1990-96, Well Care Med. Mgmt. Inc., 1992-96; exec. v.p. Well Care Mgmt. Group, Inc., 1992-97; prin. The ABER Group, 1997-98; exec. dir. Univ. Physicians Network/NYU, 1998—; bd. dirs. Wellcare Mgmt. Group Inc.; pres. Wellcare Med. Mgmt.; cons. in field. Bd. dirs. Hospice Care, Inc., Hospice of Orange Inc. Recipient Vigil Honor award Order Arrow, 1969, Eagle Scout award Boy Scouts Am., 1970. Mem. Hudson Valley Hosp. Exec. Assn. (pres., bd. dirs. 1982-85), Healthcare Fin. Mgmt. Assn., Am. Coll. Hosp. Adminstrs., Beta Gamma Soc. Home: 93 Old Castle Point Rd Wappingers Falls NY 12590-7048 Office: 9th Fl 1 Park Ave Fl 9 New York NY 10016-5802

GOFF, WILLIAM M., JR., art director, graphic designer; b. Tampa, Fla., June 21, 1959; s. Willam M. and Flora G. Goff. Degree in gen. aviation, Ala. Aviation Tech. Coll., 1983; BA, Spring Hill Coll., 1990; cert. in advanced graphic design, Chyron Corp., Melville, N.Y., 1993; cert. in animation design, Alias/Wavefront Animation, Santa Barbara, Calif., 1995. Cert. in advanced graphic design Chyron Corp. Disk jockey, mem. prodn. staff Sta. WABB-FM Radio, Mobile, Ala., 1975-78; photographer Palmer Photography, Mobile, Ala., 1978-79; mem. gen. maintenance staff Mobile Air Ctr., 1980-83; courier, mem. office svcs. staff Delchamps, Inc., Mobile, 1983-87; art dir., animator Sta. WKRG-TV 5, Inc., Mobile, 1988-98, dir. art internships, 1995-98; digital graphic cons., tech. dir., freelance animator/artist, 1998—. Art dir. (TV spl.) Someone You Know-AIDS, 1992 (AP award 1993); graphic design (documentary) Indian Blood, 1993 (award 1994). Troop leader Boy Scouts Am., Eagle Scouts, Mobile, 1977-79; past pres. Explorers Am., Mobile, 1977-78; prodr. dir. Jr. Achievement, Mobile, 1975-78. Recipient Excellence in Broadcasting award CBS, 1993, Best Sports Event award AP/Ala., 1995, 96, Best Scheduled Live Event award, 1995. Avocations: music, art, outdoor activities, writing, movies. Office: Global Village PO Box 91594 Mobile AL 36691-1594

GOFF, WILMER SCOTT, photographer; b. Steubenville, Ohio, July 11, 1923; s. Floyd Orville and Ellen Armenia (Funk) G.; m. Mary Elizabeth Fischer, Dec. 7, 1950; children: Carolyn, Christopher. BFA with honors, Ohio U., 1949. Photographer Columbus (Ohio) Dispatch, 1949-52, Warner P. Simpson, Columbus, 1952-53; owner Willy Goff Photo Studio, Grove City, Ohio, 1954-59; photographer N.Am. Rockwell, Columbus, 1953-70; supr. Transp. Rsch. Ctr. Ohio, East Liberty, 1970-89; adult edn. instr. photography Upper Arlington and Worthington Schs., 1989-99; photography instr. Columbus Coll. Art and Design, 1949-71; photography judge Ohio State Fair, 1966-68; judge Greater Columbus Film Festival, 1970-72; photographer John Glenn campaign, 1974. One man shows include 100 print exhibit Southern Hotel, Columbus, 1953. Recipient Public's Choice award Columbus Art Gallery, 1958, Photo-Pictoral 1st Pl. award Dix Newspapers, 1960, Best of Show award Balloon Show Competition, 1985. Mem. Aircraft Camera Club (pres. 1954-55), Grove City Camera CLub (pres. 1959-60). Republican. Roman Catholic. Avocations: stamp collecting, recording, cycling. Home: 6110 Darby Ln Columbus OH 43229-2628 *Personal philosophy: My philosophy of a successful life is to pursue a career of choice regardless of monetary gain. My photography career has been exciting and fullfilling. I feel I have accomplished my goals and one for which I had not planned, being included in Who's Who in the Midwest.*

GOFFART, WALTER ANDRÉ, history educator; b. Berlin, Feb. 22, 1934; emigrated to U.S., 1943, naturalized, 1959; s. Francis Leo and Andrée Juliette (Steinberg) G.; m. Ellen Horvath, May 19, 1961; children: Vivian, Andrea Judith; m. Roberta Frank, Dec. 31, 1977. AB, Harvard U., 1955, AM, 1956, PhD, 1961; postgrad., École pratique des Hautes-Études, Paris, France, 1957-58. Lectr. history U. Toronto, Ont., Can., 1961-63; asst. prof. U. Toronto, 1963-66, assoc. prof., 1966-71, prof., 1971-99, acting dir. Ctr. for Medieval Studies, 1971-72, prof. emeritus, 1999; vis. asst. prof. U. Calif. at Berkeley, 1965-66; vis. fellow Inst. Advanced Study, Princeton, N.J., 1967-68, Dumbarton Oaks Ctr. Byzantine Studies, Washington, 1973-74. Author: The Le Mans Forgeries, 1966, Caput and Colonate, 1974, Barbarians and Romans, A.D. 418-584, 1981; The Narrators of Barbarian History: Jordanes, Gregory of Tours, Bede, and Paul the Deacon, 1988, Rome's Fall and After, 1989; translator: The Origin of the Idea of Crusade (C. Erdmann), 1978. Recipient Haskins medal Medieval Acad. Am., 1991; Can. Council fellow, 1967-68; Am. Council Learned Socs. fellow, 1973-74; Guggenheim fellow, 1979-80; Connaught sr. fellow in humanities U. Toronto, 1983-84; Newberry Libr. fellow, 1989. Fellow Medieval Acad. Am. (councillor 1977-80), Royal Hist. Soc., Royal Soc. Can.; mem. Internat. Soc. Anglo-Saxonists, Haskins Soc., Can. Soc. Medievalists, Hagiography Soc., Phi Beta Kappa. Office: U of Toronto, Dept of History, Toronto, ON Canada M5S 3G3

GOFFEN, RONA, art educator; b. N.Y.C., June 7, 1944; d. William and Stella (Friedman) G. AB cum laude, Mt. Holyoke Coll., 1966; MA, Columbia U., 1968, PhD with distinction, 1974. Lectr. dept. fine arts Ind. U., Bloomington, 1971-73; lectr. dept. art and archaeology Princeton (N.J.) U., 1973-74, asst. prof. art, 1974-78; asst. prof. dept. art and art history Duke U., Durham, N.C., 1978-80, assoc. prof. art, 1980-86, chmn. dept. art and art history, 1983—, prof. art, 1986-88; Disting. prof. Rutgers U., New Brunswick, N.J., 1988-98, chmn. dept. art history, 1990-96, bd. govs. prof., 1998—; vis. assoc. prof. Barnard Coll. Columbia U., N.Y.C., fall 1980; vis. scholar Am. Acad Rome, 1976; Robert Sterling Clark vis. prof. Williams Coll., 1997. Author: Piety and Patronage in Renaissance Venice, 1986, Spirituality in Conflict, 1988, Giovanni Bellini, 1989, Titian's Venus of Urbino, 1997, Titian's Women, 1997, Masaccio's Trinity, 1998; co-editor: Life and Death in Fifteenth-Century Florence, 1989; bd. editors Renaissance Quar., Venezia Cinquecento; contbr. articles to profl. publs. Am. Philos. Soc. grantee, 1979, NEH grantee, summer 1986; Harvard U. Ctr. Italian Renaissance Studies fellow, Florence, Italy, 1976-77, Am. Council for Learned Socs. fellow, 1976-77, Nat. Humanities Ctr. fellow, Research Triangle Park, N.C., 1986-87, Guggenheim fellow, 1986-87. Mem. Coll. Art Assn., Renaissance Soc. Office: Rutgers U Dept Art History Voorhees Hall New Brunswick NJ 08903

GOFFIGAN, CHRISTOPHER WAYNE, research associate; b. Norfolk, Va., June 10, 1960; s. James Edward and Lillie Pearl (Jones) G. AAS in Mgmt., Tidewater C.C., 1982, AAS in Merchandising, 1982. Cert. in profl. communication; cert. profl. cons. Libr. aide Tidewater C.C., Virginia Beach, Va., 1980-82; inventory taxer Miller Rhodes, Virginia Beach, Va., 1984, 88; telephone sales rep. Energy Savs. Exterior Inc., Virginia Beach, Va., 1985, Sears Svc. Ctr., Virginia Beach, Va., 1985-86; credit clerical Sears Credit Ctrl., Virginia Beach, Va., 1986-87; telephone interviewer Issues Answers, Norfolk, Va., 1988; rsch. assoc. Leading Nat. Advertisers/Competitive Media Reporting, Virginia Beach, 1990—; new mem. adv. panel Am. Mktg. Assn., Chgo., 1992-93. Vol. City of Virginia Beach, 1989. Recipient Cert. of Appreciation, Mil. Mail Call, 1984, Editors Choice award Nat. Libr. Poetry, 1996, 97; named Knight Chevalier Venerable Order of the Knights of Michael the Archangel, 1992, Hon. Sgt. At Arms, Nat. Assn. Chiefs of Police, 1993, named to Internat. Poetry Hall of Fame, 1997, Inducted into Millenium Hall of Fame Am. Biog. Inst., 1998, named to Dictionary Internat. Biog. Internat. Biog. Ctr. 1998. Mem. Am. Fedn. Police and Concerned Citizens, Am. Police Hall of Fame & Mus., U.S. Marshals and Peace Officers Assn. Am., Nat. Assn. Chiefs of Police (hon. chief 1995, Good Samaritan award 1995, Gold Seal award 1995), Internat. Soc. Poets (Internat. Poet of Merit award 1996), Internat. Guild Profl. Cons. (cert.), Nat. Geographic Soc., Am. Biog. Inst. Rsch. Assn., Va. Employment Law Inst. Avocations: bowling, pool, travel, reading, shopping. Home: 740 Cason Ln Virginia Beach VA 23462-1197

GOFFMAN, THOMAS EDWARD, radiation oncologist, researcher; b. Chgo., Apr. 16, 1953; s. E. and A. (Choate) G.; divorced; 1 child, James Edward. BA, Yale U., 1975; MD, Hahnemann U., 1979. Diplomate Am. Bd. Radiology, Am. Bd. Internal Medicine, Am. Coll. Radiation Oncology. Intern, resident Georgetown U. Hosp., Washington, 1979-82; med. staff fellow, epidemiology tng. program Nat. Cancer Inst., NIH, Bethesda, Md., 1982-83; resident in radiotherapy, Joint Ctr. for Radiation Therapy Harvard U. Med. Sch., Boston, 1983-86; instr. in radiation oncology Columbia U., N.Y.C., 1986-87, asst. prof. of radiation oncology, 1987; attending in radiation oncology Washington Hosp. Ctr., 1987-89, vice chmn. dept. radiation oncology, 1988-89; asst. dir. radiation oncology Sibley Meml. Hosp., 1989; asst. clin. prof. radiation medicine Georgetown U., 1989—; assoc. prof. dept. radiation oncology/biophysics, med. dir. Eastern Va. Med. Sch., Virginia Beach, 1997—; head clin. therapy sect., radiation oncology br., Nat. Cancer Inst., Bethesda, 1989—; asst. prof. radiology USUHS, Bethesda, 1989-91; dir. radiation oncology tng. USUHS, Bethesda, 1989-92; dir. radiation oncology tng. Nat. Cancer Inst., USUHS, Bethesda, 1990-92; assoc. prof. radiology USUHS, 1991-92; dir. radiation oncology St. Agnes Hosp., Balt., 1992-93; rschr. internat. epidemiology nat. radiation NIH, 1983-84; med. dir. radiol. oncology Sentara Norfolk Gen. Hosp. Contbr. articles to profl. jours. Recipient Mosby scholarship for acad. achievement, 1979, Excellence in Medicine award, 1979, Blue Ribbon award, 1979, Nat. Rsch. Svc. award, 1983, Epidemiology Tng. fellowship Nat. Cancer Inst.-NIH, 1983. Fellow ACP; mem. AMA, AAAS, ACP, N.Y. Acad. Scis., Com. on Physicians Assn., D.c. Med. Soc. (legis. com.), Nat. Cancer Inst. (internal rev. bd. 1989-90, biol. operating com. 1991—, internat. health com. 1993-96), Balt. City Med. Soc.

GOFFMAN, WILLIAM, mathematician, educator; b. Cleve., Jan. 28, 1924; s. Sam and Mollie (Stein) G.; m. Patricia McLoughlin, Feb. 7, 1964. B.S., U. Mich., 1950, Ph.D., 1954. Math. cons., 1954-59; research asso. prof. Case Western Res. U., Cleve., 1959-71; dean Case Western Res. U. (Sch. Library Sci.), 1971-77; dir. Case Western Res. U. (Complex Systems Inst.), 1972-75. Contbr. numerous publs. to sci. jours. Served with USAAF, 1943-46. Recipient research grants NSF, research grants NIH, research grants USAF, research grants others. Fellow AAAS. Home: Ii Bratenahl Pl Bratenahl OH 44108-1183 Office: Case Western Res Univ Cleveland OH 44106

GOFORTH, MARY ELAINE DAVEY, secondary education educator; b. Barnesville, Ohio, Sept. 9, 1922; d. Frederick Richard and Lola (Knox) Davey; m. Richard Eugene Goforth, Sept. 9, 1944; 1 child, Diane Lynell Goforth-Ohning. B.M.Ed., Oberlin Coll., 1944; MA in Edn., Coll. of Mt. St. Joseph, 1987. Cert. edn. Music tchr. Leipsig, Ohio, 1944-45, Perry Local, 1945-47; English tchr. Ohio No. Univ., 1946; English and music tchr. Perry Sch., Lima, Ohio, 1945-47; English tchr. Stone Creek, Ohio, 1947-51, Barnesville, Ohio, 1952-53, Tuscarawas, Ohio, 1957-59; English tchr. Conotton Valley Sch., Bowerston, Ohio, 1960-62; English tchr. New Philadelphia, Ohio, 1964-68, Indian Valley, Midvale, Ohio, 1973-88, Indian Valley, Gnadenhetten, Ohio, 1988-93. Author poems. Pres. New Philadelphia (Ohio) Tchrs.' Assn., 1967. Named Indian Valley Tchr. of Yr., 1985, Candidate for Ohio Tchr. of the Yr., 1985; Martha Holden Jennings scholar, 1985. Home: 2123 E High Ave New Philadelphia OH 44663-3323

GOFORTH, WAYNE REID, research administrator, biologist; b. Wentzville, Mo., Feb. 13, 1932; s. Harold Franklin and Mary Elder (Reid) G.; m. Prudence Jean Osborn, Mar. 19, 1963; children: Heidi, Paul. BS, U. Mo., 1954, MA, 1963; PhD, U Mo., 1968. Prof. Iowa Wesleyan Coll., Mt. Pleasant, 1964-68; prof., unit leader U. Mo., Columbia, 1968-73; dir. No. Prairie Wildlife Rsch. Ctr. Fish and Wildlife Svc., Jamestown, N.D., 1973-80; forest environment rsch. dir. Forest Svc., Washington, 1980-83; rsch. unit supr. Fish and Wildlife Svc., Washington, 1983-93; chief div. coop. rsch. Nat. Biol. Svc., Washington, 1994-97; rsch. liaison officer U.S. Fish & Wildlife Svc., Washington, 1997—. Author: The Cooperative Fish and Wildlife Research Unit Program, 1994, also articles. Mem. Gov.'s Coun. on Wetlands, State of N.D., 1975-76. Avocations: wildlife carving, fishing, boating. Office: US Fish Wildlife Svc 4401 Fairfax Dr Arlington VA 22203-1622

GOGAN, CATHERINE MARY, dental educator; b. Buffalo, Feb. 9, 1959; d. John Francis and Mary Louise (Solomon) G. BA, SUNY, Buffalo, 1981, DDS, 1985, MS, 1995. Resident Erie County Med. Ctr., Buffalo, 1985-86, attending dentist, 1986—, dental residency coord., 1987-96, dental dir. skilled nursing facility, 1989-98; dir. dentistry Erie County Med. Ctr., 1998—; pvt. practice Buffalo, 1986—; clin. instr. SUNY, Buffalo, 1987-88, asst. prof., 1988-97, clin. assoc. prof., 1997—, dir. patient admissions, 1996-98, dir. advanced edn. in gen. dentistry, 1997-98; dir. dentistry Erie County Med. Ctr., 1998—. Editor mag. UB Dental Report, 1989-94 (Golden Scroll award); mem. editl. bd. Oral Surgery, 1997—, Oral Medicine, 1997, Oral Pathology, 1997, Oral Radiology, 1997—, Endodontics, 1997—; contbr. articles to profl. jours. Fellow Am. Assn. Hosp. Dentists; mem. ADA, Am. Assn. Dental Schs., Orgn. Tchrs. Oral Diagnosis (sec., treas.), Acad. Dentistry for Persons with Disabilities, Am. Soc. Geriat. Dentistry, U. Buffalo Dental Alumni Assn. (sec. 1988-89, v.p. 1989-90, pres. 1990-91), Mt. Mercy Acad. Alumni Assn. (bd. dirs. 1990-91), Nat. Cath. Ednl. Assn. (Disting. Grad. award 1999), Omicron Kappa Upsilon (v.p., pres.-elect chpt., pres. chpt. 1996-97). Roman Catholic. Office: Erie County Med Ctr Dept Oral Diagnostic Scis 462 Grider St Buffalo NY 14215

GOGARTY, WILLIAM BARNEY, oil company executive, consultant; b. Provo, Utah, Apr. 23, 1930; s. William B. and Zola (Walker) G.; m. Lois Gay Pritchett, Dec. 14, 1951; children: Laura Gay, Colleen, William Shaun, Kathlyn, Michael Barney. BS, U. Utah, 1953, PhD, 1959. Registered profl. engr., Colo. With Marathon Oil Co., Denver and Findlay, Ohio, 1959-86, sr. staff engr., Findlay, 1973-75, assoc. rsch. dir. prodn., Denver, 1975-86, ret. 1986; pvt. practice enhanced oil recovery cons., Littleton, Colo., 1986—; adj. assoc. prof. chem. engring. and metallurgy dept. U. Denver, 1967-73; cons. Ciba-Geigy Corp.; mem. Nat. Petroleum Coun. chem. task group Com. on Enhanced Oil Recovery, 1982-84; cons., tchr. Dept. Tech. Cooperation, UN, India, 1986, Rogaland Rsch. Inst., Norsk Hydro and Statoil, Norway, 1987, Petromer Trend Corp., Indonesia, 1988, Petrobras, Brazil, 1989; Muskat lectr. U. Utah, 1985. Contbr. articles to profl. jours.; patentee in field. Mem. Rep. precinct com., Littleton, Colo., 1984. Served to 1st lt. AUS, 1953-55. Mem. NAE, Am. Inst. Chem. Engrs., Soc. Petroleum Engrs. (fluid mechanics and oil recovery process tech. com. 1963-65, monograph com. 1971-73, chmn. monograph com. 1973, textbook com. 1974-76, chmn. textbook com. 1976, program vice chmn. 1977-78, Lester C. Uren award com. 1980-82, chmn. award com. 1982, program com. for Soc. Petroleum Engrs./U.S. Dept. Energy Enhanced Oil Recovery Symposium 1982, Disting. lectr. 1982-83, Lester C. Uren award 1987, region II dir.-elect 1988-89, bd. dirs. 1989-90, Henry Mattson Tech. Svc. award Denver petroleum sect. 1989, Enhanced Oil Recovery Pioneer award Mid-Continent region, 1990), Sigma Xi, Tau Beta Phi, Phi Kappa Phi, Alpha Chi Sigma. Mem. LDS Ch.

GOGGIN, JOAN MARIE, school system specialist; b. Boston, Nov. 15, 1956; d. Richard and Florence Muriel (Stone) G. BS in Edn., Westfield State Coll., 1978; MS in Edn., Lesley Coll., 1981; Cert. Adv. Grad. Studies in Adminstrv. Leadership, U. Mass., 1999. Spl. needs tchr. Supervisory Union # 53, Pembroke, N.H., 1978-79; grad. intern, head tchr. Ednl. Collaborative Greater Boston, Brookline, Mass., 1979-80; vocat. counselor Charles River Assn. for Retarded Citizens, Needham, Mass., 1981-83; dir. vocat. svcs. Community Assistance Corp., New Orleans, 1983-84; tchr. of pre-sch. children with severe spl. needs St. Charles Parish Pub. Schs., Luling, La., 1985-88; career placement and tng. specialist Plymouth (Mass.) Carver Regional Sch. Dist., 1988-92; inclusion facilitator Plymouth Pub. Schs., 1992—; ednl. cons. Ednl. Performance Sys., 1994—; cons. on self advocacy Mass. Assn. for Retarded Citizens, 1980-83; ednl. cons. Human Devel. Ctr., La. State U., New Orleans, 1984-85, D.K. Hollingsworth & Assocs., Metairie, La., 1984-88; vocat. cons. United Cerebral Palsy, Harahann, La., 1984-85; program coord. JTPA Project, Plymouth Sch. Dist., 1989-91, program. adminstr., 1991-93, exec. prodr. Bridging the Gap, We All Belong Together, 1991-93. Exec. prodr.: Bridging the Gap: Transition to Independence, We All Belong Together; author tng. program for paraprofls; curriculum devel. with adaptive modifications for learners with spl. needs, 1997. Active Mass. Dept. Edn. Task Force on Criteria for Spl. Edn. Svcs., 1992-93, mem. com. Individual Edn. Plan, 1990-93. Recipient Hon. Mention Tchr. of Yr. award Mass. Coun. Exceptional Children; grantee Mass. Dept. Edn., 1988—. Mem. NEA, Assn. for Severely Handicapped. Democrat. Avocations: t'ai chi, yoga, travel, reading, gourmet cooking. Office: Pupil Personnel Svcs 253 S Meadow Rd Plymouth MA 02360-4739

GOGICK, KATHLEEN CHRISTINE, magazine editor, publisher; b. N.J., Aug. 3, 1945; d. Joseph John and Emeline (Radwin) Wadowski; m. Robert Joseph Gogick, Feb. 24, 1968; 1 son, Jonathan. B.S., Fairleigh Dickinson U., Rutherford, N.J., 1967. Asst. beauty and fiction editor Cosmopolitan mag., N.Y.C., 1967-68; mdsg. and publicity coordinator Co-ed mag., N.Y.C., 1968-69; creative services coordinator Estee Lauder, Inc., N.Y.C., 1969-71; assoc. beauty and health editor Town and Country mag., N.Y.C., 1971-75; editor in chief Co-ed mag., 1976-80; editorial dir. home econs. div. Scholastic

Inc., 1981-86; pres., pub. C.M.I. (formerly Corp. Mags. Inc.), 1986—. Founder, editor: Student mag., 1989-96, College Counselor, 1993-96, Countdown to College Calendar, 1996. Trustee Fairleigh Dickinson U., 1980-89. Mem. Am. Student Assn., Inc. (founder, pres.). Club: University. Home and Office: 165 Lloyd Rd Montclair NJ 07042-1732

GOGLIA, CHARLES A., JR., lawyer; b. Phila., Aug. 26, 1931; s. Charles and Marie A. (Beckman) G.; m. Patricia A. Morrissey, July 26, 1958; children: Philip L., Catherine A. BS, St. Joseph's U., Phila., 1953; LLB, Boston Coll., 1958. Bar: Mass. 1958, U.S. Dist. Ct. Mass. 1959, U.S. Ct. Appeals (1st cir.) 1964, U.S. Tax Ct. 1977, U.S. Supreme Ct. 1993. Atty. Sheff & Gens, Boston, 1958-61, Foley, Hoag & Eliot, Boston, 1961-68; ptnr. Foley, Hoag & Eliot, 1968-74; pvt. practice Wellesley, Mass., 1974—; corporator, trustee, mem. bd. investment, exec. com. Bank Five for Savings, Burlington, Mass., 1974-92; mem. hearing com. Bd. Bar Overseers, Boston, 1984-86. Counsel Town of Nantucket, Mass., 1970-82, spl. counsel, 1982-85, Town of Weston, Mass., 1974-85, town counsel, 1986-92, spl. counsel, 1992—, mem. zoning bd. appeals, 1964-66, 74-85, mem. planning bd., 1973-74; spl. counsel Mass. Cable TV Commn., Boston, 1973-74. With USNAR, 1951-59. Mem. Wellesley Country Club (past pres.). Avocations: golf, travel. Home: 1 Hopewell Farm Rd Natick MA 01760-5570 Office: Wellesley Office Pk 65 William St Wellesley MA 02481-3802

GOGLIETTINO, JOHN CARMINE, insurance broker; b. Danbury, Conn., Sept. 5, 1952; s. Nicholas and Josephine (Staffieri) G.; m. Deborah Ann Russo, Sept. 25, 1976. BA in History, Western Conn. State Coll., 1975. Sales rep. Met. Life Ins. Co., Danbury, 1978-81; account exec. Thomas A. Settle, Inc., Danbury, 1981-88, Hodge Ins. Agy., Danbury, 1988-93; owner, mgr. John C. Goglietttino, ins. broker, Danbury, 1993—; chmn. Life Underwriters Polit. Improvement Com., to 1996. Editor: (newspaper) Yankee Doodler, 1983-84; prodr. (TV show) Cmty. Forum, 1995-99. Rec. sec. Conn. Bd. Vet. Medicine, Hartford, 1984-94; candidate Danbury Dem. Town Com., 1986, mem., 1988—, fin. chmn., 1990-92, treas., 1992-94, sec., 1996-98; active Italian Heritage Soc.; trustee, v.p. Scott-Fanton Mus., 1985-91; bd. dirs. Friends Danbury Libr., 1991-96, pres., 1994-96; mem. Environ. Impact Commn., 1991—, chmn., 1998-99; pres. coun. St. Peter's Ch., 1995-98. Recipient Statesman award Conn. Jaycees 1983, Disting. Svc. award 1990, City of Danbury 1990; named one of Outstanding Young Men of Am. Jaycees, 1982, 90, Conn. Outstanding Young Citizens award Channel 30 and Conn. Jaycees. Mem. Danbury Life Underwriters Assn. (cert., bd. dirs., pres. 1996-98), Health Underwriters Assn., Danbury Ins. Men's Orgn., Western Conn. State U. Alumni Assn. (activator memberships 1985-87), No. Fairfield County Bus. Assn. (pres. 1995, 99), Danbury Jaycees, Kiwanis (v.p. Danbury chpt. 1984-86, pres. 1989-92), Elks, Order Sons of Italy Conn. (grand trustee 1991-94). Roman Catholic. Avocations: hiking, bicycling, reading, coin collecting, stamp collecting. Home: PO Box 2598 Danbury CT 06813-2598

GOGO, GREGORY, lawyer; b. Varos, Lemnos, Greece, Oct. 6, 1943; s. Soterio and Christina (Choleva) G.; m. Paraskevi Vivi Batzaka, July 15, 1989; 1 child, Chloe. BA, U. Chgo., 1966; MA, Rutgers U., 1972; JD, Seton Hall U., 1980. Bar: N.J. 1980, U.S. Dist. Ct. N.J. 1980. Reporter The Trentonian, Trenton, N.J., 1968-69; asst. project dir. Trenton Health Ctr., 1969-71; dir. planning UPI, Trenton, 1973-77; instr. sociology Trenton State Coll., 1973-77; assoc. Merlino, Rottkamp, Trenton, 1980-83; pvt. practice Trenton, 1983—; corp. counsel Coronis Bldg. Sys. Exec. bd. dirs. ARC, Trenton, 1972-77; spl. advisor to Pres. NAACP, Trenton, 1973-74; mem. parish coun. St. George Orthodox Ch., Hamilton Twp., N.J., 1984-88, atty. for St. George, 1995—. Recipient Archon Politis award Am. Hellenic Ednl. Prog. Assn., 1981, Cert. Merit, ARC, Trenton, 1977. Mem. N.J. Bar Assn., Mercer County Bar Assn., N.J. Assn. Trial Lawyers, Hellenic Vision (founding mem. 1992, pres. 1999—). Democrat. Home: 14 Carla Way Lawrenceville NJ 08648-1500 Office: 1542 Kuser Rd Ste 1B Trenton NJ 08619-3829

GOGOLIN, MARILYN TOMPKINS, educational administrator, language pathologist; b. Pomona, Calif., Feb. 25, 1946; d. Roy Merle and Dorothy (Davidson) Tompkins; m. Robert Elton Gogolin, Mar. 29, 1969. BA, U. LaVerne, Calif., 1967; MA, U. Redlands, Calif., 1968; postgrad., U. Washington, 1968-69; MS, Calif. State U., Fullerton, 1976. Cert. clin. speech pathologist; cert. teaching and sch. adminstrn. Speech and lang. pathologist Rehab. Hosp., Pomona, 1969-71; diagnostic tchr. L.A. County Office of Edn., Downey, Calif., 1971-72, program specialist, 1972-74, cons. lang., 1975-76, cons. orgns. and mgmt., 1976-79, dir. administrv. affairs, asst. to supt., 1979-95; dep. supt., 1995—; cons. lang. sch. dists., Calif. 1975-79; cons. orgn. and mgmt. and profl. assns., Calif., 1976—; exec. dir. L.A. County Sch. Trustees Assn., 1979—; treas. L.A. County Edn. Found, 1996—. Founding patron Desert chpt. Kidney Found., Palm Desert, Calif., 1985. Doctoral fellow U. Washington, 1968; named one of Outstanding Young Women Am., 1977. Mem. Am. Mgmt. Assn., Am. Speech/Hearing Assn., Calif. Speech/Hearing Assn., Am. Edn. Research Assn. Baptist. Avocation: tennis. Office: LA County Office Edn 9300 Imperial Hwy Downey CA 90242-2813

GOGUEN, JOSEPH AMADEE, computer science educator; b. Pittsfield, Mass., June 28, 1941; s. Joseph Amadee and Helen Almira (Stratton) G.; m. Nancy Hammer (div. 1974); children: Healfdene, Heather; m. Kathleen Morrow (div. 1994); 1 child, Alice. BA, Harvard U., 1963; MA, U. Calif., Berkeley, 1967, PhD, 1968. Tutor Bur. of Study Coun. Harvard U., 1961-62; instr. dept. math. U. Calif., Berkeley, 1963-65; asst. prof. com. on info. sci. U. Chgo., 1968-73; rsch. fellow math. scis. dept. IBM T.J. Watson Rsch. Ctr., Yorktown Heights, N.Y., 1971-72; mng. dir., gen. ptnr. Structural Semantics, Palo Alto, Calif., 1978—; asst. prof. computer sci. dept. UCLA, 1973-74, assoc. prof. computer sci. dept., 1974-79, prof. computer sci. dept., 1979-81; sr. staff scientist computer sci. lab. SRI Internat., 1981-88; prof. computing sci., fellow St. Anne's Coll. Oxford (Eng.) U., 1988-96; prof. computer sci. and engring. U. Calif., San Diego, 1996—, dir. program in advanced mfg., 1996-98, dir. Lab. for Meaning and Computation, 1996—; programming and digital design technician GE Def. Electronics Div., Pittsfield, 1959, 60; scientist applied rsch. lab. Sylvania Electronic Systems, Waltham, Mass., 1962, 63; cons. Krohn-Rhodes Rsch. Inst., 1966, 67, IBM, NCR, Hughes Aircraft, Westinghouse Electric, several other corps.; acad. staff Naropa Inst., Boulder, Colo., 1974, 75, 77, 78; vis. assoc. prof. U. Colo., Boulder, 1974, 75, 77, 78; sr. vis. fellow dept. artificial intelligence U. Edinburgh, Scotland, 1976, 77. Mem. editl. bd. Math. Structures in Computer Sci., 1990—, Internat. Foundations of Computer Sci., 1988—, Cambridge Tracts in Theoretical Computer Sci., 1987—, Future Computer Sys., 1985, Jour. Computer and Sys. Scis., 1981—, Internat. Jour. Fuzzy Sets and Sys., 1977-97; editor in chief Jour. Consciousness Studies, 1993—; referee for profl. jours.; author (with others) Requirements Engineering: Social and Technical Issues, 1994, Algebraic Semantics of Imperative Problems, 1995; contbr. over 200 articles to profl. jours. Recipient NASA Cert. of Recognition, 1990. Fellow Japan Soc. for Promotion Sci.; mem. Assn. for Computing Machinery (software engring., artificial intelligence, programming langs., automata and computability theory), IEEE (tech. coms. on computer architecture, data engring., founds. of computing, com. on pub. policy), European Assn. for Theoretical Computer Sci., Math. Assn. Am., Computer Profls. for Social Responsibility, Am. Math. Soc. Buddhist. Avocations: poetry, meditation, philosophy. Office: U Calif San Diego 9500 Gilman Dr La Jolla CA 92093-0114

GOH, ANTHONY LI-SHING, business owner, consultant; b. Cleve., Apr. 14, 1954; s. Albert Goh and May Wong; m. Renee Kropat, Oct. 3, 1981; children: Anthony Tian-Fenn, Andrew Li-Shing. BSEE, U. Mich., 1975; MBA, U. Dayton, 1982. Sales engr. Toledo Scale, Mpls., 1975-76; application engr. Toledo Scale, Columbus, Ohio, 1976-77; product specialist Toledo Scale, Columbus, 1977-78, product mgr., 1978-80; internat. mktg. mgr. Toledo Scale, Benecia, Calif., 1980-82, modifications mgr., 1983; mktg. mgr. heavy capacity Toledo Scale, Columbus, 1984-86; v.p., gen. mgr. Ricton Corp., Columbus, 1987-92; owner Li-Shing Enterprises, Westerville, Ohio, 1992-95; product mgr. Mettler-Toledo, Inc., Worthington, Ohio, 1995-97, mktg. mgr., 1997—; industry rep. Nat. Bur. Standards, Washigton, 1984-85; distributors coun. Mitel Trillium Phone Systems, Boca Raton, Fla., 1990-91. Mem. Nat. Assn. Telecommunications Dealers (mem. ethics com. 1990). Avocations: squash, swimming, family activities. Home: 89 W College Ave Westerville OH 43081-2031 also: 1150 Dearborn Dr Worthington OH 43085-4766

GOH, MICHAEL PIK-BIEN, counseling, psychology educator, consultant; b. Singapore, Sept. 3, 1965; s. Fred Lam-Woo and Jessie Hwee-Wee (Tan) G.; m. Siew-Kheng Neo, June 1, 1996. BA, Ind. U., 1988, MS, 1990; PhD, U. Minn., 1995. Acad. adviser, counselor, Martin Luther King Program U. Minn., Mpls., 1990-91, counseling assoc., 1991-93; psychology intern, lectr. U. Calif., Davis, 1993-94; lectr., divsn. psychol. studies Nat. Inst. Edn., Nanyang Technol. U., Singapore, 1995-98; lectr. Coll. Edn. & Human Devel. U. Minn., 1999—; cons. psychologist Lifelinks Ltd., Singapore, 1997-98; staff counselor Nat. Inst. Edn., Singapore, 1995-98; freelance trainer/workshop facilitator, Singapore, 1995—; program coord. MA in Applied Psychology program, Singapore, 1997-98. Leader, officer Boys Brigade of Singapore, 1974-86; counselor, conf. facilitator United Way Manhood Project, Bloomington, Ind., 1989; student pres. Internat. Students, Inc., Ind. and Minn., 1986-93; adv. mem. Singapore Ministry Edn. Career Resource Com., 1995-98; vol. counselor Singapore schs., 1995—. Full lt., platoon comdr., Singapore Armed Forces, 1983-86, Singapore Armed Forces Res., 1986—. Recipient award for disting. svc., Boys Brigade of Singapore, 1981, 83. Mem. APA, ACA, Singapore Assn. Counseling, Pi Lambda Theta, Kappa Delta Pi. Home: 3259 Alden Pond Lane Eagan MN 55121

GOHDE, KURT R.D., artist; b. Cooperstown, N.Y., Sept. 29, 1973; s. Douglas James and Adrienne Lois (Bach) G. BFA, Alfred U., 1995; MFA, Syracuse U., 1998. Adj. lectr. SUNY Oneonta, 1996-97; asst. prof. sculpture, photography Transylvania U., 1998—. Home: 606 N Broadway Lexington KY 40508

GOHEEN, DEBRA ELAINE, secondary education educator; b. Beaumont, Tex., Apr. 11, 1962; d. Kenneth Charles and Doris Elaine (Berry) Cloud; m. Norman Ray Goheen, June 3, 1994. BA, Tex. A&M U., Commerce, 1986. Cert. tchr. English and History, Tex. English tchr. South Garland H.S., Garland, Tex., 1986-94; Cheerleader Coach Freshmen, 1987-90; history tchr. South Garland H.S., Garland, Tex., 1994—; Cheerleader coach junior varsity/varsity, 1990-94. Active various coms. Heather Glen Elem. PTA, Garland, pres., 1997—; dir. Pee Vee Drill Team, Garland Cheerleader Drill Team Assn., 1996-98;. Mem. Disciples of Christ. Avocations: reading, archaeology, travel, dance. Office: South Garland High Sch 600 Colonel Dr Garland TX 75043-2399

GOHEEN, ROBERT FRANCIS, classicist, educator, former ambassador; b. Vengurla, India, Aug. 15, 1919; s. Robert H.H. and Anne (Ewing) G.; m. Margaret M. Skelly, June 21, 1941; children: Anne Goheen Crane, Gertrude Goheen Swain, Stephen, Margaret Goheen Lower, Elizabeth Goheen Murphy, Charles. B.A., Princeton U., 1940, M.A. (Woodrow Wilson fellow), 1947, Ph.D. (Procter fellow), 1948; hon. degrees from 26 univs. and colls. Instr. classics Princeton U., 1948-50, asst. prof., 1950-57, prof., 1957, pres., 1957-72, emeritus, 1972—; chmn. Council on Founds., 1972-77; pres. Edna McConnell Clark Found., 1977; ambassador to India, 1977-80; sr. fellow Woodrow Wilson Sch., 1981—; dir. Mellon Fellowships in the Humanities, 1981-92; mem. adv. com. Nat. Fgn. Lang. Ctr., Ctr. for Advanced Study of India. Author: The Imagery of Sophocles' Antigone, 1951, The Human Nature of a University, 1969. Trustee Bharatiya Vidya Bhavan (USA), Nat. Humanities Ctr., Seager Fund for Hellenic Studies, Woodrow Wilson Nat. Fellowship Found., Woodrow Wilson Found. Decorated Legion of Merit, Bronze Star. Mem. Am. Philos. Soc., Coun. Fgn. Rels., Am. Acad. Arts and Scis., Am. Acad. Diplomacy, Phi Beta Kappa, Princeton Club (N.Y.C.), Century Assn. (N.Y.C.), Cosmos Club (Washington), Nassau Club (Princeton), Pretty Brook Club (Princeton), Springdale Club (Princeton), Eastward Ho Club (Mass.), Gymkhana and Delhi Golf Club (India). Address: 1 Orchard Cir Princeton NJ 08540-3025

GOHLKE, FRANK WILLIAM, photographer; b. Wichita Falls, Tex., Apr. 3, 1942. BA, U. Tex., 1964; MA, Yale U., 1966; pvt. study with Paul Caponigro, 1967-68. vis. lectr. Colo. Coll., Colorado Springs, 1979-88, Mass. Coll. Art, 1989-99, Princeton U. 1995, Harvard U., 1996-97. One-man shows include Internat. Mus. Photog., George Eastman House, Rochester, N.Y., 1974, Amon Carter Mus. Western Art, Ft. Worth, 1975, Mt. St. Helens: Work in Progress, Mus. Modern Art, 1983, Landscapes from the Middle of the World, Mus. Contemporary Photography, Chgo., 1988, DeCordova Mus., Lincoln, Mass., 1993, others; represented in permanent collections Nat. Gallery Can., Ottawa, Australian Nat. Gallery, Canberra, Bibliothéque Nat., Paris, Mus. Modern Art, N.Y.C., Cleve. Mus. Art; commd. American Images (photo works) AT&T, Washington, 1979, (photog. murals) Tulsa (Okla.) Internat. Airport, 1981, 88, Tex. Sesquicentennial (photog. survey) Tex. Hist. Found., Austin, 1984, Linea di Confine della Provincia di Reggio Emilia (photog. survey), Italy, 1994, Venice/Marghera (photog. survey), 1998, Nat. Millennium Survey (photo works); publs.: Landscapes from the Middle of the World, Chgo., 1988, Measure of Emptiness, Balt., 1992, Lindea de Confine, Parco del Gigante, Reggio Emilia, Italy, 1995, ann. report George Gund Found., Cleve., 1998. Guggenheim fellow, 1975, 84; photog. fellow Nat. Endowment Arts, 1977, 86, Artists fellow Bush Found., St. Paul, 1978. Fax: (508) 481-0117. Office: 2 Bridge St Southborough MA 01772-1962

GOIN, PETER JACKSON, art educator; b. Madison, Wis., Nov. 26, 1951; children: Kari, Dana. BA, Hamline U., 1973; MA, U. Iowa, 1975, MFA, 1976. Prof. art. U. Nev., Reno, 1984—. Author: Tracing the Line: A Photographic Survey of the Mexican-American Border, 1987, Nuclear Landscapes, 1991, Arid Waters: Photographs from the Water in the West Project, 1992, Stopping Time: A Rephotographic Survey of Lake Tahoe, 1992, Humanature, 1996, Atlas of the West, 1997; one-man shows include Nora Eccles Harrison Mus. Art, Logan, Utah, 1992, Duke U. Mus. Art, Durham, N.C., 1992, Phoenix Mus. Art, 1992, Indpls. Mus. Art, 1992, Savannah (Ga.) Coll. Art and Design, 1992, Nev. Humanities Com. Traveling Exhibit, 1992, NICA, Las Vegas, Nev., 1997, Mus. for Photographie, Braunschweig, Germany, 1997, U. Oreg. Mus. of Art, Eugene, 1997, Nev. Mus. Art, Reno, 1996, Princeton (N.J.) U. Art Mus., 1996, Whitney Mus. Am. Art, N.Y.C., 1996, among others. Recipient grant NEA, 1981, 90. Office: Univ Nev Dept Art Reno NV 89557

GOIN, ROBERT G., athletic director; m. Nancy Glastetter; 4 children. BA, Bethany Coll., 1959; MS, W.Va. U., 1962. Head baseball coach, asst. football/basketball coach, instr. Bethany Coll., 1960-63, head football coach, 1963-66, asst. athletic dir., 1996-70, athletics dir., chair phys. edn. dept., 1971-76; asst. athletics dir. W.Va. U., 1976-79; athletics dir. Calif. U. Pa., 1979-81; assoc. athletics dir. Fla. State U., 1981-90, athletics dir., 1989-94; spl. asst. pres. athletics U. North Fla., 1997; athletics dir. U. Cin., 1997—. Office: U Cin PO Box 210021 Cincinnati OH 45221-0021*

GOINS, FRANCES FLORIANO, lawyer; b. Buffalo, Jan. 30, 1950; d. William and Anita (Graziano) Floriano; m. Gary Mitchell Goins; children: Matthew W., Mark W. MusB, Cleve. Inst. Music, 1971; MusM, Case Western Res. U., 1973, JD, 1977. Bar: Ohio 1977, U.S. Dist. Ct. Ohio 1978, U.S. Ct. Appeals (6th cir.) 1979, N.Y. 1984, U.S. Ct. Appeals (2d cir.) 1984. Law clk to Hon. Frank J. Battisti U.S. Dist. Ct. (no. dist.) Ohio, Cleve., 1977-78; ptnr. Squire, Sanders & Dempsey, Cleve., 1986—; mem. vis. com. bd. overseers Case Western Res. U., Cleve., 1984—; faculty Nat. Inst. Trial Advocacy, Cleve.; faculty, lectr. trial advocacy seminar Cleve. State U. Sch. Law, 1989-90. Editor-in-chief law rev. Case Western Res. Sch. Law, 1976-77. Trustee, chairperson devel. com. Lyric Opera Cleve., 1985-92; founding trustee Shoreby Club Cleve.; v.p. bd. trustees Bay Village Montessori Sch., 1994-96. Mem. ABA (bus. law sect., bus. lit. com., subcom. on corporate governance 1995—, fed. regulation of securities com., subcom. on civil litigation and SEC enforcement matters 1992—), Ohio State Bar Assn. (ad hoc com. on bus. cts. 1994—), Cleve. Bar Assn. (com. on women and the law 1987—, ethics com. 1988-90, securities law inst., jud. selection com. 1996—). Democrat. Roman Catholic. Office: Squire Sanders & Dempsey 4900 Key Tower 127 Public Sq Ste 4900 Cleveland OH 44114-1304

GOINS, STEVEN CARTER, pediatric neurologist; b. Tulsa, May 20, 1954; s. William Lee and Norma Jean Goins; m. Candis Ring; children: Matthew, Rachel, andrew. BS, Bapt. Coll. of Charleston, S.C., 1974; MD, Med. U. S.C., 1979. Diplomate in child neurology Am. Bd. Psychiatry and Neurology, Am. Bd. Pediatrics, Nat. Bd. Med. Examiners. Rsident in pediatrics Okla. Children's Meml. Hosp., Oklahoma City, 1979-82; active staff Williamsburg County Meml. Hosp., Kingstree, S.C., 1982-84; resident in neurology U. Wis. Hosp. and Clinics, Madison, 1984-87, asst. prof. dept. neurology, 1987-88; active staff Sacred Heart Med. Ctr., Eugene, Oreg., 1988—; med. dir. Muscular Dystrophy Assocs. Clinic, Eugene, 1988—. Mem. Child Neurology Soc., Am. Acad. Neurology, Lane County Med. Soc., Oreg. Med. Assn., Lane Individual Practice Assn. (bd. dris. 1989—), Epilepsy Found. Am. Avocations: climbing, skiing. Office: Neurology Assocs Eugene-Springfield 1200 Hilyard S-420 Eugene OR 97401

GOINS, WILLIAM C., JR., engineering executive. BS in Chem. Engring., Tex. A&M U., 1942. Sr. v.p. O'Brien-Goins-Simpson & Assoc. Inc., Houston, 1977—. Mem. Nat. Acad. Engrs., Soc. Petrol Engrs. (Uren award 1983). Home: 5454 Jason St Houston TX 77096-1239 Office: O'Brien-Goins-Simpson & Assoc Inc 6430 Hillcroft St Ste 112 Houston TX 77081-3105

GOKEE, DONALD LEROY, clergyman, author; b. Lansing, Mich., Aug. 8, 1933; s. Richard Alden and June Elizabeth (Colenso) G.; m. Maxine Pawlik Adkins, Apr. 21, 1974; children: Douglas Richard, Charles Jeffrey, Mary Beth, Jessica Lynn. BA, Mich. State U. and Temple U., 1958; postgrad., George Washington U., 1960-64, Va. Theol. Sem., 1964-65, Columbia Theol. Sem., 1968, U. Edinburgh, Scotland, 1975, Frankfurt (Germany) U., 1977, U. Athens, Greece, 1978; MA cum laude, 1982, PhD magna cum luade, 1983. Ordained to ministry Presbyn. Ch., 1965. Dir. Christian edn. Ctrl. Presbyn. Ch., Chattanooga, 1958-59, Fairlington Presbyn. Ch., Alexandria, Va., 1959-66; assoc. pastor Pine Shores Presbyn. Ch., Sarasota, Fla., 1966-69; pastor Conway Presbyn. Ch., Orlando, Fla., 1969-92; ret., 1992; frequent spkr. at colls. and confs.; chaplain Orange County Juvenile Ct., 1969-73; mem. coun. Synod of Fla., 1972-75; mem. ecumenical coordinating team as rep. Presbyn. Ch. U.S., 1977-81; 1st ann. Gingerich meml. lectr. Goshen (Ind.) Coll.; vis. prof. So. Coll. Author: It's a Love-Haunted World, 1985; contbg. editor Pulpit Digest, 1986-89; poetry appears in Am. Poetry Anthology, 1986. Mem. Nat. Task Force on Criminal Justice and Prison Reform, 1976-82. Recipient cert. of merit for disting. svc. to Christ, ch. and cmty., 1970, In-God-We-Trust award Family Found. Am., 1980, Key to City, Orlando, 1981. Mem. Ministerial Assn. (past pres.). Home and Office: 3026 Carmia Dr Orlando FL 32806-5522

GOLAN, LAWRENCE PETER, mechanical engineering educator, energy researcher; b. Newark, June 20, 1938; s. Joseph and Francis (Duda) G.; m. Helen Imelda Hemko, June 30, 1962; children: Lisa Marie, Wanda Marie, Lawrence P. II. BSME, W.Va. U., 1961, MSME, 1964; PhD, Lehigh U., 1968. Mech. engr. Picatinny Arsenal, Dover, N.J., 1961-62; instr. W.Va. U., Morgantown, 1962-64, Lehigh U., Bethlehem, Pa., 1964-68; engring. assoc. Exxon Rsch. and Engring., Florham Park, N.J., 1968-86, S.C. Inst. Energy Rsch., Clemson, 1986—; prof. mech. engring. Clemson U., 1986—, chmn. 2d World Congress Chem. Engring. on Coal Utilization; cons. State of Ill. Ctr. for Coal Rsch., 1987-90; mem. S.C. Energy Products Evaluation Com.; chair Nat. HEat Transfer Conf., 1996. Contbr. articles to profl. jours. Mem. adv. com. W.Va. U., 1985—; mem. adv. com. Strom Thurmond Inst., 1996—. Mem. AIChE (exec. officer heat transfer divsn. 1973-76, 89-92, East Coast membership chmn., vice chair nat. meeting 1991, chair 1991, co-chair 1992, nat. heat transfer conf. best paper, chair AIChE Kern award 1994, chair ASME-AIChE Jakob award 1994), Am. Petroleum Inst. (chmn. sampling project 1985-89), S.C. Energy Mgrs. Roman Catholic. Avocations: jogging, woodworking. Home: 333 Lowkirk Aly Seneca SC 29672-2273 Office: SC Inst for Energy Studies 386 College Ave Ste 2 Clemson SC 29631-1475

GOLAN, ROMY, educator; b. Aug. 13, 1958. PhD, U. London, 1989. Asst. prof. Vassar Coll., Poughkeepsie, N.Y., 1986-92; asst. prof. Yale U., New Haven, Conn., 1992-98, assoc. prof., 1998—. Home: 12 East 64 St 1A New York NY 10021 Office: Dept Art History PO Box 208272 New Haven CT 06520-8072

GOLAN, STEPHEN LEONARD, lawyer; b. Chgo., Oct. 22, 1951; s. Leonard Walter and Carol (Pepper) G.; m. Sharon D. Robson, Aug. 16, 1980; children: Brianna, Jenna, Melissa. BA, Claremont (Calif.) Men's Coll., 1974; M of Mgmt., JD, Northwestern U., 1978. Bar: Ill. 1978, U.S. Dist. Ct. (no. dist.) Ill. 1978, U.S. Ct. Appeals (7th cir.) 1993. Ptnr. Seyfarth, Shaw, Fairweather & Geraldson, Chgo., 1978-93; founding ptnr. Field, Golan & Swiger, Chgo., 1993—. Mem. ABA, AICPA, Nat. Assn. JD-MBA Profls. (bd. dirs. 1984-86), Ill. Bar Assn., Chgo. Bar Assn., Tavern Club (mem. jr. com. 1984-86), Exmoor Country Club (Highland Park, Ill.), Lake Forest Caucus. Republican. Episcopalian. Office: Field Golan & Swiger 15th Fl 3 First National Plz Chicago IL 60602

GOLANY, GIDEON SALOMON, urban designer; b. Jan. 23, 1928; came to U.S., 1967, naturalized, 1975.; s. Jacob and Rajena G.; m. Esther Klein, Jan. 10, 1956; children: Ofer, Amir. BA, Hebrew U., Jerusalem, 1956, MA, 1966; PhD, 1966; MS in Environ. Design, Technion-Israel Inst. Tech., Haifa, 1965; diploma comprehensive planning, Inst. Social Studies, The Hague, Netherlands, 1965. Lectr. architecture and town planning Technion-Israel Inst. Tech., 1963-67; lectr. city and regional planning Cornell U., 1967-68; research planner Office of Research, Resources and Devel., Cornell U., 1968; assoc. prof. urban and regional planning Coll. Architecture, Va. Poly. Inst. and State U., Blacksburg, 1968-70; vis. prof. urban and regional planning Inst. Desert Research, Ben-Gurion U. of the Negev, Beer Sheva, Israel, 1975-76; prof. urban and regional planning Pa. State U., 1970-87, research prof. urban design and planning, 1987-91, Disting. prof. urban design, 1991—, chmn. grad. program, 1971-76, dir. PhD program on Environ. Design, Div. Environ. Design and Planning, 1987-89; propr. Gideon Golany Assocs., 1987-89; cons. in field; hon. prof. China Acad. Scis., China Acad. Mgmt. Sci., Tongji U., Shanghai, People's Republic China, Xian (People's Republic China) Inst. Metallurgy and Constrn. Engring. Author, editor more than 27 books including: Geography of Israel, 1962, New Town Planning and Development--A World Bibliography, 1973, Strategy for New Community Development in the United States, 1975, Innovations for Future Cities, 1976, New-Town Planning: Principles and Practice, 1976, Urban Planning for Arid Zones: American Direction and Experience, 1978, Earth-Sheltered Habitat: History, Architecture and Urban Design, 1983, Design for Arid Regions, 1983, Earth-Sheltered Dwellings in Tunisia, 1988, Urban Underground Space in China, 1989, Design and Thermal Performance, 1990, Chinese Earth-Sheltered Dwellings: Indigenous Lessons for Modern Urban Design, 1992, Ethic and Urban Design, 1995, Geo-Space Urban Design, 1996, Japan's Urban Environment, 1998; co-author: New Georgraphic Dictionary, 2 vols., 1966; co-editor: The Contemporary New Communities Movement in the United States, 1974; editor: International Urban Growth Policies, 1978, Arid Zone Settlement Planning: Israeli Experience, 1979, Housing in Arid Lands: Design and Planning, 1980, Desert Planning: International Lessons, 1982, Design for Arid Regions, 1983, Earth Sheltered Habitat: History, Architecture, and Urban Design, 1983; also articles. Mem., founder Kibbuts Baeri, communal settlement, Negev, 1946-52. Served with Hagana, 1946-48; Served with Israeli Army, 1948-50, 56, 67. Recipient prize Com. Encouragement Towards Rsch. and Higher Studies, Histadrut, Tel-Aviv, 1963, Faculty Scholar medal Pa. State U., 1987, Faculty Research/Creative Devel. award, 1987; grantee Govt. Netherlands, 1965, NSF, 1972-74; Fulbright rsch. awards, 1982, 90-91, 95-96. Mem. Assn. Engrs. and Architects Israel, Am. Underground Space Assn., Internat. New Towns Assn., Internat. Ctr. for Arid-Semi Arid Land Studies, Assn. Arid Land Studies. Home: 200 Highland Ave Apt 100 Regency Sq State College PA 16801-4929 Office: Pa State U 210 Engring Bldg Unit C University Park PA 16802

GOLASHESKY, CHRYSA ZOFIA, telecommunications company executive; b. Bayonne, N.J., Feb. 16, 1957; d. John Stanley and Margaret Walterine (Stanko) G. BS, Pa. State U., 1978; MBA, Rutgers U., 1980. Cert. Christian Founds. for Ministry. Mktg. analyst ITT - Domestic Transmission Systems, Inc., N.Y.C., 1980-81; market rsch. analyst ITT - U.S. Transmission Systems, Inc., N.Y.C., 1981-82; project mgr., market researcher ITT - U.S. Transmission Systems, Inc., Secaucus, N.J., 1982-85, mktg. mgr., 1985-86; product mgr. Metromedia Long Distance, Inc., Secaucus, 1986-87, dir. product mgmt., 1987-88, dir. mktg., 1988-89; dir. product mktg. Metromedia/ITT Long Distance, Inc., Secaucus, 1989-91; v.p. product mktg. Metromedia Communications Corp., East Rutherford, N.J., 1991-95; v.p. account rels. World Com, 1995—. Mem. edon. com. OLA Parish, Bayonne, N.J., 1986—; mem. Christian Founds. for Ministry, Irvington, N.J., 1988-91; v.p. account rels. LDDS World Com., N.E. Region

East Rutherford, 1995. Roman Catholic. Avocations: running, weight training, racquetball, craft work. Home: 101 W 24th St Bayonne NJ 07002-2701 Office: MCI/World Com 1 Meadowlands Plz East Rutherford NJ 07073-2100

GOLAY, MICHAEL WARREN, nuclear engineering educator; b. Pitts., Sept. 5, 1942; s. George Warren and Patricia (VanBustirk) G.; m. Michal-Ann Barrett, Apr. 25, 1964; children: Barrett, Geddes. BME, U. Fla., 1964; PhD, Cornell U., 1969. Rsch. assoc. Rensselaer Poly. Inst., Troy, N.Y., 1969-71; prof. nuclear engring. MIT, Cambridge, 1971—, dir. program for advanced nuclear power studies; advisor U.S. Nuclear Regulatory Commn., Dept. of Energy, Office of Tech. Assessment, Elec. Power Rsch. Inst., and pvt. industry. Contbr. articles to profl. jours. Mem. ASME, AAAS, Am. Nuclear Soc. (div. leader). Achievements include method for design simplification, software reliability, modularization, human error reduction. Office: MIT 77 Massachusetts Ave Rm 24223 Cambridge MA 02139-4307*

GOLC, JEFF, councilman; b. July 16, 1953; m. Lisa VanOort; children: Joseph, Jennifer. BA, Ind. U., 1976, MA, 1982. Mem. assoc. faculty comms. and theater dept. Ind.-Purdue U., 1981-87; recruiter Wishard Hosp., 1983-85; mgr. employment St. Francis Hosp., 1985-89; city councilman City of Indpls., 1988—; dir. employment divsn. State Personnel Dept., 1989-91; congl. aide to Dave Evans, 1982-83; dep. commr. Bur. Motor Vehicles, Ind., 1991—; instr. govt. Ritter H.S., Indpls., 1982. Mem. Assn. Cities and Towns. Democrat. Office: City Coun Office 200 E Washington St Ste 241 Indianapolis IN 46204-3310*

GOLD, ALAN B., former Canadian chief justice; b. Montreal, July 21, 1917; m. Lynn Lubin; children: Marc, Nora, Daniel. BA, Queen's U., Kingston, Ont., Can., 1938; LLD (hon.), Queen's U., 1982; LLL cum laude, U. Montreal, 1941, LLD (hon.), 1978; LLD (hon.), McGill U., 1984, Yeshiva U., 1987. Bar: Que. 1941. Lectr. Faculty of Law McGill U., Montreal, 1957-71; dist. judge, vice chmn. Labour Rels. Bd., Que., 1961-65; assoc. chief judge Provincial Ct., P.Q., 1965-70, chief judge, 1970-83, pres. Jud. Coun., 1978-83, chmn. Conseil du Referendum, 1980; chief justice Superior Ct., P.Q., 1983-92; chancellor Concordia U., 1987-92; sr. counsel, chmn. dept. alternative dispute resolution Goodman, Phillips & Vineberg, Montreal, 1992—, chair alternative dispute resolution dept.; chancellor emeritus Corcordia U., 1992—; chief arbitrator under collective labour agreements between Govt. P.Q. and Employees, 1966-83, between Shipping Fedn. Can. Inc. and Maritime Employers Assn. and Internat. Longshoremen's Assn., 1967-75; mem. multi-nat. panel Arbitration and Mediation Ctr. Ams.; spl. mediator and arbitrator in disputes concerning Fgn. Svc., Rys., Airlines, Royal Mint, Can. P.O., constrn. industry, other areas of pub., para-pub., pvt. sectors; scholar in residence McGill U. Faculty of Law, 1982; pres. Jr. Bar Assn., Montreal, 1951-52; mem. coun. Bar of Montreal, 1952-53, various other coms.; mem. bd. examiners Bar of P.Q., 1952-61, various other coms.; founder, dir., officer Legal Aid Bur., Montreal, 1956-60; mem. multinat. panel arbitrators and mediators concerning N.Am. Free Trade Agreement, Comml. Arbitration Mediation Ctr. Ams. Bd. dirs., exec. coun. Regie de la Place des Arts, 1973-82; mem., vice-chmn. Societe de la Place des Arts de Montreal, 1982—; pres. Jewish Pub. Establishments Commn., Fedn. CJA, 1993-97, bd. dirs. Fedn. CJA 1993—; pres. bd. dirs. Jerusalem Found. Can. Inc., 1980-83; bd. govs. McGill U., 1974-83, chmn. 1978-82, gov. emeritus, 1984—; gov. Soc. Pro Musica, 1970—, I Musici de Montreal, 1988—; bd. dirs. Conseil d'adminstrn. de l'orchestre, I Musici de Montreal, 1993—, chmn., 1997—. Decorated officer Ordre Nat. du Qué.; recipient Human Rels. award Can. Coun. Christians and Jews, 1985, Disting. Bora Laskin award Yeshiva U., 1987, Médaille du Premier Ministre du Qué., 1987, Montreal medal Queen's U., 1985, Bar of Québec medal, 1990-91, Nat. Assembly of Québec medal, 1992, Université de Montréal medal, 1992, Samuel Bronfman Can. Jewish Contress, 1992, Commemorative medal for 125th anniversary of Can., Case District I, Disting. Friend of Edn. award, 1993, Pres.'s award Tel Aviv U., 1998. Mem. Bar Province Quebec, Montreal Bar (various offices) Nat. Acad. Arbitrators (hon., life, U.S.), Soc. Profls. in Dispute Resolution (charter, U.S., Spl. award for excellence 1981), Corp. Professionnelle des Conseillers en Rels. Industrielles de law Province de Quebec, Conseil de l'Order (pres. 1989-91), Clin. Rsch. Inst. Montreal (chmn. ethics com. 1990-94), Phi Delta Phi. Office: 26th Fl, 1501 McGill College Ave, Montreal, PQ Canada H3A 3N9

GOLD, ALAN STEPHEN, judge, lawyer, educator; b. N.Y.C., Jan. 8, 1944; s. Frank and Geraldine (Guenzberg) G.; m. Susan Fine, May 28, 1965; children: Carol, Natalie. BA with high honors, U. Fla., 1966; JD, Duke U., 1969; M in Taxation, U. Miami, Fla., 1974. Bar: Fla., 1969, Dade County, Fla. (11th judicial cir.), 1992. Law clk. to Hon. Charles Carrol Fla. 3d Dist Ct. Appeal, Miami, 1969-71; asst. atty. Met. Dade County Atty's Office, Miami, 1971-75; ptnr. Greenberg, Traurig, Hoffman, Lipoff, Rosen & Quentel, P.A., Miami, 1975-92; apptd. judge 11th Circuit Ct., Dade County, Fla., 1992-98; appt. judge U.S. Dist. Ct. (so. dist.) Fla., Miami, 1998—. Contbr. articles to legal jours. Co-gen. counsel Fla. High Speed Rail Transp. Commn., 1985—; city atty. Village of Bal Harbour, Fla., 1976-82; spl. counsel Broward County, Fla., 1984-88; trustee Palmer Sch., Miami, 1987-88; bd. dirs. Actor's Playhouse, Miami, 1989—, South Dade Jewish Community Ctr., Miami, 1985-85; apptd. Fla. Environ. Land Mgmt. Com., 1987. Disting. scholar Fla. State U., 1990; recipient award for outstanding contbn. in field of legis. affairs South Fla. Bldrs. Assn., 1989. Mem. ABA, Fla. Bar. Assn. (com. on environment and land use law 1983-84, Disting. Svc. award 1984), Urban Land Inst. (nat. policy coun. 1988—), Greater Miami C. of C. (chmn. land use com. 1989-90), Am. Coll. Real Estate Attys. Democrat. Jewish. Avocations: trekking, vacationing, raising horses, sail fishing, reading. Office: US Dist Ct Fla 301 N Miami Ave Fl 10 Miami FL 33128-7702

GOLD, ALBERT, artist; b. Phila., Oct. 31, 1916; s. Rubin and Dora (Sklar) G.; m. Aurora Mary Vanelli, May 3, 1953; children: Madelaine, Robert. Grad., Pa. Mus. Sch. Indsl. Art, 1938. Tchr. pictoral expression Pa. Mus. Sch., Phila., 1945-48; dir. dept. illustration Phila. Mus. Coll. Arts; prof. emeritus Phila. Coll. Art; tchr. art ctrs., pvt. classes. Exhibited at maj. ann. shows including Pa. Acad. Fine Arts, Corcoran Gallery, Met. Mus., Art Inst. Chgo., Carnegie Inst., World's Fair, N.Y.C., 1939, Nat. Gallery, London, 1943, Musee Galliera, Paris, La Tausca exhbn., Burlington Acad. Galleries, 1962, Phila. Coll. Art (Alumni grant), 1968; one man shows include Pa. Acad. Fine Arts, Phila. Art Alliance, Hahn Gallery, Chestnut Hill, Pa., Wigmore Fine Arts, N.Y.C., 1991; represented in collections Libr. of Congress, Soc. Illustrators, N.Y.C., N.Y. Pub. Libr., Phila. Mus. Art, War Dept., Pentagon Bldg., U. Pa., Phila., U. Del., Newark, U. Minn., Smithsonian Instn., Atwater-Kent Mus., Phila., New Britain (Conn.) Mus. Am. Art, Forbes Collection, Ford Collection, Pa. Acad. Fine Arts, Soc. Illustrators, N.Y.C., Fogg Mus., U. Pa., Harvard U., Gimbel Pa. Collection, Free Libr. Phila., Balch Inst. for Ethnic Studies, Brown U. Libr. Mil. Collection, Phila. Mus. Art; numerous pvt. collections; commd. to paint various documentary series; illustrator various mags.; (book) The Commodore (Robert L. Abrahams), 1954; illustrator: (book) This Was Our War (Frank Brookhouser), 1961, The Court Factor, 1964, The Captive Rabbi (Lillian S. Freehof), 1965; contbr. articles to Step-By-Step Graphics. Decorated Order Brit. Empire; recipient John Gribbel Meml. prize Phila. Print Club, 1939, Prix de Rome, Am. Acad. in Rome, 1942, Geizel award Phila. Sketch Club, 1982, 83, Tiffany Found. grant, 1947-48, Jennie Sesnan Gold medal, 1950, Dorothy Kohl prize Phila. Art Alliance, 1953, Am. Artist citation Am. Water Color Soc., 1954, Am. Artists Guild award Am. Water Color Soc., 1955, Regional Water Color prize Phila. Art Alliance, 1955, Wm. W. Esty prize Am. Water Color Soc. Ann., 1961, award for series of illustrations Brandywine Ohio State U. Sch. Journalism, prize Phila. Watercolor Club, 1977, Silver Star award Phila. Coll. Art, 1979, Sawin award Phila. Watercolor Club, 1989; Woodmere Endowment Fund grantee, 1968; Tiffany Found. grantee, 1946 and 47. Mem. Artists Equity (dir.), AAUP. Selected by War Dept. as one of 12 men in U.S. Army to make pictorial record of war, 1943, spent 3 yrs. in Eng., France and Germany on project. Home: 6814 Mccallum St Philadelphia PA 19119-3001 Office: Gallery D Wigmore Fine Arts Inc 22 E 76th St New York NY 10021-2611 *I have endeavored to "be myself" in my behavior and in my work as an artist. I've always felt that the surest way to oblivion was to "follow the herd". "Style" in art should be as personal as one's handwriting.*

GOLD, ALLAN HAROLD, architect, structural engineer, educator; b. Chgo., Jan. 12, 1942; s. Melvin King and Estelle M. (Zucker) G.; m. Barbara Gail Edelstein, June 20, 1967 (div. Feb. 1989); children: Grant, Ross, Susan; m. Susan Carlucci, Dec. 30, 1989. BArch, U. Ill., Urbana, 1966, MS, 1967. Registered architect, Conn., Colo., Ill., Ind., La., Okla.; registered structural engr., Ill; registered profl. engr., Ind., La., Okla., Wis., Tex.; cert. Nat. Coun. Archtl. Registration Bds. (juor registration exam. 1985), Nat. Coun. Examiners Engrin. and Surveying Certification. Architect, project engr. various archtl., engring. cos., Chgo. area, 1963-68; project structural engr. Perkins & Will Architects, Chgo., 1968-70; structural engr. Chgo. Dept. Bldgs., 1970-73; owner, operator Allan H. Gold & Assocs., Architects/Cons. Structural Engrs., Hazel Crest, Ill., 1973-81; project mgr., sr. structural engr. HKS/Structures, Dallas, 1981-84; dir. architecture and structural engring. dept. URS Engrs., Dallas, 1984; owner, operator Allan H. Gold, Architect/Structural Engr., Dallas, 1985-88; project mgr. Hoffmann Architects, North Haven, Conn., 1988-90; prin. Allan H. Gold, Archt. & Structural Engr., Chgo., 1990-93; v.p. Salse Engrs., Northbrook, Ill., 1993-96; assoc. TT-CBM Engrs./LZA Group, Chgo., 1996—; asst. prof. archtl. tech. dept. constrn. tech. purdue U., Hammond, Ind., 1976-80; assoc. prof. architecture U. Okla., Norman, 1980-81; adj. assoc. prof. architecture U. Tex., Arlington, 1983-85; guest lectr. U. Wis. Ext., 1981. Structural engr. Century Shopping Ctr., Chgo., 1973, Phoenix Tower, Houston, 1983, Xerox II, Irving, Tex., 1984. Mem. Village of Hazel Crest Plan Commn., 1979-81. Mem. Structural Engrs. Assn. Ill., AIA, ASCE (mem. tall bldgs. com. 1983-86, std. com. design loads on structure during constrn., 1989—, std. com. design of engineered wood constrn. 1989—, editl. bd. Jour. Archtl. Engring. 1995—), Am. Arbitration Assn., Masons, Scottish Rite, Shriners (master Skokie, Ill. 1979). Jewish. Home: 360 E Randolph St # 4204 Chicago IL 60601-7341 Office: Thornton Tomasetti Engineers/LZA Tech 5 N Wabash Ave Chicago IL 60602-4703

GOLD, ARNOLD HENRY, judge; b. Santa Monica, Calif., Apr. 12, 1932; s. Louis and Rose (Shalat) G.; m. Gloria Victor; children: Jeffrey Alan, Kenneth Clarke, Susan Elizabeth. AB with distinction, Stanford U., 1953, JD, 1955. Bar: Calif. 1955, U.S. Dist. Ct. (so., ctrl. and no. dists.) Calif. 1955, U.S. Ct. Appeals (9th cir.) 1955, U.S. Supreme Ct. 1955. Law clk. to Hon. John W. Shenk Supreme Ct. of Calif., San Francisco, 1955-56; assoc. atty. Loeb & Loeb, L.A., 1956-61; pvt. practice Beverly Hills, Calif., 1961-70; ptnr. Pachter, Gold & Schaffer, and predecessors, L.A., 1970-88; judge Calif. Superior Ct. for County of L.A., 1988—, supervising judge probate dept., 1993-94; chmn. probate and mental health com. Calif. Judges Assn., 1995-96; lectr. Calif. Jud. Edn. & Rsch. Probate & Mental Health Insts., 1994-99, Civil Practice Inst., 1993, Family Law Inst., 1992; lectr. Calif. Continuing Edn. of Bar, 1969, 76-77, 79-82, 84-88, 92; mem. Calif. Atty. Gen's Com. on Charitable Reporting Standards, 1970-71, Calif. Atty. Gen.'s Task Force on Charitable Solicitation Legis., 1975-78, Calif. Judicial Coun. Probate & Mental Health Task Force, 1997—; exec. com. Stanford Law Soc. So. Calif., 1973-77. Co-author: Probate Module, California Civil Practice, 1993; contbg. author: California Family Law Handbook, California Nonprofit Corporations Handbooks; mng. editor, bd. editors Stanford Law Rev., 1954-55. Mem. ABA, State Bar Calif. (vice chmn. conf. dels. 1986-87), L.A. County Bar Assn. (trustee 1981-83), Los Angeles County Bar Found. (bd. dirs. 1985-91), Mulholland Tennis Club, Phi Beta Kappa, Alpha Epsilon Pi, Phi Alpha Delta, Delta Sigma Rho. Office: County Courthouse 111 N Hill St Los Angeles CA 90012-3117

GOLD, CAROL SAPIN, international management consultant, speaker; b. N.Y.C.; d. Cerf Saul and Muriel Louise (Fudin) Rosenberg; children: Kevin Bart Sapin, Craig Paul Sapin, Courtney Byrens Sapin. BA, U. Calif., Berkeley, 1955. Asst. credit mgr. Union Oil Co., 1956; with U.S. Dept. State, 1964-66; mem. dept. pub. rels. Braun & Co., L.A., 1964-66; corp. dir. pers. tng. Gt. Western Fin. Corp., L.A., 1967-71; pres. Carol Sapin Gold & Assocs., L.A., 1971—; bd. dirs. Marathon Nat. Bank, L.A.; cons., profl. spkr., Bath, Eng., 1987-90; cons., Can., Mex., India, Australia, New Zealand; host radio program The Competitive Edge; mem. expdn. to Syria and Jordan, 1994, to Morocco, 1995; mem. WORID Bus. Acad.; instr. Learning Annex; presenter Expertese Forum Presentations, Malaysia, Bangkok, 1997; instr. Asian program U. So. Calif., 1998. Author: Solid Gold Customer Relations; featured in tng. films Power of Words; Author: Cassette Libraries, Sound Selling. Bd. dirs. Ctr. Theatre Group, Town Hall, Music Ctr., Oddessy Theater; asst. dir. Burnhill Prodns., 1992—, Cabaret, Palisades Theatre; dir. Improv Corp.; vol. Exec. Svc. Corp., 1996—. Mem. ASTD, Am. Film Inst. Assn., Sales and Mktg. Execs., Nat. Spkrs. Assn., Nat. Platform Assn., Women in Bus., KCET Women's Coun., Exec. Svc. Corps, World Affairs Coun., Blue Ribbon, Women in Arts, Women in Film, Manuscript Soc. Forum Scotland, Plato Soc., Brandeis Univ. Women, Sierra Club (Toure de Mt. Blanc), Supreme Ct. Hist. Soc. Avocation: collecting famous manuscripts. Office: PO Box 11447 Marina Del Rey CA 90295

GOLD, CATHERINE ANNE DOWER, music history educator; b. South Hadley, Mass., May 19, 1924; d. Lawrence Frederick Dower and Marie (Barbieri) Barber; m. Arthur Gold, Mar. 24, 1994 (dec. Oct. 1998); children: Carolyn D. Gold, Judith G. Enteen. AB, Hamline U., 1945; MA, Smith Coll., 1948; PhD, The Cath. U. Am., 1968. New England rep. Gregorian Inst. Am., Toledo, 1948-49; tchr. music, organist St. Rose Sch., Meriden, Conn., 1949-53; supr. music Holyoke (Mass.) Pub. Schs., 1953-55; instr. music U. Mass., Amherst, 1955-56; prof. music Westfield (Mass.) State Coll., 1956-90, prof. emerita, 1991--; columnist and freelance writer Holyoke Transcript Telegram, 1991-93; organist St. Theresa's Ch., South Hadley, 1937-41, St. Michael's Ch., N.Y., 1945-46; concert series presenter Westfield State Coll., 1987-91, rschr. tchr.; vis. scholar U. So. Calif., 1969; vis. assoc. prof. music Herbert Lehman Coll. CUNY, 1970-71. *Catherine Gold, author of three books and numerous published articles, received many awards from the college where she taught. She was not married and had no dependents, therefore the college president said she did not need equal salary to the male faculty members. She sued the State of Massachusetts to receive better pension. A judge heard the suit and determined in her favor. She won the case! This is her contribution to the women on the state college faculties. When she won the case, those who had been members for a certain length of time recieved a stipend raising their salaries.* Author: Puerto Rican Music Following the Spanish American War, 1898-1910, 1983; (monograph) Yella Pessl, 1986, Alfred Einstein on Music, 1991, Yella Pessl: First Lady of the Harpsichord, 1993; presenter Irish Concert Springfield Symphony Orch., 1981 (plaque 1982). Pres. Coun. for Human Understanding Holyoke, 1981-83, Friends of Holyoke Pub. Libr., 1990-91; bd. dirs., chmn. nominating com. Holyoke Pub. Libr., 1987-89; bd. dirs. Holyoke Pub. Libr. Corp., 1991-94, Women's Symphony League, The Symphony Orch., 1992-94; bd. dirs., sec. Life Long Learning Soc. of Fla. Atlantic U., 1994—; presiding officer inauguration Dr. Irving Buchman pres. of Westfield State Coll.; mem. ethics com. Holyoke Hosp., 1988-94; sec. Haiti Mission, 1982-94; bd. overseers Mullen U., 1993; hon. mem. bd. Coun. Human Understanding, 1994; hon. mem. WSC Found., 1994; co-chair United Jewish Appeal/Jewish Fedn. Boca Lago Women's Divsn., South Palm Beach County, 1996-97; 1st. v.p. fin. and adminstrn. Temple Beth El Women in Reformed Judaism, Boca Raton, 1997-99. Recipient citation Academia InterAmericana de P.R., 1978, Holyoke Pub. Libr., 1983, plaque Mass. Tchrs. Assn., Boston, 1984, medal Equestrian Order Holy Sepulchre of Jerusalem, Papal Knighthood Soc., Boston, 1984, Performance award Gov. Dukakis, Mass., 1988, award for Puerto Rican Jour. Al. Margens, 1992, Human Rels. award Coun. for Human Understanding, Holyoke, 1994; named Lady Comdr., Equestrian Order of the Holy Sepulche of Jerusalem, 1987, with star, 1990, Career Woman of Yr., Quota Internat. Holyoke, Mass., 1988; Westfield State U. concert series named Catherine A. Dower Performing Arts Series in her honor, 1991; recipient 1st prize in Raddock Eminent Scholar Chair Essay Contest, Fla. Atlantic U., 1996. Mem. Am. Musicol. Soc., The Coll. Mus. Soc., Ch. Music Assn. Am. (journalist), Acad. Arts and Scis. of P.R. (medal 1977), Internat. Platform Assn., Friends of the Holyoke Pub. Libr. (pres. 1990-91), Irish Am. Cultural Inst. (chmn. bd. 1981-89), Holyoke Quota (v.p. 1976-79, pres. 1979-81, 90-92, chmn. speech and hearing com. 1987-94), B'nai B'rith of Boca Lago (sec. bd. dirs. 1994—, newsletter editor 1999—), Lifelong Learning Soc. Fla. Atlantic U. (sec. 1994-97), Women in Reform Judaism (first v.p. Temple Beth El chpt. 1997-99). Democrat. Home: 8559 Casa Del Lago Boca Raton FL 33433-2107

GOLD, EDGAR, marine affairs educator, mariner, lawyer; b. Hamburg, Fed. Republic Germany, Mar. 5, 1934; immigrated to Australia, 1951, to Can., 1961; s. Joseph and Anne Marie (Kuenn) G.; m. Judith Hammerling, June 27, 1965. B.A., Dalhousie U., N.S., Can., 1969, LL.B., 1972; Ph.D., U. Wales, 1980; diploma honor causa, Can. Coast Guard Coll., 1992. Bar: N.S. 1973. Mem. Mcht. Marine, various locations, 1951-67; ptnr. Huestis Holm, Barristers & Solicitors, Halifax, N.S., Can., 1980—; prof. faculty of law Dalhousie U., Halifax, N.S., Can., 1975-94, adj. prof. law and environ. studies, 1994—; exec. dir. Oceans Inst. Can., Halifax, 1979-90; Queen's counsel, 1995—; cons. in field; hon. consul of Fed. Republic Germany to N.S. and P.E.I., 1986—; comdr. Order of Merit, Germany, 1997; mem. Order of Can., 1997. Author: Maritime Transport, 1981 (Lilar Prize 1984), Maritime Law, 1977, Marine Pollution, 1985. Mem. Merchant Marines. Fellow Nautical Inst.; mem. Chartered Inst. Transport, Master Mariners, Can. Maritime Law Assn. (pres. 1992-94), Can. Bar Assn. (nat. coun. 1979-81, Chartered Inst. Arbitrators (assoc.). Home: 1465 Brenton St Ste 605, Halifax, NS Canada B3J 3T3 Office: Huestis Holm, 1809 Barrington St Ste 708, Halifax, NS Canada B3J 3K8*

GOLD, EDWARD DAVID, lawyer; b. Detroit, Jan. 17, 1941; s. Morris and Hilda (Robinson) G.; m. Francine Sheila Kamin, Jan. 8, 1967; children: Lorne Brian, Karen Beth. Student, Wayne State U., 1958-61; JD, Detroit Coll. Law, 1964. Bar: Mich. 1965, U.S. Dist. Ct. (ea. dist.) Mich. 1965, U.S. Ct. Appeals (6th cir.) 1965, D.C. 1966. Atty. gen. counsel FCC, Washington, 1965-66; ptnr. Conn, Conn & Gold, Detroit, 1966-67, May, Conn, Conn & Gold, Livonia, Mich., 1967-69, Hyman, Gurwin, Nachman, Gold & Alterman, Southfield, Mich., 1971-88, Butzel Long, Birmingham, Mich., 1988—; chmn. Friend of Ct. Adv. Com., Lansing, Mich., 1982-88; mem. Oakland County Criminal Justice Coordinating Coun., 1976-77; contbr. lectr. Inst. Continuing Legal Edn., Ann Arbor, Mich., 1981—, Mich. Trial Lawyers Assn. Author: Michign Family Law, 1988; contbr. articles to legal jours. Mem. Southfield Transp. Commn., 1975-77; chmn. attys.' divsn. Jewish Welfare Fedn., Detroit, chairperson atty. disp. bd. Tri-County Hearing Panel 71, 1994-98; mem. nat. young leadership cabinet United Jewish Appeal, N.Y.C., 1978-80; bd. dirs. Oakland County Legal Aid Soc., 1979-84; pres. Jewish Family Svc., Detroit, 1988-90. Tau Epsilon Rho scholar, 1963. Fellow Am. Coll. Family Trial Lawyers, Am. Acad. Matrimonial Lawyers (bd. dirs. 1986—, pres. Mich. chpt. 1992-93, nat. bd. govs. 1998—); mem. Mich. Bar Assn. (coun. real property law sect. 1973-81, coun. family law sect. 1974-75, 77-82, chmn. family law sect. 1981-82, rep. assembly 1978-82), Oakland County Bar Assn. (bd. dirs. 1984-93, pres. 1992-93), Southfield Bar Assn. (pres. 1975-76), Bar Assn. D.C., Am. Arbitration Assn., Alpha Epsilon Pi (nat. pres. 1976-77, Order of Lion award 1986). Avocation: golf. Office: Butzel Long 32270 Telegraph Rd Ste 200 Birmingham MI 48025-2457

GOLD, GEORGE MYRON, lawyer, editor, writer, consultant; b. Bklyn., June 28, 1935; s. Harry and Rose Miriam (Meyerson) G.; m. Bunny Winters, Dec. 24, 1960; 1 child, Seth Harris. A.B., U. Rochester, 1956; J.D., NYU, 1959. Bar: N.Y. 1960. Practice N.Y.C., 1960-64, 67-78; legal editor Prentice-Hall, Inc., Englewood Cliffs, N.J., 1960-62; assoc. Speiser, Shumate, Geoghan & Law, N.Y.C., 1962-64; assoc. editor Rsch. and Rev. Svc. Am., Inc., Indpls., 1964-67; dir. publs., mng. editor Estate Planners Quar., Farnsworth Pub. Co., Inc., Rockville Centre, N.Y., 1967-69; editor-in-chief Trusts & Estates, N.Y.C., 1969-76; mng. editor Trust News, N.Y.C., 1976-78; dir. news publs. and info. ABA, Chgo., 1978-83; sr. assoc. editor and dir. book divsn. ABA Jour., Chgo., 1984-87; dir. publs. and editor Trial Mag. Assn. Trial Lawyers Am., 1988-89; cons. North Potomac, Md., 1989-90; exec. sr. law editor Mead Data Cen., Dayton, 1990-93; exec. editor Stevens Pub., Washington, 1993-94; corp. editl. dir. Stevens Pub., 1994-95, v.p. editorial, 1995; cons., Ashburn, Va., 1995—. Author: The Propriety, Procedure and Evidentiary Effect of a Jury View, 1959, Investments by Trustees, Executors and Administrators, 1961, What You Should Know About Intestacy, 1962, What You Should Know About the Common Disaster, 1962, The Powers of Your Trustee, 1962, What You Should Know About the Antenuptial Agreement, 1963, Who May Be the Beneficiary of Your Will, 1963, What You Should Know About The Spendthrift Trust, 1963, Comprehensive Estate Analysis, 1966, You're Worth More Than You Think, 1966, Medicare Handbook, 1966, The ABCs of Administering Your Estate, 1966, The Will: An Instrument for Service and Sales, 1966, A Tax-Sheltered Pension Plan for the Close-Corporation Stockholder, 1968, Social Security Law in Nutshell, 1968, What You Should Know About Custodial Gifts to Minors, 1968, The Short-Term Trust and Estate Planning, 1976, The Importance of a Will, 1976, The Need for an Experienced Executor, 1976, Tax Tips-99 Ways to Reduce the Bite, 1976, Investment Management: No Job for the Amateur, 1971, Who Manages Your Securities, 1972, A Woman's Need for Financial Planning, 1972, The Lawyer's Role in the Search for Peace, 1982, True Counselors: Helping Clients Deal with Loss, 1983, Evaluating and Settling Personal Injury Claims, 1991, Cite Checking: A Guide to Validating Legal Research, 1992, The Compliance Pak for HR Managers-Book I (Hiring, Evaluation & Separation), Book II (Severance), 1993, Selling Life Insurance: Overcoming Objections, 1996; editor: Fundamentals of Federal Income Estate and Gift Taxes, 1965-67, The R & R Tax Handbook, 1965-67, Tax-Free Reorganizations, 1968, Guide to Pension and Profit Sharing Plans, 1968, A Life Underwriter's Guide to Equity Investments, 1968, The Tired Tirade, 1968, A Handbook of Personal Insurance Terminology, 1968, The 15th Anniversary Edition of Estate Planners Quar., 1968, You, Your Heirs and Your Estate, 1968, The Farnsworth Letter for Estate Planners, 1968-69, How to Use Life Insurance in Business and Estate Planning, 1969, Human Drama in Death and Taxes, 1970, Don't Bank on It, 1970, The Feldman Method, 1970, Directory of Trust Instns. (ann.), LawTalk, 1986-87, The Supreme Court and Its Justices, 1987, Aaron J. Broder on Trial: Reflections of a Famous Litigator. Mem. Soc. Law Writers (dir. 1972-75), ABA, Am. Law Inst., N.Y. State Bar Assn., Assn. Bar City N.Y., Estate Planning Council N.Y.C., Nat. Press Club, Soc. Bus. Press Editors, Soc. Human Resources Mgmt., Newsletter Publishers Assn., Washington Independent Writers, Kappa Nu, Pi Alpha Lambda. Club: KP. Office: 43325 Dovetail Pl Ashburn VA 20147-5312

GOLD, GERALD SEYMOUR, lawyer; b. Cleve., Feb. 2, 1931; s. David N. and Geraldine (Bloch) G.; 1 child, Anne; m. Rosemary Grdina, 1994. AB, Case-Western Res. U., 1951, LLB, 1954. Bar: Ohio 1954, U.S. Supreme Ct. 1961. Practiced in Cleve., 1954-60; chief asst. legal aid defender Cuyahoga County, Cleve., 1960-61; chief legal aid defender Cuyahoga County, 1961-65; assoc. Ulmer, Byrne, Laronge, Glickman & Curtis, Cleve., 1965-66; ptnr. Gold, Rotatori, Schwartz & Gibbons, Cleve., 1966—; instr. in law Case-Western Res. U., 1965-66, Cleve. State Law Sch., 1968-69, Case-Western Res. Law-Medicine Center, 1961-77; lectr. to bar assns. commr. Cuyahoga County Pub. Defender, 1977-81. Contbg. author: American Jurisprudence Trials, 1966; Contbr. articles to law revs. Fellow Am. Coll. Trial Lawyers, Am. Bd. Criminal Lawyers, Ohio State Bar Found., Internat. Soc. Barristers; mem. ABA (criminal justice coun.), Cuyahoga County Criminal Ct. Bar Assn. (chmn., Lifetime Achievement award 1995), Ohio Bar Assn. (chmn. criminal law sect. 1974-78, ho. of dels. 1986—), Greater Cleve. Bar Assn. (Merit award 1974, trustee 1978—, pres. 1982-83), Nat. Assn. Criminal Def. Lawyers (pres. 1977, Merit award 1975), Ohio Acad. Trial Lawyers (chmn. criminal law sect. 1970-75), Ohio Assn. Criminal Def. Lawyers (bd. dirs. 1990), Case-Western Res. U. Law Alumni Assn. (pres. 1974-75, Outstanding Alumnus award 1991), Soc. Benchers, Court of Nisi Prius Club, Cleve. Skating Club. Home: 33000 Pinetree Rd Pepper Pike OH 44124-5514 Office: 1500 Leader Bldg Cleveland OH 44124-3337

GOLD, GRETCHEN, painter, educator, jeweler; b. Fergus Falls, Minn., Jan. 10, 1967; m. Neal Goldberg, Dec. 17, 1996. Student, Middlesex (Eng.) Polytech., 1989; BS in Art Edn., U. Wis., Stout, 1990. Art tchr. Negril, Jamaica, 1990—, Holland Sch., Boston, Spring 1994, East Boston Social Ctr., 1996; art dir. Med-O-Lark Art Camp, Washington, Maine, 1989-96; owner, operator handmade jewelry bus., 1990—. One-woman show Milton Art Mus., 1996, Keene (N.H.) Sagendorph Gallery, 1998. Mem. Nat. Womens Caucus for Art, Womens Caucus for Art (steering com. Boston chpt. 1997, vol. coord. 1997). Democrat. Avocations: rollerblading, teaching art to children, travel. Home: 334 Beacon St Boston MA 02116-1004

GOLD, HAROLD ARTHUR, lawyer; b. Pitts., Jan. 13, 1929; m. Anita Hubert, Aug. 18, 1937; children: Howard, Bradley. BBA, U. Pitts., 1952; JD, Georgetown U., 1956. Bar: Pa. 1956, D.C. 1956. Sole practice law Pitts., 1956-64; atty. City of Pitts., 1960-69; ptnr. Baskin and Sears, Pitts., 1965-84, Reed, Smith, Shaw & McClay, Pitts., 1985-93; pres., chief exec. officer Coventry Care, Inc., Monongahela, Pa., 1970-86, chmn. bd., chief exec. officer, 1986-87; adj. prof. law Duquesne U. Pres. Young Dem. Club of Pitts., 1960-66; presdl. elector Pa., 1960; chmn. bd. Mayview State Hosp.,

Pitts., 1971-75. Served to lt. U.S. Army, 1948-49, 52-53. Mem. ABA, Pa. Bar Assn., Allegheny County Bar Assn. (real property council 1983-86). Office: The Pitt Bldg 213 Smithfield St Pittsburgh PA 15222-2224

GOLD, HYMAN, cellist; b. Cleve., Aug. 26, 1914; s. Isaac and Fanny (Liebenson) g.; m. Ruth Olgin, Feb. 4, 1936; 1 child, Ronald Kenneth; m. Sue DiCicco, Oct. 2, 1982. Student, Cleve. Inst. Music, 1932-38; studies with Victor DeGomez, Cleve., 1938-40; studies with Leonard Rose, 1941-43. Cellist Gold Trio, Cleve., 1935-46, Paul Whiteman and Cleve. Orch., 1940; musician, actor 170 films numerous studios, Los Angeles and Las Vegas, Nev., 1947—, Jack Benny TV Show, L.A., 1953-70; cellist numerous symphonies and ballet cos., L.A., 1955-65; condr. Beverly Hills (Calif.) Ensemble, Las Vegas, 1965—; cellist TV commls., L.A., 1960-73; condr. Las Vegas Pops Orch., 1977—; prin. cellist/soloist Nat. Sr. Symphony, New London, Conn., 1990-95; prin. cellist, soloist Las Vegas Civic Symphony, 1994—; pres. Gold 'N' Cello Rec. Co., 1964—. Performer numerous recs. and club shows, Los Angeles and Las Vegas, 1947—. Grantee Cleve. Inst. Music, 1935, 36, Nev. State Council for Arts, 1977-80. Mem. SAG, Am. Fedn. Musicians, B'nai B'rith. Democrat. Jewish. Club: Scrabble (Las Vegas). Avocations: gardening, tennis, bowling, travel. Home and Office: 2416 Laurie Dr Las Vegas NV 89102-2104

GOLD, I. RANDALL, lawyer; b. Chgo., Nov. 2, 1951; Albert Samuel and Lois (Rodrick) G.; m. Marcey Dale Miller, Nov. 18, 1978; children: Eric Matthew, Brian David. BS with high honors, U. Ill., 1973, JD, 1976. Bar: Ill. 1976, U.S. Dist. Ct. (no. dist.) Ill. 1976, Fla. 1979, U.S. Dist. Ct. (so. dist.) Fla. 1979, U.S. Ct. Appeals (5th and 7th cirs.) 1979, U.S. Tax Ct. 1979, U.S. Ct. Appeals (11th cir.) 1981, U.S. Supreme Ct. 1982, U.S. Dist. Ct. (mid. dist.) Fla. 1987; CPA, Ill., Fla. Tax staff Ernst & Ernst, Chgo., 1976-77; asst. state atty. Cook County, Ill., 1977-78, Dade County, Miami, Fla., 1978-82; spl. atty. Miami Strike Force U.S. Dept. Justice, Fla., 1982-87; pvt. practice Miami, 1987-92; asst. U.S. atty. U.S. Dist. Ct. (mid. dist.) Fla., 1992—; lectr. Roosevelt U., Chgo., 1976-77; vice chmn. fed. practice com. on criminal sect. Fla. Bar, 1986-88, profl. ethics com., 1992—; instr. Rollins Coll. paralegal program, 1992-97; adj. prof. criminal justice program U. Ctrl. Fla., 1994—; adj. prof. law U. Orlando, 1998—. Co-chmn. Greater Oviedo Cmty. Devel. Program, 1992-93; adviser Jr. Achievement, Chgo., 1976-78, Miami, 1982-84; coach, judge Nat. Trial Competition, U. Miami Law Sch., 1983-86, 88, 90; mentor Seminole County Sch., 1994—; coach mock trial program legal project Dade County Pub. Schs., 1985-89, 91-92, ptnr. program, 1989-92. Mem. ABA (govt. litigation counsel com., complex crimes com. litigation sect.), FBA, AICPA, ATLA, Fla. Bar, Ill. Bar Assn., Ill. Soc. CPAs, Fla. Inst. CPAs (com. on rels. with Fla. Bar 1985-86, bd. dirs. South Dade chpt. 1987-92), Orange County Bar Assn. (professionalism com., bankruptcy com.), Seminole County Bar Assn., Am. Assn. Atty. CPAs, Am. Inns of Ct. (master), U. Ill. Alumni Club (v.p.), Delta Sigma Pi. Jewish. Office: 80 N Hughey Ave Ste 201 Orlando FL 32801-2224

GOLD, JAMES PAUL, museum director; b. Seattle, Sept. 26, 1944; s. William J. and Madlyn (Hunsberger) G.; m. Cheryl Magruder, Apr. 6, 1968. BA, Hiram Coll., 1966; MA, Cooperstown Sch. SUNY, 1967. Tchr., curator Elwood Mus., Amsterdam, N.Y., 1968-71; dir. New Eng. Fire and History Mus., Brewster, Mass., 1972-74; site mgr. Senate House, N.Y. State Parks Recreation and Hist. Preservation, Kingston, 1974-77; regional historic sites supr. Bear Mountain, 1977-79; dir. N.Y. State Bur. Historic Sites and Resource Ctr., Waterford, 1979—; chair Design Rev. commn. Saratoga springs, 1992—; mem. N.Y. State Document Conservation Adv. Coun., 1984-87. Mem. Cooperstown Grad. Assn. (bd. dirs. 1983-93), N.Y. State Assn. Museums (bd. dirs. 1985-92), Am. Assn. Museums (bd. dirs. 1988-93), Am. Assn. State and Local History, Assn. Preservation Tech., Mid-Atlantic Assn. Mus. (bd. dirs. 1988-93, 94-98, pres. 1994-97). Democrat. Unitarian. Avocations: photography, architecture, gardening. Home: 197 Woodlawn Ave Saratoga Springs NY 12866-1507 Office: NY State Parks Recreation and Historic Preservation Peebles Island Waterford NY 12188

GOLD, JEFFREY MARK, investment banker, financial adviser; b. Bronx, N.Y., Jan. 7, 1945; s. Samuel L. and Sylvia E. Gold; m. Lenore N., May 29, 1966; children: Brian, Steven, Samuel. B.B.A. in Acctg, Pace U., 1967. Sr. acct. KPMG Peat, Marwick, N.Y.C., 1967-71; v.p., corp. controller Nat. Patent Devel. Corp., N.Y.C., 1971-78; exec. v.p. fin. and adminstrn., chief fin. officer Esquire, Inc., N.Y.C., 1978-84; exec. v.p. strategic planning and corp. devel. Simon & Schuster div. of Paramount Communications, N.Y.C., 1984; pres. Goldmark Advisers, Inc., N.Y.C., 1992—, Quarto Holdings, Inc., 1994—. Home: 515 E 72nd St New York NY 10021-4032 Office: Goldmark Advisers Inc 276 5th Ave Rm 205 New York NY 10001-4509

GOLD, JONATHAN M., philosophy and religion educator; b. Apr. 19, 1941. BA with honors, CUNY, Queens, 1970; PhD, SUNY, Stony Brook, 1981; MDiv, Phila. Theol. Sem., 1982. Adj. prof. philosophy Coll. N.J., Trenton, 1981-86; prof. philosophy and religion West Liberty (W.Va.) State Coll., 1986—; pastor Resurrection Life Reformed Ch., Wheelin, W.Va., 1996—. Office: West Liberty State Coll Rte 88 N West Liberty WV 26074

GOLD, JOSEPH, medical researcher; b. Binghamton, N.Y., Jan. 17, 1930; s. Leon and Gertrude J. G.; m. Judith Barbara Taylor, June 12, 1955; children: Shannon Gabriel, Skye Raphael. AB, Cornell U., 1952; MD, SUNY Health Sci. Ctr., Syracuse, 1956. Diplomate Nat. Bd. Med. Examiners. Fellow dept. pharmacology SUNY Health Sci. Ctr., Syracuse, 1961-62, rsch. asst. prof., 1962-64, asst. prof. pathology, 1964-65; dir. Syracuse Cancer Rsch. Inst., 1965—, trustee, 1965—. Author numerous articles on cancer research and therapy; contbr. chpts. to med. textbooks on ill effects of heat stress. Served with USAF, 1958-61. Recipient Presdl. citation for work in Mercury Astronaut Selection Program, 1960; USPHS postdoctoral rsch. fellow U. Calif. Sch. Medicine, 1956-58; named Disting. Grad. Binghamton Sch. Dist., 1994. Mem. Am. Assn. Cancer Rsch., Am. Assn. for Lab. Animal Sci., N.Y. Acad. Scis., Onondaga County Med. Soc., Med. Soc. State N.Y. Achievements include pioneering work in proposing gluconeogenesis as a biochemical mechanism of cancer cachexia, 1968; development of hydrazine sulfate, 1st specific anti-cachexia drug to be used in human cancer; invention of process for the synthesis and prodn. of DL-Glyceraldehyde-3-phosphate in a pure and stable form; patentee in field. Home: 127 Edgemont Dr Syracuse NY 13214-2010 Office: 600 E Genesee St Syracuse NY 13202-3111

GOLD, JUDITH HAMMERLING, psychiatrist; b. N.Y.C., June 24, 1941; d. James S. and Anne (Linder) Hammerling; m. Edgar Gold, June 27, 1965. M.D., Dalhousie U., 1965. Intern Victoria Gen. Hosp., Halifax, N.S., Can., 1964-65; resident Dalhousie U., Halifax, 1967-71; practice medicine specializing in psychiatry Halifax, 1971-97; staff psychiatrist Dalhousie U. Student Health Clinic, 1971-73; vis. colleague U. Wales Med. Sch., 1973-75; asst. prof. dept. psychiatry Dalhousie U., Halifax, 1975-78, assoc. prof., 1978-80, part-time, 1980-87; pvt. practice Brisbane, 1998—; vis. prof., reader in psychotherapy studies U. Queensland Dept. of Psychiatry, Brisbane, 1998-99. Editor: Clinical Practice Series, 1987—, 5 books; contbr. articles to profl. jours. Bd. govs. Mt. St. Vincent U., 1981-87, chmn., 1986-87. Med. Research Council Can. fellow, 1973-75; Health and Welfare Bd. Can. grantee, 1976-78. Fellow Am. Psychiat. Assn., Am. Coll. Psychiatrists (1st v.p. 1990-91, pres.-elect 1991-92, pres. 1992-93); mem. Can. Psychiat. Assn. (pres. 1981-82), Royal Coll. Phys. Surgeons Can. (exec. mem. 1992-94, coun. 1991-98), Order Can., Alpha Omega Alpha. Home: 1465 Brenton St Ste 605, Halifax, NS Canada B3J 3T3

GOLD, KEITH DEAN, advertising and design executive; b. Piqua, Ohio, Mar. 7, 1956; s. Russell D. and Sandra E. (Reid) G.; m. Karen Bell, May 28, 1977; children: Brian R., Brittany L. Student, U. Fla., Ringling Sch. Art, 1974-75; BA, U. No. Fla., 1977. Art dir. Market Assocs., Jacksonville, Fla., 1975-76, Ambrose Design, Jacksonville, 1976-77; pres. Keith Gold Advt. and Design, Atlanta, 1977-78; exec. art dir., assoc. creative dir. Garrett/Lewis/Johnson, Atlanta, 1978-81; assoc. creative dir. Price/McNabb Advt., Asheville, N.C., 1981-83; sr. v.p., dir. creative svcs., ptnr. Ensslin, Hall, Earle, Palmer and Brown Advt., Tampa, Fla., 1983-87, Group 243/Ross Roy, Ann Arbor, Mich., 1987-88; pres., creative dir. GOLD & Assocs, Ponte Vedra Beach, Fla., 1988—; exec. creative dir., mng. dir. DMB&B/Gold & Assocs., Atlanta, 1993-94; prof. Kennesaw Coll., Atlanta, 1977-80; bd. dirs., ptnr. Package Material Sales, Inc., Tampa, Fla.; guest lectr. in field. Author: Setting the Course of Excellence, 1986; featured in Kodansha Pubs. World Graphic Design; designer U.S. postage stamp, Olympic posters, numerous book and CD covers; exhibited in shows at Mus. of Modern Art, N.Y.C.; work represented in Libr. of Congress. Recipient over 800 regional, nat. and internat. awards including numerous first place awards from Advt. Club N.Y., AIGA, Clio awards, Communications Arts, Graphis, Internat. Advt. Festival of N.Y., Internat. Poster Festival, N.Y. Soc. Illustrators, Pub. Broadcasting Sys., Print Mag., Telly awards, Internat. Film and TV Festival N.Y., London Internat. Advt. and Global awards, N.Y. Art Dirs. Club, The One Show, First Place award Internat. Festivals poster competition, N.Y. Advt. Festival, N.Y. Film Festival, Graphic Design: U.S.A., Creativity, Print Mags. Design Annual, Photo Design; named one of Fla.'s Top All Time Coll. Grads. Bd. Regents, U. N. Fla. Outstanding Alumnus of the Yr., 1999, U. North Fla. Alumnus of Yr., 1999. Mem. Am. Inst. Graphic Arts. Republican. Presbyterian. Avocations: painting, writing, golf, duck hunting. Home: 136 Nandina Cir Ponte Vedra Beach FL 32082-3028 Office: Gold & Assocs Gold Bldg 6000C Sawgrass Village Cir Ponte Vedra Beach FL 32082-5026

GOLD, LEONARD SINGER, librarian, translator; b. Bklyn., July 3, 1934; s. Hyman B. and Gertrude (Singer) G.; m. Stella Schmidt, June 5, 1960; children: Yael, Dalia. BA, McGill U., 1956; MS in Libr. Service, Columbia U., 1966; MA, NYU, 1967, PhD, 1975; student, C. Redmont Art Students League. Cert. profl. librarian, N.Y. Tchr. high sch. Kiryat Hayim, Israel, 1960-61; tchr. Hugim High Sch., Haifa, Israel, 1961-63; tech. asst. N.Y. Pub. Libr., N.Y.C., 1963-66, chief Jewish div., 1971-98, Dorot chief libr. Jewish div., bibliographer Jewish studies, 1987-98, asst. dir. Jewish, Oriental and Slavonic studies, 1980-88; chmn. Jewish and Middle East studies program com. Rsch. Librs. Group, Inc., 1989-91; curator hist. exhbns. A Sign and A Witness: 2000 Years of Hebrew Books and Illuminated Manuscripts, N.Y. Pub. Libr., 1988-89, The Dead Sea Scrolls: Ancient Civilization, Modern Scholarship, N.Y. Pub. Libr., 1993-94. Translator: (Nathan Shaham) The Other Side of the Wall, 3 novellas, 1983; editor: A Sign and A Witness: 2000 Years of Hebrew Books and Illuminated Manuscripts, 1988 (Nat. Jewish Book award in Visual Arts category 1989); assoc. editor Jewish Book Annual, 1979-94; contbr. to bibliog. publs. Astor fellow, 1986-87. Mem. Assn. Jewish Librs. (pres. 1974-76, lifetime mem. award 1998), Coun. Archives and Rsch. Librs. in Jewish Studies (pres. 1978-80, disting. svc. award 1998), Jewish Book Coun. (v.p. 1980-90, pres. 1990-94), Assn. Jewish Studies, Rsch. Librs. Group (chmn. Jewish and Mid. East studies program com. 1989-91, mem. programs adv. group 1991-92), Jewish Publ. Soc. (editl. com. 1986—).

GOLD, LOIS MEYER, artist; b. N.Y.C., June 2, 1945; d. Seymour Roy and Carol (Rubin) Meyer; m. Leonard Marshall Gold, Oct. 14, 1971; 1 child, Eric Marshall. BA, Boston U., 1967; MA, Columbia U., 1970. Tchr. Lenox Sch., N.Y.C., 1972-84, Columbia Grammar Sch., N.Y.C., 1975-76; artist, free-lance N.Y.C., 1976—; represented by Lizan-Tops Gallery, Easthampton, N.Y., Ute Stebich Gallery, Lenox, Mass., Ruxetti and Gow, various, Canyon Ranch, Lenox, Mass., Martha Keats Gallery, Santa Fe. Prin. works appear in permanent mus. collections including Herbert F. Johnson Mus. Art, Ithaca, N.Y., corp. collections, including Bklyn. Union Gas Co., Canyon Ranch, Bristol Myers Squibb, Imperial Oil, others; featured artist The Artists Mag., 1993 (Landscape award 1993); pub. in: Pastel School, Reader's Digest, The Pastel Painter's Solution Book, Painting Shapes & Edges, Fresh Flower Painting, North Light Books, Burlington Books, The Best of Flower Painting; various original posters, Romm Art; featured artist Dan's Papers, 1999, Pastel Artist Internat., 1999, Decor, 1999. Recipient Artists Mag. Landscape award, 1991, 93, Pastel Soc. Am. Juried Scholarship award, 1994-95. Mem. Internat. Assn. Pastel Socs., Pastel Soc. Am., Nat. Assn. of Women Artists (Pauline Law award 1988, Works on Paper award 1988), Cassatt Pastel Soc., Studio Ctr. Artist's Assn. Avocations: tennis, skiing, biking, photography. Home: 45 E End Ave New York NY 10028-7953

GOLD, LORNE W., Canadian government official; b. Saskatoon, Sask., Can., June 7, 1928; s. Alexander Stewart and Grace Dora (Davis) G.; m. Elizabeth Joan L'Ami, Sept. 8, 1951; children: Catherine Anne, Patricia Ellen, Judith Sharon, Kenneth Robert. BSc, U. Sask., 1950; MSc in Physics, McGill U., 1952, PhD, 1970. Research officer div. bldg. research Nat. Research Coucil Can., Ottawa, Ont., 1950-52, head snow and ice sect., 1953-69, head geotech. sect., 1969-74, asst. dir. div., 1974-79, assoc. dir. div., 1979-86, chmn., assoc. com. geotech. research, 1976-83, guest worker inst. research on constrn., 1987; rschr. emeritus Nat. Rsch. Coun. of Can., Ottawa, Ont., 1988—; Canadian del. to Intern. Union of Testing and Research Labs. for Materials and Structures, 1982-87, bd. dirs. Coun. Internat. du Batiment, 1983-86; sr. visiting scientist Ctr. for Cold Oceans Resources Engring., Meml. U. of Newfoundland, 1987-88. Author: The Canadian Habbakuk Project, 1993. Fellow Royal Soc. Can. (sec. Acad. Sci. 1997—), Can. Acad. Engring., Engring. Inst. Can., Can. Soc. Civil Engrs. (Horst Leipholz medal 1991); mem. Internat. Glaciol. Soc. (pres. 1978-81), Assn. Profl. Engrs. Ont., Engring. Inst. Can. (hon. treas. 1991-96), Can. Geotech. Soc. Mem. United Ch. of Canada. Home: 1903 Illinois Ave, Ottawa, ON Canada K1H 6W5 Office: Nat Rsch Coun of Can, Inst for Rsch in Constrn, Ottawa, ON Canada K1A 0R6

GOLD, MARI S., public relations executive; b. N.Y.C., June 17, 1940; d. George B. and Natalie (Machol) Sour; m. Joel S. Ullman, May 27, 1983. BA, Vassar Coll., 1962. Coord. Family Book Svc., Meredith Pub. Co., N.Y.C., 1962-64; assoc. producer Tanglewood Theatre, Lords Valley, Pa., 1966-68; producer CasperCitron Program, N.Y.C., 1968-70; free-lance publicist N.Y.C., 1970-74; with Lobsenz-Stevens Inc., N.Y.C., 1974—, exec. v.p., 1981—, assoc. gen. mgr., 1985-92; dep. press sec. N.Y.C. Health & Hosps. Corp., 1992-93, dr. mktg. and comm., 1993-95; dir. comm. MetroPlus Health Plan, N.Y.C., 1995—. Office: MetroPlus Health Plan 11 W 42nd St New York NY 10036-8002

GOLD, MARTIN ELLIOT, lawyer, educator; b. N.Y.C., Jan. 6, 1946; s. Herman and Rose (Zippin) G.; 1 step child, Ariane. BA, Cornell U., 1967; JD, Harvard U., 1970, MPA, 1971. Bar: N.Y. 1972, U.S. Dist. Ct. (so. and ea. dists.) N.Y. 1974, U.S. Ct. Appeals (2d cir.) 1974. With Operation Crossroads Africa, The Gambia, 1965; cons. U.S. Dept. Justice, 1968; assoc. Freshfields, London, 1969; research fellow Ctr. Law and Devel. Sri Lanka, Cambridge, Mass., 1971-73; assoc. Debevoise & Plimpton, N.Y.C., 1973-78; chief econ. devel. div. N.Y.C. Law Dept., 1978-85, dir. corp. law, 1980-85; dir. N.Y.C. Indsl. Devel. Agy., 1979-85; ptnr. Brown & Wood, 1985—. adj. prof. Columbia U., 1987—; guest lectr. Fordham U., Yale U., U.S. Conf. of Mayors. Author: Law and Social Change: A Study of Land Reform in Sri Lanka, 1977; contbr. articles to profl. jours. Mem. Legal Aid Soc., 1974—; mem. Sri Lanka council Asia Soc., 1975-81, Cornell Real Estate council, 1988—; bd. dirs. Environ. Action Coalition, 1988—, INFORM, 1989—, J.F. Kennedy Sch., Tri State Coun., 1991-97; chmn. Ridgefield Coun. Lake Assns. Recipient awards Rockefeller Bros. Fund, 1979, 80, Fund for City N.Y. 1981. Mem. ABA, Am. Soc. Internat. Law , Internat. Assn. Attys. and Execs. in Corp. Real Estate, Nat. Coun. for Pub.-Pvt. Partnerships, Natural Resources Def. Coun., Common Cause, Assn. of Bar of City of N.Y. (environ. and energy and real property and housing law coms.), Cornell Club. Home: 90 Riverside Dr New York NY 10024-5306 Office: Brown & Wood 1 World Trade Ctr Fl 58 New York NY 10048-0557

GOLD, MATEA JENNY, journalist, educator; b. Northampton, Mass., Nov. 28, 1974; d. Norman Charles and Jean Bickert Gold. BA, UCLA, 1996. Editor-in-chief Daily Bruin, L.A., 1994-95; intern L.A. Times, 1996, reporter, 1996—; intern The Oregonian, Portland, 1996; instr. journalism U. Judaism, L.A., 1997-99. Recipient Sacramento Press Club awards, 1994, 95; Nat. Merit scholar, 1992. Mem. Soc. Profl. Journalists, Phi Beta Kappa. Jewish. Avocations: reading, salsa dancing, skiing. E-mail: matea.gold@latimes.com.

GOLD, MATTHEW DAVID, physician, neurologist; b. Bklyn., Feb. 26, 1951; s. Isadore Roy and Ruth Helen (Bernstein) G.; m. Karen Sue Jacobs, Jan. 16, 1983; children: Joshua Aaron, Ariel Sara. BS, Yale U., 1971; MD, Cornell U., 1975. Diplomat Am. Bd. Psychiatry and Neurology, Am. Bd. Electrodiagnostic Medicine. Intern Henry Ford Hosp., Detroit, 1975-76; resident in neurology Duke U. Med. Ctr., Durham, N.C., 1976-79; fellow aphasia, neurobehavior Boston U. Sch. Medicine, 1979-80; neurologist New Eng. Neurol. Assn., Lowell, Mass., 1980-82; pvt. practice New Eng. Neurol. Assn., Everett and Chelsea, Mass., 1982—; clin. asst. prof. Tufts Med. Sch., Boston, 1982—; chief of neurology Whidden Meml. Hosp., Everett, 1982—; site dir. Tuft Med. Sch., 1994—. Newsletter editor: Boston Computer Soc. newsletter, 1985—, Mass. Neurol. Assn. newsletter, 1989—; contbr. articles to profl. jours. and publs. Choral mem. Temple Emanuel, Andover, Mass., 1994—; coach Odyssey of the Mind, Andover, 1995—; founder, pres. emeritus The Brook House Players, Brookline, Mass., 1979-85. Fellow Am. Assn. Electrodiagnostic Medicine; mem. AMA, Am. Acad. Neurology, Behavioral Neurology Soc., Internat. Neuropsychol. Soc., Am. Acad. Clin. Neurophysiology, Am. Assn. for Study of Headaches, Am. Sleep Disorders Assn., Mass. Med. Soc., Harvard Club of Boston. Avocations: sci. fiction, GO board game, backpacking, community theatre, computer programming. Office: 111 Everett Ave Ste 1C Chelsea MA 02150-2370

GOLD, PAUL ERNEST, psychology educator, behavioral neuroscience educator; b. Detroit, Jan. 7, 1945; s. Hyman and Sylvia Gold; children: Scott David Gold, Zachary Alexander Korol-Gold. BA, U. Mich., 1966; MS, U. N.C., 1968; PhD, 1971. NIH postdoctoral fellow, lectr. psychobiology U. Calif., Irvine, 1972-76; asst. prof. U. Va., Charlottesville, 1976-78, assoc. prof., 1978-81, prof., 1981-97, Commonwealth prof., 1997—, dir. neurosci. grad. program, 1991-95. Editor Psychobiology, 1990-97, Neurobiology of Learning and Memory, 1998—; contbr. over 150 articles to sci. publs. Mem. Commonwealth of Va. Alzheimer's and Related Disorders Commn., 1998—. Recipient James McKeen Cattell award, 1983, Sesquicentennial Assn. award, U. Va., 1983, 90-93; NIH fellow, 1967. Fellow APA (com. animal rsch. & ethics), AAAS, Am. Psychol. Soc. (mem. com. 1990-91, program com. 1991); mem. Soc. for Neurosci. (com. on animals in rsch. 1993-98), NSF Adv. Panel for Behavioral and Computational Neurosci., 1993-96. Office: U Va Dept Psychology 102 Gilmer Hall Charlottesville VA 22903

GOLD, PETER FREDERICK, lawyer; b. N.Y.C., Nov. 10, 1945; s. John and Dolores (Soyer) G.; m. Dee Crafferty, June 6, 1982; children: Joshua, Katharine. BA, Cornell U., 1967; MSc, London Sch. Econs., 1968; JD, NYU, 1971. Bar: D.C. 1988, N.Y. 1972, U.S. Dist. Ct. (so. dist.) N.Y. 1972, U.S. Dist. Ct. (ea. dist.) N.Y. 1972. Assoc. atty. Paul, Weiss, Rifkind, Wharton & Garrison, N.Y.C., 1971-75; legis. dir. Senator Gary Hart, Washington, 1975-81; ptnr. Wellford, Wegman, Krulwich, Gold & Hoff, Washington, 1981-84, Winthrop, Stimson, Putnam & Roberts, Washington, 1984-94; pres. The Gold Group, Chartered, Washington, 1994—, C.G. Sloan & Co., Inc., 1995-97. Editor in chief Review of Law and Social Change, 1970. Nat. policy dir. Hart for Pres. Campaign, Washington, 1984; chmn., founder First Book, Washington, 1992—; dir. Share Our Strength, Washington, 1990—; mem. Clinton-Gore Transition Team, Washington, 1992. Recipient Disting. Visitor Program European Econ. Community, Brussels, Belgium, 1982. Mem. D.C. Bar Assn., Fed. Bar Assn., N.Y.C. Bar Assn., Kenwood Golf & Country Club, Four Streams Golf Club. Democrat. Jewish. Avocation: tennis, golf. Home: 13640 Glenhurst Rd North Potomac MD 20878-3921 Office: The Gold Group Chartered 1319 F St NW Ste 500 Washington DC 20004-1106

GOLD, PHIL, immunologist, educator, researcher; b. Montreal, Sept. 17, 1936; m. Evelyn Katz; 3 children. BSc in Physiology with honors, McGill U., Montreal, 1957, MSc, M.D., 1961, PhD in Physiology, 1965; DSc (hon.), McMaster U., 1986. Licentiate Med. Council Can. Jr. rotating intern Montreal Gen. Hosp., 1961-62, jr. asst. resident in medicine, 1962-63, sr. resident in medicine, 1965-66, jr. asst. physician, asst. and assoc. physician, 1967-73, sr. physician, 1973—, physician-in-chief, 1980-95, dir. div. clin. immunology and allergy, 1977-80, dir. McGill U. Med. Clinic, 1980-95, also sr. investigator Research Ins.; faculty dept. physiology McGill U., 1964—, mem. faculty of medicine, 1965—, prof. medicine and clin. medicine, 1973—, chmn. dept. medicine and clin. medicine, 1985-90, prof. physiology, 1974—, prof. oncology, 1989—, mem. faculty of medicine exec. com. representing clin. depts., 1985—, D. G. Cameron prof. medicine (inaugural), 1987—; exec. dir. Clin. Rsch. Ctr. Mont. Gen. Hosp. and McGill U. Hosp. Ctr., 1995—; vis. scientist Pub. Health Research Inst. N.Y.C., 1967-68; Chester M. Jones Meml. lectr. Mass. Gen. Hosp., 1974; vis. prof. U. Caracas, Venezuela, 1974; Squires Club vis. prof. Wellesley Hosp., Toronto, 1983; Cecil H. and Ida Green vis. prof., 1984 autumn lectures U. Brit. Columbia; cons. in allergy and immunology Mt. Sinai Hosp., St. Agathe des Monts, Quebec, 1975—; hon. cons. dept. medicine Royal Victoria Hosp., Montreal; cons. dept. internal medicine Douglas Hosp. Ctr., Montreal; vice chmn. med. adv. com. Council of Physicians, Dentists and Pharmacists, 1985-90; mem. Conseil d'Adminstrn., Found. Quebecoise du Cancer, 1986-88, adv. com. Burroughs Wellcome fellowship fund, 1998—; health com. mem. Centre d'Entreprises et d'Innovation de Montreal, 1996—; Sir Arthur Sims travelling prof., 1998. Mem. editorial bd. Clin. Immunology and Immunopathology, 1972—, Immunopharmacology, 1978—, Diagnostic Gynecology and Obstetrics, 1978-83, Oncodevelopmental Biology and Medicine, 1979—, Modern Medicine of Can., 1984-90, Jour. Internal Medicine, 1988—, Canadians for Health Rsch., 1989—, Current Therapeutic Rsch., 1992—, Nutrition Quar., 1992—; editorial cons. Jour. Chronic Diseases, 1981-84; mem. editorial adv. bd. Cancer Research, 1971-73, assoc. editor 1973-80; contbg. editor Practical Allergy and Immunology, 1991—; editl. bd. Can. Jour. Allergy & Clin. Immunology, 1996—; contbr. over 140 articles to med. jours. External referee Can. Red Cross Soc. Recipient Hiram Mills Gold medal, Mosby Scholarship Book award, Wood Gold medal, E.W.R. Steacie prize Nat. Research Council Can., 1973, Can. Silver Jubilee medal, 1977, Johann-Georg-Zemmerman prize for cancer research Medizinische Hochschule, Hannover, Fed. Republic Germany, 1978, Gold medal award of merit Grad. Soc. McGill U., 1979, Internat. award Gardner Found., Ernest C. Manning prize, F.N.G. Starr award Izzak Walton Killam Prize Can. Council, 1985, Tower of Hope award Israel Cancer Rsch. Fund, 1985, Sci. Achievement medal Govt. of Italy, 1990, Agora trophy Ambassador's Club, 1991, Internat. Soc.Oncodevelop. Biol. Medicine Internat. Abbott award, 1992, Commemorative medal 125th Anniversary of Can. Confedn., Govt. of Can., 1992, Carl Goresky Meml. award, 1999, Christie award Can. Assn. of Profs. of Medicine, 1999; named Most Outstanding Can. Med. Personality of the past 25 years, MacLean's Mag., 1986; decorated companion Order of Can., 1986; Great Montrealer, 1986; Knight Comdr., Sovereign Order St. John Jerusalem, Knights of Malta, 1986; MacDonald scholar, J. Francis Williams scholar, Univ. scholar; L'Ordre nat. du Quebec. Fellow AAAS; mem. Internat. Assn. Health Profls. (chmn. 1998). Achievements include discovery of Carcinoembryonic Antigen (CEA). Office: Clin Rsch Ctr Montreal Gen Hosp, 1650 Cedar Ave, Montreal, PQ Canada H3G 1A4

GOLD, PHRADIE KLING See KLING, PHRADIE

GOLD, RICHARD N., management consultant; b. Chgo., May 27, 1945; s. Irving Louis and Victoria (Saltzman) G.; m. Renee Bonnie Rein, Nov. 3, 1968; children: Jedd Steven, Amanda Caryn. BSI, U. Wis., 1967; MBA with honors, Columbia U., 1971; MA with honors, NYU, 1971. Tchr., supr. Ocean-Hill Brownsville, N.Y.C. pub. schs., 1968-71; brand mgr. packaged soap and detergent divsn. Procter & Gamble Co., Cin., 1971-76; exec. v.p. Glendinning Assocs., Westport, Conn., 1976-81; pres. R.N. Gold & Co., 1981—; producer, ptnr. Enterplan, N.Y.C., 1983-85; dir. mktg. Downtown Coun., Cin., 1975-77; bd. dirs. Hampton Products Internat. Corp., MF & A Inc., Data Nat. Corp.; bd. advs. L.A. Brewing Co., Designer Fragrances Internat., Evolve Products Inc. Mem. Pres. Assn., Am. Mgmt. Assn. Avocations: sports, theatre, collecting antique electronic musical devices. Office: RN Gold & Co 3 Indian Point Ln Westport CT 06880-2917

GOLD, RICK L., federal government executive; b. Rexburg, Idaho, June 25, 1946; s. Raymond Russell and Thelma (Lee) G.; m. Anamarie Sanone, May 14, 1988; children: Nanette Phillips, Russell. BSCE, Utah State U., 1968, MSCE, 1970. Registered profl. engr., Colo., Mont., Utah. Hydraulic engr. U.S. Bur. Reclamation, Provo, Utah, 1969-73; project hydrologist U.S. Bur. Reclamation, Durango, Colo., 1973-75; regional hydrologist U.S. Bur. Reclamation, Billings, Mont., 1975-81; spl. asst. to regional dir. U.S. Bur. Reclamation, Washington, 1981-82; asst. planning officer U.S. Bur. Reclamation, Billings, 1982-83; projects mgr. U.S. Bur. Reclamation, Durango, Colo., 1983-88; regional planning officer U.S. Bur. Reclamation, Salt Lake City, 1988-90, asst. regional dir., 1990-94, deputy regional dir., 1994—; mem. water quality com. Internat. Joint Commn. Study on Garrison Divsn. Unit, Billings, 1975-77; fed. negotiator Cost Sharing and Indian Water Rights Settlement, Durango, 1986-88; chmn. Cooperating Agy. on Glen Canyon Dam EIS, Salt Lake City, 1990-94. Contbr. articles to profl. jours.; author papers. Mem. Rotary Internat., Durango, 1985-87; bd. dirs. United Way of La Plata County, Durango, 1983-88; chmn. Combined Fed. Campaign, La Plata County, 1985. Mem. ASCE, bd. dirs. U.S. Com. on Irrigation and

Drainage. Office: US Bur Reclamation 125 S State St Salt Lake City UT 84138-1102

GOLD, SHARON CECILE, artist, educator; b. N.Y.C., Feb. 28, 1949; d. Henry Joseph and Betty (Kopan) G.; m. William McKay Watson III, July 12, 1992; 1 child, Miranda Cecile. Student, CUNY, 1967-68, Columbia U., 1968-70; BFA, Pratt Inst., 1976. Adj. prof. Art NYU, 1983; vis. artist SUNY, Purchase, 1985; assoc. prof. painting and critical theory Syracuse (N.Y.) U., 1986—; vis. artist The Art Inst. Chgo., Chgo., 1990; lectr. in field; guest critic Sch. Visual Arts, N.Y.C., 1987, N.Y. Studio Sch., 1988. Solo exhibits include Stephen Rosenberg Gallery, N.Y.C., 1987, 89, 91, 55 Mercer St., N.Y.C., 1986, John Davis Gallery, Akron, Ohio, 1986, Pam Adler Gallery, N.Y.C., 1986; group exhibits include IRIS House, N.Y.C., 1992, Everson Mus. of Art, Syracuse, 1991, ARTSTAR, L.A., 1991, Stephen Rosenberg Gallery, N.Y., 1991, Rose Art Mus. Brandeis U., 1990; performance/video works include A Video Tape 1990-1991 Stephen Rosenberg Gallery, 1991, North South Consonance St. Stephen's Ch., N.Y.C., 1984. Pratt Inst. Acad. fellow, 1974-76, NEA grantee, 1981, Penny McCall Found. grantee, 1988. Home and Studio: 10 Leonard St New York NY 10013-2929

GOLD, SIMEON, lawyer; b. Hartford, Conn., Jan. 3, 1949; s. Charles and Claire (Goldschein) G.; m. Heide Aline Turkel, Aug. 30, 1970; children: Jana, Craig. BS, Cornell U., 1970; JD, Harvard U., 1973. Bar: N.Y., U.S. Dist. Ct. (so. dist.) N.Y., U.S. Ct. Appeals (2d cir.). Assoc. Weil, Gotshal & Manges, N.Y.C., 1973-81, ptnr., 1981—; bd. dirs. Lawyers Alliance for N.Y. Contbr. articles to profl. jours. Mem. Coun. of Bus. Exec. Assn. for Help of Retarded Children, N.Y.C., Legal Aid Soc., N.Y.C.; bd. trustees Dalton Sch., 1997—. Mem. ABA, N.Y. State Bar Assn. (vice chair, exec. com., corp. law com. chair, bus. law sect.), Assn. of Bar of City of N.Y., N.Y. County Lawyers Assn., Harmonie Club, Old Oaks Country Club. Avocations: skiing, tennis, golf, travel. Office: Weil Gotshal & Manges 767 5th Ave Fl Concl New York NY 10153-0119

GOLD, STANLEY P., diversified investments executive; b. 1942. AB, U. Calif., 1964; JD, U. So. Calif., 1967. Ptnr. Gang Tyre and Brown, 1967-85, Shamrock Holdings Inc., Burbank, Calif., 1985—; pres., CEO, Shamrock Holdings, Burbank. Office: Shamrock Holdings Inc 4444 W Lakeside Dr Burbank CA 91505-4054

GOLD, SYLVIANE, entertainment editor, writer, critic; b. Paris, Feb. 17, 1948; came to U.S., 1949; d. Jack and Annette (Movermann) G.; m. Lawrence Stanley Simonberg, June 30, 1972. Student, Queens Coll., 1964-68. Prodn. asst. Village Voice, N.Y.C., 1968-70; editorial clerk, critic, reporter N.Y. Post, N.Y.C., 1970-77; arts editor Boston Phoenix, 1977-80; drama critic Wall St. Jour., N.Y.C., 1983-89; entertainment editor Newsday, 1989-95, dance critic, 1996—; freelance writer, editor, 1995—; adj. asst. prof. journalism dept. NYU, 1983-85. Contbr. stories and articles to numerous publs. including SoHo News, N.Y. Times, Elle, Boston Globe, USA Today, Vanity Fair, 1980-89. Recipient George Jean Nathan award, 1982, Penney-Missouri awards, 1992, 93. Mem. N.Y. Drama Critics Circle (emeritus), Newswomen's Club of N.Y.

GOLD, THOMAS, astronomer, educator; b. Vienna, Austria, May 22, 1920; s. Max and Josefine (Martin) G.; m. Merle Eleanor Tuberg, June 21, 1947; children—Linda, Lucy, Tanya; m. Carvel Lee Beyer, Dec. 27, 1972; 1 dau., Lauren. B.A., Cambridge (Eng.) U., 1942, M.A., 1945, Sc.D., 1969; fellow, Trinity Coll., Cambridge, 1947; M.A. (hon.), Harvard, 1957. Lectr. physics Cambridge (Eng.) U., 1948-52; chief asst. to Astronomer Royal, Gt. Britain, 1952-56; prof. astronomy Harvard, 1958, Robert Wheeler Willson prof., 1958-59; prof. astronomy, dir. Center Radiophysics and Space Research Cornell U., 1959-81, chmn. dept., 1959-68, asst. v.p. for research, 1970-71, John L. Wetherill prof., 1971-86. Contbr. articles to profl. jours. Hon. fellow Trinity Coll., Cambridge, 1986. Fellow Royal Soc. London, Am. Geophys. Union; mem. U.S. Nat. Acad. Sci., Am. Philos. Soc., Am. Acad. Arts and Scis., Royal Astron. Soc. (Gold medal 1985; past councillor), Am. Astron. Soc. Fax: (607) 257-7969. Email: tg21@cornell.edu. Home and Office: 7 Pleasant Grove Ln Ithaca NY 14850-2548

GOLD, WILLIAM ELLIOTT, health care management consultant; b. Bklyn., Oct. 21, 1948; s. Theodore David and Debra (Fridovich) G.; m. Nili Rachel Scharf, June 1, 1972; children: Avitai, Doria Michelle. BA, SUNY, Stony Brook, 1970; MSS, Hebrew U. of Jerusalem, Israel, 1972; PhD, U. Minn., 1982. Rsch. asst. Hebrew U. of Jerusalem, 1971-72; cons. Dept. Health, Mpls., 1973-74; researcher Mt. Sinai Hosp., Mpls., 1973-74; hosp. adminstrn. instr. U. Minn., Mpls., 1974-75; coord., dir. Blue Cross/Blue Shield Greater N.Y. HMO, N.Y.C., 1975-85; pres. ANCHOR, Chgo.; v.p. Rush-Presbyn. St. Luke's Med. Ctr., Chgo., 1985-88; pres. GOLD HEALTH STRATEGIES, INC., N.Y.C., 1988—; bd. dirs. N.Y. Bus. Group on Health Managed Care Task Force, chmn., 1989-95; vice chmn. The HMO Group, 1987-88; steering com. U. Mo.-KC Nat. Ctr. for Managed Care Adminstrn., Kansas City, 1986—; asst. adj. prof. Columbia U., N.Y.C., 1989—, clin. prof., Columbia U. Sch. of Pub. Health, 1999—. Founding editor Managing Employee Health Benefits. Fellowship Caldwell B. Esselstyn Found., 1991-92; mem. task force pub. health and managed care PEW Charitable Trust, 1995-96; mem. task force improving cardiovascular health Am. Heart Assn., N.Y.C., 1995-96. Avocations: clarinet, music, sports. Home: 322 W 72nd St # 14B New York NY 10023-2676 Office: GOLD HEALTH STRATEGIES INC 250 Park Ave Ste 1300 New York NY 10177-0001

GOLDANSKII, VITALII IOSIFOVICH, chemist, physicist; b. Vitebsk, USSR, June 18, 1923; s. Iosif Efimovich and Yudif' Iosifovna (Melamed) G.; m. Lyudmila Nikolaevna Semenova; children: Dmitrii, Andrei. Grad. in Chemistry, Moscow U., 1944, M of Chemistry, 1947, DSc in Physics, 1954. Scientist Inst. Chem. Physics-USSR Acad. Scis., Moscow, 1942-52, 1961—, from div. head to dir., 1988—; sr. scientist P.N. Lebedev Phys. Inst.-USSR Acad. Scis., Moscow, 1952-61; asst. prof. Phys.-Tech. Inst., Moscow, 1947-51; asst. prof., then prof. Inst. Phys. Engring., Moscow, 1951—. Author: Kinematics of Nuclear Reactions, 1959, Mössbauer Effect and its Applications in Chemistry, 1963, Physical Chemistry of Positron and Positronium, 1968, Tunneling Phenomena in Chemical Physics, 1986, many others; contbr. numerous articles and revs. to profl. jours.; patentee (numerous) in field. Chmn. Russian Pugwash Com., Moscow, 1987—; people's dep. of USSR; mem. com. fgn. affairs Supreme Soviet of USSR, 1989-92. Decorated Lenin Order, Order of October Revolution, numerous other orders and medals; recipient Lenin prize, 1980; Golden Mendeleev medal USSR Acad. Scis., 1975, Karpinsky prize Friedrich von Schiller Found., Hamburg, Germany, 1983, Boris Pregel award N.Y. Acad. Scis., 1990, Alexander von Humboldt award, Germany, 1991, Golden Semenov medal Russian Acad. Scis., 1996. Fellow Am. Chem. Soc. (hon.), Am. Phys. Soc., Am. Acad. Arts and Scis., Am. Philos Soc., Acad. Scis. German Dem. Republic, Royal Swedish Acad. Scis., Royal Danish Acad. Scis. and Lettrs, Deutsche Akademie der Naturforscher Leopoldina, World Acad. Arts and Sci., Hungarian Eotvos Lorand Phys. Soc.; mem. NAS USA (fgn., assoc.), N.Y. Acad. Scis. (life.), Russian Acad. Scis., Finnish Acad. Scis. (fgn.), Acad. Europaea, Acad. Georgia. Avocations: writing humor and aphorisms, record collecting, movies, CDs, videos. Home: Bldg 8 Apt 66, Ulitsa Zelinskogo 38, Moscow 117334, Russia Office: Russian Acad of Scis, Inst Chem Phys Ulitsa Kosygina 4, Moscow 117334, Russia

GOLDAPER, GABRIELE GAY, clothing executive, consultant; b. Amsterdam, The Netherlands, May 4, 1937; came to U.S., 1949; d. Richard and Gertrud (Sinzheimer) Mainzer; married, 1957; children: Carolyn, Julie, Nancy. BA in Econs., Barnard Coll., 1959; BS in Edn., U. Cin., 1960; postgrad., Xavier U., 1962. V.p. planning, systems and material control High Tide Swimwear div. Warnaco, Los Angeles, 1974-79; v.p., customer support cons. Silton AMS, Los Angeles, 1979-80; exec. v.p., ptnr. Prisma Corp., Los Angeles, 1980-84; exec. v.p. Mindstar Prods., Los Angeles, 1984-85; gen. mgr. Cherry Lane, Los Angeles, 1985-86; dir. inventory mgmt. Barco Uniforms, Los Angeles, 1986; mgmt. cons. to clothing industry Santa Monica, Calif., 1986—; dir. corp. operation svcs. Authentic Fitness, L.A., 1993; exec. v.p. corp. LCA Intimates, 1994—; instr. Calif. State U., 1978-79, UCLA Grad. Bus. Mgmt. Sch., 1979-86, Fashion Inst. Design and Merchandising. 1985—; chmn. data processing com. Calif. Fashion Creators, 1980; mediator Los Angeles County Bar Assn.; cons. Exec. Service Corps; lectr. various colls. Author: A Results Oriented Approach to Manufacturing Planning, 1978, Small Company View of the Computer, 1979; also articles. Elected mem. Commn. on Status Women, 1985-89. Mem. Apparel Mfrs. Assn. (mgmt. systems com. 1978-80), Calif. Apparel Industries Assn. (exec. com., bd. dirs. 1980), Am. Arbitration Assn. Home: 4342 Redwood Ave # C309 Marina Del Rey CA 90292

GOLDBECK, ROBERT ARTHUR, JR., physical chemist; b. Evanston, Ill., July 25, 1950; s. Robert Arthur Sr. and Ruth Marilyn (Nordwall) G.; m. Jennifer Jane Tollkuhn, Aug. 19, 1989; stepchildren: Jessica Kathleen Tollkuhn, Brenna Maurin Tollkuhn. BS, U. Calif., Berkeley, 1974; PhD, U. Calif., Santa Cruz, 1982. Postdoctoral fellow Stanford (Calif.) U., 1983-84, rsch. assoc., 1984-87; rsch. chemist U. Calif., Santa Cruz, 1987—; lectr. in chemistry U. Calif., 1980, 84, 86. Contbr. articles to Biophys. Jour.; contbr. articles to profl. jours. Mem. AAAS, Am. Chem. Soc., Biophys. Soc., Sigma Xi. Achievements include development of nanosecond time-resolved magnetic circular dichroism spectroscopy; research in the time-resolved MCD and natural CD of photolyzed hemeprotein-ligand complexes. Office: U Calif Dept Chemistry Biochem Santa Cruz CA 95064

GOLDBERG, ALAN MARVIN, toxicologist, educator; b. Bklyn., Nov. 20, 1939; s. William and Celia Ida (Rudman) G.; m. Helene Schoenbach, Aug. 14, 1960; children—Michael David, Naomi Jill. BS, Bklyn. Coll. Pharmacy, 1961; PhD in Pharmacology, U. Minn., 1966; DSc (hon.), L.I. U, 1995. Rsch. asst. U. Wis., 1961-62, U. Minn., 1962-66; rsch. assoc. Inst. Psychiat. Rsch. Ind. U., 1966-67, asst. prof. dept. pharmacology, 1967-69; asst. prof. environ. medicine Johns Hopkins U., Balt., 1969-71, assoc. prof., 1971-78, prof. dept. environ. health scis., 1978—, assoc. chmn. dept., 1978-80, acting dir. div. toxicology, 1979-80, dir. div. toxicology, 1980-82, dir. Ctr. Alternatives to Animal Testing, 1981—, assoc. dean rsch., 1984-94; assoc. dean corp. affairs Sch. Pub. Health, Balt., 1994—; adminstrv. head health edn. program Johns Hopkins U./Nat. Basketball Player Assn., 1990-95; cons. OECD, Paris, 1998—; prin. rsch. scientist Chesapeake Bay Inst., 1979-84; mem. health hazard evaluation team of chem. waste dumps State of Tenn., 1980; mem. rev. panel EPA, 1980-82; mem. working group on harmonization of in vitro methods Orgn. Econ. and Cmty. Devel., 1995—; organizer 1st World Congress on Alternative and Animal Use in Life Scis., 1993; scientific adv. bd. subcom. on toxicology U.S. FDA, 1996—; mem. interagy. coord. com. for validation of alternative method HHS, 1998—; bd. dirs. Xenogen, Inc. Mem. editorial bd. Jour. Am. Coll. Toxicology, assoc. editor In Vitro Toxicology; contbr. articles to profl. jours. Trustee Hildergard Doerenkamp-Gerhard & Binden Found., 1985—. Recipient award Ind. Neurol. Soc., 1967, Russell and Burch award Human Soc. of U.S., 1991; named Disting. Alumnus, L.I. Univ., 1992. Mem. AAAS, Am. Soc. Pharmacology and Exptl. Therapeutics, Soc. Neurosci. (pres. Balt. chpt. 1971-73), Am. Soc. Neurochemistry, Am. Epilepsy Soc., Assn. Univ. Tech. Mgrs., Internat. Soc. Neurochemistry, Soc. Toxicology (Ambassador Mid-Atlantic sect. 1998), Internat. Study Group on Memory Disorders, Internat. Union Pharmacology, Office of Tech. Assessment Panel on Alternatives to Animal Use in Rsch. Testing and Edn. and Frontiers in Neuroscience, Nat. Acad. Sci., Inst. for Lab. Animal Resources, Licensing Exec. Soc. Home: 2515 Boston St unit Pl Baltimore MD 21224 Office: 111 Market Pl Ste 840 Baltimore MD 21202-7113

GOLDBERG, ANNE CAROL, physician, educator; b. Balt., June 12, 1951; d. Stanley Barry and Selma Ray (Freiman) G.; m. Ronald M. Levin, July 29, 1989. AB, Harvard U., 1973; MD, U. Md., 1977. Diplomate Am. Bd. Internal Medicine, Am. Bd. Endocrinlolgy and Metabolism. Intern in medicine Michael Reese Hosp., Chgo., 1977-78; resident in medicine Michael Reese Hosp., 1978-80; fellow in endocrinology Washington U., St. Louis, 1980-83, instr. medicine, 1983-85, asst. prof. medicine, 1985-94, assoc. prof. medicine, 1994—, clin. dir. lipid reseach clinic, 1987-96. Mem. steering com. Cholesterol Coalition, St. Louis, 1988-93. Fellow ACP; mem. AMA, Am. Diabetes Assn., Am. Heart Assn., Am. Fedn. Clin. Rsch., Am. Med. Women's Assn., Alpha Omega Alpha. Democrat. Jewish. Avocations: photography, needlepoint. Office: Washington U Med Sch PO Box 8046 660 S Euclid Ave Saint Louis MO 63110-1010

GOLDBERG, ARNOLD IRVING, psychoanalyst, educator; b. Chgo., May 21, 1929; s. Morris Henry and Rose (Auerbach) G.; m. Constance Obenhaus; children: Andrew, Sarah. BS, U. Ill., 1949; MD, U. Ill., Chgo., 1953. Diplomate Am. Bd. Psychiatry and Neurology; cert. psychoanalyst. Intern Cin. Gen. Hosp., 1954-55; psychiat. resident Michael Reese Hosp., Chgo., 1957-59; tng. and supervising analyst Chgo. Inst. for Psychoanalysis, 1970—, dir., 1990-92; assoc. psychiatrist Rush Presbyterian St. Lukes Hosp., Chgo., 1982—; prof. psychiatry Rush Med. Coll., Chgo., 1982-97, Cynthia Oudejans Harris MD prof. psychiatry, 1997—. Author: Models of the Mind, 1973, A Fresh Look at Psychoanalysis, 1988, The Prisonhouse of Psychoanalysis, 1990, The Problem of Perversion, 1995, Being of Two Minds, 1999; editor: Future of Psychoanalysis: Progress in Self Psychology, Vols. 1-15, 1976-98; contbr. numerous articls to profl. jours. Capt. U.S. Army, 1955-57. Fellow Am. Psychiat. Assn. (life); mem. Am. Psychoanalytic Assn. Home: 844 W Chalmers Pl Chicago IL 60614-3223 Office: Inst for Psychoanalysis Chgo 122 S Michigan Ave Ste 1300 Chicago IL 60603-6107

GOLDBERG, ARTHUR ABBA, merchant banker, financial advisor; b. Jersey City, Nov. 25, 1940; s. Jack Geddy and Ida (Steinberg) G.; m. Jane Elizabeth Gottlieb, Aug. 10, 1968; children: Ari Matthew, Shoshana Eve, Benjamin Saul, Talia Akiva. A.B. with honors, Am. U., 1962; J.D., Cornell U., 1965; PhD (hon.), Natchez Coll., 1992, HHD (hon.), 1992. Intern, staff mem. to senator, 1962; law clk. DeSevo & Cerutti, Jersey City, 1964; pvt. practice Jersey City, 1965-89; asst. prof. law U. Conn. Sch. Law., 1965-67; cooperating atty. NAACP Legal Def. Fund, 1965-72; adminstrv. asst. to congressman Ohio, 1966-67; dep. atty. gen. N.J., counsel Dept. Community Affairs and Housing Finance Agy., 1967-70; exec. v.p., dir., mgr. mcpl. fin. dept. Matthews & Wright, Inc., N.Y.C., 1970-88; exec. v.p., dir. Landamatic Systems Corp., N.Y.C., 1982-85; vice chmn. Matthews & Wright Realty, N.Y.C., 1986-88, Matthews & Wright Pacific, N.Y.C., 1986-88; pres. New Am. Fed. Credit Union, 1981-87; dir., treas. Fedn. Community Devel. Credit Unions, 1985-88; v.p. Alfus Corp., 1958-85, Basow Corp., 1965-86; ptnr. Shayna Enterprises, York Builders, Hudson Mgmt. Svcs., 1978-87; dir. investment strategies Capital Corp., 1998—; mng. ptnr. Bank Bldg. Assocs., 1974-86, Inst. Profl. and Exec. Devel.; vis. lectr. Rutgers U., 1971-80, Practising Law Inst., 1969-76; mem. exec. com. N.J. Commn. Discrimination in Housing, 1975-80; mem. urban adv. coun. Anti-Defamation League, 1965-72; spl. cons. Exclusionary zoning Nat. Com. Discrimination in Housing, 1965-70; cons. scholarship edn. Def. Fund for Racial Equality, 1965-72; gen. counsel N.J. chpt. Mcpl. Fin. Officers Assn., N.J. chpt. Nat. Assn. Housing and Redevel. Ofcls., 1966-74, chmn. Com. for Absorption of Soviet Emigrees (CASE), 1973—; pres. CASE-UNA Cmty. Devel. Corp., 1976; v.p. Ophthalmic Mission Trust (India), 1988-91; fin. advisor Nat. Found. Manufactured Home Owners, 1994—; fin. advisor Ednl. Video Conferency, Inc., 1997—. Author: Financing Housing and Urban Development, 1975, Zoning and Land Use, 1972; adv. bd. Housing and Devel. Reporter, 1975-89; contbr. articles to law revs. Co-pres. New Synagogue, Jersey City, 1974-80; bd. dirs. Jersey City Hebrew Free Loan Assn., 1976-77; pres. Met. N.Y. Coord. Com. for Resettlement of Soviet Jewry, 1978-80; treas. Hebrew Free Loan N.J., 1977-90, pres., 1995—; bd. dirs. Hillel Acad., 1985-87; dir. Bayonne Jewish Cmty. Ctr., 1987-88, Jersey City United Jewish Appeal, 1984—, chmn. allocation com., 1994, chmn. nominating com., 1996; bd. dirs. South Bronx Cmty. Housing, Inc., 1977-81; chmn. Novy Americanitz, 1980-84; bd. dirs. Citizens Housing and Planning Coun., 1980-84, Boys Club of Jersey City, 1975-92; pres. CASE Mus. Contemporary Russian Art, 1980—; pres. Freedom Synagogue, 1982—; mem. Settlement House Fund; treas. Coun. Jewish Orgns., Jersey City, 1977; mem. bd. edn. Yeshiva of Hudson County, 1977-85; pres. Hudson Yeshiva Parents Orgn., 1980-88. Mem. Conn. Assn. Mcpl. Attys. (exec. com., editor newsletter 1965-68), Nat. Housing Conf., Am. Polit. Sci. Assn., Nat. Acad. Polit. and Social Sci., Nat. Leased Housing Assn. (nat. pres. 1972-74, chmn. emeritus 1975—), Public Securities Assn. (legis. com. 1978), Nat. Housing Rehab. Assn. (dir. 1982-89, v.p. 1985), Omicron Delta Kappa, Pi Gamma Mu, Pi Sigma Alpha, Pi Delta Epsilon, Phi Alpha Delta. Home: 83 Montgomery St Jersey City NJ 07302-3723 Office: 80 Grand St Jersey City NJ 07302-4522

GOLDBERG, ARTHUR M., gaming and fitness company executive, food products executive, lawyer; b. Newton, N.J., 1941. BA, Rutgers U., 1963; JD, Villanova U., 1966. With Transco Group Inc., 1972-81, Triangle Industries Inc., 1981-83; mng. ptnr. Arveron Investments Ltd. Partnership, 1978—; pres., CEO Internat. Controls Corp., 1985-89; chmn. bd. dirs., pres., CEO Di Giorgio Corp., Carteret, N.J., 1990—; pres., treas., bd. dirs. DIG Holding Corp.; gen. ptnr. Rose Ptnrs., L.P.; chmn., CEO, pres. Bally Mfg. Corp., 1990—; officer White Rose Foods, 1992—. Office: Di Giorgio 380 Middlesex Ave Carteret NJ 07008-3446 Address: Bally Mfg Co 26 Main St Chatham NJ 07928-2402*

GOLDBERG, BERNARD R., news correspondent; b. N.Y.C., May 31, 1945; s. Sam and Sylvia (Abovitz) G.; m. Nancy Solomon, Jan 18, 1986; children: Brian Erik, Catherine Michelle. BA, Rutgers U., 1967. Writer, reporter AP, N.Y.C., 1967-69; writer, prodr. Sta. WTVJ-TV, Miami, Fla., 1969-70; prodr., reporter Sta. WPLG-TV, Miami, 1970-72; corr. CBS News, Atlanta, San Francisco, N.Y.C., Miami, 1972—; staff corr. 48 Hours, 1988-89, spl. corr., 1988-93; corr. Eye to Eye, 1993-95; spl. corr. CBS Evening News, 1995-97; corr. Pub. Eye., 1997-98, HBO Real Sports, 1999—; corr.-at-large CBS News, 1998—. Recipient 6 Emmy awards NATAS, 1988, 89, 92, George Foster Peabody award Sch. Comm. U. Ga., 1988, Ohio State U. award, 1994, Edward R. Murrow Brotherhood award Cinema/Radio/TV unit B'nai B'rith, 1989, Cert. of Merit ABA, 1979, Silver Gavel award 1990, Cert. of Merit, 1994, Award Sigma Delta Chi, 1994. Office: CBS News 4770 Biscayne Blvd Ste 1170 Miami FL 33137-3251

GOLDBERG, BERTRAM J., social agency administrator; b. Bklyn., Oct. 23, 1942; s. Ralph Goldberg and Geraldine Janith (Herzog) Gerber; m. Lorri Ann Schwartz, Oct. 19, 1980; children: Ilissa, Andrea, Joshua, Randi. BA, Fairleigh Dickinson U., 1964; MSW, U. Pa., 1966. Diplomate Acad. of Cert. Social Workers. Tween worker Bernard Horwich Jewish Community Ctr., Chgo., 1966-68; dir. group svcs. Seattle Jewish Community Ctr., 1968-70; chief centralized intake Eastside Mental Health Ctr., Bellevue, Wash., 1970-73; coord. coll. age youth svcs. Jewish Fedn., Chgo., 1973-74; exec. dir. Jewish Family Svc., Allentown, Pa., 1974-77, Orange County, Calif., 1977-86; exec. v.p. Assn. Jewish Family and Children's Agys., Kendall Park, N.J., 1986—. Mem. NASW, Jewish Social Svc. Profls. Assn. (bd. dirs. 1977-97), Jewish Communal Svc. Assn. N.Am. (bd. dirs 1979, pres. 1994-96), World Coun. Jewish Communal Svc. (bd. dirs. 1989—). Democrat. Jewish. Avocations: computers, reading. Office: Assn Jewish Family/Childrens Agys 3086 State Route 27 Ste 11 Kendall Park NJ 08824-1658

GOLDBERG, BRADLEY JAY, artist; b. Oklahoma City, July 7, 1954; s. Burton S. and Lenisse E. (Mankoff) G.; m. Diana G. Swick, Mar. 18, 1984; children: Jason, Alex, Ian. BFA in Sculpture, B.Landscape Arch., R.I. Sch. Design, 1978. lectr. in field; vis. artist Mie (Japan) Nat. U., 1997, R.I. Sch. Design, Providence, 1989, 95, Grad. Program, Sch. Arch. and Environ. Design, U. Tex., Arlington, 1984-87. Sculpture at Forma Viva Internat. Sculpture Symposium, Kostanjevica Na Krki, Slovenija, Yugoslavia, 1976, Internat. Sculpture symposium, Liberty Hill, Tex, 1976, Lindabrunn, Austria, 1977, 79, Warrington High-rise Condominiums, Dallas, 1981, Austin Hyatt regency Hotel, 1981, Shizuki Park, Hagi, Japan, 1981-84, Baylor U., Waco, Tex., 1982, Hachioji, Tokyo, Japan, 1984, West End Oasis Restaurant, Dallas, 1984-86, Office Tower Lobbies of The Crescent, Dallas, 1987-88, Lippencott Ctr., Marlton, N.J., 1988-89, Dallas Arboretum and Bot. Soc., 1987-89, 90City of Hamamatsu, Japan, 1990-91, Dallas Area Rapid Transit Ctrl. Bus. Dist. Transit Mall Project, 1991-96, Heritage Park, Ft. Worth, 1991-92, City of St. Paul/Lowertown Redevel. Corp., 1990-93, City of Wichita (Kans.) Mus. Dist. Master Plan, 1992-94, Miyakoda Technopolis Rsch. Inst., Japan, 1992-93, Dallas Conv. Ctr. Expansion/Vertiport Project, 1990-94, Prince of Peace Cath. Cmty., Plano, Tex., 1993-94, Pegasus Plaza/Dallas City Ctr. Project, 1992-94, City Hall, Bloomington, Ind., 1994-96, Mountain View Coll., Dallas, 1995-98, tech Mus. Innovation project San Jose, 1995-98, Fine Arts Bldg., Greenhill Sch., Addison, Tex., 1996-97, Miami (Fla.) Internat. Airport Project, 1996, Criminal Justice Ctr. Project, Phoenix, 1996, Ft. Lauderdale Internat. Airport Project, 1996, Place of Origin project Aberdeenshire, Scotland, 1997, Esquire Plaza Project, sacramento, 1997, Memphis Ctr. Libr., 1997, numerous pvt. residences. Panelist broward County Pub. Art and Design Program, Ft. Lauderdale, Fla., 1996; mem. pub. art adv. com. City of Dallas, 1996. Recipient Kessler award for excellence in urban design City of Dallas, 1995, Artist/Craftsmanship award AIA, 1995, Preservation award St. Paul Preservation Com. and St. Paul chpt. AIA, 1994, Am. Soc. Landscape Artitects Honor award, 1978. Fellow Dallas Inst. Humanities and Culture. Recipient Kessler Award Excellence in Urban Design, City of Dallas, 1995, Artist/Craftsmanship award AIA, 1995, Preservation award St. Paul Preservation Com. and St. Paul chpt. AIA, 1994, Honor award Am. Soc. Landscape Architects, 1978.

GOLDBERG, DAVID ALAN, investment banker, lawyer; b. N.Y.C., Oct. 31, 1933; s. Joseph R. and Rose (Trutt) G.; m. Victoria Liebson, July 7, 1957 (div. Mar. 1976); children: Eric S., Jeremy P. A.B. magna cum laude, Harvard U., 1954, J.D., 1957, postgrad. in bus. adminstrn, 1956-57. Bar: N.Y. 1958. Counsel firm R.W. Pressprich & Co., Inc., N.Y.C., 1958-64, gen. partner, 1965-68, exec. v.p., 1968-78, also chmn. exec. com.; bd. dirs. Charterhouse Assocs., Ltd., Gen. Atomics, Gen. Atomics Techs. Corp., Newbridge, Inc. Trustee Beth Israel Med. Center, N.Y.C. Served with AUS, 1957-58. Mem. Harvard Club (N.Y.C.), Phi Beta Kappa. Home: 750 Park Ave New York NY 10021-4252

GOLDBERG, DAVID BRYAN, biomedical researcher; b. San Bernardino, Calif., Mar. 29, 1954; s. Gus and Rose (Goldrich) G.; m. Dianne Rae, Dec. 19, 1976; children: Jason, Mark, Eric, Ashley. BA, UCLA, 1976, PhD, 1987. Rsch. asst. Calif. State U., L.A., 1976-79; rsch. assoc. UCLA, 1979-82; sci. project mgr. Alpha Therapeutic Corp., L.A., 1989—; adj. prof. Chaffey Coll., Alta Loma, Calif., 1990—. Contbr. articles to N.Y. Acad. Scis., Jour. Clin. Apheresis, Proceedings of ASCO, FASEB Jour., Fedn. Preceedings, Nat. Hemophelia Found. Mem. PTA, Alta Loma, 1991. Basic Rsch. grantee, Cancer Rsch. Ctr., 1987, 88, Cancer Seed grantee 1989; Teaching fellow, UCLA, 1982-87, Rsch. fellow II, City of Hope, Duarte, Calif., 1987-89. Mem. Fedn. Am. Socs. Experimental Biology, N.Y. Acad. Sci. Achievements include patents; development of IL-2/LAK immunotherapy for the treatment of malignant melanoma; formulation chemistry; pharmaceutical product and device development. Office: Alpha Therapeutic Corp 1213 John Reed Ct La Puente CA 91745-2405

GOLDBERG, DAVID CHARLES, computer company executive; b. Los Angeles, Feb. 26, 1940; s. David and Hazel Madeline (Lucatorta) G.; m. Jolane Kay Bjork, Aug. 11, 1962 (div. Jan. 1979); children: Deborah Dawn, Jennifer Lyn. AA in Math. and Sci., Santa Monica Coll., 1969; BSBA, Sacramento State Coll., 1972. Technician Gen. Plastics, L.A., 1961-62, Honeywell Computer Control Co., L.A., 1962-65; mgr. br. customer engring. Sperry Univac, RCA, Sacramento, Calif., 1965-74; mgr. gen. svcs. comm. sys. and svcs., TRW, Hawthorne, Calif., 1974-79; mgr. west region Info. Internat. Inc., Culver City, Calif., 1979-81; v.p., gen. mgr. Data Sys. Svcs. divsn. Contel, Marina Del Rey, 1981-92; v.p. A.M. Shine Electric, Inc., Woodland Hills, Calif., 1992-95; br. mgr. Omnidata Corp., Westlake Village, Calif., 1995-97; v.p. ops. tech. scis. divsn. Pulsar Data Sys., Lanham, Md., 1997-1998; reg. man. Halifax tech. svcs., Los Alamos, N.Mex., 1998—. Pres. Gates Square Homeowners Assn., Redondo Beach, Calif., 1982-84; mem. adv. com., high tech. dept. Indian Hills C.C., Ottumwa, Iowa, computer tech. dept. Pierce Coll., Woodland Hills, Calif., 1985-92. Served with U.S. Army, 1957-66. Mem. Assn. Field Svc. Mgrs., Ind. Svc. Network Internat., Aza Club. Republican. Home: PO Box 906 Los Alamos NM 87544-0906 Office: 1627 Central Ave Ste A Los Alamos NM 87544-3018

GOLDBERG, DAVID MEYER, biochemistry educator; b. Glasgow, Scotland, Aug. 30, 1933; emigrated to Can., 1975; s. Samuel Simon and Ethel (Elyan) G.; m. Pearl Gertrude Goldberg; children: Susan Simone, Tanya Marion. BSc with honors in Biochemistry, U. Glasgow, 1959, MB, ChB, 1959, PhD, 1966, MD, 1974. Intern Stobhill Hosp., Glasgow, 1960, So. Gen. Hosp., Glasgow, 1961; resident Western Infirmary, Glasgow, 1962-66; prof. dept. clin. biochemistry U. Toronto, Can., 1975—, chmn., 1977-88; biochemist-in-chief dept. biochemistry Hosp. for Sick Children, Toronto, 1975-88; cons. chem. pathology and hon. lectr. United Sheffield Hosp., U. Sheffield, Eng., 1967-75. Joint editor-in-chief Clin. Biochemistry, 1982-94, Critical Revs. Clin. Lab. Scis., 1992—; mem. editl. bd. Enzyme, 1978-89, Clin. Chimica Acta, 1981—, Clin. Biochem. Physiology, 1982-96, Clin. Chemistry, 1986-88, Jour. Clin. Lab. Analysis, 1987—, Am. Jour. Enology

Viticulture, 1995—, Jour. Agrl. Food Chemistry, 1999—; mem. editl. bd. European Jour. Lab. Medicine, 1993, assoc. editor, 1994—. Recipient Van Slyke award Am. Assn. Clin. Chemistry, 1982; recipient Roman award Australian Assn. Clin. Chemists, 1983, Nova Idea prize Italian Soc. Clin. Pathologists, 1985, Norman Kubasick award Am. Assn. Clin. Chemistry, 1996. Mem. Can. Soc. Clin. Chemists (Ames award 1990, Beckman award 1999), Can. Assn. Med. Biochemists, Can. Soc. Clin. Investigation, Internat. Soc. Clin. Enzymology (pres. 1995—), Can. Atherosclerosis Soc. (chmn. edn. com. 1994-97). Jewish. Home: 9 Harrison Rd, Willowdale, ON Canada M2L 1V3 Office: U Toronto Banting Inst, 100 College St, Toronto, ON Canada M5G 1L5

GOLDBERG, EDWARD DAVIDOW, geochemist, educator; b. Sacramento, Aug. 2, 1921; s. Edward Davidow and Lillian (Rothholz) G.; m. Kathe Bertine, Dec. 26, 1973; children—David Wilkes, Wendy Jean, Kathi Kiri, Beck Bertine. B.S., U. Calif.-Berkeley, 1942; Ph.D., U. Chgo., 1949. Mem. faculty Scripps Instn. Oceanography, La Jolla, Calif., 1949—, prof. chemistry, 1960—; provost Revelle Coll., U. Calif. at San Diego, 1965-66; condr. research and author publs. on subjects including marine pollution, chem. composition of sea water, sediments, marine organisms, environmental management; vis. prof. chemistry U. Otago Dunedin, New Zealand, 1988. Author: (with J. Geiss) Earth Sciences and Meteorites, 1964, Guide to Marine Pollution, 1972, North Sea Science, 1973, The Sea: Marine Chemistry, vol. V, 1974, The Health of the Oceans, 1976, Black Carbon in the Environment, 1985, Coastal Zone Space: Prelude to Conflict, 1994; contbr. articles to profl. jours. Recipient B.H. Ketchum award Woods Hole Oceanographic Instn., 1984, Ruth Patrick award for environ. problem solving Am. Soc. Limnology and Oceanography, 1999; co-recipient Tyler prize U. So. Calif., 1989; Guggenheim fellow, 1961, NATO fellow, 1970; NAS exch. scholar, 1987. Fellow Am. Geophys. Union, AAAS; mem. Geochem. Soc., U.S. Acad. Scis., Sigma Xi. Home: 750 Val Sereno Dr Encinitas CA 92024-6919

GOLDBERG, EDWARD JAY, general contractor; b. Atlanta, Apr. 30, 1950; s. J. Elliott and Sarah (Spiegelman) G.; m. Susan Ellen Jacobson, Dec. 19, 1976; children: Marc Samuel, Robin Beth, Allison Gayle. BS in Fin., U. Ga., 1972. Acctg. coordinator Panasonic, Atlanta, 1972-76; account supr. Oscar Mayer Co., Birmingham, Ala., 1976-81; pres. Alscan, Inc., Birmingham, 1981—. Mem. Birminahm Mus. Art, 1987, Birmingham Symphony Orch., 1987; bd. dirs. Temple Beth-El, Young Leadership Cabinet; v.p. Birmingham Jewish Fedn., 1992-93, gen. campaign chmn., 1993-95, pres., 1998—; bd. dirs., treas. Birmingham Jewish Day Sch.; chmn. ways and means Birmingham Jewish Cmty. Ctr. Mem. Am. Soc. Indsl. Security, Associated Gen. Contractors, Ala. Alarm Assn., Birmingham C. of C., Pine Tree Country Club, B'nai B'rith (v.p. 1981-83). Jewish. Avocations: golf, organizational work. Home: 3504 Branch Mill Rd Birmingham AL 35223-1608 Office: Alscan Inc 237 Oxmoor Cir Ste 101 Birmingham AL 35209-6480

GOLDBERG, EDWARD L., financial services executive; b. Bklyn., May 27, 1940; s. Louis Goldberg and Rose (Galina) Rosenson; m. Carol Weinberg, Jan. 25, 1964; children: Ira, Seth, Erica. Grad. high sch., Bklyn., 1958. With Merrill Lynch, N.Y.C., 1961—, sr. v.p. equity markets, 1988-91, regional dir. nat. sales, 1986-88, exec. v.p. ops., svcs. and tech., 1991—. Sgt. USAR, 1961-66. Office: Merrill Lynch & Co Inc North Tower World Fin Ctr New York NY 10281-1332*

GOLDBERG, FRED SELLMANN, advertising executive; b. Chgo., Jan. 22, 1941; s. Sydney Norman and Birdie (Cohen) G.; m. Jerrilyn Toby Tager, Apr. 12, 1964; children—Robin Lynn, Susanne Joy. B.S., U. Vt., 1962; M.B.A., NYU, 1964. Mktg. research mgr. P. Ballantine & Sons, Newark, 1964-67; sr. v.p., mgmt. supr. Young & Rubicam, N.Y.C., 1967-78; sr. v.p., gen. mgr. Young & Rubicam, Los Angeles, 1978-82; exec. v.p., gen. mgr. Chiat-Day, Inc., San Francisco, 1982-85; exec. v.p., chief operation officer Chiat-Day, Advt., L.A., 1985-87; pres., chief exec. officer San Francisco office Chiat-Day, Inc., San Francisco; vice chmn. Chiat/Day Advt., Inc., L.A., 1987-90; founder, chmn., CEO Goldberg Moser O'Neill Advt., San Francisco, 1990—. Republican. Jewish. Avocations: tennis, music, running. Office: Goldberg Moser O'Neill 77 Maiden Ln San Francisco CA 94108-5414

GOLDBERG, GERALD JAY, writer, educator; b. N.Y.C., Dec. 30, 1929. BS, Purdue U., 1952; MA, NYU, 1954; PhD, U. Minn., 1958. Tchg. asst., instr. U. Minn., Mpls., 1954-57; instr., asst. prof. Dartmouth Coll., 1958-64; asst. prof. UCLA, 1964-67, assoc. prof., 1968-73, prof. English and Am. lit., 1974-91, prof. emeritus, 1991—; adv. panelist NEH TV series The Am. Short Story, 1975-81; lectr. Harvard U., 1979, U. Rennes, 1963, U. Valencia; vis. prof. Queens Coll., 1985-87, Williams Coll., 1981. Author: (fiction) Notes from the Diaspora, 1962, The National Standard, 1968, The Lynching of Orin Newfield, 1970 (N.Y. Times Book of Yr., Pulitzer prize nomination), 126 Days of Continuous Sunshine, 1972, Heart Payments, 1982; (non-fiction) (with Nancy Marmer Goldberg) The Modern Critical Spectrum, 1962, The Fate of Innocence, 1965, (with Lionel Trilling, Ihab Hassan, Karl Keller and Clifton Fadiman) American Literature Since 1945, 1971, (with Robert Goldberg) Anchors: Brokaw, Jennings, Rather and the Evening News, 1990, (with Robert Goldberg) Citizen Turner: The Wild Rise of an American Tycoon, 1995; contbr. short stories, revs. to profl. publs. Fulbright prof., 1962-63; fellow U. Calif. Inst. Arts, 1966-67, U. Calif., 1976-77;. Mem. PEN, Authors Guild.

GOLDBERG, HAROLD SEYMOUR, electrical engineer, educator; b. Bklyn., Jan. 22, 1925; s. David and Rose (Maslow) G.; m. Florence Meyerson, May 29, 1949 (dec.); children: Lawrence, Irene. BEE (Schweinberg scholar), Cooper Union, 1944; MEE, Poly. Inst. Bklyn., 1949; student, Columbia U. Engring. draftsman Cole Electric Products Co., 1944-45; radio engr. Press Wireless, Inc., 1945-47; asst. project engr. Radio Receptor Co., 1947-48; project engr. No. Radio Co., 1948-50; mgr. prodn. test, test equipment design sects. Allen B. DuMont Labs., Inc., 1950-56; mgr. engring. fabrication dept. Emerson Radio & Phonograph Corp., 1956-57; chief devel. engr. Consol. Avionics Corp., Westbury, N.Y., 1957-59; engring. mgr. data systems EPSCO, Inc., Cambridge, Mass., 1959-62; v.p. research Lexington Instruments Corp., Waltham, Mass., 1962- 66; prin. research engr. AVCO-Research div., Everett, Mass., 1966-68; ops. mgr. Orion Research Inc., 1968-70; v.p. applications Analogic Corp., Wakefield, Mass., 1970-71; ops. mgr. Data Precision Corp., Danvers, Mass., 1971-72; pres. Data Precision Corp., 1972-82; v.p. Analogic Corp., 1979-85; pres. Acrosystems Corp., Beverly, Mass., 1984-88; assoc. dean Gordon Inst., Wakefield, Mass., 1988-92; assoc. dean Gordon Inst. Tufts U., Medford, Mass., 1992-93; lectr. Tufts U., 1993—; cons. Analogic Corp., 1988—. Served with AUS, 1945-47. Recipient award of distinction Poly. Inst. N.Y., 1980, John Fluke Sr. Pioneer award, 1989, Haraden Pratt award, IEEE, 1993, Allen Ploss award Electro, 1992; N.Y. State Vets scholar, 1957. Fellow IEEE (chmn. Boston group on medicine and biology 1965-66, exec. com. Boston sect. 1967-69, vice-chmn. Boston 1969-70, chmn. Boston 1970-71, internat. bd. dirs. 1971-75, 89-90, v.p. 1975, dir. Electro 1975-89, editor Reflector 1976—, treas. tech. activities bd. 1991, chmn. tech. bd. pub. rels. com. 1992-96, citation of honor U.S. activities bd. 1978, Region 1 award 1994); mem. Instrumentation and Measurement Soc. IEEE (sec.-treas. 1983, pres. 1985-87, columnist mag. 1994—, gen. chmn. tech. conf. 1995, Disting. Svc. award 1988), Tau Beta Pi. Office: 8 Centennial Dr Peabody MA 01960-7902 *The highest achievement to which a person can aspire is that the world be a better place after he leaves it than before and that this be partly the result of his contributions to it.*

GOLDBERG, HARRIET DAVID, urban planner; b. N.Y.C., June 21, 1935; d. Henry and Sadie (Adelson) David; m. Victor J. Goldberg, June 1, 1958; children: Susan Goldberg Gevertz, Alan Jay. BA, Brown U., 1956; MA in Urban Planning, Hunter Coll., 1980. Exec. dir. YM-YWHA Neighborhood Preservation Co., Mount Vernon, N.Y., 1982-84; trustee Village of Scarsdale, N.Y., 1984-88, dep. mayor, 1987-88, chmn. planning bd., 1988-94; pres. League of Women Voters of Westchester, White Plains, N.Y., 1995-97; v.p. League of Women Voters of N.Y. State, 1997—. Trustee Scarsdale Found., 1994—; chair planning com. United Way Westchester-Putnam, White Plains, 1995—; bd. dirs. Westchester Residential Opportunities, White Plains, 1988—, Westchester Interfaith Housing Corp., Hawthorne, N.Y., 1990—. Home: 17 Chesterfield Rd Scarsdale NY 10583-1629

GOLDBERG, HARVEY, financial executive; b. Bklyn., Jan. 30, 1940; s. Joseph and Regina (Goldkrantz) G.; m. Joyce Baron, Nov. 22, 1962; children: Keith, Jodi. BS in Acctg., Bklyn. Coll., 1962; postgrad., CCNY, 1963. CPA, N.Y. Sr. acct. Schwartz, Zelin & Weiss CPA's, N.Y.C., 1962-66; mgr. fin. analysis Columbia Records div. CBS, Inc., N.Y.C., 1966-70; asst. controller Revlon, Inc., N.Y.C., 1970-71; treas. Ctrl. Textile, Inc., Jersey City, 1971-74; controller Marcade Group, Inc., Jersey City, 1974-81, v.p., controller, 1981-86; v.p., CFO Paul Marshall Products, Inc., subs. Marcade Group, Long Beach, Calif., 1982-86; v.p., CFO Player's Internat., Inc., Calabasas, Calif., 1988-93, sr. v.p., CFO, 1988-93; exec. v.p., CFO Adesso, Inc., Culver City, Calif., 1994-98; CFO, dir. Hollywood Beauty Corp., Encino, Calif., 1997-99; CFO YellowOnline.Com, L.A., 1999—. County committeeman Monmouth County Dem. Com., N.J., 1979-80; chmn. adv. bd. High Point Ctr., Marlboro, N.J., 1978-82; mem. Marlboro Twp. Bd. Edn., 1980-82, v.p., 1981-82; bd. dirs. Family Consultation Ctr., Freehold, N.J., 1982-83. Mem. AICPA, N.Y. State Soc. CPA's. Home: 19798 Greenbriar Dr Tarzana CA 91356-5442 Office: YellowOnline.Com 3700 Wilshire Blvd Ste 1020 Los Angeles CA 90010

GOLDBERG, HERB, psychologist, educator; b. Berlin, Germany, July 14, 1937; came to U.S., 1941; s. Jacob and Ella (Nagler) G.; 1 child, Amy Elisabeth. BA cum laude, CUNY, 1958; PhD, Adelphi U., 1963. Lic. psychologist, Calif. Pvt. practice, L.A., 1965—; prof. Calif. State U., L.A. Author: Creative Aggression, 1972, The Hazards of Being Male, 1976, Money Madness, 1978, The New Male, 1979, The Inner Male, 1986, The New Male/Female Relationship, 1982, What Men Really Want, 1991. Mem. APA, Phi Beta Kappa. Office: 3739 Mayfair Dr Los Angeles CA 90065-3208

GOLDBERG, HILLEL, rabbi, educator; b. Denver, Jan. 10, 1946; s. Max and Miriam (Harris) G.; m. Elaine Silberstein, May 19, 1969; children: Tehilla, Temima, Mattis, Shayna, Tiferet, Chaim. BA, Yeshiva U., 1969; MA, Brandeis U., 1972, PhD, 1978. Ordained rabbi, 1976. Lectr. Machzeke Torah Inst., Brookline, Mass., 1971-71, 75, Jerusalem Coll. for Women, 1973-75, 77, The Hebrew U., 1978-85, Jerusalem Torah Coll., 1979-82; Halakhic adviser Torah MaMidbar and Pardes Israel, Santa Fe, 1986-96; exec. editor Intermountain Jewish News, Denver, 1966—; bd. dirs. Rofeh Internat., Boston. Author: Israel Salanter: Text, Structure, Idea (Acad. Book of Yr. 1982), The Fire Within, 1987, Between Berlin and Slobodka, 1989, Illuminating the Generations, 1991; editor: In Honor of Walter Wurzburger, 1989; assoc. editor Tradition, 1988—; contbg. editor Jewish Action, 1987—; mem. editorial bd. Jewish Tradition, Jerusalem, 1990—. Vol. Head Start, Oakland, Calif., 1964-65, Harlem, N.Y., 1965-66; founder Torah Cmty. Project, Denver, 1986—; legis. com. mem. Colo. Press Assn., 1990—; sci. adv. com. mem. Nat. Assn. for Rsch. and Therapy of Homosexuality, 1997—; bd. dirs. Open Door Youth Gang Alternatives. Grantee Meml. Found. for Jewish Culture, 1972-74. Mem. Am. Hist. Assn., Am. Jewish Press Assn. (Rockower awards 1983, 85, 89, 91-94, 96-97, rec. sec. 1989-91), Rabbinical Coun. Am., Nat. Assn. Rudimental Drummers, Assn. for Jewish Studies. Office: Intermountain Jewish News 1275 Sherman St #214 Denver CO 80203

GOLDBERG, HOMER BERYL, English language educator; b. Chgo., Feb. 4, 1924; married, 1956; 2 children. AB, U. Chgo., 1947, AM, 1948, PhD in English, 1961. Instr. English U. Chgo., 1950-54, asst. prof., 1954-60; asst. prof. Haverford (Pa.) Coll., 1960-61; assoc. prof. SUNY, Stony Brook, 1961-70, prof. English, 1970-88, Disting. teaching prof., 1988—, emeritus, 1991—; Fulbright lectr., Italy, 1956-57; dir. NDEA English Inst., 1965-66; editl. cons. L.I. Rsch. Inst., 1992—. Author: The Art of Joseph Andrews, 1969; editor: Norton Critical Edition of Joseph Andrews and Shamela, 1987; contbr. articles to profl. jours. Mem. Suffolk County Campaign Fin. Bd., 1999—. Recipient Chancellor's award for Excellence in Teaching SUNY, 1973, Pres.'s award for Excellence in Teaching SUNY, 1987, others; faculty rsch. fellow SUNY, 1962, 67, 69. Mem. MLA. Office: SUNY Dept English Stony Brook NY 11794-5350

GOLDBERG, ICCHOK IGNACY, retired special education educator; b. Warsaw, Poland, Mar. 6, 1916; came to U.S., 1948, naturalized, 1958; s. Chaim and Ita (Majerczak) G; m. Diana R. Solarsh, Feb. 2, 1948; 1 child, Vivian S. Magister Philosophiae, U. Warsaw, 1938; MA, Columbia U., 1949, EdD, 1952; LHD (hon.), U. Colo., 1982. Tchr. secondary schs. Warsaw, 1937-39; press attache, info. officer Polish Consulate, Johannesburg, S.Africa, 1944-46; sales mgr. M. Golante, wholesale mcht., Johannesburg, 1946-48; instr. depts. psychol. founds. and spl. edn. Columbia Tchrs. Coll., N.Y.C., 1950-53, asst. dir. mental retardation project, 1957-61, assoc. prof. edn., 1957-63, prof. edn., 1963-79, prof. emeritus, 1979—; dir. dept. rehab. Muscatatuck State Sch., Butlerville, Ind., 1953-56; ednl. cons. Nat. Assn. Retarded Children, N.Y.C., 1956-57; lectr. Wis. State Coll., summer 1954, Ind. U., 1955-56, George Peabody Coll. for Tchrs., summer 1957, U. Kans., summer 1957; instr. Tex. Women's U., summer 1960; vis. prof. U. Alaska, 1962, Monash U., Australia, 1972, Fla. Internat. U., Miami, 1978; cons. spl. edn., vocat. rehab. Woods Sch., Longhorne, Pa.; asst. examiner N.Y.C. Bd. Edn., 1961; chmn. sub-com. edn., recreation, vocat. tng. in instns. Pres.' Panel Mental Retardation, 1961; chmn. com. couns. history Coun. for Exceptional Children, 1957-61; participant White Ho. Conf. Edn., 1965; sec.-treas. Internat. Assn. Scientific Study Mental Deficiency. Co-author: Right to Education, 1973; contbr. articles to profl. jours. Bd. dirs. United Cerebral Palsy Assn.; adv. bd. N.Y. Assn. for Help Retarded Children, Healing Community, Maimonides Inst. With Polish Forces, 1941-44. Decorated Polish Cross Valor. Fellow Am. Assn. Mental Deficiency (past pres.); mem. AAUP, Coun. Exceptional Children (life, gov.-at-large 1950-64), Phi Delta Kappa. Home: 901 S Surf Rd Apt 307 Hollywood FL 33019-2147

GOLDBERG, IRA JAY, internist, educator; b. Elizabeth, N.J., Mar. 11, 1949; m. Ina N. Cholst; children: Sarah Cholst and Jacob Cholst (twins). BS, MIT, 1971; MD, Harvard U., Boston, 1975. Diplomate Am. Bd. Internal Medicine, Am. Bd. Endocrinology and Metabolism. Intern NYU-Bellevue Hosp. Med. Ctr., N.Y.C., 1975-76, jr. and sr. resident in medicine, 1976-78; fellow in endocrinology and metabolism Mt. Sinai Sch. Medicine, N.Y.C., 1978-79, fellow in arteriosclerosis and metabolism, 1979-81, instr. medicine, 1981-83; asst. prof. medicine Columbia U. Coll. Physicians and Surgeons, N.Y.C., 1983-90, assoc. prof., 1990-96, prof., 1996—, acting dir. Inst. Human Nutrition, 1995; asst. attending physician dept. medicine Columbia-Presbyn. Med. Ctr., 1983-90, assoc. attending physician, 1990—, assoc. dir. Arteriosclerosis Rsch. Ctr., 1985—; tchr. Lipid Clinic, Overlook Hosp., 1987-91; vis. prof. U. Rennes, France, 1993; Merck Frosst-McGill lectr. lipid metabolism McGill U., Montreal, Que., Can., 1993; spkr. Gordon Conf. on Lipoprotein Metabolism, 1992, spkr., session chmn., 1996, 98; spkr. Lofland Conf. on Atherosclerosis, 1993, Gordon Conf. on Atherosclerosis, 1995; spkr. Internat. Arteriosclerosis Soc., 1994, 97, session chmn., 1997; spkr. Baker Symposium on Cardiovasc. Disease, Melbourne, Australia, 1997; also others; editl. reviewer Jour. Clin. Investigation, Jour. Biol. Chemistry, Jour. Lipid Rsch., Am. Jour. Physiology, Arteriosclerosis and Thrombosis, New Eng. Jour. Medicine; mem. editl. bd. Jour. Clin. Endocrinology and Metabolism; ad hoc reviewer grant revs. metabolism study section Nat. Heart, Lung and Blood Inst., 1992-93, 96, 97, mem. spl. rev. com. for clin. investigator and physician scientist awards, 1987, 92, 94; cons. ong rant revs. to VA Health Svcs. and Rsch. Adminstrn., 1997, also others. Contbr. over 75 articles and revs. to med. jours., also numerous chpts. to books. Recipient established scientist award N.Y. Heart Assn., 1980-94; grantee NIH-Nat. Heart, Blood and Lung Inst., 1990-95, 96—, Schering Pharm. Corp., 1990-94, Coun. for Tobacco Rsch., 1991-94, Am. Heart Assn., 1990-93. Mem. ACP, AAAS, Am. Fedn. for Clin. Rsch., Am. Soc. for Clin. Investigation, Am. Heart Assn. (fellow coun. on arteriosclerosis, nutrition com. 1997—, nat. program com. 1997—, session chmn. ann. sci. sessions 1988, 90, 91, 93, 95-97, chmn. com. on cholesterol edn. N.Y.C. affiliate, mem. coun. profl. edn. com., bd. dirs. 1993-99, chmn. peer rev. com. 1995-97, bd. dirs. heritage entity 1998—, Clinician-Scientist award 1981-86), N.Y. Lipid Club (pres. 1992-93). Fax: 212-305-5384. E-mail: IJG3@columbia.edu. Office: Columbia U Coll Phys & Surg Divsn Prev Med-Nutrition 630 W 168th St New York NY 10032-3702

GOLDBERG, IRVING HYMAN, molecular pharmacology and biochemistry educator; b. Hartford, Conn., Sept. 2, 1926; s. Morris Wolfe and Rose (Krechevsky) G.; m. Margaret Field Ziskin, Apr. 15, 1956; children: Daniel Eliot, Nancy Elizabeth. BS, Trinity Coll., 1949; MD, Yale U., 1953; PhD, Rockefeller U., 1960; AM (hon.), Harvard U., 1964. Intern Columbia-Presbyn. Med. Ctr., N.Y.C., 1953-54; asst. resident, chief resident, instr. medicine Columbia-Presbyn. Med. Ctr. (Coll. Phys. and Surgs.), 1954-57; asst. prof. medicine, biochemistry U. Chgo., 1960-64, assoc. prof., 1964; assoc. prof. medicine Med. Sch. Harvard, 1964-68; prof. medicine Med. Sch. Harvard U., 1968—, chmn. div. med. scis. Faculty Arts and Scis., 1968-70, Gustavus Adolphus Pfeiffer prof. pharmacology, 1972-83, chmn. dept. pharm., 1972-86, Otto Krayer prof. pharmacology, 1983-86, Otto Krayer prof. biol. chemistry and molecular pharmacology, 1986—; chief endocrinology-metabolism unit Beth Israel Hosp., 1964-68, physician, 1964-72, mem. bd. consultation in medicine, 1972—; cons. in pharmacology Dana-Farber Cancer Inst., Boston, 1980-87; mem. rev. panel internat. program Howard Hughes Med. Inst., 1994; cons. in clin. pharmacology Children's Hosp. Med. Ctr., Boston, 1972-91; mem. rsch. com. Med. Found., Boston, 1968-77; mem. exptl. therapeutics study sect. NIH, 1974-77; mem. com. proposed legis. to restructure FDA Assembly Life Scis., NAS-NRC, Inst. Medicine, 1976; mem. sci. adv. com. Damon Runyon-Walter Winchell Cancer Fund, 1982-86; mem. life scis. panel NRC, 1992-93. Mem. editorial bd. Endocrinology, 1964-68, Antimicrobial Agents and Chemotherapy, 1974-88; hon. editorial adv. bd. Jour. Biochem. Pharmacology, 1973-84; mem. editorial adv. bd. Biochemistry, 1986-97. Rev. panel mem. Internat. Program Howard Hughes Med. Inst., 1994. Served with USNR, 1945-46. Recipient Faculty Research award Am. Cancer Soc., 1960-71; Guggenheim fellow dept. genetics Oxford (Eng.) U., 1970-71; sr. fellow Trinity Coll., 1974-76. Mem. Inst. Medicine NAS, Am. Soc. Biochemistry and Molecular Biology, Am. Soc. Clin. Investigation, Am. Acad. Arts and Scis., Assn. of Am. Physicians, Am. Chem. Soc., Am. Soc. Pharmacology and Therapeutics (Otto Krayer award 1994), Am. Soc. Microbiology, Brit. Pharm. Soc., Phi Beta Kappa, Sigma Xi, Alpha Omega Alpha. Home: 987 Memorial Dr Apt 472 Cambridge MA 02138-5737 Office: Harvard U Med Sch 25 Shattuck St Boston MA 02115-6027

GOLDBERG, IVAN BAER, real estate executive; b. Newport News, Va., Apr. 20, 1939; s. David and Sara (Levy) G.; m. Mary Linda Caffee, Oct. 27, 1968 (div. 1978); children: Stephen Morris, Michael Scott. Student, U. Va., 1957-58, Coll. of William and Mary, 1958-60. Exec. v.p. Bedding Supply Co., Inc., Newport News, 1961-72; sec.-treas. Mut. Realty Corp., Newport News, 1972—; pres. Goldkress Corp., Newport News, 1972—; gen. ptnr. Goldkress Investment Co., Newport News, 1972—; bd. dirs. Goldkress Corp., Mut. Realty Corp. With USCGR, 1962. Mem. Newport News-Hampton Bd. Realtors, Nat. Assn. Realtors. Jewish. Home: 15 Ferguson Cv Newport News VA 23606-2016 Office: Mut Realty Corp 11116 Jefferson Ave Newport News VA 23601-2551

GOLDBERG, IVAN D., microbiologist, educator; b. Phila., May 13, 1934; s. Max and Frances Goldberg; m. Noveta McCracken, July 27, 1979; children—Micki, Judy, Lisa; stepchildren—Nick, Vikki Russell. A.B., U. Pa., 1956; Ph.D., U. Ill., 1961. Postdoctoral fellow Rutgers U., 1961-62; postdoctoral Oreg. State U., 1962-63; NRC postdoctoral research assoc. U.S. Army Biol. Labs., Frederick, Md., 1963-65, microbial geneticist, 1965-71; assoc. prof. dept. microbiology U. Kans. Sch. Medicine, Kansas City, 1971-77, prof., 1977—. Contbr. articles to profl. jours. NIH grantee; recipient Leroy D. Fothergill Sci. award, 1970. Mem. Am. Soc. Microbiology (pres. Mo. Valley br. 1974), Sigma Xi. Democrat. Jewish. Home: 14409 W 90th Ter Shawnee Mission KS 66215-2917 Office: 3901 Rainbow Blvd Kansas City KS 66160-0001*

GOLDBERG, JACK, hematologist; b. Ulm, Germany, Feb. 7, 1948; came to U.S., 1952; s. Isaac and Mary (Selitska) G.; m. Doreen, July 28, 1970; children: Joshua, Alexis. BA, Boston U., 1969; MD, SUNY, 1973. From asst. prof. medicine to prof. medicine SUNY Health Sci. Ctr., Syracuse, 1977-89; prof. medicine Robert Wood Johnson Med. Sch., Camden, N.J., 1989—, Am. Cancer Soc. prof. clin. oncology, 1992—; prof. med. Coriell Inst. for Med. Rsch., Camden, 1990—; med. dir. blood bank Cooper Hosp., Camden, 1990—, head divsn. hematology/oncology, 1989—; med. dir. CorCell, Camden, 1996—; head Cooper Cancer Inst., 1998—. V.p. N.J. divsn. Am. Cancer Soc., 1989—; vol. Leukemia Soc., Camden, 1990—. Fellow Am. Coll. Medicine. Jewish. Avocations: exercise, travel. Office: Cooper Health Sys 3 Cooper Plz Camden NJ 08103-1438

GOLDBERG, JACKIE, councilwoman; b. L.A.; 1 child, Brian. Tchr. Compton and L.A. Unified Sch. Dists.; instr. Calif. State U.; city councilwoman City of L.A., 1993—; chairwoman Personnel Com.; vice chairwoman Intergovt. Rels. Office: LA City Coun 200 N Main St Rm 408 Los Angeles CA 90012-4804*

GOLDBERG, JANE G., psychoanalyst; b. New Orleans, May 31, 1946; d. Meyer and Madeleine Malvina (Levy) Goldberg; children: Molly Malvina. BA, Washington U., 1968; postgrad., Pratt Inst., 1969-72; MA, New Sch. for Social Rsch., 1971; PhD, CUNY, 1978. Lic. psychologist, N.Y.; cert. psychoanalyst N.Y., psychoanalytic psychotherapist, N.Y. Pvt. practice psychotherapy and psychoanalysis N.Y., N.J., 1973—, pvt. practice supervision psychotherapy and psychoanalysis, 1980—; staff psychotherapist art therapy program Hillside Hosp., Queens, N.Y., 1970-72, Advanced Ctr. for Psychotherapy, Jamaica, N.Y., 1974-81; rsch. assoc. dept. psychology New Sch. for Social Rsch. Grad. Faculty, N.Y.C., 1971-72, dept. med. oncology Kingsbrook Jewish Med. Ctr., Bklyn., 1979-80; faculty psychology dept. CUNY, N.Y.C., 1972-76; faculty Fifth Ave. Ctr. for Counseling and Psychotherapy, N.Y.C., 1982-84, Ctr. for Modern Psychoanalytic Studies, N.Y.C., 1984—; mem. faculty Treatment and Referral Svc. N.Y.C., 1984—, Psychoanalytic ctr. N.J., Morristown, 1986—, Boston Ctr. Modern Psychoanalytic Studies, 1986—; lectr. in field. Author: Psychotherapeutic Treatment of Cancer Patients, 1982, Deceits of the Mind (and their effects on the body), 1991, The Dark Side of Love: the positive role of our negative emotions, 1993, The La Casa Whole Health Handbook and Cookbook, 1997, Inspirations, 1999; mng. editor: Modern Psychoanalysis; column writer: "News and Notes" in Modern Psychoanalysis; TV talk show co-host: "Schmoozing," N.Y.C.; numerous mag. and newspapers interviews; numerous TV and radio appearances; contbr. articles to profl. jours. Asst. to exec. dir. Found. for the Advancement of Cancer Therapies; dir. La Casa de Vida Natural, Rio Grande, P.R., 1987—, La Casa Day Spa, N.Y.C., 1993—. Home: 41 E 20th St New York NY 10003-1324

GOLDBERG, JAY, lawyer; b. N.Y.C., Jan. 2, 1933; s. Joseph and Lillian (Adler) G.; m. Rema, Dec. 27, 1959; children: Justin, Julie. BA, Bklyn. Coll., 1954; JD, Harvard U., 1957. Bar: N.Y. 1957, U.S. Ct. Appeals (2d, 4th and 9th cirs.) 1971, U.S. Supreme Ct. 1961. Asst. dist. atty. N.Y. County Dist. Atty. Office, N.Y.C., 1957-61; spl. asst. to atty. gen. Washington, 1961-63; spl. asst. to U.S. Atty. no. dist. Hammond, Ind., 1961-67; lawyer, sole practice N.Y.C., 1963—; lectr. trial practice Harvard Law Sch., 1976-88; com. on grievances U.S. Dist. Ct. (so. dist.) N.Y., 1989—. Editorial mgr. White Collar Crime Law Reporter, 1989—; contbr. articles to profl. jours. Recipient Merit award for Advocacy of Individual Rights for Persons Advised, N.Y. Criminal Bar Assn., 1989. Mem. Friars Club (gov. 1988-92). Home: 200 E 65th St New York NY 10021-6603 Office: 250 Park Ave New York NY 10177-0001

GOLDBERG, JOHN ROBERT, information specialist, historian, advocate; b. Indpls., Aug. 8, 1949; s. Samuel Conrad Goldberg and Rosemary Irene (Dyar) Lasky. BA in History, Northwestern U., Evanston, Ill., 1971. Unix adminstr., mgr. info. svcs., programmer Input Telecomm. Midwest Title, Indpls., 1985-90; mgr. info. svcs. Campbell, Kyle and Proffitt, Carmel, Ind., 1992—; cons. programmer Great Lakes Cons., Indpls.; cons. Networks Plus, Indpls. Author papers. Treas. Amnesty Internat., Indpls, 1986-90, fundraising com., 1997—, treas., 1998—. Mem. MENSA, Positive Change Network Host/Guide, Ctrl. Ind. Friends of Jung, Indpls. Computer Soc. Avocations: writing, dancing, guitar, traveling, swimming. Home: 6148 N Oakland Ave Indianapolis IN 46220-5121 Office: Campbell Kyle Proffitt 650 E Carmel Dr Ste 400 Carmel IN 46032-2887

GOLDBERG, JOSEPH PHILIP, government official; b. Bklyn., May 1, 1918; s. Max and Fanny (Steltzer) G.; B.S.S., CCNY, 1937; M.A., Columbia U., 1938, Ph.D., 1950; m. Selma Takiff, Aug. 22, 1943; children: Seth M., Lise A. Instr. econ. history CCNY, 1937-39; high sch. tchr., N.Y.C., 1938-42; economist Bur. Labor Stats., Washington, 1942; econ. adviser Nat. War Labor Bd. and Wage Stblzn. Bd., Washington, 1943-46; labor adviser Office of Housing Expediter, 1946-48; staff dir. joint congl. com., 1948; div. chief Bur. Labor Stats., Labor Dept., Washington, 1949-51, spl. asst. to commr. of labor stats., 1954-86; with Wage Stblzn. Bd., 1951-53; instr. Am. U., 1948-49; research asso. Harvard U., 1957, U. Mich., 1964-69, ILO Inst. Indsl. Relations Studies, 1973—; U.S. del. 22 ILO maritime and internat. labor confs., 1956-85; cons. on maritime industry U.S. Dept. Labor, 1986—. Pres., J.F. Kennedy High Sch. PTA, 1968-69, New Hampshire Estates, 1956-57, trustee schs. Montgomery County, 1957-62, 86—; arbitrator, consumer protection and Health Advocacy Specialist Md. State Atty. Gen.; mediator Washington Mediation Svc., Docent-Smithsonian Inst., 1986—. Recipient research grants Yale Fund, Harvard, U. Mich., Ford Found.; Meritorious Service award Labor Dept., 1963, 85, Commr.'s Eminent Service award, 1973. Mem. Indsl. Relations Research Assn. (pres. D.C. chpt. 1963-64, mem. nat. exec. bd. 1973-76), Am. Econ. Assn., AAAS, Phi Beta Kappa. Author: The Maritime Story, 1958; (with others) Collective Bargaining and Technological Change in American Transportation, Monograph on Modernization in the Maritime Industry, 1971; Productivity Bargaining in the Private Sector, 1975; The Law and Practice of Collective Bargaining, 1976; Frances Perkins, Isadore Lubin and the Bureau of Labor Statistics, 1980; The AFL and a National Bureau of Labor Statistics, 1983; The First One Hundred Years of the Bureau of Labor Statistics, 1985; contbr. articles to profl. jours. Home: 707 Stonington Rd Silver Spring MD 20902-1549 Office: Bicentennial Bldg Washington DC 20212

GOLDBERG, KIRSTEN BOYD, science journalist; b. San Bernardino, Calif., Oct. 29, 1963; d. Jerry Dock and Jewel Marie (Purkiss) Boyd; m. Paul Boris Goldberg, Aug. 25, 1985; children: Katherine, Sarah. BA, U. Calif., Berkeley, 1984. News editor Reston (Va.) Connection, 1985-86; reporter Edn. Week, Washington, 1986-88; assoc. editor Cancer Letter Inc., Washington, 1989-90, editor, pub., 1990—. Editor newsletter The Clin. Cancer Letter. Mem. Nat. Assn. Sci. Writers, Newsletter Pubs. Assn., Soc. Profl. Journalists (Washington Dateline award 1998), D.C. Sci. Writers Assn. Jewish. Office: Cancer Letter Inc PO Box 9905 Washington DC 20016-8905

GOLDBERG, LEE WINICKI, furniture company executive; b. Laredo, Tex., Nov. 20, 1932; d. Frank and Goldie (Ostrowiak) Winicki; student San Diego State U., 1951-52; m. Frank M. Goldberg, Aug. 17, 1952; children: Susan Arlene, Edward Lewis, Anne Carri. With United Furniture Co., Inc., San Diego, 1953-83, corp. sec., dir., 1963-83, dir. environ. interiors, 1970-83; founder Drexel-Heritage store Edwards Interiors, subs. United Furniture, 1975; founding ptnr., v.p. FLJB Corp., 1976-86, founding ptnr., sec. treas., Sea Fin., Inc., 1980, founding ptnr., First Nat. Bank San Diego, 1982. Den mother Boy Scouts Am., San Diego, 1965; vol. Am. Cancer Soc., San Diego, 1964-69; chmn. jr. matrons United Jewish Fedn., San Diego, 1958; del. So. Pacific Coast region Hadassah Conv., 1960, pres. Galilee group San Diego chpt., 1960-61; supporter Marc Chagall Nat. Mus., Nice, France, U. Calif. at San Diego Cancer Ctr. Found., Smithsonian Instn., L.A. County Mus., San Diego Mus. Contemporary Art, San Diego Mus. Art; pres. San Diego Opera, 1992-94. Recipient Hadassah Service award San Diego chpt., 1958-59; named Woman of Dedication by Salvation Army Women's Aux., 1992, Patron of Arts by Rancho Sante Fe Country Friends, 1993. Democrat. Jewish.

GOLDBERG, LUELLA GROSS, corporation executive; b. Mpls., Feb. 26, 1937; d. Louis and Beatrice (Rosenthal) Gross; m. Stanley M. Goldberg, June 23, 1958; children: Ellen Goldberg Luger, Fredric, Martha Goldberg Aronson. BA, Wellesley Coll., 1958; postgrad. in philosophy, U. Minn., 1958-59. Dir. Reliastar Fin. Corp., 1978—; bd. dirs. Northwestern Nat. Life Ins. Co., Mpls. TCF Fin. Corp., Mpls., Hormel Foods Corp., Austin, Minn., Personnel Decisions Internatl., dir. Communications System, Inc. Pres. Minn. Orch. Women's Assn., Mpls., 1972-74; bd. dirs. Minn. Orch. Assn., 1972—, chmn., 1980-83, Mpls. chpt. United Way, 1978-88, Ind. Sector, Washington, 1984-90; regent St. John's U., Collegeville, Minn., 1974-83; trustee U. Minn. Found., Mpls., 1978—, now chmn. bd. trustees, 1996-98; mem. bd. overseers Sch. Mgmt., U. Minn., Mpls., 1980—; chmn. bd. trustees Wellesley (Mass.) Coll., 1985-93, acting pres., 1993; trustee Wellesley Coll., 1978-96, emeritus, 1996—, Northwest Area Found., 1994—. Recipient Disting. Svc. award Minn. Orch. Assn., 1983, Community Svc. Leadership award Mpls. YWCA, 1986, Disting. Svc. to Higher Edn. award Minn. Pvt. Coll. Coun., 1992, Humanitarian award NCCJ, 1992. Mem. Nat. Women's Econ. Alliance, Minn. Women's Econ. Round Table, Cosmopolitan Club (N.Y.C.), Mpls. Club, Phi Beta Kappa. Avocations: water skiing, wind surfing, traveling. Home: 7019 Tupa Dr Minneapolis MN 55439-1643

GOLDBERG, MARC EVAN, biotechnology executive; b. Boston, Mar. 14, 1957; s. Ray Allan and Thelma (Englander) G.; m. Pamela Girouard, Nov. 28, 1998; children: Frederick Warren, Alyssa Rachel, Meredith Hayley. AB, Harvard U., 1979, MBA, JD, 1983. Bar: Mass. 1985. Mgr. bus. devel. Genetics Inst., Inc., Cambridge, Mass., 1983-87; v.p. fin. and corp. devel., chief fin. officer, treas. Safer, Inc., Newton, Mass., 1987-91; pres., chief exec. officer Mass. Biotech. Rsch. Inst., Worcester, Mass., 1991-97; mng. dir. BioVentures Investors LLC, Worcester, 1997—; founder Mass. Biotech. Coun., bd. dirs., 1985-97, pres., 1985-87, 90-92. Mem., prin. author Gov.'s Task Force on Biotech., 1991—; mem. pres.'s circle Beth Israel Hosp., 1985-88; trustee Worcester State Coll., 1991—, vice chmn., 1993-95, chmn., 1995-97; trustee Harvard Yearbook Pubs., 1981—; mem. exec. adv. bd. Harvard Varsity Club, 1982—; mem. adv. com. Town of Wellesley, 1992-94, mem. town meeting, 1993-95; trustee Mass. Taxpayers Found., 1993-99. Mem. Mass Bar Assn., New Eng./Israel C. of C. (trustee 1993—), Harvard Bus. Sch. Assn. Boston (bd. govs. 1993-96). Office: BioVentures Investors LLC One Innovation Dr Worcester MA 01605

GOLDBERG, MARCIA B., medical educator; b. Boston, July 29, 1957. AB in Biology summa cum laude, Harvard U., 1979, MD, 1984. Diplomate Am. Bd. Internal Medicine, Am. Bd. Infectious Diseases. Intern in primary care internal medicine Mass. Gen. Hosp., Boston, 1984-85, jr. and sr. resident in primary care internal medicine, 1985-87, clin. and rsch. fellow in medicine, 1987-90; rsch. fellow in medicine Harvard Med. Sch., Boston, 1987-90; rsch. fellow Unite de Pathogenie Microbienne Moleculaire, Inst. Pasteur, Paris, 1991-93; asst. prof. Dept. Microbiology and Immunology, Dept. Medicine divsn. Infectious Diseases Albert Einstein Coll. of Medicine, Bronx, N.Y., 1993—; mem. joint med./nursing care com. Mass. Gen. Hosp., 1986-87, benefit com. Boston Health Care for the Homeless, 1988, admissions com. Med. Scientist Tng. Program, Albert Einstein Coll. of Medicine, 1993—, assoc. dir., 1995—, mem. steering com. Med. Student Fellowship, Am. Heart Assn., Albert Einstein Coll. of Medicine, 1994—, rsch. residency com. Dept. of Medicine, 1994—, adv. com. Hybridoma/Media Facility, 1994—, divsn. rsch., 1996—. Contbr. articles and revs. to profl. jours. Hon. Nat. scholar Radcliffe Coll., 1975; Inst. Nat. de la Sante et de la Recherche Med. fellow, 1991; Moseley Traveling fellow Harvard Med. Sch., 1991-92; Fulbright scholar, 1991-92; Pew scholar, 1994—; recipient Rsch. award Fundaciion para la Edn. Superior, 1981, Proctor-Wellington Fund award, 1987, Stuart Pharms. Travel award Nat. Found. Infectious Diseases, 1990, Young Investigator award Maxwell Finland, 1991, Intersci. Conf. on Antimicrobial Agents and Chemotherapy, 1991, Established Investigator award Am. Heart Assn., 1996. Mem. Am. Soc. Microbiology, Infectious Diseases Soc. Am., Phi Beta Kappa. Office: Albert Einstein Coll of Medicine 1300 Morris Park Ave Bronx NY 10461-1926*

GOLDBERG, MARK ARTHUR, neurologist; b. N.Y.C., Sept. 4, 1934; s. Jacob and Bertha (Grushlawska) G.; 1 child, Jonathan. BS, Columbia U., 1955; PhD, U. Chgo., 1959, MD, 1962. Resident neurology N.Y. Neurol. Inst., N.Y.C., 1963-66; asst. prof. neurology Columbia U. Coll. Phys. and Surgs., N.Y.C., 1968-71; assoc. prof. neurology and pharmacology UCLA, 1971-77, prof. neurology and pharmacology, 1977—; chair dept. neurology Harbor UCLA Med. Ctr., Torrance, 1977—. Contbr. articles to profl. jours., chpts. to books. Capt. U.S. Army, 1966-68. Fellow Am. Neurol. Assn., Am. Acad. Neurology; Am. Soc. Neurochemistry, Assn. Univ. Profs. Neurology. Avocation: oriental cusine.

GOLDBERG, MARTIN, physician, educator; b. Phila., Sept. 15, 1930; s. Samuel and Esther (Shreibman) G.; m. Lynn Taksey, June 17, 1951 (dec. Aug. 31 1976); children: Meryl I., Karen L., Dara S.; m. Marion Lindblad, May 26, 1978; 1 child, David S. BA, Temple U., 1951, MD, 1955; MA (hon.), U. Pa., 1971. Diplomate: Am. Bd. Internal Medicine (chmn. nephrology com. 1976-79, bd. govs. 1976-79), Nat. Bd. Med. Examiners. Intern Phila. Gen. Hosp., 1955-56, resident, 1957-59, sr. attending physician, 1970-76; resident Cleve. Clinic, 1956-57; fellow nephrology Hosp. U. Pa., Phila., 1959-61; sr. attending physician Hosp. U. Pa., 1962-79; mem. faculty U. Pa. Sch. Medicine, 1960-79, prof. medicine, 1970-79, chief renal electrolyte sect., 1966-79, acting chmn. dept. medicine, 1975-76; sr. attending physician Phila. VA Hosp., 1968-79; Gordon and Helen Hughes Taylor prof. medicine U. Cin., 1979-86; chmn. internal medicine U. Cin. Coll. Med. and Hosp., 1979-86; prof. medicine Temple U. Sch. Medicine, Phila., 1986-96, dean, vice pres., 1986-89, prof. emeritus, 1997—, asst. to dean for computer assisted instrn., 1997—; chmn. sci. adv. com. Gen. Clin. Rsch. Ctr. Temple U. Hosp., 1993—; mem. sci. adv. bd. Nat. Kidney Found., 1970-76; chmn. kidney council Am. Heart Assn., 1973-74; study cons. NIH, 1968-72, 82-85; bd. mgrs. St. Christopher's Hosp. Children, 1986-89. Mem. editl. com. Jour. Clin. Investigation, 1969-70, Kidney Internat., 1972-74, Jour. Mineral and Electrolyte Metabolism, 1977-91; mem. editl. bd. Am. Jour. Hypertension, 1990-97; physician-editor Nephrology MKSAP Am. Coll. Physicians, 1991-94; assoc. editor MKSAP 11, MKSAP 12, ACP, 1996—. Recipient Alumni prize Temple U. Sch. Medicine, 1955, Lindback award for distinguished teaching U. Pa., 1972; Disting. Med. Scientist of Yr. award Med. Alumni Temple U. Sch. Medicine, 1985; Research Career Devel. award NIH, 1963-70, Honoree of Yr. award Greater Del. Valley Kidney Found., 1997; research grantee NIH, 1962-89; research grantee John Hartford Found., 1970-73, Centennial award Assn. Chmn. of Depts. Physiology, 1989. Fellow ACP (nat. sci. program com. 1976-81), Am. Coll. Clin. Pharmacology, Royal Soc. Medicine; mem. Assn. Am. Med. Colls. (coun. of deans 1986-89), Assn. Am. Physicians, Am. Soc. Clin. Investigation, Am. Physiol. Soc., Am. Fedn. Clin. Rsch. (chmn. ea. sect. 1967), Am. Soc. Nephrology (sec.-treas. 1975-78), Interurban Clin. Club, Internat. Soc. Nephrology (coun. 1975-84), Am. Med. Informatics Assn., Coll. Physicians Phila., Physicians for Social Responsibility (adv. bd. Phila. chpt.), Alpha Omega Alpha. Rsch. and publs. in renal physiology and disease; electrolyte and acid-base metabolism, computer-assisted instruction and diagnosis. Office: Temple U Health Scis Ctr Nephrology Parkinson Pavilion Philadelphia PA 19140

GOLDBERG, MARTIN L., federal judge; b. 1945. JD, NYU, 1969. Bar: N.Y. Acting dist. atty. Orange County, N.Y.; chief asst. U.S. atty. U.S. Dept. Justice; part-time magistrate judge for so. dist. N.Y., U.S. Magistrate Ct., Newburgh, 1992—. With U.S. Army N.G. Office: 6 Governor Dr Newburgh NY 12550-8338

GOLDBERG, MARTIN STANFORD, lawyer; b. Youngstown, Ohio, July 11, 1924; s. George and Bee (Walker) G.; m. Donna Mae Lowry, Nov. 18, 1962; children—Jeffrey A., Jeralyn Goldberg Mercer. B.A., Ohio State U., 1952, J.D., 1952. Bar: Ohio 1952, Calif. 1981. Sole practice law, Youngstown, Ohio, 1952—. Served with USAF, 1942-45, PTO. Decorated D.F.C. Mem. ABA, Calif. Bar Assn., Ohio Bar Assn., Mahoning County Bar Assn., Am. Trial Lawyers Assn. Republican. Jewish. Lodges: Masons, Lions-Friars Club. Avocations: Reading, writing, music. Home: 74513 Old Prospector Trl Palm Desert CA 92260-5624 Office: 6600 Summit Dr Canfield OH 44406-9510

GOLDBERG, MARVIN ALLEN, lawyer, business consultant; b. Phila., Jan. 9, 1943; s. Daniel and Elizabeth (Katz) G.; m. Kathryn Elizabeth Balotsky, Apr. 27, 1974; children: Robert Andrew, MaryBeth Anne. BS, Temple U., 1964, JD, 1967. Bar: Pa. 1968, U.S. Dist. Ct. (ea. dist.) Pa. 1980, U.S. Supreme Ct. 1976. Estate tax atty. IRS, Phila., 1967-68; staff atty. Legal Aid Soc. Northampton County, Easton, Pa., 1969-70, Northampton County Pub. Defender, Easton, Pa., 1969-70; pvt. practice law Phila., 1970-76; tchr. Inst. for Paralegal Tng., Phila., 1973; staff atty. Legal Aid Soc. Phila., 1974-76; CEO Goldberg & Assocs., P.C., Phila., 1976—; cons. Butcher Trade Exchange, Ft. Washington, Pa., 1982-92; dir. North Am. Resources, Phila.; pres. MAGCO, Inc., Mt. Laurel, N.J., 1989-92. Mem. Chestnut St. Assn., Phila; dir. Sr. Citizen Judicare Project, Phila., 1977. With USAF, 1967-73. Mem. ABA, Phila. Bar Assn., Phila. Trial Lawyers Assn., Assn. Trial Lawyers Am., Pa. Trial Lawyers Assn., Attys. Across Am. (founding mem.), Jewish War Vets, Beta Gamma Sigma, Phi Alpha Delta. Avocations: running, sailing, chess, Algebra, 19th century physics. Office: Goldberg & Assocs PC 1334 Walnut St Fl 5 Philadelphia PA 19107-5311

GOLDBERG, MAXWELL HENRY, retired humanities educator; b. Malden, Mass., Oct. 22, 1907; s. Felix and Zelda Janet (Kushlansky) G.; m. Shirley Alberta Bliss, Sept. 2, 1937 (div. Nov. 1957); children: Naomi Jean, Deborah Martha, Rachel Elizabeth; m. Ethel Stella Zeidman, July 29, 1962. BS, U. Mass., 1928; MA, Yale U., 1932, PhD, 1933; LHD (hon.), U. Mass., 1988. From instr. to prof., dept. head U. Mass., Amherst, 1928-61, First Commonwealth prof. humanities, 1960-61, emeritus Commonwealth prof. humanities, 1962—; prof. & dir. humanities U. Fla., Tampa, 1960-61; prof. English & humanities, assoc. dir. Humanities Ctr. for Continuing Liberal Edn. Pa. State U., State College, 1962-72, emeritus prof. English & humanities, 1972—; Helmus Disting. prof. humanities & lit. Converse Coll., Spartanburg, S.C., 1972-77, emeritus prof. humanities & lit., 1977—; lectr., author Grad. Sem. for Fed. Execs., Washington, 1962-63; dir., editor humanities project on technol. change and human values CCLE-IBM, 1962-72; lectr. Danforth Disting. Lectr. Program Assn. Am. Colls., N.Y.C., 1968-72; field reader U.S. Office HEW, Washington, 1968-72; exec. dir. Humanities Ctr. for Liberal Edn. in an Indsl. Soc., 1951-62, pres., 1963-74; chief humanities cons. Morehouse Coll., 1972-87; feature writer Spartanburg Herald-Jour., 1990—. Author: Design in Liberal Learning, 1971, Thomas Carlyle's Relationships with The 'Edinburgh Review, 1971; contbr. The University Today, Its Role and Place in Society, An International Study, 1960; author, editor: Blindness Research--The Expanding Frontiers, 1969; editor, contbr. Telics and Holistic Edn. for the Technol. Age: Internat. Jour. Innovative Higher Edn., 1985; editor: Automation, Education and Human Values, 1966, Thomas Carlyle Family Letters, 1987. Pres. Caring Coalition of Spartanburg, 1992—; bd. dirs. Spartanburg Repertory Co., 1989-94, Bicentennial Forums of Greater Spartanburg, 1973-78; mem. ednl. adv. com. S.C. Appalachian Coun. Govts., Greenville, 1989-94; bd. dirs., pres. Shepherd's Ctr. of Spartanburg, 1983-89; pres. Friends of Pub. Libr. of Spartanburg, 1980-87. Ford Found. fellow, 1959-60; recipient David W. Reid award for achievement in arts Arts Coun. Spartanburg County, 1981, Judge Davenport disting. svc. award Mental Health Assn., Piedmont, 1991; scholar Yale U., 1932-33; named disting. alumnus U. Mass. Alumni Assn., 1963, Ann. Friend of Pub. Libr. of Spartanburg County, 1985, Outstanding Older S. Carolinian Appalachian Region, 1993; U. Mass. Hillel Living and Lng. Cmty. dedicated in his honor, 1998. Mem. MLA (life), Coll. English Assn. (past v.p., exec. dir., editor 1950-59, prof. of yr. 1989), Oak Ridge Assn. Univs. (lectr., author 1965), Phi Kappa Phi (chpt. pres. 1936-37), Alpha Epsilon Pi (Gitelson meml. medallion 1945). Jewish. Avocations: gardening, photography.

GOLDBERG, MELVIN ARTHUR, communications executive; b. N.Y.C., Feb. 5, 1923; s. Louis and Anna (Bergman) G.; m. Norma N. Nertz, Oct. 18, 1956; children: Ronald, Richard, Joan Sandra. BS, CCNY, 1942; AM, Columbia U., 1950. Mem. staff Bur. Applied Social Rsch., Columbia, 1946-47; news editor, rsch. dir. TV mag., 1947-49; dir. sales planning and rsch. DuMont TV Network, 1949-52; dep. dir. Office Rsch. and Evaluation, U.S. Info. Agy., 1952-53; exec. sec. Ultra-High Frequency TV Assn., 1953-54; cons., chief of rsch. M-G Rsch., 1954-56; dir. rsch. Westinghouse Broadcasting Co., 1956-62; v.p., dir. rsch. Nat. Assn. Broadcasters, 1962-64; v.p. planning and rsch. John Blair & Co., 1964-69; pres. Melvin A. Goldberg Inc., N.Y.C., 1969-77; v.p. primary and social rsch. ABC-TV, 1977-80, v.p. news, social and tech. rsch., 1980-85; v.p. market planning, tech. and social rsch. ABC Inc.; exec. dir. Electronic Media Rating Coun., 1985-93; pres. Melvin A. Goldberg Inc., N.Y.C., 1993—; former mem. ABA Commn. on Pub. Understanding About the Law. Mem. editorial bd. TV Quar.; Contbr. articles to profl. publs. Served to capt. USAAF, 1943-45. Decorated D.F.C., Air medal with clusters. Mem. Nat. Assn. Broadcasters, TV Bur. Advt., Am. Assn. Pub. Opinion Rsch., Radio-TV Rsch. Coun., Nat. Acad. TV Arts and Scis. Home: 17 North Dr Great Neck NY 11021-1337 Office: Melvin A Goldberg Inc Comm 17 North Dr Great Neck NY 11021-1337

GOLDBERG, MELVYN, retired educator; b. Chgo., June 19, 1936; s. Sidney and Rachel (Brower) G.; m. Louise Rusch, June 23, 1957 (div. Dec. 1985); children: Robin Baden, Leslie Moss, Michael. BA, No. Ill. U., 1959; MA, Calif. State U., Long Beach, 1971. Cert. tchr., Calif., Ill., Ariz. Tchr. San Pedro (Calif.) H.S., 1959-71, Wkgn. (Ill.) H.S., 1971-94, Coll. of Lake County, Grayslake, Ill., 1987-94; ret., 1994. Author: (poetry and photography) Cyclic Path, 1989; contbr. to various books and mags. Recipient Fulbright Exch. Tchg. award in Eng., USIA, 1990-91. Mem. Assn. Am. Poets. Avocation: numismatics. Home: PO Box 2294 Sedona AZ 86339-8930

GOLDBERG, MICHAEL, artist; b. N.Y.C., Dec. 24, 1924; s. Nathan and Henriette (Goldstein) G.; stepchildren: Lucas Matthiessen, Sarah Carey Matthiessen. Student, Art Students League, N.Y.C., 1938-42, 46; pupil of, Jose de Creeft, City Coll. N.Y., 1940-42, 46-47; student, Hofmann Sch., 1941-42, 48-50. Tchr. U. Cal. at Berkeley, 1961-62, Yale, 1967, U. Minn., 1968; tchr. Sch. of Visual Arts, 1979—. One-man exhbns. include Tibor de Nagy Gallery, N.Y.C., 1953, Poindexter Gallery, N.Y.C., 1956, 58, Martha Jackson Gallery, N.Y.C., 1960, 62, 64, 66, Paul Kantor Gallery, Los Angeles, 1960, B.C. Holland Gallery, Chgo., 1961, Galerie Anderson-Mayer, Paris, 1963, Holland-Goldowsky Gallery, Chgo., two-man, 1960, Bob Keene Gallery, 1963, Paley & Lowe Gallery, N.Y.C., 1971, 72, 73, Cunningham Ward, N.Y.C., 1975, 76, Galerie Hecate, Paris, Clock tower, N.Y.C., 1976, 77, Galerie Denise Réné , N.Y.C., 1977, Galerie Sonnabend, Paris, 1978, Galerie December, Dusseldorf, W. Ger., 1978, Young-Hoffman Gallery, Chgo., 1978, Loyse Oppenheim Gallery, Geneva, 1978, Dan Weinberg Gallery, San Francisco, 1978, 79, Sonnabend, N.Y.C., 1979, 83, Thomas Segal Gallery, Boston, 1979, Turchetto/Plurimo, Milan, 1990, Galleria Plurima, Udine, Italy, 1990, numerous others; group exhbns. include 9th St. Exhbn., N.Y.C., 1951, Stable Gallery anns., N.Y.C., 1952-57, Four Younger Americans, Sidney Janis Gallery, N.Y.C., 1956, Martha Jackson Gallery, 1958, 60, 61, 63, 64, 65, 67, Turin (Italy) Art Festival, 1959, V Sao Paula (Brazil) Biennial, 1959, Documenta II, Kassel, Germany, 1959, Walker Gallery, Mpls., 1960, Am. Painters, 1960, Columbus (O.) Contemporary Am. Painting, 1960, Hans Hofmann and His Students, Mus. Modern Art, 1963-64, Musee Cantonal des Beaux Arts, Lausanne, Switzerland, 1963, I Salon Internat. des Galeries Pilotes, 1963, Gallery Modern Art, N.Y.C., 1964, Am. Fedn. Arts, 1965, Am. Art Gallery, Copenhagen, 1965, Smithsonian Instn., 1966, Mus. Modern Art, N.Y.C., 1968, Corcoran Bienale, 1969, Rykert Gallery, N.Y.C., 1969, 70, Paula Cooper Gallery, N.Y.C., 1970, 71, Whitney Ann., 1973, Corcoran Biennial, 1977, Galeri Lauter, Mannheim, Germany, 1993, Gallerie Peccolo, Livorno, Italy, 1993, Penine Hart, N.Y.C., 1993, Galeri Weinberger, Copenhagen, Denmark, 1994, numerous others; represented in permanent collections Mus. Modern Art, Chgo. Art Inst., Dayton Art Inst., Corcoran Gallery Art, Nat. Gallery, Walker Art Center, Balt. Mus. Art, Albright-Knox Gallery, Buffalo, Cornell U., De Cordova Mus., Whitney Mus., N.Y.C., Provincetown Chrysler Art Gallery, Guggenheim Mus., Smithsonian Instn., Mus. Modern Art, Israel, Mus. Modern Western Art, Tokyo. Served with U.S. Army, World War II, 1942-46. Address: 222 Bowery New York NY 10012-4216*

GOLDBERG, MICHAEL ARTHUR, land policy and planning educator; b. Bklyn., Aug. 30, 1941; s. Harold and Ruth (Abelson) G.; m. Rhoda Lynne Zacker, Dec. 22, 1963 (div. 1987); children: Betsy Anne, Jennifer Heli; m. Deborah Nelson, Sept. 7, 1991. B.A. cum laude, Bklyn. Coll., 1962; M.A., U. Calif., Berkeley, 1965, Ph.D., 1968. Acting instr. Sch. Bus. Adminstrn., U. Calif., Berkeley, 1967-68; asst. prof. Faculty of Commerce and Bus. Adminstrn., U. B.C., Vancouver, 1968-71, assoc. prof., 1971-76, prof., 1976—, assoc. dean, 1980-84, dean, 1991-97, Herbert R. Fullerton prof. urban land policy, 1981—; mem. Vancouver Econ. Adv. Commn., 1980-82, Can. dept. Fin. Deposit Ins. adv. group, 1992-94, Can. dept. Internat. Trade, Strategic Adv. Group on Internat. Trade in Fin. Svcs., 1991-96; vice chmn. B.C. Real Estate Found., 1985-87, chmn. 1987-91; mem. IFC Vancouver, 1985—, vice chmn., 1985-88, chmn., 1988-89, exec. dir., 1989-91; bd. dirs. Imperial Parking Ltd., 1991-94, VLC Properties Ltd., 1991-93, Redekop Properties, 1993—, Catamaran Ferries, Inc., 1996-97, Sinorank Petroleum, 1996-98; vice chmn. Can. Fedn. Deans of Mgmt. and Adminstrv. Scis., 1991-92, chair, 1992-94, Securities Industry Policy Adv. Con., 1995—; pub.-pvt. partnership task force, 1995-96. Author: (with G. Gau) Zoning: Its Costs and Relevance for 1980's, 1980, The Housing Problem: A Real Crisis?, 1983, (with P. Chinloy) Urban Land Economics, 1984, The Chinese Connection, 1985, (with J. Mercer) The Myth of the North American City, 1985, On Balance, 1989; editor: Recent Perspectives in Urban Land Economics, 1976, (with P. Horwood) North American Housing Markets into the Twenty-first century, 1983, (with E. Feldman) The Rites and Wrongs of Land Use Policy, 1988. Trustee Temple Sholom, 1980-84. Can. Coun. fellow, 1974-75, Social Scis. and Humanities Rsch. Coun. fellow, 1979-80, 84-85, Lincoln Inst. Land Policy fellow, 1979-80, Urban Land Inst. fellow, 1984—, Homer Hoyt Inst. fellow, 1988—; recipient Can. 125th anniversary medal for service to Can., 1993; named hon. life mem. Real Estate Inst. B.C., 1999. Mem. Canadian Regional Sci. Assn., Am. Real Estate and Urban Econs. Assn. (dir. 1978—, pres. 1984), Vancouver Bd. Trade, Real Estate Inst. British Columbia (hon.), Lambda Alpha. Home: 1986 W 15th Ave, Vancouver, BC Canada V6J 2L3 Office: U BC, Faculty Commerce & Bus, Vancouver, BC Canada V6T 1Z2 *On reflection, notions of social justice have been as important as any of the guides that I have looked to in working with others and in doing my own work. Operationally, this has meant that I have attempted to deal with students, colleagues and staff in like ways treating people with a basic respect for the inherent human dignity and abhorring those of my colleagues who have treated people in a less respectful way. It has meant that I answer my mail, respond to phone calls and remain available. The cost in the short run to my work has been high at times, but all in all well worth it.*

GOLDBERG, MITCHEL R., federal judge; b. 1943. BA, U. Colo., 1965, JD, 1968. With Rosen & Goldberg, Santa Ana, Calif., 1971-80; pvt. practice, 1981-88; apptd. bankruptcy judge cen. dist. U.S. Dist. Ct. Calif., 1988. With U.S. Army, 1969-70. Office: 3420 12th St Riverside CA 92501-3801

GOLDBERG, MORRIS, internist; b. N.Y.C., Jan. 23, 1928; s. Saul and Lena (Schanberg) G.; BS in Chemistry cum laude, Poly. Inst. Bklyn., 1951; MD, SUNY, Bklyn., 1956; m. Elaine Shaw, June 24, 1956; children: Alan Neil, Seth David, Nancy Beth. Intern, Jewish Hosp. Bklyn., 1956-57, resident, 1957-58, 61-62, renal fellow, 1958-59; practice medicine, specializing in internal medicine, N.Y.C., 1962-71, Phoenix, 1971—; instr. to asst. clin. prof. internal medicine State U. N.Y. Coll. Medicine, Bklyn., 1962-71; clin. investigator, metabolic research unit Jewish Hosp. Bklyn., 1962-71; cons. in field; mem. staff Phoenix Bapt., Maryvale Samaritan, Good Samaritan, St. Joseph's Hosp., Vets. Affairs Med. Ctr., Phoenix. Served to capt. M.C., U.S. Army, 1959-61. Diplomate Am. Bd. Internal Medicine. Fellow ACP; mem. AMA, Am. Soc. Internal Medicine, Am. Coll. Nuclear Physicians (charter mem.), Am. Soc. Nephrology, Am. Soc. Hypertension (charter mem.), Ariz. Med. Assn., 38th Parallel Med. Soc. S. Korea, Ariz., Maricopa County Med. Assn., Sigma Xi, Phi Lambda Upsilon, Alpha Omega Alpha. Contb articles to med. jours. Office: Vets Affairs Med Ctr 650 E Indian School Rd Phoenix AZ 85012-1839

GOLDBERG, MORTON EDWARD, pharmacologist; b. Phila., July 11, 1932; s. Herman and Ethel (Shill) G.; m. Janet Louise Werlin, Aug. 15, 1954; children—Shellie, Ellen, David. B.S., Phila. Coll. Pharmacy and Sci., 1954, M.S. in Pharmacology, 1955, DSc in Pharmacology, 1958. Sr. pharmacologist Abbott Labs., North Chicago, Ill., 1958-60; asst. dir. pharmacology Union Carbide Corp., Tuxedo, N.Y., 1960-69; dir. pharmacodynamics Warner Lambert Research Inst., Morris Plains, N.J., 1969-73; dir. pharmacology Squibb Inst. Med. Research, Princeton, N.J., 1973-77; v.p. biomed. research Stuart Pharms. div. ICI Americas, Wilmington, Del., 1977-84; v.p. rsch., devel., and regulatory affairs ICI Pharm. Group divsn. ICI Ams. (now Zeneca Pharm.), Wilmington, Del., 1984-92; clin. prof. pharmacology and exptl. therapeutics Dept. Pharmacology U. Pa. Sch. Medicine, Phila., 1992-96; vis. prof. toxicology Phila. Coll. Pharmacy and Sci.; vis. prof. pharmacology, Allegheny U. Med. Sch., Phila., 1978—, U. Pa. Sch. Med., Phila., 1996—; cons. to pharm. industry in drug discovery and devel., 1992—; mem. Extramural Sci. Adv. Bd., NIDA, 1993-95, nat. adv. bd. 1996—. Editor-in-chief: series Pharmacological and Biochemical Properties of Drug Substances; contbr. articles to profl. jours. Asst. scoutmaster Boy Scouts Am., Glen Rock, N.J., 1968-72. NIH grantee, 1961-64. Fellow Acad. Pharm. Sci., AAAS, N.Y. Acad. Sci.; mem. Am. Soc. Pharmacology and Exptl. Therapeutics, Behavioral Pharmacology Soc., Internat. Soc. Biochem. Pharmacology, Soc. Toxicology (charter), Sigma Xi, Rho Chi. Home: 715 Severn Rd Wilmington DE 19803-1725

GOLDBERG, MORTON FALK, ophthalmologist, educator; b. Lawrence, Mass., June 8, 1937; s. Maurice and Helen Janet (Falk) G.; m. Myrna Davidov, Apr. 6, 1968; children—Matthew Falk, Michael Falk. A.B. magna cum laude, Harvard U., 1958, M.D. cum laude, 1962; Doctoris Honoris Causa, U. Coimbra, Portugal, 1995. Diplomate Am. Bd. Ophthalmology. Intern Peter Bent Brigham Hosp., Boston, 1962-63; resident Wilmer Inst. John Hopkins Hosp., Balt., 1963-67, head dept., dir. Wilmer Inst., 1989—; prof. and head ophthalmology Eye and Ear Infirmary U. Ill. Hosp., Chgo., 1970-89. Author: (with D. Paton) Injuries of the Eye, the Lids and the Orbit: Diagnosis and Management, 1968, Management of Ocular Injuries, 1976; editor: Genetic and Metabolic Eye Disease, 1974, (with G.A. Peyman and D.R. Sanders) Principles and Practice of Ophthalmology (3 vols.), 1980; editor-in-chief Archives of Ophthalmology, Chgo., 1984-94; contbr. articles to profl. jours. Lt. comdr. USPHS, 1967-69. Recipient award for outstanding contbns. in the field of vision rsch. Alcon Research Inst., 1987, Univ. Scholar award U. Ill.-Chgo., 1986, Patz medal Macula Soc., 1999. Fellow Royal Australian Coll. Ophthalmologists (hon.), Am. Acad. Ophthalmology (sr. honor award 1985); mem. Inst. Medicine-NAS, Am. Ophthal. Soc., Chgo. Ophthal. Soc. (pres. 1985-86), Assn. Rsch. in Vision and Ophthalmology (trustee 1985-90, pres. 1989-90, Weisenfeld award 2000), Assn. Univ. Profs. Ophthalmology (trustee 1985-91, pres. 1990-91), Macula Soc. (pres. 1980-82). Avocation: snorkelling. Office: Johns Hopkins Med Insts Wilmer Eye Inst 600 N Wolfe St Baltimore MD 21287-0005

GOLDBERG, NOLAN HILLIARD, automotive company official; b. Kansas City, Mo., Apr. 1, 1960; s. Julian Angrist and Estelle Lillian (Lipton) G.; m. Elana Erin Bavel, June 5, 1988; 1 child, Nathan Julian. BA in Econs., U. Kans., 1997. Bd. marker Kansas City Bd. Trade, 1978-80; wholesale men's gift rep., Prairie Village, Kans., 1980-87; prin. Fast Lane Motoring Accessories, Prairie Village, 1987-90; new vehicle retail sales assoc. Shawnee (Kans.) Mission Ford, Inc., 1987-89, mcpl. fleet salesman, 1989-90, asst. rental mgr., 1990-98, rental mgr., 1998—. em. brotherhood bd. Temple B'nai Jehudah, Kansas City, 1987-95; mem. synagogue sanctuary com. Temple Beth Torah, Overland Park, Kans., 1994—. Exch. student to Italy, Am. Field Svc., 1978. Democrat. Avocations: motorsports (automobile crossing), bicycling, photography, self-education and improvement, violin. Home: 6200 W 76th St Prairie Vlg KS 66208-4537 Office: Shawnee Mission Ford Inc 11501 Shawnee Mission Pkwy Shawnee KS 66203-3388

GOLDBERG, NORMA LORRAINE, retired public welfare administrator; b. South Bend, Ind., May 6, 1929; d. James Albert and Minnie Sylvia (Kaplan) Seamon; m. Albert Goldberg, Apr. 19, 1959 (dec. Dec. 1976); children: Lisa Ann, Paul Ephraim. BS, Ind. U., Bloomington, 1950; post-grad. Sch. Social Work, Ind. U., Indpls., 1950-52. Social worker Indpls. Pub. Schs., 1951-53; with Marion County Dept. Pub. Welfare, Indpls., 1953-66, 71-73, asst. dir., 1961-64, dir., 1964-66, intake supr., 1971-73; asst. dir. Ind. Dept. Pub. Welfare, Indpls., 1973-79, dir., 1979-87, regional adminstr., rep. Family Support Adminstrn., Dallas, 1987-91; spl. project officer Adminstrn. Children and Families, 1991-94, asst. regional adminstr., 1994-95; steering com. Whitehouse Conf. on Children and Youth, Indpls., 1982-83; program com. Gov.'s Conf. on Children and Youth, Indpls., 1982-83. Founder Welfare Service League, Indpls., 1968, pres., 1968-71, mem., 1968—. Mem. steering com. Indpls. sect. Nat. Council Jewish Women, 1982-87; steering com. Guardian ad Litem Project; mem. Republican Round Table, Indpls., 1983-87 ; city chmn. adult bd. B'nai B'rith Youth Orgn., 1985-86. Recipient Gov.'s Voluntary Action Program Cmty. Service award Gov. of Ind., 1980. Mem. Assn. Women Execs., Dallas Council World Affairs, Dallas Women's Found., Ind. Conf. on Social Concerns (state coordinator 1963-64), Network of Women in Bus., Indpls. Council of Women (program chmn. 1968-71), The 500 Club, Inc., Meridian Hills Kiwanis, Northside Investment Club., Order Eastern Star, People of Vision, Indpls. Mus. Art.

GOLDBERG, PAMELA WINER, business manager; b. Boston, Oct. 14, 1955; d. Arthur Leonard and Marilyn (Miller) Winer; children: Frederick Warren, Alyssa Rachel, Meredith Hayley. BA, Tufts U., 1977; MBA, Stanford U., 1981. Day care dir. Community Action Inc., Haverhill, Mass., 1977-79; lending assoc. Bankers Trust Co., N.Y.C., 1980-81; mgr., bank officer, corp. fin. dept. Citicorp, N.Y.C., 1981-82; assoc. dir., mergers and acquisitions group State Street Bank, Boston, 1983-85; ind. strategic cons. Wellesley, Mass., 1986-97; dir. bus. rels. Babson Coll., Wellesley, 1998—. Bd. Friends Beth Israel Hosp., Boston, 1987-96; mem. exec. bd. trustees Temple Beth Elohim, Wellesley, 1992—, treas., 1997—; trustee Recuperative Ctr., Boston, 1988-95; bd. dirs. Wellesley League Women Voters, 1995-98; mem. Hunnewell Sch. PTO Bd., 1991-96. Avocations: swimming, tennis, singing. Home: 34 Ivy Rd Wellesley MA 02482-4554 Office: Babson Coll Babson Park MA 02457

GOLDBERG, PAUL BERNARD, gastroenterologist, clinical researcher; b. Bklyn., Apr. 11, 1950; s. Samuel and Eva (Turkenitz) G.; m. Harriet Ruth Ferrer, July 8, 1973 (div. 1987); children: Deborah Lynn, Susan Michelle; m. Mary Alice Denaro, June 23, 1990; 1 child, Laura Alicia. BA in Chemistry summa cum laude, Cornell U., 1967-71, MD, 1971-75. Diplomate Am. Bd. Internal Medicine, Am. Bd. Gastroenterology. Intern in medicine Hosp. of U. of Pa., Phila., 1975-76, resident in medicine, 1976-78, fellow in gastroenterology, 1978-80, fellow in nutritional support svc., 1979-80; med. coord. and founder nutritional support svc. Lakeland (Fla.) Gen. Hosp., 1980-81; attending physician Halifax Med. Ctr., 1980—, Ormond Meml. Hosp., 1980—, Humana Hosp., 1980—, Fish Meml. Hosp., New Smyrna Beach, Fla., 1989—, Peninsula Med. Ctr., 1989-94; pres. Sunshine Health Care Plan, Inc., 1983-86, v.p., 1986-87; chief staff Humana Hosp., Daytona Beach, 1986-88, trustee, 1986-89, mem. exec. com., 1984-91; mem. rev. bd. Coastal Instnl. Rev., 1990-93, chmn. rev. bd., 1993-96; expert reviewer Fla. Dept. Profl. Regulation, 1990—; pres. med. staff Halifax Hosp., 1996-97; clin. asst. prof. medicine dept. family medicine U. South Fla. Rschr. and author in field. Physician adv. Daytona chpt. Crohn's and Colitis Found., 1991-95. Recipient Nat. award Ford Future Scientists of Am., 1967, Westinghouse Sci. Talent Search finalist, 1967. Fellow ACP, Am. Coll. Gastroenterology; mem. Am. Gastroent. Soc., Am. Soc. Gastrointestinal Endoscopy, Am. Soc. for Parenteral and Enteral Nutrition (pres. Fla. chpt. 1991-92), Volusia County Med. Soc. (exec. com. 1991-94, co-chmn. mini internship program 1992-94), Fla. Gastrointestinal Soc., Fla. med. Assn. (alt. del. to ho. of dels. 1990-95), Fla. Assn. Nutritional Support (1st pres.), Rotary, Phi Beta Kappa, Alpha Omega Alpha. Office: Gastrointestinal Assocs 201 N Clyde Morris Blvd Ste 100 Daytona Beach FL 32114-2765

GOLDBERG, RAY ALLAN, agribusiness educator; b. Fargo, N.D., Oct. 19, 1926; s. Max and Anne G.; m. Thelma R. Englander, May 20, 1956; children: Marc E., Jennifer E., Jeffrey L. AB, Harvard U., 1948, MBA, 1950; PhD, U. Minn., 1952. Officer, dir. Moorhead (Minn.) Seed & Grain Co., 1952-62; dir. Experience, Inc., Mpls., 1963-78, Arbor Acres Farm, Inc., N.Y.C., H.K. Webster Co.; mem. faculty Harvard U. Grad. Bus. Sch., 1955—, Moffett prof. agr. and bus., 1970-97; Moffett prof. agr. and bus. emeritus, 1997—; also dir. continuing edn. programs, participant seminars Harvard U. Grad. Bus. Sch.; bd. dirs. All-Flow, Inc., RDO Equiptment, Daymon Assocs., Lion Labs.; hon. prof. Royal Agrl. Coll., Cirencester, England, 1996; vis. prof. U. Minn. Grad. Sch., summer 1960; adv. coun. Foods Multinat., Inc., 1972-77; mem. agrl. investment com. John Hancock Ins. Co., 1971-95; cons. in field, 1955—; adviser Instituto Centroamericano de Administracion de Empresa, Managua, Nicaragua, 1973—, Instituto Panamericano de Alta Direccion de Empresa, Mexico City, 1973—, U.S. Comptroller of Currency, 1975—, Food and Agr. Policy Project, Ctr. Nat. Policy, 1984—; mem. study team, subgroup chmn. world food and nutrition study NRC, 1975—; mem. com. tech. factor contbg. to nation's fgn. trade positions Nat. Acad. Engring., 1976—; chmn. agribus. adv. com. on Caribbean Basin USDA, 1982—; mem. com. on indsl. policy for developing countries Commn. on Engring. and Tech. Systems, NRC, 1982—; mem. task force on agr. Fowler-McCracken Commn., 1984—; adv. bd. The First Mercantile Currency Fund Inc., 1985—; internat. adv. bd. Atlantic Exchange Program, 1987—; mem. V.I. Lenin All-Union Acad. of Agrl. Scis., 1988—; mem. U.S. Presdl. Econ. Del. to Poland, Nov., 1989; scientific advisory bd. Sepragen Corp., 1993—, Inst. Food Technologists, 1999—; chmn. joint bus. scientific pub. policy consumer policy tech. com. U.S. Food System and Seminar, 1994—; mem. internat. bd. visitors Zamorano, 1995—; mem. adv. com. Foodfit.com., 1999—. Author numerous books, 1948— including Agribusiness Management for Developing Countries-Latin America, 1974, (with Lee F. Schrader) Farmers' Cooperative and Federal Income Taxes, 1974, (with John T. Dunlop et al) The Lessons of Wage and Price Controls-The Food Sector, 1977, (with Richard C. McGinity et al), Agribusiness Management for Devloping Countries-Southeast Asia Corn Study, 1979; editor: Research in Domestic and International Agribusiness Management, Vol. 1, 1980, Vol. 2, 1981, Vol. 3, 1982, Vol. 4, 1983, Vol. 5, 1984, Vol. 6, 1986, Vol. 7, 1987, Vol. 8, 1988, Vol. 9, 1989, Vol. 10, 1981, Vol. 11, 1995, Vol. 12, 1996; co-editor; (with Gerald E. Gaul) New Technologies and the Future of Food and Nutrition, 1991, The Emerging Global Food System: Public and Private Sector Issues, 1993; contbr. numerous articles to profl. jours.; chmn. editl. adv. bd. Agribus.: An Internat. Jour., 1983—. Bd. govs. Internat. Devel. Rsch. Ctr., Govt. of Can., 1978—; trustee Roxbury Latin Sch., Boston, 1973-76, Beth Israel Hosp., Boston, 1978—, mem. com. on patents and tech. transfer, 1982—, chmn. gerontology com., 1991—; mem. adv. com. to prep. sch. New Eng. Conservatory Music, 1974—, assoc. trustee, 1978—; vice chmn. bd. Spoleto Festival U.S.A., 1993; adv. mem. Polish Investment Fund, 1994—; chmn. adv. com. Sonoma Internat. Capital Assocs., 1994—. Recipient Outstanding Alumni award, Dept. Agrl. Econs. U. Minn., 1992. Mem. Royal Agrl. Coll. Eng. (hon. prof. 1996—), V.I. Lenin All-Union Acad. Agrl. Scis. (fgn.), Am. Agrl. Econs. Assn. (editl. coun. 1974-78, nat. agribus. edn. commn. 1988—), Internat. Agribus. Mgmt. Assn. (pres. 1990-92, bd. dirs. 1990—, chmn. Russian food mgmt. program sponsored rsch. project 1994—, coord. non-partisan ednl., govt., pvt., sci., med. and consumer group for food, safety, nutrition and environ. 1994—), Agribus. Inst. Cambridge (chmn. bd., treas. 1991-93), Am. Mktg. Assn., Am. Dairy Sci. Assn., Food Distbn. Rsch. Soc., Harvard Club (Boston and N.s. Coun. for Sustainable Devel. (adv. group for sustainable paper cycle project 1994—). Address: 975 Memorial Dr Apt 701 Cambridge MA 02138-5803

GOLDBERG, RICHARD W., federal judge; b. Fargo, N.D., Sept. 23, 1927; s. Jacob H. and Frances (Gilles) G.; m. Mary Borland, Apr. 26, 1964; children: Julie, John. B.B.A., U. Miami, Fla., 1950, J.D., 1952. Bar: Fla. 1952, N.D. 1952, D.C. 1957. Pres., chief exec. officer Goldberg Feed & Grain Co.; acting and dep. under sec. of Internat. Affairs and Commodity Program Dept. Agr., Washington, 1983-89; pvt. practice, 1989-90; judge U.S. Ct. of Internat. Trade, N.Y., 1991—. Served to capt. USAF, 1953-56. Office: US Ct of Internat Trade One Federal Plz New York NY 10007

GOLDBERG, RITA MARIA, foreign language educator; b. N.Y.C., Oct. 1, 1933; d. Abraham Morris and Hilda (Weinman) G. BA, Queens Coll., 1954; MA, Middlebury Coll., 1955; PhD, Brown U., 1968. Mem. faculty Queens Coll., N.Y.C., 1956, Oberlin (Ohio) Coll., 1957; mem. faculty St. Lawrence U., Canton, N.Y., 1957—; Dana prof. modern langs. St. Lawrence U., 1975—, chmn. dept., 1972-75, 83-91; chmn. Regional Conf. Am. Programs in Spain, 1979-81; mem. Nat. Fulbright Selection Com., 1990-92; mem. advanced placement devel. com. for Spanish, Ednl. Testing Svc., 1993—, chair, 1996-99. Spanish Ministry of Fgn. Affairs scholar, 1954-56; Danforth grantee, 1960-62, 63-64; N.Y. State Regents scholar, 1954, Brown U. scholar, 1960-62. Mem. Am. Assn. Tchrs. Spanish and Portuguese, AAUP, MLA, Am. Council Teaching of Fgn. Langs., N.E. Modern Lang. Assn., N.Y. State Assn. Fgn. Lang. Tchrs., Phi Beta Kappa, Sigma Delta Pi. Roman Catholic. Home: 45 Judson St Canton NY 13617-1146 Office: St Lawrence U Dept Modern Langs Lits Canton NY 13617

GOLDBERG, ROBERT HOWARD, forensic pathologist; b. Bklyn., May 29, 1948; s. Abraham Joeseph and Ceil R. (Platzman) G.; m. Selaura Joy Campbell, Apr. 1984 (div. Sept. 1986). BA cum laude, N.C. State U., 1976; JD, N.C. Ctrl. U., 1979; MD cum laude, World U. Sch. Medicine, Santo Domingo, Dominican Republic, 1989. Diplomate Am. Bd. Forensic/Medicine Examiners (adv. bd. 1999—). Intern Gotier Hosp., Santo Domingo, 1987-89; resident in internal medicine Aybar Hosp., Santo Domingo, 1991-92; tchg. faculty mem. Legal Aid of N.Y., N.Y.c., 1990-93; asst. prof. criminology CUNY, Bklyn., 1992-93; assoc. prof. basic sci. Life U., Marietta, Ga., 1993-97; forensic cons. U.S. Dept. Justice, 1989—; cons. Dominican Nat. Inst. Forensic Pathology, 1996—. Contbr. articles to profl. jours. Pro bono forensic expert NRA, Atlanta, 1993—, firearms instr., North Ga., 1996—, tng. counselor, 1997—. Fellow Am. Soc. Law and Medicine, 1991-98, Dominican Med. Assn., 1989-93, tchg. fellow World U. Sch. Medicine, 1986-89; book dedication Nancy Drew/Hardy Boys, 1996. Fellow Royal Soc. Medicine, Vidocq Soc.; mem. Am. Coll. Forensic Examiners (exec. bd. 1999-00), Dominican Nat. Inst. Forensic Pathology. Avocations: flying, karate (6th degree black belt), kit plane building. Home: 1600 Oakpointe Dr SW Apt D Marietta GA 30008-3707

GOLDBERG, ROBERT LEWIS, preventive and occupational medicine physician; b. Phila., Aug. 13, 1953. MD, Jefferson Med. Coll., 1976. Diplomate Am. Bd. Preventive Medicine (trustee 1995—, vice-chair occupational medicine 1997—). Resident in family medicine Scenic Gen. Hosp., Modesto, Calif., 1976-77; intensive resident occupl. medicine U. Calif., San Francisco, 1987-88; pres., med. dir. Valley Occupl. Med. Group, Modesto, 1978-98; med. dir. De la Cruz Occupl. Healthcare, Santa Clara, Calif., 1995-98; chief med. officer U.S. Healthworks of Calif., 1998—; asst. prof. family medicine Sch. Medicine U. Calif., Davis, 1997—; asst. clin. prof. medicine Sch. Medicine U. Calif., San Francisco, 1998—; mem. Inds. Med. Coun. State of Calif., 1993—. Fellow Am. Coll. Occupl. Medicine; mem. Am. Coll. Occupl. and Environ. Medicine (bd. dirs., 2d v.p., 1997, 1st v.p. 1998, pres.-elect 1999). Office: US Healthworks 1524 Mchenry Ave 500 Modesto CA 95350-4572

GOLDBERG, SAMUEL, retired mathematician, foundation officer; b. N.Y.C., Mar. 14, 1925; s. Gedalia and Fannie (Lieberman) G.; m. Marcia Chinitz, June 21, 1953; 1 son, David. B.S., CCNY, 1944; Ph.D., Cornell U., 1950. Instr., then asst. prof. math. Lehigh U., Bethlehem, Pa., 1950-53; mem. faculty Oberlin (Ohio) Coll., 1953—, prof. math., 1961-85, emeritus prof., 1985—; program officer Alfred P. Sloan Found., N.Y.C., 1985-90, cons., 1990-93; vis. assoc. prof. Harvard U. Grad. Sch. Bus. Adminstrn., 1959-60; vis. prof. U. W.Australia, 1976; mem. com. math. in social scis. Social Sci. Research Council, 1979; participant African Math. Project, Mombasa, Kenya, 1965, 68. Author: Probability: An Introduction, 1960 (translated into Greek, German and Spanish, paperback edit.), Introduction to Difference Equations, 1958 (translated into Spanish, German and Japanese, also paperback edit.), Some Illustrative Examples of the Use of Undergraduate Mathematics in the Social Sciences, 1977, Probability in Social Science, 1983. Bd. dirs. Allen Meml. Hosp., Oberlin, 1980-85, 92—. Served with AUS, 1944-46. NSF sci. faculty fellow, 1960-61, 67-68. Mem. Math. Assn. Am., Am. Math. Soc., Phi Beta Kappa, Sigma Xi.

GOLDBERG, SAMUEL IRVING, mathematics educator; b. Toronto, Aug. 15, 1923; s. Jacob L. and Rachel (Berkovitz) G.; m. Sheila Richmond, Nov. 11, 1951; children: Julia Anna, Barry Howard, Jay Michael. Student, Cambridge (Eng.) U., 1945-46; BA, U. Toronto, 1948, MA, 1949, PhD, 1951. Sci. officer Def. Research Bd., Valcartier, Que., Can., 1951-52; asst. prof. math Lehigh U., Bethlehem, Pa., 1952-55; asso. prof. Wayne State U., Detroit, 1955-61; Harvard research fellow, 1959-60; asso. prof. U. Ill., Urbana, 1960-65; prof. U. Ill., 1965—; vis. prof. U. Toronto, 1968, Israel Inst. Tech., 1972, Cambridge U., 1979, Coll. de France, 1979, U. West Indies, Kingston, Jamaica, 1991-93; Sci. Rsch. Coun. vis. fgn. scientist U. Liverpool, Eng., 1973; Lady Davis fellow Technion, Israel, 1979; Queen's Quest prof. Queen's U., Can., 1980-81; apptd. mem. Ctr. Advanced Study U. Ill., 1984-85. Author: Curvature and Homology, 1962, rev. edit., 1998, (with R.L. Bishop) Tensor Analysis on Manifolds, 1968, (with W.C. Weber) Conformal Deformations of Riemannian Manifolds, 1969. Served with Can. Army, 1943-46. Recipient medal Coll. de France, 1979. Mem. Am. Math. Soc. Home: 808 La Sell Dr Champaign IL 61820-6820 Office: U Ill Dept Math Urbana IL 61801

GOLDBERG, SETH A., lawyer; b. N.Y.C., Aug. 20, 1953; s. Seymour I. and Florence (Rovensky) G.; m. Joan E. Shapiro, July 29, 1978; children: David, Emily. BA in History, SUNY, Binghamton, 1975; JD, Stanford U., 1978. Bar: D.C. 1978, Calif. 1991. Assoc. Steptoe & Johnson, Washington, 1978-86, ptnr., 1986—. Mem. ABA, Environtl. Law Inst. Home: 8303 Whittier Blvd Bethesda MD 20817-3124 Office: 1330 Connecticut Ave NW Washington DC 20036-1704

GOLDBERG, SHERMAN I., banking company executive, lawyer; b. 1942. BA, Miami U., 1964; JD, U. Cin., 1968. Bar: Ill. 1969. With First Chgo Corp., 1968—, gen. counsel, sec., 1988—, also v.p., 1990—, exec. v.p., gen. counsel. Office: First Chgo Corp 1 First Natl Plz Chicago IL 60603-2003*

GOLDBERG, SIDNEY, editor; b. N.Y.C., Mar. 1, 1931; s. Emanuel and Florence (Fischbein) G.; m. Lucianne S. Cummings, April 10, 1966; children: Joshua John, Jonah Jacob. BA, U. Mich., 1950, MA, 1952; postgrad., NYU, 1952-53. Editor North Am. Newspaper Alliance, N.Y.C., 1957-71; editor Bell-McClure Syndicate, N.Y.C., 1957-71, pres. N. Am. Newspaper Alliance, 1971-72; reporter clk. Washington Post, 1955; fgn. editor World Week Mag., N.Y.C., 1956-57; v.p., dir. internat. newspaper ops. United Media, N.Y.C., 1972-94, sr. v.p., gen. mgr., 1994—. Pres. Newspaper Features Coun., 1999—. With AUS, 1953-55. Mem. Nat. Cartoonists Soc., Internat. Press Inst., Interam. Press Assn. Soc. of Silurians, Dutch Treat Club, Sigma Delta Chi. Jewish. Home: 255 W 84th St New York NY 10024-4321 Office: United Media 200 Madison Ave New York NY 10016-3903

GOLDBERG, STANLEY IRWIN, real estate executive; b. Newport News, Va., May 13, 1934; s. David and Sara (Levy) G.; m. Marilyn Levin, Nov. 22, 1963 (dec. Oct. 1970); 1 child, Andrew Garfield. Student, Coll. William and Mary, 1952-54, U. Va., 1954-55. Lic. real estate broker, Va. V.p. Bedding Supply Co., Inc., Newport News, 1956-59, exec. v.p., 1960-61, pres., 1962-70; gen. ptnr. Goldkress Investment Co., Newport News, 1970—, also bd. dirs.; pres. Mutual Realty Corp., Newport News, 1973—. Trustee Temple Sinai, Newport News. Served with USAF, 1957-58. Mem. Nat. Assn. Realtors, Va. Assn. Realtors, Newport News-Hampton Bd. Realtors. Lodge: Elks. Home: 19 Hopemont Dr Newport News VA 23606-2146 Office: 11116 Jefferson Ave Newport News VA 23601-2551

GOLDBERG, VICTOR JOEL, retired data processing company executive; b. Chgo., Oct. 19, 1933; s. Albert J. and Ruth R. (Rosenberg) G.; m. Harriet A. David, June 1, 1958; children—Susan A., Alan J. BS, Northwestern U., 1955, MBA, 1956. With IBM Corp., Armonk, N.Y., 1959-93; corp. dir. bus. plans IBM Corp., Armonk, 1977-78; v.p. communications IBM Corp., Armonk, N.Y., 1979-81; corp. v.p., pres. communication products div. IBM Corp., Armonk, 1981-83, pres. nat. distbn. div., 1983-86, v.p. asst. group exec. marketing, 1986-88, v.p. mgmt. systems, 1988-93; dir. Edn. Through Music, 1998—. Mem. Forum for World Affairs, 1988-97; bd. govs. Westchester chpt. Am. Jewish Com., 1976-88, v.p., 1995—; trustee Inst. Internat. Edn., 1978—, mem. exec. com., 1984—, vice chmn., 1988—; trustee Mental Health Assn., Westchester, 1984—, exec. v.p., 1997—; trustee Westchester Reform Temple, 1995—; dir. Actors Shakespeare Co., 1995—; chmn. adv. com. Long Term Care Ombudsmen Program, Westchester County, 1995—; trustee New Alternatives for Children, 1997, treas., 1998—. With U.S. Army, 1956-59. Mem. Beta Gamma Sigma.

GOLDBERG, VICTOR PAUL, law educator; b. 1941. BA, Oberlin (Ohio) Coll., 1963, MA, 1964; PhD, Yale U., 1970. From asst. to full prof. U. Calif., Davis, 1967-83; prof. Northwestern U., Evanston, Ill., 1983-88; prof., co-dir. Ctr. Law and Econ. Studies Columbia U., N.Y.C., 1988—; assoc. prof. U. Calif., Berkeley, 1977; prof. U. Va., Charlottesville, 1981; mem. Inst. for Advanced Study, Princeton, N.J., 1978-79. Fellow Ctr. for Study of Pub. Choice, Blacksburg, Va., 1975-76. Office: Columbia U Sch Law 435 W 116th St New York NY 10027-7297

GOLDBERG, WHOOPI (CARYN JOHNSON), actress; b. N.Y.C., Nov. 13, 1955; d. Robert and Emma (Harris) Johnson; m. David Claessen (div.); m. Lyle Trachtenberg, Oct. 1, 1994 (div. Oct. 1995); 1 child, Alexandrea Martin. Mem. San Diego Repertory Theatre, 1975-80, Blake St. Hawkeyes, Berkeley, Calif., 1980-84. Author: Alice; appeared in one-person show Whoopi Goldberg on Broadway, 1984-85, Living on the Edge of Chaos, 1988 (Calif. theatre award outstanding achievement); films include The Color Purple, 1985, Jumpin' Jack Flash, 1986, Burglar, 1986, Telephone, 1987, Fatal Beauty, 1987, Clara's Heart, 1988, Beverly Hills Brats, 1989 (cameo), Homer and Eddie, 1989, The Long Walk Home, 1990, Ghost, 1990 (Acad. award best supporting actress, 1991), Soapdish, 1991, House Party 2 (cameo), The Player, 1992, Sister Act, 1992, Wisecracks, 1992, Sarafina!, 1992, Made in America, 1993, National Lampoon's Loaded Weapon 1, 1993, Sister Act 2: Back in the Habit, 1993, The Lion King, 1994 (voice), The Little Rascals, 1994, Naked in New York (cameo), 1994, Corrina, Corrina, 1994, Star Trek: Generations, 1994, The Pagemaster, 1994 (voice), Boys on the Side, 1995, Bogus, 1996, The Ghost of Mississippi, 1996, Eddie, 1996, Tales from the Crypt Presents: Bordello of Blood, 1996, The Associate, 1996, An Allen Smithee Film: Burn Hollywood Burn, 1998; TV film: Kiss Shot, 1989, My Past Is My Own, Cindrella, 1997; TV series: Star Trek: The Next Generation, 1988-94, Bagdad Cafe, CBS, 1990, In The Gloaming, 1997; TV specials include: Tales from the Whoop: Hot Rod Brown, Class Clown, 1990, Happily Ever After: Fairy Tales for Ever Child, 1997 (voice), Cinderella, 1997, How Stella Got Her Groove Back, 1998, A Knight in Camelot, 1998, The Rugrats Movie, 1998, Deep End of the Ocean, 1999, Jackie's Back! 1999, Interrupted Girl, 1999, others; host TV talk show The Whoopi Goldberg Show, 1992-93; many TV appearances. Named NAACP Entertainer of the Yr., 1990, Humanitarian of Yr. Starlight Found., 1989; recipient, Hans Christian Andersen Award for outstanding achievement by a dyslexic, 1987, grammy award for album of Broadway show, 1985; nominated for Emmy, 1996. Avocation: acting. *

GOLDBERG, WILLIAM JEFFREY, accountant; b. Chgo., Jan. 18, 1950; s. Harry and Bernice Dorothy (Benson) G.; m. Brenda Liebling; children: Leslie Claire, Melissa Liebling. BA, Knox Coll., 1971; JD, Cornell U., 1974; postgrad., U. Chgo., 1976-78. Bar: Ill. 1974, U.S. Dist. Ct. (no. dist.) Ill. 1974; CPA. Fin. counseling officer Continental Ill. Nat. Bank, Chgo., 1974-79; supr. KPMG Peat Marwick, Houston, 1979-80, mgr., 1980-82, ptnr., 1982—; nat. dir. Personal Fin. Planning Svcs., 1984-93, southwest ptnr.-in-charge personal fin. planning, 1993—; instr. law Ill. Inst. Tech. Chgo. Kent Coll. Law, 1977-78. Dir. Acad. Fin. Svcs., 1988-89; trustee Jewish Fedn. Greater Houston, 1985—, Endowment Fund Jewish Cmty. Houston, 1997—. Mem. AICPA (personal fin. planning divsn., exec. com. 1986-89, 94—, chmn. exec. com. 1996-98, chmn. legis and regulation subcom. 1989-91), Tex. Soc. CPAs, Houston Estate & Fin. Forum, Houston Bus. and Estate Planning Coun., Knox Coll. Club Houston (pres. 1981-82), Westwood Country Club (bd. dirs. 1996-97), Shadow Hawk Golf Club. Office: KPMG LLP 700 Louisiana St Ste 3000 Houston TX 77002

GOLDBERGER, ARTHUR STANLEY, economics educator; b. N.Y.C., Nov. 20, 1930; s. David M. and Martha (Greenwald) G.; m. Iefke Engelsman, Aug. 19, 1957; children: Nina Judith, Nicholas Bernard. B.S., N.Y.U., 1951; M.A., U. Mich., 1952, Ph.D., 1958. Acting asst. prof. econs. Stanford U., 1956-59; assoc. prof. econs. U. Wis., 1960- 63, prof., 1963-70, H.M. Groves prof., 1970-79, Vilas research prof., 1979-98, prof. emeritus, 1998—; vis. prof. Center Planning and Econ. Research, Athens, Greece, 1964-65; Keynes vis. prof. U. Essex, 1968- 69. Author: (with L.R. Klein) An Econometric Model of the United States, 1929-52, 1955, Impact Multipliers and Dynamic Properties, 1959, Econometric Theory, 1964, Topics in Regression Analysis, 1968, Functional Form and Utility, 1987, A Course in Econometrics, 1991, Introductory Econometrics, 1998; editor: (with O.D. Duncan) Structural Equation Models in the Social Sciences, 1973, (with D.J. Aigner) Latent Variables in Socioeconomic Models, 1976; Assoc. editor: Jour. Econometrics, 1973-77; bd. editors: Am. Econ. Rev, 1964-66, Jour. Econ. Lit, 1975-77. Fulbright fellow Netherlands Sch. Econs., 1955-56, 59-60; vis. prof. U. Hawaii, 1969, 71, Stanford U., 1990, 96; fellow Ctr. for Advanced Study in Behavioral Scis., Stanford, 1976-77, 80-81; Guggenheim fellow Stanford U., 1972-73, 85. Fellow Am. Statis. Assn., Econometric Soc. (council 1975-80, 82-87), Am. Acad. Arts and Scis., AAAS; mem. Am. Econ. Assn. (Disting. fellow 1988), Nat. Acad. Scis. (foreign) Netherlands Acad. Scis. Home: 2828 Sylvan Ave Madison WI 53705-5228 Office: U Wis Dept Econs 1180 Observatory Dr Madison WI 53706-1320

GOLDBERGER, AVRIEL HORWITZ, literary translator, retired French educator; b. Phila., Feb. 23, 1928; d. Samuel and Sadie (Goldman) Horwitz; m. Arnold Goldberger; children: Lee, Ellen. BA, U. Phila., 1949; MA, Bryn Mawr Coll., 1951, PhD, 1960. Prof. French, Hofstra U., Hempstead, N.Y., 1960-93, also past chmn. dept.; ret., 1993, literary translator,, 1993—. Translator: Corinne of Italy (Mme. de Staël), 1987, A Life of Her Own (Emilie Carles) (A Life of Her Own, 1991, Delphine (Mme. de Staël), 1995

(NEH transl. and pub. grantee). Decorated chevalier Order Arts and Letters (France); Fulbright and Am. Assn. U. Women fellow, 1952; grantee Helvetia Found., Zurich, Govt. of France. Mem. MLA, Am. Lit. Translators Assn., Am. Translators Assn. (cert. in French), Am. Assn. Tchrs. French, Staël Soc., Bryn Mawr Coll. Alumni Assn. (exec. bd. rep. Grad. Sch. Arts and Scis. 1994-97). Avocations: reading, travel, theater, opera. Home: 120 Hampshire Rd Great Neck NY 11023

GOLDBERGER, BLANCHE RUBIN, sculptor, jeweler; b. N.Y.C., Feb. 2, 1914; d. David and Sarah (Israel) Rubin; m. Emanuel Goldberger, June 28, 1942 (dec. 1994); children—Richard N., Ary Louis. B.A., Hunter Coll., N.Y.C., 1934; M.A., Columbia U., 1936; Certificat d'Etudes, Sorbonne, Paris, 1936; postgrad. Westchester Arts Workshop Sculpture and Jewelry, White Plains, 1961-70, Silvermine Coll. Arts, 1962, Nat. Acad. Arts, N.Y.C., 1968. Tchr. French and Hebrew, N.Y.C. High Sch. System, Scarsdale Jr. and Sr. High Schs. One-woman shows include: Bloomingdale's, Eastchester, N.Y., 1975, Scarsdale Pub. Library, N.Y., 1976, Temple Israel, White Plains, N.Y., 1975, Greenwich Art Barn, Conn., 1972 Westlake Gallery, White Plains, N.Y., 1981; exhibited in group shows at Hudson River Mus., Yonkers, N.Y., 1978, Silvermine-New Eng. Ann., Silvermine, Conn., 1979; represented in permanent collection at Scarsdale High Sch. Library, N.Y.; sculpture commn. Jewish Community Ctr. White Plains, N.Y., 1988; commn. Manchester, Vt.; also pvt. collections. Recipient award Beaux Arts of Westchester, White Plains, N.Y., 1967, First Prize, White Plains Art Show, Holocaust Meml. Bronze Plaque for Synagogue Congregation Israel, Manchester, Vt.; various commns. for calli collis calligraphic collages. Mem. Nat. Assn. Women Artists, Nat. Assn. Tchrs. French, Scarsdale Art Assn. (bd. dirs.; first prizes for sculpture). Jewish. Avocations: lecturing on sculpture, reading contemporary lit. in Hebrew, the violin, classical music concerts, callicollies.

GOLDBERGER, MARVIN LEONARD, physicist, educator; b. Chgo., Oct. 22, 1922; s. Joseph and Mildred (Sedwitz) G.; m. Mildred Ginsburg, Nov. 25, 1945; children: Samuel M., Joel S. B.S., Carnegie Inst. Tech., 1943; Ph.D., U. Chgo., 1948. Research assoc. Radiation Lab., U. Calif., 1948-49; research assoc. Mass. Inst. Tech., 1949-50; asst.-assoc. prof. U. Chgo., 1950-55, prof., 1955-57; Higgins prof. physics Princeton U., 1957-77, chmn. dept., 1970-76, Joseph Henry prof. physics, 1977-78; pres. Calif. Inst. Tech., Pasadena, 1978-87; dir. Inst. Advanced Study, Princeton, N.J., 1987-91; prof. physics UCLA, 1991-93; prof. physics U. Calif., San Diego, 1993—, dean divsn. natural scis., 1994—; mem. President's Sci. Adv. Com., 1965-69; chmn. Fedn. Am. Scientists, 1971-73; bd. dirs. Haskel, Inc. Fellow Am. Phys. Soc., Am. Acad. Arts and Scis.; mem. Nat. Acad. Scis., Am. Philos. Soc., Council on Fgn. Relations.

GOLDBERGER, PAUL JESSE, architecture critic, writer, educator, editor; b. Passaic, N.J., Dec. 4, 1950; s. Morris and Edna (Kronman) G.; m. Susan Lynn Solomon, Feb. 17, 1980; children: Adam Hirsh, Benjamin James Solomon, Alexander David Solomon. B.A., Yale U., 1972; LHD (hon.), Pratt Inst., 1992. Staff editor The New York Times Mag., N.Y.C., 1972-73; architecture critic The New York Times, N.Y.C., 1973—, editor cultural news, 1990-94, chief cultural corr., 1994-95, freelance contbr., 1995—; vis. lectr. architecture Yale U., 1984—. Author: The City Observed: New York, An Architectural Guide to Manhattan, 1978, The Skyscraper, 1981, On the Rise: Architecture and Design in a Post-Modern Age, 1983, House of the Hamptons, 1986, Above New York, 1988; contbr. articles and essays to profl. publs. Mem. bd. overseers Parsons Sch. Design, 1986-90, 94—; bd. dirs. Jewish Found. for Christian Rescuers, 1994—, Guild Hall, East Hampton, N.Y., 1986-90. Recipient Pres. medal Mcpl. Art Soc., N.Y.C., 1984, Pulitzer prize for Disting. Criticism, 1984, Roger Starr Journalism award Citizens Housing and Planning Coun., 1987, medal of honor N.Y. Landmarks Preservation Found., 1991, Lit. Lion award N.Y. Pub. Libr., 1993. Mem. AIA (hon., medal 1981), Soc. Archtl. Historians (bd. dirs. 1977-79), Century Assn. Office: NY Times 229 W 43rd St New York NY 10036-3959*

GOLDBERGER, ROBERT D., food products company executive; b. 1935. V.p. King Foods, Inc., Newport, Minn., 1956-73; with GFI America, Mpls., 1973—, pres., CEO. Office: GFI America 2815 Blaisdell Ave Minneapolis MN 55408-2385*

GOLDBERG-SCHAIBLE, JOCELYN HOPE SCHNIER, market research consultant; b. N.Y.C., Mar. 29, 1953; d. Alex and Eileen Rosalie (Firstenberg) Schnier. AB, Princeton U., 1974; MBA, Harvard U., 1977. Statis. technician John Hancock Inc., Boston, 1974-75; product mgr. Gen. Foods Corp., White Plains, N.Y., 1977-78; strategic/tactical bus. planning analyst Bausch & Lomb Corp., Rochester, N.Y., 1979-81; mgmt. assoc. Gordon S. Black Corp., Rochester, 1981-84; pres. Rochester Rsch. Group, N.Y., 1985—; bd. dirs. M&T Bank (1st Empire State Corp.); bd. dirs. U. Rochester Med. Ctr., 1991-98; bd. dirs. JCC Greater Rochester, 1998—. Trustee Geva Theater. Recipient Achievement award Wall St. Jour., 1977. Mem. Profl. Ski Instrs. Am. (cert.). Clubs: Princeton (v.p. 1974 Princeton Class 1989-94), Harvard U. Bus. Sch. (bd. dirs.). Home: 1666 Strong Rd Victor NY 14564-9133 Office: PO Box 22954 Rochester NY 14692-2954

GOLDBLATT, BARRY LANCE, manufacturing executive; b. Palo Alto, Calif., July 29, 1945; s. Samuel and Joan Charlotte (Morton) G. BS, U. So. Calif., 1967, MBA, 1968. Supr. market rsch. for brands Procter & Gamble Co., Cin., 1968-71; mgr. market rsch. Personal Products Co. subs. Johnson & Johnson, 1971-74; assoc. dir. consumer rsch. Johnson & Johnson Baby Products Co., Skillman, N.J., 1974-87; dir. market rsch. Johnson & Johnson Dental Care Co., New Brunswick, N.J., 1987-89, Johnson & Johnson Consumer Products, Inc., Skillman, 1989-93, exec. dir. mktg. rsch. Johnson & Johnson Consumer Products Worldwide, 1994—. Bd. dirs. New Brunswick Hot Line, 1973; vol. Urban Cons. Group, 1977—. Recipient Cert. of Recognition Nat. Symposium Hispanic Bus. and Economy, Chgo., 1981, Cert. of Appreciation U. So. Calif., L.A., 1981. Mem. U. So. Calif. MBA's, U. So. Calif. Commerce Assocs., Advt. Rsch. Found., Am. Mktg. Assn., Assn. MBA Execs. (western region coun.- conf. bd.), Am. Philatel. Soc., U. So. Calif. Assocs., U. So. Calif. Alumni Club, Skull and Dagger, Zeta Beta Tau. Republican. Club: U. So. Calif. Alumni of N.J. (pres.). Home: 20 Andrews Ln Princeton NJ 08540-7633 Office: Johnson & Johnson 199 Grandview Rd Skillman NJ 08558

GOLDBLATT, EILEEN WITZMAN, foundation executive; b. N.Y.C.; d. Ben and Sylvia Witzman; m. Myron Everett Goldblatt Jr.; children: Tracy Ellen, David Laurence. BS, Russell Sage Coll., 1967; MS, Bank Street Coll, 1980. Tchr., tchr. trainer N.Y.C. Bd. Edn., 1967-73, dir. mus. and cultural programs, 1984-89; ednl. cons. Cooper-Hewitt Mus., N.Y.C., 1979-80; dir. mus., collaborative sch./cultural voucher programs Mus. Collaborative, Inc., N.Y.C., 1981-84; exec. dir. Young Audiences/N.Y., 1990-97; pres., CEO Nat. "I Have a Dream" R Found., N.Y.C., 1997—; creator N.Y.C. Arts and Cultural Edn. Network and Arts and Cultural Edn. Network Menu, 1986-90, Cultural Instn. Network Menu, 1984-85; creator N.Y.C. Cultural Instn. Network. Author: (workbook) Electroworks, 1980, (exhbn. guide) Smithsonian: A Treasure Hunt, 1979, (curriculum) The Ancient Egyptians, 1980. Trustee N.Y.C. Sch. Art League; mem. cultural del. People to People Internat., People's Republic China, 1988, 96, India Initiative, 1997; mem. Class of 1990 Leadership Am. Mem. Am. Assn. Mus., Internat. Mus. (com.), Am. Women in Enterprise, Women's City Club N.Y., City Club N.Y. Home: 500 E 83rd St New York NY 10028-7208 Office: Nat "I Have a Dream" Found 330 7th Ave Fl 20 New York NY 10001-5010

GOLDBLATT, HAL MICHAEL, photographer, accountant; b. Long Beach, Calif., Feb. 6, 1952; s. Arnold Phillip and Molly (Stearns) G.; m. Shawn Naomi Doherty, Aug. 27, 1974; children: Eliyahu Yonah, Tova Devorah, Raizel, Shoshana, Reuven Lev, Eliezer Noach, Esther Bayla, Rochel Leah, Zalman Ber, Perle Sara. BA in Math., Calif. State U., Long Beach, 1975. Owner Star Publs., Las Vegas, 1975—; treas. Goldblatt, Inc., Las Vegas, 1980—; pres. SDG Computer Svc., Las Vegas, 1985—; chief fin. officer Martin & Mills Ltd., Las Vegas, 1992-93; controller Amland Devel., Las Vegas, 1993-95; CFO Stewart Constrn., Las Vegas, 1995-96; CEO Goldblatt, Inc., Las Vegas, 1996-97; cost acct. Ameristar Casinos, Inc., Las Vegas, 1997—. Photographer: (photo essays) Mikveh Yisroel, 1978, Chassidic Fabrengen, 1979, A Day at Disneyland, 1985, Shavous Trek, 1997, Garth Brooks World Tour, 1998, Care for Kids Telethon, 1998, Chanukah - Festival of Lights, 1998; prodr., engr.: (audio cassettes) From the Heart of My Dreams, 1980, Middle Class Dreams, 1981, Uforatzta Trio, 1982. Founder, pres. Jews for Judaism, Long Beach, 1975-82, v.p., 1983—; fundraising chmn. Friends of Lubavitch, Long Beach, 1977; bd. dirs. Congregation Lubavitch, Long Beach, 1987, 91-92; treas. Actor's Repertory Theatre, 1995-98, mem. adv. bd., 1998—. Recipient Gold Press Card award Forty Niner Newspaper, 1973, 74, Floyd Durham Meml. award for Outstanding Community Svc., 1973, Georgie award Actor's Repertory Theatre, 1995, ART Disting. Svc. award, 1996. Office: Ameristar Casinos Inc 3773 Howard Hughes Pkwy Las Vegas NV 89109-5940

GOLDBLATT, STANFORD JAY, lawyer; b. Chgo., Feb. 25, 1939; s. Maurice and Bernice (Mendelson) G.; m. Ann Dudley Cronkhite, June 17, 1968; children: Alexandra, Nathaniel, Jeremy. BA magna cum laude, Harvard U., 1960, LLB magna cum laude, 1963. Bar: Ill. 1963. Law clk. U.S. Ct. Appeals, 5th Jud. Circuit, New Orleans, 1963-64; mem. firm Winston & Strawn, Chgo., 1964-67; v.p. Goldblatt Bros., Inc., Chgo., 1967-76; pres., chief exec. officer Goldblatt Bros., Inc., 1976-77, chmn. exec. com., 1977-78; ptnr. Hopkins & Sutter, 1978-97, Winston & Strawn, Chgo., 1997—; dir. MacLean-Fogg Co. Trustee U. Chgo., Louis A. Weiss Meml. Hosp., Cancer Rsch. Found., U. Chgo. Hosps. Mem. Econ. Club, Standard Club, Comml. Club. Office: Winston & Strawn 35 W Wacker Dr Ste 4200 Chicago IL 60601-1695

GOLDBLATT, STEVEN HARRIS, law educator; b. Bklyn., Apr. 30, 1947; s. J. Irving and Ethel (Epstein) G.; m. Irene P. Burns, June 12, 1981; children: Sarah P., Elizabeth G.B. BA, Franklin & Marshall Coll., 1967; JD, Georgetown U., 1970. Bar: Pa. 1970, D.C. 1981. With Phila. Dist. Atty.'s Office, 1970-81; dir. Appellate Litigation Program Georgetown U. Law Ctr., Washington, 1981-83, prof. law, dir. Appellate Litigation Progam, 1983—; chair rules adv. com. U.S. Ct. Appeals for Armed Forces. Co-author: Analysis and Commentary to the Pennsylvania Crime Code, 1973, Three Prosecutors Look at the Crimes Code, 1974, Ineffective Assistance of Counsel: Attempts to Establish Minimum Standards for Criminal Cases, 1983; reporter Criminal Justice in Crisis, 1988, Achieving Justice in a Diverse America, 1992, An Agenda for Justice: ABA Perspectives on Criminal and Civil Justice Issues, 1996. Mem. ABA (criminal justice sect. chmn. amicus curiae briefs com. 1981—, crisis in criminal justice com. 1990-91). Office: Georgetown U Law Ctr 600 New Jersey Ave NW Washington DC 20001-2075

GOLDBLITH, SAMUEL ABRAHAM, food science educator; b. Lawrence, Mass., May 5, 1919; s. Abraham and Fannie (Rubin) G.; m. Diana Greenberg, Apr. 27, 1941 (dec. June 1990); children: Errol (dec.), Judith Ann, Jonathan Mark. SB, MIT, 1940, SM, 1947, PhD, 1949; DSc (hon.), Rutgers U., 1997. Rsch. Arthur D. Little Co., Cambridge, Mass., 1940-41; mem. faculty MIT, 1949—, prof. food tech., 1959-74, Underwood Prescott prof. food sci., 1972-78, acting head dept., 1959-61, exec. officer dept., 1961-66, dep. dept. head, 1967-72, assoc. dept. head, 1972-74, dir. indsl. liaison, 1974-78, prof. food sci., 1978-89, prof. emeritus, 1989—, v.p., 1978-86, sr. advisor to pres., 1986-90; mem. coms. radiation preservation and radionuclides in foods, chmn. com. radiation preservation of foods NRC-NAS; dir. Techno Venture Co., Tokyo. Author: An Introduction to Thermal Processing of Foods, 1961, Milestones in Nutrition, 1964—, Annotated Bibliography on Microwaves in Food Preservations, Freeze Drying and Advanced Food Technology, 1975, Samuel Cate Prescott; MIT Dean and Pioneer Food Technologist, 1993, Of Microbes and Molecules: Food Technology, Applied Biology and Nutrition at MIT 1873-1988, 1995, Appetite for Life: An Autobiobraphy, 1996; also numerous sci. papers. Served to capt. AUS, 1941-46, PTO. Decorated Silver Star medal, Bronze Star with oak leaf cluster, Order of Sacred Treasure 2d class (Japan); named One of Ten Outstanding Young Men of Greater Boston, 1953; recipient Babcock-Hart award, 1969; Nicholas Appert medal, 1970. Fellow Inst. Food Technologists (chmn. N.E. sect. 1958, Monsanto Presentation award 1953, Disting. Food Scientist award N.Y. sect. 1969, Phila. sect. 1976), Inst. Food Sci. and Tech. (U.K.), AAAS; mem. Am. Chem. Soc., Royal Swedish Acad. Engring. Scis. (fgn. mem.), Swiss Acad. Engring. Scis. (corr. mem.), Am. Inst. Nutrition, Sigma Xi, Phi Tau Sigma (pres. 1958). Clubs: Cosmos (Washington), New Century (Boston) (pres. 1962-63). Lodge: Masons. Home: 6 Meadowview Rd Melrose MA 02176-2913 Office: MIT 77 Massachusetts Ave Cambridge MA 02139-4307 *My participation in the defense of the Philippines and survival of the "Bataan Death March" and subsequent events led me to my choice of graduate study and further research and teaching at MIT in food science and technology. The results of this professional career have led me into close relationship and friendship with a number of Japanese graduate students and postdoctoral fellows and have helped build bridges of friendship and understanding among us and between our countries.*

GOLDBLOOM, RICHARD BALLON, pediatrics educator; b. Montreal, Dec. 16, 1924; s. Alton and Annie Esther (Ballon) G.; m. Ruth Miriam Schwartz, June 25, 1946; children—Alan L., Barbara, David S. BSc, McGill U., 1945, MD, CM, 1949, diploma in pediat., 1953; cert. in pediat., Royal Coll. Physicians and Surgeons, Can., 1954; DLitt (hon.), U. Coll. Cape Breton, 1989. Intern Royal Victoria Hosp., Montreal, 1949-50, Montreal Children's Hosp., 1950-51; resident Children's Hosp., Boston, 1951-52; tchg. fellow dept. pediat. Harvard U., 1951-52; chief resident Montreal Children's Hosp., 1952-53, asst. physician dept. medicine, 1957, physician, assoc. dept. metabolism, 1964-67; Hosmer tchg. fellow dept. pediat. McGill U., 1953-56, demonstrator, 1957, assoc. prof., 1964-67; prof. pediat. Dalhousie U., Halifax, N.S., Can., 1967—; head dept. Dalhousie U., 1967-85; physician in chief, dir. rsch. Izaak Walton Killam Hosp. for Children, 1967-85; cons. staff St. John Regional Hosp., N.S. Rehab. Centre; chmn. task force on periodic health exam. Health and Welfare Can., 1985-94; vis. prof. Shanghai Med. U., 1985-86; Sir Arthur Sims Commonwealth traveling prof., 1986; Litchfield lectr. Oxford U., 1974; lectr. in field. Editor: International Abstracts in Pediatrics; mem. editorial bd. jour. Pediatrics; contbr. articles to profl. jours. Bd. dirs. Atlantic Symphony Orch., 1969-73, hon. dir., 1973-75, v.p., 1975-76, pres., 1976-79, chmn. med. adv. com. Can. Cystic Fibrosis Found., 1969-72; dir. Atlantic Rsch. Centre for Mental Retardation, 1967-75, 75-85; bd. dirs. Opera East, 1974, Bonny Lea Farm, N.S. Festival of Arts; trustee Queen Elizabeth II Fund for Rsch. in Diseases of Children; bd. dirs. Muscular Dystrophy Assn. Can.; v.p. Symphony of N.S., 1986-89; chmn. Rhodes Scholarship Selection Com. (Maritime Provinces); hon. dir. Symphony N.S., IWK Grace Health Ctr. Found. Decorated officer Order of Can.; recipient Queen's Jubilee medal, 1978, Can. Confedn. medal, 1993. Mem. Soc. Pediat. Rsch., Can. Soc. Clin. Investigation, Am. Pediat. Soc., Assn. Med. Sch. Pediat. Dept. Chmn., Can. Pediat. Soc. (pres. 1985-86), Am. Acad. Pediat., Can. Assn. Pediat. Hosps., Can. Med. Assn. (sr.), Halifax Med. Soc., Lunenburg Yacht Club, Bluenose Golf Club, Alpha Omega Alpha. Jewish. Home: 1465 Brenton St Ste 1106, Halifax, NS Canada B3J 3T3 Office: 5850 University Ave, Halifax, NS Canada B3J 3G9

GOLDBLUM, JEFF, actor; b. Pitts., Oct. 22, 1952; m. Patricia Gaul (div.), m. Geena Davis (div.) 11/1/93. Studied at, Neighborhood Playhouse, N.Y.C. Broadway theater debut in Two Gentlemen of Verona, 1971, also appeared in The Mooney Shapiro Songbook, 1981; off-Broadway appearances in Our Late Night, El Grande de Coca-Cola, City Sugar, 1978; films include California Split, 1974, Death Wish, 1974, Nashville, 1975, Next Stop Greenwich Village, 1976, Annie Hall, Between the Lines, 1977, Invasion of the Body Snatchers, 1978, Remember My Name, 1978, Thank God It's Friday, 1978, The Big Chill, 1983, The Right Stuff, 1983, Threshold, 1983, The Adventures of Buckaroo Banzai, 1984, Silverado, 1985, Into the Night, 1985, Transylvania 6-5000, 1985, The Fly, 1986 (Saturn award), Beyond Therapy, 1987, Vibes, 1988, Earth Girls Are Easy, 1989, The Tall Guy, 1990, The Bad Monkey, 1990, Mr. Frost, 1990, Deep Cover, 1992, The Favor, the Watch and the Very Big Fish, 1992, Fathers and Sons, 1992, Jurassic Park, 1993, Hideaway, 1995, Nine Months, 1995, Mad Dog Time, 1996, Independence Day, 1996, The Great White Hype, 1996, Lost World: The Jurassic Park, 1997, Hideaway, 1995, Nine Months, 1995, Mad Dog Time, 1996, The Great White Hype, 1996, Independence Day, 1996, Welcome to Hollywood, 1998, The Prince of Egypt (voice), 1998, Holy Man, 1998, Popcorn, 1999; TV movies include The Legend of Sleepy Hollow, 1980, Rehearsal for Murder, 1982, Ernie Kovacs: Between the Laughter, 1984, Lush Life, 1994; TV series Tenspeed and Brownshoe, 1980, host Future Quest, 1994; prodr. short action film: Little Surprises, 1995 (Acad. award nominee for best live short action film 1996). Address: care William Morris Agy Attn Peter Lemie 151 S El Camino Dr Beverly Hills CA 90212-2704*

GOLDE, DAVID WILLIAM, physician, educator; b. N.Y.C., Oct. 23, 1940. BS in Chemistry, Fairleigh Dickinson U., 1962; MD, McGill U., 1966. Diplomate: Am Bd. Internal Medicine, Am. Bd. Med. Oncology, Nat. Bd. Med. Examiners. Asst. research chemist Gen. Foods Corp., 1962; intern. U. Calif. Hosps., San Francisco, 1966-67, resident in medicine, 1970-72, fellow Cancer Research Inst., 1971-72; staff cons. continuing edn. and tng. br. div. regional med. program (NIH), 1967-68, resident in clin. pathology, 1968-70; hematology fellow NIH, 1969-70; instr. medicine U. Calif., San Francisco, 1972-73, asst. prof., 1973-74; asst. prof. medicine UCLA, 1974-75, assoc. prof., 1975-79, prof., 1979-91, chief divsn. hematology-oncology, 1981-91, prof. emeritus, 1991—, co-dir. Clin. Rsch. Ctr., 1974-87, dir., 1987-91, dir. AIDS Ctr., 1986-90; Enid A. Haupt prof. hematologic oncology Meml. Sloan-Kettering Cancer Ctr., N.Y.C., 1991—, attending physician Meml. Hosp. for Cancer and Allied Diseas, 1991—, head divsn. hematologic oncology, 1991-96; mem. Sloan-Kettering Inst. for Cancer Rsch., 1991—; prof. medicine Cornell U. Med. Coll., N.Y.C., 1991—; prof. molecular pharmacology and therapeutics Cornell U. Grad. Sch. Med. Scis., N.Y.C., 1992—; physician-in-chief Meml. Hosp. Cancer & Allied Diseases, 1996—. Mem. editl. bd. Blood, 1978-81, Peptides, 1979-83, Leukemia, 1986—;, Scandinavian Jour. Haematology (now European Jour. Haematology), 1986-99; editor: Blood Revs., 1986-93, Cytokines, Cellular & Molecular Therapy, 1997—; assoc. editor: Cancer Rsch., 1989—; contbr. numerous articles to profl. jours. With USPHS, 1967-70. Fellow ACP; mem. AAAS, Am. Assn. Cancer Rsch., Am. Fedn. Clin. Rsch., Am. Soc. Clin. Investigation, Am. Soc. Clin. Oncology, Am. Soc. Hematology, Assn. Am. Physicians, Endocrine Soc., Internat. Soc. Exptl. Hematology (councillor 1995-97), Soc. Biol. Therapy, Internat. Assn. for Comparative Rsch. on Leukemia, Soc. Exptl. Biology and Medicine, Western Soc. Clin. Investigation (pres. 1989-90), Western Soc. Clin. Rsch., Alpha Omega Alpha. Office: Meml Sloan-Kettering Ctr 1275 York Ave New York NY 10021-6007

GOLDEN, ALFRED, business owner; b. Bklyn., Apr. 24, 1917; s. Charles and Leah (Nash) G.; separated; children: Jeffrey Paul, Kenneth Todd. BA, U. Ala., 1938. Prse. Golden Press, Inc., N.Y.C., 1947-60; v.p. dir. Kinney Svcs. Corp. (now Times Warner), N.Y.C., 1961-67; pres. Riverside Funeral Chapel, 1967-84; pres., v.p. cemetery divsn. Levitt-Weinstein Meml. Chapel, 1984—. Nat. commr. Anti-Defamation League, 1948—; vice-chmn. Nat. Hillel Commn., 1992-96. With U.S. Army, 1943-45. Named Man of Yr. Anti-Defamation League, 1955; recipient numerous awards. Mem. Am. Legion, Jewish War Vets., Am. Mgmt. Assn., Jewish Funeral Dirs., Knights of Pythias. Democrat. Avocations: golf, cards, fishing. Home: 3375 N Country Club Dr Apt 708 Aventura FL 33180-1652

GOLDEN, ARTHUR F., lawyer; b. Bklyn., Apr. 14, 1946; s. Isadore and Dorothy (Schisel) G.; m. Elisabeth Lee Smith, Aug. 28, 1971; children—Frederick Tucker, James Alexander, Eliza Emerson. BS, Rensselaer Poly. Inst., 1966; JD, NYU, 1969. Bar: N.Y. 1970, U.S. Ct. Appeals (2d cir.) 1970, U.S. Dist. Ct. (so. dist.) N.Y. 1972, U.S. Supreme 1975, U.S. Ct. Appeals (D.C. cir.) 1979, D.C. 1980, U.S. Dist. Ct. D.C. 1980, U.S. Dist. Ct. (ea. dist.) N.Y. 1983, U.S. Dist. Ct. (no. dist.) Ohio 1985, U.S. Ct. Appeals (6th cir.) 1985. With firm Davis Polk & Wardwell, N.Y.C., 1969—; ptnr. Davis, Polk & Wardwell, N.Y.C., 1978—; mgmt. com., 1996—; co-founder Washington office Davis Polk, 1980-82, also bd. dirs.; mem. exec. com., chmn. compensation com. ESCO Electronics Corp., 1990-96; bd. dirs., mem. exec. and audit and fin. coms. Borg Warner Security Corp.; bd. dirs., mem. audit and pub. policy com. Allegiance Corp., 1996—. With USAR, 1968-74. Mem. ABA, Assn. of Bar of City of N.Y., N.Y. State Bar Assn., N.Y. State Communities Aid Assn. (bd. mgrs. 1986-89), New Canaan Winter Club (pres. 1988-91, bd. govs. 1987-93), Country Club New Canaan. Home: 72 Saint George Ln New Canaan CT 06840-2032 Office: Davis Polk & Wardwell 450 Lexington Ave New York NY 10017-3911

GOLDEN, BETH, Special Olympics administrator; 1 child, Molly E. Student, Eureka Coll., 1970; BA, U. N.C., Asheville, 1985; postgrad., Western Carolina U., 1993. Instr. adult basic edn. Blue Ridge C.C., Flat Rock, N.C., 1988, 90-91; tng. rep. Blue Ridge C.C., Flat Rock, 1989-90, compensatory edn. and spl. populations specialist, 1990-91, coord. spl. populations office, 1991-96; area dir. Spl. Olympics N.C., 1996—; cognitive retraining therapist Thomas Rehab. Hosp., Asheville, 1988-89, cons. in field; pvt. practice, 1997—. Chair Henderson County Mayor's Com. for Persons with Disabilities, 1992-97; chair respite care com. Parents' Assistance League, 1994-95. Recipient Lockhart Follin-Mace Advocacy award N.C. Employment Network/Divsn. Vocat. Rehab., 1998; Grantee State of N.C., 1985, Ednl. Found., 1991, 92, 93, Melvin Lane Charitable Trust, 1992, 93. Mem. N.C. Head Injury Found. (profl. coun.), Henderson County Coun. on Women (pres. 1991-93), Job Devel. Coun. Henderson County, Inter-Agy. Coun.

GOLDEN, BRUCE PAUL, lawyer; b. Chgo., Dec. 4, 1943; s. Irving R. and Anne K. (Eisenberg) G. SB in Elec. Sci. and Engring., MIT, 1965, SM in Elec. Engring., 1966; JD, Harvard U., 1969. Bar: Ill. 1969, U.S. Dist. Ct. (no. dist.) Ill. 1970, U.S. Ct. Appeals (7th cir.) 1994, U.S. Supreme Ct. 1995; cert. arbitrator. Assoc. McDermott, Will & Emery, Chgo., 1970-75, ptnr., 1976-91; of counsel Fishman & Merrick, P.C., Chgo., 1991-92, Coffield, Ungaretti & Harris, Chgo., 1992-96; Bruce P. Golden and Assocs., Chgo., 1996—; officer, dir. various corps.; speaker bank law, securities law, venture capital seminars. Contbr. articles to Banking Law Jour., contbg. editor, 1979—. Chmn. MIT Enterprise Forum Chgo.; bd. dirs. Entrepreneurship Inst. Chgo., Chgo. chpt. U.S. Entrepreneurs Network, Ill. Small Bus. Devel. Ctr., Kellogg Sch. Bus. community services com. Mem. MIT Alumni of Chgo. (dir. 1993—), Union League. Home and Office: 4137 N Hermitage Ave Chicago IL 60613-1820

GOLDEN, CAROLE ANN, immunologist, microbiologist; b. L.A., Sept. 23, 1942; d. Floyd Winfred and Betty Lee (Cantland) G. AB, Okla. Coll. Liberal Arts, 1963; MS in Microbiology, Miami U., Oxford, Ohio, 1969, PhD in Immunology, 1973. Rsch. asst. prof. medicine U. Utah Med. Sch., Salt lake City, 1973-79; sr. scientist Utah Biomed. Test Lab., Salt lake City, 1976-82; v.p., sci. dir. Microbiol. rsch. Corp., Bountiful, Utah, 1978-87; v.p. rsch. and devel. Editek Inc., Burlington, N.C., 1987-97; v.p. product devel. Xanthon Inc., Research Triangle Park, N.C., 1997—; chmn. R&D mgmt. com. Assn. Biotech. Cos., 1990-91; chmn. hand-held test kit com. NATO Indsl. Adv. Group, 1992-94. Contbr. articles to profl. jours. Recipient citation Tech. Commn., 1983. Mem. AAAS, Am. Soc. Microbiology, Am. Def. Preparedness Assn., N.Y. Acad. Sci., Soc. Leukocyte Biology, Am. Mensa, Sigma. Republican. Home: 2 White Oak St Elon College NC 27244-9106 Office: Xanthon Inc PO Box 12296 Research Triangle Park NC 27709

GOLDEN, CORNELIUS JOSEPH, JR., lawyer; b. Montreal, Que., Can., July 7, 1948; parents Am. citizens; s. Cornelius Joseph and Anna May (Gohlke) G.; m. Maureen Kay Schrader, Oct. 14, 1973; 1 child, Brendan Christopher. BA in Econs., Stanford U., 1970, JD, 1973. Bar: Calif. 1973, D.C. 1975, N.Y. 1988, U.S. Dist. Ct. D.C. 1976, U.S. Ct. Appeals (9th cir.) 1974, U.S. Ct. Appeals (D.C. cir.) 1975, U.S. Dist. Ct. (5th cir.) 1981, U.S Dist. Ct. (4th cir.) 1990, U.S. Supreme Ct. 1979. Rsch. fellow in comml. law Centre National de la Recherche Scientifique, Paris, 1974; assoc. Wilmer, Cutler & Pickering, Washington, 1974-79; assoc. Foreman & Dyess, Washington, 1980-81, ptnr., 1981-84; ptnr. D'Amico, Luedtke, Demarest & Golden, Washington, 1984-86, Chadbourne & Parke, Washington, 1986—. Contbr. articles to profl. jours. Mem. Univ. Club Wash., Lowes Island Club (Sterling, Va.). Episcopalian. Home: 971 Saigon Rd Mc Lean VA 22102-2137 Office: Chadbourne & Parke Ste 300 1200 New Hampshire Ave NW Washington DC 20036-6802*

GOLDEN, DAVID EDWARD, physicist; b. N.Y.C., May 27, 1932; s. Barnet Dade and Rose (Rosenbaum) G.; m. Paula Englander, July 18, 1962; children: Jeffrey Bertram, Leila Justine. AB, NYU, 1954, PhD in Physics, 1960. Asst. prof. NYU, 1960-61, Adelphi U., Garden City, N.Y., 1961-62; engring. specialist GTE Lab., Palo Alto, Calif., 1962-63; staff scientist Lockheed Lab., Palo Alto, 1963-68; vis. prof. U. Bari, Italy, 1968-69; sr. scientist Sylvania Electric Products, Danvers, Mass., 1969-70; prof. U. Nebr., Lincoln, 1970-75; George Lynn Gross rsch. prof., chmn. U. Okla., Norman, 1975-85; provost, v.p. acad. affairs, prof. physics U. North Tex., Denton, 1985-89, prof., dir. ctr. for materials characterization, 1989-94, regents prof., 1993—; cons. autometric divsn. Paramount Pictures, N.Y.C., 1961-62,

Tracor, Austin, Tex., 1969-74, Lawrence Radiation Lab., Livermore, Calif., 1975-78, Minn. Mining and Mftg., Mpls., 1984-86; hon. lectr. Mid-Am. State U. Assn., 1982-83; chmn. Tex. Higher Edn. Coordinating Bd. Com. on Satellite Ednl. Delivery Systems, 1986; lectr. in field. Contbr. articles to profl. jours., chpts. to books. Sr. cons. Say It Straight Found. Grantee various orgns.; fellow Centennial Edn. Program U. Nebr., 1974-75. Fellow Am. Phys. Soc. (com. mem.); mem. AAAS, MRS, Sigma Xi. Lodge: Kiwanis. Avocations: jogging, tennis.

GOLDEN, DAVID M., educator; b. Dec. 9, 1937. BS, SUNY, Oneonta, 1960, MS, 1974. Tchr. Ft. Plain (Vt.) Pub. Schs., 1961-65, Norwich (N.Y.) City Schs., 1965-68, Shenendhouse Sch., Clifton Park, N.Y., 1968—. Mem. Nat. Coun. for the Social Studies, Am. Fedn. Tchrs. (del. 1999), N.Y. State Coun. for the Social Studies, Capital Dist. Coun. for the Social Studies (editor newsletter, pres. 1984-94), N.Y. State Coun. for Social Studies (pres.-elect 1998-99, pres. 1999—). Republican. Roman Catholic. Avocations: model railroading, travel, history. Office: 4 Royal Oak Dr Clifton Park NY 12065

GOLDEN, DONA LEE, artist; b. Waterford, Minn., Mar. 13, 1931; d. Eugene and Marjorie (McCorkell) Bolin; m. Darrell Richard Golden, Feb. 21, 1959; three children. BFA, Mpls. Sch. Art & Design, 1957, U. Iowa, 1959; MEd, U. Nebr., 1980. Art tchr. K-12 Waterloo (Nebr.) Pub. Sch., 1975-89; mem. Artist Coop. Gallery, Omaha, 1989—, Nebr. Women's Caucus for Art, Period Gallery, Omaha, 1999—. Exhibited in group shows Octagon Ctr. for the Arts, Ames, Iowa, 1998, 99, McCook C.C., 1998, Shafer Gallery, Great Bend, Kans., 1998, 99; 2-person shows include St. Paul's Luth. Ch., Millard, Nebr.; group shows include Fremont, Nebr., 1998, Omaha, Nebr. Women's Caucus, 1995—. Mem. DAR, Kans. Watercolor Soc. (Wichita, signature mem.). Republican. Presbyn. Avocations: golf, genealogy, hiking, canoeing, reading. Home: 2142 S 108th St Omaha NE 68144-3101

GOLDEN, EDDIE LEE, optometrist; b. Forest, Miss., Jan. 3, 1955; s. James Madison and Hazel E. (Tucker) G.; m. Kathy Patricia Davis, Nov. 27, 1982; children: Jonathan, Heather, Jeremy, Matthew. AA, East Cen. Jr. Coll., Decatur, Miss., 1975; MS, U. Miss., 1977; OD, So. Coll. Optometry, 1982. Pvt. practice Golden Eye Clinic, Hattiesburg, Miss., 1983—. Deacon, mem. Temple Bapt. Ch., Hattiesburg; discipleship tng. dir.; missionary Bapt. Student Union, 1974, mem. state coun., 1974-75; vol. optometric missions in Cen. Am. Mem. Am. Optometric Assn. (contact lens sect., sports vision sect.), Nat. Eye Rsch. Found., Internet. CKR Soc., So. Coun. Optometry, Miss. Optometric Assn., Miss. Club (pres. 1981-82, Optometric Recognition award 1985-92), U. So. Miss. Eagle Club, Rotary. Office: Golden Eye Clinic 10336 Shrewsbury Run W Collierville TN 38017-8860

GOLDEN, E(DWARD) SCOTT, lawyer; b. Miami, Fla., Sept. 25, 1955; s. Alvan Leonard and Fay Betty (Gray) G.; m. Jane Eileen DeKlavon, June 9, 1979; children: Daniel Bryan, Kimberly Michelle. Student, So. Fla. Christian Coll., 1975-76; BS, MIT, 1978; JD, Harvard U., 1981. Bar: Fla. 1981, U.S. Dist. Ct. (so. dist.) Fla. 1982, U.S. Tax Ct. 1982, U.S. Supreme Ct. 1991, U.S. Dist. Ct. (mid. dist.) Fla. 1993. Assoc. Roberts and Holland, Miami, 1981-82, Valdes-Fauli, Richardson, Cobb & Petrey, P.A., Miami, 1982-83; v.p. Buck and Golden, P.A., Ft. Lauderdale, Fla., 1983-88; sole practice Ft. Lauderdale, Fla., 1988—; judge negotiations competition Nova Southeastern U. Editor-in-chief Harvard Jour. of Law and Pub. Policy, 1980-81; contbr. articles to profl. jours. Mem. West Lauderdale Bapt. Ch., Broward County, Fla., 1982-98, chmn. deacons, 1984-86, 87-88, elder, 1994-98; mem. MIT Ednl. Coun., 1995—; del. Fla. Rep. Conv., 1987, 90; mem. Rep. Exec. Com., Broward County, 1984-94. Named one of Outstanding Young Men of Am., 1986; nominee Order of Silver Knight; Western Electric grantee, 1972-74. Mem. Christian Legal Soc., Zeta Beta Tau. Lodge: Optimists (treas. Dade County Carol City High Sch., 1971-72). Avocations: sports, politics, Bible study. Home: 5410 Buchanan St Hollywood FL 33021-5708 Office: 644 SE 4th Ave Fort Lauderdale FL 33301-3102

GOLDEN, EDWIN HAROLD, insurance company executive; b. Corsicana, Tex., Dec. 14, 1931; s. Mace Benjamin and Sarah (Alterman) G.; m. Dolly Moskowitz, Aug. 3, 1952; children: Jeffrey L., Beth Golden Marsh. BBA, U. Tex., 1953. Agt. N.Y. Life Ins. Co., Austin, Tex., 1955-80; ptnr. Hodges, Golden & Duckworth, Austin, 1967-77; owner Ed Golden & Assocs., Austin, Tex., 1977—; pres. Golden World Travel, Austin, 1993, CEO mem. Benefits Group, Inc., 1999, Tex. Package Stores Assn., Austin, 1985—. Chmn. bd. trustees City of Austin Retirement Sys., 1975—; bd. dirs. James Dick Found. for Performing Arts, Round Top, Tex., 1979—. With U.S. Army, 1953-54. Mem. CLU (Austin chpt., certs. in pension planning and estate planning), Nat. Assn. Life Underwriters, Million Dollar Round Table (life), Top of the Table (charter), Am. Soc. Pension Actuaries, Internat. Found. Employee Benefit Plans, Shriners, Masons, Travelers' Century Club. Jewish. Avocation: travel. Office: Ed Golden and Assocs 5407 Parkcrest Dr Austin TX 78731-4911

GOLDEN, ELLIOTT, judge; b. Bklyn., June 28, 1926; s. Barnet David and Rose (Fistel) G.; m. Ana Valbuena, July 8, 1990; children: Jeffrey Stephen, Marjorie Ruth, Peter Michael (dec.); stepchildren: Robert, Elizabeth, William, John. Student, Maritime Acad., 1944-46, NYU, 1947-48; LLB, Bklyn. Law Sch., 1951. Bar: N.Y. 1952, U.S. Dist. Ct. (ea. dist.) N.Y. 1953, U.S. Tax Ct., U.S. Dist. Ct. (so. dist.) N.Y. 1953, U.S. Supreme Ct. 1961. Assoc. Golden & Golden, 1952-64; asst. dist. atty. Kings County, N.Y., 1956-64; chief asst. dist. atty. Kings County, 1964-76; acting dist. atty. Kings County, N.Y., 1968; judge Civil Ct. of City of N.Y., 1977-78; justice Supreme Ct. State of N.Y., 1979-98, jud. hearing officer, 1998—; adj. assoc. prof. N.Y.C. Tech. Coll., 1987-93; arbitrator, mediator Nat. Arbitration & Mediation, 1998—; cons. in field. Contbr. articles to profl. jours. Bd. trustees Greater N.Y. coun. Boy Scouts Am.; hon. vice chmn. March of Dimes; bd. dirs. Bklyn. Philharmonia; mem. adv. bd. Bklyn. PAL; chmn. Bklyn. Lawyers div. Fedn. Jewish Philanthropies; co-chmn. Bklyn. Lawyers div. State of Israel Bonds; assoc. trustee Temple Beth Emeth of Flatbush; mem. exec. com. Lawyers div. United Jewish Appeal; past pres. counsel Hosp. Relief Assn.; bd. dirs. Kings Bay YM-YMHA of Bklyn.; bd. dirs. Bklyn. ARC, Archway Sch. for Spl. Children, Bklyn. Sch. for Spl. Children. Recipient Cert. of Merit, Hosp. Relief Assn., numerous plaques, awards and certs. of appreciation various civic orgns. Mem. Nat. Dist. Attys. Assn. (dir. 1976-77, Disting. Svc. award), Combined Coun. Law Enforcement Ofcls. State N.Y., N.Y. State Dist. Attys. Assn. (sec. 1965-77), K.P. (supreme coun.). Avocations: golf, fishing, computers.

GOLDEN, ELOISE ELIZABETH, community health nurse; b. Hope, Ind., Nov. 20, 1938; d. John M. and Hazel E. (Gosch) Holder; m. Don Golden, Aug. 2, 1959; children: David, Susanne. Diploma, Ball State U., 1959. RN. Office nurse Columbus, Ind.; staff nurse Pub. Health Dept. Bartholomew County, Columbus; parish nurse, clinicare staff nurse, housecall coord. Bartholomew County Hosp., Columbus, intake coord. Hospice, 1991—. Lutheran. Home: 11635 E 600 N Hope IN 47246

GOLDEN, GAIL K., social worker; b. Miami Beach, Fla., July 11, 1943; d. Samuel and Ann (Posner) Kadison; m. Howard J. Golden, Sept. 11, 1966; children: Rachel, Deborah. BA, Barnard U., 1964; MSW, NYU, 1967; EdD, Fairleigh Dickinson U., 1986. Clin. dir. Vol. Counseling Svc., New City, N.Y., 1986—; pvt. practice psychotherapy New City, 1977—. Contbr. poems to journals and anthologies. Mem. NOW (corresponding sec., 1995—), Amnesty Internat. (area coord., 1994—). E-mail: peacepoet@aol.com. Home: 18 Zabella Dr New City NY 10956

GOLDEN, GERALD SAMUEL, national medical board executive; b. Newark, N.J., June 8, 1935; s. Clement Harold and Jeanette (Bellat) G.; m. Deborah Ann Berlatsky, March 22, 1959 (dec. 1984); children: Leah Rachel, Ruth Naomi; m. Constance Reisa Abramson, Jan. 26, 1985. AB, Princeton U., 1957; MD, Columbia U., 1961. Diplomate Am. Bd. Pediatrics, Am. Bd. Psychiatry and Neurology. Asst. prof. of neurology and pediatrics Albert Einstein Coll. of Medicine, Bronx, N.Y., 1967-73; assoc. prof. Albert Einstein Coll. of Medicine, Bronx, 1973-77; prof. pediatrics and neurology U. Tex., Galveston, 1977-84; prof. pediatrics and neurology, dir. ctr. for devel. disabl. U. Tenn., Memphis, 1984-92; v.p. Nat. Bd. Med. Examiners, Phila., 1993—; adj. prof. neurology U. Pa., 1993—. Author: Textbook of Pediatric Neurology; assoc. editor: Pediatric Neurology Jour., 1987-92, Jour. of Devel. and Behavioral Pediatrics, 1987—, Jour. Epilepsy, 1987-92; contbr. numerous articles to profl. jours. Bd. dirs. Harwood Day Tng. Ctr., Memphis, 1987-92 Memphis-Shelby County Assn. for Retarded Citizens, 1987-92, Memphis Oral Sch. for the Deaf, 1987-92, Temple Israel Memphis, 1989-92. Recipient fed. grant Adminstrn. on Devel. Disabilities, 1990, Dept. of Human Svcs., 1990. Fellow Am. Acad. Pediatrics (neurology sect. head 1981-83), Am. Assn. Mental Deficiency (v.p. for medicine, 1984-86); mem. Am. Assn. U. Affiliated Programs (bd. dirs. 1987-92, pres. elect 1988-89, pres. 1989-90). Democrat. Jewish. Avocations: amateur radio, travel, bird watching. Office: Nat Bd Med Examiners 3750 Market St Philadelphia PA 19104-3190

GOLDEN, GREGG HANNAN STEWART, lawyer; b. N.Y.C., Nov. 24, 1953; s. Edmond Jerome and Alvia Grace (Weinberger) G.; m. Laura Jean George, Apr. 26, 1992. Grad., Phillips Exeter Acad., 1971; AB with honors, Grinnell Coll., 1975; JD cum laude, Georgetown U., 1980. Bar: Pa. 1980, U.S. Dist. Ct. (mid. dist.) Pa. 1980, U.S. Ct. Appeals (3d and D.C. cirs.) 1981, Calif. 1982, N.J. 1983, D.C. 1984, U.S. Supreme Ct. 1984. Dep. atty. gen. State of Pa., Harrisburg, 1980-83; assoc. Hogan & Hartson, Washington, 1983-86; atty. Office of Enforcement Fed. Home Loan Bank Bd., Washington, 1986-88, assoc. dep. dir., 1988-89; assoc. dep. dir. enforcement Office Thrift Supervision U.S. Dept. Treasury, Washington, 1989-91, dist. counsel 12th Dist., 1990-91; counsel Resolution Trust Corp., Washington, 1991-94, sr. counsel, 1994-95; sr. counsel corp. affairs FDIC, Washington, 1996-99, counsel receivership ops., 1999—; trustee, sec. InterFuture, N.Y.C., 1979-89, chairing officer bd. of trustees, 1989—. Rsch. editor: American Criminal Law Review, 1979-80. Lectr. YWCA Rape Crisis Svcs. div., Harrisburg; spl. counsel Pa. State Ethics Commn., Harrisburg, 1981-82; competition judge moot ct. bd. Cath. U. of Am., Washington, 1988-89. Fellow Johnson Found., 1972, Thomas J. Watson Found., 1975. Mem. ABA, D.C. Bar (com. on ct. rules 1985—, co-chmn. com. 1987-90, com. on representation for needy civil litigants 1985-88), Fed. Bar Assn., Pa. Bar Assn. Democrat. Jewish. Office: FDIC 550 17th St NW Washington DC 20429-0001

GOLDEN, HERBERT HERSHEL, retired Romance languages educator; b. Boston, Nov. 1, 1919; s. Max and Minnie (Turetzky) G.; m. Hilda Rachel Lazerow, June 13, 1943 (dec. May 1964); children: Robert Sheman, Barry Allan, Steven Eliot; m. Evelyn Pauline Sowa, Oct. 7, 1965. BA, Boston U., 1941, MA, 1942; MA, Harvard U., 1947, PhD, 1951. Lectr. Spanish and French, Boston U., 1945-49, instr. Romance langs., 1949-53, asst. prof., 1953-57, assoc. prof., 1957-63, prof., 1963-85, prof. emeritus, 1985—; cons. for NDEA lang. insts. U.S. Office Edn., HEW, Washington, 1955-56; asst. to mng. editor Modern Lang. Jour., Nat. Fedn. Modern Lang. Tchrs. Assns., Boston, 1955-58; instr. French and Italian, Harvard U. Ext., Cambridge, Mass, 1960-79; mem., editor, mem. adv. com. on fgn. langs. Mass. Dept. Edn., Boston, 1960-69; Fulbright lectr. U. Rome, 1962-63. Co-author: Modern French Literatue and Language: A Bibliography of Homage Studies, 1953, reprinted 1971, Modern Iberian Language and Literature: A Bibliography of Homage Studies, 1958, reprinted 1971, Modern Italian Language and Literature: A Bibliography of Homage Studies, 1959, reprinted 1971, Histoire de France à Travers les Journaux du Tempe Passé)1715-1789). Lumieres et Lueurs du XVIII Siècle, 1986; editor: Studies in Honor of Samuel M. Waxman, 1969; contbr. articles and revs. to profl. jours. With U.S. Army, 1942-45, ETO. Decorated Purple Heart, Bronze Star, gold medal of cultural merit (Italy); recipient diploma of benemerenza Internat. Assn. for Study Italian Lang. and Lit., 1973; rsch. fellow Marion and Jasper Whiting Found., 1979-80. Mem. MLA (steering com. fng. lang. program 1956-59), Am. Soc. for 18th Century Studies (editor Festschriften: 18th Century Bibliography), Am. Assn. Tchrs. Italian (sec.-treas. 1959-64, pres. 1964-66), French Soc. 18th Century Studies, Masons, Phi Beta Kappa (pres. Mass. Epsilon chpt. 1970-72, cert. disting. merit 1985). Avocations: classical music, collecting French films on video, rading. Home: 29 Thorndike St Brookline MA 02446-2405

GOLDEN, HOWARD, muncipal or county official; b. Bklyn.; m. Aileen Wolsky; children: Michele, Dana. Grad., NYU; JD, Bklyn. Law Sch. Mem. N.Y.C. Coun., 1970-77; pres. Borough of Bklyn., 1977—. With USN. Fax: 718/802-3832. Office: Borough of Bklyn 209 Joralemon St Brooklyn NY 11201-3709*

GOLDEN, JAMES LESLIE, information technology executive; b. Balt., Aug. 5, 1944; s. Leslie Logan and Gladys (Kinser) G.; m. Patsy Ann Creech, June 4, 1966; children: James Brett, Courtney Leigh. BA in Math. and Edn., U. Ky., 1966; MS in Tech. of Mgmt., Am. U., Washington, 1973. Bus. sys. planning staff U.S. Postal Svc. Hdqs., Washington, 1980-83, dir. planning and devel., 1983-86, dir. data mgmt., 1986-89, dir. info. svcs., 1989-92, mgr. office and exec. info., 1992-94, info. sys. exec., 1994-97; info. sys. exec. U.S. Postal Svc., Arlington, Va., 1998—, U.S. Postal Svc. Hdqs., Arlington, Va., 1998—; exec. program dir. Year 2000 Initiative, 1997—; adj. faculty math. No. Va. C.C., 1976-77; adj. faculty Nat. Cryptologic Sch., 1993—. Coach Sterling (Va.) Youth Soccer Assn., 1980-86; pres. exec. exch. program Mobile Corp., 1979-80. Capt. USNR, 1990-99, ret. Named Ky. col., 1995—; NSF grant, 1968. Home: 117 Peyton Rd Potomac Falls VA 20165-5605 Office: US Postal Svc 4301 Wilson Blvd Ste 1003 Arlington VA 22203-1816

GOLDEN, JOHN F., packaging company executive; b. N.Y.C., Feb. 5, 1949; s. David and Sylvia G.; m. Marguerite Ann Sellars, May 30, 1981; 1 child, Rachel Jeanne. Student Bowling Green State U., 1967-69; B.A., U. Colo., 1971. Exec. v.p. Stephen Gould Paper Co., Inc., Whippany, N.J., 1973—. Office: Stephen Gould Paper Co Inc 35 S Jefferson Rd Whippany NJ 07981-1043

GOLDEN, JOHN JOSEPH, JR., information systems executive; b. New Milford, Conn., Jan. 13, 1943; s. John Joseph and Anne Munroe (Hope) G.; m. Carolyn Joan Pachesa, May 29, 1965 (div. July 1984); children: Elizabeth Susan, Jennifer Leigh, John Joseph III, Matthew Benjamin; m. Ethel M. (Piercy) O'Neill, June 8, 1991; 1 child, Michael Joseph. BS, MIT, 1966. V.p. systems devel. Quantum Computing Corp., Newton, Mass., 1968-70; mgr. computer ops. Polaroid Corp., Cambridge, Mass., 1970-75; dir. info. processing Schering-Plough Corp., Kenilworth, N.J., 1975-78; dir. info. systems Compugraphic Corp., Wilmington, Mass., 1978-80; dir. info. systems electro-optics div. Honeywell, Lexington, Mass., 1981-83; dir. adminstrn. electro-optics div. Honeywell, Wilmington, Mass., 1983-87; dir. materials electo-optics div. Honeywell, Marlboro, Mass., 1987-90; dir. ops. Micracor, Acton, Mass., 1990-96; dir. info. sys. Fresenius Med. Care, Lexington, Mass., 1996-97; mgr. computing and telecomms. U.S. Postal Svc., Washington, 1997—. With USAR, 1964-70. Mem. IEEE, Assn. for Computing Machinery, MIT alumni Orgn., Mass. Iota Tau Assn. (treas. 1970—), Sigma Alpha Epsilon. Roman Catholic. Home: 30 Marina Dr Haverhill MA 01830-4331 Office: US Postal Svc Washington DC 20260

GOLDEN, JUDITH GREENE, artist, educator; b. Chgo., Nov. 29, 1934; d. Walter Cornell and Dorothie (Cissell) Greene; m. David T. Golden, Oct. 10, 1955 (div.); children: David T. Golden III, Lucinda Golden Rizzo. BFA, Inst. Chgo., 1973; MFA, U. Calif., Davis, 1975; PhD Art, Moore Coll. Art, 1990; PhD (hon.), Moore Coll. Art. Assoc. prof. art U. Ariz., Tucson, 1981-88, prof. art, 1989-96, prof. emerita, 1996—; NEA forum pub. grants panelist, 1987; project dir. U. Calif. L.A. NEA Lecture series, 1979, 84. One woman shows include Women's Bldg., L.A., 1977, G. Ray Hawkins Gallery, L.A., 1977, Quay Gallery, San Francisco, 1979, 81, A. Nagel Galerie, Berlin, 1981, Ctr. Creative Photography, U. Ariz., 1983, Colburg Gallery, Vancouver, Can., 1985, Etherton Gallery, Tucson, 1985, 89, 91, 95, Mus. Photog. Arts, San Diego, 1986, Friends of Photography, Carmel, Calif., 1987, Tucson Mus. Art, 1987, Mus. Contemporary Photography, Chgo., 1988, Visual Arts Ctr., Anchorage, Alaska, 1990, Temple Music and Art, Tucson, 1992, 97, Scottsdale (Ariz.) Ctr. Arts, 1993, Arte de Oaxaca, Mex., 1995, Etherton Gallery, Tucson, 1995, Columbia Art Ctr., Dallas, 1997; exhibited in group shows at Centre Georges Pompidou, Paris, 1981, Security Pacific Bank, L.A., 1985, Phoenix Mus. Art, 1985, L.A. County Mus. Art, 1987, Tokyo Met. Mus. Photography, 1991, Laguna Art Mus., 1992, U. N.M. Art Mus., 1993, L.A. County Mus., 1994, Hara contemporary Mus., Tokyo, 1995, Mus. Women in Arts, Washington, 1997, Santa Barbara Mus. Art, Calif., 1997, Mus. Cont. Photography, 1998, Tucson Mus. Art, 1999, Calif. Mus. Photography, 1999, Ctr. for Creative Photography, 1999, numerous others; represented in permanent collections at Art Inst. Chgo., Calif. Mus. Photography, Ctr. Creative Photography U. Ariz., Denver Art Mus., Fed. Reserve Bank San Francisco, Fogg Mus. Art, Grunwald Ctr. Graphic Arts, Internat. Mus. Photography George Eastman House, L.A. County Mus. Art, Mpls. Inst. Arts, Mus. Photographic Arts, Newport Harbor Mus. Art, Oakland Mus. Art, Photography Mus. Osaka, Polaroid Corp., San Francisco Mus. Modern Art, Security Pacific Bank, Tokyo Met. Mus. Photography, Tucson Mus. Art, Weisman Collection, L.A., Mus. Cont. Photography, Chgo., Seattle Art Mus., Wash. Individual artist grantee Tucson Pima Arts Coun., 1987; faculty rsch. grantee U. Ariz., 1986-87, 93-94; Ariz. Found. grantee U. Ariz., 1984; fellow Ariz. Commn. Arts, 1984; individual photography fellow NEA, 1979; Regent's faculty fellow Creative Rsch. U.Calif. L.A., 1977; listed in archive to Ctr. for Creative Photography, Tucson, 1996.

GOLDEN, JULIUS, advertising and public relations executive, lobbyist, investor; b. N.Y.C., Feb. 25, 1929; s. Nathan and Leah (Michlin) G.; m. Constance Lee Carpenter, Dec. 31, 1954 (div. Mar. 1965); children: Andrew Mitchell, Juliet Deborah; m. Diana Zana George, Apr. 30, 1973; 1 child, Jeremy Philip. BA, U. N.Mex., 1952. Asst. dir. info. U. N.Mex., Albuquerque, 1952-53; writer AP, Albuquerque, part 1952-53, staff writer, 1953-55; fgn. corr. AP, S.Am., 1956-59; pres. Group West Advt./Pub. Rels. Albuquerque, 1959—; dir. Auto Lend Group, Inc., Electrical Products Co., Albuquerque. Author: A Time to Die, 1975. Active Bernalillo County Lung Assn., 1961-64; mem. Met. Crime Commn., Albuquerque, 1967-71, chmn. 1970-71; mem. Albuquerque Police Commn. Task Force, 1988-89. Served with AUS, 1945-48, PTO, Korea. Recipient Nat. Feature Writing award Sigma Delta Chi, 1952, E.H. Shaffer award N.Mex. Press Assn., 1953. Mem. Pub. Rels. Soc. (pres. N.Mex. chpt. 1972), Profl. Journalism Soc. (pres. 1969-70), Pub. Rels. Soc. N.Mex. (pres. 1972), Am. Advt. Fedn. Overseas Press of am. Club, Albuquerque Press Club, Petroleum Club, 4 Hills Country Club, Sigma Delta Chi. Democrat. Jewish. Home: 1408 Stagecoach Ln SE Albuquerque NM 87123-4429 Office: Group West 1110 Pennsylvania NE Albuquerque NM 87110

GOLDEN, KIMBERLY KAY, critical care, flight nurse; b. Munich, July 31, 1961; came to U.S., 1961; d. Henry Davis and Mary Walker G. AA, Hinds Jr. Coll., Raymond, Miss., 1980, ASN, 1984; BSN, U. Miss., Jackson, 1987, AS in EMT-Paramedic, 1990; postgrad., U. Health Scis., Antigua, W.I., 1997—. Cert. ACLS instr., PALS provider and instr.; emergency nurse, crit. care RN; cert. paramedic, Miss., Tenn. Staff nurse neuro ICU U. Miss. Med. Ctr., 1984-85, staff nurse surg. ICU, 1985-87; staff nurse emergency rm. Rankin Gen. Hosp., Brandon, Miss., 1987-88; flight nurse Lifestar Helicopter Flight Svc., 1988-91; staff nurse emergency rm., ICU Nightingale Nursing, Jackson, 1988-91, Riveroaks Hosp., Jackson, 1990-91; staff RN emergency rm., Aerovesta flight Midland Meml. Hosp., Tex., 1991-93; flight nurse Hosp. Wing BTLS, Memphis, Tenn., 1993—, U. Health Sci. Med. Sch., Antigua, West Indies, 1997—; examiner Nat. Registry EMT-P; advanced trauma life support station instr.; affiliate faculty paramedic program U. Miss. Faculty scholar Hinds Jr. Coll., 1983. Mem. AACN, Nat. Flight Assn., Emergency Nurses Assn. Baptist. Avocations: karate, skiing, horse back riding, camping. Office: PO Box 140466 Austin TX 78714-0466

GOLDEN, LEON, classicist, educator; b. Jersey City, Dec. 25, 1930; s. Nathan and Regina (Okun) G. BA, U. Chgo., 1950, MA, 1953, PhD, 1958. Instr. ancient langs. Coll. William and Mary, 1958-60, asst. prof. ancient langs., 1960-65; assoc. prof. classical langs. Fla. State U., Tallahassee, 1965-68, prof., 1968—, dir. program in humanities, 1976—, chmn. dept. classics, 1986-95; bd. dirs. Fla. Endowment for Humanities, 1983-87. Author: In Praise of Prometheus: Humanism and Rationalism in Aeschylean Thought, 1966, (with O.B. Hardison Jr.) Aristotle's Poetics, 1968, Aristotle: On Tragic and Comic Mimesis, 1992, Horace for Students of Literature, 1995. With AUS, 1953-55. Fellow coop. program humanities U.N.C. and Duke, 1964-65; fellow coop. program humanities Soc. for Religion in Higher Edn., 1971-72. Mem. Am. Philol. Assn., Archeol. Inst. Am., Classical Assn. Mid. West and South (pres. So. sect. 1972-74), Phi Beta Kappa. Office: Fla State U Dept Classics Tallahassee FL 32306

GOLDEN, LILY OLIVER, educator; b. Tashkent, Uzbekistan, USSR, July 18, 1934; d. Oliver John and Bertha Alexander (Bialik) Golden; m. Abdulla Kassim Hanga, Mar. 13, 1960 (dec. 1966); 1 child, Yelena; m. Boris Vladimirovitch Yakovlev, Aug. 14, 1979 (dec. Mar. 1997). PhD, Soviet Acad. of Sci., 1966; LHD (hon.), Chgo. State U., 1992. Jr. rschr. Inst. of Oriental Studies Acad. of Sci., Moscow, 1957-59; sr. scientific rschr. Inst. of African Studies Acad. of Sci. of Russia, 1959-60; disting. scholar-in-residence Chgo. State U., 1992—; vis. prof., lectr. Lumumba U., Moscow, Inst. of Asia and Africa, Moscow State U., Leningrad State U., Tbilici State U., History Inst. Tbilici State U., Columbia U., N.Y.C., NYU, Rutgers U., N.J., Peoria U., Ill., Loyola U., Chgo., Calif. State U., Cape Town U., South Africa, Libreville U., Gabon, Dakar U., Senegal, Zurich U., Switzerland, numerous others; presenter and lectr. in field. Author: Africans in Russia, 1966, The Tendencies of Development of African Music, 1967, Pan-Africanism, 1972, (with others) Trade Unions in Africa, 1964, Dr. Dubois-A Scholar Humanitarian and a Fighter for Freedom, 1971, USSR and Africa (also editor), 1977, Ideology of Revolutionary Democrats, 1981, Political Parties in Africa, 1964, Nationalism in Modern Africa, 1983, Marxism in Africa, 1987, African Musicology, 1984, others; editor: African Encyclopedia, Dr. Dubois-Scholar, Humanist, Fighter for Freedom, 1971, Presence Africain; contbr. articles to profl. jours. Bd. dirs. Internat. Intercultural Black Woman's Study Inst., Ctr. Am. Citizens, San Francisco, 1996—; chmn. Black-White Jews, Chgo., 1996—. Named hon. spkr. Black Caucuses U.S. Congress, Calif. State Congress; proclamation Lily Golden Day City of Mobile, Ala., City of Juno; recipient Award for Contbn. to Elimination of Racism Nat. Orgn. for Men Against Sexism, Internat. Achievement award Tau Gamma Delta; named to Educators Hall of Fame,Sacramento. Avocations: tennis, music. Home: 5530 S South Shore Dr Chicago IL 60637-1945

GOLDEN, LOUIS JOSEPH, former business news editor, newspaper executive; b. Hartford, Conn., Oct. 19, 1952; s. Merrill S. and Marjorie (Louis) G.; m. Christine Palm, June 27, 1981 (div. Dec. 1988); children: James Joseph, Daniel Louis; m. Margaret Buchanan, May 4, 1991. BA, U. Conn., 1975. Copy editor Hartford Courant, 1974-77, night city editor, 1977-79, editor Bus. Weekly, 1987-89, bus. editor, 1989—, v.p. mktg. and bus. developer, 1995—; asst. editor Weekly World News, Lantana, Fla., 1979-80, editor, 1980-81; v.p. Greater Hartford C. of C., 1981-85, Decker Guertin Cheyne, Hartford, 1985-87. Office: Hartford Courant 285 Broad St Hartford CT 06115-2510*

GOLDEN, OLIVIA A., health and science agency administrator; b. N.Y.C., Jan. 23, 1955. BA in Philosophy and Govt., Harvard U., MPP, PhD. Budget dir. office human svcs. State of Mass., 1983-85; lectr. in pub. policy J.F. Kennedy Sch. Govt. Harvard U., Cambridge, Mass., 1987-91; dir. programs and policy Children's Def. Fund, Washington, 1991-93; commr. on children, youth and families HHS, Washington, 1993-97, prin. dep. asst. sec. on children, youth and families, 1997, asst. sec. on children and families, 1997—; mem. adv. com. children and youth City of Cambridge. Author: Poor Children and Welfare Reform, 1992. Candidate for senator, Mass. Office: Office Asst Sec Aerospace Bldg 6th Fl 370 L'Enfant Promenade SW Washington DC 20447

GOLDEN, REYNOLD STEPHEN, geriatrician; b. Herkimer, N.Y., Jan. 11, 1937; s. Harold Theodore and Ethel Anne (Myers) G.; m. Gale Holtz, Nov. 26, 1959 (div. May 1978); children: Nathan Myers, Jennifer Lynn (dec.), Laura Beth (Lieba); m. Ellen Jean Moore, Sept. 9, 1978; children: Melissa Nan, Benjamin Harold. AB cum laude, Harvard Coll., 1958; MD, SUNY, Syracuse, 1962. Diplomate Am. Bd. Family Practice, Am. Bd. Internal Medicine; cert. added qualifications in geriatrics. Intern Lankenau Hosp., Phila., 1962-63; resident in internal medicine SUNY, Syracuse, 1963-66; pvt. practice Utica, N.Y., 1966-78; dir. family practice residency St. Elizabeth Hosp., Utica, 1978-92, St. Francis Hosp., Poughkeepsie, N.Y., 1992-95; clin. assoc. prof. dept. family medicine SUNY, Syracuse, 1991-96; chief of geriatrics Unity Med. Group (formerly Rochester Park Med. Group), 1995—; med. dir. continuing care svcs. Park Ridge Health Sys. (now Unity Health Sys.), Rochester, 1995—; clin. asst. profl. dept. ent. medicine U. Rochester, 1999—; cons. residency assistance program, Kansas City, Mo.,

1988-96; charter mem. N.Y. State Coun. on Grad. Med. Edn., N.Y.C., 1987-89. Editor N.Y. Family Physician, 1987-92. Mem. N.Y. State Acad. Family Physicians (chmn. bd. dirs. 1988-89, pres. 1992-93, Presdl. Citation 1985, 86, 88), Cen. N.Y. Acad. Medicine (pres. 1977-79, Golden Torch award 1989). Jewish. Avocations: travel, computers, music, theater, skiing. Office: 2300 Buffalo Rd Bldg 600 Rochester NY 14624-1368

GOLDEN, ROBERT CHARLES, financial services executive; b. Bklyn., July 12, 1946; s. Charles Joseph and Audrey (Griffin) G. BS in Acctg., Fordham U., 1968, MBA in Fin., 1978. V.p. internal audit Walston & Co., Inc., N.Y.C., 1969-73; v.p.-fin. Acan X-Ray Co., Inc., Detroit, 1973-76; exec. v.p. Prudential Securities Inc., N.Y.C., 1976-97, Prudential Ins. Co. Am., Inc., Roseland, N.J., 1997—. Bd. dirs. HeartShare Human Svcs. of N.Y., 1985—; trustee Xaverian H.S., Bklyn., 1987-93. Recipient citation Coun. of City of N.Y., Franciscan Heritage award Franciscan Sisters of the Poor at Pla. Hotel, 1987, Apple award Prudential Pacesetters, 1989, St. Francis Xavier Soc. award Xaverian Bros., 1990, Thomas J. Cuite award, Irish Am. Heritage Wk. Com. of N.Y.C. Hall, 1991, Crystal Shield award Salvation Army, 1992, Disting. Alumni award Xaverian H.S., 1993; named Educator of Yr. Assn. of Tchrs. of N.Y., 1986, Cath. Guardian Soc. Humanitarian of Yr., 1985, Chief Brehon of the Great Irish Fair, 1992; named to Diocesan Ct. of Honor, Diocese of Bklyn., Knight of the Sovereign Mil. Order of Malta, 1995, Assembly of Stewarts, Diocese of N.Y., 1995, Knights of the Equestrian Order of Holy Sepulchre, 1998. Mem. Securities Industry Assn., Mcpl. Club Bklyn., St. Patrick Soc. Bklyn., Emerald Assn. L.I. (past pres.), Ft. Hamilton Hist. Soc., Acad. Magical Arts, The Friendly Sons St. Patrick City N.Y., Cathedral Club of Bklyn. (past pres., Man of Yr. 1994), Bay Ridge Men's Club, Fordham U. Pres. Club, Bishop's Coat of Arms Club, Ancient Order of Hibernians (divsn. 22), KC, Bayfort Benevolent Assocs. (past pres.). Roman Catholic. Home: 33 Columbia Ave Staten Island NY 10305-3739 Office: Prudential Ins Co Am 80 Livingston Ave Roseland NJ 07068-1798

GOLDEN, SOMA, newspaper editor; b. Washington, Aug. 27, 1939; m. William Behr; 2 children. BA, Radcliffe Coll.; MA, Columbia U. Mem. econs. staff Bus. Week Mag., Washington, 1962-73; with The New York Times, 1973—, mem. editorial bd., 1977-82, editor Sunday bus. sect., 1982-87, nat. news editor, 1987-93, asst. mng. editor, 1993—; adj. prof. Columbia U., N.Y.C., 1961-76; final judge Gerald Loeb awards, 1995—. Office: The New York Times Co 229 W 43rd St New York NY 10036-3959

GOLDEN, T. MICHAEL, state supreme court justice; b. 1942. BA in History, U. Wyo., 1964, JD, 1967; LLM, U. Va., 1992. Bar: Wyo. 1967, U.S. Dist. Ct. 1967, U.S. Ct. Appeals (10th cir.) 1967, U.S. Supreme Ct. 1970. Mem. firm Brimmer, MacPherson & Golden, Rawlins, Wyo., 1971-83, Williams, Porter, Day & Neville, Casper, Wyo., 1983-88; justice Wyo. Supreme Ct., Cheyenne, 1988—, chief justice, 1994—, assoc. justice; mem. Wyo. State Bd. Law Examiners, 1977-82, 86-88. Capt. U.S. Army 1967-71. Office: Wyo Supreme Ct Bldg PO Box 1737 2301 Capitol Ave Cheyenne WY 82002

GOLDEN, THOMAS RUTLEDGE, psychotherapist, author; b. Washington, Feb. 14, 1951; s. Thomas Simeon and Margaret P. Golden; m. Dorothy Altland, Jan. 31, 1981; children: Julia Terra, Luke Andrew. BS, U. Md., 1973; MSW, U. Md., Balt., 1978. Lic. social worker, Md. Grief therapist St. Francis Ctr., Washington, 1979-90; pvt. practice Kensington, Md., 1985—; spkr., trainer Golden Healing, 1994—. Author: Swallowed by a Snake, 1996; author booklets. Bd. dirs. Hospice Caring, Gaithersburg, Md., 1996; mem. nat. adv. bd. Men Web, Seattle, 1996. Mem. NASW, Assn. Death Edn. & Counseling. Avocations: music, gardening. Office: 149 Little Quarry Rd Gaithersburg MD 20878-5683

GOLDEN, WILLIAM C., lawyer; b. N.Y.C., Oct. 27, 1936; s. Edwin and Sue (Lipman) G.; m. Rachel Epstein; children: Rebecca, Naomi, Nathaniel, David. BS, Wharton Sch., U. Pa., 1957; LLB, Columbia U., 1960. Bar: N.Y. 1961, Ill. 1967. Atty. Dept. Justice, Tax Div., Washington, 1960-61, Dept. Treasury, Washington, 1962-65; assoc. prof. of law Ind. U., Bloomington, 1965-67; assoc., then ptnr. Sidley and Austin, Chgo., 1967—; bd. dirs. ALAMCO, Clarksburg, W.Va., 1980-85. Author: Attorneys' Guide to Charitable Giving, 1967. bd. dirs. Self Help Ctr., Evanston, Ill., 1985-86; chmn. Info. Tech. Resource Ctr., Chgo., 1987—. Mem. ABA, Chgo. Bar Assn. (chmn. fed. tax com. 1979-80). Office: Sidley & Austin 1 First Natl Plz Chicago IL 60603-2003

GOLDEN, WILLIAM THEODORE, trustee, corporate director; b. N.Y.C., Oct. 25, 1909; s. S. Herbert and Rebecca (Harris) G.; m. Sibyl Levy, May 2, 1938 (dec. 1983); children: Sibyl Rebecca, Pamela Prudence. AB, U. Pa., 1930, LLD (hon.), 1979; postgrad. bus. adminstrn., Harvard U., 1930-31; DSc (hon.), Poly. Inst. N.Y., 1975, Bard Coll., 1988; MA, Columbia U., 1979, LLD (hon.), 1986; LLD (hon.), Hamilton Coll., 1987; DHL (hon.), CUNY, 1997. Lic. amateur radio operator, 1922—, station 2AEN. Asst. to pres. Cornell, Linder & Co., N.Y.C., 1931-34; with Carl M. Loeb & Co., Carl M. Loeb, Rhoades & Co., 1934-41; dir. Woodward Iron Co., 1940-68; asst. to commr. AEC, Washington, 1946-50, cons., 1950-58; chmn. bd. Nat. U.S. Radiator Co. (and successor cos.), 1952-74; dir. Pitts. Railways Co., 1952-63, United Carbon Co., 1957-63, Crowell-Collier and Macmillan, Inc., 1964-71, Paribas Corp., 1965-69; trustee Mitre Corp., 1958-72, 76-85; trustee System Devel. Corp., 1957-66, chmn. bd. trustees, 1961-66; spl. cons. on rev. govt. sci. activities Pres. Truman, Washington, 1950-51; advisor on NSF to dir. Bur. Budget, 1950-51; mem. mil. procurement task force Commn. on Orgn. Exec. Br. Govt., Hoover Commn., 1954-55; mem. adv. com. on pvt. enterprise in fgn. aid, U.S. State Dept., 1964-65; pub. mem. Hudson Inst., 1964-94; mem. commn. on delivery personal health services Mayor's Piel Commn., 1966-68; mem. adv. council Sch. Gen. Studies, Columbia U., N.Y.C., 1966—; mem. vis. com. on astronomy Princeton (N.J.) U., 1969—, chmn., 1976-89; mem. vis. com. on engring. and applied physics and on medicine and dental medicine Harvard U., Cambridge, Mass., 1969-77, mem. vis. com. on astronomy, 1976-90; mem. vis. com. Assn. Univs. for Research in Astronomy, 1973-76, dir. at large, 1988-91, Disting. advisor, 1991—; mem. vis. com. Space Telescope Sci. Inst., 1982-87; mem. adv. panel on space transp. ops. NASA, 1976-77; mem. adv. panel U.S. Postal Service, 1981-83; vice chmn. Mayor's Commn. on Sci. and Tech., 1983-91, hon. chair, 1992—, Commn. Coll. Retirement, 1984-88, Scientists Inst. Pub. Info., 1985-94; co-chmn. Carnegie Commn. on Sci., Tech. and Govt., 1988-96; bd. dirs. Verde Exploration, Ltd., Inc., Block Drug Co., Inc.; bd. dirs. emeritus Gen. Am. Investors Co. Editor, co-author: Science Advice to the President, 1980, 2d rev. edit., 1993, Science and Technology Advice to the President, Congress and Judiciary, 1988, 2d rev. edit., 1993, Worldwide Science and Technology Advice to the Highest Levels of Governments, 1991; contbr. articles on govt. and sci. to various publs. Trustee Hebrew Free Loan Soc., 1935—, treas., 1985—, United Neighborhood Houses, 1952-61, Associated Hosp. Service N.Y., 1959-74, Univ. Corp. for Atmospheric Research, 1965-74, Riverside Research Inst., 1967-76, N.Y.C-Rand Inst., 1969-75, Ctr. for Advanced Study Behavioral Scis., 1970-76, Bennington Coll., 1971-76, Haskins Labs., 1971-92, SIAM Inst. Math. and Soc., 1973-91, Columbia U. Press, 1974-77, John Simon Guggenheim Meml. Found., 1976-81, Nat. Humanities Ctr., 1978-90, emeritus, 1990—; trustee The Population Council, 1979-89, Catskill Ctr. for Conservation and Devel., 1981—, U. Pa. Press, 1985—; mem. Marine Biology Lab., Woods Hole, Mass., 1968—, trustee, 1968-87, trustee emeritus, 1987; trustee Mt. Sinai Hosp., N.Y.C., 1955—, vice chmn., 1977—; mem. governing council Courant Inst. Math. Scis., NYU, 1962-91, vice chmn., 1962-86, chmn., 1986-91; trustee Mt. Sinai Med. Sch., 1963—, vice chmn., 1977—; trustee N.Y. Found., 1963-84, treas., 1974-78; chmn. bd. trustees City Univ. Constrn. Fund, 1967-71; mem. exec. com. Health Research Council, City of N.Y., 1968-75; trustee Am. Mus. Natural History, 1968—, v.p., 1971-88, vice chmn., 1988-89, chmn., 1989-94, chmn. emeritus, 1994—; trustee Carnegie Instn. Washington, 1969—, sec., 1971—; trustee Barnard Coll., 1973—, vice chmn., 1975-79, 86-92, treas. 1980-83, hon. vice chmn., 1992-98, emeritus, 1998—; trustee N.Y. Council for Humanities, 1975-78, chmn., 1976-78; bd. overseers Sch. Arts and Scis., U. Pa., Phila., 1976-97, emeritus, 1997—; mem. council Rockefeller U., 1978—; mem. bd. visitors Grad. Sch. and Univ. Ctr., CUNY, 1979-96, mem. bd. Grad. Ctr. Found., 1996—; trustee Am. Trust for Brit. Library, 1980-92, 98—, vice chmn., 1985-92, co-chmn., treas., 1998—; trustee Neurosci. Research Found., 1981—, chmn., 1981-87; bd. dirs. Grad. Sch. of Arts and Sci. Alumni Assn., Columbia U., 1984-93, vice chmn. 1984-91; chmn. Black Rock Forest Consortium, 1988—; mem. adv. bd. Johns Hopkins Sch. Hygiene and Pub. Health, 1995-98; bd. dirs. Internat. Univ. Exch., Inc., 1996—. Served to lt. comdr. USNR, 1941—. Recipient Letters of Commendation with ribbon Sec. of Navy and chief Bur. Ordnance for invention of naval gunfire device used in WWII, Pub. Svc. award Mus. City of N.Y., 1981, Disting. Pub. Svc. award NSF, 1982, Tribute of Appreciation, Nat. Sci. Bd., 1991, Pub. Welfare medal NAS, 1996; Benjamin Franklin fellow Royal Soc. Arts (London). Fellow AAAS (treas., bd. dirs. 1969—), N.Y. Acad. Scis. (mem. bd. govs. 1977—, pres. 1988, chmn. 1989, life gov. 1991), Am. Acad. Arts and Scis., New York Acad. of Medicine; mem. Nat. Acad. Pub. Adminstrn., Am. Philos. Soc. (mem. coun. 1985-91, v.p. 1992—, Benjamin Franklin award for disting. pub. svc. 1995), History of Sci. Soc., Coun. Fgn. Rels., Army and Navy Club, Cosmos Club (Washington), Century Assn., Down Town Assn. Home: 730 Park Ave New York NY 10021-4945 Office: 40 Wall St Rm 4201 New York NY 10005-2301

GOLDENBERG, CHARLES LAWRENCE, real estate company executive; b. N.Y.C., Sept. 4, 1933. BSBA, NYU, 1955, JD, 1958. Associated with Brown, Harris, Stevens, Inc., 1955-75, officer, 1960-75, sr. v.p., dir. fin. dist. office; pres., CEO Sylan Lawrence Co., Inc., N.Y.C., 1975—; former adj. prof. real estate NYU; cons., lectr. in field. Contbr. articles to N.Y. Times, Real Estate Weekly, and other profl. jours. Mem. Nat. Assn. Real Estate Bds., Internat. Real Estate Fedn., Real Estate Bd. N.Y. Inc. (gov.). Office: Sylvan Lawrence Co 100 William St Fl 12 New York NY 10038-4552 also: 375 Park Ave New York NY 10152-0002

GOLDENBERG, DAVID MILTON, experimental pathologist, oncologist; b. N.Y.C., Aug. 2, 1938; s. Leo and Lillie (Spivak) G.; m. Hildegard Gruenbaum, Apr. 28, 1961 (div. 1996); children: Eva, Deborah, Marc, Denis, Neil, Lee; m. Cynthia Sullivan, Aug. 13, 1997. Student, Shimer Coll., 1954-56; BS, U. Chgo., 1958; ScD, U. Erlangen-Nuremberg, Fed. Republic of Germany, 1965; MD, U. Heidelberg, Fed. Republic of Germany, 1966. Assoc. rsch. prof. pathology U. Pitts. Med. Sch., 1968-70; assoc. prof. pathology Temple U. Med. Sch., Phila., 1970-72, U. Ky. Med. Ctr., Lexington, 1972-73; prof., dir. div. exptl. pathology U. Ky., Lexington, 1973-83; pres. Ctr. for Molecular Medicine and Immunology, Newark, 1983—, Garden State Cancer Ctr., Belleville, N.J., 1992—; adj. prof. surgery N.J. Med. Sch., U. of Medicine and Dentistry of N.J., Newark, 1983—; adj. prof. microbiology immunology N.Y. Med. Coll., Valhalla, 1993—; mem. VA Merit Rev. Bd. for Oncology, Washington, 1974-77; exec. dir. Ephraim McDowell Cmty. Cancer Network, Lexington, 1975-80; pres. Ephraim McDowell Cancer Rsch. Foun., 1978-80; sec., treas. Ky. Cancer Commn., Frankfort, 1978-80; mem. sci. adv. bd. German Fund for Cancer Rsch., Bonn, 1980—; chmn. bd. Immunomedics, Inc., Morris Plains, N.J., 1983—; mem. exptl. immunology study sect. NIH, Bethesda, Md., 1980-83. Author more than 1000 articles, book chpts., abstracts, 1962—; mem. editl. bd. Tumor Biology, Antibody, Immunoconjugates and Radiopharms., Jour. Nuclear Medicine and Allied Scis., Cancer, Qtly. Jour. Nuclear Medicine, Tumor Targeting. Outstanding Investigator grantee Nat. Cancer Inst., 1985, 92; recipient Rsch. Found. award U. Ky., 1978, N.J. Pride award in sci. and tech. N.J. Monthly, 1986, Excellence in Cancer Rsch. award N.J. Legis., 1986, Herz Meml. lectureship Tel Aviv U., 1991, 3M/Mayneord Meml. lectureship Brit. Inst. Radiology, 1991, Abbott prize Internat. Soc. Oncodevelopmental Biol. Medicine, 1994, Vikram Sarabhai Meml. Oration award, Soc. Nuclear Medicine, India, 1994, Ted Bloch Meml. lectr. Southwestern chpt. Soc. Nuc. Medicine, 1999. Hon. mem. Argentine Cancer Assn. Jewish. Achievements include more than 30 patents in field. Office: Garden State Cancer Ctr 520 Belleville Ave Belleville NJ 07109-1308

GOLDENBERG, GEORGE, retired pharmaceutical company executive; b. N.Y.C., Mar. 12, 1929; s. Gersh and Rose (Kolpacci) G.; m. Arlene Sandra Yudell, May 22, 1955; children: Steven Alan, Heidi Michele Goldenberg Handelsman, Jeffrey Evan Student, Blkyn. Coll., 1946-47; BS, Bklyn. Coll. Pharmacy of L.I. U., 1951. Pharmacist Dolcorts Pharmacy, N.Y.C., 1951-56; export mgr. Chem. Specialties Co., Inc., N.Y.C., 1956-58; sales mgr. Syntex Chem. Co., Inc., N.Y.C., 1958-60; asst. to pres. Syntex Labs., Inc., N.Y.C., 1960-61; gen. sales mgr. Panray-Parlam Corp., Englewood, N.J., 1961-63; v.p. Ormont Drug & Chem. Co., Inc., Englewood, 1963-64, exec. v.p., dir., 1964-66, pres., dir., 1966-81; sec., dir. Goldleaf Pharmacal Co., Inc., Englewood, N.J., 1966-81; pres., dir. Moleculon, Inc., 1982-88; pres., chief exec. officer, dir. Argus Pharmaceuticals Inc., The Woodlands, Tex., 1988-92; bd. dirs. Fed. Pharmacal Co., Ft. Lauderdale, Fla., Bedford Acme Surg. Co., Inc., Bklyn., Lawton Labs., Inc., Englewood, Ormont Diagnostics Ltd., London. Trustee L.I. U., Bklyn. Coll. Pharmacy. Mem. Bklyn. Coll. Pharmacy Alumni Assn. (pres.), Fedn. Alumni Assns. L.I. U. (pres.), Am. Pharm. Assn., Englewood Jr. C. of C., Young Pres. Orgn., Am. Mgmt. Assn., Drug and Allied Trades Assn., Delta Sigma Theta. Club: B'nai B'rith, The Polo Club of Boca Raton (pres. bd. govs.). Home: 16730 Colchester Ct Delray Beach FL 33484-6946

GOLDENBERG, KIM, university president, internist. BS, SUNY, Stonybrook, 1968; MS, Polytech. Inst. N.Y., 1972; MD, Albany (N.Y.) Med. Coll., 1979. Test engr. lunar lander and naval jets Grumman, N.Y., 1968-75; resident internl medicine Western Res. Care Sys., Youngstown, Ohio, 1979-82; dir. gen. internal medicine Wright State U. Sch. Medicine, Dayton, Ohio, 1983-89, vice chair medicine, 1988-89, assoc. dean for students and curriculum, 1989-90, dean, 1990-98, pres., 1998—. Office: Wright State U Office of Pres Dayton OH 45435

GOLDENBERG, MARVIN MANUS, pharmacologist, pharmaceutical developer; b. N.Y.C., July 7, 1935; s. Jacob and Sarah Goldenberg; m. Esther K. Gelman, Sept. 8, 1957; children: Sol Jeffrey, Lisa Shari. BS, Bklyn. Coll. Pharmacy, 1957; MS, Temple U., 1959; PhD, Med. Coll. Pa., 1965. Lic. pharmacist, N.Y., Pa. Group leader Procter & Gamble Pharms., Norwich, N.Y., 1965-80; dir. immunopharmacology rsch. Merck Sharp & Dohme, Rahway, N.J., 1980-85, asst. dir. clin. rsch., 1985-88; dir. ophthalmic R&D Am. Cyanamid, Pearl River, N.Y., 1988-89, dir. ophthalmic rsch., 1989-91; v.p. pharm. product devel. and mfg. Reed and Carnrick div. Block Drug Co., Jersey City, N.J., 1991-92; v.p. pharmacology & clin. design, 1992-93; v.p. pharmacology clin. design, pres. Mt. Sinai Med. Ctr., N.Y.C., 1994—; investigational drug mgr. drugs internal rev. bd.; grant reviewer NIH and DRG, Bethesda, Md., 1978-95, fellowship reviewer, 1984-89; cons. in field. Author: The Role of Arachidonic Acid Oxygenation Products, 1984, Gastric Cytoprotection with Prostaglandins, 1985, Critical Review of Losartan, 1995, Analysis of the Asthma Drug Zileuteon, 1996, Critical Drug Appraisal: Mesalamine in IBD Fundamentals of the Clinical Trial, 1997, Critical Drug Appraisal: Misoprostol in NSAID-Induced Gastrontestinal Injury, 1998; sect. editor New Drugs: Jour. Clin. Therapeutics; column editor New Drugs: Jour. Pharmacy and Therapeutics; mem. editl. bd. Clin. Therapeutics; med. writer New Drugs: Clin. Trials; contbr. numerous articles to profl. jours.; inventor on numerous patents. Pres. Temple, Norwich, N.Y., 1972. Fellow Am. Soc. for Pharmacology, Am. Gastroent. Assn., Inflammation Rsch. Assn., Soc. of Clin. Pharmacology; mem. Am. Assn. Pharm. Scientists, N.Y. Soc. Health Care Specialists, Masons (pres. Norwich, N.Y. 1975). Achievements include patents relating to use of chemical entities in inflammation, pain and gastrointestinal disorders. Office: Mt Sinai Med Ctr One Gustave L Levy Pl New York NY 10029 also: 721 Shackamaxon Dr Westfield NJ 07090-3407

GOLDENBERG, MYRNA GALLANT, English language and literature educator; b. Bklyn., Mar. 8, 1937; d. Harry and Fay (Solomon) Gallant; m. Neal Goldenberg, Jan. 27, 1957; children: Elizabeth, David Brian, Eve Lisa. BS cum laude, CCNY, 1957; MA, U. Ark., 1961; PhD, U. Md., 1987. Faculty dept. English Montgomery Coll., Rockville, Md., 1971—, chair dept., 1979-81, coord. gen. edn., 1981-90, coord. women's studies program, 1990-94, dir. Paul Peck Humanities Inst., 1997—; adj. faculty humanities dept. Johns Hopkins U., judaic studies, women's studies, honors coll. English U. Md.; English grad. dept. adj. faculty, U. Va.; dir. project to integrate scholarship on women and minorities into the curriculum Ford Found., 1993-94; co-dir. project integrating scholarship of women in curricula of selected Md. C.C.s, FIPSE, 1988-90; chmn. Montgomery County Commn. on Humanities, 1984-91; chmn. Title IX adv. com. Montgomery County Pub. Schs., 1985-89; lectr. in field. Contbr. author/author: Common and Uncommon Concerns: The Complex Role of Community College Department Chairpersons/Enhancing Department Leadership, 1990, Different Horrors/Same Hell: Women Remembering the Holocaust, Thinking the Unthinkable: Human Meanings of the Holocaust, 1990, Writing Everybody In: Two-Year College English: Essays for a New Century, 1994, Testimony, Narrative and Nightmare: Experience of Jewish Women in the Holocaust: Active Voices/Women and Jewish Culture, 1995, Lessons Learned from Gentle Heroism: Women's Holocaust Narratives, 1995;The Beautiful Days of My Youth, 1997, Memoirs of Auschwitz Survivors: The Burden of Gender, 1998; contbg. editor: Belles Lettres, 1989-98; editor: C.C. Humanities Rev., Community College Guide to Curriculum Change, 1990; contbr. articles to profl. jours. Bd. dirs. Jewish Cmty. Coun., 1997—, Md. Humanities Coun., 1997—, Jewish Hist. Soc. Greater Washington, 1997—. Recipient Disting. Humanities Educator award C.C. Humanities Assn., 1989, Outstanding Faculty Mem. award Montgomery Coll., 1990, Teaching award Md. Assn. for Higher Edn., 1991; Acad. Adminstrn. fellow Am. Coun. on Edn., 1981-82; Lowenstein Wiener fellow U. Md.; 1983; recipient William H. Meardy Faculty award Assn. of Comm. Coll. Trustees, 1996. Mem. MLA (sec.), Nat. Women's Studies Assn. (sec.), Assn. Jewish Studies, Nat. Coun. Tchrs. English, Jewish Hist. Soc. Greater Wash. (bd. dirs. 1997—), Phi Kappa Phi. Avocations: walking, travel, writing, reading, cooking. Office: Montgomery Coll 51 Mannakee St Rockville MD 20850-1101

GOLDENBERG, ROBERT L., obstetrician; b. N.Y.C., Jan. 23, 1943. BS, Columbia U., 1964; MD, Duke U., 1968. Intern Duke U. Sch. Med, N.C., 1968; resident Duke U. Sch. Med, 1968-69; resident in OB-Gyn. Columbia U., N.Y.C., 1969-70; fellow Endocrine-Infertility sec. Nat. Inst. Child Health NIH, Bethesda, Md., 1970-72; resident Yale U. Sch. Med., New Haven, Conn., 1972-74; asst. prof. Yale U. Sch. Med., 1974-76; from asst. prof. to prof. U. Ala. Sch. Med., Birmingham, 1976-88; assoc. prof. Sch. Pub. Health U. Ala. Sch. Med., 1981-89, dir. MCH Training prog., 1989-91, dir. Ctr. Obstetric Rsch., 1984—, Charles E. Flowers prof., 1988—, prof. Dept. Pub. Health, 1989-96; dir. Yale Infertility Clinic, 1974-76; dir. Bur. Maternal & Child Health, Ala. Dept. Pub. Health, 1977-81; fellow Maternal-fetal medicine Dept. Ob-gyn., U. Ala., 1983-85; mem. study sec. Off. Maternal & Child Health, Dept. HHS, 1983-86; dir. Obstetric Svcs. Cooper Green Hosp., 1986-87; chmn. Dept. Ob-gyn., 1987-91; mem. child health advisory panel Off. Tech. Assessment, U.S. Congress, 1986-88; mem. Maternal & Child Health Rsch. Com. Nat. Inst. Child Health and Human Devel., NIH, 1990-95. Mem. Inst. Med. Nat. Acad. Sci., Am. Assn. Maternal & Neonatal Health, Am. Col. Ob-gyn., Am. Gyn. and Obstetric Soc., Am. Pub. Health Assn., Nat. Perinatal Assn., Soc. Perinatal Obstetricians. Office: Dept Obstetrics and Gynecology 618 20th St S Rm 560 Birmingham AL 35233-2010

GOLDENTHAL, NATHAN DAVID, physician; b. Toronto, Can., Sept. 13, 1951; m. Elaine Zaifman, May 26, 1977. MD, U. Toronto, 1975; MPH, U. N.C., 1990. Diplomate Am. Bd. Forensic Examiners, Am. Bd. Forensic Medicine, Am. Bd. Preventive Medicine. Med. dir. Peoria (Ariz.) Med. Clinic, 1977-85; pvt. cons. Peoria, 1985-89; med. developer U. N.C., Chapel Hill, 1989-90; chief profl. svcs. USAF Logistics Command, Dayton, Ohio, 1990-92; dir. Ariz. Inst. Occupl. Safety and Health, Phoenix, 1992—; site physician TRW-Air Bag Safety, Mesa, Ariz., 1995—. Author: Understanding the American with Disabilities, 1993; manuscript reviewer Am. Indsl. Hygiene Jour., 1994-95; contbr. articles to profl. jours. Med. dir. Lyons Aquatic Rehab. Program, Phoenix, 1994-95; mem. tech. com. State Govern ACERP Project, Phoenix, 1994-95; chmn. occupl. health coun. Dept. Def., Dayton, Ohio, 1991-92, chmn. dept. strategic planning, 1991-92. Recipient Nat. Med. fellowship U. N.C., 1989, Pub. Health traineeship U. N.C., 1989. Fellow Am. Coll. Preventive Medicine; mem. Am. Coll. Occupl. Environ. Medicine, Maricopa County Med. Soc. Avocations: investigative and information acquisition. Office: Ariz Inst Occupl Safety & Health 333 E Virginia #204 Phoenix AZ 85004

GOLDER, LEONARD HOWARD, lawyer, writer; b. Boston, June 6, 1950; s. Hershel and Pauline (Glass) G.; 1 child, Robert. BA, Clark U., 1972; JD, New Eng. Sch. Law, 1980. Bar: Mass. 1981, U.S. Dist. Ct. Mass. 1981, U.S. Ct. Appeals (1st cir.) Mass. 1981, U.S. Supreme Ct. 1984; lic. notary pub., Mass.; lic. real estate broker, Mass. Assoc. Law Offices Jacob Shair, West Roxbury, Mass., 1982-85; dir. collections unit Mass. Dept. Pub. Welfare, Boston, 1985-87; pvt. practice Stow, Mass., 1987—. Creator: (polit. game) Compromise, 1987; contbr. articles to profl. jours. Social worker Tufts Mental Health, Boston, 1973-81; selectman Town of Stow, Mass., 1997, chmn. Stow Bd. Selectmen, 1994; chmn. Stow Dem. Com., 1994—; adv. mem. Stow Master Plan, 1997; chmn. Stow Dem. Com., 1997; mem. Middlesex County adv. bd., Cambridge, Mass., 1997. Mem. Boston Bar Assn. Avocations: collecting sports and polit. memorabilia, reading, travel. Home and Office: 67 Old Bolton Rd Stow MA 01775-1212

GOLDES, JORDAN, legislative staff member; b. Manhattan, N.Y.. Student, N.Y. Inst. Tech., 1985-86; BA in Comm., SUNY, Oswego, 1989. Freelance tv prodr. Nat. Video Ctr., N.Y.C., 1988-89; prodr., asst. prodr. 1010 WINS Radio, N.Y.C., 1989-93, on air reporter, 1992-94; press sec., media advisor U.S. Congressman Gary Ackerman, Queens, L.I., N.Y., 1994—; freelance on air reporter Radio Pacific, 1993—, Can. Broadcasting Corp., 1993—. Avocations: bike riding, roller blading, Internet surfing, amateur video/photography, music. Home: 28 Vista Hill Rd Great Neck NY 11021

GOLDEY, JAMES MEARNS, physicist; b. Wilmington, Del., July 3, 1926; s. Robert Perkins and Ellen (Mearns) G.; m. Jeanne Calvert Potts, June 29, 1951; children: James P., Kristina. B.S. with honors, U. Del., 1950; Ph.D. in Physics, M.I.T., 1955. Mem. tech. staff Bell Labs. (now Lucent Techs.), Murray Hill, N.J., 1954-56, supr., 1956-59, head integrated cir. and silicon transistor dept., 1959-60; dir. integrated cir. customer svc. lab. Bell Labs., Allentown, Pa., 1981-84; dir. linear and high voltage integrated cir. lab Bell Labs., Reading, Pa., 1984-89; devel. v.p. high performance integrated cir. devel. AT&T Microelectronics, Reading, 1988-89, ret., 1989. Contbr. articles in field to profl. jours. Served with U.S. Army, 1944-46. Fellow IEEE. Republican. Presbyterian. Patentee in field. Home: 3930 Azalea Rd Allentown PA 18103-9743

GOLDFARB, BERNARD SANFORD, lawyer; b. Cleve., Apr. 15, 1917; s. Harry and Esther (Lenson) G.; m. Barbara Brofman, Jan. 4, 1966; children—Meredith Stacey, Lauren Beth. A.B., Case Western Res. U., 1938, J.D., 1940. Bar: Ohio bar 1940. Since practiced in Cleve.; sr. ptnr. firm Goldfarb & Reznick, 1967-95; pvt. practice Cleve., 1997—; spl. counsel to atty. gen. Ohio, 1950, 71-74; mem. Ohio Commn. Uniform Traffic Rules, 1973—. Contbr. legal jours. Served with USAAF, 1942-45. Mem. Am., Ohio, Greater Cleve. bar assns. Home: 39 Pepper Creek Dr Pepper Pike OH 44124-5279 Office: 55 Public Sq Ste 1500 Cleveland OH 44113-1998

GOLDFARB, IRENE DALE, financial planner; b. Newark, N.J., Jan. 13, 1929; d. Philip and Lucie (Mintz) Dale; m. Samuel Goldfarb, Jan. 28, 1951; children: Ruth Goldfarb Koizim, David Alan, Sally Fay, Judith Valerie. BS in Chemistry, Rutgers U., 1950; MBA, U. Pa., 1979. CFP. Asst. to assoc. provost Princeton (N.J.) U., 1968-70, asst. to provost, 1970-72, tech. staff, 1972-74, mgr. pers. svcs., 1974-75, asst. dir. pers. svcs., 1975-84; fin. planner, mgr. A.L. Herst Assocs., Inc., Princeton, 1984-86; pvt. practice Princeton, 1986-90; v.p. A.L. Herst Assocs., Inc., Princeton, 1990-92; fin. planner Glenmede Trust Co. N.J., Princeton, 1992—; cons. in field. Mem. Internat. Assn. Fin. Planning (founding officer Princeton-Western N.J. chpt. 1986-98, pres. 1988-89, chmn. 1989-90), Inst. Cert. Fin. Planners, Assoc. Alumnae Douglass Coll. (chmn. ann. fund 1982-84, v.p. adminstrn. 1988-94), Phi Beta Kappa. Avocations: music, gardening, travel. Home and Office: 69 Balsam Ln Princeton NJ 08540-5326 Office: 16 Chambers St Princeton NJ 08542-3708

GOLDFARB, LISA MICHELE, psychiatrist; b. N.Y.C., Oct. 2, 1963; d. Herbert Allen and Beverly Susan (Rozman) G.; m. Steve Martin Chaiken, Jan. 8, 1994; 1 child, Jackson Archer. BS in life scis., MIT, 1985; MD, Columbia U., 1989. Diplomate Am. Bd. Psychiatry and Neurology. Intern St. Luke's-Roosevelt Med. Ctr., N.Y.C., 1989-90; resident in psychiatry N.Y. State Psychiat. Inst., Columbia-Presbyn. Hosp., N.Y.C., 1990-93; fellow in divsn. alcoholism and drug abuse, dept. psychiatry NYU Sch. Medicine, N.Y.C., 1993-95; clin. instr. NYU Med. Ctr., N.Y.C., 1994-96; clin. asst. prof. psychiatry NYU Med. Ctr., 1997—; doctoral candidate Columbia U., Ctr. for Psychoanalytic Tng. & Rsch., N.Y.C., 1995—; med. staff Bellevue Hosp., N.Y.C., 1994—; med. staff with admitting privileges Tisch Hosp., NYU Med. Ctr., 1996—; homebound elderly program of Columbia-Presbyn. Hosp., 1993; assoc. med. staff Regent Hosp., 1991-93. Contbr. articles to profl. jours. Mem. Am. Psychiat. Assn. (com. on treatment svcs. for addicted patients 1996—), Am. Acad. Psychiatrists in Alcoholism and Addiction, Am. Med. Women's Assn. Office: 3 E 65th St New York NY 10021-6527

GOLDFARB, MARTIN, sociologist; b. Toronto, Ont., Can., May 6, 1938; s. David and Sonia (Silverstein) G.; m. Joan Freedman, June 7, 1961; children—Alonna, Baila, Rebecca, Daniel, Avi. BA, U. Toronto, 1961, MA, 1965. Tchr. North York Bd. Edn., Toronto, 1965-67; chmn., pres. CEO The Goldfarb Corp., Toronto, 1987—; chmn., CEO Goldfarb Cons., 1967—; co-chmn. The Kantar Group; bd. govs. York U., Toronto; bd. dirs. CLC Downsview Inc., Fleming Packaging Corp., Noma Industries Ltd., Axia Multimedia Corp.; chmn. SMK Speedy Internat., Inc. Author: The Goldfarb Report, 1981-97, Marching to a Different Drummer, 1988; contbr. articles to profl. jours. Past bd. dirs. Toronto Symphony Orch., Shaw Festival, Niagara-on-the-Lake, Can. Coun. Christians and Jews, Can. Opera Co., Toronto, Coun. for Can. Unity; trustee The Martin Goodman Trust for Canadian Nieman Fellows. Avocations: skiing; tennis. Office: The Goldfarb Corp, 4950 Yonge St, Toronto, ON Canada M2N 6K1

GOLDFARB, MARVIN AL, retired civil engineer; b. Memphis, Tenn., Dec. 12, 1928; s. Al Bohne and Melba (Pollock) G.; m. Lorene Shelton, June 13, 1965 (div. 1974); children: David Al, Julie Lin. BSCE, U. Tenn., 1950; MS in Engring. Mgmt., U. Mo., 1971. Registered profl. engr., Ala., Mo. Field engr. Inter-Am. Geodetic Survey, Panama, 1950-53; engr., supr. Rust Engring. Co., Birmingham, Ala., 1956-64; engr., prin. Monsanto Co., St. Louis, 1964-90, ret., 1990. Author: An Owner's Approach to Project Scheduling, 1975. Chmn. troop com. Boy Scouts Am., 1980—; councilman City of Maryland Heights, Mo., 1985-86, mem. Planning and Zoning Commn., chmn., 1986-98. Mem. VFW, Mo. Soc. Profl. Engrs. (pres. 1985-86), Profl. Engrs. Industry (regional vice chmn. 1980-82), Am. Legion (comdr. post 213 1991-93). Jewish. Home: 1474 Glenmeade Dr Maryland Heights MO 63043

GOLDFARB, MURIEL BERNICE, marketing and advertising consultant; b. Bklyn., Mar. 29, 1920; d. Barnett Goldfarb and May (Steinberg) Goldfarb Oshman; BA, U. Miami, Coral Gables, Fla., 1942; postgrad. CCNY, 1950. Pub. info. asst. UNESCO, Paris, 1946-47; advt. mgr. Majestic Specialties Co., N.Y.C., 1947-50; retail promotion mgr. Glamour Mag., 1955-61; advt. dir. Country Tweeds Co., N.Y.C., 1961-65; advt. dir. S. Augstein & Co., N.Y.C., 1966-72, Feature Ring Co., Inc., Gotham Ring Co., Inc., Fidco Inc., N.Y.C., 1972-77; dir. advt. and promotion Wasko Gold Products Corp., N.Y.C., 1977-81; advt. and mktg. cons. specializing in promotions and sale of vintage jewelry and Bric à Brac. Lt. WAVES, 1943-46. Mem. Fashion Group N.Y. Inc., Women's Jewelry Assn. (corr. sec. 1983-85). Jewish.

GOLDFARB, RONALD LAWRENCE, lawyer; b. Jersey City, N.J., Oct. 16, 1933; s. Robert S. and Aida J. (Weintraub) G.; m. Joanne Jacob, June 9, 1957; children: Jody, Nicholas, Maximilian Goldfarb. AB, Syracuse U., 1954, LLB, 1956; LLM, Yale, 1960, JSD, 1962. Bar: N.Y. 1956, Calif. 1959, D.C. 1962, U.S. Supreme Ct. 1965. Spl. asst. to U.S. atty. gen. (organized crime sect.), 1961-64; ptnr. Goldfarb and Assocs. and predecessor law firms, 1966—; Dir. Brookings Instn. program on cts. and adminstrn. Justice, 1966-67; mem. staff counsel com. on law and social action Am. Jewish Congress, 1960-61; cons. Pres.'s Poverty Program, 1964, Riots Commn., 1967-68. Author: The Contempt Power, 1963, Ransom: A Critique of the American Bail Systems, 1965, (with Alfred Friendly) Crime and Publicity, 1967, (with Linda Singer) After Conviction--A Review of the American Correction System, 1973, Jails: The Ultimate Ghetto, 1975, Migrant Farm Workers: A Caste of Despair, 1981, (with James Raymond) Clear Understandings: A Guide to Legal Writing, 1983, (with Gail Ross) The Writer's Lawyer: Essential Legal Advice for Writers and Editors in All Media, 1989, Perfect Villains, Imperfect Heroes: Robert F. Kennedy's War Against Organized Crime, 1995, TV or Not TV: Courts, Television and Justice, 1998. Served to capt. JAG Corps USAF, 1957-60. Arthur Garfield Hays fellow N.Y.U., 1960-61; Woodrow Wilson fellow. Mem. ACLU, ABA, D.C. Bar Assn., N.Y. Bar Assn., Calif. Bar Assn., Sigma Alpha Mu., Phi Delta Phi. Office: 1501 M St NW Washington DC 20005

GOLDFARB, STANLEY, internist, educator; b. N.Y.C., Dec. 18, 1943; s. Robert Melvin and Mary Ann (Siegel) G.; m. Rayna Lynne Block, Aug. 30, 1970; children: Rachael, Michael. AB, Princeton U., 1965; MD, U. Rochester, 1969; MS, U. Pa., 1986. Intern Hosp. U. Pa., Phila., 1969-70, resident, 1970-73; asst. prof. U. Pa., Phila., 1974-84, assoc. prof., 1984-88, prof. medicine, 1988—; mem. nephrology bd. Am. Bd. Internal Medicine, Phila., 1988—. Editor: Hormones, Autocoids and Kidney, 1991. Bd. dirs, bd. regents ACP; bd. dirs. Nat. Kidney Found. Pa., Phila, 1988-90. NIH grantee, Washington, 1984-88; recipient Vol. award Nat. Kidney Found., N.Y.C., 1990. Mem. Am. Soc. Clin. Investigation. Avocation: golf. Home: 801 Muirfield Rd Bryn Mawr PA 19010-1940 Office: Hosp of the U of Pa 3400 Spruce St Philadelphia PA 19104-4204*

GOLDFARB, TIMOTHY MOORE, hospital administrator; b. Jerome, Ariz., Dec. 15, 1949; married. B, Ariz. State U., 1975, MHA, 1978. Adminstrv. resident Univ. Med. Ctr., Tucson, 1977-78, mgr. patient accts., 1978-79; asst. adminstr. Tucson Gen. Hosp., 1979; asst. adminstr. Univ. Med. Ctr., Tucson, 1979-83, assoc adminstr., 1983-84; assoc. hosp. dir. Oreg. Health Scis. Univ. Hosp., Portland, 1984-89, health care sys. dir., 1989—. Office: Oreg Health Scis Univ Hosp 3181 SW Sam Jackson Park Rd Portland OR 97201-3011*

GOLDFARB, WARREN (DAVID), philosophy educator; b. N.Y.C., Aug. 25, 1949; s. Norman J. and Ella (Kaback) G. A.B., Harvard U., 1969, A.M., 1971, Ph.D., 1975. Asst. prof. philosophy Harvard U., Cambridge, Mass., 1975-80, assoc. prof., 1980-82, prof., 1982—, Pearson prof. math. logic, 1995—; chmn. dept. philosphy Harvard U., 1984-91, 93-94; vis. prof. U. Calif.-Berkeley, 1984. Author: (with Burton Dreben) The Decision Problem, 1979; editor: Jacques Herbrand, Logical Writings, 1971. Mem. Am. Philos. Assn., Assn. Symbolic Logic (exec. com. 1982-84). Office: Harvard U Dept Philosophy Cambridge MA 02138

GOLDFIELD, EDWIN DAVID, statistician; b. N.Y.C., Oct. 26, 1918; s. Maurice and Sarah (Spears) G. BS, CUNY, 1939; MA, Columbia U., 1940; postgrad., Am. U., 1940-46. Rsch. assoc. dept. investigation N.Y.C., 1938-39; statis. adviser Ct. Spl. Sessions, N.Y.C., 1939; with Bur. Census, Washington, 1940-75, asst. dir., 1967-71, chief internat. programs, 1971-75; with NAS, Washington, 1975—, study dir., 1975-78, exec. dir. com. on nat. statis., 1978-87, sr. assoc., 1987—; cons. in field, 1951—; staff dir. subcom. census and statistics Ho. of Reps., 1959-60, 67. Contbr. articles. Editor: Papers on Labor Force Statistics in the United States, 1952. Recipient Meritorious Svc. award Dept. Commerce, 1954. Fellow Am. Statis. Assn.; mem. Washington Statis. Soc. (past pres.), Am. Econ. Assn., Population Assn. Am., Inter-Am. Statis. Inst., Internat. Assn. Survey Statisticians, Internat. Statis. Inst., Phi Beta Kappa. Home: 4131 23rd Pkwy Apt 1102 Temple Hills MD 20748-4462 Office: NAS 2101 Constitution Ave NW Washington DC 20418-0007

GOLDFIELD, EMILY DAWSON, finance company executive, artist; b. Bklyn., May 31, 1947; d. Martin and Renee (Solow) Dawson; m. Stephen Gary Goldfield, June 17, 1973; children: Stacy Rose, Daniel James. BS, U. Mich., 1969; MEd, Pa. State U., 1971; PhD, U. So. Calif., 1977. Chmn. bd. Union Home Loan, Inc. Author: The Value of Creative Dance, 1971; Development of Creative Dance, 1977. U. Mich. scholar, 1969; Pa. State U. fellow, 1970, U. So. Calif. fellow, 1972. Mem. PTA, Mortgage Assn. of Calif., Calif. Trust Deed Brokers Assn., South Orange County Assn. of Realtors, Am. Small Bus. Assn., Nat. Assn. Realtors, Calif. Assn. Realtors, Visual Arts Assn., Friend of the Orange County Performing Arts Ctr., U.S. Tennis Assn., Am. Horse Show Assn., Sierra Club, Nat. Audobon Soc., Golf and Racquet Club, Ferrari Owners Club. Office: 23586 Calabasas Rd Ste 201 Calabasas CA 91302

GOLDFISCHER, JEROME D., cardiologist; b. N.Y.C., Mar. 14, 1930; s. Sidney and Bella (Bernstein) G.; m. Joan Lila Goldfarb, June 28, 1953 (dec. Oct. 1996); children: Mindy Ann, Robin Lisa, Cathi Sue, Marilyn Lori. BS in Biology, Rutgers U., 1951; MD, NYU, 1955. Diplomate Am. Bd. Internal Medicine, Am. Bd. Cardiology. Researcher Polio Found. Irvington (N.J.) House, 1953; intern Montefiore Hosp., N.Y.C., 1955-56, jr. asst. resident in medicine, 1956-57, asst. resident in medicine, 1959-60, resident in cardiology, 1960-61, USPHS postdoctoral rsch. fellow in cardiology, 1961-63, rsch. asst. cardiology; attending medicine physician Montefiore Hosp., N.Y.C., N.J., 1963—; pvt. practice cardiology Ft. Lee, N.J.; mem. attending staff Englewood (N.J.) Hosp., 1963—; mem. electrocardiography dept. Montefiore Hosp., 1961—; chmn. cardiac care com. Englewood Hosp., 1976-91, dir. coronary care unit, 1963-81, acting chief cardiology, 1966-71, chief cardiology, 1971-81, chief medicine, 1981-92, dir. electrocardiography dept., 1966—; instr. medicine Albert Einstein Coll. Medicine, 1967-77, asst. clin. prof., 1978—. Contbr. articles to profl. jours. Mem. Bergen County Cmty. Coun., 1973-81. Capt. USAF, 1957-59. Fellow ACP, Am. Coll. Cardiology, Am. Heart Assn. (coun. clin. cardiology 1976, bd. dirs. Bergen County chpt. 1966-81, exec. com. 1969-81, chmn. cardiopulmonary resuscitation com. 1966-79, chmn. com. emergency coronary care 1973-80, other offices); mem. Assn. Advancement of Med. Instrumentation, Bergen County Med. Soc., Bergen County Heart Assn. Office: 1555 Center Ave Fort Lee NJ 07024-4612

GOLDFRANK, LEWIS ROBERT, physician; b. N.Y.C., Sept. 8, 1941; s. Herbert John and Helen (Colodny) G.; m. Susan M. Harrington, Aug. 29, 1964; children: Michelle, Andrew, Jennifer, Rebecca. BA, Clark U., 1963; MD, U. Brussels, Belgium, 1970. Diplomate Am. Bd. Med. Toxicology (dir., chmn. 1985-90). Resident Montefiore Hosp., Bronx, N.Y., 1971-73; dir. emergency medicine Morrisania Hosp., Bronx, 1973-76, North Cen. Bronx Hosp., 1976-79, Montefiore Hosp., 1976-79, Bellevue Hosp., Manhattan, N.Y., 1979—, NYU Med. Ctr., Manhattan, 1979—; dir. N.Y. City Poison Ctr., Manhattan, 1979—; bd. dirs. Soc. Acad. Emergency Medicine, 1990-96. Author, editor: Goldfrank's Toxicologic Emergencies, 1978, 6th edit., 1998, Emergency Doctor, 1987, Diagnostic Testing in the Emergency Department, 1984, 2d edit., 1995. Recipient Am. Med. Writer's Assn. Hon. Mention, 1988, Hal Jayne Acad. Excellence award Soc. Acad. Emergency Medicine, 1990. Fellow Am. Coll. Emergency Physician, Am. Acad. Clin. Toxicology, Am. Coll. Physicians; mem. NAS (Inst. Medicine). Avocation: gardening. Home: 55 Grace Ln Ossining NY 10562-2129 Office: Bellevue Hosp Ctr First Ave # 27th St New York NY 10016

GOLDGAR, BERTRAND ALVIN, literary historian, educator; b. Macon, Ga., Nov. 17, 1927; s. Benjamin Meyer and Annie (Shapiro) G.; m. Corinne Cohn Hartman, Apr. 6, 1950; children: Arnold Benjamin, Anne Hartman. BA, Vanderbilt U., 1948, MA, 1949; MA, Princeton U., 1957, PhD, 1958. Instr. in English Clemson (S.C.) U., 1948-50, asst. prof., 1951-52; instr. English Lawrence U., Appleton, Wis., 1957-61, asst. prof., 1961-65, assoc. prof., 1965-71, prof. English, 1971—, John N. Bergstrom prof. humanities, 1980—; mem. fellowship panel NEH, 1979. Author: The Curse of Party: Swift's Relations with Addison and Steele, 1961, Walpole and the Wits: The Relation of Politics to Literature, 1722-1742, 1976; editor: The Literary Criticism of Alexander Pope, 1965, Henry Fielding's The Covent-Garden Jour., 1988, Henry Fielding's Miscellanies, Vol. 2, 1993, Vol. 3, 1997; adv. editor: 18th Century Studies, 1977-82. With AUS, 1952-54. Fellow, Am. Coun. Learned Socs, 1973-74, NEH, 1980-81. Mem. Am. Soc. 18th Century Studies, Johnson Soc. Cen. Region. Home: 914 E Eldorado St Appleton WI 54911-5536 Office: Lawrence U Dept English Appleton WI 54912

GOLDHABER, GERALD MARTIN, communication educator, author, consultant; b. Brookline, Mass., Jan. 23, 1944; s. Robert and Ruth Irene G.; m. Marylynn Blaustein, Aug. 17, 1969; children—Michelle, Marc. B.A., U. Mass., 1965; M.A., U. Md., 1967; Ph.D., Purdue U., 1970. Asst. prof. communication U. N.Mex., 1970-74; assoc. prof., assoc. chmn. dept. communication SUNY, Buffalo, 1974-78; chmn. dept. SUNY, 1979-88; owner Goldhaber Research Assocs., Buffalo, 1975—; polit. analyst N.Y. Post, CKO-Radio Can., WEBR Radio, Buffalo, WGRZ-TV, Buffalo, WBEN Radio, Buffalo, WIVB-TB, Buffalo; cons. polit. candidates, pollster. Author: Organizational Communication, 1974, 6th edit., 1993, (with B. Peterson and R.W. Pace) Communication Probes, 1974, 3d edit., 1982, (with L. Rosenfeld and V. Smith) Experiments in Human Communication, 1975, (with M.B. Goldhaber) Transactional Analysis, 1976, (with E. Zannes) Stand Up and Speak Out, 1978, 2d edit., 1982, (with H. Dennis, G. Richetto and O. Wilo) Information Strategies: New Pathways to Corporate Power, 1979, 2d edit., 1983, (with D. Rogers) Auditing Organizational Communication Systems: The ICA Communication Audit, 1979, (with G. Barnett The Handbook of Organizational Communication, 1988; contbg. author numerous books; rev. editor: Orgnl. Communication Abstracts; contbr. articles to profl. jours. Bd. dirs. Temple Beth El, Buffalo, 1980—, pres., 1992-94; bd. dirs. Rep. polit. pollster, Erie County, N.Y. Recipient Disting. Alumnus award U. Mass., 1983, numerous teaching awards and grants. Fellow Inst. Internat. Sociol. Research (life); mem. Internat. Communication Assn. (v.p., dir. 1974-76), Am. Mktg. Assn., Mktg. Research Assn., Council of Communication Mgmt., Human Factors Soc., Am. Assn. Public Opinion Research. Home: 48 Jamstead Ct Buffalo NY 14221-4642 Office: SUNY-Buffalo Dept Communication Buffalo NY 14260 *I have always believed that the search for excellence should govern the lives of all people. There is virtually nothing that a human being cannot achieve if he or she lives in accordance with this standard and possesses a strong sense of morality and a good sense of humor. I have lived my entire life according to these precepts and owe much to those who have stood with me for excellence.*

GOLDHABER, GERSON, physicist, educator; b. Chemnitz, Germany, Feb. 20, 1924; came to U.S., 1948, naturalized, 1953; s. Charles and Ethel (Frisch) G.; m. Judith Margoshes, May 30, 1969; children—Amos Nathaniel, Michaela Shally, Shaya Alexandra. M.Sc., Hebrew U., Jerusalem, 1947; Ph.D., U. Wis., 1950; PhD honoris causus, U. Stockholm, 1986. Instr. Columbia U., N.Y.C., 1950-53; acting asst. prof. physics U. Calif., Berkeley, 1953-54, asst. prof., 1954-58, assoc. prof., 1958-63, prof. physics, 1963-92, prof. physics emeritus, 1992—; Miller research prof. Miller Inst. Basic Sci. U. Calif.-Berkeley, 1958-59, 75-76, 84-85, prof. Grad. Sch., 1994—; Morris Loeb lectr. in physics Harvard U., 1976-77. Named Calif. Scientist of Yr., 1977, Sci. Assoc., CERN, 1986; Ford Found. fellow CERN, 1960-61; Guggenheim fellow CERN, 1972-73. Fellow AAAS, Am. Phys. Soc. (Panofsky prize 1991), Sigma Xi; mem. Royal Swedish Acad. Sci. (fgn.), Nat. Acad. Sci. Fax: 510-486-6738. E-mail: gerson@lbl.gov. Office: EO Lawrence Berkeley Nat Lab Dept Physics MS 50-208 Berkeley CA 94720

GOLDHABER, JACOB KOPEL, retired mathematician, educator; b. Bklyn., Apr. 12, 1924; s. Joseph and Shirley (Heller) G.; m. Ruth Last, Dec. 25, 1951; children: Doreet, David, Aviva. BA, Bklyn. Coll., 1944; MA, Harvard, 1945; PhD, U. Wis., 1950. Instr. math. U. Conn., Storrs, 1950-53; instr. Cornell U., Ithaca, N.Y., 1953-54; asst. prof. Washington U., St. Louis, 1954-59, assoc. prof., 1959-61; assoc. prof. U. Md., College Park, 1961-62, prof., 1962-93, chmn. math. dept., 1968-77, acting dean grad. studies and rsch., 1984-86, 87-92, acting v.p. acad. affairs, provost, 1992-93, prof. emeritus, 1993—; exec. sec. Office Math. Scis., NRC, 1976-82; vis. rsch. assoc., NSF sci. faculty fellow U. London, 1966-67. Author: (with Gertrude Ehrlich) Algebra, 1970; contbr. papers to profl. jours. Mem. AAAS, Am. Math. Soc., Math. Assn. Am., Sigma Xi. Home: 2801 New Mexico Ave NW Washington DC 20007-3921

GOLDHABER, MAURICE, physicist; b. Lemberg, Austria, Apr. 18, 1911; came to U.S., 1938, naturalized, 1944; s. Charles and Ethel (Frisch) G.; m. Gertrude Scharff, May 24, 1939; children: Alfred S., Michael H. PhD, Cambridge U., Eng., 1936; PhD (hon.), Tel Aviv U., 1974; Dr. (hon.), U. Louvain-La-Neuve, Belgium, 1982; DSc (hon.), SUNY, Stony Brook, 1983, U. Notre Dame, 1992. Bye fellow Magdalene Coll., Cambridge, 1936-38; asst. prof. physics U. Ill., 1938-43, assoc. prof., 1943-45, prof., 1945-50; sr. sci. Brookhaven Nat. Lab., 1950-60, chmn. dept. physics, 1960-61, dir., 1961-73, distinguished scientist emeritus, 1973—; cons. labs. AFC; Morris Loeb lectr. Harvard U., 1955, 93, Rabi Scholar lectr., 1995; adj. prof. physics SUNY, Stony Brook, 1965—, Royal Soc. Rutherford Meml. lectr., Can., 1987; nuclear sci. com. NRC. Assoc. editor: Phys. Rev. 1951-53; Contbr. articles on nuclear physics to sci. jours. Bd. govs. Weizmann Inst. Sci., Rehovoth, Israel, Tel Aviv U.; trustee Univs. Rsch. Assn. Recipient citation for meritorious contbns. U.S. AEC, 1973, J. Robert Oppenheimer meml. prize, 1982, Nat. Medal Sci., 1983, Am. Acad. Achievement award, 1985, Wolf Found. prize in physics (Jerusalem), 1991, Enrico Fermi award in physics, 1998; co-recipient Rossi prize Am. Astron. Soc., High Energy Astrophysics div., 1989. Fellow AAAS, Am. Phys. Soc. (pres. 1982), Am. Acad. Arts and Scis.; mem. NAS, Am. Philos. Soc. (Tom W. Bonner prize in nuclear physics 1971). Office: Brookhaven Nat Lab Bldg 510 Upton NY 11973

GOLDHABER, PAUL, dental educator; b. N.Y.C., Mar. 16, 1924; m. Ethel Gurland, 1949; children: Samuel Zachary, Joshua Irving. DDS, NYU, 1948; BS, CCNY, 1954; MA (hon.), Harvard U., 1962. Diplomate Am. Bd. Periodontics. Asst. ophthalmology rsch. Harvard Med. Sch., Boston, 1948-50; asst. dentist Sch. Dental and Oral Surgery Columbia U., N.Y.C., 1950; rsch. fellow dental medicine Harvard Sch. Dental Medicine, Boston, 1954-55, rsch. assoc. oral pathology, 1955-56, assoc., 1956-59, from asst. prof. to assoc. prof., 1959-62, from assoc. prof. to prof., 1962-66, dir. postdoctoral studies, 1962-68, dean, 1968-90, prof. periodontics, 1966—, emeritus dean, 1990—; emeritus dean Harvard Sch. Dental Medicine, 1990—; vis. rsch. fellow Sloan-Kettering Inst. Cancer Rsch., 1954-55, rsch. fellow, 1955-56, USPHS sr. rsch. fellow, 1956-61; chmn. dental study sect. NIH, 1968-71. Mem. Am. Assn. Dental Rsch. (pres. 1973-74), Inst. Medicine, Internat. Assn. for Dental Rsch. (pres. 1985-86). Office: Harvard U Sch Dental Medicine 188 Longwood Ave Boston MA 02115-5819

GOLDHAMER, DAVID J., medical educator, researcher. BS in Biology, Purdue U., 1979; PhD in Devel. Biology, Ohio State U., 1988; postgrad., Marine Biol. Lab., Woods Hole, Mass., 1984. Rsch. assoc. lab. renewable resources engring. Purdue U., 1979-82; grad. tchg. asst. Ohio State U., 1982-87; asst. instr. embryology Marine Biol. Lab., Woods Hole, Mass., 1985; postdoctoral fellow U. Va., 1988-91; rsch. assoc. Inst. for Cancer Rsch. Fox Chase Cancer Ctr., 1991-92; asst. prof. dept. cell and devel. biology U. Pa. Sch. Medicine, 1993—. Contbr. articles to profl. jours.; reviewer: Biochimica and Biophysica Acta, Devel., Devel. Biology, Differentiation, DNA and Cell Biology, Molecular and Cellular Biology, Trends in Cardiovasc. Rsch.; lectr. in field. Recipient Grad. Student Alumni Rsch. award, 1987, Established Investigatorship award Am. Heart Assn., 1996—; NIH Tng. grantee, 1984, Sigma Xi grantee, 1986; Presdl. fellowship Ohio State U., 1987-88, MDA Postdoctoral fellowship, 1988-89, MDA Jere Thompson Neuromuscular Rsch. fellowship, 1989-91. Mem. AAAS, Soc. for Devel. Biology, John Morgan Soc., Pa. Muscle Inst. (co-organizer seminar series on muscle devel. 1994, co-organizer ann. retreat 1995). Office: U Pa Sch Medicine Dept Cell & Developmental Biology 1111 BrB2 Anatomy Chem Bldg Philadelphia PA 19104*

GOLDIE, RAY ROBERT, lawyer; b. Dayton, Ohio, Apr. 1, 1920; s. Albert S. and Lillian (Hayman) G.; m. Dorothy Roberta Zafman, Dec. 2, 1941; children: Marilyn, Deanne, Dayle, Ron R. Student, U. So. Calif., 1943-44, JD magna cum laude, 1957; student, San Bernardino Valley Coll., 1950-51. Bar: Calif. 1957; cert. specialist estate planning, trusts and probate law, Calif. Bd. Legal Specialization. Elec. appliance dealer various locations, 1944-54; dep. atty. gen. State Bar of Calif., L.A., 1957-58, 1957-58; pvt. practice San Bernardino, Calif., 1958-87, Rancho Mirage, Calif., 1987—; pres. Trinity Acceptance Corp., 1948-53. Mem. World Peace Through Law Ctr., 1962—; regional dir. Legion Lex U. So. Calif. Sch. Law 1959-75; chmn. San Bernardino United Jewish Appeal, 1963; v.p. United Jewish Welfare Fund, San Bernardino, 1964-66; Santa Anita Hosp., Lake Arrowhead, 1966-69; bd. dirs. San Bernardino Med. Arts Corp.; trustee McCallum Theater, Bob Hope Cultural Ctr., 1996-99, Friends of Cultural Ctr. Found.; bd. dirs. Palm Canyon Theater, 1998—; legal counsel Lake Arrowhead Skating Found., 1998. Fellow Internat. Acad. Law and Sci.; mem. ABA, Assn. Naval Aviation Desert Storm Sqdn. (adminstrv. officer, sec.), San Bernardino County Bar Assn., Riverside County Bar Assn., State Bar Calif. (cert. specialist estate planning, probate and trust law), Am. Judicature Soc., Am. Soc. Hosp. Attys., Calif. Trial Lawyers Assn. (v.p. chpt. 1965-67, pres. 1967-68), Am. Arbitration Assn. (nat. panel arbitrators), Coachella Valley Desert Bar Assn. (chmn. taxation and estate planning, trusts, wills and probate com. 1992-94), Order of the Coif, Lake Arrowhead Country Club (pres. 1972-73, 80-81), Lake Arrowhead Yacht Club, Club at Morningside (CFO 1992-93, sec. 1993-94), Nu Beta Epsilon (pres. 1956-57). Home and Office: 1 Hampton Ct Rancho Mirage CA 92270-2585

GOLDIN, DANIEL S., federal agency administrator; b. N.Y.C., July 23, 1940; m. Judith Linda Kramer; children: Ariel, Laura. BS in Mech. Engring., CCNY, 1962; PhD (hon.), Case Western Res. U., Cen. State U., CCNY, Fla. Inst. of Tech., Framingham State U., Poly. U. of N.Y., U. Ariz., U. Md., U. Mich. Rsch. scientist Lewis Rsch. Ctr., NASA, Cleve., 1962-67; with TRW, from 1967, mem. tech. staff, 1967; v.p., gen. mgr. Space & Tech. Group, TRW, Redondo, Calif., 1987-92; adminstr. NASA, Washington, 1992—. Recipient 1996 Chmn. award Am. Assn. Engring. Societies, 1997, Civilian Kitty Hawk Sands of Time award, Goddard Quality award, Heald award Ill. Inst. of Tech., Nelson P. Jackson Aerospace award Nat. Space Club, Internat. Von Karman Wings award Aerospace Hist. Soc., Meritorious award (2) Nat. Assn. of Small and Disadvantaged Businesses, President's medal N.Y. Inst. of Tech., Nat. award for Space Achievement, Rotary, Space Pioneer award Nat. Space Soc.; named one of 100 Most Influential in Govt. Nat. Jour., One of 40 Most Influential Def. Industry Leaders, Def. Bus. mag. Fellow AIAA (Piper Gen. Aviation award), Am. Astronom. Soc. (John F. Kennedy Astronautics award), Inst. for Advancement of Engring. Achievements during his tenure at TRW include the building of 13 spacecraft, the launch and operation of NASA tracking and Data Relay Satellite-5 and the Compton Gamma Ray Observatory. The group also has worked on other NASA programs including the successfull grinding and testing of the worlds two largest X-ray mirrors for the Advanced X-ray Astrophysics Facility. Office: NASA Office of Adminstr 300 E St SW Washington DC 20546-0005*

GOLDIN, JACOB ISAAK, software executive; b. Leningrad, Russia, Aug. 29, 1958; came to U.S., 1990; s. Isaak and Tamara (Rozhetsky) G.; m. Marina I. Vaynstein, May 17, 1983; children: Daniel, Simon. BS in Computer Sci., Leningrad Inst. Tech., 1978, MS in Chem. Engring., 1980; PhD in Chem. Engring., Leningrad Acad. Wood Chemistry, 1987. Programmer/analyst All-Union Hydrolysis Corp., Leningrad, 1979-83, chem. engr., 1983-84, sr. chem. engr., 1984-87, sr. rschr., 1987-90; pres., owner Jacob's Chem. Assoc., Livingston, N.J., 1993—; sr. programmer, analyst Givaudan-Roure Corp., Clifton, 1995-96; gen. project mgr. Reed-Elsevier, 1998—; cons. Atlas Refinery, 1993-96, ACIMI Corp., 1992-96; specialist in design and implementation of object-oriented multi-tier software architectures. Author software packages for analytical chemistry; contbr. articles to profl. jours. in phys. chemistry and software engineering. Mem. AIChE, Am. Oil Chem. Soc., NRA. Avocation: computer programming.

GOLDIN, JUDAH, Hebrew literature educator; b. N.Y.C., Sept. 14, 1914; s. Gerson David and Rachel (Robkin) G.; m. Grace Avis Aaronson, June 21, 1938; children: Robin Elinor (dec.), David Lionel. BSS, CCNY, 1934; diploma, Sem. Coll., 1934; MA, Columbia, 1938; MHL, Jewish Theol. Sem., 1938, DHL, 1943, HLD, 1968; MA, Yale, 1958; DD, Colgate U., 1973; HLD, Jewish Inst. Religion, Hebrew Union Coll., 1986. Ordained rabbi, 1938. Lectr., vis. assoc. prof. Jewish lit. and history Duke, 1943-45; assoc. prof. religion U. Iowa, 1946-52; dean, assoc. prof. Agada Sem. Coll., Jewish Theol. Sem., 1952-58; adj. prof. religion Columbia, 1955-58; prof. Jewish studies Yale, 1958-62, prof. classical Judaica, 1962-73; prof. postbibl. Hebrew lit. U. Pa., Phila., 1973-85, prof. emeritus, 1985—; hon. Moses Dropsie fellow Annenberg Rsch. Inst., U. Pa., 1994-95. Author: The Two Versions of Abot de Rabbi Nathan, 1945, Hillel the Elder, 1946, The Period of the Talmud, 1949, The Fathers, 1955, The Living Talmud, 1957, The Three Pillars of Simeon the Righteous, 1958, A Philosophical Session in a Tannaite Academy, 1965, The End of Ecclesiastes, 1966, The Song at the Sea, 1971, Profile of Aqiba ben Joseph, 1976, The First Pair, 1980, Freedom and Restraint of Haggadah, 1986; editor: The Jewish Expression, 1970, The Munich Mekilta, 1980. Am. Philos. Soc. grantee, 1957, 71; Guggenheim fellow, 1958; Fulbright fellow, 1958, 64-65; Am. Council Learned Socs., 1978. Fellow Am. Acad. Jewish Research, Am. Acad. Arts and Scis.; mem. Am. Schs. Oriental Research, Conn. Acad. Arts and Scis., Oriental Club Pa., Phi Beta Kappa. Home: C202 3300 Darby Rd Apt C202 Haverford PA 19041-1062 Office: U Pa Oriental Studies Dept Philadelphia PA 19104*

GOLDIN, LEON, artist, educator; b. Chgo., Jan. 16, 1923; s. Joseph P. and Bertha (Metz) G.; m. Meta Solotaroff, July 30, 1949; children: Joshua,

Daniel. BFA, Art Inst. Chgo., 1948; MFA, U. Iowa, 1950. From instr. to assoc. prof. Columbia U., N.Y.C., 1964-82, prof., 1982-92, prof. emeritus, 1992—, 1992—; former tchr. Calif. Coll. Arts and Crafts, Phila. Coll. Art, Queen's Coll., Cooper Union; vis. prof. painting Stanford, summer 1973. One-man shows Oakland Art Mus., 1955, Felix Landau Gallery, L.A., 1956, 57, 59, Galleria L'Attico, Rome, 1958, Kraushaar Galleries, N.Y.C., 1960, 64, 68, 72, 84, 88, 90, 93, 96, 98, U. Houston, 1981; represented in permanent collections Bklyn. Mus., City Mus. St. Louis, Worcester Mus., Addison Gallery Am. Art, Pa. Acad. Fine Arts, L.A. County Mus., Santa Barbara Mus., Oakland Art Mus., Munson Proctor Inst., Va. Mus. Fine Arts, Portland (Maine) Mus., Everson Mus., U. Ark., Okla. Art Ctr., Cleve. Mus. Fine Art. Served with AUS, 1943-46, ETO. Recipient Prix de Rome, Am. Acad. Rome, 1955-58, Jennie Sesnan Gold medal Pa. Acad. Fine Arts, 1966, Benjamin Altman Landscape prize Nat. Acad. Design, 1993; Tiffany grantee, 1951; Fulbright scholar to France, 1952; Guggenheim fellow, 1959, Nat. Endowment for Arts grantee, 1967, 80; Nat. Inst. Arts and Letters grantee, 1968; N.Y. Caps grantee, 1981. Mem. NAD. Home: 438 W 116th St New York NY 10027-7203

GOLDIN, MARION FREEDMAN, television news producer, reporter; b. N.Y.C., Sept. 5, 1940; d. Milton I. and Alice S. Freedman; m. Norman W. Goldin, Mar. 19, 1967 (dec. Sept. 1992). BA, Barnard Coll.; MA, Harvard U. Sec./researcher Eric Sevareid, 1963-69; researcher/assoc. producer CBS Morning News, 1969-72; producer "60 Minutes" CBS News, 1972-82, 84-88; sr. producer, asst. to exec. producer "20/20" ABC News, 1982-84; sr. producer "Expose" NBC News, 1990-91; pres. Marigold Unltd., 1988-90, 92—. Avocations: tennis, art, music.

GOLDIN, MARTIN BRUCE, financial executive, consultant; b. Teaneck, N.J., May 18, 1938; s. Arthur Daniel and Shirley Edith (Holland) G.; m. Joyce Anne Rossin, Aug. 22, 1960; children: Melissa Beth, Julie Amber, Kevin James, Sabrina Nicole. BBA, U. Miami, 1960; postgrad., Detroit Coll. Law, 1967. Fin. analyst Chrysler Corp. Detroit, London, Eng., 1967-70; chief fin. officer Chrysler de Mex., Mexico City, 1971-77, Chrysler Australia Ltd., Adelaide, 1978-80, Internat. Harvester De Mex., Mexico City, 1980-85; compt. Citicorp Diners Club, Denver, 1985-87; chief fin. officer, exec. v.p. Citicorp Diners Club, Chgo., 1988-96; v.p. fin. Deluxe Corp., Shoreview, Minn., 1997-98; fin. cons. Rossin-Goldin, Detroit, 1960—, La Torre de Acapulco (Mex.), 1980-88. Office: Rossin-Goldin Co 4710 Bouleau Rd White Bear Lake MN 55110-3355

GOLDIN, PAUL RAKITA, history educator; b. N.Y.C., Apr. 1, 1972; s. Frederick and Dione (Rakita) G. BA, MA, U. Pa., 1992; PhD, Harvard U., 1996. Asst. prof. history U. Pa., Phila., 1996—. Author: Rituals of the Way, 1999; contbr. articles to profl. jours. Mem. Soc. for Study Early China, Assn. Asian Studies (project grantee 1997). Office: U Pa 817 Williams Hall Philadelphia PA 19104

GOLDIN, SOL, marketing consultant; b. N.Y.C., Mar. 5, 1909; s. Isaac and Fanny (Barr) G.; m. Doris Margaret Curley, Nov. 26, 1930; children—Richard Thomas, Barbara (Mrs. James MacDonald), Kenneth Lee, Arlene (Mrs. Paul Cavaness), Steven Edward. B.B.A., Bryant Coll., 1928. With Sears Roebuck & Co., Chgo., 1933-49; buyer appliances Goldblatt Bros., Chgo., 1949-51; sales mgr. Henry N. Clark Co., Boston, 1951-52; buyer, mgr. appliances and TV Strawbridge & Clothier, Phila., 1952-55; with Whirlpool Corp., Benton Harbor, Mich., 1955-74; pres. Mktg. Affiliates Corp., Benton Harbor, 1974—; Lectr. in, U.S., France, Belgium, Australia.; Chmn. bd., chmn. exec. com. Brand Names Found., N.Y.C., 1971—. Writer: column Home Appliance Builder mag., 1961-67; Contbr. articles to profl. jours. Recipient Appreciation certificate Am. U., 1964, Nat. Alumni Council award Bryant Coll., 1964; Torch of Truth award Indpls. Advt. Club, 1972. Mem. Home Furnishings Industry Inst. (chmn. trustees 1971—), Nat. Appliance-Radio-TV Dealers Assn. (Man of Year award 1963), Nat. Account Mktg. Assn. (co-founder, bd. dirs. 1962-66), Inst. Appliance Mfrs. (Statesmanship award 1963, pres. 1965-67), Sales Execs. Club N.Y.C., Whirlpool Mgmt. Club (pres. 1966). Home and Office: 819 Suffield Sq Lincolnshire IL 60069-3433

GOLDING, ALAN CHARLES, English educator; b. London, Oct. 4, 1952; came to U.S., 1974; s. Charles and Dorothy Margaret (Marshall) G.; m. Lisa Beth Shapiro, May 19, 1984; 1 child, Chase Joshua Louis. BA, U. Exeter, Eng., 1974; MA with honors, U. Chgo., 1975, PhD with honors, 1980. Lectr. Dept. English, Kishwaukee Coll., Malta, Ill., 1976; instr. Dept. English, Roosevelt U., Chgo., 1977-79; vis. lectr. writing programs UCLA, 1980-84; asst. prof. Dept. English, U. Miss., Oxford, 1984—. Contbr. numerous articles in field to profl. jours.; book reviewer Am. Poetry mag., Am. Lit. mag., South Cen. Rev., others. Whiting Found. fellow, 1979. Mem. MLA, N.E. Modern Lang. Assn. (sec.), South Cen. Modern Lang. Assn. (poetry sect.), South Atlantic Modern Lang. Assn., D.H. Lawrence Soc. Avocations: soccer, squash, racquetball, camping, hiking. Office: U Miss Dept English University MS 38677

GOLDING, BRAGE, former university president; b. Chgo., Apr. 28, 1920; s. Leon M. and Viola B. (Brage) G.; m. Hinda F. Wolf, Dec. 21, 1941; children: Brage, Susan, Julie. BS, Purdue U., 1941, PhD, 1948; LLD, Wright State U., 1975. Assoc. dir. research Lilly Varnish Co., Indpls.; also research assoc. Purdue U., 1948-57; vis. prof. engring. Purdue U., dir. research Lilly Varnish Co., 1957-59; head Sch. Chem. Engring. Purdue U., 1959-66; v.p. Ohio State U. and; Miami U., 1966-67; pres. Wright State U., Dayton, Ohio, 1967-72, San Diego State U., 1972-77, Kent State U., 1977-82, Met. State Coll., Denver, 1984-85; acting pres. Western State Coll., Gunnison, Colo., 1985—; cons. Dept. Higher Edn., Pa. and N.J. Author: Polymers and Resins, 1959; Contbr. articles to profl. jours. Fellow AAAS; mem. Am. Chem. Soc., Phi Beta Kappa (hon.). Address: 12179 Branicole Ln San Diego CA 92129-5037

GOLDING, CAROLYN MAY, former government senior executive, consultant; b. Essex County, N.J., July 1, 1941; d. Wesley Irwin and Florence Grace (Smith) G.; m. Gary Anthony Derosa, Oct. 18, 1975 (div. Sept. 1982). BA, Duke U., 1963, postgrad., 1965-66. English tchr. Parkersburg (W.Va.) H.S., 1963; asst. to registrar Duke U., Durham, N.C., 1963-65; mgmt. intern Dept. Labor, Washington, 1966-67; various other positions Dept. Labor, 1967-72; dep. assoc. regional adminstr. Employment and Tng. Adminstrn., San Francisco, 1972-77; comptroller Employment and Tng. Adminstrn., Washington, 1977-78; regional adminstr. Employment and Tng. Adminstrn., San Francisco, 1979-82; dir. Unemployment Ins. Svc. Employment and Tng. Adminstrn., Washington, 1982-87, adminstr. employment security, 1987-88, dep. asst. sec. employment and tng., 1988-96; cons. on mgmt., labor force, long-range planning, workforce edn. issues and exec. coaching, 1996—. Recipient Disting. Career Svc. award Dept. Labor, 1979, Fed. Women's Career award Sec. Labor, 1983, Presdl. Meritorious rank, 1987, 95, Philip Arnow award Dept. Labor, 1988. Mem. Internat. Women's Forum of Washington, Coun. for Excellence in Govt. (prin.). Episcopalian.

GOLDING, MARTIN PHILIP, law and philosophy educator; b. N.Y.C., Mar. 30, 1930; s. Sidney Israel and Mildred (Lewis) G.; m. Naomi Holtzman, Apr. 8, 1951; children—Shulamith, Belinda, Joshua. B.A., UCLA, 1949, M.A., 1952; Ph.D., Columbia U., 1959. From asst. to assoc. prof. philosophy Columbia U., 1957-70, adj. prof., 1971-80; prof. philosophy John Jay Coll. Criminal Justice, City U. N.Y., 1970-76; prof. philosophy and law Duke U., Durham, N.C., 1976—; vis. prof. jurisprudence Faculty Law, Bar-Ilan U., Israel, 1971-72. Author: The Nature of Law, 1966, Philosophy of Law, 1975, Legal Reasoning, 1984, Jewish Law and Legal Theory, 1994, also articles. Mem. Am. Soc. Polit. and Legal Philosophy, Internat. Soc. Legal and Social Philosophy, Am. Philos. Assn. Jewish. Office: Duke U Philosophy Dept Durham NC 27708

GOLDING, SUSAN, mayor; b. Muskogee, Okla., Aug. 18, 1945; d. Brage and Hinda Fay (Wolf) G.; children: Samuel, Vanessa. Cert. Pratique de Langue Francaise, U. Paris, 1965; BA in Govt. and Internat. Rels., Carleton Coll., 1966; MA in Romance Philology, Columbia U., 1974. Asssoc. editor Columbia U. Jour. of Internat. Affairs, N.Y.C., 1968-69; teaching fellow Emory U., Atlanta, 1973-74; instr. San Diego Community Coll. Dist., 1978; assoc. pub., gen. mgr. The News Press Group, San Diego, 1978-80; city council mem. City of San Diego, 1981-83; dep. sec. bus., transp., housing State of Calif., Sacramento, 1983-84; county supr. dist. 3 County of San Diego, 1984-92; mayor City of San Diego, 1992—; chmn. San Diego Drug Strike Force, 1987-88, Calif. Housing Fin. Agy., Calif. Coastal Commn.; bd. dirs. San Diego County Water Authority; trustee So. Calif. Water Com., Inc.; founder Mid City Comml. Revitalization Task Force, Strategic Trade Alliance, 1993, Calif. Big 10 City Mayors, 1993; mem. Gov. Calif. Mil. Base Reuse Task Force, 1994; established San Diego World Trade Ctr., 1993, San Diego City/State/County Regional Permit Assistance Ctr., 1994; mem. adv. bd. U.S. Conf. of Mayors, 1994; chair Gov. Wilson's Commn. on Local Governance for 21st Century. Bd. dirs. Child Abuse Prevention Found., San Diego Conv. and Vis. Bur., Crime Victims Fund, United Cerebral Palsy, San Diego Air Quality Bd., San Diego March of Dimes, Rep. Assocs.; adv. bd. Girl Scouts U.S.; trustee So. Calif. Water Comm.; mem. Rep. State Cen. Com.; co-chair com. Presidency George Bush Media Fund, Calif.; chair San Diego County Regional Criminal Justice Coun., race rels. com. Citizens Adv. Com. on Racial Intergration, San Diego Unified Sch. Dist.; hon. chair Am. Cancer Soc's. Residential Crusade, 1988. Recipient Alice Paul award Nat. Women's Polit. Caucus, 1987, Calif. Women in Govt. Achievement award, 1988, Willie Velasquez Polit. award Mex. Am. Bus. and Profl. Assn., 1988, Catalyst of Chance award Greater San Diego C. of C., 1994, Woman Who Means Bus. award San Diego Bus. Jour., 1994, Internat. Citizen award World Affairs Coun., 1994; named One of San Diego's Ten Outstanding Young Citizens, 1981, One of Ten Outstanding Rep. County Ofcls. in U.S.A., Rep. Nat. Com., 1987, San Diego Woman of Achievement Soroptimists Internat., 1988. Mem. Nat. Assn. of Counties (chair Op. Fair Share, mem. taxation and fin. com.), Nat. Women's Forum. Jewish. Office: Office of the Mayor City Administration Bldg 11th Fl 202 C St San Diego CA 92101-4806*

GOLDINGER, SHIRLEY ANNE, elementary education educator. Spl. edn. tchr. La Esperanza Sch., San Juan, P.R. Name P.R. State Spl. Edn. Tchr. of Yr., 1993.

GOLDMAN, AARON, foundation executive, writer; b. Washington, June 8, 1913; s. Hymen and Sadie (Cohen) G.; m. Cecile A. Saloman, Nov. 26, 1939 (dec.); children: Phyllis Goldman Margolius, Michael D.; m. Paula S. Kruglak, Oct. 2, 1994. BS, Georgetown U., 1934. With Macke Co., Washington, 1934, pres., chmn. bd., 1946-75, chmn. emeritus, 1975-80. Contbr. numerous articles to profl. jours. Gen. chmn. Greater Washington Cmty. Chest Campaign, 1954; pres. Jewish Cmty. Coun. Greater Washington, 1953-56; chmn. D.C. Coun. Human Rels., 1958-63, Nat. Jewish Cmty. Rels. Adv. Coun., 1964-67, Washington Ctr. for Met. Studies, 1973-75, Washington Ednl. TV Assn., 1980-83, Washington Inst. Jewish Leadership, 1992; hon. pres. Jewish Hist. Soc. Greater Washington, 1991—; mem. bd. regents Georgetown U.; mem. D.C. Cable Design Commn. Lt. comdr. USNR, 1942-45. Recipient Nat. Brotherhood award NCCJ, 1958, Meritorious Pub. Svc. award Govt. of D.C., 1963, Stephen S. Wise Medallion award Am. Jewish Congress, 1964, John Carroll award Georgetown U., 1968, Nat. Humanitarian award B'nai Brith, 1976, Interfaith Conf. Met. Washington award, 1998; Brandeis U. fellow. Mem. Nat. Automatic Merchandising Assn. (pres. 1951-53, bd. dirs.), Am. Vets. Com., Am. Jewish Congress, Woodmont Country Club, Phi Beta Kappa. Home: 2801 New Mexico Ave NW Washington DC 20007-3921 *This is an old Jesuit motto, I wish I could claim it: A great deal of good can be done in the world if one is not too careful who gets the credit.*

GOLDMAN, ALAN IRA, investment banking executive; b. N.Y.C., July 29, 1937; s. Julius and Florence (Blum) G.; m. Joanne T. Marren. AB, Cornell U., 1958; MBA, NYU, 1962; grad., Stonier Grad. Sch. Banking, 1967. Methods analyst, personnel-researcher Fed. Res. Bank of N.Y., N.Y.C., 1958-62; platform asst. Bankers Trust Co., N.Y.C., 1962-63; asst. mgr. Bankers Trust Co., 1963-64, mgr., 1964-65, asst. treas., 1965-66, asst. v.p., 1967-69; assoc. investment banking dept. Lehman Bros., N.Y.C., 1969-70; v.p. fin., chief fin. officer, treas. Interway Corp., N.Y.C., 1970-74; mgmt. cons. Montclair, N.J., 1974-75; v.p. fin. Mgmt. Assistance Inc., N.Y.C., 1975-80; sr. v.p. fin. Mgmt. Assistance Inc., 1980-85; ind. investment banker, bus. cons., 1985—; pres. Goldmark Capital, 1987-88; lectr., adv., examiner Stonier Grad. Sch. Banking, 1968-71; lectr. Am. Inst. Banking, 1968-69; vice chair adv. bd. Columbia U. Sch. Pub. Health. Co-chmn. Montclair chpt. campaign ARC, 1970-73; chmn. Cornell Funds' N.Y. Area Phonathons, 1972-74, UN Week, Montclair, 1973; trustee, treas. Cocteau Repertory Theatre; bd. dirs. Planned Parenthood Fedn. Am., 1986-88, Planned Parenthood Met. N.J., Montclair ARC, vice-chair; adv. coun., vice chair Columbia U. Sch. of Pub. Health; dir. Productivity Technologies Corp. Mem. West Point Soc. N.Y., Orange Lawn Tennis Club, Nutley Tennis Club, Univ. Club (N.Y.C.), Phi Beta Kappa, Phi Kappa Phi, Zeta Beta Tau.

GOLDMAN, ALAN JOSEPH, mathematician; b. N.Y.C., Mar. 2, 1932; married; 1 child. BA, Bklyn. Coll., 1952; MA, Princeton U., 1954, PhD in Math., 1956. Instr. Princeton U., 1955-56; mathematician Nat. Bur. Standards, 1956-61, chief ops. rschr., 1961-79, dep. chief. Applied Math Divsn., 1968-78; prof. math. sci. Johns Hopkins U., 1979—; lectr. Am. U., 1956-57, Cath. U., 1957-63; mathematician Nat. Inst. Stanards and Tech., 1979—. Mem. Nat. Acad. England, Math Assn. Am., Inst. Ops. Rsch. and Mgmt. Sci., Sigma Xi. Office: Johns Hopkins U Dept Math Sci 104 Whitehead Hall Baltimore MD 21218*

GOLDMAN, ALFRED EMANUEL, marketing research consultant; b. Bklyn., Dec. 19, 1925; s. Samuel and Julia (Schwartz) G.; m. Adele Lieb, Mar. 30, 1952; children: Julia Madelaine, Marshall Scott. BS, CCNY, 1949, MA, cert. in clin. sch. psychology, 1950; PhD in Clin. Psychology, Clark U., 1955. Research clin. psychologist Boston State Hosp., 1953-54; asst. prof. Northeastern U., Boston, 1954-55; research assoc. Sch. Public Health, Harvard U., 1955-56; asst. dir. psychol. services Norristown (Pa.) State Hosp., 1956-60; dir. rsch. devel. Nat. Analysts Inc., 1960-64, exec. v.p., dir. rsch., 1964-70; pres. Nat. Analysts div. Booz Allen and Hamilton Inc., 1970-82, sr. v.p., 1982-91; pvt. practice mktg. rsch. cons. Bryn Mawr, Pa., 1991—; founding chmn. Coun. Am. Survey Rsch. Organs, 1975-77. Author: The Group Depth Interview: Principles and Practice, 1986; contbr. articles in field to various publs. Served with USAAF, 1944-46. Fellow Am. Psychol. Assn.; mem. Phi Beta Kappa.

GOLDMAN, ALLAN BAILEY, lawyer; b. Auburn, N.Y., Jan. 1, 1937; s. Charles and Rose Hortense (Abrahams) G.; m. Eleanor Ruth Levy, May 26, 1963; children; Jennifer Brooke Horwitz, Andrea Allison Gellert. AB magna cum laude, Harvard U., 1958, JD, 1963; LHD (hon.), Hebrew Union Coll.-Jewish Inst. Religion, 1992. Bar: Calif. 1964, D.C. 1977, U.S. Supreme Ct. 1977. Assoc. Wyman, Bautzer, Kuchel & Silbert, Beverly Hills, Calif., 1963-67; ptnr. Wyman, Bautzer, Kuchel & Silbert, L.A., 1967-91, Katten Muchin & Zavis, L.A., 1991—; judge pro-tem Calif. Mcpl. and Small Claims Cts.; arbitrator Calif. Superior Ct. Contbr. articles to profl. jours. Chmn. Attys. for Brown for Gov., officer Brown for Pres., 1976; founder L.A. Com. for Civil Rights Under Law, Mus. Contemporary Art., L.A., Fraternity of Friends of L.A. Music Ctr.; trustee Calif. Mus. Sci. and Industry, 1981-89, St. John's Hosp. and Health Ctr. Found., 1978—, exec. com., 1979-89, bd. dirs., 1989-95, treas., 1990-94, chmn., 1994-95; chmn. nat. bd. trustees Union of Am. Hebrew Congregations, 1987-91; bd. govs. Hebrew Union Coll.-Jewish Inst. Religion, 1988—, bd. overseers L.A. campus, 1981-85, 88—; trustee SKirball Cultural Ctr., 1997—; pres. Leo Baeck Temple, L.A., 1975-77, Coun. of Synagogue Assn. of Greater L.A., 1983—; mem. Conf. Pres.'s Major Jewish Orgns., 1987-91; mem. synagogue funding com. Jewish Fedn. Coun. of Greater L.A., 1979, chmn., 1985-88. Lt. USNR, 1958-60. Mem. ABA, Calif. Bar Assn., D.C. Bar Assn., Regency Club. Democrat. Jewish. Avocations: trekking, running, tennis. Home: 347 Conway Ave Los Angeles CA 90024-2603 Office: Katten Muchin & Zavis Ste 1400 1999 Avenue Of The Stars Los Angeles CA 90067-6115

GOLDMAN, ALLEN MARSHALL, physics educator; b. N.Y.C., Oct. 18, 1937; s. Louis and Mildred (Kohn) G.; m. Katherine Virginia Darnell, July 31, 1960; children—Matthew, Rachel, Benjamin. AB, Harvard U., 1958; PhD, Stanford U., 1965. Rsch. asst. Stanford U., Calif., 1960-65, rsch. assoc., 1965; asst. prof. physics U. Minn., Mpls., 1965-67, assoc. prof., 1967-73, prof., 1974—, inst. tech. prof., 1992—, dir. Ctr. for Sci. and Application of Superconductivity, 1989—, head Sch. of Physics and Astronomy, 1996—; co-chmn. Gordon Conf. on Quantum Liquids and Solids, 1981; dir. NATO Advanced Study Inst., 1983; mem. materials rsch. adv. com. NSF, 1985-88; mem. vis. com. Francis Butter Nat. Magnet Lab., 1986-89, chmn., 1987-89; mem. vis. com. Nat. Nanofabrication Facility at Cornell, 1988-90, mem. user com., 1997—; mem. vis. com. U. Chgo. Materials Program of Argonne Nat. Lab., 1992-98, chmn. 1995; mem. Buckley prize com., 1994-95, London prize com., 1994-98; mem. Helium Res. com. NAS/NRC, 1998-99. Mem. publs. oversight com. Am. Phys. Soc., 1996-99, chair 1997; mem. pub. policy com. Am. Inst. Physics, 1999—, assoc. editor Revs. of Modern Physics, 1999—; contbr. articles to profl. jours. Com. of vis. divsn. materials rsch. NSF, 1999. Alfred P. Sloan Found. fellow, 1966-70. Fellow AAAS, Am. Phys. Soc. (divisional councilor divsn. condensed matter physics 1994-96). Jewish. Home: 1015 James Ct Mendota Hts MN 55118-3640 Office: U Minn Sch Physics and Astronomy 116 Church St SE Minneapolis MN 55455-0149

GOLDMAN, ALVIN LEE, lawyer, educator; b. N.Y.C., Feb. 27, 1938; s. Joseph I. and Emma (Berger) G.; m. Elisabeth C. Paris, Nov. 23, 1956; children—Paula, Douglas. A.B., Columbia U., 1959; LL.B., NYU, 1962. Bar: Ky. 1969. Assoc. Parker, Chapin & Flattau, N.Y.C., 1962-65; mem. faculty U. Ky., Lexington, 1965—, prof. law, 1972—; prof. in residence NLRB Zagoria staff, 1967-68; vis. scholar Inst. for Labor Law, U. Lueven, 1973; vis. prof. U. Calif., Davis, 1976-77. Author: Processes for Conflict Resolution, 1972, The Supreme Court and Labor-Management Relations Law, 1975, Labor Law and Industrial Relations in the USA, 2d edit., 1983, (with R. Covington) Legislation Protecting the Individual Employee, 1982, (with M. Finkin, C. Summers) Legal Protection for the Individual Employee, 1989, 2d edit., 1995, Settling for More: Mastering Negotiating Strategies and Techniques, 1991, Labor and Employment Law in the United States, 1996. Bd. dirs. Central Ky. Jewish Assn., 1978-80, 81-84. Mem. Ky. Bar Assn., Soc. Am. Law Tchrs., Nat. Acad. Arbitrators (bd. govs. 1994-97), Labor Law Group Trust (chmn. 1988-94), Indsl. Rels. Rsch. Assn., Internat. Soc. Labor Law (exec. bd. U.S. br. 1982-85, 88—, vice-chair 1995—), Internat. Indsl. Rels. Assn. Democrat. Home: 2063 Bridgeport Dr Lexington KY 40502-2615 Office: U Ky Coll of Law Lexington KY 40506

GOLDMAN, ARNOLD IRA, biophysicist, statistical analyst; b. Chgo., Mar. 13, 1945; s. Morton Irving and Rita Mae (Satten) G.; m. Sandra Gail Lipman, Aug. 8, 1971; children: Jennifer Lauren, Lesley Anne. MS in Radiol. Health, U. Pitts., 1968; PhD in Biophysics, Med. Coll. Va., 1974. Postdoctoral fellow Jules Stein Eye Inst., UCLA, 1974-75; staff fellow Nat. Eye Inst., NIH, Bethesda, Md., 1975-79; asst. prof. Med. Coll. Wis., Milw., 1979-82; rsch. v.p. otorhinolaryngol. and ophthal. divsn., dir. MIS Biomatrix, Inc., Ridgefield, N.J., 1983—; ind. statis. cons., Milw., 1980-83. Contbr. to profl. publs. including Science. Lt. (j.g.) USPHS, 1968-70. Mem. Assn. Rsch. in Vision and Ophthalmology. Home: 15 Stockbridge Ave Suffern NY 10901-7222 Office: Biomatrix Inc 65 Railroad Ave Ste 2 Ridgefield NJ 07657-2176

GOLDMAN, BARBARA DEREN, film and theatrical producer; b. Bridgeport, Conn., Dec. 22, 1949; m. James Goldman, Oct. 25, 1975. Pres. Barbara Deren Assocs., N.Y.C., 1975—, Raoulfilm Inc., N.Y.C., 1979—; co-pres. Magellan Entertainment, 1994—; v.p. Trans-Internat. Revisions, 1980—. Co-author: Where to Eat in America, 1987; contbr. to book Feast of Wine and Food, 1987; producer Tolstoy, London, 1996.

GOLDMAN, BENJAMIN EDWARD, lawyer; b. N.Y.C., Feb. 25, 1940; s. William Wolfe and Blanche (Kallenburg) G.; m. Lynda Ann Schwartz, July 27, 1950; children: Brian Edward, Victoria Beth, Adam Edward. BS, NYU, 1965; JD, Fordham U., 1968; LLM, Georgetown U., 1970. Bar: N.Y. 1968, D.C. 1972, U.S. Dist. Ct. D.C., U.S. Ct. Appeals (D.C., 4th, 5th and 9th cirs.), Calif. 1986, U.S. Dist. Ct. (cen. dist.) Calif. 1986. Atty., advisor to chmn. NLRB, Washington, 1968-72; assoc. Arent, Fox, Kitner, Plotkin, Kahn, Washington, 1972-75; ptnr. Feldman, Krieger, Goldman, Tisch, Washington, 1976-83, Memel, Jacobs, Pierno, Gersh & Ellsworth, L.A., 1984-87, Graham and James, L.A., 1987—; mem. com. on devel. law under NLRB Act, 1968—; speaker Healthcare Fin. Mgmt. Assn., Calif., 1987, Nat. Health Edn. Conf. on AIDS, 1987, Inst. Corp. Counsel, 1986, Hosp. Coun. N. Calif., 1985, others. Contbr. articles to profl. jours. Mem. ABA (forum com. on health law 1983, mem. labor and employment law sect. 1968—), Nat. Health Lawyers Assn. (speaker ann. healthlaw update 1985), Calif. Bar Assn., N.Y. Bar Assn., D.C. Bar Assn., Am. Acad. Hosp. Attys. Office: Graham & James LLP 801 S Figueroa St Fl 14 Los Angeles CA 90017-2573

GOLDMAN, BERT ARTHUR, psychologist, educator; b. N.Y.C., Apr. 4, 1929; children: Lisa, Linda. B.A., U. Md., 1951; M.Ed., U. N.C., 1956; Ed.D., U. Va., 1960. Mem. faculty U. N.C., Greensboro, 1965—, prof. ednl. psychology, 1971-85, dean acad. advising, 1970-85, prof. higher ednl. adminstrn., 1985—, acting chair dept. ednl. adminstrn., higher edn. and ednl. rsch., 1987-88, dept. coord., 1991-92. Served with U.S. Army, 1951-53. Mem. APA, Am. Coun. Measurement Edn., N.C. Assn. for Rsch. in Edn., Am. Ednl. Rsch. Assn. Office: U NC at Greensboro Dept Ednl Leadership PO Box 26171 Greensboro NC 27402-6171

GOLDMAN, BRIAN ARTHUR, lawyer, accountant; b. Balt., June 30, 1946; s. Marvin L. and Edythe R. Goldman; m. Eileen G. Safro, Aug. 22, 1970; children—Jonathan S., Evan M. B.S. in Real Estate Planning, Am. U., 1968; J.D., U. Md., 1971. Bar: Md. 1972, U.S. Dist. Ct. Md. 1972, U.S. Tax Ct. 1977, U.S. Supreme Ct. 1977, Acct., Balt., 1974—; mem. Burke, Gerber & Wilen, 1972-77, Sapero & Sapero, 1977-78; pvt. practice, 1978-83; ptnr. firm Goldman and Fedder, P.A., Balt., 1983-85, Fedder & Garten, P.A., 1986-88, Goldman & Vetter, P.A., 1989—; asst. prof. income taxation U. Balt., 1974-75. Mem. ABA, Md. Bar Assn., Balt. City Bar Assn., Md. Assn. CPAs, Ctr. Club, Suburban (Balt.) Club, Woodholme. Office: Goldman & Vetter PA 36 S Charles St Ste 2401 Baltimore MD 21201-3108

GOLDMAN, CHARLES, electromechanical engineer; b. N.Y.C., Sept. 19, 1968; s. Ira and Marilyn Goldman. BSME, Rutgers U., 1995; BSEE, Ariz. State U., 1999. Chem. coater Nat. Starch Corp., Bridgewater, N.J., 1992-93, engring. asst., 1994; engring. asst. Rsch. Devel. and Engring. Ctr., Dover, N.J., 1995. Tutor math and physics CCM Ambs., 1992-93, video mgr., 1992-93. Rsch. Coun. N.J. engring. scholar, 1993, Coll. Morris scholar, 1992. Mem. NSPE, ASME, AIAA, The Planetary Soc., Am. Phys. Soc., Phi Theta Kappa, Tau Alpha Pi. Avocations: travel, space science, astrophysics. Home: PO Box 64371 Phoenix AZ 85082-4371

GOLDMAN, CHARLES NORTON, retired corporate lawyer; b. N.Y.C., Feb. 15, 1932; s. Morris and Mary Celia (Tames) G.; m. Jane Barbara Webbink, July 21, 1968; children: Alexander Daniel, Jeffrey David. AB with honors, Columbia U., 1953, LLB, 1955. Bar: N.Y. 1956. Practiced in N.Y.C., 1955-60; atty.-advisor AID, Washington, 1960-62; regional legal advisor for India, Nepal and Ceylon AID mission to India, New Delhi, 1962-64; asst. gen. counsel for Latin Am. AID, 1965-68, dep. gen. counsel, 1968-69; staff counsel for Latin Am. ITT, N.Y.C., 1969-72; sr. counsel, asst. to gen. counsel ITT, 1972-74, sr. counsel for Latin Am., 1974-75; v.p., gen. counsel ITT Europe Inc., Brussels, 1975-81; v.p. ITT, 1976-95, assoc. gen. counsel, 1981-95; mem. Overseas Devel. Coun., 1988-95, Bretton Woods Com., 1992-95. Bd. dirs. Alliance of Resident Theatres, N.Y.C., 1996—, Shakespeare Globe Ctr. Inc., 1996—. Mem. Coun. on Fgn. Rels., Mid-Atlantic Club N.Y. Inc. (pres. 1996—), Univ. Club. Phi Beta Kappa.

GOLDMAN, DONALD HOWARD, lawyer; b. N.Y.C., July 18, 1942; s. Leon and Jean (Burke) G.; m. Madeleine Blane, July 23, 1967; children: Diane, David. B.B.A., CCNY, 1964; J.D., Bklyn. Law Sch., 1967. Bar: N.Y. 1968, Fla. 1977. Pvt. practice, N.Y.C., 1974—; assoc. prof. real estate Pace U., Hofstra U. Mem. N.Y. State Bar Assn., Nassau County Bar Assn., Bklyn. Law Sch. Alumni Assn., City Coll. Alumni Assn. Home: 331 W Broadway Long Beach NY 11561-3936 Office: 382 S Oyster Bay Rd Hicksville NY 11801-3529 *In order to succeed one must be prepared to risk.*

GOLDMAN, ED, broadcast executive; b. July 7. Degree in econ., George Washington U. V.p., gen. mgr. Sta. WBZ-TV, Boston, 1997—. Office: Sta WBZ-TV 1170 Soldiers Field Rd Boston MA 02134-1004*

GOLDMAN, EDWARD MERRILL, musician; b. July 2, 1917. Diploma, Longy Sch. Music, Cambridge, Mass., 1943; cert., Juilliard Sch. Music, N.Y.C., 1952, U. Grenoble, France, 1945. Tchr. piano Goldman Sch. Music and Art, Bayonne, N.J., 1945-79; condr. Bayonne Little Symphony, 1958-65; metal sculptor Bayonne, 1970-85; poet Poets & Writers, N.Y.C., 1986—;

composer of religious works for voice, orch., Sabbath svcs. Avocation: sea shell painting. Home: 43 W 32nd St Bayonne NJ 07002

GOLDMAN, ERIC SCOT, lawyer; b. Quincy, Mass., Mar. 5, 1957; s. Terry and Harriet (Goldstein) G.; m. Lora Anderson, June 18, 1983; children: William, Daniel, Leigh. BA, Boston Coll., 1979; MSc in Criminal Justice, Northeastern U., 1980; JD, Suffolk U., 1987. Bar: Mass. 1987, U.S. Dist. Ct. Mass. 1987, U.S. Mil. Ct. Appeals. Adminstr. McLean Hosp., Belmont, Mass.; caseworker Norfolk County Dist. Atty.'s Office, Dedham, Mass.; atty. McDermott & Padis, Milton, Mass., 1983-93; assoc. Lynch & Lynch, South Easton, Mass., 1993-98, Lang & Morgera, Boston, 1998—; mediator Norfolk-Plymouth County; bd. dirs. Criminal Justice Scis. Inst., Washington. Recipient Cert. of Recognition, Norfolk County Dist. Atty., Commonwealth of Mass. Dist. Ct. Mem. Mass Acad. Trial Attys., Norfolk, Plymouth and Bristol County Bar Assn., Braintree Rifle and Pistol Club (pres. 1988—). Avocations: scuba diving, karate, music, firearms training. Home: 36 Forge Way Duxbury MA 02332-4743 Office: Finnera Byrne & Dreschler 50 Redfield St Boston MA 02122

GOLDMAN, ETHAN HARRIS, retail executive; b. Boston, Jan. 2, 1956; s. Marshall Irwin and Merle Dorothy (Rosenblatt) G.; m. Julie Ellen Hurwitz, Sept. 11, 1982; children: Jessica, Todd, David, Lauren. BA, U. Pa., 1978, BS in Econs., 1978; MBA, Harvard Coll., 1982. CPA, Md. Pub. acct. Touche Ross, Balt., 1979-80, Coopers and Lybrand, Boston, 1982-84; mgr. fin. planning Hit or Miss Stores subs. Zayre Corp., Stoughton, Mass., 1984-86; asst. v.p. ops. planning/new bus. ventures Zayre Stores subs. Zayre Corp., Framingham, Mass., 1986-88, asst. v.p. mdse. logistics, 1988-89; housewares buyer Ames Stores, Rocky Hill, Conn., 1989-90, dir. mdse. planning and adminstrn., 1990-91, dir. pull replenishment, 1991-93, divisional mdse. mgr., 1993-95; dir. fin. analysis ADVO, Inc., Windsor, Conn., 1995—, dir. strategic bus. devel., 1999—. Coach West Hartford Youth Soccer. 2d lt. U.S. Army, 1978-79, maj. Res., 1979—. Mem. No. Conn. Harvard Bus. Sch. Club (bd. dirs.-at-large 1992—). Jewish. Avocations: distance running, soccer, stamp collecting, tennis, history. Home: 9 Vardon Rd West Hartford CT 06117-2848 Office: ADVO Inc PO Box 755 One Univac Ln Windsor CT 06095-0755

GOLDMAN, GARY CRAIG, lawyer; b. Phila., Dec. 28, 1951; s. Ronald Walter and Connie Sylvia (Stein) G.; m. Diane Rose Lane, Oct. 1, 1977; children: Justin Edward, Gregory David. BA magna cum laude, Temple U., 1973; JD, Villanova U., 1976. Bar: Pa. 1976, U.S. Dist. Ct. (ea. dist.) Pa. 1981. Jud. law clk. Common Pleas Ct., Northampton County, Pa., 1976-77; asst. atty. gen. office of legal counsel Pa. Dept. Pub. Welfare, Phila., 1977-81, asst. counsel, 1981-84; staff counsel CDI Corp., Phila., 1984-86, v.p., assoc. gen. counsel, 1986—; mem. faculty, planning chmn. Nationwide Comml. Real Estate Leasing Programs. Author: Drafting a Fair Office Lease, 1989, 2d edit., 1999; contbg. author: The Commercial Real Estate Tenant's Handbook, 1987, The Practical Real Estate Lawyer's Manual, 1987, Commercial Tenants' Leasing Transactions Guide, 1991, Office Planning and Design Desk Reference, 1992, Negotiating and Drafting Office Leases; assoc. editor: Villanova Law Rev., 1974-76; contbr. articles to legal jours. Mem. Am. Corp. Counsel Assn., ABA, Phila. Bar Assn. Republican. Jewish. Avocations: golf, coaching little league. Home: 210 Fox Hollow Dr Langhorne PA 19053-2477 Office: CDI Corp 1717 Arch St Fl 35 Philadelphia PA 19103-2713

GOLDMAN, GERALD HILLIS, beverage distribution company executive; b. Omaha, July 26, 1947; s. Lester Jack and Lilyan Haykin (Weiskopf) G.; m. Cathy Evelyn Brightman, Dec. 15, 1973; children: Lori, Jeffrey. BSBA, U. Nebr., 1969; MBA, U. So. Calif., 1975. C.P.A., Calif., Nebr. Sr. acct. Arthur Andersen & Co., Los Angeles, 1969-72; exec. v.p., CFO CORE-MARK Internat., Inc., Richmond, B.C., Can., 1972-86, exec. v.p., 1986-87; pres. Gen. Acceptance Corp., Los Angeles, 1986-87; CFO, sr. v.p. Alaska Distbrs., Inc., Seattle, 1987—. Mem. AICPA, Calif. Soc. CPAs, Fin. Execs. Inst.

GOLDMAN, IRA STEVEN, gastroenterologist; b. Bronx, N.Y., May 19, 1951; s. George David and Belle (Hans) G.; m. Niki Ellen Kantrowitz, Jan. 20, 1980; children: Zachary, Joshua. BA, U. Rochester, 1973; student, Oxford U., 1972; MD, Columbia U., 1977. Diplomate Am. Bd. Internal Medicine, Am. Bd. Gastroenterology. Intern Columbia Presbyn. Med. Ctr., N.Y.C., 1977-78, resident in internal medicine, 1978-80; fellow in gastroenterology and liver diseases U. Calif. Sch. Medicine, San Francisco, 1980-83; instr. in anatomy Columbia U., N.Y.C., 1978; asst. prof. medicine U. Calif., San Francisco, 1983-85, Cornell U. Med. Coll., N.Y.C., 1985-91; assoc. prof. clin. medicine Cornell U. Med. Coll., 1991-96; attending physician North Shore Univ. Hosp., Manhasset, N.Y., 1985—; assoc. prof. clin. medicine NYU Sch. Medicine, 1996—; physicians adv. bd. Am. Liver Found., Greater N.Y. chpt., 1985—; mem. sci. adv. commn. L.I. chpt. Nat. Found. for Ileitis and Colitis, 1985-91; vice chair clin. practice sec. Am. Gastroent. Assn., 1995-97, chair, 1997—. Reviewer jours. Gastroenterology; contbr. articles, book chapts. to profl. jours. Rsch. fellow Am. Liver Found., 1982, Clin. Investigator award NIH, 1983. Fellow ACP, Am. Coll. Gastroenterology; mem. Am Fedn. for Clin. Rsch., Am. Assn. for Study of Liver Diseases, Med. Soc. State of N.Y., Nassau County Med. Soc., Nassau County. Acad. Medicine, N.Y. Soc. for Gastrointestinal Endoscopy (pres. 1996-97), Alpha Omega Alpha. Avocations: sailing, tennis. Office: 310 E Shore Rd Great Neck NY 11023-2432

GOLDMAN, JAMES, playwright, screenwriter, novelist; b. Chgo., June 30, 1927; s. M. Clarence and Marion (Weil) G.; married, 1962 (div. 1972); m. Barbara Deren, Oct. 25, 1975. PhB, U. Chgo., 1947, MA, 1950; postgrad., Columbia U., 1950-52. Writer screenplays, drama, novels, N.Y.C., 1954—; author: (plays) (with William Goldman) Blood, Sweat and Stanley Poole, 1961, (with William Goldman and John Kander) Family Affair (musical), 1962; They Might Be Giants, 1961; (play) The Lion in Winter, 1966, also screenplay (Am. Screenwriters award, Acad. award, Brit. Screenwriters award), Tolstoy, London, 1996; (novels) Waldorf, 1965, The Man from Greek and Roman, 1974, Myself as Witness, 1980, Fulton County, 1989; (screenplays) They Might Be Giants, 1970, Nicholas and Alexandra, 1971, Robin and Marian, 1976; co-writer: (film) White Nights, 1985, (musical) Evening Primrose, 1967; adaptation Oliver Twist, CBS-TV, 1982; writer: (TV movie) Anna Karenina, 1985; (TV miniseries) Anastasia: The Mystery of Anna Anderson, 1986 (WGA nomination); (musical) Follies, 1971 (Drama Critics award for best musical); author: Musical Follies, London, New Book, 1987 (Drama Mag. award, Evening Standard award, Olivier award, Plays and Players award best musical); contbr. articles to various mags. Served with U.S. Army, 1952-54. Mem. Dramatists Guild (council 1966—), Authors League Am. (council 1966—), Acad. Motion Picture Arts and Scis., PEN, Nat. Acad. Rec. Artists, French Acad. Playwrights. Address: care Barbara Deren Assocs Inc 965 5th Ave New York NY 10021-1709

GOLDMAN, JAY, industrial engineer, educator, former dean; b. Norfolk, Va., Apr. 15, 1930; s. Louis H. and Rose O. (Oser) G.; m. Renitta Librach, Dec. 20, 1959. BSME, Duke U., 1950; MSME, Mich. State U., 1951; DSc in Indsl. Engring., Washington U., St. Louis, 1955. Registered profl. engr., Mo. Lectr. indsl. engring. Washington U., 1952-56, asst. prof., 1956-64, acting chmn. human and orgn. factors, 1963-64; dir. dept. indsl. engring. Jewish Hosp., St. Louis, 1960-64; research assoc. dept. hosp. adminstr. U. N.C., Chapel Hill, 1964-68; prof., grad. adminstr. dept. indsl. engring. N.C. State U., Raleigh, 1964-68; prof., chmn. dept. indsl. engring. U. Mo., Columbia, 1968-84, prof. bioengring., 1969-75, prof. bioengring. and advanced automation, 1975-84; dean, prof. U. Ala., Birmingham, 1984—; cons. to fed., state agys., pvt. industry. Contbr. to textbooks, profl. jours.; producer 6 tech. motion pictures; patentee in field. V.p. Boone County Cmty. Svcs. Coun., 1973-76; v.p., exec. com., treas. Cmty. Rels. Coun.; bd. dirs. Birmingham Jewish Fedn.; vice-chmn., bd. dirs. Sloss Furnaces Nat. Hist. Landmark, bd. dirs., treas. Jewish Family Svcs. Recipient Editl. award Hosp. Mgmt. mag., 1969, U. Mo. Faculty Alumni award, 1981; named Ala. Engr. of Yr., Outstanding Engr. Educator in State, ASPE. Fellow Inst. Indsl. Engrs. (trustee, exec. v.p., regional v.p., chpt. pres., v.p. edn. and profl. devel., editl. bd. Trans., Health Svcs. Devel. award 1981), Accreditation Bd. Engring. and Tech. (dir., treas.); mem. NSPE, Soc. Health Sys. (bd. dirs., pres.), Nat. Coun. Indsl. Engrs. Acad. Dept. Heads (chmn.), Ala. Soc. Profl. Engrs., Am. Soc. Engring. Edn., Sigma Xi, Alpha Pi Mu, Tau Beta Pi, Phi Kappa Phi, Omicron Delta Kappa. Home: 4631 Pine Mountain Rd Birmingham AL 35213-1834 Office: U Ala-Birmingham Sch Engring 1075 13th St S Ste 310 Birmingham AL 35205-3408

GOLDMAN, JERRY STEPHEN, lawyer; b. Bklyn., Sept. 7, 1951; s. Bernard I. and Charlotte (Emerling) G.; children by previous marriage: Rachel Dawn, Samantha. BA with honors, NYU 1973; JD, Boston U., 1976; LLM in Taxation, Temple U., 1983. Bar: Mass. 1977, N.Y. 1977, U.S. Dist. Ct. (ea. and so. dists.) N.Y. 1980, U.S. Dsit. Ct. (Mass.) 1997, U.S. Supreme Ct. 1981, Pa. 1982, U.S. Tax Ct. 1983, U.S. Ct. Appeals (3d cir.) 1983, U.S. Dist. Ct. (ea. dist.) Pa. 1983, U.S. Ct. Appeals (2d cir.) 1996, U.S. Ct. Appeals (1st cir.) 1997, U.S. Dist. Ct. Mass. 1997. Sr. asst. dist. atty. Kings County Dist. Atty.'s Office, Bklyn., 1976-82; pvt. practice, N.Y.C. and Phila., 1982—; dir., pres. Huntingdon Brook Community Assn., Bucks Co, Pa., 1985-89. Mem. bd., counsel Citizen's Crime Commn., Phila., 1983-95; atty. Phila. Vol. Lawyers for the Arts, 1983—; chmn. Upper Southampton Planning Commn., 1984-90. Mem. ABA, N.Y. State Bar Assn., Mass. Bar Assn., Pa. Bar Assn., Phila. Bar Assn. Jewish. Avocations: cross-country skiing, music. Office: 1520 Locust St Philadelphia PA 19102-4403 also: 111 Bronty 13th Fl New York NY 10006

GOLDMAN, JOEL J., retired lawyer; b. N.Y.C., Sept. 7, 1940; s. Myron and Pearl (Jacobs) G.; m. Jane I. Stalker, July 23, 1973; children: Elizabeth Ann, Rebecca Lynn. BS, U. Va., 1962, JD, Syracuse U., 1965. Bar: N.Y. 1966, U.S. Dist. Ct. (we. dist.) N.Y. 1966. Law clk. Myron Goldman, N.Y.C., 1965; staff atty., chief trial counsel Legal Aid Soc. Rochester, N.Y., 1966-73; ptnr. Kaman, Berlove, Marafioti, Jacobstein & Goldman, Rochester, 1973-97; ret., 1997; lectr. family law; spl. investigator N.Y. State Spl. Commn. on Attica, 1972; mem. panel arbitrators Am. Arbitration Assn.; mem. faculty Nat. Bus. Inst., 1985-97. Referee, Ea. Assn. Inter-Collegiate Football Ofcls., 1974-95, v.p. Empire chpt., 1988, pres. 1989, Observer, Ea. Coll. Athletic Conf., 1996—, Inductee Jewish Athletes Sports Hall of Fame, 1996. Fellow Am. Acad. Matrimonial Lawyers (ret.); mem. ABA, N.Y. State Bar Assn. (exec. com. family law sect. 1982, mem. exec. com. 1981-97), Monroe County Bar Assn. (chmn. family law sect. 1982, exec. com. 1981-86), Assn. Trial Lawyers Am. Jewish. Author continuing edn. materials. Contbg. editor Bender's Forms for Civil Practice, 1986, Medina's Bostwick, 1986. Home: 67 Mountain Rd Rochester NY 14625-1816 also: 21 Bluebill Ave Apt 1005B Naples FL 34108-1765

GOLDMAN, JOHN ABNER, rheumatologist, immunologist, educator; b. Cin., June 9, 1940; s. Leon and Belle (Hurwitz) G.; children from previous marriage: Joey, Beth; m. Deborah J. Staples, Aug. 1, 1993; children: Shelley, Michael. BS, U. Wis., 1962; MD, U. Cin., 1966. Diplomate Am. Bd. Internal Medicine, subspecialty in rheumatology, allergy-immunology, advanced achievement in internal medicine, 1987. Intern, U. Oreg. Med. Sch., Portland, 1966-67; resident U. Cin. Med. Center, 1967-69, postdoctoral fellow in rheumatology and immunology, 1969-71 clin. prof. medicine Emory U. Sch. Medicine, Atlanta, 1973—. Contbr. numerous articles to sci. jours. Bd. dirs. Atlanta Arthritis Found.; med. adv. com. Lupus Erythematosus Found, Inc. Maj. U.S. Army, 1971-73. Fellow ACP, Am. Soc. Lasers in Medicine and Surgery (bd. dirs.), Am. Coll. Rheumatology (chair CORC SE network); mem. Ga. Soc. Rheumatology (pres. 1974-75), Med. Assn. Atlanta, Med. Assn. Ga. (council of splty. socs.), Met. Atlanta Rheumatology Soc. (pres.), Am. Soc. Clin. Densitometry (cert.). Office: Med Quarters Ste 293 5555 Peachtree Dunwoody Rd NE Atlanta GA 30342-1711

GOLDMAN, JOSEPH ELIAS, advertising executive; b. N.Y.C., Nov. 26, 1923; s. A. Milton and Caroline (Elias) G.; m. Barbara Van Gelderen, Mar. 22, 1947; children: Carlee Georgette Goldman Paddock, Richard Jonathan. Student, Pratt Inst. Sch. Fine Art, 1941-42, 47-48. Gen. artist, designer Maxon, Inc., N.Y.C., 1948-50; officer, creative dir. Gamut, Inc., Garden City, N.Y., 1952-64; pres., chmn. bd. Adways, Inc., Jericho, N.Y., 1965-74; pres. Goldman Van Gelderen, Inc., Greenville, S.C., 1974-80; also bd. dirs.; pres. Gamut Agy., Inc., Hempstead, N.Y., 1975-77; v.p. Graphics Plus, Inc., Greenville, 1983-86; ret., 1986. Bd. dirs. Urban League L.I., 1976-77. With USMCR, 1942-46. Mem. League Advt. Agys. (pres. 1964-65), Art Dirs. Club L.I. (co-founder, pres. 1971-72, 72-73), Greenville Artists Guild (pres. 1986, bd. dirs. 1987), Blue Ridge Art Assn., Upstate Visual Artists, Nat. Caricaturists Network, Alpha Delta Sigma.

GOLDMAN, LARRY, public relations executive. Pres. Bender, Goldman & Helper/Show Case Entertainment, Beverly Hills. Office: Bender Goldman & Helper 11500 W Olympic Blvd Ste 655 Beverly Hills CA 90210*

GOLDMAN, LAWRENCE H., construction company executive. BA, U. Ill., 1982; MBA, DePaul U., 1986. Asst. project mgr. Babco Constrn. Co., 1983-84, project mgr., 1984-97, pres., 1997—. Office: 1723 Howard St Evanston IL 60202

GOLDMAN, LAWRENCE SAUL, lawyer; b. Phila., Mar. 25, 1942; s. Ephraim Lederer and Belle Joan (Finkelstein) G.; m. Kathi Sue Schleifer, June 20, 1965; children: Carolyn, Jonathan. BA, Brandeis U., 1963; JD, Harvard U., 1966. Bar: N.Y. 1966. Asst. dist. atty. New York County, N.Y.C., 1966-71; asst. gen. counsel N.Y. State Commn. To Investigate N.Y.C., 1971-72; ptnr. Goldman & Hafetz, N.Y.C., 1972—; cons. N.Y.C. Commn. on Police Corruption, 1972. Contbg. author: Criminal Trial Advocacy, 1980—. Trustee Congregation Rodeph Sholom, N.Y.C., 1983-92; bd. dirs. William F. Ryan Comty. Health Ctr., N.Y.C., 1986-88, Bronx Defenders, 1997—; mem. N.Y. State Commn. on Jud. Conduct, 1990—, mem. adv. com. on the criminal law, 1992—. Recipient Man of Yr. award Hogan Assocs., 1984. Mem. NACDL (chmn. ethics adv. com. 1988-92, white collar com. 1992-97, Robert C. Heeney award 1998, v.p. 1999—), N.Y. State Assn. Criminal Def. Lawyers (pres. 1987-89, Thurgood Marshall award 1999), N.Y. Criminal Bar Assn. (pres. 1982-85, Outstanding Practitioner award 1994), N.Y. State Bar Assn. (Outstanding Practitioner award criminal justice sect. 1996), Harvard Club. Democrat. Office: 500 Fifth Ave New York NY 10110-0002

GOLDMAN, LEO, psychologist, educator; b. Kingston, N.Y., June 13, 1920; s. Morris and Tillie (Kushner) G.; m. Elsie Kamber, June 25, 1950 (div. 1982); children—Deborah Maxine, Amy Beth. BS, CCNY, 1940; MA, Columbia U., 1947, PhD in Counseling Psychology, 1950. Diplomate Am. Bd. Profl. Psychology (trustee 1966-71, v.p. 1969-71). Psychometrist Stevens Inst. Tech., 1947-48; vocat. counselor VA, N.Y.C., 1948-49; from asst. prof. to assoc. prof. psychology and edn. U. Buffalo, 1950-58; assoc. prof. Bklyn. Coll., 1958-64; prof. CUNY Grad. Sch., 1964-82, assoc. Ctr. for Advanced Study in Edn., 1982—; cons. Lorge Sch., 1982-88; prof. Fordham U. Grad. Sch. Edn., 1982-91, adj. prof., 1993-94; adj. prof. Hunter Coll. CUNY, 1991-95; adj. prof. NYU, N.Y.C., 1996—; Fulbright lectr. U. Amsterdam, Netherlands, 1965-66; vis. prof. Syracuse U., U. Wis., U. Pa., Rutgers U., Columbia U., Hebrew U. of Jerusalem, Israel; mem. coms. Ednl. Testing Service, Coll. Entrance Examination Bd.; adv. editor John Wiley & Sons Inc., 1975-78. Author: Using Tests in Counseling, 1961, 2nd edit., 1971, Research Methods for Counselors, 1978; editor Jour. Counseling and Devel. (formerly Pers. and Guidance Jour.); mem. editorial bd. The Counseling Psychologist, Profl. Psychology; contbr. articles to profl. jours. Staff sgt. USAAF, 1942-46. Fellow APA (sec. divsn. 1966-69, coun. 1984-87, pres. divsn. counseling psychology 1989-90); mem. Assn. for Assessment in Counseling (pres. 1967-68), ACA (Rsch. award 1962, exec. coun. 1966-68), Nat. Career Devel. Assn. Home: 321 W 29th St Apt 6B New York NY 10001-4749 Office: CASE/CUNY 25 W 43rd St Rm 620 New York NY 10036-7406

GOLDMAN, LOUIS BUDWIG, lawyer; b. Chgo., Apr. 11, 1948; s. Jack Sydney and Lorraine (Budwig) G.; m. Barbara Marcia Berg, Oct. 2, 1983; children: Jacqueline Ilyse, Annie Dara, Michael Louis. BA magna cum laude, U. Calif., Berkeley, 1970; JD cum laude, U. Chgo., 1974. Bar: Calif. 1975, U.S. Dist. Ct. (no. dist.) Calif. 1975, U.S. Ct. Appeals (9th cir.) 1975, N.Y. 1976, U.S. Dist. Ct. (so. and ea. dists.) N.Y. 1976, U.S. Ct. Appeals (2nd cir.) 1976, Ill. 1991, Czech Republic, 1997. Law clk. U.S. Dist. Ct., San Francisco, 1974-75; assoc. Cleary, Gottlieb, Steen & Hamilton, N.Y.C. and Paris, 1975-81; assoc. Edwards & Angell, N.Y.C., 1981-83, ptnr., 1986-88; ptnr. Wald, Harkrader & Ross, N.Y.C., 1983-86, Altheimer & Gray, Chgo., 1989—; mng. dir. Abacus & Assocs. Inc., N.Y.C.; supervisory bd. Pudliszki S.A. Contbr. articles to profl. jours. Mem. Chgo.-Prague Sister Cities Com., Chgo.-China Sister Cities Com.; bd. dirs. Lyric Opera Ctr. for Am. Artists, New Trier Swim Club; sec. class of 1970, U. Calif., Berkeley; bd. trustees The Ravinia Festival. Mem. ABA (com. on privatization), Calif. Bar Assn., N.Y. State Bar Assn. (com. on internat. banking, securities and fin. transactions), Assn. of the Bar of City of N.Y., N.Y. County Lawyers Assn., Chgo. Bar Assn., Ill. State Bar Assn., Internat. Bar Assn., U. Chgo. Law Rev., Order of Coif, Phi Beta Kappa, Chgo. China Sister Cities Comm. Home: 465 Grove St Glencoe IL 60022-1844 Office: Altheimer & Gray 10 S Wacker Dr Ste 4000 Chicago IL 60606-7407

GOLDMAN, LYNN ROSE, medical educator; b. Galveston, Tex., Apr. 24, 1951; d. Armond Samuel and Barbara Jean (Bangert) G.; m. Douglas George Hayward. BS, U. Calif., 1976; MPH, Johns Hopkins U., 1981; MS, U. Calif., Berkeley, 1979; MD, U. Calif., San Francisco, 1981. Diplomate Am. Bd. Pediatrics; lic. physician, Calif. Resident pediatrics Children's Hosp. Med. Ctr., Oakland, Calif., 1985; resident preventive medicine U. Calif., Berkeley, 1985; public health medical officer Calif. Dept. Of Health Svcs., Berkeley, 1985-91; public health medical adminstrator Calif. Dept. of Health Svcs., Berkeley, 1991-93; asst. adminstr. Office of Prevention, Pesticides and Toxic Substances EPA, Washington, 1993-98; vis. scholar Sch. Hygiene and Pub. Health Johns Hopkins U., Balt., 1999—. Democrat. Office: Johns Hopkins University Sch Hygiene/Public Health 111 Market Pl Ste 850 Baltimore MD 21202

GOLDMAN, MARC L., federal judge; b. 1948. BA, U. Mich., 1969; JD, Wayne State U., 1973. Atty. State Appellate Defender Office, 1973-74, Washtenaw County Pub. Defender, Ann Arbor, Mich., 1974-76; asst. U.S. atty. U.S. Dist. Ct. (ea. dist.) Mich., 1980-83; magistrate judge U.S. Dist. Ct. (ea. dist.) Mich., Flint, 1983—; asst. prof. Wayne State U. Law Sch., 1973-74; vis. asst. prof. U. Mich. Law Sch., 1979-80. Fax: (810) 341-7859. Office: US Dist Ct Ea Dist Mich 104 Fed Bldg 600 Church St Flint MI 48502

GOLDMAN, MARVIN GERALD, lawyer; b. L.A., June 1, 1939; s. Harry Eli Goldman and Esther Cynthia Brodsky; m. Marilynn Sue Cohen, Oct. 11, 1964; children: Daniel, Sharon, Haviva. AB, UCLA, 1960, JD, 1963; LLM in Comparative Law, NYU, 1964. Bar: Calif. 1964, N.Y. 1966, D.C. 1981. Assoc. Reid & Priest, N.Y.C., 1965-73; ptnr. Thelen Reid & Priest, N.Y.C., 1974—. Author: El Al: Star in the Sky, 1990; editor Thelen Reid & Priest Internat. Bus. Transactions Newsletter, 1983—. Trustee Hebrew Acad. of Nassau County, Uniondale, N.Y., 1981-88. Ford Found. grantee NYU Sch. Law, 1963-64; Fulbright grantee U.S. Govt. Mexico, 1964-65; UCLA Law Rev. award 1963. Mem. ABA (sect. internat. law and practice, chmn. internat. com. arbitration com. 1979-83), Internat. Bar Assn. (internat. constrn. projects com.), Am. Fgn. Law Assn., World Airline Hist. Soc. Avocations: civil aviation history, antique airline postcards, ethnomusicology, philately, fluorescent minerals. Office: Thelen Reid & Priest LLP 40 W 57th St New York NY 10019-4097

GOLDMAN, MIA, film editor; b. N.Y.C., Sept. 26, 1954; d. Bo Goldman and Mab Ashforth. BA, Vassar Coll., 1977. Film editor Choose Me, 1984, 2010, 1984, Silverado, 1985, The Big Easy, 1986, Cross My Heart, 1987, Dead Man Out, 1989, Crazy People, 1990, Prisoner of Honor, 1991, Untamed Heart, 1992, Flesh and Bone, 1994, Something to Talk About, 1995, Dick, 1999. Mem. Am. Cinema Editors, Acad. Motion Picture Arts and Scis.

GOLDMAN, MICHAEL P., lawyer; b. Chgo., June 10, 1960; s. William J. and Judith Ann (Holleb) G.; m. Karla Sue Berman, June 26, 1983; children: Joshua, Adam, David. BS in Accountancy, U. Ill., 1982; JD cum laude, Loyola U. Chgo., 1985. Bar: Ill. 1985, U.S. Dist. Ct. (no. dist.) Ill. 1985; CPA, Ill. Acct. L. Karp & Sons Inc., Elk Grove Vill., Ill., 1979-81; tax analyst Beatrice Foods Corp., Chgo., 1981-84; ptnr. Katten Muchin & Zavis, Chgo., 1984—; lectr. in field. contbr. articles to profl. jours. Bd. dirs. K.I.D.S.S. for Kids (auxiliary of Children's Meml. Hosp., Chgo.), 1993—. Mem. ABA (tort and ins. and bus. law sects.), Chgo. Bar Assn.(ins. and corp. lawcoms.), Ill. CPA Soc. (chmn ins. co. com.), Soc. Fin. Ins. Examiners. Republican. Jewish. Avocations: skiing, handball. Office: Katten, Muchin & Zavis 525 W Monroe St Ste 1600 Chicago IL 60661-3693

GOLDMAN, NORMAN LEWIS, chemistry educator; b. Bklyn., Aug. 11, 1933; s. Sam and Rose (Schrager) G. BS, CCNY, 1954; AM, Harvard U., 1956; PhD, Columbia U., 1959, Postdoctoral NSF fellow, 1959-60; NIH postdoctoral fellow, Columbia U., N.Y.C., 1960-61. Mem. faculty Queens Coll., CUNY, 1961—, prof. chemistry, 1976-98; prof. chemistry emeritus Queens Coll., 1998—; chmn. dept. Queens Coll., CUNY, 1972-77, acting assoc. dean faculty, 1977-78, acting dean faculty, div. math. and natural scis., 1978-79, dean faculty, div. math. and natural scis., 1979-98. Contbr. articles to profl. jours. Mem. Am. Chem. Soc., Royal Soc. Chemistry (London), N.Y. Acad. Sci. (vice chair chem. sci. sect. 1998-99, chair 1999—), Sigma Xi, Phi Beta Kappa. E-mail: normanúgoldman@qc.edu. Home: 75-10 Grand Central Pky Forest Hills NY 11375-5562 Office: CUNY Queens Coll 120 Remsen Hall Flushing NY 11367-1597

GOLDMAN, PETER, nutrition and clinical pharmacology educator; b. N.Y.C., May 23, 1929; married, 1959; 2 children. BEngPhys, Cornell U., 1952; MA, Harvard U., 1953; MD, Johns Hopkins U., 1957. Rsch. assoc. biochemistry Nat. Heart Inst., Washington, 1959-63; sr. investigator biochem. pharmacology Nat. Inst. Arthritis, Metabolism and Digestive Diseases, Washington, 1963-72; prof. clin. pharmacology Harvard Med. Sch., Boston, 1972-76; prof. health sci. dept. nutrition Harvard Sch. Pub. Health, Boston, 1982—, acting chmn. dept., 1984-90, Maxwell Finland prof. clin. pharmacology, 1976—. Office: Harvard U 643 Huntington Ave Boston MA 02115-6021

GOLDMAN, RACHEL BOK, civic volunteer; b. Phila., Mar. 28, 1937; d. W. Curtis and Nellie Lee (Holt) Bok; m. James Nelson Kise, Dec. 20, 1958 (div. May 1974); children: Jefferson B, C. Curtis; m. Allen S. Goldman, Nov. 28, 1981; stepchildren: Jonathan, Benjamin Allen, Adam Louis. Student, Sweet Briar (Va.) Coll., 1955-57; BA in Art History, U. Pa., 1977. Bd. dirs. Arts Exchange mag., 1977-79, chmn. bd. dirs., 1977-79. Mem. collector's circle Pa. Acad. Fine Arts, 1983-85, exhbn. selection com. Morris Gallery, 1979-82; mem. Rittenhouse Sq. Women's Com. Pa. Orchestra, 1979-85; mem. Indian com. Pa. Yearly Meeting, 1971-75; mem. ladies' com. Powel House, 1965-69; founder, pres. Friends of Curtis Inst. Music, 1982—, chmn. 1982-85; bd. dirs. Mary Louis Curtis Bok Found., 1982—, The Curtis Inst. Music, 1982—, The Buten Mus., 1982-84, Brady Cancer Rsch. Inst. 1983—, Settlement Music Sch., 1984-87, The Phila. Award, 1970—, Elfreth's Alley Assn., 1962-65, sec. 1963-65; bd. dirs. The Am. Found., 1955-83, sec.-treas., 1980-83; bd. dirs. The Community Sch. of Phila., 1971-74, chmn. bd. dirs., co-founder, adminstr.; bd. dirs. Women in Transition, 1973-78, div. counselor, 1974-76; bd. dirs. Friends of Phila. Mus. Art, 1977-83, sec., 1979-81, program chmn., 1981-82, co-chmn., 1982-83; bd. dirs. Samuel Yellin Found., 1977-86, co-founder, sec., 1977-84; mem. com. Soc. for Contemporary Art, Art Inst. Chgo., 1988-90, exhibitrix-selection subcom., 1987-88; collectors' group Mus. Contemporary Art, Chgo., 1986-92; bd. dirs. Art Resources in Teaching (A.R.T.), 1987-93, Craniofacial Ctr., 1989-95, AboutFace, 1993-95, Bay Chamber Concerts Inc. 1993-95. Mem. Camden (Maine) Yacht Club, Cosmopolitan Club of Phila. (house com. 1981-84). Democrat. Avocations: art, sailing, music, reading, travelling, gardening.

GOLDMAN, RALPH FREDERICK, research physiologist, educator; b. Boston, Mar. 3, 1928; s. Harry and May (Field) G.; m. Joan R. Krinsky, May 27, 1957; children: Harry, Ellen. BS in Chemistry, U. Denver, 1949; MA in Physiology, Boston U., 1951, PhD in Physiology, 1954; MS in Engring., Northeastern U., Boston, 1962. Rsch. physiologist Natick (Mass.) Labs., U.S. Army, 1955-61; dir. div. environ. medicine U.S. Army Rsch. Inst., Natick, 1961-82; prin. cons. Dept. of Army for Environ. Physiology, Natick, 1971-82; chief scientist Multi-Tech Corp., Natick, 1982-88; chief scientist, R&D, clothing and human comfort Comfort Tech., Inc., Natick, 1989—; sr. cons. tech. and product devel. Arthur D. Little, Inc., Cambridge, Mass., 1993-97; adj. prof. Boston U., 1970—, N.C. State U., 1989—; lectr. MIT, Cambridge, 1974-94; vis. scientist Peoples Rep. of China, 1981—; vis. scholar lectr. Springfield (Mass.) Coll., 1977, Ohio State U., 1977, 88; chmn. rsch. group biomed. effects of clothing, NATO, 1981-86. Author 2 books; contbr. over 500 articles, abstracts and tech. reports to profl. publs., 15 chpts. to books. Scoutmaster Boy Scouts Am., Framinginham, Mass., 1956-90, exec. bd., 1991—; mem. town meeting Town of Framingham, 1983-88. Recipient Meritorious Civilian Svc. award U.S. Army R&D Command,

1963, Exceptional Civilian Svc. award Sec. of Army, 1976, Sr. Exec. Svc. award U.S. Civil Svc., 1979, Silver Beaver award Boy Scouts Am., 1981. Fellow ASHRAE (bd. dirs. 1982-85, assoc. editor Internat. Jour. HVAC&R Rsch. 1995—, Disting. Fellow award 1992), Am. Coll. Sports Medicine (editl. bd. 1979-85), Ergonomics Soc. (hon.); mem. IEEE (AEMB coun. 1978-84), ASTM, Am. Physiol. Soc. (editl. bd. 1972-78), Assn. Mil. Surgeons U.S., Framingham Amateur Radio Assn. (treas. 1970-84), Cape Cod Yacht Club (Falmouth, Mass.), Pelican Isle Yacht Club (Naples, Fla.). Jewish. Avocations: piano, gardening, camping, duplicate bridge, tennis. Office: Comfort Tech PO Box 847 Framingham MA 01701-0847

GOLDMAN, RALPH MORRIS, political science educator; b. Bklyn., May 14, 1920; s. Benjamin and Rose (Smotritski) G.; m. Joan Alicia Walsh, Oct. 20, 1953 (div. Feb. 1990); children: Peter Timothy, Marjorie Edythe; m. Barbara Elizabeth Alban, Mar. 24, 1990. BA, NYU, 1947; MA, U. Chgo., 1948, PhD, 1951. Rsch. assoc. Brookings Instn., Washington, 1953-56; asst. prof., then assoc. prof. Mich. State U., East Lansing, 1956-62; prof. San Francisco State U., 1962-86, prof. emeritus, 1987—, dir. Inst. for Rsch. on Internat. Behavior, 1964-67, dean faculty rsch., 1965-67, chmn. dept. polit. sci., 1971-74; pres. Ctr. for Party Devel., Washington and Seattle, 1992—; dir. Congrl. Studies Program Cath. U., Washington, 1992-96; vis. prof. Am. U., Washington, 1955, 85, 90, U. Chgo., 1961-62, U. Calif., Berkeley, 1963, Stanford (Calif.) U., 1966, U. Calif., San Diego, 1979; cons. rsch. divsn. Dem. Nat. Com., Washington, 1952, 86; cons. Ednl. Testing Svc., Princeton, N.J., 1976-77, CEELI ABA, 1993-96; commentator on pub. affairs Voice of Am., Washington, 1985-86; sr. cons. Nat. Dem. Inst. for Internat. Affairs, Washington, 1986-89. *Upon returning from military service in World War II, Ralph Goldman decided to devote his professional life to the study of the political processes that produce non-violent resolutions of conflict. This focus led him to the investigation of normally disparate topics: conflict theories, arms control, international peacekeeping, political behavior, democracy, and political party systems. He has concluded that competitive party systems are the institutional alternative to warfare, as indicated in his published works. In the arena of international affairs, he anticipates that a transnational party system will eventually render this service to humankind.* Author: Contemporary Perspectives on Politics, 1972, Behavioral Perspectives on American Politics, 1973, Search for Consensus: The Story of the Democratic Party, 1979, Arms Control and Peacekeeping: Feeling Safe in This World, 1982, Dilemma and Destiny: The Democratic Party in America, 1986, The National Party Chairmen and Committees: Factionalism at the Top, 1990, From Warfare to Party Politics: The Critical Transition to Civilian Control, 1990, How to Build and Maintain a Democratic Party System, 1993; co-author: The Politics of National Party Conventions, 1960, Political Science Concept Inventory, 1979, Building Trust: An Introduction to Peace Keeping and Arms Control, 1997; also contbr. chpts. to books and encys.; editor: Transnational Parties; Organizing the World's Precincts, 1983; co-editor: Presidential Nominating Politics in 1952, 1954, Promoting Democracy: Opportunities and Issues, 1988; contbg. editor: Encyclopedia of American Political Parties and Elections, 1991; mem. editorial com. Background jour., 1963-66; mem. editorial bd. Ctr. for Study of Armament and Disarmament, 1984—; founding editor Party Devels., 1993—. Bd. dirs. Frederic Burk Found. for Edn., San Francisco, 1967-78, chmn. bd., 1968-71; coord. Peace Force Proposition Campaign, San Francisco, 1972-73. Capt. U.S. Army, 1946. Edward Hillman fellow U. Chgo., 1948-49, Social Sci. Rsch. Coun. fellow, 1949-50, Air Force Office of Sci. Rsch., 1958; grantee U.S. Office of Naval Rsch., 1968, NSF, 1968-69. Mem. Am. Polit. Sci. Assn. (life), Internat. Polit. Sci. Assn., Internat. Studies Assn., Assn. to Unite the Democracies (bd. dirs. 1989-95). Democrat. Avocation: ballroom dancing. Home: 6825 117th Ave NE Kirkland WA 98033-8451

GOLDMAN, RICHARD HARRIS, lawyer; b. Boston, June 17, 1936; s. Charles M. and Irene M. (Marks) G.; m. Patricia Grollman, June 21, 1959; children: Elaine, Stephen. BA, Wesleyan U., 1958; LLB, NYU, 1961. Bar: Mass. 1961, U.S. Dist. Ct. Mass. 1961. Mem. Slater & Goldman, Boston, 1961-76, Widett, Slater & Goldman, PC, Boston, 1976-93; Sullivan & Worcester LLP, 1993—; past trustee, chmn. audit com. Grove Bank. Co-author: The Ritual Dance Between Lessee and Lender; contbr. articles to profl. jours. Trustee, v.p. Temple Israel; former chmn. Newton (Mass.) Human Rights Commn. Mem. ABA, Mass. Bar Assn., Boston Bar Assn. (chmn. leasing com. 1996-97, lectr., chmn. seminar comml. real estate fin. 1997, real estate steering com. 1997—, co-chair real estate sect. 1999—), Mass. Conveyancers Assn., Belmont Country Club (past v.p., sec.). Home: 47 Vaughn Ave Newton MA 02461-1038 Office: Sullivan & Worcester LLP 1 Post Office Sq Ste 2300 Boston MA 02109-2129

GOLDMAN, RICHARD MARTIN See GOULD, R(ICHARD) MARTIN

GOLDMAN, RICHARD N., foundation administrator; b. San Francisco, Apr. 16, 1920; s. Richard and Alice Goldman; m. Rhoda Haas (dec.); children: Richard (dec.), John, Douglas, Susan. BA, U. Calif., Berkeley, 1941, postgrad. Chmn. Goldman Ins. Svcs.; pres. Richard and Rhoda Goldman Fund; former mem. port commn., pub. utilities commn., chief of protocol City and County of San Francisco. Trustee World Fine Arts Mus. San Francisco, Nat. Symphony, U. Calif.-Berkeley Berkeley Found., Washington Inst. for Near East Policy, World Affairs Coun. No. Calif.; bd. dirs. Am. Jewish History Soc., Internat. House, Berkeley, Jerusalem Found., League to Save Lake Tahoe, San Francisco Ballet; mem. coun. Yosemite Fund; mem. exec. com. Bay Area Internat. Forum; mem. dv. com. Bus. Execs. for Nat. Security; bd. visitors Inst. for Internat. Studies, Stanford U.; bd. dirs., former pres. Jewish Cmty. Fedn., San Francisco; mem. adv. coun. Pacific Grad. Sch. Psychology; mem. governing coun. Save-the-Redwoods League; mem. pres.' adv. coun. San Francisco State U. With U.S. Army, 1942-46. Mem. San Francisco Planning and Urban Renewal Assn. (mem. adv. coun.), Concordia-Argonaut Club, The Family, Villa Taverna, Calif. Tennis Club. Office: Richard and Rhoda Goldman Fund 1 Lombard St Ste 303 San Francisco CA 94111

GOLDMAN, RICHARD PAUL, educational administrator; b. N.Y.C., Mar. 31, 1935; s. Edward and Dorothy (Myer) Goldman; m. Claire Elaine Taylor, Aug. 16, 1975; stepchildren: Lisa Backe, Nina Backe. BA magna cum laude, Yale U., 1956; MA, Middlebury Coll., 1965. Tchr., adminstr. Wilbraham (Mass.) Acad., 1959-72; asst. headmaster Germantown Friends Sch., Phila., 1972-92, interim head, 1992-93, assoc. head, 1993—; cons. The Franklin Group, 1985-92. Editor: (book) Sportswriters' Choice, 1959, (mag.) Studies in Education, 1972—; author: Profession at Risk, 1988; contbr. articles to profl. jours. Trustee Wilbraham and Monson Acad. Mem. Council for Advancement and Support of Edn., Phi Beta Kappa. Democrat. Jewish. Club: Yale. Avocations: reading, travel, walking. Home: 107 W Allens Ln Philadelphia PA 19119-4101

GOLDMAN, ROBERT DAVID, cell biologist, educator; b. Port Chester, N.Y., July 23, 1939; married; two children. B.A., U. Vt., 1961, M.S., 1963; Ph.D. in Biology, Princeton U., 1967. With Royal Postgrad. Med. Sch., London, 1967-69; with Med. Research Council Great Britain, Glasgow, Scotland, 1967-69; asst. prof. biology Case Western Res. U., 1969-74; prof. biology Mellon Inst. Sci., Carnegie-Mellon U., 1974-81; prof., chmn. dept. cell biology and anatomy Northwestern U. Med. Sch., Chgo., 1981-89, prof., chmn. dept. cell and molecular biology, 1989—. *

GOLDMAN, SHERRY ROBIN, public relations executive; b. Queens, N.Y., Mar. 2, 1958; d. Daniel and Alice (Epstein) G. BA, Hofstra U., 1980. Assoc. editor Gralla Publs., N.Y.C., 1980-84; account supr. G.S. Schwartz & Co. Publs., N.Y.C., 1984-87; v.p. Ruder-Finn, Inc., N.Y.C., 1987-95, sr. v.p., 1992-95; cons., 1995—; sr. v.p. The Rowland Co., 1995-96; pres. Goldman Comms.Group, 1996—. Mem. Pub. Rels. Soc. Am. (bd. dirs. N.Y. chpt. 1993—, Silver Anvil award 1991), Nat. Assn. Profl. Environ. Communicators, Women Execs. in Pub. Rels. Avocations: music, sports. *

GOLDMAN, SIMON, broadcasting executive; b. Carthage, N.Y., Jan. 18, 1913; s. Isaac and Ida (Slavin) G.; m. Meurice H. Finer, Jan. 4, 1948 (dec. Aug. 1972); children: Richard Michael, Gail Meurice, Paul Simon; m. Marilyn Gross Fink, Feb. 7, 1976; stepchildren: Shelley Simon, Ronna Fink. BS magna cum laude, Syracuse U., 1935. Various sales positions, 1931-36; mgr. sales James Broadcasting Co., Jamestown, N.Y., 1936-40, v.p., gen. mgr., 1940-43, 45-55, owner, pres., 1955—; pres. Sta. WDOE, Dunkirk, N.Y., 1957-85, Sta. WLKK, Erie, Pa., 1961-85, Sta. WVMT, Burlington, Vt., 1961—, Sta. WTOO, Bellefontaine, Ohio, 1968-71, Stas. WSYB/WRUT, Rutland, Vt., 1970-87, Sta. WXXX-FM, Burlington, Vt., 1990—; owner Goldman Group, Jamestown, 1955—; charter mem. bd. govs. ABC; mem. adv. bd. Erie County Savs. Bank, 1976-86; mem. Broadcast Rating Coun., 1964-72. Mem. adv. bd. St. Bonventure U. Sch. Journalism, 1966-85; mem. exec. bd. Jamestown chpt. NCCJ, 1960-68; mem. nat. coun., Jamestown Areas rep. USO, 1959—; active United Fund, United Negro Coll. Fund, YMCA, Better Jamestown Com.; pres. Ops. Jobs, Jamestown, 1964-80; trustee Fredonia Coll. Found., 1977-81; mem. Blue Cross-Blue Shield Task Force, Mayor's Com. Indsl. Expansion, Roger Tory Peterson Inst. Community Coun.; bd. dirs. Western N.Y. Anti-Defamation League, Chautauqua coun. Boy Scouts Am.; trustee Jamestown Community Coll., 1964-79, chmn. bd., 1968-72; pres. congregation Temple Hesed Abraham, Jamestown, 1951-56; mem. adv. coun. Roger Tory Peterson Inst.; charter mem. media adv. coun. SUNY at Fredonia. Corp. Signal Corps, U.S. Army, 1943-44, ETO. Recipient Brotherhood award NCCJ, 1974, Outstanding Broadcaster of Western N.Y. award Buffalo Pioneers, 1998; named Communicator of the Yr. N.Y. state Broadcasters Assn., 1992. Mem. Radio Advt. Bur. (founder, dir., officer 1951-58), Nat. Assn. Broadcasters (chmn. com. on small market stas. 1947-49, dir. 1956-62, 68-72, mem. copyright com. 1983), Am. Entertainment Network Affiliates Assn. (sec. 1980-88), Community Broadcasters Assn. (dir. 1970-85), Fenton Hist. Soc. (trustee), Am. Legion. Jewish. Avocations: golf, bridge. Home: 2153 Winch Rd Lakewood NY 14750-9628 Office: James Broadcasting Co 2 Orchard St # We Jamestown NY 14701-3710 *If you are going to be a garbage collector, be the best; if you are going to be a broadcaster, teacher, whatever you strive to do, do your best and it will lead to your goal.*

GOLDMAN, STANFORD MILTON, medical educator; b. Salt Lake City, Nov. 28, 1940; s. Osher and Mirian (Soloman) G.; m. Harriet Kaplow, Apr. 2, 1965; children: Etan, Nava. BA, Yeshiva U., 1961; MD, Einstein Coll. Medicine, 1965. Intern Jefferson U. Sch. Medicine, Phila., 1965-66; resident Einstein Coll. Medicine, Bronx, 1966-69; chmn. dept. radiology USPHS Phoenix Indian Med. Ctr., 1969-71; asst. prof. radiology Einstein Coll. Medicine, Bronx, 1971-72; from instr. to asst. prof. radiology Johns Hopkins U. Sch. Medicine, Balt., 1972-79; from asst. prof. to assoc. prof. U. Md., Balt., 1975-81; assoc. prof. Johns Hopkins U., 1979-86; clin. prof. Uniformed Svcs. U., Bethesda, Md., 1981-94; prof. radiology Johns Hopkins U., 1986-94, prof. urology, 1988-93; prof., chmn. radiology U. Tex. Med. Sch., Houston, 1993—, prof. urology, 1995—; adj. prof. radiology and urology Baylor Coll. Medicine, Houston, 1994—; med. dir. radiology Houston C.C., 1994; prof. radiology M.D. Anderson Cancer Ctr., Houston, 1995. Editor: Computed Tomography of Kidneys & Adrenals, 1983, CT & MRI of the Genitourinary Tract, 1990, Tc E Rm Del Trattos Genito-Urinario, 1994; assoc. editor: Urologic Radiology, 1982-85, Radiology, 1986-94; cons. editor Urology, 1998—. Mem. Radiation Control Adv. Bd., Md., 1989-93. Lt. comdr. USPHS, 1969-71. Recipient Albert Einstein Disting. Alumni Assn. award, 1996. Mem. AMA (CPT adv. bd. 1995—), Am. Assn. for History Medicine, Am. Coll. Radiology (alt.-counselor from Tex. 1995-96, counselor from Tex. 1996—, mem. com. on coding and nomenclature of commn. on econs. 1996—, intersoc. com.), Am. Roentgen Ray Soc., Am. Soc. Emergency Medicine (sec.-treas., nominating com., 2002 site selection com., bd. dirs. 1994—, mem. indsl. com. 1994—, chmn. audit com. 1995-99, fin. com. 1996-98, mem. abstract com. 1995-97, chmn. sci. program com. 1996—, mem. site com. 1996-98, vice chair program com. 1996—, mem. ad hoc audit com. 1996—, sec.-treas. 1998—), Am. Urological Assn. (chmn. hematuria guidelines panel 1998—, Radiological Soc. N.Am. (pub. info. bd. 1991—, expert rev. panel for genitourinary radiology exhibits for radiographics 1993-97, chmn. program coms. subcom. on gu radiology 1996—, chmn. sci. exhibits awards com. 1996—, chmn. spl. focus session 1998—), Soc. Uroradiology (ethics com., bd. dirs. 1992-98), Tex. Med. Soc., Tex. Med. Found., Tex. Radiological Soc. (mem. program com. 1994-96, chmn. long range planning com. 1996-97, fellowship nominating com. 1998—, bd. dirs. 1996—, exec. com.), Houston Med. Soc., Houston Radiological Soc., European Soc. Urogenital Radiology, Assn. Univ. Radiologists, Johns Hopkins Med. and Surg. Assn., Soc. Nuclear Medicine, GynecoRadiology Soc., Soc. Chmn. Acad. Radiology Depts. (mem. com. on edn. and tng. 1996—), Assn. U. Radiologists (rep. AMA CPT adv. bd. 1995—, nominating com. 1997-98, ethics com. 1997), U. Md. Alumni Assn. (assoc.), Albert Einstein Disting. Alumni Assn. (bd. dirs. 1991—, award 1996), U.S.-Israel Bi-Nat. Sci. Found. Jewish. Avocations: swimming, music. Office: U Tex Med Sch Dept Radiology 6431 Fannin St Ste 2-132 Houston TX 77030-1501

GOLDMAN, STEPHEN LEWIS, occupational physician; b. Bklyn., Aug. 31, 1949; m. Rita D. Goldman, June 8, 1975; children: Marci, Jared, Daniel, Andrea. BS, Muhlenberg Coll., 1971; MD, Temple U., 1975. Diplomate Am. Bd. Family Practice, Am. Bd. Preventive Medicine, Med. Rev. Officer Cert. Coun. Dir. student health Muhlenberg Coll., Allentown, Pa., 1978-83; pvt. practice Allentown, 1978-90; corp. med. dir. Mack Trucks, Allentown, 1990-94; chief med. officer CSX Transp., Jacksonville, Fla., 1994—. Fellow Am. Acad. Family Practice; mem. Am. Coll. Occupl. and Environ. Medicine. E-mail: SteveuGoldman@csx.com. Home: 7565 Founders Way Porte Vedra Beach FL 32082 Office: CSX Transp 500 Water St J-290 Jacksonville FL 32202

GOLDMAN, STEVEN JASON, lawyer, accountant; b. Boston, Nov. 11, 1947; s. Philip Charles and Selma Laura (Goldblatt) G. BSBA, Northeastern U., Boston, 1970, MBA, 1974; JD, New Eng. Sch. Law, 1987. Bar: R.I., 1987, U.S. Dist. Ct. R.I. 1988, U.S. Tax Ct. 1987; CPA, R.I. Staff auditor CPA firms, Boston and Providence, 1970-72; sr. accountant Peat, Marwick, Mitchell & Co., Providence, 1972-73; contr. Warwick Fed. Savs. & Loan Assn. (R.I.), 1974, v.p., 1975-79, exec. v.p., 1980-82; pres. Fin. Adv. Svcs., Unltd., 1982-87; pvt. practice, Warwick, 1987—. Fellow AICPA; mem. ABA (taxation div.), Nat. Soc. Tax Profls., R.I. Soc. CPAs, R.I. Bar Assn. (taxation com.), Turk's Head Club, Aircraft Owners and Pilots Assn., Edgewood Yacht Club. Jewish. Avocations: flying, sailing, tennis. Office: 1009 Post Rd Warwick RI 02888-3362

GOLDMAN, WILLIAM, writer; b. Chgo., Aug. 12, 1931; s. M. Clarence and Marion (Weil) G.; m. Ilene Jones, Apr. 15, 1961; children: Jenny, Susanna. B.A., Oberlin Coll., 1952; M.A., Columbia U., 1956. Author: (novels) The Temple of Gold, 1957, Your Turn to Curtsy, My Turn to Bow, 1958, Soldier in the Rain, 1960, Boys and Girls Together, 1964, No Way to Treat a Lady, 1964, The Thing of It Is, 1967, Father's Day, 1971, The Princess Bride, 1973, Marathon Man, 1974, Wigger, 1974, Magic, 1976, Tinsel, 1979, Control, 1982, The Silent Gondoliers, 1983, The Color of Light, 1984, Heat, 1985, Brothers, 1987, (non-fiction) The Season: A Candid Look At Broadway, 1969, Adventures in the Screen Trade, 1983, (with Mike Lupica) Wait Until Next Year, 1988, Hype and Glory, 1990, Four Screenplays, 1995, Five Screenplays, 1997; (play, with James Goldman) Blood Sweat and Stanley Poole, 1961; (musical comedy, with James Goldman and John Kander) A Family Affair, 1962; (screenplays) Masquerade, 1965, Harper, 1966, Butch Cassidy and The Sundance Kid, 1969 (Acad. award best original screenplay 1970), The Hot Rock, 1972, The Stepford Wives, 1974, The Great Waldo Pepper, 1975, Marathon Man, 1976, All the President's Men, 1976 (Acad. award best screenplay adaptation 1977), A Bridge Too Far, 1977, Magic, 1978, The Princess Bride, 1987, Heat, 1987, Misery, 1990, The Year of the Comet, 1992, Memoirs of an Invisible Man, 1992, Chaplin, 1992, Maverick, 1994, Ghost and the Darkness, 1996, Absolute Power, 1997. Recipient Laurel Award for Lifetime Achievement in Screenwriting, 1983. Office: c/o CAA 9830 Wilshire Blvd Beverly Hills CA 90212-1804

GOLDMANN, JAMES ALLEN, healthcare consultant; b. Milw., Feb. 26, 1952; s. Allen Abraham and Ruth Lois (Kolbur) G.; m. Pamela Anne McCole, June 6, 1980; children: Michael, Elissa, Kerry. AB, Harvard Coll., 1974; MHA, Washington U., St. Louis, 1979. V.p. Riverside Meth. Hosp., Columbus, Ohio, 1980-85; COO Children's Med. Ctr., Dallas, 1986-92; cons. APM, Inc., N.Y.C., 1993-96; ptnr. Arthur Andersen, Dallas, 1996—. Bd. dirs. Hope Cottage, Dallas, 1989-93; scout leader Boy Scouts Am., Columbus and Grapevine, Tex., 1980-84, 92, 93. Fellow Am. Coll. Healthcare Execs. Office: Arthur Andersen 901 Main St Ste 5600 Dallas TX 75202-3799

GOLDMANN, MORTON AARON, cardiologist; b. Chgo., July 11, 1924; s. Harry Ascher and Frieda (Cohon) G.; m. Doris-Jane Tumpeer, July 18, 1951; children: Deborah, Jory, Erica, Leslie. BS, U. Ill., 1943, MD, 1946. Diplomate Am. Bd. Internal Medicine. Intern Cook County Hosp., Chgo., 1946-47, resident physician, 1949-52; practice medicine specializing in internal medicine and cardiology Skokie, Ill., 1952—; chief of medicine Rush North Shore Med. Ctr. (formerly Skokie Valley Hosp.), 1964-65, also trustee, 1968—, pres. med. staff, 1968-69, attending physician, med. dir. heart sta. and cardiac rehab. unit, 1973-96, bd. dirs., 1970—; former attending physician Ill. Research Hosp.; former assoc. prof. Abraham Lincoln Sch. Medicine, U. Ill., Chgo.; prof. Cook County Grad. Sch. Medicine; pres. Heart Assn. North Cook County, 1978-81, North Suburban Assn. Health Resources, 1974-77. Contbr. numerous articles to profl. jours. Capt. M.C., AUS, 1947-49, PTO. Fellow ACP, Inst. Medicine Chgo., Am. Coll. Cardiology; mem. AMA, Am. Soc. Internal Medicine, Am. Heart Assn., Ill. Med. Soc., Chgo. Med. Soc., Chgo. Heart Assn. (bd. govs., bd. dirs. 1978-87, bd. trustees 1979-83). Office: 667 Carriage Hill Dr Glenview IL 60025-5402

GOLDMANN, PETER DANIEL, editor; b. N.Y.C., June 25, 1953; s. Robert Berthold and Eva (Petchek) G.; m. Barbara Wohler, June 20, 1982; children: Benjamin J.H., Leah F. BA, U. Mich., 1975; MSc, London Sch. Econs., 1976. Editor German Am. C. of C., N.Y.C., 1976-79, Seatrade Publs., N.Y.C., 1979-85, Bottom Line/Bus., N.Y.C., 1985—. Mem. N.Y. Assn. Bus. Economists. Office: Boardroom Reports 55 Railroad Ave Greenwich CT 06830-6378

GOLDMAN-RAKIC, PATRICIA SHOER, neuroscience educator. AB cum laude, Vassar Coll., 1959; PhD, UCLA, 1963; AM (hon.), Yale U., 1979. USPHS predoctoral fellow dept. psychology UCLA, 1961-63, USPhS postdoctoral fellow dept. psychiatry, 1963-64; rsch. assoc. dept. animal behavior Am. Mus. Natural History, N.Y.C., 1964-65; staff fellow sect. neuropsychology NIMH, Bethesda, Md., 1965-68, rsch. physiologist Lab. Neuropsychology, 1978-78, chief sect. devel. neurobiology, 1978-79; prof. neurosci. sect. neurobiology Yale U. Sch. Medicine, New Haven, 1979—, joint appointment dept. psychology, 1991-96, dir. grad. studies sect. neuroanatomy, 1981-86, acting chmn. sect. neurobiology, 1986-87; USPHS postdoctoral trainee dept. psychiatry NYU, N.Y.C., 1964-65; vis. scientist MIT, Cambridge, 1974-75; Edward Sacher lectr. Columbia U., 1992; Herbert Birch meml. lectr. Internat. Neuropsychobiology Soc., 1981; Plenary lectr. Union Swiss Socs. for Exptl. Biology, 1983; Sigma Xi lectr. Brown U., 1984, SUNY Downstate Med. Sch., Bklyn., 1988; Kendon Smith meml. lectr. U. N.C., 1985; Bernard Sachs meml. lectr. Child Neurology Soc., Memphis, 1985; Frontiers of Sci. lectr. Am. Psychiat. Assn., 1988; Sally Harrington Goldwater lectr. Barrow Neurol. Inst., Phoenix, 1990; 4th Hillarp lectr. European Neurosci. Soc., 1990; Rushton lectr. Fla. State U., 1990; Lanier lectr. U. Ill., 1991; Hal Robinson disting. lectr. U. N.C., 1992; Jock Cleghorn meml lectr. McMaster U., 1994; mem. sci. adv. bd. Ency. Neurosci., 1994—; mem. Nat. Adv. Mental Health Coun., 1993—; numerous others; participant sems., confs., symposia, and workshops throughout world. Editor-in-chief Cerebral Cortex; mem. adv. bd. Advances in Neurosci., Behavioral Brain Rsch., Behavioral Neurosci., Brain Rsch., Brain Rsch. Bull., Concepts in Neurosci., Devel. Brain Rsch., Devel. Neuropsychology, Devel. Psychobiology, Exptl. Neurology, Jour. Neurosci., Progress in Brain Rsch., Trends in Neurosci., Sci., Critical Revs. in Neurobiology, Biol. Psychiatry, Neuropsychopharmacology, Jour. Comparative and Physiol. Psychology. Recipient Lieber award Nat. Alliance for Rsch. on Schizophrenia and Depression, 1991, award Robert T. and Claire Pasarow Found., 1993, prize in neurosci. Fyssen Found., Paris, 1990, Alden Spencer award Columbia U., 1982, Karl Spencer Lashley prize Am. Philos. Soc., 1996; grantee NIMH, 1980-2000. Fellow AAAS (John P. McGovern award 1993), APA (Disting. Sci. Contbn. award 1991), Am. Psychopath. Assn., N.Y. Acad. Scis.; mem. NAS, Soc. for Neurosci. (councilor 1984-88, young investigator award selection com. 1985-87, pres. 1989-90), Internat. Soc. for Devel. Psychobiology, Am. Anat. Assn. (Krieg Cortical Discoverer award Cajal Club 1989), Internat. Neuropsychology Symposium, Internat. Brain Rsch. Orgn., Am. Acad. Arts and Scis., Inst. Medicine. Home: 253 Saint Ronan St New Haven CT 06511-2313 Office: Yale U Sch Medicine Sect Neurobiology SHMC303 333 Cedar St Box 208001 New Haven CT 06520-8001*

GOLDMARK, PETER CARL, JR., publishing executive; b. N.Y.C., Dec. 2, 1940; s. Peter Carl and Frances Charlotte (Trainer) G.; Aliette Marie Misson, Nov. 7, 1964; children: Lara, Karin, Sandra. BA in Govt., Harvard Coll., 1962. Tchr. history Putney (Vt.) Sch., 1962-64; program analyst, then asst. to dep. dir. OEO, Washington, 1965-66; exec. asst. to dir. budget of N.Y.C., 1966-67; acting chief program planning unit N.Y.C., 1966-68; asst. dir. N.Y.C. budget, 1968-70, exec. asst. to N.Y.C. mayor, 1970; sec. human svcs. Commonwealth of Mass., 1971-74; dir. budget State of N.Y., Albany, 1975-77; exec. dir. Port Authority of N.Y. & N.J., 1977-85; sr. v.p. Times Mirror Co., 1985-88; pres. Rockefeller Found., N.Y.C., 1988-97; chmn., CEO, Internat. Herald Tribune, Paris, 1998—; dir. Knight-Ridder Co., 1991-98. Overseer Harvard U., 1984-90. With USAR, 1965-70. Office: Internat Herald Tribune, 181 Ave Charles de Gaulle, 92521 Neuilly Cedex France*

GOLDNER, SHELDON HERBERT, export-import company executive; b. Bklyn., Aug. 3, 1928; s. David and Esther (Maskowsky) G.; m. Lila Diane Silber, Aug. 14, 1954; children: Jonathan Shepard, Jeffrey Scott, Barbara Jill. B.S. in acctg., L.I. U., 1950. C.P.A., N.Y. Acct. S.H. Goldner & Co., N.Y.C., 1950-59; v.p. fin. Connell Rice & Sugar Co., Inc., Westfield, N.J., 1959-89, ret., 1989. Pres., trustee Temple Israel, Union, N.J. Served with U.S. Army, 1946-47, PTO. Mem. AICPA, N.Y. State Soc. CPAs, Halloween Yacht Club (Stamford, Conn.), Royal Veere (Netherlands) Yacht Club, Dartmouth Yacht Club (Devon, Eng.), Miles River Yacht Club (St. Michaels, Md.).

GOLDOFF, ANNA CARLSON, public administration educator; b. N.Y.C., Feb. 3, 1948; d. Edwin Olavi and Sylvia Amanda Carlson; m. Barry Goldoff, June 2, 1968; children: David, William, Jacqueline. BA, Hunter Coll., 1969; PhD, CUNY, 1974. Asst. prof. pub. adminstrn. John Jay Coll. Criminal Justice, N.Y.C., 1974-80, assoc. prof. pub. adminstrn., 1980—; mem. editl. bd. Public Adminstrn. & Mgmt.; an Interactive Jour., Internat. Jour. of Orgn. Theory & Behavior. Author, editor: The Essence of Decision Redux Crisis Decision Making, 1999. Bd. dirs. St. Christopher's, Inc., N.Y.C., 1997—; elder Rye (N.Y.) Presbyn. Ch., 1994-97. Mem. Am. Polit. Sci. Assn., Am. Soc. Pub. Adminstrn., Women's Coalition. Democrat. Avocations: reading, swimming, walking.

GOLDRICH, STANLEY GILBERT, optometrist; b. N.Y.C., Sept. 22, 1937; s. Joseph and Doris (Stelzner) G. BA, Queens Coll., 1959, MA, 1965; PhD, CUNY, 1966; OD, Mass. Coll. Optometry, 1974. Lic. optometrist, N.Y., Calif. Rsch. assoc. U. Wis. Primate Ctr., Madison, 1965-67; asst. prof. Ohio State U., Columbus, 1967-72; assoc. clin. prof. SUNY Coll. Optometry, N.Y.C., 1974—; cons. U. Optometry Assocs., N.Y.C. Contbr. articles to profl. jours.; inventor in field. With USAR, 1960-65. NSF grantee, 1967. Fellow Am. Acad. Optometry; mem. Am. Psychol. Assn., Am. Optometric Assn., N.Y. State Optometric Assn. Jewish. Avocation: piano. Home: 150 Lexington Ave New York NY 10016-8108 Office: SUNY 100 E 24th St New York NY 10010-3676

GOLDRING, NORMAN MAX, advertising executive; b. Chgo., June 22, 1937; s. Jack and Carolyn (Wolf) G.; m. Cynthia Lois Garland, Dec. 20, 1959; children: Jay Marshall, Diane. BS in Bus., Miami (Ohio) U., 1959; MBA, U. Chgo., 1963. Advt. account mgr. Edward H. Weiss & Co., Chgo., 1959-61; sr. v.p., dir. mktg. svcs. Stern, Walters & Simmons, Inc., Chgo., 1961-68; chmn. Goldring & Co., Inc., Chgo., 1968-89; pres., CEO CPM, Inc., 1969-93, chmn., 1994—; pres. CPO Inc., 1994-98; bd. dirs. Root Mktg. Inc.; dir. Creative Works, Inc.; instr. mktg. and advt. mgmt. Roosevelt U., 1965-68. Mem. editorial bd. Jour. Media Planning. Commr. Ridgeville Park Dist., Evanston, Ill., 1971-75, pres. 1974-75; bd. dirs., v.p. Mus. Broadcast Comm., 1983-92; dir. Chgo. Chamber Musicians 1988—; dir. Chgo. Metro History Fair, 1990. Mem. Am. Mktg. Assn. (speaker), Advt. Coun. Inc. (Midwest adv. bd. 1983-90), Am. Mgmt. Assn. Home: 855 Beverly Pl Lake Forest IL 60045-3901 Office: CPM Inc 515 N State St Ste 2200 Chicago IL 60610-4300

GOLDSAMT, BONNIE BLUME, lawyer; b. N.Y.C., July 31, 1946; d. Frank and Evelyn (Tobias) Blume; m. Jay S. Goldsamt, June 25, 1967; children: Seth, Kathryn, Deborah. BA, Sarah Lawrence Coll., 1967; MA, NYU, 1971; JD, Rutgers U., 1979. Bar: N.J. 1979, N.Y. 1990, U.S. Dist. Ct. N.J. 1979, U.S. Supreme Ct. 1987. Law sec. to judge Superior Ct. N.J. Chancery Family Part, Newark, 1979-80; assoc. Cole, Schotz, Bernstein, Meisel and Forman, Rochelle Park, N.J., 1980-82; asst. county counsel govtl. affairs Essex County, Newark, 1982-84; assoc. Rose & DeFuccio, Hackensack, N.J., 1984-87; sr. assoc. Steven Morey Greenberg, Hackensack, 1987-89; pvt. practice Hackensack, 1989—, Verona, 1992—; speaker Women Bankers Assn., Hackensack, 1982, Seton Hall Law Sch., Newark, 1983; appointed mem. family practice com. N.J. Supreme Ct., 1990-92, ct. apptd. contract arbitrator, Essex County, 1996—, Task Force on Alternative Work Arrangements, State Bar Assn. Dispute Resolution Com.; asst. clin. prof. law Seton Hall Law Sch. Bd. dirs. Downtown Bklyn. Planning Bd., 1974-75; committeeperson Essex County Com., 1987-96; ward co-chair Dem. County Com., Montclair, 1988-91, ward chair, 1993-96; fundraiser, speaker, chair women's issues No. N.J. Clinton Campaign; fin. com. Clinton/Gore campaign; chair women's issues Women's Coalition for Clinton/Gore; surrogate speaker Clinton for Pres. campaign; active Dem. Nat. Conv., Women's Leadership Forum. Named one of Bklyns. Women of the Yr., Bklyn. NOW, 1974. Mem. ABA, Am. Arbitration Assn. (arbitrator 1990—), Essex and Bergen County Comml. Bar Assns. (trustee Bergen County 1988-97, com. mem.), N.J. State Bar Assn. (chair dispute resolution sect. 1999—, family law exec. com., chair child abuse protocol com., elder law com., state bar family law exec. com., exec. com., judicial adminstrn. programming, pro bono com., sec. gen. coun. 1996-97), N.J. Assn. of Profl. Mediators (2nd vice-chair), Women Lawyers in Bergen County (pres. 1985-87, trustee Jean Robertson Found. 1987-88, dir. at large 1987-88, Merit award 1987), N.J. Assn. Profl. Mediators (sec. bd. dirs. 1997-98), Bergen County Bar Found. (trustee 1990-95), Nat. Acad. Elder Law Attys., Acad. of Family Mediators (practitioner mem.), Hadassah. Democrat. Jewish. Avocations: reading, travel. Office: Ste 14 1 University Plaza Dr Hackensack NJ 07601-6207 also: 25 Pompton Ave Verona NJ 07044-2934

GOLDSBOROUGH, ROBERT GERALD, publishing executive, author; b. Chgo., Oct. 3, 1937; s. Robert Vincent and Wilma (Janak) G.; m. Janet Elizabeth Moore, Jan. 15, 1966; children: Suzanne Joy, Robert Michael, Colleen Marie, Bonnie Laura. BS, Northwestern U., 1959, MS with honors, 1960. Reporter A.P., 1959, City News Bur., Chgo., 1959; with Chgo. Tribune, 1960-82, reporter neighborhood news sect., asst. editor Sunday mag. and TV sect., 1963-66, editor TV Week mag., 1966-67, asst. to features editor, 1967-71, asst. to editor, 1971-72, Sunday editor, 1972-75, editor Sunday mag., 1975-82; exec. editor Advt. Age Mag., Chgo., 1982-88, spl. projects dir., 1988-91; corp. projects editor Crain Communications, Chgo., 1991-96, spl. projects dir., 1997—. Author: Great Railroad Paintings, 1976, The Crain Adventure, 1992, Nero Wolfe Mysteries: Murder in E-Minor, 1986, Death on Deadline, 1987, The Bloodied Ivy, 1988, The Last Coincidence, 1989, Fade to Black, 1990, Silver Spire, 1992, The Missing Chapter, 1994. Served with AUS, 1961. Mem. Arts Club. Presbyterian. Office: 740 N Rush St Chicago IL 60611-2546

GOLDSCHMID, HARVEY JEROME, law educator; b. N.Y.C., May 6, 1940; s. Bernard and Rose (Braiker) G.; m. Mary Tait Seibert, Dec. 22, 1973; children: Charles Maxwell, Paul MacNeil, Joseph Tait. AB, Columbia U., 1962, JD, 1965. Bar: N.Y. 1965, U.S. Supreme Ct. 1970. Law clk. to judge 2d Circuit Ct. Appeals, N.Y.C., 1965-66; assoc. firm Debevoise & Plimpton, N.Y.C., 1966-70; asst. prof. law Columbia U., 1970-71, assoc. prof., 1971-73, prof., 1973-84, Dwight prof. law, 1984—, founding dir. Ctr. for Law and Econ. Studies, 1975-78; of counsel Arnold & Porter, N.Y.C., 1995-98; cons. in field to pub. and pvt. orgns.; mem. planning and program com. 2d Cir. Jud. Conf., 1982-85; reporter 2d Cir. Jud. Conf. Evaluation Com., 1980-82, 88-89; mem. legal adv. com. N.Y.S.E., 1997-98, chmn. subcom. on corp. governance; gen. counsel Securities and Exch. Commn., 1998—. Author(with others) Cases and Materials on Trade Regulation, 1975, 4th edit., 1997; editor: (with others) Industrial Concentration: The New Learning, 1974, Business Disclosure: Government's Need to Know, 1979, The Impact of the Modern Corporation, 1984. Chmn. bd. advisors program on philanthropy and the law NYU Sch. Law, 1992-94; bd. dirs. Nat. Ctr. on Philanthropy and the Law, 1996—; nat. bd. visitors U. Ariz. Coll. Law, 1996—; bd. dirs. Greenwall Found., 1996—, vice chair, 1999—. Fellow Am. Bar Found.; mem. ABA (task force on lawyers polit. contbrns. 1997-98), Am. Law Inst. (reporter part IV, duty of care and the bus. judgment rule, corp. governance project 1980-93), N.Y. State Bar Assn., Assn. Bar City N.Y. (v.p. 1985-86, chmn. exec. com. 1984-85, chmn. com. on antitrust and trade regulation 1971-74, nominating com. 1986-87, com. on the 2d century, chmn. com. on securities regulation 1992-95, chmn. audit com. 1988-96, chmn. com. on corp. takeover legislation 1985-86, 88-92, treas., mem. exec. com. 1996-98), Assn. Am. Law Schs. (chmn. sect. antitrust and econ. regulation 1976-78), Am. Assn. Internat. Commn. Jurists (sec.-treas., bd. dirs.), Century Assn., Riverdale Yacht Club (bd. dirs. 1987-90), Phi Beta Kappa. Office: Securities and Exch 450 5th St NW Washington DC 20001-2739

GOLDSCHMIDT, ARTHUR EDUARD, JR., history educator, author; b. Washington, Mar. 17, 1938; s. Arthur Eduard and Elizabeth (Wickenden) G.; m. Louise Robb, June 17, 1961; children: Stephen Robb, Paul William. A.B., Colby Coll., Waterville, Maine, 1959; A.M., Harvard U., 1961, Ph.D., 1968. Asst. prof. history Pa. State U., University Park, 1965-73, assoc. prof., 1974-89, prof. Middle East History, 1989— ; vis. assoc. prof. middle east history Haifa U., Israel, 1973-74; vis. prof. Semester at Sea, 1987, vis. rsch. fellow Durham U., 1989, 90; acad. dean N.J. Scholars, Lawrenceville, 1985. Author: Concise History of the Middle East, 1979, 6th edit., 1999, Modern Egypt, 1988;, The Memoirs and Diaries of Muhammad Farid: An Egyptian Nationalist Leader (1868-1919), 1992, Historical Dictionary of Egypt, rev. edit., 1994, Biographical Dictionary of Modern Egypt, 1999; contbr. AHA Guide to Historical Literature, 3d edit., 1995, American National Biography, 1999, Understanding the Contemporary Middle East, 1999; cons., contbr. The Encyclopedia of the Modern Middle East, 1996; editor: Articles on the Middle East, 1947-71, 1980. Trustee Unitarian-Universalist Fellowship, State College, 1977-80, 85-87. Recipient AMOCO Teaching award Pa. State U., 1981; Fulbright research fellow, 1981-82; faculty fellow Am. Rsch. Ctr. Egypt, 1998. Mem. Middle East Studies Assn., Am. Research Ctr. Egypt. (bd. govs. 1989-92), Am. Hist. Assn, Central Pa. Torch Club (pres. 1993), Voices of Ctrl. Pa. (founding pres. 1993-97). Democrat. Avocations: cooking, reading. Home: 1173 Oneida St State College PA 16801-5938 Office: 303 Weaver Bldg University Park PA 16802-5503

GOLDSCHMIDT, CHARLES, advertising agency executive; b. N.Y.C., June 15, 1921; s. Harry and Adele (Safir) G.; m. Patricia Nevins, Jan. 17, 1951; children: Richard Walter, Jane, Peter. BA, NYU, 1941. Advt. copywriter Warner Bros. Pictures Co., 1946-48, Buchanan & Co., N.Y.C., 1948-49, Ray Austrian Assocs., N.Y.C., 1949-52; founder, ptnr. Daniel & Charles Inc., N.Y.C., 1952; chmn. bd. dirs. LCF&L, Inc., 1952—. Author fiction, play, articles. Served to lt. USNR, 1941-46. Mem. Beach Point Club (Mamaroneck, N.Y.), Phoenix Country Club. Democrat. Home: 710 The Cres Mamaroneck NY 10543-4531 Office: LCF&L Inc 260 Madison Ave New York NY 10016-2401

GOLDSCHMIDT, LYNN HARVEY, lawyer; b. Chgo., June 14, 1951; d. Arthur and Ida (Shirman) H.; m. Robert Allen Goldschmidt, Aug. 27, 1972; children: Elizabeth Anne, Carolyn Helene. BS with honors, U. Ill., 1973; JD magna cum laude, Northwestern U., 1976. Bar: Ill. 1976. Ptnr. Hopkins & Sutter, Chgo., 1976—. Articles editor Northwestern U. Law Rev. Mem. Airport Coun. Internat., N. Am., Order of Coif. Office: Hopkins & Sutter 3 1st National Plz Ste 4100 Chicago IL 60602

GOLDSCHMIDT, PETER GRAHAM, physician executive, business development consultant; b. Cardiff, Wales, Feb. 18, 1945; came to U.S., 1970; s. Heinz Joachim Siefried and Marjorie (Sweet) G. DMS, U. Westminster, 1968; MB, BS, U. London, 1970; MPH, Johns Hopkins U., 1971, DPH, 1980. Rsch. assoc. Johns Hopkins U. Sch. Hygiene and Pub. Health, Balt., 1972-75; v.p., dir. Policy Rsch. Inc., Balt., 1974-81; dir. health svcs. R&D svc. VA, Washington, 1981-86; v.p., dir. Quality Standards in Medicine, Inc., Boston, 1986-90; pres. World Devel. Group, Inc., Bethesda, Md., 1986—; bd. dirs. Quality Standards in Medicine, Inc., Boston, 1986-96; pres. Health Improvement Inst., Bethesda, 1991—, Med. Care Mgmt. Corp., Bethesda, 1992—. Author: Quality Management in Health Care, 1995; contbr. numerous articles to profl. jours. Bd. dirs. Policy Rsch. Inst., Balt., 1978-87. Recipient various grants. Mem. AMA, APHA, Balt.-Washington Venture Group. Office: Med Care Mgmt Corp 5272 River Rd Ste 650 Bethesda MD 20816-1405

GOLDSCHMIDT, ROBERT ALPHONSE, financial executive; b. Cin., July 3, 1937; s. Alphonse Francis and Lillian Mary (Ashbrock) G.; m. Karen Ann Koehnemann, June 10, 1961; children: Diane, Kristine, Linda, Mark, Erik. BA, U. Notre Dame, 1959, BSME, 1960; MS in Indsl. Mgmt., Purdue U., 1961. CPA; registered profl indsl. engr. Mgmt. cons. Touche Ross & Co., N.Y.C., 1961-66; mgr. planning and control Litton Med. Group, Des Plaines, Ill., 1966-68; v.p. fin. Bell TV, N.Y.C., 1968-70; pres., chief exec. officer Living Industries, Farmingdale, N.Y., 1971-72; asst. to pres. Gen. Instrument Corp., N.Y.C., 1972-73; v.p. ops. Jackson Communications, Dayton, Ohio, 1973-74; v.p., chief fin. officer Esterline Corp., Darien, Conn., 1974-87; v.p. fin. controls The Dyson-Kissner-Moran Corp., N.Y.C., 1987-93; CFO The Archdiocese of New York, 1994—. Treas. YMCA, Tarrytown, N.Y., 1980-82. Republican. Roman Catholic. Club: Sleepy Hollow Country (Scarborough, N.Y.) (treas. 1982-84). Home: 226 River Rd Briarcliff Manor NY 10510-2414 Office: The Archdiocese of New York 1011 1st Ave New York NY 10022-4106

GOLDSCHMIDT, WALTER ROCHS, anthropologist, educator; b. San Antonio, Feb. 24, 1913; s. Hermann and Gretchen (Rochs) G.; m. Beatrice Lucia Gale, May 27, 1937; children: Karl Gale, Mark Stefan. B.A., U. Tex., 1933, M.A., 1935; Ph.D., U. Calif. at Berkeley, 1942. Social scientist Bur. Agrl. Econs., 1940-46; mem. faculty UCLA, 1946—, prof. anthropology, 1956—, chmn. dept., 1964-69, prof. anthropology and psychiatry, 1970-83, prof. emeritus, 1983—; Vis. lectr. Stanford, summer 1945, U. Calif. at Berkeley, 1949, Harvard, 1950. Dir. radio program: Ways of Mankind, 1951- 53, Culture and Ecology in E. Africa, 1960-68. Spl. editor: World of Man Series, Aldine Pub. Co., 1966-75. Author: Small Business and the Community, 1946, As You Sow, 1947, 2d edit., 1978, Nomlaki Ethnography, 1951, Ways to Justice, 1953, Man's Way, 1959, Exploring the Ways of Mankind, 1960, 3d edit., 1977, Comparative Functionalism, 1966, Sebei Law, 1967, Kambuya's Cattle, The Legacy of an African Herdsman, 1968, On Being an Anthropologist, 1970, Culture and Behavior of the Sebei, 1976, The Sebei: A Study in Cultural Adaptation, 1986; The Human Career: The Self in The Symbolic World, 1990; co-author: Haa Aani, Our Land: Tlingit and Haida Land Rights and Use, 1998; editor: The U.S. and Africa, rev, 1963, French edit., 1965, The Anthropology of Franz Boas, 1959, (with H. Hoijer) The Social Anthropology of Latin America, 1970, The Uses of Anthropology, 1979, Anthropology and Public Policy: A Dialogue, 1986, Am. Anthropologist, 1956-59; founding editor: Ethos, 1972-79. Fulbright scholar U.K., 1953; grantee Social Sci. Rsch. Coun., 1953; grantee Wenner-Gren. Found., 1953; NSF postdoctoral fellow, 1964-65; fellow Center Advanced Study Behavioral Scis., 1964-65; sr. sci. fellow NIMH, 1970-75; disting. lectr. U. Indonesia, 1993. Fellow Am. Anthrop. Assn. (pres. 1975-76), African Studies Assn. (founding, bd. dirs. 1957-60); mem. AAAS, Southwestern Anthrop. Assn. (pres. 1950-51), Am. Ethnol. Soc. (pres. 1969-70), Phi Beta Kappa, Sigma Xi. Home: 978 N Norman Pl Los Angeles CA 90049-1535

GOLDSMITH, AARON CLAIR, federal government executive; b. Kalamazoo, Feb. 4, 1946; s. Richard Samuel and Vivian Jean (Davis) G.; m. Wilma June Long, July 19, 1969; children: Philip, Kristin, Karen. BA, Bob Jones U., Greenville, S.C., 1969; MBA, Embry-Riddle Aero. U., 1995. Cert. govt. fin. mgr. Intern Tank Automotive and Armaments Command, Warren, Mich., 1969-71; sys. analyst U.S. Army Gen. Material and Petroleum Ctr., New Cumberland, Pa., 1971-76, Depot Sys. Command, Chambersburg, Pa., 1976-79; logistician TACOM, Warren, 1979-84, chief, Abrams Tank br., 1984-89, chief, budget and policy br., 1989-91, chief, plans, policy and program divsn., 1991-93, dir., bus. and planning office, 1993—; advisor Faith Christian Sch., Clinton Twp., Mich., 1993-99, Calvary Christian Sch., Roseville, 1993—. Deacon and trustee Faith Baptist Ch., Warren, Mich., 1995-97, Calvary Baptist Ch., Roseville, Mich., 1981-92; founding bd. edn. Tri-County Christian H.S., Mechanicsburg, Pa., 1971. Mem. Assn. U.S. Army, Am. Soc. Mil. Comptr., Bob Jones U. Alumni Assn. Baptist. Avocations: traveling, reading, golf. E-mail: gold19@juno.com, acg46@worldnet.att.net. Office: TACOM 11 Mile Rd Warren MI 48397

GOLDSMITH, ARTHUR AUSTIN, magazine editor; b. Merrimac, Mass., July 7, 1926; s. Arthur Austin and Daisy (Bishop) G.; m. Carolyn Milford, Sept. 2, 1948; children: Arthur, James, Susan, Amy. Student, U. N.H., 1946-47; B.S. in Journalism, Northwestern U., 1951, M.S., 1951; MA in History, Western Conn. State U., 1995. Asst. editor to exec. editor Popular Photography, N.Y.C., 1951-60; picture editor This Week, N.Y.C., 1960-62; editor, head of instrn. Famous Photographers Sch., Westport, Conn., 1962-69, pres., dir., 1969-72; editorial dir. Popular Photography, N.Y.C., 1972-85; photography columnist Nat. Geog. Traveler, 1988-95; lectr., moderator Internat. Ctr. Photography, N.Y.C., 1974-75; co-chmn. Focus on Electronic Photography, 1992; mem. faculty Focus 82, 83, New Sch. Social Rsch.; panelist Photography at the Summit, 1988-89. Contbr.: photography Ency. Brit. Yearbook, 1974—, Compton's Ency., 1987; author: How To Take Better Pictures, 1956, The Photography Game, 1971, The Nude in Photography, 1975, The Camera and Its Images, 1979, (with Alfred Eisenstadt) The Eye of Eisenstaedt, 1969; editor: Photojournalism: The World Gallery of Photography, 1983. Photography chmn. Wilton (Conn.) Arts Coun., 1982-89. Served with USN, 1944-46. Recipient Harrington award Medill Sch. Journalism, Northwestern U., 1951, Photokina Eye award City of Cologne, Germany, 1980, Photokina Obelisk, 1982, 84, Editor of Yr. award United Jewish Appeal, 1982, Spl. Appreciation Award Photog. Adminstrs., Inc., 1998. Mem. German Photog. Soc., Chinese Photographers Assn., Photog. Adminstrs. Inc. (v.p. 1995), Dutch Treat Club, Kappa Tau Alpha, Phi Alpha Theta.

GOLDSMITH, BARBARA, author, social historian, journalist; d. Joseph I. and Evelyn (Cronson) Lubin; children: Andrew Goldsmith, Alice Elgart, John Goldsmith. BA, Wellesley Coll., 1958; DLitt (hon.), Syracuse U., 1980; LHD (hon.), Pace U., 1982, Lake Forest Coll., 1996. Entertainment editor Woman's Home Companion, N.Y.C., 1954-57; contbr. N.Y. Herald Tribune, Esquire Mag., 1957-64; founder, contbg. editor N.Y. Mag., 1968—; sr. editor Harpers Bazaar Mag., N.Y.C., 1970-74; lectr. NYU, 1969, 75. Spl. writer TV documentaries and entertainments; author: (novel) The Straw Man, 1975; (non-fiction) Little Gloria . . . Happy at Last, 1980, Johnson v. Johnson, 1987, Other Powers, 1998, The Age of Suffrage, Spiritualism and the Scandalous Victoria Woodhull, 1998. Mem. jr. coun. Mus. Modern Art, N.Y.C., 1951-73; bd. dirs. Parks Coun. N.Y.C., 1965-82; mem. acquisitions com. Friends of Whitney Mus. Art, 1964-69; mem. pres.'s coun. Mus. City N.Y., 1970—; bd. dirs. Nat. Dance Inst., 1979—, Goldsmith Found., 1981—; exec. bd. PEN Am. Ctr., 1984-96, chmn. permanent paper com.; founder Ctr. for Learning Disabilities, Albert Einstein Coll. Medicine; trustee N.Y. Pub. Libr., 1985—; mem. N.Y. Pub. Libr. Rsch. Librs., 1985—; mem. exec. com. N.Y. Pub. Libr., trustee, 1987—; trustee N.Y. Soc. Libr.; gubernatorial appointee N.Y. State Coun. on Arts, 1990; bd. dirs. permanent paper task force Nat. Libr. Medicine, 1989—, Com. for Preservation and Access, 1990-95; commr. Pres. Commn. Celebration of Women in Am. History, 1998—; founder PEN Freedom to Write award. Recipient Brandeis U. Library Trust award, 1980, Albert Einstein Spirit of Achievement award, 1988; Permanent Paper citation N.Y. Pub. Libr.; Lit. Lions N.Y. Pub. Libr., 1988, Pubs. 1st Ann. award Lit. Market Place, 1990, Nat. Libr. Medicine Lit. award, 1991, Nat. Archives award, 1991, NYU Presdl. Citation award, 1993; elected Guild Hall Acad. of Arts, 1985—. Mem. Authors Guild, Inc., Century Assn. Office: Janklow & Nesbit Attn Ms Lynn Nesbit 598 Madison Ave New York NY 10021

GOLDSMITH, BARBARA CECILE, sculptor, curator; b. Chgo., June 8, 1938; d. Arthur and Sarah (Emmerman) Gitler; m. Morton Goldsmith, Sept. 12, 1959; children: Marc Richard, Lesley Sue Nemzoff. BFA, U. Ill., 1960; cert., Sch. Art Inst. Chgo., 1990; student, Evanston (Ill.) Art Ctr., 1976-80, U. Minn., 1989. Cert. tchr., Ill. Art tchr. mid. and secondary schs., 1960-65; curator Noyes Cultural Art Ctr. Gallery, 1983—, Evanston Art Ctr., 1976; with Art Advance, Inc., 1992; bd. dirs. Skokie (Ill.) Northshore Sculpture Park, 1993—; com. mem. Evanston Art Coun., 1983—; mem. exhbn. com. Evanston Arts Ctr., 1986—. One-woman shows include North-care Ctr., Evanston, 1981, Loyd Shin Gallery, Wilmette, Ill., 1987; exhibited in group shows at Spertus Mus. Judaica, 1981-82, 88, 90, Dellora A. Norris Cultural Arts Ctr., St. Charles, Ill., 1982, Livertyville Art Ctr., 1982-83, Countryside Gallery, 1982, Peace Mus., Chgo., 1984, Grove St. Gallery, Evanston, 1984, Minn. Art Inst., 1984, U. Wis., 1984, Burpee Art Mus., Rockford, Ill., 1985, Triton Coll., River Grove, Ill., 1985, Alliance Gallery, Ft. Wayne, Ind., 1986, 87, 88, 89, 90, David Adler Cultural Ctr., 1988, 90, Noyes Cultural Arts Ctr. Gallery, Evanston, 1988, 93, 96, South Bend (Ind.) Art Ctr., 1988, 89, 90, Arc Gallery, Chgo., 1990, Spertus Mus., Chgo., 1990, Galesburg (Ill.) Art Ctr., 1990, Evanston Art Ctr., 1990, 94, Elgin (Ill.) Coll., 1991, Signature Gallery, Stoughton, Wis., 1991, 92, 93, 94, Uhlein Peters Gallery, Milw., 1992, Calumet City (Ill.) Gallery, 1993, Northwest Cultural Coun. Gallery, Rolling Meadows, Ill., 1994, Suburban Fine Arts Ctr., Highland Park, Ill., 1994, 96, Sch. Art Inst. Chgo., 1994, Friendship Village Corp. Gallery, Schaumberg, Ill., 1995, Norris Gallery, St. Charles, 1996, Noyes Cultural Art Ctr., Evanston, 1996, 97, Chgo. Cultural Ctr., 1998, The Three Arts Club, Chgo., 1998, Time-Life Bldg., Chgo., 1998, Gallery 510, Decatur, Ill, 1999, James R. Thompson Ctr., Chgo., 1999, others; commd. Stockholm, 1993, Lake Geneva, Wis., 1993, Skokie Northshore Sculpture Park, 1994; also pvt. and corp. collections. Recipient award for extraordinary dedication and profl. curatorial experties Evanston Arts Coun., 1997, Mayors Arts awards, Evanston. Home: 9055 Keystone Ave Skokie IL 60076-1723

GOLDSMITH, BILLY JOE, real estate broker; b. Blum, Tex., Nov. 6, 1933; s. John T. and Gladys Aileen (Curlee) G.; m. Jean Elizabeth Wendel, Oct. 20, 1962; 1 child, Anne. BS, Tex. A&M U., 1955. Asst., county agrl. agt. Harris County Tex. Extension Svc., Houston, 1957-64; mgr. Rice Coun., Houston, 1964-75, exec. v.p., 1975-95, ret., 1995; owner, broker real estate co. Houston, 1995—; owner Goldsmith Realty, Houston, Bill Goldsmith Agrl. Consulting. Arena dir. Houston Livestock Show and Rodeo, 1966-73; pres. Houston br. Prevent Blindness Tex. With U.S. Army, 1955-57. Internat. Rice Festival honoree, 1992. Mem. Tex. Cattle Raisers Assn., Southwestern Cattle Raisers Assn., Nat. Cattlemen's Assn., Houston Livestock Show and Rodeo Rancher, Res. Officer Assn., Harris County Ext. Bd. Advisors. Home: 5826 Cheena Dr Houston TX 77096-5928

GOLDSMITH, BRAM, banker; b. Chgo., Feb. 22, 1923; s. Max L. and Bertha (Gittelsohn) G.; m. Elaine Maltz; children: Bruce, Russell. Student, Herzl Jr. Coll., 1940, U. Ill., 1941-42. Asst. v.p. Pioneer-Atlas Liquor Co., Chgo., 1945-47; pres. Winston Lumber and Supply Co., East Chicago, Ind., 1947-50; v.p. Medal Distilled Products, Inc., Beverly Hills, Calif., 1950-75; pres. Buckeye Realty and Mgmt. Corp., Beverly Hills, 1952-75; exec. v.p. Buckeye Constrn. Co., Inc., Beverly Hills, 1952-75; chmn. bd., CEO City Nat. Corp., Beverly Hills, 1975-95; CEO City Nat. Bank, 1975-96, chmn., 1975-95; chmn. CNC, 1995—. Mem., bd. dirs. L.A. Philharm. Assn.; bd. dirs. Cedars/Sinai Med. Ctr.; pres. Jewish Fedn. Coun. Greater L.A., 1969-70; nat. chmn. United Jewish Appeal, 1970-74; regional chmn. United Crusade, 1976; co-chmn. bd. dirs. NCCJ; chmn. Am. com. Weizman Inst. Sci. With signal corps U.S. Army, 1942-45. Mem. Masons, Hillcrest Country Club, Balboa Bay Club. Office: City Nat Corp 400 N Roxbury Dr Beverly Hills CA 90210-5021

GOLDSMITH, CAROLINE L., arts executive; b. N.Y.C., Nov. 25, 1925; d. Reuben and Gladys (Garf) Steinholz; m. Mortimer M. Lerner, Dec. 1, 1946 (div. Nov., 1968); children: Lawrence, David; m. John F. Goldsmith, Dec. 1973. BA, Cornell U., 1946. Pres. dir. Gallery Passport Ltd., N.Y.C., 1960-66; sr. v.p. Ruder Finn Arts and Comm. Counselors, N.Y.C., 1966—; exec. dir. Arttable, Inc., N.Y.C., 1980-94. Mem. Cmty. Bd., N.Y.C., 1987-95. Mem. Am. Assn. Mus., Am. Fedn. Arts, Internat. Coun. Mus. Coll. Art Assn., Smithsonian Inst., Century Assn., Internat. Women's Forum (bd. dirs.). Democrat. Jewish. Avocations: theater, museums. Home: 375 W End Ave New York NY 10024-6568 Office: Ruder Finn Inc 301 E 57th St New York NY 10022-2900

GOLDSMITH, CATHY ELLEN, special education educator; b. N.Y.C., Feb. 18, 1947; d. Eli D. and Gertrude A. G. BS, NYU, 1968, MA in Elem. Edn., 1971, MA in Ednl. Psychology, 1974. Cert. phys. handicapped, K-6 elem. edn. tchr., N.Y. 2d grade tchr. N.Y.C. Bd. Edn., 1968-69, tchr. learning disabled students (spl. edn.), 1969-86, tchr. emotionally disturbed learning disabled students, 1986-87, tchr. learning disabled students, 1987-88, tchr. trainable retarded students, 1988—. Represented in permanent collections Bobst Libr. NYU. Recipient Charles Oscar Maas Essay award in Am. History, 1968, Disting. Alumni Svc. award NYU, 1987. Mem. Internat. Profl. Assn. in Edn., Coun. for Exceptional Children, Coun. for Learning Disabilities, Found. for Exceptional Children, Orton Dyslexia Soc., N.Y. State-N.Y.C. Assn. Tchrs. Handicapped, NYU Alumni Assn. (past rec. sec., v.p.), NYU Alumni Assn., NYU Alumnae Club (v.p.), Pi Lambda Theta (past pres., past historian). Home: 3 Washington Sq Village New York NY 10012-1836

GOLDSMITH, CLIFFORD HENRY, former tobacco company executive; b. Leipzig, Germany, Sept. 6, 1919; came to U.S., 1940, naturalized, 1943; s. Conrad and Elise (Stahl) G.; m. Katherine W. Kaynis; children: Corinne Elizabeth Goldsmith Dickinson, Audrey Jane Goldsmith Kubie, Alexandra Eve. Grad., Bradford (Eng.) U., 1939. Technologist, Glenside Mills Corp., Skaneateles, N.Y., 1940-41; supt. Falls Yarn Mills, Woonsocket, R.I., 1941-42, Aldon Spinning Mills, Talcotville, Conn., 1942-43; with Benson & Hedges Co., 1945-53, plant mgr., 1945-53; with Philip Morris, Inc., 1954-84, pres., 1978-83, vice chmn., 1983-84; now prin. Prendel Co. Chmn. emeritus Nat. Multiple Sclerosis Soc.; trustee, treas. Mt. Sinai-NYU Med. Ctr. and Health Sys.; vice chmn. Poly. Univ.; chmn. FOJP Svc. Corp. With inf. AUS, 1943-45. Mem. Textile Inst. (Manchester, Eng., assoc.), Commonwealth Club (Richmond), Univ. Club (N.Y.), Century Club (N.Y. Office: 900 Park Ave New York NY 10021-0231

GOLDSMITH, DALE CAMPBELL, university official; b. Chgo., May 3, 1937; s. Oliver and Evangeline (Carlson) G.; m. Catherine Mae Choguill, Oct. 13, 1959; children: John, Katherine, Janet, Joy. AB, Princeton U., 1959; MA, U. Chgo., 1964, PhD, 1973. Ordained to ministry Presbyn. Ch., 1963. Prof. biblical langs., lit. Bapt. Sem. Mex., Mexico City, 1966-68; prof. philosophy, religion McPherson (Kans.) Coll., 1969-86, v.p. academics, 1986-94; v.p. acad. affairs Okla. Panhandle State U., Goodwell, 1996—. Author: New Testament Ethics, 1988. Mem. Soc. Biblical Lit. Home: 3 Pheasant Run Goodwell OK 73939-9734 Office: Okla Panhandle State U Goodwell OK 73939

GOLDSMITH, ETHEL FRANK, medical social worker; b. Chgo., May 31, 1919; d. Theodore and Rose (Falk) Frank; m. Julian Royce Goldsmith, Sept. 4, 1940; children: Richard, Susan, John. BA, U. Chgo., 1940. Lic. social worker, Ill. Liaison worker psychiat. consultation service U. Chgo. Hosp., 1964-68; med. social worker Wyler Children's Hosp., Chgo., 1968—. Treas. U. Chgo. Service League, 1958-62, chmn. camp Brueckner Farr Aux., 1966-72; pres. Bobs Roberts Hosp. Service Commn., 1962; bd. dirs. Richardson Wildlife Sanctary, 1988—; mem. Field Mus. Women's Bd., 1966—; bd. dirs. Hyde Park Art Ctr., 1964-82, Chgo. Commons Assn., 1967-77, Alumni Assn. Sch. Social Service Adminstrn., 1976-80, Self Help Home for Aged, 1985—. Recipient Alumni Citation Pub. Service, U. Chgo., 1972. Mem. Phi Beta Kappa. Home: 5631 S Blackstone Ave Chicago IL 60637-1827

GOLDSMITH, HOWARD, writer, consultant; b. N.Y.C., Aug. 24, 1945; s. Philip and Sophie (Feldman) G. B.A. with honors, CUNY, 1965; M.A. with honors, U. Mich., Ann Arbor, 1966. Research psychologist Mental Hygiene Clinic, Detroit, 1966-70; freelance writer Ency. Britannica Ednl. Corp., Chgo., 1970; writer, pvt. practice editorial cons. Flushing, N.Y., 1970—; editorial cons. Mountain View Ctr. for Environ. Edn., U. Colo., Boulder, 1970-85. Author poetry, plays, numerous short stories, books, novels including: The Whispering Sea, 1976, What Makes a Grumble Smile?, 1977, The Shadow and Other Strange Tales, 1977, Terror by Night, 1977, Spine-Chillers, 1978, Sooner Round the Corner, 1979, Invasion: 2200 A.D., 1979, The Ivy Plot, 1981, Three-Ring Inferno, 1982, Plaf Le Paresseux, 1982, Ninon, Miss Vison, 1982, Toufou Le Hibou, 1982, Fourtou Le Kangourou, 1982, The Tooth chicken, 1982, Mireille l'Abeille, 1982, Little Dog Lost, 1983, Stormy Day Together, 1983, The Sinister Circle, 1983, Shadow of Fear, 1983, Treasure Hunt, 1983, The Square, 1983, The Circle, 1983, The Contest, 1983, Welcome, Makoto!, 1983, Helpful Julio, 1984, The Secret of

Success, 1984, Pedro's Puzzling Birthday, 1984, Rosa's Prank, 1984, A Day of Fun, 1984, The Rectangle, 1984, Kirby the Kangaroo, 1985, Ollie the Owl, 1985, The Twiddle Twins' Haunted House, 1985, Young Ghosts, 1985, Von Geistern Besessen, 1987, The Further Adventures of Batman, 1989, Visions of Fantasy, 1989, The Pig and the Witch, 1990, The Mind-Stalkers, 1990, Spooky Stories, 1990, Little Quack and Baby Duckling, 1991, The Proust Syndrome, 1992, The President's Train, 1993, Thomas Edison Had A Bright Idea, 1993, The Day My Dad and I Got Mugged, 1993, Evil Tales of Evil Things, 1993, The Christmas Star, 1994, The Curiosity Kid, 1994, Tales of the Batman, 1995, Dream Weavers, 1996, The Gooey Chewy Contest, 1997, Science Through Stories, 1997, The Twiddle Twins' Music Box Mystery, 1997, The Twiddle Twins' Amusement Park Mystery, 1998, Science Through Stories (series), 1998, The Twiddle Twins' Single Footprint Mystery, 1999; contbg. editor: Children's Magic Window, 1987-90. Rackham predoctoral fellow U. Mich., 1966; recipient Phi Sigma Sci. award, 1966. Mem. Poets and Writers, Sci. Fiction Writers of Am., Soc. Children's Book Writers and Illustrators, Phi Beta Kappa, Psi Chi, Sigma Xi, Phi Kappa Phi. Avocations: classical music, book collecting, chess, old movies. Home: 41-07 Bowne St Apt 6B Flushing NY 11355-5629

GOLDSMITH, JACK LANDMAN, former retail company executive; b. Memphis, Apr. 10, 1910; s. Fred and Aimee (Landman) G.; m. Dorothy Metzger, Feb. 9, 1960; children—Joan Goldsmith Marks, Jack Landman; stepchildren—Larry, Melvin. Grad., Memphis Law Sch.; student, Washington U., St. Louis, N.Y. U. Dir. First Nat. Bank, 1946-71; With Federated Dept. Stores, Inc., 1959—, v.p., 1961—; ret. chmn. bd., chmn. exec. com. Goldsmith's Dept. Store; past dir. world trade adv. com. Dept. Commerce; mem. U.S. Trade Mission to Greece, 1957, to Austria, 1958; past pres. Cavendis Trading Corp., N.Y.C. Former trustee Brooks Art Gallery, Memphis; pres. Goldsmith Found.; past bd. dirs. Bapt. Hosp., Memphis; del. to Tenn. Constnl. Conv., 1953. Served to maj. USAR, 1931-41, U.S. Army, 1942-45. Mem. Nat. Retail Mchts. Coun. (past pres.), Tenn. Retail Mchts. Coun., Downtown Assn. (pres.). Clubs: Rotary (Memphis) (past dir.), One Hundred (Memphis). Home: 601 Putting Green Ln Longboat Key FL 34228-3523

GOLDSMITH, JERRY, composer; b. L.A., Feb. 10, 1929; m. Carol Sheinkopf. Student, Los Angeles City Coll.; studies with, Jakob Gimpel, Mario Castelnuovo-Tedesco; MusD, Berklee Coll. Music, 1990. Composer: (radio scores) Romance, Suspense, CBS Radio, (TV scores) Twilight Zone, Gen. Elec. Theatre, Doctor Kildare, Gunsmoke, Climax, Playhouse 90, Studio One, Star Trek: Voyager (Emmy award, 1995), (film scores, partial list) (debut) Black Patch, 1956, Lonely Are The Brave, 1961, Freud (Acad. award nomination), 1962, The Stripper, 1962, Lilies of the Field, 1963, The Prize, 1963, Seven Days in May, 1963, In Harm's Way, 1964, The Man From UNCLE, 1965, Von Ryan's Express, 1965, A Patch of Blue (Acad. award nomination), 1965, The Blue Max, 1965, Our Man Flint, 1965, Seconds, 1965, Stagecoach, 1965, The Sand Pebbles (Acad. award nomination), 1966, In Like Flint, 1967, Planet of the Apes (Acad. award nomination), 1968, The Ballad of Cable Hogue, 1969, Tora! Tora! Tora!, 1970, Patton (Acad. award nomination), 1970, Wild Rovers, 1971, The Other, 1972, The Red Pony (Emmy award), 1972, Papillon (Acad. award nomination), 1973, QB VII (Emmy award), 1974, Chinatown (Acad. award nomination), 1974, The Reincarnation of Peter Proud, 1974, Logans Run, 1975, The Wind and the Lion (Acad. award nomination), 1976, The Omen (Acad. award winner, Grammy award nomination, two N.B. nominations), 1976, Islands in the Stream, 1976, Mac Arthur, 1977, Coma, 1977, The Boys from Brazil (Acad. award nomination), 1978, Damien-Omen II, 1978, Alien, 1979, Babe (Emmy award), Masada (Emmy award), 1981, Star Trek: The Motion Picture (Acad. award nomination), 1979, The Final Conflict, 1981, Outland, 1981, Raggedy Man, 1981, Mrs. Brisby: The Secret of NIMH, 1982, Poltergeist (Acad. award nomination, Edgar Allan Poe award), 1982, First Blood, 1982, Twilight Zone-The Movie, 1983, Psycho II, 1983, Under Fire (Acad. award nomination), 1983, Gremlins (Saturn award), 1984, Legend (European version), 1985, Explorers, 1985, Rambo: First Blood II, 1985, Poltergeist II: The Other Side, 1986, Hoosiers (Acad. award nomination), 1986, Innerspace, 1987, Extreme Prejudice, 1987, Rambo III, 1988, Criminal Law, 1989, The 'Burbs, 1989, Leviathan, 1989, Star Trek V: The Final Frontier, 1989, Total Recall, 1990, Gremlins 2: The New Batch, 1990, The Russia House, 1990, Not Without My Daughter, 1991, Sleeping With the Enemy, 1991, Medicine Man, 1991, Love Field, 1992, Mom and Dad Save the World, 1992, Basic Instinct, 1992 (Acad. award nomination, Golden Globe nomination), Mr. Baseball, 1992, Forever Young, 1992, Matinee, 1992, The Vanishing, 1993, Dennis the Menace, 1993, Malice, 1993, Rudy, 1993, Six Degrees of Separation, 1993, Angie, 1994, Bad Girls, 1994, The Shadow, 1994, I.Q., 1994, The River Wild, 1994, First Knight, 1995, Congo, 1995, Powder, 1995, City Hall, 1995, Executive Decision, 1996, Chain Reaction, 1996, The Ghost and the Darkness, 1996, Star Trek: First Contact, 1996, Fierce Creatures, 1996, L.A. Confidential, 1997, Air Force One, 1997, The Edge, 1997, Deep Rising, 1997, U.S. Marshals, 1998 (Golden Globe nomination), Small Soldiers, 1998, Star Trek: Insurrection, 1998, The Mummy, 1999, The 13th Warrior, 1999, The Haunting of Hill House, 1999; debuted as concert condr. with Christus Apollo, So. Calif. Chamber Symphony, 1969; guest condr. Royal Philharm. Orch., London, 1975, 87, Glendale Symphony, 1975, USAF Band, 1976, 83, Okla. Symphony Orch., 1983, San Diego Pops Orch., 1985, London Philharmonia, 1987, Pitts. Symphony, 1988, Ala. Symphony, 1988, Nat. Symphony, Washington, 1988, Indpls. Symphony, 1989, Ft. Worth Symphony, 1989, Detroit Symphony, London Symphony, 1989, Utah Symphony, 1990, El Paso (Tex.) Symphony, 1990, Syracuse Symphony, 1990, Toronto (Ont., Can.) Symphony, 1990, Balt. Symphony, 1990, New World Symphony, Miami, Fla., 1991, Cin. Symphony, 1991, Utah Symphony, 1991, Memphis Symphony, 1992, Milw. Symphony, 1993, Detroit Symphony, 1993, Oulu (Finland) City Orchestra, 1993, Colo. Symphony, 1993, Madrid (Spain) Symphony, 1993, BBC Concert Orchestra, Eng., 1994, San Diego Symphony Orchestra, 1994, Toledo Symphony, 1995, San Jose Symphony, 1997, Pasadena POPS Orch., 1997, New York FILMharmonic Orchestra., 1998, Seville (Spain) Symphony, 1998, Kanagawa (Japan) Philharmonic Orchestra., 1998, Royal Scottish National Orchestra, 1999, London Symphony Orchestra, 1999; ballet scores include Othello, 1971, A Patch of Blue, 1970, Capricorn One, 1989; premier Music For Orchestra with St. Louis Symphony, 1971-72. Recipient Max Steiner award Nat. Film Soc., 1982, 1st ann. Richard Kirk award BMI, 1987, Golden Score award Am. Soc. Music Arrangers, 1990, Career Achievement award Soc. for Preservation of Film Music, 1993, 1st Am. Music Legend award from Variety, 1995, 17 Acad. award nominations, 8 Emmy award nominations, 7 Grammy award nominations, 8 Golden Globe nominations. Office: c/o Savitsky & Co 1901 Ave Of Stars Ste 1450 Los Angeles CA 90067-6087

GOLDSMITH, JOCELYN STONE, state employment professional; b. Columbus, Ohio, Aug. 26, 1933; d. Roy J. Stone and Lillian (Bedwinek) Stone Friedland; m. Daniel J. Goldsmith, Mar. 15, 1953 (div. Nov. 1972); children: Debra Ann Goldsmith Wilson, Jeffrey Robert (dec.), David Michael; m. Chester G. Bandman, Sept. 20, 1972 (dec. Jan. 1995). BS in Bus., Franklin U., 1980, BS in Employee Assistance Counseling, 1989. User svcs. coord. R.G. Barry Corp., Columbus, 1974-82; claims mgr. Ohio Bur. Employment Svcs., Columbus, 1983—; Adopt-A-Sch. coord. Columbus Pub. schs., Greater Columbus C. of C., 1979—. Recipient plaque Ohio Sch. Partnership, 1995. Mem. Am. Soc. Women Accts., Internat. Assn. Personnel in Employment Security. Jewish. Avocations: reading, enjoying plays, concerts and ballet. Office: Ohio Bur Employement Svcs 145 S Front St Columbus OH 43215-4116

GOLDSMITH, JOHN ANTON, linguist, educator; b. N.Y.C., Nov. 7, 1951; s. Simon Albert and Thelma Margaret (Ettesvold) G.; m. Jessie Elizabeth Pinkham, Nov. 20, 1982; children: Elizabeth, Paul, Julia. BA, Swarthmore Coll., 1972; PhD, MIT, 1976. Asst., assoc. then prof. Ind. U., Bloomington, 1976-84; prof. U. Chgo., 1984—, Edward Carson Waller Disting. Svc. prof., 1997—; bd. dirs. U. Chgo. Press, 1990-94. Author: Autosegmental and Metrical Phonology, 1990, (with G. Huck) Ideology and Linguistic Theory, 1995; editor, translator Syntax and Human Experience, 1991; editor: The Last Phonological Rule, 1993, Handbook of Phonological Theory, 1995. Mem. Linguistics Soc. Am. (mem. exec. com. 1988-91). Office: U Chgo Dept Linguistics 1010 E 59th St Chicago IL 60637-1512

GOLDSMITH, JOHN H., investment company executive. Chmn. bd., CEO Tucker Anthony Inc., N.Y.C. Office: Tucker Anthony Inc 200 Liberty St Fl 3 New York NY 10281-1073*

GOLDSMITH, JULIAN ROYCE, geochemist, educator; b. Chgo., Feb. 26, 1918; s. Mitchel and Cecelia (Kallis) G.; m. Ethel J. Frank, Sept. 4, 1940; children—Richard, Susan (Mrs. Kent Wooldridge), John. S.B., U. Chgo., 1940, Ph.D., 1947. Research chemist Corning Glass Works, N.Y., 1942-46; mem. faculty U. Chgo., 1946 —, prof. geochemistry, 1958—, assoc. dean div. phys. scis., 1960-72, chmn. dept. geophys. scis., 1963-71, Charles E. Merriam Distinguished Service prof., 1969-88, educator emeritus, 1988—; Mem. earth-sci.-panel NSF, 1958-60, chmn., 1960, mem. nat. sci. bd., 1964-70; mem. U.S. Nat. Com. on Geology, 1972-75; cons. Lawrence Radiation Lab., U.S. Geol. Survey; mem. Gov.'s Sci. Adv. Com., 1989—. Author articles in field.; Co-editor: Jour. Geology, 1957-62; cons. editor: Ency. Sci. and Tech. Chmn. of gov. bd. Lab. Schs. U. Chgo., 1959-60. Fellow AAAS, Mineral. Soc. Am. (counsellor 1960-62, award 1955, v.p. 1968-69, pres. 1970-71, Roebling medal 1988), Geol. Soc. Am. (counsellor 1968-71, v.p. 1973-74, pres. 1974-75), Am. Geophys. Union (Harry H. Hess medal 1987), Am. Acad. Arts and Scis.; mem. Geochem. Soc. (charter v.p. 1955, pres. 1965-66), Renaissance Soc. (pres. 1966- 68), Am. Chem. Soc., Am. Crystallographic Assn., Am. Ceramic Soc., Mineral. Soc. Gt. Brit., Phi Beta Kappa, Sigma Xi. Club: Quadrangle (v.p. 1973, pres. 1974). Home: 5631 S Blackstone Ave Chicago IL 60637-1827 Office: U Chgo Dept Geophys Scis 5734 S Ellis Ave Chicago IL 60637-1434

GOLDSMITH, LEE SELIG, lawyer, physician; b. N.Y.C., Nov. 18, 1939; s. Isidore L. and Elsie (Friedman) G.; m. Arlene F. Applebaum, June 10, 1962; children: Ian Lance, Helena Ayn, Jordan Seth. B.S. with honors, N.Y. U., 1960, M.D., 1964, LL.B., 1967. Bar: N.Y. 1968, N.J. 1974. Assoc. clk. Speiser, Shumate, Geoghan Krause & Rheingold, 1965-70; individual practice law, 1970-72; mem. firm Lea, Goldberg, Goldsmith & Spellen, N.Y.C., 1972-74; of counsel Newark, 1974-77; mem. firm Goldsmith, Cohen & Simon, 1976-77, Goldsmith & Cohen, 1977-80, Greenstone, Greenstone, Naishuler & Goldsmith, Newark, 1981, Goldsmith & Richman, P.C., N.Y.C., 1981—, Goldsmith & Richman, P.A., Englewood, N.J., 1981—; adj. prof. law Fordham U., 1976-88 ; spl. counsel N.Y. State Senate health com., 1971; lectr. Practicing Law Inst.; chmn. Am. Bd. Law in Medicine, 1984-85. Author: Malpractice Made Easy, 1976, Hospital Liability Law, 1972, 2d edit. 1979; editor: Jour. Legal Medicine, 1978-81, Legal Aspects of Med. Practice, 1981—, Medical Malpractice, Guide to Medical Issues, 7 vols., 1986; contbr. articles to various publs. Fellow Am. Coll. Legal Medicine (bd. govs. 1982, pres.-elect 1986-87, pres. 1987-88, chmn. com. legis. rev.), N.Y. Acad. Medicine; mem. AMA, N.Y. Med. Soc., N.Y. County Med. Soc., Assn. of Bar of City of N.Y. (sec. sci. and law com. 1985—), Assn. Trial Lawyers Am. (sec. N.J. chpt. 1988-89, treas. 1989-90, 2d. v.p. 1990-91, 1st v.p. 1991-92, pres. 1993-94, treas. N.J. PAC 1996—), N.Y. Bar Assn., N.Y. Trial Lawyers Assn. Home: 1 Kelwynne Rd Scarsdale NY 10583-4507 Office: Goldsmith & Richman PA 747 3rd Ave New York NY 10017-2803 also: 140 Sylvan Ave Englewd Clfs NJ 07632-2502

GOLDSMITH, MERWIN, actor, theater director; b. Detroit, Aug. 7, 1937; s. Max Harold and Alice Flora (Singer) G.; m. Susan Leigh Benson, Mar. 1966 (div. 1969); m. Barbara Parry, July, 1996. BA in Theater, UCLA, 1960; student, Bristol Old Vic Theatre Sch., Bristol. Appeared in (stage prodns.) Auntie Mame, 1958, License to Murder, 1964, The Tempest, Trap for a Lonely Man, Phaedra, Gentlemen Prefer Blondes, 1965, Billy Budd, 1967, Fiddler on the Roof, 1968-69, Minnie's Boys, 1970, Much Ado About Nothing, Pal Joey, 1973, Last of the Red Hot Lovers, 1974, Hedda Gabler, 1975, Dirty Linen, 1977, Oklahoma!, 1978, Death of a Salesman, The Importance of Being Ernest, 1982, Hello Dolly!, 1983, La Boheme, 1984, The Taming of the Shrew, 1985, Hamlet, 1986, Me & My Girl, 1988, 89, Grand Hotel, The Musical, 1991, Merry Widow, 1991, Learned Ladies, 1991, Ain't Broadway Grand, 1993, The Little Prince, 1993, An Imaginary Life, 1993, Beau Jest, 1994, After-Play, 1995, By Jeeves, 1996; (films) Shamus, 1972, Boardwalk, 1979, So Fine, 1981, Blue Heaven, 1984, Making Mr. Right, 1986, Cadillac Man, 1991, Cop Gives Waitress Two Million Dollar Tip, 1993, Quiz Show, 1993, Rounders, 1998, Lazarus and The Hurricane, 1998, Company Man, 1999, Joe Gould's Secret, 1999, (TV) All My Children, Ryan's Hope, The Guiding Light, Search for Tomorrow, As the World Turns, Another World, Wide World of Mystery, The Connection; dir. Vanities, 1980. Served with USAFR. Nominated Best Actor in a Mus. award Variety Critics Poll, 1972, Best Supporting Actor in a Mus. award, 1973; nominee Best Actor Mus., Joseph Jefferson Awards, 1972. Mem. AFTRA, SAG, NARAS (Grammy awards voter), Actors Equity Assn., The Players Club, The Century Assn. Avocations: photography, studying French and Hebrew. Office: Silver & Massetti & Szatmary Ltd 145 W 45th St New York NY 10036-4008

GOLDSMITH, MICHAEL ALLEN, oncologist, educator; b. Bronx, N.Y., Jan. 28, 1946; s. Walter and Bertha (Tannenberg) G.; m. Judith Harriet Plaut, June 6, 1971; children: Sharon, Esther, Eva, Steven. BA, Yeshiva U., 1967; MD, Albert Einstein Coll. Medicine, 1971. Diplomate Am. Bd. Internal Medicine. Intern Bronx Mcpl. Hosp. Ctr., 1971-72; staff assoc. Nat. Cancer Inst., Bethesda, Md., 1972-74; resident in medicine Mt. Sinai Hosp., N.Y.C., 1974-75, fellow in neoplastic diseases, 1975-77, asst. clin. prof. medicine and neoplastic diseases, 1977—; attending physician Oncology Consultants, P.C., N.Y.C., 1977—; reviewer Jour. AMA, 1988-90, New Eng. Jour. Medicine, 1995—. Contbr. articles to med. jours. Vice-pres. Congregation Orach Chaim, N.Y.C., 1978-83. Lt. comdr. USPHS, 1972-74. Fellow ACP; mem. Am. Soc. Clin. Oncology, Am. Assn. Cancer Rsch. Achievements include research in new anticancer drugs. Office: Oncology Cons PC 1045 5th Ave New York NY 10028-0138

GOLDSMITH, PAUL FELIX, physics and astronomy educator; b. Washington, Nov. 5, 1948; s. Raymond William and Selma Evelyn (Fine) G.; m. Sheryl E. Reiss, June 5, 1988. AB, U. Calif., Berkeley, 1969, PhD., 1975. Mem. tech. staff AT&T Bell Labs., Holmdel, N.J., 1975-77; asst. prof. U. Mass., Amherst, 1977-82, assoc. prof., 1982-85, prof. physics and astronomy, 1985-92; prof. astronomy, dir. Nat. Astronomy and Ionosphere Ctr. Cornell U., Ithaca, N.Y., 1993—; cons. MIT Lincoln Lab., Lexington, Mass., 1977-80; v.p. R & D Millitech Corp., South Deerfield, Mass., 1983-92. Author: Quasioptical Systems, 1998; editor: Instrumentation and Techniques for Radio Astronomy, 1988; contbr. articles on radio astronomy and millimeter and submillimeter wavelength tech. to profl. jours. Fellow IEEE; mem. Microwave Theory Tech. Soc. of IEEE (mem. spkr.'s bur. 1989-90, Disting. lectr. 1992-93), Am. Astron. Soc. Office: Nat Astronomy & Ionsphere Ctr Cornell University Space Sciences Building Ithaca NY 14853

GOLDSMITH, ROBERT LEWIS, youth association magazine executive; b. N.Y.C., Jan. 9, 1928; s. Arthur and Elizabeth (Kohn) G.; m. Joan M. Hartman, 1976. B.S., NYU, 1950. Advt. promotion mgr. Esquire, Inc., N.Y.C., 1952-53; advt. dir. Schine Hotels, N.Y.C., 1953; promotion dir. Dell Pub. Co., N.Y.C., 1953-58, Outdoor Life Mag., N.Y.C., 1958-65; assoc. dir. mag. div. Boy Scouts Am., N.Y.C., 1965-89, ret., 1989; N.Am. rep. Ea. Art Report, London, 1991—. Bd. dirs. Inst. Asian Studies, N.Y.C., 1981—, assoc. dir., 1989—, pres., 1995-99; mem. Friends of Asian Art, Met. Mus. Art, Oriental Art Coun. Bklyn. Mus., Indpls Mus. Art, life trustee. Mem. N.Y. Sales Execs. Club, Mktg. Comms. Execs. Assn., Am. Mktg. Assn., Asia Soc., Japan Soc., China Inst. Am., NYU Club (bd. govs., v.p. exec. com.). Office: 141 E 44th St New York NY 10017-4006 *The general purpose I have had in mind is to leave the world no worse a place than I found it, and to try in my own way to make improvements wherever possible. To help people, to teach them to help themselves, to combat ignorance, to give material and emotional support to those who need, to the extent that is possible... are all factors of great importance. I have tried to learn about a wide variety of subjects and to use that knowledge to make both my business life and my personal life more satisfying and more productive.*

GOLDSMITH, STANLEY ALAN, lawyer; b. N.Y.C., Oct. 18, 1956. AB magna cum laude, Dartmouth Coll., Hanover, N.H., 1977; JD, Vanderbilt U., 1980. Bar: Ohio 1980, U.S. Dist. Ct. (so. dist.) Ohio 1980, Fla. 1983, U.S. Ct. Appeals (6th cir.) 1983, U.S. Dist. Ct. (mid. dist.) Fla. 1984, U.S. Ct. Appeals (11th cir.) 1984, U.S. Supreme Ct. 1990. Assoc. Porter, Wright, Morris & Arthur, Dayton, Ohio, 1980-83; pvt. practice, Sarasota, Fla., 1983—. Mem. ABA, Fla. Bar, Sarasota County Bar Assn. Avocations: swimming, bicycling, travel, cooking. Office: 1605 Main St Ste 1001 Sarasota FL 34236-5861

GOLDSMITH, STANLEY JOSEPH, nuclear medicine physician, educator; b. Bklyn., Aug. 17, 1937; s. Jack and Mae (Greenzweig) G.; m. Miriam Schulman, June 6, 1959; children: Ira, Arthur, Beth, Mark. BA, Columbia U., 1958; MD, SUNY-Downstate Med. Ctr., 1962. Diplomate: Am. Bd. Internal Medicine (endocrinology and metabolism), Am. Bd. Nuclear Medicine (bd. dirs. 1990-96, treas. 1995-96). Intern SUNY-Kings County Med. Center, Bklyn., 1962-63, resident, 1965-66, chief resident, 1966-67; fellow in endocrinology Mt. Sinai Hosp., N.Y.C., 1967-68, dir. physics nuclear medicine, 1973-92; Clin. Dir. Nuclear Medicine, Meml. Sloan Kettering Cancer Ctr., N.Y.C., 1992-95; dir. nuclear medicine N.Y. Hosp.-Cornell Med. Ctr., 1995—; rsch. assoc. radioisotope svc. Bronx (N.Y.) VA Hosp., 1968-69; dir. nuclear medicine, asst. dir. endocrine dept. Nassau County Med. Ctr., East Meadow, N.Y., 1969-73; asst. prof. medicine radiology SUNY-Stony Brook Health Sci. Ctr., 1971-73, asst. prof. medicine Mt. Sinai Sch. Medicine, 1973-76, assoc. prof., 1976-84, prof. clin. medicine, 1985-91, prof. radiology and medicine, 1991-92, Cornell U. Med. Coll., 1993—, prof. radiology, medicine; bd. dirs. Capintec, Inc., Ramsey, N.J.; rsch. collaborator Brookhaven Nat. Labs., Upton, N.Y., 1971-75; cons. nuclear medicine; cons. dept. health State of N.Y., 1973-77, Health Svcs. Adminstrn., N.Y.C., 1976; mem. radiopharm. adv. com. FDA, 1987-90, low level radioactive waste diposal site commn., N.Y., 1987-95. Assoc. editor Newline 1984-93, Jour. Nuclear Medicine, editor-in-chief, 1993-98; mem. editorial bds. Am. Jour. Cardiology, 1978-82, European Jour. Nuclear Medicine, 1993-98; Cancer Biotherapy and Radiopharm., 1998—, reviewer: Israeli Jour. Med. Scis., 1979, Jour. AMA, 1983-92, Jour. Am. Coll. Cardiology, 1984-94, Jour. Nuclear Medicine, 1989-93. Capt. U.S. Army, 1963-65. Fellow Am. Coll. Cardiology, ACP, Am. Coll. Nuclear Physicians (chmn. nuclear med. tech. affairs, chmn. Washington oversight com.), N.Y. Acad. Medicine; mem. AAAS, Am. Fedn. Clin. Rsch., Am. Coll. Radiology, Endocrine Soc., N.Y. Acad. Scis., Radiol. Soc. N.Am., Soc. Nuclear Medicine (trustee 1982-84, pres.-elect 1984-85, pres. 1985-86, chmn. govt. rels. com. 1991-93, sec. Greater N.Y. chpt. 1975-78, pres. 1979-80, chmn. govt. rels. com. 1991-93). Home: 72 Ivy Way Port Washington NY 11050-3817 Office: NY Hosp Cornell Med Ctr 525 E 68th St New York NY 10021-4885

GOLDSMITH, STEPHEN, mayor; b. Indpls., Dec. 12, 1946; s. Joseph F. and Marjorie (Holmes) G.; m. Margaret McDaniel, June 15, 1988; children: Reid, Elizabeth, Devereaux, Olivia; AB, Wabash Coll., 1968, hon. LLD, 1993, JD with honors, U. Mich., 1971. Pvt. practice atty., 1972-78, 91; dep. corp. counsel, City of Indpls., 1974-75; chief trial dep., City of Indpls., 1976-78; pros. atty., Marion County, Ind., 1979-90; mayor Indpls., 1991—; chmn. Ctr. Civic Innovation, Manhattan Inst.; adv. bd. Bur. Justice and Stats.; chmn. Indpls. & Ctrl. Ind. Tech. Partnership; co-chmn. domestic strategy group, Aspen Inst.; hon. co-chmn. Nat. Coun. Pub.-Pvt. Partnerships; mem. def. reform group, Dept. Def.; various adv. and peer rev. bds., Nat. Inst. Justice; adv. bd. Office Juvenile Justice and Delinquency; adv. bd. Pres.'s Commn. on Missing and Exploited Children; vice chmn. Pres.'s Commn. on Model State Drug Laws; rsch. fellow in criminal justice & mgmt., Harvard U. Kennedy Sch. Govt.; asst. and adj. prof. I.U.,; adj. fellow The Manhattan Inst.; adj. faculty, Columbia U. Author: The Twenty-first Century City; editor (jour.) Prosecutor's Perspective; contbr. Jerusalem Post, Harvard Bus. Rev., Wall St. Jour., others. USAR, 1968-74. Office: Office of Mayor 2501 City-County Bldg 200 E Washington St Indianapolis IN 46204-3307*

GOLDSMITH, WERNER, mechanical engineering educator; b. Düsseldorf, Rhineland, Germany, May 23, 1924; came to U.S., 1938; s. Siegfried and Margarethe (Grunewald) G.; m. Adrienne Kessler (div.); children: Stephen M., Andrea Jo; m. Penelope I. Alexander, Oct. 5, 1973; 1 child, Remy M. BSME, U. Tex., 1944, MSME, 1945; PhDME, U. Calif., Berkeley, 1949. Registered mech. and safety engr., Calif. Engr. Westinghouse Electric Co., Pitts. and Phila., 1945-47; instr. div. engrng. design U. Calif., Berkeley, 1947-49, asst. prof., 1949-55, assoc. prof. dept. mech. engrng., 1955-60, prof., 1960-87, prof. emeritus in active svc., 1988-97, prof. Grad. Sch., 1997—; mech. engr. U.S. Naval Weapons Ctr., China Lake, Calif., 1951—; instr. math. U. Pitts., 1945-46; lectr. in engrng. U. Pa., Phila., 1946-47; engrng. cons. govt., industry, legal profession, Berkeley, 1953—; chmn. head injury com. NIH, Bethesda, Md., 1966-70; cons. Fuze div. U.S. Army, Picatinny Arsenal, N.J., 1970-76; panel mem. Nat. Rsch. Coun. Rev. Armanent and Materials Disectorate of Army Rsch. Labs.; vis. prof. Technion, Haifa, Israel, Nat. Poly. U., Athens, Greece, Tokyo Inst. Tech., East China Inst. Tech., Nanjing, 1968—, T.H., Eindhoven, Holland, Inst. Su. Matériaux et Construction Mécanique, St. Ouen, France. Author: A History of the Department of Mechanical Engineering, University of California, Berkeley, 1997; (monograph) Impact, 1960, reprint, 1999; co-author, co-editor: Introduction to Bioengineering, 1996; contbr. over 225 articles on impact, wave propagation, rock mechanics, biomechanics, head and neck injuries, protective devices, exptl. mechs. to profl. jours.; also numerous tech. reports. Guggenheim fellow, 1953-54, Fulbright rsch. fellow U.S. Dept. State, 1974-75, 81-82, Lady Davies fellow Lady Davies Trust Fund, 1986. Fellow ASME (life, chair West Coast applied mechanics divsn. 1960, honoree 1988, honoree 3-day symposium Applied Mechanics/Materials divsn. 1995, Hon. Mem. 1997), Am. Acad. Mechanics (spl. issue internat. jour. Impact engrng honoring 70th birthday 1994); mem. NAE, Faculty Club (Berkeley). Avocations: tournament bridge, collecting old maps, stamp collecting, classical music. Fax: (510) 486-8050. E-mail: goldsmith@me.berkeley.edu. Home and Office: 450 Gravatt Dr Berkeley CA 94705-1506 Office: U Calif Dept Mech Engring Berkeley CA 94720

GOLDSMITH, WILLIAM WOODBRIDGE, city and regional planning educator; b. San Francisco, June 6, 1941. BS in Civil Engring., U. Calif., Berkeley, 1963; PhD in Regional Planning, Econ. Theory and Devel., Pub. Adminstrn., Cornell U., 1968. Mem. faculty dept. city and regional planning Cornell U., Ithaca, N.Y., 1967—, dir. program on internat. studies in planning, 1970-95, chair dept. city and regional planning, 1983-88; dir. undergrad. program, mem. grad. fields City and Regional Planning, Urban Studies, Pub. policy, Regional Sci., Latin Am. Studies, Internat. Devel., mem. econ. faculty U. Cartegena, Colombia, 1973; mem. archtl. faculty U. Andes and U. Javeriana, Bogota, Colombia, 1973; instr. short course on regional devel. coll. engring. U. Guatemala/Orgn. Am. States, Guatemala City, 1975; mem. faculty grad. sch. econs. U. Brasilia and Fed. U. Ceara, Fortaleza. Author: (with Edward J. Blakely) Separate Societies: Poverty and Inequality in U.S. Cities, 1992; editor: (with Pierre Clavel and John Forester) Urban and Regional Planning in an Age of Austerity, 1980; contbr. numerous articles to profl. jours. Mem. Assn. Collegiate Schs. Planning, Am. Econ. Assn., Am. Planning Assn., Latin Am. Studies Assn., Planners Network, Regional Sci. Assn. Office: Cornell U Dept City and Regional Planning W Sibley Hall Ithaca NY 14853*

GOLDSMITH, WILLIS JAY, lawyer; b. Paris, Feb. 21, 1947; came to U.S., 1949; s. Irving and Alice (Rosenfeld) G.; m. Marilynn Jacobson, Aug. 12, 1973; children: Andrew Edward, Helene Sara. AB, Brown U., 1969; JD, NYU, 1972. Bar: N.Y. 1973, U.S. Ct. Appeals (2d cir.) 1975, D.C. 1978, U.S. Ct. Appeals (4th cir.) 1979, U.S. Ct. Appeals (D.C. cir.) 1979, U.S. Supreme Ct. 1980, U.S. Ct. Appeals (6th cir.) 1985, U.S. Ct. Appeals (7th cir.) 1989, U.S. Ct. Appeals (3d cir.) 1991, U.S. Ct. Appeals (5th cir.) 1998. Atty. Dept. Labor, Washington, 1972-74; assoc. Guggenheimer & Untermyer, N.Y.C., 1974-77; assoc. Seyfarth, Shaw, Fairweather & Geraldson, Washington, 1977-79, ptnr., 1979-83; ptnr. Jones, Day, Reavis & Pogue, Washington, 1983—, chmn. labor and employment law practice, 1991—; adj. prof. law Georgetown U., 1988-91; fellow Coll. Labor and Employment Law, 1997—. Contbg. editor Employee Rels. Law Jour., 1983-91; assoc. editor Occupl. Safety and Health Law; mem. editl. adv. bd. Benefits Law Jour., 1991—. Mem. ABA (sect. labor and employment law com. on employee benefits, com. on occupl. safety and health), NYU Ctr. for Labor and Employment Law (bd dirs. 1997—), D.C. Bar Assn., Met. Club (Washington), Kenwood Golf and Country Club (Bethesda, Md.). Democrat. Jewish. Home: 6409 Elmwood Rd Chevy Chase MD 20815-6621 Office: Jones Day Reavis & Pogue 51 Louisiana Ave NW Washington DC 20001

GOLDSON, ALFRED LLOYD, oncologist, educator. BS, Hampton Inst., 1968; MD, Howard U., Washington, 1972. Diplomate Am. Bd. Therapeutic

Radiology; med. lic. D.C.; cert. Ga. state med. bd. Resident in radiation therapy Howard U. Hosp., Washington, 1972-75; fellow Meml. Sloan-Kettering Cancer Ctr., N.Y.C., 1975-76; clin. instr. radiation therapy coll. medicine Howard U., 1976, from asst. prof. to assoc. prof., 1977-79, chmn. dept. radiotherapy, 1979—, prof., 1984; clin. assoc. prof. radiation oncology coll. medicine Georgetown U., Washington, 1979; chmn. radiation therapy Greater Southeastern Cmty. Hosp., 1991; chmn. Howard U. Cancer Com., 1985—; interim dir. Howard U. Cancer Ctr., 1991, exec. com., 1979—; chmn. adv. bd. Howard U. Coll. Allied Health Scis. Radiation Therapy Tech., 1977—; appt. to Nat. Cancer Adv. Bd., 1994—. Contbr. articles to profl. jours. Chmn. D.C. Cancer Consortiu,; chmn. trial com. Nat. Cancer Inst., 1984-86, patient data query editl. bd., 1984-86; program com. nat. conf. Am. Cancer Soc., 1984, trustee, 1979—; mem. Nat. Cancer Adv. Bd., 1994—. Jr. Faculty Clin. fellow Am. Cancer Soc., 1977-79. Mem. Am. Soc. Therapeutic Radiology (scientific program com. 1982-85), Am. Coll. Radiology (com. radiotherapy rsch. and devel. 1982-85), Am. Soc. Clin. Onocology, Nat. Med. Assn., Radiologic Soc. North Am., Mid-Atlantic Soc. Radiation Onocologists, N.Y. Acad. Scis., Meml. Sloan-Kettering Radiation Therapy Dept. Alumni Assn. (pres. 1989). Home: 4015 28th Pl NW Washington DC 20008-3801 Office: Howard U Dept Radiotherapy 2041 Georgia Ave NW Dept Washington DC 20060-0002

GOLDSON, AMY ROBERTSON, lawyer; b. Boston, Jan. 16, 1953; d. Irving Edgar and E. Emily (Lippman) Robertson; m. Alfred Lloyd Goldson, June 29, 1974. BA magna cum laude, Smith Coll., 1973; JD, Cath. U., 1976. Bar: D.C. 1976, U.S. Dist. Ct. D.C. 1976, U.S. Ct. Appeals (D.C. and 4th cirs.) 1976. Atty. office of chief counsel, tax ct. litigation div. IRS, Washington, 1976-77; assoc. Smothers, Douple, Gayton & Long, Washington, 1977-82; sole practice Washington, 1982—. Gen counsel Congl. Black Caucus Found., Inc., Washington, 1977—. Mem. ABA, Nat. Bar Assn., Washington Bar Assn., D.C. Bar Assn., Phi Beta Kappa. Democrat. Roman Catholic. Club: Links (Washington). Avocations: swimming, skiing, tennis. Home and Office: 4015 28th Pl NW Washington DC 20008-3801

GOLDSPIEL, ARNOLD NELSON, real estate executive; b. N.Y.C., Aug. 4, 1949; s. Julius and Minna (Nelson) G. BA in Econ., Rutgers U., 1971. Elec. data processing auditor Chubb and Son, Inc., Short Hills, N.J., 1972-74; audit coord., tech. support Merrill Lynch and Co., N.Y.C., 1974-76; sr. EDP auditor Hoffman-LaRoche, Inc., Nutley, N.J., 1976-78; sr. EDP auditor then EDP audit assoc. Mut. Benefit Life Ins. Co., Newark, 1978-82, asst. comptr. corp. data security, 1982-85; sr. EDP auditor Bristol-Myers Co., N.Y.C., 1985-88; sales rep. Century 21 Valerius Realty, Belleville, N.J., 1989-90, Century 21 Stanford Agy., Nutley, N.J., 1990—; sr. EDP auditor Borg-Warner Security Corp., 1994—. Mem. Info. Mgmt. System com. IBM Share-Audit Project, 1980-81. Mem. citizens planning adv. com. Nutley Sch. Bd., 1978. Staff sgt. N.J. Air N.G., 1968-74. Mem. Info. Sys. Audit and Control Assn. (cert.), Inst. Internal Auditors, Nat. Assn. Realtors, Bloomfield, Glen Ridge, Nutley and Belleville Bd. Realtors.

GOLDSTEIN, ABRAHAM S., lawyer, educator; b. N.Y.C., July 27, 1925; s. Isidore and Yetta (Crystal) G.; m. Ruth Tessler, Aug. 31, 1947 (dec. Feb. 1989); children: William Ira, Marianne Susan; m. Sarah Feidelson, May 7, 1995. B.B.A., CCNY, 1946; LL.B., Yale U., 1949, M.A. (hon.), 1961; M.A. (hon.), Cambridge (Eng.) U., 1964; LL.D. (hon.), N.Y. Law Sch., 1979, DePaul U., 1987. Bar: D.C. bar 1949. Law clk. to judge U.S. Ct. Appeals, 1949-51; partner firm Donohue & Kaufmann, Washington, 1951-56; mem. faculty Yale Law Sch., 1956—, prof. law, 1961—, dean, 1970-75, Sterling prof. law, 1975—; vis. prof. law Stanford Law Sch., summer 1963; vis. fellow Inst. Criminology, fellow Christ's Coll. Cambridge U., 1964-65; faculty Salzburg Seminar in Am. Studies, 1969, Inst. on Social Sci. Methods on Legal Edn., U. Denver, 1970-72; vis. prof. Hebrew U., Jerusalem, 1976, UN Asia and Far East Inst. for Prevention Crime, Tokyo, 1983, Tel Aviv U., 1986; cons. Pres.'s Com. Law Enforcement, 1967; mem. Conn. Bd. of Parole, 1967-69, Conn. Commn. Revise Criminal Code, 1966-70; mem. of the Conn. Planning Com. on Criminal Adminstrn., 1967-71; sr. v.p. Am. Jewish Congress, 1977-84, mem. exec. com., 1977-89, gov. coun., 1989-94. Author: The Insanity Defense, 1967, The Passive Judiciary, 1981, (with L. Orland) Criminal Procedure, 1974, (with J. Goldstein) Crime, Law and Society, 1971; contbr. numerous articles and revs to profl. jours. Served with AUS, 1943-46. Guggenheim fellow, 1964-65, 75-76, Am. Acad. Arts & Scis., 1975—. Office: Yale Law Sch PO Box 208215 New Haven CT 06520-8215

GOLDSTEIN, ALFRED GEORGE, retail and consumer products executive; b. N.Y.C., Sept. 22, 1932; s. Milton and Pauline M. G.; m. Hope D. Perry, July 5, 1959; children: Mark, Robert. AB, CCNY, 1953; MS, Columbia U., 1954. With Sears, Roebuck & Co., Chgo., 1956-79, v.p. mdse, group nat. mdse. mgr., 1976-79; sr. v.p. consumer bus. Am. Can Co., Greenwich, Conn., 1979-81, sr. v.p. waste recovery bus., 1981-82, exec. v.p. plastics packaging bus., 1982-83, pres. splty. retailing sector, 1983-87; pres. splty. merchandising and direct mktg. group, Sears Logistics Svc. Sears, Roebuck & Co., Chgo., 1987-93; pres., CEO AG Assocs., Chgo., 1993 —; bd. dirs. Sears Mdse. Group, Sears Can., Ltd.; former vice chmn., CEO, bd. dirs. Fingerhut Corp.; chmn. bd. dirs. Pickwick Internat.; chmn., CEO, Musicland Group; bd. dirs. Gander Mountain Corp., 1994. Exec. editor: Internat. Jour. Addictions, 1975-80. Trustee Archeus Found., 1978-90; bd. dirs., mem. exec. com. United Negro Coll. Fund, 1991—, Columbia U. Grad. Sch. Bus. Alumni Assn., 1980-85, Am. Can Co. Found.; mem. mktg. com. bd. trustees Art Inst., Chgo., 1988—; mem. adv. bd. J.L. Kellogg Sch. Mgmt. Ctr. Study Ethical Issues in Bus., Northwestern U., 1992—, Gozuieta Bus. Sch. Ctr. Leadership and Career Studies, Emory U., 1990-97; bd. dirs. Art Americana, 1996. With AUS, 1954-56. Mem. Am. Arbitration Assn. (arbitrator).

GOLDSTEIN, ALLAN LEONARD, biochemist, educator; b. Bronx, N.Y., Nov. 8, 1937; s. Morris and Miriam (Siegel) G.; m. Linda Jo Tish, Dec. 23, 1975; children: Jennifer Joy, Dawn Eden, Adam Lee. BS, Wagner Coll., 1959; MS, Rutgers U., 1961, PhD, 1964; DSc (hon.), Wagner Coll., 1997. Teaching asst. Rutgers U., New Brunswick, N.J., 1959-61; asst. instr. biology, 1961-63, instr. physiology, 1963-64; research fellow Albert Einstein Coll. Medicine, 1964-66, instr. biochemistry, 1966-67, asst. prof., 1967-71, asso. prof., 1971-72; prof., dir. div. biochemistry U. Tex. Med. Br., Galveston, 1972-78; acting dir. multidisciplinary research program in mental health U. Tex. Med. Br., 1973-78; prof., chmn. dept. biochemistry and molecular biology George Washington U. Sch. Medicine, Washington, 1978—, pres., sci. dir. Inst. for Advanced Studies in Immunology and Aging, , 1985-95; chmn. bd. Alpha 1 Biomeds., 1982—; cons. Syntex Rsch., 1972-74, Hoffmann-LaRoche, 1974-82; spl. cons. bd. sci. counselors Nat. Inst. Allergy and Infectious Diseases, 1975; mem. med. rsch. svc. rev. bd. in oncology VA, 1977-80; cons. mem. decisive network com. Biol. Response Modifiers program Div. Cancer Treatment, Nat. Cancer Inst., 1982-84; mem. sci. adv. com. to pres. Papanicolaou Cancer Rsch. Inst. Miami, Inc., 1981-84; mem. AIDS task force adv. com. Nat. Cancer Inst., 1983-84; mem. sci. bd. Alliance for Aging Rsch., 1986—. Discoverer (with Abraham White) Thymosins, hormones of thymus gland and HGP-30 a "core" based p17 AIDS Vaccine currently undergoing Phase I human testing. Decorated Chevalier des Palmes Academiques (France), 1993; recipient Career Scientist award N.Y.C. Health Rsch. Coun., 1967, Alumni Achievement award Wagner Coll., 1974, Gordon Wilson medal Am. Clin. and Climatol Soc., 1976, Disting. Faculty Rsch. award U. Tex. Sch. Biomed. Scis., 1976, Van Dyke award in pharmacology Columbia Coll. Physicians and Surgeons, 1984; vis. prof. award Burroughs Wellcome Found., FASEB, 1986, Fernnandez-Cruz award, 1989, Martin Rubin award Am. Coll. Advancement in Medicine, 1990, Michele Fodera Internat. prize for Biomed. Rsch., 1990. Mem. AAAS, Endocrine Soc., Am. Soc. Biol. Chemists and Molecular Biologists, Am. Assn. Immunologists, Internat. Soc. Immunopharmacology (coun. mem. 1985-94), Assn. Med. Sch. Chm. of Depts. Biochemistry, AAUP, Acad. Medicine of Washington, Toastmasters Internat. (pres. N.Y. chpt. 1971), Sigma Xi. Home: Apt 1005 800 25th St NW Washington DC 20037 Office: George Washington U Med Ctr Dept Biochemistry/Molecular Biology 2300 I St NW Washington DC 20037-2336

GOLDSTEIN, ALVIN, lawyer; b. N.Y.C., Nov. 21, 1929; s. Abraham and Florence (Bruckner) G.; m. Eleanor Kronish, Dec. 27, 1959; children—Eric, Michael, Eileen. B.S.S., Coll. City N.Y., 1950; LL.B., Bklyn. Law Sch., 1953, S.J.D. magna cum laude, 1960. Bar: N.Y. State 1953, U.S. Supreme Ct. Asso. firm Levine & Berman, N.Y.C., 1955-59; partner Levine & Berman, 1963; practiced in N.Y.C., 1960-62; partner firm Berman, Paley, Goldstein, Kannry, N.Y.C., 1964—. Contbr. articles to profl. publs. Served with AUS, 1953-55. Mem. N.Y. State Bar Assn., Assn. Bar City of N.Y. Home: 1 Chester Ter Hastings Hdsn NY 10706-3907 Office: Berman Paley Goldstein & Kannry 500 5th Ave New York NY 10110

GOLDSTEIN, ARTHUR LOUIS, liquid purification company executive; s. David and Henrietta (Frankfort) G.; m. Vida F. Fishbach; children: Jonathan M., Susanne B., James A. BSChE, Rensselaer Poly. Inst., 1957; MSChE, U. Del., 1959; MBA, Harvard U., 1960. Pres., chmn., CEO Ionics, Inc., Watertown, Mass., 1990—; bd. dirs. State St. Boston Corp., State St. Bank and Trust Co., Cabot Corp. Bd. dirs. Jobs for Mass., Inc.; trustee Calif. Inst. Tech., Mass. Gen. Physicians Orgn., Inc.; mem. vis. com. Harvard Bus. Sch.; mem. vis. com. Harvard Sch. Pub. Health, mem. cardiovascular adv. coun., Harvard Environ. Health Coun.; exec. com. CEOs for Fundamental Change in Edn., Inner-City Scholarship Fund; chmn. Mass. High Tech. Coun., 1985-87, bd. dirs., mem. exec. com.; past pres. Rensselaer Coun. Mem. Nat. Acad. Engring. Achievements include 8 patents related to purification and processing of liquids. Office: Ionics Inc PO Box 9131 Watertown MA 02471-9131 also: 65 Grove St Watertown MA 02472-2826

GOLDSTEIN, AVRAM, pharmacology educator; b. N.Y.C., July 3, 1919; s. Israel and Bertha (Markowitz) G.; m. Dora Benedict, Aug. 29, 1947; children—Margaret, Daniel, Joshua, Michael. A.B., Harvard, 1940, M.D., 1943. Intern Mt. Sinai Hosp., N.Y.C., 1944; successively instr., assoc., asst. prof. pharmacology Harvard U., 1947-55; prof. dept. pharmacology Stanford U., Palo Alto, Calif., 1955-89, exec. head dept., 1955-70, prof. emeritus, 1989—; dir. Addiction Research Found., Palo Alto, Calif., 1973-87. Author: Biostatistics, Principles of Drug Action, 1965, ADDICTION: From Biology to Drug Policy, 1994. Served from 1st lt. to capt., M.C. AUS, 1944-46. Mem. AAAS, NAS and Inst. Medicine, Am. Acad. Arts and Scis., Am. Soc. Pharmacology and Exptl. Therapeutics, Am. Soc. Biol. Chemists. Home: 735 Dolores St Palo Alto CA 94305-8427*

GOLDSTEIN, BARRY BRUCE, biologist, food company executive, lawyer; b. N.Y.C., Aug. 2, 1947; s. George and Pauline (Kolodner) G.; m. Jacqueline Barbara Aboulafia, Dec. 21, 1968; children: Joshua, Jessica. BA, Queens Coll., 1968; MA, CCNY, N.Y.C., 1974; PhD, CUNY, N.Y.C., 1980; JD, U. N.Mex., 1994. Microbiologist CPC Internat., Yonkers, N.Y., 1968-71; rsch. scientist U. Tex., Austin, 1977-80; v.p. SystemCulture Inc., Honolulu, 1980-83; bioenergy/aquaculture program mgr. N.Mex. Solar Energy Inst., Las Cruces, 1983-89; pres. Ancient Seas Aquaculture Inc., Roswell, N.Mex., 1989-92, Desert Seas Aquaculture Inc., Roswell, 1990-92, Hawaii Shellfish Co., Las Cruces, 1991—; prin. mem. tech. staff Sandia Nat. Labs., Carlsbad, N.Mex., 1994—. Editl. bd. Natural Resources Jour.; contbr. articles to profl. jours. Recipient Nat. Energy Innovation award Dept. Energy, Washington, 1985; Grad. fellow CUNY, 1971, Jesse Smith Noyes fellow, 1975, Regents scholar SUNY, 1964. Mem. World Aquaculture Soc., Am. Bar Assn., N.Mex. State Bar Assn. Avocations: aquaculture, gardening, reading, inventing. Office: PO Box 1349 Carlsbad NM 88221-1349

GOLDSTEIN, BERNARD, transportation and casino gaming company executive; b. Rock Island, Ill., Feb. 5, 1929; s. Morris and Fannie (Borenstein) G.; m. Irene Alter, Dec. 18, 1949; children: Jeffrey, Robert, Kathy, Richard. BA, U. Ill., 1949, LLB, 1951. Bar: Iowa 1951. With Alter Co., Bettendorf, Iowa, 1951—, chmn. bd., 1979—; chmn. bd. Valley Corp., Bettendorf, 1984—; chmn. bd. Isle of Capri Casinos, Inc., Biloxi, Miss., 1992—, chmn. CEO, 1997—. Pres. Quad City Jewish Fedn., 1975. Jewish.

GOLDSTEIN, BERNARD DAVID, physician, educator; b. Bronx, N.Y., Feb. 28, 1939; m. Russellyn Carruth, May 5, 1995; children: Lara, Ross. B.S., U. Wis., 1958; M.D., NYU, 1962. Diplomate Am. Bd. Toxicology, Am. Bd. Internal Medicine, Am. Bd. Hematology. Intern, asst. resident, resident 3d and 4th (NYU) med. divs. Bellevue Hosp., N.Y.C., 1962-65; mem. faculty depts. environ. medicine and medicine NYU Med. Ctr., N.Y.C., 1968-80; attending physician Bellevue and Univ. Hosps., N.Y.C., 1968-80; prof., chmn. dept. environ. and community medicine U. Medicine and Dentistry, N.J.-Robert Wood Johnson Med. Sch., Piscataway, 1980—; acting dean Sch. Pub. Health of N.J., Piscataway, 1998-99; dir. grad. program in pub. health U. Medicine and Dentistry, N.J.-Robert Wood Johnson Med. Sch., Piscataway, 1982-89, dir. environmental and occupational health scis. inst., 1985—; asst. adminstr. for research and devel. EPA, Washington, 1983-85; dir. Nat. Inst. Environ. Health Scis. Ctr. of Excellence, 1988-94; chmn. clean air sci. adv. com. EPA, 1982-83; mem. toxicology study sect. NIH, 1980-84, chmn., 1982-84; mem. bd. sci. dirs. Risk Sci. Inst., 1986—; chmn. com. molecular markers NAS, 1986-89, on risk assessment methodology, 1990-93, on role of physician in occupational an environ. medicine Inst. Medicine, 1986-87, on enhancing role of primary care practitioners in environ. and occupational health Inst. Medicine, 1989-91; chmn. ad hoc com. on dioxin, EPA, 1988-89; vice chmn., chmn. sci. group on methodology for sci. evaluation chems., 1989—; chmn. mem. working group on Air Quality Guidelines for Major Urban Air Pollutants, 1985; mem. health rev. com., chmn. health rsch. com. Health Effects Inst., 1987—; mem. nat. adv. environ. health effects coun. NIH, 1987-91; bd. dirs. Lovelace Inst., 1988-96, Internat. Life Sci. Inst., Roy F. Weston, Inc. Fellow ACP, Am. Coll. Preventive Medicine; mem. NAS Inst. Medicine (chmn. sect. pub. health, biostats and epidemiology 1996—), Am. Soc. Clin. Investigation. Office: Rutgers University UMDNJ Enviro & Occupational Health Scis Inst Piscataway NJ 08855-1179

GOLDSTEIN, BRENDA IRIS, retired elementary school educator; b. Bklyn., Mar. 18, 1940; d. Joseph and Gladys Gordon Goldstein. BA, Bklyn. Coll., 1960, MS, 1969. Ret. tchr. Bklyn., 1996; profl. reader, internet rschr. CIA, 1997—. Polit. writer, 1997—. Mem. Libr. of Congress Assocs. Congregationalist. Avocations: reading history and classic novels, listening to contemporary and classical music. Home: 73 Bay 22 St Brooklyn NY 11214-3854

GOLDSTEIN, BRIAN ALAN, lawyer, physician; b. Bronx, N.Y., Oct. 24, 1959; s. Stanley Irving and Hortense (Silverstein) G.; m. Eva Rubinstein, June 19, 1988; children: Ariel Petra, Adam Izak. MD, Ctr. Tech. U., Santo Domingo, Dominican Republic, 1980; JD magna cum laude, SUNY Buffalo, 1995. Diplomate Am. Bd. Surgery; bar: N.Y., U.S. Dist. Ct. (we. dist.) N.Y., U.S. Dist. Ct. (ea. dist.) Mich., 1997 (we. dist.) 1999. Resident N.Y. Meth. Hosp., Bklyn., 1981-86; surgeon Hadassah Med. Ctr., Jerusalem, 1988-91; cardiothoracic surgeon Tygerburg Hosp., Capetown, South Africa, 1992; assoc. Michael Doran & Assocs., Buffalo, 1994—; instr. surgery Hebrew U., Jerusalem, 1989-91, U. Stellenbosch, South Africa, 1992. Contbr. articles to profl. jours. Fellow Interam. Coll. Physicians and Surgeons; mem. ABA, Internat. Soc. Cardiothoracic Surgeons, Assn. Trial Lawyers Am., N.Y. State Bar Assn., Erie County Bar Assn. (health law com. 1996). Office: Michael Doran & Assocs 1234 Delaware Ave Buffalo NY 14209-1430

GOLDSTEIN, BURTON BENJAMIN, JR., communications executive; b. Atlanta, Mar. 11, 1948; s. Burton B. and Grace Goldstein; m. Kathleen N. Gurley, Aug. 22, 1970; children: Katherine Claire, Alexander Max. AB, U. N.C., 1970; MEd, U. Mass., 1973; JD with honors, U. N.C., 1976. Bar: Ga. 1976. Assoc. dir. urban internat. Yale U., New Haven, 1970-72; assoc. Long, Aldridge & Norman, Atlanta, 1976-80; gen. counsel Solinet, Atlanta, 1980-81; pres. Info. America, Atlanta, 1981-98, Networth Ptnrs., Atlanta, 1998—; ex-officio dir. Info. Industry Assn., Washington, 1992-93. Bd. dirs. SciTrek, Atlanta, 1988—, High Mus. of Art, 1996—; chmn. adv. bd. Inst. for Arts & Humanities, Chapel Hill, N.C., 1991—; chmn. Info. Industry Assn. Investment Conf., N.Y.C., 1992-93; v.p. Atlanta chpt. Am. Jewish Com. Named Fast Tech 50, Arthur Andersen, Atlanta, 1988—, Runner-up Entrepreneur of Yr., Ernst & Young & INC Mag., 1991, Entrepreneur of the Yr., Info. Industry, 1991. Mem. ABA, Ga. Bar Assn., Am. Jewish Com., The Temple, Chancellor's Club U. N.C., Phi Beta Kappa. Democrat. Jewish. Avocation: running. Office: Information America 245 Peachtree Center Ave NE Atlanta GA 30303-1222*

GOLDSTEIN, BURTON JACK, psychiatrist; b. Balt., Sept. 23, 1930; s. Hyman and Roz (Levin) C.; m. Linda; children: Howard, Herbert, Brian, Esther, Leonard, Mark. B.S. in Pharmacy, U. Md., 1953, M.D., 1960. Diplomate Am. Bd. Psychiatry and Neurology (bd. examiner). Intern Jackson Meml. Hosp., Miami, Fla., 1960-61; NIMH fellow in psychiatry Jackson Meml. Hosp., 1961-63, chief resident, 1963-64; dir. div. clin. psychopharmacology, dept. psychiatry U. Miami, 1964—, chief div. research, 1964-71, prof. pharmacology, 1973—, prof. psychiatry, 1973—, acting chmn. dept. psychiatry, 1983-85; sr. cons. in psychopharmacology Mt. Sinai Med. Ctr., Miami Beach, 1993—; dir. psychiat. consultation liaison svc. Mt. Sinai Hosp., Miami Beach, 1993—; bd. advs. Fla. Mental Health Inst. U. South Fla.; cons. in psychiat. rsch. South Fla. State Hosp., West Hollywood; cons. indsl. security program Dept. Def.; cons. VA Psychiatry Svc., Miami; chmn. panel on neuropharmacologic drugs U.S. Pharmacopeial Conv., Inc., mem. exec. com.; mem. faculty Health Svcs. Ctr., U. Miami, 1996. Mem. editorial bd. Miami Medicine, Clin. Advancement in Treatment of Depression; contbr. chpts. to books, articles to profl. publs. Served to maj. AUS, 1953-62. Fellow Am. Psychiat. Assn. (life), Am. Coll. Psychiatrists, Am. Coll. Clin. Pharmacology, Am. Coll. Neuropsychopharmacology; mem. Fla. Med. Assn., Dade County Med. Assn., Royal Soc. Health, Am. Assn. Clin. Pharmacology and Chemotherapy, Am. Soc. Addiction Medicine, Collegium Internationale Neuropsychopharmacologium, South Fla. Psychiat. Soc. Office: U Miami Sch Medicine Health Svcs Rsch Ctr 1400 NW 10th Ave Ste 1103 Miami FL 33136-1000*

GOLDSTEIN, CHARLES ARTHUR, lawyer; b. N.Y.C., Nov. 20, 1936; s. Murray and Evelyn V. Goldstein; m. Judith Stein, Sept. 29, 1962 (div. 1982); 1 child, Deborah Ruth; m. Carol Sager, Nov. 10, 1990 (div. 1995). A.B., Columbia U., 1958; J.D. cum laude, Harvard U., 1961. Bar: N.Y. 1962. Law clk. U.S. Ct. Appeals (2d cir.), 1961-62; assoc. Fried, Frank, Harris, Shriver & Jacobson, N.Y.C., 1962-69; ptnr. Schulte Roth & Zabel, N.Y.C., 1969-79; ptnr. Weil, Gotshal & Manges, N.Y.C., 1979-83, counsel, 1983-85; ptnr. Shea & Gould, N.Y.C., 1985-94, Sutherland, Asbill & Brennan, N.Y.C., 1994-95; counsel Squire, Sanders & Dempsey, N.Y.C., 1996—; lectr. Columbia U. Law Sch. Gen. counsel to Citizens Budget Commn., 1980-87; mem. Temp. Commn. on City Fins., 1975-77; mem. Gov.'s Task Force on World Trade Ctr. Mem. Am. Coll. Real Estate Lawyers. Republican. Home: 220 E 65th St New York NY 10021-6620 Office: Squire Sanders & Dempsey 350 Park Ave New York NY 10022-6022

GOLDSTEIN, CHARLES HENRY, architect, consultant; b. Winthrop, Mass., Mar. 23, 1938; s. Daniel and Rose (Shulman) G.; m. Marilyn Binda, July 6, 1958; (div. Apr. 1971); children: Brent R., Scott H.; m. Janet Harrison, Oct. 12, 1973; children: Nathan H., Lindsay H., Vanessa H. Cert., Boston Archtl. Ctr., 1965. Registered architect, Mass., N.H., Conn. Chief designer Milo Hart Assocs., Lynnfield, Mass., 1970-72; prin. C.H. Goldstein Assocs., Methuen, Mass., 1972-73; ptnr. Sarver & Goldstein, Saugus, Mass., 1973-75; chief architect A.D. Maclaren Assocs., Andover, Mass., 1975-80, Allen & Demurjian, Boston, Mass., 1980-83; prin. Archtl. Energies, North Hampton, N.H., 1983—, North Andover, Mass., 1983—; guest lectr. Wentworth Inst., Boston, 1982—, Merrimack Coll., North Andover, Mass.1978—, U. Debrecen, Hungary, 1992. Mem. bd. selectmen, bd. of health Town of Tewksbury (Mass.), 1969-72; mem. sch. coms., Merrimac and West Newbury, Mass., 1983—. Recipient Honorable Mention award Interval Internat., 1982, N.H. Sam awards (5) for design, 1989-91; Boston Soc. Architects scholar, 1960; John Worthington Ames scholar, 1964; Rotch scholar finalist, 1964. Mem. Nat. Council Archtl. Registration Bds., Boston Soc. Architects, AIA. Office: Archtl Energies 200 Sutton St North Andover MA 01845-1656

GOLDSTEIN, DEBRA HOLLY, judge; b. Newark, Mar. 11, 1953; d. Aaron and Erica (Schreier) Green; m. Joel Ray Goldstein, Aug. 14, 1983; children: Stephen Michael, Jennifer Ann. BA, U. Mich., 1973; JD, Emory U., 1977. Bar: Ga. 1977, Mich. 1978, D.C. 1978, Ala. 1984. Tax analyst atty. Gen. Motors Corp., Detroit, 1977-78; trial atty. U.S. Dept. Labor, Birmingham, Ala., 1978-90; U.S. adminstrv. law judge office hearing and appeals Social Security Adminstrn., Birmingham, 1990—; new judge faculty U.S. adminstrv. law judges Social Security Adminstrn., 1991, 93—; co-chair Pluralism Think Tank, 1999. Mem. editorial bd. The Ala. Lawyer, 1994—, The Addendum, 1995—. Chairperson Women's Coordinating Bur., Birmingham, 1983-85; active United Way, Birmingham, 1983, 87, 90, 98, mem. vis. allocation team, 1998, active adult edn. Temple Beth-El, bd. dirs., 1993-94, co-chair workshop initiative group, 1993-94; program chmn. Sisterhood, 1987-88, adminstrv. v.p., 1989-90, 90-92; scholarship chairperson Nat. Coun. Jewish Women, 1986; mem. steering com. Birmingham Bus. and Profl. Women Fedn., 1987-88, 95—; leader Brownie Troop, 1992—, bd. dirs. Cahaba Girl Scout Coun., 1996—, mem. enrichment com. Cherokee Bend Sch., 1992-93, 94-95, chmn. enrichment com., 1995-96, mini-grants co-chmn. 1997-98; mem. edn. com. Temple Emanu-El, 1995-97; mem. Leadership for Diversity Initiative, 1995-96, Leadership Birmingham, 1997-98, Women's Network, 1997—. Mem. ABA, Ga. Bar Assn., D.C. Bar Assn., Mich. Bar Assn., Birmingham Bar Assn. (mem. law day com., scholarship com. 1994—, mem. women's liaison and project coms. 1998-99, bd. dirs. women's sect. 1999—, liaison com. 1998-99, chmn. Long Range Planning com. 1999—), Ala. Bar Assn., Zonta (v.p. 1983-84, bd. dirs. 1988-89, 90-92, intercity chmn. 1995, co-pres. 1996-98), B'nai B'rith Women (chair S.E. region 1984-86, counselor 1986-88, Women's Humanitarian award 1981), Hadassah (local bd. dirs. 1979-83, adminstrv. v.p. 1989-90, 90-92). Jewish. Office: Social Security Adminstrn 1910 3rd Ave N Birmingham AL 35203-3513

GOLDSTEIN, DONALD MAURICE, historian, educator; b. N.Y.C., Dec. 15, 1932; s. Max A. and Jean M. Goldstein; m. Mariann Norma Zinck, Aug. 5, 1961; children: Tammie, Timmie, Tommie, Teri. BA, U. Md., 1954, MA, 1962; MS, Georgetown U., 1963; MPA, George Washington U., 1965; PhD, U. Denver, 1970; grad. War Coll., 1973, Air Command and Staff Coll., 1965. Commd. 2d lt. U.S. Air Force, 1955, advanced through grades to lt. col., 1972; comdr. missile site, Taiwan, 1958-59; staff officer U.S. Strike Command, 1961-64; rsch. assoc. Airstaff Pentagon; assoc. prof. history USAF Acad., 1965-71, asst. track coach, 1965-71; ret., 1977; assoc. prof. history Troy (Ala.) State U., 1971-74; prof. aerospace studies U. Pitts., 1975-77, assoc. prof. pub. and internat. affairs, 1975-92, prof. 1993, dir. placement and alumni, 1977-85, assoc. dean, 1985-88. Decorated Soldiers medal, Meritorious Svc. medal with 2 oak leaf clusters, Joint Service Commendation medal, Air Force Commendation medal with oak leaf cluster. Mem. Am. Hist. Assn., Internat. Studies Assn., Am. Soc. Pub. Adminstrs., Am. Polit. Sci. Assn., Air Force Assn., Omicron Delta Kappa, Phi Kappa Phi, Phi Alpha Theta, Sigma Nu. Roman Catholic. Club: Toastmasters. Author: Ennis C. Whithead Aerospace Commander, 1970; Adolph Hitler in the Perspective of the American Press, 1961; Adolph Hitler Adminstrator of a Society, 1965; (with others) Miracle at Midway, 1982, Target Tokyo: The Story of the Surge Spy Ring in Japan, 1984; collaborator: At Dawn We Slept: The Untold Story of Pearl Harbor, 1981; Pearl Harbor: The Verdict of History, 1985, December 7, 1941: the Day the Japanese Attacked Pearl Harbor, 1988, God's Samurai Lead Pilot at Pearl Harbor, 1990, Fading Victory: The Diary of Matome Ugaki, 1991, The Way it Was: A Pictorial History of Pearl Harbor, 1991, The Williwar War: The Arkansas National Guard in World War II, 1992, The Pearl Harbor Paper, 1993, Classics in International Affairs with Others, 1993, 2d edit., 1998, D Day: A Pictorial History, 1994, Nuts: The Battle of the Bulge, 1994, Security in Korea: War, Stalemate and Negotiation, 1994, Rain of Ruin: A Photographic History of Hirosima and Nagasaki, 1995, Amelia Earhart: A Biography, 1997, Vietnam: A Pictorial History, 1997, The Spanish American War: A Centennial History, 1998; asst. editor papers on fgn. policy for House Com. on Internat. Affairs, 1947-54; contbr. articles on def. policy and nat. security affairs to profl. jours. Home: 2146 Meadowmont Dr Upper St Clair Pittsburgh PA 15241 Office: U Pitts Grad Sch Pub Int Affairs Dean's Office Forbes Complex 3J-11 Pittsburgh PA 15260

GOLDSTEIN, DORA BENEDICT, pharmacologist, educator; b. Milton, Mass., Apr. 25, 1922; d. George Wheeler and Marjory (Pierce) Benedict; m. Avram Goldstein, Aug. 29, 1947; children: Margaret E. Wallace, Daniel P., Joshua S., Michael B. Student, Bryn Mawr Coll., 1940-42, Stanford U., 1945; M.D., Harvard U., 1949. Research assoc. Stanford U., 1955-70, sr. research assoc., 1970-74, adj. prof., 1974-78, prof. pharmacology, 1978-92, prof. pharmacology emerita, 1992—, co-dir. faculty mentoring program sch. medicine, 1994—. Author: Pharmacology of Alcohol, 1983; contbr. articles to sci. jours. Mem. Research Soc. Alcoholism (pres. 1979-81, award for excellence), Am. Soc. Pharmacology and Exptl. Therapeutics, Am. Soc. Biol. Chemists, Internat. Soc. Biomed. Research on Alcoholism. Office: Stanford U Stanford U Sch Medicine Stanford CA 94305

GOLDSTEIN, E. ERNEST, lawyer; b. Pitts., Oct. 9, 1918; s. Nathan E. and Annie (Ginsberg) G.; m. Peggy Janet Rosenfeld, June 22, 1941; children: Susan M. Goldstein Lipsitch, Daniel F. A.B. cum laude, Amherst Coll., 1939; student, U. Chgo. Law Sch., 1940-42; LL.B., Georgetown U., 1947; S.J.D., U. Wis., 1956. Bar: D.C. 1947, Tex. 1958, U.S. Supreme Ct. 1967, conseil juridique, France 1973-79. Pvt. practice Washington, 1947; with Dept. Justice, also War Claims Commn., 1947-50; assoc. counsel crime com. U.S. Senate, 1950-51; gen. counsel antitrust subcom. jud. Ho. of Reps., 1951-52; restrictive trade practices specialist Office U.S. Spl. Rep., Paris; also U.S. rep. productivity and applied research com. OEEC, 1952-54; prof. law U. Tex., 1955-65; spl. asst. to Pres. U.S. Lyndon B. Johnson, 1967-69; counsel Coudert Freres, Paris, 1966-67, ptnr., 1969-79; cons. CBS, Inc., 1980-85; advisor Ransom Humanities Rsch. Ctr. U. Tex., 1995—; cons. on antitrust European coal and steel cmty., Luxembourg, 1956, on trade regulation Justice Sec., P.R., 1962; internat. law cons. Naval War Coll., 1962, 64; lectr. Inst. Advanced European Studies, U. Nice, France, 1967, Free U. Brussels, 1967, Europa Inst., Amsterdam, 1970; vis. prof. U. P.R. Law Sch., 1962; prof. Am. sem., Salzburg, Austria, 1963, 79; adj. prof. law U. Tex., 1993-95; chmn. Internat. Lawyers Ann. Conf. Mgmt. Ctr., Europe, 1971-79. Author: Patent, Trademark and Copyright Law, 1959, American Enterprise and Scandinavian Antitrust Law, 1962; contbr. author: LBJ: To Know Him Better, 1995, procs. of The Conference on Global Responsibility of Law Librarians, 1990; founder Tex. Internat. Law Jour., 1963, mem. adv. bd., 1983—. Membership chair Am. Vets. Com., Washington, 1946-47; chmn. S.W. regional adv. bd. Anti-Defamation League, 1964-65; bd. dirs. Am. C. of C. in France, 1970-79, Ctr. Internat. Formation Européene, 1971—; trustee Leadership Enrichment Arts Program, 1996—; dir. Bus. Alliance for Vietnamese Edn., 1996—, chmn. adv. bd., 1994, co-chmn. adv. bd., 1995—; bd. govs. Am. Hosp. Paris, 1972-79, sec., 1974-79; chmn. fund raising Dem. Party Com. in France, 1973-77; mem. nat. com. Lyndon B. Johnson Meml. Grove, 1972-74; mem. nat. fin. coun. Dem. Nat. Com., 1975-77. With AUS, 1942-46. Decorated Legion of Merit; chevalier Légion d'Honneur, 1971; chevalier Ordre des Arts et des Lettres, 1981; recipient Carl Fulda Internat. Law award U. Tex., 1978; Medal of Honor, Am. C. of C., Paris, 1984; Carnegie Found. fellow, 1954-55, Ford. Found. Internat. Studies fellow, 1959, 60. Mem. Am. Club Paris (pres. 1976-78), Philos Soc. of Tex., Tex. Internat. Law Soc. (founder), Headliners Club, Austin Town and Gown Club, Order of Coif, Phi Delta Phi. Home: 1619 Northumberland Rd Austin TX 78703-3143 Office: U Tex Harry Ransom Humanities Rsch Ctr PO Box 7219 Austin TX 78713-7219

GOLDSTEIN, EDWARD DAVID, lawyer, former glass company executive; b. N.Y.C., July 12, 1927; s. Michael and Leah (Kirsh) G.; m. Rhoda Gordon, Apr. 18, 1950; children: Linda, Ellen, Ruth, Michael. BA, U. Mich., 1950, JD with distinction, 1952. Bar: Calif. 1952. Assoc. Orrick, Dahlquist, Herrington & Sutcliffe, San Francisco, 1952-54, Johnston & Johnston, San Francisco, 1954-56; with legal dept. Ohio Match Co., Hunt Foods & Industries, 1956-58; asst. gen. mgr., sales mgr. Glass Containers Corp., Fullerton, Calif., 1958-62; v.p., gen. mgr. Glass Containers Corp., 1962-68, pres., CEO, 1968-83; chmn. bd. Knox Glass Co., Fairmount Glass Cos., 1967-68; gen. counsel FHP, Internat., FHP, Inc., 1985-87. Chmn. bd. trustees St. Jude Hosp., Fullerton, 1984-88. Served with USNR, 1945-46. Mem. ABA, State Bar Calif., Orange County Bar Assn., Nat. Health Lawyers Assn., Am. Coll. Legal Medicine (assoc.-in-law), Calif. Soc. Healthcare Attys. Home: 2230 Yucca Ave Fullerton CA 92835-3320 Office: 110 E Wilshire Ave Fullerton CA 92832-1900

GOLDSTEIN, ELEANOR, artist, social worker; b. N.Y.C., May 2, 1935; d. Benjamin and Gertrude (Bober) Kronish; m. Alvin Goldstein, Dec. 27, 1959; children: Eric, Michael, Eileen. BA, Bennington (Vt.) Coll., 1957; MSW, Columbia U., 1981. Cert. social worker, N.Y. Asst. dir. Westchester Student Adv. Coalition, White Plains, N.Y., 1981-82, exec. dir., 1982-85; artist Hastings-on-the-Hudson, N.Y., 1985—. Exhibited in group shows at Mus. of Fine Arts, Springfield, Mass., 1989, Salmagundi Club, N.Y.C., 1989, Lever House Gallery, N.Y.C., 1989, 92, N.J. Bergen Mus. Arts, Paramus, 1991, Nat. Arts Club, N.Y.C., 1991, 98, Hammond Mus., North Salem, N.Y., 1992, Pen and Brush Club, N.Y.C., 1992, Westbeth Gallery, N.Y.C., 1994, Am. Embassy, Sanaa, Yemen, 1995-98, Sch. House Gallery, Croton Falls, N.Y., 1997-98, Cornell Med. Libr., 1998; permanent collections include IBM, Pepisco, Pfizer & Co., The Cathedral of St. John the Devine, N.Y.C., Std. & Poor; selected for U.S. Dept. State Art in Embassies Program. Organizer Hastings Com. for Youth, Inc., 1976-79. Recipient Pastel Soc. Am. award. Mem. N.Y. Artists Equity Assn., Pastel Soc. of Am. Home and Studio: 1 Chester Terr Hastings On Hudson NY 10706

GOLDSTEIN, ELLIOTT, lawyer; b. Atlanta, Oct. 23, 1915; s. Max Fullmore and Sarah Ray (London) G.; m. Harriet Weinberg, Oct. 24, 1942; children: Lillian, Ellen. Student, Ga. Sch. Tech., 1932-33; B.S., U. Ga., 1936; LL.B., Yale U., 1939. Bar: Ga. 1938, D.C. 1977. Asso. firm Little, Powell, Reid & Goldstein, Atlanta, 1939-40; partner firm Powell, Goldstein, Frazer & Murphy, Atlanta, 1946-77, 80—, Washington, 1977-80; spl. counsel com. on standards ofcl. conduct U.S. Ho. of Reps., 1978; mem. legal adv. com. N.Y. Stock Exchange, 1982-85. Author: Counselling the Board of Directors in its Structure, Functions and Compensation, 1985, Georgia Corporation Law and Practice, 1989; contbr. articles to profl. jours. Hon. v.p. Am. Jewish Com.; chmn. Atlanta Hist. Soc., 1990-94. Lt. col. F.A., U.S. Army, 1941-46, ETO. Decorated Bronze Star. Fellow ABA Found.; mem. ABA (chmn. com. corp. laws 1979-84, chmn. ad hoc com. ALI Corp. governance project 1982-86, mem. coun. sect. corp. banking and bus. law 1983-86, sr. del. ho. of dels. 1986-94), Am. Law Inst., Ga. Bar Assn., Atlanta Bar Assn., Lawyers Club Atlanta, Commerce Club, Standard Club. Democrat. Home: 2660 Peachtree Rd NW Atlanta GA 30305-3673 Office: Powell Goldstein Frazer & Murphy Fl 16 191 Peachtree St NE Fl 16 Atlanta GA 30303-1740

GOLDSTEIN, FRANK ROBERT, lawyer; b. Balt., July 31, 1943; s. Morris Herman and Maxine (Herzfeld) G.; m. Phyllis Ellen Levy, Jan. 26, 1967; children—Matthew Alexander, Andrew Stephen. A.B., Duke U., 1964; LL.B., U. Md., 1967. Bar: Md. 1967, D.C. 1981, Mass. 1985. Clk. to chief judge U.S. Dist. Ct. Md., Balt., 1967-68; assoc. Piper & Marbury, Balt., 1968-74, ptnr., 1974-88; ptnr. Morgan, Lewis & Bockius, LLP, 1989-96, Brown & Wood LLP, Washington, 1997—. Author: Mournful Numbers, 1995; co-author: District of Columbia Limited Liability Company Forms and Practice Manual, 1995. Bd. govs. Reconstructionist Rabbincal Coll., Wyncote, Pa. 1992-94; bd. dirs. Washington-Balt. Regional Assn., 1984-93, Al Marah Neighborhood Assn., Bethesda, Md., 1982-85, Paine Webber Mortgage Fin. Inc., Columbia, Md., 1987-93; pres. Adat Shalom Reconstructionist Congregation, Bethesda, 1990-92, Meadowbrook Neighborhood Assn., Potomac, 1990-93, Tidesfall Neighborhood Assn., Columbia, Md., 1972. Fellow Am. Bar Found.; mem. ABA, D.C. Bar Assn. (chmn. ptnr. com. 1985-86, treas. 1988-89), Balt. Bar Assn., Md. State Bar Assn. (chmn. ptnr. com. 1980-82, chmn. sect. legal edn. and admission to bar com. 1975, chmn. D.C. corp. code rev. project 1989—), Order of Coif. Jewish. Home: 11516 Big Piney Way Potomac MD 20854-1365 Office: Brown & Wood LLP 815 Connecticut Ave NW Washington DC 20006-4004

GOLDSTEIN, GARY SANFORD, executive recruiter; b. Rochester, N.Y., Nov. 29, 1954; s. Perry Leon and Joyce Lorraine (Hoffman) G.; m. Lisa Ann Bernstein, Sept. 24, 1977 (div. 1980); m. Alicia de la Caridad Lazaro, Jan. 3, 1983 (div. 1992); children: Jessica Leigh, Vanessa Kyle; m. Jill Allyson Brooke, June 11, 1995; 1 child, Parker Leon. BS in Acctg., Canisius Coll., 1976. Acct. Arthur Andersen & Co., N.Y.C., 1976-79; mng. dir. A-L Assocs., N.Y.C., 1979-84; chmn., pres. The Whitney Group, N.Y.C., 1984—; chmn., CEO Headway Corp. Resources, 1992—. Coun. mem. The Brookings Instn., Washington, 1990—; mem. bd. dirs. Rippowam Cisqa Sch., 1992—. Mem. Young Pres. Orgn. Avocations: horseback riding, tennis, collecting photorealistic art, basketball. Home: 161 Buxton Rd Bedford Hills NY 10507-2310 Office: Headway Corp Resources 850 3rd Ave New York NY 10022-6222

GOLDSTEIN, HOWARD BERNARD, investment banker, advertising and marketing executive; b. Bronx, N.Y., Dec. 4, 1943; s. Maurice and Matilda Goldstein; student, Bernard Baruch City Coll. N.Y., 1962-63; B.F.A., Pratt Inst., 1970; m. Susan Nadine Goldberg, June 25, 1967; children: Jill Alecya, Brett Adam. Art dir. Fairfax Advt. div. Ogilvy & Mather, Inc., N.Y.C., 1968-72; creative dir. Hoffman Advt., N.Y.C., 1972-80, Miller, Addison, Steele, Inc., N.Y.C., 1980-82; pres. Gould Advt., Cliffside Park, N.J., 1969—; registered securities broker, 1984, br. officer tax shelter coordinator E.F. Hutton & Co., Inc., 1983-85; registered security broker, sr. v.p., mem chmn.'s coun., dir.'s coun. Lehman Bros. Shearson Lehman Bros., Inc., 1985-94, mem. guided portfolio mgmt. program Lehman Bros. Shearson Lehman Bros., Inc., 1985-94; registered securities broker, sr. v.p. Gruntal & Co., 1994—. V.p. bd. dirs. Winston Tower 200, Condominium Assn.; mem. Internat. Assn. Fin. Planning, Inst. Cert. Fin. Planners, Coll. Cert. Fin. Planners, Denver Grad. Police & Fire Acad. of Bergen County, N.J., June 12, 1986. Fin. officer N.J. State Police Office of Emergency Mgmt., Cliffside Park, 1986; spl. police officer Cliffside Park Police Dept., N.J. State Police Benevolent Assn., 1986—, Montclair State Coll. World of Computers, 1981; mem. steering com. Coalition Bus., Labor and Community Orgns. of N.Y., 1992, mem. exec. com., chmn. fin., 1992—; bd. advisor to UN Nat. Com. for Habitat, 1993—; first Am. invesment banker to coord. private bus. coun. meeting N.Y.C. with His Excellency Saparmurad A. Niyazov (1st elected pres. The Rep. of Turkismanistan, previously part of USSR) and cabinet of minsters, 1993; mem. Rep. Senatorial Inner Circle, 1992.; mem. Graphic Artists Guild, 1976-80, Bronx County Hist. Soc., 1968-71, Cliffside Park Baseball Assn., 1979—, coach, 1981, 83; sponsor Project High Frontier, U.S. Govt., 1986, sustaining mem. Rep. Nat. Com., 1981—; preferred mem. U.S. Senatorial Club, 1984—; majority mem. Nat. Republican Senatorial Com., 1984—; mem. Heritage Found., 1990—, Nat. Republican Congressional Com., 1984—, N.J. Republican State Com., 1994—, The City Club N.Y.C. (govt. ops. com.); Sachs art scholar, 1955; Designed Seal for art svcs. for Am. Red Cross, 1961, Exhibited Bronx Hist. Soc. photo show, N.Y.C., 1970; paintings at Soc. of Illustrators show, 1971-72; numerous other shows; represented in permanent collection Smithsonian Inst. Recipient medal for art service Youth Friends Assn., 1961, Ga. Pacific award, 1978, Scholastic Mixed media award Scholastic Mag., 1961. Mem. Citizens Against Govt. Waste, The City Club N.Y., Tenafly Rifle and Pistol Club Inc., Nat. Rifle Assn. Jewish. Clubs: Fort Lee Racquetball. Lodge: Bnai Brith. Address: 200 Winston Dr Cliffside Park NJ 07010-3235

GOLDSTEIN, HOWARD SHELDON, lawyer; b. Apr. 22, 1952; s. Jerome Harold and Goldie G.; m. Amy Ruth, Aug. 24, 1980. BA, CUNY, 1974; JD, Bklyn. Law Sch., 1977. Bar: N.Y. 1978, U.S. Dist. Ct. (so. and ea. dists.) N.Y. 1978. Assoc. Loew & Cohen, Esquires, N.Y.C., 1976-82, ptnr., 1982-87; ptnr. Cohen & Goldstein, N.Y.C., 1988—. Contbr. articles to profl. jours. Mem. N.Y. State Bar Assn. (family law com., legis. com.), N.Y. County Lawyers Assn., Nassau County Bar Assn., N.Y.C. Bar Assn. (legal referral svcs.). Republican. Jewish. Office: Cohen & Goldstein Esqs LLP 32 Broadway Rm 1700 New York NY 10004-1670

GOLDSTEIN, HOWARD WARREN, lawyer; b. N.Y.C., Mar. 29, 1949; s. Murray and Claire (Millrod) G.; m. Wendy Jo Zacharius, Sept. 9, 1973; children: Lindsay Rebecca, Amanda Mikael, Justin Zacharius. BA, Northwestern U., 1970; JD, NYU, 1973. Bar: N.Y. 1974, U.S. Dist. Ct. (so. and ea. dists.) N.Y. 1974, U.S. Ct. Appeals (2d cir.) 1975, U.S. Ct. Appeals (10th cir.) 1984, U.S. Ct. Appeals (6th cir.) 1985, U.S. Ct. Appeals (3d cir.) 1997, U.S. Supreme Ct. 1984, U.S. Claims Ct. 1988. Law clk. to judge U.S. Dist. Ct. (ea. dist.) N.Y., 1973-74; assoc. Cravath, Swaine & Moore, N.Y.C., 1974-76; asst. U.S. atty. Office of U.S. Atty. (so. dist.) N.Y., N.Y.C., 1976-80; assoc. Mudge, Rose, Guthrie, Alexander & Ferdon, N.Y.C., 1980-81, ptnr., 1982-90; ptnr. Fried, Frank, Harris, Shriver & Jacobson, N.Y.C., 1990—. Author: Grand Jury Practice, 1998; co-author: The Rights of Crime Victims, 1985, RICO: Civil and Criminal, Law and Strategy, 1989, Corporate Sentencing Guidelines, 1993, Grand Jury Practice, 1998. Mem. Fed. Bar Coun., Assn. of Bar of City of N.Y., Nat. Assn. Criminal Def. Lawyers, N.Y. Coun. Def. Lawyers, Order of Coif, Phi Beta Kappa. Jewish. Office: Fried Frank Harris Shriver & Jacobson One New York Plz New York NY 10004

GOLDSTEIN, IRVING ROBERT, mechanical and industrial engineer, educator, consultant; b. Jersey City, N.J., Apr. 28, 1916; s. David and Anna (Krug) G.; m. Natalie E. Glattstein, Jan. 30, 1949; children: Barbara Joy, David Lee. BSME, Newark Coll. Engring., 1939; MSME, Stevens Inst. Tech., 1947. Registered profl. engr., N.J., Calif. Field worker N.J. Dept. Edn., 1938-39; indsl. engr. Maidenform Co., 1939-40; cost analyst William Bal Corp., 1940-41; resident insp. N.Y. Ordnance Dist., War Dept. U.S. Army, 1941-43; sales rep. Eagle Hosiery Co., 1946-47; instr. dept. indsl. and mgmt. engring. N.J. Inst. Tech., 1947-50, asst. prof., 1950-55, assoc. prof., 1955-70, prof., 1970-81, prof. emeritus, 1981—; prof. dept. info. sci. and sys. Fairleigh Dickinson U., 1992; cons. engr. Irving R. Goldstein, P.E., Springfield, N.J., 1967—; lectr. in field; examiner profl. engring. exam State of N.J., 1967-82; rep. Am. Nat. Stds. Inst., 1970-83, Engr. Joint Coun. Com. for Am. Bicentennial, 1975-78; vice-chmn. N.J. Engrs. Com. for Student Guidance, 1981-83, state meetings coord., 1974-81, treas., 1983-86. Contbr. articles to profl. jours. With U.S. Army, 1943-46, ETO. Fellow Inst. Indsl. Engrs. (dir. work measurement and method engring. div. 1970-73, conf. chmn. 1973-81, publs. chmn. 1966-70, Phil Carroll Achievement award 1975, pres. Met. N.J. chpt. 1977-78, v.p. rsch. and edn. 1968-73, 75-76, 79-81, chmn. bd. gov.'s Metro N.J. chpt. 1966-68, 81-82, faculty advisor N.J. Inst. Tech. U. chpt. 1962-77, Disting. Svc. award Met. N.J. chpt. 1970, 76, 85, Walter Salabun award 1989, author, historian Metro N.J. chpt. 1982—, dir. student affairs Dist. 2, 1989-90, life mem.); mem. NSPE, ASME (life), Informs, Am. Soc. Metals, Prodn. Ops. Mgmt. Soc., N.Y. Acad. Scis., Order of Engr., Alpha Pi Mu, Pi Tau Sigma. Home and Office: 21 Janet Ln Springfield NJ 07081-2714

GOLDSTEIN, IRVING SOLOMON, chemistry educator, consultant; b. Bronx, N.Y., Aug. 20, 1921; s. Jacob and Jennie (Rathsprecher) G.; m. Helen Haft, Dec. 16, 1945; children: Ardath Ann, Darra Jane, Jared. BS in Chemistry, Rensselaer Poly. Inst., 1941; MS in Chemistry, Ill. Inst. Tech., 1944; PhD in Organic Chemistry, Harvard U., 1948. Teaching asst. Ill. Inst. Tech., Chgo., 1941-42; teaching fellow Harvard U., Cambridge, Mass., 1946-48; rsch. chemist N.Am. Rayon Corp., Elizabethton, Tenn., 1948-51; mgr. wood chemistry rsch. Koppers Co., Inc., Pitts., 1951-63; sr. rsch. scientist Nalco Chem. Co., Chgo., 1963-66; mgr. paper rsch. Continental Can Co., Chgo., 1966-68; prof. forest sci. Texas A&M U., College Station, 1968-71; prof., head wood and paper sci. dept. N.C. State U., Raleigh, 1971-78, prof. wood chemistry, 1978-92; prof. emeritus, 1992—. Editor: Wood Technology: Chemical Aspects, 1977, Organic Chemicals From Biomass, 1981, Composition and Structure of Wood, 1991; contbr. articles to profl. jours.; 15 inventions in field. Lt. USNR, 1942-46, ATO, PTO. Fellow Internat. Acad. Wood Sci.; mem. AAAS, Am. Chem. Soc. (chmn. cellulose div. 1982), Tech. Assn. Pulp and Paper Industry, Forest Products Rsch. Soc., Soc. Wood Sci. and Tech. Office: NC State U Dept Wood & Paper Sci Raleigh NC 27695-8005

GOLDSTEIN, IRWIN JOSEPH, medical research executive; b. Newark, N.J., Sept. 8, 1929; 2 children. BA, Syracuse U., 1951; PhD in Biochemistry, U. Minn., 1956. Rsch. fellow, dept. agrl. biochemistry U. Minn., St. Paul, 1956-59; asst. prof., dept. biochemistry State U. N.Y., Buffalo, 1961-65; assoc. prof., dept. biological chemistry U. Mich., Ann Arbor, 1965-72, prof., dept. biological chemistry, 1972—, mem. comprehensive Cancer Ctr.; cons. Ann Arbor Community, 1968-71, Procter & Gamble Co., 1968-90; assoc. dean Rsch. and Grad. Studies U. Mich., 1986-98; mem. rsch com. Henry Ford Hosp., 1983—. Editorial bd.: Journal of Biological Chemistry, 1983-88, 1991-96, Plant Physiology, 1983-86, Carbohydrate Research, 1984-87, Glycoconjugate Journal, 1985-88, Archive Biochemistry and Biophysics, 1989-95. Rsch. bd. United Fund, Buffalo, N.Y., 1963-65; bd. dirs. Guild House U. Mich., 1975-80. Recipient Kaiser Permanente Pre Clinical Teaching award, 1980, Claude S. Hudson Carbohydrate Chemistry award Am. Chem. Soc., 1993; Guggenheim fellow, 1959-60, NIH fellow, 1960-61. Mem. Am. Heart Assn., Biochemical Soc., Chem. Soc., Am. Soc. Biological Chemists, Am. Chem. Soc., Soc. Complex Carbohydrates (exec. com. 1987—), Sigma Xi, Phi Lambda Upsilon. Achievements include research in carbohydrate-protein interactions; isolation, purification and characterization of lectins (carbohydrate-binding proteins); use of lectins to study cell-surface phenomena; studies on the structure and biosynthesis of glycoproteins; immunochemistry of carbohydrates. Office: U Mich Med Sch Deans Office 7319 Med Sci I 1301 Catherine St Ann Arbor MI 48109-0600

GOLDSTEIN, JACK, health science executive, microbiologist; b. N.Y.C., June 7, 1947; s. Arnold L. and Rachel (Vogel) G.; m. Laurie Ann Sacks, Aug. 28, 1969; 1 child, Justin T. BA, Rider Coll., Trenton, N.J., 1969; MS, St. John's U., Jamaica, N.Y., 1974, PhD, 1976. Diplomate Am. Bd. Med. Microbiology. Asst. dir. microbiology Queens Hosp. Ctr., Jamaica, 1976-81; dir. diagnostic labs. API div. Sherwood Med. Co., Plainview, N.Y., 1981-83; v.p. research and devel. MicroScan div. Baxter Travenol, Sacramento, 1983-86; group v.p. Ortho Diagnostic Systems Inc. div. Johnson & Johnson Co., Raritan, N.J., 1986-88; group v.p., gen. mgr. infectious disease bus. Ortho Diagnostic Systems, Inc. div. Johnson & Johnson Co., Raritan, N.J., 1988-92; exec. v.p. worldwide Ortho Diagnostic Sys. Inc. divsn. Johnson & Johnson Co., Raritan, N.J., 1992-93, pres. Ortho Diagnostic Sys. Inc. divsn., 1993-97; pres., CEO Applied Imaging Corp., Santa Clara, Calif., 1997—; mem. exam. com. Am. Bd. Med. Microbiology, Washington, 1984-91. Mem. editl. bd. Jour. Clin. Microbiology, Wasington, 1983-91; contbr. articles to profl. jours. Mem. Am. Soc. Microbiology, Am. Soc. Clin. Chemistry, Beta Beta Beta. Avocations: reading, skiing. Office: Applied Imaging Corp 2380 Walsh Ave Santa Clara CA 95051-1301

GOLDSTEIN, JACK CHARLES, lawyer; b. Ft. Worth, May 11, 1942; s. Bennie Harrison and Rae (Shanblum) G.; m. Leslie P. Silber, July 3, 1965; children: Jason Brent, Jill Paige. BSME, Purdue U., 1964; JD with honors, George Washington U., 1968. Bar: Ill. 1968, Tex. 1968, D.C. 1969, U.S. Dist. Ct. D.C. 1969, U.S. Dist. Ct. (no. and so. dists.) Tex. 1971, U.S. Dist. Ct. (we. dist.) Tex. 1974, U.S. Dist. Ct. (ea. dist.) Tex. 1975, U.S. Dist. Ct. (no. dist.) Miss. 1980, U.S. Dist. Ct. (no. dist.) Calif. 1992, U.S. Dist. Ct. (so. dist.) Calif. 1993, U.S. Ct. Appeals (5th cir.) 1970, U.S. Ct. Appeals (7th cir.) 1974, U.S. Ct. Appeals (2d cir.) 1975, U.S. Ct. Appeals (11th cir.) 1981, U.S. Ct. Appeals (fed. cir.) 1982, U.S. Patent and Trademark Office 1968, U.S. Supreme Ct. 1972. Patent examiner U.S. Patent and Trademark Office, Washington, 1964-67; patent advisor Office Naval Rsch., Silver Spring, Md., 1967-68; law clk. to judge U.S. Ct. Customs and Patent Appeals, Washington, 1968-69; adj. prof. S. Tex. Coll. of Law, Houston, 1974-84; atty. Arnold, White & Durkee, Houston, 1969-97; v.p. The Whitaker Corp., Wilmington, Del., 1998, pres., 1998—; mem. intellectual property adv. bd. U. Houston Law Ctr., 1991—; mem. adv. com. U.S. Ct. Appeals for Fed. Cir., Washington, 1984-92; copyright adv. com. Libr. of Congress, Washington, 1981-82; mem. adv. bd. Patent, Trademark & Copyright Jour., Washington, 1978—. Bd. editors The Intellectual Property Law Strategist, 1994—; contbr. articles to profl. publs. Bd. dirs. Found. For A Creative Am., Washington, 1989-94. Recipient Alumni Svc. award George Washington U., 1985, G. Rose Meml. Comp. award John Marshall Law Sch., 1986, Jour. Finalist award Tex. Bar Found., 1981; Jacob Burns award for extraordinary svc. to the Law Sch., George Washington U., 1996. Fellow Tex. Bar Found. (life), Houston Bar Found. (charter life); mem. ABA (chair, sect. intellectual property law 1992-93), FBA, Am. Intellectual Property Law Assn. (pres. 1988-89), Fed. Cir. Bar Assn. (pres. 1987-88), Copyright Soc. U.S.A. (trustee 1979-82), Bar Assn. D.C., D.C. Bar, Houston Intellectual Property Law Assn. (pres. 1979-80, Pres.'s award 1988), State Bar Tex. (chair intellectual property law sect. 1988-89, Chair's award 1992), Coll. State Bar Tex., Internat. Assn. Protection Indsl. Property, Intellectual Property Owners Assn. (bd. dirs. 1998—), Internat. Intellectual Property Assn. (exec. com. 1996—), Assn. Former CAFC Law Clks. and Tech. Advisors (pres. 1979-80), George Washington Law Alumni Assn. (bd. dirs. 1980-84, 93—), Patent and Trademark Office Soc., Order of Coif, Pi Tau Sigma. Home: 116 Yardley Pl Hockessin DE 19707-8910 Office: The Whitaker Corp Ste 450 4550 New Linden Hill Rd Wilmington DE 19808-2952

GOLDSTEIN, JACOB HERMAN, retired physical chemist; b. Atlanta, Dec. 18, 1915; s. David and Jennie (Levine) G.; m. Audrey Jones, Dec. 26, 1952. A.B., Emory U., 1942, M.S., 1944; M.A., Harvard U., 1947, Ph.D., 1949. Phys. chemist Manhattan Project, 1944-46; asst. prof. Emory U., Atlanta, 1949-51; asso. prof. Emory U., 1951-57, prof., 1958-60, Candler prof. chemistry, 1960-86; cons. industry and govt. Contbr. 200 articles to profl. jours. NRC fellow, 1946-49; recipient Charles Herty medal, 1981; Charles H. Stone award, 1984. Fellow Am. Phys. Soc.; mem. Math. Assn. Am., Am. Chem. Soc., Phi Beta Kappa, Sigma Xi. Jewish. Home: 1671 S Pontz Ln Atlanta GA 30307-1210*

GOLDSTEIN, JEROME ARTHUR, mathematics educator; b. Pitts., Aug. 5, 1941; s. Morris and Henrietta (Vogel) G.; children: Maurice Roland, David Jonathan, Devra. B.S., Carnegie-Mellon U., 1963, M.S., 1964, Ph.D., 1967; S.M.D. (hon.), Internat. Boswell Inst., Loyola U., New Orleans, 1973. Mem. Inst. Advanced Study, Princeton, N.J., 1967-68; asst. prof. math. Tulane U., New Orleans, 1968-71, assoc. prof., 1971-75, prof., 1975-91; prof. Math. Sci. Rsch. Inst. U. Calif., Berkeley, 1990-91; prof. math. La. State U., Baton Rouge, 1992-96, U. Memphis, 1996—. Author: Semigroups of Linear Operators and Applications, 1985; editor: P.D.E. and Related Topics, 1975, Mathematics Applied to Science, 1988, Differential Equations in Biology, Physics and Engineering, 1991, Semigroups of Operators and Applications, 1993, Stochastic Processes and Functional Analysis, 1997, Semigroup Forum, 1982—, Applied and Compositional Mathematics, 1983—. Differential and Integral Equations, 1988—, Electronic Jour. Differential Equations, 1992—, Advances in Differential Equations, 1995—, Communications in Applied Analysis, 1995—, Positivity, 1996—, Jour. Math. Analysis and Applications, 1998—, Jour. of Computational Analysis and Applications, 1998—; contbr. articles to profl. jours. Recipient Faculty Excellence in Research award Coll. Arts and Scis., Tulane U., 1985; NSF grantee, 1968-96. Mem. Am. Math. Soc., Math. Assn. Am., Soc. Indsl. Applied Math., London Math. Soc. Soc. Math. Brazil, Edinburgh Math. Soc., Assn. Women in Math., Sigma Xi (Rsch. award 1972). Jewish. Office: U Memphis Dept Math Scis Memphis TN 38150

GOLDSTEIN, JEROME CHARLES, professional association executive, surgeon, otolaryngologist; b. Nov. 4, 1935; m. Rochelle Jacobs; children: Harry Glenn, Bradley John, Brian Louis. AB, U. Rochester, 1957; MD, SUNY, Syracuse, 1963. Diplomate Am. Bd. Otolaryngology (bd. dirs. 1982—). Intern Phila. Gen. Hosp., 1963-64; resident in gen. surgery Bronx Mcpl. Hosp. Ctr., N.Y.C., 1964-65; resident in otolaryngology SUNY, Syracuse, 1965-68; asst. prof. Northwestern U. Med. Sch., Chgo., 1968-71; pvt. practice Glens Falls, N.Y., 1971-74; prof. surgery, head div. otolaryngology Albany (N.Y.) Med. Coll., 1974-83; exec. v.p. Am. Acad. Otolaryngology-Head and Neck Surgery, Washington, 1984-94, sr. exec. v.p., 1995-96, exec. v.p. emeritus, 1997—; otolaryngologist-in-chief Albany Med. Ctr. Hosp., 1974-83; prof. dept. otolaryngology, head and neck surgery Johns Hopkins Med. Sch., 1986—, Georgetown Med. Sch., 1990; pres. Centurions of Deafness Rsch. Found., N.Y.C., 1987-88. With USAFR, 1965-70. Fellow ACS, Royal Coll. Surgeons Edinburgh, Am. Acad. Facial, Plastic and Reconstructive Surgery, Triology Soc., Am. Laryngol. Assn., Am. Soc. for Head and Neck Surgery (pres. 1982-83), Soc. Head and Neck Surgeons, Am. Neurotol. Soc. (hon.), Am. Bronchoesoph. Soc., Nat. Assn. Physicians for the Environment (founding pres. 1993-95); mem. AMA, Am. Otol. Soc. (hon.), Internat. Fedn. Otorhino-Laryngol. Socs. (regional sec. for N.Am.), Coun. of Med. Specialty Socs. (pres. 1996). Fax: (561) 649-9412. E-mail: JCGMD@aol.com. Home and office: Am Acad Otolaryngology Head and Neck Surgery 4119 Manchester Lek Dr Lake Worth FL 33467

GOLDSTEIN, JILL M., psychiatric epidemiologist, clinical neuroscientist, psychiatry educator; b. New Haven, Sept. 18, 1954; d. Paul and Betty (M.) G.; m. Phillip S. Freeman, Sept. 23, 1984; children: Sonya, Eliana. AB with honors, Brown U., 1976; MPH, Columbia U., 1979, MPhil, 1984, PhD, 1985. Rsch. scientist N.Y. State Psychiat. Inst., N.Y.C., 1976-81, 81-84; rsch. fellwo Columbia U., N.Y.C., 1984-85; sr. rsch. assoc. Brandeis U., Mass., 1985-89; instr. psychiatry Harvard Med. Sch., Boston, 1986-89, cons. psychiat. rsch. project, 1987—, asst. prof. psychiatry, 1989-95, assoc. prof. psychiatry, 1996—; mem. exec. com. Harvard Med. Sch./Mysell, Boston, 1992—; mem. NIMH sci. rev. com. Behavioral Sci. Track Awards for Rapid Transition, 1994—; exec. mem. rsch. com. Mass. Mental Health Ctr., Boston, 1995—. Reviewer, ad hoc jour. referee Am. Jour. Med. Genetics, Neuropsychiat. Genetics, Am. Jour. Psychiatry, Archives of Gen. Psychiatry, Biol. Psychiatry, Hosp. and Cmty. Psychiatry, Jour. Nervous and Mental Disease, Jour. Psychiat. Rsch., Psychiatry, Psychiatry Rsch., Schizophrenia Bull., Schizophrenia Rsch.; guest editor Schizophrenia Bull., 1990; contbr. articles to profl. jours. Grant reviewer Needham (Mass.) Edn. Found., 1992-94; fundraiser Countryside Sch., Newton, Mass., 1996—. NIMH fellow in psychiat. epidemiology, 1980-84; recipient Investigator award Nat. Alliance Rsch. on Schizophrenia and Depression, 1989, Investigator award Internat. Congress on Schizophrenia Rsch., 1989-91, NIMH Scientist Devel. award,

1992-94. Mem. AAAS, Phi Beta Kappa. Avocations: tennis, skiing, violin. Office: Harvard Med Sch/Mass Mental Health Ctr 74 Fenwood Rd Boston MA 02115-6113

GOLDSTEIN, JONATHAN AMOS, ancient history and classics educator; b. N.Y.C., July 19, 1929; s. David Aaron and Rose Frances (Berman) G.; m. Helen Charlotte Tunik, Feb. 1, 1959; children—Rise Belle, Rachel Sarah. AB cum laude, Harvard U., 1950, AM, 1951; M of Hebrew Lit., Jewish Theol. Sem., 1955, D of Hebrew Letters (hon.), 1987; PhD, Columbia U., 1959. Instr. Columbia U., N.Y.C., 1960-62; prof. U. Iowa, 1962—. Author: The Letters of Demosthenes, 1968, I Maccabees, 1976, II Maccabees, 1983, Semites, Iranians, Greeks, and Romans, 1990. Pres. Congregation Agudas Achim, Iowa City, 1969-70. Fulbright scholar U.S. State Dept., Israel, 1959-60; sr. faculty fellow U. Iowa, 1984. Fellow Am. Acad. for Jewish Research; mem. Am. Philol. Assn., Assn. Ancient Historians, AAUP, Archaeol. Inst. Am., Phi Beta Kappa. Democrat. Jewish. Avocations: singing; Jewish community activities. Home: 312 Windsor Dr Iowa City IA 52245-6044 Office: U Iowa Dept History Schaeffer Hall Iowa City IA 52242

GOLDSTEIN, JOSEPH, law educator; b. Springfield, Mass., May 7, 1923; s. Nathan E. and Anna (Ginsberg) G.; m. Sonja Lambek, Aug. 3, 1947; children: Joshua, Anne, Jeremiah, Daniel. AB, Dartmouth Coll., 1943; PhD, London Sch. Econs., 1950; LLB, Yale U., 1952, postgrad., 1968. Bar: Va. 1953. Law clk. to judge U.S. Ct. Appeals D.C., 1952-53; acting asst. prof. Stanford Law Sch., 1954-56; Russell Sage resident, vis. scholar Harvard Law Sch., 1955-56; assoc. prof. Yale Law Sch., 1956-59, prof., 1959—, Justus S. Hotchkiss prof. law, 1968, Walton Hale Hamilton prof. law, sci. and social policy, 1970, prof. Child Study Center, Med. Sch., 1976—, Sterling prof. law, 1978-93, Sterling prof. law emeritus, 1993—, Ruttenberg profl. lectr. in law, 1993—; exec. sec., research dir. Gov. Conn. Prison Study Com., 1956-57; cons. devel. neighborhood legal service Community Progress, Inc., New Haven, 1963-64; mem. U.S. atty. gen. com. poverty and adminstrn. criminal justice, 1962-63; cons. Legal Assistance Assos., Inc., New Haven, 1964-73; pres., bd. dirs. Friends of Legal Services South Central Conn., 1981—; bd. dirs. Vera Inst. Justice, 1966—, Sigmund Freud Archives, 1968—; mem. life scis. and social policy com. NRC, 1968; on legal services Office Econ. Opportunity, 1965, Council on Biology in Human Affairs, Salk Inst., 1969. Author: The Government of a British Trade Union, 1953, (with others) Criminal Law, 2d edit., 1962, The Family and the Law, 1965, Psychoanalysis, Psychiatry and Law, 1967, Crime, Law and Society, 1971, (with Anna Freud and Albert J. Solnit) Beyond the Best Interests of the Child, 1973, 2d edit., 1979, Criminal Law-Theory and Process, 1974, Before the Best Interests of the Child, 1979, (with Burke Marshall and Jack Schwartz) The My Lai Massacre and Its Coverup: Beyond the Reach of Law, 1976, (with Anna Freud, Albert J. Solnit and Sonja Goldstein) In the Best Interests of the Child, 1986, The Intelligible Constitution, 1992, (with Albert J. Solnit and Sonja Goldstein) The Best Interest of the Child-The Least Detrimental Alternative, 1996. Served with AUS, 1943-46. Fulbright scholar, 1949-50; law fellow U. Wis., 1958; Fulbright sr. lectr., 1973; Guggenheim fellow, 1982. Fellow Am. Acad. Arts and Scis.; mem. New Haven Legal Assistance Assn.

GOLDSTEIN, JOSEPH IRWIN, materials scientist, educator, b. Syracuse, N.Y., Jan. 6, 1939; s. Louis and Sylvia (Scharfeld) G.; m. Barbara Hammond, June 30, 1963; children—Steven, Anne. BS in Metallurgy, MIT, 1960, MS, 1962, ScD in Metallurgy, 1964. Instr. metallurgy dept. MIT, 1960-63; phys. metallurgist Smithsonian Astron. Obs., Cambridge, Mass., 1963-64; aerospace technologist NASA-Goddard Space Ctr., Greenbelt, Md., 1964-68; lectr. chem. engring. U. Md., 1966-68; asst. prof., metall. and materials sci. Lehigh U., Bethlehem, Pa., 1968-70, assoc. prof., 1970-75, prof., 1975-93, T.L. Diamond Dist. prof., 1976-79, asst. v.p. rsch. 1979-83, v.p. research, 1983-90, R.D. Stout prof. materials sci. and engring., 1990-93, dean Engring., U. Mass. Amherst, 1993—. Author, editor 8 books. Contbr. over 200 articles to profl. jours. Recipient Nat. Environ. Research Council award, Britain, 1974. Fellow Am. Soc. for Metals; mem. Microbeam Analysis Soc. (pres. 1977-78, Sci. award 1991, Svc. award 1984), Meteoritical Soc. (council mem. 1979-81, treas., 1995—). Republican. Jewish. Home: 49 Sheerman Ln Amherst MA 01002-1584 Office: U Mass Office of the Dean Coll of Engineering Amherst MA 01003

GOLDSTEIN, JOSEPH LEONARD, physician, medical educator, molecular genetics scientist; b. Sumter, SC, Apr. 18, 1940; s. Isadore E. and Fannie A. Goldstein. BS, Washington and Lee U., Lexington, Va., 1962; MD, U. Tex., Dallas, 1966; DSc (hon.), U. Chgo., 1982, Rensselaer Poly. Inst., 1982, Washington and Lee U., 1986, U. Paris, 1988, U. Buenos Aires, 1990, So. Meth. U., 1993, U. Miami, 1996, U. Miami, 1006. Intern, then resident in medicine Mass. Gen. Hosp., Boston, 1966-68; clin. assoc. NIH, 1968-70; postdoctoral fellow U. Wash., Seattle, 1970-72; mem. faculty U. Tex. Southwestern Med. Ctr., Dallas, 1972—, Paul J. Thomas prof. medicine, chmn. dept. molecular genetics, 1977—, regental prof., 1985—; Harvey Soc. lectr., 1977; mem. sci. rev. bd. Howard Hughes Med. Inst., 1978-84, mem. med. adv. bd., 1985-90, chmn. med. adv. bd., 1995—; nonresident fellow Salk Inst., 1983-94; chmn. Albert Lasker Med. Rsch award jury, 1996—; mem. bd. sci. govs. Scripps Rsch. Inst., 1996—. Co-author: The Metabolic Basis of Inherited Disease, 5th edit., 1983; editorial bd. Jour. Biol. Chemistry, 1981-85, Cell, 1983—, Jour. Clin. Investigation, 1977-82, Ann. Rev. Genetics, 1980-85, Arteriosclerosis, 1981-87, Sci. 1985-98. Mem. bd. trustees Rockefeller U., 1994—; mem. sci. adv. bd. Welch Found., 1986—; bd. dirs. Passano Found., 1985—. Recipient Heinrich-Wieland prize, 1974, Pfizer award in enzyme chemistry Am. Chem. Soc., 1976; Passano award Johns Hopkins U., 1978; Gairdner Found. award, 1981; award in biol. and med. scis. N.Y. Acad. Scis., 1981, Lita Annenberg Hazen award, 1982; Rsch. Achievement reward Am. Heart Assn., 1984; Louisa Gross Horwitz award, 1984; 3M Life Scis. award, 1984, Albert Lasker award in Basic Med. Rsch., 1985; Nobel Prize in Physiology or Medicine, 1985, Trustees' medal Mass. Gen. Hosp., 1986, U.S. Nat. medal of Sci., 1988. Mem. NAS (Lounsbery award 1979, coun. 1991—), ACP (award 1986), Assn. Am. Physicians, Am. Soc. Clin. Investigation (pres. 1985-86), Am. Soc. Human Genetics (William Allan award 1985), Amer. Acad. Arts and Scis., Am. Soc. Biol. Chemists, Am. Fedn. Clin. Research, Am. Philos. Soc., Inst. Medicine, Royal Soc. London (fgn. mem.), Tex. Philos. Soc., Phi Beta Kappa, Alpha Omega Alpha. Home: 3831 Turtle Creek Blvd Apt 22B Dallas TX 75219-4415 Office: U Tex Southwestern Med Ctr 5323 Harry Hines Blvd Dallas TX 75235-9046

GOLDSTEIN, JOYCE, special education educator; b. Bklyn., July 7, 1949; d. George and Eleanor (Mittleman) Kluback; m. Charles Irwin Goldstein, May 31, 1975; children: Andrew, Roger. BA, CUNY, Queens, 1971; MS, C W Post, 1975, C W Post, 1990. Sci. tchr. IS 151, Bronx, N.Y., 1972-76; spl. edn. tchr. of emotionally handicapped Bd. Coop. Ednl. Svcs. 2, Sayville, N.Y., 1989-91; spl. edn. tchr. emotionally handicapped Bd. Coop. Ednl. Svcs., West Islip, N.Y., 1991—. Contbr. articles to profl. jours. V.p. Young Republicans, Queens, 1969-71. Mem. Coun. for Exceptional Children. Avocations: reading, fishing, traveling. Home: 49 Empress Pines Dr Nesconset NY 11767-3128

GOLDSTEIN, KATHERINE H., technology educator, computer consultant; b. N.Y.C., Oct. 17, 1968; d. Leon and Patricia (Chambers) G. BA, CUNY, 1991; MA, Columbia U., 1995. Lic. pub. h.s. tchr., N.Y.C.; lic. pub. h.s. tchr., N.Y. State. Acctg. asst. Biller & Schnyer, N.Y.C., 1984-89; salesperson retail electronics Crazy Eddie, N.Y.C., 1986-87; tchr. Hebrew sch. Larchmont (N.Y.) Temple, 1987-93; youth dir. United Synagogue Youth Forest Hills JCC, Kane St. and Town & Village Synagogue, N.Y., 1988—; computer tech. coord. Middle Coll. H.S. at LaGuardia Coll., Long Island City, N.Y., 1994—; computer tchr. Murry Bergtraun Adult Edn., N.Y.C., 1996—; computer instr. Monroe Coll., Bronx, 1996—. Adminstr. Camp Ramah, Nyack, N.Y., summer 1985-92, 96, 97; counselor, staff USY Pilgramage, Israel, and Poland sem. summer 1993-95; educator AIDS Ctr. Queens County, Queens, 1990-93; vol. Nat. Jewish Dem. Coun., N.Y.C., 1995—; vol., educator, mentor United Synagogue of Am., N.Y.C., 1987—. Mem. NOW, ACM, Coalition for Advancement of Jewish Edn., Delta Kappa Phi, Kappa Delta Phi. Democrat. Jewish. Avocations: rollerblading, swimming, traveling, woodworking. Office: Middle Coll HS at LaGuardia Coll Rm L101 31-10 Thomson Ave Long Island City NY 11101

GOLDSTEIN, KEITH STUART, family practice physician, emergency physician; b. Bronx, N.Y., July 4, 1955; s. Stanley Irving and Horty (Silverstein) G.; m. Staci Marta Willner; 1 child, Lara Jacquelyn. BS in Biology with honors, Tulane U., 1976; MD with honors, Ross U., 1982; postgrad., Med. Coll. Wis., 1991—. Resident in gen. surgery Brookdale Hosp. Med. Ctr., Bklyn., 1982-83; resident in family practice Niagara Falls (N.Y.) Meml. Med. Ctr., 1984-86; attending physician dept. emergency medicine Scranton (Pa.) State Gen. Hosp., 1987-89, attending physician dept. family practice, 1988—; attending physician dept. emergency medicine Towanda (Pa.) Meml. Hosp., 1988-94, med. dir. wellness program, 1992-94; pvt. family practice Scranton, 1987-89; med. dir. Bettis Atomic Power Lab., 1994—; med. dir. Tri-Twp. Ambulance, 1990-94, Wyalusing Ambulance, 1991-94, Canton Ambulance, 1991-94, Endless Mountains (Bradford County) Tri-Athlon, 1990-91, Scranton Plasma Ctr., 1988-94, Bradford County Fall Run, 1991; team physician asst. All Bradford County Pa. Sch. Teams, 1988-94; asst. sports medicine clinic Towanda Meml. Hosp., 1988-94; lectr. in field; vis. prof. anatomy Niagara County C.C. Sch. Nursing, Sanborn, N.Y., 1985. Mem. editorial bd. Jour. Contemporary Surgery, 1987—; contbr. articles to profl. publs. Mem. AMA (Physician Recognition award 1991, 93, 95, 97), Am. Assn. Physician Specialists-Emergency Medicine, Am. Med. Assn. Sports Medicine Physicians, Am. Acad. Family Physicians, Am. Coll. Sports Medicine, Am. Coll. Emergency Physicians, Pa. Med. Soc., Am. Assn. Trauma Specialists, Nat. Assn. Emergency Med. Technicians, B'nai B'rith. Avocations: flying, amateur radio, scuba diving, computer programming, writing poetry. Home: 3200 Cambridge Ct Murrysville PA 15668-1411 Office: PO Box 79 West Mifflin PA 15122-0079

GOLDSTEIN, KENNETH B., lawyer; b. Bklyn., Sept. 16, 1949; s. Nathan and Isabella (Solow) G. BA, Tulane U., 1973, JD, 1974; postdoctoral, Fordham U., 1979. Bar: N.Y. 1977, U.S. Dist. Ct. (so. and ea. dist.) N.Y. 1980, U.S. Ct. Appeals (D.C. cir.) 1981. Gen. mgr., v.p. Middletown (N.Y.) Window Cleaning Co., Inc., 1974; tchr. various schs., Middletown and Chester, N.Y., 1975-77; asst. sr. v.p., dir. mktg. Saks Fifth Ave, N.Y.C., 1977-79; sr. asst. dist. atty. Orange County, Goshen, N.Y., 1979-81; assoc. Zola & Zola, N.Y.C., 1981-83, Freedman, Weisbein & Samuelson P.C., Garden City, N.Y., 1983-85, Jaffe & Asher, N.Y.C., 1985-91, Raoul Lionel Felder P.C., N.Y.C., 1991—; bd. dirs. Middletown Window Cleaning Co., Inc. Bd. dirs. New Orleans Jazz and Heritage Found., 1972-74. Named one of Outstanding Young Men in Am., 1980. Mem. ABA, N.Y. State Bar Assn., Middletown Bar Assn., Orange County Bar Assn., Order of DeMolay. Republican. Jewish. Avocations: swimming, art, dance, opera. Home: 145 E 35th St Apt 2me New York NY 10016-4121 Office: Raoul Lionel Felder PC 437 Madison Ave New York NY 10022-7001

GOLDSTEIN, KENNETH F., entertainment executive, software executive; b. Detroit, Mar. 10, 1962; s. Earl Goldstein and Sarita (Bow) Snow. BA in Philosophy and Theater, Yale U., 1984. Freelance writer, TV and film producer L.A., 1984-89; writer, producer Cinemaware Corp., Westlake Village, Calif., 1989-91; designer, producer Philips Interactive Media, L.A., 1991-92; exec. publisher Carmen Sandiego series Broderbund Software, Inc., Novato, Calif., 1992-96; v.p. entertainment, gen. mgr. divsn. Red Orb Entertainment Myst, Riven Series Broderbund Software, Inc., Novato, 1996-98; Journeyman Project series, Warlords series Broderbund Software, Inc., 1996-98; sr. v.p., gen. mgr. Disney Online, 1998—. Author: (screenplays) 8, 1992-95; designer (software programs) Carmen Sandiego: Jr. Detective Edition, 1994 (Software Publs. Assn. award 1995), Reading Galaxy, 1994 (Family PC, Mac World awards 1996), In the 1st Degree, 1995 (Software Publs. Assn. award 1996). Vol. Olive Crest Treatment Ctr., 1986, Free Arts for Abused Children, 1988; sec. bd. trustees Full Circle Programs, Marin County, Calif., 1992-98. Recipient Pub. Svc. awards, Olive Crest Treatment Ctrs., 1986, Free Arts for Abused Children, 1988; named one of Top 100 Multimedia Producers, Multimedia Producer Mag., 1995, Best of What's New in Computers, Electronics, Popular Sci. Mag., 1995, Upside Mag. Elite 100, Honorable Mention Digital Entertainment, 1998. Mem. Writers Guild of Am. West, Acad. Interactive Arts and Scis (founding mem., bd. govs. L.A.), Yale Univ. Alumni (schs. com. 1988—), Computer Game Developers Assn. Avocations: skiing, health and fitness, reading lit. and non-fiction. Office: Disney Online 500 S Buena Vista St Burbank CA 91521-7710

GOLDSTEIN, LAURENCE ALAN, trade association executive; b. Milw., June 4, 1948; s. Henry David and Sylvia (Sadowsky) G.; m. Carolyn Frances Chamoy, Sept. 6, 1981; children: Justin Chamoy, Doran Alisa, Shira Kate. BA, U. Wis., Milw., 1970, MA, 1971. Assoc. dir. State of Israel Bonds, Milw., 1977-81; exec. dir. Wis. region Jewish Nat. Fund, Milw., 1981-84; ptnr. Chamoy Goldstein & Assocs., Milw. and Washington, 1984-93; dir. pub. rels. Nat. Aggregates Assn., Silver Spring, Md., 1993-97; publs. specialist Washington Gas, 1998—. Author: (periodical) Aggregates For Tomorrow: The Sand Gravel and Crushed Stone Industry, 1994, 50 Fascinating Facts About Aggregates, 1994; editor, reviser (periodicals) How to Plan and Conduct an Aggregates Industry Open House, 1993, The Year 2000 and You, 1999; producer and writer (video slide show) Aggregates: The Fundamental Resource For The Future, 1995. Bd. dirs. Jewish Nat. Fund of Nat. Capitol Region. Mem. Pub. Rels. Soc. Am. (accredited mem.), Am. Planning Assn., Urban Land Inst., Am. Soc. Landscape Architects, Masons, Shriners. Republican. Avocations: reading, music, historical research, family activities. Office: Washington Gas 900 Spring St Washington DC 20080

GOLDSTEIN, LEONARD BARRY, dentist, educator; b. Seaford, N.Y., Feb. 6, 1944; s. Jacob Martin and Adele (Pelzner) G.; m. Phyllis Lynn Kerwin, June 25, 1967; children: Marcie Ilene, Sherri Elysse. Student, Ind. U., 1961-63; DDS, Case Western Reserve U., 1967; Cert. in Orthodontics, Dewey Sch. Orthodontics, N.Y.C., 1969; PhD in Electro-Medicine, City U., Los Angeles, 1988. Diplomate Am. Acad. of Pain Mgmt., Am. Bd. Forensic Medicine, Am. Bd. Forensic Dentistry. Gen. practice dentistry Smithtown, N.Y., 1969—; attending orthodontist Abe Stark Philanthropies Dental Clinic, Bklyn., 1970-77; med. dir. TMJ Facial Pain Ctr. Southside Hosp., Bay Shore, N.Y.; guest prof. Dept. Phys. Edn. Queens Coll., N.Y., 1979—; guest lectr. Dept. Phys. Edn. Queensboro (N.Y.) Community Coll., 1980—; dir. dental services Good Samaritan Profl. Services, St. James, N.Y., 1979—, v.p. med. bd., 1979—; attending dental staff St. John's Episc. Hosp., 1980—, Community Hosp. Western Suffolk, 1980—; bd. dirs. L.I. Ctr. for Cranio-Facial Pain, Smithtown; med. dir. TMJ/Facial Pain Ctr., Southside Hosp. Contbr. articles to profl. jours. Served to capt. Dental Corps, U.S. Army, 1967-69. Recipient fellowship in removeable prosthetics U.S. Army Dental Corps, 1967. Fellow Acad. Stress and Chronic Disease, Acad. Gen. Dentistry, Am. Endodontic Soc., Internat. Coll. Dentists; mem. Am. Equilibration Soc., Am. Coll. Sports Medicine, Internat. Acad. Preventive Medicine, Cranial Acad. of Am. Osteopathic Soc., Am. Orthodontic Soc., Internat. Soc. Orthodontists, Am. Dental Soc., Cronio-Mandibular Study Club of N.Y., L.I. Gnathological Study Club, Northeastern Gnathological Soc. Home: PO Box 217 178 Alexander Ave Nesconset NY 11767-1602 Office: 50 Route 111 Smithtown NY 11787-3700

GOLDSTEIN, LIONEL ALVIN, personal financial and investment advisor; b. Bklyn., Oct. 19, 1932; s. Alexander and Ruth (Spitzer) G.; m. Judy Calk, May 19, 1973; children: Alex Nolan, Sharon Anne. Student, So. Meth. U., 1965; MS, U. Dallas, Irving, Tex., 1977; cert. fin. planner, Coll. Fin. Planning, 1983; PhD, Golden State U., 1986. CPA, Tex.; CFP; cert. personal fin. specialist; accredited estate planner; accredited investment mgmt. cons. V.p. fin., treas. Arrow Industries, Inc, Carrollton, Tex., 1965-76; pres. Goldstein & Co., CPA, Dallas, 1976-87; prin., co-founder Quest Capital Mgmt., Inc., Dallas, 1987-89; owner, mgr. Goldstein & Assocs., Dallas, 1989—; dir. MBA program fin. planning services U. Dallas Grad. Sch. Mgmt., 1985-88. Served with U.S. Army, 1951-53. Mem. AICPA, Tex. Soc. CPAs. (com. chmn. Dallas chpt. 1978-80), Nat. Assn. Accts. (internat. bd. standards and practices for cert. fin. planners, bd. examiners 1988), Inst. CFPs (pres. Dallas chpt. 1987-88, chmn. Dallas chpt. 1988-89), Inst. Investment Mgmt. Cons., North Tex. Estate Planning Coun. Republican. Jewish. Avocation: wood working. Home: 2627 Valley Creek Trl Mc Kinney TX 75070-4337 Office: 1216 N Central Expy Ste 101 Mc Kinney TX 75070-3314

GOLDSTEIN, LISA JOY, writer; b. L.A., Nov. 21, 1953; d. Harry George and Miriam (Roth) G.; m. Douglas Andrew Asherman, Jan. 12, 1986. BA, UCLA, 1975. Author: The Red Magician, 1982 (Am. Book award for best paperback 1983), The Dream Years, 1985, paperback edit., 1986, A Mask for the General, 1987, paperback edit., 1988, Tourists, 1989, paperback edit., 1994, Author's Choice Monthly: Daily Voices, 1989, Strange Devices of the Sun and Moon, 1993, paperback edit., 1994 (Sci. Fiction Book Club selection), Summer King, Winter Fool, 1994, paperback edit., 1995, Travellers in Magic, 1994, paperback edit., 1997, Walking the Labyrinth, 1996, paperback edit., 1998, Dark Cities Underground, 1999 (Sci. Fiction Book Club selection). Office: care Tor Books 175 5th Ave New York NY 10010-7703

GOLDSTEIN, MANFRED, retired consultant; b. Vienna, Austria, Jan. 30, 1927; came to U.S., 1939, naturalized, 1945; s. Isidore and Anna (Hahn) G.; m. Shirley Marie Lavine, Aug. 27, 1950; children: Cindy Marie, Lynn Alyse. Student Manhattan Trade Center, 1947; E.E., Capitol Radio Engring. Inst., 1963; student L.I. U., 1961, Indsl. Coll. Armed Forces, 1967-68. Sr. technician Bklyn. Radio, 1953-55, Budd Stanley, Inc., Long Island City, N.Y., 1955; lead engr. telephone equipment Precision Indsl. Design Newark, 1955-57; project engr., contract adminstr., sales mgr. Lieco, Inc., Syossett, N.Y. 1957-65, v.p., 1964-65; mgmt. and engring. cons., 1965-91, ret.; pres. Positive Cons. Inc., Bellmore, N.Y., 1967-86, Lake Luzerne, N.Y., 1986-91, 95—; owner Lake Luzerne (N.Y.) Seaplane Base, 1969—. Mem. small bus. adv. com. to Congressman Thomas J. Downey, 1977-91; mem. small bus. adv. council L.I. Assn. Commerce; founder NCMA L.I. Scholarship Fund. Served with AUS, 1945-46. Fellow Nat. Contract Mgmt. Assn. (bd. dirs. L.I. chpt., v.p. 1983-85); mem. IEEE (sr.), Soc. Plastics Engrs., Am. Indsl. Preparedness Assn. (exec. bd. mgmt. div.), ABA (assoc.), Air Force Assn., Capitol Radio Engring. Inst. Alumni (sr.), Nat. Pilots Assn., Aircraft Owners and Pilots Assn., Internat. Platform Assn. Inventor torpedo fire control cable and connector for Polaris, high pressure seals for Polaris submarine antennae. Home: 18 Bay Rd Lake Luzerne NY 12846-2601

GOLDSTEIN, MARC, microsurgeon, urology educator, administrator; b. N.Y.C., Mar. 22, 1948. BS cum laude, CUNY, Bklyn., 1968; MD summa cum laude, SUNY, Bklyn., 1972. Diplomate Nat. Bd. Med. Examiners, Am. Bd. Urology. Surgical intern Columbia-Presbyn. Med. Ctr., N.Y.C., 1972-73, surgical resident, 1973-74; asst. instr., resident, chief resident dept. urology Downstate Med. Ctr. SUNY, Bklyn., 1977-80, asst. prof. urology dept. urology Downstate Med. Ctr., 1980-82; asst. attending surgeon Univ. Hosp., SUNY Downstate Med. Ctr., and Kings County Hosp. Ctr., Bklyn., 1980-82; fellow-in-residence Population Coun. Rockefeller U., N.Y.C., 1980-82, rsch. assoc., 1980-83; assoc. physician Rockefeller U. Hosp., N.Y.C., 1980-86, vis. assoc. physician, 1986-87; asst. attending surgeon urology N.Y. Hosp., N.Y.C., 1982-88; asst. prof. surgery Cornell U. Med. Ctr., N.Y.C., 1982-88; staff scientist Population Coun. Ctr. Biomed. Rsch., N.Y.C., 1982—; dir. divsn. male reproductive medicine and microsurgery, dept. urology N.Y. Hops.-Cornell Med. Ctr., N.Y.C., 1982—; assoc. attending surgeon N.Y. Hosp., N.Y.C., 1988-94; assoc. prof. surgery Cornell U. Med. Coll., N.Y.C., 1988-94; attending surgeon N.Y. Hosp., 1994—; prof. urology Cornell U. Med. Coll., N.Y.C., 1994—, dir. ctr. for male reproductive medicine and microsurgery, 1982—; mem. adv. com. Assn. Voluntary Surgical Contraception, 1984—; participant concept clearance meeting NIH, 1989; mem. editorial bd. Microsugery, 1983—, Jour. of Andrology, 1991-93, Andrology Report, 1992—. Author: (with M. Feldberg) The Vasectomy Book: A Complete Guide to Decision Making, 1982, 2d edit., 1985, (with G. Berger, M. Fuerst) The Couples Guide to Fertility, 1989, 2d edit., 1995, (with Doubleday Co.) Surgery of Male Infertility, 1995, Atlas of the Urology Clinics: Surgery for Male Infertility, 1999; contbr. chpts. to books, articles to profl. jours.; patentee in field. Maj. USAF, 1974-77, USAFR, 1977-90. Honor scholar Downstate Med. Ctr., 1969; Summer Rsch. fellow Downstate Med. Ctr., 1969-70, Ferdinand C. Valentine fellow N.Y. Acad. Medicine, 1980-82; recipient Ferdinand C. Valentine Urology prize N.Y. Acad. Medicine and N.Y. sect. Am. Urological Assn., 1981, Best Movie award Am. Fertility Soc. and Can. Fertility and Andrology Soc., 1986, 96, Excellence in Video Prodn. award Video Urology, 1987, 90; commd. Ky. Col., Commonwealth of Ky., 1988. Fellow ACS; mem. AMA, Am. Soc. Andrology (mem. various coms.), Am. Fertility Soc., Am. Urological Assn. (scholar 1980-82, mem. various coms.), N.Y. County Med. Soc., Internat. Microsurgical Soc., Soc. Study Reproduction, Soc. Reproductive Surgeons (fellowship com. 1989—), Soc. for Male Reproduction and Urology (pres. 1996), Alpha Omega Alpha, N.Y. Rd. Runners Club (completed 14 N.Y.C. marathons), Brit. Mountaineering Coun. E-mail: mgoldst@mail.med.cornell.edu. Office: NY Hosp-Cornell Med Ctr Dept Urology 525 E 68th St Dept Urology New York NY 10021-4885

GOLDSTEIN, MARCIA LANDWEBER, lawyer; b. Bklyn., Aug. 7, 1952; d. Jacob and Sarah Ann (Danovitz) Landweber; m. Mark Lewis Goldstein, June 3, 1973. AB, Cornell U., 1973, JD, 1975. Bar: N.Y. 1976, U.S. Dist. Ct. (so. and ea. dists.) N.Y., U.S. Ct. Appeals (2d, 3d, 5th, 7th and 9th cirs.). Assoc. Weil, Gotshal & Manges, N.Y.C., 1975-83, ptnr., 1983—; adv. bd. Colliers on Bankruptcy, 15th edit.; vis. lectr. Yale Law Sch.; lectr. Practicing Law Inst. ALI-ABA, NYU bankruptcy worksop. Mem. ABA (com. on creditors' rights, corp. counse. com.), Assn. of Bar of City of N.Y. (chair bankruptcy and reorgn. com.), Nat. Bankruptcy Conf., Am. Coll. Bankruptcy. Office: Weil Gotshal & Manges 767 5th Ave Fl Concl New York NY 10153-0119

GOLDSTEIN, MARGARET ANN, biologist; b. Sinton, Tex., Mar. 13, 1939; d. Daniel Archibald and Sarah Elizabeth (Tegg) McNeill; m. Alexander Goldstein, Jr., Feb. 14, 1959; 1 child, David William. BA magna cum laude, Rice U., Houston, 1965; PhD, Rice U., 1969. Lab instr. biology Rice U., 1965-69; instr. biology U. Tex./M.D. Anderson Hosp., Houston, 1969-70; asst. prof. biology U. Tex., Houston, 1969-77; instr. cell biophysics and medicine Baylor Coll. Medicine, Houston, 1970-73; asst. prof. cell biophysics and medicine Baylor Coll. Medicine, 1973-77, asst. prof. medicine and cell biology, 1977-79, assoc. prof. medicine and cell biology, 1979-89, prof. medicine and cell biology, 1989—; ccons. NHLBI, NIH, 1986-94, NRC, 1996—; exec. com. basic scis. coun. Am. Heart Assn., Dallas, 1987-94, assembly del., 1995-98; biol. dir. Microscopy Soc. Am., 1990-92, chair internat. com., 1993-95, pres., 1995-96; liaison officer to AAAS/CAIP, 1990-95, resp. to AAAS bd., 1993-96. Contbr. articles to profl. jours. V.p., bd. dirs. Tex. Chamber Orch., Houston, 1982-86; bd. dirs. River Oaks Women's Breakfast Club, 1980-85, Houston Friends of Music, 1991—, Rice U. Shepherd Soc. Governing Coun., 1995—; mem. award com. YWCA Outstanding Houston Women, 1991-96; adv. bd. mem. Houston Grand Opera, 1995-96. Recipient Outstanding Houston Woman in Sci. and Tech. award YWCA, Houston, 1990, Order of Silver Thistle, Scottish Heritage Found., Houston, 1990, NASA Achievement award for Cosmos 2044, 1991, for Cosmos 2G, 1994; NIH grantee, 1974—. Mem. AAAS (affiliate bd. consortium of affils. for internat. programs), Microscopy Soc. Am. (biol. dir. 1990-92, pres. 1995-96), Tex. Soc. for Electron Microscopy (pres. 1981-82, exec. coun. 1977-83), Am. Soc. Cell Biology, Assn. for Women in Sci. (v.p. 1979-80), Coun. Sci. Soc. Pres.'s (exec. bd. dirs. 1997). Avocations: music, gardening, physical fitness. Office: Baylor College Medicine Dept Medicine Houston TX 77030-3498

GOLDSTEIN, MARJORIE TUNICK, special education educator; b. Port Chester, N.Y., Oct. 20, 1940; d. Abraham and Gertrude (Gluckman) Tunick; m. Herbert Goldstein, May 27, 1973. BA, Syracuse U., 1961; MA, George Washington U., 1968; PhD, Yeshiva U., N.Y.C., 1979. Spl. edn. tchr. Lancaster (Pa.) City Pub. Schs., 1962-63, Hempfield Union Schs., Landisville, Pa., 1963-64, Montgomery County (Md.) Pub. Schs., 1964-65; edn. specialist U.S. Office Edn., Washington, 1965-69; coord. field ops. Curriculum R&D Ctr., Yeshiva U., N.Y.C., 1969-78; supr. spl. edn. E. Ramapo Cen. Sch. Dist., Spring Valley, N.Y., 1978-79; adj. asst. prof. Herbert Lehman Coll., Bronx, 1980-83; spl. edn. coord. Ednl. Improvement Ctr./NE, W. Orange, N.J., 1981-83; prof. William Paterson U. of N.J., Wayne, N.J., 1983—; spl. needs book reviewer Instr. mag., N.Y.C., 1984-90; co-developer entry level cert. tests Pa. Ednl. Testing Svc., Princeton, 1985-88. Cons. editor Career Devel. for Exceptional Individuals, 1988-97. Contbr. articles to profl. jours. Office Spl. Edn. and Rehab. Svc./Dept. Edn. grantee, 1987-90; named Educator of Yr., Morris County ARC, 1991, N.J. Assn. Retarded Citizens, 1991. Mem. ASCD, Coun. Exceptional Children (sec. N.J. div. on career devel. 1988, pres. 1992-93), Am. Assn. Mental Deficiency, Am. Ednl. Rsch. Assn., N.J. Assn. Supervision and Curriculum Devel. (assoc. exec. dir. 1984-85, 86-87, 89-91). Office: William Paterson Univ NJ 300 Pompton Rd Wayne NJ 07470-2103

GOLDSTEIN, MARK ALLAN, pediatrician, adolescent medicine specialist; b. Washington, Jan. 8, 1947; s. Samuel and Jean (Epstein) G.; m. Myrna chandler, Dec. 27, 1970; children: Brett Jonathan, Samantha Anne. BS, U. Md., 1968; MD, Georgetown U., 1972. Lic. physician, Mass. Intern in pediats. Boston City Hosp., 1972-73; resident in pediats. Mass. Gen. Hosp., Boston, 1975-77; fellow in adolescent and young adult medicine Children's Hosp., Boston, 1977-78; acad. practice and med. rsch. Cambridge, Mass.; chief pediats. and student health MIT, Cambridge, 1978—; asst. clin. prof. pediats. Harvard Med Sch., Boston, 1990—. Author: Definitive Guide to Medical School Admission, 1996, 2d edit., 1998; editor: Our Baby: The First Year, 1997. co-chair Presdl. Working Group on Dangerous Drinking, MIT, 1997—. Fellow Soc. for Adolescent Medicine, Am. Acad. Pediats.; mem. Mass. Med. Soc. (chmn. com. student health and sports medicine 1998—), New Eng. Pediat. Soc. Jewish. Avocation: historic preservation. Office: MIT 77 Massachusetts Ave Cambridge MA 02139-4307

GOLDSTEIN, MARVIN EMANUEL, aerospace scientist, research center administrator; b. Cambridge, Mass., Oct. 11, 1938; s. David and Evelyn (Wilner) G.; m. Priscilla Ann Beresh, July 5, 1965; children: Deborah, Judy. BS in Mech. Engring., Northeastern U., 1961; MS in Mech. Engring., MIT, 1962; PhD in Mech. Engring., U. Mich., 1965. Engr. Arthur D. Little, Inc., Cambridge, 1958-61; rsch. asst. MIT, Cambridge, 1961-63, rsch. assoc., 1965-67; aerospace engr. Lewis Rsch. Ctr., NASA, Cleve., 1967-79, chief scientist, 1980—; adj. prof. math dept. Case Western Res. U., 1998—. Author: Aeroacoustics, 1976; contbr. articles to profl. jours. Fellow AIAA (assoc. editor jour. 1977-79, chmn. aeroacoustics tech. com., 1979-81, mem. publs. com. 1980-83, Aeroacoustics award 1983, Pendray award 1983), Am. Phys. Soc. (exec. com. div. fluid dynamics 1991-93, Otto Laporte award in fluid mechanics 1997); mem. NAE. Avocation: automobile racing and rebuilding. Office: NASA Lewis Rsch Ctr MS 3-17 21000 Brookpark Rd Cleveland OH 44135-3191

GOLDSTEIN, MARVIN MARK, lawyer; b. Bklyn., Jan. 24, 1944; s. Abraham and Regina (Winkler) G.; m. Linda Ann Sinkoff, Aug. 4, 1969; 1 child, Randal Ian. BS, Cornell U., 1966; JD, Boston U., 1969. Bar: N.Y. 1969, N.J. 1972. Corp. labor counsel Gen. Cable Corp., N.Y.C., 1970-72; assoc. Grotta, Oberwager & Glassman, Newark, N.J., 1972-76; ptnr. Grotta, Glassman & Hoffman P.A., Roseland, N.J., 1976—; resident, ptnr. Proskauer Rose LLP, Newark, N.J., 1999—. Asst. sec. Hackensack (N.J.) Med. Ctr., 1987-93, mem. exec. com., 1987-96; bd. trustees United Jewish Community Bergen County, N.J., 1984-90. Mem. ABA (chmn. subcom. fair labor standards act labor law sect.), N.J. Bar Assn. (chmn. adminstrv. law sect. 1987-89, legis. liaison labor law sect. 1986). Avocation: cross country skiing. Office: Proskauer Rose LLP 1 Newark Ctr Newark NJ 07102

GOLDSTEIN, MARVIN NORMAN, physician; b. Balt., Aug. 10, 1940; s. Manuel Quezon and Sylvia (Wagenheim) G.; m. Athene Schiffmann, July 1, 1962; children: Joshua, Claire. AB summa cum laude, Western Md. Coll., 1960; MD, U. Md., 1964. Diplomate Am. Bd. Psychiatry and Neurology. Intern in internal medicine U. Chgo. Hosp., 1964-65; resident in neurology Strong Meml. Hosp., U. Rochester, N.Y., 1965-68; chief resident in neurology Strong Meml. Hosp., U. Rochester, 1967-68; asst. attending neurologist, instr. U. Md. Hosp., Balt., 1968-69, Johns Hopkins Hosp., Balt., 1969-70; asst. prof. neurology and anatomy U. Rochester Sch. Medicine and Dentistry, 1970-74, clin. asst. prof. neurology and anatomy, 1974-78, clin. assoc. prof. neurology and anatomy, 1978-97; sr. attending neurology The Genesee Hosp., Rochester, 1978—, dir. neurology unit, 1996—; clin. prof. neurology, 1997—; instr. in neurology and anatomy U. Rochester Sch. Medicine and Dentistry, 1965-68, Sch. Medicine, Georgetown U., Washington, 1968-70; staff neurologist U.S. Naval Hosp., Bethesda, 1968-70; med. staff exec. com. The Genesee Hosp., Rochester, 1989-90. Contbr. articles to profl. jours. Bd. dirs. Rochester Area Multiple Sclerosis, Rochester, 1972-78; adult edn. com. Temple Beth El, Rochester, 1985-90. Lt. comdr. USNR, 1968-70. Grantee NIH, 1972-74. Fellow Am. Acad. Neurology, Royal Soc. Medicine; mem. Am. Epilepsy Soc., Am. Acad. Clin. Neurophysiology, Sigma Xi. Avocations: gardening, canoeing, model shipbuilding, fishing. Home: 20 Varinna Dr Rochester NY 14618-1508 Office: 222 Alexander St Rochester NY 14607-4039

GOLDSTEIN, MARY KANE, physician; b. N.Y.C., Oct. 24, 1950; d. Edwin Patrick and Mary Kane; m. Yonkel Noah Goldstein, June 24, 1979; children: Keira, Gavi. Philosophy degree, Columbia U., 1973, MD, 1977; MS in Health Svcs. Rsch., Stanford U., 1994. Resident Duke U. Med. Ctr., Durham, N.C., 1977-80; asst. prof. medicine U. Calif., San Francisco, 1980-84; staff physician Cowell Student Health Ctr. U. Calif., Santa Cruz, 1984-85; clin. instr. dept. family and cmty. preventive medicine Stanford U., Santa Cruz, 1984-85; staff physician Mid-Peninsula Health Svc., Palo Alto, Calif., 1986-88; dir. grad. med. edn. divsn. gerontol. Stanford (Calif.) U., 1986-93, Agy. for Health Care Policy Rsch. fellow Sch. Medicine, 1991-94, asst. prof. med., 1996—; acting program dir. primary care policy sect. Stanford U., 1998—; sect. chief for gen. internal medicine Palo Alto (Calif.) VA Med. Ctr., 1994-96; rsch. assoc. health svcs. R&D Palo Alto (Calif.) VA Med. Ctr., Palo Alto, 1996—; dir. Geriatrics Clin., The Geriatric Rsch. Edn. and Clinical Ctr., Palo Alto, 1999—; editor Computer Ctr. Pubs., N.Y.C., 1971-72; computer programmer Columbia U., N.Y.C., 1972-73; governing coun. evidence-based practice ctr. U. Calif., Stanford, 1998—. Author chpt. to book; contbr. articles to profl. jours. Recipient Rsch. award Far West Health Svcs. R&D, 1990, Cost Implications award Hartford Found. Geriat. Ctr., 1991, Preference Assessment in Geriat. award Palo Alto Inst. for Rsch. and Edn., 1992, Clin. Practice Guildelines for Hypertension, 1997. Fellow Am. Geriat. Soc. (bd. dirs. 1996—); mem. Am. Bd. Family Practice (bd. dirs. 1993-98), Am. Fedn. Clin. Rsch., Geriatric Test Com. Office: VA Palo Alto Health Care Sys GRECC 182B 3801 Miranda Ave Palo Alto CA 94304-1207

GOLDSTEIN, MELVYN C., anthropologist, educator; b. N.Y.C., Feb. 8, 1938; s. Harold and Rae (Binen) G.; 1 son, Andre. B.A., U. Mich., 1959, M.A., 1960; Ph.D., U. Wash., 1968. Asst. prof. Case Western Res. U., Cleve., 1968-71; asso. prof. Case Western Res. U., 1971-76, prof., chmn. dept. anthropology, 1976—, dir. ctr. rsch. on Tibet, 1987-91, J.R. Harkness prof., 1991—. Author: Modern Spoken Tibetan, 1970, Modern Literary Tibetan: A Grammar and Reader, 1973, Tibetan English Dictionary of Modern Tibetan, 1975, Tibetan for Travellers and Beginners, 1980, English-Tibetan Dictionary of Modern Tibetan, 1984, Tibet Phrasebook, 1987, A History of Modern Tibet, 1913-1951: The Demise of the Lamist State, 1989, 2d edit., 1991, Nomads of Western Tibet, The Survival of a Way of Life, 1990, Essentials of Modern Literary Tibetan: A Reading Course and Reference Grammar, 1991, The Changing World of Mongolian Nomads, 1994, The Struggle for Modern Tibet: The Autobiography of Tashi Tsering, 1997, The Snow Lion and the Dragon: China, Tibet and the Dalai Lama, 1997, Buddhism in Contemporary Tibet: Religious Revival and Cultural Identity (with Matthew Kapstein), 1998; editor Jour. Cross-Cultural Gerontology; contbr. articles to profl. jours. Grantee Am. Council Learned Socs., 1973-74, NIH, 1976-77, 80-82, NEH, 1980-82, 84-85, 89—, Dept. Edn., 1980-82, Smithsonian Instn., 1981-83, Nat. Geographic Soc., 1980-81, Nat. Inst. Child Health and Human Devel., 1981-83, NSF, 1982-83, Com. for Scholarly Exchange with People's Republic China, 1985-86, 87-88, Nat. Geog. Soc., 1986-88, 90-91, Dept. of Edn., 1986-87, IREX, 1990-92. Mem. Assn. Asian Studies, Am. Anthropol. Assn., Soc. Applied Anthropology, Soc. Med. Anthropology, Assn. for Anthropology and Gerontology. Home: 50 E 252d St Euclid OH 44132-3901 Office: Case Western Res Univ 236 Mather Memorial Cleveland OH 44106

GOLDSTEIN, MICHAEL, retail executive. Formerly exec. v.p., treas., CFO Toys R Us Inc., Rochelle Park, N.J., exec. v.p. fin. and adminstrn., vice chmn., CEO, chmn. bd., 1998—. Office: Toys R Us Inc 461 From Rd Ste 2 Paramus NJ 07652-3524

GOLDSTEIN, MICHAEL AARON, finance educator; b. Winchester, Mass., Oct. 9, 1964; s. Norman and Sheila Judith Goldstein. BS, U. Pa., 1986, MBA, 1991, MA in Fin., 1992, PhD in Fin., 1993. Investment banker Merrill Lynch Capital, N.Y.C., 1986-88; rsch. assoc. WhartonSch, U. Pa., Phila., 1988-93; adviser Ministry of Privatization, Warsaw, Poland, 1990; asst. prof. U. Colo., Boulder, 1993—; vis. economist NYSE, 1997-98; various appearances on CNN, PBS, N.Y. Times, CNNfn, News Hour with Jim Leher, BBC, others. Contbr. articles to scholarly and profl. jours., including Jour. of Fin. Treas., CFO Boulder County Dems., Boulder, Colo., 1996; contr. Boulder County Clinton/Gore, 1995-96; bd. dirs. Hillel of Colo., Denver, 1993-96, chair, Boulder, 1994-96. Recipient Tchg. award U. Colo., 1994; GeeWax Terker fellow, 1988-91. Mem. Am. Fin. Assn., Fin. Mgmt. Assn. (reviewer/referee 1996—), Wharton Club of Colo., Phi Beta Kappa, Beta Gamma Sigma, Delta Sigma Pi. Democrat. Jewish. Avocations: skiing, hiking, travel, flying, running in N.Y.C. and Boston marathons, others. Office: Coll Bus U Colo Boulder PO Box 419 Boulder CO 80309-0419

GOLDSTEIN, MICHAEL B., lawyer; b. N.Y.C., Sept. 29, 1943; s. Isaac and Betty (Friedman) G.; m. Jinny M. Loewenthal, Dec. 18, 1966; 1 child, Eric Loren. BA in Govt., Cornell U., 1964; JD, NYU, 1967. Bar: N.Y. 1967, Ill. 1974, D.C 1978. Spl. asst., dep. mayor Office of Mayor, N.Y.C., 1965-66, asst. city adminstr., dir. univ. rels., 1969-72; dir. N.Y.C. Urban Corps, 1966-69; assoc. vice chancellor for urban and govtl. affairs, assoc. prof. urban scis. U. Ill., Chgo., 1972-78; mem. Dow, Lohnes & Albertson PLLC, Washington, 1978—; practice leader Edn. Inst. Pub. Policy and Govt. Rels.; chmn. task force on pub. policy Commn. on Higher Edn. and Adult Learner Am. Coun. on Edn.; mem. bd. advisors Stanford Forum for Coll. Financing. Contbr. articles to profl. texts and jours. Pres. Nat. Ctr. for Pub. Svc. Internship Programs, 1975-77; bd. dirs., officer Washington Ctr. Internships and Acad. Seminars, 1977—; bd. dirs. and gen. counsel Washington Ballet, 1978—; bd. dirs. Greater Washington Rsch. Ctr., 1982-96, Chgo. Urban Corps, 1972-75; trustee Fielding Inst., 1989-94, 98—; trustee, chmn. fin. com. Mt. Vernon Coll., 1991-96; dir. Am.-Russian Cultural Cooperation Found., 1995—; bd. visitors Mt. Vernon Coll., 1996-98, WETA, 1997—. Wall St. Jour. Newspaper Fund fellow, 1963, Loeb fellow Harvard U., 1972. Mem. ABA (chmn. edn. law com. 1991-92), FBA (co-chmn. edn. grants com. 1985-86, 91-92), Nat. Assn. Coll. and Univ. Attys. (mem. ctrl. office com. 1986-88, vice chmn. pvt. bar com. 1989-90), Nat. Soc. Internships and Exptl. Edn. (pres. 1972), Am. Assn. Higher Edn. (dir. 1997—). Democrat. Jewish. Office: Dow Lohnes & Albertson 1200 New Hampshire Ave NW Washington DC 20036-6802*

GOLDSTEIN, MICHAEL GERALD, lawyer; b. St. Louis, Sept. 21, 1946; s. Joseph and Sara G. (Findelstein) G.; m. Ilene Marcia Ballin, July 19, 1970; children: Stephen Eric, Rebecca Leigh. BA, Tulane U., 1968; JD, U. Mo., 1971; LLM in Taxation, Washington U., 1972. Bar: Mo. 1971, U.S. Dist. Ct. (ea. dist.) Mo. 1972, U.S. Tax Ct. 1972, U.S. Ct. Appeals (8th cir.) 1974, U.S. Supreme Ct. 1976. Atty. Morris A. Shenker, St. Louis, 1972-78; ptnr. Lashly, Caruthers, Baer & Hamel and predecessor, St. Louis, 1979-84, Suelthaus & Kaplan, P.C. and predecessors, St. Louis, 1974-91; pres., CEO 1st Fin. Resources, 1999—; ptnr., chmn. dept. tax & estate planning Husch & Eppenberger; adj. prof. tax law Washington U. Sch. Law; bd. dirs. Anchor Floor Co., Maritz Inc., 1986-89, Connector Castings Inc., 1971-96; mem. planning com. Mid-Am. Tax Confs., chmn. ALI/ABA Tax Seminar; lectr. taxation field. Author: BNA Tax Mgmt. Portfolios; contbr. numerous articles to profl. jours. and publs. Bd. dirs. Jewish Family and Children's Svc. St. Louis, 1980—, pres., 1986-88; bd. dirs. Jewish Fedn. of St. Louis; trustee United Hebrew Temple, 1986-88; grad. Jwish Fedn. St. Louis Leadership Devel. Coun.; co-chmn. lawyers divsn. Jewish Fedn. St. Louis Campaign, 1981-82, Leadership St. Louis, 1988-89. Capt. USAR, 1970-78. Fellow Am. Coll. Tax Counsel, Am. Coll. Trust and Estate Counsel; mem. ABA (chmn. tax seminar, group editor newsletter for taxation sect.), Am. Law Inst., Mo. Bar Assn., Bar Assn. Met. St. Louis, St. Louis county Bar Assn. Home: 201 Yacht Mischief Newport Beach CA 92660 Office: 695 Town Center Dr 7th Fl Costa Mesa CA 92626

GOLDSTEIN, MICHAEL L., neurologist; b. Chgo., June 14, 1945; s. Charles and Dorothy (Mack) G.; m. Barbara Joan Kaplan, June 18, 1967; children: Rachel, Elizabeth, Adam. AB, Princeton, 1966; MD, U. of Chgo., 1970. Intern Stanford U., 1970-71; resident in neurology Beth Israel Hosp., Boston, 1971-74; fellow in neurology Harvard U. Med. Sch., 1971-74; chief resident in neurology Children's Hosp., Boston, 1973-74; with Western Neurol. Assoc., Salt Lake City; cons. Soc. Sec., Balt., 1990-91; bd. dirs., edn. comm. chmn. Rowland Hall, St. Marks Sch., Salt Lake City, 1986-92; examiner Am. Bd. Psychiatry and Neurology, 1987—; clin. assoc. prof. U. Utah Med. Sch., Salt Lake City, 1977—. Co-author: Managing Attention Disorders, 1990, Parent's Guide to ADD, 1993; co-producer: Educating Inattentive Children, 1992, It's Just Attention Disorder, 1993. Pres. synagogue, Salt Lake City, 1985-86. Fellow Am. Acad. Pediat., Am. Acad. Neurology (chair practice com, 1995—). Office: Western Neurol Assn 1151 E 3900 S Salt Lake City UT 84124-1216

GOLDSTEIN, MILTON, art educator, printmaker, painter; b. Holyoke, Mass., Nov. 14, 1914; s. Jacob Bernard and Sarah (Peskin) G.; m. Mollie Brick. Student, Northeastern U., 1934-35, Art Students League, 1939-41, 46-49. Part-time instr. Art. Students League, N.Y.C., 1948-65; instr. graphics arts dept. Adelphi U., Garden City, N.Y., 1953-56, asst. prof., 1956-59, assoc. prof., 1959-65, prof., 1965-85, prof. emeritus, 1985. Represented in permanent collections Mus. Modern Art, Pila. Mus. Art, Met. Mus., Bklyn. Mus., Smithsonian Nat. Mus., Libr. Congress., Mil. Mus. of War Dept., Washington, U.S. Army Ctr. of Mil. History, Washington, and other pub. and pvt. collections in Am. and Europe; several one-man shows (nat. prizes and purchase awards); inventor color printing method for making color etchings. With U.S. Army, 1942-45. Guggenheim fellow, 1950. Fellow Royal Soc. Arts; mem. Soc. Am. Graphic Artists, Art Student League (life). Avocations: refinishing old furniture, fixing broken objects, sports. Home and Office: 56-16 219th St Flushing NY 11364-1918

GOLDSTEIN, MORRIS, entertainment company executive; b. Pitts., Feb. 2, 1945; s. Irving and Clara (Caplan) G.; m. Diane Donna Davis, Aug. 21, 1966 (div. Nov. 1985); children: Jonathan, Julie; m. Kathy Evelyn Niemeier, July 7, 1990. BS, Carnegie Inst. Tech., 1967; MBA, U. Pa., 1979. Sales rep. computer divsn. RCA, Cherry Hill, N.J., 1968-70; sales mgr. Sedgwick Printout Sys., Princeton, N.J., 1970-76, pres., 1976-80; v.p. Courier-Jour. Louisville Times, 1980-81; mgr. bus. devel. Ziff-Davis Pub., N.Y.C., 1982—; pres. Information Access Corp. divsn., Foster City, Calif., 1982—; pres., COO Imagination Network Inc., Oakhurst, Calif., 1994; sr. v.p. Ziff-Davis Pub., Foster City, Calif., 1994; CEO Info. Access Co., A Thomson Corp. Co., Foster City, Calif., 1995-96, Thomson Tech. Ventures, San Mateo, Calif., 1997; pres., CEO Alliance Gaming Inc, Las Vegas, Nev., 1997—. Dep mayor Mt. Laurel Twp., N.J., 1974-78. Home: 2217 Chatsworth Ct Henderson NV 89014-5310 Office: Alliance Gaming Inc 6601 Bermuda Rd Las Vegas NV 89119-3605

GOLDSTEIN, MURRAY, health organization official; b. N.Y.C., Oct. 13, 1925; s. Israel and Yetta (Zeigen) G.; m. Sue Mary Michael, June 13, 1957; children: Patricia Sue Robertson, Barbara Jean Warner. BA, NYU, 1947; DO, Des Moines Still Coll. Osteo. Medicine, 1950; MPH, U. Calif., 1959; DSc (hon.), Kirksville Coll. Osteo. Medicine, 1970, U. New Eng., 1984, Ohio U., 1986, U. Osteo. Medicine and Health Scis., 1990; LLD (hon.), N.Y. Inst. Tech., 1982; Dr. honoris causa, Med. Univ. Pecs, Hungary, 1985; LHD (hon.), Coll. Osteo. Medicine Pacific, 1988; Dr. honoris causa, Med. Sch. U. Lund, Sweden, 1994. Diplomate Am. Osteo. Bd. Preventive Medicine (sec.-treas. 1987-88, vice chmn. 1988-92). Rotating intern Still Coll. Osteo. Hosp., Des Moines, 1950-51, resident internal medicine, 1951-53; commd. corps USPHS, 1953, advanced through grades to asst. surgeon gen., 1980, ret., 1993; asst. to chief, then asst. chief, grants and tng. br., Nat. Heart Inst. NIH, Bethesda, Md., 1953-58, dir. epidemiology and biometry tng. grant program, divsn. rsch. grants, 1956-58; asst. chief rsch. grants rev. br., divsn. rsch. grants, 1959-60; exec. sec. joint coun. subcom. cerebrovascular disease Nat. Inst. Neurol. Diseases and Stroke and Nat. Heart and Lung Inst., NIH, Bethesda, Md., 1961-67, 69-75; dir. extramural programs Nat. Inst. Neurol. and Communicative Disorders and Stroke, NIH, Bethesda, Md., 1961-76, dir. stroke and trauma program, 1976-78, dep. dir., 1978-81, acting dir., 1981-82, dir., 1982-93; pub. health trainee epidemiology Calif. State Dept. Pub. Health, Berkeley, 1958, acting chief sect. virus diseases ctrl. nervous system, Bur. Acute Communicable Disease, 1958; med. dir. United Cerebral Palsy Rsch. and Edn. Found., Washington, 1993—, bd. dirs., 1972-93; clin. prof. neurol. medicine N.Y. Coll. Osteo. Medicine, 1977—; sr. lectr. dept. neurology Uniformed Svcs. U. Health Scis., 1986—; bd. dirs. Nat. Stroke Assn., Burke Rsch. Inst., Robarts Rsch. Inst.; adj. prof. pub. health Nova-Southeastern U., 1995—; chmn. Commd. Corps Adv. Com. to NIH dir., 1990-93, WHO Task Force on stroke and other vascular cerebral disorders, 1986-89; dir. WHO Neurosci. Collaborating Ctr., Bethesda, 1981-93; liaison, mem. sci. adv. bd. Kent Waldrep Nat. Paralysis Found., 1989-94; vis. prof. med. rsch. Semmelweis Med. U., Budapest, Hungary, 1975; vis. sci. sect. neurology Mayo Clinic and grad. sch., Rochester, Minn., 1967-68; vis. scholar Henry Ford Hosp., 1979-80; v.p. Eisenhower Inst. Stroke Rsch., 1975-88; cons. bur. rsch. Am. Osteo. Assn., 1990—; lectr., cons. in field. Assoc. editor Stroke: A Journal of Cerebral Circulation, 1976-91, consulting editor, 1992—; mem. editl. bd. Osteo. Annals, 1973-85, 87-88, Internat. Jour. Neurology, 1980—, Jour. Neuroepidemiology, 1981-90, Hosp. and Community Psychiatry, 1980—, Alzheimer Disease: An Internat. Jour., 1985-93, Cerebralvascular and Brain Metabolism Revs., 1985-93; contbr. articles to profl. jours. Bd. dirs. Bapt. Home for Children and Adults, 1999—. With U.S. Army, 1943-45. Decorated DSM, Silver Star, Purple Heart; recipient USPHS Disting. Svc. medal with oak leaf cluster, Surgeon Gen.'s Exemplary Svc. medal, Surgeon Gen.'s medallion, Founders Day medal U. Osteo. Medicine and Health Scis., 1983, Patenge Pub. Svc. medal Mich. State U., 1987, Marjorie Guthrie award The Huntington's Disease Soc. Am., 1988, Burke award Buke Found., 1988, Spl. Leadership award United Cerebral Palsy Rsch. & Ednl. Found., 1989, Phillips Pubs. Svc. medal Ohio U., 1990, others. Fellow Am. Acad. Neurology (mem. long range planning com. 1972-75, mem. manpower com. 1979-85, mem. neurology in govtl. svcs. and insts. com. 1979-85, chmn. 1981-83, 93-95, mem. internat. affairs com. 1981-90, chmn. 1981-83, mem. com. govt. rels. 1983-85, ANA-AAN del to World Fedn. Neurology 1983-85, mem. AAN com. on pub. comm. and legislation 1983-85, mem. ad hoc com. for soc. neurology liaison 1987-89, sr. advisor uniformed svcs. orgn. neurologists com. 1987-93, bd. dirs. 1993—), United Cerebral Palsy Assn. (interim dir. 1998), Am. Acad. Cedrebral Palsy and Devel. Medicine, NIH Alumni Assn. (v.p. bd. dirs. 1999—), others. Avocations: gardening, golf, swimming. Home: 6210 Swords Way Bethesda MD 20817-3349 Office: United Cerebral Palsy Rsch & Ednl Found 1660 L St NW Ste 700 Washington DC 20036-5616

GOLDSTEIN, NAOMI, psychiatrist; b. N.Y.C., Apr. 24, 1932; d. Eli and Caroline (Kleppner) G.; m. Franklin Feldman, June 3, 1956; children: Sarah, Eve, Jacob. AB, Vassar Coll., 1952; MD, N.Y. Med. Coll., 1956. Diplomate in psychiatry Am. Bd. Psychiatry and Neurology. Pvt. practice N.Y.C., 1960-98; staff psychiatrist Criminal Ct. Psychiat. Clinic, 1961-68; psychiat. adminstr. N.Y.C. Probation Methadone Clinic, Bernstein Inst., 1970-72; dir. Supreme and Criminal Ct. Psychiat. Clinics, 1968-72; staff psychiatrist Liaison Svc. Bellevue Hosp., 1972-74; chief psychiatry Met. Correction Ctr. Fed. Bur. Prisons, N.Y.C., 1974-78; attending psychiatrist Bellevue Hosp., 1978-90; clin. prof. psychiatry NYU Med. Sch., N.Y.C., 1990—; pres. Am. Bd. Forensic Psychiatry, Balt., 1988-89; mem. N.Y. State Bd. Profl. Med. Conduct, Albany, 1978—, chmn., 1982-84; lectr. law Columbia U., N.Y.C., 1988; bd. advisors Fed. Correctional Instn., Otisville, N.Y., 1980-85. Contbr. articles to profl. jours. Fellow AMA, Am. Psychiat. Assn. (life, trustee-at-large 1982-85, pres. N.Y. County dist. br. 1985-86), N.Y. Acad. Medicine (chmn. psychiatry sect. 1993-94), Am. Acad. Psychiatry and the Law, Assn. Women Psychiatrists, Am. Med. Women's Assn., Acad. Hon. Soc. N.Y. Med. Coll., Phi Beta Kappa. Jewish.

GOLDSTEIN, NEIL WARREN, filmmaker; b. Washington, June 3, 1950; s. Alfred Frank and Tillie Goldstein; m. Janice Posatery Burke, Mar. 28, 1981; 1 child, Evan Benjamin. BA, Washington U., St. Louis, 1972, MA, 1974. Dir. instl. tech. Childrens Hosp., L.A., 1975-82; chief exec. officer Corp. Disabilities and Telecommunication, L.A., 1982-88; chmn. East Coast chpt. Corp. Disabilities and Telecommunication, Phila., 1988-92; pres. Neil Goldstein & Assocs., 1992—; pres. Ctrl. Coast Cmty. TV, L.A., 1982, Concept Works, Inc., L.A., 1980-82; co-founder Lyme Project, Phila., 1988-92; vice chmn. Pub. Health Planning Group, Phila., 1988; instr. Montgomery County C.C., 1992—, Drexel U., 1997—; comm. cons. U. of the Arts, Phila., 1998-99. Dir., prodr. film festival Superfest, 1976-88 (CC Robinson award 1987); exec. prodr. TV spl. Superfest, 1982-89 (Emmy 1986, Gov. award 1989); dir., prodr. TV spl. Breaking Ground, 1987 (Gov. award 1988, Presdl. Commendation 1988, Emmy nominee), Amnesty KTLA-TV, 1988, Lyme Disease: In Our Own Backyard, N.J. Network, 1991, Shattered Lives: Composing an Identity After a Traumatic Brain Injury, 1994, Barriers, The Montgomery County Neighborhood Youth Corps, 1995 (Best H.S. Documentary, Tusculum Videofest, 1995, Best Practice, 1998, A Chance to Hear, 1998. Vol. Westside YMCA, West Los Angeles, Calif., 1982-84; bd. dirs. Ranch Owners Assn., Tehachapi, Calif., 1984-88; adv. com. Sch. Bd. Upper Moreland Twp., 1990-91; co-chair health issues adv. com. Montgomery County, 1992. Grantee Corp. Pub. Broadcasting, L.A., 1987, Am. Film Inst., L.A., 1988. Mem. Soc Motion Picture and TV Engrs., Dirs. Guild, Acad. TV. Avocations: reading, writing, walking, biking. Home: 1930 Cathedral Rd Huntingdon Valley PA 19006-5006

GOLDSTEIN, NILES ELLIOT, rabbi, author; b. Chgo., Feb. 5, 1966; s. Melvin Joel and Lois Ann (Rakita) G. BA, U. Pa., 1988; MA in Hebrew Letters, Hebrew Union Coll., 1993. Ordained rabbi, 1994. Jewish educator Jewish Cmty. Ctr. of Staten Island, N.Y., 1994-95; asst. rabbi Temple Israel, New Rochelle, N.Y., 1995-97; Steinhardt fellow CLAL: The Nat. Jewish Ctr. for Learning and Leadership, N.Y.C., 1996-97, sr. fellow, 1997-98; prgm. officer/educator Jewish Life Netowrk, N.Y.C., 1998—; bd. dirs. Union of Couns., Washington, 1996—; mem. com. on interreligious affairs Union Am. Hebrew Congregations, 1993—; spkr., presenter in field. Author: Forests of the Night, 1996, Judaism and Spiritual Ethics, 1996; editor: Duties of the Soul, Spiritual Manifestos, 1999. Nat. Jewish chaplain Fed. Law Enforcement Officers Assn., 1994—; chaplain Drug Enforcement Adminstrn., N.Y.C., 1996—. 1st lt. USAR, 1991-97. Fellow Bd. Jewish Edn., 1994-96. Mem. Ctrl. Conf. Am. Rabbis, N.Y. Bd. Rabbis, Shelley Soc. N.Y., Acad. Am. Poets, Assn. for Jewish Studies. Avocations: hiking, dogsledding, karate. Home: 196 8th Ave Apt 8 Brooklyn NY 11215-2615 Office: Jewish Life Network 6 E 39th St New York NY 10016

GOLDSTEIN, NORM, editor, writer; b. N.Y.C., Mar. 24, 1939; s. Michael David and Minna (Shaffer) G.; m. Ruth Weiss, Sept. 15, 1963 (div. 1975), m. Jeannette Reilly, July 15, 1975; 1 child, Frank Parker. BA, Bklyn. Coll., 1959; MA, Pa. State U., 1960. Assoc. editor Ind. Film Jour., N.Y.C., 1960-61; writer, editor AP, Phila., 1963-66; writer, editor AP, N.Y.C., 1966-72, dir. ednl. svcs., 1972-84, editor, spl. editions, 1984-91, dir. spl. projects, 1991—. Author: Joyn Wayne: A Tribute, 1979, Frank Sinatra: Ol' Blue Eyes, 1982, Henry Fonda, 1982, History of Television, 1991, Marshal: The Story of the U.S. Marshals, 1991, Kim Dae Jung, 1998; editor: Footprints on the Moon, 1969, Seventy-Six, 1976, 444 Days, 1981, Eyewitness History of the Vietnam War, 1983, Moments in Time, 1984, Moments in Sports, 1985, Front Page, 1985, Moments in Space, 1986, World War II: A 50th Anniversary History, 1989; project dir.: 20th Century America: A Primary Source Collection From the Associated Press, 1995; editor AP Stylebook and Libel Manual, 1986—. With USAR. Avocation: softball. Home: 450 E 20th St New York NY 10009-8238 Office: Assoc Press 50 Rockefeller Plz Fl 5 New York NY 10020-1666

GOLDSTEIN, SIR NORMAN, dermatologist; b. Bklyn. July 14, 1934; s. Joseph H. and Bertha (Docteroff) G.; B.A., Columbia Coll., 1955; M.D., SUNY, 1959; m. Ramsay, Feb. 14, 1980; children: Richard, Heidi. Intern, Maimonides Hosp., N.Y.C., 1959-60; resident Skin and Cancer Hosp., 1960-61, Bellevue Hosp., 1961-62, NYU. Postgrad. Center, 1962-63 (all N.Y.C.); ptnr. Honolulu Med. Group, 1967-72; practice medicine specializing in dermatology, Honolulu, 1972—; clin. prof. dermatology U. Hawaii Sch. Medicine, 1973—; bd. dirs. Pacific Laser. Bd. dirs. Skin Cancer Found., 1979—; trustee Dermatol. Found., 1979-82, Hist. Hawaii Found., 1981-87; pres. Hawaii Theater Ctr., 1985-89, Hawaii Med. Libr., 1987; mem. Oahu Heritage Council, 1986-94. Served with U.S. Army, 1960-67. Recipient Henry Silver award Dermatol. Soc. Greater N.Y., 1963; Husik award NYU, 1963; Spl. award Acad. Dermatologia Hawaiiana, 1971, Outstanding Scientific Exhibit award Calif. Med. Assn., 1979, Special award for Exhibit Am. Urologic Assn., 1980, Svc. to Hawaii's Youth award Adult Friends for Youth, 1991, Nat. Cosmetic Tattoo Assn. award, 1993, Cmty. Svc. award Am. Acad. Dermatology, 1993; named Physician of Yr., Hawaii Med. Assn., 1993. Fellow ACP, Am. Acad. Dermatology (Silver award 1972), Am. Soc. Lasers Medicine & Surgery, Royal Soc. Medicine; mem. Internat. Soc. Tropical Dermatologists (Hist. and Culture award), Soc. Investigative Dermatologists, AAAS, Am. Soc. Photobiology, Internat. Soc. Cryosurgery, Am. Soc. Micropigmentation Surgery, Pacific and Asian Affairs Council, Navy League, Assn. Hawaii Artists, Biol. Photog. Assn., Health Sci. Communication Assn., Internat. Pigment Cell Soc., Am. Med. Writers Assn., Physicians Exchange of Hawaii (bd. dirs.), Am. Coll. Cryosurgery, Internat. Soc. Dermatol. Surgery, Am. Soc. Preventive Oncology, Soc. for Computer

Medicine, Am. Assn. for Med. Systems and Info., Japan Am. Soc. Hawaii (bd. dirs.), Pacific Telecom Council, Hawaii State Med. Assn. (mem. public affairs com.), Hawaii Dermatol. Soc. (sec.-pres.), Hawaii Public Health Assn., Pacific Dermatol. Assn., Pacific Health Research Inst., Honolulu County Med. Soc. (gov.), Nat. Wildlife Fedn., C. of C., Preservation Action, Am. Coll. Sports Medicine, Rotary, Hemlock Soc. USA (med. bd.), Hawaii Govs. Blue Ribbon Panel on Living and Dying with Dignity, Ancient Gaelic Nobilitary Soc. (named Knight of the Niadh Nask, 1995), Outrigger Canoe Club, Plaza Club (pres. bd. dirs. 1990-92), Chancellor's Club, Oahu Country Club. Editor: Hawaii Med. Jour.; contbr. articles to profl. jours. Office: Tan Sing Bldg 1128 Smith St Honolulu HI 96817-5197

GOLDSTEIN, NORMAN RAY, international trading company executive, consultant; b. Chgo., Nov. 20, 1944; s. Max and Rose (Weiner) G.; m. Bonnie A. Brod, Aug. 31, 1969; children: Russell, Matthew, Jamie. AA, Wright Jr. Coll., 1965; BS in Fin., No. Ill. U., DeKalb, 1967; MS in Acctg. cum laude, Roosevelt U., 1986. Gen. bus. mgr. Greenstreet Corp., Whiting, Ind., 1967; wholesale credit mgr. Atlantic Richfield Co., Chgo., 1968-74; v.p. fin., treas. Barton Inc. (Barton Brands, Ltd.), Chgo., 1974-96; chmn., CEO Gold Internat., 1996—; spl. master U.S. Dist. Ct., 1998; chmn. ABC Fin. Communications Forum, Chgo., 1987-88; v.p., bd. dirs. Consort Corp., Chgo., 1971-80; spl. master U.S. Dist. Ct., 1998; speaker on treasury and fin. mgmt. Contbg. author: Handbook of Cash Flow and Treasury Management, 1987; contbr. articles to profl. publs. Bd. dirs. Maine Twp. Jewish Congregation Shaare Emet, Des Plaines, 1986—, pres. 1989-91. Named Outstanding Credit Exec. of Yr., Nat. Assn. Credit Mgmt., 1987, Disting. Alumnus Coll. of Bus. No. Ill. U., 1998. Fellow Nat. Inst. Credit; mem. Treasury Mgmt. Assn., Fin. Mgrs. Assn. Chgo. (treas. 1991-92), Treasury Mgmt. Assn. Chgo. (chmn. ednl. scholarship com. 1995—), Distillers Imports and Vintners (chmn. 1980-82), N.Y. Credit and Fin. Mgmt. Assn., Chgo. Midwest Credit Mgmt. Assn. (bd. dirs. 1984-87).

GOLDSTEIN, NORMAN ROBERT, safety engineer; b. Boston, June 5, 1928; s. Myer and Janet Katherine (Bornstein) G.; BSc, Northeastern U., 1951; MSc, Franklin and Marshall Coll., 1956, PhD Columbia Pacific U., 1994; m. Charlotte Lipson, Sept. 15, 1948; children—Sue Ellen, David, Julie. Registered prof. engr. N.J., Pa., Mass. Various engring. positions RCA, Lancaster, Pa., 1951-67, mem. tech. staff David Sarnoff Research Center, 1967-70; co-founder, v.p. Engineered Inspection System, Inc., Robbinsville, N.J., 1970-89; founder, prin. N.R. Goldstein & Assocs., Robbinsville, 1989—; lectr. various local colls.; instr. Realtor's Inst.; mem. standards panel Commn. on Consumer Product Safety. Pres., Men's Club, Temple Beth El, Lancaster, 1958, Eden Civic Assn., 1960; bd. dirs. Jewish Community Center, Lancaster, Princeton Jewish Center, Temple Beth Chaim, West Windsor, N.J.; conciliator N.J. HOW Program; dist. commr. Boy Scouts Am., 1973-76. Served with C.E., U.S. Army, 1945-47. Recipient award of merit Stony Brook dist. George Washington coun. Boy Scouts Am., 1976. Fellow Nat. Acad. Forensic Engrs.; mem. ASTM, NSPE, N.J. Soc. Profl. Engrs., Am. Soc. Safety Engrs. (profl. grade), World Safety Orgn. (cert. safety specialist, cert. safety exec.), Bldg. Ofcls. and Code Adminstrs., South. Bldg. Conf., Voices of Safety Internatl., Sigma Pi Sigma. Republican. Clubs: Engineers (Trenton). Lodges: Lions (past pres. West Windsor, past gov. internat. dist. 16B, editor jour.), K.P., B'nai B'rith. Contbr. numerous articles to profl. jours.; patentee in U.S. and fgn. countries. Office: N R Goldstein & Assoc 1200 US Highway 130 Robbinsville NJ 08691-1002

GOLDSTEIN, PAUL, lawyer, educator; b. Mount Vernon, N.Y., Jan. 14, 1943; s. Martin and Hannah (Shimberg) G.; m. Jan Thompson, Aug. 28, 1977. B.A., Brandeis U., 1964; LL.B. Columbia U., 1967. Bar: N.Y. 1968, Calif. 1978. Asst. prof. law SUNY-Buffalo, 1967-69, assoc. prof., 1969-71, prof., 1972-75; vis. assoc. prof. Stanford U., Calif., 1972-73, prof. law, 1975—, Stella W. and Ira S. Lillick prof. law, 1985—; of counsel Morrison and Foerster, San Francisco, 1988—. Author: Changing the American Schoolbook--Law, Politics and Technology, 1978, Real Estate Transactions--Cases and Materials on Land Transfer, Development and Finance, 1980, 3d edit. (with G. Korngold), 1993, Real Property, 1984, Copyright: Principles, Law and Practice, 4 vols., 2d edit., 1996, Copyright, Patent, Trademark and Related State Doctrines--Cases and Materials on the Law of Intellectual Property, Rev. 4th edit., 1999, Copyright's Highway: FromGutenberg to the Celestial Jukebox, 1995. Mem. Assn. Litteraire et Artistique Internationale, Copyright Soc. U.S.A. Office: Stanford U Law Sch Nathan Abbott Way Stanford CA 94305

GOLDSTEIN, PEGGY R., sculptor; b. N.Y.C., Jan. 16, 1921; d. Francis Mortimer and Ruth (Schram) Rosenfeld; m. E. Ernest Goldstein, June 22, 1941; children: Susan Lipsitch, Daniel Frank. AB, Smith Coll., 1941; student, Art Inst. Chgo., 1941-42, Corcoran Sch. Art, 1951-52, Acad. de la Grand Chaumière, Paris, 1952-53, Atelier 17, Paris, 1953, 66-67, Acad. de Peinture Orientale, Paris, 1973-75. tchr. Anacostia Neighborhood Mus., Smithsonian Instn., Washington, 1967-68, Am. Coll., Paris, 1976-77. One woman shows include Creative Gallery, N.Y.C., 1951, 53, Springfield Mus. Fine Arts, Mass., 1956, SW Tex. State Coll., San Marcos, 1960, Laguna Gloria, Austin, 1956, 61, Maison du Décor, Washington, 1968, Gottesman and Ptnrs., London, 1976, Galerie Lambert, Paris, 1970, 73, 77, 78, Galerie de la Cathédrale, Fribourg, 1981, Galerie Cimaise, Lausanne, 1983, Galerie Cardas, Lausanne, 1983, Galerie Valentine, Bex, 1984, Galerie Farel, Aigle, 1982, 85, Le Vieux Bourg, Denges, 1987, Galerie Motte, Geneva, 1989, Animalart, Austin Tex., 1995; exhibited in group shows at Salon de la Jeune Sculpture, 1961, 71-76, Salon de Mai, 1970, 72, 73, 77, Galerie Horizon, 1978—, Galerie Picpus, Montreux, 1981, Biennale of Fedn. Internat. de la Médaille, 1983, 85, 87, Création 85, Montreux, 1986, France-Chine, Marseille, 1987, Gravure, Paris, 1987, Galerie Siret, Paris, 1987-88, U. Fribourg, 1988, La Fondation Taylor, Paris, 1990, Galerie Les Hirondelles, Coppet, 1990, Bibliothèque Nationale, Paris, 1992; U.S. Info. Agy. exhbns. Latin Am.; represented in permanent collections Bibliothèque Nationale, Paris, Nat. Archives, Washington, Musée Jenisch, Vevey, Bibliothèque Nationale, Berne; also pvt. collections; executed bronze outdoor sculpture, Nat. Hdqrs. Am. Camping Assn., Ind., 1987, 2 bronze mural sculptures, Austin, 1988, outdoor sculpture Andrews Elem. Sch., Austin; designer 20 medals Adminstrn. des Monnaies et Médailles, Ministère de Fin., Paris, 1973-86; illustrator: At Home After 1840, 1965; author, calligrapher: Lóng is a Dragon: Chinese Writing for Children, 1990 (Gold award Parents Choice 1991); author, calligrapher, illustrator: Hu is a Tiger, An Introduction to Chinese Writing, 1995; contbr. articles to jours. Recipient Sculpture prize Soc. Washington D.C. Artists, 1954, Small Sculpture award Ball State Tchrs. Coll., 1961, Prize UPFS Concours de Masque, 1977; Prèfecture de Paris grantee, 1971; nominated Outstanding Ptnr., Ptnrs. in Edn., Austin Adopt-a-Sch., 1995-96. Fellow Tex. Fine Art Assn., Headliners Club (Austin, Tex.), Austin Visual Arts Assn. Home: 1619 Northumberland Rd Austin TX 78703-3143

GOLDSTEIN, PHYLLIS ANN, art historian, educator; b. Chgo., Apr. 27, 1926; d. Frederick and Belle Florence (Hirsch) Jacoby; m. Seymour Goldstein, Nov. 19, 1947 (dec. 1980); children: Arthur Bruce, Kathy Susan Goldstein Maultasch. BA, Hunter Coll., 1948; MA, Hofstra U., 1985. Tchr. home econs. Cin. Pub. Schs., 1948-50; nutrition instr. Brandeis U. Nat. Women's Com., Westbury, N.Y., 1975-78, instr. art history, 1984-91; lectr. art history Brandeis U., Westbury, N.Y., 1985-92; instr. art history Herricks Adult Community Edn. Program, 1990-91. Camp counselor, troop leader Girl Scouts U.S., N.Y.C., Cin., 1942-51; cub leader Boy Scouts Am., Westbury, 1963-64; active Sisterhood of Temple Beth Avodah, Westbury, 1958-70, pres. 1964-65; active Sisterhood of Temple of Beth Am., Merrick, N.Y., 1980-91; life mem. Brandeis U. Nat. Women's Com., lectr. art history, 1992—, Meadowbrook chpt. pres., 1985-87, South Dade chpt., 96-98, mem. Fla. regional bd., 1998-99; vol. Fairchild Tropical Gardens, 1994—. Mem. Jewish Mus. N.Y., Williamsburg Mus., Mus. Modern Art N.Y., Mus. Art Ft. Lauderdale, Met. Mus. Art N.Y., Hadassah (life). Democrat. Avocations: sewing, swimming, needlework, quilting, travel.

GOLDSTEIN, RICHARD A., consumer products company executive; b. 1942; married. BBA, U. Mass.; LLB, Boston U.; LLM, Harvard U. Atty. Choate Hall & Stewart, 1968-70; spl. asst. to cabinet mem. U.S. Govt., Washington, 1970-73; assoc. Arnold & Porter, Washington, 1973-75; staff atty., gen. couns. Lever Bros. Co., 1975-80, v.p. adminstrv. asst. to chmn., 1980-84; pres., CEO Unilever Can. Ltd., 1984; exec. v.p., COO Unilever U.S., N.Y.C., 1988; pres., CEO Unilevel U.S., 1989; chmn., CEO Unilever Can. Ltd., 1989-97; pres., CEO Unilever N.Am. Foods, 1996—; chmn. Lipton, 1996—. Office: Unilever US Inc 390 Park Ave New York NY 10022-4606*

GOLDSTEIN, RICHARD JAY, mechanical engineer, educator; b. N.Y.C., Mar. 27, 1928; s. Henry and Rose (Steierman) G.; m. Barbara Goldstein; children: Arthur Sander, Jonathan Jacob, Benjamin Samuel, Naomi Sarith. BME, Cornell U., 1948; MS in Mech. Engring., U. Minn., 1950, MS in Physics, 1951, PhD in Mech. Engring., 1959; DSc (hon.), Israel Inst. Tech., 1994; Dr. honoris causa, U. Lisbon, 1996; hon. doctorate, A.V. Luikov Heat and Mass Transfer Inst., Minsk, Belarus, 1997. Instr. U. Minn., Mpls., 1948-51, instr., rsch. fellow, 1956-58, mem. faculty, 1961—, prof. mech. engring., 1965—, head dept., 1977-97, James J. Ryan prof., 1989—, Regents' prof., 1990—; devel. rsch. engr. Oak Ridge Nat. Lab., 1951-54; sr. engr. Lockheed Aircraft, 1956; asst. prof. Brown U., 1959-61; vis. prof. Technion, Israel, 1976, Imperial Coll., Eng., 1984; cons. in field, 1956—; chmn. Midwest U. Energy Consortium; chmn. Coun. Energy Engring. Rsch.; NSF sr. postdoctoral fellow, vis. prof. Cambridge (Eng.) U., 1971-72; Prince lectr., 1983, William Gurley lectr., 1988, Hawkins Meml. lectr., 1991; disting. lectr. Pa. State U., 1992; mem. acad. com. internat. bd. govs. Technion; hon. mem. sci. bd. A.V. Luikov Heat and Mass Transfer Inst., Minsk, 1997. Editorial adv. bd. Experiments in Fluids, Heat Transfer-Japanese Rsch., Heat Transfer-Soviet Rsch., Bull of the Internat. Centre for Heat andMass Transfer, Internat. Archives of Heat and Mass Transfer; hon. editorial adv. bd. Internat. J. Heat and Mass Transfer, Internat. Communications in Heat and Mass Transfer. 1st U.S. Army lt. AUS, 1954-55. Recipient NASA award for tech. innovation, 1977, MUEC Dist. Svc. award, 1986, George Taylor Alumni Soc. award, 1988, A.V. Lykov medal, 1990, Max Jakob Meml. award ASME/AICE, 1990, Nusselt-Reynolds prize, 1993, Dr. Scientiarum Honoris Causa award Technion-Israel Inst. Tech., 1994, Thermal Engring. Internat. award Japan Soc. Mech. Engring.; NATO fellow, Paris, 1960-61, Lady Davis fellow Technion, Israel, 1976. Fellow AAAS, ASME (Heat Transfer Meml. award 1978, Svc. award 1978, Centennial medallion 1980, BEG v.p. 1984—, 50th anniv. award of heat transfer divsn. 1988, sr. v.p. 1989-93, hon. mem. 1992, BOG 1993—, pres. 1996—), Am. Soc. Engring. Edn., Assembly for Internat. Heat Transfer Confs. (pres. 1986-90), Internat. Ctr. for Heat and Mass Transfer (exec. com. 1985—, chmn. 1992, pres.), Am. Phys. Soc.,Japan Soc. Promotion of Sci.; mem. Am. Phys. Soc., Minn. Acad. Sci., Nat. Acad. Engring., Nat. Acad. Engring.-Mex. (corr. 1991), Golden Key Nat. Honor Soc., Sigma Xi, Tau Beta Pi, Pi Tau Sigma. Achievements include research and publications in thermodynamics, fluid mechanics, heat transfer, optical measuring techniques. Home: 4241 Bassett Creek Dr Golden Valley MN 55422-4257 Office: U Minn Dept Mech Engring 111 Church St SE Minneapolis MN 55455-0150

GOLDSTEIN, ROBERT DAVID, plastic surgeon, educator; b. Nov. 5, 1951. BS, Wilkes U., 1973; MD, Pa. State U., 1977. Dir. plastic surgery Weiler Hosp. Montefiore Med. Ctr., Bronx, 1989—; assoc. prof. plastic surgery Albert Einstein Coll. Medicine, Bronx, N.Y., 1993—. Mem. ACS (pres. Bronx chpt. 1994-95). Home: 1625 Poplar St Bronx NY 10461-2608 Office: 1515 Jarrett Pl Bronx NY 10461-2606

GOLDSTEIN, ROBIN, lawyer; b. Bklyn., Sept. 23, 1957; s. Jerome and Edna (Cohen) G. SB, MIT, 1979, M of City Planning, 1980; JD, Union U., 1983. Bar: N.Y. 1984, U.S. Patent Office 1984, U.S. Dist. Ct. (ea. and so. dists.) N.Y. 1985, Mass. 1992, U.S. Supreme Ct. 1992, Ct. of Appeals for Fed. Cir. 1992. Patent clk. Internat. Paper Co., N.Y.C., 1982; assoc. Blum, Kaplan, Friedman, Silberman & Beran, N.Y.C., 1983; patent atty. Digital Equipment Corp, Maynard, Mass., 1984-86; patent counsel SONY Corp Am., Park Ridge, N.J., 1986-91; of counsel Schiller & Kusmer, Boston, 1991-93; pvt. practice Palo Alto, Calif., 1993-95, 97—; sr. counsel Apple Computer, Inc., Cupertino, Calif., 1995-97; gen. counsel Newton, Inc., 1997; talk show host Stas. KSCO-KOMY, 1998—. Mem. ABA, Am. Intellectual Property Law Assn. (mem. group 220 oversight com.), N.Y. Patent Law Assn., Sigma Phi Epsilon. Home: 4842 National Ave San Jose CA 95124-4919

GOLDSTEIN, SANDU, biotechnology executive, researcher; b. Iasi, Romania, May 22, 1936; s. Moise and Perla Goldstein; m. Sylvia Vainstein, Sept. 30, 1967; 1 child, Miron. MSc, Poly. Inst. Iasi, 1958, PhD in Chemistry and Chem. Engring., 1974. Registered profl. engr., profl. chemist. Rsch./devel. engr. Antibiotice, Iassy, Romania, 1958-75; dir. sci. and regulatory affairs ICN Pharms., Montreal, Que., Can., 1976-86; dir. rsch. adminstrn. and planning Merck Frosst Ctr. for Therapeutic Rsch., Montreal, 1986-93, dir. indsl., acad. and govt. affairs, 1993-94; dir. bioprocess engring. sector Biotech. Rsch. Inst. of Nat. Rsch. Coun. of Can., Montreal, 1994—. Patentee in field; contbr. articles to profl. jours. Fellow Chem. Inst. Can. (chairperson Montreal sect. 1987—, mem. mgmt. com. Can. Chem. News 1990-94), Royal Soc. Chemistry (Eng.), Can. Rsch. Mgmt. Assn. (bd. dirs. 1993-97); mem. Am. Chem. Soc., Can. Soc. Chemistry (bd. dirs. 1996—), Ordre des Ingenieurs (Que.), Ordre des Chimistes (Que.). E-mail: sandu.goldstein@nrc.ca. Office: Biotech Rsch Inst, 6100 Royalmount Ave, Montreal, PQ Canada H4P 2R2

GOLDSTEIN, SIDNEY, pharmaceutical scientist; b. Phila., Mar. 27, 1932; s. Israel and Gertrude (Stein) G.; m. Janice Levy, June 19, 1955; children: Rhonda, David, Nina. BSc in Pharmacy, Phila. Coll. Pharmacy & Sci., 1954, MSc in Pharmacy, 1955, DSc in Pharmacy, 1958. Cardiovascular unit head Eaton Labs, Norwich, N.Y., 1958-59; anti-inflammatory unit head Lederle Labs, Pearl River, N.Y., 1959-61; with Merrell Dow Rsch. Inst., Cin., 1961-93; v.p. global pharm. and analytical scis. Marion Merrell Dow Inc., Kansas City, Mo., 1991-93; v.p. sci. and tech. Duramed Pharm., Inc., Cin., 1994—; adj. assoc. prof. U. Cin. Coll. Pharmacy, 1984—, mem. dean's adv. coun., 1998—; lectr. pharmacology Phila. Coll. Pharmacy, 1967-70; chiar PQRI-drug product tech. com. AAPS, 1997—; mem. So. Ohio Life Sci. Task Force, 1999—. Contbr. articles to profl. jours. Bd. trustees Glen Manor Home for Aged, Cin., 1983-89. Recipient Award for Nicoderm, R&D Mag., 1992. Mem. Am. Assn. Pharm. Scientists, Am. Soc. Clin. Pharmacology and Therapeutics, Soc. Exptl. Biology and Medicine, Am. Soc. Pharmacology and Exptl. Therapeutics, B'nai B'rith (chpt. v.p. 1978). Home: 1125 Fort View Pl Cincinnati OH 45202-1713 Office: Duramed Pharmaceuticals 5040 Duramed Dr Cincinnati OH 45213-2520

GOLDSTEIN, SIDNEY, sociology educator, demographer; b. New London, Conn., Aug. 4, 1927; s. Max and Bella (Hoffman) G.; m. Alice Dreifuss, June 21, 1953; children: Beth Leah, David Louis, Brenda Ruth. BA, U. Conn., 1949, MA, 1951; PhD, U. Pa., 1953. Instr. sociology U. Pa., 1953-55; mem. faculty Brown U., Providence, 1955—, prof. sociology, 1960—, George Hazard Crooker univ. prof., 1977—, prof. emeritus, 1993—, rsch. prof. population studies, 1997—, chmn. dept. sociology and anthropology, 1963-70, dir. Population Studies and Tng. Ctr., 1965-89; demographic advisor Chulalongkorn U., Bangkok, 1968-69; research fellow Inst. Contemporary Jewry, Hebrew U. Jerusalem, 1969—; sr. fellow East-West Population Inst., Honolulu, 1976, 82, 90; scholar-in-residence Rockefeller Study Ctr., Bellagio, 1990; sr. vis. scholar Hebrew U., 1990; fellow Inst. of Advanced Study, Indiana U., 1995; vis. fellow Australian Nat. U., Canberra, 1977; cons. UN Econ. and Social Commn. for Asia and Pacific, 1971-72, 77-82, Nat. Ctr. Health Stats., 1970-77, Internat. Program Population Analysis, Smithsonian Instn., 1971-76; mem. U.S. Bur. Census Adv. Com., 1965-71, Rand Corp., 1975-83; mem. nat. com. research on 1980 census Social Sci. Research Council, 1981-88; mem. governing bur. Com. Internat. Cooperation in Nat. Research in Demography, 1981-98, treas., 1994-98; mem. com. on population Nat. Research Council of Nat. Acad. of Scis., 1983-87; chmn. nat. tech. adv. com. on Jewish population studies Council Jewish Fedns., 1984-95; co-chmn. internat. sci. com. on 1990 census surveys of world Jewry, Jerusalem, 1988-92. Author: Patterns of Mobility, 1910-1950, 1958, Consumption Patterns of the Aged, 1960, The Norristown Study: An Experiment in Interdisciplinary Research Training, 1961, (with K.B. Mayer) The First Two Years: Problems of Small Business Growth and Survival, 1961, Migration and Economic Development in Rhode Island, 1958, (with Calvin Goldscheider) Jewish Americans, 1968, Urbanization in Thailand, 1947-1960, 1970, The Demography of Bangkok, 1972, (with V. Prachuabmoh and A. Goldstein) Urban-Rural Migration Differentials in Thailand, 1974, (with A. Speare and W. Frey) Residential Mobility, Migration and Metropolitan Change, 1975, Circulation in the Context of Total Mobility in Southeast Asia, 1978; editor: (with D.F. Sly) Basic Data Needed for the Study of Urbanization, 1975, The Measurement of Urbanization and the Projection of Urban Population, 1975, Patterns of Urbanization: Comparative Country Studies, 1977, (with wife) A Test of the Potential Use of Multiplicity in Research on Population Movement, 1979, Population Mobility in the People's Republic of China, 1985, Surveys of Migration in Developing Countries: A Methodological Review, 1981, Migration and Fertility in Peninsular Malaysia, 1983, Urbanization in China, 1985, (with wife) Migration in Thailand: A Twenty-Five Year Review, 1986, (with C. Goldscheider) The Jewish Community of Rhode Island: A Social and Demographic Survey, 1988, Comparative Migration Patterns to Shanghai and Bangkok, 1989, Urbanization in China, 1982-1987, The Role of Migration and Reclassification, 1990, (with wife) Permanent and Temporary Migration Differentials in China, 1991, Demographic Issues and Data Needs for Mega-City Research, 1994, The Impact of Temporary Migration on Urban Places, 1993, (with R. Neupert) Urbanization and Population Redistribution in Mongolia, 1994, (with wife) Jews on the Move, 1996, (with Gang Liu) Migrant-Non Migrant Fertility in Anhui China, 1996, (with Dang Anh) Internal Migration and Development in Vietnam, 1997, (with wife and Michael White) Migration Futility and State Policy in Hubei Province, China, 1997, (with wife) Lithuanian Jewry, 1993: A Demographic and Sociocultural Profile, 1997, (with wife) Conservative Jewry in the United States: A Sociodemographic Profile, 1998. Bd. dirs. Jewish Fedn. R.I., 1964-68, 78-82, 85— . Bur. Jewish Edn., Providence, 1959-82, 94— ; bd. dirs. Council of Jewish Fedns., 1987-94, Guggenheim fellow, 1961-62; Harrison fellow, 1953; Social Sci. Research Council fellow, 1961-62; Fulbright scholar, Denmark, 1961-62; recipient Disting. Svc. medal Chulalongkorn U., 1969, Disting. Svc. medal Mahidol U., 1992, Disting. Leadership award Coun. Jewish Federations, 1992, Lifetime Achievement award Assn. Social Sci. Study of Jewry, 1992; sr. research awardee NAS, 1983. Mem. Am. Sociol. Assn., Population Assn. Am. (pres. 1975-76), Assn. Jewish Demography and Stats. (dir.), Internat. Union Sci. Study of Population (chair com. urbanization and population distbn. 1971-76), Assn. Sociol. Study of Jewry, Phi Beta Kappa. Home: 95 Kiwanee Rd Warwick RI 02888-4040 Office: Brown U Sociology Dept 79 Waterman St Providence RI 02912-9079

GOLDSTEIN, STANLEY P., retail company executive; b. Woonsocket, RI, 1934; married. Grad., Wharton Sch., U. Pa., 1955. V.p. Mark Steven, Inc., 1955-61, Francis I. DuPont, 1961-63; exec. v.p. Consumer Value Stores, 1963-69; pres. CVS div. Melville Corp., Harrison, N.Y., 1969-71, corp. v.p., pres. CVS div., 1971-85, then corp. exec. v.p., 1985-87, pres., 1986—, chmn., CEO, 1987-96, also bd. dirs.; chmn., CEO CVS Corp., Woonsocket, R.I., 1996-98, chmn. bd., 1998—. Office: CVS 1 Cvs Dr Woonsocket RI 02895-6195*

GOLDSTEIN, STANLEY PHILIP, engineering educator; b. Bklyn., Feb. 3, 1923; s. Max and Rose (Ahrenstein) G.; m. Wanda Rouse, June 6, 1949; children—Bruce, Richard. B.S., U. Okla., 1949; M.S., NYU, 1956; Ph.D. in Astronautics, Poly. Inst. Bklyn., 1969. Engr. Vapor Recovery Systems Corp., Compton, Calif., 1950-52; project engr. Alderson Research Labs., N.Y.C., 1952-54; mem. faculty Hofstra U., Hempstead, N.Y., 1954—; prof. engring. Hofstra U., 1957-84, prof. emeritus, 1984—, chmn. engring. sci. dept., 1956-68, 70-72, 80-83, dir. acad. computer center, 1970-72; assoc. dean Hofstra U. (Coll. Arts and Scis.), 1973-74, 77, assoc. provost for planning, budgeting and instl. research, 1974-76; pres. Techmark Enterprises, Inc.; Alcorn Combustion Co., N.Y.C. Transit Authority, Hofstra Internat. Trade & Devel. Corp.; dir. Collegiate Sci. and Tech. Entry Program Hofstra U., 1987-89. Served to 1st lt. USAAF, 1942-45, ETO. Decorated D.F.C., Air medal with 4 oak leaf clusters, 6 Battle Stars. Mem. Sigma Xi. Home: 18 Millers Ln Kingston NY 12401-4426 Office: Hofstra U Engring Dept Hempstead NY 11550

GOLDSTEIN, STEVEN, lawyer; b. St. Louis, Sept. 8, 1950; s. Alexander Julius and Dorothy Lea (Matier) G.; m. Laura Lou Staley, July 20, 1980. BS in Speech, Northwestern U., Evanston, Ill., 1972; JD, U. Mich., 1975. Bar: Mo. 1975. Prin. Goldstein & Vouga, P.C., St. Louis, 1993—. Mem. ABA, Mo. Bar Assn. (chmn. bankruptcy com. 1983-85), Bar Assn. of Met. St. Louis. Home: 712 Swarthmore Ln Saint Louis MO 63130-3618 Office: Goldstein & Vouga PC 121 Hunter Ave Ste 101 Saint Louis MO 63124-2082

GOLDSTEIN, STEVEN ALAN, medical and engineering educator; b. Reading, Pa., Sept. 15, 1954; m. Nancy Ellen Gehr, Aug. 22, 1976; children: Aaron Michael, Jonathan David. BS in Mech. Engring., Tufts U., 1976; MS in Bioengring., U. Mich., 1977, PhD in Bioengring., 1981. Rsch. investigator dept. surgery U. Mich., Ann Arbor, 1981-83, asst. prof. surgery, 1983-88, assoc. prof. surgery, 1988-92, prof. surgery, 1992—; co-dir. orthopaedic biomechanics lab. U. Mich., 1981-82, dir. orthopaedic rsch. labs. U. Mich., 1982—; adj. asst. prof. mech. engring. and applied mechanics, 1988-92, prof. mech. engring. and applied mechanics, 1992—, rsch. dir., advisor, 1981—, mem. faculty bioengring. program, 1982-96, prof. biomed. engring., 1996—, interim chmn., 1985-89, rsch. scientist inst. gerontology, 1993—, asst. dean rsch. & grad. studies U. Mich. Med. Sch., 1993-98, assoc. dean, 1999—; rsch. asst. bioengring. ctr. Tufts New England Med. Ctr., 1974-76; mem. calcium homeostasis adv. group NASA, 1987-89; cons. Libbey-Owens Ill., Gen. Tire & Rubber, Upjohn, Ethyl Corp., Norwich Eaton, KMS Fusion, Whitby Pharmaceuticals, Norian Corp., Genetics Inst., Therics Inc., Osteo Biologics Inc., Matrigin Inc.; chair NIH study sect. on orthopaedics and musculoskeletal diseases, 1993-95. Author: Advances in Engineering, 1991; author (with others) Biomechanics of Diathrodial Joints, 1990, Molecular Biology of the Cardiovascular System, 1991, Surgery: Scientific Principles and Practice, 1993, Limb Development and Regeneration, 1993, Accidental Injury: Biomechanics and Prevention, 1993; reviewer Math. Bioscis., 1982—, Annals of Biomed. Engring., 1983—, Clin. Orthopaedics and Related Rsch., 1983—, Jour. Rehab. Rsch. and Devel., 1987—; reviewer Jour. Biomechanics, 1982—, editorial cons., 1992—; reviewer Jour. Biomech. Engring., 1982—, assoc. editor, 1991-97; reviewer Jour. Orthopaedic Rsch., 1984—, mem. bd. assoc. editors , 1992—; reviewer Jour. Bone and Joint Surgery, 1987—, mem. bd. assoc. editors for rsch., 1989—; reviewer, mem. study section NIH, NSF, NASA, Nat. Inst. Occupational Health & Safety, 1983—; contbr. more than 100 articles to profl. jours. Recipient Young Rsch. Investigator award 3M Corp., 1984, Nicolas Andre award Assn. Bone & Joint Surgeons, 1987-88. Mem. ASME (chair program com. 1989-92, sec.-elect 1993, exec. com. bioengring. divsn. 1989—, chair bioengring. divsn. 1995-96, Y.C. Fung Young Investigator award 1987), Am. Soc. Biomechanics (exec. bd. 1984-85), Am. Acad. Orthopaedic Surgeons (com. biomed. engring. 1991—, Kappa Delta award 1989-90), Orthopaedic Rsch. Soc. (adj. program com. 1990-91, program com. 1992, sec. 1997—), Biomed. Engring. Soc., Engring. Soc. Detroit (Young Engr. of Yr. award 1987), The Knee Soc. Achievements include patents (with other) for Intracone Reamer, Instacone Prosthetic Surface, Flexible Connecting Shaft for Intramedullary Reamer, Tissue Pressure Measurement Transducer System, Continuous Flow Tissue Pressure Measurement Transducer System, Prosthesis Interface Surface and Method of Implanting, Direct Gene Transfer in Wounds. Office: U Mich Orthopaedic Rsch Labs 400 N Ingalls St Rm G161 Ann Arbor MI 48109-2003

GOLDSTEIN, STEVEN EDWARD, psychologist; b. Bronx, N.Y., Nov. 25, 1948; s. Maurice and Matilda (Weiss) G.; BS in Psychology, CCNY, 1970, MS in Sch. Psychology, 1971; EdD in Sch. Psychology, U. No. Colo., 1977. Tchr., N.Y.C. Public Schs., 1970-71; 72-73, tchr., counselor, 1974; extern in sch. psychology N. Shore Child Guidance, 1972; sch. psychologist Denver Pub. Schs., 1975; asst. prof. psychology Northeastern Okla. State U., Tahlequah, 1976-78; coord. inpatient, emergency svcs. Winnemucca (Nev.) Mental Health Center, 1978-80; dir. Desert Devel. Ctr., Las Vegas, Nev., 1980-82; sr. psychologist Las Vegas Mental Health Ctr., 1982-92; pvt. practice psychology, Las Vegas, 1983—; sr. psychologist Desert Regional Ctr., 1992—; participant NSF seminar on biofeedback, 1977. Sec. grad. coun. CUNY, 1971; pres. grad. coun. in edn. CCNY, 1971. Lic. psychologist, Nev.; cert. sch. psychologist, N.Y., Calif. Mem. APA (Nev. coord. office of pvt. practice 1987-88), Biofeedback Soc. Nev. (membership dir. 1982-90), Nev. Soc. Tng. and Devel. (dir. 1982-83), So. Nev. Soc. Cert. Psychologists (pres. 1984-86), Jewish Fedn. Las Vegas (bus. & profl. com. 1995—). Presenter papers to profl. confs. Office: 1391 S Jones Blvd Las Vegas NV 89146-1200 also: 3180 W Sahara Ave Ste C-25 Las Vegas NV 89102-6073

GOLDSTEIN, STUART WOLF, lawyer; b. Buffalo, N.Y., Sept. 9, 1931; s. Joseph and Esther (Wolf) G.; m. Myra Saft Stuart, June 1960 (dec. Aug.

1981); children: Jeffrey, Jonathan, Meryl; m. Nancy Baynes Lux, 1993. Student, U. Buffalo, 1949-52, JD, 1955; postgrad., U. Va., 1956. Bar: N.Y. 1956, Fla. 1974, Ariz. 1977, U.S. Supreme Ct. 1960, U.S Dist. Ct. (we. dist.) N.Y. 1956, U.S. Ct. Mil. Appeals 1957, U.S. Ct. Appeals (2d cir.) N.Y., 1978, U.S. Dist. Ct. Ariz. 1981. Sole practice Buffalo, 1960-79, 82-85, Phoenix, 1980-82, 85—. Pres., founder Cystic Fibrosis Found., Buffalo, 1960; fund-raiser United Fund, United Jewish Appeal; pres. Boys League; active Erie County Spl. Task Force on Energy, Buffalo, 1978. 1st lt. JAG, U.S. Army, 1956-60. Fellow Ariz. Bar Found.; mem. ATLA, Ariz. State Bar Assn., N.Y. Trial Lawyers Assn., Erie County Trial Lawyers, Ariz. Trial Lawyers Assn. (Ariz. real property sect.), N.Y. State Bar Assn., Fla. Bar Assn., Am. Arbitration Assn., Maricopa County Bar Assn., Buffalo Skating Club, Curling Skating Club (legal counsel). Avocations: swimming, jogging. Office: 2700 N 3rd St Ste 2010 Phoenix AZ 85004-4602

GOLDSTEIN, WALTER, economics educator; b. London, Aug. 16, 1930; s. Israel and Dora Goldstein; m. Batya Goldstein, Dec. 14, 1958 (dec. Aug. 1993); children: Miriam, Marc, David; m. Irene Gilbert. BSc in Econs., London Sch. Econs., 1955; MA, Northwestern U., 1956; PhD, U. Chgo., 1961. Asst. prof., then assoc. prof. Bklyn. Coll., CUNY, 1959-66; prof. Rockefeller Coll., SUNY, Albany, 1968-95, prof. emeritus, 1995—; vis. prof. London Sch. Econs., INSEAD, Paris, Johns Hopkins (SAIS), Bologna, Italy, Columbia U., N.Y.C., NYU, N.Y.C.; sr. fellow Rockefeller Inst., Albany; cons. MITRE, Washington, Ford Found., N.Y.C. and Paris, IBM, N.Y.C., Brussels and Tokyo; chair seminar on tech. and social change Columbia U., 1964-87. Author: Planning, Politics and the Public Interest, 1978, Fighting Allies, 1986, Europe After Maastricht, 1992, Europe Stalling, 1992; mem. editl. bd. jours. Energy Policy, Resources Policy, 1980-91. Mem. Gov.'s Task Force on Higher Edn., N.Y., 1974, Gov. Carter's Task Force on the Economy, 1976; exec. dir. N.Y. Forum, N.Y.C., 1998—. Home: 343 E 30th St New York NY 10016-6417

GOLDSTEIN, WILLIAM MARKS, lawyer; b. Phila., Aug. 28, 1935; s. David and Estelle (Marks) G.; m. Lilia E. Demchuk; 1 child, Laura; children by previous marriage: Adam, Benjamin, Daniel. AB, Princeton U., 1957; JD magna cum laude, Harvard U., 1960. Bar: Pa. 1961, D.C. 1977. Law clk. to judge U.S. Ct. Appeals, Phila., 1960-61; assoc. firm Morgan Lewis & Bockius, Phila., 1961-66; ptnr. Morgan Lewis & Bockius, 1967-75, 77-82, Drinker, Biddle & Reath LLP, Phila., 1982—; dep. asst. sec. for tax policy Dept. Treasury, Washington, 1975-76. Contbr. numerous articles on fed. taxation to law publs. Mem. Democratic Party Com. Lower Merion, Pa., 1965-68; candidate for Sch. Bd. Lower Merion, 1965, for state legis., 1966. Mem. ABA, Pa. Bar Assn., Phila. Bar Assn., D.C. Bar Assn., Am. Law Inst., Am. Coll. Tax Counsel. Jewish. Home: 787 Trephanny Ln Wayne PA 19087-1931 Office: Drinker Biddle & Reath LLP 1345 Chestnut St Ste 1300 Philadelphia PA 19107-3496

GOLDSTICK, THOMAS KARL, biomedical engineering educator; b. Toronto, Ont., Can., Aug. 21, 1934; came to U.S., 1955; s. David and Iva Sarah (Kaplan) G.; m. Marcia Adrienne Jenkins, July 4, 1982. BS, MIT, 1957, MS, 1959; PhD, U. Calif., Berkeley, 1966, U. Calif., San Francisco, 1966-67. Asst. prof. Northwestern U., Evanston, Ill., 1967-71, assoc. prof. chem. engring. and biol. sci., 1971-81, prof. chem. engring., neurobiology and physiology, 1981-85; prof. chem. engring., biomed. engring., neurobiology and physiology Northwestern U., Evanston, 1985—; spl. research fellow U. Calif.-San Diego, LaJolla, 1971-73; adj. prof. ophthalmology U. Ill., Chgo., 1981-91. Editor: Oxygen Transport to Tissue V, 1983, VII, 1985, X, 1988, XI, 1989, XII, 1990, XIII, 1992. Research grantee NIH, 1968—. Mem. Internat. Soc. Oxygen Transport to Tissue (sec. 1980-86, exec. com. 1986-93), Biomed. Engring. Soc. (bd. dirs. 1983-86, chmn. publs. bd. 1985-86). Home: 2025 Sherman Ave Apt 504 Evanston IL 60201-3269 Office: Chem Engring Dept Northwestern U Evanston IL 60208-3120

GOLDSTINE, STEPHEN JOSEPH, college administrator; b. San Francisco, Nov. 16, 1937; s. Edgar Nathan and Regina Thelma (Benno) G.; m. Emily Raechel Miller Keeler, Apr. 12, 1981; children: Rachel, Bettina, Simone Massimiliana. Student, Calif. Sch. Fine Arts, 1951, 58; B.A., U. Calif., Berkeley, 1961, postgrad. in philosophy, 1962-67. Teaching asst. rhetoric dept. U. Calif., Berkeley, 1963-66; asst. prof. St. Mary's Coll., Moraga, Calif., 1964-70; chmn. art dept. St. Mary's Coll., 1969-70; cons. Freeman & Gossage, San Francisco, 1967-69; dir. neighborhood arts program Art Commn. City and County San Francisco, 1970-77; exec. sec. Mayor's Interagency Com. for Arts, San Francisco, 1971-75; founding dir. Performing Arts for the Third Age, San Francisco, 1973; co-dir. Rockefeller Tng. Fellowships in Mus. Edn., San Francisco, 1975; pres. San Francisco Art Inst., 1977-86; dir. grad. programs Calif. Coll. Arts and Crafts, 1986—; visiting faculty San Francisco State U.; sr. cons. Daniel Solomon Architects and Planners, 1988; mem. chancellor's adv. bd. Univ. Art Mus., U. Calif., Berkeley, 1979—, exec. com., trustee San Francisco Arts Edn. Found., 1985—; mem. prominent orgns. panel Calif. Arts Coun., 1981, vice chmn., 1983, chmn., 1985-87; chmn. invited session Am. Philos. Assn. (pacific div.), 1986, lectr. UCLA, 1976, Stanford U., 1966, Harvard U., 1976, 71; docent Lycee Internat. Franco-Americain, 1993—. Editor: Western Round Table on Modern Art, 1993; co-prodr., co-dir. (film) Walz um die Wände hoch zu gehen, 1999. Conductor The Art Orch., Calif. Palace of the Legion of Honor, 1997. Democrat. Jewish. Home: 1331 Green St San Francisco CA 94109-1926 Office: Calif Coll Arts and Crafts 5212 Broadway Oakland CA 94618-1426

GOLDSTON, STEPHEN EUGENE, community psychologist, educator, consultant; b. N.Y.C., Apr. 19, 1931; s. Michael Louis and Molly Ruth (Rothenberg) G.; children—Beth Karen, Lisa Robin. BA, NYU, 1952; MSPH, Columbia U., 1953, MA, 1957, EdD, 1958. Lectr., instr. Columbia U., N.Y.C., 1956-58; asst. to dir. Westchester County Cmty. Mental Health Bd., White Plains, N.Y., 1958-60; chief mental health edn. unit, dir. mental health consultation program N.Y.C. Cmty. Mental Health Bd., 1960-62; staff asst. to assoc. dir. extramural programs NIMH, Rockville, Md., 1962-63, tng. specialist pilot and spl. grants sect. Tng. and Manpower Resources br., 1963-65, tng. specialist exptl. and spl. tng. br., 1966-67, chief pub. health sect. exptl. and spl. tng. br., 1967-69, spl. asst. to dir. for preventive programs, 1967-71, coord. primary prevention program, 1972-80, chief primary prevention service programs, Div. Mental Health Service Program, 1980-81, dir. office of prevention, 1981-85; cons. in preventive psychiatry Neuropsychiat. Inst., UCLA, 1985-87; assoc. dir. UCLA Preventive Psychiatry Ctr., 1987-89, chair ann. nat. conf., 1987, 88; staff dir. Mayor's Citizen's Task Force on Cen. City East, Los Angeles, 1986-88; pres. Goldston & Assocs., Chgo., 1986—; chmn. nat. conf. UCLA Preventive Psychiatry Ctr., 1987-88; coord. nat. conf. Mental Health in Pub. Health Tng., 1967-68; lectr. Bar-Ilan U. Sch. Soc. Work, Ramat Gan, Israel, 1996-98, The Hebrew U. Sch. Soc. Work, Jerusalem, Israel, 1997—; sr. editor NIMH Prevention Publ. Series, 1976-85; assoc. editor coun. Am. Assn. Applied and Preventive Psychology, 1991—. Mem. editl. bd. Jour. Preventive Psychiatry, Jour. Primary Prevention; contbr. articles to profl. jours. With U.S. Army, 1953-55, USPHS, 1957-85. Recipient Sustained High Quality Peformance award HEW, 1968, 72, 76; Superior Work Performance award HEW, 1970; Outstanding Contbn. to Prevention in Mental Health award Nat. Council Community Mental Health Ctrs., Washington, 1985. Fellow Am. Psychol. Assn. (Disting. Profl. Contbns. award 1984), Am Psychol. Soc. (charter mem.), Am. Pub. Health Assn. (chmn. com. on prevention, mental health sect. 1974-77, Am. Assn. Applied and Preventive Psychology (founding).

GOLDSTONE, JACK ANDREW, sociologist; b. San Francisco, Sept. 30, 1953; s. Jack Robert and Ursula (Weinberg) G.; m. Gina Belinda Saleman, Feb. 9, 1992; children: Alexander, Simone. AB, Harvard U., 1976, AM, 1979, PhD, 1981. Asst. prof. Northwestern U., Evanston, Ill., 1981-84; assoc. prof. Northwestern U., 1984-88; prof. U. Calif., Davis, 1989—; dir. ctr. for comparative rsch., U. Calif., Davis, 1989-91. Author: Revolution and Rebellion, 1991 (disting. pub. award Am. Sociol. Assn. 1993); editor: Encyclopedia of Political Revolutions, 1998. ACLS fellow, 1983-84, Ctr. for Advanced Studies fellow Stanford U., 1993-94. Mem. Am. Sociol. Assn., Sociol. Rsch. Assn. Office: U Calif Sociology Dept Davis CA 95616

GOLDSTONE, JAMES, film, television and stage director; b. Los Angeles, June 8, 1931; s. Jules C. and Anita (Rosenberg) G.; m. Ruth Liebling; children: Peter, Jeffrey, Barbara. BA in English Lit., Dartmouth Coll., 1953; MA in Drama, Bennington Coll., 1959. Ind. film and TV dir., 1958—; mem. film adv. bd. Dartmouth Coll., 1991—; vis. prof. Sch. of the Arts Grad. Film Divsn. Columbia U., 1996-97. Dir. numerous TV show episodes including Amos Burke, It's A Man's World, Death Valley Days, Bat Masterson, Outer Limits, The Man From UNCLE, Doctor Kildare, Route 66, Perry Mason, Rawhide, The Eleventh Hour, The Fugitive, The Lieutenant, The Chrysler Theater, (TV show pilots) Star Trek, The Senator, (also writer) Ironsides, (also creator) Iron Horse, (TV films) Scalplock, 1966, Shadow Over Elveron, 1967, A Clear and Present Danger, 1970 (Emmy award nomination), Cry Panic, 1974, Things in Their Season, 1974, Journey from Darkness, 1975 (Christopher award), Eric, 1975 (Internat. Film Festival award), Studs Lonigan miniseries, 1979, Kent State, 1982 (Emmy award Best Dir., Gold medal N.Y. Film Festival), Charles & Diana: A Royal Love Story, 1982, Calamity Jane, 1983, The Sun Also Rises miniseries, 1984, Dreams of Gold, 1986, Earth*Star Voyager miniseries, 1987, (feature films) Jigsaw, 1968, A Man Called Gannon, 1968, Winning, 1969, Brother John, 1971, Red Sky at Morning, 1971, The Gang That Couldn't Shoot Straight, 1972, They Only Kill Their Masters, 1973, Swashbuckler, 1976, Rollercoaster, 1977, When Time Ran Out, 1980. Pres. Bennington Area Arts Coun., 1991-95; trustee Vt. Arts Coun., 1995—; founding mem., bd. dirs. Vt. Film Commn., 1997—. Mem. Dirs. Guild Am. (co-chmn. pres's. com. 1986—, mem. dirs. coun. nat. bd.), Writers Guild Am., Film Editors Union, Acad. TV Arts and Scis. (bd. govs. 1966-68, mem. awards adv. com., Emmy award 1981), Acad. Motion Picture Arts and Scis. (mem. dirs's. exec. com. 1985—).

GOLDSTONE, JEFFREY, physicist; b. Manchester, Eng, Sept. 3, 1933; came to U.S., 1977; m. Roberta Gordon; 1 child, Andrew. BA, Cambridge U. Eng., 1954, PhD, 1958. Fellow Trinity Coll., Cambridge, Eng., 1956-60, 62-82; lectr., reader U. Cambridge, Cambridge, 1961-76; MIT, Cambridge, 1977—, Cecil and Ida Green prof. physics, 1983—. Recipient Dannie Heineman prize Am. Phys. Soc., 1981, Guthrie medal Inst. Physics, 1983, Dirac prize Internat. Centre for Theoretical Physics, 1991. Mem. Royal Soc., Am. Acad. Arts and Scis. Office: MIT 77 Massachusetts Ave # 6-313 Cambridge MA 02139-4307

GOLDSTONE, MARK LEWIS, lawyer; b. Phila., Apr. 12, 1959; s. George Ronald and Jacqueline Suzanne (Yentis) G.; m. Mindy Ann Lieberman, Nov. 10, 1984. BA, Lafayette Coll., 1981; postgrad., Tel Aviv (Israel) U., 1982; JD, Temple U., 1984. Bar: Pa. 1985, D.C. 1985, Md. 1991. Fgn. affairs and def. researcher Mondale-Ferraro Campaign, Washington, 1984; legal intern Senator Joseph R. Biden Jr., Washington, 1985; pvt. practice Washington, 1985—; gen. counsel London Fog Corp., Eldersburg, Md., 1990-94; corp. counsel, asst. sec. London Fog Corp., Eldersburg, 1994-95; instr. Inst. for Legal Studies, Arlington, Va., 1988. Contbg. author: Almanac of the Unelected, 1988; contbr. articles to profl. jours. and mags. Pro bono lawyer various peace, justice and social welfare orgns., Washington, 1985—; vol. lawyer Ams. for Harkin, 1991-92. Mem. ABA, Pa. Bar Assn., Nat. Lawyers Guild (bd. dirs. D.C. chpt.), D.C. Bar Assn., Md. Bar Assn., Supreme Ct. Bar Assn. Home and Office: 9419 Spruce Tree Cir Bethesda MD 20814-1654

GOLDSTONE, SANFORD, psychology educator; b. N.Y.C., July 17, 1926; s. Albert and Anna (Steckel) G.; children: Susan Beth, Arthur Craig, Nancy Lynn; stepchildren: Peter B., Anthony A., Jane P., Elisabeth W.; m. Lois Adams. B.S., CCNY, 1947; Ph.D., Duke U., 1953. Intern Duke Sch. Medicine, 1949-51; chief clin. psychologist Duke Sch. Medicine (Psychiat. Out-Patient Clinic), 1951-54, lectr. psychology, 1953-54, asso. dept. psychiatry, 1953-54; asst. prof. to prof. psychiatry, chief psychologist, program dir. Baylor U. Coll. Medicine, 1955-67; prof., head div. psychology dept. psychiatry Cornell U. Med. Coll., 1967-79; prof. psychology field neurobiology Cornell U. Med. Coll. (Grad. Sch. Med. Scis.), 1969-79; prof., dir. clin. tng., dept. psychology U. Maine, Orono, 1979-86, prof. psychology emeritus, 1986—; cons. VA Hosps., Durham, N.C., 1953-54, Houston, 1959-67, Temple, Tex., 1964-67, Montrose, N.Y., 1968-79, Togus, Maine, 1979-88; mem. profl. staff Eastern Maine Med. Center and; Bangor Mental Health Inst., 1980-86; trustee Miles Meml. Hosp., Damariscotta, Maine, 1990-99; cons. criminal law sect. Am. Bar Assn., 1967-69, Westchester County Probation Dept., 1968-71, Community Service Bur., N.Y. State Tng. Schs., 1969-75; head div. psychology Houston State Psychiat. Inst., 1958-67, acting bus. mgr., 1959-60, head div. crime and delinquency, 1966-67; clin. asso. prof. to clin. prof. U. Houston, 1958-67; dir. mental health services Harris County Probation Dept., Houston, 1963-67; cons. Silver Hill Found., 1974-81; psychologist-in-chief Payne Whitney Psychiat. Clinic, 1967-74, Westchester div. N.Y. Hosp., 1967-74; attending psychologist N.Y. Hosp., 1967-79; head, community cons. services outpatient dept. Payne Whitney Psychiat. Clinic, 1970-73; head community cons. services Westchester div. N.Y. Hosp.-Cornell Med. Center, 1973-75. Contbr. numerous articles to profl. jours. Served with USAAF, 1945. USPHS grantee, 1955-65, 79-86. Fellow APA (life); mem. Am. Psychopath. Assn. (life). Home: PO Box 282 East Boothbay ME 04544-0282 Office: U Maine Psychology Little Hall Orono ME 04469

GOLDSTONE, STEVEN F., consumer products company executive; b. N.Y.C., Jan. 30, 1946; s. Milton Harold and Beatrice (Chase) G.; m. Elizabeth Caravella; children: Elissa Eve, Margaret Chase. BA, U. Pa., 1967; JD, NYU, 1970. Bar: N.Y. 1971, U.S. Dist. Ct. (so. dist.) N.Y. 1972, U.S. Ct. Appeals (2d cir.) 1971). Assoc. Davis, Polk & Wardwell, N.Y.C., 1970-78, ptnr., 1978-95; gen. counsel RJR Nabisco, Inc., 1995; chmn., CEO, bd. dirs. RJR Nabisco Inc., 1995—; also bd. dirs. Nabisco Holdings, Inc., 1997—. Office: RJR Nabisco Inc Rm 900 1301 Avenue Of The Americas Fl 33 New York NY 10019-6054*

GOLDSTRAND, DENNIS JOSEPH, business and estate planning executive; b. Oakland, Calif., July 12, 1952; s. Joseph Nelson and Frances Marie (Royce) G.; m. Judy A. Goldstrand. BSBA, Calif. State U., Chico, 1975; CLU, Am. Coll., 1986, CFC, 1988. Accredited estate planner, Nat. Assn. Estate Planners Couns. Asst. mgr. Household Fin. Corp., San Leandro, Calif., 1975-76; registered rep. Equitable Fin. Svcs., San Francisco, 1976-79, dist. mgr., 1979-85; ptnr. Goldstrand & Small Ins. and Fin. Svcs., Stockton, Calif., 1986-89; owner Goldstrand Fin. & Ins. Svcs. (now Goldstrand Planning Group), Stockton, 1989—; spkr. taxation course Law Sch. Humphreys Coll., 1997, 98, 99. Spkr. Calif. Assn. Life Underwriters, 1986, 95, San Joaquin chpt. Calif. CPA Soc., 1997; contbr. articles to Life Ins. Selling mag., 1986, 88. Mem. Stockton Estate Planning Coun., bd. dirs. 1995—, pres. 1998-99, spkr., 1996, 97; past pres. United Way San Joaquin County Endowment Found., Inc., 1994, bd. dirs. Keel Club; mem. endowment devel. com. U. Pacific; charter mem. planned giving com. U. of Pacific; assoc. mem. scholarship adv. coun. Bldr.'s Exch. of Stockton. Mem. Nat. Assn. Life Underwriters, pres. Stockton chpt. 1990-91, chair ethics com. 1993-94, Life Underwriter of Yr. 1994, Soc. Fin. Svc. Profls. (formerly Soc. CLU ChFC, pres. Stockton chpt. 1989-90), Calif. Assn. Life Underwriters (trustee 1995-96), Calif. Restaurant Assn. (assoc.), Million Dollar Round Table, Greater Stockton C. of C., Rotary, Golden Key Soc. Avocation: tennis. Home: 9215 Stony Creek Ln Stockton CA 95219-4910 Office: Goldstrand Planning Group 2800 W March Ln Ste 326 Stockton CA 95219-8218

GOLDWASSER, EDWIN LEO, physicist; b. N.Y.C., Mar. 9, 1919; s. I. Edwin and Edith (Goldstein) G.; m. Elizabeth Weiss, Oct. 27, 1940; children: Michael, John, Katherine, David, Richard. BA, Harvard U., 1940; PhD, U. Calif., Berkeley, 1950. Rsch. asst. and rsch. assoc. U. Calif., Berkeley, 1946-51; rsch. assoc., prof. physics U. Ill., Urbana, 1951-88; dep. dir. Fermi Nat. Accelerator Lab., Batavia, Ill., 1967-78; vice chancellor for rsch. U. Ill., Urbana, 1978-80, vice chancellor acad. affairs, 1979-86, acting dir. internat. programs, 1988-89, acting dir. Computer-based Edn. Rsch. Lab., 1989-92; assoc. dir. Superconducting Super Collider Cen. Design Group, Berkeley, 1986-88; disting. fellow Calif. Inst. Tech., 1993-94; mem., chmn. Nat. Rsch. Coun. div. Phys. Scis., Washington, 1961-69; chmn. sci. policy com. Stanford (Calif.) Linear Accelerator Ctr., 1980-84; chmn. sci. and ednl. adv. com. U. Calif., Berkeley, 1986-92. Author: Optics, Waves, Atoms and Nuclei, 1965; contbr. articles to profl. jours. Westinghouse fellow, 1949-50; Guggenheim fellow, 1957-58; Fulbright fellow, 1957-58. Fellow Am. Acad. for Arts and Scis.; mem. Phi Beta Kappa, Sigma Xi, Phi Kappa Phi. Avocations: tennis, swimming, opera. Home: 612 W Delaware Ave Urbana IL 61801-4805 Office: U Ill Dept Physics 1110 W Green St Urbana IL 61801-3003

GOLDWASSER, EUGENE, biochemist, educator; b. N.Y.C., Oct. 14, 1922; s. Herman and Anna (Ackerman) G.; m. Florence Cohen, Dec. 22, 1949 (dec.); children—Thomas Alan, Matthew Laurence, James Herman; m. Deone Jackman, Feb. 15, 1986. B.S., U. Chgo., 1943, Ph.D., 1950; ScD (hon.), N.Y. Med. Coll. Am. Cancer Soc. fellow U. Copenhagen, Denmark, 1950-52; rsch. assoc. U. Chgo., 1952-61, mem. faculty, 1962—, prof. biochemistry, 1963-91, prof. emeritus biochemistry and molecular biology, 1991—, chmn. com. on devel. biology., 1976-91, chmn. biochemistry and molecular biology, 1994-98. Served with AUS, 1944-46. Recipient Esther Langer medal for cancer rsch. Internat. Soc. Blood Purification, 1987, Simpson award Wayne State U., Lucerne award Fedn. European Physiol. Soc., Karl Landsteiner award Am. Assn. of Blood Banks; Guggenheim fellow Oxford (Eng.) U., 1966-67. Fellow AAAS, Am. Acad. Arts and Scis.; mem. Am. Soc. Biol. Chemists, Biochem. Soc., Internat. Soc. Exptl. Hematology, Am. Soc. Hematology, Sigma Xi. Achievements include purification of human erythropoietin; rsch. in biochemistry and red blood cell formation. Home: 5656 S Dorchester Ave Chicago IL 60637-1706

GOLDWATER, BERT M., federal judge. Apptd. bankruptcy judge U.S. Dist. Ct. Nev., 1995. Office: Fed Bldg and US Courthouse 300 Booth St Ste 1167 Reno NV 89509-1300

GOLDWATER, JOHN LEONARD, publisher, writer; b. N.Y.C., Feb. 14, 1916; s. Daniel and Edna (Bogart) G.; m. Gloria Freibrun; children—Jonathan, Jared; 1 child from previous marriage: Richard. Litt.D. (hon.), William Penn Coll., Oscaloosa, Iowa, 1981. Pub. Archie Comic Publs., Inc., N.Y.C., 1947-83; pres. Archie Comic Publs., Inc., 1947-83, Periodicals for Export, Inc., N.Y.c., 1940-98. Creator: syndicated comic character Archie; Collaborator: Best of Archie, 1980, animated TV series, 1969-77; author: Americana in Four Colors, 1973. Commr., nat. exec. com. Anti-Defamation League; pres. N.Y. Soc. for the Deaf, 1974-77. Mem. Comics Mag. Assn. Am. (pres. 1954-79, award 1979, 86, 94, chmn. bd.), Nat. Libr. Poetry. Republican. Jewish. Clubs: Old Oaks Country, Friars.

GOLDWATER, LESLIE RACHEL, business communications consultant; b. N.Y.C., Nov. 7, 1955; d. Melvin and Ruthe Goldwater; m. David W. Nelson, Sept. 2, 1979; children: Robert, Benjamin. AB in Comparative Lit., Brown U., 1977; MS, Columbia U., 1978. News editor UP Internat., Atlanta, 1978-79; rsch. dir. Norback and Co., Princeton, N.J., 1979-81; ea. regional editor Iron Age mag., Radnor, Pa., 1981-83; comm. specialist McKinsey & Co. Inc., Atlanta and N.Y.C., 1983-88; v.p. J.P. Morgan Securities, Inc., N.Y.C., 1988-92; pres. Communication Strategies, Inc., Canton, Ohio, 1992—. Office: Communication Strategies Inc 6632 Scarborough Rd NW Canton OH 44718-3830

GOLDWEITZ, JULIE, lawyer. Assoc. counsel Reed Publishing USA. Office: 275 Washington St Newton MA 02458-1646*

GOLDWYN, RALPH NORMAN, financial company executive; b. Chgo., Jan. 24, 1925; s. Herman and Rissie F. Goldwyn; m. Joan J. Snyder, Dec. 25, 1954; children: Bob, Greg, Lisa. BS, UCLA, 1948. Ptnr. Arc Loan Co., L.A., 1948-52; v.p. Arc Discount Co., L.A., 1952-73; pres. Arc Investment Co., L.A., 1952-73; ptnr. First Factors, L.A., 1960-78; pres. First Comml. Fin., L.A., 1978—; dir. Roy J. Maier, Inc. Trustee, mem. bd. govs., audit com., fin. com. UCLA Found.; grustee, mem. fin. com., icon com. UCLA Ctr. on Aging; mem. UCLA Arts and Architecture. Lt. (j.g.) USN, 1943-46. Named to UCLA Hall of Fame. Mem. UCLA Bruin Bench, UCLA Alumni Assn., World Affairs Coun., Anti-Defamation League, Town Hall of Calif. Club (life), Jazz Bakery, Brentwood Country Club of L.A. Jewish. Office: First Comml Fin 4221 Wilshire Blvd Ste 260 Los Angeles CA 90010-3537*

GOLEC, JENNIFER JANE, insurance underwriter; b. Hartford, Conn.; d. Edward John and R. Jane (Bancroft) G. BA, Ctrl. Conn. State U., 1987; MBA, U. Conn., 1990; postgrad., U. Mo., 1994—. Tax analyst The Travelers, Hartford, Conn., 1987-90, auditor, 1990-91; fin. planner The Travelers, Farmington, Conn., 1991-92; customer svc. rep. The Travelers, Walnut Creek, Calif., 1992-94; underwriter, mem. sales staff The Travelers, Overland Park, Kans., 1994—. Mem. Mothers Against Drunk Drivers, Conn., 1989-92. Avocations: photography, rock climbing, sailing. Office: Travelers 7500 College Blvd Overland Park KS 66210-1855

GOLECKI, ILAN, physicist, researcher, educator; b. Haifa, Israel; came to U.S., 1978; s. Moshe and Rebecca (Lazarovici) G. BS cum laude in Physics, Technion, Israel Inst. Tech., Haifa, Israel, 1970, MS in Physics, 1974; PhD in Physics, U. Neuchâtel, Neuchâtel, Switzerland, 1978. Rsch. fellow Calif. Inst. Tech., Pasadena, Calif., 1978-79, vis. assoc., 1979-86; mem. tech. staff Rockwell Internat. Corp., Anaheim, Calif., 1979-85, Thousand Oaks, Calif., 1985-86; ind. cons. Thousand Oaks, Calif., 1986-87; sr. rsch. physicist Allied-Signal, Inc., Morristown, N.J., 1987-93, rsch. scientist, 1993-96, prin. scientist, 1997—; organizer, chmn. of session on silicon-on-insulators, SPIE Conf., L.A., 1986; chem. vapor infiltration session co-chair ECS Conf., Paris, 1997; co-chair, organizer and procs. editor Engring. Found. Conf. on High-Temperature Electronics, San Diego, 1998; referee of jour. articles in field. Contbr. over 60 articles to sci. jours., including archival review papers. Mem. IEEE, Soc. Adv. Materials & Process Engring., Am. Assn. for Crystal Growth, Am. Carbon Soc., Am. Vacuum Soc., Böhmische Phys. Soc., Electrochem. Soc., Materials Rsch. Soc., Am. Ceramic Soc. Achievements include 6 patents concerning the processing of silicon-on-sapphire. SiC epitaxial growth by chemical vapor deposition, rapid densification of carbon-carbon composites by chemical vapor infiltration; in-situ densification monitor; development of new silicon-on-insulator technologies; co-discovery of ion beam induced epitaxial regrowth effect in silicon; development of apparatus enabling ion channeling measurements at elevated pressure; research interests include growth and analytical characterization of thin films and densification of porous composites by chemical vapor deposition and infiltration; intelligent in-situ densification monitor; ion beam analysis by Rutherford backscattering and channeling; vacuum science and technology and apparatus design and fabrication. Home: 100 Vail Rd Apt N-5 Parsippany NJ 07054-1337 Office: Allied Signal Inc CTC-1 101 Columbia Rd Morristown NJ 07960-4658

GOLEMBE, CARLA DRU, artist; b. Boston, June 20, 1951; d. Stanley Norman and Thelma (Levowich) G.; m. Joseph H. Eudovich, July 12, 1981. BA, Bennington Coll., 1972; MFA, U. Guanajuato, Mex., 1979. Instr. Newbury Coll., Brookline, Mass., 1981-96, Md. Coll. Art and Design, Silver Spring, 1998—. Author, illustrator: Annabelle's Big Move, 1999, Dog Magic, 1997; illustrator children's books: Why the Sky Is Far Away, 1992, the Creation, 1993, How Night Came from the Sea, 1994, People of Corn, 1995, the Woman in the Moon, 1996; one-woman shows at Cove Gallery, Wellfleet, Mass., 1988, 90-95, Kolbo, Brookline, 1988, 93, Wheelock Coll., Boston, 1991, Galeria Prin. Altos de Chavon, Dominican Republic, 1994, Designs for Living, Boston, 1995, Spirit Echoes Gallery, Austin, Tex., 1996, Soho Gallery, Pensacola, Fla., 1996, Golden Pacific Gallery, San Diego, 1997; exhibited in group shows at Fuller Art Mus., Brockton, Mass., 1988, Artists Found. Gallery at Cityplace, Boston, 1989, Boston Ctr. for Arts, 1989, Estampe du Rhin, Strasbourg, France, 1990, U. Mass. Med. Ctr. Gallery, Worcester, 1990, Galeria Mesa, Ariz., 1990, Zenith Gallery, Washington, 1990, 91, 93, 94, 98, Stamford (Conn.) Mus., 1990, boston Pub. Libr., 1992, soc. Illustrators, N.Y.C., 1992, Saga Graphics, N.Y.C., 1993, Fletcher Priest Gallery, Worcester, 1994, Muse Gallery, Kansas City, Mo., 1995, Soho Gallery, 1996, Cove Gallery, 1996, Stoughton (Mass.) JCC Gallery, 1997, Boston U. Art Gallery, 1997, Starr Gallery, Newton, Mass., 1998; represented in numerous permanent collections at Bessamer Venture Ptnrs., Goldstein and Monello, Boston Pub. Libr., Hyatt Corp., Med. Coll. Va. Hosps., McCormack and Dodge, Peabody and Brown, others. Recipient Jones award Faber Birren Color Show, 1990, Best Illustrated Children's Book award N.Y. Times, 1992, Picture Book honor Parents Choice, 1995, Aesop Accolade Am. Folklore Soc., 1996. Mem. Lee Art Ctr. Printmaking Studio, Wash. Children's Book Guild. Avocations: dance, drumming, travel. Home: 9129 Sudbury Rd Silver Spring MD 20901-3525

GOLEMBESKI, JEROME JOHN, wire and cable company executive; b. Nanticoke, Pa., Mar. 16, 1931; s. Edward and Mary Ellen (Grozio) G.; m. June Beverly Chadwick, Aug. 9, 1958; children—Dale, Gary, Gregg, Cheryl, Kim. BS, U. Conn., 1957. Auditor Price Waterhouse & Co., Hartford, Conn., 1957-59; mem. controller's staff Insilco Corp., Meriden, Conn., 1959-86; Times Fiber Comm. Inc. Times Wire & Cable Co., Wallingford, Conn., 1959-86; contr., treas. Uniset Inc., Wallingford, 1986—. Served with USNR,

1949-53. Mem. Nat. Assn. Accountants (Cost Accounting award Hartford chpt.). Office: Uniset Inc 85 Legend Hill Rd Madison CT 06443-1879

GOLEMO, TIMOTHY FRANKLIN, urban planner; b. June 26, 1972. BA in Urban Planning, U. Ill., Urbanna, 1994; MPA, U. Ill., Springfield, 1999. program analyst Ill. Dept. Transp., Springfield, Ill., 1998—; city planner City of Champaign, Ill., 1992-94; exec. asst. to bds. of commn. Gov.'s Office, Springfield, Ill., 1994-98. E-mail address: golemotf@nt.dot. Home: 6907 Montrose Ct Springfield IL 62707

GOLEMON, RONALD KINNAN, lawyer; b. Atlanta, Tex., Nov. 22, 1938; s. William Layton and Avis (Bogle) G.; m. Jacqueline Alice Burst, Sept. 2, 1966; children: Donald Brent, Jennifer Alice. BS in Indsl. Mgmt. Engring., U. Okla., 1961; LLB, U. Tex., 1967. Bar: Tex. 1967, U.S. Ct. Appeals (5th cir.) 1970, U.S. Dist. Ct. (so. dist.) Tex. 1968, U.S. Dist. Ct. (we. dist.) Tex. 1981, U.S. Dist. Ct. (no. dist.) 1986. Engr. asst. Tex. Water Pollution Control Bd., Austin, 1964-67; assoc. Keys, Russell, Watson & Seaman, Corpus Christi, Tex., 1967-71; ptnr. Keys, Russell, Watson & Seaman, 1971-73, Brown McCarroll & Oaks Hartline, Austin, 1974—; mng. ptnr. Brown McCarroll & Oaks Hartline, 1989-94. Contbg. author The Southwestern Legal Foundation, 40th Annual Institute on Oil and Gas Law and Taxation, 1989, The Southwestern Legal Foundation, 43rd Annual Institute on Oil and Gas Law and Taxation, 1992; contbr articles to profl. jours. Alt. mem. RCRA permit adv. com. U.S. EPA, 1983; mem. Gov.'s Hazardous Waste Task Force, 1984-85; v.p. St. Stephen's Sch. PTA, 1985-86, pres., 1986-87; mem. cmty. adv. bd. Ronald McDonald House, Austin, 1990—. Mem. ABA (mem. standing com. membership & liaison 1997—, mem. market rsch. task force 1995-96, chmn. sect. natural resources, energy and environ. law 1994-95, chmn.-elect 1993-94, vice-chmn. 1992-93, mem. coun. liaison environ. group 1989-91, chmn. air quality com. 1986-89, vice chmn. 1982-86), State Bar Tex. (chmn. environ. law sect. 1971-72), Tex. Mining and Reclamation Assn. (dir. 1988—), Travis County Bar Assn., U. Tex. Law Alumni Assn. (pres. 1984-85, mem. exec. bd. 1984-86). Avocations: hunting, skiing, golf. Office: Brown McCarroll & Oaks Hartline 111 Congress Ave Ste 1400 Austin TX 78701-4043

GOLER, MICHAEL DAVID, lawyer; b. Cleve., June 29, 1952; s. George G. and Harriet (Zellen) G.; m. Jacqueline, June 8, 1975; children: Jonathan A. Jennifer S. BA in Classics, Union Coll., 1974; JD, Case We. Reserve U., 1977. Bar: Ohio 1977, U.S. Dist. Ct. Ohio 1977, U.S. Ct. Appeals (6th cir.) 1982. Assoc. Persky, Marken, Konigsbert & Shapiro, Cleve., 1977-81; assoc. counsel Cardinal Fed. Savings Bank, Cleve., 1981-84; assoc. Arter & Hadden, Cleve., 1984-86; ptnr. Kohrman, Jackson & Krantz, Cleve., 1986-94; of counsel Goodman Weiss & Miller, Cleve., 1994-95, ptnr., 1996—. Mem. ABA (sect. real property probate and trust law, chmn. com. enforcement of creditor's rights and bankruptcy, 1991-95, vice chair com. on economics, tech. and practice methods 1995-97, chair 1997—), Cleve. Bar Assn. (founder, chmn. environ. law sect. 1991-95, chmn. real estate sect. 1989-90). Avocations: music, golf, squash, bicycling, skiing. E-mail: mdgoler@ix.netcom.com. Home: 32200 Shaker Blvd Cleveland OH 44124-4928 Office: Goodman Weiss Miller LLP 100 Erieview Plz Fl 27 Cleveland OH 44114-1824

GOLER, ROBERT I., museum curator; b. Cleve., Aug. 20, 1956; s. George G. and Harriet E. (Zellen) G. AB, Yale U., 1979; MA, Case Western Res. U., 1984. Cert. Mus. Mgmt. Inst. Asst. curator Western Res. Hist. Soc., Cleve., 1979-80; curator collections Frances Tavern Mus., N.Y.C., 1981-88, acting dir., 1986-88; curator Chgo. Hist. Soc., 1988-93; exec. adminstr. Nat. Mus. Health & Medicine, Washington, 1993—; adj. faculty New Sch., N.Y.C., 1986-87. Author: The Legacy of Lafayette, 1983, The Heating Arts in Early America, 1984, Capital City-New York After the Revolution, 1985; co-author: A City Comes of Age-Chicago in the 1890s, 1991; editor: Federal New York: A Symposium, 1992, AIDS Education: A Handbook, 1994. Bd. mem. Md. Inst. Traditional Chinese Medicine, Bethesda, 1997—. Recipient Lawrence Redway award Med. Soc. N.Y. State, N.Y.C., 1988, rsch. fellowship The Wintethur (Del.) Mus., 1992-93. Office: Nat Mus Health and Medicine 6825 16th St NW Washington DC 20306-6000

GOLIGHTLY, DOUGLAS RAYMOND, artist; b. Milw., Feb. 13, 1931; s. William Bruce and Dorothy Agnes (Klein) G.; m. Patricia Anne Jelinek, June 20, 1959; children: Christine Marie Golightly Richter, William James. BS in Art, U. Wis., 1957, MS in Art, 1959, MFA, 1960. Instr. Layton Sch. Art, Milw., 1964-65. *Mr. Golightly's work is oil painting which is in varying degrees symbolic, allegorical, fantasy, surrealism, mythological and magic realism, using the forms of nature, often emphasizing the human form. In the last five years the subject matter is "man's inhumanity to man." Technical emphasis is on solid development of the illusion of three dimensional forms in a two dimensional medium. The oil technique accommodates sharp focus and detail.* One-man shows Bradley Galleries, Milw., 1962, 66, 69, Wustum Mus. Art, Racine, Wis., 1968, Madison Art Ctr,, 1968, Rahr Civic Ctr. and Pub. Mus., 1968, Manitowoc, Wis., Kenosha (Wis.) Pub. Mus., 1968, Hardy Gallery, Door County, Wis., 1969, Santa Cruz (Calif.) Art League, 1986-87, Sunset Cultural Ctr., Carmel, Calif., 1989, C.L. Clark Gallery, Bakersfield, Calif., 1993, Kings Art Ctr., Hanford, Calif., 1994; 3-person show Sun Gallery, Hayward, Calif., 1985; exhibited in group shows Milw. Art Inst., 1950, 55, U. Wis. Meml. Libr., Madison, 1960, Milw. Art Ctr., 1960, 61, 66, 67, 68, Capitol Ct., Milw., 1961, 62, C.W. Post Coll., L.I., N.Y., 1962 (hon. mention), Nat. Arts Club, N.Y.C., 1962, Long Beach (N.Y.) Art Assn., 1962, Madison Gallery, N.Y.C., 1962, Lynn Kottler Galleries, N.Y.C., 1964, Layton Sch. Art, 1965, Wis. State Fair, Milw., 1967, Mus. Fine Art, Springfield, Mass., 1968, Las Vegas (Nev.) Art Roundup, 1968, Butler Inst. Am. Art, Youngstown, Ohio, 1972, Janacek Atelier, Madison, 1978, Milw. Symphony Showcase, 1980, Santa Cruz Art League, 1987, 88, Gallery Imago, San Francisco, 1987, Tulare County Fair, Tulare, Calif., 1989-94 (3d prize for oil 1989, 1st and 2d prizes for oils 1990, 92, Best in Show award 1991, 1st prize for oil 1993, 94), Visions Gallery, Reedley, Calif., 1989, 93 (hon. mention 1993) Fanny Garver Gallery, Madison, 1989, 90, 91, C.L. Clark Galleries, 1990, 91, 92, Mus. Fine Arts, Mus. N.Mex., Santa Fe, 1991, La. State U., Baton Rouge, 1992, Kings Art Ctr., Northlight Gallery, West Los Angeles, Calif., 1994, Hanford, Calif., 1995-98, also others; represented in permanent collections Milw. Jour., Wis., Milw. Pub. Libr.; represented in pvt. collections C.L. Clark, Bakersfield, Calif., Ms. Jane Doud, Elm Grove, Wis., many others. With U.S. Army, 1953-55, Korea. Recipient purchase award Milw. Pub. Libr., 1961. Mem. Kings Art Ctr. Avocations: philosophy, theology, ethics, Hebrew and Greek linguistics. Home and Studio: 1155 W Brown Ave Porterville CA 93257

GOLINKIN, WEBSTER FOWLER, media executive; b. N.Y.C., Aug. 3, 1951; s. Joseph Webster and Ruth Forman (Fowler) G.; m. Allison Ann Willeford, Apr. 19, 1985; children: Joseph Webster, George Willeford. BA, Harvard U., 1973. V.p. Geer, DuBois Advtg., N.Y.C., 1976-79; sr. v.p. Reeves Entertainment Group, 1986-88; v.p. Reeves Communication Corp., 1979-88; pres. Reeves Corp. Svcs., N.Y.C., 1979-88; co-chmn., CEO Am. Med. Comms., Houston, 1988-93; chmn., CEO America's Health Network, Orlando, Fla., 1993-. Mem. Young Presidents' Orgn. Home: 5660 Longmont Dr Houston TX 77056-2345 Office: Americas Health Network 2500 Universal Studios Plz Orlando FL 32819-7610

GOLIS, PAUL ROBERT, lawyer; b. San Francisco, Sept. 25, 1954. BA with high distinction, Calif. State U., Long Beach, 1977; JD, Syracuse U., 1981. Bar: Fla. 1984, U.S. Dist. Ct. (so. dist.) Fla. 1985. Assoc. Russell L. Forkey, P.A., Ft. Lauderdale, Fla., 1984-85, Josias & Goren, P.A., Ft. Lauderdale, 1985-88; sr. trial atty. State of Fla. Dept. Transp., Ft. Lauderdale, 1988-90; asst. county atty. Palm Beach County, West Palm Beach, Fla., 1990-91; assoc. Scott, Royce, Harris, Bryan & Hyland, Palm Beach Gardens, Fla., 1991-93, Watterson, Hyland & Klett, Palm Beach Gardens, 1993-98; sole practice, Boca Raton, Fla., 1998—. Bd. dirs. Aid to Victims of Domestic Assault, Inc., 1990-99, v.p., 1993-97, pres. 1997-99. Mem. ABA, Fla. Bar Assn. (eminent domain com. 1989—), Palm Beach County Bar Assn. (vice chmn. environ., land use and eminent domain CLE com. 1993-95, chmn. 1995—, jud. rels. com. 1996—). Office: 1200 N Federal Hwy Ste 200 Boca Raton FL 33432

GOLISANO, B. THOMAS, finance company director, human resources director; b. Irondequoit, N.Y., 1941. BS, SUNY, Alfred, 1961. Founder, chmn., CEO Paychex, Inc., Rochester, N.Y., 1971—. Mem. exec. com. Prevention Ptnrs; founder B. Thomas Golisano Found; chmn. capital campaign for Sch. of the Holy Childhood; trustee Rochester Inst. Tech., past mem. bd. dirs. Rochester Gen. Hosp. and St. John Fisher Coll.; founding mem. Independence Party. Named to INC mag.'s Dream Team of the Eighties list, Entrepreneur of the Decade, Rochester Bus.; Paychex listed with 200 Best Growth Cos. by Fin. World, among the 1000 Most Valuable in Am. by Forbes; recipient Herbert W. VanderBrul Entreprenurial award, 1987, Humanitarian of Yr. award, Boy's Town of Italy, 1993, Commerce and Industry award, Rochester C. of C., 1993, Shumway Disting. Svc. award, 1995. Office: Paychex Inc PO Box 25397 Rochester NY 14625-0397*

GOLITZ, LOREN EUGENE, dermatologist, pathologist, clinical administrator, educator; b. Pleasant Hill, Mo., Apr. 7, 1941; s. Ross Winston and Helen Francis (Schupp) G.; MD, U. Mo., Columbia, 1966; m. Deborah Burd Frazier, June 18, 1966; children: Carrie Campbell, Matthew Ross. Intern, USPHS Hosp., San Francisco, 1966-67, med. resident, 1967-69; resident in dermatology USPHS Hosp., Staten Island, N.Y., 1969-71; dep. chief dermatology, 1972-73; vis. fellow dermatology Columbia-Presbyn. Med. Ctr., N.Y.C., 1971-72; asst. in dermatology Coll. Physicians Surgeons, Columbia, N.Y.C., 1972-73; vice-chmn. Residency Rev. Com. for Dermatology, 1983-85. Earl D. Osborne fellow dermal. pathology Armed Forces Inst. Pathology, Washington, 1973-74; assoc. prof. dermatology, pathology Med. Sch. U. Colo., Denver, 1974-88, prof., 88-97, clin. prof. patholoigy, dermatology, 1997—; chief dermatology Denver Gen. Hosp., 1974-97; med. dir. Ambulatory Care Ctr., Denver Gen. Hosp., 1991-97. Diplomate Am. Bd. Dermatology, Nat. Bd. Med. Examiners. Fellow Royal Soc. Medicine; mem. Am. Soc. Dermatopathology (sec., treas. 1985-89, pres.-elect 1989, pres. 1990), Am. Acad. Dermatology (chmn. coun. on clin. and lab. svcs., coun. sci. assembly 1987-91, bd. dirs. 1987-91, chmn. 1991, chmn. task force dermatopathology, 1998—), Soc. Pediatric Dermatology (pres. 1981), Soc. Investigative Dermatology, Pacific Dermatol. Assn. (exec. com. 1979-89, sec.-treas. 1984-87, pres. 1988), Noah Worcester Dermatol. Soc. (publs. com. 1980, membership com. 1989-90), Colo. Dermatol. Soc. (pres. 1978), Am. Bd. Dermatology Inc. (chmn. part II test com. 1989—, exec. com. 1993—, v.p. 1994, pres.-elect 1995, pres. 1996, dir. Emeritus, cons. to bd. 1997—), Colo. Med. Soc., Denver Med. Soc., AMA (residency rev. com. for dermatology 1982-89, dermatopathology test com. 1979-85), Denver Soc. Dermatopathology, Am. Dermatol. Assn. Editorial bd. Jour. Cutaneous Pathology, Jour. Am. Acad. Dermatology, Advances in Dermatology (editorial bd. Current Opinion in Dermatology), Women's Dermatologic Soc., So. Med. Assn., Internat. Soc. Pediatric Dermatology, Am. Contact Dermatitis Soc., Am. Soc. Dermatologic Surgery, Physicians Who Care, Am. Bd. Med. Specialties (del.), N.Y. Acad. Scis., AAAS, Brit. Assn. Dermatologists (hon.), Brazilian Soc. Dermatology (hon.), U. Mo. Med. Alumni Orgn. (bd.govs. 1993—); contbr. articles to med. jours. Home: 130 S Elm St Denver CO 80246-1131 Office: Dermatopathology Svc PO Box 6218 Denver CO 80206-0218

GOLL, PAULETTE SUSAN, secondary education educator; b. Cleve., June 5, 1947; d. Ferdinand Paul and Lillian Clarice (Mehalko) G. BA in English, Cleve. State U., 1969, MEd, 1974; MA in English, U. Bridgeport, Conn., 1979; PhD in English, Case Western Res. U., 1987. Cert. secondary tchr., English tchr., asst. supr., secondary prin., Ohio. Part-time instr. U. Bridgeport, 1978-79, Case Western Res. U., Cleve., 1985-87; tchr. English, Cleve. Pub. Schs., 1969—, chmn. dept., coord. Ohio Proficiency Test, 1991-96; advisor Students Against Drunk Drivers, 1985-86; coord. project success Lincoln-West H.S., Cleve., 1987-90. Co-author: Shakespearean Comedies, 1985. Mem. com. on human rels. Cleve. Partnerships, 1989-92; co-chmn. High Schs. for Future, 1985-86; liaison MetroHealth/Lincoln-West Partnership, 1989-92. Named Master Tchr., Martha Holden Jennings Found., 1988; recipient Congl. Commendation Mary Rose Oaker, 1988, Award of Excellence, Rotary, 1989, British Petroleum Tchr. of Year, 1997; NEH fellow, 1985, NEH Ind. Studies in Humanities fellow, 1993; Jennings scholar, 1985, 88. Mem. ASCD (presenter), Nat. Coun. Tchrs. of English, North Cen. Assn. (chairperson vis. team 1991, 93), Phi Delta Kappa (v.p. programs 1993, ACT vis. tchr. 1999). Republican. Roman Catholic. Avocations: travel, music, needlepoint, writing fiction, camping. Home: 11366 Clarke Rd Columbia Station OH 44028 Office: Lincoln-West High Sch 3202 W 30th St Cleveland OH 44109-1582

GOLLADAY, MARY JEAN, statistician; b. Spokane, Wash., Oct. 12, 1942; d. James T. Albertson and Gladys I. Graves; m. Frederick L. Golladay Aug. 22, 1965; children: Addison, Kendall, Ann, Catherine. BA with honors, U. Puget Sound, 1964; MAT, Northwestern U., 1965, PhD, 1970. Tchr. secondary sch. Evanston Twp. (Ill.) H.S., 1965-68; instr. edn. adminstrn. U. Wis., Madison, 1969, project assoc., 1969-74; statistician U.S. Dept. Edn., Washington, D.C., 1975-84, NSF, Arlington, Va., 1984—; cons. Nat. Acad. Science, Washington, 1984—, U.S. Dept. Edn., Washington, 1984—. Editor: (book) Women, Minorities and Persons With Disabilities in Science and Engineering, 1994, (statistical report) Condition of Education, 1975, 76, 77, 78. Named Disting. Lectr. The MITRE Corp., 1993. Mem. Am. Statistical Assn., Am. Ednl. Rsch. Assn., Assn. for Institutional Rsch., Math. Assn. Am. Office: National Science Foundation Social Behavioral & Economc Sci 4201 Wilson Blvd Arlington VA 22230-0002

GOLLANCE, ROBERT BARNETT, ophthalmologist; b. N.Y.C., Oct. 25, 1937; s. Harvey and Sarah (Chinitz) G.; m. Carmen Côté Gollance, Nov. 8, 1969; 1 child, Stephen Andrew. BA cum laude, Harvard Coll., 1958; MD, Columbia Coll., 1962. Diplomate Am. Bd. Ophthalmology, Nat. Bd. Med. Examiners. Intern in medicine Bellevue-NYU, 1962-63, resident and chief resident in ophthalmology, 1963-66; fellowship NIH, 1964-69; sec.-treas. Ophthalmology Assocs., Wayne, N.J., 1970-93; pres. Eye Assocs. of Wayne, 1993—; lectr. in ophthalmology Columbia U., N.Y.C., 1998-99; chmn. ophthalmology Chilton Meml. Hosp., Pompton Plains, N.J., 1987-89, pres. med. staff, 1991; mem. great hands adv. com. Becton Dickinson Corp., Franklin Lakes, N.J., 1990—; mem. adv. com. Bausch & Lomb Corp., Rochester, N.Y., 1980-83; mem. faculty various courses on cataract surgery and lens implantation. Contbr. articles to profl. jours. Chmn. parent's fund raising Loomis Chaffee Sch., Windsor, Conn., 1989-90. Capt. U.S. Army, 1966-68. Recipient Letter of Appreciation Korean Opthalmology Soc., 1967, Cath. Med. Ctr., 1967. Fellow ACS, Am. Soc. Cataract and Refractive Surgery, Am. Acad. Ophthalmology, European Soc. Cataract and Refractice Surgery. Office: Eye Assocs of Wayne 968 Hamburg Tpke Wayne NJ 07470-3225

GOLLATA, JAMES ANTHONY, library director; b. Manitowoc, Wis., Aug. 18, 1945; s. Anthony Francis and Evelyn Marion (Terens) G.; children: Davis, Adrian. BS, U. Wis., 1969, MA, 1973. Libr. dir. Mt. Senario Coll., Ladysmith, Wis., 1974-87, U. Wis., Richland Center, 1987—; pres. Wis. Ctr. for the Book, Madison, 1997-98, bd. dirs. Author numerous poems; contbr. articles to profl. jours. Mem. Wis. Libr. Assn. (newsletter editor 1986—, Literary award 1984-87, 96-99), Wis. Acad. Scis., Arts and Letters (chmn. Gordon MacQuarrie com. 1997). Avocations: music, art, book collecting, theater, acting. Home: 489 S Ira St Richland Center WI 53581-2617 Office: Univ Wis 1200 US Hwy 14 W Richland Center WI 53581-1316

GOLLEHER, GEORGE, food company executive; b. Bethesda, Md., Mar. 16, 1948; s. George M. and Ruby Louise (Beecher) G.; div.; 1 child, Carly Lynn. BA, Calif. State U., Fullerton, 1970. Supr. acctg. J.C. Penney, Buena Park, Calif., 1970-72; systems auditor Mayfair Markets, Los Angeles, 1973, v.p., CFO, 1982-83; controller Fazio's, Los Angeles, 1974-78; group controller Fisher Foods, Ohio, 1978-79; v.p. fin. Stater Bros. Markets, Colton, Calif., 1979-82; sr. v.p., CFO Boys Markets Inc., Los Angeles, 1983—; CEO Ralph Grocery Co., Compton, Calif., 1995—. Office: Ralph Grocery Co 1100 W Artesia Blvd Compton CA 90220-5108*

GOLLIN, ALBERT EDWIN, media research executive, sociologist; b. Chgo., Dec. 8, 1930; s. Morris and Ida (Coopersmith) G.; m. Gillian M. Lindt, Aug. 15, 1959 (div. 1987); children: Karin, Mark; m. Ann K. Stern, June 1, 1991. BA, Queens Coll., 1952; Cert. in Clin. Psychology, US Army Med. Corps, 1953; PhD, Columbia U., 1967. Research assoc. Bureau of Applied Social Research, Columbia U., N.Y.C., 1958-63; research assoc., dir. Washington Survey Bureau of Social Sci. Research, Washington, 1963-77; v.p. rsch. Newspaper Assn. Am. (formerly Newspaper Advt. Bur.), N.Y.C., 1977-94; pres. Gollin Rsch., 1995—; adj. prof. Howard U., Washington, 1969-71; vis. prof. Am. U., Washington, 1971-74, Queens Coll. (CUNY), 1985; cons. research and evaluation Peace Corps, State Dept., Washington, 1966-71. Author: Education for National Development, 1970; editor: Polls and the News Media, 1980, Monitoring Revolutionary Change, 1992; mem. editl. bd. Newspaper Rsch. Jour., 1979—, Pub. Opinion Quar., 1981-85, Am. Sociologist, 1986-91, Sociol. Practice Rev., 1989-92, Sociol. Forum, 1996—; contbr. articles to profl. and trade jours., chpts. to books. Chmn. Lafayette Modernization Com., Washington, 1972-77; v.p. D.C. Citizens for Better Pub. Edn., 1974-77; dep. dir. D.C. Carter-Mondale Presdl. Campaign, Washington, 1976, D.C. Dem. Ctrl. Com., 1976-77; chmn. Adv. Neighborhood Com. 3G, Washington, 1976-77; pres. 11-69 Owners Corp., N.Y.C., 1993-98. Recipient Zarwell award Newspaper Rsch. Coun., Des Moines, 1983, Pres.'s award Internat. Circulation Mgrs. Assn., Nashville, 1989, NAA Rsch. Career award San Diego, 1994; AAAS fellow, 1994, sr. fellow Freedom Forum Media Studies Ctr., 1995-96; U.S. Fulbright Commn. scholar, 1957; rsch. grantee NIMH, 1967, NSF, 1970. Mem. Am. Assn. Pub. Opinion Rsch. (sec. treas. 1980-82, pres. 1984-85, councillor 1994-96, Award 1998), Am. Sociol. Assn. (chmn. sociol. practice sect. 1981-82, Career award com. 1984-86, Disting. career award sociology practice sect. 1989, Disting. career award sociology nat. 1996), D.C. Sociol. Soc. (pres. 1976-77), Ea. Sociol. Soc. (treas. 1990-92), Market Rsch. Coun., Rsch. Industry Coalition (chmn. 1993), Phi Beta Kappa. Office: Gollin Rsch 400 W End Ave New York NY 10024-5750

GOLLIN, STUART ALLEN, accountant; b. Bronx, N.Y., Aug. 7, 1941; s. Samuel and Suggie (Schreiber) G.; m. Harriet Joy Friedlander, Aug. 16, 1964; children: Deborah Lynn, Mark David, Adam Douglas, Seth Craig. BBA, CCNY, 1963. CPA, N.Y., N.J. Ptnr., nat. dir. retailing Touche Ross & Co., Newark, 1963-80; ptnr., nat. dir. retailing, nat. dir. bankruptcy and insolvency, dir. litigation and ins. cons. svcs. Laventhol & Horwath, N.Y.C., 1980-90; ptnr. in charge bankrupty litig. support and ins. cons. David Berdon & Co., N.Y.C., 1990-92; v.p. insolvency Buccino & Assocs., N.Y.C., 1993-94; dir. litig. and appraisal svcs. J.H. Cohn & Co., N.Y.C., 1994-96; mng. dir. corp. transactions KPMG Peat Marwick, N.Y.C., 1996-97, Morrison & Gollin LLP, N.Y.C., 1999—; s. Bd. dirs. Dad's Club of Hartsdale, Mid-Westchester YM/YMHA; treas. Am. Liver Found.; bd. dirs. The Transplant Living Ctr.; pres. Scarsdale Sports Assn. Mem. AICPA, N.Y. State Soc. CPAs, Am. Bankruptcy Inst., Nat. Cert. Insolvency & Reorgn. Acct., N.J. Soc. CPAs (acctg. and auditing stds., rels. with bankers, rels. with fin. writers coms., rels. with credit unions, chmn. bankruptcy and involvency com., litig. support com.), Nat. Assn. Accts. (dir. Westchester chpt.), Turnaround Mgmt. Assocs., Nat. Retail Mchts. Assn., Nat. Mass Retailers Inst., N.J. Retail Mchts. Assn., Met. Retail Fin. Execs. Assn., White Plains Jaycees, Bergen County C. of C., Ardsley Swim Club (dir.), Ridgeway Country Club, Beta Alpha Psi. Home: 34 Benedict Rd Scarsdale NY 10583-7340

GOLLINGS, RUTH ERICKSON, community health nurse; b. Oakland, Calif., July 19, 1944; d. Merland Walter and Astrid Christine (Sundberg) Erickson; m. Richard Haworth Gollings, Jan. 15, 1977; children: Eric Haworth, Sara Joy. Diploma, Mounds Midway, 1965; BSN, U. Colo., 1967; cert., Multnomah Sch. of the Bible, 1969; MA in Nursing, U. Wash., 1976. RN, Calif. Instr. in nursing Mesa Coll., Grand Junction, Colo.; asst. prof. nursing Seattle Pacific U.; lectr. in nursing Calif. State U., L.A.; missionary nurse Bapt. Gen. Conf. Global Ch. Planting, Arlington Heights, Ill.

GÖLLNER, MARIE LOUISE, musicologist, educator; b. Ft. Collins, Colo., June 27, 1932; d. Francis Gilbert and Gertrude Valentine (Steele) Martinez; m. Theodor W. Göllner, Sept. 30, 1959; children: Katharina, Philipp. B.A., Vassar Coll., 1953; postgrad., Eastman Sch. Music, 1953-54, U. Heidelberg, Germany, 1954-56; Ph.D. summa cum laude, U. Munich, 1962, Dr. phil. habil., 1975. Research asst. Bavarian State Library, Munich, 1964-67; lectr. Coll. Creative Studies, U. Calif., Santa Barbara, 1968; asst. prof. UCLA, 1970-74, assoc. prof., 1974-78, prof. musicology, 1978—, chmn. dept. music, 1976-80, chmn. dept. musicology, 1985-89. Author: Die Musik des frühen Trecento, 1963, Katalog der Musikhandschriften der Bayerischen Staatsbibliothek München, vol. 2, 1979, vol. 1, 1989, Joseph Haydn, Symphonie 94, 1979, Orlando di Lasso: Sämtliche Werke, Neue Reihe, Das Hymnarium, (1580-82), 1980, Eine neue Quelle zur italienischen Orgelmusik des Cinquecento, 1982, The Manuscript Cod. lat. 5539 of the Bavarian State Library (Musicological Studies & Documents 43), 1993; contbr. articles to profl. jours. NEH grantee, 1983, Fulbright grantee, 1954-55, 55-56; Gordon Anderson Meml. lectr. U. New Eng., Armidale, Australia, 1984. Mem. Internat. Assn. Music Libraries, Am. Musicol. Soc., Internat. Musicol. Soc., Medieval Acad. Am. Episcopalian. Home: 817 Knapp Dr Santa Barbara CA 93108-1941 Office: Univ Calif Dept Musicology Los Angeles CA 90024-1623

GOLLOB, HERMAN COHEN, retired publishing company, editor; b. Waco, Tex., July 7, 1930; s. Abe and Ruybe (Cohen) G.; m. Barbara Kowal, Apr. 9, 1961; children: Emily, Jared. B.A., Tex. A & M U., 1951. Lit. agt. MCA, Beverly Hills, Calif., 1956-58, William Morris, N.Y.C., 1958-59; editor Little, Brown & Co., Boston, 1959-64, Atheneum Pubs., N.Y.C., 1964-68; v.p., editor-in-chief Atheneum Pubs., 1971—; editor-in-chief Harper's Mag. Press, N.Y.C., 1968-71; v.p., editorial dir. The Literary Guild, N.Y.C., 1979-81; v.p., sr. editor Simon & Schuster, N.Y.C., 1981-86; sr. v.p., editor-in-chief Doubleday Pub. Co., 1986-90, editor-at-large, 1990-95; ret., 1995. Served to lt. USAF, 1951-53. Home: 40 Frederick St Montclair NJ 07042-4106 Office: Doubleday 1540 Broadway New York NY 10036-4039

GOLLOBIN, LEONARD PAUL, chemical engineer; b. N.Y.C., July 2, 1928; s. Morris and Jennie (Levine) G.; m. Charlotte Weissman, Jan. 21, 1951; children: Michael L., Susan D. Brown. BSChemE, CUNY, 1951; MS, Kans. State U., 1952; grad. mgmt. program, Harvard U., 1975. Design engr. Foster Wheeler Corp., N.Y.C., 1952-55; mfg. engr. Gen. Electric Co., Waterford, N.Y., 1955-58; program dir. ORI, Inc., Silver Spring, Md., 1958-63; chmn, chief exec. Presearch, Inc., Fairfax, Va., 1963—; U.S. del. NATO Indsl. Avd. Group, 1989, chmn., 1992-93, chmn. emeritus, 1994—; bd. visitors Nat. Def. U., Washington, 1989-98. Bd. dirs. Cultural Alliance Greater Washington, 1980-88; trustee Washington Opera, 1988-90. Recipient NSIA Adrm. Charles Weakley award, 1986, Meritorious Pub. Svc. award U.S. Dept. Navy, 1987, U.S. Marine Corps, 1989. Mem. Nat. Security Indsl. Assn. (exec. com. 1986—, chmn. antisubmarine warfare com. 1981-84, chmn. amphibious warfare com. 1986-89, chmn. environ. com. 1990-92, chmn. internat. com. 1991-93, vice chmn. exec. com. 1993, chmn. 1994, chmn. bd. trustees 1994-95), Nat. Def. Indsl. Assn. (chmn. fin. com. 1998—), Naval Undersea Warfare Found. Mus. (v.p. 1982—), Loudon Golf and Country Club (Purcellville, Va.). Home: 6710 Bradley Blvd Bethesda MD 20817-3045 Office: Presearch Inc 8500 Executive Park Ave Fairfax VA 22031-2223

GOLLUB, JERRY, academic administrator. Provost, prof. Haverford (Pa.) Coll., 1987—. Office: Haverford Coll Office of the Provost 754 College Ave Stokes #113 Haverford PA 19041*

GOLOBY, GEORGE WILLIAM, JR., environmental scientist, ornithologist, aviculturist; b. Franklin, Ky., Mar. 21, 1949; s. George William Sr. and Katherine Jacqueline (Panchot) G.; m. Diane Grayson, Dec. 29, 1974; children: Amy Vanessa, George William III. BS in Wildlife Sci., Tex. A&M U., 1971. Zookeeper of birds Houston Zool. Gardens, 1971-72; warehouseman, driver Houston Ind. Sch. Dist., 1972-76; lab. mgr. Empak Inc., Houston, 1976-80; asst. sect. chief City of Houston Dept. Pub. Works, 1980-90; environ. quality specialist III City of Houston Dept. Pub. Works & Engring., 1990—; founder, owner Penfeathers Tours, Houston, 1984—; instr. Houston Arboretum and Nature Ctr., 1999—. Editor (newsletters) Water Environment Assn. Tex. (WEAT) Pipeline, 1984—, Tex. Ornithol. Soc. Newsletter, 1989-99, Penfeathers Newsletter, 1986—, Panchot Paper, 1989-93, Houston Audubon Soc., 1977-80, The Naturalist, 1986-89; asst. editor (books) Houston, 1978, Encyclopedia of American Cities, 1979. Mem. Houston Proud, 1986, Cy-Fair Houston C. of C., 1986, Greater Houston Conv. and Vis. Bur., 1986-88. Mem. Water Environ. Assn. Tex. (com. chmn. 1984—), Tex. Water Utilites Assn., Houston Audubon Soc. (v.p. adminstrv. affairs 1986-89), Am. Birding Assn., Outdoor Nature Club, Parrot People Club (v.p. Houston chpt. 1985-86), Purple Martin Conservation Assn., Whooping Crane Conservation Assn., Tex. Nature Conservancy. Office: City Houston 4545 Groveway Houston TX 77087

GOLODNER, JACK, labor association official; b. N.Y.C., Nov. 2, 1931; s. Maurice S. and Regina (Gaber) G.; m. Linda Louise Fowler, June 14, 1964; children: Dean Dovid, Daniel Dimmick, Jonathan Wilmot. B.S., Cornell U., 1953; J.D., Yale U., 1958. Labor arbitrator Washington, 1958-60; exec. asst. to U.S. Congressman Giaimo, 1960-62; cons. pub. affairs, 1962-80; exec. sec. Council AFL-CIO Unions for Profl. Employees, 1967-77; dir. dept. for profl. employees AFL-CIO, 1977-89, pres., 1989—. V.p. bd. trustees Ford's Theater, Washington, 1973-79, Actors Studio, N.Y., 1982-87; bd. dirs. Nat. Theatre, 1978—; mem. gen. bd. Am. Coun. for the Arts, 1981-96; mem. adv. coun. Nat. Info. Infrastructure, 1994-96; mem. adv. coun. nat. orgns. Corp. Pub. Broadcasting, 1973-79; mem. Labor Adv. Com. for Multilateral Trade Negotiations of Dept. of Labor, 1975—; mem. arts and humanities com. Pres.'s Commn. on Internat. Women's Year, 1975-76; mem. U.S. del. UNESCO govtl. experts meeting, Paris, 1980; U.S. del. to adv. com. on salaried and profl. workers Internat. Labor Orgn., 1981, 85, 94, U.S. labor del. Plenary Confs., 1981, 82; chmn. labor del. tripartit meeting on salaried authors and inventors, 1987; mem. coun. Cornell U., 1987-93; chmn., mem. adv. coun. N.Y. State Sch. of Indsl. and Labor Rels., 1980-88, 90-94, mem. outside rev. com., 1986-87; mem. U.S. govt. delegation Diplomatic Conf. on Certain Copyright and Neighboring Rights Questions, World Intellectual Property Orgn., Geneva, 1996. Capt. USAF, 1953-55. Recipient William B. Groat award Cornell U., 1979. Mem. Indsl. Rels. Rsch. Assn. (exec. bd. 1993-96), Internat. Secretariat Arts, Mass Media and Entertainment Trade Unions (world v.p. 1987-93), Media and Entertainment Internat. (1st v.p. 1993-97), Nat. Policy Assn. (exec. com. New Am. Realities Program 1987—), Phi Kappa Phi. Home: 1739 Q St NW Washington DC 20009-2407 Office: AFL-CIO Dept Profl Employees 815 16th St NW Ste 209 Washington DC 20006-4145

GOLOMB, FREDERICK MARTIN, surgeon, educator; b. N.Y.C., Dec. 18, 1924; s. Jacob J. and Hannah (Loewy) G.; m. Joan E. Schneider, Nov. 28, 1954; children: James Bradley, Susan Lynn. B.S., Yale U., 1945; M.D., U. Rochester, 1949. Diplomate: Am. Bd. Surgery. Intern Johns Hopkins Hosp., 1949-50; resident NYU Hosp., 1950-56; pvt. practice specializing in surgery N.Y.C.; mem. staff NYU Med. Center, 1950—, dir. chemoimmunotherapy divsn. tumor svc. dept. surgery, 1967-96; attending surgeon Tisch Hosp., Beth Israel North Hosp.; cons. in gen. surgery Manhattan VA Hosp.; cons. surgeon Cabrini Health Care Center; vis. surgeon Bellevue Hosp.; mem. faculty NYU Sch. Medicine, 1956—, prof., clin. surgery, 1977—; cons. N.Y.C. div. Am. Cancer Soc., 1968—; mem. clin. trials rev. com. Nat. Cancer Inst., 1976-79; chmn. melanoma com. Eastern Coop. Oncology Group, 1978-80; prin. investigator Central Oncology Group, 1969-77, exec. com., 1976-77; mem. met. med. com. Chemotherapy Found.; co-prin. investigator Ea. Coop. Oncology Group NYU, 1978-95. Editorial adv. bd., contbg. editor Oncology News; contbr. articles to profl. jours. Served with M.C. AUS, 1953-54, Korea. Recipient John E. Sullivan award Beth Israel Med. Ctr., 1993. Fellow ACS; mem. AMA, Soc. Head and Neck Surgeons, Soc. Surgery Alimentary Tract, Am. Assn. Cancer Rsch., Am. Soc. Clin. Oncology, N.Y. Cancer Soc. (pres. 1974-75), N.Y. Surg. Soc., N.Y. State Med. Soc., N.Y. County Med. Soc., Soc. Surg. Oncology, George Hoyt Whipple Soc., Brit. Assn. Surg. Oncology (editl. adv. panel 1980-85), Pan Am. Med. Soc., Am. Alpine Club, Explorers Club, Sigma Xi. Office: NYU Sch Medicine 530 1st Ave New York NY 10016-6481

GOLOMB, HARVEY MORRIS, oncologist, educator; b. Pitts., Feb. 13, 1943; s. Russell Austin and Dorothy (Simon) G.; m. Lynne Rooth, Dec. 28, 1965; children: Adam, Sara. BA, U. Chgo., 1964; MD, U. Pitts., 1968. Diplomate Am. Bd. Internal Medicine, Am. Bd. Med. Oncology. Intern Boston City Hosp., 1968-69; resident Johns Hopkins U., Balt., 1971-72, fellow, 1972-73; fellow U. Chgo., 1973-75, asst. prof. dept. medicine, 1975-79, assoc. prof., 1979-83, prof., 1983—, chief sect. hematology/oncology, 1981-98, chmn. dept. medicine, 1998—; chmn. subspecialty bd. med. oncology Am. Bd. Internal Medicine, 1991-95. Contbr. over 300 articles, papers to profl. publs.; co-editor: Lung Cancer, 1988. Capt. U.S. Army, 1971-73. Mem. Am. Soc. Hematology (bd. dirs. 1987-91), Am. Soc. Oncology (pres. elect 1989-90, pres. 1990-91). Office: U Chgo MC 6092 5841 S Maryland Ave Chicago IL 60637-1463

GOLOMB, HERBERT STANLEY, dermatologist; b. N.Y.C., Sept. 6, 1933; s. Morris and Ida (Schwartz) G.; AB, U. Pa., 1955; MD, State U. N.Y., Bklyn., 1960; m. Suzanne Nazer, Dec. 20, 1964; children: Meredith, Valerie. Intern, Ohio State U. Hosp., Columbus, 1960-61; resident in dermatology State U. N.Y.-Kings County Med. Center, 1961-62, N.Y. U. Skin and Cancer Unit and Bellevue Hosp., N.Y.C., 1962-64; pres. Falls Church Med. Ctr., 1963-64; practice medicine specializing in dermatology, Falls Church, Va., 1964-66, 68—; mem. staff George Washington U., Fairfax (Va.), Arlington hosps.; instr., then clin. assoc. prof. dermatology George Washington U. Sch. Medicine, 1964—; cons. USPHS Dermatology Clinic, 1964-66; chmn. Atlantic Dermatol. Conf., 1978. Pres. Dermatology Found. No. Va., 1972-99, bd. dirs., 1978-79. Served with USPHS, 1966-68. Diplomate Am. Bd. Dermatology. Fellow Am. Acad. Dermatology; mem. AMA, Soc. Investigative Dermatology, Internat. Soc. Tropical Dermatology, Med. Soc. Va., D.C., Fairfax County med. socs., D.C., Va. dermatol. socs. Clubs: Tuckahoe Swim and Tennis. Home: 1910 Woodgate Ln Mc Lean VA 22101-5441 Office: 6060 Arlington Blvd Falls Church VA 22044-2943

GOLOMB, MYRA J., nurse; b. Pa., Sept. 29, 1967; d. Arnold and H. Jolene (Campbell) Stackhouse; m. John Golomb; children: Dylan, Dagaen, Kaytiona. Diploma, Geisinger Sch. Nursing, 1987; BSN, Bloomsburg U., 1993; cert. in sch. nursing, Lycoming Coll., 1996. RN, Pa. Staff registered nurse Pa. State Geisinger Health Sys., Danville, 1987—; substitute sch. nurse; mem. Geisinger 2000 Design Team; presenter to various groups of children and teens on health topics. Sch. vol., 4-H Club vol.

GOLOMB, RICHARD MOSS, lawyer; b. Phila., Oct. 24, 1958; m. Marci Cohen. BS in Polit. Sci., Am. U., 1980; JD, Nova U., 1983. Bar: Pa. 1984, N.J. 1984, U.S. Dist. N.J. 1984. Law clk. to presiding justice Camden, N.J., 1983-84; assoc. Romisher & Phillips, Phila., 1984-85, Kreithen Baron & Miller, Phila., 1985-89; ptnr. Kreithen, Baron, Villari & Golomb, Phila., 1989-96, Villari & Golomb, Phila., 1996-97, Villari, Golumb & Honik, Phila., 1997—; hearing officer Disciplinary Bd. of Supreme Ct. of Pa., 1994—. Mem. Phila. Dem. Exec. Com., 1983-85; vice chair. young lawyers divsn. Fedn. Allied Jewish Appeal, 1989, chair chai divsn. 1990-92; mem. Nat. Young Men's Cabinet, 1992-94; bd. dirs. Young Leadership Coun., 1990—; chmn. Camapign for Qualified Judiciary, 1993-95; sec. State Civil Jud. Procedures, 1994. Fellow Acad. Advocacy; mem. ABA, ATLA, Pa. Bar Assn., Phila. Bar Assn. (chair state civil com., trustee 1997—, bd. govs. 1997—), Pa. Trial Lawyers Assn. (bd. govs. 1999), Phila. Trial Lawyers Assn. (bd. govs. 1990—, asst. sec. 1995-96, v.p. 1997-98, pres.-elect 1998—, pres. 1999), Phila. Bar Found. (trustee 1996—). Jewish. Home: 205 Wiltshire Rd Wynnewood PA 19096-3332 Office: Villari Golomb & Honik 121 S Broad St Philadelphia PA 19107-4533

GOLOMB, SOLOMON WOLF, mathematician, electrical engineer, educator, university official; b. Balt., May 31, 1932; s. Elhanan Hirsh and Minna (Nadel) G. A.B., Johns Hopkins U., 1951; M.A., Harvard U., 1953, Ph.D., 1957; postgrad., U. Oslo, 1955-56; DSc (hon.), Dubna Internat. U., Russia, 1995; DHL (hon.), Hebrew Union Coll., L.A., 1996. Mem. faculty Boston U., 1954-55, Harvard U., 1954-55, UCLA, 1957-61, Calif. Inst. Tech., 1960-62; sr. research engr. Jet Propulsion Lab., Pasadena, Calif., 1956-58, research group supr., 1958-60, asst. chief telecommunications research sect., 1960-63; assoc. prof. U. So. Calif., Los Angeles, 1963-64, prof. elec. engring. and math., 1964—; vice provost for research U. So. Calif., 1986-89; univ. prof., 1993—; dir. tech. Annenberg Ctr. for Comms. U. So. Calif., L.A., 1995-98; cons. to govt. and industry. Author: Digital Communications with Space Applications, 1964, 81, Polyominoes, 1965, rev. edit., 1994, Shift Register Sequences, 1967, 82, Basic Concepts in Information Theory and Coding, 1994; contbr. articles to profl. jours. Recipient Presdl. medal U. So. Calif., 1985, Lomonosov medal Russian Acad. Sci., 1994, Kapitsa medal Russian Acad. Natural Scis., 1995. Fellow IEEE (Shannon award Info. Theory Soc. 1995), AAAS; mem. NAE, AAUP, Internat. Sci. Radio Union, Russian Acad. Natural Scis. (fgn.), Am. Math. Soc., Math. Assn. Am., Soc. Indsl. and Applied Math., Golden Key, Phi Beta Kappa, Sigma Xi, Pi Delta Epsilon, Eta Kappa Nu, Phi Kappa Phi. Office: U So Calif Univ Park Dept Elec Engring EEB 504A Los Angeles CA 90089-2565

GOLOMSKI, WILLIAM ARTHUR, consulting company executive; s. John Frank and Margaret Sophie (Glisczinski) G.; m. Joan Ellen Golomski; children: Gretchen, William. Registered profl. engr., Calif. Prin. W.A. Golomski & Assocs., Algoma, Wis., 1949—, pres., 1971—; sr. lectr. Grad. Sch. Bus. U. Chgo., 1990—. Author chpts. in books; co-editor A Quality Revolution in Manufacturing, 1989; founding editor Quality Mgmt. Jour., 1993. Mem. Avoca Sch. Bd., Wilmette, Ill.; adv. bd. Milw. Sch. Engring. U. Wis., 1967-72, 83-87, indsl. engring. com. Hon. mem. Philippine Soc. Quality Control, 1992. Fellow AAAS, Am. Soc. Quality Control (Eugene L. Grant award 1991, Edwards medal, William A. Golomski rsch. award named in his honor 1986, Am. Deming medal met. sect., hon. mem. 1993), N.Y. Acad. Scis., Royal Soc. Health, Am. Statis. Assn., Inst. Indsl. Engrs. (judge Malcolm Baldrige nat. quality award 1988, bd. overseers 1989-91), Nat. Acad. Engring. Achievements include devel. of world class orgns.; first jour. for quality mgmt. and quality in higher edn. Office: N 9690 County Rd U Algoma WI 54201-9528

GOLSBY, MARSANNE, press secretary. BA, N.E. La. U., 1977. Press sec. La. Press Office, Baton Rouge, 1996—. Office: Press Office State Capitol 4th Fl Baton Rouge LA 70804

GOLSHANI, FOROUZAN, computer science and engineering educator; b. Mashhad, Iran, Oct. 27, 1953; came to U.S., 1984; s. Azizullah and Khadijeh (Momtaz) G.; m. Rezvanieh Mazloom, Apr. 7, 1984; children: Ashkahn Edward, Afsaneh Aimee, Andrew Arian. BS, Arya Mehr U. Tech., Tehran, 1976; MS, U. Warwick, Coventry, Eng., 1979, PhD, 1982. Project mgr. Gen. Sys., Tehran, 1976-78; rsch. fellow Imperial Coll., London, 1982-84; from asst. prof. to assoc. prof. Ariz. State U., Tempe, 1984-95, prof., 1995—; cons. Bull Worldwide Info. Sys., Phoenix, Ariz., 1988-97, Honeywell, Mpls., 1993-96, Frost & Sullivan, London, 1995-97, Motorola, Phoenix, 1997—. Co-founder Corp. Enhancement Group, Phoenix, 1995, roz Software Sys., Inc., Scottsdale, Ariz., 1997. Mem. IEEE (sr., Disting. Spkr. 1990-93), Computer Sci. Accreditation Bd. (team chair 1995—), Corp. Enhancement Group Phoenix (co-founding). Baha'i. Achievements include 9 inventions in field. Avocations: music, literature, sports. Office: Ariz State U Dept Computer Sci Tempe AZ 85287-5406

GOLSON, GEORGE BARRY, editor; b. Lynn, Mass., Dec. 12, 1944; s. George Albert and Beverly Margaret G.; m. Thia Anne MacKenzie, Aug. 24, 1968. B.A., Yale U., 1967; postgrad., Stanford U., 1967-68. Columnist, mng. editor Atlas World Press Rev., 1969-71; sr. editor Playboy mag., 1974-76, exec. editor, 1976-89; exec. editor TV Guide mag., N.Y.C., 1991-95; editor-in-chief Yahoo Internet Life, 1995—. Editor: The Playboy Interview, 1981; contbr. articles on politics, satire and travel to various publs. Ford fellow, 1968. Mem. Am. Soc. Mag. Editors, Am. Soc. Journalists and Authors. Office: Ziff Davis Corp Yahoo Internet Life 1 Park Ave New York NY 10016-5802*

GOLSTON, JOAN CAROL, psychotherapist; b. Vancouver, B.C., Can., Aug. 10, 1947; came to U.S., 1958; d. Stefan and Lydia Barbara (Fruchs) G. Student, Reed Coll.; BA, U. Wash., 1977, MSW, 1979. Cert. social worker; bd. cert. diplomate in clin. social work Am. Bd. Examiners in Clin. Social Work. Clin. supr. Crisis Clinic, Seattle, 1975-77; psychiatric social worker Valley Gen. Hosp., Renton, Wash., 1979-82; psychotherapist pvt. practice, Seattle, 1981—; sch. counselor Northwest Sch., Seattle, Seattle Acad.; clin. cons. outpatient dept. Valley Cities Cmty. Mental Health, Renton, 1991, Seattle Counseling Svcs., 1991-96, emergency svcs., 1975-89; cons., trainer and presenter in field. Contbr. articles to profl. jours. Bd. dirs. Open Door Clinic, Seattle, 1975-76, Northwest Family Tng. Inst., Seattle, v.p., 1990, pres., 1991, mem. exec. com., 1988-91; mem. adv. bd. Ctr. Prevention of Sexual and Domestic Violence, 1993—, AIDS Risk Reduction Project Sch. Social Work U. Wash., 1988-93. Nat. Merit scholar, 1964. Mem. NASW (diplomate), Wash. State chpt. NASW (chmn. com. on inquiry ethics 1996—, mem. com. 1992—), Internat. Soc. Study of Dissociation, Internat. Soc. Trauma Stress Studies, Acad. Cert. Social Workers. Avocations: athletics, antiquities. Office: 726 Broadway Ste 303 Seattle WA 98122-4337

GOLTER, CHRISTINA RITA, marketing specialist, consultant; b. Aurora, Ill., Apr. 24, 1966; d. Hermann and Rita Marie Anne (Bauernfeind) G. BA in Internat. Studies, Am. U., 1988; MBA, Northwestern U., 1992. Intern in cultural svcs. Embassy of France, Washington, 1985; intern Office of Fgn. Policy U.S. Senator Edward Kennedy, Washington, spring 1986; intern security and fgn. policy German Fed. Govt., Bonn, fall 1986; intern Blue Danube Radio Austrian Fed. Broadcast Sys., Vienna, 1987; account exec. Lufthansa German Airlines, Chgo., 1988-93; dir. world capitals programs Am. U., Washington, 1993-94; market devel. mgr. Ragold Inc., Chgo., 1994-96; sr. mktg. analyst/account mgr. Lee Hill Inc., Chgo., 1996-97; supr. worldwide mktg.and resource svcs. Draft Worldwide, Chgo., 1997—. Host com. vol. World Cup Soccer '96, Chgo., 1993, Nat. Dem. Conv., Chgo., 1996. Recipient Cert. of Appreciation, Golden Kiwanis, 1996. Mem. Am. Mktg. Assn., Am. Mgmt. Assn., Nat. Assn. for Female Execs., Chgo. Assn. Direct Mktg. Kellogg Exec. Mgrs. Program Alumni Club, Phi Kappa Phi. Avocations: cooking, playing piano, language tutoring in German, French, and Spanish. Home: 300 N State St Apt 5131 Chicago IL 60610-4837 Office: Draft Worldwide 633 N Saint Clair St Chicago IL 60611-3234

GOLTZ, ROBERT WILLIAM, physician, educator; b. St. Paul, Sept. 21, 1923; s. Edward Victor and Clare (O'Neill) G.; m. Patricia Ann Sweeney, Sept. 27, 1945; children: Leni, Paul Robert. *Dr. Goltz has been married to Patricia Ann (Sweeney) Goltz since 1945. They have two children, Leni Wilcox, a health care executive in Minneapolis, and Paul, in charge of foreign sales for the Hach Chemical Company in Loveland, Colorado. They have four grandchildren.* B.S., U. Minn., 1943, M.D., 1945. Diplomate: Am. Bd. Dermatology (pres. 1975-76). Intern Ancker Hosp., St. Paul, 1944-45; resident in dermatology Mpls. Gen. Hosp., 1945-46, 48-49, U. Minn. Hosp., 1949-50; practice medicine specializing in dermatology Mpls., 1950-65; clin. instr. U. Minn. Grad. Sch., 1950-58, clin. asst. prof., 1958-60, clin. assoc. prof., 1960-65, prof., head dept. dermatology, 1971-85; prof. medicine and dermatology U. Calif., San Diego, 1985—, acting chair divsn. dermatology, 1995-97; prof. dermatology, head div. dermatology U. Colo. Med. Sch., Denver, 1965-71. Former editorial bd.: Archives of Dermatology; editor: Dermatology Digest. Served from 1st lt. to capt., M.C. U.S. Army, 1946-48. Mem. Assn. Am. Physicians, Am. Dermatol. Assn. (dir. 1976-79, pres. 1985-86), Am. Soc. Dermatopathology (pres. 1981), Am. Dermatologic Soc. Allergy and Immunology (pres. 1978-83), AMA (chmn. sect. on dermatology 1973-75), Dermatology Found. (past dir.), Minn. Dermatol. Soc., Soc. Investigative Dermatology (pres. 1972-73, hon. 1988), Histochem. Soc., Am. Acad. Dermatology (pres. 1978-79, past dir.) (hon.), Brit. Assn. Dermatology (hon.), Chilean Dermatology Soc. (hon.), Colombian Dermatol. Soc. (corr. mem.), Can. Dermatol. Soc. (hon. mem.), Pacific Dermatol. Soc. (hon.-mem.), S. African Dermatol. Soc. (hon. mem.), N.Am. Clin. Dermatol. Soc., Assn. Profs. Dermatology (sec.-treas. 1970-72, pres. 1973-74), West Assn. Physicians. Home: 6097 Avenida Chamnez La Jolla CA 92037-7404 Office: U Calif-San Diego Med Ctr Divsn Dermatology H-8420 200 W Arbor Dr San Diego CA 92103-1911

GOLTZMAN, DAVID, endocrinologist, educator, researcher; b. Montreal, Que., Can., Sept. 22, 1944; s. Jack and Lily (Roth) G.; m. Naomi Lyon, Dec. 29, 1968; children: Jonathan, Rebecca, Daniel. BSc, McGill U., 1966, MD, 1968. Diplomate Am. Bd. Internal Medicine, Am. Bd. Endocrinology and Metabolism. Med. intern Royal Victoria Hosp., Montreal, 1968-69; med. resident Columbia U. Coll. Physicians and Surgeons, N.Y.C., 1969-71; clin. and rsch. fellow in endocrinology Mass. Gen. Hosp., Boston, 1971-75; instr. medicine Harvard Med. Sch., Boston, 1974-75; asst. prof. medicine McGill U., Montreal, 1976-78, assoc. prof., 1978-83, prof., 1983—, chmn. physiology, 1988-93, dir. calcium rsch. lab., 1981—, hosmer prof. physiology, 1992-93, Massabki prof. medicine, 1994—; chmn. medicine, 1994—; sr. physician dept. medicine Royal Victoria Hosp., 1987-94, physician-in-chief, 1994-98; physician-in chief, McGill U. Hlth. Ctr., 1998—; chmn. exptl. medicine com. Med. Rsch. Coun. Can., Ottawa, Ont., 1984-88; mem. gen. medicine B study sect., NIH, Bethesda, Md., 1987-91; active Exec. Med. Rsch. Coun. Can., 1993—. Author: (with others) Principles of Bone Biology, 1996, Primer of Metabolic Bone Disease and Disorders of Mineral Metabolism, 1996, 1989, Principles and Practice of Endocrinology and Metabolism, 1995; editl. bd. Endocrinology Jour., 1985-90, Jour. Bone Mineral rsch., 1985-90, Bone and Mineral, 1991-94, Osteoporosis Internat., 1991-94, Assoc. Edn. Bone, 1989-94; assoc. editor: Jur. Bone Mineral research, 1995—; contbr. numerous articles to profl. jours. Recipient Chercheur Boursier award Que. Med. Rsch. Coun., 1980-83, Scientist award Med. Rsch. Coun. Can., 1983-88, Andre Lichtwitz prize Nat. Inst. for Med. Rsch., France, 1987. Fellow Royal Coll. Physicians and Surgeons, Royal Soc. Canada; mem. Can. Soc. Endocrinology and Metabolism (pres. 1990-92), Am. Soc. for Bone and Mineral Rsch. (chmn. program com. 1989-90), Am. Assn. Physicians, Endocrine Soc. (program com. 1989-91), Can. Soc. Clin. Investigation (councillor 1986-89, pres. 1998-99) Am. Soc. Clin. Investigation, Am. Assn. Physicians, Canadian Assn. Profs. of Medicine (pres. 1998-99). Avocations: classical music, gardening, tennis. Office: Royal Victoria Hosp, 687 Pine Ave W, Montreal, PQ Canada H3A 1A1

GOLUB, GERALD LEONARD, accounting company executive; b. Bklyn., 1939. BS in Acctg., CUNY, 1962. CPA, N.Y. Owner, mgr. Gerald L. Golub & Co., N.Y.C., 1967-71; with Goldstein, Golub, Kessler & Co. (merger with above co. 1971), N.Y.C., 1971-98, mng. ptnr., pres., 1981-98, also bd. dirs., til 1998; mng. ptnr. Goldstein Golub Kessler LLP, 1998—. Office: Goldstein Golub Kessler LLP 1185 Avenue Of The Americas New York NY 10036-2601*

GOLUB, HARVEY, financial services company executive; b. N.Y.C., Apr. 16, 1939. Student, Cornell U., 1956-58; BS, NYU, 1961. Jr. ptnr. McKinsey & Co. Inc., N.Y.C., 1967-74, sr. ptnr., 1977-83; pres. Shulman Air Freight, N.Y.C., 1974-77; chmn., pres. IDS Fin. Svc., Mpls., 1984-90; chmn., CEO IDS Fin. Svcs. (name changed to Am. Express Fin. Advisors), Mpls., 1990—; vice chmn., dir. Am. Express Co., N.Y.C., 1990-91, pres., 1991-93; CEO, chmn. bd. dirs. Am. Express Co., 1993—; chmn., CEO Am. Express Travel Related Svcs. Co. Inc., N.Y.C., 1991. Bd. dirs. Am. Enterprise Inst., Columbia Presbyn. Hosp., Carnegie Hall, N.Y.C. Partnership, N.Y. C. of C. and Industry, United Way of N.Y.C.; mem. Bus. Roundtable, Bretton Woods Com.; apptd. mem. Pres.'s Com. for Arts and Humanities, Pres.'s Adv. Trade and Policy Negotiations. Mem. World Travel and Tourism Coun. (exec. com., chmn.-elect). Office: Am Express Co Tower C 3 World Fin Ctr 200 Vesey St New York NY 10285-1000*

GOLUB, LEWIS, supermarket company executive; b. 1931. BS, Mich. State U., 1953; LHD (hon.), SUNY--Empire State Coll., 1998. With Golub Corp., 1953—, v.p., 1963-71, exec. v.p., 1971-72, pres., treas., 1972-82, chmn. bd., 1982—; also chief exec. officer, dir. Golub Corp., Schenectady; bd. dirs. Taylor Made Co., CIES; mem. regional adv. bd. Chase Bank. Advisor MBA program Russell Sage Coll.; mem. adv. coun. grad. mgmt. inst. Union Coll.; bd. dirs. Empire State Coll. Found., Saratoga Performing Arts Ctr., Proctor's Theatre, Food Mktg. Inst.; chmn. The N.Y. State Bus. Coun.; Paul Harris hon. fellow Rotary Internat., 1992; active Found. SUNY. Served with U.S. Army. Recipient Marketer Exec.-Citizen award Sales and Mktg. Execs. Ea. N.Y., 1988, Disting. Citizen award SUNY, 1989, Dr. Norman D. Kathan Cmty. Svc. award YMCA, 1990, Tree of Life award Jewish Nat. Fund, 1992, Disting. Cmty. Svc. award Chinese Cmty., 1993, Cmty. Svc. award Inter-Faith Cmty. of Schenectady, 1993, Cmty. Svc. accolate Northeastern N.Y. chpt. Arthritis Found., 1993, Achievement award Am. Diabetes Assn., 1994, Disting. Citizen Laureate award U. Albany Found., 1994, John J. O'Connor Excellence in Leadership award United Way, 1995, Disting. Citizen award Boy Scouts Am., 1995, N.Y. State Chiefs of Police, 1995, Cmty. Svc. awar Office of Aging, 1996, Legends of the Industry award N.Y. State Food Mchts. Assn., 1996; named Man of Yr., Am. Jewish Com., 1981, Exec. of Yr., The Capital Dist. Bus. Rev., 1989; named to Hall of Fame, Capital Region Bus., 1997, Jr. Achievement, 1997. Office: Golub Corp 501 Duanesburg Rd Schenectady NY 12306-1092

GOLUB, SHARON BRAMSON, psychologist, educator; b. N.Y.C., Mar. 25, 1937; m. Leon M. Golub, June 1, 1958; children: Lawrence E., David B. Diploma, Mt. Sinai Hosp. Sch. Nursing, 1957; BS, Columbia U., 1959, MA, 1966; PhD, Fordham U., 1974. Head nurse Mt. Sinai Hosp., N.Y.C., 1957-59; contbg. editor RN Mag., Oradell, N.J., 1967-74; asst. prof. psychology Coll. New Rochelle, N.Y., 1974-79, assoc. prof., 1979-86, prof., 1986-98; prof. emeritus Coll. New Rochelle, $D, $D, 1998—; dir. women's studies Coll. New Rochelle, N.Y., 1978-79, chmn. dept. psychology, 1979-82; pvt. practice individual and group psychotherapy Harrison, N.Y., 1976—; adj. prof. psychiatry N.Y. Med. Coll., Valhalla, 1980-94. Editor: Menarche, 1983 (Assn. Women in Psychology Disting. Pub. award 1984, Book of Yr. award Am. Jour. Nursing 1984), Lifting the Curse of Menstruation, 1983, Health Care of the Female Adolescent, 1984, Health Needs of Women as They Age, 1984, PERIODS from Menarche to Menopause, 1992; (with Rita Jackaway Freedman) Psychology of Women: Resources for a Core Curriculum, 1987; editor Women and Health, 1982-86, mem. editorial bd., 1986—; mem. editorial bd. Psychology of Women Quar., 1989—. Grantee Nat. Libr. Medicine, 1983-84; NIH rsch. fellow, 1971-74. Fellow Am. Psychol. Assn. (chmn. task force on teaching psychology of women 1980-83), Am. Psychol. Soc., Am. Assn. Applied and Preventive Psychology; mem. Soc. for Menstrual Cycle Rsch. (pres. 1981-83, bd. dirs. 1981-93), Assn. Women in Psychology, Phi Beta Kappa, Sigma Xi, Psi Chi. Office: Coll New Rochelle Dept Psychology New Rochelle NY 10805

GOLUSIN, MILLARD R., obstetrician and gynecologist; b. Detroit, Feb. 14, 1947; s. Raddie and Joan (Lalich) G.; m. Yvonne Marie Cronovich, Sept. 29, 1974; children: Milan, Marko, Matthew. BS with honors, Wayne State U., 1968, MS, 1970, MD, 1975. Diplomate Am. Bd. Obstetrics and Gynecology. Intern, then resident William Beaumont Hosp., Royal Oak, Mich., 1975-78; practice medicine specializing in obstetrics and gynecology Village Gynecologic and Obstetric Assocs., P.C., Southfield and Troy, Mich., 1978-92; pvt. solo practice specializing in obstetrics and gynecology Troy, Mich., 1992—; mem. quality assurance com. William Beaumont Hosp., Royal Oak, Mich., 1979—, mem. gynecol. quality assurance com., 1993—; charter mem., pres. Preferred Ob-Gyn. Mgmt. Group L.L.C. Trustee United Beaumont Physicians Group, 1993—. Served with U.S. Army, 1969-71. Fellow ACOG; mem. Am. Soc. Reproductive Medicine, Mich. State Med. Soc., Am. Inst. Ultrasound Medicine, Serbian Singing Soc., Ravanica (musical dir. 1967—, pres. 1981-82). Republican. Serbian Eastern Orthodox. Avocations: music, golf. Office: 1050 Wilshire Dr Ste 100 Troy MI 48084-1526

GOMBERG, EDITH S. LISANSKY, psychologist, educator; b. N.Y.C., Jan. 14, 1920; d. Barnet and Dorothy (Resnick) Silverglied; m. Henry Jacob Gomberg, June 24, 1967; children: Stephen, Judith, Eugene, Richard, Robert. M.A., Columbia U., 1940; Ph.D., Yale U., 1949. Lectr., rsch. asst., rsch. assoc. Center Alcohol Studies, Yale U., New Haven, 1949-67; assoc. prof. dept. psychology U. P.R., 1968-71; prof. Sch. Social Work, U. Mich., Ann Arbor, 1974-90; prof. psychology, dept. psychiatry U. Mich., Ann Arbor, 1988—. Author: Gender and Disordered Behavior, 1979, Alcohol, Science and Socity Revisited, 1982, Current Issues in Alcohol/Drug Studies, 1989, Drugs and Human Behavior: A Sourcebook for the Helping Professions, 1991, Women and Substance Abuse, 1993, Alcohol and Aging, 1995; contbr. chpts. to books, articles to profl. jours. Mem. Rep. Town Meeting, Hamden, Conn., 1964-65; mem. Blue Ribbon Study Commn. on Alcoholism and Aging, Nat. Council on Alcoholism, 1979-82; chmn. panel on prevention, study to assess sci. opportunities of alcohol-related research Inst. Medicine, Nat. Acad. Sci.; mem. alcohol psychosocial research rev. com. Nat. Inst. Alcohol Abuse and Alcoholism, 1981-82. Mary E. Ives fellow, 1944; AAUW Elizabeth Avery Colten fellow, 1955. Mem. Psychonomic Soc., Sociedad Interamericana de Psicologia, Rsch. Soc. on Alcoholism, Sigma Xi. Jewish. Home: 430 Hillspur Rd Ann Arbor MI 48105-1049 Office: U Mich Alcohol Rsch Ctr 400 E Eisenhower Pkwy Ann Arbor MI 48108-3308

GOMBERG, SYDELLE, dancer educator; m. Ralph Gomberg. Student, Met. Opera Ballet Sch.; studies with Pierre Vladimiroff, Anatale Oboukoff, Edward Caton, Anatole Vilzak, Vincenzo Celli, Margaret Craske. Dir. Boston Ballet Sch., until 1993; faculty mem. Boston Conservatory of Music; resident master teacher Walnut Hill School, Natick, Mass., 1993-96; guest tchr., mem. adv. bd. Walnut Hill Sch., Natick, Mass., 1996—. Performed with Met. Opera Ballet, Radio City Ballet; soloist (Broadway play) Lute Song starring Mary Martin and the Late Yul Brynner. Founder dance dept. All Newton Music Sch., Walnut Hill Sch., 1971-85, apptd. dean arts, trustee, adv. bd. mem.; regional sec. Royal Acad. Dancing; mem. dance panel Mass.

Coun. on the Arts and Humanities; chmn. spl. com. Dance Edn. Home: 264 Mill St Newtonville MA 02460-2436

GOMBOCZ, ERICH ALFRED, biochemist; b. Vienna, Austria, Aug. 29, 1951; came to U.S., 1990; s. Erich and Maria (Mayer) G.; m. Gisela M. Dorner, June 12, 1973 (div. Apr. 1992); 1 child, Manfred Alexander (dec.). Cert., T.U., Vienna, 1970-75. With Fed. Inst. for Food Analysis and Rsch., Vienna, 1975-90, head of sect. dept. biochem. analysis, 1980-90, contbr. Cen. Lab. Info. Mgmt. System, 1987-90; chmn. scientific adv. bd. LabIntelligence, Inc., Menlo Park, Calif., 1989-99, COO, v.p. R & D, 1989-99; chief sci. officer NucleoTech Corp., San Mateo, Calif., 1999—; speaker and lectr. in field. Editor: Computers in Electrophoresis; contbr. articles to profl. jours.; patentee in field. Postdoctoral Rsch. award NIH, Bethesda, Md., 1985-86, 88. Mem. Internat. Assn. for Cereal Chemistry, Internat. Electrophoresis Soc., Am. Electrophoresis Soc. Roman Catholic. Office: NucleoTech Corp Ste 510 1400 Fashion Island Blvd San Mateo CA 94404

GOMER, ROBERT, chemistry educator; b. Vienna, Mar. 24, 1924; m. Anne Olah, 1955; children: Richard, Maria. B.A., Pomona Coll., 1944; Ph.D. in Chemistry, U. Rochester, 1949; AEC fellow chemistry, Harvard, 1949-50. Instr. dept. chemistry James Franck Inst. U. Chgo., 1950-51, asst. prof., 1951-54, assoc. prof., 1954-58, prof., 1958-96, Carl William Eisendrath Disting. Service prof., 1984-96, prof. emeritus, 1996—; dir. James Franck Inst. U. Chgo., 1977-83. Bd. dirs. Bull. Atomic Scientists, 1960-84. Served with AUS, 1944-46. Recipient Kendall award in surface chemistry Am. Chem. Soc., 1975, Davisson Germer prize Am. Phys. Soc., 1981, Medard W. Welch award Am. Vacuum Soc., 1989, Arthur W. Adamson award Am. Chem. Soc., 1996; Sloan fellow, 1958-62, Guggenheinm fellow, 1969-70; Bourke lectr. Eng., 1959. Mem. Leopoldina Acad. Scis., Nat. Acad. Scis., Am. Acad. Arts and Sci. Home: 4824 S Kimbark Ave Chicago IL 60615-1916 Office: 5640 S Ellis Ave Chicago IL 60637-1433

GOMERY, DOUGLAS, communications educator, writer; b. N.Y.C., Apr. 5, 1945; s. John Edgar and Julia (Halsted) G.; m. Marilyn L. Moon, Jan. 13, 1973. BS, Lehigh U., 1967; MA, U. Wis., 1970, PhD, 1975. Asst. prof. mass communication U. Wis., Milw., 1974-79, assoc. prof., 1980; assoc. prof. U. Md., College Park, 1981-87, prof., 1987—; sr. rschr. media studies project Woodrow Wilson Ctr. for Internat. Scholarship, Washington, 1988-92; vis. prof. Northwestern U., Evanston, Ill., 1980, U. Iowa, Iowa City, 1982, U. Utrecht, The Netherlands, 1990, 92; cons. Am. Film Inst., Washington, 1982-90. Author: High Sierra, 1979, Media in America, 1998, (with Annette Michelson) The Art of Moving Shadows, 1989; (with Robert C. Allen) Film History: Theory and Practice, 1985; The Hollywood Studio System, 1986; (with Phil Cook and L.W. Lichty) American Media, 1988; Movie History: A Survey, 1991, Shared Pleasures, 1992 (Am. Theater Libr. Assn. Book award 1992); editor: The Will Hays Papers, 1987, The Future of News, 1992, Media in America, 1998; mem. editorial bd. Cinema Jour., 1983-92, Jour. Media Econs., 1989—, Jour. Film and Video, 1983-92; contbg. editor Screen, London, 1984-89, Iris, Paris, 1983-89, Jour. of Comm., 1995—; editor Marquee, 1991; columnist Am. Journalism Rev., 1995—; author more than 500 articles. Cons. Joint Com. on Landmarks Washington, 1983, 85, 86, 90, NEH, 1980—, Nat. Endowment Arts, 1980—, Md. State Hist. Preservation Office, 1988, Voice of Am., Nat. Gallery Art., Wis. Dept. Revenue, 1978; trustee Am. Film Inst., 1986-89. Mem. Theatre Hist. Soc. (chmn. Weiss award com. 1984-87, bd. dirs. 1987-89, Weiss prize 1988), Soc. Cinema Studies, Univ. Film and Video Assn. (editorial bd. jours. 1983-92), Broadcast Edn. Assn., Assn. for Edn. in Journalism and Mass Comm., Internat. Comm. Assn. Avocation: economics. Home: 4817 Drummond Ave Chevy Chase MD 20815-5428 Office: U Md Coll Journalism College Park MD 20742

GOMES, EDWARD CLAYTON, JR., construction company executive; b. Terre Haute, Ind., Nov. 15, 1933; s. Edward Clayton Sr. and Jewel Margaret (James) G.; m. Pamela Thompson, Jan. 11, 1958; children: Hilary T., Valerie C. BBA, Washington U., St. Louis, 1955, MBA, 1968. Pres. Mo. Petroleum Products Co., St. Louis, 1969-80; pres., CEO Lionmark Constrn. Cos., St. Louis, 1980—; bd. dirs. Martin K. Eby Constrn., Inc., Wichita, Magna Bank, St. Louis, Rightchoice Managed Care, Inc., 1994—; internat. dir. Young Pres.'s Orgn., N.Y.C., 1975-80; trustee Blue Cross Blue Shield Mo., 1991-94. Bd. dirs. Acad. of Sci., St. Louis, 1977-80; trustee St. Louis Art Mus., 1988-92, The Hawthorne Found., Jefferson City, Mo., 1983-86; commr. St. Louis Sci. Ctr., 1980-83. Mem. World Bus. Coun., Chief Execs. Orgn. (bd. dirs.), Whittemore House, St. Louis Club, Beta Gamma Sigma. Episcopalian. Avocations: swimming, tennis, reading, travel. Office: Lionmark Inc 1620 Woodson Rd Saint Louis MO 63114-6129

GOMES, NORMAN VINCENT, retired industrial engineer; b. New Bedford, Mass., Nov. 7, 1914; s. John Vincent and Georgianna (Sylvia) G.; grad. U.S. Army Command and Gen. Staff Coll., 1944; BS in Indsl. Engring. and Mgmt., Okla. State U., 1950; MBA in Mgmt., Xavier U., 1955; m. Carolyn Moore, June 6, 1942 (dec. Apr. 1983); m. Helen Groesbeck Kuzava, April 22, 1995. Asst. chief engr. Leschen divsn. H.K. Porter Co., St. Louis, 1950-52; staff mfg. cons. Gen. Electric Co., Cin., 1952-57: lectr. indsl. mgmt. U. Cin., 1955-56; vis. lectr. indsl. mgmt. Xavier U. Grad. Sch. Bus. Adminstrn., 1956-57; staff indsl. engr. Gen. Dynamics, Ft. Worth, 1957-60; chief ops. analysis Ryan Electronics, San Diego, 1960-64; sr. engr., jet propulsion lab. Calif. Inst. Tech., Pasadena, 1964-67, mem. tech. staff, 1967, mgr. mgmt. sys., 1967-71; industry rep. and cons. U.S. Commn. on Govt. Procurement, Washington, 1970-72; adminstrv. officer GSA, Washington, 1973-78, program dir., 1979; vis. lectr. mgmt. San Antonio Coll., 1982-85. Active Serra, Internat., v.p. membership San Antonio chpt., 1991-92, mem. Drug and Alcohol Adv. Coun. N.E. Ind. Sch. Dist., San Antonio, 1989-95. 2d lt. to maj. C.E., AUS, 1941-46; engring. adviser to War Manpower Bd., 1945. Decorated Army Commendation medal, Armed Svcs. Res. medal; recipient Apollo Achievement award, 1969; Outstanding Performance award GSA, 1974- 75, 76, 77, 79. Mem. Am. Inst. Indsl. Engrs. (nat. chmn. prodn. control research com., 1951-57; bd. dirs. Cin., Fort Worth, San Diego, Los Angeles, San Antonio chpts. 1954-84, pres. Cin. chpt. 1956-57, pres. Los Angeles 1970-71, nat. dir. community services 1969-73), Ret. Officers Assn. U.S. (chpt. pres. 1968-69, recipient Nat. Pres. certificate Merit 1969), Nat. Security Indsl. Assn. (mgmt. systems subcom. 1967-69), Vis. Nurse Assn. of San Antonio (mem. adv. coun. 1988-95), Freedoms Found. at Valley Forge (v.p. edn. and youth leadership programs San Antonio chpt. 1987-89), Pillars San Fernando Cathedral, Old Dartmouth Hist. Soc., Equestrian Order of the Holy Sepulchre of Jerusalem (knight comdr. with star). Republican. Roman Catholic. Club: K.C. (4th deg.). Home: 24834 Shining Arrow San Antonio TX 78258-2744

GOMES, PETER JOHN, clergyman, educator; b. Boston, May 22, 1942; s. Peter L. and Orissa Josephine (White) G. AB, Bates Coll., Lewiston, Maine, 1965; STB (Rockefeller fellow 1967-68), Harvard U., 1968; DD (hon.), New Eng. Coll., 1974; LHD (hon.), Waynesburg Coll., 1978; HumD (hon.), Gordon Coll., 1985; LittD (hon.), Knox Coll., 1987; DD (hon.), U. South, 1989, Bates U., 1997; LHD (hon.), Duke U., 1997, U. Nebr., 1997. Ordained to ministry Am. Bapt. Ch., 1968. Instr. history, dir. freshmen exptl. program Tuskegee (Ala.) Inst., 1968-70; asst. minister, then acting minister Meml. Ch. Harvard U., 1970-74, minister Meml. Ch., 1974—, Plummer prof. Christian morals, 1974—; nat. chaplain Am. Guild Organists, 1978-82; hon. fellow Emmanuel Coll., U. Cambridge, Eng.; vis. prof. Duke U., Durham, N.C., 1993-94; Brecher lectr. Yale Divinity Sch., 1998. Author: Proclamation Series Commentaries, Lent, 1985, Proclamation Series Lent, 1995, History of Harvard Divinity School, 1992, Good Book, 1996, Sermons, 1998, Sundays at Harvard, 1995, 96, 97, 98; co-author: Books of the Pilgrims; editor: Parnassus, 1970, History of the Pilgrim Society, 1970; editor: Harvard Divinity School History, 1992; edtl. bd. Pulpit Digest. Trustee Bates Coll., 1973-78, 80-94, Pilgrim Soc., 1970—, pres. 1989, 93, Charity of Edward Hopkins, 1974—, Donation to Liberia, 1973—, Plimoth Plantation, 1977—, Roxbury Latin Sch., 1982—, Wellesley Coll., 1985—, Boston Found., 1985—, Plymouth Pub. Libr., 1985—; acting dir. W.E.B. DuBois Inst. for Afro-Am. History Harvard U., 1990—. Fellow Royal Soc. Arts; mem. Royal Soc. Ch. Music, Colonial Soc. Mass., Mass. Hist. Soc., Handel and Hayden Soc. (trustee), New Eng. Conservatory (trustee), Signet Soc. (pres.), Country Day Sch. Headmasters Assn. (hon.), Phi Beta Kappa. Club: Tavern. Home: Sparks House 21 Kirkland St Cambridge MA 02138-2001 Office: Harvard U Meml Ch Cambridge MA 02138

GOMES, WAYNE REGINALD, academic administrator; b. Modesto, Calif., Nov. 15, 1938; s. Frank C. and Mary (Rogers) G.; m. Carol L. Gerlach, Sept. 2, 1964; children: John Charles, Regina Carol. BS, Calif. Poly. State U., 1960; MS, Wash. State U., 1962; PhD, Purdue U., 1965. Asst. prof. dairy sci. Ohio State U., Columbus, 1965-69, assoc. prof. dairy sci., 1969-72, prof. dairy sci., 1972-81; prof., head dept. dairy sci. U. Ill., Urbana, 1981-85, prof., head dept. animal scis., 1985-89, acting dean Coll. Agr., 1988-89, dean, 1989-95; v.p. agr. and natural resources U. Calif. System, Oakland, 1995—; Fulbright prof. Zagreb U., Yugoslavia, 1974; vis. scholar Kyoto U., Japan, 1980. Editor: The Testis, Vols. 1-4, 1970-77; contbr. over 100 articles to jours. and chpts. to books. Mem. Council for Agrl. Sci. and Tech., Am. Soc. of Animal Sci., Am. Dairy Sci. Assn., Soc. for Study of Reproduction, Endocrine Soc., others. Lodge: Rotary. Office: U Calif 1111 Franklin St Oakland CA 94607-5201

GOMEZ, ANDREA HOPE, artist; b. Phila., June 2, 1950; d. Eugene Barton Sharf and Sylvia Molly Troppauer; m. Joseph Anthony Gomez, Mar. 20, 1976; children: Jodi Ann, Jason Anthony, Sasha Rose, Joel Isaac. BFA, Temple U., 1972; grad. cert., Wayne State U., 1988. Prof. animation Wayne State U., Detroit, 1980-88, Ctr. for Creative Studies, Detroit, 1982-88. One-woman shows include Tyndall Galleries, 1993, Carteret Gallery Contemporary Art, Morehead City, N.C., 1993; two-person shows include Wilson (N.C.) Art Ctr., 1991, others; juried exhbns. include New Works Artspace, Raleigh, N.C., 1988-99, Durham Art Guild, 1990-99, Henley Spectrum, Winston-Salem, N.C., 1990, Wake Visual Annual Exhibit, 1990-91, Smithsonian Inst. Portrait Gallery, 1992; represented in permanent collections Biogens, IBM, SAS, Glaxo; films screened at Kennedy Ctr., Washington, 1985, 92d St. Y, N.Y.C., 1981, Pacific Film Archive, 1980. Juror for student art Wake County Schs., Raleigh, N.C., 1997-98. Recipient Filmmaker Fellowship award Am. Film Inst., 1977, award USA Film Festival, 1983, award Ann Arbor Film Festival, 1976, 83; Filmmaker grantee Ctr. for New TV, 1984, artist grantee Mich. Coun. for the Arts, 1984-85. Mem. Artspace Artists Assn., Durham Art Guild. Home: 527 N Boundary St Raleigh NC 27604-1952

GOMEZ, DAVID FREDERICK, lawyer; b. Los Angeles, Nov. 19, 1940; s. Fred and Jennie (Fujier) G.; m. Kathleen Holt, Oct. 18, 1977. BA in Philosophy, St. Paul's Coll., Washington, 1965, MA in Theology, 1968; JD, U. So. Calif., 1974. Bar: Calif. 1975, U.S. Dist. Ct. (cen. dist.) Calif. 1975, U.S. Dist. Ct. (ea. dist.) Calif. 1977, Ariz. 1981, U.S. Dist. Ct. Ariz. 1981, U.S. Ct. Claims 1981, U.S. Ct. Appeals (9th cir.) 1981, U.S. Supreme Ct. 1981; ordained priest Roman Cath. Ch., 1969. Staff atty. Nat. Labor Relations Bd., Los Angeles, 1974-75; ptnr. Gomez, Paz, Rodriguez & Sanora, Los Angeles, 1975-77, Garrett, Bourdette & Williams, San Francisco, 1977-80, Van O'Steen & Ptnrs., Phoenix, 1981-85; pres. David F. Gomez, PC, Phoenix, 1985—; faculty Practicing Law Inst., 1989; instr. contracts law Peoples Coll. Law., L.A., 1975-76, Nat. Lawyers Guild; mem. Missionary Soc. St. Paul the Apostle (Paulist Fathers), 1963-75. Author: Somos Chicanos: Strangers in Our Own Land, 1973; co-author: Advanced Strategies in Employment Law, 1988, Arizona Employment Law Handbook, Vol. 2, 1995. Fellow Ariz. Bar Found.; mem. ABA, Maricopa County Bar Assn., Los Abogados Hispanic Bar Assn., Nat. Employment Lawyer's Assn., Calif. State Bar Assn., Ariz. Employment Lawyers Assn. (bd. dirs. 1996—), Ariz. State Bar Assn. (com. on rules of profl. conduct 1991-97, civil jury instructions com. 1992-94, peer rev. com. 1992—). Democrat.

GOMEZ, EDWARD CASIMIRO, physician, educator, vintner; b. Key West, Fla., Nov. 30, 1938; s. Edward C. and Francisca (Pijuan) G.; m. Barbara Jeanne Wilson, 1960 (div. 1979); 1 child, Marielle Elise; m. Ellen Elizabeth Mack, 1980. AB in Biol. Scis., Johns Hopkins U., 1960; MD, U. Miami, 1965, PhD, 1971. Diplomate Am. Bd. Dermatology; bds. cert. spl. competence in dermopathology. Pediatric intern U. Miami, Fla., 1966-67, resident in dermatology, 1969-72; research coordinator Dept. Dermatology Mt. Sinai Med. Ctr., Miami Beach, Fla., 1972-75, dermatopathology fellow, 1976-77; assoc. prof. dermatology NYU, 1977-80; prof. dermatology Sch. Medicine U. Calif., Davis, 1980-91, prof. emeritus, 1991—, assoc. dean for affiliate programs, 1983-86, assoc. dean for clin. affairs, 1987-90; regional chief of staff VA Western Region, San Francisco, 1991-93; assoc. chief staff No. Calif. Sys. Clinics, Pleasant Hill, 1993-99; CEO Russian Hill Estate Winery, Windsor, Calif., 1998—; asst. chief to chief dematology sect. VA Med. Ctr., N.Y.C., 1977-80; assoc. chief to chief of staff, VA Med. Ctr., Martinez, Calif., 1983-86; mem. VA Dermatology Field Adv. Group, Washington, 1978-80, task force on Chloracne, 1979-84; cons. U.S. Army Med. Research and Devel. Command, Frederick, Md., 1979-80, Johnson and Johnson Corp., New Brunswick, N.J., 1979-80; expert witness FDA, Washington, 1978; Gov.'s appointee Med. Quality Rev. Com., Alameda and Contra Costa counties, Calif., 1984-87. Editor 1 book; contbr. articles to profl. jours. Served to lt. comdr., USNR, 1967-69. Fellow Soc. Investigative Dermatology, Am. Acad. Dermatology; mem. Am. Fedn. Clin. Research, Am. Soc. Dermatopathology, Am. Coll. Physician Execs., Alpha Omega Alpha, Phi Kappa Psi. Republican. Avocations: skiing, computers, electronics, woodblock prints. Office: Russian Hill Estate 4525 Slusser Rd Windsor CA 95492

GOMEZ, IVAN A., lawyer; b. Cuba, Sept. 13, 1955; s. Severino and Adelina Gomez. BBA in Acctg., Fla. Internat. U., 1977; JD, Loyola U., 1980; LLM in Taxation, U. Miami, 1984. Bar: Fla. 1980, U.S. Dist. Ct. (so. dist.) Fla. 1980, U.S. Tax Ct. 1980, U.S. Ct. Claims 1980, U.S. Ct. Appeals (5th and 11th cirs.) 1980; CPA, Fla.; bd. cert. tax atty. Trial atty., dist. counsel IRS, 1979; assoc. Wood, Lucksinger & Epstein, Miami, Fla., 1984-86, English, McCaughan & O'Bryan, Fort Lauderdale, Fla., 1986-89; pvt. practice Miami, 1989—. Mem. Cuban Am. Bar Assn., Fla. Bar Assn. (co-chair tax sect. com. on internat. tax, gratuitous transfers 1994-95), South Fla. Tax Litigation Assn., Cuban Am. CPA., Greater Miami C. of C., Latin C. of C. Broward County (past pres.), Interam. Businessmen's Assn. Broward County, Inc. Office: 601 Brickell Key Dr Ste 507 Miami FL 33131-2652

GOMEZ, LUIS CARLOS, manufacturing executive; b. San Jose, Costa Rica, June 17, 1943; came to U.S., 1961; s. Luis and Julietta (De Blanco) G.; children: Robert, Marie; m. Donna J. Lewis; children: Terri Munoz, Mikell Simmons. Grad., San Jose High Sch., 1959. Pres. Vitalizer, Hialeah, Fla. Patentee for retro fit device to lower emissions and save fuel The Vitalizer III. Roman Catholic. Avocations: beach, boating, environment. Office: 2344 W 77th St Hialeah FL 33016-1868

GOMEZ, LUIS OSCAR, Asian and religious studies educator; b. Guayanilla, P.R., Apr. 7, 1943; s. Manuel Gomez and Lucila Rodriguez; m. Ruth Cedenia Maldonado, Dec. 24, 1963; children: Luis Oscar, Jr., Miran Ruth. BA, U. P.R., 1963; PhD Asian Langs. and Lit., Yale U., 1967; MA in Clin. Psychology, U. Mich., 1991, PhD, 1998. Lic. clin. psychologist. Vis. asst. prof. U. P.R., Rio Piedras, 1967, lectr., 1969-70, assoc. prof., 1970-73; assoc. prof. dept. Asian langs. and cultures U. Mich., Ann Arbor, 1973-80, prof. Buddhist studies, dept. Asian langs. and cultures, 1980—, chmn. dept., 1981-89; adj. prof. psychology dept. psychology, 1995—; vis. asst. prof. U. Wash., Seattle, 1967-68; Evans-Wentz Disting. lectr. Stanford (Calif.) U., 1983, vis. prof., 1985; vis. prof. Otani U. Kyoto, Japan, 1991-94. Author: The Land of Bliss, 1996; co-editor: Barabudur, Problemas de Filosofia, Studies in the Literature of the Great Vehicle, 1989. Mem. Am. Psychol. Assn., Soc. for Sci. Study Religion, Am. Acad. Religion, Internat. Assn. Buddhist Studies (gen. sec. 1986-89), Assn. Asian Studies. Home: 3204 Lockridge Dr Ann Arbor MI 48108-1722 Office: U Mich Dept Asian Langs & Cultures 105 S State St Ann Arbor MI 48109-1285

GOMEZ, MANUEL RODRIGUEZ, physician; b. Minaya, Spain, July 4, 1928; came to U.S., 1952, naturalized, 1961; s. Argimiro Rodriguez Herguedas and Isabel Gomez Torrente; m. Joan A. Stormer, Sept. 25, 1954; children: Christopher, Gregory, Douglas, Timothy. M.D., U. Havana, Cuba, 1952; M.S. in Anatomy, U. Mich., 1956. Intern Michael Reese Hosp., 1952-53, asst. resident in pediatrics, 1953-54; resident in neurology U. Mich., 1954-56; fellow in pediatric neurology U. Chgo. Med. Sch., 1956-57; instr. neurology U. Buffalo Med. Sch., 1957-58, 59-60; clin. clk. neurology Inst. Neurology, U. London, 1958-59; asst. prof., then assoc. prof. neurology Wayne State U. Med. Sch., 1960-64; mem. faculty Mayo Med. Sch., Rochester, Minn., 1964—; prof. pediatric neurology Mayo Med. Sch., 1975—; emeritus prof. pediatric neurology Mayo Med. Sch., Rochester, Minn., 1994—; cons. pediatric neurology, head sect. Mayo Clinic, 1964-84, sr. cons. 1992—; vis. prof. King Faisal Hosp., Riyjadh, Saudia Arabia, 1994, Children's Hosp. Miami, 1995, Seville, Spain, 1995. Author: Tuberous Sclerosis, 1979, 2nd edit., 1988, 3d edit., 1999, Neurocutaneous Diseases, 1987; co-editor: Tuberous Sclerosis and Allied Disorders, 1991, Neurologia y Neuropsicologia Pediatrica, 1996; adv. bd. Brain and Devel., Pedriatrika. Recipient Ramón y Cajal award Academia Iberoamericana de Neuropediatria, 1995. Mem. Am. Acad. Neurology, Am. Neurol. Assn., Child Neurology Assn. (founder, former pres., Hower award 1989), N.Y. Acad. Scis., Philippine Pediatric Soc. (hon.), Sociedad Española de Neurologia (hon.), Sociedad Española de Neuropediatria (hon.), Assn. Research Nervous and Mental Disease, Orton-Dyslexia Soc. (adv. bd.), Am. Epilepsy Soc., Internat. Child Neurology Soc. (founder), Cen. Soc. Neurol. Research, Nat. Tuberous Sclerosis Assn. (hon. profl. advisor, Leadership award 1994), Sociedad Centroamericana de Neurologia y Neurociugia, Colombian Neurologic Soc. (hon.), Soc. Psiquiatría y Neurologia de Infancia y Adolescencia Chile (hon.), Costarican Neurol. Sci. Soc. (hon.), soc. Argentina de Neurologia Infantil (hon.). Home: 4225 Meadow Ridge Dr SW Rochester MN 55902-6640 Office: Mayo Clinic 200 1st St SW Rochester MN 55902-3008

GÓMEZ, RICARDO JUAN, philosophy educator; b. Buenos Aires, Jan. 23, 1935; came to U.S., 1976; s. Inocencio A. and Maria T. (Pianzola) G.; m. Maria J. Proaño. MA, Ind. U., 1978, PhD, 1982. Prof. U. LaPlata, Argentina, 1967-76; prof. methodology U. Buenos Aires, 1970-76, prof. logic, 1970-74; prof. philosophy of sci. U. Quito, 1978-82; prof. philosophy and sci. Nat. U., Mex., 1978, 82 summer; asspc. prof. philosophy Calif. State U., L.A., 1983-87, prof., 1987—; dir. Inst. of Logic of Philosophy of Sci., La Plata, 1970-76; dean Sch. of Arts and Letters, La Plata, 1973-74. Author: Scientific Theories, 1977, Neoliberalism and Pseudoscience, 1995; contbr. articles to profl. jours. Recipient Konex's prize, Argentina, 1996, Outstanding Prof. award Colo. State, 1996. Mem. Philosophy of Sci. Assn., Am. Philos. Assn., N.Am. Kant Soc., Soc. for Philosophy Tech., Honors Soc. for Internat. Scholars, Sociedad Filosofia Iberoamericana. Office: Philosophy Dept Calif State U 5151 State University Dr Los Angeles CA 90032-4226

GOMEZ, SYLVIA, pediatric critical care nurse; b. L.A., July 27, 1960; d. Antonio and Belia (Rubalcava) G. AA, East L.A. Coll., 1980; BSN, Calif. State U., L.A., 1985. Cert. pediatric nurse, Pediatric CCRN. RN staff relief Personal Care Home Health Care, San Gabriel, Calif., 1984-86; RN staff nurse LAC/USC Pediatric Pavilion, L.A., 1985-86; RN relief nurse Care Visions Corp., Encino, Calif., 1990-93; RN staff nurse/PICU Huntington Meml. Hosp., Pasadena, Calif., 1986-96, RN extra-help/NICU, 1996-98; RN clin. nurse II/CTICU Children's Hosp. L.A., 1994—. Mem. ANA, AACN (L.A. chpt.), AHA (mem. coun. cardiovascular nursing), Nat. Assn. Neonatal Nurses, Soc. Pediatric Nurses, Calif. State U. L.A. Nursing Alumni Assn., Calif. State U. L.A. Alumni Assn., Alpha Tau Delta Phi Pi (chpt. historian 1994-95). Democrat. Roman Catholic. Avocations: photography, travel, music. Home: 273 E Markland Dr Monterey Park CA 91755-7206

GÓMEZ LANCE, BETTY RITA, sciences and foreign language educator, writer; b. San Jose, Costa Rica, Aug. 28, 1923; came to U.S., 1942; d. Joaquín Gómez-Fernández and Blanca Castillo-Salazar De Gómez; children: Edward T., Harold Elliott. BS, Ctrl. Mo. State U., 1944; MA, U. Mo., 1947; PhD, Washington U., St. Louis, 1959. Cert. tchr., Costa Rica, Mo. Rsch. asst. U. Mo., Columbia, 1944-47; tchg. asst. Washington U., 1955-59; asst. prof. U. Ill., Urbana, 1959-61; prof. Kalamazoo (Mich.) Coll., 1961-88, prof. emeritus, 1988—. Author short stories and poetry. Mem. Friends of Libr., Kalamazoo, 1961—, Kalamazoo Inst. Arts, 1961—, Nature Ctr., Kalamazoo, 1961—, Environ. Concerns Com., Kalamazoo, 1988—. Mem. Poets and Writers Am., Am. Assn. Tchrs. Spanish and Portuguese, Assn. Prometeo De Poesía, Assn. Iberoamericana De Poesía, Assn. De Escritores Costarricenses, and others. Avocations: hiking, nature activities, knitting. Home: 1562 Spruce Dr Kalamazoo MI 49008

GOMOLL, ALLEN WARREN, cardiovascular pharmacologist; b. Chgo., July 10, 1933; s. Herbert Fredrick and Sara Evelyn (Cowan) G.; m. Elaine L. Kirkpatrick, Sept. 17, 1955; children: Gary A., Lisa E. BS in Pharmacy, U. Ill., Chgo., 1955, MS, 1958, PhD, 1961. Instr. U. Ill. Coll. Medicine, Chgo., 1960-61, asst. prof., 1961-66; group leader Mead Johnson, Evansville, Ind., 1966-70, sect. leader, mgr., 1970-81; prin. rsch. scientist Bristol-Myers, Evansville, 1981-84; rsch. fellow Bristol-Myers, Wallingford, Conn., 1984-90; sr. rsch. fellow Bristol-Myers Squibb, Princeton, N.J., 1990—. Reviewer Life Scis., 1973—, Jour. Med. Chemistry, 1975—, Circulation, 1989—; contbr. sci. articles to profl. jours. Fellow Am. Coll. Cardiology, Am. Heart Assn. Coun. Circulation and Basic Sci. Coun.; mem. Am. Soc. Pharmacology & Exptl. Therapy, Internat. Soc. Heart Rsch., Sigma Xi. Office: Bristol-Myers Squibb PRI PO Box 4000 Princeton NJ 08543-4000

GOMORY, RALPH EDWARD, mathematician, manufacturing company executive, foundation executive; b. N.Y.C., N.Y., May 7, 1929; s. Andrew L. and Marian (Schellenberg) G.; m. Laura Dumper, 1954 (div. 1968); children: Andrew C., Susan S., Stephen H. BA, Williams Coll., 1950, ScD (hon.), 1973; postgrad., Kings Coll., 1950-51, Cambridge U., Eng., 1950-51; PhD, Princeton U., 1954; LHD (hon.), Pace U., 1986; DSc (hon.), Poly. U., 1987, Syracuse U., 1989, Worcester Poly. U., 1989, Carnegie-Mellon U., 1989. Rsch. assoc. Princeton U., 1951-54, asst. prof. math., Higgins lectr., 1957-59; with IBM, Yorktown Heights, N.Y., 1959-86, dir. math. scis., rsch. div., 1965-67, 68-70, dir. rsch., 1970-86, v.p., 1973-84, sr. v.p., 1985-89, sr. v.p. for sci. and tech., 1986-89, also mem. corp. mgmt. bd., 1983-89, dir. Asia Pacific Group, 1982-88; pres. Alfred P. Sloan Found., N.Y.C., 1989—; Andrew D. White prof.-at-large Cornell U., 1970-76; bd. dirs. Bank of N.Y., Lexmark Internat., Inc., Washington Post Co., Ashland Inc., Polaroid Corp.; mem. adv. coun. dept. math. Princeton (N.J.) U., 1982-85, chmn., 1984-85; mem. adv. coun. Sch. Engring. Stanford (Calif.) U., 1978-85; chmn. vis. com. divsn. applied scis. Harvard U., Cambridge, Mass., 1987-91, mem. vis. com. Grad. Sch. Bus., 1995—; mem. White House sci. coun., 1986-89, Coun. on Fgn. Rels.,; chmn. adv. com. to Pres. on High Temperature Superconductivity, 1987-88; mem. coun. on grad. sch. Yale U., New Haven, 1988-93; mem. vis. com. elec. engring. and computer sci. MIT, Cambridge, 1988-90; mem. Pres.' Coun. Advisors on Sci. and Tech., 1990-93; rschr. in integer and linear programming, non-linear differential equations and internat. econs. Trustee Hampshire Coll., 1977-86, Princeton U., 1985-89, Alfred P. Sloan Found., 1988-89; mem. governing bd. NRC, 1980-83, 97—, chmn. com. on mandatory retirement in higher edn., 1989-91. With USN, 1954-57. Recipient Lanchester prize Ops. Rsch. Soc. Am., 1964, Harry Goode Meml. award Am. Fedn. Info. Processing Socs., 1984, John Von Neumann Theory prize Ops. Rsch. Soc. Am. and Inst. Mgmt. Scis., 1984, IRI medal Indsl. Rsch. Inst., 1985, Engring. Leadership Recognition award IEEE, 1988, Nat. Medal of Sci., 1988, Arthur M. Bueche award NAE, 1993; IBM fellow, 1964. Fellow Econometric Soc., Am. Acad. Arts and Scis., NAS (coun. 1977-78, 80-83, 97—, com. sci. engring. and pub. policy 1985—); mem. Nat. Acad. Engring. (coun. 1986-92), Am. Philos. Soc. (coun. 1986-92), IEEE (hon.). Home: 260 Douglas Rd Chappaqua NY 10514-3100 Office: Alfred P Sloan Found 630 5th Ave Ste 2550 New York NY 10111-0100*

GONANO, J. ROLAND, technology research and development manager; b. Winchester, Va., Jan. 21, 1939; s. Lezelle and Mary (Fuss) G.; m. Joyce Dove, Aug. 22, 1959; children: Gina Gonano Bickish, Dawn, John R. Jr. BS in Physics, W.Va. U., 1960; PhD in Physics, Duke U., 1966. Postdoctoral fellow U. Fla., Gainesville, 1966-68; physicist U.S. Nat. Bur. Standards, Washington, 1968-71, U.S. Army Belvoir R&D Ctr., Ft. Belvoir, Va., 1971-82; R&D mgr. U.S. Army Material Command, Alexandria, Va., 1982-85; R&D br. chief U.S. Army Lab. Command, Adelphi, Md., 1985-87; chief advanced concepts & tech. U.S. Army Rsch. Lab., Adelphi, 1987-92; dep. chief R&D integration U.S. Army Material Command, Alexandria, 1992-93; army tech. transfer mgr. U.S. Army Rsch. Lab., Adelphi, 1993-95; R&D mgmt. and tech. transfer consulting Gonano Tech. Portfolios, Clarksburg, Md., 1996—; pres. F-G Farms, Hedgesville, W.Va., 1975—. Recipient Bronze medal for outstanding paper Army Sci. Conf., 1974. Mem. Am. Phys. Soc., Army Acquisition Corps, Sigma Xi, Sigma Pi Sigma. Office: 10401 Regina Ct Clarksburg MD 20871-8525

GONCAROVS, GUNTI, radiation chemist; b. Seneca Falls, N.Y., Sept. 5, 1956; s. Olegs and Skaidrite (Krebs) G.; m. Joan Margaret Sherman, Dec. 29, 1979; children: Kristina, Rebekah, Nina. BS in Chemistry, Charter Oak Coll., 1983. Chemistry technician Conn. Yankee Atomic Power, Haddam Neck, 1981-82, chemistry supr., 1982-83, chemist, 1983-91, sr. chemist, 1991-

92, acting chemistry dept. mgr., 1992-93; chemistry dept. mgr. Conn. Yankee Atomic Power Co., Haddam Neck, 1992-95; radiation protection dept. mgr. Conn. Yankee Atomic Power Co., East Hampton, Conn., 1995-96; chemistry dept. mgr. Conn. Yankee Atomic Power Co., Haddam Neck, 1996-97, Millstone Nuclear Power Sta., Waterford, Conn., 1997-99; tech. assessor Shearon Harris Nuclear Power Sta., New Hill, N.C., 1999—; chmn. Sorrento Electronics Radiation Monitoring Systems Users Group, 1991-93. Contbr. articles to Nuclear Technology, 1993. Mem. Electric Coun. New Eng. (chemistry com. 1986-95, vice chmn. 1993-95), Edison Electric Inst. (chemistry subcom.), Am. Nuclear Soc., Am. Chem. Soc., Assn. Ofcl. Analytical Chemists. Achievements include derivation of new technique to evaluate radiochemical data for nuclear fuel evaluation using combination of radioactive noble gas and radioiodines. Office: Shearon Harris Nuclear Power Sta PO Box 165 New Hill NC 27562

GONDER, SHARON, special education educator; b. Princeton, Mo., Aug. 1, 1943; d. Raymond Dale and V. Juanita (Wharton) Hagan; m. Glen William Gonder, Oct. 18, 1985; 1 child, Patricia; stepchildren: Gil, Gailen, Gary, Geoffrey, Gregory, Douglas. BS in Edn., U. Mo., 1968, MEd in Spl. Edn., 1971; MEd in Counseling, Lincoln U., Jefferson City, Mo., 1978. Cert. elem. edn., behavioral disorders, learning disabilities, mentally handicapped, orthopedic handicapped, counseling, psychol. exam., adaptive phys. edn.. Instr. Mental Health Ctr., Columbia, Mo., 1969-71; diagnostician staffing coord. Non-Pub. By-Pass Program, Jefferson City, 1976-89; psychol. examiner Disabilities Determ, Dept. Elem. and Sec. Edn., Jefferson City, 1981-84; coord. Project Lift-Up Lincoln U., Jefferson City, 1984-86; diagnostician Metro Bus. Coll., Jefferson City, 1987-89; tchr., psychol. examiner Jefferson City Pub. Schs., 1968-97; program cons. Lincoln U., Jefferson City, 1980—, adj. prof., 1985—; sec., spl. programming cons. Osage Bend Pub. Co., 1989—; bd. dirs. Ednl. Resources Info. Ctr. Leader 4-H, Jefferson City, 1978-81; non-registered lobbyist Mo. State Tchrs. Assn., 1987-97; deacon, tchr. Sunday sch. First Christian Ch., 1985—; mem. task force to establish area at risk programs Jefferson City C. of C., 1993-97. Named Mo. State Spl. Edn. Tchr. of Yr., Mo. Fedn. Coun. for Exceptional Children, 1991. Mem. Coun. for Exceptional Children (legis. chmn., sec.-treas. subdivsns. learning disabilities and mentally retarded 1988—, bd. rep. Mo. coun. 1973-88, state fedn. pres. 1984-86, internat. del. 1974, 85, non-registered lobbyist 1983—, profl. devel. standing com. internat. coun. 1998—, Internat. Spl. Edn. Tchr. of the Yr. 1992), Learning Disabilities Assn. (chpt. pres., exec. bd. dirs. 1975-91), Gen. Fedn. Women's Clubs, Delta Kappa Gamma (spkr. nat. circuit 1991—, author nat. publs. 1992—, bd. dirs. Ednl. Resource Info. Ctr. 1993—). Avocations: traveling, camping, crafts, gardening. E-mail: obpc@socket.net. Office: Osage Bend Pub Co Inc 213 Belair Dr Jefferson City MO 65109-0703

GONET, JUDITH JANU, pediatric nurse, consultant; b. Cleve., Sept. 27, 1947; d. John D. Sr. and Betty J. (Kurtz) Janu. Diploma in nursing, Mt. Sinai Hosp., Cleve., 1969; BSN, Ursuline Coll., Cleve., 1991; postgrad., Notre Dame Coll., Cleve., 1995. Cert. neonatal intensive care nurse, neonatal resuscitation, instr. Asst. head nurse adolescent medicine U. Hosps. of Cleve., 1970-73; staff nurse maternity surgery Fairview Gen. Hosp., Cleve., 1975-77; staff nurse pediatric ICU, Univ. Hosps. of Cleve., 1977-79; nurse mgr. spl. care nursery Meridia Hillcrest Hosp., Mayfield Heights, Ohio, 1980-92; legal nurse cons., 1994-95; supr. Patient Access Svcs., 1995—; legal nurse cons., 1994—; quality disease care mgr. Univ. Hosps. of Cleve., 1997—. Mem. AWHONN, Am. Assn. Legal Nurse Cons., Nat. Assn. Neonatal Nurses. Home: 1137 Orchard Heights Dr Cleveland OH 44124-1727

GONG, CAROLYN LEI CHU, real estate agent; b. Visalia, Calif., July 10, 1949; d. Robert C. and Lynn P. (Low) G. BA in Health Sci., Calif. State U., Long Beach, 1973; MA in Sociology, Calif. State U., L.A., 1980. Cert. jr. coll. tchr., Calif. Social worker County of L.A., El Monte, Calif., 1974-76, children treatment counselor, 1976-81; children svcs. worker County of L.A., Norwalk, 1981-89; real estate agt. Coldwell Banker, Diamond Bar, Calif., 1989-90, First Team Real Estate, Dana Point, Calif., 1991-92, Grubb & Ellis Real Estate, Dana Point, Calif., 1994—, 1994-95, San Clemente, Calif., 1995—. Active March of Dimes Walk-a-Thon, Toys for Tots, Sugar Plum Tree, Am. Cancer Soc., Am. Heart Assn., Disabled Vet., Easter Seal. Mem. AAUW, Nat. Assn. Realtors (Mult-million Prodn. award 1989—, Relocation award 1995), Calif. Assn. Realtors, Tennis Connection, Orchid Soc. Republican. Avocations: tennis, piano, reading, traveling, plays. Home: 1330 Crestmont Dr Diamond Bar CA 91765-4302

GONG, EDMOND JOSEPH, lawyer; b. Miami, Fla., Oct. 7, 1930; s. Joe Fred and Fayline G.; m. Sophie Vlachos, July 25, 1957 (dec.); children: Frances Fayline, Peter Joseph (dec.), Madeleine, Joseph Fred, II, Edmond Joseph; m. Dana Leigh Clay, Dec. 7, 1988. AB cum laude, Harvard U., 1952, postgrad. in law, 1954-55; JD, U. Miami, 1960. Bar: Fla. 1960. Spl. writer Hong Kong Tiger Standard, 1955-56; staff writer Miami Herald, 1958-59; assoc. firm Helliwell, Melrose and DeWolf, 1960-61; asst. U.S. atty. So. Dist. Fla., 1961-62; mem. Fla. Ho. of Reps., 1963-66, Fla. Senate, 1966-72; trustee Fla. Gulf Realty Trust, 1974-80; pres. Inflahedge Resources Fund, Edmond Gong and Co., Inc., 1979-85, Pub. Policy Cons. Inc., 1988—; sr. pub. policy analyst and legal counsel Everett Clay Assocs., Inc., 1988—; chmn. Fla. Land Sales Advisory Council, 1974-76; vice chmn. Bd. Bus. Regulation, State of Fla., 1976-77; fellow Inst. Politics John Fitzgerald Kennedy Sch. Govt., Harvard U., 1969-70, assoc. dir., 1971-72. Mem. Harvard 350th Commn., 1984-86; mem. com. on univ. resources, bd. overseers and pres. and fellows Harvard Coll., 1984-86; mem. North Key Largo Habitat Conservation Planning Study Com., 1984-88; regional chmn. Selection Com. for Anglo-Am. Conf., Johns Hopkins Sch. Advanced Internat. Studies, 1985; mem. Fairbanks Ctr. Com., Fairbank Ctr. for East Asian Research, Harvard U., 1987-90. Mem. ABA, Fla. Bar, Harvard U. Alumni Assn. (dir.-at-large), Miami City Club, Harvard Club (Miami), Fla. Audubon Soc. (bd. dirs. 1990-93). Episcopalian. Office: Pub Policy Cons 6161 Blue Lagoon Dr #270 Miami FL 33126

GONG, HENRY, JR., physician, researcher; b. Tulare, Calif., May 23, 1947; s. Henry and Choy (Low) G.; m. Janice Wong; children: Gregory, Jaimee. BA, U. of the Pacific, 1969; MD, U. Calif., Davis, 1973. Diplomate Am. Bd. Internal Medicine, 1977, Pulmonary Disease subspecialty bd., 1980. Resident in medicine Boston U., 1973-75; fellow in pulmonary medicine UCLA Med. Ctr., 1975-77; asst. prof., then assoc. prof. Sch. Medicine UCLA, 1977-89, prof. medicine, 1989-93; assoc. chief pulmonary div. UCLA Med. Ctr., 1985-92; chief Environ. Health Svc. Rancho Los Amigos Med. Ctr., 1993—; prof. medicine U. So. Calif., 1993—, prof. preventive medicine, 1997—; dir. Environ. Exposure Lab., UCLA, 1988-93; chmn. dept. medicine Rancho Los Amigos Med. Ctr., 1996—; mem. pub. health and socio-econs. task force South Coast Air Quality Mgmt. Dist., El Monte, Calif., 1989-90. Contbr. over 300 articles to rsch. publs., chpts. to books; editorial bd. Jour. Clin. Pharmacology, 1983—, Heart and Lung Jour., 1984-92, Am. Jour. Critical Care, 1992—. Elder on session Pacific Palisades Presbyn. Ch., 1984-86, 89-91. Fellow Am. Coll. Chest Physicians (pres. Calif. chpt. 1991-92), Am. Coll. Clin. Pharmacology; mem. Am. Thoracic Soc., Am. Fedn. Clin. Rsch., Western Soc. Clin. Investigation, Air and Waste Mgmt. Assn., Phi Eta Sigma, Phi Kappa Phi. Avocation: travel. Office: Environ Health Svc Rancho Los Amigos Med Ctr 7601 Imperial Hwy Downey CA 90242-3456

GONICK, HARVEY CRAIG, nephrologist, educator; b. Winnipeg, Man., Can., Apr. 10, 1930; s. Joseph Wolfe and Rose (Chernick) G.; m. Gloria Granz, Dec. 16, 1967; children: Stefan, Teri. BS in Chemistry, UCLA, 1951; MD, U. Calif., San Francisco, 1955. Diplomate Am. Bd. Internal Medicine, Am. Bd. Nephrology. Intern Peter Bent Brigham Hosp., 1955-56; fellow in nephrology Mass. Meml. Hosp., 1956-57; fellow in nephrology, resident in internal medicine Wadsworth VA Hosp., Los Angeles, 1959-61, clin. investigator, 1961-64, chief metabolic balance unit, 1964-67; instr. medicine Sch. Medicine, UCLA, 1961-64, asst. prof., 1964-69, assoc. prof., 1969-72, adj. assoc. prof., 1972-76, adj. prof., 1976—, assoc. chief div. nephrology, 1965-72, co-dir. Bone and Stone Clinic, 1972-76, coordinator postgrad. nephrology edn., 1975-78; mem. staff St. John's Hosp., Santa Monica, Calif.; mem. staff Century City Hosp., L.A., med. dir. dialysis unit, 1972-79, chief medicine, 1978-79; mem. staff Cedars-Sinai Med. Ctr., L.A., dir. trace element lab., 1979-96, clin. chief nephrology, 1983-85, coord. renal tng., dir. hypertension rsch., 1996—; practice medicine specializing in nephrology Los Angeles, 1972-94; co-founder, med. dir. Berkeley East Dialysis Unit, Santa Monica, 1971-75; co-founder, cons. Kidney Dialysis Care Units Inc., Lynwood, Calif., 1971-78; co-dir. Osteoporosis Prevention and Treatment Ctr., Santa Monica, 1987-93; mem. numerous adv. coms. to state and fed. agys., 1969-83. Contbr. articles to profl. jours.; editor: Current Nephrology, 1977-96. Served to capt. M.C., USAF, 1957-59. Fellow Charles Nelson Fund, Kaiser Found., NIH; recipient Oliver P. Douglas Meml. award Los Angeles County Heart Assn., 1959, Vis. Scientist award Deutscher Academischer Austauschendienst, 1978. Fellow ACP; mem. AMA, AAAS, Internat. Soc. Nephrology (organizing com. internat. cong. 1984), Am. Soc. Nephrology, European Dialysis and Transplant Assn., Soc. Exptl. Biology and Medicine, Calif. Med. Assn., Los Angeles County Med. Assn., Nat. Kidney Found. (active ann. conf. 1963-65, sec. nat. med. adv. coun. 1969-70, regional rep. and legis. com. nat. med. adv. coun. 1970-73, grantee 1963), So. Calif. Kidney Found. (chmn. sci. adv. coun. 1968-70, co-chmn. legis. com. 1970-73, bd. dirs. 1974-83, honoree 1979), Am. Soc. Bone and Mineral Rsch., Am. Coll. Toxicology, Soc. Toxicology, Am. Heart Assn. (renal sect. of coun. on circulation), Am. Fedn. Clin. Rsch., Western Soc. Clin. Rsch., Western Assn. Physicians, Phi Beta Kappa, Sigma Xi, Alpha Omega Alpha, Phi Eta Sigma, Alpha Mu Gamma, Phi Lambda Upsilon. Avocation: tennis. Office: Cedars-Sinai Med Ctr Becker Bldg Rm 227 8700 Beverly Blvd Los Angeles CA 90048-1865

GONICK, PAUL, retired urologist; b. Bklyn., July 5, 1930; s. Benjamin and Yetta (Shedrofsky) G.; m. Angela M. Furlong, Mar. 24, 1963; children—Brian Michael, Peter Benjamin, Julia Nancy. B.A., N.Y. U., 1951; M.D., Yale U., 1955. Diplomate: Nat. Bd. Med. Examiners. Intern Albany (N.Y.) Hosp., 1955-56; resident VA Hosp. and U. Minn., Mpls., 1958-62; instr. urology Wayne State U., Detroit, 1964-65; asst. prof. urology Wayne State U., 1965; asst. clin. prof. urology Columbia U., N.Y.C., 1966-69; asso. prof. urology Hahnemann Med. Coll. and Hosp., Phila., 1969-74; prof. urology Hahnemann Med. Coll. and Hosp., 1974-95, dir. div. urology, 1969-80; practice medicine specializing in urology Phila., 1969-95; chief urology sect. VA Hosp., Dearborn, Mich., 1963-66; acting asso. chief staff for research and edn. VA Hosp., 1964-65; jr. attending physician Detroit Receiving Hosp., 1964-65; chief urology sect. VA Hosp., Bronx, 1966-69; asst. urologist Presbyn. Hosp., N.Y.C., 1966-69; dir. div. urology Presbyn. Hosp., Phila., 1992-95; cons. urology Harlem Hosp., 1967-69, Radiol. Therapy Oncology Group, numerous hosps. Contbr. numerous articles to med jours. Served to capt. USAF, 1956-58. James Hudson Brown fellow, 1953. Fellow ACS; mem. AMA, Yale Med. Soc., Am. Urol. Assn., Vets. Urol. Assn. (treas. 1969), Soc. Univ. Urologists, Phila. Urol. Soc. (pres. 1994-95), Pa. Med. Soc., Philadelphia County Med. Soc., Phila. Acad. Surgery, Caducean Soc., Phi Beta Kappa, Mu Chi Sigma, Beta Lambda Sigma. Home: 341 Conshohocken State Rd Gladwyne PA 19035-1348

GONNELLA, JOSEPH SALVATOR, medical educator, university dean and official, consultant, researcher; b. Pescopagano, Italy, Apr. 5, 1934; s. John and Mary Gonnella; m. Linda G. Rapp, Jan. 19, 1963; children—John, Mary, Robert. B.A., Dartmouth Coll, 1956; M.D., Harvard U., 1959. Intern U. Ill. Research and Ednl. Hosps., Chgo., 1959-60, resident in internal medicine, 1960-64, chief resident in internal medicine, 1964-65; instr. medicine U. Ill., Chgo., 1965-66; asst. dean, asst. prof. medicine Hahnemann Med. Coll., Phila., 1966-67; asst. prof. medicine Jefferson Med. Coll., Phila., 1967-70, assoc. prof. medicine, 1970-77, prof. medicine, 1977—, asst. dean, 1967-70, assoc. dean, dir. acad. programs, 1969-83, dir. Office Med. Edn., 1969-83, dean for ednl. programs, 1983-84, dir. Ctr. for Research in Med. Edn. and Health Care, 1983—, acting dean, 1983-84, dean, v.p., 1984-88, dean, sr. v.p., 1989—; cons. HHS, 1972—, WHO, Geneva, 1974—, Ministry Pub. Health, People's Republic China, 1982—. Editor: Clinical Criteria for Disease Staging, 1983. Served to capt. U.S. Army, 1961-63. W.K. Kellogg Found. grantee, 1984—. Mem. Am. Assn. Med. Colls. (chmn. editorial bd. jour. 1985—). Roman Catholic. Avocations: reading; gardening; swimming; tennis. Home: 211 W Country Club Ln Media PA 19086-6507 Office: Jefferson Med Coll Thomas Jefferson Univ 1025 Walnut St Philadelphia PA 19107-5001*

GONNELLA, NINA CELESTE, biophysical chemist; b. Phila., Dec. 22, 1953; d. Anthony and Antoinette E. Gonnella. BA, Temple U., 1975; PhD, U. Pa., 1979; postdoctoral, Calif. Inst. Tech., 1979-81; Columbia U., 1981-83; research assoc., Yale U., 1984. Sr. rsch. scientist CIBA Geigy Pharm. Co., Summit, N.J., 1983-88, staff scientist II, 1989-93, rsch. fellow I, 1993-94, mgr., 1994-97; sr. fellow Novartis Pharm. Corp., Summit, 1997—; vis. rsch. fellow Yale U., 1984; invited lectr. CCNY, City Coll. Grad. Ctr., 1999, CIBA Geigy, Basel, Temple U., Varian Assocs., Internat. Soc. Magnetic Resonance Conf. Contbr. articles to profl. jours. NSF fellow, 1976-79. Mem. AAAS, ACS, Phi Lambda Upsilon. Office: Novartis Pharm Corp 556 Morris Ave Summit NJ 07901-1398

GONNERING, RUSSELL STEPHEN, ophthalmic plastic surgeon; b. Milw., Nov. 21, 1949; s. Russell Richard and Virginia Mary (Mlinar) G.; m. Sandra Lynne Brubaker, Aug. 6, 1971; children: Julie Kathleen, Stephen Russell, Scott Duncan. Student, U. Vienna, Austria, 1969-70; AB in History cum laude, Boston Coll., 1971; MD, Med. Coll. Wis., 1975. Diplomate Am. Bd. Ophthalmology; lic. physician, Wis. Intern St. Luke's Hosp., Milw., 1975-76; fellow in ophthalmic plastic and reconstructive surgery U. Wis., Madison, 1980-81, asst. clin. prof. dept. ophthalmology, 1981-92, assoc. clin. prof. dept. ophthalmology, 1992-96, clin. prof. dept. ophthalmology, 1996—, Kambara lectr., 1997; resident in ophthalmology Med. Coll. Wis., Milw., 1977-80, asst. clin. prof. dept. ophthalmology, 1985—; ophthalmologist Children's Hosp. Wis., Milw., St. Joseph's Hosp., Milw.; ophthalmologist St. Luke's Hosp., Milw., chief ophthalmologist, 1983-94, 97-99; pvt. practice Ophthalmic Plastic & Reconstructive Surgery, 1981—; rsch. assoc. in corneal physiology Med. Coll. Wis., 1976-77; rsch. advisor to fellowship in ophthalmic plastic and reconstructive surgery U. Wis., Madison, 1983—. Author: (with others) Infections of the Eye and Ocular Adnexa, 1986, Oculoplastic, Orbital and Reconstructive Surgery, 1988, Oculoplastic and Orbital Emergencies, 1990, Ophthalmic Plastic, reconstructive and Orbital Surgery, 1997, Ophthalmic Surgery: Principles and Techniques, 1999; sect. editor: Principles and Practice of Ophthalmic Plastic and Reconstructive Surgery, 1995; contbr. numerous articles to profl. jours.; presenter in field. Recipient George K. Kanbara award U. Wis., 1997. Fellow ACS (coun. Wis. chpt. 1996—), Am. Acad. Ophthalmology (basic and clin. sci. course com. 1986-92, chmn. 1988-92, Honor award 1990, Ruedemann lectr. 1994), Am. Soc. Ophthalmic Plastic and Reconstructive Surgery (editl. bd. 1987-99, edn. com. 1988—, vice chmn. edn. com. 1995-97, chmn. edn. com. 1997—, Marvin H. Quickert award 1982, Rsch. award 1982); mem. AMA, Internat. Soc. Orbital Disorders, European Soc. Ophthalmic Plastic and Reconstructive Surgery, Internat. Dacryology Soc., Assn. for Rsch. in Vision and Ophthalmology, Med. Soc. Wis., Milw. County Med. Soc. (del. to state med. soc. 1987-90, bd. dirs. 1989-94, Dirs. citation 1994), Milw. Acad. Medicine, Milw. Ophthalmol. Soc. (treas. 1989-90, sec. 1990-91, v.p. 1991-92, pres. 1992-93), Am. Soc. Ocularists (med. adv. bd. 1987—), Nat. Soc. to Prevent Blindness (med. adv. bd. Wis. chpt. 1987-88). Avocations: sailing, skiing, Tai Kwon Do. Office: Oculoplastic & Orbital Cons 2600 N Mayfair Rd Ste 950 Milwaukee WI 53226-1307

GONSER, THOMAS HOWARD, lawyer, former bar association executive; b. Berkeley, Calif., May 8, 1938; s. William Adam and Alice Gertrude (Lease) G.; m. Stephanie Jane Griffiths, Nov. 27, 1960; children: Thomas Howard, Catherine Ruth. AA, U. Calif., Berkeley, 1958, BA in Polit. Sci., 1960, JD, 1965. Bar: Calif. 1965, Idaho 1970. Atty. S.P. Co., San Francisco, 1965-68; asst. gen. counsel Boise Cascade Corp., Idaho, 1969-72, assoc. gen. counsel, 1972-81, asst. sec., 1972-81; exec. dir. ABA, Chgo., 1981-87, exec. v.p., COO, 1987, also bd. dirs. Author: The Bar Foundation, 1979. Served with U.S. Army, 1960-62. Fellow Am. Bar Found.; mem. Internat. Bar Assn. (dep. sec. gen. 1982-86), Am. Law Inst., Nat. Conf. Bar Founds. (pres. 1980-81), Nat. Ctr. Preventive Law (trustee 1988—), ABA (chmn. task force on preventive law 1996—), Econ. Club Chgo. Methodist. Office: T H Gonser & Associates 4841 E Harbor Dr Friday Harbor WA 98250-9322*

GONSHAK, ISABELLE LEE, nurse; b. Newark, Apr. 4, 1932; d. Robert John and Clara Kate (Cooperman) McClelland; m. David M. Gonshak, Aug. 8, 1953; children: Evan J., Brett A., Kathryn Susan. RN, N.J. Nurse Newark City Hosp., 1953. Tchr. Ideal Sch. for Nurse's Aides, Miami, Fla., 1972-74; vocal soloist numerous TV and social affairs; photographer multiple media, multi-faceted subjects. Bd. dirs. Miami Beach Symphony, 1971—, pres. 1978-79; bd. dirs. South Fla. Symphony; mem. Opera Guild Soc. Ft. Lauderdale (life); active Statue of Liberty Refinishing Com. Mem. Greater Miami Opera Assn., Hadassah (life). Jewish. Home: 1700 SW 72nd Ave Plantation FL 33317-5037

GONSON, S. DONALD, lawyer; b. Buffalo, June 13, 1936; s. Samuel and Laura Rose (Greenspan) G.; m. Dorothy Rose, Aug. 28, 1960; children: Julia, Claudia. A.B., Columbia U., 1958; J.D., Harvard U., 1961; postgrad., U. Bombay, India, 1961-62. Bar: Mass. 1962. With Hale and Dorr, Boston, 1962—, sr. ptnr., 1972—; lectr. Fin. Times (U.K.), Instl. Investors, New Eng. Law Inst., Mass. Soc. C.P.A.s; co-chmn. Speech-Tech., N.Y.C., 1987; instr. in law Boston U., 1963-65, bd. trustees Boston Five Cents Savs. Bank, 1978-83, bd. advisors, 1983-88; bd. dirs. Colonial Penn Group, Inc., 1982-86. Chmn. Mass. Comty. Devel. Fin. Corp., 1976-82; pres. Cambridge Ctr. for Adult Edn., 1985-88; bd. dirs. Boston Psychoanalytic Soc. and Inst., 1994—, chair Internat. Law Sect. Boston Bar Assn., Fellow, Am. Bar. Found., 1998—. Fulbright scholar, 1961-62. Mem. ABA, Internat. Bar Assn., Mass. Bar Assn., Boston Bar Assn. (chmn. internat. law sect. 1998—), Harvard Club. Home: 32 Hubbard Park Rd Cambridge MA 02138-4731

GONSOULIN GHATTAS, WENDY ANN, choreographer, dancer; b. New Iberia, La., Jan. 14, 1965; d. Claude Cleaveland and Margaret Ann Gonsoulin; m. Rony Joseph Ghattas, June 26, 1987; 1 child, Eliott Joseph. BFA, U. Southwestern La., 1988, postgrad. in speech-language pathology. Sales assoc. Zales Jewelers, LaFayette, La., 1986-92; choreographer The Performing Art Cons., Ltd., New Iberia, 1989—; instr. creative dance Cathy's Daycare Ctr., New Iberia, 1990—; dance movement instr. Daspit Elem., Iberia Parish Sch. Bd. Prin. dancer (musical) Cajun Odyssey, 1990, (concert with symphony) An Evening with the Acadiana and State of La Danse, 1991. Dance instr. for deaf students Daspit Elem. Sch., New Iberia, 1990—; bd. dirs. New Iberia Community Concert, 1991—; mem. svc. commn. Our Lady of Wisdom Cath. Ch., LaFayette, 1991—; founder PAC Reperatory Ensemble Modern Dance Co. Mem. Am. Bus. Women Assn. (nominee Outstanding Young Woman award 1991), Profl. Dance Tchr. Assn., Nat. Student Speech-Lang.-Hearing Assn., Top 10 Bus. Women, New Iberia Downtown Merchants Assn., Iberia Gen. Hosp Adv. bd., 1996, Cofounder Dance Teachers Alliance, 1996, Grant recipient for inner sch. Art Program, Dance Educators Am., Delta Delta Delta (libr. 1983-84, marshall 1984-85), mem. Gama Beta Phi. Democrat. Avocations: costume designing, studying sign language. Home: 19251 Preston Rd Apt 1604 Dallas TX 75252-8506 Office: The Performing Arts Cons Lt 101 Julia St PO Box 9125 New Iberia LA 70562-9125

GONTARZ, MICHAEL JOSEPH, school psychologist; b. Berwyn, Ill., June 20, 1959; s. Thaddeus M. and Gertrude (Szerlag) G.; m. Frances M. Lecheler, July 18, 1987; children: Danielle, Christian, Jonathan. BA in Psychology, U. Dallas, 1981; MSEd in Sch. Psychology, U. Wis., LaCrosse, 1984, Cert. Adv. Grad. Study, 1985; doctoral intern in Neuropsychology, Med. Coll. Wis., 1996. Nat., Wis. cert. sch. psychologist. Sch. psychologist D.C. Everest Area Schs., Schofield, Wis., 1986—; lic. pvt. practice sch. psychologist Wausau, Wis., 1988—; lic. pvt. prac. sch. psych. Wausau, WI, 1988—; lic. prof. counselor Wausau, Wis., 1996—; adv. bd. mem. Learning Disabilities Assn. Wis., Neceedah, 1997—; edn. adv. com. mem. Children of ADHD Assoc. Wis., Wausau, 1990-91; chair pupil svcs. self eval. D.C. Everest Area Schs., Schofield, 1994—. Pres. pastoral coun. St. Michael's Ch., Wausau, 1995-96, mem. religious edn. com., 1995-96, liturgical min., 1998—; mem. Christian Family Movement Diocese of LaCrosse, 1993—. Mem. Nat. Acad. Neuropsychology, Nat. Assn. Sch. Psychologists, Internat. Sch. Psychology Assn., Wis. Sch. Psychology Assn., Christian Assn. Psychol. Studies, Cath. Soc. Social Scientists, Cath. Soc. for Soc. Scientists. Roman Catholic. Avocations: photography, writing, reading, classical music, traveling. Home: 630 Franklin St Wausau WI 54403-4726 Office: DC Everest Area Schs. 6300 Alderson St Schofield WI 54476-3906

GONTHIER, CHARLES DOHERTY, Canadian supreme court justice; b. Montreal, Que., Can., Aug. 1, 1928; s. Georges and Kathleen (Doherty) G.; m. Mariette Morin, June 17, 1961; children: Georges, François, Pierre, Jean-Charles, Yves. BA, Coll. Stanislas, Montreal, 1947; BCL, McGill U., Montreal, 1951, LLD (hon.), 1990. Queen's counsel, 1971. Atty. Hackett, Mulvena and Laverty, Montreal, 1952-57, Laing, Weldon, Courtois, Clarkson, Parsons, Gonthier & Tetrault (name now McCarthy & Tetrault), Montreal, 1957-74; judge Superior Ct. Que., Montreal, 1974-88, Que. Ct. Appeal, Montreal, 1988-89; puisne judge Supreme Ct. Can., Ottawa, Ont., 1989—; sec. Montreal br. Can. Inst. Internat. Affairs, 1957-58; bd. dirs. Montreal Legal Aid Bur., 1959-69; pres. Jr. Bar Montreal, 1960-61; pres. jr. bar sect. Can. Bar Assn., 1961-62, sec. Que. div., 1963-64; bd. dirs. Montreal Bar, 1961-62; mem. Com. on Bldg. Contracts Que. Civil Code Rev., 1969-72; mem. com. on discipline Bar Que., 1973-74; chmn. Commn. for Nat. Judges, 1st World Conf. on Independence of Justice, Montreal, 1983; pres. Can. Inst. for Adminstrn. Justice, 1986-87; pres. Can. Judges Conf., 1988-89. Chmn. Assn. Anciens Coll. Stanislas, Montreal, 1954-55; hon. sec. Montreal Mus. Fine Arts, 1961-76; bd. dirs. McCord Mus. Can. History, Montreal, 1976-89; chmn. bd. Coll. Stanislas, Montreal, 1984-90; mem. Internat. Commn. Jurists, 1989. Decorated knight L'Ordre des Palmes académiques (France). Fellow Am. Coll. Trial Lawyers (hon.); mem. Univ. Club (Montreal). Roman Catholic. Office: Supreme Ct Can, Wellington St Supreme Ct Bldg, Ottawa, ON Canada K1A 0J1

GONTIER, JEAN ROGER, medicine and physiology educator; b. Lens, France, Mar. 8, 1927; s. Paul Maurice and Marie Jeanne (Tricoche) G.; m. Sylviane Prevost, Dec. 8, 1968; children: Sylviane, Yannick, Jean-Yves, Yann. BA magna cum laude, Arras Coll., France, 1944; BS summa cum laude, Etampes Coll., Paris, 1946; MS magna cum laude, Coll. Scis., Paris, 1948; MD summa cum laude, Sch. Medicine, Paris, 1965. Prof., chair dept. physiology UGSEL, Paris, 1957-62; instr. in medicine Sch. Medicine, Paris, 1960-65; resident Hop Cochin, Paris, 1964; assoc. prof. medicine Hop Bicetre, Paris, 1966; dir. physiology Sch. Medicine, Reims, 1966-68; prof. physiology U. Montreal, 1970-78; cons. in internal medicine Paris, 1979—; prof. physiology Bicetre U. Hosp., Paris, 1967-68; cons. editor various pubs., N.Y.C., 1975-78, Paris, 1969-73, Montreal, 1986-89; rsch. in diving physiology in man. Author: (textbooks) Hormones, Nervous System and Digestion, 1968, Respiration, 1971, 77, Digestion, 1969, 82, Textbook of Medical Physiology, 1980, Human Physiology, 1989. Recipient Silver medal Sch. Medicine, Paris, 1965. Mem. AAAS, Am. Physiol. Soc. (teaching physiology/respiration/cardiovascular/history sects.), Can. Physiol. Soc., N.Y. Acad. Scis., French Physiol. Soc., Cercle de l'Etrier Club, La Baule Country Club. Roman Catholic. Achievements include research in diving physiology in man. Avocation: sailing. Home and Office: 133 Rue Michel Ange, F75016 Paris France

GONWA, THOMAS ARTHUR, nephrologist, transplant physician; b. Chgo., Sept. 2, 1949; s. George Joseph and Darline (Sears) G.; m. Mary Alice Westrick, Sept. 28, 1974; children: Claire, Charlotte. BS, St. Joseph's Coll., 1971; MD, U. Ill., 1975. Diplomate Am. Bd. Internal Medicine, Nephrology, Critical Care Medicine. Resident Bowman Gray, Winston-Salem, N.C., 1975-78, renal fellow, 1978-80; postdoctoral rsch. fellow U. Calif., San Francisco, 1980-82, instr., 1982-83; asst. prof. U. Iowa, Iowa City, 1983-86; staff physician Dallas Nephrology, 1986—; assoc. dir. transplant Baylor U. Med. Ctr., Dallas, 1987—; clin. assoc. prof. medicine Southwestern Med. Sch., 1993—. Assoc. editor Jour. Immunology, 1985-86; editl. bd. Transplantation, Graft; contbr. more than 100 articles to profl. jours. Recipient rsch. award VA, 1984. Fellow ACP; mem. Am. Soc. Transplant Physicians (sec., treas. 1990-93, pres. 1994-95, Upjohn award 1983), Am. Soc. Nephrology, Am. Assn. Immunologists, Transplantation Soc., Nat. Kidney Found. (head coun. transplantation 1998—, bd. dirs. 1998—). Office: Dallas Nephrology 3801 Swiss Ave Dallas TX 75204-6225

GONYEA, BRUCE EDWARD, mortgage company executive; b. Flint, Mich., Feb. 13, 1944; s. George M. Gonyea and Leona M. (Cooper) Mudd; m. Carol A. Gonyea (div. Nov. 7, 1987); children: Burce E. Jr., Gwen J.; m. Della Telghemti Gonyea, Dec. 7, 1991. Assoc. in Bus., Baker Coll., 1978. Pres. Pioneer Mortgage, Las Vegas, 1981-88, Westwind Mortgage, Las Vegas, 1988—, Pro-File Mortgage, Henderson, Nev., 1989—. Mem. Rep. Men's Club, Las Vegas, 1981—, past bd. dirs. Home: 376 Viewmont Dr Henderson NV 89015-7715 Office: Pro-File Mortgage Corp 376 Viewmont Dr Henderson NV 89015-7715

GONYNOR, FRANCIS JAMES, lawyer; b. Cambridge, Mass., Nov. 6, 1959; s. James Francis and Beverly Joan (Lintz) G.; m. Deborah Lynn Snyder, July 25, 1981; children: Brian Christopher, Caroline Jane, Madeline Marie. AA, U. Fla., 1978, BA, 1980; JD, U. Houston, 1983. Bar: Tex. 1983, U.S. Dist. Ct. (so. dist.) Tex. 1983, U.S. Ct. Appeals (5th cir.) 1983. Assoc. Eastham Watson Dale & Forney, Houston, 1983-88, ptnr., 1988—; mediator Am. Arbitration Assn., 1992. Contbr. articles to profl. jours. Mem. Maritime Law Assn., Houston Bar Assn., Coll. of the State Bar of Tex., Galveston Bay Found. Home: 3327 Spring Trail Dr Sugar Land TX 77479-3050 Office: Eastham Watson Dale Forney 808 Travis St Fl 20 Houston TX 77002-5706

GONZALES, DANIEL RICHARD, defense and technology analyst; b. L.A., Mar. 6, 1956; s. Daniel Richard Jr. and Clotidla (Jeske) G.; m. Kate Tapley. BS in Physics, Stanford U., 1979; PhD in Physics, MIT, 1985. Analyst Inst. for Def. Analyses, Alexandria, Va., 1985-89, Rand Corp., Santa Monica, Calif., 1989—. Mem. AIAA. Avocations: running, sailing. Office: Rand Corp 1333 H St NW Washington CA 20005

GONZALES, PABLO, pharmacist; b. Nuevo Laredo, Mex., Apr. 19, 1949; came to U.S., 1949; s. Pablo and Zulema (Montemayor) G.; m. Diana Laura Vargas, Aug. 28, 1976; children: Cynthia Yvonne, Pablo Rafael, Araceli Marie. BS in Pharmacy, U. Tex., 1971. Pharmacist, co-owner Dilley (Tex.) Drug L.C., Gaddis Pharmacy L.C., Cotulla, Tex. Bd. dirs., pres. bd. edn. Cotulla Ind. Sch. Dist., 1980-85; bd. dirs., chmn. Cotulla C. of C., 1986-88; mayor City of Cotulla, 1996—. Democrat. Roman Catholic. Avocation: golf. Home: 708 Johnston Cotulla TX 78014-2543 Office: Gaddis Pharmacy LC 302 N Main St Cotulla TX 78014-2198

GONZALES, RICHARD L., fire department chief. AA in Fire Sci. Tech., Red Rocks C.C., 1988; BS summa cum laude in Bus. Adminstrn., Regis U., 1991; MA, Harvard U., 1991; student, U. Colo. Firefighter Denver Fire Dept., 1972-75, mem. fire prevention bureau, dist. 5 roving officer, 1976-79, mem. training divsn., 1980-81, dist. roving officer firefighter, 1981-82, capt. firefighter pumper 2 and 27, 1982-85, asst. chief, 1985-87, chief fire dept., 1987—; Mem. Nat. Fire Protective Assn. Urban Fire Forum, Internat. Assn. Fire Chiefs, Metro Fire Chiefs Assn., Denver Metro Fire Chiefs Assn., Colo. State Fire Chiefs Assn., Urban Fire Forum, IAFF Local 858 Negotiating Team; bd. trustees Nat. Fire Protection Assn., 1992-95. Mem. adv. bd. U. Colo. Denver Sch. of Pub. Affairs, Red Rocks C.C., Denver Ptnrs., KAZY Denver Marathon; bd. trustees Nat. Multiple Sclerosis Soc.; bd. dirs. Rocky Mountain Poison Drug Found., Chic Chicana, Golden Gloves Charity. Recipient Outstanding Achievement award Hispanics of Colo., 1987; named Young Firefighter of the Yr., 1981. Office: Denver Fire Dept 745 W Colfax Ave Denver CO 80204-2612

GONZALES, RICHARD ROBERT, academic administrator; b. Palo Alto, Calif., Jan. 12, 1945; s. Pedro and Virginia (Ramos) G.; m. Jennifer Ayres; children: Lisa Dianne, Jeffrey Ayres. AA, Foothill Coll., 1966; BA, San Jose (Calif.) State U., 1969; MA, Calif. Poly. State U., San Luis Obispo, 1971; grad. Def. Info. Sch., Def. Equal Opportunity Mgmt. Inst. Counselor student activities Calif. Poly. State U., San Luis Obispo, 1969-71, instr. ethnic studies, 1970-71; counselor Ohlone Coll., Fremont, Calif., 1971-72, coord. coll. readiness, 1971; counselor De Anza Coll., Cupertino, Calif., 1972-78, mem. community speakers bur., 1975-78; counselor Foothill Coll., Los Altos Hills, Calif., 1978—, mem. community speakers bur., 1978—; instr. Def. Equal Opportunity Mgmt. Inst., 1984—. Mem. master plan com. Los Altos (Calif.) Sch. Dist., 1975-76; vol. worker, Chicano communities, Calif.; active mem. Woodside (Calif.) Recreation Commn. With Calif. Army N.G., now maj. Adj. Gen. Corps, USAR. Recipient Counselor of Yr. award Ohlone Coll., 1971-72; Masters and Johnson Inst. fellow. lic. marriage family child counselor, Calif. Mem. ACA, Am. Coll. Counseling Assn., Calif. Assn. Marriage and Family Therapists, Calif. Community Coll. Counselor Assn. (former pres.), Calif. Assn. Counseling and Devel. (former pres. Hispanic Caucus), Calif. Assn. for Humanistic Edn. and Devel., Calif. Assn. for Multi-Cultural Counseling, Res. Officers Assn., La Raza Faculty Assn. Calif. Community Colls., Nat. Career Devel. Assn., Phi Delta Kappa, Chi Sigma Iota. Republican. Office: Foothill Coll Los Altos CA 94022

GONZALES, RICHARD STEVEN, broadcast executive; b. San Diego, Apr. 25, 1954; s. Lawrence Avila and Catalina Victoria (Salvaterra) G.; m. Tara Norcross Siler, Oct. 12, 1991; 1 child, Diego Siler. BA in Psychology, Harvard U., 1976. Pub. affairs dir. KPFA-FM, Berkeley, Calif., 1980-86; fgn. affairs corr. Nat. Pub. Radio, Washington, 1986-90, White House corr., 1990-93, congl. corr., 1993-95; reporter, nat. corr. Nat. Pub. Radio, San Francisco, 1995—. Co-founder Familias Unidas, Richmond, Calif., 1980. Recipient Media award World Hunger Inc., N.Y.C., 1988, Thomas Starke award World Affairs Coun. No. Calif., San Francisco, 1984; John S. Knight fellow Stanford U., 1994-95. Office: Nat Pub Radio 635 Massachusetts Ave NW Washington DC 20001-3752*

GONZALES, RON, mayor, former county supervisor; b. San Francisco; m. Alvina Gonzales; 3 children: Miranda, Rachel, Alejandra. BA in Community Studies, U. Calif., Santa Cruz. Formerly with Sunnyvale (Calif.) Sch. Dist., City of Santa Clara, Calif.; then human resource mgr. Hewlett-Packard Co.; market program mgmt. cons. state and local govts.; mem. city coun. City of Sunnyvale, 1979-87, mayor, 1982, 87; mem. bd. suprs. Santa Clara County, 1989-96; edn. program mgr. Hewlett Packard Co., 1996-98; mayor San Jose, Calif., 1999—; bd. chair, 1993; bd. transit suprs. Santa Clara County, 1989—; bd. dirs. Joint Venture: Silicon Valley, The Role Model Program, Bay Area Biosci. Ctr., Am. Leadership Forum, Santa Clara County. Office: Office of the Mayor City Hall 801 N 1st St Rm 600 San Jose CA 95110-1704*

GONZALES, SAM C., protective service official; b. Aug. 24, 1941; married; 2 children. BS in Criminal Justice, Abilene Christian Coll., 1975; grad., FBI Nat. Acad., 1979; grad. Sr. Mgmt. Inst. for Police, Harvard U., 1989; grad., U.S. Secret Svc. Dignitary Protection Sch., 1990; grad. Nat. Exec. Inst., FBI Sch. Mgmt., 1991. Spl. investigator organized crime unit La. State Police, 1969-70; patrol officer Dallas Police Dept., 1963-67, investigator narcotics, vice, and organized crime unit Intelligence Unit, 1967-69, investigator vice divsn., 1970-71, police sgt. detention svcs. divsn., supervisory sgt. Internal Affairs and Patrol, 1971-75, police lt. cmty. svcs. divsn. and auto theft sect., 1975-79, police capt., exec. officer S.E. and S.W. patrol divsns., identification divsn., and detention svcs. divsn., 1979-87, dep. chief divsn. commdr. N.W. patrol divsn., 1987-88, asst. chief of police patrol east, 1988-90, exec. asst. chief of police office of spl. svcs., 1990, acting chief of police, 1990, 1st exec. asst. chief of police, 1990-91; chief of police Oklahoma City Police Dept., 1991—; presenter drug initiatives and cmty. policing S.W. Law Enforcement Inst., 1989, Cmty. Policing and Drugs Conf., Mich. State, 1990, Ala. Mayor's Conf., 1990. Bd. dirs. New Horizons Ranch for Disadvantaged Youth; mem. Criminal Justice Task Force; mem. steering com. Edna McConnell Clark Found.; mem. adv. commn. Truth in Sentencing. Recipient Spl. Recognition award City Coun., 1990, Excellence in Svc. award City Mgr., 1990, Presdl. commendation, 1990, Neighborhood Initiative Program award City Mgr., 1992. Mem. Internat. Assn. Chiefs of Police, Police Exec. Rsch. Forum (presenter drug initiatives and cmty. policing 1989), Major Cities Chiefs Assn. Office: Police Department 701 Couch Dr Oklahoma City OK 73102-2211*

GONZALES, STEPHANIE, state official; b. Santa Fe, Aug. 12, 1950; 1 child, Adan Gonzales. Degree, Loretto Acad. for Girls. Office mgr. Jerry Wood & Assocs., 1973-86; dep. sec. of state Santa Fe, 1987-90, sec. of state, 1991; state dir. rural devel. U.S. Dept. of Agriculture, Albuquerque, 1999—; bd. dirs. N.Mex. Pub. Employees Retirement, N.Mex. State Convassing Bd., N.Mex. Commn. Pub. Records. Mem. exec. bd. N.Mex. AIDS Svc.; mem. Commn. White House Fellowships. Mem. Nat. Assn. Secs. State, United League United Latin Am. Citizens (women's coun.), Nat. Assn. Latino Elected and Appointed Ofcls. Office: Rural Devel State Office 6200 Jefferson St NE Rm 255 Albuquerque NM 87109

GONZALEZ, ALAN FRANCIS, lawyer; b. Tampa, Fla., Nov. 28, 1951; s. Frank R. and Maria (Font) G.; m. Hilda Martinez, July 28, 1973 (div. May 1982); 1 child, Adria; m. Yolanda Alvarez, Mar. 28, 1986; 1 child, Carly. BA in Mktg., U. South Fla., 1973; MBA, Samford U., Birmingham, Ala., 1977; JD, Samford U., 1977; LLM, U. Fla., 1978. Bar: Fla. 1977, U.S. Tax Ct. 1977, U.S. Ct. Claims 1978, U.S. Dist. Ct. (mid. dist.) 1977, U.S. Ct. Appeals (5th cir.) 1977, U.S. Ct. Appeals (11th cir.) 1995. Assoc. Salem, Salem, Musial & Morse P.A., Tampa, Fla., 1978-79; ptnr. Gonzalez & Scaglione, Attys. at Law, Tampa, 1979-90; pvt. practice Tampa, 1990-92; ptnr. Sierra, Gustafson & Gonzalez, Tampa, 1992-95; pvt. practice Tampa, 1995—; instr. Royalton Coll., South Royalton, Vt., 1973-74, Rollin Coll., 1993; adj. prof. Ala. Christian Coll., Birmingham, 1975-76, Hillsborough C.C., Tampa, 1978-81; asst. prof. U. Ctrl. fla., 1990-92. Author: (Fla. student pocket accompaniment text) Civil Litigation for the Paralegal, 1992; contbr. articles to profl. jours. Mem. ABA, Fla. Acad. Trial Lawyers, Hillsborough County Bar Assn. Avocations: weight training, tennis. Home: 10243 Woodford Bridge St Tampa FL 33626-1819

GONZALEZ, ANTONIO, academic administrator, mortgage company executive; b. Edinburg, Tex., Mar. 14, 1943; s. Manuel Gonzalez and Natalia Torres; m. Elma De Luna, Oct. 10, 1975; 1 child, Julissa Priscilla. BA, U. Md., Balt., 1971; MA, U. Tenn., 1973; JD, Miles Coll., 1979. Law clk. Crain Caton James & Oberwetter, Houston, 1979-81; instr. U. Houston, 1981-83, asst. dir., 1983-86; instr. Houston C.C., 1982-85, 95; assoc. dir. No. Ill. U., Dekalb, 1986-88; adminstr. Prairie View (Tex.) A&M U., 1988-95; instr. Houston Internat. U., 1988-89, pres., CEO, 1989-90; pres., CEO Am. Fidelity Mortgage & Title Co., Houston, 1992-95; instr. North Harris Coll., Houston, 1994-95, Wharton County Jr. Coll., 1996—; mem. adv. com. Houston C.C., 1994-95. Editor: Mexican-American Musicians, 1987; mem. editl. bd. Jour. Minority Issues, 1993-94. Chair tng. and devel. LULAC Dist. 18, Houston, 1994-96; dir. Inst. Chicano Culture, Houston, 1995; mem. SER Jobs for Progress, Houston, 1994-96; Dem. candidate Tex. Ho. Reps. Dist. 130, 1994; mem. Tejano Ctr. for Cmty. Concerns. With USAF, 1966-70, Vietnam. Named Man of Yr. LULAC, Ill., 1987. Mem. AAUP, ABA, VFW, Am. Hist. Assn., Tex. Assn. Chicanos in Higher Edn., Tex. Assn. Coll. Admissions Counselors, Tex. C.C. Tchrs. Assn., Tex. Assn. Mortgage Brokers, Tex. Fgn. Lang. Assn., Nat. Bar Assn., Tex. Assn. Coll. Univ. Student Pers. Adminstrs., Phi Delta Kappa, Delta Theta Phi. Roman Catholic. Avocations: writing, research. Home: 16614 Dounreay Dr Houston TX 77084-3410 Office: Wharton County Jr Coll 911 E Boling Hwy Wharton TX 77488-3252

GONZALEZ, ARTHUR J., federal judge; b. 1947. BS, Fordham U., 1969, JD, 1982; MS, CUNY, 1974; LLM, NYU, 1990. Bar: N.Y. Sr. staff atty. Office Dist. Counsel, IRS, N.Y.C., 1983-88; assoc. Pollner, Mezan, Stolzberg & Berger, P.C., N.Y.C., 1988-90, Gaston & Snow, N.Y.C., 1990-91; asst. U.S. trustee for region 2 U.S. Bankruptcy Ct., N.Y.C., 1991-93, U.S. trustee for region 2, 1993-85, bankruptcy judge for so. dist. N.Y., 1995—. Office: US Bankruptcy Ct 517 US Custom House One Bowling Green New York NY 10004-1408

GONZALEZ, ARTHUR PADILLA, artist, educator; b. Sacramento, July 22, 1954; s. John and Rita (Padilla) G.; m. Christine Carol Ciavarella, Feb. 11, 1988; stepchild, Nick Port. BA, Calif. State U., Sacramento, 1977, MA, 1979; MFA, U. Calif., Davis, 1981. Vis. artist La. State U., Baton Rouge, 1982-83, U. Ga., Athens, summer 1984, R.I. Sch. Design, Providence, 1985; asst. prof. U. Calif., Davis, 1985-86, Berkeley, 1987-88; vis. artist, instr. San Francisco Art Inst., 1990-91; assoc. prof. art Calif. Coll. Arts & Crafts, Oakland, 1991—; mem. adv. bd. Calif. Craft Mus., San Francisco, 1994-95; juror Sacramento Met. Arts Commn., 1994-95. One-person shows include Sharpe Gallery, N.Y.C., 1984, 85, 86, 88, Phyllis Kind Gallery, N.Y.C., 1995, Susan Cummins Gallery, Mill Valley, Calif., 1997. Recipient awards Nat. Endowment for Arts, 1982, 84, 86, 90, Virginia Groot award, 1997. Democrat. Avocation: Polynesian dance. Home: 1713 Versailles Ave Alameda CA 94501-1650 Office: Calif Coll Arts & Crafts 5212 Broadway Oakland CA 94618-1426

GONZALEZ, CHARLES A., congressman; b. San Antonio, Tex.; s. Henry B. and Bertha G.; m. Becky Whetstone; children: Leo Gonzalez, Benjamin and Casey Schmidt. BA in Govt., U. Tex., Austin; JD, St. Mary's Sch. Law, San Antonio. 5th grade tchr. Kindred Elem. Sch. So. San Antonio Sch. Dist.; pvt. practice San Antonio, 1972-82, mcpl. ct. judge; county ct. at law judge, 1983-87, dist. judge, 1989-97; mem. U.S. Congress from 20th Tex. dist., 1999—; appointed regional whip for the Dem. Caucus; elected v.p. freshman class for 106th Congress; as mem. of Congl. Hispanic Caucus, named chair of Census Task Force; co-chair Census Task Force for Dem. Caucus; mem. Ho. Com. on Banking and Fin. Svcs., Small Bus. Com. Succeeded father (Hon. Henry B. Gonzalez) as congressman from 20th dist. Fatherserved from 1961-99. Served bd. dirs. Arthritis Found., Literacy Coun., YMCA Metroboard, Camp Fire Girls, March of Dimes, Easter Seals. As a sitting judge was recognized as one of the highest rated trial judges; responsible for introducing the latest in tech. into the courtroom and streamlining the dockets; earned reputation as ardent mediator. Office: 327 Cannon HOB Washington DC 20515*

GONZALEZ, EDGARDO ANTONIO, lawyer; b. Ponce, PR; s. Antonio and Herminia (Torres) G.; m. Olga Alvarez, July 14, 1972; children: Beatriz, Olga. BBA cum laude, U. P.R., 1964, JD, 1967. Bar: P.R. 1967, U. S. Dist. Ct. P.R. 1968, U.S. Ct. Appeals (1st cir.) 1968, U.S. Supreme Ct. 1973, U.S. Ct. Mil. Appeals 1985. Commd. 2d lt. U.S. Army, 1964, advanced through grades to brig. gen.; staff judge advocate 7581st U.S. Army Garrison, Ft. Buchanan, P.R., 1980-82; comdr. 346th Transp. Bn., Ft. Buchanan, 1982-85, 169th Judge Advocate Gen.'s Detachment, 1985-87; comdg. gen. U.S. Army Res. Forces P.R., 1987-91; prin. Gozalez & Torres, P.S.C., San Juan, P.R., 1967—; chmn. promotion com. Caribbean Basin Initiative Task Force, 1986; chmn. bd. dirs. San Juan Bus. Devel. Ctr., 1985-86; pres. P.R. Products Assn., 1985-86; mem. Com. for Devel. of P.R. Industries, 1985; mem. Adv. Com. to Sec. of Commerce P.R., 1985-86; commr. Commn. for Hearing Grievances Against Employees for the Municipality of San Juan, 1969-71; mem. trade missions to various states of U.S. and several Caribbean and Latin Am. countries, 1969—; mem. Dept. of Def. Com. for Employers Support for Guard and Res., 1987—; panelist radio and TV programs, guest spkr. in profl. confs. relating to econ. and indsl. devel. P.R., 1984—; guest spkr. civilian and mil confs. on behalf of U.S. Army; mem. adv. com. P.R. Products Assn., 1994—. Decorated Legion of Merit, Meritorious Svc. medal, Army Commendation medal, Army Achievement medal, Nat. Def. Svc. medal, Army Res. Components Achievement medal with 4 oak leaf clusters; recipient Spl. Recognition Ho. of Reps. of Commonwealth P.R., 1987, Spl. Recognition award Data Processing Mgmt. Assn., 1993; named Disting. Mem. Transp. Corps. Regiment, 1991. Mem. ABA, P.R. Bar Assn., P.R. Products Assn., P.R. Mfrs. Assn., P.R. C. of C., (award for pub. svcs. during ops. Desert Shield/Storm 1991), Nat. Small Bus. Assn., Assn. U.S. Army (v.p. P.R. chpt.), Res. Officers Assn., Mil. Order World Wars, Caparra County Club, Banker's Club P.R., Phi Eta Mu. Home: K-17 Villa Caperra Guaynabo PR 00957*

GONZALEZ, EDUARDO, federal agency administrator; b. Tampa, Fla., Oct. 24, 1940; married Marina Gonzalez; three children. BA in Criminal Justice, Fla. Internat. U., 1974; grad., FBI Nat. Acad. From patrol officer to dep. dir. Metro-Dade Police Dept., Miami, Fla., 1965-92; chief of police City of Tampa, Fla., 1992-93; dir. U.S. Marshals Svc., 1993—. Mem. Hispanic Am. Police Command Officers Assn., Internat. Assn. Chiefs Police, FBI Nat. Exec. Inst. Assocs., Police Exec. Rsch. Forum. Office: US Marshals Svc 600 Army Navy Dr Arlington VA 22202-4221*

GONZALEZ, EFREN, airport executive. Acting aviation dir. City of San Antonio Aviation Dept. San Antonio Internat. Airport. Office: San Antonio Internat Airport Dept of Aviation 9800 Airport Blvd San Antonio TX 78216-4888*

GONZALEZ, EMILIO BUSTAMANTE, rheumatologist, educator; b. Asuncion, Paraguay, Jan. 9, 1949; came to U.S., 1974; s. Emilio Gonzalez-Jovellanos and Clara (Bustamante) Gonzalez; m. Elizabeth Ferreira, Jan. 4, 1973; 1 child, Daniel. BS in Scis. and Humanities, C.A.L. Coll., Asuncion, 1972; MD summa cum laude, Nat. U., Asuncion, 1972. Diplomate Am. Bd. Internal Medicine, Am. Bd. Rheumatology, Am. Bd. Allergy and Immunology. Intern Univ. Hosp., Asuncion, 1973-74; resident Danbury (Conn.) Hosp., 1975-78; teaching fellow allergy/clin. immunology U. Pitts. Sch. Medicine/VA Med. Ctr., 1978-79; mem. staff allergy/clin. immunology Nat. Jewish Hosp. and U. Colo. Affiliated Hosps., Denver, 1979-80; mem. staff clin. immunology/rheumatology U. Tex. Med. Br., Galveston, 1980-81, clin. instr. dept. medicine, 1981-82, asst. prof. medicine, 1982-89, assoc. prof. medicine, 1989—; chief rheumatology svc. Grady Meml. Hosp./Emory U. Sch. Medicine, Atlanta, 1989—; attending physician rheumatology sect. med. svc. VA Med. Svc., Emory U., Decatur, Ga., 1989—; attending physician divsn. rheumatology Emory U. Hosp., Atlanta, 1989—; cons., part-time mem. divsn. rheumatology The Emory Clinic/Emory U., Atlanta, 1989—; dir. rheumatology Ga. Baptist Med. Ctr., Atlanta, 1998—; bd. dirs. Arthritis Found., Ga., sci. com., 1993—; presenter in field. Contbr. numerous articles to profl. jours.; nat. manuscript reviewer jours. in field. Fellow ACP, Am. Coll. Rheumatology; mem. AMA, Am. Acad. Allergy and Immunology, Ga. Rheumatism Soc. (program chmn. 1993-94), Ga. Soc. Rheumatology (pres. 1995-96), Sigma Xi. Office: Atlanta Med Ctr Box 423 303 Parkway Dr NE Atlanta GA 30312

GONZALEZ, EUGENE ROBERT, investment banker; s. Eugenio Tomas and Alice Marie (Macdonald) Gonzalez-Mandiola. BA in Internat. Rels., Yale U., 1952; postgrad., Georgetown U., 1954; postgrad. sem. in advanced mgmt., Internat. Mgmt. Devel. Inst., Lausanne, Switzerland, 1967; postgrad., Georgetown U., 1994. Econ. officer Dept. Defense, Washington, 1954-57; project fin. officer Devel. Loan Fund (now AID), Washington, 1957-58; fin. mgr. RCA Internat., N.Y.C., 1958-61; fin. instns. specialist Interam. Devel. Bank, Washington, 1961-62; fin. officer Interam. Devel. Bank, 1962-63; dep. regional rep. for Europe Interam. Devel. Bank, Paris, 1964; exec. v.p. Adela Investment Co., Luxembourg, 1964-74; pres., chief exec. officer Adelatec Mgmt. Cons. Co., 1969-72; mng. dir. Adela Investment Co., 1974-75, pres., chief exec. officer, 1975-76; adviser, regional coordinator Ibero Am. Morgan Stanley Internat., N.Y.C., 1977-89; sr. v.p., head internat. pvt. banking Barclays Bank, N.Y.C., 1989-91; mng. dir. Kidder, Peabody & Co., N.Y.C., 1992-94; pres. Quasar Capital Corp., S.A., 1995—. Author: International Sources of Financing, 1961. Served with U.S. Army, 1952-54. Fellow Internat. Bankers Assn. (disting.); mem. Nat. Com. on Am. Fgn. Policy, Internat. Assn. Fin. Planners, Am. Soc. Profl. Cons., Presidents Assn., Americas Soc., Spanish Inst., Met. Club (Washington), City Tavern Club (Washington), Brook Club (N.Y.C.), River Club (N.Y.C.), Racquet and Tennis Club (N.Y.C.), Meadow Club (Southampton, N.Y.), Yale Club (N.Y.C.), Union Club (San Francisco), Zeta Psi Soc. N.Am. Home: 165 E 66th St # 6B New York NY 10021-6132

GONZALEZ, HECTOR HUGO, nurse, educator, consultant; b. Roma, Tex., Mar. 9, 1937; s. Amadeo Lorenzo and Carlotta (Trevino) G. BSN, Incarnate Word Coll., 1963; MSN, Cath. U. Am., 1966; PhD in Edn., U. Tex., 1974. RN, Tex. Staff nurse Santa Rosa Med. Ctr., San Antonio, 1962-65; asst. dir. nursing divsn. Incarnate Word Coll., San Antonio, 1968-72; prof., chmn. dept. nursing San Antonio Coll., 1972-92, dir. Ctr. for Assoc. Degree Edn. Rsch. and Svc., 1987-92, prof. and chmn. emeritus, 1993—; cons. NIMH, 1973, FDA, 1989-93, numerous ednl. instns. and hosps. in U.S., Mex., P.R., Kuwait; mem. Nat. Adv. Coun. on Alcohol Abuse and Alcoholism, 1976-80; mem. nat. adv. coun. nurses edn. and practice, 1992-96; mem. panel on nursing practice U.S. Pharmacopeia, 1985—. Contbr. articles to profl. jours.; peer reviewer Nursing Outlook, 1983, Advancing Clinical Care. Mem. legis. affairs adv. com. State Senator Glen Kothman, San Antonio, 1983; bd. dirs. Family Svcs. Assn. San Antonio; mem. multidisciplinary academic external com. U. Autonoma de Nuevo Leon, Mex., 1986-88. Capt. nurse corps U.S. Army, 1966-68. Recipient cert. of appreciation Citizens of Bexar County, San Antonio, 1970, Nat. Student Nurses Assn., 1977. Mem. ANA (mem. adv. bd. minority fellowship program 1976-80), Nat. Assn. Hispanic Nurses (pres. 1982-84, bd. dirs. 1995-97, CEO San Antonio chpt. 1998—, project dir. breast cancer tng. grant Am. Cancer Soc. and Nat. Assn. Hispanic Nurses 1992-96), Nat. League for Nursing (bd. dirs. 1973-81). Democrat. Roman Catholic. Home: 114 Magnolia Dr San Antonio TX 78212-3115

GONZALEZ, HENRY BARBOSA, former congressman; b. San Antonio, Tex., May 3, 1916; s. Leonides and Genevieve (Barbosa) G.; m. Bertha Cuellar, 1940; children: Henry B., Rosemary, Charles, Bertha, Stephen, Genevieve, Francis, Anna Marie. LLB, St. Mary's U., 1943, LLD (hon.), 1943, JD, 1967; HHD, Our Lady of Lake U., 1984; LLD (hon.), U. D.C., 1984. Formerly with father's translating co., dep. dir. San Antonio Housing Authority; chief probation officer Bexar County, 1946; exec. sec. Jr. Deps. of Am. (predecessor Pan Am. Progressive Assn.); mem. San Antonio City Coun., 1953-56, mayor pro-tem, 1955-56; state senator, 1956-61; mem. 87th-105th Congresses from 20th Tex. Dist., Washington, D.C., 1961-98; chmn. bank, fin. and urban affairs com. 1989-94, ranking mem. banking and fin. svcs. com., 1998-98. Civilian cable and radio censor Army and Naval Intelligence, World War II. Recipient Philip Hart Pub. Svc. award Consumer Fedn. Am., 1993, Outstanding Govt. Svc. award Am. Fedn. Trial Lawyers, 1993, Outstanding Govt. Svc. award Am. Numismatic Assn., 1993, Amicus award ATLA, 1993, John F. Kennedy Profile in Courage award John F. Kennedy Libr. Found., 1994, Wayne Morse Integrity in Politics award Wayne Morse Hist. Park Corp., 1994. Mem. Order Mil. Med. Merit (hon.). Democrat. Home: 238 W Kings Hwy San Antonio TX 78212-2964*

GONZALEZ, I. MILEY, agriculture administrator; b. Yaleta, Tex., July 30, 1946. BS in Agrl. Edn., U. Ariz., MS in Agrl. Edn.; PhD in Agrl. and Ext. Edn., Pa. State U. Tchr. vocat. agr. Parker (Ariz.) H.S., 1970; asst. dir. Office of Resident Instrn., Coll. Agr., U. Ariz., 1976; asst. dir. internat. agr. programs Coll. Agr., Iowa State U., 1988-91; prof., head dept. agrl. and ext. edn. Coll. Agr. and Home Econs., N.Mex. State U., asst. dean, dep. dir. Coop. Ext. Svc., 1994-96, assoc. dean, dir. acad. programs; under sec. agr. for rsch., edn. and econs. USDA, Washington, 1997—; 4-H specialist Pa. State U., 1980; mem. N.Mex. State U. leadership team Hispanic Assn. of Colls. and Univs. Recipient Am. Farmer degree Future Farmers of Am., Disting. Svc. award Am. Assn. Agrl. Edn. FAX: 202-690-2842. Office: US Dept Agr 1400 Independence Ave SW Washington DC 20250-0002

GONZALEZ, IRMA ELSA, federal judge; b. 1948. BA, Stanford U., 1970; JD, U. Ariz., 1973. Law clk. to Hon. William C. Frey U.S. Dist. Ct. (Ariz. dist.), 1973-75; asst. U.S. atty. U.S. Atty. Office Ariz., 1975-79, U.S. Attys. Office (ctrl. dist.) Calif., 1979-81; trial atty. antitrust divsn. U.S. Dept. Justice, 1979; assoc. Seltzer Caplan Wilkins & McMahon, San Diego, 1981-84; judge U.S. Magistrate Ct. (so. dist.) Calif., 1984-91; ct. judge San Diego County Superior Ct., 1991-92; dist. judge U.S. Dist. Ct. (so. dist.) Calif., San Diego, 1992—; adj. prof. U. San Diego, 1992; trustee Calif. Western Sch. Law; bd. visitors Sch. Law U. Ariz. Mem. Girl Scout Women's Adv. Cabinet. Mem. Lawyers' Club San Diego, Thomas More Soc., Inns of Ct. Office: Edward J Schwartz US Courthouse 940 Front St Ste 5135 San Diego CA 92101-8994

GONZALEZ, JOHN M., educator; b. Harlingen, Tex., June 30, 1966; s. Juan H. and Matiana M. Gonzalez. AB, Princeton U., 1988; MA, Stanford U., 1991, PhD, 1998. Asst. prof. U. Mich., Ann Arbor, 1996—. Doctoral fellow Andrew Mellon Found., Stanford U., 1989, Predoctoral fellow Ford Found., Stanford U., 1991, Pres. Postdoctoral fellow U. Calif., Santa Cruz, 1995. Mem. MLA (del. 1991—), Nat. Assn. Chicano/a Studies, L.Am. Studies Assn., Am. Studies Assn. E-mail: gonzalez@alumni.princeton.edu. Fax: 734-763-3128. Office: U Mich 3187 Angell Hall Ann Arbor MI 48109-1003

GONZALEZ, JORGE E., psychologist, researcher; b. Weslaco, Tex., Dec. 6, 1962; s. Eduardo P. and Maria (Cantu) G. BA, U. denver, 1985; MA, U. Tex., Edinburg, 1994. With May D&F, Denver, 1985-88; account exec. MCI, McAllen, Tex., 1988-90; bus. analyst Dunn & Bradstreet, Tucson, 1990-92; tchg. asst. U. Tex.-P.A., Edinsburg, 1992-94; grad. asst. U. Nebr., Lincoln, 1994-95; rsch. asst. Buros Inst., Lincoln, 1995—. Vol. Helping Hands, Lincoln, 1997—, Daywatch, Lincoln, 1997—. Fellow Ednl. Testing Svcs., Princeton, N.J., 1993, 94, Larson Minority fellow U. Nebr., 1995—, Outstanding Stud. Psychologist Awd., 1998. Mem. Sch. Psychology Students Assn. (pres. 1996—, ethnic minority affairs com. leader 1996—). Avocations: writing, cooking. Home: 819 S 12th #2 Lincoln NE 68508

GONZALEZ, JOSE ALEJANDRO, JR., federal judge; b. Tampa, Fla., Nov. 26, 1931; s. Jose A. and Luisa Secundina (Collia) G.; m. Frances Frierson, Aug. 22, 1956 (dec. Aug. 1981); children—Margaret Ann, Mary Frances; m. Mary Sue Copeland, Sept. 24, 1983. B.A., U. Fla., 1952, J.D., 1957; LLD, Nova Southeastern U., 1998. Bar: Fla. 1958, U.S. Dist. Ct. (so. dist.) Fla. 1959, U.S. Ct. Appeals 1959, U.S. Supreme Ct. 1963. Practice in

Ft. Lauderdale, 1958-64; claim rep. State Farm Mut., Lakeland, Fla., 1957-58; assoc. firm Watson, Hubert and Sousley, 1958-61, ptnr., 1961-64; asst. state atty. 15th Cir. Fla., 1961-64; cir. judge 17th Cir. Ft. Lauderdale, 1964-78, chief judge, 1969-70; assoc. judge 4th Dist. Ct. Appeals, West Palm Beach; U.S. dist. judge So. Dist. Fla., 1978—, sr. judge, 1996—. Bd. dirs. Arthritis Found., 1962-72; bd. dirs. Henderson Clinic Broward County, 1964-68, v., 1967-68. Served to 1st lt. AUS, 1952-54. Recipient Kupferman award Laymen's Nat. Bible Assn., 1991; named Broward County Outstanding Young Man, 1967, one of Fla.'s Five Outstanding Young Men, Fla. Jaycees, 1967, Broward Legal Exec. of Yr., 1978. Mem. ABA, Am. Judicature Soc., Fed. Bar Assn., Fla. Bar Assn., Broward County Bar, Ft. Lauderdale Jaycees (dir. 1960-61), Fla. Blue Key, Sigma Chi (Significant Sig), Phi Alpha Delta. Democrat. Club: Kiwanian (pres. 1971-72). Home: 631 Intracoastal Dr Fort Lauderdale FL 33304-3618 Office: US Dist Ct 205 US Courthouse 299 E Broward Blvd Fort Lauderdale FL 33301-1944

GONZALEZ, JUAN (ALBERTO VAZQUEZ), professional baseball player; b. Vega Baja, Puerto Rico, Oct. 16, 1969. Outfielder Tex. Rangers, 1989—. Named Am. Assn. MVP, 1990; named to Am. League Silver Slugger Team, 1992-93, Sporting News Am. League All-Star team, 1993, 96. Named Am. League MVP, Baseball Writer's Assn. of Am., 1996. Leader Am. League home runs, 1992-93. Office: Tex Rangers 1000 Ballpark Way Arlington TX 76011-5168*

GONZALEZ, MANUEL JOHN, investment broker, international trade executive; b. Miami, Fla., Dec. 19, 1963; s. Manuel and Maria (Gomez) G. AA in Bus. Adminstrn., Miami-Dade Coll., 1983; BA in Internat. Affairs, George Washington U., 1986. Sr. account exec. Southeastern Fin. Group, Miami, 1986-88; pres. First Fidelity Mgmt., Inc., Coral Gables, Fla., 1988-92; sr. account resident mgr. Advantage Capital Corp., Miami, 1990-91; exec. dir. City of Miami Trade Bd., 1992-97, internat. trade and commerce coord., 1997—; bd. dirs. City of Miami Internat. Trade Bd., 1988—. Active City of Miami Youth Adv. Bd., 1987-89; exec. com. bd. Dade County Rep. Party, Miami, 1988-90; pub. relations comm. chmn. City of Miami Internat. Orgns. Comm., 1989—. Roman Catholic. Home: 3271 SW 16th Ln Miami FL 33145-1809 Office: Office of Mayor Dupont Plaza Center 111 NW 1st St Ste 2910 Miami FL 33128-1930*

GONZALEZ, MICHAEL JOE, multimedia producer; b. North Hollywood, Calif., Mar. 6, 1959. AA in Journalism, L.A. Valley Coll., Van Nuys, Calif., 1984; postgrad. in mgmt., Master's U., 1998—; student, Master's Coll., 1998—. Cert. graphic designer. Pub. Martial Arts Mag., North Hollywood, 1982-87; tng. instr. Great Western Bank, Northridge, Calif., 1987-92; multimedia prodr. Calif. Fed. Bank, L.A., 1992-96; prodr. Martial Arts Entertainment, Valencia, Calif., 1995—; multimedia prodr. Blue Cross Calif., Woodland Hills, 1996—; art dir. Scott Advt., Van Nuys, Calif., 1984-87. Author: Monkey Kung-Fu Book, 1984, Monkey Kung-Fu Book, Vol. Z, 1998; freelance writer Inside Kung-Fu Mag., 1983—, Black Belt Mag., 1983—, Whu Shu Kung-Fu Mag., 1998—; art dir. Traveling Times mag., 1982-84. Recipient hon. black belt Universal Soc. Martial Arts, 1986. Mem. Am. Film Inst., Nat. Assn. Photoshop Profls., Internat. Interactive Comm. Soc., Tau Alpha Epsilon. Avocations: Kung-Fu instr., studying martial arts. E-mail: Michael.Gonzalez@wellpoint.com. Office: Blue Cross Calif 21555 Oxnard St 3J Woodland Hills CA 91367-4943

GONZALEZ, RAFAEL CEFERINO, electrical engineering educator; b. Havana, Cuba, Aug. 26, 1942; came to U.S., 1958; s. Emerito R. and Mercedes (Gonzalez) G.; m. Corinne Fuller, Aug. 14, 1965; children: Ralph, Rob. BSEE, U. Miami, Coral Gables, Fla., 1965; MEE, U. Fla., 1967, PhDEE, 1970. Design engr. GTE, Tampa, Fla., 1966-67; grad. asst. U. Fla., Gainesville, 1967-70; asst. prof. U. Tenn., Knoxville, 1970-73, assoc. prof., 1973-78, prof., 1978-81, IBM prof., 1981—, Disting. Svc. prof., 1984—; pres., chmn. bd. Perceptics Corp., Knoxville, 1982-92; cons. Oak Ridge (Tenn.) Nat. Lab., 1972-82, Lockheed Corp., Sunnyvale, Calif., 1981-84, Tex. Instruments, 1984-87. Co-author: Pattern Recognition Principles, 1974, Digital Imaging Processing, 1977, 2d edit., 1987, Syntactic Pattern Recognition, 1978, Robotics, 1987. Recipient M.E. Brooks Disting. Prof. award U. Tenn., 1981, Albert Rose Nat. award, 1988, B. Otto Wheeley award, 1989, Entrepreneur of Yr. award Coopers and Lybrand, 1989; named Disting. Svc. Prof., U. Tenn., 1984, Disting. alumnus, U. Miami, 1985; Magnavox Engring. professorship, 1980, IBM professorship, 1981, Nathan Dougherty award, 1992, Aut. Imaging Assn. award 1993. Fellow IEEE (Outstanding Engr. award 1992); mem. Pattern Recognition Soc., Sigma Xi, Eta Kappa Nu, Phi Kappa Phi, Tau Beta Pi. Republican. Roman Catholic. Avocations: flamenco guitar, piano, reading. Office: U Tenn EE Dept Ferris Hall Knoxville TN 37996-2100

GONZALEZ, RAQUEL MARIA, pharmacist; b. Veguitas, Oriente, Cuba, June 1, 1952; d. Ernesto Esteban and Evora Cristina (Ramirez) G. BS in Biology, Ga. Coll., 1974; BS in Pharmacy, Mercer U., 1977. Registered pharmacist, Ga., Fla., Tenn.; registered pharmacist cons., Fla. Staff pharmacist Cobb Gen. Hosp., Austell, Ga., 1978; staff pharmacist VA Hosp., Nashville, 1978-79, Decatur, Ga., 1979-81; staff pharmacist Lewisburg (Tenn.) Community Hosp., 1981-89; pharmacist Pharmacy Staffing Svcs. Inc., Brentwood, Tenn., 1989—; chief pharmacist Super D Drug Store # 50, Fayetteville, Tenn., 1989-93; chief of pharmacy Fred's Discount Pharmacy, Lewisburg, Tenn., 1993—; relief pharmacist Farmer's Market Pharmacy (Kroger), Nashville, 1989—. Mem. Tenn. Pharmacist Assn., Ducks Unltd., Atlanta Ski Club. Republican. Roman Catholic. Avocations: piano, white water rafting, snow skiing, snorkeling, gardening. Home: RR 1 Box 35 Belfast TN 37019-9801 Office: Fred's Discount Pharmacy 1800 Mooresville Hwy Lewisburg TN 37091-2010

GONZALEZ, RAUL A., state supreme court justice; b. Weslaco, Tex., Mar. 22, 1940; s. Raul G. and Paula (Hernandez) G.; m. Dora Blanca Champion, Dec. 22, 1963; children—Celeste, Jaime, Marco, Sonia. BA in Govt., U. Tex., Austin, 1963; JD, U. Houston, 1966; LLM, U. Va., 1986. Bar: Tex. 1966. Asst. U.S. atty. U.S. Dist. Ct. (so. dist.) Tex., Brownsville, 1969-73; atty. Gonzalez & Hamilton, Brownsville, 1973-78; judge 103d Dist. Ct. Tex., Brownsville, 1978-81, U.S. Dist. Ct. Appeals (13th cir.), Corpus Christi, Tex., 1981-84; justice Tex. Supreme Ct., Austin, 1984—; of counsel Locke Liddell & Sapp LLP. Bd. dirs. Brownsville Boy's Club, Brownsville Community Devel. Corp., So. Tex. Rehab. Ind. Sch. Dist.; U.S. Recipient Outstanding Performance Rating award Dept. Justice, 1972, Toll fellow, 1987. Mem. Christian Legal Soc., Christian Conciliation Service, ABA, Tex. Bar Found. Lodge: Rotary. Avocations: jogging; racquetball. Home: 2300 Pebble Beach Dr Austin TX 78747-1615 Office: Locke Liddell & Sapp LLP 100 Congress Ave Ste 300 Austin TX 78701-4042

GONZALEZ, RICARDO, surgeon, educator; b. Buenos Aires, June 26, 1943; s. Salvador Maria and Clyde Alcira (Prevettoni) G.; children: Diego Andres, Carlos Ricardo. BA, Coll. Nat. San Isidro, Buenos Aires, 1959; MD, U. Buenos Aires, 1965. Diplomate Am. Bd. Urology. Resident in surgery Hosp. Militar Cen., Buenos Aires, 1966-68; intern in surgery U. Minn., 1969-70; resident (med. fellow) in urologic surgery, 1970-74; from instr. to prof. urology U. Minn., Mpls., 1974-85, prof. urology 1985-94, prof. pediat., 1993-94; chief, pediat. urology Children's Hosp. of Mich., Detroit, 1994; prof. urology Wayne State U., Detroit, 1995; pres. Pediat. Urology P.C., Detroit, 1995—; vis. prof. Harvard U., Cambridge, Mass., 1994, Johns Hopkins U., Balt., 1995, U. Washington, Seattle, 1995, U. Calif., San Francisco, 1996, Cornell U., N.Y., 1998; presenter in field. Contbr. over 160 articles to profl. jours., over 50 chpts. to books; editor 2 books. Am. Acad. Pediat. fellow, 1981, Nat. Kidney Found. rsch. fellow 1974-76; co-prin. investigator USPHS cancer grant 1976-78. Fellow Am. Acad. Pediat. (mem. exec. sect. on urology com. 1995-98); mem. Am. Urologic Assn., Mex. Coll. Urology (hon.). Venezuelan Soc. for Spina Bifida, Argentine Confedn. Urology, Société Internat. d'Urologie, Ibero-Am. Soc. Pediat. Urology (pres. 1995-98), Soc. for Pediatric Urol. Surgeons (by invitation). Avocations: opera, music, language, reading, writing. Office: Pediatric Urology PC 3901 Beaubien St Detroit MI 48201-2119

GONZALEZ, RICHARD, quality performance professional; b. Dec. 7, 1966. Father Valentin Gonzalez retired as a 1st Sergeant from the U.S. Army. Mother Margarita Crespo is a homemaker. Richard's parents currently reside in Moca, Puerto Rico, and own/operate a small grocery store. Richard's two sisters, Maria Teresa and Brenda, reside in Puerto Rico. BA

in Spanish with honors, U. Minn., 1991; BA in Polit. Sci., 1991; MPA, Fla. Atlantic U., 1998. Regulatory project officer, analyst USCG Hdqtrs., Washington, 1992-93; divsn. head, supply dept., deck watch officer CGC Courageous, Panama City, Fla., 1993-95; chief, uninspected vessel safety sect. (7th Dist.) USCG, Miami, 1995-98, quality performance cons., 1998—. With USCG, 1987—. Decorated Nat. Def. Svc. medal, numerous commendation medals USCG, others. Mem. Am. Soc. for Quality, Am. Soc. Pub. Adminstrn., Phi Gamma Delta, Alpha Phi Omega, Alpha Mu Gamma, Pi Alpha Alpha, Pi Gamma Mu. Home: # 217 5901 Palm Tree Landing Dr Davie FL 33314-1846

GONZALEZ, RICHARD THEODORE, photographer; b. Trona, Calif., Nov. 9, 1939; s. Alfonso Contreras and Mary (Duarte) G.; m. Gerry Price, Oct. 30, 1958 (div. 1972); children: Richard K., Debra G., Maria E., Felicia F.; m. Yolanda Quijano, Apr. 18, 1991; 1 child, Andrea. Degree in profl. still photography, N.Y. Inst. Photography, 1962. Photographer Kerr McGee Chem. Corp., Trona, 1962-86, San Bernadino, Calif., 1987-89; founder Gonzalez's Modeling Agy., Midwest City, Okla., 1996—; newspaper photographer Trona Argonaut, 1962-86; freelance photographer, Trona, 1962-86. Democrat. Roman Catholic. Home: 769 NW 1st St Moore OK 73160-2329 Office: 700 S Air Depot Blvd Ste D-366 Midwest City OK 73110-4833

GONZALEZ, ROLANDO NOEL, secondary school educator, religion educator, photographer; b. Rio Grande City, Tex., Sept. 10, 1947; s. Ubaldo and Beulah (Gutierrez) G. BA, U. Tex., 1968; MA, Tex. A & I U., 1972. Cert. tchr. all scis., guidance and counseling. Tchr., head sci. dept. Roma (Tex.) Jr. High Sch., 1968-71; migrant/Title I counselor Roma Elem. and Roma Jr. High Sch., 1972-76; head sci. dept. Rio Grande High Sch., Rio Grande City, Tex., 1976-78; tchr., head sci. dept. Ringgold Jr. High Sch., Rio Grande City, 1982-83, Pharr-San Juan-Alamo High Sch., Pharr, Tex., 1986—; seminarian Diocese of Brownsville, San Antonio, 1979-82; pastoral asst. Our Lady, Queen of Angels Ch., La Joya, Tex., 1982-83; coord., lay ministries Brownsville Diocese, McAllen, Tex., 1983-85; lectr., tchr. on scripture Perpetual Help Ch., McAllen, 1986-88, Holy Spirit Ch., McAllen, 1989—; scripture tchr., lectr. St. Mary Margaret Ch., Pharr, 1988; instr. history of chemistry U. Tex.-Pan Am., Edinburg, 1990; wedding and portrait photographer, 1973—. Contbr. articles to profl. jours. tchr. scripture, lectr. Sts. Mary and Margaret Ch., Pharr, 1988, Sacred Heart Ch., Mercedes, Tex., 1990. Recipient Appreciation award Sacred Heart Ch., 1990, Tchr. of Yr. award Rio Grande Valley Sci. Assn., 1996-97. Home: 2800 W Iris Ave Mcallen TX 78501-6200 Humans are so resilient and basically optimistic. I marvel at how humans reach for the stars even though they see around them a planet full of woes.

GONZALEZ, ROSE A-NAVARRO, artist; b. Granada, Nicaragua, May 22, 1936; d. Manuel Navarro and Candelaria (Guerrero) Martinez; m. Simeon Gonzalez, Oct. 15, 1959. Diploma. Nat. Inst. Orient, Granada, Nicaragua, 1956, Sch. Art and Design, N.Y.C., 1964, Abbey Sch. N.Y., 1972; postgrad., Art Student's League, 1972-73. Group exhbns. include Empire Savs. Bank, 1973, Mus. City of N.Y., 1977, 82, Cayman Gallery, 1977, New Rochelle Gallery, 1978, Los Sures Gallery, 1978, Bklyn. Mus. Gallery, 1979, Louis Aborns Arts for Living Ctr., 1979, Studio 54, 1983, Keanne Mason Gallery, 1983, Queen's Coll., 1984, St. Sabastian Parish Ctr., 1991, Latino Open-Air and Cultural Festival, 1992, SUNY, 1992, Agora Gallery, N.Y.C., 1993, Progress Gallery, N.Y.C., 1993-94, 98, Dist. Coun. 37, N.Y.C., 1994, 95, New Rochelle Pub. Libr., 1996, Goya Gallery, 1997, Colombian Consulate, 1997, Aguilar Libr., 1997, Oller Campeche Gallery, 1997, Taller Romano Gallery, Madrid, 1998. Mem. coun. Eisenhower Commn., Rep. Nat. Com., Washington, 1995. Recipient Spl. prize Friends of Puerto Rico; Comision awarded Hispana Pro-Obra Ruben Dario, 1999; nominated Rep. Senatorial Medal of Freedom, 1999. Mem. Lions Club Internat. (v.p. 1995—, Melvin Jones award 1993-94). Republican. Roman Catholic. Home: 1121 Morrison Ave Bronx NY 10472-4235

GONZALEZ, SALVADOR HINOJOSA, electronics executive, municipal official; b. Falfurrias, Tex., Sept. 29, 1930; s. Clemente and Josefa (Hinojosa) G.; m. Esperanza Hinojosa Gonzalez, Jan. 29, 1956; children: Xavier, Melissa Kathy, Salvador Jr. Grad., De Vry Tech., 1954. Lic. radio telephone operator, FCC. Foreman Electronics Svc. Co., Falfurrias, Tex., 1954-62; owner Falfurrias Radio and TV Svc., Falfurrias, Tex., 1962-98. Commr. Brooks County, Falfurrias, 1991-99, Housing Authority Commr., 1980-86; mem. workforce bd. State of Tex., Corpus Christi, 1994-97. Recipient Cert. State of Tex., 1997. Mem. VFW, KC. Democrat. Roman Catholic. Avocations: hunting, fishing, watching sports. Home: 802 W. Stockton St Falfurrias TX 78355-4150

GONZÁLEZ-ALEXOPOULOS See CHRYSOSTOMOS

GONZALEZ ARIAS, VICTOR HUGO, management executive; b. Guayaquil, Ecuador, July 12, 1955; s. Porfirio Alfredo and Ernestina Perpetua (Arias) G.; children: Victor Christopher, Andres Alfredo; m. Rosa Amalia Hernandez; 1 child, Victor Hugo Jr. BA in Econ. and Internat. Svcs., Cath. U., 1980; MBA, U. D.C., 1983. Utility specialist Water & Sewer Dept., Washington, 1981-83; pres., founder hispanic student assn. U. D.C., Washington, 1982-83; gen. mgr. Inter-High Connection Entrepreneurship Program, a tng. program on how to manage and operate a small bus., Washington, 1983—; v.p. Hispanic Festival, Washington, 1987-88; commr. for Columbia Heights Mayor's Office, Washington, 1987-88; ptnr. Victor H. Gonzalez & Assocs., Washington, 1994—; mktg. cons. Small Bus. Adminstrn., Washington, 1981-82. Activist Hispanic Community Coalition, Washington, 1973—; mem. Coun. hispanic Agencies, Washington, 1976-81, Change, Inc., Washington, 1976-78, Latino Students Assn. Cath. U., Washington, 1976-78. Mem. Nat. Soc. Accts., Tax Refund Express, Am. Vocat. Assn., Am. Mgmt. Assn., Nat. Soc. Tax Profls., Sheraton Internat. Democrat. Roman Catholic. Office: 5502 Kenilworth Ave Ste 100 Riverdale MD 20737-3123

GONZALEZ-CERON, OSCAR, visual artist; b. Bogota, Colombia, Mar. 20, 1956; came to U.S., 1996; s. Jorge Enrique and Ligia (Ceron) Gonzalez; m. Amparo Molina, Dec. 20, 1974 (div. Jan. 1981); children: Catalina, Juliana; m. Lilian Patricia Mejia, Apr. 14, 1994; 1 child, Maria Alejandra. BS, Federico Herbart, Bogota, 1972; MFA, Nat. U. of Colombia, 1981; postgrad., U. London, 1984-85. Art prof. Sch. of Fine Arts, Cartagena, Colombia, 1981-82, J.T.L. U. of Bogota, 1983-85, Nat. U. of Colombia, Bogota, 1990-91; dir. Cooperartes Ltda., Bogota, 1993-94; art prof. U. of the Andes, Bogota, 1987-95; dir. Gonzalez Ceron Print Workshop, Bogota, 1981-96; master printer Pyramid Atlantic, Riverdale, Md., 1997—; art. prof. The Corcoran Sch. of Art, Washington, 1999. Solo exhbns. include: Mansion Art Gallery, Rockville, Md., 1999, A.T. Gallery of Contemporary Art, Bogota, 1996, Sala de Proyectos, Bogota, 1995, Espacio Alterno Gallery, Bogota, 1987, Enrique Echandi Gallery, San Jose, Costa Rica, 1986, Mus. of Modern Art, Cartagena, 1982, Circulo Gallery, Bogota, 1981, Banco de Colombia, Bogota, 1980, Aexandes Gallery, Bogota, 1979, Fra Angelico Gallery, Bogota, 1978, Luis Angel Arango Libr., Bogota, Colombia, 1977; numerous group shows include: Balt. Mus. of Art, Balt., 1998, The Arts Club of Washington, 1998, Howard County for the Arts, Ellicot City, Md., 1998, Evergreen House, Balt., 1999, McLean Project for Arts, McLean, Va., 1999, HBO Corp. Gallery, N.Y.C., 1997, 96, Northpark Ctr., Dallas, 1994, Colombian Consulate Gallery, Washington, 1993, Arte Moderno Gallery, Bogota, 1993, Brit. Coun., Bogota, 1993, others. Recipient Brit. Coun. scholarship for postgrad. studies in Britain, 1984; finalist Internat. Senefelder Prize '87, Germany, 1987, others. Home: 1526 12th St NW #6 Washington DC 20005

GONZALEZ-DEL-VALLE, LUIS TOMAS, Spanish language educator; b. Nov. 19, 1946. BA in Spanish cum laude, Wilmington Coll.-U. N.C., Wilmington, 1968; MA in Spanish and Spanish-Am. Lits., U. Mass., 1972; Phd in Spanish and Spanish-Am. Lits. five coll. coop. program, Amherst Coll., Hampshire Coll., Mt. Holyoke Coll., Smith Coll., U. Mass., 1972. Asst. prof. modern langs. Kans. State U., 1972-75, assoc. prof. modern langs., 1975-77; assoc. prof. modern langs. and lits. U. Nebr., Lincoln, 1977-79, prof. modern langs. and lits., 1979-86; prof. Spanish and Portuguese U. Colo., Boulder, 1986—, chmn. dept. Spanish and Portuguese, 1986—; reading cons. South-Western Pub. Co., Inc., 1974, Eliseo Torres & Sons, 1974; dir. Ibero-Latin Am. Studies Ctr., 1987—; lectr. in field. Author: La

nueva ficción hispanoamericana a traves de M.A. Asturias y G. Garcia Marquez, 1972, La ficción breve de Valle-Inclán, 1990, El Canon: Reflexiones Sobre la Recepción Literaria-Teatral, 1993; co-author: Luis Romero, 1979; gen. editor: Anales de la literatura española contemporánea, 1975—, Siglo xx/20th Century, 1985—; editor: Jour. Spanish Studies: 20th Century, 1972-80, Studies in 20th Century Lit., 1975-79, Annual Bibliography of Post-Civil War Spanish Fiction, 1977-82, Ecos de Cuba, 1997; co-editor: La generacion de 1898 ante España, 1997; contbr. articles, essays, book revs. to profl. jours. Recipient Postdoctoral Rsch. award Coun. for Internat. Exch. Scholars, 1984, 500th Rsch. Award Spanish Fgn. Ministry, 1992; grantee Coun. on Rsch. and Creative Work, U. Colo., 1986-87, Com. for Ednl. & Cultural Affairs, U. Nebr.-Lincoln, Chancellor's Rsch. Initiation Fund, U. Nebr.-Lincoln, 1980-81, Rsch. Coun., U. Nebr.-Lincoln, 1978, 79; Sr. Faculty Summer Rsch. fellow Rsch. Coun., U. Nebr.-Lincoln, 1978, Woodrow Wilson Dissertation fellow, 1971-72, Univ. fellow U. Mass., 1968-69, 70-72, Grad. fellow, 1969-70. Mem. Conf. Editors of Learned Jours. (bd. dirs. 1987—), MLA, Spain's Pen Club (founding 1984), Assn. Colegial de Escritores (spl. rep. to U.S., v.p.), Assn. de Escritores y Artistas Espanoles (U.S. rep.), Fgn. Lang. Adminstrs. of Colo., North Am. Acad. of Spanish Lang. (corrs. mem.), Assn. Europea de Profesores de Espanol, Am. Assn. Tchrs. Spanish and Portuguese (Excellence in Tchg. award Colo. chpt. 1996), Soc. Spanish and Spanish-Am. Studies (bd. dirs. 1975—), 20th Century Spanish Assn. (exec. sec. 1982—), Circulo de Cultura Panamericano (exec. coun. 1972), Castilian Assn. Writers (hon.), Cervantes Soc., Am. Nebr. Fgn. Lang. Assn., Phi Kappa Phi, others. Home: 1875 Del Rosa Ct Boulder CO 80304-1800 Office: U Colo Dept Spanish/Portuguese Boulder CO 80309

GONZALEZ-PITA, J. ALBERTO, lawyer; b. Havana, Cuba, Aug. 20, 1954; came to U.S., 1960; s. Benigno Jesus and Maria Modesta (Diaz) G.P.; m. Suzanne J. Martin, Apr. 7, 1984; children: Roberto Martin, Antonio Martin. AA, Miami-Dade Community Coll., 1973; BA, U. Miami, 1974; JD, Boston U., 1977. Bar: Fla. 1977, U.S. Dist. Ct. (so. dist.) Fla. 1977, U.S. Ct. Appeals (5th cir.) 1977, U.S. Ct. Appeals (11th cir.) 1981. Assoc. Walton, Lantaff, Schroeder & Carson, Miami, Fla., 1977-80; assoc. Patton & Kanner, Miami, 1980-82, ptnr., 1982-86, mng. ptnr., 1986-89; ptnr. McDermott, Will & Emery, Miami, 1989-91, White & Case, Miami, 1991-99; chair Worldwide Privatization Practice Group; co-chair Latin Am. Practice Group, vice pres., gen. couns., Bell South, Inc., 1999—. Mem. Acad. for Community Edn., Miami, 1980-90; bd. dirs. Inst. Innovative Intervention, Miami, 1980-90; trustee St. Thomas U., Miami, 1991-96. Mem. ABA, Internat. Bar Assn., Inter-Am. Bar Assn., Internationale des Avocats, Cuban-Am. Bar Assn., Maritime Law Assn. U.S. Roman Catholic. Office: Bell Soutn Internatl Inc 1100 Peachtree St NE Atlanta GA 30309-4599

GONZALEZ-SCARANO, FRANCISCO ANTONIO, neurologist; b. Ponce, P.R., Mar. 23, 1950; s. Francisco and Genoveva (Scarano) Gonzalez-Hernandez; m. Barbara Jean Turner, June 23, 1979; children: Genevieve Carre, Stephanie Katharine, Lisa Frances. BA, Yale U., 1971; MD, Northwestern U., Chgo., 1975; MA, U. Pa., Phila., 1988. Diplomate Am. Bd. Neurology. Intern Hosp. U. Pa., 1975-76, resident in neurology, 1976-79; fellow U. Pa., Phila., 1979-82; NIMR, London, 1981-82; asst. prof. depts. neurology and microbiology U. Pa., Phila., 1982-88, assoc. prof., 1988-94, prof., 1994—; vice-chair for rsch. neurology dept. U. Pa., 1998—; co-dir. Pa. Ctr. for HIV and AIDS, 1998—; chmn. bd. sci. counselors Nat. Inst. Neurol. Diseases and Stroke, Bethesda, Md., 1991-97. Assoc. editor Viral Pathogenesis, 1997; editl. bd. Jour. Neurovirology, 1996—, Virus Rsch., 1997—, AIDS, 1995—. Bd. trustees Swarthmore Presbyn. Ch., 1997—. Harry Weaver scholar Multiple Sclerosis Soc., N.Y.C., 1982-87. Mem. Am. Neurol. Assn., Am. Acad. Neurology (mem. sci. issues com. 1985-89, profl. and pub. issues com. 1987-93), Am. Soc. Clin. Investigation, John Morgan Soc., Penn Club. Presbyterian. Avocations: photography, skiing. Office: U Pa Dept Neurology CRB 415 Curie Blvd Philadelphia PA 19104-6146

GONZALEZ-VALES, LUIS ERNESTO, historian, educational administrator; b. Rio Piedras, P.R., May 11, 1930; s. Ernesto and Carmen (Vales) G.; B.A. with honors, U. P.R., 1952; M.A., Columbia U., 1957; doctorate (hon.) Pontifical Catholic U. P.R., 1995; m. Hilda Gonzalez, July 16, 1952; children—Carmen L., Luis E., Antonio S., Maria G., Rosa Maria, Gerardo, Rosario, Hildita. Instr. humanities U. P.R., Rió Piedras, 1955-58, asst. prof. humanities, 1958-64, assoc. prof. humanities, 1964-67, assoc. prof. history, 1967, prof. history, 1983, asst. dean faculty gen. studies, 1960-65, asso. dean faculty gen. studies, 1965-67. Author: Gabriel Gutierrez de Riva: Albores del Siglo XVIII en Puerto Rico, 1990. Dir. P.R. Acad. History, 1992—; exec. sec. Council on Higher Edn., 1967-83; exec. sec. Commonwealth Post Secondary Commn., 1973-83; chancellor P.R. Jr. Coll., 1985-87; bd. dirs Inst. Puerto Rican Culture; mem. Collegiate Ednl. adv. panel Cadet Command, U.S. Army, 1986-96. Served as 1st lt. inf. U.S. Army, 1952-55, adj. gen. P.R. N.G., 1983-85, ret. maj. gen. U.S. Army, 1990. Appointed Ofcl. Historian P.R., P.R. Legislature and Gov., 1977. Mem. Am. Hist. Assn., Acad. Polit. Scis., P.R. Acad. History, Am. Acad. Polit. and Social Scis., Latin Am. Studies Assn., Assn. U.S. Army, N.G. Assn., Mil. Order World Wars, Res. Officers Assn., P.R. Acad. of Arts and Scis. Phi Alpha Theta (pres. 1962-63). Roman Catholic. Author: Alejandro Ramirez: La Vida de un Intendente Liberal, 1972; contbg. author: Puerto Rico: A Political and Cultural History, 1983; contbr. articles on Puerto Rican history (in Spanish) to hist. jours.; editorial bd. Revista Historia, 1960-67.

GOO, ABRAHAM MEU SEN, retired aircraft company executive; b. Honolulu, May 21, 1925; s. Tai Chong and Lily En Wui (Dai) G.; m. Shin Quon Wong, June 12, 1950; children: Marilynn, Steven, Beverly Cardinal. BSEE U. Ill., 1951; postgrad. MIT, 1975. With The Boeing Co., Seattle, 1951-73; B-1 avionics program mgr. Boeing Aerospace Co., Seattle, 1974-75, v.p., gen. mgr. aircraft armament div., 1975-77; v.p. mil. systems Boeing Mil. Airplane Co., Wichita, Kans., 1977-79, exec. v.p., 1979-84, pres., 1984-87; pres. Boeing Advanced Systems, Seattle, 1987-89. With USAAF, 1946-47. Recipient Chinese-Am. Engrs. and Scientists of So. Calif. Achievement award Sci. and Engring., 1989, Pioneer award Assn. for Unmanned Vehicle Systems, 1989. Home: 18909 SE 282nd Ct Kent WA 98042-5458

GOO, VINCE, women's collegiate basketball coach; m. Gay; children: Cappy, Kippy, Kasey, Kimi. BS in Health & Phys. Edn., U. So. Oreg., 1969. Boy's jr. varsity basketball coach Castle H.S., 1969-71, head coach boy's varsity basketball coach, 1971-79; head coach boy's varsity basketball coach Kaiser H.S., 1979-83; from asst. coach to head coach women's basketball U. Hawaii, 1983—. Office: U Hawaii Women's Athletic Dept 1337 Lower Campus Rd Honolulu HI 96822-2370

GOOCH, ANTHONY CUSHING, lawyer; b. Amarillo, Tex., Dec. 3, 1937; s. Cornelius Skinner and Sidney Seale (Crawford) G.; m. Elizabeth Melissa Ivanoff, May 27, 1963 (div. Nov. 1983); children: Katherine C., Jennifer C., Melissa G., Andrew E.; m. Linda B. Klein, Nov. 7, 1987. BA, U. of South, 1959; diploma, Coll. of Europe, 1960; JD, NYU, 1963, M in Comparative Law, 1964. Bar: N.Y. 1963. Assoc. Cleary, Gottlieb, Steen & Hamilton, N.Y.C., Paris, Brussels, 1963-72; ptnr. Cleary, Gottlieb, Steen & Hamilton, Rio de Janeiro, 1973-78, N.Y.C., 1978—. Co-author: Loan Agreement Documentation, 1982, 2d edit., 1991, Swap Apreement Documentation, 1987, 2d edit., 1988, Documentation for Derivatives, 1993, Credit Support Supplement, 1995, Documentation for Loans, Assignments and Participations, 1996; articles editor NYU Law Rev., 1962-63. Mem. ABA, Inter-Am. Bar Assn., N.Y. State Bar Assn., Assn. Bar City N.Y., New York County Lawyers Assn., Down Town Assn. Democrat. Episcopalian. Home: Seven Mine Hill Rd Redding CT 06896-2701 Office: 1 Liberty Plz New York NY 10006-1404*

GOOCH, BRAD, writer; b. Kingston, Pa., Jan. 31, 1952. BA magna cum laude, Columbia Coll., 1973, MA in Comparative Lit. with honors, 1977, MPhil, 1979, PhD in English/Comparative Lit., 1986; cert. of french lang. and civilization, Sorbonne, 1974. Instr. English LaGuardia Cmty. Coll., 1979-81; sr. preceptor in English Columbia Coll., 1983-86; asst. prof. Columbia U., 1986; assoc. prof. English William Paterson U., 1992—; adj. lectr. NYU, 1985. Author: City Poet: The Life and Times of Frank O'Hara, 1993 (Book-of-the-Month Club selection 1994), The Golden Age of Promiscuity, 1996, Scary Kisses, 1992, Jailbait and Other Stories, 1984, Germany, 1992, Finding the Boyfriend Within, 1999, (Book-of-the-Month Club Quality Paperback selection); contbr. poems, stories, articles and revs. to profl. publs. Recipient Poetry prize Acad. of Am. Poets, 1977; pres. fellow Columbia U.,

1977-78, 80-81. Mem. PEN Am. Ctr., Poetry Soc. Am., The Authors Guild, Phi Beta Kappa. Office: c/o The Joy Harris Agy 156 Fifth Ave Ste 617 New York NY 10016

GOOCH, CAROL ANN, psychotherapist consultant; b. Meridian, Miss., Apr. 17, 1950; d. James Tackett and Chris M. Page; (div.); 1 child, Aaron Patrick Gooch. BS, Fla. State U., 1972, DS, 1975; MS, Troy State U., 1974. Lic. profl. counselor, Tex.; lic. chem. dependency counselor, Tex.; lic. marriage and family therapist, Tex.; cert. chem. dependency specialist, Tex.; cert. compulsive gambling counselor, Tex.; cert. tobacco addiction counselor ACP, Tex. Tchr. Okaloosa Sch. Dist., Fort Walton, Fla., 1972-77; counselor USAF, Osan AFB, Korea, 1977-79; sch. counselor Tomball (Tex.) Sch. Dist., 1983-90; cons. Montgomery (Tex.) Sch. Dist., 1992—; psychotherapist pvt. practice, Houston, 1990—; cons. school systems, Houston, 1990—; coord. sr. program Forest Springs Hosp., Houston, 1993—, Cypress Creek Hosp., 1994—. Vol. cons. PTO, Woodlands, Tex., 1990. Recipient fellowship Fla. State U., Tallahassee, 1973, Nat. Disting. Svc. award Ex Coun. U.S. Pubs., N.J., 1989; named Outstanding High Sch. Counselor, Tomball Ind. Sch. Dist., 1989. Mem. AAUW, ACA, ASCD, Tex. Sch. Counselors Assn., Am. Mental Health Counselors Assn., Tex. Mental Health Counselors Assn., Am. Bus. Women's Assn., Fla. State U. Alumni Assn., Kappa Delta Pi. Avocations: travel, dancing, boating. Home and Office: Carol A Gooch MS LPC PO Box 1308 Montgomery TX 77356-1308

GOOCH, NANCY JANE, realtor, mortgage executive; b. Ann Arbor, Mich., Dec. 19, 1941; d. Donald B. and Marjorie (Gilchrist) G. BA, Western Mich. U., 1963; MA, Ea. Mich. U., 1987. Lic. real estate broker, Fla., Mich. Tchr. Broward County Schs., Ft. Lauderdale, Fla., 1968-73; v.p. Chinelly Real Estate, Inc., Miramar, Fla., 1973-83; closing exec. Cenville Devel. Co., Hollywood, Fla., 1983-85; mortgage originator Empire of Am., Southfield, Mich., 1987-90; dir. Am. Mortgage Tng. Co., Garden City, Mich., 1990—; founder First Fin. Mortgage Corp. Editor Bridlepath mag., 1983-84, The Saddlebred Mag., 1989-95; contbr. numerous articles to various publs. Pres. Broadway Area Neighborhood Assn., Ann Arbor, 1985-86. Recipient honors S. Fla. Trail Riders Broward County, 1983. Mem. Wayne-Oakland Bd. Realtors, Am. Saddlehorse Assn. (bd. dirs. Mich. chpt. 1990-95, sec. 1994-95, editor The Saddlebred, 1989-95), Women's Econ. Club. Republican. Avocations: equestrian, photographer. Office: BMAC 325 E Eisenhower Pkwy Ann Arbor MI 48108-3355

GOOCH, STANFORD RONDALL, Air Force Operations research analyst; b. Selmer, Tenn., Feb. 15, 1944; s. Tolbert Johnson and Eula Demillus (Wilson) G.; m. Linda Lee Hunt; 1 child, Aimee Marie. BS, Memphis State U., 1967; MA, Auburn U., 1980. Chief svcs. br. 7th Bomb Wing, Carswell AFB, Tex., 1967-68; arc light 4133 Bomb Wing, Anderson AFB, Guam, 1968; chief, main supr. 7th Bomb Wing, Carswell AFB, 1968-69, 305th Bomb Wing, Grissom AFB, Ind., 1969-70; maj. comdr. mcpl. staff ofcl. Strategic Air Command, Offutt AFB, Nebr., 1970-72; br. chief, svcs. br. 307th Mcpl. Maintenance Squadron, U. Tapao, Thailand, 1972-73; maj. comdr. mcpl. program mgr. Strategic Air Command, Offutt AFB, 1973-79; air comdr. and staff col. Air U., Maxwell AFB, Ala., 1979-80; comdr. 10th equipment maintenance squadron RAF Alconbury, Eng., 1980-83; chief, sys. info. br. Def. Nuclear Agy., Alexandria, Va., 1983-86; mgr. nuclear weapon acquisitions Strategic Air Command, Offutt AFB, 1986-91; program analyst Strategic Air Command, 5, 1991-92; program analyst U.S. Strategic Command, 5, 1992-97, ops. rsch. analyst, 1997—; mem. CINCSTRAT posture team U.S. Strategic Command, Offutt AFB, 1993—, mem. stockpile assessment team, 1996; leader weapons team Plans & Policy Directorate, Offutt AFB, 1994—. Vol. Meals-on-Wheels, Easter Nebr. Office on Aging, 1992-93. Recipient Bronze Star medal USAF, 1973, Def. Meritorious Svc. medal Dept. of Def., 1986, USAF Meritorious Svc. medal USAF, 1979, 83, 90, USAF Commendation medal (2), 1970, 72, Viet Nam Svc. medal w/4 Bronze stars USAF, 1973, Superior Performance awards (6) U.S. Strategic Commn, 1992-97, Cert. of Recognitiion (3), U.S. Strategic Command, 1992, 93, 95, Performer of Yr. award, 1995, Exemplary Civilian Svc. award, 1995, Letter of Appreciation (2), 1993, 96, Meritorious Civilian Svc. award, 1998. Mem. Nat. Polit. Sci. Honor Soc. Republican. Avocations: reading, music. Home: 501 Kent Dr Papillion NE 68046-4145 Office: USSTRATCOM/J533 901 Sac Blvd Ste 2E9 Offutt A F B NE 68113-6500

GOOD, DAVID P., federal agency administrator. BA, SUNY, Stony Brook, 1970. Trainee fgn. svc. tng. USIA, Washington, 1970-71; jr. officer U.S. Embassy USIA, New Delhi, 1971-72; program officer Am. Consulate, Calcutta, India, 1972-76, USIA, Washington, 1976-78; asst. dir. Am. Embassy USIA, Abu Dhabi, United Arab Emirates, 1978-79; cultural affairs officer Am. Embassy USIA, Amman, Jordan, 1979-82; dir. Am. Embassy USIA, Kuwait, 1982-85; dir. Am. Consulate USIA, Jerusalem, 1985-89; pub. affairs advisor to asst. sec. NEA U.S. Dept. State, Washington, 1989-91; dep. dir. North Africa, Near East and South Asian affairs USIA, Washington, 1991-93; dir. Am. Embassy USIA, Tel Aviv, 1993-97; dir. North Africa, Near East and South Asian affairs USIA, Washington, 1997-99; consul-gen. Am. Consulate, Bombay, 1999—. Office: Am Consulate Gen N Africa Near East So Asia care US Dept of State Washington DC 20521-6240

GOOD, IRVING JOHN, statistics educator, mathematician, philosopher of science; b. London, Dec. 9, 1916; came to U.S., 1967; s. Morris Edward and Sophia (Polikoff) G. ScD, Cambridge (Eng.) U., 1963; DSc, Oxford (Eng.) U., 1964. Scientific officer Fgn. Office, Bletchley, Eng., 1941-45; lectr. math. and electronic computing Manchester (Eng.) U., 1945-48; sr. prin. sci. officer Govt. Communications Hdqrs., Cheltenham, Eng., 1948-59; spl. merit dep. chief sci. officer Admiralty Rsch. Lab., Teddington, Middlesex, Eng., 1959-62; sr. rsch. fellow Trinity Coll., Oxford U. and Atlas Computer Lab., Didcot, Berkshire, Eng., 1964-67; Univ. disting. prof. stats, adj. prof. philosophy Va. Poly. Inst. and State U., Blacksburg, 1967—; prof. emeritus; adj. prof. Ctr. Study of Sci. in Society; mem. comm. theory com. Ministry Supply, London, 1953-56; mem. comm. com. electronics rsch. com. Ministry Aviation, London, 1960-62; mem. rsch. sect. com. Royal Statis. Soc., London, 1965-67. Author: Probability and the Weighing of Evidence, 1950, The Estimation of Probabilities, 1965, Good Thinking, 1983; editor: The Scientist Speculates, 1962 (also French and German translations); chpt. in The Codebreakers, 1994; also 5 chpts. in Festschriften; contbr. 800 articles to profl. jours. Grantee NIH, 1970-89; recipient Smith's prize, Cambridge, Eng., 1940. Fellow Am. Acad. Arts and Scis., Va. Acad. Scis., Inst. Math. Stats., Am. Statis. Assn.; mem. IEEE Computer Soc. (Pioneer award 1998), Internat. Statis. Inst. (hon.), Internat. Order Merit. Home: 1309 Lynn Dr Blacksburg VA 24060-3001 Office: Va Poly Inst and State U Dept Stats Blacksburg VA 24061-0439

GOOD, JANE ELIZABETH, history educator; b. Akron, Ohio, Mar. 24, 1948; d. William Carl and Marjorie Jean (Hoover) G.; m. James Andrew Malloy, Jr., Nov. 13, 1976; children: Alexander Good, Nicholas Good. BA, Wittenberg U., Springfield, Ohio, 1970; MA in Teaching, Brown U., 1972, PhD, Am. U., 1979. Peace corps vol., Morocco, 1970-71; editor Am. Assn. for State and Local History, Nashville, 1972-73; asst. prof. Mt. Vernon Coll., Washington, 1977-79; assoc. prof. U.S. Naval Acad., Annapolis, Md., 1979—; mem. U.S. Naval Acad. Admissions Bd. Contbr. articles to profl. jours. Recipient Meritorious Civilian Service medal Dept. Navy, 1988, Disting. Civilian Svc. medal, 1994. Mem. Am. Assn. for Advancement Slavic Studies, So. Conf. Slavic Studies. Home: 27 Steele Ave Annapolis MD 21401-2840 Office: US Naval Acad Dept History Annapolis MD 21402

GOOD, JEFFREY, journalist. Grad., St. Michael's Coll., Cochester, Vt. Editor Public Citizen mag., D.C.; assoc. editor Vt. Vanguard Pr.; editorial writer St. Petersburg (Fla.) Times; now capital bureau chief Burlington (Vt.) Free Press, 1991—; now dir. centennial history project; writer, tchr. St. Michael's Coll., Colchester, 1999—. Co-author: (with Susan Goreck) Poison Mind, 1995. Recipient Pulitzer Prize for editorial writing, 1995. Office: Burlington Free Press Capital Bur PO Box 307 Montpelier VT 05601-0307

GOOD, JOSEPH COLE, JR., lawyer; b. Columbia, S.C., Sept. 18, 1945; s. Joseph Cole and Virginia (Williams) G.; m. Virginia St. Claire Craver, Apr. 5, 1969; children: Joseph III, Katharine. AB, Wofford Coll., 1967; JD, U. S.C., 1970. Bar: S.C., 1970. Asst. atty. gen. State of S.C., Columbia, 1970-73; atty. S.C. Electric & Gas Co., Columbia, 1973-83; dir. corp. and civic affairs S.C. Electric & Gas Co., Charleston, 1983-85; gen. counsel Med. U. S.C., Charleston, 1987—, faculty mem., 1988—; lectr. S.C. Higher Edn. Assn. Pres. Charleston Navy League, 1987; exec. bd. Low Country Council Girl Scouts U.S.A., 1987. Mem. ABA, S.C. Bar Assn. (state chmn. lawyers caring about lawyers com. 1987), Edison Electric Inst., Charleston Hibernian Soc., Carolina Yacht Club, The Charleston Club. Presbyterian. Avocations: tennis, golf. Home: 883 Parrot Creek Way Charleston SC 29412-9055 Office: 171 Ashley Ave Charleston SC 29425-0001

GOOD, LARRY IRWIN, physician, consultant; b. N.Y.C., Feb. 8, 1948; s. Samuel and Lillie (Sternlight) G.; m. Judy Chafetz, Aug. 16, 1969; children: Adam Eric, Lauren Elyse, Bryan Scott, Allison Jill. BA, Colgate U., 1969; MD, Med. U. of S.C., 1973. Diplomate Am. Bd. Internal Medicine, Am. Bd. Gastroenterology. Intern in medicine Teaching Hosp. Med. U. of S.C., 1973-74, resident in medicine Teaching Hosp., 1974-75, chief resident in medicine Teaching Hosp., 1975-76; fellow in gastroenterology U. Pa., 1976-78; with Hempstead (N.Y.) Gen. Hosp., 1978—, Nassau County Med. Ctr., East Meadow, N.Y., 1978—; with South Nassau Communities Hosp., Oceanside, N.Y., 1978—, chief div. gastroenterology dept. medicine, 1989; asst. prof. Sch. of Medicine, SUNY, Stony Brook, 1978; mem. health adv. bd. Hofstra Health Dome Uniondale, N.Y., 1983; with Lydia E. Hall Hosp., Freeport, N.Y., 1978-86, Mercy Hosp., Rockville Centre, N.Y., 1978-80. Contbr. articles to Am. Jour. Gastroenterology, The Papilla Vateri and its Diseases, Med. Times, New Eng. Jour. Medicine., Gastroenterology, Alpha Omega Alpha. Trustee, dir. Little Village Sch. & House, Garden City, N.Y., 1985—. Recipient Rsch. Svc. award NIH, 1977. Fellow Am. Coll. Gastroenterology; mem. AMA, ACP, L.I. Gastroenterologic Assn., Am. Gastroenterologic Assn. Jewish. Office: 999 Franklin Ave Garden City NY 11530-2913

GOOD, LAURANCE FREDERIC, office director; b. Wheeling, W.Va., Sept. 26, 1932; s. Sidney Samuel and Jeannette (Berg) G.; m. Barbara S. Mayer, Oct. 18, 1959; children: Philip (dec.), Jay, Paul, Jenny, Heidi. BA, Brown U., 1954; postgrad., U. Va., 1955. CLU, ChFC, cert. employee benefits specialist, health ins. assoc.; registered health underwriter. V.p., gen. mdse. mgr. L.S. Good & Co., Wheeling, 1961-69, exec. v.p., 1969-80, vice chmn., sec. bd., 1961-80; pres. Personal History Systems, Inc.; life underwriter Equitable Life Assurance Soc. Am., 1983-89; health and welfare cons. Mockenhaupt, Mockenhaupt, Cowden & Parks, 1989; employee benefit specialist, life underwriter Lincoln Fin. Svcs., Inc., Pitts., 1990; exec. dir. Wheeling Works, Inc., Wheeling, W.Va., 1993-95; dir. Office of Gift Planning Med. Park Found., Wheeling, W.Va., 1995—; mem. Million Dollar Roundtable, 1985-86. Producer: Wheeling Rediscovered; Author: My Lifetime Book. Mem. bd. Wheeling Symphony Soc., 1964-67, 68-73; active Ohio Valley Indsl. & Bus. Devel. Corp., Wheeling, 1971; area chmn. Brown U. Alumni Program, 1954-88; Christmas seals chmn. Tb Assn. Ohio Valley, 1973; co-chmn. United Jewish Appeal, 1971-73; v.p., chmn. fin. com. Temple Shalom, 1986-89; co-founder Good Zoo; also pres. Good Zoo Friends, 1974-78; chmn. establishment com. Wheeling Devel. Conf.; bd. found. W. Liberty State Coll., 1971; creator Kraft-Good Archives; bd. dirs. Wheeling Hosp., 1972-87, hon. bd. dirs., 1988-96; bd. visitors Bethany Coll., 1972-77; trustee Oglebay Inst., 1972-90; mem. Estate Planning Coun. of Ohio Valley and Pitts.; co-chair Greater Wheeling/Bel-o-Mar Empowerment Zone/Enterprise Community Initiative, 1994; campaign dir. Toward the Next Century, Wheeling Hosp., 1998. With USN, 1955-57. Decorated South China Sea medal; recipient Disting. West Virginian award, 1976. Fellow Life Tng. Underwriters Coun.; mem. Nat. Retail Mchts. Assn. (dir. merchandising div. 1966-71, del. conf. 1969), Am. Technion Soc. (trustee Pa. chpt. 1965), Ohio Valley Assn. Life Underwriters (pres. 1987), W.Va. Assn. Life Underwriters (regional dir. 1988). Office: Med Park Found Office Gift Planning One Medical Pk Wheeling WV 26003

GOOD, LEONARD PHELPS, artist; b. Chickasha, Okla., June 25, 1907; s. Jacob Calvin and Belle (Leonard) G.; m. Nancye Dooley, July 15, 1932 (dec. May 1969); 1 son, Leonard Jacob; m. Yoshie Tobe, Nov. 26, 1970. BFA, U. Okla., 1927; postgrad., Art Students' League, N.Y.C., 1930, Clarence White Sch. Photography, N.Y.C., 1937, State U. Iowa, 1940. Tchr. pub. sch. art depts. Tex. and Okla., 1927-30; mem. faculty U. Okla. Sch. Art, 1930-50, U. Wis., 1950-52; prof., head dept. art Drake U., 1952-68, prof. art dept., 1968-77, emeritus prof., 1977—; curator paintings Mus. Art, U. Okla., 1935-50; vis. artist-in residence Iowa State U., Ames, 1966, Shenandoah (Iowa) Community High Sch. for Nat. Endowment for Arts, 1970-71, Central Coll., Pella, Iowa, 1984. Exhibited paintings nat. exhbns. Am. Art Met. Mus., N.Y., 1936, 37, Am. Painters in Paris, 1975-76, Sigurd Anderson Gallery at Drake U., Des moines, 1997, USAO Art Gallery, 1998, 99, OU Fine Art Sch., 1999; traveling exhbns., Am. Fedn. Art, 1940-41; represented in permanent collections Oklahoma City Art Mus., Okla. Hist. Soc., Philbook Art Ctr., Tulsa, Kans. Fedn. Arts, Brunnier Mus., Iowa State U., Ames, Milw. Art Ctr., Des Moines Art Ctr., Mabee-Gerrer Mus. Art, Shawnee, Okla., Iowa Hist. Mus., Springville (Utah) Mus. Art, Schoen Collection, New Orleans, Charles H. MacNider Mus. Art, Mason City, Iowa, Kenichi Muto U. Tokyo High Energy Lab., Tsukuba, Japan, Urasenke Internat. Found., Kyoto, Japan, Anderson Gallery, Des Moines, Iowa, 1997, U. Chickasha, Okla., 1998, Coll. Fine Art U. Okla., Norman, 1999, Main Libr. U. Okla Campus, 1999; retrospective exhbn. Leonard Good: Eight Decades at U. Okla. Fred Jones Jr. Mus. of Art, 1993; juror nat. exhbns.; one-man exbhn. The Firehouse Art Ctr., Norman, Okla., 1995; contbr. to Chronicles of Okla., 1992. Trustee Mabee-Gerrer Mus. Art, Shawnee, Okla., 1978-95. Leonard Good Day proclaimed by State of Okla., Jan. 17, 1993. Mem. Omicron Delta Kappa (hon.), Delta Phi Delta (nat. pres. 1958-60). Home: 1320 W Oregon Ave Chickasha OK 73018-4106 Address: PO Box 2181 Chickasha OK 73023-2181

GOOD, LINDA LOU, elementary education educator; b. Zanesville, Ohio, May 30, 1941; d. John Robert and Alice Laura (Fulkerson) Moore; B.S. in Elem. Edn., Ohio U., 1964; m. Larry Alvin Good, Jan. 11, 1964; children—Jason (dec.), Alicia and Tricia (twins), Amy Jo. Tchr., West Muskingum Sch. Dist., 1962-64; 1st grade tchr., Bellevue, Ohio, 1964-68, 2d grade tchr., Zanesville Sch. System, 1970—; head tchr. Munson Sch., Zanesville. Co-chmn. Zane Trace Commemoration; pres. Munson-Garfield Schs. PTA; mem. Trinity Presbyn. Ch. Mem. NEA, Ohio Edn. Assn., Zanesville Edn. Assn., Eastern Ohio Tchrs. Assn. Presbyterian.

GOOD, MARY LOWE (MRS. BILLY JEWEL GOOD), investment company executive, educator; b. Grapevine, Tex., June 20, 1931; d. John W. and Winnie (Mercer) Lowe; m. Billy Jewel Good, May 17, 1952; children: Billy, James. BS, Ark. State Tchrs. Coll., 1950; MS, U. Ark., 1953, PhD, 1955, LLD (hon.), 1979; DSc (hon.), U. Ill., Chgo., 1983, Clarkson U., 1984, Ea. Mich. U., 1986, Duke U., 1987; hon. degree, St. Mary's Coll., 1987, Kenyon Coll., 1988, Stevens Inst. Tech., 1989, Lehigh U., 1989, Northeastern Ill. U., 1989, U. S.C., 1989, N.J. Inst. Tech., 1989; hon. law degree, Newcomb Coll. of Tulane U., 1991; LLD (hon.), Coll. of William and Mary, 1992; DSc (hon.), Manhattan Coll., 1992, Ind. U., 1992, SUNY, Binghamton, 1994, Rensselaer Polytechnic Inst., 1994, Monmouth U., 1995, La. State U., 1995, Ill. Inst. Tech., 1997, Ill. Inst. Tech., 1997, Mich. State U., 1997, U. Mich., 1998; DEng (hon.), Mich. State U., 1997, U. Mich., 1998. Instr. Ark. State Tchrs. Coll., Conway, summer 1949; instr. La. State U., Baton Rouge, 1954-56, asst. prof., 1956-58; assoc. prof. La. State U., New Orleans, 1958-63, prof., 1963-80; Boyd prof. materials sci., divsn. engring. rsch. La. State U., Baton Rouge, 1979-80; v.p., dir. rsch. UOP, Inc., Des Plaines, Ill., 1980-84; pres. Signal Rsch. Ctr. Inc., 1985-87; pres. engineered materials rsch. divsn Allied-Signal Inc., Des Plaines, Ill., 1986-88; sr. v.p.-tech. Allied-Signal Inc., Morristown, N.J., 1988-93; under sec. of commerce for technology Dept. of Commerce, Washington, DC, 1993-97; mng. mem. Venture Capital Investors LLC, Little Rock, 1997—; Donaghey Univ. prof. U. Ark., Little Rock, 1998—; chmn. Pres.'s Com. for Nat. Medal Sci., 1979-82; mem. Nat. Sci. Bd., 1980-91 (chmn. 1988-91), chair, 1988-90; adv. bd. NSF Chemistry Sect., 1972-76; com. medicinal chemistry NIH, 1972-76, Office of USAF Rsch., 1974-78, chemist divsn. Brookhaven and Oak Ridge Nat. Labs., 1973-83, chem. tech. divsn. Oak Ridge Nat. Lab., catalysis program Lawrence-Berkeley Lab.; catalysis program coll. engring. La. State U.; vice chair Nat. Sci. Bd., 1984, chair, 1988-90; bd. dirs. Biogen, IDEXX Labs., Lockheed-Martin Energy Rsch. Corp., Whatman plc. Contbr. articles to profl. jours. Mem. Nat. Sci. Bd., 1980-91; mem. Pres.' Coun. Advisors for Sci. and Tech., 1991-93, chair, 1988-91. Recipient Agnes Faye Morgan rsch. award, 1969, Disting. Alumni citation U. Ark., 1973, Scientist of Yr. award Indsl. R&D mag., 1983, Delmer S. Fahrney medal Franklin Inst., 1988, N.J. Women of Achievement award Douglass Coll., Rutgers U., 1990, Indsl. Rsch. Inst. medal, 1991, Disting. Svc. award NSF, 1992, Roe award ASME, 1993, Gold medal SME, 1995, Earle Barnes award ACS, 1996, Priestley medal, 1997, UCLA Glenn T. Seaborg medal, 1996, Nat. Materials Advancement award Fedn. Materials Socs., 1996, Othmer medal award Chem. Heritage Found., 1998; AEC tng. grantee, 1967, NSF Internat. travel grantee, 1968, NSF rsch. grantee, 1969-80, Albert Fox Demers award, 1992. Fellow AAAS (Abelson award 1999), Am. Inst. Chemistry (Gold medal 1983), Chem. Soc. London, Royal Soc. Chemistry (hon.); mem. NAE, Swedish Acad. Engring., Am. Chem. Soc. (1st woman dir. 1971-74, regional dir. 1972-80, chmn. bd. 1978, 80, pres. 1987, Garvan medal 1973, Herty medal 1975, award Fla. sect. 1979, Charles Lathrop Parsons award 1991), Internat. Union Pure and Applied Chmistry (pres. inorganic div. 1980-85), Zonta (past pres. New Orleans club, chmn. dist. status of women com. and nominating com., chmn. internat. Amelia Earhart scholarship com. 1978-88, pres. internat. Found. 1988-93, mem. internat. bd. 1988-90), Rotary Internat., Phi Beta Kappa, Sigma Xi, Iota Sigma Pi (regional dir. 1967-93, hon. mem. 1983). Home: 13824 Rivercrest Dr Little Rock AR 72212-1521 Office: Venture Capital Investors LLC Office Tech Admn 400 W Capitol Ave Ste 1845 Little Rock AR 72201-3436 also Office: U Ark at Little Rock Coll Info Sci/Sys Engring 2801 S University Ave Little Rock AR 72204-1000

GOOD, REBECCA MAE WERTMAN, learning and behavior counselor, grief and loss counselor, hospice nurse, therapeutic touch practitioner, educator; b. Barberton, Ohio, May 13, 1943; d. Frederick Daniel Wertman and Freda Beam Wertman Lombardi; m. William Robert Good Jr., Aug. 15, 1964; children: William Robert III, John Joseph, Matthew Stephan. RN diploma, Akron Gen. Med. Ctr., Ohio, 1964; BS in Psychology, Ramapo Coll., Mahwah, N.J., 1986; MA in Counseling, NYU, 1990. RN, Utah; nat. cert. counselor; cert. psychiat. and mental health nurse; lic. profl. counselor, AIDS cert. RN. Staff nurse Green Cross Gen. Hosp., Cuyahoga Falls, Ohio, 1965-68; staff nurse, relief supr., psychiat. nurse F.D.R. VA Hosp., Montrose, N.Y., 1971-72; geriatric staff and charge nurse Westledge Extended Care Facility, Peekskill, N.Y., 1972-77; infirmary and ICF nurse St. Dominics Home, Orangeburg, N.Y., 1981-83; allergy and immunology nurse Dr. Andre Codispoti, Suffern, N.Y., 1979-89; rsch. asst. counselor NYU, N.Y.C., 1989-90; Rockland advocate Student Advocacy Inc., White Plains, N.Y., 1989-90; exec. dir. Rockland County Assn. for Learning Disabled, Orangeburg, 1990-91; life skills counselor Bd. Coop. Edn., West Nyack, N.Y., 1991-93; learning and behavior disorders counselor, Suffern, 1991-93, Salt Lake City, 1994—; hospice nurse United Hospice Rockland, 1991-93; assessment and referral counselor/case mgr. CPC Olympus View Hosp., Salt Lake City, 1994-97; practitioner, tchr. Therapeutic Touch, 1990—; outcomes coord. U. Utah Med. Ctr., 1997—. Co-chmn. Rockland County Coordinating Coun. for Devel. Disabled Offenders, New City, N.Y., 1990-93; bd. visitors Rockland Children's Psychiat. Ctr., Orangeburg, 1991-93, sec., 1992; mem. U.S. Congressman Benjamin Gilman's Handicapped Adv. Com., Rockland County, 1985-94; pres. Ramapo Ctrl. Sch. Dist. Spl. Edn. PTA, 1982-86. Ramapo Coll. of N.J. Pres.'s scholar, 1986. Mem. ACA, Utah Counselors Assn., Children and Adults with Attention Deficit Disorders (coord. Rockland chpt. 1992-93), Hospice Nurses Assn., Nurse Healers Profl. Assn., Internat., Inc. (trustee, Utah networker), Learning Disabilities Assn. of Utah (profl. adv. bd. 1997—), Assn. Nurses in AIDS Care. Episcopalian. Avocations: gardening, nature, golf, skiing, choir. Office: 1100 E Quicksilver Dr Salt Lake City UT 84405

GOOD, ROBERT ALAN, physician, educator; b. Crosby, Minn., May 21, 1922; s. Roy Homer and Ethel Gay (Whitcomb) G.; m. Noorbibi K. Day, 1986; children from previous marriage: Robert Michael, Mark Thomas, Alan Maclyn, Margaret Eugenia, Mary Elizabeth. BA, U. Minn., 1944, MB, 1946, PhD, 1947, MD, 1947, DSc (hon.), 1989; MD (hon.), U. Uppsala, Sweden, 1966; DSc (hon.), N.Y. Med. Coll., 1973, Med. Coll. Ohio, 1973, Coll. Medicine and Dentistry N.J., 1974, Hahnemann Med. Coll., 1974, U. Chgo., 1974, St. John's U., 1977, U. Health Scis., Chgo. Med. Sch., 1978, Miami Children's Hosp., 1986, Med. Sch., U. Minn., 1989, U. Rome, Rome. Teaching asst. dept. anatomy U. Minn., Mpls., 1944-45; instr. pediatrics U. Minn. (Med. Sch.), 1950-51, asst. prof., 1951-53, asso. prof., 1953-54, Am. Legion Meml. research prof. pediatrics, 1954-73, prof. microbiology, 1962-72, Regents prof. pediatrics and microbiology, 1969-73, prof., head dept. pathology, 1970-72; intern U. Minn. Hosps., 1947, asst. resident pediatrics, 1948-49; pres., dir. Sloan-Kettering Inst. for Cancer Research, 1973-80, mem., 1973-81; prof. pathology Sloan-Kettering div. Grad. Sch. Med. Scis. Cornell U., 1973-81, dir., 1973-80; adj. prof., vis. physician Rockefeller U., 1973-81; prof. medicine, pediatrics and pathology Cornell U. Med. Coll., 1973-81; dir. research Meml. Sloan-Kettering Cancer Ctr., v.p., 1980-81; dir. research Meml. Hosp. for Cancer and Allied Diseases, 1973-80, also attending physician depts. medicine and pediatrics; attending pediatrician N.Y. Hosp., 1973-81; mem., head cancer research program Okla. Med. Research Found., 1982-85; prof. pediatrics, research prof. medicine, Okla. Med. Rsch. Found. prof. microbiology and immunology U. Okla. Health Scis. Ctr., 1982-85; attending physician, head div. immunology Okla. Children's Meml. Hosp., 1982-85; attending physician in internal medicine Okla. Meml. Hosp., 1983-85; physician-in-chief All Children's Hosp., St. Petersburg, Fla., 1985—; prof., chmn. dept. pediatrics U. South Fla., St. Petersburg, 1985-91, prof. depts. pediatrics, microbiology, immunology and medicine, 1985—; head allergy and clinical immunology, dept. pediatrics U. South Fla./All Childrens Hosp., St. Petersburg, 1985—; disting. rsch. prof. U. South Fla., St. Petersburg, 1989—; vis. investigator Rockefeller Inst. for Med. Rsch., N.Y.C., 1949-50, asst. physician to Hosp., 1949-50; attending pediatrician Hennepin County Gen. Hosp., 1950-73, cons., 1960-73; mem. Unitarian Svc. Commn. Med. Exch. Team to France, Germany, Switzerland and Czechoslovakia, 1958; cons. VA Hosp., Mpls., 1959-60; cons., sci. adviser Nat. Jewish Hosp., Denver, Children's Asthma Rsch. Inst. and Hosp., Denver, 1964-69; mem. study sects. USPHS, 1952-69; mem. expert adv. panel on immunology WHO, 1967—; cons. Merck & Co., N.J., 1968-72, Nat. Cancer Inst., 1973-74; mem. ad hoc com. Pres.'s Sci. Adv. Coun. on Biol. and Med. Sci., 1970, Pres.'s Cancer Panel, 1972; mem. Lyndon B. Johnson Found. awards com., 1972; mem. adv. com. Bone Marrow Transplant Registry, 1973—; chmn. Internat. Bone Marrow Registry, 1977-79; bd. dirs. Nat. Marrow Donor Program, 1987-94; fgn. adv. Acad. Med. Scis., People's Republic of China, 1980—; chmn. Fla. Gov.'s Task Force on AIDS, 1985-87, mem., 1988-94. Author, editor numerous books; contbr. many articles to profl. jours. Mem. adv. council Childrens Hosp. Research Found., Cin., 1954-58; bd. dirs. Allergy Found. Am., 1973; bd. sci. advisers Jane Coffin Childs Meml. Fund Med. Research, 1972-74, Merck Inst. Therapeutic Research, 1972-76; trustee Eleanor Naylor Dana Charitable Trust, 1982—. Recipient Borden Undergrad. Research award U. Minn. Med. Sch., 1946, E. Mead Johnson First award, 1955, Theobald Smith award, 1955, Parke-Davis 6th Ann. award, 1962, Rectors medal U. Helsinki, 1963-64, Pemberton Lectureship award, 1966, Gordon Wilson Gold medal, 1967, R.E. Dyer Lectureship award, 1967, Clemens Von Pirquet Gold medal 9th Ann. Forum on Allergy, 1968, Presidents medal U. Padua, Italy, 1968, Robert A. Cooke Gold medal Am. Acad. Allergy, 1968, John Stewart Meml. award Dalhousie U., 1969, Borden award Assn. Am. Med. Colls., 1970, Howard Taylor Ricketts award U. Chgo., 1970, Gairdner Found. award, 1970, City of Hope award, 1970, Am. Acad. Achievement golden plate award, 1970, Albert Lasker award for clin. and med. research, 1970, ACP award, 1972, Am. Coll. Chest Physicians award, 1974, Lila Gruber award Am. Acad. Dermatology, 1974, award in cancer immunology Cancer Research Inst. N.Y., 1975, Outstanding Achievement award U. Minn., 1978, award Am. Dermatological Soc. Allergy and Immunology, 1978, 1st Sarasota Med. award, 1979, sect. on mil. pediatrics award Am. Acad. Pediatrics, 1980, recipient Univ. medal Hacettepe U., Ankara, Turkey, 1982, Pres.' medal U. Lyon, France, 1986, Merieux Found. award Internat. Soc. Preventive Oncology, 1987, Claude Bernard prize World Med. Communications, Inc., 1987, Disting. Med. Sci. of Fla. award Fla. Soc. Pathologists, 1989, Gold-Headed Cane award Dept. Pediatrics U. Minn., 1990, Askounes-Ashford Disting. Scholar award, USF, 1990, Excellence award Ronald McDonald Children's Charities, 1991, Councill C. Rudolph award, All Children's Hosp., 1991, Merit award for outstanding and superior res., Dept. Health and Human Services, Md., 1992, Lifetime Achievement award Immune Deficiency Found., Md., 1992, Asthma and Allergy Found. Am. award 1993, Univ. Rsch. medallion award Disting. Rsch. Prof. U. South Fla., 1993, Immune Deficiency Found. award, 1993, Internat. Nutritional Immunology Group award, 1993, Paul Harris Fellow award Rotary Found. of Rotary Internat., 1994, Steven C. Beering award Indiana U., 1996, Internat. Bone Marrow Transplant Registry award, 1997, Gold and Silver Star The Order of the Sacred Treasure, 1998, Disting. Scientist award, Turkey Acad. Scis., 1999, numerous others; named one of top physicians in U.S., The Best Doctors in Am., 1992, 94-95; Endowment chair named in honor Children's Hosp. and U. South Fla., 1994; Fellow Nat.

Found. for Infantile Paralysis, 1947, Helen Hay Whitney Found. fellow, 1948-50; Markle Found. scholar, 1950-55. Fellow AAAS, Am. Coll. Physicians (award 1993), Royal Soc. Medicine, Acad. Multidisciplinary Research, N.Y. Acad. Sci., Am. Acad. Arts and Scis., Am. Coll. of Allergy and Immunology (hon., John P. McGovern Lectureship award 1993, Schering Jaros Lecture award 1993), Am. Acad. Pediat. (1st hon. fellow sect. on allergy and immunology), The Philippine Pediat. Soc. (hon.); mem. NAS, Am. Soc. Transplant Surgeons (hon.), Am. Assn. History of Medicine, Am. Fedn. Clin. Research, Am. Assn. Anatomists, Am. Assn. Immunologists (past pres.), AAUP, Am. Pediatric Soc. (John Howland award 1987), Mpls. Pediatric Soc., Northwestern Pediatric Soc., Am. Rheumatism Assn., Am. Soc. Clin. Investigation (past pres.), Am. Soc. Exptl. Pathology (past pres.), Am. Soc. Microbiology, Assn. Am. Physicians, Central Soc. Clin. Research (past pres.), Harvey Soc., Infectious Disease Soc. Am. (Squibb award 1968), Internat. Soc. Nephrology, Internat. Acad. Pathology, Internat. Soc. for Transplantation Biology, Minn. State Med. Assn., NAS Inst. Medicine (charter), Reticuloendothelial Soc. (past pres.), Soc. for Exptl. Biology and Medicine (past pres.), Soc. for Pediatric Research, Am. Clin. and Climatol. Assn. (Gordon Wilson Gold medal 1967), Detroit Surg. Assn. (McGraw medal 1969), Internat. Soc. Blood, Transfusion, Practitioners' Soc., Am. Assn. Pathologists, Internat. Soc. Exptl. Hematology (award in pioneering leadership and accomplishments 1994), Transplant Soc., Western Assn. Immunologists, Internat. Soc. Immunopharmacology (founding mem.), Am. Soc. Transplant Surgeons, Pioneer, Internat. Bone Marrow Transplant Registry (charter), Phi Beta Kappa, Sigma Xi, Alpha Omega Alpha. Office: All Children's Hosp 801 6th St S Saint Petersburg FL 33701-4899

GOOD, SHELDON FRED, realtor; b. Chgo., June 4, 1933; s. Joseph and Sylvia (Schwartz) G.; student Drake U., 1951; children: Steven, Todd; m. Susan Forman, Dec. 22, 1990. BBA, U. Ill., 1955. Sales mgr. Baird & Warner Real Estate, Chgo., 1957-65; chmn. Sheldon F. Good & Co. Realtors, Chgo., 1965—; guest lectr. Northwestern U., U. Chgo., U. Calif., Wharton Grad. Sch., U. Pa., Stanford U., Vanderbilt U., U. Ill.; staff instr. Central YMCA City Coll., Chgo.; guest spkr. Wall St. Week UN, 1993 cons. in field. Chmn. United Settlement Appeal, Chgo., YMCA Edn. Libr. Drive, Chgo., Chgo. Jewish United Fund. Bd. dirs. Child, Inc.; pres. Gastrointestinal Research Found., U. Chgo., 1979; chmn. Chgo. Assn. Realtors Hall of Fame, 1996-97; bd. dirs. U. Ill. Found., 1995-97. Served with AUS, 1955-57. Recipient Levi Eshkol Premier medal State Israel, 1967, Crown of A Good Name award Jewish Nat. Fund, 1972, Chgo. Realtor of Yr. award, 1991; First recipient of Richard W. Dewees Meml. award, 1998; named one of 10 outstanding young men Chgo., 1968, Chgo. Man of Yr., 1998, Illini of Yr. Chgo. Assn. Realtors, 1999. Mem. Chgo. Real Estate Bd. (treas., pres. 1988-89), Nat. Assn. Real Estate Bds., Nat. Assn. Realtors (chmn. nat. auction com. 1990, RTC task force), State of Ill. Internat. Real Estate Fedn. (FIABCI exec. com., pres. 1991, pres. FIABCI-USA, 1994-95, world pres.-elect FIABCI-Internat., 1995-96, world pres. 1996-97, pres., Prix D'Excellence Awd. Contest, 1998-99), Chgo. Better Bus. Bur., Chgo Assn. Commerce and Industry, Alpha Epsilon Pi (Outstanding Alumnus award 1996), Lambda Alpha, Omega Tau Rho. Club: Bryn Mawr Country (pres. 1988), Hundred of Cook County (bd. dirs.). Author: How to Sell Apartment Buildings; Techniques of Investment Property Exchanging; How to Lease Suburban Office Buildings; The Real Estate Auction as a Marketing Tool. Home: 180 E Pearson St Chicago IL 60611-2130 Office: 333 W Wacker Dr Chicago IL 60606-1220

GOOD, WALTER RAYMOND, investment executive; b. Oak Park, Ill., Sept. 9, 1924; s. Walter William and Elsie Sophia (Lussow) G.; m. Jean S. Stockman, Feb. 5, 1949; children: Elizabeth, Deborah, William. Ph.B., U. Chgo., 1947, M.B.A., 1949. Buyer fats and oils Procter and Gamble, Cin., 1949-52; dir. research Brown Bros. Harriman, N.Y.C., 1952-70; exec. v.p., dir. Lionel D. Edie, N.Y.C., 1970-80; v.p. Continental Group Inc., Stamford, Conn., 1980-85; mng. ptnr. Actively Managed Universes, Darien, Conn., 1985-86; pres. Mellon Universe Mgmt. Group, Stamford, 1986-90; mng. ptnr. Capital Market Systems, Darien, 1990-98; mem. investment adv. panel Pension Benefit Guaranty Corp., Washington, 1980-83; dir., mem. exec. com. Retirement Systems for Savs. Instns., N.Y.C., 1985-86; mem. investment adv. council N.Y.C. Retirement Funds, 1980-85; mem. Pension Execs. Conf., 1981-85, chmn., 1983, mem. fin. adv. panel The Aerospace Corp., 1986—. Author: (with D. Love) Managing Pension Assets: Pension Finance and Corporate Financial Goals, 1990, (with R. Hermansen and J. Meyer) Active Asset Allocation: Gaining Advantage in a Highly Efficient Stock Market, 1993, (with R. Hermansen) Index Your Way to Investment Success, 1998; assoc. editor Fin. Analysts Jour., 1972-97. Served with USAAF, 1943-46. Recipient Graham and Dodd Scroll Fin. Analysts Fedn., 1979. Mem. Inst. Chartered Fin. Analysts (council examiners 1980-86), N.Y. Soc. Security Analysts, Stamford Soc. Investment of Analysts.

GOOD, WILLIAM ALLEN, professional society executive; b. Oak Park, Ill., May 29, 1949; s. Fred Clifton and Dorothy Helen (Stockdale) G.; m. Julianne Doggett, Jan. 8, 1972 (div. Apr. 1980); m. Paulette Edith Gordon, Apr. 23, 1983 (div. Apr. 1991); m. Laura Elizabeth Wellbank, Sept. 25, 1993. MBA, U. Chgo., 1992. Supr. Dun & Bradstreet, Inc., Chgo., 1972-73; gen. mgr. Nat. Roofing Contractors Assn., Chgo., 1973-85, exec. v.p., Rosemont, Ill., 1987—; dir. mktg. Rand Devel. Corp., San Antonio, 1985-86; co-owner GT Communications, Inc., Dallas, 1985-87. Mem. Am. Soc. Assn. Execs. (cert.), Inst. for Orgn. Mgmt. (chmn. 1990-91), Chgo. Soc. Assn. Execs. (pres. 1996-97). Republican. Presbyterian. Avocations: tennis, photography. Office: Nat Roofing Contractors Assn 10255 W Higgins Rd Rosemont IL 60018-5606

GOODALE, JAMES CAMPBELL, lawyer, media executive, television producer/host; b. Cambridge, Mass., July 27, 1933; s. Robert Leonard and Eunice (Campbell) G.; m. Toni Krissel, May 3, 1964; children: Timothy Fuller, Ashley Krissel; foster child: Joseph Clayton Akiwenzie. Grad., Pomfret Sch., 1951; BA, Yale U., 1955; JD, U. Chgo., 1958. Bar: N.Y. 1960. Assoc. Lord, Day and Lord, N.Y.C., 1959-63; gen. atty. N.Y. Times Co., 1963-67, gen. counsel, 1967-72, sr. v.p., 1972-73, exec. v.p., 1973-79, vice-chmn., 1979-80; ptnr. Debevoise and Plimpton, 1980-93, founder, head media-comm. and intellectual property sect., 1980—, mem. exec. com., 1981-84, of counsel, 1994-96; co-prodr., host The Telecom. and Info. Revolution, Ch. 25 WNYE, N.Y.C., 1995—; with Cmty. Law Office, East Harlem, 1968-70; vis. lectr. Yale U. Law Sch., 1977-80; adj. prof. NYU Sch. Law, 1983-86, Fordham Law Sch., 1986—; affiliated scholar N.Y. Law Sch., 1995—; mem. N.Y. State Privacy and Security Com., 1976-79; 2nd cir. Commn. Reduction of Burdens and Costs in Civil Litigation, 1977-80; vice chmn. N.Y. State Jud. Commn. on Minorities, 1987-90, chmn., 1990-91, bd. dirs. com. to protect journalist, 1989—, chmn., 1989-94; mem. adv. bd. Comm. and the Law, 1980—; pres., owner Midtown Skating Corp., 1981-90; chmn. bd. Cable TV Law and Fin., 1981—; trustee N.Y.C. Citizens Budget Commn., 1990-98; advisor U.S. Supreme Ct. Jud. Conf. Com. on the Judiciary, 1980-89; chmn., founder PLI Comm. Law Seminar, 1972—. Author: All About Cable, 1987; compilor, editor: The New York Times Company vs. U.S., 1971; bd. editors: Media Law Reporter (co-founder), Nat. Law Jour., 1983—; columnist nat. and N.Y. law jours.; contbr. articles on comms. law to profl. jours. Mem. rules com. Dem. Nat. Conv., 1988; chmn. N.Y. lawyer com. for Dukakis, 1988; former bd. dirs. N.Y. Times, N.Y. Times Neediest Cases Fund, N.Y. Times Found.; former trustee Pomfret Sch., Gunnery Sch., St. Bernard's Sch., Boys' Club N.Y., Salzburg Seminar, Fed. Bar Coun.; mem. vis. com. U. Chgo. Law Sch., 1977-80; bd. dirs. Human Rights Watch, 1994-96, Sky Rink Scholarship Fund, Inc., 1990—, Citizens Pub. Utilities, 1996—, Internat. Ctr. Journalists, 1998—. With AUS, 1958-59, Res., 1959-64. Named one of 200 Rising Leaders in U.S., Time mag., 1974, with 100 Most Influential Lawyers in U.S., Nat. Law Jour., 1991-97, one of Best Lawyers in Am., 1991-99; William Brinckerhoff Jackson scholar, 1954-55, Nat. Honor scholar U. Chgo. Law Sch., 1955-58. Fellow Inst. Judicial Adminstrn., N.Y. State Bar Assn. (chmn. spl. com. on pub. access to info. and proc. 1979-84, spl. com. on media law 1985-92); mem. N.Y.C. Bar Assn. (chmn. comm. law com. 1978-83, mem. corp. law com. 1977-81), ABA (governing bd. comm. law forum, commn. on pub. understanding about law 1979-82), Fed. Bar Coun. (trustee 1980-84), Columbia U. Seminars on Media and Society. Clubs: Yale (gov. 1964-67), Century Assn, Economic, St. Elmo, Elihu (gov. 1966-70), Washington Corp. (gov. 1972-78). Office: Debevoise & Plimpton 875 3rd Ave Fl 23 New York NY 10022-6256

GOODALE, RALPH E., Canadian government minister; b. Regina, Sask., Can., Oct. 5, 1949; s. Thomas Henry and Winnifred Claire (Myers) G.; m. Pamela Jean Kendel, Feb. 8, 1986. BA, U. Regina, 1971; LLB, U. Sask., 1972. M.P. from Assiniboia, Sask. Ho. of Commons, Ottawa, 1974-79; leader Sask. Liberal Party, 1981-88; mem. Legis. Assembly from provincial riding Assiniboia-Gravelbourg, Sask., 1986-88; corp. sec. Pioneer Life Ins. Co., 1989-90, Soveriegn Life Ins. Co., 1990-93; M.P. from Wascana Ho. of Commons, Ottawa, 1993—; min. Nat. Resources Can., Can. Wheat Bd., Ont., 1997—; also min. Agr. and Agri-Food Com., Ottawa, 1993-97; fed. interlocutor for Metis and Non-States Indians, 1997—; parliamentary sec. to Min. Transport, Min. Wheat Bd., Pres. Privy Coun., 1974-79. Active polit. coms. Mem. Law Soc. Sask. Lutheran. Office: Natural Resources Canada, 407 Confederation Bldg, Ottawa, ON Canada K1A 0A6

GOODALE, TONI KRISSEL, development consultant; b. N.Y.C., May 26, 1941; d. Walter DuPont and Ricka Krissel; m. James Campbell Goodale, May 3, 1964; children: Timothy Fuller, Ashley Krissel, Clayton A. (Ward). AB cum laude, Smith Coll., 1963; student, U. Geneva, 1962-63; postgrad., Hunter Coll., 1964-65. Congl. intern Senator Keating U.S. Senate, Washington, 1963; broadcast analyst FCC, Washington, 1963-64; adminstrv. asst., dir. grant rsch. dept. Ford Found., N.Y.C., 1964-67, cons. pub. edn. dept., 1968-69; N.Y. rep. Smith Coll., N.Y.C., 1975-78, asst. dir. devel., 1978-79; pres. Goodale Assocs., N.Y.C., 1979-92, chmn., CEO, 1992—; mem. NYC 2000 Millennium Coun.; vis. com. continuing edn. New Sch. Social Rsch.; lectr., writer in field; mem. bd. advs. First Women's Bank; bd. dirs. N.Y. Outward Bound., mem. exec. com., chmn. alumni com. Columnist Fund Raising Mgmt. Bd. dirs. N.Y. Pub. Libr.; bd. dirs., mem. exec. com. Pen Am. Ctr.; mem. Women's Fgn. Policy Group; lectr. U.S. Naval Acad.; mem. alumnae fund com. Smith Coll., v.p. class, chmn. 25th reunion, Women's Forum; trustee, alumnae fund chmn., mem. alumnae coun.; bd. dirs. Brearley Sch.; mem. exec. com. Parents' Assn., St. Bernard's Sch.; mem. benefit com. N.Y. Philharmonic; trustee, bd. govs. Churchill Sch.; co-chmn. spl. events com. Carnegie Hall, The Joffrey Ballet Opening Gala; chmn. Coro Benefit Dinners; trustee N.Y. Inst. Child Devel.; mem. women's divsn. Legal Aid Soc.; mem. N.Y. com. Joffrey Ballet; mem. benefit com. Grosvenor House; vice chmn. N.Y.C. Opera Benefit, Peir Ctr. Benefit; mem. com. Sch. Am. Ballet; active Women's Forum. Mem. Am. Coun. Arts (vice-chmn. bd., exec. com., chmn. nat. patrons commn., chair long range planning com.), Nat. Cultural Alliance (bd. dirs.), Am. Assn. Fund-Raising Counsel (bd. dirs. trust for philanthropy), Nat. Assn. Fund Raising Execs., Assn. Healthcare Philanthropy, Brearley Sch. Alumnae Assn., Smith Coll. Alumnae Assn., Cosmopolitan Club, Smith Club, Washington Club, Seventh Regiment Armory Club, Doubles Internat. Club, Women's Forum. Office: 009 Madison Ave Ste 1112 New York NY 10022-4208

GOODALL, JACKSON WALLACE, JR., restaurant company executive; b. San Diego, Oct. 29, 1938; s. Jackson Wallace and Evelyn Violet (Koski) G.; m. Mary Esther Buckley, June 22, 1958; children: Kathleen, Jeffery, Suzanne, Minette. BS, San Diego State U., 1960. With Foodmaker, Inc., San Diego, 1963—, pres., 1970—, CEO, 1979—, also chmn. bd. dirs.; founder, bd. dir. Grossmont Bank, La Mesa, Calif.; bd. dirs. Thrifty Drug Stores Inc., Van Camp Seafood Inc., Ralcorp.; owner, dir., bd. dirs. San Diego Padres Baseball Club. Bd. dirs. Greater San Diego Sports Assn.; mem. Pres.'s Coun. San Diego State U.; chmn. Child Abuse Prevention Found.; dir. San Diego Hall Champions. Recipient Golden Chain award, 1982, Silver Plate award Internat. Foodsvc. Mfg. Assn., 1985; named Disting. Alumni of Yr. San Diego State U., 1974, 89, Golden Chain Operator of Yr. Multi Unit Food Svc. Operators, 1988, State of Israel Man of Yr., 1987, Citizen of Yr. City Club of San Diego, 1992, Marketer of Yr. Acad. Mktg. Sci., 1992, Manchester Cmty. Svc. award, 1997; inducted into San Diego Bus. Hall of Fame, 1992. Mem. Am. Restaurant Assn., Fairbanks Ranch Country Club (founder), Univ. Club of San Diego, San Diego Intercollegiate Athletic Coun., Kadoo Club of N. Am., La Jolla Country Club. Republican. Office: Foodmaker Inc 9330 Balboa Ave San Diego CA 92123-1598

GOODALL, JANE, anthropologist; b. London, Apr. 3, 1934; d. Mortimer Herbert and Vanne (Joseph) Morris-Goodall; m. Hugo Van Lawick, 1964 (div. 1974); one child, Hugo Eric Louis; m. Derek Bryceson, 1975 (dec. 1980). PhD, Cambridge U., Eng., 1965. Asst., sec. to Dr. Louis S. B. Leakey Coryndon Meml. Mus. Nat. History, Olduvai Gorge, Tanzania; rschr. in animal behavior, sci. dir. Gombe Stream Rsch. Ctr., Tanzania, 1960—; vis. prof. psychiatry, human biology Stanford U., 1970-75; hon. vis. prof. zoology U. Dar Es Salaam, Tanzania; lectr. Yale U., 1973; disting. adj. prof. occupl. therapy and anthropology U. So. Calif., 1990—; Andrew D. White prof.-at-large Cornell U., 1996—. Author: In the Shadow of Man, 1961, My Friends, the Wild Chimpanzees, 1967, The Chimpanzees of Gombe, 1986, Through a Window, 1990, (with Dale Peterson) Visions of Caliban: On Chimpanzees and People, 1993; contbg. author: Primate Behavior, 1965, Primate Ethology, 1967, American Handbook of Psychiatry, 1976, Understanding Chimpanzees, 1990. Recipient conservation award N.Y. Zool. Soc., Franklin Burr award Nat. Geographic Soc. (2), Kyoto prize, 1976, Centennial award, 1988, Hubbard Medal, 1995, Tanzanian medal, 1996, Pub. Svc. awrd Nat. Sci. Bd., 1998, John Hay award Orion Soc., 1998. Mem. Am. Acad. Arts. and Scis. (hon. fgn.). Office: Jane Goodall Inst PO Box 14890 Silver Spring MD 20911-4890*

GOODALL, LEONARD EDWIN, public administration educator; b. Warrensburg, Mo., Mar. 16, 1937; s. Leonard Burton and Eula (Johnson) G.; m. Lois Marie Stubblefield, Aug. 16, 1959; children: Karla, Karen, Greg. BA, Central Mo. State U., 1958; MA, U. Mo., 1960; PhD (Kendrick C. Babcock fellow), U. Ill., 1962; AA (hon.), Schoolcraft Coll., 1977. Asst. prof. polit. sci., asst. dir. Bur. Govt. Research, Ariz. State U., Tempe, 1962-65; bur. dir. Bur. Govt. Research, Ariz. State U., 1965-67; assoc. prof. polit. sci., assoc. dean faculties U. Ill. at Chgo. Circle, 1968-69, vice chancellor, 1969-71; chancellor U. Mich., Dearborn, 1971-79; pres. U. Nev., Las Vegas, 1979-85; prof. mgmt. and pub. adminstrn. U. Nev., 1985—; cons. Ariz. Acad., Phoenix, 1964-67; dir. Peace Corps tng. program for Chile, 1965; vice chmn. bd. Comml. Bank of Nev., 1993—. Contributing editor, Canadian Moneysaver, 1997—; Author: The American Metropolis: Its Governments and Politics, 1968, rev. edit., 1975, Gearing Arizona's Communities to Orderly Growth, 1965, State Politics and Higher Education, 1976, When Colleges Lobby States, 1987, Managing Your TIAA-CREF Retirement Accounts, 1990, The World Wide Investor, 1991, Nevada Government and Politics, 1996; editor: Urban Politics in the Southwest, 1967. Mem. univ. exec. com. United Fund, 1966-67; v.p. Met. Fund, Inc.; mem. Mich. Gov.'s Commn. Long Range Planning, 1973-75, Tempe Planning and Zoning Commn., 1965-67, New Detroit Com., 1972-79; mem. Wayne County (Mich.) Planning Comm., 1973-79, vice chmn., 1976-79; mem. exec. bd. Clark County chpt. NCCJ, 1979-86; bd. dirs. Nev. Devel. Authority, 1980-86, Boulder Dam coun. Boy Scouts Am., 1980-89; bd. dirs. Nev. Power Co. Consumer Adv. Coun., 1984-90, chmn., 1986-89. Served with AUS, 1959. Mem. Am. Polit. Sci. Assn., Am. Soc. Pub. Adminstrn. (chpt. pres. 1989-90), Western Govtl. Rsch. Assn. (exec. coun. 1966-68), Dearborn C. of C. (dir. 1974-79), Phi Sigma Epsilon, Phi Kappa Phi Found. (bd. dirs. 1994-96). Lodge: Rotary. Home: 6530 Darby Ave Las Vegas NV 89146-6518 Office: U Nev Dept Pub Adminstrn Las Vegas NV 89154

GOODBERRY, DIANE JEAN (OBERKIRCHER), mathematics educator, tax accountant; b. Buffalo, June 24, 1950; d. Ralph Arthur and Muriel Carol (Glaeser) O.; m. Lawrence D. Goodberry, Sr. BS in Math. Edn., State Univ. Coll., Brockport, N.Y., 1972, MS in Ednl. Adminstrn., 1974. Cert. in secondary math. edn., N.Y. Uni-Pay clk. Marine Midland Bank, Buffalo, 1968-72; asst. registrar State Univ. Coll., Brockport, 1972-74; home instrn. tutor Clarence (N.Y.) Ctrl. Sr. H.S., 1974-75; part-time inst. Erie C.C., Buffalo, 1975-86; instr. math. Ednl. Testing Methods, Buffalo, 1984-90, Buffalo Pub. Sch. System, 1974—; mem. curriculum devel. com. Buffalo Pub. Schs., 1988, 92—, yearbook advisor 1994—; cooperating tchr. BRIET-U. Buffalo, 1990-96; part-time tax acct. Vol., World Univ. Games, Buffalo, 1993. Mem. AAUW, Women Tchrs. Assn. (bd. dirs., v.p. 1993-94, pres. 1994-96, rec. sec. 1996-98, treas. 1998—), Assn. Math. Tchrs. N.Y. State (conf. spkr.), Theodore Roosevelt Rough Riders, Nat. Coun. Math. (conf. spkr.). Republican. Methodist. Avocations: crafts, reading, travel, sports. Home: 10644 Crump Rd Holland NY 14080-9303 Office: South Park HS 150 Southside Pkwy Buffalo NY 14220-1552

GOOD-BLACK, EDITH ELISSA (PEARL WILLIAMS), writer; b. Hollywood, Calif., Jan. 10, 1945; d. Jack Brian and Rose Marie (Miller) Good; m. Michael Lawrence Black, Dec. 18, 1986. BA in English, Calif. State U., Northridge, 1974. Author, pub. Gull Press, L.A., 1990-95, Tal-San Pub./Distributing, Glendale, Ariz., 1995—; participant numerous dance, art, music and lit. classes; dancer Hajde Dance Troop, Berkeley, Calif., 1962-66; artist/one-woman shows in L.A., 1962-95; art collected in Libr. of Congress, Washington, 1990-95; singer coffee houses, cafe, night clubs, half-way houses, librs., others., L.A., 1986-96; contbr. poetry to numerous publs. and radio and internet broadcasts; author: (pseudonym Pearl White) The Trickster of Tarzana, 1992, Short Stories, 1995, Mad in Craft, 1995, Missives, 1995, others. Supporter Westside Women's Ctr., Venice, Calif., 1971-79; fundraiser, del. to local convs. Beverly Hills and Marina del Ray, Calif. Dem. Clubs, 1974-79. Mem. Mensa, Am. Soc. Composers, Authors, and Pubs. Home: 335 N Stanley Ave # 220 Los Angeles CA 90036-6205

GOODBY, JEFFREY, advertising agency executive. Grad., Harvard Univ., 1973. Political reporter Boston; began advt. career with J. Walter Thompson; with Hal Riney & Ptnrs. San Francisco; co-chmn., creative dir. Goodby, Silverstein & Ptnrs., San Francisco, 1983—.

GOODCHILD, ROSINA ANN, community health nurse; b. Streator, Ill., Nov. 28, 1963; d. David Floyd and Reita Mae (Keith) Allen; m. Robert Joseph Goodchild, June 4, 1988; children: Christopher Robert, Matthew James, Nathan Charles. AAS in Nursing, Ill. Valley Community Coll., 1984; BSN, Bradley U., 1988. RN, Ill. Camp nurse, counselor YMCA/CETA, Streator, 1983; pvt. duty nurse Streator, 1982-85; staff nurse emergency/trauma dept. St. James Hosp., Pontiac, Ill., 1984-88; charge nurse, preceptor ARC, Peoria, Ill., 1988-94; immunization nurse La Salle County Health Dept., Ottawa, Ill., 1992-94; mem. nursing adv. com. Heart of Ill. Blood Svcs., ARC, 1985-88. Spl. events coord. Village of Grand Ridge, Ill., 1995—; feature and staff writer for "Round the Ridge," 1995—; youth choir dir., 1995—; mem. Boy Scouts Am., 1998—, local charter rep., com. chairperson, 1998—, Tiger Cub coach, 1998—, day camp mgmt. dir., 1999—. Mem. ANA, Ill. Nurses Assn., Emergency Nurses Assn. Home: PO Box 233 400 Sylvan Ave Grand Ridge IL 61325-0233

GOODE, ANN, civil rights administrator. Staff assoc. com. on minorities in engring. NRC; work on nat. civil rights policy issues U.S. Commn. on Civil Rights, 1980-86; assoc. dir. Office of Civil Rights, EPA, various position Office of Air and Radiation, dir. human resources, chief of staff, acting dep. asst. adminstr., dir. civil rights,; instr. Morgan State U., Am. U.; dir. career devel. and spl. projects Howard. U. Sch. Comm. Office: EPA 401 M St SW # Mc1201 Washington DC 20460-0002

GOODE, BARRY PAUL, lawyer; b. N.Y.C., Apr. 11, 1948; s. Hy and Charlotte (Langer) G.; m. Erica Tucker, Sept. 1, 1974; children: Adam, Aaron. AB magna cum laude, Kenyon Coll., 1969; JD cum laude, Harvard U., 1972. Bar: Mass. 1972, Calif. 1975, Hawaii 1995, U.S. Dist. Ct. Mass. 1972, U.S. Dist. Ct. (no. dist.) Calif. 1975, U.S. Dist. Ct. (ctrl. dist.) Calif. 1983, U.S. Ct. Appeals (9th cir.) 1976, U.S. Ct. Appeals (6th cir.) 1999, U.S. Supreme Ct. 1986. Spl. asst. Sen Adlai E. Stevenson III, Washington, 1972-74; assoc. McCutchen, Doyle, Brown & Enersen, San Francisco, 1974-80, ptnr., 1980—. Co-author: Federal Litigation Guide, 1985. Advisor Gov.'s Com. to Review Water Law, San Francisco, 1979; bd. dirs. Stanford Pub. Interest Law Found., 1979-82; bd. dirs. Coro No. Calif., 1997—. Mem. San Francisco Bar Assn. (exec. com. environ. law sect. 1989-91). Office: McCutchen Doyle Brown & Enersen 3 Embarcadero Ctr San Francisco CA 94111-4003

GOODE, CLEMENT TYSON, retired English language educator; b. Richmond, Va., July 10, 1929; s. Clement Tyson and Bessie Mae (Trimble) G.; m. Jane Anderson, Aug. 19, 1952; children: Sara Elizabeth, Robert Clement. BA, Hendrix Coll., 1951; MA, Vanderbilt U., 1953, PhD, 1959. Instr. English Vanderbilt U., Nashville, 1954-56; instr. English, Baylor U., Waco, Tex., 1957-58; asst. prof., 1958-60, asso. prof., 1960-63, prof., 1963-97; prof. emeritus Baylor U., Waco, Tex., 1997—; Exchange prof. Seinan Gakuin U. Fukuoka, Japan, 1972-73. Author: (with Oscar Santucho) A Comprehensive Bibliography of Secondary Materials in English: George Gordon, Lord Byron with a Review of Research, 1976, George Gordon, Lord Byron: A Comprehensive, Annotated Research Bibliography of Secondary Materials in English 1973-1994, 1997. Mem. adv. bd. Salvation Army, Waco, 1968-69; deacon First Bapt. Ch., 1970—. So. Fellowship Fund grantee, 1956-57; named Outstanding Tchr., Student Congress, Baylor U., 1971; recipient Outstanding Tchr. award Baylor U., 1985. Mem. MLA, South Central MLA, Coll. Conf. Tchrs. English, Byron Soc., Keats Shelley Assn., Nat. Council Tchrs. English. Democrat. Home: 2720 Braemar St Waco TX 76710-2119

GOODE, DAVID RONALD, transportation company executive; b. Vinton, Va., Jan. 13, 1941; s. Otto and Hessie M. (Maxey) G.; m. Susan Skiles, June 22, 1963; children: Christina, Martha. AB, Duke U., 1962; JD, Harvard U., 1965. Bar: Va. 1965. Tax atty. Norfolk & Western Ry., Roanoke, Va., 1965-66, asst. gen. tax atty., 1967, gen. tax atty., 1968-70, dir. taxation, 1971-81; asst. v.p. taxation Norfolk So. Corp., Roanoke, 1982-85, v.p. taxation, 1985-91, exec. v.p. adminstrn., 1991, pres., 1991-92, chmn., pres., CEO, dir., 1992—; bd. dirs. Assn. Am. R.R., Bus. Com. for Arts Caterpillar, Inc., C. of C. of U.S.A., Ga.-Pacific Corp., Tex. Instruments, Inc., TRINOVA Corp., Va. Econ. Devel. Partnership. Bd. trustees Gen. Douglas MacArthur Meml. Found., Hollins Coll., Va. Found. Ind. Colls.; bd. visitors Fuqua Sch. Bus., Duke U.; mem. Am. Soc. Corp. Execs., Bus. Adv. Coun. Northwestern U., Bus. Roundtable, Coal Industry Adv. Bd.; Gov.'s Adv. Coun. on revenue Estimates: co-chair Hampton Road's Partnership; vice-chmn. Kennedy Ctr. Corp. Fund Bd.; Nat. Freight Transp. Assn., Nat. Grain Car Coun., Norfolk Mil./Civilian Liaison Group, Transp. Rsch. Bd. Exec. Com., Va. Bus. Coun., Va. Bus. Higher Edn. Coun. Mem. ABA, Va. Bar Assn., Roanoke Bar Assn., Norfolk Bar Assn., Bayville Golf Club, East Lake Golf Club, Princess Anne Country Club, Harbor Club, Hunting Hills Country Club, Laurel Valley Golf Club, The Links, Met. Club, Norfolk Yacht and Country Club, Shenandoah Club, Town Point Club, Virginian Golf Club. Democrat. Presbyterian. Avocations: golf, tennis. Home: 7301 Woodway Ln Norfolk VA 23505-3149 Office: Norfolk So Corp 3 Commercial Pl Norfolk VA 23510-2108*

GOODE, ERICA TUCKER, internist; b. Berkeley, Calif., Mar. 25, 1940; d. Howard Edwin and Mary Louise (Tucker) Sweeting; m. Bruce Tucker (div. 1971); m. Barry Paul Goode, Sept. 1, 1974; children: Adam Nathaniel, Aaron Benjamin. BS summa cum laude, U. Calif., Berkeley, 1962, MPH, 1967; MD, U. Calif., San Francisco, 1977. Diplomate Am. Bd. Internal Medicine. Chief dietitian Washington Hosp. Ctr., Washington, 1968; pub. health nutritionist Dept. Human Resources, Washington, 1969-73; intern Children's Hosp. (now Calif. Pacific Med. Ctr.), San Francisco, 1977-78, resident, 1978-80, chief med. resident internal medicine, 1979-80; pvt. practice internal medicine San Francisco, 1980—; expert witness med.-legal issues, Calif., 1990—; lectr., tchr. med. house staff C.P.M.C. Hosp., 1982—; assoc. prof. medicine U. Calif., San Francisco, 1984—. Contbr. articles to profl. publs. Co-chair Physicians for Clinton, No. Calif., 1992, 96. Mem. AMA, ACP, Calif. Med. Assn., Calif. Soc. Internal Medicine, San Francisco Med. Soc., U. Calif. Alumni Assn. (del.), Alpha Omega Alpha (named Best Doctor's list 1996-98). Office: Goode Brayer Dobrow Watanabe & Liberman 3801 Sacramento St # 100 San Francisco CA 94118-1625

GOODE, JEAN, publishing company executive; b. Phila., Nov. 12, 1927. BA in Edn., U. Pa., 1949. Profl. musician, 1943-70; v.p. Whitson Pub. Co. Inc., Troy, N.Y., 1969-78; chmn., pres. Whitson Pub. Co. Inc., Troy, N.Y., 1978—. Former bd. dirs. Rensselaer County Coun. for the Arts, Rensselaer County Hist. Soc., Troy Pub. Libr. Recipient 1st Place award Nat. Piano Tchrs. Assn. Contest for Young Artists, 1948. Office: Whitson Pub Co Inc PO Box 958 Troy NY 12181-0958*

GOODE, JOHN MARTIN, manufacturing company executive; b. Chgo., Sept. 24, 1934; s. Robert C. and Alyce (Belz) G.; children: John Martin, Sue Ellen, James Edward, Leslie Maureen. B Commerce, DePaul U., 1960; MBA, U. Chgo., 1966; EdD, No. Ill. U., 1984. CPA, Ill.; CMA, Ill. Contr. farm equipment div. Allis Chalmers, Milw., 1966-69; v.p., contr. Maremont Corp., Chgo., 1969-73; sr. v.p. Whittakers Corp., Chgo., 1973-75; assoc. dean DePaul U., Chgo., 1976-78, asst. prof., 1975-80; sr. v.p. fin. and corp. planning J.I. Case Co., Racine, Wis., 1980-85; chmn. bd., chief exec. officer Prestolite Electric Inc., Toledo, 1986-91; dean Sch. Mgmt. and Bus. Nat. U.,

San Diego, 1991-93; investor, 1993—; chmn. bd. dirs., CEO K&W Products, LLC, Bloomington, Ind., 1996—; bd. dirs. A.P. Labs, Inc., San Diego, Ohmite Mfg. Co., Chgo., Rescue Industries Inc., San Diego, Integrated Insights, San Diego, Internat. Forum for Corp. Dirs., San Diego. Mem. San Diego Yacht club, Univ. Club, Del Mar Country Club. Home: 5050 La Jolla Blvd Apt 3-c San Diego CA 92109-1709

GOODE, PAUL, educational consultant, psychologist; b. Bklyn., Nov. 14, 1937; s. Arthur and Bertha (Rose) G.; m. Judith Granich, June 22, 1960; children: Lawrence J., Andrew P., Joshua S. BA in Psychology, Bklyn. Coll., 1959; MA in Sch. Psychology (rsch. asst.), Syracuse U., 1962; EdD in Sch. Psychology (doctoral fellow 1967-68), Temple U., 1972. Unemployment ins. claims examiner N.Y. State Employment Service, Cortland, 1961-62; sch. psychologist Steuben County Bd. Coop. Ednl. Services, Bath, N.Y., 1962-66, Camden (N.J.) Bd. Edn., 1966-67; sch. psychologist Delaware County Bd. Sch. Dirs., Media, Pa., 1967-68, intern psychologist, 1968-69 ; sch. psychologist specialist Phila. Non-Public Elem. Schs., 1969-70; assos. dir. clin. ednl. services project King of Prussia (Pa.) Intermediate Unit # 23, 1970-73; coordinator suburban unit Nat. Regional Resource Center of Pa., King of Prussia, 1971-74, asso. dir., 1974-75; dir. Pa. Area Learning Resources Center, Doylestown, 1975-77; dir. IEP devel. program Bucks County (Pa.) Intermediate Unit # 22, Doylestown, 1977-79, coordinator fed. programs in spl. edn., 1979-81; acting dir. spl. edn., 1980-81; asst. exec. dir. and dir. spl. edn., 1981-93; mem. adj. faculty Temple U., Phila., 1988—; pvt. practice Melrose Park, Pa., 1993—; vis. prof. Universidad de Antioquia (Colombia), 1964-65; part-time instr. Corning (N.Y.) Community Coll., 1965-66, Cabrini Coll., Radnor, Pa., 1972; instr. diagnosis of ednl. disabilities Pa. State U., Ogontz, 1972-84. Treas., Cub Scout pack 190, 1970-80; mgr. Old York Rd. Little League, 1970-80. Recipient Alumni award Temple U., 1980. Fellow Pa. Psychol. Assn. (editor divsn. newsletter 1975-77, pres. sch. psychology divsn. 1978-79, pres. 1981-82); mem. APA (divsn. 16), Coun. Exceptional Children, Coun. Orgn. Edn. (pres. 1989-90), Pa. Assn. Sch. Adminstrs., Pa. Assn. Pupil Personnel Adminstrs., Phi Delta Kappa. Asso. editor Archives, newsletter NRRC/P, 1970-72. Home and Office: 7610 Montgomery Ave Elkins Park PA 19027-2901

GOODE, RICHARD BENJAMIN, economist, educator; b. Ft. Worth, July 31, 1916; s. Flavius M. and Laura Nell (Carson) G.; m. Liesel Gottscho, June 23, 1943. A.B., Baylor U., 1937; M.A., U. Ky., 1939; Ph.D., U. Wis., 1947. Economist U.S. Bur. Budget, 1941-45, Treasury Dept., 1945-47; asst. prof. econs. U. Chgo., 1947-51; with IMF, Washington, 1951-59, 65-81, dir. fiscal affairs dept., 1965-81; mem. staff Brookings Instn., Washington, 1959-65, guest scholar, 1981-87; professorial lectr. Sch. Advanced Internat. Studies, Johns Hopkins U., 1981-88; cons. Treasury Dept., 1947-51, UN, 1950, World Bank, 1964. Author: The Corporation Income Tax, 1951; The Individual Income Tax, 1964, rev. edit., 1976; Government Finance in Developing Countries, 1984; Economic Assistance to Developing Countries through the IMF, 1985. Editor Nat. Tax Jour, 1948-51. Mem. Am. Econ. Assn., Royal Econ. Soc., Nat. Tax Assn. (Holland medal for contbns. to study and practice of pub. fin. 1997), Internat. Inst. Pub. Fin., Cosmos Club. Home: 5420 Connecticut Ave NW Washington DC 20015-2813

GOODE, STEPHEN HOGUE, publishing company executive; b. Charlotte, N.C., Dec. 25, 1924; s. Henry Grady and Marie Louella (Creamer) G.; m. Jean Cameron Advena, Oct. 16, 1953; children: Elizabeth Whitston Joane Downe, Polly Turpin Dulcinea Hogue. B.A., U. Md., 1948; M.A., U. Pa., 1954, Ph.D., 1958. Asst. prof. English Rensselaer Poly. Inst., 1958-59; asst. prof. Fairleigh Dickinson U., 1960-65; dir. libraries, asso. prof. English Russell Sage Coll., 1965-78; pres., chmn. bd. Whitston Pub. Co., Troy, N.Y., 1968-81, Turpin Book Corp., Troy, 1973-80; pres. Penkevill Pub. Co., Greenwood, Fla., 1982—; dir. Trenowyth Pub. Co., Penkivil Book Co. Author: Index to Little Magazines, 1943-47, 1965, Index to Little Magazines, 1940-42, 1967, Index to Commonwealth Little Magazines, 1966-67, 68, plus, biennial, Index to American Little Magazines, 1920-39, 1969, 1900-1919, 1974; editor: Studies in 20th Century, 1968-75; founding editor Am. Humanities Index, 1978-82. Served with AUS, 1943-46, 49-52. Decorated Purple Heart, Bronze Star with oak leaf cluster. Mem. MLA, Am. Hist. Assn., Bibliog. Soc. (London), Bibliog. Soc. Am., Bibliog. Soc. U. Va., Index Soc. (London). Club: Grolier (N.Y.C.).

GOODE, VIRGIL H., JR., congressman; m. Lucy D. Dodson; 1 child, Catherine S. BA, U. Richmond, 1969; JD, U. Va., 1973. Mem. Va. Senate, 1973-97, 105th-106th Congress from 5th Va. dist., 1997—; mem. agr. com. 105th Congress from 5th Va. dist., mem. small bus. com. Recipient Outstanding Legis. Svc. award Va. State Sheriffs' Assn., Outstanding Svc. award Vol. Rescue Squads, 1994. Mem. Phi Beta Kappa, Omicron Delta Kappa, Lambda Chi Alpha, Phi Alpha Delta. Baptist. Office: Ho of Reps 1520 Longworth HOB Washington DC 20515-4605*

GOODE, WILLIAM JOSIAH, sociology educator; b. Houston, Aug. 30, 1917; s. William J. and Lillian Rosalie (Bare) G.; m. Josephine Mary Cannizzo, Dec. 22, 1938 (div. 1946); children: Brian Erich, Rachel (dec.), Barbara Nan; m. Ruth Siegel, Oct. 20, 1950 (div. 1971); 1 son, Andrew Josiah. B.A., U. Tex., 1938, M.A., 1939; Ph.D., Pa. State U., 1946; D.Sc. (hon.), Upsala U., 1970. Instr. sociology Pa. State U., 1941-43; social sci. analyst Inter-Am. Statis. Inst., 1943-44; asst. prof. Wayne State U., 1946-50; asso. research dir. Columbia U., 1950-52, asso. prof. sociology, 1952-56, prof., 1956-74, Giddings prof. sociology, 1975-77; prof. Stanford U., 1977-86, prof. emeritus, 1986—; assoc. Harvard U., 1986-92; vis. prof. Hebrew U., Jerusalem, 1992-93; rsch. assoc. sociology George Mason U.; prof. Free U. Berlin, 1954; vis. fellow Wolfson Coll., Oxford U., 1980; U.S. del. UN Conf. Aid to Tech. Undeveloped Nations, 1963; bd. dirs., sec. Social Sci. Research Council; gov., asso. dir. Bur. Applied Social Research; mem. behavioral scis. tng. com. Nat. Inst. Gen. Med. Scis., NIMH, 1966-67; vis. scholar Nat. Acad. Scis., China, 1986; vis. prof. Hebrew U., Jerusalem, 1992-93. Author: Religion Among the Primitives, 1951, Methods in Social Research, 1952, After Divorce, 1956, Struktur Der Familie, World Revolution and Family Patterns, 1963, The Family, 1964, 82, Family and Society, 1965, Dynamics of Modern Society, 1966, Explorations in Social Theory, 1973, (with L. Mitchell and F. Furstenberg) Willard Waller: On the Family, Education and War, 1970, Principles of Sociology, 1977, The Celebration of Heroes: Prestige as a Social Control Process, 1979, World Changes in Divorce Patterns, 1993; co-author: The Other Half, 1971, Social Systems and Family Patterns, 1971; editor: series Sociol, 1953; assoc. editor: Marriage and Family Living, 1956; contbr. articles to profl. jours. Served with USNR, 1944-45. Guggenheim fellow, 1965-66, 83-84; sr. scientist career grantee NIMH, 1969-74; Russell Sage Found. fellow, 1983-84; recipient MacIver award Am. Sociol. Soc., 1965, Burgess award Nat. Council Family Relations, 1969, Merit award Eastern Social Soc., 1992. Fellow Am. Acad. Arts and Scis.; mem. Am. Sociol. Soc. (exec. com., council 1959-62, pres. 1971-72), Eastern Sociol. Soc. (pres. 1959-60, exec. com. 1959-61), ACLU (dir.), Sociol. Research Assn. (exec. council, pres. 1967—). Home: 5427 Ladue Ln Fairfax VA 22030-4620

GOODE-HADDOCK, CELIA ROSS, title company executive; b. Bryan, Tex., May 22, 1950; d. Phillip Barron and Sara June (Council) Goode; m. Wallace Leonard Williams, Jan. 13, 1968 (div. 1969); 1 child, Quinn Williams; m. Robert Sherman Stallings, Aug. 19, 1972 (div. 1986); children: Ashley, Leigh; m. Billy Dan Haddock, Dec. 11, 1994. BS, Tex. A&M U., 1972. Sec. Univ. Title Co., College Station, Tex., 1972-77; mgr. Univ. Title Co., 1977-83; pres., 1983—; adv. com. Ticor Title Ins., Dallas, 1988-90; mem. adv. com. for continuing edn. State Bd. Ins., Austin, 1989-91. Election judge Brazos County, Tex., 1983—; mem. loan com. Community Devel. Loan Com., College Station, 1988-91; commr. Brazos County Ctrl. Appraisal Dist., 1985-95; mem. adv. com. Congressman Joe Barton, 1987-92; bd. dirs. Humana Hosp. of Brazos Valley, 1988-91, Tex. A&M U. Pvt. Enterprise Rsch. Ctr., 1996—, Tex. A&M 12th Man Found., 1988-97, Tex. A&M/Bryan Coll. Sta. Coun., 1995—; legisleader Tex. A&M U., 1997; bd. dirs. Columbia Hosp. Brazos Valley, 1994-96, vice chmn. bd., 1996; pres. Brazos Valley Devel. Coun. Revolving Loan Fund; publicity chmn. Family Outreach, 1988-90, bd. dirs., 1995—; pres. bd. trustees Christ Meth. Ch., 1996—; vol. Sta. KAMU-TV, 1979—, active in past numerous civic and polit. orgns.; mem. Operation Child Save Task Force, 1990-92; mem. Real Estate Rsch. Adv. Com., 1997—; divsn. leader Brazos County United Way, others. Winner Newman 10 award Bryan Rotary Club; recipient Rotary Internat. Jean Harris award, 1998. Mem. Tex. Land Title Assn. (legis. chmn. 1990—, Outstanding Young title Person 1982), Bryan/College Station Bd. Realtors (Affiliate of Yr. 1985), Bryan College Station Homebuilders Assn., Bryan/College Station C. of C. (v.p. for leadership 1994-96, v.p. adminstrn. 1996-97, chmn. elect 1997-98, chmn. 1998—), Tex. A&M/Bryan College Station Coun Bd., Opera and Performing Arts Guild (chmn.), Leadership Brazos Alumni Assn. (Outstanding Alumni award for Leadership 1996). Methodist. Avocations: reading, movies, theater, dancing, singing. Office: Univ Title Co 1021 University Dr E College Station TX 77840-2120

GOODELL, JOHN DEWITTE, electromechanical engineer; b. Omaha, Nebr., Sept. 20, 1909; s. Edwin Dewitte and Vera May (Watts) G.; m. Bernadette Michel, Apr. 27, 1943; children: Mary, Greg, Thomas, Caroline, Daniel. Cons. engr. N.Y.C., 1931-41; tech. dir. U.S. Army Detroit Signal Lab., 1941-43; dir. engring. Minn. Electronics, St. Paul, 1946-57; mgr. new product design CBS Lab., Stamford, Conn., 1957-60; dir. engring. Robodyne, U.S.Industries, Silver Spring, Md., 1960-61; corp. tech. dir. U.S. Industries, N.Y.C., 1962-63; producer Goodell Motion Pictures, St. Paul, 1964-75; cons. engr. New Product Design, St. Paul, 1976-90; exhibit prototyper Sci. Mus. of Minn., St. Paul, 1990-93; dir. engring. Tomorrow's World, St. Paul, 1993—. Author: The World of Ki, 1967; writer, dir. (motion picture) Always a New Beginning, 1973, (acad. nominated best documentary 1973), (TV documentary) Wisdom and Change, 1992; dir. Challenge for Tomorrow, 1964 (indsl. Oscar); inventor: automatic mail handler, automatic manipulator, magnetic pulse controlling device, conditioned reflex teaching machines and others, 1954—; editor Jour. of Computing Systems, 1965-70. With U.S. Navy, 1943-46, S. Pacific. Recipient Master Design award, Product Engring., 1962. Mem. IEEE (sr.), Soc. Motion Picture and TV Engrs. Avocations: Oriental Game of Go (capt. U.S team 2nd place winners Internat. Go Cong., 1964). Home: 751 Mt Curve Blvd Apt 5 Saint Paul MN 55116-1113

GOODELL, JOSEPH EDWARD, manufacturing executive; b. El Paso, Tex., Aug. 18, 1937; s. Joseph Edward and Grace Louise (Beck) g.; m. Margaret Rives, Aug. 12, 1961 (di. June 1978); children: Marian, Margaret Trout, Martha, Maryellen Olszyk; m. Mary Ellen Hager, Sept. 17, 1993. BSME, MIT, 1959; MBA, Harvard U., 1961. Project engr. Bechtel Corp., San Francisco, 1961-65; mfg. engr. Chase Brass and Copper Co., Cleve., 1965-67; adminstrv. mgr. Montpelier, Ohio, 1967-69, Waterbury, Conn., 1969-71; v.p., gen. mgr. Montpelier, 1971-76; group v.p. Chase Brass and Copper Co., Cleve., 1976-79, Pangborn div. Carborundum, Hagerstown, Md., 1979-81; v.p. planning Standard Oil Ind. Products, Cleve., 1981-82, sr. v.p., 1982-85; pres., chief exec. officer Am. Brass Co., Buffalo, N.Y., 1985-94; chmn. bd. West Tex. and Buffalo Steam Ship & Rwy. Co., N.Y., 1991—; bd. dirs. Nitto Metals, Tokyo, 1974-79, TWI Properties, El Paso, Tex., 1975-93, Tech. Devel. Corp., Buffalo, Tech. Bldg. Corp., Boston. Active Boy Scouts Am., Waterbury, Conn.; past chmn. Buffalo Health Care Coalition; vice chmn. Greater Buffalo Partnership; chmn. Horizons Waterfront Commn.; dir. Downtown Devel., Inc.; dir. Buffalo State Coll. Found.; exec. dir. Buffalo Philharm. Orch.; chmn., CEO West Tex. and Buffalo Steamship and Railway Co.; chmn. planning com. Buffalo Expo Pan Am. 2001. Recipient Spl. award Buffalo Philharm. Orch., 1999; named Citizen of Yr. Buffalo, 1996. Mem. Country Club of Buffalo, Buffalo Club. Home: 6746 Lakeshore Dr Dearby NY 14047

GOODELL, SOL, retired lawyer; b. St. Louis, Aug. 24, 1906; s. Abram and Jennie (Silverberg) G.; m. Beatrice Cholden, Feb. 24, 1946 (dec. Mar. 1998); children: Thomas C., Susan Jean. LLB, U. Tex., 1929. Bar: Tex. 1929. Asso. prof. law U. Tex. Law Sch., 1929-30; asso., then mem. firm Thompson & Knight, and predecessors, Dallas, 1930-76, of counsel, 1976—. Former chmn. bd. Greenhill Sch., Dallas; former trustee bd. devel. U. Tex., Dallas; former trustee, v.p. Excellence in Edn. Found.; former sec., trustee Goals for Dallas; former trustee Dallas Grand Opera Assn.; former pres. Found. for Callier Ctr. and Communication Disorders. Served to capt. AUS, 1942-46. Mem. ABA, Dallas Bar Assn., State Bar Tex., Columbian Country Club. Jewish (trustee, past pres. temple). Home: 5927 Joyce Way Dallas TX 75225-1626 Office: 1700 Pacific Ave Ste 3300 Dallas TX 75201-4656

GOODEN, BENNY L., school system administrator. Supt. Ft. Smith (Ark.) Pub. Schs. State finalist Nat. Supt. Yr. award, 1993. Office: Ft Smith Pub Schs 3205 Jenny Lind Rd Fort Smith AR 72901-7101

GOODEN, DWIGHT EUGENE, professional baseball player; b. Tampa, Fla., Nov. 16, 1964; s. Dan and Ella Mae G.; m. Monica Colleen Harris, Nov. 21, 1987. Pitcher minor league teams, Kingsport, Little Falls and Lynchburg, 1982-83, N.Y. Mets, Nat. League, 1984-96, Cleveland Indians, 96-; mem. Nat. League All-Star Team, 1984-86, 88. Named Pitcher of Yr., Carolina League, 1983, Rookie of Yr., Nat. League, 1984, Rookie Pitcher of Yr., Nat. League, 1984; winner Cy Young award Nat. League, 1985; first major league pitcher to record 200 strikeouts in each of first 3 seasons. Office: Cleveland Indians 2401 Ontario St Cleveland OH 44115

GOODEN, PAMELA JOYCE, lawyer; b. Tuscaloosa, Ala., Nov. 21, 1954; d. Robert Joseph and Betty Jo (Bullock) G.; m. Johnnie Wade Hope, Apr. 26, 1980 (div. Feb. 1984); m. James Douglas Cook, Aug. 3, 1985; children: Cullen, Connor. BA, Judson Coll., 1975; JD, U. Ala., 1978. Bar: Ala. 1978, U.S. Dist. Ct. (mid. dist.) Ala. 1980, U.S. Ct. Appeals (11th cir.) 1993. Staff atty. Legal Svcs. of Ala., Montgomery, 1978-80; assoc. Segrest & Pilgrim, Montgomery, 1980-82; ptnr. Pilgrim & Gooden, Montgomery, 1983-92; pvt. practice Montgomery, 1992—. Mem. ABA, Ala. Bar Assn., Soroptimist Internat. (2d v.p. 1981-82, 1st v.p. 1984-85, pres. 1985-86, corr. sec. 1989-90), So. States Llama Assn., Alpaca and Llama Show Assn. Baptist. Avocations: camping, hiking, fishing, travel, gourmet cooking, llama farming. Fax: (334) 834-5331. E-mail: gooden@earthlink.net. Home: 2443 Belcher Dr Montgomery AL 36111-2147 Office: Pamela J Gooden Atty at Law 1138 S McDonough St Montgomery AL 36104-5044

GOODENBERGER, DANIEL MARVIN, medical educator; b. McCook, Nebr., Apr. 24, 1948; s. Marvin Eugene and Mary Ellen (Marshall) G.; m. Janet Ann King, July 30, 1979; children: James Michael, Katherine Elizabeth. BS, U. Nebr., 1970; MD, Duke U., 1974. Diplomate Am. Bd. Internal Medicine, Am. Bd. Emergency Medicine (examiner 1983-95), Am. Bd. Pulmonary Disease, Am. Bd. Critical Care Medicine. Intern Peter Bent Brigham Hosp., Boston, 1974-75, resident in internal medicine, 1975-76; clin. assoc. Nat. Cancer Inst., Bethesda, Md., 1976-78; fellow pulmonary and critical care medicine Boston U. Med. Ctr., 1985-88; assoc. dir. emergency dept. Arlington (Va.) Hosp., 1979-82; edn. dir. emergency dept. Georgetown U. Hosp., Washington, 1982-85; dir. emergency svcs. U. Hosp., Boston, 1986-87; dir. pulmonary and critical care fellowship Washington U. Med. Schs., St. Louis, 1989-93; dir. pulmonary cons. svcs. Barnes Hosp., St. Louis, 1990-93, dir. internal medicine residency program, 1992—; assoc. prof. medicine Washington U., St. Louis, 1995—; dir. divsn. med. edn. Washington U. Sch. Medicine, St. Louis, 1998—; chief Wood-Moore Firm, Barnes-Jewish Hosp., 1996—. Editor Careers, 1996-98. Lt. comdr. USPHS, 1973-78. Winthrop Breon and Am. Coll. Chest Physicians scholar, 1987. Fellow ACP, Am. Coll. Chest Physicians; mem. AMA, Am. Thoracic Soc., Assn. Program Dirs. Internal Medicine (nominating and publs. com. 1991-98), St. Louis Met. Med. Soc. (councilor 1997—), Phi Beta Kappa, Alpha Omega Alpha. Methodist. Avocations: theatre, symphony music, travel. Home: 4615 Lindell Blvd Saint Louis MO 63108-3726 Office: Washington U Sch Medicine Box 8121 660 S Euclid Ave Saint Louis MO 63110-1010

GOODENOUGH, ANDREW LEWIS, publishing executive; b. Norwalk, Conn., Aug. 21, 1955; s. James Hinchman and Gloria (Cleworth) G.; m. Susan Whitton, Oct. 4, 1980; children: Kathryn, Kyle, James. BA in Econs. and Am. Lit., Middlebury (Vt.) Coll., 1977; MBA in Fin., NYU, 1982. Spl. asst. to gen. mgr. Perkin-Elmer Corp., Norwalk, 1977; mktg. mgr. Cleworth Pub. Co., Cos Cob, Conn., 1977-83, pub. Financial Computing mag., 1983-85; pub. U.S. Banker mag., Greenwich, Conn., 1985-91; pres. Kalo Comms. Inc., Greenwich, Conn., 1985-92; exec. v.p. Faulkner & Gray, N.Y.C., 1993—; pub. U.S. Banker. Past pres. bd. trustees Rye (N.Y.) Presbyn. Ch. Mem. Fin. Communications Soc. (bd. dirs.), Assn. Bus. Pubs., Westchester Country Club (Rye). Republican. Home: 25 Mohawk St Rye NY 10580-1715

GOODENOUGH, JOHN BANNISTER, engineering educator, research physicist; b. Jena, Germany, July 25, 1922; came to U.S., 1922; parents Am. citizens.; s. Erwin Ramsdell and Helen Meriam (Lewis) G.; m. Irene Johnston Wiseman, June 16, 1951. AB, Yale U., 1943; MS, U. Chgo., 1951, PhD, 1952; D honoris causa, U. Bordeaux, France, 1967; MA (hon.), U. Oxford, Eng., 1976. Rsch. engr. Westinghouse Rsch. Corp., 1951-52; rsch. scientist, group leader Lincoln Lab., MIT, 1952-76; prof., head inorganic chem. lab. U. Oxford, Eng., 1976-86; centennial prof. engring. U. Tex., Austin, 1986—; cons. numerous firms in U.K. and U.S.; trustee, fellow Neuroscis. Rsch. Program, 1962-76; Centenary lectr. Royal Soc. Chemistry, 1976; vis. Raman prof. Indian Inst. Sci., 1983; hon. prof. Northwestern U., Changchun, China, 1996, Jilin U., Shenyang, China, 1996. Author: Magnetism and the Chemical Bond, 1963, Les Oxydes des métaux de transition, 1973; assoc. editor Materials Rsch. Bull., 1966—, Jour. Solid State Chemistry, 1968—, Structure and Bonding, 1977—, Solid State Ionics, 1980—, Superconductor Sci. and Tech., 1987, Jour. Materials Chem., 1991—, Chem. of Materials, 1989-92; mem. exec. editorial bd. Jour. Applied Electrochemistry, 1982-89, European Jour. Solid State and Inorganic chemistry, 1992—, contbr. over 500 articles to profl. jours. Capt. USAAF, 1942-48. Recipient Solid State Chemistry prize Chem. Soc. U.K., 1980, Sr. Rsch. award Am.Soc. for Engring. Edn., 1990; professorial fellow St. Catherine's Coll., Oxford U., 1976; recipient medal for disting. achievement U. Pa., 1996, John Bardeen award Minerals, Metals & Materials Soc., 1997. Fellow AAAS, Royal Soc. Chemistry, Am. Phys. Soc. (profl.), Indian Acad. Scis. (fgn. assoc.), Nat. Acad. Engring., Academie des Scis. L'Institut de France, Materials Rsch. Soc. (hon.); mem. Am. Chem. Soc., Materials Rsch. Soc. (Von Hippel award 1989), Japanese Phys. Soc., Ashmolean Club (Oxford), Skull and Bones, Phi Beta Kappa, Sigma Xi. Episcopalian. Home: 4311 Greystone Dr Austin TX 78731-1240 Office: U Tex. ETC 9.102 Austin TX 78712-1063

GOODENOUGH, WARD HUNT, anthropologist, educator; b. Cambridge, Mass., May 30, 1919; s. Erwin Ramsdell and Helen Miriam (Lewis) G.; m. Ruth Gallagher, Feb. 8, 1941; children: Hester G. Goodenough Gelber, Deborah L. Goodenough Gordon, Oliver R., Garrick G. Grad., Groton (Mass.) Sch., 1937; AB, Cornell U., 1940; PhD, Yale U., 1949. Instr. anthropology U. Wis., 1948-49; mem. faculty U. Pa., Phila., 1949—, prof. anthropology, 1962-89, university prof., 1980-89, emeritus univ. prof., 1989—, chmn. dept. anthropology, 1976-82; vis. prof. Cornell U., Ithaca, N.Y., 1961-62, vis. lectr., summer 1950; vis. lectr. Swarthmore Coll., spring 1955, Bryn Mawr Coll., fall 1955, U. Hawaii, summer 1959, 75-77; vis. prof. U. Wis., Milw., summer 1967, Yale U., New Haven, spring 1969, Colo. Coll., spring 1979, U. Hawaii, 1982-83; anthrop. studies in Truk, 1947, 64-65, Gilbert Islands, 1951, New Guinea, 1951, 54; Pacific Sci. bd. Nat. Acad. Scis.-NRC, 1962-66; standing com. anthropology and social scis. Pacific Sci. Assn., 1962-66; cons. Office Sci. and Tech., 1961-62. Author: Property, Kin and Community on Truk, 1951, Cooperation in Change, 1963, Explorations in Cultural Anthropology, 1964, Description and Comparison in Cultural Anthropology, 1970, Culture, Language and Society, 1971, Trukese-English Dictionary, 1980, 90. Bd. dirs. Human Rels. Area Files, Inc., 1964-86, chmn., 1971-81; bd. dirs. East Rock Inst., 1986-98, sec., 1995-98. With AUS, 1941-45. Fellow Center Advanced Study Behavioral Scis., 1957-58; Guggenheim fellow, 1979-80; Fulbright lectr. St. Patrick's Coll., Ireland, 1987. Mem. NAS, AAAS (v.p., chmn. sect. H 1971, bd. dirs. 1972-75), Am. Philos. Soc., Am. Acad. Arts and Scis., Royal Anthrop. Inst., Am. Anthrop. Assn. (editor 1966-70, Disting. Svc. award 1986), Am. Ethnol. Soc. (pres. 1962), Soc. Applied Anthropology (pres. 1963), Linguistics Soc. Am., Inst. on Religion in an Age of Sci. (pres. 1987-89), Polynesian Soc., Assn. Social Anthropology in Oceania, Phi Beta Kappa, Sigma Xi, Phi Kappa Phi. Office: Univ Penn Univ Museum Philadelphia PA 19104-6398

GOODENOW, ROBERT W., labor union administrator. Exec. dir. Nat. Hockey League Player's Assn., Toronto, ON, Canada. Office: Nat Hockey League Players Assn, 777 Bay St Ste 2400, Toronto, ON Canada M5G 2C8*

GOODES, MELVIN RUSSELL, retired manufacturing company executive; b. Hamilton, Ont., Can., Apr. 11, 1935; s. Cedric Percy and Mary Melba (Lewis) G.; children: Melanie, Michelle, David. B in Commerce, Queen's U., Kingston, Ont., Can., 1957; MBA, U. Chgo., 1960. Rsch. assoc. Can. Econ. Rsch. Assocs., Toronto, Ont., 1957-58; market planning coord. Ford Motor Co. Can., Oakville, Ont., 1960-64; asst. to v.p. O'Keefe Breweries, Toronto, 1964-65; mgr. new product devel. Adams Brands div. Warner-Lambert Can., Scarborough, Ont., 1965-68; area mgr. Warner-Lambert Internat., Toronto, 1968-69; regional dir. confectionary ops. Warner-Lambert Europe, Brussels, 1969-70; pres. Warner-Lambert Mex., 1970-76; pres. Pan-Am. zone Warner-Lambert Internat., Morris Plains, N.J., 1976-77, pres. Pan-Am. and Asian zone, 1977-79; pres. consumer products div. Warner-Lambert Co., Morris Plains, N.J., 1979-81, sr. v.p., pres. consumer products group, 1981-83, exec. v.p., pres. U.S. ops., 1984-85, pres., COO, 1985-91, chmn., CEO, 1991-99, also bd. dirs.; bd. dirs. Ameritech Corp., Chase Manhattan Bank, Unisys; mem. exec. adv. coun. Nat. Ctr. Ind. Retail Pharmacy, 1984-85. Bd. dirs. Coun. on Family Health, N.Y.C., 1981-86, Advt. Edn. Found., N.Y.C., 1989-91; mem. fin. com. Nat. Coun. on Econ. Edn., 1984—, mem. exec. com., 1986—; mem. Internat. Exec. Svc. Corps., 1989—; mem. adv. coun. Sch. of Bus. Queen's U., Kingston, Ont., Can., 1980-84; trustee Drew U., Madison, N.J., 1985-88, Queen's U., 1988—. Fellow Ford Found., 1958, Sears, Roebuck Found., 1959. Mem. Nat. Wholesale Druggists Assn. (assoc. adv. com.), Nat. Assn. Retail Druggists (exec. adv. coun. 1983-85), Pharm. Mfrs. Assn. (bd. dirs. 1989-91), Proprietary Assn. (v.p. 1983-88, bd. dirs., exec. com. 1981-88), Nat. Alliance Bus. (bd. dirs. 1984-86), Plainfield Country Club (N.J.), Pine Valley Golf Club (N.J.). Unitarian. Avocations: golf, tennis. Office: care Warner-Lambert Co 201 Tabor Rd Morris Plains NJ 07950-2693*

GOODEY, ILA MARIE, psychologist; b. Logan, Utah, Feb. 1, 1948; d. Vernal P. and Leona Marie (Williams) Goodey. BA with honors in English and Sociology, U. Utah, 1976; Grad. Cert. Criminology, U. Utah, 1976, MS in Counseling Psychology, 1984, PhD in Psychology, 1985. Speech writer for dean of students U. Utah, Salt Lake City, 1980-89, psychologist Univ. Counseling Ctr., 1984—; cons. Dept. Social Services, State of Utah, Salt Lake City, 1983—; pvt. practice psychology Consult West, Salt Lake City, 1985-86; pub. relations coordinator Univ. Counseling Ctr., 1985—; cons. Aids Project, U. Utah, 1985—; pvt. practice psychology, Inscapes Inst., Salt Lake City, 1987-88; writer civic news Salt Lake City Corp., 1980—; mem. Senator Orrin Hatch's Adv. Com. on Disability Oriented Legis., 1989—. Author book: Love for All Seasons, 1971, Poemspun, 1994, Echoes, 1995, Rapture, 1996; play: Validation, 1979; musical drama: One Step, 1984. Contbr. articles to profl. jours. Chmn. policy bd. Dept. State Social Service, Salt Lake City, 1986—; campaign writer Utah Dem. Party, 1985; appointed to Utah State Legis. Task Force on svcs. for people with disabilities, 1990; chmn. bd. Utah Assistive Tech. Program, 1990—. Recipient Creative Achievement award Utah Poetry Soc., 1974, English SAC, U. Utah, 1978, Leadership award YWCA, 1989, Nat. Golden Rule award J.C. Penny, Washington, 1989, 90, Volunteerism award State of Utah, 1990; Ila Marie Goodey award named in honor. Mem. AAUW, Am. Psychol. Assn., Utah Psychol. Assn., Internat. Platform Assn., Mortar Board, Am. Soc. Clin. Hypnosis, Utah Soc. Clin. Hypnosis, Soc. Psychol. Study Social Issues, League of Women Voters, Phi Beta Kappa, Phi Kappa Phi, Alpha Lambda Delta. Mormon. Clubs: Mormon Theol. Symposium, Utah Poetry Assn. Avocations: theatrical activities, creative writing, travel, political activities. Office: U Utah Counseling Ctr 2450 SSB Salt Lake City UT 84112

GOODFRIEND, HERBERT JAY, lawyer; b. N.Y.C., Sept. 9, 1926; s. Sidney and Blanche (Prager) G.; m. Barbara Gottlieb, Oct. 12, 1952; children: Sandra, Beth Ann. AB, NYU, 1947, LLB, 1950, LLM in Taxation, 1953. Bar: N.Y. 1950, U.S. Dist. Ct. (so. dist.) N.Y. 1951, U.S. Dist. Ct. (ea. dist.) N.Y. 1982, U.S. Ct. Appeals (2nd cir.) 1953, U.S. Tax Ct. 1954. Assoc. Otterbourg, Steindler Houston & Rosen, N.Y.C., 1950-55, ptnr., 1955-86; counsel Summit, Solomon & Feldesman, 1986-93, N.Y.C.; counsel Philips, Nizer, Benjamin, Krim & Ballon, 1993—; counsel N.Y. Bd. Trade, N.Y.C., 1981-87, bd. dirs., 1982-88; spl. master Supreme Ct. New York County, N.Y.C., 1977-79; vice chmn., bd. dirs. Jones Apparel Group, Inc., 1990-98., sec., 1990—. Columnist N.Y. Law Jour., 1977-79. With U.S. Army, 1945-46. Fellow Am. Bar Found., Coll. Law Practice Mgmt.; mem. ABA (chmn. econs. law practice sect. 1984-85, ho. of dels. 1994-97), N.Y. State Bar Assn. (chmn. com. on law office econ. and mgmt. 1983-85), N.Y. County Lawyers Assn. (com. on arbitration 1974-87), NYU Club (v.p. exec. com. 1976-80), Landmark Club, Adelphi U. Inst. for Paralegal Tng. (adv. bd. 1976-96), Am. Apparel Mfg. Assn. (fin. mgmt. com.), Tau Delta Phi (nat. pres. 1952-57). Avocations: golf; computers. Home: 176 E 71st St

New York NY 10021-5159 Office: Jones Apparel Group Inc 1411 Broadway New York NY 10018

GOODGAME, GORDON CLIFTON, minister; b. Jones County, Miss., Oct. 8, 1934; s. J. Clyde and Eloise Hertha (Smith) G.; m. Dianne Fraser, July 29, 1961; children: Gordon Clifton Jr., Gregory Carson, Cathey. BS in Law and Bus., U. Tenn., 1955; MDiv, Emory U., 1958; STM, San Francisco Theol. Sem., 1970, STD, 1974. Sr. min. 1st United Meth. Ch., Pulaski, Va., 1973-74; leader devel. cons. Holston Conf. Coun. Ministries, Johnson City, Tenn., 1974-77; sr. min. 1st United Meth. Ch., Oak Ridge, Tenn., 1977-81, 1st-Centenary United Meth. Ch., Chattanooga, 1981-90; dir. Holston Conf. Coun. Ministries, Johnson City, 1990-93; exec. dir. Southeastern Jurisdictional Adminstrv. Coun., Lake Junaluska, N.C., 1994—; del. United Meth. Gen. Conf., 1976, 80, 84, 88, 92, 96, Southeastern Jurisdictional Conf., United Meth. Ch., 1972, 76, 80, 84, 88, 92, 96; dir. United Meth. Bd. Global Ministries, N.Y.C., 1980-88; mem. World Meth. Coun., 1986-96; mem. United Meth. Gen. Coun. Ministries, 1992—. Bd. dirs. Chattanooga United Way, 1983-89, Hospice Chattanooga, 1982-90; trustee Hiwassee Coll., Madisonville, Tenn., 1979-90, pres. bd. trustees; trustee Meth. Med. Ctr. Oak Ridge, 1977-81. Mem. Emory U. Alumni Assn. (bd. govs.), Candler Sch. Theology Alumni Assn. (pres., Svc. award 1992), Rotary (sgt. at arms 1989-90). Democrat. Home: 2775 Lakeshore Dr Lake Junaluska NC 28745-8709 Office: SEJ Adminstrv Coun PO Box 67 Lake Junaluska NC 28745-0067 *The present day is the most fantastic of the ages. A growing sense of world interdependence is developing alongside an increased concern for justice and universal peace, while enhanced technology raises the possibility of a true world community. If we can only claim the highest truth and live faithfully by grace, humankind can become what God intends.*

GOODHEART, ADAM K., journalist; b. Phila., June 5, 1970; s. Bernard J. and Harriet G. (Kaufman) G. AB, Harvard Coll., 1992. Assoc. editor Civilization mag., Washington, 1994-96, sr. editor, 1996-97, sr. editor, writer, 1997-98; contbg. editor, columnist Civilization mag., N.Y.C., 1998—; bd. contbr. USA Today, Arlington, Va., 1998—; bd. incorporators, contbg. editor, Harvard Mag., Cambridge, 1996—. Editl. bd. The Am. Scholar, Washington, 1997—; acting deputy op-ed editor: The N.Y. Times, 1999; adv. editor: Preservation Mag., Washington, 1999—. Recipient Henry Russell Shaw fellowship Harvard U., 1992-93, Berta Greenwald Ledecky fellowship, 1991-92, McCord Writing prize, 1998; Nat. Merit scholar, 1988. Mem. Nat. Book Critics Circle. Home and Office: 1715 15th St NW Apt 16 Washington DC 20009-3876

GOODHEART, EUGENE, English language educator; b. Bklyn., June 26, 1931; s. Samuel and Miriam G.; m. Patricia Somer, Aug. 13, 1960 (div. July 1973); children: Eric, Jessica; m. Joan Bamberger, July 8, 1977. B.A., Columbia U., 1953, Ph.D. in English and Comparative Lit, 1961; M.A. in English, U. Va., 1954; postgrad. (Fulbright fellow), Sorbonne, U. Paris, 1956-57. Instr., then asst. prof. English, Bard Coll., 1958-62; asst. prof. U. Chgo., 1962-66; asso. prof. Mt. Holyoke Coll., 1966-67; asso. prof., then prof. MIT, 1967-74; prof., chmn. dept. English Boston U., 1974-83; Edytha Macy Gross prof. humanities Brandeis U., 1983—; vis. prof. Wesleyan U. Summer Sch., 1963, 64, 66, 69; Gauss seminarist Princeton U., 1972. Author: The Utopian Vision of D.H. Lawrence, 1963, The Cult of the Ego, 1968, Culture and the Radical Conscience, 1973, The Failure of Criticism, 1978, The Skeptic Disposition in Contemporary Criticism, 1984, Pieces of Resistance, 1987, Desire and Its Discontents, 1991, The Reign of Ideology, 1996. Fellow Am. Coun. Learned Socs., 1965-66, Guggenheim Found., 1970-71, NEH, 1980-81, Nat. Humanities Ctr., 1987—; resident Rockefeller Found., Bellagio. Mem. MLA, PEN. Home: 25 Barnard Ave Watertown MA 02472-3412

GOODHUE, MARY BRIER, lawyer, former state senator; b. London, 1921; naturalized, 1942; d. Ernest and Marion H. (Hawks) Brier; m. Francis A. Goodhue, Jr., May 15, 1948 (dec. Sept. 1990); 1 child, Francis A. III. BA, Vassar Coll., 1942; LLB, U. Mich., 1944. Bar: N.Y. 1945. Assoc. Root, Clark, Buckner & Ballantine, N.Y.C., 1945-48; asst. counsel N.Y. State Crime Commn., N.Y.C., 1951-53, Moreland Commn., N.Y.C., 1953-54; mem. firm Goodhue, Arons & Neary and predecessors, Mt. Kisco, 1955—; mem. N.Y. State Assembly from 93d Dist., 1975-78, N.Y. State Senate, 1979-92. Trustee Katonah Mus. Art, Vis. Nurse Assn., Hudson Valley, John Jay Homestead, St. Peter's Cmty. Outreach Ctr., Inc., Rep. Pro-Choice Alliance Polit. Action Com.; N.Y. del. Nat. Women's Conf., Houston, 1977. Mem. ABA, West Bar Assn., No. Westchester Bar Assn. Office: 126 Barker St Mount Kisco NY 10549-1502 also: Rock Gate Farm Rd Mount Kisco NY 10549

GOODHUE, PETER AMES, obstetrician and gynecologist, educator; b. Ft. Fairfield, Maine, Feb. 26, 1931; s. Lawrence and Zylpha (Ames) G.; m. Edith Ann Helfenstein, June 21, 1958; children: Lisa Grace, Scott Ames. BA, Amherst Coll., 1954; MD, U. Vt. 1958. Diplomate Am. Bd. Ob-Gyn. Intern Bellevue Hosp., N.Y.C., 1958-59; resident Yale-New Haven Med. Center, 1959-62; practice medicine specializing in ob-gyn, Stamford, Conn., 1964—; assoc. clin. prof. ob-gyn N.Y. Med. Coll. Contbr. articles to profl. jours. Served to capt. USAF, 1962-64. Recipient Carbee prize, U. Vt., 1958. Fellow ACS, Am. Fertility Soc., Am. Coll. Obstetricians and Gynecologists (chmn. Conn. sect. 1976-76, pres. Conn. sect. 1973-76), Am. Soc. For Colposcopy and Cervical Pathology, Am. Assn. Of Gynecologic Laproscopists; mem. Conn. Med. Soc., Conn. Soc. Am. Bd. Obstetricians and Gynecologists (pres. 1973-76), Fairfield County Med. Soc., Fairfield County Gynecol. and Obstet. Soc., Stamford Med. Soc. (pres. 1989-90). Republican. Episcopalian. Office: Stamford Gynecology PC 70 Mill River St Stamford CT 06902-3725

GOODIN, EVELYN MARIE, writer; b. Fullerton, Calif.; d. Theodore Hopper and Nellie Mary (Henger) DeWitt; m. Robert Delmer Goodin, Feb. 23, 1950; 1 child, Michael Warren. AA, Fullerton Jr. Coll., 1942; BA, U. Calif., Santa Barbara, 1946. Tchr. Bakersfield (Calif.) City Schs., 1947-50, Stockton (Calif.) City Schs., 1950-58, San Juan Unified Schs., Carmichael, Calif., 1958-82. Author: (poetry) The Young West Sings, 1940, (children's book) The Greatest Living Scientist, 1993; editor: (poetry anthology) First the Blade, 1942; writer radio show Uncle Punkle Show, 1951. Registrar Selective Svc. Sys., Bakersfield, 1948; vol. tchr. Sacramento Safety Ctr., 1985; sec. Suburban Writers Club, Sacramento, 1986-87; mem. Fremont Presbyn. Fremont Presbyterian Inspiration Recreation Svc., 1992-96; with Friendship Inspiration Recreation Svc. Recipient First Prize in Poetry, Creative Arts Coun. Fullerton Jr. Coll., 1942, Recognition award for extended profl. svc. San Juan Tchrs. Assn., 1982; named Disting. mem. Internat. Soc. Poets, 1998. Mem. Whitney Lunch Bunch, Calif. Ret. Tchrs. Assn. (mailing com. N.E. sect. 1994-96), Sports Leisure Travel Club. Avocations: music, reading, politics, decorating, travel. Home: 5705 River Oak Way Carmichael CA 95608-5549

GOODING, CHARLES ARTHUR, radiologist, physician, educator; b. Cleve., Feb. 28, 1936; s. Joseph J. and Florence G. (Pitt) G.; m. Gretchen Wagner, June 19, 1961; children: Gunnar, Justin, Britta. BA, Western Res. U., 1957; MD, Ohio State U., 1961. Intern Ohio State U. Hosp., 1961-62; resident in radiology Peter Bent Brigham Hosp., Children's Hosp. Med. Center, both Boston, 1963-65; rsch. fellow radiology Harvard Med. Sch., Boston, 1962; tchg. fellow Harvard Med. Sch., 1965-66; Harvard Med. Sch. fellow Hosp. for Sick Children, London, Karolinska Hosp., Stockholm, 1966; faculty U. Calif. Med. Center, San Francisco, 1967—; prof. radiology and pediatrics U. Calif. Med. Center, 1976—, exec. vice-chmn. dept. radiology, 1974—; pres. Radiology Rsch. and Edn. Found., 1973—, Radiology Outreach Found., 1988—; hon. mem. faculty Francesco Maroquin U. Sch. Medicine, Guatemala City. Contbr. chpts. to books.; Editor: Pediatric Radiology, 1973—; editor: Diagnostic Radiology, 1972—; contbr. articles to profl. jours. Capt. M.C. USAR, 1967-68. Recipient Outstanding Alumni award Brigham Women's Hosp. Harvard Med. Sch., Disting. Alumnus award Ohio State U., 1986, Case Western Res. U., 1999, Beclere medal Internat. Soc. Radiology; named to Disting. Alumni Hall of Fame Cleve. Heights H.S., 1999. Fellow Am. Coll. Radiology, Coll. Radiologists (hon.), Royal Coll. Radiologists London (hon.), Armenian Radiol. Soc. (hon.); mem. Am. Roentgen Ray Soc., Assn. Univ. Radiologists, European Soc. Pediat. Radiologists (hon.), Pacific Coast Pediat. Radiologists Assn., Radiol. Soc. N.Am., Polish Radiology Soc. (hon.), Hungarian Radiology Soc. (hon.), San Francisco Med. Soc., Soc. Pediat. Radiology (v.p. 1994, pres. 1997 pres. SPR rsch. and edn. found. 1993-96, chmn., bd. dirs. 1998), Rocky Mountain Radiol. Soc. (hon.), Australian Soc. for Pediatric Imaging (hon.), Chinese Radiol. Soc. (hon.), Swiss Radiol. Soc. (hon.), Malaysian Radiol. Soc. (hon.), French Soc. of Radiology (hon.), Indian Radiol. and Imaging Soc. (hon.), Radiol. Soc. of Pakistan (hon.), Indonesian Radiol. Soc. (hon.), Mongolian Nat. Radiol. Assn. (hon.), Nepal Radiol. Soc. (hon.), Armenian Med. Diagnostic Assn. (hon.). Home: 8 Overhill Rd Mill Valley CA 94941-1378 Office: U Calif Med Ctr Dept Radiology San Francisco CA 94143

GOODING, CHARLES THOMAS, psychology educator, retired college provost; b. Tampa, Fla., Nov. 18, 1931; s. Charles T. and Gladys (Bingman) G.; m. Shirley Ann Puckett, June 7, 1953; children: Steven Thomas, Carol Ann, David Lee, Mark Charles. B.A., U. Fla., 1954, M.Ed., 1962, Ed.D., 1964; postgrad., U. Tampa, 1956-58. Tchr. Meml. Sch., Tampa, 1956-58; asst. prin., then prin. St. Mary's Sch., Tampa, 1958-62; grad. fellow U. Fla., Gainesville, 1962-63, instr., 1963-64; assoc. prof., then prof. SUNY, Oswego, 1964-79, prof. psychology, 1980—, assoc. dean grad. studies, 1982-89, dean grad. studies and rsch., 1989-95, provost, v.p. for acad. affairs, 1995-98, emeritus, 1998—; vis. prof. U. Liverpool, Eng., 1979-80; mem. SUNY Chancellor's Task Force on Tchr. Edn., 1984; grad. fellow U. Fla., Gainesville, 1962-63. Author: Learning Theories in Educational Practice, 1971; contbg. author: Florida Studies in the Helping Professions, 1969, Questioning and Discussion: A Multidisciplinary Study, 1988, Research Matters to the Science Teacher, 1992; contbr. articles to profl. jours. Bd. dirs. Oswego County unit Am. Cancer Soc., N.Y., 1972-74, 82-84; mem. commn. on ordination Episcopal Diocese Central N.Y., 1980-95; bd. dirs. Lancaster Career Devel. Ctr., 1984-95, Oswego Coll. Found., 1996—. Served to 1st lt. USAR, 1954-56. SUNY Rsch. Found. grantee, 1966, 69, 70; N.Y. State Dept. Edn. grantee, 1971-72, 88-94; NSF grantee, 1980-81, 85-88, 90-95. Mem. AAAS, APA, Ea. Ednl. Rsch. Assn. (v.p. 1979-81, treas., dir. 1983-85, pres.-elect 1987-88, pres. 1989-91, editorial bd. 1991-98), Brit. Ednl. Rsch. Assn., Am. Ednl. Rsch. Assn. (chair ednl. enterprises SIG, 1994-96), Nat. Assn. for Rsch. in Sci. Teaching. Avocation: antique and classic automobiles, Jaguar sports cars specialist. Home: 2861 W River Rd 603 Wild Pine Way Venice FL 34292-4618 Office: SUNY Provost's Office 702 Culkin Hall Oswego NY 13126-3500

GOODING, CUBA, JR., actor; b. Bronx, N.Y., Jan. 2, 1968; s. Cuba, Sr. and Shirley Gooding. Films include: Coming to America, 1988, Sing, 1989, Boyz N the Hood, 1991, Gladiator, 1992, A Few Good Men, 1992, Hitz, 1992, Judgement Night, 1993, Lightning Jack, 1994, Losing Isaiah, 1995, Outbreak, 1995, Jerry Maguire, 1996 (Golden Globe nomination, Academy award for Best Supporting Actor, 1997), The Audition, 1996, As Good As It Gets, 1997, What Dreams May Come, 1998, A Murder of Crows, 1999, Instinct, 1999; TV movies include: Kill or Be Killed, 1990, Murder with Motive: The Edmund Perry Story, 1992, Daybreak, 1993. Office: Rogers & Cowan 1888 Century Park E Ste 500 Los Angeles CA 90067-1709*

GOODING, DAVID MICHAEL, lawyer, mediator; b. Jacksonville, Fla., June 10, 1952; s. Marion William and Eunice (Drawdy) G.; m. Cathy Rhoden, Aug. 3, 1974; chidlren: Sara Lynn, John Thomas Gooding. BA, U. Fla., 1974; JD, U. Miami, 1988. Asst. state atty. Office of State Atty., Jacksonville, Fla., 1988-89; assoc. Penland & Penland, P.A., Jacksonville, 1989-92; shareholder Kent, Ridge & Crawford, Jacksonville, 1992-97, Kent, Crawford & Gooding, Jacksonville, 1997—; bd. dirs. Anastasia Advertising Art, Inc., St. Augustine, Fla., 1990-97, Samaritan Counseling Ctr., Jacksonville, 1990-94. Bd. dirs. Girls, Inc., Jacksonville, 1997—, Southside United Meth. Preschool, Jacksonville, 1995-97; adult tchr. Christ Ch., 1994-96—, nursery vol., 1991-94; elder South Jacksonville Presbyn. Ch., 1991-94. Mem. ABA, Fla. Bar, Fla. Trial Lawyers Assn., Jacksonville Trail Lawyers Assn., Masons, Scottish Rite of Freemasonery, Royal Order of Jesters, Shriners (1998 imperial conv. com. counsel 1995—), Christian Legal Soc. (trustee 1997—). Democrat. Presbyerian. Avocations: running. Office: Kent Crawford & Gooding 225 Water St Ste 900 Jacksonville FL 32202-5142

GOODING, JUDSON, writer; b. Rochester, Minn., Oct. 12, 1926; s. Arthur Faitoute and Frances (Judson) G.; m. Françoise Ridoux, June 21, 1952; children: Anthony, Amélie, Timothy. Grad. with honors, Yale U., 1948; diplome d'Études Françaises, U. Paris, 1950. Staff writer Dept. Army, Hdqrs. EUCOM, Germany, 1950-52; script writer Affiliated Film Producers, N.Y.C., 1952-53; news writer WCCO-CBS, Mpls., 1953; reporter Mpls. Tribune, 1953-57, Life mag., N.Y.C., 1957-60; fgn. corr. Life mag., Paris, 1960-62, Time mag., Paris, 1962-65; chief of bur. Time-Life News Service, San Francisco, 1966-68; edn. editor Time mag., N.Y.C., 1968-69; assoc. editor Fortune mag., 1969-73; v.p. Urban Research Corp.; also editor Trend Report, Chgo., 1973-75; mng. partner Trend Analysis Assocs., 1975—; exec. editor Next Mag., N.Y.C., 1979-81; contbg. editor Next Mag., 1981-82; counselor for pub. affairs U.S. Permanent Del. to UNESCO, 1982-84; vis. lectr. in journalism U. Paris, Ecole Nationale d'Administration, also Togo, Kenya, Zaire, Senegal and Nigeria; writing cons. UN, Ford Found., Am. Assembly, also corps.; vis. lectr. in journalism, Barbados, Grenada, Dominica, Haiti and Martinique. Author: The Job Revolution, 1972; contbr. to: American Dreams, The Environment, The Hippies, The Survival Equation, The Failure of Success; Contbr. articles to popular mags. and profl. jours. Bd. patrons Wilson Ctr., Faribault, Minn.; mem. program com. Internat. Found. for Cultural Cooperation, Courchevel, France; trustee Friends of John Jay Homestead, Walpole Hist. Soc. Served with USNR, 1944-46. Recipient 1st place award U. Mo. Sch. Journalism Penney-Mo., 1980, hon. certificate Program Mgmt. Devel. Harvard U. Grad. Sch., Disting. Alumnus award Middlesex Sch., 1994. Mem. Inst. Current World Affairs (elected), Common Cause, World Future Soc., Nat. Trust Hist. Preservation, Am. Soc. Journalists and Authors, Mensa. Clubs: Elizabethan (New Haven); Century Assn. (N.Y.C.), Yale (N.Y.C.); Bedford Bicycle Polo (founder, co-capt.); Polo de Paris, The Travellers (Paris). Office: Old North Main St PO Box 745 Walpole NH 03608-0745

GOODING, ROBERT C., engineering administrator; b. New Orleans, June 27, 1918. BS, U.S. Naval Acad., 1941; MS, MIT, 1946. Commd. ensign USN, 1940; ret., 1976, cons., 1976—; chmn. Columbia Rsch. Corp., Arlington, Va., 1980—; instr. calculus Pratt Inst., Bklyn., 1958-62/. Recipient Gold medal Am. Soc. Naval Engrs., 1988, Saunders award ASME, 1989. Mem. NAE, Sigma Xi. E-mail: rgooding@columbiaresearch.com. Office: Columbia Rsch Corp 2531 Jefferson Davis Hwy Arlington VA 22202-3905*

GOODKIN, MICHAEL JON, publishing company executive; b. N.Y.C., June 10, 1941; s. Harold and Rose (Mostkoff) G.; m. Helen Graham Fairbank, Oct. 1, 1971; children: Graham Laird, Nathalie Fairbank. BA, Harvard U., 1963; postgrad., U. Chgo., 1964. Trainee Random House, N.Y.C., 1964-65; asst. dir. Simulmatics, N.Y.C., 1966-67; account exec. World Book Ency., Inc., Chgo., 1967-70; rsch. dir. World Book Ency., Inc., 1970-73, v.p. mktg., 1973-76, v.p., gen. mgr. mail order div., 1976-78, pres., chief operating officer, 1978-86, chmn., chief exec. officer, pres., dir., 1983; exec. v.p. World Book Inc., 1978-84, pres., 1984-86, sr. v.p., 1979-80; exec. v.p., corp. dir. mktg., dir. World Book Internat. Inc., 1983-84; dep. dir. World Book Pty. Ltd., Australia, 1983-86; pres. World Book Life Ins. Co., 1983; prin. Chgo. City Capital Group, 1987-91; chmn. Med. Holdings, Inc., Chgo., 1987-91; sr. v.p. mktg. internat. P.F. Collier, N.Y.C., 1992-94, pres., 1994-96; pres.-dir. KT holdings, 1988—. Mem. editl. adv. bd. Jour. Interactive Mktg. Bd. dirs. Chgo. Area Project; pres. aux. bd. Art Inst. Chgo., 1975-77, trustee, 1975—, chmn. mktg. com., mem. 20th century com., mem. devel. com., long range planning com.; trustee Modern Poetry Assn.; trustee Latin Sch. Chgo., 1983-92, chmn. ednl. policy com., sec., 1988, pres., 1990-92, mem. long range com., com. on trustees, 199-93; trustee DMA Edn. Found., 1983-94, mem. exec. com., 1988-94; mem. vis. com. visual arts U. Chgo. With Army N.G., 1963-69. Mem. Direct Mktg. Assn. (internat. coun. steering com. 1983), Direct Selling Assn. (internat. com. 1982-86), Racquet Club, Harvard Club (N.Y.C.), Harvard Club (Boston), Csino Club, Saddle and Cycle Club (Chgo.). *

GOODKIN, RICHARD ELLIOT, French educator, writer; b. Chgo., Sept. 15, 1953; s. Ben Goodkin and Minnie (Becker) Green. BA, Swarthmore Coll., 1975; MA, Princeton U., 1979, PhD, 1981. Asst. prof. French Yale U., New Haven, Conn., 1980-86; assoc. prof. French Yale U., New Haven, 1986-89; assoc. prof. French U. Wis., Madison, 1989-92, prof. French, 1992—; cons. in field. Author: The Symbolist Home and The Tragic Home, 1984, The Tragic Middle, 1991, Around Proust, 1991; editor: Autour de Racine, 1989; translator: Proust Between Two Centuries, 1992; contbr. articles to profl. jours. Recipient Whiting Humanities fellowship, 1979-80, Ind. Rsch. fellowship NEH, 1984-85, Sidonie Miskimin Clauss prize for tchg. excellence Yale Coll., 1987. Mem. MLA, N.Am. Soc. for French Seventeenth Century Lit., Phi Beta Kappa. Avocations: swimming, cycling, photography. Office: U Wis Dept French Italian 618 Van Hise Hall 1220 Linden Dr Madison WI 53706-1525

GOODKIND, CONRAD GEORGE, lawyer; b. Arlington, Va., Aug. 8, 1944; s. Bernard Arthur and Sylvia (Lieber) G.; m. Sandra Timme, Aug. 27, 1966; children: Carley M., Adam B., Erica L., Anne G. BS, U. Wis., 1966, JD, 1969. Bar: Wis. 1969, U.S. Dist. Ct. (ea. and we. dists.) Wis. 1969. Assoc. Kivett & Kasdorf, Milw., 1969-71; counsel Citizens' Study Com. on Jud. Orgn., Madison, Wis., 1971-73; dep. commr. securities State of Wis., Madison, 1973-79; assoc. Quarles & Brady, Milw., 1979-81, ptnr., 1981—; adj. prof. securities law U. Wis. Law Sch., Madison, 1975-79, Marquette U. Law Sch., Milw., 1981-83; mem. Gov.'s Bus. Cts. Task Force, 1994—, state regulation com. Nat. Assn. Securities Dealers, Inc., Washington, 1986-92; bd. dirs. Able Distbg. Corp.; bd. dirs., sec. Cade Industries, Inc., 1989—. Bd. dirs. Milw. Repertory Theatre, 1995—, exec. com. mem., 1997—. Mem. ABA (vice chmn. state regulation securities com. 1986-89, chmn. 1989-92), Wis. Bar Assn. (chmn. securities com., 1981-95, bd. dirs. sect. bus. law 1991—, vice chair sect. bus. law 1996-98, chair 1998—). Office: Quarles & Brady 411 E Wisconsin Ave Ste 2550 Milwaukee WI 53202-4497

GOODKIND, LOUIS WILLIAM, lawyer; b. St. Paul, Aug. 29, 1914; s. Leo and Grace (Goldsmith) G.; m. Jean Wald Morgenthau, Apr. 8, 1942 (dec. July 1975); children: Barbara Goodkind Pepper, Mary Goodkind Garner, Kathryn Goodkind Boyle; m. Carol Eaton Bourquin, Oct. 30, 1976; stepchildren: Philip F. Eaton, Dorothee R. Bourquin Caulfield. BA, Yale U., 1936, JD, 1939. Bar: N.Y. 1939, D.C. 1951. Pvt. practice N.Y.C., 1939-40; asst. U.S. atty. So. Dist. N.Y., 1940-43; with CAB, Washington, 1943-52; sr. atty. CAB, 1943-46; assoc. dir. Bur. Econ. Regulation, 1946-51; dep. dir. Bur. Air Operations, 1951-52; chief econ. def. div. Dept. State, Washington, 1952-56; ptnr. Zimet, Haines, Friedman & Kaplan (and predecessor firms), 1956-78, of counsel, 1979-95; guest lectr. air transp. Am. U., 1946-51; acting village justice, Irvington, N.Y., 1971-72; mem. U.S. delegations 3d Session Facilitation div. Internat. Civil Aviation Orgn., Buenos Aires, 1951, Consultative Group, Paris, 1954, Four Power Fgn. Ministers Meeting, Geneva, 1955. Mem. Village Dem. Com., Irvington, N.Y., Town Dem. Com., Greenburgh, N.Y., County Dem. Com., Westchester, N.Y., 1964-71; past pres., trustee Green Acres Sch., Rockville, Md.; corp. mem., past dir. and corp. sec. Neighborhood Playhouse, Inc., N.Y.C.; sec. Yale Law Sch. Class of 1939, 1939-93, class agt. Yale Law Sch. Fund.; mem. exec. com. Yale Law Sch. Assn., 1981-85, v.p., 1986-88; mem. exec. com. Yale Coll. Class of 1936. Mem. Phi Beta Kappa, Phi Delta Phi, Yale Club (N.Y.C.). Home: 5 Daisy Ln Irvington NY 10533-2016

GOODLAD, JOHN INKSTER, education educator, author; b. North Vancouver, B.C., Can., Aug. 19, 1920; s. William James and Mary (Inkster) G.; m. Evalene M. Pearson, Aug. 23, 1945; children: Stephen John, Mary Paula. Teaching certificate, Vancouver Normal Sch., 1939; BA, U. B.C., 1945, MA, 1946; PhD, U. Chgo., 1949; DPS (hon.), Brigham Young U., 1995; LHD (hon.), Nat. Coll. Edn., 1967, U. Louisville, 1968, So. Ill. U., 1982, Bank Street Coll. Edn., 1984, Niagara U., 1989, SUNY Coll. Brockport, 1991, Miami U., 1991, Linfield Coll., 1993, W.Va. U., 1998; LLD (hon.), Kent State U., 1974, Pepperdine U., 1976, Simon Fraser U., 1983, U. Man., 1992; DEd (hon.), Eastern Mich. U., 1982, U. Victoria, 1998; LittD (hon.), Montclair State U., 1992; PedD (hon.), Doane Coll., 1995. Tchr. Surrey Schs., B.C., 1939-41; prin. Surrey Schs., 1941-42; dir. edn. Provincial Sch. For Boys, B.C., 1942-46; cons. curriculum Atlanta Area Tchr. Edn. Service, 1947-49; assoc. prof. Emory U., 1949-50; prof., dir. div. tchr. edn. Agnes Scott Coll. and Emory U., 1950-56; prof., dir. U. Chgo. Center Tchr. Edn., 1956-60; prof., dir. Univ. Elem. Sch. UCLA, 1960-85, dean Grad. Sch. Edn.., 1967-83; prof. U. Wash., Seattle, 1985-91; prof. emeritus, 1991—; dir. Ctr. for Ednl. Renewal U. Wash., Seattle, 1986—; pres. Inst. for Ednl. Inquiry, Seattle, 1992—; chmn. Coun. on Coop. Tchr. Edn., Am. Coun. Edn., 1959-62; dir. rsch. Inst. for Devel. of Ednl. Activities, 1966-82; mem. governing bd. UNESCO Inst. for Edn., 1971-79. Author: (with others) The Elementary School, 1956, Educational Leadership and the Elementary School Principal, 1956, (with Robert H. Anderson) The Nongraded Elementary School, 1959, rev. edit., 1963, reprinted, 1987, (with others) Computers and Information Systems in Education, 1966, Looking Behind the Classroom Door, 1970, rev. edit., 1974, Toward a Mankind School, 1974, The Conventional and the Alternative in Education, 1975, Curriculum Inquiry: The Study of Curriculum Practice, 1979, Planning and Organizing for Teaching, 1963, School Curriculum Reform, 1964, The Changing School Curriculum, 1966, School, Curriculum and the Individual, 1966, The Dynamics of Educational Change, 1975, Facing the Future, 1976, What Schools Are For, 1979, A Place Called School, 1983, Teachers for Our Nation's Schools, 1990, Educational Renewal: Better Teachers, Better Schools, 1994, In Praise of Education, 1997; author, editor: The Changing American School, 1966, (with Harold S. Shane) The Elementary School in the United States, 1973, (with M. Frances Klein and Jerrold M. Novotney) Early Schooling in the United States, 1973, (with Norma Feshback and Alvima Lombard) Early Schooling in England and Israel, 1973, (with Gary Fenstermacher) Individual Differences and the Common Curriculum, 1983, The Ecology of School Renewal, 1987, (with Kenneth A. Sirotnik) School-University Partnerships in Action, 1988, (with Pamela Keating) Access to Knowledge, 1990, (with others) The Moral Dimensions of Teaching, 1990, Places Where Teachers Are Taught, 1990, (with Thomas C. Lovitt) Integrating General and Special Education, 1992, (with Timothy J. McMannon) The Public Purpose of Education and Schooling, 1997; mem. bd. editors Sch. Rev, 1956-58, Jour. Tchr. Edn, 1958-60; contbg. editor: Progressive Edn, 1955-58; mem. editorial adv. bd. Child's World, 1952-80; chmn. editorial adv. bd. New Standard Ency, 1953—; chmn. ednl. adv. bd. Ency. Brit. Ednl. Corp, 1966-69; contbr. chpts. to books, articles to profl. jours. Recipient Disting. Svc. Medal Tchrs. Coll., Columbia U., 1983, Outstanding Book award Am. Ednl. Rsch. Assn., 1985, Disting. Contbns. to Ednl. Rsch. award 1993; named Faculty Rsch. Lectr. U. Wash., 1987-88, faculty of High Distinction, UCLA, 1987; Edward C. Pomeroy award, Amer. Assn. of Coll. for Teacher Edn., 1995, Disting. Svc. award Coun. Chief State Sch. Officials, 1997. Fellow Internat. Inst. Arts and Letters; mem. Nat. Acad. Edn. (charter; sec.-treas.), Am. Ednl. Rsch. Assn. (past pres., award for Disting. Contbns. to Ednl. Rsch. 1993), Nat. Soc. Coll. Tchrs. Edn. (past pres.), Nat. Soc. for Study of Edn. (dir.), Am. Assn. Colls. for Tchr. Edn. (pres. 1989-90). Office: U Wash Coll of Edn PO Box 353600 Seattle WA 98195-3600

GOODLATTE, ROBERT WILLIAM (BOB GOODLATTE), congressman, lawyer; b. Holyoke, Mass., Sept. 22, 1952; m. Maryellen Flaherty; children: Jennifer, Robert. BA, Bates Coll., 1974; JD, Washington & Lee U., 1977. Bar: Mass. 1977, Va. 1978, U.S. Ct. Appeals (4th cir.) 1981. Dist. mgr. congressman M. Caldwell Butler U.S. Ho. of Reps., Washington, 1977-79; pvt. practice Roanoke, Va., 1979-81; ptnr. Bird, Kinder & Huffman, Roanoke, 1981-93; mem. 103d-106th Congresses from 6th Va. dist., Washington, 1993—, asst. majority whip, chmn. agriculture subcom., dept. ops., nutrition and forestry, mem. jud. com., co-chair of Congl. Internet Caucus, mem. Rep. Policy com., chmn. Ho.Rep. High Tech Working Group. Mem. bldg. better bds. adv. com. United Way of Roanoke Valley, Roanoke, 1988-92; chmn. Roanoke City Rep. Com., 1980-83, 6th Cong. Dist. Rep. Com., Va., 1983-88. Mem. Civitan (pres. Roanoke chpt. 1989-90). Avocations: tennis, travel, swimming. Office: US Ho of Reps 2240 Rayburn HOB Washington DC 20515-4606

GOODLING, WILLIAM F., congressman; b. Loganville, Pa., Dec. 5, 1927; m. Hilda Wright; children: Todd, Jennifer. BS, U. Md.; MS, Western Md. Coll.; doctoral studies, Pa. State U. Various tchg. positions including prin. West York Area H.S.; supt. Spring Grove Area Schs.; supr. student tchrs. Pa. State U.; mem. 94th-106th Congresses from 19th Pa. Dist., 1975—; chmn. com. on edn. and the workforce, mem. internat. rels. com. Served with Armed Forces, 1946-48. Mem. Lions. Republican. Methodist. Office: US House Reps 2107 Rayburn Washington DC 20515-3819

GOODMAN, ALAN PAUL, academic administrator, business educator; b. N.Y.C., Oct. 20, 1949; s. Edward I. and Grace (Burstein) G. AB cum laude, Rutgers U., 1971; MEd, Ohio U., 1972; PhD, Ohio State U., 1984. Guidance counselor Southeastern Ohio Upward Bound Project, Athens, summer 1972, assoc. dir. for guidance, summer 1973, resident dir., summers 1978-79; dir. counseling svcs. W.Va. Inst. Tech., Montgomery, 1973-77; exec. intern Continential Ins. co., Cranbury, N.J., 1990-91; social responsibility bus. lectr. Cath. U. Am., Washington, 1993-95, dir. career svcs., 1981—; bus. ethics and soc. instr. U. Md., College Park, 1997—; mgmt. cons. Beckley Coal Co., Glen Daniel, W.Va., 1974-77, BOMI Inst., Arnold, Md., 1994-95. Author: (with others) Ethics is Good Business, 1996; contbr. articles to profl. jours. Mem. Nat. Assn. Colls. and Employers (chairperson principles for profl. conduct com. 1995—, principles for profl. conduct com. 1990-93, 95—), Mid. Atlantic Placement Assn. (chairperson ethics com. 1988-90), Phi Kappa Phi. Avocation: photography. E-mail: goodman@cua.edu. Office: Cath U Am Career Svcs Office 100 St Bonaventure Washington DC 20064

GOODMAN, ALFRED, composer, musicologist; b. Berlin, Mar. 1, 1920; came to U.S., 1940; s. Oskar and Paula Guttman. Student, Stern's Conservatory, Berlin, 1938; BS, Columbia U., 1952, MA, 1953; PhD, Tech. U. Berlin, 1972. Instr. Henry St. Settlement, N.Y.C., 1956-60; editor Westminster Records, N.Y.C., 1955; freelance music editor Bavarian Broadcasting Service, Munich, 1961, music editor, 1971-85; instr. State Coll. Music, Munich, 1976-90; music critic N.Y. Weekly, Aufbau, 1956-61. Composer, accompanist theatre group in London; occasional scoring for BBC, 1939-40; arranger for Jimmie Lunceford and Charlie Barnet, 1944-50, for Buddy Rich, Noro Morales, Benny Goodman, and several other dance bands, N.Y.C., 1946-50; composer, arranger for: Movie Tone, 1957-60; incidental music for: Broadway play Bride in the Morning, 1960; Composer: 5 Inventions for Strings & Piano, 1946, String Quartet in C, 1947, Uptown-Downtown for Symphony Orchestra, 1947, The Audition; opera, 1948; Psalm XII for Baritone Solo, Women's Chorus and Organ, 1949, Divertimento for 3 Saxophones, 1949, Symphony No. 1, 1949, 7 Sketches for Piano, 1950, Cycle of 10 Songs for Tenor and Piano, 1950, Prelude 51 for Symphony Orchestra, 1950, Sinfonietta for Orchestra, 1951, Piano Pieces for Young People, 1951, Sonata for Trumpet and Piano, 1954, 5 Songs from the Bronx for Soprano, Woodwind Ensemble and Harpsichord, 1954, Sonata for Violin and Piano, 1955, 3 Madrigals Without Words for Mixed Chorus, 1956, 3 Sonatinas for Harpsichord, 1956, 4 Songs for Soprano Voice and Piano, 1956, 3 Odes for Mixed Chorus, 1956, String Quartet No. 2, 1959, Mayfair Overture for Symphony Orchestra, 1960, Prelude and Fugue for Organ, 1960, 4 Pieces for Organ, 1961, 7 Essays on Poems by Dylan Thomas for Alto, Tenor and Guitar, 1961, 3 Bagatelles for Piano, 1961, 3 Pictures for Tenor Voice and Big Band, 1961, Concerto for Clarinet and Orchestra, 1961, 3 Chants for Voice, Saxophone and Cembalo, 1962, Suite for Soprano-Alto Saxophone, Double Bass, Cembalo, 1963, Brass Quintet in Seven Rounds, 1963, 3 Meditations on Israel for Piano, 1965, 3 Monologues for Violoncello, 1965, Chamber Concerto for Violoncello, Doublebass and Keyboard Instrument, 1965, Little Suite for Flute, Oboe and Clarinet, 1966, Symphony No. 2, 1966, Quintet for Woodwind Ensemble, 1966, Seven Studies for String Trio Opera, 1967, The Runner, 1972, Pro Memoria, 1973, Duo for Alto Saxophone and Harpsichord, 1972, 3 Ornaments for Voice, Flute and Piano, 1971, Individuation for Vocal and Orchestra, 3 Chants for Soprano and 8 Instruments, Aphorism for 2 Woodwind Quartets, 3 Meditations for Mixed Chorus, 1975-77, 2 Soliloquies for Double Bass, Across the Board for Brass Ensemble, 1977-78, 3 1/2 Moments for Flute, Viola, Guitar, 1980, Models for Big Band, 1980, Checking In for Voice and Piano, 1980, Ad Absurdum for Voice and Piano, 1980, The Lady and the Maid, P'opera, Brassology for Eleven, Direction LA for 4 Trumpets and 4 Trombones, Three Thoughts over the Blues: For Trombone and Orch., 1986, Guitaresque, 1987, Flutes & Harpsichord, 1987, Constellations I, II, 1987, Signatures, Spirituals for Organ with Brass or Flute, Saxology for 4 Saxophones, 1987, 3 Chapters for Keyboard, 1988, Universe of Freedom Orchestrology, 1991, Orchestrette in 7 parts, 1992, Nine for Nine, Nonett Ensemble, 1993, A Little School Music for Orchestra, 1995/96, Reflections: Manhattan Survey for Sazophones and Orchestra, 1997, others; arranger: Olympic Hymn, 1972; also other music for Olympics.; Author: Musik in Blut, 1968, Music from A-Z, 1970, Die Amerikanischen Schueler Franz Liszt's, 1972, Dictionary of Musical Terms, 1982. Served with AUS, 1942-44. Address: Kurfuerstendamm 162/6, 10709 Berlin Germany *Music as a universal language has served and is obligated in serving for any understanding between peoples around the globe without discrimination of race, creed or color. Music has the task to contribute peaceful co-existence between mankind. There is no more glorious interpretation than the musical sound to be absorbed by the living.*

GOODMAN, ALFRED NELSON, lawyer; b. N.Y.C., Jan. 21, 1945; s. Bernard R. and Mildred (Schlanger) G. BS in Mech. and Aerospace Scis., U. Rochester, 1966; JD, Georgetown U., 1969. Bar: N.Y. 1970, D.C. 1971, U.S. Supreme Ct. 1974. Patent examiner U.S. Patent Office, Washington, 1969-71; assoc. Roylance, Abrams, Berdo & Goodman, Washington, 1971-74, ptnr., 1975—. Mem. Am. Patent Law Assn., ABA, Bar Assn. of D.C. (chmn. patent, trademark and copyright law sect. 1984-85, bd. dirs. 1985-86). Home: 4948 Sentinel Dr Bethesda MD 20816-3557 Office: Roylance Abrams Berdo & Goodman Ste 315 1225 Connecticut Ave NW Washington DC 20036-2680

GOODMAN, ALLEN CHARLES, economics educator; b. Cleve., Oct. 28, 1947; s. Nathan and Pearl (Dorfman) G.; m. Janet Hankin, July 22, 1984; 1 child, Sara. AB, U. Mich., 1969; PhD, Yale U., 1976. Asst. prof. Lawrence U., Appleton, Wis., 1975-78; rsch. scientist Johns Hopkins U., Balt., 1978-86; economist Dept. Housing and Urban Devel., Washington, 1985-86; assoc. prof. Wayne State U., Detroit, 1986-88, prof. econs., 1988—, chmn. dept., 1988-96. Author: Changing Downtown, 1987, Economics of Housing Markets, 1989, Economics of Health and Health Care, 1993, 2d edit., 1997. Mem. Mayor's Coord. Coun. on Criminal Justice, Balt., 1984-86. Mem. APHA, Am. Econs. Assn., Am. Real Estate and Urban Econs. Assn., Rsch. Soc. Alcoholism. Office: Wayne State U Dept Econs Detroit MI 48202

GOODMAN, ALVIN S., engineering educator, consultant; b. N.Y.C., Mar. 14, 1925; s. Solomon and Dora Goodman; m. Nettie Leef Gilson, Sept. 9, 1951; children—Sandra, Lynn, Nancy, Sally. B. Civil Engring., CCNY, 1944; M.S. in Civil Engring., Columbia U., 1948; Ph.D., NYU, 1966. Registered profl. engr. N.Y., Mass., Conn., N.C.; profl. hydrologist, NIH. Engr. Interstate Sanitation Commn., N.Y.C., 1950-51; project engr. Tippetts-Abbett-McCarthy-Stratton, N.Y.C., 1951-62; staff cons. water resources, 1962-85 ; prof. civil engring. Northeastern U., Boston, 1962-69, NYU, 1969-73; prof. civil engring. Poly. U., Bklyn., 1973—, head dept., 1985-90; cons. engring. firms, edni. instns., 1970—. Author: Principles of Water Resources Planning, 1984. Contbr. articles to profl. jours., papers and reports to confs. Served to 1st lt., C.E., U.S. Army, 1944-47; ETO. Fellow ASCE; mem. Am. Water Resources Assn., Internat. Water Resources Assn., Am. Geophys. Union, Water Environ. Fedn., Am. Soc. Engring. Edn., Sigma Xi, Tau Beta Pi, Chi Epsilon. Office: Poly U Dept Civil & Environ Engring 6 Metrotech Ctr Brooklyn NY 11201-3840

GOODMAN, BEATRICE MAY, real estate professional; b. Rehoboth, Mass., Nov. 12, 1933; s. Manuel Silva and Mercy Elizabeth (Mayers) Bettencourt; m. Sam R. Goodman, Sept. 15, 1957; children: Mark, Stephen, Christopher. BS, Marymount Coll., 1980. Pres. Bettencourt Draperies, Rehoboth, Mass., 1955-56; asst. mgr. Leo H. Spivack Furniture, L.I., N.Y., 1956-57; asst. designer Lillian Decorators, L.I., N.Y., 1957-58; asst. buyer Macy's N.Y., N.Y.C., 1958-59; pres. Beatrice & Beverly, Mt. View, Calif., 1980-82; realtor Coldwell Banker, Menlo Park, Calif., 1984—; pres. The Added Touch, Atherton, Calif., 1984-91; realtor Cornish & Carey Realtors, Menlo Park, Calif., 1991—. Den mother Boy Scouts Am., N.Y.C., 1970-76; active Peninsula Vols., Palo Alto, 1974—, Internat. Friendship Force. Mem. Nat. Bd. Realtors, Orgn. for Rehab. Tng. Avocations: gardening, travel, physical fitness activities, vol. work for the arts. Home: 60 Shearer Dr Atherton CA 94027-3957 Office: Coldwell Banker 1000 El Camino Real Ste 150 Menlo Park CA 94025-4327

GOODMAN, BERNARD, physics educator; b. Phila., June 14, 1923; s. Louis and Fannie (Solomon) G.; m. Joyce Janet Willoughby, Mar. 3, 1950; children—David Nathan, Jonathan Bernard, Mark William. AB, U. Pa., 1943, PhD, 1955. Stress analyst Internat. Harvester Co., Chgo., 1947-52; research assoc. U. Mo., 1952, asst. prof. physics, 1954-58, assoc. prof., 1958-64, prof., 1964—; prof. physics U. Cin., 1965-93, prof. emeritus, 1993—; vis. sci. Argonne Nat. Lab., 1956-57, 61-62, 65-66, 70, Brookhaven Nat. Lab., 1960, Bell Telephone Lab., 1967, Ohio U., 1969; Nordita guest prof. Inst. Theoretical Physics, Uppsala, Sweden, 1962-63, Gothenberg, Sweden, 1971-72; vis. prof. Inst. Theoretical Physics, Gothenberg, 1985. Guggenheim fellow, 1962-63, Gordon Godfrey fellow U. NSW, Sydney, Australia, 1990; Fulbright scholar Inst. Theoretical Physics, Trieste, Italy, 1979-80. Fellow Am. Phys. Soc.; mem. AAAS, Phi Beta Kappa, Sigma Xi. Rsch. on condensed matter theory. Home: 3411 Cornell Pl Cincinnati OH 45220-1501 Office: U Cin Dept Physics Cincinnati OH 45221

GOODMAN, CAROL M., lawyer; b. Rye Brook, N.Y., May 11, 1965; d. Melvin Jay and Ethel Belle Friedman; m. Robert I. Goodman, Dec. 5, 1997; children: Amanda Rachel, Joanna Lorynn. BBA, Emory U., 1987; JD, Fordham U., 1990. Bar: N.Y., U.S. Ct. Appeals (2d cir.), U.S. Ct. Appeals (D.C. cir.), U.S. Dist. Ct. (so. and ea. dists.) N.Y. Assoc. Phillips, Nizer, Benjamin, Krim & Ballon, N.Y.C., 1990-93, Herrick, Feinstein LLP, N.Y.C., 1993—; pro bono in-house clinic Fordham Law Sch., 1989-90; pro bono Lawyers for Children, 1991-92. Editor: Urban Law Jour., 1989-90. Mem. Bar City N.Y. Office: Herrick Feinstein LLP 2 Park Ave New York NY 10016

GOODMAN, CHARLES DAVID, physicist, educator; b. N.Y.C., May 9, 1928; s. Jacob and Libby (Freed) G.; m. Joan Louise Wright, June 11, 1952; children: Henry N., Diana R. AB, Clark U., 1949; PhD, U. Rochester, 1955. Rsch. scientist Oak Ridge (Tenn.) Nat. Lab., 1955-80; prof. physics Ind. U., Bloomington, 1980-98, prof. emeritus, 1999—; vis. scientist Weizmann Inst. Sci., Rehovot, Israel, 1966; vis. prof. U. Colo., Boulder, 1972-73; guest scientist Los Alamos (N.Mex.) Nat. Lab., 1979-94, Lawrence Berkeley (Calif.) Lab., 1980—, Lawrence Livermore (Calif.) Lab., 1980—, Laboratoire Nat Saturne, Saclay, France, 1982-91. Contbr. articles to profl. jours. Recipient Humboldt Found. Rsch. award, Germany, 1991. Fellow AAAS, Am. Phys. Soc. (Tom W. Bonner Prize 1983); mem. IEEE, Sigma Xi. Achievements include mapping of Gamow-Teller strength function; patent on neutron detector. Office: Ind U Milo Sampson Ln Bloomington IN 47401

GOODMAN, CHARLES SCHAFFNER, marketing educator; b. Detroit, Apr. 5, 1916; s. Lawrence Manche and Carolyn Jeanette (Schaffner) G.; m. Dorothy Ruth Irvin, Dec. 4, 1943; children: Suzanne Goodman Hogsett, Charles Schaffner. B.S., UCLA, 1938, M.A., 1940; Ph.D., U. Mich., 1948. Lectr. mktg. Wharton Sch., U. Pa., Phila., 1946-48, asst. prof., 1948-53, asso. prof., 1953-57, prof., 1957-86, prof. emeritus, 1986—; chmn. dept. mktg. Wharton Sch., U. Pa., 1974-78. Author: (with Reavis Cox) Distribution in a High-Level Economy, 1965, Management of the Personal Selling Function, 1971, La Force de Vente, 1973; contbr. articles to profl. jours. Served to comdr. USNR, 1942-46. Recipient Alpha Kappa Psi award for best article in Jour. Mktg., 1968. Mem. Am. Mktg. Assn. (proc. mng. editor 1960-68), Beta Gamma Sigma, Pi Gamma Mu. Home: 11740 Wilshire Blvd Apt A-402 Los Angeles CA 90025-6536 Office: U Penn Wharton Sch Business Dietrich Hall Philadelphia PA 19104

GOODMAN, COREY SCOTT, neurobiology educator, researcher; b. Chgo., June 29, 1951; s. Arnold Harold and Florence (Friedman) G.; m. Marcia M. Barinaga, Dec. 8, 1984. BS, Stanford U., 1972; PhD, U. Calif., Berkeley, 1977. Postdoctoral fellow U. Calif., San Diego, 1979; asst. prof. dept. biol. scis. Stanford (Calif.) U., 1979-82, assoc. prof., 1982-87; prof. neurobiology and genetics U. Calif., Berkeley, 1987—; investigator Howard Hughes Med. Inst., 1988—, head neurobiology div., 1992—. Mem. editl. bd. Cell, Neuron; assoc. editor Devel.; contbr. more than 180 articles to profl. jours. Recipient Charles Judson Herrick award, 1982, Alan T. Waterman award Nat. Sci. Bd., 1983, Javits Neurosci. Investigator award NIH, 1985, 92, NIH Merit award, 1985, Found. IPSEN Neuronal Plasticity prize, 1996, J. Allyn Taylor Internat. prize in medicine, 1996, Gairdner Found. Internat. award for achievment in med. sci., 1997, Ameritec Found. Basic Rsch. Toward Cure Paralysis prize, 1997, Wakeman award for rsch. in neuroscis., 1998. Fellow Am. Acad. Arts and Scis.; mem. NAS, Am. Philos. Soc. Office: U Calif Howard Hughes Med Inst Dept Molecular & Cell Biology Life Sci Addition Rm 519 Berkeley CA 94720

GOODMAN, DAVID BARRY POLIAKOFF, physician, educator; b. Lynn, Mass., June 1, 1942; s. Nathan and Eva (Poliakoff) G.; m. J. Kathleen Greenacre, 1994; children: Derek, Alex. A.B., Harvard Coll., 1964; M.D., U. Pa., 1968, Ph.D., 1972. Intern dept. pathology U. Pa. Hosp., Phila., 1971-72; assoc. pediatrics and biochemistry U. Pa. Sch. Medicine, Phila., 1972-73, research asst. prof., 1973-76, assoc. prof., 1980-82, prof. pathology and lab. medicine, 1982—, dir. div. lab. medicine, 1980-83; dir. endocrinology-oncology lab., 1984—; asst. prof. internal medicine Yale U. Med. Sch., New Haven, 1976-79, assoc. prof., 1979-80; cons. NSF, VA, Ctr. Oral Health Research, U. Pa. Contbr. numerous articles to profl. jours.; mng. editor: Metabolic Bone Disease and Related Rsch., 1981-90; editor Hormonal Regulation Epithelial Transport Ions and Water, 1981, Technology Impact: Potential Directions for Laboratory Medicine, 1984. Recipient Achievement award Upjohn Co., 1968; Roland Jackson scholar, 1964-68; Pa. Plan scholar, 1968-72. Fellow N.Y. Acad. Scis. (Lamport award 1981); mem. Acad. Clin. Lab. Physicians and Scientists, AAAS, Am. Assn. Pathologists, Am. Fedn. Clin. Research, Am. Heart Assn., Am. Physiol. Soc., Am. Soc. Bone and Mineral Research, Soc. Devel. Biology, Soc. Neurosci. Home: 1201 Grenox Rd Wynnewood PA 19096-2218 Office: U Pa Hosp Dept Path & Lab Med 3400 Spruce St Philadelphia PA 19104-4204

GOODMAN, DAVID BRYAN, musician, educator; b. Akron, Ohio, Nov. 24, 1953; s. Jason Jones and Louise (Campbell) G. MusB, Oberlin Coll., 1975; MA in Music, U. Calif., Berkeley, 1977, PhD in Music, 1982. Instr. U. Calif., Berkeley, 1976-82; asst. prof. Pomona Coll., Claremont, Calif., 1982-89; pianist UCLA Extension Film Sch., 1989-91; vis. prof. music UCLA, 1993-96; prof. theory, composition and music tech. Santa Monica Coll., 1997—; affiliate Broadcast Music, Inc., N.Y.C., 1982—; orchestrator film and TV projects, L.A., 1989—. Composer Piano Quartet, 1999, Dolphin Dance for orch., 1998, Three Songs on Poems of Michael Altman, 1997, Sinfonia Domestica, 1992, Child's Play, 1991, River's Edge, 1989, Reina de la Selva, 1989, Miroirs, 1987-88, Jody's Ride, 1988, Canto de Esperanza, 1987, A Day in Two Lives, 1984, Village Echoes, 1984, Caged Bird, 1984, Tides of Lemuria, 1982, Lucy's Samba for Latin Big Band, 1996, Darkness Into Light PBS Documentary Film score, numerous others. Artist-in-residence Na-Bolom Found., Chiapas, Mex., 1987, 88; Charles Ives scholar Am. Acad. Inst. Arts, Letters, 1978. Mem. Broadcast Music Inc., Assn. for Promotion of New Music, Soc. Composers and Lyricists, Am. Fedn. Musicians, Coll. Music Soc., Soc. Composers and Lyricists. Avocations: sailing, cooking, foreign travel, foreign languages. Home and Office: 10959 Rochester Ave Apt 202 Los Angeles CA 90024-7717

GOODMAN, DAVID GORDON, Japanese, comparative literature educator, writer; b. Racine, Wis., Feb. 12, 1946. BA, Yale U., 1969; PhD, Cornell U., 1982. Asst. prof. U. Kans., Lawrence, 1981-82; prof. U. Ill., Champaign, 1982—. Author: After Apocalypse, 1986, Japanese Drama and Culture, 1988, Hashiru (Running), 1989, Jews in the Japanese Mind, 1995; editor, translator: Long Long Autumn Nights, 1989; editor, pub. Concerned Theatre Japan, 1969-73. Univ. scholar U. Ill., 1992; Fulbright fellow 1980, 90; NEH grantee, 1985, NEA, 1993; recipient Translation Ctr. award Columbia U., 1990. Office: U Ill 608 S Mathews Ave Urbana IL 61801-3602

GOODMAN, DAVID WAYNE, research chemist, educator; b. Glen Allen, Miss., Dec. 14, 1945; s. Henry G. and Anniebelle G.; m. Sandra Faye Hewitt, June 9, 1967; 1 child, Jac Hewitt. BS, Miss. Coll., 1968; PhD, U. Tex., 1974. NATO postdoctoral fellow Tech. Hochschule, Darmstadt, Fed. Republic of Germany, 1974-75; NRC postdoctoral fellow NBS, Washington, 1975-76, mem. research staff, 1976-80; mem. research staff Sandia Labs., Albuquerque, 1980-85, head surface sci. div., 1985-88; prof. chemistry, Tex. A&M U., College Station, 1988-94, head phys. and nuc. divsn., 1991-94, Welch prof., 1994—, Welch chair, 1998—; lectr. Texas A&M U., 1987, U. Tex. 1990, Northwestern U., 1993, Am. Chemical Soc., 1993. Recipient Yarwood Medal, 1994, Humboldt Rsch. award, 1995; named Disting. Alumnus, Miss. Coll., 1992. Mem. Am. Chem. Soc. (treas. div. colloid and surface sci. 1980-83, vice chair 1983, chmn. 1984, Colloid or Surface Chemistry award 1993, Langmuir Disting. Lectr. award, 1991, Ipatieff prize, 1983), Am. Vacuum Soc. (mem. exec. council 1981, 85-87). Office: Tex A&M University Dept Chemistry PO Box 30012 College Station TX 77842-3012

GOODMAN, DONALD C., university administrator; b. Chgo., Nov. 24, 1927; s. Alexander Goodman and Freda (Mermelstein) G.; m. Martha Huggins, July 3, 1968; children: Brian and Eric (twins), Michael and Susan (twins), Elaine, Alison; stepchildren: Bruce, Adam, Mitchell. B.S., U. Ill., 1949, M.S., 1950, Ph.D., 1954. Instr. U. Pa., 1954-56; mem. faculty U. Fla., 1956-68, prof., 1963-68, chmn. dept. anatomical scis., 1965-68; co-dir. Center Neurol. Sci., 1964-68; prof. anatomy, chmn. dept. SUNY Med. Center, Syracuse, 1968-82; dean Coll. Grad. Studies, SUNY Med. Center, 1973-82, interim dean med. scis., 1975-76, v.p. acad. affairs, 1975-78, v.p. research and acad. affairs, 1978-82; v.p. acad. affairs East Tenn. State U., 1982; dean health related professions SUNY-Syracuse Health Scis. Ctr., 1983-95, v.p. acad. affairs, 1983-86, provost, 1986-95, interim pres., 1992; mem. interdisciplinary studies adv. coun. Fla. Gulf Coast U., 1997. Author books and articles; editor: Brain, Behavior and Evolution. Mem. study sect. NIH. Served with AUS, 1946-48. Recipient Annual Research award Fla. chpt. Sigma Xi; fellow award Assn. Schs. Allied Health Professions, 1993. Fellow Am. Soc. Allied Health Professions; mem. Am. Assn. Anatomists (exec. com. 1978-82), Nat. Coun. Univ. Rsch. Adminstrs., Soc. Neurosci., Am. Assn. Higher Edn., Sigma Xi. Home: 401 Via Esplanade Punta Gorda FL 33950-6400

GOODMAN, EDMUND NATHAN, surgeon, pain management consultant; b. N.Y.C., July 14, 1908; s. Benjamin Harry and Sophia (Schweisheimer) G.; m. Marian Powers, Mar. 9, 1950; children: Wendy, Tonne, Edmund Jr., Stacy. BS, CCNY, 1928; MD, Columbia U., 1933, MEd, DSc, 1942; postgrad. Cambridge U., 1935-36. Intern in surgery Columbia-Presbyn. Hosp., N.Y.C., 1936-38, asst. resident, then resident in surgery, 1938-41, instr. in surgery, 1941, asst. clin. prof. surgery, 1950-65, assoc. clin. prof., 1965-81; attending surgeon Mt. Sinai Hosp., N.Y.C., 1947-49; practice medicine specializing in pain mgmt., Roslyn, N.Y., 1982-96. Lt. comndr. USN, 1941-46. Mem. ACS, N.Y. Surg. Soc., N.Y. Acad. Med., Am. Bd. Surgery. Home and Office: 35 Sterling Ln Sands Point NY 11050-1239

GOODMAN, ELIZABETH ANN, lawyer; b. Marquette, Mich., Aug. 11, 1950; d. Paul William and Pearl Marie Goodman; m. Herbert Charles Gardner, Sept. 24, 1977. Student, U. Munich, 1970-71; BA cum laude, Alma (Mich.) Coll., 1972; JD cum laude, U. Mich., 1977. Bar: Minn. 1978, Mich. 1978, U.S. Dist. Ct. Minn. 1979. Cert. real property law specialist, real property sect. Minn. Bar Assn. High sch. tchr. Onaway (Mich.) High Sch., 1973-74; assoc. Dorsey & Whitney LLP, Mpls., 1978-82; ptnr. Dorsey & Whitney, Mpls., 1983—. Mem. ABA (natural resource, energy and environ. law sect., real property, probate and trust law sect.), Minn. Bar Assn., Hennepin County Bar Assn. Office: Dorsey & Whitney LLP 220 S 6th St Ste 2200 Minneapolis MN 55402-1498

GOODMAN, ELLEN HOLTZ, journalist; b. Newton, Mass., Apr. 11, 1941; d. Jackson Jacob and Edith (Weinstein) Holtz; m. Robert Levey; 1 dau., Katherine Anne. B.A. cum laude, Radcliffe Coll., 1963; hon. degrees, Mt. Holyoke Coll., Amherst Coll., U. Pa., U. N.H. Researcher, reporter Newsweek Mag., 1963-65; feature writer Detroit Free Press, 1965-67; feature writer columnist Boston Globe, 1967-74, assoc. editor, 1986—; syndicated columnist Washington Post Writers Group, 1976—; radio commentator Spectrum, CBS, 1978-80, NBC, 1979-80; commentator NBC Today Show, 1979-81; vis. prof. Stanford U., 1995. Author: Close to Home, 1979, Turning Points, 1979, At Large, 1981, Keeping in Touch, 1985, Making Sense, 1989, Value Judgments, 1993. Trustee Radcliffe Coll. Nieman fellow Harvard U., 1974; named New Eng. Newspaper Woman of Year New Eng. Press Assn., 1968; recipient Catherine O'Brien award Stanley Home Products, 1971, Media award Mass. Commn. Status Women, 1974, Columnist of Year award New Eng. Women's Press Assn., 1975, Pulitzer Prize for Commentary, 1980, prize for column writing Am. Soc. Newspaper Editors, 1980, Hubert H. Humphrey Civil Rights award, 1988, William Allen White award 1995. Office: Globe Newspapers Co 135 Morrissey Blvd Dorchester MA 02125-3310

GOODMAN, ELLIOT RAYMOND, political scientist, educator; b. Indpls., Sept. 3, 1923; s. Lazure L. and Esther (Miller) G.; m. Norma B., Mar. 1, 1947; children—Laura Goodman Humphrey, Jordan, Roger. A.B., Dartmouth Coll., 1948; M.A. and cert. Russian Inst., Columbia U., 1951, Ph.D., 1957; M.A. (hon.), Brown U., 1960. Ford teaching intern Brown U., Providence, 1955-56; instr. Brown U., 1956-58, asst. prof., 1958-60, asso. prof., 1960-70, prof. polit. sci., 1970-87, prof. emeritus, 1987—. Author: The Soviet Design for a World State, 1960, The Fate of the Atlantic Community, 1975; contbr. numerous articles to profl. jours. Served with U.S. Army, 1943-46. Guggenheim fellow, 1962-63; NATO research fellow, 1962-63. Mem. Internat. Inst. Strategic Studies (London), Atlantic Council U.S. (politico-mil. com. 1971-74, acad. assoc. 1985—), New Eng. Polit. Sci. Assn., Am. Polit. Sci. Assn., Am. Assn. Advancement of Slavic Studies, Com. Atlantic Studies (N. Am. sect.). Home: 45 Amherst Rd Cranston RI 02920-6010 Office: Brown U Dept Polit Sci Providence RI 02912

GOODMAN, ELLIOTT I(RVIN), lawyer; b. Chgo., Mar. 28, 1934; s. Sidney W. and Jean (Strauss) G.; m. Sybil J. Shapiro, Dec. 25, 1957; children: Jessica, Paul, Jonathan. BS, Northwestern U., 1955, JD, 1958. Bar: Ill. 1958, U.S. Dist. Ct. (no. dist.) Ill. 1959; CPA, Ill. With Gottlieb & Schwartz, Chgo., 1959-90, ptnr., 1966-90, mng. ptnr., 1981-88; ptnr. D'Ancona and Pflaum, Chgo., 1990-95; exec. v.p. ATI Carriage House, Inc., Lombard, Ill., 1995—; permanent arbitrator Amalgamated Social Benefit Ins. Plan. Sec., bd. dirs. Ind. Basketball Players Assn., 1971-74, Abe Saperstein Found., Athletes for Better Edn. Found., 1975-79; mem. Highland Park Housing Commn. (Ill.), 1980-87. Mem. ABA (labor law com. 1977-97, environ. law com. 1988-97), Chgo. Bar Assn. (past chmn. Am. citizenship com. 1967-69, mem. labor law com. 1971—, environ. law com. 1988-97), Human Resource Mgmt. Assn. Chgo., Lake Geneva Yacht Club. Home: 211 Rivershire Ln Apt 201 Lincolnshire IL 60069-3817 Office: ATI Carriage House Inc 1111 N Ridge Ave Lombard IL 60148-1212

GOODMAN, ERIC KEITH, writer, educator; b. Bklyn., May 29, 1953; s. Sidney M. and Dorothy (Lees) G.; m. Susan Jennifer Morgan, May 8, 1982; childen: Ethan, Seneca. BA in English, Yale U., 1975; M in English, Stanford U., 1979. Free-lance journalist, 1976—; asst. prof. Miami U., Oxford, Ohio, 1991-95, assoc. prof., 1995—, dir. creative writing external programs, 1996—. Author: High on the Energy Bridge, 1980, The First Time I Saw Hall, 1983, In Days of Awe, 1991. Local event organizer Share Our Strength, Oxford, 1994—; youth soccer coach North Avondale Soccer Am. for Youth, Cin., 1994—. Recipient Individual Artist award Ohio Arts Coun., 1995; Mirrielees fellow in fiction Stanford U., 1976, Atherton fellow in fiction Breadloaf Writers' Conf., Middlebury, Vt., 1983. Fellow Writers Guild Am. West. Democrat. Jewish. Avocations: softball, golf, old home restoration, Thai cooking, travel. Office: Dept English Miami Univ Oxford OH 45056

GOODMAN, ERIK DAVID, engineering educator; b. Palo Alto, Calif., Feb. 14, 1944; s. Harold Orbeck and Shirley Mae (Lillie) G.; m. Denise Rowand Dyktor, Aug. 10, 1968 (div. 1976); m. Cheryl Diane Barris, Aug. 27, 1978; 1 child, David Richard. BS in Math., Mich. State U., 1966, MS in Systems Sci., 1968; PhD in Computer Communication Sci., U. Mich., 1972; Hon. Doctorate, Dneprodzerzhinsk State Tech U., Ukraine, 1996. Asst. prof. elec. engring. Mich. State U., East Lansing, 1972-77, assoc. prof. elec. engring., 1977-84, dir. case ctr. for computer aided engring. and mfg., 1983—, prof. elec. engring., dir., 1984—, prof. mech. engring., 1992—; dir. Mich. State U. Mfg. Rsch. Consortium, 1993—; pres. Tech. Gateway, Inc., East Lansing; cons. Chinese Computer Comms., Inc., Lansing, 1988—; gen. chair First Internat. Conf. on Evolutionary Computation and its Applications, Moscow, 1996, Seventh Internat. Conf. on Genetic Algorithms, 1997; gen. co-chmn. Internat. Computer Graphics Conf., Detroit, 1986. Author: (with others) SYSKIT: Linear Systems Toolkit, 1986; patentee in field. Academician, Internat. Informatization Acad. (Russia), 1993—. Mem. AIAA (chair rsch. and future dirs., subcom. CAD/CAM tech. com. 1987-89, Outstanding Svc. 1990), IEEE Computer Soc., Soc. Mfg. Engrs., Aircraft Owners and Pilots Assn., Internat. Soc. for Genetic Algorithms (exec. com. 1997—). Avocations: musician, tennis, studying Chinese. Office: Mich State U Case Ctr Coll Engring 2325 Engring Bldg East Lansing MI 48824-1226

Mutually beneficial use of European and Asian technological capabilities is a significant opportunity for U.S. firms today.

GOODMAN, ERIKA, dancer, actress; b. Phila.; d. A. Allan and Laura (Baylin) G. Student, Sch. of Am. Ballet, 1961-63; BA in Theatre and Dance, Empire State Coll., 1993; master classes, Princeton Ballet, 1994, Hartford Ballet Co., 1995, Va. Intermont Coll., 1995—. Mem. faculty Actors and Dirs. Lab., N.Y.C., 1979—; founding mem. ensemble theater co. The Barrow Group, N.Y.C., 1986—; mem. dance faculty CCNY, 1990; mem. dance faculty CCNY, 1990; guest tchr. ballet Balettakademein, Stockholm, 1986, 89; instr. master classes Rutgers U., East Carolina U., 1989, Hofstra U., U. Kans., 1990, Harvard U., summer 1993, Cornell U., Skidmore Coll., Vassar Coll., 1992—, Conn. Coll.; vis. prof. ballet, head ballet dept. CCNY, 1992—, lectr. world arts, 1993—. Dancer N.Y.C. Ballet Co., 1964-65, prin. dancer Joffrey Ballet, N.Y.C., 1966-75; performer (with Barrow Group) Seymour in the Heart of Winter, Perry St. Theatre, N.Y.C., 1986, When You Comin' Back Red Rider, 1987, Feather Hat, Three Sisters, 1989; casting dir. (films) Hazing in Hell, Neon Red; dir. ballet rehearsal Ballet Hispanico. Richard Porter Leach fellow, 1992-93. *In my life as with my art, I have strived to achieve purity, truth and beauty—to preserve my integrity when it was challenged, and never to compromise the dictates of my heart.*

GOODMAN, ERNEST MONROE, air force officer; b. Casper, Wyo., May 14, 1955; s. Gordon Lee and Georgia Lee (Lent) G.; m. Songkran Sana, Sept. 30, 1976 (div. Feb. 1995). BSEE, U. Okla., 1982; MBA in Mgmt., Cen. State U., Edmond, Okla., 1986. Registered profl. engr., Okla. Avionics technician USAF, N.D., Okla., and S.E. Asia, 1973-78, USAFR, Tinker AFB, Okla., 1978-83; project engr., mgr. engring. Okla. City Air Logistics Ctr., Tinker AFB, 1982-90, 90—; commd. 2nd lt. USAF, 1983, advanced through grades to maj.; engring. officer USAFR, Tinker AFB, 1983—. Mem. NSPE, Okla. Soc. Profl. Engrs., Air Force Assn., Res. Officers Assn., Tinker Mgmt. Assn., Toastmasters Internat. Democrat. Lutheran. Avocations: photography, fishing, hunting, hiking, jogging. Home: 1313 SW 22d St Moore OK 73170-7483 Office: USAF OC-ALC/LASKF Bldg 3220 Tinker AFB OK 73145

GOODMAN, GARY A., lawyer; b. N.Y.C., Mar. 8, 1948; s. Nathaniel and Edith (Rosen) G.; m. Susan Schachter, Aug. 13, 1972; children: Max, Jonah, William, Zachary, Holden. AB in History summa cum laude, Economics with honors, U. Rochester, 1970; JD, NYU, 1973. Bar: N.Y. 1974, U.S. Dist. Ct. (so. dist. and ea. dist.) N.Y. 1974, U.S. Dist. Ct. Guam, 1975, U.S. Ct. Appeals (2d cir.) 1975, Calif. 1996, Tex. 1996. Ptnr. Akin, Gump, Strauss, Hauer & Feld, L.L.P., N.Y.C., 1996—, co-head estate practice group. Contbr. numerous articles to profl. jours.. Mem. bd. edn. Locust Valley (N.Y.) Ctrl. Sch. Dist., 1995-96, v.p., 1996-97, pres., 1997-98. Mem. ABA (vice chmn. internat. investment in real estate com. 1983-90, chmn. Pacific Rim trans. subcom. real estate financing com. 1987-88), N.Y. State Bar Assn. (chmn. fgn. investment in U.S. real estate com. 1987-88), Assn. of Bar of City of N.Y. (uniform state laws com. 1978-80, real property law com. 1991-94, 97—, land use com. 1994-97), Internat. Coun. Shopping Ctrs. (task force environ. issues 1987-90, law com. 1991-94), Real Estate Bd. N.Y. Office: Akin Gump Strauss Hauer & Feld LLP 590 Madison Ave New York NY 10022-4616

GOODMAN, GARY ALAN, lawyer; b. Memphis, Nov. 27, 1947; s. Louis H. and Margie (Evensky) G.; m. Teresa E. Berry, July 2, 1987. AB, Cornell U., 1969; JD, Columbia U., 1972. Bar: N.Y., 1973, U.S. Dist. Ct. (so. dist.) N.Y. 1973, Ill. 1979, U.S. Dist. Ct. (no. dist.) Ill. 1979, U.S. Cir. Ct. (2d cir.), U.S. Cir. Ct. (7th cir). Assoc. Sullivan & Cromwell, N.Y.C., 1972-79; ptrn., gen. counsel Winston & Strawn, Chgo., 1979—. bd. dirs. Lyric Opera Chgo., 1998—. Home: 219 E Lake Shore Dr Chicago IL 60611-1352 Office: Winston & Strawn 35 W Wacker Dr Ste 4200 Chicago IL 60601-1695

GOODMAN, GEORGE JEROME WALDO (ADAM SMITH), author, television journalist, editor; b. St. Louis, Aug. 10, 1930; s. Alexander Mark and Viola (Cremer) G.; m. Sallie Cullen Brophy, Oct. 6, 1961; children: Alexander Mark, Susannah Blake. AB magna cum laude, Harvard U., 1952; AB Rhodes scholar, Oxford (Eng.) U., 1952-54. Reporter Barron's, 1957; contbg. editor, assoc. editor Time and Fortune mags., 1958-60; portfolio mgr., v.p. Lincoln Fund, 1960-62; co-founder New York mag., 1967, contbg. editor, v.p., 1967-77; exec. editor, then cons. Esquire, 1978-81; 1st editor, exec. v.p., bd. dirs. Instl. Investor, 1967-72; chmn. Continental Fidelity Group, 1980—, also dir.; exec. v.p., dir. Instl. Investor Systems, 1969-72; dir. USAIR, Inc., 1978—, Hyatt Hotels, 1977-81, Cambrex, Inc., 1981—, Providentia Ltd., Sweden, 1984-86; bd. dirs. New Eng. Life; lectr. Harvard Bus. Sch., Princeton; commentator NBC News, 1974, PBS, 1981—; creator, host, editor-in-chief Adam Smith's Money Game, PBS, 1984-97; 1st U.S. pub. affairs TV broadcast in Russia, 1990—; host, editor-in-chief Adam Smith's Money Gene, PBS, 1998—; editorial chmn. N.J. Monthly, 1976-79; adv. com. publs. U.S. Tennis Assn., 1978-83. Screenwriter, L.A., 1962-65, screenplay The Wheeler Dealers; author: The Bubble Makers, 1955, A Time for Paris, 1957, Bascombe, The Fastest Hound Alive, 1958, A Killing in the Market, 1958, The Wheeler Dealers, 1959; under pseudonym Adam Smith: The Money Game, 1968 (#1 bestseller), Supermoney, 1971 (#1 bestseller), Powers of Mind, 1975, Paper Money, 1981, The Roaring 80's, 1988; mem. editl. bd. N.Y. Times, 1977; contbr. articles to profl. jours. Trustee Glassboro (N.J.) State Coll., 1967-71, co-chmn. presdl. selection com., 1968; trustee C.G. Jung Found., 1981-88; mem. adv. council econs. dept. Princeton U., 1970-89, chmn., 1975-77; rep. com. on shareholder responsibility Harvard U., 1971-74, mem. vis. com. psychology and social relations dept., 1974-80—, mem. vis. com. Middle East Inst.; mem. adv. council Sloan Fellowships, Princeton U., 1976-79, Ctr. for Internat. Studies, Princeton U., 1990—; trustee The Urban Inst., 1986-96, Found. for Child Devel., 1986-88. Served with AUS, 1954-56. Recipient G.M. Loeb award for distinguished achievement bus. and fin. writing U. Conn., 1969, Media award for econ. understanding with TV documentary Amos Tuck Sch., Dartmouth Coll., 1978, Overseas Press award, 1997; Ind. award Brown U., 1993; nominee 8 Emmy awards, 1985-97, winner Best Interview 1995, winner 3 Emmys, graphics, 1985-94. Mem. Coun. Fgn. Rels., Authors League Found. (v.p.), Authors Guild (bd. dirs. 1975—), Assn. Harvard Alumni (bd. dirs. 1972-75), Harvard Club, Century Club, Knickerbocker Club. Office: Adam Smith's Money World 26 E 63rd St New York NY 10021-8030

GOODMAN, GERTRUDE AMELIA, civic worker; b. El Paso, Tex., Oct. 24, 1924; d. Karl Perry and Helen Sylvia (Pinkiert) G. BA, Mills Coll., 1945. Pres. El Paso chpt. Tex. Social Welfare Assn., 1963-65, bd. dirs. 1965-70, state bd. dirs., 1965-70; state bd. dirs. Pan-Am. Round Table, El Paso, 1966—, bd. dirs. 1970-71, sec., 1973-74, life mem.; founder, 1st chmn. El Paso Mus. Art Mem. Guild, 1962-68; bd. dirs. Mus. Art Assn., 1962-69, also v.p.; chmn. dir. El Paso C. of C. women's Dept., 1976-77; bd. dirs. Rio Grande Food Bank, 1988-94; bd. dirs. El Paso Pub. Libr., 1972-80, pres. bd. dirs., 1978-80; pres. El Paso County Hist. Soc., 1981-82, bd. dirs., 1986-92; mem. planning com. El Paso United Way, 1953—; mem. El Paso Mus. Art Bd. Coun. Recipient Hall of Honor award El Paso County Hist. Soc., Nat. Human Rels. award NCCJ, 1981, numerous awards for civic vol. work. Avocations: tennis, travel, art, books. Home: 905 Cincinnati Ave El Paso TX 79902-2435

GOODMAN, GWENDOLYN ANN, nursing educator; b. Davenport, Iowa, Aug. 7, 1955; d. Merle Erwin and Loraine Etta (Mahannah) Langfeldt; m. Mark Nathan Goodman, Oct. 24, 1982; children: Zachary Aaron, Alexander Daniel. BS in Nursing, Ariz. State U., 1977. RN, Ariz. Staff nurse surg. fl. and intensive care unit St. Luke's Hosp. and Med. Ctr., Phoenix, 1977-81; staff nurse intensive care unit Yavapai Regional Med. Ctr., Prescott, Ariz., 1981-82; instr. nursing Yavapai Coll., Prescott, 1982-88, cons., 1986; part-time staff nurse Ariz. Poison Control Ctr., Phoenix, 1980-81; mem. profl. adv. com. Home Health Agy. Yavapai Regional Med. Ctr., 1988-93. Mem. Sigma Theta Tau. Democrat. Home: PO Box 450 Prescott AZ 86302-0450

GOODMAN, HAROLD S., lawyer; b. St. Louis, Aug. 17, 1937; s. David and Eva Katherine (Wasserman) G.; m. Karen K. Mauldin, Aug. 5, 1979; 1 child, James Richardson. AB, U. Mo., 1960; LLB, JD, Washington U., St. Louis, 1963. Bar: Mo. 1963. Assoc. firm Bishop & Goodman, St. Louis, 1963-70; v.p., gen. counsel, sec. World Color Press, Inc., St. Louis, 1970-75; pvt. practice St. Louis, 1975-81; ptnr. Gallop, Johnson & Neuman, L.C., St. Louis, 1981—. Mem. St. Louis County CSC, 1976-80; trustee Cystic Fibrosis Found., 1971—, pres., 1975; mem. Mo.-St. Louis Met. Airport Authority, 1980-86; trustee-at-large Nat. Cystic Fibrosis Found., 1984-90; mem. Laumeier Sculpture Park, 1996—, Cmty. in Partnership., 1986-88. Mem. ABA, Mo. Bar Assn., Bar Assn. St. Louis, Washington U. Law Alumni Assn. (pres. 1976-77), Zeta Beta Tau (pres. trustee corp. 1964-69), Phi Delta Phi. Home: 340 Falling Leaves Ct Saint Louis MO 63141-7405 Office: Gallop Johnson & Neuman LC 101 S Hanley Rd Ste 1600 Saint Louis MO 63105-3489

GOODMAN, HERBERT IRWIN, petroleum company executive; b. Pitts., Mar. 11, 1923; s. Meyer Irwin and Bessie (Crossof) G.; m. Mary Katherine Schilken, Aug. 12, 1978; children: Michael Christopher, Anne Katheryn, Nancy Hjortshoj, Sara Elizabeth, Mary Ellen. BS, U. Pitts., 1943; cert., U. Besancon, 1945; MBA, Harvard U., 1949, AM, 1950. Commd. officer U.S. Fgn. Service, 1951; served in U.S. Fgn. Service, Copenhagen, 1951-53, Vietnam, 1953-54, Cambodia, 1954-55; intelligence research officer Dept. State, 1956-57; with Gulf Oil Corp., 1957-84; coordinator European sales Gulf Oil Corp., London, 1957-59; gen. mgr. Pacific Gulf Oil, Tokyo, 1960-64; coordinator crude oil dept. Pacific Gulf Oil, Pitts., 1964-66, coordinator Far East, 1966-70; pres. Gulf Oil Co. South Asia, Singapore, 1970-72, Gulf Oil Trading Co., Pitts., 1972-80, Gulf Trading and Transp. Co., Houston, 1980-84, GOTCO USA, Inc., Houston, 1984-87, SARMAR Corp., Houston, 1987—; bd. chmn. Applied Trading Systems, Houston, 1988-96, IQ Holdings, Inc., Houston, 1996—; bd. dirs. Houston Livestock Show and Rodeo, Genesis Energy L.P. Bd. dirs., chmn. internat. adv. bd. Tex. A&M U.; bd. dirs. U. Houston Coll. Bus., U. St. Thomas Sch. Bus. 1st lt. U.S. Army, 1943-46. Decorated Bronze Star; médaille de la Réconnaissance (France). Mem. Am. Petroleum Inst., Am. Mgmt. Assn., Coun. on Fgn. Rels., Assn. Asian Studies, Mid East Inst., Asia Soc. N.Y. (corp. coun.), Assn. Internat. Petroleum Negotiators, Harvard Club (N.Y.C.), Lakeside Country Club, Racquet Club, Univ. Club, Petroleum Club. Office: SARMAR Corp 16212 State Highway 249 Houston TX 77086-1014

GOODMAN, JAMES A., federal judge; b. Mar. 21, 1936; s. Samuel Solomon and Hilda (Lipman) G.; m. Marjogie Sara Golden, June 14, 1960; children: Lisa, Joseph, David, Samuel. LLB, Boston U., 1961. Bar: Maine 1961, U.S. Dist. Ct. Maine 1962. Pvt. practice, 1961-68; ptnr. Goodman & Goodman, Bangor, Maine, 1968-78, Goodman, Goodman & Kornreich, Bangor, 1978-81. Fellow Am. Coll. Bankruptcy, Am. Bankruptcy Inst., Nat. Conf. Bankruptcy Judges, Comml. Law League, Maine Bar Assn. Office: US Bankruptcy Ct 537 Congress St Fl 2 Portland ME 04101-3318

GOODMAN, JERRY L(YNN), judge; b. Mangum, Okla., Apr. 17, 1939; s. A.O. and Viola Louise (Bogart) G.; m. Donna L. Rudy, Dec. 16, 1961; children: Courtney L., Polly K., Mallory E., Benjamin R. BA, U. Tulsa 1961; JD, Georgetown U., 1964. Bar: Okla. 1964. Law clk. antitrust div. Dept. Justice, 1962-63; legis. asst. to U.S. Senator J. Howard Edmondson, 1963-64; assoc. David M. Thornton, Atty.-at-Law, 1964-65; asst. city atty. City of Tulsa, 1965-68; ptnr. Owens & Goodman, Tulsa, 1968-70; gen. counsel OTASCO Stores, Tulsa, 1970-74, v.p., gen. counsel, 1974-85, chmn., CEO, 1985-89; bd. dirs. Bank of Okla., spl. counsel, 1989-90; pres., gen. counsel The Sigma Asset Mgmt. Group, Inc., 1991—; sec. policy and mgmt., COO Office of Gov., State of Okla., Tulsa, 1992; judge Okla. Ct. Civil Appeals, Tulsa, 1994—. Bd. dirs. United Way, 1984-87; chmn., bd. trustees Univ. Ctr. at Tulsa, 1992. Served to lt. USNR, 1964-70. Mem. Met. Tulsa C. of C. (chmn. 1988). Presbyterian. Home: 3417 E 87th St Tulsa OK 74137-2628 Office: Okla Ct Civil Appeals 601 State Office Bldg 440 S Houston Ave Tulsa OK 74127-8922

GOODMAN, JOAN FRANCES, avionics manufacturing executive; b. N.Y.C., Oct. 25, 1941; d. Jack and Evelyn (Fine) G.; m. Stephen Gordon Glatzer, Oct. 2, 1982 (dec. Dec. 1987). BS, Alfred U., 1963; MA, NYU, 1967. RN, N.Y. Psychiat. liaison nurse Hosp. Albert Einstein Coll. Medicine, N.Y.C., 1968-73; nursing care coord. United Hosp., Port Chester, N.Y., 1974-80; asst. to pres. Glatzer Industries, New Rochelle, N.Y., 1980-87; pres., CEO Glatzer Industries Corp., New Rochelle, 1987—, Emergency Beacon Corp., New Rochelle, 1987—, ELTS Ltd., Inc., New Rochelle, 1987—. Mem. ANA, Nat. League Nursing, Westchester Assn. Women Bus. Owners, Am. Women's Econ. Corp., Nat. Bus. Aviation Assn., Women in Aviation Internat. Office: Glatzer Industries Corp 15 River St New Rochelle NY 10801-4351

GOODMAN, JOHN, actor; b. St. Louis, June 20, 1952; m. Annabeth Hartzog, 1989; 1 daughter. Student, Meramac Community Coll.; BFA in Theater, S.W. Mo. State U., 1975. Performer dinner and children's theater prodns., off-Broadway plays; appeared on Broadway in Loose Ends, 1979, Big River, 1985; TV credits include Mystery of the Moro Castle,, Face of Rage, Heart of Steel, Moonlighting, Chiefs, The Paper Chase, Murder Ordained, The Equalizer; series regular, Roseanne, 1988-96 (Emmy award nominations outstanding lead actor in comedy series, 1989, 90, 93, 94); film credits include The Survivors, 1983, Eddie Macon's Run, 1983, Revenge of the Nerds, 1984, C.H.U.D., 1984, Maria's Lovers, 1985, Sweet Dreams, 1985, True Stories, 1986, The Big Easy, 1987, Burglar, 1987, Raising Arizona, 1987, The Wrong Guys, 1988, Everybody's All-American, 1988, Punchline, 1988, Sea of Love, 1989, Always, 1989, Stella, 1990, Arachnophobia, 1990, King Ralph, 1990, Barton Fink, 1991, The Babe, 1992, Matinee, 1993, Born Yesterday, 1993, The Flintstones, 1994, Kingfish: A Story of Huey P. Long, 1995, Mother Night, 1996, Fallen, 1997, Combat!, 1997, The Borrowers, 1997, The Big Lebowski, 1998, Blues Brothers 2000, 1998, Dirty Work, 1998, The Runner, 1999, Bringing Out the Dead, 1999; tv movies include The Jack Bull, 1999; appeared in numerous commls. Office: Creative Artists Agency c/o Fred Specktor 9830 Wilshire Blvd Beverly Hills CA 90212-1825*

GOODMAN, JOHN M., construction executive; b. Omaha, 1947. BS in Acctg., Calif. State U., Long Beach, 1970; JD, Pepperdine U., 1974. CPA, Calif.; cert. real estate broker, Calif.; cert. ins. agt., Calif.; lic. contractor, Calif. Sr. v.p., CEO, dir. Lewis Homes Mgmt. Corp., Upland, Calif. Office: Lewis Operating Corp PO Box 670 Upland CA 91785-0670*

GOODMAN, JOSEPH WILFRED, electrical engineering educator; b. Boston, Feb. 8, 1936; s. Joseph and Doris (Ryan) G.; m. Hon Mai Lam, Dec. 5, 1962; 1 dau., Michele Ann. B.A., Harvard U., 1958; M.S. in E.E., Stanford U., 1960, Ph.D., 1963; DSc (hon.), U. Ala., 1996. Postdoctoral fellow Norwegian Def. Rsch. Establishment, Oslo, 1962-63; rsch. assoc. Stanford U., 1963-67, asst. prof., 1967-69, assoc. prof., 1969-72, prof. elec. engring., 1972—; vis. prof. Univ. Paris XI, Orsay, France, 1973-74; dir. Info. Sys. Lab. Elec. Engring. Stanford U., 1981-83, chmn. dept. of elec. engring., 1988-96, William E. Ayer prof. elec. engring., 1988—, sr. assoc. dean engring., 1996-98; cons. to govt. and industry, 1965—; v.p. Internat. Comm. for Optics, 1985-87, pres., 1988-90, past pres., 1991-93. Author: Introduction to Fourier Optics, 1968, 2nd edit. 1996, Statistical Optics, 1985, (with R. Gray) Fourier Transforms: An Introduction for Engineers; editor: International Trends in Optics, 1991; contbr. articles to profl. jours. Recipient F.E. Terman award Am. Soc. Engring. Edn., 1971, Frederic Ives Medal, 1990, Optical Soc. Am., Ester Hoffman Beller award Optical Soc. of Am., 1995. Fellow AAAS, Optical Soc. Am. (dir. 1977-83, editor jour. 1978-83, Max Born award 1983, Frederick Ives award 1990, Esther Hoffman Beller medal 1995, v.p. 1990, pres.-elect 1991, pres. 1992, past pres. 1993), IEEE (edn. medal 1987), Soc. Photo-optical Instrumentation Engrs. (bd. govs. 1979-82, 88-90, Dennis Gabor award 1987), Am. Acad. Arts & Scis.; mem. NAE, Electromagnetics Acad. Home: 570 University Ter Los Altos CA 94022-3523 Office: Stanford U Dept Elec Engring Dept Elec Engring Stanford CA 94305

GOODMAN, LAWRENCE EUGENE, structural analyst, educator; b. N.Y.C., Mar. 12, 1920; s. Joseph John and Dorothy (Goldberger) G.; m. Katherine Cecilia Lewis, Sept. 16, 1951; children: Jennifer Robin, Jeanne, Alice. AB, Columbia U., 1939, BSCE, 1940; MS in Applied Mechanics, U. Ill., 1942; PhD, Columbia U., 1948. Registered profl. engr. Lectr. Columbia U., N.Y.C., 1946-48; assoc. prof. civil engring. U. Ill., Urbana, 1948-54; prof. applied mechanics U. Minn., Mpls., 1954-65, dept. head civil engring., 1965-72, Record prof. civil engring., 1975-88, Record prof. emeritus, 1988—; cons. Xerxes Corp., Mpls., 1988; vis. prof. Tex. A&M U., College Station, 1991-92. Co-author: Statics, 1963, Dynamics, 1963; contbr. articles to profl. jours. Lt. U.S. Navy, 1943-46, PTO. Recipient Disting. Teaching award Regents of U. Minn. NSF sr. fellow, 1962-63. Fellow ASCE (Newmark Gold medal 1990), Am. Soc. of ME, 1970. Jewish. Home: 1589 Vincent Ave Saint Paul MN 55108-1324

GOODMAN, LINDSEY ALAN, furniture manufacturing executive, architect; b. L.A., Nov. 17, 1957; s. Ira and Wilma Carolyn (Sanders) G.; m. Joan Frances Radditz, July 7, 1990; children: Alexandra Isabelle, Andrew Nicholas. BA, UCLA, 1980; MArch, Calif. State Poly. U., Pomona, 1983. Registered architect. Project designer Bertram Berenson, Architect, Claremont, Calif., 1983; job capt. Architecture & Planning, San Rafael, Calif., 1985-86, Barry Archtl. Design Group, Santa Barbara, Calif., 1986-87; project architect Architects West, Santa Barbara, 1987-89; prin. L.A. Goodman, Architect, Santa Barbara, 1989-91; v.p. IWI/Internat., Chino, Calif., 1992—; CFO Gourmet Artists Inc., Santa Barbara, 1995—; ptnr. IWI/Capital Devel., Chino, 1991—; bd. advisors Human Race, Inc., Santa Barbara, 1997-98. Author: (poem) The Camargue, 1987. Mem. adv. coun. Santa Barbara Mus. Natural History, 1988-89, 95-96, trustee, 1989-95, v.p. bd. trustees, 96-98, pres., 1998—; patron Santa Barbara Civic Light Opera, 1992—; mem. Young Pres.'s Orgn., 1995—. Recipient Richard J. Neutra Meml. award, 1983. Mem. Coun. on Fgn. Rels. Avocations: tennis, international travel, reading, attending musicals and plays. Office: IWI/Internat 15044 La Palma Dr Chino CA 91710-9669

GOODMAN, LOUIS ALLAN, lawyer; b. Providence, Nov. 13, 1943; s. Jacob and Frieda (Feldman) G.; m. Phebe Silver, June 9, 1968; children: Jonathan J., Rebecca A. AB, Columbia U., 1965; MA, Harvard U., 1966, JD, 1969. Bar: N.Y. 1970, Mass. 1973. Assoc. Skadden, Arps, Slate, Meagher & Flom LLP, 1970-72, 73-77, ptnr., 1978—. Home: 59 North St Newton MA 02460-1065 Office: Skadden Arps Slate Meagher & Flom LLP 1 Beacon St Boston MA 02108-3107

GOODMAN, MAJOR MERLIN, botanical sciences educator; b. Iowa, Sept. 13, 1938; s. Jarrett Wilson and Mable Ollie (Michael) G.; m. Sheila Balfour Dail; children: Sean Balfour Dail, Andrew Scot Dail. BS, Iowa State U., 1960; MS, N.C. State U., 1963, PhD, 1965. Rsch. asst. N.C. State U., Raleigh, 1960-61, NSF coop. fellow, 1961-65; NSF postdoctoral fellow Inst. de Genetica Escola Superior de Agricultura, Piracicaba, Sao Paulo, Brazil, 1965-67; vis. asst. prof. N.C. State U., Raleigh, 1967-68, asst. prof., 1968-70, assoc. prof., 1970-76, prof. crop sci., statistics, genetics, botany, 1976-88, W.N. Reynolds disting. univ. prof., 1988—. Co-author: Races of Maize in Brazil and Adjacent Areas, 1977; author numerous tech. artilces. Recipient research awards Sigma Xi, 1973, N.C. State U. Alumni Assn., 1982, O.M.Gardner award, 1987; named Outstanding PhD Phi Sigma and Phi Kappa Phi, 1965. Mem. Crop Sci. Soc. Am., Soc. for Econ. Botany, Soc. for Systematic Botany, Nat. Acad. Scis. Achievements include clarification of genetics of numerous isozyme loci in maize including chromosomal localizations; devel. of several commercially used parental inbred lines of corn. Office: NC State Univ Box 7620 Crop Sci Dept Raleigh NC 27695

GOODMAN, MARGARET GERTRUDE, government administrator; b. East Troy, Wis., Aug. 29, 1947; d. Andrew J. and Florence M. (Zinn) G.; 1 child, Mary Zinn. BA, Beloit Coll., 1969; MA, Johns Hopkins U., 1971. Legis. asst. to Rep. Clement J. Zablocki Ho. of Reps., Washington, 1971-73, staff cons. Com. Fgn. Affairs, 1977-93; fgn. policy analyst Congl. Rsch. Svc., Libr. Congress, Washington, 1973-77; regional dir. for Asia and Pacific Peace Corps, Washington, 1993-97; country dir. Peace Corps, Bangladesh, 1998—. Mem. Soc. Internat. Devel. (pres. Washington chpt. 1982-84, internat. v.p. 1988-91), Women in Fgn. Policy Assn., Asia Soc. Democrat. Office: Peace Corps 1990 K St NW Rm 7616 Washington DC 20006-1103*

GOODMAN, MARK, journalist, educator. B in Journalism with honors, U. Mo., 1982; JD, Duke U., 1985. Lectr. U. Md. Univ. Coll., College Park, 1987-88; exec. dir. Student Press Law Ctr., Washington, 1985—; mem. faculty Inst. Study Ednl. Policy, U. Wash., Seattle, 1987; instr. summer journalism workshops Ball State U., Muncie, Ind., 1988, U. Iowa, Iowa City, 1991, 92, 93, 94, Mich. State U., East Lansing, 1991, 93; adj. guest lectr. Sch. Mass Comm., Bowling Green (Ohio) State U., 1990; mem. faculty coll. newspaper advisers seminar Poynter Inst. Media Studies, St. Petersburg, Fla., 1989, 90, 92; media law com. Coll. Media Advisers, Inc.; panelist Danforth Found., 1988, 89, Assn. Edn. in Journalism and Mass Comm., 1987, 88; guest lectr. Sch. Comm. Am. U., Washington, 1989, 90, 94. Contbr. articles to profl. jours. Recipient Golden Quill award Garden State Scholastic Press Assn., 1987, Disting. Svc. award Mich. Interscholastic Press Assn., 1987, Ind. Scholastic Journalism award Ball State U., 1988, Disting. Svc. award So. Interscholastic Press Assn., 1988, Presdl. citations Coll. Media Advisers, Inc., 1987, 88, 89, Disting. Svc. award Fla. C.C. Press Assn., 1989, Knight award, Earl English Scholastic Journalism award Mo. Interscholastic Press Assn./Mo. Journalism Edn. Assn., 1992, Cert. of Merit, Soc. Collegiate Journalists, 1989, Gold Key award Columbia U. Scholastic Press Assn., 1988, Carl Towley award Journalism Edn. Assn., 1992. Mem. Kappa Tau Alpha. Home: 1636 Florida Ave NW Washington DC 20009-2603 Office: Student Press Law Ctr 1101 Wilson Blvd Ste 1910 Arlington VA 22209-2248*

GOODMAN, MARK N., lawyer; b. Phoenix, Jan. 16, 1952; s. Daniel H. and Joanne Goodman; m. Gwendolyn A. Langfeldt, Oct. 24, 1982; children: Zachary A., Alexander D. BA, Prescott Coll., 1973; JD summa cum laude, Calif. Western Sch. Law, 1977; LLM, U. Calif., Berkeley, 1978. Bar: Ariz. 1977, U.S. Dist. Ct. Ariz. 1978, U.S. Ct. Appeals (9th cir.) 1978, U.S. Supreme Ct. 1981. Practice Law Offices Mark N. Goodman, Prescott, Ariz., 1978-79, 81-82, Mark N. Goodman, Ltd., Prescott, 1983-86; ptnr. alward and Goodman, Ltd., Prescott, 1979-81, Perry, Goodman, Drutz & Musgrove, Prescott, 1986-87, Goodman, Drutz & Musgrove, Prescott, 1987-88, Sears & Goodman, P.C., Prescott, 1988-92, Goodman Law Firm, P.C., Prescott, 1992—. Author: The Ninth Amendment, 1981; contbr. articles to profl. jours.; notes and comments editor Calif. Western Law Rev., 1976. Bd. dirs. Yavapai Symphony Assn., Prescott, 1981-84, N. Ariz. chpt. Alzheimer's Assn., 1995-97. Mem. ABA, Def. Rsch. Inst., State Bar Ariz. (fee arbitration com. vice chmn. 1988—), Yavapai County Bar Assn. (v.p. 1981-82). E-mail: mng@goodmanlaw.com. Office: Goodman Law Firm PC PO Box 2489 Prescott AZ 86302-2489

GOODMAN, MARK PAUL, physician; b. N.Y.C., Mar. 6, 1967; s. Leonard Carl and Alice Belle (Barnum) G. BS in Biology cum laude, UCLA, 1989, MD, 1993. Diplomate Am. Bd. Internal Medicine. Resident physician UCLA Med. Ctr., 1993-96, internist, 1996—; mem. risk mgmt. com., ethics com. UCLA Med. Ctr.; mem. morbidity and mortality com. UCLA Dept. Medicine. Author: The Physician in Sherlock Holmes: The Anatomy of a Legend, 1993 (Donald O'Malley award in med. history). Founder, 1st pres. UCLA Regents Scholar Soc., 1989. U. Calif. Regents scholar, U. Calif. Alumni scholar, L.A. County Med. Assn. scholar. Mem. AMA (nat. patient safety found., western steering com.), ACP, Los Angeles County Med. Assn., UCLA Med. Alumni Assn., Golden Key Honor Soc., Phi Eta Sigma. Avocations: nature, photography, music and the arts, travel, marine fish, skiing. Office: 9400 Brighton Way Ste 201 Beverly Hills CA 90210-4709

GOODMAN, MAX A., lawyer, educator; b. Chgo., May 24, 1924; s. Sam and Nettie (Abramowitz) G.; m. Marlyene Monkarsh, June 2, 1946; children: Jan M., Lauren A. Packard, Melanie Murez. AA, Herzl Jr. Coll., 1943; student, Northwestern U., 1946-47; JD, Loyola U., 1948. Bar: Calif. 1948; cert. family law specialist, 1980, 85, 90. Pvt. practice L.A., 1948-53; ptnr. Goodman, Hirschberg & King, L.A., 1953-81; prof. Southwestern U. Sch. Law, L.A., 1966—; lectr. Calif. Continuing Edn. of the Bar, 1971—; editorial cons. Bancroft Whitney, San Francisco, 1986—. Contbr. articles to profl. jours. Served to cpl. U.S. Army, 1943-45. Mem. ABA (chmn. law sch. curriculum com. family law sect. 1987-88, family law sect. 1987-88, 97-98), State Bar Calif. (del. conf. dels. 1972, 80-87, 91, exec. com. family law sect. 1981-85), Los Angeles County Bar Assn. (chmn. family law sect. 1971-72, editor family law handbook 1974-89). Avocation: contract bridge. Office: Southwestern U Sch of Law 675 S Westmoreland Ave Los Angeles CA 90005-3905

GOODMAN, MICHAEL B(ARRY), communications educator; b. Dallas, July 10, 1949; s. Harold A. and Dora (Einhorn) G.; m. Karen E. Kailenta, June 4, 1977; children: 1 stepchild, Craig Cook, 1 child, John David. BA, U. Tex., 1971; MA, SUNY, Stony Brook, 1972, PhD, 1979. Adj. instr. SUNY,

Old Westbury, 1976-79; adj. asst. prof. N.Y. Inst. Tech., N.Y.C., 1976-82, N.Y.U., 1979-81; asst. prof. SUNY, Stony Brook, 1979-81, Northea. U., Boston, 1982-86; prof., dir. MA in Corp. Comm. program Fairleigh Dickinson U., Madison, N.J., 1986—; cons. in communications to numerous orgns. in U.S.; conducts seminars and workshops on written communication, 1979—; conf. chmn. Internat. Profl. Communication Conf., Phila., 1993, New Orleans, 1999; lectr. Moscow, 1992, U. Alaska, 1996; founder Ann. Conf. on Corp. Comm., 1988—. Author: William S. Burroughs: An Annotated Bibliography, 1975, Contemporary Literary Censorship: The Case History of Burroughs Naked Lunch, 1981, Write to the Point: Effective Communication in the Workplace, 1984, William S. Burroughs: A Research Guide, 1990, Corporate Communication: Theory and Practice, 1994, Working in a Global Environment—Understanding, Communicating, and Managing Transnationally, 1995, Corporate Communications for Executives, 1998; contbr. articles and revs. to profl. jours., encys. and lit. mags.; assoc. editor Issues in Corp. Comm., IEEE Transactions on Profl. Comm., 1990—; editl. bd. mem. N.J. Jour. Comm.; cons. reader for Coll. English. V.p. Friends Sem. PTA, N.Y.C., 1990-91. Named to Resident Faculty Nat. Faculty Excellence in Teaching English Program, Vassar Coll., 1984. Mem. Profl. Comm. Soc. of IEEE (sr., mem. adminstrv. com., Alfred Goldsmith award 1994), MLA, Nat. Coun. Tchrs. of English, Soc. for Tech. Comm. (sr.), Am. Mgmt. Assn., Assn. for Bus. Comm., Authors Guild, Authors League. Avocations: hiking, skiing, running, cycling. Home: 28 W 38th St Apt 11W New York NY 10018-6235 Office: Fairleigh Dickinson U 285 Madison Ave Madison NJ 07940-1099

GOODMAN, NORMAN, sociologist, researcher; b. N.Y.C., Feb. 19, 1934; s. Jack Goodman and Hannah (Hoffman) Brodsky; m. Marilyn Goldberg, Dec. 26, 1954; children: Jack, Susan, Carolyn. BA, Bklyn. Coll., 1955; MA, NYU, 1961, PhD, 1963. Social investigator N.Y.C. Dept. of Welfare, Bklyn., 1957-58; instr. sociology Columbia U. Tchrs. Coll., N.Y.C., 1961-62; from lectr. to asst. prof. Queens Coll. CUNY, 1962-64; from asst. to assoc. prof. SUNY, Stony Brook, 1964-73, prof., chmn. sociology dept., 1973-89, Disting. Teaching prof. sociology, 1986—, Disting. Svc. prof., 1990—; reviewer proposals NSF, 1975-76, Social Scis. and Humanities Council of Can., 1981-86; reviewer manuscripts numerous pubs., N.Y.C., 1970—. Author: (with others) Personality and Decision Processes, 1962, (with others) Society Today, 3d edit., 1978, 4th edit., 1982; (with other) Marriage, Family and Intimate Relationships, 1980, (with other) Social Roles and Social Institutions, 1991, Introduction to Sociology, 1992, Marriage and the Family, 1993, (with other) Test Yourself in Introduction to Sociology, 1996, (with others) Extending Self-Esteem Theory and Research: Sociological and Psychological Currents, 2000. Served with U.S. Army, 1955-56. Mem. Am. Sociol. Assn., Eastern Sociol. Soc., Soc. for Study of Symbolic Interaction, Nat. Council on Family Relations. Jewish. Avocations: classical and operatic music, sports. Office: SUNY At Stony Brook Dept Sociology Stony Brook NY 11794-4356

GOODMAN, NORMAN LOYAL, microbiologist, educator; b. Milburn, Okla., Sept. 29, 1931; s. James Loyal and Jocie Lee (Clemons) G. ;m. Markita Marie Staton; children: James, Cathryn. BS, Southeastern State U., Durant, Okla., 1954; MS, U. Okla., 1960, PhD, 1965. Diplomate Am. Bd. Med. Microbiology, Am. Bd. bioanalysis. Microbiologist USPHS, Norman, Okla., 1962-68; asst. prof., dir. bacteriology lba. Med. U. S.C., Charleston, 1968-71; from assoc. prof. to prof. dept. pathology, dir. mycology U. Ky. Coll. Medicine, Lexington, 1971—; cons. Bur. Lab. Svcs. S.C. Bd. Health, Columbia, 1969-71. Fellow Am. Acad. Microbiology (bd. govs. 1983-86); mem. Am. Soc. Microbiology (chmn. continuing edn. com. 1975-79, chmn. mycology divsn. 1976-77), Mycol. Soc. Am. (pres. 1982), Internat. Union Microbiol. Socs. (chmn. mycology divsn. 1982-86), South Ctrl. Assn. Clin. Microbiology (pres. 1992). Home: 2153 Lakeside Dr Lexington KY 40502-3073 Office: U Ky Coll Medicine 800 Rose St Lexington KY 40536

GOODMAN, ROBERT MERWIN, microbiologist, plant biologist, educator; b. Ithaca, N.Y., Dec. 30, 1945; s. Robert Browning and Janet Edith (Pond) G.; 1 child, Nathan Mansfield. Student, Johns Hopkins U., 1963-65; B.Sc., Cornell U., 1967, Ph.D., 1973. Vis. rsch. fellow John Innes Inst., Norwich, Eng., 1973-74; asst. prof. U. Ill., Urbana, 1974-78; assoc. prof. U. Ill., 1978-81, prof., 1981-83; exec. v.p. R&D Calgene, Inc., Davis, Calif., 1982-90; sr. scholar-in-residence NRC, 1990-91; vis. prof. U. Wis., Madison, 1990-91, prof., 1991—, prof., chair undergrad. program molecular biology, 1993—; mem. Bd. on Agr., NRC, 1986-91, chair com. on exam. plant sci. rsch. programs U.S., 1990-92, Commn. on Life Sci.; bd. dirs. Cornell Rsch. Found., Inc.; mem. NSF Task Force: Biology, Behavioral and Social Scis. Looking to 21st Century, 1990-91; cons. W.K. Kellogg Found., 1990-94; chmn. oversight com. collaborative crop rsch. program McKnight Found. Editor: Expanding the Use of Soybeans, 1976; assoc. editor Virology, 1976-94; mem. editl. bd. Plant Molecular Biology-Molecular Breeding, 1994—. Pres. Channing-Murray Found., Urbana, Ill., 1976-78; bd. dirs. Sacramento Sci. Ctr., 1989-90. NSF-NATO postdoctoral fellow, 1973. Mem. AAAS, Am. Chem. Soc., Internat. Soc. Plant Molecular Biology, Internat. Soc. Molecular Plant Microbe Interactions, Am. Soc. Microbiology, Soc. Gen. Microbiology. Office: U Wisconsin Russell Laboratories 1630 Linden Dr Madison WI 53706-1520*

GOODMAN, ROGER MARK, television director; b. Chgo., Apr. 28, 1945; s. David and Bette (Goldfinger) G.; m. Sharon Ann Dosh, July 5, 1975; children: Danielle Lynn, Gregory Michael. Student, Tarkio Coll. Prodn. assoc. WBKB, Chgo., 1964-65; prodn. assoc. ABC Sports, N.Y.C., 1965-68, assoc. dir., 1968-76, dir., 1976-80; dir. prodn. devel. ABC News and Sports, N.Y.C., 1980-85, dir. prodn. and design, 1985-95; sr. dir. ABC News, N.Y.C., 1996—; exec. dir. spl. projects ABC TV Network, N.Y.C., 1992—. Recipient 21 Emmy awards, Silver award Internat. Film and 3 Cine TV Festival, 1982, Gold award Internat. Film and TV Festival, 1983, Desi award, 1983, Creativity award, 1983, 85, Typographic Excellence award, 1984, Gold Baton Alfred I. DuPont Awards, 1985. Office: ABC News 47 W 66th St Fl 6 New York NY 10023-6201*

GOODMAN, ROY MATZ, state senator, business executive; b. N.Y.C., Mar. 5, 1930; s. Bernard A. and Alice (Matz) G.; m. Barbara Christine Furrer, June 28, 1955; children: Claire Goodman Pellegrini Cloud, Leslie Alice, Randolph Bernard. BA cum laude, Harvard U., 1951, MBA with distinction, 1953; DHL (hon.), Pratt Inst., 1994. Assoc. buying and new bus. dept. Kuhn, Loeb & Co. Investment Bankers, 1955-60; pres. Drug Devel. Corp., Ex-Lax, Inc., Roycemore, Inc., 1962-71; mem. N.Y. State Senate, 1966—; dep. majority leader for policy, chmn. investigations, taxation and govt. ops. com.; chmn. Senate spl. com. on arts and cultural affairs; mem. Senate task force on def. spending, AIDS, vandalism, religious desecration and bigotry, and econ. recovery and devel.; mem. fin., rules, cities, edn., crime and correction and transp. coms., subcom. on libraries chmn. legis. com. on pub. pvt., coop., 1985-88; chmn. housing and urban devel. com., 1968-76; pres. Goodman Family Found.; bd. dirs. M & T Bank Corp.; adv. bd. Chemical Bank, 1963-65; commr. fin., fin. adminstr. City of N.Y., 1966-68; mem. N.Y.C. Banking Commn., 1966-68; trustee N.Y.C. Police Pension Fund, N.Y.C. Fire Dept. Pension Fund, 1966-68; mem. Mayor's Cabinet and Supercabinet, N.Y.C. Treasurer, 1966-68; Chmn. State Charter Revision Commn. for N.Y.C., 1972-76; adj. prof. pub. admin. Baruch Coll. CUNY, 1975; mem. Mayor Guiliani Transition Team, 1993, Gov. Pataki Transition Team, 1994; pres. Roycemore Inc., 1968-70, also bd. dirs.; pres. Drug Devel. Corp., 1968-70, bd. dirs.; bd. dirs. 1st Empire State Corp.; mem. Bklyn. adv. bd. Chem. Bank N.Y. Trust Co., 1963-65; commr. fin., fin. adminstr. City of N.Y., 1966-68; mem. mayor's cabinet and supercabinet, 1966-68; chmn. Housing and Urban Devel. Com., 1968-76, State Charter Revision Commn. for N.Y.C., 1972-76; adj. prof. pub. adminstrn. Baruch Coll. CUNY, 1975; mem. Gov. Pataki Transition Team, 1994, Mayor Giuliani Transition Team, 1993. Mem. N.Y.C. Banking Commn., 1966-67; past trustee N.Y.C. Police Pension Fund, N.Y.C. Fire Dept. Pension Fund; trustee Dalton Schs.; past mem. bd. Brotherhood-In-Action; trustee Heart Research Found.; exec. asst. to chmn. N.Y. State Assembly Jud. Com., 1963-64; asst. to atty. gen. State N.Y., 1960; pres. 9th A.D. Rep. Club, 1963-64; del. N.Y. State Rep. Convs., 1966-94, Rep. Nat. Conv., 1968, 72, 76, 80, 84, 88, 92. 96, Presdl. Elector, 1984; chmn. N.Y. County Rep. Com., 1981—, treas., 1965; mem. N.Y. Rep. State Com., exec. com.; N.Y. State co-chmn. Bush-for-Pres. campaigns, 1988, 92, Bush-Quayle Nat. Fin. Com., 1988, 92; candidate for Mayor of N.Y.C., 1977; trustee Carnegie Hall Soc., Inc., Carnegie Hall Corp., past trustee Barnard Coll., Columbia Coll. Pharm. Scis., L.I. Coll. Hosp., N.Y. Com. Young Audiences, United Jewish Appeal, Tel Aviv U., Freedom House, Dalton Schs. Brotherhood-In-Action, Heart Rsch. Found.; presdl. appointee to Nat. Commn. Fine Arts, 1985-89, Nat. Coun. Arts, 1989-96; amb. arts NEA; fellow Met. Mus. Art; patron Met. Opera; sponsor N.Y. Philharm. Soc.; mem. Regents vis. com. N.Y. State Mus.; trustee Temple Emanu-El; bd. dirs. N.Y. Legis. Svc., Inc., 1990; past bd. dirs. Freedom House, Dalton Sch.; mem. council advisors N.Y. Com. for Young Audiences, Harvard Com. on Univ. Resources,; mem. com. Harvard U. Overseers visitors com. John F. Kennedy Sch. Govt. & Harvard com. Univ. Resources. Lt. USNR, 1953-56. Recipient Disting. Service award (Young Man of Yr.) Jaycees, 1966, Mt. Scopus citation Hebrew U., Jerusalem, 1968, Scroll of Honor United Jewish Appeal, 1970, Kennedy Ctr. award for Disting. Leadership in Arts-in Edn., Nat. Arts Club Citation of Merit, Medal of Merit City U., 1972, Man of Yr. award Brotherhood-in-Action, 1972, Humanitarian award Soc. for Prevention Cruelty to Children, 1976, citation for community service Odyssey House, 1976, Our Town newspaper award for leadership in City Charter revision, 1976, Fiorello H. LaGuardia Meml. award, 1979-80, citation for outstanding service N.Y. Young Rep. Club, 1982, Disting. Alumni award Hunter Coll. Elem. Sch. Parents Assn., 1985, Service awards N.Y. Police Found. and N.Y. Fire Safety Found., 1986, Patriotic Service award U.S. Treasury Dept.; named to honor scroll Columbia Assn. of N.Y.C. Police Dept., 1979, N.Y. State Rep. of Yr. Ripon Soc., 1972, Cmty. Activist award Lenox Hill Neighborhood Assn., Inc., 1995, Artists fellowship award, John LaFarge Meml. award for interracial justice, Local Hero award Stanley Isaacs Assn., Playwrights Horizon award, 1995, Gari Melchers Meml. medal Artists Fellowship, Inc., 1995, South Street Seaport Mus. award, 1995, Friend of the Arts award Town Hall Found., 1995, Legacy of Hope award N.Y. Foundling Home, Carnegie Hall, 1996, Margaret Sanger award Family Advs. N.Y., 1997; named Statesman Father of Yr. award, 1984, named to Econ. Hon. Soc. St. John's U., 1991. Mem. Anti-Defamation League (bd. govs. N.Y.), Am. Young Pres.'s Orgn., Fin. Analysts Fedn., N.Y. Soc. Security Analysts, Council Fgn. Relations, Assn. Harvard Alumni (past dir.), Harvard Club (gov.), Century Assn., Century Country Club, Dutch Treat Club, Senate Club (pres.), Harvard Bus. Sch., City Club, Fort Washington, Omicron Delta Epsilon (hon.). Clubs: City, Century Assn., Harvard Bus. Sch. (N.Y.C.); Senate of N.Y. State; Harvard (gov.); Century Country (Purchase, N.Y.); Fort Orange (Albany, N.Y.); Dutch Treat. Home: 1035 Fifth Ave New York NY 10007-0135 Office: 633 Third Ave 31st Fl New York NY 10017 also: NY State Senate Legislative Office Bldg Rm 913 Albany NY 12247

GOODMAN, SAM RICHARD, electronics company executive; b. N.Y.C., May 23, 1930; s. Morris and Virginia (Gross) G.; m. Beatrice Bettencourt, Sept. 15, 1957; children—Mark Stuart, Stephen Manuel, Christopher Bettencourt. BBA, CCNY, 1951; MBA, NYU, 1957, PhD, 1968. Chief acct. John C. Valentine Co., N.Y.C., 1957-60; mgr. budgets and analysis Gen. Foods. Corp., White Plains, N.Y., 1960-63; budget dir. Crowell Collier Pub. Co., N.Y.C., 1963-64; v.p., chief fin. officer Nestle Co., Inc., White Plains, 1964; chief fin. officer Aileen, Inc., N.Y.C., 1973-74, Ampex Corp., 1974-76; exec. v.p. fin. and adminstrn. Baker & Taylor Co. div. W.R. Grace Co., N.Y.C., 1976-79, Magnuson Computer Systems, Inc., San Jose, Calif., 1979-81; v.p., chief fin. officer Datamac Computer Systems, Sunnyvale, Calif., 1981; pres. Nutritional Foods Inc., San Francisco, 1983-84; chmn., chief exec. officer CMX Corp., Santa Clara, Calif., 1984-88; dir., sr. v.p. Masstor Systems Corp., Santa Clara, 1988—; pvt. cons. Atherton, Calif., 1990—; sr. mgmt. cons. Durkee/Sharlit, 1991—; pres. Mayfair Packing Co., 1991—; mng. dir. Quincy Pacific Ptnrs., L.P., 1992—; pres., CEO Mayfair Packing Co., San Jose, Calif., 1991-94; pvt. cons. SRG Assocs., 1994—; lectr. NYU Inst. Mgmt., 1965-67; asst. prof. mktg. Iona Coll. Grad. Sch. Adminstrn., 1967-69; prof. Golden Gate U., 1974—; prof. fin. and mktg. Pace U. Grad. Sch. Bus. Adminstrn., 1969-79. Author 7 books, including Controller's Handbook; contbr. articles to jours. Lt. (j.g.) USNR, 1951-55. Mem. Fin. Execs. Inst., Nat. Assn. Accts., Am. Statis. Assn., Am. Econs. Assn., Planning Execs. Inst., Am. Arbitration Assn., Turnaround Mgmt. Assn. Home and Office: 60 Shearer Dr Atherton CA 94027-3957

GOODMAN, SEYMOUR EVAN, computer science and international studies educator, researcher, consultant; b. Chgo., June 19, 1943; s. Paul S. and Shirley (Young) G.; m. Diane Margot Samuel, Dec. 18, 1966; children: Richard Michael, Steven Neal. BS, Columbia U., 1965, MS, 1966; PhD, Calif. Inst. Tech., 1970. Asst. prof. applied math. U. Va., Charlottesville, 1970-75, assoc. prof. applied math. and computer sci., 1975-81; prof. mgmt. info. sys. U. Ariz., Tucson, 1981—; prof. Sam Nunn Sch. Internat. Affairs Ga. Inst. of Tech., Atlanta, 1999—; vis. prof. pub. and internat. affairs, Princeton (N.J.) U., 1977-79, rsch. fellow, 1978-79; vis. scholar U. Chgo., 1979; mem. Mid. Ea. Ctr., 1992—; Carnegie Sci. fellow Ctr. Internat. Security and Arms Control, Stanford U., 1994-97; dir. program info. tech. and nat. security, 1996-98, dir. Consortium for Rsch. on Info. Security and Policy, Stanford U., 1998—, vis. prof. dept. engring. econ. sys. and ops. rsch., 1998-99; mem. adv. com. Internat. Trade Adminstrn., Dept. Commerce, 1979-82; mem. adv. com. Def. Sci. Bd., Dept. Def., 1981-84, Def. Intelligence Agy., 1983-87, NRC coms., 1985-92, Dept. State, 1987-89; chmn. NRC com. Internat. Devel. in Computer Sci. and Tech., 1987-88; chmn. computer tech.-subpanel NRC panel on Future Design and Implementation of U.S. Nat. Security Export Controls, 1989-91; cons. govtl. agys. Danforth Assoc., 1977-82; Sesquicentennial Assoc. State of Va., 1977. Editor: Technology and Transnational Political Issues, International Information Systems, 1991-93; adv. bd. PRIISM, 1995-97; adv. editor Jour. Global Info. Tech. Mgmt., 1997—; contbr. numerous articles to profl. jours. NSF grantee, 1978-79, 83; numerous grant and rsch. contracts Office Tech. Assessment, U.S. Congress, 1979-81, Los Alamos Nat. Lab., USAF, Battelle Meml. Labs., IBM, Nat. Coun. for Soviet and East European Rsch., Dept. Commerce, Dept. Def.; U.S. participant U.S.-USSR IREX program, 1988-96. Mem. Assn. for Computing Machinery (nat. lectr. 1981-82, com. computing and pub. policy 1981-83, 93—, contbg. editor Internat. Perspectives, Comms. 1991—), Am. Assn. for Advancement of Slavic Studies, Computer Soc. of IEEE (com. on pub. policy 1987-95), Highlands Forum. Office: Ga Inst Tech Sam Nunn Sch Internat Affairs Habersham Bldg Atlanta GA 30332

GOODMAN, SHERRI WASSERMAN, lawyer; b. N.Y.C., Apr. 9, 1959; m. John B. Goodman, Aug. 8, 1987. BA, Amherst (Mass.) Coll., 1981; JD, MPP, Harvard U., 1987. Bar: Mass. 1988, D.C. 1990. Analyst Sci. Applications, Inc., McLean, Va., 1981-83; counsel Senate Armed Svcs. Com., Washington, 1987-90; assoc. Goodwin, Procter & Hoar, Boston, 1990-93; dep. und. sec. of def., Env. Security D.O.D., Washington, 1993—; cons. Def. Nuclear Facilities Safety Bd., Washington, 1990—, PEW Faculty Fellowship in Internat. Affairs, Cambridge, Mass. Author: The Neutron Bomb Controversy, 1983, Weapons Acquisition, 1988; contbr. articles to profl. jours. Vol. Mayor's Youth Leadership Corps, Boston, 1990-91. Mem. Coun. on Fgn. Rels. Office: 3400 Defense Rm 3E792 Pentagon Washington DC 20301-3400

GOODMAN, STANLEY, lawyer; b. Cin., June 16, 1931; s. Sol and Ethel (Barsman) G.; m. Diane Elaine Kassel, Apr. 15, 1956; children: Julie Lerner, Jeffrey Stephen, Richard Paul. BA, U. Cin., 1953, JD, 1955. Bar: Ohio 1955, Ky. 1976. Ptnr. Goodman & Goodman, Cin., 1955—; dir. Cin. Boss Co., Winbco Tank Co., Ottumwa, Iowa; lectr. Ohio Bar Continuing Legal Edn. Series. Mem. ABA, Am. Health Lawyers Assn., Ohio Bar Assn., Ky. Bar Assn., Cin. Bar Assn., Bankers Club, Losantiville Country Club. Jewish. Office: 123 E 4th St Cincinnati OH 45202-4003

GOODMAN, STANLEY LEONARD, advertising executive; b. N.Y.C., Jan. 21, 1920; s. Abraham and Leah (Fellman) G.; m. Anita Davis, Aug. 30, 1960; children—Patricia, Laurence; stepchildren—Marilyn Rice, Stuart Rice. B.S. in Econs, Wharton Sch. U. Pa., 1941; certificate electronics, U. Richmond, 1943. Asst. to pres. Decca Records, Inc., N.Y.C., 1941-56; v.p., mktg. dir. Grayson Robinson Stores, N.Y.C., 1956-61; club plan creative dir. Popular Mdse. Co., Inc., Passaic, N.J., 1961-62, dir. mktg., 1962-64; pres. Elliot, Goodman & Russell, Inc., advt., N.Y.C., 1964, EGR Travel Promotion, Inc., N.Y.C., 1969-80, EGR Mktg., Inc., N.Y.C., 1968-80, EGR Communications, Inc., Detroit, 1969-80; chmn. Consol. Tech. Industries, Northvale, N.J., 1987—; pres., dir. EGR Communications, Inc., N.Y.C., 1968—; dir. Pub. Service Mut. Ins. Co., N.Y.C.; Lectr. Am. Mgmt. Assn., 1964-82; instr. mktg. dept. Pace Coll.; chmn. Consolidated Tech. Industries, Inc., 1988—. Contbr. articles to sales mags. Bd. trustees Westchester Philharmonic Orch., 1996—, Union Am. Hebrew Congs., 1996—. Mem. Sales Promotion Execs. Assn. (Sales Promotion Man of Year N.Y. 1959, internat. pres. 1960-62, honored Stanley Goodman grant 1954—), Direct Mail Advt. Assn., Council Sales Promotion Agys. (pres. 1969-71), Am. Mktg. Assn., Hundred Million Club, Westchester Alumni Assn. U. Pa. (v.p. 1966—). Home: 46 Crosshill Rd Hartsdale NY 10530-3013 Office: 157 Veterans Dr Northvale NJ 07647-2301

GOODMAN, STEPHEN MURRY, lawyer; b. Phila., Oct. 8, 1940; s. Edward and Jean (Landau) G.; m. Janis Freeman, Jan. 8, 1983; children: Carl, Rachel. BS cum laude, U. Pa., 1962, LLB magna cum laude, 1965. Bar: D.C. 1967, Pa. 1969. Law clerk to Hon. David Bazelon U.S. Ct. Appeals (D.C. cir.), Washington, 1965-66; law clk. to Hon. William J. Brennan Jr. U.S. Supreme Ct., Washington, 1966-67; ptnr. Goodman & Ewing, Phila., 1970-83, Wolf, Block, Schorr & Solis-Cohen, Phila., 1983-94, Morgan, Lewis & Bockius LLP. Mem. Order of Coif. Democrat. Jewish. Avocation: profl. jazz pianist. Office: Morgan Lewis & Bockius LLP 1701 Market St Philadelphia PA 19103-2921

GOODMAN, STEVEN ROY, educational consultant, lawyer; b. Queens, N.Y., Aug. 12, 1963; s. Wallace Kalman Goodman and Pearl Iris (Rosenberg) Taylor. BA, Duke U., 1985; MS in Higher Edn., U. Pa., 1989; JD, U. So. Calif., 1989. Bar: Pa. 1990, D.C. 1991, N.Y. 1997. Assoc. Kynazis & Assocs., Phila., 1989-96; admissions cons. L.A., Phila., Washington, 1986—; assoc. Kynazis & Assocs., Phila., 1989-96; adj. lectr. The Wharton Sch., 1994-95, 95-96; cons. Eisenhower Exch. Fellowships, Phila., 1993; legal rschr. U. Western Cape, South Africa, 1992; bd. dirs. Assn. Interactive Media, Washington, 1994-98; bd. trustees Phila. Bar Assn. Internat. Human Rights Fund, 1993—; U.S. spkr. U.S. Info. Svc., Liberia, 1997, profl.-in-residence, U.S. Info. Svc., Tanzania, 1995, 96. Election observer South African Elections, Kwa Zulu, Natal, South Africa, 1994. Recipient Cert. of Attendance, Hague Acad. Internat. Law, The Netherlands, 1994. Mem. Phila. Com. Fgn. Rels, Charlottesville Com. Fgn. Rels. Avocations: tennis, travel, college admissions, ballroom dance. Home: Schuyler Arms 705 1954 Columbia Rd NW Washington DC 20009-5040

GOODMAN, SUSAN, English language educator; b. Boston, Mar. 20, 1951; d. Ralph and Rhoda (Cohen) R.; m. Carl Dawson, July 28, 1995. BA, U. N.H., 1972, MEd, 1974, MA, 1985, PhD, 1988. English tchr. various sch. dists., Maine, N.H., 1972-83; asst. to assoc. prof. English Calif. State U., Fresno, 1989-94, U. Del., Newark, 1994—. Author: Edith Wharton's Women: Friends and Rivals, 1990, Edith Wharton's Women, 1994, Ellen Glasgow: A Biography, 1998. Resident fellow Va. Ctr. for the Humanities, 1991. Mem. MLA, Ellen Glasgow Soc., Edith Wharton Soc., Soc. for the Study of So. Lit. Office: U Del Dept English Newark DE 19716

GOODMAN, SUSAN KATHLEEN, charitable organization administrator, educator; b. Seattle, Dec. 29, 1952; d. Robert S. and Barbara J. (Tseka) Campbell. BA with honors in Music, Wash. State U., 1976, BA with honors in Elem. Edn., 1976. Dir. St. Francis Episcopal Youth Brass Choir, Tex., 1976-79; pvt. music tchr. Bend, Oreg., 1979—; devel. assoc. St. Charles Med. Ctr. Found., Bend, 1992-96, dir. devel., 1997—; music dir. Trinity Episcopal Church, 1979-89; adj. prof. French horn Ctrl. Oreg. C.C., 1979-89; substitute tchr. Bend LaPine (Oreg.) schs., 1980-82; team tchr. band Cascade (Oreg.) Jr. H.S., 1982; exec. dir. Cascade Festival Music, 1982-92; mgmt. cons. Oreg. Coast Music Festival, Coos Bay, 1989, Wash. Music Educators Assn., spkr. bd. dirs. retreat, 1993; project dir. Regional Arts Coun. Ctrl. Oreg., 1995; tutor Friends of Thompson Sch., 1992-94. musician Houston Civic Symphony, 1976-79; prin. hornist, mgr. Ctrl. Oreg. Symphony; prin. hornist Brass and Woodwind Quintets, 1979-89; conductor, arranger, performer, then head coach orchestral ministries Westside Ch., Bend, Oreg., 1995—. Co-chair fundraising banquet, Young Life Ctrl. Oreg.; team leader Family Kitchen; music dir., choirmaster Trinity Episcopal Ch., 1980-89; juror touring programs Oreg. Arts Commn.; alumnus Leadership Bend, 1994—; bd. dirs. Ctrl. Oreg. Youth Choir, 1997—. Recipient Alumni of Yr. Woodway Sr. H.S., 1989, Cmty. Svc. award Ctrl. Oreg. Arts Soc., 1990. Mem. Cursillo Cmty. Ea. (rec. sec. 1995), Bend (Oreg.) C. of C. (mem. leadership com., ambassador 1995), Ctrl. Oreg. Avocations: pastoral music ministry, music performance, youth ministry. Office: St Charles Med Ctr Found 2500 NE Neff Rd Bend OR 97701-6015

GOODMAN, SYLVIA KLUMOK, volunteer; b. Moorhead, Miss., June 19, 1940; d. Sol Harry and Fannie Ida (Davidson) Klumok; m. Carl Gerald Goodman, June 5, 1960; children: Lisa Wynne Goodman Stone, Gary Steven, Jeffrey David. BS in Zoology with honors, Newcomb Coll., 1962; M in Zoology, Tulane U., 1963; postgrad., Harvard U., summer 1990. Tchr. Midway Jr. H.S., Shreveport, La., 1963-68; instr. biology La. State U., Shreveport, 1967-68; instr. physiology, asst. coord. plans La. State U. Med. Ctr., Shreveport, 1970-74. Mem. Shreveport Mayor's Women's Commn., 1986-90; vice-chair La. State Mineral Bd., Baton Rouge, 1988-92; chmn. Food Project, Shreveport, 1990-92; chair beautification com. Shreveport Regional Airport, 1990-94; bd. dirs. Sci-Port Discovery Ctr., Shreveport, 1990—, pres., 1993-95; bd. dirs. La. Endowment Humanities, 1996—; pres. Shreveport Jewish Fedn., 1982-83; trustee Shreveport-Bossier Cmty. Found., vice chmn., 1993—; bd. dirs. Meadows Art Mus., 1991-97, vice chmn., 1995; chancellor's adv. com. LSU-S, 1996-99; mem. Red River Refuge Com., 1999. Recipient Humanitarian award NCCJ, Humanitarian award Caddo Commn., 1991, Vol. Fundraiser award Nat. Fedn. Fundraising Execs., 1996, Angel award Blue Cross Blue Shield, 1998; named Women Who Made a Difference Shreveport Celebration of Women Week, 1996, Best-Dressed Woman of No. La. Shreveport Times, 1998. Mem. Jr. League Shreveport (Sustainer of Yr. award 1995, Blue Cross Angel award 1998), Mensa, Phi Beta Kappa, Alpha Epsilon Phi. Jewish. Avocations: theater, piano, dance, taking courses, movies. Home: 409 Southfield Rd Shreveport LA 71106-2213

GOODMAN, THOMAS BLACKBURN, III, regional processor specialist; b. West Jefferson, N.C., Jan. 1, 1969; s. Thomas Blackburn and Clara Lorettra (Mash) G.; m. Anne Elizabeth Cargill, May 18, 1995 (div. June 1996). BED, Tex. A&M Univ., 1994. V.p. sales & market Positive Images Design, Dallas, 1989-94; v.p. sales & mktg. Jones & Assocs., Dallas, 1994-95; region acct. exec. Viskase Corp., Chgo., 1995-98; regional processor specialist Bunzl Distbn., Inc., Carrollton, Tex., 1998—. Mem. Am. Inst. Architects, Nat. Broiler Coun., Nat. Turkery Fedn., S.W. Meat Assn., La. Meat Assn., Golden Key Nat. Hon. Soc. Republican. Baptist. Avocations: golfing, scuba, snow skiing, wine collecting, racing nascar, hunting. Home: 18778 Vista del Sol Dallas TX 75287 Office: Bunzl Distbn Inc 1615 Diplomat Ste 120 Carrollton TX 75287

GOODMAN, VALERIE DAWSON, psychiatric social worker; b. Bluefield, W.Va., Feb. 2, 1948; d. Francis Carl and Lesly (Collett) Dawson; m. David William Goodman, June 9, 1985; 1 child, Amanda Lynn. BS, W.Va. U., 1970, MS, 1972; MSW, U. Md., 1980. Lic. clin. social worker, Md. Social worker Md. Children's Aide Family Svcs. Soc., Balt., 1972-78; social worker III Montgomery County Dept. Social Svcs., Rockville, Md., 1980-81; clin. social worker Johns Hopkins Hosp., Balt., 1981-83; pvt. practice Suburban Psychiat. Assoc. Hopkins at Greenspring Station, Balt., 1986—; supr. Johns Hopkins Hosp., 1983-86, chair Brogden com., 1984-85, spl. events com. depression and related affective disorders dept. psychiatry, 1994; spkr. in field. Parent vol. Park Sch. Mem. Kappa Delta. Avocations: reading, piano, gourmet cooking, weightlifting. Home: 54 Bellchase Ct Pikesville MD 21208-1300 Office: Suburban Psychiat Svc Md Adult Ctr ADD Johns Hopkins at Greenspring Sta Falls Concourse Falls Rd Ste 306 Lutherville MD 21093

GOODMAN, WALTER, author, editor; b. N.Y.C., Aug. 22, 1927; s. Hyman and Sadie (Rybakof) G.; m. Elaine Egan, Feb. 10, 1951; children: Hal, Bennet. B.A. magna cum laude, Syracuse U., 1949; M.A., Reading (Eng.) U., 1953. Editor N.Y. Times, N.Y.C., 1974—; mem. editorial bd. N.Y. Times, 1977—, critic, 1983—; sr. writer, 1996—; exec. editor WNET, 1979-80, dir. humanities programming, 1980-83; lectr. Salzburg Seminar in Am. Studies, Breadloaf Writers Conf., Columbia U. Sch. Journalism. Author: The Committee, 1968, All Honorable Men, 1963, The Clowns of Commerce, 1957, Black Bondage, 1969, A Percentage of the Take, 1971; also numerous articles. Pulitzer prize finalist, 1990; Guggenheim fellow, 1974. Mem. ACLU, P.E.N. Home: 4 Crest Dr White Plains NY 10607-2702

GOODMAN, WILLIAM BEEHLER, editor, literary agent; b. Bklyn., July 1, 1923; s. Philip Howard and Anne Louise (Landersman) G.; m. Lorraine Rappaport, Nov. 24, 1948; children: Jonas Robert, Sara Emily. B.A., Washington Sq. Coll., NYU, 1948; M.A., U. Mich., 1952. Editor coll. and trade Harcourt Brace Jovanovich Inc., N.Y.C., 1956-76; gen. editor Harvard Univ. Press, Cambridge, Mass., 1976-79; editorial dir. David R. Godine Pub., Inc., Boston, 1979-90, editor, lit. agt., 1990; tutor history and lit. Harvard U., 1953-54, lectr. in English, 1982-83, 84-85. Contbr.: essay Reading in the 1980's, 1983. Trustee Warner Library, Tarrytown, N.Y., 1973-75. Served with U.S. Army, 1943-44. Club: Harvard (N.Y.C.). Home: 26 Pickman Dr Bedford MA 01730-1005

GOODMAN, WILLIAM RICHARD, insurance adjusting company executive; b. Staunton, Va., Sept. 19, 1930; s. Harry and Ruth (Meyer) G.; m. Alice Helene Katzenstein, June 13, 1954; children: Harvey, Laurie, Barry. BS, U. Md., 1952; JD, U. Balt., 1955. Cert. profl. pub. adjuster FPPA. Pub. ins. adjuster, lawyer Goodman-Gable-Gould Co., Balt., 1952-73, v.p., 1973-85, pres., 1985-97, CEO, 1985—, chmn. bd., 1989—. Chmn. Baltimore County Indsl. Devel. Commn., 1967-69; mem. Met. Transit Authority, Balt., 1969-71, bd. rev. Dept. Transp., Md., 1971-76, Md. Racing Commn., 1984. Mem. Nat. Assn. Pub. Ins. Adjusters (dir., v.p., pres., chmn. bd. dirs., Disting. Svc. award 1987, Man of Yr. 1995), B'nai B'rith (v.p. Menorah Lodge 1992-94, pres. 1996-98). Democrat. Jewish. Avocation: collector of toy trains and antique cars. Home: 7811 Park Heights Ave Baltimore MD 21208-4322 Office: Goodman Gable Gould Co 6 Reservoir Cir Ste 202 Baltimore MD 21208-7310

GOODNER, JACOB B., JR. (JAY GOODNER), marketing professional; b. Birmingham, Ala., Feb. 23, 1954; s. Jacob B. and Mary Elizabeth (Logan) G.; m. Julie Lynn Payne, Oct. 22, 1988. BA in English, U. Ala., 1976, BA in German, 1977, Ednl. Specialist magna cum laude, 1991, PhD in Adminstrn. Higher Edn., 1992; MA in Linguistics, U. Ga., 1981. Computer mktg. mgr., ednl. specialist Tandy Corp., Birmingham, 1984-87; mktg. rep. Computer Products Group Control Data Corp., Mpls., 1987-91; project mgr., implementation cons. Dynamic Maintenance System and IMMPower System Revere Tech., Inc., Birmingham, 1992—; mason Goodner Constrn. Co., Birmingham, 1970-81; mem. collegiate faculty So. Coll., Chattanooga, So. Jr. Coll., Birmingham, Jefferson State C.C., Birmingham, 1980-86. Mem. Am. Dialect Soc., Am. Prodn. and Inventory Control Soc., Am. Union Bricklayers and Allied Craftsman, Phi Kappa Phi, Kappa Delta Pi, Alpha Mu Gamma. Home: 2212 Great Rock Rd Birmingham AL 35216-2122 Office: Revere Inc Ste 2305 One Perimeter Park South Birmingham AL 35243

GOODNER, NORMAN WESLEY, governmental relations specialist; b. Fort Smith, Ark., Apr. 16, 1969; s. Charles E. and Sharron A. (Langston) G. BS in Pub. Adminstrn., U. Ark., 1990, student, 1991-92. Govt. rels. Auditor of State's Office, Little Rock, 1992—. Bd. dirs. Scott County Friends of Libr., Waldron, Ark., 1988; asst. coord. Little Rock Town Hall Meeting On Africa, 1997; constituent liaison Ark. Senate Adv. Com., Waldron, 1983—. Recipient Capitol citation Ark. Sec. of State, 1986. Democrat. Baptist. Avocations: hiking, reading. Office: Auditor States Office Rm 230 State Capitol Bldg Little Rock AR 72201

GOODNICK, PAUL JOEL, psychiatrist; b. Phila., Sept. 29, 1950. BA magna cum laude, U. Pa.; MD with honors, SUNY Downstate Med. Ctr., Bklyn. Diplomate Am. Bd. Psychiatry and Neurology. Resident Washington U., St. Louis, Mo., Columbia U., N.Y.C.; fellow Mt. Sinai Hosp., N.Y.C.; asst. prof. psychiatry Wayne State U., Detroit, 1980-81, U. Chgo., 1981-84, Columbia U., N.Y.C., 1984-87; asst. prof. psychiatry U. Miami, Fla., 1987-89, clin. assoc. prof. psychiatry, 1989-90, assoc. prof., 1990-93, prof., 1993—, dir. mood disorders program, dept. psychiatry, 1989—; dir. outpatient svcs. and affective disorders program Fair Oaks Hosp., Boca/Delray, Fla., 1987-90; cons. APA, 1991. Assoc. editor jour. Lithium, 1989-94; editor: Chronic Fatigue and Related Immune D eficiency Syndromes, 1993, Predictors of Response in Mood Disorders, 1996, Mania, 1998. Mem. nat. adv. bd. Jerusalem Health Ctr. Recipient Clin. Excellence award N.Y. Alliance for Mentally Ill, 1987. Fellow Am. Psychopathological Assn., Am. Psychiat. Assn.; mem. Soc. Biol. Psychiatry, N.Y. Acad. Sci., AAAS, Am. Acad. Clin. Psychiatry, KP. Office: U Miami Dept Psychiatry 1400 NW 10th Ave Ste 304 Miami FL 33136-1020

GOODNIGHT, JAMES, software company executive; b. Wilmington, N.C.. PhD in Statistics, N.C. State U., 1971. Faculty N.C. State U., 1972-76; pres. SAS Inst. Inc., Cary, N.C., 1976—; adj. prof. N.C. State U., 1976—. Fellow Am. Statis. Assn. Office: SAS Inst Inc 100 Sas Campus Dr Cary NC 27513-8617*

GOODPASTER, ANDREW JACKSON, retired army officer; b. Granite City, Ill., Feb. 12, 1915; s. Andrew Jackson and Teresa Mary (Mrovka) G.; m. Dorothy Dulaney Anderson, Aug. 28, 1939; children: Susan Dulaney, Anne Morgan. Student, McKendree Coll., 1931-33; BS, U.S. Mil. Acad., 1939; MS in Engring., Princeton U., 1949, MA, 1949, PhD in Internat. Rels., 1950. Commd. 2d lt., C.E. U.S. Army, 1939, advanced through grades to gen., 1968; comdg. officer 48th Engr. Combat Bn., World War II, strategic and policy staff duty War Dept. Gen. Staff, 1944-47, mem. Joint Adv. Study Com., 1950, spl. staff asst. SHAPE, 1950-54; dist. engr. C.E. San Francisco, 1954; def. liaison officer and staff sec. to Pres. U.S., 1954-61, asst. div. comdr. 3d Inf. Div., 1961, div. comdr. 8th Inf. Div., 1961-62, asst. to chmn. Joint Chiefs Staff, 1962-66, dir. Joint Staff, 1966-67; dir. spl. studies Office Chief of Staff U.S. Army, 1967; sr. U.S. Army mem. mil. staff com. UN, 1966-68; comdt. Nat. War Coll., 1967-68; mem. U.S. Del. Paris negotiations with N.Vietnam, 1968; dep. comdr. U.S. forces Vietnam, 1968-69; comdr.-in-chief U.S. forces, supreme allied comdr. Europe, 1969-74; ret., 1974, recalled, 1977-81; supt. U.S. Mil. Acad., 1977-81, ret., 1981; chmn. Am. Battle Monuments Commn., 1985-90; pres. Inst. Def. Analyses, 1983-85, trustee, 1981-89; sr. fellow security and strategic studies Woodrow Wilson Internat. Ctr. for Scholars, 1975-76; prof. govt. and internat. studies The Citadel, Charleston, S.C., 1976-77; chmn. adv. bd. Eisenhower Inst.; chmn. Atlantic Coun. of U.S., 1985-97; spl. cons. to Vice Pres. U.S., Commn. Orgn. Govt. for Conduct Fgn. Policy, 1975. Author: For the Common Defense, 1977. Chmn. George C. Marshall Found.; mem. numerous adv. groups on strategy, security, internat. affairs, mgmt. and orgn. Decorated U.S. Medal of Freedom, D.S.C., Def. D.S.M. with oak leaf cluster, Army D.S.M. with 3 oak leaf clusters, Navy D.S.M., Air Force D.S.M., Silver Star, Legion of Merit with oak leaf cluster, Purple Heart with oak leaf cluster; numerous fgn. decorations including; Italian Mil. Cross of Valor, Korean Order Mil. Merit, Vietnamese Cross Valor, Grand Cross Mil. Order Aviz Portugal, Grand Cordon Order Leopold Belgium, Grand Cross with Swords Order Orange-Nassau Netherlands, Grand Cross 1st class Order of Merit Fed. Republic Germany, Disting. Service medal Turkish Armed Forces, Disting. Pub. Service award Dept. Def.; recipient James Madison award Princeton U. Fellow Am. Acad. Arts Scis.; mem. Nat. Acad. Pub. Adminstrn., Coun. Fgn. Rels., Soc. Am. Mil. Engrs., Army and Navy Club, Sigma Xi, Phi Kappa Phi. Home: Knollwood Apt 345 6200 Oregon Ave NW Washington DC 20015

GOODPASTURE, JUDY GAIL ASHMORE, English language educator, administrator; b. Wichita, Kans., May 22, 1943; d. A. L. and Nadine McFaddin Ashmore; m. Hewitt C. Goodpasture, Aug. 20, 1964; children: Emily Lynn Goodpasture Ottaway, Timothy Hewitt. BA in English, Mills Coll., 1965; MA in English Lit., U. Mo., Kansas City, 1968. Cert. tchr., Kans. Tchr. English Barstow Sch., Kansas City, Kans., 1965-68; tchr. freshman English U. Mo., Kansas City, 1968-69; tchr. English S.E. H.S., Wichita, 1985-94; tchr. English, chair English dept. Ind. H.S., Wichita, 1994—. Comty. v.p. Wichita Jr. League; pres. Episcopal Ch. Women, St. Stephens Episcopalian Ch., Wichita, 1996-97. Named NEA-Wichita Tchr. of Yr., 1990. Mem. Kans. Assn. Tchrs. of English (bd. dirs. 1992-98, v.p. 1998, pres. 1999—). Avocations: writing, sewing, painting. Home: 8803 Clubside Cir Wichita KS 67206-4039 Office: Ind H S 8301 E Douglas Ave Wichita KS 67207-1213

GOODPASTURE, PHILIP HENRY, lawyer; b. Lisbon, Portugal, Sept. 16, 1960; s. Henry McKennie and Ellen Ingabor (Moller) G.; m. Paige Everett Hargroves, June 25, 1994. BA with high distinction, U. Va., 1982, JD, 1985. Bar: Va. 1985, U.S. Dist. Ct. (ea. dist.) Va. 1985. Assoc. Christian & Barton and predecessor firm, Richmond, Va., 1985-92, ptnr., 1993—, vice-chmn. corp. team, 1994-97, mem. exec. com., 1998. Dir. Downtown Presents Inc., Richmond, 1993—, Va. League for Planned Parenthood, Richmond, 1989-95, Vol. Emergency Famlies for Children, Richmond, 1998—; dir. parliament City of Richmond, 1997-98; mem. Leadership Metro Richmond, 1994; mem. leadership devel. coun. ARC, 1995. Mem. Va. Bar Assn., Richmond Bar Assn. Office: Christian & Barton 909 E Main St Ste 1200 Richmond VA 23219-3013

GOODREDS, JOHN STANTON, newspaper publisher; b. Buffalo, July 7, 1934; s. V. Spencer and Pansy (Nisbet) G.; m. Helen Walter, Aug. 11, 1962 (dec. May 1991); children—John, Cynthia; m. Susan T. Bromley, May 23, 1997. B.A. in Econs. with honors, Colgate U., 1956; M.B.A. in Fin, Syracuse (N.Y.) U., 1970; HHD, Thiel Coll., 1984. Mgmt. trainee GE, Syracuse, 1956-60; with Bristol Labs., Syracuse, 1960-70; budget mgr. Bristol Labs., 1968-70; treas. Ottaway Newspapers, Inc., 1970, fin. v.p., 1971-77, v.p. fin. and devel., 1978, sr. v.p., 1978; exec. v.p. Ottaway Newspapers, Inc., Campbell Hall, N.Y., 1980-85; pres. Ottaway Newspapers, Inc., 1985-92; newspaper cons., 1992—; bd. dirs. Am. Press Inst., Reston, Va., 1985-94, treas., 1991—; mem. Dow Jones Mgmt. Commn., 1989-92; bd. dirs. Kendall Comm., Inc., Bruedan Corp. Bd. dirs. Arden Hill Hosp., Goshen, N.Y., 1978—, Arden Hill Life Care Ctr., Arden Hill Svcs.; chmn., treas. Glen Arden Retirement Community; mem. Colgate U. Alumni Bd., 1997—. With AUS, 1957-58. Mem. Internat. Newspaper Fin. Execs., N.Y. Newspaper Pubs. Assn., Newspaper Advt. Bur. (N.Y.C., bd. dirs. 1989-92), Newspaper Assn. Am. (bd. dirs. 1992), Goshen Rotary (chmn. scholarship found.), Orange Country Golf Club (pres. 1979). Episcopalian. Home and Office: 43 Gregory Dr Goshen NY 10924-1014

GOODRICH, GAIL CHARLES, JR., retired basketball player; b. L.A., Apr. 23, 1943. Basketball player L.A. Lakers, 1965-68, 70-73, Phoenix Suns, 1968-70. Named to Basketball Hall of Fame, 1996; mem. NBA Championship Team, 1972. Office: Naismith Mem Basketball Hall of Fame PO Box 179 1150 W Columbus Ave Springfield MA 01105*

GOODRICH, GEORGE HERBERT, judge; b. Charleston, W.Va., June 19, 1925; s. Edgar Jennings and Beulah Etta (Lenfest) G.; m. Nancy Ann Needham, Sept. 3, 1949; children: George Herbert, Craig N., Thomas A. B.A., Williams Coll., 1949; LL.B., U. Va., 1952. Bar: D.C. 1953, Md. 1958. Gen. practice law Washington, also, Md., 1953-69; asso. judge D.C. Superior Ct., 1969-91, sr. judge, 1991—; lectr. law Am. U., 1969-74. Pres. Homemakers Service, 1962-63; v.p. Hillcrest Children's Center, 1963-69; mem. community adv. com. Jr. League D.C., 1969-73; bd. dirs. ARC. Served with USNR, 1943-46. Mem. D.C. Bar Assn., Delta Psi. Republican. Presbyterian. Club: Chevy Chase. Home: 6003 Corbin Rd Bethesda MD 20816-3402 Office: DC Superior Ct 500 Indiana Ave NW Ste 1 Washington DC 20001-2191

GOODRICH, HERBERT FUNK, JR., lawyer; b. Phila., Dec. 14, 1942; s. Herbert Funk and Mary (Dern) G.; m. Virginia Page, Sept. 10, 1966; children: Cynthia Dern, Matthew Page, Steven Withington. AB, Dartmouth Coll., 1964; LLB, Harvard U., 1967. Bar: Pa. 1967, U.S. Dist. Ct. (ea. dist.) Pa. 1967. Assoc. Dechert Price & Rhoads, Phila., 1967-74; resident ptnr. Dechert Price & Rhoads, Brussels, 1974-78; ptnr. Dechert Price & Rhoads, Phila., 1978—; vis. lectr. Villanova (Pa.) U., 1985—; faculty participant Pa. Bar Inst., Harrisburg, 1980—. Bd. dirs. Episc. Cmty. Svcs., Phila., 1988—; trustee Chestnut Hill Healthcare Corp., Phila., 1993—, vice chmn., 1995—. Mem. ABA, Phila. Bar Assn., Pa. Bar Assn., Am. Law Inst. Republican. Office: Dechert Price & Rhoads 4000 Bell Atlantic Tower 1717 Arch St Philadelphia PA 19103-2793

GOODRICH, ISAAC, neurosurgeon, educator; b. Milledgeville, Ga., Sept. 19, 1939; s. Ellis and Frieda (Bergman) G.; m. Dianne L. Brittain, Aug. 28, 1965; children: Mindy Anne, Scott David, Jennifer Gale. AA, Ga. Mil. Coll., 1959; BS, U. Ga., 1961; MD, Med. Coll. Ga., 1964. Cert. Am. Bd. Neurol. Surgery. Intern Columbia-Presbyn. Med. Ctr., N.Y.C., 1964-65; resident in neurosurgery Yale-New Haven Med. Ctr., 1967-71; practice medicine specializing in neurosurgery New Haven, 1971—; instr. neurosurgery, Yale U. Med. Sch., 1970-71, asst. clin. prof., 1978-86; assoc. clin. prof., 1986—; attending neurosurgeon Yale-New Haven Hosp., 1973—, Hosp. St. Raphael, 1971—; mem. courtesy staff Milford Hosp., 1986—; cons. staff Vets. Meml. Med. Ctr., 1986—, VA Hosp., West Haven, 1990—, Griffin Hosp., 1992—, St. Mary's Hosp., 1995-99, courtesy staff, 1999—. Contbr. articles to profl. jours. Capt. U.S. Army, 1955-67. Decorated Bronze Star, Air Medal; recipient Disting. Alumni award Ga. Mil. Coll., 1980; named Hon. Citizen, Boys Town, Nebr., 1971. Fellow ACS, Internat. Coll. Surgeons, Royal Soc. Medicine; mem. AMA (Physicians Recognition award for Continuing Med. Edn. 1969, 72, 75, 78, 81, 85, 88, 91, 94, 97), AAAS, Congress Neurol. Surgeons, New Eng. Neurosurg. Soc. (pres. 1997-99), Pan Pacific Surg. Assn., Soc. Med. Cons. to Armed Forces, Soc. 1st Inf. Divsn., 28th Inf. Assn., Am. Assn. Neurol. Surgeons, Conn. State Neurol. Soc., Conn. State Med. Soc., New Haven City (pres. 1989-90), New Haven County Med. Assn. (pres. 1998-99), N.Y. Acad. Scis. Jewish. Home: 264 Rimmon Rd Woodbridge CT 06525-1847 Office: 60 Temple St New Haven CT 06510-2716

GOODRICH, JAMES TAIT, neuroscientist, pediatric neurosurgeon; b. Portland, Ore., Apr. 16, 1946; s. Richard and Gail (Josselyn) G.; m. Judy Loudin, Dec. 27, 1970. Student, Golden West Coll., 1971-72; A.A., Orange Coast Coll., 1972; B.S. cum laude, U. Calif.-Irvine, 1974; M.Phil., Columbia U., 1979, Ph.D., 1970 M.D., 1980; Diplomate Am. Bd. Neurological Surgery. Neuroscientist, pediatric neurosurgeon N.Y. Neurol. Inst., N.Y.C., 1981-86; dir. div. pediatric neurosurgery Albert Einstein Coll. Medicine, N.Y.C., 1986—, prof. neurol. surgery, pediatrics, plastics and reconstructive surgery, 1992-98; prof. neurosurgery U. Palermo, Italy, 1997—. Contbr. articles to profl. jours. Recipient Roche Labs. award in neuroscis, 1978, Mead-Johnson award, 1978, Bronze medal Alumni Assn. Coll. Physicians and Surgeons, 1980, Sandoz award for outstanding research, 1980; Willamette Industries scholar; NIH grantee. Fellow Royal Soc. Medicine (London); mem. Internat. Soc. Pediatric Neuro-Surgeons, Worshipful Soc. Apothecaries (London), N.Y. Acad. Medicine (Melicow award 1980), Am. Assn. History of Medicine (Sir William Osler medal 1977-78), AMA, Brit. Brain Research Assn., European Brain Research Assn., Friends of Columbia U. Libraries, Friends of Osler Library of McGill U., N.Y. Acad. Scis., Am. Assn. Neurol. Surgeons, Am. Assn. Neurological Surgery (chmn. sect. on history of neurological surgery), Congress Neurol. Surgeons, Med. History Soc. N.J., ISIS History of Sci. Soc., Soc. for Bibliography of Natural History (London), Columbia Presbyn. Med. Soc., U. Calif. Alumni Assn., Soc. Ancient Medicine, AAAS, Am. Osler Soc., Les Amis du Vin, South Coast Wine Explorers Club (past chmn.), Friends of Bacchus Wine Club (past chmn.), Dionysius Council of Presbyn. Hosp. of N.Y.C., Sigma Xi, Alpha Gamma Sigma. Research on neuronal regeneration, brain reconstruction and craniofacial reconstruction. Home: 125 Tweed Blvd Nyack NY 10960-4913 Office: Albert Einstein Coll Medicine Montefiore Med Ctr Div Pediatric Neurosurgery Bronx NY 10467

GOODRICH, JAMES WILLIAM, historian, association executive; b. Burlington, Iowa, Oct. 31, 1939; s. Martin Glenn and Marion Elizabeth (Prasse) G.; m. Linda Marlyse Andreoli, Aug. 31, 1963 (div. Aug. 1989); children: Anne Marlyse, Kimberly Ann. BS in Edn., Cen. Mo. State U., 1962; MA, U. Mo., 1964, PhD, 1974. Archivist Sec. of State, Mo., 1966; asst. then assoc. editor State Hist. Soc. Mo., Columbia, 1967-78, assoc. dir., 1978-85, dir., 1985—; cons. USDA Soil Conservation Svc., Columbia, 1976, Mus. History and Sci., Kansas City, Mo., 1978, Mo. State Mus., 1989; mem. Mo. Hist. Records Adv. Bd., Jefferson City, 1985—, State Records Commn., Jefferson City, 1984—; dir. Western Hist. Manuscript Collection, 1985—; adj. prof. history U. Mo., Columbia, 1988—. Co-author: Historic Missouri, 1988; editor: Report on a Journey to North America, 1980; assoc. editor Mo. Hist. Rev., 1967-85, editor 1985—; co-editor: German-American Experience in Missouri, 1986; co-editor, contbr. Marking Missouri History, 1998; contbr. articles to profl. jours. Mem. Planning and Zoning Commn., Columbia, 1975-77; councilman City of Columbia, 1977-79, 79-81; chmn. city audit com., Columbia, 1981-88; v.p. Friends of Mo. St. Archives, 1989-94; mem. 13th Jud. Cir. Bar Rev. Com., 1991-97; bd. dirs. Mo. Mansion Preservation Inc., 1991—; bd. dirs. Boone County Cmty. Trust, 1992—; mem. exec. com. Mo. State U Alumni Assn., 1988-92, pres. 1991; mem. 6th Regional Disciplinary Com. Mo. Judiciary, 1997—; mem. Mo. Lewis and Clark Bicentennial Com., 1997—. Mem. Orgn. Am. Historians, Western History Assn., Am. Assn. for State & Local History, Conservation Fedn. Mo., Ducks Unlimited, Mo. Mus. Assn., Mo. Press Assn., Wild Canid Survival and Rsch. Ctr. Avocations: decoy collecting, waterfowl hunting, orinthoscopy. Office: State Hist Soc Mo 1020 Lowry St Columbia MO 65201-7207

GOODRICH, JOHN BERNARD, lawyer, consultant; b. Spokane, Wash., Jan. 4, 1928; s. John Casey and Dorothy (Koll) G.; m. Therese H. Vollmer, June 14, 1952; children—Joseph B., Bernadette M., Andrew J., Philip M., Thomas A., Mary Elizabeth, Jennifer H., Rosanne M. J.D., Gonzaga U., 1954. Bar: Ill. bar 1955, Wash. bar 1954. Indsl. traffic mgr. Pacific N.W. Alloys, Spokane, 1950-54; asst. to gen. counsel Cromium Mining & Smelting Corp., Chgo., 1954-56; with Monon R.R., 1956-69, atty., gen. solicitor, 1956-66, sec., 1957-69, treas., 1959-66, v.p. law, 1966-69; also dir.; sec.-treas. I.C.G.R.R., Chgo., 1970-79; sec., gen. atty. I.C.G.R.R., 1979-85; gen. counsel Ill. Devel. Fin. Authority, Chgo., 1985-92, spl. counsel, 1993; atty., cons. pvt. practice, Park Forest, Ill., 1994—. Mem. Park Forest Traffic and Safety Commn., 1963-66; mem. Park Forest Recreation Bd., 1966-77, chmn., 1969-70; trustee Village of Park Forest, 1977-80; mem. bd. Sch. Dist. 163, 1984-89; pres. South Cook Orgn. for Pub. Edn., 1988-89; conf. and meeting planner The Compassionate Friends, Inc., Oak Brook, Ill., 1991-94; bd. dirs. Park Forest Art Ctr., 1993-95, Ill. Philharm. Orch., 1994—, treas., 1995—; mem. adv. bd. Chgo. Self Help Ctr., 1993-94; bd. dirs. Ill Self Help Coalition, 1994-96; treas. Bereaved Parents of the U.S.A., 1995—; trustee Chgo. South Suburban Mass Transit Dist., 1996—. Inducted into Park Forest Hall of Fame, 1998. Mem. The Parkforesters, Inc. (pres. 1998—), KC. Republican. Roman Catholic. Home and Office: 35 Cunningham Ln Park Forest IL 60466-2094

GOODRICH, KENNETH PAUL, retired college dean; b. Elkhorn, Wis., 1933; s. Kenneth Potter and Helene (Keller) G.; m. Elaine L. Ashby, June 12, 1954; children—Laurel Lynn, David Kenneth, Paul Ashby, Karen Elaine. A.B. Oberlin Coll, 1955; M.A., U. Ia., 1958, Ph.D., 1959. Mem. faculty U. Pa. Phila., 1959-63; lectr., project assoc. U. Wis., Madison, 1963-65; mem. faculty psychology Macalester Coll., St. Paul, 1965-73; chmn. dept. psychology Macalester Coll., 1965-67, dean coll., 1967-69, dean and dir. ednl. resources, 1969-71, v.p. for acad. affairs and provost, 1971-73; dean Coll. Arts and Scis., prof. psychology Syracuse (N.Y.) U., 1973-78; provost Ohio Wesleyan U., Delaware, 1978-83; v.p. acad. affairs, dean of faculty Linfield Coll., McMinnville, Oreg., 1983-94, spl. asst. to pres. for instnl. rsch. and planning, 1994-95. Bd. dirs. Group Health Plan, Inc., St. Paul, 1970-73, Yamhill County (Oreg.) United Way, 1991-95, McMinnville Area Habitat for Humanity, 1993-95; vol. staff writer Otterbein Coll., 1996—.

GOODRICH, LEON RAYMOND, lawyer; b. Denver, Oct. 29, 1936; s. Leon Raymond and Maude Lavina (Farrar) G.; m. Katherine Jean Gulliksen, Dec. 30, 1960; children: James, Aileen, Daniel. AB, Dartmouth Coll., 1958; JD, Harvard U., 1961. Bar: Mo. 1962, Minn. 1964, U.S. Dist. Ct. Minn. 1968, U.S. Supreme Ct. 1986. Atty. Monsanto Chem. Co., St. Louis, 1961-63; instr. U. Mich. Law Sch., Ann Arbor, 1963-64; assoc. Oppenheimer Wolff & Donnelly LLP, St. Paul, 1964-68, ptnr., 1969—. Contbr. articles to legal jours. Mem. bd. mgmt. Camp Widjiwagan, St. Paul, St. Paul YMCA, 1983-90. Mem. ABA, Ramsey County Bar Assn., Minn. Bar Assn. (co-chmn. antitrust sect. 1983-85), Rotary. Mem. Unitarian Ch. Avocations: piano, jogging, golf.

GOODRICH, NORMA LORRE (MRS. JOHN H. HOWARD), French and comparative literature educator; b. Huntington, Vt., May 10, 1917; d. Charles Edmund and Edyth (Riggs) Falby; m. J.M.A. Lorre, Dec. 10, 1943 (div. June 1946); 1 son, Jean-Joseph; m. John Hereford Howard, Jan. 20, 1964. BS cum laude, U. Vt., 1938; postgrad. (U. Vt. fellow), U. Grenoble, France, 1938-39; PhD (Ellis fellow), Columbia U., 1965; LittD, U. Vt., 1993. Tchr. high schs., Vt., 1939-43, Bentley Sch., N.Y.C., 1943-47; owner dir. Am. Villa in Normandy, Trouville, France, 1947-53; tchr. Fieldston Sch., N.Y.C., 1954-63; asst. prof. French U. So. Calif., 1964-66, assoc. prof., 1966-71; dean faculty Scripps Coll., Claremont, Calif., 1971-72; prof. French and comparative lit. Claremont Colls., 1972, prof. emeritus, 1982—; vis. scholar Calif. Luth. Coll., 1965, Isle of Man, U.K., 1986, Claremont McKenna Coll., 1986; vis. prof. John Carroll U., Cleve., 1987, Calif. State U., Long Beach, 1986, 87, 88, Cal Arts, Pasadena, 1989, Calif. Poly. U., Pomona, 1992, Southwestern Coll., 1993, Riverside Bapt. Coll., 1994, Scripps Coll., Claremont, 1994; lectr. Arthurian Soc., Carlisle, Cumbria, Eng., 1994, 96, 97, Santa Anita (Calif.) Ch., 1995, Trinity Episc. Ch., Redlands, Calif., 1996. Author: Ancient Myths, 1959, rev. edit., 1977, 94, Medieval Myths, 1960, rev. edit., 1977, 94, Doctor and Maria Theresa, 1961, Myths of the Hero, 1961, Ways of Love, 1963, Charles of Orleans: A Study of Themes in His French and English Poetry, 1967, Giono: Master of Fictional Modes, 1973, Afterword for the Man Who Planted Trees (Jean Giono), 1985 (New Eng. Book award), London edit., 1989, King Arthur, 1986, 2d edit., 1989, Merlin, 1987, 2d edit., 1989, Il Mito della Tavola Rotonda (transl. of King Arthur), 1989, Le Roi Arthur, 1989, Die Ritter von Camelot, 1994, 95 (transl. of King Arthur), Castle Epstein (transl. of Alexander Dumas), 1989, Priestesses, 1989, Guinevere, 1991, The Holy Grail, 1992, Il Mito di Merlino, 1992 (transl. of Merlin), Heroines, 1993, Il Mito di Ginevra (transl. Guinevere), 1995; editor: Bullfinch Mythology, The Age of Fable, 1995, Bullfinch Mythology, The Age of Chivalry, 1995, Il Santo Graal, 1997, (boxed edit.) Hors Commerce, 1997; contbr. articles to internat. profl. jours.; guest appearances various TV and radio shows, Eng., 1986, 94, U.S., 1986-90, 93, 94. Mem. pub. rels. staff Worthington Corp., N.Y.C., 1953-54; bd. dirs. patron West End Opera Assn., 1973-74, program dir., 1975-76; guest lectr. Flower Festival, Arthuret Ch., Longtown, Cumbria, Eng., 1991, guest preacher, 1992. Recipient Good Citizen medal SAR, 1989, Martha Washington medal, 1992, Wallace award Am. Scottish Found., 1990; invested as Dame Knights Templar, Commandery of Nova Scotia, in the Rosslyn Chapel, Scotland, 1990; reinvested as Knight Templar, Dame and Officer with the rank of comdr. in Teampull of Sion, Edinburgh, Scotland, 1990, St. Mary's Cath., Edinburgh, Order of St. George, 1993, Mil. Order Fgn. Wars, 1994, Calif. Commandery medal, 1997. Fellow Soc. Antiquarians, Nat. Inst. Social Scis.; mem. Assn. Study of Dada and Surrealism (sec. 1970-72), Philol. Assn. Pacific Coast (nominating com. 1971-72), MLA (mem. del. assembly's election com. 1975), The Prehistoric Soc., Am. Assn. Tchrs. French, Medieval Assn. Pacific, Medieval Acad. Am., Nat. Soc. DAR (vice-regent 1996-97), Columbia U. Alumni Assn., Dante Soc., Pierport Morgan Libr., Clan MacArthur, Clan MacKay (hon.), 78th Fraser's Highlanders 2d Bn. of Foot Am. (lt.), Tordarroch Trust (Scotland and U.S.), Met. Opera Guild, Order of the Crown of Charlemagne in the U.S.A. (life), Phi Kappa Phi. Avocations: gymnastics, gardening, dressmaking. Home: 620 Diablo Dr Claremont CA 91711-1616 *I believe in the creative power of certain individuals who, because of this power or gift, must be allowed by society to be alone, work alone, and alone to perfect their work. Our education must be more lenient to these individuals and more understanding of that individual who does not conform to the average.*

GOODRICH, ROBERT LAWRENCE, JR., educator, accountant; b. Tacoma, Wash., May 24, 1952; s. Robert L. and Hazel E. (Snyder) G.; m. Melinda Luker Schaefer, Dec. 11, 1971 (div. 1980); children: Michelle D. Bain, Stacy L.; m. Anita Louise Waite, Aug. 7, 1982; children: Russel N. Waite, Shawn R. Goodrich. AA, Orange Coast Coll., Costa Mesa, Calif., 1975; BA, Calif. State U., Fullerton, 1977; MA in Edn., Chapman U., Orange, Calif., 1992. Ryan profl. clear multisubject credential. Acct. Avco Fin. Svcs., Newport Beach, Calif., 1976-80; corp. acctg. mgr. Kratos, Inc., La Jolla, Calif., 1980-81; sch. dir. Airco Ednl. Svcs., Chgo., 1982-87; tchr., educator Moreno Valley (Calif.) Unified Sch., 1990—. Sgt. USMC, 1970-74. Mem. NEA, Inst. Mgmt. Accts., Calif. Tchrs. Assn., Moreno Valley Educators Assn. Repubican. Mem. Ch. of Jesus Christ of Latter-day Saints. Avocations: bowling, archery, automobiles.

GOODRICH, THOMAS MICHAEL, lawyer, engineering and construction executive; b. Milan, Tenn., Apr. 28, 1945; s. Henry Calvin and Billie Grace (Walker) G.; m. Gillian Comer White, Dec. 28, 1968; children: Michael, Braxton, Charles, Grace. BSCE, Tulane U., 1968; JD, U. Ala., 1971. Bar: Ala. 1971. Adminstrv. asst. Supreme Ct. Ala., Montgomery, 1971-72; various mgmt. positions BE & K, Inc., Birmingham, Ala., 1989-95, pres., CEO, 1995—, also bd. dirs.; bd. dirs. First Comml. Bank, Birmingham. Bd. dirs. Birmingham Civil Rights Inst., Constrn. Industry Inst., Birmingham

Area coun. Boy Scouts Am., U. Ala. Health System; trustee Nat. Bldg. Mus., Elsenhowen Exchg. Fellow. Capt. U.S Army, 1970-72. Mem. TAPPI, ABA, Ala. State Bar Assn., Assn. Builders and Contractors (pres. 1990), Constrn. Industry Roundtable. Presbyterian. Avocations: hunting, jogging. Office: B E & K Inc PO Box 2332 2000 Internat Park Dr Birmingham AL 35243

GOODRIDGE, ALAN GARDNER, research biochemist, educator; b. Peabody, Mass., Apr. 2, 1937; s. Lester Elmer and Gertrude Edith (Gardner) G.; m. R. Ann Funderburk, Aug. 19, 1960; children—Alan Gardner Jr., Bryant C. BS in Biology, Tufts U., 1958; MS in Zoology, U. Mich., 1963, PhD in Zoology, 1964. Rsch. fellow dept. biochemistry Harvard Med. Sch., Boston, 1964-66; asst. prof. physiology U. Kans. Med. Ctr., Kansas City, 1966-68; assoc. prof. Banting and Best dept. med. rsch. U. Toronto, Ont., Can., 1968-76; prof. Banting and Best dept. med. rsch. U. Toronto, 1976-77; prof. pharmacology and biochemistry Case Western Res. U., Cleve., 1977-87; prof., head dept. biochemistry U. Iowa, 1987-96; prof. biochemistry, dean coll. biol. scis. Ohio State U., 1996—. Assoc. editor Jour. Biol. Chemistry, 1990—, Ann. Rev. of Nutrition, 1994-99, Jour. Lipid Rsch., 1995-99; contbr. numerous articles to profl. jours. Served with USN, 1958-61. Grantee Med. Rsch. Coun. Can., 1968-77, NIH, 1966-68, 77-97; Josiah Macy Jr. faculty scholar, 1975-76, USDA, 1986-90, 93-97. Mem. AAAS, Am. Soc. Biochemistry and Molecular Biology, Thyroid Assn. Home: 844 W Orange Rd Delaware OH 43015-7978 Office: Ohio State U Coll Biol Scis 484 W 12th Ave Columbus OH 43210-1214

GOODRIDGE, ALLAN D., lawyer; b. Bucharest, Romania, June 12, 1936; s. Benjamin F. and Fanny M. (Weissman) G.; m. Lora, Sept. 12, 1965; children: Jeremy P., Andrew P. BA, Harvard U., 1957; JD, Columbia U., 1960. Bar: N.Y., U.S. Dist. Ct. (so. dist., ea. dist. N.Y.), U.S. Ct. Appeals (2d circuit). Assoc. Wickes, Riddell, Bloomer, Jacobi & McGuire, N.Y.C., 1960-64, Spitzer & Feldman, N.Y.C., 1965; assoc. Demov, Morris & Hammerling, N.Y.C., 1965-70, ptnr., 1970-85; ptnr. Schnader, Harrison, Segal & Lewis, N.Y.C., 1985—. Mem. ABA, N.Y. Bar Assn. Club: Harvard (N.Y.C.). Home: 336 Central Park W New York NY 10025-7111 Office: Schnader Harrison 330 Madison Ave Fl 14 New York NY 10017-5092

GOODSELL, CHARLES T., educator; b. July 23, 1932. BA, Kalamazoo Coll., 1954; MPA, Harvard U., MA, PhD, 1961. Asst. prof. U. P.R., Rio Piedras, 1961-64; prof. So. Ill. U., Carbondale, 1966-78, Va. Tech., Blacksburg, 1978—. E-mail: goodsell@vt.edu. Office: 509 College View Dr Blacksburg VA 24060

GOODSON, CAROL FAYE, librarian; b. Detroit, Mar. 28, 1947; d. Norman Elwood and Wilma Mary (Harmon) G.; m. Lawrence J. Price, May 10, 1974 (div. 1977). BA, SUNY, Buffalo, 1970, MLS, 1972; MA, State U. West Ga., 1996. Libr. SUNY, Buffalo, 1970-72, St. Louis Pub. Libr., 1973-77; community sch. dir. St. Louis Bd. Edn., 1977-80; reference libr. Ga. Dept. Edn., Atlanta, 1981-84; head pub. svcs. Atlanta campus Mercer U., Chamblee, Ga., 1985; mem. Dominican Sisters of Nashville, 1985-90; asst. dir. Clayton County Libr. System, Jonesboro, Ga., 1990-91; coord. off-campus libr. svcs. State U. West Ga., Carrollton, 1991-96, head libr. access svcs., 1996—; state coord. Ga. Summer Reading Club, 1991; owner and moderator, ALA-PLAN listserv., FISC-L listserv and WOODY-L listserv. Editor Ga. Conf., AAUP Summary, 1996-98, Jour. Libr. Svcs. Distance Edn., 1997—; author: The Complete Guide to Performance Standards for Library Personnel, 1997; contbr. articles to profl. jours. Pres. Tower/Literacy Vols. Am., Clayton County, 1991; with Leadership Clayton, 1990-91. Mem. AAUP (exec. com. 1994-98), ALA, Ga. Libr. Assn., Libr. Info. Tech. Assn. (program planning com. 1992-97, sec. 1993-95), Assn. Coll. Rsch. Librs. (clip notes com. 1992-96, extended campus libr. svcs. sect., comm. com. 1994-98), Beta Phi Mu, Phi Kappa Phi, Omicron Delta Kappa, Sigma Tau Delta. Avocations: photography, computers. Home: 210 Oak Ave Carrollton GA 30117-3726 Office: State U West Ga Ingram Libr 1500 Maple St Carrollton GA 30117-4233

GOODSON, RAYMOND EUGENE, business educator, former automotive executive; b. Canton, N.C., Apr. 22, 1935; s. Lon R. and Ruby M. (Goodson); m. Susie Elisabeth Tweed, Aug. 10, 1957; children: Kathryn, Kenneth. AB, Duke U., 1957, BSME, 1959; MSME, Purdue U., 1961, PhD, 1963. Registered profl. engr., Ind. Mem. faculty Purdue U., West Lafayette, Ind., 1963-81; chief scientist U.S. Dept. Transp., Washington, 1973-75; dir. Interdisciplinary Inst., Purdue U., 1975-80, assoc. dean rsch., 1980-81; chmn. bd., CEO GLN, Inc., West Lafayette, 1971-81; v.p., gen. mgr. Hoover Universal, Ann Arbor, Mich., 1981-85; group v.p. Automotive Systems Group Johnson Controls, Inc., Milw., 1985-90; chmn. bd., CEO, Oshkosh (Wis.) Truck Corp., 1990-97; adj. prof. U. Mich. Sch. Bus. Adminstrn., Ann Arbor, 1998—; bd. dirs. Donnelly Corp., Holland, Mich., Knowles Electronics, Inc., Itasca, Ill., Am. Indsl. Ptnrs., N.Y.C. Patentee in field; contbr articles to tech. jours. Named Disting. Engring. Alumnus, Duke U., 1984, Purdue U., 1991. Fellow ASME. Republican. Presbyterian.

GOODSON, SHANNON LORAYN, behavioral scientist, author; b. Beaumont, Tex., May 26, 1952; d. James Ernest and Lorayn (Miller) G. BS in Psychology, Lamar U., 1974, MS in Organizational Psychology, 1977. Co-founder, pres., CEO Behavioral Scis. Rsch. Press, Inc., Dallas, 1979-92, pres., 1992—; presenter in field; guest on various radio talk shows. Co-author: (with G.W. Dudley) Earning What You're Worth?, 1992, Psychology of Call Reluctance, 1986; contbr. articles to profl. jours. and periodicals. Mem. APA, S.E. Psychol. Assn. Achievements include pioneering research into inhibited contact initiation; discovery of 12 diagnostic categories and subclassifications; devel. of formal diagnostic/assessment procedures (with G.W. Dudley); research on female executives and the glass ceiling. Office: Behavioral Scis Rsch Press 12803 Demetra Dr Ste 100 Dallas TX 75234-6169

GOODSTEIN, AARON E., federal magistrate judge; b. Sheboygan, Wis., Apr. 28, 1942. BA, U. Wis. Madison, 1964; JD, U. Wis., 1967. Bar: Wis. 1967, U.S. Dist. Ct. (ea. and we. dists.) Wis. 1967, U.S. Ct. Appeals (7th crct.) 1968. Law clk. to Hon. Myron L. Gordon U.S. Dist. Ct., Ea. Dist. Wis., 1967-68; shareholder Chernov, Croen & Goodstein, S.C., Milw., 1968-79; U.S. magistrate judge Ea. Dist. Wis., Milw., 1979-87, reapptd., 1987-95, 95—; panelist Current Issues Relating to the Fourth, Fifth and Sixth Amendments, Jud. Conf. of 7th Cir., 1991; speaker fed. ct.'s class Marquette Law Sch., 1992; moderator probation and pretrial svcs. divsn. U.S. Cts., 1992; former chair magistrate judges edn. com. Fed. Jud. Ctr., mem. magistrate judges com. of Jud. Conf. of U.S.; adv. com. local rules and practice Ea. Dist. Wis., mem. adv. panel under Civil Justice Reform Act 1990; faculty mem. in field. Prodr: (video) Complaints, Warrants for Arrest and Search Warrants, 1992, Administrative Matters Pertaining to Magistrate Judges and Their Staff, 1993; mem. editl. adv. panel Handbook of Federal Civil Discovery and Disclosure, 1998; contbr. articles to profl. jours. Bd. dirs. Milw. Legal Aid Soc., 1974-79, Milw. Jewish Coun., 1977-79; pres. Milw. Forum, 1979-80, alumni mem.; pres. Congregation Shalom, 1990-92. Recipient Pro Bono award Gene and Ruth Posner Found., 1988. Mem. ABA (former chair magistrate judges com. Nat. Conf. Fed. Trial Judges), Fed. Magistrate Judges Assn., State Bar Wis. (pres. young lawyer's divsn. 1975-76, bd. govs. 1975-77), Milw. Bar Assn. (exec. bd. 1978-79, sec. 1979-82), Order Coif, Phi Kappa Phi. Office: US Magistrate Judge 258 US Courthouse 517 E Wisconsin Ave Milwaukee WI 53202-4500

GOODSTEIN, BARNETT MAURICE, lawyer; b. Dallas, Oct. 1, 1921; s. Arthur Louis and Viola Esther (Levy) G.; m. Mira Brodsky, Jan. 26, 1947; children—Pamela Renee, Heather Ann, Robin Leslie. Student, Rice Inst., 1938-40; B.A., U. Tex., Austin, 1942, M.A., 1942; postgrad., U. Wis., 1949-51; J.D., So. Meth. U., 1957. Bar: Tex. 1957, U.S. Dist. Ct. (no. dist.) Tex. 1963, U.S. Supreme Ct. 1971. Acting dir. case analysis Wage Stblzn. Bd., Dallas, 1951-53; practice of law Dallas, 1957—; ptnr. Goodstein & Starr, P.C., 1977-91, Goodstein, Starr & Pascoe, P.C., 1991—; adminstrv. law judge City of Dallas, 1994—; lectr. econs. So. Meth. U., Dallas, 1946-48, 51-60; lectr. Massey Realty Coll., Real Estate Inst., Dallas; labor arbitrator, 1953—; former permanent arbitrator City of San Antonio, Police Officers' Assn.; mem. permanent arbitration panel Tinker AFB, Okla., 1984-88, Am. Fedn. Govt. Employees, 1984-90, SW Bell Telephone, AT&T, CWA, IBEW, 1988—, FAA, 1993—, Nat. Assn. Air Traffic Specialists, 1994—, Ga. Pacific, 1994—, UPIU, 1994—, also various VA Med. Facilities, paper and copper industries, others; mem. permanent panel Dallas Area Rapid Transit Sys., 1988-90, 94-96; adminstrv. law judge City of Dallas, 1994-96. Hearing officer work suspensions appeals bd. City of Dallas, 1981-83; trustee Dallas County Sch. Bd., 1980—, v.p., 1990-91; past trustee Temple Emanu-El; mem. legal representation com. Nat. Acad. Arbitrators, 1992-96, chmn. legal affairs com. 1997—. Served with USAAF, 1942-46, China, 1945-46. Mem. ABA, Tex. Bar Assn., Nat. Acad. Arbitrators (chmn., S.W. region 1987-88), Indsl. Rels. Rsch. Assn. (pres. North Tex. chpt. 1985-86, neutral mem. bd. dirs. North Tex. chpt. 1990-92), Am. Arbitration Assn. (Southwestern adv. coun. 1985-92). Home: 6427 Forest Creek Dr Dallas TX 75230-2814 Office: Law Offices of Barnett M Goodstein Ste 315 4230 Lyndon B Johnson Fwy Dallas TX 75244-5803

GOODSTEIN, DAVID LOUIS, physics educator; b. Bklyn., Apr. 5, 1939; s. Sam and Claire (Axel) G.; m. Judith R. Koral, June 30, 1960; children: Marcia, Mark. BS, Bklyn. Coll., 1960; PhD, U. Wash., 1965. Research instr. U. Wash., Seattle, 1965-66; research fellow Calif. Inst. Tech., Pasadena, 1966-67; asst. prof. Calif. Inst. Tech., 1968-71, asso. prof., 1971-76, prof., 1976—, vice-provost, 1987—, Frank J. Gilloon disting. teaching and svc. prof., 1995—; vis. scientist Frascati Nat. Lab., Italy, 1971—. Author: States of Matter, 1975, (with J. Goodstein) Feynman's Lost Lecture, 1996; mem. editl. bd. Il Nuovo Cimento, 1987—; contbr. articles to profl. jours.; project dir., host physics TV course The Mechanical Universe. Bd. dirs. Calif. Coun. Sci. and Tech., 1989—; sci. adv. com. David and Lucille Packard Found., 1988—. NSF postdoctoral fellow, 1967-68; Sloan Found. fellow, 1969-71; recipient Oersted medal, 1999. Fellow AAAS; mem. Am. Phys. Soc., Am. Inst. Physics. Office: Calif Inst Tech Dept Physics Pasadena CA 91125

GOODSTEIN, LES, newspaper publishing executive. V.p.-advertising The Daily News, N.Y.C., 1991—, exec. v.p. assoc. pub., 1996—. Office: The Daily News 450 W 33rd St Fl 3 New York NY 10001-2681*

GOODSTEIN, RICHARD GEORGE, sales executive; b. Bronx, N.Y.; s. Julius Goodstein and Alice Anita (Hochberg) Sanchez-Claypool-Weiser; m. Janis M. Gilmore, Aug. 23, 1970; children: Samuel, Benjamin, Joshua, Abigail, Maegan, Jacob. BS in Edn., Nat. Lewis U., 1971; cert. in Spl. Edn. Visually Impaired, Cranleigh Sch., 1978. Various sales positions Chgo., Des Moines, 1972-77; cons., trainer, nat. sales mgr. Blvd. Bus. Systems, Canberra, Australia, 1977-82; salesperson, trainer Johnson & Johnson, Piscataway, N.J., 1982-85; dir. mgmt. and sales devel. team Bristol Myers Squibb-Zimmer, Warsaw, Ind., 1986-93; pres. Monolith, Ft. Lauderdale, 1993—; cons. ACT Schs. Auth., Canberra, 1977-80, Rank Xerox, 1980-81, AT&T Internat., Morristown, N.J., 1984-85. Author mgmt. curriculum; contbr. articles to profl. jours. Bd. dirs. Evatt (Australia) Elem. Sch., 1980-82, Beaman House, Warsaw, 1989—; com. mem. Boy Scouts Am., 1988. Mem. ASTD, Am. Mgmt. Assn., Meeting Planners Internat., Internat. Conf. of Police Chaplains. Home: 415 Cambridge Ln Fort Lauderdale FL 33326-3567

GOODSTEIN, SANDERS ABRAHAM, scrap iron company executive; b. N.Y.C., Oct. 3, 1918; s. Samuel G. and Katie (Lipson) G.; m. Rose Laro, June 28, 1942; children: Peter, Esther, Jack, Rachel. Student, Wayne State U., 1934-36; AB, U. Mich., 1938, MBA, 1939, JD, 1946; postgrad., Harvard, 1943. Bar: Mich., 1946. Sec. Laro Coal & Iron Co., Flint, Mich., 1946-60, pres., 1960—; owner, operator Paterson Mfg. Co., Flint, 1953—; gen. ptnr. Indianhead Co., Pontiac, Mich., 1955-70, pres., 1965-70; sec. Amatac Corp., Erie, Pa., unitl 1969; chmn. bd. Gen. Foundry & Mfg. Co., Flint, 1968—, pres., 1970-92; pres. Lacron Steel Co., Providence, 1975-80, ETL Corp., Flint, 1983-91, Can. Blending and Processing, Windsor, 1988-97; mem. corp. body Mich. Blue Shield, 1970-76. Served to lt. comdr. USNR, 1942-46. Mem. Fed. Bar Assn., Am. Bar Assn., Bar Mich., Am. Pub. Works Assn., Am. Foundrymen's Soc., Order of Coif, Beta Gamma Sigma, Phi Kappa Phi. Jewish. Home: 2602 Parkside Dr Flint MI 48503-4662 Office: 6301 N Dort Hwy Flint MI 48505-2348

GOODSTONE, EDWARD HAROLD, retired insurance company executive; b. N.Y.C., July 19, 1934; s. Abraham and Gladys (Lande) G.; m. Harriet Jill Pearle, Oct. 16, 1955; children: Marjorie Faith, Michael Stuart. B.A., CUNY, 1956; C.L.U., Coll. Life Underwriters, 1973. Agt. Penn. Mut. Ins. Co., N.Y.C., 1957-67, assoc. gen. agt., 1971-72; agy. mgr. Lincoln Nat. Life of N.Y., N.Y.C., 1967-71; 2d v.p., dir. advanced markets Lincoln Nat. Life of N.Y., Pearl River, N.Y., 1972-75; v.p. U.S. Life Ins. Co., N.Y.C., 1975-78; sr. v.p. USLIFE Corp., N.Y.C., 1978-95; exec. v.p. USLIFE Corp., 1984-90, U.S. Life Ins. Co. (now am. Gen. Corp.), N.Y.C., 1990-95; ret., 1995. Mem. Am. Soc. C.L.U.s, Nat. Assn. Life Underwriters, Life Underwriters Assn. N.Y. Jewish. Home: 66 Shadom Ln East Hampton NY 11937-2082 Office: USLIFE Corp 125 Maiden Ln New York NY 10038-4912

GOODWILL, GEORGE WALTON, hospital administrator; b. Montego Bay, Jamaica, Sept. 17, 1938; came to U.S., 1954; s. John Goodwill and Daisy (Rodney) Scott. BA, Fordham U., 1980; postgrad., Aubrey Cohen Coll., N.Y.C. Asst. contr. G.H. & E. Freydberg divsn. Genesco, N.Y.C., 1970-73; assoc. dir. Harlem Hosp. divsn. Health and Hosps. Corp., N.Y.C., 1973—; mem. Regional Emergency Med. Asst. Corp., N.Y.C. Bd. dirs. St. Mary's Ctr., N.Y.C.; com. mem. Fire Dept./Emergency Med. Svcs., N.Y.C.; apptd. to Cmty. Bd. # 9, Manhattan Borough, 1997—. Episcopalian. Avocation: collecting art and antiques. Home: 458 W 152nd St New York NY 10031-1814 Office: Harlem Hosp Ctr 506 Lenox Ave New York NY 10037-1802*

GOODWIN, ALFRED THEODORE, federal judge; b. Bellingham, Wash., June 29, 1923; s. Alonzo Theodore and Miriam Hazel (Williams) G.; m. Marjorie Elizabeth Major, Dec. 23, 1943 (div. 1948); 1 son, Michael Theodore; m. Mary Ellin Handelin, Dec. 23, 1949; children: Karl Alfred, Margaret Ellen, Sara Jane, James Paul. B.A., U. Oreg., 1947; J.D., 1951. Bar: Oreg. 1951. Newspaper reporter Eugene (Oreg.) Register-Guard, 1947-50; practiced in Eugene until, 1955; circuit judge Oreg. 2d. Jud. Dist., 1955-60; assoc. justice Oreg. Supreme Ct., 1960-69; judge U.S. Dist. Ct. Oreg., 1969-71; judge U.S. Ct. Appeals for (9th cir.), Pasadena, Calif., 1971-88, chief judge, 1988-91, sr. judge, 1991—. Editor Oreg. Law Rev., 1950-51. Bd. dirs. Central Lane YMCA, Eugene, 1956-60, Salem (Oreg.) Art Assn., 1960-69; adv. bd. Eugene Salvation Army, 1956-60, chmn., 1959. Served to capt., inf. AUS, 1942-46, ETO. Mem. Am. Judicature Soc., Am. Law Inst., ABA (ho. of dels. 1986-87), Order of Coif, Phi Delta Phi, Sigma Delta Chi, Alpha Tau Omega. Republican. Presbyn. Club: Multnomah Athletic (Portland, Oreg.). Office: US Ct Appeals 9th Cir PO Box 91510 125 S Grand Ave Pasadena CA 91105-1621

GOODWIN, ANDREW WIRT, II, radiologist; b. Oil City, Pa., Feb. 4, 1932; s. Frank Bert and Florence Bickford (Green) G.; m. Anita Faye Adkins, May 27, 1987; children: Andrew, Victoria, Mary Elizabeth, Mark H., Martha J., Lisa R. BA, Colgate U., 1953; MD, U. Mich., 1957. Intern Mary Hitchcock Meml. Hosp., Hanover, N.H., 1957-58; resident in radiology Mayo Clinic, Rochester, Minn., 1958-61, resident, 1958-61; radiologist Associated Radiologists, Inc., Charleston, W.Va., 1961-86, Radiol. Assocs., Fairmont, W.Va., 1988—; pvt. practice, $D; pvt. practice. Republican. Episcopalian. Home: 205 Whispering Way Charleston WV 25304 Office: Radiol Cons Assn 700 Village Dr Fairmont WV 26554-2409

GOODWIN, BECKY K., secondary education educator. Sci. tchr. Kansas Sch for the Deaf, Olathe, Kans. Christa McAuliffe fellowship grantee State of Kans., 1992, 94, 97; named Kans. Tchr. of Yr., 1995; recipient Presdl. award for Excellence in Sci. and Math. Secondary Sci. for Kans., 1992, Outstanding Biology Tchr. award Nat. Assn. Biology Tchrs., 1992, Sci. Teaching Achievement Recognition Star award NSTA, 1993, Milken Nat. Educator award, 1995, Tandy Tech. Tchr. award, 1998. Office: Kansas Sch For the Deaf 450 E Park St Olathe KS 66061-5410

GOODWIN, BRUCE KESSELI, retired geology educator, researcher; b. Providence, Oct. 14, 1931; s. Thomas William and Lizetta Christina (Kesseli) G.; m. Joan Marilyn Horton, June 9, 1956; children: Stephen Bruce, Susan Joan, Jennifer Anne. AB, U. Pa., 1953; MS, Lehigh U., 1957, PhD, 1959. Grad. asst. Lehigh U., Bethlehem, Pa., 1956-59; geologist Vt. Geol. Survey, Burlington, 1956-58; instr. U. Pa., Phila., 1959-63; asst. prof. geology Coll. William and Mary, Williamsburg, Va., 1963-66, assoc. prof. geology, 1966-71, prof. geology, 1971-96, chmn. dept. geology, 1970-76, 82-88, 92-96; tchr. geology Math.-Sci. Ctr., Richmond, Va., 1968-70; with Va. Bd. Geology, 1982-88, chair, 1983; mem. Va. Geologic Mapping Adv. Com., 1993—. Contbr. articles to profl. jours. Pres. Lafayette Ednl. Fund, Inc., Williamsburg, Va., 1976-79, Lafayette High Sch. PTA, Williamsburg, Bruton Heights PTA, Williamsburg; mem. com. Va. Jr. Acad. Sci., 1971-73. Recipient Thomas Jefferson Teaching award Coll. William and Mary, 1971; cert. of merit Math.-Sci. Ctr. Fellow Geol. Soc. Am. (edn. com. 1994-96); mem. AAAS, Nat. Assn. Geology Tchrs. (pres. eastern sect. 1982), Va. Acad. Sci. (chmn. geology sect. 1970, 98), Am. Inst. Profl. Geologists (sec., treas. Va. sect. 1989, pres. Va. sect. 1990), St. Andrews Soc., Coun. on Undergrad. Rsch (geology councilor 1988-94), Kiwanis, Delta Upsilon, Sigma Xi. Republican. Presbyterian. Avocations: fishing, sailing, geology, travel, ballroom dancing. Home: 103 Wakerobin Rd Williamsburg VA 23185-4441

GOODWIN, CLAUDE ELBERT, lawyer, former gas utility executive; b. Ripley, W.Va., Aug. 9, 1910; s. Claude Earl and Marie (Vail) G.; m. Ireta Joy Watson, Aug. 15, 1931; 1 dau., Judith. A.B., W.Va. Wesleyan Coll., 1931; LL.B., W.Va. U., 1940; grad. student speech, Northwestern U., 1932. Bar: W.Va. 1940. Mem. firm Goodwin & Goodwin, Ripley, 1941-47, 73—; prof. W.Va. U. Coll. Law, 1947-48; sec., counsel United Fuel Gas Co., 1963-67; v.p., gen. counsel, dir. Charleston group companies Columbia Gas System, Inc., 1967-73; dir. United Nat. Bank Ripley, 1949—; bd. dirs. United Bank Shares, Inc. Editor-in-chief: W.Va. Law Rev, 1939-40; Contbr. legal articles to publs. Past pres., bd. dirs., mem. alumni exec. coun.ss W.Va. U.; past pres., bd. dirs. Charleston (W.Va.) Area Med. Ctr. Found., 1977—; trustee Sunrise Mus., Charleston, 1971-73. Served with USNR, 1943-46. Decorated Commendation ribbon. Mem. ABA, W.Va. Bar Assn., Order of Coif. Episcopalian. Home: Evans Rd Ripley WV 25271 Office: Goodwin & Goodwin One Valley Sq Charleston WV 25301

GOODWIN, CRAUFURD DAVID, economics educator; b. Montreal, Que., Can., May 23, 1934; came to U.S., 1962; s. George G. and Roma (Stewart) G.; m. Nancy Virginia Sanders, June 7, 1958. B.A., McGill U., 1955; Ph.D., Duke U., 1958. Econ. research asst. Courtauld's Can., Ltd., 1955; lectr. econs. U. Windsor, Ont., 1958-59; exec. sec. Commonwealth Studies Center, Duke U., also; vis. asst. prof., 1959-60; hon. research fellow Australian Nat. U., 1960-61; asst. prof. econs. York U., Toronto, 1961-62; asst. prof. econs., asst. to provost Duke U., Durham, N.C., 1962-63; assoc. prof. econs., sec. to Univ., asst. to provost Duke U., 1963-64, assoc. prof. econs., sec. Univ., asst. provost, 1964- 66, assoc. prof. econs., asst. provost, dir. internat. studies, 1966-68, prof. econs., vice provost for internat. studies, 1968-69, prof. econs., vice provost, dir. internat., 1969-72, prof. econs., 1971-74, James B. Duke prof. econs., 1974—, dean Grad. Sch., vice provost for research, 1980-86; Smuts vis. prof. Cambridge U., 1967-68; officer in charge European and internat. affairs Ford Found., 1971-76. Author: Canadian Economic Thought: The Political Economy of a Developing Nation 1814-1914, 1961, Economic Enquiry in Australia, 1966, The Image of Australia, 1974, (with M. Nacht) Absence of Decision, 1983, Fondness and Frustration, 1984, Decline and Renewal, 1986, Abroad and Beyond, 1988, Missing the Boat, 1991; editor: (with W.B. Hamilton and Kenneth Robinson) A Decade of the Commonwealth 1955-64, 1966, (with I.B. Holley) The Transfer of Ideas, 1968, (with R.D.C. Black and A.W. Coats) The Marginal Revolution in Economics, 1973, Exhortation and Controls, 1975, Energy Policy in Perspective, 1981, Economics and National Security, 1991, International Investment in Human Capital, 1993, (with Alan Smith, Ulrich Teichler, and Peggy Blumenthal) Academic Mobility in a Changing World: Regional and Global Trends, 1996, (with M. Nacht) Beyond Government, 1995, Talking to Themselves, 1995, Art and the Market, 1998; editor: (jour.) History of Political Economy, 1969—, (series) Historical Perspectives on Modern Economics, 1981—. Guggenheim fellow, 1967-68. Home: PO Box 957 Hillsborough NC 27278-0957

GOODWIN, DANIEL L., real estate company executive; b. 1943. BS, No. Ill. U., De Kalb, 1964, MA, 1966. Chmn. bd., CEO The Inland Group Inc., Oak Brook, Ill. Office: The Inland Group Inc 2901 Butterfield Rd Oak Brook IL 60523-1190*

GOODWIN, DORIS HELEN KEARNS, history educator, writer; b. Rockville Centre, N.Y., Jan. 4, 1943; d. Michael Alouisius and Helen Witt (Miller) Kearns; m. Richard Goodwin, 1975; three sons. BA magna cum laude, Colby Coll., 1964; PhD, Harvard U., 1968. Intern Dept. State, D.C., 1963, Ho. of Reps., D.C., 1965; rsch. assoc. U.S. Dept. Health, Edn., and Welfare, D.C., 1966; spl. asst. to Willard Wirtz U.S. Dept. Labor, D.C., 1967; spl. asst. to President Lyndon B. Johnson, 1968; asst. prof. Harvard U., Cambridge, 1969-71, assoc. prof. govt., 1972, historian; spl. cons. to President Johnson, 1969-73; asst. dir. Inst. Politics, 1971—; hostess "What's the Big Idea", WGBH-TV, Boston, 1972; polit. analyst news desk, WBZ-TV, Boston, 1972; mem. Women's Polit. Caucus, Mass., 1972, Faculty Coun. Harvard U., 1971, Dem. Party Platform Com., 1972; trustee Wesleyan U., Colby Coll., Robert F. Kennedy Found. Author: Lyndon Johnson and the American Dream, 1976, The Fitzgeralds and the Kennedys: An American Saga, 1987, No Ordinary Time: Franklin and Eleanor Roosevelt-The Homefront in World War II, 1994 (Pulitzer Prize for history 1995); contbr.: Telling Lives: The Biographer's Art, 1979; forward: Mortal Friends: A Novel, 1992. Named Fulbright fellow, 1966, White House fellow, 1967. Mem. Am. Polit. Sci. Assn., Coun. Fgn. Relations, Women Involved, Group for Applied Psychoanalysis, Signet Soc., Phi Beta Kappa (outstanding young women of yr. award 1966), Phi Sigma Iota. Roman Catholic. Office: c/o Dori Lawson Soldier Creek Asso 642 Gladstone St Sheridan WY 82801-5109*

GOODWIN, DOUGLAS IRA, steel trading company executive; b. New Haven, Feb. 17, 1946; s. Samuel and Daisy (Avrick) G.; m. Evelyne Mathes, 1978; 1 child, David. BA, Franklin and Marshall Coll., 1968; postgrad., So. Conn. State U., 1968-70. Elem. sch. tchr. Attleboro, Mass., 1968-71; prodn. engr. Ea. Steel & Metal Co., Milford, Conn., 1971-73, inside salesman, 1973-74, from v.p. sales and mktg. to pres., 1974-90; v.p. Dynamic Metals Inc., Piscataway, N.J., 1990-98, Duferco, Laurence Harbor, N.J., 1998—; advisor, mgmt. cons. Douglas Indsl. Supply, Milford, Conn., Kirk Ea., Gardner, Mass., 1980-94. Bd. dirs. Jewish Cmty. Ctr., New Haven, 1983-87; bd. dirs. Jewish Home for Aged, New Haven, 1986-89, chmn. Adult Day Care Ctr., 1985-97, chmn. Goodwin-Levine Adult Day Care Ctr.; advisor Conn. Joint Coun. on Econ. Edn., 1986-88, bd. dirs., 1988-89; basketball coach Bliss Sch., Attleboro, Mass., 1970-72; lacrosse coach Noble and Greenough Schs., Dedham, Mass., 1971—, mem. Men's Sr. Baseball League, 1990-97. Recipient Pres.'s award Assn. Steel Distbrs., 1977, Presdl. Citation Jewish Community Ctr., 1987, Kvod Soc. award Jewish Cmty. Ctr., 1988, Disting. Alumni award Milford Acad., 1986, Mens. Sr. Baseball League U.S. Nat. Champion, 1996. Avocations: golf, softball, baseball, photography. Home: 125 Mountain Brook Cir Cheshire CT 06410-3563 Office: Duferco 100 Metropark South Laurence Harbor NJ 08879*

GOODWIN, EVERETT CARLTON, minister; b. L.A., July 28, 1944; s. Carlton Byron and Pauline (Freeman) G.; m. Jane Gray, Sept. 3, 1966; children: Elizabeth Jane, Leah Grace. BA in Polit. Sci., U. Chgo., 1966; MDiv, Andover Newton Theol. Sch., 1969; MA in History, Brown U., 1971, PhD, 1979. Ordained to ministry Am. Bapt. Chs. in U.S.A., 1971. Asst. chaplain Harvard U. No. Bapt. Edn. Soc., Cambridge, Mass., 1968-69; asst. pastor Quidnick Bapt. Ch., Coventry, R.I., 1969-71; pastor Peoples Bapt. Ch., Cranston, R.I., 1971-78; pastor 1st Bapt. Ch., Meriden, Conn., 1978-81, Washington, 1981-93; chaplain The Flint Hill Sch., Oakton, Va., 1994-98; pastor Bapt. Fellowship of Met., Washington, 1995—; sr. min. Scarsdale (N.Y.) Cmty. Bapt. Ch., 1998—; chmn. United Ministries in Higher Edn., R.I. State Coun. Chs., 1976-78; bd. dirs. Am. Bapt. Chs. R.I., Am. Bapt. Chs. Conn.; mem. exec. coun. D.C. Bapt. Conv., 1981—; mem. statements of concern com. Am. Bapt. Chs., 1993-97, chair 1995-97. Author: The Magistracy Rediscovered, 1980, Baptists in the Balance: The Tension Between Freedom and Responsibility, 1997, The New Hiscox Guide for Bapt. Chs., 1995; contbr. revs. to profl. jours; revisions editor: Diary of Isaac Backus, 1974. Mem. United Way S.E. New Eng., Providence, 1974-76, chmn. appeals com., 1977; trustee Cranston Pub. Libr., 1976-78; bd. dirs. Nat. Rainbow Coalition; vice chmn. No. Va. Youth Symphony Assn., 1992—. Recipient Religious Leadership award Order Ea. Star, Providence, 1976;

Brown U. fellow, 1971, Woodrow Wilson Found. fellow, 1971-73. Mem. Inter-ch. Club D.C. (pres. 1988-90), Am. Bapt. Mins. Assn., Bapt. World Alliance (program com. 1985-90, chair, budget and fin. com. 1990-95), Am. Bapt. Hist. Soc. (v.p. 1993—), Westchester County Hist. Soc. (bd. dirs. 1999—). Address: 5 Autenrieth Rd Scarsdale NY 10583 *The former structures of church and denomination are in decline. Now we come full circle to again value the significance of the individual as teacher and spiritual guide.*

GOODWIN, FELIX LEE, retired educational administrator, retired army officer; b. Nov. 24, 1919; s. Felix and Lucille Marie (Lee) G.; m. Esther Brown, Nov. 1, 1941 (dec.); children: Cheryl Washington, Sylvia, Judith Barnes; m. Barbara Gilpin, Aug. 15, 1988. BS, U. Md., 1958; M of Pub. Adminstrn., U. Ariz., 1965, EdS, 1974, EdD, 1979. Enlisted U.S. Army, 1939, advanced through grades to lt. col., 1963; ret., 1969; asst. prof. army mil. sci. dept. U. Ariz., Tucson, 1968-69, asst. to pres., 1969-83. Chmn. Pima County Merit Sys. Commn., 1975-77, 79-82, Pima County Law Enforcement Merit Coun., 1973-82; mem. Ariz. Bicentennial Commn., 1974-77, chmn., 1976-77. Decorated Legion of Merit, Army Commendation medal with 2 oak leaf cluster, Meritorious Svc. medal; recipient Cert. of Appreciation, City of Tucson, 1967, 83, Man of Yr. award Una Noche Plateada, Tucson, 1976, Leadership award Tucson Urban League, 1975, IRS award, 1981; named Hon. Citizen, Sierra Vista, Ariz. Mem. NEA, NAACP (life), DAV (life), NRA, Nat. Alliance Black Sch. Educators (life), Soc. Ethnic and Spl. Studies Assn. U.S. Army, Am. Legion, Amvets, Ret. Officers Assn., Kiwanis (life), K.C., VFW, Phi Delta Kappa, Alpha Phi Alpha (life), Pi Lambda Theta, Alpha Delta Delta, Beta Gamma Sigma. Roman Catholic.

GOODWIN, FREDERICK KING, psychiatrist; b. Cin., Apr. 21, 1936; s. Robert Clifford and Marion Cronin (Schmadel) G.; m. Rosemary Powers, Oct. 19, 1963; children: Kathleen Kelly, Frederick King, Daniel Clifford. B.S., Georgetown U., 1958; philosophy fellow, St. Louis U., 1958-59, M.D., 1963. Intern medicine and psychiatry SUNY, Syracuse, 1963-64; resident psychiatry U. N.C., Chapel Hill, 1964-65; commd. med. officer USPHS, 1965; clin. assoc. adult psychiatry br. NIMH, 1965-67; research fellow Lab. Biochemistry, Nat. Heart Inst., NIH, Bethesda, Md., 1967-68; chief sect. on psychiatry NIMH, Bethesda, 1970-77; chief clin. psychobiology br. NIMH, 1970-81, sci. dir., 1981-88; apptd. by Pres. adminstr. Alcohol, Drug Abuse and Mental Health Adminstrn., Washington, 1988-92; pvt. practice medicine, specializing in psychiatry Bethesda, 1967—; dir. NIMH, Rockville, Md., 1992-94; dir. Ctr. on Neurosci. Med. Progress on Soc. George Washington U. Med. Ctr., Washington, 1994—; faculty George Washington U. Sch. Medicine, Washington Sch. Psychiatry, Uniformed U. Sch. Health Scis.; vis. prof. U. Calif., Irvine, U. Wis., Boston U., U. So. Calif., Duke U.; cons. AMA Council on Drugs; AIDS coordinator Alcohol, Drug Abuse and Mental Health Adminstrn., 1986-88; participant pub. edn. programs on local and network television and radio. Author: (with K.R. Jamison) Manic-Depressive Illness, 1990 (Best Med. Book award 1990 Assn. Am. Pubsd.); editor in chief Psychiatry Research, 1979-97; mem. editorial bd. Archives of Gen. Psychiatry, 1977—, Psychopharmacology, 1976-79; contbr. articles to med. jours.; host (pub. radio program) The Infinite Mind, 1998—. Mem. adv. bd. Max Planck Inst., Munich, W. Ger. Recipient Psychopharmacology Research prize Am. Psychol. Assn., 1971, Internat. Anna Monica prize for research in depression, 1971, Taylor Manor award, 1976, Adminstrs. award HEW, 1977, Superior Service award USPHS, 1980, Strecker award, 1983, Sr. Exec. Service Presdl. Meritorious Rank award, 1982, Disting. Rank award, 1986, Disting. Exec. Service award Sr. Exec. Assn. Profl. Devel. League, 1986, Best Tchr. in Am. Psychiatry award CME Inc., 1989, Svc. to Sci. award Nat. Assn. for Biomed. Rsch., 1990, Pub. Svc. award. Fed. Am. Socs. for Exptl. BNiologhy, 1990, 1st recipient of Fawcett Humanitarian award NDMDA, 1990, McAlpin award NMHA, 1991; NIMH Spl. fellow, 1967-68. Fellow Am. Psychiat. Assn. (chmn. com. on protection of human subjects, task force on research tng., Hofheimer prize for research 1971, chmn. task force on future of psychiat. research), Am. Coll. Neuropsychopharmacology (chmn. com. on problems of public concern); mem. Inst. Medicine, Nat. Acad. Scis., AAAS, Am. Psychosomatic Soc., Soc. Biol. Psychiatry (A.E. Bennett award 1970), Am. Acad. Psychoanalysis, Soc. for Neuroscience, Psychiat. Rsch. Soc. (pres. 1998—), Washington Psychiat. Soc. Fax: 202-994-6377. Home: 5712 Warwick Pl Bethesda MD 20815-5502 Office: George Washington U Med Ctr Dept Psychology 2150 Pennsylvania Ave NW Washington DC 20037-3201 *Many aspects of one's innerself contribute to shaping a career, most, I suspect, evolving and changing along the way. For me, one characteristic stands out as unchanging - the capacity to derive genuine pleasure and a special sense of satisfaction from the successes and the growth of those whose careers you have helped - in a sense, your professional "children.".*

GOODWIN, GEORGE EVANS, public relations executive; b. Atlanta, June 20, 1917; s. George and Carrie (Clark) G.; m. Lois Milstead, Nov. 2, 1940; children: Clark, Allen. AB with cert. in journalism, Washington and Lee U., 1939, HDL, 1997. Reporter Atlanta Georgian, 1939, Charleston (S.C.) News and Courier, 1940, Washington Times-Herald, 1940-41, Miami Daily News, 1941-42; staff writer Atlanta Jour., 1945-52; exec. dir. Central Atlanta Improvement Assn., 1952-54; v.p. First Nat. Bank of Atlanta, 1954-64; exec. v.p. Bell & Stanton, Inc., 1965-76; pres. Manning, Selvage & Lee, Atlanta, 1976-85; sr. counselor Manning, Selvage & Lee, 1985—; exec. sec. Ga. Senatorial Transit Study Com., 1954. Chmn. Atlanta Bicentennial Commn., 1974-76; trustee emeritus Oglethorpe U.; life dir. Alliance Theater; dir. Atlanta Com. for Pub. Edn.; elder Presbyn. Ch. Decorated Purple Heart, Navy Unit Commendation; recipient Pulitzer prize for local reporting, 1948, Pall Mall Big Story award, 1949, Sigma Delta Chi award for gen. reporting, 1948. Mem. SAR, Pub. Rels. Soc. Am., Rotary Internat., Delta Tau Delta, Soc. Profl. Journalists/Sigma Delta Chi (award for gen. reporting on vote fraud 1948), Omicron Delta Kappa. Home: 3302 Ivanhoe Dr NW Atlanta GA 30327-1528 Office: Manning Selvage & Lee 400 Colony Sq NE Ste 500 Atlanta GA 30361-6303

GOODWIN, IRWIN, magazine editor; b. Chgo., Aug. 19, 1929; s. Albert and Sarah Esther (Wallen) G.; m. Mary Margaret Revell, Apr. 21, 1966 (div. 1987). AB, Roosevelt U., Chgo., 1948; MA, U. Mich., 1949. Reporter City News Bur., Chgo., 1949-50; reporter, asst. editor Newsweek, Chgo. and N.Y.C., 1952-58; dir. pub. info. Sci. Rsch. Assocs., Chgo., 1958-60; corr. Newsweek, London, 1960-70; Caribbean corr. Washington Post, San Juan, P.R., 1970-72; spl. asst. to dir. Smithsonian Instn., Washington, 1972-73; sr. editor Nat. Acad. Scis., Washington, 1973-82; editor Washington bur. Physics Today, Washington, 1983-93, sr. editor Washington bur., 1993—. Co-author: Physics and Nuclear Arms Today, 1991; editor: Paying for America's Health Care, 1973, Energy and Environment: Collision of Crises, 1974; contbr. articles to profl. jours. Sgt. maj. U.S. Army, 1950-52. Recipient News Writing award Overseas Press Club, 1971, 72, Pub. Svc. Group Achievement award NASA, 1981. Mem. AAAS, Nat. Assn. Sci. Writers, Fedn. Am. Scientists, D.C. Sci. Writers Assn., Nat. Press Club, Phi Beta Kappa. Office: Physics Today 1050 National Press Bldg 529 14th St NW Washington DC 20045-1000

GOODWIN, JARRAD, otolaryngologist, educator. MD, Albany Med. Coll., 1972. Prof., chmn. dept. otolaryngology U. Miami, Fla., 1989—; dir. Sylvester Comprehensive Cancer Ctr. U. Miami Hosp. and Clinic, 1993—. Mem. Am. Acad. Otolaryngology/Head and Neck Surgery (Disting. S c. award 1996). Office: 1611 NW 12th Ave Miami FL 33136

GOODWIN, JEAN MCCLUNG, psychiatrist; b. Pueblo, Colo., Mar. 28, 1946; d. Paul Stanley and Geraldine (Smart) McClung; m. James Simeon Goodwin, Aug. 8, 1970; children: Laura (dec.), Amanda Harding Goodwin, Robert Caleb, Paul Joshua, Elizabeth Cronin Goodwin. BA in Anthropology summa cum laude, Radcliffe Coll., 1967; MD, Harvard U., 1971; MPH, UCLA, 1972. Diplomate Am. Bd. Psychiatry and Neurology, Am. Bd. Forensic Psychiatry; added qualifications in forensic psychiatry, psychoanalytic tng. Resident in psychiatry Georgetown U. Hosp., Washington, 1972-74; resident in psychiatry U. N.Mex. Sch. Medicine, 1974-76, asst. dir., dir. psychiat. residents tng., 1979-85; prof. Med. Coll. Wis., 1985-92; prof. U. Tex. Med. Br., Galveston, 1992-98, prof. clin. psychiatry, 1998—; pvt. practice in gen. and forensic psychiatry; from instr. to assoc. prof. dept. psychiatry U. N.Mex. Sch. Medicine, 1976-85; cons. protective services Dept. Human Services, N.Mex., 1976-84; lectr. profl. groups. Author: Effects of High Altitude on Human Birth, 1969, Sexual Abuse: Incest Victims and Their Families, 1982, 2d edit., 1989, Rediscovering Childhood Trauma: Historical Casebook and Clinical Applications, 1993, Mischief and Mercy, 1993; co-author (with Reina Attibo) Splintered Reflections: Images of the Body in Trauma, 1999; mem. editl. bd. Jour. Traumatic Stress, 1985-93, Dissociation, 1988-98; contbr. numerous articles on child abuse to profl. jours. Chmn. work group on child sexual abuse Surgeon Gen.'s Conference on Violence and Pub. Health, Leesburg, Va., 1985; mem. adv. bd. Nat. Resource Ctr. on Child Sexual Abuse, 1989-96. Recipient Esther Haar award Am. Acad. Psychoanalysis, 1990, Cornelia Wilbur award Internat. Soc. for Study of Dissociation, 1994; Nat. Cen. Child Abuse and Neglect grantee, 1979-82, Nat. Inst. Aging grantee, 1980-85. Fellow Internat. Soc. Study Dissociation (exec. com. 1991-96), Am. Psychiat. Assn. (dist. br. treas., sec. N.Mex. br. 1980-82, exhibits and programs subcoms. 1985-91); mem. Am. Profl. Soc. on Sexual Abuse in Children (bd. dirs. 1986-90), Am. Med. Women's Assn. (state dir. N.Mex. 1978-80). Democrat. Roman Catholic. Fax: (409) 762-1163. Office: # 510 4925 Ft Crockett Blvd Galveston TX 77551

GOODWIN, JOSEPH R., judge; b. 1942. BS, W.Va. U., 1965, JD, 1970. Ptnr. Goodwin & Goodwin, 1970-95; judge U.S. Dist. Ct. (so. dist.) W.Va., Charleston, 1995—. Editor W.Va. Law Rev. Mem. W.Va. U. Bd. Advisors, 1981-86; bd. visitors W.Va. U. Coll. Law, 1995-98, chmn., 1998. With USAR, 1965-67. Mem. ABA, W.Va. State Bar Assn., Jackson County Bar Assn., 4th Cir. Jud. Conf. Office: US Dist Ct So Dist WVa PO Box 2546 Charleston WV 25329-2546

GOODWIN, MARTIN BRUNE, radiologist; b. Vancouver, B.C., Can., Aug. 8, 1921; came to U.S., 1948; m. Cathy Dennison, Mar. 7, 1980; 1 child, Suzanne; stepchildren: Chuck Glikas, Dianna; 1 child from previous marriage, Nancijane Goodwin Hilling. *Stepson Chuck Glikas is an excellent wild life artist. He was featured prominently for 3 years on the PBS TV series "Images in Watercolor", which was broadcast elsewhere via satellite.* BSA in Agriculture, U. B.C., 1943, postgrad., 1943-44; MD, CM, McGill U. Med. Sch., Montreal, Can., 1948. Diplomate Am. Bd. Med. Examiners, lic. Med. Coun. Can.; cert. diagnostic and therapeutic radiology Am. Bd. Radiology; cert. Am. Bd. Nuclear Medicine. Intern Scott & White Hosp., Temple, Tex., 1948-49; fellow radiology Scott & White Clinic, 1949-52, mem. staff, 1952-53; instr. U. Tex., Galveston, 1952-53; radiologist Plains Regional Med. Ctr., Clovis, N.Mex.; radiologist Plains Regional Med. Ctr., Portales, N.Mex., pres. med. staff; chief radiology De Baca Gen. Hosp., Ft. Sumner, N.Mex.; cons. Cannon AFB Hosp., Clovis; pvt. practice radiology Clovis, Portales, Ft. Sumner and Tucumcari, 1955—; adj. prof. health scis. Ea. N.Mex. U., 1976-77; adj. clin. prof. health scis. We. Mich. U., 1976-78. *Dr. Goodwin gave DuPont the idea to use a higher definition single screen with single coated film for better detail in Mammography. Preliminary work was done in his office and later confirmed by Universities who checked and developed the process. The paper was presented to the International Congress of Radiology in Madrid, Spain. It was not orally presented, but it was filed in their archives.* Apptd. N.Mex. Radiation Tech. Adv. Coun., N.Mex. Bd. Pub. Health; former chmn. N.Mex. Health and Social Svcs. Bd.; mem. Regional Health Planning Coun.; treas. Roosevelt County Rep. Ctrl. Com. Capt. U.S. Army M.C., 1953-55; Col. USAF M.C., 1975-79. Fellow AAAS, Am. Coll. Radiology, Am. Coll. Radiology (past councillor); mem. Am. Soc. Thoracic Radiologists (founder), Radiol. Soc. of N.Am. (past councillor), N.Mex. Med. Soc. (various coms., chmn. joint practice com., councillor bd. dirs.), N.Mex. Radiol. Soc. (past pres.), N.Mex. Thoracic Soc. (past pres.), N.Mex. Med. Review Assn. (bd. dirs. 1970-93), N.Mex. Med. Soc. Found. for Med. Care (bd. dirs. 1975—, former v.p., former treas.), County Med. Soc. (past pres., past v.p., past sec.), Clovis C. of C. (chmn. civic affairs com., bd. dirs.), Clovis Elks Lodge (past exalted ruler), Clovis Noonday Lions Club (past sec.). Republican. Presbyterian. Home: 505 E 18th St Portales NM 88130-9201

GOODWIN, MARYELLEN, state legislator; b. Providence, Sept. 27, 1964. Student, R.I. Coll. mem. 12th Ward Dem. Com., R.I. Young Dems. Mem. state senate State of R.I., 1986—. Roman Catholic. Home: 325 Smith St Providence RI 02908-3759 Office: RI State Senate State House Rm 318 Providence RI 02903*

GOODWIN, NANCY LEE, corporate executive; b. Peoria, Ill., Aug. 11, 1940; d. Raymond Darrell and Mildred Louise (Brown) G. B.A. (Nat. Meth. scholar, Nat. Merit scholar), MacMurray Coll., 1961; M.A., U. Colo., 1963; Ph.D., U. Ill., 1971. Tchr. Roosevelt Jr. High Sch., Peoria, 1961-62; counselor U. Ill., Urbana, 1963-66; staff assoc., asst. prof. edn. measurement U. Ill., Chgo., 1967-71; asst. v.p., assoc. prof. stats. Fla. Internat. U., Miami, 1971-78; pres. Greenfield (Mass.) Community Coll., 1978-82, Arapahoe Community Coll., Colo., from 1982; corp. owner MTF Enterprises; prof. Nat. U.; owner C.A.T.S. Inc., 1987—; corp. mgr. DRM Enterprises; dir. Cons. Mid-Am. Computer Corp., First Chance Network U.S. Office Edn., 1972-78. Mem. Com. on Ill. Govt., Higher Edn. Task Force; mem. Vol. Action Center, Miami, 1972-78; active Girl Scouts U.S.A.; mem. Franklin/Hampshire Area Service Planning Team, 1978; incorporator Franklin County (Mass.) United Way, Farren Meml. Hosp.; adv. Franklin County Public Hosp.; bd. dirs. Women's Inst. Fla., Franklin County Arts Council, Franklin County Devel. Corp., Western Welcome Week, Inc.; bd. dirs., mem. fin. monitoring com. New Eng. Soy Dairy, 1980. Recipient Merit award Chgo. Tchrs. Assn., 1969; citation Girl Scouts U.S.A., 1973. Mem. NEA, Am. Assn. Higher Edn., Am. Ednl. Research Assn., Assn. Instl. Research, Centennial C. of C. (dir. 1983). Home: 5228 Del Rey Ave Las Vegas NV 89146-1414

GOODWIN, NEVA R., economist; b. N.Y.C., June 1, 1944; children: David Kaiser, Miranda Kaiser; m. Bruce Mazlish. BA, Harvard Coll., 1962; MPA, Kennedy Sch. of Govt., 1982; PhD, Boston U., 1987; BA (hon.), Coll. of the Atlantic, Bar Harbor, Maine, 1990. Dir. Program for Study of Sustainable Change and Devel. Tufts U., Medford, Mass., 1991-94, co-dir. Global Devel. And Environment Inst., 1994—. Author: Social Economics: An Alternative Theory, 1991; series editor: (6 books) Frontier Issues in Economic Thought, 1995; editor: As If the Future Mattered: Translating Social and Economic Theory into Human Behavior, 1996; editor jour. spl. issue World Devel., 1991. Trustee Winrock Internat. Inst. for Agrl. Devel., 1986—; mem. task force on population and consumption Pres.'s Coun. on Sustainable Devel., 1995; mem. adv. coun. Coll. of the Atlantic, 1996—; vice chair bd. Coll. of the Atlantic, Bar Harbor, 1981-90; founding trustee World Game Inst., Phila., 1986—. Avocations: gardening, cooking, bicycling, hiking. Home: 11 Lowell St Cambridge MA 02138-4725*

GOODWIN, PHILLIP HUGH, hospital administrator; b. Paragould, Ark., Sept. 10, 1940; s. Ray H. and Helen L. (Griffin) G.; m. Pamela J. Davis, June 24, 1962; children: Philip Grey, Julie Ann. BA in Bus. and Econs., Hendrix Coll., 1962; M in Hosp. Adminstrn., Washington U., St. Louis, 1968; LLD (hon.), U. Charleston, 1995. Bus. mgr. Stuttgart (Ark.) Meml. Hosp., 1962-64; asst. adminstr. Union Meml. Hosp., El Dorado, Ark., 1964-67; adminstrv. asst. to assoc. adminstr. Hillcrest Med. Ctr., Tulsa, 1968-77, v.p., adminstr., chief operating officer, 1977-82; exec. v.p. Charleston (W.Va.) Area Med. Ctr., 1982-87, pres., chief exec. officer, 1987-97; pres., CEO Camcare, Inc., Charleston, W.Va., 1998—; adj. faculty Wash. U., St. Louis, W.Va. U., Med. Coll. Va., W.Va. Coll. Grad. Studies; bd. dirs. Auther B. Hodges Nursing Home, Charleston, One Valley Bank N.A., Charleston, One Valley BanCorp of W.Va.; frequent speaker ednl., profl. and bus. assns. Co-author: Time Management for Hospital Administrators; contbr. articles to profl. publs. Bd. dirs. Kanawha Hospice Inc., Charleston, 1987-89, W.Va. Bus. Roundtable, Wellness Coun. Am., Nat. Com. for Quality Health Care; vol. Mgmt. Assistance Program, Charleston, 1987-89, Nat. Inst. Chem. Studies, Charleston, 1988-91, Charleston Renisance Corp., Bus. and Industry Coun. of W.Va., Pvt. Industry Coun. of W.Va.; pres. Civitan Club, Tulsa, 1970. Fellow Am. Coll. healthcare Execs.; mem. W.Va. Hosp. Assn. (pres. 1987, 88), Am. Hosp. Assn. (ho. of dels. 1988—), Vol. Hosps. Am. (bd. dirs. 1978-82, bd. Wellness Coun. of Am. 1994), Charleston Ranaisance Soc., W.Va. C. of C., Charleston C. of C., Ducks Unltd., Berry Hill Country Club. Republican. Methodist. Avocations: hunting, golf, rafting, sports. Office: Charleston Area Med Ctr PO Box 1547 Charleston WV 25326-1547

GOODWIN, RICHARD CLARKE, military analyst; b. Hancock, Mich., Mar. 24, 1949; s. Robert Clement and Jean (Gibson) G.; m. Linda Wells, Oct. 30, 1971; children: Katherine E., James G. BS in Nuclear Engring., U.S. Mil. Acad., 1971; MS in Systems Mgmt., U. So. Calif., 1977; MS in Nuclear Engring., Air Force Inst. Technology, 1978; D of Pub. Adminstrn., U. Ala., 1991. Asst. prof., physicist Dept. Physics, U.S. Mil. Acad., West Point, N.Y., 1978-81; asst. flight comdr. 441 Bomb Squadron, KI Sawyer AFB, Mich., 1981-84; rsch. fellow CADRE/ACSC, Montgomery, Ala., 1984-85; dep. chief, combat ops. 2nd Bomb Wing/DOXX, Bossier City, La., 1986-87; rsch. fellow CADRE, Montgomery, 1987-88; chief strategy & policy bd. Hdqrs. USAF, Studies & Analysis, Washington, 1988-90; mil. advisor for theater affairs Arms Control & Disarmament Agy., Washington, 1990-91; ret. USAF, 1991; with Logicon/RDA, SHAPE, Mons, Belguim, 1991-95; program mgr. Logicon, Arlington, Va., 1995—; cons. Allied Force Structure Requirement; cons. on counterproliferation strategy and requirements for Def. Nuclear Agy. and US European Command; cons. Joint/Navy Theater Missle Defense; cons AEGIS weapons system; vis. asst. prof. U. So. Ill., Carbondale, 1987; presenter studies at profl. confs.; mem. sci. and adv. working groups NATO. Contbr. articles to profl. jours. Mem. Am. Nuclear Soc., Am. Soc. Naval Engrs., Soc. Am. Mil. Engrs. (past pres. 1978), Am. Soc. Pub. Adminstrs., Mil. Ops. Rsch. Soc., Pi Sigma Alpha. Home: 4358 Huntley Ct Woodbridge VA 22192-5111 OFFICE: SYSCON 2341 JEFFREY DAVIS HIGHWAY 104 Arlington VA 22202

GOODWIN, RICHARD HALE, botany educator; b. Brookline, Mass., Dec. 14, 1910; s. Harry Manley and Mary Blanchard (Linder) G.; m. Esther Bemis, Oct. 12, 1936; children: Mary G. Wetzel, Richard H. Jr. AB, Harvard U., 1933, MA, 1934, PhD, 1937. Fellow Am.-Scandinavian Found., U. Copenhagen, 1937-38; instr. botany U. Rochester, N.Y., 1938-41, asst. prof., 1941-44; prof. Conn. Coll., New London, 1944-76, prof. emeritus, 1976—; dir. conn. Arboretum, New London, 1944-65, 67-68; pres. Conservation and Rsch. Found., Boston, 1953-94; treas. Inst. Ecology, Washington, 1975-77. Co-author: Inland Wetlands of the U.S. Fellow AAAS, Am. Acad. Arts and Scis.; mem. Nat. Com. Plant Sci. Socs. (coord. 1961-62), Am. Inst. Biol. Scis. (governing bd. 1967-71), Nature Conservancy (pres. 1956-58, 64-66), Conservation and Rsch. Found. (pres. 1953-94), Am. Soc. Plant Physiology, Ecol. Soc. Am., New Eng. Bot. Soc., Bot. Soc. Am., Torrey Bot. Club, Country Club (Brookline). Democrat. Unitarian-Universalist. Achievements include rsch. in plant morphogenesis, growth inhibitors, fluorescent constituents of plants, long range vegetation studies, effects of prescribed burning. Office: Conn Coll Conservation & Rsch Box 5261 New London CT 06320

GOODWIN, ROBERT, human resources specialist; b. Paterson, N.J., July 1, 1937; s. Herbert and Lodia (Czajkowski) Jackson; m. Paula Flo Wininger, Dec. 15, 1959 (div. Dec. 1980); children: Robert, Roger, Richard; m. Bertha Ann Walker, Apr. 14, 1984; stepchildren: Susan, Kerry. BS, U. of the State of N.Y., 1986. Tng. system analyst U.S. Navy, NATOPS coord.; air program mgr., surface program mgr., dir. tng. divsn. Naval Tng. Systems Ctr. Regional Office, 1983-87; tech. tng. equipment officer U.S. Atlantic Fleet, 1987-88, tng. systems advisor, 1988-94; tech. advisor, mem. steering com. IEEE Stds. for DIS, 1994-95; L.Am. mktg. cons. Goodwin Assocs., Virginia Beach, Va., 1995—. With U.S. Navy, 1955-73. Mem. Fleet Res. Assn., Navy League (life), Assn. Naval Aviation (life), Surface Navy Assn. (charter). Home and Office: Goodwin Assocs 909 Pillow Dr Virginia Beach VA 23454-2624

GOODWIN, ROBERT CRONIN, lawyer, consultant; b. Cleve., Mar. 17, 1941; s. Robert Clifford and Marion (Schmadel) G.; m. Judith Mary Baxter, June 7, 1968; children: Anne, Helen, Sharon, Katherine. AB, Fordham U., 1963; JD, Georgetown U., 1969. Bar: D.C. 1970, Md. 1990. Vol., Peace Corps, Thailand, 1964-65; asst. community devel. advisor AID, Thailand, 1965-66; atty. advisor Office Gen. Counsel, Dept. Commerce, 1969-74; dep. asst. gen. counsel internat. and resource devel. programs Fed. Energy Adminstrn., Washington, 1974-77, asst. gen. counsel internat. conservation and resource devel. programs, 1977; asst. gen. counsel internat. trade and emergency preparedness Dept. Energy, 1977-79; ptnr. Thompson, Hine & Flory, 1979-82; v.p., gen. counsel China Energy Ventures, Washington, 1982-86; ptnr. Goodwin & Soble, 1986-90, pvt. practice 1990-92; exec. v.p., gen. counsel, dir. U.S.-China Indsl. Exchange, Inc., 1992—; guest lectr. internat. petroleum contracts East China Petroleum Inst. Beijing, 1985; frequent lectr. on internat. contracts and Chineses legal and bus. issues; adj. assoc. prof. internat. mgmt. progam, U. Md., 1990—. Editor-in-chief Law and Policy in International Business, 1968-69; co-editor Legal Environ. for Fgn. Direct Investment in U.S., 1994; contbr. articles to profl. jours. Mem. pvt. sch. bd. 1980-83. Recipient cert. of Merit Fed. Energy Adminstrn., 1974, cert. Spl. Achievement, 1974, 76. Mem. ABA, D.C. Bar Assn., Thai-Am. Assn. (chmn. bus. com. 1991, pres. 1995), Nat. Council for U.S. China Trade (chmn. legal com. 1987), Am. Corp. Counsel Assn., Md.-China Bus. Coun. (bd. dirs.). Home: 3710 Bradley Ln Chevy Chase MD 20815-4257 Office: 7201 Wisconsin Ave Ste 703 Bethesda MD 20814-4850

GOODWIN, RODNEY KEITH GROVE, international bank and trade company executive; b. Emsworth, Hants., Eng., Nov. 9, 1944; s. Richard John Grove and Joan Avril (Gamon) G.; m. Lynda Elaine Brown, May 19, 1967; children—Keith Randal Grove, Kathryn Julie, Kara Dawn. Student, Eastbourne Coll., Sussex, Eng., NYU, Abilene Christian U.; B.A., SW Mo. State U.; M.A., U. Mo., 1972. Passenger rep. Grace Line Inc., N.Y.C., 1963-66; univ. youth coordinator Lausanne, Switzerland, 1966-68; asst. instr. French U. Mo., 1971-72; internat. sales rep. Mueller Internat. Sales Corp. subs. Paul Mueller Co., Springfield, Mo., 1973-76; v.p. internat. Peabody Tec Tank, Parsons, Kans., 1976-78; group dir. exports water/fluids group Peabody Internat. Corp., 1976-80, dir. exports, 1980—; v.p. exports/trading, 1980-84; sr. v.p., pres. Peabody World Trade.; chief mktg. officer, exec. dir. HSBC Equator Bank PLC and Equator Trade Svcs. Ltd., Hartford, Conn., 1984—; sr. v.p., exec. dir. HSBC Equator USA Inc., Glasonbury, Conn., 1984—; bd. dirs. Equator Holdings Ltd. Mem. U.S.-Angola C. of C. (co-founder, bd. dirs.). Address: HSBC Equator USA Inc 45 Glasonbury Blvd Glastonbury CT 06033

GOODWIN, SHARON ANN, academic administrator; b. Little Rock, May 19, 1949; d. Jimmy Lee and Eddie DeLois (Cluck) G.; m. Mitchell Shayne Mick, May 4, 1968 (div. Mar. 1973); 1 child, Heather Michelle; m. Raymond Eugene Vaclavik, June 24, 1974 (div. Aug. 1982); 1 child, Tasha Rae Vaclavik. BA in Psychology, U. Houston-Clear Lake, 1980; MEd in Higher Edn. Adminstrn., U. Houston, 1990. Various clerical positions Gen. Telephone Co., Dickinson, Tex., 1969-80; state dir. Challenge, Inc., Oklahoma City, 1980-82; gen. mgr. Mr. Fix It, Houston, 1982-85; assoc. dir. admissions U. Houston, Tex., 1985-92; adminstr. Inst. for the Med. Humanities U. Tex. Med. Br., Galveston, 1992—. Contbr. poetry to World of Poetry Anthology, 1986, 87, 90, 91, Nat. Libr. of Poetry Anthology, 1997, SOL Mag., 1997, 98, Lucidity Jour., 1997, New Winds Jour., 1997, Galveston Writers Anthology, 1998, Nat. Poetry Guild Anthology, 1998. Mem. legis. com. Comm. Workers, Dickinson and Austin, 1975; mem. centennial choir U. Tex. Med. Br., Galveston, 1992—; vol. Dickens on the Strand, Galveston, 1993—. Recipient award of merit World of Poetry Anthology, 1986, 91, Golden Poet award, 1987, Silver Poet award, 1990, rd 1990, Golden Poet award, 1991, hon. mention SOL Mag., 1997, 98, 1st pl., 1998, 2d pl., 1998; named to Internat. Poetry Hall of Fame, 1997. Mem. AAUW, Assn. of Am. Med. Colls.-Group on Institutional Planning. Avocations: travel, music, sports, books, movies. Home: 917 Avenue K Galveston TX 77550-6232 Office: Univ Tex Med Br Inst for the Med Humanities 301 University Blvd Galveston TX 77555-5302

GOODWIN, TODD, banker; b. Rochester, N.Y., Aug. 6, 1931; s. Philip Curtis and Ellen Laura (Todd) G.; m. Jacqueline Haswell, Nov. 27, 1987; children: Alexandra, Leslie, Ian, Elizabeth, Amanda. AB, Harvard Coll., 1954. With Bankers Trust, N.Y.C., 1954-57; banker White, Weld & Co., N.Y.C., 1957-78, Merrill Lynch, N.Y.C., 1978-84, Gibbons, Goodwin, Van Amerongen, N.Y.C., 1984—; bd. dirs. Wells Aluminum, Balt., Rival Co., Kansas City, Schult Homes, Middlebury, Ind., Johns Manville Corp., Denver, U.S. Energy, West Palm Beach, Fla. Home: 195 Toylsome Ln Southampton NY 11968-5020 Office: Gibbons Goodwin Van Amerongen 600 Madison Ave New York NY 10022-1615*

GOODWIN, WILLIAM DEAN, consulting company executive; b. Independence, Kans., Aug. 3, 1937; s. William Brice and Rozella Delia (Lillibridge) G.; m. Jane Louise Varnum, Oct. 23, 1960 (div. 1973); children: Deborah Diane, Laura Louise; m. Linda Ann Booth, July 26, 1980; 1 child,

William D. II. BS in Advt. and Bus., U. Kans., 1961. Editor Marshall County News, Marysville, Kans., 1961-63; dir. pub. relations U.S. Jaycees, Tulsa, 1963-67; account exec. Carl Byoir & Assocs., Chgo., 1967-68, Holder, Kennedy & Co., Nashville, 1968-70; press sec. U.S. Senator Bill Brock, Washington, 1970-74; exec. v.p. Nat. Energy Corp., Nashville, 1974-78, Tenn. Land & Exploration, Nashville, 1979-80; pres. Commerce Oil Co., Nashville, 1980-83; pvt. practice oil producer Crossville, Tenn., 1984-91; v.p. Tom Jackson & Assocs., Nashville, 1991-96; prin. Akins & Tombras, Nashville, 1996-97, Target Market Devel., Nashville, 1997—; treas. Tenn. Oil Producers Polit. Action Com., Nashville, 1983-88. Editor-in-chief Future mag., 1966-67; editor Nat. Young Reps. mag., 1971-72, The Oilpatch newsletter, PLS News mag. Chmn. Davidson County Reps., Nashville, 1979; nominee Candidate for U.S. Congress 5th Dist. Tenn., 1978; cons. Nat. Rep. Senatorial Com., Washington, 1973; dir. publicity Com. to Reelect the Pres., 1972; vice chmn. Tenn. Commn. on Status of Women, 1979-80. Served with USN, 1956-57. Mem. Nat. Assn. Royalty Owners Assn. (life, bd. govs. 1986—), Tenn. Oil and Gas Assn. (exec. v.p. 1975-82, named Tenn. Oil Man of Yr. 1981), VFW, Nashville City Club, Downtown Kiwanis (pres.). Methodist. Club: Lake Tansi (Crossville). Avocation: oil and gas exploration and production consulting. Home: 900 Hawthorne Ct Franklin TN 37069-4134 Office: Two Brentwood Commons 750 Old Hickory Blvd #170 Brentwood TN 37027

GOODWIN, WILLIAM MAXWELL, financial executive; b. Muncie, Ind., Oct. 13, 1939; s. Donald Dunkin and Beth Virginia (Maxwell) G.; m. LaDonna Sherry Erickson, June 9, 1962; children: Lauri Michelle, Lisa Dianne. AB, Ind. U., 1961, MBA, 1966. CPA, Ind. Staff acct., supr. Ernst & Whinney (now Ernst & Young), Indpls., 1966-72; contr. Lilly Endowment, Inc., Indpls., 1972-82, treas., sec., 1983-95, v.p. cmty. devel., 1996—; advisor Sch. Bus., Ind. U., Bloomington, Ind., 1980-95; fin. advisor U.S. Gymnastic Fedn., Indpls., 1983-89; treas., dir. Nat. Gymnastics Found. Inc., Indpls., 1988-89. Contbr. articles to profl. jours. Treas., dir. Ind. Sports Corp., Indpls., 1979-88; dir. Youth Works, Inc., Indpls., 1977-85, Greater Indpls. Progress Com., 1996—; treas. Nat. Sports Festival, Indpls., 1982; treas., mem. exec. com. 1987 Pan Am. Games, Indpls.; chmn. AAU Sullivan Award Dinner, Indpls., 1983-94, mem. award selection com., 1993—. Capt. U.S. Army, 1962-64. Mem. AICPA, Ind. Assn CPA's, Beta Gamma Sigma, Delta Phi Alpha. Republican. Methodist. Home: 3586 Inverness Blvd Carmel IN 46032-9380 Office: Lilly Endowment Inc PO Box 88068 Indianapolis IN 46208-0068

GOODY, JOAN EDELMAN, architect; b. N.Y.C., Dec. 1, 1935; d. Beril and Sylvia (Feldman) Edelman; m. Marvin E. Goody, Dec. 18, 1960 (dec. 1980); m. Peter H. Davison, Aug. 11, 1984. BA, Cornell U., 1956; MArch, Harvard U., 1960. Registerd architect, Mass., Conn., Maine, Md., N.Y., R.I. Prin. Goody, Clancy & Assocs., Inc., Boston; asst. prof., design critic Harvard U., Cambridge, Mass., 1973-80, Eliot Noyes vis. critic, 1985; faculty Mayors Inst. for Design, 1989—; lectr. in field. Mem. Boston Landmarks Commn., 1976-87; chair Boston Civic Design Commn.; bd. dirs. Historic Boston, Sta. WGBH-TV, Historic Mass. Fellow AIA (hon. award 1980), Boston Soc. Architects (bd. dirs. 1983-85, design awards), Boston Archtl. Ctr. (hon.), Internat. Women's Forum, Saturday Club, Tavern Club. Office: Goody Clancy & Assocs Inc 334 Boylston St Fl 3 Boston MA 02116-3866

GOODY, RICHARD MEAD, geophysicist; b. Welwyn-Garden-City, Eng., June 19, 1921; came to U.S., 1958, naturalized, 1966; s. Harold Earnest and Lilian (Rankine) G.; m. Elfriede Koch, Sept. 11, 1946; 1 dau., Brigid. Ph.D., Cambridge U., 1949; M.A. (hon.), Harvard U., 1958. With Brit. Civil Service, 1942-46; fellow St. John's Coll., Cambridge, 1950-53; reader London U., 1953-58; prof. div. applied scis. Harvard U., 1958-91; dir. Blue Hill Obs., 1958-70, Center for Earth and Planetary Physics, 1970-71. Author: Physics of the Stratosphere, 1947, Atmospheric Radiation, 1964, rev. edit., 1989, Atmospheres, 1974, The Principles of Atmospheric Physics and Chemistry, 1995. Mem. Royal Meteorol. Soc. (Buchan prize 1955), Am. Meteorol. Soc. (50th Anniversary medal 1970, Cleveland Abbé award 1977), Nat. Acad. Scis., Am. Philos. Soc., Am. Geophys. Union (William Bowie medal 1998). Home: 101 Cumloden Dr Falmouth MA 02540-1609

GOODYEAR, AUSTIN, electronics and retail company executive; b. Buffalo, Nov. 18, 1919; s. Charles W. and Grace (Rumsey) G.; m. Louisa Robins, mar. 30, 1940 (dec. July, 1992); children: Grace R. (Mrs. Franklin D. Roosevelt III), Thomas R., Cullen C.; m. Sara Suleri, July, 1993. Student, Yale U., 1939-40. With Hewitt-Robins Inc. div. Litton Industries, Stamford, Conn., 1941-53, from apprentice machinist to v.p., 1953-56, pres., 1958-70; sr. v.p. Litton Industries, 1967-70; pres. Ellsworth Falls Lumber Co. Inc., Maine, Ellsworth Builders Supply Inc. Office: EBS Bldg Supplies State St Ellsworth ME 04605

GOODYEAR, JULIE ANN, marketing and fundraising specialist; b. Lafayette, Ind., Dec. 10, 1956; d. Charles Robert and Leona Mae (Widmer) Stroop; m. Michael Clark Goodyear, May 31, 1986; children: Elizabeth, Katharine, (twins) Charles and David. BA, Purdue U., 1983; MA, U. N.D., 1985. Asst. mktg. dir. Mo. Repertory Theater, Kansas City, 1985-88; dir. mktg. and pub. rels. Northlight Theater, Chgo., 1988-91; membership mgr. Chgo. Bot. Gardens, Glencoe, Ill., 1991-92; mgr. rel. mktg. Evanston (Ill.) Hosp. Corp., 1992-93, sr. devel. officer, 1993—. Active Dawes Elem. Sch. PTA, Evanston, 1992—; pres. Ctrl. Evanston ChildCare Parents Bd., 1993-94; bd. dirs. Evanston Arts Ctr. Design winner for poster Saks 5th Ave., 1986. Mem. Nat. Soc. Fundraising Execs., Assn. Healthcare Philanthropy, Jr. League of Evanston-North Shore. Avocations: reading, arts, cooking. Home: 1804 Cleveland St Evanston IL 60202-1902

GOODYEAR, NANCY L., biology educator; b. Silver City, N.Mex., Oct. 13, 1945; d. Howard R. and Audrey Willella (Lee) G. BA, MacMurray Coll., 1967; MS, U. Wis., 1967; EdD, Auburn U., 1976. Secondary tchr. Fgn. Mission Bd. So. Bapt. Conv., Richmond, Va., 1969-71; secondary sci. tchr. Pine Bluff (Ark.) Sch. Sys., 1971-74, 75-76; prof. biology Bainbridge (Ga.) Coll., 1976—; adj. prof. biology Tallahassee C.C., 1993—. Contbr. articles to profl. jours.; author poetry. Grantee Ga. Endowment for the Humanities, 1984; recipient Original Poetry award Bahamian Art and Drama Festival, 1971. Mem. Assn. for Biology Lab. Edn. (mem. 1982—, mem.-at-large 1998—), St. Marks Wildlife Refuge Assn., Delta Kappa Gamma (treas. 1983-96). Avocations: reading, gardening, travel, large cross-stitching, collecting tin/frog memorabilia. Home: 1439 Lloyds Cove Rd Tallahassee FL 32312-9688 Office: Bainbridge Coll 2500 E Shotwell St Bainbridge GA 31717-8400

GOODYKOONTZ, CHARLES ALFRED, newspaper editor, retired; b. Radford, Va., Dec. 29, 1928; s. Charles A. and Claudine (Noell) G.; m. Jean Shirley Beasley, Sept. 17, 1955; 1 child, Charles Alfred III. Student, Emory and Henry Coll., 1946-48. Sports editor Radford News Jour., 1948-50; mem. staff Richmond (Va.) Times-Dispatch, 1952-81, mng. editor, 1969-81; v.p., exec. editor Richmond (Va.) Times-Dispatch and The Richmond News Leader, 1982-93, ret., 1993; former chmn. Va. AP, UPI. Bd. trustees Emory and Henry Coll., 1985-92; chmn. Trinity United Methodist Ch., Richmond, 1995-97, bd. trustees; bd. govs. Va. Home for Boys, 1995. With AUS, 1950-52. Recipient George Mason award for service to Va. journalism, 1973; inducted into Va. Comm. Hall of Fame, 1992. Mem. AP Mng. Editors Assn. (treas. 1988-90), Va. Press Assn. (bd. dirs. 1986-89, life), Soc. Profl. Journalists, Sigma Delta Chi (regional dir. 1971-74, nat. officer 1975-79, pres. 1978, Wells Key award 1982, pres. Found. 1985-87), Va. Inst. of Pastoral Care (bd. dirs. 1995, v.p. 1997). Home: 8207 Shannon Hill Rd Richmond VA 23229-4911

GOOGASIAN, GEORGE ARA, lawyer; b. Pontiac, Mich., Feb. 22, 1936; s. Peter and Lucy (Chobanian) G.; m. Phyllis Elaine Law, June 27, 1959; children—Karen Ann, Steven George, Dean Michael. B.A., U. Mich., 1958; J.D., Northwestern U., 1961. Bar: Mich. 1961. Assoc. Marentay, Rouse, Selby, Fischer & Webber, Detroit, 1961-62; asst. U.S. Atty. U.S. Dept. Justice, Detroit, 1962-64; assoc. Howlett, Hartman & Beier, Pontiac and Bloomfield Hills, Mich., 1964-81; ptnr. Googasian Hopkins Hohauser & Forhan, Bloomfield Hills, Mich., 1981-96, The Googasian Firm, Bloomfield Hills, 1996—; bd. law examiners State of Mich., 1997—. Author: Trial Advocacy Manual, 1984, West Groups Michigan Practice Torts, vols. 14, 15, 1998. Pres. Oakland Parks Found., Pontiac, 1984-89; chmn. Oakland County Dem. party, Pontiac, 1964-70; state campaign chmn. U.S. Senator Philip A. Hart, Detroit, 1970; bd. dirs. Big Bros. Oakland County, 1968-73. Fellow Am. Bar Found., Am. Coll. Trial Lawyers, Internat. Acad. Trial Lawyers; mem. ABA (del. 1992-93, exec. coun. nat. conf. bar pres. 1993-96), ATLA, Am. Bd. Trial Advocates, State Bar Mich. (pres. elect 1991-92, pres. 1992—), Oakland County Bar Assn. (pres. 1985-86), Mich. State Bar Found., Oakland Bar Found. (pres. 1990-92). Presbyterian. Club: U. Mich. Club Greater Detroit. Home: 3750 Orion Rd Oakland MI 48363-3029 Office: 6895 Telegraph Rd Bloomfield Hills MI 48301-3138

GOOGINS, LOUISE PAULSON, financial planner; b. Iola, Wis., June 14, 1941; d. Walter August and Helen Veronica (Waldoch) Paulson; m. James R. Googins, June 19, 1965 (div. 1978); children: Michael James, Shane Paul. BS, Stevens Point State U., 1963; MA, U. Wis., 1976, Coll. Fin. Planning, Denver, 1984. Cert. fin. planner. Recreational therapist Cen. Wis. Colony, Madison, Wis., 1966-69; tchr. mentally retarded Madison Schs., Madison, 1969-71; supr. student tchrs. U. Wis., Madison, 1972-76; tchr. learning disabled Monona, Wis., 1976-78; rep. FPC Secs. & Charter Securities, Madison, 1978-83; prin., pres. Googins & Co. Inc., Madison, 1983—. Bd. dirs. REBOS House, Madison, 1982-95, pres. 1987-90; bd. dirs. Benedictine Life Found., 1996—; pres. S. Rotary Found., 1998-99. Mem. Inst. CFPs, Madison South Rotary (bd. dirs. 1993—, sgt. at arms 1990-91, pres. 1997-98). Office: Googins & Co Inc 437 S Yellowstone Dr Ste 110 Madison WI 53719-1096

GOOKIN, THOMAS ALLEN JAUDON, civil engineer; b. Tulsa, Aug. 5, 1951; s. William Scudder and Mildred (Hartman) G.; m. Sandra Jean Andrews, July 23, 1983. BS with distinction, Ariz. State U., 1975. Registered profl. engr., Calif., Ariz., Nev., land surveyor Ariz., hydrologist. Civil engr., treas. Gookin Engrs. Ltd, Scottsdale, Ariz., 1968—. Chmn. adv. com. Ariz. State Bd. Tech. Registration Engrng., 1984—. Recipient Spl. Recognition award Ariz. State Bd. Tech. Registration Engrng., 1990. Mem. NSPE, Ariz. Soc. Profl. Engrs. (sec. Papago chpt. 1979-81, v.p. 1981-84, pres. 1984-85, named Young Engr. of Yr. 1979, Outstanding Engrng. Project award 1988), Order Engr., Ariz. Congress on Surveying and Mapping, Am. Soc. Civil Engrs., Ariz. Water Works Assn., Tau Beta Pi, Delta Chi (Tempe chpt. treas. 1970-71, sec. 1970, v.p. 1971), Phi Kappa Delta (pres. 1971-73). Republican. Episcopalian. Avocations: Disneyana, science fiction, computer gaming. Home: 10760 E Becker Ln Scottsdale AZ 85259-3868 Office: Gookin Engrs Ltd 4203 N Brown Ave Ste A Scottsdale AZ 85251-3990

GOOLD, FLORENCE WILSON, occupational therapist; b. Chgo., Aug. 26, 1912; d. Frank Elmer and Marie Louise (Walker) Wilson; m. Robert Charles Goold, Dec. 28, 1938; children: Frances Louise Goold Felty, Nancy Jean Goold Magurno, Elizabeth Jane Ill, Robert Charles, Jr. Student, U. Wis., 1934; BA, Boston Sch. Occupational Therapy, 1936. Occupational therapist Ypsilanti (Mich.) State Hosp., 1936-40, Michael Reese Hosp., Chgo., 1940-42, DuPage County Easter Seal Ctr., Villa Park, Ill., 1959-62; dir. occupational therapy Hinsdale (Ill.) Sanitarium and Hosp., 1962-71, Marianjoy Rehab. Hosp., Wheaton, Ill., 1971-73, Cen. DuPage Hosp., Winfield, Ill., 1972-73, Royal Oak Convalescent Home, Oak Park, Ill., 1973, Highland House Nursing Home, Downers Grove, Ill., 1973-75, St. Charles Med. Ctr., Aurora, Ill., 1975-78, Westmont (Ill.) Health Ctr., 1978-80, Americana Health Care Ctr., Naperville, Ill., 1981-84, Med. Pers. Pool, Chgo., 1985-89, Midwest Rehab. Svcs., Hinsdale, 1986-95. Pres. bd. dirs. DuPage County Easter Seal Ctr., Villa Park, 1942-59; bd. dirs. Community Adult Day Care, Downers Grove, 1985-95. Named Citizen of Yr., Downers Grove, 1987. Mem. PEO, Am. Occupational Therapy Assn., Ill. Occupational Therapy Ass. (past pres., Occupational Therapist of Yr. 1988), Phi Mu. Episcopalian. Home: 6582 Willowwood Ct Downers Grove IL 60516-3045 Office: Ill Occupational Therapy Assn 715 Lake St Ste 710 Oak Park IL 60301-1416 *Personal philosophy: Having been brought up in a cleryman's home, the Parable of the Talents and the Golden Rule, in that order, have been my greatest guidelines for my life, both in my marriage and with my children, and in my professional life. Using my talents and education with basic principles of good relationship with others through courtesy, kindness and respect for people have all helped me achieve my successes in my chosen profession.*

GOOLDY, PATRICIA ALICE, retired elementary education educator; b. Indpls., Nov. 23, 1937; d. Harold Emanuel and Emma Irene (Wade) Van-Treese; m. Walter Raymond Gooldy, May 4, 1968. BS, U. Indpls., 1959; MS, Butler U., 1963. Tchr. Franklin Twp. Cmty. Schs., Indpls., 1959-68, 72-99, USA Dep. Schs., Bad Kreuznach, Germany, 1969-72; ret., 1999; co-owner Ye Olde Genealogie Shoppe, Indpls., 1972—; lectr. in field. Author: 21 Things I Wish I'd Found, 1984; editor: Indiana Wills to 1880: Index to Indiana Wills, 1987; co-editor: Indiana Manual For Gen, 1991, Illinois Manual For Gen, 1994. Mem. Franklin Twp. Geneal. Soc. (founder), Ind. Geneal. Soc. (chartered). Office: Ye Olde Genealogie Shoppe PO Box 39128 Indianapolis IN 46239-0128

GOOLDY, WALTER RAYMOND, genealogist; b. Ellettsville, Ind., May 4, 1932; s. Donovan Oral and Catherine Lois (Frantz) G.; m. Patricia Alice Van Treese, May 4, 1968. Grad. h.s., Ellettsville, Ind., 1952. Advanced through grades to sgt. U.S. Army, 1952-72; clk. Ind. Ins. Co., Indpls., 1973-76; owner, CEO Ye Olde Genealogie Shoppe, Indpls., 1975—. Author: Manual For Indiana Genealogical Research, 1991, Manual For Illinois Genealogical Research, 1994, 3 others. Office: Ye Olde Genealogie Shoppe PO Box 39128 Indianapolis IN 46239-0128

GOOLKASIAN, PAULA A., psychologist, educator; b. Methuen, Mass., Aug. 9, 1948; d. Paul K. and Sadie T. (Touma) G.; m. Francis C. Martin, July 29, 1978; 1 child, Christopher. BA, Emmanuel Coll., 1970; MS, Iowa State U., 1972, PhD, 1974. Asst. prof. U. N.C., Charlotte, 1974-79, assoc. prof., 1979-85, prof. psychology, 1985—, pres. faculty, 1989—; cons. in field. Contbr. articles to profl. jours. Nat. Def. Ednl. Act. fellow, 1971-74; grantee NSF, NIH, and numerous others. Mem. AAAS, APA, Psychonomics Soc., Ea. Psychol. Assn., Internat. Soc. Psychophysics, Soc. for Computers in Psychology (sec.-treas. 1989-91, pres. 1994), Sigma Xi, Phi Kappa Phi. Home: 20125 River Chase Dr Cornelius NC 28031-7175 Office: U NC Dept Psychology Charlotte NC 28223

GOOLRICK, ROBERT MASON, lawyer, consultant; b. Fredericksburg, Va., Mar. 25, 1934; s. John T. and Olive E. (Jones) G.; m. Audrey J. Dippo (div.); children—Stephanie M., Meade A. B.A. with distinction, U. Va., 1956; J.D., 1959. Bar: Va. 1959, D.C., 1959, U.S. Dist. Ct. D.C. 1961, U.S. Ct. Appeals (D.C. cir.) 1961. Assoc. Steptoe & Johnson, Washington, 1959-65, ptnr., 1965-79; sole practice, Alexandria, Va., 1979-83; cons. bus., oil and gas fin.; instr. U. Va. Law Sch. Mem. ABA (corps. sect.), Jefferson Soc., Raven Soc., Order of Coif, Phi Beta Kappa. Author: Public Policy Toward Corporate Growth, 1978; Corporate Mergers and Acquisitions under Federal Securities Laws, 1978. Home: Ste 22 3320 Woodburn Vill Dr Annandale VA 22003-6860

GOOLSBY, CHARLES WILLIAM, artist, educator; b. Trenton, Mich., Sept. 11, 1958; s. William Lyman and Helen May (Richardson) G. BFA in Art, Radford U., 1980; MFA in Art, James Madison U., 1994. Art instr. Pulaski County H.S., Dublin, Va., 1980-87, Augusta County Schs., Fishersville, Va., 1987-88, Waynesboro (Va.) H.S., 1988-90; adj. instr. art Blue Ridge C.C., Weyers Cave, 1989-90; grad. tchg. asst. James Madison U., Harrisonburg, 1991-94; asst. prof. art Emory & Henry Coll., Emory, 1994—. One-person shows include Danville (Va.) Mus. Fine Arts, 1986, James Madison U.,1 994, Washington and Lee U., Lexington, Va., 1991, Roanoke Coll., Salem, Va., 1992, Berea (Ky.) Coll., 1997, Ralston Fine Arts, Johnson City, Tenn., 1997, William King Regional Arts Ctr. Abingdon, Va., 1998, Spartanburg (S.C.) Mus. Art, 1998; exhibited in group shows at Butler Inst. Am. Art, Youngstown, Oho, Ctrl. Mo. State U., Warrensburg, Appalachian State U., Boone, N.C., Md. Fedn. Art, Annapolis, others; represented in collections at Appalachian State U., Blue Ridge C.C., Weyers Cave, Va., Roanoke County Courthouse, Salem, Va., Radford (Va.) U., Roanoke Times and World News, others. Fellow Va. Mus. Fine Arts, 1997, Marie Walsh Sharpe Art Found., 1989; Liquitex-Binney & Smith Inc. grantee, 1992. Mem. So. Graphics Coun., Coll. Art Assn. Avocations: bicycling, hiking, tennis.

GOON, GILBERT, software consultant; b. N.Y.C., Oct. 7, 1946; s. Fook Mun and Nellie (Eng) G.; m. Susan R. Lishinsky, May 23, 1982; 1 stepchild, Deborah F. Rosenblum; 1 child, Michael Francis. BA, Princeton U., 1967; MA, Columbia U., 1972, MPH, 1975. Assoc. engr. Sperry Systems Mgmt., Great Neck, N.Y., 1972-75; sr. staff analyst Loral Electronic Systems, Yonkers, N.Y., 1975-81; cons. ITT Avionics Div., Nutley, N.J., 1981-86, Norden Sys., Norwalk, Conn., 1986; staff cons. Lockheed Martin Fairchild Sys., Yonkers, 1986—. Named Princeton U. chess champion, 1964-67, N.Y.C amateur chess champion, 1967. Mem. World Tae Kwon Do Assn. (3rd degree black belt), Harley Owners Group (charter mem. White Plains, N.Y. chpt.). Democrat. Lutheran. Avocations: Tae Kwon Do, motorcycling, chess, flute. Office: Lockheed Martin Fairchild Sys Ridge Hill Yonkers NY 10710

GOONREY, CHARLES W., retired lawyer. BA, Northwestern U., 1958, JD, 1961. Bar: Il. 1961, Pa. 1985. Asst. sec. Sunbeam Corp., 1970-83; v.p., gen. legal counsel AMP Inc., Harrisburg, Pa., 1987-98; ret., 1998. Office: AMP Inc PO Box 3608 Mail Stop 17641 470 Friendship Rd Harrisburg PA 17111-1203

GOOS, ROGER DELMON, mycologist; b. Beaman, Iowa, Oct. 29, 1924; s. Gus and Georgiana Bertha (Witt) G.; m. Mary Lee Engel, Sept. 21, 1946; children: Marinda Lee, Suzanne Maurine. B.A., U. Iowa, 1950, Ph.D., 1958. Mycologist United Fruit Co., Norwood, Mass., 1958-62; scientist USPHS, NIH, Bethesda, Md., 1962-64; curator of fungi Am. Type Culture Collection, Rockville, Md., 1964-68; assoc. researcher, vis. assoc. prof. botany U. Hawaii, Honolulu, 1968-70; assoc. prof. botany U. R.I., Kingston, 1970-72, chair dept. of botany, 1971-86, prof. botany, 1972-95, prof. emeritus, 1995—; trustee Am. Type Culture Collection, Rockville, Md., 1977-82; vis. rschr. U. B.C., 1977, U. Hawaii, 1977, U. Exeter, U.K., 1984, Bishop Mus., 1990. Served with U.S. Army, 1944-46, 50-51. Decorated Bronze Star, Purple Heart, Combat Infantry badge; Indo-Am. fellow, U. Madras, India, 1981; Fulbright scholar U. Lisbon, 1993. Mem. AAAS, Mycol. Soc. Am. (sec.-treas. 1980-83, v.p. 1983-84, pres.-elect 1984-85, pres. 1985-86), Bot. Soc. Am., Am. Soc. Microbiology, Am. Phytopath. Soc., Mycol. Soc. Japan, Brit. Mycol. Soc., Mycol. Soc. India. Home: 4 Tanglewood Trl Narragansett RI 02882-1034 Office: U RI Ranger Hall Dept Biol Scis Kingston RI 02881

GOOTEE, TARA RENEE, educational counselor, family therapist; b. Louisville, Jan. 11, 1973; d. Harry Ray Koons and Janice Marie (Lone) Koons Tucker; m. John Phillip Gootee, July 1991. BA in Psychology, Purdue U., West Lafayette, Ind., 1995; MS in Marriage and Family Therapy, Purdue U.-Calumet, Hammond, Ind., 1998. Introductory psychology tchr. Purdue U. Calumet, Hammond, Ind., 1995-97; acad. advisor Purdue U. Calumet, Hammond, 1997-98; ednl. counselor Kentuckiana Coll. Access Ctr., Louisville, 1998—; speaker in field; presenter state and nat. confs. Contbr. chpts. to books. Vol., blood donor ARC, North Vernon, Ind., 1990-93. O. Bundrants and J. Eubanks ednl. grantee, 1991-97; Purdue U.-Calumet grantee, 1997. Repblican. Baptist. Avocations: arts and crafts, movies, reading, home decorating.

GOOTNICK, MARGERY FISCHBEIN, lawyer; b. Rochester, N.Y., Oct. 24, 1927; d. Morris R. and Regina (Kroll) Fischbein; m. Lester T. Gootnick, Mar. 1, 1952; children—Jonathon, David, Amy. B.A., Harvard U., 1949; J.D., Cornell U., 1952. Bar: N.Y. 1952. Assoc. Stone & Hoffenberg, Rochester, N.Y., 1952-55; sole practice, Rochester, 1968—; permanent arbitrator Am. Airlines and Assn. Profl. Flight Attendants, NW Airlines and Teamsters Local 2000, Presbyn. Hosp.-N.Y. State Nurses Assn., U. Rochester and U. Rochester Security Guards Union, numerous others; chmn. Fgn. Service Impasse Disputes Panel, Washington, 1983-97; apptd. fgn. svc. grievance bd. U.S. State Dept., 1997; mem. exec. com. N.Y. State Bar, 1998. Mem. Rep. Jud. Screening Com., Rochester, 1976—. Mem. ABA, Fed. Bar Assn., Nat. Acad. Arbitrators (v.p. 1992-94, chair membership com. 1988-91, exec. com. 1987, bd. govs. 1983-86), N.Y. State Bar Assn. (labor and employment sect. chair elect 1994—, exec. com. 1982—), Soc. Fed. Labor Rels. Profls. (1st v.p. 1993—), Am. Arbitration Assn. (upstate N.Y. labor adv. panel). Home and Office: 46 Knollwood Dr Rochester NY 14618-3513

GOOTT, ALAN F(RANKLIN), lawyer; b. Washington, Aug. 6, 1947. BA, George Washington U., 1969; JD cum laude, Harvard U., 1973. Bar: N.Y., 1974, U.S. Dist. Ct. (so., ea. dists.) N.Y. 1974, U.S. Ct. Appeals (2d cir) 1974. Assoc. Kaye, Scholer, Fierman, Hays & Handler, LLP, N.Y.C., 1973-82, ptnr., 1982—. Office: Kaye Scholer Fierman et al 425 Park Ave New York NY 10022-3506*

GOOTT, DANIEL, government official, consultant; b. N.Y.C., Apr. 23, 1919; s. Hyman and Min (Novak) G.; m. Sylvia Blousman, Aug. 29, 1940; children: Alan F., Eugene M. BSS, CCNY, 1940; postgrad., Columbia U., 1940-41; diploma, Sch. Internat. Studies, Geneva, 1946. Assoc. chief labor rels. br. War Prodn. Bd., 1942-43; spl. asst. internat. labor affairs to under sec. state U.S. Dept. State, Washington, 1956-61; dep. coord. internat. labor affairs Office Sec. State, Washington, 1961-62; 1st sec., labor attache Am. Embassy, Paris, 1962-65; chief spl. profl. affairs Office Dep. Undersec. of State for Adminstrn., Washington, 1965—; labor and UN advisor Bur. European Affairs; mem. U.S. del. 7th spl. and 30th regular sessions UN Gen. Assembly, 1975; pvt. cons. internat. labor and bus. affairs, 1980. With AUS, 1943-46. Decorated Bronze Star. Mem. Am. Econ. Assn., Indsl. Rels. Rsch. Assn., Am. Fgn. Svc. Assn., Am. Acad. Polit. and Social Sci., American. Club. Home: 15101 Interlachen Dr Apt 917 Silver Spring MD 20906-5620

GOOZNER, MERRILL, journalist; b. N.Y.C., 1950. Degree in History, U. Cin., 1975; MS in Journalism, Columbia U., 1982. Journalist Hammond (Ind.) Times, 1982-83, Crain's Chgo. Bus., 1983-87; bus. reporter, Tokyo bur. chief Chgo. Tribune, 1987—, chief Asia corr., 1991-95, nat. corr., 1995-98, chief econs. corr., 1998—. Office: Chgo Tribune Washington Bur 1325 G St NW Ste 200 Washington DC 20005-3104*

GORA, DANIEL MARTIN, lawyer; b. Chgo., Oct. 27, 1969; s. Martin O. and Jacqueline K. (Lancaster) G. BS, No. Ill. U., 1992; JD, Hamline U., 1995; MBA, U. St. Thomas, Mpls., 1996, MSS, 1999. Bar: Minn. 1995, Ill. 1996. Assoc. Spence, Ricke & Thurmer, St. Paul, 1992-96; ptnr. Weatherman, Wolters & Gora, Roseville, Minn., 1995-96; pvt. practice Gora Law Offices, St. Paul, 1997-98; info. counsel Dayton-Hudson Corp., 1998, Carlson Cos. Inc., Mpls., 1998—; mem. faculty Minn. Sch. Bus., Brooklyn Center, 1996—, Met. State U., Mpls., 1997—; counsel N.E. Metro Bus. Network, Maplewood, Minn., 1997. Judge Am. Mock Trial Assn., Minn., 1994-99. Dean's Law scholar Hamline U., 1992, Ill. Gen. Assembly scholar, 1988. Mem. ABA, Minn. Bar Assn., Ill. Bar Assn., Fed. Bar Assn., Chgo. Bar Assn., Acad. Polit. Sci., Golden Key Nat. Honor Soc., Phi Sigma Alpha. Avocations: golf, basketball, reading, theater.

GORA, JOANN M., academic administrator. BA, Vassar Coll.; M in Sociology, D in Sociology, Rutgers U. Various adminstrv. positions univ.-level, 1980—; dean Coll. Arts and Scis., sr. dean Madison campus Fairleigh Dickinson U.; provost, v.p. for acad. affairs, prof. sociology Old Dominion U., Norfolk, Va., 1992—. Author: The New Female Criminal: Empirical Reality or Social Myth?; co-author: Emergency Squad Volunteers: Professionalism in Unpaid Work; contbr. numerous articles to profl. jours. Office: Old Dominion U 5215 Hampton Blvd Norfolk VA 23529-1000

GORALSKI, DONALD JOHN, public relations executive, counselor; b. Buffalo, Apr. 21, 1957; s. John Bernard and Irene (Kazmierczak) G. BA, Canisius Coll., 1980. Cmty. svc. rep. western N.Y. chpt. March of Dimes Birth Defects Found., Buffalo, 1981-82, pub. rels. dir. western N.Y. chpt., 1982-83; pub. rels. dir. no. Jersey chpt. March of Dimes Birth Defects Found., Fairfield, N.J., 1983-84; pub. rels. dir. Ellis Singer, Greve, St. Paul, Minn., 1984-87, Buffalo, 1984-87; sr. pub. rels. officer Multidisciplinary Ctr. for Earthquake Engrng. Rsch., Buffalo, 1987—; guest lectr. U. Buffalo, Buffalo State Coll., Medaille Coll., 1984-88, 95, Canisius Coll., 1990, 95, 97, 99. Mem. spl. events com. Am. Cancer Soc., Western N.Y. chpt., 1985-86; mem. mktg. subcom. St. Mary's Sch. for Deaf, 1987; mentor Pub. Rels. Student Soc. of Am., Buffalo, 1989-91; mem. Allied Comm. Talent for Literacy, Buffalo, 1990-91; mem. meeting and event planners coun. Univ. at Buffalo, 1992; mem. comm. com. World Assn. Vet. Athletes 1995 Games, 1994-95; mem. ad coun. we. N.Y., 1993—; mem. comms. com. Buffalo Alliance for Edn., 1993—; mem. Mayor's Advisory Com. for a City Vision, Buffalo, N.Y., 1994-95; trustee Turner/Carroll H.S., 1996-97; mem. Dr.

Marilyn G.S. Watt scholarship com. Canisius Coll., 1997—, May C. Randazzo Meml. scholarship com., 1997—; liaison State Employees Federated Appeal/United Way, 1998. Mem. Pub. Rels. Soc. Am. (bd. dirs. Buffalo-Niagara chpt. 1987-91, pres.-elect 1992, pres. 1993, past pres. 1994-95, accredited, 1995, assembly del. 1997—, N.E. dist. sec./treas. 1999, Cert. Recognition 1993, Nat. Chpt. Banner award Buffalo/Niagara chpt. 1993), Pub. Rels. Assn. Western N.Y. (treas. 1986-87, v.p. 1987-88, pres. 1989), Western N.Y. Pub. Rels. and Comm. (exec. steering com. 1987-90, 92-94, chmn. 1994). Avocations: golf, football, reading, current events, on-line computer networks/services. Home: 14 Spindrift Ct #8 Williamsville NY 14221 Office: Multidisciplinary Ctr Quake Engring Rsch U Buffalo Red Jacket Quad Buffalo NY 14261

GORAY, GERALD ALLEN, investor, business executive, lawyer; b. Detroit, Aug. 22, 1939; s. James A. and Lucille (Rankin) G.; m. Donna Marie Belian, Apr. 26, 1958; children: Brian M., Gregory D. BBA magna cum laude, U. Detroit, 1963; JD, U. Mich., 1965. Bar: Mich. Atty. Parsons, Tennant et al, Birmingham, Mich., 1966-70, U.S. Dept. of Housing, Detroit, 1970-71, Rodgers & Goray, Southfield, Mich., 1971-75; pres. Goray Devel. Co., Boca Raton, Fla., 1975—; bd. dirs. Monroe (Mich.) Bank & Trust, 1968-70; ptnr. Nat. Self-Storage Equities Fla., Tucson, 1984—; pres. Stonemark Devel. Co., Boca Raton, 1988—. Vice-chmn. Lathrup Village (Mich.) Zoning Bd. Appeals, 1981. Mem. Village Athletic Club (pres. 1975-76). Office: Goray Devel Co 621 NW 53rd St Ste 255 Boca Raton FL 33487-8281

GORBATY, JAN, pianist, music educator; b. Woloczysk, Russia; came to U.S., 1950; s. Julius and Maria (Tafler) G.; m. Judith Weiss, July 6, 1940; 1 child, Susan Zosia. Grad. with highest honors, Conservatory Higher Music Edn., Lwow, Poland, 1938. Prof. musit N.Y. Coll. Music, NYU, Lehman Coll., Kingsborough (N.Y.) C.C. Contbr. articles to profl. publs. Founder, pres. Chopin Found. Coun. of N.Y., 1983—. Recipient Cavalier Cross of Merit, Pres. Lech Walesa, Poland, 1995, Medal of Recognition Min. Art and Culture, Rep. Poland. Mem. Internat. Leshetizky Orgn. (v.p.). Home: 67-64 Fleet St Forest Hills NY 11375

GORBATY, MARTIN LEO, chemist, researcher; b. Bklyn., Nov. 17, 1942; s. Julius and Florence (Birnbach) G.; m. Dianne Morse, June 30, 1968; children: Howard M., Matthew J., Lisa R. BS in Chemistry with honors, City Coll. of N.Y., 1964; PhD in Organic Chemistry, Purdue U., 1969. Rsch. chemist Esso Agrl. Products Lab. Esso Rsch. and Engring. Co., Linden, N.J., 1969-70; sr. rsch. chemist Corp. Rsch. Lab. Exxon Rsch. and Engring. Co., Linden, 1970-73; sr. rsch. chemist Baytown (Tex.) R & D divsn. Corp. Rsch. Lab. Exxon Rsch. and Engring. Co., 1973-75; group head Corp. Rsch. Labs. Corp. Rsch. Lab. Exxon Rsch. and Engring. Co., Linden, 1975-78, lab. dir. corp. rsch., 1978-84; sr. rsch. assoc. Corp. Rsch.-Resource Chemistry Lab. Corp. Rsch. Lab. Exxon Rsch. and Engring. Co., Annandale, N.J., 1984—; mem. internat. editorial bd. Fuel, 1983—; chmn. Gordon Conf. Fuel Sci., 1988. Editor 5 books on synthetic crudes and coal sci.; contbr. some 65 articles to profl. jours. Recipient R.A. Glenn award Bituminous Coal Rsch., Inc., 1990, Disting. Alumnus award Sch. of Sci. Purdue U., 1993. Mem. AAAS, Am. Chem. Soc. (chmn. divsn. petroleum chemistry 1983-84, program com. 1978—, councilor 1988—, divsn. fuel chemistry, adv. bd. ACS books 1984-87, editorial bd. Chemtech 1986—, Henry H. Storch award 1993), N.Y. Acad. Scis., Soc. Sigma Xi, Phi Lambda Upsilon. Achievements include invention of 4 new classes of highly active broad spectrum insecticides, include inexpensive cosolvent system for producing high diene butyl rubber economically, new class of low molecular weight high diene isobutylene based polymers and sulfonated derivatives useful for coatings and thermoplastic elastomers, first catalyst recovery scheme for Exxon's catalytic coal gasification process; invention and development of solution for critical problem during coal liquifaction; development and implementation of strategic research plan that led to several new proprietary approaches for utilization of heavy oils, oil shale and coal; research on building structure-reactivity relationships for coals, oil shales and heavy petroleum; 43 patents, 9 patents pending. Office: Exxon Rsch & Engring Co PO Box 998 Annandale NJ 08801-0998

GORBELL, MICHAEL RANDALL, federal agency and business management executive; b. L.A., Oct. 23, 1953; s. Frederick John and Elsie Klemm; m. Deborah Kay Rasberry, Oct. 15, 1988. BS, U. So. Calif., 1974, MS, 1980; postgrad., Oxford (Eng.) U., 1998. Adminstr. officer Am. Embasssy, San Salvador, El Salvador, Cairo, Beirut, Lebanon, 1982-88; chmn. AEEA Am. Embasssy, London, 1991-93; dir. fin. and adminstrn. Ogden Allied Facility Mgmt., Inc., N.Y.C., 1988-89; dir. travel and relocation svcs. CIA, Washington, 1989-91, chief adminstrv. officer external, 1994-99; bus. mgmt. cons., 1988—. *Michael Gorbel was a professional intelligence officer for over 22 years, appointed to U.S. Senior Intelligence Service in 1997. He is recognized as one of the intelligence community's foremost experts in commercial business operations, a proven corporate leader with global business, government, and military exposure. Since 1999, he has been a corporate affairs/business operations executive and consultant well known for optimizing results with limited resources, successfully applying his his skills and experience in such diverse fields as financial and human resource management, contract and material management, security and asset protection, and information systems applications.* Capt. USMC, 1974-82. Mem. Nat. Eagle Scout Assn., Spl. Forces Club. Avocations: travel, aviation, auto racing. E-mail: gorbell@msn.com.

GORBY, WILLIAM GUY, anesthesiologist; b. Clarksburg, W.Va., Apr. 6, 1950; s. William Darrell and Sara Lucille (Harner) G.; m. Sharyn Louise Reitz; children: William Michael, Chad Robert, Brenna Lynn. BS cum laude, W.Va. U., 1972, MS, 1974; DO magna cum laude, W.Va. Sch. Osteo. Medicine, 1978; JD, Pa. State Law Sch., Carlisle, 1995—. Diplomate Osteo. Bd. of Anesthesiology. Intern Met. Gen. Hosp., Pinellas Park, Fla., 1978-79; resident in anesthesia Cuyahoga Falls (Ohio) Gen. Hosp., 1979-81; fellow pain mgmt. Cleve. Clinic Found., 1981-82; dir. pain mgmt. Geisinger Med. Ctr., Danville, Pa., 1982-85; dir. anesthesia Washington County Hosp., Hagerstown, Md., 1985-92; assoc. prof. anesthesia W.Va. Sch. Osteo. Medicine, Lewisburg, 1992-93; part-time emergency rm. anesthesiologist Wetzel County Hosp., New Martinsville, W.Va., 1993—, War Meml. Hosp., Berkley Spring, W.Va., 1993-98; emergency medicine Stonewall Jackson Hosp., Weston, W.Va.; anesthesiologist Alleghany U. Hahneman Hosp., 1998—; assoc. prof. pulmonary medicine W.Va. Sch. Osteo. Medicine, 1982-90. Staff writer On the Trail mag.; contbr. articles to profl. jours. Mem. ABA (student mem.), Am. Coll. Osteo. Anesthesiology, Am. Osteo. Assn., Aircraft Owners and Pilots Assn. Avocations: flying (comml. lic.), camping, canoeing, art. Home: 49 Brian Dr Carlisle PA 17013-4326

GORCHEFF, NICK A., controller; b. Salem, Ohio, Sept. 20, 1958; s. Albert N. and Jean A. (Felger) G. BS, Youngstown State U., 1981. Acct., computer programmer RE Gibson Contractor Inc., Lisbon, Ohio, 1981-85; v.p., contr. The Traichal Construction Co., Niles, Ohio, 1985-98; officer Plant Indsl. Sales Co., 1989-92; v.p. Fowler Ctr. A & C Inc., 1989-91; pres. Austintown Mgmt. Corp., 1991—; v.p., treas. Royal Palms Mgmt. Inc., 1995-98, pres. 1998—; v.p. Cloud 9 Limousine Inc., 1996-98. Office: Royal Palms Mgmt Inc 447 E Beacon Dr Austintown OH 44515-4064

GORCHOV, RON, artist; b. Chgo., Apr. 5, 1930; s. Herman and Grace (Bloomfield) G.; children: Michael, Jolie. Prof. emeritus Hunter Coll. CUNY, N.Y.C., 1998—. Address: 532 La Guardia Pl # 673 New York NY 10012

GORDAN, GILBERT SAUL, physician, educator; b. San Francisco, July 8, 1916; s. Gilbert Saul and Sadie (Joseph) G.; m. Cynthia Vaughan, Feb. 2, 1978. A.B., U. Calif., 1937, M.D., 1941, Ph.D., 1947. Intern U. Calif. Hosp., San Francisco, 1940-41; resident U. Calif. Hosp., 1941-42; mem. faculty U. Calif., San Francisco, 1946-85; prof. medicine U. Calif., 1962-85, prof. emeritus, 1985—; prof. medicine U. Calif., Davis, 1985-88; Lady Davis vis. prof. Hebrew U., Jerusalem, 1978; assoc. chief of staff for edn. VA Med. Ctr., Martinez, Calif., 1985-88; cons. in field. Author: Endocrinology in Clinical Practice, 1953, The Parathyroids, 1971, Clinical Management of the Osteoporoses, 1976; editor: Yearbook of Endocrinology, 1951-63; contbr. numerous articles to profl. jours. Served with M.C. AUS, 1942-45. Decorated Bronze Star; recipient Disting. Achievement award Nat. Osteoporosis Found., 1992; Commonwealth fellow, 1947-48, 62-63; Guggenheim fellow, 1967-68. Fellow ACP, AAAS; mem. Assn. Am. Physicians, Am. Soc. Clin. Investigation, Endocrine Soc., Royal Soc. Medicine (hon.). Democrat. Jewish. Co-discoverer assay for anabolic steroids and other growth stimulants; pioneer in clin. application of metabolic properties of sex hormones and hormone replacement therapy.

GORDEN, PHILLIP, federal agency administrator. Dir. Nat. Inst. Diabetes, Digestive and Kidney Diseases, HHS, Bethesda, Md. Office: Nat Inst Diabetes Digestive & Kidney Diseases Bldg 31 Rm 9A52 31 Center Dr MSC 2560 Bethesda MD 20892-0001*

GORDENKER, LEON, political sciences educator; b. Detroit, Oct. 7, 1923; s. Samuel and Anna (Posalsky) G.; m. Belia Emilie Strootman, Aug. 16, 1956 (dec. Apr. 1984); children: Robert Jan Mario, Hendrik Willem Paul, Emilie Elise Saskia. AB, U. Mich., 1943; student, Inst. d'Etudes Politiques, Paris, 1951-52; MA, Columbia U., 1954, PhD, 1958; postgrad., Acad. Internat. Law, Hague, The Netherlands, 1958. Journalist AP, 1943, Detroit Free Press, 1944-45; info. officer Nat. War Labor Bd., 1945; pub. info. officer UN, 1945-53; instr. Dartmouth U., 1956-58; mem. faculty Princeton U., 1958—, prof. politics, 1966-86, faculty assoc. Ctr. Internat. Studies, 1963—, prof. emeritus, 1986—, sr. rsch. polit. scientist, 1990-94; prof. Institut Universitaire de Hautes Internationales, Geneva, 1986-89, vis. prof., 1979-80; dir. Centre de Recherches sur les Institutions Internationales, Geneva, 1986-89; vis. prof. Columbia U., 1961, 67, Makerere U., Uganda, 1969-70, U. Pa., 1971, 74, U. Witwatersrand, South Africa, 1976, Leiden U., 1984-85, 93, Erasmus U., 1985, CUNY, 1989, 90, 92, 95, Inst. Social Studies, The Hague, 1993-97; rsch. fellow Ralph Bunche Inst. on UN, CUNY, 1989—. Author: The United Nations and the Peaceful Unification of Korea, 1959, The UN Secretary-General and the Maintenance of Peace, 1967, The United Nations in the International System, 1971, International Aid and National Decisions, 1976, The International Executive, 1978, (with W.P. Davison) Resolving Nationality Conflicts, 1980, (with P.R. Baehr) The United Nations: Reality and Ideal, 1984, Refugees in International Politics, 1987, (with T.G. Weiss) Soldiers, Peacekeepers and Disasters, 1991, (with P.R. Baehr) The United Nations in the 1990s, 1992, 94, De Verenigde Naties: Werkelijkheid en Ideaal, 1992, 94, 96, (with Benjamin Rivlin) The Challenging Role of the UN Secretary-General, 1993, (with others) International Cooperation in Response to AIDS, 1995, (with T.G. Weiss) NGOs, the UN and Global Governance, 1996. Fellow The Netherlands Inst. Advanced Study, 1972-73, 96-97. Mem. Acad. Coun. on UN, Princeton Club of N.Y. Office: Princeton U Ctr Internat Studies Princeton NJ 08544

GORDER, STEVEN F., business executive; b. Bottineau, N.D., Feb. 4, 1951; s. Walter F. and Wilma E. (Myles) G.; m. Randy Sue Greenwood, Aug. 20, 1972; children: S. Kelsey, Corey J. AS/BA, N.D. State U.; Bottineau, 1971; BA, Minot (N.D.) State U., 1973. Br. mgr., loan officer Farm Credit Svcs., Morris, Minn., 1973-87; realtor Coldwell Banker First Realty, Fargo, N.D., 1987-89; supt., treas. Internat. Peace Garden, Dunseith, N.D., 1989-96; office mgr. WOLD Engring. PE, Bottineau, 1996—. Office: 23 Lake Metigoshe Park Bottineau ND 58318-8041

GORDEVITCH, IGOR, publishing company executive; b. Kaunas, Lithuania, Dec. 17, 1924; s. Alexander Michael and Militsa (de Nikitin) G.; came to U.S., 1950, naturalized, 1955; ed. Institut Sillig, Vevey, Switzerland, 1937-39, Royal U., Rome, 1939-40; m. Margaret Boomer; children—Alexandra, Tatiana; m. 2d, Carin Roechling, Oct. 7, 1960. Sr. adminstrv. asst. Allied Mil. Govt., Europe, 1944-45; corr. N.Y. Herald Tribune, 1945-50; Washington bur. chief Vision Inc., N.Y.C., 1950-56, editor, 1957-64, chief exec. officer, Latin Am. ops., Sao Paulo, Brazil, 1964-67, pub., exec. v.p., dir. Vision Group of Cos., N.Y.C., 1967-76, pres., 1973-77, mng. dir., chmn. Vision/Europe, Paris, 1970-77; pres. Publi-Communications Inc., N.Y.C., 1977-83; exec. v.p., dir. Gruner & Jahr USA, Inc., N.Y.C., 1979-83; also pub. dir. GEO mag. 1979-81; pres. U.S. Investment Pub., 1983-89; pres. ECO Inc, 1990-96; dir. PHP Inst. Am., Inc.; edit. dir., pub. Impact 21 mag., 1996; pub. cons.; lectr. in field. Mem. Pan Am. Soc. U.S., Council of Ams., Akin Hall Assn. Republican. Eastern Orthodox. Club: Knickerbocker (N.Y.C.), Coral Beach and Tennis (Bermuda), Nat. Press (Washington). Home: 144 Quaker Hill Rd Pawling NY 12564-1814 Office: 216 E 49th St New York NY 10017-1546

GORDIMER, NADINE, author; b. Republic of South Africa, Nov. 20, 1923; d.Isidore and Nan (Myers) Gordimer; m. Reinhold Cassirer, Jan. 29, 1954; children: Oriane, Hugo. Ed., Convent Sch., Springs, Republic of South Africa. Author: (story collections) Face to Face, 1949, The Soft Voice of the Serpent, 1952, Six Feet of the Country, 1956, Friday's Footprint, 1960 (W.H. Smith and Son Literary award 1961), Not for Publication, 1965, Livingstone's Companions, 1971, Selected Stories, 1975, Some Monday for Sure, 1976, A Soldier's Embrace, 1980, Something Out There, 1984, Crimes of Conscience, 1991, Jump, 1991, Why Haven't You Written?, 1992; (polit. and lit. essays) The Essential Gesture, 1988, Three in a Bed, 1991, Living in Hope and History: Notes From Our Century, 1999; (literary criticism) The Black Interpreters, 1973, Writing & Being: Charles Eliot Norton Lectures, 1995; (essays) Living in Hope and History: Notes from Our Century, 1999; (novels) The Lying Days, 1953, A World of Strangers, 1958, Occasion for Loving, 1963, The Late Bourgeois World, 1966, A Guest of Honour, 1970 (James Tait Black Meml. prize 1973), The Conservationist, 1974 (Booker prize for fiction Eng. 1974), Burger's Daughter, 1979, July's People, 1981, A Sport of Nature, 1987, My Son's Story, 1991, None to Accompany Me, 1994, The House Gun, 1998; (other) On the Mines, 1973, Lifetimes Under Apartheid, 1986; editor: (with Lionel Abrahams) Southern African Writing Today, 1967. Decorated comdr. de l'Ordre des Arts et des Lettres (France), 1986; recipient Thomas Pringle award English Acad. South Africa, 1969, CNA award, 1974, 79, 81, 91, Grand Aigle d'Or, 1975, Disting. Svc. in Lit. Commonwealth award, 1981, MLA award, 1982, Nelly Sachs prize (Germany), 1985, Malaparte award (Italy), 1986, Bennett award, 1986, Benson medal, 1990, Nobel Prize for Literature, 1991; Neil Gunn fellow Scottish Arts Coun., 1981. Fellow Royal Soc. Lit.; mem. AAAS, Com. European Authors, Am. Acad. (hon.), Inst. Arts and Letters (hon.), PEN (v.p).

GORDIN, DEAN LACKEY, retired agricultural products executive; b. Jamestown, Ohio, Dec. 28, 1935; s. Arnett Jordan and Elizabeth Louise (Lackey) G.; m. Marilyn Katherine Welch, Sept. 2, 1961 (div. 1984); children: Jana Lynn, Deana Lynn; m. Martha Ann Duvall, Jan. 12, 1986. BS, Ohio State U., 1957, MS, 1959. Faculty staff agrl. dept. Wilmington (Ohio) Coll., 1964-66; regional mgr. Buckeye Farm Records Svc., Columbus, Ohio, 1968; v.p., gen. mgr. Gordin Homestead Farms, Inc., Cedarville, Ohio, 1963-71, pres., chief exec. officer, 1971-90, ret., 1990; mem. support coun. Ohio Agrl. R&D Ctr., 1980—, mem. exec. com., 1984-88; midwest regional dir. Dole for Pres. Com., 1987-88, Dole for Pres. Expl. Com., 1995; bd. elections Ohio Dole for Pres. Com., 1995—; co-chmn. Agr. for Voinovich-DeWine, 1990. Pres. Ohio Rep. Agrl. Coun., Columbus, 1974-77; bd. dirs., exec. chmn. Greene County Rep. Party, Xenia, Ohio, 1987-92; regional v.p. Ohio Rep. County Chmn.'s Assn., 1987-92; trustee Rep. Heritage Found., Inc., Washington, 1988; S.W. coord., Bush/Quayle Com. Ohio, 1988, 92; mem. Greene County Bd. Elections; life mem. Rep. Presdl. Task Force, 1984—; mem. Nat. Rep. Senate Inner Circle, 1989—. Recipient Ohio Jaycees award, 1970, citation Ohio Commodore, 1987; named Outstanding Young Farmer, Greene County, 1970; honoree Golden Heart Club, Order of the Purple Heart Assn., 1995. Mem. Am. Soc. Farm Mgrs. and Rural Appraisers, Ohio Soc. Farm Mgrs. and Rural Appraisers, Ohio Corn Growers Assn. (pres., CEO 1986-88), Nat. Corn Growers Assn. (nat. dir.), Nat. Assn. Rev. Appraisers and Mortgage Underwriters (cert.), Cin. Agri-Bus. Coun., Columbus Farmers Club, U.S. Senatorial Club, Capitol Hill Club (Washington), Wilmington Coll. Aggie Club (hon.), Lions Internat. Club (chmn. community svc. award), U.S. Capitol Hist. Soc. (trust mem.), Nixon Presdl. Libr. Cabinet Coun., Gamma Sigma Delta. Republican. Presbyterian. Avocations: photography, travel, history, music, art. Home: 5264 Lackey Rd Cedarville OH 45314-9552*

GORDIN, MISHA, photographer; b. Riga, Latvia, Mar. 12, 1946; came to U.S., 1974; s. Boris and Hasia (Geskin) G.; m. Rosa Dritz, 1969 (dec. June 1985); 1 child, Margarita; m. Vitamin Gordin, Apr. 7, 1993; children: Boris, Uma. BA in Engring., Aviation Coll., Riga, 1969. One person shows include Foto Gallery, N.Y., 1976, Gilbert Gallery, Chgo., 1980, 81, Blixt Gallery, Ann Arbor, Mich., 1980, Images Gallery, Cin., 1982, Jesse Besser Mus., Alpena, Mich., 1982, Xochipilli Gallery, Birmingham, Mich., 1984, Nagase Photo Salon, Tokyo, 1984, New Gallery, Bemis Project, Omaha, 1985, 90, Habatat Galleries, Bay Harbor Islands, Fla., 1986, Mark Masuoka Gallery, Las Vegas, 1990, 91, Klein Art Works, Chgo., 1991, Bentley/Tomlinson Gallery, Scottsdale, Ariz., 1992, Dennas Mus. Ctr., Northwestern Mich. U., Traverse City, Mich., 1993, N.D. Mus. Art, Grand Forks, 1994; exhibited in group shows Internat. Foto Salon, Belgium, 1976, Weston Gallery, Carmel, Calif., 1980, Daniel Wolf Gallery, N.Y., 1981, Gallery Des Beaux-Arts, Bordeaux, France, 1982, Detroit Inst. Arts, 1983, Musee St. Denis, Reims, France, 1984, Klein Art Works, Chgo., 1991, 92, 93; represented in permanent collections Art Inst. Chgo., Dennas Mus. Ctr., Northwestern Mich. U., Traverse City, Everson Mus. Art, Syracuse, N.Y., Internat. Mus. Photography, George Eastman House, Rochester, N.Y., Krannert Art Mus., U. Ill., Champaign-Urbana, Nat. Mus. Modern Art, Kyoto, Japan, Toledo Mus. Art; works included in publs. Creative Camera, Photoworks, American Photographer, New Photography, Saturday Rev., Afterimage. Recipient 2d prize 27th Salon of Art Photography, Strasbourg, France, 1972, Gold medal Mich. Photography Exhbn., Detroit, 1977, P.S.A. Gold medal 22d Internat. Salon of Photography, Bordeaux, 1979, F.I.A.P. medal 24th Internat. Salon Photography, Bordeaux, 1979, Niepce medal Salon Internat. D'Art Photographique, Reims, 1983, F.I.A.P. Gold medal Salon Internat. D'Art Photographique, Musee St. Denis, Reims, 1984, Gold medal and Niepce medal Salon Internat. D'Art Photographique, Demain, France, 1985, Mich. Arts award Arts. Found. Maine, 1987; creative artist grantee Mich. Coun. for Arts, 1985, 88, visual artist fellowship grantee Nat. Endowment for Arts, 1986. Home: 15257 Fruit Farm Rd Saint Joseph MN 56374-9627

GORDINIER, TERRI KLEIN, speech-language pathologist; b. Inglewood, Calif., Aug. 20, 1959; d. Jerome Lee Klein and Justina Dean (Woodard) Popp; m. Terry Lee Gordinier, July 23, 1988; children: Cory James, Collin William. MA, Ea. Mich. U., 1989; BS in Edn. cum laude, Columbus (Ga.) Coll., 1985. Cert. speech-lang. tchr., Mich. Instr. in sign lang. Main Post Office, Columbus, 1983-84, Columbus Coll., 1984-85; speech pathology intern Buena Vista (Ga.) Elem. Sch., 1985; tchr. speech-lang. impaired Burger devel. learning program Wayne County Progrma for Autistically Impaired, Garden City, Mich., 1986-90; speech lang. pathologist Mich. Sch. for the Deaf, Flint, 1991-94; instr. Ann Arbor Cmty. Edn. and Recreation, 1995—; speech lang. pathologist Ann Arbor Pub. Schs., 1997—; asst. instr. swimming Listening Eyes Presch. for Deaf, Columbus, 1983-84; program coord., counselor outdoor freedon camporee Ala. Soc. for Crippled Children and Adults, 1983-85; speech clinician Columbus Coll., 1982-85; asst. interpreter for deaf Packard Road Bapt. Ch., Ann Arbor, 1985-86; teaching asst. Key Elem. Sch., Columbus, 1982-84; lectr. in field. Fellow Am. Speech-Lang.-Hearing Assn., Libr. of Spl. Edn. Pathology, Alliance for Speech Communication; mem. Communication Disorders Assn. (sec., treas. 1984-85), Communications Disorders Assn. Fall Conf. (exec. coun. rep. 1984-85), Ea. Mich. U.'s Fall Conf. (student rep. 1986-87), Mich. Speech Lang. Hearing Assn. Baptist. Avocations: swimming, sailing, white water canoeing, camping. Home: 5196 Sutton Rd Ann Arbor MI 48105-9538

GORDIS, DAVID MOSES, academic administrator, rabbi; b. N.Y.C., June 4, 1940; s. Robert and Fannie (Jacobson) G.; m. Felice Witztum, Sept. 3, 1962; children: Lisa, Elana. BA, Columbia U., 1960, MA, 1966; MHL, Jewish Theol. Sem., 1962, PhD, 1980. Ordained rabbi, 1964. Dean of students Tchrs. Inst., Jewish Theol. Sem., N.Y.C., 1966-72; exec. dir. Found. for Conservative Judaism, 1981-84; assoc. prof., v.p. U. of Judaism, L.A., 1972-84; v.p. Jewish Theol. Sem., N.Y.C., 1981-84; exec. v.p. Am. Jewish Com., N.Y.C., 1984-87; v.p. U. Judaism, L.A., 1988-92, dir. Wilstein Inst. of Jewish Policy Studies, 1988—, adj. assoc. prof. Talmud, 1988-92, dir. inst. rsch.; pres. Hebrew Coll., 1993—. Mem. edit. bd. Tikkun, 1988—. Bd. dirs. Interns for Peace, N.Y.; pres., prof. rabbinics Hebrew Coll., 1993—; exec. com. Am. Found. for Polish-Jewish Studies, 1988—; trustee Am. Jewish Hist. Soc., 1993—, vice-chair Archives for Hist. Documentation, 1995—; chair United Synagogue Coun. on Jewish Edn., 1973-82. Mem. Rabbinical Assembly Am., Assn. Colls. of Jewish Studies. Avocation: cello.

GORDIS, ENOCH, science administrator, internist; b. N.Y.C., Feb. 21, 1931; s. Robert and Fannie (Jacobson) G. BA, Columbia U., 1950, MD, 1954. Fellow Dazian Found., N.Y.C., 1958-59; clin. fellow Mt. Sinai Hosp., N.Y.C., 1959, chief resident dept. medicine, 1960; assoc. prof. dept. medicine Mt. Sinai Sch. Medicine, N.Y.C., 1971-79, prof. medicine, 1979—; guest investigator Rockefeller U., N.Y.C., 1961-62, rsch. assoc., 1962-63, assoc. prof., 1965-71, adj. prof., 1971—; dir., mem. treatment prevention study sect. Nat. Inst. on Alcohol Abuse and Alcoholism, Rockville, Md., 1986—; extensive pub. appearances in U.S. and abroad on topics related to alcoholism and addiction. Author: (with others) Controversies in Clinical Care, 1981, Current Therapy in Gastroenterology and Liver Disease, 1986; manuscript reviewer Annals Int. Medicine, Butterworth Inc., Clin. Textbook of Addictive Disorders, European Jour. Clin. Investigation, Jour. Clin. Investigation, Jour. Lipid Rsch., Jour. Studies in Alcohol, Med. Letter, others; assoc. editor Alcoholism: Clin. and Exptl. Rsch., 1979—; mem. editorial bd. U. Medicine and Dentistry of N.J., N.J.Med. Sch.; contbr. articles, abstracts to profl. jours. Corr. Com. on Human Rights, 1988-89. Capt. M.C., U.S. Army, 1955-57. Fellow ACP; mem. Adv. Group on Fellowships in Alcohol and Drug Abuse, Am. Coll. Neuropsychopharmacology, Am. Fedn. for Clin. Rsch., Am. Gastroent. Assn., Am. Soc. Addiction Medicine, Am. Physiol. Soc., Inst. of Medicine of NAS (corr. com. human rights 1988-89), Rsch. Soc. on Alcoholism, Sigma Xi, Phi Beta Kappa. Office: Dept HHS NIH Nat Inst Alcohol Abuse Alcoholism 6000 Executive Blvd Bethesda MD 20892-7003

GORDIS, LEON, physician; b. N.Y.C., July 19, 1934; s. Robert and Fannie (Jacobson) G.; m. Hadassah Cohen, June 14, 1955; children: Daniel, Elihu, Jonathan. B.A., Columbia, 1954; B.H.L., Jewish Theol. Sem., 1954; M.D., SUNY, 1958; M.P.H., Johns Hopkins U., 1966, Dr.P.H., 1968. Intern, then resident in pediatrics Jewish Hosp., Bklyn., 1958-61; fellow in pediatrics Sch. Medicine Johns Hopkins U., 1962-66, instr. Sch. Medicine, 1966-68, assoc. prof. epidemiology, Sch. Hygiene and Pub. Health, 1971-73; asst. med. dir. ambulatory care Sinai Hosp., Balt., 1966-68; chief dept. community medicine Sinai Hosp., 1968-69; prof. epidemiology Johns Hopkins, 1973—, chmn. dept. epidemiology, 1975-93; prof. pediatrics, 1992—; assoc. dean admissions & Acad. affairs Johns Hopkins Sch. Medicine, 1993-99; vis. prof. med. ecology Hebrew U., Jerusalem, 1969-71. Served with USPHS, 1961-65. Fellow Am. Acad. Pediatrics, AAAS; mem. Inst. Medicine, Nat. Acad. Sci., Soc. Epidemiologic Research (pres. 1979-80), Am. Epidemiol. Soc. (pres. 1983-84), Am. Pediatric Soc., Soc. Pediatric Research, Am. Public Health Assn., Am. Heart Assn., Assn. Tchrs. Preventive Medicine. Home: 105 Swanhill Ct Baltimore MD 21208-1608 Office: 615 N Wolfe St Baltimore MD 21205-2103

GORDLEY, JAMES RUSSELL, law educator; b. 1946. BA, U. Chgo., 1967, MBA, 1968; JD, Harvard U., 1970. Fellow U. Florence Inst. Law, Italy, 1970-71; assoc. Foley, Hoag & Eliot, Boston, 1971-72; fellow comparative law Harvard U., Cambridge, Mass., 1973-78; acting prof. U. Calif., Berkeley, 1978-81, prof., 1981—, Shannon Cecil Turner prof. jurisprudence, 1995—. Fellow Deutsche Forschungsgemeinschaft, 1983, sr. NATO fellow, 1991, Guggenheim fellow, 1995-96, Fulbright fellow, 1996. Office: U Calif Sch Law Boalt Hall Berkeley CA 94720*

GORDLY, AVEL LOUISE, senator, community activist; b. Portland, Oreg., Feb. 13, 1947; d. Fay Lee and Beatrice Bernice (Coleman) G.; 1 child, Tyrone Wayne Waters. BS in Adminstrn. of Justice, Portland State U., 1974; Grad. John F. Kennedy Sch. Govt., Harvard U., 1995; grad., U. Oreg. Pacific Program, 1998. Phone co. clk. Pacific West Bell, Portland, 1966-70, mgmt. trainee, 1969-70; work release counselor Oreg. Corrections Divsn., Portland, 1974-78, parole and probation officer, 1974-78; dir. youth svcs. Urban League of Portland, 1979-83; dir. So. Africa program Am. Friends Svc. Com., Portland, 1983-89, assoc. exec. sec., dir. Pacific N.W. region, 1987-90; freelance writer Portland Observer, Portland, 1988-90; program dir. Portland House of Umoja, 1991; mem. Oreg. Ho. of Reps., Portland, 1991-96, mem. joint ways and means com., adv. mem. appropriations com., rules and reorgn. com., low income housing com., energy policy rev. com., others; mem. Senate, 1997—, mem. crime and corrections com., trades econ. devel. com., 1997, mem. joint ways and means com. on pub. safety, 1997, mem. joint ways and means com. on edn., 1999; mem. joint ways and means com.

on edn., mem. gov. drug and violent crime policy bd., mem. Oreg. liquor control commn. task force, mem. sexual harrassement task force, mem. Hanford waste bd., mem. Gov.'s Commn. for Women, Gov.'s Drug and Violent Crime Policy Bd.; originator, producer, host Black Women's Forum, 1983-88; co-producer, rotating host N.E. Spectrum, 1983-88. Mem. corrections adv. com. Multnomah Cmty.; mem. adv. com. Oregonians Against Gun Violence; mem. Black Leadership Conf.; treas., bd. dirs. Black United Fund; co-founder, facilitator Unity Breakfast Com.; co-founder Sisterhood Luncheon; past project adv. bd. dirs. Nat. Orgn. Victims Assistance; past citizen chmn. Portland Police Bur.; past mem. coordinating com. Portland Future Focus Policy Com.; past coord. Cmty. Rescue Plan; past vice chmn. internat. affairs Black United Front; past sec. Urban League Portland, past vice chmn. and exec. com.; past adv. com. Black Ednl. Ctr.; past vice chmn. Desegregation Monitoring; also past adv. com., past chmn. curriculum com., founder African Am. Leg. Issues Roundtable; founder Black Women Gathering; other past orgn. coms.; elected state senate African Am. Women Orgn., 1996. Recipient Outstanding Cmty. Svc. award NAACP, 1986, Outstanding Women in Govt. award YWCA, 1991, Girl Scout-Cmty. Svc. award, 1991, N.W. Conf. of Black Studies-Outstanding Progressive Leadership in the African-Am. Cmty. award, 1986, Cmty. Svc. award Delta Sigma Theta, 1981, Joint Action in Cmty. Svc.-Vol. and Cmty. Svc. award, 1981, Quality of Life Photography award Pacific Power & Light Co., 1986, Am. Leadership Forum Sr. fellow, 1988, Equal Opportunity award, Urban League, 1996, Outstanding Alumni, 1996, PSU, Causa '98 En Defensa de la Comunidad award, 1997, Matrix award Assn. for Women in Comm., 1999, Pres.'s award Portland Oreg. Visitors Assn., 1999. Mem. NAACP. Avocations: reading group, mentoring, photography, walking.

GORDON, A. POPE, federal judge; b. 1922. Judge Ala. Bankruptcy Ct., Montgomery, 1985—. Fax: 334-206-6374. Office: One Ct Sq Montgomery AL 36102-1248

GORDON, ALAN LEE, psychiatrist; b. N.Y.C., Nov. 26, 1936; s. Abe and Fan Gordon; m. Lois Goldfein; 1 child, Robert Michael. AB, Columbia Coll., 1957; MD, U. Wis., 1963. Resident Albert Einstein Coll. Medicine, N.Y.C., 1964-66, 68-69; dir. of aftercare Riverdale Mental Health Clinic, N.Y.C., 1969-78; clin. instr. Mt. Sinai Sch. of Medicine, N.Y.C., 1982-90; psychiatrist divsn. of post-institutional svcs. Human Resources Adminstrn.-City of N.Y., 1986—; psychiatrist Bowery Residence Com., CSS Program, N.Y.C., 1990—; lectr. in field; TV, radio interviewer; spkr. in field. Author: Columbia Chronicles of America Life, 1960-92, 1995, American Chronicle: Seven Decades of American Life 1920-89, 1990, American Chronicle: Six Decades in American Life, 1920-79, 1987, American Chronicle: Year by Year through the Twentieth Century, 1999; contbr. poetry to various jours. and sci. jours. Capt. U.S. Army, 1966-68. Mem. Alpha Omega Alpha. Democrat. Jewish. Avocations: history, literature, sports. Office: 300 Central Park W New York NY 10024-1513

GORDON, ALICE JEANNETTE IRWIN, secondary and elementary education educator; b. Detroit, Mar. 18, 1934; d. Manley Elwood and Jeannette (Coffron) Irwin; m. Edgar George Gordon, Feb. 4, 1967; children: David Alexander, John Scott. BA in Elem. Edn., Mich. State U., 1956; MA in Child Devel., U. Mich., 1959, EdS in Ednl. Psychology, 1967, MA in Reading, 1990. Cert. K-12 tchr., Mich.; cert. K-12 reading specialist. Elem. tchr. Detroit Pub. Schs., 1956-67, reading tchr., 1967-68; secondary tchr. English and reading Parchment Pub. Schs., 1989-94; secondary reading specialist Kalamazoo Pub. Schs., 1994-96; jr. high reading specialist South Middle Sch., Kalamazoo, 1996-99; reading therapist Western Mich. U., Kalamazoo, 1992-97; participant Ednl. Leadership Acad., 1998-99. Mem. alumni bd. Mich. State U. Coll. Edn., 1992-96; chmn. Century Ball, Nazareth Coll., Kalamazoo, 1987; co-chmn. Evening of Nte, Kalamazoo Symphony, 1989; precinct del. Kalamazoo Rep. Com., 1989, 92, 96, 99; mem. Mich. Adult Edn. Practitioner Inquiry Project, 1994, 95, 96. Fellow U. Mich., 1963, 65-66; coop. learning grantee Mich. Dept. Edn., 1990, Excellence in Edn. grantee, 1997, Kalamazoo Pub. Edn. Found. grantee, 1997, 98, Arts Coun. Greater Kalamazoo mini-grantee, 1997, Kalamazoo Pub. Edn. Found., 1998; Third Coast Writing fellow, 1998. Mem. Internat. Reading Assn., Mich. Reading Assn., Homer Carter Reading Assn., P.E.O., Jr. League, Lawyers Wives Auxillery, Kappa Delta Pi, Phi Delta Kappa (pres. 1998—), Alpha Omega Pi. Presbyterian. Avocations: miniatures, antiques, reading, genealogy, public education. Home: 4339 Lakeside Dr Kalamazoo MI 49008-2802 Office: Kalamazoo Pub Schs 1220 Howard St Kalamazoo MI 49008-3610

GORDON, ALVIN JOSEPH, cardiologist; b. N.Y.C., Jan. 26, 1915; s. Isaac and Jennie (Perla) G.; m. Elaine Isaacson, Dec. 1, 1939; children: Melissa, Todd. AB, Columbia U., 1934, MD, 1938. Diplomate Am. Bd. Internal Medicine, Am. Bd. Cardiovascular Diseases. Intern Mt. Sinai Hosp., N.Y.C., 1938-41, asst. in morbid anatomy, 1941-42, resident in ward medicine, 1942-43, head cardiac catheterization, 1947-61, attending cardiologist, 1961—, clin. prof. medicine emeritus; chief cardiology Beth Israel North, N.Y.C., 1990-95. Author: (with Kirschner and Moscovitz) Hemodynamics of Aortic and Mitral Valve Disease, 1961; contbr. articles to profl. publs. Lt. USN, 1943-46, PTO. Recipient Jacobi Medallion, Mt. Sinai Alumni, 1973, H. Mason Hicks award for disting. svc. to Doctors Hosp., 1989. Fellow ACP, Am. Coll. Cardiology, Am. Heart Assn. Avocations: photography, computers. Office: 70 E 77th St New York NY 10021-1811

GORDON, ANN MARIE, pharmacist; b. Manitowoc, Wis., May 18, 1956; d. Raymond and Mary Jean (Wertheimer) Wiersig; m. Larry Charles Gordon, May 1, 1982; two children. BS, Purdue U., 1979. Pharmacist Marsh Drugs, Anderson, Ind., 1979-81, Reliable Drugs, Whiteland, Ind., 1981-86; pharmacy mgr. Drug Emporium, Greenwood, Ind., 1986-95; asst. pharmacy mgr. Walmart Pharmacy, Franklin, Ind., 1995-97; mng. pharmacist Henderson Drugs, LLC, Franklin, 1997—, owner, 1999&.

GORDON, ANNE KATHLEEN, editor; m. Phillip L. Berman. BA, U. Denver, 1979; postgrad., Columbia Grad. Sch. Journalism, 1983. Fin. writer Rocky Mountain Bus. Jour., Denver, 1981; fin. writer Sun-Tattler, Hollywood, Fla., 1982-83, fin. editor, 1983; asst. bus. editor Ft. Lauderdale (Fla.) News, 1983-85; bus. editor The Denver Post, 1985-88, asst. mng. editor, 1988; news cons. Sta. KCNC-TV, Denver, 1988-89, assignment mgr., 1989-90; editor Jackson Hole News, 1990-92; aeditor Sunday Mag. The Plain Dealer, Cleve., 1993-99; arts and entertainment editor The Phila. Inquirer, 1999—. Author: A Book of Saints, 1994. Recipient Best of Show award Colo. Press Assn., 1981, 86, Woman of Yr. award Broward County Bus. and Profl. Women's Assn., 1983, 1st Pl. Spot News award Colo. Associated Press, 1986, 1st Pl. Breaking News award Colo. Press Assn., 1986, Gen. Excellence award Wyo. Press Assn., 1991, Gen. Excellence award Nat. Newspaper Assn., 1992. Home: 149 Fairview Rd Penn Valley PA 19072 Office: The Philadelphia Inquirer 400 N Broad St Philadelphia PA 19000

GORDON, ARNOLD MARK, arbitrator, lawyer; b. Norwich, Conn., Oct. 2, 1937; s. Barney and Rose (Bilsky) G.; m. Carolyn. BSBA, Wayne State U., Detroit, 1959, JD, 1962. Bar: Mich. 1962. With Gordon & Gordon P.C. and predecessor firms, Southfield, Mich.; arbitrator Am. Arbitration Assn., 1969—; lectr. in field. Mem. Am. Coll. Trial Lawyers, State Bar Mich. (chmn. med.-legal com. 1976—, negligence sect. 1977-78, pub. negligence sect. bull.), Detroit Bar Assn. (co-chmn. trial advocacy program continguing legal edn. 1972—), Assn. Trial Lawyers Am. (exec. bd. Mich. 1967—), Mich., Detroit trial lawyers assns., Tau Epsilon Rho. Club: Masons. Office: Gordon & Gordon PC 18411 W 12 Mile Rd Ste 200 Southfield MI 48076-2663

GORDON, BARON JACK, stockbroker; s. George M. and Rose (Salsbury) G.; midshipman U.S. Naval Acad., 1946; BS, Lynchburg Coll., 1953; m. Ellin Bachrach, Aug. 20, 1954; children: Jonathan Ross, Rose Patricia, Alison. V.p. Consol. Ins. Agy., Norfolk, 1948-55; asst. treas. Henry Montor Assos., Inc., N.Y.C., 1956; v.p., sec. Propp & Co., Inc., N.Y.C., 1957-58; ptr. Koerner, Gordon & Co., N.Y.C., 1959-62; sr. ptnr. Gordon, Kulman Perry, and predecessor firm, N.Y.C., 1962-71, pres., chmn. bd., 1971-74; pres., chmn. bd. Palison, Inc., mem. N.Y. Stock Exch., White Plains, N.Y., 1974—; chmn. bd. Rojon, Inc., real estate and investments, Williamsburg, Va., 1979—. Mem. Harrison (N.Y.) Archtl. Rev. Bd., 1970-72, Harrison Planning Bd., 1975-77; bd. dirs. Montefiore Hosp. Assn., YM-YWHA, Lafayette Ednl. Fund., Inc., 1986-92; internat. adv. coun. Mus. of Am. Folk Art, 1990—; naval aide-de-camp to gov. State of Va., 1989—. Lt. USNR, 1953-55, capt., 1989. Mem. Folk Art Soc. (bd. dirs. 1987-95, mem. nat. adv. bd. 1996—), U.S. Naval Acad. Alumni Assn. (life). Clubs: Stock Exch. Luncheon (N.Y.C.), Kingsmill Sports (Williamsburg, Va.), Buttonwood, N.Y. Stock Exch. Home: 113 Elizabeth Meriwether Williamsburg VA 23185-5107 Office: Drawer JG Williamsburg VA 23187

GORDON, BARRY JOEL, investment advisor; b. N.Y.C., July 16, 1945; s. Ned and Beatrice (Brahms) G.; m. Joan Shirley Busch, Jan. 27, 1968; children: Jill, Jeffrey. B.B.A. in Mktg., U. Miami, 1967; M.B.A. in Fin., Hofstra U., 1970. Analyst Ea. Air Lines, N.Y.C., 1967-69; cons. R. Dixon Speas Assocs., Manhasset, N.Y., 1969-71; pres. NCS-Select-A-Coll., N.Y.C., 1971-72; securities analyst N.Y. Hanseatic Corp., N.Y.C., 1972-73; exec. v.p. Am. Fund Advisors, Inc., N.Y.C., 1978-80, chmn., pres., 1980—, pres., dir., 1982—; exec. v.p. John Hancock Nat. Aviation & Tech. Corp., N.Y.C., 1973-83, pres., 1983-95; exec. v.p. John Hancock Global Tech. Fund, Inc., N.Y.C., 1982-83, pres., 1983—; chmn., pres. Nat. Value Fund, N.Y.C., 1986-92; chmn., CEO minor league baseball team N.J. Cardinals, 1991—; chmn., chief exec. officer minor league baseball team Norwich Navigators affiliate N.Y. Yankees, 1992—; bd. dirs. Winfield Capital Corp., Robecom Sys., Inc., John Hancock Nat. Aviation and Tech. Fund, N.Y.C., 1978-95, John Hancock Global Tech. Fund, Boston, 1983—; chmn., pres. Nat. Value Fund, N.Y.C., 1986-92; dir. N.Y.-Pa. League Profl. Baseball, Ea. League Profl. Baseball, v.p. Bd. dirs. Chanteclaire at Muttontown Homeowners Assn., N.Y., 1973-77, Brooklyn Sports Found.; com. mem. New Leadership div. North Shore Hosp., Manhasset, 1991. With USAR, 1968-73. Named L.I. Entrepreneur of Yr., 1992. Mem. AIAA, N.Y. Soc. Securities Analysts (chmn. transp. com., industry group coord.), Am. Stock Exch. (arbitrator), Soc. Aerospace Analysts, Soc. Airline Analysts (pres. 1976-81), Wings Club, Glen Head Country Club, Addison Res. Country Club. Democrat. Jewish. Avocations: golfing, tennis, baseball memorabilia. Office: Am Fund Advisors Inc 1415 Kellum Pl Ste 205 Garden City NY 11530-1604

GORDON, BARTON JENNINGS (BART GORDON), congressman, lawyer; b. Murfreesboro, Tenn., Jan. 24, 1949; s. Robert Jennings and Margaret Louise (Barton) G. B.S., Middle Tenn. State U., 1971; J.D., U. Tenn., 1973. Bar: Tenn. 1974. Congressman 99th-105th Congresses from 6th Tenn. dist., Washington, D.C., 1985—; mem. energy and power com., mem. commerce and sci. com., mem. telecom, trade and consumer protection com., mem. tech., space subcoms. Mem. Tenn. Democratic Exec. Com., 1974-83, exec. dir., 1979-81, chmn., 1981-83; bd. dirs. Middle Tenn. State U. Found.; chmn. Rutherford County United Givers Fund, Rutherford County Cancer Crusade. Mem. Rutherford County C. of C. (bd. dirs.). Methodist. Office: US Ho of Reps 2368 Rayburn Bldg Washington DC 20515-0005

GORDON, BASIL, mathematics educator; b. Balt., Dec. 23, 1932; s. Basil and Helen (Williams) G. MA, Johns Hopkins, 1953; PhD, Calif. Inst. Tech., 1956. Instr. Calif. Inst. Tech., 1956-57; asst. prof. math. U. Calif. at Los Angeles, 1959-63, assoc. prof., 1963-67, prof., 1967-93; prof. emeritus, 1993—. Editor: Pacific Jour. Mathematics, 1969-70, 72-73, Jour. Combinatorial Theory, 1970—, Ramanujan Jour., 1997—; contbr. articles to profl. jours. Served with AUS, 1957-59. Alfred P. Sloan fellow, 1962-64. Mem. Math. Assn. Am., Pi Mu Epsilon. Rsch. on number theory, combinatorics, group theory, and function theory. Home: 526 Palisades Ave Santa Monica CA 90402-2722 Office: 405 Hilgard Ave Los Angeles CA 90095-9000

GORDON, BENJAMIN, physical therapist; b. N.Y.C., June 18, 1929; s. Charles and Ida Gordon; m. Betty Kerin Kenyon, Nov. 11, 1962; 1 child, Robert Eric Kenyon. BS in Phys. Edn., L.I. U., 1949; MEd, Springfield (Mass.) Coll., 1952; cert. in phys. therapy, NYU, 1955. Phys. therapist St. Charles Hosp., Bklyn., 1955-59, Sailors Snug Harbor Clinic, S.I., N.Y., 1960-63; chief phys. therapist S.I. Univ. Hosp., 1963-78, phys. therapist, 1978—. With inf. U.S.Army, 1943-45, PTO. Mem. Am. Phys. Therapy Assn. Avocations: tennis, stamp collecting, religious studies, reading philosophy and psychology, travel. Office: SI Univ Hosp 475 Seaview Ave Staten Island NY 10305

GORDON, BENJAMIN DICHTER, medical executive, pediatrician; b. Bklyn., Mar. 4, 1927; s. Abraham S. and Selma F. (Dichter) G.; m. Ellen M. Nimaroff, June 10, 1951; children: Wendy, Marcy, Amanda. AB, Amherst Coll., 1947; MD, U. Md., 1951. Diplomate Am. Bd. of Pediatrics. Rotating intern Kings County Hosp., Bklyn., 1951-52, asst. resident in pediatrics, 1953-54; asst. resident in pediatrics Maimonides Hosp., Bklyn., 1952-53; research fellow Irvington House, Irvington-on-Hudson, N.Y., 1954-55; practice medicine specializing in pediatrics Stratford & Bridgeport, Conn., 1955-73; assoc. attendant, emergency dept. Bridgeport Hosp., 1973-78; asst. dir. emergency dept. Danbury (Conn.) Hosp., 1978-82; clin. dir. Union Carbide Corp., Danbury, 1982-87; med. dir Chesebrough-Ponds, Inc., Trumbull, Conn., 1987-90; asst. prof. occupational medicine Yale U.; chmn. Rheumatic Fever com. Conn. State Heart Assn.; cons. to cosmetic industry and product-testing labs.; attending occupl. med. clinic Milton (Mass.) Hosp. Author: Practical Guide for New Parents, 1970; contbr. articles to profl. jours. Served with USNR, 1945-46. Fellow Am. Acad. Pediats., Am. Coll. Occupational and Environ. Medicine, Am. Acad. Dermatology (spl. affiliate); mem. Conn. State Med. Soc. (past chmn. comty. pub. health), Fairfield County Med. Soc. (past chmn. pub. health com.), Occupational Med. Assn. Conn. (pres. 1987-88), Williams Club (N.Y.C.), Mass. Med. Soc., Barnstable Dist. Med. Soc. (com. on violence). Jewish. Avocations: music, dance, skiing, reading, history, golf. Home: 14 Hillsea Rd Yarmouth Port MA 02675-1111

GORDON, BERNARD M., computer company executive; b. 1927. Pres., CEO, chmn. Analogic Corp., Peabody, Mass., 1967-94, CEO, chmn., 1994—. Recipient Nat. Medal Tech., 1986, John Fulke Sr. Meml. award, 1993. Fellow IEEE (Leadership Recognition award 1992); mem. Nat. Acad. Engrs. Office: Analogic Corp 8 Centennial Dr # B-1 Peabody MA 01960-7987*

GORDON, BETTY L., health services administrator; b. Sayre, Pa., Apr. 4, 1947; d. Manley and Helen (Featherman) Rockman; m. Alan F. Gordon, Dec. 29, 1972. BSN, Russell Sage Coll., 1964; postgrad., Boston U., 1973-74; MPH in Health Svcs. Adminstrn., John Hopkins U., 1981. RN, Mass., N.Y. Gen. staff nurse Robert Packer Hosp., Sayre, Pa., 1968; staff nurse, team leader Vis. Nurse Assn. Allegheny County, Pa., 1968-71; nurse pub. health Vis. Nurse Assn. Boston, 1971; staff continuing care coord. Faulkner Hosp., Jamaica Plain, Mass., 1972-74; nurse pub. health, home health coord. Arlington County Dept. Human Resources, Va., 1974-78; dir. patient care svcs. Hospice Met. Denver, 1978-80; project site dir. long term care channeling demonstration City Balt., 1981-83; sr. v.p. clin. svcs. Kimberly Quality Care, Boston, 1983-94; v.p. Simione Ctrl., Inc., Westboro, Mass., 1994—. Home: 125 Coolidge Ave Apt 606 Watertown MA 02472-2875 Office: 1700 W Park Dr Ste 300 Westborough MA 01581-3941

GORDON, BRIDGETTE, professional basketball player; b. Apr. 27, 1967. Degree in polit. sci., U. Tenn., 1989. Basketball player Como Tean, Casnate, Italy, 1990-97; forward Sacramento Monarchs, (WNBA), 1997-99, New York Liberty, (WNBA), 99-. Gold medalist, tournament MVP Olympic Fesitval, 1986; Gold medalist U.S. Olympic Team, 1988; winner with Como team European Cup Championship, 1993, 95. Avocations: riding four-wheelers, swimming, hanging out. Office: New York Liberty 2 Penn Plaza New York NY 10121

GORDON, CAREY NATHANIEL, lawyer, federal agency administrator; b. Cleve., Mar. 11, 1950; s. Murray Byron and Pearl Miriam (Jackson) G.; m. Lois Elizabeth Bradshaw, Nov. 28, 1981. BA, Ohio State U., 1972; MA, U. London, 1973; postgrad., Cambridge (Eng.) U., 1973-74; JD, Cleve. State U., 1977. Bar: Ohio 1977, D.C. 1978, U.S. Supreme Ct. 1983. Assoc. Rippner Schwartz & Carlin, Cleve., 1977-80, ptnr., 1980-84; spl. advisor Atty. Gen.'s Chambers, Khartoum, Sudan, 1984-85; contract advisor U.S. Agy. for Internat. Devel., Khartoum, Cairo, Kinshasa, Islamabad, 1986-94; contracting officer U.S. Agy. for Internat. Devel., Abidjan, Ivory Coast, 1995-97, Phnom Penh, Cambodia, 1997—; vis. lectr. U. Khartoum, 1984-85. Mem. Fed. Bar Assn., Am. Soc. Internat. Law, Cleve. Bar Assn., African Studies Assn. Office: USAID Cambodia Box P APO AP 96546

GORDON, CAROLANN, oncological nurse, community health nurse; b. Hackensack, N.J., May 8, 1947; d. Henry Alfred and Irene Anne (Bielawski) Prell; m. Bruce Anthony Gordon, Mar. 3, 1967. LPN, Bergen Pines Hosp., Paramus, N.J., 1966; AAS, Dutchess C.C., Poughkeepsie, N.Y., 1985; BSN, SUNY, New Paltz, 1993. Staff nurse Columbia Presbyn. Hosp., N.Y., 1972-73, Alexander Linn Hosp., Sussex, N.J., 1974-75, Vassar Bros. Hosp., Poughkeepsie, 1978-86; asst head nurse, oncology No. Westchester Hosp. Ctr., Mt. Kisco, N.Y., 1987-93; nurse St. Francis Home Care Agy., Poughkeepsie, 1993—. Mem. Oncology Nurse Soc., Nat. Oncology Nurse Soc. (Hudson Valley chpt.), Dutchess C.C. Alumni Assn., SUNY New Paltz Nursing Alumni Assn. Office: St Francis Home Care Aby Rte 9G Poughkeepsie NY 12601

GORDON, COREY LEE, lawyer; b. Mpls., Aug. 22, 1956; s. Jack I. and LaVerne (Shedlov) G.; m. Ciel Schaeffer, Aug. 29, 1982; children: Jared Isaac, Lian Miriam. BA, Macalester Coll., 1976; JD cum laude, U. Minn., 1980. Bar: Minn. 1980, U.S. Dist. Ct. Minn. 1981, U.S. Ct. Appeals (8th cir.) 1983, U.S. Supreme Ct. 1983, Wis. 1987, U.S. Dist. Ct. (ea. and we. dists.) Wis. 1987, N.Y. 1991, U.S. Dist. Ct. (so. dist.) N.Y. 1991, U.S. Ct. Appeals (3d cir.) 1992, Ill. 1993, U.S. Dist. Ct. (no. dist.) Ill. 1995, Fla. 1995. Assoc. Fried, Frank, Harris, Shriver & Jacobson, N.Y.C., 1980-81; ptnr. Shapiro, Lavintman & Gordon P.A., Mpls., 1982-85; assoc. Robins, Zelle, Larson & Kaplan, St. Paul, 1986-88; ptnr. Robins, Kaplan, Miller & Ciresi, Mpls., 1989—; bd. dirs. Jewish Family and Children's Svc. of Mpls., 1992-96, Mpls. Fedn. for Jewish Svc., 1994—. Treas. The H.H.H. Fund, Minn., 1984-89; bd. dirs., sec.-treas. Minn. Humane Soc., 1985-86; active Dem. Farm Labor Party; trustee Bet Shalom Synagogue, 1992-93, v.p., 1993-97, pres., 1997-99. Mem. ABA, ATLA (co-chair inadequate security litigation group 1992-95). Jewish. Avocations: folk music, scuba diving, photography. Home: 2640 Glenhurst Pl Saint Louis Park MN 55416-3957 Office: Robins Kaplan Miller & Ciresi 2800 LaSalle Pla 800 Lasalle Ave Ste 2800 Minneapolis MN 55402-2015

GORDON, CRAIG JEFFREY, oncologist, educator; b. Detroit, Feb. 10, 1953; s. Maury Allen and Shirley Phoebe (Jacoby) G.; m. Susan Ann Blase, Aug. 3, 1980; children: Sari, Scott, Brittany. BS, Oakland U., 1978; DO, U. Osteopathic Medicine and, Health Scis./Des Moines, 1983. Diplomate Am. Bd. Internal Medicine, Am. Bd. Med. Oncology. Intern-chief Botsford Gen. Hosp., Farmington Hills, Mich., 1983-84, resident, 1984-87; fellow in hematology and oncology Wayne State Univ. (affiliated Hosp.'s Prog.), Detroit, 1987-90, fellow-chief, 1989-90; clin. asst. prof. dept. medicine Wayne State U., Detroit, 1990—; dir. divsn. hematology and oncology Botsford Hosp., Livonia, Mich., 1992—; med. dir. Angela Hospice, 1993—; mem. extrarenal transplantation com. Mich. Dept. Pub. Health; physician advisor Gilda's Club Mich.; mem. Greater Detroit Area Health Care Coun. on Cancer Care. Contbr. articles to profl. jours. Named Intern of the Yr. Botsford Hosp. Staff, 1984, Resident of the Yr., 1985-87; clin. fellow Am. Cancer Soc., 1987-90. Fellow Am. Coll. Osteo. Internists; mem. Am. Osteo. Assn., Assn. Adminstrs. and Cancer Execs., Mich. Assn. Osteo. Physicians and Surgeons, Mich. Soc. Hematology and Oncology, Assn. Cancer Execs., S.W. Oncology Group, Am. Soc. Clin. Oncologists, Oakland County Osteo. Assn. Avocations: sports, popular music, astronomy, electronics. Office: Botsford Gen Hosp 28595 Orchard Lake Rd Ste 300 Farmington Hills MI 48334

GORDON, CYRUS HERZL, Orientalist, educator; b. Phila., June 29, 1908; s. Benjamin Lee and Dorothy (Cohen) G.; m. Joan Elizabeth Kendall, Sept. 22, 1946 (dec. 1985); children: Deborah J. Gordon Friedrich, Sarah Y. Gordon Krakauer, Rachel K. Gordon Bernstein, Noah D., Dan K; m. Constance Victoria Wallace, Oct. 18, 1986. AB, U. Pa., 1927, MA, 1928, PhD, 1930; D Hebrew Letters (hon.), Balt. Hebrew Coll., 1981; DHL (hon.), Hebrew Union Coll., 1985; LittD (hon.), Boston Hebrew Coll., 1995; D Hebrew Laws (hon.), Gratz Coll., 1996. Instr. semitics U. Pa., 1930-31; field archaeologist, fellow Am. Schs. Oriental Research, Near East, 1931-35; tchg. fellow Oriental Sem., Johns Hopkins U., 1935-38; lectr. Bible, Smith Coll., 1938-39, 40-41; mem. Inst. Advanced Study, Princeton, N.J., 1939-40, 41-42; prof. Assyriology and Egyptology, Dropsie U., Phila., 1946-56; prof. Near Eastern studies Brandeis U., Waltham, Mass., 1956-73, prof. emeritus, 1973—, also chmn. dept. Mediterranean studies, 1958-73, dir. Grad. Sch., 1957-58, assoc. dean faculty, 1957-58; Gottesman prof. Hebrew studies NYU, 1973-89, prof. emeritus, 1989—; dir. Ctr. Ebla Rsch., NYU, 1982—; vis. fellow humanities U. Colo., 1967; Gay lectr. Simmons Coll., 1970; vis. prof. NYU, 1970-73; vis. fellow Japan Found., 1974; vis. prof. history and anthropology U. N.Mex., 1976; vis. prof. humanities S.W. Mo. State U., 1977-79; Disting. vis. prof. N.Mex. State U., Las Cruces, 1979-80; vis. prof. Judaic studies SUNY, Albany, 1981-82, U. Hawaii, Honolulu, 1988; Del Grauer lectr. U. B.C., Vancouver, 1988; vis. Brownstone prof. Dartmouth Coll., 1990; vis. prof. Maritime Civilizations, U. Haifa, Israel, 1993; elected Soc. Scholars, Johns Hopkins U., 1990—; archeol. expdns.; lectr. Cornell U., 1992. Author: Ugaritic Grammar, 1940, Ugaritic Handbook, 1947, Ugaritic Manual, 1955, The Living Past, 1941, Adventures in the Nearest East, 1957, Ugaritic Literature, 1949, Smith College Tablets, 1952, Introduction to Old Testament Times, 1953, Hammurapi's Code, 1957, The World of the Old Testament, 1958, rev. as The Ancient Near East, 1965, rev., expanded edition (by C.H. Gordon and G.A. Rendsburg), 1997, Before the Bible, 1963, rev. as The Common Background of Greek and Hebrew Civilizations, 1965, Ugaritic Textbook, 1965, rev. with supplement, 1967, 2nd rev. printing, 1998, Ugarit and Minoan Crete, 1966, Forgotten Scripts, 1968, rev. edit., 1971, rev. and enlarged edits., 1982, 87, Before Columbus, 1971, Riddles in History, 1974, The Pennsylvania Tradition of Semitics, 1986, The Background to Jewish Studies in the Bible and in the Ancient East, 1994; contbg. author, editor Pub. Ctr. for Ebla Rsch., vol. 1, 1987, vol. 2, 1990, vol. 3, 1992; also numerous articles; contbg. editor Am. Jour. Archaeology, 1938-45; edtl. coun. Encounter, 1956; internat. adv. coun. Jewish Quar. Review, 1979-82. Trustee, Boston Hebrew Coll.; corr. mem. Inst. Antiquity and Christianity Claremont Grad. Sch. and Univ. Center; trustee Internat. Council Etruscan Studies of Order of Holy Cross; mem. mng. com. Am. Sch. Classical Studies, Athens, 1958-73. Served as officer U.S. Army, 1942-46; col. USAF Res., ret.; flight comdr. Boston Air Res. Center 1958-61; moblzn. assignee Hdqrs. U.S. Army, 1961-67. Harrison scholar U. Pa., 1928-29; Harrison fellow, 1929-30; Am. Council Learned Socs. fellow, 1932-33; Am. Scandinavian Found. fellow, 1939; recipient Alumni award Gratz Coll., Phila., 1961, cert. of merit Acad. for Jewish Religion, 1991; honored 4 Festschriften: Orient and Occident: Essays presented to Cyrus H. Gordon on the Occasion of his 65th Birthday, 1973, The Bible World: Essays in Honor of Cyrus H. Gordon, 1980, A Synthesis of Cultures: Essays on the Major Contributions of Cyrus Gordon, 1996, Boundaries of the Ancient Near Eastern World: A Tribute to Cyrus H. Gordon—Four Score and Ten, 1998. Fellow Am. Acad. Arts and Scis., Royal Asiatic Soc. (hon.), Am. Acad. Jewish Rsch., Explorers Club; mem. Am. Hist. Assn., Am. Oriental Soc. (exec. com. 1964-67), Am. Philol. Assn., Archaeol. Inst. Am., Soc. Bibl. Lit. and Exegesis, Soc. for Nr. Ea. Studies in Japan (hon.). *My road to discovery is to follow facts to their inescapable conclusions. This imposes on us practical risks for we live in a world of consensus which demands political correctness if our goal is worldly success. Luckily I am spending my life in the quest for truth and surviving long enough to win recognition for doing what I love.*

GORDON, DAN, food service executive. CEO Gordon Food Svc. Inc., Grand Rapids, Mich. Office: Gordon Food Svc Inc PO Box 1787 Grand Rapids MI 49501-1787*

GORDON, DARRIEN X. JAMAL, professional football player; b. Shawnee, Okla., Nov. 14, 1970. Student, Stanford U. Cornerback, punt returner San Diego Chargers, 1993-97; with Denver Broncos, 1997-98, Oakland Raiders, 1998—. Mem. AFC Championship Tesm, 1994; leader in punt return average AFC, 1994. Office: c/o Oakland Raiders 1220 Harbor Bay Pky Alameda CA 94502*

GORDON, DAVID, playwright, director, choreographer; b. N.Y.C., July 14, 1936; m. Valda Setterfield; 1 child, Ain. Dir. Pick Up Performance Co., Inc., N.Y.C., 1978—. Playwright, dir. dance, theater, music prodn. The Mysteries and What's So Funny?, 1991; writer, dir. TV program (1992-93) and theatrical work (1996) Punch and Judy Get Divorced; co-writer, dir.: (with Ain Gordon) The Family Business, 1994-95; dir. Shlemiel The First, Am. Repertory Theater, 1994-95; dir., choreographer: The Firebugs, The Guthrie Theater, 1995; co-writer, dir. (with Ain Gordon) First Picture Show,

1999. Guggenheim fellow, 1981, 87. Office: Pick Up Performance Co 47 Great Jones St # 2 New York NY 10012-1118

GORDON, DAVID ELIOT, lawyer; b. Santa Monica, Calif., Mar. 8, 1949; s. Sam and Dee G.; m. Mary Debora Lane, Mar. 5, 1978. BA, Harvard U., 1969, JD, 1972. Bar: Calif. 1972. Ptnr. O'Melveny & Myers, L.A., 1980—. Founder, editor ERISA Litigation Reporter; contbr. articles on tax and employee benefits to profl. jours. Trustee Ctr. for Early Edn., 1997—. Fellow Los Angeles County Bar Found. (life, pres. 1984-85, bd. dirs. 1980-86); mem. ABA (employee benefits com. 1986—), Am. Coll. Tax Counsel, Los Angeles County Bar Assn. (tax sect., pres. 1990-91), Nat. Assn. Bond Lawyers (bd. dirs. 1982-84). Republican. Avocations: tennis, squash, racquetball. Office: O'Melveny & Myers 400 S Hope St Los Angeles CA 90071-2899

GORDON, DAVID JAMIESON, tenor; b. Phila., Dec. 7, 1947; s. David William and Lois Irene (Lukens) G.; m. Barbara Jean Bixby, June 14, 1969. Student, Coll. of Wooster, 1965-68, McGill U., Montreal, Que., Can., 1968-70; student of Dale Moore, 1965—. Prin. tenor soloist Bach Festival, 1990-97; mem. faculty Esalen Inst., 1996—. Debut with Lyric Opera Chgo., 1973; leading tenor Landestheater Linz (Austria), 1975-79; prin. roles with San Francisco Opera, Houston Grand Opera, Met. Opera, Hamburg Staatsoper, Washington Opera, Mostly Mozart Festival, Salzburg Festival; concert soloist with Bach Festivals: Carmel, Calif., Bethlehem, Pa., Festival Casals, Stuttgart, Tokyo, Buenos Aires, Eugene, Oreg., Boston Symphony, Berlin Philharm., Czech Philharmonic, Vienna Symphony, St. Louis Symphony, San Francisco Symphony, L.A. Philharm., Seattle Symphony, Phila. Orch., Cleve. Orch., Nat. Symphony Washington, Baltimore Symphony; appears in opera, concerts, chamber music, recitals throughout U.S. and Europe as performer, lectr., and tchr.; specialist in music of J.S. Bach; performing artist for Delos, Dorian, Telarc, London Records, Decca Records, Smithsoniam Collection of Recs., RCA Red Seal, Nonesuch Records. E-mail: david@spiritsound.com. Home & Studio: 535 Bellevue Ave Apt 17 Oakland CA 94610*

GORDON, DAVID ZEVI, retired lawyer; b. Bklyn., Mar. 2, 1943; s. Isidore and Yaffa S. (Stern) G.; m. Karen Baranker, Apr. 25, 1971; children: Ilana, Naomi. BA magna cum laude, Yeshiva U., 1964; JD cum laude, MBA, Columbia U., 1969. Bar: N.Y. 1970, U.S. Dist. Ct. (so. dist.) N.Y. 1973, U.S. Ct. Appeals (2d cir.) 1973. Assoc. Spear and Hill, N.Y.C., 1969-71; sr. assoc. LeBoeuf Lamb Lieby & McRae, N.Y.C., 1971-77; ptnr. Finley Kumble Heine & Underburg, N.Y.C., 1977-78, David Z. Gordon and Assocs., N.Y.C., 1978-81; mng. ptnr. Moroze Sherman Gordon & Gordon, P.C., N.Y.C., 1981-96. Trustee, exec. com. Stern Coll. for Women, 1990-96; co-chmn. United Jewish Appeal, Operation Exodus, 1991-96, Project Renewal, 1987-96, exec. com. Israel econ. devel.; chmn. Israel Bonds, Bronx, 1988-96. Recipient Heritage award Yeshiva U., 1988. Mem. ABA, N.Y. State Bar Assn., N.Y.C. Bar Assn. (mem. com. condemnation and tax certiorari), Real Estate Tax Bar Assn. Democrat.

GORDON, DEBRA GWEN, music educator; b. Clinton, Iowa, Apr. 5, 1951; d. Otto Edward and Edna Firm (Griffin) Bruhn; m. Roger L. Gordon, July 30, 1983. BA in Music Edn., U. Iowa, 1973; MA in Music Edn., U. No. Iowa, 1985, EdD in Curriculum and Instrn., 1997. Cert. music tchr. Elem. music tchr. Lincoln Community Schs., Mechanicsville, Iowa, 1973-76; elem. music tchr., German tchr. Hudson (Iowa) Community Schs., 1976-93; asst. prof. music edn., chair music edn. U. No. Iowa, 1993—; mem. North Ctrl. Accredidation Team, 1980—; clinician, presenter at various convs., 1977—; mem. musician's del. to China and Kazakhstan, 1992; condr. Iowa Opus Concert, 1997, various choral festivals; master tchr. Heartland Choral Festivals, Des Moines, 1996, 98; presenter Internat. Music Edn. Symposium, Tasmania, 1999. Contbr. to Teaching Examples: Ideas for Music Educators, 1994, Strategies for Teaching K-4 General Music, 1996; contbr. articles to profl. publs. Grantee Iowa Dept. Edn., 1985, 87. Mem. Iowa Music Educators (bd. dirs., exec. sec. 1984—), Am. Choral Dirs. Assn., Pi Delta Kappa, Pi Kappa Lambda. Democrat. Lutheran. Avocations: sewing, painting. Office: U No Iowa 121 Russell Hall Cedar Falls IA 50614-0246

GORDON, DOLORES JOAN, retired emergency medical technician; b. Cicero, Ill., Mar. 21, 1935; d. Harry Lewis and Louise Eva Marie (Uxa) G.; m. Joseph Delbert Ebert, Mar. 29, 1968 (div. Aug. 1977); children: Mark Harry Louis, Gloria Louise Dolores. Student, Mundelein Coll., 1953-54. Cert. EMT, Am. Coll. Surgeons. Floral designer, office mgr. E.T. Will Landscaping and Florist, Berwyn, Ill., 1964-67; co-owner, EMT Ebert's Ambulance Svc., Berwyn, 1968-76; with invoicing dept. Turner Mfg. Co., Chgo., 1957-58. Author: A Nanny's Memoirs, 1994; co-author: God's Country, 1996. Named Woman of Yr. Hon. Mention Morton Twp. Women's History Com., 1997. Mem. Betsy Ross Lodge. Roman Catholic. Achievement: 1st woman in 5 states to become EMT cert. by ACS. Avocation: writing. Home: 6506 Pershing Rd Berwyn IL 60402-4046

GORDON, DOUGLAS, artist; b. Glasgow, Scotland, 1966. Student, Glasgow Sch. Art, 1984-88, Slade Sch. Art, London, 1988-90. One-man shows include Mus. d'Art Moderne de la Ville de Paris, 1993, Tramway, Glasgow and Kunst-werke, Berlin, 1993, Lisson Gallery, London, 1994, Rooseum Espresso, Malmö, 1995, Ctr. Georges Pompidou, Paris, 1995, Van Abbe Mus., Eindhoven, 1995, the Agy., London, 1995, Kunstlerhaus, Stuttgart, 1995, Tate Gallery, London, 1996, Galerie Walchenturm, Zurich, 1996, Mus. Gegenwartskunst, Zurich, 1996, Canberra Contemporary Art Space, 1996, Galleria Bonoma, Rome, 1996, Uppsala Konstmus., 1996, FRAC Languedoc-Roussillion, Montpellier, France, 1996, Deutsches Mus. Bonn, 1997, Kunstverein Hannover, 1997, Biennale de Lyon, 1997, Gandy Gallery, Prague, 1997, Galerie Mot & Van den Boogaard, Brussels, 1997, Munster Skulptur Projekt, 1997, Galerie Micheline Swajcer, Antwerp, 1997, Bloom Gallery, Amsterdam, 1997, Galleri Nicolai Wallner, Copenhagen, 1997, others; exhibited in group shows at Hayward Gallery, London, 1996, Transmission Gallery, Glasgow, 1996, Soros Contemporary Art Gallery, Kiev, 1997, Southampton City Art Gallery, 1997, Ashiya City Mus. Art and History, 1998, Guggenheim Mus. SoHo, N.Y., 1998, numerous others. Recipient Turner prize, 1996, Premio 2000 award Venice Biennale, 1997. Fax: 212-228-2878. Office: care Gagostan Gallery 136 Wooster St New York NY 10012

GORDON, EDMUND WYATT, psychologist, educator; b. Goldsboro, N.C., June 13, 1921; s. Edmund Tayloe and Mabel (Ellison) G.; m. Susan Elizabeth Gitt, Nov. 6, 1948; children: Edmund T., Christopher W., Jessica G., Johanna S. BS, Howard U., 1942, BD, 1945, LHD (hon.), 1997; MA, Am. U., 1950; EdD, Columbia U., 1957; MA (hon.), Yale U., 1979; LHD (hon.), Yeshiva U., N.Y.C., 1986, Brown U., 1989, Bank St. Coll., 1992; DS, Mt. Holyoke Coll., 1994. Asst. dean men Howard U., Washington, 1946-50; from assoc. prof. to prof. Yeshiva U., N.Y.C., 1961-68; prof., chmn. dept. guidance Columbia U., N.Y.C., 1968-78, Richard March Hoe prof. psychology and edn., 1978-79; John M. Musser prof. of psychology Yale U., New Haven, 1979-91; John M. Musser prof. of psychology emeritus Yale U., 1991; disting. prof. ednl. psychology CUNY, N.Y.C., 1992-96. Author: Compensatory Education for the Disadvantaged: Programs and Practices, 1966; editor: Equality of Educational Opportunity: Handbook for Research, 1974, Human Diversity and Pedagogy, 1989; editor Am. Jour. Orthopsychiatry, 1978-83, Rev. of Rsch. in Edn., 1983-85, Ednl. Resilience in Inner City America, 1994; contbr. articles to Am. Jour. Orthopsychiatry, Am. Jour. Mental Deficiency, Am. Zoologist, Jour. of Genetic Psychology, Am. Child, others. Pres. Rockland County NAACP. Fellow AAAS, APA, Am. Orthopsychiatric Assn., Am. Psychol. Soc.; mem. Am. Ednl. Rsch. Assn., Nat. Assn. Black Psychologists, Nat. Acad. Edn., N.Y. Acad. Sci. Achievements include research in human diversity, cultural hegemony, culture and cognitive development, and education of low status populations; responsible for and one of the founders and the 1st director of research for Project Head Start, 1965-67. Home and Office: 3 Cooper Morris Dr Pomona NY 10970-3309

GORDON, EDWARD EARL, management consultant; b. Evergreen Park, Ill., Feb. 28, 1949; s. Earl and Estelle (Biehn) G.; m. Elaine Huarisa, Aug. 6, 1983. BA in History, Edn., DePaul U., 1971, MA in History, 1972; postgrad., U. Chgo., 1972-73; PhD in History of Edn./Psychology, Loyola U., 1988. Founding pres. Imperial Edn. Corp., Oak Lawn, Ill., 1968—; exec. dir. North Am. Inst. for Tng. and Ednl. Rsch., 1972—; arbitrator Am. Arbitration Assn., Chgo., 1973—, Coun. Better Bus. Burs., Chgo., 1977—, Ill. Bd. Edn., 1986—; lectr. Sch. Edn., DePaul U., Chgo., 1979-92, instr. dept. history, 1989-91; mem. adv. coun. U. Ill., Chgo., 1989—; adj. prof., dir. grad. program in tng. and devel. Roosevelt U., Chgo., 1990-91; instr. adult corp. instrn. mgmt. program Loyola U., Chgo., 1992—; mem. Conf. Bd. Bus. Edn. Conf., 1996; keynote spkr. Partnerships in Learning at Work program U. B.C., Vancouver, Can., 1990, ednl. conf. Assn. Legal Adminstrs., 1999, Corp. Univ. Forum, Chgo., 1996, Measuring Performance and Profit for Workforce Edn. Programs, Palm Springs, Calif., 1996; presenter profl. confs. Author: Educators' Consumer Guide to Private Tutoring Services, 1989, Centuries of Tutoring: A History of Alternative Education in America and Western Europe, 1990, Closing the Literacy Gap in American Business: A Handbook for Trainers and Human Resources Development Specialists, 1991, The Need for Work Force Education, 1993, FutureWork: The Revolution Reshaping American Business, 1994, Ethics for Training and Development, 1995, Enhanceing Learning in Training, 1996, Opportunities in Training and Development Careers, 1996, Skill Wars: Winning the Battle for Productivity and Profit, 1999; contbr. articles to profl. jours.; mem. editl. adv. bd., columnist Corp. Univ. Forum Mag., 1995—. Bd. dirs. Ill. Literacy Resource Devel. Ctr., BBB of Chgo. and No. Ill., 1996—; mem. bus.-edn. partnerships bd. Ill. Bd. Edn., 1995—; mem. Pvt. Industry Coun. of Cook County, 1994—. Mem. ABA, ASTD (pres.-elect. Chgo. chpt. 1989-90, dir. manuscript rev. bd. 1988—), Orgnl. Devel. Network, Am. Ednl. Rsch. Assn., Am. Hist. Assn., Internat. Reading Assn., Am. Mgmt. Assn. (presenter New Strategic Corp. Model 1993), Am. Man. Assn., Nat. Soc. Perform and Instrn., Midwest History of Edn. Soc. (pres.), Phi Delta Kappa (pres. DePaul U. chpt. 1986-88). Roman Catholic. Office: Imperial Consulting Corp 10341 Lawler Ave Oak Lawn IL 60453-4714

GORDON, ELLEN RUBIN, candy company executive; d. William B. and Cele H. (Travis) Rubin; m. Melvin J. Gordon, June 25, 1950; children: Virginia, Karen, Wendy, Lisa. Student, Vassar Coll., 1948-50; B.A., Brandeis U., 1965; postgrad., Harvard U., 1968. With Tootsie Roll Industries, Inc., Chgo., 1968—, corp. sec., 1970-74, v.p. product devel., 1974-76, sr. v.p., 1976-78, pres., COO, 1978—, pres.; v.p., dir. HDI Investment Corp.; bd. dirs. Bestfoods (formerly CPC Internat., Inc.); mem. coun. on divsn. biol. scis. and Pritzker Sch. Medicine U. Chgo. Mem. dean's coun. J.L. Kellogg Grad. Sch. Mgmt. at Northwestern U.; mem. adv. coun. Stanford U. Grad. Sch. Bus.; mem. bd fellows Harvard U. Med. Sch.; mem. univ. resources and overseers com. Harvard U.; trustee, mem. Com. for Econ. Devel., Northwestern U. Assocs.; active Pres. Export Coun., Radcliffe Coll. Ptnrs.; bd. advisors Women Inc. Recipient Kettle award, 1985. Mem. Nat. Confectioners Assn. (bd. dirs.). Office: Tootsie Roll Industries Inc 7401 S Cicero Ave Chicago IL 60629-5885*

GORDON, ERNEST, clergyman; b. Greenock, Scotland, May 31, 1916; naturalized, 1960; s. James and Sarah Rae (Macmillan) G.; m. Helen McIntosh Robertson, Dec. 17, 1945 (dec. Feb. 1997); children: Gillian Margaret, Alastair James. BD, Hartford Theol. Sem., 1948, STM, 1949; postgrad., U. Glasgow, 1950-51; LLD, Bloomfield Coll., 1957; DCL (hon.), Bishop's U. of Can., 1966; LHD (hon.), Marshall U., 1973; DD (hon.), St. Andrews U., Scotland, 1976; DLitt (hon.), Grove City Coll., 1988. Ordained to ministry Ch. of Scotland, 1950. Dep. minister Paisley Abbey, 1950-52; supply minister Amagansett and Montauk chs., 1953-54; Presbyn. chaplain Princeton U., 1954-55, dean univ. chapel, 1955-81; ret. pres. Christian Rescue Effort for Emancipation of Dissidents, 1991-96; Danforth lectr. Davis and Elkins Coll., 1968; Turnbull preacher Melbourne, Australia, 1969; Staley distinguished scholar, 1972-96; tchr. in residence Presbyn. Ch., Houston, 1983; vis. prof. King Coll., Tenn., 1985; lectr. Inst. of History Princeton U., U. St. Andrews, 1987; vis. lectr. Moscow State Open Univ., 1993; lectr. Hall of Scientists, Moscow; vis. lectr. Internat. Christian U., Tokyo, 1996. Author: A Living Faith for Today, 1956, Through the Valley of the Kwai, 1962, Miracle on the River Kwai, 1963, Meet Me at the Door, 1969, A Guidebook for the New Christian, 1972, Solan, 1973, Islands Apart, 1977, Me, Myself & Who?, 1980. Contbr. articles to periodicals and publs. in USSR. Capt. 93d Highlanders, 1939-46, PTO, prisoner of war, 1942-45. Recipient Amy Found. award for lit., 1986, Faith and Freedom award Presbyn. Com. for Religion and Democracy, 1987, Am. Coptic Assn. award, 1989, Helsinki Internat. Fedn. award, 1991. Fellow Victoria Inst. London; mem. Royal Inst. Philosophy (London), Ch. Service Soc. Am. (founder). Clubs: Highland Brigade (London); Burma Star, Brit. Officers.; Nassau-Princeton. Home: 206 E Stanworth Dr Princeton NJ 08540-3122 also: Bendigo Rd Amagansett NY 11850

GORDON, EUGENE ANDREW, judge; b. Guilford County, N.C., July 10, 1917; s. Charles Robert and Carrie (Scott) G.; m. Virginia Stoner, Jan. 1, 1943; children: Eugene Andrew, Rosemary Anne. AB, Elon Coll., 1938, LLD (hon.), 1982; LLB, Duke U., 1941. Bar: N.C. 1941. Practiced law, 1946-64; mem. firm Young, Young & Gordon, Burlington, 1947-64; solicitor Alamance Gen. County Ct., 1947-54; county atty. Alamance County, 1954-64; U.S. judge Middle Dist. N.C., 1964-82, sr. judge, 1982—; instr. U.S. Atty. Gen.'s Sch. Former chmn. adv. bd. Salvation Army.; Former nat. committeeman N.C. Young Democrats; former pres. Alamance County Young Democrats; chmn. Alamance County Dem. Exec. Com., 1954-64; mem. U.S. Jud. Conf. Adv. Com. on Criminal Rules, 1976-84. Capt. AUS, 1942-46, N.C. Army N.G., 1946-47. Mem. Greensboro Bar Assn., Assn. U.S. Dist. Judges (past pres.). Office: Middle Dist Ct PO Box 3285 US Post Office & Ct House Greensboro NC 27402*

GORDON, EZRA, architect, educator; b. Detroit, Apr. 5, 1921; s. Abraham and Rebecca (Reimer) G.; m. Jeanette Greenberg, Oct. 8, 1942; children: Cheryl P. Gordon Van Ausdal, Rana Gordon Oremland, Judith Gordon Eichhorn. Roosevelt Coll., 1946-48; BS in Architecture, U. Ill., 1951. Draftsman Pace Assos. Architects, 1951-53; sr. planner Chgo. Plan Commn., 1953-54; project architect Harry Weese & Assos., 1954-61; ptnr. Gordon-Levin & Assocs., Chgo., 1961-84, Gordon & Levin, Inc., Chgo., 1984-95; cons. Dept. Urban Renewal City Chgo., Council for Jewish Elderly, Chgo. Jewish Fedn.; prof. emeritus U. Ill.-Chgo. Sch. Architecture; former mem. Mayor's Adv. Coun. on Bldg. Code Amendments; master juror Nat. Coun. Archtl. Registration Bds. Works include Long-Kogan Office Bldg., 1957, 5401 Hyde Park Apt. Bldg., Chgo., 1962, South Commons, Chgo., 1968, The Commons Townhouse Devel., Chgo., 1968, Hyde Park West Apts., Chgo., 1969, IBM Office bldgs., Kalamazoo, 1969, Moline, Ill. 1970, Jefferson City, Mo., Omaha, 1971, Eastwood Tower Apts., Chgo., 1970, Wexler Pavilion and Siegel Inst., Michael Reese Hosp., Chgo., 1971, Arbor Trails Apts. and Townhouses, Park Forest, Ill., 1972, Kenmore Plaza Apts. Sr. Housing, 1972, Kennaly Sq. Warehouse Apts. 19972-74, Pontiac Office Bldg., Mich., 1972, Concourse Office Towers, Skokie, 1972, Belle Plaine Apts., Chgo., 1972, Newberry Plaza, Chgo., 1973, Greenwood Park Apts., Chgo., 1974, River Plaza, Chgo., 1976, Elm St. Plaza, Chgo., 1976, Dearborn Park, Twin Tower Apts., Chgo., 1979, Huron Plaza, Chgo., 1981, 400 E. Ohio Condominiums, Streeterville, Chgo., 1983, East Bank Club, Chgo., 1983, Dearborn-Elm Apts., Chgo., 1986-87; designer World Trade Ctr. Apts., 1989, Lachman Montisorri Sch. for Hearing Impaired Children, Deerfield, Ill., 1990, Elm Street Apts., 1990, restoration of 1130 S. Michigan Ave., 1991, Montissori Sch. for the Hearing Impaired, 1991, Love residence, Glencoe, Ill., 1991, Drs. Barak & Oremland offices, Skokie, Ill., 1991, Oral Rehab. Ctr., Skokie, 1992, residence addition, Glencoe, 1998. Former mem. bd. dirs. Hyde Park-Kenwood Cmty. Conf., Astor St.-Lake Shore Dr. Assocs.; former v.p. Harper Ct. Found.; trustee Chgo. Athenaeum Mus. Archtl. Art and Urban Studies; mem. Art Inst. Chgo., Mus. Sci. and Industry, Spertus Mus., Mus. Contemporary Art, Chgo. Hist. Soc.; mem. Landmarks Preservation Coun., Chgo. Archtl. Found. Decorated Croix de Guerre with palm; recipient Honor award Dept. Housing and Urban Devel., 1967, Honor award AIA-Chgo. C. of C., 1967, award AIA-House & Home Mag., 1967, Distinguished Bldg. award AIA, 1957, 63, 69, 71, 73, 75, award City of Chgo. Beautification, 1969, 75, award of excellence Concrete Post Tensioning Inst., 1984, Silver Circle award for excellence in teaching U. Ill., Chgo., 1985. Fellow AIA (past bd. dir. Chgo. chpt.); mem. AIA, Labor Zionist Alliance, Am. Profs. for Peace in Middle East, Am. Jewish Congress, Chgo. Archtl. Found., Lambda Alpha. Jewish. Club: Cliff Dwellers.

GORDON, FRAN DILUSTRO, writer; b. Bklyn., 1965; d. Frank Joseph diLustro and Rose Cotilda Gualtieri; m. Richard Haden Gordon IV, 1992. BSChemE, U. Va., 1986; MFA in Creative Writing, Vt. Coll., 1996. bd. govs. Nat. Arts Club, N.Y.C. Author: (novel) Paisley Girl, 1999. Mem. Madre, N.Y.C. Recipient Award for Precocious Youth, Johns Hopkins, Gold medal Nat. Arts Club Can.; Yaddo fellow; fiction scholar Wesleyan U. Writers Conf. Mem. SAG, Nat. Writers Union, Writers Room.

GORDON, FRANK JEFFREY, medical educator; b. Washington, Dec. 5, 1948; married; 2 children. Attended, Case Western Reserve U., 1966-69; BS in Biology, N.Mex. State U., 1972, MA in Psychology, 1974; PhD in Biopsychology, U. Iowa, 1980. Interdisciplinary rsch. fellow U. Iowa, Iowa City, 1978-80, postdoctoral rsch. fellow Dept. Internal Medicine, 1980-81, rsch. scientist, 1981-82; asst. prof. Dept. Pharmacology Emory U. Sch. Medicine, Atlanta, 1982-88, assoc. prof., 1988—; spkr. in field. Editl. bd. Am. Jour. Physiology, 1989-93. Mem. com. on risk factors Iowa Heart Assn., 1982. USPHS pre-doctoral fellow, 1978-80, post-doctoral fellow, 1980-82; rsch. starter grantee Pharm. Mfgs. Assn. Found., 1983-85. Fellow Coun. High Blood Pressure Rsch.; mem. Am. Physiol. Soc., Am. Soc. Pharmacology and Exptl. Therapeutics, Am. Heart Assn. (rsch. investigatorship Ga. affiliate 1987-88, AHA established investigator 1989-94), Soc. Neurosci., Sigma Xi. Achievements include research in brain and spinal cord regulation of peripheral cardiovascular systems in normal and pathological states. Office: Dept Pharmacology Rm 5011 Rollins Rsch Ctr Atlanta GA 30322

GORDON, FREDERICK, marine engineer; b. N.Y.C., Nov. 10, 1956; s. Roy and Ethel G.; m. Claire McKechnie; children: James, William. BS, Webb Inst. Naval Architecture, Glen Cove, N.Y., 1978; MS, Columbia U., 1987. From naval architect to project mgr. Navios Corp., N.Y.C., 1978-86; pres. Heuristics Internat., Cos Cob, Conn., 1986—; project mgr. Sonmez Denizcilik, Istanbul, Turkey, 1990-92; v.p. Energy Transp. Group, N.Y.C., 1993—; pres. ETG Romania, Inc., Del., 1997—; bd. adminstrn. Blacksea LPG Romania, S.A., Bucharest, 1998—. Mem. Soc. Naval Architects & Marine Engrs. Office: Energy Transportation Group Inc 11th Fl 625 Madison Ave New York NY 10022

GORDON, GILBERT, chemist, educator; b. Chgo., Nov. 11, 1933; s. Walter and Catherine Gordon; m. Joyce Elaine Masura; children: Thomas, Lyndi. B.S., Bradley U., 1955; Ph.D., Mich. State U., 1959. Postdoctoral research asso. U. Chgo., 1959-60; asst. prof. U. Md., College Park, 1960-64; asso. prof. U. Md., 1964-67, prof., 1967; prof. chemistry U. Iowa, Iowa City, 1967-73; prof., chmn. dept. Miami U., Oxford, Ohio, 1973-84; Volwiler Disting. Research prof. Miami U., 1984—; Mem. editl. bd. synthesis inorganic metal, organic chemistry; contbr. articles to chem. jours. Editor: catalysis kinetics sect. Chem. Abstracts, 1970—; editorial bd. synthesis inorganic metal, organic chemistry: catalysis kinetics sect. Ohio Jour. Sci, 1971—; contbr. articles to chem. jours. Named Cin. Chemist of Yr., 1981. Mem. Am. Chem. Soc., Chem. Soc. London, Faraday Soc., Sigma Xi, Phi Kappa Phi. Home: 190 Shadowy Hills Dr Oxford OH 45056-1441 Office: Miami U Dept Chemistry Oxford OH 45056 *My objectives have been to investigate meaningful areas of chemistry in an attempt to better understand chemical phenomena affecting our everyday lives (such as better and less expensive ways to purify drinking water), and to work diligently with students while helping to educate them to be better citizens and aware of the exciting potential of science.*

GORDON, GRANVILLE HOLLIS, church official; b. Reayune, Miss., Oct. 12, 1922; s. Thomas and Eugenia (Landrum) G.; m. Miriam C. Culpepper, Sept. 6, 1942; children: Tessa Eileen, Gerald Keith, Cathy Annette, Connie Jean, Donna Lynn. Student, Jacksonville Bapt. Coll. & Sem., 1950-52. Ordained to ministry Bapt. Ch., 1950. Pastor Friendship Bapt. Ch., Jewett, Tex., 1950-51, Little Flock Bapt. Ch., Jewett, 1950-51, Rural Shade Bapt., Kerens, Tex., 1951-52, Ogden Ave. Bapt., Mobile, Ala., 1952-54, Stanton Way Bapt., Mobile, 1954-58, Creston Hills Bapt., Jackson, Miss., 1958-65, 1st Bapt. Shady Grove, Laurel, Miss., 1965-74, Creston Hills Bapt., Jackson, Miss., 1974-84, Rolling Hills Bapt., Jacksonville, Fla., 1984-86, Temple Bapt. Ch., Lucedale, Miss., 1986-89, Highland Pk. Bapt., Hattiesburg, Miss., 1990-96, Shiloh Bapt. Church, Mt. Olive, Miss., 1996-98; Pastor Pear Orchard Bapt. Ch., Jackson, Miss., 1998—. With USAF, ETO. Mem. Miss. Bapt. Assn. (rec. clk. 1961-70), Bapt. Missionary Assn. (rec. clk. 1975-94). Office: Baptist Missionary Assoc of Am 193 Old Campton Dr Jackson MS 39211*

GORDON, HAROLD P., manufacturing executive; b. Montreal, Can., 1937. BA, Sir. George Williams U., 1961; B Civil Law, McGill U., 1964, B Comm, 1958. Atty. Stikeman Elliott, Montreal, Can., 1967-75, ptnr., 1975-95; vice-chmn. Hasbro, Inc., Pawtucket, R.I., 1995—; apptd. Queen's Coun., Montreal, 1985. Bd. dirs. Alliance Comm. Can. Office: Hasbro Inc 1027 Newport Ave Pawtucket RI 02861-2539*

GORDON, HARRISON J., lawyer; b. Newark, Aug. 21, 1950; s. Carl and Rose (Katz) G.; children by previous marriage: Caryn Rachel, Robert Jonathan. BS, U. Bridgeport, 1972; JD, U. Miami, 1975. Bar: N.J. 1976, D.C. 1995, U.S. Dist. Ct. N.J. 1976, U.S. Supreme Ct. 1980. Sole practice West Orange, N.J., 1976-78, Montclair, N.J., 1978-83; ptnr. Gordon & Gordon, West Orange, 1983-87, Gordon, Gordon & Haley, West Orange, 1987-90, Gordon & Gordon, PC, West Orange, 1990—; adj. prof. Montclair State Coll., Upper Montclair, N.J., 1979. Mem. N.J. State Bar Assn. (exec. com. young lawyers div. 1981-83), Assn. Trial Lawyers Am. (chmn. automobile and premises liability sect.), N.J. Trial Lawyers Assn. (bd. govs. 1987-90, sec. 1990-91, treas. 1991-92, 3d v.p. 1992-93, 2d v.p. 1993-94, 1st v.p. 1994-95, pres.-elect 1995—, assoc. editor mag. 1987—, pres. 1996-97), Am. Arbitration Assn. (arbitrator), Soc. Bar and Gavel, Optimists Club (pres. 1981-82), Psi Chi, Phi Alpha Theta. Democrat. Office: Gordon & Gordon PC 80 Main St West Orange NJ 07052-5414

GORDON, HARRY THOMAS, architectural firm executive; b. Albany, N.Y., Apr. 10, 1950. BS, Rensselaer Poly. Inst., 1973, BArch, 1973. Registered architect, Pa.; cert. NCARB. Gen. mgr. energy divsn. Burt Hill Kosar Rittelmann Assocs., Butler, Pa., 1977-80; gen. mgr. Washington office Burt Hill Kosar Rittelmann Assocs., Washington, 1980-81, prin. in charge Washington office, 1982—; cons. U.S. Depts. Energy, Def., HUD, Agr., GSA, Nat. Bur. Stds., N.E. Solar Energy Ctr. Author: Solar Energy Systems Design Handbook, 1978; prin. author: Commercial Building Design-Integrating Climate, Comfort and Cost, 1987; contbg. author: Retrofitting of Commercial, Institutional and Industrial Buildings for Energy Conservation, 1984, Advances in Solar Energy, Vol. 3, 1986, The Changing Office Workplace, 1986; cons. editor energy sect. AIA Archtl. Graphic Standards, 8th edit.; contbr. articles to profl. jours., papers to profl. confs. Mem. AIA (founding mem., chmn. com. on environment, Coll. Fellows), Am. Solar Energy Soc., Potomac Region Solar Energy Assn. (founder), U.S. Green Bldg. Coun. Office: Burt Hill Kosar Rittelmann Assoc 1056 Thomas Jefferson St NW Washington DC 20007-3813

GORDON, HELEN HEIGHTSMAN, English language educator, writer, publisher; b. Salt Lake City, Sept. 7, 1932; d. Fred C. and Florence Isabel Heightsman; m. Norman C. Winn, Aug. 10, 1950 (div. Sept. 1972); children: Bruce Vernon Winn, Brent Terry Winn, Holly Winn Willner; m. Clifton Beverly Gordon, Feb. 17, 1974. Student, U. Utah, 1959-62; BA in English and Edn., Calif. State U., Sacramento, 1964, MA in English, 1967; EdD, Nova U., 1979. Cert. tchr., Calif.; lic. counselor, Calif. Stenographer, payroll clk. Associated Food Stores, Inc., Salt Lake City, 1951-59; part-time instr. in remedial English U. Utah, Salt Lake City, 1960-61; tchr. high sch. Rio Americano High Sch., Sacramento, 1965-66; assoc. prof., counselor Porterville (Calif.) Coll., 1967-74; prof., counselor Bakersfield (Calif.) Coll., 1974-95; chair lang. arts divsn. Porterville Coll., 1971-74; coord. women's studies Bakersfield Coll., 1977-78, adminstrv. intern, 1982-83; dir. region V, English Coun. of Calif. Two Yr. Colls., 1990-92; articulation coord. Bakersfield Coll., 1992-93; pres., pub. Anacade Internat. Ednl. Books and Games, 1998—. Author: (textbook) From Copying to Creating, 2d edit., 1983, Developing College Writing, 1989, Wordforms, Book I & II, 2d edit., 1990, Interplay: Sentence Skills in Context, 1991, (novel) Voice of the Vanquished: The Story of the Slave Marina and Hernan Cortes, 1995 (memoirs) First Captured, Last Freed: Memoirs of a P.O.W. in World War II Guam and Japan, 1995; pub.: (game) Anagrabber, the Word Game for All Ages, 1998 (poetry book) Life, Love and Laughter, 1998. Founder, 1st pres. Writers of Kern, Bakersfield, 1993; guest mem. editl. bd. Bakersfield Californian Newspaper, 1988; past pres. Unitarian Fellowship of Kern County, Bakersfield, 1976-78. Calif. Fund for Instruction grantee, 1978; U. Utah scholar, 1959-62. Mem. NEA, AAUW (pres. Santa Barbara chpt. 1997-98), Am. Assn. Women in Cmty. and Jr. Colls. (founder Bakersfield chpt., pres., program chair 1988-91), Nat. Coun. Tchrs. of English, Faculty Assn. Calif. Cmty.

Coll., Text and Acad. Authors Assn. (charter, columnist Acad. Author 1996—), LWV (pres. Bakersfield chpt. 1981-83, 89-90), Calif. Writers Club, Pi Lambda Theta. Democrat. Avocations: poetry, personal computer, travel, bowling, theatre. Home: 3775 Modoc Rd Apt 135 Santa Barbara CA 93105-4462

GORDON, HOWARD LYON, advertising and marketing executive; b. Chgo., Oct. 8, 1930; s. Milton Arthur and Bess Z. (Ginsburg) G.; BS, U. Ill., 1953; MS, Northwestern U., 1954, MBA, 1962; m. Lois Jean Kaufman, Aug. 21, 1955; children: Carolyn Ann, Leslie Meredith. Mktg. rsch. mgr. Marsteller Inc., advt., Chgo., 1960-68, v.p. mktg. services Marsteller Inc. and Burson Marsteller, Chgo., 1968-76; dir. client service Britt and Frerichs Inc., mktg. research and advt. cons., Chgo., 1977-78, sr. v.p., 1978—, prin., 1979—, ptnr., 1986—; lectr. advt. and mktg. Northwestern U., 1963—, vis. prof. Medill grad. studies in advt., 1981—; advt. prof. in residence No. Ill. U., DeKalb, 1974-76; lectr., seminar leader Am. Mgmt. Assn., 1965-72; bd. dirs. Bus. Advt. Rsch. Coun., 1985—, chmn. life style rsch. com. Advt. Rsch. Found., 1991—; bd. dirs. Advt. Rsch. Found., Media Comm. Coun.; mem. alumni awards com. Medill Sch. Northwestern U., 1986, fund-raising com. Kellogg Grad. Sch. Northwestern U., 1986—; presenter 17th World Advt. Congress, Amsterdam, 1992; mem. publs. bd. U. Ill., 1997—. Co-author: Marketing Manager's Handbook, 3d edit., 1994; contbr. articles to profl. publs. Regional chmn. Crusade of Mercy, Evanston, Ill., 1969; founding dir. Alumni Assn. Medill Sch., 1984—; adv. council athletic dept., Northwestern U., 1985—. With AUS, 1954-56. Recipient award Dept. Def., 1956, Alumni Award Northwestern U., 1989. Mem. Am. Mktg. Assn. (dir., v.p. mktg. mgmt.), Northwestern U. Faculty, Kellogg Alumni Assn. (program com., exec. bd. dirs.), Direct Mktg. Assn., Assn. Consumer Rsch., Sigma Delta Chi. Contbr. articles to profl. publs. and mktg. texts. Office: 400 E Randolph Dr Chicago IL 60601-7329

GORDON, INGRID THORNGREN, gerontology, home health nurse; b. Salem, Mass., Mar. 8, 1954; d. Richard Henry and Martha O. (Gale) Thorngren; m. Paul C. Gordon, Oct. 4, 1980. BS cum laude in Psychology, Tufts U., 1975; AS in Nursing, Catherine Laboure Jr. Coll., 1978. Cert. gerontol. nurse; cert. community health nurse. DON SRT Med.-Staff Internat., Milw.; supr. Michael J. Neville Manor, Cambridge, Mass.; home care coord. Kimberly Quality Care, Boston; DON Med-Care Nursing Svc., Inc., Portland, Oreg.; primary case nurse HomeCare Southwest, Vancouver, Wash. Mem. ANA, Wash. Nurses Assn. E-mail: mapickle@teleport.com. Home: 6239 SW 40th Ave Portland OR 97221-3321 Office: HomeCare Southwest PO Box 2369 Vancouver WA 98668-2369

GORDON, IRENE MARLOW, radiology educator; b. White County, Tenn., May 21, 1943; d. Paul Terah and Mary Eva (Holloway) Marlow; m. Shigern Chino, July 14, 1969 (div.); children: Hatsuyo Mary Chino, Kazumi Elaine Chino, Junzo Paul Chino, Hazuki Carol Chino, Fumiko Catherine Chino; m. James Robert Gordon, Sept. 6, 1979. BS, U. Dayton, 1966; MD, Ohio State U., 1970, MS, 1974. Intern in medicine and pediat. St. Lukes Hosp., San Francisco, 1970-71; resident in gen. radiology Ohio State U. Hosp., 1971-74; fellow in radiation and oncology U. Calif., Irvine, Irivne; clin. instr. dept. radiology Ohio State U., Columbus, 1971-74; asst. clin. prof. divsn. radiation therapy U. Calif., Irvine, 1976-78, acting chief divsn. radiation therapy, 1976-77; asst. clin. prof. divsn. radiation therapy Harbor-UCLA Med. Ctr., L.A., 1981-82; clin. asst. prof. radiology, radiation oncology Ind. U. Med. Ctr., Indpls., 1992-95; bd. dirs. Health Talents Internat., Sentinel Med. Rev. Orgn., sec., 1985-89, Hoosier Oncology Group, mem. exec. com., 1993-96; mem. staff St. Joseph & Children's Hosp., Orange, Calif., 1974-82, Long Beach Meml. Med. Ctr., 1979-82; dir. radiation oncology St. Elizabeth Hosp. and Med. Ctr. Regional Treatment Ctr., Lafayette, Ind., 1982—. Translator for deaf Ouabache Ch. of Christ, Lafayette, 1993—; bd. dirs. Tippecanoe County chpt. ARC, 1992—. Mem. AMA, Am. Coll. Radiology (cert.), Am. Soc. Therapeutic Radiology and Oncology, Radiology Soc. N.Am., Am. Endocurie Soc., Am. Coll. Radiation Oncology, Am. Soc. Clin. Oncology, Tippecanoe County Med. Assn. (pres. 1994), Ind. 9th Dist. Med. Assn. (pres. 1994). Avocations: collecting Japanese dolls, coins, stamps. Office: Regional Treatment Ctr 1116 N 16th St Lafayette IN 47904-2119*

GORDON, JACK DAVID, senator, foundation executive; b. Detroit, June 3, 1922; s. A. Louis and Henrietta (Rodgers) G.; m. Myra L. MacPherson; children from previous marriage: Andrew Louis, Deborah Mary Jonathan Henry; stepchildren: Leah Siegel, Michael Siegel. BA, U. Mich., 1942. Engaged in real estate and ins. businesses Miami Beach, Fla., 1946-52; founding dir., pres., chief mng. officer Washington Savs. & Loan Assn., Miami Beach, 1952-80; vice chmn. bd. Washington Savs. & Loan Assn., 1980-81; founding dir. Jefferson Nat. Bank of Miami Beach, 1962-77, past chmn. exec. com.; dir. Inst. Pub. Policy and Citizenship Studies Fla. Internat. U.; pres. The Hospice Found. of Am., Miami; mem. Fla. Senate, 1972-92; housing fin. cons. Dept. State and; expert cons. UN Tech. Assistance Program in Costa Rica, Nicaragua, Panama, Ethiopia, Somali Republic, Nigeria, 1959-63; cons. to ROCAP, 1962-64, Eastern Nigerian Housing Corp., 1963; contract supr. AID Housing Guaranty Program in Latin Am., 1966-69; chmn. Miami Beach Housing Authority. 1947-56. Author: (with others) A Survey of New Home Financing Institutions in Latin America, 1969. Mem. Dade County Bd. Pub. Instrn., 1961-68. Served with AUS, 1943-46. Mem. Am. Jewish Congress, Am. Friends of Hebrew U., ACLU. Democrat. Office: 777 17th St Ste 401 Miami Beach FL 33139-1854

GORDON, JAMES POWER, optics scientist; b. N.Y.C., Mar. 20, 1928. BS, MIT, 1949; MA, Columbia U., 1951, PhD in Physics, 1955. Asst. physics dept. Columbia U., 1953-55; mem. tech. staff electronics rsch. AT&T Bell Labs., Holmdel, N.J., 1955-59; head quantum electronics rsch. dept. AT&T Bell Labs., Murray Hill, N.J., 1959-80; sr. tech. staff cons. Lucent Technologies, Murray Hill, N.J., 1980—. Recipient Max Born award, 1991, Optical Soc. Am. Fellow Am. Phys. Soc., Optical Soc.; mem. IEEE (sr.), Nat. Acad. Engring., Nat. Acad. Scis. Achievements include demonstration of lot MASER, research in quantum electronics, interaction of electromagnetic waves with matter and soliton theory, communication theory. Office: Lucent Bell Labs Crawfords Corner Rd Holmdel NJ 07733

GORDON, JAMES S., lawyer; b. N.Y.C., Feb. 15, 1941; s. George S. and Sylvia A. (Wolfson) G.; m. Marcia G. Gordon, Dec. 22, 1968 (dec.); children: Daniel, Sarah; m. Debbie S. Pase, June 15, 1996. BA with high honors, U. Fla., 1962; LLB, Yale U., 1965. Bar: Ill. 1965, Fla. 1966, U.S. Supreme Ct. 1974. Asst. prof. Ind. U. Sch. Law, Bloomington, 1967-68, assoc. prof., 1969; ptnr. Feiwell, Galper & Gordon, Chgo., 1970-72; sole practice Chgo., 1972-80; pres. James S. Gordon, Ltd., Chgo., 1981-93; chmn. Gordon, Glickman, Flesch & Woody, 1994—. Editor Yale Law Jour., 1963-65; contbr. articles to profl. jours. Mem. Winnetka Caucus, 1981-82. Ford Found. grantee, 1965-66. Mem. Chgo. Bar Assn., Yale U. Law Alumni Assn. (exec. com. 1987-94), Order of Coif, Phi Beta Kappa, Phi Alpha Delta, Legal Club, Birchwood Club (Highland Park, Ill.). Office: 140 S Dearborn St Ste 404 Chicago IL 60603-5202

GORDON, JAMES SAMUEL, psychiatrist; b. N.Y.C., Oct. 12, 1941; s. Jules David and Cynthia (Hymanson) G. AB magna cum laude, Harvard U., 1962, MD, 1967. Diplomate Am. Bd. Psychiatry and Neurology. Tchg. fellow gen. edn. Harvard U., Cambridge, Mass., 1963-67; NIH rsch. fellow, tchg. asst. dept. pathology Cornell Med. Coll., N.Y.C., 1964-65; intern Mt. Zion Hosp., San Francisco, 1967-68; resident in psychiatry Albert Einstein Coll. Medicine, Bronx, N.Y., 1968-70, chief resident, clin. instr. psychiatry, 1970-71; research psychiatrist NIMH, Rockville, Md., 1971-82, cons. alternative forms of svc., 1974-82, dir. spl. study Pres.'s Commn. Mental Health, 1977-78; chief adolescent svcs. St. Elizabeth's Hosp., Washington, 1980-82; clin. prof. Georgetown U. Med. Sch., Washington, 1980—; dir. Ctr. for Mind-Body Medicine, Washington, 1991—; chair program adv. coun. Office of Alternative Medicine NIH, 1994-97; dir. Ctr. for Mind-Body Medicine, Washington; sr. cons. L.Am. Youth Ctr., Washington, 1984—; mem. cancer adv. panel NIH, 1998—; vis. scholar Aurora Assocs., Washington, 1982-84; rsch. psychiatrist divsn. spl. mental health programs NIMH, 1980-82; med. cons. wellness program Walter Reed Army Med. Ctr., Washington, 1980-82; sr. cons. on adolescence divsn. child and adolescent svcs. St. Elizabeth's Hosp., Washington, 1979-80; Blanche Ittleson cons. Group for Advancement of Psychiatry, 1979; dir. spl. study on alternative svcs. Pres.' Commn. on Mental Health, 1977-78; vis. lectr. Cmty. Therapy Tng. Ctr., Washington, 1975, Cath. U. Am., Washington, 1974; lectr. in field. Author: The Golden Guru, 1987, Holistic Medicine, 1988, Transforming Medicine, 1996, Manifesto for a New Medicine, 1996; editor: Health for the Whole Person (Med. Self Care Book award 1980), Mind, Body and Health: Towards and Integral Medicine, 1984; contbr. articles to profl. jours. Commdr. USPHS, 1971-82. Recipient award Ford Found., 1982. Fellow Am. Assn. Social Psychiatry; mem. Am. Psychiat. Assn., Am. Holistic Med. Assn. (founding mem. 1980, trustee 1980-86), Am. Assn. Med. Acupuncture (founding mem. 1987), Physicians for Social Responsibility (exec. com. 1984-86). Office: Ste 414 5225 Connecticut Ave NW Washington DC 20015-1845

GORDON, JAY F(ISHER), lawyer; b. N.Y.C., Feb. 5, 1926; s. Harry Schuyler and Sylvia (Fisher) G.; m. Eleanor T. Gordon, Sept. 8, 1946 (dec. Mar. 1988); children: Patricia (dec.), Amy, Irving, Cindy; m. Barbara Brooks Bell, Nov. 20, 1988. Student, City Coll., N.Y.C., 1941-43, Cornell U., 1943-44; JD, St. Johns U., 1948. Bar: N.Y. 1949, U.S. Dist. Ct. (so. dist.) N.Y. 1949, U.S. Ct. Appeals (2d cir.) 1954, U.S. Dist. Ct. (no. dist.) N.Y. 1956, U.S. Dist. Ct. (ea. dist.) N.Y. 1963, U.S. Supreme Ct. 1965, U.S. Ct. Appeals (D.C. cir.) 1977, U.S. Dist. Ct. (ea. dist.) Mich. 1984, U.S. Ct. Appeals (3d and 5th cirs.) 1986. From assoc. to ptnr. Harte & Natanson, N.Y.C., 1949-54; ptnr. Natanson, Gordon & Reich, N.Y.C., 1954-68, Gordon, Goldman, Cooperman & Buchalter, Hempstead, N.Y., 1969-71; ptnr. Phillips, Nizer, Benjamin, Krim & Ballon, N.Y.C., 1972-95, of counsel, 1996—. Mem. Bd. Bldg. Design, 1961-63, bd. trustees, 1964-66; mayor Village of Lawrence (N.Y.), 1966-69. With U.S. Army and USN, 1943-46. Mem. Nassau County Bar Assn., The Woodmere Club. Avocation: golf. Home: 285 Central Ave Apt A5 Lawrence NY 11559-1574 Office: Phillips Nizer Benjamin 600 Old Country Rd Garden City NY 11530-2001

GORDON, JEFF, race car driver; b. Pittsboro, Ind., Aug. 4, 1971; m. Brooke Sealy. Stock race car driver DuPont Chevrolet, 1993—; Season highlights: winner NASCAR Winston Cup, 1994, 1997, winner Busch Clash, 1994, finished fourth Daytona 500, 1994, winner Winston Select Open, won the pole for Coca-Cola 600, 1994, winner Brickyard 400, 1994, winner Goodwrench 500, 1995, winner Purolator 500, 1995, winner Food City 500, 1995, winner Pepsi 400, 1995, winner Slick 50 300, 1995, winner Mountain Dew Southern 500, 1995, winner MBNA 500, 1995, winner Daytona 500, 1997, others. Winner Daytona 500, 1999; named to McDonald's All-star team, 1994, 95; 1993 Maxx Race Cards Rookie of the Yr., 2d youngest Winston Cup Champion NASCAR ever at age 24. E-mail: JGFAN@Primenet.com. Office: NASCAR PO Box 2875 Daytona Beach FL 32120-2875 Office: Jeff Gordon Nat. Fan Club 514 E Route 66 Williams AZ 86046-2704*

GORDON, JERRY ARTHUR, retired family services organization administrator; b. Rochester, N.Y., Apr. 27, 1939; s. Philip R. and Grace (Itkin) G.; m. Susan G. Gerring, July 11, 1940; children: Julie, Lili. BS, Ithaca Coll., 1962; MS, Syracuse U., 1966; EdD, U. Buffalo, 1979. Film editor WOKR-TV, Rochester, N.Y., 1962-63; tchr. Wayne Ctrl. Sch., Walworth, N.Y., 1963-65; dir. Westhill Ctrl. Sch., Syracuse, N.Y., 1965-66; instr. Fredonia (N.Y.) State Coll., 1966-69; assoc. prof. Alfred (N.Y.) State Coll., 1969-82; dir. U. Calif. Media Resources, Riverside, 1982-95; exec. dir. Jewish Family Svcs., Riverside, 1996-97; cons. radio, telecom. and tech. Riverside, 1995-98. Mem. Dirs. of Ednl. Tech., Calif. Higher Edn. (pres. 1987-88), Riverside Agy. Exec. Assn. Avocations: gardening, travel. Home: 375 Two Trees Rd Riverside CA 92507-3225

GORDON, JOAN IRMA, lawyer; b. N.Y.C., Nov. 1, 1945; d. Morris and Dora (Mittman) G. BA in Polit. Sci., Vassar Coll., 1967; MA in Polit. Sci., Brown U., 1969; JD, Am. U., 1974. Bar: Md. 1974, D.C. 1975, U.S. Dist. Ct. Md., 1976, U.S. Supreme Ct. 1978, N.Y. 1981. Intern N.Y. State Pub. Adminstrn., Albany, 1969-70; adminstrv. asst. to asst. commr. N.Y. State Health Dept., Albany, 1970-71; staff counsel Washington Suburban San. Commn., Hyattsville, Md., 1975-80; legal counsel and govt. affairs officer Montgomery C.C., Rockville, Md., 1980-84, gen. counsel, 1984—; rsch. cons. Inst. Studies in Justice and Soc. Behavior, Am. U. Law Sch., Washington, 1974. Contbr. Maryland Criminal Jury Instructions and Commentary, 1975. Mem. prospective students com. Vassar Coll., Washington, 1975-83; vice-chmn. precinct Dem. Com. Montgomery County, 1976-82, Montgomery County coun. Task Force on Problems of Homeowners Assn., Condominiums and Cooperatives, 1989; mem. archtl control com. Redland Crossing Homeowners Assn., Derwood, Md., 1982-84, bd. dirs., 1984-88, pres. bd. dirs. 1986-87, v.p. 1987-88; mem. Montgomery County Commn. on Common Ownership Communities, 1992-95. Recipient Am. Jurisprudence award, 1972, 73. Mem. ABA, Am. Corp. Counsel Assocs., Nat. Assn. Coll. and Univ. Attys. (chair continuing legal edn. com. 1989-91, bd. dirs. 1987-90), Md. Bar Assn., N.Y. State Bar Assn., Montgomery County Bar Assn. Jewish. Home: 15909 Yukon Ln Rockville MD 20855-2632 Office: Montgomery CC 900 Hungerford Dr Rockville MD 20850-1740

GORDON, JOHN CHARLES, forestry educator; b. Nampa, Idaho, June 10, 1939; s. John Nicholas and Ada Elizabeth (Scheuermann) G.; m. Helka Lehtinen, Aug. 6, 1964; 1 child, Sean Nicholas. BS, Iowa State U., Ames, 1961, PhD, 1966; postgrad., U. Helsinki, Finland, 1961-62; MA (hon.), Yale U., New Haven, 1984. Instr. forestry Iowa State U., Ames, 1965-66; plant physiologist U.S. Forest Service, Rhinelander, Wis., 1966-70; prof. forestry Iowa State U., Ames, 1970-77; prof., head dept. forestry Oreg. State U., Corvallis, 1977-83; prof., dean forestry and environ. studies Yale U., New Haven, 1983-92, 97-98, Pinchot prof. forestry and environ. studies, 1991—, acting dir. Inst. for Biospheric Studies, 1994-95, 96; founding ptnr. Interforest LLC, 1996—; chmn. Commn. on rsch. and Resources Mgmt. in Nat. Parks, 1988-89; chmn. com. on forestry rsch. NAS, 1989—; lectr. Syracuse U., 1990, Oreg. State U., 1993, U. Fla., 1994, U. Mont., 1998. Editor: Symbiotic Nitrogen Fixation, 1983; author (books) Agroforestry Research, 1991, Environmental Leadership, 1993; contbr. articles to profl. jours. Bd. dirs. Friends of Gray Towers, Milford, Pa., 1983-87, Yale U. Alumni Fund, 1985-92, Tropical Forest Found., 1991-94, Wintock Internat., 1993-95; vis. com. Harvard U., 1985-92; pres. C.V. Riley Found., N.Y.C., 1985, 92-94, Conn. Fund for Environ., 1986-92; mem. rsch. adv. com. U.S. AID, 1988-92; co-chmn. 7th Am. Forest Congress, 1994-97. Fulbright scholar, 1961, 84; hon. sr. fellow U. Glasgow, Scotland, 1975-76; Green vis. prof. U. B.C., Vancouver, 1985; named Conservationist of the Yr., Pacific Rivers Coun., 1992; fellow Timothy Dwight Coll., Yale U.; disting. svc. award Am. Forests, 1996. Mem. SAAS, Soc. Am. Foresters, Am. Forestry Assn. (Disting. Svc. award 1996), Sigma Xi (hon.), Phi Kappa Phi (hon.). Presbyterian. Clubs: Yale (N.Y.C.), Morys (New Haven), Cosmos (Washington). Avocations: hiking; fishing; writing short stories. Home: RR 3 Box 129A Plymouth NH 03264-9123 Office: Yale U Sch Forestry 360 Prospect St New Haven CT 06511-2104

GORDON, JOHN L., JR., historian, educator; b. Elizabethtown, Ky., July 14, 1942; s. John L. and Rose (Kemph) G.; m. Susan L. Cooper, Sept. 1963; 1 child, Sarah Elizabeth. AB History and Mathematics, Western Ky. U., 1963; MA, Vanderbilt U., 1965, PhD, 1972. From instr. to assoc. prof. history U. Richmond, Va., 1967-90, prof. history, 1990—, interim v.p., provost, 1983, interim dean faculty arts and scis., 1981-82, assoc. dean faculty arts and scis., 1980-87, dean grad. studies, 1980-87, chair dept. history, 1989—; spkr. in field; rschr. in field, England, Ireland, Can. contbr. numerous articles to profl. jours. Grantee Can. Studies Faculty Enrichment Program, 1987; Duke Alberta Rsch. fellow, 1984; faculty summer rsch. fellow, grantee U. Richmond, 1977, 88, 95. Mem. Am. Hist. Assn., Assn. Can. Studies in U.S., Can. Hist. Assn., Carolinas Symposium Brit. Studies, N.Am. Conf. Brit. Studies, S.E. Coun. Can. Studies (exec. com., pres. 1993-96), So. Conf. Brit. Studies (exec. coun., program chair 1993, 94), So. Hist. Assn., Omicron Delta Kappa, Phi Alpha Theta. Home: 4 Bostwick Ln Richmond VA 23226-3107 Office: U Richmond Ryland Hall Richmond VA 23173

GORDON, JONATHAN DAVID, psychologist, lawyer; b. Watertown, N.Y., Nov. 5, 1949; s. Morton Lawrence and Anna (Lesser) G.; m. Doris Susan Perkel, Jan. 16, 1972 (div.); 1 child, Pamela Michelle; m. Janet S. Levick, Nov. 25, 1984; children: Lisa Danielle, Sharon Rachelle, Jaclyn Gabrielle. BA, Fairleigh Dickinson U., 1971, MA, 1973; PhD, Hofstra U., 1976; JD, Fordham U., 1998. Diplomate Child Custody Evaluation Am. Coll. Forensic Examiners, Am. Bd. Med. Psychotherapists, Internat. Acad. Behavioral Medicine, Am. Acad. Pain Mgmt., Nat. Registry Neurofeedback Providers. Team supr., psychologist dept. ambulatory care Mt. Sinai Med. Ctr., N.Y.C., 1976-80; pvt. practice clin. psychology Teaneck, N.J., 1978-97; chief psychologist, coord. profl. svcs. Holley Child Care and Devel. Ctr. Youth Consultation Svc., Hackensack, N.J., 1980-85; staff psychologist div. psychol. svcs. Fairleigh Dickinson U., Hackensack, 1982-85, acting dir., 1989; dir. adult outpatient psychiatry Jersey City Med. Ctr., 1985-87; dir. Bergen Biofeedback and Psychotherapy Ctr., Teaneck, 1986—; dep. atty. gen. N.J. Div. Law, Newark, 1999—; sch. cons. Leonia (N.J.) High Sch., 1987-88. Mem. ABA, ATLA, APA, N.Y. State Bar Assn., N.J. Bar Assn., N.J. Psychol. Assn., N.Y. State Psychol. Assn., Bergen County Assn. Lic. Psychologists, Assn. Applied Psychophysiology and Biofeedback, Biofeedback Cert. Inst. Am. (cert.), Perineometer Rsch. Inst. (cert.). Office: PO Box 480 124 Halsey St PO Box 45029 Newark NJ 07101

GORDON, JOSEPH ELWELL, university official, educator; b. Deatsville, Ala., July 2, 1921; s. Joseph Elwell and Martha (Berry) G.; m. Doris Elizabeth Smith, June 5, 1948; children—Cecile Lizabeth, Joseph Elwell, Melissa Innes. AB, Birmingham-So. Coll., 1942; MS, Auburn U., 1949; PhD, U. Chgo., 1951. Tchr. math. Montgomery, Ala., 1946-48; instr. math. Auburn U., 1948-49; research asst. North Central Assn. Colls. and Secondary Schs., Chgo., 1949-51; program analyst Air U., Maxwell AFB, 1951-54; mem. faculty Tulane U., 1954—, asst. prof. edn., 1958—, assoc. dean admissions, 1957-63, dean Coll. Arts and Scis., 1964-84, dir. found. rels., 1984-86, spl. asst. to v.p. devel., 1986-90, univ. historian, 1990-96, vice provost, 1996-97. Served to lt. USNR, 1942-46. Mem. Omicron Delta Kappa, Phi Delta Kappa, Pi Kappa Alpha. Democrat. Presbyterian. Home: 1108 Lowerline St New Orleans LA 70118-5205

GORDON, JOSEPH HAROLD, lawyer; b. Tacoma, Mar. 31, 1909; s. Joseph H. and Mary (Obermiller) G.; m. Jane Wilson, Sept. 12, 1936 (dec.); children: Joseph H., Nancy Jane; m. Eileen (Rylander) Rademaker, Jan. 7, 1967. BA, Stanford, 1931; LLB, U. Wash., 1935, JD, 1935. Bar: Wash. 1935. Since practiced in Tacoma; ptnr. Gordon & Gordon, Tacoma, 1935-50, Henderson, Carnahan, Thompson & Gordon, Tacoma, 1950-57, Carnahan, Gordon & Goodwin, Tacoma, 1957-70, Gordon, Thomas, Honeywell, Malanca, Peterson & Daheim, Tacoma, 1970—. Mem. ABA (ho. dels., bd. govs. 1962-72, treas. 1965-72), Wash. State Bar Assn., Tacoma Bar Assn. (past pres.). Presbyn. (elder). Clubs: Rotary, Tacoma, Tacoma Golf and Country. Home: 2819 N Junett St Tacoma WA 98407-6345 Office: Gordon Thomas et al PO Box 1157 2200 Wells Fargo Plz Tacoma WA 98401-1157

GORDON, JUDITH, communications consultant, writer; b. Long Beach, Calif.; d. Irwin Ernest and Susan (Perlman) G.; m. Lawrence Banka, May 1, 1977. BA, Oakland U., 1966; MS in Libr. Sci., Wayne State U., 1973. Researcher Detroit Inst. of Arts, 1968-69; libr. Detroit Pub. Libr., 1971-74; caseworker Wayne County Dept. Social Svcs., Detroit, 1974-77; advt. copywriter Hudson's Dept. Store, Detroit, 1979; mgr. The Poster Gallery, Detroit, 1980-81; mktg., corp. communications specialist Bank of Am., San Francisco, 1983-84; mgr., consumer pubs. Bank of Am., 1984-86; prin. ACTIVE VOICE, San Francisco, 1986—. *Judith Gordon brings a singular combination of capabilities to ACTIVE VOICE, a company she founded in 1986. Since then, she has provided editorial, project management, consulting, and marketing services to diverse clients nationwide. Gordon is the former manager of consumer publications at Bank of America where she directed an award-winning publications program within strict time and cost constraints. Among the publications were the bank's account disclosures, considered models of plain language. The name of Gordon's company reflects its key focus: to communicate clearly and compellingly to specialists and laypersons alike. Her company's primary emphasis is financial services collateral, consumer information/education materials, and customer documents that satisfy legal, compliance, and marketing objectives. For these efforts, Gordon has received frequent recognition.* Contbr. edit. The Artist's Mag., 1988-93; contbr. to book Flowers: Gary Bukovnik, Watercolors and Monotypes, Abrams, 1990. Vol. From the Heart, San Francisco, 1992, Bay Area Book Festival, San Francisco, 1990, 91, Aid & Comfort, San Francisco, 1987, Save Orch. Hall, Detroit, 1977-81, NOW sponsored abortion clinic project. Recipient Nat. award Merit. Soc. Consumer Affairs Profls. in Bus., 1986, Bay Area Best award Internat. Assn. Bus. Communicators, 1986, Internat. Galaxy awards, 1992, 95, 97, Internat. Mercury awards, 1995. Mem. AAUW, Internat. Assn. Bus. Communicators, Nat. Writers Union, Freelance Editl. Assn., Clarity, Achenbach Graphics Arts Coun., Women's Nat. Book Assn., Assn. for Women in Comms., FIMA West (bd. dirs.), ZYZZYVA (bd. dirs., v.p.). Office: 899 Green St San Francisco CA 94133-3756

GORDON, JULIE PEYTON, foundation administrator; b. Jacksonville, Fla., June 21, 1940; d. Robert Benoist Shields and Bessie (Cavanaugh) Peyton; m. Robert James Gordon, June 22, 1963. BA, Boston U., 1963; MA, Harvard U., 1965, PhD, 1969. Asst. prof. English Ill. Inst. Tech., Chgo., 1968-75, assoc. prof., 1975-77, asst. dean students, 1975-78; asst. dean acad. affairs Northwestern U., Evanston, Ill., 1978-80, lectr. English, Univ. Coll., 1978—, assoc. dean Univ. Coll., 1980-85, sec. Econometric Soc., 1975—, exec. dir. Econometric Soc., 1985—; mem. nat. adv. com. ALA, Chgo., 1983-86. Author: Seasons in the Contemporary American Family, 1984. Grantee NEH, 1971-73; project scholar NEH, 1983-86. Mem. Phi Beta Kappa. Avocation: writing fiction and poetry. Home: 202 Greenwood Evanston IL 60201-4714 Office: Northwestern U Dept Econs Econometric Soc Evanston IL 60208-2600

GORDON, KENNETH ANTONY, publisher; b. Lewes, Sussex, Eng., June 28, 1937; s. Colin Fraser Gordon and Sidney Eileen (Short) Walker; m. Valerie Anne McMullen, June 7, 1937; children: Una Elizabeth, Jane Alice, Sarah Anne, Colin Patrick. Asst. product mgr. Reader's Digest Assn. of Can., Montreal, 1960-65, mgr. music div., 1965-69; subscription sales mgr. Reader's Digest, Pleasantville, N.Y., 1969-72; v.p., mktg. dir. Nat. Sales Incentives, Toronto, Ont., 1972-73; v.p., gen. mgr. Nat. Sales Incentives, N.Y.C., 1973-74; internat. circulation dir. Reader's Digest, Pleasantville, 1974-78, internat. sales dir., 1978-81, mktg. dir. books and music div., 1981-83, v.p., dir. books and music div., 1983-85, publisher, 1985-97; bd. dirs. Compucard Internat., Stamford, Conn., Reader's Digest of Finland, Italy, Switzerland, and Portugal. Bd. dirs. Operation Enterprise, Hamilton, N.Y., 1986—; bd. dirs. Madison Sq. Boys Club, N.Y.C., 1986—; trustee Leukemia Assn. of Westchester, White Plains, N.Y., 1986—; bd. dirs. Wallace Funds, N.Y.C., 1987—. Mem. Mag. Pubs. Assn. (bd. dirs., exec. com.), Am. Mgmt. Assn., Direct Mail Assn. Republican. Episcopalian. Club: Sky, Manhattan Rugby (N.Y.C.); Wanderers Rugby (Montreal) (capt. 1962-64, pres. 1967-69). Avocations: sailing, skiing, theater. *

GORDON, KEVIN DELL, lawyer; b. Oklahoma City, June 23, 1958; s. James Dell and Mary Lurana (Tracewell) G.; m. Janice Linn Mathews, Aug. 4, 1979; children: Tracewell, Elise. BA cum laude, Westminster Coll., 1981; JD, Washington U., 1984. Bar: Okla. 1984, U.S. Dist. Ct. (we., no. and ea. dists.) Okla. 1984, U.S. Ct. Appeals (10th cir.) 1985, U.S. Supreme Ct. Shareholder, dir. Crowe & Dunlevy, Oklahoma City, 1984—; adj. prof. health law U. Okla. Law Sch., 1997—. Editor Washington U. Law Quarterly, 1982-84. Trustee, past pres. Youth Svcs. Oklahoma County, 1986—; chair adv. com. Okla. Assn. Youth Svcs., 1994-98. Mem. ABA (ins. coverage com. 1990—), Okla. Bar Assn. (uniform laws com. 1994—, membership com. 1999—, coord./moderator ann. ins. law update 1999—), Assn. Trial Lawyers Am., Am. Health Lawyers Assn., Oklahoma County Bar Assn. (legal aid com. 1990-98, comty. svc. com. 1997—), Ruth Bader Ginsberg Am. Inn of Ct. (chair mentoring com. 1996-99, chair membership com. 1999—, Master of Yr. 1998), Order of Coif. Avocations: sports, gardening, guitar, reading. Home: 8309 Glenwood Ave Oklahoma City OK 73114-1111 Office: Crowe & Dunlevy Suite 1800 20 N Broadway Ave Ste 1800 Oklahoma City OK 73102-8273

GORDON, LARRY JEAN, public health administrator and educator; b. Tipton, Okla., Oct. 16, 1926; s. Andrew J. and Deweylee (Stewart) G.; m. Nedra Callender, Aug. 26. 1950; children: Debra Gordon Dunlap, Kent, Gary. Student, U. Okla., 1943-44; BS, U. N.Mex., 1949, MS, 1951; MPH, U. Mich., 1954. High sch. sci. tchr. N.Mex., 1949-50; various positions N.Mex. Dept. Health, 1950-55; commd. officer USPHS, 1957—, advanced through grades to Dir. Grade (Navy capt.), dir. Albuquerque Environ. Health Dept., 1955-68, 82-86; dir. Environ. Improvement Agy., Santa Fe, 1968-73; adminstr. for health and environ. programs N.Mex. HHS Dept.,

Santa Fe, 1976-78; dir. N.Mex. Sci. Lab. System, Albuquerque, 1973-76; dep. sec. N.Mex. Health and Environ. Dept., Santa Fe, 1978-82, sec., 1987-88; vis. prof. pub. adminstrn. U. N.Mex., Albuquerque, 1988—, adj. prof. polit. sci., 1997—, sr. fellow Inst. for Pub. Policy, 1997—; chmn. N.Mex. Water Quality Commn., 1971-73. Asst. editor Jour. Environ. Health, 1975-78; cons. editor Environ. News Digest, 1970-82; editl. cons. Jour. Pub. Health Policy, 1980-96, Underwriters Labs., 1996; contbr. over 200 articles to profl. jours. Recipient Samuel J. Crumbine award for Outstanding Devel. of Comprehensive Program for Environ. Sanitation, 1959 and 65, Sanitarians Disting. Service award Internat. Assn. Milk, Food, and Environ. Sanitarians, 1962, Outstanding Contrbn. award N.Mex. Assn. Pub. Health Sanitarians, 1967, Boss of Yr. award Santa Fe chpt. Nat. Secs. Assn., 1970, Walter F. Snyder award For Achievement in Environ. Quality, 1978, Commendation for Leadership in Health Care N.Mex. Hosp. Assn., 1981, N.Mex. Outstanding Pub. Svc. award, 1988, Zimmerman award U. N.Mex. Alumni, 1993, L.A. County Breslow award L.A. County Dept. Health Svcs., 1994, Outstanding Leadership in Environ. Adminstrn. award Am. Soc. for Pub. Adminstrn., 1994. Mem. APHA (exec. bd. 1975-82, pres. 1980-81, John J. Sippy Meml. award 1962, other coms., Sedgwick award 1987), Am. Acad. Sanitarians (founder, David Calvin Wagner Excellence award 1984), N.Mex. Pub. Health Assn. (past pres., Disting. Svc. award 1970, Spl. award, 1978, D.A. Larrazola award 1989), N.Mex. Environ. Health Assn., (past pres.), Am. Lung Assn. N.Mex. (bd. dirs. 1982-94, Clinton P. Anderson award for Oustanding Contbn. to Lung Health 1987), Nat. Accreditation Coun. Environ. Health Curricula, Nat. Audubon Soc. (pres. coun. 1982-86), U. Mich. Sch. Pub. Health Alumni Assn. (bd. govs. 1985-88, Outstanding Alumnus award 1995), Royal Soc. Promotion of Health, London (hon.), N.Mex. Soc. Pub. Adminstrn. (Disting. Pub. Adminstr. award 1996), Delta Omega, Phi Kappa Phi, Phi Sigma. Republican. Avocations: fishing, boating, golf. Home: 1674 Tierra Del Rio NW Albuquerque NM 87107-3259 Office: Polit Sci Dept Univ NMex Albuquerque NM 87131

GORDON, LAWRENCE ALLAN, accounting educator; b. Bklyn., Apr. 15, 1943; s. Seymour and Jessie (Killion) G.; m. Hedy Hellen Ambrozy, Nov. 23, 1968; children: Lauren Allison, Marc Elliot. BS, SUNY, Albany, 1966, MBA, 1967; PhD, Rensselaer Poly. Inst., 1973. Cert. cost analyst. Asst. prof. acctg. Clarkson Coll. Tech., 1971-72; asst. prof. acctg. McGill U., Montreal, Can., 1972-74, assoc. prof. acctg., 1974-76; assoc. prof. acctg. U. Kans., Lawrence, 1976-79, prof. acctg., 1979-80; prof. acctg. U. Md., College Park, 1980-81, Ernst & Young Alumni prof. managerial acctg., 1981—; coord. PhD program in acctg. U. Md., 1980-96, dir. PhD program Coll. Bus. and Mgmt., 1996—, chairperson acctg. faculty, 1982-87, chairperson numerous univ. and profl. coms., 1972—; cons. IBM, 1984-91, U.S. Dept. Labor, 1985-87, U.S. Gen. Acctg. Office, 1978-84, N.Y. State Tchr.'s Retirement System, 1968-69; mgmt. acctg. cons./lectr. Dept. of Supplies and Svcs., Ottawa, Can., 1974-79; mem. audit staff Peat, Marwick, Mitchell & Co., N.Y.C., 1966; presenter in field. Co-editor Jour. Acctg. and Pub. Policy, 1982—; assoc. editor Jour. Bus. Fin. and Acctg., 1991—; editorial bd. mem. Acctg. Rev., 1981-82, Mgmt. Internat. Rev., 1982—, Contemporary Acctg. Rsch., 1984-92; ad-hoc reviewer Jour. Fin. and Quantitative Analysis, Acctg., Orgns. and Soc., Acctg. Rev., Jour. Bus. and Econ. Stats.; author: (with others) Improving Capital Budgeting: A Decision Support System Approach, 1984, The Pricing Decision, 1981, others; author: Managerial Accounting: Concepts and Empirical Evidence, 1998 (4th edit); author articles. Rsch. grantee U. Md. Coll. Bus. and Mgmt., 1980-90, Am. Acctg. Assn., 1976, summer rsch. grantee U. Kans., 1977, grantee Arthur Andersen & Co., 1977, Nat. Assn. Accts. and the Soc. Mgmt. Accts., 1976-80, McGill U., 1975, 75-76, U. Western Ont., 1974, expense grantee for rsch. McGill U., 1973, grantee (with others) U.S. Dept. Labor, 1978-80. Mem. Am. Acctg. Assn., Am. Econ. Assn., Am. Fin. Assn., Inst. Mgmt. Accts., Inst. for Cost Analysis. Office: Coll Bus and Mgmt U Md College Park College Park MD 20742

GORDON, LEONARD, sociology educator; b. Detroit, Dec. 6, 1935; s. Abraham and Sarah (Rosen) G.; m. Rena Joyce Feigelman, Dec. 25, 1955; children: Susan Melinda, Matthew Seth, Melissa Gail. B.A., Wayne State U., 1957; M.A., U. Mich., 1958; Ph.D., Wayne State U., 1966. Instr. Wayne State U., Detroit, 1960-62; research dir. Jewish Community Council, Detroit, 1962-64; dir. Mich. area Am. Jewish Com., N.Y.C., 1964-67; asst. prof. Ariz. State U., Tempe, 1967-70, assoc. prof., 1970-77, prof., 1977—, chmn. dept. sociology, 1981-90, assoc. dean for acad. programs Coll. Liberal Arts and Scis., 1990—; cons. OEO, Maricopa County, Ariz., 1968. Author: A City in Racial Crisis, 1971, Sociology and American Social Issues, 1978, (with A. Mayer) Urban Life and the Struggle To Be Human, 1979, (with R. Hardert, M. Laner and M. Reader) Confronting Social Problems, 1984, (with J. Hall and R. Melnick) Harmonizing Arizona's Ethnic and Cultural Diversity, 1992. Sec. Conf. on Religion and Race, Detroit, 1962-67; mem. exec. bd. dirs. Am. Jewish Com., Phoenix chpt., 1969-70. Grantee NSF, 1962, Rockefeller found., 1970, 84. Fellow Am. Sociol. Assn.; mem. AAUP, Pacific Sociol. Assn. (v.p. 1978-79, pres. 1980-81), Soc. Study Social Problems (chair C. Wright Mills award com. 1988, treas. 1989-96), Ariz. State U. Alumni Assn. (faculty dir. 1981-82). Democrat. Jewish. Home: 13660 E Columbine Dr Scottsdale AZ 85259-3753 Office: Ariz State U Coll Liberal Arts and Scis Office for Acad Programs Tempe AZ 85287

GORDON, LEONARD VICTOR, psychologist, educator emeritus; b. Montreal, Que., Aug. 15, 1917; came to U.S., 1936, naturalized, 1938; s. Peter Z. and Bessie Victoria (Kirsch) G.; m. Katharine Ann Burton, Nov. 30, 1946; children: John Christopher (dec.), Jeffrey Burton. BA, UCLA, 1940; MA, Ohio State U., 1947, PhD, 1950. Instr. Ohio State U., Columbus, 1947-49, rsch. assoc., 1949-50; assoc. dir. office rsch. svcs. Boston U., 1950-51; vis. asst. prof. U. N.Mex., Albuquerque, 1951-52; divsn. dir. Naval Pers. Rsch. Activity, San Diego, 1952-62; lab chief U.S. Army Pers. Rsch. Office, Washington, 1962-66; prof. ednl. psychology and stats. SUNY, Albany, 1966-87, prof. emeritus, 1987—; pres. Intertest, Guilderland, N.Y, 1985—; Disting. vis. prof. Wilford Hall U.S. Air Force Med. Ctr., Lackland AFB, Tex., 1977-79; rsch. adv. com. Office of Edn., 1969-70; advisor European Test Publishers Group, 1992—; adv. com. Ednl. Psychologist, 1973-74; grant referee NIE, 1972-73, Can. Coun., 1975-77, NSF, 1977-78; external examiner U. West Indies, 1978-81, Patna U., 1969-75, India Inst. Tech., 1977-81; lectr., cons. in field. Author: (with Ross L. Mooney) Mooney Problem Check Lists, 1950, Gordon Personal Profile, 1953, (rev. edit. 1993), 1978, Gordon Personal Inventory, 1956, (rev. edit. 1993), 1978, Global edit., 1992, Survey of Interpersonal Values, 1960, (rev. edit.), 1976, Gordon Occupational Check List, 1963, (rev. edit.), 1981, Work Environment Preference Schedule, 1973, Measurement of Interpersonal Values, 1975, (with Akio Kikuchi) Social Psychology of Values, 1975, (rev. edit. with Akio Kikuchi), 1981, Survey of Personal Values, 1967, (rev. edit.), 1984, School Environment Preference Survey, 1978; mem. editl. bd. Jour. Applied Psychology, 1971-82; contbr. articles to profl. jours. Rsch. coord. Peace Corps, Washington, 1964-65; internat. steering com. Evaluation Rsch. Soc., 1976-77. With USAAC, 1941-44. Univ. Exchange scholar SUNY, 1969-71. Fellow Am. Psychol. Assn., AAAS; mem. Internat. Assn. Applied Psychology, Am. Ednl. Research Assn., Nat. Council Measurement in Edn., Author's Guild. Home: 385 Highland Dr Schenectady NY 12303-5727 Office: Intertest PO Box 27 Guilderland NY 12084-0027

GORDON, LESLIE PEYTON, executive recruiting consultant; b. Asheville, N.C., July 15, 1962; d. William Madison and Grace Baker Peyton; m. Barton Jennings Gordon, June 27, 1998. BA in Econ. (with honors), U. N.C., 1984; MBA, U. Va., 1989. Assoc. Bankers Trust Co., N.Y.C., 1988-92; v.p. then sr. v.p. The Whitney Group, N.Y.C., 1992-96; mng. dir. Korn/Ferry Internat., N.Y.C., 1996—. Com. chair N.Y. Jr. League, N.Y.C., 1994-97. Recipient YWCA Acad. Women Achievers award, 1996. Mem. Congl. Club, Univ. Club (N.Y.C.). Democrat. Episcopalian. Fax: 212-661-2547. E-mail: gordonl@kornferry.com. Office: Korn/Ferry Internat 200 Park Ave New York NY 10166

GORDON, LOIS GOLDFEIN, English language educator; b. Englewood, N.J.; d. Irving David and Betty (Davis) Goldfein; m. Alan Lee Gordon, Nov. 13, 1961; 1 son, Robert Michael. B.A. (Nat. Merit supplementary scholar, Barbour scholar), U. Mich., 1960; postgrad., Columbia U., 1960-61; M.A., U. Wis., 1962, Ph.D. (Dissertation Completion fellow), 1966. Teaching asst. U. Wis., 1962-64; lectr. CCNY, 1964-66; asst. prof. U. Mo., Kansas City, 1966-68; asst. prof. English Fairleigh Dickinson U., Teaneck, N.J., 1968-71; assoc. prof. Fairleigh Dickinson U., 1971-75, prof., 1975—, chmn. dept. English and comparative lit., 1982-90; vis. exch. prof. Rutgers U., 1994; cons. U. Mo. Press, 1968-69, Doubleday Inc., 1974, Fairleigh Dickinson U. Press, 1975—, Prentice Hall, 1977—, Duke U. Press, 1986—, U. Wis. Press, Rutgers U. Press, Cambridge U. Press, Harper Collins. Author: Stratagems To Uncover Nakedness: The Dramas of Harold Pinter, 1969, Donald Barthelme, 1981, Robert Coover: The Universal Fiction-Making Process, 1983, American Chronicle: Six Decades in American Life, 1920-79, 1987, Seven Decades in American Life, 1920-89, 1990, Harold Pinter: A Casebook, 1990, The Columbia Chronicles of American Life, 1910-1992, 1995, The World of Samuel Beckett, 1906-1946, 1996, American Chronicle: Year by Year Through the Twentieth Century, 1999; asst. editor Lit. and Psychology, 1968-71; contbr. book revs. to profl. jours. and newspapers. Research grantee U. Mo., 1968, Fairleigh Dickinson U., 1985, 89. Mem. MLA, PEN, Internat. Bach Soc., Internat. League Human Rights, Authors Guild, Acad. Am. Poets, Harold Pinter Soc., Samuel Beckett Soc. Jewish. Home: 300 Central Park W New York NY 10024-1513 Office: Fairleigh Dickinson U Dept English Teaneck NJ 07666

GORDON, LORI HEYMAN, psychotherapist, author, educator; b. S.I., N.Y., Jan. 31, 1929; d. Julius and Bertha (Hahn) Heyman; m. Morris Gordon, Sept. 5, 1982; children: Beth, Jonathan, David, Seth. *Her deceased parents emigrated from Vilna, Lithuania. Her father's mother's ancestry dates back to the Katzenellengogen family which includes rabbinical leaders dating back to the 14th century. The famed Golem legend can be traced here. Ancestry includes Martin Buber, Karl Marx and Felix Mendelsohn. Her father graduated from Columbia University as a surgeon dentist. She was raised in Staten Island. Husband, Rabbi Morris Gordon, is a prominent community leader. Son Jonathan is a vice president and associate counsel of Merrill Lynch. Son, David, is vice president of John Hancock Investments. Son, Seth, is CEO and partner in PAIRS INTERNATIONAL, Inc. She is grandmother of nine.* BS, Cornell U., 1950; MSW, Cath. U. Am., 1963; PhD, Summit U. La., 1993. Lic. clin. social worker, accredited supr., Va. Founder/dir. Family Rels. Inst., Falls Church, Va., 1969; condr. psychoednl. tng. seminars nat. and internat. PAIRS (Practical Application Intimate Relationship Skills), Falls Church; instr. family therapy Am. U. Grad. Sch. Counseling Edn., Washington; field supr. Cath. U. Am. Sch. Social Work, Washington; presenter profls. cons. Am. Assn. Marriage and Family Therapy Conf., 1988-91, Va. Assn. Marriage and Family Therapy Conf., 1989, ABA Family Law divsn. ptnrs. program, 1994; founder Ctr. for Separation and Divorce Mediation, 1980; founder, dir. PAIRS Ltd., 1984, PAIRS Inst., 1990; founder, exec. dir. PAIRS Found., Ltd., 1991, dir. tng., 1995; founder, pres., tng. dir. PAIRS Internat., Inc. *She is an internationally recognized marriage and family therapist. She created a series of clinical and educational programs designed to prevent marital breakdown and enhance marital relationships. Noted for creating a new paradigm for relationships in the 21st century through her conceptual and skill-based PAIRS psychoeducational program, a model of peer relationships for both sexes. Television appearances include the Today Show, Geraldo, Gordon Elliott, Sonya Live, CNN, CBS and NBC news. Interviews have appeared in Time, Newsweek, Cosmopolitan, Ladies Home Journal and Psychology Today among others. She is noted for her humor and deep insights into modern day relationship issues.* Author: Love Knots-How To Untangle Daily Frustrations, 1990, Passage to Intimacy, 1993, If You Really Loved Me..., 1996; contbr. articles to profl. jours. and mags. Mem. Am. Assn. Marriage and Family Therapists, Acad. Cert. Social Workers, Internat. Human Lng. Resource Network, Avanta-The Va. Satir Tng. Orgn., Inst. Noetic Scis., Coalition Marriage, Family and Couples Edn. (bd. dirs.). E-mail: pairsline@aol.com. Office: PAIRS Found Ltd 1056 Creek Ford Dr Weston FL 33326

GORDON, MALCOLM STEPHEN, biology educator; b. Bklyn., Nov. 13, 1933; s. Abraham and Rose (Walters) G.; m. Diane M. Kestin, Apr. 16, 1959 (div. Sept. 1973); 1 child, Dana Malcolm; m. Marjorie J. Weinzweig, Jan. 28, 1976 (dec. Mar. 1990); m. Carol A. Cowen, July 19, 1992. BA with high honors, Cornell U., 1954; PhD, Yale U., 1958. Instr. UCLA, 1958-60, asst. prof., 1960-65, assoc. prof., 1965-68; prof. biology, 1968—, dir. Inst. Evolutionary and Environ. Biology,, 1971-76, chmn. interdept. com. Environ. Sci. Engring. Program,, 1984-88; asst. dir. rsch. Nat. Fisheries Ctr. and Aquarium, U.S. Dept. of Interior, Washington, 1968-69; vis. prof. zoology Chinese U. Hong Kong, 1971-72; mem. panel on marine biology, panel on oceanography Pres.'s Sci. Adv. Com., 1965-66; mem. nat. adv com. R/V Alpha Helix, Scripps Inst. Oceanography, 1969-73; mem. com. on Latimeria, NAS, 1969-72; mem. tech. adv. com. Santa Monica Bay Restoration Project, EPA, 1988—; mem. tech. adv. group on milkfish reprodn. AID, 1984-92; chmn. Commn. on Comparative Physiology, Internat. Union Physiol. Sci., 1993—; co-founder Inst. of Environment, UCLA, 1997. Author coll. textbooks, technical books; mem. editorial bd. Fish Physiol. Biochem. Jour., 1986—, Jour. Exptl. Zool., 1990-93; contbr. articles to sci. jours. Active community orgns. on environ., civil liberties. NSF fellow Yale U., 1958; Fulbright fellow U.K., 1957-58; Guggenheim fellow Italy and Denmark, 1961-62; Sr. Queen's fellow in marine sci. Australia, 1976. Fellow AAAS; mem. Am. Physiol. Soc. (mem. exec. com. pub. affairs 1989-92), Am. Soc. Ichthyologists and Herpetologists, Soc. Integrative Comparative Biology (chmn. divsn. ecology 1979-80, chmn. divsn. comparative biochem. physiology 1988-89), Soc. for Exptl. Biology. Home: 2801 Glendower Ave Los Angeles CA 90027-1118 Office: UCLA Dept Organismic Biology PO Box 951606 Los Angeles CA 90095-1606

GORDON, MARC STEWART, pharmacist, scientist; b. Cleve., June 13, 1958; s. Eugene and Eileen (Israel) G.; m. Diane Southwell, Aug. 11, 1985; children: Evan, Emma. BS in Pharmacy, U. Mich., 1982. Registered pharmacist, Calif. Staff rschr. II, mgr. Syntex Rsch., Palo Alto, Calif., 1982-95; sr. scientist Inhale Therapeutic Systems, Palo Alto, Calif., 1995—. Contbr. numerous articles to profl. jours.; patentee pharmaceuticals. Mem. Am. Assn. Pharm. Scientists, Am. Pharm. Assn., No. Calif. Pharm. Discussion Group, Rho Chi. Avocations: reading, hiking. Home: 1474 Samedra St Sunnyvale CA 94087-4054 : 150 Industrial Rd San Carlos CA 94070-6256

GORDON, MARJORIE, lyric coloratura soprano, opera producer, teacher; b. N.Y.C.; d. Theodore and Minnie (Glantz) Fishberg; m. Nathan Gordon; children: Maxine, Peter Jon. BA cum laude, Hunter Coll. Prof. voice Duquesne U., 1957-59, Wayne State U., 1961-91, Nat. Music Camp, Interlochen, 1963-65, Meadowbrook Sch. Music, 1966-71, U. Mich., 1970, Mich. State U., 1971; soloist, tchr. Am. U.-Wolf Trap Program, Washington, 1973; spl. edn. cons. Detroit Grand Opera Assn.; adj. prof. Oakland (Mich.) C.C. Solo debut N.Y. Philharm. Symphony, 1950, soprano soloist, N.Y.C. Opera, 1955-57, Chautauqua Opera Co., 1949-61, Pitts. Opera, 1956; dir. Detroit Opera Theatre, 1960-72, Piccolo Opera Co., 1961—; soloist with orchs., opera cos., summer stock, on radio and TV; recitals U.S., Greece, Europe, Can., Israel; editor: Opera Study Guide, 1968—. Mem. music adv. panel Mich. Arts Coun.; mem. Palm Beach County Cultural Coun.; opera producer Blue Lake Fine Arts Camp, 1993—. Recipient resolution honoring 25th Anniversary Piccolo Opera Co., Mich. Senate; established voice scholarship in perpetuity Nat. Opera Assn. Mem. AFTRA, Internat. Platform Assn., Fla. Music Tchrs. Assn., Mich. Music Tchrs. Assn. (voice chmn. 1970-76), Am. Guild Mus. Artists, Music Tchrs. Nat. Assn., Nat. Opera Assn., Nat. Assn. Tchrs. of Singing, Cen. Opera Svc., Met. Opera Guild, Boca Raton Music Study Club, Broward County Music Club, Intracoastal Chpt. Nat. Assn. Tchrs. Singing, Mu Phi Epsilon. Avocations: handcrafts, swimming, reading, sketching.

GORDON, MARK, actor, theater director, theater educator; b. N.Y.C., May 19, 1926; s. Jacob and Sarah (Benin) G.; m. Barbara Glenn, Oct. 13, 1955; 1 child, Keith. Student, Theater Sch. Dramatic Arts, N.Y.C., 1946-47, Actors Lab., Los Angeles, 1947-50, Am. Theater Wing, N.Y.C., 1950-54, Drama Lab., N.Y.C., 1954-55. Workshop dir., actor Compass Players, Chgo., 1955-56; ind. theatrical and film actor, 1955—, ind. theatrical dir., 1969—; guest prof. theater Carnegie-Mellon Univ., Pitts., 1969-70, Columbia Univ., N.Y.C., 1970-71, High Sch. Performing Arts, N.Y.C., 1970-72, Finch Coll., N.Y.C.; head M.B.K. Prodns., N.Y.C., 1982—. Playwight: (with others) Glorious Age, 1975; actor numerous Broadway prodns. including Desire Under the Elms, Of Mice and Men, Mr. Roberts, The Devils, off-Broadway prodns. include The Iceman Cometh, The Man Who Never Died...Joe Hill, TV appearances include Mary Tyler Moore, Hawaii 5-O, Kojack, Dick Van Dyke, film appearances include Take the Money and Run, A New Leaf, Don't Drink the Water, Ninth Configuration; dir. Broadway prodn.: Before You Go (named Best Comedy Dir. on Broadway 1969), off-Broadway prodns. for Los Angeles Actors Theater, Carnegie Recital Hall, Playwrites Horizon, participating dir. Actors Studio; dir. numerous TV commls. Recipient numerous Andy awards, Clio nominations, Contribution to Comedy in Chgo. medal Univ. Chgo.; Rockefeller grantee Ctr. Opera of Mpls., 1963-64; scholar Am. Theater Wing. Mem. AAUP, AFTRA, Dirs. Guild Am.; Screen Actors Guild, Actors Equity Assn., Nat. Acad. TV Arts and Scis., Soc. Stage Dirs. and Choreographers. Avocations: violin, scuba diving, photography. Office: MBK Prodns 323 W 83rd St New York NY 10024-4835

GORDON, MARK, II, film producer; b. 1957. Prodr. films including: Sawdust, 1988, Brothers in Arms, 1989, Opportunity Knocks, 1990, traces of Red, 1992, Fly by Night, 1993, Swing Kids, 1993, Speed, 1994, Trial by Jury, 1994, A Pyromaniac's Love Story, 1995, Broken Arrow, 1996, The Relic, 1997, Speed2: Cruise Control, 1997, The Jackal, 1997, A Simple Plan, 1998, Hard Rain, 1998, Paulie, 1998, Black Dog, 1998, Saving Private Ryan, 1998, To the Moon, 1999, Virus, 1999; TV movies include: Out of Step, 1983, One Too Many, 1983, How to be a Perfect Person in Just Three Days, 1983, War Between the Classes, 1985, Double Switch, 1987, Lightning Field, 1991, Love Kills, 1991, The Man Who Wouldn't Die, 1995, Children Remember the Holocaust, 1995, The Ripper, 1997; dir. film: Children Remember the Holocaust, 1995. Winner Daytime Emmy award for outstanding children's spl. for War Between the Classes, 1985, Motion Picture Prodr. of the Yr. award for Saving Pvt. Ryan, 1999. Office: Mutual Film Co Raleigh Studios 650 N Bronson Ave Los Angeles CA 90004*

GORDON, MARY CATHERINE, author; b. L.I., N.Y., Dec. 8, 1949; d. David and Anna (Gagliano) G.; m. James Brain, 1974 (div.); m. Arthur Cash, 1979; children: Anna Gordon, David Dess Gordon. BA, Barnard Coll., 1971; MA, Syracuse U., 1973. Tchr. English Dutchess Community Coll., Poughkeepsie, N.Y., 1974-78, Amherst (Mass.) Coll., 1979-80, Barnard Coll., 1988—. Author: (novels) Final Payments, 1978, The Company of Women, 1981, Men and Angels,1985, The Other Side, 1989, The Rest of Life, 1993, Spending, 1998, (short stories) Temporary Shelter, 1987, Good Boys and Dead Girls and Other Essays, 1991, The Rest of Life: Three Novellas, 1993. Recipient Kafka prize for Fiction, 1979, 82. Roman Catholic. Office: Viking Penguin Publicity Dept 375 Hudson St New York NY 10014-3658 also: Barnard Coll Dept of English 3009 Broadway New York NY 10027-5706*

GORDON, MAXWELL, pharmaceutical company executive; b. Kamenka, Ukraine, Feb. 13, 1921; came to U.S., 1923; s. Abraham and Sarah Gordon; m. Ethel Mayer, June 5, 1949 (dec. Sept. 1980); m. Barbara Ullman, Apr. 10, 1983; children: Alan Michael, Sandra Lynn, Anthony Ullman, Claudia Marie Ullman. B.S., Phila. Coll. Pharmacy and Sci., 1941; M.A., U. Pa., 1946, Ph.D., 1948; D.I.C., Imperial Coll. Sci., London, 1953. Rsch. fellow NIH, Zurich, Switzerland, 1948-49; fellow AEC U. Calif., Berkeley, 1949-50; exchange fellow Am. Cancer Soc. Imperial Coll., London, 1950-51; Research assoc. Squibb Inst. for Med. Research, New Brunswick, N.J., 1951-55; assoc. dir. research Smith Kline & French Labs., Phila., 1955-70; sr. v.p. sci. and tech. group Bristol-Myers Co., N.Y.C., 1970-87; chmn. bd., CEO Lenti-Chemico Pharm. Lab., Inc. subs. Ajinomoto Co., Inc., Tokyo, 1988-93; pres., CEO Ajinomoto Pharmaceuticals, USA, Inc., Teaneck, N.J., 1993-97; cons. Ajinomoto Pharmaceuticals, USA, Inc., Tokyo, 1997—; mem. com. on chem. documentation NRC, 1960-66; assoc. com. on problems of drug dependence NAS/NRC, 1960-64. Author: Handbook of Toxicology-Tranquilizers, 1959; editor: Psychopharmacological Agents, 1960, Bristol-Myers Symposium Series in Cancer Research, vols. 1-8, 1977-85. Fellow NIH, AEC. Fellow AAAS; mem. Am. Chem. Soc., Chem. Soc. London, Austrian Chem. Soc., Swiss Chem. Soc., Chem. Soc. Japan. Avocations: photography, electronics. Office: Ajinomoto Co Inc Glenpointe Ctr W Teaneck NJ 07666

GORDON, MICHAEL MACKIN, lawyer; b. Boston, Apr. 15, 1950; s. Lawrence H. and Gladys (Mackin) G.; m. Linda Lowry, June 8, 1991; children: Alexandra, Harrison. AB, Vassar Coll., 1972; JD, Columbia U., 1976. Bar: N.Y. 1977, U.S. Dist. Ct. (so. and ea. dists. N.Y. 1977), D.C. 1980, U.s. Ct. Appeals (2d cir.) 1985, U.S. Supreme Ct. 1985, U.S. Claims Ct. 1991, U.S. Ct. Appeals (3d cir.), 1992, U.S. Dist. Ct. (no. dist.), Tex. 1993, U.S. Ct. Appeals (5th cir.) 1995, U.S. Dist. Ct. (ea. dist.) Tex. 1996. Assoc. Seward & Kissel, N.Y.C., 1977-79; assoc. Cadwalader, Wickersham & Taft, N.Y.C., 1979-85, ptnr., 1985—. Mem. ABA, N.Y. State Bar Assn., N.Y. County Lawyers Assn. Club: Vassar (N.Y.C.). Home: 12 W 72nd St New York NY 10023-4163 Office: Cadwalader Wickersham & Taft 100 Maiden Ln New York NY 10038-4818

GORDON, MILTON ANDREW, academic administrator; b. Chgo., May 25, 1935; s. Herrmann Andrew Gordon and Ossie Bell; m. Margaret Faulwell, July 18, 1987; children: Patrick Francis, Vincent Michael; 1 stepchild, Michael Faulwell. BS, Xavier U. La., New Orleans, 1957; MA, U. Detroit, 1960; PhD, Ill. Inst. Tech., 1968; postgrad., Harvard U., 1984. Teaching asst. U. Detroit, 1958-59; mathematician Lab. Applied Scis. U. Chgo., 1959-62; part-time tchr. Chgo. Pub. Sch. System, 1962-66; assoc. prof. math. Loyola U., Chgo., 1966-67; dir. Afro-Am. Studies Program Loyla U., Chgo., 1971-77; dean Coll. Arts and Scis., prof. math. Chgo. State U., 1978-86; v.p. acad. affairs, prof. math. Sonoma State U., Rohnert Park, Calif., 1986-90; pres., former prof. math. Calif. State U., Fullerton, 1990—; bd. dirs. Associated We. Univs., Inc.; hon. admissions counselor United States Naval Acad., 1979; mem. exec. coun. Calif. State U., 1990; rep. for Calif. univs.Am. Assn. State Colls. and Univs., 1992; commn. on leadership devel. Am. Coun. on Edn., 1992; nat. task force on gender equality Nat. Collegiate Athletic Assn., 1992-94, pres.'s commn., 1994—; commr. joint commn. on accoutability reporting project Am. Assn. of State Colls. and Univs./Nat. Assn. of State Univs. and Land Grant Colls., 1994—, Am. Assn. Applied Ethics. Contbr. articles to profl. jours. Chmn. Archdiocese of Chgo. Sch. Bd., 1978-79; bd. govs. Orange County Community Found., Costa Mesa, Calif., 1990—, NCCJ, 1991—; bd. dirs. United Way of Orange County, Irvine, Calif., 1991, Pacific Symphony Orch., Santa Ana, 1993—; bd. adv. St. Jude Med. Ctr., Fullerton, Calif., 1992, Partnership 2010, Orange County, 1994, Black Leadership in Orange County, 1995—; bd. dirs. Orange County Bus. Coun., 1996—. Recipient cert. of appreciation Community Ch. Santa Rosa, Calif., 1988, Tree of Life award Jewish Nat. Fund, 1994, Humanitarian of Yr. award North Orange County YMCA, 1995; named Adminstr. of Yr., Chgo. State U., 1979. Mem. Am.conf. Acad. Deans (chmn. bd. dirs. 1983-85), Am. Assn. Univ. Adminstrs. (bd. dirs. 1983-86), Calif. Coalition of Math., Sigma Xi, Phi Beta Delta. Roman Catholic. Avocations: photography, sports, walking, movies. Office: Calif State Univ 800 N State College Blvd Presidents Office Lh900 Fullerton CA 92834-6810

GORDON, MILTON PAUL, biochemist, educator; b. St. Paul, Feb. 8, 1930; s. Abraham and Rebecca (Ryan) G.; m. Elaine Travis, Jan. 1, 1955; children—David, Karen, Nancy, Peter. B.A. summa cum laude, U. Minn., 1950; Ph.D., U. Ill., 1953. Upjohn Co. fellow U. Ill., 1950-51; Am. Cancer Inst. fellow Sloan-Kettering Inst. for Cancer Research, N.Y.C., 1953-55; research asst. Sloan-Kettering Inst. for Cancer Research, 1955-57; lectr. Bklyn. Coll., 1955-57; asst. research biochemist Virus Lab., U. Calif. at Berkeley, 1957-59; mem. faculty U. Wash., Seattle, 1959—; prof. U. Wash., 1966—, acting chmn., 1984-85; Sec., treas. Pacific Slope Biochem. Conf., 1964-68, pres., 1968; vis. scholar Max Planck Inst., Tübingen, Fed. Republic Germany, 1975; sci. adv. bd. Ctr. forExcellence in Molecular Biology, Lahore, Pakistan; founding organizer Verdant Technologies. Assoc. editor Biochemistry, 1960-91. Mem. Am. Chem. Soc., AAAS, Am. Soc. Biol. Chemists. Rsch. and publs. on plant tumorogenesis and plant transformation, research on phytoremediation. Home: 7111 Linden Ave N Apt 404 Seattle WA 98103-5169

GORDON, MORRIS AARON, medical mycologist, microbiologist; b. Waterbury, Conn., Apr. 3, 1920; s. Samuel and Anna (Rubinstein) G.; m. Ruth Kathryn McKee, May 22, 1945 (div. 1970); children: Barbara Jean, David Spencer, Sarah Elizabeth. BS, City Coll. N.Y., N.Y.C., 1940; MS, U. Chgo., 1942; PhD, Duke U., 1949. Diplomate Am. Bd. Microbiology; cert. lab. dir., N.Y. Lab. officer Regional Hosp., U.S. Army, Camp Blanding, Fla., 1945-46; mycologist Communicable Disease Ctr., Atlanta, 1949-54; biol. warfare specialist Chem. Corps Training Command, Fort McClellan, Ala., 1954-55; assoc. prof. microbiology Med. Coll. S.C., Charleston, 1955-59; sr. to prin. rsch. scientist, dir. mycology labs. N.Y. State Dept. Health, Albany, 1959-87, dir. clin. microbiology & mycology labs., 1983-87, dir. emeritus clin. microbiology and mycology labs., 1987—; study sect. NIH, Washington, 1971-75; adv. com. Brown-Hazen Awards, N.Y.C., 1974-78;

cons. VA Hosp., Albany, 1959-96; rsch. prof. Albany Med. Coll., 1975-90. Author: Laboratory Identification of Pathogenic Fungi, 1970; founder/editor Bull. Med. Mycol. Soc. Ams., 1976-94; contbr. articles to numerous profl. jours. Lt. comdr. USPHS, 1949-54. Recipient various rsch. grants NIH, teaching fellowship Duke U., 1947-49; Fulbright professor, 1978, Inter-Am. fellow La. State U., 1959. Mem. Med. Mycol. Soc. Ams. (pres. 1978-79, Benham award 1988), Internat. Soc. Human and Animal Mycology (v.p. 1982-85, Georg award 1991), Am. Soc. Microbiology (pres. mycology sect.), Phi Beta Kappa, Sigma Xi (pres. Albany chpt. 1972). Achievements include invention of latex test for cryptococcosis; initiation of diagnostic immunofluorescence for human fungal diseases; cultured pathogenic lipophilic yeasts; establishment of first presence in North America and first presence in humans of Dermatophilus infection. Address: 501 Penncross Dr Raleigh NC 27610-2176

GORDON, MYRON L., federal judge; b. Kenosha, Wis., Feb. 11, 1918; m. Peggy Gordon, Aug. 16, 1942 (dec. Mar. 1973); children: Wendy, John, Polly; m. Myra Gordon, Mar. 30, 1979. BA, MA, U. Wis., 1939; LLB, Harvard U., 1942. Judge U.S. Ct. Appeals, Milw., 1951-62, Wis. State Supreme Ct., Madison, 1966-67, U.S. Dist. Ct., Milw., 1967—; now sr. judge. Office: US Dist Ct 271 US Courthouse 517 E Wisconsin Ave Milwaukee WI 53202-4500*

GORDON, NEIL ALAN, facial plastic surgeon; b. Bklyn., Mar. 3, 1964; s. George H. and Sandra (Eisenberg) G.; m. Stephanie Hack, Oct. 13, 1991. BS magna cum laude, SUNY, Albany, 1986; MD, Albert Einstein Coll. Medicine, 1990. Diplomate Am. Bd. Otolaryngology. Intern in gen. surgery Yale U. Sch. Medicine, New Haven, 1990-91, resident in otolaryngology, head and neck surgery, 1991-95; fellow in facial plastic surgery Tulane U. Sch. Medicine, New Orleans, 1995-96; mem. staff Bridgeport (Conn.) Hosp., 1996—, Charity Hosp., New Orleansl; pvt. practice Greenwich and Westport, Conn., 1996—; med. dir. New Eng. Surg. Ctr., LLC, Westport, Conn., 1997—; clin. instr. Yale U. Sch. Medicine. Contbr. articles to profl. publs. Mem. Face to Face domestic violence program, Westport, 1996. Fellow Am. Acad. Otolaryngology-head and Neck Surgery; mem. Am. Acad. Facial Plastic and Reconstructive Surgery, Yale Surg. Soc. (Disting. Svc. award 1995), Alpha Omega Alpha. Address: 116 Mason St Greenwich CT 06830-6629 also: 208 Post Rd W Westport CT 06880-4604

GORDON, NICHOLAS, broadcasting executive; b. Chgo., Apr. 12, 1928; s. Jacques and Ruth (Janeway) G.; m. Gladys Sack, Apr. 10, 1950 (div. 1976); children: Catherine, Christopher, Susan; m. Julie E. Miles, Aug. 12, 1977. Ph.B., U. Chgo., 1946. Reporter City News Bur., Chgo., 1948; radio-TV analyst William Weintraub Agy., N.Y.C., 1949-50; dir. rsch. and sales planning Keystone Broadcasting Sys., N.Y.C., 1951-52; with NBC, 1953-74, mgr. rates and program evaluation, 1956-58, mgr. sales devel. NBC-TV Sales, 1959-60, dir. sales devel. NBC-TV Sales, 1960-63, account exec. TV sales, 1964-68, v.p. Ea. sales, 1968-70; v.p. radio network sales NBC, N.Y.C., 1970-74; pres. Keystone Broadcasting Sys., N.Y.C., 1974-85, chmn., 1985—. Vice chmn. Riverdale Cmty. Coun., 1968-71; mem. N.Y.C. Planning Bd., Riverdale, 1969-75, vice chmn., 1972-74; pres. Riverdale Cmty. Planning Assn., 1972-76; mem. vol. corps N.Y.C. Dept. Commerce, 1968-70; bd. dirs. Wave Hill Ctr. Environ. Studies, 1969-80, exec. v.p., 1970-80; mem. Bronx Democratic County Com., 1968; bd. dirs. Music Mountain, Inc., Falls Village, Conn., 1970—, pres., 1974—; bd. dirs. Riverdale Neighborhood House, Bronx, N.Y., 1970-74, Bronx Coun. Arts, 1970-72, Phila. Orch. Media Inst., 1998—; trustee St. Hilda's and St. Hugh's Sch., 1965-76. Decorated chevalier l'Ordre des Arts et Lettres (France). Mem. Century Assn., Univ. Club, Explorers Club (N.Y.C.), Tavern Club, Cliff Dwellers Club (Chgo.), East India Club (London). Office: Keystone Broadcasting Syst PO Box 1739 Sharon CT 06069-1739

GORDON, NORMAN BOTNICK, psychology educator; b. N.Y.C., Feb. 12, 1921; s. Moses and Molvine (Botnick) G.; m. Diana Jean Drews, July 27, 1974; children: Jane Ellen, Judith Ann, Marc Daniel, Aaron Drew. B.A., Bklyn. Coll., 1942; M.A., New Sch. Social Research, 1951; Ph.D., NYU, 1957. Research psychologist U.S. Naval Tng. Device Ctr., Port Washington, N.Y., 1951-58; assoc. prof. psychology Yeshiva U., N.Y.C., 1959-68, prof., 1968-74; guest investigator Rockefeller U., N.Y.C., 1964-77; prin. rsch. scientist N.Y. State Office of Drug Abuse Svcs., 1974-77; prof. SUNYCO-Oswego, 1977—, chmn. dept. psychology, 1977-86, prof. emeritus, 1988—; adj. prof. SUNY-Oswego, 1988-97, rsch. assoc., 1997—. Served with U.S. Army, 1942-46. Grantee USPHS, 1966-74, 64-67. Mem. Am. Psychol. Assn., AAAS, Eastern Psychol. Assn., Sigma Xi. Home: 900 County Route 20 Oswego NY 13126-5672 Office: SUNY Coll Dept Psychology Oswego NY 13126

GORDON, PAMELA ANN WENCE, piano teacher; b. Dayton, Ohio, Apr. 28, 1943; d. Arthur Elbert and Melva C. (Coleman) Wence; m. Clifford Elwood Gordon, Oct. 23, 1971. BS, Ind. State U., Terre Haute, 1966. Self-employed piano tchr., 1957—; round dance leader, 1973—. Recipient CitHonors Recital award Interlochen Music Camp, 1958, honor Internat. Hon. Music Frat., 1962, Appreciation award Rock Eights, 1985. Mem. ROUNDALAB (charter mem., chair survey com. 1985-86, Maestro trophy 1998), Round Dance Tchrs. Assn. Greater D.C. Area (v.p.), Nat. Capital Area Sq. Dance Leaders Assn. (treas.), Washington Music Tchrs. Assn. (treas.). Avocations: camping, violin, reading, caring for box turtles. Home: 5215 Newton St Bladensburg MD 20710-2340

GORDON, PAUL, metallurgical educator; b. Hartford, Conn., Jan. 1, 1918; s. Charles Dana and Anne Mabel (Hirshberg) G.; m. Evelyn Rubin, Oct. 16, 1941; children—Dana Charles, Jane Ellen. Student, Wesleyan U., Middletown, Conn., 1935-37; B.S. in Metallurgy, Mass. Inst. Tech., 1939, M.S., 1940, Sc.D., 1949. Research asso. metallurgy Mass. Inst. Tech., 1941-42; group leader Manhattan Project, 1942-47; mem. faculty Ill. Inst. Tech., 1949-50, 54—, prof. metall. engring., 1957—, chmn. dept., 1966-76; asst. prof. Inst. Study Metals, U. Chgo., 1951-54. Author: Principles of Phase Diagrams in Materials Systems, 1968; Contbr. articles to profl. jours., chpts. to books. Recipient Albert Easton White Disting. Tchr. award ASM Internat. 1993. Fellow Am. Soc. for Metals; mem. Am. Inst. Mining and Metall. Engrs. (Mathewson gold medal 1957), Inst. Metals, AAAS, Am. Soc. Engring. Edn., Engrs. Council Profl. Devel., Am. Soc. for Testing and Materials, Sigma Xi. Home: 1220 Park Ave W Apt 116 Highland Park IL 60035-2242

GORDON, PAUL JOHN, management educator; b. N.Y.C., Oct. 14, 1921; s. Arthur L. and Georgiana (McDonough) G.; m. Mary Brigid Keany, Jan. 28, 1950; children: Brian Joseph, Peter Christopher, Martha Ann, Hugh John, Paul John. BBA, CCNY, 1945; MBA, Cornell U., 1949; PhD, Syracuse U., 1958. With Brooks Bros., N.Y.C., 1941-43, Lago Oil & Transp. Co., Ltd., Netherlands W. Indies, also Bayway Refinery, Linden, N.J. and Standard Oil Co. N.J., 1943-48; asst. prof. Cornell U., Ithaca, N.Y., 1949-54; prof., chmn. dept. mgmt. Sch. Bus. Duquesne U., Pitts., 1954-55; rsch. cons. Sloan-Kettering Meml. Ctr. for Cancer, N.Y.C., 1955-56; assoc. prof., planning dir. grad. program hosp. adminstrn. Sch. Bus. Adminstrn. Emory U., Atlanta, 1956-59; assoc. prof. Grad. Sch. Bus. Ind. U., 1959-63, prof., chmn. dept. mgmt. adminstrv. studies Grad. Sch. Bus., 1963-67, prof. mgmt. Grad. Sch. Bus., 1963-89, chmn. adminstrv. and behavioral studies Grad. Sch. Bus., 1980-83, prof. emeritus mgmt. Grad. Sch. Bus., 1989—; disting. prof. mgmt. St. John's U., N.Y.C., 1990-93; Fulbright/FLAD chair in strategic mgmt. Tech. U. Lisbon, Portugal, 1997; chief U.S. Dept. State-Ford Found. party Ljubljana U., Yugoslavia, 1967; vis. prof. Trinity Coll., Dublin, 1967; vis. prof., Fulbright lectr. Instituto Post-Universitario Per Lo Studio Dell Organizzazione Aziendale, Turin, Italy, 1963; Fulbright lectr., cons. Nat. U. Republic Uruguay, 1970; disting. guest Systems Rsch. Inst., Polish Acad. Scis., 1980; vis. Fulbright prof. Helsinki Sch. Econs. and Bus. Adminstrn., Finland, 1990; mem. U.S. AID Mgmt. Edn. Reconnaissance Survey, India, also Pakistan, 1971; cons. IRS, 1956-63, Am. Coll. Hosp. Adminstrs., 1957—; with Inst. Higher Studies of Adminstrn., Caracas, Venezuela, 1973-79. Editor Acad. Mgmt. Jour, 1964-66, mem. editorial bd., 1961-75; editorial cons. adv. bd.: Bus. Horizons, Hosp. Adminstrn, W.B. Saunders Co.; contbr. articles to profl. jours. Mem. Cath. Commn. on Intellectual and Cultural Affairs, 1973—, chmn., 1980-81; chmn. UNESCO multi-nat. bus. conf. Ind. U., 1972; chmn. adv. screening com. in bus. mgmt. Coun. for Internat. Exch. of Scholars, Fulbright-Hays Program, 1979-80, 90-93, chmn., 1991-93; bd. dirs. Ind. Newman Found., 1971-82; mem. adv. bd. Abbey Press, St. Meinrad, Ind., 1991-95. Ford Found. grantee, 1963, 66, 70; IBM fellow, 1964. Fellow Acad. Mgmt. (v.p. program 1967, pres. 1969, Disting. Svc. award 1992), Internat. Acad. Mgmt., Am. Acad. Med. Adminstrs. (hon.); mem. Fulbright Assn. (life). Home: 1422 S Winfield Rd Bloomington IN 47401-6152

GORDON, PETER LOWELL, immigration and naturalization administrator; b. Powell, Wyo., Feb. 16, 1953; s. John Eric Gordon and Carol Mae (Peterson) Olson; m. Mitsuko Natsume, Sept. 18, 1993. BA in Polit. Sci., Criminal Justice, Calif. State U., L.A., 1975. Asst. cook Country Kitchen, LaCrosse, Wis., 1970-71; asst. mgr. Ky. Fried Chicken, Tujunga, Calif., 1975-76, Parasol Restaurant, Alhambra, Calif., 1976-77; border patrol agt. Immigration and Naturalization Svc., Dept. Justice, San Diego, 1977-80; immigration insp. Immigration and Naturalization Svc., Dept. Justice, Anchorage, 1980-83; immigration examiner Immigration and Naturalization Svc., Dept. Justice, L.A., 1983-87; legalization mgr. Immigration and Naturalization Svc., Dept. Justice, Laguna Niguel, Calif., 1987-90, immigration mgr., 1990-98; dep. dist. dir. Immigration and Naturalization Svc., Dept. Justice, Anchorage, Ala., 1998—. Co-developer (nat. data base) Legalization Adjustment Processing System, 1987 (Commr.'s award 1987); co-designer Calif. Svc. Ctr., 1989; co-author Calif. Svc. Ctr. Guidelines, 1989. Spkr. Am. Immigration Lawyers Assn., So. and Northern Calif. chpts.; contbr. Dedication and Everlasting Love to Animals. Mem. Nat. Space Soc., Fedn. for Am. Immigration Reform. Republican. Lutheran. Avocations: coin and stamp collecting, baseball and softball, reading, hiking.

GORDON, REVA JO, retired librarian; b. Martinsville, Mo., Feb. 16, 1928; d. Earl G. and Claudia Olive (Goodwin) Kerns; m. Roland Gordon, Nov. 24, 1949; children: Gary Paul, Gloria Gay Gordon Zuber. BS, N.W. Mo. State U., 1949; postgrad., State U. Iowa, 1951; MA in Libr. Sci., U. Mich., 1970. Ordained elder and deacon Presbyn. Ch. Bus. tchr. LeRoy (Iowa) H.S., 1948; bus./English tchr. Malvern (Iowa) Consolidated Schs., 1949-51; English tchr. Flushing (Mich.) Cmty. Schs., 1959-64, libr., media dir., 1964-86, ret., 1986. Author: The Goodwins and Hensleys, 1990; contbr. articles to newspapers and mags. Mem. Mich. Assn. Retired Sch. Personnel (W. Genesee County chpt.), Flushing Hist. Soc., Flushing Book Club, Royal Quarter. Avocations: writing, lecturing. Home: PO Box 406 Flushing MI 48433-0406

GORDON, RICHARD M. ERIK, retailing executive, educator; b. Atlanta, 1949; s. David Albert and Harriet Sonya G. V.p. The Original Gt. Am. Chocolate Chip Cookie Co., Inc., Atlanta, 1984-85, sr. v.p., CEO, 1985—, pres., 1990—; dir. Ctr. for Retailing Edn. and Rsch. U. Fla., Gainesville, 1996—; adj. prof. Ga. State U. Coll. Bus. Adminstrn., 1994-96; bd. dirs. Morgan-Revere Co., Scarsdale, N.Y., Alpha Omega Techs., Punta Gorda, Fla., dir. Audubon Venture Fund-II, Atlanta; mem. industry adv. coun. internat. franchise studies program U. Nebr., Lincoln. Mem. NATAS, IEEE, Am. Mgmt. Assn., Am. Mktg. Assn., Assn. for Consumer Rsch., Acad. Advt., Internat. Franchise Assn. (edn., internat. and legis. coms., bd. dirs.), Inst. for Ops. Rsch. and Mgmt. Sci., Assn. Computing Machinery, Fin. Mgmt. Assn., Ga. State U. Retailing Roundtable, Acad. Mktg. Sci. Office: U Fla 200 Bryan Hall PO Box 117153 Gainesville FL 32611-7153

GORDON, ROBERT BOYD, geophysics educator; b. Orange, N.J., Dec. 25, 1929; s. Myron Boyd and Catherine (Rote) G.; m. Joan Parke Ruttiger, Sept. 13, 1952; children: Penelope, Margaret. BS, Yale U., 1952, DEng, 1955. Asst. prof. Sch. Mines, Columbia U., 1955-57; mem. faculty Yale U., 1957—, assoc. prof. applied sci., 1960-68, prof. geophysics and applied mechanics, 1968—, chmn. dept. geology and geophysics, 1979-82. Author: Physics of the Earth, 1972, Structure and Properties of Engineering Materials, 1977, (with others) Toward a New Iron Age?, 1987, (with P.M. Malone) The Texture of Industry, 1994, American Iron, 1607-1900, 1996. Smithsonian Regents' fellow, 1991. Mem. Am. Phys. Soc., Am. Geophys. Union, Am. Inst. Mining and Metall. Engrs., Phi Beta Kappa. Home: 485 Whitfield St Guilford CT 06437-3443 Office: Kline Geol Lab PO Box 208109 New Haven CT 06520-8109

GORDON, ROBERT BRUCE, mechanical engineer; b. Phila., May 5, 1931; s. Hans Cochrane and Sarah Elizabeth (Hall) G.; m. Elinor Mildred Cloud, May 8, 1954; children: Bruce Cloud, Lisa Diane. BS, Ursinus Coll., 1953; postgrad., U. Md., 1956, Widener U., 1958, Temple U., 1960. Test and devel. engr. Naval Air Materials Ctr., Phila., 1953-55; design engr. RCA Corp., Camden, N.J., 1957, 58-64, Tatnall Measuring Sys. Co., Phoenixville, Pa., 1957-58; devel. engr. Martin Marietta Co., Orlando, Fla., 1964; project devel. engr. Eastman Kodak Co., Rochester, N.Y., 1964-65; prin. engr., unit mgr. RCA Corp. (GE), Camden, 1965-92; sr. staff cons. Marconi AES, Inc., Lansdale, Pa., 1992—. Patentee in field. Com. chmn. Troop 419 Boy Scouts Am., Springfield, Pa., 1969-74. With U.S. Army, 1955-57. Recipient Cert. of Recognition for Creative Tech., NASA, Huntsville, Ala., 1977. Mem. IEEE (sr.), Masons (Richmond lodge), Shriners. Republican. Lutheran. Home: 492 Thatcher Rd Springfield PA 19064-2912

GORDON, ROBERT DANA, transplant surgeon; b. N.Y.C., Jan. 25, 1945; s. Gerson George and Muriel Ruth (Danish) G.; m. Linda Susan Svirsky, July 9, 1970; children: David Charles, Daniel Lawrence. BA, Amherst Coll., 1966; MD, Cornell U., 1971. Diplomate Am. Bd. Surgery. Intern in surgery Mass. Gen. Hosp., Boston, 1971-72, resident in surgery, 1972-74, 77-78; vis. scientist transplantation biology unit Clin. Rsch. Ctr., Harrow, U.K., 1974-76; rsch. fellow Mass. Gen. Hosp./Harvard Med. Sch., Boston, 1974-76; clin. fellow Harvard Med. Sch., Boston, 1977-78; asst. prof. surgery U. Colo., Denver, 1979-83; asst. prof. surgery U. Pitts., 1983-88, assoc. prof., 1988-92; prof. surgery, chief liver transplant svc. Emory Univ., Sch. Medicine, Atlanta, 1992-98; med. dir. transplantation Roche Labs., Nutley, N.J., 1999—; attending surgeon Egleston Children's Hosp., Atlanta, 1992-98; attending surgeon, co-dir. organ transplant svcs., Emory U. Hosp., Atlanta, 1992-98; chmn. fgn. rels. com. United Network Organ Sharing, Richmond, Va., 1987-90. Bd. dirs. Pitts. chpt. ARC; mem. Corp. of Jackson Lab., Bar Harbor, Maine, 1994—. Fellow ACS; mem. Internat. Soc. Cardiovasc. Surgery, Ctrl. Surg. Assn., Soc. Univ. Surgeons, Am. Soc. Transplant Surgeons, Am. Soc. Transplant Physicians, Transplantation Soc., Internat. Liver Transplantation Soc., Am. Assn. for Study Liver Diseases, Pan Am. Med. Assn. (pres. sect. organ transplantation 1992), Ga. Surg. Soc., Pa. Soc. Biomed. Rsch. (bd. dirs. 1991-92). Avocations: computer science, skiing, hiking, cycling, organ music. Office: Roche Labs Bldg 1/5 340 Kingsland St Nutley NJ 07110-1199

GORDON, ROBERT JAMES, economics educator; b. Boston, Sept. 3, 1940; s. Robert Aaron and Margaret (Shaughnessy) G.; m. Julie S. Peyton, June 22, 1963. A.B., Harvard U., 1962; M.A., Oxford U., Eng., 1969; Ph.D., MIT, 1967. Asst. prof. econs. Harvard U., 1967-68; asst. prof. U. Chgo., 1968-73; prof. econs. Northwestern U., Evanston, Ill., 1973—, Stanley G. Harris prof. social scis., 1987—; chair econs. dept. Northwestern U., Evanston, 1992-96; rsch. assoc. Nat. Bur. Econ Rsch., 1968—; mem. Brookings Panel Econ. Activity, 1970—; co-chmn. Internat. Seminar Macroecons., 1978-94; mem. exec. com. Conf. Rsch., Income and Wealth, 1978-83; mem. panel rev. productivity measures NAS, 1977-79; cons. bd. govs. Fed. Res. Sys., 1973-83, U.S. Dept. Treasury, 1967-80, U.S. Congl. Budget Office, 1996—; mem. Nat. Commn. on Consumer Price Index, 1995-97. Author: Macroeconomics, 1978, 7th edit., 1998, Milton Friedman's Monetary Framework, 1974, Challenges to Interdependent Economies, 1979, The American Business Cycle: Continuity and Change, 1986, The Measurement of Durable Goods Prices, 1990, International Volatility and Economic Growth, 1991, The Economics of New Goods, 1997; editor Jour. Polit. Economy, 1970-73. Marshall fellow, 1962-64; fellow Ford Found., 1966-67; grantee NSF, 1971—; fellow Guggenheim Meml. Found., 1980-81; rsch. fellow German Marshall Fund, 1985-86. Fellow AAAS, Econometric Soc. (treas. 1975—); mem. Am. Econ. Assn. (bd. editors 1975-77, mem. exec. com. 1981-83), Phi Beta Kappa. Office: Northwestern U Dept Econs Evanston IL 60208-2600

GORDON, RONALD CLAYTON, biomedical engineer; b. Petersburg, Va., Aug. 13, 1933; s. Robert Lee and Georgia Frank (Clayton) G.; m. Vivian Verdell, Jan. 27, 1957 (div. 1987); children: Ronald Jr., Susan; stepchildren: Yasmin, Taslim, Karim; m. Zarina Watkin, Mar. 27, 1989. BS, Va. State Coll., 1955, MS, 1968; PhD, U. Va., 1978. Physicist Nat. Bur. Standards, Washington, 1957-64; rsch. engr. McDonnell Douglas, Santa Monica, 1964-68; asst. prof. U. Va. Sch. Medicine, Charlottesville, 1979-82; fgn. sci. technologist U.S. Army, 1982-92; asst. prof. U. Va. Sch. Medicine, 1992-94; commr. Dept. Rehab. Svc., Richmond, Va., 1994-95; dir. Va. Neuro Trauma, Crozet, 1995—. NIH fellow, 1972-76. Home: 2635 White Hall Rd Crozet VA 22932-2402

GORDON, RONNI ANNE, journalist; b. N.Y.C., Aug. 24, 1954; d. Alfred O. and Lynne (Lewin) G.; children: Benjamin, Joseph, Katherine. BA in English, Vassar Coll., 1976; MS in Journalism, Boston U., 1979. Feature writer, reporter Holyoke (Mass.) Transcript-Telegram, 1979-80, editor, 1981; feature writer Springfield (Mass.) Union-News and Sunday Republican, 1982—. Office: The Republican Co 1860 Main St Springfield MA 01103-1000

GORDON, ROY GERALD, chemistry educator; b. Akron, Ohio, Jan. 11, 1940; s. Nathan Gold and Frances (Teitel) G.; m. Myra Sheila Miller, Dec. 24, 1961; children: Avra Karen, Emily Francine, Steven Eric. A.B. summa cum laude, Harvard, 1961, A.M. in Physics, 1962, Ph.D. in Chem. Physics, 1964. Jr. fellow Soc. of Fellows, Harvard, 1964-66, mem. faculty, 1966—, prof., 1969—. Sloan Found. fellow, 1966-69, Einstein fellow, Israel, 1985. Fellow Am. Phys. Soc.; mem. Am. Chem. Soc. (award in pure chemistry 1972, Baekeland award 1979, Esselen award 1996) R & D award 1991, Faraday Soc., Union of Concerned Scientists, NAS, Am. Acad. Arts and Scis., Phi Beta Kappa, Sigma Xi. Achievements include inventions in solar energy, energy conservation and microelectronics, theoretical research discovering forms of forces between molecules, the way molecules collide with each other, motion of molecules in liquids and solids. Office: Harvard U Dept Chemistry 12 Oxford St Cambridge MA 02138

GORDON, RUBY DANIELS, retired nursing educator, counselor; b. Camden, Ark., Dec. 28, 1927; d. Fred Jewell and Etta Matilda (Watson) Daniels; m. DeVore Basil Gordon, Sept. 1, 1946 (div. 1950); children: Sally Ann Gordon, Lynne Gordon. Diploma, St. Monica's Hosp., Phoenix, 1949; BS, Ariz. State U., 1959, MA, 1962, PhD, 1975. Instr. basic scis. St. Joseph Hosp. Sch. Nursing, Phoenix, 1962-67; chairperson dept. nursing Glendale (Ariz.) C.C., 1967-80; prof. Phoenix Coll., 1980-92; counselor Glendale C.C., 1993-98; ret., 1998.

GORDON, SANDY GALE COMBS, medical surgical nurse, community health nurse; b. Lafollette, Tenn., Sept. 8, 1950; d. Wise and Edna Leona (Boshears) Combs; m. Ralph William Gordon, Aug. 30, 1975 (dec. Feb. 1998). Diploma, Middletown Hosp., 1971. RN, Ohio. Pub. health nurse Bur. Pub. Health, Middletown, Ohio, 1979-82; staff nurse Middletown Hosp., 1971-79. Named Internat. Women of Yr., 1994-95. Mem. Middletown Hosp. Alumni Assn. E-mail: sgordon@erinet.com. Home: 1107 Ellen Dr Middletown OH 45042-3341

GORDON, SANFORD DANIEL, economics educator; b. Newark, June 23, 1924; s. Harry Louis and Beatrice (Safris) G.; m. Alice Lillian Pressman, May 27, 1948; children—Ellen Ann, Eric Alan. Student, Tulane U., 1942; B.S. magna cum laude, NYU, 1947, M.A., 1948, Ph.D., 1953. Instr. econ. NYU, 1948-50; mem. faculty State U. Coll., Oneonta, N.Y., 1950—; prof. econs. State U. Coll., 1957—, chmn. dept., 1960—; asst. vice chancellor for policy and planning State U. N.Y. Central Adminstrn., 1972-76, provost for policy analysis, 1976-79; exec. dir. N.Y. State Coun. on Econ. Edn., 1979-89; prof. econs. Russell Sage Coll., 1979-89; adj. prof. econs. U. So. Fla., 1989—; econ. editor Kennikat Press, Inc., Port Washington, N.Y., 1970—; cons. govt., industry, banks, pub. schs., 1954—; vis. prof. State U. N.Y., Buffalo, 1965, U. Miami, 1967. Author: (with J. Witchel) An Introduction to the American Economy, 1967, A Visual Analysis of the American Economy, 1968, (with G. Dawson) The American Economy, 1969, Introductory Economics, 1972, 7th edit., 1991; (with Conover and Ramstadder) Business Dynamics, 1982, 2d edit., 1988, The Economy of New York State, 1987, Basic Economic Principles, 1988, Economics U$A: A Resource Guide for Teachers, 1988, (with A. Stafford) Applying Economic Principles, 1994; lectr., writer: pub. TV series The American Economy, Conversations on Economic Issues, 1970—. Mem. Parks Commn., also Charter Revision Commn., Oneonta, 1957—; v.p. Oneonta Brotherhood, 1958; Dem. candidate for 13th Congl. Dist., Fla., for U.S. Ho. of Reps. Served to sgt. USAAF, 1942-44. Recipient Kazajian Found. award, 1967, Bessie B. Moore Service award , 1987. Mem. N.Y. Econ. Assn. (past pres.), AAUP (past pres. N.Y. conf.). Home: 7127 Fairway Bend Ln Sarasota FL 34243-3608 *Success has less to do with innate ability than with self-confidence, motivation, and perhaps most important, resiliancy.*

GORDON, STEPHEN MAURICE, manufacturing company executive, rancher; b. Chgo., Aug. 20, 1942; s. Milton A. and Elinor (Loeff) G.; m. Helene Lindow, Feb. 11, 1978 (div. Mar. 1998); 2 children: Hallie Lindow, Lacey Edison; m. Marilee Ann Enright, Mar. 21, 1998. Student, Middlebury Coll., 1960-61; B.A., U. Chgo., 1964; J.D., N.Y. U., 1967; D.I.L., Cambridge (Eng.) U., 1968. Bar: N.Y. State 1968. Aide to Vice Pres. Hubert Humphrey, Democratic Nat. Com., Washington, 1968; assoc. firm Marshall, Bratter, Greene, Allison & Tucker, N.Y.C., 1968-70; sr. rsch. assoc. Halle & Stieglitz, Inc., N.Y.C., 1970-72; v.p. Halle & Stieglitz, Inc., 1972-75, pres., 1975-79; pres., chief exec. officer Irvin Industries Inc., N.Y.C., 1979-89; pres. Diamond G Ranch Inc., Dubois, Wyo.; chmn. bd. dirs. Vincennes Steel Corp. Mem. Nat. Wildlife Art Mus. (dir., treas.), MacLean-Fogg (dir.), Am. Red Angus Assn., Young Pres.' Orgn., Beta Gamma Sigma, Psi Upsilon. Home: Diamond G Ranch Dunoir Rd Dubois WY 82513 Office: PO Box 25009 Jackson WY 83001-7000

GORDON, STEVEN B., chemist; b. Brookline, Mass., Nov. 10, 1948; s. Samuel N. and Dora I. (Resnick) G.; m. Cathy J. Hopewell, Oct. 20, 1973; children: Robin N., Jeffrey A. AB, Boston U., 1970; MA, Clark U., 1973. Chemist Reed Plastics Corp., Holden, Mass., 1972-74, adminstr. tech. svcs., 1974-80, corp. tech. mgr., 1980-84, tech. dir., 1984-88; dir. tech. Masterbatches divsn. (formerly ReedSpectrum) Clariant Corp., Holden, Mass., 1988—. Mem. Am. Chem. Soc., Soc. Plastics Engrs. (tech. program com. 1976-79). Achievements include contributions to plastics coloring technology. Office: Clariant Corp Masterbatches Divsn Holden Indsl Park Holden MA 01520

GORDON, SUSAN J., writer; b. N.Y.C., Nov. 12, 1943; m. Kenneth Gordon, Nov. 21, 1965; children: Edward, Peter. BA in Am. Studies, Queens Coll., 1964; MA in Am. Studies, NYU, 1967. vis. artist Westchester (N.Y.) Arts Coun., 1983—. Author: Wedding Days: When and How Great Marriages Began, 1998. Mem. Am. Soc. Journalists and Authors, Authors Guild. Home: 11 Avondale Rd White Plains NY 10605-4101

GORDON, SYDNEY MICHAEL, research chemist; b. Pretoria, South Africa, Apr. 18, 1939; came to U.S., 1977; s. Cyril and Ida (Goldberg) G.; m. Patricia C. Hammerschlag, Sept. 1963 (div. Feb. 1982); children: Danielle, Anna K., Stephanie; m. Maria Hawryluk, Mar. 9, 1984; 1 child, Andrew M. BSc, U. Pretoria, 1959, MSc, 1962, DSc, 1964. Chief chemist Atomic Energy Bd., Pelindaba, South Africa, 1964-77; sci. advisor Ill. Inst. Tech. Rsch. Inst., Chgo., 1977-91; rsch. leader Battelle Meml. Inst., Columbus, Ohio, 1991—. Contbr. articles to profl. jours., chpts. to books. Mem. Am. Chem. Soc., Am. Soc. Mass Spectrometry, Internat. Soc. Exposure Analysis. Office: Battelle Meml Inst 505 King Ave Columbus OH 43201-2681

GORDON, THELMA HUNTER, state official. Sec. Aging Dept., Topeka. Office: Kans Dept on Aging New Eng Bldg 503 S Kansas Ave Topeka KS 66603-3404

GORDON, THOMAS CHRISTIAN, JR., former justice; b. Richmond, Va., July 14, 1915; s. Thomas Christian and Ruth Nelson (Robins) G. B.S., U. Va., 1936, LL.B., 1938. Bar: Va. bar 1937. Assoc. Parrish, Butcher & Parrish, Richmond, 1938-40; assoc., then partner McGuire, Woods & Battle (and predecessors), Richmond, 1940-65, 72-83; justice Supreme Ct. Va., 1965-72; lectr. Law Sch., U. Va., 1970-72, Marshall-Wythe Sch. Law, 1979-81. Bd. editors: Va. Law Rev, 1937-38. Trustee, past pres. Childrens Hosp., Richmond. Served to maj. AUS, 1941-45. Fellow Am. Bar Found.; mem. Am. Bar Assn., Va. Bar Assn. (pres. 1963-64). Episcopalian (vestry, sr. warden). Home: 1435 Floyd Ave Richmond VA 23220-4663 Office: One James Ctr 4th Fl Richmond VA 23219

GORDON, THOMAS JOSEPH, psychologist; b. Boston, Sept. 15, 1943; s. Thomas J. and Margaret M. G.; m. Janet A. Cusick; children: Thomas J., Karen M., Joseph M. BS cum laude, Boston Coll., 1965, PhD with distinction, 1970. Psychologist Tri City Mental Health Ctr., Malden, Mass., 1970-79, Carney Hosp., Boston, 1978—, Arbor Hosp., Boston, 1978—, Milton (Mass.) Hosp., 1984—; adj. prof. Boston Coll., Chestnut Hill, Mass., 1970-74. Mem. APA, Mass. Psychol. Assn., Mass. Neuropsychol. Soc. Avocations: golf, travel, boating, music. Home: 2001 Marina Dr Apt 304W Quincy MA 02171-1544 Office: Carney Hosp 2100 Dorchester Ave Ste 4437 Boston MA 02124-5666

GORDON, TOM LEE, education educator; b. Pitts., June 20, 1946; s. Edward P. and Ruth (Wein) G.; divorced; children: Dana, Erick, Gordon. PhD, U. N.C., Greensboro, 1987. Instr. Montgomery Tech. Coll., Troy, N.C., 1979-86; founder McIver Street Child Care, Greensboro, N.C., 1985-91; assoc. prof. edn. Slippery Rock (Pa.) U., 1992—; mem. presch. screening bd. Devel. Evaluation Ctr., Greensboro, 1988-92; cons., founder Tom Gordon & Assoc., Pitts., 1993—. Contbr. articles to profl. jours. Coun. mem., officer Butler (Pa.) County Heat Start, 1993—. Slippery Rock U. grantee, 1994. Mem. Assn. Childhood Edn. Internat., Nat. Assn. Edn. Young Children. Avocations: canoeing, scuba diving, bicycling. Home: 422 Lloyd St Pittsburgh PA 15208-2829 Office: Slippery Rock U McKay Edn Bldg Slippery Rock PA 16057

GORDON, WALTER KELLY, retired provost, English language educator; b. Bklyn., Jan. 25, 1930; s. William Benjamin and Grace Adele (Kelly) G.; m. Lydia Caroline Fruchtman, Aug. 29, 1959; 1 child, Karyn Gay. A.B., Clark U., 1950; M.A., U. Pa., 1956, Ph.D., 1961. Instr. Cedar Crest Coll., 1959-61; faculty Rutgers U., Camden, 1961-97; prof., dean coll. Rutgers U., 1974-81, acad. dean, provost Camden campus, 1981-97; ret., 1997; cons. Campbells Soup Co., 1976-94. Author: (with J.L. Sanderson) Exposition and the English Language, 1963, 2d edit., 1968, Literature in Critical Perspectives, 1969. Bd. dirs. Walt Whitman Internat. Poetry Center, 1974-77. Served to lt. USNR, 1951-56. Recipient Lindback award for disting. teaching, 1970. Home: 2803 Salem Dr Riverton NJ 08077-4027 Office: Rutgers U Camden Coll Arts & Scis 379 Armitage Hall Camden NJ 08102

GORDON, WILLIAM A., lawyer; b. Bklyn., Feb. 6, 1940; m. Joyce Kahler, Aug. 26, 1962; children: Kyle Robert, Michael Stuart, David Andrew. BS, Northwestern U., 1960; LLB, Harvard U., 1963. Bar: Ill. 1963, U.S. Dist. Ct. (no. dist. trial bar) Ill. 1965, U.S. Ct. Appeals (7th cir.) 1971, U.S. Supreme Ct. 1971, U.S. Tax Ct. 1971, U.S. Ct. Appeals (2nd cir.) 1983, U.S. Ct. Appeals (6th cir.) 1987. Law clk. U.S. Dist. Ct. (no. dist.) Ill., 1963-66; ptnr. Mayer, Brown & Platt, Chgo., 1970—. Office: Mayer Brown & Platt 190 S La Salle St Ste 3100 Chicago IL 60603-3441

GORDON, WILLIAM C., college administrator; m. Kathryn Gordon; children: Jason, Scott, Kate, Jonathan. Bachelor's degree, Master's degree, Wake Forest U.; PhD in Exptl. Psychology, Rutgers U. Asst. prof. psychology SUNY, Binghamton, 1973-78; tchr. psychology dept. U. N.Mex., Albuquerque, 1978, chair psychology dept., 1990; interim dean Coll. Arts and Scis. U. N.Mex., 1992, dean, 1993, provost, v.p. for acad. affairs, 1996, interim pres., 1998—. Office: U N Mex Albuquerque NM 87131-0001

GORDON, WILLIAM EDWIN, physicist, engineer, educator, university official; b. Paterson, N.J., Jan. 8, 1918; s. William and Mary (Scott) G.; m. Elva Freile, June 22, 1941; children:Larry Scott, Nancy Lynn. BA, Montclair (N.J.) State Coll., 1939, MA, 1942; MS, NYU, 1946; PhD, Cornell U., Ithaca, N.Y., 1953. Registered profl. engr., Tex. Assoc. prof. Cornell U., 1953-59, prof., 1959-65; Walter R. Read prof. engring. Arecibo Ionospheric Obs., P.R., 1965; prof. elec. engring. and space physics and astronomy Rice U., Houston, 1966-86, dean engring. and sci., 1966-75, dean Sch. Natural Scis., 1975-80, provost, v.p. Sch. Natural Scis., 1980-86; fgn. sec. NAS, 1986-90; conceived, directed design constrn and early operation of Arecibo Obs. and 1000 foot antenna, 1960-65; chmn. bd. trustees Upper Atmosphere Rsch. Corp., 1971, 73-78, Univ. Corp. for Atmospheric Rsch., 1979-81, 86-89, 91-92; trustee Cornell U., 1976-80; mem. Arecibo Obs. Adv. Bd., 1977-80, 90-93. Bd. dirs. Taping for the Blind, Houston, 1994—. Capt. USAAF, 1942-46. Recipient Balth. Vander Pol award for disting. research in radio sci., 1966; 50th Anniversary medal Am. Meteorol. Soc., 1969; Guggenheim fellow, 1972-73, Arktowski Medal, 1984. Fellow IEEE (chmn. profl. group on antennas and propagation 1964-65), Am. Geophys. Union; mem. AAAS, NAS, NAE, Am. Acad. Arts and Scis., Internat. Sci. Radio Union (v.p. 1975-81, pres. 1981-84, hon. pres. 1990—), Internat. Coun. Sci. Unions (v.p. 1988-93), Am. Meteorology Soc., Philos. Soc. Tex., Cosmos Club, Sigma Xi, Tau Beta Pi, Kappa Delta Pi, Sigma Kappa Nu, Phi Kappa Phi. Spl. rsch. radio scattering. Office: Rice U Dept Space Physics PO Box 1892 Houston TX 77251-1892

GORDON-SPEARMAN, FLORIDA LEE, nursing educator; b. Marks, Miss., Sept. 26, 1934. AA, Malcolm X Coll., 1971; BA, Logos Bible Coll., N.Y.C., 1984; MA, Logos Grad. Sch., Brandon, Fla., 1988; MS, Nat. Louis U., 1992. CNA, Chgo. LPN instr. Dawson Skills Ctr., Chgo., 1974-77; supr. CNA's Metro Home Health, Inc., Chgo., 1979-87; pvt. duty hi-tech. specialist VNA-Caring Touch, Chgo., 1988-89; clin. coord., instr. P.T.C. Career Inst., Chgo., 1989-94; advance CNA instr. Ill. Med. Tng., Chgo., 1990-92; case mgr. for home health Staff Builder Nursing Registry, 1996-98; instr. Logos, Bible Coll, 1985—, Career Coll. Assn., Chgo., 1989-94, Harold Washington Coll., 1994—; bd. dirs. House of Daniel. Author: Women in Ministry, 1992; narrator WCFC-TV, WYCA, Chgo., 1976—. Ordained min. Monument of Faith Ch., Chgo., 1987—; mentor for young adult women on home mgmt., career planning, spiritual devel., 1983—. Mem. Nat. Louis U. Alumni Assn., Logos Bible Coll. Alumni Assn. (lay counselor).

GORDY, BERRY, entrepreneur, record company executive, motion picture executive; b. Detroit, Nov. 28, 1929; m. Grace Eaton, July 17, 1990; children: Berry IV, Hazel Joy, Terry James, Kerry A., Kennedy W., Stefan K. Founder Motown Record Corp., from 1961; chmn. bd. dirs. The Gordy Co.; exec. producer motion pictures; chmn. bd. dirs. West Grand Media, 1998—. Dir. motion picture Mahogany, 1975; exec. producer films Lady Sings the Blues, 1972, Bingo Long Traveling All-Stars and Motor Kings, 1975, The Last Dragon, 1984; author: To Be Loved: The Music, the Magic, the Memories of Motown, 1994. Recipient Bus. Achievement award Interracial Coun. for Bus. Opportunity, 1967, 2d Ann. Am. Music award for outstanding contbn. to mus. industry, 1975, Whitney M. Young Jr. award L.A. Urban League, 1980, NARAS Trustees award, 1991, Am. Legen award ASCAP Pop Music Awards, 1998; named one of Five Leading Entrepreneurs of Nation Babson Coll., 1978; inducted into Rock and Roll Hall of Fame, 1988, Jr. Achievement Nat. Bus. Hall of Fame, 1998; Gordon Grand fellow Yale U., 1985. Mem. Guild Am. (bd. dirs.). Office: West Grand Media 6255 W Sunset Blvd Ste 1100 Los Angeles CA 90028-7412*

GORE, ALBERT, JR., Vice President of the United States; b. Washington, DC, Mar. 31, 1948; s. Albert and Pauline (LaFon) G.; m. Mary Elizabeth Aitcheson, May 19, 1970; children: Karenna, Kristin, Sarah, Albert III. BA cum laude (Univ. scholar), Harvard U., 1969; postgrad., Grad. Sch. of Religion, Vanderbilt U., 1971-72, Law Sch., 1974-76. Investigative reporter, editorial writer The Tennessean, 1971-76; mem. 95th-98th Congresses from Tenn., 1977-85; U.S. senator from Tenn., 1985-93; homebuilder and land developer Tanglewood Home Builders Co., 1971-76; livestock and tobacco farmer, from 1973, V.P. of U.S., 1993—. Author: Earth in the Balance: Ecology and the Human Spirit, 1992. Served with U.S. Army, 1969-71, Vietnam. Mem. Farm Bur., Tenn. Jaycees. Democrat. Baptist. Clubs: Am. Legion, VFW. Office: The White House Office of Vice President Old Executive Office Bldg NW Washington DC 20501*

GORE, DAVID CURTISS, investment banker, consultant; b. Conway, S.C., Dec. 4, 1964. BS in Fin., U. S.C., 1986. Co-owner, v.p. Gem-Clarke Co., Inc., Columbia, S.C., 1985-89; cons. Columbia, S.C., 1989-95; exec. Tomlin & Co. Inc.; investment banker Venture Capital Investments, Columbia, S.C., 1995—. Mem. Lambda Chi Alpha (treas. 1984-85). Republican. Baptist. Office: PO Box 7304 Columbia SC 29202-7304

GORE, DONALD RAY, orthopedic surgeon; b. Michigan City, Ind., Mar. 13, 1936; s. Clarence Bernard and Susan Leone (Fuller) G.; m. Jacqueline Marie Kraabel, Aug. 25, 1956; children: Donald, Daniel, Jennifer, Elizabeth. BS, U. Ill., 1958, MD, 1960; MS, Marquette U., 1967. Cert. Am. Bd. Orthopaedic Surgery. Intern Milw. County Gen Hosp., 1960-61; resident gen. surgery Marquette U. Sch. Medicine, Milw., 1961-64, resident orthopaedic surgery, 1964-67; fellow Biomechanics Lab U. Calif., San Francisco, 1967-68; practice medicine specializing in orthopaedic surgery Sheboygan (Wis.) Orthopaedic Assocs., S.C., 1968—; clin. prof. dept. orthopaedic surgery Med. Coll. Wis., Milw., 1980—; staff St. Nicholas Hosp., Sheboygan, Sheboygan Meml. Hosp.; cons. surgery Wood (Wis.) VA Hosp., 1970—; asst. instr. dept. surgery Med. Coll. Wis., 1964-68, clin. instr. dept. surgery, 1969-72, asst. clin. prof., 1972-73, assoc. clin. prof., 1973-80; research assoc. VA Med. Ctr., Milw., 1970—, co-investigator kinesiology research lab., 1970-84. Mem. bd. editors Jour. Orthopaedic Surg. Techniques, 1985—; contbr. articles to profl. jours. Served to capt. USAF, 1962-63. Fellow Am. Acad. Orthopaedic Surgeons (bd. councilors 1985—); mem. AMA, Mid-Am. Orthopaedic Soc., Clin. Orthopaedic Soc., Wis. Orthopaedic Soc. (pres. 1982-84), Milw. Orthopaedic Soc., Wis. Arthritis Found. (bd. dirs. 1974-82), Sierra Cascade Trauma Soc., Cervical Spine Research Socs. Republican. Lutheran. Avocations: skiing, fishing, tennis, golf, backpacking. Home: 2528 N 3rd St Sheboygan WI 53083-5007 Office: Sheboygan Orthopaedic Assocs SC 2920 Superior Ave Sheboygan WI 53081-1944

GORE, GENEVIEVE WALTON, company executive; b. Salt Lake City, Mar. 23, 1913; d. Thaddeus and Ethel May (Arnold) Walton; m. Wilbert Lee Gore, Jan 1, 1935 (widowed July 1986); children: Robert, Susan, Virginia, David, Elizabeth. Student, U. Utah, 1933, Henninger Bus. Coll., 1935; HHD in Humanities, Westminster Coll., 1982; D in Bus. Adminstrn., Goldey-Beacom Coll., 1991. Sec., treas. W.L. Gore & Assoc., Inc., Newark, Del., 1958—; dir. W.L. Gore & Assoc., Scotland, West Germany, India, Del. State C. of C., Wilmington. Co-founder W.L. Gore & Assoc., Inc., 1958. Bd. counselors Goldey-Beacom Coll., Wilmington, Del., 1991; bd. govs. Winterthur (Del.) Mus., 1991. Recipient Medal Distinction, U. Del., Newark, 1983, Bavarian Order of Merit, Germany, 1988, Disting. Performance in Mgmt. award Widener U., Wilmington, 1986; named Del. Women's Hall of Fame, Dover, 1989, Del. Bus. Leaders Hall of Fame, 1991. Mem. Girl Scouts Pres.Adv. Coun., Chesapeake Bay Girl Scouts, Independence Sch., Boy Scouts Am. Avocations: mountain climbing, swimming, music, world travel. Home: PO Box 9329 Newark DE 19714-9329 Office: WL Gore & Associates Inc PO Box 9329 Newark DE 19714-9329*

GORE, JAMES ARNOLD, biology educator, aquatic ecologist, hydrologist; b. Los Alamos, N.Mex., Sept. 3, 1949; s. James Kenneth and Margaret Emma (Arnold) G.; m. Gertrude Morron, Aug. 21, 1971 (div. 1978); children: Sarah Elizabeth, James Matthew; m. Ellen Diane O'Quinn, Mar. 8, 1980 (div. 1994); 1 child, Erin Kathleen. BA, U. Colo., 1971; MA, U. Mont., 1976, PhD, 1981. Rsch. aquatic biologist Wyo. Water Resources Res. Inst., Laramie, 1978-80; rsch. assoc. Tenn. Coop. Fisheries Res. Unit, Cookeville, Tenn., 1980-81; assoc. prof. U. Tulsa, 1981-90; prof., dir. Ctr. for Field Biology Austin Peay State U., Clarksville, Tenn., 1990-92; eminent scholar chair in environ. sci. Troy (Ala.) State U., 1992-94; dir. environ. protection The Conservancy, Naples, Fla., 1994-96; prof., dir. environ. sci. grad. program Columbus (Ga.) State U., 1996—; guest prof. Zoologishes Inst. U., Karlsruhe, Fed. Republic of Germany, 1985; rsch. ecologist Waterways Experiment Sta., Vicksburg, Miss., 1986-88; vis. prof. U. Cape Town, South Africa, 1989. Author and editor: The Restoration of Rivers and Streams, 1985, Alternatives in Regulated River Management, 1989. With USN, 1971-74, Vietnam. Fulbright scholar, South Africa, 1989. Mem. AAAS, Am. Inst. Biol. Scis., N.Am. Benthological Soc., South African Soc. Aquatic Scientists, N.Z. Limnological Soc. Achievements include research in hydraulic stream ecology. Office: Columbus State Univ Sch of Science Environ Sci Program Columbus GA 31907

GORE, ROBERT W., electronics executive. Pres., CEO W.L. Gore & Assocs., Newark, Del. Office: W L Gore & Assocs PO Box 9329 Newark DE 19714-9329*

GORE, TIPPER (MARY ELIZABETH GORE), wife of the vice president of the United States; b. Washington, Aug. 19, 1948; m. Albert Gore Jr., May 19, 1970; children: Karenna, Kristin, Sarah, Albert III. BA in Psychology, Boston U., 1970; MA in Psychology, Vanderbilt U., 1975. Freelance photographer; mental health policy advisor to pres. Author: Raising PG Kids in an X-Rated Society, 1987, Picture This: A Visual Diary, 1996; coprodr. (with Nat. Mental Health Assn.) Homeless in America: A Photographic Project. Co-founder Parents Music Resource Ctr., Arlington, Va., 1985; founder Tenn. Voices for Children, 1990; co-chair Am. Goes Back to Sch. Initiative, 1996—; chair Congl. Wives Task Force, 1978-79. Office: Old Exec Office Bldg Rm 200 Washington DC 20501*

GORE, WILLIAM JAY, political science educator; b. Medford, Oreg., Feb. 23, 1924; s. Jay Ish and Gertrude (Moore) G.; m. Dorothy Elaine Mathson, Sept. 24, 1947; children: Edmond J., Kathleen J., Brian J. BA, U. Wash., 1948; M of Pub. Adminstrn., U. So. Calif., 1950, DPA, 1952. Instr. U. Wash., Seattle, 1951-56, prof. polit. sci., 1966-89, prof. emeritus, 1989—; asst. prof. polit. sci. Kans. U., Lawrence, 1956-57, 58-61, Cornell U., Ithaca, N.Y., 1957-58; assoc. prof. polit. sci. Ind. U., Bloomington, 1961-66; asst. dir. Govt. Rsch. Ctr. Kans. U., 1958-61; cons. U. So. Calif. (NASA Project), 1967-69, Nat. Safety Council, Chgo., Il., 1962-66, USPHS, 1980-81. Author: Administrative Decision-Making, 1964, (with Dyson) The Making of Decision, 1964, Change in the Small Community, 1967. Ford Career Devel. grantee, 1959-61; HEW grantee, 1956-58; Washington Com. for Humanities grantee, 1979-81. Mem. Am. Soc. Pub. Adminstrn. (jour. editor 1967-70), Western Polit. Sci. Assn. (bd. dir. 1953-56). Methodist. Home: 4130 NE 43rd St Seattle WA 98105-5104 Office: U Wash Dept Polit Sci Seattle WA 98195 *The determination to lay bare the dilemmas and contradictions that once dogged us, and seek thereby to transcend them, is one of the proper expressions of the creative intellect.*

GORELICK, JAMIE SHONA, lawyer; b. N.Y.C., May 6, 1950; d. Leonard and Shirley (Fishman) G.; m. Richard E. Waldhorn, Sept. 28, 1975; children: Daniel H., Dana E. BA, Radcliffe Coll., 1972; JD, Harvard U., 1975. Bar: D.C. 1975, U.S. Dist. Ct. D.C. 1976, U.S. Tax Ct. 1976, U.S. Ct. Claims 1976, U.S. Ct. Appeals (D.C. cir.) 1976, U.S. Ct. Appeals (5th cir.) 1977, U.S. Supreme Ct. 1979, U.S. Ct. Appeals (Fed. cir.) 1982, U.S. Ct. Internat. Trade 1984, U.S. Dist. Ct. Md. 1985, U.S. Ct. Appeals (4th cir.) 1986, U.S. Ct. Appeals (3d. cir.) 1988. With Miller, Cassidy, Larroca & Lewin, Washington, 1975-79, 81-93; asst. to sec., counselor to dep. sec. U.S. Dept. Energy, Washington, 1979-80; gen. counsel Dept. Def., Washington, 1993-94; dep. atty. gen. Dept. Justice, Washington, 1994-97; vice chair Fannie Mae, Washington, 1997—; mem. chmn.'s adv. coun. U.S. Senate Jud. Com., 1988-93; tchg. mem. trial advocacy workshop Harvard Law Sch., Cambridge, Mass., 1982, 84; vice chair task force evaluation of audit investigative inspection components Dept. Def., Washington, 1979-80; mem. sec.'s transition team Dept. Energy, Washington, 1979; bd. dirs. Fannie Mae, Fannie Mae Found., D.C. Coll. Access, Am.'s Promise-Alliance for Youth, Nat. Park Found., Carnegie Endowment, Nat. Women's Law Ctr., Bazelon Ctr. Mental Health Law, Washington Legal Clinic for Homeless, Local Initiatives Support Corp., Nat. Legal Ctr. for the Pub. Interest; coun. mem. Am. Law Inst., D.C. Bar Found.; co-chair adv. com. Presdl. Commn. on Critical Infrastructure Protection; mem. Nat. Commn. Support Law Enforcement, Washington, 1995—. Mem. editl. bd. Corp. Criminal Liability Reporter, 1986-93, Destruction of Evidence, 1989; contbr. articles to profl. jours. Mem. overseers com. to visit Harvard Coll., 1989-93. Fellow Am. Bar Found.; mem. ABA (chair complex crimes litigation com. litigation sect. 1984-87, vice-chair complex crimes litigation com. 1983-84, Nat. Commn. to Support Law Enforcement, 1995—, sec. litigation sect. 1988-90, coun. mem. 1990-93, com. on profl. discipline, ho. of dels. 1991-93, 97—), D.C. Bar (pres. 1992-93, bd. govs. 1982-88, sec. bd. govs. 1981-82, bar found. advisors 1985-93, legal ethics com.), Womens Bar Assn., Am. Law Inst. (coun.), Coun. on Fgn. Rels. Office: Fannie Mae 3900 Wisconsin Ave NW Washington DC 20016-2892

GORELIK, ALLA, piano educator; b. Chernobyl, Ukraine, Oct. 9, 1949; came to U.S., 1992; d. Simon and Eugena (Ben) Tsoiref; m. Roman Gorelik, June 16, 1971 (div. Apr. 1978); m. Valentin Stadnik, Dec. 26, 1979; children: Regina, Vladislav. BA, State Mus. Coll., Kiev, Ukraine, 1970. Piano and theory tchr. Music Sch. #5, Kiev, 1970-91; accompanist Fort Myers, Fla., 1992—; organist Temple Beth El, Fort Myers, 1993—; music instr. Learning Tree, Fort Myers, 1994—; piano and theory tchr. Fort Myers, 1992—; children musical program dir. North Shore Child Care, Fort Myers, 1993-95; youth art dir. Music Sch. #5, Kiev, 1986-90. Vol., performer Jewish Fedn., Fort Myers, 1992—, Hadassah, Fort Myers, 1993—; vol., accompanist Temples Beth-El and Judea, Fort Myers, 1992—. Recipient Labor Merit medal Ministry of Culture, 1990. Mem. Nat. Music Tchrs. Assn. Avocations: travel, cooking, reading. Home: 18257 Huckleberry Rd Fort Myers FL 33912-5234

GORENBERG, CHARLES LLOYD, financial services executive; b. Phila., Mar. 1, 1938; s. Abraham and Esther (Freedman) G.; m. Roslyn Grobman, May 22, 1960; children: David M., Kenneth M. BA, Franklin & Marshall Coll., 1960; MS, The Am. Coll., Bryn Mawr, Pa., 1981. Cert. Employee Benefit Specialist, CLU, ChFC. Sales assoc. Landis & Co., Phila., 1960-62; agt. Phoenix Mut. Life, Phila., 1962-64, supr., 1964-67; dir. tng. Rittenhouse Assocs., Phila., 1967-75; exec. v.p. Corp. Pension Actuaries, Phila., 1975-91; pres. Delta Fin. Group, Phila., 1991-97, Chaslyn Fin. Group, Marlton, N.J., 1997—. Co-editor: (book) Planning for Business Owners and Professionals, 1988; contbr. over 35 articles to mags. Mem. Internat. Soc. Cert. Employee Benefit Specialists, Am. Soc. CLUs and ChFCs (various offices), Am. Soc. Pension Actuaries. Avocation: golf. Office: Chaslyn Fin Group 2001 Lincoln Dr W Ste B Marlton NJ 08053-1531

GORENBERG, NORMAN BERNARD, aeronautical engineer, consultant, retired; b. St. Louis, May 18, 1923; s. Isadore and Ethel G.; m. Lucille Richmond, June 10, 1947; children: Judith Allyn Gorenberg Stein, Carol Ann Gorenberg, Gershom Gorenberg. BSME, Washington U., St. Louis, 1949. Registered profl. engr., Mo. Aero. engr. USAF Wright Air Devel. Ctr., Dayton, Ohio, 1949-51; aerodynamicist McDonnell Aircraft Corp., St. Louis, 1951-59; supervisory engr. Boeing Co., Vertol Div., Phila., 1959-62; R & D engr. Lockheed Corp., Burbank, Calif., 1962-89; vertical takeoff and landing aircraft cons. Dana Point, Calif., 1989-94; ret., 1994. Contbr. articles to profl. reports. With USAAF, 1943-46. Mem. AIAA, ASME, Am. Helicopter Soc. (chmn. St. Louis sect. 1955-56, nat. aerodyns. com. 1969-70, tech. dir. western region 1969-70), Nat. Mgmt. Assn. (life). Jewish.

GORENCE, PATRICIA JOSETTA, judge; b. Sheboygan, Wis., Mar. 6, 1943; d. Joseph and Antonia (Marinsheck) G.; m. John Michael Bach, July 11, 1969; children: Amy Jane, Mara Jo, J. Christopher Bach. BA, Marquette U., 1965, JD, 1977; MA, U. Wis., 1969. Bar: Wis. 1977, U.S. Dist. Ct. (ea. and we. dists.) Wis. 1977, U.S. Ct. Appeals (7th cir.) 1979, U.S. Supreme Ct. 1980. Asst. U.S. atty. U.S. Atty.'s Office, Milw., 1979-84, 1st asst. U.S. Atty., 1984-87, 89-91, U.S. Atty., 1987-88; dep. atty. gen. State of Wis. Dept. Justice, Madison, 1991-93; assoc. Ginbel, Reilly, Guerin & Brown, Milw., 1993-94; U.S. magistrate judge U.S. Dist. Ct. Wis., Milw., 1994—. Bd. dirs. U. Wis.-Milw. Slovenian Arts Coun., 1989—, treas., 1989—, Milw. Dance Theatre, 1993-98. Recipient Spl. Commendation, U.S. Dept. Justice, 1986, IRS, 1988. Mem. ABA, Am. Law Inst., Am. Judicature Soc., Nat. Assn. Women Judges, Fed. Magistrate Judges Assn. (cir. dir. 1997—), Milw. Bar Assn. (Prosecutor of Yr. 1990), State Bar Wis. (chair professionalism com. 1988—, vice chair legal edn. commn. 1994-96, Pres. award 1995), 7th Cir. Bar Assn. (chair rules and practices com. 1991-95), Assn. for Women Lawyers, Profl. Dimensions.

GORENSTEIN, DAVID G., chemistry and biochemistry educator; b. Oct. 6, 1945; s. Ben and Shirley (Adelberg) G.; m. Deborah H. Joseph, June 11, 1967; 1 child, Jennifer. BS in Chemistry, M.I.T., 1966; MA in Chemistry, Harvard U., 1967, PhD in Chemistry, 1969. Asst. prof. U. Ill., Chgo., 1969-73, assoc. prof., 1973-76, prof., 1976-85; prof. chemistry Purdue Univ., West Lafayette, Ind., 1985-94; dir. Purdue Biochem. MRI Lab., West Lafayette, Ind., 1985-94, NSF Nat. Biol. Facilities Ctr., West Lafayette, 1987-93, NMR and Structural Biology Cores, West Lafayette, 1988-94; dep. dir. NIH Designated AIDS Rsch. Ctr., West Lafayette, 1993-94; prof. human biol. chemistry and genetics U. Tex. Med. Sch., Galveston, 1994—; sr. investigator Sealy Ctr. Molecular Sci. U. Tex. Med. Br., Galveston, 1994—; dir. Nuclear Magnetic Resonance Ctr. U. Tex. Med. Br., Galveston, dir. Sealy Ctr. for Structural Biology, 1995—, dep. dir. NIEHS Ctr., 1996—, Charles Marc Pomerat Disting. Prof. of biology, 1997—; vis. assoc. prof. U. Wis., Madison, 1975; vis. prof. Oxford U., 1977-78, U. Calif., San Francisco, 1986; adj. prof. Biomed. Engring. U. Tex., Austin, 1996—; cons. Baxter Travenol, 1985-95, Merck and Co., 1988, Eli Lilly, 1987-89, Ill. Tool Works, 1973-85, Chronomatic Inc., 1973-85, U.S. Dept. of Labor, 1975, Continental Group, Inc., 1982-84; active numerous univ. coms.; lectr. in field. Editor Bull. of Magnetic Resonance, 1982—; mem. editorial bd. Magnetic Resonance Revs., 1983-93, Jour. Magnetic Resonance, 1992—, Biophys. Jour., 1992-98; pub. abstracts; contbr. articles to profl. jours. Grantee: NSF, 1987-93, NIH, 1970—, Eli Lilly, 1988-94 and numerous others; tchg. fellow Harvard U., 1966-69, trainee summer fellow NSF, 1966, predoctoral fellow NIH, 1967-69, Alfred P. Sloan fellow 1975-79, Sr. Rsch. fellow Fulbright, 1977-78, Guggenheim fellow, 1986; recipient Internat. Lectr. award Fulbright, 1978. Fellow AAAS; mem. Am. Soc. for Biochemistry and Molecular Biology, Am. Chem. Soc. (program chmn. divsn. biol. chemistry 1985-87, vice chmn. Purdue sect. 1990-91, chmn. 1991-92), Midwest NMR Group, Internat. Soc. of Magnetic Resonance (organizing com. VIIIth meeting 1983, exec. bd. XIth meeting 1992), Biophys. Soc., Protein Soc., Sigma Xi, Phi Lambda Upsilon. Achievements include patent in process for Preparing Dithiophosphate Oligonucleotide Analogs via Nucleoside Thiophosphoramidite Intermediates; research in applications of NMR spectroscopy and other physical techniques to biological systems, theoretical bio-organic chemistry, biomolecular design; cancer and AIDS drugs development; development of high quality NMR solution structures of biopolymers, NMR method for understanding the detailed structure of proteins bound as a monolayer to a solid support and the detailed structure of proteins in non-aqueous media; development of 3D Hybrid Hybrid relaxation matrix of biomolecular structure. Address: 3922 Crown Ridge Ct Houston TX 77059-3711 Office: U Tex Med Br Sealy Ctr Structural Biology Galveston TX 77555-1157

GORENSTEIN, EDWARD, employment services executive; b. Bklyn., Apr. 10, 1936; s. David and Deborah (Jablow) G.; m. Helene Clarke, Mar. 12, 1961; children: Robin, Fran, Andrew. BBA in Mktg., Hofstra U., 1958. Founder Career Employment Svcs., Inc., Woodbury, N.Y., 1960—. Contbr. articles to bus. jours. Trustee Temple Emanuel, East Meadow, 1980—; mem. L.I. Com. for Soviet Jewry, 1983-86; chmn. Nassau C.C. Adv. Coun., Garden City, N.Y., 1983—, bd. dirs. Nassau C.C. Found., 1988—; program chmn. Dist. Citizen award dinner Nassau County Coun. Boy Scouts Am., 1985; bd. dirs. L.I. March of Dimes, 1989—, Symphony of L.I., 1993-94; mem. corp. devel. com. Hofstra U., 1989—. With USAFR, 1958-64. Recipient Svc. award, L.I. Employment Agy. Coun., 1977, Ohio Assn. of Pers. Cons., 1980, Outstanding Contbn. award, N.J. Assn. of Pers. Cons., 1982. Mem. Nat. Assn. Pers. Svcs. (mem. speakers bur. 1977—, bd. dirs. 1968—), Assn. of Pers. Cons. (N.Y. bd. dirs. 1968—, Svc. award 1983), Nat. Assn. Temporary Svcs., Cert. Pers. Cons. Soc., Hofstra U. Alumni Assn., L.I. Assn., East Meadow C. of C., Am. Diabetes Assn. Home: 260 Foxhunt Crescent Syyosset NY 11791-1708

GORES, CHRISTOPHER MERREL, lawyer; b. N.Y.C., Aug. 27, 1943; s. Guido James and Mary (Callaway) G.; children: Ellen, Eugenia, James. AB, Princeton U., 1965; LLB, Columbia U., 1968. Bar: N.Y. 1968, Tex. 1973, U.S. Dist. Ct (no. dist.) Tex. 1977. Assoc. Akin, Gump, Strauss, Hauer & Feld, LLP, Dallas, 1973-79, ptnr., 1979—. Bd. dirs. Shakespeare Festival of Dallas, 1982-88. Lt. USNR, 1969-72. Office: Akin Gump Strauss Hauer & Feld LLP 1700 Pacific Ave Ste 4100 Dallas TX 75201-4675

GORES, GARY GENE, credit union sales manager; b. Wildrose, N.D., Mar. 7, 1940; s. Orville Jerome and Irene Constance G.; m. Gail H. Gores, 1963 (div. Dec. 1989); m. Terre Jenice, June 29, 1991; children: Leslie, Christopher. AA, Grays Harbor Coll., Aberdeen, Wash., 1961; BA in Bus., Seattle U., 1969. V.p. 7 Up Bottling Co., Aberdeen, 1955-69, Capitol Savs. & Loan, Olympia, Wash., 1970-75; CEO Wash. State Employees Credit Union, Olympia, 1975-83; br. mgr. Nat. Consumer Coop. Bank, Seattle, 1983-86; CEO Chetco Fed. Credit Union, Brookings, Oreg., 1986-89; pres. Gt. Am. Herb Co., Olympia, 1989-90; pres., CEO Ohio Credit Union League & Svc. Corp., Columbus, 1990—; bus. cons., 1997—; sales mgr. Freeman

Marine, Goldbeach, Oreg., 1998—. Pres. Capitol Area Assn. Performing Arts, Olympia, 1975-86; dist. chair Boy Scouts Am., Brookings, Oreg., 1987-89. With U.S. Army, 1962-68. Home: 28336 Hunter Creek Gold Beach OR 97444-2055

GORES, THOMAS C., lawyer; b. Milw., Sept. 24, 1948; s. Kenneth W. and Carolyn (Camblin) G.; m. Ann P. Pacelli, June 13, 1970; children: Lauren, Jake, Kathryn. BA, U. Notre Dame, 1970, JD, 1973; LLM, U. Miami, 1977. Bar: Wash. 1973, U.S. Tax Ct. 1973. Assoc., then ptnr. Bogle & Gates, Seattle, 1973-78, ptnr., 1978-93; ptnr. Gores & Blais, Seattle, 1993—. Fellow Am. Coll. Trust and Estate Counsel; mem. Wash. State Bar Assn., Seattle Estate Planning Coun. (pres.). Office: Gores & Blais 1420 5th Ave Ste 2600 Seattle WA 98101-1357

GOREWITZ, RUBIN LEON, accountant, financial consultant; b. Bklyn., June 7, 1924; s. Isadore Asa and Esther (Tickotzki) G.; children: Shalom, Heshi, Marian Esther. BBA, CCNY, 1951. CPA, N.Y. Acct. J. Sherago & Co., CPAs, N.Y.C., 1942-48; sr. acct. Leonard A. Shair, CPA, N.Y.C., 1948-56; contr. Herold Radio & Electronics Co., Mt. Vernon, N.Y., 1956-59; pvt. practice acctg. and fin. cons. N.Y., 1959—; cons. Mollen Haurer & Eitel, CPAs, N.Y.C.; staff acct., cons. N.Y. State Coun. Arts; founder, former treas., dir. Midsummer, Inc., Expts. in Art & Tech., Inc., The Real U. of Sts., The Real Gt. Soc.; treas. 21c Corp.; bd. dirs. Robert Rauschenberg, Inc., Untitled Press, Inc., Cloud Mgmt. Internat., Inc., Change, Inc.; cons. new bus. ventures; controller, advisor, fin. cons. Peter Max. Founder, past treas., dir. Abstract Ballet Comtempo, Inc.; founder, past dir. Storytime Dance Theatre, Inc.; founder, treas., dir. Jazz Composers Orch., Found. for Devel. and Preservation of Cultural Arts, Opera Today, Inc., Inst. for Chamber Music, Inc., Traditional Jazz Band Co., Inc., Found. for Vital Arts, Creative Dance Found., Modern Dance Artists, Inc., Seamus Murphy Dance Found., Yuriko Dance Found., Daniel Nagrin Dance Found., Intermedia Found.; founder, dir. Cunningham Dance Found.; treas. Lightyears, Inc.; founder, fin. advisor Martha Graham Ctr., Chimera Dance Found., New World Workshop, Dance Theatre Found., Search, Inc.; Ctrs. for Change; chmn. bd. Dance Notation Bur.; bd. dirs. Dance Theatre Workshop, Change Inc. Concert Artists Guild; founder, pres. Artists' Rights Today, Inc.; fin. advisor Performance Group, Living Theatre, Open Theatre, Found. Contemporary Performing Arts, Music Drama Theatre, Cantor's Assembly Am., Anthology Film Archives; adv. dir. Modern Dance Found., Hackensack; lectr., writer and lobbyist on rights of artists. With AUS, 1943-45, ETO. Mem. AICPA, N.Y. State Soc. CPAs, Nat. Assn. Cost Accts. (past dir. N.Y.C. chpt.), Rochester (N.Y.) C. of C. (pres.). E-mail: rubing@aol.com. Home: 30 W 63rd St Apt 5R New York NY 10023-7108 Office: Mollenhaurer & Eitel CPAs 36 E 20th St New York NY 10003

GOREY, EDWARD ST. JOHN, author, artist; b. Chgo., Feb. 22, 1925; s. Edward Leo and Helen Dunham (Garvey) G. BA, Harvard U., 1950. Author: The Unstrung Harp, 1953, The Doubtful Guest, 1957, The Hapless Child, 1961, The Willowdale Handcar, 1962, The Wuggly Ump, 1963, The Remembered Visit, 1965, The Gilded Bat, 1966, The Blue Aspic, 1968, The Other Statue, 1968, The Epiplectic Bicycle, 1969, The Awdrey-Gore Legacy, 1972, Amphigorey, 1972, The Glorious Nosebleed, 1975, Amphigorey Too, 1975, The Broken Spoke, 1976, The Loathsome Couple, 1977, The Dwindling Party, 1982, The Water Flowers, 1982, Amphigorey Also, 1983, The Raging Tide, 1987, The Helpless Doorknob, 1989, The Betrayed Confidence, 1992, The Pointless Book, 1993, Figbash Acrobate, 1994, The Just Dessert, 1997, The Deadly Blotter, 1997, The Haunted Tea-cosy, 1998, The Headless Bust, 1999; (theatre) Tinned Lettuce, 1985, Lost Shoelaces, 1987, Useful Urns, Stuffed Elephants, 1990, Flapping Ankles, 1991, Crazed Teacups, 1992, Amphigorey: The Musical, 1992, Blithering Christmas, 1992, Chinese Gossip, 1994, Inverted Commas, 1995, Stumbling Christmas, 1995, Epistolary Play, 1997, others. Served with AUS, 1943-46. Address: PO Box 146 Yarmouth Port MA 02675-0146

GORGES, HEINZ AUGUST, retired research engineer; b. Stettin, Germany, July 22, 1913; came to the U.S., 1959; s. Gustav and Marga (Benda) G.; m. Sapienza Teresa Coco, Sept. 2, 1957. ME, Tech. U. Dresden, Germany, 1938; PhD, Tech. U. Hannover, 1946. Registered profl. engr., D.C. Group leader LFA Aero Rsch. Establishment, Braunschweig, Germany, 1940-45; with Royal Aircraft Establishment, Farnborough, Eng., 1946-49; prin. sci. officer Weapons Rsch. Establishment, Adelaide, Australia, 1949-59; sci. asst. George C. Marshall Space Flight Ctr., NASA, Huntsville, Ala., 1959-61; dir. advanced projects Cook Technol. Ctr., Morton Grove, Ill., 1961-62; sci. adviser Ill. Inst. Tech. Rsch. Inst., Chgo., 1962-66; asst. v.p. environ. and phys. scis. Tracor, Inc., Austin, Tex., 1966-99; ret.; prof. Redstone ext. U. Ala., 1960; v.p. Tracor-Jitco Inc., Rockville, Md., 1972-75. Fellow AIAA (assoc.); mem. ASME, Acoustical Soc. Am., Cosmos Club. Achievement include research super and hypersonics, resources management, environmental sciences, system engineering and analysis. Address: 3705 Sleepy Hollow Rd Falls Church VA 22041-1021

GORHAM, BRADFORD, lawyer; b. Providence, Mar. 7, 1935; s. Sayles and Ruth C. (Campbell) G.; m. Diann Gebow, Aug. 1, 1959; children: Christopher, Nicholas, Joshua, Jane, Nancy. Degree, Dartmouth Coll., 1957, Harvard U., 1964. Bar: R.I. 1964. Ptnr. Gorham & Gorham, Scituate, R.I., 1964—; state rep. R.I. State Ho. of Reps., Providence, 1969-70, 77-90; state senator R.I. State Senate, Providence, 1991-97. Capt. USMC, 1957-60. Named Legislator of Yr. Nat. Conf. State Legislatures, 1985, Outstanding Legislator Am. Legion Exch. Coun., 1986. Republican. Home: 11 Cucumber Hill Rd Foster RI 02825-1211 Office: Gorham & Gorham 25 Danielson Pike Scituate RI 02857-1801

GORHAM, EVILLE, ecologist, biogeochemist; b. Halifax, N.S., Can., Oct. 15, 1925; s. Ralph Arthur and Shirley Agatha (Eville) G.; m. Ada Verne MacLeod, Sept. 29, 1948; children: Kerstin, Vivien, Jocelyn, James. BSc in Biology with distinction, Dalhousie U., 1945, MSc in Zoology, 1947, LLD (hon.), 1991; PhD in Botany, U. London, Eng., 1951; DSc (hon.), McGill U., 1993, U. Minn., 1999. Lectr. botany U. Coll., London, Eng., 1951-54; sr. sci. officer Freshwater Biol. Assn., Ambleside, Eng., 1954-58; lectr., asst. prof. botany U. Toronto, 1958-62; assoc. prof. botany U. Minn., Mpls., 1962-65; prof. U. Minn., 1966-75, head dept., 1967-71, prof. ecology, 1975-84, Regents' prof. ecology and botany, 1984-98, Regents' prof. emeritus, 1999—; prof., head dept. biology U. Calgary, Alta., Can., 1965-66; mem. for Can., Internat. Commn. on Atmospheric Chemistry and Radioactivity, 1959-62; mem. vis. panel to rev. toxicology program NAS-NRC, 1974-75, mem. com. on inland aquatic ecosys. Water Sci. and Tech. Bd., 1994-96, mem. com. to evaluate indicators for monitoring aquatic and terrestrial environments Water Sci. and Tech. Bd., 1997—, mem. com. on hydrologic sci. bd. on Atmospheric Scis. and Climate, 1998—; mem. coordinating com. for sci. and tech. assessment environ. pollutants Environ. Studies Bd., 1975-78; mem. com. on med. and biologic effects of environ. pollutants Assembly Life Scis., 1976-77; mem. com. on atmosphere and biosphere Bd. Agr. and Renewable Resources, 1979-81; mem. panel on environ. impact diesel impact study com. NAE-NRC, 1980-81; mem. U.S.-Can.-Mex. joint sci. com. on acid precipitation Environ. Studies Bd., NAS-NRC, Royal Soc. Can., Mex. Acad. Scis., 1981-84; mem. health and environ. rsch. adv. com. U.S. Dept. Energy, 1992-94; mem. Water Sci. and Tech. Bd. NAS-NRC, 1996—; mem. coun. sci. advisors Marine Biol. Lab., Woods Hole, Mass., 1996—. Mem. editl. bd. Ecology, 1965-67, Limnology and Oceanography, 1970-72, Conservation Biology, 1987-88, Ecol. Applications, 1989-92, Environ. Revs., 1992—; contbr. articles on limnology, ecology, and biogeochemistry to profl. jours. Bd. dirs. Acid Rain Found., 1982-87, sec. treas. 1982-84. Recipient Regents' medal U. Minn., 1984; Royal Soc. Can. rsch. fellow State Forest Rsch. Inst., Stockholm, Sweden, 1950-51; grantee NSF, AEC, NIH, ERDA, NASA, Dept. of Energy, NRC Can., Environment Can., Office Water Resources Rsch., Dept. Interior, Andrew W. Mellon Found., N.Y.C. Fellow AAAS, Royal Soc. Can., Am. Acad. Arts and Scis.; mem. NAS, Am. Soc. Limnology and Oceanography (G. Evelyn Hutchinson medal 1986), Ecol. Soc. Am., Internat. Assn. Theoretical and Applied Limnology, Soc. Wetland Scientists, Swedish Phytogeog. Soc. (hon.), Gown in Town Club. Home: 1933 E River Ter Minneapolis MN 55414-3673

GORHAM, FRANK DEVORE, JR., petroleum company executive; b. St. Louis, June 4, 1921; s. Frank DeVore and Lillian (Hawley) G.; m. Marie Ellis Kelly, Sept. 1, 1947; children—Frank DeVore III, Daniel Kelly, Timothy Walker, Robert Hawley II, Mark Linton. AB, U. Mo., 1943. Petroleum geologist Creole Petroleum Co., Venezuela, 1946-49; dist. geologist Pure Oil Co., Denver, 1949-50; chief geologist Pubco Petroleum Corp., Albuquerque, 1950-60; exec. v.p. Pubco Petroleum Corp., 1960-65, pres., 1965-73; pres. Questa Petroleum Inc., 1973—; owner Cuesta Prodn. Co., 1973—, Riva Ridge Ranch, 1979—; mng. ptnr. Sindbad Partnership, 1990—. Served to capt. AUS, 1943-46, MTO. Decorated Silver Star. Fellow Geol. Soc. Am., Explorers Club, Am. Assn. Petroleum Geologists (pres. Rocky Mountain sect. 1959). Home: 218 16th St SW Albuquerque NM 87104 Office: Ste 1300 Sandia Savs Bldg Albuquerque NM 87102

GORHAM, GEORGE H., playwright, lyricist; b. Morris, Ill., Nov. 29; s. Charles H. and Edith Cecilia (Hayes) G. BS, So. Ill. U., 1977. mem. BMI Music Theatre Workshop, 1992—. Writer, lyricist (book, lyrics) Holiday Waltz, 1981, A Change in the Heir, 1988, on Broadway, 1990.

GORHAM, WILLIAM, organization executive; b. N.Y.C., Dec. 14, 1930; s. Jack and Fay (Blank) G.; m. Gail Wiley Finsterbusch, 1973; children from previous marriage: Sarah, Nancy, Kim, Jennifer, Becky. Student, MIT, 1949-50; BA, Stanford U., 1952; LLD (hon.), Trinity Coll., 1996. Mem. rsch. staff RAND Corp., 1953-62; dep. asst. sec. def. U.S., 1962-65, asst. sec. health, edn. and welfare, 1965-68; co-chmn. (with Daniel Bell) Pres.'s Panel Social Indicators, 1967-68; chmn. Pres.'s Task Force on Child Devel., 1966; pres. Urban Inst., Washington, 1968—; bd. dirs. Insituform Group Ltd., 1986-92, chmn., 1987-92; bd. dirs Insituform Techs., Inc., 1992-97; mem. Internat. Commn. on Edn. for 21st Century, Delors Commn., UNESCO, 1992-97; mem. U.S. adv. com. Internat. Inst. Applied Sys. Analysis, 1974-82; bd. dirs.-at-large Social Sci. Rsch. Coun. Editor: (with Nathan Glazer) The Urban Predicament, 1976; mem. bd. editors Policy Scis, 1969—, Jour. Policy Analysis and Mgmt., 1980—. Recipient Disting. Civilian Svc. award U.S. Dept. Def., 1965. Mem. Nat. Acad. Pub. Admisntrn., Assn. Pub. Policy Analysis and Mgmt. (policy coun. 1979-85), Cosmos Club (Washington). Office: Urban Institute 2100 M St NW Ste 401 Washington DC 20037-1264

GORIA, ELLEN THERESA, professional society administrator; b. Mt. Holly, N.J., Mar. 3, 1969; d. John Gordon and Margaret Mary (Rau) McGinley; m. Timothy Keith Goria, Sept. 10, 1994. BSBA in Acctg., U. Scranton, 1991. CPA N.Y., N.J. Staff acct. Coopers & Lybrand, N.Y.C., 1991-96; tech. mgr. AICPA, Jersey City, N.J., 1996-98, sr. tech. mgr., 1998—. Chmn. blood dr. N.Y. Blood Svcs., N.Y.C., 1995-96. Mem. AICPA. Roman Catholic. Avocations: golf, tennis, skiing. Office: AICPA Harborside Fin Ctr 201 Plaza Three Jersey City NJ 07311-3881

GORIN, GEORGE, retired chemistry educator; b. Como, Italy, Aug. 19, 1925; came to U.S., 1939, naturalized, 1946; s. Victor and Piera (Jahn) G.; m. Helen S. Surber, June 16, 1952; children—Sarah A., Victor W. A.B., Bklyn. Coll., 1944; M.S., Princeton, 1947, Ph.D., 1949. Chemist Heyden Chem. Corp., Garfield, N.J., 1945; instr. Rutgers U., New Brunswick, N.J., 1948-50; postdoctoral fellow Purdue U., Lafayette, Ind., 1950-51; asst. prof. U. Ore., Eugene, 1952-55, Okla. State U., Stillwater, 1955-58; asso. prof. Okla. State U., 1958-61, prof., 1962-90, prof. emeritus, 1991—. Contbr. sci. papers on sulfur compounds, proteins, radiation damage to profl. jours. Recipient NIH Career Devel. award, 1963-73. Mem. Am. Chem. Soc. (chmn. Okla. sect. 1968), Am. Soc. Biol. Chemists. Home: 1302 S Western Rd Stillwater OK 74074-6830

GORING, DAVID ARTHUR INGHAM, chemical engineering educator, scientist; b. Toronto, Ont., Can., Nov. 26, 1920; s. George Ingham and Susan Edna (Jones) G.; m. Elizabeth Dodds Haswell, Aug. 24, 1948; children—James, Rosemary, Christopher. B.Sc., U. London, 1942; Ph.D., McGill U., Montreal, Que., 1949, Cambridge U., 1953. Scientist NRC, Halifax, N.S., Can., 1951-55; with PAPRICAN, Pointe Claire, Que., Can., 1955-85, dir. research, 1971-77, v.p. sci., 1977-83, v.p. acad., 1983-85; prof. U. Toronto, 1986—; research assoc. McGill U., 1955-69, sr. research assoc., 1969-86. Contbr. chpts. to books and articles to profl. jours. Patentee in field. Served as flying officer RAF, 1943-46. Recipient Le Sueur Meml. Lecture award Can. Sect. Soc. Chem. Industry, 1988. Fellow Royal Soc. Can., Chem. Inst. Can., TAPPI (Gunnar Nicholson Gold medal 1986), Internat. Acad. Wood Sci.; mem. Can. Pulp and Paper Assn. (tech. sect., cert. appreciation 1986, John Bates Meml. Gold medal 1995), Am. Chem. Soc. (cellulose paper textile chemistry div., Anselm Payen award 1973). Anglican. Avocations: fishing, music. Home: 14 1/2 Ottawa St, Toronto, ON Canada M4T 2B6 Office: U Toronto, Dept Chem Engring Applied Chem, Toronto, ON Canada M5S 3E5

GORINSON, STANLEY M., lawyer; b. Bklyn., May 30, 1945; s. Rubin and Lena (Shulman) G.; m. Barbara Jorgenson, Jan. 28, 1983; children: Ross Evan, Hunter Lloyd. BA cum laude, Bklyn. Coll., 1967; JD with honors, Rutgers U., 1973. Bar: N.Y. 1974, U.S. Dist. Ct. (so. dist.) N.Y. 1976, U.S. Ct. Appeals (2nd cir.) 1976, Md. 1984, D.C. 1984, U.S. Dist. Ct. D.C. 1984, U.S. Ct. Appeals (D.C. cir.) 1985, U.S. Dist. Ct. (ea. dist.) Mich. 1986, U.S. Ct. Appeals (6th cir.) 1988, U.S. Supreme Ct. 1979. Atty. judgments sect. U.S. Dept. Justice, Washington, 1973-76, asst. chief transp. sect., 1977-80; chief spl. regulated industries U.S. Dept. Justice, 1980-84; assoc. Wachtell, Lipton, Rosen & Katz, N.Y.C., 1976-77; chief counsel Pres. Com. on Three Mile Island, Washington, 1979; ptnr. Pillsbury, Madison & Sutro, Washington, 1984-91, Winthrop, Stimson, Putnam & Roberts, Washington, 1991-93, Preston Gates Ellis & Rouvelas Meeds, Washington, 1993—. Contbg. author: Report on Regulatory Reform, 1985; also articles. Cons. NSF, Washington, 1982-83. Mem. ABA (bd. editors Antitrust Law Devels. 1984-87, chmn. comms. subcom. antitrust sect. 1985-88, chmn. criminal practice subcom. litigation sect. 1985-89, adminstrv. law sect., chmn. industry regulation com. antitrust sect. 1988-92, mem. edn. com. dispute resolution sect. 1994—), Fed. Comm. Bar Assn., N.Y. State Bar Assn. Office: Preston Gates Ellis & et al 1735 New York Ave NW # 500 Washington DC 20006-5209

GORLIN, RENA ANN, writer; b. Bklyn., Dec. 27, 1957; d. Philip and Sylvia (Levy) G.; m. Raymond R. Plante, 1991. BA magna cum laude, Brandeis U., 1979; JD, Am. U., 1982. Legal editor and reporter U.S. Law Week, Washington, 1983-86; legal editor and reporter BNA's Patent, Trademark and Copyright Jour. Bur. Nat. Affairs, Inc., Washington, 1983, sr. copywriter, 1986-96, coord. copywriting, 1996—; freelance editor and copywriter, Washington area, 1986—. Author: Codes of Professional Responsibility: Ethics Standards in Business, Health, and Law, 1986, 4th edit. 1999. Mem. law com. Anti-Defamation League B'nai Brith, Washington, 1980; vol. Big Sisters, Waltham, Mass., 1976-78; moot ct. judge Cath. U. Law Sch. competitions, Washington, 1985-95. Recipient 1st place award for direct mail campaign Info. Industry Assn. Mktg. Awards, 1995. Mem. Washington Ind. Writers, Am. Soc. for Bioethics and Humanities. Avocation: photography. Office: BNA Sales and Mktg Div 1231 25th St NW Washington DC 20037-1157

GORLIN, ROBERT JAMES, medical educator; b. Hudson, N.Y., Jan. 11, 1923; s. James Alter and Gladys Gretchen (Hallenbeck) G.; m. Marilyn Alpern, Aug. 24, 1952; children: Cathy, Jed. AB, Columbia U., 1943, postgrad., 1947-50; DDS, Washington U., St. Louis, 1947; MS, State U. Iowa, 1956; DSc (hon.), U. Athens, Greece, 1982, U. Thesalonike, Greece, 1993. Oral pathologist VA Hosp., Bronx, N.Y., 1950-51; instr. dentistry Columbia U., N.Y.C., 1950-51; dental dir., pathologist Op. Blue Jay, Thule, Greenland, 1951-52; mem. exec. faculty, chmn. oral pathology and genetics Sch. Dentistry U. Minn., Mpls., 1956-90, assoc. prof. div. oral pathology Sch. Dentistry, 1956-58, prof. Sch. Dentistry, 1958-93, prof. pathology and dermatology Sch. Medicine, Sch. Dentistry, 1971-93; prof. pediatrics, ob-gyn, otolaryngology Sch. Medicine U. Minn., 1973-93; Regents' prof. oral pathology U. Minn., Mpls., 1978-93; Fulbright exch. prof., Guggenheim fellow Royal Dental Coll., Copenhagen, 1961; 1st Lingamfelter lectr. dermatology U. Va., 1971; 1st Boyle lectr. Case Western Res. U. Med. Ctr., Cleve., 1972; vis. prof. UCLA-Harbor Gen. Hosp., 1972; asst. chief dental service Glenwood Hills Med. Ctr., 1959-61, chief, 1962-64, cons., 1969-73; Regents' prof. emeritis U of Minn. Sch. of Dentistry, Mpls, 1994-; cons. pediatrics and oral pathology U. Minn. Hosps., 1956—; cons. oral pathology Mpls. VA Hosp., 1958—, Mt. Sinai Hosp., Mpls., 1958-91; cons. pediatrics Hennepin County Gen. Hosp., St. Paul's Children's Hosp., Ramsey County Gen. Hosp., Mpls. Children's Hosp., Gillette State Hosp. Crippled Children; mem. Minn. Adv. Com. Human Genetics, 1959-73; Minn. mem. U.S. Congl. Liaison Com. for Dentistry, 1963-80 ; mem. Ctr. Histologic Nomenclature and Classification of Odontogenic Tumors and Allied Lesions, WHO, 1966-80 ; mem. adv. com. periodontal disease and soft tissue study NIH, 1967-78 , mem. dental sect., 1970-73; mem. adv. com. Nat. Found. Clin. Rsch., 1974—; vis. prof. Tel Aviv U., 1980, Sch. Dentistry, Jerusalem, Israel, 1981; 2nd Edward Sheridan lectr., Dublin, Ireland, 1989; Windermere lectr. Brit. Paediatric Assn., 1990; founder, bd. dirs. Found. for Developmental and Medical Genetics, 1994. Author: (with J. Pindborg and M. Cohen) Syndromes of the Head and Neck, 1964, 76, 90, (with R. Goodman) The Face in Genetic Disorders, 1970, 77, The Malformed Infant and Child, 1983, (with B. Konigsmark) Genetic and Metabolic Disorders, 1977, Hereditary Hearing Loss and Its Syndromes, 1995; co-contbr.: Computer Assisted Diagnosis in Pediatrics, 2d edit., 1971; editor: (with H. Goldman) Thoma's Oral Pathology, 1970, Chromosomes and Human Cancer (J. Cervenka and B. Koulischer), 1972; editorial cons. Jour. Dental Rsch., Geriatrics, Archives of Oral Biology, Jour. Pediats., Pediats., Am. Jour. Diseases of Children, Syndrome Identification, Radiology; editor oral pathology Oral Surgery, Oral Medicine, Oral Pathology, Clin. Pediats.; assoc. editor Am. Jour. Human Genetics, 1970-73, Jour. Oral Pathology, 1972-83, Jour. Maxillofacial Surgery, 1973—, Cleft Palate Jour., 1976—, Clin. Pediats., 1985—; mem. bd. Excerpta Medica, 1976-80, Jour. Craniofacial Genetic Devel. Biology, 1980—, Jour. Clin. Dysmorphology, 1982-86, Gerodontics, 1984-86, Birth Defects Ency., 1986—, Dysmorphology Clin. Genetics, 1987—; cons. editor Stedman's Med. Dictionary, 1959—; contbr. numerous articles to profl. jours. Bd. dirs. Minn. div. Am. Cancer Soc., 1959-60, mem. nat. clin. fellowship com., 1962-65. With U.S. Army, 1943-44; lt. USNR, 1953-55. Columbia U. fellow, 1947-48, NIH fellow 1948-49, Nat. Insts. Dental Rsch. fellow, 1949-50; recipient Fredrick Birnberg Rsch. award Columbia U., 1987, Lifetime Achievement award March of Dimes, 1989, Am. Cleft Palate Assn. award, 1993, Spinoza chair U. Amsterdam, 1995, Norton Ross prize ADA, 1995, Washington U. Disting. Alumni award, 1997, Goldhaber award Harvard U., 1997, Premio Anni Verdi award in med. genetics, Spoleto, Italy, 1997. Fellow Am. Acad. Oral Pathology (v.p. 1957-58, 64-65, sec. 1958-64, pres. 1966-67, award 1993), Am. Coll. Genetics (hon.), Am. Bd. Oral Pathology, Am. Bd. Med. Genetics (hon.), Royal Soc. Surgeons of Ireland, Royal Soc. Surgeons of Eng.; mem. ADA (cons. coun. dental edn. 1967—), Internat. Assn. Dental Rsch. (sec. Minn. div. 1958-59, pres. 1959-60), Minn. Soc. Pathologists, Am. Soc. Human Genetics, Am. Acad. Oral Pathology (pres. 1966-67, 75-76, diplomate, bd. dir. 1970-76, v.p. 1974-75), Inst. Medicine of NAS (sr.), Royal Soc. Medicine London (Burrough Welcome fellow 1991, R. Abercrombie award in med. genetics 1994), Internat. Acad. Oral Pathology (assoc.), Skeletal Dysplasia Soc. (hon.), Internat. Skeletal Soc., Internat. Soc. Craniofacial Biology (bd. dir. 1966-67, v.p. 1967-68, pres. 1969-70), Hollywood Acad. Medicine (hon.), Sigma Xi, Omicron Kappa Upsilon. Office: U Minn 16-206 Health Sci Unit A Minneapolis MN 55455

GORMAN, BRIAN, umpire; b. Whitestone, N.Y., June 11, 1959; m. Marsha Traeger, Nov. 3, 1990. Umpire N.Y.-Pa. League, Fla. State League, So. League Triple Alliance, Am. Assn., Nat. League, 1993—; second-base umpire 69th All-Star Game, Nat. League, 1998. Office: Nat League 350 Park Ave New York NY 10022 Office: Umpires Union 1735 Market St Philadelphia PA 19103

GORMAN, CHRIS, lawyer; b. Frankfort, Ky., Jan. 22, 1943; m. Vicki Lynn Beekman; two sons. Grad., U. Ky. Bar: Ky., 1967. Former ptnr. Conliffe, Sandman, Gorman, and Sullivan, Louisville; former dir. civil div. Jefferson County Attys. Office; atty. gen. Ky., 1992-95; gen. counsel Taylor Bldg. Corp. Am., Louisville, 1996—; ptnr. Sheffer, Hutchinson, Kinney, Louisville. Address: Nat City Tower 101 South Fifth St Ste 1600 Louisville KY 40202

GORMAN, CLIFF, actor; b. N.Y.C.; m. Gayle Stevens. Student, U. N.Mex., UCLA; BS in Edn., NYU. Mem. Jerome Robbins' Am. Theatre Lab., 1966-67. N.Y.C. appearances include Hogan's Goat, 1965, Ergo, 1968, Boys in the Band, 1968 (Obie award), Lenny, 1972-73 (Drama Desk award, Toni award), Chapter Two, 1977, Doubles, 1985; stage appearance in Social Security, 1986; film appearances in Justine, 1969, The Boys in the Band, 1970, Cops and Robbers, 1973, An Unmarried Woman, 1978, Night of the Juggler, 1979, All That Jazz, 1979, Angel, 1984, Night and the City, 1992, Hoffa, 1993, Ghost Dog, 1999; TV appearances in The Trial of the Chicago Seven, 1970, Class of 63, 1973, The Bunker, 1981, Double Take, 1985, Internal Affairs, 1988, Howard Beach, 1989, Murder in Black and White, 1990, Vestige of Honor, 1990, Murder Times Seven, 1990, Terror on Track 9, 1992, Return of Ironside, 1993, Silent Betrayal, 1994, Forget-Me-Not Murders, 1994, Down Came a Blackbird, 1995; TV shows include Law and Order, Police Story, Hawaii Five-O, Streets of San Francisco, Trapper John, Murder She Wrote, Friday the 13th-The Series, Cagney and Lacey, Spenser for Hire. Recipient La Guardia Meml. award, 1972, Show Bus. award, 1972. Mem. Honor Legion N.Y.C. Police Dept., Friends George Spelvin (life).

GORMAN, GERALD WARNER, lawyer; b. North Kansas City, Mo., May 30, 1933; s. William Shelton and Bessie (Warner) G.; m. Anita Belle McPike, June 26, 1954; children: Guinevere Eve, Victoria Rose. AB cum laude, Harvard U., 1954, LLB magna cum laude, 1956. Bar: Mo. 1956. Assoc. firm Dietrich, Tyler, Davis, Burrell & Dicus, Kansas City, 1956-62; ptnr. Dietrich, Davis, Dicus, Rowlands, Schmitt & Gorman, 1963-90; dir. Slagle, Bernard & Gorman, P.C., 1990—; bd.dirs. Musser-Davis Land Co., Curry Investment Co. Bd. govs. Citizens Assn. Kansas City, 1962—; trustee Harvard/Radcliffe Club Kansas City Endowment Fund, chmn. bd. trustees, 1977-83; trustee Kansas City Mus., 1967-82; chmn. bd. trustees Avondale Meth. Ch., 1969-92; mem. Citizens Bond Com. of Kansas City, 1973—, chmn. 7th jud. cir. citizens com., 1982-84; chmn. Downtown Coun. Allis Plaza Reconstrn., 1983-85; bd. dirs. Spofford Home for Children, 1972-77, Clay County Econ. Devel. Commn., 1989-94, mem. exec. com., 1991-93. With U.S. Army, 1956-58; capt. USAR, 1958-64. Mem. Lawyers Assn. Kansas City (exec. com. 1968-71), ABA, Mo. Bar Assn., Kansas City Bar Assn., Clay County Bar Assn., Harvard Law Sch. Assn. Mo. (pres. 1973), Harvard Club (pres. 1966), Univ. Club (bd. dirs. 1983-86, 88-93, pres. 1990-91), Kansas City Club (bd. dirs. 1993-97), 611 Club (bd. dirs. 1987-91, pres. 1990), Kansas City Country Club, Old Pike Country Club, River Club. Republican. Home: 917 NE Vivion Rd Kansas City MO 64118-5317 Office: 4600 Madison Ave Ste 600 Kansas City MO 64112-3012

GORMAN, JAMES CARVILL, pump manufacturing company executive; b. Mansfield, Ohio, Apr. 16, 1924; s. James Carville and Ruth (Barnes) G.; m. Marjorie Newcomer, Apr. 10, 1950; children: Jeff, Gayle. BS, Ohio State U., 1949. Sales engr. Gorman Rupp Co., Mansfield, Ohio, 1949-58, sales mgr., 1958-64, pres., 1964-89, chmn., CEO, 1989-99, chmn., 1999—; pres. Manairco, Inc., 1952-85, chmn. bd., 1985—; chmn. Mansfield Airport Commn., 1954—; treas. EAA Aviation Found., Oshkosh, Wis., 1980—. Capt. USAAF, 1942-46. Mem. Constrn. Industry Mfrs. Assn. Episcopalian. Home: PO Box 2599 Mansfield OH 44906-0599 Office: Gorman Rupp 305 Bowman St Mansfield OH 44903-1600

GORMAN, JAMES FRANCIS, systems analyst; b. Phila., July 28, 1945; s. William James and Alvina Frances (Thompson) G.; m. Linda Ann Bell, Mar. 21, 1970; children: Julie Lynn, Timothy James, Thomas Matthew. BS in Systems Analysis, U. Miami, Oxford, Ohio, 1972; MA in Personnel Mgmt., Ctrl. Mich. U., 1977; MBA, U. North Fla., 1985. Commd. ensign USN, 1972, advanced through grades to lt. comdr.; ret., 1985; sr. AIREM analyst Summit Rsch., Jacksonville, Fla., 1985—. Contbr. articles to profl. jours. Scoutmaster troop 412 Boy Scouts Am., Orange Park, Fla., 1985-89, asst. scoutmaster, 1989—. Mem. Sertoma. Avocations: genealogy, scouting. Home: 5396 Orchard St Orange Park FL 32065-7248 Office: COMHSWINGLANT PO Box 91 Jacksonville FL 32212-0091

GORMAN, JOHN R., auxiliary bishop. Ordained priest Roman Cath. Ch., 1952. Aux. bishop Roman Cath. Ch., Chgo., appointed aux. bishop, titular bishop of Catula, 1988—, consecrated, 1988—. Home and Office: Archdiocese of Chgo-Vicariate V 2330 W 118th St Chicago IL 60643-4710

GORMAN, JOSEPH GREGORY, JR., lawyer; b. Chgo., Sept. 27, 1939; s. Joseph Gregory Sr. and Genevieve C. (Smith) G.; m. Mary (Molly) O'Donovan, Mar. 23, 1968; children: Jennifer Ann Gorman Patton, Joseph Gregory III. BA, U. Calif., Berkeley, 1961; MBA, UCLA, 1963, JD, 1966. Bar: U.S. Dist. Ct. (cen. dist.) Calif. 1967, U.S. Ct. Appeals (9th cir.) 1967, U.S. Tax Ct. Assoc., ptnr. Sheppard, Mullin, Richter & Hampton LLP, L.A., 1966—; chair death and gift tax com. Los Angeles County Bar Assn., 1974-76, probate & trust law sect., 1980-81; chair death and gift tax com.

Calif. State Bar, 1976-77; co-founder U. So. Calif. Probate & Trust Conf., 1974—; mem. adv. bd. Miami Inst. Estate Planning, 1978—. Contbr. articles to profl. jours. Served with USAR, Calif. NG, 1962-68. Fellow Am. Coll. Trust and Estate Counsel, Academician, The Internat. Acad. of Estate and Trust Law. Republican. Roman Catholic. Clubs: Annandale Golf (Pasadena); Jonathan (Los Angeles). Office: Sheppard Mullin Richter & Hampton LLP 333 S Hope St Fl 48 Los Angeles CA 90071-1448

GORMAN, JOSEPH TOLLE, corporate executive; b. Rising Sun, Ind., 1937. BA, Kent State U., 1959; LLB, Yale U., 1962. Assoc. Baker, Hostetler & Patterson, Cleve., 1962-67; with legal dept. TRW Inc., Cleve., 1968-69, asst. sec., 1969-70, sec., 1970-72, v.p. sr. counsel automotive worldwide ops., 1972-73, v.p., asst. gen. counsel, 1973-76, v.p., gen. counsel, 1976-80, acting head communications function, 1978, exec. v.p. indsl. and energy sector, 1980-84, exec. v.p., asst. pres., 1984-85, pres., chief operating officer, 1985-88, chmn., CEO, 1988—, also bd. dirs.; bd. dirs. Aluminum Co. Am., Procter & Gamble Co.; mem. adv. bd. BP Am. Inc.; bd. dirs. U.S.-China Bus. Coun., bd. dirs.; mem. Bd. of The Prince of Wales Bus. Leaders Form; mem. hon. com. Fedn. Internat. des Soc. d'Ingenieurs des Tech. de l'Automobile; mem. Def. Industry Initiative Steering Com.; chmn. Internat. Trade and Investment Task Force; mem. strengthening of Am. Initiative Ctr. for Strategic and Internat. Studies; adv. com. Nat. Security Telecom.; mem. Conf. Bd., Bus. Coun., Trilateral Commn., Bus. Roundtable's Policy Com., Coun. on Fgn. Rels., Pres.'s Export Coun., Coun. on Competitiveness. Trustee New Ohio Inst., Cleve. Tomorrow, Mus. Arts Assn., Cleve. Inst. Art, United Way Svcs., Cleve. Clinic Found., Com. for Econ. Devel., com. for econ. devel. and the Malcolm Baldrige Nat. Quality Award Found.; mem. Ohio Gov.'s Edn. Mgmt. Coun., Kent State U. Found.; bd. mem. The New Am. Schs. Devel. Corp., The Bus.-Higher Edn. Forum, Civic Vision 2000 and Beyond. Recipient Japan Prime Minister's Trade award, 1994. E-mail: cgal@mindspring.com. Fax: (212) 334-2463.

GORMAN, JOYCE J(OHANNA), lawyer; b. N.Y.C., Aug. 23, 1952; d. Peter J. and Jane M. (Kelly) G. Student, Williams Coll., 1972-73; BA, Smith Coll., 1974; JD with honors, U. Md., 1977. Bar: Md. 1977, D.C. 1988. Assoc. Miles & Stockbridge, Balt., 1977-84, ptnr., 1984-87; ptnr. Miles & Stockbridge, Washington, 1987-88, Ballard, Spahr, Andrews & Ingersoll, Washington, 1988-94, Piper & Marbury, Washington, 1994-98; spl. counsel Cadwalader, Wickersham & Taft, Washington, 1998—. Bd. dirs. Va. Opera, 1994—. Mem. Md. Bar Assn. (sec. corp. banking and bus. sect. 1983-84, vice chmn. 1984-85, chmn. 1985-86), Merchants Club (Balt. bd. dirs. 1980-87), City Club (Washington). Democrat. Roman Catholic. Avocations: swimming, scuba, horseback riding, gourmet cooking, knitting. Home: 9492 Lynnhall Pl Alexandria VA 22309-3064 Office: Cadwalader Wichersham & Taft Ste 700 1333 New Hampshire Ave NW Washington DC 20036-1511*

GORMAN, LAWRENCE JAMES, banker; b. Albany, N.Y., Mar. 22, 1948; s. Lawrence Edward and Olive Gertrude (MacDowell) G.; m. Barbara J. Pisarek, Aug. 4, 1973; children: Ryan Patrick, Michael Patrick. BS, Syracuse U., 1970; JD, Union U., 1973; grad., Nat.Grad.Trust Sch., 1980. Bar: N.Y. 1976. Assoc. Grasso,Rivizzigno & Woronov, Syracuse, 1973-76; asst. v.p. Trust and Investment divsn. Lincoln 1st Bank NA, Syracuse, 1976-79; v.p. 1st Va. Banks Inc., 1983-88; pres. Retirement Plan Svcs. Inc., 1988-98; adminstrv. dir. retirement planning Lord, Abbett & Co., 1998—; adj. prof. Onondaga County C.C.; faculty N.Y. State Bar, 1980-81. Dir. Our Town Fredericksburg, 1985-89, pres., 1986-87; mem. investment com. Am. Cancer Soc., N.Y. state chpt.,1981-93; trustee N.Y.C. chpt. Leukemia Soc. Am., 1982-83. Mem. N.Y. State Bar Assn., Onondaga County Bar Assn. (chmn. bank liaison com. 1980-82). Home: 3 Russell Rd Fredericksburg VA 22405-2301 Office: 767 Fifth Ave New York NY 10153

GORMAN, LEO JOSEPH, priest; b. Far Rockaway, N.Y., June 11, 1929; s. Joseph J. and Helen Cecilia (Lally) G. BA in Philosophy, Passionist Monastic Sem., 1953, MA in Theology, 1957. Ordained priest Roman Cath. Ch., 1957. Itinerant preacher Eastern U.S. and Can., 1957-59, 61-64; assoc. pastor St. Mary's Parish, Dunkirk, N.Y., 1959-61, assoc. dir., 1961-64; assoc. dir. retreats Our Lady of Fla. Monastery, North Palm Beach, Fla., 1964-67, resident retreat preacher, 1967-69; dir. Passionist Retreat House, West Springfield, Mass., 1969-74; vice rector St. Gabriel's Monastery, Brighton, Mass., 1974-76; exec. producer The Sunday Mass program WNYW-TV, Pelham, N.Y.; sec. Passionist Communications, Pelham, 1976—; v.p., sec. That's The Spirit Prodns., Inc., 1980-90; substitute chaplain Kennedy Meml. Hosp. for Children, 1974-76; moderator Cath Young Adult Club, West Palm Beach, 1963-68; vol. counselor Palm Beach County Juvenile Ct., 1963-69; panelist TV program Face to Face, Palm Beach, 1968-69; mem. Springfield Clergy Task Force on Drugs, 1970-74; co-chmn. West Springfield Clergy Assn., 1971-73; founding pres. Hope Home Western Mass., Inc., 1972-74; chaplain NYAC Yacht Club, 1993-99, Pelham Police Dept., 1999—. V.p. Big Brothers, 1968-69; pres. Community Health Commn., West Springfield, 1971-72; bd. dirs. YMCA, Palm Beach County Mental Health Assn. Mem. Nat. Assn. Cath. Broadcasters, Fla. Sheriffs Assn. (hon.). Home: 190 Mt Tom Rd Pelham NY 10803-3309 Office: PO Box 440 Pelham NY 10803-0440

GORMAN, LEON A., mail order company executive; b. Nashua, N.H., Dec. 20, 1934. Mdse. trainee Filene's of Boston, 1956; with L.L. Bean, Inc., Freeport, Maine, 1960—, v.p., treas., 1967, pres., 1967—; dir. Central Maine Power Co., Depositors Corp., Carroll Reed Ski Shops. Mem. Alumni Coun. Bowdoin Coll.; bd. dirs. Pine Tree Coun. Boy Scouts Am.; trustee Hurrican Usland Outward Bound Sch.; corp. Maine Med. Ctr.; adv. trustee Maine Audubon Soc. Lt. USNR, 1957-60. Mem. C. of C. Greater Portland (dir.). Office: L L Bean Inc Casco St Freeport ME 04033*

GORMAN, LILLIAN R., human resources executive; b. N.Y.C., July 4, 1953; d. Helmuth H. and Ida A. (Malitsch) Degen; m. Mark R. Gorman, Oct. 23, 1976. BA in Psychology, Lehman Coll., CUNY, 1975; MA in Indsl. Psychology, Case Western Res. U., 1978, PhD in indsl. Psychology, 1979; MBA in Corp. Fin., U. So. Calif., 1986. Econ. benefits asst. Girl Scouts U.S.A., N.Y.C., 1971-75; psychologist Pers. Rsch. Svcs., Cleve., 1975-79; cons. psychologist Pers. Rsch. & Devel. Corp., Cleve., 1977-78; mgr. pers. rsch. 1st Interstate Bank, L.A., 1979-82, v.p., mgr. human resource planning and devel., 1982-85; v.p., mgr. human resource planning and exec. devel. 1st Interstate Bancorp, L.A., 1985-86; sr. v.p., human resources dir. 1st Interstate Bank of Calif., 1986-90; v.p. human resources Edison Internat., Rosemead, Calif., 1996-99, sr. v.p. human resources, 1999—; cons. psychology; mem. bd. advisors Claremont Grad. Sch. Econs. and Politics, 1999—. Bd. dirs. INROADS/L.A., 1986—; bd. advisors Andrus Gerontology Ctr., 1990—, EXED LLC, 1997—; mem. pub. policy bd. United HealthCare, 1997—; mem. conf. bd. Human Resources Coun., 1996—. Mem. APA, Soc. for Psychologists in Mgmt. (bd. dirs. 1993-97), Orgn. for Women Execs., Soc. for Human Resources Mgmt., Soc. for Indsl. and Orgnl. Psychology. Home: 1332 Allenford Ave Los Angeles CA 90049-3612

GORMAN, MAUREENU., foundation administrator; b. Stamford, Conn.. B in English, Sacred Heart U.; M in Bus., Columbia U. Reporter Bridgeport Post; with Hydraulic Co., Pitney Bowes; mgr. comm. projects GTE Products and Systems Group, 1982-89; dir. corp. social responsibility, v.p. GTE Found., Stamford, Conn., 1989-91, v.p., 1991—. Mem. Coun. on Founds.; mem. corp. com. Contbns. Coun. of conf. Bd.; bd. trustees Long Wharf Theatre; mem. corp. adv. coun. ARC; mem. devel. coun. Nat. Alliance Bus.; mem. adv. com. Found. for Ind. Higher edn.; GTE rep. Nat. Gallery art Collectors Com. Bd. mem., TREE Found., NSF Corp. and Found. Alliance, Pub. Rels. Soc. Am., Internat. Assn. Bus. Communicators. Office: GTE Found 1255 Corporate Dr Irving TX 75038

GORMAN, MICHAEL JOSEPH, library director, educator; b. Witney, Oxfordshire, Eng., Mar. 6, 1941; came to U.S. 1977; s. Philip Denis and Alicia F. (Barrett) G.; m. Anne Gillett, Mar. 6, 1962 (div. 1992); children—Emma, Alice. Student, Ealing Sch. Librarianship, 1964-66. Dir. gen. services dept. Univ. Library U. Ill., Urbana, 1977-88, acting univ. librarian, 1986-87; prof. library adminstrn. U. Ill., Urbana, 1977-88; vis. prof. U. Chgo. Library Sch., 1984, 86-88, U. Calif., Berkeley, 1989-91; dean libr. svcs. Calif. State U., Fresno, 1988—; vis. lectr. U. Ill. Grad. Sch. Library Sci., Urbana, 1974-75; bibliog. cons. Brit. Library Planning Secretariat, 1972-74; head cataloguing Brit. Nat. Bibliography 1969-72. Author: A Study of the Rules for Entry and Headings in the Anglo-American Cataloguing Rules, 1967, 68, Format for Machine Readable Cataloguing of Motion Pictures, 1973, Concise AACR2, 1980, 2d edit., 1990, Technical Services Today and Tomorrow, 1990, 2nd edit., 1998, (with Walt Crawford) Future Libraries, 1995, Our Singular Strengths: Meditations for Librarians, 1998, others; editor: Anglo-American Cataloguing Rules, 2d edit., 1978, rev., 1988, Catalogue and Index, 1973, Non Solus, 1981, Crossroads, 1986, Convergence, 1990; contbr. articles to profl. jours., chpts. to books. Recipient Blackwell scholarship award, 1997. Fellow Brit. Libr. Assn.; mem. ALA (Margaret Mann citation 1979, mem. coun. 1991-95, Melvil Dewey medal 1992), Libr. Info. and Tech. Assn. (mem.-at-large exec. bd. 1982-85). Office: Calif State U Henry Madden Libr 5200 N Barton Ave Fresno CA 93740-8014

GORMAN, MICHAEL STEPHEN, construction executive; b. Tulsa, Aug. 3, 1951; s. Lawrence Matthew and Mary Alice (Veith) G.; m. Sheryl Lane McGee, Feb. 19, 1972; children: Kelley Lane, Michael Ryan. Student, Colo. State U., 1970, 71. With McGee Constrn. Co., Denver, 1972-74, with sales and estimating dept., 1974-78, gen. mgr., 1978-80, pres., owner, 1980-91; pres. Wisor Group, Boulder, 1990—; cons., author, columnist in remodeling and custom home building; mortgage banker, ins. cons., 1995—; presenter seminars in field. Mem. Nat. Assn. Remodeling Industry (chmn. membership svcs. com. 1987-91, bd. dirs. 1982-91, regional v.p. 1987-89, nat. sec. 1990-91, Man of Yr. 1982, Regional Contractor of Yr. 1988). Avocations: running, racquetball, sailing, skiing, pilot.

GORMAN, PATRICIA JANE, editor; b. Oak Ridge, Tenn., Feb. 28, 1950; d. Joseph Francis and Ruth (Kommedahl) G.; m. Adrian Thomas Higgins, Apr. 22, 1978; children: Mary Catherine, Patrick Edward. BJ, U. Mo., 1972. Feature writer, copy editor Northamptonshire Evening Telegraph, Eng., 1972-76; asst. editor Am. Tchr. newspaper Am. Fedn. Tchrs., AFL-CIO, Washington, 1976-82, editor, 1982—, mng. editor Am. Educator mag., 1978-83; mem. delegation of labor editors to Israel, AFL-CIO, Washington, 1983. Author TV study guides for tchrs., 1979-83. Mem. Internat. Labor Communications Assn. Democrat. Roman Catholic. Office: Am Fedn Tchrs 555 New Jersey Ave NW Washington DC 20001-2029*

GORMAN, ROBERT SAUL, architect; b. N.Y.C., June 28, 1933; s. Philip and Lillian (Weiss) G.; B.Arch., M.Arch., Yale U., 1966; m. Judith Alice Albaum, July 2, 1965; children—Melissa, Sasha William Shannon. Apprentice to Frank Lloyd Wright, 1953-56; designer Eero Saarinen, Hamden, Conn., 1961-67; architect, planner Victor Gruen Assos., N.Y.C., 1967-69, Juster/Pope, Architects, Shelburne Falls, Mass., 1977-78; architect Robert Gorman Assos., Architects, Planners, Solar Energy Cons., Richmond, N.H., 1969-80; founder, prin. Rawson Place Architects, 1980-89; founder, prin. Green River Architects, 1989—; cons. Bklyn. Coll., 1967-69. Served with AUS, 1956-58. Frank Lloyd Wright Found. fellow, 1953-56. Mem. AIA (Design award 1972). Achievements include pioneering work in solar energy archtl. applications. Home: Richmond Rd Richmond NH 03470 Office: Green River Architects RR 4 Box 817 Brattleboro VT 05301-9202

GORMAN, RUSSELL WILLIAM, marketing executive, consultant; b. Glen Ridge, N.J., Aug. 17, 1927; s. William Francis and Emily (Weldon) G.; m. Mieko Deguchi, June 19, 1956. BS, U.S. Merchant Marine Acad., 1949. Lic. mcht. marine, chief mate. Lic. officer Moore McCormack Lines Inc., N.Y., 1949-53; dir. tng. Chevron Shipping Co., San Francisco, 1957-77; mgr. orgn., adminstrn. Utah Internat. Corp., San Francisco, 1977-84; pres. Lumier Inc., San Francisco, 1984-85; v.p. John F. Perry Assocs., Concord, Calif., 1986; pres. Market Devel. Assocs., Danville, Calif., 1986-92; sr. v.p. Aegis Fin. Svcs., 1993—; pres., dir. Perfect Wash US, 1993-96; ptnr. Two Star Internat., Oakland, Calif., 1993—; bd. dirs., v.p. Norlock Tech. Inc., San Mateo, Calif., 1989—; bd. dirs. INTA, Inc., Santa Clara, Calif., 1986—. Chmn. Calif. Vets. Coalition for Bush, 1988; mem. Sec. of Def. Adv. Bd. on Naval History, 1990-97; vice chmn. Sec. of Interior Adv. Commn. on San Francisco Maritime Hist. Park, 1992—; chmn., CEO U.S.S. Missouri and Allied Forces Meml., 1995—; adv. speaker Peter Wilson for Senate Campaign, 1988; bd. dirs. Calif. Mil. Mus., Sacramento, 1996—; trustee VFW Post 75, 1997—. Lt. USN, 1954-57, rear adm. USNR, 1980-87. Decorated Legion of Merit with gold star, Navy Commendation medal. Mem. VFW (trustee 1998—, adjutant post 75 1998—), Navy League of U.S. (v.p. Pacific Ctrl. region 1989—), Res. Officer Assn. of U.S. (v.p. Navy sect. 1990-92, chmn. long range planning 1992-97), Naval Res. Assn. (nat. v.p. surface/subsurface 1990-95, co-chair long range plan 1995—), Oakland C. of C. (vice chmn. mil. affairs com. 1990-95), Am. Legion (sr. vice comdr. post 246 1999—), M.C. League (post 942 1998—). Republican. Methodist. Home: 46 Willowview Ct Danville CA 94526-1945

GORMAN, WILLIAM DAVID, artist, graphic artist; b. Jersey City, June 27, 1925; s. William Daniel and Margaret (Johnson) G.; m. Janice Echols Gary, Feb. 9, 1957. Grad., Newark Sch. Fine and Indsl. Arts, 1949. art evaluator N.J. Council of Arts, 1975. Contbr. articles to art mags.; One-man shows, Jersey City Mus., 1962, Revel Gallery, N.Y.C., 1963, East Side Gallery, N.Y.C., 1970, Madison (N.J.) Library, 1975, Caldwell (N.J.) Coll., 1976, SUNY, Alfred, 1977, Martin (Tenn.) Arts Commn., 1978, Old Bank Gallery, Port Washington, N.Y., 1981, The Academy/N.J. State Dept. Edn., Edison, 1987; group shows include, Davenport (Iowa) Mcpl. Art Gallery, 1975, Canton (Ohio) Art Inst., 1971, NAD, 1971-81, Am. Acad. and Inst. Arts and Letters, N.Y.C., 1979, 80, Internat. Waters invitational traveling exhbn., Can., U.S., U.K., 1991-93, U.S./China/Australian Watermedia Exposition, Taiwan, 1994; represented in permanent collections, U.S. State Dept., NAD, N.Y.C., Newark Mus., Montclair (N.J.) Art Mus., Springfield (Mo.) Art Mus., Colorado Springs Fine Arts Center, Syracuse (N.Y.) U., Butler Inst. Am. Art, Ohio. Served with U.S. Army, 1943-44, ETO. Recipient Artist's Mag. award, 1991. Mem. Allied Artists Am. (v.p. 1975-78, pres. 1978-81, hon. life pres. 1983, dir. watercolor 1981-84, Gold medal of honor 1973, De Maree award, 1981, FitzGerald Meml. award, 1982, 91, Diana Kan award, 1983, Bainbridge award 1985, Silver medal of Honor, 1986, John Young-Hunter award 1989), Am. Watercolor Soc. (hon. mem., 1st v.p. 1981-86, pres. 1986-93, Emily Lowe meml. award 1984, Ogden Pleissner meml. award 1988, Four Winds medal 1989, Mary S. Litt medal 1992, Silver Medal of Honor award 1993), Audubon Artists (exhbn. chmn. 1974-77, dir. 1977-80), Nat. Soc. Painters in Casein and Acrylic (Shiva award 1987), N.J. Water Color Soc. (pres. 1957-59, Grumbacher Silver medal 1982, Warga award 1983), Artists Fellowship, Am. Vets. Soc. Artists, Garden State Watercolor Soc. (award 1985), Hudson Artists (founder 1955), Jersey City Mus. Assn. (dir. 1953-60), NAD (NA full academician, Henry Ward Ranger Fund purchase awards 1965, 71), Old Bergen Art Guild (pres. and dir. 1962—), Salmagundi Club (hon.), Australian Watercolor Inst. (hon.), Mexican Watercolor Soc. (hon.). Home and Studio: 43 W 33rd St Bayonne NJ 07002-3907 also: Am Watercolor Soc 47 5th Ave New York NY 10003-4303

GORMÈZANO, KEITH, arbitrator, writer, marketer; b. Madison, Wis., Nov. 22, 1954; s. Isadore and Miriam Gormèzano; m. Emma Lee Rogers, Aug. 17, 1986 (div. Nov. 1990). BGS, U. Iowa, 1977, postgrad. in pub. affairs, 1979-80; postgrad. in law, U. Puget Sound, 1984-86. Pub. Le Beacon Presse, Seattle, 1980-89; real estate agt. Jim Stacy Realty, Seattle, 1988-89; owner A Better Temporary, 1989—; arbitrator Better Bus. Bur. Greater Seattle, 1987-93; arbitrator Puget Sound Multi-Listing Assn., 1988-89, Nat. Assn. Securities Dealers, 1989-92, Ford Consumer Appeals Bd., 1991-93, Harborview Med. Ctrs., 1990-91, 92-93, Up. Improvement Found., 1980-81; joint labor mgmt. com. Puget Fin. Svcs., U. Wash. Med. Ctr., 1990-91, 92-93; pub. info. officer; vol. VISTA, 1982-83; dir. ACJS, Inc., 1981-82; mem. steering com. Seattle Polyfidelity Group, 1994-98, mem. No Safeword Writers Group, 1996-98. Editor M'godolim, 1980-81, Funding Bull. U. Wash. Health Scis. Grantseekers, 1991; pub., editor Beacon Rev., 1980-89. Vice chmn. Resource Conservation Commn., Iowa City, 1979-80; bd. dirs. Seattle Mental Health Inst., 1981-83, Youth Advocates, Seattle, 1984, Atlantic St. Ctr., 1984; mem. City of Seattle Animal Control Commn., 1984-86, vice chmn., 1985-86, chmn., 1986; mem. Selective Svc. System, 1982—, vice chmn. civilian rev. bd. 742, 1985—; mem. Wash. State Local Draft Bd. # 18, 1982-84, controlled choice appeals bd. Seattle Sch. Dist., 1989; patient collection rep. U. Wash., 1990-91, Harborview Med. Ctrs., 1990-91, 92-93; mem. Ford Consumer Appeals Bd., 1991-93, Ford Motor Co. Dispute Settlement Bd., 1991-93, Joint Labor-Mgmt. Com., Patient Fin. Svcs., U. Wash. Med. Ctr., 1990-91, 92-93, Temple B'nai Torah, 1986-96, Congregation Eitz Or, Phinney Neighborhood Assn.; mem. coordinating com. edn. after dark program Jewish Fedn. Greater Seattle, 1991-92, young leadership divsn.; mem. exec. bd. thirty-something plus Jewish Community Ctr., 1991-92; coord. Seattle BiPolar Support Group, 1992-93; coordinating chair Seattle BiPolar Disorder Support Grop, 1992-93; co-facilitator Polyfidelity Group, 1995-98; amb. Wash. State Basic Health Program, 1996—. Named Citizen of the Day Sta. KIXI Radio, 1982. Mem. Am. Assn. for Nude Recreation, Self Help for the Hard of Hearing, The Naturist Soc., Hosteling Internat., League United Latin Am. Citizens Amigos (chair 1984-86), U. Iowa Alumni Assn., No Safeword Writers' Group, Wandering Jews Hiking Club, Seattle Cmty. Network Assn., Mensa, Sierra Club. Democrat. Jewish. E-mail: bb822@scn.org. Office: 501 N 36th St PMB 330 Seattle WA 98103-8653

GORMLEY, FRANCIS XAVIER, JR., social worker; b. Boston, Apr. 27, 1953; s. Francis Xavier and Catherine Caroline (Ireland) G. Student, Massasoit Community Coll., 1973; BA in Psychology, U. Mass., Boston, 1981; MSW, U. Wash., 1984. Lic. social worker, Hawaii. Coordinator Gerontology Career Program Elder Fest, Chico, Calif., 1981; mgr. Arnold's Restaurant, Cardiff, Wales, 1981-82; med. social worker Harborview Med. Ctr., Seattle, 1983-84; psychotherapist Seattle Counseling Svc., 1982-88; clin. social worker Pain Ctr. Swedish Hosp., Seattle, 1984-88, Valley Med. Ctr., Renton, Wash., 1987-88; clin. social worker AIDS program, virology clinic Univ. Hosp., Seattle, 1988-94; mgr. clin. ops. dept. social work The Queen's Med. Ctr., Honolulu, 1994—; speaker U. Wash Sch. Social Work Graduation Class, 1984, Social Sensitivity in Health Care U. Wash., 1985—; coord. Coping with AIDS Swedish Hosp. Tumor Inst., 1985; participant Coun. of Internat. Fellowship Italia, Placement Servizi Socio-Sanitari AIDS-Roma, 1991; guest speaker Sta. KIRO-TV, Seattle, 1985, Sta. KPLZ, Seattle, 1985; presentor psychosocial aspects HIV/AIDS Northwest AIDS Edn. & Tng. Ctr. Program, U. Wash. Med. Ctr., 1992, clin. mgmt. of patient with HIV/AIDS El Rio Health Ctr., Pima Colo. Pub. Health Dept., 1992, Queen's Cancer Inst. Symposium, 1996; cons. Assn. Workers Resources, Seattle, 1985—; practicum instr. U. Wash. Seattle Sch. Social Work, 1989—; preceptor, intern Residency Tng. Project Sch. of Medicine/Health Scis., Univ. Wash; HIV/AIDS planning coun. Seattle/King County Pub. Health Dept., 1993; com. for the 25th health scis. open house U. Wash; trainer, cons. Queen's Med. Ctr. Mind/Body Med. Inst. Editor abstract form Comprehensive Multi-Disciplinary Documentation, Western U.S.A. Pain Soc., 1986; contbr. articles to profl. jours. Mem. Seattle Aids Network, 1985—. Mem. NASW (bd. dirs. Wash. chpt. 1988-90), Occupl. Social Work Orgn. of NASW, Acad. Cert. Social Workers, Leukemia Soc. Am. (co-facilitator family support group Hawaii chpt., trustee San Diego/Hawaii chpt., Man and Woman of Yr. com. 1997), Coun. Internat. Fellowship, U. Wash. Alumni Assn., U. Mass. Alumni Assn., Green Key Soc. Democrat. Avocations: travel, reading, swimming. Office: Queen's Med Ctr Social Work Dept 1301 Punchbowl St Honolulu HI 96813-2413

GORMLEY, GAIL F., mental health nurse; b. Evanston, Ill., Nov. 9, 1953; d. Frank M. and Arline W. (Husband) G. Diploma, Newton-Wellesley Hosp., 1978; AB in Psychology magna cum laude, Boston Coll., 1976. Staff nurse, inpatient psychiat. unit Bournewood Hosp., Brookline, Mass. Home: 197 Highgate St Needham MA 02492-3937

GORMLEY, R(OBERT) JAMES, retired lawyer; b. Oak Park, Ill., July 23, 1921; s. James Reilly and Mary Elizabeth (McGann) G.; m. Mary Adele Howard, Feb. 26, 1921; children: Philip V., Monica L. BSC, Northwestern U., 1942, MBA, 1950, JD, 1950. Bar: Ill.1950; CPA, Ill. Acct. Baumann, Finney & Co., Chgo., 1941-42, 46-47; lectr. fin. Northwestern U., Chgo., 1947-49; mem. Bell, Boyd & Lloyd, Chgo., 1950-91, of counsel, 1992—. Author: The Law of Accountants and Auditors, 1981; contbr. articles to Law Rev. Lt. Supply Corps/USNR, 1942-46 PTO. Mem. ABA, AICPA, Chgo. Bar Assn., Univ. Club. Chgo. Democrat. Roman Catholic. Home: 1641 Hinman Ave Evanston IL 60201-4509*

GORMLEY, ROBERT JOHN, book publisher; b. Lynn, Mass., Oct. 14, 1939; s. Ernest Raymond and Catherine Louise (Maitl) G.; m. Beatrice LeCount, Sept. 4, 1966; children: Catherine, Jennifer. B.A., Williams Coll., 1961; M.A., U. Calif. at Berkeley, 1964. With Wadsworth Inc., 1964-85; pres., pub. PWS Pubs. (encompassing various divs. Wadsworth, Inc.), Boston, 1980-85; pres. Duxbury Press, Boston, 1971-80; corp. v.p. Wadsworth, Boston, 1981-83, Ea. group v.p., 1983-85; exec. dir. Orbis Books, Maryknoll, N.Y., 1986-98; pub. Chatham (N.J.) House, 1998—; ptnr. Seven Bridges Press, Chappaqua, N.Y., 1998—. Bd. dirs. Mayflower Mental Health Assn.; trustee Duxbury Free Library; pres. Greater Boston Irish Children's Fund, Inc. Served with U.S. Army, 1964-69. Mem. Cath. Book Pubs. Assn. (pres.). Democrat. Roman Catholic. Home: 50 Pinesbridge Rd Ossining NY 10562-2115 Office: Chatham House Pub PO Box 1 Chatham NJ 07928-0001

GORNEY, RODERIC, psychiatry educator; b. Grand Rapids, Mich., Aug. 13, 1924; s. Abraham Jacob Gorney and Edelaine (Roden) Harburg; m. Carol Ann Sobel, Apr. 13, 1986. BS, Stanford U., 1948, MD, 1949; PhD in Psychoanalysis, So. Calif. Psychoanalytic Inst., 1977. Diplomate Am. Bd. Psychiatry and Neurology. Pvt. practice psychiatry San Francisco, 1952-62; asst. prof. UCLA, 1962-71, assoc. prof., 1971-73, prof. psychiatry, 1980—, dir. psychosocial adaptation and the future program, 1971—; faculty So. Calif. Psychoanalytic Inst. Author: The Human Agenda, 1972. Served with USAF, 1943-46. Fellow AAAS, Acad. Psychoanalysis, Am. Psychiatric Assn. (essay prize 1971), Group for Advancement of Psychiatry. Avocations: trail riding, guitar, singing. Office: UCLA Neuropsychiatric Inst 760 Westwood Plz Los Angeles CA 90095-8353

GÓRNIAK-KOCIKOWSKA, KRYSTYNA STEFANIA, philosopher, educator; b. Potczyn Zdrój, Poland, Oct. 10, 1947; came to U.S., 1989; d. Kazimierz and Stefania Wiktoria (Jagielska) Górniak; m. Andrzej-Bogdan Kocikowski, Aug. 3, 1974; 1 child, Mikotaj. MA in German philology, Adam Mickiewicz U., Poznań, Poland, 1973, PhD in philosophy, 1981; MA in Religion, Temple U., 1992. Lectr. philosophy dept. Adam Mickiewicz U., 1976-81, sr. lectr., 1981-89; lectr. Internat. Ctr. for Postgrad. Studies, Dubrovnik, Yugoslavia, 1983; adj. prof. La Salle U., Phila., 1989-92; sr. lectr. U. R.I., Kingston, 1990-92, 92-97; asst. prof. philosophy dept. So. Conn. State U., New Haven, 1992—; assoc. prof. So. Conn. State Univ., New Haven, 1997—. Co-author: On Selected Problems in Contemporary Ethics, 1979, From The History of German Mental Culture, 1985 (Minister Higher Edn. award 1986). Rsch. and Travel grantee Kosciuszko Found., 1990-91, Metaphilosophy Found., 1995; grantee NEH, 1992; scholar Temple U., 1989-92. Mem. Polish Philos. Soc., Am. Philos. Assn., Am. Acad. Religion (co-chair group on religion in Ea. Europe and former USSR 1996—), Karl Jaspers Soc. N.Am., Internat. Hegel Soc., European Bus. Ethics Network, Internat. Soc. for the Study of European Ideas, Group on Religion in Ea. Europe and Former USSR. E-mail: gorniak@scsu.ctstateu.edu. Office: So Conn State U 501 Crescent St New Haven CT 06515-1330

GOROG, WILLIAM FRANCIS, corporate executive; b. Warren, Ohio, Sept. 2, 1925; s. Frank and Margaret R. G.; m. Gretchen Elizabeth Meister, June 11, 1949; children: Robin, Jonathan, William Christopher, Lesley Anne, Jennifer, Peter. B.S., U.S. Mil. Acad, 1949; M.S., Ohio State U., 1951. Mktg. mgr. Bulova Watch Co., N.Y.C., 1954-55; exec. v.p. Data Corp., Dayton, Ohio, 1956-63, chmn., chief exec. officer, 1963-75; v.p. Mead Corp., Dayton, Ohio, 1972-75; dep. asst. to pres. The White House, Washington, 1975; exec. dir. White House Council on Internat. Econ. Policy, 1976; pres., chief exec. officer Mag. Pubs. Am., N.Y.C., 1982-87; chmn., chief exec. officer Arbor Internat., Vienna, Va., 1987-90; chmn., founder InteliData, Herndon, Va., 1990—; chmn. Worldcorp, Herndon, Va., 1993-97; bd. dirs. Nations Bank, C & S Sovran Corp., Verifone Inc., Fiskars, Helsinki, Finland, Chief Execs. Orgn. Chmn. adv. bd. Georgetown U. Grad. Sch. of Bus., 1982, chmn. Washington campus. Capt. USAF, 1949-53. Republican. Roman Catholic. Clubs: Maroon Creek (Aspen, Colo.), Bay Colony (Naples, Fla.), Georgetown Club (Washington). Office: InteliData 11600 Sunrise Valley Dr Reston VA 20191

GORONKIN, HERBERT, physicist; b. Pitts., Jan. 9, 1936; s. Sander (Tammie) and Mae (Shulman) G.; children: David, Jeffrey, Michael; m. Pamela Louise Cooper, Oct. 4, 1980; children: Rebecca Louise, Theresa Louise, James David. BA, Temple U., 1961, MA, 1962, PhD, 1973. Physicist Internat. Resistance Co., Phila., 1963-65; sr. research physicist

Honeywell Inc., Ft. Washington, Pa., 1965-66; sect. head Am. Electronic Labs., Colmar, Pa., 1966-69; project engr. Gen. Electric Co., Syracuse, N.Y., 1969-75; mgr. semiconductor ops. Varian Assocs., Beverly, Mass., 1975-77; from mgr. high speed devices to chief scientist Phoenix copr. rsch. labs. Motorola Inc., Phoenix, 1977—, mgr. to dir. phys. rsch. lab., 1988—; v.p. phys. labs., Phys. Scis. Rsch. Labs., Phoenix, 1999—; chmn. Workshop on Compound Semicondr. Microwave Materials and Devices, 1984-86, Quantum Electronics, Quantum Functional Devices and Compound Semicondr. Devices, 1986, Advanced Hetrostructure Workshop, 1994; program chair Internat. Symposium on Compound Semicondrs., 1994, gen. chair, 1997. Contbr. articles to profl. jours., chpts. to books; patentee in field. Served with USAF, 1954-57. Recipient Motorola Disting. Innovator award, 1993, Motorola Master Innovator award, 1995, Motorola Dan Noble fellow, 1996; named IEEE Phoenix Sect. Sr. Engr. of Yr., 1993. Fellow IEEE (IEDM compound semiconductor tech. program com. 1983-86); mem. Am. Phys. Soc., Sigma Xi. Avocations: hiking, Japanese, cooking. Home: 8641 S Willow Dr Tempe AZ 85284-2523 Office: Motorola Inc 2100 E Elliot Rd Tempe AZ 85284-1806

GORR, ELAINE GRAY, therapist, elementary education educator; b. Pitts., Oct. 3, 1949; d. Elmer and Elizabeth Gray; m. Joseph Charles Bonasorte, June 20, 1969 (div. 1972); 1 child, Leah Christine Bonasorte; m. Arthur Richard Gorr, Aug. 12, 1983; children: Arthur, Stephen, Ellen, Bruce, Matthew, Leah, Carl. BS in Psychology, U. Pitts., 1972; MA in Counseling/Psychology, Norwich U., 1993; postgrad., Walden U., 1992-99. Cert. elem. sch. counselor, Pa., elem. tchr., Pa. Tchr. Pitts. Pub. Schs., 1973-89; outpatient therapist Mercy Behavioral Health, Pitts., 1992—. Nat. bd. dirs. Children and Adults with Attention Deficit Disorders. Mem. ASCD, APA, ACA, Am. Sch. Counseling Assn., PPA.

GORR, LOUIS FREDERICK, investment consultant; b. North Platte, Nebr., Aug. 1, 1941; s. Ernest Frederick and Eileen Bethel (Green) G.; m. Madeleine Zangla, Dec. 12, 1967; 1 dau., Michaela. B.A., U. Nebr., 1963, M.A., 1967; postgrad., U. Md., 1972; M.B.A., U. Dallas, 1981; mgmt. and real estate courses, So. Meth. U. Spl. asst. to dir. Nat. Mus. Am. History and Tech., Smithsonian Instn., Washington, 1969-73; dir. div. museums and historic preservation Fairfax (Va.) County Govt., 1973-77; dir. Dallas County (Tex.) Heritage Soc., 1977-79, Dallas Mus. Natural History, 1979-86, Dallas Aquarium, 1979-86; dep. dir. fin and adminstrn., treas. Winterthur (Del.) Mus. and Gardens, 1986-89; owner East End Devel. Corp., 1984-86; pres. Janus Mgmt. Advisors, 1985-86; exec. dir. Mus. of the Confederacy, Richmond, Va., 1989-92; investment cons. Branch Cabell & Co., Richmond, Va., 1993-96; fin. planner Lincoln fin. advs. Profl. Fin. Planning Corp., Richmond, 1996—; pres. Harbor Fin. Advisors, LLC, Richmond, 1996—; real estate broker, Tex.; cons., lectr. mus. and mgmt. fields, 1970—; adj. prof. mus. studies U. Okla., 1982-93; mem. bd. commerce Dallas Nat. Bank, 1980-84; dir., mem. exam. and shareholder rels. coms. Fidelity Nat. Bank, 1985-86, advisory dir., 1986-88—; chmn. bd. commerce Republic Bank Dallas East, 1983-84. Author numerous articles, revs. in field; columnist Inside Bus., 1995—. Pres. Fairfax Symphony Orch., 1976-77; bd. dirs. No. Va. Youth Symphony, 1975-77, Met. Washington Cultural Alliance, 1976, Prince George's County (Md.) Arts Council, 1973, Fairfax County Assn. Civic Orgns., 1976-77; bd. dirs. Cen. Va. Pub. Broadcasting, 1990-93; mem. arts and culture adv. com. Dallas Ind. Sch. Dist., Leadership Dallas, 1983; leadership devel. trainer United Way, 1980-83; mem. adv. bd. March of Dimes Found.; mem. community adv. bd. Med. Coll. Va., 1991-93. Served with USAF, 1963-64. Research fellow Smithsonian Instn., 1971; Research fellow Naval Inst. Mem. Am. Assn. Mus. (bd. dirs. 1982-83), Va. Assn. Mus. (bd. dirs. 1989-93), Tex. Assn. Mus. (pres. 1981-83, dir.), Assn. Sci. Mus. Dirs. (v.p. 1983), Dallas Bus. League, Dallas 40, Dallas C. of C., East Dallas C. of C., Leadership Dallas Alumni Assn., Bus. Workout Coun., Internat. Assn. Fin. Planning, Inst. CFPs, Internat. Assn. of Registered Fin. Cons., Masons (32 degree), Shriners, Sigma Iota Epsilon, Lambda Chi Alpha. Republican. Home: 2310 E Marshall St Richmond VA 23223-7147 Office: 9011 Arboretum Pkwy Ste 250 Richmond VA 23236-3496

GORRIN, EUGENE, lawyer; b. Irvington, N.J., Apr. 22, 1956; s. Harry and Ruth (Goldberg) G. BA, Rutgers U., 1978; JD, George Washington U., 1981; LLM in Taxation, NYU, 1982. Bar: N.J. 1981, U.S. Dist. Ct. N.J. 1981, U.S. Tax Ct. 1982, U.S. Supreme Ct. 1985. Assoc. Ozzard, Rizzolo, Klein, Mauro & Savo, Somerville, N.J., 1982-83; Assoc. Levine, Furman & Davis, East Brunswick, N.J., 1984-88; ptnr. Cole, Schotz, Meisel, Forman & Leonard, P.A., Hackensack, N.J., 1988-98; corp. adv. specialist Family Office Group Merrill Lynch Trust Co., Plainsboro, N.J., 1999—. Contbr. articles to profl. pubs. Mem. ABA (taxation sect.), N.J. Bar Assn. (taxation sect.), U.S. Supreme Ct. Hist. Soc., Phi Alpha Delta. Home: 2607 Frederick Ter Union NJ 07083-5603 Office: Merrill Lynch Trust Co Family Office Group 800 Scudders Mill Rd 1F Plainsboro NJ 08536

GORRY, G. ANTHONY, medical educator. BSE, Yale U., 1962; MS, U. Calif., Berkeley, 1962; PhD in Computer Sci., MIT, 1967. From asst. prof. to assoc. prof. Sloan Sch. Mgmt., 1967-73, assoc. prof. computer sci., 1973-75; from assoc. prof. cmty. medicine to prof. health mgmt. Baylor Coll. Medicine, Houston, 1975-85, prof. divsn. neurosci., v.p. info. tech., 1986-89; dean tech., v.p. for info. tech. Rice U., Houston, 1989—; assoc. faculty Oper. Rsch. Ctr., MIT, 1971-75; lectr. dept. med. Tufts U. Sch. Med., 1971-75; adj. assoc. prof. math. sci. Rice U., 1975-78, adj. prof. dept. computer sci., 1985—; adj. prof. bus. and econ. Tex. Womens U., 1978-79; com. mem. Nat. Libr. Med., 1984-88; dir. W.M. Keck ctr. computer biology Baylor Coll. Med. and Rice U.; dir. evaluation rsch. group Nat. Heart and Blood Vessel Rsch. and Demonstration Ctr., 1975-82, dir. health mgmt. rsch., 1978-80; adj. prof. neurosci. and cmty. medicine Baylor Coll. Med. Fellow Am. Coll. Med. Informatics; mem. Inst. Med.-Nat. Acad. Sci. Office: Rice University PO Box 1892 6100 South Main Houston TX 77251*

GORSKE, ROBERT HERMAN, retired lawyer; b. Milw., June 8, 1932; s. Herman Albert and Lorraine (McDermott) G.; m. Antonette Dujick, Aug. 28, 1954; 1 child, Judith Mary (Mrs. Charles H. McMullen). Student, U. Wis., Milw., 1949-50; B.A. cum laude, Marquette U., 1953, J.D. magna cum laude, 1955, MS in Clin. Psychology, 1996; LL.M. (W.W. Cook fellow), U. Mich., 1959; student, Hague Acad. Internat. Law, The Netherlands, 1981. Bar: Wis. bar 1955, D.C. bar 1975, U.S. Supreme Ct. bar 1970. Assoc. firm Quarles, Spence & Quarles, Milw., 1955-56; atty. Allis-Chalmers Mfg. Co., West Allis, Wis., 1956-62; instr. law U. Mich. Law Sch., Ann Arbor, 1958-59; lectr. law Marquette U. Law Sch., Milw., 1963; assoc. firm Quarles, Herriott & Clemons, Milw., 1962-64; atty. Wis. Electric Power Co., Milw., 1964-67, gen. counsel, 1967-94, v.p., 1970-72, 76-94, dir., 1991-94; mem. firm Quarles & Brady, Milw., 1972-76; gen. counsel Wis. Energy Corp., Milw., 1981-94; tutor in psychiatry Med. Coll. Wis., 1995. Contbr. articles to profl. jours.; Editor-in-chief: Marquette Law Rev, 1954-55. Bd. dirs. Guadalupe Children's Med. Dental Clinic, Inc., Milw., 1976-86; bd. dirs. Milw. Urban League, 1991-94, treas., 1993-94; trustee Ronald McDonald House, Wauwatosa, Wis., 1987-94. Mem. State Bar Wis., Edison Electric Inst. (vice chmn. legal com. 1975-77, chmn. 1977-79), Am. Arbitration Assn. (panelist comml. arbitrators 1985—), Ctr. for Pub. Resources (com. on alt. dispute resolution 1985-94, exec. com. 1991-94, panel disting. neutrals 1991-94). Home: 12700 Stephen Pl Elm Grove WI 53122-1964

GORSKI, DANIEL ALEXANDER, art educator; b. Cleve., Oct. 26, 1939; s. Alexander and Theodora (Krajewski) G.; m. Bonnie Allen Printz (div. 1987); children: Kalika Theodora, Elektra Printz. Diploma, Cleve. Inst. Art, 1961; BFA, Yale U., 1962, MFA, 1964. Assoc. prof. design and painting Sch. of Visual Arts, N.Y.C., 1964-67; assoc. prof. design and painting Ithaca Coll., Ithaca, N.Y., 1967-68, Drexel U., Phila., 1969-71; prof. design and painting, chmn. painting dept. Md. Inst. Coll. Art, Balt., 1971-90; dir. Glassell Sch. Art, Mus. Fine Arts, Houston, 1990-96; artist, cons. Houston, 1996—; vis. artist Tex. Christian U., Ft. Worth, Pratt Inst., N.Y.C., 1989. One-man shows at Franz/Bader Gallery, Washington, 1989, Barbara Davis Gallery, Houston, 1993, 95. Home: 4134 Blue Bonnet Blvd Houston TX 77025-1705

GORSKI, JACK, biochemistry educator; b. Green Bay, Wis., Mar. 14, 1931; s. John R. and Martha (Kenney) G.; m. Harriet M. Fischer, Sept. 9, 1955; children: Michael, Jo Anne. Student, Calif. Poly. Coll., 1949-50; B.S., U. Wis., 1953; postgrad., U. Utah, 1957; M.S., Wash. State U., 1956, Ph.D., 1958. NIH postdoctoral fellow U. Wis., 1958-61; asst. prof., asso. prof. physiology U. Ill., Urbana, 1961-66; prof. physiology U. Ill., 1967—, prof. biochemistry, 1969—; prof. biochemistry and animal scis. U. Wis., Madison, 1973—; Wis. Alumni Research Found. prof. U. Wis., 1985; NSF research fellow Princeton, 1966-67; mem. endocrinology study sect. NIH, 1966-70, molecular biology study sect., 1977-81; mem. biochemistry adv. com. Am. Cancer Soc., 1973-76, mem. personnel for research com., 1983—. Contbr. articles to profl. jours. Recipient NIH Merit award, 1986. Fellow Am. Acad. Arts and Sci.; mem. NAS, Am. Soc. Biol. Chemists, Endocrine Soc. (Oppenheimer award 1971, Disting. Leadership award 1987, pres. 1990-91, F.C. Koch award 1995). Democrat. Unitarian. Office: U Wis Dept Biochemistry 433 Babcock Dr Madison WI 53706-1544

GORSKI, ROGER ANTHONY, neuroendocrinologist, educator; b. Chgo., Dec. 30, 1935; s. Casimir Michael and Mary (Wajrowski) G.; m. Judith Ann Bentley, Sept. 6, 1959 (dec. 1992); children: Denise May, Kevin Bentley, Brian Michael. B.S., U. Ill., 1957, M.S., 1959; Ph.D., U. Calif. at Los Angeles, 1962. Asst. prof. dept. neurobiology Sch. Medicine, U. Calif. at Los Angeles, 1962-66, asso. prof., 1966-70, prof., 1970—, vice chmn. grad. affairs, 1967-74, chmn., 1980-92; vis. prof. dept. animal sci. Cornell U., 1968; dir. lab. Neuroendocrinology, UCLA Brain Research Inst., 1981—. Editorial bd.: Neuroendocrinology, 1967-75, Anatomical Record, 1968-77, Endocrinology, 1973-77, Biology of Reprodn, 1974-78; Contbr. articles profl. jours. Recipient Lederle Med. Faculty award, 1966, Profl. Achievement award UCLA Alumni Assn., 1982, Disting. Teaching award, 1986, Med. Sci. award, 1998. Mem. AAAS, Am. Acad. Arts and Sci., Am. Assn. Anatomists, Am. Physiol. Soc., Endocrine Soc. (Ernst Oppenheimer award 1976), Internat. Soc. Neuroendocrinology, Japan Endocrine Soc. (hon.), Soc. Exptl. Biology Medicine, Soc. Neurosci., Internat. Brain Rsch. Orgn., Soc. for Study Reprodn. (sec. 1973-77, pres. 1978, Rsch. award 1983), Phi Beta Kappa., Sigma Xi. Home: 3832 Minerva Ave Los Angeles CA 90066-4023 *There is one almost certain route to success: Always do your absolute best.*

GORSKI, TIMOTHY N., obstetrician-gynecologist, educator; b. Milw., Dec. 22, 1957; s. Roger J. and Donna J. (Thompson) G.; m. Deborah A. Boak, 1976; children: Genevieve, Imogene, Franklin, Frederick, Adelaide. BA in Biochem. Scis., Harvard U., 1978; MD, U. Wis., 1982. Diplomate Am. Bd. Ob-Gyn. Intern and resident in ob-gyn. U. Colo. Health Scis. Ctr., Denver, 1986; mem. staff Ob-Gyn. Ltd., Las Vegas, Nev., 1986-87; pvt. practice Dallas/Ft. Worth, 1987—; asst. clin. prof. U. N. Tex. Health Scis. Ctr., Arlington, 1991—; mem. staff Arlington Meml. Hosp., HCA South Arlington Med. Ctr., Dallas/Ft. Worth Med. Ctr., Grand Prairie, Harris-Meth. Ft. Worth. Nursery Rhymes for the 3rd Millenium, 1992; assoc. editor Sci. Rev. Alternative Medicine; contbr. articles to profl. jours. Founder, pastor North Tex. Ch. Freethought, Dallas-Ft. Worth, 1994—. Fellow ACOG; mem. AMA, AAAS, Tex. Med. Assn. (med. review panel for Tex. dept. health), Tarrant County Med. Soc. (med. legislation com., publs. com., contbr. monthly jour.), Am. Soc. Reproductive Medicine, Tex. Health Care Anti-Fraud Assn., Nat. Coun. Against Health Fraud, Fedn. of State Med. Bds. (advisor to ad hoc com. 1996—), Am. Coun. Sci. and Health (bd. sci. and policy advisors). Republican. Office: 1001 N Waldrop Dr Ste 815 Arlington TX 76012-4704

GORSLINE, STEPHEN PAUL, security firm executive; b. Washington, Aug. 22, 1954; s. Robert William and Patricia Ann (Ketchum) G. AAS in Criminal Justice, Coll. of Lake County, 1987; BS in Criminal Justice, Madonna U., 1998. Dir. safety/security ops. Thielenhaus Corp., Novi, Mich., 1998—. Vol. Nat. Rep. Com., Washington, 1992. Staff sgt. USAF, 1977-82. Mem. Safety/Security Mgmt. Assn. (exec. dir. 1996—), Fraternal Order Police. Roman Catholic. Avocations: collecting stamps, old coins and postcards.

GORSUCH, EDWARD LEE, chancellor. Degree in Econ. & Cmty. Devel., U. Mo. Dir. Inst. Social and Econ. Rsch., 1976-94; dean Sch. Pub. Affairs U. Alaska, Anchorage, 1988-94, chancellor, 1994—; commr. U.S. Arctic Rsch. Commn.; bd. dirs. Commonwealth North; mem. adv. bd. Alaska Airlines Anchorage Cmty.; mem. civilian adv. bd. ALCOM; mem. Fiscal Policy Coun. Alaska. Office: Office of Chancellor Univ AK Anchorage 3211 Providence Dr Anchorage AK 99508-8060

GORT, MICHAEL, economics educator; b. Minsk, USSR, Sept. 30, 1923; came from China to U.S., 1937; m. Elizabeth Ann Mitchell, June 15, 1957; children: William Henry, Adam Michael. AB, Bklyn. Coll., CUNY, 1943; AM, Columbia U., 1951, PhD, 1954. Lectr. in econs. U. Calif., Berkeley, 1951-54; mem. research staff Nat. Bur. Econ. Research, N.Y.C., 1954-57; assoc. prof. fin. U. Chgo., 1957-62; cons. Dept. Commerce, Washington, 1962-63; prof. econs. SUNY, Buffalo, 1963—; vis. prof. econs. Northwestern U., Evanston, Ill., 1967-68; sr. research staff mem. and dir. research program in indsl. orgn. Nat. Bur. Econ. Research, N.Y.C., 1971-75; pres. Michael Gort Assocs., Buffalo, 1977—. Author: Diversification and Integration in American Industry, 1962, Changes in the Size Standard of Business Firms, 1964; contbr. articles to profl. jours. Mem. adv. com. U.S. Bur. of the Census. Fellow Social Sci. Research Council, 1950-51. Mem. Am. Econ. Assn. Royal Econ. Assn. Home: 71 Smallwood Dr Buffalo NY 14226-4028 Office: SUNY Dept of Econs North Campus Buffalo NY 14260

GORTATOWSKI, MELVIN JEROME, retired chemist; b. Chgo., Oct. 30, 1925; s. Walter Harry and Anna Martha (Santowski) G. BS, U. Ill., 1950, PhD, 1956; MS, Wash. State U., 1952. Research instr. biochemistry U. Utah, Salt Lake City, 1955-58, research assoc. psychiatry, 1958-59, research instr. biochemistry, chemist VA Hosp., 1959-65; assoc. investigator, asst. rsch. prof. pediatrics, biochemistry U. So. Calif. Children's Hosp., Los Angeles, 1965-71; dir. bur. clin. chemistry Utah State Health Lab., Salt Lake City, 1971-87, safety officer, 1980-87. Contbr. articles to jours. Served with U.S. Army, 1944-46. Eastman Kodak fellow U. Ill., 1954. Mem. Am. Chem. Soc., Mineral Collectors Utah, Utah Numismatic Soc. (bd. dirs. 1976-77), Sigma Xi, Phi Lambda Upsilon. Roman Catholic. Avocations: photography, philatelics, music, mineral collecting, swimming. Home: 4045 Foubert Ave Salt Lake City UT 84124-3410

GORTER, JAMES POLK, investment banker; b. Balt., Dec. 10, 1929; s. T. Poultney and Swan (Deford) G.; m. Audrey Fentress; children: James Jr., David F., Mary H. A.B., Princeton U., 1951; postgrad., London Sch. Econ., 1951-52. Ptnr. Goldman, Sachs & Co., 1956-88, ltd. ptnr., 1989—; chmn. Baker, Fentress & Co., Chgo., 1987—; bd. dirs. Caterpillar Inc., Consol. Tomoka Land Co. Trustee Lake Forest Coll. Served with USN, 1952-55. Clubs: Chicago Commonwealth, Chicago, Economic, Commercial. Office: Baker Fentress & Co 200 W Madison St Ste 3510 Chicago IL 60606-3417

GORTON, NATHANIEL M., federal judge, lawyer; b. 1938; m. Jodi Linnell; children: Kerry, Craig, Nan. AB, Dartmouth Coll., 1960; LLB, Columbia U., 1966. Bar: Mass. 1966, U.S. Dist. Ct. Mass. 1967, U.S. Ct. Appeals (5th cir.) 1975, U.S. Ct. Appeals (9th cir.) 1977, U.S. Ct. Appeals (1st cir.) 1979, U.S. Ct. Appeals (11th cir.) 1990. Assoc. Nutter, McClennen & Fish, Boston, 1966-69; assoc. Powers & Hall, P.C., Boston, 1970-74, ptnr., dir., 1975-92; district judge Mass., 1992—. Trustee Buckingham Browne & Nichols Sch., Cambridge, Mass., 1984-93, chmn., 1989-93; mem. corp. Boston Children's Svcs., 1991—; mem. Wellesley Town Meeting, 1971-86; sr. warden All Saints Episcopal Ch., Brookline, Mass., 1975-80; apptd. Mass. Citizens Commn. on Gen. Ct., 1976; mem. com. Modern Legis., 1967-69; coach Wellesley Little League and Youth Hockey, 1983-87; bd. dirs. Rep. Club Mass., 1991-92; mem. fin. com. Citizens for Joe Malone, 1989-90; mem. Weld/Cellucci Com., 1989-90; program chmn. Boston chpt. Ripon Soc., 1967-68. (Lt. (j.g.) USN, 1960-62. Mem. Boston Bar Assn. (law day classroom program, 1987-93, litigation, adminstrn. justice sect.). Avocations: hockey, tennis, skiing, sailing, mem. Boston Atoms Hockey N.Am.- (nat. finalist 1988, 91). Office: Dist Judge Mass US Dist Ct 595 Main St Worcester MA 01608-2025

GORTON, SLADE, senator; b. Chicago, Ill., Jan. 8, 1928; s. Thomas Slade and Ruth (Israel) G.; m. Sally Jean Clark, June 28, 1958; children: Tod, Sarah Jane, Rebecca Lynn. AB, Dartmouth Coll., 1950; LLB with honors, Columbia U., 1953. Bar: Wash. 1953. Assoc. law firm Seattle, 1953-65; ptnr. law firm, 1965-69; atty. gen. State of Wash., Olympia, 1969-81; U.S. senator from Wash., 1981-87, 89—; ptnr. Davis, Wright & Jones, Seattle, 1987-89; mem. Wash. Ho. of Reps., 1959-69, majority leader, 1967-69, nat. Rep. senatorial com., Indian affairs, budget com., appropriations com., commerce/sci. and transp. com., energy and natural resources com.; chmn. commerce, sci. and transp. subcom. on aviation, chmn. com. on appropriations subcom. on interior. Trustee Pacific Sci. Center, Seattle, found. mem., 1977-78; mem. Pres.'s Consumer Adv. Council, 1975-77; mem. Wash. State Law and Justice Commn., 1959-80, chmn., 1969-76; mem. State Criminal Justice Tng. Commn., 1969-80, chmn., 1969-76. Served with AUS, 1946-47; to 1st lt. USAF, 1953-56; col. USAFR (ret.). Mem. ABA, Wash. Bar Assn., Nat. Assn. Attys. Gen. (pres. 1976-77, Wyman award 1980), Phi Delta Phi, Phi Beta Kappa. Clubs: Seattle Tennis, Wash. Athletic (Seattle). Office: US Senate 730 Hart Senate Bldg Washington DC 20510

GORUM, JACQUELYNE W., dean, social work educator; b. Pitman, N.J., July 20, 1941; d. John Emerick and Evelyn Carretta (Weekes) W.; m. Wendell J.L. Gorum, Nov. 24, 1964; children: W. Jay, Guy, Marc. MSW, U. Denver, 1965; postgrad., Pa. State U.; DSW, Howard U., 1983. Asst. prof. Sch. Social Work Howard U., Washington, 1980-84, dir. admissions, recruitment and fin. aid dir., undergrad., 1983-84; asst. prof. Sch. Social Work SUNY, Stony Brook, 1984-89; assoc. prof., dir. undergrad. programs Dept. Social Work Del. State U., Dover, 1989-91, dean Sch. Edn. and Profl. Studies, 1991—. Active Del. Perinatal Bd., Dover, 1996—, Del. Health Care Commn., Dover, 1994—; liaison, mem. program bd. Leadership Alliance, 1991—. Recipient Beyond War award Peace Inst., 1987. Mem. Black Women in Higher Edn. (bd. dirs. 1997—, award 1993), Nat. Black Alcoholics and Addictions Coun. (exec. bd. dirs. 1991—), Coun. Social Work Edn. (site vis., Svc. award 1991), Pioneer Peace Corps Vol., Delta Sigma Theta (chair program and planning devel.). Avocations: travel, swimming, reading. Office: Del State U 1200 N Dupont Hwy Dover DE 19901-2202

GORUP, GREGORY JAMES, marketing executive; b. Kansas City, Kans., Mar. 27, 1948; s. Mike and Helen F. Gorup; m. Kathleen Susan Grogan, Apr. 12, 1986 (div.); children: Michael Thomas, Ryan Nicholas. BA in Econs., St. Benedict Coll., 1970; MBA, U. Pa., 1972. Market analyst product planning and devel. dept. Citibank, N.Y.C., 1972-73, market planning officer corp. product mgmt. div., 1973-74, product mgr. securities services, 1974-75; v.p., dir. product devel. Irving Trust Co. N.Y.C., 1975-80, mgr. product mgmt. dept., 1980-81; v.p. mktg. Credit Suisse, U.S. area, 1981-84; sr. cons. Wesley, Brown and Bartle, N.Y.C., 1985-86; bank mktg. mgr. Digital Equipment Corp., N.Y.C., 1986-87; money mktg. mgr. Reuters N.Am., 1987-88; pres. Gorup Assocs., 1989-91; dist. v.p. Nat. Computer Systems, N.Y., 1991-94; regional mgr. Soc. Worldwide InterBank Fin. Telecommunications, 1994-96, sr. regional mgr. 1996—. Mem. Rep. Nat. Com., Nat. Rep. Senatorial Com., U.S. Shooting Team. Mem. NRA (life), West Point Soc. N.Y., Wharton Bus. Sch. Club, Princeton Club N.Y., Orienta Beach Club, Willow Wood Gun Club, Army "A" Club, U.S. Naval Inst., Naval League of the U.S., Air Force Assn. Roman Catholic. Home: 910 Stuart Ave # 2-0 Mamaroneck NY 10543-4134 Office: 200 Park Ave Fl 38 New York NY 10166-3899

GOS, MICHAEL WALTER, English educator, author; b. East Chicago, Ind., Apr. 23, 1950; s. Walter S. and Anne S. (Kalutz) G.; m. Patricia A. Motley, Aug. 5, 1996. BA, Purdue U., 1972, MA, 1986, PhD, 1992. CEO SRC, Inc., Lafayette, Ind., 1980-88; grad. instr. Purdue U., West Lafayette, Ind., 1983-92; prof. U. Houston Downtown Campus, 1992-98, Lee Coll., Baytown, Tex., 1998—. Author: (books) The Brackish Aquarium, 1979, Waxbills, 1981, Lories, 1981, Doves, 1981, Unwelcome Guests: Working Class Students in the American Universities, 1999. Sam Walton fellow Students in Free Enterprise, Kansas City, Kans., 1996. Mem. Nat. Coun. Tchrs. of English, Conf. on Coll. Composition and Comm., Assn. Tchrs. of Tech. Writing, Soc. for Technical Comm., Am. Cuture Assn. (area chair tech. writing), Two Year Coll. English Assn. Office: Lee Coll Dept English Houston TX 77002-1014

GOSE, CELESTE MARLENE, writer; b. Laramie, Wyo., Jan. 2, 1959; d. Richard Vern Gose and Agnes Jean (Allen) McGreggor. Student, U. UNA, Belo Horizonte, Brazil, 1982; BS, U. Wyo., 1984; student, U. UNA, Belo Horizonte, Brazil, 1982. Freelance writer Santa Fe, 1990—; mng. editor Imprintables Today; writer, mng. editor Virgo Pub.; mng. editor Virgo Pub., Scottsdale, 1995-96. N.Mex. prodn. coord. (feature movies) Twins, 1988, Young Guns, 1988, (cable) The Tracker, 1987; asst. prodn. coord. (feature movies) Outrageous Fortune, The Sunday Disney Movie; asst. unit publicist The Milagro Beanfield War, 1986; casting asst. (TV) Lonesome Dove, 1988, Sparks, 1989, The Fantasticks, 1995; author: Your Daggar or Mine?, 1991, (song lyrics) Awake Inside a Dream, 1990, Caught in Eternity, 1990, Drum Sticks on the Moon, 1990, Of A Different Spirit, 1994, After Paradise, 1994, Coyotes Don't Bark, 1995, The Reluctant Actress, 1995, Have No Regrets, 1995; writer, prodr. (screenplay) The Silent War; mng. editor Imprintables Today; asst. editor Embroidery Business News and Flat Bus. Quar. Mem. Internat. Arabian Horse Assn., Brazilian Inst. Ariz., Master Foxhounds Assn. of Am. Avocations: Arabian horse owning/training, antique collecting, interior design, scuba diving. Home and Office: PO Box 762 Tesuque NM 87574-0762

GOSE, RICHARD VERNIE, lawyer; b. Hot Springs, S.D., Aug. 3, 1927. MS in Engring., Northwestern U., 1955; LLB, George Washington U., 1967; JD, George Washington U., 1968. Bar: N.Mex. 1967, U.S. Supreme Ct. 1976, Wyo. 1979; registered prof. engr., Wyo.; children: Beverly Marie, Donald Paul, Celeste Marlene. Exec. asst. to U.S. Senator Hickey, Washington, 1960-62; mgr. E.G. & G., Inc., Washington, 1964-66; asst. atty. gen. State of N.Mex., Santa Fe, 1967-70; pvt. practice law, Santa Fe, 1967—, Santa Fe/Prescott, 1989—; assoc. prof. engring. U. Wyo., 1957-60; owner, mgr. Gose & Assocs., Santa Fe, 1967-78; pvt. practice law, Casper, Wyo., 1978-83; pres. Argosy Internat., Inc., 1994—; ranch mgr., foreman, 1945-49; mem. Phoenix com. on fgn. rels., 1980—; co-chmn. Henry Jackson for Pres., M.Mex., 1976, Wyo. Johnson for Pres., 1960. With U.S. Army, 1950-52. Mem. N.Mex. Bar Assn., Wyo. Bar Assn., Yavapai County Bar Assn., Masons, High Country Hounds, Phoenix Com. Foreign Rels., High Country Hounds, Phi Delta Theta, Pi Tau Sigma, Sigma Tau. Methodist. Home and Office: PO Box 3998 Prescott AZ 86302-3998

GOSFIELD, MARGARET, educator, educational administrator, consultant, editor; b. Marshall County, Minn., Mar. 9, 1942; d. William Jay and Evelyn Pearl (Anderson) Wayne; m. Amor Gosfield, Aug. 21, 1964. BA in History, U. Calif., Santa Barbara, 1966, secondary tchrs. credential, 1968, MA in Edn., 1976. Cert. tchr., Calif. Tchr. Ventura (Calif.) Unified Sch. Dist., 1969-89, coord. gifted and talented edn. program, 1982-97; cons. gifted edn. Author: History of the Wayne Family, 1983; editor: Meeting the Challenge: A Guidebook for Teaching Gifted Students, 1996; jour. editor The Communicator, 1998—. Named Calif. Outstanding Educator, Johns Hopkins U., 1994; recipient Ednl. Achievement award Phi Delta Kappa, 1997. Mem. Calif. Assn. for the Gifted (regional rep. 1990-94, v.p. 1994-96, pres. 1996-98, Tchr. of Yr. 1985), Santa Barbara Mus. of Art. Avocations: travel, writing, family historical research, gardening. Home: 3136 Calle Mariposa Santa Barbara CA 93105-2775 Office: Calif Assn for Gifted Ste 1670 5777 W Century Blvd Los Angeles CA 90045

GOSLAWSKI, VIOLET ANN, nurse, substance abuse counselor; b. Bangor, Mich., Aug. 31, 1929; d. George and Ethel Pikal; m. Stephen T. Goslawski, Jan. 18, 1975; children: John F. Cappetto, Steve Goslawski, Carol Smurawski. AAS in Nursing, Morton Coll., 1986; AAS in Mental Health, Loop Coll., 1987. RN, Fla., Ill.; clin. nurse specialist; cert. substance abuse counselor; nat. cert. addictions counselor, internat. cert. addictions counselor. Psychiat. nurse and addictions counselor HCA Riveredge Hosp., Forest Park, Ill., 1987-90; psychiat. nurse, counselor Choices of Pinellas Cmty. Hosp., Choices of Pinellas Park, Fla., 1990-96, Charter Psychiat. Hosp., Largo, Fla., 1990—, Rader Inst., Seminole, 1990-96.

GOSLEE, PATRICIA CLAIRE, artist, graphic artist; b. San Diego, Apr. 13, 1960; d. John William and Virginia Claire (Parker) G.; m. Michael Patrick O'Sullivan, Jan. 10, 1998. BFA in Graphic Design, U. Ga., 1982; MFA in Painting, Cath. U., 1988. Graphic artist Nat. Geog. Soc., Washington, 1983-89; typographer Phil's Photo, Washington, 1989-90; graphic artist Greenhorne & O'Mara, Greenbelt, Md., 1990-91; design cons. U.S. Postal Svc., Washington, 1991—. One woman shows include Night Gallery, Athens, Ga., 1981, Landon Sch., Bethesda, Md., 1988, Mt. Rainier (Md.) City Hall, 1996, eklektikos gallery, Washington, 1997, Dance Pl., Washington, 1997, U. D.C., 1998, Kramerbooks, Washington, 1998; exhibited at numerous group shows, including Arlington (Va.) Arts Ctr., 1987, Alex Agllery, Washington, 1988, D.C. Arts Ctr., 1998, Fifth Column, Washington, 1990, Peninsula Fine Arts Ctr., Newport News, Va., 1991, Foundry Gallery, Washington, 1991, 92, Target Gallery, Alexandria, Va., 1992, In Time Art Salon, Washington, 1992, Kristin Johnson Gallery, Washington, 1993, D.C. Arts Ctr., 1993, 94, 95, 96, 97, Clark & Co. Gallery, Washington, 1993, On-the-Hill Arts Ctr., Yorktown, Va., 1993, MOCA, Washington, 1994, 95, 96, Arlington Arts Ctr., 1996, Fells Point MAP, Balt., 1997, eklektikos galley, 1997, St. Mary's Coll. Md. Boyden Gallery, 1997, Kalit Kala Acad., New Delhi, 1998, Montgomery Coll., Rockville, Md., 1998, others; contbr. revs. to profl. publs. Recipient 1st Pl. Purchase award U. Ga., 1982, Best Emerging Artist of Washington award KOAN/Mus. Contemporary Art, 1993, 94, Hon. Mention award Ctrl. Pa. Festival Arts, 1995. Mem. D.C. Arts Ctr., Arlington Arts Ctr., McLean Project for Arts, Washington Project for Arts, Peninulsa Fine Arts Ctr. (award of distinction 1991), Smithsonian Resident Assocs. Democrat. Avocations: swimming, yoga, reading, music, theater. E-mail: mookiedome@aol.com. Home: 1502 Columbia Rd NW Washington DC 20009-4214

GOSLIN, DAVID ALEXANDER, research administrator, sociologist; b. N.Y.C., Oct. 27, 1936; s. Omar Pancoast and Ryllis Clair (Alexander) G.; m. Ann Compter, Sept. 6, 1958 (div. 1963): 1 child, Jean Davis; m. Nancy Jean McGirr, Oct. 10, 1982; children: David Pancoast, Christopher Stratton. BA, Swarthmore Coll., 1958; MA, Yale U., 1960, PhD, 1962. Sociologist Russell Sage Found., N.Y.C., 1961-74; adj. prof. of edn. Tchrs. Coll., Columbia U., N.Y.C., 1966-74; exec. dir. Commn. on Behavioral and Social Scis. and Edn., Nat. Acad. of Scis., Washington, 1974-87; pres. Am. Insts. for Rsch., 1987—; bd. dirs. Coun. on Basic Edn., Washington, Sci. Svc. Inc., Washington. Author: The Search for Ability, 1962, The School in Contemporary Society, 1965, Teachers and Testing, 1967; editor: Handbook of Socialization Theory and Research, 1969; author articles: Social effects of standardized testing. Active Yale U. Coun., 1988-93. Recipient Nat. Rsch. Coun. Prof. Staff award for Disting. Svc., Nat. Acad. of Scis, 1986. Fellow AAAS; mem. Am. Sociological Assn., Yale Club (N.Y.C.). Office: Am Insts Rsch Behavioral Scis 3333 K St NW Washington DC 20007-3500*

GOSLIN, GERALD HUGH, concert pianist, educator; b. Detroit, Jan. 7, 1947; s. Hugh Jennings and Helen Margaret (Senauit) G. Student, Wayne State U., Detroit, 1966-69. Music tchr. Peralta Music, Farmington, Mich., 1965-80, Hammell Music, Livonia, Mich., 1980-83; prof. music Oakland C.C., Farmington Hills, Mich., 1983—; host The Piano Hour Sta. WHNDAM, Oak Park, Mich., 1985; recitalist Allen, Rodgers and Baldwin Organs, Detroit, 1975—; judge Leontyne Price Vocal Competition, 1986—, Verdi Opera Assn. Vocal Competition, 1995—. Block capt. Rogers Park Residents Assn., Redford, 1995-96; choirmaster-organist Littlefield Presbyn. Ch., Dearborn, Mich., 1997—. Mem. Detroit Fedn. of Musicians Local #5, Am. Choral Dir. Assn., Am. Guild of Organists. Home and Office: 19782 Olympia Redford MI 48240-1334

GOSLIN, THOMAS B., career officer. BA in Polit. Sci., La. State U., 1970; grad., Officer Tng. Sch., 1970; student pilot tng., Columbus AFB, Miss., 1971-72; student, Squadron Officer Sch., 1974; MA in Guidance and Counseling, La. Tech U., 1975; student, Air Command and Staff Coll., 1975, Air War Coll., 1980, Armed Forces Staff Coll., 1981, Can. Nat. Def. Coll., 1988, Duke U., 1995. Commd. 2d lt. USAF, 1970, advanced through grades to brig. gen., 1996; forward air controller Tan Son Nhut Air Base, S. Vietnam, 1972-73; pilot, instr. pilot 71st Air Refueling Squadron, Barksdale AFB, La., 1973-76; air staff tng. officer, intelligence threat assessment Pentagon, Washington, 1976-77, various positions, 1993-94; pilot, instr. pilot, flight comdr. 62d Bomb Squadron, Barksdale AFB, 1977-80; stationed at Hdqs. USAF, Pentagon, Washington, 1981-84, 94-95, now dep. dir. programs, dep. chief staff plans and programs; fighter lead-in tng. Holloman AFB, N.Mex., 1984; pilot 162d Tactical Fighter Group Air NG, Tucson, 1984; various comdr. assignments, 1984-93; asst. dir. ops. Hdqs. Air Combat Command, Langley AFB, Va., 1995-96; comdr. 509th Bomb Wing, Whiteman AFB, Mo., 1996—. Decorated Legion of Merit, D.F.C. with oak leaf cluster, Air medal with seven oak leaf clusters, Rep. Vietnam Gallantry Cross. Office: HQ USAF/XPP 1070 Air Force Pentagon Washington DC 20330-1070

GOSS, DONALD DAVIS, consultant, author, lecturer; b. Marblehead, Mass., May 18, 1923; s. Donald Chapin and Ruth Alden (Johnson) Goss; m. Marilyn Elizabeth Riddle, Jan. 1, 1948; children: Daniel Griffith, Cynthia Davis, Charles Chapin. Student, Chauncy Hall Sch., Boston; grad., Sch. Practical Art Boston. Freelance comml. artist; art dir. various advt. agys. and comml. printers; advt. mgr., dir. mktg. Vogue Dolls Inc., until 1958; founder consulting firm Ideation, 1958—; founder Goss Galleries, Inc., Dallas, until 1990. Author: Problem Solving Through Innovation, Imaginative Skills Development, Take Time to Think, Turning Problems Into Profits. With U.S. Army, WW II. Home and Office: Ideation 1404 Carrollton Ave Metairie LA 70005-1811

GOSS, GEORGIA BULMAN, translator; b. N.Y.C., Dec. 1, 1939; d. James Cornelius and Marian Bright (McLaughlin) Bulman; m. Douglas Keith Goss, Dec. 21, 1957; children: Kristin Anne, David. BA, U. Mich., 1961. Libr., High Altitude Obs., Boulder, Colo., 1963-64, U.S. Bur. Standards, Boulder, 1964-65; cons. editor Spanish lang. pilots' tng. manual, 1981-82; freelance translator, 1982—. Mem. U. Mich. Alumni Assn., Phi Sigma Iota. Republican. Episcopalian. Home and Office: 200 Hancock St Apt 706 Bangor ME 04401-6570

GOSS, JAMES WALTER, oil company executive; b. Farmerville, La., Mar. 18, 1924; s. Walter Frank and Lovie (Hollis) G.; m. Mertie Henry, Jan. 1, 1953; children: James Walter, Kimberly. BS, La. State U., 1949. With Gen. Am. Oil Co. Tex., Dallas, 1949—, v.p. charge land dept., 1960—, exec. v.p., dir., mem. exec. com., 1970—, chief oper. officer, 1979-83; oil and gas cons., 1983—. Lt. comdr. USNR, 1943-46, Res., ret. Mem. Ind. Petroleum Assn. Am. (exec. com., past v.p.), Dallas (past pres., dir.), Assns. Petroleum Landmen, Midcontinent Oil and Gas Assn., Am. Petroleum Inst., Dallas Athletic, Petroleum, Brook Hollow Golf, Lambda Chi Alpha. Home: 3509 Centenary Ave Dallas TX 75225-5014 Office: Meadows Bldg Dallas TX 75206

GOSS, JAMES WILLIAM, lawyer; b. London, Ont., Can., Mar. 10, 1941; s. Joseph Allen and Virginia Ruth (Farrah) G.; m. Rita Meyer, Aug. 2, 1969; children: Anne Candace, Jennette Courtney. BBA, West Mich. U., 1966; MS, U. Ill., 1972; JD, Georgetown U., 1974. Bar: Mich. 1974, U.S. Dist. Ct. (ea. dist.) Mich. 1974, U.S. Ct. Appeals (6th cir.) 1974. Sr. acct. Price Waterhouse & Co., Washington, 1969-71; assoc. Miller, Canfield, Paddock & Stone, Detroit, 1974-82, James W. Goss P.C., Southfield, Mich., 1982-88; ptnr. Dean & Fulkerson, Troy, Mich., 1988-95, James W. Goss P.C., Grosse Pointe Farms, Mich., 1995—; adj. lectr. U. Mich. Law, Ann Arbor, 1978-82. Bd. dirs. Old Newsboys Goodfellow Fund of Detroit, 1990-96, Adrian Coll., 1991-96; bd. dirs., v.p. Svc. to Older Citizens, Grosse Pointe, Mich., 1997—; bd. dirs. Grosse Pointe Hist. Soc., 1998-99; bd. govs. William L. Clements Libr., U. Mich., 1998—. Named Outstanding Goodfellow, Old Newsboys Goodfellows of Detroit, 1991; recipient Disting. Alumni award Western Mich. U., 1995. Mem. ABA, Mich. Bar Assn., Assn. Def. Trial Attys., Georgetown U. Law Alumni Assn., Grosse Pointe Yacht Club, Georgetown Club of Mich., Old Club, Commanderie de Bordeaux, Hundred Club, Rotary, Masons. Presbyterian. Avocations: philately, wine collecting, cartographic collecting. Home: 398 Rivard Blvd Grosse Pointe MI 48230-1629 Office: 230 Punch and Judy Bldg 21 Kercheval Ave Grosse Pointe MI 48236-3698

GOSS, J.B., psychopharmacologist; b. Bklyn., June 1, 1956; s. Bernard David and Catherine (Marino) G.; m. Linda M. Goss, Dec. 28, 1979; children: Catherine, Jessica, Joseph S. B in Pharmacology, St. John's U., 1982; PhD in Psychology, LaSalle U., 1994. Diplomate Am. Bd. Psychopharmacology and Psychotherapy. Prof. Union U., Albany, 1985-96; dir. pharmacy O'Connor Hosp., Delhi, N.Y., 1985; v.p. for pharmacy svcs. Advanced Med. Cons., N.Y.C., 1987-93; psychiatric pharmacotherapeutics Stratton VA Med. Ctr., Albany, 1993-96; regional dir. Med. Pharmacology Rsch. Unit, Albany, 1993-96; reimbursement mgr. N.E. region Janssen Rsch. Found., 1996—; med. dir. A.E.C.H.O., Malta, N.Y., 1994-98; chair mental health N.Y. State Coun. of Hosp. Pharm., Albany, 1995—; mem. regional IRB Albany Med. Coll., 1993, others; mem. Freund's Scholarly Rsch. Group Think Tank, 1994—. Author: Hydroponic Workbook, 1985; adv. bd. mags., 1987-94. Avocation: patron of arts.

GOSS, JEROME ELDON, cardiologist; b. Dodge City, Kans., Nov. 30, 1935; s. Horton Maurice and Mary Alice (Mountain) G.; m. Lorraine Ann Sanchez, Apr. 20, 1986. BA, U. Kans., 1957; MD, Northwestern U., 1961. Diplomate Am. Bd. Internal Medicine, Am. Bd. Cardiology (fellow, bd. govs. 1981-84). Intern Met. Gen. Hosp., Cleve., 1961-62; resident in internal medicine Northwestern U. Med. Ctr., Chgo., 1962-64; fellow in cardiology U. Colo., Denver, 1964-66; asst. prof. medicine U. N.Mex., Albuquerque, 1968-70; pvt. practice N.Mex. Heart Clinic, Albuquerque, 1970—; bd. alumni counsellors Northwestern U. Med. Sch., 1977-89, nat. alumni bd., 1991-97; chief dept. medicine Presbyn. Hosp., Albuquerque, 1978-80, exec. com., 1980-82, dir. cardiac diagnostic svcs., 1970-96. Contbr. articles to profl. jours. Bd. dirs. Presbyn. Heart Inst., Ballet West N.Mex., N.Mex. Symphony Orch.; pres. Albuquerque Mus. Found. Lt. comdr. USN, 1966-68. Nat. Heart Inst. research fellow, 1965-66; named one of Outstanding Young Men Am., Jaycees, 1970; recipient Alumni Service award Northwestern U. Med. Sch., 1986, Disting. Achievement award Albuquerque Mus. Found., 1997. Fellow ACP, ACC, Coun. Clin. Cardiology of Am. Heart Assn., Soc. Cardiac Angiography; mem. Albuquerque-Bernalillo County Med. Soc. (sec. 1972, treas. 1975, v.p. 1980), Alpha Omega Alpha. Republican. Methodist. Office: NMex Heart Clinic 1001 Coal Ave SE Albuquerque NM 87106-5205

GOSS, JOEL FRANCIS, writer; b. Pawnee, Okla., Nov. 15, 1955; s. William Richard and Mary Ann (Webb) G.; m. Cat Guthrie, 1992; 1 child, William Keaton Guthrie-Goss. BA, U. Tenn., 1985. Staff writer Sta. WDXB, Chattanooga, 1970-73, Sta. WGOW, Knoxville, Tenn., 1973-75; writer, dir. V.T. Films, Knoxville, 1974-76; writer Hi-Test Films, Knoxville, 1976; freelance writer N.Y.C., 1976-80; writer, mgr. Improvisation, Inc., N.Y.C., 1980-84; writer, producer CB Prodns., N.Y.C., 1984; mng. dir. Albuquerque '49, N.Y.C., 1983—; v.p. Buster Keaton Archive, N.Y.C., 1985—; cons. Rohauer Films, London, 1985-88, Am. Theatre Wing, N.Y.C., 1987; film instr. Brown Sch., Knoxville, 1976; chmn. Film com., Knoxville, 1974-76. Author: Albuquerque '49, 1973, (with Michael Kaluta) The Shadow, 1992, Coils of Leviathan, 1993; screenplays: The Prairie Traveler, 1986, Manhattan Underground, 1987, Bard of Broadway, 1988, Sandhogs, 1991, Battling Butler, 1991; translator tng. manuals: Construzione Aeronauticle, 1973; co-screenwriter (with Raymond Rohauer), researcher Buster Keaton-A Hard Act to Follow, 1987; writer Spectacular Days of Radio, 1990, (with Martin Connor) Madame Sherry, 1989, Cat Guthrie in Concert, 1992, The Rich Conaty Radio Show, 1992; writer (with others) The Rocketeer, The Shadow, 1994, The Shadow & the Mysterious 3, 1994, (with M. Kaluta and Gary Gianni) Hell's Heat Wave, 1994, Buster Keaton: Genius In Slapshoes, 1995, Cut To The Chase: Buster Keaton, 1995, The Sound of Buster Keaton, 1995, Complete Films of BK; restored dialog to film (with Bruce Goldstein) The Donovan Affair (1929), 1992, Cliff Edwards--Fascinatin' Rhythm, 1996, (with Eliot Camaren) That's Funny, 1997, Killing Time; co-producer Am. Hepatitis Assn. Benefit, 1989; promotions writer CNN Headline News, Sandy Hook Found.; editor: Brio Technology, 1999. Vol. Nat. Music Theatre Network, N.Y.C., Washington, 1985, 87, Nat. Theatre Wing, N.Y.C., 1987, Muscular Dystrophy Assn., N.Y.C., 1987; signings for St. Jude's Children's Hosp., 1994. Grantee U. Tenn., 1975, CB Prodns., 1984. Mem. Buster Keaton Soc., CVPO Assn.

GOSS, KAY COLLETT, government official. BA in Polit. Sci. and Pub. Adminstrn., U. Ark., 1963, MA in Polit. Sci. and Pub. Adminstrn., 1966; postgrad., W.Va. U., N.W. Mo. State U., San Diego State U., Harvard U., Am. U., 1998—. Cert. emergency mgr. Internat. Assn. Emergency Mgrs. Instr. govt., polit. sci., geography, history and sociology Westark C.C., Ft. Smith, Ark.; instr. govt., polit. sci., geography, history and sociology U. Ark., Fayetteville; instr. govt., polit. sci., geography, history and sociology U. Ark., Little Rock, adj. asst. prof. Ark. govt. and politics; adminstrv. asst. to Reps. Thornton, Schroeder and Mills, U. S. Ho. of Reps., Washington; chief dep. auditor of state State of Ark., Little Rock, sr. asst. for intrgovtl. rels. Office of Gov.; assoc. dir. for preparedness Fed. Emergency Mgmt. Agy., Washington, 1994—; former project coord. Assn. Ark. Counties; chmn. Emergency Food and Shelter Nat. Bd.; mem. President's Interagy. Coun. on Women, President's Interagy. Coun. on Homeless, Nat. Security Steering Group; co-chmn. Joint U.S.-Russian Com. on Emergencies, U.S. Sr. Interagy. Coordination Group for Counter Terrorism, 1996-98; mem. nat. adv. com. Natural Hazards Rsch. and Applications Info. Ctr., U. Colo., Boulder; mem. project steering com. Vice President's Global Disaster Information Network; mem. govt. rels. com. Oklahoma City Meml. Found.; mem. nat. adv. bd. fire and emergency mgmt. program Okla. State U., Stillwater; mem. nat. adv. coun. for emergency adminstrn. and mgmt. program Ark. Tech. U., Russellville. Author: Wilbur D. Mills: The People's Congressman, The Arkansas Constitution: A Reference Guide, The City Manager Plan in Arkansas, Political Paradox: Constititional Revision in Arkansas. Bd. dirs. Opera Co. Boston, Wilbur D. Mills Meml. Found., Wilbur D. Mills Treatment Ctr. for Alcoholism and Drug Abuse, Ark. Women's History Inst.; mem. career svcs. adv. bd. Kennedy Sch. Govt., Harvard U., also mem. Washington area regional alumni coun. Mem. Ark. Polit. Sci. Assn. (past pres.), Harvard U. John F. Kennedy Sch. Govt. Alunni Assn. (former mem. exec. coun.), U.S. Capitol Host. Soc., Nat. Archives, Ark. Hist. Assn., William Jefferson Clinton Birthplace Found., William Jefferson Clinton Presdl. Libr., John F. Kennedy Presdl. Libr., Sam Rayburn Meml. Found., White House Hist. Soc., U.S. House Adminstrv. Assts. Alumni Assn., Nat. Fallen Firefighter's Meml., Libr. of Congress Assocs., Am. Polit. Items Collectors, Bill Clinton Polit. Items Collectors, Kennedy Polit. Items Collectors, Ark. State Soc. Office: Fed Emergency Mgmt Agy 500 C St SW Ste 622 Washington DC 20472-0001

GOSS, KAY GENTRY COLLETT, federal official; b. Fayetteville, Ark., Aug. 7; d. Kirby and Susan Elizabeth (Sutton) Collett; m. Oscar Eugene Goss, Apr. 25, 1975 (dec. April 1991); 1 child, Susan Laura. BA in Polit. Sci., U. Ark.-Fayetteville, 1963, MA in Polit. Sci., 1966; postgrad. W.Va. U., 1968-69, San Diego State U. 1982, Harvard U. 1983; secondary teaching cert. in social scis. NW Mo. State U., 1964. Instr. social sci. Westark C.C., 1966-68; asst. prof. polit. sci. U. Ark., Fayetteville, 1969-73; legis. asst. to Congressman Ray Thornton, 1973-74; mgr. re-election campaign hdqrs. Congressman Wilbur Mills, 1974; adminstrv. asst. Congresswomen Patricia Schroeder, 1974-75; project coord., spl. sch. fin. study Ark. Legis., 1977-78; rsch. dir. Constitl. Conv., Little Rock, 1978-80; project dir. Assn. Ark. Counties, Little Rock, 1979-81; chief dep., state auditor, 1981-82; sr. asst. intergovtl. rels. to gov. State of Ark., Little Rock, 1983-94; assoc. dir. preparedness, tng. & exercises FEMA, 1994—. Mem. editl. bd. Midsouth Polit. Sci. Jour., 1983—. Bd. dirs., chmn. pers. com. Ark. Cmty. Found., 1978-85, bd. dirs. Wilber D. Mills Treatment Ctr.; founding dir. The Wilber D. Mills Mem. Found., mem. Nat. Adv. Com. Opera Co. of Boston; mem. assoc. friends of John F. Kennedy Ctr. for Performing Arts, 1976—; mem. govs. rep. Little Rock Air Force Base Cmty. Coun., 1983—; bd. dirs., sec. Fire Tng. Acad. Bd., So. Ark. U. Tech Br., 1983-85; mem. exec. com. Pulaski County Dem. Cen. Com., 1982-84; sec.-treas. Cmty. Theater of Little Rock Guild, 1985-86, also bd. dirs. 1987—. Fellow John F. Kennedy Presdl. Libr.; mem. Ark. Polit. Sci. Assn. (pres. 1985-86), U. Ark. Alumni Assn. (life), John F. Kennedy Sch. Govt. Alumni Assn. (exec. coun. 1989—), Pi Sigma Alpha (pres. 1988—). Methodist. Home: PO Box 1250 Conway AR 72033-1250 Office: Gov's Office State Capitol Little Rock AR 72201-1088

GOSS, LAURENCE EDWARD, JR., geographer, educator; b. Greenfield, Mass., Dec. 9, 1944; s. Laurence Edward and Anna Louise (Oliver) G.; m. Sharon Margaret Ripp, June 9, 1968; children: Laura Marie, Peter Edward. AB, Dartmouth Coll., 1966; MA, U. Wash., 1969, PhD, 1973. Registered planner, Am. Inst. Cert. Planners. Adminstr., lectr. Dartmouth Coll., Hanover, N.H., 1970-71; asst. prof. SUNY, Oswego, 1971-76; asst. dir. Office of State Planning, Concord, N.H., 1976-86; project dir. Provan & Lorber, Inc., Contoocook, N.H., 1986-91; prin. No. Econ. Planners, Concord, 1991—; assoc. prof. Salem (Mass.) State Coll., 1996—; pres. Frontiers of Knowledge Lyceum, Concord, 1996. Lead author: Garvins Falls Devel. Strategy for City of concord, N.H., 1996 (Tech. Merit award for Maine, N.H. and Vt. 1997 No. New Eng. chpt. Am. Planners Assn.). Recipient Letter of Commendation Nat. award HUD, Washington, 1986. Mem. Am. Planners Assn. (pres. no. New Eng. chpt. 1989-91, Profl. Planner of Yr. 1993, Project of Yr. award 1995), New Eng.-St. Lawrence Valley Geog. Soc. (bd. dirs. 1992-94), N.H. Planners Assn. (pres. 1982-83), N.H. Natural Resources Forum (treas. 1993—). Congregationalist. Office: Dept Geography Salem State Coll Salem MA 01970

GOSS, MARY E. WEBER, sociology educator; b. Chgo., May 8, 1926; m. Albert E. Goss, 1945; 1 son, Charles. B.A. in Sociology with distinction (Univ. Merit scholar 1946-47, Chi Omega Sociology prize 1947), U. Iowa, 1947, M.A., 1948; Ph.D. (Gilder fellow 1951-52), Columbia U., 1959. Rsch. asst. U. Iowa, 1947-48, Amherst Coll., 1949; instr. Smith Coll., 1949-50; instr. U. Mass., 1950-51, 55-56, adj. mem. grad. faculty, 1961-66; rsch. assoc. Bur. Applied Social Rsch., Columbia U., 1952-53; cons. sociology, mem. rsch. staff, rsch. coord. N.Y. Hosp.-Cornell U. Med. Center, N.Y.C., 1957-66; mem. faculty dept. medicine Cornell U. Med. Coll., 1959-72, prof. sociology in pub. health, 1973-92, prof. emerita, 1992—. Author: Physicians in Bureaucracy, 1980; also numerous articles; editor: Jour. Health and Social Behavior, 1976-78; co-editor: Comprehensive Medical Care and Teaching: A Report on the N.Y. Hospital-Cornell Medical Center Program, 1967; mem. editorial bd. profl. jours. Fellow APHA, N.Y. Acad. Medicine; mem. AAAS, AAUP, Am. Sociol. Assn., Assn. Tchrs. Preventive Medicine, Assn. Health Svcs. Rsch., Internat. Sociol. Assn., Ea. Sociol. Soc., Phi Beta Kappa, Sigma Xi. Office: Cornell U Med Coll Dept Pub Health 411 E 69th St New York NY 10021-5603

GOSS, PORTER J., congressman; b. Waterbury, Conn., Nov. 26, 1938; m. Mariel Robinson; children: Leslie, Chauncey, Mason, Gerrit. BA, Yale U., 1960. Clandestine svcs. officer CIA, 1962-71; co-founder newspaper Island Reporter, Sanibel, Fla., 1973; mayor City of Sanibel, coun. mem., 1974-82; commr. County of Lee, Fla., 1982-88, chmn. commn., 1985; mem. 100th-106th Congresses from 14th Fla. Dist., 1988—, mem. intelligence com., chair rules com.; port commr. S.W. Fla. Regional Airport. Dir. Lee County Mental Health Ctr., J.N. "Ding" Darling Found.; dir. chmn. Sanibel-Captiva Conservation Found.; chmn. bd. Canterbury Sch.; mem. S.W. Fla. Mental Health Dist. Bd. Intelligence officer U.S. Army, 1960-62. Republican. Presbyterian. *

GOSS, REBECCA O., lawyer, pharmaceutical company executive. BS, Ind. U., 1970, JD, 1975. Bar: Ind. 1975. Lectr. Ind. U. Sch. Bus., 1979-80; counsel Nat. Ins. Assn., 1980-81; atty. Eli Lilly and Co., Indpls., 1981-83, sec., gen. counsel Elanco Products co. divsn., 1983-88, sec., gen. counsel Pharm. divsn., 1988-93, dep. gen. counsel, asst. sec., 1993-95, v.p., gen. counsel, 1995-98, now sr. v.p., gen. counsel, 1998—. Office: Eli Lilly and Co Lilly Corp Ctr Indianapolis IN 46285

GOSS, RICHARD HENRY, lawyer; b. Worcester, Mass., Oct. 24, 1935; s. George Lee and Marion Bernadine (Henry) G.; children: Margaret Elizabeth, Richard Henry Eric, Emily Charlotte; m. Eleanor Kirsten Berg, Nov. 28, 1971. Student, Mich. State U., 1952-54; BA in Econs., Clark U., 1956; JD, Northwestern U., 1959. Bar: Ill. 1959, U.S. Supreme Ct. 1970. Asst. cashier Nat. Blvd. Bank of Chgo., 1959-61; v.p. Paul D. Speer & Assocs. Inc., Mcpl. Fin. Cons., Chgo., 1962-68; mng. ptnr. Chapman and Cutler, Attys. at Law, Chgo., 1968-95. Bd. dirs. Japan Am. Soc. Chgo., 1987-96, v.p., chmn. mem. com., 1988-90; chmn. bd. dirs. Brays Island Plantation Colony, Inc., 1995-97. Mem. ABA, Chgo. Bar Assn. (chmn. com. on local govt. 1978-80), Pub. Securities Assn. (com. on fed. legislation and regulation 1982-93), Govtl. Fin. Officers Assn. U.S. and Can. (lectr. 1972-79), Sunset Ridge Country Club (chmn. skeet and trap com. 1986-88), Northbrook Sports Club (bd. dirs. 1985-90), Hanover (Ill.) Farm Hunt Club (sec. 1979-83), Chgo. Athletic Assn. (entertainment com. 1979-81), Michigan Shores Club, Beaufort (S.C.) Yacht Club. Republican. Episcopalian. Avocations: hunting, skeet, sporting clays and trap shooting, travel, Oriental studies. Home: 1 Pocotaligo Pl Brays Island Plantation Sheldon SC 29941 also: 7 Par Brae Eastman Grantham NH 03753

GOSS, WILLIAM ALLAN, author, speaker; b. Summit, N.J., Apr. 23, 1955; S. Eugene Joseph and Barbara Tennyson (Dacey) G.; m. Margaret Mary Goss, Apr. 10, 1980; children: Brian William, Christina Marie. BA, Rutgers Coll., New Brunswick, N.J., 1980; MBA, N.H. Coll., 1988. Pilot USN, 1980-95; author, spkr. pvt. practice, Jacksonville, Fla., 1994—; cons. Goshawk Internat., Jacksonville, Fla., 1994-96. Author: The Luckiest Unlucky Man ALive, 1997; contbg. author: Chicken Soup for the Soul, 1997, Earth Angels, 1997. Vol. self def. instr. Battered Women Shelters, Jacksonville, Fla., 1994-97; contbr. HawkWatch, N.Mex., 1993-97, Jacksonville Zoo, 1992-97. Lt. Comdr. USN, 1980-97. Named Navy Officer of Yr., Navy League, Corpus Christi, tex., 1987, Writer of Yr., Navy Flying Mag., Washington, 1988. Mem. Nat. Spkrs. Assn., North Fla. Spkrs. Assn. Avocations: flying, writing, scuba diving, hiking, self-defense. Office: PO Box 7060 Orange Park FL 32073

GOSSAGE, JOHN RALPH, photographer; b. S.I., Mar. 15, 1946; s. John and Edith (Giefer) G.; m. Terri L. Weifenbach, Aug. 21, 1992. Student, Walden Sch., 1965-67. Rep. by Leo Castelli Castelli Graphics, N.Y.C.; mgr. Charles Pratt Award Ctr. for Creative Photography. One-man shows photography Camera Infinity Gallery, N.Y.C., 1963, Hinckley Brohel Gallery, Washington, 1968, Ohio. U., 1971, Pyramid Gallery, Washington, 1972, Jefferson Place Gallery, Washington, 1974, Castelli Graphics, N.Y.C., 1976, 78, 80, 87, Werkstaat fur Photographie der VHS Kreuzberg, Berlin, 1982, Forum Stadtpart, Graz, Austria, 1982, Gallerie Lange-Irschl, Munich, 1982, Mus. of Art, Hannover, 1982, Castelli Gallery, 1983, 87, Jones Troyer Gallery, Washington, 1987, Mus. Contemporary Phototgraphy, 1990, C. Grimaldis Gallery, Balt., 1993; group shows N.Y. Coliseum Photo Expo, 1975, Lever House, 1975, Washington Gallery Modern Art, Corcoran Gallery, 1975, San Francisco Art Inst., 1975, Pasadena Mus. Art, 1975, Balt. Mus. Art, 1975, Newport Harbor Mus., 1975, LaJolla Mus. Contemporary Art, 1972, Walker Art Center, 1975, Ft. Worth Art Mus., 1975, Phila. Print Club, 1976, Broxton Gallery, 1976, U. N.M. Art Gallery, 1976, Castelli Uptown, 1976, Houston Mus. Fine Art, Internat. Photography, Mus. Modern Art, City of Paris, Nd. Art Gallery, Mus.; Nice (France), MIT, 1977, Chgo. Ctr. Contemporary Photography, Mus. Modern Art Strasbourg (France), U. Mass. Gallery, 1978, Addison Gallery Am. Art, Santa Barbara Mus. Art, Corcoran Gallery Art, Cranbrook Acad., Mus. Contemporary Art, Chgo., Corcoran Gallery, 1979, Internat. Center Photography, Washington Art Consortium, Hoffer Meml. Photography Collection, Colgate U., Seattle Art Mus., 1980, George Eastman House, Inst. Contemporary Art, U. Pa, Castelli Photography, Oakland Mus., Arlington Arts Ctr., 1981, Impressions Gallery, Boston, 1982, Fotografie Biennale, Rotterdam, 1992; permanent collections Smithsonian Instn., Mus. Modern Art, N.Y.C., Pasadena Mus., Nat. Endowment for Arts, Library of Congress, Princeton U., Pan Am. Union, Houston Mus. Fine Art, Corcoran Gallery Art, Phila. Mus. Art, Walker Art Ctr., Siemens Corp., Munich, Jai Chiat, N.Y.C.; represented Bibliotheque Nationale, Paris, Addison Gallery Am. Art, Australian Nat. Gallery, Canberra, Oakland Mus. Art, San Francisco Mus. Art, others; author: (with Walter Hopps) Gardens, 1978; The Pond, photographs, 1985, Stadt des Schwarz, 1987, LAMF, 1988, There and Gone, 1997, The Things That Animals Care About, And, 1998; contbr. articles to profl. jours. Washington Gallery Modern Art Fund fellow, 1969, 70; Nat. Endowment Arts grantee, 1973, 74, 78, Stern Family Fund grantee, 1974. Address: 2070 Belmont Rd NW Apt 502 Washington DC 20009-5407

GOSSAGE, WAYNE, library director, management consultant, entrepreneur, executive recruiter; b. Bellingham, Wash., June 13, 1926; s. Coy Dell and Sadie Fay (Campbell) G.; m. Grace Villella, July 3, 1950; children: Leslie Anne, Gordon. BS, U. Wash., 1947; MS, Columbia U., 1951, MA, 1969. Asst. head adult svcs. East Orange (N.J.) Pub. Libr., 1951-54; head adult svcs. Levittown (N.Y.) Pub. Libr., 1954-55; dir. Warner Libr., Tarrytown, N.Y., 1956-63; asst. libr. Tchrs. Coll., Columbia U., N.Y.C., 1964-67; dir. Bank St. Coll. Edn. Libr., N.Y.C., 1967-80; pres. Gossage Regan Assocs., Inc., N.Y.C., 1980—; libr. cons. Gossage Regan Assocs., Inc., N.Y.C., 1980—; cons. to corp. librs., univs., assns., founds., chs., pubs., govt. agys. *Wayne Gossage was the first executive search consultant, from 1983, for directors of public library systems and for university deans of libraries. Earlier, in 1980, Wayne Gossage and Muriel Regan had formed Gossage Regan Associates for library management consulting. It became also, in 1980, the first library personnel firm specializing in library temporary services.* Contbr. articles to profl. jours. Vice pres. Hist. Soc. Tarrytown, 1960-61; trustee Harvard Libr., N.Y., 1978—; mem. alumni trustee nominating com. Columbia U., 1974-76; bd. advisors Pratt Inst. Sch. Info. and Libr. Sci., 1988—. With USNR, 1944-46. Coun. on Libr. Resources fellow, 1978-79; recipient Disting. Community Svc. award Tarrytown, 1962. Mem. ALA (notable books coun. 1961-62, ACRL bd. dirs. 1975-76, chmn. edn. and behavioral sci. sect. 1975-76, Ralph Shaw award for libr. lit. jury 1975-76, chmn. Wilson indexes com. 1978-81, Mudge citation com. 1985-87), N.Y. Libr. Assn. (v.p. resources and tech. svcs. sect. 1974-75, legis. com. 1974-75, pres. coll. and univ. librs. sect. 1978-79), N.Y. Libr. Club (pres. 1990-91), Spl. Libr. Assn. (chmn. div. social sci. 1975-76), Columbia U. Sch. Libr. Svcs. Alumni Assn. (sec.-treas. 1974-76, pres. 1977-78), Archons of Colophon (convenor 1989-90). Avocations: reading, writing, walking, travel. Home: 382 W Clinton Ave Irvington NY 10533-2132 Office: Gossage Regan Assocs Inc Ste 812 25 W 43d St New York NY 10036-7406

GOSSARD, ARTHUR CHARLES, physicist; b. Ottawa, Ill., June 18, 1935; s. Arthur Paul and Mary Catherine (Lineberger) G.; m. Marsha Jean Palmer, Jan. 8, 1965; children: Girard Christopher, Elinore Suzanne. B.A., Harvard U., 1956; Ph.D., U. Calif., Berkeley, 1960. Solid state physicist, disting. mem. tech. staff AT&T Bell Labs., Murray Hill, N.J., 1960-87; prof. materials and electrical and computer engring. U. Calif., Santa Barbara, 1987—. Mem. editorial bd. Jour. Applied Physics and Applied Physics Letters, 1988-92; author tech. papers magnetic resonance, magnetism, transition metals, molecular beam epitaxy, quantum structures, semiconductors. NSF postdoctoral fellow, 1962-63. Fellow Am. Phys. Soc. (Oliver Buckley condensed matter physics prize 1984); mem. Nat. Acad. of Engring. Office: U Calif Materials Dept Santa Barbara CA 93106

GOSSARD, EARL EVERETT, physicist; b. Eureka, Calif., Jan. 8, 1923; s. Ralph Dawson and Winifred (Hill) G.; m. Sophia Poignand, Nov. 21, 1948; children: Linda Margaret, Kenneth Earl, Diane Winifred. BA, UCLA, 1948; MS, U. Calif., San Diego, 1951; PhD in Phys. Oceanography, Scripps Instn. Oceanography, 1956. Meteorologist Navy Electronics Lab., San Diego, 1949-55, head radio meteorol. sect., 1955-61; head radio physics div. Navy Electronics Lab. (name now Naval Ocean Systems Ctr.), San Diego, 1961-71; chief geoacoustics program Wave Propagation Lab., NOAA, Boulder, Colo., 1971-73, chief meteorol. radar program, 1973-82; sr. rsch. assoc. Coop. Inst. for Rsch. in Environ. Scis. U. Colo., Boulder, 1982-98; sr. rsch. assoc. Sci. and Tech. Corp., Colorado Springs, Colo., 1998-99; emeritus sr. scientist Environment Rsch. Lab. of NOAA. Co-author: (with Hooke) Waves in the Atmosphere (Disting. Authorship award Dept. Commerce 1975), 1973; (with Strauch) Radar Observation of Clear Air and Clouds (Disting. Authorship award Dept. Commerce 1985); editor: Radar Observation of the Clear Air, 1980; contbr. over 74 articles to profl. jours. 1st lt. USAAF, 1943-46, CBI. Recipient Silver medal Dept. Commerce, 1976, Citation Am. Geophys. Union, 1986. Fellow Am. Meteorol. Soc.; mem. Nat. Acad., Internat. Union Radio Sci. (past chmn. U.S. Commn. F.). Republican. Presbyterian. Home: 1088 Kelly Rd W Sugarloaf Star Rt Boulder CO 80302 Office: Environ Tech Lab-NOAA 325 Broadway Boulder CO 80303

GOSSELL, TERRY RAE, advertising agency executive, small business owner; b. Rockford, Ill., Jan. 24, 1947; d. Virgil Houston and Wilma Beatrice (Cox) Pierce; m. Ronald Richard Gossell, Mar. 3, 1979 (div. Apr., 1983); children: Cameo Ann Elliott, Ronica Rae. Grad. high sch., Loves Park, Ill.; arts cert., U. Kans., 1962. Artist Rockford (Ill.) Silk Screen Process, 1967-72, Grocery Co-op Advt., Ocala, Fla., 1973-74; art dir. Carlson & Co. Advt., Rockford, Ill., 1975; co-owner R.S.S.P. Graphics & Typesetting, Rockford, 1975-76; owner Graphic Comm., Inc., Rockford, 1976-79, T.R. Gossell Advt., Rockford, 1979-82, TR Gossell Advt. & Mktg. Svcs., Phoenix, 1982-88, 97—, The Gossell Agy., Rockford, 1988-97. Author, artist: (comic book) The Gang from Carl Hayden High Sch., 1986-87. Advisor No. Ill. Advt. Coun. Explorer Post #423, Rockford, 1990-92. Recipient Merit and 1st Place awards Rockford Advt. Club, 1978, 79, 1st Place award of Excellence, Nat. Assn. Pers. Cons., San Diego, 1985, Cert. of Merit, BMA Tower awards, 1994. Mem. Am. Advt. Fedn., No. Ill. Advt. Coun. (pres. 1992-94, merit, 1st and 2nd pl. awards 1980, 81, 91, 93, 94, 95, 96, 97), Greater Rockford Ad Club (bd. dirs. 1996-98). Democrat. Lutheran. Avocations: fishing, photography, horses, outdoors, classic cars. Office: TR Gossell Advt & Mktg Svcs 5131 N 6th St Phoenix AZ 85012

GOSSEN, EMMETT JOSEPH, JR., motel chain executive, lawyer; b. Kenosha, Wis., Aug. 23, 1942; s. Emmett J. and Julia (Tribur) G.; m. Patricia E. Zele, June 14, 1968; children: André, Nicole. BA, Case Western Res. U., 1965; PhD, Yale U., 1970; JD, Harvard U., 1974. Bar: Mass. 1974, D.C. 1975. Assoc. Hale and Dorr, Boston, 1974-77; counsel The Sheraton Corp., Boston, 1977-83, sr. v.p., dir. devel., 1983-86; exec. v.p. corp. devel. Inter-Continental Hotels, Montvale, N.J., 1988-90; sr. v.p., dir. devel. Motel 6, L.P., Santa Barbara, Calif., 1986-88; exec. v.p. corp. affairs and devel. Motel 6, L.P., Dallas, 1990—. Office: Motel 6 LP 14651 Dallas Pkwy Ste 500 Dallas TX 75240-8807

GOSSETT, FORREST SCOTT, publishing executive; b. Atlanta, Aug. 19, 1955; s. James H. and Geraldine B. Gossett. BA in Communications, Am. U., 1979. Reporter Lake County News-Herald, Willoughby, Ohio, 1979-81; assoc. editor Crain's Cleve. Bus., 1981-84; bus. reporter Wichita Eagle, 1984-89; chief Capitol corr. Wichita Eagle, Topeka, 1989-92; mktg. dir. Allen, Gibbs & Houlik, Wichita, 1992-94; pub. Wichita Bus. Jour., 1994-98, Tampa Bay Bus. Jour., 1998—. Pres. Crime Stoppers Wichita, 1997-98; mem. campaign exec. cabinet United Way Plains, Tampa, 1998—; dir. Jr. Achievement Wichita, 1995-98; bd. dirs. Fla. orch., 1999—, Jr. Achievement of Tampa, 1999—. Mem. Am. Mktg. Assn., Am. Advt. Fedn. Wichita, Soc. Profl. Journalists (regional dir. 1989-92), Rotary. Avocation: golf. Home: 10384 Carrollwood Ln #276 Tampa FL 33618 Office: Tampa Bay Bus Jour 4350 W Cypress Ste 400 Tampa FL 33603

GOSSETT, JANINE LEE, middle school educator; b. Carlsbad, N.Mex., Jan. 22, 1950; d. William Adair and Anita Jeanne (Hilty) G. BS, N.Mex. State U., 1974, MA, 1992. Tchr., dir. Sunshine Sch., Parker, Ariz.; tchr. spl. edn. Lubbock (Tex.) State Sch.; tchr. regular and accelerated lang. arts Carlsbad Mcpl. Schs.; tchr. 7th & 8th gr. advanced ednl. placement Carlsbad Mcp. Schs. Mem. Nat. Coun. Tchrs. English, Nat. Mid. Sch. Assn., N.Mex. Coun. Tchrs. English (past treas., directory/membership chair). Office: 408 N Canyon St Carlsbad NM 88220-5812

GOSSETT, KATHRYN MYERS, language professional, educator; b. Baltimore, Ohio; d. Charles Edgar and Vera Mae (Good) Myers; m. William Thomas Gossett, June 30, 1984. BA summa cum laude, Ohio U., 1931, MA, 1936. Cert. tchr., Ohio, Pa., Mich. Latin and English tchr. Beccaria Twp. High Sch., Coalport, Pa., 1931-32; French, Latin and English tchr. Buford (Ohio) High Sch., 1932-36; tchr. fgn. langs. Oak Hill (Ohio) High Sch., 1936-42; critic tchr. Ohio U. and Athens High Sch., 1942-43; English and Spanish tchr. Eastern High Sch., Lansing, Mich., 1943-45; French tchr. Kingswood/Cranbrook Pvt. Sch., Bloomfield Hills, Mich., 1945-55, chmn. fgn. lang., 1955-75; Fulbright tchr. Lycée de Jeunes Filles, Annecy, France, 1953-54. Contbr. articles to profl. jours. Decorated chevalier des Palmes Academiques (France); recipient Cranbrook Founders medal, 1976; U. Besancon (France) scholar. Mem. AAUW, Am. Assn. Ret. Persons, Eastern Star, Bloomfield Hills Country Club, The Ocean Club of Fla. (Ocean Ridge), The Little Club (Gulf Stream, Fla.), The Village Club (Bloomfield Hills), Phi Beta Kappa. Republican. Episcopalian. Avocations:art, music, history.. Home: 1276 Covington Rd Bloomfield Hills MI 48301-2365

GOSSETT, LOUIS, JR., actor; b. Bklyn., May 27, 1936; s. Louis and Helen (Wray) G.; m. Cyndi Jones-Reese, 1987; 1 adopted child, Sharron. B.A., N.Y. U., 1959; studied with, Frank Silvera, Nola Chilton, Eli Rill, Lloyd Richards. Made Broadway debut in Take a Giant Step, 1953; other stage performance include The Charlatan; appeared: motion pictures including A Raisin in the Sun, 1961, The Landlord, 1970, The Bushbaby, 1970, Skin Game, 1971, Travels with My Aunt, 1972, The Laughing Policeman, 1973, The White Dawn, 1974, The River Niger, 1976, J.D.'s Revenge, 1976, The Deep, 1977, The Choirboys, 1977, An Officer and a Gentleman, 1982 (Acad. award for Best Supporting Actor), Jaws 3-D, 1983, Finders Keepers, 1984, Enemy Mine, 1984, Iron Eagle, 1985, Firewalker, 1986, The Principal, 1987, Iron Eagle II: Battle Beyond the Flag, 1988, The Punisher, 1990, Cover Up, 1991, Toy Soldiers, 1991, Aces: Iron Eagle III, 1992, Diggstown, 1992, Monolith, 1993, A Good Man in Africa, 1994, Blue Chips, 1994, Iron Eagle IV, 1995, Inside, 1996, Managua, 1996, Legend of the Mummy, 1997, Y2K, 1999, The Highwayman, 1999; TV films: It's Good to Be Alive, 1974, Side Kicks, 1974, Delancey Street: The Crisis Within, 1975, Little Ladies of The Night, 1977, Roots, 1977, (Emmy award Nat. Acad. TVC Arts and Scis. 1977), The Critical List, 1978, To Kill a Cop, 1978, This Man Stands Alone, 1979, Backstairs at the White House, 1979, Don't Look Back, 1981; Benny's Place, 1982, Sadat, 1983, The Guardian, 1984, A Gathering of Old Men, 1987, The Father Clements Story, 1987, Roots: The Gift, 1988, Goodbye Miss 4th of July, 1988, El Diablo, 1990, Sudie and Simpson, 1990, The Josephine Baker Story, 1991, Carolina Skeletons, 1991, Keeper of The City, 1992, Father and Son: Dangerous Relations, 1993, Return to Lonesome Dove, 1993, Ray Alexander: A Taste for Justice, 1994, Flashfire, 1994, A Father for Charlie, 1995, Zoo Man, 1995, Curse of The Starving Class, 1995, A Father for Charlie, 1995, Captive Heart: The James Mink Story, 1996, In His Fathers Shoes, 1997, To Dance with Olivia, 1997; also various TV series, including The Young Rebels, 1970-71, The Lazarus Syndrome, 1979, The Powers of Matthew Star, 1982-83, Gideon Oliver, 1989, (voice) Captain Planet and The Planeteers, 1990, Nitecap, 1992; singer in nightclubs, 1960's. Mem. Acad. Motion Picture Arts and Scis., Actors Equity, Screen Actors Guild, AFTRA, Am. Guild Variety Artists, Am. Fed. Musicians, Negro Actors Guild Am., Alpha Phi Alpha. *

GOSSETT, PHILIP, musicologist; b. N.Y.C., Sept. 27, 1941; s. Harold and Pearl (Lenkowsky) G.; m. Suzanne Solomon, Aug. 4, 1963; children: David, Jeffrey. BA summa cum laude, Amherst Coll., 1963; student, Columbia U., 1961-62; MFA, Princeton U., 1965, PhD, 1970; LHD, Amherst Coll., 1993. Asst. prof. music and humanities U. Chgo., 1968-73, assoc. prof., 1973-77, prof., 1977-84, Robert W. Reneker Disting. Svc. prof. music, 1984—, dean divsn. humanities, 1989-99; vis. assoc. prof. Columbia U., 1975, Inst. de Musicologie Universite de Paris, 1988, Gauss seminars, Princeton U., 1991; cons. in field. Gen. editor: The Works of Giuseppe Verdi, Opera Omnia di Gioachino Rossini; mem. editorial bd. Am. Musicol. Soc., 1972-78; cons. editor: Critical Inquiry, 1974—, Ninteenth Century Music, 1976—, Cambridge Opera Jour., 1987—; translator Treatise on Harmony (Jean-Philippe Rameau), (with Charles Rosen) Early Romantic Opera, Anna Bolena and the Maturity of Gaetano Donizetti, 1985, Il Barbiere di Siviglia, 1993, Don Pasquale, 1999, also numerous critical edits.; prepared vocal ornamentation for operas in Milan, Rome, Bologna, Pesaro, Chgo., Miami, St. Louis, N.Y. Trustee Chgo. Symphony Orch., 1991—, Ct. Theatre, Chgo., 1994—. Decorated Gold medal 1st class (Italy), 1985, Grande Ufficiale della Rep. (Italy), 1997, Order Rio Branca, Brazil, 1998, Cavaliere di gran Croce (Italy), 1998; Woodrow Wilson fellow, 1963-64, 66-67; Fulbright scholar Paris, 1965-66; Martha Baird Rockefeller fellow, 1967-68; Guggenheim fellow, 1971-72; NEH sr. scholar, 1982-83; Deems Taylor award of ASCAP, 1986. Fellow AAAS, Academia Filarmonica of Bologna (hon.); mem. Am. Musicol. Soc. (coun. 1972-74, bd. dirs. 1974-76, v.p. 1986-88, Albert Einstein award 1969, pres. 1994-96), Internat. Musicol. Soc., Am. Inst. Verdi Studies (bd. dirs.), Societa Italiana di Musicologia, Soc. Textual Scholarship (pres. 1993-95), Premio Paolo Borciani (pres. 1997). Home: 5810 S Harper Ave Chicago IL 60637-1843 Office: U Chgo Dept Music Chicago IL 60637

GOSSETT, ROBERT FRANCIS, JR., merchant banker; b. San Antonio, Tex., Nov. 19, 1943; s. Robert Francis and Anne Elizabeth (Donnell) G.; m. Pauline Washington Gillespie, June 27, 1964; children: Robert Francis III, Frank Morgan Gillespie. BA, U. Tex., 1964; JD, Georgetown U., 1967; MBA, U. Pa., 1969. Assoc., investment bank div. Merrill Lynche, Pierce, Fenner & Smith, N.Y.C., 1969-74; v.p. Oppenheimer Properties, Inc., N.Y.C., 1974-78; exec. v.p., dir. Loeb Rhoades Hornblower Capital Corp., N.Y.C., 1978-81; chmn. bd., pres. Vance Capital Corp., N.Y.C., 1981—; gen. ptnr. First San Bernardio Assoc., Ltd., Long Beach, Calif., 1979—, First Riverside (Calif.) Assoc., 1980—, First Portland Assoc., Beaverton, Oreg., 1980—, Corp. Realty Income Fund I, Ltd., N.Y.C., 1986—, Vance, Teel & Co. Ltd., San Antonio, 1998—; chmn. bd. dirs. 1345 Realty Corp., N.Y.C., 1994—, Minn. Street Assoc., Inc., St. Paul, 1988—; gen. ptnr. Hoopes Assocs., Ltd., Rockport, Tex., 1989—, Teel Land and Cattle Co., LLC, Yancey, Tex., 1997—. Mem. bd. regents Georgetown U., 1993—. Mem. Campfire Club, The Mashomack Preserve Club. Office: Vance Capital Corp 406 E 85th St New York NY 10028-6302

GOSSICK, LEE VAN, consultant, executive, retired air force officer; b. Meadville, Mo., Jan. 23, 1920; s. Clark and Myrtle (Staats) G.; m. Ruth Matter, Apr. 29, 1942; children: Roger V., Cynthia L. B.S. in Aero. Engring, Ohio State U., 1951, M.S., 1951; grad., Air War Coll., 1959, Advanced Mgmt. Program, Harvard, 1961. Aviation cadet, 1941-42; commd. 2d lt. USAAF, 1942; advanced through grades to maj. gen. USAF, 1968; fighter pilot (87th Fighter Squadron), North Africa, 1942- 43; various R & D posts, 1951-64; comdr. Arnold Engring. Devel. Center, 1964-67; dep. for F-111 Aero. Systems div., Wright-Patterson AFB, Ohio, 1967-68; vice comdr. Aero. Systems Div., 1968-69, comdr., 1969-70; dep. chief staff systems Hdqrs. Air Force Systems Command, Andrews AFB, Md., 1970-71, chief of staff, 1971-73, ret., 1973; asst. dir. regulation AEC, Washington, 1973-74; exec. dir. ops. Nuclear Regulatory Commn., Washington, 1975-79; v.p., dep. gen. mgr. Sverdrup Tech. Inc., Tullahoma, Tenn., 1980-89. Decorated D.S.M. with oak leaf cluster; Legion of Merit with oak leaf cluster; D.F.C.; Air medal with 9 oak leaf clusters; named Distinguished Alumnus Ohio State U., 1960, Centennial Achievement award, 1970; recipient Vandenberg trophy Arnold Air Soc., 1967, Distinguished Service award AEC, 1974. Fellow Am. Inst. Aeros. and Astronautics, AEDC. Home: 106 Blantonwood Drr Tullahoma TN 37388-5801

GOSSLING, HARRY ROBERT, orthopaedic surgeon, educator; b. Phila., July 20, 1922. MD, Temple U., 1947; MSc in Orthopaedic Surgery, U. Tenn. Intern Hartford Hosp., 1947-48, res. gen. surgery, 1948-49, sr. attending, dir. dept. orthopaedic surgery, 1965-76; orthopaedic surgeon Campbell Clinic, Memphis, 1950-51, 53-55; chief div. orthopaedics Conn. Health Ctr., Farmington, 1975-84; prof. orthopaedic surgery U. Conn. Sch. Medicine, Farmington, 1975—; chmn. dept. orthopaedic surgery U. Conn. Sch. Orthopaedics, 1975-90, Gray Gossling prof. orthopaedic surgery, 1990-92, prof. emeritus, 1992—; assoc. orthop. surgery, corporator Conn. Children's Med. Ctr.; corporator Hartford Sem., 1983—, Corporator Hartford Hosp., 1996—; chmn. parent co. Hosp. for Spl. Care (formerly New Britain Meml. Hosp.), 1992-96, bd. dirs., 1996—; bd. dirs. Fidelco Guide Found.; chair Parent Co., 1992-99; cons. orthop. surgery Manchester Meml. Hosp. Editor-in-Chief Complications in Orthopaedic Surgery, 1986—. Capt. U.S. Army, 1951-53. Fellow AMA, ACS, ASOS, La Soc. Internationale Re Chirurgie Orthopedique et de Traumatologie; mem. Am. Orthopaedic Assn. (v.p. 1987-88), Orthopaedic Rsch. Soc., Ea. Orthopaedic Assn. (pres. 1987), Am. Acad. Orthopaedic Surgeons, Orthopaedic Rehab. Assn. (exec. com. 1997—). Office: U Conn Sch Medicine Dept Orthopaedic Surgery 10 Talcott Notch Rd Dept Surgery Farmington CT 06034-4037

GOSSMAN, FRANCIS JOSEPH, bishop; b. Balt., Apr. 1, 1930; s. Frank M. and Mary Genevieve (Steadman) G. BA, St. Mary Sem., Balt., 1952; S.T.L., N. Am. Coll., Rome, 1955; J.C.D., Cath. U. of Am., 1959. Ordained priest Roman Cath. Ch., 1955; asst. pastor Basilica of the Assumption, Balt., 1959-68; asst. chancellor Archdiocese of Balt., 1959-65, vice chancellor, 1965-68; pro-synodal judge Balt. Tribunal, 1961; vice officialis Tribunal of Archdiocese of Balt., 1962-65, officialis, 1965-68; made papal chamberlain with title Very Rev. Monsignor, 1965; elected to Senate of Priests of Archdiocese, 1967-68; adminstr. Cathedral of Mary Our Queen, 1968-70; named aux. bishop of Balt. and titular bishop of Agunturn, 1968-75, apptd. vicar gen., 1968; apptd. to Bd. Consultors, 1969; urban vicar Archdiocese of Balt., 1970-75; bishop of Raleigh N.C., 1975—; Mem. Balt. Community Relations Commn., 1969-75; mem. exec. com. Md. Food Com., Inc., 1969-75. Bd. dirs. United Fund Central Md., 1974-75. Mem. Canon Law Soc. Am., Nat. Conf. Cath. Bishops, U.S. Cath. Conf. Home: 1601 Westbridge Ct Raleigh NC 27606-2656 Office: 715 Nazareth St Raleigh NC 27606-2108*

GOSTIN, LAWRENCE, lawyer, educator; b. N.Y.C., Oct. 19, 1949; s. Joseph and Sylvia (Berkman) G.; m. Jean Catherine Allison, July 30, 1977; children: Bryn Gareth, Kieran Gavin. JD, Duke U., 1974; BA summa cum laude, SUNY-Brockport, 1971, LLD (hon.). Bar: N.Y., Council Europe. Fulbright fellow U. Oxford, 1974-75; vis. prof. social policy McMaster U., Hamilton, Ont., Can. 1978-79; legal dir. Nat. Assn. Mental Health, London, 1975-82; vis. fellow U. Oxford Ctr. for Criminological Research, 1982-83; gen. sec. Nat. Council Civil Liberties, London, 1983-85; sr. fellow in health law Harvard U. Sch. Public Health, 1985—; exec. dir. Am. Soc. Law, Medicine, and Ethics, Boston, 1987-94; adj. assoc. prof. Sch. Pub. Health Harvard U., 1988—, lectr. Law Sch., 1990—; adj. prof. Sch. Pub. Health Harvard U., 1990—; vis. prof. Georgetown U. Law Ctr., 1993-94, assoc. prof., 1994-95, prof., 1996—; prof. Johns Hopkins Sch. Hygiene and Pub. Health, 1994—; co-dir. Georgetown/Johns Hopkins Program on Law and Pub. Health; legis. council U.S. Senate Labor and Human Resources Com., Washington, 1987, 88; bd. dirs., nat. exec. com. Am. Civil Liberties Union, 1987—; assoc dir. Harvard U. WHO Internat. Collaborating Ctr. on Health Legis., 1989—. Mem. legal affairs com. Internat. League Socs. for Mentally Handicapped, Brussels, 1980—. Western European editor Internat. Jour. Law and Psychiatry, London, 1978-81; editor in chief: Law Medicine & Health Care; exec. editor: Am. Jour. Law and Medicine; sect. editor Jour. Am. Med. Assn.; editor: Secure Provision, 1985, AIDS and the Health Care System, 1990, Surrogate Motherhood: Politics and Privacy, 1990, Implementing the Americans with Disabilities Act, 1993; co-editor: Law, Science and Medicine 2d edit., 1996; author: Human Rights and Public Health in the AIDS Pandemic, 1997, The Rights of Persons with HIV Disease, 1996, Mental Health Services: Law and Practice, 1986; Institutions Observed, 1986; Mental Health: Tribunal Procedure, 1984, 2nd edit., 1992; A Human Condition, 1975, 2d vol., 1977, Civil Liberties in Conflict, 1988. Trustee, Cobden Trust, London, 1983-85; chmn. Advocacy Alliance, London, 1981-84; sec. All Party Parliamentary Civil Liberties Group, London, 1984-85; bd. dirs. ACLU, 1986—, exec. com. 1988—; mem. com. experts drafting conventions on human experientation UN, Siracusa, Italy 1980-82. Recipient Rosemary Delbridge Meml. award Nat. Consumer Council U.K., 1983; fellow Kennedy Inst. of Ethics, 1994—. Avocations: climbing; vegetable growing. Home: 10413 Masters Ter Potomac MD 20854-3862 Office: Georgetown U Law Ctr 600 New Jersey Ave NW Washington DC 20001-2075

GOSZCZYNSKI, STEFAN, chemistry educator; b. Radomsko, Poland, Apr. 14, 1924; came to U.S., 1987; s. Tadeusz and Zofia (Nowak) G.; m. Hanna Jaroslawska, June 28, 1953; children: Peter, Thomas. MSc, Silesian Tech., Gliwice, Poland, 1950; PhD, Silesian Tech., 1960, DSc, 1964. Asst., reader Silesian Tech. U., 1948-60, from asst. to assoc. prof., 1962-68; postdoctoral fellow Birmingham (Eng.) U., 1960-61; from assoc. prof. to prof. Poznan (Poland) Tech. U., 1968-87; vis. prof. U. Idaho, Moscow, 1987—; dir. Inst. Tech. and Engring. Poznan Tech. U., 1968-70, head dept., 1977-80. Patentee in field. Named to Order of Merit Polonia Restituta, 1978, Disting. Prof. Republic of Poland, 1980; recipient medal Nat. Edn. Com., 1984. Home: 115 S Lilley St Apt 201 Moscow ID 83843-2082 Office: U Idaho Food Rsch Ctr 103 Moscow ID 83843

GOTBAUM, BETSY, historical society director; m. Victor Gotbaum; 1 child. BA, Barnard Coll., 1961; MA, Columbia U., 1968. Asst. edn. City N.Y.; exec. dir. N.Y.C. Police Found., 1977-82, Nat. Alliance Against Violence, 1982-86, N.Y. Hist. Soc., N.Y.C., 1994-98; assoc. Prospect Group, 1986-90; commr. N.Y.C. Parks & Recreation, 1990-94; pres. N.Y. Hist. Soc., 1998—. Office: NY Hist Soc 2 W 77th St New York NY 10024-5101*

GOTCHER, JACK EVERETT, JR., oral and maxillofacial surgeon; b. Wichita Falls, Tex., May 11, 1949; s. Jack Everett Sr. and Josephine Caroline (Kruh) G.; m. Kathyanne Mary King, Dec. 30, 1972; children: Elizabeth Gayle, Jeffrey Everett. BS in Chemistry and Biology, Midwestern U., 1971; DMD magna cum laude, Harvard U., 1975; PhD, U. Utah, 1979. Diplomate Am. Bd. Oral and Maxillofacial Surgery, 1984. Resident in oral and maxillofacial Surgery U. Tenn., Knoxville, 1982; asst. prof. Emory State U., Atlanta, 1982-83; assoc. prof. U. Tenn., Knoxville, 1983—; cons. Proctor and Gamble Co., Cin., 1977, VA Hosp., Atlanta, 1982-83, The Upjohn Co., Kalamazoo, Mich., 1984-88, Am. Assn. Oral and Maxillofacial Surgery, Chgo., 1986—. Contbr. articles profl. jours. Chmn. profl. edn. com. Am. Cancer Soc., Knoxville, 1988—. Recipient Am. Inst. Chemists award, 1971; NIH fellow, 1975-78, Am. Cancer Soc. fellow, 1978-79. Fellow Am. Assn. Oral and Maxillofacial Surgeons (del. 1988—); mem. ADA, Tenn. Dental Assn. (del. 1989—), Am. Cleft Palate-Craniofacial Assn. Presbyterian. Avocations: fishing, hiking, photography. Home: 1409 Kensington Dr Knoxville TN 37922-6039 Office: U Tenn Med Ctr PO Box I 1928 Alcoa Hwy Knoxville TN 37920-1502*

GOTCHER, JAMES RONALD, lawyer; b. Dallas, Jan. 18, 1947; s. James Bentley and Elga Audra (Dyess) G.; m. Satoko Hata, June 20, 1970; 1 son, James Kensuke. BA in History magna cum laude, Calif. State U., Long Beach, 1972; postgrad., U. Hawaii, 1972-73; JD, Loyola U., L.A., 1976. Bar: Calif. 1976 (cert. legal specialist immigration and nationality law), U.S. Supreme Ct. 1980. Assoc. Gruber & Kelman, 1976-77; ptnr. Gotcher & Shapiro, 1977-81, Aberson, Lynes & Gotcher, 1982-89; counsel Coudert Brothers, 1989-93; prin. Law Offices of James R. Gotcher, 1993—; lawyer; b. Dallas, Jan. 18, 1947; s. James Bentley and Elga Audra (Dyess) G.; m. Satoko Hata, June 20, 1970; 1 son, James Kensuke. B.A. magna cum laude in History, Calif. State U.-Long Beach, 1972; postgrad. U. Hawaii, 1972-73; J.D., Loyola U., Los Angeles, 1976. Bar: Calif. 1976 (cert. legal specialist immigration & nationality law), U.S. Supreme Ct. 1980. Assoc. Gruber & Kelman, 1976-77; ptnr. Gotcher & Shapiro, 1977-81; ptnr. Aberson, Lynes & Gotcher, 1982-89; counsel Coudert Brothers, 1989-93; prin. Law Offices of James R. Gotcher, 1993—. Mem. Town Hall of Los Angeles. Served with USAF, 1965-68. Decorated Bronze Star. Mem. Los Angeles County Bar Assn. (chmn. immigration law sect. 1983-84), Am. Immigration Lawyers Assn., ABA. Clubs: University (Los Angeles). Author: Comprehensive guide to U.S. Nonimmigrant Visas, 1983; contbr. articles to legal jours. Author: Comprehensive Guide to U.S. Nonimmigrant Visas, 1983; contbr. articles to legal jours. Mem. Town Hall of L.A. With USAF, 1965-68. Decorated Bronze Star. Mem. ABA, Los Angeles County Bar Assn. (chmn. immigration law sect. 1983-84), Am. Immigration Lawyers Assn., Univ. Club (L.A.). Address: Ste 507 15300 Ventura Blvd Sherman Oaks CA 91403-3110

GOTHARD, DONALD LEE, retired auto company executive; b. Madison, Wis., Dec. 2, 1934; s. William Henry and Lorraine Marie (Williams) G.; m. Doris Marie Lockhart, May 27, 1990; children from previous marriage: children: Donald Lee Jr., Ann Marie. BSEE, U. Notre Dame, 1956. Elec. engr. AC Spark Plug div. Milw. GM, 1956-62; systems engr. AC Electronics div. GM, Wakefield, Mass., 1962-63, Oak Creek, Wis., 1963-67; sr. project engr., supr. Delco Electronics div. Oak Creek, Bethpage, N.Y., 1967-71; systems engr., asst. mgr. engring. staff GM Tech. Ctr., Warren, Mich., 1971-75; asst. staff engr., then staff engr. Chevrolet Engring. div. Warren, 1975-82; chief engr. GM Truck & Bus. Engring., Pontiac, Mich., 1982-85; exec. engr. GM Truck & Bus. Engring., Auburn Hills and Troy, Mich., 1985-90; dir. rsch. and adminstrv. svcs. GM Rsch. and Environ. Activities Staff, Warren, 1990-92; exec. prototype, process engring. GM Design Ctr., GM Tech. Ctr., Warren, 1992-93; dir. quality and mfg. engrs. GM N.Am. Ops. N.Am. Tech. Ctr., Warren, 1993-96; cons. United Technologies Automotive, 1996. Chmn. fin. com. adv. coun. Utica (Minn.) Cmty. Schs., 1975; mem. Shelby Twp (Mich.) Cable TV Coordinating Com., 1980; mem. engring. adv. coun. U. Notre Dame, 1988—, mem. minority engring. program adv. coun., 1994—; bd. dirs. Sci. Engring. Fair Met. Detroit, 1992—; chmn. ch. fin. com., 1996—. 1st lt. U.S. Army, 1956-58. Recipient Cert. of Commendation MIT, 1969, Apollo Achievement award NASA, 1969, Disting. Svc. award Utica Cmty. Schs., 1976, Cert. of Recognition Coun. of Engring. Deans of Historically Black Colls., Mobil Corp. and U.S. Black Engr. Mag., 1991; team leader, internat. land speed records with Pickup Truck, Internat. Motor Sports Assn./So. Calif. Timing Assn., 1989, U. Notre Dame Coll. of Engring. Honor award, 1994, Rev. Edward Williams Svc. award U. Notre Dame Black Alumni, 1994. Mem. Soc. Automotive Engrs. (excellence in oral presentation award 1987, Black Engr. of Yr. award for lifetime achievement-industry 1995), Black Alumni Assn. U. Notre Dame (coord.-at-large exec. bd. 1987-94). Avocations: photography, bicycling, exercising. Home: 5510 Brookside Ln Washington MI 48094-2683

GOTHOLD, STUART EUGENE, school system administrator, educator; b. L.A., Sept. 20, 1935; s. Hubert Eugene and Adelaide Louise (Erickson) G.; m. Jane Ruth Soderberg, July 15, 1955; children: Jon Ernest, Susan Louise, Eric Arthur, Ruth Ann. BA, Whittier Coll., 1956, MA in Edn., 1961, LLD (hon.), 1988; EdD, U. So. Calif., 1974. Tchr. grades 1-9 El Rancho Sch. Dist., Pico Rivera, Calif., 1956-61, prin. jr. h.s., 1961-66; curriculum cons. L.A. County Office Edn., 1966-70; asst. supt. South Whittier (Calif.) Sch. Dist., 1970-72, supt., 1972-77; asst. supt. L.A. County Office Edn., Downey, 1977-78, chief dep. supt., 1978-79, supt., 1979-94; clin. prof. U. So. Calif.,

L.A., 1994—; mem. adv. bd. Nat. Ctr. Fgn. Lang., 1984—; charter mem. Edn. Insights, Detroit, 1990—; bd. dirs. Fedco, KCET. Author: (book) Inquiry, 1970, Decisions-A Health Edn. Curriculum, 1971. Recipient Alumni Merit award USC, 1993, Alumni Achievement award Whittier Coll., 1986; named Dist. Educator Calif. State U., 1993. Republican. Roman Catholic. Avocations: tennis, choral singing, photography, hiking. Home: 10121 Pounds Ave Whittier CA 90603-1649 Office: U So Calif WPH 902c Los Angeles CA 90089-0031

GOTIAN, RUTH, educational program administrator; b. Beer-sheva, Israel, Dec. 9, 1970; came to U.S., 1975; d. Arthur James and Dina Ginsburg; m. Amnon Gotian, Aug. 22, 1995. BS, SUNY, Stony Brook, 1992, MS, 1994. Cert. in labor mgmt., N.Y. Asst. dir. residence hall SUNY, Stony Brook, 1992-94; asst. dir./housing Cornell U. Med. Coll., N.Y.C., 1993-94; investments cons. Bank Leumi Le-Israel, Tel Aviv, 1994-96; program coord. Cornell/Rockefeller/Sloan-Kettering Tri Instnl. MD-PhD Prog., N.Y.C., 1996-98, program mgr., 1998—; co-chair Nat. MD-PhD Program Adminstrs. Conf., Aspen, Colo., 1999; cons. adv. bd. Nat. Minority Rsch. Conf., San Diego, 1998-99. Mem. Nat. Assn. Student Pers. Adminstrs. Jewish. Avocations: reading, movies. Email: rgotian@mail.med.cornell.edu. Office: Tri-Instnl MD-PhD Program 1300 York Ave Rm D-115 New York NY 10021-4896

GOTLIEB, ALLAN E., former ambassador; b. Winnipeg, Man., Can., Feb. 28, 1928; s. David Phillip and Sarah (Schiller) G.; m. Sondra Kaufman, Dec. 20, 1955; children: Rebecca, Marcus, Rachel. B.A., U. Calif., 1949; LL.B., Harvard U., 1954; M.A., B.C.L. (Vinerian Law scholar), Oxford U., 1956; LLD (hon.), various schs. Bar: Eng. 1956. Fellow Wadham Coll. and univ. lectr. in law Oxford U., 1954-56; joined Can. Dept. External Affairs, 1957; asst. under sec. for external affairs and legal adviser, 1967-68, dep. minister communications, 1968-73, dep. minister manpower and immigration, 1973-76; chmn. Can. Employment and Immigration Commn., 1976-77; under sec. Dept. External Affairs, 1977-81; Can. ambassador to U.S., Washington, 1981-89; chmn. Can. Coun., Ottawa, 1989-94; vis. fellow All Souls Coll., Oxford, 1975-76; William Lyon Mackenzie King vis. prof. Harvard U., 1989, Claude Bissell vis. prof. U. Toronto, 1989; former gov. Internat. Devel. Rsch. Ctr., Nat. Film Bd.; co-chmn. of bd., hon. pub. Saturday Night Mag.; bd. dirs. Alcan, Hollinger Inc., Champion Internat. Corp., Livent Inc., Peoples Jewellers Ltd.; mem. adv. bd. The Investment Co. Am., Nestle Canada, Inc.; sr. advisor Julius Baer Investment Adv. (Canada) Ltd.; hon. sec. Hollinger Internat. Inc.; N.Am. vice chmn. Trilateral Commn.; chmn. Donner Canadian Found., Ont. Heritage Found., Crown Found. Art Gallery Ont.; mem. coun. Internat. Inst. Strategic Studies, Senior; cons. Stikeman, Elliott, Toronto. Author: Disarmament and International Law, 1965, Canadian Treaty-Making, 1968, Impact of Technology on the Development of International Law, 1982, I'll Be With You In A Minute, Mr. Ambassador, 1991; editor: Human Rights, Federalism and Minorities, 1979; editor: Harvard Law Rev., 1950-51. Chmn. Ont. Heritages Found., Cronon Found Art Gallery Ont. Decorated companion Order of Can.; recipient outstanding achievement award Govt. of Can., 1983, Haas internat. award U. Calif. Bd. Regents, 1985. Office: Commerce Court West, PO Box 85 Ste 5300, Toronto, ON Canada M5L 1B9

GOTLIEB, CALVIN CARL, computer scientist, educator; b. Toronto, Ont., Can., Mar. 27, 1921; s. Israel and Jennie (Sherman) G.; m. Phyllis Fay Bloom, June 12, 1949; children: Leo, Margaret, Jane. BA, U. Toronto, 1942, MA, 1944, PhD, 1947; D in Math. (hon.)., U. Waterloo, Can., 1968; D in Engring. (hon.), N.S. Tech. U., 1985; LLD (hon.), U. Toronto, 1996. Faculty U. Toronto, 1949—; dir. Inst. Computer Sci., 1962-70, chmn. dept. computer sci., 1964-67, prof. computer sci., 1962—, emeritus, 1986—; pres. C.C. Gotlieb Cons. Ltd., 1978—; cons. info. scis. to various govts., internat. orgns., indsl. cos., 1969—; McKay vis. prof. U. Calif., Berkeley, 1981; chmn. tech. com. 9 on relationship between computers and soc. Internat. Fedn. for Info. Processing, 1975-81. Author: (with J.N.P. Hume) High-Speed Data Processing, 1958, (with A. Borodin) Social Issues in Computing, 1973, (with L.R. Gotlieb) Data Types and Structures, 1978, Economics of Computers, 1985; editor, editor-in-chief, contbr. various Can., Netherlands, U.S. sci. jours. Recipient Silver Core award Internat. Fedn. of Info. Processing Socs., 1974, Auerbach award, 1994; rsch. grantee Nat. Sci. and Engring. Rsch. Coun. Can., 1955-90, C.M. Order of Can., 1996. Fellow Royal Soc. Can., Brit. Computer Soc., Assn. Computing Machinery; mem. Can. Info. Processing Soc. (hon.). Jewish. Clubs: Faculty (U. Toronto); Nat. Yacht (Toronto). Home: 19 Lower Village Gate PH 06, Toronto, ON Canada M5P 3L9 Office: U Toronto, Dept Computer Sci, Toronto, ON Canada M5S 3G4

GOTO SABAS, JENNIFER, state official. BA, U. Hawaii, 1983; JD, Georgetown U., 1986. Bar: Va. 1986. Legal rsch. and writing instr. Cath. U. Law Sch., 1986-87; legis. asst. Joint Chief of Staff-Office US Senator Daniel K. Inouye, Washington, 1987-90, dep. chief of staff, 1990-91; chief of staff Joint Chief of Staff-Office US Senator Daniel K. Inouye, Honolulu, 1993—; adj. instr. legal rsch. and writing Am. U. Sch. of Law, 1988. Office: Office Sen Daniel K Inouye Prince Kuhin Bldg Fed Bldg Rm 7325 Honolulu HI 96850

GOTSCH, AUDREY ROSE, environmental health sciences educator, researcher; b. Milw., May 30, 1939; d. Carlos Louis and Florence Olga (Clausing) Grandy; m. Thomas Gotsch, June 20, 1959; children: Christine Anne Robinson, Allison Lorraine. BS, Ind. U., 1963; MPH, U. Mich., 1966; DrPH, CHES, Columbia U., 1976. Pvt. practice as dental hygienist Lafayette, Ind., 1962-63, Springfield, Ill., 1963-65; health educator Ill. Dept. Health, Springfield, 1966-67, N.J. State Dept. Health, Trenton, 1968; assoc. prof., chief dept. environ. and cmty. medicine U. Medicine and Dentistry N.J. Robert Wood Johnson Med. Sch., Piscataway, 1978-93, prof. dept. environ. and cmty. medicine, 1993—, acting chair dept. environ. and cmty. medicine, 1994-95, vice-chair dept. environ. and cmty. medicine, 1997—; dir. pub. edn. and risk com. divsn. Environ. and Occupational Health Scis. Inst., 1983—; interim dean Sch. Pub. Health U. Medicine and Dentistry of N.J., Piscataway, 1999—; cons. Nat. Hospice Demonstration Programs, 1980, Hospice of Ctrl. N.Y., Syracuse, 1980, Nat. Cancer Inst., 1981—, Fox Chase Cancer Ctr., Phila., 1983, Medcom, Inc., Calif., 1985, NIH, Heart, Lung and Blood Inst., Bethesda, Md., 1985—, and others; assoc. mem. grad. faculty, Rutgers U., New Brunswick, N.J., 1984—; mem. Outreach Task Force, The Cancer Inst. N.J., 1991—; assoc. mem. Inst. for Health, Health Care Policy and Aging Rsch., Rutgers, 1992; councilor, Coun. on Edn. for Pub. Health, 1990-96, pres. 1993-96; chair ednl. programs com. Environ. Health Found., 1995—; mem. steering com. Cmty. Environ. Health Assessment, NACCHO and Nat. Ctr. Environ. Health, CDC, 1995—; chair sch. health edn. com. Nat. Ctr. for Health Edn., 1997; mem. adv. bd. Joint NIEHS/NIH Office of Sci. Edn. Project. Author: (with others) Communication of Risk, 1992, Education for Health: Strategies for Change, 1978, The Environment and the Community: Environmental Health Lessons for Grades 10-12, 1990, Occupational Health Awareness: Lessons for Vocational Students in Secondary Schools, 1990, Healthy Environment--Healthy Me for Kindergarten-Sixth Grade, 1991, 92, Environmental Decision Making, 1995, Advanced Decision Making: Solid Waste Issues in Businesses, Schools and the Community, 1996, and others; mem. editl. bd. Health Edn. Quar., 1986-89; editor-in-chief INFOletter: Environmental and Occupational Health Briefs, 1988-96; contbr. reports, articles and abstracts to profl. jours. and newspapers; videos Alexandria's Clean-Up Fix-Up Parade, 1988, Alu-man the Can, 1987 (Sci. Commendation Cath. Audio Visual Educators 1991), A Breath of Fresh Air: Improving Air Quality in Your Office, 1989, Take Charge! Jobs or Health: A Town's Dilemma, 1989, Safety Sense, 1989, Sam's Safety Star Award, 1988, Down the Drain, 1989, Keeping the Lid on Air Pollution, 1989 (Cable award Programming Excellence CTN N.J. 1990), Inside Story on Air Pollution, 1990, What To Do With All Our Garbage?, 1990, PEOSH & RTK: What's It All About?, 1990, Talkin' Trash, 1992, Enviro-Decisions: Solid Waste, 1996, Environ-Decisions: Living with Toxins, 1997, ToxRAP: Toxicology, Risk Assessment and Air Pollution, 1998 (Nat. Environ. Edn. Achievement award 1997); bd. of assoc. editors: Am. Assn. for Health Edn., 1997-2001; contbr. numerous articles to profl. jours. Mem. N.J. Pub. Health Coun., Trenton, 1987—, sec., 1992-94, vice chair, 1994-96, chair, 1996-98; task force Gov.'s Conf. on Aging, 1980-81; mem. State Health Planning Bd., 1996—; bd. govs. Sch. Pub. Health Alumni Soc., U. Mich., 1996—; bd. dirs. Nat. Ctr. for Health Edn., 1996—. Recipient sec.'s award HHS, 1988, 94, statewide faculty recognition award N.J. Bd. Higher Edn., 1989, Spl. Recognition award Commr. N.J. Dept. Health and Sr. Svcs., 1998, Virginia S. Dehan Lecture award on Health Promotion and Edn., Rollins Sch. Pub. Health, Emory U., 1998; USPHS fellow, 1965-66, 72-74; grantee Nat. Inst. Environ. Health Scis., 1987—, NSF, 1991-95, N.J. Bus. Roundtable, 1989-92, N.J. Dept. Edn., 1991-92, EPA, 1991-96, N.J. Dept. Environ. Protection and Energy, 1991-92, numerous others; C.V. Mosby scholar, 1962. Mem. APHA (pres.-elect 1997-98, Disting. Career award 1996), Assn. for Social Scis. in Health, Assn. Tchrs. Preventive Medicine, Soc. for Pub. Health Edn. (subcom. on environ. outreach and svc. Greater N.Y. and N.J. chpts.), Internat. Union for Health Edn., Soc. Toxicology (Pub. Comm. award 1997), Nat. Hospice Orgn., N.J. Hospice Orgn. (bd. trustees 1980-82), N.J. Pub. Health Assn. (state health planning bd. 1996—, Dennis J. Sullivan award 1997), Soc. for Risk Analysis, Sigma Xi, Sigma Phi Alpha. Lutheran. Avocations: sailing, tennis, swimming, church choir, theater. Office: U Medicine and Dentistry NJ Sch Pub Health EOHSI 170 Frelinghuysen Rd Piscataway NJ 08854

GOTSCH, SUSAN D., academic administrator, dean; b. Oak Park, Ill., Aug. 9, 1942; d. Richard E. and Mildred (Peckat) G.; m. Ronald B. Thomson, June 10, 1973; 1 child, Jessica Jin Hwa. BA, Valparaiso (Ind.) U., 1964; MA, Bryn Mawr Coll., 1974, PhD, 1977. Asst. prof. sociology Tuskegee (Ala.) U., 1977-80; assoc. prof. sociology Glassboro (N.J.) State Coll., 1980-89; assoc. dean Beaver Coll., Glenside, Pa., 1989-93; v.p., dean academic affairs Hartwick Coll., Oneonta, N.Y., 1993—. Contbr. articles to profl. jours., chpt. to books. Mem. sch. bd. Gateway Regional H.S., Woodbury Heights, N.J., 1988-93. Grantee 3M Corp., Assn. Am. Colls. Univs., 1990, 91, 93, Consortium for Advancement of Higher Edn., 1996. Mem. Am. Conf. Acad. Deans (bd. dirs.). Avocations: sailing, sewing, swimming, reading. Office: Hartwick Coll Oneonta NY 13820

GOTSCHLICH, EMIL CLAUS, physician, educator; b. Bangkok, Thailand, Jan. 17, 1935; came to U.S., 1950, naturalized, 1955; s. Emil Clemens and Magdalene (Holst) G.; m. Kathleen-Anne Haines, May 24, 1975; children: Emil Christopher, Hilda Christina, Emil Chandler, Emily Claire. BA, NYU, 1955, MD, 1959. Intern Bellevue Hosp., N.Y.C., 1959—; mem. faculty Rockefeller U., N.Y.C., 1960—, prof. microbiology, 1978—, sr. physician, 1978—. Capt. M.C., U.S. Army, 1966-68. Decorated Army Commendation medal; recipient Squibb award Am. Soc. Infectious Disease, 1974; Lasker award Albert and Mary Lasker Found., 1978. Mem. NAS, Am. Assn. Immunologists, Assn. Am. Physicians, Am. Soc. for Clin. Investigation, Peripatetic Club, Sigma Xi, Alpha Omega Alpha. Office: Rockefeller U Dept Bacterial Pathogenesis 1230 York Ave Dept New York NY 10021-6399

GOTSHALL, CORDIA ANN, publishing company executive, distributing executive; b. Greenwood, Ark., Jan. 21, 1931; d. Harrison Wages and Mabel Magdalene (Boswell) Wages Moreland; m. Daniel W. Gotshall, Apr. 12, 1952. AA with honors, Foothill Jr. Coll., Los Altos Hills, Calif., 1966; BA magna cum laude, Humboldt State U., Arcata, Calif., 1969; student, Humboldt State U., 1969-71. Clk., typist Indentification Bur. Stanislaus County Sheriff's Office, Modesto, Calif., 1950-55; credit dept. mgr. Brizard's Dept. Store, Arcata, 1955-56; sec.-coord. City of Eureka (Calif.) Recreation Dept., 1956-60; seasonal aide State of Calif. Dept. Fish and Game, Palo Alto, 1961; owner, v.p. Sea Challengers Pub. Co., Monterey, Calif., 1976-83, pres., 1983—; co-editor (with Daniel W. Gotshall) Fishwatcher's Guide, 1977; U.S. rep. Moscow Internat. Book Fair, 1985. Mem. Chi Sigma Epsilon. Avocations: reading, travel, hiking, nature studies, exploring.E-mail: ANNGOT@AOL.COM. Office: 4 Sommerset Rise Monterey CA 93940-4112

GOTT, J. RICHARD, III, astrophysicist; b. Louisville, Feb. 8, 1947; s. J. Richard and Marjorie (Crosby) G.; m. Lucy Jennifer Pollard, June 10, 1978; 1 child, Elizabeth. AB summa cum laude, Harvard U., 1969; PhD, Princeton U., 1973. Postdoctoral fellow Calif. Inst. Tech., Pasadena, 1973-74; vis. fellow Cambridge U., Eng., 1975; asst. prof. astrophysics Princeton U., 1976-80, assoc. prof., 1980-87, prof., 1987—; chmn. of the judges Nat. Westinghouse Sci. Talent Search, Washington, 1986—; chmn. Hayden Planetarium vis. com., 1992-93. Contbr. articles to profl. jours. Recipient R. J. Trumpler award, Astron. Soc. of Pacific, 1975; Alfred P. Sloan fellow, 1977-81. Mem. Am. Astron. Soc., Internat. Astron. Union, Phi Beta Kappa. Achievements include rsch. in theory that the universe will continue to expand forever; solution to Einstein's field equations for the gravitational field around cosmic strings. Office: Princeton U Dept Astrophys Sci Princeton NJ 08544*

GOTT, MARJORIE EDA CROSBY, conservationist, former educator; b. Louisville; d. Alva Baird and Nellie (Jones) Crosby; m. John Richard Gott, Jr., Mar. 12, 1946 (dec. Sept. 1993); 1 child, J. Richard III. AB in Math., U. Louisville, 1934; postgrad., U. Ky., 1938-42. Nationally accredited flower show judge, landscape design critic and judge. Underwriter Commonwealth Life Ins. Co., Louisville, 1934-37; tchr. English Hikes Sch., Buechel, Ky., 1937-43; civilian chief statis. control unit Materiel Command, Army Air Force, Dayton, Ohio, 1943-46; tchr. psychology Bapt. Hosp. and Gen. Hosp., Louisville, 1950-52; dedicated Ky.'s Floral Clock to All Kentuckians Who Take Pride in the Beauty of Their State Commonwealth of Ky.,1961. Author: (booklet) How a Garden Club Beautifies a City, 1967. Pres. Young Women's Rep. Club of Louisville and Jefferson County, 1938-40; pres. Beautification League Louisville and Jefferson County, 1963-64; co-chair Keep Ky. Cleaner-Greener, 1963-68; bd. dirs. Scenic Ky., Inc., 1989—, Nat. Coun. State Garden Clubs, 1961-83. Recipient Conservation award of merit Commonwealth of Ky., 1963, Landscape Design Critics award Nat. Coun. State Garden Clubs, 1979. Mem. Woman's Club of Louisville (pres. 1973-75, hon. 1991—), Garden Club of Ky. (pres. 1961-63), Nat. Assn. Parliamentarians (founder, pres. Louisville unit 1961-63), Louisville Astron. Soc. (hon.). Presbyterian. Avocations: travel, bridge, cooking. Home: 136 Indian Hills Trl Louisville KY 40207-1541

GOTTA, ALEXANDER WALTER, anesthesiologist, educator; b. Bklyn., Apr. 10, 1935; s. A. Walter and Helen C. (Bruskewic) G.; m. Colleen A. Sullivan, July 17, 1965; 1 child, Nancy C. BS summa cum laude, St. Johns's U., 1956; MD, NYU, 1960. Diplomate Am. Bd. Anesthesiology, Am. Bd. Med. Examiners. Intern, U. Chgo., 1960-61; resident Boston City Hosp., 1961-62, N.Y. Hosp.-Cornell U., N.Y.C., 1962-64; instr. anesthesiology Cornell U., 1964-66, asst. prof., 1978-79; dir. anesthesia St. Mary's Hosp., Bklyn., 1968-78; asst. prof. SUNY, Bklyn., 1968-78, assoc. prof., 1978-85, prof., 1985-97, prof. emeritus 1997—; dir. anesthesia L.I. Coll. Hosp., Bklyn., 1983-90; dir. anesthesia Kings County Hosp. Ctr., 1990-97; spkr. in field. Editor: Anesthesiology Clinics Trauma, 1996; contbr. articles to profl. jours. Capt. U.S. Army, 1966-68, Vietnam. Fellow N.Y. Acad. Medicine (chmn. anesthesia sect. 1990), Am. Coll. Anesthesiologists, Am. Soc. Anesthesiologists (ho. of del. 1986-97, chmn. refresher course com. 1995); mem. N.Y. Soc. Anesthesiologists (bd. dirs. 1983-97, chmn. sci. program com. 1991-93, chmn. PGA 1994-96, v.p. 1994, pres.-elect 1995, pres. 1996), N.Y. Soc. Critical Care Medicine (pres. 1985), Assn. Univ. Anesthesiologists, Acad. Anesthesia. Republican. Roman Catholic. Avocation: history. Home: 29 Ascot Ridge Rd Great Neck NY 11021-2912 Office: Kings County Hosp Ctr 451 Clarkson Ave Brooklyn NY 11203-2097

GOTTEMOELLER, ROSE E., federal agency administrator. BS in Russian Lang. and Linguistics, Georgetown U.; MA in Sci. Tech. and Pub. Policy, George Washington U. Sr. def. analyst RAND; dir. Clinton-Gore transition team Arms Control and Disarmament Agy., 1992; dir. Russian Ukrainian and Eurasian affairs Nat. Security Coun., 1993-94; dep. dir. Internat. Inst. Strategic Studies, London, 1994; asst. sec. nonproliferation and nat. security U.S. Dept. of Energy, Washington, 1997—. Office: Dept Energy 1000 Independence Ave SW Washington DC 20585-0002

GOTTESMAN, DAVID SANFORD, investment executive; b. N.Y.C., Apr. 26, 1926; s. Benjamin and Esther (Garfunkel) G.; m. Ruth Levy, Aug. 17, 1950; children: Robert, Alice, William. B.A., Trinity Coll., 1948; M.B.A., Harvard U., 1950; LHD (hon.), Yeshiva U., 1988. Ptnr. Hallgarten & Co., N.Y.C., 1950-64; mng. ptnr. First Manhattan Co., N.Y.C., 1964—; bd. dirs. Sequa Corp. Trustee Am. Mus. Natural History; vice chmn. Mt. Sinai Hosp.; chmn. bd. Yeshiva U., N.Y.C. Mem. N.Y. Soc. Security Analysts, Econs. Club, Harmonie Club, Lyford-Cay Club, Century Country Club. Office: First Manhattan Co 437 Madison Ave New York NY 10022-7001

GOTTESMAN, IRVING ISADORE, psychology educator; b. Cleve., Dec. 29, 1930; s. Bernard and Virginia (Weitzner) G.; m. Carol Applen, Dec. 23, 1970; children—Adam M., David B. B.S., Ill. Inst. Tech., 1953; Ph.D., U. Minn., 1960. Diplomate in clin. psychology and psychol. assessment; lic. psychologist Minn., Calif., Va. Intern clin. psychology VA Hosp., Mpls., 1959-60; lectr. dept. social relations Harvard U., 1960-63; USPHS fellow in psychiat. genetics Inst. Psychiatry, London, 1963-64; assoc. prof. psychiat. & genetics, dept. psychiatry U. N.C., 1964-66; prof. dept. psychology, psychiatry and genetics U. Minn., 1966-80; prof. dept. psychiatry and genetics Washington U., St. Louis, 1980-85; Commonwealth prof. psychology U. Va., Charlottesville, 1985-94, Sherrell J. Aston prof. psychology, prof. clin. pediats., 1994—; cons. NIMH, Washington, 1975-79, 92-96, NIMH Nat. Plan for Schizophrenia, 1988-89; mem. Pres.'s Commn. on Huntington Disease, 1977; tng. cons. VA, Washington, 1968-85; fellow Ctr. for Advanced Studies in the Behavioral Scis., Stanford, Calif., 1987-88; Inst. of Medicine Com. cons. Vietnam War Experience Study, 1987-88; NRC cons. Workshop on Schizophrenia, 1995-96. Author: Schizophrenia and Genetics, 1972 (Hofheimer prize), Schizophrenia The Epigenetic Puzzle, 1982, Schizophrenia Genesis: The Origins of Madness, 1991 (transl. into Japanese and German, William James Book award, Phi Beta Kappa U. Va. Book award 1992), Schizophrenia and Genetic Risks, 1992, Schizophrenia and Manic Depressive Disorder: Biological Roots of Mental Illness Revealed by Study of Identical Twins, 1994, transl. into Japanese, 1998, Seminars in Psychiatric Genetics, 1994; editor: Man, Mind and Heredity, 1971, Vital Statistics, Demography and Schizophrenia, 1989. Served with USNR, 1949-53, 56-61; USN, 1953-56. Guggenheim fellow U. Copenhagen, 1972; recipient R. Thornton Wilson prize Ea. Psychiat. Rsch. Assn., 1965, Stanley Dean award Am. Coll. Psychiatrists, 1988, Eric Stromgren medal Danish Psychiat. Soc., 1991, Kurt Schneider prize, Bonn, 1992, Alexander Gralnick prize Am. Assn. Suicidology, 1992, Jonathan Logan award Nat. Alliance for Mentally Ill, 1995; David C. Wilson lectr. U. Va. Sch. Medicine, 1967, Lifetime Achievement award Internat. Soc. for Psychiat. Genetics, 1997; Parker lectr. Ohio State U. Sch. Medicine, 1983, 93. Fellow APA (Disting. Scientist award divsn. 12, sect. 3 1994), AAAS, Am. Psychopathol. Assn., Royal Coll. Psychiatrists (hon.), Am. Psychol. Soc. (human capital initiative task force for psychopathology rsch. agenda 1993-96); mem. Minn. Human Genetics League (v.p. 1969-71), Soc. Study Social Biology (v.p. 1976-80), Behavior Genetics Assn. (pres. 1976-77, T. Dobzhansky award 1990), Am. Soc. Human Genetics (editl. bd. 1967-72), Soc. Rsch. in Psychopathology (pres. 1993). Home: 245 Terrell Rd W Charlottesville VA 22901-2168 Office: Univ Va Gilmer Hall Charlottesville VA 22903

GOTTFELD, GUNTHER MAX, retired urban mass transit official, consultant; b. Berlin, June 13, 1934; came to U.S., 1941; s. William James and Charlotte Jeanette (Less) G.; m. Linda Stratton Keene, Oct. 26, 1969 (div. Jan. 1976); children: Deborah Charlotte, David William; m. Ann Richmond, July 13, 1985. BS, Shepherd Coll., 1958; MA, Am. U., 1960. Transp. planner Nat. Capital Trnasp. Agy., Washington, 1961-63; cons. Stockholm Transit Authority, 1963-64; fed. liaison officer Mass. Bay Transp. Authority, Boston, 1965-70; sr. transp. planner Md. Mass Transit Adminstrn., Balt., 1970-74, intergovtl. coordinator, 1974-94. Mem. Am. Pub. Transit Assn. (mem. legis. com. 1981—), Md. Mass Transit Adminstrn., Am. Rd. and Transp. Builders Assn. (mem. pub. transit council 1986-94, mem. legis. watch com. 1986-94), Internat. Union Pub. Transport (rail transit new starts com. 1992—). Democrat. Jewish. Avocations: European travel, cross-country skiing, hiking, classical music. Home: 5301 Hesperus Dr Columbia MD 21044-1808

GOTTFREDSON, DON MARTIN, criminal justice educator; b. Sacramento, Sept. 25, 1926; s. Don Angus and Marion Dorothy (Williams) G.; m. Betty Jane Hunt, Oct. 9, 1946; children: Gary Don, Stephen David, Michael Ryan, Eric Bert, Ronald Lee. B.A., U. Calif.-Berkeley, 1951; M.A., Claremont Grad. Sch., 1955, Ph.D., 1959. Project dir. Inst. for Study Crime and Delinquency, Sacramento, 1962-66; dir. Nat. Council on Crime and Delinquency Research Ctr., Davis, Calif., 1965-73; prof. Sch. Criminal Justice, Rutgers U.-Newark, 1973—, dean, 1973-86, Richard J. Hughes prof. criminal justice, 1987-94; prof. emeritus Rutgers U.-Newark, 1994—; chmn. N.J. State Criminal Disposition Commn., 1984-94; pres. Justice Policy Rsch. Corp., 1985—. Author: (with Wilkins and Hoffman) Guidelines for Parole and Sentencing, 1978, (with Gottfredson) Decisionmaking in Criminal Justice, 1980, 88; exec. editor: Jour. Research in Crime and Delinquency, 1965-73; editor: Criminal Justice and Behavior, Newark, 1981-86. Mem. bd. fellows Nat. Ctr. Juvenile Justice, Pitts., 1973-93; mem. adv. bd. Nat. Inst. Justice, Washington, 1980; trustee N.J. Assn. on Corrections, Trenton, 1983. Served with U.S. Army, 1944-46. Recipient Outstanding Nat. Contbns. to Criminal Justice Adminstrn. award Am. Soc. Pub. Adminstrn., 1978, Donald Cressey award Nat. Coun. Crime and Delinquency, Paul Tappan award Western Soc. Criminology, Ron Beattie award Assn. for Correctional Rsch. and Info. Mgmt., Richard A. McGee award Am. Justice Inst. Fellow Am. Soc. Criminology (v.p. 1976-78, pres.-elect 1985-86, pres. 1986-87, August Vollmer award). Democrat. Home: 23 Axios River Ct Sacramento CA 95831-4829

GOTTFRIED, BENJAMIN FRANK, retired manufacturing exeuctive; b. Phila., Apr. 13, 1939; s. Harry Nathan and Sylvia (Chernow) G.; m. Nancy L. Prunty, June 24, 1994; 1 child from previous marriage, Hal. Student, U. Md., 1973-74, 79-80, Cen. Tex. Coll., 1974-75. Enlisted U.S. Army, 1959; served as chief warrant officer U.S. Army Engrs., 1959-79, ret., 1979; regional maintenance mgr. Avis Truck Leasing, Balt., 1979-82; svc. mgr. Hale Truck and Trailer Equipment, Marlton, N.J., 1982-85; sr. dir. svc. Iveco Trucks N.Am., Bensalem, Pa., 1985-95; ret., 1995. Author: (with others) Fleet Equipment, 1986, Transport Topics, 1987. Decorated Purple Heart, Bronze Star, Commendation Medal, Meritorious Svc. Medal, Cross of Gallantry. Mem. DAV (life), Vietnam Vets. Am. (life), Warrant Officers Assn., Hon. Order Ky. Cols., Fraternal Order Police, Mil. Order of The Purple Heart (life). Jewish. Avocations: remote control car racing, camping, pool, exercise. Home: 303 N Elmwood Rd Marlton NJ 08053-3307

GOTTFRIED, BYRON STUART, engineering educator; b. Detroit, May 24, 1934; s. Sidney and Faye Gottfried; m. Marcia Faye Singer, June 21, 1959; children: Sharon, Gail, Susan. B.S., Purdue U., 1956; M.S., U. Mich., 1958; Ph.D., Case-Western Res. U., 1962. Assoc. engr. Westinghouse Electric Corp., Pitts., 1958-59; assoc. engr. Lewis Research Ctr., NASA, Cleve., 1959-62; research engr. Gulf Research & Devel. Co., Pitts., 1962-65; supr. Gulf Research & Devel. Co., 1968-70; asst. prof. dept. mech. engring. Carnegie-Mellon U., Pitts., 1965-68; assoc. prof. dept. indsl. engring. U. Pitts., 1970-75, prof., dir. energy resources program, 1975-76, prof. indsl. engring., 1975—; cons. Systems Modeling Corp., U.S. Dept. Interior Bur. Mines, Dept. Energy. Author: Programming with Fortran IV, 1972, 83, 84 (with Joel Weisman) Introduction to Optimization Theory, 1973, Data Processing, 1974, Programming with Basic, 1975, 82, 86, Introduction to Engineering Calculations, 1979, Elements of Stochastic Process Simulation, 1984, Programming with Pascal, 1985, 94, Programming with C, 1990, 96, Programming with Structured Basic, 1993, Spreadsheet Tools for Engineers, 1996, 98; (with Sepulveda and Souder) Engineering Economics, 1984; contbr. articles to profl. jours. Served with Signal Corps, AUS, 1958. Mem. Am. Soc. Engring. Edn., Soc. for Computer Simulation. Home: 129 Old Suffolk Dr Monroeville PA 15146-4800 Office: U Pitts Indsl Engring Dept Pittsburgh PA 15261

GOTTFRIED, EUGENE LESLIE, physician, educator; b. Passaic, N.J., Feb. 26, 1929; s. David Robert and Rose (Chill) G.; m. Phyllis Doris Swain, Aug. 16, 1957. AB, Columbia U., 1950, MD, 1954. Cert. Nat. Bd. Med. Examiners, Am. Bd. Internal Medicine. Intern Presbyn. Hosp., N.Y.C., 1954-55, asst. resident in medicine, 1957-58; resident Bronx (N.Y.) Mcpl. Hosp. Ctr., 1958-59, fellow in medicine, 1959-60; asst. instr. medicine Albert Einstein Coll. Medicine Yeshiva U., N.Y.C., 1959-60, instr., 1960-61, assoc., 1961-65, asst. prof., 1965-69; assoc. prof. medicine Cornell U. Med. Coll., N.Y.C., 1969-81, assoc. prof. pathology, 1975-81; clin. prof. dept. lab. medicine U. Calif., San Francisco, 1991-93, prof., 1993-99, vice chmn. dept. lab. medicine, 1981-98, prof. emeritus, 1999—; hosp. appointments include asst. vis. physician Bronx Mcpl. Hosp. Ctr., 1960-66, assoc. attending physician, 1966-69; assoc. attending physician N.Y. Hosp., N.Y.C., 1969-81, assoc. attending pathologist, 1975-81, dir. lab. clin. hematology, 1969-81; chief lab. medicine San Francisco Gen. Hosp. Med. Ctr., 1981-98, dir. clin. labs., 1981-98. Assoc. editor Jour. Lipid Research, 1971-72, 75-77; mem. editorial bd. Jour. Lipid Research, 1972-77. Lt. comdr. USNR, 1955-57. Recipient Career Scientist award Health Research Council City of N.Y., 1964-72. Fellow ACP, Am. Soc. Hematology, Internat. Soc. Hematology,

Acad. Clin. Lab. Physicians and Scientists; mem. Nat. Com. for Clin. Lab. Stds., Phi Beta Kappa, Alpha Omega Alpha.

GOTTFRIED, IRA SIDNEY, management consulting executive; b. Bronx, N.Y., Jan. 4, 1932; s. Louis and Augusta (Champagne) G.; m. Judith Claire Rosenberg, Sept. 19, 1954; children: Richard Alan, Glenn Steven, David Aaron. BBA, CCNY, 1953; MBA, U. So. Calif., 1959. Lic. airline transport pilot. Sales mgr. Kleerpak Plastics, North Hollywood, Calif., 1956-57; head sys. and procedures Hughes Aircraft Co., Culver City, Calif., 1957-60; mgr. corp. bus. sys. The Aerospace Corp., El Segundo, Calif., 1960-61; dir. adminstrn. Eldon Industries, Inc., Hawthorne, Calif., 1962; mgr. info. sys. Litton Industries, Inc., Woodland Hills, Calif., 1963-64; exec. v.p. Norris & Gottfried, Inc., L.A., 1964-69; pres. Gottfried Cons., Inc., L.A., 1970-85; exec. ptnr. PriceWaterhouseCoopers, LLP, L.A., 1985-88, ret., 1988; v.p. Cresap/Towers Perrin, 1988-90; pres., dir. Gottfried Cons. Internat. 1990—; vice chmn. ACME Inc., 1984-85; dir., mem. exec. com. Blue Cross of Calif., 1968-77. Contbr. articles to profl. jours. Bd. dirs. ARC, Westside Amateur Radio Bluc, Univ. Synagogue, 1986-92. With USNR, 1953-56. Recipient Pres.'s award United Hosp. Assn. Mem. Inst. Mgmt. Cons. (life), Am. Arbitration Assn., Assn. Info. Tech. Profls. (life), Alpha Phi Omega (life), Brentwood Country Club, Palm Valley Country Club. Jewish. Avocations: amateur radio operator (K6IRA), model railroading. Home: 12118 La Casa Ln Los Angeles CA 90049-1530

GOTTFRIED, KURT, physicist, educator; b. Vienna, Austria, May 17, 1929; came to U.S., 1952, naturalized, 1965; s. Salomon and Augusta (Werner) G.; m. Sorel B. Dickstein, June 26, 1955; children: David M., Laura S. B.Eng., McGill U., 1951, M.S., 1952; Ph.D., MIT, 1955. Jr. fellow Soc. Fellows, Harvard, 1955-58; research fellow Inst. Theoretical Physics, Copenhagen, 1958-59; research fellow Harvard, 1959-60, asst. prof. physics, 1960-64; assoc. prof. physics Cornell U., Ithaca, N.Y., 1964-68, prof. physics, 1968—, chmn. dept., 1991-94; prof. physics emeritus Cornell U., Ithaca; staff mem. European Orgn. for Nuclear Research, Geneva, Switzerland, 1970-73. Author: Quantum Mechanics, 1966, Concepts of Particle Physics, Vol. 1, 1984, Vol. 2, 1986; co-editor: Crisis Stability and Nuclear War, 1988. Fellow AAAS, Am. Acad. Arts and Scis., Am. Phys. Soc. (chmn. div. particles and fields 1981, councillor 1990-94), Union Concerned Scientists (bd. dirs. 1978—, vice-chair 1997—, chair 1999—), Coun. on Fgn. Rels. Office: Newman Lab Nuclear Studies Cornell U Ithaca NY 14853

GOTTFRIED, LEON ALBERT, English language educator; b. Ames, Iowa, Nov. 6, 1925; s. Samuel and Louise G.; children: Laura, Ann. A.B., U. Ill., 1948, M.A., 1951, Ph.D. (Univ. fellow), 1958. Teaching asst. U. Ill., 1948-50; instr. English U. Conn., 1953-54, Washington U., St. Louis, 1954-58; asst. prof. Washington U., 1958-63, assoc. prof., 1963-69, prof., 1969-81, chmn. dept. art and archaeology, 1972-76; dean Washington U. (Faculty Arts and Scis.), 1976-78; prof., chmn. dept. English Purdue U., 1981-1990, prof., 1981-98, prof. emeritus, 1998—; Fulbright prof. U. Malaya, 1970-71. Author: Matthew Arnold and the Romantics, 1963; Contbr. articles to profl. jours. Served with USNR, 1944-46, PTO. Am. Philos. Soc. grantee, 1966, 71. Office: Purdue U Dept English West Lafayette IN 47907

GOTTHEIMER, GEORGE MALCOLM, JR., insurance executive, educator; b. Orange, N.J., Mar. 26, 1933; s. George Malcolm Sr. and Rosalie Kahn Zugsmith; m. Patricia Ann Savarese, Apr. 30, 1966; children: Nancy Lorraine, Kerry Suzannne. BSBA, Edison State Coll., Princeton, N.J., 1978; MBA, The Coll. of Ins., N.Y.C., 1980; PhD, Calif. Coast U., 1983. Cert. assoc. in reinsurance. Sec. Am. Internat. Group, N.Y.C., 1958-66; pres. Reinsurance Agy. Mgmt. Corp., Bala Cynwyd, Pa., 1966-69; v.p. Occidental Life Ins. Co., Raleigh, N.C., 1969-72, Midland Ins. Co., N.Y.C., 1972-77; exec. v.p. John D. Ryan & Co. Inc., N.Y.C., 1977-82; v.p. Gen. Re Group, 1982-84; sr. v.p. Pro Re of Am., Inc., N.Y.C., 1984-86; pres. Kernan Assocs., Inc., Berkeley Heights, N.J., 1986—; adj. asst. prof. ins., reinsurance mgmt. The Coll. Ins., N.Y.C., 1972-80, adj. assoc. prof., 1980-97, assoc. prof., 1997—; adj. prof. Baruch Coll. CUNY. Contbr. articles to profl. jours. Research fellow Harry J. Loman Found., Malvern, Pa., 1982. Mem. Chartered Property Casualty Underwriters (cert. 1957, nat. dir. 1983-86, regional v.p. 1985-86, pres. N.Y. chpt. 1980-81, Eugene A. Toale Meml. award 1985), CLU's (cert. 1973). Home: 6 Oechsner Ct Berkeley Heights NJ 07922-1731

GOTTHOFFER, LANCE, lawyer; b. N.Y.C., June 23, 1949; s. Joel Sidney and Muriel (Diamond) G. BA, Monmouth Coll., 1971; JD, Georgetown U., 1974. Bar: N.Y. 1975, U.S. Dist. Ct. (so. dist.) N.Y. 1975, U.S. Ct. Appeals (2nd, 3rd, 5th, 6th and 9th cirs.) 1981, U.S. Ct. Internat. Trade 1986, U.S. Supreme Ct. 1987. Legal asst. Office of N.Y.C. Coun. Pres., N.Y.C., 1970-73; assoc. Mudge, Rose, Guthrie & Alexander, N.Y.C., 1974-77; ptnr. Marks & Murase, N.Y.C., 1977-94, Oppenheimer, Wolff & Donnelly, N.Y.C., 1994—; guest lectr. Grad. Sch. Bus., Baruch Coll., N.Y.C.; speaker in field. Mem. ABA. Office: Oppenheimer Wolff & Donnelly 153 E 53rd St New York NY 10022-4611

GOTTIER, RICHARD CHALMERS, retired computer company executive; b. Columbus, Ohio, Oct. 12, 1918; s. Chalmers M. and Grace (Eisnaugle) G.; m. Mary S. Hiatt, Nov. 13, 1965; children: Barbara, Diane, Richard Chalmers, Penny. B.S. in Bus. Adminstrn, Ohio State U., 1939; postgrad., Northwestern U. Grad. Sch. Bus., 1969. Spl. agt. FBI, Washington, 1940-51; with RCA, Indpls., 1951-59; dir. Magnavox Co., Ft. Wayne, Ind., 1959-70; sr. v.p. Control Data Corp., Mpls., 1970-80; chmn., gen. ptnr. Minn. Seed Capital, Inc., 1980-97. Home: 4735 Sparrow Rd Minnetonka MN 55345-2438

GOTTLEIB, KARLA LEWIS, writer, college official; b. Miami, Fla., Oct. 3, 1966; d, Norman Lee and Marilyn Patricia (Roberts) Gottlieb-Roberts, . BA, Yale U., 1984; MA, San Francisco State U., 1994. Student mentor San Francisco State U., 1992, tutorial supr. FSMP program, 1992-94; campus organizer Fla. PIRG, Miami, 1995; translator, jr. rschr. Ind. Project, Senegal, West Africa, 1995; assoc. producer The Passing Project Visco, Miami, Fla., 1995; tutor Ednl. Resources, Miami, 1995-96; translator, rschr. Ind. Project, Mali, West Africa, 1996; intake advisor Miami (Fla.)-Dade C.C., 1996-97, coord. vocat. programs, 1997, campus dir. svc.-learning program, 1997—. Author: (book) The Mother of Us All. Activist Am. Indian Movement, San Francisco, 1991-92. Recipient Elinor C. Backman English award Ransom-Everglades Sch., Miami, 1984, Writing award Bar Coll., N.Y.C., 1984. Avocations: swimming, diving, polit. activism, yoga, African dance. Home: 800 Lenox Ave Apt 5 Miami Beach FL 33139-5621

GOTTLIEB, A(BRAHAM) ARTHUR, medical educator; b. Dec. 14, 1937; m. Marise S. Gottlieb, 1958; children: Mindy, Joanne. AB summa cum laude, Columbia Coll., 1957; MD, NYU, 1961. Med. house officer Peter Bent Brigham Hosp., Boston, 1961-62, asst. resident, 1962-63; rsch. fellow in chemistry, tutor in chemistry Harvard U., Peter Bent Brigham Hosp., Boston, 1965-67; assoc. in medicine Harvard U., Peter Bent Brigham Hosp., 1968; asst. prof. medicine Harvard Med. Sch., 1969; assoc. prof. microbiology Inst. Microbiology, Rutgers U., New Brunswick, N.J., 1969-72, prof. microbiology, 1972-75; prof., chmn. microbiology and immunology Tulane U. Sch. Medicine, New Orleans, 1975—, prof. medicine, 1975—; pres., sci. dir. IMREG, Inc., New Orleans, 1981-96; cons. in field; vis. prof. Walter and Eliza Hall Inst. Med. Rsch., Melbourne, Australia, 1979, Wakayama Med. Coll. and Gunma Med. Coll., Japan, 1980; vis. prof. medicine and pharmacology Shanghai Med. U., People's Republic of China, 1991-92. Mem. editorial adv. bd. several profl. publs. Mem. sci. adv. bd. Cancer Assn. Greater New Orleans, 1979-84; mem. tech. rev. bd. U. New Orleans, 1984-90. Recipient Frances Stone Burn award Am. Cancer Soc., 1968, Rsch. Career Devel. award Nat. Inst. Gen. Med. Scis., 1968-69; Macy Inst. Med. Edn. fellow Harvard U., 1995-96. Fellow ACP, Am. Assn. Cancer Rsch., Am. Assn. Immunologists, Am. Chem. Soc., Am. Soc. Biol. Chemists, Am. Soc. Cell Biology, Am. Soc. Clin. Investigation, Am. Soc. Microbiology, Am. Acad. Microbiology, Internat. Assn. Comparative Rsch. on Leukemia and Related Diseases, N.Y. Acad. Scis., Reticulendothelial Soc. (chmn. publs. com.), Assn. Med. Sch. Microbiology (chmn.), AAAS, Phi Beta Kappa, Sigma Xi, Alpha Omega Alpha. Office: Tulane U Sch Medicine 1430 Tulane Ave # Sl38 New Orleans LA 70112-2699*

GOTTLIEB, ALAN MERRIL, advertising, fundraising and broadcasting executive, writer; b. L.A., May 2, 1947; s. Seymour and Sherry (Schutz) G.; m. Julie Hoy Versnel, July 27, 1979; children: Amy Jean, Sarah Merril, Alexis Hope, Andrew Michael. Grad. Georgetown U., 1970; BS, Nuclear Engring., U. Tenn., 1971. Press sec. Congressman John Duncan, Knoxvill, Tenn., 1971, regional rep., Young Ams. for Freedom, Seattle, 1972, nat. dir. Young Ams. for Freedom, Washington, 1971-72; nat. treas. Am. Conservative Union, Washington, 1971—, bd. dirs., 1974—; pres. Merril Assocs., 1974—; chmn. Citizens Com. for Right to Keep and Bear Arms, Bellevue, Wash., 1972—, exec. dir., 1973; pres. Ctr. Def. of Free Enterprise, Bellevue 1976—, Second Amendment Found., Bellevue, 1974—; pub. Gun Week, 1985—, The Gottlieb-Tartaro Report, 1995—; bd. dirs. Nat. Park User Assn., 1988—, Am. Polit. Action Com., 1988—, Coun. Nat. Policy, bd. govs., 1985—, Svc. Bureau Assn., pres., dir., 1974—, Chancellor Broadcasting, Inc, Las Vegas, Nev., 1990-93; pres. Sta. KBNP Radio, Portland, 1990—, Pres. Station KZTY Radio, Las Vegas, NV, Evergreen Radio Network, Bellevue, 1990-93, Westnet Broadcasting Inc., Bellevue, 1990, Sta. KSBN Radio, Spokane, 1995—; chmn. Talk Am. Radio Networks, 1994—. With U.S. Army, 1968-74. Recipient Good Citizenship award Citizens Home Protective Assn., Honolulu, 1978, Cicero award Nat. Assn. Federally Licensed Firearms Dealers, Fla., 1982, Second Amendment award Scope, 1983, 91, Outstanding Am. Handgunner award, Am. Handgunners Award Found., Milwaukee, Wisc., 1984, Roy Rogers award, Nat. Antique Arms Collectors Assn., Reno, Nev., 1987, Golden Eagle award, Am. Fedn. Police, Washington, 1990. Mem. NRA. Republican. Author: The Gun Owners Political Action Manual, 1976, The Rights of Gun Owners, 1981, Rev. edit., 1991, The Gun Grabbers, 1988, Gun Rights Fact Book, 1989, Guns For Women, 1988, The Wise Use Agenda, 1989, Trashing the Economy, 1993, Things You Can Do To Defend Your Gun Rights, 1993, Alan Gottlieb's Celebrity Address Book, 1994, More Things You Can Do To Defend Your Gun Rights, 1995, Politically Correct Guns, 1996, She Took a Village, 1998.

GOTTLIEB, ANITA FAYE, management consultant; b. Norfolk, Va., Apr. 20, 1946. B in Sociology, George Washington U., 1966, D in Pub. Adminstrn., 1975; MBA, Old Dominion U., 1970. Programmer analyst Group Hospitalization, Inc., Washington, 1966-67; campaign coord. U.S. Congl. Campaign of Joseph T. Fitzpatrick, Norfolk, 1970; instr. quantitative scis. in bus. and econ. Old Dominion U., 1971-72; asst. prof. bus. administrn. Am. U., 1974-76; mentor, asst. prof. Empire State Coll., SUNY, Albany, 1976-77; nat. rep. Nat. Treas. Employees Union, Washington, 1977-79; staff dir. subcom. human resources, com. post office and civil svc. U.S. Ho. of Reps., 1979-83; asst. v.p. univ. rels. Am. U., 1983-92; sr. v.p. ops. Defenders of Wildlife, Washington, 1992-94; v.p. fin. and adminstrn. Washington Coll., Chestertown, Md., 1994-95; judge Nat. Women in Comm. awards program, 1990; cons. Ctr. for Women in Govt. SUNY, 1979-82; mem. program rev. team Am. Coun. Edn., 1978; mem. exec. steering com. N.Y. Higher Edn. Assn., 1976-77; trainer N.Y. Sch. Indsl. and Labor Rels. COrnell U., 1977; cons., lectr. state and local govt. fin. U.S. Civil Svc. Commn. Bur. Tng., 1973-75; panelist, spkr. in field. Book reviewer in pub. administrn. Thomas Y. Crowell Co., Inc., 1976; contbr. articles to profl. jours. Co-chair Eleanor Roosevelt Fund of Dem. Nat. Com.; cons. Slaughter for Congress Campaign, 1986, 88; mem. Va. Dem. State Ctrl. Com., chair rsch. and leadership tng., mem. com. to revise Dem. Party Plan of Va., 1972-76; bd. dirs. Earth Share, Environ. Fedn. Am., 1992-94, Planned Parenthood Met. Washington, mem. spl. task force on healthcare reform, chair nominating com., 1991-97; treas. D.C. Rape Crisis Ctr., 1997—. Office: 1832 Biltmore St NW Apt 3 Washington DC 20009-1933

GOTTLIEB, DANIEL SETH, lawyer; b. Los Angeles, Sept. 19, 1954; s. Seymour and Blanche Joyce (Kaufman) G.; m. Marilynn Jeanne Payne, July 21, 1985; children: Gwendolyn Z., Rebecca Lucinda. BA summa cum laude, Columbia U., 1976; JD, Harvard U., 1980. Bar: Wash. 1980, U.S. Dist. Ct. (we. dist.) Wash. 1980. Assoc. Riddell, Williams, Bullitt & Walkinshaw, Seattle, 1980-86, ptnr., 1986-95; prin. Graham & James LLP/Riddell Williams P.S., Seattle, 1996-97; mem. Gottlieb, Fisher & Andrews, PLLC, Seattle, 1997—; coord. S.E. Legal Clinic, Seattle, 1984-86. Mem. Seattle Fremont Adv. Com. Recipient Achievement award Seattle-King County Econ. Devel. Coun., 1990. Mem. ABA, Nat. Assn. Bond Lawyers, Wash. State Bar Assn., King County Bar Assn. (treas. 1993-95, 2d v.p. 1995-96, 1st v.p. 1996-97, pres. 1997-98, bd. dirs. young lawyers divsn. 1987-90, treas. 1987-88, vice-chmn. 1988-89, chmn. 1989-90, chmn. legal info. and referral cliics com. 1986-87), Wash. State Assn. Mcpl. Attys., Wash. Coun. Sch. Attys., Wash. State Soc. Hosp. Attys., Bainbridge Island-North Kitsap Jewish Chavurah (v.p. and sec. 1993-95). Jewish. Avocations: tuba, hiking, bicycling. Home: 4880 NE N Tolo Rd Bainbridge Island WA 98110-3461 Office: Gottlieb Fisher & Andrews PLLC 1325 Fourth Ave Ste 1200 Seattle WA 98101-2531

GOTTLIEB, GIDON ALAIN GUY, law educator; b. Paris, Dec. 9, 1932; m. Antoinette Rozoy Countess de Roussy de Sales, May 12, 1965. LLB with honors, London Sch. Econs., 1954, Cambridge (Eng.) U., 1956; diploma in comparative law, Cambridge (Eng.) U., 1958; LLM, Harvard U., 1957, SJD, 1962. Bar: Called to bar Lincoln Inn, London 1958. Lectr. govt. Dartmouth Coll., 1960-61; assoc. firm Shearman & Sterling, N.Y.C., 1962-65; mem. faculty N.Y. U. Law Sch., 1965-76; Leo Spitz prof. internat. law and diplomacy U. Chgo. Law Sch., 1976—; UN rep. Amnesty Internat., 1966-72; mem. founding com. World Assembly Human Rights, 1968; adv. bd. Internat. League Rights of Man; disting. vis. fellow Hoover Instn., Stanford, Calif., 1991-94, 97—. Author: The Logic of Choice: An Investigation of the Concepts of Rule and Rationality, 1968, Nation Against State, 1993. Fellow N.Y. Coun. on Fgn. Rels. (sr. fellow, dir., Middle East Peace Project 1988-94); mem. Am. Soc. Internat. Law, Century Assn. (N.Y.C.). Office: U Chgo Law Sch 1111 E 60th St Chicago IL 60637-2776*

GOTTLIEB, GILBERT, psychobiologist, educator; b. Bklyn., Oct. 22, 1929; s. Leo and Sylvia Sherman; m. Nora Lee Willis, Feb. 38, 1961; children: Jonathan Brian, David Herschel, Aaron Lee, Marc Sherman. AB, U. Miami, 1955, MS, 1956; PhD, Duke U., 1960. Clin. psychologist Dorothea Dix Hosp., Raleigh, N.C., 1959-61; rsch. scientist N.C. Divsn. Mental Health, Raleigh, 1961-82; head dept. psychology U. N.C., Greensboro, 1982-86, Excellence Found. prof., 1982-95; mem. faculty Carolina consortium human devel. U. N.C., Chapel Hill, 1988—, rsch. prof. dept. psychology, 1995—; guest Czechoslovak Acad. Scis., 1967, USSR Acad. Scis., 1989; advisor German NSF, 1977; U.S. del. Internat. Ethnological Congress com., 1977-83; mem. exec. com. NIMH Ctr. for Devel. Sci., U. N.C., 1993—; vis. lectr. Inst. Child Devel., U. Minn., 1975; vis. scholar Ctr. Interdisciplinary Rsch., U. Bielefeld, Germany, 1977; disting. vis. prof. psychology dept. U. Colo., Boulder, 1985; vis. fellow The Neuroscis. Inst., San Diego, 1996; disting. vis. lectr. dept. psychology U. Alta., 1996, Clark U., 1999. Author: Development of Species Identification in Birds, 1971, Individual Development and Evolution: The Genesis of Novel Behavior, 1992, Synthesizing Nature-Nurture: Prenatal Roots of Instinctive Behavior, 1997 (APA Book award 1998); editor: Behavioral Embryology, 1973, Aspects of Neurogenesis, 1974, Neural and Behavioral Specificity, 1976, Early Influences, 1978, Measurement of Audition and Vision in the First Year of Postnatal Life, 1985; assoc. editor Jour. Comparative and Physiol. Psychology, 1974-80; editl. cons. various sci. jours. and pub. houses. Recipient Disting. Sci. Contbn. awad for child devel. Soc. Rsch. Child Devel., 1997; NSF grantee, 1963, 85-88; Nat. Inst. Child Health grantee, 1964-85; NIMH grantee, 1989—. Mem. Internat. Soc. Devel. Psychobiology (pres. 1986-87), Internat. Conf. Infant Studies. Home: 4908 Forestville Rd Raleigh NC 27616-9683 Office: U NC Ctr Devel Sci Chapel Hill NC 27599-8115

GOTTLIEB, H. DAVID, podiatrist; b. Washington, Mar. 2, 1956; s. Julius J. and Charlotte G.; m. Wendy Ilene Weisbard, June 17, 1979; children: Jason, Cheryl. BA, Cornell U., 1978; DPM, Pa. Coll. Podiatric Medicine, 1982. Diplomate Nat. Bd. Podiatry Examiners, Am. Acad. Pain Mgmt., Am. Coun. Cert. Podiatric Physicians and Surgeons, Am. Bd. Podiatric Orthopedics and Primary Podiatric Medicine. Podiatrist Dr. Julius J. Gottlieb, P.C., Washington, 1982-91; prin. H. David Gottlieb, DPM, P.C., Washington, 1991—. Author (book chpt.) Laser Surgery of the Foot, 1988. Mem. Chevy Chase (D.C.) Citizens Assn., 1982—; den master Cub Scouts Am., Gaithersburg, Md., 1991-93; pres. Young Couples Club Gaithersburg Hebrew Congregation, 1982-85. Fellow Acad. Ambulatory Foot Surgery, Am. Med. Athlete Assn.; mem. Am. Assn. Podriatric Physicians and Surgeons, Am. Running and Fitness Assn. Avocations: karate, gardening, marine reef aquaria. Office: 5480 Wisconsin Ave Ste 225 Chevy Chase MD 20815-3503

GOTTLIEB, JAMES RUBEL, federal agency administrator, lawyer; b. N.Y.C., July 2, 1947; s. Robert J. Gottlieb and Mildred C. Blaufox; m. Roberta James, 1974; children: Zoe, Zachary. BA, Mich. State U., 1969; MA, NYU, 1970; JD, N.Y. Law Sch., 1974. Bar: N.Y. 1974, D.C. 1983. Trial asst. Fuchsberg & Fuchsberg, 1971-74, assoc., 1974-77; adminstrv. asst., legis. dir., counsel for rep. Ted Weiss U.S. House of Reps., 1977-83, staff dir., chief counsel Human Resources & Intergovt. Rels. Subcom., 1983-93; chief counsel, staff dir. Senate Com. on Vets. Affairs, Washington, 1993-94; minority chief counsel, staff dir. Senate Com. Vets. Affairs, Washington, 1995—. Office: Senate Com on Vets Affairs 202 Hart Senate Office Washington DC 20510

GOTTLIEB, JERROLD HOWARD, advertising executive; b. N.Y.C., Aug. 25, 1946; s. Saul and Sylvia (Siegel) G.; m. June L. Brownstein, June 18, 1978; children: Steven Andrew, Melissa Eve. B.A., Mich. State U., 1968; M.B.A., Am. U., 1969. Sales rep. Gen. Foods Corp., White Plains, N.Y., 1969-71; v.p., account mgr. J. Walter Thompson, N.Y.C., 1971-75; sr. product mgr. Gen. Foods Corp., White Plains, 1976-78; v.p., account mgr. Batten, Barton, Durstein & Osborn, N.Y.C., 1978-80; sr. v.p. N.Y.O., account dir. J. Walter Thompson, N.Y.C., 1980-82, sr. v.p. U.S.A., mng. dir., 1982-84, sr. v.p. U.S.A., worldwide mng. dir., 1984-87, sr. v.p. worldwide, dir. account mgmt., 1987-90; exec. v.p. Backer Spielvogel Bates Inc., N.Y.C., 1991-92, exec. v.p., mng. dir. office of chmn., 1992-94; pres. Lane Gottlieb Advt., N.Y.C., 1994-96; ptnr. McCaffery Ratner Gottlieb & Lane Inc., N.Y.C., 1997—; bd. dirs. Advt. Hall of Fame, N.Y.C., U.J.A. Fedn. N.Y. Founder Washington Saturday Coll., 1969; chmn. Am. U. campus, Washington, 1969; mem. adv. coun. ARC, Washington, 1981-86; vice chmn. mktg. UJA Fedn., N.Y.C., 1987-91, chmn., 1992-96, bd. dirs., 1994—. Mem. Metropolis Club (admissions com.). Home: 1095 Park Ave New York NY 10128-1154 Office: McCaffery Ratner Gottlieb & Lane 370 Lexington Ave New York NY 10017-6503

GOTTLIEB, JULIUS JUDAH, podiatrist; b. Jersey City, May 27, 1919; s. Joseph Uziel and Gussie (Farber) G.; m. Charlotte Papernik, Oct. 18, 1942; children: Sheldon, Cynthia, Lorinda, David, Jonathan. Student, NYU, 1938-39, Ill. Coll. Podiatric Medicine, 1940-42; DPM, Ohio Coll. Podiatric Medicine, 1943. Diplomate Am. Podiatric Med. Specialties Bd. Pvt. practice podiatric medicine Washington, 1943-92; pres. Chevy Chase Profl. Cons., 1993-96; past cons. Army Footwear Clinic. Co-inventor fiberglass foot prosthetics and plastic shoe lasts. Podiatry dir. Greater Washington Hebrew Home for the Aged, 1963; pres. Franklin Knolls Citizens Assn., 1963, Ridgefield Citizens Inc., 1994-96, 97—; chmn. com. Nat. Capital Area coun. Boy Scouts Am., 1969-73; pres. Active Retirees of Kehilat Shalom, 1996-98. Recipient Shofar award Boy Scouts Am. Fellow Acad. Ambulatory Foot Surgeons (region 8 sci. chmn. 1987-88); mem. Am. Podiatric Med. Assn. (life), Am. Pub. Health Assn., Am. Podiatric Circulatory Soc., Am. Bd. Foot Surgeons (founding diplomate), D.C. Podiatric Med. Soc. (past pres.), Am. Assn. Foot Specialists (past pres., Foot Specialist of the Yr. 1973), Am. Assn. Individual Investors, Internat. Platform Assn., Am. Physicians Fellowship Inc. for Medicine in Israel, Columbia Heights Bus. Men's Assn. (past pres., Man of Yr. 1964), Parents Assn. U. Md. (co v.p. parents fund 1980-81, co-recipient Outstanding Svc. Award), B'nai B'rith. Republican. Jewish. Home: 15812 Ancient Oak Dr Darnestown MD 20878-2110

GOTTLIEB, LEONARD SOLOMON, pathology educator; b. Boston, May 26, 1927; s. Julius and Jeanette (Miller) G.; m. Dorothy Helen Apt, Mar. 23, 1952; children: Julie Ann, William Apt, Andrew Richard. AB cum laude, Bowdoin Coll., 1946; MD, Tufts U., 1950; MPH, Harvard U., 1969. Diplomate Am. Bd. Anatomic Pathology. Intern in surgery Boston City Hosp., 1950-51, resident Mallory Inst. Pathology, 1951-55; assoc. pathologist Mallory Inst. Pathology, Boston, Mass., 1957-66; assoc. dir. Mallory Inst. Pathology, Boston, 1966-72, dir., 1972—; asst. chief pathology U.S. Naval Hosp., Chelsea, Mass., 1955-57; chief pathology dept. Boston U. Med. Ctr. Hosp., 1973-96; prof. pathology & lab. medicine Sch. Medicine Boston U., 1970—, chmn. dept., 1980—; dir. Mallory Inst. Pathology Found., 1980—; pathologist-in-chief divsn. pathology Boston City Hosp., 1994-96; pathologist-in-chief, divsn. pathology Boston Med. Ctr., 1996—; lectr. Harvard Med. Sch., 1963—; dir. student faculty exch. program Boston U. and Hebrew U., Hadassah Med. Sch., 1988—. Gen. editor Biopsy Pathology Series, Chapman and Hall, 1981-93, editor emeritus, 1993—; mem. editl. bd. Am. Jour. Surg. Pathology; author or co-author approximately 180 publs. and abstracts and 14 book chpts. dealing primarily with exptl. and human diseases of the liver and gastrointestinal tract. Assoc. mem. bd. govs. Hebrew U. Jerusalem, 1991-95, mem. bd. govs., 1995—; pres. New Eng. region Am. Friends of Hebrew U., 1989-97, coun. trustees, 1992—, founder, 1991—; mem. sci. adv. bd. Boston chpt. Israel Cancer Rsch. Fund, 1991-92; co-chair and chair Physicians divsn. Greater Boston chpt. State of Israel Bonds Cabinet, 1991-98; pres. Am. Physicians Fellowship for Medicine in Israel, 1990-93; class sec. 1977 Program for Health Sys. Mgmt., Harvard Bus. Sch., 1995-97. Lt. M.C. USNR, 1955-57, lt. comdr. res. ret. 1963. Recipient Stanley L. Robbins award for excellence in teaching, 1986, Jerusalem City of Peace award Boston chpt. State of Israel Bonds, 1992, Disting. Bowdoin Educator award, 1995, Torch of Learning award Am. Friends of The Hebrew U., 1997, Lion of Judah award State of Israel Bonds, 1998; named hon. mem. faculty medicine Hebrew U., 1987; James Bowdoin scholar, 1945, Bingham scholar, 1944-50. Mem. Am. Soc. for Investigative Pathology, Am. Assn. for Study of Liver Diseases, U.S.-Can. Acad. Pathology, Coll. Am. Pathologists, Am. Soc. Cell Biology, Am. Gastroenterol. Assn., Am. Soc. Clin. Pathologists, Am. Coll. Physician Execs., New Eng. Soc. Pathologists (pres. 1968-69), Mass. Med. Soc., Charles River Med. Soc., Assn. Pathology Chairs, N.Y. Acad. Sci., Alpha Omega Alpha (faculty mem.). Office: Boston U Sch Medicine Dept Path and Lab Medicine 80 E Concord St Boston MA 02118-2307

GOTTLIEB, LESTER M., entrepreneur; b. N.Y.C., May 3, 1932; s. Samuel and Eva (Schoenfeld) G.; children: Cynthia, Curtis, Mark, Alyssa, Adine. BA, CCNY, 1954; postgrad. NYU, 1956. With IBM, 1956-69, mgr. bus. planning for systems devel. div., 1967-69; pres. Data Dimensions, Inc. 1969-84, vice chmn., 1984-90; pres. CAMAC Securities, Ltd., Greenwich, Conn., 1981-91, also chmn. bd. dirs., 1991—; pres. CAMAC Equities, Ltd., 1981—; chmn. bd. dirs. Safe, Inc., Stamford, Conn., Elite Health, Peekskill, N.Y., Ripe and Ready Music, Inc., YPY Group, Stamford; adj. asst. prof. econs. U. Bridgeport; nat. lectr. Assn. Computing Machinery. bd. dirs. Ctr. for Internat. Mgmt. Studies. Nat. Bd. YMCA's 1972-90, Greater N.Y. YMCA; bd. dirs., treas. City Coll. Fund, 1990, v.p., 1996-99. With AUS, 1954-56. Recipient Leo Klauber award, Mark Asa Abbott award; named Vol. of Yr. Greater N.Y. YMCA, 1994. Mem. Am. Arbitration Assn. (comml. arbitrator 1981—), CCNY Alumni Assn. (bd. dirs. 1983, pres. alumni varsity assn. 1987-88, Alumni Svc. award, Athletic Hall of Fame). Republican. Home: 1 Byram Dock St Greenwich CT 06830-6901

GOTTLIEB, MORTON EDGAR, theatrical and film producer; b. Bklyn., May 2, 1921; s. Joseph William and Hilda (Newman) G. BA, Yale U., 1941. Asst. press rep. Theatre Inc., N.Y.C., 1945, bus. mgr., 1946; gen. mgr. Cape Playhouse, Dennis, Mass., 1947-48, New Stages, N.Y.C., 1947-48; mgr. to Robert Morley during Australian prodn., Theatre Royal, Sydney, 1949; gen. mgr. Gilbert Miller Prodns. and Henry Miller's Theatre, N.Y.C., 1948-53; guest lectr. Emerson Coll., Yale U., Columbia U., Northwestern U., Queens Coll., Harvard U., Wesleyan U. Singer charity show: Go Home and Tell Your Mother, Bklyn. Acad. Music, 1928; producer, Broadway, London shows, 1954-62; gen. mgr.: Sail Away, 1961, The Affair, 1962, The Hollow Crown, 1963; co-producer: (with Helen Bonfils) Enter Laughing, 1963, Chips With Everything, 1963, The White House, 1964, The Killing of Sister George, 1966, The Promise, 1967, Lovers, 1968, We Bombed in New Haven, 1968, The Mundy Scheme, 1969, Sleuth, 1970; producer: (films) Sleuth, 1972, Same Time Next Year, 1978, Romantic Comedy, 1982, (plays) Veronica's Room, 1973, Same Time Next Year, 1975, Tribute, 1978, Faith Healer, 1979, Romantic Comedy, 1979, Special Occasions, 1982, Dancing in the End Zone, 1985, Of Thee I Sing-Let 'Em Eat Cake, 1987, Bklyn. Acad. Music; contbr. articles to popular mags. Mem. League N.Y. Theatres. Clubs: Yale; Players. (N.Y.C.). Office: 26 W 9th St Apt 2E New York NY 10011-8923 *My early life was spent dreaming about some day working in the Broadway Theatre, and the rest of my life has been spent living out my youthful fantasies on Broadway. Whether the times have been Ups or Downs, they've all been worth while —and the only way I want to live.*

GOTTLIEB, PAUL, publishing company executive; b. N.Y.C., Jan. 16, 1935; s. Vitaly Matthew and Liza (Rabinowitz) G.; m. Linda Ellen Salzman, June 19, 1960 (div. Nov. 1989); children: Nicholas, Andrew; m. Elisabeth Lohman Scharlatt, Jan. 27, 1990; 1 stepchild Nicholas T. Scharlatt. B.A., Swarthmore Coll., 1956. Lit. agt. William Morris Agy., N.Y.C., 1956-57, 59-60; asst. to pres. Omni Products Corp., N.Y.C., 1960-62; with Am. Heritage Pub. Co. Inc., N.Y.C., 1962-75; pres. Am. Heritage Pub. Co. Inc., 1970-75; chmn. bd. Fulfillment Corp. Am.; pres. Paul Gottlieb Assos., Inc., 1975—, Thames and Hudson Inc., 1976-79; pres., pub., editor-in-chief Harry N. Abrams, Inc., N.Y.C., 1980—; dir. Tanya Corp.; pub. cons., 1967. Guide U.S. exhbns., Moscow, 1959, 61; vice chmn. E. Harlem Coll. and Career Counseling Program, 1971-74; trustee Mus. Modern Art, Dalton Sch.; bd. dirs. Nat. Found. Depressive Illness, Pub. Ctr. for Cultural Resources, N.Y. Studio Sch. Drawing, Painting and Sculpture, Acad. Am. Poets. Mem. Assn. Am. Pubs., Chevalier des Artes et des Lettres. Clubs: Coffee House (N.Y.C.), Century Assn. (N.Y.C.). Home: 1 Fifth Ave New York NY 10003 Office: Harry N Abrams Inc 100 5th Ave Fl 6 New York NY 10011-6999

GOTTLIEB, PAUL MITCHEL, lawyer; b. N.Y.C., Mar. 30, 1954; s. Henry Gottlieb and Thelma Ethel (Friedman) Miller; m. Helene Manya Roiter, Apr. 3, 1982; children: Jordan Seth, Zachary Michael. BA, Hobart Coll., 1976; JD, MBA, Washington U., St. Louis, 1980. Bar: Ill. 1980, U.S. Dist. Ct. (no. dist.) Ill. 1980, N.Y. 1988. Assoc. Rudnick & Wolfe, Chgo., 1980-81; ind. trader Chgo. Bd. of Trade, 1981-83; staff atty. Chgo. Merc. Exch., 1983-84; v.p. market regulation Chgo. Merc. Exchange, 1984-87; commodity counsel Morgan Stanley and Co. Inc., N.Y.C., 1987-89; spl. counsel commodities, futures and derivative products Skadden, Arps, Slate, Meagher & Flom, N.Y.C., 1989-92; ptnr., chair derivative products practice group Seward & Kissel, N.Y.C., 1992-96; dir., sr. counsel structured products & commodities Union Bank of Switzerland, N.Y.C., 1996-98; sr. v.p., dep. gen. counsel PaineWebber Inc., N.Y.C., 1998—; Eisenhower Exch. fellow to New Zealand, 1992; adj. prof. Ctr. for Tech. & Fin. Svcs. Polytechnic U.; adviser risk mgmt. adv. bd. Stern Sch. of Bus., NYU. Contbr. chpts. to books, articles to profl. jours. Mem. Futures Industry Assn. (law and compliance divsn.), Securities Industry Assn. (law and compliance divsn.), Bond Market Assn. Jewish. Avocations: coaching youth hockey and lacrosse, tennis, golf. Home: 11 Highpoint Pl West Windsor NJ 08550 Office: PaineWebber Inc 1285 Ave of the Americas New York NY 10019

GOTTLIEB, RICHARD DOUGLAS, media executive; b. Davenport, Iowa, June 12, 1942; s. David and Elaine Gottlieb; m. Harriet Barg; children: Michael, Jason, Allison, Meghan. BS, U. Ariz., 1964. Mgr.-in-tng. Madison (Wis.) Newspapers, Inc., 1965-68, prodn. coordinator, 1968-72, treas., dir., 1972-80, gen. mgr., 1973-80; pub. Racine (Wis.) Journal-Times, 1980-85; v.p. Lee Enterprises, Inc., Davenport, 1985-86, pres., chief oper. officer, 1986—; bd. dirs. Madison Newspapers, Inc., NAPP Systems, Inc., San Marcos, Calif., Newspaper Advt. Bur., Washington. Avocations: hunting, tennis. Office: Lee Enterprises Inc 215 N Main St Ste 400 Davenport IA 52801-1924*

GOTTLIEB, RICHARD MATTHEW, psychiatrist, consultant; b. N.Y.C., Aug. 26, 1943; m. Josephine L. Wright; 2 children. BS (hon.), U. Chgo., 1965; MD, U. Chgo. Sch. Medicine, 1969. Lic. N.Y., Conn., Calif. Asst. dir. Outpatient Svcs. Bronx Mcpl. Hosp. Ctr., N.Y., 1973-1974; attending psychiatrist Montefiore Hosp. and Med. Ctr., 1977-82; asst. attending physician Montefiore Hosp. Ctr., 1974—; adjunct attending physician St. Luke's/Roosevelt Hosp. Ctr., 1990—; attending physician Dept. Psychiatry Bronx Mcpl. Hosp. Ctr., 1973-74; cons. Housatonic Mental Health Ctr., Lakeville, Conn., 1988—; psychiatric cons. The Marvelwood Sch., Cornwall, Conn., 1979—, The Salisbury Sch., Lakeville, Conn., 1986—, The Indian Mountain Sch., 1994—; consulting staff The Sharon (Conn.) Hosp., 1988—; assoc. clin. prof. The Albert Einstein Coll. of Medicine, Bronx, N.Y., 1996—; faculty The Psychoanalytic Inst. of the Sch. Medicine of N.Y. U., 1989—, The N.Y. Psychoanalytic Inst., 1991—; sec. N.Y. Psychoanalytic Soc.; chmn. Scientific Program Com., N.Y. Psychoanalytic Soc., A.A. Brill award Lecture Com. N.Y. Psychoanalytic Soc.; nat. treas. Coun. for Advancement of Psychoanalytic Edn.; keynote spkr. Ind. Schs. Health Assn., 1997. Contbr. numerous papers and presentations in field. Recipient Heinz Hartmann award N.Y. Psychoanalytic Inst., 1994. Mem. Am. Psychoanalytic Assn., N.Y. Psychoanalytic Soc., Psychoanalytic Assn. N.Y., Internat. Psychoanalytical Assn., Am. Soc. for Adolescent Psychiatry, N.Y. Soc. for Adolescent Psychiatry, N.Y. Psychoanalytic Inst. (Heinz Hartmann award com.). Home: 170 Fairchild Rd Sharon CT 06069-2440

GOTTLIEB, ROBERT ADAMS, publisher; b. N.Y.C., Apr. 29, 1931; s. Charles and Martha (Keen) G.; m. Maria Tucci, Apr. 26, 1969; children—Roger, Elizabeth, Nicholas. B.A., Columbia, 1952; postgrad., Cambridge (Eng.) U., 1952-54. Editor-in-chief, v.p. Simon & Schuster, 1955-68; editor-in-chief Alfred A Knopf, Inc., N.Y.C., 1968-87, exec. v.p., 1968-73, pres., 1973-87; editor New Yorker mag., 1987-92. Author: Reading Jazz, 1996. Mem. Phi Beta Kappa. Home: 237 E 48th St New York NY 10017-1538

GOTTLIEB, SHERRY GERSHON, author, editor; b. L.A., Apr. 6, 1948; d. Harry L. and Evelyn Jellen) Gershon; m. David Neil Gottlieb, Aug. 12, 1971 (div. 1973). BA in Dramatic Arts, U. Calif., Berkeley, 1969. Exec. sec. Budget Films, L.A., 1970-72; script reader United Artists, L.A., 1971-74; owner A Change of Hobbit bookstore, L.A. and Santa Monica, Calif., 1972-91; class coord. UCLA Extension, 1982. Author: Hell No, We Won't Go! Evading the Draft During the Vietnam War, 1991, Love Bite, 1994. Named Spl. Guest of Honor, Westercon, 1979. Mem. PEN USA. Democrat. Avocations: reading, cooking, Scrabble, Trivial Pursuit, travel.

GOTTO, ANTONIO MARION, JR., internist, educator; b. Nashville, Tenn., Oct. 10, 1935; s. Antonio M. and Reather (Gray) G.; m. Anita Louise Safford, July 21, 1959; children: Jennifer, Gillian, Teresa. B.A. magna cum laude, Vanderbilt U., 1957, M.D., 1965; D. Phil., Oxford (Eng.) U., 1961; LL.D. (hon.), Abilene Christian U., 1979; M.D. (hon.), U. Bologna, 1982. Diplomate: Am. Bd. Internal Medicine. Intern Mass. Gen. Hosp., Boston, 1965-66, resident, 1966-67; practice medicine specializing in internal medicine, 1967—; head molecular disease br. Nat. Heart and Lung Inst. NIH, Bethesda, Md., 1969-71; dir. and prin. investigator Lipid Research Clinic, Houston, 1971-77; prof. medicine, chief dir., arteriosclerosis and lipoprotein rsch. Baylor Coll. Medicine, Houston, 1971-96; dir., prin. investigator specialized center rsch in arteriosclerosis Nat. Heart, Lung and Blood Inst., 1971-96; dir., prin. investigator Spl. Ctr. Rsch. Arteriosclerosis Nat. Heart, Lung, and Blood Inst., 1971-96; J.S. Abercrombie prof. Baylor Coll. Medicine, 1976-96, Disting. Service prof., 1985-96; sci. dir. Meth. Hosp. and Baylor Nat. Research and Demonstration Center, 1974-83, 87-90; Bob and Vivian Smith prof. and chmn. dept. medicine Baylor Coll. Medicine, 1977-96; chief internal medicine svcs. The Meth. Hosp., 1977-96; dean Cornell Univ. Medical Coll., 1997—; provost medical affairs Cornell Univ., 1997—; hon. guest lectr. various med. socs., schs. and hosps., 1972—; mem. nat. diabetes adv. bd. HEW (now HHS), 1977-84; mem. steering com. Italian-Am. com. on cardiovascular disease NIH, 1978—; mem. adv. council Nat. Heart, Lung and Blood Inst., 1987-91; hon. prof. U. Buenos Aires, 1985. Author: (with Michael E. DeBakey), The Living Heart, 1977, The Living Heart Diet, 1984, The New Living Heart Diet, 1996, The New Living Heart, 1997; contbr. articles on biochem and cardiovascular rsch. to profl. publs.; mem. editorial bd. Jour. Biol. Chemistry, 1976-81, Advanced in Lipid Rsch., 1973-78, Am. Heart Jour., 1981—, Arteriosclerosis, 1981-89, Circulation Rsch., 1974-79, Cardiovascular Rsch. Ctr. Bull., 1972—; co-editor Atherosclerosis Rev. Series, 1976-92, Jour. Cardiovascular Risk, 1994—. Mem. sci. adv. bd. Fondation Cardiologique Princesse Liliane, Brussels, Belgium, 1976—, Lorenzini Found., Milan, Italy, Fritz Thyssen Found., Cologne, Germany; mem. Mission of Houston Econ. Devel. Council, 1985. Served with USPHS, 1967-69; walkathon chmn. Juvenile Diabetes Found., 1986. Decorated knight Order of Merit (Italy); Order of the Lion (Finland); recipient Albert Weinstein award, 1965, Laurea ad Honorem, U. Bologna, Seale Harris award So. Med. assn., 1995; John A. Hartford Found. grantee, 1971-75; named hon. cons. Adm. Bristol Hosp., Istanbul, Turkey, Houston Internat. Exec. Yr., 1987. Fellow Am. Coll. Cardiology; mem. Inst. Medicine of NAS, Am. Soc. Clin. Investigation (v.p. 1980-81), So. Soc. Clin. Investigation, Internat. Soc. of Atherosclerosis (Achievement award 1982, pres. 1985—), Am. Assn. Physicians, Am. Soc. Biol. Chemists, Am. Diabetes Assn., Am. Heart Assn. (pres. 1983-84, past pres. 1984-86, Paul Ledbetter award for Disting. Service, Paul Dudley White award for Outstanding Contbns., Gold Heart award 1989), Am. Bd. Internal Medicine, Am. Assn. of Rhodes Scholars, Am. Longevity Assn., Alpha Omega Alpha. Mem. Ch. of Christ. Club: River Oaks Country. Home: 435 E 70th St Apt 31 J K New York NY 10021-5351 Office: Weill Med of Cornell U Med Coll 1300 York Ave Rm F 105 New York NY 10021-4805*

GOTTRON, FRANCIS ROBERT, III, small business owner; b. Youngstown, Ohio, Dec. 26, 1953; s. Francis R. Jr. and Norma J. (Giba) G.; m. Joyce L. Garling, Nov. 25, 1975. BSBA cum laude, Youngstown State U., 1978. With Commonwealth Land Title Youngstown, Inc., 1972-87, Lender's Svc., Inc., 1979—, Title Agy. Michaels, 1984—; examiner delinquent tax Mahoning County Prosecutor's Office, 1989—; owner, prin. Mahoning County Recorder's Office, Youngstown, 1978—; examiner Fed. Title Agy., 1982—; pres. M&G Title Search Inc.; appraiser Probate Ct., 1989—. Democrat. Lutheran. Avocations: fantasy baseball, camping, forestry, environment. Home: 9165 New Rd North Jackson OH 44451-9707 Office: PO Box 268 Youngstown OH 44501-0268

GOTTS, ILENE KNABLE, lawyer; b. Phila., Nov. 25, 1959; d. Harry Lee and Ethel Beatrice (Teitelman) Knable; m. Michael D. Gotts, May 25, 1986; children: Isaac, Samuel. BA magna cum laude with hon., U. Md., 1980; JD cum laude, Georgetown U., 1984. Bar: D.C. 1984, N.Y., 1997, U.S. Dist. Ct. D.C. 1986, U.S. Ct. Appeals (D.C. cir.) 1985, U.S. Dist. Ct. Md. 1987, U.S. Ct. Appeals (fed. cir.) 1989, U.S. Supreme Ct. 1988. Staff atty. FTC, 1984-86; assoc. Foley & Lardner, Washington, 1986-92, ptnr., head legis./adminstrv. group, antitrust practice group, 1992-96; ptnr. Wachtell, Lipton, Rosen & Katz, N.Y.C., 1996—; adj. prof. George Washington U. Law Ctr., 1995-96. Mem. editorial bd. The Practical Lawyer, 1994—; mem. editorial adv. bd. The Antitrust Counselor, 1995—; contbr. articles to profl. jours. Recipient Sklar award; Mary Elizabeth Robey scholar. Mem. ABA (health care com. antitrust sect. 1988—, vice chair intellectual property com. 1994-97, consumer protection com. 1994—, vice chair Clayton Act com. 1997-98, chmn. 1998—), FBA (chair health care com. of antitrust sect. 1991-95, chair antitrust and trade regulation sect. 1995-97), D.C. Bar (steering com., antitrust and trade regulation com. 1994-95), N.Y. Bar Assn. (task force of women and the law), Am. Law Inst., Washington Coun. Lawyers (exec. com. and bd. dirs. 1988-97, pres. 1994-95), Mortar Board, Phi Beta Kappa, Phi Kappa Phi, Pi Sigma Alpha, Phi Alpha Theta. Democrat. Jewish. Office: Wachtell Lipton Rosen & Katz 51 W 52d St New York NY 10019

GOTTSCHALK, ALEXANDER, radiologist, diagnostic radiology educator; b. Chgo., Mar. 23, 1932; s. Louis R. and Fruma (Kasden) G.; m. Jane Rosenbloom, Aug. 13, 1960; children: Rand, Karen, Amy. B.A. magna cum laude, Harvard U., 1954; M.D., Washington U., St. Louis, 1958. Diplomate: Am. Bd. Radiology, Am. Bd. Nuclear Medicine. Intern U. Ill. Research and Edn. Hosps., Chgo., 1958-59; resident U. Chgo., 1959-62, asst. prof., 1964-66, assoc. prof., 1966-68, prof. radiology, 1968-74, chmn. dept. radiology, 1971-72; research assoc. Donner Lab., Lawrence Radiol. Lab., Calif., 1962-64; dir. Franklin McLean Meml. Research Hosp., 1967-74; prof. and dir. nuclear medicine Sch. Medicine Yale U., New Haven, 1974-77, acting chmn. radiology, 1980-81, vice-chmn. radiology, 1977-89; prof. radiology Mich. State U., East Lansing, 1990—. Contbr. chpts. to books, articles to publs. in field. Fleischner lectr., 1983. Fellow Am. Coll. Radiology, Am. Coll. Chest Physicians; mem. Radiol. Soc. N.Am. (2d v.p. 1977), Assn. Univ. Radiologists (pres. 1971), Soc. Nuclear Medicine (pres. 1974-75), Am. Roentgen Ray Soc., Fleischner Soc. (treas. 1978-83, pres. 1989-90), Phi Beta Kappa, Alpha Omega Alpha. Home: 4246 Van Atta Rd Okemos MI 48864-3137 Office: Radiology Bldg Rm 120 Mich State U East Lansing MI 48824-1303

GOTTSCHALK, ALFRED, college chancellor; b. Oberwesel, Germany, Mar. 7, 1930; came to U.S., 1939, naturalized, 1945; s. Max and Erna (Trum-Gerson) G.; m. Deanna Zeff, 1977; children by previous marriage: Marc Hillel, Rachel Lisa. AB, Bklyn. Coll., 1952; MA with honors, Hebrew Union Coll.-Jewish Inst. Religion, 1957; PhD, U. So. Calif., 1965, STD (hon.), 1968, LLD (hon.), 1976; LLD (hon.), U. Cin., 1976, Xavier U., 1981, Mt. St. Joseph Coll., 1995, No. Ky. U., 1996; DHL (hon.), U. Judaism, 1971, Jewish Theol. Sem., 1986, Bklyn. Coll., 1991, Trinity Coll., 1996; LittD (hon.), Dropsie U., 1974, St. Thomas Inst., 1982; D Religious Edn. (hon.), Loyola-Marymount U., 1977; DD (hon.), NYU, 1985. Ordained rabbi, 1957;. Dir. Hebrew Union Coll., Jewish Inst. Religion, L.A., 1957-59, dean, 1959-71, prof. Bible and Jewish intellectual history, 1965—, pres., 1971-95, chancellor, 1996—; hon. fellow Hebrew U., Jerusalem, 1972, Oxford Ctr. for Hebrew and Jewish Studies, 1994. Author: Your Future as a Rabbi-A Calling that Counts, 1967, (translator) Hesed in the Bible, 1967, The Man Must be the Message, 1968, Jewish Ecumenism and Jewish Survival, 1968, Ahad Ha-Am, Maimonides and Spinoza, 1969, Ahad Ha-Am as Bible Critic, 1971, A Jubilee of the Spirit, 1972, Israel and the Diaspora: A New Look, 1974, Limits of Ecumenicity, 1979, Israel and Reform Judaism: A Zionist Perspective, 1979, Ahad Ha-Am and Leopold Zunz: Two Perspectives on the Wissenschaft Des Judentums, 1980, Hebrew Union College and Its Impact on World Progressive Judaism, 1980, Diaspora Zionism: Achievements and Problems, 1980, What Ecumenism Means to a Jew, 1981, Introduction: Religion in a Post-Holocaust World, 1982, Problematics in the Future of American Jewish Community, 1982, Introduction to the American Synagogue in the Nineteenth Century, 1982, A Strategy for Non-Orthodox Judaism in Israel, 1982, Our problems and Our Future: Jews and America, 1983, From the Kingdom of Night to the Kingdom of God: Jewish Christian Relations and the Search for Religious Authenticity after the Holocaust, 1983, The Making of a Contemporary Reform Rabbi, 1984, Is Yom Kippur Obsolete?, 1985, Ahad Ha-am: Confronting the Plight of Judaism, 1987, To Learn and To Teach, Your Future as a Rabbi, 1988, Preface to Gezer V: The Field I Caves, 1988, The American Reform Rabbinate Retrospect and Prospect, A Personal View, 1988, The German Pogrom of November 1938 and the Reaction of American Jewry, 1988, Building Unity in Diversity 1989, Ahad Ha'am and the Jewish National Spirit (Hebrew), 1992; contbr. to Studies in Jewish Bibliography, History, and Literature, 1971, The Yom Kippur War: Israel and the Jewish People, 1974, The Image of Man in Genesis and the Ancient Near East, 1976, The Public Function of the Jewish Scholar, 1978, The Reform Movement and Israel: A New Perspective, 1978, The Use of Reason in Maimonides--An Evaluation by Ahad Ha-Am, 1993; also numerous articles to profl. jours. Mem. Pres. Johnson's Com. on EEO, 1964-66, Gov.'s Poverty Support Corps Program, 1964-66, Pres.'s Commn. on Holocaust, 1979, U.S. Holocaust Meml. Coun., 1980-92, 96— (exec. com., 1980-87, 96—, chmn. edn. com., 1987-88, chmn. acad. com., 1988—, com. on conscience, 1996—); chmn. N.Am. Assocs. Internat. Ctr. Univ. Teaching of Jewish Civilization, 1982-93; bd. trustees Am. Sch. Oriental Rsch., Albright Inst. Archaeol. Rsch.; bd. govs. Oxford Ctr. for Hebrew and Jewish Studies, 1995; exec. com. Nat. Underground Railroad Freedom Ctr., 1997, Nat. Adv. Ctr. Bd., Nat. Underground Freedom Ctr., 1996—; mem. coun. World Union Jewish Studies, 1997. Recipient award for contbns. to edn. L.A. City Coun., 1971, Human Relations award Am. Jewish Com., 1971, Tower of David award for cultural contbn. to Israel and Am., 1972, Gold medallion Jewish Nat. Fund, 1972, Alumnus of Yr. award Bklyn. Coll., 1972, Myrtle Wreath award Hadassah, 1977, Brandeis award Z.O.A., 1977, Nat. Brotherhood award NCCJ, 1979, Alfred Gottschalk Chair in Communal Svc. HUC, 1979, Jerusalem City of Peace award 1988, Defender of Jerusalem award honoree, 1990, Isaac M. Wise award, 1991, Heritage award Jewish Club of 1933, 1991, Nat. award NCCJ, 1994, Shanghai Acad. Social Scis. award, 1994, others, Xavier Medallion, Xavier U., 1996; grantee State Dept./Smithsonian Instn., 1963, 67. Mem. AAUP, NEA, Union Am. Hebrew Congregations and Ctrl. Conf. Am. Rabbis (exec. com., bd. govs. Hebrew Union Coll.), Soc. Study Religion, Am. Acad. Religion, Soc. Bibl. Lit. and Exegesis, Internat. Conf. Jewish Communal Svc., Israel Exploration Soc., So. Calif. Assn. Liberal Rabbis (past pres.), So. Calif. Jewish Hist. Soc. (hon. pres.), World Union Jewish Studies (internat. coun.), World Union Progressive Judaism (gov. bd.), Coun. for Initiatives in Jewish Edn. (bd. dirs.). Home: 2401 Ingleside Ave Apt 12G Cincinnati OH 45206-2118 Office: Hebrew Union College Jewish Inst 3101 Clifton Ave Cincinnati OH 45220-2488 *I value the need for the individual to feel unique and for the collective to remain hospitable to diversity. I believe in unity without uniformity and in humanity's capacity to redeem himself.*

GOTTSCHALK, CHARLES M., international energy consultant; b. Bochum, Germany, Feb. 2, 1928; emigrated to U.S., 1941, naturalized, 1949; s. Josef and Elsbeth Gottschalk; m. Marianne Ida Besser, Dec. 24, 1948; children: Diane Linda, Leslie Anne. B Engring. Scis., Cleve. State U., 1950; MA, Pa. State U., 1951; MLS, Catholic U., 1966. Research analyst Library of Congress, 1951-54, phys. sci. adminstr., head reference sect., sci. and tech. div., 1956-62, chief stack and reader div., 1962, head systems identification and analysis sect., 1962-63; instrumentation physicist Nat. Bur. Standards, 1954-56; information systems specialist Atomic Energy Comm., 1963-66, dir. libraries, 1966-69; sr. officer Internat. Atomic Energy Agy., Vienna, Austria, 1969-73, Energy Research and Devel. Adminstrn., Washington, 1973-77, Dept. Energy, 1977-79; sr. ofcl. UNESCO, Paris, 1979-88, cons., expert, 1988-94; cons., expert CMG Internat. Energy Consultancy, Paris and Washington, 1994—; liaison officer/registrar Internat. Tech. U., London and Paris, 1989-93; liaison officer World Fedn. Engring. Orgns., London and Paris, 1995-96; lectr. Dept. Agr. Grad. Sch., 1964-66; cons. Arctic Inst. N.Am., 1954-59; rsch. asst. Ohio State U., 1958-59; exec. sec. oper. com. Fed. Coun. Sci. and Tech. Com. on Sci. and Tech. Info., 1965, exec. sec. panel edn. and tng., 1965-66, mem. panel info. scis. and tech., 1966-68, mem. nuclear cross sect. adv. group, 1965-69; mem. com. on terminology World Energy Conf., 1980—. Author articles, monographs. Served with AUS, 1946-47; Served with USMCR, 1947-51. NSF grantee, 1961-62. Mem. World Energy Coun., Assn. Energy Engrs., Mensa, Beta Phi Mu.

GOTTSCHALK, FRANK KLAUS, real estate company executive; b. Berlin, Jan. 25, 1932; came to U.S. 1947, naturalized 1953; s. Richard and Grete Johanna (Singer) G.; m. Ellen Ruth Meinhardt, June 16, 1957. Student N.Y. Inst. Banking & Fin., N.Y.C., 1952-53, NYU, 1955-56. Lic. comml. real estate broker. Trainee, investment securities Newborg & Co. mem. N.Y. Stock Exchange, N.Y.C., 1951-52; fin. analyst Bendix Luitweiler & Co. Investment Bankers, N.Y.C., 1952-53; assoc. broker, v.p., dir. Peter F. Pasbjerg & Co., Inc., Mortgage Bankers, Newark, N.J., 1955-62; v.p., dir. Baldwin Bros., Inc. Real Estate Investors, Erie, Pa., 1962—; pres., treas., dir. The Baldwin-Gottschalk Group, Investment Real Estate, asset. mgmt. cons., Erie, Pa., Charleston, W.Va., 1994—; pres. Baldwin-Gottschalk, Inc. Real Estate and Mortgage Financing, N.Y.C., Erie, Charleston, 1962—; pres., treas., dir. Baldwin Gottschalk Properties, Erie, 1967—, Balgot Realty Corp., Erie, 1963—, Balgot Bldg. Corp., Erie, 1967—; pres. The Kanawha Realty Investment Group, Investment Real Estate, Charleston, Erie, 1990—; pres., treas., dir. Kanawha Realty & Devel. Corp., Charleston, 1959—, Associated Properties Holdings, Inc., Charleston, 1962—; pres. Assoc. Properties Holdings Pension Trust, Charleston, W. Va., 1982—; pres., dir. APH Securities, Charleston, W. Va., 1990—; trustee Assoc. Properties Holding Retirement Trust, Charleston, 1982—; mng. ptnr. Kanawha-Monarch Holdings, Erie, 1980—, Balgot-Kanawha Holdings, Erie, Pa., 1994—. Trustee, Erie Philharm., 1971-90; corporator Gannon U., 1980—. Served with U.S. Army, 1953-55, ETO. Mem. Internat. Real Estate Inst., Erie Club, Aviation Country Club Erie, Addison Reserve Country Club, Delray Bch., Fla. Office: Baldwin Gottschalk Inc 5 W 10th St Erie PA 16501-1492

GOTTSCHALK, KEITH EDWARD, journalist; b. Willoughby, Ohio, Nov. 19, 1962; s. Edward and Constance (Tanski) G.; children: Eric, Karl; m. Veronica Lynn Worley, Oct. 4, 1997. BA, Cleve. State U., 1986. Sportswriter The News-Herald, Willoughby, 1980-81, The Cleve. Press, 1981-82; asst. sports info. dir. Cleve. State U., 1982-83; sportswriter The Geauga Times-Leader, Chardon, Ohio, 1983; asst. editor The Kirtland Enterprise, Willoughby, 1984-85; pub. rels. asst. U.S. Army Recruiting, Cleve., 1987-89, 91-96; contbg. writer The News-Herald, 1989-90; editor Dwight (Ill.) Star & Herald, 1996-97; Bloomington bur. reporter The Peoria (Ill.) Jour.-Star, 1997—; talk show host WJBC-AM, Bloomington, Ill., 1999—. V.p. Pub. Svc. Consortium Greater Cleve., 1995; mem. Fedn. Cmty. Planning, Cleve., 1994-96. Mem. Soc. Profl. Journalists. Home: 1102 S University St Normal IL 61761-3536

GOTTSCHALK, SISTER MARY THERESE, nun, hospital administrator; b. Doellwang, Germany, June 21, 1931; came to U.S., 1953, naturalized, 1959; d. John and Sabina (Dietz) G. BS in Pharmacy, Creighton U., 1960; M.H.A., St. Louis U., 1970. Joined Sisters of the Sorrowful Mother, Roman Catholic Ch, 1952. Dir. pharmacy St. Mary's Hosp., Roswell, N.Mex., 1960-68; chief exec. officer St. Mary's Hosp., 1972-74; asst. adminstr. St. John Med. Ctr., Tulsa, 1970-72; chief exec. officer St. John Med. Ctr., 1974—; pres. St. John Health Sys., 1982—, Marian Health Sys., 1989—. Vol. ARC, United Way. Fellow Am. Coll. Hosp. Adminstrs.; mem. Cath. Health Assn. (bd. dirs.), Am. Hosp. Assn. (ho. of dels., regional policy bd.), Okla. Hosp. Assn. (pres. 1984), Tulsa Hosp. Coun. (past pres.), Okla. Conf. Cath. Hosps. (past pres.), Tulsa C. of C. Office: St John Med Ctr 1923 S Utica Ave Tulsa OK 74104-6502*

GOTTSCHALK, MILTON JOE, management consultant; b. Albany, N.Y., May 21, 1947; s. Karl and Liesel (Nussbaum) G.; m. Emily Jennifer Garr, Sept. 2, 1990; children: Eric, Marc. BS, Cornell U., 1969, M in Engring., 1970; MBA, U. Houston, 1976. Chem. engr. Rohm and Haas Co., Deer Park, Tex., 1971-78; raw material purchasing specialist Rohm and Haas Co., Phila., 1978-80, process planning mgr., 1980-83, ops. planning project mgr., 1983-86, bus. devel. mgr., 1986-88, distbn. and packaging dept. mgr., 1991-97; bus. mgr. Plaskon Corp., Phila., 1988-91; prin. cons. Gottschalk and Assocs., Voorhees, N.J., 1997—. V.p. Chanticleer Hill Houses, Cherry Hill, N.J., 1990-91, bd. mem., 1988-91. Mem. Am. Inst. Chem. Engrs., Coun. Logistics Mgmt., Am. Assn. Individual Investors, Warehouse Edn. Rsch. Coun. Avocation: sailing. Home and Office: Gottschalk and Assocs 41 Covington Ln Voorhees NJ 08043-4107

GOTTSCHALK, STEPHEN ELMER, lawyer; b. Rochester, Minn., Oct. 9, 1947; s. Elmer H. and Ruth F. (Thurley) G.; m. Lorilyn J. Dopp, Feb. 14, 1970; children: Andrew Stephen, Stephanie Beth, Lorissa Christine, Michael Donald. BS, Valparaiso U., 1969, JD, 1972. Bar: Minn. 1972, U.S. Dist. Ct. (Minn.) 1972. Judicial clk. Minn. Supreme Ct., St. Paul, 1972-73; assoc. Dorsey & Whitney, Minn., 1973-78, ptnr., 1979—, dept. head employee benefits dept., 1986-91, 98—; adj. prof. employee benefits Sch. Law U. Minn. Mem. pres. adv. coun., Valparaiso U., 1983—; bd. dirs. Twin Cities Habitat for Humanity, Inc. Recipient Service award Valparaiso Alumni Assn., 1986. Mem. Midwest Pension Conf. Avocation: squash. Home: 4339 Fremont Ave S Minneapolis MN 55409-1720 Office: Dorsey & Whitney 220 S 6th St Ste 2200 Minneapolis MN 55402-1498

GOTTSCHALK, THOMAS A., lawyer; b. Decatur, Ind., July 5, 1942; s. John Simson and Edith (Liechty) G.; m. Barbara J. Risen, Aug. 28, 1965; children: Deborah, Diane. AB, Earlham Coll., 1964; JD, U. Chgo., 1967. Bar: Ill. 1967, D.C. 1986, U.S. Supreme Ct. Assoc. Kirkland & Ellis, Chgo., 1967-73, ptnr., 1973-94; sr. v.p., gen. counsel Gen. Motors Corp., 1994—. Trustee Earlham Coll., Richmond, Ind., 1972—, chmn., 1985-91. Mem. ABA (mem. litigation, antitrust and criminal law sects.), D.C. Bar Assn., Chgo. Coun. of Lawyers, Conf. Bd. Coun. of Chief Legal Officers. Office: Gen Motors Corp PO Box 33122 Detroit MI 48232-5122*

GOTTSCHALK, WALTER HELBIG, mathematician, educator; b. Lynchburg, Va., Nov. 3, 1918; s. Carl and Lula (Helbig) G.; m. Margaret Hemsworth, Aug. 27, 1952; children: Heather, Steven. B.S., U. Va., 1939, M.A., 1942, Ph.D. in Math, 1944; M.A. (hon.), Wesleyan U., Middletown, Conn., 1964. From instr. to prof. math. U. Pa., 1944-63, chmn. dept., 1955-58; prof. math. Wesleyan U., 1963-82, prof. emeritus, 1982—, chmn. dept., 1964-69, 70-71; Mem. Inst. Advanced Study, Princeton, 1947-48; research assoc. Yale U., 1960-61. Author: (with G.A. Hedlund) Topological Dynamics, 1955; Mem. editorial bd.: Math. Systems Theory, 1967-75; Contbr. articles to profl. jours. Mem. Am. Math. Soc. (asso. editor proc. 1954-56, asso. sec. for East 1971-76), Math. Assn. Am., Soc. Indsl. and Applied Math., AAUP, Phi Beta Kappa, Sigma Xi. Democrat. Unitarian. Home: 500 Angell St Apt 414 Providence RI 02906-4455

GOTTSCHALL, EDWARD MAURICE, graphic arts company executive; b. N.Y.C., Dec. 28, 1915; s. Myer and Stephanie (Kraus) G.; m. Lee Beatrice Natale, Feb. 6, 1943 (dec. 1984); 1 child, Robert J.; m. Alice J. Wise, Jan. 20, 1985. B.S., CCNY, 1937; M.S., Columbia U., 1938. Mng. editor Graphic Arts Prodn. Yearbook, Colton Press, 1937-51; editor Art Direction, 1952-69; sr. editor Popular Merchandising Co., Passaic, N.J., 1964-67; co-pub., editorial dir. Advt. Trade Publs., Inc., 1967-69; exec. dir. Am. Inst. Graphic Arts, N.Y.C., 1969-75; exec. v.p. Internat. Typeface Corp., N.Y.C., 1975-86; vice chmn. Internat. Typeface Corp., 1986-90; editor U & lc, 1981-89, cons. editor, 1990—; v.p. Design Processing Internat., Inc., 1977-85; U.S. rep. Assn. Typographique Internat., 1978-89, chmn. world conf. on typographic communication, 1988; lectr. Pratt Inst. Evening Art Sch., 1947-64, N.Y. U., 1955-64. Author: (with F.C. Rodewald) Commercial Art as a Business, 3d edit., 1972, Vision '80s, 1980, Graphic Communication '80s, 1981, Typographic Communications Today, 1988, reprinted 1992; co-editor: Advertising Directions, vols. 1-4, 1960-64, Editor Typographic i, 1969-79; cons. editor: Graphic Arts Manual, 1973-80; contbr. essay to Contemporary Masterworks, 1992. Served with USAAF, 1942-45, ETO. Mem. Type Dirs. Club (past pres., Spl. award 1963), N.Y. Club of Printing House Craftsmen (Fellowship award 1993), Phi Delta Pi. Club: Masons. Home: 63 Highland Ave Eastchester NY 10707-3627 Office: 2 Dag Hammarskjold Plz New York NY 10017-2905 *Knowledge is never enough. One must be able to evaluate, to judge, to have taste, and to make decisions.*

GOTTSCHALL, JOAN B., judge; b. Oak Ridge, Tenn., Apr. 23, 1947; d. Herbert A. and Elaine (Reichbaum) G. BA cum laude, Smith Coll., Mass., 1969; JD, Stanford Univ., Calif., 1973. Bar: Ill. 1973. Assoc. Jenner & Block, 1973-76, 78-81, ptnr., 1981-82; staff atty. Fed. Defender Program, 1976-78, Univ. of Chgo., Office of Legal Counsel, 1983-84; magistrate judge U.S. Dist. Ct. (no. dist.) Ill., Chgo., 1984-97, judge, 1997—; mem. vis. com. Divinity Sch., Univ. of Chgo.; mem. vis. com. on coll. and student activities Univ. of Chgo., co-vice-chmn. Chgo. Bar Assn. Alliance for Women; bd. dirs. Just the Beginning Found.; mem. com. Seventh Cir. Judicial Conf. Mem. Am. Bar Assn., Chgo. Bar Assn., Law Club of the City of Chgo., Am. Inns of Ct., Am. Law Inst. Office: Everett McKinley Dirksen Bldg ste 1978 219 S Dearborn St Chicago IL 60604-1801*

GOTTSCHLICH, GARY WILLIAM, lawyer; b. Dayton, Ohio, Aug. 27, 1946; s. William Frederick and Rosemary Teresa G.; m. Sharon Melanie Plunkett, Oct. 7, 1978; children: David W., Andrew J., Thomas M. BS, U. Dayton, 1968; cert., Univ. Coll., London, 1970; J.D., U. Notre Dame, 1971. Bar: Ohio 1971. Asst. pros. atty. Montgomery County, Dayton, 1971-73; assoc. Young, Pryor, Lynn & Jerardi, 1973-80, ptnr., 1980-84; ptnr. Louis & Froelich, Dayton, 1984-87; ptnr. Porter, Wright, Morris & Arthur, Dayton, 1987-97, Gottschlicl & Protune, 1997—. Served to capt. USAR. Mem. ABA, Assn. Trial Lawyers Am., Ohio Bar Assn. (bd. govs. litigation sect.), Dayton Bar Assn. (treas. 1981-82), Miami Valley Trial Lawyers Assn. (founding). Roman Catholic. Avocations: golf, sailing, squash. Home: 5260 Little Woods Ln Dayton OH 45429-2124 Office: Gottschlich & Portune LLP 110 N Main St Ste 900 Dayton OH 45402-1786

GOTTSTEIN, BARNARD JACOB, retail and wholesale food company executive, real estate executive; b. Des Moines, Dec. 30, 1925; s. Jacob B. and Anna (Jacobs) G.; children: Sandra, James, Ruth Anne, David, Robert; m. Rachel Landau, July, 1986. BA in Econs. and Bus., U. Wash., 1949; LLD (hon.), U. Alaska, Fairbanks, 1991. Pres. J.B. Gottstein & Co., Anchorage, 1953-90; chmn. bd. Carr-Gottstein Inc., Anchorage, 1974-90; ret., 1990—; dir. United Bank Alaska, Anchorage, 1975-86. Commr. Alaska State Human Rights Commn., 1963-68; del. Dem. Nat. Conv., 1964, 68, 76, 88, 92; committeeman Dem. Nat. Com., 1976-80; v.p. State Bd. Edn., Alaska, 1983-87, pres., 1987-91. Served with USAF, 1944-45. Jewish. Office: Carr-Gottstein Properties 550 W 7th Ave Ste 1540 Anchorage AK 99501-3567

GOTTWALD, BRUCE COBB, chemical company executive; b. Richmond, Va., Sept. 28, 1933; s. Floyd Dewey and Anne Ruth (Cobb) G.; m. Nancy Hays, Dec. 22, 1956; children: Bruce Cobb Jr., Mark Hays, Thomas Edward. BS, Va. Mil. Inst., 1954; postgrad., U. Va., Inst. Paper Chemistry, Appleton, Wis., U. Richmond; LLD (hon.), Va. Union U., 1990. Chemist Albemarle Paper Mfg. Co., Richmond, Va., from 1956, asst. sec., 1960; v.p. Ethyl Corp., Richmond, Va., 1962-64, sec., 1962-69, exec. v.p., 1964-69, pres., COO, 1969-92, pres., CEO, 1992-94, chmn., CEO, 1994—; bd. dirs. James River Corp., CSX Corp., Tredegar Industries, First Colony Corp. Former pres. Va. Mus. Fine Arts; bd. visitors Va. Mil. Inst.; bd. govs. Va. Coun. Econ. Edn. Named Outstanding Industrialist, Sci. Mus. Va., 1990. Office: Ethyl Corp PO Box 2189 Richmond VA 23218-2189*

GOTTWALD, BRUCE COBB, JR., treasurer analyst; b. Richmond, Va., Dec. 6, 1957; s. Bruce C. and Nancy (Hays) G.; m. Kimberly Clifton, Dec. 29, 1984; children: Nancy, Caroline, Bruce III. BA, Va. Mil. Inst., 1980; MBA, William & Mary Coll., 1984. Mktg. dir. Ethyl Plastics, Richmond, 1981-84, fin. analyst, 1984-85; treasury analyst Ethyl Corp., Richmond, 1985-87, mgr. banking & fgn. currency, 1987-88, asst. treas., 1988-89, v.p., treas., 1989-92; product devel. analyst First Colony Life, Lynchburg, Va., 1984-85; chmn., CEO First Colony Corp. (formerly Ethyl Corp.), Richmond, 1992-96; mng. dir. Jonah LLC, Richmond, Va., 1996—. Bd. dirs. Athletic Club Va. Mil. Ins., Lexington, 1985; trustee Va. Mus. Fine Arts. Presbyterian. Office: Jonah LLC Riverfront Towers West 901 E Byrd St Ste 1350 Richmond VA 23219*

GOTTWALD, FLOYD DEWEY, JR., chemical company executive; b. Richmond, Va., July 29, 1922; s. Floyd Dewey and Anne (Cobb) G.; m. Elisabeth Morris Shelton, Mar. 22, 1947; children: William M., James T., John D. BS, Va. Mil. Inst., 1943; MS, U. Richmond, 1951. With Albemarle Paper Co., Richmond, 1943-62, sec., 1956-57, v.p., sec., 1957-62, pres., 1962; exec. v.p. Ethyl Corp., Richmond, 1962-64, vice chmn., 1964-68, chmn., 1968-94, CEO, 1970-92, chmn. exec. com., 1970-94, vice chmn., 1994-96; bd. dirs. Tredegar Industries, Inc.; chmn., CEO Albemarle Corp. Past bd. dirs. Nat. Petroleum Coun.; trustee U. Richmond; mem. River Rd. Bapt. Ch.; past trustee V.M.I. Found., Inc.; mem. bd. visitors Coll. William and Mary, 1993-97; pres. bd. trustees Va. Mus. Fine Arts, 1994-96. Decorated Bronze Star, Purple Heart. Mem. NAM (former bd. dirs.), Am. Petroleum Inst. (bd. dirs.) Chem. Mfrs. Assn. (former bd. dirs.), Internat. Game Fish Assn. (trustee 1992—), Alfalfa Club, Country Club Va., Commonwealth Club. Office: Albemarle Corp PO Box 1335 Richmond VA 23218-1335

GOTTWALD, GEORGE J., bishop; b. St. Louis, May 12, 1914. Student, Kenrich Sem., Mo. Ordained priest Roman Catholic Ch., 1940. Ordained titular bishop of Cedamusa and aux. bishop St. Louis, 1961-88. Office: Cath Ctr 4445 Lindell Blvd Saint Louis MO 63108-2497*

GOUDY, JAMES JOSEPH RALPH, electronics executive, educator; b. Bloomfield, Iowa, Nov. 3, 1952; s. Charles Jacob and Marjorie Ethel (Morten) G.; m. Diane Marie Guenther, Nov. 24, 1978; children: Megan Joanne, Monica Victoria, Mitchell Thaddeus. BS, Wayne State Coll., 1976; AAS, Indian Hills C.C., Ottumwa, Iowa, 1978; MA, N.E. Mo. State U., 1980; BA, Iowa Wesleyan Coll., 1986. Cert. sr. engring. technician Nat. Inst. Certification Engring. Technicians. Sr. electronic comm. cons. ANR Pipeline Co., Fairfield, Iowa, 1978—, instr. high tech., 1987—; sr. electronics technician ANR Pipeline Co., Birmingham, Iowa, 1991—; owner Advanced Tech. Cons., 1993—; temp. instr. Wayne (Nebr.) State Coll., 1976-77; instr. VA program Indian Hills C.C., Ottumwa, 1978, mem. high tech. programs adv. com., 1992—; instr. Iowa Wesleyan Coll., Mt. Pleasant, 1986. Bd. dirs. Wapello County Agrl. Fair, Eldon, 1988—, Ottumwa Area Translator Sys.; participant Nat. Runners Health Study, U. Calif. Mem. Radio Club Am., Masons, Shriners, Order Ea. Star, Toastmasters, Optimists. Avocations: amateur radio, running. Home: 702 S 32nd St Fairfield IA 52556-4704 Office: ANR Pipeline Co PO Box 9 Birmingham IA 52535-0009

GOUDY, JOSEPHINE GRAY, social services administrator; b. Des Moines, Nov. 30, 1925; d. Gerald William and Myrtle Maria (Brooks) Gray; BA, State U. Iowa, 1954, MSW, 1966; cert. in gerontology U. Ill.; m. John Winston Goudy, June 5, 1948; children: Tracy Jean, Paula Rae. Clin. social worker, Iowa, Ill.; diplomate in Clin. Social Work; lic. ind. social worker, Iowa. Child welfare supr. Iowa Dept. Social Svcs., 1960-68; psychiat. social worker Community Mental Health Ctr. Scott County (Iowa), 1966-71; social work instr. Palmer Jr. Coll., Davenport, Iowa, 1967-70; psychiat. social worker, chief social svcs. Jacksonville (Ill.) State Mental Hosp., 1971-74; coord. community mental health outpatient services McFarland Mental Health Ctr., Springfield, Ill., 1974; exec. dir. Macoupin County Mental Health Ctr., Carlinville, Ill., 1974-98, Youth attention Ctr., Jacksonville, Ill., 1998—; chmn. Human Svcs. Edn. Coun., Springfield, 1979-81; bd. mem. Alzheimer's Disease and Related Disorders Assn., Springfield Ill. Area Chpt., past exec. Davenport Community Welfare Coun.; adj. prof. dept. psychiatry So. Ill. U., Springfield. Mem. APA, Nat. Assn. Social Workers (Social Worker of Yr. Central Ill. area 1983), Acad. Cert. Social Workers, Am. Psychotherapy Assn., AAUW (br. pres. 1964-66, mem. state bar 1966-68, br. grantee 1975), Internat. Fedn. U. Women, U. Iowa Alumni Assn., Bus. and Profl. Women (Woman of Yr. 1983), Delta Kappa Gamma, Kappa Delta Pi. Republican. Methodist. Club: Carlinville Women's (pres. 1975-77, 96-98). Home: 364 W Tremont St Waverly IL 62692-1073 Office: 100 N Side Sq Carlinville IL 62626-1748

GOUGE, BETTY MERLE, family therapist; b. Colbert, Okla., Nov. 8, 1937; d. Clifford Carlton and Cleo (Sims) Gage; m. W. Frank Wolfenbarger, July 26, 1980; children: Carol Gouge-Blanchard, Jeff Gouge, Gretchen Wolfenbarger-Doll. BS, Tex. Womans U., 1968, MS, 1971, PhD, 1975. workshop leader shcs. and profl. orgns. Co-author: Choices! Choices! Choices!, 1985, Wonderful You, 1985, My Feelings and Me, 1985, Let's Share, 1985, Land of Listening, 1985, The Feeling Fun House, 1985, A Lasting Friend, 1985, Rules at my House, 1986, An Island Adventure, 1986. Mem. DGPA, AGPA, DAMFT, Am. Assn. Marriage and Family Therapy. Office: Family Counseling Ctr Ste 280 2925 Lyndon B Johnson Fwy Dallas TX 75234-7614

GOUGE, RUBY LEE, textiles company administrator; b. Brunsville, N.C., Jan. 18, 1947; d. Carl and Lena (Williams) Grindstaff; m. Robert Earl Gouge, Mar. 26, 1965; children: Robert Delon, Carlyn Melena. Grad. H.S., Burnsville, N.C. Materials inspector Am. Thread, Marion, N.C., 1965-85; systems scheduler Coats Am., Marion, N.C., 1985—. Democrat. Baptist. Avocations: writing, reading, sewing, painting, hiking. Home: 1840 Halls Chappel Rd Burnsville NC 28714-6733

GOUGÉ, SUSAN CORNELIA JONES, microbiologist; b. Chgo., Apr. 18, 1924; d. Harry LeRoy and Gladys (Moon) Jones; student Am. U., Washington, 1942-43, La. Coll., 1944-45; BS, George Washington U., 1948; postgrad. Georgetown U., 1956-58, 66-69, Vt. Coll. of Norwich U., M.A. in Pub. Health, 1984, Walden U., 1996—; m. John Oscar Gougé, Aug. 7, 1943; children: John Ronald, Richard Michael (dec.), Claudia Renée Gougé Carr. Med. technician Children's Hosp. Research Lab., Washington, 1948-49; bacteriologist George Washington U. Research Lab., D.C. Gen. Hosp., 1950-53; med. microbiologist Walter Reed Army Inst. Research, Washington, 1953-61; research asst. Dental Research, Walter Reed Army Med. Ctr., 1961-62; microbiologist antibiotics div. FDA, 1962-63; supr. quality control John D. Copanos Co., Pharms., Balt., 1963-64; research tng. asst. infectious diseases and tropical medicine Howard U. Med. Sch., 1964-65; research assoc. Georgetown U. Lab. Infectious Diseases, D.C. Gen. Hosp., 1966-69; mycologist Georgetown U. Hosp. Lab., 1969-70; microbiologist Research Found. of Washington Hosp. Ctr., 1971-73; dir. quality control Bio-Medium Corp., Silver Spring, Md., 1973-76; microbiologist Alcolac, Inc., Balt., 1976-77; microbiologist div. labs., dept. human resources Community Health and Hosps. Adminstrn., Washington, 1978-79; microbiologist div. ophthalmic devices, Office Device Evaluation, Ctr. for Devices and Radiol. Health, FDA, Rockville, Md., 1979—; alt. contact on U.S. Pharmacopoeia Divsn. Stds. Devel. Microbiology subcom., 1996—, FDA observer on Nat. Com. Clin. Lab. Stds. com. abbreviated bacterial identification, 1994-98, alt. liaison to Assn. Advancement Med. Instrumentation sterilization stds. com., 1996—; alt. contact Ctr. of Devices and Radiol. Health, U.S. Pharmacopacia divsn. Std. and Devel. microbiology subcom., 1996—; FDA observer Nat. Com. Clin. Lab. Stds. com. on abbreviated bacterial identification, 1994—; alt. liaison to Assn. Advancement Med. Instrumentation Sterilization stds. com., 1996—. Sec. to exec. bd. Bethesda Project Awareness, 1970-71; vol. lead poisoning detection testing project, D.C. Office Vols. Internat. Tech. Assistance, 1970-71; vol. Zacchaeus Free Clinic, Washington, 1979-84, Winchester Med. Ctr., 1994—. Mem. Nat. Capital Harp Ensemble, 1941-65; mem. parish social concerns com. Roman Cath. Ch., 1972-84; mem. Winchester Med. Ctr. Aux., 1994—. Recipient medal cmty. svc.; registered microbiologist Nat. Registry Microbiologists; specialist microbiologist Am. Acad. Microbiology. Mem. AAAS, VITA, IEEE (engring. in medicine and biology soc.), LWV (v.p. Winchester-Frederick County chpt. 1997-98), Am. Soc. for Microbiology, Am. Inst. Biol. Scis., Am. Chem. Soc., Internat. Union Pure and Applied Chemistry, N.Y. Acad. Scis., Am. Pub. Heath Assn., Bus. and Profl. Women (Capital Club, rec. sec. 1973-74, 1st v.p. 1974-75, pres. 1975-76), Winchester Bus. and Profl. Women, Winchester-Frederick County League Women Voters (v.p. 1997-98), World Affairs Council of Washington D.C., Winchester-Frederick County Hist. Soc., Toastmasters Internat. (charter sec. BMD Club #3941 1979-80), Pi Kappa Delta, Sigma Xi. Methodist. Office: FDA Div Ophthalmic Devices Office Device Evaluation 9200 Corporate Blvd Rockville MD 20850-3223

GOUGELMAN, PAUL REINA, lawyer; b. Chgo., Mar. 16, 1951; s. Paul Reina Gougelman and Jayne Bohus. BA, Fla. Internat. U., Miami, 1975; JD, Nova Law Sch., Ft. Lauderdale, 1980. Bar: Fla. 1981, U.S. Ct. Appeals (11th cir.) 1981, US. Dist. Ct. (mid. dist.) Fla. 1983. Atty. 1st Dist. Ct. Appeals, Tallahassee, 1980-83; ptnr. Holland & Knight LLP, Melbourne, Fla., 1996-99; city atty. Indialantic, Fla., 1989—, Melbourne Beach, Fla., 1990—, Melbourne, Fla., 1996—, Cocoa Beach, Fla., 1998-99; spl. counsel for land use and growth mgmt. City of Maitland, 1984-88; spl. counsel for code enforcement bd. City of Longwood, Fla., 1985-87; cons. growth mgmt. City of Lake Mary, Fla., 1985-87; gov.'s appointee East Ctrl. Fla. Regional Planning Coun., 1986-98; mem. Seminole County Charter Adv. Com., 1987-88; gen. counsel City of Cocoa Redevel. Agy., 1990-99, Brevard Met. Planning Orgn., 1993—, Space Coast League of Cities, 1991—; adv. coun. Fla. Met. Planning Orgn., 1994—. Active Orange County Bar Task Force, 1985, Brevard County Planning and Zoning Bd., 1989-92, chmn., 1991-92; chmn. Brevard County Charter Com., 1993-94; chmn. bd. dirs. Harbor City Vol. Ambulance Squad, 1994-97. Mem. ABA, Fla. Bar (local govt. law sect., elected exec. coun. environ. and land use law sect.). Republican. Presbyterian. Office: Holland & Knight LLP 1499 S Harbor City Blvd Melbourne FL 32901-3245

GOUGEON, LEN GIRARD, literature educator; b. Northampton, Mass., Aug. 8, 1947; s. William Louis and Helen Ann (Murphy) G.; m. Deborah Jean Zagorski, Feb. 21, 1980; children: Elliott, Nadia, Wesley. BA, St. Mary's U., Halifax, N.S., Can., 1969; MA, U. Mass., 1972, PhD, 1974. Asst. prof. Am. lit. U. Scranton, Pa., 1974-78, assoc. prof. Am. lit., 1978-82, prof. Am. lit., 1982—. Author: Virtue's Hero: Emerson, Antislavery and Reform, 1990; editor: Emerson's Antislavery Writings, 1995; contbr. articles to lit. publs. NEH fellow, 1981, grantee, 1996. Mem. MLA, Am. Lit. Assn., Ralph Waldo Emerson Soc. (pres.-elect 1997), Thoreau Soc. Office: Univ Scranton Dept English Scranton PA 18510

GOUGH, CAROLYN HARLEY, library director; b. Paterson, N.J., Sept. 23, 1922; d. Frank Ellsworth and Mabel (Harrison) Harley; m. George Harrison Gough, Sept. 21, 1944; children: Deborah Ann Gough Bornholdt, Douglas Alan. BA, Coll. William and Mary, 1943; MLS, Drexel U., 1966. Rsch. asst. Young and Rubicam, Inc., N.Y.C., 1943-44; libr. dir., asst. prof. Cabrini Coll., Radnor, Pa., 1966-81; chmn. Palm Beach County Libr. Bd., 1984-86; mem. resources study com. Tredyffrin Twp. Libr., 1964-65; docent Henry Morrison Flagler Mus., 1982-92. Mem. AAUP, DAR (Palm Beach chpt.), Tri-State Coll. Libr. Coop. (v.p. 1973-74, pres. 1974-75), Assn. Coll. and Rsch. Librs. (dir. 1978-81), Questers, Inc. (1st nat. v.p. 1964-66), Atlantis Golf Club, Atlantis Women's Club (co-pres. 1982-83), Sir Robert Boyle Soc., Beta Phi Mu, Kappa Delta. Republican. Episcopalian. Home: 458 S Country Club Dr Atlantis FL 33462-1238

GOUGH, CLARENCE RAY, retired designer, educator; b. Denton County, Tex., Dec. 7, 1919; s. Herman Lang and Gertrude (Page) G.; m. Georgia Belle Leach, Feb. 7, 1975. BS in Art, U. North Tex., Denton, 1940, MS in Art, 1941; BArch, Ill. Inst. Tech., 1950. Art tchr. Edinburg (Tex.) Ind. Sch. Dist., 1941; interior designer Contemporary House, Dallas, 1950; environ. designer Gough Assocs., Denton, 1951-90; prof. U. North Tex., Denton, 1951-88; juror Nat. Coun. Interior Design Qualifications; chmn. accreditation com. Found. Interior Design Rsch. Illustrator: Modern Dance for the Youth of America, 1944. Exhbn. chmn. U. North Tex., Denton, 1950-63; curator exhbns. Greater Denton Arts Coun., 1997-98. Lt. USNR, 1942-46, PTO. Recipient Career Educator award Am. Soc. Interior Designers, Dallas, Svc. award Gov.'s Conf. on the Arts, Denton. Avocations: photography, collecting art. Home: 1813 Willowwood St Denton TX 76205-6992

GOUGH, DENIS IAN, geophysics educator; b. Port Elizabeth, Cape, South Africa, June 20, 1922; came to Can., 1966; s. Frederick William and Ivy Catherine (Hingle) G.; m. Winifred Irving Nelson, June 2, 1945; children—Catherine Veronica, Stephen William Cyprian. B.Sc., Rhodes U., Grahamstown, Republic of South Africa, 1943, M.Sc., 1947, D.Sc. (hon.), 1990; Ph.D., U. Witwatersrand, Johannesburg, Republic of South Africa, 1953. Research officer Nat. Phys. Lab., Johannesburg, S. Africa, 1947, sr. research officer; lectr. Univ. Coll. Rhodesia, Salisbury, 1958, sr. lectr.; assoc. prof. geophysics Southwest Ctr. for Advanced Studies, Dallas, 1964-66; prof. geophysics U. Alta., Edmonton, Can., 1966-87, prof. emeritus, 1987—, dir. Inst. Earth and Planetary Physics, 1975-80. Contbr. numerous articles to profl. jours. Royal Soc. Can. fellow, 1972. Fellow Royal Astron. Soc. (Chapman medal 1988), Am. Geophys. Union; Geol. Assn. Can.; mem. Can. Geophys. Union (past pres., J. Tuzo Wilson medal 1983), Internat. Assn. Geomagnetism and Aeronomy (pres. 1983-87), S. African Geophys. Assn. (Rudolf Krahmann medal 1989). Avocations: reading, music, poetry. Office: Univ Alta, Dept Physics, Edmonton, AB Canada T6G 2J1

GOUGH, EUGENE V., vocational education educator; b. Salt Lake City, Apr. 3, 1931; s. Frank and Veneda Carrie (Stewart) G.; m. Penny Diane Fry, Dec. 28, 1956; children: Liane, Loren Jay, Noel Dion. BA, San Jose State U., 1959; M of Indsl. Edn., Brigham Young U., 1979; postgrad., U. Utah, 1962-80. Cert. secondary edn. tchr., vocat. edn./drafting and carpentry, Utah, Calif. Tchr., dept. chmn. Mapusaga High Sch., Tutuila, Am. Samoa, 1959-62, Butte Valley High Sch., Dorris, Calif., 1962-64; tchr. Skyline High Sch., Salt Lake City, 1966-67, Bonneville Jr. High Sch., Salt Lake City, 1967-70; tchr., co-op edn. coord. Cottonwood High Sch., Salt Lake City, 1970-81; tchr., dept. chmn. Taylorsville High Sch., Salt Lake City, 1981-91; dist. Boy Scout exec., Snake River Coun., Boy Scouts Am., Twin Falls, Idaho, 1962-64. Sgt. U.S. Army, 1953-55. Named Vocat. Tchr. of Yr., Granite Sch. Dist., Salt Lake City, 1987. Mem. NEA, Am. Vocat. Assn., Utah Edn. Assn., Granite Edn. Assn., Vocat. Indsl. Clubs of Am. (advisor 1970-91). Republican. Mormon. Avocations: woodworking, landscaping, gardening, fly fishing. Home: 6227 S 1200 E Salt Lake City UT 84121-1921

GOUGH, JOHN FRANCIS, lawyer; b. Phila., Nov. 28, 1934; s. John Joseph and Honora Veronica (Garrity) G.; m. Natalie Smith, Mar. 8, 1984; children: David, Robert, J. Joseph II, Richard, Jonathan, Kristin. AB cum laude, St. Joseph's U., 1957; JD, Yale Law Sch., 1960. Bar: Pa. 1961, N.J. 1994, U.S. Dist. Ct. (ea. dist.) Pa. 1961, U.S. Ct. Appeals (3d cir.) 1966, U.S. Supreme Ct. 1967. Assoc. Erskine, Barbieri & Sheer, Phila., 1960-65, White and Williams, Phila., 1965-68; ptnr. White and Williams, 1968-80, Toll, Ebby & Gough, Phila., 1980-87; ptnr., chmn. corp. dept. Abrahams & Loewenstein, Phila., 1987-88; ptnr. Hoyle, Morris & Kerr, Phila., 1988-92; ptnr. Montgomery, Mccracken, Walker & Rhoads, LLP, Phila., 1992-98, co-chair bus. bankruptcy sect., 1998; ptnr. Hoyle, Morris & Kerr LLP, Phila., 1998—; exec. com. Ea. Dist Bankruptcy Conf., 1989—; faculty co-chmn. and lectr. Temple Grad. Sch. Law C.L.E. Program, 1989-92; lectr. U. Pa. Grad. Sch., Temple Law Sch., 1990—. Contbr. to Temple Law Quar.; author course materials for profl. and ednl. orgns. Pres. Highfield Sch. PTA, Plymouth, Pa., 1966-68, Greene Towne Montessori Sch., Phila., 1979-80; v.p., exec. com. Schuylkill River Devel. Coun. Mem. ABA, Am. Law Inst., Phila. Bar Assn. (pres. Jr. Bar Assn. 1964-65), Hosp. Attys. S.E. Pa. (pres. 1977-79), Am. Bankruptcy Inst. (bd. cert. in bus. bankruptcy), Yale Club Phila. Avocations: tennis, fitness. Office: Hoyle Morris and Kerr LLP One Liberty Pl Ste 4900 Philadelphia PA 19103

GOUGH, PAULINE BJERKE, magazine editor; b. Wadena, Minn., Jan. 7, 1935; d. Luther C. and Zita Pauline (Halbmaier) Bjerke; BA, U. Minn., Mpls., 1957; BS, Moorhead (Minn.) State Coll., 1970; MS, Ind. U., Bloomington, 1972, EdD, 1977; children: Mary Pauline, Sarah Elizabeth, Philip Clayton. Reporter women's page San Jose (Calif.) Mercury-News, 1957-58; with rsch. dept. Campbell-Mithun Advt., Mpls., 1958-60; tchr. Univ. Elem. Sch., Bloomington, 1970-79; freelance writer Agy. Instructional TV, Bloomington, 1974-80; mem. adj. faculty Ind. U.-Purdue U., Indpls., summers 1976, 77; asst. editor Phi Delta Kappan, Bloomington, 1980-81, mng. editor, 1981-88; editor, 1988—; mem. profl. staff Phi Delta Kappa, 1981—, also leader insts. on writing for publ. Recipient Disting. Alumna award Moorhead State U., 1982. Mem. Phi Beta Kappa, Phi Delta Kappa. Author articles in field. Home: 3570 S Oakridge Dr Bloomington IN 47401-8926 Office: Phi Delta Kappa PO Box 789 408 N Union St Bloomington IN 47405-3800

GOUGHER, RONALD LEE, foreign language educator and administrator; b. Allentown, Pa., July 27, 1939; s. Samuel Franklin and Beatrice Dorothy (Shanaberger) G.; 1 child, Robert. BA, Muhlenberg Coll., 1961; MA, Lehigh U., 1964; postgrad., Albright Coll., 1962, Stanford U., 1963, Harvard U., 1964, U. Pa., 1964-75; advanced cert., Goethe Inst., Munich, 1969. Chmn. fgn. lang. dept. Parkland H.S., Allentown, Pa., 1961-65; tchr. German Moravian Sem. for Girls, 1965-69; instr. German Lehigh U., 1965-69; assoc. prof. German West Chester (Pa.) U., 1969—, dir. internat. edn., 1974-83, chmn. dept. fgn. langs., 1977-96, campus dir. Expt. in Internat. Living, 1972-92; treas. Pa. Consortium Internat. Edn., 1978-83, pres., 1983-86, World Learning Inc., 1992—; coord.-chairperson Assn. Depts. Fgn. Langs., State Sys. Higher Edn., Pa., 1984-88, del. First Joint Conf. Chinese and Am. Edn. Great Hall of People, Beijing, 1992; citizen amb. Linguistics del. to China, 1991, 92, lectr. in field, cons. Franklin Mint, 1992—; cons., program dir. Chester Conty Intermediate Unit; guest lectr. Ufa, Ivanova, Russia, 1993, Czestochowa, Poland, Ufa, Russia, Sendai, Japan, Jurmala, Riga, Valmiera, Latvia, 1994, 95, 96, Kaunus, Lithuania, 1995; participant Hungarian Parliament Sessions, Budapest, 1994; dir. Am.-European studies program, West Chester U. and Soros Found., Latvia, Lithuania, Czech Republic, Slovakia, Hungary, Romania, Yugoslavia, Bulgaria, Croatia, Slovenia, Macedonia, 1994, Moldova, 1995, Estonia, 1996, Albania, Bosnia, Kyrgystan, Mongolia, 1997—, Kazakhstan, 1998—, Azerbaijan, 1999; dir. Internat. Sch.-U. Partnership Program, West Chester U. and Chester County Intermediate Unit, 1988—. Co-editor, Individualization Fgn. Lang. Learning in Am., 1970-75; author numerous publs. in German lang. and lit., individualizing instrn. in fgn. langs. Bd. dirs. Peters Valley Crafts Ctr., U.S. Info. Agy., 1988-95; active Congress-Bundestag Youth Exch. Program, 1988-96, Citizen Amb. Program, China, 1991, 92. Fulbright travel grantee, 1963, 69, travel grantee Soros Found., 1990-94; travel and study grantee, Finland and Leningrad, USSR, 1990; travel grantee to Poland, Slovakia, Romania, 1991-92, Russia, 1993, 95, Bulgaria, Slovenia, 1994, Kagoshima, Japan and Taipei, Taiwan, 1996, Croatia, Latvia, Lithuania, Slovenia, 1996, Hungary, Bulgaria, Macedonia, 1999, Mongolia, 1999; Fed. Fgn. Lang. Assistance Act grantee, 1992-96, dir. Internat. Sch.-U. Ptnrs. program Chester County Intermediate Unit and West Chester U., 1991-97, Soros Found. grantee internat. program devel. Latvia, Lithuania, Czech Republic, Slovakia, Hungary, Slovenia, Yugoslavia, Romania, Bulgaria, Macedonia, Moldova, Estonia, Mongolia, Kyrgystan, Bosnia, Albania, 1994—; Open Soc. grantee, 1994-96, 97, 98, 99; recipient numerous grants for fgn. langs. and internat. studies programs, pub. and pvt. founds., NEH, Rockefeller Found.; recipient Chapel of Four Chaplins award, 1981. Mem. Am. Assn. Tchrs. German, Am. Coun. Tchg. Fgn. Langs., N.E. Conf. Tchg. Fgn. Langs., Internat. Platform Assn., Smithsonian Instn. Republican. Lutheran. Home: 3309 Windsor Ln Thorndale PA 19372-1038 Office: West Chester U Dept Fgn Langs West Chester PA 19380

GOUIN, SERGE, corporate executive; b. Montreal, Mar. 6, 1943; came to U.S., 1984; s. Jean-Marie and Mariette (Champoux) G.; m. Ginette DuPuy, Aug. 22, 1964 (div.); children: Sophie, Philippe, Simon. BA, U. Western Ont., 1966, BBA, 1965, MBA, 1966. Mgmt. cons. Currie, Cooper & Lybrand, Montreal, 1968-73; gen. mgr. Nat. Cablevision Ltd., Montreal, 1973-76; exec. v.p. Can. Devel. Corp., Toronto, Ont., Can., 1976-83; chmn. Savin Corp., Stamford, Conn., 1983-86, also bd. dirs.; pres., CEO TéLé-Métropole Inc., 1987-91, chmn. bd., 1991-96; pres., COO Le Groupe Vidéotron Ltée, 1991-96; pres. Sofimon Inc., Outremont, Que., 1997; vice chmn. Salomon Smith Barney Can. Inc., Montreal, 1998—; bd. dirs. Cott Beverages Ltd., Onex Corp., Toronto, Toon Boom Tech. Inc., Montreal, Astral Comms., Montreal, DF Albums Ltd., Montreal, Siemens Can., Inc., Toronto; vice chmn. Salomon Smith Barney, Can. Mem. Mt. Royal Club (Montreal), Quail Ridge Country Club (Boynton Beach, Fla.). Roman Catholic. Avocations: hunting, cross country skiing, golfing. Home: 740 Pratt, Outremont, PQ Canada H2V 2T6 Office: Ste 4345, 1250 René Linesque Blvd, Montreal, PQ Canada H3B 4W8

GOUK, JAMES WILLIAM, government official; b. Toronto, Ont., Can., Apr. 15, 1946. Mem. House of Commons, Ottawa, Ont., 1997—. Office:

House of Commons, 930 Confederation Bldg, Ottawa, ON Canada K1A 0A6*

GOULART, JANELL ANN, elementary education educator; b. Merced, Calif., July 29, 1936; d. James Riddoch and Rowena Janell (Futrell) Mitchell; m. Frank Goulart, May 19, 1956; children: Robert, Frank, Sharon. BA, Fresno (Calif.) State U., 1972, postgrad.; postgrad., Fresno Pacific Coll., Irvine U. Cert. elem. sci. tchr., Calif.; cert. Calif. Assn. for Gifted. Sci. staff developer, K-12 alliance staff developer Calif. Sci. Implementation Network, Irvine, Calif., 1989-96; tchr. Royal Oaks Sch., Visalia, Calif., 1972-99; tchr. sci. Visalia (Calif.) Unified Sch. Dist., 1995; co-dir. Ctrl. Valley HUB program K-12 Alliance, 1998-99; trainer Calif. Learning Assessment System state testing; sci. and math mentor for Visalia Unified Sch. Dist. Mem. Nat. Sci. Tchrs. Assn., Calif. Sci. Tchrs. Assn., Ctrl. Calif. Sci. Tchrs. Assn., Tulare County Reading Coun., Kappa Delta Pi. Home: 1546 River Way Dr Visalia CA 93291-9212 Office: Royal Oaks Sch 1323 S Clover St Visalia CA 93277-4299

GOULAZIAN, PETER ROBERT, retired broadcasting executive; b. N.Y.C., Apr. 17, 1939; s. G.B. and Alice Goulazian; m. Mary C. Holland, Dec. 19, 1965; children: Cindy Anne, Peter Robert. B.A., Columbia U., 1962. With media and programming dept. Dancer-Fitzgerald-Sample, Inc., N.Y.C., 1963-67; v.p., mktg. dir. Katz Communications, Inc., N.Y.C., 1967-79; v.p. broadcasting Katz Communications, Inc., 1980-81; pres. Continental TV div., 1981-84, pres. TV group, 1985-91; pres., CEO Katz Media Corp., 1992-94; bd. dirs. The TV Bur., Seltel, Inc., Cable Media Corp., Katz International. Trustee Standardbred Retirement Found. Mem. Varsity "C" Club, N.Y. Athletic Club, Nantucket Anglers Club, Columbia U. Club. Home: 36 Welsh Rd Lebanon NJ 08833-4316

GOULD, ALAN BRANT, academic administrator; b. Aug. 2, 1938; m. Mary Nell; children: Adam, Charles, Christopher. BA in History cum laude, Marshall U., 1961, MA in History, 1962; PhD in Am. History, W.Va. U., 1969. Grad. instr., dept. history W.Va. U., Morgantown, 1962-65; instr., dept. history D.C. Tchrs. Coll., 1965-66; asst. prof. history No. Va. Community Coll., 1966-69; prof., dept. history Marshall U., Huntington, W.Va., 1969—, sr. v.p., 1988-89, provost, 1989-92, interim pres., 1990-91, v.p. for acad. affairs, 1991-94, dean Coll. Liberal Arts, 1980-88, acting v.p. acad. affairs, 1984-86, asst. to pres. for spl. projects, 1986, chmn. dept. history, 1977-80, asst. to v.p. acad. affairs, 1976-77, coord. Regents BA degree program, 1976-80, 86-94; exec. dir. John Deavin Drinko Acad. John Deaver Drinko Acad., 1994—; adj. prof. history W.Va. Coll. Grad. Studies, 1976-86; lectr. Ohio U., Ironton, 1970-74; vis. lectr. for Project Newgate, Fed. Youth Correction Inst., Summit, Ky., fall 1970. Contbr. articles to hist. jours, also conf. papers. Chmn. Cabell County Hist. Landmark Commn., 1983-92; trustee Huntington Mus. Art, 1983-93, chmn. edn. com., mem. exec. com.; pres. River Cities Cultural Coun., 1985-91; bd. dirs. W.Va. Humanities Coun., 1986-90, v.p., 1989-91, pres., 1991-94, W.Va. Coalways, Inc., 1987—; mem. Mayor of Huntington's Main St. Project, 1987-92, Marshall U. Rsch. Corp., 1988, mem., 1982-86; mem. W.Va. Antiquities Commn., 1975-77, Cabell County Commn. on Crime, Delinquency and Corrections, 1982-86, statewide steering com. Ideas That Built Am., 19856, Carter G. Woodson Meml. Commn., 1986—; mem. steering com. Ethics W.Va. Program, 1983-84, chmn. Great Books Program; mem. affirmative action bd. City of Huntington, 1989-91, mem. Cabell County (W.Va.) hist. landmark commn., 1989-91, 94—; bd. trustees W. Va. Ednl. Found., Inc., 1993—; mem. W.Va. Libr. Commn., 1997—. Inducted into Huntington East High Sch. Hall of Fame, Class of 1986, City of Huntington (W.Va.) Wall of Fame, 1997; recipient Charles Daugherty Humanities award W.Va. Humanities Coun., 1996. Mem. Am. Hist. Assn. (com. on status of history in schs. 1974-76), Orgn. Am. Historians (state rep.), W.Va. Hist. Assn. (sec. 1974, v.p. 1975, pres. 1976), W.Va. Assn. Acad. Deans (mem. exec. bd. 1982-86), W.Va. Bd. Regents (univ. rep., acad. affairs adv. com. 1984-86), Soc. Yeager Scholars (steering com. 1986-87), W.Va. Humanities Ctr. (exec. com. 1987—), Gamma Theta Upsilon, Omicron Delta Kappa, phi Alpha Theta, Phi Eta Sigma, Pi Sigma Alpha. Avocation: tennis. Office: Marshall U John Deaver Drinko Acad 400 Hal Greer Blvd Huntington WV 25755-0003

GOULD, ALVIN R., international business executive; b. Seattle, May 16, 1922; s. Charlie I. and Laura (Klos) G.; m. Ruth Nelson, May 25, 1946; children: Stephen Charles, Jon Patrick. Grad. pub. schs. Mem. engring. dept. Pacific Car & Foundry Co., Renton, Wash., 1943-45, asst. mgr. indsl. sales, 1945-48, mgr. indsl. sales, 1948-55, gen. sales mgr., 1956-60; gen. sales mgr. Peterbilt Motors Co., Newark, Calif., 1961-64; v.p., dir., gen. sales mgr. Honolulu Iron Works Co., 1964-66, exec. v.p., dir., chief operating officer, 1966, pres., dir., chief exec. officer, 1966-71; group pres. Food Equipment Group Ward Foods Inc., N.Y.C., 1970-71; v.p. merchandising Dillingham Corp., Honolulu, 1972-75, v.p. mining and merchandising, 1973-75, group v.p. mining and merchandising, mem. exec. mgmt. com.; pres. Truck Center Corp., Seattle, 1976-90, co-owner, sec.-treas., 1991-95; pvt. practice in personal investments, 1995—. Mem. nat. export expansion Council Dept. Commerce, 1969-74, chmn. regional export expansion council, 1969-74; mem. Western Regional Export Council; chmn. Honolulu Export Council, 1975-77; Chmn. bd. trustees Hawaii Pacific Coll., 1973-77; bd. dirs. Center for International. Bus. Mem. Hawaii C. of C. (chmn. trade com. 1968-69), Hawaii World Trade Assn. (mem. exec. com. 1968-69), Hawaii Assn. Industries (v.p., dir. 1975-76), Navy League (dir.). Clubs: Rotary, Meridian Country, Outrigger Canoe, Rainier. Home: 8464 W Mercer Way Mercer Island WA 98040-5633

GOULD, ANNE AUSTIN, special education educator; b. Detroit, Jan. 5, 1961; d. John David and Jane Brown (Austin) G. BS in Edn. magna cum laude, Lesley Coll., Cambridge, Mass., 1983; MA summa cum laude, Appalachian State U., 1988. Cert. spl. edn. tchr., elem. tchr. Spl. edn. tchr. Northwest Ministries Devel. Day Sch., Winston-Salem, N.C., 1983-84, Winston-Salem/Forsyth County Schs., 1984—; tutor, Winston-Salem, 1988—; respite provider, 1986—; cons., 1988-94; habilitation, technician/respite provider Substitute Horizons Residential Care Rural Hall, N.C., 1991-92. Treas. Winston-Triad chpt. Lupus Assn., 1983-84; Rites of Christian Initiation of Adults sponsor Holy Family Cath. Ch., Clemmons, N.C., 1989-90; vol. Cath. Hispanic Ctr., East Bend, N.C., 1989; active Mar-Don Hills Homeowners Assn., 1987-92, mem. at large, 1990-92. Mem. NEA, Coun. for Exceptional Children (newsletter editor 1989-90, polit. action coord. 1990-92), Beta Sigma Phi (corr. sec. 1990-91, v.p. Upsilon chpt. 1991-92), Xi Delta Gamma (rec. sec. 1994-95). Democrat. Avocations: crafts, reading, computers, horseback riding, walking. Home: 105 Bradford Lake Ct Lewisville NC 27023-8662

GOULD, BONNIE MARINCIC, realtor; b. Cleve., Sept. 3, 1947; d. Edward Louis and Frances (Dee (Pavlovich) Marincic. Student, John Carroll U. Asst. prodn. mgr. Nelson Stern Advt., Cleve., 1966-73; sec. acctg. S. James Dubin & Assocs., Eastlake, Ohio, 1976-78; sec., atty. James Todoroff, Andrews & Todoroff, Eastlake, 1977-78; realtor sales Century 21-Baur, Euclid, Ohio, 1978-82; relocations dir., mgr. Century 21, Euclid, 1979-82; realtor assoc., relocation dir. Century 21-Malone, Inc., Willowick, Ohio, 1982-83, Century 21-William T. Byne, Willowick, 1983-84, Smythe, Cramer Co., Willowick, 1984-86; sr. v.p., treas., corp. mgr. Acacia Realty Profls. Inc., 1986-98; pres., treas., interior design coord. Acacia Design and Trade Profls. Inc. Gen. Contractors, 1990—; pres., CEO Acacia Design Fine Homes and Properties, 1999—. Mem. Realtors Polit. Action Com., Cleve., 1981—; vice chmn. local taxation and legislation com. Cleve. Area Bd. Realtors, 1983-84, vice chmn. polit. affairs, 1987—, chmn. home and flower 1986, mem. enlarged legis. com., 1986-97, internat. rules and fin. com., 1993-95, chmn. 1995; sec., trustee Euclid Gateway Found., 1987—. Recipient Disting. Svc. award Cleve. Bd. Realtors, 1983-87, 96, Woman of Yr. award 1990. Mem. Cleve. Bd. Realtors (dir. 1984-86, 93—, 2d v.p. 1994, treas. 1995, gov. Northern Ohio multiple listings svc. 1992—, contract and fin. com., 1992—), Ohio Assn. Realtors (trustee 1981-97), Nat. Assn. Realtors (treas. Cleve. chpg. 1986-87, v.p. 1987-88, pres. 1989, chmn. nominating com. 1990, Woman of Yr. 1990), North East Roundtable (sec. 1980, chair 1981), Euclid C. of C. (trustee). Republican. Roman Catholic. Office: Acacia Design & Fine Homes & Properties 293 E 266th St Cleveland OH 44132-1552 also: Acacia Design & Trade Profls Inc 20851 Lake Shore Blvd Euclid OH 44123-1820

GOULD, CHARLES PERRY, lawyer; b. Los Angeles, Mar. 11, 1909; s. Thomas Charles and Viola Frank (Keeney) G.; m. Mary Dalrymple, Sept. 1, 1932; children—Thomas Charles, Mary (Mrs. Robert Lancefield), Anne (Mrs. Thomason). Student, Pomona Coll., 1926-28; Ph.B., U. Chgo., 1930; LL.B., U. So. Calif., 1932. Bar: Calif. bar 1932. Asso. firm Frankley & Spray, Los Angeles, 1932- 35; mem. firm Spray, Gould & Bowers, 1935—; dir. Gould Music Co. Served to lt. comdr. USNR, 1942-45. Mem. Am. Bar Assn., Internat. Assn. Ins. Counsel, Am. Judicature Soc. (dir. 1979), Nat. Club Assn. (pres. 1962, dir.), World Affairs Council, Navy League U.S., Legion Lex, Delta Theta Phi. Republican. Episcopalian. Clubs: Elk. (Los Angeles), Jonathan (Los Angeles), Town Hall (Los Angeles), Los Angeles (Los Angeles); Balboa Bay (Balboa, Calif.); Calif. Book (San Francisco). Home: 1200 Old Mill Rd San Marino CA 91108-1842 Office: 3530 Wilshire Blvd Los Angeles CA 90010-2328

GOULD, DAVID, lawyer; b. L.A., Feb. 19, 1940; s. Erwin and Beatrice (Altman) G.; m. Bonnie Becker, Feb. 12, 1967; children: Julie M., Michael. AB, U. Calif., L.A., 1962; LLB, U. Calif., Berkeley, 1965. Bar: Calif. 1965, U.S. Dist. Ct. (cen., so., ea. and no. dists.) Calif. 1966, U.S. Ct. Appeals (9th cir.) 1967, U.S. Supreme Ct. 1995. Dep. atty. gen. Calif. Dept. of Justice, L.A., 1965-68; assoc. Loeb & Loeb, L.A., 1968-73; assoc. Danning, Gill, Gould, Diamond & Spector, L.A., 1974-76, ptnr., 1976-92; ptnr. McDermott, Will & Emery, L.A., 1992—; adj. assoc. prof. Southwestern U. Sch. of Law, L.A., 1978-80; adj. prof. Pepperdine U. Sch. of Law, Malibu, Calif., 1982. Co-author: Local Bankruptcy Practice Manual for the Central District of California, 2d edit., 1990—. Fellow Am. Coll. Bankruptcy; mem. ABA (bus. bankruptcy com. sect. on bus. law 1982—, vice chair rules subcom. 1986-92, chair 1992—), Calif. Bar Assn. (debtor/creditor rels. and bankruptcy com. 1984-87, chair 1987-88, advisor 1988-89, uniform comml. code com. 1988-92, bankruptcy cons. group bd. legal specialization 1989-93), L.A. County Bar Assn. (fed. cts. com. 1987—, chair bankruptcy 1989-90), Calif. Bankruptcy Forum (bd. dirs. 1995—, treas. 1998-99, sec. 1999—), L.A. Bankruptcy Forum (bd. trustees 1989, sec. 1990—, pres. 1993-94, lawyer rep. cen. dist. Calif. to 9th cir. jud. conf.). Avocations: trap and skeet shooting. Office: McDermott Will & Emery 2049 Century Park E Ste 3400 Los Angeles CA 90067-3208

GOULD, DOUGLAS C(HESTER), communications executive; b. Rockville Centre, N.Y., Sept. 22, 1951; s. Chester T. and Barbara Anne (Everett) G.; Stephanie Petrillo, July 31, 1982; children: Benjamin, Amanda. BA, Iowa Wesleyan Coll., 1973. Asst. dir. Responsible Social Involvement Iowa Wesleyan Coll., Mt. Pleasant, 1973-75; exec. dir. Planned Parenthood of Southeast Iowa, Mt. Pleasant, 1975-77; assoc. exec. dir. Planned Parenthood of N.Y.C., 1977-85; v.p. communications Planned Parenthood Fedn. of Am., N.Y.C., 1985-90; pres. Douglas Gould & Co., Larchmont, N.Y., 1990—. Mme. conservation adv. com. Town of Mamaroneck. Mem. Am. Pub. Health Assn., LWV, Nat. Press Club. Democrat. Office: Douglas Gould & Co 1865 Palmer Ave Ste 103 Larchmont NY 10538-3037

GOULD, ELEANOR LOIS (ELEANOR GOULD PACKARD), editor, grammarian; b. Newark, N.Y., Oct. 3, 1917; d. Wilson Mosher and Eleanor (Loveland) G.; m. Frederick A. Packard, Dec. 7, 1946 (dec.); 1 child, Susan Hathaway Packard. *Descended on mother's side from 3 Mayflower passengers: Francis Cooke, Isaac Allerton, and John Warren. Father ran as candidate for Congress in upstate New York for Theodore Roosevelt's Progressive Party in 1912 and lost (as all Progressive candidates did). Two grandsons of hers sailed around the world in their father's boat as preteenagers and are now the heads of their school classes at Wycliffe College in England.* BA summa cum laude, Oberlin Coll., 1938. Editor D. Appleton Century, Inc., N.Y.C., 1939-44, Duell, Sloan and Pearce, N.Y.C., 1944, Creative Age Press, N.Y.C., 1944-45; editor, grammarian The New Yorker, N.Y.C., 1945—; freelance editor, N.Y.C., 1940—. *Eleanor Louis Gould Packard is approaching her 55th year as editorial grammarian for The New Yorker, having worked for its founder, Harold Ross; then, from 1952 to 1987, for his successor, William Shawn; and for shorter periods for Robert Gottlieb, his successive editor, Tina Brown, more recently for its present editor, David Remnick. At age 81, she is the only member of the editorial staff remaining from those early days.* Mem. Phi Beta Kappa. Democrat. Avocations: reading, puzzles, activities for the deaf. Home: 415 Central Park W Apt 7D New York NY 10025-4812 Office: The New Yorker 20 W 43rd St Fl 16 New York NY 10036-7400

GOULD, ELLIOTT, actor; b. Bklyn., Aug. 38, 1938; s. Bernard and Lucille (Raver) Goldstein; m. Barbra Streisand, Mar. 21, 1963 (div.); 1 son, Jason; m. Jennifer Bogart; children—Molly, Sam. Student, Profl. Children's Sch., N.Y.C., 1955; pupil of, Jerome Swinford, Sonya Box, Bill Quinn, Colin Romoff, Charles Lowe, Eugene Lewis, Matt Mattox. Theatrical appearances include Rumple, 1957, Say, Darling, 1958, Irma La Douce, 1960, I Can Get It For You Wholesale, 1962, On The Town, 1963, The Fantastiks; appeared in films: Bob & Carol & Ted & Alice, 1969, M*A*S*H, 1970, I Love My Wife, 1970, Getting Straight, 1970, Move, 1970, The Touch, 1971, Little Murders, 1971, The Long Goodbye, 1973, Spys, 1974, Busting, 1974, California Split, 1974, Nashville, 1975, Whiffs, 1975, I Will, I Will . . . For Now, 1976, Harry & Walter Go to N.Y, 1976, Mean Johnny Barrows, 1976, A Bridge Too Far, 1977, Capricorn One, 1978, Matilda, 1978, The Silent Partner, 1979, Escape to Athena, 1979, The Lady Vanishes, 1979, The Muppet Movie, 1979, Falling in Love Again, 1980, The Devil and Max Devlin, 1981, Dirty Tricks, 1981, The Brooklyn Bridge, 1984, The Naked Face, 1984, Inside Out, 1987, Dead Men Don't Die, 1989, Strawanser, The Lemon Sisters, 1990, Bugsy, 1991, The Player, 1992, Johns, 1996, American History X, 1998, The Big Hit, 1998; TV appearance in Once Upon A Mattress, 1964, Come Blow Your Horn, 1981; star TV series E.R., 1984, Together We Stand, 1986, Friends (15 episodes), 1998, Getting Personal, 1998, It's Like You Know (3 episodes), 1998; other TV appearances include: (film) The Rules of Marriage, Saturday Night Live (6 segments), Shelly Duvall's Fairy Tale Theater prodn. of Jack and the Beanstalk, 1983, Tall Tale of Casey at the Bat, 1986, (film) Vanishing Act, 1986, Sessions, 1991, Bloodlines: Murder in the Family, 1993, Hoffman's Hunger, 1993, The Dangerous, 1995, Touched by an Angel, 1997, The Shining, 1997. Mem. Actor's Equity Assn., AFTRA, SAG. Office: 1900 Ave Of Stars Ste 1640 Los Angeles CA 90067-4407

GOULD, GLENN HUNTING, marketing professional, consultant; b. Martinsburg, W.Va., June 15, 1949; s. Glenn Hunting Sr. and Margaret Alice (Otto) G.; m. Marilyn Kay Jones, July 12, 1953; 2 children: Courtney Lynn, Angela Pace. BA in Sociology, W.Va. U., 1973, MS in Indsl. Relations, 1974. Mgr. human resources Hillenbrand Ind., Batesville, Ind., 1979-81; mgr. human resources, MIAD div. Bausch & Lomb, Balt., 1981-82; dir. human resources Universal Security Inst., Balt., 1982-83; chief exec. officer M.K. Jones & Assocs., Largo, Fla., 1983—; bd. dirs. Pitts. Inst. Mortuary Soc.; cons. Colombian Fin. Group, 1995-96, Wilbert Inc. Contbg. author: Successful Funeral Service Practice, 1987. Served as sgt. USAF, 1967-71, Vietnam. Named one of Outstanding Young Men Am., 1980. Mem. Soc. Human Resource Mgmt. (cert. sr. profl.), Alpha Kappa Delta. Democrat. Presbyterian. Avocations: antiques, tennis, reading, skiing. Office: 1501B Belcher Rd S Largo FL 33771-4505

GOULD, HAROLD, actor; b. Schenectady, N.Y., Dec. 10, 1923; m. Lea Shampanier, Aug. 1950; children: Deborah, Joshua David, Lowell Seth. BA, SUNY, Albany, 1947; MA, Cornell U., 1948, PhD, 1953. Asst. prof. drama Randolph Macon Woman's Coll., 1953-56, U. Calif., Riverside, 1956-60. Films include Two for the Seesaw, Harper, Inside Daisy Clover, Marnie, The Arrangement, The Lawyer, Where Does It Hurt?, The Sting, The Strongest Man in the World, Gus, The Big Bus, Love and Death, The Front Page, Silent Movie, The One and Only, Seems Like Old Times, Romero, Killer, Patch Adams, My Giant; TV appearances include Columbo, L.A. Law, The Virginian, The Twilight Zone, Perry Mason, The Fugitive, Get Smart, Hogan's Heroes, The Big Valley, The Wild, Wild West, The F.B.I., Mission Impossible, I Dream of Jeannie, Cannon, The Rockford Files, Felicity, The Outer Limits, Lois & Clark: The New Adventures of Superman, The Long Hot Summer, Washington-Behind Closed Doors, Soap, Love Boat, Feather and Father, Rhoda (Emmy nomination), Gunsmoke, Petrocelli, Lou Grant, Double Solitaire, Streets of San Francisco, Hawaii Five-O, Mary Tyler Moore Show, The 11th Victim, Aunt Mary, Police Story (Emmy nomination), Man in the Santa Claus Suit, Insight/Holy Moses, The Gambler, Moviola (Emmy nomination), King Crab, Never Too Late, St. Elsewhere, Mrs. Delafield Wants to Marry (Emmy nomination), Night Court, Dallas, Empty Nest, The Golden Girls, Midnight Caller, Ray Bradbury Theatre (Emmy nomination and ACE award 1989), The Sunset Gang, Touched by an Angel, For Hope; appeared in Broadway plays including Fools, 1980, Grown Ups, 1982, Artist Descending a Staircase, 1989, Mixed Emotions, 1993, and others; also appeared in other plays including King Lear, 1958, Rhinoceros, 1962, Much Ado About Nothing, 1958, Merchant of Venice, 1964, Troilus and Cressida, 1958, JB, 1965, Seidman and Son, 1964, Once in a Lifetime, 1975, The Miser, 1968, The Devils, 1967, The Birthday Party, 1986, House of Blue Leaves, 1971, The Price, The World of Ray Bradbury, 1964, Life with Father, 1982, Skin of Our Teeth, 1982, I'm Not Rappaport, 1985, Through Roses, 1987, I Never Sang for My Father, 1988, one man show Freud, 1990, Love Letters, 1990, King Lear, 1992, Incommunicado, 1993 (L.A. Drama Critics award 1994), Old Business, 1995-95, The Tempest, 1995, Substance of Fire, 1996, Death of a Salesman, 1997; off-Broadway appearance in Increased Difficulty of Concentration (Obie award), 1969. Recipient Centennial Alumnus award SUNY Albany, Nat. Assn. State Univs. and Land-Grant Colls., 1987. *

GOULD, HARRY EDWARD, JR., industrialist; b. N.Y.C., Sept. 24, 1938; s. Harry Edward and Lucille (Quartucy) G.; m. Barbara Clement, Apr. 26, 1975; children: Harry Edward III, Katharine Elizabeth. Student, Oxford U., 1958; BA cum laude, Colgate U., 1960; postgrad., Harvard Bus. Sch., 1960-61; MBA, Columbia U., 1964. Assoc. in corp. fin. dept. Goldman, Sachs & Co., N.Y.C., 1961-62; exec. asst. to sr. v.p. ops. Universal Am., N.Y.C., 1964-65; sec., treas. Young Spring & Wire Corp., Detroit, 1965-67, exec. v.p., COO, 1967-69, also bd. dirs.; v.p. adminstrn. and fin. Universal Am. Corp., 1968-69; mem. exec. com., v.p., sec.-treas. Daybrook-Ottawa Corp., Bowling Green, Ohio, 1967-69; dir., mem. exec. com. Am. Med. Ins. Co., N.Y.C., 1966-74; chmn., pres., CEO Gould Paper Corp., N.Y.C., 1969—, also chmn. bd. dirs.; chmn. bd., dir. Vrisimo Mfg., Inc., Ceres, 1974—; chmn. bd. Lewis & Gould Paper Co., Inc., Northfield, Ill., 1975-78; chmn., pres., CEO, Signature Comm. Ltd., L.A. and N.Y.C., 1986—; chmn. bd. Legion Paper West Corp., Commerce, Calif., 1997—; chmn. bd. dirs. Samuel Porritt & Co., East Peoria, Ill., Ingalls Mfg., Inc., Ceres, Calif., McNair Mfg., Inc., Chico, Calif., Hawthorne Paper Co., Kalamazoo, Weiss Mfg., Inc., Chico; bd. dirs. Reinhold Gould GmbH, Hamburg, Germany; ltd. ptnr. Hardy & Co., N.Y.C., 1973-78; chmn. exec. com., bd. dirs. Richard Lewis Paper Corp., Northfield, Ill., 1992-97; bd. dirs., mem. environ. and health and safety com. Domtar Inc., Montreal, 1995—. Co-chmn. Pacesetter's com. Boy Scouts Am., 1966-69; participant as U.S. Pres.'s rep. UN E-W Trade Devel. Commn., 1967; mem. N.Y. Gov.'s Task Force on N.Y. State Cultural Life and Arts, 1975—; pres. Harry E. Gould Found., N.Y.C., 1971—; mem. nat. coun. Colgate U., 1973-76, trustee, mem. budget, devel., fin. and student affairs com., 1976-82; mem. vis. com. Sch. Dramatic Arts of The New Sch., 1995—; mem. adv. bd. Columbia U. Grad. Sch. Bus., 1980—; bd. dirs. United Cerebral Palsy Rsch. and Ednl. Found., 1976—, Nat. Multiple Sclerosis Soc., 1977—, Housing Devel. Corp., 1977—, USO of Met. N.Y., 1981—; bd. dirs. Housing N.Y. Corp., 1986—, vice chmn., 1987—; bd. dirs., chmn. exec. com. Cinema Group, Inc., L.A., 1979-86, chmn., pres., 1982-86; mem. Dem. Nat. Fin. Coun., 1974-78, also vice chmn. exec. com., chmn. budget and audit coms.; treas. N.Y. State Dem. Com., 1976-77; mem. mayor's citizens com. Dem. Nat. Conv., 1976; mem. U.S. Pres.'s Export Coun. (exec. com., chmn. export expansion subcom., mem. export promotion subcom.), 1979-82; mem. exec. br. Acad. Motion Picture Arts and Scis., 1985—; nat. trustee, mem. exec. com. Nat. Symphony Orch., Washington, 1978—; trustee Riverdale Country Sch., 1990—; bd. dirs. Residential Mortgage Ins. Corp., 1992—. Mem. Nat. Paper Trade Assn. (dir., mem. printing paper com. 1973—), Paper Mchts. Assn. N.Y. (dir. 1972—), Paper Distbn. Coun. (chmn. 1993—), Young Pres. Orgn., Am. Mgmt. Assn. (trustee, mem. audit com.), Paper Club N.Y., Fin. Execs. Inst., Columbia U. Grad. Sch. Bus. Alumni Assn. (dir. 1980—), Phi Kappa Tau. Clubs: Pres.'s N.Y. (co-chmn. assocs. div. 1964-68), City Athletic, Harvard, Harvard Business, Friars, Marco Polo (N.Y.C.); Les Ambassadeurs (London); Rockrimmon Country (Stamford, Conn.). Home: 25 Sutton Pl S New York NY 10022-2441 also: Cherry Hill Farm 429 Taconic Rd Greenwich CT 06831-2829 Office: Gould Paper Corp 11 Madison Ave New York NY 10010-3629 *In business the most difficult problem to resolve is blending the profit goals with the dignity of human relations. In the long run, it is probably best to forego some of the profits in order to successfully meld the economic and human sides of business.*

GOULD, HOWARD RICHARD, physician; b. N.Y.C., May 21, 1931; m. Barbara Ann Paretti, Oct. 6, 1956; children: Susan, Carolyn, Richard, Joanne, Anthony, MaryJean, Eileen, Laura, Margaret. Student, Fordham U., 1949-52; MD, SUNY, 1956. Diplomate Am. Bd. Radiology, Am. Bd. Nuclear Med., Nat. Bd. Med. Examiners. Resident in radiology St. Vincent's Hosp., N.Y.C., 1957-60; assoc. dir. St. Vincent's Hosp., 1974-79; chief radiology 811th Med. GP, Loring AFB, Maine, 1960-62, USAF Hosp., Wiesbaden, Germany, 1962-65; radiologist St. Vincent's Hosp., N.Y.C., 1965-79; dir. diagnostic radiology Clin. Sci. Ctr. U. Wisc., Madison, 1979-84, U. Tenn. Med. Ctr., Knoxville, 1984-95; sr. radiologist U. Tenn. Med. Ctr., 1995—; clin. asst. prof. N.J. Coll. Med., 1965-69; clin. assoc. prof. N.Y. U. Sch. Med., N.Y.C., 1969-79; prof. radiology U. Wisc., Madison, 1979-84, U. Tenn., 1984—; sec. v.p., pres. elect, pres. med. staff St. Vincent's Hosp., 1969-76; chief staff elect, chief staff U. Tenn. Med. Ctr., 1993, 94; sec. N.Y. Celtic Med. Soc., N.Y.C., 1969-73; examiner, oral examinations Am. Bd. Radiology, 1979. Author various book chpts.; contbr. articles to profl. jours. Major USAF, 1957-65. Fellow Am. Coll. Radiology; mem. AMA, Radiological Soc. N.A., Am. Coll. Radiology, N.Y. Roentgen Soc. (sec., v.p., pres. 1971-78), Assn. U. Radiologists, Am. Roentgen Ray Soc., Alpha Omega Alpha (honor med. soc., SUNY, 1955). Roman Catholic. Avocations: reading, woodworking, flying. Office: U Tenn Med Ctr 1924 Alcoa Hwy Knoxville TN 37920-1511

GOULD, JAMES L., biology educator; b. Tulsa, July 31, 1945; s. James L. and Doris Mae (Frazier) G.; m. Carol Holly Grant, June 6, 1970; children: Grant Frazier, Clare Holly. BS, Calif. Inst. Tech., 1970; PhD, Rockefeller U., 1975. Asst. prof. Princeton (N.J.) U., 1975-80, assoc. prof., 1980-84, prof. biology, 1984—. Author: Ethology, 1982, Biological Science, rev. edit., 1996, The Honey Bee, 1988, Sexual Selection, 1989, The Animal Mind, 1994; contbr. more than 100 articles to profl. jours. With U.S. Army, 1967-68. Guggenheim Found. fellow, 1987, AAAS fellow, 1988, Animal Behavior Soc. fellow, 1992; grantee NSF, 1976, 79, 82, 85, NIH, 1976, Nat. Geogrphic Soc., 1984; named Prof. of Yr. Carnegie Found. N.J., 1996, Tchr. of Yr. Animal Behavior Soc., 1997. Presbyterian. Achievements include research in animal behavior. Office: Princeton U Dept Ecol Evol Biology Princeton NJ 08544-1003

GOULD, JAMES SPENCER, financial consultant; b. Albany, N.Y., Oct. 18, 1922; s. James Spencer and Elsie May (Spiegel) G.; m. Shirley Joan Burrett, June 12, 1948 (div. Oct. 1985); children: Deborah Ann, Jeffrey George, Douglas Spencer; m. Mary White Tredennick, Sept. 6, 1986. BS cum laude, Syracuse U., 1944; grad. advanced mgmt. program, Harvard U., 1958. C.P.A., N.Y., Calif. Ptnr. Ernst & Young, Buffalo and L.A., 1949-65, N.Y.C., 1966-82; chief fin. officer, v.p. fin. Stanley Works, New Britain, Conn., 1982-87, v.p., 1987; free-lance cons., 1987—. Served to 1st lt. inf. U.S. Army, 1943-46, ETO, 1st lt. Fin. Corps, 1951-52, Korea. Recipient Disting. Merit award Syracuse U. Sch. Mgmt., 1982, Alumnus of Yr. award, 1987. Mem. AICPA, Manchester (Vt.) Country Club. Home: 790 Boylston St Apt 18B Boston MA 02199-7917

GOULD, JAY MARTIN, economist, consultant; b. Chgo., Aug. 19, 1915; s. Max and Ida (Dolger) G.; m. Paula Halpern, Nov. 10, 1942 (div.); children: Diana, Emily; m. Jane S. Auerbach, Nov. 17, 1970. B.A., Bklyn. Coll., 1936; M.A., Columbia U., 1938, Ph.D., 1946. Economist McGraw-Hill, N.Y.C., 1946-48; mng. dir. Market Statistics, N.Y.C., 1948-66; pres. Econ. Info. Systems, N.Y.C., 1966-81; cons. economist Winston and Strawn, Chgo., 1960-80; cons. Dept. Justice, Washington, 1954-55; exec. cons. Control Data Corp., Mpls., 1981—; dir. Ctr. Internat. Mgmt. Studies, Chgo., 1978—, Feminist Press, Woodbury, N.Y., 1980—, Inst. Policy Studies, Washington, 1982—. Author: Productivity Trends in U.S. Public Utilities, 1946, The Technical Elite, 1966, Input-Output Databases, 1979, Structure of U.S. Business, 1980, Quality of Life in American Neighborhoods, 1986, (with Benjamin Goldmay) Deadly Deceit: Low Level Radiation High Level Cover Up, 1990, The Enemy Within: The High cost of Living Near Nuclear

Reactors, 1995. Dir. radiation and pub. health project. Home: 302 W 86th St New York NY 10024-3141

GOULD, JOHN JOSEPH, communications executive; b. Chelsea, Mass., June 10, 1930; s. James Thomas and Mary Margaret (Cullen) G.; m. Mary Christine Houlihan, Feb. 2, 1957; children: Michael Joseph, Eileen Rose Marie. AA, Boston U., 1975; postgrad., Suffolk U., 1959. Reporter, polit. writer Herald-Traveler Corp., Boston, 1955-60; pub. affairs dir. Associated Industries of Mass., Boston, 1960-64, pres, CEO, 1988—; v.p., account exec. Newsome and Co., Boston, 1964-65; sr. v.p. corp. comms. Shawmut Corp., Boston, 1966-88. Mem. bd. visitors Northeastern U., Boston; mem. adv. bd. U. Mass., 1993-96; mem. Boston Sch. Com., 1993-96; chair Mass. Soc. Prevention of Cruelty to Children. Mem. Pub. Rels. Soc. of Am. (accredited pub. rels. practioner). Roman Catholic. Avocations: photography, golf. Office: Associated Industries of Mass 222 Berkeley St Boston MA 02116-3748*

GOULD, JOHN PHILIP, economist, educator; b. Chgo., Jan. 19, 1939; s. John Philip and Lillian (Jicka) G.; children: John Philip III, Jeffrey Hayes; m. Kathleen A. Carpenter. BS with highest distinction, Northwestern U., 1960; MBA, U. Chgo., 1963, PhD, 1966. Faculty U. Chgo., 1965—, prof. econs., 1974—, disting. service prof. econs., 1984—, dean Grad. Sch. Bus., 1983-93, v.p. planning, 1988-91; Steven G. Rothmeier prof., disting. svc. prof. econs., 1996—; exec. v.p. Lexecon Inc., 1994—; vis. prof. Nat. Taiwan U., 1978; spl. asst. econ. affairs to sec. labor, 1969-70; spl. asst. to dir. Office Mgmt. and Budget, 1970; past chmn. econ. policy adv. com. Dept. Labor; bd. dirs. DFA Investment Dimensions Group, Harbor Capital Advisors, First Prairie Funds, 1985-96; chmn. Pegasus Funds, 1996—, Milw. Mutual, 1997—, Unext.com, 1999—. Author: (with E. Lazear) Microeconomic Theory, 6th edit, 1989; contbg. author: Microeconomic Foundations of Employment and Inflation Theory, 1970; editor: Jour. of Bus., 1976-83, Jour. Fin. Econs., 1976-83, Jour. Accounting and Econs., 1978-81; contbr. articles to profl. jours. Bd. dirs. United Way/Crusade of Mercy, 1986-91, Lookingglass Theatre Co., 1994-96. Recipient Wall St. Jour. award, 1960, Am. Marketing Assn. award, 1960; Earhart Found. fellow. Mem. Am. Econs. Assn., Econometric Soc. (chmn. local arrangements 1968), Econ. Club of Chgo., Comml. Club of Chgo., Beta Gamma Sigma. Home: 100 E Huron St Apt 2105 Chicago IL 60611-5903 Office: U Chgo Grad Sch Bus 1101 E 58th St Chicago IL 60637-1511

GOULD, LILIAN, writer; b. Phila., Apr. 19, 1920; d. Reuben Barr and Lilian Valentine (Scott) Seidel; m. Irving Gould, Nov. 16, 1944; children: Mark, Scott, Paul, John. Student, U. Pa., Charles Morris Price Sch. of Advt. and Journalism, Phila. Copywriter, mgr. advt. agys., Phila. Author: Our Living Past, 1969, Jeremy and the Gorillas, 1977 (award 1977). Mem. Authors Guild, Phila. Children's Reading Roundtable, Phila. Writers Orgn. Home: 772 Newtown Rd Villanova PA 19085-1121

GOULD, MARTHA BERNICE, retired librarian; b. Claremont, N.H., Oct. 8, 1931; d. Sigmund and Gertrude Heller; m. Arthur Gould, July 29, 1960; children: Leslie, Stephen. BA in Edn., U. Mich., 1953; MS in Library Sci., Simmons Coll., 1956; cert., U. Denver Library Sch. Community Analysis Research Inst., 1978. Childrens librarian N.Y. Pub. Libr., 1956-58; adminstr. library services act demonstration regional library project Pawhuska, Okla., 1958-59; cons. N.Mex. State Libr., 1959-60; childrens librarian then sr. childrens librarian Los Angeles Pub. Libr., 1960-72; acctg. dir. pub. srvices, reference librarian Nev. State Libr., 1972-74; pub. services librarian Washoe County (Nev.) Libr., 1974-79, asst. county librarian, 1979-84, county librarian, 1984-94; ret., 1994; cons. Nev. State Libr. and Archives, 1996—; part-time lectr. in libr. adminstrn. U. Nev.; cons. Nev. State Libr. and Archives; acting dir. Nev. Ctr. for the Book. Contbr. articles to jours. Exec. dir. Kids Voting/USA, Nev., 1996; treas. United Jewish Appeals, 1981; bd. dirs. Temple Sinai, Planned Parenthood, 1996-97, Truckee Meadows Habitat for Humanity, 1995—; trustee RSVP, North Nevadans for ERA; No. Nev. chmn. Gov.'s Conf. on Libr., 1990; mem. bd. Campaign for Choice, No. Nev. Food Bank, Nev. Women's Fund (Hall of Fame award 1989); mem. No. Nev. NCCJ, Washoe County Quality Life Task Force, 1992—; chair Sierra (Nev.) Comty. Access TV; presdl. appointee vice-chair Nat. Comn. on Librs. and Info. Sci., 1993—; mem. adv. bd. Partnership Librs. Washoe County; co-chair social studies curriculum adv. task force Washoe County Sch. Dist.; mem. Nev. Women's History Project Bd.; chair Downtown River Corridor Com., 1995-97; vice chair Dem. Party Washoe Dem. Party. Recipient Nev. State Libr. Letter of Commendation, 1973, Washoe County Bd. Commrs. Resolution of Appreciation, 1978, ACLU of Nev. Civil Libertarian of Yr. 1988, Freedom's Sake award AAUW, 1989, Leadership in Literacy award Sierra chpt. Internat. Reading Assn., 1992, Woman of Distinction award 1992, Nev. Libr. Assn. Libr. of Yr., 1993. Mem. ALA (bd. dirs., intellectual freedom roundtable 1977-79, intellectual freedom com. 1979-83, coun. 1983-86), ACLU (bd. dirs. Civil Libertarian of Yr. Nev. chpt. 1988, chair gov.'s conf. for women 1989), Nev. Libr. Assn. (chmn. pub. info. com. 1972-73, intellectual freedom com. 1975-78, govt. rels. com. 1978-79, v.p., pres.-elect 1980, pres. 1981, Spl. Citation 1978, 87, LIbr. of Yr. 1993).

GOULD, MARTY LEON, minister, writer, composer; b. Salina, Kans., May 26, 1949; s. Aubrey Fredrick and Patricia Jolene (Johnson) G.; m. Roberta Joan Butler, May 25, 1973; children: Jeremy Alan, Brandon Matthew, Chad Austin. BA in Bible, Cen. Bible Coll., Springfield, Mo., 1972. Ordained to ministry Assemblies of God, 1976. Min. music Bethel Temple, Hampton, Va., 1972-74, Cen. Assembly, Wichita, Kans., 1974, Bethel Ch., Quincy, Ill., 1974-76, Cen. Assembly, Muskogee, Okla., 1977-78, Bethel Temple, Tampa, Fla., 1978-80, 82-89, Calvary Assembly, North Huntingdon, Pa., 1980-82, Calvary Temple, Springfield, Mo., 1989-91, Cen. Assembly, Cumberland, Md., 1991-95, Evangel Temple, Jacksonville, Fla., 1995-97; dist. music dir. Pa./Fla. Assemblies of God, Lakeland, Fla., 1984-86; mem. nat. music com. Assemblies of God, Springfield, 1987-89, local liaison music com., 1989—; seminar speaker Nat. Assemblies of God. Contbr. articles to religious jours.; TV producer and dir.; composer songs. Organist Revivaltime choir and radio broadcast C.M. Ward; spkr., 1969-72. Republican. Avocations: writing, photography, collecting out of print books on theater. Home: 333 W Ellsworth Ave #611 Denver CO 80223

GOULD, PETER ROBIN, geographer, educator; b. Coulesdon, Eng., Nov. 18, 1932; came to U.S., 1940; s. Ralph Graham and Helene Beatrice (Hanson) G.; m. Johanna Stuyck, July 10, 1956; children: Katherine, Richard, Andrew. BA, Colgate U., 1956; MA, Northwestern U., 1957, PhD, 1960; DSc (hon.), U. Strasbourg, 1982. Asst. prof. Syracuse U., 1960-63; assoc. prof., 1963-68, prof., 1968-86; Evan Pugh prof. Penn. State, University Park, 1986-98, prof. emeritus, 1998—; cons. Dept of State, Portugal, ERA and others. Author: 17 books and monographs, 160 articles and essays. Lt. Gordon Highlanders, Brit. Army, 1951-53, Scotland, Malaya. Recipient award for meritorious contbn. Assn. Am. Geographers, 1975, Scholar's medal Pa. State U., 1981, St. Dié internat. prize Geography, 1993, Retzius Gold medal Swedish Acad. Scis., 1997. Mem. Amnesty Internat., Greenpeace, Phi Beta Kappa. Avocations: reading, walking, music, wine. Office: Penn State 306 Walker Bldg State College PA 16802-5011

GOULD, PHILLIP, defense planner, engineer; b. N.Y.C., Feb. 19, 1940; s. Isaac and Blanche (Handler) G.; m. Elizabeth West Ratigan, Nov. 29, 1980; children: David Elliot, Jessica Ann. B.S.M.E., CCNY, 1961; M.S., MIT, 1963, ScD, 1965. Asst. prof. mech. engring. MIT, Cambridge, 1965-67; mem. staff Inst. for Def. Analyses, Alexandria, Va.; asst. dir. Inst. for Def. Analyses, Alexandria, 1984—; dir. Def. Sci. Study Group, 1998—. Author: Missile Defense Study, 1980, NATO Air Basing Study, 1981, NATO Counterair Study, 1984 (Excellence In Rsch. award 1985), Planning U.S. Conventional Forces, 1986, JCS Forces Planning Study, 1988, Low Observables and Counter Low Observables, 1993, Combating the Proliferation of Weapons of Mass Destruction, 1995, Scenarios for the 2010 to 2015 Time Frame, 1997, Explosive Ordnance Disposal, 1999. Ford fellow, 1965. Fellow AAAS; mem. N.Y. Acad. Scis., Inst. for Ops. Rsch. and Mgmt. Sci., Am. Soc. for Engring. Edn., Soc. for Humanistic Judaism (dir., exec. com.), Sigma Xi. Home: 4590 Indian Rock Ter NW Washington DC 20007-2567 Office: Inst Def Analyses 1801 N Beauregard St Alexandria VA 22311-1733

GOULD, PHILLIP LOUIS, civil engineering educator, consultant; b. Chgo., May 24, 1937; m. Deborah Paula Rothholtz, Feb. 5, 1961; children: Elizabeth; Nathan, Rebecca, Joshua. BS, U. Ill., 1959, MS, 1960; PhD, Northwestern U., 1966. Structural designer Skidmore, Owings & Merrill, Chgo., 1960-63; prin. structural engr. Westenhoff & Novick, Chgo., 1963-64; NASA trainee Northwestern U., Evanston, Ill., 1964-66; asst. prof. civil engring. Washington U., St. Louis, 1966-68, assoc. prof., 1968-74, prof., 1974—, chmn. dept. civil engring., 1978-98, Harold D. Jolly prof. civil engring., 1981—; vis. prof. Ruhr U., Fed. Republic Germany, 1974-75, U. Sydney, Australia, 1981, Shanghai Inst. Tech., Peoples Republic of China, 1986; dir. Earthquake Engring. Rsch. Inst., exec. coun. Internat. Assn. for Shelland Spatial Structures, pres. Great Lakes chpt. and New Madrid chpt. Earthquake Engring. Rsch. Inst. Author: Static Analysis of Shells: A Unified Development of Surface Structures, 1977, Introduction to Linear Elasticity, 1984, Finite Element Analysis of Shells of Revolution, 1985, Analysis of Shells and Plates, 1987, 2d edit., 1999; co-author: Dynamic Response of Structures to Wind and Earthquake Loading, 1980; co-editor: Environmental Forces on Engineering Structures, 1979, Natural Draught Cooling Towers, 1985; editor: Engineering Structures, 1979—. Dir. Earthquake Engring. Rsch. Inst., 1993-95; vice chmn. Mo. Seismic Safety Commn.; St. Louis regional dir. Mid-Am. Earthquake Ctr. Recipient Sr. Scientist award Alexander von Humboldt Found., Fed. Republic Germany, 1974-75. Fellow ASCE (bd. dirs. St. Louis sect. 1985-87, Otto Nutli award); mem. Am. Soc. Engring. Edn., Internat. Assn. Shell Structures, Structural Engrs. Assn. Ill., Mo. Soc. Profl. Engrs. (Outstanding Engr. in Edn. award), Civil Engring. Alumni Assn. U. Ill., Urbana-Champaign (Disting. Alumnus award). Home: 102 Lake Frst Saint Louis MO 63117-1303 Office: Washington U Dept Civil Engring PO Box 1130 Saint Louis MO 63188-1130

GOULD, R(ICHARD) MARTIN (RICHARD MARTIN GOLDMAN), marketing consultant, researcher; b. Auburn, N.Y., Aug. 19, 1941; s. Max and Lillian (Kanter) Goldman. Grad., Auburn East H.S., 1959; student, U. Buffalo, 1961; AB, Ohio No. U., 1963, JD, 1966; postgrad., U. Ariz., 1966. Dir. response mktg. Rep. Orgn., Tucson, 1966-67; legal rschr. ICC, Washington, 1967; asst. bank examiner Comptr. of the Currency, N.Y.C., 1967-68; pub. bond securities salesman Henry Harris & Sons, Inc., N.Y.C., 1968-69; pub. bond salesman Chester Harris & Co., Inc., N.Y.C., 1970-93; land surveyor Interstate Gen. Corp., San Juan, P.R., 1969; with Gen. Devel. Corp., San Juan, 1969; marketer, new bus. rep. Canadaigua Enterprises, Inc., Farmington, N.Y.; assoc. Law Offices of Max Goldman, Auburn, N.Y., 1972-77; sales mktg. cons. G. Enterprises, Gould & Assocs., San Rafael, Calif., 1972—, pub. rels. exec., 1993-96, sales mktg. cons., 1996—. Mem. Internat. Platform Assn., Alpha Epsilon Pi, Phi Alpha Delta, Phi Beta Lambda. Humanist. Avocations: walking, tennis, table tennis, golf, reading. Home and Office: Gould Consultants PO Box 6701 128 La Perdiz Ct San Rafael CA 94903-3541

GOULD, RONALD, lawyer; b. Newark, Oct. 22, 1945. BSEE, N.J. Inst. Tech., 1967; MS, Northwestern U., 1970; JD, U. Ariz., 1973. Bar: N.J. 1973, U.S. Dist. Ct. N.J. 1973, U.S. Ct. Appeals (3d cir.) 1979, U.S. Ct. Appeals (D.C. cir.) 1980, U.S. Supreme Ct. 1980, N.Y. 1981, U.S. Dist. Ct. (so. and ea. dists.) N.Y. 1984, U.S. Ct. Appeals (fed. cir.) 1984, U.S. Patent and Trademark Office. With Shanley & Fisher, P.C., Morristown, N.J. Mem. ABA, IEEE, N.J. State Bar Assn.. *

GOULD, ROY WALTER, engineering educator; b. Los Angeles, Apr. 25, 1927; s. Roy Walter Gould and Rosamonde Belle (Stokes) Terman; m. Ethel Stratton, Aug. 23, 1952; children: Diana Stratton, Robert Clarke. BS, Calif. Inst. Tech., 1949, PhD, 1956; MS, Stanford U., 1950. With Calif. Inst. Tech., Pasadena, 1955—, exec. officer for applied physics, 1972-79, chmn. div. engring. and applied sci., 1979-84, Simon Ramo prof. engring., 1979-96, prof. emeritus, 1996—; dir. div. controlled thermonuclear research U.S. Energy Research Devel. Agy., Washington, 1970-72. Contbr. 85 research papers to profl. pubs. Served with USN, 1945-46. Fellow IEEE, Am. Phys. Soc. (James Clerk Maxwell prize in plasma physics 1994); mem. NAS, Am. Acad. Arts and Scis., Nat. Acad. Engring. E-mail: rwgould@caltech.edu. Office: Calif Inst Tech Dept Engring Applied Sci MS 128-95 Pasadena CA 91125

GOULD, SAMUEL HALPERT, pediatrics educator; b. Balt., June 14, 1922; s. Herman and Theresa Gould; m. June Linda Walter, June 17, 1952; children: Hallie, Phyllis, Cynthia, Nancy. MD, State U. Iowa, 1951. Diplomate Am. Bd. Pediat. Intern Balt. City Hosp., 1951-52, Johns Hopkins Hosp., Balt., 1952-53; resident U. Iowa Hosps., Iowa City, 1953-54; pvt. practice, Benton Harbor, Mich., 1957-86; assoc. prof. pediat. U. Chgo., 1986—, chief sect. gen. pediat., 1993—. Mem. Alpha Omega Alpha. Home: 1555 N Astor St Chicago IL 60610-1673 Office: U of Chgo Pritzker Sch of Medicine 5841 S Maryland Ave MC 1057 Chicago IL 60637-1463*

GOULD, STEPHEN JAY, paleontologist, educator; b. N.Y.C., N.Y., Sept. 10, 1941; s. Leonard and Eleanor (Rosenberg) G.; m. Deborah Ann Lee, Oct. 3, 1965; children: Jesse, Ethan. AB in Geology, Antioch Coll., Yellow Springs, Ohio, 1963; PhD, Columbia U., 1967; DHL (hon.), Marlboro Coll., 1982; DSc (hon.), Bucknell U., 1982; LLD (hon.), Antioch Coll., 1983; LHD (hon.), Colgate U., 1984, Pace U., 1984, Suffolk U., 1984, New Sch. for Social Rsch., 1986, Hofstra U., 1987, Bank Street Coll. of Edn., 1988, Westfield State Coll., 1989, Miami U., Oxford, Ohio, 1992; DSc (hon.), Bucknell U., 1982, MacAlester Coll., 1983, Denison U., 1984, U. Md., 1984, Williams Coll., 1985, Bard Coll., 1986, Kalamazoo U., 1986, SUNY, 1986, L.I. U., 1986, Union Coll., 1987, Rutgers U., 1987, Bates Coll., 1987, Pomona U., 1988, Dickinson Coll., 1988, Duke U., 1989, U. Mo., Saint Louis, 1990, Clark U., 1990, Am. U., 1991, Ripon Coll., 1991, U. Pa., 1991, Wheaton Coll., 1992, CUNY, 1992, Leeds U., England, 1992. Asst. prof. geology, asst. curator Invertebrate Paleontology Harvard U., Cambridge, Mass., 1967-71, assoc. prof. geology, assoc. curator Invertebrate Paleontology, 1971-73, prof. geology, 1973—, curator Invertebrate Paleontology Mus. Comparative Zoology, 1973—, Alexander Agassiz prof. zoology, 1982—, mem. com. profs. dept. biology, adj. mem. dept. history sci., 1973—; Tanner lectr. Cambridge U., 1984, Stanford U., 1989; Terry lectr. Yale U., 1986; Mila Manfield lectr., Tokyo, 1989; inaugural lectr. for Isaiah Berlin annual lectureship, Wolfson Coll., Oxford U., England; mem. Smithsonian Council, 1976—; bd. dirs. biol. scis. curriculum study, 1976-79; adv. bd. Children's TV Workshop, 1978-81; adv. bd. TV program NOVA, 1980—. Author: Ontogeny and Phylogeny, 1977, Ever Since Darwin, 1977, The Panda's Thumb, 1980 (Am. Book award Sci. 1981, Nat. Book award for sci., 1981), The Mismeasure of Man, 1981 (1981 Nat. Book Critics Circle award for gen. non-fiction 1982, Outstanding Book award Am. Ednl. Rsch. Assn. 1983, Iglesias prize for Italian transl., 1991), rev. edit., 1995, (with S.E. Luria and S. Singer) A View of Life, 1981, Hen's Teeth and Horse's Toes, 1983 (Phi Beta Kappa book award in Sci. 1983), The Flamingo's Smile, 1985, Illuminations, A Bestiary, 1986, Time's Arrow, Time's Cycle, 1987, An Urchin in the Storm, 1987, Wonderful Life, 1989 (Forkosch award for best book on humanistic subject, 1990, Phi Beta Kappa book award in sci., 1990, Rhone-Poulenc prize, 1991), Bully for Brontosaurus, 1991, (with R.W. Purcell) Finders, Keepers, 1992, Eight Little Piggies, 1993, Dinosaur in a Haystack, 1995, Full House, 1996, Questioning the Millenium, 1997; gen. editor, preface The Book of Life, 1993; assoc. editor Evolution, 1970-72; editorial bd. Systematic Zoology, 1970-72, Paleobiology, 1974-76, Am. Naturalist, 1977-80; bd. editors Science mag.; also numerous articles, mo. col. This View of Life (Nat. Mag. award 1980), others. Mem. coun. Nat. Portrait Gallery, Washington, 1989—; mem. NASA Space Exploration Coun., 1989-91; bd. dirs. British Mus. Internat. Found., 1992—. Recipient Scientist of Yr. award Discover Mag., 1981, Medal of Excellence Columbia U., 1982, F.V. Haydn medal Phila. Acad. Scis., 1982, J. Priestley award and medal Dickinson Coll., 1983, Neil Miner award for excellence in teaching Nat. Assn. Geology Tchrs., 1983, Disting. Service award Am. Humanists' Assn., 1984, Silver medal Zool. Soc. London, 1984, Founders Coun. award of merit Field Mus. of Natural History, chgo., 1984, Meritorious Service award Am. Assn. Systematics Collections, 1984, Bradford Washburn award and Gold medal Mus. Sci. Boston, 1984, John and Samuel Bard award in Medicine and Sci. Bard Coll., 1984, Creative Arts award Brandeis U., 1986, Glenn T. Seaborg award for contribution to public interest in sci. Internat. Platform Assn., 1986, In Praise Of Reason award CSICOP, 1986, H.D. Vursell award AAAL for recent writing in book form that merits recognition for quality of prose, 1987, Anthropology in Media award Am. Anthrop. Assn., 1987, History of Geology award Geol. Soc. Am., 1988, T.N. George medal U. Glasgow, Scotland, 1989, Sue T. Friedman medal Geol. Soc. London, 1989, Disting. Svc. award Am. Inst. Profl. Geologists, 1989, Edinburgh medal City of Edinburgh, 1990, Britannica award and gold medal, 1990, Disting. Svc. award Nat. Assn. Biology Tchrs., 1991, Homer Smith medal NYU Sch. Medicine, 1992, Disting. Svc. medal Tchrs. James H. Shea awd., Nat. Assn. of Geology Teachers, 1992, Coll. Columbia U., 1992, UCLA medal, 1992, 1st recipient Commonwealth award State of Mass., 1993, J.P. McGovern award and medal in sci. Cosmos Club, 1993; named Humanist Laureate Acad. of Humanism, 1983; Buwalda lectr. Calif. Inst. Tech., 1985; McArthur Found. prize fellow 1981-86; subject of film profile for TV program NOVA, 1985 (Westinghouse Sci. Film award to producers 1985); prin. investigator numerous grants NSF, 1969—; NSF fellow, Woodrow Wilson hon. fellow, Columbia U. hon. fellow, 1963-67, Lilly lectr. Royal Coll. Physicians, London, 1993; Human Talk lectr. Muratec, Kyoto, Japan, 1993. Fellow Am. Acad. Arts and Scis., European Union Geosciences (hon.), AAAS (mem. council 1974-76, com. council affairs 1976-77), Royal Soc. Edinburgh, European Union Geoscis. (hon. fgn.); mem. NAS, Paleontol. Soc. (pres. 1985—, Schuchert award for excellence in paleontol. research (under age 40) 1975), Soc. Study Evolution (v.p. 1975), Soc. Systematic Zoology, Am. Soc. Naturalists (pres. 1977-80), Paleontol. Soc. U.K., Soc. Vertebrate Paleontology, Linnean Soc. (Silver medal 1992), History of Sci. Soc., Soc. for Study Evolution (pres. 1990), Soc. Am. Baseball Rsch., Soc. Study Sports History, Bermuda Biological Station (trustee 1988—), Galerie de l'Evolution Mus. d'Histoire Naturelle, Paris (internat. bd. advisors 1989—), Sigma Xi (sec. treas. Harvard-Radcliffe chpt. 1968-70). Office: Harvard U Mus Comparative Zoology Cambridge MA 02138*

GOULD, W. SCOTT, financial administrator; b. Boston, July 19, 1957; m. Michèle A. Flournoy; 1 child, Alexander. AB, Cornell U., 1979; MBA, U. Rochester, EdD. Commd. ensign USN, advanced through grades; mgmt. cons. TB&A, 1988-90, mng. assoc., 1990-91; asst. receiver, dir. ops. City of Chelsea, Mass., 1991-93; spl. asst. to chmn. Export-Import Bank of U.S., Washington, 1993-94; spl. asst. White House Chief of Staff, Washington, 1993-94; dep. asst. sec. Dept. Treasury, Washington; CFO, asst. sec. adminstrn. Dept. Commerce, Washington; mem. adv. bd. Simon Sch. Bus.; class agt. Roxbury Latin Sch. Ann. Fund; mentor Cornell U. Extern Program. Comdr. USNR. Mem. Inst. Mgmt. Consultants (assoc.), Kappa Delta Pi. Office: Dept of Commerce 15th and Constitution NW Washington DC 20230

GOULD, WESLEY LARSON, political science educator; b. Cleve., May 15, 1917; s. Francis E. and Helen M. (Larson) G.; m. Jean Sarah Barnard, Jan. 24, 1946; children: Francis Barnard, Sarra Marie Gould Marshall, Margaret Elizabeth Gould Pope, Leona Larson Gould-McElhone. AB, Baldwin-Wallace Coll., 1939; MA, Ohio State U., 1941; postgrad, U. Calif., Berkeley, 1941-42; PhD, Harvard U., 1949. Instr. Northeastern U., Boston, 1946-49; asst. prof. polit. sci. Purdue U., Lafayette, Ind., 1949-58; assoc. prof. Purdue U., 1958-61, prof., 1961-67; vis. prof. Northwestern U., 1963-64; prof. Wayne State U., Detroit, 1967-83, prof. emeritus, 1984—; cons. internat. law study U.S. Naval War Coll., summer 1960, Detroit City Charter Revision, 1972-73, Can. Rev. of Studies in Nationalism, 1973-74; PhD examiner Patna U., India, 1963-64; vis. scholar U. Winnipeg, summer 1979. Author: An Introduction to International Law, 1957, (with L. Erades) International and Municipal Law in the Netherlands and the U.S, 1961, (with M. Barkun) International Law and Social Sciences, 1970; contbr. articles to profl. jours. Mem. adv. council on community service of continuing edn. programs Mich. Dept. Edn., 1971-72; mem. regional structure, transp. and communications coms. Regional Citizens Project, Met. Fund, Inc., 1973-74; del. Mich. Dem. Conv., 1971-72; bd. dirs. Citizens Council for Land Use Research and Edn., 1974-79, 86-89. Served with U.S. Army, 1942-45, PTO. Recipient Alumni Merit award Baldwin-Wallace Coll., 1984; fellow U. Liverpool, 1974-75; Am. Soc. Internat. Law grantee, 1964, Wayne U. research grantee, 1970, Earhart Found. grantee, 1974, Social Sci. Research Council grantee, 1957. Mem. Am. Polit. Sci. Assn., Internat. Polit. Sci. Assn., Midwest Polit. Sci. Assn., Acad. Polit. Sci., Am. Soc. Legal and Polit. Philosophy, Internat. Assn. Philosophy of Law and Social Philosophy, Am. Soc. Internat. Law (exec. council 1959-62), Ind. Acad. Social Scis. (bd. dirs. 1958-60), Am. Assn. Higher Edn., Soc. Gen. Systems, Law and Society Assn., Detroit Council World Affairs, Internat. Studies Assn. (exec. com.), AAUP, Assn. Can. Studies U.S., Pi Sigma Alpha. Democrat. Episcopalian. Club: Harvard of Eastern Mich. Home: 693 Partington Ave, Windsor, ON Canada N9B 2N6 Office: Wayne State U Dept Polit Sci Detroit MI 48202 *A scholar's life should be a search for the unknown either through finding hard-to-get information, or by seeking new techniques for extracting the deeper meanings of data. Even if one discovers that a seemingly effective path toward better use of knowledge is a dead end, that in itself is worth discovering so that others will not attempt what does not work.*

GOULD, WILLIAM BENJAMIN, IV, lawyer, educator, federal agency administrator; b. 1936. AB, U. R.I., 1958; LLB, Cornell U., 1961; postgrad. London Sch. Econs., 1962-63; LLD (hon.) U. R.I., 1986, D.C. Sch. Law, 1995, Stetson U., 1996, LLD Capital U., 1997, Rutgers U., 1998. Bar: Mich. 1962. Asst. gen. counsel UAW, AFL-CIO, Detroit, 1961-62; atty. NLRB, Washington, 1963-65; assoc. Battle, Fowler, Stokes & Kheel, N.Y.C., 1965-68; prof. Wayne State U., 1968-71, Stanford (Calif.) U. Law Sch., 1972—; chmn. Nat. Labor Rels. Bd., Washington, 1994-98, Coun. Adminstrv. Conf. U.S., Washington, 1994-95; vis. prof. Harvard U., 1971-72; overseas fellow and vis. prof. Churchill Coll., Cambridge, Eng., 1975; vis. scholar U. Tokyo, 1975; vis. scholar, 1978; Fulbright-Hays Disting. lectr. Kyoto Am. Studies Summer Seminar; Charles A. Beardsley prof. Stanford Law Sch., 1984; vis. fellow Australian Nat. U. Faculty of Law, 1985; vis. prof. European U. Inst., Florence, Italy, 1988; vis. prof. U. Witwatersrand, Johannesburg, South Africa, 1991; Rockefeller Found. fellow, 1975; Guggenheim fellow, 1978. Mem. Nat. Acad. Arbitrators, ABA (sec. labor and employment law sect.), Internat. Soc. for Labor Law and Social Security (exec. com. U.S. nat. br.).; lectr. Am. and fgn. indsl. relations, labor law, U.S., Europe, Japan, S.E. Asia, Africa, Ea. Europe. Office: National Labor Relations Board Office of the Chairman 1099 14th St NW Washington DC 20570

GOULDEN, JOSEPH CHESLEY, author; b. Marshall, Tex., May 23, 1934; s. Joe C. and Lecta M. (Everitt) G.; m. Leslie Cantrell Smith, 1979; children by previous marriage: Joseph C., Jim Craig. Student, U. Tex., 1952-56. Reporter Marshall News Messenger, 1956, Dallas News, 1958-61, Phila. Inquirer, 1961-68; dir. media analysis Accuracy in Media, 1989-98. Books include The Curtis Caper, 1965, Monopoly, 1968, Truth Is the First Casualty, 1969, The Money Givers, 1971, Meany, 1972, The Superlawyers, 1972, The Benchwarmers, 1974, The Best Years, 1976, The Million Dollar Lawyers, 1978, Korea: The Untold Story of the War, 1982, Jerry Wurf: Labor's Last Angry Man, 1982, The Death Merchant, 1984, (as Henry S.A. Becket) The Dictionary of Espionage, 1986, Fit to Print: A.M. Rosenthal and His Times, 1988; author: (with Paul Dickson) There Are Alligators in Our Sewers, 1983, (with Paul Dickson) Myth-Informed, 1993, (with Reed Irvine and Cliff Kincaid) The News Manipulators, 1993; editor: books include Mencken's Last Campaign, 1976. Served with U.S. Army, 1956-58. Mem. Tex. Inst. Letters, Washington Ind. Writers, H.L. Mencken Soc., Assn. Former Intelligence Officers, Phi Kappa Tau. Home: 1534 29th St NW Washington DC 20007-3060 Office: Brandt & Brandt 1501 Broadway New York NY 10036-5601

GOULDER, GERALD POLSTER, retail executive, management consultant, lawyer; b. Columbus, Ohio, Apr. 30, 1953; s. Norman Ernest and Betty (Polster) G.; children: Gavrielle, Nathaniel. *Wife Debra, daughter of Dr. Robert and Rascha Kriegsman is Executive Director ofCollege Hill Child Care Coop, Greensboro. Rascha Kriegsman, trustee Witherspoon Art Gallery, UNC-Greensboro. Robert Kriegsman, BA UNC-Chapel Hill, Fellow American College of Dentistry. Mother, Betty Norman Goulder, BA Case Western, President, Perhar Corporation. Father Norman Goulder, BA Oberlin, MD Harvard, Fellowship University of Chicago, former Major USAF, first board certified cardiologist in Columbia, Associate Professor, Ohio State University Medical School. Brother Eric, BA Oberlin, MD Ohio State University, Director Riverside Hospitals Cardiac Rehabilitation Center, Fellow American College of Cardiology. Sister Marcey, BA Ohio State University, broadcast journalist, WBNS-TV, WCMH-TV, Columbus.* BA, Ohio State U., 1975; JD, Washington U., 1978. Bar: Ohio 1978, N.C. 1985; cert. mediator N.C. Supreme Ct., N.C. Indsl. Commn. Spl. prosecutor office state atty. gen. Divsn. Medicaid Fraud Control, Columbus, 1979-80; spl. prosecutor Antitrust Divsn., Columbus, 1981-83; atty. James M. Schottenstein & Assocs., Columbus, 1983-84; chmn., CEO Carolina Drug Distbrs., Inc. and Emporium Stores, Ltd., Greensboro, N.C., 1984-96; CEO, dir. Planetemall.com, 1999—; dir. Greensboro Pvt. Adjudication Ctr., 1998—.

Assoc. editor Washington U. Urban Law Ann., 1977-78; contbr. articles to profl. jours. Trustee Wexner Heritage Village, Columbus, 1983-84, bd. dirs. Eastern Music Festival, Greensboro, 1991-94, U. N.C.-Greensboro Spartan Club, 1991-95; v.p. Beth David Synagogue, Greensboro, 1992-95, pres., 1996; participant Leadership Greensboro, 1985, Triad Leadership, 1991; mem. Crime Study Commn., Greensboro, 1992, Greensboro Devel. Corp., 1993-95. Mem. Am. Arbitration Assn., Am. Intellectual Property Lawyers Assn., N.C. Bar Assn., Greensboro Bar Assn., Columbus Bar Assn., Ohio Bar Assn., Leadership Greensboro Alumni Assn., Equestrian Dispute Resolution Assn. (bd. dirs. 1999—). E-mail: goulder@MEDIAT8.net. Office: Greensboro Pvt Adjudication Ctr 1006 N Holden Rd Greensboro NC 27410-4826

GOULDEY, GLENN CHARLES, manufacturing company executive; b. N.Y.C., July 28, 1952; s. George Howard and Jeannette Ruth Williamson; m. Leslie Jeanne Ruth, Oct. 2, 1982; children: Jeremy Charles, Nicholas Glenn, Alexander James George. BS in Bus., Coll. N.J., 1976; postgrad. Portland State U., 1980; MBA Rider U., 1981; postgrad. Dartmouth Coll., 1994-95. Cert. in purchasing mgmt. Purchasing Mgrs. Assn. Sr. planner Eaton Corp., Flemington, N.J., 1975-77, pricing mgr., distbn., 1977-79, inventory control mgr., 1979-80, materials mgr., purchasing, Beaverton, Oreg., 1980-81, mfg. and materials mgr., 1981-83, mktg. and materials mgr., 1983-87, plant and gen. mgr., 1987-88, v.p. sales and mktg., Carol Stream, Ill., 1988-89, mgr. ops. div., 1989-93, gen. bus. mgr., 1993-95, pres., gen. mgr., LECTRON Products Divsn./EATON, Rochester Hills, Mich., 1995—; bd. advisors Oakland U. Bus. Sch. Patentee in field. Mem. Am. Prodn. Inventory Control Soc. (cert. in prodn. and inventory control), Nat. Youth Sports Coaches Assn. (cert.), Soc. Automotive engrs. Internat. Republican. Lutheran. Office: Lectron Products Eaton Corp 1400 S Livernois Rd Rochester MI 48307-3362

GOULDING, NORA See CLARK, SUSAN

GOULDTHORPE, KENNETH ALFRED PERCIVAL, publisher, state official; b. London, Jan. 7, 1928; came to U.S., 1951, naturalized, 1956; s. Alfred Edward and Frances Elizabeth Finch (Callow) G.; m. Judith Marion Cutts, Aug. 9, 1975; children: Amanda Frances, Timothy Graham Cutts. Student U. Westminster (formerly Regent St. Poly.), 1948-49, Bloomsbury Tech. Inst., 1949-50; diploma City and Guilds of London, 1949; student, Washington U., 1951-52. Staff photographer Kentish Mercury, London, 1949-50, St. Louis Post-Dispatch, 1951-55, picture editor, 1955-57; nat. and fgn. corr. Life mag., Time, Inc., N.Y.C., 1957-61, Paris Bur., 1961-65, regional editor Australia-New Zealand, 1966-68, editorial dir. Latin Am., 1969-70; editor Signature mag., N.Y.C., 1970-73; mng. editor Penthouse mag., N.Y.C., 1973-76, pub. cons., 1976-79; editor, exec. pub. Adventure Travel mag., Seattle, 1979-80; sr. ptnr. Pacific Pub. Assocs., Seattle, 1981-83; editor, pub. Washington mag., 1984-89; vice chmn. Evergreen Pub. Co., 1984-89; dir. tourism, State of Wash., 1989-91; pub./cons., writer, 1991—; dir. Grand Fir Pub. Corp., 1994—; tchr. design, editorial techniques Parsons Sch. Design, N.Y.C.; lectr., contbr. elementary schs. lit. progs. Served with Royal Navy, 1946-48. Decorated Naval Medal and bar; recipient awards of excellence Nat. Press Photographers Assn., AP and UP, 1951-57, Pres.' medal Ea. Wash. U., 1986; certs. excellence, Am. Inst. Graphic Arts, 1971, 72, 73, Communication Arts, 1980, 81, 84; spl. award, N.Y. Soc. Publs. Designers, 1980. Mem. Regional Pubs. Assn. (v.p., pres., Best Typography award 1985, Best Spl. Issue 1989), Western Publs. Assn. (Best Consumer Mag. award, Best Travel Mag. awards, 1980, Best Regional and State Mag. award 1985, 86, 88, Best New Publ. award 1985, Best Column award 1985, Best Signed Essay 1986, 87, Best Four-Color Layout 1985, Best Four Color Feature Design), City and Regional Mag. Assn. (William Allen White Bronze awards), Time/Life Alumni Soc., Assn. Washington Gens. (gen. of state 1995, bd. dirs.), Sigma Delta Chi. Episcopalian. Nominated for Pulitzer Prize for coverage of Andrea Doria disaster, 1956; contbr. articles, photographs to nat. mags., books by Life mag.; author: Design for Music, 1998. Home: 3049 NW Esplanade Seattle WA 98117-2624

GOULET, CHARLES RYAN, retired insurance company executive; b. Fond du Lac, Wis., Oct. 13, 1927; s. Charles N. and Irene (Ryan) G.; m. Jeanne Comfort, Aug. 18, 1951; 1 child, Christopher Robert. B.A., Beloit Coll., 1951; M.B.A., U. Chgo., 1953. Adminstrv. resident Jefferson-Hillman Hosp., Birmingham, Ala., 1952-53; adminstrv. asst., asst. supt. Cleve. City Hosp., 1953-55; asst. prof. U. Pitts., 1955-58; asso. dir. Johns Hopkins Hosp., 1958-62; dir. U. Chgo. Hosps. and Clinics, 1962-69; prof. hosp. adminstrn. U. Chgo., 1962-69, assoc. dir. program in hosp. adminstrn., 1962-69; prin. Cresap, McCormick and Paget, Inc.; mgmt. cons., Chgo., 1969-71; v.p. Blue Cross-Blue Shield, Chgo., 1971-75; exec. v.p. Blue Cross-Blue Shield, 1975-88; vice chmn., dir. H.M.O. Ill. Inc., 1980-88; exec. sec. Assn. U. Programs in Hosp. Adminstrn., 1962-65, pres. Chgo. Hosp. Council, 1968; pres. HMO Ill., Inc., 1976-82; treas. Ill. Hosp. Assn., 1969; mem. exec. com. Council Teaching Hosps., Assn. Am. Med. Colls., 1966-69. Mem. adv. coun. Kellogg Found., 1965-67; bd. dirs. Hyde Park Dept. YMCA, 1966-68, Coop. Blood Replacement Plan, Home for destitute Crippled Children, 1965-69, Chgo. Home for Incurables, 1966-69, Harvard-St. George Sch. Chgo., 1968-72, Hosp. Planning Coun. Met. Chgo., 1968-69, Comprehensive Health Planning, Chgo., 1968-71, Ill. Regional Med. Program, 1967-69, Am. Blood Commn., 1976-89, v.p., 1978-83, Geneva (Ill.) Cmty. Chest, 1990, 93-96, pres., 1975-76; mem. governing commn. Cook County Hosp., 1969-70; mem. Ill. Health Fin. Authority, 1979-82, Ill. Health Care Cost Containment Com., 1984-96; trustee Alexian Bros. Med. Ctr., Elk Grove Village, Ill., 1993-94; bd. govs. Alexian Bros. Health Sys., 1995—; dir. Alexian Bros. Health Providers, 1996—. 1st lt. Med. Adminstrn. Corps AUS, 1946-47. Recipient Bachmeyer award U. Chgo., 1953; Disting. Service award Beloit Coll., 1976. Fellow Am. Coll. Hosp. Adminstrs.; mem. Am. Hosp. Assn., Phi Kappa Psi, Skyline Club (Chgo.), Big Foot Country Club (Fontana, Wis.), Quadrangle Club (Chgo.), Oasis Country Club (Palm Desert, Calif.). Home: 1001 S Batavia Ave Geneva IL 60134-3012

GOULET, DENIS ANDRÉ, development ethicist, writer; b. Fall River, Mass., May 27, 1931; s. Fernand Joseph and Lumena (Bouchard) G.; m. Ana Maria Reynaldo, Nov. 21, 1964; children: Andrea, Sinane. BA in Philosophy, St. Paul's Coll., Washington, 1954, MA in Philosophy, 1956; MA in Social Planning, Institut de Recherche et de Formation en Vue du Développement, Paris, 1960; PhD in Polit. Sci., U. São Paulo, Brazil, 1963. Laborer France, Spain, Algeria, 1956-59; planning advisor AID, Recife, Brazil, 1964-65; vis. prof. U. Sask., Regina, Can., 1965-66; assoc. prof. Ind. U., Bloomington, 1966-68; vis. fellow Ctr. for Study of Dem. Instns., Santa Barbara, Calif., 1969; fellow Ctr. for Study Devel. & Social Change, Cambridge, Mass., 1970-74; vis. prof. U. Calif., San Diego, 1969-70; sr. fellow Ctr. for Study Devel. and Social Change, Cambridge, Mass., 1970-74; vis. fellow Overseas Devel. Coun./OAS, Washington, 1974-76; sr. fellow Overseas Devel. Coun., Washington, 1976-79; O'Neill chair in edn. for justice, dept. econs. U. Notre Dame, Ind., 1979—; faculty fellow Kellogg Inst. for Internat. Study, Krock Inst. for Internat. Peace Studies; vis. prof. U. Warsaw, Poland, 1989-90. Author: The Cruel Choice, 1971, The Uncertain Promise, 1977, Mexico: Development Strategies for the Future, 1983, Incentives for Development: The Key to Equity, 1989, Development Ethics: A Guide to Theory and Practice, 1995. Exec. bd. Internat. Dev. Ethics Assn.; editl. bd. Jour. of Health and Population in Developing Countries; hon. editl. bd. Encyclopedia of Life Support Sys.; internat. adv. coun. TODA Inst. for Global Peace and Policy Rsch.; internat. adv. bd. Internat. Centre for Islamic Political Economy. Decorated chevalier Odre Nat. du Cedre (Lebanon), 1960; OAS grantee, 1961-62, Fulbright grantee, 1986; recipient Reinhold Niebuhr award U. Notre Dame, 1988. Democrat. Roman Catholic. Avocations: racquetball, piano. Home: 825 Ashland Ave South Bend IN 46616-1307 Office: U Notre Dame 119 Hesburgh Ctr Notre Dame IN 46556-5677

GOULET, WILLIAM DAWSON, marketing professional; b. Hartford, Conn., Sept. 24, 1941; s. Henry J.K. and Elizabeth Bryne (Dawson) G. BA in English, Marietta Coll., 1963. Field service rep. Conn. Gen. Life Ins. Co., Hartford, 1963-65; sales promotion assoc. Phoenix Mut. Life Ins. Co., Hartford, 1965-69; dir. sales promotion Pacific Nat. Life Ins. Co., San Francisco, 1969-70; v.p. sales and mktg. E.F. Hutton Life Ins. Co., San Francisco, 1970-79; sr. v.p., fin. planning Prudential-Bache, San Francisco, 1979; v.p. GUMP's, San Francisco, 1980-91, mem. exec. com., 1981-91, mktg. cons., 1991-94; pres. Campton Advt. Agy., 1980-91; dir. mktg. Asian Art Mus. of San Francisco, 1994—; dean ins. faculty Life Ins. Industry Sch., Williamsburg, Va., 1974; mktg. cons. U. of the Pacific, Stockton, Calif., 1972-80. Bd. dirs. Mus. Soc. San Francisco, 1984-90, Friends of Recreation and Parks, 1980-95, v.p. bd. dirs., 1986, sch. internat. studies U. Pacific, 1997—; mem. adv. bd. The McLean Home, Simsbury, Conn., 1985; mem. hon. bd. govs. The World Corp. Games, San Francisco, 1988; trustee Performing Arts Libr. and Mus., 1990-98, v.p. bd. 1991, pres. bd. 1992-95, Asian Art Mus. Found., 1992-94. Sgt. USAR, 1963-69. Recipient Lawrence award Life Advertisers Assn., Vancouver, B.C., Can., 1979, Disting. Alumni Lectr. award Marietta Coll., 1985. Mem. San Francisco Grand Prix Assn. (adv. bd. 1986), Western Retail Mktg. Assn. (bd. dirs. 1989). Democrat. Roman Catholic. Avocations: gardening, travel. Home and Office: PO Box 155 Ross CA 94957-0155

GOULIANOS, KONSTANTIN, physics educator; b. Salonica, Greece, Nov. 9, 1935; came to U.S., 1958, naturalized, 1967; s. Achilles and Olga (Nakopoulou) G. Student, U. Salonica, 1953-58; Ph.D., Columbia U., 1963. Research assoc. Columbia U., N.Y.C., 1963-64; instr. physics Princeton U., N.J., 1964-67, asst. prof., 1967-71; assoc. prof. physics Rockefeller U., N.Y.C., 1971-81, prof., 1981—. Patentee electronic device of analysis of radioactivitively labeled gel electrophoretograms. Fulbright scholar, 1958-59. Home: 11 W 69th St Apt 4A New York NY 10023-4700 Office: Rockefeller U Lab Expt High-Energy Physics 1230 York Ave New York NY 10021-6399

GOUMNEROVA, LILIANA CHRISTOVA, physician, neurosurgeon, educator; b. Jakarta, Indonesia, Sept. 27, 1956; came to U.S., 1988; d. Christo Todorov and Jeanne Dimitrova (Petkova) G. BSc, Faculty of Medicine, Sofia, Bulgaria, 1977; MD, U. Toronto, 1980. Intern U. Toronto, 1980-81; resident in neurosurgery U. Ottawa, Can., 1981-86; fellow in pediatric neurosurgery Hosp. Sick Children, Toronto, 1987-88, assoc. staff neurosurgeon, 1987-88; assoc. staff surgeon Ottawa (Can.) Civic Hosp., 1986-87; Dana fellow in neurosurgery U. Pa., Phila., 1988-90; assoc. in neurosurgery Children's Hosp., Boston, 1990—, dir. clin. pediat. neurosurg. oncology, 1999—; assoc. in neurosurgery Brigham & Women's Hosp., Boston, 1990—; cons. neurosurgeon Dana Farber Cancer Inst., Boston, 1990—, dir. clin. pediat. neurosurg. oncology, % ; asst. prof. surgery Sch. Medicine Harvard U., Boston, 1990—. Mem. Am. Assn. Neurol. Surgeons (Young Investigator award 1996). Office: Childrens Hosp 300 Longwood Ave Boston MA 02115-5737

GOUNARIDOU, KIKI, theater educator. PhD, U. Calif., Davis, 1992. Prof. U. Pitts., 1992—. E-mail: kikigo @pitt.edu. Office: U Pitts Theater Dept Cathedral of Learning 1617 Pittsburgh PA 15260

GOUNARIS, ANNE DEMETRA, biochemistry educator, researcher; b. Boston, Oct. 27, 1924; d. Demetrios Themistocles and Kaliope (Gouvalaris) G. R.N. Mass. Gen. Hosp., 1946; A.B., Boston U., 1955; Ph.D., Harvard U., 1960. Research assoc. Brookhaven Nat. Lab., Upton, N.Y., 1960-62, Carlsberg Lab., Copenhagen, 1962-64, Rockefeller U., N.Y.C., 1964-66; prof. Vassar Coll., Poughkeepsie, N.Y., 1966-90, prof. emeritus, 1990—; vis. fellow Mass. Gen. Hosp., Boston, 1978-83; vis. scientist Strangeways Research Lab., Cambridge, Eng., 1980-81. Contbr. articles to profl. jours. NIH grantee, 1968-71, 1972-76; Ann Horton Fellow, 1980-81; named Collegium Disting. Alumnae, Boston U., 1974. Mem. AAAS, AAUP, Am. Chem. Soc., Am. Soc. for Biochemistry and Molecular Biology, Phi Beta Kappa, Sigma Xi.

GOUNLEY, DENNIS JOSEPH, lawyer; b. Phila., Jan. 29, 1950; s. George Gerard and Elizabeth Mary (Maggioncalda) G.; m. Martha Ann Zatezalo, Sept. 25, 1976. B.A., St. Joseph's Coll., Phila., 1971; J.D., Dickinson Sch. Law, 1974. Bar: Pa. 1974, U.S. Dist. Ct. (we. dist.) Pa. 1995, U.S. Ct. Appeals (3d cir.) 1976, U.S. Supreme Ct. 1977. Sole practice, Greensburg, Pa., 1974-83, 1990—; ptnr. Gounley & O'Halloran, Greensburg, 1984-90; Westmoreland County mental health rev. officer, 1991—. Council mem. Franklin Towne Condominium Assn., Murrysville, Pa., 1976-79. Mem. Pa. Bar Assn., Westmoreland Bar Assn., Rotary. Republican. Roman Catholic. Home: 3590 N Hills Rd Murrysville PA 15668-1438 Office: 15 E Otterman St Greensburg PA 15601-2543

GOURAIGE, HERVÉ, lawyer; b. Port-au-Prince, Haiti, Feb. 12, 1950; came to U.S., 1962; s. Frantz and Altagracia (Rodriguez) G.; m. Carla J. Edwards, Oct. 21, 1989; 1 child, Sophia India. BA, Boston U., 1972, Oxford (Eng.) U., 1974; MA, Oxford (Eng.) U., 1982; JD, Harvard U., 1977. Bar: N.Y. 1978, U.S. Dist. Ct. (ea. and so. dists.) N.Y. 1978, U.S. Ct. Appeals (2d, 3d and 9th cirs.) 1982, U.S. Supreme Ct. 1982, N.J. 1991, U.S. Dist. Ct. N.J. 1991. Assoc. Mudge Rose Guthrie Alexander & Ferdon, N.Y.C., 1977-84; asst. U.S. atty. for so. dist. N.Y. U.S. Dept. Justice, N.Y.C., 1984-91; of counsel Crummy, Del Deo, Dolan, Newark, 1991-94, Latham & Watkins, Newark, N.J., 1994—. Trustee Newark Community Sch. Arts, 1992—. Rhodes scholar, 1972. Mem. ABA, Am. Law Inst., Assn. Bar City N.Y. Democrat. Roman Catholic. Avocations: tennis, soccer, reading. Office: Latham & Watkins One Newark Center Newark NJ 07101-3174

GOURAN, DENNIS STEPHEN, communications educator; b. Peoria, Ill., Oct. 30, 1941; s. Rolland James and Helen Catherine (Rogers) G.; m. Marilyn Kamman, Aug. 31, 1963; children: David Scott, Darren Shea. BS, Ill. State U., 1963, MS, 1965; PhD, U. Iowa, 1968. Prof. communication Ind. U., Bloomington, 1968-84; prof. communications, head dept. speech communication Pa. State U., University Park, 1984-98, prof. speech comm./labor and indsl. rels., 1998—. Author: Discussion: The Process of Group Decision Making, 1974, Making Decision in Groups: Choices and Consequences, 1983, contbr. book chpts. and articles to profl. publs.; editor Cen. State Speech Jour., 1978-82. Mem. Internat. Communication Assn., Speech Communication Assn. (Scholar 1985), Cen. States Speech Assn. (pres. 1984-86, Teaching award 1973), Acad. Polit. Sci. Home: 538 Brittany Dr State College PA 16803-1420 Office: Pa State U Dept of Speech Comm University Park PA 16802*

GOURAS, MARK STEVEN, lawyer; b. Seattle, Apr. 21, 1961; s. Robert N. and Suzanne Marie Gouras; m. Elvira Pilar Lipio, July 27, 1984. BA in English, U. Wash., 1983; JD, U. Puget Sound, 1986. Bar: Wash. 1986, U.S. Dist. Ct. (we. dist.) Wash. Assoc. Albert & Slater, P.S., Federal Way, Wash., 1986-88, Taylor, Kiefer & Bartlett, Seattle, 1988-93; pvt. practice Seattle, 1993-96; ptnr. Hillman & Gouras, LLP, Tukwila, Wash., 1997—. Mem. ABA, Wash. State Bar Assn., Seattle-King County Bar Assn. Republican. Office: 16040 Christensen Rd Ste 215 Tukwila WA 98188-2966

GOURAUD, JACKSON S., energy company executive; b. N.Y.C., Sept. 7, 1923; s. Powers St. George and Irma (Hunt) G.; m. Sheila Marguerite McCowan, Jan. 31, 1942; children: Irma Marguerite, George Edward; m. Betty Buffum, 1996. BS in Econs., U. Pa., 1945. Asst. dir. establishment div. Remington Rand, 1946-52; dir. vet. and animal health div. Pfizer, 1952-58; div. mgr. Joseph E. Seagrams, 1958-60; assoc. founding ptnr., exec. v.p. Bragarnick, N.Y.C., 1960-67; gen. mgr. mktg. Liggett and Myers,, 1968-70; chmn. bd. dirs., chief exec. officer On-Line Decisions, N.Y.C. and London, 1970-78; dep. under sec. Dept. Energy, Washington, 1978-80; pres., chief exec. officer Energy Clinic Co., 1980—; chmn., chief exec. officer Quantum Pharmics, 1986-87; lectr. Yale U., 1958-68; bd. dirs. Brady and Sun, Worcester, Mass.; chmn. bd. dirs. Presto/Tek, Vinal Therm West; chmn. Window/Tech., Austin, Tex., Alten Ozone. Chmn. Ark. initiative com. Interfaith Alliance, Washington, 1995-96, chmn. adv. com.; chmn. adv. com. Citizens Coalition for Nursing Home Reform; bd. dirs. Gundersen Med. Found. Col. AUS, 1941-78. Decorated Bronze star, Purple Heart, Legion of Merit, Combat Inf. badge. Mem. AARP (chmn. congl. contact com., chmn. Calif. vote, chmn. Calif. legis. network), Solar Energy Industries Assn. (chmn., pres. 1983-89), Bucks Club (London), Dorsett Field Club (Vt.), Rockefeller Club, Army-Navy Club (N.Y.C., Washington), Squadron A Club, Internat. Club (Washington). Democrat. Episcopalian. Home: Kissing Camels Country Club 3445 Hill Cir Colorado Springs CO 80904-1004 Office: Alten Ozone 3788 Fabian Way Palo Alto CA 94303-4601 *One develops a value chronolgy as he moves through life. I suspect it depends very much on one's age at the time of development, but clearly mine now is: health, family, money.*

GOUREVITCH, JACQUELINE, artist; b. Paris, Oct. 28, 1933; came to U.S., 1940; d. Henry and Sophie (Eliasberg) Herrmann; m. Victor Gourevitch, June 18, 1954; children: Marc, Philip. BA, U. Chgo., 1954; student, Black Mountain (N.C.) Coll., 1950, Art Inst. Chgo., 1955-57. Vis. artist Wesleyan U., Middletown, Conn., 1967-71/2, Hartford (Conn.) Art Sch., 1973-78; vis. artist, lectr. U. Calif., Berkeley, 1974, Vassar Coll., Poughkeepsie, N.Y., 1977; prof. painting and drawing Wesleyan U., 1978-89; adj. faculty Cooper Union, N.Y.C., 1989-92; vis. prof. Mt. Holyoke Coll., South Hadley, Mass., 1995. Solo exhbns. at Eleanor Rigelhaupt Gallery, Boston, 1967, 69, Tibor DeNagy, N.Y.C., 1971, 72, 73, Wadsworth Atheneum, Matrix Gallery, Hartford, 1975, Gallery Marina Dinkler, Berlin, 1988, New Britain Mus. Am. Art, New Britain, Conn., 1994, Paesaggio Gallery, West Hartford, Conn., 1993, 96, 99; represented in pub. collections at Wadsworth Atheneum, Menil Collection, Houston, De Cordova Mus., Lincoln., Mass., U.Calif., Berkeley, others. NEH grantee, 1976; Conn. Commn. on Arts grantee, 1983; Tamarind Inst. fellow, 1973. Home: 120 Duane St New York NY 10007-1113

GOURGEY, KAREN LUXTON, special education educator; b. Bklyn., Oct. 20, 1947; d. William Collin and Eleanor (Neubert) Luxton; m. Charles Steven Gourgey, May 9, 1993. BA in Psychology, Oberlin Coll., 1969; MAT in Secondary Edn., NYU, 1971; EdD in Spl. Edn., Columbia U., 1983. Ednl. cons. N.Y. Assn. for the Blind, N.Y.C., 1970-71; English tchr. Woodland (Calif.) H.S., 1972-75; instr. dept. spl. edn. Tchrs. Coll. Columbia U., N.Y.C., 1976-77, project counselor program for handicapped coll. students, 1977-78, coord. student svcs. program for handicapped coll. students, 1978-79; assoc. dir. rsch. and devel. computer ctr. visually impaired Baruch Coll., N.Y.C., 1980-83, dir. computer ctr. visually impaired people, 1983—; ednl. cons. Nat. Theater Workshop of Handicapped, N.Y.C., 1982—, Theater Workshop of Handicapped, N.Y.C.; chair subcom. on centralized info. Gov.'s Task Force on Tech. and Disability, N.Y.C., 1987-88; peer reviewer Office Spl. Edn. and Rehab. Svcs., 1990, NSF, Washington, 1995—. Co-prodr. (monthly radio series) Disabled in Action Speaks Sta. WBAI-FM, 1977. Trustee, chair cmty. adv. coun. Jewish Guild for the Blind, N.Y.C., 1984—; v.p. Ctr. Ind. of Disabled N.Y., 1988-90. Included in Manhattan Profile New York Newsday, 1990; recipient Access award Am. Found. for the Blind, 1990. Mem. Assn. for the Edn. and Rehab. of the Blind and Visually Impaired. Avocations: musical performance in duo Folkspirit, acting, walking, swimming. Home: 55 W 14th St Apt 4A New York NY 10011-7400

GOURLEY, DICK R., college dean; b. Franklin, Ky., Dec. 26, 1944; m. Greta Ann Kimbrough, Dec. 7, 1968; 1 child, Kristin Marie. BS in Pharmacy, U. Tenn., 1969, D of Pharmacy, 1970. Lic. pharmacist Tenn., Ga., Nebr. Asst. prof. clin. pharmacy Mercer U., Atlanta, 1970-72, prof., dean., 1984-89; prof., dean. Coll. Pharmacy, U. Tenn., Memphis, 1989—; asst. prof., chmn. dept. pharmacy practice U. Nebr., Omaha, 1972-73, assoc. prof., chmn., 1973-81, prof. chmn., 1981-84; vis. prof. U. Sydney, Australia, 1978; vis. tutor Ctrl. Inst. Tech., Upper Hutt, New Zealand, 1978; bd. dirs. Internat. Fedn. for Pharmacy Edn.; cons. Eli Lilly Co., 1983-85, Australian Nat. Health and Med. Rsch. Coun., 1982—, Lancaster County Bd. Lancaster Manor Nursing Home, 1981-82, Nebr. State Dept. Pub. Instns., 1976-84, Family Health Care, Inc., Omaha, 1975-84, Tri-County Meml. Hosp., Lexington, Nebr., 1975-76, Pharmacy and Therapeutics Com. Luth. Med. Ctr., Omaha, 1975, Henderson-Floyd Drugs and Shannondale Nursing Home, Knoxville, Tenn., 1971-72, Dr.'s Meml. Hosp. Atlanta, 1971-72, Ga. Narcotic Treatment Program, 1971-72, Grady Meml. Hosp., Atlanta, 1971-72, and numerous others; active Bd. Pharm Specialists, 1993—, vice chmn., 1994, chair 1995, 96, 97). Author: (with J. McHan) Laboratory Manual for Introductory Pharmacy, Physical Pharmacy and Pharmacy Technology, 1971; (with others) Practicing Pharmacist Handbook: Guidlines for the Establishment of High Blood Pressure Control Services by the Practicing Pharmacist, 1977, various chpts. in Pharmacy Technicians' Manual, 1988, Applied Therapeutics for Clinical Pharmacists, 1983, Clinical Pharmacy and Therapeutics, 1982, Pharmaceutics and Pharmacy Practice, 1981, Sourcebook on Clinical Pharmacy, 1980, Clinical Pharmacy and Therapeutics, 1979, Handbook of Non-Prescription Drugs, 1979, Handbook for Institutional Pharmacy Practice, 1979; editor: A Study Guide for the PCAT Examination, 1983, 3d edit., 1998; co-editor: Clinical Pharmacy and Therapeutics, 4th edit., 1988, 5th edit., 1992, Tectbook of Therapeutics: Drug and Disease Management, 6th edit., 1996; mem. editorial bds. Topics in Hosp. Mgmt., Clin. Rsch. Practices and Drug Regulatory Affairs, World Pharmacy Sci., Am. Jour. Managed Care; published audio-visual ednl. materials; contbr. articles to profl. jours. Chmn. UNMC Coll. Pharmacy United Way Campaign, 1979-81; judge Greater Nebr. Sci. and Engring. Fair, 1973-79. Grantee Eli Lilly and Co., 1996, 97, 98, U. Nebr-Lincoln, 1979, HEW, 1976-80, Area Health Edn. Ctr., 1974, 73, Robert Wood Johnson Found., 1973-76, Novartis, 1994, 95, 96, 97, 98, Sishering Plough, 1997, SKB, 1997, Ruche, 1997; fellow Internat. Ctr. for Pharmacy Edn. and Rsch., 1988, U. Nebr., 1978. Mem. Am. Coun. Pharm. Edn. (mem. site team), Am. Soc. Hosp., Pharmacists (chmn., vice chmn. ASHP-ANA Joint Com., 1977-79, bd. dirs. 1981-84, del. Ho. Delegates, 1977, 78, 82, 83, 84, bd. liaison Coun. on Legal and Pub. Affairs, 1983-84, Coun. Edn. and Manpower 1982-83, Coun. Organizational Affairs, 1981-82, mem. several other coms.), Am. Assn. Colls. of Pharmacy (chmn. Sect. Teachers of Clin. Instrn. 1977-79, chmn. Coun. of Sects. 1995—, chmn. Standing Rules of Procedure Com., 1974-76, mem. several other coms.), Am. Pharm. Assn. (del. Ho. Delegates, 1977, 88-94), Nebr. Soc. Hosp. Pharmacists (chmn. Program Com. 1979-81, co-chmn. 1976-77, Spl. Svc. to Hosp. Pharmacy award 1984), Ga. Pharmaceutical Assn., Greater Omaha Pharmacists Assn. (bd. dirs. 1974-77), Nebr. Pharmacists Assn., Tenn. Pharmacists Assn., Internat. Found. for Pharmacy Edn. (pres. 1992—), Fedn. Internat. Pharm., Soc. Hosp. Pharmacists Australia, Pan Pacific Found. (program coord. II Conf. 1979-82, III Conf. 1982—, IV Conf. 1987, chmn. V Conf. exec. v.p. 1982-92), Blue Lodge, Shriners, Phi Delta Chi (v.p. collegiate affairs 1973-78), Rho Chi (counselor region V 1976-78). Office: U Tenn Coll Pharmacy 847 Monroe Ave Memphis TN 38103-4901

GOURLEY, EVERETT HAYNIE, educator; b. Hammond, Ind., Apr. 14, 1952; m. Cheryl Maureen McGuire, Sept. 25, 1974 (dec. Oct. 1978); m. Sandra Jean Lentz, Dec. 28, 1990. AA, Delta Coll., 1972; BS, Ea. Mich. U., 1974, MA, 1978. Instr. English Dowagiac (Mich.) Schs., 1975—; counselor Madison Ctr., Mishawaka, Ind., 1981-89; adj. instr. speech Southwestern Mich. Coll., Dowagiac, 1979-81, Lake Mich. Coll., Benton Harbor, 1982-87, adj. instr. interpersonal theory Notre Dame U., South Bend, Ind., 1983-91; advisor interpersonal studies Lake Mich Coll., 1985-88, Purdue U., Westville, Ind., 1986-88; cons. in field. Author of poems. Founder strides for life Am. Cancer Soc., Southwestern Mich., 1978-87. Mem. Nat. Coun. Tchrs. English, Nat. Coun. Tchrs. Speech, Bay Striders Running Club (dir., pres.). Taoist. Avocations: ultra marathons, writing. Home: 2286 Thunderbird Dr Niles MI 49120-8806 Office: Dowagiac Union Schs 701 Ptairie Ronde Dowagiac MI 49047

GOURLEY, FRANK A., JR., engineering educator; b. Danville, Va., June 24, 1940; s. Frank Arnett and Georgia Davis (Bousman) G.; m. Mary Joyce Pass, June 17, 1967 (div. 1997); children: Elizabeth, F. Austin. BSME, Va. Poly. Inst. & State U., 1962; MS in Tech. Edn., N.C. State U., 1970, EdD in Occupl. Edn., 1984. Profl. engr., N.C. Instr. engring. Va. Poly. Inst. & State U., Danville, 1962-65; rsch. asst. N.C. State U., Raleigh, 1965-66; asst. dir. engring. tech. programs N.C. Dept. C.C.'s, Raleigh, 1966-80; from coord. tech. devel. to sr. safety engr. Carolina Power & Light Co., Raleigh, 1980-90; dir. divsn. engring. tech. W.Va. U. Inst. Technology, Montgomery, 1990—; bd. dirs. Kanawha Valley Mining Inst., Charleston, W.Va.; commr. tech. accreditation Commn. Accreditation Bd. Engring. Tech., 1995—. Author: Engineering Technology—An ASEE History, 1995, Directory of Engineering Technology Institutes and Programs, 1995; contbr. articles to profl. jours. Mem. Am. Soc. Engring. Edn. (numerous offices), ASME, Rotary. Avocations: music, crafts, skiing, canoeing, travel. Office: WVa U Inst Technology 218 Davis Hall Montgomery WV 25136

GOURLEY, JAMES LELAND, editor, publishing executive; b. Mounds, Okla., Jan. 29, 1919; s. Samuel O. and Lodema (Scott) G.; m. Vicki Graham Clark, Nov. 24, 1976; children: James Leland II, Janna Lynn Gourley, Kelly Clark, Brandon Clark. BA in Liberal Studies, U. Okla., 1963. Editor, pub., pres. Daily Free-Lance, Henryetta, Okla., 1946-73; editor Oklahoma City Friday, 1974—; chmn. Nichols Hills Pub. Co., 1974—; pres. Suburban Graphics, Inc., 1991-93; pres. Central Okla. Newspaper Group, 1987, 90, 93,

96, 98, 99; pres. Sta. KHEN, KHEN-FM, Henryetta, 1955-63; pres. Hugo (Okla.) Daily News, 1953-63; chief of staff gov. Okla., 1959-63; chmn., pres. State Capitol Bank, 1962-69; v.p. sta. KXOJ Sapulpa, 1972-75; treas. Sta. KJEM-FM, Oklahoma City, 1962-67. Mem. Pres. Nat. Pub. Advisory Com. to Sec. Commerce, 1963-66; exec. dir. Gov's Comm. Higher Edn., 1960-61; Dem. candidate for gov. Okla., 1966. Dist. chmn. Boy Scouts Am., 1963-65; bd. dirs. So. Regional Edn. Bd., 1959-67, Okla. Symphony Soc., 1976-88, Oklahoma City Crimestoppers, 1982—, Salvation Army, Oklahoma City, 1985-87, Okla. Goodwill Industries, 1989-91; mem. Gov.'s Reform Com., 1984; bd. trustees Okla. City Univ., 1993—; bd. dirs. Okla. City Edn. Round Table, 1992—. Maj. AUS, 1942-46, ETO. Recipient Best Okla. Small Daily newspaper awards, 1949-58, 69-72, Best Large City Weekly newspaper awards, 1977-80, 83-85, 87-91, 94-95, 97, 98; inducted into Okla. Journalism Hall of Fame, 1980. Bd. trustees Okla. City Univ., 1993—; bd. dirs. Okla. City Edn. Round Table, 1992—. Mem. UP Internat. Editors Okla. (pres. 1958-59), Okla. Disciples of Christ Laymen (pres. 1964-65), Suburban Newspapers Am. (dir. 1980-89), Nat. Newspaper Assn., Okla. Press Assn. (pres. 1988-89, treas. 1991-93), Oklahoma City C. of C. (dir. 1975—), Henryetta C. of C. (pres. 1955), Oklahoma City Golf and Country Club (bd. dirs. 1991-95), Econ. Club Okla., Oklahoma City Com. of 100, Rotary (pres. Oklahoma City club 1992-93), Mil. Order of World Wars, The Ret. Officers Assn., Pi Kappa Alpha. Republican. Home: 6449 Grandmark Dr Oklahoma City OK 73116-6535 Office: 10801 Quail Plaza Dr Oklahoma City OK 73120-3123

GOURLEY, RONALD ROBERT, architect, educator; b. St. Paul, Oct. 5, 1919; s. Robert Thomas and Eva Irene (Cardle) G.; m. Phyllis Mary McDonald, Apr. 10, 1950; children: Robert McDonald, Karen Ellen, Geoffrey James. BArch, U. Minn., 1943; MArch, Harvard U., 1948. Instr. architecture MIT, Cambridge, 1948-53; vis. prof. Royal Acad., Copenhagen, Denmark, 1952; prof. architecture Harvard U., 1953-70; ptnr., co-founder Sert, Jackson & Gourley, Cambridge, 1958-64, Integrated Design Svcs. Group, Cambridge, 1966-72; ptnr. Gourley/Richmond, 1972-76, Gourley, Richmond & Mitchell, 1976-82; tech. coord. Boston Archtl. Ctr., 1976-77; prof. architecture U. Ariz., Tucson, 1977-90, dean Coll. Architecture, 1977-87, pres. Architecture Lab., 1986-89; dean, prof. emeritus U. Ariz., 1990—, disting. vis. prof. architecture, 1990—; pvt. practice Cambridge, 1954-58, 64-66, Tucson and Chilmark, 1990—. Prin. works include U. N.H. Meml. Union Bldg., Harvard U. Married Student Housing (Nat. Honor award AIA 1965), Cunningham Found. Bldg., Radcliffe Coll. Faculty Housing (Nat. Honor award AIA 1973), Brookline (Mass.) Pub. Libr., Kingston Housing for Elderly, Wheaton Coll. Libr., Mass. Hosp Sch. Recreation Bldg. With AUS, 1944-46. Inducted to Hall of Fame, The Humboldt Complex, St. Paul, 1995. Fellow AIA; mem. Boston Archtl. Ctr. (hon.). Home: 2522 E 3rd St Tucson AZ 85716-4115 also: Box 177 Middle Road Martha's Vineyard Chilmark MA 02535 Office: U Ariz Coll Architecture Tucson AZ 85721

GOUSE, S. WILLIAM, JR., engineering executive, scientist; b. Utica, N.Y., Dec. 15, 1931; s. S. William and Charlotte Virginia G.; m. Jacqueline Ann McLaughlin, Aug. 6, 1955; children: Linda Ellen, S. William III. S.B., S.M., Mass. Inst. Tech., 1954, Sc.D., 1958; Assoc. degree, Aspen Inst., 1996. Registered profl. engr., Mass. Instr. mech. engring. MIT, 1956-57, asst. prof., 1957-61, 62-65, assoc. prof., 1965-67, lectr., 1967-68; prof. mech. engring., prin. rsch. engr. Transp. Rsch. Inst., Carnegie-Mellon U., 1967-69; staff mem. Office Sci. and Tech. of Exec. Office of the Pres., Washington, 1969-70; assoc. dean Carnegie Inst. Tech. and Sch. Urban and Pub. Affairs Carnegie-Mellon U., 1971-73, dir. Environ. Studies Inst., 1971-73, adj. prof. engring. and pub. policy, 1980-90; dir. Office R&D, sci. advisor to sec. U.S. Dept. Interior, 1973-75; acting dir. Office Coal Rsch., 1974-75; dep. asst. adminstr. fossil energy ERDA, 1975-77; chief scientist MITRE Corp., 1977-79, v.p., 1979-80, v.p., gen. mgr. Ctr. for Civil Systems, 1980-84, sr. v.p., gen. mgr. Ctr. for Civil Systems, 1984-90, 1990-92, sr. v.p., 1992-94; mng. dir. Energy Sys. and Tech., 1994—; cons. and mem. panels various industry and govt. agys. including U.S. Dept. Commerce, U.S. Office Sci. and Tech., NSF; mem. rsch. adv. com. Electric Power Rsch. Inst., 1973-76; chmn. rev. adv. bd. on coal liquefaction Internat. Energy Agy., Paris, 1981-82; mem. energy engring. bd. NRC, 1985-88; U.S. rep. to com. energy conservation in indsl. processes World Energy Conf., 1984-89; mem. com. on environ. and energy aspects of waste handling World Energy Coun., vice chmn. com. on efficient use of energy utilization using high tech.; mem. adv. bd. Aspen Inst. Humanistic Studies Com. Pub. Policy Issues Energy and Resources, 1982-95; internat. adv. bd. World Energy Coun.; dir. Colshire Group, 1997; tech. advisor AB Volvo, 1976—. Editorial bd. Internat. Jour. Environ. Studies, 1971-81; editor-in-chief Energy Systems and Policy, 1973-93; assoc. editor Energy Sources, 1994—; contbr. to books, profl. jours., and congl. testimony. Mem. vis. com. mech. engring. dept. MIT, 1978-85. Served with ordnance AUS, 1961-62. Visking Corp. fellow, 1954-55; GE W. Rice Jr. fellow, 1955-56; recipient Ralph Teetor award Soc. Automotive Engrs., 1966; Sir A.L. Mudslior lectr in tech. Al Alagappa Chettiar Coll. Tech., U. Madras, 1969; Disting lectr. mech. engring. Pa. State U., 1980; recipient Outstanding Svc. award No. Area Environ. Coun., Allegheny County, Pa., 1973, Meritorious Svc. award ERDA, 1976, 60th Lord Melchett Medal Lectr. Inst. Energy London, 1994. Fellow ASME, AIAA (assoc.); mem. AAAS, SAE, Am. Soc. Engring. Edn., U.S. Energy Assn. (bd. dirs. 1987-88, 91-92), Internat. Assn. Energy Economists, Internat. Com. Coal Rsch., Cosmos Club, Explorers Club.

GOUTERMAN, MARTIN PAUL, chemistry educator; b. Phila., Dec. 26, 1931; s. Bernard and Melba (Buxbaum) G.; 1 child, Mikaelin BlueSpruce. B.A., U. Chgo., 1951, MS, 1955, Ph.D. in Physics (NSF Predoctoral fellow), 1958. Faculty Harvard U., Cambridge, Mass., 1958-66; postdoctoral fellow to asst. prof. chemistry dept. Harvard U., Cambridge; mem. faculty U. Wash., Seattle, 1966—, prof. chemistry, 1968—. Fellow Am. Inst. Physics; mem. Am. Chem. Soc., Sigma Xi. Achievements include research and publications in spectroscopy and quantum chemistry of porphyrins and their use as luminescence sensors for biomedical and aeronautical application, in particular pressure sensitive paint; developed BS degree program in biochemistry and a chemistry minors program. Office: U Wash Chemistry Box 351700 Seattle WA 98195-1700

GOUTMAN, LOIS CLAIR, retired drama educator; b. Clairton, Pa., Apr. 14, 1923; m. Dolya Goutman, Mar. 10, 1947; children: Andrew, Christopher, Thomas. BFA in Drama, Carnegie-Mellon U., 1944. Tchr., head drama dept. Baldwin Sch., Bryn Mawr, Pa.; ret.; dir. St. Thomas Players, Circle Theatre, L.A., Carnegie Tech. Drama Sch.; asst. dir. Actors' Lab., L.A., Arlington Films; presenter workshops in field; instr. theatre studies program Rosemont Coll. Forum, Pa. Appeared in various theatrical prodns., including The Tempest; writer, performer of one woman play Edith Wharton. Stanford U. fellow, Nat. Theatre Conf. alt. fellow, 1947; recipient Olmsted prize Williams Coll., Williamstown, Mass., 1992; holder first Rosamond Cross Chair in Teaching, The Baldwin Sch., 1991; teaching chair endowed in her honor Baldwin Sch. Mem. Am. Edn. Theatre Assn., Am. Alliance for Theatre and Edn., Theatre Edn. Assn., Actors' Equity. Avocations: theatre, concerts, reading, art exhibitions. Home: 314 Williams Rd Bryn Mawr PA 19010-1214

GOVAN, GLADYS VERNITA MOSLEY, retired critical care and medical/surgical nurse; b. Tyler, Tex., July 24, 1918; d. Stacy Thomas and Lucy Victoria (Whitmill) Mosley; m. Osby David Govan, July 20, 1938; children Orbrenett K. (Govan) Carter, Diana Lynn (Govan) Mosley. Student, East Los Angeles Coll., Montebello, Calif., 1951; lic. vocat. nurse, Calif. Hosp. Med. Ctr., L.A., 1953; cert., Western States IV Assn., L.A., 1978. Lic. vocat. nurse, Calif.; cert. in EKG. Intravenous therapist Calif. Hosp. Med. Ctr., cardiac monitor nurse; ret. Past pres. PTA, also hon. mem., 1963—; charter mem. Nat. Rep. Presdl. Task Force.

GOVE, SAMUEL KIMBALL, political science educator; b. Walpole, Mass., Dec. 27, 1923. Student, Mass. State Coll., 1941-43; B.S. in Econs, U. Mass., 1947; M.A. in Polit. Sci, Syracuse U., 1951. Research asst. govt. and pub. affairs U. Ill., 1950-51, research asso., 1951-54, mem. faculty, 1954—, prof. polit. sci., 1966-89, prof. emeritus, 1989—; dir. Inst. Govt. and Pub. Affairs, 1967-85, dir. emeritus, 1987—; Staff asst. Nat. Assn. Assessing Officers, 1949; mem. research staff Ill. Commn. Study State Govt., 1950-51; staff fellow Nat. Municipal League, 1955-56; exec. asst. Ill. Auditor Pub. Accounts, 1957; program coordinator Ill. Legis. Staff Intern Program, 1962-70; mem. com. financing higher edn. Ill. Master Plan Higher Edn., 1963; mem. Ill. Commn. Orgn. Gen. Assembly, 1965-69, 70-73, Ill. Commn. State Govt., 1965-67; cons. elections ABC, 1964, 66, 68; chmn. Champaign (Ill.) County Econ. Opportunity Council, 1966-67; state legis. research fellow Am. Polit. Sci. Assn., 1966-68; cons. Am. Council Edn., 1966-67; sec. Local Govts. Commn., 1967-69; staff dir. Ill. Constn. Study Commn., 1968-69; exec. sec. Gov. Ill. Constn. Research Group, 1969-70; mem. Ill. Constn. Study Commn., 1969-70; chmn. Citizens Task Force on Constl. Implementation, 1970-71; mem. Gov. Elect's Task Force on Transition, 1972, 91-92; adv. coun. Ill. Dept. Local Govt. Affairs, 1969-79, Gov.'s Human Resources 1991-93, Ill. Commn. on Regulatory Rev., 1994-98, Ill. Bd. Higher Edn., 1998—; Ill. Issues Bd. 1974— (chmn. bd. dirs. 1974-85); adj. scholar Ctr. for Study of Federalism, Temple U. Author numerous books, monographs and articles. Chmn. Champaign-Urbana Study Commn. on Intergovtl. Coop., 1976-78. Served to lt. (j.g.) USNR, 1943-46. Fellow Nat. Acad. Pub. Adminstrn.; mem. AAUP (past chpt. pres., mem. nat. com. R 1969-75, 78-84, nat. coun. 1978-80), Am. Polit Sci. Assn., Am. Soc. Pub. Adminstrn. (past chpt. chmn.; chmn. univs. govtl. rsch. conf. 1969-71), Govtl. Rsch. Assn. (dir. 1969-71), Ill. Hist. Soc., Midwest Polit. Sci. Assn. (v.p. 1978-80), Nat. Mcpl. League (council 1972-80, 81-84, 85), Nat Civic League (coun. advisors 1987-89), Cosmos Club. Home: 2006 Bruce Dr Urbana IL 61801-6419 Office: 1007 W Nevada St Urbana IL 61801-3812

GOVE, WALTER R., sociology educator; b. June 8, 1938; married; 2 children. BS, SUNY, Syracuse, 1960; MA in Sociology, U. Wash., 1967, PhD in Sociology, 1968. From asst. prof. to assoc. prof. Vanderbilt U., Nashville, 1968-75, prof. sociology, 1975—, dir. grad. studies, 1985-86; dir. NIMH Grad. Tng. Program, 1972-76; organizer confs., symposia in field; participant profl. confs., presenter in field. Author: (with Michael Geerken) At Home and at Work: The Family's Allocation of Labor, 1983; (with Michael Hughes) Household Crowding: Social and Structural Determinants of Its Effects, 1983; editor: Deviance and Mental Illness, 1982, co-editor: Labelling Deviant Behavior: Evaluating a Perspective, 1975, 2 edit., 1980, The Fundamental Connection Between Nature and Nurture, 1982, A Feminist Perspective in the Academy, 1983; adv. editor Social Forces, 1971-74; cons. editor Am. Jour. Sociology, 1974-76, Women and Politics, 1978-86; assoc. editor Social Sci. Rsch., 1974—, Social Psychology Quarterly, 1978-80, Jour. Health and Social Behavior, 1981-83, 97—, Jour. Family Issues, 1984-92; contbr. articles to profl., non-profl. jours., book revs. Recipient Reuben Hill award Nat. Coun. Family Rels., 1979; grantee PHS, 1963-65, 71-76, 79-82, NSF, 1973-77, 93, Dept. Justice, 1984-85, Okla. Dept. Corrections, 1993-94, Ethel Mae Wilson Found., 1980-81, Shell Found., 1974, others. Fellow AAAS; mem. Soc. Study of Social Problems (Outstanding Scholarship and Svc. to Psychiatric Sociology award 1989), Sociology Rsch. Assn., Am. Soc. Criminology, Am. Sociological Assn. (liaison com. to AAAS 1990-94), Southern Sociological Soc. (pres.-elect 1992-93, pres. 1993-94, exec. coun., program com. 1986). Avocation: numerous first ascents as mountaineer, primarily in Alaska. Office: Vanderbilt U PO Box 1811 Nashville TN 37235-1811

GOVEDARE, PHILIP BAINBRIDGE, artist, educator; b. Yuba City, Calif., Oct. 5, 1954; s. Philip Wright and Virginia (Pease) G.; m. Christine Lambert; 1 child, Eloise. BFA, San Francisco Art Inst., 1980; MFA, Tyler Sch. of Art, Phila., 1984. Instr. Tyler Sch. of Art, Phila., 1985-88, asst. prof., 1988-91; asst. prof. Univ. of Wash., Seattle, 1991-96, assoc. prof., 1996—; mem. program com. Sch. of Art Wash. U., 1993—; chmn. painting U. Wash.,1993-95. Recipient fellowship NEA, Washington, 1993; grantee Pa. Coun. on the Arts, Harrisburg, 1988, Pollock Krasner Found., N.Y.C., 1991. Home: 4702 35th Ave NE Seattle WA 98105-3004 Office: Univ of Wash Sch of Art M-10 Seattle WA 98103

GOVER, ALAN SHORE, lawyer; b. Lyons, N.Y., Sept. 5, 1948; s. Norman Marvin and Beatrice L. (Shore) G.; m. Ellen Rae Ross, Dec. 4, 1976; children: Maxwell Ross, Mary Trace. AB, Tufts U., 1970; JD, Georgetown U., 1973. Bar: Tex. 1973, D.C. 1980, U.S. Dist. Ct. (so. dist.) Tex. 1974, U.S. Dist. Ct. (we. dist.) Tex. 1976, U.S Dist. Ct. (no. dist.) Tex. 1988, U.S. Dist. Ct. (ea. dist.) Tex. 1990, U.S. Ct. Appeals (5th cir.) 1974, U.S. Ct. Appeals (D.C. cir.) 1977, U.S. Dist. Ct. (we. dist.) 1979, U.S. Ct. Appeals (2d cir.) 1979, D.C. 1980, U.S. Ct. Appeals (9th and 11th cirs.) 1981, U.S. Ct. Appeals (8th cir.) 1981, U.S. Supreme Ct. 1976. Assoc. Baker & Botts, Houston, 1973-80, ptnr., 1981-85; ptnr. Weil, Gotshal & Manges, Houston, 1985—. Co-author: The Texas Nonjudicial Foreclosure Process, 1990; editor, chmn. editorial bd. P.L.I. Oil and Gas and Bankruptcy Laws, 1985. Trustee Congregation Beth Israel, Houston, 1980-86, v.p., 1996—; trustee Houston Ballet, 1986—, v.p., 1993-96; chmn. ann. fund St. John's Sch., Houston, 1993-95; trustee Retina Rsch. Found., Houston, St. John's Sch., Houston, 1996—. Fellow Tex. Bar Found.; mem. ABA, Coronado Club, N.Y. Athletic Club, The Argyle (San Antonio). Jewish. Office: Weil Gotshal & Manges 700 Louisiana St Ste 1600 Houston TX 77002-2784

GOVER, RAYMOND LEWIS, newspaper executive; b. Somerset, Ky., Dec. 5, 1927; s. Raymond Bolen and Leslie Fay (Silvers) G.; m. Frieda Jane McGill, July 27, 1957; children: Janine Gover Park, Mark H., Janet L., Matthew R. BA, U. Mich., Ann Arbor, 1951; PhD (hon.), Shippensburg U., 1996. Reporter Port Huron Times, Mich., 1951-54; reporter, asst. city editor, city editor The Jour., Flint, Mich., 1954-70, editor, 1976-78; editor, pub. The News, Saginaw, Mich., 1970-76, 78-81; pub. The Patriot News, Harrisburg, Pa., 1981-97; pres. Patriot News Co., Harrisburg, 1997—. Bd. dirs. Ctrl. Pa. Econ. Devel. Corp., Harrisburg, 1983-93, Harrisburg Hosp., 1984—, YMCA, Harrisburg, 1984-90, Harrisburg Symphony Orch.; v.p. Tri-County United Way, Harrisburg; mem. bd. adv. Pa. State U., Harrisburg; trustee Pa. Newspaper Pubs. Found., Pine St. Presbyn. Ch., Harrisburg, Greater Harrisburg Found. Mem. Newspaper Assn. Am., Pa. Newspaper Assn. (bd. dirs. 1987—, pres. 1990-91), Am. Soc. Newspaper Editors, Mich. Press Assn. (bd. dirs. 1978-81), Soc. Profl. Journalists, West Shore Country Club (mem. bd. govs. 1991-95), Tuesday Club, Masons. Avocations: golf; fishing; hunting. Home: 905 Grandon Way Mechanicsburg PA 17055 Office: Patriot-News Co PO Box 2265 812 Market St Harrisburg PA 17101-2827

GOVETT, BRETT CHRISTOPHER, lawyer; b. Corpus Christi, Tex., May 17, 1965; s. Raymond Weston and Martha Lenora (Barton) G.; m. Cynthia Lynn Rowell, June 5, 1993. BA in Chemistry cum laude, The Citadel, 1987; JD cum laude, Tex. Tech U., 1990. Bar: Tex. 1990, U.S. Ct. Appeals (5th cir.) 1990, U.S. Dist. Ct. (so. dist.) Tex. 1990, U.S. Dist. Ct. (no. dist.) Tex. 1991, U.S. Supreme Ct. 1998. Jud. clk. for Judge Reynaldo G. Garza U.S. Ct. Appeals (5th cir.), Brownsville, Tex., 1990-91; assoc. Fulbright & Jaworski L.L.P., Dallas, 1991-98, ptnr., 1999—. Note editor Tex. Tech. Law Rev., 1989-90, contbr. articles. Mem. Southwestern Legal Found. Mem. ABA, Tex. Bar Assn., Dallas Bar Assn., Order of Coif. Office: Fulbright & Jaworski LLP 2200 Ross Ave Ste 2800 Dallas TX 75201-2784

GOVIER, GORDON OLIVER, radio news broadcaster, consultant; b. Lancaster, Wis., Nov. 16, 1951; s. Vernon and Geraldine Amanda (Olson) G.; m. Anne Marie Stommel, Mar. 29, 1980; children: Brian, Andrew, Sara, Samuel. BA in Journalism, U. Wis., 1973. Announcer Sta. WPRE, Prairie du Chien, Wis., 1971-73; news reporter Sta. WOSH, Oshkosh, Wis., 1973-75; news dir. Sta. WYFE, Rockford, Ill., 1975; news reporter Sta. WISM, Madison, Wis., 1975-80; news anchor and reporter Sta. KLMS, Lincoln, Nebr., 1980-82; news dir. Sta. WNWC, Madison, 1982—; exec. producer weekly radio program on bibl. archeology The Book and the Spade, 1983—; contbr. UPI Radio Network, Washington, 1982—, Voice of Am., Washington, 1984—, Internat. Media Service, Washington, 1982-90; tour host Internat. Broadcasters, Ctr. Fgn. Journalists, Washington, 1987-91. Founder, editor: (newsletter) SCRIBE, 1987, QV, 1994; editor: Artifax newsletter Inst. for Bibl. Archeology Newsletter; religion columnist The Capitol Times Daily, 1988—; contbr. articles to mags. Recipient Angel award Religion in Media, 1988, Mad City Radio Hero award Wis. State Jour., Madison, 1987. Mem. Radio TV News Dirs., Madison Orgn. Reporters and Editors, Soc. Profl. Journalists (pres. 1995—). Methodist. Avocation: photography. Home: 6305 Bridge Rd Madison WI 53716-3425 Office: Sta WNWC 5606 Medical Cir Madison WI 53719-1204

GOVIL, NARENDRA KUMAR, mathematics educator; b. Aligarh, India, Jan. 5, 1940; came to U.S., 1983; s. Panna Lal and Kamla Devi (Agrawal) G.; m. Urmila Agrawal, Feb. 1, 1964; children: Sanjay, Sandeep. BSc, Agra (India) U., 1957; MSc, Aligarh (India) U., 1959; PhD, U. Montreal, Que., Can., 1968. Lectr. Concordia U., Montreal, 1967-68, asst. prof., 1968-70; asst. prof. Indian Inst. Tech., New Delhi, 1970-78, assoc. prof., 1978-80, prof., 1980-85; assoc. prof. Auburn (Ala.) U., 1985-86, prof., 1986—; vis. scientist Dalhousie U., Halifax, Can., 1980; vis. prof. U. Alta., Edmonton, 1981, Auburn U., 1983-85; mem. exec. com. Forum Interdisciplinary Math., Delhi, 1989-91. Co-editor 2 books; contbr. numerous articles to profl. jours.; reviewer for Math. Reviews. Mem. exec. India Cultural Assn. East Ala., Auburn, 1986, 96-97. Fellow Nat. Acad. Scis. India (life); mem. Indian Math. Soc. (life), Am. Math. Soc., India Cultural Assn. East Ala. (pres. Auburn 1991). Avocations: music, reading. Home: 523 Owens Rd Auburn AL 36830-2513 Office: Auburn Univ Dept Math Auburn AL 36849

GOVINDJEE, biophysics and biology educator; b. Allahabad, India, Oct. 24, 1933; came to U.S., 1956, naturalized, 1972; s. Vishveshvar Prasad and Savitri Devi Asthana; m. Rajni Varma, Oct. 24, 1957; children: Anita Govindjee, Sanjay Govindjee. BSc, U. Allahabad, 1952, MSc, 1954; PhD, U. Ill., 1960. Lectr. botany U. Allahabad, 1954-56; grad. fellow U. Ill., Urbana, 1956-58; research asst. U. Ill., 1958-60, USPHS postdoctoral trainee biophysics, 1960-61, mem. faculty, 1961—, assoc. prof. botany and biophysics, 1965-69, prof. biophysics and plant biology, 1969-99, disting. lectr. Sch. Life Scis., 1978, emeritus prof. biophysics, plant biology and biochemistry, 1999—. Author: Photosynthesis, 1969; editor: Bioenergetics of Photosynthesis, 1975, Photosynthesis: Energy Conversion by Plants and Bacteria Carbon Assimilation and Plant Productivity, 2 vols., 1982 (Russian transl. 1987), The Oxygen evolving system of photosynthesis, 1983, Light Emission by Plants and Bacteria, 1986, Excitation Energy and Electron Transfer in Photosynthesis, 1989, Molecular Biology of Photosynthesis, 1989, Photosynthesis: From Photoreactions to Productivity, 1993, Concepts in Photobiology" Photosynthesis and Photomorphogenesis, 1999; editor Hist. Corner: Photosynthesis Rsch., 1989—; guest editor spl. issue Biophys. Jour., 1972, Photochemistry and Photobiology, 1978, Photosynthesis Research, 1996; editor-in-chief Photosynthesis Rsch., 1985-88; series editor: Advances in Photosynthesis, vol. 1, 1994, vol. 2, 1995, vols. 3, 4 and 5, 1996, vols. 6 and 7, 1998, Vols. 8 and 9, 1999; contbr. articles to profl. jours., also Sci. Am. Fulbright scholar, 1956-61, 96-97. Fellow AAAS, NAS (India); mem. Am. Soc. Plant Physiologists, Biophys. Soc. Am., Am. Soc. Photobiology (coun. 1976, pres. 1981), Internat. Photosynthesis Soc. (exec. com., publ. com. 1995-98), Sigma Xi. Home: 2401 Boudreau Dr Urbana IL 61801-6655

GOW, CHRISTOPHER RADFORD GUTHRIE, sea shell and sculpture specialist; b. Eng., Aug. 3, 1962; came to U.S., 1987; s. Derek William and Joan Shirley (Thomas) G. BS in Botany, Durham (Eng.) U., 1983; diploma in gen. history of art, Ecole du Louvre, Paris, 1987; MBA, So. Meth. U., 1989. Curator Trammell Crow Co., Dallas, 1987-88; 19th European paintings specialist Sotheby's, N.Y.C., 1989-93, sculpture specialist, 1993—; mem. Internat. Sculpture Ctr., Washington, 1989—; ptnr. Ruzzetti & Gow Italian Silver Coated Sea Shells, N.Y.C., 1995—. Mem. Nat. Sculpture Soc. (coun. 1995—), Conchologists Am., Am. Malacological Union, Inc. Home: 34 W 37th St New York NY 10018-7412

GOW, LINDA YVONNE CHERWIN, travel executive; b. Plymouth, N.H., Dec. 15, 1948; d. Roger and Alice Mary (Theriault) Carignan; m. James T. Gow Jr., Aug. 29, 1987; 1 child, Alison. Student Rivier Coll., 1966-68, Whittemore Sch. Bus., 1976-79. Asst. mgr. Travel New Horizons, Peterborough, N.H., 1972-76; mgr. Garnsey Bros. Travel, Sanford, Maine, 1976-77; gen. mgr. R-W Travel, Dover, N.H., 1977-84; pres., owner The Travel Pro, Somersworth, N.H., 1984—; owner Cruise Quarters, Somersworth, 1988—. Sponsor Internat. Children's Festival, Somersworth, N.H., 1985—; mem. Gov.'s Pvt. Industry Council, 1987, 88. Mem. Am. Retail Travel Agts. Assn., Cruise Lines Internat. Assn., Rochester C. of C., Somersworth C. of C., Rotary Internat. (Somersworth N.H. chpt.). Office: The Travel Pro 394 High St Somersworth NH 03878-1420

GOW, OLIVIA GRECO, public official, former English language educator; b. Chgo., Oct. 13; d. Annunciato and Beatrice (Scarpelli) Greco; m. John Eldred Gow, Dec. 30, 1961; children: John, Anne. Postgrad. summer fellow, Boston Coll., 1959; postgrad. fellow, Williams Coll., 1960; BA, DePauw U., 1954; MA, Northwestern U., 1956. Cert. tchr., Ill. Tchr. English Elmwood Park (Ill.) H.S., 1955-60, Wright Jr. Coll., Chgo., 1960-66; instr. Elmhurst (Ill.) Coll., 1967, Morton Coll., Berwyn, Ill., 1968-69, MacCormac Coll., Elmhurst, 1979-81; alderman City of Elmhurst, 1983-91; mem. DuPage County Bd., Wheaton, Ill., 1992—; commr. DuPage Forest Preserve, Wheaton, Ill., 1992—; commr., v.p. Northeastern Ill. Planning Commn., Chgo., 1993—. Chmn. Sch. Dist. 205 Caucus, Elmhurst, 1976-80; pres. Sandburg Jr. High Music Club, Elmhurst, 1980-82; vol. Coalition for Polit. Honesty, Oak Park, Ill., 1975-85; tchr. Sunday sch. Immaculate Conception Ch., Elmhurst, 1979-89. Mem. Phi Beta Kappa. Avocations: writing, reading, walking, attending plays. Office: DuPage County Bd 421 N County Farm Rd Wheaton IL 60187-3989

GOWANS, JAMES LEARMONTH (SIR), science administrator, immunologist; b. Sheffield, Eng., May 7, 1924; s. John Gowans and Selma Ljung; m. Moyra Leatham, July 28, 1956; children: William, Jenny, Lucy. MB, BS, U. London, 1947; MA, DPhil, Oxford U., 1953; ScD (hon.), Yale U., 1966; DSc (hon.), U. Chgo., 1971, U. Birmingham, Eng., 1978, U. Rochester, 1987; MD (hon.), U. Edinburgh, Scotland, 1979; DM (hon.), U. Southampton, Eng., 1987; LLD, U. Glasgow, Scotland, 1988. Rsch. prof. sch. pathology Oxford U., Eng., 1962-77, dir. med. rsch. coun. cellular immunology unit, 1963-77; sec., CEO U.K. Med. Rsch. Coun., 1977-87; cons. WHO Global Program on AIDS, Geneva, Switzerland, 1987-88; rsch. programs adv. com. Nat. Multiple Sclerosis Soc., N.Y.C., 1988-90; sec.-gen. Human Frontier Scis. Program, Strasbourg, France, 1989-93; chmn. European Med. Rsch. Coun., 1985-87; mem. governing coun. Internat. Agy. for Rsch. on Cancer, Lyon, France, 1980-87; mem. awards assembly GM Cancer Rsch. Found., N.Y.C., 1988-92; dir. European Iniatívie for Communicators of Sci., Munich, Germany, 1995-99. Contbr. articles on cellular immunology to profl. jours. Recipient Gairdner Found. award, 1968, Paul Ehrlich prize, 1974, Feldberg award, 1979, Wolf prize in medicine, 1980, Medawar prize, 1990. Fellow Royal Soc. (Royal Medal 1976); mem. NAS (fgn. assoc.), Am. Assn. Immunologists (hon.), Am. Assn. Anatomists (hon.). Avocations: music, gardening, old books. Home: 75 Cumnor Hill, Oxford OX2 9HX, England

GOWDA, NARASIMHAN RAMAIAH, financial consultant; b. Mallasandra, Karnataka, India, Nov. 21, 1949; came to U.S., 1982; s. Ramaiah and Kamalamma Gowda; m. Padma Gowda, Oct. 11, 1981; children: Shyla, Shilpa. BS, Bangalore U., India, 1971, MS, 1975; MBA, Armstrong U., 1985, U. Cin., 1986, Clayton U., 1989. Sales exec. Elys Chem. Lab., Bangalore, 1975-80; mgr. Health Clinic, Cin., 1982-87; account exec. Stuart James Co., Cin., 1987-88; fin. cons. Quest Capital Strategies, Inc., Cin., 1988-90; pres. Gowda Fin. Svcs., 1988-97, Investors Funding Group, 1989-97; sr. v.p. Gowda Glass & Assocs., 1990-97; fin. cons. Merrill Lynch, Pierce, Fenner & Smith, Inc., 1991-92, Montano Securities Corp., Orange, Calif., 1993-97, Remax Realty Svcs., 1997—; prof. fin. Shepherd's Coll., 1992-93. Adminstr. Rural Devel. Program, Bangalore, 1985—; pres. Indian Developers Bangalore, 1995—, Remax Realty Svcs., 1997—. Mem. Real Estate Investors Assn., Internat. Assn. Registered Fin. Planners, Inc., Assn. MBA Execs., U.S. Golf Assn., Cmty. Assns. Inst., Internat. Policy Inst., Potomac C. of C., Scandinavian Health Club, Bally's Health Club. Republican. Avocations: tennis, golf, jogging, social activities. E-mail: info@naragowda.com, www.maragowda.com. Home: PO Box 60345 Potomac MD 20859-0345

GOWDY, CURTIS, sportscaster; b. Green River, Wyo., 1919; m. Jerre Dawkins, June 1949; children: Cheryl Ann, Curtis, Trevor. BS, U. Wyo., 1942, LLD, 1972. Radio sta. broadcaster Cheyenne, Wyo., Oklahoma City; with Mel Allen broadcast N.Y. Yankees Baseball Team games, 1949-51; announcer for Boston Red Sox Baseball Team games, 1951-66; broadcaster Am. Football League games, 1961—; sports broadcaster NBC-TV, Major League Baseball Game of Week, World Series, Profl. Game of Week, Rose Bowl, Super Bowl, 1961-79; sports broadcaster NFL Football, Sports Spectacular CBS-TV, 1979—; host Am. Sportsman Outdoor Series for ABC-TV; owner radio stas. KOWB, Laramie, Wyo. Pres. Basketball Hall of Fame; overseer Boston Mus. Fine Arts. Served with USAAF, 1942-43. Named Sportscaster of Yr., Nat. Assn. Sportswriters and Sport Broadcasters, 1965, 67; named to Sports Broadcasters Hall of Fame, 1981, Baseball Hall of Fame, 1984, Am. Sportscasters Hall of Fame, 1985, Okla. Sports Hall of Fame, 1992, Pro Football Hall of Fame, 1993; recipient George Foster

Peabody award, 1970, 6 Emmy awards as host and co-prodr. Am. Sportsman, Fisherman of Yr. award Sport Fishing Inst. Washington, 1991, Life Time Achievement award NATAS, 1992. Office: KOWB 3525 Soldier Spring Rd Laramie WY 82070*

GOWDY, FRANKLIN BROCKWAY, lawyer; b. Burlington, Iowa, Dec. 27, 1945; s. Franklin Kamm and Dorothy Faye (Brockway) G.; m. Jennifer June McKenrick, Nov. 27, 1982; stepchildren: Jeffrey F. Hammond, Tracy Lawrence, Jonathan R. Hammond, Julie E. Rawls. BA in Polit. Sci., Stanford U., 1967; JD, U. Calif., Berkeley, 1970. Bar: U.S. Dist. Ct. (no. dist.) Calif. 1971, U.S. Ct. Appeals (9th cir.) 1971, U.S. Supreme Ct. 1979, U.S. Dist. Ct. (cen. dist.) Calif. 1984. Assoc. Brobeck, Phleger & Harrison, San Francisco, 1971-78, ptnr., 1978—. Fellow Am. Coll. Trial Lawyers; mem. ABA, Calif. Bar Assn., San Francisco Bar Assn., Assn. Bus. Trial Lawyers (bd. govs.). Home: 3428 Shangrila Rd Lafayette CA 94549-2423 Office: Brobeck Phleger Harrison LLP Spear St Tower 1 Market Plz San Francisco CA 94105-1420

GOWEN, KAY S., communications educator. BA, Harding U., 1968; MS in Mass Communications, Ark. State U., 1986. Dir. coll. affairs Crowley's Ridge Coll., Paragould, Ark., 1980-82; dean of women Harding U., Searcy, Ark., 1989-91; assoc. prof. comm., dir. student publ. Harding U., Searcy, 1991—. Mng. editor Ch. & Family Mag., 1998—. E-mail: gowen@harding.edu.

GOWEN, RICHARD JOSEPH, electrical engineering educator, academic administrator; b. New Brunswick, N.J., July 6, 1935; s. Charles David and Esther Ann (Hughes) G.; m. Nancy A. Applegate, Dec. 28, 1955; children: Jeff, Cindy, Betsy, Susan, Kerry. BS in Elec. Engring., Rutgers U., 1957; MS, Iowa State U., 1961, PhD, 1962. Registered profl. engr., Colo. Rsch. engr. RCA Labs., Princeton, N.J., 1957; commd. USAF; ground electronics officer Yaak AFB, Mont., 1957-59; instr. USAF Acad., 1962-63, rsch. assoc., 1963-64, asst. prof., 1964-65, assoc. prof., 1965-66, tenured assoc. prof. elec. engring., 1966-70, tenured prof., 1971-77, dir., prin. investigator NASA instrumentation group for cardiovascular studies, 1968-77; mem. launch and recovery med. team Johnson Space Ctr., NASA, 1971-77; v.p., dean engring., prof. S.D. Sch. Mines and Tech., Rapid City, 1977-84, pres., 1987—; pres. Dakota State U., Madison, 1984-87; prin. investigator program in support space cardiovascular studies NASA, 1977-81; co-chmn. Joint Industry, Nuclear Regulatory IEEE, Am. Nuclear Soc. Probabilistic Risk Assessment Guidelines for Nuclear Power Plants Project, 1980-83; mem. Dept. Def. Software Engring. Inst. Panel, 1983. Contbr. articles to profl. jours.; patentee in field. Bd. dirs. St. Martins Acad., Rapid City, S.D., Journey Mus., 1998—, Greater Rapid City Econ. Devel. Partnership, 1991—; mem. U.S. Web Edn. Commn., 1999—. Fellow IEEE (Centennial Internat. pres. 1984, bd. dirs., 1976-75), USAB/IEEE Disting. Contbns. to Engring. Professionalism award 1986); mem. Am. Assn. Engring. Socs. (bd. dirs., 1983-87, chmn. 1988), Rapid City C. of C. (bd. dirs. 1998—), Rotary, Sigma Xi, Phi Kappa Phi, Tau Beta Phi, Eta Kappa Nu (bd. dirs., 1994, pres. 1998—) Pi Mu Epsilon. Roman Catholic. Home: 1609 Palo Verde Dr Rapid City SD 57701-4461 Office: SD Sch Mines & Tech Office of Pres Rapid City SD 57701*

GOWENS, WALTER, II, financial and business services executive; b. Tampa, Fla., Sept. 30, 1954; s. Walter and Bessie (Bridges) G. BS, Ariz. State U., 1975; MBA, Ind. U., 1977. CFP; registered investment advisor. Fin. analyst Am. Can Co., Greenwich, Conn., 1977-79; cons. Norman Jaspan Assocs., N.Y.C., 1979; pvt. cons. practice N.Y.C., 1979-80; mgr. fin. reporting YMCA Greater N.Y.C., 1980-81; sr. fin. analyst Met. Transp. Authority, N.Y.C., 1981-83; pres. Prudential Vanguard Cos., Inc., N.Y.C., 1983—; portfolio mgr., lic. stockbroker, lic. ins. broker, N.Y.C., 1986—. founder, editor Prudential Vanguard Tax & Investment newsletter, 1986-89. Recipient Entrepreneurial Skills award C.A. C. of C., 1987; Consortium Grad. Study fellow, 1975. Mem. Inst. Cert. Fin. Planners, Am. Assn. Individual Investors, Nat. Soc. Tax Profls. Avocations: attending N.Y.C. theaters, tennis, exploring N.Y.C. Office: Prudential Vangurad Cos Inc 2790 Broadway New York NY 10025-2846

GOWER, BOB G., gas and oil industry executive; b. 1937. With Atlantic Richfield Co., L.A., 1963-88; pres., CEO, bd. dirs. Lyondell Petrochem. Co., Houston, 1988-97; chmn., owner Specified Fuel & Chems., Channel View, Tex., 1997—. Office: Specified Fuel & Chems 1201 Sheldon Rd Channelview TX 77530-3519*

GOWER, CINDY ELAINE LONES, electronic technician; b. Springfield, Ohio, Nov. 27, 1960; d. James K. Lones and Catherine May (Dellinger) Oldfield; m. George W. Gower Jr., July 11, 1981 (div. 1986); children: Natasha May, Matthew W. AAS in Electronic Engring., Columbus State C.C., 1993. HVAC electronic control tech. Creative Control Designs, Inc., Columbus, 1993-96; owner Gower's Tax Svc., Columbus, 1992—; tax cons. Mem. Nat. Assn. Tax Profls., Am. Inst. Profl. Bookkeepers, WIBC. Republican. Avocations: pencil drawing, reading, bowling, electronics, philosophy. Office: 1632 Harrisburg Pike Columbus OH 43223-3614

GOYAK, ELIZABETH FAIRBAIRN, retired public relations executive; b. Chgo., Oct. 7, 1922; d. Lewis Howard and Berenice Marie (Bowers) Fairbairn; m. Edward Anthony Goyak, May 20, 1951. BEd, So. Ill. U., 1943; MA, No. Ill. U., 1979. Reporter Internat. News Svc., Chgo., 1945-49, Chgo. Tribune, 1949-52; writer Gardner & Jones, Chgo., 1954-59, Aaron Cushman & Assocs., Chgo., 1959-60; v.p. Daniel J. Edelman, Chgo., 1960-76; mgr. pub. rels. Stone Container Corp., Chgo., 1976-82; pres. pub. rels. Firm Chgo. Connection, Matteson, Ill., 1982-98. Dir. pub. rels. Ill. Dem. Women for Adlai Stevenson, 1952; founder, pres. bd. dirs. Matteson Pub. Libr., 1958-87; chmn. Matteson Bicentennial Commn., 1973-76. Mem. Pub. Rels. Soc. Am. (accredited, Silver anvil award 1975), Publicity Club Chgo. (sec., bd. dirs. 1964-76, Golden Trumpet award 1965, 66, 75), Chgo. Press Vets. Mem. United Ch. Christ. Home: 21310 Butterfield Pkwy Matteson IL 60443-2460

GOYAL, RAJ KUMAR, medical educator; b. Hissar, India, May 6, 1937; came to U.S., 1967; m. Prem Jain Goyal; children: Anish, Sunita. B Medicine, MS, Punjab U., Amristar, India, 1960; MD, Maulana Azad Med. Coll., New Delhi, 1965; AM (hon.), Harvard U., 1982. Diplomate Am. Bd. Internal Medicine. Intern Irwin Hosp. Med. Coll., New Delhi, 1961-62, resident, 1964-67; resident Hosp. St. Raphael, New Haven, 1967-68; instr. medicine Yale U. Sch. Medicine, New Haven, 1969-70; asst. prof. medicine Baylor U. Coll. Medicine, Houston, 1971-73; assoc. prof. medicine U. Tex. Health Ctr., Dallas, 1977, prof., 1977-78; prof. U. Tex. Health Ctr., San Antonio, 1978-81; Mallinckrodt prof. medicine Harvard U. Med. Sch., Boston, 1981—, Charlotte F. and Irving W. Rabb prof. medicine, 1984-95; chief dept. gastroenterology Beth Israel Hosp., Boston, 1981—; cons. West Roxbury (Mass.) VA Hosp., 1982—, Brockton (Mass.) VA Hosp., 1982—. Editor: Symposium on Esophageal Motility, 1976, Barrett's Esophagus, 1985; editor in chief Gastroenterology jour., 1986—. Recipient Merit award NIH, 1986, Gen. MEDA, Div. Rsch. grants, NIH, 1994—. Mem. Am. Gastroenterology Assn., Am. Fedn. Clin. Rsch., Am. Soc. Clin. Invest, Am. Assn. Physicians. Office: VA Med Ctr R&D 151 1400 Vfw Pkwy West Roxbury MA 02132-4927

GOYAN, JERE EDWIN, business executive, former university dean; b. Oakland, Calif., Aug. 3, 1930; s. Gerald H. and Lucille (Johnson) G.; m. Patricia B. Mesirow, Aug. 24, 1952 (div.); children: Pamela, Terrence H., Andrea; m. Linda Lloyd Hart, Mar. 25, 1988. B.S., U. Calif. Sch. Pharmacy, 1952, Ph.D., 1957. Asst. prof. pharmacy U. Mich., 1956-61, assoc. prof., 1961-63; assoc. prof. pharmacy and pharm. chemistry U. Calif. at San Francisco, 1963-65, prof., 1965-79, 81-92; assoc. dean Sch. Pharmacy, 1966-67, dean, 1967-79, 81-92; pres., COO Alteon, Inc., Ramsey, N.J., 1993-97; pres. Goyan & Hart Assocs., 1999—; commr. FDA/HHS, 1979-81. Fellow AAAS; mem. Inst. Medicine of NAS, N.Y. Acad. Scis., Am. Pharm. Assn., Acad. Pharm. Scis., Am. Assn. Pharm. Scientists (pres. 1990), Calif. Pharm. Assn., Am. Assn. Colls. Pharmacy (pres. 1978-79), Sigma Xi, Rho Chi, Phi Lambda Upsilon.

GOYAN, MICHAEL DONOVAN, stockbroker, investment executive; b. Eureka, Calif., Sept. 18, 1938; s. Gerald Hazen and Lucille (Johnson) G.; children: Michael Donovan, Kevin Lee. A.B., Occidental Coll., 1960. Stockbroker, allied mem. William R. Staats, Los Angeles, 1961-74; ptnr., stockbroker Crowell, Weedon & Co., L.A., 1974-89; sr. v.p. investments PaineWebber Inc., L.A., 1989—; mem. hearing bd. N.Y. Stock Exchange, 1970—. Bd. dirs. Inst. Internat. Edn., Los Angeles and N.Y.C., 1972-78, West Coast nat. trustee. Mem. Newcomen Soc., Long Beach Yacht Club, L.A. Bond Club (bd. dirs. 1970—, pres. 1983-84), Calif. Club, Ingomar Club (Eureka), Kappa Beta Phi (bd. dirs. 1985—).

GOYER, ROBERT ANDREW, pathology educator; b. Hartford, Conn., June 2, 1927; s. Andrew R. and Cecelia P. (Castonquay) G.; m. Mary Ellen Wilke, Feb. 4, 1955; children—Barbara, John, Peter, Ellen. B.S., Holy Cross Coll., 1950; M.D., St. Louis U., 1955. Diplomate: Am. Bd. Pathology. Intern St. Francis Hosp., Hartford, 1955-56; resident in pathology St. Louis U. Hosps., 1956-60; practice medicine specializing in pathology St. Louis, 1956-65; instr. pathology St. Louis U., 1960-62, asst. prof., 1962-65; asst. prof. Sch. Medicine, U. N.C., Chapel Hill, 1965-68; assoc. prof. Sch. Medicine, U. N.C., 1968-71, prof. pathology, 1971-74, adj. prof. pathology, 1979-87; clin. pathologist Cardinal Glennon Meml. Hosp. for Children, St. Louis, 1961-62; dir. labs. Cardinal Glennon Meml. Hosp. for Children, 1962-64; staff pathologist N.C. Meml. Hosp., Chapel Hill, 1965-74; chief pathology U. Hosp., London, Ont., Can., 1974-79; prof. pathology Health Scis. Centre, U. Western Ont., Can., 1974-79, 87-92; prof. emeritus Health Scis. Centre, U. Western Ont., 1992—; dept. dir. Nat. Inst. Environ. Health Scis., Research Triangle Park, N.C., 1979-87; pvt. cons. health effects, toxic metals Chapel Hill, N.C., 1992—. Contbr. articles to profl. jours.; mem. editorial bd. Yearbook Pathology, 1979-88, AMA Archives of Pathology, 1973-82. Served with USN, 1945-47. Nat. Found. fellow, 1959-60. Mem. Coll. Am. Pathology, Am. Assn. Pathologists, Internat. Acad. Pathology, Soc. Exptl. Biology and Medicine. Roman Catholic. Rsch. in exptl. pathology and metal toxicology. Office: 6405 Huntingridge Rd Chapel Hill NC 27514-7867

GOYER, ROBERT STANTON, communication educator; b. Kokomo, Ind., Oct. 7, 1923; s. Clarence V. and Genevieve M. (Sober) G.; m. Patricia Ann Stutz, Aug. 12, 1950; children: Karen, Susan, Linda, Amy. BA, DePauw U., 1948; MA, Miami U., Oxford, Ohio, 1950; PhD, Ohio State U., 1955. Instr. Miami U., Oxford, 1949-51; instr., then asst. prof. Ohio State U., Columbus, 1955-58, rsch. assoc., cons. rsch. found., 1956-63; from asst. to assoc. to prof. Purdue U., Lafayette, Ind., 1958-66; prof. Ohio U., Athens, 1966-81, dir. ctr. communication studies, 1966-74, 79-81, assoc. dean grad. coll., 1978, dean grad. coll., acting dir. rsch., 1979, acting assoc. provost grad. and rsch. programs, 1979, prof. emeritus, 1981—; prof., chmn. dept. communication Ariz. State U., Tempe, 1981-89, prof., 1989-94, prof. emeritus, 1994—; cons. in field. Author books; contbr. articles to profl. jours. 1st lt. U.S. Army, 1943-46, 52-53. Decorated Bronze Star. Fellow AAAS, Internat. Comm. Assn.; mem. APA, Nat. Comm. Assn. Presbyterian. Home: 517 W Summit Pl Chandler AZ 85225-7799

GOYER, VIRGINIA L., accountant; b. Troy, N.Y., July 19, 1942; d. Clarence Archie and Edna Alice (Toussaint) G.; m. James Cobb Stewart, May 17, 1986. BS, Rochester Inst. Tech., 1975, MBA, 1976. Tax mgr. Deloitte Haskins & Sells, Rochester, N.Y., 1976-82; pres. Lamanna & Goyer, PC, CPAs, Rochester, 1982-89; owner Goyer & Assocs., CPAs, Rochester, 1989-93; pres. Virginia L. Goyer, CPA, P.C., Rochester, 1993—. Mem. adv. bd. Salvation Army, Rochester, 1985-88, Rochester Inst. Tech. Deferred Giving, 1988-89; mem. bd. Nat. Women's Hall of Fame. Mem. AICPA (nat. coun. 1995-98), Fla. Inst. CPAs, N.Y. State Inst. CPAs (bd. dirs. 1990-93, v.p. 1994-95, 1st woman pres. Rochester chpt. 1988-89), Rochester Women's Network, Nat. Assn. Women Bus. Owners (bd. dirs. 1992-93), Estate Planning Coun. (bd. dirs. 1987-89), NOW. Office: 354 Westminster Rd Rochester NY 14607-3233

GOYETTE, GEOFFREY ROBERT, sales executive; b. Rice Lake, Wis., Dec. 11, 1948; s. Robert William and Anne (Gorshek) G.; children: Nano E., Lynne M. Student, Marquette U., 1967-71. Sales rep. Xerox Corp., Milw., 1972-74, sales plan mgr., 1975-76, product specialist, 1976-77; sales mgr. Xerox Corp., Chgo., 1977-81; region mgr. Kohinoor Rapidograph, Chgo., 1981-83, Automatic Data Processing, Chgo., 1983-87; br. mgr., dir. sales Automatic Data Processing, Milw., 1988-94; dir. nat. acct. sales ADP, San Francisco, 1994-96; area sales exec. for N.Y. State ADP, Syracuse, 1996-97, v.p. sales ctrl. and western N.Y. State, 1997-98; dir. SIS, 1999—; baseball agt. 10th Man, Inc., Chgo., 1985-89. Vol. Big Bros., San Francisco, Syracuse. Mem. Soc. Human Resource Mgrs., Milw. Athletic Club. Avocations: golf, reading, collecting sports memorabilia, bass fishing. Home: 250 Athania Pkwy Metairie LA 70001-5204

GOZ, HARRY G., actor, singer; b. St. Louis, June 23, 1932; s. Isadore and Helen (Becker) G.; m. Margaret O. Avsharian, May 3, 1958; children: Michael P., Melissa S. , Geoffrey C. Student, Washington U., St. Louis, 1950-51, St. Louis Inst. Music, 1954-56. Toured with Boris Goldovsy Co. in 1959, sang in operas Don Giovanni, St. Louis, 1955, La Boheme, St. Louis, 1955; singer, actor: (Broadway shows) Bajour, 1964, Fiddler on the Roof, 1965-70, Two by Two, 1970, Prisoner of Second Ave, 1972, Born Yesterday, 1976, Hocus Pocus Dominocus, 1978, To Bury A Cousin, 1980, Ferocious Kisses, 1981, Chess, 1988, (other stage prodns.) Cafe Crown, Kiss of the Spider Woman; (films) Mommie Dearest, Bill, Bill on His Own, Marathon Man, Looking Up, Rapping, Darrow, Kennedy, (stock) over 40 appearances in musicals, comedies, dramas, operas; (TV): Search for Tomorrow, The Guiding Light, The Edge of Night, All My Children, L.A. Law, Wise Guy, The Ed Sullivan Show, Ned & Stacy, Law and Order; co-prodr.: Brother Champ (42nd St. Theatre) 1976, The Importance of Being Oscar, 1998; rep. over 1200 products and comml. campaigns TV and radio voice overs and on camera appearances. With U.S. Army, 1952-54.

GOZANI, TSAHI, nuclear physicist; b. Tel Aviv, Nov. 25, 1934; came to U.S., 1965; s. Arieh and Rivcca (Meiri) G.; m. Adit Soffer, Oct. 14, 1958; children: Mor, Shai Nachum, Or Pinchas, Tal. BSc, Technion-Israel Inst. Tech., Haifa, 1956, MSc, 1958; DSc, Swiss Fed. Inst. Tech. (ETH), Zurich, Switzerland, 1962. Registered profl. nuclear engr., Calif.; accredited nuclear material mgr. Rsch. physicist Israel Atomic Energy Commn., Beer-Sheva, 1962-65; rsch. assoc. nuclear engring. dept. Rensselaer Poly. Inst., Troy, N.Y., 1965-66; sr. staff scientist General-Atomic & IRT, San Diego, 1966-70, 71-75; prof. applied physics Tel Aviv U., 1971; chief scientist, divsn. mgr. Sci. Applications Internat. Corp., Palo Alto and Sunnyvale, Calif., 1975-84; v.p., chief scientist Sci. Applications Internat. Corp., Sunnyvale, 1984-87; corp. v.p. Sci. Applications Internat. Corp., Santa Clara, Calif., 1987-93, sr. v.p., 1993-97; pres., CEO Ancore Corp., Santa Clara, 1997—; Lady Davis vis. prof. Technion-Israel Inst. Tech., 1983-84; bd. dirs. Radiation Sci. Inst., San Jose State U. Author: Active Non-Destructive Assay of Nuclear Materials, 1981; co-author: Handbook of Nuclear Safeguards Measurement Methods, 1983; contbr. over 170 articles to profl. jours. Recipient 1989 Laurel award Aviation Week Jour., R&D 100 award, 1988, Most Innovative New Products. Fellow Am. Nuclear Soc.; mem. Am. Phys. Soc., Inst. Nuclear Materials. Achievements include patents for explosive detection system, explosive detection system using an artificial neural system, multi sensor explosive detection system, composite cavity structure for an explosive detection system, apparatus and method for detecting contraband using fast neutron activation, contraband detection system using direct imaging pulsed fast neutrons; invention of method to measure nuclear reactor's reactivity. Office: Ancore Corp 2950 Patrick Henry Dr Santa Clara CA 95054-1813

GOZEMBA, PATRICA ANDREA, women's studies and English language educator, writer; b. Medford, Mass., Nov. 30, 1940; d. John Charles and Mary Margaret (Sampey) Curran; m. Gary M. Gozemba, Sept. 4, 1967 (div. Feb. 1975). BA, Emmanuel Coll., Boston, 1962; MA, U. Iowa, 1963; EdD, Boston U., 1975. Tchr. Waltham (Mass.) High Sch., 1963-64; prof. Salem (Mass.) State Coll., 1964—; vis. fellow East-West Ctr., 1995; vis. prof. U. Hawaii, 1997-98. Editor: New England Women's Studies, 1977-87; mem. editorial bd. Thought and Action, 1990-93; contbr. articles to profl. jours. Mem. NEA (standing com. 1982-93), NOW, NAACP, Nat. Women's Studies Assn. (gov. bd. 1977-89), Nat. Coun. Tchrs. English, Nat. Gay and Lesbian Task Force, Mass. State Coll. Assn. (editor 1982-90, 92-97), Herb Soc. Am. Democrat. Avocations: walking, tennis, gardening, photography. Home: 17 Sutton Ave Salem MA 01970-5728 Office: Salem State Coll English Dept Salem MA 01970

GOZONSKY, EDWIN O. O., investment broker; b. Laconia, N.H., Mar. 31, 1930; s. Archie and Ida G.; m. Dorothy Adelson, Feb. 28, 1965; children: Judith, Diane. BA, Yale U., 1952; MBA, Harvard U., 1954. With Eastman Dillon, Union Securities (merged with Paine Webber 1980), Boston, 1959—, v.p. Boston office, 1971—; pres. Variable Annuities Provide Personal Security, 1979—; lectr. in retirement income, sales variable annuities, bonds, 1979—. With U.S. Army, 1954-56. Mem. Bulldog Soc. (provisional dir.), Harvard Bus. Sch. Alumni (class sec. 1988—), Dist. Com. 11 Nat. Assn. Securities Dealers. Home: 118 Irving Ave Providence RI 02906-4510 Office: Paine Webber 265 Franklin St Fl 13 Boston MA 02110-3196

GOZUM, MARVIN ENRIQUEZ, internist; b. Phila., July 19, 1960; s. Filemon Tizon and Teresita Ver G. BS in Biology, Ateneo de Manila, The Philippines, 1980; MD, Fatima Coll. of Medicine, The Philippines, 1984. Intern The Bklyn.-Caledonian Hosp. div. Downstate Med. Ctr., N.Y., 1984-85, resident in internal medicine, 1985-87; attending physician Thomas Jefferson U. Hosp., Phila., 1987—; clin. instr. Jefferson Med. Coll., Phila., 1987-89, rsch. assoc. Ctr. for Rsch., 1989—, clin. asst. prof. medicine, 1989—, chief med. informatics div. internal medicine, 1989—; med. cons. Wills Eye Hosp., Phila., 1987—, chief med. cons., 1990—; adv. bd. computers in medicine com. Thomas Jefferson U. Hosp., 1987—; adv. bd. computer com. Wills Eye Hosp., 1987; adv. bd. curriculum devel. com. Thomas Jefferson U., Phila., 1988; adv. bd. Continuing Med. Edn. Com. Internal Medicine, 1991—. Developer: (computer programs) Diagnosticon Computer Assisted Diagnosis, 1982, Fluid/Electrolyte Calculator, 1984, Preoperative Evaluation, 1987; co-developer: (computer program) VACAD Image Processor, 1987. Named to Osteoporosis Project, Health Sci. Inst., 1990. Mem. AAAS, Am. Med. Informatics Assn., Soc. Gen. Internal Medicine. Achievements include development of computer assisted preoperative evaluation, automated report generation for preoperative evaluations, automated medical diagnosis, pocket intensive care calculator. Office: Jefferson Med Coll 1025 Walnut St Philadelphia PA 19107-5001

GRAB, FREDERICK CHARLES, lawyer; b. N.Y.C., Aug. 1, 1946; s. Daniel Justin and Elizabeth (Kam) G. BS in Aerospace Engring., Polytech U. N.Y., 1967; JD, U. So. Calif., 1977. Bar: Calif. 1978, U.S. Dist. Ct. (cen. dist.) Calif. 1978, U.S. Supreme Ct. 1988, U.S. Ct. Appeals (9th cir.) 1989. Deputy atty. gen. Calif. Atty. Gen., L.A., 1977—. Contbr. articles to profl. jours. Avocations: playwright, author, composer, musican.

GRABAR, OLEG, art educator; b. Strasbourg, France, Nov. 3, 1929; came to U.S., 1948, naturalized, 1960; s. Andre and Julie (Ivanova) G.; m. Terry Ann Harris, June 9, 1951; children—Nicolas Howard, Anne Louise. B.A. magna cum laude, Harvard, 1950; licence d'Histoire, U. Paris, 1950; Ph.D., Princeton, 1955. Instr. U. Mich., 1954-55, asst. prof., 1955-59, assoc. prof., 1959-64, prof., 1964-69; dir. Am. Sch. of Oriental Research, Jerusalem, Jordan, 1960-61; v.p. Am. Sch. of Oriental Rsch., Jerusalem, 1968-75; prof. fine arts Harvard U., 1969-81; Aga Khan prof. Islamic art Harvard, 1981-90; with sch. hist. studies Inst. For Advanced Study, Princeton, 1990—; dir. Mich.-Harvard U. excavations in Syria, 1964-71. Author: Coinage of Tulunids, 1957, Islamic Architecture and its Decoration, 1967, Sasanian Silver, 1967, The Formation of Islamic Art, 1973, the Alhambra, 1978, City in the Desert, 1978, Epic Images, 1982, Illustrations of the maqamat, 1984, Islamic Art, 1987, Great Mosque of Isfahan, 1989, The Mediation of Ornament, 1992, The Shape of the Holy, 1996; editor: Ars Orientalis, 1957-71; contbr. articles to profl. jours. Mem. Coll. Art Assn. (dir. 1968-72), Archeol. Inst. Am., Mediaeval Acad. Am., German Archeol. Inst., Middle Eastern Studies Assn., Am. Acad. Arts and Scis., Am. Philosophy Soc., Brit. Acad. (hon.), Austrian Acad. (hon.). Home: 43 Maxwell Ln Princeton NJ 08540-4931 Office: Inst for Advanced Study Princeton NJ 08540

GRABARZ, DONALD FRANCIS, pharmacist; b. Jersey City, Sept. 18, 1941; s. Joseph and Frances (Zotynia) G.; m. Joan Isoldi, Aug. 13, 1966; children: Christine, Robert, Danielle. BPharm, St. Johns U., N.Y.C., 1964. Lic. pharmacist, N.Y., Vt. Dir. qualtiy control and assurance Johnson and Johnson Co., New Brunswick, N.J., 1965-72; dir. quality assurance and regulatory affairs Bard Parker div. Becton Dickinson, Franklin Lakes, N.J., 1972-76; asst. corp. dir. regulatory affairs Becton Dickinson, 1976-80; corp. dir. regulatory affairs C.R. Bard Inc., Murray Hill, N.J., 1980-85; v.p. regulatory affairs, qualtiy assurance Symbion Inc., Salt Lake City, 1985-86; cons., pres. DFG & Assocs., Inc., Salt Lake City, 1986—; mem., mng. dir. Internat. Regulatory Consultants, L.C., Sale Lake City, 1987—; adj. prof. Salt Lake C. C., 1993—; lectr. Inst. for Applied Tech., Inst. Internat. Rsch., Ernst & Young, Salt Lake C.C. Co-author, technical advisor, editor Inspection and Recall Film; co-author: Science, Technology, and Regulation in a Competetive Environment, 1990; contbr. articles to profl. jours. Bd. dirs. v.p., asst. treas. Am. Lung Assn., N.J., 1972-75; chmn. Drug Edn., DuPage County, Ill., 1968. Mem. Health Industry Mfg. Assn. (chmn. Legal and Regulatory commn. 1983), Regulatory Affairs Profl. Soc. (lectr.), Am. Soc. Quality Control, Am. Mfr. Med. Instrumentation Assn., Am. Pharm. Assn., Food and Drug Law Inst., Cottonwood Country Club (bd. dirs., treas. 1995—, v.p. 1996—, pres. 1997). Avocations: soccer, tennis, baseball, skiing, music. Office: Internat Regulatory Cons, LC PO Box 17801 Salt Lake City UT 84117-0801

GRABAU, LARRY J., crop physiologist, educator; b. Spring Valley, Minn., Nov. 4, 1954; s. Joseph Jerome and Flora Roberta (Anderson) G.; m. Mary Jo K. Adams, July 31, 1981; children: Joseph Lawrence, Laura Grace, Jonathan David. BS, U. Minn., 1979; MS, U. Mo., 1981, PhD, 1985. Asst. prof. U. Ky., Lexington, 1984-90, assoc. prof., 1990-96, prof., 1997—. Assoc. editor Jour. Nat. Resource Life Sci. Edn., 1990-96, editor 1997—; contbr. articles to profl. jours. Mem. Am. Soc. Agronomy, Crop Sci. Soc. Am., Coun. Agr. Sci. Tech., Sigma Xi, Gamma Sigma Delta. Republican. Methodist. Office: U Ky N106A Agrl Sci N Lexington KY 40546-0091

GRABBE, CROCKETT LANE, physicist, researcher, writer; b. Silverton, Tex., Mar. 12, 1951; s. Warner Brooks and Opal Dean (Chappell) G. BS with highest honors, U. Tex., 1972, MA, 1973; PhD, Calif. Tech. Inst., 1978. Postdoctoral fellow Calif. Tech. Inst., Pasadena, 1977-78; vis. asst. prof. U. Tenn., Knoxville, 1978-79; rsch. scientist Sci. Applications, Alexandria, Va., 1979-81; assoc. rsch. scientist U. Iowa, Iowa City, 1981-88, rsch. scientist, 1988—; pub. spkr. and spkr. in field. Author, editor: Plasma Waves and Instabilities, 1986; author: Space Weapons and Strategic Defense Initiative, 1991; co-author: Advances in Space Plasma Physics, 1985, Trends in Geophysical Research, vol. 2, 1993; contbg. author: Physics and the Ultimate Significance of Time, 1986. Recipient Outstanding Sr. award Am. Chem. Soc., 1971, postdoctoral fellowship NSF, 1977-78; Rsch. grantee NSF, 1983-88, 92, 94-2000, NASA, 1982-89. Mem. Am. Phys. Soc., Am. Assn. Physics Tchrs., Internat. Union of Radio Sci., Am. Geophys. Union. Avocation: tournament bridge (regional championships 1988, 89, 90, 92). Office: Univ Iowa Dept Physics and Astronomy Iowa City IA 52242

GRABEMANN, KARL W., lawyer; b. Chgo., Apr. 27, 1929; s. Karl H. and Trude (Stockram) G.; m. Mary Darr, Dec. 6, 1958; children: Robert S., Lisa D. B.S., Northwestern U., 1951, J.D., 1956. Bar: Ill. 1957, U.S. Supreme Ct. 1960, U.S. Ct. Appeals for D.C. 1957, U.S. Ct. Appeals for 7th Circuit 1957, U.S. Ct. Appeals for 5th Circuit 1967, U.S. Dist. Ct. for D.C. 1957, U.S. Dist. Ct. for No. Dist. Ill. 1957. Atty. NLRB, Chgo., 1956-60; ptnr. firm Turner, Hunt & Woolley, Chgo., 1960-69, Keck, Mahin & Cate, Chgo., 1969-79, McDermott, Will & Emery, Chgo., 1979-89; of counsel Murphy, Smith & Polk, Chgo., 1990—. Mem. ABA, Ill. Bar Assn., Chgo. Bar Assn. Republican. Club: Metropolitan (Chgo.).

GRABER, DORIS APPEL, political scientist, editor, author; b. St. Louis, Nov. 11, 1923; d. Ernest and Martha (Insel) Appel; m. Thomas M. Graber, June 15, 1941; children: Lee Winston, Thomas Woodrow, Jack Douglas, Jim Murray, Susan Doris. AB, Washington U., St. Louis, 1941, MA, 1942; PhD, Columbia U., 1947. Feature writer St. Louis County Observer, Univ. City Tribune, St. Louis, 1939-41; civilian dir. U.S. Army Ednl. Reconditioning Program, Camp Maxey, Tex., 1943-45; editor legal mags. Commerce Clearing House, Chgo., 1945-46; lectr. polit. sci. Northwestern U., 1948-49; lectr. polit. sci. U. Chgo., 1950-51, rsch. assoc. Ctr. for Study Am. Fgn. and Mil. Policy, 1952-71; lectr. polit. sci. North Park Coll., 1952; mem. faculty U. Ill., Chgo., 1964—, assoc. prof. polit. sci., 1964-69, prof., 1970—; editor textbooks Harper & Row, Evanston, 1956-63; vis. prof. Harvard U., 1996. Author: The Development of the Law of Belligerent Occupation, 1949, 68,

Crisis Diplomacy: A History of U.S. Intervention Policies and Practices, 1959, Public Opinion, The President and Foreign Policy, 1968, Verbal Behavior and Politics, 1976, Mass Media and American Politics, 1980, 84, 89, 93, 96, Crime News and the Public, 1980, (with others) Media Agenda Setting in a Presidential Election, 1981, Processing the News: How People Tame the Information Tide, 1984, 88, 94, Public Sector Communication: How Organizations Manage Information, 1992; editor, contbr. The President and the Public, 1982; editor: Media Power in Politics, 1984, 90, 94, Political Comm., 1992-98, (with others) The Politics of News: The News of Politics, 1998; book rev. editor Polit. Psychology, 1998—; contbr. articles to profl. jours. Mem. LWV, Am. Assn. Pub. Opinion Rsch., Midwest Assn. Pub. Opinion Rsch. (program chmn. 1978-79, pres. 1980-81), Midwest Polit. Sci. Assn. (past pres.), Am. Polit. Sci. Assn. (coun. 1978-79, v.p. 1980-81, program chmn. 1984, 89-90, chmn. polit. comm. sect. 1989-91, chmn. editl. bd. P.S. 1992-94), Internat. Polit. Sci. Assn., Internat. Commn. Assn. (divsn. program chmn. 1978-80, divsn. chmn. 1980-82), Assn. Edn. for Journalism, Acad. Polit. Sci., Am. Acad. Polit. and Social Sci., Internat. Soc. Polit. Psychology (coun. 1992-93, co-program chmn. 1993-94, pres. 1995-96), Phi Beta Kappa (pres. Iota of Ill. chpt. 1991-92), Pi Sigma Alpha, Pi Alpha Alpha. Home: 2895 Sheridan Pl Evanston IL 60201-1725 Office: U Ill 1007 W Harrison St Chicago IL 60607-7135

GRABER, EDWARD ALEX, obstetrician, gynecologist, educator; b. Chgo., July 24, 1914; s. Irving D. and Grace (Davis) G.; m. Sylvia H. Hess, Nov. 24, 1938; 1 son, Fredric Jay. MD, Emory U., 1936. Diplomate: Am. Bd. Gyn. Assoc. dir. ob-gyn Lenox Hill Hosp., N.Y.C., 1972-75; attending obstetrician-gynecologist N.Y. Hosp., 1975-88; prof. ob-gyn Med. Sch. Cornell U., N.Y.C., 1975—, emeritus Med. Sch., 1988; hon. attending physician N.Y. Hosp.-Cornell Med. Ctr., N.Y.C., 1971—. Author: Gynecologic Endocrinology, 1961, (with Barber) Are The Pills Safe?, Obstetric and Gynecology Procedures, 1969, Gynecological Oncology, 1970, Surgical Disease in Pregnancy, 1974, (with G. Schaefer) Complications of Gynecological Surgery, 1982; contbr. articles to profl. jours. Fellow Am. Coll. Ob-Gyn, ACS, N.Y. Acad. Medicine (pres. ob-gyn sect. 1971-72), N.Y. Gynecol. Soc. (pres. 1972-73); mem. AMA. Home: 130 E 75th St New York NY 10021-3277 *Three words have had a marked influence on my life. They are excellence, responsibility, and love.*

GRABER, SUSAN P., judge; b. Oklahoma City, July 5, 1949; d. Julius A. and Bertha (Fenyves) G.; m. William June, May 3, 1981; 1 child, Rachel June-Graber. BA, Wellesley Coll., 1969; JD, Yale U., 1972. Bar: N.Mex. 1972, Ohio 1977, Oreg. 1978. Asst. atty. gen. Bur. of Revenue, Santa Fe, 1972-74; assoc. Jones Gallegos Snead & Wertheim, Santa Fe, 1974-75, Taft Stettinius & Hollister, Cin., 1975-78; assoc., then ptnr. Stoel Rives Boley Jones & Grey, Portland, Oreg., 1978-88; judge, then presiding judge Oreg. Ct. Appeals, Salem, 1988-90; assoc. justice Oreg. Supreme Ct., Salem, 1990-98; judge U.S. Ct. Appeals (9th cir.), Portland, 1998—. Mem. Gov.'s Adv. Coun. on Legal Svcs., 1979-88; bd. dirs. U.S. Dist. Ct. of Oreg. Hist. Soc., 1985—, Oreg. Law Found., 1990-91; mem. bd. visitors Sch. Law, U. Oreg., 1986-93. Mem. Oreg. State Bar (jud. adminstrn. com. 1985-87, pro bono com. 1988-90), Ninth Cir. Jud. Conf. (chair exec. com. 1987-88), Oreg. Jud. Conf. (edn. com. 1988-91, program chair 1990), Oreg. Appellate Judges Assn. (sec.-treas. 1990-91, vice chair 1991-92, chair 1992-93), Am. Inns of Ct. (master), Phi Beta Kappa. Office: US Ct Appeals 9th Cir Pioneer Courthouse 555 SW Yamhill St Portland OR 97204-1336

GRABER, THOMAS M., orthodontist; b. St. Louis, May 27, 1917; Diplomate Am. Bd. Orthodontics (Reconition award 1990, Dewel award 1992); Fellow Royal Coll. Surgeons (Eng.). DMD, Washington U., St. Louis, 1940; MS in Dentistry, Northwestern U., 1946, PhD in Anatomy, 1950; Doctorate (hon.), U. Gothenberg, 1989; DSc (hon.), Washington U., 1991, U. Mich., 1994, U. Kunming, 1996. Diplomate Am. Bd. Orthodontics (Recognition award 1990, Dewel award, 1992). Mem. faculty Northwestern U. Dental Sch., 1946-58, assoc. prof. orthodontics, 1954-58; dir. research Northwestern U. Dental Sch. (cleft lip and palate Inst.), 1947-58; assoc. attending orthodontist Children's Meml. Hosp., Chgo., 1951-58; vis. lectr. U. Mich. Dental Sch., 1958-67; dir. Kenilworth Research Found., Ill., 1967—; prof. orthodontics Zoller Dental Clinic; pediatrics research assoc. prof. anthropology and anatomy U. Chgo., 1969-80, assoc. prof. plastic and reconstructive surgery, 1980-82; research scientist ADA Research Inst., Chgo., 1980-90; dir. G.V. Black Inst. for Continuing Edn., 1967—; vis. prof. U. Mich., 1984-94; clin. prof. orthodontics U. Ill. Coll. Dentistry, Chgo., 1994—; Northcroft lectr., Birmingham, Eng., 1989; cons. in field. Author textbooks, articles; editor-in-chief Am. Jour. Orthodontics, 1985—. Served as capt. Dental Corps AUS, 1941-45. Recipient Alumni Merit award Northwestern U., 1977; named Disting. Alumnus Washington U., 1980; NIH grantee, 1954, 56-60, 76, 77, 79, 80, 85, 86. Fellow Royal Coll. Surgeons (Eng.), Am. Coll. of Dentists, Internat. Coll. of Dentists; mem. Am. Dental Soc., Ill. Dental Soc., Am. Assn. Orthodontists (gen. chmn. 1960, 77, 80, founding mem., chmn. coun. on orthodontic edn. and audio visual com. 1962, 67, gen. chmn. jour. 1977, trustee, Grieve Meml. award 1964, 84, Disting. Service award 1970, Ketcham award 1975, Salzmann award 1979, 75th Anniversary citation 1990, Mershon award 1989, Horace Hayden award 1991, Jarabak Internat. Teaching and Rsch. award 1994, Heritage award 1998, 99), Internat. Assn. Research (chmn. Chgo. sect. 1973-74), Chgo. Orthodontists Assn. (pres. 1961-62), European Orthodontists Soc., Ill. Orthodontists Soc. (pres. 1969-70), Angle Soc. (pres. 1968), Japan Orthodontists Soc., SAR. Republican. Presbyterian. Home: 2895 Sheridan Pl Evanston IL 60201-1725 Office: U Ill Coll Dentistry MC842 801 S Paulina St # Mc842 Chicago IL 60612-7210

GRABNER, GEORGE JOHN, manufacturing executive; b. Muskogee, Okla., Aug. 25, 1918; s. George and Helen (Leitch) G.; m. Martha Ebright, Oct. 2, 1993; children: George John, Jan, Heidi, John, Thomas. B.A., Western Res. U., 1939; postgrad., Harvard Grad. Sch. Bus. Adminstrn., 1940. CPA, Ohio. Asst. mgr. Ernst & Ernst (CPAs), Cleve., 1946-57; v.p., dir. Cyrus Eaton Interests, 1957-58; fin. v.p., treas. Weatherhead Co., Cleve., 1958-63; exec. v.p. Weatherhead Co., 1963-65, pres., dir., 1965-70; pres., dir. Weatherhead Co. Can., Ltd., 1966-70, LPG Leasing Corp., Cleve., 1958-70; pres., chief exec. officer Lamson & Sessions Co., 1970-98, chmn. bd., 1978-84, chmn. exec. com., 1985-90; ret., 1998; trustee 1st Union Realty, 1967-91. Chmn. bd. Greater Cleve. Growth Assn., 1966-69; chmn. Cleve. Devel. Found., 1966-69, Fin. Supervisory Commn. of City of Cleve., 1980-88; trustee S.A. Horvitz Testamentary Trust. 1st lt. USAAF, 1942-45. Mem. Ohio Soc. CPAs, Am. Ordinance Assn. (past pres., dir.), Union Club, Pepper Pike Country Club, Hole in the Wall Club, The Everglades Club, The Ocean Club. Home: 32515 Creekside Dr Pepper Pike OH 44124

GRABOIS, NEIL ROBERT, association executive, former college president; b. N.Y.C., Dec. 11, 1935; s. Lazarus Lawrence and Florence (Graber) G.; m. Miriam Blau, Aug. 19, 1956; children: Adam, Daniel. BA, Swarthmore Coll., 1957; MA, U. Pa., 1959, PhD, 1963; LLD (hon.), Williams Coll., 1988. Asst. instr. math. U. Pa., Phila., 1957-61; instr. math. Lafayette Coll., Easton, Pa., 1961-63; mem. faculty Williams Coll., Williamstown, Mass., 1963-88; prof. math. Williams Coll., 1972-88, dean coll., dean faculty, then provost, 1970-80, chmn. dept. math. scis., 1981-83, provost, 1983-88; pres. Colgate U., Hamilton, N.Y., 1988-99; v.p. for strategic planning, program coord. Carnegie Corp. N.Y., N.Y.C., 1999—; treas. Roper Ctr., Storrs, Conn., 1979-88. Co-author: Linear Algebra and Multivariable Calculus, 1970. Chmn. edn. subcom. Gov.'s Task Force for No. Berkshires, North Adams, Mass., 1985-87; bd. trustees Swarthmore Coll., 1991—; mem. ACE Commn. on Leadership Devel. Mem. Am. Math. Soc., Math. Assn. Am. (vis. lectr. 1971), AAAS, N.Y. Acad. Scis. Democrat. Avocations: squash, tennis, clarinet, recorder. Office: Carnegie Corp NY 437 Madison Ave New York NY 10022 *Without the support of our fellows, there can be no success; without understanding, and compassion, ideas have shape but may lead only into darkness; without honesty and clarity, and a willingness to hear the other side, tactics may succeed but the right path will be lost; no person sees the whole truth but the leader can help us find our way.*

GRABOW, RAYMOND JOHN, mayor, lawyer; b. Cleve., Jan. 27, 1932; s. Joseph Stanley and Frances (Kalata) G.; BSBA, Kent State U., 1953; JD, Western Res. U., 1958; m. Margaret Jean Knoll, Nov. 27, 1969; children: Rachel Jean, Ryan Joseph. Bar: Ohio 1958. Counsel, No. Ohio Petroleum Retailers Assn., Cleve., 1965-78; counsel, trustee Alliance of Poles Fed. Credit Union, 1972, also gen. counsel Alliance of Poles of Am.; councilman City of Warrensville Heights (Ohio), 1962-68, mayor, 1969-98; sec. Space Comfort Co., S.S.K., Inc.; fed. panelist U.S. Dist. Ct.; active Dem. Exec. Com., Cuyahoga County, 1966-98, precinct com., 1966-80; trustee Brentwood Hosp., Nat. League Cities, Brentwood Found.; bd. govs. Meridia Southpoint Hosp., 1996-99; pres. West Harbor Lagoons Assn. Mem. Ohio Jud. Conf. (life), Ohio State Bar Assn., Cuyahoga County Bar Assn., Cleve. Bar Assn., U.S. Conf. of Mayors, Am. Legion, PLAV Vets, Cleve. Soc., Warrensville Heights C. of C. (trustee 1989-98), Ohio Assn. Pub. Safety Dirs., Ohio Mcpl. League, Mcpl. Treas. Assn., Order of Alhambra, Fraternal Order of Eagles. Home: 20114 Gladstone Rd Cleveland OH 44122-6644 Office: 5005 Rockside Rd Cleveland OH 44131-2194

GRABOW, STEPHEN HARRIS, architecture educator; b. Bklyn., Jan. 15, 1943; s. Philip and Ida (England) G.; 1 child, Nicole Elizabeth. BArch., U. Mich., 1965; MArch., Pratt Inst., 1966; postgrad., U. Calif.-Berkeley, 1966-67; PhD, U. Wash., 1973. Architect-planner U.S. Peace Corps, Tunisia, 1967-69; regional planning cons. Teheran, Iran, 1969; asst. prof. architecture U. Ariz., 1969-70; teaching assoc. U. Wash., 1970-72; lectr. town and regional planning Duncan of Jordanstone Coll. Art, U. Dundee, Scotland, 1972-73; asst. prof. architecture and urban design U. Kans.-Lawrence, 1973-76, assoc. prof., 1976-82, prof., 1982—, dir. architecture, 1979-82, 83-86; vis. fellow U. Calif.-Berkeley, 1977; research and design cons. Design Build Architects, Lawrence; bd. dirs. Assn. Collegiate Schs. Architecture, 1982-87; vis. lectr. Royal Danish Acad. Fine Arts, Copenhagen, 1987-88. Author: Christopher Alexander and the Search for a New Paradigm in Architecture, 1983; mem. editorial bd.: Jour. Archtl. Edn., 1982-84. Recipient award Nat. Endowment for Arts, 1974, citation for excellence in design rsch. NEA, 1980, Biennial Svc. award Denmark's Internat. Studies Program, 1997; Fulbright Scholar award, 1987-88; NEH fellow, 1976-77. Mem. Nat. Archtl. Research Council (appointee 1986-87). Home: 1518 Crossgate Dr Lawrence KS 66047-3504 Office: U Kans Sch Architecture & Urban Design 205 Marvin Hall Lawrence KS 66044-7532

GRABSKI, DANIEL ALEXIS, psychiatrist; b. Cleve., May 22, 1928; s. Alex Jacob and Pauline Josephine (Rutkowski) G.; m. Rosemarie Karl, Dec. 24, 1950; children: Daniel Jacob, Daryl Jeffry. BS, Baldwin-Wallace Coll., 1948; MD, St. Louis U., 1952. Diplomate Am. Bd. Psychiatry and Neurology. Exec. dir. Kern County Mental Health Dept., Bakersfield, Calif., 1962-66, 72-86; chief dept. psychiatry Kern County Med. Ctr., Bakersfield, 1972-81; asst. dep. dir. Calif. Dept. Mental Hygiene, Sacramento, 1966-72; med. dir. Weil Meml. Child Guidance Clinic, Bakersfield, 1986-97; sr. cons. Weil Child Guidance Clinic, Bakersfield, 1997—. Capt. USAR, 1954-56. Fellow Am. Psychiat. Assn. (life, spkr. assembly 1977); mem. AMA, Calif. Med. Assn., Ctrl. Calif. Psychiat. Soc., Kern Med. Soc., Flying Physicians Assn., Am. Med. Fly Fishing Assn. (pres.-elect, pres. 1998). Avocations: airline transport rating, private pilot, fly fishing. Office: Weill Child Guidance Clinic 3628 Stockdale Hwy Bakersfield CA 93309-2153

GRABURN, NELSON HAYES HENRY, anthropologist, educator; b. London, Nov. 25, 1936; s. Henry Long Kingsforth and Cecily Marion (Finch) G.; m. Katherine Kazuko Yaguchi, June 25, 1966; children: Eva Mariko, Cecily Atsuko Ring. B.A., Cambridge (Eng.) U., 1958; M.A., McGill U., 1960; Ph.D., U. Chgo., 1963. Research anthropologist Govt. of Can., 1959-60; research asso. Northwestern U., Evanston, Ill., 1963-64; mem. faculty dept. anthropology U. Calif., Berkeley, 1964—, prof., 1974—, chmn. dept., 1981-84, 96; curator N.Am. Ethnology, P.A. Hearst (Lowie) Mus., 1975—; co-chmn. Can. studies program N. Am. ethnology Lowie Mus., 1986—; cons. NSF, NIMH, Can. Council. Author: Lake Harbour N.W.T., 1963, Taqagmiut Eskimo Kinship Terminology, 1964, Eskimos Without Igloos, 1969, Readings in Kinship and Social Structure, 1971, Circumpolar Peoples, 1973, Ethnic and Tourist Arts, 1976, To Pray, Pay and Play: The Cultural Structure of Japanese Domestic Tourism, 1983, Tourism Social Sciences, 1991, Catalogue Raisonne of the Alaska Commercial Company Collection, 1996; co-editor: Working Papers in Traditional Arts, 1976-81, Annals of Tourism Research, 1977—. Served with Brit. Army, 1953-55. Recipient Nat. Mus. Can. award, 1976; grantee NSF 1967-69, 79-80, NEH, 1987-88, Alaska Humanities Forum grantee; sr. fellow in Can. studies, 1985-86; NEH grantee, 1987-88; vis. professorship Nat. Mus. Ethnology, Osaka, Japan, 1989-90. Mem. Royal Anthropol. Inst., Am. Anthropol. Assn., Can. Ethnology Soc., Internat. Acad. Study of Tourism (founding). Office: Univ of Calif Dept Anthropology Berkeley CA 94720-3710

GRACE, BETTE FRANCES, certified public accountant; b. Hanford, Calif., Apr. 16, 1957; d. Boyd Lowell Sharp and Janet Praria; m. Clyde Jon Nold, May 4, 1974 (div. 1987); children: Mandolin P., Christopher J.; m. Michael E. Grace, Feb. 14, 1996. AA in Bus., Gavilan Coll., Gilroy, Calif., 1992; BS in Bus./Acctg., San Jose State U., 1994, postgrad., 1994—. CPA, Calif. Fin. controller Hollister (Calif.) Disposal, Inc., 1984-92; owner, operator Hollister Bookkeeping and Tax Svc., 1985-98; acct. mgr. Ridgemark Golf & Country Club, Hollister, 1992-98; CPA, owner Grace & Assocs CPAs, Hollister, 1998—; fin. controller John Smith Landfill, Inc., Hollister, 1986-92, Ajax Portable Svc., Hollister, 1987-92. Supporter Monterey County (Calif.) Symphony Guild, 1991—; parent mem. Calif. High Sch. Rodeo Assn., Hollister, 1991—; dir. 33rd Dist. Agrl. Assn., San Benito County Fair Bd., 1992-96; fin. chmn. AT&T Pebble Beach Nat. Pro-Am. Mem. AICPA, El Gabilan Young Ladies Inst. Republican. Roman Catholic. Avocations: water and snow skiing. Office: Grace & Assocs CPAs PO Box 1352 Hollister CA 95024-1352

GRACE, BRIAN GUILES, lawyer; b. Lawrence, Kans., Dec. 26, 1942; s. Bernard and Theola Avida (Guiles) G.; m. Carol Diane Seaver, June 9, 1967; children: Kevin A., Jeff S., Brady A. BBA, U. Kans., 1964, JD, 1967. Bar: Kans. 1967, U.S. Dist. Ct. Kans. 1967, U.S. Ct. Appeals (10th cir.) 1974, U.S. Supreme Ct. 1991. Assoc., ptnr. Curfman, Harris, Stallings, Grace & Snow and predecessor firm, Wichita, Kans., 1967-84; ptnr. Grace Unruh & Pratt and predecessor firms, Wichita, 1984—; mem. Fed. Bench and Bar Comm., 1992-96. Bd. dirs. Leukemia Soc. Kans. Inc., Wichita, 1974-77; chmn. bd. edn. Desegretion Com., 1990-95. Mem. ABA (vice chmn. constn. litigation com. 1974-76), Assn. of Trial Lawyers of Am., Kans. Bar Assn. (bench and bar com. 1991—, chmn. 1993-96), Kans. Trial Lawyers Assn. (editor jour. 1989-91). Avocations: golf, tennis, bridge. Home: 36 Stratford Rd Wichita KS 67206 Office: 501 N Market St Wichita KS 67214-3513

GRACE, HELEN KENNEDY, retired foundation administrator; b. Beresford, S.D., Mar. 30, 1935; d. Walter James and Ethel Elvira (Soderstrom) Kennedy; m. Elliott A. Grace, Nov. 20, 1961; 1 child, Elizabeth Ann. BSN, Loyola U., Chgo., 1963; MSN, U. Ill., Chgo., 1966; PhD in Sociology, Northwestern U., 1969; LLD, Valparaiso U., 1992; DSc (hon.), S.D. State U.; LHD honoris causa, Loyola U., 1993, Northeastern U., 1994. Nursing adminstr. Ill. Dept. Mental Health, 1963-67; instr. Coll. Nursing, U. Ill., Chgo., 1967-69, asst. prof., 1969-71, assoc. prof., 1971-73, prof., assoc. dean for grad. study, 1973-76, dean Coll. Nursing, 1977-82; program dir. W.K. Kellogg Found., Battle Creek, Mich., 1982-86, coord. health programs, 1986-91, v.p. program, 1991-95, spl. asst. to pres./CEO, 1995-98. Author: Mental Health Nursing: A Psychosocial Approach, 1977, 2d edit., 1981; Families Across the Life Cycle: Family Studies for Nursing, 1977; The Development of a Child Psychiatric Treatment Program, 1971; Current Issues in Nursing, 1981, 5th edit., 1997. Recipient Disting. Alumnus award Loyola U. Coll. Nursing U. Ill., Centennial Alumni award Am. State and Land Grand Univs. Mem. ANA, Nat. League for Nursing (governing bd. 1978-86), Am. Acad. Nursing (governing coun. 1976-80), Am. Sociol. Assn.

GRACE, JASON ROY, advertising agency executive; b. N.Y.C., Dec. 5, 1936; s. Jack and Mitzi (Goldstick) G.; m. Marcia Jean Bell, May 16, 1966; children: Jessica Bell, Nicholas Bell. Student, Cooper Union, 1955-56, 58-62. Art dir. Benton & Bowles Inc., N.Y.C., 1962-63, Grey Advt., N.Y.C., 1963-64; sr. v.p., creative mgmt. supr. Doyle Dane Bernbach Inc., N.Y.C., 1964-72; creative dir., exec. v.p. Gilbert, Grace & Stark, N.Y.C., 1972-75; creative dir., exec. v.p. Doyle Dane Bernbach Inc., 1975-79, exec. v.p., exec. creative dir., 1979—, vice chmn., 1981-86, chmn. bd. U.S., exec. creative dir., 1986—; chmn. bd. Grace and Rothschild; film dir., 1970—. Elected art dirs. Hall of Fame, 1986—; trustee Cooper Union, 1987—; bd. dirs. Nat. Mus. Am. History, Smithsonian Inst., 1988—. With U.S. Army, 1956-58. Recipient 8 Andy awards Advt. Club N.Y., 28 Clio awards Am. Film Festival, 5 Gold Lion awards, 3 Silver Lion awards Cannes Film Festival, 9 Gold medals Art Dirs. Club, Best TV Comml. of Last 20 Yrs. award; recipient Internat. Broadcasting award, 1980, St. Gaudens medal Cooper Union Alumni Assn., 6 commls. named in Clio Hall of Fame, Outstanding Alumnus Sch. Art and Design, 1987; 4 commls. placed in permanent collection Mus. Modern Art; elected to Creative Hall of Fame, The One Club, 1994, 97; 2 commls. in Advtg. Age's 50 Best TV Commls. of All Time, 3 of Top 10 in TV Guide's List of Best 50 Commls. of All Time. Mem. Dirs. Guild Am. Home: 55 W 85th St New York NY 10024-4106 Office: 114 5th Ave New York NY 10011-5604

GRACE, JOHN EUGENE, business forms company executive; b. Dundee, Ill., Nov. 22, 1931; s. Arnold Victor and Louise Joan (Boncosky) G.; m. Janice Rae Fohey, June 30, 1956; children: Gregory Alan, Michael Brian, Michele Marie. BS in Bus. Adminstrn. with high honors, U. Ill., 1958; MSBA in Fin., No. Ill. U., 1976. Gen. acctg. mgr. Elgin Watch Co., Ill., 1958-60; corp. controller Newell Cos., Freeport, Ill., 1960-68; controller jewelry div. Josten's, Inc., Owatonna, Minn., 1968-71; v.p. fin., chief fin. officer, asst. sec. Duplex Products Inc., Sycamore, Ill., 1971-87; cons. Duplex Products Inc., 1987-97; cons. in field. Active local United Fund, Little League, YMCA. Served with USAF, 1951-53. Mem. Fin. Execs. Inst. (past pres., dir. Fox-Rock chpt.), IMA (past dir.), Adminstrv. Mgmt. Soc. (past dir.), Jaycees, C. of C., Beta Alpha Psi. Republican. Methodist. Clubs: Elks. Home and Office: 405 Timber Ln Palm Harbor FL 34683-3737

GRACE, JOHN ROSS, chemical engineering educator; b. London, Ont., Can., June 8, 1943; s. Archibald John and Mary Kathleen (Disney) G.; m. Sherrill Elizabeth Perley, Dec. 20, 1964; children—Elizabeth, Malcolm. B.E.Sc., U. Western Ont., 1965; Ph.D., Cambridge (Eng.) U., 1968. From asst. prof. to prof. chem. engring. McGill U., Montreal, Que., 1968-79; sr. research engr. Surveyor Nenniger & Chenevert Inc., 1974-75; prof. chem. engring. U. B.C., Vancouver, 1979—, head dept. chem. engrin., 1979-87, dean faculty grad. studies, 1990-96; cons. in field. Co-author: Bubbles, Drops and Particles, 1978; co-editor: Fluidization, 1980, Fluidization VI, 1989, Circulating Fluidized Beds, 1997; editor Chem. Engring. Sci., 1984-90; contbr. articles to profl. jours. NRC sr. indsl. fellow; Athlone fellow; Can. Coun. Killam Res. fellow, 1999. Fellow chem. Inst. Can. (v.p. 1994-95, pres. 1995-96); mem. Can. Soc. Chem. Engring. (pres., Erco award, R.S. Jane award), Assn. Profl. Engrs. B.C., Instn. Chem. Engrs., Nat. Scis. and Engring. Rsch. Coun. of Can. Office: 2216 Main Mall, Vancouver, BC Canada V6T 1Z4

GRACE, JOHN WILLIAM, electrical company executive; b. Swissvile, Pa., May 29, 1921; s. Joseph and Ruth Margaret (Bailey) G.; student Am. TV Inst. Tech., 1950; BEE, Drexel U., 1960; m. Ruth Delores Schroeder, Nov. 25, 1950; children: Martha, Joan, Nancy, John William. Technician missiles and surface radar div. RCA, Moorestown, N.J., 1950-56, design engr., 1956-60, project engr., 1960-66; mgr. engring. and sci. exec. EG & G, Inc., Las Vegas, Nev., 1966-73, mgr. bus. devel. operational test and evaluation, Albuquerque, 1973-77; engring. mgr. Instrumentation div., Idaho Falls, Idaho, 1977-79, mgr. systems project office, 1979, mgr. instrumentation program office, 1979-82, mgr. engring. spl. products div., 1982-84, dir. tech. resources, 1984-91, retired 1991. Active Boy Scouts Am., 1969-71. Served with USNR, 1941-45. Mem. IEEE, Instrument Soc. Am. (dir. sci. instrumentation and research div.), Assn. Old Crows, Am. Legion (post adj. vice comdr. 1950). Episcopalian (pres. couples retreat 1969-70). Patentee contradirectional waveguide coupler. Home: 8311 Loma Del Norte Dr NE Albuquerque NM 87109-4901 Office: EG&G Spl Projects Divsn PO Box 93747 Las Vegas NV 89193-3747

GRACE, JULIANNE ALICE, investor relations firm executive; b. Riverdale, N.Y., Oct. 29, 1937; d. Arthur Edward and Julia May (McCarthy) Thompson; m. Daniel Vincent Grace, July 2, 1960; children: Daniel Vincent III, Deirdre Elizabeth Beck. BA, Marymount Manhattan Coll., 1959; MA, Fordham U., 1960. Dir. admissions Marymount Manhattan Coll., N.Y.C., 1966-72; mgr. human resources The Perkin-Elmer Corp., Norwalk, Conn., 1972-78, dir. human resources, 1978-81, asst. sr. v.p. semiconductor equipment, 1981-83, asst. pres., 1983-85, v.p., asst. to chief exec. officer, 1985-86; v.p. adminstrn. The Perkin-Elmer Corp., Norwalk, 1986-90, v.p. corp. rels., 1990-95; pres. The Jagcom Group, New Canaan, Conn., 1995—. Bd. dirs. Norwalk and Wilton chpts. ARC, 1975-85, Metropool, 1991—; pres., bd. dirs. Waveny (Conn.) Care Ctr.; trustee Norwalk YMCA, 1986-94; active Norwalk C.C. Found., 1986-90, Fairfield 2000; mem. corp. cabinet U. Conn. Downstate Initiative, 1995-98. Woodrow Wilson Nat. Found. fellow, 1959-60. Mem. Econ. Soc. Conn., Nat. Investor Rels. Inst. (sr. exec. roundtable), Fairfield Pub. Rels. Assn., Assn. Women in Comm., Regional Plan Assn. (com.), Sports Car Club Am., Wolfpit Running Club, Saugatuck Harbor Yacht Club (mem. bd. govs.). Home and Office: 54 Louises Ln New Canaan CT 06840-2120

GRACE, MARCELLUS, pharmacy educator, university dean; b. Selma, Ala., Oct. 17, 1947; s. Capp and Mary (Davis) G.; m. Laura Dunn, Sept. 8, 1973; children: K'Chebe M., Syreeta L., Marcellus Jr. BS in Pharmacy, Xavier U. La., 1971; MS in Hosp. Pharmacy, U. Minn., 1975, PhD in Pharmacy Adminstrn., 1976. Registered pharmacist, La., Ohio, Calif., Minn., D.C. Hosp. pharmacy resident USPHS Hosp., Balt., 1971-72; staff pharmacist USPHS Hosp., Boston, 1972-73, Thrifty Drug Stores, L.A., 1973; asst. dir. pharmacy Bethesda Hosps., Cin., 1975; dir. pharmacy svcs. Tulane U. Med. Ctr., New Orleans, 1976-77; assoc. prof., asst. dean Howard U., Washington, 1979-82; assoc. prof. clin. pharmacy Xavier U. La., New Orleans, 1976-78, prof. pharmacy adminstrn., dean, 1983—; mem. adv. coun. Nat. Heart Lung and Blood Inst., NIH, Bethesda, 1990-93; mem. Walgreens Pharmacy adv. coun., 1993-97; chair pharmacy panel Peer Health Professionscommn., 1991-92; bd. dirs. New Orleans Regional Med. Complex, 1993—, Ernest N. Morial Asthma and Respiratory Disease Ctr., 1995—, La. Cancer and Lung Trust Fund, 1995—, Alton Ochsner Med. Found., 1996—. Contbr. articles and abstracts to profl. jours. Recipient cert. appreciation Nat. Assn. Bds. Pharmacy, 1983. Mem. Am. Assn. Colls. Pharmacy (bd. dirs. 1992-94), N.Y. Acad. Scis., Assn., Rho Chi. Democrat. Baptist. Avocations: automobile restoration, flying. Office: Xavier U La Coll Pharmacy 7325 Palmetto St New Orleans LA 70125-1056

GRACE, MARCIA BELL, advertising executive; b. Pitts., July 29, 1937; d. Daniel Henry and Gertrude Margaret (Loew) Bell; m. Roy Grace, May 16, 1966; children: Jessica Bell, Nicholas Bell. AB, Harvard U., 1959. V.p., assoc. creative dir. Doyle Dane Bernbach, N.Y.C., 1964-77; sr. v.p., creative dir. Wells, Rich, Greene, Inc., N.Y.C., 1977-85, exec. v.p., creative dir., 1986-90; cons. Marcia Grace & Co., N.Y.C., 1990—. Represented in permanent collection Mus. Modern Art. Recipient 1st Pl. ANDY award Advt. Club N.Y., 1968, 70, 72, 75, 1st Pl. Gold award The One Show, 1973, 78, Hall of Fame award The Clio Show, N.Y.C., 1982, 86. Avocations: horseback riding, gardening.

GRACE, MARK EUGENE, baseball player; b. Winston-Salem, N.C., June 28, 1964. Student, Saddleback C.C., San Diego State U. First baseman Chgo. Cubs, 1988—; mem. Nat. League All-Star Team, 1993, 95. Recipient Golden Glove award, 1992-93; named Sporting News Rookie Player of Yr., MVP Ea. League, 1987; assist leader for 1st basemen, 1990-92; ranked 1st in Nat. League for put-outs, 1991-92. Office: Chgo Cubs Wrigley Field 1060 W Addison St Chicago IL 60613-4305*

GRACE, PRISCILLA ANNE, labor union executive; b. Ft. Worth, Mar. 20, 1943; d. John Paul and Pauline (Greer) G.; children: K. C. Caldwell Jr., George E. Caldwell, Kristina Caldwell Henry. Grad. pvt. sch., Our Lady of Victory Sch., Ft. Worth. Telephone operator Southwestern Bell Telephone, Ft. Worth and Houston, 1968-70; letter carrier U.S. Postal Svc., Humble, Tex., 1973-85; officer local 283, Nat. Assn. Letter Carriers, Houston, 1984-98, pres., 1998—; chmn. bd. dirs. Houston Postal Credit Union, 1990—; mem. exec. bd. Harris County AFL-CIO, Houston, 1988-98. Editor Houston Letter Carrier Newsletter, 1978-84. Mem. Tex. AFLCIO (v.p. 1997—), Nat. Assn. Letter Carriers. Lutheran. Avocations: genealogy research, needlework, travel, reading. Office: Nat Assn Letter Carriers 2414 Broadway St Houston TX 77012-3812

GRACE, RENÉ EARLE, physician; b. Aberdeen, S.D., Dec. 28, 1940; s. Cyril Winfield and Sara Vivian Grace; m. Susan Linda Smith (div. Feb. 1992); 1 child, Susan Leslie Grace Miller; m. Marilyn Kay Smith, Feb. 24, 1994; 1 child, René Ethan. Grad., U. S.D., 1962; MD, George Washington

U., 1966. Pvt. practice family medicine Clinton, Md., 1969—. Piano recitalist, 1961—; composer piano music. Vol. Cath. Clinic Health Ptnrs., Waldorf, Md., 1994—; bd. dirs. Jude House, Bel Alton, Md., 1998—. Lt. M.C., USN, 1967-69, Vietnam. H.M. Cook scholar U. S.D., 1959-61. Mem. Phi Eta Sigma. Avocations: music, gardening, tennis. Office: 9131 Piscataway Rd Clinton MD 20735

GRACE, THOMAS LEE, healthcare administrator, nurse; b. Huntingdon, Pa., Mar. 29, 1955; s. Robert Leroy and Mary Elizabeth (Isenberg) G.; m. Renee Lee Ramsey, Oct. 20, 1979; children: Elliott, Amanda. ASN, Robert Morris Coll., 1978; diploma in nursing, Sewickley (Pa.) Valley Hosp., 1979; BSN, LaRoche Coll., 1984; M in Pub. Mgmt., Carnegie Mellon U., 1985; PhD in Mgmt., Cambridge State U., 1999. RN, Pa. Staff nurse ortho dept. McKeesport (Pa.) Hosp., 1979-80; staff nurse emergency rm. Allegheny Gen. Hosp., Pitts., 1980-81; flight nurse Life-Flight-Allegheny Gen. Hosp., Pitts., 1981-85; chief flight nurse Aries-Fairfax Hosp., Falls Church, Va., 1985-86; coord. emergency svcs. Fairfax Hosp., Falls Church, 1986-87; flight program dir. Pennstar U. Pa. Med. Ctr., Phila., 1987-91; asst. adminstr. Hosp. of U. Pa., Phila., 1991-96; dir. safety mgmt. U. Pa. Health Sys., 1996—. Inventor crico ventilation device; contbr. articles to profl. jours. Citizen rep. Upper Merion Twp. (Pa.) Emergency Svc. Bd., 1994-97; mem. Huntingdon Vol. Fire Dept., 1972—, Valley Ambulance Authority, Corapolis, Pa., 1977-79; bd. dirs., citizen rep. Lafayette Ambulance Svc., King of Prussia, Pa., 1996—, treas., 1998—; del. Ctrl. Dist. Fireman's Assn., Tyrone, Pa., 1983—; scoutmaster Sewickley Math. Ch. troop Boy Scouts Am., 1978-79. With U.S. Army, 1973-76. Mem. Emergency Nurses Assn., Nat. Flight Nurses Assn. (past pres.), Am. Phys. Plant Adminstrs., Am. Legion. Democrat. Avocations: fishing, skiing. Home: 594 Forest Rd Wayne PA 19087-2322

GRACE, WALTER CHARLES, prosecutor; b. Elmira, N.Y., Mar. 4, 1947; s. Claude Henry and Grace Anne (Richardson) G.; m. Barbbara Lynn Eaglen, Oct. 3, 1981; children: Katherine Anne, Charles Brigham. BA History, Duke U., 1969; JD, U. Tenn., 1972. Bar: Ill., 1972; U.S. Dist. Ct. (ea. and so. dists.) Ill., 1972. Asst. state's atty. Jackson County, Murphysboro, Ill., 1972-73; assoc. Donald R. Mitchell Law Office, Carbondale, Ill., 1973-74; atty. Jackson County Pub. Defender, Murphysboro, 1974-77; ptnr. Lockwood & Grace, Carbondale, 1977-78; pvt. practice Lockwood & Grace, 1978-79; ptnr. Hendricks, Watt & Grace, Murphysboro, 1979-82; assoc. Feirich, Schone, Mager, Green & Assocs., Carbondale, 1982-83, Feirch, Schoen, Mager, Green & Assocs., Carbondale, 1983-88; state's atty. Jackson County State's Atty., Murphysboro, 1988-93; U.S. Atty. U.S. Atty.'s Office, Fairview Heights, Ill., 1993—; chmn. Jackson County Child Advocacy Adv. Bd., 1988-93; adv. bd. Ill. State Violent Crime Victim's Adv. Bd., 1988-90; com. mem. Jackson County Juv. Justice Task Force, 1988-93; exec. com. Ill. State's Atty.'s Assn., 1991-93; legis. com. Ill. Sate's Atty.'s Assn., 1992-93; co-chmn. Jackson County SAFE Policy/Gang Policy Interagy. Steering Com. Adv. Bd., 1991-93; master So. Ill. Am. Inn. of Ct., 1992—; others. Active NAACP,, Carbondale; mem. Jackson County Heart Fund Campaign, 1976-77; bd. dirs. Carbondale United Way, 1978-80, capt. campaign drive, profl. div., 1980; mem. planning com. John A. Logan Coll.-Jackson County Bar Assn. Continuing Edn. Programs; mem. adv. com. to Corrections and Law Enforcment Programs, So. Ill. U. Sch. of Tech. Careers, 1978-89; mem. Hill House Board, Inc., 1979-84; pres. 1980-82; lector St. Francis Xavier Ch., Carbondale. Mem. Jackson County Bar Assn. (sec. 1978-79, pres. 1980-81), Ill. State Bar Assn. (mem. criminal law sect., family law sect., tort law sect.), ABA (family law and criminal law sects.), Assn. Trial Lawyers of Am., Nat. Legal Aid and Defender Assn., Ill. Pub. Defenders Assn., So. Ill. Am. Inns of Ct. (barrister 1993-95). Democrat. Roman Catholic. Avocations: golf, swimming, cooking, enology. Home: 431 Phillips Rd Carbondale IL 62901-7459 Office: US Attys Office 9 Executive Dr Ste 300 Fairview Heights IL 62208-1344*

GRACEY, DOUGLAS ROBERT, physician, physiologist, educator; b. Fort Dodge, Iowa, Aug. 7, 1936; s. Warren Robert and Areta Mary (Thompson) G.; m. Edith Ann Haas, Dec. 23, 1961; children—Laura, Douglas Robert. B.A., Coe Coll., 1958; M.D., Northwestern U., 1962; M.S., U. Minn., 1968. Diplomate Am. Bd. Internal Medicine. Intern Cook County Hosp., Chgo., 1962-63; resident Mayo Grad. Sch. Medicine, 1963-66, 68-69; asst. prof. medicine Northwestern U. Med. Sch., 1969-75; assoc. prof. medicine Mayo Med. Sch., Rochester, Minn., 1975-83; prof. Mayo Med. Sch., 1983—, vice chmn. pulmonary div., 1982-87; vice chmn. for practice dept. medicine Mayo Clinic, Rochester, 1983-93, dir. critical care medicine div., 1985-89, chmn. revenue systems com., chmn. divsn. pulmonary and critical care medicine. Author: (with W.W. Addington) Tuberculosis, 1972; editor: Pulmonary Diseases in the Adult, 1981; contbr. articles to profl. jours. Trustee Coe Coll., 1976-92. Served to capt. M.C., USAF, 1966-68. Am. Thoracic Soc. tng. fellow, 1968-69. Fellow ACP, Am. Coll. Chest Physicians, AMA. Republican. Lodges: Masons, Shriners. Office: Mayo Clinic Chmn Div Pulmonary & Critical Care Med Rochester MN 55901

GRACEY, JAMES STEELE, corporate director, retired coast guard officer, consultant; b. Newton, Mass., Aug. 24, 1927; s. Ernest James and Edna Alicia (Steele) G.; m. Dorcas Randall Neal, June 15, 1949; children: Kevin S., Cheryl A., Pamela R. B.S., U.S. Coast Guard Acad., 1949; M.B.A., Harvard U., 1956. Commd. ensign USCG, 1949, advanced through grades to adm.; comptroller 2d Coast Guard Dist., St. Louis, 1962-65; dep. Governors' Island (N.Y.) project and Coast Guard Base, 1965-69; chief programs div. Chief of Staff's Office, Washington, 1969-74; chief of staff 5th Coast Guard Dist., Portsmouth, Va., 1974; comdr. 9th Coast Guard Dist., Cleve., 1974-77; chief of staff Coast Guard Hqtrs., Washington, 1977-78; comdr. Coast Guard Pacific Area and 12th Coast Guard Dist., San Francisco, 1978-81, Coast Guard Atlantic Area and 3d Coast Guard Dist., N.Y.C., 1981-82; commandant of USCG, Washington, 1982-86; sr. fellow Inst. for Higher Def. Studies, Capstone, 1986—; chmn. Fed. Exec. Bd. Cleve., 1976-77; coord. regional emegency transp. Fed. Region IX, 1978-81; bd. dirs. Marine Spill Response Corp., chmn. audit com.; bd. dirs. Maguire Group, Inc., Maguire Group Conn., Inc., chmn., 1993-98; advisor New Sulzer Diesel Group, 1991-95; cons. Mitre Corp., 1987-92; vis. lectr. Nat. Def. U., Navy, Air and Army war colls., Fgn. Svc. Inst., Presdl. Classroom, Sloane Fellows, MIT, Kennedy Sch. Govt., Harvard U., 1982-86; bd. mgrs. Am. Bur. Shipping, 1982-86; bd. dirs. Nat. Cargo Bur., 1981-86; leader U.S. del. to Internat. Maritime Orgn., UN Assembly, 1983, 85; bd. visitors Mich. Maritime Acad. Mem. world bd. govs. USO, 1982-91; bd. trustees, vice chmn. Calvary United Meth. Ch. Decorated Legion of Merit with gold star, D.S.M. with gold star; named Bay Stater of Yr., Maritime Man of Yr., San Diego NL Man of the Yr.; recipient Michelob Schooner award, San Francisco Honor medal. Mem. Ret. Officers Assn. (bd. dirs. 1986-92), Am. Soc. Naval Engrs., Coast Guard Found. (bd. dirs. 1982—), Internat. Platform Assn., Navy League, Nat. Mil. Family Assn. (advisor 1986—), Assn. for Rescue at Sea (bd. dirs., vice chmn. 1988-97, chmn. 1997—), Army-Navy Country Club. Home and Office: 1411 21st St S Arlington VA 22202-1507

GRACIA, BRENDA LEE, poet; b. Uvalde, Tex., Nov. 16, 1970; d. Irma Duran Martinez, July 14, 1990; m. Armando V. Quiroz Jr., July 14, 1990; 1 child, Armando Gracia III. Diploma, Knippa (Tex.) H.S., 1989. Contbr. poetry to lit. publs. Recipient Hon. Mention award World Poetry Soc., 1990. Avocations: writing stories and poetry, drawing, dance, singing, reading, Greek mythology. Home: 101 Washington St PO Box 114 Knippa TX 78870

GRACIA, JORGE JESUS EMILIANO, philosopher, educator; b. Camaguey, Cuba, July 18, 1942; s. Ignacio Jesus Loreto and Leonila (Otero) G.; m. Norma Elida Silva, Sept. 3, 1966; children: Leticia Isabel, Clarisa Raquel. BA, Wheaton Coll., Ill., 1965; MA, U. Chgo., 1966; MSL, Pontifical Inst. Mediaeval Studies, Toronto, 1970; PhD, U. Toronto, 1971. From asst. prof. to prof. SUNY, Buffalo, 1971-95, Disting. prof., 1995—, assoc. chmn. dept. philosophy, 1974-76, chmn. dept., 1980-85, acting chmn., 1988-89, Samuel P. Capen prof. philosophy, 1998—; magister Schola Lullistica Maioricensis, Palma de Mallorca, 1976-96. Author: Suárez on Individuation, 1982, Introduction to the Problem of Individuation, 1984, 2d edit., 1986, Individuality: An Essay in the Foundations of Metaphysics, 1988, Philosophy and Its History: Issues in Philosophical Historiography, 1991, A Theory of Textuality: The Logic and Epistemology, 1995, Texts: Ontological Status, Identity, Author, Audience, 1996, Metaphysics and Its Task: The Search for the Categorial Foundation of Knowledge, 1999, Hispanic/Latino Identity: A Philosophical Perspective, 1999; editor: Man and His Conduct, 1980, El Hombre y los valores, 1975, Com Usar Be de Beure e Menjar, 1977; (with others) Philosophical Analysis in Latin America, 1984, Latin American Philosophy in the XXth Century, 1986, Risieri Frondizi: Ensayos Filosoficos, 1986, Filosofia e Identidad Cultural, 1987, The Metaphysics of Good and Evil, 1989, Philosophy and Literature in Latin America, 1989, Directory of Latin American Philosophers, 1988, Social Sciences in Latin America, 1989, Latin American Philosophy Today, 1989, Individuation in Scholasticism, 1994; (with K. Barber) Individuation and Identity in Early Modern Philosophy, 1994, Filosofía hispánica: Concepto, origen y foco hisforiográfico, 1998, Concepciones de la Metafísica, 1998. NEH grantee, 1981-82, N.Y. Coun. for Humanities, 1987, John N. Findlay prize Metaphysical Soc. Am., 1992. Mem. Am. Philos. Assn. (com. internat. cooperation 1981-84, chmn. com. for Hispanics in philosophy 1991-95, chmn. prog. com. 1993-94, exec. com. 1996-2000, Am. Cath. Philos. Assn. (exec. com. 1983-86, chmn. program com. 1987, v.p. 1996-97. pres. 1997-98), Soc. for Iberian and Latin Am. Thought (exec. com. 1982—, v.p. 1984-85, pres. 1986-88), Soc. for Medieval and Renaissance Philosophy (exec. com. 1986-97, chmn. program com. 1989-91, v.p. 1989-91, pres. 1991-93, chmn. nominating com. 1993-95), Soc. de Filosofia Iberoamericana (exec. com. 1985—), Internat. Fedn. Latin Am. and Caribbean Studies (pres. 1987-89), Metaphy. Soc. Am. (program com. 1992-93, councillor 1995—, chmn. Findlay prize com. 1995, v.p. 1999—), Soc. Internat. pour Etude de Philos. Medievale (orgn. com. 1992, program com. 1996), Internat. Fedn. Philos. Socs. (program com. 1994-98). E-mail: gracia@acsu.buffalo.edu. Home: 420 Berryman Dr Buffalo NY 14226-4640 Office: Univ at Buffalo Dept Philos 681 Baldy Hall Buffalo NY 14260-0104

GRACY, DAVID BERGEN, II, archivist, information science educator, writer; b. Austin, Tex., Oct. 25, 1941; married; 3 children. BA, U. Tex., Austin, 1963, MA, 1966; PhD in History, Tex. Tech. U., 1971. Cert. archivist. Archivist S.W. Collection Tex. Tech. U., 1966-71; from asst. prof. to assoc. prof. urban life Ga. State U., 1971-77; archivist So. Labor Archives, 1971-77; dir. Tex. State Archives, 1977-86; Gov. Bill Daniel prof. in archival enterprise U. Tex., Austin, 1986—, assoc. dean Grad. Sch. of Libr. and Info. Sci., 1991-95; interim dir. preservation and conservation dept. U. Tex.; gen. ptnr. David B. Gracy II & Assocs., 1989—; adj. prof. history De Kalb C.C., 1973-74; instr. Ga. Archives Inst., Grad. Sch. Libr. and Info. Sci. U. Tex., Austin, Modern Archives Inst. Nat. Archives of U.S., Rare Books Sch. Columbia U., Soc. Am. Archivists, Soc. S.W. Archivists, Spl. Librs. Assn., Tex. State Libr., Trinity U., U.S. Info. Agy. for U. Philippines, Presdl. Commn. on Culture and Arts, Philippines, Univ. Republic, Uruguay, Utah State Archives, Western Archives Inst.; cons. N.Mex. State Archives and Libr. Bldg. project, 1994—, Nat. Episc. Ch. Archives, 1978, Oral Roberts U., 1978, Archives Civil Rights, M.L. King Ctr., Atlanta, 1976-81, Am. Heritage Ctr. U. Wyo., 1988-89, San Antonio Pub. Libr., 1988, Nat. Assn. for Preservation and Perpetuation of Storytelling, Jonesborough, Tenn., 1988-89, Jet Propulsion Lab., Pasadena, Calif., 1987-89, King Ranch, Kingsville, Tex., 1987; coord. Tex. Hist. Records Adv. Bd., 1979-86; mem. Ga. Hist. Records Adv. Bd., 1976; mem. Nat. Hist. Publs. and Rec. Commn., 1980-85; lectr. U. Tex., Austin, 1980-81, sr. lectr., 1982-86. Author: Littlefield Lands: Colonization on the Texas Plains, 1912-1920, 1968, Archives and Manuscripts: Arrangement and Description, 1977, It's Your Heritage: The Archives of Texas, 1977, An Introduction to Archives and Manuscripts, 1981, Moses Austin: His Life, 1987; co-author: Ships of the Texas Navy, 1979; bibliography advisor Handbook of Texas, 1988—; mem. editl. bd. Libraries and Culture, 1985—, Am. Archivist, 1976-79; founder, editor Ga. Archive (subsequently Provenance), 1972-76; contbr. to Reflections of Western Historians, 1969; assoc. editor Tex. Mil. History, 1962-88; editl. asst. Southwestern Hist. Quar., 1963-66; contbr. articles to profl. jours. Bd. dirs. Nat. Achives Episcopal Ch., 1986—, vice chair, 1995—; bd. dirs. Task Force on Preservation Edn., Commn. on Preservation and Access, 1989-90, mem., 1991-97; chmn. task force on archives Summerlee Commn. on Tex. History, 1989-93, Tex. Preservation Task Force, 1988-90; sec. Coun. on Libr. and Info. Resources, 1997—. Named Disting. Alumnus Dept. History Tex. Tech. U., 1987; recipient award of merit Am. Assn. for State and Local History, 1969, Disting. Svc. award Organized Labor and Workmen's Circle, Atlanta, 1976, Cert. Merit Soc. Ga. Archivists, 1976, Soc. S.W. Archivists, 1978, Tex. Excellence in Teaching award Grad. Sch. Libr. and Info. Sci. U. Tex. at Austin, 1987, San Jacinto award, 1993. Fellow Soc. Am. Archivists (v.p., pres. 1982-84, award of merit 1975), Tex. State Geneal. Soc., Tex. State Hist. Assn.; mem. Tex. Bar Hist. Found., Am. Assn. State and Local History (award of merit 1968), Internat. Coun. Archives (v.p. sect. on archival edn. and tng., editor Edn. and Devel. News 1989-96, listmaster sect. archival edn. & tng. listserv 1996—), Assn. Records Mgrs. and Adminstrs. (pres. Austin chpt. 1980-81, cert. award 1981), Pan Am. Inst. Geography and History (U.S. rep. archives com. 1982—), Acad. Cert. Archivists (bd. regents 1990-93), Soc. Ga. Archivists (pres. 1972-74, cert. merit 1976). Office: U Tex Grad Sch Libr Info Sci Austin TX 78712-1276

GRAD, BONNIE L., art historian, educator; b. N.Y.C., June 1, 1949; d. Julius and Sue (Roberts) Grad; m. Gary Wolf, June 21, 1980; children: Alexander, Theodore. BA cum laude, Cornell U., 1971; PhD, U. Va., 1977. Art instr. Cin. Art Mus., 1967, 68; tchg. asst. U. Va., Charlottesville, 1973-74; collections asst., graphic arts collection Princeton (N.J.) Univ. Libr., 1976-77; asst. prof. art history Clark U., Worcester, Mass., 1977-83, assoc. prof., 1983—; bd. dirs. New Eng. Fulbright Assn., 1997—; grant reviewer Nat. Endowment for Humanities, 1997, The Bunting Inst., 1991; vis. scholar Pollock-Krasner Home and Studies Ctr., 1994, 97. Curator exhbns. including The Princeton U. Graphic Arts Collection, Worcester Arts Mus., Nat. Gallery of Art, Simmons Coll., Rose Art Mus.; author: Milton Avery, 1981, Robert Richenburg, 1993; co-author: Visions of City and Country, 1982; contbr. articles to profl. jours. Mem. Weston (Mass.) Arts Coun., 1988-94. Fulbright-Hays grantee, 1974-75, Nat. Endowment for Humanities grantee, 1980-83, Mellon grantee, 1984-87, Higgins grantee, 1989-95, Richard A. Florsheim Art Fund grantee, 1993-94, Seymour N. Logan fellow, 1992-94. Mem. Coll. Art Assn. Office: 950 Main St Worcester MA 01610-1400

GRAD, FRANK PAUL, law educator, lawyer; b. Vienna, May 2, 1924; came to U.S., 1939, naturalized, 1943; s. Morris and Clara Sophie (Scher) G.; m. Lisa Szilagyi, Dec. 6, 1946; children: David Anthony, Catharine Ann. B.A. magna cum laude, Bklyn. Coll., 1947; LL.B., Columbia U., 1949. Bar: N.Y. 1949. Assoc. in law Columbia U. Law Sch., N.Y.C., 1949-50, asst. dir. Legis. Drafting Research Fund, 1953-55, assoc. dir., 1956-68, dir., 1969-95, mem. faculty, 1954—, prof., 1969—, Joseph P. Chamberlain prof. legis., 1982-95, Joseph P. Chamberlain prof. emeritus legis. and spl. lectr., 1995—; mem. legal adv. com. U.S. Council Environ. Quality, 1970-73; mem. N.Y. Deptl. Com. Ct. Adminstrn., Appellate Div., 1st Dept., 1970-74; counsel N.Y. State Spl. Adv. Panel Med. Malpractice, 1975; legal counsel Nat. Mcpl. League, 1967-88; cons. in field, 1955—; reporter U.S. Superfund Study group, 1981-82; dir. rsch. N.Y.C. Charter Revision Commn., 1982-83; N.Y. State-City Commn. on Integrity in Govt., 1986. Author: Public Health Law Manual, 1st edit., 1965, 2d rev. edit., 1990, The Drafting of State Constitutions, 1963, Environmental law: Sources and Problems, 3d edit., 1985, Treatise on Environemntal Law, 8 vols., 1973-99; co-author other legal reports; contbr. legal jours.; draftsman mcpl. codes and state legislation. Served with AUS, 1943-46. 10th Horace E. Read Meml. lectr. Dalhousie Law Sch., 1984. Mem. ABA, APHA, Assn. of Bar of City of N.Y., N.Y. Bar Assn., Am. Law Inst., Am. Soc. Law and Medicine, World Conservation Union (commn. on environ. law 1991—), Human Genome Orgn., Internat. Coun. Environ. Law, N.Y.. Soc. Med. Jurisprudence. Office: Columbia U Sch Law 435 W 116th St New York NY 10027-7297

GRADDICK, CHARLES ALLEN, lawyer; b. Mobile, Ala., Dec. 10, 1944; s. Julian and Elvera (Smith) G.; m. Corinne Whiting, Aug. 19, 1966; children: Charles Allen, Herndon Whiting, Corinne. J.D., Cumberland Sch. Law, 1970. Bar: Ala. 1970. Clk. Ala. Supreme Ct., 1970; asst. dist. atty. County of Mobile, Ala., 1971-75, dist. atty., 1975-79; atty. gen. State of Ala., Montgomery, 1979-87; ptnr. Thorton, Farish and Gaunt, Montgomery, 1987-89, Anderson, Graddick and Nabors, P.C., Montgomery, 1989-90; dist. atty. Montgomery County, Montgomery County, Ala., 1991-93; ptnr. Graddick & Belser, P.C., Montgomery and Mobile, 1993—. Served with USNG, 1969-96. Named Outstanding Young Man of Mobile, Mobile Jaycees, 1976, State Conservationist of Yr., Ala. Wildlife Fedn.; recipient cert. appreciation Ala. Peace Officers, 1978, Appreciation award Optimists, 1978. Mem. ABA, ATLA, Ala. Bar Assn., Mobile Bar Assn., Montgomery Bar Assn., Ala. Trial Lawyers Assn., Ala. Dist. Attys. Assn., Nat. Dist. Attys. Assn., Nat. Assn. Attys. Gen. Republican. Episcopalian. Office: Graddick and Belser PC 138 Adams Ave Montgomery AL 36104-4224 also: Graddick and Belser PC 1 St Louis St Ste 2000 Mobile AL 36602-3926

GRADE, JEFFERY T., manufacturing company executive; b. Chicago, 1943. BS, Ill. Inst. Tech., 1966; MBA, DePaul U., 1972. With Plasto Mfg. Corp., 1965-66, Motorola Inc., 1966-67, Bell and Howell, 1967-68, Ill. Cen. Gulf R.R., 1968-73; v.p. fin. IC Industries, 1973-83; with Harnischfeger Corp., Milw., 1983—, pres., COO, bd. dirs., 1986—, CEO, 1991—, also chmn., CEO. Served with USN, 1865-66. Office: Harnischfeger Industries 3600 S Lake Dr Saint Francis WI 53235-3716*

GRADELESS, DONALD EUGENE, secondary education educator; b. Warsaw, Ind., Apr. 17, 1949; s. Harmon Willard and Donna Maxine (Mort) G. BS in Acctg., U. Wis., Stevens Point, 1972; MS in Teaching, U. Wis., Eau Claire, 1975; PhD in Edn., Pacific Western U., 1988. Cert. in data edn. Tchr. high schs. Racine, Wis., 1972-77; mgr. constrn. Computer Control Corp., Milw., 1977; indsl. engr. Weatherhead div. Dana Corp., Columbia City, Ind., 1977-78; instr. bus. edn. Elmbrook pub. schs., Brookfield, Wis., 1978—; coordinator instructional data processing Racine Unified Schs., 1973-77. Author geneal. books. Fellow Am. Coll. Genealogists; mem. NEA, NRA (golden eagles, life mem.), SAR (sec., host. 1977, registrar 1975-76, publs. chmn. 1975-77, pres. 1976-77, 95-96, Nat. Soc. Mem. awards 1976-78, Silver Good Citizenship edal 1978, mem. Ind. soc.), S.R. (chmn. 1975-79, pres. 1979-83, registrar 1979-82, 84-87, sec. 1983—, Gen. Pres.'s Spl. Commendation award 1985, Outstanding Svc. award 1982, mem. various state bds. mgrs.), Nat. Bus. Edn. Assn., Wis. Bus. Edn. Assn., Children Am. Revolution (sr. registrar 1976-77, 80-83, sr. v.p. 1984-86, sr. pres. 1986-90, hon. sr. state pres. 1990—), Sons and Daus. of Pilgrims (counselor 1979-80, 2d dep. govs. 1989-90, 1st dep. gov. 1990-92, gov. Wis. 1992—), Soc. Colonial Wars (dep. sec. Wis. chpt. 1978-79, registrar 1994-96, lt. gov. 1975-77), Studebaker Family Nat. Assn. (life mem.), Soc. of the War of 1812 (v.p. 1994-95, pres. 1995—, life mem.), Huguenot soc. (registrar 1975-77, chaplain 1993—), Wis. State Old Cemetery Soc., U.S. Postal Svcs. Racine (customer adv. com. 1992—), Mensa, Whitley County Hist. Soc., Soc. Ind. Pioneers, Sons of Union Vets of Civil War, Children Am. Revolution, Nat. Officers Club (patron award 1993), Sons of Am. Colonists (gov. 1996—), Delta Phi Epsilon. Lodge: Masons (32 degree), K.T. Home: 2655 Fairview Ln Brookfield WI 53045-4117 Office: Brookfield Ctrl High Sch 16900 Gebhardt Rd Brookfield WI 53005-5138

GRADER, PATRICIA ALISON LANDE, editor; b. L.A., Mar. 23, 1960; d. Frederick and Irma Rose (Davidson) L.; m. Scott P. Grader, Feb. 11, 1995. Student, Washington U., St. Louis, 1977-79; BA with high distinction, U. Calif., San Diego, 1982. Editl. asst. Crown Pubs., N.Y.C., 1982-83; asst. editor St. Martin's Press, N.Y.C., 1983-84; editor Atheneum Pubs., N.Y.C., 1984-87; v.p., sr. editor Simon & Schuster, Inc., N.Y.C., 1987-91; v.p., dir. IMG-The Julian Bach Literary Agy., N.Y.C., 1992-95; exec. editor Avon Books, N.Y.C., 1995—; mentor internship program Simon & Schuster, 1991; mem. adminstrv. com. IMG, 1992-95; speaker in field. Mem. Pi Beta Phi. Office: Avon Books 1350 Avenue Of The Americas New York NY 10019-4702

GRADINGER, GILBERT PAUL, plastic surgeon; b. Waterloo, Iowa, 1930. MD, Wash. U., 1956. Diplomate Am. Bd. Plastic Surgery (sec.-treas. 1993, chmn. 1994). Intern U. Calif. Hosp., San Francisco, 1956-57, resident in surgery, 1957-59, chief resident in plastic surgery, 1960-61; resident in plastic surgery Franklin Hosp., San Francisco, 1959-60; plastic surgeon Peninsula Hosp. Med. Ctr., Burlingame, Calif.; clin. prof. plastic surgery U. Calif., San Francisco; pvt. practice Burlingame. Fellow ACS; mem. Am. Assn. Plastic Surgeons, Am. Soc. Plastic and Reconstructive Surgery, Calif. Soc. Plastic Surgeons. Office: 1750 El Camino Real Ste 405 Burlingame CA 94010-3217

GRADO, ANGELO JOHN, artist; b. N.Y.C., Feb. 17, 1922; s. Pasquale and Rose (Valenti) G.; m. Justine Barbara Johnson, June 26, 1943; children: Barbara, Paul, John, Frank, Richard. Student Art Students League. Comml. artist N.Y. Jour.-Am., N.Y.C., 1946-52; art dir. Harrison Publs., N.Y.C., 1952-55; art dir., owner advt. agy. N.Y.C., 1955-70; artist oils and pastels, 1970—; tchr. Nat. Art League, N.Y., Naples Art League, Von Lebig Art Ctr., Naples, Fla.; lectr., Europe and U.S. Author: Mastering the Craft of Painting, 1985. Served with USAAF, 1943-46. Recipient 78 nat. awards, 1957—; recipient Best in Show-Newington award, 1980. Mem. Am. Artists Profl. League (pres. N.Y. 1977-88, pres. emeritus 1988—), Hudson Valley Art Assn. (Best Portrait award 1994), Pastel Soc. Am. (elected master pastelist), Am. Watercolor Soc., Salmagundi Club. Home: 641 46th St Brooklyn NY 11220-1410

GRADO-WOLYNIES, EVELYN (EVELYN WOLYNIES), clinical nurse specialist, educator; b. N.Y.C., Apr. 2, 1944; d. Joseph Frederick and Evelyn Marie (Ronning) Grado; m. Jon Gordon Wolynies, July 12, 1964; children: Jon Andrew, Kristine Elisabeth. AAS, Burlington County Coll., 1990; AS, Camden C.C., 1990; BSN cum laude, Thomas Jefferson U., 1991, MSN summa cum laude, 1992; postgrad., Johns Hopkins U., 1993-95. RN, N.J., Pa., cert. clin. nurse specialist. Charge nurse Hampton Hosp., Westampton, N.J., 1990-92; adjunct clin. instr. psychiat. nursing Burlington County Coll., Pemberton, N.J., 1992-93; project leader Alzheimer's disease clin. drug study Olsten Health Care, Cherry Hill, N.J., 1992-95, psychiat. case mgr., 1992-94; CNS neuropsych in Huntingtons Disease Dr. Allen Rubin, Camden, N.J., 1992; psychiat. case mgr. Moorestown (N.J.) Vis. Nurses Assn., 1992; charge nurse, group therapist, rschr. Friends Hosp., Phila., 1994—; clin. mgr. The Caring Link partial geriatric outpatient program Frankford Hosp., Phila., 1996—; pvt. practice hypnotherapy/psychotherapy; cons. psychiat. care, Alzheimer's Disease, RN/home health aide instr. Olsten-Kimberly Home Care; clin. preceptor U. Pa. Sch. NSG, MSN, GNP and Adult Mental CS Programs. Contbr. articles to nursing jours. Mem. Burlington County Coll. Alumni Bd.; founder, dir. Support Group for Adult Children with Aging Parents; Developed music therapy/exercise program for Geriatric Psych patients. Recipient Juanita Wilson award, 1991, Farber fellowship, 1991-92; Nurse in Washington intern, 1992; named to Burlington County Coll. Hall of Fame, 1994. Mem. Am. Assn. of Neuroscience Nurses, Am. Psychiat. Nurses Assn., N.J. State Nurses Assn., Sigma Theta Tau (Delta Rho chpt.), Phi Theta Kappa. Home: PO Box 3604 Cherry Hill NJ 08034-0550

GRADY, GREGORY, lawyer, banker; b. Takoma Park, Md., Oct. 10, 1945; s. Francis Joseph Grady and Deane (McGehee) Black; m. Carol Love Harrison, Feb. 25, 1978; children: Olivia Love, Blake McGregor, Harrison Edwards. BA in Econs., U. Va., 1969; JD, Tulane U., 1972. Bar: D.C. 1973, U.S. Ct. Appeals (D.C. cir.) 1973, U.S. Ct. Appeals (4th cir.) 1975, U.S. Supreme Ct. 1976, U.S. Ct. Appeals (5th cir.) 1977, U.S. Ct. Appeals (10th cir.) 1979, U.S. Ct. Appeals (11th cir.) 1981, U.S. Ct. Appeals (6th cir.) 1982, U.S. Dist. Ct. 1988. Staff atty., supervisory atty. FPC, Washington, 1972-74; assoc. Littman, Richter, Wright & Talisman, P.C., Washington, 1974-79; mem. Wright & Talisman, P.C., Washington, 1979—, pres., chmn. bd. dirs., chmn. exec. com., 1997-98, mng. mem., 1999—; bd. dirs. Bank of Franklin, Miss., D.R. McGehee Ins. Agy., Inc., Miss. Mem. Fed. Energy Bar Assn., D.C. Bar Assn., Congl. Country Club. Republican. Episcopalian. Home: 666 Live Oak Dr Mc Lean VA 22101-1569 Office: Wright & Talisman PC 1200 G St NW Ste 600 Washington DC 20005-3838

GRADY, HUGH H., English educator; b. Savannah, Ga., Oct. 6, 1947; s. Hugh Hartridge Sr. and Laura Duggan Grady; m. Susan Wells, June 9, 1969; children: Laura Rose, Constance. BA magna cum laude, Fordham U., 1969; MA in English, U. Tex., 1972, PhD in Comparative Lit., 1978. English and French H.S. tchr. Houston, 1970-71; tchg. asst., asst. instr. Tex., 1973-78; lectr. U. Louisville, 1979-80; instr. U. Tex., Austin, 1980-81; sr. asst. editor Shakespearean Criticism Gale Rsch. Co., Detroit, 1982-83; instr. Detroit Coll. Bus., 1983-85; vis. asst. prof. English Temple U., Phila., 1985-87; asst. prof. English Beaver Coll., Glenside, Pa., 1987-92, chmn. dept. English, comms. and theater arts, 1989-92, assoc. prof. English, 1992—; vis. asst. prof. English Temple U. Japan, 1992-93; presenter, spkr. in field; reader/cons. Johns Hopkins Press, 1996; outside reader McGill U., 1997, 98. Author: the Modernist Shakespeare: Critical Texts in a Material World, 1994, Shakespeare's Universal Wolf: Studies in Early Modern Reification, 1996; contbr. numerous articles, revs. to profl. publs. Vol. Vista, 1969-70.

GM scholar, 1965-69; Nat. Def. Fund fellow, 1972-74. Mem. MLA (co-chair spl. session 1994), Shakespeare Assn. Am. (chair/co-chair seminars), Phi Beta Kappa, Phi Kappa Phi. Democrat. Office: Beaver Coll Dept English Glenside PA 19038

GRADY, JAMES THOMAS, novelist; b. Shelby, Mont., Apr. 30, 1949; s. Thomas and Donna Jane (Martin) G.; m. Bonnie Joy Goldstein, 1985; children: Rachel, Nathan. BA, U. Mont., 1972. Research analyst Mont. Constl. Conv., Helena, 1971-72; youth worker-researcher Youth Devel. Bur., Helena, 1972-73; freelance writer, Helena and Missoula, Mont., 1973-74; legis. aide to Senator Lee Metcalf U.S. Senate, Washington, 1974; investigative reporter Jack Anderson's column, Washington, 1975-80; freelance writer, Washington, 1980—. Novelist: Six Days of the Condor, 1974, Shadow of the Condor, 1975, The Great Pebble Affair, 1975, Catch the Wind, 1980, Runner in the Street, 1985, Razor Game, 1986, Hard Bargains, 1986, Just a Shot Away, 1987, Steeltown, 1988, River of Darkness, 1991; scriptwriter D.C. Cop, 1986; story editor Top of The Hill, 1989 (1st pl. short fiction awards 1988, 2d pl. award, 1991). Mem. PEN, Writers Guild Am., Mystery Writers Am.

GRADY, JOHN F., federal judge; b. Chgo., May 23, 1929; s. John F. and Lucille F. (Shroder) G.; m. Patsy Grady, Aug. 10, 1968; 1 child, John F. BS, Northwestern U., 1952, JD, 1954. Bar: Ill. 1955. Assoc. Sonnenschein, Berkson, Lautmann, Levinson & Morse, Chgo., 1954-56; asst. U.S. atty. No. Dist. Ill., 1956-61, chief criminal divsn., 1960-61; assoc. Snyder, Clarke, Dalziel, Holmquist & Johnson, Waukegan, Ill., 1961-63; practice law Waukegan, 1963-76; judge U.S. Dist. Ct. (no. dist.) Ill., Chgo., 1976-86, chief judge, 1986-90, sr. judge, 1994—; mem. com. criminal law U.S. Jud. Conf., 1982-87, adv. com. civil rules, 1984-90, chair, 1987-90; mem. bench book com. Fed. Jud. Ctr., 1988-93; mem. Nat. State-Fed. Jud. Coun., 1990-92, Jud. Panel on Multidist. Litigation, 1992—. Assoc. editor: Northwestern U. Law Rev. Mem. Phi Beta Kappa. Office: US Dist Ct 2286 Dirksen Bldg 219 S Dearborn St Chicago IL 60604-1702*

GRADY, KEVIN E., lawyer; b. Charlotte, N.C., Jan. 19, 1948; s. Thomas F. and Rosemary (Loughran) G.; m. Mary Beth O'Brien, Dec. 27, 1975; children: Martin E., Donald F. BA, Vanderbilt U., 1969; JD, Harvard U., 1974. Bar: Ga. 1974, U.S. Dist. Ct. (no. dist.) Ga. 1975, U.S. Ct. Appeals (11th cir.) 1981, U.S. Supreme Ct. 1990. Assoc. Jones, Bird & Howell, Atlanta, 1974-76; trial atty. Antitrust divsn. U.S. Dept. Justice, Atlanta, 1976-77; ptnr. Alston & Bird, Atlanta, 1977—. Editor: Georgia Hospital Law Manual, 1997. Mem. bd. trust Vanderbilt U., 1995-97. Recipient Top Hat award St. Vincent de Paul Soc., 1995. Mem. ABA (mem. coun. antitrust sect. 1995-98, publs. officer 1998—), Ga. Acad. Healthcare Attys. (pres. 1997-98), Am. Health Lawyers Assn. (vice chair antitrust program 1992-99, chair 1999—), Am. Counsel Assn. (dir. 1991—, pres. 1995), State Bar Ga. (vice chair health law sect. 1998-99). Democrat. Roman Catholic. Avocations: running, racketball, reading. Office: Alston & Bird 1201 W Peachtree St NW Ste 4200 Atlanta GA 30309-3424

GRADY, LEE TIMOTHY, pharmaceutical chemist; b. Chgo., Mar. 21, 1937; s. Thomas Aloysius and Lentella Kathryn (Eibel) G.; m. Ann Marie Gill, Aug. 8, 1964; children: Patricia Ann, Meghan Elizabeth. BS in Pharmacy with high honors, U. Ill., 1959, PhD in Chemistry, 1963. Registered pharmacist, Ill., Va., Md. Sr. rsch. pharmacologist Merck Inst. Therapeutic Rsch., West Point, Pa., 1965-68; dir. drug standards lab. Am. Pharm. Assn. Found., Washington, 1968-74; dir. drug rsch. and testing lab. U.S. Pharmacopeia, Rockville, Md., 1975-78; v.p., dir. stds. devel., dir. drug stds., 1979-99; mem. expert coms. WHO, Geneva, 1980-87; temp. advisor Pan Am. Health Orgn., Washington, 1984; observer Internat. Conf. Harmonization, 1990—; mem. Pharmacopeial Discussion group, U.S., Japan, Europe, 1989—. Contbr. articles to sci. jours.; sci. editor U.S. Pharmacopeia National Formulary, 1980—. Recipient rsch. award Am. Soc. Hosp. Pharmacists, 1982. Fellow AAAS, Am. Assn. Pharm. Scientists; mem. Am. Pharm. Assn. (J.L. Powers rsch. achievement award 1990), Am. Chem. Soc., Internat. Pharm. Fedn., Cath. Acad. Scis. (U.S.), Order of Holy Sepulchre, Rho Chi, Phi Kappa Phi. Roman Catholic. Avocations: swimming, hiking. E-mail: ltg@usp.org. Office: US Pharmacopoeia 12601 Twinbrook Pkwy Rockville MD 20852-1790*

GRADY, MAUREEN FRANCES, lawyer; b. N.Y.C., Oct. 6, 1960; d. Frank J. and Pauline (Laberge) G. BA, Manhattan Coll., 1982; JD, Georgetown U., 1985. Bar: N.Y. 1986, U.S. Dist. Ct. (so. and ea. dists.) N.Y. 1987, U.S. Ct. Appeals (2d cir.) 1990. Assoc. Griffin, Scully & Savona, N.Y.C., 1985-87, Morris & Duffy, N.Y.C., 1987-88, Summit, Rovins & Feldesman, N.Y.C., 1988-89; asst. gen. counsel N.Y.C. Transit Authority, 1989-92; trial atty. Fireman's Fund Ins. Co., N.Y.C., 1992-97; sr. assoc. DeCicco Gibbons & McNamara, P.C., N.Y.C., 1998-99; assoc. Kral Clerkin Redmond Ryan Perry & Girvan, N.Y.C., 1999—. Recipient Bur. Nat. Affairs award. Mem. Assn. of Bar of City of N.Y. (young lawyers com. 1987-90, constrn. law com. 1991-92, spl. com. on alcoholism and substance abuse 1994-97, sec. spl. com. on alcoholism and substance abuse 1995-97, product liability com. 1995-98), Phi Beta Kappa, Epsilon Sigma Pi, Phi Alpha Theta.

GRADY, PATRICIA A., health institute director, researcher. Diploma in nursing, St. Francis Hosp. Sch. Nursing, 1964; BSN, Georgetown U., 1967; MS, U. Md., 1968, PhD, 1977, D of Pub. Svc. (hon.), 1996; cert. in sr. mgrs. in govt., John F. Kennedy sch. Govt., Cambridge, 1994. Instr. Sch. Nursing Washington Hosp. Ctr., 1966-67; from instr. to rsch. asst. prof. Sch. Nursing U. Md., Bethesda, 1968-88, rsch. assoc., 1976-77; health sci. administrator Nat. Inst. Neurol. Disorders and Stroke NIH, Bethesda, 1988-92, asst. dir. Nat. Inst. Neurol. Disorders and Stroke, 1992-93, acting dir., dep. dir. Nat. Inst. Neurol. Disorders and Stroke, 1993-94, dep. dir. Nat. Inst. Neurol. Disorders and Stroke, 1994-95, dir. Nat. Inst. Nursing Rsch., 1995—; cons., spkr., presenter in field. ad hoc reviewer SCIENCE; reviewer Physiol. Measurement in Nursing; reviewer, editor all sci. statements, press releases, policy statements, manuscripts, and confl. corr. Nat. Insts. Neurol. Disorders and Stroke; mem. editl. bd. STROKE; contbr. articles to profl. jours., chpts. to books. NIH fellow, 1973-76; NIN(C)DS grantee, 1976-88; recipient Sol Greenberg award for leadership ability and clin. excellence St. Francis Hosp., 1964, Rozella M. Schlottfeld Disting. Lecture award Case Western Reserve U., 1996. Fellow Am. Acad. Nursing, Am. Heart Assn. (excellence in nursing lectr. award 1995); mem. AAAS, ANA, Am. Lung Assn., Am. Soc. Profl. and Exec. Women, Am. Acad. Neurology (lectr. 1993-95), Am. Neurol. Assn., Soc. Neurosci., N.Y. Acad. Scis., Neurotrauma Soc., Sigma Theta Tau (award 1966). Fax: (301) 594-3405. Office: Nat Inst Nursing Rsch NIH Bldg 31 Rm 5B10 31 Center Dr Bethesda MD 20892

GRADY, SEAN MICHAEL, writer; b. Palo Alto, Calif., Oct. 3, 1965; s. Michael Wilmont and Naomi Jane (Gladstone) G. BA, U. So. Calif., 1988. Bus. writer Daily Press, Victorville, Calif., 1988-89; bus. editor The Olympian, Olympia, Wash., 1989-90; freelance writer, 1990-98; writer, asst. editor Mag. Divsn. Reno Gazette-Jour., 1998—; instrnl. asst. Truckee Meadows C.C., Reno, 1992, part-time instr., 1993. Author: Plate Tectonics: Earth's Shifting Crust, 1991, Ships: Crossing the World's Oceans, 1992, The Importance of Marie Curie, 1992, Submarines: Probing the Ocean Depths, 1994, Illiteracy, 1994, Explosives: Devices of Controlled Destruction, 1995, Virtual Reality: Computers Mimic the Physical World, 1998. Mem. Soc. Profl. Journalists, Soc. Children's Book Writers and Illustrators (Sierra Nev. chpt.). Home and Office: 1555 Ridgeview Dr #229 Reno NV 89509 Office: 955 Kuenzli St PO Box 22000 Reno NV 89520-2000

GRADY, THOMAS J., retired bishop; b. Chicago, Ill., Oct. 9, 1914; s. Michael and Rose (Buckley) G. S.T.L., St. Mary of Lake Sem., Mundelein, Ill., 1938; student, Gregorian U., Rome, 1938-39; MA in English, Loyola U., Chgo., 1944. Ordained priest Roman Cath. Ch., 1938. Prof. Quigley Prep. Sem., Chgo., 1939-45; procurator St. Mary of Lake Sem., 1945-56; dir. Nat. Shrine Immaculate Conception, Washington, 1956-67; titular bishop Vamalla, aux. bishop Chgo., 1967-74; pastor St. Hilary Ch., Chgo., 1968-74, St. Joseph Ch., Libertyville, Ill., 1974; bishop of Orlando, Fla., 1974-90; Chgo. Archdiocesan dir. seminaries and post-ordination priestly tng., 1967-74; chmn. Chgo. Archdiocesan Liturg. Commn., 1968-74; dir. program Permanent Diaconate, Chgo., 1969-74; cons. Bishops' Com. on Priestly Formation, from 1967, chmn., 1969-72; mem. Ad Hoc Com. on Priestly Life and Ministry, 1971-73; chmn. Bishops' Com. on Priestly Life and Ministry, from 1973. Address: Diocese of Orlando PO Box 1800 421 E Robinson St Orlando FL 32801-1916*

GRADY, WAYNE J., government official; b. Halifax, N.S., Can., Dec. 15, 1943; s. Joseph Myles and Helen Virginia (McNeil) G. B.Comm., St. Mary's U., Halifax, 1973; MHA, U. Alta., Edmonton, 1975. Cons. Health Commn., Halifax, 1975-78; asst. to dep. minister Dept. of Health, Halifax, 1978-87, dep. minister health, 1987-91; dep. miniter Dept. of the Environment, Halifax, 1991-96, ret., 1996. Roman Catholic. Home: Site 8 Box 48 RR 1, Waverley, NS Canada B0N 2S0

GRAEBNER, JAMES HERBERT, transportation executive; b. New Castle, Pa., Aug. 5, 1940; s. Herbert Conrad and Mildred Elizabeth (Fessel) G.; children: Karla Elizabeth, Michael Conrad, James Conrad, David Fessel, Mildred Ann. BA, Valparaiso U., 1962; MBA, Case Western Res. U., 1970. Assoc. W.C. Gilman & Co., Inc. (transit cons.), Cleve., 1967-71; with Regional Transp. Dist., Denver, 1971-75; gen. mgr. R.I. Public Transit Authority, Providence, 1975-78; dir. Santa Clara County Transp. Agy., Calif., 1978-84; dir. product devel. UTDC, 1984-86; pres. Lomarado Group, Denver, 1986—; chief operating officer Transit Constrn. Authority, Denver, 1987-89; v.p. San Jose Historic Trolley Corp.; vis. prof. Northeastern U., 1979; guest. lectr. at numerous univs.; bd. dirs Denver Rail Heritage Soc. Mem. Am. Public Transit Assn. (pres. 1983-84), Calif. Assn. Publically Owned Transit Systems (vice chmn. 1984), Regional Transit Assn. Bay Area (past pres.). Lutheran.

GRAEBNER, NORMAN ARTHUR, history educator; b. Kingman, Kans., Oct. 19, 1915; s. Rudolph William and Helen (Brauer) G.; m. Laura Edna Baum, Aug. 30, 1941; m. Jane Shannon, Jan. 3, 1998. B.S., Milw. State Tchrs. Coll., 1939; M.A., U. Okla., 1940; Ph.D., U. Chgo., 1949; Litt.D., Albright Coll., 1976; M.A., Oxford (Eng.) U., 1978; D.H.L., U. Pitts., 1981, Valparaiso U., 1981, Eastern Ill. U., 1986, U. Wis., Milw., 1997; D of Pedagogy, Marshall U., 1993. Asst. prof. Okla. Coll. for Women, 1942-43, 46-47; from asst. prof. to prof. Iowa State Coll., 1948-56; prof. history U. Ill., Urbana, 1956-67; chmn. dept. history U. Ill., 1961-63; Edward R. Stettinius prof. modern Am. history U. Va., 1967-82, Randolph P. Compton prof., Miller Ctr. Pub. Affairs, 1982—; vis. prof. Stanford U., 1952-53, summers 1959, 72, U. Colo., summer 1968, Concordia Tchrs. Coll., summer 1971, U.S. Mil. Acad., West Point, N.Y., 1981-82, Beloit Coll., spring 1987, Va. Mil. Inst., fall 1987, Coll. of William and Mary, spring 1988, Marshall U., spring 1989; Commonwealth Fund lectr. U. Coll., London, 1958; Fulbright lectr. U. Queensland, Brisbane, Australia, 1963, U. Sydney, Australia, 1983, U. Heidelberg, Germany, 1998-99; disting. vis. prof. history Pa. State U., 1975-76; Harmsworth prof. Am. history Oxford U., 1978-79; Phi Beta Kappa vis. scholar, 1981-82; Thomas Jefferson vis. scholar Downing Coll., Cambridge U., 1985; disting. vis. prof. Nat. War Coll., 1994-95. Author: Empire on the Pacific, 1955, The New Isolationism, 1956, Cold War Diplomacy, 1962, rev. edit., 1977, The Age of Global Power, 1979, America As a World Power: A Realist Appraisal from Wilson to Reagan, 1984, Foundations of American Foreign Policy: A Realist Appraisal from Franklin to McKinley, 1985; co-author: A History of the United States, 2 vols, 1970, A History of the American People, 1970, 2d edit., 1975, Recent United States History, 1972; Editor: The Enduring Lincoln, 1959, Politics and the Crisis of 1860, 1961, An Uncertain Tradition: American Secretaries of State in the Twentieth Century, 1961, The Cold War: A Conflict of Ideology and Power, 1963, rev. edit., 1976, Ideas and Diplomacy, 1964, Manifest Destiny, 1968, Nationalism and Communism in Asia: The American Response, 1977, Freedom in America: A 200-Year Perspective, 1977, American Diplomatic History before 1900, 1978; Traditions and Values: American Diplomacy, 1790-1865, 1985, 1865-1945, 1985; The National Security: Its Theory and Practice, 1945-1960, 1986; contbr. articles to hist. jours. Dir. bicentennial program Pa. State U., 1975-76. Served to 1st lt. U.S. Army, 1943-46. Recipient Thomas Jefferson award U. Va., 1985. Mem. Am., So. hist. assns., Orgn. Am. Historians, Soc. Am. Historians, Soc. Historians Am., Fgn. Rels. (pres. 1972), Am. Acad. Arts and Scis., Mass. Hist. Soc., Phi Beta Kappa. Home: 11 Ednam Vlg Charlottesville VA 22903-4636 *One should never demand more of society than society can grant to all without suffering chaos or disintegration.*

GRAEDEL, THOMAS ELDON, chemist, researcher; b. Portland, Oreg., Aug. 23, 1938; s. Philip Edward and Helen Beatrice (Peterson) G.; m. Susannah Grace Ketchum, July 23, 1966; children: Laura, Martha. B-SChemE, Wash. State U., 1960; MA in Physics, Kent State U., 1964; MS in Astronomy, U. Mich., 1967, PhD in Astronomy, 1969. Tech. staff Bell Labs., Murray Hill, N.J., 1969-84; disting. mem. tech. staff AT&T Bell Labs., Murray Hill, N.J., 1984-96; prof. indsl. ecology Yale U., 1997—; bd. dirs. Am. Inst. Physics; exec. com. Bd. Atmospheric Scis. and Climate Nat. Rsch. Coun.; convener Global Emission Inventory Project Internat. Global Atmospheric Chem. Programme; chmn. Chem. Rsch. Applied to World Needs Poster Session, NAS panel to review U.S. High Speed Civil Transport Rsch. Program, 1993; bd. adv. Bowers Medals of the Franklin Inst., Phila.; chmn. sci. adv. com. Rutgers U. Ozone Rsch. Ctr., Air/Ocean Chemistry Experiment; mem. NAS Panel to Review the FY 1991 U.S. Global Change Rsch. Program. Author: Chemical Compounds in the Atmosphere, 1978; co-author: Atmospheric Chemical Compounds: Sources, Occurrence and Bioassay, 1986, Atmospheric Change: An Earth System Perspective, 1993, Industrial Ecology, 1995, Atmosphere, Climate and Change, 1995, Design for Environment, 1996, Indsl. Ecology and Automobile, 1997, Streamlined Life Cycle Assessment, 1998; assoc. editor Atmospheric Environment, 1979-82, Rev. of Geophysics, 1987-91, Jour. Geophys. Rsch., 1989-92; author/co-author more than 200 tech. papers and articles for profl. jours. Chmn. Environ. Commn., Mendham, N.J., 1971-74; ruling elder First Presbyn. Ch., Mendham, 1989-91. Capt. Armed Svcs., 1960-62. Fellow AAAS, NRC (mem. exec. com. bd. on atmospheric scis and climate 1989-93), Am. Geophys. Union; mem. Conn. Acad. of Sci. and Engring, Am. Chem. Soc., Electrochem. Soc. Presbyterian. Achievements include patents for composition useful for detecting H2S and for protection of devices; research on sulfur chemistry in lower atmosphere, on trends in atmospheric "greenhouse" gases, on atmospheric compounds, on chemistry in atmospheric droplets, on effects of atmosphere on materials, on the formation of copper patinas in the atmosphere, on the implications of trends in atmospheric composition, and on theoretical and practical foundations of industrial ecology. Office: Yale U Sch Forestry Envir Studies 205 Prospect St New Haven CT 06511-2106

GRAEFF, DAVID WAYNE, maintenance executive, consultant; b. West Reading, Pa., Oct. 24, 1946; s. Wayne Samuel and Sara (Spohn) G.; m. Linda Ruth Lohrke, Aug. 17, 1968; children—Hether, Rebecca, Matthew. B.S.M.E., Ind. Inst. Tech., 1969. Lic. in sewage treatment plant and waterworks, Pa. Maintenance engr. Central Soya, Decatur, Ind., 1969-71; mfg. engr. Nat. Seal div. Fed. Mogul, Van Wert, Ohio, 1971-73; facilities engr. Kawecki Berylco div. Cabot, Van Wert, Ohio, 1973-76; plant engr. Willson Products div. E.S.B., Reading, 1976-78; facilities and environ. health/safety mgr. Brush-Wellman Inc., Reading, 1978—; maintenance cons. Maintenance Inc., Fleetwood, Pa., 1976—. Vice comr. USCG Aux., Reading, 1983-84, cert. marine examiner, 1982—, info. system officer, 1984. Mem. AICE, Soc. Mfg. Engrs., Am. Water Works Assn., Am. Inst. Plant Engrs., Am. Assn. Energy Engrs., Am. Chem. Soc., Environ. Engrs. & Mgrs. Inst., Pa. Soc. Profl. Engrs., Wire Assn. Internat., Ducks Unltd., Moose, Theta Xi. Republican. Lutheran. Avocations: boating; woodworking. Home: 815 N Forest St Fleetwood PA 19522-1021 Office: Brush-Wellman Inc Shoemakersville Rd Shoemakersville PA 19555-1414 also: PO Box 973 Reading PA 19603-0973

GRAESSLE, WILLIAM RUDOLF, pediatrician, educator; b. Point Pleasant, N.J., Jan. 29, 1964; s. Frederick William and Marilyn Ann (Meyer) G.; m. Tracy Lynn Roscoe; children; Rebecca Lynn, William Ryan. BS, Trenton State Coll., 1986; MD, U. Medicine and Dentistry N.J., 1991. Intern Univ. Hosp., Newark, 1991-92; resident in pediat. St. Christopher's Hosp., Phila., 1992-94; clin. instr. Cooper Hosp., Camden, N.J., 1994-98; asst. prof. Allegheny U. Hosps.-Med. Coll. Pa., Phila., 1996—. Fellow Am. Acad. Pediats.; mem. Phila. Pediat. Soc. Avocations: cycling, hiking. Home: 30 Tall Timber Ln Burlington NJ 08016-9758 Office: Allegheny U Hosps Med Coll Pa 3300 Henry Ave Philadelphia PA 19129-1121*

GRAESSLEY, WILLIAM WALTER, retired chemical engineering educator; b. Muskegon, Mich., Sept. 10, 1933; s. William Walter and Mary Iva (Isler) G.; m. Helen Lorraine Carlsen, June 13, 1953; children: Kathryn Lorraine, William W., Laurie Jo. BS, U. Mich., 1956, BS in Engring, 1956, MS in Engring, 1957, PhD, 1960. With Air Reduction Co., 1959-63, group leader, 1962-63; mem. faculty Northwestern U., Evanston, Ill., 1963-82, assoc. prof. chem. engring. and materials sci., 1966-70, prof., 1970-81, Walter P. Murphy prof., 1981-82, asst. dir. Materials Research Ctr., 1968-69; sr. sci. advisor Exxon Research and Engring. Co., 1982-87; prof. chem. engring. Princeton U., 1987-98; sr. vis. fellow Cambridge U., 1979-80; disting. lectr. various univs. Asst. editor Trans. Soc. Rheology, 1969-75; mem. editorial adv. bd. Jour. Polymer Sci., 1979—, Rubber Revs., 1981-85, Macromolecules, 1983-85; contbr. articles to profl. jours. NSF fellow, 1956-59; Bingham medalist Soc. Rheology. Fellow Am. Phys. Soc. (exec. com., div. high polymer physics 1975-78, high polymer physics prize awardee); mem. Soc. Rheology (exec. com. 1971-73), Am. Inst. Chem. Engrs., Am. Chem. Soc., Nat. Acad. of Engring. Rsch. in synthetic polymers. E-mail: graessle@princeton.edu.

GRAEVE, PETER JOHN, county official; b. Bayshore, N.Y., June 15, 1962; s. George William and Marie Therese (Rizzo) G.; m. Heather Love Riedl, Oct. 5, 1991; children: Holland Love, Nicholas Ruger. BA in History, U. Fla., 1984; postgrad., Fla. Atlantic U., 1998—. Constrn. laborer family owned bus. U.S. and V.I., 1969-84; exec. v.p. Boynton Beach, Fla., 1994-95; mgr.-in-tng. Amoco Corp., Boca Raton, Fla., 1994; flatwork supr. Nat. Linen Svc., West Palm Beach, Fla., 1994-95; mgr. vet. svc. office Palm Beach Bd. County Commrs., West Palm Beach, Fla., 1995—. Co-author: Emergency Operations Center Deployment Plan for Operation Just Cause, 1989, Standard Operating Procedures for Light Tacfire, 1991. Mem. Cmty. Svcs. Adv. Bd., West Palm Beach, 1996—. Maj. U.S. Army, 1984-93; maj. USAR. Mem. County Vet. Svc. Officer Assn. (area v.p. 1998). Lutheran. Avocations: traveling, military battle site tours.

GRAF, ARNOLD HAROLD, employee benefits executive, financial planner; b. Buffalo, Oct. 30, 1930; s. John Edward and Rose Ruth (Tyman) G.; m. Joan Nensel, Sept. 1, 1956 (div. Apr. 1980); children: Jenny, David, Laurie, Paul, Ellen, Amy; m. Rita Mary DiFlorio, Aug. 3, 1981; stepchildren: Patricia, William, Kathleen, Stephan. Student, Rutgers U., 1955-58; BS in Econs., U. Pa., Phila., 1968; postgrad., Command-Gen. Staff Coll., 1966; MA in Internat. Rels., Army War Coll., 1973-75; JD, Weidner U., 1985. CLU, CFP ChFC. Commd. 2d lt. U.S. Army, 1952, advanced through grades to col., 1975, served in Korea, served in Vietnam, ret., 1983; shift supr. Campbell Soup Co., Camden, N.J., 1956-57; pers. dir. Container Corp. of Am., Phila., Oaks, Pa., 1957-59; special agt. Provident Mut. Life Ins. Co., Phila., 1959-60; dist. and regional mgr. Franklin Life Ins. Co., Phila., 1960-68; field mktg. dir. Nat. Liberty Corp., Frazier, Pa., 1968-70; regional mgr. Southland Life Ins. Co., King of Prussia, Pa., 1970-72; sr. supt. agys. Ins. Co. N.Am., Phila., 1972-75; career gen. agt. Aetna Life Ins. Co., Phila., 1975-80; pres. Nat. Employee Benefit Svcs. Inc., Newtown Square, Pa., 1980—. Contbr. articles to profl. jours. Dir. sch. bd. Marple/Newtown Sch. Dist., 1995—. Paul Harris fellow Rotary Found., 1988, fellow Guntaker Found., 1990; recipient Humanitarian award Chapel of Four Chaplains, 1996. Mem. Rotary Internat. (pres. Newton Sq. club 1987-88, R.I. dist. gov. 1990-91), Masons (32 degree), Del. County Assn. Life Underwriters (pres.), Serra Internat. (gov. dist. 28 1996-98, trustee found. 1998—). Republican. Roman Catholic. Avocations: bowling, golf, walking, reading. Home: 4107 Meadow Ln Newtown Square PA 19073-1611 Office: Nat Employee Benefits Svcs Inc PO Box 397 Newtown Square PA 19073-0397

GRAF, DOROTHY ANN, business executive; b. Nashville, Mar. 21, 1935; d. Henry George and Martha Dunlap (Hill) Meek; student Montgomery Coll., 1979—; m. Peter Louis Graf, Oct. 28, 1971; children—Sidney E. Pollard, Deborah Lynn Pollard, Robert George Pollard, Michelle Joy Graf. Office mgr. Pa. Life Ins. Co., Miami and Dallas, 1957-72; exec. sec. to med. dir. Pitts. Children's Hosp., 1974; sec. G.E./TEMPO, Washington, 1974-76; adminstrv. asst. to sr. v.p. Logistics Mgmt. Inst., Washington, 1976-81, dir. adminstrv. svcs., 1981-97, dir. recruiting and tng., 1995-97, dir. human resources, 1997-99, cons. human resources specialist, 1999—; dir. KHI Svcs., Inc. Mem. Washington Tech. Personnel Forum. Democrat. Baptist. Home: 20404 Remsbury Pl Montgomery Village MD 20886-4369 Office: 2000 Corporate Rdg Mc Lean VA 22102-7805

GRAF, ERVIN DONALD, municipal administrator; b. Crow Rock, Mont., Mar. 9, 1930; s. Emanuel and Lydia (Bitz) G.; m. Carolyn Sue Robinson, Mar. 15, 1956 (div. 1958); m. Eleanor Mahlein, Apr. 13, 1959 (dec. Oct. 1990); children: Debra, Belinda, Corrina, Melanie (dec.), Ervin Jr. (dec.). Enlisted U.S. Army, 1948; served two tours of duty in Vietnam; ret. U.S. Army, 1972; with office and maintenance staff Greenfields Irrigation Dist., Fairfield, Mont., 1972-77, sec. to Bd. Commrs., 1977-95; ret., 1995. Decorated Bronze star with oak leaf cluster. Mem. Am. Legion (all offices Post #80 and Dist. 8 incl. dist. comdr.). Democrat. Lutheran. Avocations: bowling, coin collecting, fishing, camping. Home: 211 6th St N Fairfield MT 59436-0565

GRAF, HANS, conductor; b. Austria, Feb. 15, 1949. Studied with Franco Ferrera and Arvid Jonsons. Music dir. Mozarteum Orch., Salzburg, Austria, 1984-94, Calgary Philharm. Orch., 1995—; guest condr. Vienna Symphony, Vienna Philharm., Orchestre Nat. de France, Leningrad Philharm., Pitts. Symphony, Boston Symphony. Office: Calgary Philharmonic Orchestra, 205 8th Ave SE, Calgary, AB Canada T2G 0K9*

GRAF, PETER GUSTAV, accountant, lawyer; b. Vienna, Austria, June 19, 1936; came to U.S. 1940, naturalized, 1945; m. Rosalie Greenbaum, Apr. 6, 1963; 1 child, Paul Evan. B.S. in Econs., U. Pa., 1957; LL.B., NYU, 1960, LL.M., 1962. Bar: N.Y. 1960; C.P.A., N.Y. Tax acct. J.K. Lasser & Co., N.Y.C., 1961-62; with Joseph Graf & Co., N.Y.C., 1962—, ptnr., 1966—; v.p., founder, dir. AGS Computers Inc., N.J., 1967—; ptnr., founder, treas., dir. Nardin Gallery, Inc., Somers, N.Y.; founder Cable Sys. USA Assocs., W.Va., Pa. and Ohio; founder USA Mobile Commn., Inc., Cellular USA Inc., USA Ventures Ltd.; chmn. Phonetel Technologies, Inc., 1995—. Mem. AICPA, N.Y. State Soc. CPA, N.Y. State Bar Assn. Home: 87 Holly Pl Briarcliff Manor NY 10510-2107 Office: Joseph Graf & Co 6 E 43rd St Fl 18 New York NY 10017-4647

GRAF, ROBERT ARLAN, retired financial services executive; b. Bethlehem, Pa., Dec. 8, 1933; s. Rudolph Bernard and Edith May (Crossman) G.; m. Bernice Irene Garman, Dec. 21, 1957; 1 child, R. Mark. AB, U. Pa., 1955; JD, Temple U., 1958. Bar: Mass. 1963. Mgr. annuities The Paul Revere Life Ins. Co., Worcester, Mass., 1960-68; v.p. mass coverage adminstrn. Bankers Security Life Ins. Soc., Washington, 1968; regional dir. group pension Participating Annuity Life Ins. Co., McLean, Va., 1968-69; pres. LNC Equity Sales Corp., Ft. Wayne, Ind., 1969-84; 2d v.p. Lincoln Nat. Corp., Ft. Wayne, Ind., 1969-84; sr. v.p. personal fin. services mktg. and tng. The No. Trust, Chgo., 1984-86; sr. v.p. Kemper Fin. Services Inc., Kemper Investors Life Ins. Co., Chgo., 1986-90; pres. Investors Brokerage Svcs., Inc., Chgo., 1987-90; v.p. fin. instns. div. Rollins Spity. Group, Chgo., 1990-91; nat. sales dir. fin. instns. Paul Revere Ins. Group, Worcester, Mass., 1991-99; ret., 1999. Vol. Boy Scouts Am., Ft. Wayne, Sci. Ctrl., Ft. Wayne; vol. fundraiser United Way, Ft. Wayne, 1982-83, Fine Arts Found., Ft. Wayne, 1984. Served with USMC, 1958-60. Mem. Life Ins. Mktg. and Rsch. Assn. (chmn. investment products com. 1981-83, mem. mktg. through supplemental distbn. systems com.), Nat. Assn. Securities Dealers (prin.), Chgo. Bar Assn. (employee benefits com., fin. svcs. com., ins. com.), Bank Mktg. Assn., Fin. Instns. Ins. Assn., Assn. of Banks in Ins., Met. Club Chgo., Chgo. Shell Club, Masons, Delta Tau Delta, Phi Delta Phi. Presbyterian. Avocations: collecting specimen seashells, tennis, reading. Office: 127 W Berry St Ste 1200 PO Box 1367 Fort Wayne IN 46801-1367

GRAF, STEFFI, professional tennis player; b. 1969; d. Peter and Heidi Graf. Winner numerous profl. women's tennis tournaments including Italian Open, 1987, French Open, 1987, The Golden Grand Slam (Australian Open, French Open, Wimbledon, U.S. Open, Olympics), 1988, Berlin Open, 1988, Wimbledon, 1989, 91, 93, 95, German Open, 1989, 91, 94, U.S. Open, 1989, 91, 92, 93, 95, 96, U.S. Hardcourt Championship, 1989, 91, Australian Open, 1990, 94, Players Challenge, 1990, French Open, 1993, 95, 96, 99; Paris Open, 1995, Lipton Open, 1995; State Farm Evert Cup, 1996, Chase Champ,

1996, WTA Tour Champ, 1995; ranked no. 1 in world for more consecutive weeks than any other player in tennis history. *

GRAF, TRUMAN FREDERICK, agricultural economist, educator; b. New Holstein, Wis., Sept. 18, 1922; s. Herbert and Rose (Sell) G.; m. Sylvia Ann Thompson, Sept. 6, 1947; children: Eric Kindley, Siri Lynne, Peter Truman. BS, U. Wis., 1947, MS, 1949, PhD, 1953. Mktg. specialist, coop. agt. USDA and U. Wis., 1948-50; instr. agrl. econs. U. Wis., Madison, 1951-53, asst. prof., 1953-56, assoc. prof., 1956-61, prof., 1961-85, prof. emeritus, 1985—; expert witness, 1982—; mem. Gov.'s Com. on Wis. Dairy Mktg.; mem. 3-man team to make mktg. analysis in Nigeria, USDA, 1962, made U.S. milk mktg. study, 1971; made mktg. analyses in 13 Carribbean countries, 1964; made mktg. analysis U. Wis., Mex., 1965; made mktg. analyses U.S. Ednl. Found., Finland, 1970, Rumanian Ministry Edn., U.S. Dept. State, Rumania, USSR, 1976, France, 1981, Russia, 1992, Ukraine, 1992, 98, Bulgaria, 1992, 93, Hungary, 1993, Poland, 1993, Zimbabwe, Africa, 1994, Ukraine, 1998; rschr. for internat. agrl. mktg. agys., Kazakhstan, 1999, U. Tchg. on Internat. Trade., 1963-93. Contbr. articles to profl. jours. Active Cub Scouts; bd. dirs. Univ. Houses Assn., 1955-56, Univ. Hill Farm Assn., 1958-59, Univ. Hill Farm Swim Club, 1959-60, Oakwood Retirement Homes. Recipient Uhlman award Chgo. Bd. Trade, 1952, recipient Man of Yr. award World Dairy Expn., 1976, Disting. Svc. award U. Wis. Extension, 1981, Coop. Builder award Fedn. Coops., 1982, Internat. Trade Spl. award Gov. Wis., 1983. Mem. AARP (econ. security adv. com.), Am. Agrl. Econs. Assn. (Published Rsch. award 1974), Am. Mktg. Assn., Madison Naval Res. Assn. (pres. 1968—), Am. Econ. Assn., Hist. Soc., United Dairy Industries Assn. (adv. com.), Wis. Fedn. Coops., Lakeshore Federated Dairy Coop., Wis. Ret. Educators Assn. (bd. dirs.), Wis. Coalition of Annuitants (vice chair), Civil War Club. Lutheran. Applied rsch. study for dairy firms, orgns. state ed. regulatory agys. and agrl. bus. firms. Home: 5007 Prairie Rose Ct Middleton WI 53562-2385 Office: U Wis Dept of Agr Madison WI 53706

GRAF, WILLIAM J., entrepreneur; b. Phila., July 16, 1948; s. William J. and Margaret (Plenskofski) G.; m. Cecilia Ann Vogt, Sept. 18, 1971; children: David William, Paul. BA, Temple U., 1969. Agt. Mutual of N.Y., Phila., 1972-74; owner William J. Graf & Assocs., Phila., 1974-76; v.p. Nat. Equity Life Ins. Co., N.Mex., 1976-78, Pa. Physician Plan, Media, Pa., 1982-86; pres., CEO Graco Triad Group, Phila., 1986-90, Sales Success Inst., Phila., 1986-90, Graco Ins. Group, Bensalem, Pa., 1990—, Worldwide Mktg. Sys., Bensalem, 1995—; CEO, Internat. Comm. Network, Bensalem, 1997—; instr. Life Assn. Tng. Coun., Washington, 1991-92; exec. dir. Nat. Assn. Master Athletes; founder, pub. Master Athlete Mag., 1993—. Author: Goals - The Dynamics of Life, 1989, Seven Steps to Successful Selling, 1994, Honesty, the Last Virtue, 1995; contbr. articles to profl. jours. 2nd lt. U.S. Army, 1969-71. Mem. Metro. Life Million Dollar Club, Nat. Assn. Life Underwriters (Million Dollar Round Table, Nat. Quality award 1972), Life Underwriters Tng. Coun., Pa. Assn. Life Underwriters, Buck County Estate Planning, Coun., Nat. Assn. Profl. Salespersons (pres. 1982), Phila. Masters Track Assn., Buck County Paces (pres. 1990-92), U.S. Track and Field Assn., Internat. Platform Assn. Republican. Roman Catholic. Home: 3968 Bainbridge Ct Bensalem PA 19020-4817

GRAFE, WARREN BLAIR, cable television executive; b. N.Y.C., June 22, 1954; s. Warren Edward and Maree Lee (Ahn) G.; m. Pamela Arden Rearick, Mar. 8, 1980 (div. Nov. 1982). Student, Kendall Coll., 1974-75, U. Wis., Platteville, 1975-76; BA, Ind. U., 1979. Sales rep. Sta. WGTC-FM, Bloomington, Ind., 1979-84, account exec., coop. cord., 1980-84; nat. sales rep. Stas. WTTS-WGTC, Bloomington, 1984; sales rep. Sta. KLFF-KMZK, Phoenix, 1985; account exec. Rita Sanders Advt. and Pub. Rels. Agy., Tempe, Ariz., 1985, Am. Cable TV, Phoenix, 1985-86, Dimension Media Svcs., Phoenix, 1986-89, Greater Phoenix Interconnect, 1989-95, CableRep/Phoenix, 1995—. Recipient Nat. Sales awards, Cable TV Advt. Bur., 1986, 87, 91, 94, 96, 98, finalist, 1995; named one of Cable's Best Top Ten Cable Advt. Sales Reps. in Country, Cable Avails, 1995. Mem. Tempe C. of C. (ambassador 1986), Chandler (Ariz.) C. of C., Mesa (Ariz.) C. of C. Home: 9616 N 26th Pl Phoenix AZ 85028-4708 Office: CableRep/Phoenix 2020 N Central Ave Ste 400 Phoenix AZ 85004-4510

GRAFF, DARRELL JAY, physiology educator; b. Cedar City, Utah, Sept. 8, 1936; s. Glen Reber and Wanda Russell G.; m. Joyce Richens, June 16, 1962; children: Michael, Darla Kaye, Janenne Joyce, Christina Lynn. BS, Utah State U., 1958, MS, 1960; PhD, UCLA, 1963. Post doctoral fellow Rice U., Houston, Tex., 1963-65; prof. Physiology Weber State U., Ogden, Utah, 1965—; cons. Albion Laboratories, Clearfield, Utah, 1969-96; bd. mem. Med. Interpretations, Ogden, Utah, 1970-72. Author: Laboratory Manual Physiology, 1967, Intestinal Absorption, 1985; represented U.S. as guitarist at Internat. Folk Dance Festivals in Holland, 1998, Spain, 1999. Avocation: stringed instruments. Office: Weber State U 3750 Harrison Blvd Ogden UT 84408-0001

GRAFF, DAVID AUSTIN, chiropractor; b. Mpls., Sept. 24, 1949; s. Austin Joseph and Aleen Marie (O'Donnell) G.; m. Barbara Ruth Paterson, Jan 15, 1983. Student, U. Wis., Stevens Point, 1967-70; D Chiropractic Medicine, Palmer Coll., 1974; postgrad., Nat. Coll. of Chiropractic, Lombard, Ill., 1988-91. Diplomate Nat. Bd. Chiropractic Examiners. Extern Caputo Chiropractic Clinic, Plainview, N.Y., 1975; chiropractor Bahan & Bahan Chiropractic Health Ctr., Derry, N.H., 1976—; instr. N.Y. Chiropractic Coll., Old Brookville, 1975; nutritional cons. Floyd & Graff, Profl. Corp., Derry, N.H., 1976—, treas., 1984—. Editor: Textbook on spinal X-Rays, 1975. Mem. N.H. Chiropractic Assn., Whole Health Inst. Avocations: gourmet cooking, dog training, cross country skiing, golfing. Office: Floyd & Graff Chiropractic Health Ctr 33 Crystal Ave Derry NH 03038-1711

GRAFF, GEORGE LEONARD, lawyer; b. Bklyn., Sept. 6, 1940; s. Charles M. and Nettie (Starr) G.; m. Judith S. Udell, Apr. 20, 1963; children: David, Peter, Matthew. AB, Columbia U., 1962, LLB magna cum laude, 1967. Bar: N.Y. 1967, U.S. Dist. Ct. (so., ea. and no. dists.) N.Y. 1970, U.S. Ct. Appeals (2d, 3rd, 9th and Fed. cirs.) 1975, U.S. Ct. Claims, 1980, U.S. Supreme Ct. 1985. Law clk. to Hon. Stanley H. Fuld N.Y. Ct. Appeals, Albany, 1967-70; assoc. Nickerson, Kramer, Lowenstein, Nessen & Kamin, N.Y.C., 1970-74; member Milgrim, Thomajan & Lee, P.C., N.Y.C., 1974-92; ptnr. Paul, Hastings, Janofsky & Walker, N.Y.C., 1992—. Lt. comdr. USNR, 1962-64. Mem. ABA (advisor to drafting com. uniform computer info. transactions act 1994—, sci. and tech. sect. 1999—), Assn. of Bar of City of N.Y. (chmn. state legislation com. 1973-75). Home: 112 Holly Pl Briarcliff Manor NY 10510-2107 Office: Paul Hastings Janofsky & Walker 399 Park Ave Fl 31 New York NY 10022-4614

GRAFF, GEORGE STEPHEN, aerospace company executive; b. N.Y.C., Mar. 16, 1917; s. George Russell and Marjory Eleanor (Dolan) G.; m. Mary Rita Shaughnessy, Oct. 3, 1942 (dec.); children: Mary Ann, George Stephen, James Russell, Thomas Gerald, Maureen Rita; m. Marjory V. Kassabaum, Apr. 4, 1987; stepchildren: Douglas George, Ann Denise, Karen Jane. A.B. cum laude, DeSales Coll., Toledo, 1939; B.Aero. Engring., U. Detroit, 1942. Draftsman Continental Aviation & Engring. Corp., Detroit, 1940-42; with McDonnell Aircraft Co., 1942-82, dir. system tech., 1961-64, v.p. engring. tech., 1964-68, v.p. engring., 1968-70, exec. v.p., 1970-71, pres., 1971-82, also dir.; v.p. McDonnell Douglas Corp., 1971-82, mem. exec. com., 1974-87, also bd. dirs.; Mem. subcom. stability and control NACA, 1951-56; mem. subcom. aerodynamic stability and control NASA, 1956-58, com. missile and spacecraft aerodynamics, 1959-61, com. aircraft aerodynamics, 1964-65, chmn. aircraft aerodynamics com., 1965-67, mem. research and tech. adv. com. on aeros., 1967-71. Mem. industry com. Parks Coll., St. Louis, 1950-58; chmn. bd. trustees Fontbonne Coll., 1977-87; bd. dirs. Jr. Achievement of Mississippi Valley, Inc. Recipient trophy for design excellence Continental Aviation and Engring. Corp., 1942; Outstanding Engring. Alumnus of Yr. award U. Detroit, 1973. Fellow AIAA (regional dir., chmn. com. aircraft design 1964-67, fellow grade com. 1975-76); mem. Nat. Acad. Engring., Tau Beta Pi. Home: 761 Kent Rd Saint Louis MO 63124-1657

GRAFF, HENRY FRANKLIN, historian, educator; b. N.Y.C., Aug. 11, 1921; s. Samuel F. and Florence Babette (Morris) G.; m. Edith Krantz, June 16, 1946; children: Iris Joan (Mrs. Andrew R. Morse), Ellen Toby (Mrs. Martin A. Fox). BSS magna cum laude, Coll. City N.Y., 1941; MA, Columbia, 1942, PhD, 1949. Fellow history Coll. City N.Y., 1941-42, tutor history, 1946; lectr. history Columbia U., N.Y.C., 1946-47, instr. to asso. prof., 1946-61, prof. history, 1961-91, prof. emeritus, 1991—, chmn. dept. history, 1961-64; sr. fellow Freedom Forum Media Studies Ctr., N.Y.C., 1991-92; disting. lectr. Med. Sch. Columbia U., N.Y.C., 1992; lectr. Vassar Coll., 1953; chmn. advanced placement com. Am. History Coll. Entrance Exam. Bd., 1959-63; presdl. appointee Nat. Hist. Publs. Commn., 1965-71; mem. hist. adv. com. to sec. Air Force, 1972-80; acad. cons. Gen. Learning Corp., Time-Life Books; cons. editor Alfred A. Knopf, Inc.; hist. adviser to CBS for Bicentennial TV Series The American Parade, 1973-76, Presdl. Portraits, 1987-88; hist. adviser to ABC for TV series Our World, 1986-87, 20th Century Project, 1993—; presdl. appointee J.F.K. Assassination Records Rev. Bd., 1993-98; humanities lectr. Med. Sch. Yale U., 1993; Richard W. Cooper lectr. Phi Beta Kappa Assocs., 1996. Author: Bluejackets with Perry in Japan, 1952, (with Jacques Barzun) The Modern Researcher, 1962, rev. edit., 1970, 3d edit., 1977, 4th edit., 1985, 5th edit., 1992, (with Clifford Lord) American Themes, 1963, (with John A. Krout) The Adventure of the American People, 3d edit., 1973, The Free and the Brave, 4th edit., 1980, Thomas Jefferson, 1968, American Imperialism and the Philippine Insurrection, 1969, The Tuesday Cabinet, 1970; (with Paul J. Bohannan) The Call of Freedom, 1978, The Promise of Democracy, 1978, This Great Nation, 1983, The Presidents: A Reference History, 1984, 2d edit., 1996, paperback, 1997, America: The Glorious Republic, 1985, rev. edit., 1990; cons. editor: Life's History of the United States, 1963-64; contbr. articles to profl. jours. 1st lt. AUS, 1942-46. Recipient citation War Dept., Townsend Harris medal CCNY, 1966, Mark Van Doren award Columbia U., 1981, Gt. Tchr. award Columbia U., 1982, Kidger award New Eng. History Tchrs. Assn., 1990; Am. Coun. Learned Socs. fellow, 1942, Presdl. medal George Washington U., 1997, James Madison award ALA, 1999. Mem. Orgn. Am. Historians, Am. Hist. Assn., Coun. Fgn. Rels., Author's Guild, P.E.N., Soc. Am. Historians, Soc. Historians Am. Fgn. Rels., Mass. Hist. Soc. (corr.), Century Assn. (N.Y.C.), Sunningdale Country Club, Phi Beta Kappa (former pres. Gamma chpt.), Phi Beta Assocs. (hon.). Home: 47 Andrea Ln Scarsdale NY 10583-3115

GRAFF, PAT STUEVER, secondary education educator; b. Tulsa, Mar. 24, 1955; d. Joseph H., Sr. and Joanne (Schneider) Stuever; m. Mark A. Rumsey; children: Earl, Jr., Jeremy. BS in Secondary Edn., Okla. State U., 1976; postgrad., U. N.M., 1976-87. Cert. tchr. lang. arts, social studies, journalism, French, N.Mex. Substitute tchr. Albuquerque Pub. Schs., 1976-78; tchr. Cleveland Middle Sch., Albuquerque, 1978-86, La Cueva High Sch., Albuquerque, 1986—; adviser award winning lit. mag. El Tesoro, sch. newspapers The Edition, Huellas del Oso; instr. journalism workshops, N.Mex. Press Assn., Ind. U., Bloomington, Nat. Scholastic Press, Mpls., 1987—, Kans. State U., Manhattan, Interscholastic Press League, Austin, Tex., St. Mary's U., San Antonio; keynote spkr. at numerous confs. in Ohio, Ind., Kans., S.C., Okla., N.Mex., Tex., and N.Y.; reviewer of lang. and textbooks for several cos.; instr. Homework Hotline, Dial-A-Tchr., N.Mex., 1991—; textook evaluator Holt Pub., Inc., 1991. Author: Journalism Text, 1983; contbg. author: Communication Skills Resource Text, 1987, Classroom Publishing/Literacy, 1992; contbr. articles to profl. jours. Troop leader Girl Scouts U.S., 1979-90, coord. various programs, asst. program com. chmn. Chaparral Coun., 1988-89, chmn. adult recognition task force, 1991-96, bd. dirs., 1991-98; active PTA Gov. Bent Elem. Sch., 1983-86, v.p., 1985-86, Osuna Elem. Sch., 1986-92, N.Mex. PTA, 1994—; pub. various children's lit. mags., 1987—, writer parent's newsletter, 1986—; newsletter layout editor Albuquerque Youth Soccer Orgn., 1985-88; active YMCA youth and govt. model legis., faculty advisor La Cueva del., 1986—, press corps advisor, 1987—; asst. den. leader Cub Scouts, Boy Scouts Am., 1987-88, den leader, 1988-91. Recipient Innovative Teaching award Bus. Week mag., 1990, Svc. commendatin Coll. Edn. Alumni Assn., Okla. State U., 1990, Alumni Recognition award, 1993, Mem. Yr. Svc. award Bernalillo County Coun. Internat. REading Assn., Thanks to Tchrs. award Apple Computers, 1990, Spl. Recognition Albuquerque C. of C., 1992; named Spotlighted Mem. Phi Delta Kappa, 1990, Spl. Recognition Advisor Dow Jones Newspaper Fund, 1990, Nat. H.S. Journalism Tchr. of Yr., 1995, Disting. Advisor, 1991, U.S. West Tchr. Yr. finalist, 1991, N.Mex. Pubs. Adviser of Yr., 1991, N.Mex. State Tchr. of Yr., 1993, finalist Nat. Tchr. Yr., 1993, finalist Am. Tchr. Awards, Disney, 1998; grantee Phi Delta Kappa 1989, 91, Geraldine R. Dodge Found., 1990, 92, 95, 96, 97. Mem. ASCD (Focus on Excellence award 1990, editor newsletter 1991-92, focus on excellence awards com. 1992-94), Nat. Coun. Tchrs. English (nat. chair com. English Tchrs. and Pubs. 1988-91, nat. chair assembly for advisors of student pubs., regional rep. Tex., La., N.Mex., standing com. affiliates 1991-94, nat. chair, 1995-98), Nat. Sch. Pub. Rels. Assn. (Zia chpt., contest winner 1991-94, Pres.'s award 1993), Nat. Fedn. Press Women, Journalism Edn. Assn. (judge nat. contests 1988—, mem. nat. cert. bd. 1989—, presenter nat. convs. 1989—, cert. journalism educator 1990, master journalism educator 1991, issues seminar planning com. 1990, chair 1991, nat. conf. chmn. 1997-99), Journalism Edn. Assn. (nat. bd.), N.Mex. Coun. Tchrs. English (regional coord. Albuquerque 1983-86, chair state confs. 1985-87, editl. bd. N.Mex. English Jour. 1986-88, adv. mgr. 1989-90, state pres. 1987-88, chair English Humanities expo com. 1988—, chair facilities for Fall conf. 1988-93, Svc. award 1989, Outstanding H.S. English Tchr. N.Mex. 1991), N.Mex. Scholastic Press Assn. (state v.p. 1985-89, coord. workshop 1986, editor newsletter 1986-89, asst. chair state conf. 1988, 89, state bd. dirs. 1991—, state v.p. 1992-95, state pres. 1995-97), N.Mex. Press Women (state scholarship chair 1994, publicity chair 1995-96, state treas. 1996-1998, state v.p., 1998-99), Albuquerque Press Women (Communicator of Achievement award 1993, v.p. 1994, pres. 1995), Quill & Scroll (adv. La Cueva chpt. 1986—, judge nat. newspaper rating contest 1988—), AAUW (chpt. newsletter editor 1995-97, local v.p. 1997-99, state program v.p. 1997-99), Pi Lambda Theta (Ethel Mary Moore award Outstanding Educator 1993), N.M. Goals 2000 (panel mem. 1994-97). Roman Catholic. Avocations: soccer, running, hiking, travel, skiing. Home: 8101 Krim Dr NE Albuquerque NM 87109-5223 Office: La Cueva High Sch 7801 Wilshire Ave NE Albuquerque NM 87122-2807

GRAFF, RANDY, actress; b. Bklyn., May 23, 1955. Grad., Wagner Coll. Profl. theater debut in Gypsy, Village Dinner Theater, Raleigh, N.C.; appeared in Godspell, Raleigh; other appearances include Pins and Needles, Roundabout Theatre, N.Y.C., 1978, Something Wonderful, Westchester Regional Theatre, Harrison, N.Y., 1979, Sarava, Mark Hellinger Theatre, N.Y.C., 1979, Coming Attractions, Playwrights Horizons, Mainstage Theatre, N.Y.C., 1980, Keystone, McCarter Theatre, Princeton, N.J., 1981, A...My Name is Alice, Village Gate Theatre, N.Y.C., 1984, Amateurs, Playhouse in the Park, Cin., 1985, Fiorello!, Goodspell Opera House, East Haddam, Conn., 1985, Absurd Person Singular, Phila. Drama Guild, Phila., 1986, Les Miserables, Broadway Theatre, N.Y.C., 1987, City of Angels, Va. Theatre, N.Y.C., 1989 (Drama Desk award Featured Actress in Musical 1989, Tony award Supporting of Featured Actress in Musical 1990), Falsettos, 1993, Laughter on the 23rd Floor, 1993, Moon Over Buffalo, Martin Beck Theatre, 1995-96; (TV shows) include Mad About You, Law & Order, Love & War, Pros & Cons; (films) Key's to Tulsa, 1995. Recipient Drama Desk award, 1990, Antoinette Perry award for best featured actress in musical, 1990.

GRAFF, ROBERT ALAN, computer consultant; b. Detroit, Nov. 13, 1953; s. Jack and Irene Bertha (Horowitz) G.; m. Karen Elaine Morgan, Dec. 21, 1985; 1 child, David. BS in Physics, Wayne State U., 1976, MS in Computer Engring., 1981. Office automation specialist Burroughs Corp., Detroit, 1977-78; optical engr. Energy Conversion Devices Co., Troy, Mich., 1978-80; ind. contract programmer Southfield, Mich., 1981; sr. programmer/analyst Comprehensive Health Planning Coun. Southeastern Mich., Detroit, 1981-86; pres., computer cons. Data Concepts, Bloomfield Hills, Mich., 1983—; adj. instr. Walsh Coll., 1987—, Detroit Coll. Bus., 1990—; instr. U. Detroit, 1994—, Marygrove Coll., 1997—. Contbr. articles for devel. custom software for acctg. oriented micro computer applications, network analysis and adminstrn.; custom tng. on software products; topical computer topics. Mem. Assn. Computing Machinery, IEEE, Nat. Computer Soc. Democrat. Jewish. Office: Data Concepts 984 S Reading Rd Bloomfield Hills MI 48304-2044

GRAFFAM, WARD IRVING, lawyer; b. Portland, Maine, Sept. 2, 1940; s. Irving Hall and Mary Earl (Williams) G.; m. Linda Lewsen, June 10, 1967; children: Ward Jr., Kristen, Jerome. Bar: Maine 1967, U.S. Dist. Ct. Maine 1967. Lawyer Unum Life Ins. Co., Portland, 1968-70, assoc. counsel, 1970-75, counsel, 1975-80, v.p. ltd. products, 1980-83, v.p. employee benefits mktg., 1983-85, v.p. reins ops., 1985-86, v.p. flexible benefits, 1986, v.p., counsel, 1986-88, v.p. internat. ops., 1988-90; chmn. NEL Britannica Life Assurance, 1990-92; pres., mng. dir. Unum European Holding Co. Ltd. (London), 1990-97, sr. v.p. internat. ops., 1992-97; COO Young Am. America's Cup Syndicate; chmn. Unum Ltd., U.K., 1992-95, Maine Internat. Trade Ctr.; vice chmn. bd. dirs. Maine World Trade,Internat. Ins. Coun., Found. for Blood Rsch.; chmn. ACLI Internat. Life Ins. Co.; mem. bd. visitors U. Maine Law Sch., bd. mem., treas. Marine Maritime Acad. Author: (with others) The Mutual Company, 1971; editor-in-chief U. Maine Law Rev., 1966-67. Chmn. bd. South Portland HUD, 1973-75; mem. Gov.'s Coun. on Alcohol and Drug Abuse, Augusta, Maine, 1980-82; bd. dirs. Cumberland unit Am. Cancer Soc., Portland, 1976-78, Vis. Nurses Assn., Portland, 1971-72, YMCA, Portland, 1984-89; bd. dirs. Maine World Affairs Coun., Maine Maritime Mus.; mem. Gov.'s Internat. Adv. Bd., 1995-96; treas., bd. dirs. Maine Maritime Acad. Recipient 1st Place award Moot Ct. Competition U. Maine Sch. Law, Dist. Alumni award. Mem. ABA, Am. Corp. Counsel Assn., Maine State Bar Assn., Cumberland Bar Assn. (award), Portland Country Club, Portland Yacht Club (commodore 1983-84), Woodford Club, Masons. Home: 29 Orchard St Portland ME 04102-3613 Office: Unum Life Ins Co 2211 Congress St Portland ME 04102-1941

GRAFFEO, MARY THÉRÈSE, music educator, performer; b. Mineola, N.Y., Jan. 20, 1949; d. Michael Joseph and Florence Marie (Lonette) G. BA in Music Edn., Adelphi U., 1972; MusM in Vocal Performance, Kent State U., 1982. Cert. music tchr. N.Y. Tchr. music, therapist Nassau County Bd. Coop. Ednl. Svcs., Westbury, N.Y., 1972-85; tchr. music, developer curricula Great Neck (N.Y.) Pub. Schs., 1985-87; tchr. music Syosset (N.Y.) Pub. Schs., 1987-88, 89-90, Jericho (N.Y.) Pub. Schs., 1988-89; tchr. music, developer creative programs Lawrence (N.Y.) Pub. Schs., 1990-92; tchr. music Herricks Pub. Schs., New Hyde Park, N.Y., 1992-93, Hempstead (N.Y.) Pub. Schs., 1993—; music dir. summer programs Friends Acad., Locust Valley, N.Y., 1989-94. Author: (curriculum) Music for the Trainable Mentally Retarded, 1973, (book) Creative Enrichment Programs/America: The First 200 Years in Song, 1990; co-author: The Remediation of Learning Discrepancies Through Music, 1980; composer: (mus. play) Red Riding Hood's Day, 1993, The Bell of Atri, 1994, The Children's Song, 1995. Cultural adv. bd. Lawrence Pub. Schs., 1990-92, Hempstead Pub. Schs., 1993—; founding mem. United We Stand Am., Dallas, 1992—. Scholar Adelphi U., 1968-72, Blossom Festival Sch., Kent, Ohio, 1978-79. Mem. NEA, Music Educators Nat. Conf., N.Y. State United Tchrs., N.Y. State Sch. Music Assn., Nassau Music Educators Assn. Democrat. Roman Catholic. Avocations: aviculture, needlework, travel, photography, concerts. Home: 300 Edwards St Roslyn Heights NY 11577-1140 Office: Early Childhood Ctr 436 Front St Hempstead NY 11550-4212

GRAFFIS, JULIE ANNE, entrepreneur, retail consultant, interior designer; b. Houston, Jan. 4, 1960; d. Robert B. and Dorothy Gean (Weempe) Hyde; m. William B. Graffis, May 29, 1988; 1 child, Aaron James Hehr. Student, U. St. Thomas, Houston, 1977, Portland C.C., The Dalles, Oreg., 1984-85; AA, North Seattle C.C., 1987. Cert. window fashions profl. assoc., specialist, master Window Fashions Cert. Program. Co-owner Mosier (Oreg.) Shell Svc., 1981-85; quality control mgr. Town & Country Jeep-Eagle, Seattle, 1986-87; cons. Giovi Ford-Mercury, Pullman, Wash., 1988-89; prin., CEO, Interiors by JAG, Houston, 1990—; mem. Allied Bd. of Trade; cons. Habitat for Humanity, Vancouver, 1992-93; lectr., presenter interior design workshops; retail cons. Bus. ptnr. Hough Elem. Found. and Sch.; patron Pilchuck Glass Sch. Mem. NAFE, Window Fashions Edn. and Design Resource Network, Greater Vancouver C. of C. (liaison bus. and edn. partnership 1992—, amb. 1993-95), Inst. Managerial and Profl. Women. Avocations: furniture and landscape design, jewelry design, classic automobiles, art collecting, travel, architecture, interior renovations.

GRAFFIUS, RICHARD STEWART, II, middle school educator; b. Punxsutawney, Pa., May 27, 1948; s. Richard S. and Adeline L. (Piquet) G.; m. Rose M. Ingham, Apr. 13, 1974; children: Alissa, Lindsay, Emily. BS in Elem. Edn., Ind. U. Pa., 1970; MEd in Ednl. Adminstrn., Pa. State U., 1975, EdD in Ednl. Adminstrn., 1993. Cert. elem. tchr., elem. and secondary prin., asst. supt., Pa. Sci. tchr. Punxsutawney (Pa.) Area Middle Sch., 1970—. Author (coloring book) The Official Punxsutawney Phil Coloring Book, 1978. Councilman, v.p. Borough of Punxsutawney, 1981-85; consistory mem. St. Peter's United Ch. of Christ, Punxsutawney, 1993-96. Mem. NEA, ASCD, Pa. State Edn. Assn., Pa. Coun. for Social Studies, Punxsutawney Area Ednl. Assn. Avocations: skiing, hunting, fishing, antique and classic car restoration. Home: 102 Pleasant Ave Punxsutawney PA 15767-1708

GRAFFMAN, GARY, pianist, music educator; b. N.Y.C., Oct. 14, 1928; s. Vladimir and Nadia (Margolin) G.; m. Naomi Helfman, Dec. 5, 1952. Student, Curtis Inst. Music, 1936-46, Columbia U., 1947-48; studied with Vladimir Horowitz, Rudolf Serkin; MusD (hon.), Juilliard Sch., 1993, Moravian Coll., 1995. Dir. Curtis Inst. Music, Phila., 1986-95, pres., dir., 1995—. Soloist debut, Phila. Orch, 1947; first tours U.S., 1951, S.Am., 1955, Europe, 1956, Asia-Australia, 1958, South Africa, 1961; solo appearances with N.Y. Philharmonic, Boston, Chgo., Cleve., San Francisco, Los Angeles, London, Cape Town symphony orchs., Philharmonia London, Halle Orch. of Manchester, Royal Liverpool, Berlin, Lisbon, Oslo, Warsaw philharmonic orchs., Johannesburg, Sydney, Melbourne orchs., others; rec. artist with N.Y., Phila., Boston, Cleve., Chgo., San Francisco orchs., also solo recs.; author: I Really Should Be Practicing, 1981. Fulbright scholar, 1950; Ford Found. fellow, 1962; recipient Rachmaninoff Fund. spl. award, 1948, Leventritt award, 1949, Pa. Gov. Excellence in Arts award, 1991. Office: Curtis Inst Music Office of Director 1726 Locust St Philadelphia PA 19103-6187 also: ICM Artists Ltd 40 W 57th St New York NY 10019

GRAFSTEIN, BERNICE, physiology and neuroscience educator, researcher. BA, U. Toronto, Ont., Can., 1951; PhD, McGill U., Montreal, Que., Can., 1954. Vincent and Brooke Astor Disting. prof. in neurosci., prof. physiology and biophysics Cornell U. Med. Coll., N.Y.C. Office: Cornell U Med Coll Weill Med Coll Dept Physiology New York NY 10021

GRAFTON, ANTHONY THOMAS, history educator; b. New Haven, May 21, 1950; s. Samuel and Edith (Kingstone) G.; m. Louise Erlich, May 13, 1972; children: Samuel David, Anna Temma Rachel. BA, U. Chgo., 1971, MA, 1972, PhD, 1975. Instr. Cornell U., Ithaca, N.Y., 1974-75; from asst. prof. to assoc. prof. Princeton (N.J.) U., 1975-85, prof., 1985—, Andrew Mellon prof., 1988-93, Dodge prof. of history, 1993—; Meyer Schapiro lectr. Columbia U., 1996-97; exhibit curator N.Y. Pub. Libr., N.Y.C., 1992, Libr. of Congress, Washington, 1993. Author: Joseph Scaliger, 1983-93, Defenders of the Text, 1991, New Worlds, Ancient Texts, 1992, The Footnote: A Curious History, 1997, Commerce with the Classics, 1997. Recipient L.A. Times prize for history, 1993; Danforth fellow, 1971-75, Guggenheim fellow, 1988-89, Fairchild fellow Calif. Tech. Inst., 1988-89, Behrman fellow Princeton U., 1994-95. Mem. Am. Philos. Soc., Brit. Acad., Berlin-Brandenburgische Akad. der Wissenschaften (corr.). Democrat. Jewish. Avocations: walking, reading. Office: Princeton U Dickinson Hall History Dept Princeton NJ 08544

GRAFTON, SUE, novelist; b. Louisville, Apr. 24, 1940; d. Cornelius Warren and Vivian Boisseau (Harnsberger) G.; children: Leslie, Jay, Jamie; m. Steven Humphrey, Oct. 1, 1978. BA, U. Louisville, 1961. lectr. L.A. City Coll., Long Beach (Calif.) City Coll., U. Dayton (Ohio) Writers Conf., Midwest Writers Conf., Canton, Ohio, Calif. Luth. Coll., Thousand Oaks, Santa Barbara (Calif.) Writers Conf., L.A. Valley Coll., Antioch Writers Conf., Yellow Springs, Ohio, S.W. Writers Conf., Albuquerque, Smithsonian Campus on the Mall, Washington, and others. Author: (novels) Keziah Dane, 1967, The Lolly-Madona War, 1969, "A" is for Alibi, 1982 (Mysterious Stranger award 1982-83), "B" is for Burglar, 1985 (Shamus award 1986, Anthony award 1987), "C" is For Corpse, 1986, "D" is for Deadbeat, 1987, "E" is for Evidence, 1988 (Doubleday Mystery Guild award 1989), "F" is for Fugitive, 1989 (Doubleday Mystery Guild award 1990, The Falcon award 1990), "G" is for Gumshoe, 1990 (Doubleday Mystery Guild award 1991, Anthony award 1991, Shamus award 1991), "H" is for Homicide, 1991 (Doubleday Mystery Guild award 1992), "I" is for Innocent, 1992 (Doubleday Mystery Guild award 1992, Mystery Scene Am. Mystery award 1993), Kinsey and Me, 1992, "J" is for Judgement, 1994, "K" is for Killer, 1994 (Shamus award 1994), "L" is For Lawless, 1995, "M" is For Malice, 1996, "N" is for Noose, 1998, "O" is for ..., 1999; editor: Writing Mysteries,

1992; author short fiction, short stories, screenplay, teleplay TV episodes. Mem. Writers Gild Am. West, Mystery Writers Am. Inc. (pres. 1994), Private Eye Writers Assn. (pres. 1989-90), Crime Writers Assn. Address: care Henry Holt and Co 115 West 18th St New York NY 10011*

GRAFTON, W. ROBERT, professional services company executive. Degree, W. Va. U. With Arthur Andersen, L.L.P., 1963—; past mng. ptnr. Arthur Andersen, L.L.P., Balt.; past mng. ptnr. audit and bus. adv. practice Arthur Andersen, L.L.P., Washington; past mng. ptnr. southeast region Arthur Andersen, L.L.P., Washington; now mng. ptnr., chief exec. Andersen Worldwide, N.Y.C., also bd. ptnrs.; past mem. adv. bd. Sch. Bus. Towson State U.; past mem. exec. coun. Coll. Bus. James Madison U. Past trustee Hampden-Sydney Coll., past mem. exec. com., past chmn. budget and audit com.; past bd. dirs. United Way, Md., past chmn. profl. firms com. Washington United Way Campaign. Mem. Nat. Assn. Accts. (past nat. dir., past pres. Washington chpt.), D.C. Inst. Cert. Pub. Accts. (past chmn. S.E.C. com.),. Office: care Andersen Worldwide 1345 Avenue Of The Americas New York NY 10105-0302

GRAGER, STEVEN PAUL, life insurance and trust consultant; b. Everett, Wash., July 18, 1964; s. Clara A. Grager; m. Courtney A. Van Detta, June 27, 1987; children: Emma, Camille. BA in Mktg. magna cum laude, Seattle Pacific U., 1986; MBA in Fin., U. Chgo., 1991. CLU, ChFC, CFP. Fin. cons. H.D. Vest Fin. Svcs., Irving, Tex., 1987-89; mktg. dir. Mut. of N.Y., San Francsico, 1991-92; fin. planner Mut. of N.Y., Bellevue, Wash., 1992-94; regional v.p. Pacific Mut., Seattle, 1994-98; divsnl. v.p. Paine Webber, San Francisco, 1998—; investment advisor Steven P. Grager & Assocs., Seattle, 1992-96. Co-chmn. Giving Something Back, Chgo., 1989-91; v.p. Toastmasters, Chgo., 1990-91. Arthur Andersen scholar Seattle Pacific U., 1984; Student Activities grantee U. Chgo., 1990. Mem. Nat. Assn. Life Underwriters, Internat. Assn. Fin. Planners, Am. Soc. CLU, Am. Assn. Individual Investors, Commonwealth Club San Francisco. Republican. Presbyterian. Avocations: skiing, travel. Office: PaineWebber 555 California St 32d Fl San Francisco CA 94104 Address: PO Box 1987 Danville CA 94526-6987

GRAGG, KARL LAWRENCE, lawyer; b. Watertown, N.Y., Sept. 25, 1946; s. Karl Lawrence and Pauline (Sykes) G.; m. Maureen Gilluly, Dec. 13, 1975; children: Meaghan Christina, Erika Lawrence, Jenny Camille. BS, Fla. State U., 1968; JD, U. Fla., 1974, LLM in Taxation, 1975. Bar: Fla. 1975, U.S Dist. Ct. (so. dist.) Fla., U.S. Tax Ct., U.S. Ct. Appeals (5th cir.). Assoc. Mershon, Sawyer, Johnson, Dunwoody & Cole, Miami, Fla., 1975-80, ptnr., 1980-82; ptnr. Gunster, Yoakley, Criser & Stewart, Palm Beach, Fla., 1982-84, Walker Ellis Gragg & Deaktor, Miami, 1984-86, White & Case, Miami, 1987—; adj. prof. law U. Miami, 1978-89; mem. tax com. Fla. Ho. of Reps., Tallahassee, 1983. Contbr. articles to U. Fla. Law Rev. Vol. Miami United Way, 1977-80. Mem. ABA (taxation sect.), Nat. Assn. State Bar (chmn. 1986), Am. Coll. Tax Counsel, Fla. Bar Assn. (tax sect., chmn. tax sect. 1991, chmn. coun. of sect.), Nat. Assn. Indsl. and Office Parks (bd. dirs. 1989-91), Ctr. for Health Techs., Inc. (bd. dirs. 1992-98), Japan Soc. South Fla. (bd. dirs. 1990-98). Office: White & Case 200 S Biscayne Blvd Ste 4900 Miami FL 33131-2352

GRAGLIA, LINO ANTHONY, lawyer, educator; b. Bklyn., Jan. 22, 1930; s. Pasquale and Antoinette (Romeo) G.; m. F. Carolyn Pennington, July 17, 1954; children: Donna, Carol, Laura. BA, CCNY, 1952; LLB, Columbia U., 1954. Bar: N.Y. 1954, D.C. 1957, Tex. 1980, U.S. Supreme Ct. Atty. U.S. Dept. Justice, Washington, 1954-57; pvt. practice law Washington and N.Y.C., 1957-66; prof. law U. Tex., Austin, 1966—. Author: Disaster by Decree: The Supreme Court Decisions on Race and the Schools, 1976. Recipient George Washington medal Freedoms Foundation at Valley Forge, 1989. Republican. Avocations: tennis, biking, hiking, billiards. Office: U Tex Sch Law 727 E 26th St Austin TX 78705-3224

GRAHAM, ALAN MORRISON, surgeon; b. Perth, Scotland, Mar. 23, 1953; m. Michiko P. Graham; children: George A., Mie I, Fraser S. Queen's U., Kingston, Ont., 1973-75, MD, 1979. Diplomate Am. Bd. Surgery, Am. Bd. Gen. Surgery and Vascular Surgery. Internship Kingston Gen. Hosp. Queen's U., 1979-80; residency Royal Victoria Hosp. McGill U., 1980-84; fellowship U. Chgo., 1984-85; asst. prof. dept. surgery Montreal Children's Hosp., 1985-91, Royal Victoria Hosp., 1985-91; asst. prof. dept. surgery McGill U., 1985-91, assoc. prof., 1991-92; assoc. prof. dept. surgery Royal Victoria Hosp., 1991-92; assoc. prof., chief div. vascular surgery Robert Wood Johnson Medical Sch., 1992—, program dir. vascular fellowship program, 1992—. Author numerous book chapters; contbr. articles to profl. jours. Recipient Edgar Forrester scholarship, 1977, W.W. Near scholarship, 1977, Alice Pierce Waddington scholarship, 1977, Prof. prize in Surgery, 1979, Neil Currie Polson Meml. prize, 1979, Outstanding Tchr. award U. Chgo., 1985, E.J. Wylie Travelling fellowship, 1989, numerous grants. Fellow ACS, Royal Coll. Physicians and Surgeons; mem. Soc. Univ. Surgeons, Soc. Vascular Surgery, Ea. Vascular Soc., Can. Assn. Gen. Surgeons, Assn. Acad. Surgeons, Assn. Internat. Vascular Surgery, Can. Soc. Vascular Surgery, Peripheral Vascular Surgery Soc., Internat. Soc. Cardiovascular Surgery, Soc. Clin. Vascular Surgery, Phoenix Alliance, Inc., Vascular Soc. N.J. (pres.), Internat. Fedn. Surg. Colls., Soc. of Surgeons of N.J. Office: Robert Wood Johnson Med Sch 1 Robert Wood Johnson Pl New Brunswick NJ 08901-1928

GRAHAM, ALBERT DARLINGTON, JR., educational administrator; b. Camden, N.J., July 28, 1948; s. Albert Darlington and Betty Jane (Belancin) g.; m. Susan K. Tomarchio, July 30, 1994; children: Jason Carl, Jayme Lynn. BS cum laude, Union Coll., Barbourville, Ky., 1970, MA, 1973; EdM, Johns Hopkins U., 1977; EdD, Calif. Western U., 1980; MA, Rowan U., 1991; PhD, LaSalle U., 1992. Cert. supt., prin., supr., sch. bus. adminstr., secondary social studies tchr., in student personnel svcs., N.J. Tchr. social studies Penns Grove (N.J.) Mid. Sch., 1970-82, coord. career edn., 1974-75, chmn. social studies dept., 1978-82; athletic dir. Penns Grove H.S., Carneys Point, N.J., 1983-85, coord. gifted and talented program, 1986-87, dir. guidance, vice prin. in charge curriculum, fin.-instrn., 1982-92, dir. spl. projects, 1992—. Mem. Carneys Point Twp., 1979-84, 81-91; mayor Carneys Point Twp., 1992, 96, 99; mem. Salem County (N.J.) Bd. Chosen Freeholders, 1985-87, N.J. Gov.'s Coun. on Phys. Fitness and Sports, 1986—; chmn. Carneys Point Sewerage Authority, 1981-85, 91—; pres. Salem County Selective Svc. Bd., 1982—; pres. Salem County Assn. Local Govt., 1983-84, Village Arms Sr. Citizens Complex, Carneys Point, 1984—; pres. Carneys Point Rep. Club, 1981-84; trustee Salem C.C., 1987-91, Union Coll., 1992—. Recipient Gov. James D. Black Sr. award for acad. excellence, Balckwell Meml. award in polit. sci., medal for excellence in edni. adminstrn., Disting. Cmty. Svc. award Carneys Point Twp. Com., 1983, Disting. Leadership award Salem County Assn. Local Govt., 1986, Salem County recognition award Salem County Bd. Chosen Freholders, 1987, Citizen of Yr. Penns Grove VFW, 1993; named to Personal Achievement Hall of Fame, Penns Grove H.S., 1994, Educators Hall of Fame, Union Coll., 1998. Mem. ASCD, N.J. Pins. and Suprs. Assn. (svc. and leadership award 1984), N.J. League Municipalities (svc. and leadership award 1984), South Jersey Assn. Freeholders (svc. and leadership award 1985), Penns Grove High Sch. Alumni Assn. (treas. 1975—, Personal Achievement Hall of Fame 1994), Penns Grove Exch. Club (pres. Penns Grove 1984-85, Exchangite of Yr. 1984, Cmty. Svc. award 1985), Masons (32d degree), Elks (leading knight Penns Grove 1986-87), Mensa, Phi Delta Kappa, Iota Sigma Nu, Gamma Beta Phi, Phi Delta Gamma. Methodist. Avocations: reading, sports, coin collecting, working on 1929 Mercedes. Home: 58 N Norman Ave Carneys Point NJ 08069-1546 Office: Penns Grove-Carneys Point Sch Dist Adminstrv Offices 113 W Harmony St Penns Grove NJ 08069-1322

GRAHAM, ANITA LOUISE, correctional and community health nurse; b. Casa Grande, Ariz., Sept. 17, 1959; d. Therman Louis (dec. 1995) and Annie Clessie (Dornan) Nichols; m. Richard Arthur Christy, Aug. 27, 1990; children: Amanda Sue Foster-Wells, Kristi Lynn Foster. AS in Practical Nursing, Ctrl. Ariz. Coll., 1982; AAS, RN, Gateway C.C., Phoenix, 1985, Degree in Health Svc. Mgmt., 1992. RN, Ariz., Okla.; cert. BLS, ACLS, Chemotherapy. Cert. nursing asst. Hoemako Hosp., Casa Grande, 1977-82; lic. practical nurse Mesa (Ariz.) Luth. Hosp., 1982-85; RN Mesa Gen. Hosp., 1985-86, East Mesa Care Ctr., 1986-88; RN, case mgr. Interim Healthcare, Phoenix, 1988-93; RN, nurse clinician PDR Carum Care, Phoenix, 1991-97; correctional RN Ariz. Dept. Corrections, Florence, 1993-95; IV nurse clinician Signature Home Care, 1994-97; RN, unit mgr., home health IV specialist Select Care, Globe, Ariz., 1997—; mem. RN adv. bd. Interim Healthcare, 1990-93. Mem. Ariz. Nurses Assn., Internat. Platform Assn. Republican. Avocations: stitchery, reading. Home: 1646 N Pennington Dr Chandler AZ 85224-5115

GRAHAM, ANNA REGINA, pathologist, educator; b. Phila., Nov. 1, 1947; d. Eugene Nelson and Anna Beatrice (McGovern) Chadwick; m. Larry L. Graham, June 29, 1973; 1 child, Jason. BS in Chemistry, Ariz. State U., 1969, BS in Zoology, 1970; MD, U. Ariz., 1974. Diplomate Am. Bd. Pathology. With Coll. Medicine U. Ariz., Tucson, 1974—, asst. prof. pathology, 1978-84, assoc. prof. pathology, 1984-90, prof. Pathology, 1990—. Fellow Am. Soc. Clin. Pathologists (bd. dirs. Chgo. chpt. 1993—, sec. 1995—), Internat. Acad. Pathology, Internat. Acad. Telemedicine, Coll. Am. Pathologists; mem. AMA (alt. del. Chgo. chpt. 1992—), Ariz. Soc. Pathologists (pres. Phoenix chpt. 1989-91), Ariz. Med. Assn. (treas. Phoenix chpt. 1995-97). Republican. Baptist. Avocations: motorcycles, piano, choir. Office: Ariz Health Scis Ctr Dept Pathology Tucson AZ 85724-5108

GRAHAM, B. ALASDAIR, government official; b. Dominion, N.S., Can., May 21, 1929; m. Jean Elizabeth MacDonald, 1952; 10 children. BA, St. Francis Xavier U. Apptd. to Senate Ottawa, 1972; dep. leader Govt. of Senate, Ottawa, 1995-97, leader, 1997—. Office: Senate of Canada Rm 279-S, Parliament Hill Centre Blk, Ottawa, ON Canada K1A 0A4*

GRAHAM, BEARDSLEY, management consultant; b. Berkeley, Calif., Apr. 24, 1914; s. Reuben Jacob and Kate Ellen (Beardsley) G.; m. Frances Rose McSherry, June 17, 1951 (div. Mar. 1967); children: McSherry, Heather; m. Lorraine Juliana Shaw, Oct. 22, 1973. BS in Chemistry, Physics and Math., U. Calif., Berkeley, 1935; postgrad. in Electronics, U. Calif., 1938-40, Columbia U., 1941-42; postgrad. in Chemistry, Tufts U., 1942-43. Registered profl. engr., Ariz., Calif., Ky.; lic. real estate broker, Calif. Instr. Edison Elec. Sch., Berkeley; frameman Pacific Tel. & Tel. co., San Francisco, 1937-39; chief engr. Golden Gate Internat. Expn. RCA Mfg. Co., 1939-40; devel. engr. NBC, Hollywood, Calif., N.Y.C., 1940-42; staff mem. radiation lab MIT, Cambridge, 1942-44; chief engr., head dept. spl. products devel. labs. Eclipse-Pioneer div. Bendix Aviation Corp., Teterboro, N.J., and Pacific div., Detroit, 1946-51, chief engr. rsch. labs., tech. cons. to v.p. rsch.; asst. chmn. engring. dept. Stanford Rsch. Inst., Menlo Park, Calif., 1951-56; pres. Spindletop Rsch., 1961-67; exec. v.p. Sequoia Process Corp., Redwood City, Calif., 1956-57; spl. asst. comml. satellites Lockheed Aircraft Corp., Palo Alto and Sunnyvale, Calif., 1957-61, mgr. satellite systems planning Air Force Satellite Systems Program, mgr. specialty sales dept.; pres. Spindletop Rsch. Inc., Lexington, Ky., 1961-67; cons. Lockheed Aircraft Corp., Palo Alto and Sunnyvale, Calif., 1967—; pvt. practice mgmt. cons. Bend, Oreg., 1967—; pioneer in fields of new techs. and svcs. including econ. devel., air pollution and environ. qualities, nuclear weapons and power, satellite systems; bd. dirs., incorporator (selected by Pres. Kennedy) Communication Satellite Corp., 1962-64; founding chmn. bd. Videorecord Corp. Am.; mem. adv. com. on isotope and radiation devel. AEC, Ky., Atomic Energy and Space Authority, Ky. adv. com. on nuclear energy; rsch. prof. elec. engring. U. Ky., 1965; active in Microwave Communications Inc. (now MCI), Aetna Life Inc., numerous other. Papers on file at Bancroft Libr., U. Calif. at Berkeley. V.p. Bend Urban Area Planning Commn., 1983-87; vice chmn. engring. tech. adv. com. Cen. Oreg. Community Colls., 1983—, Citizens Com. for Cityhood, Yucca Valley, Calif., 1977; mem. energy adv. com. League Oreg. Cities, 1983-87; active various other civic orgns.; treas., bd. govs. ocm. for art Stanford U., 1956; mem. Bend Traffic-Saftey Com., 1987, Cent. Oreg. Coun. on Higher Edn., 1983—. Named to Hon. Order Ky. Cols. Fellow IEEE (life), AIAA (assoc.); mem. Internat. Solar Energy Soc. (founding sec., bd. dirs. 1953-66), Solar Energy Assn. Oreg. (parliamentarian 1986, exec. bd.), International Club (Washington), Arizona Club, University Club (L.A.). Democrat. Home and Office: 214 Hillcrest Pl Baker City OR 97814-4132

GRAHAM, BILLY See **GRAHAM, WILLIAM FRANKLIN**

GRAHAM, BRAUN H., plastic surgeon; b. July 29, 1952. MD, Ind. U., 1977. Diplomate Am. Bd. Plastic Surgery. Pres. Sarasota (Fla.) Plastic Surgery, 1990—. Mem. Am. Soc. Aesthetic Plastic Surgery, Southea. Soc. Plastic and Reconstructive Surgeons. E-mail: bhgra@home.com. Office: 2255 S Tamiami Trail Sarasota FL 34239

GRAHAM, BRENDA J., nurse; b. Savannah, Ga., July 30, 1944; d. Herman James and Dotha Lee Johnson; 1 child, La Trelle Denise Jackson. AAS, Bronx Community Coll., 1971; BS, Savannah State Coll., 1987; MEd, U. Ga., 1993. Cert. RN, Ga., N.Y., S.C. Retired staff nurse Athens (Ga.) Regional Med. Ctr./Hosp.; lead tchr. nursing instrn. South Coll., Savannah; dir. of nursing Pleasantview Nursing Home, Metter, Ga.; collection supr. Am. Red Cross, Savannah; program coord. Savannah (Ga.) State Coll.; retired, 1993; facilitator Athens Sickle Cell Support Group.

GRAHAM, CHARLES, research psychologist; b. Atlantic City, N.J., Nov. 21, 1937; s. Charles Leroy and Margery (Kaplan) G.; m. Sally Jones, Dec. 8, 1962 (div. Apr. 1974); children: Ronna, Christopher, Glen; m. Mary R. Cook, May 18, 1996; 1 child, Sheri J. BS, U. Md., 1966; MS, Pa. State U., 1968, PhD, 1970. Rsch. assoc. Inst. Pa. Hosp., Phila., 1970-74; instr., lectr. dept. psychiatry U. Pa., Phila., 1970-74; sr. exptl. psychologist Midwest Rsch. Inst., Kansas City, 1974-78; prin. exptl. psychologist Midwest Rsch. Inst., 1979-94, sr. advisor for life scis., 1994—; mgr. Bioelectromagnetics Rsch. Program, 1998—; tech. review panel Dept. of Energy, EPA, NIH, WHO, Internat. Commn. on Non-Ionizing Radiation Protection. With U.S. Army, 1960-62. NIH grantee, 1975—. Mem. Am. Psychol. Assn., Soc. Psychophysiol. Rsch., Claude Bernard Soc., Bioelectromagnetics, Sigma Xi. Avocations: travel, photography, gardening. Office: Midwest Rsch Inst 425 Volker Blvd Kansas City MO 64110-2299

GRAHAM, CHARLES JOHN, university educator, former university president; b. Peru, Ill., May 29, 1929; s. John William and Pauline (Powell) G.; m. Florence Yvonne Ure, Sept. 2, 1951; children: John Charles, James Spencer, David Powell. A.B., U. Ill., 1950, M.A., 1951, Ph.D., 1955. Mgmt. intern Navy Dept., 1953-54; contract negotiator Bur. Ships, 1954; from instr. to prof. polit. sci. Wis. State U., River Falls, 1954-63, chmn. dept. social scis., 1962-63; vis. lectr. U. Wis., summer 1957, U. Ill., summer 1959; legislative asst. to Senator Proxmire, 1960-61; dean Coll. Art and Scis., Wis. State U., Whitewater, 1963-70; asst. to pres. for fed. programs Coll. Art and Scis., Wis. State U., 1965-68, acting chmn. dept. polit. sci., 1970-71; pres. St. Cloud (Minn.) State U., 1971-81, Hamline U., St. Paul, 1981-87; sr. v.p. Minn. Pvt. Coll. Council/Fund, 1987-88; interim pres. Met. State U., St. Paul, 1988-89; disting. svc. prof. Minn. State U. System, 1989-95; pres. emeritus Hamline U.; St. Cloud, State U. Bd. dirs., Minn. Inst. for Talented Youth; bd. dirs. Indianhead coun. Boy Scouts Am., St. Paul Rotary Club (pres.). Recipient Alumni Achievement award U. Ill., 1995; James W. Garner fellow polit. sci., 1951-52, 52-53. Mem. Rotary, Phi Beta Kappa, Phi Kappa Phi. Methodist. Home: 1675 Ridgewood Ln S Saint Paul MN 55113-5625

GRAHAM, CHARLES PASSMORE, retired army officer; b. Seward, Alaska, Dec. 19, 1927; s. Thomas Phillip and Lynnie Ethel (Passmore) G.; m. Alice Ann Chandler, Nov. 20, 1954; children: Susan Kay, Edwin C., Richard C. B.S., U.S. Mil. Acad., 1950; M.S. in Engring, U. Mich., 1957. C. Commd. 2d lt. U.S. Army, 1950, advanced through grades to lt. gen., 1977; dir. force programs and structure, office of dep. chief of staff for ops. Hdqrs. Dept. Army Washington, 1975-77; comdg. gen. 2d Armored Div. Ft. Hood, Tex., 1977-80; dep. chief of staff for ops. Hdqrs. U.S. Army Forces Command Ft. McPherson, Ga., 1980-81; chief of staff Hdqrs. U.S. Army Forces Command, 1981-83; comdg. gen. 2d U.S. Army Ft. Gillem, Ga., 1983-85; mgmt. cons., 1985—; mediator Justice Ctr. of Atlanta, 1993—. Exec. dir. Ga. Internat. Cultural Exch., Inc., prodr. of fine arts and cultural exhbns., 1994-95; trustee Kiwanis Found. Atlanta, Chattahoochee Nature Ctr. Decorated D.S.M., Legion of Merit, Bronze Star. Mem. Assn. U.S. Army, Armor Assn., Assn. Grads U.S. Mil. Acad., Assn. Grads Army War Coll., 2d Armored Divsn. Assn. Presbyterian. Lodge: Kiwanis. Home: 134 Warbler Way Georgetown TX 78628 *Guided by the principle of "Duty, Honor, Country" learned as a cadet at West Point, my goal was to do my very best in every assignment I was given, remembering that what was best for the United States, best for the U.S. Army, and best for the American soldier was the proper solution to each problem. With that goal, success would come naturally.*

GRAHAM, CYNTHIA ARMSTRONG, banker; b. Charlotte, N.C., Jan. 3, 1950; d. Beverly Weller and Katherine (Anderson) Armstrong; m. Walter Raleigh Graham Jr., May 23, 1970. AB in Chemistry, Bryn Mawr Coll., 1971; MBA in Fin. with distinction, U. Pa., 1976. Computer programmer Philco-Ford, Ft. Washington, Pa., 1973-74; asst. dir. admissions Wharton Sch., U. Pa., Phila., 1974-76; asst. v.p. N.C. Nat. Bank, Charlotte, 1976-80; v.p. Barclays Am. Corp., Charlotte, 1980-86; sr. v.p. Barclays Bank Del., N.A., Wilmington, 1986-87, Barnett Banks, Inc., Jacksonville, Fla., 1987-97; chmn., pres. Barnett Mcht. Svcs., Inc., Jacksonville, 1987-89, TeleCheck Southcoast, 1987-89, Barnett Card Svcs. Corp., Jacksonville, 1989-97; exec. v.p. retail databased mktg. Nat. City Corp., Cleve., 1998—; bd. advisors Nat. DAta Corp., Atlanta, 1987-88; delivery sys. advisor VISA U.S.A., Inc., San Mateo, Calif., 1987-91; mcht. svcs. advisor MasterCard, Internat., N.Y.C., 1989-92; mem. U.S. regional bus. com. MasterCard, 1992-97; card products advisor VISA U.S.A., Inc., San Mateo, 1991-94, VISA Internat., 1994, mem. mktg. com., 1994-97; bd. dirs. Interlink Network, Inc., U$A Value Exchg., 1995-97. Mem. Jacksonville Women's Network, 1988-92, bd. dirs., 1991-92, treas., 1992; mem. bd. suprs. Spaceport Fla., 1990-92. Mem. Am. Bankers Assn. (exec. com. card divsn. 1991-94, vice chmn. 1993, chmn. 1994), Jacksonville C. of C.

GRAHAM, D. ROBERT (BOB GRAHAM), senator, former governor; b. Coral Gables, Flor., Nov. 9, 1936; m. Adele Khoury; children: Gwendolyn Patricia, Glynn Adele, Arva Suzanne, Kendall Elizabeth. BA, U. Fla., 1959; LLB, Harvard U., 1962. Atty.; cattle and dairy farmer; real estate developer; mem. Fla. Ho. of Reps., 1966-70, Fla. Senate, 1970-78; gov. State of Fla., Tallahassee, 1978-86; U.S. senator from Fla. Washington, 1986—; chmn. Edn. Commn. of the States, 1980-81, Caribbean/Central Am. Action, 1980-81, U.S. intergovtl. adv. council on edn.; mem. So. Growth Policies Bd., chmn., 1982-83; chmn. So. Govs.' Assn.; chmn. com. trade and fgn. affairs Nat. Govs.' Assn.; energy & natural resources, environ. & pub. works com., fin. com., VA affairs/intelligence com., senate Dem. steering & coord. com.; ranking mem. long-term growth, debt and deficit reduction com., com. on fin., 1997—; mem. com. environment and pub. works, ranking mem. clean air, wetlands, pvt. property and nuc. safety com., 1995—; mem. com. energy and natural resources, ranking mem. energy rsch., devel., prodn. and regulation subcom., 1997—. Active 4-H Youth Found., Nat. Commn. on Reform Secondary Edn., Nat. Found. Improvement Edn., Nat. Com. for Citizens in Edn., Sr. Centers of Dade County, Fla.; chmn. So. Regional Edn. Bd., 1979-81. Named one of 5 Most Outstanding Young Men in Fla. Fla. Jaycees, 1971; recipient Allen Morris award for outstanding 1st term mem. senate, 1972, Allen Morris award for most valuable mem. senate, 1973, Allen Morris award for 2d most effective senator, 1976. Mem. Fla. Bar Assn. Democrat. Mem. United Ch. of Christ. Office: US Senate 524 Hart Senate Bldg Washington DC 20510*

GRAHAM, DAVID BOLDEN, food products executive; b. Miami Beach, Fla., Feb. 10, 1927; s. Robert Cabel and Bertha Eugenia (Hack) G.; m. Stuart Hill Smith, Sept. 1, 1956; children: Bird, Ellen, Darnall, Lamar, Lyle, Gerard, Barbara, David Bolden. Student, Colegio de san Bartolome, Bogota, Colombia, 1946; BS, Georgetown U., 1949; postgrad., Harvard Bus. Sch., 1950. Chmn. Graham Farms, Inc., Washington, Ind., 1950-99, Graham Cheese Corp., Washington, 1950—; sec. Bal Harbour Square, Fla., 1956-57, Graham Bros., Inc., Washington, 1950-72; dir. German Am. Bancorp. Contbr. articles on agr., transp., early fur traders to various publs. Past pres. Washington Planning Commn., Regional Planning Commn.; past bd. dirs. Hist. Landmarks Found., Ind.; mem. revolving fund com., mem. rural preservation com.; past mem. Ind. Agrl. Adv. Coun.; past mem. adv. coun. Bur. Water and Mineral Resources; past mem. Natural Resources Commn.; dir. Ind. Regional Hwy. Coalition; v.p. I-69 Mid-Continent Hwy. Coalition; past pres. Nat. Turkey Fedn.; mem. Olympic Yachting Staff, 1996; active Coast Guard Aux., Lic. Master Great Lakes or Inland Waters, FCC Marine Radio Lic. Lt. col. USAF Res., 1949-77. Mem. Columbia Club (Indpls.), Rotary (past pres., Paul Harris fellow), Atlantic Cruising Club, Inland Yacht Club, Elks. Republican. Roman Catholic. Home and Office: Graham Farms PO Box 391 Washington IN 47501-0391

GRAHAM, DAVID BROWNING, lawyer; b. Wildwood, N.J., Dec. 20, 1942; s. William Browning and Mary Graham; m. Linda Lea Beasley, Feb. 20, 1971; children: Owen, Mary. BS, La. State U., 1966, JD, 1969. Bar: La. 1969, U.S. Ct. Appeals (D.C. cir.) 1972, Ill. 1980, U.S. Dist. Ct. Ill. 1980, U.S. Supreme Ct. 1980. Atty. U.S. EPA, Washington, 1972-73; corp. counsel Nat. Rural Elec. Coop. Assn., Washington, 1973-77; dir. office hearing and appeals U.S. Dept. Interior, Arlington, Va., 1977-79; dep. gen. counsel Velsicol Chem. Corp., Chgo., 1979-84; ptnr. Freedman, Levy, Kroll & Simonds, Washington, 1984-89, Kaye, Scholer, Fierman, Hays & Handler, Washington, 1989-92, Howrey & Simon, Washington, 1992-98, Baker & Hostetler, Cleve., 1998—; mem. bd. advisors Toxics Law Reporter, Washington, 1987—, Chem. Waste Litigation Reporter, Washington, 1986—. Co-author: Environmental Justice and Underlying Societal Problems, 1997; contbr. articles to profl. jours. Mem. ABA (officer sect. natural resources, energy & environ. law), D.C. Bar Assn. Presbyterian. Avocations: running, skiing. Office: Baker & Hostetler 1900 E 9th St 3200 National City Ctr Cleveland OH 44114-3485*

GRAHAM, DAVID F., lawyer; b. Chgo., Sept. 14, 1953. BA with high honors, Haverford Coll., 1975; JD, U. Chgo., 1978. Bar: Ill. 1978. Law clk. to Hon. Charles Levin Mich. Supreme Ct., 1978-79.; Bigelow teaching fellow, lectr. on law U. Chgo., 1979-80; ptnr. Sidley & Austin, Chgo. Office: Sidley & Austin 1 First Natl Plz Chicago IL 60603-2003*

GRAHAM, DAVID GREGORY, preventive medicine physician, psychiatrist; b. Nov. 17, 1949; s. Thomas and Catherine G.; m. Katherine A. Graham; children: Brigitte, John. BA magna cum laude, Walsh U., 1971; MD, U. Puerto Rico, 1980; MPH, Columbia U., 1985. Diplomate Am. Bd. Preventive Medicine, Am. Bd. Clin. Psychiatry. Intern, then resident in psychiatry SUNY, Stony Brook, 1980-84, resident in preventive medicine, 1984-86, asst. prof. preventive medicine, 1985—; attending physician VA Med. Ctr., Northport, N.Y., 1985—; chief, Bur. Preventive Svcs. Suffolk County (N.Y.) Dept. Health Svcs., 1986—. Author: Medieval Minds, 1985, Profiles in Protest, 1987, Statistics, 1987, Mental Status Manual, 1989. Fellow Am. Coll. Preventive Medicine; mem. APHA, Am. Psychiatric Assn., Am. Assn. Pub. Health Physicians, Alumni Assn. Columbia U. Avocations: gardening, antiques, tennis, reading, outdoor recreation. Office: PO Box 5711 Hauppauge NY 11788-0152

GRAHAM, DAVID RICHARD, orthopedic surgeon; b. Detroit, May 15, 1940; s. Lewis J. and Elberta Y. (Frees) G.; m. Dorothy T. Young, June 11, 1966; children: Rebecca, Jeffrey. BA cum laude, Harvard U., 1962; MD, U. Rochester, 1966. Diplomate Am. Bd. Orthop. Surgery. Intern Highland Hosp., Rochester, N.Y., 1966-67, resident in surgery, 1967-68; resident in orthopaedic surgery Henry Ford Hosp., Detroit, 1970-72; orthopaedic surgeon Elmira (N.Y.) Orthopaedic Assocs., P.C., 1972-96; pres. Elmira (N.Y.) Orthop. Assocs., P.C., 1992—; pres. Arnot Ogden Med. Staff, Elmira, 1990; clin. assoc. Sch. Medicine & Dentistry U. Rochester, 1992—. Lt. cmmdr. U.S. Navy, 1968-70. Fellow Am. Coll. Surgeons, Am. Acad. Orthop. Surgeons; mem. AMA, Med. Soc. State N.Y., Ea. Orthop. Assn., Am. Coll. Sports Medicine, Chemung County Med. Soc. (pres. 1993-94), Elmira Torch Club (pres. 1990). Republican. Presbyterian. Home: 690 W Clinton St Elmira NY 14905-2226 Office: Elmira Orthop Assocs 722 W Water St Ste 1 Elmira NY 14905-2488

GRAHAM, DAVID YATES, gastroenterologist; b. Balboa, Panama, Dec. 24, 1940; came to U.S., 1941; s. Harry Edward and Helen Graham; m. Janet Susan Butel, Mar. 31, 1967; children: Kathleen, David. BS, U. Notre Dame, 1963; MD with honors, Baylor U., 1966. Diplomate Am. Bd. Internal Medicine, Am. Bd. Gastroenterology. Intern Ban Taub Gen. Hosp., VA Hosp., Houston, 1966-67; resident internal medicine Baylor Affiliated Hosps., Houston, 1969-71, fellow gastroenterology, 1972-73; from asst. prof. to prof. medicine Baylor Coll. Medicine, Houston, 1973—, chief gastroenterology sect. VA Med. Ctr., 1976—, from assoc. prof. to prof. virology, 1981-89, prof. molecular virology, 1989—; chief gastroenterology sect. Meth. Hosp., Houston, 1988—; dir. gastroenterology fellowship program Ben Taub Gen. Hosp., Houston, 1975-80, 88—; chief div. digestive disease dept. medicine Baylor Coll. Medicine, Houston, 1988—; planning com. 10th World Congresses of Gastroenterology, 1991-94; advisor to Japanese Rsch. Soc. for Helicobacter pyloria Related Gastroduodenal Diseases, 1995; editor-in-chief of jour. Helicobacter. Contbr. 60 chpts. in 28 books, numerous articles to profl. jours. With U.S. Army, 1967-69. Recipient Joseph B. Kirsner award Am. Gastroenterology Assn., 1994, Michael E. DeBakey, M.D. award for Excellence in Rsch., 1994, Janssen award for Special Achievement in Gastroenterology, 1995. Fellow Am. Coll. Physicians, Am. Coll. Gastroenterology (Henry Baker Lecture award 1983, pres. 1990-91), Infectious Diseases Soc. Am.; mem. Am. Gastroent. Assn., Am. Soc. Gastrointestinal Endoscopy, Tex. Soc. for Gastrointestinal Endoscopy, Houston Gastroent. Soc., Gastrointestinal Rsch. Group, Alpha Omega Alpha. Office: Vet Affairs Med Ctr 2002 Holcombe Blvd Houston TX 77030-4211 also: Baylor Coll of Medicine Dept of Medicine One Baylor Plaza Houston TX 77030-3498

GRAHAM, DENIS DAVID, marriage and family therapist, educational consultant; b. Santa Rosa, Calif., Oct. 21, 1941; s. Elbert Eldon and Mildred Bethana (Dyson) G.; m. Margaret Katherine Coughlan, Aug. 31, 1968; children: Kathleen Ann, Todd Cameron (dec.). BS in Edn., U. Nev., 1964, MEd, 1973, MA, 1982. Cert. for ednl. pers.; lic. marriage and family therapist, Nev.; nat. cert. counselor. Tchr. vocat. bus. edn. Earl Wooster H.S., Reno, 1964-66, chmn. dept. bus. edn., 1966-67; stare supr. bus. and office edn. Nev. Dept. Edn., Carson City, 1967-70, adminstr. vocat. edn. field svcs., 1970-74, asst. dir., 1974-78, vocat. edn. cons., 1978-85; edn. curriculum specialist Washoe County Sch. Dist., Reno, 1985-89, curriculum coord., 1989-94, ret., 1994; pres. Midpoint Inc., 1995—; marriage and family counselor Severance & Assocs., Carson City, 1983-85, Mountain Psychiat. Assocs., 1985-87; mem. tng. and youth employment coun. S.W. Regional Lab. for Ednl. R&D, Los Alamitos, Calif., 1982, mem. career edn. coun., 1980-81. Editor Coun. of Chief State Sch. Officers' Report: Staffing the Nation's Schools: A National Emergency, 1984; contbr. articles to profl. jours. Bd. dirs. U. Nev.-Reno Campus Christian Assn., 1988-90, 97; mem. adv. com. Truckee Meadows C.C., Reno, 1988-94; mem. Gov.'s Crime Prevention Com., Carson City, 1979-83, Atty. Gen.'s Anti-Shoplifting Com., Carson City, 1974-78, Gov.'s Devel. Disabilities Planning Coun., Carson City, 1977-79; bd. dirs. Jr. Achievement No. Nev., 1989-92, sec., mem. exec. com., 1990-91; bd. dirs. Friends of the Coll. of Edn., U. Nev., Reno, 1995—. Recipient award for svc. Bus. Edn. Assn. No. Nev., 1973, Svc. award YMCA, 1962, 63, Helping Hand award Procter R. Hug H.S., 1993-94. Mem. ACA, Am. Vocat. Assn., Nat. Assn. Vocat. Edn. Spl. Needs Pers. (Outstanding Svc. award Region V 1982), Am. Assn. Marriage and Family Therapy, Nev. Vocat. Assn. (Outstanding Svc. award 1991, Bill Trabert Meml. award Excellence in Occup. Edn. 1994), Internat. Assn. Marriage and Family Counselors, U. Nev. Reno Alumni Assn. (exec. com. 1971-75), Phi Delta Kappa, Phi Kappa Phi. Democrat. Methodist. Home: 3056 Bramble Dr Reno NV 89509-6901 Office: PO Box 33034 Reno NV 89533-3034

GRAHAM, DIANE E., newspaper editor; b. Gary, Ind., June 29, 1953; d. William M. and Mary Jane (Shreve) G.; m. Daniel Kevin Miller, Oct. 18, 1986. Bachelor's degree, Drake U., 1974. Reporter Des Moines Tribune, 1974-78; reporter Des Moines Register, 1978-84, bus. editor, 1984-86, dep. mng. editor, 1986-95, mng. editor, 1995—; pres. Iowa Freedom of Info. Coun., Des Moines, 1992-93; chair adv. bd. Drake U. Sch. Journalism, Des Moines, 1995—. Davenport fellow for bus./econ. reporting U. Mo., 1983. Avocations: pipe-organ playing, gardening. Office: Des Moines Register 715 Locust St Des Moines IA 50309-3767*

GRAHAM, DONALD EDWARD, publisher; b. Balt., Apr. 22, 1945; s. Philip L. and Katharine (Meyer) G.; m. Mary L. Wissler, Jan. 7, 1967. B.A., Harvard U., 1966. Formerly with Newsweek mag.; with The Washington Post, 1971—, asst. mng. editor sports, 1974-75, asst. gen. mgr., 1975-76, exec. v.p., gen. mgr., 1976-79, pub., 1979—; pres., CEO The Washington Post Co., 1991-93, CEO, 1991—, chmn., CEO, 1993—; dir. Washington Post Co. Trustee Fed. City Council, 1976. Served with U.S. Army, 1966-68. Mem. Am. Antiquarian Soc. Office: Washington Post 1150 15th St NW Washington DC 20071-0002*

GRAHAM, DONALD LYNN, federal judge; b. Salisbury, N.C., Dec. 15, 1948; s. Ernest Jethro and Mildred (Donald) G.; m. Brenda Joyce Savage, Sept. 27, 1969; 1 child, Sherrian Lynne. BA magna cum laude, W.Va. State Coll., 1971; JD, Ohio State U., 1974. Bar: Ohio 1974, U.S. Ct. Mil. Appeals, 1974, Fla. 1980, U.S. Dist. Ct. (so. dist.) Fla. 1980, Supreme Ct. 1980, U.S. Ct. Appeals (5th and 11th cirs.) 1981. Asst. U.S. atty. U.S. Dist. Ct. (so. dist.) Fla., Miami, 1979-84; ptnr. Raskin & Graham, Miami, 1984-91; judge U.S. Dist. Ct. (so. dist.) Fla., 1991—; instr. U. Md., Hanau, Fed. Republic Germany, 1977-78, Embry Riddle U., Homestead, Fla., 1978-79. Served to Maj., asst. staff judge adv. U.S. Army, 1974-79. Recipient Arthur S. Fleming award Washington Jaycees, 1982, Superior Performance award U.S. Dept. Justice; named One of Outstanding Young Men of Am., 1984. Mem. Assn. Trial Lawyers Am., Nat. Bar Assn., Fed. Bar Assn. (so. Fla. pres. 1984-85, treas. 1982-83), Fla. Bar Assn., N.Y. Bar Assn., Ohio Bar Assn., NAACP, Alpha Phi Alpha. Democrat. Baptist. Avocation: fishing, reading. Office: US Courthouse 99 NE 4th St Rm 1067 Miami FL 33132-2138*

GRAHAM, DOUGLAS JOHN, museum curator, banker, artist, poet; b. Dunfermline, Scotland, July 6, 1934; came to U.S., 1959, naturalized, 1965; s. Hugh Merton and Ellen Charlotte (Baroness Podmaniczky) G.; children: Robert, Christopher, Anabel, Isis. MBA, N.Y. Inst. Fin., 1961. Ptnr. Mitchell, Hutchins & Co., N.Y.C., William D. Witter Inc., N.Y.C., 1959-72; founder, chmn. bd. trustees The Turner Mus., Denver, 1973—; pres. Internat. Bank Holdings Ltd., 1979-95; bd. dirs. Turner Soc. London, patron H.R.H. The Prince of Wales, 1978—. Author: Turner's Cosmic Optimism, 1990, Turner's Angels, 1991, Turner's Rainbows, 1992, Turner's Children-So Much Love, 1993, Turner's Powerful Allegories, 1994. Life mem. St. Andrew's Soc. Colo. Served with M.I., Brit. Army, 1952-59. Office: The Turner Mus 5747 Summerside Ln Sarasota FL 34231-8370 *Personal philosophy: We are on this planet to do the will of God...during our journey here we come to realize what the ultimate truth is...we are all brothers and sisters...the children of a loving Father of limitless resources.*

GRAHAM, FRANCES KEESLER (MRS. DAVID TREDWAY GRAHAM), psychologist, educator; b. Canastota, N.Y., Aug. 1, 1918; d. Clyde C. and Norma (Van Surdam) Keesler; m. David Tredway Graham, June 14, 1941; children: Norma, Andrew, Mary. BA, Pa. State U., 1938; PhD, Yale U., 1942; DSc (hon.), U. Wis., 1996. Acting dir. St. Louis Psychiat. Clinic, 1942-44; instr. Barnard Coll., 1948-51; research assoc. Sch. Medicine, Washington U., St. Louis, 1942-48, 53-57, U. Wis., Madison, 1957-64; asso. prof. pediatrics and psychology U. Wis., 1964-68, prof., 1968-86, Hilldale research prof., 1980-86; prof. U. Del., Newark, 1986-89, prof. emerita, 1989—; Disting. faculty lectr., U. Del., Newark, 1989; cons. Nat. Inst. Neurol. Diseases and Blindness perinatal research br.; mem. exptl. psychology research review com. NIMH, 1970-74, NRC, 1971-74; mem. bd. sci. counselors NIMH, 1977-81, chmn., 1979-81; mem. Pres.'s Commn. for Study of Ethical Problems in Medicine and Biomed. and Behavioral Research, 1980-82. Mem. editorial bd. Jour. Exptl. Child Psychology, 1964-67, Child Devel., 1966-68, Jour. Exptl. Psychology, 1968-73, Psychophysiology, 1968-73; contbr. articles to profl. jours. Recipient Rsch. Scientist award NIMH, 1964-89, Disting. Alumna award Pa. State U., 1983, Wilbur L. Cross medal Yale U., 1992, Gold medal Am. Psychol. Found., 1995. Fellow AAAS (chmn. sect. psychology 1979, mem. nominations com. 1992-95), APA (coun. 1975-77, pres. div. physiol. and comparative psychology 1978-79, G. Stanley Hall award 1982, Disting. Scientist award 1990); mem. NAS, Am. Psychol. Soc. (William James fellow 1990), Soc. Rsch. Child Devel. (council 1965-71, pres. 1975-77, Disting. Sci. Contbns. award 1991), Soc. Psychophysiol. Rsch. (dir. 1968-71, 72-75, pres. 1973-74, Disting. Contbns. award 1981), Soc. Exptl. Psychologists, Soc. Neurosci., Fedn. Behavioral Psychol. and Cognitive Scis. (exec. com. 1991-94), Psychonomic Soc., Acoustical Soc. Am., Internat. Soc. Devel. Psychobiology, Phi Beta Kappa, Sigma Xi. Home: 311 Dove Dr Newark DE 19713-1211

GRAHAM, GEORGE ADAMS, political scientist, emeritus educator; b. Cambridge, N.Y., Dec. 23, 1904; s. Andrew Allen and Anna Katherine (Adams) G.; m. Rosanna Grace Webster, Aug. 20, 1930 (dec. Mar. 1985); children: Andrew Allen, Lora Katherine Graham Lunt, Mary Graham Jenne; m. Elisabeth Childs Rowse, June 25, 1986. A.B., Monmouth Coll., 1926, LL.D., 1959; A.M., U. Ill., 1927, Ph.D., 1930; LL.D., Nova U., 1985. Instr. Monmouth Coll., 1927-28; asst. U. Ill., 1929-30; faculty Princeton, 1930-58, instr., 1930-31, asst. prof., 1931-39, asso. prof., 1939-45, prof., 1945-58, chmn. dept. politics, 1946-49, 52-55; dir. govtl. studies Brookings Inst., 1958-67; exec. dir. Nat. Acad. Pub. Adminstrn., 1967-72, sr. social scientist, 1972-73; prof. pub. adminstrn. Nova U., Ft. Lauderdale, Fla., 1974-85; prof. emeritus Nova U., 1985—; mem. staff Detroit Bur. Govt. Research, 1929-30; with U.S. Bur. Budget, 1942-46, as adminstrn. cons., 1942-43, chief war supply sect., 1943-45; sec. Com. on Records War Adminstrn., 1944-45; chief Govt. Orgn. Br. and asst. chief Div. Adminstrv. mgmt., 1945; cons., 1945-46; chmn. com. on Indian Affairs, Hoover Commn. on Orgn. Exec. Br. Govt., 1948, staff dir., task force on personnel and civil service, 1953-54; cons. Senate subcom. Ethics in Govt., 1951; dir. pub. affairs program Ford Found., 1956-57. Author: books including Education for Public Administration, 1941, (with Henry Reining) Regulatory Administration, 1943; Morality in American Politics, 1952, America's Capacity to Govern, 1960. Mem. Nat. Acad. Pub. Adminstrn., Theta Chi. Presbyterian. Club: Cosmos. Home: 120 Kenan St Chapel Hill NC 27516-2528

GRAHAM, GEORGE GORDON, physician; b. Hackensack, N.J., Oct. 4, 1923; s. Charles Stewart and Angelica (Gomez de la Torre) G.; m. Simone H. Custer, Mar. 3, 1949; children—Marianne, Alexander, Monica, Carol. A.B., U. Pa., 1941, M.D., 1945. Diplomate: Am. Bd. Pediatrics, Am. Bd. Nutrition. Intern, resident Brit. Am. Hosp., Lima, Peru, 1946-48; staff pediatrics Brit. Am. Hosp., 1948-50, 52-55, dir. research, 1960-71; dir. research Instituto de Investigacion Nutricional, Lima, Peru, 1971-83, pres., 1987-89; rsch. U. Pa. Hosp., 1951; resident pediatrics Balt. City Hosp., 1955-56, asso. chief pediatrician, 1965-68; assoc. prof. pediatrics Johns Hopkins U., 1965-78, prof., 1978—, prof. human nutrition, 1968-91, prof. emeritus, 1992—, dir. nutrition program, 1976-85; staff pediatrician Cleve. Clinic, 1957-59; mem. com. amino acids Food and Nutrition Bd. of NRC, 1966-71, com. internat. nutrition programs, 1978-79; mem. Food and Nutrition Bd., 1981-84; cons. nutrition AID, GAO, NIH; mem. nutrition study sect. NIH, USPHS, 1971-75, chmn., 1973-75, mem. cancer control intervention program rev. com., 1985-86; mem. Pres.'s Commn. on Food Assistance, 1983-84. Mem. editorial bd. Jour. Nutrition, 1968-73, Am. Jour. Clin. Nutrition, 1969-74. Decorated Orden al Merito Agricola Peru; Orden Hipolito Unanue; recipient Joseph Goldberger award AMA, 1972; Borden award Am. Acad. Pediatrics, 1977. Fellow Am. Inst. Nutrition; mem. Am. Soc. Clin. Nutrition (coun. 1980-84), Soc. Pediatric Rsch., Am. Pediatric Soc. Rsch. on infantile malnutrition, its long-term effects, its prevention by new protein sources. Office: Johns Hopkins U 615 N Wolfe St Baltimore MD 21205-2103

GRAHAM, GEORGE J., JR., political scientist, educator; b. Dayton, Ohio, Nov. 12, 1938; s. George J. and Mary Elizabeth (McBride) G.; m. Scarlett Gower, Sept. 10, 1966 (div. 1991); 1 child, Carmen Michelle. BA in History, Wabash Coll., 1960; PhD, Ind. U., 1965. Instr. Vanderbilt U., Nashville, 1963-64, asst. prof., 1965-71, assoc. prof., 1971-77, prof. polit. sci., 1977—, assoc. dean, 1986-88, 97—, chair dept. polit. sci., 1988-92; series editor Chatham (N.J.) House Pub., 1978—, Greenwood/Praeger Presses, N.Y., 1989—; Fulbright John Marshall chair Budapest U. of Econ. Studies, 1995-96. Author: Methodological Foundations, 1971; author, editor: Post-Behavioral Era, 1972, Founding Principles, 1977; contbr. articles to profl. jours. Chair Mt. Juliet (Tenn.) Sewer Commn., 1985-86; sec. Zoning Commn., Mt. Juliet, 1988-89. Guggenheim fellow, 1973-74, NEH fellow New Haven Nat. Humanities Inst., 1976-77; Fulbright John Marshall chair in Budapest, Hungary, 1995-96. Mem. Am. Polit. Sci. Assn. (founder Found. Polit. Theory sect. 1975—), So. Polit. Sci. Assn. (mem. coun. 1987-90), Midwest Polit. Sci. Assn., Internat. Polit. Sci. Assn., Com. Conceptual Analysis (chair). Avocations: painting, golf, guitar, travel. Office: Vanderbilt U PO Box 1814-B Nashville TN 37235-1814

GRAHAM, GLORIA FLIPPIN, dermatologist; b. Durham, N.C., Mar. 3, 1935; d. James Meigs and Ida Mae (Boyd) F.; m. Douglas Graham (div.); 1 child, Wayne Meigs; m. James Herbert Graham, July 29, 1989. BS, Wake Forest U., 1957; MD, Bowman-Gray Sch. Medicine, 1961. Diplomate Am. Bd. Dermatology. Intern Sch. Medicine Vanderbilt U., 1961-62; resident, dermatology U. Va. Med. Ctr., Charlottesville, 1962-65; pvt. practice Columbia, S.C., 1965-66; physician, owner Wilson (N.C.) Dermatology Clinic, 1966-94; physician, pres. Grahams Dermatology Svcs., Morehead City, N.C., 1992—; cons. Carteret Gen. Hosp., Morehead City, 1986—; clin. attending prof. Bowman Gray Sch. Medicine, Winston-Salem, N.C., 1991—; adj. clin. prof. U. N.C. Sch. Medicine, Chapel Hill, 1995—. Co-exhibitor: Two Hereditary Osseocutaneous Syndromes, Acad. Dermatology, 1965 (Silver award), So. Med. Assn. Exhibit Hereditary Acrokeratotic Poikiloderma, 1970 (Third Place award); presenter in field. Named Woman of Yr., Womens Residence Coun. Wake Forest U., 1982, Practitioner of Yr. Dermatology Found., 1998. Mem. World Congress Dermatology (co-chmn. cryosurgical symposium 1997), North Am. Clin. Dermatologic Soc. (bd. dirs. 1995—), Am. Acad. Dermatology (bd. dirs. 1991-96, audit com. 1996—, ethics com. 1996—), Am. Dermatologic Assn. (elect), Women's Dermatologic Soc. (pres. 1997-98). Avocations: traveling, fishing. Office: Grahams' Dermatology Svcs PA 3604 Medical Park Ct Morehead City NC 28557 also: PO Box 2804 Atlantic Beach NC 28512

GRAHAM, HARDY MOORE, lawyer; b. Meridian, Miss., Oct. 21, 1912; s. Sanford Martin and Mary Emma (Hardy) G.; Cora Lee Poindexter, Oct. 26, 1938; children: Hardy Poindexter, Richard Newell. Student, U. So. Calif., 1932; BA, LLB, U. Miss., 1934. Bar: Miss. 1934, Tenn. 1946, U.S. Ct. Appeals (D.C. cir.) 1943, U.S. Dist. Ct. Miss. 1934, U.S. Supreme Ct. 1943, U.S. Dist. Ct. (we. dist.) Tenn. 1952. Ptnr. Graham & Graham, Meridian, 1934-43; atty. FTC, Washington, 1943-44; pvt. practice Union City, Tenn., 1946—; city judge City of Union City, 1950-58; bd. dirs., 1st v.p. Meridian Coca-Cola Bottling Co., 1964-97; ptnr. Union City Coca-Cola Bottling Co.; v.p. Coca-Cola Coin Caterers Corp. 7-Up Bottler; pres. Tenn. Soft Drink Assn., 1963-65. Mayor City of Union City, 1950-58; pres. Union City C. of C., 1948-50, bd. dirs.; chmn. March of Dimes, Obion County Tenn., 1947; mem. Union City Sch. Bd., 1958-66, vice chmn., 1958-60, chmn., 1964-66; chmn. indsl. bd. Union City, 1968-97; bd. dirs. Tenn. Mcpl. League, 1950-58, pres., 1956-57; former trustee Union U., Jackson, Tenn., 1st Bapt. Ch., Union City; pres. U. Tenn. Martin Devel. Com., 1970-72; mem. U. Tenn., Knoxville Devel. Coun., 1970-75, 82-85, bd. dirs. U. Miss. Found., 1987-93. Lt. USNR, 1944-46, ETO. Named Law Alumnus of Yr., U. Miss. Law Sch., 1984, Young Man of Yr., Union City, 1948; recipient Disting. Svc. award U. Tenn., Martin, 1989, U. Miss. Hall of Fame Disting. Alumnus award, 1989; Union City named Graham Park in his honor, 1986. Mem. ABA, Tenn. Bar Assn., Miss. Bar Assn., Union City-Obion County Bar Assn., (pres. 1948-49, past. bd. dirs.), Meridian Country Club, Union City Country Club, Rotary (pres. Union City 1963-64, Paul Harris fellow). Republican. Baptist. Avocation: international travel. Home: 630 E Main St Union City TN 38261-3515 Office: 1915 E Reelfoot Ave Union City TN 38261-6007

GRAHAM, HAROLD STEVEN, lawyer; b. Kansas City, Mo., Feb. 1, 1950; s. Martie Sydney and Elsie Helen (Bradford) G.; m. Deborah Ruth Glick, Apr. 8, 1973; children: Elizabeth, Jonathan, Joshua, Lauren. BS with distinction, U. Wis., 1972; JD, U. Chgo., 1976. Bar: Mo. 1976. Assoc. Lathrop, Koontz & Norquist, Kansas City, 1976-81; mem. Lathrop & Norquist, L.C., Kansas City, 1982-95, Lathrop & Gage L.C., Kansas City, 1996—. Active Kansas City Tomorrow Alumni Assn. Year X; bd. dirs. Hyman Brand Hebrew Acad., Kansas City, 1985—, Beth Shalom Synagogue, Kansas City, 1983-88, Jewish Community Campus, 1992-98. Mem. ABA (sect. on real property and trust law, mem. Forum on Affordable Housing), Mo. Bar Assn. (property law com.), Kansas City Met. Bar Assn. Avocations: tennis, running. Office: Lathrop & Gage LC 2345 Grand Blvd Ste 2600 Kansas City MO 64108-2617

GRAHAM, HEATHER, actress; b. Milw., Jan. 29, 1970. Motion picture actress. Films include License to Drive, 1988, Drugstore Cowboy, 1989, I Love You to Death, 1990, Guilty as Charged, 1991, Diggstown, 1992, 6 Degrees of Separation, 1993, Don't Do It, 1994, Swingers, 1996, Boogie Nights, 1997 (MTV movie award 1998), Scream 2, 1997, Kiss & Tell, 1999, Austin Powers: The Spy Who Shagged Me, 1999, Bowfinger, 1999; T.V. series include Twin Peaks, 1990, 92. Recipient ShoWest award for Female Star of Tomorrow, 1999. *

GRAHAM, HOWARD BARRETT, publishing company executive; b. Boston, Dec. 7, 1929; s. Robert M. and Belle (Brown) G.; m. Rita J. Mahony; children: Ronni M., Erica. B.A., Syracuse U., 1951. Gen. mgr. sch. supply div., sales mgr. ednl. div. Milton Bradley Co., Springfield, Mass., 1954-63; gen. mgr. jr. book div. McGraw-Hill Co., 1964-69; pres., dir. Franklin Watts Inc., N.Y.C., 1970-87; also chmn. bd. Franklin Watts Ltd.; sr. v.p. mktg/product devel., dir. Grolier, Inc., 1983-89, exec. v.p., 1988-89; pres. Grolier Internat., 1986-89; chmn., chief exec. officer Graham Internat. Pub. and Rsch., Inc., 1989—; ptnr. SMG Assocs., 1990; dir., v.p. The Millbrook Press, 1990-96, chmn. bd. dirs., 1997—; pres., CEO Chambers Kingfisher Graham, Publishers Inc., 1994-96; mem. adv. bd. Internat. Exec. Svc. Served with USAF, 1951-53. Mem. Mensa, Save the Children (adv. bd. mem.). Home: PO Box 77 Sagaponack NY 11962-0077 Office: 27 Main St # A Southampton NY 11968-4808

GRAHAM, HOWARD HOLMES, financial executive; b. Greensburg, Pa., Apr. 24, 1947; s. Howard B. and Dorothy (Holmes) G.; m. Roberta A. Grant, June 8, 1968 (div. Feb. 1984); m. Linda A. Cossarek, Mar. 14, 1987; children: Christina Ross, John Howard. BS, Carnegie Mellon U., 1968; MBA, U. Chgo., 1973. CPA, Ill. Various positions Zenith Electronics Corp., Glenview, Ill., 1973-81, dir. acctg., 1981-82, v.p. fin. svcs., 1982-87, v.p. fin., 1987-88; sr. v.p. fin. Wyse Tech. Inc., San Jose, Calif., 1988-90, Informix Corp., Menlo Park, Calif., 1990-96; sr. v.p. fin. and adminstrn., CFO, Siebel Sys., San Mateo, Calif., 1997—. Capt. U.S. Army, 1968-71, Vietnam. Decorated Bronze Star; recipient Elijah Watt Sells award Am. Inst. CPA's, 1982. Mem. La Rinconada Country Club, Beta Gamma Sigma. Office: Siebel Systems 1855 S Grant St San Mateo CA 94402-7016

GRAHAM, HOWARD LEE, SR., corporate executive; b. Monroe, Mich., May 26, 1942; s. Carl Lee and Myrtle Leota (Manis) G.; m. Bobbie Jo Hamilton; children: Kimber Lee, Howard Lee Jr., Jacquelyn Leota, John-Nathan Howard. Grad., Dake Bible Sch., Atlanta, 1960-62; student, Cen. Bible Coll., Springfield, Mo., 1964-67; grad., Internat. Sem., 1993, DD, 1996. Debit agt. Met. Life Ins. Co., Colorado Springs, Colo., 1963-64; agt. Met. Life Ins. Co., Allen Park, Mich., 1964-67, 68; agy. mgr. Preferred Risk Life Ins. Co., Allen Park, 1968-72; agy. owner Howard Graham Ins. Agy., Taylor, Mich., 1972-85; spl. agt., rep. Prudential Ins. Co., Cleve., 1985-89; regional mgr. Primerica Fin. Svcs., Abingdon, Va., 1995—; pres. Graham & Graham Canvas Shoppe, Inc., 1976-95, CEO, 1995—; pres. Graham Enterprises, Cleve., 1985—; CEO Graham & Graham Canvas Shoppe, Inc., 1976; nat. and regional sales leader Preferred Risk Ins. Co., Des Moines, 1969-72. Life mem. Full Gospel Bus. Men's Fellow, Detroit, 1963-85, officer, 1974-80, officer, Cleve., 1985—; active Gideons Internat., Cleve., 1963—; pres. Truth Alive, Inc., 1988—. Named Central Region Agt. of Yr., 1985; admitted to Million Dollar Round Table, 1985, Hall of Honor, 1986. Mem. Indsl. Fabrics Assn. Internat., Am. Coll., Nat. Assn. Life Underwriters, Internat. Platform Assn. Republican. Mem. Pentecostal Ch. Avocations: sports, Bible research. Home: 14009 Vintage Vw Abingdon VA 24210-7794 Office: PO Box 1805 Abingdon VA 24212-1805

GRAHAM, HUGH DAVIS, history educator; b. Little Rock, Sept. 2, 1936; s. Otis L. and Lois (Patterson) G.; m. Ann Clary, June 11, 1966 (div. 1976); children: Hugh Patterson (dec.), Holter Ford; m. Janet Gorman, Feb. 5, 1978. BA magna cum laude, Yale U., 1958; MA, Stanford U., 1961, PhD, 1964. Instr. history Foothill Coll., Los Altos, Calif., 1962-64; asst. prof. San Jose State Coll., Calif., 1964-65; tng. officer, regional dir. Peace Corps, Washington, 1965-66; vis. asst. prof. history Stanford U., 1966-67; assoc. prof. history, assoc. dir. Inst. So. History Johns Hopkins U., Balt., 1967-71, acting dir. Inst. So. History, 1969-70; assoc. prof. History, chmn. divsn. social scis. U. Md.-Baltimore County, 1971-72, prof. History, 1972-91, dean div. social scis., 1972-77, dean grad. studies and rsch., 1982-85; Holland N. McTyeire prof. history Vanderbilt U., Nashville, 1991—, chmn. dept. history, 1994-97; reporter Nashville Tennessean, 1960. Author: Crisis in Print, 1967 (Award of Merit 1968), Since 1954: Desegregation, 1972, (with Numan V. Bartley) Southern Politics and The Second Reconstruction, 1975 (V.O. Key award 1976), The Uncertain Triumph, 1984, The Civil Rights Era, 1990 (jury nominee Pulitzer prize 1991), Civil Rights and the Presidency, 1992, (with Nancy Diamond) the Rise of American Research Universities, 1997; co-editor: Violence in America, 1969, rev. edit., 1979, Southern Elections, 1978, The Carter Presidency, 1998; editor: Huey Long, 1970, Violence, 1971, American Politics and Government, 1975, Civil Rights in the United States, 1994. Co-dir. history task force Nat. Com. on Causes and Prevention of Violence, 1968-69; commr. Howard County Commn. Human Rights, Md., 1980-83. Served to 1st lt., arty. USMCR, 1958-60. Woodrow Wilson fellow, 1960-61, 63-64, Guggenheim fellow, 1970-71; recipient Merit award Am. Assn. State and Local History, 1968; V.O. Key award for best book on So. politics So. Polit. Sci. Assn., 1975; Wilson Ctr. fellow Smithsonian Instn., 1985-86; Sr. fellow NEH, 1989-90. Mem. Am. Hist. Assn., Am. Polit. Sci. Assn., So. Hist. Assn., Orgn. Am. Historians., Phi Beta Kappa. Home: 1231 Nichol Ln Nashville TN 37205-4419 Office: Vanderbilt U Dept History Nashville TN 37235

GRAHAM, JAMES A., state commissioner; b. Cleveland, N.C., Apr. 7, 1921; s. James T. and Laura G. Graham; m. to Helen Ida Kirk; children: Alice Underhill, Connie Brooks. BS, N.C. State U., 1942. Agr. tchr. Iredell County, 1942-45; supt. Upper Mountain Rsch. Sta., 1946-52; gen. mgr. Raleigh Farmers Mkt., 1956-64; owner farm N.C.; commr. N.C. Dept. Agr., Raleigh, 1964—; mem. N.C. Coun. State. Former trustee AT&T Univ., Greensboro, N.C.,past. pres.,Southern United Trade Assn., Past pres., Former bd. mem. Raleigh C. of C., bd. of Adv., Camnpbell U. Recipient Gov. award N.C. Wildlife Fedn., 1983, Spl. Svc. award Park Prodrs. Assn., 1983, Disting. Svc. award Poultry Fedn., 1983, Disting. Svc. award N.C. Crop Improvement Assn., and numerous others; named Man of Yr. Progressive Farmers Mag., 1970. Mem. Nat. Assn. Market Mgrs., N.C. Hereford Breeders Assn., Ashe County Wildlife Club (sec./treas., former pres.), Kiwanis (former pres.), Shriners, Raleigh C. of C., United Cerebral Palsy. Baptist. Office: NC Agr Dept PO Box 27647 2 W Edenton St Raleigh NC 27611

GRAHAM, JAMES E., federal judge; b. 1949. JD, Mercer U., 1977. Office: US Courthouse 801 Gloucester St Brunswick GA 31520-7075

GRAHAM, JAMES HERBERT, dermatologist; b. Calexico, Calif., Apr. 25, 1921; s. August K. and Esther (Choudoin) G.; m. Anna Kathryn Luiken, June 30, 1950 (dec. May 1987); children: James Herbert, John A., Angela Joann; m. Gloria Boyd Flippin, July 29, 1989. Student, Brawley Jr. Coll., 1941-42; AB, Emory U., 1945; MD, Med. Coll. Ala., 1949. Diplomate: Am. Bd. Dermatology (dir. 1977-87, v.p. 1985-86, pres. 1986-87, Disting. Service medal 1987); diplomate in dermatopathology Am. Bd. Dermatology and Am. Bd. Pathology. Intern Jefferson-Hillman Hosp., Birmingham, Ala., 1949-50; resident in dermatology VA Center and UCLA Med. Center, 1953-56; clin. asst. instr. in medicine UCLA, 1954-56; Osborne fellow and NRC fellow in dermal pathology Armed Forces Inst. Pathology, Washington, 1956-58; vis. scientist Armed Forces Inst. Pathology, 1958-69, chmn. dept. dermatopathology, 1980-88; registrar Registry of Dermatopathology, Armed Forces Inst. Pathology, 1980-88, also program dir. dermatopathology, 1979-88; program dir. dermatopathology Walter Reed Army Med. Center, Washington, 1979-88; asst. prof. dermatology and pathology Temple U., 1958-61, assoc. prof., 1961-65, prof. dermatology, 1965-69, assoc. prof. pathology, 1965-67, prof. pathology, 1967-69; prof. medicine, chief div. dermatology, prof. pathology, dir. sect. dermal pathology and histochemistry U. Calif., Irvine, 1969-78; chief dermatology U. Calif. Med. Ctr., Irvine, 1977-78; prof. emeritus Coll. Medicine, U. Calif., 1978—; head sect. dermatology Orange County (Calif.) Med. Center, 1969-73; cons. dermatology VA Hosp., Long Beach, Calif., 1969-73; chief dermatology sect. VA Hosp., 1973-78, acting chief med. service, 1976; cons. dermatology, dermal pathology Regional Naval Med. Center, San Diego, 1969-82, Long Beach, 1969-78, Camp Pendleton, Calif., 1972-78; cons. dermatology, dermal pathology Meml. Hosp. Med. Center, Long Beach, 1972-86, Fairview State Hosp., Costa Mesa, Calif., 1969-78; cons. for career devel. for rev. clin. investigator applications VA Central Office, Washington, 1973-78; Disting. Eminent physician VA physician and dentist-in-residence program, 1980-88; mem. organizational com. Am. Registry Pathology, Armed Forces Inst. Pathology, Washington, 1976-77; mem. exec. com. Am. Registry Pathology, Armed Forces Inst. Pathology, 1977-78; prof. dermatology, clin. prof. pathology Uniformed Services U. of Health Scis., Bethesda, Md., 1979-88, prof. emeritus, 1989—;

program dir. dermatopathology Naval Hosp. and Scripps Clin. and Rsch. Found., San Diego, 1991-94; head divsn. dermatopathology, dept. pathology Scripps Clinic and Rsch. Found., LaJolla, Calif., 1988-94, ret., 1994. Sr. author: Dermal Pathology, 1972; contbr. articles to profl. publs. Served with M.C. USNR, 1949-53. Named Disting. Alumnus, Med. Coll. Ala., 1994. Mem. AMA (accreditation coun. for grad. med. edn., 1977-87, residency rev. com. for dermatology 1977-87, chmn. 1984-87, cert. of merit 1960), Soc. Investigative Dermatology (life), U.S. and Can. Acad. Pathology (life), Am. Soc. Investigative Pathology (life, emeritus mem. 1995), Am. Dermatol. Assn. (essay award 1958, v.p. 1986-87), Am. Soc. Dermatopathology (pres. 1975-76, Founder's award 1990, rep. to bd. of mem. Am. Registry Pathology 1988-92), Dermatopathology Club (pres. 1980-81), Assn. Mil. Dermatologists (life), Am. Acad. Dermatology (life, dir. 1974-77, 82, v.p. 1980-81, rep. to bd. mems. Am. Registry Pathology 1977-78), N.Am. Clin. Dermatologic Soc. (hon.), 1973, Pa. Acad. Dermatology, Pacific Dermatol. Assn. (dir. 1972-75, hon. mem. 1981), Dermatology Found. (Leader's Soc. and Annenberg Circle), Washington Dermatol. Soc. (spl. hon.), Phila. Dermatol. Soc. (pres. 1967-68, hon mem. 1994), San Diego Dermatol. Soc., Cutaneous Therapy Soc., Alpha Omega Alpha, Cosmos Club. *I have achieved far more than I dreamed possible but it could only happen in America. Being generally optimistic, enthusiastic and persistent has resulted in my serving society in a positive way.*

GRAHAM, JAMES LOWELL, federal judge; b. 1939. BA, JD summa cum laude, Ohio State U., 1962. Pvt. practice law Crabbe, Brown, Jones, Potts & Schmidt, Columbus, Ohio, 1962-69, Graham, Dutro, Nemeth, and predecessors, Columbus, 1969-86; judge U.S. Dist. Ct. (so. dist.) Ohio, Columbus, 1986—; faculty Ohio Jud. Coll., Ohio Legal Inst. Chmn. Ohio Bar Examiners, 1974, Devel. Commn. City of Columbus, 1976-77; mem. legal svcs. Salvation Army of columbus, 1967-77, legal sect. United Way Campaign, 1976-80. Fellow Am. Coll. Trial Lawyers; mem. Capital U. Coll. of Law Assn. (dean's coun.), Ohio State U. A;umni Assn. Office: US Dist Ct 169 US Courthouse 85 Marconi Blvd Columbus OH 43215-2823

GRAHAM, JAMES MILLER, physiology researcher; b. St. Louis, Oct. 16, 1945; s. Alvin Rudd and Edrie (Miller) G.; m. Linda Kay Edwards, May 3, 1969; children: Michael Edwards, Melissa Edwards. MA, U. Mich., 1968, PhD, 1979. Postdoctoral scholar environ. engrng. U. Mich., Ann Arbor, 1979-80; lectr. zoology U. Wis., Madison, 1981-82, rsch. assoc. physiology, 1983-88, lectr. botany, 1987-88, physiology researcher, 1988—; reviewer Phycological Soc. Am., Jour. Great Lakes Rsch., Microbial Ecology. Contbr. chpt. to Periphyton of Freshwater Ecosystems, 1983; contbr. articles to profl. jours. With U.S. Army, 1969-72. Mem. AAAS, Am. Soc. Limnology and Oceanography, Phycological Soc. Am., Phi Beta Kappa, Sigma Xi. Office: U Wis Dept Physiology 1300 University Ave Madison WI 53706-1510

GRAHAM, JAN, state attorney general; b. Salt Lake City. BS in Psychology, Clark U., Worcester, Mass., 1973; MS in Psychology, U. Utah, 1977, JD, 1980. Bar: Utah. Ptnr. Jones, Waldo, Holbrook & McDonough, Salt Lake City, 1979-89; soliciter gen. Utah Atty. Gen.'s Office, Salt Lake City, 1989-93; atty. gen. State of Utah, 1993—; adj. prof. law U. Utah Law Sch.; bar commr. Utah State Bar, 1991; master of bench Utah Inns Ct. VII; mem. Utah Commn. on Justice in 21st Century; bd. dirs. Jones, Waldo, Holbrook & McDonough; bd. trustees Coll. Law U. Utah (pres.). Fin. devel. chair YWCA; chair Ctrl. Bus. Improvement Dist.; mem. Salt Lake City Olympic Bid Com. 1988 Games. Named Woman Lawyer Yr. Utah, 1987. Mem. Am. Arbitration Assn. (nat. panel arbitrators), Women Lawyers Utah (co-founder, mem. exec. com.). Office: Office of Attorney General 236 State Capitol Building Salt Lake City UT 84114-1202*

GRAHAM, JESSE JAPHET, II, lawyer; b. Kingston, N.Y., May 16, 1950; s. Kelsey D. and Florence M. (Smith) G.; m. Margaret Mary Breuer, Aug. 18, 1973; children: Courtney E., Michael B., Peter A. BA, Rider Coll., 1972; JD, Bklyn. Law Sch., 1975; LLM, George Washington U., 1979. Bar: N.Y. 1976, D.C. 1978, U.S. Ct. Mil. Appeals 1978, U.S. Customs Ct. 1979, U.S. Ct. Claims 1979, U.S. Ct. Customs and Patent Appeals 1979, U.S. Tax Ct. 1979, U.S. Supreme Ct. 1979. Assoc. Campbell, Currior & C'Connor, Eastcester, N.Y., 1979-80; ptnr. Bower & Gardner, N.Y.C., 1980-94, Parker Chapin Flattau & Klimpl LLP, N.Y.C., 1994—; mem. faculty various seminars in field; mem. faculty Practising Law Inst., N.Y.C., 1986-95. Contbg. author: Hospital Liability, 1980-94; guest commentator Court TV, NewsTalk TV and radio stas., including CNN, FOX 5, and FOX News, 1994—. Lt. USNR, Judge Advs. Gen. Corps., 1976-79. Home: 4 Pine Glen Dr Blauvelt NY 10913-1150 Office: Parker Chapin et al Ste 1700 1211 Avenue Of The Americas New York NY 10036-8735*

GRAHAM, JEWEL FREEMAN, social worker, lawyer, educator; b. Springfield, Ohio, May 3, 1925; d. Robert Lee and Lula Belle Freeman; m. Paul N. Graham, Aug. 8, 1953; children: Robert, Nathan. BA, Fisk U., 1946; student, Howard U., 1946-47; MS in Social Svc. Adminstrn., Case Western Res. U., 1953; JD, U. Dayton, 1979; LHD (hon.), Meadville-Lombard Theol. Sch., 1991. Bar: Ohio; cert. social worker. Assoc. dir. teenage program dept. YWCA, Grand Rapids, Mich., 1947-50; coord. met. teenage program YWCA, Detroit, 1953-56; dir. program for interracial edn. Antioch Coll., Yellow Springs, Ohio, 1964-69, from asst. prof. to prof., 1969-92, prof. emeritus, 1992—; mem. Ohio Commn. on Dispute Resolution and Conflict Mgmt., 1990-92. Mem. exec. com. World YMCA, Geneva, 1975-83, 87—, pres., 1983; bd. dirs. YWCA of the U.S.A., 1970-89, pres., 1979-85; bd. dirs. Antioch U., 1994-96. Named to Greene County Women's Hall of Fame, 1982, Ohio Women's Hall of Fame, 1988; named 1 of 10 Outstanding Women of Miami Valley, 1987; recipient Ambassador award YWCA of the U.S.A., 1993. Mem. ABA, Nat. Assn. of Social Workers (charter), Nat. Coun. of Negro Women (life), Alpha Kappa Alpha. Democrat. Unitarian Universalist. Avocations: bicycling, swimming, walking, needlework. Office: Antioch Coll Livermore 51 Yellow Springs OH 45387

GRAHAM, JOHN BORDEN, pathologist, writer, educator; b. Goldsboro, N.C., Jan. 26, 1918; s. Ernest Heap and Mary (Borden) G.; m. Ruby Barrett, Mar. 23, 1943; children: Charles Barrett, Virginia Borden, Thomas Wentworth. B.S., Davidson Coll., 1938, D.Sc. (hon.), 1984; M.D., Cornell U., 1942. Asst. Cornell U., 1943-44; medical corps U.S. Army, 1944-46; mem. faculty U. N.C., Chapel Hill, 1946—; Alumni Disting. prof. pathology U. N.C., 1966—, chmn. genetics curriculum, 1963-85, assoc. dean medicine for basic scis., 1968-70, coordinator interdisciplinary grad. programs in biology, 1968—, dir. hemostasis program, 1974-87; vis. prof. haematology St. Thomas's Hosp. Med. Sch., London, 1972; vis. prof. Teikyo U. Med. Sch., Tokyo, 1976; mem. selection com. NIH research career awards, 1959-62; genetics tng. com. USPHS, 1962-66, chmn., 1967-71; mem. genetic basis of disease com. Nat. Inst. Gen. Med. Scis., 1977-80; mem. pathology test com. Nat. Bd. Med. Examiners, 1963-67; mem. research adv. com. U. Colo. Inst. Behavioral Genetics, 1967-71; mem. Internat. Com. Haemostasis and Thrombosis, 1963-67; chmn. bd. U. N.C. Population Program, 1964-67; sec. policy bd. Carolina Population Center, 1972-78; cons. Environ. Health Center, USPHS, WHO, Bolt, Beranek & Newman, Inc.; mem. med. and sci. adv. council Nat. Hemophilia Found., 1972-76; hon. cons. in genetics Margaret Pyke Centre, London, 1972—. Author: Sand in the Gears, 1992, How It Was, 1896-1973, 1996, Coping with Old Age: An Odyssey, 1998; mem. editl. bd. N.C. Med. Jour., 1949-66, Am. Jour. Human Genetics, 1958-61, Soc. Exptl. Biology and Medicine, 1959-62, Human Genetics Abstracts, 1962-72, Haemostasis, 1975-80, Christian Scholar, 1958-60. Recipient O. Max Gardner award U. N.C., 1968, Disting. Svc. award U. N.C. Med. Sch., 1992; Markle scholar in med. sci., 1949-54. Mem. AMA, AAAS, Elisha Mitchell Sci. Soc. (pres. 1963), AAUP, Soc. Exptl. Biology and Medicine, Am. Soc. Exptl. Pathology, Assn. Univ. Pathologists, Am. Assn. Pathologists and Bacteriologists, Am. Soc. Human Genetics (sec. 1964-67, pres. 1972), Genetics Soc. Am., Internat. Soc. Hematology, Am. Inst. Biol. Sci., Royal Soc. Medicine (London), Med. Soc. N.C., Mayflower Soc., Cosmos Club, Sigma Xi. Democrat. Presbyterian. Achievements include publs. on blood clotting, inherited diseases in humans, human population dynamics, medical history; co-discoverer blood coagulant Factor X (Stuart factor). Home: 108 Glendale Dr Chapel Hill NC 27514-5910

GRAHAM, JOHN DALBY, public relations executive; b. Maryville, Mo., Aug. 24, 1937; s. Kyle T. and Irma Irene (Dalby) G.; m. Linda Mills Graham, Dec. 21, 1996; children: Katherine Elizabeth, David Landon. B.J., U. Mo., 1959. Editor Hallmark Cards, Inc., Kansas City, Mo., 1959-62; dir. pub. relations St. Louis Met. YMCA, 1962-66; chmn., chief exec. officer Fleishman-Hillard, Inc., St. Louis, 1966—; chmn. Fleishman-Hillard Europe; bd. dirs. Fleishman-Hillard/U.K. Ltd. Trustee St. Louis U.; mem. exec. bd. St. Louis Area coun. Boy Scouts Am. Capt. U.S. Army, 1959-66. Fellow Pub. Rels. Soc. Am.; mem. Internat. Pub. Rels. Assn., Nat. Investor Rels. Inst., Round Table, Arthur Page Soc., Log Cabin Club. Home: 7 Lorenzo Ln Saint Louis MO 63124-1997 Office: Fleishman Hillard Inc 200 N Broadway Ste 1800 Saint Louis MO 63102-2796*

GRAHAM, JOHN H. IV, health science association administrator. BA, Franklin and Marshall Coll., 1971. Mem. Valley Forge coun. Boy Scouts Am., 1971-79; exec. dir. Am. Diabetes Assn., Phila., 1979-83; dir. devel. divsn. Am. Diabetes Assn., N.Y.C., 1983-85; asst. exec. v.p. Am. Diabetes Assn., Alexandria, Va., 1985-88, dep. exec. v.p., 1988-90, CEO, 1990—. Mem. Am. Soc. Assn. Execs., Nat. Health Coun., Greater Washington Soc. Assn. Execs., Ind. Sector, Combined Health Appeal. Office: Am Diabetes Assn 1660 Duke St Alexandria VA 22314-3427*

GRAHAM, JOHN ROBERT, JR., financial executive; b. Chgo., Oct. 11, 1930; s. John Robert and Grace Beatrice (Strangeman) G.; m. Bettina Abigail Hoffman, Sept. 6, 1958 (div. June 1975); children: Jonathan, Karl; m. Beverly Criley, Dec. 31, 1975. BS, U.S. Mcht. Marine Acad., 1952; MBA, Harvard U., 1959. Ship officer Moore-McCormack Lines, N.Y.C., 1952-53, 55-58; asst. v.p., loan officer Hartford (Conn.) Nat. Bank, 1959-67; asst. treas. Heublein, Inc., Hartford, 1967-68, treas., 1968-74; sr. v.p. fin. and adminstrn. Sikorsky Aircraft Co., Stratford, Conn., 1974-80; v.p. fin., CFO Planning Rsch. Corp., Washington, 1980-82; v.p., CFO Uniroyal Inc., Middlebury, Conn., 1982-88, Uniroyal Holding, Inc., Waterbury, Conn., 1982-88; also bd. dirs.; v.p. fin., CFO, treas., dir. Healthware Corp., Seattle, 1989-92; bd. dirs. Uniroyal Goodrich Tire Co., Akron, Ohio, U.S. Mcht. Marine Acad. Found.; trustee CDU Holding, Inc. Liquidating Trust, N.Y.C., 1986—. Co-author: Nonwoven Textiles-An Unbiased Appraisal, 1959. Corporator Middlesex Hosp., Middletown, Conn., 1964-85; v.p., treas. Conn. Valley YMCA, Deep River, 1962-64; pres. Essex (Conn.) Bus. Assn., 1964-65; bd. dirs. U.S. Mcht. Marine Acad. Found., 1987—. Lt. (j.g.) USNR, 1953-55, PTO, Korea. Mem. Harvard Club (N.Y.C.), Masons. Avocations: sailing, skiing. Home: 82 Cascade Key Bellevue WA 98006-1030

GRAHAM, JOHN STUART, III, lawyer; b. N.Y.C., Dec. 21, 1944; s. John Stuart and Alma Agnes (Tofty) G.; m. Cynthia Jean Haslam, Aug. 20, 1988; children from previous marriage: Elizabeth Love, Nicola Stuart, BA, Washington and Lee U., 1967; BPhil, U. St. Andrews (Scotland), 1969; JD, Yale U., 1974. Bar: Va. 1974, D.C. 1975, Md. 1992, U.S. Dist. Ct. (ea. dist.) Va. 1975, U.S. Dist. Ct. (Md.) 1996, U.S. Ct. Appeals (4th cir.) 1976, U.S. Supreme Ct. 1993, U.S. Tax Ct., 1994. Mem. Alston, Miller & Gaines, Washington, 1974-75, Browder, Russell, Morris & Butcher, Richmond, Va., 1975-90, McGuire Woods Battle & Boothe, Richmond and Balt., 1990-98, Akin, Gump, Strauss, Hauer & Feld, L.L.P., Washington, 1998—; sec., bd. dirs. World Trade Ctr. Inst., Balt. Trustee, mem. exec. com. Living Classrooms Found., Balt., 1992—; trustee B&O Railroad Mus., 1995—; active Balt. Mayor's Com. on Hispanic Affairs. Mem. ABA, Va. Bar Assn., Fed. Bar Assn., Md. Bar Assn., D.C. Bar Assn., Internat. Bar Assn., Am. Arbitration Assn. (nat. energy panel 1997—), Inter-Am. Bar Assn. Democrat. Clubs: Commonwealth (Richmond); Md. Club (Balt.). Fax: 202-887-4288. E-mail: jgraham@akingump.com. Home: 216 Springdale Ave Severna Park MD 21146 Office: Akin Gump Strauss Hauer & Feld LLP 1333 New Hampshire Ave NW Ste 400 Washington DC 20036

GRAHAM, JOHN W., advertising executive; b. 1946. With Richfield (Ohio) Properties, 1969-83; with Nationwide Advt. Svc., Cleve., 1983—, pres., CEO. Office: Nationwide Advt Svc Inc 1228 Euclid Ave Ste 600 Cleveland OH 44115-1845*

GRAHAM, JORIE, author; b. N.Y.C., May 9, 1950; d. Curtis Bell and Beverly (Stoll) Pepper; m. James Galvin. BFA, NYU, 1973; MFA, U. Iowa, 1978. Asst. prof. Murray (Ky.) State U., 1978-79, Humboldt State U., Arcata, Calif., 1979-81; instr. Columbia U., N.Y.C., 1981-83; mem. staff U. Iowa, Iowa City, 1983—, prof. English, dir. poetry workshop, 1999—; poetry editor Crazy Horse, 1978-81; Bayelston chair Harvard U., 1998-99. Author: Hybrids of Plants and of Ghosts, 1980 (Great Lakes Colls. Assn. award 1981), Erosion, 1983, The End of Beauty, 1987, Region of Unlikeness, 1991, Materialism, 1993, The Dream of the Unified Field: Selected Poems 1974-94, 1995, The Errancy, 1997, Swarm, 1999; editor: Earth Took of Earth: 100 Great Poems of the English Language, 1996; editor: (with David Lehman) The Best American Poetry 1990, 1990. Recipient Am. Acad. Poets award, 1977, Young Poet prize Poetry Northwest, 1980, Pushcart prize, 1980, 82, American Poetry Review prize, 1982, Pulitzer prize in poetry, 1996, Lavan award Acad. Am. Poets, 1991, Martin Zaubel award Acad. and Inst. of Arts and Letters, 1992; Bunting fellow Radcliff Inst., 1982, Guggenheim fellow, 1983, John D. and Catherine T. MacArthur Found. fellow, 1990; grantee Ingram-Merrill Found., 1981. Office: U Iowa 102 Dey House 507 N Clinton St Iowa City IA 52245*

GRAHAM, JUL ELIOT, lawyer, educator; b. Bklyn., June 14, 1953; s. Arnold Harold and Roselle (Lesser) G.; m. Sherry Robin Goldberg, Nov. 2, 1980. BA in Polit. Sci. cum laude, NYU, 1975; JD magna cum laude, N.Y. Law Sch., 1978. Bar: N.Y. 1979, U.S. Supreme Ct. 1984. Cons. Consumer Law Tng. Ctr., N.Y. Law Sch., 1976, mem. adj. faculty, 1980—; prin. appellate law rsch. asst. appellate div. 1st Dept., Supreme Ct. of State of N.Y., N.Y.C., 1978-79, staff atty., 1979-82, assoc. atty., 1982-83, law asst. to the justices, 1983-88, exec. sec. deptl. adv. com. to family ct., 1979-82, editor criminal trial advocacy handbook, 1980—, prin. appellate ct. atty. to the justices, 1988—, 1st Dept., 1990—; Assoc. editor N.Y. Law Sch. Law Rev., 1976-78, contbg. author, 1975. Guest lectr. Joe Franklin Show, WOR-TV, 1982—. Mem. N.Y. County Lawyers Assn. (com. on communications and entertainment law 1980—, com. on penal and correctional reform 1980— , spl. com. on practical legal edn. 1979—), Am. Arbitration Assn. (arbitrator 1985—), Internat. Radio and TV Soc., Am. Film Inst., Phi Delta Phi, Phi Sigma Alpha. Home: 249 Adelaide Ave Staten Island NY 10306-3949 Office: NY State Supreme Ct Appellate Div 1st Jud Dept 27 Madison Ave New York NY 10010-2201

GRAHAM, KATHARINE, newspaper executive; b. N.Y.C., June 16, 1917; d. Eugene and Agnes (Ernst) Meyer; m. Philip L. Graham, June 5, 1940 (dec. 1963); children: Elizabeth Morris Graham Weymouth, Donald Edward, William Welsh, Stephen Meyer. Student, Vassar Coll., 1934-36; AB, U. Chgo., 1938. Reporter San Francisco News, 1938-39; mem. editorial staff Washington Post, 1939-45, mem. Sunday circulation and editorial depts., pub., 1969-79; pres. Washington Post Co., 1963-73, 77, chmn. bd., 1973-93, CEO, 1973-91, chmn. exec. com., 1993—; co-chmn. Internat. Herald Tribune; ind. trustee Reuters Founders Share Co. Ltd.; vice chmn. bd. dirs. Urban Inst.; mem. Coun. on Fgn. Rels., Overseas Devel. Coun.; past chmn. N.Y. Pubs. Assn. Life trustee U. Chgo.; hon. trustee George Washington U.; mem. collectors com. The Nat. Gallery of Art, Washington. Recipient Pulitzer prize for biography, 1998. Fellow Am. Acad. Arts and Scis.; mem. Am. Soc. Newspaper Editors, Nat. Press Club, Coun. Fgn. Rels., Overseas Devel. Coun., Met. Club, Cosmopolitan Club, 1925 F Street Club. Office: Washington Post Co 1150 15th St NW Washington DC 20071-0002

GRAHAM, KATHLEEN MARGARET (K. M. GRAHAM), artist; b. Hamilton, Ont., Can., Sept. 13, 1913; d. Charles and G. Blanche (Leitch) Howitt; m. J. Wallace Graham, Dec. 17, 1938; children: John Wallace, Janet Howitt. B.A., U. Toronto, Ont., 1936. Solo shows include Carmen Lamanna Gallery, Toronto, 1967, Trinity Coll., U. Toronto, 1968, Founders Coll., York U., Toronto, 1970, Pollock Gallery, Toronto, 1971, 73, 75, Art Gallery Cobourg, Ont., 1973, City Hall, Toronto, 1974, David Mirvish Gallery, Toronto, 1976, Klonaridis, Inc., Toronto, 1978, Watson-Willour Gallery, Houston, 1980, Downstairs Gallery, Edmonton, Alta., 1980, 82, Lillian Heidenberg Gallery, N.Y.C., 1981, 86, Klonaridis, Inc., Toronto, 1981-85, 87, 88, 90, ELCA London Gallery, Montreal, Que., Can., 1983, MacDonald-Stewart Art Centre, Guelph, Ont., 1984, Glenbow Mus., Calgary, 1984, Concordia Gallery, Montreal, 1984, Hart House Gallery, Toronto, 1985, Lillian Heidenberg Gallery, N.Y.C., 1986, Klonaridis Inc., Toronto, 1985, 87, 88, 90, 91, Feheley Fine Arts, Toronto, 1989, Douglas Udell Gallery, Vancouver, 1993, Meml. Art Gallery, St. Johns, N.F., 1994, Beaverbrook Gallery, Fredericton, N.B., 1994, Costin and Klintworth, Toronto, Ont., 1994, 95, The Art Gallery of Ont., 1997; group shows include Montreal Mus. Fine Arts, 1976, Hirshhorn Mus., Washington, 1977, Edmonton (Alta., Can.) Art Gallery, 1977, Norman MacKenzie Art Gallery, Regina, Sask., Can., 1977, David Mirvish Gallery, Toronto, Watson De Nagy Gallery, Houston, Galerie Wentzel, Hamburg, Fed. Republic of Germany, Beaverbrook Gallery, Fredericton, N.B., Associated Am. Artists, N.Y.C., 1986, 88, Elca London, Montreal, 1987, Klonaridis Inc., Toronto, 1987, 91, Douglas Udell Gallery, Vancouver, 1987, Associated Am. Artists, N.Y.C., 1988; travelling shows include CanadaxTen, 1974, The Can. Canvas, 1975-76, Changing Visions, 1976-77, The Shell Canada Collection, 1977, The Fauve Heritage, 1997, 14 Canadians Hirschhorn Mus., Washington, 1977, Certain Traditions, 1978, 79, Bolduc Fournier Graham, 1981, The Heritage of Jack Bush, 1981-82, Selections from the Westburne Collection, 1982-83; represented in permanent collections Nat. Gallery Can., Ottawa, Edmonton Art Gallery, Art Gallery Ont., Art Gallery Hamilton, Ont., MacDonald-Stewart Art Gallery, Guelph, Ont., Toronto City Hall, The Brit. Mus., London, Art Gallery of Vancouver, Agnes Etherington Art Centre, Kingston, Ont., Can., Musée d'Art Contemporarin Montre Beaverbrook Art Gallery, Frederickton, N.B., Art Gallery Nfld. and Labrador, Art Gallery, Peterborough, Ont., Robert McLaughlin Gallery, Oshawa, Ont., Kitchener Waterloo Art Gallery, McMichael Can. Art Gallery, Hart House Art Gallery, Toronto, also numerous corp. collections. Trinity Coll. fellow, U. Toronto, 1988. Mem. Royal Can. Acad.

GRAHAM, KENNETH JOHN EMERSON, English language educator; b. Waltham, Mass., Feb. 22, 1960; s. William A. G. Graham and Sydna L. Cantelon; m. Elizabeth A. Crawford, July 30, 1988; 1 child, James. BA (honors), U. Alta., Edmonton, Can., 1981; MA, U. Toronto, Ont., Can., 1982; PhD, U. Calif., Berkeley, 1990. Asst. prof. English U. Wyo., Laramie, 1990-91; Kaplan postdoctoral fellow U. Alta, Edmonton, 1991-93; asst. prof. English Dalhousie U., Halifax, N.S., Can., 1993-94; asst. prof. English N.Mex. State U., Las Cruces, 1994-98, assoc. prof. English, 1998—. Author: (book) The Performance of Conviction, 1994. Fellow NEH, 1998-99. Mem. MLA, Shakespeare Assn. Am., Rocky Mountain Medieval and Renaissance Assn. (sec. (1995-98). Office: NMex State U Dept English # 3E Las Cruces NM 88003

GRAHAM, KENT HILL, philanthropist, museum guide; b. Winston-Salem, N.C., May 16, 1937; d. Charles Gideon and Nancy Critz (O'Hanlon) Hill; m. William Thomas Graham, Feb. 1, 1958; children: William Thomas, Ashton Cannon. Student, Duke U., 1955-58, U. Hawaii, 1958. Chmn. of vols., sec., sec. to exec. bd. Forsyth County chpt. ARC, asst. to nat. chmn. vols. Am. Nat. Red. Cross, Washington; bd. dirs. Centenary United Meth. Ch. Day Care Ctr.; bd. dirs. Am. Cancer Soc., Forsyth County, Little Theatre, Child Guidance Clinic, Carolina Ballet, 1996-97, Wake County Libr., 1996—, Forsyth County Libr., 1970-77, chmn., 1975-77; Rep. candidate for alderman West Ward, Winston-Salem, 1965; vice chmn. N.C. Battleship Commn., 1973-77; bd. dirs. Winston-Salem Debutante Com., 1984-86, pres., 1985, nominating chmn., 1986; mem. exec. bd. Historic Winston, Inc.; trustee N.C. Sch. Arts, 1986-87; mem. N.C. Sentencing and Policy Adv. Com., 1990-93, Celebration N.C. Fin. Com. Capt. N.C. Naval Militia. Mem. Jr. League Nat. Fedn. Rep. Women, Order of the Long Leaf Pine, Twin City Garden Club (treas., 1st v.p., pres.), Garden Club Am. (zone VIII, bull. editor 1975-77, vice chmn. 1977-80, nominating com. 1979-80, water conservation coord. 1980-83), Baha Vista Club (bd. dirs. 1995—). Avocations: horseback riding, travel, historic preservation, collecting early southern antiques. Home: 3421 Williamsborough Ct Raleigh NC 27609-6368

GRAHAM, LAUREL DIANE, sociology educator; b. Aberdeen, S.D., May 16, 1963; d. Rodney Walter and Virginia (Olinger) G. BA, Moorhead State U., 1985; PhD, U. Ill., 1992. Asst. prof. dept. sociology U. South Fla., Tampa, 1992-98, assoc. prof., 1998—. Author: Managing on Her Own: Dr. Lillian Gilbreth and Women's Work in the Interwar Era, 1998; contbr. articles to profl. jours. Mem. Am. Sociol. Assn., Soc. for Study Symbolic Interactn, Midwest Sociol. Soc. Avocation: member brass band. E-mail: lagraham@luna.cas.usf.edu. Office: U South Fla Dept Sociology 4202 E Fowler CPR 107 Tampa FL 33620

GRAHAM, LAURIE, editor, writer; b. Evanston, Ill., Nov. 22, 1941; d. Thomas Harlin and Mary Elisabeth (Stoner) Graham; m. George McKay Schieffelin, Dec. 12, 1980 (dec. Jan. 1988); m. Robert Dale Shearer, Apr. 6, 1994. Student, Mt. Holyoke Coll., 1959-61; BA, U. Colo., 1963. Editor Charles Scribner's Sons, N.Y.C., 1969-87. Author: Rebuilding the House, 1990, Singing the City, 1998; mem. editl. bd. Creative Nonfiction, 1994—, (press series) Emerging Writers in Creative Nonfiction, Duquesne U., 1994—. Mem. PEN, N.Y. Jr. League, Colony Club. Home: 1000 Grandview Ave Pittsburgh PA 15211-1362

GRAHAM, LAWRENCE OTIS, lawyer, writer, television personality; b. N.Y.C., Dec. 25, 1961; s. Richard Charles and Betty Johnyce (Walker) G.; m. Pamela Alexis Thomas, Feb. 15, 1992. AB, Princeton U., 1983; JD, Harvard U., 1988. Bar: N.Y. Corp. atty. Weil, Gotshal & Manges, N.Y.C., 1988-93; pres. Progressive Mgmt. Assocs., Inc., White Plains, N.Y., 1993—; asst. prof. Fordham U., N.Y.C., 1993—; legal corr. Sta. WNBC-TV, N.Y.C., 1994; adj. lectr. Dutchess C.C., Poughkeepsie, N.Y., 1997—. Author: 10 Point Plan for College Acceptance, 1980, Jobs in the Real World, 1981, Conquering College Life, 1982, Your Ticket to Law School, 1983, Your Ticket to Business School, 1984, Your Ticket to Medical School, 1984, Flyers: Fun Loving Youth En Route to Success, 1985, (with Betty Graham) Teenager's Ask and Answer Book, 1986, (with Lawrence Hamdan) Youth-Trends, 1987, Best Companies for Minorities, 1993, Member of the Club, 1995, Proversity: Getting Past Face Value, 1997, Our Kind of People: Inside America's Black Upper Class, 1999; columnist Gannett Westchester Newspapers, White Plains, 1988-91; contbg. editor U.S. News and World Report, 1997—; assoc. prodr. Warner Bros. Studios, Burbank, Calif. Bd. dirs. Princeton (N.J.) Ctr. for Leadership Tng., 1993—, Westchester County African Am. Adv. Bd., White Plains, 1994-96, Manhattanville Coll. Entrepreneurial Inst., Purchase, N.Y., 1987-91, White Plains br. NAACP, 1990-93, Westchester Civil Liberties Union, 1994-96, Westchester Holocaust Commn., 1996—, White Plains Pub. Libr., 1995—, Coun. on Economic Priority, N.Y.C., 1996—; mem. Coun. of Fgn. Rels., Urban League, 1996—; chair Westchester County Police Bd. Named one of 10 Most Interesting Young Men in Am. by Mademoiselle Mag., 1985. Mem. ABA, Nat. Bar Assn. (Young Lawyer of Yr. 1993), N.Y. State Bar Assn., Assn. Bar City N.Y., Westchester County Bar Assn., Harvard Club (N.Y.C.). Office: Progressive Mgmt Assocs Inc PO Box 80 Chappaqua NY 10514*

GRAHAM, LESTER LYNN, radio journalist; b. Carlinville, Ill., Aug. 16, 1960; s. Lyndal L. and Betty L. (Cottingham) G.; m. Evelyn Elaine Epperson, Aug. 4, 1979; children: Joshua Nathanael, Alayna Renee. AAS, Lewis & Clark Coll., 1985. News dir. Metroplex Comm. Sta. WBGZ, Alton, Ill., 1985; news dir. Midwest Comm. Stas. WPMB and WKRV, Vandalia, Ill., 1986-87; news dir. Seith-Serafin Comm. Stas. WSDR and WSSQ, Sterling, Ill., 1987-88; news dir. No. Ill. U. Stas. WNIU and WNIJ, Rockford, Ill., 1988-94; news dir. U. of Mo.-St. Louis Stas. KWMU, 1994-98; prodr. Great Lakes Radio Consortium, Mich. Radio U. Mich., 1998—. Co-writer, co-prodr. (radio documentary) Whistle-Stops: The 1948 Presidential Campaign, 1998; editor (revised) Pronunciation Guider for Illinois Place Names, 1998. Recipient Nat. Individual Achievement award UPI 1990, John Stewart Meml. Broadcasting award Lewis and Clark Coll., 1985, Alumnus Yr. award, 1997. Mem. Pub. Radio News Dirs. Inc. (Nat. Spot News Coverage award 1990, 1994, Nat. Use of Medium award 1991, Nat. Breaking News Coverage award 1994, bd. dirs., large staff rep. 1996-97), Radio and TV News Dirs. Assn. (News Series Documentary award 1992, Spot News award 1994, Use of Sound award 1994, Investigative Reporting award 1997, News Documentary award 1998), Ill. News Broadcasters Assn. (v.p. 1996-97, bd. dirs. 1991-96, pres. 1997-98), Lewis and Clark Radio Adv. (bd. dirs.). Soc. Profl. Journalists (v.p. St. Louis chpt. 1996). Avocations: amateur Ill. historian. E-mail: graham@gtec.com. Home and Office: 213 Goodrich St Jerseyville IL 62052-2213

GRAHAM, LINDSEY O., congressman; b. Pickens County, S.C., July 9, 1955; s. E. J. and Millie Graham. BA in Polit. Sci. in Psychology, U. S.C., 1977, JD, 1981. Area def. counsel Shaw AFB, 1982-84; cir. trial counsel USAF Europe, 1984-88; asst. county atty. County of Oconee, S.C., 1988-92; pvt.

practice, 1989—; city atty. Central, S.C., 1990-94; mem. S.C. Ho. of Reps., 1992-94, 104th-106th Congress from 3rd S.C. dist., 1995—; mem. edn. and workforce, nat. sec./jud. com. With USAF, 1990, Desert Shield/Desert Storm. Lt. col. Air Force Reserves. Republican. Office: US Ho of Reps 1429 Longworth Ho Off Bldg Washington DC 20515-4003

GRAHAM, LOIS CHARLOTTE, retired educator; b. Denver, Mar. 20, 1917; d. James Washington and Martha Wilhemina (Raukohl) Brewster; m. Milton Clinton Graham, June 30, 1940 (dec.); children: Charlotte, Milton, Charlene, James. Student, Okla. City U., 1935-36; AB, Ouachita Bapt. U., 1939; postgrad., U. Nev., Reno, 1953, 63, 68, Ark. State U., 1954, 59. Cert. tchr., Colo., Nev., Ark. Tchr. Fairmount Sch., Golden, Colo., 1939-40, Melbourne (Ark.) Sch., 1940-41, Blytheville (Ark.) Jr. H.S., 1944-45, Hawthorne (Nev.) Elem. Sch., 1952-81; substitute tchr. Mineral County Sch. Dist., Hawthorne, 1988-94; sr. resource cons. dept. geriatrics U. Nev.-Reno Med. Sch., 1988-90, del. to Rural Health Conf., Hawthorne, 1990; officer Mineral County Tchrs. Assn., 1955-65; ad hoc com. Nev. State Tchrs., 1965. Mem. Mineral County Emergency Planning Com., 1991—; asst. to pres. High Sch. PTA, Hawthorne, 1958, Elem. PTA, Hawthorne, 1961; pianist, choir dir., tchr. various chs., 1927—; active Older Am. Friends of Libr. Recipient Disting. Svc. award. Mem. AAUW (membership v.p. 1988-91, pres. 1991-92, 94-96), AARP (pres. 1995-98), Ret. Pub. Employees of Nev. (membership v.p. 1994-96, pres. 1995—), Older Ams., Friends Libr., Delta Kappa Gamma (v.p. 1991-92). Republican. Baptist. Avocations: volunteer work, reading, writing, knitting, crochet. Home: PO Box 1543 Hawthorne NV 89415-1543 *I was raised in a Christian home with Christian morals and ideals. I was very aware of children and their needs, because of this I became a teacher. I have always tried to be a good example both to my children and the ones I taught.*

GRAHAM, LOREN RAYMOND, historian, educator; b. Hymera, Ind., June 29, 1933; s. Ross Raymond and Hazel Mae (McClanahan) G.; m. Patricia Parks Albjerg, Sept. 6, 1955; 1 child, Marguerite Elizabeth. B.S., Purdue U., 1955, D.Letters (h.c.), 1986; M.A., Columbia U., 1960, Ph.D., 1964; postgrad., Moscow U., 1960-61. Gandy-dancer Pa. R.R., 1950-51; research chem. engr. Dow Chem. Co., 1955; lectr. dept. history Ind. U., 1963-64, asst. prof., 1965-66; vis. asst. prof. dept. public law and govt. Columbia U., 1965-66, assoc. prof., dept. history, 1967-72, prof., 1972-78, adj. prof., 1978-89; mem. Russian Inst., 1966-78; assoc., mem. exec. com. Davis Ctr. for Russian Studies/Harvard U., 1980—, acting dir., 1995-96; vis. prof. dept. history of sci. Harvard U., 1985—; prof. MIT, 1978—; vis. scholar U. Chgo., 1991-92; mem. adv. bd. Internat. Sci. Found., 1992-96,. Author: The Soviet Academy of Sciences and The Communist Party, 1967, Science and Philosophy in the Soviet Union, 1972, Between Science and Values, 1981, Sci. Philosophy and Human Behavior in the Soviet Union, 1987, Science in Russia and the Soviet Union: A Short History, 1993, The Ghost of the Executed Engineer: Technology and the Fall of the Soviet Union, 1993, A Face in the Rock: Tale of a Grand Island Chippewa, 1995, What Have We Learned About Science and Technology From the Russian Experience?, 1998; editor (with others) Functions and Uses of Disciplinary History, 1983, (with R. Stites) Red Star: The First Bolshevik Science Utopia, 1983, Science and the Soviet Social Order, 1990; contbr. numerous articles to profl. jours.; narrator, cons. Nova TV, 1987. Served with USN, 1955-58. Woodrow Wilson fellow, 1958-59; Danforth fellow, 1958-63; Fulbright Hayes fellow, 1966; Guggenheim fellow, 1969-70; Rockefeller fellow, 1976-77; Smithsonian Instn. fellow, 1981-82. Fellow AAAS, Am. Acad. Arts and Scis., Am. Philos. Soc.; mem. Acad. Natural Scis. (fgn.; Moscow), Acad. Humanitarian Scis. (fgn.; Moscow), Am. Hist. Assn., Am. Assn. Advancement of Slavic Studies, History of Sci. Soc. (Sarton medal 1996), Soc. History of Tech., Soc. Social Study of Sci. Home: 7 Francis Ave Cambridge MA 02138-2009 Office: MIT E51-163 77 Massachusetts Ave Cambridge MA 02139-4307

GRAHAM, MATT PATRICK, minister, librarian; b. Colorado City, Tex., Sept. 28, 1950; s. Matt Noe and Mary Edna (Frizell) G.; m. Doris Jean Mickey, Jan. 1, 1971; children: Jennifer, Abigail, Joy, Crystal. BA, Abilene Christian U., 1973, MA, 1974, MDiv, 1976; PhD, Emory U., 1983; M in Libr. Info. Sci., U. Tex., 1990. Ordained to ministry Ch. of Christ, 1971. Min. Druid Hills Ch. of Christ, Atlanta, 1979-82; asst. prof. Columbia Christian Coll., Portland, Oreg., 1983-85, Inst. for Christian Studies, Austin, Tex., 1985-88; dir. of libr. Pitts Theology Libr., Atlanta, 1988—. Author: The Utilization of I and II Chronicles in the Reconstruction of Israelite History in the Nineteenth Century, 1990. Mem. Soc. Bibl. Lit., Am. Schs. Oriental Rsch., Am. Theol. Libr. Assn. Office: Emory U Pitts Theology Libr Atlanta GA 30322*

GRAHAM, MICHAEL PAUL, lawyer; b. Leavenworth, Kans., May 15, 1948; s. K.L. and Norma D. (Whiteside) G.; m. Pamela Jeanne Haymes, Feb. 21, 1976; children—Sarah Kathryn, Patrick Edward. A.B., Dartmouth Coll., 1970; J.D., Harvard, 1973. Bar: Tex. 1973. Assoc., Baker & Botts, Houston, Tex., 1973-80, ptnr., 1981—; bd. govs. Texans for Lawsuit Reform. Mem. Houston Bar Assn., Houston Bar Found. Office: Baker & Botts 3000 One Shell Plz 910 Louisiana St Ste 3000 Houston TX 77002-4991*

GRAHAM, OTIS LIVINGSTON, JR., history educator; b. Little Rock, Ark., June 24, 1935; s. Otis Livingstone and Lois (Patterson) G.; m. Ann Zemke, Sept. 5, 1959 (div. 1981); children—Ann Kathryn Lakin, Wade Livingston; m. Delores Yochum, Apr. 24, 1982. B.A., Yale U., New Haven, 1957; M.A., Columbia U., N.Y.C., 1961, Ph.D., 1966. Asst. prof. history Mt. Vernon Coll, Washington, 1962-64, Calif. State U., Hayward, 1965-66; prof. history U. Calif., Santa Barbara, 1966-80, 89—; disting. univ. prof. history U. N.C., Chapel Hill, NC, 1980-89; vis. prof. Hunter Coll., 1962, George Washington U., 1965, Columbia U., 1967, U. Hawaii, 1967; mem. editorial bd. U. Calif. Press, 1991-95. Author: An Encore for Reform: The Old Progressives and the New Deal, 1967; The Great Campaigns: Reform and War in America 1900-1928, 1971; The New Deal: The Critical Issues, 1971; Toward a Planned Society: From Roosevelt to Nixon, 1977, Losing Ground: The Industrial Policy Debate, 1992, A Limited Bounty: The U.S. Since World War II, 1996; editor The Pub. Historian, 1989—; contbr. chpts. to books, articles to profl. jours. Chair policy bd. Ctr. for Immigration Studies. Served with USMC, 1957-60. Am. Philos. Soc. grantee, 1966; NEH sr. fellow, 1972; Guggenheim fellow, 1977; Woodrow Wilson Internat. Ctr. for Scholars fellow, 1983; recipient Robert Kelley prize Nat. Coun. Pub. History, 1999. Fellow Soc. Am. Historians, Ctr. for Advanced Study in the Behavioral Scis.; mem. Am. Hist. Assn., Orgn. Am. Historians (program chmn. 1977, nominating bd. 1993-95), Ctr. Study Democratic Instns. (assoc. 1975—, program dir. 1976-79), Fedn. Am. Immigration Reform (nat. bd. dirs. 1978—), NEH, Woodrow Wilson Ctr., Soc. Am. Historians (chmn. Parkman prize com. 1974, 80). Avocation: sailing. Office: U N C Dept History Wilmington NC 28403

GRAHAM, PAMELA SMITH, artist, distributing company executive; b. Winona, Miss., Jan. 18, 1944; d. Douglas LaRue and Dorothy Jean (Hefty) Smith; m. Robert William Graham, Mar. 6, 1965 (div.); children: Jennifer, Eric; m. Thomas Paul Harley, Dec. 4, 1976; stepchildren: Tom, Janice. Student, U. Colo., 1962-65, U. Cin., 1974-76. Profl. artist, craft tchr., internat. art known artist, 1968—; property mgmt. and investor Cin., 1972-77; acct., word processor Borden Chem. Co. divsn.. Borden, Inc., Cin., 1974-78; owner, pres. Hargram Enterprises, Cin., 1977-81; owner Sagebrush Studio, 1985—; tchr.; cons. County committeewoman Bergen County, N.J., 1972, clk. of session, 1975-79, conv. chmn., 1981; campaign chmn. United Appeal, 1977; lifeline telephone counselor Suicide Hotline, 1985—; coord. program svcs. and victim advisor Abusive Men Exploring New Directions, 1986-91. One woman shows include U. Colo. Health Scis. Ctr. Denison Libr., 1992—, Jefferson County Nature Ctr., 1998-99, Mt. Vernon County Club, 1998-99, Colo. Symphony, 1998; exhibited in group shows at Colo. Audubon Soc., 1989, Evergreen Artists Assn. Fine Arts Fair, 1988—, River Sage, 1989, Evergreen Naturalists Audubon Soc., 1988-91, Foothills Art Ctr., 1989, 93, Gilpin County Arts Assn., 1989-94, Greenwood Springs Art Guild, 1989-90, Hilton Head Art League; featured in Spree mag., 1989, Weekend Arts sect. Denver Post, 1998; included in Ency. of Living Artists, 11th edit., 1999; represented in permanent collections at Univ. Hosp., AMEND, U. Colo. Health Scis. Ctr. Chancellor's Office, U. Colo. at Boulder Waldenburg Health Ctr., Willis Corroon Corp., Dean Witter Reynolds, Inc., others. Recipient awards for art exhibits including People's Choice award Evergreen Artists Assn. Mem. NAFE, Profl. Artists Assn., Denver Art Mus., Denver Mus. Natural History, Mus. Modern Art N.Y., United Sales Leaders Assn., Nat. Mus. Women in Arts, Colo. Artists Assn., Evergreen Artists Assn. (bd. dirs., pres. 1990-91, People's Choice award 1993), Hilton Head Art League, Coo. Calligraphers Guild, Gilpin County Arts Assn., Foothills Art Ctr., Mt. Vernon Country Club, Queen City Racquet Club, Alpha Gamma Chi, Kappa Kappa Gamma. Office: Graham & Harley Enterprises 818 Logan St # 903 Denver CO 80203 Studio: Sagebrush Studio 818 Logan St # 903 Denver CO 80203

GRAHAM, PARKER LEE, II, computer systems manager; b. Shelby, Ohio, Aug. 6, 1957; s. Parker Lee, Sr. and Shelvy Jean (Schwall) G.; m. Renee Marie MacCartney, Sept. 4, 1976; children: Tella Marie, Kami Nicole. Grad. high sch., Shelby. Parts insp. Essex Wire, Lexington, Ohio, 1974-76; supr. shipping dept. Supreme Distbr., Detroit, 1978-79; driver Everrett Delivery Service, Detroit, 1979-81; field supr. Wesco Energy Systems, Warren, Mich., 1981-82; mgr. shipping Kemar Inc., Sterling Heights, Mich., 1982-84; pres., chief exec. officer Metro Cartage Co., Romulus, Mich., also bd. dirs., 1984-90; salesman Swad Chevrolet, Columbus, Ohio, 1991-92; computer systems mgr. MBA Mktg. Corp. dba "Just for Feet", Dublin, Ohio, 1992-93; customer edn. specialist CAM Data Systems, Inc., Fountain Valley, Calif., 1993-96; sys. adminstr. Donatos Pizza, Inc., Columbus, 1996-97; sys. engr. CAM Data Sys., Inc., Fountain Valley, Calif., 1997—.

GRAHAM, PATRICIA ALBJERG, education educator, foundation executive; b. Lafayette, Ind., Feb. 9, 1935; d. Victor L. and Marguerite (Hall) Albjerg; m. Loren R. Graham, Sept. 6, 1955; 1 child, Marguerite Elizabeth. BS, Purdue U., 1955, MS, 1957, DLett (hon.), 1980; PhD, Columbia U., 1964; MA (hon.), Harvard U., 1974; DHL (hon.), Manhattanville Coll., 1976; LLD (hon.), Beloit Coll., 1977, Clark U., 1978; DPA (hon.), Suffolk U., 1978, Ind. U., 1980; DLitt (hon.), St. Norbert Coll., 1980; DH (hon.), Emmanuel Coll., 1983; DHL (hon.), No. Mich. U., 1987, York Coll. of Pa., 1989, Kenyon Coll., 1991, Bank St. Coll. Edn., 1993; LLD (hon.), Radcliffe Coll., 1994, Salem State Coll., 1998. Tchr. high sch. Norfolk, Va., 1955-56, 57-58, N.Y.C., 1958-60; lectr., asst. prof. Ind. U., 1964-66; asst. prof. history of edn. Barnard Coll. and Columbia Tchrs. Coll., N.Y.C., 1965-68; assoc. prof. Barnard Coll. and Columbia Tchrs. Coll., 1968-72, prof., 1972-74; dean Radcliffe Inst., 1974-77; also v.p. Radcliffe Coll., Cambridge, Mass., 1976-77; prof. Harvard U., Cambridge, Mass., 1974-79, Warren prof., 1979—; dean Grad. Sch. Edn., 1982-91; pres. Spencer Found., Chgo., 1991—; dir. Nat. Inst. Edn., Washington, 1977-79, trustee Northwestern Mut. Life., 1980—. Author: Progressive Education: From Arcady to Academe, 1967, Community and Class in American Education: 1865-1918, 1974, S.O.S. Sustain Our Schools, 1992. Bd. dirs. Dalton Sch., 1973-76, Josiah Macy, Jr. Found., 1976-77, 79—; trustee Beloit Coll., 1976-77, 79-82, Found. for Teaching Econs., 1980-87; dir. Spencer Found., 1983—, Johnson Found., 1983—, Hitachi Found., 1985—, Carnegie Found. for Advancement of Teaching, 1984-92. Am. Council on Edn. fellow Princeton U., 1969-70. Mem. AAAS (coun. 1993-96, v.p. 1998—), Sci. Rsch. Assocs. (dir. 1980-89), Nat. Acad. Edn. (pres. 1985-89), Am. Hist. Assn. (v.p. 1985-89), Am. Philos. Soc., Phi Beta Kappa. Episcopalian. Office: The Spencer Found 875 N Michigan Ave Chicago IL 60611 also: Harvard U Grad Sch Edn Cambridge MA 02138

GRAHAM, PATRICK SAMUEL, air transportation executive; b. Savannah, Ga., May 25, 1949; s. Preston John and Beatrice Eliza (Canady) G.; m. Vikki Lynn Hancock, Nov. 10, 1973 (div. Nov. 1989); children: Kathleen Denise, Kristen Diane. BBA in Acctg., Armstrong State Coll., 1977; MA in Bus. Adminstrn., Ctrl. Mich. U., Savannah, 1983. CPA; accredited airport executive; cert. pvt. pilot. Cost acct. woodlands divsn. Union Camp Corp., 1977-79; various positions bldg. products divsn. Continental Forest Industries, 1979-85; dep. dir. adminstrn./fin. Savannah Airport Commn., 1985-87, dep. exec. dir., 1988-91; exec. dir. Savannah Airport Commn., Savannah, GA, 1992—. Active Alee Shrine Patrol Unit, Savannah Conv. & Visitors Bur. Mem. AICPA, Ga. Soc. CPAs, Savannah Area C. of C. (bd. dirs.), Southside Savannah Jaycees (life, past pres.), Rotary. Office: Savannah Airport Commn 400 Airways Ave Savannah GA 31408-8000*

GRAHAM, REINA LYNN, rehabilitation counselor; b. Aug. 15, 1970. BS in Human Svcs. Counseling, Old Dominion U., 1992; MA in Rehab. Counseling, Gallaudet U., 1994; postgrad., U. Md., 1996—. Rehab. specialist Md. State Dept. Edn. Divsn. Rehab. Svcs., 1993-97; tchg. asst. U. Md., College Park, 1997—. Home: 15076 Copper Turtle Pl Woodbridge VA 22193-5832

GRAHAM, R(ICHARD) NEWELL, soft drink bottling company executive; b. Union City, Tenn., June 15, 1947; s. Hardy Moore and Cola Lee (Poindexter) G.; m. Bettie Rene Young, Dec. 28, 1968; children: Richard, Stanford. BA, U. Miss., 1969. Operating ptnr., chief exec. officer Union City Coca-Cola Bottling Co., 1972—; sec., treas. C.C. Coin Caterers Corp., Union City, 1972-93, pres., 1993—; pres. ReelFoot Ordnance Inc., 1996—; bd. dirs. First State Bank, Union City, Meridian (Miss.) Coca-Cola Bottling Co. Pres. Union City Arts Coun., 1978-79; mem. devel. com. U. Tenn., Martin, 1980-95, vice chmn. devel. coun., 1990-93; treas. St. James Episcopal Ch., Union City, 1987—. With USN, 1969-72. Recipient Project of Yr. award Tenn. Jaycees, Nashville, 1974, Friend of Edn. award Obion County Schs., Union City, 1980. Mem. Assn. Coca-Cola Bottlers Tenn. (pres. 1989-91), Tenn. Soft Drink Assn. (bd. dirs. 1985—), Obion County C. of C. (bd. dirs. 1989-93), Union City Jaycees (pres. 1975, Outstanding Young Man award 1976), Chaine des Rotisseurs (chavalier 1989—), Union City Rotary Club. Republican. Avocations: wine, food, hunting, fishing, gardening. Office: Union City Coca-Cola Bottling Co 1915 E Reelfoot Ave Union City TN 38261-6007

GRAHAM, ROBERT, sculptor; b. Mexico City, Aug. 1938. Study, San Jose (Calif) State Coll., 1961-63, San Francisco Art Inst., 1963-64. Prin. works include Whitney Mus. Am. Art & Mus. Modern Art, N.Y., Hirshhorn Mus. & Sculpture Garden, L.A. County Mus., Dallas Mus. Fine Art, Kunstmus., Cologne, Germany; commd. Fed. Res. Bank San Francisco, 1983, San Jose Fed. Bldg., 1984, L.A. Olympic Organizing Com., 1984, Joe Louis Meml., Detroit, Duke Ellington Meml., Central Park, N.Y., 1992, and others; exhbited in group shows at Galerie Neuendorf, Hamburg, Germany, 1979; one-man shows include Walker Art Ctr., 1981, L.A. County Mus. Art, 1988, Dorothy Rosenthal Gallery, 1981, Sch. Visual Arts, N.Y., 1981; Robert Miller Gallery, N.Y., 1982, 89, 90, 92, Whitney Mus. Am. Art, 1983, 84, 86, 88, 89, Mus. Fine Arts, Houston, 1987-89, Contemporary Arts Ctr., New Orleans, 1990; author: (bibliography) Maurice Tuchman, The Duke Ellington Meml. In Progress, L.A. County Mus. Art, 1989, John McEwen, Robert Graham Statues, Frankfurt, Galerie Neuendorf, Twenty-one Figures, N.Y., Robert Miller Gallery. Office: care Robert Miller Gallery 41 E 57th St Fl 2 New York NY 10022-1908*

GRAHAM, ROBERT, medical association executive; b. Pueblo, Colo., Feb. 15, 1943; married. AB, Earlham Coll., 1965; MD, U. Kans., 1970. Asst. adminstr. agy. goals Health Svc. & Mental Health Admn. Dept. Health Edn. & Welfare, Washington, 1970-73; asst. dir. divsn. edn. Am. Acad. Family Physicians, Kansas City, Mo., 1973-76; dep. dir. Bur. Health Manpower, Health Resources Adminstrn. Dept. Health Edn. & Welfare, 1976-78, dep. adminstr., 1978-79; profl. staff mem. subcom. health & sci. rsch. Comty. Labor & Human Resources, U.S. Senate, 1979-80; acting adminstr. health resources adminstrn. Dept. Health & Human Svc., 1981-82, adminstr., 1982-85; exec. v.p. Am. Acad. Family Physicians, Kansas City, Mo., 1985—; resident family practice Bapt. Meml. Hosp., 1974-75; staff Prog. Health Mgmt., Baylor Coll. Medicine, 1976; exec. sec. Grad. Med. Edn. Nat. Adv. Com., 1978-79; bd. dirs. Alliance for Health Referendum, 1994—, Sun Valley Forum Nat. Health. Mem. AMA, Inst. Medicine-NAS, Assn. Am. Med. Colls., Am. Acad. Family Physicians, Am. Acad. Med. Dirs., Am. Assn. Med. Soc. Execs., Am. Soc. Assn. Execs. Office: Am Acad Family Physicians 8880 Ward Pkwy Kansas City MO 64114-2762*

GRAHAM, ROBERT ALBERT, research physicist; b. Dallas, Feb. 11, 1931; s. John Mark and Eleanor Ball (Evans) G.; m. Lettie Barbara Umphres, Sept. 1, 1951; children: Stephanie Ann Graham Farrow, Mark Lee, Stuart Russell; m. Nell Heard Griffin, Apr. 6, 1996. AA Allen Jr. Coll., 1951; BS in Civil Engring., U. Tex., 1954, MS in Engring. Mechanics, 1958; DSc in Materials Sci. and Engring. by spl. invitation Tokyo Inst. Tech., 1990. Rsch. eng. S.W. Rsch. Inst., San Antonio, 1956-57; staff mem. Sandia Labs., Albuquerque, 1958-83; disting. mem. tech. staff. Sandia Nat. Labs., Albuquerque, 1983-96; dir. rsch. Tome Group, 1996—; adviser NAS, Washington, 1982—, Ctr. for Explosives Tech. Rsch., Socorro, N.Mex., 1983-88, U. N.Mex., Albuquerque, 1988—. Editor: Procs. 1981 Shock Conference; Procs. 1983 Shock Conference; N.Mex. Genealogist, 1974-75, High Pressure Expl. Processing of Ceramics Trans. Tech., 1987; author: Solids Under High Pressure Shock Compression: Mechanics, Physics and Chemistry, 1993; mng. editor, Shock Waves, an Inter-Jour., 1991—; editor-in-chief Springer-Verlag book series on Shock Compression of Condensed Matter, 1988—. Contbr. articles to profl. jours. Patentee in field. Vice pres. Amigos de las Ams., Albuquerque, 1968-70; host family Am. Field Service, Albuquerque, 1969. 1st. lt. U.S. Army, 1954-56. Recipient Excellence award Dept. Energy, 1983; G.B. Sawyer Meml. award Sawyer Rsch. Products, 1984, Am. Phys. Soc. Shock Compression Sci. award, 1993. Fellow AAAS, Am. Phys. Soc.; mem. IEEE, Am. Chem. Soc., Materials Rsch. Soc., Tau Beta Pi, Chi Epsilon, Phi Theta Kappa. Republican. Home and Office: 383 La Entrada Rd Los Lunas NM 87031-7617

GRAHAM, ROBERT CLARE, III, lawyer; b. Albuquerque, Mar. 24, 1955; s. Robert C. Jr. and Helen (Hoagland) G.; children: Jennifer, Jessica, Kourtney, Kate. BA, DePauw U., 1977; JD magna cum laude, Pepperdine U., 1980. Bar: Mo. 1980, Ill. 1981, U.S. Dist. Ct. (ea. dist.) Mo. 1981. Assoc. Shephard, Sandberg & Phoenix, St. Louis, 1980-82, Suelthaus & Kaplan, PC and predecessors, St. Louis, 1982-91, Armstrong, Teasdale, Schlafly & Davis, St. Louis, 1991—. Chmn. Kirkwood (Mo.) Greentree Festival, 1985. Named one of Outstanding Young Men in Am. Jaycees, 1981; recipient Outstanding Service to the Community of Kirkwood award. Mem. ABA, Ill. Bar Assn., Mo. Bar Assn., Bar Assn. Met. St. Louis, St. Louis County Bar Assn. Republican. Presbyterian. Office: Armstrong Teasdale Schlafly & Davis 1 Metropolitan Sq Ste 2600 Saint Louis MO 63102-2740

GRAHAM, ROGER JOHN, photography and journalism educator; b. Phila., Feb. 16; s. William K. and Peggy E. (Owens) G.; divorced; children: John Roger, Robb Curt; m. Debbie Kenyon, Dec. 28, 1991. AA, Los Angeles Valley Coll., 1961; BA, Calif. State U., Fresno, 1962, MA, 1967; postgrad, UCLA, 1976. Cert. in elem., jr. high, high sch., cmty. coll., counseling and adminstrn. Tchr. Riverdale (Calif.) Sch., 1963, Raisin City (Calif.) Sch., 1964; tchr., counselor Calif. State Prison, Jamestown, 1966; tchr. trainer UCLA's Western Ctr., 1967; chmn. media arts dept. Los Angeles Valley Coll., Van Nuys, Calif., 1968—; vis. prof. Pepperdine U., Malibu, Calif., 1976, Calif. Luth. Coll., Thousand Oaks, 1973, South Africa, 1997; vis. prof. Chapman U., Orange, Calif., 1996, GAIN prof., 1998; del. Calif. Fedn. Tchrs. Conv., 1997; dir. Photography Seminar, Spain, summer 1990. Author: Observations on the Mass Media, 1976, (jour) Jr. Coll. Jour., 1972; photo illustrator: The San Fernando Valley, 1980; contbr. articles to profl. jours.; display advertiser Turlock (Calif.) jour., 1962, Fresno Guide, 1963. Mem. Hayden's Com. for Schs., Santa Monica, Calif., 1984, YMCA, Pacific Palisades, Calif.; pres. Pacific Palisades Dem. Club, 1992; rep. to 41st assembly dist. Calif. Dem. Party State Ctrl. Com., 1993, sec. srs. caucus, 1993—. With USN, 1957. NEH scholar 1981; recipient Mayor's Outstanding Citizen award Los Angeles Mayor's Office, 1974, Extraordinary Service award UCLA, 1971; named one of Outstanding Young Men Am., 1971. Mem. C.C. Journalism Assn. (nat. pres. 1978—, Nat. Dedication Journalism award 1972-76), Journalism Assn. C.C. (pres. Calif. sect. 1972—), Calif. Srs. Caucus (state sec. 1993—), L.A. Prof.'s Club, Dem. Club Pacific Palisades (pres. 1992-93), L.A. Valley Coll. Retirees Assn. (pres. 1999), Am. Legion (sgt. at arms 1986—, Palisades post 238 adminstrv. officer 1996—), Sons of the Desert, Sigma Delta Xi, Phi Delta Kappa, Pi Lambda Theta. Avocation: hiking. Home: 7878 Naylor Ave Los Angeles CA 90045-2909 Office: Los Angeles Valley Coll 5800 Fulton Ave Van Nuys CA 91401-4062

GRAHAM, RONALD LEWIS, mathematician; b. Taft, Calif., Oct. 31, 1935; s. Leo Lewis and Margaret Jane (Anderson) G.; children: Cheryl, Marc. Student, U. Chgo., 1951-54; BS, U. Alaska, 1958; MA, U. Calif., Berkeley, 1961, PhD, 1962; LLD (hon.), Western Mich. U., 1984; DSc, St. Olaf Coll., 1985, U. Alaska, 1988. Mem. tech. staff Bell Labs., Murray Hill, N.J., 1962—, head dept. discrete math., 1968—, dir. Math. Scis. Rsch. Ctr., 1983—, adj. dir. rsch., info. scis. divsn., 1987-95; prof. Rutgers U., 1987—; chief scientist AT&T Labs. Rsch., Florham Park, N.J., 1996-98, chief scientist emeritus, 1999—; Regents' prof. UCLA, 1975; vis. prof. computer sci. Stanford U., 1979, 81, Princeton (N.J.) U., 1987, 89; Irwin and Joan Jacobs prof. computer sci. U. Calif. San Diego, La Jolla, 1998—. Author: Ramsey Theory, 1980, Concrete Mathematics, 1989, Erdös on Graphs, 1998. Served with USAF, 1955-59. Recipient Polya prize, 1975; Euler prize, 1993; named Scientist of Yr. World Book Encyclopedia, 1981; scholar Ford Found., 1958, Fairchild Found. Disting. scholar Calif. Inst. Tech., 1983; fellow NSF, 1961, Woodrow Wilson Found., 1962. Fellow AAAS, N.Y. Acad. Scis., Assn. Computing Machinery; mem. NAS (treas. 1996—), Am. Math. Soc. (pres. 1993-94), Math. Assn. Am., Soc. Indsl. and Applied Math., Am. Acad. Arts and Scis., Internat. Jugglers Assn. (past pres.). Office: AT&T Labs 180 Park Ave Florham Park NJ 07932-1004 Office: CSE Univ Calif San Diego La Jolla CA 92093-0114

GRAHAM, SAM DIXON, urologist; b. Norton, Va., Nov. 5, 1920; s. Sam G. and Ruth Cleveland Flanary; m. Jane Warwick O'Neill, Mar. 28, 1946; children: San D. Jr., Gordon Craig, Richard Warwick, Sallie Trigg. MD, U. Va., 1946. Resident U. Va., Charlottesville, 1950-53; chief urology Kings Daus. Hosp., Staunton, Va., 1953—; clin. prof. urology U. Va. Med. Sch., Charlottesville, 1982-89; cons. in field. Co-author: (chpt.) Physical Medicine and Rehabilitation Approaches in Spinal Cord Injury, 1979; contbr. articles to profl. jours. Bd. trustees Mary Baldwin Coll., Staunton; mayor Town of Staunton; chmn. bd. Planters Bank & Trust, Staunton. Lt. USNR, 1941-49. Mem. Am. Urol. Assn. (pres.). Episcopalian. Avocation: golf. Home: 10010 Cedarfield Ct Richmond VA 23233

GRAHAM, (LLOYD) SAXON, epidemiology educator; b. Buffalo, Jan. 14, 1922; s. Lloyd S. and Kathryn (Graser) G.; m. Caroline Lee Morgan, June 19, 1948; children: Robin Porter, Saxon Parker, Morgan Graser. BA, Amherst Coll., 1943; MA, Yale U., 1949, PhD, 1951; DSc (hon.), SUNY, Buffalo, 1996. Asst. prof. Chatham Coll., Pitts., 1951-53; asst. prof. biostats. U. Pitts., 1953-56; from asst. prof. to prof. epidemiology dept. sociology and dept. social and preventive medicine SUNY, Buffalo, 1957—, chmn. dept. social and preventive medicine, 1981-91, prof. emeritus, 1992—; assoc. to prin. cancer rsch. scientist Roswell Pk. Cancer Inst., Buffalo, 1956-65, prof. SUNY div., 1967—; mem. epidemiology and disease control sect. NIH, Bethesda, Md., 1966-70; cons. WHO, Switzerland, 1965-66; dir. demographic studies, Kabul, Afghanistan, 1970-74; chmn. adv. com. to study long-term effects of plutonium Los Alamos (N.Mex.) Nat. Lab., 1976-86; mem. coun. advisors divsn. cancer rsch., resources and ctrs. Nat. Cancer Inst., Bethesda, 1973-77, mem. bd. sci. councillor divsn. cancer prevention and control, 1982-86; mem. sci. coun. Internat. Agy. Rsch. on Cancer, Lyon, France, 1986-90. Author: American Culture, 1957; contbr. numerous articles to profl. jours. Spl. agt. Counter Intelligence Corps, U.S. Army, 1943-46, PTO. Nat. Cancer Inst. grantee, 1969-91. Fellow Am. Coll. Epidemiology, Am. Pub. Health Assn., Am. Sociologic Assn.; mem. Soc. Epidemiologic Rsch. (pres. 1987-88), Am. Epidemiol. Soc., Planned Parenthood, Nat. Abortion Rights League, Orchard Pk. Country Club, Concord Ski Club (Ellicottville, N.Y.), Scriptores (Buffalo). Republican. Avocations: piano, oil painting, alpine skiing, golf. Home: 32 Stonehenge Rd Orchard Park NY 14127 Office: SUNY Dept Social & Preventive Medicine 270 Farber Hall Buffalo NY 14214-2648

GRAHAM, SELDON BAIN, JR., lawyer, engineer; b. Franklin, Tex., Apr. 14, 1926; s. Seldon Bain and Lillian Emma (Struwe) G.; m. Patricia Gene Noah, Feb. 14, 1953; children—Seldon Bain, Kyle, Laurie. B.S., U.S. Mil. Acad., 1951; J.D., U. Tex., 1970. Registered profl. engr., Tex. Bar: Tex. 1970, U.S. Dist. Ct. (so. dist.) Tex. 1980, U.S. Ct. Appeals (5th cir.) 1983; cert. in oil, gas and mineral law Tex. Bd. Legal Specialization. Commd. 2d lt. U.S. Army, 1946; advanced through grades to col., 1979; with Office of Dep. Chief of Staff for Personnel, 1979; ret., 1979; area reservoir engr. ARCO, Okla., 1954-60; div. regulatory engr. Mobil Oil Co., Corpus Christi, 1961-67; counsel Exxon Co. USA, Houston, 1970-85. Decorated Legion of Merit. Mem. Soc. Petroleum Engrs. Methodist. Home and Office: 4713 Palisade Dr Austin TX 78731-4516

GRAHAM, STEPHEN MICHAEL, lawyer; b. Houston, May 1, 1951; s. Frederick Mitchell and Lillian Louise (Miller) G.; m. Joanne Marie Sealock, Aug. 24, 1974; children: Aimee Elizabeth, Joseph Sealock, Jessica Anne. BS, Iowa State U., 1973; JD, Yale U., 1976. Bar: Wash. 1977. Assoc. Perkins Coie, Seattle, 1976-83, ptnr., 1983—. Bd. dirs. Wash. Spl. Olympics, Seattle, 1979-83, pres., 1983; mem. Seattle Bd. Ethics, 1982-88, chmn., 1983-88, Seattle Fair Campaign Practices Commn., 1982-88; trustee Cornish Coll. of the Arts, 1986-91, exec. com., 1988; trustee Epiphany Sch., 1987-93, exec. com., 1989-91; bd. trustees Arboretum Found., 1994-96—; mem. exec. com. Sch. Law Yale U., 1988-92, 93-97; bd. dirs. Perkins Coie Cmty. Svc. Found., 1988-91; trustee Seattle Repertory Theatre, 1993-95; trustee Seattle Children's Theatre, 1996-98, mem. exec. com., 1997-98; bd. dirs. Wash. Biotech. and Biomed. Assn., 1996—, mem. exec. com., 1997—. Mem. ABA, Wash. State Bar Assn., Seattle-King County Bar Assn., Wash. Athletic Club, Rainier Club. Episcopalian. Office: Perkins Coie 1201 3rd Ave Fl 40 Seattle WA 98101-3000

GRAHAM, SUSETTE RYAN, retired English educator; b. Plattsburgh, N.Y., Aug. 31, 1929; d. Andrew Warren Ryan and Lillian Grace MacDougall; m. James H. Graham, July 1, 1950; children: Marguerite, Andrea, James Jr., Martha, Amy, Matthew. BA, Wellesley Coll., 1950; MA, U. Rochester, 1967, PhD, 1987. Prof. English Nazareth Coll., Rochester, N.Y., 1963-93; prof. emerita Nazareth Coll., Rochester, 1993; ret. Contbr. articles, revs. to profl. jours. Fulbright sr. lectr., Poland, 1992-93. Mem. AAUW, MLA, Am. Acad. Poets. Democrat. Avocations: travel, reading, genealogical research. Home: 10 Arbor Ct Fairport NY 14450 also: 603 Pipers Ln Myrtle Beach SC 29575

GRAHAM, SYLVIA ANGELENIA, wholesale distributor, retail buyer; b. Charlotte, N.C., Mar. 27, 1950; d. John Wesley and Willie Myrl (Ray) White; m. James Peter Cleveland Fisher, Apr. 23, 1967 (div. Sept. 1972); 1 child, Wesley James Fisher; m. Harold Walker Graham, Sept. 14, 1972 (dec. June 1994); 1 child, Angelique Jane Graham. Cert., Naval Reserve Force Detachment Mgmt. Sch., 1985; air cargo specialist cert., Air U., 1987. Store owner Naval Air Terminal/Naval Transp. Support Unit, Norfolk, Va., 1985—; fleet liaison technician Naval Material Transp. Orgn., Norfolk, 1988-93; passenger svc. rep. Naval Transp. Support Unit Naval Material Transport Orgn., Norfolk, Va., 1996—; distbr. Blair Divsn. of Merchants, Lynchburg, Va., 1988—; distbr. Mason Shoe Co., Chippewa Falls, Wis., 1988—, mem. dealer adv. bd., 1997—; driver Greater Charlotte Transp. Co., 1988—, Watkins Products, Winona, Minn., 1992—, Citizens Def. Products, St. Joseph, Mo., 1993—; dealer Creative Card Co., Chgo., 1995—, Home Showcase Products, Lynchburg, 1995—; jewelry dealer Merlite Industries, N.Y.C., 1994; dealer Creative Cards, Chgo., 1995—; mem. Nat. Safety Coun., Charlotte, 1988—, "C" team Watkins Products, Lincoln, Nebr., 1992—; sec. Popular Club Plan, Dayton, N.J., 1990—; pub. Citizens Def. Products, 1993—; sponsor The Paralyzed Vets. Am., Wilton, N.H., 1994—; mem. RBC Ministries, Grand Rapids, Mich., 1998—. Crusader Cancer Ctr. for Detection and Preventin Drive, Seattle, 1991—; blcok chmn. Easter Seal Soc., 1988—. With USN, 1991, Persian Gulf; USNR, 1992, Somolian Relief Effort; USN, 1993-94. Named Top Dealer, Home Showcase Products, Lynchburg, Va. Mem. NAFE, Nat. Enlisted Res. Assn., Naval Enlisted Res. Assn., Nat. Pk. and Conservation Assn., Nat. Trust Hist. Preservation, Direct Selling Assn., Navy League of the U.S., Libr. of Congress Assocs., Nature Conservancy, Nat. Audubon Soc. Democrat. Pentecostal. Avocations: stamp collecting, reading, bicycling, dancing, painting. Home: PO Box 16066 Charlotte NC 28297-6066

GRAHAM, THOMAS, JR., lawyer; b. Louisville, Oct. 9, 1933; s. Thomas and Charlotte (Henriques) G.; m. Clover Nicholas, Aug. 10, 1968 (div. Dec. 1982); children: Elizabeth Malcolm, Thomas Lawrence, Clover Chace; m. Christine Coffey Ryan, Sep. 26, 1983; stepchildren: Thomas Coffey Ryan, Mary Christine Ryan. AB, Princeton U., 1955; postgrad., L'institute des Sciences Politiques, 1955-56; JD, Harvard U., 1961. Bar: Ky. 1961, D.C. 1963, N.Y. 1966. Law clk. U.S. Cir. Ct. Appeals (D.C. cir.), 1961-62; chief counsel U.S. Ho. Reps. Com. on Banking and Currency, Washington, 1962-63; counsel to compt. of currency Treasury Dept., Washington, 1963-64; assoc. Wyatt, Grafton & Sloss, Louisville, 1964-66, Shearman & Sterling, N.Y.C., 1966-69; lawyer Office of Sec. USAF, Washington, 1969-70; asst. gen. counsel U.S. Arms Control and Disarmament Agy., Washington, 1970-73, dep. gen. counsel, 1973-77, gen. counsel, 1977-81, 83-94, dir. Congl. rels. and pub. affairs, 1981-83, acting dir., 1993, acting dep. dir., 1993-94; spl. rep. of Pres. (amb.) Arms Control, Non-Proliferation and Disarmament, 1994-97; ret., 1997; legal advisor U.S. SALT II del., Geneva, 1974-79; legal advisor U.S. del. to rev. conf. Nonproliferation Treaty, Geneva, 1980; sr. arms control advisor, legal advisor U.S. del. to negotiations on Intermediate Range Nuclear Forces, 1981-82; legal advisor U.S. del. to Conf. Disarmament, Geneva, 1985; legal advisor U.S. del. to negotiation on nuc. and space arms, Geneva, 1985-88, U.S. del. to ABM Treaty Rev. Conf., Geneva, 1988; sr. arms control advisor, legal advisor U.S. del. Conventional Armed Forces in Europe negotiation, 1989-90; legal advisor U.S. del. START Negotiation, 1991, START II Negotiation, 1992; chmn. U.S. del. ABM Treaty rev. conf., 1993, U.S. rep. Nonproliferation Treaty Ext. Conf., 1993-95; chmn. U.S. Del. Conventional Armed Forces Europe rev. com., 1996; chmn. bd. dirs. Mex. Energy Corp., 1997—; lectr. U. Va. Law Sch., 1984-91; adj. prof. Georgetown U. Law Ctr., 1991-93, Georgetown Sch. Fgn. Svc., 1991-94; pres. Lawyers Alliance for World Security, Washington, 1997—; bd. dirs. Radetsky Thorium Power Corp. Spl. asst. to chmn. United Citizens for Nixon-Agnew, Washington, 1968. With U.S. Army, 1956-58, 1st lt. U.S. Army Res., 1958-61. Mem. ABA (chmn. com. on arms control 1986-94), D.C. Bar Assn., N.Y. State Bar Assn., Ky. Bar Assn., Coun. on Fgn. Rels., Chevy Chase Club, Cosmos Club, Met. Club, Louisville Country Club, Ausable Club. Republican. Episcopalian. Avocations: tennis, golf, skiing, hiking. Office: Lawyers Alliance World Security 1901 Pennsylvania Ave NW Washington DC 20006-3405

GRAHAM, THOMAS PEGRAM, JR., pediatric cardiologist; b. Charlotte, N.C., Mar. 1, 1937; s. Thomas P. and Margaret (Martin) G.; m. Carol Ann Noggle, June 1, 1960; children: Bethany, Brent, Brooke. A.B., Duke U., 1959, M.D., 1963. Diplomate Am. Bd. Pediatrics. Resident in pediatrics Children's Hosp., Boston, 1963-65; research assoc. Nat. Heart Inst., Bethesda, Md., 1965-67; fellow in pediatric cardiology Duke U., Durham, N.C., 1967-69, asst. prof. pediatrics, 1969-71; dir. pediatric cardiology, prof. pediatrics Vanderbilt U., Nashville, 1971—, vice chmn. pediat. dept., 1989—. Contbr. articles to profl. jours. Fellow Am. Acad. Pediatrics (exec. com. 1972-74), Am. Coll. Cardiology (chmn. pediatric cardiology subcom. 1979-86, bd. trust 1996—), Am. Heart Assn. (chmn. council on cardiovascular disease in the young 1981-83). Presbyterian. Office: Vanderbilt Med Ctr Div Ped & Cardiology D2220 Med Ctr N Nashville TN 37232 also: 21st S At Garland Ave S Nashville TN 37232*

GRAHAM, THOMAS RICHARD, lawyer; b. Shelbyville, Ind., Nov. 23, 1942; s. Kermit A. and Esther L. (Thompson) G.; m. Rosemond Eve Toner, June 12, 1965; children: Rachel Christina, Thomas Ian. BA, Ind. U., 1965; JD, Harvard U., 1968. Bar: D.C. 1970, U.S. Supreme Ct. 1973. Exec. asst. to pres. Ford Motor de Venezuela, Caracas, 1968-70; vis. prof. law U. Catolica Andres Bello, Caracas, 1968-70; legal officer UN, Geneva, 1970-73; dep. gen. counsel Office U.S. Trade Rep., Washington, 1974-79; vis. prof. U. N.C., Chapel Hill, 1979-80; assoc. Patton, Boggs & Blow, Washington, 1980-81; counsel, ptnr. Kilpatrick & Cody, Washington, 1981-85; ptnr. Skadden, Arps, Slate, Meagher & Flom, Washington, 1985—; adj. prof. law Georgetown U., Washington, 1977-85, 95—; vis. fellow Brookings Instn., Washington, 1978-79; sr. assoc. Carnegie Endowment, Washington, 1979-80. Co-editor: Managing Trade Relations in the 1980's, 1983, Trade and Environment, 1982; contbr. articles to profl. jours. Chief advisor on internat. trade John Glenn Presdl. Campaign, 1984. Mem. ABA (chmn. subcom. exports 1985-89), Am. Soc. Internat. Law (chmn. internat. econ. law sect. 1981-83). Avocations: history, sports. Home: 6115 33rd St NW Washington DC 20015-2403 Office: Skadden Arps et al 1440 New York Ave NW Ste 1000 Washington DC 20005-6000

GRAHAM, TINA TUCKER, psychiatric and pediatrics nurse; b. Cherry Pointe, N.C., Jan. 16, 1962; d. Jerry Keith and Masako (Sueshita) Tucker. AAS, Shelby State Community Coll., 1985. RN, Tenn.; cert. CPR, crisis intervention, psychiat. and mental health nurse, pediatric advanced life support. Civff nurse newborn ICU, IMC Memphis Regional Med. Ctr., 1986-87; nurse team leader MidSouth Hosp., Memphis, 1986-87, charge nurse, 1987-89, nurse mgr. adolescent unit, 1989-90; dir. infection control/employee health/emergency responder, 1990-91; nurse mgr. child unit, acting out program dir. MidSouth Hosp., Memphis, 1991-92, program dir. child svcs., 1993-99; staff nurse oper. rm. LeBonheur-Childrens Med. Ctr., Memphis, 1993-99, nurse, clin. educator perioperative svcs., 1999—; mem. safety team LeBonheur-Childrens Med. Ctr., 1998, clin. educator perioperative svcs., 1999—; cons. in field; clin. specialist in ORSOS Zeiss navigational and frameless stercotaxy computers. Named Nurse of Yr., MidSouth Hosp., 1989. Mem. ANA, AORN, Assn. for Practitioners Infection Control, Phi Theta Kappa. Office: LeBonheur Childrens Med Ctr 50 N Dunlap St Memphis TN 38103-2800

GRAHAM, TONI, writer; b. San Francisco, June 24, 1945; d. Joseph Foster and Maxine E. (Johnson) Avila; m. J. Richard Graham, Nov. 23, 1972 (div. 1987); 1 child, Salvatore Z. BA, New Coll. Calif., 1989; MA in English, San Francisco State U., 1992, MFA in Creative Writing, 1995. Lectr. creative writing San Francisco State U., 1992, 98; adj. prof. MA writing program U. San Francisco, 1994—; lectr. U. Calif., Santa Cruz, 1995-97, Chabot Coll., 1996-97, Dominican Coll., 1996-97, Santa Clara U., 1997-98, Calif. State U., Chico, 1999—. Author: The Daiquiri Girls, 1998; contbr. short fiction to mags., including Playgirl, Am. Fiction 88, Five Fingers Rev., Miss. Rev., Ascent, Clockwatch Rev., Miss. Mud, SFSU Rev., Worcester Rev., ZIPZAP mag., Green Mountain Rev., Chiron Rev., others. Harrold scholar, 1986; recipient Calif. Short Story Competition award, 1987, Herbert Wilner Meml. Short Story award, 1994; story Shadow Boxing cited in Pushcart Prize XIV-Best of the Small Presses, 1989; recipient Associated Writing Programs Fiction award 1997. Mem. MLA, Assoc. Writing Programs, Hemingway Soc., Golden Key Honor Soc. Home: 345 Prospect Ave San Francisco CA 94110-5509

GRAHAM, TONY M., lawyer; b. 1949. BS, U. Mo., Rolla; JD, U. Tulsa. Bar: Okla. 1977. Judge Tulsa County Dist. Ct., Tulsa, 1978-87; U.S. atty. U.S. Dist. Ct. (no. dist.) Okla., 1987-93; ptnr. Feldman, Franden, Woodard & Farris, 1993—. Office: 525 S Main St Ste 1000 Tulsa OK 74103-4504

GRAHAM, VICTOR ERNEST, French language educator; b. Calgary, Alta., Can., May 31, 1920; s. William John and Mary Ethel (Wark) G.; m. Mary Helena Faunt, Aug. 1, 1946; children: Ian Robert, Gordon Keith, Miriam Elizabeth, Ross William. BA, U. Alta., 1946; BA (Rhodes scholar), Oxford U., 1948, MA, 1952, DLitt, 1968; PhD, Columbia U., 1953. Asst. prof. French and English U. Alta. Calgary br., 1948-52, assoc. prof. French, 1952-57, prof., 1957-58, asst. to dir., 1952-58; assoc. prof. French U. Toronto, Ont., 1958-60; prof. U. Toronto, 1960-85, chmn. grad. dept. French, 1965-67; assoc. dean U. Toronto (Sch. Grad. Studies), 1967-69; vice prin. Univ. Coll., 1969-70; vis. prof. U. Mich., 1954-55, U. Victoria, 1980-81; mem. governing council U. Toronto, 1973-76. Author: Critical Edition of the Poetry of Philippe Desportes, 7 vols., 1958-63, The Imagery of Proust, 1966, Rymes, Pernette du Guillet, 1968, (with W. McAllister Johnson) Le Recueil des Inscriptions 1558, 1972, The Paris Entries of Charles IX and Elisabeth of Austria 1571, 1974, The Royal Tour of France by Charles IX and Catherine de'Medici (1564-1566), 1979, Bibliographie des etudes sur Marcel Proust et son oeuvre, 1976, The Art of the Chinese Snuff Bottle: The J&J Collection, 1993, (with Hugh Moss and Ka Bo Tsang) A Treasury of Chinese Stuff Bottles, Vol. 1 Jade, 1995, Vol. 2 Quartz, 1998, Vol. 3, Stones Other than JAde and Quartz, 1998, others. Columbia U. open fellow, 1948; Can. Council sr. fellow, 1963; Guggenheim fellow, 1970; Connaught sr. research fellow in humanities, 1978. Fellow Royal Soc. Can. Home: 100 Glenview Ave, Toronto, ON Canada M4R 1P8 Office: U Toronto, 185 Univ Coll, Toronto, ON Canada M5S 3H7

GRAHAM, WALTER S., environmental engineer; b. Phila., Feb. 3, 1948; s. Daniel and Ruth G.; m. Karen R. Mesisca, Apr. 13, 1985; 3 children. BA in Biology and Chemistry, U. Del., 1970, MA in Environ. Engring., 1974. Rsch. asst. L. Brown Labs, Upper Darby, Pa., 1970; rsch. biologist Alfred I. DuPont Inst., Wilmington, Del., 1972-74; environ. engr. U.S. EPA, Phila., 1975—, supr. engr., 1989, program mgr. design, constrn., 1995; v.p. ops. Mktg. 2000, Wilmington, Del., 1992-98; sr. DOD liaison to State of Del.-USAR, Wilmington, 1993-96; sr. emergency prepardness liaison FEMA, Phila., 1996—. 1st lt. med. svc. U.S. Army, 1970-72, res., 1974—. Recipient 1st Nat. Supr. of Yr., EPA. Mem. Disaster Preparedness and Emergency Response Assn., Retired Officers Assn., Elks. Avocations: teaching nature studies, hiking, photography, woodworking. Home: 206 Plymouth Rd Wilmington DE 19803-3117 Office: US EPA 1650 Arch St Philadelphia PA 19103-2029

GRAHAM, WARREN KIRKLAND, dentist; b. Albuquerque, July 22, 1938; s. Warren Reno and Alice Barbara (Eller) G.; m. Nancy Lou White, Apr. 2, 1966; children: John Warren, Jason Kirkland. BS, U. N.Mex., 1960; DDS, Baylor U., 1964. Pvt. practice dentistry, Albuquerque, 1965-89; dental dir. Farmington Cmty. Health Ctr., 1989—; corp. dir. Presbyn. Med. Svcs., 1994—; adj. asst. prof. Coll. Dentistry, Baylor U., 1995—; clin. instr. dental programs U. N.Mex., 1968-73, adj. asst. prof. dental programs, 1996—; vice chair N.Mex. Bd. Dental Health Care, 1997—; examiner Western Regional Exam. Bd., 1998—; implementor area sr. citizens' dental program, 1985. Bd. dirs. N.Mex. Coun. on Smoking and Health, 1969-71; mem. N.Mex. Medicaid Adv. Bd., 1972-77, Mid Rio-Grande Health Planning Coun., 1972-76; chmn. N.Mex. Health Sys. Agy. Subarea Coun., Dist. II, 1977-78. Capt. USAF, 1964-65. Fellow Am. Coll. Dentists, Acad. Gen. Dentistry (pres. Albuquerque chpt. 1976; mem. ADA, N.Mex. Acad. Gen. Dentistry (pres. 1990-91), N.Mex. Dental Assn. (sec.-treas. 1982-86, v.p. 1986-87, pres. 1988-89), Albuquerque Dist. Dental Soc. (pres. 1976), Pierre Fouchard Acad., Sigma Chi, Delta Sigma Delta. Republican. Mem. LDS Ch. Office: Presbyn Med Svcs Farmington Cmty Health Ctr PO Box 3239 Farmington NM 87499-3239

GRAHAM, WILLIAM ALBERT, religion educator, history educator; b. Raleigh, N.C., Aug. 16, 1943; s. William Albert and Evelyn (Powell) G.; m. Barbara Stecconi, Aug. 26, 1983; 1 child, Powell Louis. Student, U. Goettingen, Fed. Republic Germany, 1964-65; BA summa cum laude, U. N.C., 1966; AM, Harvard U., 1970, PhD, 1973. Lectr. Islamic religion Harvard U., Cambridge, Mass., 1973-74, asst. prof., 1974-79, Allston Burr sr. tutor, 1975-77, assoc. prof., 1979-81, sr. lectr. history of religion, 1981-85, prof. history of religion and Islamic studies, 1985—, chmn. Study of Religion, 1987-90, dir. Ctr. for Middle Eastern Studies, 1990-96; master Currier House Harvard Coll., 1991—; Mem. Joint Com. on Comparative Study of Muslim Socs., Social Sci. Rsch. Coun., Am. Coun. Learned Socs., 1988-93; mem. adv. coun. dept. religion Princeton (N.J.) U., 1982-96, chmn. Coun. on Grad. Studies in Religion, 1993-96; vis. lectr. Friedrich-Wilhelms U., Bonn, 1982-83; chmn. Near Ea. Langs. and Civilizations, Harvard U., 1997—. Author: Divine Word and Prophetic Word in Early Islam, 1977 (Am. Coun. Learned Socs. book prize 1978), Beyond the Written Word, 1987, 93; co-author: Heritage of World Civilizations, 1986, 90, 93, 98; co-editor: Islamfiche: Readings from Islamic Primary Sources, 1987; mem. editl. bd. jours. and ency.; contbr. articles and revs. to profl. jours. Woodrow Wilson Found. grad. fellow Harvard U., 1966-67, Danforth Found. grad. fellow Harvard U., 1966-73, John Simon Guggenheim Found. fellow, Germany, India, 1982-83, Alexander von Humboldt Found. fellow, Germany, 1982-83. Mem. Am. Soc. for Study of Religion, Am. Acad. Religion, Middle East Studies Assn., Am. Oriental Soc., Am. Alpine Club, Phi Beta Kappa. Democrat. Avocation: tech. mountaineering. Home: Currier House 64 Linnaean St Cambridge MA 02138-1502 Office: Harvard U Currier Masters Office 64 Linnaean St Cambridge MA 02138-1502

GRAHAM, WILLIAM AUBREY, JR., real estate broker; b. Montgomery, Ala., Dec. 7, 1930; s. William Aubrey and Nina Judson (Jenkins) G.; m. Carol Fletcher, Aug. 15, 1953; children: William G., Carol Anne. BS in Bldg. Constrn., Auburn U., Ala., 1956. Lic. real estate broker, gen. contractor. V.p. Meadow Corp., Montgomery, Ala., 1956-60; pres. Graham Constrn. Co., Montgomery, 1960-65; engr. Portland Cement Assn., Orlando, Fla., 1965-69; gen. mgr. bldg. Punta Gorda Isles, Inc., Punta Gorda, Fla., 1969-72; sales mgr. Punta Gorda Isles, Inc., Punta Gorda, 1972-78; pres. Punta Gorda Realty, Inc., 1978—; chmn. bd. dirs. Southwest Fla. Bank N/A; bd. dirs. v.p. Coral Harbor Enterprises, Punta Gorda, 1978—; pres. Judson Corp., Punta Gorda, 1980—. Bd. dirs., pres. YMCA, Charlotte County, Fla., 1978-88, United Way, Charlotte County, 1979-90, Fla. Internat. Air Show, Charlotte County, 1981—, pres., 1983-96, chmn. bd. dirs., 1996—; bd. dirs., v.p. Spl. Tng. and Rehab., Charlotte County, 1983—, chmn., 1990—, bd. dirs. U.S. Selective Svc. System, 1983, chmn. 1997—. Mem. Nat. Assn. Realtors, Fla. Assn. Realtors, Nat. Assn. Home Builders, Charlotte County Home Builders Assn., VFW, Am. Legion, Elks, Kiwanis (bd. dirs., pres. Punta Gorda 1979—, Citizen of Yr. award 1983, Kiwanian of Yr. award 1990, 98). Republican. Episcopalian. Avocations: golf, tennis. Home: 500 Bal Harbor Blvd Punta Gorda FL 33950-5291 Office: Punta Gorda Realty Inc 1601 W Marion Ave Punta Gorda FL 33950-3202

GRAHAM, WILLIAM B., pharmaceutical company executive; b. Chgo., July 14, 1911; s. William and Elizabeth (Burden) G.; m. Edna Kanaley, June 15, 1940 (dec.); children: William J., Elizabeth Anne, Margaret, Robert B.; m. Catherine Van Duzer, July 23, 1984. SB cum laude, U. Chgo., 1932, JD cum laude, 1936; LLD, Carthage Coll., 1974, Lake Forest Coll., 1983; LLD (hon.), U. Ill., 1988; LHD, St. Xavier Coll. and Nat. Coll. Edn., 1983; LHD (hon.), Barat Coll., 1997, DePaul U., 1998. Bar: Ill. 1936. Patent lawyer Dyrenforth, Lee, Chritton & Wiles, 1936-40; mem. Dawson & Ooms, 1940-45; v.p., mgr. Baxter Internat., Inc., Deerfield, Ill., 1945-53, pres., 1953-71; CEO Baxter Internat., Inc., Deerfield, 1960-80; chmn. bd. Baxter Internat., Inc., Deerfield, Ill., 1980-85, sr. chmn., 1989-95, chmn. emeritus, 1995—; prof., chair Weizmann Inst. Sci., Rehoboth, Israel, 1978; lectr. U. Chgo., 1981-82. Chmn. bd. dirs. Lyric Opera Chgo.; bd. dirs. Big Shoulders, Wendy Will Care Fedn., Chgo. Hort. Soc.; trustee Orchestral Assn., U. Chgo., Evanston (Ill.) Hosp.; past pres. Cmty. Fund of Chgo. Recipient V.I.P. award Lewis Found., 1963, Disting. Citizen award Ill. St. Andrew Soc., 1974, Decision Maker of Yr. award Am. Statis. Assn., 1974, Marketer of Yr. award AMA, 1976, Found. award Kidney Found., 1981, Chicagoan of Yr. award Chgo. Boys Club, 1981, Bus. Statesman of Yr. award Harvard Bus. Sch. Club Chgo., 1983, Achievement award Med. Tech. Svcs., 1983, Disting. Fellows award Internat. Ctr. for Artificial Organs and Transplantations, 1982, Chgo. Civic award DePaul U., 1986, Internat. Visitors Golden Medallion award U. Ill., 1988, Chgo. medal U. Chgo., 1992, Laureate award Lincoln Acad. Ill., 1992, Lyric Opera Carol Fox award, 1992, Good Scout award N.E. Coun. Boy Scouts Am., 1993, Making History award Chgo. Hist. Soc., 1996, Depaul U. Dr. Humane Letters award, 1998; recognized for pioneering work Health Industry Mfrs. Assn., 1981; inducted Jr. Achievement Chgo. Bus. Hall of Fame, 1986, Modern Healthcare Hall of Fame, 1994. Mem. Am. Pharm. Mfrs. Assn. (past pres.), Ill. Mfrs. Assn. (past pres.), Pharm. Mfrs. Assn. (past chmn., award for spl. distinction leadership 1981), Chgo. Club (past pres.), Commonwealth Club, Comml. Club, Indian Hill Club, Casino Club, Old Elm Club, Seminole Club, Everglades Club, Bath and Tennis Club, Links Club, Phi Beta Kappa, Sigma Xi, Phi Delta Phi. Home: 40 Devonshire Ln Kenilworth IL 60043-1205 Office: Baxter Internat Inc 1 Baxter Pkwy Deerfield IL 60015-4625

GRAHAM, WILLIAM EDGAR, JR., lawyer, retired utility company executive; b. Jackson Springs, N.C., Dec. 31, 1929; s. William Edgar and Minnie Blanch (Autry) G.; m. Jean Dixon McLaurin, Nov. 24, 1962; children: William McLaurin, John McMillan, Sally Faircloth. AB, U. N.C., 1952, JD with honors, 1956. Bar: N.C. bar. Law clk. U.S. Ct. Appeals 4th Circuit, 1956-57; individual practice law Charlotte, N.C., 1957-69; judge N.C. Ct. Appeals, 1969-73; sr. v.p., gen. counsel Carolina Power & Light Co., Raleigh, N.C., 1973-81, exec. v.p., 1981-85, vice chmn., 1985-93; counsel Hunton & Williams, 1994—. Served with USAF, 1952-54. Mem. ABA, N.C. Bar Assn., Wake County Bar Assn. Presbyterian. Home: 761 Bishops Park Dr Raleigh NC 27605-3234 Office: Hunton & Williams PO Box 109 Raleigh NC 27602-0109

GRAHAM, WILLIAM FRANKLIN (BILLY GRAHAM), evangelist; b. Charlotte, N.C., Nov. 7, 1918; s. William Franklin and Morrow (Coffey) G.; m. Ruth McCue Bell, Aug. 13, 1943; children: Virginia Leftwich, Anne Morrow, Ruth Bell, William Franklin, Nelson Edman. BA, Wheaton Coll. (Ill.), 1943; ThB, Fla. Bible Inst., Tampa, 1940; ThB numerous hon. degrees, including, Houghton (N.Y.) Coll., Baylor U., The Citadel, William Jewell Coll. Ordained to ministry So. Baptist Conv., 1939; minister First Bapt. Ch., Western Springs, Ill., 1943-45; 1st v.p. Youth for Christ, Internat., 1945-50; pres. Northwestern Coll., Mpls., 1947-52; founder World Wide Pictures, Inc., Burbank, Calif.; worldwide evangelistic campaigns, 1949—; speaker weekly Hour of Decision radio program, 1950—; also periodic Crusade Telecasts; founder Billy Graham Evangelistic Assn.; hon. chmn. Lausanne Congress World Evangelization, 1974. Author: Peace with God, 1953, World Aflame, 1965, The Jesus Generation, 1971, Angels: God's Secret Agents, 1975, How To Be Born Again, 1977, The Holy Spirit, 1978, Till Armageddon, 1981, A Biblical Standard for Evangelists, 1984, Approaching Hoofbeats, 1983, Unto the Hills, 1986, Facing Death and The Life After, 1987, Answers to Life's Problems, 1988, Hope for the Troubled Heart, 1991, Storm Warning, 1992, (autobiography) Just As I Am, 1997; also writer of daily newspaper column. Recipient numerous awards, including Bernard Baruch award, 1955, Humane Order of African Redemption, 1960, Gold award George Washington Carver Meml. Inst., 1964, Horatio Alger award, 1965, Internat. Brotherhood award NCCJ, 1971, Sylvanus Thayer award Assn. Grads. U.S. Mil. Acad., 1972, Franciscan Internat. award, 1972, Man of South award, 1974, Liberty Bell award, 1975, Templeton prize for Progress in Religion, 1982, Presdl. Medal of Freedom, 1983, William Booth award Salvation Army, 1989, Congl. Gold Medal, 1996. Office: Billy Graham Evangelistic Assn PO Box 9313 Minneapolis MN 55440-9313

GRAHAM, WILLIAM HENRY, lawyer; b. Newark, Jan. 6, 1946; s. Robert and Ruth Ellen (McElroy) G.; m. Lorraine Majeski, Mar. 23, 1969; 1 child, Allison. BA, Ohio State U., 1968; JD, Rutgers U., 1973; LLM in Corp. Law, NYU, 1978, LLM in Trade Regulation Law, 1980. Law clk. Connell Foley & Geiser, Roseland, N.J., 1971-73; atty. Connell Foley & Geiser, Roseland, 1973-77; atty. Bethlehem (Pa.) Steel Corp., 1977-79, sr. atty., 1979-81, gen. atty., 1981-85, asst. gen. counsel, 1985-89, asst. gen. counsel, asst. sec., 1989-92, gen. counsel, 1992-95, v.p., gen. counsel, sec., 1995—. Bd. dirs. Atlantic Legal Found., N.Y.C., 1986—; bd. mem. Pa. Civil Justice Coalition, Harrisburg, Pa., 1987—; chmn. Pa. Task Force on Product Liability, Harrisburg, 1989—. 1st lt. U.S. Army, 1969-71, Vietnam. Mem. ABA, N.J. Bar Assn., Pa. Bar Assn., Trial Attys. N.J., Am. Iron and Steel Inst., Assn. Gen. Counsel. Lutheran. Office: Bethlehem Steel Corp 1170 8th Ave Bethlehem PA 18016-7600

GRAHAM, WILLIAM JAMES, packaging company executive; b. Johnstown, Pa., Sept. 20, 1923; s. John Ellis and Margaret (Euwer) G.; m. Natalie Joan Stolk, Feb. 17, 1951; children: Susan, Margaret, John, Elizabeth, Joan, Catherine. B.A. cum laude, Amherst Coll., 1948. Salesman, Owens-Ill., Inc., 1953-60, closure sales mgr., 1960-66, v.p. sales Pacific region, 1966-69, v.p., gen. mgr. Pacific region, 1969-72, v.p. sales and mktg., 1972-75; v.p., gen. mgr. plastic products div. Owens-Ill., Inc., Toledo, 1975-82; group v.p. plastics and closures Owens-Ill., Inc., 1982-85, sr. v.p. West, 1985-88, ret., 1988; bd. dirs. G.W. Plstics, Garden Grow Co., Inc. Trustee, pres. Filoli, 1990-96; trustee Strybing Arboretum, 1996—. Served to 1st lt. U.S. Army, 1943-46, 50-51. Mem. Soc. Plastics Industry (dir.-at-large, exec. com.), Plastic Bottle Inst. (chmn. 1983-86), Mgmt. Policy Council (exec. com.). Republican. Presbyterian. Clubs: Menlo Country, Foothills Tennis. Home: 8 Hawk View Portola Valley CA 94028-8037

GRAHAM, WILLIAM PATTON, III, plastic surgeon, educator; b. Plainfield, N.J., Apr. 30, 1934; s. William Patton and Mary Alice (Bucher) G.; m. Susan Ames Fox, Nov. 27, 1968; children: Susan Patton, Elizabeth Ames. AB, Princeton U., 1955; MD, U. Pa., 1959. Diplomate Am. Bd. Surgery, Am. Bd. Plastic Surgery (chmn. 1985-86). Intern U. Colo. Med. Ctr., Denver, 1959-60; resident in surgery VA Hosp., Denver, 1960-61, U. Calif., San Francisco, 1961-64; chief resident in surgery U. Calif., 1964-65; resident and instr. plastic surgery U. Pa., Phila., 1965-67; asst. prof. surgery U. Pa., 1967-70; assoc. prof. surgery Pa. State U., Hershey, 1971-74; prof. surgery Pa. State U., 1974-85, chmn. divsn. plastic surgery, 1971-85, 1996—, clin. prof. surgery, 1985-96; prof. surgery U. Colo., 1994—; chmn. Plastic Surgery Research Council, Hershey, 1979-80. Co-author: The Hand-Surgical and Non-Surgical Management, 1977, Practical Points in Plastic Surgery, 1980. Trustee Harrisburg Acad., 1980-85. Maj. USAR, 1960-73. USPHS research grantee, 1974-76; advanced clin. fellow Am. Cancer Soc. Phila., 1969-70. Fellow ACS; mem. Am. Surg. Assn., Am. Assn. Plastic Surgeons (trustee 1983-86, 91-94), Am. Soc. Surgery of Hand (mem. coun. 1989-92), Soc. Head and Neck Surgeons, Am. Soc. Aesthetic Plastic Surgery (pres.

1992-93), Northeastern Soc. Plastic Surgeons (pres. 1988-89, Newport R.I.), Robert H. Ivy Soc. (pres. Hershey 1974-75), Sigma Xi (full), Alpha Omega Alpha, Nu Sigma Nu, Tower Club (Princeton, N.J.). Republican. Office: Aesthetic & Reconst Surgery 816 Belvedere St Carlisle PA 17013-4001

GRAHAM, WILLIAM PIERSON, investment banker, entrepreneur; b. East St. Louis, Ill., Feb. 19, 1935; s. William Schley and Opal Elizabeth (Gray) G.; m. Margaret Newton McDowell, Sept. 30, 1961; children: Lisa, Heather, Jennifer. BS, U. Ill., 1956. With IBM Corp., 1956-69, asst. to pres., 1967-68, dir. mktg. comml. industries data processing div., 1968-69; exec. v.p. EDP Tech., Inc., Washington, 1969-71, pres., chief exec. officer, 1971-73; pres. Washington Profl. Group, 1973-81; pres. SRC Corps., Equisource Corps.; mng. dir. Pierce Investment Banking, Inc.; dir., mem. exec. com. Cornerstone R.E.I.T., 1993-96; chmn. bd. Synthesis Internat., Inc., Paradigm Integration Corp., Empowernet, Inc. Asst. for domestic programs White House, Washington, 1966-67; chmn. bd. dirs. Congl. Mgmt. Found.; mem. fgn. service profl. devel. rev. group Dept. State, 1976; mem. U.S. Adv. Com. Vocat. Edn., 1968-69, U.S. Fed. Adv. Com. Employment Security, 1968-71, Com. for Excellence in Govt.; panel cons. Edn. Profl. Devel. Act, HEW, 1969-71; del. German Am. Forum, Bonn, Berlin, 1975; chmn. parents assn. Sidwell Friends Sch., Washington, 1976-78; vice chmn. fin. adv. com. Nat. Com. for Effective Congress, 1976-77. Served with AUS, 1957. White House fellow, 1966-67. Mem. White House Fellows Assn. (pres. Assn. and Found. 1973-74). Home and Office: 3238 O St NW Washington DC 20007-2842

GRAHAM, WILLIAM THOMAS, lawyer; b. Waynesboro, Va., Oct. 24, 1933; s. James Monroe and Margaret Virginia (Goodwin) G.; m. Kent Hill, Feb. 1, 1958; children: Ashton Cannon, William Thomas Jr. AB in Econs., Duke U., 1956; JD, U. Va., 1962. Bar: N.C. 1962, Va. 1962, D.C. 1970, U.S. Supreme Ct. 1970. Assoc. Craige, Brawley and predecessor firms, Winston-Salem, N.C., 1962-64; ptnr. Craige, Brawley, Horton & Graham, Winston-Salem, 1965-69; asst. gen. counsel HUD, Washington, 1969-70; ptnr. Billings & Graham, Winston-Salem, 1971-75; judge N.C. Superior Ct., 1975-79; pvt. practice Winston-Salem, 1981-87; commr. of banks State of N.C., Raleigh, 1987-95; counsel Patton Boggs, LLP, Raleigh, 1995-98. Chmn. Forsyth County Reps., Winston-Salem, 1966-69, 73-75, George Bush for Pres., N.C., 1988. With U.S. Army, 1957-58. Mem. Old Town Club. Methodist. Avocation: travel. Home: 3421 Williamsborough Ct Raleigh NC 27609-6368

GRAHM, CHARLES MORTON, sales executive; b. Orting, Wash., Aug. 15, 1914; s. Ralph R. and Jane Ethel (Morton) G. BBA, U. Miami, 1947-50. Sales agt., supr. Pan Am. World Airways, Miami, Fla., 1946-77, ret., 1977. With USMCR, 1943-45, PTO. Decorated two Purple Hearts, USMC. Mem. DAV (life). Republican. Avocations: fishing, cutting gemstones. Home: 1280 W 29th St Hialeah FL 33012-5527

GRAHMANN, CHARLES V., bishop; b. Halletsville, Tex., July 15, 1931. Student, Assumption-St. John's Sem., Tex. Ordained priest Roman Catholic Ch., 1956. Ordained titular bishop Equilium and aux. San Antonio, 1981-82; 1st bishop Victoria, Tex., 1982-89; coadjutor biship Dallas, 1990; bishop Diocese of Dallas, Dallas, Tex., 1990—. Office: Diocese of Dallas Chancery Office PO Box 190507 Dallas TX 75219-0507*

GRAHN, BARBARA ASCHER, publisher; b. Chgo., Mar. 26, 1929; d. Harry L. and Eleanor (Simon) Ascher; m. Robert D. Grahn, Dec. 23, 1952; children: Susan Grahn Gantz, Nancy Lee, Wendy Grahn O'Brien. BA, Miami U., Oxford, Ohio, 1950. Promotion dir. George Williams Coll., Chgo., 1950-52; sales mgr. Chatham Mfg., Chgo., 1952-54; research asst. Standard Rate and Data Service, Skokie, Ill., 1968-70, adminstr. editorial services, 1970-75, asst. editor, 1975-77; editor Wilmette, Ill., 1977-87; assoc. pub. Std. Rate and Data Svc., Wilmette, Ill., 1987-95, quality assurance mgr., 1995-96, mgr. support svcs., 1996-98, mgr. data acquisition, 1998—. Precinct capt. Ill. Reps., 1956-58; pres. Cmty. Club of Jewish Women, Skokie, 1958-60; bd. dirs., treas. North Shore Towers Condo Assn., Skokie, 1986-90, 93—. Mem. NAFE, Chgo. Ad Club, Alpha Epsilon Phi. Avocations: choreography, swimming, spending time with grandchildren. Office: SRDS 1700 E Higgins Rd Ste 500 Des Plaines IL 60018-5610

GRAINGER, MARY MAXON, civic volunteer; b. Arlington, Va., Apr. 14, 1957; d. Fred J. and Grace A. (Ziel) Maxon; m. Bradley R. Grainger, Aug. 18, 1979; children: Aileen, Maura, Erin. BS, Cornell U., 1979, MPS, 1987. Dir. pub. rels. Cazenovia (N.Y.) Coll., 1979-80; assoc. dir. admissions Cornell U., Ithaca, N.Y., 1980-85; v.p. Cornell Class of 1979, 1984—. Bd. dirs. Sciencenter, devel. com., 1993—; com. chair 1st Congl. Ch., comms. com., 1985—; editor Cayuga Heights PTA, 1994-98; leader Girl Scouts, 1991—; com. chair Boynton Mid. Sch. PTA, equity com., 1997—; adv. Cayuga Heights Sch., literary mag., 1996—. Mem. Tompkins Girls Hockey Assn. (sec. bd. dirs.). Fax: 607-257-0483. E-mail: mmgithaca@aol.com. Home: 421 Highland Rd Ithaca NY 14850

GRALA, JANE M., securities firm executive; b. Phila.; d. Stanley Frank and Anna Stephanie Grala. BS, Rutgers U., Camden, 1976; MBA, Winthrop U., 1979; postgrad., Am. Mgmt. Assn., N.Y.C., 1980-82, Am. Inst. Real Estate Appraisers, Chgo., 1985. Mgr. acctg. dept. NDI Engring. Co., Pennsauken, N.J., 1968-72, project mgr., 1972-76; rep. sales Am. Cyanamid, Wayne, N.J., 1976-80; dist. mgr. Am. Appraisal Assocs., Phila., 1980-86; assoc. v.p. investments Prudential Securities Incorporated, Clearwater, Fla., 1986—; adj. prof. fin. area Tampa (Fla.) Coll., 1995. Mem. Nat. Assn. Accts. (dir. advt. So. Jersey chpt. 1983-86), Assn. MBA Execs., Bus and Profl. Women's Assn., Nat. Assn. for Female Execs., Chi Delta, Phi Chi Theta. Republican. Avocation: archeology. Office: Prudential Securities Inc 28100 Us Highway 19 N Ste 100 Clearwater FL 33761-2660

GRALEN, DONALD JOHN, lawyer; b. Oak Park, Ill., Mar. 18, 1933; s. Oliver Edwin and Rosalie Marie (Buskens) G.; m. Jane Walsh, Dec. 29, 1956; children: Alana, Mark, Paul, Ann, Sarah. BS, Loyola U., Chgo., 1956; JD with honors, Loyola U., 1957. Bar: Ill. 1958. Assoc. Sidley & Austin, Chgo., 1959-65; ptnr. Sidley & Austin, 1966-94, counsel, 1994—. Co-author chpts. in books. Trustee Village of LaGrange, Ill., 1973-77; chmn. LaGrange Zoning Bd., 1971-73, LaGrange Econ. Devel. Com., 1982, Cmty. Meml. Found., 1995—; bd. dirs. Carson Pirie Scott Found., Chgo., 1980-89, Jr. Achievement, 1978-88, Met. Housing and Planning Coun., 1982-89, Cmty. Family Svc. and Mental Health Assn., 1983-87, Chgo. Youth Conservation Corps, 1988-92, LaGrange Meml. Found., 1990-95, YMCA Met. Chgo., 1990—. 1st lt. U.S. Army, 1957-59. Mem. Ill. Bar Assn., Am. Coll. Real Estate Lawyers, Univ. Club, Big Foot Country Club. Home: 42 Durham Ct Burr Ridge IL 60521-7938 Office: Sidley & Austin 1 First Natl Plz Chicago IL 60603-2003

GRALLA, EUGENE, natural gas company executive; b. N.Y.C., May 3, 1924; s. Jacob and Anna Ruth (Kleiman) G.; m. Beverly Dorman, Apr. 7, 1946; children: Rhona Gralla Spilka, Steven Stuart. B.S., U.S. Naval Acad., 1945; M.B.A., Harvard U., 1947. Commd. ensign USN, 1945, advanced through grades to comdr., 1961; served sea duty, 1947-49, 54-56; control officer (Naval Supply Depot, Guantanamo Bay), Cuba, 1959-61; with (Office Asst. Sec. Def. for Installations and Logistics), 1961-64; ret., 1966; dir. data systems planning Trans World Airlines, N.Y.C., 1966-68; corp. dir. mgmt. info. systems Internat. Paper Co., N.Y.C., 1968; v.p. electronic data processing Columbia Gas System Service Corp., Wilmington, Del., 1969-73; sr. v.p. Columbia Gas Distbn. Cos., Columbus, Ohio, 1973-86, pres., 1986-89, ret., 1989. Mem. U.S. Naval Inst., Navy League of the U.S., Harvard Bus. Sch. Club, Palm Beach Club, Ret. Officers Assn., Masons. Home: 7641 La Corniche Cir Boca Raton FL 33433-6007

GRALLA, HOWARD IRWIN, graphic designer; b. Bklyn., Nov. 29, 1946; s. Reuben and Charlotte (Rothbardt) G.; m. Linda Jo Schultz, Aug. 29, 1993. BS, Rochester Inst. Tech., 1968; MFA, Yale U., 1975. Tchr. graphic arts Bassick H.S., Bridgeport, Conn., 1968-69; instr. sch. printing Rochester Inst. of Tech., 1969-73; staff designer Yale U. Printing Svc., New Haven, 1975-76; book designer Howard Gralla Book Design, New Haven, 1977—; tchr., critic in graphic design Yale U. Sch. of Art, New Haven, 1978-93. Designer: American Windsor Chairs, 1996 (AIGA award 1997), 50 Books in the Boston Athenaeum, 1994 (New Eng. Book Show 1994), East Asian Lacquer, 1991 (AAUP award 1992). Mem. Am. Printing History Assn., Bookbuilders of Boston, Columbiad Club of Conn., Printing Hist. Soc. (London), The Typophiles (N.Y.), The Soc. of Printers. Avocations: gardening, reading, theatre, listening to opera. Home: 45 Mumford Rd New Haven CT 06515-2431 Office: Howard Gralla Book Design 45 Mumford Rd New Haven CT 06515-2431

GRALLA, LAWRENCE, publishing company executive; b. Bronx, N.Y., June 24, 1930; s. Meyer and Julia (Barnett) G.; m. Yvette Glickenstein, Dec. 24, 1952; children—Adele, Heidi. B.S., CCNY, 1951. V.p. Nationwide Trade News Service, N.Y.C., 1951-55; pres. Gralla Publs., N.Y.C., 1955-87, exec. cons., 1987—; founding pub. Kitchen Bus., 1955, Bank Systems & Equipment, 1964, Multi-Housing News, 1966, Meeting News, 1977, Comml. Property News, 1988. Pres. Woodlands Community Temple, White Plains, N.Y., 1979-81. Recipient Govt. Israel Spl. Trade award 1980. Jewish. Office: Miller Freeman Inc One Penn Plaza New York NY 10119

GRALLA, MILTON, publisher; b. Bklyn., Jan. 28, 1928; s. Meyer and Julia (Barnett) G.; m. Shirley Edelson, Aug. 31, 1950; children—Edward, Karen, Dennis. B.A. in Journalism, CCNY, 1948; LHD (hon.), Yeshiva U., 1991. News reporter, 1948-51; co-founder nat. bus. news agy. N.Y.C., 1951-55; co-founder, exec. v.p. Gralla Pubs., N.Y.C., 1955-93; adj. prof. journalism NYU, Ramapo Coll., Yeshiva U., 1989—; del. leader Reawakening 1990-91, Moscow, 1990. Author: How Good Guys Grow Rich, 1995. Candidate for Congress, N.J., 1974; chmn. Israel Salute parade, 1993-94. Recipient major awards (trade) Govt. of Israel, (community service) Brandeis U., United Jewish Appeal, Orgn. Rehab. Through Tng., NCCJ. Mem. Friars Club, 24 Karat Club. Republican. Jewish.

GRAMATTE, JOAN HELEN, graphic designer, art director, photographer; b. Chgo., Dec. 12, 1942; d. Ernest H. and A. Helen (Gill) G. AAS, So. Seminary Coll., 1962; BFA, R.I. Sch. Design, 1965. Graphic illustrator Contis Studio, Boston, 1965-66; designer, illustrator Graham Assocs., Inc., Washington, 1966-69; art dir. Stanisbury Design, Washington, 1969-71; founder, art dir. Nuestro Grafico, Inc., Washington, 1971-77; co-founder, exec. art dir. Nuestro Mag., bd. dirs. Nuestro Grafico, Inc., N.Y.C., 1977-81; owner Joan Gramatte Design, N.Y.C., 1981—. Recipient First Pl. award aerodynamic kite design Smithsonian Inst., 1970, Addy award Advt. Club of Met. Washington, 1971, First Pl. award Art Dirs. Club, Met. Washington, 1972, Silver medal Art Dirs. Club Met. Washington, 1979, Achievement award N.Y. Soc. Illustrators, 1980, award of excellence Printing Industries of Am., 1991. Home and Office: 429 E 52nd St New York NY 10022-6430

GRAMM, WILLIAM PHILIP (PHIL GRAMM), senator, economist; b. Fort Benning, Ga., July 8, 1942; s. Kenneth Marsh and Florence (Scroggins) G.; m. Wendy Lee, Nov. 2, 1970; children: Marshall Kenneth, Jefferson Philip. BA, U. Ga., 1964, PhD, 1967. Mem. faculty dept. econs. Tex. A&M U., College Station, 1967-78, prof., 1973-78; ptnr. Gramm & Assocs., 1971-78; mem. 96th-98th Congresses from 6th Tex. Dist.; U.S. senator from Tex., 1985—; chmn. Banking, Housing, and Urban Affairs Com., Fin. Com., Budget Com.; chmn. Nat. Rep. Senatorial Com., 1991-95; chmn. Senate Steering Com. Contbr. articles to profl. jours., periodicals. Republican. Episcopalian. Office: US Senate 370 Senate Russell Bldg Washington DC 20510

GRAMMATER, RUDOLF DIMITRI, retired construction executive; b. Detroit, Nov. 29, 1910; s. D.M. and Amelia (Busse) G.; m. Fredricka W. Cook, Aug. 18, 1943, 1 child, Douglas. Student, Pace Inst., 1928-32; LLB, Lincoln U., 1937. Bar: Calif. 1938; CPA, Calif. With Bechtel Corp., San Francisco, 1941-73, treas., v.p., 1955-62, v.p., 1962-71, dir., 1960-73, cons., 1973, v.p., dir. subsidiaries, 1955-71. Mem. ABA, AICPA, Calif. Soc. CPAs, Calif. Bar Assn., Menlo Country Club. Home: The Peninsula Regent # 819 One Baldwin Ave San Mateo CA 94401-3852

GRAMMER, FRANK CLIFTON, oral surgeon, researcher; b. El Dorado, Ark., Aug. 12, 1943; s. Norman Alexander and Lillie Mae (Martin) G.; m. Ann Marie Beller, Feb. 8, 1964 (div. Feb. 1980); children: William Cody, Tamara Ann; m. Sandra Lanier Boyd, July 5, 1980; 1 child, Jeremy Boyd. BS, Washington U., St. Louis, 1966, DDS summa cum laude, 1968; MSD, U. Minn., 1972, PhD, 1973. Diplomate Am. Bd. Oral and Maxillofacial Surgery. Research fellow U. Minn., Mpls., 1968-73; practice dentistry specializing in oral surgery, Fayetteville, Ark., 1973—; cons. Cambridge Hosp., Minn., 1972-73; instr. U. Ark., Fayetteville, 1978-79; asst. prof. U. Tenn., Memphis, 1979-80; mem. adv. com. Am. Bd. Oral and Maxillofacial Surgery, Chgo., 1979-85; bd. govs. Antaeus Research Inst., Fayetteville, 1979-85; mem. coun. on sci. affairs ADA, 1997—. Editor Arkansas Dentistry, 1992—; contbr. articles to profl. jours. Recipient Research award Am. Soc. Oral Surgeons, 1973. Fellow Am. Coll. Oral and Maxillofacial Surgeons, Am. Dental Soc. of Anesthesiologists, Internat. Coll. Dentists, Am. Coll. Dentists; mem. Ark. Soc. Oral and Maxillofacial Surgeons (pres. 1982-84), Ark. State Dental Assn. (v.p. 1988-89, pres. 1990-91), N.W. Dist. Dental Soc. (pres. 1983-84). Republican. Presbyterian. Club: Fayetteville Country (pres. 1980-81, 94—). Avocations: golf, tennis, hunting. Home: 359 Fairway Ln Fayetteville AR 72701-7159 Office: PO Box 1807 Fayetteville AR 72702-1807

GRAMMER, KELSEY, actor; b. St. Thomas, V.I., Feb. 21, 1955; s. Allen and Sally Grammer. Studied, Juilliard Sch., N.Y.C. Actor (films) Toy Story 2 (voice), 1999, 15 Minutes, 1999, New Jersey Turnpikes, 1999, Standing on Fishes, 1999, The Real Howard Spitz, 1998, Down Periscope, 1996, (voice) Anastasia, 1997, (TV series) Cheers, 1984-93, Frasier, 1993— (Best New Comedy award Viewers Quality TV, Favorite Male in New TV Series award 20th Ann. People's Choice Awards, Best Actor in Comedy Series nomination 51st Ann. Golden Globe Awards, Lead Actor Emmy award - Comedy Series, 1994, 1995, 98, other awards); appeared in (Off-Broadway prodns.) Plenty, A Month in the Country, Sunday in the Park with George, Quartermaine's Terms, (Broadway prodns.) Macbeth, Othello, TV appearances include Kate and Allie (premiere episode), Wings, Tracy Ullman Show, The Simpsons, mini-series include Kennedy, 1983, George Washington, 1984, Crossings, 1986; TV movies include Dance 'til Dawn, 1988, Beyond Suspicion, 1993, (also exec. prodr.) The Innocent, 1994, London Suite, 1996, The Pentagon Wars; exec. prodr. (TV series) Fired Up, 1997. also: The Artists Agency 10000 Santa Monica Blvd Ste 305 Los Angeles CA 90067-7007*

GRAMMIG, ROBERT JAMES, lawyer; b. Oceanside, Calif., June 15, 1956; s. Richard Adolf and Mary Elizabeth (Spisak) G.; m. Laurel Jean Lenfestey, Aug. 10, 1996. BA, U. Pa., 1978, MA, 1978; JD, Harvard U., 1981. Bar: Fla. 1982, D.C. 1986, U.S. Dist. Ct. (mid. dist.) Fla. 1982, U.S. Ct. Appeals (11th and 5th cirs.) 1982, U.S. Supreme Ct. 1985. Law clk. to Hon. Thomas A. Clark U.S. Ct. Appeals (5th and 11th cirs.), Atlanta, 1981-82; assoc. Holland & Knight, Tampa, Fla., 1982-88, ptnr., 1989—. Bd. dirs. Child Abuse Coun., Tampa, 1993-97; mem. Leadership Tampa, 1994-95; Sec. Tampa Bay Internat. Trade Coun., 1994, vice chmn., 1995. Mem. Tampa Bay Coun. on Fgn. Rels., German Am. C. of C., U.S.-Austrian C. of C., Phi Beta Kappa. Republican. Roman Catholic. Home: 21 Bahama Cir Tampa FL 33606-3317 Office: Holland & Knight 400 N Ashley Dr Ste 2300 Tampa FL 33602-4322

GRAMS, BETTY JANE, minister, educator, writer; b. Lead, S.D., Mar. 13, 1926; d. Harold C. and Elizabeth Amanda (Vaughn) Haas; m. Monroe David Grams, May 1, 1949; children: MonaRe' Grams Shields, Rocky Vaughn, Rachel Jo Grams Schaible. Student, North Cen. Bible Coll., 1945-48, Diploma in Theology, 1963; BA in Edn. and Theology, Assemblies of God Theol. Sch., 1978. Ordained to ministry Assemblies of God, 1957. Asst. pastor local ch. Huron, S.D., 1948-49; co-pastor local ch. Cataract, Wis., 1949-51; missionary to Latin Am. Assemblies of God Ch., Springfield, Mo., 1951—; sec. women's orgn. Assemblies of God, various South Am. countries, 1972-77, missionary educator, Bolivia, Argentina, 1951-91; prof. North Cen. Bible Coll., Mpls., 1963-64, 68-70; speaker Pentecostal Fellowship of N.Am., 1st Hispanic Congress, Can. *God uses men and women to make miracles happen. Teaching is "being." Learning results through "seeing."* Author: Women of Grace, 1978, Families Can Be Happy, 1981, Solving Ministry's Toughest Problems, 1985, Familia, Fe, y Felicidad, 1985, Ministering Through Music, 1990; (music theory) Ministrando Con Musica, 1960—; contbr. articles to various publs. Musician, dir. choirs, Bolivia and Argentina. Home: 611 Manchester Ln Davie FL 33331-2970 Office: Assemblies of God 1448 N Boonville Ave Springfield MO 65802-1806

GRAMS, RODNEY D., senator, former congressman; b. 1948. Student, Anoka-Ramsey Jr. Coll., Brown Inst., Minneapolis, Minn., Carroll Coll., Helena, Mont. Engring. cons. Orr-Schelen Mayeron & Assoc., Mpls.; anchor, producer Sta. KFBB-TV, Great Falls, Mont., Sta. WSAU-TV, Wausau, Wis., Sta. WIFR-TV, Rockford, Ill., Sta. KMSP-TV, Mpls.; mem. 103d Congress from 6th Minn. Dist., 1993-94; U.S. Senator Minn., 1995—; pres., CEO Sun Ridge Builders. Republican. Office: US Senate SD-257 Dirksen Senate Office Bldg Washington DC 20510

GRANADE, FRED KING, lawyer; b. Mobile, Ala., Mar. 3, 1950; s. Joe C. and Lucille (Williams) G.; m. Callie Virginia Smith, Oct. 9, 1976; children: Taylor Rives, Milton Smith, Joseph Kee. BA, Auburn U., 1972; JD, Washington and Lee U., 1975. Bar: Ala. 1975, Fla. 1976, U.S. Dist. Ct. (so. and mid. dists.) Ala., 1977, U.S. Supreme Ct. 1979, U.S. Ct. Appeals (5th and 11th cirs.) 1981. Law clk. to presiding justice Ala. Ct. of Criminal Appeals, Montgomery, 1975-76; ptnr. Stone, Granade & Crosby P.C., Bay Minette, Daphne, Ala., 1986—; bd. dirs. First Community Bank, Chatom, Ala., S.W. Bancshares, Mt. Vernon, Ala. Bd. dirs. Historic Blakeley Authority, Ala., 1983-85, North Baldwin Hosp.; chmn. profl. div. North Baldwin United Fund, Bay Minette, 1987. Mem. Ala. Bar Assn., Fla. Bar Assn., Baldwin County Bar Assn., Omicron Delta Kappa, Foley (Ala.) Club, Optimist. Presbyterian. Office: Stone Granade & Crosby 34 N Pine St Bay Minette AL 36507-3202

GRANADY, JUANITA H., retired religious organization administrator. Asst. stated clerk of the gen. assembly Dept. Stated Clerk of Presbyn. Ch., USA, Louisville; dir. Dept. Stated Clerk of Presbyn. Ch., USA, until 1998; ret., 1998. Office: Presbyterian Church 100 Witherspoon St Louisville KY 40202-6300

GRANATA, LINDA M., lawyer; b. Montreal, June 9, 1951; d. Albert Joseph and Marylka (Aksamit) G. BS in Broadcasting, U. Fla., 1974; JD, Nova U., 1988. Bar: Fla. 1988, U.S. Dist. Ct. (so. dist.) Fla. 1989, U.S. Ct. Appeals (11th cir.) 1990, U.S. Tax Ct. 1990. Pres. Mkt. Makers, Inc., Miami, Fla., 1978-88, Ethylene Eaters, Inc., North Miami, Fla., 1981-88, 92—; law clk. to Hon. Paul M. Marko III 17th Cir. Ct., Ft. Lauderdale, Fla., 1986-87; corp. counsel Quantum Assocs., Inc., Miami Beach, 1988-89; assoc. Richard C. Fox, P.A., Boca Raton, Fla., 1989-90; pvt. practice North Miami, 1990-93; corp. counsel World Trade Consortium, Inc., Miami, 1993-99; arbitrator Nat. Assn. Securities Dealers, Ft. Lauderdale, 1990—, Nat. Futures Assn., Ft. Lauderdale, 1990-95; guardian ad litum 17th Cir. Ct. Broward County, 1996-99. Mem. Am. Arbitration Assn., Nat. Panel Consumer Arbitrators. Office: 20101 NE 16 Pl Ste 200 Miami FL 33179

GRANATO, CATHERINE (CAMMI GRANATO), hockey player; b. Downers Grove, Ill., Mar. 25, 1971. Student, Providence Coll., R.I., 1989-93, Concordia U., 1994-97. Hockey player U.S. Nat. Team, 1992—. Recipient ice hockey Gold medal Olympic Games, Nagano, Japan, 1998. Office: USA Hockey Inc 1775 Bob Johnson Dr Colorado Springs CO 80906-4090*

GRANATO, JESSE D., alderman; b. Dec. 30, 1958; s. Blas B. and Maria (Salinas) G.; m. Avril; 2 children. Student, Roosevelt U. Asst. Ho. of Reps., 1980-88, Vice-Mayor's Office, Chgo., 1988-94; alderman ward 1 City of Chgo., 1994—; ward committeeman, del. Dem. Nat. Conv., 1996—. Office: 1951 W Division St Chicago IL 60622-3148*

GRANATSTEIN, JACK LAWRENCE, history educator; b. Toronto, May 21, 1939; s. Benjamin and Shirley (Geller) G.; m. Mary Elaine Hitchcock, 1961; children: Carole, Michael (dec.). BA, Royal Mil. Coll., Kingston, Ont., 1961; MA, U. Toronto, 1962; PhD, Duke U., 1966; DLitt (hon.), Meml. U., 1993; LLD (hon.), U. Calgary, 1994, Ryerson Polytech. U., 1999. Historian Dept. Nat. Def., Ottawa, Ont., 1965-66; prof. history York U., 1966-95, Disting. rsch. prof. history emeritus, 1995—; Rowell Jackman fellow Canadian Inst. of Internat. Affairs, 1995-98; commr. Spl. Commn. on the Restructuring of the Can. Forces Reserves, 1995; CEO, dir. Can. War Mus., 1998—. Author: Politics of Survival, 1967, Canada's War, 1975, Broken Promises, 1977, Ties That Bind, 1977, American Dollars-Canadian Prosperity, 1978, A Man of Influence, 1981, The Ottawa Men, 1982, Twentieth Century Canada, 1983, The Great Brain Robbery, 1984, Canada 1957-67, 1986, Sacred Trust? Brian Mulroney and the Conservatives in Power, 1986, The Collins Dictionary of Canadian History, 1988, Marching to Armageddon, 1989, How Britain's Weakness Forced Canada into the Arms of the United States, 1989, A Nation Forged in Fire, 1989, Pirouette: Pierre Trudeau and Canadian Foreign Policy, 1990, Mutual Hostages: Canadians and Japanese in the Second World War, 1990, Spy Wars, Espionage and Canada from Gouzenko to Glasnost, 1990, For Better or Worse: Canada and the U.S. to the 1990's, War and Peacekeeping, 1991, English Canada Speaks Out, 1991, Oxford Dictionary of Canadian Military History, 1992, The Generals: The Canadian Army's Senior Commanders in the Second World War, 1993, Empire to Umpire: Canada and the World to the 1990's, 1994, The Good Fight: Canadians and World War II, 1995, Victory 1945: Canadians From War to Peace, 1995, Yankee Go Home? Canadians and Anti-Americanism, 1997, The Canadian 100, 1997, Petrified Campus: The Crisis of Canada's Universities, 1997, The Veterans Charter and Post World War II Canada, 1998, Who Killed Canadian History?, 1998. Bd. govs. Royal Mil. Coll., 1996—. Served to lt. Can. Army, 1956-66. Recipient Tyrrell medal for Can. history, 1992, J.W. Dafoe prize, 1993, medal for biography U. B.C., 1993, Vimy award Conf. Def. Assns. Inst., 1996; Killam rsch. fellow Can. Coun., 1982-84, 91-93; rsch. grantee Can. Dept. External Affairs, 1978-80, Can. Dept. Nat. Def., 1987-88, Social Sci. and Humanities Rsch. Coun. Can., 1978-79, 82-84, 85-89, 91-97; named officer Order of Can., 1997. Fellow Royal Soc. Can.; mem. Can. Inst. Internat. Affairs. Home: 53 Marlborough Ave, Toronto, ON Canada M5R 1X5

GRANATSTEIN, VICTOR LAWRENCE, electrical engineer, educator; b. Toronto, Feb. 8, 1935; s. Charles Samuel and Bella (Godfrey) G.; m. Bethie Mills, Sept. 4, 1955; children—Rebecca Miriam, Abraham Solomon, Annie Sara Khaya. B.S., Columbia U., 1960, M.S., 1961, Ph.D., 1963. Research staff physicist Bell Telephone Labs. Murray Hill, N.J., 1964-72; head high power electromagnetic radiation br. Naval Research Lab., Washington, 1972-83; prof. elec. engring. U. Md., College Park, 1983—; acting dir. Inst. for Plasma Research, 1986-88; dir. 1988-98. Vis. lectr. Hebrew U., Jerusalem, 1969-70; vis. prof. Tel Aviv U., 1994; cons. BDM Corp., McLean, Va., 1981-83, Sci. Applications Corp., McLean, 1983—, Omega-P Inc., New Haven, 1983—, Pulse Scis. Inc., San Leandro, 1985-88, Jet Propulsion Lab., Pasadena, 1987-91. Patentee microwave devices; contbr. articles to profl. jours.; editor Wave Heating and Current Drive in Magnetic Plasmas, 1985, High Power Microwaves, 1987, Applications of High Power Microwaves, 1994. Pres., Bethesda Chevy Chase Jewish Community Group, 1983-84. Recipient R.D. Conrad Award Sec. Navy, 1981, Superior Civilian Service award, Office Naval Research, 1980, E.O. Hulbert award Naval Research Lab., 1980, Robert L. Woods award Sec. Def., 1998; Fulbright sr. scholar award, 1993-94. Fellow Am. Phys. Soc., IEEE (vice chmn. plasma sci. com. 1984-85, Plasma Sci. and applications award 1991). Democrat. Avocations: folk dancing; swimming. Home: 13508 Rippling Brook Dr Silver Spring MD 20906-3177 Office: U Md Inst Plasma Rsch College Park MD 20742-3511

GRANCHELLI, RALPH S., company executive; b. Framingham, Mass., Jan. 2, 1955; s. Ralph S. and Avon L. (Chadwick) G. ASEE, Wentworth Inst. Tech., Boston, 1975; postgrad., U. Mass., 1975-78. Nat. sales mgr. Teledyne Semiconductor Co., Mountain View, Calif., 1981-85; v.p. Elantec, Inc., Milpitas, Calif., 1985—. Office: Elantec Inc 1996 Tarob Ct Milpitas CA 95035-6824*

GRANDE, ALEXANDER, IV, artist; b. Sellersville, Pa., Oct. 20, 1970; s. Alexander Grande III and Mary Alice (Bowman) Kern. BFA in Printmaking, Kutztown U., 1994. Printmaker Silverdale, Pa., 1994—; guest lectr. Albright Coll., Reading, 1998. Contbr. prints: International Typographic Design, 1994; contbr. prints to profl. jours. Recipient 1st place color abstract print Reading (Pa.) Fair, 1996, 2d place abstract mixed media print graphics and pastels category, 1996, 1st place black and white abstract print in graphics and pastels category; Scenic River Days Juried Art Show, Reading, 1993, 3d place original prints category Gallery in the Park Festival, Sellersville, Pa., 1992, 1st pl. award for black and white abstract print Reading Fair Juried Art Show, 1997, 1st pl. award for computer/mixed media print, 1997, 1st place award black/white abstract print Reading (Pa.) Fair Juried Art Show, 1998, 3rd place award abstract mixed media print, 1998. Mem. New Arts Program, Print Ctr., Nat. Campaign for Freedom of Expression. Avocations: exercise, movies, music, reading. Home: 124 Baringer Ave Silverdale PA 18962

GRANDERATH, WALTER JOSEPH, tax administrator; b. Albany, N.Y., Aug. 10, 1943; s. Werner Josef and Maria (Wimmer) G.; m. Beverly Ann Bonebright, June 27, 1964; 1 child, Daniel John. Grad., Siena Coll., 1995. Svc. mgr. Abele Tractor, Albany, 1965-70; tax examiner trainee N.Y. State Dept. of Tax and Fin., Albany, 1970-72, sr. tax examiner, 1970-77, assoc. tax examiner, 1977-79, prin. tax examiner, 1979-84, tax processing adminstr., 1984—. With USAF, 1962-65. Mem. NRA, Tax Processing Mgrs. Assn. (funder, pres. bd. dirs. 1989—), N.Am. Hunters Club, Waukesha Hunting Club, U.S. Table Tennis Assn., Nat. Chevelle Owners Assn., Elks. Republican. Roman Catholic. Avocations: hunting, table tennis, collector of cars, choral group singing, camping. Home: 26 Cardinal Ave West Sand Lake NY 12196-2101 Office: NY State Dept Tax and Fin Bldg 8 Rm 680 State Campus Albany NY 12227

GRANDIN, TEMPLE, livestock equipment designer, educator; b. Boston, Aug. 29, 1947; d. Richard McCurdy and Eustacia (Cutler) G. BA in Psychology, Franklin Pierce Coll., 1970; MS in Animal Sci., Arizona State U., 1975; PhD in Animal Sci., U. Ill., Urbana, 1989. Livestock editor Ariz. Farmer Ranchman, Phoenix, 1973-78; equipment designer Corral Industries, Phoenix, 1974-75; ind. cons. Grandin Livestock Systems, Urbana, 1975-90, Fort Collins, Colo., 1990—; lectr., asst. prof. animal sci. dept. Colo. State U., Fort Collins, 1990—; chmn. handing com. Livestock Conservation Inst., Madison, Wis., 1976—; surveyor USDA. Author: Emergence Labelled Autistic, 1986, Recommended Animal Handling Guidelines for Meat Packers, 1991, Livestock Handling and Transport, 1993, Thinking in Pictures, 1995, Genetics and the Behavior of Domestic Animals, 1998; contbg. editor Meat and Poultry mag., 1987-98; contbr. articles to profl. jours. Recipient Meritorious Svcs. award Livestock Conservation, Madison, Wis., 1986, Disting. Alumni award Franklin Pierce Coll., 1989, Industry Innovators award Meat Mktg. and Tech. Mag., 1994, Brownlee award for internat. leadership in sci. publ. promoting respect for animals Animal Welfare Found. of Canada, 1995, Harry Roswell award Scientists Ctr. for Animal Welfare, 1995, Humane Ethics in Action award Geraldine R. Dodge Found., 1998, Forbes award Am. Meat Assn., 1998; named One of Processing Stars of 1990 Nat. Provisioner, 1990, Woman of Yr. in Svc. to Agr. Progressive Farmer, 1999. Mem. Autism Soc. Am. (bd. dirs. 1988—, Trammel Crow award 1989), Am. Soc. Animal Sci. (Animal Mgmt. award 1995), Am. Soc. Agrl. Cons. (bd. dirs. 1981-83), Am. Soc. Agrl. Engrs., Am. Meat Inst. (supplier mem., Industry Advancement award 1995), Am. Registry of Profl. Animal Scis. Republican. Episcopalian. Achievements include design of stockyards and humane restraint equipment for major meat packing companies in the U.S., Canada and Australia. Home: Grandin Livestock Systems 2918 Silver Plume Dr C-3 Fort Collins CO 80526 Office: Colo State U Animal Sci Dept Fort Collins CO 80523

GRANDINETTI, MICHEAL LAWRENCE, marketing executive; b. Bklyn., Mar. 7, 1960; s. Francis Mario and Mary Ann (Yelapi) G. BS in Mech. Engrng. magna cum laude, Rutgers U., 1983; MBA, Yale U., 1989. With Hewlett Packard, Wallingford, Conn., 1983-85; mgr. market devel. Hewlett Packard, Ft. Collins, Colo., 1985-87; mgmt. cons. McKinsey and Co., N.Y.C., 1989-91; dir. worldwide field ops. Viewlogic Systems, Marlborough, Mass., 1991-95; v.p. mktg. Raptor Systems, Waltham, Mass., 1995-97; v.p. mktg. and bus. devel. Connected Corp., 1997-99, Marketsoft Corp., Lexington, Mass., 1999—. Advisor Jr. Achievement. Named to Nat. Dean's List; Jess Morrow Johns Meml. scholar Yale U. Mem. Nat. Engrng. Honor Soc., Nat. Mech. Engrng. Honor Frat., Am. Mgmt. Assn., Nat. Assn. Corp. Dirs. (adv. bd.), Yale Sch. Mgmt. Alumni Assn., Mass. Software Coun., Mass. Telecomm. Coun., Yale Club (N.Y.C.), Toastmasters, MIT Enterprise Forum, Tau Beta Pi, Pi Tau Sigma. Roman Catholic. Avocations: bicycling, lap swimming, skiing, travel, arts.

GRANDIZIO, LENORE, social worker; b. N.Y.C., Apr. 20, 1952; d. Louis and Angelina (Prez de Garcia) G. BA, SUNY, Geneseo, 1973; MSSW, Columbia U., 1978. Cert. social worker, N.Y.; cert. child psychiatry and child guidance; diplomate clin. social work. Assoc. staff mem. Child, Adolescent and Family Clinic Postgrad. Ctr. for Mental Health, N.Y.C., 1981-83, assoc. staff mem. Adult Clinic, 1984-87; social worker East Harlem Consultation Svc., N.Y.C., 1983-84; sr. worker Jewish Bd. Family and Children's Svcs., Bklyn., 1984-85; sch. social worker N.Y.C. Bd. Edn., 1985—; co-chair regional staff devel. com. N.Y.C. Bd. Edn., 1996-98; presenter in field, N.Y.C., 1995-97. Mem. NAFE, NASW. Home: 229 W 105th St Apt 53 New York NY 10025-3918

GRANDMAISON, J. JOSEPH, federal agency executive. Grad., Burdett Coll. V.p. Weil & Howe; with U.S. Trade and Devel. Agy., Washington, dir., 1993—; adj. instr. Sch. Pub. Comm., Boston U.; fellow Harvard U./John F. Kennedy Sch. Govt.; cons. in field. Fed. co-chair New Eng. Reg. Commn., 1977-80; chmn. Fed. Reg. Coun.; Dem. nominee for Gov. N.H., 1990; chmn. N.H. Dem. Party, 1987-90. Office: Trade & Devel Agy 1621 N Kent St Ste 200 Arlington VA 22209-2131

GRANDSTRAND, RUTH HELENA, retired community health and gerontology nurse; b. Shafer, Minn., Jan. 28, 1916; d. Gustav Furman and Edna Gertrude (Paulson) Hawkinson; m. Clifford J. Grandstrand, Aug. 28, 1943; children: Mark Clifford, Lois Ruth, Gail Louise (dec.). Diploma, Bethesda Sch. Nursing, St. Paul, 1937; postgrad., U. Minn., 1938-39. Cert. in hospice mgmt. Surg. nursing supr. Asbury Hosp., Mpls., 1939-41; instr. nursing arts Bethesda Hosp., 1941-43; dir. insvc. edn. Margaret S. Parmly Residence, Chisago City, Minn., 1977-85; home care nurse Meml. Enterprises, Freeport, Ill., 1985-94; ret., 1994; home care nurse, Freeport. 2d lt. Army Nurse Corps, 1941-43. Mem. Minn. Nurses Assn., Ill. Nurses Assn.

GRANDY, FRED, foundation administrator, former congressman, former actor; b. Sioux City, Iowa, June 29, 1948; s. William Frederick and Bonnie Grandy; m. Catherine Mann, 1987; children: Marya, Charlie, Monica. B.A. in English, Harvard U., 1970. Founder improvisational group The Proposition, Harvard U.; mem. 100th-104th Congresses from 6th (now 5th) Iowa Dist., 1987-94; mem. standards of official conduct com., mem. ways and means com.; CEO Goodwill Industries Internat. Inc., 1995—. Appeared in play Green Julia, N.Y.C., Joe Papp's In The Boom Boom Room, until 1974; collaborator rev.: in play Pretzels; film appearances include Close Encounters of the Third Kind; television films include The Girl Most Likely To, 1973, Blind Ambition, 1979, Love Boat II, Love Boat III; television series: The Monster Squad, 1976-77, The Love Boat, 1977-86; other television appearances include Welcome Back Kotter. Office: Goodwill Industries Internat 9200 Rockville Pike Bethesda MD 20814-3896*

GRANDY, WALTER THOMAS, JR., physicist, educator; b. Phila., June 1, 1933; s. Walter Thomas and Margaret Mary (Hayes) G.; m. Patricia Josephine Langan, Dec. 27, 1955; children: Christopher, Neal, Mary, Jeanne. BS, U. Colo., 1960, PhD, 1964. Physicist Nat. Bur. Standards, Boulder, Colo., 1958-63; mem. faculty U. Wyo., Laramie, 1963—; prof. physics U. Wyo., 1969-98, head dept., 1971-78; prof. emeritus, 1998—; Fulbright lectr. U. Sao Paulo, Brazil, 1966-67, vis. prof., 1982; vis. prof. U. Tubingen, W. Germany, 1978-79, U. Sydney, Australia, 1988. Author: Introduction to Electrodynamics and Radiation, 1970, Foundations of Statistical Mechanics: Volume I, Equilibrium Theory, 1987, Vol. II, Nonequilibrium Phenomena, 1988, Relativistic Quantum Mechanics of Leptons and Fields, 1991. Served with USNR, 1953-57. Fellow AAAS; mem. Am. Phys. Soc., Brasilian Phys. Soc., Am. Assn. Physics Tchrs., Sigma Xi, Sigma Pi Sigma. Achievements include research on statis. mechanics, electrodynamics, quantum theory. Home: 604 S 18th St Laramie WY 82070-4304

GRANET, KENNETH M., internist; b. Manhasset, N.Y., Mar. 22, 1957; s. Irving and Arlene Granet; m. Wendy Granet. BA summa cum laude, Hofstra U., Hempstead, N.Y., 1979; MD, SUNY-Downstate Med. Ctr., Bklyn., 1984. Diplomate Am. Bd. Internal Medicine. Intern/resident in medicine North Shore Univ. Hosp., Manhasset, 1984-87, Meml. Sloan Kittering Cancer Ctr., N.Y.C., 1984-87; pvt. practice L.I., N.Y., 1987-93, Eatontown, N.J., 1993—; asst. program dir. dept. medicine Monmouth Med. Ctr., Long Branch, N.J., 1993—; clin. asst. prof. medicine Hahnemann U. Sch. Medicine, Phila., 1993—; med. dir. Cerebral Palsy, Monmouth, 1993—; lectr. in field. Contbr. articles to profl. jours. Organizer/founder 5 mile Spring Health Run, North Shore Univ. Hosp., 1987-92. Recipient Dean's Spl. award for excellence in clin. teaching Hahnemann U. Sch. Medicine, 1995; named Attending of the Yr., Dept. Medicine, Monmouth Med. Ctr., 1993-94. Fellow ACP (preceptor/mentor program); mem. N.J. Med. Soc., Monmouth County Med. Soc. (exec. com. 1994—), Phi Beta Kappa. Office: Victoria Plz 615 Hope Rd Eatontown NJ 07724-1277

GRANGAARD, DANIEL ROBERT, psychologist; b. Fond du Lac, Wis., Jan. 7, 1950; s. Lawrence Robert and Dorothy Ruth (Giove) G.; m. Becky Anne Byas, June 16, 1979; children: Dawn Michelle, Scott Robert. BA, Baylor U., 1972, MS, 1974, EdD, 1976. Lic. psychologist; lic. specialist in sch. psychology. Teaching fellow Baylor U., Waco, Tex., 1974-76; assoc. sch. psychologist Edn. Svc. Ctr. Region XII, Waco, 1976-77; sch. psychologist Austin (Tex.) Ind. Sch. Dist., 1977-85; psychologist in pvt. practice Austin, 1985-89; dir. testing, internship tng. Minirth-Meier Tunnell & Wilson Clinic, Austin, 1989-94; pvt. practice, psychologist Austin, 1994—; psychologist Genesis unit Shoal Creek Hosp., Austin, 1987-92, 94-95; cons. psychologist Charter Hosp., Austin, 1984-94, United Cerebral Palsy Assn., 1992-98, Genesis Behavioral Health Clinic, Austin, 1994-95, Austin Child Guidance Ctr., 1995-96; instr. psychology Austin C.C., 1995—; adj. prof. psychology St. Edwards U., 1997—. Contbr. chpts. to books, articles to profl. jours. Westcreek rep. Austin Neighborhood Coun., 1980; coach YMCA Little League Baseball, 1995—; dir. counseling First Evangel. Free Ch., Austin, 1994-95, elder, 1993-96. Mem. Am. Psychol. Assn., Tex. Psychol. Assn., Tex. Cmty. Coll. Tchrs. Assn. Republican. Mem. Evangelical Free Ch. Avocations: softball, golf, tennis, model railroading, fly fishing. Office: Austin CC Rio Grande Campus 1212 Rio Grande Austin TX 78701

GRANGER, BRUCE INGHAM, retired English language educator; b. Phila., Feb. 28, 1920; s. Percival Harkness and Caroline Scovel (Gibbons) G.; m. Rosemary Ingham Jemne, Oct. 14, 1944 (dec. June 1988); children: Percival Harkness III (dec.), Adam Lewis; m. Eleanor Goltz Huzar, Oct. 11, 1991. BA, Cornell U., 1942, MA, 1943, PhD, 1946. Instr. in English U. Wis., Madison, 1946-50; asst. prof. U. Denver, 1950-53; assoc. prof. U. Okla., Norman, 1953-61, prof. English, 1961-82, ret., 1982; Fulbright lectr. U. Vienna, Austria, 1968-69. Author: Political Satire in The American Revolution, 1960, Benjamin Franklin: An American Man of Letters, 1964, American Essay Serials from Franklin to Irving, 1978; editor: Washington Irving's Old Style—Salmagundi, 1977. Grantee-in-aid Am. Philos. Soc., 1955, 58, 66, 67, 78, NEH, 1975. Mem. MLA (pres. South Ctrl. chpt. 1978-79), Phi Beta Kappa. Home: 1375 Burcham Dr East Lansing MI 48823-3671

GRANGER, FRANK, III, assessor; b. Baton Rouge, La., Oct. 13, 1958; m. Dottia Kent; children: Lauren, Melissa. Chief dep. assessor City of Baton Rouge, 1980-85, assessor, 1985—. Mem. Internat. Assn. Assessing Officer, La. Assessor Assn. (past chmn. legis. com.). Office: Office of Assessor 222 Saint Louis St Baton Rouge LA 70802-5817

GRANGER, HARVEY, JR., retired manufacturing company executive; b. Savannah, Ga., Sept. 9, 1928; s. Harvey and Marion (Rauers) G.; m. Barbara Brandt, Sept. 8, 1951; children: Harvey, Matthew Brandt, Barbara James. B in Indsl. Engrng., Ga. Inst. Tech, 1951. Indsl. engr. Union Camp Paper Co., Savannah, 1950-56; indsl. engr. Great Dane Trailers, Savannah, 1956-61, plant mgr., 1961-71, v.p. mfg., 1971-78, exec. v.p., chief operating officer, 1978-84, pres., chief exec. officer, 1984-91; cons. Savannah, 1992-96, ret., 1996; city adv. bd. dirs. Nations Bank, Savannah, 1979-95. Mem. adv. bd. Sch. Engrng. Ga. Inst. Tech., 1985-91; mem. bd. trustees St. Joseph's Hosp., Savannah, 1988-97, vice-chmn. 1995, chmn. 1996-97; chmn. bd. trustees St. Joseph's-Candler Health Sys., Savannah, 1997—; dir. vol. trustees Not-For-Profit Hosps., Washington, 1995—, mem. exec. com., 1997, sec., 1998, vice chmn., 1999—. With USN, 1945-47. Mem. Truck Trailer Mfrs. Assn. (chmn. 1986-87). Clubs: Oglethorpe (Savannah) (pres. 1984-85), Savannah Golf. Avocations: golf, fishing. Home: 405 Coveview Dr Savannah GA 31406-3204

GRANGER, KAY, congresswoman; b. Greenville, Tex., Jan. 18, 1943; children: John Dean, Chelsea, Brandon. BA, Tex. Wesleyan U., 1964; DHL, Tex. Wesleyan U., Arlington, 1993. Mem. zoning com. City of Ft. Worth, 1980-88; mem. pvt. industry coun., 1988-89; councilwoman City of Ft. Worth, 1989-91, mayor, 1991-95; mem. 105th-106th Congress from 12th Tex. dist., 1996—; owner G&R Ins. Agy., Ft. Worth; owner Kay Granger & Assocs. Recipient Leadership award state of Tex., 1986, Woman of Yr. award, 1987, Bus. and Profl. Woman award, 1987. Mem. Am. Planning Assn., Internat. Sister Cities Assn., Women's Policy Forum (bd. dirs.), East Ft. Worth Bus. and Profl. Assn. (bd. dirs.), Ft. Worth Bus. and Estate Planning Coun., Meadowbrook Bus. and Profl. Womens Assn., East Ft. Worth C. of C. (vice chmn.). Methodist. *

GRANGER, LUC ANDRE, university dean, psychologist; b. St. Jean, Que., Can., Apr. 8, 1944; s. Andrew and Georgette (Lacasse) G. B.A., U. Montreal, 1962, B.Sc., 1964, L.P.S., 1966, Ph.D., 1969. Asst. prof. psychology U. Montreal, 1969-73, assoc. prof., 1973-79, prof., 1979—, head dept., 1979-83, 90—, assoc. dean, 1983-87. Author: Apprentissage et Therapie, 1972, La Therapie Behaviorale, 1976, La Communication dans le Couple, 1979. Postdoctoral fellow U. Lille, France, 1969. Mem. Can. Psychol. Assn. (sec.-treas. 1982-85, pres. 1992-95), Corp. des Psychologues (treas. 1974-78, pres. 1986-90). Office: U Montreal Dept Psychology CP 6128 Succa Sentre Ville, Montreal, PQ Canada H3C 3J7

GRANGER, PHILIP RICHARD, minister; b. Detroit, June 19, 1943; s. Myrl Richard and Alvirta May (Kling) G.; m. Karen Elizabeth Draper, Feb. 20, 1965 (div. 1972); children: Mark, Leslie; m. Susan Kay Alderfer, Mar. 4, 1973; children: Randall, Candace. AA, Jackson Jr. Coll., 1963; BA, MBA, Mich. State U., 1965, 67; MDiv, No. Bapt. Theol. Sem., Lombard, Ill., 1978; D of Ministry, Oral Roberts U., 1986. Ordained deacon United Meth. Ch., 1977, ordained elder, 1980; CPA, Mich. Audit staff, cons. Ernst & Ernst, Detroit, 1967-71; mem. contrs. staff Assocs. Corp., South Bend, Ind., 1971-73; v.p., contr. 1st Fed. Savs. and Loan, Chgo., 1973-76; pastor Mokena (Ill.) United Meth. Ch., 1976-82; dir. fin. No. Ind. Conf. United Meth. Ch., Marion, 1982-86; sr. pastor St. Lukes United Meth. Ch., Kokomo, Ind., 1986-89, Trinity United Meth. Ch., Huntington, Ind., 1989-94; dist. supt. Kokomo (Ind.) Dist. United Meth. Ch., 1994-99; sr. pastor Coll. Ave. United Meth. Ch., Muncie, Ind., 1999—; mem. adj. faculty Huntington Coll., 1990-94; new life missioner Gen. Bd. Discipleship, Nashville, 1980—; bd. dirs. Good News, Wilmore, Ky., Samaritan Ctr., Inc., Huntington, Found. for Mission and Ministry, Inc., Marion. Author: Discerment Planning, 1986. Founding mem. Tri-Village Crisis Intervention Ctr., Mokena, 1978-81; treas. Village of Mokena, 1978-82; bd. dirs. Mental Health Assn. Ill., Chgo., 1974-75. Mem. Am. Assn. Christian Counselors, Rotary Internat., Delta Sigma Pi, Beta Gamma Sigma, Beta Alpha Psi. Avocations: reading, travel, personal computers. Home: 4011 Coventry Dr Mongie IN 47304 Office: Coll Ave United Meth Ch 1968 Main St Muncie IN 47303 *To experience life requires more than experiencing the simple joys and pleasures that life provides. To really experience life is to experience the Christian community of caring and sharing that only occurs when we are truly one in Christ.*

GRANGER, ROBERT ALAN, mechanical and aerospace engineering educator, consultant, publisher; b. Evanston, Ill., Aug. 7, 1928; s. Robert Alan and Kathleen (Buehr) G.; m. Ruth Nickerson, Oct. 7, 1951; children: Eric Carl, Erin Alyson. B.A., Pomona Coll., 1955; M.S. Drexel Inst. Tech., 1959; Ph.D., U. Md., 1970. Sr. research scientist Martin Co., Balt., 1955-60; prin. engr. Boeing Co., Renton, Wash., 1975; prof. mechanical and aerospace engrng. U.S. Naval Academy, Annapolis, Md., 1960—, discipline dir., 1972-75; fellow (hon.) Cambridge (England) U., 1991; pub., CEO Sci. Archives, Inc., 1997; cons. NASA, Boeing Co.; vis. prof. U. Petroleum and Minerals, Saudi Arabia, 1977-79, U. Zurich, Switzerland, 1978, Yale U., 1989; dir. Vortex Dynamics Symposium von Karman Inst., Brussels, Belgium; dir., prin. lectr. Introduction to Wing Flutter Symposium, 1991. Author: Fluid Mechanics, 1985, Unified Method of Aeroelasticity, 1986, Experiments in Fluid Mechanics, 1986, Design of Spacecraft, 1988, Introduction to the Flutter of Winged Aircraft, 1992, Experiments in Heat Transfer and Thermodynamics, 1994, Fluid Mechanics, 1994, Life on Mars, 1997. Contbr. over 400 technical papers. Served with U.S. Army, 1950-52, Korea. Ford Found. fellow, 1965; recipient USN Meritorious Civilian award, 1996. Hon. mem. Inst. Modern Physics (Athens, Greece); mem. AIAA, Kappa Mu Epsilon, Alpha Gamma Sigma. Republican. Avocations: composing, mountain climbing, writing, tennis, swimming. Home: 31 Hickory Head Hammock Lady Lake FL 32159-8868 Office: US Naval Acad Mech Engrng Dept Annapolis MD 21402

GRANHOLM, JENNIFER MULHERN, state attorney general; b. Vancouver, B.C., Can., Feb. 5, 1959; came to U.S., 1962; d. Civtor Ivar and Shirley Alfreda (Dowden) G.; m. Daniel Granholm Mullhern, May 23, 1986; children: Kathryn, Cecelia, Jack. BA, U. Calif., Berkeley, 1984; JD, Harvard U., 1987. Bar: Mich. 1987, U.S. Dist. Ct. (ea. dist.) Mich. 1987, U.S. Ct. Appeals (6th cir.) 1987. Jud. law clk. 6th Cir Ct. Appeals, Detroit, 1987-88; exec. asst. Wayne County Exec., Detroit, 1988-89; asst. U.S. atty. Dept. Justice, Detroit, 1990-94; corp. counsel Wayne County, Detroit, 1994—; elected atty. gen., 1999; gen. counsel Detroit/Wayne County Stadium Authority, 1996—. Contbr. articles to profl. jours. V.p., bd.dirs. YWCA, Inkster, Mich., 1995—; del. Dem. Nat. Conv., Chgo., 1996; chair sel. com. U.S. Sen., Detroit, 1997; mem. LEadership DEtroit, 1990—. Mem. Detroit Bar Assn., Women's Law Assn., Inc. Soc. Irish Lawyers. Roman Catholic. Avocations: running, family, laughing. Office: Atty Gen PO Box 30212 Lansing MI 48909-1454*

GRANIK, RUSSELL T., sports association executive; m. Joyce Granik; children: Daniel, Erynn. Grad. magna cum laude, Dartmouth Coll., 1969; law degree cum laude, Harvard U., 1973. With Breed, Abbott & Morgan, N.Y.C.; staff atty. NBA, 1976-78, asst. gen. counsel, 1978-80, gen. counsel, 1980-84, exec. v.p., 1984-90, dep. commr., 1990—; v.p. USA Basketball, 1989-96, pres. 1996—. Trustee, mem. exec. com. Naismith Meml. Basketball Hall of Fame. Office: Nat Basketball Assn Olympic Tower 645 5th Ave 15th Fl New York NY 10022-5986

GRANIRER, EDMOND ERNEST, mathematician, educator; b. Constanza, Romania, Feb. 19, 1935; s. Jacob G. M.Sc., Hebrew U., Jerusalem, 1959, Ph.D., 1962. Mem. faculty dept. math. U. Ill., 1962-64, Cornell U., 1964-65, U. B.C., Vancouver, 1965-66, 67—; prof. math. U. B.C., 1970-97, prof. emeritus, 1997—; faculty U. Montreal, 1966-67. Contbr. articles to profl. jours. Grantee NSERC, 1996. Fellow Royal Soc. Can.; mem. Can. Math. Soc., Am. Math. Soc. Office: U BC, Dept Math, Vancouver, BC Canada V6T 1Z2

GRANLUND, THOMAS ARTHUR, engineering executive, consultant; b. Spokane, Wash., Mar. 1, 1951; s. William Arthur and Louise (Urie) G.; m. Jean MacRae Melvin, May 25, 1974 (div. Feb. 1991). BS, Wash. State U., 1973, BA, 1973; MBA, Gonzaga U., 1982. Engrng. adminstr. Lockheed Aeronautical Systems Co., Burbank, Calif., 1978-91; mgmt. cons., 1991—. Co-author: (screenplay) Identities, 1988, Flash, 1989. 1st lt. USAF, 1973-78. Mem. Wash. State U. Alumni Assn. Avocations: skiing, golf, tennis. Home: 20924 Ben Ct Santa Clarita CA 91350-1418

GRANN, PHYLLIS, publisher, editor; b. London, Sept. 2, 1937; d. Solomon and Louisa (Bois-Smith) Eitingon; m. Victor Grann, Sept. 26, 1962; children: Alison, David, Edward. B.A. cum laude, Barnard Coll., 1958. Sec. Doubleday Pubs., N.Y.C., 1958-60; editor William Morrow Inc., N.Y.C., 1960-62, David McKay Co., N.Y.C., 1962-70, Simon & Schuster Inc., N.Y.C., 1970; v.p. Simon & Schuster Inc., 1976; pres., pub. G. P. Putnam's & Sons., N.Y.C., 1976-86; pres. Penguin Putnam, Inc., N.Y.C., 1986-96, CEO, 1987-96, chmn., 1997—. Office: Penguin Putnam Inc 375 Hudson St New York NY 10014*

GRANNEMAN, VERNON HENRY, lawyer; b. Chico, Calif., Aug. 2, 1953; s. Vern Henry and Mary Elizabeth (Riley) G.; m. Stephanie Sampson, Aug. 19, 1978; children: Kelly, Michael. BA, Santa Clara U., 1975, JD, 1978. Bar: Calif. 1978, U.S. Dist. Ct. (no. dist.) Calif. 1978, U.S. Dist. Ct. (cen. dist.) Calif. 1984, U.S. Dist. Ct. (so. and ea. dists.) Calif. 1985. Assoc. atty. Ruffo Ferrari & McNeil, San Jose, Calif., 1978-81; assoc. atty. Pillsbury, Madison & Sutro (merger with Ruffo Ferrari & McNeil), San Jose, 1981-85, ptnr., 1986-96; ptnr. O'Donnell, Rice, Davis, Alexander & Granneman, San Jose, 1996-97, Genesis Law Group, LLP, San Jose, 1997-99, Skjerven, Morrill, MacPherson, Franklin & Friel, San Jose, 1999—. Mem. ABA, Internat. Found. Employee Benefit Plans (arbitration com. 1991-94), Santa Clara County Bar, Santa Clara Univ. Law Alumni (bd. dirs. 1986-92). Democrat. Roman Catholic. Office: Skjerven Morrill MacPherson Franklin & Friel 25 Metro Dr Ste 700 San Jose CA 95110*

GRANNUCI, LEO, marketing professional. Sr. v.p. mktg. and sales Core-Mark Internat., South San Francisco, Calif. Office: Core-Mark Internat 395 Oyster Point Blvd Ste 415 South San Francisco CA 94080-1932*

GRANOF, MICHAEL H., accounting educator; b. N.Y.C., June 16, 1942; s. David H. and Diana (Simon) G.; m. Dena Gloria Hirsch, Aug. 27, 1972; children: Leah, Joshua. AB, Hamilton Coll., 1963; MBA, Columbia U., 1965; PhD, U. Mich., 1972. CPA, Tex. Sr. acct. Coopers & Lybrand, N.Y.C., 1966-68; asst. prof. to prof. acctg. U. Tex., Austin, 1972-84, Ernst & Young disting. centennial prof., chmn. acctg. dept., 1984-88; mem. Nat. Council on Govtl. Acctg., 1982-84, Govtl. Acctg. Standards Adv. Council, Norwalk, Conn., 1984-90; Fulbright prof. Council for Internat. Exchange Scholars, Hebrew U., Jerusalem, 1978-79; vis. prof. U. Tel Aviv, 1981. Author: How To Cost Your Labor Contract, 1973, Financial Accounting: Principles and Issues, 1977, 4th edit., 1990, Accounting for Managers and Investors, 1983, 2d edit., 1993, Government and Not-for-Profit Accounting, 1998; co-editor: Government Accounting and Auditing Update, 1989-97. Co-pres. Congregation Agudas Achim; treas. Austin Area Urban League. With USCG, 1965-66. Erskine fellow U. Canterbury, Christchurch, N.Z., 1983. Mem. AICPAs (com. on govt. acctg. and auditing), Am. Acctg. Assn. (chmn. pub. sector sect. 1981-82), Tex. Soc. CPAs (chmn. govt. acctg. standards com.), Govt. Fin. Officers Assn., Assn. Govt. Accts. Jewish. Home: 7310 Valburn Dr Austin TX 78731-1146 Office: U Tex Dept Acctg CBA 4M 202 Austin TX 78712

GRANOFF, GAIL PATRICIA, lawyer; b. Phila., July 25, 1952; d. Jerome Claymont and Jean (Kessler) G.; m. Stanley B. Edelstein; children: Jessica, Jonathan. A.B., Temple U., 1973; J.D., U. Pa., 1976. Bar: Pa. 1976, U.S. Dist. Ct. (ea. dist.) Pa. 1977, U.S. Ct. Appeals (3d cir.) 1977, U.S. Supreme Ct. 1981. Law clk. to Judge Kalodner U.S. Ct. Appeals (3d cir.), Phila., 1976-77; assoc. Pepper Hamilton & Scheetz, Phila., 1977-84; counsel Rohm and Haas Co., Phila., 1984-86, sr. counsel, 1987-90, corp. sec., sr. counsel, 1990-93, asst. gen. counsel and corp. sec., 1993—. Mem. ABA (chair Reporting Cos. Under the '34 Act, Fed. Securities Com., Bus. Law sect. 1995—), Phila. Bar Assn. (exec. young lawyers sect. 1983-86, sec. 1984-86, commn. on jud. selection and retention investigative divsn. 1985-95, exec. com. bus. law sect. 1998—), Am. Corp. Counsel Assn. Office: Rohm & Haas Co 100 Independence Mall W Philadelphia PA 19106-2399*

GRANOFF, GARY CHARLES, lawyer, investment company executive; b. N.Y.C., Feb. 2, 1948; s. N. Henry and Jeannette (Trum) G.; m. Leslie Barbara Resnick, Dec. 21, 1969; children: Stephen, Robert, Joshua. BBA in Acctg., George Washington U., 1970, JD with honors, 1973. Bar: N.Y., 1974, Fla., 1974, U.S. Dist. Ct. (so. dist.) N.Y., 1976. Assoc. Dreyer & Traub, N.Y.C., 1973-75; ptnr. Ezon, Langberg & Granoff, N.Y.C., 1975-78, Granoff & Walker, N.Y.C., 1982-92, Granoff, Walker & Forlenza P.C., N.Y.C., 1993—; pvt. practice N.Y.C., 1978-81; pres., also bd. dirs. Elk Assocs. Funding Corp., N.Y.C., 1979—, GCG Assocs., Inc., N.Y.C., 1982—; pres., dir. Gemini Capital Corp., 1996—; atty. del. to U.S.-China Joint Session on Trade, Investment and Econ. Law, Beijing, 1987; mem. dean's adv. bd. George Washington U. Law Sch., 1993-. Campaign vol. Mondale for Pres., N.Y.C., 1984; fundraiser Robert Garcia for Congress, N.Y.C., Dem. Senatorial Campaign Com., N.Y.C., 1987-88; active N.Y. Lawyers for Dukakis com., 1988; chmn. N.Y.C. chpt. George Washington U. Nat. Law Ctr. Leadership Gifts Com.; mem. dean's adv. bd. Law Sch. George Washington U., 1994—; bd. trustees George Washington U., 1998. Mem. ABA, N.Y. State Bar Assn., Fla. Bar Assn., Assn. of Bar of City of

N.Y., People to People Internat., Nat. Assn. Investment Cos. (legis com.), George Washington U. Alumni Assn. (chmn. N.Y.C. chpt., bd. dirs. law sch. alumni assn., alumni com. 21 century, bd. trustees), bd. trustees George Washington U., North Shore Country Club (chmn. legal com., bd. govs. 1994-96, 98-99). Avocations: golf, tennis, skiing. Office: Granoff Walker & Forlenza P 747 3rd Ave Fl 4 New York NY 10017-2803

GRANOFF, MICHAEL, investment agency manager; b. N.Y.C., Oct. 17, 1968; s. Martin Jay and Perry Barbara (Kasper) G. BA, Tufts U., 1991; JD, Northwestern U., 1997, MM, 1997. Summer assoc. Squadron Ellenoff, N.Y.C., 1994; mgr. Maniv Investments, Hasbrouck Heights, N.J., 1997; pres. Kehilat Orach Eliezer, N.Y.C., 1996—; bd. govs. Hillel Founds., Washington, 1997—. Jewish coord. Clinton/Gore '92, N.Y.C., 1992. Democrat. Jewish. Avocations: Jewish learning, Broadway musicals, harness racing, marathon running. Fax: (201) 727-1418. E-mail: mikejg2@aol.com. Office: Maniv Investments # 305 411 Rte 17 S Hasbrouck Heights NJ 07604

GRANSTROM, MARVIN LEROY, civil and sanitary engineering educator; b. Anaconda, Mont., Sept. 25, 1920; s. Carl August and Alida Sophia (Eckstrom) G.; m. Ruth Maybelle Olsen, Jan. 1, 1944; children—David Marvin, Kay Ruth, Chris Carl. B.S., Morningside Coll., 1942; B.S. in Civil Engring, Iowa State Coll., 1943; M.S. in San. Engring, Harvard, 1947, Ph.D., 1955. Engring. aide Soil Conservation Service, Whiting, Iowa, 1939; cons. engr. Sioux Falls, S.D., 1946; instr. civil and san. engring. Case Inst. Tech., 1947-49; assoc. prof. san. engring. U. N.C., 1949-58; prof. civil engring. Rutgers U., New Brunswick, N.J., 1958-83, prof. emeritus, 1983; research participant Oak Ridge Nat. Labs., 1954; cons. Nat. Engring. Sch., Lima, Peru, 1955-57, WHO, 1966—; cons. in hydrology, 1970—. Author articles in field. Served with USMCR, 1943-46. Research grantee N.C., 1953; Research grantee NIH, 1954-58; Research grantee NSF, 1954-63; Research grantee Army Chem. Center, 1961-64; Research grantee surgeon gen. U.S. Army, 1962; Research grantee Office Water Resources Research, Dept. Interior, 1965-76; Research grantee N.J. Dept. Environ. Protection, 1957—; fellow Nat. Found., 1946-47; fellow USPHS, 1952-53. Mem. Am. Chem. Soc., ASCE, Am. Water Works Assn., Am. Water Resources Assn., Am. Acad. Environ. Engrs., Tau Beta Pi, Sigma Xi, Delta Omega, Chi Epsilon. Home: 931 Oakwood Pl Plainfield NJ 07060-3437

GRANT, ALAN J., business executive, educator; b. Chgo., Dec. 18, 1925; s. Hugo Bernard and May (Gardner) G.; m. Margaret Stewart, Dec. 21, 1946; children: Pamela Rose, Deborah May, Bruce David. BSEE, Ill. Inst. Tech., 1946, MSEE, 1948; EdD, U. San Diego, 1992. Instr. elec. engring. Ill. Inst. Tech., Chgo., 1946-49; with N.Am. Aviation, Inc. (Autonetics), Anaheim, Calif., 1949-64; v.p., gen. mgr. computer and data systems div. N.Am. Aviation, Inc. (Autonetics), 1962-64; pres. Lockheed Electronics Co. div. Lockheed Aircraft Corp., Plainfield, N.J., 1965-69; also v.p. parent co.; exec. v.p. Aerojet-Gen. Corp., El Monte, Calif., 1970-74; chmn., pres. Wavecom Industries, Sunnyvale, Calif., 1974-78, Primark Corp., San Mateo, Calif., 1975-80; chmn., chief exec. officer Internat. Rotex, Inc., Reno, Nev., 1980-86; dir. UNC Resources Inc, Falls Church, Va., 1974-81; chmn. Atasi Corp., San Jose, Calif., 1982-85; gen. ptnr. EMC Venture Ptnrs., San Diego, 1984-86; pres. Grant Venture Mgmt. Co., Coronado, Calif., 1986-96; chmn. Am. Innovision, San Diego, 1986-92, SalePoint Systems Corp., San Diego, 1987-92; adj. prof. managerial scis. U. Nev., Reno, 1976-87, mgmt. San Diego State U., 1986-90; dir. Onward Svcs., Inc., 1996—; pres. Corp. Mgmt. Assocs., 1996—. Paul T. Babson prof. entrepreneurship Babson Coll., Babson Park, Mass., 1992-94; trustee Sierra Arts Found., Reno, 1981-85. Mem. Am. Electronics Assn. (chmn. 1973, dir. 1970-74). Office: Corp Mgmt Assocs PO Box 845 Cypress CA 90630-0845

GRANT, ALEXANDER MARSHALL, ballet director; b. Wellington, New Zealand, Feb. 22, 1925; s. Alexander Gibb and Eleather May (Marshall) G. Ed., Wellington Coll.; scholarship student, Sadler's Wells Sch., London, 1946-46. Mem. Sadler's Wells Ballet (now Royal Ballet), London, 1946-76, prin. dancer, 1950-76, co-dir. Ballet for All touring co., 1970-71, dir., 1971-76; artistic dir. Nat. Ballet Can., 1976-83; frequent judge internat. ballet competitions, Jackson, Miss., Moscow, Varna, Bulgaria, Helsinki, Paris, Budapest, Hungary. Prin. dancer London Festival Ballet (now English Nat. Ballet), 1985-91; guest artist Royal Ballet, Joffrey Ballet, English Nat. Ballet; numerous leading roles on stage, also in film Tales of Beatrice Potter, others. Decorated comdr. Brit. Empire, 1965.

GRANT, BARRY M(ARVIN), judge; b. Detroit, Jan. 16, 1936; s. Daniel and Pauline (Dantzig) G.; m. Lisa Geffen, Jan. 31, 1960; children: James D., Nanci J., L. Scott. B.A., Mich. State U., 1957; J.D., Wayne State U., 1960; postgrad., Northwestern U., 1964, Harvard U. Bar: Mich. 1961, U.S. Supreme Ct. 1961, U.S. Ct. Appeals. Probate clk. Oakland County, Mich., 1960; legal investigator (Mental Health div.); asst. pros. atty. Oakland County, 1961-64, probate ct. referee, 1962-63, 71, 74; chmn. Oakland County Condemnation Commn., 1964, 73; trial atty. Oakland County, from 1961; acting circuit judge Oakland County, 1980-85; chief judge Oakland County Probate Ct., 1977—; traffic safety commr., 1964; chief judge pro tem Oakland County Probate Ct., 1996—; sec., state jud. coordinator Spl. Com. on Ct. Reorgn.; mem. Jud. Tenure Com. State of Mich., 1985—, probate rep., 1986—; mem. exec. com. State Bar Mud. Coun.; chmn. Mich. Jud. Tenure Commn., sec.; chmn. Oakland County Election Commn., Mich. Jud. Commn., 1991-93; pres., probate judge Nat. Coll. columnist Detroit Free Press; weekly columnist Judge Grant column Detroit News. Mem. Parent-Youth Guidance Commn., 1963-64; chmn. Oakland County Lawyers United Found. Torch Drive, 1968, 71; exec. sec. Southfield Beautification Com., 1963; trustee Wm. Beaumont Hosp.; treas. Southfield Bd. Edn., Oakland County Sch. Bd. Assn., 1968, also trustee; mem. spl. planning com. Nat. Conf. on Mental Health, 1990—; mem. exec. com., bd. dirs. Camp Oakland, Mich. Soc. Mental Health, Oakland County Hist. Soc., Mich. Cancer Found., March of Dimes, Boy Scouts Am. Mem. ABA, ATLA, Mich. Bar Assn. (rep. assembly), Nat. Coll. Probate Judges (exec. com. 1988—, editor-in-chief newsletter, conf. chmn. 1994, pres.-elect 1995—), Nat. Coun. Juvenile Ct. Judges, Mich. Probate and Juvenile Judges Assn. (bd. dirs., pres. 1988—), Oakland County Bar Assn., Mich. Probate Judges Assn. (v.p. 1986, pres.-elect, pres. 1988—), Oakland County Law Enforcement Assn., Oakland County Judges Assn. (pres. 1991), Mich. State U. Club, Oakland County Club. Office: Oakland County Probate Ct 1200 N Telegraph Rd Pontiac MI 48341-1032

GRANT, BRIAN WADE (GENERAL GRANT), professional basketball player; b. Columbus, Ohio, Mar. 5, 1972. Degree in Organizational Comms., Xavier, 1994. Forward Sacramento Kings, 1994-97, Portland Trailblazers, 1997—. Active Sacramento charities, Kings Cmty. Found. Named NBA Schick Rookie of the Month, Jan. 1995. Avocation: watching movies. Office: Portland Trailblazerz 1 Center Ct Ste 200 Portland OR 97227-2103*

GRANT, BUD (HARRY PETER GRANT), retired professional football coach; b. Superior, Wis., May 20, 1927. Student, U. Minn. Basketball player Mpls. Lakers, NBA, 1949-51; football player Phila. Eagles, NFL, 1951-52, Winnipeg Blue Bombers, Canadian Football League, 1953-56; head coach Winnipeg Blue Bombers, CFL, 1957-66, Minn. Vikings, NFL, 1967-84, 85. Coach Can. Football League championships, 1958-59, 61-62. Coached in Super Bowls IV, VIII, IX, XI, NFL; NFL Coach of the Year, The Sporting News, 1969; NFL Hall of Fame, 1994. Earned nine varsity letters in football, basketball and baseball at U. Minn. after having overcome polio at the age of ten. Office: Prof Football Hall of Fame 2121 George Halas Dr NW Canton OH 44708-2699*

GRANT, BURTON FRED, lawyer; b. Chgo., Mar. 16, 1938; s. Louis Z. and Ruth (Kaplan) G.; m. Joan Carolyn Friedman, July 11, 1965; children: Robin, Steven, Lauren. BA, De Paul U., 1959, JD, 1962; LLM, John Marshall U., 1965. Bar: Ill. 1963, U.S. Dist. Ct. (no. dist.) Ill. 1963. Sole practice Chgo., 1963-73; ptnr. Grant, Kaplan & Grant, Chgo., 1973-76, Grant, Grant & Stein, Chgo., 1977-81; prin. Grant & Grant, Chgo., 1981—; adj. prof. De Paul U. Sch. Law, Chgo., 1979-83. Contbr. articles to profl. jours. Named one of Leading Attorneys at Law in Family Law in State of Ill., (pub.) Law and Leading Attorneys, one of 20 Top Divorce Lawyers North Shore Mag., 1997. Fellow Am. Acad. Matrimonial Lawyers (cert.); mem. ABA, Ill. Bar Assn., Chgo. Bar Assn., N.W. Suburban Bar Assn. (cert. appreciation 1986), North Suburban Bar ASsn. (bd. mgrs. 1992—), Lake County Bar Assn., Phi Alpha Delta. Avocations: travel, photography. Office: Grant & Grant 180 N La Salle St Ste 2400 Chicago IL 60601-2787 also: 707 Skokie Blvd Ste #600 Northbrook IL 60062

GRANT, CARL N., communications executive; b. Sharon, Pa., July 10, 1939; s. Carl and Hedwig Theresa Nothhaft; m. Carol Ann Pasacic, June 12, 1965; children: Carl, Kevin, Heather Lee. BA, Kent State U., 1963, MA, 1966; PhD, Ohio State U., 1972. With various radio, TV stas., Ohio and Mich., 1962-67; asst. news dir. Sta. WLWC-TV, Columbus, Ohio, 1967-69; news and pub. affairs dir. Sta. WKBS-TV, Phila., 1969-72; exec. staff dir., nat. com. employer support and guard Dept. Def., Washington, 1972-73; dir. Pres. Com. on White House Fellows, Washington, 1973-74; dir. news and pub. affairs Kaiser Broadcasting Corp., Washington, 1974; assoc. dir. and editor Def. Manpower Commn., Washington, 1974-76; dir. pub. affairs Gen. Svcs. Adminstrn., Washington, 1976-77; sr. v.p. membership devel. U.S. C. of C., Washington, 1977—; CEO, chmn. PrimePower, Inc., 1995—. Recipient Investigative Reporting award AP, 1968, 69, Emmy award nomination NATAS, 1968, George Washington medal Freedoms Found., 1989, William Taylor Disting. Alumnus award Kent State U., 1991, Legion of Merit award, 1994. Avocations: running, weight training, cycling. Office: US C of C 1615 H St NW Washington DC 20062-0001

GRANT, CYNTHIA D., writer; b. Brockton, Mass., Nov. 23, 1950; d. Robert Cheyne and Jacqueline Ann (Ford) G.; m. Daniel Heatley; 1 child: Morgan; m. Erik Neel; 1 child, Forest. Author: Joshua Fortune, 1980 (Woodward Park Sch. annual book award 1981), Summer Home, 1981, Big Time, 1982, Hard Love, 1983, Kumquat May, I'll Always Love You, 1986, Phoenix Rising, 1989 (Mich. Libr. Assn. Young Adult Caucus best book of yr. 1990, PEN/Norma Klein award 1991, Detroit Pub. Libr. Author Day award 1992), Keep Laughing, 1991, Shadow Man, 1992, Uncle Vampire, 1993 (ALA best books for young adults list 1994), Mary Wolf, 1995, The White Horse, 1998. Recipient Book of Distinction award Hungry Mind Review, 1993, 94. Mem. PEN (Norma Klein award 1991), Soc. Children's Book Writers and Illustrators. Avocations: reading, volunteer work, CLOVERSTOCK. Home: PO Box 95 Cloverdale CA 95425-0095 Office: care Atheneum Children's Books 1230 Avenue Of The Americas New York NY 10020-1513

GRANT, DANIEL GORDON, information services company executive; b. Taplow, Bucks, Eng., June 28, 1957; came to U.S., 1981; s. Victor Daniel and Annie (McKeown) G.; m. Gaynor Kerry Swainson, Aug. 8, 1981; children: Andrew Douglas, Alexander Daniel, Megan Louise. BS in Computer Sci. with commendation, Portsmouth (Eng.) Polytech., 1979; postgrad., Carnegie Mellon U., 1994-95. Chartered engr. info. scis.; cert. EMT, Nat. EMS registry. Cons. in computers London, 1979-80; applications cons. Tymshare, U.K., London, 1980-81; from cons. to dep. pres. Tangent Internat., N.Y.C., 1981-90, pres., 1990—, pres., CEO, 1991-94, also bd. dirs.; owner, pres., COO DXI Inc., Pitts., 1994-95, also bd. dirs.; CEO, bd. dirs. Lecor Inc, Pitts., 1995-96; owner, pres., CEO Parallel Tech. Corp., Livingston, N.J., 1996—. Contbr. articles to profl. jours. V.p. Upper Saddle River Vol. Ambulance Corps. Named Chevalier, Conte de Poznan, 1986, Hon. Col. U.S. Army, 1986. Mem. Brit. Computer Soc., Knights of St. John of Jerusalem. Roman Catholic. Club: Franklin Lakes Rangers (N.J.) (capt. 1981). Avocations: basketball, soccer, Scottish history, Pittsburgh Dynamos. Office: Parallel Tech Corp Two Peachtree Hill Rd Livingston NJ 07039

GRANT, DANIEL HOWARD, author; b. Westport, Conn., Sept. 5, 1954; s. Howard Alexander and Marjorie Grant; m. Alexandra Louise Chesner, Oct. 28, 1984; children: Sarah, Emma. BA, Northwestern U., 1976. Asst. dir. Found. for Cmty. of Artists, N.Y.c., 1976-84; art critic Comml.-Appeal, Memphis, 1984-86; artists' advisor Amherst, Mass., 1986—; prof. Greenfield (Mass.) C.C., 1992—; lectr. in field. Author: The Business of Being an Artist, 1991, How to Start and Succeed as an Artist, 1993, The Artist's Resource Handbook, 1994, The Writer's Resource Handbook, 1997, The Fine Artist's Career Guide, 1998. Chmn. Amherst Cultural Coun., 1992-94, Amherst Pub. Arts Com., 1998—. E-mail: danhg@aol.com. Home and Office: 19 Summer St Amherst MA 01002

GRANT, DANIEL ROSS, retired university president; b. Little Rock, Aug. 18, 1923; s. James Richard and Gracie (Sowers) G.; m. Betty Jo Oliver, June 17, 1947; children: Carolyn, Shirley, Ross. B.A., Ouachita Bapt. U., 1945; M.A., U. Ala., 1946; Ph.D., Northwestern U., 1948. Asst. prof. polit. sci. Vanderbilt U., 1948-54, assoc. prof., 1954-63, prof., 1963-70, dir. Urban and Regional Devel. Ctr., 1968-70; pres. Ouachita Bapt. U., 1970-88, pres. emeritus, 1988—; bd. dirs. TCBY Enterprises, Inc.; vis. prof. mcpl. govt. and planning Thammasat U., Bangkok, 1958-59; cons. U.S. Adv. Commn. Intergovtl. Rels., 1962-67; assoc. dir. Harris County Home Rule Commn., Houston, 1957; mem. adv. com. federalism and met. govt. Nat. Com. Econ. Devel., 1969-73. Author: The Christian and Politics, 1968, (Lloyd Omdahl) State and Local Government in America, 6th edit., 1993, (with others) The States and the Metropolis, 1968, Metropolitan Surveys: a Digest, 1958, Government and Politics: an Introduction to Political Science, rev. edit., 1971, Plan of Metropolitan Government for Nashville and Davidson County, 1956. Active So. Bapt. Found., 1959-60; active Ark. Bapt. Found., 1991-97, vice chmn., 1995-96, chmn., 1996-97; mem. commn. on religious liberty and human rights Bapt. World Alliance, 1971-95, vice chmn., 1985-90; mem. edn. commn. So. Bapt. Conv., 1973-80, chmn., 1978-80; mem. regional rev. panel Harry S. Truman Scholarship Found., 1982-96, chmn., 1984-96; pres. Assn. So. Bapt. Colls. and Schs., 1984-85, bd. dirs., 1997—; 1st v.p. Ark. Bapt. State Conv., 1989-91; active Ark. Postsecondary Edn. Planning Commn., 1980-89; chmn. Coop. Svcs. Internat. Edn. Consortium (name now Consortium for Global Edn.), 1987-88, cons., 1988-90, pres., 1990-98; mem. Ark. Higher Edn. Coordinating Bd., 1997—. Mem. Am., So. polit. sci. assns., Am. Soc. Pub. Adminstrn. Club: Rotary (pres. 1986-87). Home: 4 Glendale Pl Arkadelphia AR 71923-3529 Office: Ouachita Bapt Univ PO Box 3636 Arkadelphia AR 71998-3636

GRANT, DAVID JAMES WILLIAM, pharmacy educator; b. Walsall, Eng., Mar. 26, 1937; came to U.S., 1988; s. James and Attie Hilda May (Stringer) G. BA in Chemistry with 1st class honors, Oxford U., Eng., 1961, MA, DPhil in Phys. Chemistry, 1963, DSc in Phys. Sci., 1990. Lectr. chemistry U. Coll. of Sierra Leone, Freetown, 1963-65; lectr. then sr. lectr. pharm. chemistry U. Nottingham, Eng., 1965-81; prof. phys. pharmacy Sch. Pharmacy, U. Toronto, Ont., Can., 1981-88, assoc. dean grad. studies and rsch., 1984-87; endowed prof. pharmaceutics Coll. Pharmacy, U. Minn., Mpls., 1988—; bd. dirs. Hosokawa Micron Internat., Inc.; mem. grants com. for pharm. sci. Med. Rsch. Coun. Can., Ottawa, 1983-87; mem. com. on health rsch. Ont. Univs., Toronto, 1985-87; vis. prof. Med. Rsch. Coun. Can.; mem. adv. panel of phys. test methods-functionality for U.S. Pharmacopeia, 1991—; cons. to numerous chem. and pharm. cos. Coauthor: Physical Chemistry for Students of Pharmacy and Biology, 1977, Solubility Behavior of Organic Compounds, 1990; mem. editl. bd. Jour. Pharm. Scis., 1990-93, assoc. editor, 1994—; mem. editl. adv. bd. Pharm. Devel. and Tech., 1995—, Kona, 1996—; contbr. over 120 articles to sci. jours. Lt. Brit. Army, 1955-57. Recipient Rsch. award Leverhulme Found., U.K., 1969, Pharmaceutics award of excellence PhRMA Found., 1999; grantee rsch. couns. and indsl. cos., U.K., Can., U.S. Fellow Royal Soc. Chemistry, Am. Assn. Pharm. Scientists (sustaining charter mem. 1986—); mem. Am. Inst. Chem. Engrs., Am. Pharm. Assn., Am. Chem. Soc., Am. Assn. Coll. Pharmacy. Achievements include showing how small amounts of additives or impurities modify the physical properties of crystalline drugs and excipients; development of crystal engineering of pharmaceutical substances. Office: U Minn Weaver-Densford Hall 308 Harvard St SE Minneapolis MN 55455-0353

GRANT, DENNIS, newspaper publishing executive. Dir. advt. Chgo. Tribune. Office: Chgo Tribune Co 435 N Michigan Ave Chicago IL 60611-4066*

GRANT, D(ORIS) JEAN, writer; b. Traverse City, Mich., Jan. 1, 1934; d. Robert James and Lillias Naoma Grant. BA, U. Calif., Berkeley, 1955. Cert. clin. lab. technologist, Calif. Clin. lab. technologist, 1960-93, novelist, 1992—. Author: The Revelation, 1993, The Promise of the Willows, 1994, The Promise of Peace, 1995, The Promise of Victory, 1995, The Promise of Harvest, 1996. Mem. Romance Writers of Am. Mem. Christian and Missionary Alliance Ch. Avocation: travel.

GRANT, EILEEN GERARD, medical/surgical nurse; b. St. Louis, Mar. 20, 1953; d. Thomas Richard and Eileen Mary (Hanley) G. Diploma, Jewish Hosp. Sch. Nursing, St. Louis, 1974; MSN, St. Louis U., 1991, postgrad. Charge nurse, asst. head nurse Jewish Hosp., St. Louis, 1974-89; asst. head nurse Barnes Hosp., St. Louis, 1989-90, clin. nurse specialist surg. unit, 1990-96, mgr. nursing practice, 1996—. Mem. Mo. Nurses Assn., St. Louis U. Sch. Nursing Alumni Assn., Jewish Hosp. Sch. Nursing Alumni Assn., Sigma Theta Tau.

GRANT, ELIZABETH JANE THURMOND, graphic design educator, consultant; b. Jacksonville, Fla., Nov. 16, 1950; d. Lloyd Turner and Mildred Anna (Suggs) Thurmond; m. Joseph Curtis Grant, Sept. 30, 1972; children: Elizabeth Ashley, Daniel Thurmond. AA, Fla. Community Coll., Jacksonville, 1970; BS in Advt., U. Fla., 1972, MEd in Instrn. Design and Ednl. Media, 1986. Coord. merchandising Bryant Air Conditioning Co., Indpls., 1972-73; freelance designer GE, Pittsfield, Mass., 1973-74; mgr. prodn. Multi-Media Advt., Inc., Gainesville, Fla., 1974; info. specialist III, editor U. Fla. Alumni Assn., Gainesville, 1974-77; dir. mktg. and advt. The Hope Cos., real estate developers, Gainesville, 1977-80; prof. graphic design Sante Fe C.C., Gainesville, 1980—, program dir., 1980-94, mem. exec. com. senate, 1981-94; mem. adj. faculty pub. rels. dept. U. Fla., Gainesville, 1988-90; pres., chief exec. officer Grant, Grant and Assocs., Inc., Alachua, Fla., 1989—; contest judge Fla. Mag. Assn., Gainesville, 1988-89; v.p., co-owner High Rock Sportswear Inc.; appointed juror Fla. Design Arts Award, 1998. Vol. Am. Cancer Soc., Vol. Action Ctr., United Way, Chris Collingsworth Fund Raise for Alachua County; troop leader Brownies, Alachua, 1987-89; v.p. Alachua Elem. Sch. PTA, 1987-90; coach Santa Fe Babe Ruth Softball, Alachua, 1987-94; graphic design, printing and mailing cons. Rep. Party of Fla., Tallahassee, 1990—. Recipient 1st place award for menu design and direct mail, 2d place award for direct mail 4th Dist. Am. Advt. Fedn., 1978, cert. of distinction, 1980. Mem. Fla. Assn. Community Colls., Alachua County Vocat. Assn., Gainesville Advt. Fedn. (bd. dirs., treas. 1978-80), Gainesville Area Postal Customer Coun. (sec. 1979-81), Alpha Sigma Delta, Phi Theta Kappa, Kappa Delta Pi, Chi Omega. Republican. Episcopalian. Avocations: Gator fan, baseball fan, family travel, desktop publishing. Fax: 904-4542733. E-mail: hiroc@aol.com. Home: 16104 NW 188th St Alachua FL 32615-5239 Office: Santa Fe C C 3000 NW 83rd St #N-308 Gainesville FL 32606-6210

GRANT, GRETCHEN GULLICKSEN, artist; b. Elmhurst, Ill., Dec. 5, 1958; d. Spencer Ole and Dorothy Margery (Bohmer) Gullicksen; m. Stephen Lawrence Grant, Sept. 6, 1980; children: Mason G., Claire M. art instr. various pub. schs., Kenilworth, Ill., 1991-93, Barrington, Ill., 1993-97. One-woman shows include Friendsof the Arts,Chgo., Barrington Libr. Gallery, 1999; group shows include Barrington Area Arts Coun. Gallery, 1998, 99; muralist. Vol. PTO, Kenilworth, 1991-93, Barrington Hills, 1994—, Citizens Conservation, 1994—; mem. Barrington Hist. Soc., 1994—; assoc. dir. N. Cook County Soil and Water Conservation, 1998—. Mem. Art. Inst. Chgo., Barrington Area Arts Coun., Chgo. Area Lace Guild (editor corr. 1992). Avocation: making bobbin lace. E-mail: thechicago4@earthlink.net.

GRANT, H(ARRY) ROGER, history educator; b. Ottumwa, Iowa, Nov. 28, 1943; s. Harry Roger Grant and J. Marcella (Dinsmore) Dearinger; m. Martha Farrington, June 12, 1966; 1 child, Julia Dinsmore. BA, Simpson Coll., 1966; MA, U. Mo., 1967, PhD, 1970. Asst. prof. to prof. history U. Akron, Ohio, 1970-96; prof. history, chair history dept. Clemson (S.C.) U., 1996—. Author 20 books, including: The Corn Belt Route: A History of the Chicago Great Western Railway, 1985 (Railroad History Book award Rlwy. & Locomotive Hist. Soc.), Spirit Fruit: A Gentle Utopia, 1988, Living in the Depot: The Two-Story Railroad Station, 1993, Erie Lackawanna: Death of an American Railroad, 1938-1992, 1994, The North Western: A History of the Chicago and North Western Railway System, 1996; contbr. over 150 articles to profl. jours., chpts. to books. Mem., chair Ohio Historic Site Preservation adv. bd., Columbus, 1990-96; mem. S.C. Archives and History Commn., Columbia, 1996—; reader, table leader, chief reader Advanced Placement Exams., Ednl. Testing Svc., Princeton, N.J., 1977—. Democrat. Home: 123 Hickory Ridge Rd Central SC 29630-9461 Office: Clemson U Dept History 100 Hardin Hall Clemson SC 29634-1507

GRANT, HUGH, actor; b. London, Sept. 9, 1960. BA in English Lit. with honors, Oxford (Eng.) U., Eng., 1982. Debuted on stage at Nottingham Playhouse; formed revue group The Jockeys of Norfolk, 1985; appearences include (films) Privileged, 1982, Maurice, 1987, White Mischief, 1988, The Lair of White Worm, 1988, The Dawning, 1988, Remando al Viento, 1988, La Nuit Bengali, 1988, Impromptu, 1991, Crossing the Line, 1991, Bitter Moon, 1992, The Remains of the Day, 1993, Four Weddings and a Funeral, 1994, Sirens, 1994, Restoration, 1994, The Englishman Who Went Up a Hill But Came Down a Mountain, 1995, Nine Months, 1995, An Awfully Big Adventure, 1995, Sense and Sensibility, 1995, Extreme Measures, 1996, Notting Hill, 1999, Woody Allen Spring Project, 1999; actor, dir.: Mickey Blue Eyes, 1999; guest appearances include A Very Peculiar Practice, 1986. Office: Creative Artists Agency c/o Josh Lieberman 9830 Wilshire Blvd Beverly Hills CA 90212-1825*

GRANT, IAN STANLEY, engineering company executive; b. Auckland, New Zealand, Apr. 1, 1940; came to U.S., 1969; s. Edmund William and Tui (Hadfield) G.; m. Josephine Anne McHardy, Apr. 23, 1962 (div. June 1972); children: Megan Anne, Philippa Jane; m. Joan McCabe, Apr. 28, 1973. BEng, U. New Zealand, 1962; MEng, U. New South Wales, Sydney, Australia, 1968. Engr. Electricity Commn. New South Wales, Sydney, 1962-69, GE, Pittsfield, Mass., 1969-72; with Power Techs. Inc., Schenectady, N.Y., 1972—, dept. mgr., 1986—, v.p., 1989-94; exec. v.p. Power Techs. Inc., 1994—, exec. v.p. internat. ops. Contbr. articles to profl. jours. Fellow IEEE; mem. Conf. Internat. des Grandes Reseaux Electriques (convenor 1986—). Republican. Episcopalian. Avocations: antique automobiles, music, tennis. Home: 1163 Avon Rd Schenectady NY 12308-2405 Office: Power Techs Inc 1482 Erie Blvd Schenectady NY 12305-1005*

GRANT, JAMES COLIN, banker; b. N.S., Can., Jan. 24, 1937; s. Jack Danial and Isabel G.; m. Sonia Chicorli, July 3, 1965; 1 dau., Allison Lee-Anne. Student, St. Francis Xavier U., 1954-57, Dal/Tech., 1957-59. Engr. Dept. Transport, Fed. Govt., 1959-65; mgr. tech. support Gulf Oil Ltd., Toronto and Montreal, 1965-69; mgr. tech. design Royal Bank of Can., Montreal, 1969-72; dir. ops. Royal Bank of Can., 1972-75, asst. gen. mgr. systems, 1975-79, v.p. systems, 1979-81, v.p. strategic planning, retail banking, 1981-84, sr. v.p. ops. and systems, 1984-87, exec. v.p. ops. and systems, 1987-88, exec. v.p. systems and tech., 1988-92; pres. C.G. James & Assocs., Internat. Adv. Svcs., 1992—; mem. sectorial adv. group on internat. trade Govt. of Can., chmn. Can. info. productivity awards judging com.; bd. dirs. Rogers Cantel Mobile Comm., Inc., Newstar Techs. Inc., ORI Inc.; chmn. Connect It: com. mem. scholarships and fellowship Natural Sci. and Engring. Rsch. Coun. Can.; mem. exec. coun. info. mgmt. and tech. G.A.O. U.S. Govt. Bd. dirs. Tech. U. N.S., 1974-78. Recipient award for achievement in mng. info. tech. Carnegie Mellon U. Grad. Sch. Indsl. Adminstrn./Am. Mgmt. Systems Inc., 1989, Quality System award C.I.O. Mag., 1991, Pres. award contbn. telecomm. in Can. Canadian Telecomm. Alliance, 1992. Mem. Order Profl. Engrs. Ont., Can. Info. Processing Soc. (Outstanding Achievement in Information Processing award 1993), Internat. C. of C. (Can. del., commn. on computing, telecommunications and info. policies).

GRANT, JAMES DENEALE, health care company executive; b. Washington, July 9, 1932; s. Deneale and Frances (Hoskins) G.; m. Bonnie Carol Johnson, June 14, 1955; children: Glenn James, Bruce William, Scott Stockman. B.S., William and Mary Coll., 1954; M.B.A., Wharton Sch. U. Pa., 1956; postgrad. (Pub. Affairs fellow), Stanford U., 1963-64. Mem. staff AEC, Washington, 1956-64; v.p. Nat. Inst. Pub. Affairs, Washington, 1964-69; dep. dir. White House Conf. Food, Nutrition and Health, 1969-70; dep. commr. FDA, Washington, 1970-72; asst. to chmn. CPC Internat. Inc., Englewood Cliffs, N.J., 1972-73, v.p., 1973-86; chmn., chief exec. officer T Cell Scis., Inc., 1986-92, chmn., 1992-97; bd. dirs. Targeted Genetics Corp., Internat. Biotech. Trust, U.K., Biocompatibles, Ltd., U.K., Biocompatibles, Inc. (U.S.A.); cons. U.S. Bur. Budget, 1965-69, U.S. Civil Svc. Commn. (Office Pers. Mgmt.), 1965-69; mem., vice chmn., sec. adv. com. HHS, FDA, 1990-91. Chmn. Bergen County United Fund, 1974-75; trustee Nutrition Found., 1973-78; chmn. adv. group to sec. gen. UN Conf. on Sci. and Tech. for Devel., 1979. Recipient U.S. Govt. Career Edn. award, 1963. Mem.

Omicron Delta Kappa. Presbyterian. Club: Univ. (N.Y.C.). Home: 860 5th Ave New York NY 10021-5856

GRANT, JAMES MARTIN, academic administrator; b. Dec. 17, 1941. BA, Toccoa Falls Coll., 1963; BA with honors, Samford U., 1968; MA, U. Ga., 1969, PhD, 1976. Pres. Simpson Coll., Redding, Calif., 19963—; prof., adminstr. Toccoa (Ga.) Falls Coll., 1969-80; dir. editl. svcs. Christian Publs., Camp Hill, Pa., 1980-82. Sr. pastor York (Pa.) Christian and Missionary Alliance Ch., 1982-63. E-mail: president@Simpsonca.edu. Office: 2211 College View Dr Redding CA 96003

GRANT, JOAN JULIEN, artist, poet; b. Cornwall, Ont., Can., Apr. 15, 1934; d. John Duncan Julien and Winnifred Josephine McCormick; m. Douglas MacDougal Grant, Sept. 24, 1955; children: Stephen John, Ann Elizabeth, D. Arakaki, Abigail Jennifer, David King. *Great-grandparents were of French and Irish lineage. Joseph Julien, born in 1863and Maria Louise LaRivier were married in Quebec, Canada. Great-grandparents of Irish descent were Jeremiah McCormick and Polly Lex. Richard Julien is currently tracing the descendants for a complete genealogical chart.* AA, West L.A. C.C., 1975; BFA, Otis Art Inst., 1977, MFA, 1979. Instr. Plymouth (N.H.) State Coll., 1998. *Joan Julien Grant, MFA and BFA, 1979, Otis Art Institute, Los Angeles, California, has exhibited fine art nationally and internationally as well as teaching and lecturing. First influenced by her father who painted in oils, she studied sculpture under the direction of R. Fenci, California, and Dr. P. Rhylands, Art Theory in Venice, Italy. Her work is represented in private collections throughout the United States, Canada and Hong Kong. She is currently involved in sculpture and writing poetry.* Author, editor: Terrestis, 1995; prin. works include sculpture for Nat. Sculpture Soc. Mem. CLCC Citizens for a Livable Culver City, 1998-99. Avocations: reading, book discussion groups, walking, hiking. Home: 9999 Braddock Dr Culver City CA 90232

GRANT, JOANNE CUMMINGS, film company executive; b. N.Y.C., Oct. 12, 1947; d. Ivan Moxley and Antoinette Marie (Lomuscio) Chapman; m. Frank Bernard Cummings, Aug. 16, 1969 (div. Mar. 1977); 1 child, Matthew Colin; m. Rodney Clay Grant (div. May 1991). BA in Speech and History, Marshall U., 1969, MA in Speech Broadcasting, 1976. Adminstrv. asst. Gallup Orgn., Princeton, N.J., 1970; dir. prodn., continuity Sta. WGNT Radio, Huntington, W.Va., 1970-75, dir. news, 1976-78; asst. dir. Huntington Civic Ctr., 1978-82; mgr. bookings Orange County Conv. Ctr., Orlando, Fla., 1982-84; asst. dir. Ocean Ctr., Daytona Beach, Fla., 1984-87; mgr. events Orlando Centroplex, 1987-90, dir., 1990-94; pres. Jade Consulting Group, Inc., Orlando, 1994—; exec. dir. Weekends of Greater Orlando, Inc., 1996-98; dir. entertainment prodn. Universal Studios, Orlando, 1998—; adj. prof. Valencia C.C., 1995-97; bd. dirs. Orlando/Orange County Conv. Bur., World Cup USA. Bd. dirs. Women's Resource Ctr., Light Up Orlando, co-chmn.; mem. Coun. Agy. Execs., 1996; pres. Downtown Orlando Partnership, 1994; met. bd. dirs. Ctrl. Fla. YMCA, 1998—; bd. dirs. Ctrl. Fla. Civic Theatre, Harbor House. Named Downtown Woman of Yr. in Govt. Women's Exec. Coun., 1991, Facility Mgr. Yr. Performance Mag., 1993. Mem. Internat. Assn. Auditorium Mgrs. (chmn. exhibits and advt. com. 1984-85, 85-86, publs. and pub. rels. com. 1986-87, arenas com. 1987-88, 91-94, bd. dirs. dist. V 1990-91, 93-94, long range planning com. 1992-93, bd. dirs. 1994—, exec. com. 1994—), Am. Soc. Assn. Execs., Fla. Assn. Assn. Execs., Ctrl. Fla. Soc. Assn. Execs., Fla. Citrus Sports Assn. (exec. com., bd. dirs.). Democrat. Roman Catholic. Avocations: reading, beach, music. Home: 1243 Lake Willisara Cir Orlando FL 32806-5584 Office: 1000 Universal Studios Plz Orlando FL 32819-7601

GRANT, JOHN THOMAS, retired state supreme court justice; b. Omaha, Oct. 25, 1920; s. Thomas J. and Mary Elizabeth (Smith) G.; m. Marian Louise Saner, Dec. 27, 1947 (dec. 1995); children: Martha Grant Bruckner, John P., Susan J., Joseph W., Timothy K.; m. Zella Forehead, June 16, 1997. LLB, JD, Creighton U., 1950. Bar: Nebr. 1950. Sole practice law Omaha, 1950-74; judge State Dist. Ct., Omaha, 1974-83; justice Nebr. Supreme Ct., Lincoln, 1983-92. Served with Signal Corps, U.S. Army, 1942-45, PTO. Home: 912 S 118th Plz Omaha NE 68154-3404

GRANT, JOSEPH D., business administrator, executive director; b. Dec. 19, 1966. BA in Econs., BA in Polit. Sci., U. Minn., Mpls., 1989; MBA, U. S.D., 1999. HR/compliance officer Western Nat. Bank, Duluth, Minn., 1992-96; bd. pres. RSI, Inc., Duluth, 1996-98; analyst Norwest Svcs., Inc., Duluth, 1997-98; bus. adminstr. 1st Luth. Ch., Sioux Falls, S.D., 1998-99; exec. dir. NHS Duluth, Minn., 1999—. E-mail: josgrant@aol.com.

GRANT, JOSEPH MOORMAN, finance executive; b. San Antonio, Oct. 30, 1938; s. George William and Mary Christian (Moorman) G.; m. Sheila Ann Peterson, Aug. 26, 1961; children: Mary Elizabeth, Steven Clay. BBA, So. Meth. U., 1960; MBA, U. Tex., 1961, PhD, 1970. Banking officer Citibank, N.Y.C., 1961-65; sr. v.p., economist Tex. Commerce Bank (N.A.) also Tex. Commerce Bancshares, Houston, 1970-73; pres., dir. Tex. Commerce Bank, Austin, 1974-75; chmn., CEO Tex. Am. Bankshares/Ft. Worth, 1986-89; pres. Tex. Am. Bank/Ft. Worth, 1976-89, chmn., CEO, 1983-89; exec. v.p., CFO Electronic Data Systems, Dallas, 1990-98; chmn., CEO Tex. Capital Bancshares, 1998—; bd. dirs. Houston Industries, Wingate Ptnrs., Metamor Worldwide, World Pres.' Orgn. Author: (with Lawrence L. Crum) The Development of State-Chartered Banking in Texas, 1978, The Great Texas Banking Crash, 1996. Trustee Tex. Christian U., 1989-94, So. Meth. U., 1980-89; chmn. adv. coun. Coll. Bus. Adminstrn. Found., U. Tex., Austin; trustee Edwin L. Cox Sch. Bus. Exc. Bd., Dallas County C.C.; bd. dirs. Dallas Mus. of Art, North Tex. Commn., 1976-86, chmn., 1981-82; trustee Paul Quinn Coll., 1995-98. Recipient Man of Yr. award Anti-Defamation League B'nai B'rith, 1988; named to Disting. Alumni, U. Tex. at Austin, Coll. Bus. Adminstrn., 1982. Mem. Ft. Worth C. of C. (past chmn.), Young Pres. Orgn. (bd. dirs. 1980-89, internat. pres. 1987-88, exec. com.), Blue Key, Ft. Worth Club, Exch. Club, Sigma Alpha Epsilon. Episcopalian. Home: 3510 Turtle Creek Blvd Apt 6C Dallas TX 75219-5543

GRANT, LEE (LYOVA HASKELL ROSENTHAL), actress, director; b. N.Y.C., Oct. 31, 1931; d. A.W. and Witia (Haskell) Rosenthal; m. Arnold Manoff (dec.); 1 dau., Dinah; m. Joseph Feury; 1 dau., Belinda. Student, Julliard Sch. Music, Neighborhood Playhouse Sch. Theatre, Met. Opera Ballet Sch. Stage debut as child in: L'arocolo, Met. Opera House, N.Y.C., 1934; Broadway appearances include Detective Story (Critics Circle award 1949), Lo and Behold, A Hole in the Head, Wedding Breakfast; toured with The Maids (Obie award), Electra, Silk Stockings, St. Joan, Arms and The Man, Prisoner of Second Avenue; with road co. Two for the Seesaw, The Captains and the Kings, N.Y. Shakespeare Festival; motion pictures include Detective Story, 1952 (best actress Cannes Film Festival), Storm Fear, 1956, Middle of the Night, 1959, Affair of the Skin, The Balcony, 1963, Divorce American Style, 1967, Valley of the Dolls, In The Heat of the Night, 1968, Marooned, 1970, There Was a Crooked Man, 1970, The Landlord, 1970, Plaza Suite, 1971, Shampoo, 1975 (Acad. award for best supporting actress), Voyage of the Damned, 1976, Airport '77, 1977, The Swarm, 1978, The Mafu Cage, 1978, Damien-Omen II, 1978, When You Comin' Back, Red Ryder, 1979, Little Miss Marker, 1980, Charlie Chan and the Curse of the Dragon Queen, 1981, Visiting Hours, 1982, Teachers, 1984, The Big Town, 1987, Defending Your Life, 1991, It's My Party, 1996; TV series include Search for Tomorrow, 1953-54, Fay, 1975, Peyton Place (Emmy award for best supporting actress 1966); TV movies include Night Slaves, 1970, The Respectful Prostitute (BBC), Neon Ceiling (Emmy award), Ransom for a Dead Man, Lieutenant Shuster's Wife, 1972, Partners in Crime, 1973, What Are Best Friends For?, 1973, Perilous Voyage, 1976, The Spell, 1977, The Million Dollar Face, 1981, For Ladies Only, 1981, Thou Shalt Not Kill, 1982, Bare Essence, 1982, Will There Really Be A Morning?, 1983, The Highjacking of the Achille Lauro, 1989, She Said No, 1990, Something to Live For: The Allison Gertz Story, 1992, In My Daughter's Name, 1992, Citizen Cohn, 1992 (Emmy nomination, Supporting actress - miniseries, 1993); dir. TV spl. Shape of Things, 1973; dir. play Private View, 1983; dir. documentary When Women Kill, 1983, What Sex Am I?, 1984, Battered, 1989; dir. (feature film) Tell Me A Riddle, 1980, Women of Willmar, 1982, Feature A Matter of Sex, 1983, Nobody's Child, 1986 (Dirs. Guild Am. award), Down and Out in America, 1987 (Acad. award), No Place Like Home, 1989, (feature comedy) Staying Together, 1989; dir. documentary Women on Trial, 1992, Breast Cancer Say it! Fight it! Cure It!, 1997; dir. TV film Season's of the Heart, 1994, Reunion, 1994, Sing Me The Blues, Lena, 1994. Recipient Congl. Arts Caucus award U.S. Govt., 1983, Lifetime Achievement award Women in Film, 1989. *The prescription for success is the same as for failure. When one is conflicted between fear and desire, choose desire.**

GRANT, LEONARD TYDINGS, clergyman; b. Lakewood, N.J., May 8, 1930; s. Allaire Harrison and Edith Dorothy (MacEntee) G.; m. Nancy Elisabeth MacKerell, June 21, 1958; children: Scott Alexander, Elisabeth Tydings, Constance Allaire. BA, Rutgers U., 1952; BD, Princeton Theol. Sem., 1955; STM, Temple U., 1958; PhD, U. Edinburgh, 1961. Ordained to ministry Presbyn. Ch. U.S.A., 1955; pastor 4th Presbyn. Ch., Camden, N.J., 1955-58, Meml. Presbyn. Ch., Wenonah, N.J., 1961-65; instr. Rutgers U., 1956-58; lectr. Conwell Sch. Theology, Phila., 1962-65; prof. history Indpls. Univ., 1965-76; grad. dean Indpls. U., 1966-76, acad. dean, 1974-76; pres. Elmira (N.Y.) Coll., 1976-87; pres. emeritus, 1987—; pres. Independent Coll. Fund N.Y., 1987-95; assoc. pastor Presbyn. Ch., Westfield, N.J., 1995-97, Ctrl. Presbyn. Ch., Summit, N.J., 1997—. Author: Prayers and Devotions of Richard Baxter, 1965; contbr. articles on edn., history and religion to jours. Former mem. adv. com. Am. Inst. of Banking, Arnot-Ogden Hosp., Coun. Ind. Colls., Ind. Coll. Fund N.Y., Sullivan Trail coun. Boy Scouts Am., Coun. Elizabeth Presbytery, Found. for Indep. Higher Edn. Mem. Rotary, Princeton Club (N.Y.C.), Alpha Sigma Lambda, Phi Alpha Theta, Phi Delta Kappa.

GRANT, LINDA SUSAN, nursing consultant; b. Seattle, Apr. 27, 1953; d. Richard Elton and Dorothy June (Crawford) Grant; m. Stephen Alan Boruchowitz, Sept. 16, 1989; 1 child, Grant Stephen Boruchowitz. BSN, Seattle U., 1975; MBA, City U. Tacoma, 1989. Instr. practical nursing South Puget Sound C.C., Olympia, Wash., 1976-79; charge nurse short stay unit St. Peter Hosp., Olympia, 1980-85; health care practice investigator Dept. Licensing, State of Wash., Olympia, 1985; occupl. nurse cons. supr. dept. Wash. Dept. Labor and Industries, Olympia, 1986-90; supr. utilization mgmt. Dept. Labor & Industries, State of Wash., 1990-92; provider referral nurse Dept. of Labor and Industries, State of Wash., Olympia, 1992—. Mem. Capital City Nurses Assn. (past 1st v.p.), Sigma Theta Tau, Alpha Sigma Nu.

GRANT, M. DUNCAN, lawyer; b. Madison, Wis., Apr. 22, 1950; s. David Evans and Margaret Jane (Bloomfield) G.; m. Marcia Joan Cox, Sept. 18, 1970 (div. Dec. 1975); 1 child, Thomas David; m. Margaret Ann MacDonald, Mar. 24, 1990 (div. Jan. 1995). AB, Princeton U., 1972; JD, U. Pa., 1975. Bar: Pa. 1975, Del. 1991, U.S. Dist. Ct. (ea. dist.) Pa. 1976, U.S. Ct. Appeals (3d cir.) 1977, U.S. Dist. Ct. (Del.) 1992, U.S. Ct. Appeals (10th cir.) 1986, U.S. Ct. Appeals (11th cir.) 1996, U.S. Supreme Ct. 1980. Law clk. to judge U.S. Ct. Appeals (3d cir.), Phila., 1975-76; assoc. Pepper Hamilton LLP, Phila., 1976-83, ptnr., 1983—. Am. fellow Salzburg Seminar, 1986. Mem. ABA, Pa. Bar Assn., Phila. Bar Assn., Del. State Bar Assn. Democrat. Avocations: baseball, wine, golf. Home: 221 W Allens Ln Philadelphia PA 19119-4103 Office: Pepper Hamilton LLP 3000 Two Logan Sq 18th & Arch Sts Philadelphia PA 19103-1083

GRANT, MERRILL THEODORE, producer; b. N.Y.C., July 9, 1932; s. Samuel and Rae (Renko) G.; m. Barbara Rosner, May 24, 1961; children: Andrea, Jonathan Samuel. BBA, CCNY, 1953; MS, Columbia U., 1954. V.p., dir. programming Benton & Bowles, N.Y.C., 1957-70; sr. v.p., dir. radio and TV Grey Advt., N.Y.C., 1970-72; v.p. Viacom Internat., N.Y.C., 1972-74; pres. Don Kirshner Prodns., N.Y.C., 1974-78, Grant Case McGrath, N.Y.C., 1978-79, Grant-Reeves Entertainment, N.Y.C., 1979-85; chmn., CEO Reeves Entertainment, N.Y.C., 1985-93; co-chmn. Koslow-Grant Assocs., N.Y.C., 1994—. Served with AUS, 1954-56.

GRANT, MICHAEL ERNEST, educational administrator, institutional management educator; b. L.A., June 6, 1952; s. Ernest Grant and Shirley Ruth (George) G. BA in Spanish, Calif. State U., Long Beach, 1974, MA in Edn. Adminstrn., 1978; EdD, Pepperdine U., 1984. Cert. elem., secondary, and community coll. tchr., bilingual and cross-cultural edn., adminstr. Tchr. kindergarten through adult edn. Long Beach Unified Sch. Dist., 1975-83, tchr. 5th grade, 1975, tchr. 6th grade, 1975-76, bilingual multicultural specialist, 1976-78, tchr. 6th, 7th and 8th grades, 1978-79, mgmt. program specialist, 1979-80, adminstr., program specialist, 1980-81, vice prin., 1981-83; asst. prof. tchr. edn. Calif. State U., San Bernardino, 1986-88; prin. dir. IMPACT/TEACH, assoc. prof. edni. psychology and adminstrn. Calif. State U., Long Beach, 1988-91; pres., founder Mykulphone Teleteach, Long Beach, 1991—; Spanish instr. Calif. Disting. Sch., Beverly Hills, 1993-98; asst. part-time instr. tchr. edn. Grad. Sch. Edn., Calif. State U., Long Beach, 1983-86; pres., CEO Mykulphone, 1999—. Contbr. articles to profl. jours. Pepperdine U. scholar, 1983-84; Calif. State U. grantee, 1988-89, 89-90, 89-91. Mem. NEA, Assn. Calif. Sch. Adminstrs., Nat. Assn. Tchr. Educators, Nat. Coun. States In-Svc. Edn., Nat. Black Congress Faculty, Calif. Faculty Assn., Calif. State Intersegmental Coordination Coun., Calif. Black Faculty and Staff Assn., Calif. Assn. Tchr. Educators, Calif. Edn. Rsch. Assn., Intersegmental Coordinating Coun. Democrat. Baptist. Avocations: Shotokon karate (black belt), acting, dancing, singing, songwriting. Home and Office: Ste 1220 270 N Cañon Dr Beverly Hills CA 90210-9999

GRANT, MICHAEL PETER, electrical engineer; b. Oshkosh, Wis., Feb. 26, 1936; s. Robert J. and Ione (Michelson) G.; m. Mary Susan Corcoran, Sept. 2, 1961; children: James, Steven, Laura. B.S., Purdue U., 1957, M.S., 1958, Ph.D., 1964. With Westinghouse Research Labs., Pitts., summers 1953-57; mem. tech. staff Aerospace Corp., El Segundo, Calif., 1961; instr. elec. engring. Purdue U., West Lafayette, Ind., 1958-64; sr. engr. Combustion Engring. Corp., Columbus, Ohio, 1964-67, mgr. advanced devel. and control systems, 1967-72, mgr. control and info. scis. div., 1972-74, asst. gen. mgr. indsl. systems div., 1974-76, mgr. system design, 1976-87; v.p., chief scientist SynGenics Corp., Columbus, 1987—; dir. Nat. Ctr. for Mfg. Scis., Ann Arbor, MIch., 1987-95. Contbr. articles to profl. jours.; holder 8 patents in field of automation. Mem. IEEE, Sigma Xi, Eta Kappa Nu, Pi Mu Epsilon, Tau Beta Pi. Home: 4461 Sussex Dr Columbus OH 43220-3857

GRANT, PATRICK ALEXANDER, lawyer, association administrator; b. Denver, Nov. 14, 1945; s. Edwin Hendrie and Mary Belle (McIntyre) G.; m. Carla Clyde Yancey, Aug. 16, 1975; children: Mary Cameron, Sara Mansur, Alexis Hendrie. BA with honors, Colgate U., 1967; MBA, Denver U., 1973; JD, Drake U., 1976. Bar: Colo. 1977. Law clk. to Judge Donald P. Smith, Jr. Colo. Ct. Appeals, Denver, 1976-77; assoc. Grant, McHendrie, Haines & Crouse, PC, Denver, 1977-83, ptnr., v.p., 1984-91, also bd. dirs.; state rep. Colo. Gen. Assembly, Denver, 1984-92, vice-chmn. fin. com., 1987-88, chmn. audit com., 1989-90, chmn. judiciary com., 1988-92, chmn. legal svcs. com., 1988-89; mem. Colo. Coun. Elected Ofcls. for Soviet Jewry, Denver, 1985-92, Colo. Spl. Task Force Tort Liability and Ins., Denver, 1985; bd. dirs. Colo. Sports Hall of Fame, Colo. State U. Livestock Leader Coun. Upper sch. chmn. parents divsn. Kent Denver Leadership Fund, 1996-97; mem. Denver Cmty. Mental Health Commn., 1985-86; mem. exec. coun., planning com. St. Joseph Hosp., Denver, 1985-88; mem. Denver Bd. for Developmentally Disabled, 1987-88; vestryman, jr. warden St. Barnabas Parish, Denver, 1979-84; mem. adv. com. Nat. Ctr. Preventive Law, 1987-90; bd. dirs. Colo. Jud. Inst., 1990-96; mem. exec. bd. Parents Assn., Gettysburg (Pa.) Coll.; exec. bd. Denver coun. Boy Scouts Am., 1997—. Gates Found. fellow John F. Kennedy Sch. Govt. Harvard U., 1985, Toll Fellow Coun. of State Govts., 1987; recipient Outstanding Alumni award Kent Denver Country Day Sch., 1986, Colo. Wildlife Fedn. Appreciation award, 1987, Disting. Svc. to Higher Edn. award U. Denver, 1988, Bus. Legis. of Yr., award Colo. Pub. Affairs Coun., 1989, Outstanding Achievement award EPA, 1989, award of honor Hist. Denver, 1989, Stephen H. Hart award Colo. Hist. Soc., 1990, Spl. Recognition award AIA; named one of Outstanding Young Men in Am., U.S. Jaycees, 1980, Legislator of Yr. Associated Builders and Contractors, 1991, Gen. Heritage award for Former Legislator, 1997. Mem. Colo. Med. Soc. Found. (bd. dirs., pres. 1997-99, pres. emeritus 1999—), Western Stock Show Assn. (exec. com., bd. dirs. 1984—, exec. v.p. and CEO 1990-91, pres. and CEO 1991—), Metro Denver C. of C. (chmn. econ. devel. coun. 1995-96, chmn. pub. affairs coun. 1999—), Roundup Riders of Rockies (scout show chmn. 1999—). Republican. Episcopalian. Avocation: wood chopping, horseback riding. Home: 5 Parkway Ln Englewood CO 80110-4228 Office: 4655 Humboldt St Denver CO 80216-2818

GRANT, PAUL BERNARD, industrial relations educator, arbitrator; b. Chgo., Mar. 18, 1931; s. Paul B. and Catherine (Flyke) G.; m. Madeleine Grant, Aug. 15, 1959; children: Maura, Elizabeth, Paul, Francis, Timothy. BS, Loyola U., Chgo., 1952; MS, Inst. Indsl. Rels., Chgo., 1954. Asst. prof. Loyola U., Chgo., 1959-89, assoc. prof. indsl. rels., 1989-96, asst. v.p., 1977-85, dir. employee rels., 1967-76, sec. retirement com., 1967-95; expert witness Employment Matters, Chgo., 1993—; prof. emeritus Loyola U., Chgo., 1996—; labor arbitrator Am. Arbitration Assn., Chgo., 1972—, Fed. Mediation Conciliation Svc., Washington, 1976—, Ill. Labor Rels. Bd., Chgo., 1984—, Ill. Ednl. Labor Rels. Bd., Chgo., 1987—, Nat. Mediation Bd., Chgo., Washington, 1988—; mediator Ctr. for Employment Dispute Resolution, 1993—; U.S. arbitrator, del. N.Am. Agreement on Labor Cooperation, 1993—; expert witness employment and civil rights. Author: Cutting Health Care Costs, 1987. Sgt. U.S. Army, 1954-56. Mem. Am. Arbitration Assn., Soc. Profls. in Dispute Resolution, Indsl. Rels. Rsch. Assn., Am. Legion, Ill. Labor History Soc. Roman Catholic. Avocation: history. Home and Office: 3300 W Rance Ter Lincolnwood IL 60645-3831

GRANT, PAULA DIMEO, lawyer, nursing educator; b. Bridgeport, Conn., Aug. 3, 1943; d. Samuel Peter and Emilie Alyce (DiChiera) DiMeo; m. James Mullett Grant, Nov. 26, 1975. AS in Nursing, U. Bridgeport, 1973; BSN cum laude, Boston Coll., 1975; JD, No. Va. U., 1982; MA in Nursing, NYU, 1994. Bar: D.C. 1985, U.S. Ct. Appeals (D.C.) 1985, U.S. Dist. Ct. D.C. 1985, U.S. Supreme Ct. 1989, U.S. Dist. Ct. Md. 1995. RN, Conn. Coronary care nurse Cornell Med. Ctr., N.Y.C., 1969-70; with Trans World Airlines, Chgo. and N.Y.C., 1970-79; nursing cons., law clk. Andrew R. Bensi Law Offices, Garden City, N.Y., 1980-84; pvt. practice, Washington, 1986-98; of counsel Ross & Hardies, Washington, 1998—; bd. dirs. So. Conn. Dialysis Unit, Bridgeport, 1986-92; mediator Superior Ct. D.C., 1991—; clin. asst. prof. cmty. and preventive medicine N.Y. Med. Coll., 1992-96; adj. prof. dept. nursing Columbia U. Tchrs. Coll., N.Y.C., 1993, 1994, adj. asst. prof. nursing Sacred Heart U., Fairfield, Conn., 1998—. Mem. ABA, ATLA, D.C. Bar Assn., Am. Assn. Nurses Attys. (co-chmn. legis. affairs com. 1987-91, bd. dirs. N.Y. Met. chpt. 1986-88, sec. 1986-87, nat. bd. dirs. 1996, pres. Found. 1998-99), Conn. Nurses Assn. (chmn. cabinet on econ. and gen. welfare 1985-88), Sigma Theta Tau, Kappa Delta Pi. Roman Catholic. Avocations: reading, theater, music. Office: 888 16th St NW Ste 400 Washington DC 20006-4103

GRANT, RAYMOND THOMAS, arts administrator; b. Yonkers, N.Y., Nov. 1, 1957; s. Kieran J. and Rita B. (Benedek) G.; m. Susan Mary McLoughlin, Nov. 6, 1993; children: 1 child, Kieran John. B of Music Edn., U. Kans., 1980; MA in Arts Adminstrn., NYU, 1984. Cert. music edn. tchr. Intern John F. Kennedy Ctr. for the Performing Arts, Washington, 1980; band dir. Lawrence (Kans.) Pub. Schs., 1980-81; dir. spl. projects 92nd St. YM-YWHA, N.Y.C., 1983-85; gen. mgr. Am. Symphony Orch., N.Y.C., 1985-91; pres. Raymond T. Grant, Ltd., 1989-93; dir. Tisch Ctr. for the Arts of the 92d St. Y, N.Y.C., 1991-92; mgr. program devel. performing arts and film The Disney Inst., Celebration, Fla., 1993-96; programming cons. Walt Disney Attractions, Inc., 1996-98; dir. arts and culture Salt Lake Organizing Com. for Olympic Winter Games of 2002, 1998—; guest lectr., spkr. King's Coll., NYU, N.Y.C., 1990, The Hartt Sch., U. Hartford, U. No. Iowa, Ind. U., 1997, The Sch. of the Art Inst. of Chgo., 1998, Va. Tech., 1998; mem. adv. com. Carnegie Hall Profl. Tng. Workshops, 1990-91; programming cons. Imperial Tombs of China Exhbn., Orlando (Fla.) Mus. Art, 1997—. Bd. dirs. Kans. Alliance for Arts Edn., Lawrence, 1981, Concerts for Young People, Lawrence, 1981, Negro Spiritual Scholarship Found., Orlando, Fla., 1997—; mem. adv. bd. N.Y. Youth Symphony, 1986; panel mem. presenting and commissioning program, challenge grant program NEA, 1993, site visitor presenting and commissioning program, 1994; mem. music orgn. panel divsn. cultural affairs Fla. Dept. State, 1994, 95, 96; facilitator, mem. panel Martin Luther King, Jr. Forum, Diocese of Orlando, Orlando Mus. Art, 1997, 98. Power Found. scholar U. Kans., 1979; Stella Wolcott Aten grantee U. Kans., 1978, Scholarship Found. grantee, N.Y.C., 1980. Mem. Rocky Mountain Elk Found., Blue Mountain Sportsman Ctr., Ducks Unltd. Roman Catholic. Avocation: handgun shooting. Office: Salt Lake Organizing Com for Olympic Winter Games of 2002 257 E 200 S Ste 600 Salt Lake City UT 84111-2081 Home: 2188 Wilson Ave Salt Lake City UT 84108-3022

GRANT, RICHARD W., lawyer; b. Oct. 25, 1945. AB, Brown U., 1968; JD, Boston U., 1971. Bar: D.C. 1972, Pa. 1984. Assoc. dir. divsn. investment mgmt. SEC, Washington, 1981-83; ptnr. Morgan, Lewis & Bockius, LLP, Phila. Office: Morgan Lewis & Bockius LLP 1701 Market St Philadelphia PA 19103-2903*

GRANT, ROBERT E., federal judge; b. 1954. BA, Wabash Coll., 1977; JD, Dickinson Coll., 1980. Bar: Ind. Atty. Baker & Daniels, 1980-87; bankruptcy judge U.S. Dist. Ct. (no. dist.) Ind., Ft. Wayne, 1987—. Office: 2128 Federal Bldg 1300 S Harrison St Fort Wayne IN 46802-3495

GRANT, ROBERT MCQUEEN, humanities educator; b. Evanston, Ill., Nov. 25, 1917; s. Frederick Clifton and Helen McQueen (Hardie) G.; m. Margaret Huntington Horton, Dec. 21, 1940; children: Douglas McQueen, Peter Williams, Susan Hardie, James Frederick. AB, Northwestern U., 1938; postgrad., Episcopal Theol. Sch., 1938-39, Columbia U., 1939-40; BD, Union Theol. Sem., 1941; STM, Harvard U., 1942, ThD, 1944; DD, Seabury-Western Theol. Sem., 1969, U. Glasgow, 1979; LHD, Kalamazoo Coll., 1979; DD, Ch. Div. Sch. Pacific, 1992. Ordained to ministry Episcopal Ch., 1942. Minister St. James Ch., South Groveland, Mass., 1942-44; instr. to prof. N.T. U. of South, 1944-53, acting dean, 1947; vis. lectr. U. Chgo., 1945, research assoc., 1952-53, assoc. prof., 1953-58, prof., 1958-87, emeritus, 1988—, Carl Darling Buck prof. humanities, 1973-87, Carl Darling Buck prof. emeritus, 1988—; vis. lectr. Vanderbilt U., 1945-47, Seabury-Western Theol. Sem., 1954-55, 89, Augustinianum (Rome), 1990; lectr. Am. Council Learned Socs., 1957-58; vis. prof. Yale U., 1964-65, Fla. State U., 1989. Author: Second-Century Christianity, 1946, The Bible in the Church, 1948, rev. edit. (with David Tracy), 1984, Miracle and Natural Law, 1952, The Sword and the Cross, 1955, The Letter and the Spirit, 1957, Gnosticism and Early Christianity, 1959, 63, Gnosticism: An Anthology, 1961, The Earliest Lives of Jesus, 1961, Historical Introduction to the New Testament, 1963, The Apostolic Fathers, vol. I, 1964, vol. II (with H. H. Graham), 1965, vol. IV, 1966, U-Boats Destroyed 1914-1918, 1964, The Formation of the New Testament, 1965, History of Early Christian Literature (revision from E. J. Goodspeed), 1966, The Early Christian Doctrine of God, 1966, After the New Testament, 1967, U-Boat Intelligence 1914-1918, 1969, Augustus to Constantine, 1970, Theophilus of Antioch Ad Autolycum, 1970, Early Christianity and Society, 1977, Eusebius as Church Historian, 1980, Christian Beginnings: Apocalypse to History, 1983, Gods and the One God, 1986, Greek Apologists of the Second Century, 1988, Jesus after the Gospels, 1989, Heresy and Criticism, 1993, Irenaeus of Lyons, 1997; author: (with D. N. Freedman) The Secret Sayings of Jesus, 1960, (with G. Menzies) Joseph's Bible Notes, Hypomnestikon, 1996, Early Christians and Animals, 1999; assoc. editor Vigiliae Christianae. Fulbright research prof. U. Leiden, 1950-51; Guggenheim fellow, 1950, 54, 59. Fellow Am. Acad. Arts and Scis.; mem. Soc. Bibl. Lit. (pres. 1959), Am. Soc. Ch. History (pres. 1970, co-editor 1962-87), Chgo. Soc. Bibl. Research (pres. 1963-64, editor 1956-61), Phi Beta Kappa, Alpha Delta Phi. Home: 5807 S Dorchester Ave Apt 11E Chicago IL 60637-1776

GRANT, ROBERT NATHAN, lawyer; b. Newburgh, N.Y., Mar. 7, 1930; s. Henry and Helen (Berkowitz) Grusky; m. Barbara Weil, Feb. 10, 1952; children—Susan, Elizabeth Grant Ellerton, Nancy Grant Gray. BA, Yale U., 1951; LLB, Harvard U., 1956. Bar: Ill. 1956, N.Y. 1990; registered fgn. lawyer, U.K. Assoc. Sonnenschein Nath & Rosenthal, Chgo., 1956-65; ptnr. Sonnenschein, Nath & Rosenthal, Chgo., 1965—; sec. UNR Industries, Inc., Chgo., 1979-90; sec. San Diego Padres Prof. Baseball Team, 1974-78. Contbr. articles to ABA Jour., Ill. Bar Assn. Jour. Mem. Winnetka (Ill.) Bd. Edn., 1974-81, pres., 1980-81; mem. Winnetka Planning Commn., 1975-77, Winnetka Village Caucus, 1975-77; mem. New Trier Twp. Caucus, 1974; bd. dirs. United Charities, 1984-94; mem. legal aid com., 1982—, vice chmn., 1986-87, chmn., 1987-94; pres. Legal Aid Soc. Ill., 1988-94; trustee The Nature Conservancy-Ill., 1978-88; pres. Winnetka Pub. Schs. Found., 1995-98. 1st lt. USAF, 1951-53. Recipient William H. Avery award for 10 yrs. svc. as chmn. Legal Aid Soc., 1994. Mem. ABA (vice chmn. commercial leasing com.), Scholarship and Guidance Assn. (bd. dirs. 1968-92, pres. 1979-

83), Harvard Law Sch. Spl. Gifts, Yale Alumni Recruiting Com., Standard Club, Yale Club (N.Y.C.), Phi Beta Kappa. Avocations: tennis; jogging; travel; reading. Home: 1165 Hamptondale Ave Winnetka IL 60093-1811 Office: Sonnenschein Nath & Rosenthal 233 S Wacker Dr Ste 8000 Chicago IL 60606-6342

GRANT, ROBERT ULYSSES, retired manufacturing company executive; b. Laramie, Wyo., Sept. 19, 1929; s. Guy Reid and Martha Clotilda (Krehmke) G.; m. Patricia Anne Towle, Feb. 12, 1955; children—Elizabeth, Sheila, Guy, Wilson, Mary. B.S. in Civil Engring., U. Wyo., 1951; M.B.A., Harvard U., 1957. Fin. analyst, dir. acquisition analysis, v.p. mgmt. services, sr. v.p. corp. devel. Lear Siegler, Inc., Santa Monica, Calif., 1964-87. Served to lt. USNR, 1952-55. Democrat. Lutheran. Club: Jonathan (Los Angeles). Lodge: Masons. Avocations: sailing; jogging. Home: 6549 Via Lorenzo Palos Verdes Peninsula CA 90275-6571

GRANT, STEPHEN ALLEN, lawyer; b. N.Y.C., Nov. 4, 1938; s. Benton H. and Irene A. Grant; m. Anne. K. Bagley, Feb. 11, 1961 (div. Nov. 1975); children: Stephen, Katharine, Michael; m. Anne-Marie Laignel, Dec. 8, 1975; children: Natalie, Elizabeth, Alexandra. AB, Yale U., 1960; LLB, Columbia U., 1965. Bar: N.Y. 1965, U.S. Supreme Ct. 1969. Law clk. to judge U.S. Ct. Appeals (2d cir.), N.Y.C., 1965-66; assoc. Sullivan & Cromwell, N.Y.C., 1966-73, ptnr., 1973—. Mem. Japan-U.S. Friendship Commn., U.S.-Japan Conf. on Cultural and Ednl. Interchange, 1989-92. Lt. (j.g.) USNR, 1960-62. Mem. ABA, N.Y. State Bar Assn., Assn. of Bar of City of N.Y., Coun. Fgn. Rels. Clubs: Down Town, Links. Home: 1021 Park Ave New York NY 10028-0959 Office: Sullivan & Cromwell 125 Broad St Fl 28 New York NY 10004-2489

GRANT, SUSAN IRENE, lawyer; b. N.Y.C., Apr. 27, 1953; d. Walter Arnold and Beatrice L. (Thalheimer) G.; m. Brian A. King, June 24, 1990; 1 child, Alexander Grant King. BA, NYU, 1974; JD, Columbia U., 1977. Bar: N.Y. 1978, U.S. Dist. Ct. (so. and ea. dists.) N.Y. 1978. Assoc. Law Offices of Rita Eredics, Esq., Flushing, N.Y., 1977-78; staff atty. The Dreyfus Corp., N.Y.C., 1978-85; asst. gen. counsel Prudential-Bache Securities Inc., N.Y.C., 1985-89, asst. v.p., 1986-89; asst. gen. counsel, assoc. v.p. Prudential Mut. Fund Mgmt., Inc., N.Y.C., 1987-89; asst. counsel First Investors Corp., N.Y.C., 1989-94; sr. counsel, chief compliance officer Quest Adv. Corp., N.Y.C., 1994-96; sr. atty. Van Eck Assocs. Corp., N.Y.C., 1996-98, Weil, Gotshal & Manges LLP, N.Y.C., 1998—. Mem. ABA, N.Y. State Bar Assn. Home: 11045 Queens Blvd Forest Hills NY 11375-5501 Office: Weil Gotshal & Manges LLP 767 Fifth Ave New York NY 10153

GRANT, SYDNEY ROBERT, educator; b. N.Y.C., Feb. 3, 1926; s. Herman S. and Ethel H. (Hymes) G.; m. Margarita Henderson, Sept. 4, 1951. EdB cum laude, CCNY, 1950; MA in Spanish Letters, Nat. U. Mex., Mexico City, 1951; EdD, Columbia U. Tchrs. Coll., 1961. Cert. tchr., N.Y.; cert. gen. supr., N.J., Wash. Program asst. Sch. Gen. Studies CCNY, 1951-52, instr. Spanish Sch. Gen. Studies evening program, 1952-64; tchr. Spanish and common brs. N.Y.C. Bd. Edn., 1952-60; dir. of instrn. K-12 Verona (N.J.) Pub. Schs., 1961-64; assoc. chief of party, assoc. prof. Columbia U. Tchrs. Coll., US/AID contract team, Lima, Peru, 1964-68; assoc. supt. for curriculum Bellevue (Wash.) Pub. Schs., 1968-69; dir. office internat. edn. Coll. Edn. Fla. State U., Tallahassee, 1969-72, assoc. prof., dir. Ctr. for Ednl. Tech., 1972-75, assoc. dean for grad. studies Coll. Edn., 1975-78, prof. Coll. Edn., 1972—, prof., head dept. ednl. founds. and policy studies, 1986-89, prof. internat.-intercultural devel. edn., 1979-85, prof. emeritus, 1994—; cons. U.S./AID, UN Devel. Program, UNESCO, Fundacion Natura, Fla. State U., Latin Am., S.E. Asia, Africa, 1969-90; sr. resident tech. adv. Min. Edn. and Culture, Fla. State U., Windhoek, Namibia, 1991-93. Cpl. U.S. Army, 1944-46, ETO. Recipient Esso award Esso Standard Oil Co., 1960, Palmas Magisteriales Peruvian Ministry of Edn., 1967, Pres.'s Teaching award Fla. State U., 1978; Downer scholar CCNY, 1950. Mem. Nat. Soc. for Study Edn., Comparative and Internat. Edn. Soc., Common Cause, Amnesty Internat., Phi Delta Kappa. Democrat. Roman Catholic. Avocations: short wave radio, reading. Office: 1503 Belleau Wood Dr Tallahassee FL 32312-3411

GRANT, VERNE EDWIN, biology educator; b. San Francisco, Oct. 17, 1917; s. Edwin and Bessie (Swallow) G.; m. Alva Day, June 12, 1946 (div. Aug. 1959); children: Joyce Grant Mixon, Brian, Brenda Grant Aley; m. Karen Alt, Nov. 3, 1960. AB, U. Calif., Berkeley, 1940, PhD, 1949. Teaching asst. botany U. Calif., Berkeley, 1946-49; NRC fellow Carnegie Inst., Stanford, Calif., 1949-50; geneticist Rancho Santa Ana Bot. Garden, Claremont, Calif., 1950-67; asst. prof. Claremont Grad. Sch., 1951-53, assoc. prof., 1953-57, prof., 1957-67; prof. biology Inst. Life Sci., Tex. A&M U., College Station, 1967-68; prof., dir. Boyce Thompson Southwestern Arboretum U. Ariz., Superior, 1968-70; prof. botany U. Tex., Austin, 1970-87, prof. emeritus, 1987—. Author: Natural History of the Phlox Family, 1959, The Origin of Adaptations, 1963, The Architecture of the Germplasm, 1964, (with Karen Grant) Flower Pollination in the Phlox Family, 1965, (with Karen Grant) Hummingbirds and Their Flowers, 1968, Plant Speciation, 1971, 2d edit., 1981, Genetics of Flowering Plants, 1975, Organismic Evolution, 1977, The Evolutionary Process, 1985, 2d edit., 1991, The Edward Grant Family and Related Families in Massachusetts, Rhode Island, Pennsylvania, and California, 1997; mem. editorial bd. Ency. Americana, 1955-64, Brittonia, 1957-62, Evolution, 1960-62, Am. Naturalist, 1964-67, Biologisches Zentralblatt, 1974-97; contbr. numerous articles to profl. jours. Recipient Sci. award Phi Beta Kappa, 1964. Fellow Am. Acad. Arts and Scis.; mem. NAS, Am. Soc. Naturalists, Soc. for Study of Evolution (pres. 1968), Bot. Soc. Am. (cert. of merit 1971), Internat. Soc. Plant Taxonomists, Am. Soc. Plant Taxonomists, Genetics Soc. Am. Home: 2811 W Fresco Dr Austin TX 78731-5028 Office: U Tex Dept Botany Austin TX 78712

GRANT, WALTER MATTHEWS, lawyer, corporate executive; b. Winchester, Ky., Mar. 30, 1945; s. Raymond Russell and Mary Mitchell (Rees) G.; m. Ann Carol Straus, Aug. 5, 1967; children—Walter Matthews II, Jean Ann, Raymond Russell II. ABJ, U. Ky., Lexington, 1967; JD, Vanderbilt U., 1971. Bar: Ga. 1971, Tenn. 1992. Assoc. Alston & Bird, Atlanta, 1971-76, ptnr., 1976-83; v.p., gen. counsel, sec. Contel Corp., Atlanta, 1983-91; sr. v.p., gen. counsel Smith & Nephew N.Am., Memphis, 1991-93; sr. v.p., gen. counsel, sec. The Actava Group Inc., Atlanta, 1993-96, Bruno's Inc., Birmingham, Ala., 1996—. Editor in chief Vanderbilt Law Rev., 1970-71, Ga. State Bar Jour., 1979-82. Baptist. Home: 23 Rose Gate Dr NE Atlanta GA 30342-4161 Office: Bruno's Inc PO Box 2486 Birmingham AL 35201-2486

GRANT, WILLIAM FREDERICK, geneticist, educator; b. Hamilton, Ont., Can., Oct. 20, 1924; s. William Aitken and Myrtle Irene (Taylor) G.; m. Phyllis Kemp Harshaw, July 23, 1949; 1 son, William Taylor. BA, McMaster U., Hamilton, 1947, MA, 1949; PhD, U. Va., Charlottesville, 1953. Botanist, geneticist under Colombo Plan to Dept. Agr., Malaysia, 1953-55; asst. prof. McGill U., Montreal, Que., 1955-61, assoc. prof., 1961-66, prof. depts. plant sci. and biology, 1967-90, prof. emeritus, 1990—; mem. joint WHO and Internat. Program on Chem. Safety Collaborative Study on Short Term Tests for Genotoxicity and Carcinogenicity, 1984-94; environ. contaminants adv. com. Ministers of Environ. and Nat. Health and Welfare, Ottawa, Ont., 1978-86; co-dir. workshop on higher plant mutagen bioassays, UN Environ. Program, Quingao (China) Ocean U., 1995. Editor Lotus Newsletter, 1970-85, Can. Jour. Genetics and Cytology, 1974-82; mem. editl. bd. Mutation Rsch., 1978-85, Plant Species Biology, 1985-92, Revista Internacional de Contaminacion Ambiental, 1991—; hon. editor Plant Species Biology, 1993—. Recipient Andrew Fleming award, 1953, Gov. Gen. silver medal commemorating 25th Ann. Accession of H.M. Queen Elizabeth to Throne, 1977, disting. alumni/alumnae scholar award McMaster U., 1990; inducted into Alumni Gallery, McMaster U., 1996; Blandy rsch. fellow, 1950-53. Fellow AAAS, Linnean Soc. London, Royal Soc. Can.; mem. Internat. Orgn. Plant Biosystematists (life, pres. 1981-86), Genetics Soc. Can. (life, pres. 1975, archivist 1984—, Presdl. citation 1991), Environ. Mutagen Soc., Can. Bot. Assn. (George Lawson medal 1989), Am. Soc. Plant Taxonomists, Soc. for Study Evolution (v.p. 1972), Biol. Council Can. (treas. 1974-78), Sigma Xi (chpt. pres. 1975). Home: 43 St Andrews Rd, Baie d'Urfe, PQ Canada H9X 2T9 Office: McGill U Macdonald campus, Box 4000 Dept Plant Sci, Sainte Anne de Bellevue, PQ Canada H9X 3V9

GRANT, WILLIAM PACKER, JR., banker; b. Orange, N.J., July 18, 1942; s. William Packer and Ruth Katherine (Dwyer) G.; m. Maureen Ann Mele; May 20, 1972; children: William Packer III, Michael Charles. Student, U. Pa., 1960-63. Adminstrv. asst. fiscal svcs. Fed. Res. Bank N.Y., N.Y.C., 1972-76, spl. asst. fiscal services, 1976-85, chief safekeeping div., 1985-86, chief automated payments div., 1986-87, spl. asst. electronic payments, 1987-93, oper. support specialist electronic payments, 1993—; pres. WPG Enterprises, 1990—. Editor newsletter Update, 1987-90. Mem. Comdr.'s Club DAV, Washington, 1983—, Am. Space Frontier Com., Washington, 1984-88, Ams. for the High Frontier, 1988-94, Rep. Nat. Com., Washington, 1981—; commr. Little Falls Youth Wrestling, 1988-90; co-founder, dir. Hornets Wrestling Club, 1990; mem. The Cato Inst. With U.S. Army, 1964-66. Recipient Spl. Commendation in connection with internat. direct deposit program Social Security Adminstrn. Mem. Am. Security Coun., Internat. Platform Assn., Little Falls Athletic Club, Deer Lake Club, Am. Legion, Phi Sigma Kappa. Republican. Roman Catholic. Home: 159 Main St Apt G Little Falls NJ 07424-1440 Office: Fed Res Bank NY 33 Liberty St New York NY 10045-1003

GRANT, WILLIAM WEST, III, banker; b. N.Y.C., May 9, 1932; s. William West and Katherine O'Connor (Neelands) G.; m. Rhondda Lowery, Dec. 3, 1955. BA, Yale U., 1954; postgrad., NYU Grad. Sch. Bus., 1958, Columbia U. Grad. Sch. Bus., 1968, Harvard U. Grad. Sch. Bus., 1971. With Bankers Trust Co., N.Y.C., 1954-58; br. credit adminstr. Bankers Trust Co., 1957-58; with Colo. Nat. Bank, Denver, 1958-93; pres. Colo. Nat. Bank, 1975-86, chmn. bd., 1986-93; chmn. bd. Colo. Capital Advisors, 1989-94; bd. dirs. Barrett Resources Corp. Trustee Denver Mus. Natural History, Gates Found. Denver, Midwest Rsch. Inst., Kansas City, Episc. Ch. Found., Nat. Trust for Hist. Preservation; bd. dirs. Mountain State Employers Coun., World Trade Ctr. Mem. Colo. Bankers Assn., Metro. Denver C. of C. (dir. Internat. Gateway Com.). Episcopalian. Clubs: Denver Country, Denver. Home: 545 Race St Denver CO 80206-4122 Office: KRMA-TV 1089 Bannock St Denver CO 80204-4066

GRANTER, SHARON SAVOY, restaurateur, caterer; b. Hammond, Ind., Oct. 21, 1940; d. Theodore Grummer and Marie Theresa (Vincent) Kocur; m. John Albert Savoy, Aug. 14, 1959 (div. Nov. 1974); children: Renee Savoy Heuss, Jennifer Lynn Savoy, Elizabeth Anne Savoy, Ericca Marie Savoy, Caroline Savoy Sanders; m. Donald Ralph Granter, Feb. 10, 1979. Student, Ohio State U., 1958-59; grad., Lancaster Bus. Coll., 1959. Sec., bookeeper Manpower, Inc., Albany, N.Y., 1960-64; owner, operator, caterer Granter's Deli Catering Svc., Mansfield, Ohio, 1979-94; restaurateur, operator Perkins of Mansfield, 1989-94; co-owner, operator Paisley Park Gourmet Deli and Granter's Catering, Mansfield, 1996—; co-owner EZ Meals, Inc., Mansfield, 1998—. Editor newsletter NCO Rehab. Ctr., 1971-74. Vocalist Ohio State U. Jazz Forum Big Band, 1955-59; founder, dir. New Start Seminar, Mansfield, 1973-79; sec. Miss Ohio Scholarship Pageant, Mansfield, 1974-80, traveling companion, 1974-80, judge, 1974-86; mem. procurement com. Mansfield Gen. Hosp., 1973-74; pres. aux. AMA Riverside Hosp., Columbus, 1972; bd. dirs. Am. Cancer Soc. Mem. Nat. Restaurant Assn., Ohio Restaurant Assn. Republican. Home: 660 Brae Burn Rd Mansfield OH 44907-1916 Office: 1400 Park Ave E Mansfield OH 44905

GRANTHAM, CHARLES EDWARD, broadcast engineer; b. Andalusia, Ala., Mar. 15, 1950; s. J.C. and Geraldine (Brooks) G. Student, Enterprise State Jr. Coll., 1968-69; AA, Lurleen B. Wallace Coll., 1979; m. Sandra J. Mosley, Mar. 9, 1973; 1 child, Christopher Charles. Sales engr., draftsman S.E. Ala. Gas Co., Andalusia, 1968-70; asst. mgr., engr. Sta. WAAO, Andalusia, 1972-78; engr. Ala. Public TV, WDIQ-TV, Dozier, Ala., also chief technician Sta. WAAO, Andalusia, 1978—; South Ala. microwave engr. APTV, 1980-93; asst. dir. broadcasting ops., APTV, 1993—. Notary pub., Ala.; bd. dirs. Carolina Vol. Fire Dept., sec./treas., 1985-91; pres. Andalusia Men's Ch. Softball, 1985-86; youth dir. Cedar Grove Ch., 1987-89, deacon 1993—; pres. Andalusia High Sch. Band Boosters, 1990-91; coach Andalusia Little League, 1982-83; active Lt. Govs. Commn. on Youth and Violence, 1995-96. With inf. U.S. Army, 1970-72. Named Civitan Outstanding Young Am., 1967. Mem. IEEE, I.S.C.E.T., S.M.P.T.E., Assn. Cert. NABER Technicians (sr. mem.), N.A.R.T.E. (master endorsement), Internat. Soc. Cert. Electronic Technicians, Am. Film Inst., Nat. Rifle Assn., Ala. State Employees Assn. (bd. dirs., pres. local chpt. 1991-99), Country Music Assn., Nat. Assn. Bus. and Ednl. Radio, Soc. Broadcast Engrs., Country Music Disc Jockey Assn., Rotary Club, Phi Theta Kappa. Mem. Ch. of Christ. Home: RR 5 Box 48-w Andalusia AL 36420-9296 Office: Sta WDIQ-TV RR 2 Dozier AL 36028-9802

GRANTHAM, DEWEY WESLEY, historian, educator; b. Manassas, Ga., Mar. 16, 1921; s. Dewey W. and Ellen (Holland) G.; m. Virginia Burleson, Dec. 26, 1942; children: Wesley, Clinton, Lauren. B.A., U. Ga., 1942; M.A., U. N.C., 1947, Ph.D., 1949. Asst. prof. history North Tex. State Coll., 1949-50; asst. prof. history Womans Coll., U. N.C., 1950-52, Vanderbilt U., Nashville, 1952-55; assoc. prof. Vanderbilt U., 1955-61, prof., 1961—, Harvie Branscomb Disting. prof., 1971-72, Holland N. McTyeire prof. history, 1977-91, prof. emeritus, 1991—; dir. NEH Seminar Tchrs., summer 1975, 1976-77; Douglas Southall Freeman Prof. History U. Richmond, Va., 1993; Lewis P. Jones prof. history Wofford Coll., 1997; vis. prof. Coe Inst. SUNY, Stony Brook, summer 1970. Author: Hoke Smith and the Politics of the New South, 1958, The Democratic South, 1963, Contemporary American History: The United States since 1945, 1975, The United States since 1945: The Ordeal of Power, 1976, The Regional Imagination: The South and Recent American History, 1979, Southern Progressivism: The Reconciliation of Progress and Tradition, 1983, Recent America: The United States Since 1945, 1987,, 2d edition, 1998, The Life & Death of the Solid South: A Political History, 1988, The South in Modern America: A Region at Odds, 1994; editor: Following the Color Line: American Negro Citizenship in the Progressive Era, 1964, The South and the Sectional Image: The Sectional Theme since Reconstruction, 1967, Theodore Roosevelt, 1970, The Political Status of the Negro in the Age of FDR, 1973; gen. editor: Twentieth-Century America series, 1975-95. Chmn. regional selection com. Woodrow Wilson Nat. Fellowship Program, 1957-59; mem. advanced placement exam com. in Am. history Coll. Entrance Exam. Bd., 1966-67. Served with USCG, 1942-46. Recipient Sydnor award for best book in So. history, 1959; Ford Found. fellow, 1955-56; Social Sci. Research Council faculty fellow, 1959; John Simon Guggenheim Meml. fellow, 1960; Huntington Library research fellow, 1968-69; Fulbright-Hays vis. lectr. U. Provence, 1978-79; Nat. Humanities Ctr. fellow, 1982-83; NEH sr. research fellow, 1986-87. Mem. Am. Hist. Assn. (council 1969-71, bd. editors 1975-77, chmn. com. on program 1977), Orgn. Am. Historians (exec. bd. 1965-68, chmn. com. on program 1973), Am. Studies Assn., AAUP, So. Hist. Assn. (exec. council 1960-62, chmn. com. on program 1959, pres. 1966), Phi Beta Kappa. Democrat. Unitarian-Universalist. Home: 3510 Echo Hill Rd Nashville TN 37215-2010 Office: Vanderbilt U Dept History Nashville TN 37235

GRANTHAM, DONALD JAMES, engineer, educator, author; b. Grantham, N.C., Aug. 1, 1916; s. James Clarence and Nannie (Rose) G.; children: David S., Philip L. BA in Chemistry, U. N.C., 1939. Radio announcer, 1940-42, radio programmer, sta. gen. mgr., 1946-50; founder, pres. Grantham Coll. of Engring., L.A., 1951-90; with Grantham Edn. Corp.; Grantham edn. CEO Grantham Edn. Corp., Slidell, 1992—. Office: 34641 Grantham College Dr Slidell LA 70460-6815 also: 10609 Staghound Trl Zebulon NC 27597-6948

GRANTHAM, JARED JAMES, nephrologist, educator; b. Dodge City, Kans., May 19, 1936; married, 1958; 4 children. AB, Baker U., 1958; MD, U. Kans., 1962. Assoc. prof. med. U. Kans., Kansas City, 1969-76, head nephrology sect., 1970-96, prof., 1976-96, disting. prof., 1996—. Founder and chmn. Polycystic Kidney Rsch. Found. Fellow NIH, 1964-66; grantee Nat. Inst. Diabetes Digestive and Kidney Diseases, 1969—; recipient Homer Smith award Am. Soc. Nephrology and Am. Heart Assn., David Hume award Nat. Kidney Found. Mem. Am. Soc. Nephrology, Am. Soc. Clin. Investigation, Am. Physiol. Soc., Am. Fedn. Clin. Rsch., Assn. Am. Phys. Achievements include research in fluid and electrolyte metabolism, electrolyte transport, mechanism of action of antidiuretic hormone and polycystic kidney disease. Office: U Kans Dept Medicine/ Nephrology 3901 Rainbow Blvd Kansas City KS 66160-0001

GRANTHAM, JOSEPH MICHAEL, JR., hotel executive, management and marketing consultant; b. Smithfield, N.C., Aug. 23, 1947; s. Joseph Michael and Anne Laurie (Hare) G.; student Oak Ridge Mil. Inst., 1965-66, East Tenn. State U., 1966-70; m. Wilsie Moss Hartman, Nov. 3, 1973 (div. 1982); children: Molly Meade, Joseph Michael III; m. Jean Marie Scully, 1986; children: William Warner, Stewart Michael. With Grand Hotel, Mackinac Island, Mich., 1966-78, v.p. sales, 1973-74, v.p. and mgr., 1974-78; dir. resort ops., gen. mgr. Pinehurst (N.C.) Hotel and Country Club, 1978-80; pres., chmn. bd. Ind. Fin. Investments, Pinehurst, 1980—; pres., chmn. bd. Carolina Hotels, Inc., 1982—; pres., chmn. Asset Mgmt. & Mktg., Inc., 1986—. Vice chmn. No. Mich. Conv. and Visitors Bur., Mackinac Island; commr. scouting Boy Scouts Am., Pinehurst, 1978—; bd. dirs., mem. exec. com., chair legal and risk mgmt. com. Sandhills Hospice, Inc. With USNG, 1970-76. Mem. Mackinac Island C. of C. (dir. 1976-79), Mich. Lodging Assn. (dir. 1976-79), Meeting Planners Internat., Hotel Sales Mgmt. Assn. Internat., Am. Hotel and Motor Hotel Assn., N.C. Restaurant Assn., N.C. Hotel and Motel Assn., Nat. Tour Brokers Assn., Chgo. Assn. Execs., N.C. Innkeepers Assn. (dir. 1978-80), Travel Council of N.C. (dir. 1978-80), Pinehurst Bus. Guild (bd. dirs., pres. 1986), Turnaround Mgmt. Assn., Sandhills Area C. of C. (dir. 1984—), Kappa Alpha. Methodist. Lodges: Shriners (bd. dirs. Moore County club, 1982—, pres. 1986—), Masons. Home and Office: PO Box 1479 Pinehurst NC 28370

GRANTHAM, KIRK PINKERTON, lawyer, insurance company executive; b. Tupelo, Miss., Oct. 12, 1941; s. Homer Kirk and Lucile (Pinkerton) G.; m. Damaris Falkner, Aug. 25, 1964 (div. 1980); 1 child, Dodson Kirk; m. Cheryl Mellinger, Apr. 25, 1983; 1 child, Tyler Kirk. B in Pub. Adminstrn., U. Miss., 1963, JD, 1966. Bar: Miss. 1966, Fla. 1971; cert. real property law and wills, trusts and estate planning. Estate tax atty. IRS, W. Palm Beach, Fla., 1966-72; ptnr. Day, Grantham & Hess, Lake Worth, Fla., 1972-81; assoc. Shutts & Bowen, Lake Worth, 1981-86; pvt. practice, West Palm Beach, 1986—; pres. Std. Title Ins. Agy., Inc., West Palm Beach. Pres. Palm Beach County Heart Assn., 1991. Sgt. USAR, 1966-72. Recipient Leadership award YMCA, 1987. Mem. Fla. Bar Assn., ABA, Miss. Bar Assn., Lake Worth Bar Assn. (pres. 1978), Tuskawillow Club. Republican. Episcopalian. Office: 1860 Forest Hill Blvd West Palm Beach FL 33406-6022

GRANTHAM, RICHARD ROBERT, real estate company consultant; b. Ogden, Utah, July 25, 1927; s. Arthur and Dorothy (Taylor) G.; m. Charlotte Blackwood, Aug. 10, 1951; children: Robert Arthur, Scott Ford, Ann Margaret, Susan Marie. B.S. magna cum laude, Claremont Men's Coll., 1950. C.P.A., Calif. Acct., Price Waterhouse & Co., Los Angeles, 1950-57; asst. controller Cyprus Mines Corp., Los Angeles, 1957-64; div. controller Cyprus Mines Corp., 1964-65, budget dir., 1965-72, v.p., treas., 1972-74, sr. v.p., treas., 1975-79, sr. v.p., controller, 1979-81; controller Amoco Minerals Co., Denver, 1980-81; sr. v.p., treas. Trust Co. of the West, L.A., 1982-88; sec., treas. TCW Convertible Securities Fund, Inc., 1986-89; mng. dir. Trust Co. of the West, L.A., 1989, cons. on oil and gas matters, 1989-92; sr. ptnr., chief adminstrv. officer TCW Realty Advisors, 1989-95; cons. earthquake repair and ins. matters Westmark Realty Advisors, 1995—; lectr. in field. Trustee Claremont McKenna Coll., 1965-68, 74—, vice chmn., 1976-96; dir. Pasadena (Calif.) Symphony Assn., 1995—, v.p. finance 1996-99, exec. v.p., 1999—. Mem. San Marino Men's Republic Club (pres. 1967), Calif. Soc. C.P.A.s, Am. Inst. C.P.A.s, Claremont Men's Coll. Alumni Assn. (pres. 1956), Republican Assocs. Clubs: California, Valley Hunt. Home: 1660 Oak Grove Ave San Marino CA 91108-1109

GRANTHAM, SHONNETTE DENISE, mental health nurse, care facility supervisor; b. Bklyn., July 23, 1961; d. Willie Clemons and Johnice Grantham. BS, Atlantic Christian Coll., Wilson, N.C., 1983. Lead nurse O'Berry Ctr., Goldsboro, N.C., 1983-88; lead nurse Cherry Hosp., Goldsboro, 1988-89, admission screening nurse, 1989, nurse supr., 1989-98, nurse B, 1998—; co-adminstr. Goldsboro Disciple Rest Home, 1983-90. Pres. nurses aid unit Elm Grove Ch. of Christ, Pikeville, N.C.; ch. youth hour tchr. Mem. Alpha Kappa Alpha.

GRANTUSKAS, PATRICIA MARY, elementary education educator; b. Irvington, N.J., Jan. 17, 1952; d. Albert L. and Mary D. (Gradeckis) G. BA summa cum laude, Kean Coll., Union, N.J., 1973, MA, 1977 and 1993, supr.'s cert., 1980. Cert. prin. supr., tchr., reading specialist, elem. tchr. Reading clinician Reading Inst., Kean Coll., 1977-80; instr. reading Newark Acad., Livingston, N.J., 1983—; reading specialist, test and basic skills coord. Garwood (N.J.) Bd. Edn., 1977-89; reading instr. Summer Clinic Pingry Sch., N.J., 1977-82; reading specialist, coord. basic skills Harrington Park (N.J.) Bd. Edn., 1989—; remedial reading tchr. Garwood (N.J.) Pub. Schs., 1973-77; pvt. tutor. Mem. YMCA. chairperson award of Excellence. Mem. ASCD, N.J. ASCD, Nat. Coun. Tchrs. English, Internat. Reading Assn. (hon. coun., Pres.'s Club), N.J. Edn. Assn., N.J. Reading Assn. (bd. dirs. 1991-94, sec. bd. dirs. 1989-90), Garwood Tchrs. Assn., Harrington Park Edn. Assn., Suburban Reading Coun. (past pres., bd. dirs.), Delta Kappa Gamma, Kappa Delta Pi, Phi Kappa Phi. Office: Harrington Park Sch 191 Harriot Ave Harrington Park NJ 07640-1400

GRANZIG, WILLIAM WALKER, clinical sexologist, educator; b. Greenwich, Conn.; s. William Alvin and Edna M. (Walker) G. BS, Loyola U., 1967, PhD, 1971. Diplomate Am. Bd. Sexology. Dir. of edn. Am. Coll. Ob-Gyn., Washington, 1972-86; clin. prof. U. Ill. Med. Sch., Chgo., 1976-81; pvt. practice as clin. sexologist Winter Park, Fla., 1986—. Co-author: The Parent Test, 1978; editor: Jour. Sex Edn. and Therapy, 1976-78; cons. editor: Jour. Sex and Marital Therapy, 1992—; contbg. editor: Brit. Jour. Sexual Medicine; appeared on more than 30 TV talk shows. V.p. Planned Parenthood, Washington, 1985-86; sec. Rotary Club, Washington, 1984. Fellow Am. Acad. Clin. Sexologists (life, pres. 1992-96); mem. Am. Assn. Sex Edn., Counseling, Therapy (bd. dirs. 1976-82, exec. dir. 1980-82, pres. 78-80), N.Y. Acad. Sci., Masons, Conquistadors Motorcycle Club (pres. 1995-96), Medinah Shrine. Republican. Episcopalian. Avocations: sports, research, motorcycles. Home: 120 Lake Sue Ave Winter Park FL 32789

GRANZOW, ROBERT FREDERICK, III, security firm executive; b. Harrisburg, Pa., July 7, 1961; s. Robert Frederick Granzow Jr. and Grace Marie Straub; m. Robin Michelle Freundel, Nov. 17, 1984 (div. 1998); children: Mandy L., Leidra M., Robert F. IV. AA in Police Adminstrn., Harrisburg (Pa.) C.C., 1981; BS in Criminal Justice, York Coll. Pa., 1983; MS in Criminal Justice, St. Joseph's U., Phila., 1994. Asst. corp. security mgr., asst. v.p. Dauphin Deposit Banks, Harrisburg, 1988-96; chief of police Paxtang Borough Police Dept., Harrisburg, 1996-98; sr. security specialist AMP Inc., Harrisburg, 1998—. Named Outstanding Young Am., 1981. Mem. Am. Soc. for Indsl. Security (chmn. Ctrl. Pa. chpt. 1991—), Assn. Cert. Fraud Examiners (cert. fraud examiner, v.p. Ctrl. Pa. chpt. 1993—), Free & Accepted Masons, Valley Harrisburg Scottish Rite Consistory. Republican. Roman Catholic. Avocations: sporting clays, archery, mountain biking. E-mail: rfg1@mindspring.com. Fax: 717-592-4355. Home: 994 E Maple St Palmyra PA 17078 Office: AMP Inc PO Box 3608 Harrisburg PA 17105

GRAPER, WILLIAM PETER, cardiac surgeon; b. Owen Sound, Ont., Can., Jan. 16, 1948; s. William Fredrick and Beatrice Shara Ileen Graper; m. Grace Louise Arnold, Feb. 4, 1975 (div. Apr. 1994); children: Lauren, Meghan, Kathryn, William, Kent; m. Rhonda Louise Grimes, Sept. 14, 1996. BSc, U. Toronto, 1970; MD, McMaster U., 1973. Diplomate Am. Bd. Surgery, Am. Bd. Thoracic Surgery. Intern in surgery Duke U., Durham, N.C., 1973-74, resident in surgery, 1974-75, 77-81; fellow in surgery Harvard U. Sch. Medicine, Boston, 1975-77; tchg. scholar in surgery Duke U., Durham, 1981-82; chief cardiac surgery Watson Clinic, Lakeland, Fla., 1982-87; pvt. practice Melbourne, Fla., 1987-89, Sarasota, Fla., 1989—; prin. co-investigator surg. robotics. Fellow ACS, Am. Coll. Cardiology; mem. ACCP, Soc. Thoracic Surgery, So. Thoracic Surg. Assn., David C. Sabiston Jr. Surg. Soc. Avocation: enology. E-mail: wpgmd@home.com. Office: Heart Surg Group 1921 Waldemere St #814 Sarasota FL 34239

GRAPIN, JACQUELINE G., journalist; b. Paris, Dec. 15, 1942; came to U.S., 1985; d. Jean and Raymonde (Ledru) G.; m. Michel Le Goc, June 4, 1971; children: Claire, Julien. Degree, Institut d'Etudes Politiques, Paris, 1966; Degree in Law, U. Paris, 1967; Auditeur, Inst. des Hautes Etudes de Def. Nat., Paris, 1980. Staff writer LeMonde, Paris, 1967-81; dir.-gen. Interavia Pub. Group, Geneva, 1982-86; pres. The European Inst., Washington, 1989—; econ. corr. Le Figaro, Washington, 1987—; prof. Inst. d'Etudes Politiques, Paris, 1974-77. Author: Guerre Civile Mondiale, 1977, Radioscopie des Etats-Unis, 1980, Fortress America, 1984, Pacific America, 1987; assoc. editor World Paper, Boston, 1980-93; contbr. articles to profl. jours. Trustee Aspen Inst. for Humanistic Studies, N.Y.C., 1981-96; bd. dirs. Internat. Women's Media Found., Internat. Action Against Hunger. Recipient Prix Vauban Inst. des Hautes-Etudes, Paris, 1977, Ordre de la Legion d'Honneur, 1993. Mem. Internat. Inst. Strategic Studies Longon, Swiss Soc. of the French Legion of Honor, Pen Club, Nat. Press Club, Kenwood Golf Club (Washington),. Home: 4745 Massachusetts Ave NW Washington DC 20016-2345 Office: The European Inst 5225 Wisconsin Ave NW Ste 200 Washington DC 20015-2014

GRAPNER-MITCHELL, PAMELA KAY, primary education educator; b. Celina, Ohio, Nov. 28, 1946; d. Eldon Leroy and Mildred Katherine (Koldewey) Grapner; m. E. Eldon Mitchell, July 18, 1992; 1 child, Trey Eldon. BS in Edn., Capital U., 1969; MEd, Nat. Lewis U., 1991. Cert. elem. tchr. Tchr. Columbus (Ohio) State Inst., 1970-72, West Jefferson (Ohio) Schs., 1972-74; with Dept. of Def. Schs., 1974-79, Okinawa, Japan, 1974-76, Bremerhaven, Germany, 1976-79; tchr. ethnic dancing, 1980-81; tchr. Keflavik, Iceland, 1981-82, Kitzingen, Germany, 1982-93, Schweinfurt, Germany, 1993-96, Kaiserslauten, Germany, 1996—; tchr. gifted children Camp Enquire, Celina, Ohio, summers 1985-88. Contbr. articles to profl. jours. Performer ethnic folk dance Community Arts Coun., Celina, 1978; guest folk dance artist Jay County Coun., Portland, Ind., 1979, Pkwy. Elem., Rockford, Ohio, 1979. Mem. NEA, Ohio Edn. Assn., Overseas Edn. Assn., Kitzingen Edn. Assn. Avocations: public speaking, traveling, dancing, skiing, reading. Home: 630 N Buckeye St Celina OH 45822-1511

GRAPPE, HAROLD HUGO, civil engineer; b. Portland, Oreg., Feb. 21, 1970; s. Donald Eugene and Anna Elizabeth (Rexroth) G. BSCE, Portland State U., 1994. Registered engr.-in-tng., Oreg. Engring. technician Bonneville Power Adminstrn., Portland, 1990-91, trainee in civil engring., 1991-94, civil engr., 1994-97, structural engr., 1997—. Team guide Dept. Energy Regional Sci. Bowl, Portland State U., 1995, U. Portland, 1996, 97. Recipient Appreciation cert. for leadership in support of the Rose Festival and a spirit of teamwork Portland Rose Festival Assn., 1996, 97, 98. Mem. ASCE, Am. Concrete Inst. Avocations: skiing, hiking, basketball, playing drums, travel, racquetball. Home: 8510 SW 42nd Ave Portland OR 97219-3522 Office: Bonneville Power Adminstrn 905 NE 11th Ave Portland OR 97232-4170

GRAPPONE, WILLIAM EUGENE, clinical social worker, gerontologist, consultant; b. Bklyn., July 31, 1942; s. Generoso Eugene and Sabina Mary (Fescina) G.; m. Frances Ann Cecere, Mar. 19, 1968 (div. Aug., 1973) children: Matthew, Rachele. BA, Adelphi U., 1966; MSW, Syracuse U., 1978, cert. in gerontology, 1978. ACSW; CSW-R. Dir. children's svcs. Syracuse (N.Y.) Assn. of Workers for the Blind, Inc., 1972-86; psychiat. social worker pvt. practice, Syracuse, 1986-87, '89—; staff social worker Wayne County Mental Health, Lyons, N.Y., 1987-89; cons. family support svcs. program dir. Cortland (N.Y.) Mental Health Dept., 1989-90; psychiat. social worker (affiliated) Psychiat. Dept. Community Gen. Hosp., Syracuse, 1990—; staff social worker Delaware County Mental Health, Walton, N.Y., 1991-92; therapist/cons. PPC Inc., Vestal, N.Y., 1992-94; social worker sch.-based program Family Health Network, Cortland, N.Y., 1990-91; psychiat. clin. social worker/clin. gerontologist in pvt. practice, Oneonta, N.Y., 1992—; cons. social worker At Home Care, Oneonta, 1992—. With U.S. Navy, 1967-71, Vietnam. Mem. NASW. Achievements include research in child psychotherapy and play therapy, geriatric psychiatry. Avocations: lepidoptera, stamp collecting, photography, swimming, walking. Home: 10 Telford St Oneonta NY 13820-1238 Office: 34 Main St # 7 Oneonta NY 13820-1586

GRASER, BERNICE ERCKERT, elementary school principal; b. Buffalo, May 5, 1933; d. George Snead Sr. and Ada Louise (Sheasley) Erckert; m. Stanley Richard Graser, May 8, 1953; children: Deberah Dawn Walvoord Rogers. BA magna cum laude, Coll. Gordon & Barrington, 1963; MA, R.I. Coll., 1965; postgrad., Boston U., 1969-71. Cert. elem., pre-sch.-high sch. handicapped tchr.; cert. spl. edn. adminstr.; cert. sch. psychologist. Spl. edn. instr. United Coll. Gordon (Mass.) & Barrington; prin. Pleasant View Sch. for Handicapped Children, Providence; spl. edn. supr. Meeting Street Sch., East Providence; prin. Wm. D'Abate Meml. Elem. Sch., Providence; established State Model Child Opportunity Zone at Wm. D'Abate Sch.; cons. on ednl. reform; spkr. on critical ednl. issues; presenter workshops and confs. Producer TV broadcast Internat. Celebrations of Cultures; contbr. articles to profl. jours. Named Sch. Adminstr. of Yr., State of R.I., 1993; grantee: U.S. Govt. Dept. Edn.1971—, 1991-93; Very Spl. Arts, State of R.I., 1985-87. Avocations: world travel, photography, videography, business economics, volunteer church work. Home: 45 Clarke Rd Barrington RI 02806-4037

GRASHOF, AUGUST EDWARD, lawyer; b. Rochester, N.Y., Aug. 3, 1932; s. Carl Henry and Mary Elizabeth (Shinn) G.; m. Anita Synnöve Leppänen, June 19, 1957; children: Carl, Anna, Amanda. AB, Brown U., 1953; LLB, U. Pa., 1959. Bar: N.Y. 1960, U.S. Dist. Ct. (so. and ea. dists.) N.Y. 1961, U.S. Ct. Appeals (2d cir.) 1961, U.S. Ct. Appeals (5th cir.) 1971, U.S. Supreme Ct. 1972, U.S. Dist. Ct. Conn. 1983, U.S. Ct. Appeals (4th cir.) 1987, (6th cir.) 1995. Ptnr. Winthrop, Stimson, Putnam & Roberts, N.Y.C., 1970-99. With U.S. Army, 1953-56. Mem. Assn. of Bar of City of N.Y., Fed. Bar Coun. Episcopalian. Avocations: stamp collecting, bridge, fishing. Home: 7 Jensen Ct Chatham NJ 07928-1618 Office: Winthrop Stimson et al 1 Battery Park Plz New York NY 10004-1405

GRASMICK, NANCY S., superintendent of schools; b. Balt.; m. Louis J. Grasmick. BS in Elem. Edn., Towson State U., 1961; MS in Deaf Edn., Gallaudet U., 1965; PhD in Communicative Scis. with distinction, Johns Hopkins U., 1979; LHD (hon.), Towson State U., 1992, Goucher Coll., 1992, U. Balt., 1996, Villa Julie Coll., 1998. Tchr. deaf William S. Baer Sch., Balt., 1961-64; tchr. hearing and lang. impaired children Woodvale Sch., Balt., 1964-68; supr. Office Spl. Edn. Balt. County Pub. Schs., 1968-74; prin. Chatsworth Sch., Balt., 1974-78; asst. supt. Balt. County Pub. Schs., 1978-85, assoc. supt., 1985-89; sec. juvenile svcs. Dept. Juvenile Svc., Balt., 1991; spl. sec. children, youth and families Gov.'s Exec. Office, Balt., 1989-94; supt. schs. Md. Dept. Edn., Balt., 1991—; mem., chmn. interagy. com. on sch. constrn. Gov.'s Subcabinet for Children, Youth and Families; mem. Gov.'s Workforce Investment Bd.; mem. profl. stds. and tchr. edn. bd. Md. Assocs. for Dyslexic Adults and Youth; mem. State Bd. Edn. profl. adv. bd. Met. Balt. Assn. Learning Disabled Children. Trustee Md. Retirement and Pension Sys.; active Women Execs. in State Govt.; mem. adv. coun. Scholastic, Inc. Recipient Medallion award Jimmy Swartz Found., 1989, Louise B. Makofsky Meml. award Md. Conf. Social Concern, 1990, Child Advocacy award Am. Acad. Pediat., 1990, Humanitarian award March of Dimes, 1990, Disting. Citizen's award Md. Assn. Non-pub. Spl. Edn. Facilities, 1991, Women of Excellence award Nat. Assn. Women Bus. Owners, 1991, Andrew White medal Loyola Coll., 1992, Nat. Edn. Adminstr. of Yr. award Nat. Assn. Ednl. Office Profls., 1992, Nat. award computing to asst. persons with disabilities Johns Hopkins U., 1992, Vernon E. Anderson Disting. Lecture award for outstanding leadership in edn. Coll. Edn., U. Md., 1992, DuBois Circle Award of Honor, 1992, Disting. Alumna of Yr. award Johns Hopkins U., 1992, Pub. Affairs award Md. C. of C., 1994, Educator of the Yr. award Am. Coun. on Rural Spl. Edn., Profl. Legal Excellence-Advancement of Pub. Understanding of Law award Md. Bar Found., Inc., Pressley Ridge award, Victorine Q. Adams Humanitarian award; named Communicator of Yr. by Speech and Hearing Agy., 1990, Marylander of Yr. by Advt. and Profl. Club of Balt., 1990, Marylander of Yr. by The Balt. Sun, 1997, Most Disting. Woman Girl Scouts Ctrl. Md., 1994, Cmty. Honoree 9th Ann. Heartfest Johns Hopkins Hosp., 1999; selected as one of Md.'s Top 100 Women, Warfields Bus. Record, 1996, 98. Fellow Nat. Assn. Pub. Adminstrs.; mem. Phi Delta Kappa (Excellence in Edn. award), Pi Lambda Theta. Office: Md Dept Edn 200 W Baltimore St Baltimore MD 21201-2502

GRASS, ALEXANDER, retail company executive; b. Scranton, Pa., Aug. 3, 1927; s. Louis and Rose (Breman) G.; m. Lois Lehrman, July 30, 1950; children: Linda Jane, Martin L., Roger L., Elizabeth Ann; m. Louise B. Gurkoff, Apr. 26, 1974. LLB, U. Fla., 1949. Bar: Fla. 1949, Pa. 1953. Pvt. practice Miami Beach, Fla., 1949-51; v.p. Rite Aid Corp., Shiremanstown, Pa., 1952-66; pres. Rite Aid Corp., 1966-69, 77-89, chmn., chief exec. officer, 1969-95, chmn. exec. com., 1995—; chmn., CEO Super Rite Foods, Inc., 1983-95; bd. dirs. Hasbro Industries; chmn. bd. Gov. Hebrew U. of Jerusalem, 1996—. Mem. nat. exec. com. United Jewish Appeal, 1968-79, nat. vice chmn., 1970-79, gen. chmn., 1984-86, chmn. bd. trustees, 1986-88, mem. bd. trustees, 1988—; pres. Harrisburg (Pa.) Jewish Fedn., 1970-72; chmn. Israel Edn. Fund, 1975-78; bd. dirs. Pa. Right to Work Found., 1972-74, Harrisburg Hosp., 1977-81; vice chmn. Harrisburg Hosp., 1988-95; bd. dirs. Pinnacle Health Sys., 1995—; mem. Pa. Coun. Arts, 1982; bd. dirs. Keystone State Games, 1982-92, Israel Ctr. Social and Econ. Studies, 1983; trustee Jerusalem Inst. Mgmt., 1983; mem. exec. com. Jewish Agy. for Israel, 1984-88, bd. govs. 1984-90; treas. United Israel Appeal, 1986-90. With USNR, 1945-46. Recipient Disting. Alumnus award U. Fla., 1992, Nat. Scopus award Hebrew U., 1993, Americanism award Anti Defamation League, 1995. Mem. Nat. Am. Wholesale Grocers Assn. (bd. dirs. 1971-73), Nat. Assn. Chain Drug Stores (bd. dirs. 1972-95, chmn. 1985-86, Nat. Achievement award 1995). Jewish (dir. temple). Home: 4025 Crooked Hill Rd Harrisburg PA 17110-9458 Office: Rite Aid of NY Inc 30 Hunter Ln Camp Hill PA 17011-2410

GRASS, GEORGE MITCHELL, IV, pharmaceutical executive; b. Bryn Mawr, Pa., Dec. 31, 1957; s. George Mitchell III and Irma Lucy (Schaffer) G. PharmD, U. Nebr., Omaha, 1980; PhD, U. Wis., 1985. Lic. pharmacist. Staff rschr. Syntex Rsch., Palo Alto, Calif., 1985-91; pres. Precision Instrument Design, Tahoe City, Calif., 1987-96, NaviCyte Inc., San Diego, 1996—; cons. Costar Corp., Cambridge, Mass., 1990-96, various pharm. cos., 1991—; co-founder Raptor Graphics, Snohomish, Wash. Contbr. numerous articles to profl. jours. Recipient Ebert prize Jour. Pharm. Sci., 1989. Mem. AAAS, Am. Assn. Pharm. Scientists, Sigma Xi. Avocations: skiing, bicycling, music.

GRASSA, ROSEMARIE LUCIA, massage therapist; b. Boston, Nov. 9, 1950; d. Peter Cesar and Laura Marie (O'Neill) G.; m. Theodore Thomas, Apr. 30, 1968 (div. June 1970); children: James W., Christina M., Carol L., Richard A., Peter C.; m. William McCormic, June 6, 1971 (div. 1980). Student, Pondville Sch. Nursing, Mass., 1980-81, Sch. Shiatsu and Massage, Calif., 1990-91. Owner, operator Treetop Nursery, Foxboro, Mass., 1979-80, Rosemarie's Sweet Things, Foxboro, 1980-83, Rosemarie's Nursing Svcs., Forestville, Calif., 1985-89, Guerneville (Calif.) Washboard, 1987-90, Rosemarie's Therapeutic Massage Ctr., Guerneville, 1990-98, River Run Weekender, Guerneville, 1996—, Rosemarie's Russian River Spa and Massage, Guerneville, 1998—; tchr. Sch. Shiatsu and Massage, Middletown, Calif., 1990-92. Bd. dirs. Met. Cmty. Ch., Guerneville, 1984; bd. dirs., social dir. Met. Cmty. Ch., Santa Rosa, 1992-94; pres. bd. dirs. Sonoma County Lesbian and Gay Pride, Santa Rosa, 1992-95; elected town rep. N. Attleboro, Mass., 1977-78. Named Vol. of Yr. Met. Cmty. Ch. of Redwoods, Guerneville, 1992, Woman of Yr. Raudy Roland, Santa Rosa, 1995. Avocations: dancing, hiking, music, cooking, baking. Office: Rosemarie's Russian River Spa and Massage 16370 1st St Guerneville CA 95446-1195

GRASSANO, THOMAS DAVID, minister; b. Greenwood, S.C., June 19, 1961; s. Thomas and Atha Elizabeth (Watts) G.; m. Lidia Angélica Minay, Aug. 20, 1983; children: Gabrielle Angélica, Thomas David Jr. MusB, Furman U., 1983; MusM, U. S.C., 1984; MusD, Fla. State U., 1988. Ordained to ministry Ch. of God, 1981. Evangelist Ch. of God, 1980-85; assoc. pastor Pkwy. Ch. of God, Tallahassee, Fla., 1985-86; instr. music Fla. State U., Tallahassee, 1986-88; campus min. Fla. State U., 1986-88; min. youth and music Br. St. Ch. of God, Tallahassee, 1987-88; dir. worship, campus pastor Univ. Ch. of God, Tampa, Fla., 1988-89; coord. short-term missions and collegiate ministry internat. dept. youth and Christian edn. Ch. of God, 1989-94; founder, dir. Urban Harvest Ministries, N.Y.C., 1994—; pastor Harvest Ch., Bronx, N.Y., 1995—; lectr. Internat. Bible Schs., Mex., Guatemala, Chile, Argentina, 1981—; founder Alpha Omega Campus Outreach Ministry, Ch. of God. Cmty. svc. chaplain, 1996—. Mem. Southeastern Composers League, Nat. Assn. Composers, Promise Keepers, March for Jesus. Republican. E-Mail: UrbanNY@aol.com. Office: Urban Harvest Ministries PO Box 143 East Meadow NY 11554-0143 *Success is not found through position, money or power. True success is found when selfish ambitions are pushed aside to accomplish the will of Christ.*

GRASSELLI, MARGARET MORGAN, curator; b. Worcester, Mass., Mar. 1, 1951; d. Paul Shepard and Anne Piersol (Murray) Morgan; m. Nicholas Eugene Grasselli, May 24, 1981; children: James, Juliana, Anne Regina. AB magna cum laude, Radcliffe Coll., 1973; AM in Fine Arts, Harvard U., 1977, PhD, 1987. Curatorial asst. drawing dept. Fogg Art Mus., Cambridge, Mass., 1974-75, curatorial asst. print dept., 1977-78; asst. curator prints and drawings Nat. Gallery of Art, Washington, 1984-89, curator of Old Master Drawings, 1989—; tutor fine arts dept. Harvard U., Cambridge, Mass., 1977; guest curator exhbn. Nat. Gallery of Art, Washington, 1980-84; professorial lectr. Georgetown U., Washington, 1988. Author: (exhbn. catalogs) Eighteenth-Century Drawings from the Collection of Mrs. Gertrude Laughlin Chanler, 1982; co-author: (exhbn. catalogs) Renaissance and Baroque Drawings from the Collection of John and Alice Steiner, 1977, Old Master Drawings and Bronzes from the Cottonian Collection, 1979, Watteau 1684-1721, 1984-85, Master Drawings from the Armand Hammer Collection, An Inaugural Celebration, 1989, Art for the Nation, Gifts in Honor of the 50th Anniversary of the National Gallery of Art, 1991, Dürer to Diebenkorn: Recent Acquisitions of Art on Paper, 1992, Drawings from the O'Neal Collection, 1993, The Touch of the Artist: Master Drawings from the Woodner Collections, 1995; mem. editl. bd. Master Drawings, 1994—; contbr. articles to profl. jours. Agnes Mongan Travelling fellow Harvard U., 1978-79, Samuel H. Kress Pre-doctoral fellow Samuel H. Kress Found., 1979-80, Ailsa Mellon Bruce Curatorial fellow Ctr. for Advanced Study in Visual Arts, 1989-90. Mem. Print Coun. Am. (bd. dirs. 1993-96). Office: Nat Gallery of Art 4th & Constitution Ave NW Washington DC 20565-0001

GRASSER, GEORGE ROBERT, lawyer; b. Staten Island, N.Y., Oct. 21, 1939; s. George J. and Anita F. (Spinetta) G.; m. Cecelia Frizziola, July 13, 1968; children: Mark, Eric. BBA, Iona Coll., 1960; JD, Fordham U., 1964. Asst. office mgr. Chgo. Title Ins. Co., N.Y.C., 1966-67; assoc., then ptnr. Moot & Sprague, Buffalo, 1967-75; ptnr. Willig, Grasser & Sheffer, Williamsville, N.Y., 1975-77; prin. Albrecht, Maguire, Heffern & Gregg, Buffalo, 1977-85, Law Offices of George R. Grasser, Buffalo, 1985-87; ptnr. Phillips, Lytle, Hitchcock, Blaine & Huber, Buffalo, 1987—; adv. bd. Ticor Title Guarantee Co., Buffalo, 1981—. Contbg. author: Condominium Development, 1990; bd. editors N.Y. Land Report, Albany, 1980-83; contbr. articles to profl. jours. Mem. N.Y. State Bar Assn. (condominium and coop. com. 1978—, co-chmn. 1990-96), N.Y. State Builders Assn. (trustee legal def. fund 1987—, dir. 1989—), Erie County Bar Assn. (chmn. real estate com. 1978-82), Niagara Frontier Builders Assn. (bd. dirs. 1978-80, 89—, sec. 1980-81, v.p. 1981, Svc. award 1977-98), Cmty. Assns. Inst. (trustee 1988-90, Svc. award 1986), Coll. Cmty. Assn. Lawyers (bd. govs. 1996-99). Roman Catholic. Office: Phillips Lytle Hitchcock et al 3400 Marine Midland Ctr Buffalo NY 14203-2887

GRASSHOFF, ALEX, writer, producer, director; b. Boston. Student, Tufts Coll., U. So. Calif. Writer, producer, dir.: TV series Rockford Files, CHiPs, Nightstalker. Recipient Acad. award nomination for Really Big Family, 1966; recipient Acad. award nomination for Journey to the Outer Limits, 1974, Acad. award for documentary Young Americans, 1968, Emmy award for Journey to the Outer Limits, 1974, Emmy award for The Wave, 1982. Office: 7845 Torreyson Dr West Hollywood CA 90046-1228

GRASSI, JAMES EDWARD, Christian ministry executive director; b. Oakland, Calif., Nov. 19, 1943; s. Dante Carlos and Mae Johanna (Condon) G.; m. Mary Louise Etter, Apr. 10, 1965; children: Daniel James, Thomas William. BS in Recreation Adminstrn., Calif. State U., Hayward, 1966; MPA, Calif. State U., 1971. Ordained to ministry Evangelical Ch.,1992. Recreation supr. Oakland (Calif.) Pks. & Recreation, 1964-66; adminstrv. asst. East Bay Regional Pk. Dist., Oakland, 1966-76; dep. town mgr. Town of Moraga, Calif., 1976-86; exec. dir. Let's Go Fishing & FOCAS Ministries, 1986—; dir. Calif. Recreational Fisheries Coun., Sacramento, 1968-74; trustee Christian Heritage Coll. Bd., El Cajon, Calif., 1989-91; nat. spkr. on bldg. strong families. Author: (booklet) Ultimate Fishing Challenge, 1990, (books) Promising Waters, 1996 (also audio cassette 1998), Heaven on Earth, 1997, In Pursuit of the Prize, 1998 (Silver Angel award Excellence in Media 1998), (pamphlet) Anchoring Your Lives in Christ, 1990; co-host TV program Fishing Tales, 1988-91; contbr. articles to profl. jours.; freelance writer on outdoor sports. Bd. dirs. Rotary Internat., 1976-86, YMCA, Hayward, 1977-70. Recipient Legis. Resolution Appreciation and Accomodation, Disting. Employee award Moraga Town Counsel, 1986, Presdl. plaque Calif. Pks. & Recreation Soc., 1980, Faith & Freedom award Religious Heritage Am., 1996. Mem. U.S. Trout Farmers Aquaculture Assn., Nat. Assn. Evangs. Republican. Evangelical. Avocations: fishing, boating, water skiing, writing, time with family. Home: 309 S Madison Rd Post Falls ID 83854-9458 Office: Lets Go Fishing PO Box 3303 Post Falls ID 83866-3303

GRASSI, LOUIS C., accountant; b. Bklyn., Sept. 25, 1955; s. Salvatore R. and Lena (Cestone) G.; m. Kathy Siciliano, July 3, 1982; 1 child, Alessandra. BBA, Queens Coll., 1977. CPA, N.Y. Staff acct. Pustorino, Puglisi & Co., N.Y.C., 1977-79; sr. acct. Peat Marwick Mitchell & Co., N.Y.C., 1979-81; mng. ptnr. Castellano, Grassi & Co., Westbury, N.Y., 1981-87; pres., CEO, Biscotti, Grassi & Co., Valley Stream, N.Y., 1987-95; pres., CEO, mng. ptnrs. Grassi & Co. CPAs P.C., Lake Success, N.Y., 1995—; chmn. bd. EAC, Inc., Mineola, N.Y., 1987-96; frequent speaker to profl. and trade groups. Editor Jour. of Constrn. Acctg. and Taxation; contbr. articles to profl. jours. Mem. N.Y. State Soc. CPAs (exec. bd., dir.), Constn. Fin. Mgmt. Assn. (bd. dirs. 1989—), Profl. Liability Commn. (chmn. 1990—), Associated Acctg. Firms Internat. (exec. bd. 1988—), bd. mem., Flushing Savings Bank, 1998—, Nassau Cty. comptroller transition team, 1994—, bd. mem. North Hills County Club, 1998—, Strathmore Vandervilt Country Club (past pres.). Republican. Roman Catholic. Avocations: golf, music. Office: Grassi & Co 2001 Marcus Ave New Hyde Park NY 11042-1011

GRASSLE, JUDITH PAYNE, marine biology educator; b. Brisbane, Australia, Dec. 4, 1936; came to U.S., 1960; d. Thomas Basil and Helena (Ripley) Payne; m. John Frederick Grassle, Nov. 21, 1964; 1 child, John Thomas. BSc, U. Queensland, Brisbane, 1958, BSc with 1st class honours, 1960; PhD, Duke U., 1968. Rsch. asst. Duke U., Durham, N.C., 1960-67; rsch. assoc. U. Queensland, 1968-69; rsch. assoc. Marine Biol. Lab., Woods Hole, Mass., 1970, ind. investigator, 1972-85, sr. scientist, 1986-89; prof. marine biology Rutgers U., New Brunswick, N.J., 1989—. Fellow AAAS. Home: 113 Cleveland Ln Princeton NJ 08540 Office: Rutgers U Inst Marine and Coastal Sci 71 Dudley Rd New Brunswick NJ 08901-8521

GRASSLEY, CHARLES ERNEST, senator; b. New Hartford, Iowa, Sept. 17, 1933; s. Louis Arthur and Ruth (Corwin) G.; m. Barbara Ann Speicher; children: Lee, Wendy, Robin, Michele, Jay. BA, U. No. Iowa, 1955, MA, 1956; postgrad., U. Iowa, 1957-58. Farmer; instr. polit. sci. Drake U., 1962, Charles City Community Coll., 1967-68; mem. Iowa Ho. of Reps., 1959-75, 94th-96th Congresses from 3d Iowa Dist.; U.S. senator from Iowa, 1981—. Mem. Am. Farm Bur., Iowa Hist. Soc., Masons, Pi Gamma Mu, Kappa Delta Pi. Republican. Baptist. Office: US Senate 135 Hart Senate Bldg Washington DC 20510

GRASSMUCK, GEORGE LUDWIG, political science educator; b. Nebraska City, Nebr., Sept. 17, 1919; s. Ralph O. and Katherine (Ballard) G.; m. Barbara Lois Lamb, Sept. 6, 1953; children: Janice Ballard Grassmuck Lilja, Karen Elizabeth Grassmuck Kraushaar, Terri Ellen Grassmuck Millson. A.B., UCLA, 1941, M.A., 1943; Ph.D., Johns Hopkins U., 1949. Instr. polit. sci. Boston U., 1949-50; vis. asst. prof. U. Cal. at Los Angeles, 1951-53; assoc. prof. Am. U., Beirut, Lebanon, 1953-57; dept. chmn. Am. U., 1955-57; mem. faculty U. Mich., Ann Arbor, 1957—; prof. polit. sci. U. Mich., 1964-90, prof. emeritus, 1990—, asst. v.p. internat. programs, 1967-69; cons. internat. divsn. Ford Found., 1968-69; guest lectr. USAF Acad., 1989-90, part. SCUSA USMA, West Point, 1994; student conf. U.S. Affairs # 46; co-chair roundtable on domestic influences. Author: Sectional Biases in Congress on Foreign Policy, 1951, Reformed Administration in Lebanon, 1964, also articles.; editor: Before Nomination: Our Primary Problems, 1985, others. Spl. cons. to Vice Pres. of U.S., 1959-61; spl. asst. internat. affairs to sec., also dir. Office of Internat. Affairs, Dept. Health, Edn. and Welfare, 1969-70; exec. asst. White House staff, 1970-72; chmn. adv. com. on accreditation and instnl. eligibility U.S. Commr. Edn., 1973-76; cons. examiner North Central Assn., Colls. and Secondary Schs., 1966-79; chmn. dedication Gerald R. Ford Library, 1981; trustee Gerald R. Ford Found., 1982—, sec., 1982-87; Chmn. Blue Ribbon Com. Fiscal Reform, Ann Arbor, 1967-68; dir. research Republican presdl. campaign, 1960; cons. critical issues council, Rep. Citizens Com., 1963. Served to lt. USNR, 1943-46. Fulbright research grantee, 1965-66; guest scholar Brookings Instn., 1975; recipient Amoco Found. teaching award, 1983. Mem. Am. Assn. Middle Eastern Studies (charter), others.

GRASSO, ANTHONY ROBERT, priest, educator; b. Boston, Feb. 23, 1951; s. Leonard Joseph and Nancy Antoinette (Solazzo) G. BA in English Lit., U. Notre Dame, 1973, MTh, 1977; MA in English, U. Toronto, Ont., Can., 1980, PhD in English, 1985. Joined Congregation Holy Cross, ordained priest Roman Catholic Ch., 1978. Tchr. English, Notre Dame Cath. High Sch., Fairfield, Conn., 1973-74; teaching asst. theology U. Notre Dame, South Bend, Ind., 1975-76; tchr. English, St. Mark's High Sch., Wilmington, Del., 1978-79; asst. Most Holy Trinity Ch., Saco, Maine, 1977-78; teaching asst. English, Erindale Coll. U. Toronto, 1981-82; dir. Holy Cross Sem., Toronto, 1982-85; pastoral asst., cons. St. Ann's Ch., Toronto, 1979-85; assoc. prof. English, King's Coll., Wilkes Barre, Pa., 1985—, chairperson English dept., 1996—, humanities rep. Faculty Coun., 1987-89, chmn. Bd. Student Communications Media, 1987-92, moderator Delta Epsilon Sigma, Campion Soc., writing cons. ACT 101 program; mem. Profl. Acad. Affairs Com. and adv. bd. Honors Program. Author poems and articles; mem. editorial adv. bd. Collegiate Press, Poetry. Fellow Sch. Grad. Studies, U. Toronto, 1981-82, 82-83; Charles Gordon Heyd fellow, 1984-85. Mem. MLA, Tennyson Soc., Nat. Coun. Tchrs. English, N.E. Regional Conf. on Christianity and Lit. (exec. com. 1991—, chmn. N.E. region 1991-92), Victorians Inst., N.E. Victorian Studies Assn., Assn. Lit. Scholars and Critics, Pa. State Poetry Soc., N.E. Pa. Writing Teachers' Conf., Delta Epsilon Sigma (mem. nat. exec. com. 1992-97, v.p. 1998—). *Ironically, human beings devote a good deal of time to dodging complex issues. Yet complexity is what denotes us from other creatures; it is the source of our uniqueness and diversity.*

GRASSO, JAMES ANTHONY, public relations executive, educator; b. Providence, Jan. 12, 1954; s. Eleanor Marie (D'Angelo) Grasso; m. Kimberly I. Maher, Sept. 14, 1986. BS in Pub. Communication cum laude, Boston U., 1976, MS in Pub. Relations, 1983. Land and pub. relations rep. Algonquin Gas Transmission Co., Boston, 1978-83, asst. mgr., 1983-85, mgr. land, pub. relations, govt. relations, 1985-94, dir. pub. & govt. rels., 1994-97; v.p. pub. & govt. affairs Providence (R.I.) Energy Corp./Providence Gas Co., 1997—; mem. adj. faculty Coll. Communications, Boston U., 1987-98. Bd. dirs. New Eng. Coalition for Clean Air, New Eng. Can. Bus. Coun., Narragansett Coun. Boy Scouts Am., Christmas in April. Mem. Pub. Relations Soc. Am., Interstate Natural Gas Assn. Am. Gas Assn. (natural gas industry exec. rep. World's Fair 1982), New England Council, New Eng.-Can. Bus. Council, New Eng. Broadcasting Assn., Pub. Utilities Communicators Assn., Italian Ams. in Communication, Publicity Club Boston, Radio-TV News Dirs. Assn., Capitol Hill Club, Pub. Affairs Coun., Utility Comms. Internat., New Eng. Gas Assn. Roman Catholic. Office: Providence Energy Corp 100 Weybosset St Providence RI 02903-2822

GRASSO, MARY ANN, theater association executive; b. Rome, N.Y., Nov. 3, 1952; d. Vincent and Rose Mary (Pupa) Grasso. BA in Art History, U. Calif., Riverside, 1973; MLS, U. Oreg., 1974. Dir. Warner Rsch. Collection, Burbank, Calif., 1975-84; mgr. CBS TV/Docudrama, Hollywood, Calif., 1984-88; v.p. Nat. Assn. Theatre Owners, North Hollywood, Calif., 1988—; instr. theatre arts UCLA, 1980-85, Am. Film Inst., L.A., 1985-88. Screen credits: The Scarlet O'Hara Wars, This Year's Blonde, The Silent Lovers, A Bunnies Tale, Embassy. Apptd. commr. Burbank Heritage Commn. Mem. Nat. Assn. Theatre Owners (v.p., Friend of Tripod award 1999), Bus. and Profl. Women's Assn. (Woman of Achievement award 1983), Retinitis Pigmentosa Internat. (The Vision award 1996), Acad. Motion Picture Arts and Scis., Found. of the Motion Picture Pioneers, Phi Beta Kappa. Democrat. Avocations: traditional music and dance, environ. activities, tennis. Office: Nat Assn Theatre Owners 4605 Lankershim Blvd Ste 340 North Hollywood CA 91602-1875

GRASSO, RICHARD A., stock exchange executive. BS in Acctg., Pace U., D in Comml. Sci. (hon.); postgrad. cert. advanced mgmt., Harvard U., 1985; JD (hon.), Fordham U. Mem. staff N.Y. Stock Exch., 1968-73, dir. listing and mktg., 1973-77, v.p. corp. svcs., 1977-81, sr. v.p. corp. svcs., 1981-83, exec. v.p. mktg. group, 1983-86, exec. v.p. capital markets, 1986-88; pres., chief operating officer N.Y. Stock Exchange, 1988-93; exec. vice-chmn., pres. N.Y. Stock Exchange, N.Y.C., 1993-95, chmn., CEO, 1995—; overseer ops. N.Y. Future Exchange; coord. Depository Trust Co., Nat. Securities Clearing Corp.; bd. dirs. Securities Industry Automation Corp. Past chmn. bd. trustees Jr. Achievement N.Y; trustee Securities Industry Found. Econ. Edn., N.Y.C. Police Found., Inc., YMCA Greater N.Y.; bd. dirs. Nat. Italian Am. Found., Police Found., Washington, Centurion Found.; metro N.Y. regional chmn. U.S. Olympic Com.; chmn. N.Y.C. Columbus Quincentennial Commn., 1992; hon. chmn. Friends of Statue of Liberty Nat. Monument/Ellis Island Found. Recipient Humanitarian of Yr. award Tomorrows Children's Fund, Spl. Achievement award Nat. Italian Am. Found., Ellis Island medal of honor Nat. Ethnic Coalition of Orgs., Good Scout award Greater N.Y. Couns. Boy Scouts Am., Brotherhood award NCCJ; named Man of Yr., Cath. Big Brothers, 1994. Office: NY Stock Exch 11 Wall St Fl 6 New York NY 10005-1974*

GRATALO, JOHN, JR., mortgage banker, business owner; b. Sommerville, N.J., May 2, 1963; s. John and Anna Mae (Tylka) G. BS in Fin., DePaul U. Banker Sears Mortgage Corp., Libertyville, Ill., 1987-94; sr. loan officer Lincoln Home, Bloomingdale, Ill., 1994—; owner The Cichlid Hideout, Northbrook, Ill.; loan officer First Chgo. Mortgage, 1994—. Mem. Philipino-Am. C. of C. (officer 1996—), Indak Dance Club. Roman Catholic. Avocation: rare exotic tropical fish. Home: 1108 Whitfield Rd Northbrook IL 60062-3947

GRATCH, SERGE, mechanical engineering educator; b. Monte San Pietro, Italy, May 2, 1921; s. Isaak F. and Tatiana (Dermaner) G.; m. Rosemary Delay, June 30, 1951; children: Susan, Mary, Lucia, Karen, Elizabeth, Ann, Barbara, Amy, Ellen, Thomas Charles. BSChemE, U. Pa., 1943, MS, ME, 1945, PhD, ME, 1950. Instr., U. Pa., 1943-45, asst. prof., 1945-50, assoc. prof., 1950-51; research scientist Rohm & Haas Co., Phila., 1951-59; assoc. prof. mech. engring. Northwestern U., Evanston, Ill., 1959-61; supr. processes and devices Ford Motor Co., Dearborn, Mich., 1961-62; mgr. chem. processes and devices Ford Motor Co., 1963-69, asst. dir. engring. sci., 1969-72, dir. chem. sci. lab., 1972-85, dir. vehicles and component research lab., 1985-86; prof. mech. engring. GMI Inst., Flint, Mich., 1986-96; prof. emeritus Kettering U. (formerly GMI Inst.), Flint, 1999—; mem. adv. bd. Coll. Engring. U. Iowa, 1969-73, Coll. Engring. U. Detroit, 1971-88; adv. bd. dept. mech. engring. U. Pa., 1973-88; chmn. air pollution rsch. adv. com. Coord. Rsch. Coun., 1983-85; mem. Nat. Alcohol Fuels Commn., 1979-81. Regional editor Internat. Jour. Fracture, 1965-91; contbr. articles to profl. jours. Mem. ASME (hon., past v.p. rsch., past pres., John Fritz medal 1992), NAE, AAAS, Am. Soc. Engring. Edn., Am. Chem. Soc., Engring. Soc. Detroit (past pres.), Soc. Automotive Engrs. (chmn. lubricant rev. bd. 1982-83), Sigma Xi, Tau Beta Pi, Sigma Tau. Roman Catholic. Home: 32475 Bingham Rd Bingham Farms MI 48025-2427

GRATHWOL, JAMES NORBERT, lawyer; b. St. Paul, Dec. 19, 1930; s. John E. and Bozena R. (McKeon) G.; m. Lael Dudley, Aug. 2, 1954; children: Robert, John, Joan, James, Katharine, Margaret. BA, Coll. of St. Thomas, 1952; LLB, William Mitchell Coll. of Law, 1958. Bar: Minn. 1958, U.S. Supreme Ct., 1966. Pvt. practice Minn., 1958-99. Bd. dirs. Friends of Southshore Sr. Ctr., Shorewood, Minn., 1996-99; Lake Minnetonka Conservation Dist., Wayzata, Minn., 1967-76, 88-95; mem. city coun. City of Excelsior, Minn. 1st lt. USAF, 1954-56. Mem. ABA, Minn. State Bar Assn., Hennepin County Bar Assn., Rotary (pres. Excelsior chpt. 1978-79). Office: 216 Water St Excelsior MN 55331-1825

GRATTAN, GEORGE GILMER, IV, lawyer; b. Harrisonburg, Va., Nov. 13, 1933; s. George Gilmer III and Elizabeth (Conover) G.; m. Martha Townes, Aug. 27, 1955; children—Rebecca, Kathleen, G. Stuart, David. B.A., U. Va., 1955, J.D., 1960. Bar: Va. 1960. Ptnr. Christian, Barton, Epps, Brent & Chappell, Richmond, Va., 1960-74; legal adviser U. Va., Charlottesville, 1974-88. Former pres. Big Bros. Richmond; former bd. dirs. Big Bros. Am. Served as 1st lt. U.S. Army, 1955-57. Fellow Va. Law Found., Am. Bar Found.; mem. Va. Bar Assn. (pres. 1984-85), SPEBSQSA, Inc. (barbershop Quartet & chorus). Presbyterian. Home and Office: 5250 Advance Mills Rd Earlysville VA 22936-1830

GRATTAN, PATRICIA ELIZABETH, art gallery director; b. Sault Ste. Marie, Ont., Can., Sept. 19, 1944; d. David Andrew and Virginia (Graham) G.; m. Ian Bowmer, June 29, 1968. BA with honours, U. Western Ont., London, 1966; BFA, Concordia U., Montreal, 1974; grad., Mus. Mgmt. Inst., Berkeley, Calif., 1995. Exhbns. coord. Art Gallery, Meml. U. Nfld., St. John's, 1978-80, acting curator, head visual and performing arts, 1980-81; acting chief curator Nfld. Mus., Govt. Nfld. and Labrador, St. John's, 1981-82; curator Art Gallery, Meml. U. Nfld., St. John's, 1982-88, dir., 1988-94; exec. dir. Art Gallery Nfld. and Labrador, St. John's, 1994—; chmn. adv. com. Art Purchase Program, Govt. Nfld. and Labrador, 1984-89; mem. The Can. Coun., 1995-98. Author: (exhbn. catalogues) 25 Years of Art in Newfoundland, 1986, Flights of Fancy: Yard Art in Newfoundland, 1983, David Blackwood: Prints' 1960-1985, 1986, Pam Hall: The Coil, 1994. Bd. dirs. Resource Ctr. for Arts, St. John's, 1981-82, Arts Atlantic Mag., 1982-95, Anna Templeton Ctr., St. John's, 1997—; treas. St. Michael's Printshop, 1985-87; mem. Provincial Govt. Spl. Anniversaries and Celebrations Com. Lakecrest Ind. Sch., 1987-89. Mem. Can. Mus. Assn. (nat. councillor 1987-89), Can. Art Mus. dirs. Orgn. (pres. 1993-95). Office: Art Gallery Nfld-Labrador, PO Box 4200, Saint John's, NF Canada A1C 5S7 Office: Art Gallery Nfld-Labrador, PO Box 4200, Saint John's, NF Canada A1C 5S7

GRATTON, PATRICK JOHN FRANCIS, oil company executive; b. Denver, Aug. 28, 1933; s. Patrick Henry and Lorene Jean (Johnson) G.; m Jean Marie McKinney, June 10, 1955; children: Sara, Vivian, Patrick, Lizabeth (dec.). BS in Geology, U. N.Mex., 1955, MS in Geology, 1958. Geologist Westvaco Mineral Devel. Corp., Grants, N.Mex., 1955; mining engr. Utah Internat., Denver, 1956; geologist Shell Oil Co., Roswell, N.Mex. and Tyler, Tex., 1957-62; adminstrv. asst. Delhi-Taylor Oil Corp., Dallas, 1962-64; exploration mgr., ptnr. Eugene E. Nearburg, Dallas, 1965-70; ind. geologist Dallas, 1970—; pres. Patrick J.F. Gratton, Inc., Dallas, 1976—. Contbr. articles to profl. jours. Bd. dirs. U. N.Mex. Found., 1992—. Served with USCG, 1951-53, U.S. Army, 1956-57. Named Disting. Alumnus in Geology, U. N.Mex., 1989; recipient Diplomacy and Innovation Spl. award Assn. Engring. Geologists, 1991. Mem. Am. Assn. Petroleum Geologists (v.p. S.W. sect. 1976-77, del. 1978-81, 91—, chair ho. of del. 1996-97, pres. profl. affairs 1989-90, hon. life mem. profl. affairs 1993, adv. bd. divsn. environ. geoscientists 1993-96, Disting. Svc. award 1998), Soc. Ind. Profl. Earth Scientists (v.p. 1976-77, pres. 1977-78, Outstanding Svc. award 1990, hon. mem. 1998), Tex. Ind. Producers and Royalty Owners Assn. (exec. com. 1985-97, 99—), Dallas Geol. Soc. (hon. life, Pub. Svc. award 1985, Profl. Svc. award 1992), Petroleum Club Dallas, Explorers Club (Tex. chpt. chmn. 1987-88), N.Y. Athletic Club. Roman Catholic. Office: 3232 Mckinney Ave # LB54 Dallas TX 75204-2429

GRATTON, ROBERT, diversified financial services company executive; b. Montreal, Que., Can., Oct. 23, 1943; s. Bernard and Judith (Dufour) G.; m. Nicole Marcil, Aug. 1966; 3 children. LLL, U. Montreal; LLM, London Sch. Econs. & Polit. Sci.; MBA, Harvard U. Bar: Que. 1967. Asst. to Hon. Paul Gérin-Lajoie Quebec City; with Credit Foncier, COO, pres., CEO; chmn., pres., CEO Montreal Trust; pres., CEO Power Fin. Corp., 1989—, also bd. dirs.; chmn. Great-West Life & Annuity, U.S., Investors Group Inc.; bd. dirs. Power Corp. Can., Great-West Life, London Ins. Group, London Life Assurance Co., Pargesa Holding S.A. Mem. Mt. Royal Club, St.-James's Club, St.-Denis Club. Office: Power Fin Corp, 751 Victoria Sq, Montreal, PQ Canada H2Y 2J3

GRATWICK, JOHN, management consulting executive, writer, consultant; b. Langley, Eng., Mar. 2, 1923; emigrated to Can., 1956, naturalized, 1970; s. Ernest Frank and Doris Hilda (Shepherd) G.; m. Dorothy Shirley Vincent, Aug., 1945 (div. 1957); children: Jane Mary, Paul Vincent; m. Gwendoline Johnston, Mar. 23, 1957; 1 son, Adrian. Cert. in Physics, London U., 1942, B.Sc., 1948. Chmn. Transp. Devel. Agy., Montreal, 1970-72; v.p. research and devel. Canadian Nat., Montreal, 1972-76, corp. v.p., 1980-82; pres. CN Marine, Montreal, 1976-80; prof. Sch. Bus. Adminstrn. Dalhousie U., Halifax, NS, 1983-87; dir. Can. Marine Transp. Ctr. Dalhousie U., Halifax, N.S., 1983-86, exec. dir. Internat. Inst. Transp. & Ocean Policy Studies, 1986-88; chmn. Halifax Industries Ltd., 1978-84; pres. Gratwick Hickling Inc., 1985-98; dir. Oceans Inst. Can., 1989-91; ptnr. Hickling Corp., Ottawa; bd. dirs. CPCS Transcom Ltd.; chmn. Ctr. for Marine Vessel Design and Rsch., Tech. U. N.S., 1989-91; chmn. Halifax-Dartmouth Port Devel. Commn., 1991-96. Gov. Mt. St. Vincent U., 1989-98; mem. Nat. Transp. Act Rev. Commn., 1992-93. Recipient Achievement award Nat. Transp. Week, 1990. Fellow Royal Statis. Soc., Chartered Inst. of Transport; mem. Can. Operational Rsch. Soc. (pres. 1969-70), Can. Transp. Rsch. Forum (hon. life mem., pres. 1971-72), Internat. Fedn. Operational Rsch. Socs. (v.p. 1977-79). Fax: 902-422-6215. E-mail: johngrat@netcom.ca. Home: 984 Bellevue Ave, Halifax, NS Canada B3H 3L7

GRATZ, CINDY CARPENTER, dance educator, choreographer; b. Corpus Christi, Tex., Nov. 20, 1958; d. Regan and Sara (Medellin) Carpenter; m. Robert David Gratz, Dec. 30, 1995. BA, UCLA, 1980, MA, 1982; PhD, NYU, 1990. Adj. instr. dance NYU, N.Y.C., 1987-90, adj. asst. prof., 1990-91; asst. prof. dance Sam Houston State U., Huntsville, Tex., 1991-97, assoc. prof. dance, 1997—; artist-in-residence Dan-Ching Acad., Taiwan City, Taiwan, 1986, Brenau Coll., Gainesville, Ga., 1988, U. Nebr., Lincoln, 1989; dir. Washington Square Repertory Dance Co., N.Y.C., 1990-91; founder, dir. Janus Dance Projects, N.Y.C., 1986-91, Prime Time: Srs. in Motion Dance Co., Huntsville, 1992—, The Cindy Carpenter Dance Co., Huntsville, 1995—. Choreographer, performer Afterimages, 1992; choreographer, dir. Post Post Dances: Another Artist Slips Away, 1995; dir., choreographer, performer (play) Stepping Out, 1995; choreographer Cheval, 1995, Prelude: Gathering of the Misfits, 1996, Starving, 1997, Excerpts from the Point, 1998; elephant rider, showgirl Ringling Bros. and Barnum and Bailey Circus, 1977-78. Mem. exec. bd. Huntsville Cmty. Theatre, 1994-97. Grantee Chi Tau Epsilon, 1994, Huntsville Arts Commn., 1994-97. Mem. AAUP (pres. local chpt. 1994-97), AAUW (officer 1994-96), Sam Houston State U. Women (officer 1991-96). Avocations: swimming, horses, tennis, scuba diving. Home: 2223 Mustang Ln San Marcos TX 78666-1120 Office: Sam Houston State U PO Box 2269 Huntsville TX 77341-2269

GRATZ, DONALD BURR, educational administrator, writer, consultant; b. Ithaca, N.Y., Jan. 31, 1950; s. Kenneth Leroy and Joan Esther (Bradley) G.; m. Frances Murray Wheeler, June 4, 1983; children: Jennifer Leigh, Julia Lindsay. BA, Wesleyan U., 1972; EdM, Harvard U., 1976; PhD, Boston Coll., 1998. Children's program dir. Russell Libr., Middletown, Conn., 1972-75; dir. after sch. programs South Shore Day Care Svcs., Quincy, Mass., 1976-77; adminstrv. coord. Jackson/Mann Cmty. Sch., Boston, 1977-79; gen. mgr., dir. programs and exhibits Boston's Mus. of Transp., 1979-83; exec. dir. Ford Hall Forum, Boston, 1983-88; exec. dir., continuing edn. Quincy (Mass.) Coll., 1988-92; sr. assoc., coord. Nat. Sch. Reform Programs Cmty. Tng. and Assistance Ctr., Boston, 1992—. Author: Advise & Consent: A Study of Collaborative Decision-Making in Denver, 1999, The Road Not Taken: The Evolution of a Municipal Junior College, 1998; contbr. articles to profl. jours. Bd. clk., founder Cmty. Tng. and Assistance Ctr., Boston, 1979—; v.p. Jamaica Plain Neighborhood Devel. Corp., Boston, 1983-91; pres. Cmty. Action for Greater Middletown, 1972-75. Fax: 617-423-4748. E-mail: gratzdb@aol.com. Home: 330 Central Ave Needham MA 02494 Office: Cmty Tng and Assistance Ctr 30 Winter St Boston MA 02108

GRAU, GARRY LEE, business educator; b. Indpls., Sept. 13, 1946; s. Leroy Harry and Mary Virginia (Beard) G.; m. Junita Kaye Mullers (div.); children: Amanda Kaye Grau Roark; m. Diane Augustine, Nov. 23, 1995. BS in Edn., Ctrl. Mo. State U., 1968; M History, Wash. State U., 1973; MBA, Stetson U., 1984; ABD, East Tenn. State U., 1999. Cert. prodn. and inventory control mgr. Product planner Harris Satellite Comm., Melbourne, Fla., 1981-82; supr. material ops. Def. Comm. divsn. ITT, Cape Canaveral, Fla., 1982-87; adminstrv. mgr. Software Productivity Solutions, Indialantic, Fla., 1987-91; ops. mgr. Fleming Mfg., Cuba, Mo., 1991-93; asst. prof., head bus. mgmt. dept. N.E. State Tech. C.C., Blountville, Tenn., 1993—. Office: Northeast State Tech CC PO Box 246 Blountville TN 37617-0246

GRAU, JEAN ELIZABETH, retired insurance agent; b. New Orleans, June 8, 1932; d. Adolph Eugene and Katherine Caroline (O'Nion) Grau; divorced; children: Steven, Marilyn, Laurence, Lorraine. BEd, Loyola U. of New Orleans, 1953, MS, 1972. Cert. tchr., La. Tchr. French and English Notre Dame Acad., Washington, 1954-55; tchr. French Orleans Parish Pub. Sch. Dist., New Orleans, 1953-54, 72-86; pvt. ins. agt., New Orleans, 1980-95; tchr. gifted students Plaquemines Parish Pub. Schs., 1987-89; tchr. French East Baton Rouge, La., 1989-90, St. Charles Parish, La., 1990-91; registered rep. Jackson Nat. Fin. Svcs., New Orleans, 1993-95, ret., 1995. Author numerous poems, contbr. poetry to Scimitar and Song Anthology, Yearbook Modern Poetry, Reflections of Light Anthology, Nat. Libr. Poetry Anthologies, Word of Mouth Anthology, newspapers, mags. Pres. Aurora-Hyman-Kabel Civic Orgn., New Orleans, 1982—, del. Pres.' Council of Civic Orgns., 1984—; adv. bd. Algiers Community Network, 1985-86; active Algiers Priorities Conv., 1986, Non-Pack Police Support Group, West Bank Action Com. Mem. Codofil, France-Amerique, Am. Assn. Tchrs. French, La. Edn. Assn., L'Athenee Louisinais, Internat. Platform Assn., New Orleans Poetry Forum, La. Poetry Soc., Kappa Kappa Iota (hon.), Delta Epsilon Sigma (hon.), Kappa Delta Pi (hon.). Republican. Roman Catholic. Avocations: ham radio, violin, sewing, bicycling, gardening. Home and Office: 1601 Kabel Dr New Orleans LA 70131-3633

GRAU, JOHN MICHAEL, trade association executive; b. St. Joseph, Mich., May 22, 1952; s. Otto R. and Esther P. (Spitzer) G.; m. Gayle Luedeman, May 7, 1983 (div. Nov. 1996); m. Kristine Sweeney, Aug. 30, 1997. BBA, U. Mich., 1974. Realty specialist HUD, Washington, 1974-75; field rep. Nat. Elec. Contractors Assn., San Mateo, Calif., 1975-76, chpt. mgr., Milw. chpt., 1976-85, asst. exec. v.p., Bethesda, Md., 1985-86, exec. v.p., CEO, 1986—; chmn., trustee Nat. Elec. Benefit Fund, Washington, 1986—; co-chmn. Coun. Indsl. Rels., Washington, 1986—; bd. mem. Plan for Settlement Jurisdictional Disputes in Constrn. Industry, Washington, 1986—; co-chmn. Nat. Joint Apprenticeship and Tng. Com. for Elec. Industry, Washington, 1986—; trustee Associated Specialty Contractors, Washington, 1987—. V.p. Elec. Contracting Found., Bethesda, 1989—; bd. dirs. Nat. Elec. Safety Found., Rosslyn, Va., 1996—, treas., 1996-98; trustee Nat. Labor-Mgmt. Coop. Com., Washington, 1997—. Fellow Acad. Elec. Contracting (bd. mem. 1986—); mem. Am. Soc. Assn. Execs. (key industries assn. com. 1987—), Internat. Assn. Elec. Contractors (assoc. bd. dirs. 1993—), U.S. C. of C. (Com. of 100 1990—). Lutheran. Home: 4805 Jamestown Rd Bethesda MD 20816-2710 Office: Nat Elec Contractors Assn 3 Bethesda Metro Ctr Ste 1100 Bethesda MD 20814-6302

GRAU, MARCY BEINISH, real estate broker, former investment banker; b. Bklyn., Aug. 7, 1950; d. Joseph Beinish and Gloria (Rosenbaum) Bennett; m. Bennett Grau, Nov. 19, 1978; 3 children. AB with high honors, U. Mich., 1971; postgrad., Columbia U., 1972, N.Y. Inst. Fin., 1973. Asst. to chmn. Bancroft Convertible Fund, N.Y.C., 1973-75; precious metals trader J. Aron & Co., N.Y.C., 1975-81, mgr. metals mktg., 1981-83; v.p. Goldman, Sachs & Co/J. Aron, N.Y.C., 1983-88; investment banking cons., N.Y.C., 1988-90; real estate broker Fox Residential Group, 1998—. Editor Precious Metals Rev. and Outlook, 1980—; contbr. article to profl. jours. Vol. worker pediatrics dept. Lenox Hill Hosp., N.Y.C., 1978-79; asst. The Holiday Project, The Hunger Project, N.Y.C., 1978-83; vol. Yorkville Common Pantry, N.Y.C., 1984; tutor Yorkville Neighborhood Assn., N.Y.C., 1984; assoc. Child Devel. Ctr., N.Y.C.; trustee Congregation B'Nai Jeshurun, 1989—, pres., 1991-94, chair, 1994-97; trustee Ethical Fieldston Fund, 1994—. Mem. Phi Beta Kappa. Democrat. Jewish. Avocations: interior design, fashion, cooking, piano. Home and Office: 300 W End Ave New York NY 10023-8156

GRAU, SHIRLEY ANN (MRS. JAMES KERN FEIBLEMAN), writer; b. New Orleans, July 8, 1929; d. Adolph and Katherine (Onion) G.; m. James Kern Feibleman, Aug. 4, 1955; children: Ian, James, Nora Miranda, William, Katherine. BA, Tulane U., 1950. Author: (short stories) The Black Prince and Other Stories, 1955, The Hard Blue Sky, 1958, The House on Coliseum Street, 1961, The Keepers of the House, 1964 (Pulitzer prize for fiction 1965), The Condor Passes, 1971, The Wind Shifting West and Other Stories, 1973, Evidence of Love, 1977, Nine Women, 1986, Roadwalkers, 1994; writer publs. including Holiday, New Yorker, New World Writing, Mademoiselle, Saturday Evening Post, Atlantic, The Reporter, 1954—. Mem. Phi Beta Kappa. Office: 210 Baronne St Ste 1120 New Orleans LA 70112-4179

GRAUBARD, SEYMOUR, lawyer; b. N.Y.C., Mar. 8, 1911; s. John and Edna (Kiesler) G.; m. Blanche Kazon, Aug. 24, 1941; 1 child, Katherine (Mrs. William Calvin). A.B., Columbia U., 1931, LL.B., 1933. Bar: N.Y. 1933. Legislative asst. to bd. aldermen N.Y.C., 1934-35; ptnr. Joseph D. McGoldrick, N.Y.C., 1936-37; law sec. to comptroller N.Y.C., 1937-41; sec. to justice Supreme Ct. N.Y. County, 1942, 45-46; practice in N.Y.C., 1949-75; counsel Graubard, Mollen & Miller, 1975-91; lectr. municipal govt. N.Y. U., New Sch. Social Research, 1938-40. Co-author: Building Regulation in New York City, 1944. Mem. N.Y.C. Commn. Govtl. Operations, 1959-61, Coordinating Council Criminal Justice, 1967-70; Nat. chmn. Anti-Defamation League, B'nai B'rith, 1970-76; pres. ADL Found., 1976-80; chmn. bd. dirs. Fund for N.Y.C., to, 1978; bd. dirs. Palm Beach Civic Assn., 1996—. Served to maj. U.S. Army, 1942-45. Mem. Assn. Bar City N.Y. (past chmn. com. city cts.), N.Y. State Bar Assn., N.Y. County Lawyers Assn. Clubs: City (trustee past pres.), Harmonie (N.Y.C.). Home: 2784 S Ocean Blvd Palm Beach FL 33480-5506

GRAUBARD, STEPHEN RICHARDS, history educator, editor; b. N.Y.C., Dec. 5, 1924; s. Harry and Rose (Polk) G.; m. Margaret Cavendish-Bentinck Georgiades, Aug. 5, 1978; stepsons: William J. Georgiades, David C. Georgiades. AB, George Washington U., 1945; AM, Harvard U., 1946, PhD, 1951; DHL, Providence Coll., 1971, Suffolk U., 1984, Union Coll., 1987; DLitt, U. Vt., 1990. Instr. history and gen. edn. Harvard U., 1952-55, asst. prof., 1955-60, lectr., 1960-63, exec. sec. com. on gen. edn., 1952-59, research assoc. in internat. affairs, 1963-65; vis. prof. history Brown U., 1965-66, prof. history, 1966-94, prof. history emeritus, 1994—; mng. editor Daedalus, 1960-61, editor, 1961—; asst. editor Confluence, 1952-55; dir. studies Assembly on Univ. Goals and Governance, 1969-75. Author: British Labour and the Russian Revolution, 1956, Burke, Disraeli and Churchill: The Politics of Perseverance, 1961, Kissinger, Portrait of a Mind, 1973, Mr. Bush's War: Adventures in the Politics of Illusion, 1992; editor: (with G. Holton) Excellence and Leadership in a Democracy, 1962, A New Europe?, 1964, (with G. Ballotti) The Embattled University, 1970 (with F. Gilbert) Historical Studies Today, 1972, (with S.N. Eisenstadt) Intellectuals and Tradition, 1973, (with F. Cavazza) Il Caso Italiano, 1974, A New America?, 1979, Generations, 1979, The State, 1980, Reading in the 1980s, 1983, Australia: The Daedalus Symposium, 1985, Art and Science, 1987, The Artificial Intelligence Debate, 1989, In Search of Canada, 1990, Living with Aids, 1990, Showa: The Japan of Hirohito (with Carol Gluck), 1992, The Research University in a Time of Discontent (with Jonathan R. Cole and Elinor G. Barber), 1994, (with Daniel Bell) Toward the Year 2000, 1997, A New Europe for and Old, 1998. Served with AUS, 1943. Social Sci. Research Council fellow, 1948-50. Fellow Am. Acad. Arts and Scis. (editor 1963—), Council on Fgn. Relations, Mass. Hist. Soc. Clubs: Century, Signet. Home: 8 Maple Ave Cambridge MA 02139-1116 Office: Am Academy of Arts & Sciences Nortons Woods 136 Irving St Cambridge MA 02138-1929

GRAUER, DOUGLAS DALE, civil engineer; b. Marysville, Kans., June 27, 1956; s. Norman Wayne and Ruth Ann (Schwindaman) G.; m. Bette Lynn Bohnenblust, Aug. 16, 1980; children: Diana Kathryn, Laura Jaclyn. Student, Baker U., 1976; BSCE, Kans. State U., 1979. Registered profl. engr., Iowa, Kans., Nebr., Okla. Pipeline engr. Cities Service Pipeline Co., Shreveport, La., 1979-80; products terminal engr. Cities Service Co., Braintree, Mass., 1980-81; project engr. Cities Service Co., Tulsa, 1981-83; staff engr. Cities Service Oil and Gas Corp., Tulsa, 1983-85; asst. products pipeline and terminal supt. Nat. Coop. Refinery Assn., Blue Rapids, Kans., 1985-90, supt. products pipeline and terminal, 1990—. Mem. ASCE, NSPE, Nat. Assn. Corrosion Engrs., Kans. Engring. Soc., Chi Epsilon. Republican. Avocations: golf, fishing, woodworking. Home: 1321 Ranch Rd Mcpherson KS 67460-2313 Office: Nat Coop Refinery Assn PO Box 1404 Mcpherson KS 67460-1404

GRAULE, RAYMOND (SIEGFRIED), metallurgical engineer; b. Phila., Feb. 7, 1932; s. Oscar P. and Elizabeth Keim (Merkle) G.; m. Beatrice D. Miller, Sept. 4, 1954 (div. Nov. 1982); children: Melissa, Jon; m. Marlys Ann Sunkle, Sept. 21, 1985 (div. Jan. 1995); children: Troy, Tara, Tiffany. BSChemE, N.J. Inst. Tech., Newark, 1955; MS in Metallurgy, Stevens Inst. of Tech., Hoboken, N.J., 1961. Process engr. Wilbur B. Driver Co., Newark, 1954-62; supr. of prod. engring. G.T.E. Corp., Newark, 1962-77; engring. mgr. Amax Corp., Parsippany, N.J., 1977-84; sr. mfg. engr. Carpenter Tech. Corp., Orangeburg, S.C., 1984—; adj. instr. Essex County Coll., Newark, 1979-81, Orangeburg Calhoun Tech. Coll., 1984-87. County committeeman Rep. Party, Parsippany, 1965-81; advisor Bd. of Edn., 1969-73. With U.S. Army, 1956-58. Mem. Rep. Club (Parsippany), Goodyear Blimp Club, Exptl. Aviation Assn., Orangeburg Pilots Assn. Avocations: woodworking, flying, boating. Home: 433 Gue Rd NW Orangeburg SC 29115-4128 Office: Carpenter Splty Wire Products PO Box 1467 144 Old Elloree Rd Orangeburg SC 29115

GRAUPE, DANIEL, electrical and computer engineering educator, systems and biomedical engineer; b. Jerusalem; came to U.S., 1970, naturalized, 1976; s. Heinz M. and Hella N. (Neumann) G.; m. Dalia Smilansky, July 9, 1968; children: Menachem-Henny, Pelleg-Pinhas, Oren. BSME, Technion, Israel Inst. Tech., Haifa, 1958, BSEE, 1959, Dipl. Ing. Elec. Engring., 1960; PhDEE, U. Liverpool, Eng., 1963. Lectr. U. Liverpool, Eng., 1963-67; sr. lectr. Technion, Israel Inst. Tech., Haifa, 1967-70; assoc. prof. elec. engring. Colo. State U., Ft. Collins, 1970-74, prof. elec. engring., 1974-78; prof. elec. and computer engring. Ill. Inst. Tech., Chgo., 1978-84, Bodine chair disting. prof. elec. and computer engring., 1984-85; Sr. U. Ill. scholar U. Ill., Chgo., 1988—; prof. elec. engring., computer sci., 1991—; adj. prof. rehab. medicine U. Ill., Chgo., 1985—; vis. prof. elec. engring. Notre Dame U., Ind., 1976; Springer vis. chair prof., dept. mech. engring. U. Calif.-Berkeley, 1977; vis. prof. Sch. Medicine, Tel Aviv U., summers 1982, 83, 84, Swiss Fed. Inst. Tech., Zurich, 1988, 89, 91, 92, 96; vis. prof. Northwestern U., Evanston, Ill., 1995-96; founder, v.p. Intellitech Inc., Northbrook, Ill., 1982-88; founder, chief scientist, bd. dirs. Sigmedics Inc., Northfield, Ill., 1988-95; bd. dirs. GS Systems Inc., Skokie, Ill. Author: Identification of Systems (transl. into Russian and Serbo-Croat), 1972, 2d edit., 1976, Time Series Analysis Identification and Adaptive Filtering, 1984, 2d edit., 1989, Chinese translation, 1987; (with K.H. Kohn) Functional Electrical Stimulation for Ambulation by Paraplegics, 1994, (Spanish transl.), 1998, Principles of Artificial Neural Networks, 1997; assoc. editor Internat. Jour. Software Engring. and Knowledge Engring., 1996—, Neurol. Rsch., 1998—, Psychline, 1998—; contbr. articles to profl. jours.; patentee in field. Trustee Knowledge Systems Ins., Skokie, Ill., 1988—; chmn. Chgo. chpt. Leo Baeck Inst., 1992—. With Israel Air Force, 1952-55. Recipient Anna Frank prize Hebrew U. Jerusalem and Technion, Haifa, 1961. Fellow IEEE; mem. IEEE Cirs. and Systems Soc. (chmn. tech. com. on image and signal processing in medicine 1988-92, assoc. editor IEEE Transactions on Cirs. and Systems 1989-92), Internat. Orgn. Neurol. Socs. (mem. internat. adv. bd. 1999—), N.Y. Acad. Scis. Jewish. Avocations: reading; history; philosophy. E-mail: graupe@eecs.uic.edu. Home: 496 Hillside Dr Highland Park IL 60035-4826 Office: U Ill Dept Elec Engring and Sci 851 S Morgan St Chicago IL 60607-7042

GRAUPNER, SHERYLL ANN, elementary education educator; b. Independence, Mo., Sept. 19, 1947; d. Horace Alvin and Estelle (LeJeune) G. BS in Edn., Ctrl. Mo. State U., 1969; MEd, U. Mo., Kansas City, 1972. Tchr. Independence Pub. Schs., 1969—; head tchr. Procter Sch., Independence, 1995—; chmn. Procter Sch. North Ctrl., Independence, 1982, 97, co-chmn., 1989; tchr. math. connection Mo. Ednl. Incentive Grant, Independence, 1987, 94. Mem. NEA, Internat. Reading Assn., Nat. Congress Parents and Tchrs.

GRAUSAM, JEFFREY LEONARD, lawyer; b. Newark, Sept. 21, 1943; s. John G. and Angela (D'Addario) G.; m. Anne Jenks Boynton, Dec. 20, 1969; children: Daniel Carpenter, Elizabeth Wiley. BA, Wesleyan U., 1965; JD, U. Chgo., 1968; LLM in Taxation, NYU, 1975. Bar: Calif. 1969, N.Y. 1970, U.S. Supreme Ct. 1981. Law clk. to chief justice Roger J. Traynor Supreme Ct., State of Calif., San Francisco, 1968-69; assoc. Debevoise,

Plimpton, Lyons & Gates, N.Y.C., 1969-75; officer, mem. firm Tuttle & Taylor, Inc., L.A., 1975-89; ptnr. Morgan, Lewis & Bockius, LLP, L.A., 1989—. Editor-in-chief law rev. U. Chgo., 1967-68. Dir. Libr. Found. L.A., 1993-98, 99—. Mem. L.A. County Bar Assn. (exec. com. taxation sect. 1994-95), Order of Coif. Avocation: cycling. Office: Morgan Lewis & Bockius LLP 300 S Grand Ave 22nd Fl Los Angeles CA 90071-3132

GRAUSMAN, PHILIP, sculptor; b. N.Y.C., July 16, 1935; 1 child, David. Studetn, Sch. Painting and Sculpture, Skowhegan, Maine, 1956-57; BA cum laude, Syracuse U., 1957; studetn, Art Students' League, 1959; MFA, Cranbrook Acad. Art, 1959. Critic of archtl. drawing Grad. Sch. Architecture, Yale U., New Haven, 1974—; instr. design Cooper Union, 1965-67; instr. design and drawing Pratt Inst., 1965-69; artist-in-residence Dartmouth Coll., 1972; instr. sculpture and drawing Skowhegan Sch. Painting and Sculpture, 1973; vis. asst. prof. art Yale U., 1974-76. Solo exhbns. include Borgenicht Gallery, N.Y.C., 1966, 74, 79, Alpha Gallery, Boston, 1968, 75, Dartmouth Coll., Hanover, N.H., 1972, U. Conn., 1976, Pa. State U., 1977, Washington Art Assn., Washington Depot, Conn., 1978, 82, Robert Schoelkopf Gallery, N.Y.C., 1983, 87, Babcock Galleries, N.Y.C., 1993; exhibited in group shows at Whitney Mus. Am. Art, Am. Acad. in Rome, Ohio State U., Boston Coliseum, Wadsworth Atheneum, Chgo. Arts Club, Fine Arts Mus. San Diego, U. N.C., Paris/N.Y./Kent Gallery, Kent, Conn., numerous others; represented in collections at Vassar Coll., U. Mich., U. Mass., U. Conn., Newark Mus., Met. Mus. Art, Jewish Mus., N.Y.C., De Cordova Mus. Art, Lincoln, Mass., Cornell U., Bklyn. Mus., Rose Art Mus./Brandeis U., Balt. Mus. Art, Akron Art Mus., others. Recipient Gold medal of honor in sculpture Audubon Artists, 1956, Alfred G.B. Steel Meml. prize Pa. Acad. Fine Aarts, 1962, Solon H. Borgliem award Silvermine Guild, Conn., 1980, Albert JacobsonMeml. award Silvermine Guild, 1984, others; Huntington Hartford fellow, 1957, Louis Comfort Tiffany Found. grantee, 1959, Nat. Inst. Arts and Letters grantee, 1961, Prix de Rome fellow, 1962-65. Fellow Am. Acad. in Rome; mem. NAD (Dessie Greer prize 1981, Gold medal in sculpture 1988, cert. of merit in sculpture 1993. Office: Yale U Sch of Architecture New Haven CT 06520

GRAVATT, CLAUDE CARRINGTON, JR., research and development executive; b. Washington, Dec. 12, 1939; s. Claude Carrington and Martha Loretta (Bost) G.; m. Ann Lee Sullivan, June 20, 1964; children: Lee Carrington, Arn English. BS, U. Richmond, 1962; PhD, Duke U., 1966. Postdoctoral rsch. assoc. Cornell U., Ithaca, N.Y., 1965-67; mem. tech. staff Bell Telephone Labs., Murray Hill, N.J., 1967-69; rsch. chemist Nat. Bur. Standards, Gaithersburg, Md., 1969-73; program analyst, Office of the Dir. Nat. Bur. Standards, Gaithersburg, 1973-75, dep. dir. Ctr. for Analytical Chemistry, 1975-78, chief Office of Environ. Measurements, 1978-80, dep. dir. for progs., 1980-82, dep. dir. Nat. Measurement Lab., 1982-89; dep. assoc. dir. for strategic planning Nat. Inst. Standards and Tech. (formerly Nat. Bur. Stand.), Gaithersburg, 1989-90, dir. tech. commercialization, 1990-94; dir. manufacturing competitiveness Dept. Commerce, Washington, 1994-95; visiting prof. Ga. Inst. Tech., Atlanta, 1995-96; dir. Mfg. Competitiveness Office Undersec. Tech., Gaithersburg, Md., 1996—; dir. mfg. competitiveness Office of Under-Sec. of Tech. Contbr. articles to profl. jours. and procs., chpts. to books. Fellow AAAS (Indsl. Sci. and Tech. sec., chair Nominations com.); mem. Optical Soc. Am., Am. Physical Soc., Soc. Automotive Engrs., Nat. Conf. of the Advancement of Rsch. Achievements include patents on light scattering instruments for chemical and physical characterization of particulates. Home: 7064 Wolftree Ln Rockville MD 20852-4355 Office: Office Undersec Tech 100 Bureau Dr Stop 8101 Gaithersburg MD 20899-8101

GRAVELLE, JOHN DAVID, secondary education educator. Tchr. math, Eng. grades 10-12 Merrill (Wis.) High Sch., to 1997, technology coord., 1997—. Recipient State Tchr. of Yr. Math/Eng. award Wis., 1992. Office: Merrill High Sch 120 N Sales St Merrill WI 54452*

GRAVENSTEIN, JOACHIM STEFAN, anesthesiologist, educator; b. Berlin, Germany, Jan. 25, 1925; came to U.S., 1952, naturalized, 1959; m. Alix Trutschler, Aug. 27, 1949; children—Nikolaus, Alix, Frederike, Stefan, Ruprecht, Dietrich, Constanze, Katharina. MD, U. Bonn, Germany, 1951, Harvard, 1958; MD (hon.), U. Graz, Austria, 1988. Resident and staff appointments anesthesia Mass. Gen. Hosp., 1952-58; fellow, tchr. Harvard Med. Sch., 1952-58; chief anesthesiology Coll. Medicine, U. Fla., 1958-69; prof. anesthesiology, chmn. dept. Case Western Res. Med. Sch., 1969-79; grad. research prof. Coll. Medicine, U. Fla., Gainesville, 1979-96, prof. emeritus, 1996—. Mem. Am. Soc. Anesthesiology. Home: 3421 SW 79th Ter Gainesville FL 32608-3668 Office: U Fla Coll Medicine Gainesville FL 32610*

GRAVER, JACK EDWARD, mathematics educator; b. Cin., Apr. 13, 1935; s. Harold John and Rose Lucille (Miller) G.; m. Yana Regina Hanus, June 3, 1961; children: Juliet Rose, Yana-Maria, Paul Christopher. BA in Math., Miami U., Oxford, Ohio, 1958; MA in Math., Ind. U., 1961, PhD in Math., 1964. Instr. Ind. U., Bloomington, 1964; John Wesley Young Rsch. instr. Dartmouth Coll., Hanover, N.H., 1964-66; asst. prof. math. Syracuse (N.Y.) U., 1966-69, assoc. prof., 1969-76; vis. prof. U. Nottingham (Eng.), 1971-72; prof. math. Syracuse U., 1976—, chmn. dept. math., 1979-82. Co-author: (books) (with M. Watkins) Combinatorics with Emphasis on Graph Theory, 1977, Locally Finite, Planar, Edge-Transitive Graphs, 1997, (with J. Baglivo) Incidence and Symmetry in Design and Architecture, 1982, (with B. and H. Servatius) Combinatorial Rigidity, 1993; contbr. articles to profl. jours. With USN, 1953-55. Fellow Inst. Combinatories and its Applications; mem. Soc. Indsl. and Applied Math., Nat. Coun. Tchrs. of Math., Assn. Math. Tchrs. N.Y. State, Math. Assn. Am. (bd. govs. 1985-88, Seaway sect. chair 1995-97), Am. Math. Soc. Home: 871 Livingston Ave Syracuse NY 13210-2935 Office: Syracuse Univ Dept Math Syracuse NY 13244

GRAVER, LAWRENCE STANLEY, English language professional; b. N.Y.C., Dec. 6, 1931; s. Louis and Rose (Pearlstein) G.; m. Suzanne Levy, Jan. 28, 1960; children—Ruth, Elizabeth. B.A., CCNY, 1954; M.A., U. Calif., Berkeley, 1959, Ph.D., 1961. Asst. prof. English UCLA, 1961-64; asst. prof. English, Williams Coll., Williamstown, Mass., 1964-67; assoc. prof. English Williams Coll., 1967-72, prof. English, 1972—; William R. Kenan, Jr. prof. English, Williams Coll., 1977-81, John H. Roberts prof., 1981-97, Roberts prof. emeritus, 1997—. Author: Conrad's Short Fiction, 1969, Carson McCullers, 1969; editor: Mastering the Film, 1977, Samuel Beckett, 1979, (Landmarks of World Lit. series) Waiting for Godot, 1989, An Obsession With Anne Frank: Meyer Levin and the Diary, 1995. Served with U.S. Army, 1954-56. Nat. Endowment for Humanities fellow, 1980-81. Mem. MLA, AAUP. Democrat. Home: 117 Forest Rd Williamstown MA 01267-2028 Office: Williams Coll Dept English Williamstown MA 01267

GRAVES, ADAM, professional hockey player; b. Toronto, Ont., Can., Apr. 12, 1968. With Detroit Red Wings, 1986-88, 88-89, 89-90, Edmonton Oilers, 1990-91; left wing N.Y. Rangers, 1991—; mem. Stanley Cup Championship Team, 1990, 94; player NHL All-Star game, 1994. Recipient King Clancy Meml. trophy, 1993-94; named Sporting News All-Star first team, 1993-94. Office: NY Rangers Madison Sq Garden 2 Penn Plz New York NY 10121-2819*

GRAVES, BENJAMIN BARNES, business administration educator; b. Jones County, Miss., Nov. 5, 1920; s. Thomas Cannon and Velma (Barnes) G.; m. Hazeline Wood, May 25, 1946; children—Benjamin Barnes, Janis Elizabeth, Cynthia Wood. B.A., U. Miss., 1942; M.B.A., Harvard, 1947; Ph.D., La. State U., 1961; LL.D., U. Ala., 1970. Staff and supervisory positions Exxon Co., 1947-60; spl. lectr. Coll. Bus. Adminstrn., La. State U., 1959-60, asst. prof., 1960-62; assoc. prof. U. Va., 1962-64; Milner prof. indsl. econs. U. Miss., 1964-65; pres. Millsaps Coll., Jackson, Miss., 1965-70; prof. bus. adminstrn. U. Ala. in Huntsville, 1970-90, pres., 1970-79, prof. emeritus, 1990—; guest lectr. Mid-South Exec. Devel. Program, La. State U., 1962-68, also asso. dir. program, 1961-62; guest lectr. mgmt. program Natural Resources Mgrs., Pa. State U., 1962-72, Va.-Md. Sch. Banking, U. Va., 1962-73; vis. prof. bus. adminstrn. U. N.C. at Charlotte, 1976-77. Author articles in field. Pres. Miss. Found. Ind. Colls., 1967-68; mem. com. human investigation U. Miss. Sch. Medicine, 1964-70; v.p. Miss. Jr.-Sr. Coll. Conf., 1968-69; pres. Miss. Assn. Colls., 1969-70; mem. exec. com. Ind. Coll. Funds Am.; mem. adv. com. Am. Council on Edn.'s Inst. for Coll. and U. Adminstrs.; mem. Am. Assn. Schs. and Colls. univ. pres.'s del. to People's Republic of China, 1975, Republic of China, 1976; Pres. Huntsville Research Park Adv. Bd., 1973; Mem. exec. bd. Andrew Jackson council Boy Scouts Am., 1966—; bd. dirs. Jackson Symphony Assn., 1965-70; mem. pres.'s coun. U. Ala., Huntsville. Served to lt. (s.g.) USNR, 1942-46. Paul Harris fellow Rotary Internat. Mem. Acad. Mgmt., Am. Mktg. Assn., Southwestern Social Sci. Assn., So. Econ. Assn., A.I.M. (pres.'s council), Jackson C. of C., Pi Kappa Alpha (mem. centennial com. 100), Phi Kappa Phi, Omicron Delta Kappa. Methodist. Club: Rotarian (dir. Huntsville 1973). Home: 302 Kensington Ct SW Huntsville AL 35802-4516

GRAVES, CAROL KENNEY, construction company executive; b. Boise, Idaho, May 3, 1937; d. Elmer Kenney and M. Elizabeth (Rogers) Kenney Stolquist; m. Philip L. Graves, Aug. 6, 1955; children: Steven P., Kenton L., Cynthia M. Owner Carols, Peoria, Ill., 1975-78; realtor Clifton-Strode E.R.A., Peoria, 1978-83; pres. Little Red Hen Outlets Inc., Peoria, 1983-87, Asbestos Enviro-Clean Inc., Bartonville, Ill., 1988-93; CEO Graves Environ. Safety, Bartonville, 1989—; pres. Enviro-Care Ins., Inc., 1988-93, Twice Over Clean, Inc., 1988-97. Rep. precinct committeeperson, Peoria, 1983—, funds dir. YWCA, Oconomowoc, Wis., 1965; active Girl Scouts U.S., Ill., 1963—; mem. Kickapoo Twp. Assn., bd. dirs., 1984-88. Mem. Downtown Bus. Assn. (bd. dirs., pres. 1987-90), Heart of Ill. Food Svc. Assn., Nat. Radon Assn., Midwest Asbestos Coun., Nat. Lead Abatement Coun., Nat. Asbestos Coun., Profl. Assn. for Asbestos Control, Nat. Lead Assn., Steel Structures Painting Coun., Nat. Air Duct Cleaners Assn. (cert.), Nat. Assn. Demolition Contractors, Ctrl. Ill. Builders Contractor Assn., Environ. Info. Assn., Environtl. Info. Assn. Roman Catholic. Avocation: breeding Red Angus cattle. Office: Graves Environ Safety 4322 Entec Dr Bartonville IL 61607-2777

GRAVES, CHARLES C., III, city planning director. BA in Polit. Sci. and Urban Planning, Hampton U.; MS in Cmty. Econ. Devel., N.H. Coll. With city planning depts. various cities; dir. planning and devel. City of Appleton, Wis.; dir. planning dept. City of Balt., 1993—. Office: City Planning Dept 8th Fl 417 E Fayette St Ste 8 Baltimore MD 21202-3431*

GRAVES, DEIDRA NICOLE, international tax consultant; b. Dallas, Dec. 19, 1966; d. Claude Raymond, Jr. and Barbara Jean (Cowherd) Wilson; 1 child, Caitlin Buchanan; m. William S. Graves, Sept. 5, 1998. AB, Duke U., 1988; JD, So. Meth. U., 1998. CPA, Tex. Auditor Coopers and Lybrand, Dallas, 1988-91; tax acct. Ernst & Young, LLP, Wichita, Kans., 1992-96; internat. tax. mgr. PricewaterhouseCoopers, LLP, Dallas, 1996—. Mem. Jr. League of Dallas, 1997—. Mem. Tex. Soc. of CPAs. Republican. Episcopalian. Avocations: vol. work, hunting, horseback riding. Office: PricewaterhouseCoopers LLP 2001 Ross Ave Ste 1800 Dallas TX 75201-2959

GRAVES, DENYCE ANTOINETTE, mezzo-soprano; b. Washington, Mar. 7, 1964; d. Charles Graves and Dorothy (Middleton) Graves-Kenner; m. David Paul Perry, Sept. 8, 1990. Student, Oberlin Coll. Conservatory, 1981-84; MusB, artists diploma, New Eng. Conservatory, 1988. Appeared as Hansel in Hansel and Gretel, 1989, and as Suzuki in Madame Butterfly, 1990, Houston Grand Opera; as Maddalena in Rigoletto, Washington D.C. Opera, 1991, as Carmen in Carmen, Minnesota Opera, 1991, as Baba the Turk in The Rake's Progress, Châtelet, Paris, Charlotte in Werther, Genova, Cuniza in Oberto, Covent Garden, as. Dalila in Samson et Dalilia, Chgo. Symphony, 1991, as Antigene in Antigene, Teatra Massimo, Palermo, 1992, as Leonora in La Faverita, Teatre Bellini, Catania, as high priestess in La Vestala, La Scala, 1993, as Ginlette in Les Contes d'Hoffmann, La Scala, as Adalgisa in Norma, Opernhous Zurich, as Dorabella in Castfay tutti, Opera Co. Phila, as Dalila at the Met. Opera, 1998, Washington Opera, 1999; appeared at San Francisco Opera, Vienna State Opera, Covent Garden, L.A. Opera, Geneva Opera, Opera Co. Phila., Deutsche Opera Berlin, Maggio Musicale, Florence, Italy, Paris Opera Bastille, Houston Grand Opera, Buenos Aires Teatro Cdon, Opernhaus Zurich, Bavarian State Opera, Washington D.C. Opera, Arena di Verona, Met. Opera, Dallas Opera, Royal Opera Housel London, Minn. Orch., ; solo performances include Mass., N.Y., Calif., Fla., N.H., Tex., Ohio; soloist with Orquesta Sinfonia de Sevilla, Orch. Philharmonique de Monte Carlo, Nat. Symphony, Atlanta Symphony Orch., Boston Pops, Israel Philharmonic, Bonn's Orchster der Beethovenhasle, Houston Symphony, City of Burlington Symphony Orch., L.A. Philharmonic; performer numerous PBS programs, 1990-91; TV panel mem. Black Entertainment TV, 1990; actress various TV commls.; solo recital at Kennedy Ctr. Concert Hall, 1997, White House, Supreme Ct. Participant ednl. outreach programs Opera Grand Rapids, Mich., 1991, Opera Theatre of St. Louis, 1990, Houston Grand Opera, 1990; panel mem. Washington Opera Open Forum, 1991; active supporter African Nat. Congress, Boston, 1985. Recipient Nat. Endowment for the Arts grant, 1990, Ceremonial Resolution Dist. Columbia, 1991, Grand Prize Councours de Chant de Paris, 1990, Met. Opera grant, N.Y.C., 1990, Richard Jacobson grant Richard Tucker Music Found., N.Y.C., 1990, Eleanor Steber award Opera Columbus, Ohio, 1990, various other awards; nat. finalist Met. Opera, N.Y.C., 1988. Mem. Am. Guild Musical Artists. Avocations: aerobics, metaphysical meditations, creative writing. *

GRAVES, EARL GILBERT, publisher; b. Bklyn., 1935; s. Earl Godwin and Winifred (Sealy) G.; m. Barbara Kydd, July 2, 1960; children: Earl Gilbert, John, Michael. BA in Econs., Morgan State U., Balt., 1958, LLD (hon.), 1973; LLD (hon.), Rust Coll., 1974, Wesleyan U., 1982; LHD (hon.), Dowling Coll., 1980; LLD (hon.), Va. Union U., 1976, Fla. Meml. Coll., 1978, J.C. Smith U., 1979; LittD (hon.), Hampton Inst., 1979; PhDBA (hon.), Bryant Coll., 1983; LLD (hon.), Talladega Coll., 1983, Baruch Coll., 1984; LittD (hon.), St. Josephs, N.Y., 1985; LLD (hon.), Ala. State U., 1985; HHD (hon.), Morehouse Coll., 1986; LLD (hon.), Mercy Coll., 1986, Iona Coll., 1987, Elizabeth City State U., 1987; DCS (hon.), Suffolk U., 1987; LLD (hon.), Brown U., 1987, Lincoln U., 1988, Cen. State U., 1988; LittD (hon.), Meharry Med. Coll., 1989; LLD (hon.), Howard U., 1989, Livingstone Coll., 1989, Northwood Inst., 1991, U. D.C., 1991, Tougaloo U., 1992; DCL (hon.), Univ. South, 1993, U. Vt., 1994; degree (hon.), N.C. Ctrl. U., 1997, Manhattanville Coll., 1998. Adminstrv. asst. to Senator Robert F. Kennedy, 1965-68; owner mgmt. cons. firm, 1968-70; editor, pub. Black Enterprise Mag., N.Y.C., 1970—; chmn., CEO Pepsi-Cola of Washington, L.P., chmn. customer adv. and ethnic mktg. com.; pres. Earl G. Graves Pub. Co., Inc.; bd. dirs. Rohm & Haas Corp., DaimlerChrysler Corp., Mag. Pub. Assn., N.Y. State Urban Devel. Corp., Nat. Supplier Devel. Coun., New Am. Schs. Devel. Corp., Glass Ceiling Commn., TransAfrica Forum, Aetna Life & Casualty Co., Federated Dept. Stores, Inc., AMR Corp. (Am. Airlines); keynote spkr. for small and large corps., pub. and non-profit sectors of bus. in Am. Author: How to Succeed in Business Without Being White, 1997 (finalist Fin. Times/Booz-Allen & Hamilton Global Bus. Book award 1997). Mem. adv. coun. Character Edn. Partnership; bd. dirs. New Am. Schs. Devel. Corp., TransAfrica Forum, Steadman-Hawkins Sports Medicine Found., Am. Mus. Natural History and Planetarium, trustee; nat. commr. scouting Boy Scouts Am.; bd. trustees Howard U., Washington; mem. vis. com. Harvard U. John F. Kennedy Sch. Govt.; mem. Pres.'s Com. Small and Minority Bus.; mem. nat. adv. bd. Nat. Underground R.R. Freedom Ctr.; trustee Howard U., Com. for Econ. Devel.; mem. pres.'s coun. for bus. adminstrn. U. Vt. Capt. U.S. Army, 1958-60. Recipient Silver Beaver award Boy Scouts Am., 1969, Scroll of Honor, Nat. Med. Assn., 1971, Nat. award of excellence U.S. Dept. Commerce, 1972, Pub. for Freedom award Operation PUSH, Black Achiever award Talk mag., 1972, Key award Nat. Assn. Black Mrs., 1972, Chgo. Econ. Devel. Corp. award, 1974, Nat. Alliance Black Sch. Educators award, 1974, Silver Antelope award Boy Scouts Am., 1988, Silver Buffalo award Boy Scouts Am., 1988, Free Enterprise award Internat. Franchise Assn., 1991, Entrepreneurial Excellence award Dow Jones & Co., 1992, Ernst & Young N.Y.C. Entrepreneur of Yr. award, 1995, Sci. and Industry Divsn. award Bklyn. Pub. Libr.'s Centennial Celebration, 1997, award DRUM Orgn./Bell Atlantic Corp., 1998, Marietta Tree award for pub. svc., Citizens Com. for N.Y.C., Inc., 1998, Charlse Evans Hughes gold medal NCCJ, 1998, Ronal H. Brown Leadership award Dept. Commerce Minority Bus. Devel. Agy., 1998, N.Y. Black 100 award Schomburg Ctr. for Rsch. in Black Culture/Black New Yorkers/Black N.Y. Consortium, 1998, Merrick-Moore Spaulding Nat. Achievement award N.C. Mut. Life Ins. Co.-100th Anniversary, 1998, Legacy award Rush Philanthropic Arts Found./Rush Comm., 1998; named One of Ten Most Outstanding Minority Businessman in Country by Pres. U.S., 1973, Outstanding Citizen of Yr., Omega Psi Phi, 1974, also one of 200 Future Leaders of Country, Time mag., Outstanding Black Businessman, Nat. Bus. League, one of 100 influential Blacks, Am. Ebony mag.; Poynter fellow Yale U., 1978; inducted Nat. Sales Hall of Fame, 1995, Morgan State U. Hall of Fame, 1998. Mem. NAACP (bd. dirs. spl. contbns. fund), SCLC, Am. Inst. for Pub. Svc. (bd. selectors), Interracial Coun. Bus. Opportunity (award), Young Pres. Orgn., Mag. Pubs. Assn. (dir.), Advt. Coun., Bus. Mktg. Corp. N.Y.C., N.Y. Econs. Club (trustee), Sigma Pi Phi, Omega Psi Phi. Democrat. Episcopalian. Club: N.Y. Econ. (trustee). Office: Black Enterprise Mag and Earl G Graves Pub Co Inc 130 Fifth Ave New York NY 10011-4306

GRAVES, ERNEST, JR., retired army officer, engineer; b. N.Y.C., July 6, 1924; s. Ernest and Lucy (Birnie) G.; m. Nancy Herbert Barclay, May 12, 1951; children: Ralph Henry, Robert Barclay, William Hooper, Emily Birnie. B.S., U.S. Mil. Acad., 1944; Ph.D., M.I.T., 1951; postgrad., Engr. Sch., Ft. Belvoir, Va., 1954-55, Command and Gen. Staff Coll., Ft. Leavenworth, Kans., 1957-58, Army War Coll., Carlisle Barracks, Pa., 1964-65, Harvard Bus. Sch., 1968. Commd. 2d lt. U.S. Army, 1944, advanced through grades to lt. gen., 1978, ret., 1981; with (SHAPE), Paris, 1951-54, (Army Package Power Reactor), Ft. Belvoir, 1955-57; comdr. (44th Engr. Constrn. Bn.), Korea, 1958-59; dir. (Army Nuclear Cratering Group, Lawrence Radiation Lab.), Livermore, Cal., 1962-64; exec. to sec. army Washington, 1967-68; comdr. (34th Engr. Group), Vietnam, 1968-69; div. engr. (U.S. Army Engr. Div., N. Central), Chgo., 1970-73; asst. gen. mgr. for mil. application U.S. AEC, Washington, 1973-75; dir. civil works Office Chief Engrs., Washington, 1975-77; dep. chief engr. Office Chief Engrs., 1977-78; dir. Def. Security Assistance Agy., Washington, 1978-81; sr. advisor Ctr. for Strategic and Internat. Studies, Washington, 1982—. Contbr. articles profl. jours. Decorated D.S.M., Legion of Merit, Bronze Star, Air medal. Mem. Soc. Am. Mil. Engrs. Home: 2328 S Nash St Arlington VA 22202-1548 Office: 1800 K St NW Washington DC 20006-2202

GRAVES, FRED HILL, librarian; b. Rockdale, Tex., Feb. 11, 1914; s. Fred Hill and Etta Sherman (Loper) G. B.A., Southwest Tex. State Coll., San Marcos, 1935; postgrad., U. Tex., 1938, 41, U. Chgo., 1943-46; M.S., Columbia U., 1954, advanced cert. in librarianship, 1973. Successively tchr. English, librarian, prin. Rockdale (Tex.) High Sch., 1935-43; asst. librarian Bemidji (Minn.) State Coll., 1943-44; acting librarian Hardin-Simmons U., 1944-45; librarian Tex. A. and I. U., Kingsville, 1945-51; asst. to dean Sch. Library Service, Columbia U., 1952-54, vis. lectr., spring terms 1968, 69, 70, 71, 72, 73, 76; vis. lectr. Sch. Library Service, Columbia, summer terms 1979, 80, 81, 82; asst. prof. Grad. Sch. Library Service, Rutgers U., 1954-60; vis. instr. So. Conn. State Coll., New Haven, fall 1960; head librarian Cooper Union, N.Y.C., 1960-78. Editor: Tex. Library Jour, 1948-49. Mem. Jamestowne Soc., ALA, N.Y. Library Assn., N.Y. Tech. Services Librarians (exec. bd. 1960-66, pres. 1965-66). Home: 360 E 55th St New York NY 10022-4163

GRAVES, H. BRICE, lawyer; b. Charlottesville, Va., Sept. 1, 1912. B.S., U. Va., 1932, M.S., 1933, Ph.D., LL.B., 1938. Bar: N.Y. 1940, Va. 1949. Assoc. Cravath, Swaine & Moore, N.Y.C., 1938-42, 45-48; ptnr. Hunton & Williams, Richmond, Va., from 1949; planning com. U. Va. Ann. Tax Conf., 1971-82, trustee emeritus, 1989—; lectr. in field. Contbr. articles to profl. jours. Mem. Richmond Bar Assn., Va. Bar Assn. (chmn. taxation com. 1971-73), ABA (chmn. com. exempt orgns. tax sect. 1963-65, com. mem. 1975-77), Am. Law Inst., Richmond Estate Planning Council, Am. Coll. Tax Counsel. Home: Cottage 20 10,000 Cedarfield Ct Richmond VA 23233 Office: Hunton & Williams PO Box 1535 Richmond VA 23218-1535

GRAVES, HOWARD DWAYNE, army officer, academic administrator, educator; b. Roaring Springs, Tex., Aug. 15, 1939; s. Tommy J. and Velma Lee (Clifton) G.; m. Gracie Pauline Newman, June 29, 1963; children: Gigi Reneé Graves Kail, Gregory Howard. BS in Mil. Sci., U.S. Mil. Acad., West Point, N.Y., 1961; BA, Oxford (Eng.) U., 1963, MA, 1968, M of Letters, 1971. Commd. 2d lt. U.S. Army, 1961, advanced through grades to lt. gen., 1989; instr., then asst. prof. and assoc. prof. dept. social scis. U.S. Mil. Acad., West Point, 1970-73; mil. asst. to sec. def. Washington, 1973-76; comdr. 54th Engr. Bn., V Corps, U.S. Army Europe, 1976-78; student U.S. Army War Coll., Carlisle Barracks, Pa., 1978-79, spl. asst. to dep. comdt., 1979; comdr. 20th Engr. Brigade, XVIII Airborne Corps, Ft. Bragg, N.C., 1980-82; asst. div. comdr. 1st Inf. Div., Ft. Riley, Kans., 1982-83; dep. chief of staff, engr. U.S. Army Forces Command, Ft. McPherson, Ga., 1983-84; dep. dir. strategy plans and policy directorate Office Dep. Chief of Staff for Ops. and Plans; asst. army ops. dep. Orgn. Joint Chiefs of Staff, Washington, 1984-86, vice dir. joint staff, 1986-87; comdt. U.S. Army War Coll., Carlisle Barracks, 1987-89; asst. to chmn. Joint Chiefs of Staff, Washington, 1989-91; supt. U.S. Mil. Acad., West Point, 1991-96; assoc. The Internat. Found., Washington, 1996-97; rsch. fellow U. Tex., Austin, 1997-98, vis. prof. LBJ Sch. Pub. Affairs, 1998-99. Decorated D.S.M., Def. D.S.M. with oak leaf cluster, Legion of Merit with oak leaf cluster, Bronze Star with 2 oak leaf clusters, Air medal (5), Meritorious Svc. medal with oak leaf cluster. Avocations: golf, reading, fishing. Office: PO Box Y Austin TX 78713-8925

GRAVES, JERRELL LOREN, demographic studies researcher; b. Humansville, Mo., Feb. 10; s. Loren Silas and Edith Lucille (Childress) G. AA, San Jose City Coll., 1986. Lic. gen. contractor, Calif. Farm laborer Guy McDaniel, Bolivar, Mo., 1952-54; laborer Standard Milk Co., Bolivar, 1952-55; constrn. worker Local Union # 676, Springfield, Mo., 1957-59; wood worker Bolivar Wood Products, 1959-61; rschr. life cycles and coop. living, coord. S.W. Dem. Studies, Half Way, Mo., 1961—; instr. hatha yoga San Jose City Coll., 1973. coord. Caring and Sharing, San Jose, 1977-81, San Jose Coop., Inc., 1985-87; vol. Getting out the Vote Friends of John Vasconselles, San Jose, 1980. Mem. ACLU, UN Assn. U.S.A., World Federalists Assn., Common Cause, Greenpeace, World Watch, World Future Soc., Self-Realization Fellowship, Internat. Platform Assn., Rosicrucian. Avocations: studying mysticism and metaphysics, swimming, yoga. Home and Office: SW Demographic Studies 4280 Highway P Half Way MO 65663-9133

GRAVES, KAREN LEE, high school counselor; b. Twin Falls, Idaho, Dec. 9, 1948; d. Isaac Mason and Agnes Popplewell; m. Frederick Ray Graves, Apr. 2, 1987. BA, Idaho State U., 1971; MEd, Coll. of Idaho, 1978. Cert. tchr. secondary edn., english 7-12, vocat. home econs. 7-12, pupil pers. svcs. K-12, Idaho. Tchr. Filer (Idaho) Sch. Dist., 1971-74, 76-80, Twin Falls (Idaho) Sch. Dist., 1974-76; counselor Mountain Home (Idaho) Sch. Dist., 1980—, dept. chairperson, dir.; bldg. coord. student assistance program, parent newsletter. Sponsor mem. Rocky Mountain Elk Found.; support person Donor Network. Mem. NEA, ACA, ASCD, Am. Sch. Counseling Assn., Idaho Counseling Assn., Idaho Sch. Counseling Assn., Idaho Edn. Assn., Idaho Affiliation Supervision and Curriculum Devel. Avocations: painting ceramics, crafting, reading, crossword puzzles. Home: 1105 Maple Dr Mountain Home ID 83647 Office: Mountain Home H S 300 S 11th E Mountain Home ID 83647-3263

GRAVES, KATHRYN LOUISE, dermatologist; b. Kansas City, Kans., Mar. 9, 1949; d. Jack Clair and Ruth Marjory (Prentice) Schroll; m. Jeffery Jackson Graves, Mar. 31, 1973; children: Jeffery Justin, Jonathon Tyler, Kathryn Camille. BA, U. Kans., 1971; MD, U. Kans., Kansas City, 1974. Diplomate Am. Bd. Dermatology. Intern St. Lukes Hosp., Kansas City, 1975-76, resident in internal medicine, 1976; resident dermatology Sch. Medicine U. Kans., Kansas City, 1976-79; dermatologist Hutchinson (Kans.) Clinic P.A., 1979—; mem. med. staff Hutchinson Hosp., 1979—. Fellow Am. Acad. Dermatology; mem. AMA, Kans. Dermatology Soc., Kans. Med. Assn., Reno County Med. Assn., Hutchinson C. of C., Gamma Phi Beta (standards chair 1973—). Republican. Methodist. Avocations: reading, walking, golf, jetskiing. Home: 130 Hyde Park Dr Hutchinson KS 67502-4457 Office: Hutchinson Clinic 2101 N Waldron St Hutchinson KS 67502-1197

GRAVES, LORRAINE ELIZABETH, dancer, educator, coach; b. Norfolk, Va., Oct. 5, 1957; d. Thomas Edward and Mildred Fayette (Odom) G. BS, Ind. U., 1978. Dancer, Regisseuse Dance Theatre of Harlem, N.Y.C., 1978—, ballet mistress, 1980—, prin. dancer, 1982-96, artistic asst., 1998—; artistic advisor Va. Ballet Theatre, 1997—; tchr./coach Dance Theatre of Harlem, 1998—; guest tchr. N.C. Sch. of Arts, Winston-Salem, 1987, 93, Gov.'s Sch. for Arts, U. Richmond, 1990-98, Carlton Johnson Acad. of Dance, 1991-95, Okla. Summer Arts Inst., 1993-94, The Flint Sch. Performing Arts, Dance Theatre of Harlem, Kennedy Ctr. Residency Program, 1993-95, 98, Worcester Sch. Performing Arts, 1997; resident guest tchr. Gov.'s Sch. for Arts, Norfolk, Va., 1988-91, mem. faculty, 1996—;

guest tchr. Worcester Sch. Performing Arts, 1997; resident guest tchr. S.C. Gov.'s Sch. for Arts, 1995-97; guest tchr. Va. Ballet Theatre, 1996-98, artistic advisor, 1998—; guest tchr. Va. Sch. for the Arts, 1997-99; educator, judge Dance Olympus, 1997-98; judge Internat. Dance Challenge, 1998-99; guest faculty Mid-States Regional Dance Festival, 1999. Appeared with Dance Theatre of Harlem as Princess of Unreal Beauty in live TV prodn. of Firebird, 1982, as Myrta, Queen of the Willis in NBC prodn. of Creole Giselle, 1987; performed at White House, 1981, also at the closing ceremonies of the 1984 Olympics, toured with Dance Theatre of Harlem, USSR, 1988, South Africa, 1992; guest artist Young People's Concert series, N.Y. Philharm., 1988, Detroit Symphony, 1989, River City Ballet, Memphis, 1991, 92, N.W. Fla. Ballet, 1994, Va. Ballet Theatre, Norfolk, 1996—; regisseuse Dance Theatre of Harlem, 1989, 98. Fellow Am. Guild Mus. Artists. Episcopalian. Avocations: modeling, teaching younger dancers.

GRAVES, MARIE MAXINE, public relations executive, OSHA consultant; b. Cullman, Ala., Feb. 15, 1957; d. Hugh Max and Nellie Marie (Elliott) G. AS in Psychology, Wallace State Coll., Hanceville, Ala., 1977; student, OSHA courses, 1993—. Sales clk. Rexall Drugs, Hanceville, 1973-78; office mgr., pub. rels. Hanceville Tire Co., 1978-83, Warren Supply Co., Hanceville, 1983-86; office mgr., pub. rels., rsch., OSHA cons. Hanceville Dental Clinic, 1986-92; office mgr., pub. rels. Conn Surveyors, Cullman, Ala., 1992-97; office mgr. pub. rels. Rural Enterprises, Hayden, Ala., 1997—; part time OSHA cons. Hanceville Dental Clinic, 1992-95. Beat committeman Dem. Exec. Com., Hanceville, 1980—; exec bd. pub. rels., fin., Cullman County Dems., 1980—; mem. Cullman County Dem. Women, pres. 1993-94; founder, sponsor Cullman County Young Dems.; steering com. Dem. Nat. Com., Washington, 1990—. Mem. NOW (pres. Greater Birmingham chpt., sec. Ala.). Baptist. Avocations: sculpting, calligraphy, watercolor pens. Home: 414 Blountsville St NE Hanceville AL 35077-5659 Office: 11900 State Highway 160 Hayden AL 35079-4262

GRAVES, MAUREEN ANN, counselor, minister; b. Sioux City, Iowa, July 10, 1946; d. Jack Milford and Elizabeth Mildred (St. George) Dryden; m. Thomas Darrel Graves, Oct. 9, 1965; children: Michael James, Lorrie Michelle. Grad. 1-yr. program, Gestalt Inst. Iowa, 1980. Cert. drug and alcohol counselor, Nebr.; cert. profl. asst., U. S.D.; cert. hypnotherapist, The Wellness Inst., Seattle; Reiki Master (healing touch), 1998. Counselor Siouxland Coun. on Alcoholism and Drug Abuse, Sioux City, 1979-81; counselor, co-founder New Hope Alcohol and Addiction Ctr., South Sioux City, Nebr., 1981-98; Reiki practitioner, 1997—; cons. St. Luke Hosp. Addiction Ctr., Sioux City, 1987—; trainer Va. Satir-Internat. Tng. Inst., Crested Butte, Colo., 1988-89. Vol. co-facilitator Siouxland Coun. on Alcoholism and Drug Abuse, Sioux City, 1976-79; mem. exec. team couple World Wide Marriage Encounter, N.E. Nebr., 1979-82; trainer Va. Satir-Internat. Tng. Inst., Crested Butte, Colo., 1992; co-leader Satir Family Camp, 1997, 98, San Jose, 1992, 93, 94, 95, 96; mem. Avanta Faculty Governing Coun., 1994-97, 98, 99. Mem. ACA, Avanta Network, Am. Mental Health Counselors Assn., Moscow Inst. for Profl. Devel. of Psychologists and Social Workers (founding). Roman Catholic. Avocation: Reiki master. Home: 14811 Manderson Plz Apt 104 Omaha NE 68116-8209 Office: New Hope Alcoholism & Addiction Ctr Inc PO Box 35 South Sioux City NE 68776-0035

GRAVES, MAXINE, medical and surgical nurse; b. Mobile, Ala., July 16, 1941; d. Leon Sr. and Mary E. (McDaniel-Lane) Grove; m. Perry R. Graves. Oct. 29, 1966; children: Dennis, Anita Graves Ricks. AD, Delaware County Community Coll, Media, Pa., 1972; BSN, Gwynedd Mercy Coll., Gwynedd Valley, Pa., 1983. Tchrs. aide Chester (Pa.)-Upland Sch. Dist.; simulation lab. instr. Delaware County Community Coll.; ambulatory care staff nurse Crozer-Chester Med. Ctr.; nurse mgr. Crozer Internal Medicine Assocs., Upland, Pa.; staff nurse transitional care ctr. Crozer Chester Med. Ctr., Upland, case mgr. nurse, 1998—. Editor newsletter Sleuth, 1989. Mem. ANA, Pa. Nurses Assn. (past. chmn. membership com.). Office: Croze Home Care 1 Medical Center Blvd Upland PA 19013

GRAVES, MICHAEL, architect, educator; b. Indpls., July 9, 1934; s. Thomas Browning and Erma Sanderson (Lowe) G.; children by previous marriage; Sarah Browning, Adam Daimhin; stepchildren: Anne Gilbert, Liza Gilbert. BS in Architecture, U. Cin., 1958, DFA (hon.), 1982; MArch, Harvard U., 1959; postgrad. (Acad. fellow), Am. Acad. in Rome, 1960-62; LHD (hon.), Boston U., 1984; HHD (hon.), Savannah Coll. Art and Design, 1986; DFA (hon.), RISD, 1990, N.J. Inst. Tech., 1991; LHD (hon.), Rutgers U., 1994, U. Colo., 1995. Lectr. architecture Princeton (N.J.) U., 1962-67, assoc. prof., 1967-72, Schirmer prof. architecture, 1972—; pres. Michael Graves, Architect, Princeton, 1964—; architect in residence Am. Acad. in Rome, 1979. Exhibited in group shows Mus. Modern Art, N.Y.C., 1967, 68, 75, 78, 79, 80, 81, 84, Cooper-Hewitt Mus., N.Y.C., 1976, 78, 79, 80, 82, 85, 87, Triennale, Milan, Italy, 1973, 85, Roma Interrotta, Rome, 1978, Venice Biennale, Italy, 1980, Met. Mus. of Art, 1985, 86, 87, Emory U. Mus. Art and Archaeology, Atlanta, 1985; one-man shows include U. So. Calif., 1981, No. Ill. U., 1982, Inst. for Architecture and Urban Studies, N.Y.C., 1982, Colby Coll., Maine, 1983, Moore Coll. Art, Phila., 1983, Fla. Internat. U., Miami, 1983, Pa. State U., University Park, 1984, Royal Inst. Brit. Archs., Heinz Gallery, London, 1984, Wadsworth Athenaeum, Hartford, Conn., 1984, Carleton Coll., Northfield, Minn., 1986, W.Va. U., 1986, Hamilton Coll., Clinton, N.Y., 1987, Archivolto Gallery, Milan, Italy, 1987, U. Va.-Charlottesville, 1987, U. Md.-College Park, 1988, Duke U. Mus. Art, Durham, N.C., 1988, Butler Inst. Art, Youngstown, Ohio, 1989, Deutsches Architekturmuseum, Frankfurt, Dem. German Republic, 1989, Washington Design Ctr., 1989, Syracuse U. Sch. Architecture, 1990, Kunsternes Hus, Oslo, 1990, Mikimoto Hall, Tokyo, 1992, Pitts. Cultural Trust, 1993, Richard Stockton Coll., 1993; Clark County Libr., 1994; Thessaloniki Design Mus., Greece, 1996; Princeton Arts Coun., 1996, 99; U. Cinn. Aronoff Ctr. Design and Art, 1996; designer archtl. projects: Newark Mus., 1968, Rockefeller House, 1969 (Progressive Architecture Design award 1970), Hanselmann House, 1967 (AIA Nat. Honor award 1975), Gunwyn Ventures Office, 1971 (AIA Nat. Honor award 1979), Snyderman House, 1972 (Progressive Architecture Design award 1976), Crooks House, 1976 (Progressive Architecture Design award 1977), Schulman House, 1976 (AIA Nat. Honor award 1982), Fargo (N.D.)-Moorhead (Minn.) Cultural Ctr., 1977-79 (Progressive Architecture Design award 1979), Chem-Fleur Inc., 1977 (Progressive Architecture Design award 1978), Warehouse Renovation (Graves House), 1977, 85 (Progressive Architecture Design award 1978), Plocek House, 1978 (Progressive Architecture Design award 1979), pvt. residence in Green Brook, N.J., 1978 (Progressive Architecture Design award 1980), Sunar Showrooms, N.Y.C., 1979, Chgo., 1979, Houston, 1980, L.A., 1980, N.Y.C., 1981 (Interiors award 1981), London, 1985, Loveladies Beach House, 1979 (Progressive Architecture Design award 1980), Environ. Edn. Ctr., 1980 (Progressive Architecture award 1983), Portland (Oreg.) Bldg., 1980 (AIA Nat. Honor award 1983), Pub. Library, San Juan Capistrano, Calif., 1980 (AIA Nat. Honor award 1985), Newark Mus. Master Plan and Renovation, 1982 (AIA Nat. Honor award 1992), Humana Bldg., Louisville, 1982 (Interiors award 1985, AIA Nat. Honor award 1987), Emory U. Mus. Art and Archaeology, 1982 (Interiors award 1985, AIA Nat. Honor award 1987), Riverbend Music Ctr., 1983, Whitney Mus. Am. Art, N.Y.C., 1984, Diane Von Furstenberg Boutique, 1984, Clos Pegase Winery, Calif., 1984 (AIA Nat. Honor award 1990), Sotheby's Tower, N.Y.C., 1985, Aventine Devel., La Jolla, Calif., 1985, Shiseido Health Club, Tokyo, 1985, Disney Co. Corp. Office Bldg., Burbank, Calif., 1985, Crown Am. Hdqrs., Johnston, Pa., 1985, Walt Disney World Dolphin and Walt Disney World Swan Hotels, Fla., 1986 (Progressive Architecture award 1989), Youngstown (Ohio) Hist. Ctr. Industry and Labor, 1986 (Progressive Architecture Design award 1987), 10 Peachtree Place, Atlanta, 1987, Henry House, Rhinebeck, N.Y., 1987 (Progressive Architecture award 1989), U. Va. Arts and Sci. Bldg., Charlottesville, 1987, Portside Dist. Condominium Tower, Yokohama, Japan, 1987, Momochi Dist. Apt. Bldg., Fukuoka, Japan, 1987, Portside Dist. Condominium Tower, Yokohama, Japan, 1987, Momochi Dist. Apt. Bldg., Fukuoka, Japan, 1987, Metropolis Master Plan, L.A., 1988, Stores and Galleries for Lenox, Tysons Corner, 1988, Palm Beach, 1988, N.Y., 1988, Mpls., 1988, Costa Mesa, 1989, Frankfurt, 1989, Phila., 1989, Nashville, 1989, Midousuji Minami Office Bldg., Osaka, 1988, Fed. Triangle Devel. Site Competition, Washington, 1988, Tajima Office Bldg., Tokyo, 1988, Hotel N.Y., Euro Disneyland, France, 1988, Inst. for Theoretical Physics U. Calif. at Santa Barbara, 1989, Detroit Inst. of Arts Master Plan, 1989, Indpls. Art Ctr., 1989, Emory U. Mus. of Art and Archaeology Addition, Atlanta, 1989, Fukuoka Internat. Office Project, 1990, Kasumi Group Rsch. and Tng. Ctr., Tsukuba City, Japan, 1990, Isetan Dept. Store, Yokohama, Japan, 1990, Clark County Libr., Las Vegas, 1990, U. Cin. Sci. and Engring. Rsch. Ctr., 1990, Richard Stockton State Coll. Arts and Scis. Bldg., Pomona, N.J., 1991, Denver Cen. Libr., 1991, Astrid Park Plz. Hotel and Bus. Ctr., Antwerp, Belgium, 1992, Thomson Consumer Electronics Hdqs., Indpls., 1992, Rome Reborn Vatican Exhibit, Libr. Cong., 1992 (Casebook award Print Mag. 1993), Pitts. Cultural Trust Theater and Office Bldg., 1992, Del. River Port Authority Hdqs., 1992, Taiwan Mus. Pre-History, Taipei, 1993, Archdiocesan Ctr., Newark, 1993, Internat. Fin. Corp. Hdqs., Washington, 1993, 1500 Ocean Drive Condominiums, Miami, 1994, St. Martin's Coll. Libr., Lacey, Wash., 1994, Topeka (Kans.) and Shawnee County Pub. Lib., 1995, Abu Dhabi Bank Competition, 1995, Miramar Hotel, Southern Egypt, 1995, Residence Hall, N.J. Inst. Tech., 1995, Jiang-to Blvd. Master Plan, Xiamen, China, 1995, Shanghai Xingli-Pu Banking Tower, 1996, Alexandria (Va.) Ctrl. Libr., 1996, U.S. Courthouse Annex, Washington, 1996, Life Mag. Dream House, 1996, Lake Hills Country Club, Seoul, Korea, 1996, World Trade Exch., Manila, 1996, Washington Monument Restoration Scaffolding and Interior Design, Washington, 1997, New Residence Hall, Drexel U., Phila., 1997, Dongwha Hoiyhun Mixed-Use Project, Seoul, 1997, Richardson (Tex.) Internat. Ctr. Master Plan, 1997, Miele Appliances Hdqs. Bldg., Princeton, Hotel Makati (Philippines), 1997, Acacia Hotel, Southern Egypt, 1997, Hdqs. & Hall of Champions, Indpls., 1998, Impala Bldg., N.Y.C., 1998, NCAA 2000 Hdqs. and Hall of Champions, Indpls., Cin. Art Mus. Renovation, numerous others; designer furniture, textiles artifacts, and consumer products: Sunar, 1980-83, V'Soske, 1979-80, Alessi, 1981—, Baldinger Archtl. Lighting, 1983—, Swid Powell, 1985—, Steuben, 1986—, Tiffany, 1986, Munari, 1986—, WMF, 1987—, Atelier Internat., 1987—, Vorwerk, 1987—, Tajima, 1987, Dunbar Furniture, 1989, Arkitektura, 1989—, Moeller Internat. Design, 1992—, Duravit, 1992—, Dornbracht, 1992—, Valli & Valli, 1992—, Target Stores, 1998—; monographs include Michael Graves, Academy Editions, 1979, Michael Graves: Buildings and Projects, 1966-1981, 1981, Michael Graves: Buildings and Projects 1982-89, 90, Michael Graves: Design Monograph, 1994, Michael Graves: Buildings and Projects, 1990-1994, 1995; illustrator: The Great Gatsby, 1984, Mr. Chas and Lisa Sue Meet the Pandas, 1994. Trustee Am. Acad. Rome. Recipient Rome prize Am. Acad. in Rome, 1960-62, Arnold W. Brunner-Meml. prize in architecture, 1981, Silver Spoon award Boston U., 1984, Euster award, 1984, Ind. Arts award, 1984, Henry Hering Meml. medal Am. Sculpture Soc., 1986, N.J. Gov.'s Pride award, 1991, Walt Whitman Creative Arts award, 1991, also 57 N.J. Soc. Archs. AIA awards, 15 Progressive Architecture Design awards; named Interior Designer of Yr., 1981. Fellow AIA (9 awards), Soc. Fellows Am. Acad. in Rome (trustee); mem. Am. Acad. Inst. Arts and Letters. Office: Michael Graves & Assocs 341 Nassau St Princeton NJ 08540-4602

GRAVES, MORRIS COLE, artist; b. Fox Valley, Oreg., Aug. 28, 1910; s. Edwin Lyman and Helen (Malson) G. Works exhibited: Seattle Art Mus., 1936-56, Mus. Modern Art, 1942, Arts Club Chgo., 1943, Calif. Palace Legion of Honor, 1948, Whitney Mus. Am. Art, 1956; retrospective exhbns.: in 1956, in Mus. Fine Arts, Boston, Whitney Mus., N.Y.C., De Young Meml. Mus., San Francisco, retrospective show at, Brussels Fair, 1958 (Recipient 1st purchase prize Seattle Art Mus. 1933), also the, Brussels Fair, 1958 (Harris medal Art Inst. Chgo. 1947), Brussels Fair, 1958 (Blair prize 1948, purchase prize U. Ill. 1955), U.S. State Dept. travelling show, Europe, Asia, 1957, Pavilion Gallery, Balboa, Calif., 1963, retrospective exhbns.: Sch. Visual Arts, N.Y.C., 1978, Greenville County Mus. Art, S.C., 1983, Whitney Mus. Am. Art, 1983, Oakland Mus. Art, 1983, Oakland Mus. Art, 1984, Seattle Art Mus., 1984, San Diego Mus. Art, 1984, others, one-man shows, Willard Gallery, N.Y.C., 1942, 44, 45, 48, 53, 54, 55, 59, 71, 73, 76, 78, 81, 82, Univ. Gallery, Mpls., 1943, Detroit Inst. Art, 1943, Phillips Gallery, Washington, 1943, 54, Santa Barbara Mus. Art, 1948, Los Angeles County Mus., 1948, Art Inst Chgo., 1948, Beaumont (Tex.) Art Mus., 1952, Oslo (Norway) Kunstforening, 1955, Bridgestone Gallery, Tokyo, 1957, Charles Campbell Gallery, San Francisco, 1982, annual exhibitions, Philadelphia Art Alliance, 1946, N.Y. World's Fair, 1939, Art Inst. Chgo., 1947, Tate Gallery, London, 1946, 56, Solomon R. Guggenheim Mus., N.Y.C., 1956, others; works represented in permanent collections, Art Inst. Chgo., Balt., Cleve., San Francisco museums of art, Detroit, Milw. art insts., Mus. Modern Art, Phillips Gallery, Museum of Contemporary Art, Dublin, Ireland, also the, Whitney Mus. Am. Art, Tate Gallery London, and others. Guggenheim fellow, 1946; Windsor award, 1957; grantee Nat. Inst. Arts and Letters, 1956. Mem. Nat. Inst. Arts and Letters. Office: Schmidt-Bingham Gallery 41 E 57th St # 5fl New York NY 10022-1908*

GRAVES, PATRICK LEE, lawyer; b. Pasadena, Calif., Sept. 16, 1945; s. James Edward and Virginia (Dudley) G.; children: Carrie Kathleen, Michael Patrick. AS, Citrus Jr. Coll., Glendora, Calif., 1969; BS, Calif. State Polytechnic U., 1973; BS in Law, Western State U., 1973, JD, 1975. Bar: Calif. 1975, U.S. Dist. Ct. (cen. dist.) Calif. 1976, U.S. Ct. Appeals (9th cir.) 1978, U.S. Supreme Ct. 1980. Assoc. Lynberg & Watkins, Los Angeles, 1975-80, ptnr., 1981-93; ptnr. Graves & King, Riverside, Calif., 1993—; settlement officer Los Angeles Superior Ct., 1988—, arbitrator, 1981—; arbitrator San Bernardino Superior Ct., 1990—; mediator L.A. Superior Ct., 1993—, Riverside Superior Ct., 1996—, AAA-Inland Empire, 1996—. judge pro tem L.A. Superior Ct., 1992—. Sustaining mem. Rep. Nat. Com., Washington, 1979—; mem. Nat. Rep. Congl. Com., 1980—. Mem. ABA, San Bernardino County Bar Assn., Assn. So. Calif. Def. Counsel (chmn. 1988, bd. dirs. 1996—), Def. Rsch. Inst., Upland (Calif.) C. of C. Avocations: flyfishing, golf. Home: 424 Monterey Ln # B San Clemente CA 92672-5329 Office: Graves & King 3610 14th St Fl 2D Riverside CA 92501-3843

GRAVES, PETER, actor; b. Mpls., Mar. 18, 1926; s. Rolf C. and Ruth E. (Duesler) Aurness; m. Joan E. Endress, Dec. 16, 1950; children: Kelly Jean, Claudia King, Amanda Lee. Ed., U. Minn., 1949. Engaged in motion pictures and TV, 1951—; star: TV series Mission Impossible, 1966-73, Discover: The World of Science (Pub. TV), New Mission: Impossible, 1988-90; TV miniseries: War and Rembrance, 1988; TV films include: Winds of War, If It's Tuesday, It Still Must Be Belgium, (host/narator: Discover! The World of Science, 1985-90, Biography 1987—; (Recipient Outstanding Achievement award U. Minn. 1968, honoree Am. Acad. Achievement 1972). Hon. Calif. chmn. Am. Cancer Soc., 1968, hon. nat. crusade chmn., 1974; celebrity chmn. Arthritis Found., 1990-91. With USAAF. Mem. Phi Kappa Psi. Address: care Barman Mgmt Co 9777 Wilshire Blvd Ste 215 Beverly Hills CA 90212-1908

GRAVES, RAY, lawyer; b. Seattle, Feb. 23, 1924; s. Ralph Raymond and Naomi (Capron) G.; m. Joan Catherine Kikkert, May 19, 1946; children: Valerie Ann, Jon Carlton. BA, Wash. State Coll., 1950; JD, Duke U., 1952. Bar: Wash. 1952. Pvt. practice Tacoma, 1952-60; of counsel McGavick, Graves, P.S. (and predecessor), 1960—; mem. Wash. Bd. Bar Examiners, 1968-76. Contbr. articles to profl. jours. Served with USMCR, 1943-46. Mem. Wash. Bar Assn., Order of Coif, Tacoma Club. Republican. Presbyterian. Club: Tacoma Country and Golf. Home: 1040 Wilson Rd NW Olympia WA 98502-9416 Office: 1102 Broadway Tacoma WA 98402-3525

GRAVES, RAY REYNOLDS, judge; b. Tuscumbia, Ala., Jan. 10, 1946; s. Isaac and Olga Ernestine (Wilder) G.; children: Claire Elisé, Reynolds Douglass. BA, Trinity Coll., Hartford, Conn., 1967; JD, Wayne State U., 1970. Bar: Mich. 1971, U.S. Dist. Ct. (ea. dist.) Mich. 1971, U.S. Ct. Appeals (6th cir.) 1972, U.S. Supreme Ct. 1976, D.C. 1977. Defender, Legal Aid and Defender Assn., Detroit, 1970-71; assoc. Liberson, Fink, Feiler, Crystal & Burdick, 1971-72, Patmon, Young & Kirk, 1972-73; ptnr. Lewis, White, Clay & Graves, 1974-81; mem. legal dept. Detroit Edison Co., 1981; judge U.S. Bankruptcy Ct., Eastern Dist. Mich., Detroit, 1982—, chief judge U.S. Bankruptcy Ct., 1991-95; Mem. U.S. Ct. Com., State Bar Mich. bd. dirs. Mich. Cancer Found.; trustee Mich. Opera Theatre, 1986-88; vestry Christ Ch. Episcopal, Grosse Pointe, Mich., 1994-97; del. Diocesan Conv. of the Episcopal Ch., Mich., 1997. Fellow Am. Coll. Bankruptcy, 1993; mem. Nat. Conf. Bankruptcy Judges (bd. govs. 1984-88), World Assn. Judges, World Peace Through Law Conf., Assn. Black Judges Mich., Wolverine Bar Assn., Detroit Bar Assn., D.C. Bar Assn., Delta Kappa Epsilon, Sigma Pi Phi, Iota Boulé. Episcopalian. Office: US Bankruptcy Ct 211 W Fort St Ste 1900 Detroit MI 48226-3211

GRAVES, REBECCA O., public health nurse, consultant; b. Nashville, Jan. 25, 1941; d. Earl T. and Anna (Davis) Odom; m. Edward L. Graves, Dec. 22, 1964; children: Angela R., Alison R. BSN, Tuskegee U., 1965. RN, Tenn.; cert. intravenous therapy critical care nurse. Staff nurse med.-surg. L. Richardson Meml. Hosp., Greensboro, N.C.; coord. health svcs. Shaw U., Raleigh, N.C.; med. svcs. nurse disability det. sect. State of N.C., Raleigh; intravenous therapy nurse, clin. coord. IV therapy Hubbard Hosp., Nashville; pub. health nurse cons. State of Tenn., Nashville. Mem. Intravenous Nurses Soc., Tenn. Nurses Assn., Tenn. Pub. Health Assn. Home: 4111 Dalemere Ct Nashville TN 37207-1211

GRAVES, ROBERT LAWRENCE, mathematician, educator; b. Chgo., Sept. 1, 1926; s. Lawrence Murray and Josephine (Wells) G.; m. Barbara Junette Sward, Oct. 20, 1951; children—Susan Johanna, Julia Lowell, Christine Craig, Virginia Anne. B.A., Oberlin Coll., 1947; M.A., Harvard U., 1948, Ph.D., 1952. Teaching fellow Harvard U., 1949-51; supervisory and rsch. positions Standard Oil Co., Ind., 1951-58; mem. faculty Grad. Sch. Bus. U. Chgo., 1958—, prof. applied math., 1965—, assoc. dean Grad. Sch. Bus., 1972-73, 75-81, dep. dean, 1981-85, assoc. dean for PhD studies, 1990-94, assoc. provost computing and info. systems, 1985-87, assoc. provost, 1987-90; on leave as dir. European Inst. Advanced Studies in Mgmt., Brussels, Belgium, 1973-75. Author: (with H.B. Thorelli) INTOP, The International Operations Simulation, 1964, (with L.G. Telser) Functional Analysis in Economics, 1972; editor: (with Philip Wolfe) Recent Advances in Mathematical Programming, 1963. Served to ensign USNR, 1944-46. Mem. Am. Math. Soc., Math. Assn. Am., Operations Research Soc., Inst. Mgmt. Sci. (mem. council 1971-73), Assn. Computing Machinery (co-chmn. spl. interest group for math. programming 1961-63). Episcopalian. Club: Quadrangle (U. Chgo.). Home: 830 Park Dr Flossmoor IL 60422-1145 Office: Univ Chgo Grad Sch Business Chicago IL 60637

GRAVES, RUTH PARKER, educational executive, educator; b. Port Arthur, Tex., Oct. 19, 1934; d. Thomas B. and Eunice Parker; m. Glenn R. Graves, Aug. 8, 1956; 1 child, Christopher. BA, Baylor U., 1956; MA, U. Tex., 1961; postgrad., George Washington U., 1963-64. Migrant labor advisor Tex. State AFL-CIO, Austin, 1959-61; pub. info. officer Pres.'s Com. on EEO, Washington, 1961-63; tchg. fellow George Washington U., Washington, 1963-64; labor desk coord. Dem. Nat. Conv., Washington, 1965-67; program analyst U.S. OEO, Washington, 1965-67, dir. migrant divsn., 1967-72; pres. emerita Reading is Fundamental, Inc., Washington, 1998; nat. adv. coun. Ctr. for the Book, Libr. of Congress, 1977-97; adv. bd. Kidwave Radio Network, Phila., 1990-97; bd. advisors Ednl. Pub. Group, 1994-97; faculty Salzburg Seminar, 1998—; lectr. in field. Mem. editl. bd. Child Mag., N.Y.C., 1989-97; adv. coun. Ednl. Pub. Group, 1994-97; editor: The RIF Guide to Encouraging Young Readers, 1987; contbr. articles to profl. jours. Recipient William A. Jump award, U.S. Govt., 1971, Jeremiah Ludington Literacy Leadership award Ednl. Paperback Assn., 1982, Manhattan Literacy Coun. award, 1986, Internat. Reading Assn. Literacy award, 1987, As They Grow award Parents Mag., 1991; named Bookwoman of the Yr. Woman's Nat. Book Assn., 1987. Avocations: reading, theater, design and production of craft items. Office: Reading is Fundamental 600 Maryland Ave SW # 600 Washington DC 20024-2520

GRAVES, SID FOSTER, JR., retired library and museum director; b. Memphis, May 11, 1946; s. Sidney Foster and Sarah Susan (Peterson) G.; m. Laura Charjean Laughlin; 1 child from previous marriage, Martha Abigail. BA, Millsaps Coll., Jackson, Miss., 1968; MA, U. Miss., Oxford, 1971; MLS, Peabody Coll., 1973. Archtl. reporter Dodge div. McGraw Hill, Jackson, 1968-69; instr. English U. Miss., 1968-72; dir. South Miss. Regional Libr., Columbia, 1973-76; exec. dir. Carnegie Pub. Libr./Delta Blues Mus., Clarksdale, Miss., 1976-95; ret., 1995; guest lectr. U. Ala. Grad. Sch. Libr. Scis., Tuscaloosa, 1979; mem. Miss. Humanities Coun., 1988—, project dir., 1983, Miss. Libr. Com., Jackson, 1983;. Chmn. Tennessee Williams Festival Com., 1992, 93. Recipient Keeping the Blues Alive in Edn. award Blues Found. Memphis, 1987, Keeping the Blues Alive in Hist. Preservation, 1989, Early Wright award Sunflower River Blues Assn., 1993, Gov.'s Arts award for Career in the Arts, 1995, 96. Mem. ALA (notable books coun. 1990-94), Miss. Mus. Assn. (pres. 1985), Miss. Libr. Assn. (pres. 1989, Outstanding Achievement award 1980, Past Pres.'s award 1976), Governor's award for lifetime career in the arts, 1996.

GRAVES, THOMAS ASHLEY, JR., educational administrator; b. Buffalo, July 3, 1924; s. Thomas Ashley and Esther (Brittain) G.; m. Zoe Ann Wasson, June 12, 1962; children: Thomas, Stephen, Mary, Andrew, Elizabeth. BA, Yale U., 1945; MBA, Harvard U., 1949, DBA, 1958; LLD, U. Pa., 1975; LittD(hon.), Coll. of Charleston, 1976; LLD, Christopher Newport Coll., 1986, Wesley Coll., 1990. Asst. dean, assoc. dir. doctoral program Harvard. Grad. Sch. Bus. Adminstrn., 1950-60; dir. IMEDE, Internat. Mgmt. Devel. Inst., Lausanne, Switzerland, 1960-64; assoc. dean, dir. Internat. Center for Advancement of Mgmt. Edn., Stanford Grad. Sch. Bus., 1964-67; assoc. dean Harvard Grad. Sch. Bus., 1967-71; pres. Coll. William and Mary, Williamsburg, Va., 1971-85; dir., chief exec. officer, trustee Henry Francis du Pont Winterthur Mus., Garden and Libr., Del., 1985-92; exec. dir. Grand Opera House, Wilmington, Del., 1992-93; pres. Grand Opera House, 1993-94; co-chmn. Grand Opera House, Wilmington, Del., 1994-97; chmn. Del. Arts Stabilization Fund, 1993—; cons. MBNA Am. Bank N.A., 1994—. Served with USNR, 1943-46. Mem. Phi Beta Kappa (hon.), Phi Sigma (hon.), Beta Gamma Sigma. Home: 2305 W 11th St Wilmington DE 19805-2605

GRAVES, THOMAS BROWNING, investment banker; b. Indpls., Feb. 1, 1932; s. Thomas Browning and Erma Sanderson (Lowe) G.; m. Betty Lee MacLeod, June 12, 1954; children: Russell Evan, Bruce Ryan, Jill Graves, Jeffrey Hall. BS, Ind. U., 1954; M in Pub. Adminstrn., Harvard U., 1975. Asst. v.p. Penn Cen. Corp., Phila., 1968-72, Union Pacific R.R., Omaha, 1972-77; v.p. fin. and adminstrn. Union Pacific Corp., Omaha, 1977-84; exec. dir. Merrill Lynch, N.Y.C., 1984-85; pres. Pvt. Capital Ptnrs., Inc., N.Y.C., 1985—; CEO Consumer Credit & Debt Counseling, Vineland, N.J., 1995-98; trustee-in-bankruptcy U.S. Dept. of Justice, Newark, N.J., 1991—, cons. Credit & Budget Counseling, Marmora, NJ, 1998—. Maj. U.S. Army, 1955-57, 61-62. Club: Somers Point Yachting & Sportman Assn., Somers Point, NJ. Home: 120 E Wilmont Ave Somers Point NJ 08244-2736 Office: Consumer Credit & Budget Counseling 299 S Shore Rd Marmora NJ 08223-1210

GRAVES, THOMAS VINCENT, sculptor; b. Marblehead, Mass., Jan. 22, 1954; s. Robert G. and Nancy (Simpson) G.; m. Winnett Hope Sellers, Aug. 11, 1996; children: Suddha, Varsha, Sara, Dina, Vincent. Commd. to sculpt a bust of Pope John Paul II for Vatican Art Collection, Rome, 1987, drawing to commemorate the Columbus Quincentennial, Kent, Washington, 35-foot heoric outdoor sculpture/Palace of Gold, Limestone, W.Va., 1991, six-foot outdoor sculpture, Valley Brook Meml. Garden, Moundsville, W.Va., 1989, Sitting Jesus/life-size statue, New Vrindaban Community, Moundsville, 1988, others; pub. collections of work include Vatican Art Collection, Vatican City, 1992, City of Kent Art Collection, 1992; exhbns. include: The Sanctuary, N.Y.C., 1998, Lynn Arts Coun., Mass., 1997, Mass. Coll. of Art, Boston, 1996, The State House, Boston, 1995, The Copley Soc. of Boston, 1994, Marblehead Arts Assn. Arts in Bloom, Mass., 1994, Marblehead Festival of the Arts, 1994, Grand Mondnock Arts Coun., Keene, N.H., 1994, numerous others. Mem. Nat. Sculpture Soc., Internat. Sculpture Ctr., Copley Soc. of Boston, Marblehead Arts Assn. Home: 25 1st Ave Apt 2W New York NY 10003-9459

GRAVES, VASHTI SYLVIA, computer analyst, EDP auditor, consultant; b. Detroit, Mar. 22, 1967; d. James Graves and Sandra Horne Mcleod Graves Lewis. Student computer programming, Cass Tech. Sch., Detroit, 1981-85; BS in Computer Info. Systems, DeVry Inst. Tech., Chgo., 1988. Gen. officer worker Lenzip Mfg. Co., Chgo., 1985-86; programmer Safer Found., Chgo., 1986-89; programmer, user systems analysts Am. Automotive Assn., Dearborn, Mich., 1989-94; project adminstr. Comerica, Auburn Hills, Mich., 1994-96; EDP auditor Comerica, Inc., Detroit, 1996—; cons. GSA Advt., Chgo., 1988; owner, cons. Maze Advisors, Detroit, 1993; patron Internat. Inst. Active Alliance Française of Mich., 1995. Mem. Am. Mgmt. Assn., Air Courier Assn., Info. Systems Audit Control Assn. (Detroit chpt.). Home: # 303 340 1st St Apt 303 Rochester MI 48307-2673 Office: 3128 Walton Blvd PMB # 141 Rochester Hills MI 48309

GRAVES, WALLACE BILLINGSLEY, retired university executive; b. Ft.Worth, Feb. 10, 1922; s. Ellery George and Edith (Billingsley) G.; m. Barbara Jeanne Abey, Nov. 20, 1943; children: David W., Emily Graves Hay, John R., Julie Graves Williams. BA, U. Okla., 1943; MA, Tex. Christian U., 1947; PhD, U. Tex., 1953; LLD (hon.), Ind. State U., 1970, Valparaiso U., 1972; LHD (hon.), Morningside Coll., 1971, U. Evansville, 1989. Teaching fellow Tex. Christian U., Ft. Worth, 1946-47, U. Tex., Austin, 1947-50; prof. polit. sci. DePauw U., Greencastle, Ind., 1950-58; Armstrong prof. govt., dean of men Tex. Wesleyan Coll., Ft. Worth, 1958-63, asst. to pres., 1963-65; acad. v.p. U. Pacific, Stockton, Calif., 1965-67; pres. U. Evansville, Ind., 1967-87, chancellor, 1986-89; pres. emeritus U. Evansville, 1989—; vis. prof. Butler U., summer 1956; bd. dirs. Citizens Nat. Bank, Evansville, Herrburger Brooks P.L.C., Nottingham, Eng. Author: The United Nations, Great Britain and the British Non-Self Governing Territories, 1954, The One Semester Course in International Relations, 1956, Harlaxton College: The Camelot of Academe, 1990; contbr. articles to profl. jours. Mem. exec. bd. Tarrant County chpt. ARC, 1960-65, chmn. home svc. com.; chmn. ARC of Southwestern Ind., 1994—; bd. dirs. Ft. Worth Assn. Retarded Children, 1963-65; mem. Met. Ft. Worth Devel. Coordinating Com., World Affairs Coun., Chgo. and Stockton, adv. bd. Supplementary Edn. Ctr., Stockton; v.p. Buffalo Trace coun. Boy Scouts Am., Evansville, 1968, exec. bd., 1968-74, adv. coun, 1974—; bd. dirs. Jr. Achievement Inc., Evansville, 1968-73; mem. commn. ecumenical affairs United Meth. Ch., Evansville, 1968-72, univ. senate, 1972-76, Ind. area study commn., 1972-74; bd. dirs. Evansville Day Sch., 1967-76; mem. Ind. State Scholarship Commn., 1969-77, adv. bd. St. Mary's Med. Ctr., Evansville, 1970—, Evansville's Future Inc., 1967—, pres., 1974-77; bd. dirs. Ind. Health Careers Inc., 1974-75; mem. Govs. Adv. Com. Pub. Health, 1971-72; bd. dirs. Leadership Evansville, 1975-71, Evansville Mus., 1978—, Lincolnland Hist. Trust, 1978—; pres. Beethoven Found., Indpls., 1980-88; mem. organizing com. Pan Am. Games, 1987; bd. dirs. Sta. WNIN Pub. TV, Evansville, 1973—, chmn. bd., 1982-84. With U.S. Army, 1943. Recipient Best Tchr. award DePauw U., 1954, medal of honor U. Evansville, 1977, Medal of merit Govt. Thailand, 1984; Wallace B. Graves Day named in his honor Office Mayor City Evansville, 1977; rsch. scholar U. Tex., 1947; Ford Found. fellow, summer 1951, 55; Paul Harris (Rotary) fellow, 1995. Mem. AAUP, Am. Assn. Acad. Deans, Am. Coll. Pub. Relations Assn., Am. Polit. Sci. Assn., Ind. Colls. and Univs. Ind. Inc. (pres. 1970-71, 76-77), North Cen. Assn. Colls. and Secondary Schs. (cons., investigator), Am. Assn. Pres. Ind. Colls. and Univs. (exec. com. 1969-70), Am. Assn. Colls. (various coms.), Associated Colls. Ind. (pres. 1972-74), Carl Duisberg Soc. (pres. Am. assn. 1973-74), Internat. Assn. Univ. Pres. (bd. dirs. N.Am. council 1975-87), Ind. Consortium Computer and High Tech. Edn., Ft. Worth C. of C. (chmn. econ. edn. com. 1963-64), Gold Key, Blue Key, Phi Kappa Phi, Phi Mu Alpha, Alpha Sigma Lambda, Pi Sigma Alpha, Sigma Nu. Clubs: Knife and Fork (pres. 1964-65) (Ft. Worth); Commonwealth (San Francisco); Columbia (Indpls.); Petroleum; Evansville Country, Kennel (Evansville). Lodge: Rotary (pres. Ft. club 1964-65).

GRAVES, WILLIAM PRESTON, governor; b. Salina, Kans., Jan. 9, 1953; s. William Henry and Helen (Mayo) G.; m. Linda Richey, Apr. 1990; 1 child, Katie. BBA, Kans. Wesleyan U., Salina, 1975; postgrad., U. Kans., 1978-79. Dep. asst. sec. of state State of Kans., Topeka, 1980-85, asst. sec. of state, 1985-87, sec. of state, 1987-95; gov. State of Kans., 1995—; mem. Competitiveness Policy Coun. Mem. Kans. Cavalry; trustee Kans. Wesleyan U., 1987—; bd. trustes Sunflower State Games. Named Outstanding Young Alumnus, Kans. Wesleyan U., 1978, to Athletic Hall of Fame, 1986; named Outstanding Young Kansan, Salina Jaycees and Kans. Jaycees, 1986. Mem. Kans. C. of C. and Industry. Republican. Methodist. Avocations: running, reading, traveling. Office: Office of Gov 2nd Fl State Capitol Topeka KS 66612

GRAVITT, NANCY CANUP, realtor; b. Gainesville, Ga., Jan. 8, 1950; d. Samuel Edward Canup and Martha Aretta (Rich) Meeks; m. Robert Sherman Gravitt, Oct. 30, 1963; children: Robie G. Collins, Rusty B., Rynna G. Philyaw, Richalle G. Thomas. Owner/designer The Flower Nook, Gainesville, 1972-78; ptnr., mgr. Bob gravitt Heating and Air Conditioning, Gainesville, 1982-90; co-owner, mgr. End of the Rainbow, Gainesville, 1986-87; designer Bennett's Nursery, Lilburn, Ga., 1993; owner Fancy Nancy's, Gainesville, 1995—; realtor Northside Realty, Gainesville, 1997—. Group leader Campfire Girls, Gainesville, 1972-83; advisor Johnson H.S. Band Flagettes, Gainesville, 1981-89; v.p. Hall County Exchangette Club, Gainesville, 1980-83; co-pres. Johnson H.S. Touchdown Club, Gainesville, 1984-85. Recipient Knight award Johnson High Football Program Coaches and Players, 1984. Mem. Hall County Bd. Realtors. Baptist. Avocations: flowers, sewing, painting, grandchildren. Home: 3678 Whiting Rd Gainesville GA 30504-9207 Office: Northside Realty 675 Ee Butler Pkwy Gainesville GA 30501-4546

GRAW, LEROY HARRY, purchasing-contract management company executive; b. Dupree, S.Dak., Jan. 10, 1942; s. Harry Fred and Luella (Eichmann) G.; m. Kyong Hee Yuk, Sept. 25, 1969 (div. Feb. 1979); 1 child, Natasha; m. Anat Harari, July 3, 1981; children: Byron, Karen. BS, U.S. Mil. Acad., 1964; M Commerce, U. Richmond, 1974; EdD, U. So. Calif., 1980. Govt. contracting officer worldwide, 1971-88; mgr. govt. contracts Fluor Corp., Dallas, 1988-89; mgr. contracts Superconducting Super Collider, Dallas, 1989-95; dir. contract adminstnr. Los Angeles County MTA, L.A., 1995-96; pres. Internat. Resource Mgmt. Assocs., Upland, Calif., 1996—; ccons., Dallas, 1991-95; adj. prof. U. Dallas, 1990-95, U. Calif., Riverside, 1996—, UCLA, Westwood, 1996—, Keller Grad. Sch., 1997—. Author: Service Purchasing, 1994, Cost/Price Analysis, 1994; editor: Global Purchasing, 1990; contbr. articles to profl. jours. Dist. commr. Boy Scouts Am., Portland, Oreg., 1987, mem. troop com. troop 608, La Crescenta, 1997. Capt. U.S. Army, 1964-70, Vietnam. Recipient dist. award of merit Boy Scouts Am., Honolulu, 1985. Fellow Nat. Contract Mgmt. Assn. (cert., chpt. pres. 1997—); mem. Nat. Assn. Purchasing Mgmt. (cert., nat. officer 1992—). Avocations: skiing, hiking, camping, chess. Home and Office: 1667 N Vallejo Way Upland CA 91784-1934

GRAY, ALFRED ORREN, retired journalism educator, communications specialist; b. Sun Prairie, Wis., Sept. 8, 1914; s. Charles Orren and Amelia Katherine (Schadel) G.; m. Nicolin Jane Plank, Sept. 5, 1947; children—Robin, Richard. B.A., U. Wis.-Madison, 1939, M.A., 1941. Reporter-correspondent-intern U. Wis.-Madison and Medford newspapers, 1937-39; free-lance writer, 1938-41, 51-57; intelligence investigator U.S. Ordnance Dept., Ravenna, Ohio, 1941-42; hist. editor, chief writer U.S. Office Chief Ordnance Service, ETO, Paris and Frankfurt, Germany, 1944-46; asst. prof. journalism Whitworth Coll., Spokane, Wash., 1946-48, assoc. prof., 1948-56, head dept. journalism, adviser student publs., 1946-80, prof., 1956-80, prof. emeritus, 1980—, chmn. div. bus. and communications arts, 1958-66, chmn. div. applied arts, 1978-79; rschr. writer Spokane, 1980—; dir. Whitworth News Bur., 1952-58; prin. researcher, writer 12 hist. and ednl. projects. Author: The History of U.S. Ordnance Service in the European Theater of Operations, 1942-46, Not by Might, 1965, Eight Generations From Gondelsheim: A Genealogical Study, 1980; co-author: Many Lamps, One Light: A Centennial History, 1984; editor: The Synod Story, 1953-55; mem. editl. adv. bd. Whitworth Today mag., 1989-90; contbr. articles to newspapers, mags., jours.; reader Am. Presbyns.: The Jour. of Presbyn. History, 1992-94. Scoutmaster Troop 9, Four Lakes Coun., Boy Scouts Am., Madison, Wis., 1937-41; chmn. Pinewood Addition Archtl. Com., Spokane, 1956—; dir. Inland Empire Publs. Clinic, Spokane, 1959-74; mem. ho. of dels. Greater Spokane Council of Chs., 1968-71; judge Goodwill Worker of Yr. awards Goodwill Industries Spokane County, 1972; vice-moderator Synod Wash.-Alaska, Presbyn. Ch. (U.S.A.), 1966-67; bd. dirs. Presbyn. Hist. Soc., 1984-90, 91-94, exec. com., 1986-90, chmn. hist. sites com., 1986-90; mem. Am. Bd. Mission Heritage Commn. for Sesquicentennial of Whitman Mission, 1986; elder Spokane 1st Presbyn. Ch., 1962—, clk. of session, 1984-86, mem. Inland Empire Presbytery Com. for Bicentennial of Gen. Assembly, 1988-89; mem. com. justice and peacemaking Presbytery of the Inland Northwest, 1988-95; mem. Care and Equipping of Congregations Com., 1995—; Dem. precinct official, Spokane, 1988-92. Served with AUS, 1942-46. Decorated Bronze Star and Army Commendation medals; recipient Printers Ink trophy Advt. Assn. West, 1953, citation Nat. Coun. Coll. Publ. Advisers, 1967, Outstanding Teaching of Journalism award Whitworth Coll. Alumni Assn., 1972; named Disting. Newspaper Adviser in U.S. among colleges and univs., Nat. Coun. Coll. Publ. Advisers, 1979. Mem. Assn. for Edn. in Journalism and Mass Comms., Ea. Wash. Hist. Soc., Coll. Media Advisors (hon.), Ea. Wash. Geneal. Soc., N.Am. Mycol. Assn., U. Wis. Alumni Assn. Half Century Club, Phi Beta Kappa (pres. profl. chpt. 1949-50, 67-68, 70-71), Sigma Delta Chi, Phi Eta Sigma. Democrat. Avocations: genealogy, travel. Home: 304 W Hoerner Ave Spokane WA 99218-2124

GRAY, ANTHONY ROLLIN, capital management company executive; b. Des Moines, Nov. 26, 1939; s. James W. and Pauline (Frink) G.; m. Janet Eicher, June 26, 1971 (div. Mar. 1987); m. Barbara Lacey Whittaker, June 14, 1991. BA, Grinnell Coll., 1961; MS, U. Iowa, 1963. Securities analyst Lincoln Nat. Life Ins. Co., Ft. Wayne, Ind., 1966-69; dir. rsch. lst Wis. Trust, Milw., 1969-71; chief investment officer Oak Park (Ill.) Trust, 1971-74; asst. v.p. Union Cen. Life Ins. Co., Cin., 1974-79; dir. rsch. Sun Banks, Orlando, Fla., 1979-85; past pres. Sun Bank Capital Mgmt. Co., Orlando, now chmn. bd., CEO. Capt. USPHS, 1963-66. Avocation: biking, golf. Office: Sun Bank Capital Mgmt PO Box 3786 Orlando FL 32802-3786*

GRAY, ARTHUR, JR., investment counselor; b. N.Y.C., Dec. 21, 1922; s. Arthur and Beatriz (Lerner) G.; m. Adele Hall, Dec. 1944 (div. 1954); children—Michael H., Kathleen W., John M., Wendy L.; m. Betty Johnson; children—Lydia B., Elisabeth C. Asso. Student, Lawrenceville (N.J.) School, 1937-40, Mass. Inst. Tech., 1941-42. With Kuhn, Loeb & Co., 1945-53; pres. Michael Myerberg Prodns., 1953-57; exec. v.p., dir. A.M. Kidder & Co., Inc., 1957-59; sr. partner Gray & Co.; mem. N.Y. Stock Exchange, 1959-75; 1st v.p. Mitchell, Hutchins; chmn. Tallasi Mgmt. Co., N.Y.C., 1975-80; mng. dir. Dreman Gray & Embry, 1981-83; pres., chief exec. officer Dreyfus Personal Mgmt., 1984-93; mng. dir. Cowen Asset Mgmt., N.Y.C., 1993—; chmn. Christine Valmy, Inc.; bd. dirs. Prudential Lines, Inc., Seventh Generation, Inc., GeneLabs, Inc. Pres. bd. Boys Athletic League, 1960-64, Speech and Hearing Inst., 1970-74; chmn. spl. events Citizens for Eisenhower-Nixon, 1952; trustee Am. Mus. Natural History; pres. Lerner-Gray Found.; bd. dirs. ICD Internat. Ctr. for Disabled, Smithsonian Nat. Mus. of Natural History; trustee Woodlwan Cemetery. Served to 1st lt. USAAF, 1942-45. Decorated D.F.C., Air medal with 4 oak leaf clusters. Mem. Am. Arbitration Assn. (dir.), Sigma Alpha Epsilon. Presbyn. (trustee). Clubs: Union, University (N.Y.C.). Home: Bliss Tavern Haverhill NH 03765 Office: S G Cowen Investment Counselors 545 Madison Ave New York NY 10022-4219

GRAY, AUGUSTINE HEARD, JR., computer consultant; b. Long Beach, Calif., Aug. 18, 1936; s. Augustine Heard Gray and Elizabeth (Dubois) Jordan Gray; m. Averill Forneret, Dec. 27, 1959. SB, MIT, 1959, SM, 1959; PhD, Calif. Inst. Tech., 1964; MBA, Pepperdine U., 1981. Asst. prof. dept. elec. and computer engring. U. Calif., Santa Barbara, 1964-68, assoc. prof., 1968-75, prof., 1975-80; v.p. Signal Tech. Inc., Santa Barbara, 1980-88; v.p. SmartStar Corp., Goleta, Calif., 1988-90, sr. scientist, 1990-92; owner A.H. Gray Cons., 1993—. Co-author: Linear Prediction of Speech, 1976; contbr. articles to profl. jours. Fellow IEEE. Democrat. Avocations: amateur radio, computers. Home: 88039 Leeward Dr Florence OR 97439-9003*

GRAY, BRADFORD HITCH, health policy researcher; b. Greenwich, Conn., Dec. 31, 1942; s. John Bradford and Joyce (Hitch) G.; m. Anne Morgan, Aug. 6, 1966 (div. 1980); children: Carrie Elizabeth, Joshua Bradford; m. Helen Darling, Jan. 15, 1983. BS, Okla. State U., 1964; PhD, Yale U., 1973. Asst. prof. U. N.C., Chapel Hill, 1971-74; staff sociologist Nat. Commn. for the Protection of Human Subjects of Rsch., Washington, 1975-77; study dir. Inst. of Medicine NAS, Washington, 1977-88; prof. pub. health Yale Sch. Medicine, New Haven, 1989-96; exec. dir. Program on Non-Profit Orgns. Yale U., New Haven, 1989-96; dir. Inst. for Social and Policy Studies Yale U., 1992-96; dir. divsn. health and sci. policy N.Y. Acad. Medicine, N.Y.C., 1996—. Author: Human Subjects in Medical Experimentation, 1975, The Profit Motive and Patient Care, 1991; editor: New Health Care for Profit, 1983, For-Profit Enterprise in Health Care, 1986. Grantee Lilly Endowment, Indpls., 1990, Ford Found., N.Y., 1989, Rockefeller Bros. Fund, N.Y., 1989, Robert Wood Johnson Found., 1989, 93, 96, Commonwealth Fund, 1997. Mem. Yale Club of N.Y. Home: 93 Buttery Rd New Canaan CT 06840-5002 Office: New York Academy of Medicine 1216 5th Ave New York NY 10029-5202*

GRAY, BRUCE F(RANK), lawyer; b. Memphis, Jan. 18, 1937; s. Bruce Frank and Billie Raiford (McCall); m. Linda Dare Faught, Nov. 11, 1962; children: B. Frank III, Holly E. BBA, U. Miss., 1960; JD, U. Memphis. Bar: Tenn. 1965. Spl. counsel, v.p. Mdeicenters Am., Inc., Memphis, 1965-72; pres., lawyer Omega Properties Inc., Memphis, 1972-75; pvt. practice, Memphis, 1975—; bd. dirs. Security Title Inc., Memphis. Pres. Mid South Mil. M, Covington, Tenn., 1994—. Mem. Tenn. Bar Assn., Memphis Bar Assn. Episcopalian. Avocations: motorcycling, collecting WWII military trucks. Office: Ste 100 6489 N Quail Hollow Rd Memphis TN 38120-1305

GRAY, BRUCE GORDON, sculptor; b. Nov. 14, 1956. BFA, U. Mass., 1983. Sculptor L.A., 1989—. E-mail: Bgrayart@aol.com. Home and Office: 688 S Avenue 21 Los Angeles CA 90031-2891

GRAY, CAROL HICKSON, chemical engineer; b. Atlanta, Jan. 3, 1958; d.Ronald Allen and Charlotte Patricia (Blitch) Hickson; m. Randy Lee Gray, June 25, 1983; children: Amanda Christine, Stephanie Lee, Jamie Noel. BSChemE, Ga. Inst. Tech., 1979. Process engr. Air Products and Chems., Inc., Calvert City, Ky., 1979-83, sr. process engr., 1983-86, sr. prodn. engr., 1986-87, prin. prodn. engr., 1987-89; engring. supr. Air Products and Chems., Inc., Pasadena, Tex., 1990-92; lead engr. Air Products and Chems., Inc., Calvert City, Ky., 1992-93, area supr., 1993-95; area supt. Westvaco Corp., Wickliffe, Ky., 1996—. Mem. NAFE, Internat. Platform Assn. Avocations: bicycling, photography. Office: Westvaco Corp 2025 Beech Grove Rd Wickliffe KY 42087-9010

GRAY, CHARLES AGUSTUS, chemical company research executive; b. Washington, Oct. 15, 1938; s. Joseph Alexander and Meriam (Chandler) G.; m. Rachel Davis, May 22, 1965; children: Elizabeth, Douglas, James. B-ChemE, Cornell U., 1961; PhD, MIT, 1965. Rsch. engr. FMC Corp., Princeton, N.J., 1965-68; mgr. process rsch., inorganic chemical divsn. R&D FMC Corp., Carteret, N.J., 1968-71; tech. supt. inorganic chemical divsn. FMC Corp., South Charleston, W.Va., 1971-74; project mgr. inorganic chemical divsn. R&D FMC Corp., Carteret, 1974-75; spl. project mgr. agrl. chemical divsn. R&D FMC Corp., Princeton, 1975-76, dir. process R&D, 1976-81; dir. comml. devel. FMC Corp., Phila., 1981-83; chief technologist Chem. Products Group FMC Corp., Princeton, 1983-90; v.p. tech. Cabot Corp., Billerica, Mass., 1990—. Author: Explorations in Chemistry, 1965 (Thomas Edison award 1965); contbr. articles to profl. jours.; patentee in field. Bd. dirs. Mass. Sci. Fair, Boston, 1991-96. Presbyterian. Office: Cabot Corp Billerica Tech Ctr 157 Concord Rd Billerica MA 01821-4698

GRAY, CHARLES AUGUSTUS, banker; b. Syracuse, N.Y., Sept. 16, 1928; s. Charles William and Elizabeth Marie (Koch) G. Cert., Am. Inst. Banking, 1958, Sch. Bank Adminstrn., 1961. Cert. internal auditor. With Mchts. Nat. Bank & Trust Co. of Syracuse, 1946-77, auditor, 1959-77, v.p., 1970-77; N.Y. State dir. Bank Adminstrn. Inst., 1970-72; regional auditor cen. N.Y. region Irving Bank Corp., 1977-82, v.p. cen. N.Y. region, 1982-89. Treas. Upper N.Y. Synod, Luth. Ch. in Am., 1966-87, Upstate N.Y. Synod, Evang. Luth. Ch. in Am., 1988—; treas. Luth. Found. Upstate N.Y., 1977-78, bd. dirs., 1980—; pres. Interfrat. Alumni Coun., Syracuse U., 1980-83; treas. N.Y. State Coun. Deliberation, 1997—. Mem. Bank Adminstrn. Inst. (pres. central N.Y. chpt. 1970-72), Inst. Internal Auditors (treas. cen. N.Y. chpt. 1974-76, pres. 1985-86), Lions (pres. local club 1973-75), Masons, Shriners. Republican. Home and Office: 1321 Westmoreland Ave Syracuse NY 13210-3436

GRAY, CHARLES ELMER, lawyer, rancher, investor; b. Elvins, Mo., July 23, 1919; s. Grover P. and Martha Elizabeth (Sullivan) G.; m. Beulah Henrich Gray, July 4, 1942; children—Karen Lee, Cecilia Jean, Bette Sue, Marsha Dawn. Student, Flat River Jr. Coll., 1937-38, U. Hawaii, 1940-41; LL.B., Washington U., St. Louis, 1947. Bar: Mo. 1947. Pvt. practice St. Louis, 1947—; ptnr. Gray and Ritter; gen. counsel, dir. United Mo. Bank, St Louis; mem. Mo. Appellate Jud. Commn.; mem. rules com. Supreme Ct. Mo., 1970-81. Served to capt. USAF, 1939-45. Fellow Internat. Acad. Trial Lawyers (dir.), Am. Coll. Trial Lawyers, Internat. Soc. Barristers (state chmn., dir.); mem. ABA, Mo. Bar Assn., St. Louis Bar Assn., Lawyers Assn. St. Louis (v.p. 1954, bd. govs., Honor award 1977), Harbour Ridge Yacht Club (commodore 1991-92), Phi Delta Phi. Home: The Regency PHI 8650 S Ocean Dr Jensen Beach FL 34957 also: PO Box 709 Farmington MO 63640-0709 Office: Gateway One on the Mall 701 Market St Fl 8 Saint Louis MO 63101-1850

GRAY, CHARLES ROBERT, lawyer; b. Kirksville, Mo., Aug. 22, 1952; s. George Devon and Bettie Louise (McCormick) G.; m. Dana Elizabeth Kehr, June 1, 1974; children: Jennifer, Jessica, Marcus, Gregory, Victoria. BS, N.E. Mo. State U., 1974; JD, U. Mo., Kansas City, 1978. Bar: Mo. 1978, Va. 1993, U.S. Dist. Ct. (we. dist.) Mo. 1978, U.S. Ct. Appeals (fed. cir.) 1992, U.S. Ct. Appeals (4th cir.) 1995, U.S. Supreme Ct. 1981; cert. mediator; cert. hearing officer Va. Supereme Ct., 1997. Pvt. practice Parkville, Mo., 1978-81; asst. pub. defender 5th Judicial Cir. Ct. Mo., St. Joseph, 1978-79; pub. defender 6th Judicial Cir. Ct. Mo., Platte City, 1981; asst. dist. counsel Army Corps of Engrs., Kansas City, 1981-82, Vicksburg, Miss., 1982-83; chief counsel space shuttle, MX missile U.S. Army, Vandenberg AFB, Calif., 1983-85; chief counsel troop support agy. U.S. Army, Ft. Lee, Va., 1985-87; fraud counsel Def. Gen. Supply Ctr. Dept. of Def., Richmond, Va., 1987-93; pvt. practice, Chester, Va., 1993—; owner Pvt. Jud. Svcs., Inc., Chester, 1993—; adj. prof. St. Leo Coll., Ft. Lee, 1986-91, John Tyler Coll., Chester, Va., 1994—. Mem. Selective Svc. Draft Bd., Brookfield, Mo., 1972-74; pres. Old Towne Parkville Assn., 1979-81, Chester (Va.) Youth Sports Boosters, 1989-91; den leader Boy Scouts Am., Chester, 1991—. Victor Wilson honor scholar, 1977; recipient Am. Jurisprudence award Coop-Bancroft-Whitney, 1989. Mem. ATLA, Am. Arbitration Assn. (mem. nat. panel arbitrators 1994—, mem. govt. disputes panel 1995—, mem. constrn. panel 1995—, mem. comml. panel 1995—), Def. Rsch. Inst. (approved mem. panel on mediation and arbitration), Mo. Bar Assn., Va. Bar Assn., Va. Trial Lawyers Assn. Methodist. Avocations: coaching youth sports, cub scouts, softball, tennis, basketball. Home: PO Drawer B Chester VA 23831 Office: Pres/Presiding Ofcl Pvt Jud Svcs PO Drawer B Chester VA 23831-0317

GRAY, CHRISTOPHER DONALD, software researcher, author, consultant; b. Brookville, Pa., May 18, 1951; s. Donald Garrison and Patricia Lee (Huffman) G.; m. Allison Selby Farragher, Oct. 12, 1974 (div. 1989); children: Patrick Xanthe, Colin Christopher; m. Leah Carene Lanzillo, Feb. 7, 1998. BA in Math., Washington and Jefferson Coll., 1973; MS in Math., Carnegie-Mellon U., 1975. Mfg. systems analyst Ohaus Scale Corp., Florham Park, N.J., 1974-76; systems rep. Software Internat. Corp., Florham Park, N.J., 1976-77, cons. mfg. systems, 1977-78, mktg. rep., 1978-79; v.p. Mfg. Software Systems, Inc., Essex Junction, Vt., 1979-85, pres., 1985; pres. Oliver Wight Software Research, Inc., Essex Junction, Vt., 1985-88, Gray Rsch., Exeter, N.H., 1988—; pres., pub. Gray Media, Inc., 1992—, Monochrome Press, Inc., 1992—; bd. dirs. Ptnrs. for Excellence, Inc.; assoc. R.D. Garwood, Inc., 1988-92, Oliver Wight Edn. Assocs., Newbury, 1982-88; cons. Oliver Wight Video Prodns., Essex Junction, Vt., 1980-84; advisor mfg. applications Software News, Sentry Pub. Co., Hudson, Mass., 1983-89. Author: The Right Choice: The Complete Guide to Evaluating, Selecting and Installing MRP II Software, 1987; co-author MRP II Standard System, 1983 (rsch. report), MRP II Standard System: A Handbook for Manufacturing System Survival, 1989, MRP II Standard System Workbook, 1989; contbr. rsch. reports, articles and conf. papers to tech. lit. Fellow Am. Prodn. and Inventory Control Soc. (cert. fellow prodn. and inventory mgmt.; chpt. program chmn. 1978-79, v.p. 1979-80, pres. 1980-81); mem. Phi Beta Kappa. Republican. Presbyterian. Avocations: gardening, landscaping, house restoration, furniture building. Home: 270 Pinewood Shores East Wakefield NH 03830 Office: Gray Rsch PO Box 424 Exeter NH 03833-0424

GRAY, CHRISTOPHER JOHN, history educator, human rights activist; b. Natick, Mass., Apr. 21, 1958; s. John Richard and Doris (Chaffee) G.; m. Kisanga Hortense Salama, Sept. 14, 1990; children: Zuula-Jenine Maluguza, Alex A.N., Brendan M.L. BA, U. Mass., 1980; MA, U. London, 1987; PhD, Ind. U., 1995. Substitute tchr. Medway (Mass.) Sch. Sys., 1980-81; bookseller Waldenbooks, Seattle, 1981-82; vol. U.S. Peace Corps, Republic of Gabon, 1982-84, Republic of Senegal, 1984-86; assoc. instr. Ind. U., Bloomington, 1988-95; asst. prof. African history Fla. Internat. U., Miami, 1995—; cons. pre-election evaluation team Internat. Found. for Election Sys., Gabon, 1998. Author: Conceptions of History in the Works of C.A. Diop and T. Obengs, 1989; contbr. articles to profl. jours. Coord. for Congo, Amnesty Internat. U.S.A., 1992-93; human rights activist. MacArthur scholar Ind. Ctr. Global Change and World Peace, 1992-93; John H. Edwards fellow Ind. U., 1994-95; Fulbright fellow in France, Gabon, Congo-Brazzaville, 1990-91. Mem. African Studies Assn., Am. Hist. Assn., French Colonial Hist. Soc., Francophone Africa Rsch. Group, Assn. Third World Studies, World History Assn. Office: Fla Internat U History Dept University Park DM 397 Miami FL 33199

GRAY, CLARENCE JONES, foreign language educator, dean emeritus; b. Red Bank, N.J., June 21, 1908; s. Clarence J. Sr. and Elsie (Megill) G.; m. Jane Love Little, Aug. 25, 1934 (dec. June 1998); children: Frances Gray Adams, Kenneth Stewart. BA, U. Richmond, 1933, LLD, 1979; MA, Columbia U., 1934; postgrad. Centro de Estudios Historicos, Madrid, summer 1935; EdD, U. Va., 1962. Underwriter Aetna Life and Casualty, 1925-30; instr. Spanish, Columbia U., 1934-38; gen. sec., mem. exec. council Instituto de las Espanas en los Estados Unidos, 1934-39; instr., sec. dept. Romance langs. Queens Coll., N.Y.C., 1938-46 (on mil. leave 1943-46); dean students U. Richmond (Va.), 1946-68, assoc. prof. modern langs., 1946-62, prof., 1962-79, emeritus, 1979—, dean administrv. svcs., 1968-73, exec. asst. to pres., 1971-79, dean adminstrn., 1973-79, emeritus, 1979—, spl. cons. to pres., 1979-91, spl. cons. to chancellor, 1991—, editor bull., 1968-74, moderator U. Richmond-WRNL Radio Scholarship Quiz Program, mem. bd. Univ. Assos. Cons., Commn. on Colls., So. Assn. Colls. and Schs. Trustee' Inst. Mediterranean Studies. Contbr. articles to profl. jours. Served from lt. to lt. comdr., USNR, 1943-46. Recipient Nat. Alumni award for disting. svc. U. Richmond. Mem. MLA, NEA, Am. Assn. Tchrs. Spanish, Am. Assn. for Higher Edn., Newcomen Soc. N.Am., Inst. Internat. Edn. (cert. meritorius svc.), English-Speaking Union, Legion of Honor, Order of De Molay, Country Club of Va., Colonnade Club, Masons, Rotary, Phi Beta Kappa (sec. emeritus, historian), Phi Delta Kappa, Kappa Delta Pi, Omicron Delta Kappa (nat. sec. gen. council 1966-72, Disting. Svc. key 1968, nat. chmn. scholarship awards 1972-78), Alpha Psi Omega, Phi Gamma Delta (award for disting. and exceptional svc.), Alpha Phi Omega, Phi Beta Kappa Assocs. (life). Baptist. Home: Dogwood Tower P-18 1711 Bellevue Ave Richmond VA 23227-3964

GRAY, CLAYLAND BOYDEN, lawyer; b. Winston-Salem, N.C., Feb. 6, 1943; s. Gordon and Jane (Craige) G. J.D. with high honors, U. N.C., 1968; B.A. in History magna cum laude, Harvard U., 1964. Bar: D.C. 1970, N.C. Law clk. to chief justice Earl Warren, 1968; assoc. Wilmer, Cutler & Pickering, 1969, partner, 1976-81; counsel and dep. chief of staff to Vice Pres. George Bush, Washington, 1981-85; counsellor Vice Pres. George Bush, 1985-89; counsel to the Pres., 1989-93; ptnr. Wilmer, Cutler & Pickering, Washington, 1993—; chmn. Citizens for a Sound Economy, 1993—, Summit Comms., Inc., Atlanta, 1982-89. Mem. com. to visit coll. and com. on univ. devel., Harvard U.; pres. trustees St. Mark's Sch. With USMC, 1964-70. Mem. ABA, D.C. Bar Assn., N.C. Bar Assn., Fed. Bar Assn. Republican. Episcopalian. Clubs: Met, Chevy Chase, Alibi. Home: 1534 28th St NW Washington DC 20007-3058 Office: Wilmer Cutler & Pickering 2445 M St NW Ste 500 Washington DC 20037-1487*

GRAY, DARLENE AGNES, nurse; b. Prince Frederick, Md., June 10, 1957; d. Reynold Jerome Gray and Ellen (Madaglene) Cooke. AA, Charles County Community Coll., 1988; student, U. Md., Balt., 1982. RN; cert. med. asst. Secretarial aide U. Md. Ea. Shore, Princess Anne, Md., 1979-82; med. surg. technician Calvert Meml. Hosp., Prince Frederick, Md., 1982—; nurse Homecall, Prince George, Md., 1985-88, night supr., 1988—, health care giver, 1996—. Mem. NAACP, Alpha Kappa Alpha, Alpha Beta Kappa. Avocations: poetry, writing.

GRAY, DAVID LAWRENCE, retired air force officer; b. Portland, Oreg., Aug. 19, 1930; s. Thomas Graham and Helen Lee (Brown) G.; m. Nelda Joyce Ryan, Nov. 17, 1951 (dec. June 1987); children: David Scott, Vicki Lynn Gray Copeland, Steven Mark; m. Patricia F. Umstead, Mar. 22, 1991. BS, U. Colo., 1958; M.B.A., George Washington U., 1962. Registered rep. United Services Planning Assn. & Ind. Research Agy.,

Montgomery, Ala., 1982-83; dist. agt. United Services Planning Assn. & Ind. Research Agy., Charleston, S.C., 1983-86; exec. dir. Air Force Assn., Arlington, Va., 1986-87. Host: TV talk show Def. Issues, 1982-83. Exec. dir. Air War Coll. Found., 1982-94. Maj. gen. USAF, 1951-82; Korea, Vietnam. Mem. Air Force Assn. (pres. Charleston chpt. 1985-86, nat. exec. dir. 1986-87), Daedallians. Republican. Avocations: golf, boating.

GRAY, DAWN PLAMBECK, work-family consultant; b. Chgo., Aug. 23, 1957; d. Raymond August and Eunice Eve (Fox) Plambeck; m. Richard Scott Gray, Apr. 13, 1985; children: Zachary, Rae. BS, Northwestern U., 1979. Desk asst. Sta. WCFL, Chgo., 1979-80; writer UPI Internat., Chgo., 1980; asignment editor Cable News Network, Chgo., 1980-81; account exec. Aaron Cushman and Assoc., Chgo., 1981-83; account exec. Ruder Finn & Rotman, Chgo., 1983-84, account supr., 1984-86, dir. consumer group, 1986-87; dir. pub. rels. Tassani Communications, Chgo., 1987-90; v.p. Marcy Monyek & Assoc., Chgo., 1990; pres. Moments Inc., Chgo., 1991—. Avocation: dance. Office: Moments Inc 1028 W Monroe St Chicago IL 60607-2604

GRAY, DEBORAH DOLIA, business writing consultant; b. Elmo, Mo., Jan. 25, 1952; d. Gerald Lee and Rosalie (Thompson) G. BS in Music and Journalism cum laude, U. Nebr., 1976; MFA, Columbia U., 1988. Reporter The Lincoln (Nebr.) Star, 1975-78; spl. writer, feature projects The Fort Lauderdale (Fla.) News, 1978-79; reporter Miami (Fla.) News, 1979-80; curriculum specialist John Jay Coll. Criminal Justice, N.Y.C., 1980-84; tng. specialist Mgmt. Devel. Systems Inc., N.Y.C., 1985—; writing cons. various non-profit agys. and corps. Contbr. articles to profl. jours. Hollingsworth fellow Columbia U., 1985. Avocations: songwriter, keyboard player, poet. Home: 120 Bennett Ave Apt 6N New York NY 10033-2325

GRAY, DEBORAH MARY, wine importer; b. Sydney, N.S.W., Australia, Feb. 4, 1952; came to U.S., 1973; d. Anthony Eric and Mary Patricia (O'Mullane) Gray. Student, St. Petersburg Jr. Coll., 1973-85, Eckerd Coll., 1988-90. Fin. counselor Wuesthoff Meml. Hosp., Rockledge, Fla., 1973-75; admintrv. dir. Dresden & Ticktin, MDs, P.A., St. Petersburg, Fla., 1976-80; exec. dir., v.p. Am. Med. Mgmt., Inc., Clearwater, Fla., 1980-90; pres., dir. All Women's Health Ctr., Inc., various locations, Fla., 1980-90, Lakeland Women's Health Ctr., Fla., 1980-90, Ft. Myers Women's Health Ctr., Fla., 1980-90, Nat. Women's Health Svcs., Inc., Clearwater, Fla., 1983-90, Women's Ob-Gyn. Ctr. Countryside, Inc., 1984-90, D.M.S. of Ft. Myers, Inc., 1985-90; treas., v.p., dir. Birthing Mgmt. Inc., 1985-90; healthcare cons., 1990-92; N.Am. mgr. Cowra Wines, Australia, 1991-95; owner, sole proprietor The Australian Wine Connection, Breckenridge, Colo., 1992—; bd. dirs. Australian Trade Commn., N.Y., 1996—; pres., dir. Alternative Human Svcs., 1979; dir. Perinatal Ctr. Ga. Bapt. Med. Ctr., 1990-92. Mem. bd. agy. that facilitates hard to place children adoptions One Ch. One Child, 1990-94.

GRAY, DIANE, dancer, choreographer; b. Painesville, Ohio, May 29, 1941; d. Gordon Dallas and Bettie (Kerr) G.; m. James William Viera, May 15, 1971; 1 child, James William II. BS, Juilliard Sch., 1963; MS in Edn., Hunter Coll., 1987. Chorus dancer Martha Graham Dance Co., N.Y.C., 1963-69, soloist, 1969-71, prin. dancer, 1972-79, assoc. artistic dir., 1993—; artist-in-residence various Univs., worldwide, 1965-97; tchr. Martha Graham Sch., N.Y.C., 1963-97; also dir. Martha Graham Sch., 1983-97; dir. Dances by Diane Gray, N.Y.C., 1979-83. Mem. Kappa Delta Pi. Avocations: traveling, reading, cooking.

GRAY, DONALD LYMAN, orchard owner; b. Newkirk, Okla., Oct. 10, 1929; s. Lyman Otto and Mara Frances (Leven) G.; m. Clara Mae Groden, June 25, 1949 (dec. Feb. 1967); children: Linda, Donald, William, James, Elaine, Janet, Thomas, Robert, Michael; m. Michel Bridget Gavin, Sept. 2, 1977. Student, Okla. State U., 1968-74. Supr. Conoco, Inc., Ponca City, Okla., 1949-77; dir. Conoco Pipeline Co., Houston, 1977-85; owner, cons. Little Cabin Pecan Co., Vinita, Okla., 1985—. Co-author: (nat. computer network) Petroex, 1969; co-author Terminal Automation System, 1981. Named to Hon. Order Ky. Cols., 1976, Okla. Pecan Grower of Yr., 1989. Mem. Nat. Wool Growers Assn., Okla. Wool and Sheep Producers, Okla. Pecan Growers Assn. (officr 1986—), Nat. Pecan Mktg. Coun., Vinita C. of C., Okla. Route 66 Assn. (v.p.), Elks. Republican. Roman Catholic. Avocation: landscaping. Home: PO Box 246 Disney OK 74340-0246 Office: Little Cabin Pecan Co RR 2 Box 22 Vinita OK 74301-9802

GRAY, DONALD MELVIN, molecular and cell biology educator; b. Milton, Pa., Apr. 4, 1938; s. Harry Seal and Edith Sophia (Larrison) G.; m. Carla Christine Winlund, Sept. 10, 1970. BA, Susquehanna U., 1960; MS, Yale U., 1963, PhD, 1967. Postdoctoral fellow U. Calif., Berkeley, 1967-70; asst. prof. molecular and cell biology U. Tex. at Dallas, Richardson, 1970-76, assoc. prof., 1976-83, prof., 1983—; program head, 1989-95. Contbr. over 80 articles to profl. jours. Fogarty Sr. Internat. fellow European Molecular Biology Lab., Heidelberg, Fed. Republic of Germany, 1977-78; NIH grantee U. Tex. at Dallas, 1972-93, NSF grantee, 1994-98, Welch Found. grantee, 1972—. Fellow AAAS; mem. Am. Chem. Soc., Biophys. Soc. Office: Univ Tex at Dallas Molecular and Cell Biology PO Box 830688 Richardson TX 75083-0688

GRAY, DOROTHY LOUISE ALLMAN POLLET, librarian; b. Billings, Mont., Dec. 17, 1945; d. Lee F. and Ruth H. (Behner) Allman; m. Michael Haslam Gray, Aug. 11, 1980; children: M. Alexander, Timothy Haslam. BA, U. Colo., 1969; MSLS, Syracuse U., 1972. Reference libr., bibliographer Libr. of Congress Div. Blind and Physically Handicapped, Washington, 1972-75; reference specialist Libr. of Congress Gen. Reference and Bibliography Div., Washington, 1975-77; ednl. liaison officer nat. programs Libr. of Congress, Washington, 1977-82; rsch. assoc. Nat. Commn. on Librs. and Info. Sci., Washington, 1982-88; info. ctr. mgr. Nat. Assn. Inveterate and Obdurate Politicos, Arlington, Va., 1988-92; libr. dir. Nat. Sch. Bds. Assn., Alexandria, Va., 1992—. Editor: Sign Systems for Libraries, 1979; editor Leads, the newsletter of Internat. Rels. Roundtable, ALA, 1979-82; cons. editor: The Bowker Annual of Library and Book Trade Information, 1986-88. Recipient Superior Svc. award Libr. of Congress, Washington, 1981. Mem. ALA, CEC, Spl. Librs. Assn. Avocations: music, calligraphy. Office: Nat Sch Bds Assn 1680 Duke St Ste 100 Alexandria VA 22314-3493

GRAY, DUNCAN MONTGOMERY, JR., retired bishop; b. Canton, Miss., Sept. 21, 1926; s. Duncan Montgomery and Isabel (McCrady) G.; m. Ruth Miller Spivey, Feb. 9, 1948; children: Duncan Montgomery, Anne Gray Finley, Lloyd Spivey, Catherine Gray Clark. B.E.E., Tulane U., 1948; M.Div., U. South, 1953, D.D. (hon.), 1972. Ordained priest Episcopal Ch., 1953, bishop, 1974; priest-in-charge Calvary Ch., Cleveland, Miss. and Grace Ch., Rosedale, Miss., 1953-57, Holy Innocents Ch., Como, Miss., 1957-60; rector St. Peter's Ch., Oxford, Miss., 1957-65, St. Paul's Ch., Meridian, Miss., 1965-74; bishop coadjutor Diocese of Miss., Jackson, 1974; bishop Diocese of Miss., 1974-93; chmn. Standing Commn. on Constn. and Canons of Gen. Conv. of Episc. Ch., 1977-83, House of Bishops' Com. Canons, 1975-89; pres. Province IV Episc. Ch., 1984-88, chmn. com. on rules, 1989-93; mem. advice council to the Presiding Bishop, 1984-88; vice chmn. Bd. Archives Episc. Ch. Contbr. articles in field to religious publs. Chmn. bd. trustees All Saints Episc. Sch., Vicksburg, 1975-77; trustee U. South, Sewanee, Tenn., 1974-97, regent, 1981-87, chancellor, 1991-97; chmn. Miss. Religious Leadership Conf., 1977-79, So. Regional Council, 1967-73; mem. Miss. Mental Health Assn., 1968-73; bd. dirs. Miss. Council on Human Relations, 1962-93, pres., 1963-67; mem. Miss. Adv. Com. to U.S. Commn. on Civil Rights, 1975-90. Recipient Nat. Speaker of Year award Tau Kappa Alpha, 1962. Home: 3775 Old Canton Rd Jackson MS 39216-3519

GRAY, D'WAYNE, retired marine corps officer; b. Navarro County, Tex., Apr. 9, 1931; s. Henry Oliver and Myrtle Daisy (Lee) G.; m. Mary Joan Sobieck, Oct. 11, 1955; children: Stephen D'Wayne, Elizabeth Joan Gray Hendrickson, Theresa Mary Gray Croghan. Student, N. Tex. Agrl. Coll., 1948-49; B.A., U. Tex., 1952; M.S. in Internat. Affairs, George Washington U., 1971; postgrad., Naval War Coll., 1970-71, Harvard U., 1980. Commd. 2d lt. USMC, 1952, advanced through grades to lt. gen., 1983; combat svc. Korea, 1953, Vietnam, 1965, 71-72; asst. div. comdr. 1st Marine Div. Camp Pendleton, Calif., 1977-79; dir. plans Hdqrs. Washington, 1979-80, dir. ops. Hdqrs., 1980-81, dir. personnel mgmt. Hdqrs., 1981-83, chief of staff Hdqrs., 1983-85; comdg. gen. Fleet Marine Force, Pacific; comdr. Marine Corps Bases, Pacific, Camp H.M. Smith, Hawaii, 1985-87; ret., 1987, ind. cons., 1987-89; exec. dir. Montgomery County Revenue Authority, Rockville, Md., 1989-90; undersec. veterans affairs for benefits Dept. Vet. Affairs, Washington, 1990-93; del. Inter-Am. Def. Bd., 1980; bd. dirs. U.S. Naval Inst., 1980-85; mem. bd. govs. Uniformed Svcs. Benefit Assn. Kansas City, 1982-83, 85-88; mem. sec. of state's Adv. Panel on Overseas Security, 1984-85. Chmn. editorial bd., U.S. Naval Inst., 1980-83. Mem. maritime policy study group Ctr. for Strategic and Internat. Studies, Georgetown U., 1981-85. Decorated D.S.M., Legion of Merit with gold star and V, Bronze Star medal with V., Meritorious Svc. medal with gold star, Air medal with bronze numeral 5, Joint Svc. Commendation medal with V, Navy Commendation medal with V. Mem. Marine Corps Assn., U.S. Naval Inst., Marine Corps Heritage Found., Ret. Officers Assn. (bd. dirs. 1994—, 1st vice chmn. 1998—), Cath. War Vets. Roman Catholic. Home: 3423 Barger Dr Falls Church VA 22044-1202 *The military way of life is not for everyone. But, to those for whom it is right, it offers an unequalled opportunity for both personal adventure and service to one's fellow Americans. I wish I could do it all again!.*

GRAY, ELIZABETH MARIE, biologist; b. South Bend, Ind., June 29, 1965; d. Henry Froehlich and Joan (Griglun) G. AB, Harvard U., 1987; PhD, U. Wash., Seattle, 1994. Rsch. asst. Monteverde Res., Costa Rica, 1987-88, Punta Tombo Res., Argentina, 1988; asst. molecular biologist U. Ky., Lexington, 1990-93; prof. biology U. Nev., Reno, 1995-96, postdoctoral rsch. assoc., 1996—; sci. cons. Wash. State Dept. Wildlife, Olympia, 1991-93; ind. investigator Indonesia, 1995. Reviewer sci. jours.; contbr. articles to profl. jours. Grantee Ctr. Wildlife Conservation, 1992-93. Mem. AAUW, Am. Ornithologists' Union, Assn. Women in Sci., Animal Behavior Soc., Soc. Conservation Biology. Democrat. Avocations: hiking, riding, soccer, camping, reading. Office: USGS-BRD-PIERC PO Box 44 Hawaii National Park HI 96718

GRAY, FESTUS GAIL, electrical engineer, educator, researcher; b. Moundsville, W.Va., Aug. 16, 1943; s. Festus P. and Elsie V. (Rine) G.; m. Caryl Evelyn Anderson, Aug. 24, 1968; children: David, Andrew, Daniel. BSEE, W.Va. U., 1965, MSEE, 1967; PhD, U. Mich., 1971. Instr. W.Va. U., Morgantown, 1966-67; asst. prof. Va. Poly. Inst. and State U., Blacksburg, 1971-77, assoc. prof., 1977-82, prof., 1983—; vis. scientist Rsch. Triangle Inst., N.C., 1984-85; faculty fellow NASA, 1975; cons. Inland Motors, Radford, Va., 1980, Rsch. Triangle Inst., 1987—; researcher Rome Air Devel. Ctr., N.Y., 1980-81, Naval Surface Weapons Ctr., Dahlgren, Va., 1982-83, Army Rsch. Office, 1983-86, NSF, 1991-93, 98—, ARPA, 1993—; publs. chmn. Internat. Symposium on Fault Tolerant Computing, Ann Arbor, Mich., 1985. Co-author: Structured Logic Design with CHDL, 1993, 2d edit., 1999; contbr. articles to sci. jours. Assoc. treas. Northside Presbyn. Ch., Blacksburg, 1986—, bd. deacons, 1980-83; coach S.W. Va. Soccer Assn., Blacksburg, 1980-86; asst. scoutmaster Boy Scouts Am., 1990—. Grantee NSF, Office NAval Rsch., NASA, Adv. Rsch. Projects Agy; Teaching fellow U. Mich., 1967-70. Mem. IEEE (chpt. chmn. 1979-80), Computer Soc. IEEE, Sigma Xi. Democrat. Achievements include research on fault tolerance, diagnosis, testing and reliability issues for VLSI, disturbed and multiprocessor computer architectures, modeling and synthesis with VHOL, modeling and design with hardware description languages. Home: 304 Fincastle Dr Blacksburg VA 24060-5036 Office: Va Poly Inst and State U Blacksburg VA 24061-0111

GRAY, FRANCINE DU PLESSIX, author; b. Warsaw, Poland; came to U.S., 1941, naturalized, 1952; d. Bertrand Jochaud and Tatiana (Iacovleff) du Plessix; m. Cleve Gray, Apr. 23, 1957; children: Thaddeus Ives, Luke Alexander. B.A., Barnard Coll., 1952; Litt.D. (hon.), CUNY, Oberlin Coll., U. Santa Clara, St. Mary's Coll., U. Hartford. Annenberg fellow Brown U., 1997; disting. vis. prof. CCNY, 1975; vis. lectr. Yale U., New Haven, 1981-82; Ferris prof. Princeton U., 1986. Author: Divine Disobedience: Profiles in Catholic Radicalism, 1970 (Nat. Cath. Book award), Hawaii: The Sugar-Coated Fortress, 1972 , Lovers and Tyrants, 1976, World Without End, 1981, October Blood, 1985, Adam & Eve and the City, 1987, Soviet Women: Walking the Tightrope, 1989, Rage and Fire: A Life of Louise Colet, 1994, At Home with the Marquis de Sade: A Life, 1998. Guggenheim Found. fellow, 1991-92. Mem. Am. P.E.N., Am. Acad. Arts and Letters. Democrat. Roman Catholic.

GRAY, FRANCIS CAMPBELL, bishop; b. Manila, Apr. 27, 1940. Grad., Rollins Coll., Winter Park, Fla., 1966; BD, Nashota House, SJM, 1979; attended, St. George's Coll., Jerusalem. Ordained priest Roman Cath. Ch., 1969. Asst. St. Wilfred's Ch., Sarasota, Fla., 1969-70; chaplain Manatee Jr. Coll., 1970-74; rector St. John's Ch., Melbourne, Fla., 1979-87, Emmanuel Ch., Orlando, Fla., 1986-87; bishop co-adjutor Diocese of No. Ind., South Bend, 1986-87, bishop, 1987-98; asst. bishop Diocese of Va., Richmond, 1998—. With USMC. Office: Diocese of Virginia 110 W Franklin St Richmond VA 23220*

GRAY, FRANK C., bishop. Bishop of Northern Indiana The Episcopal Church, South Bend, Ind., 1987-98; asst. bishop Diocese of Va., Richmond, 1998—. Office: Diocese of Virginai 110 W Franklin St Richmond VA 23220*

GRAY, FRANK TRUAN, lawyer; b. Prince Frederick, Md., Oct. 22, 1920; s. John B. and Aimée Atlee (Truan) G.; m. Sally A. Jackson, Dec. 31, 1976; children: John W., Edward A., Philip L., Theodora R. A.B., Princeton U., 1942; student, Cambridge (Eng.) U., 1945; LL.B., Harvard U., 1948. Bar: Md. 1949. Assoc. firm Piper & Marbury, Balt., 1948-56; ptnr. Piper & Marbury, 1957-90; asst. atty. gen., State of Md., 1955-56; pres. Balt. Estate Planning Council, 1975-76. Editor: Harvard Law Rev, 1947-48. Pres. Citizen's Planning and Housing Assn., Balt., 1960-62, bd. dirs. Balt. Neighborhoods, Inc., 1959-85, Balt. Bar Found., 1985-93; trustee Provident Hosp., Inc., 1961-74. Fellow Am. Bar Found. (chmn. Md. 1993-98), Md. Bar Found.; mem. ABA, Md. Bar Assn., Balt. Bar Assn., Am. Law Inst. Office: Piper & Marbury LLP 36 S Charles St Baltimore MD 21201-3020

GRAY, FREDERICK THOMAS, JR. ('RICK GRAY), actor, educator; b. Hopewell, Va., Mar. 22, 1951; s. Frederick Thomas and Evelyn (Helms) Johnson Gray. BA with distinction, U. Va., 1972, JD, 1975, MEd, 1990, postgrad., 1991-94; postgrad., U. Richmond, 1981-82. Bar: Va. 1976. Law clk. Williams, Mullen & Christian, Richmond, Va., 1975-76, assoc., 1976-78; sec. Commonwealth of Va., Richmond, 1978-81; high sch. tchr., 1982-89, asst. prin., 1991-92. Appeared in TV series In the Heat of the Night, profl. stage prodns. My Fair Lady, Macbeth, To Kill a Mockingbird, A Midsummer Night's Dream, also others. Mem. SAG, Raven Soc. (U. Va.). Address: 4701 Bermuda Hundred Rd Chester VA 23836-3257

GRAY, F(REDERICK) WILLIAM, III, lawyer; b. Niagara Falls, N.Y., Aug. 6, 1944; s. Frederick William Jr. and Doris May (Nelson) G.; m. Molly Glennie, May 31, 1969; children: Andrew Glennie, Susan Elizabeth. Student, Gettysburg Coll., 1962-63; BA, Johns Hopkins U., 1966; JD, Cornell U., 1969. Bar: N.Y. 1970. With N.Y. State Urban Devel. Corp., Rochester, Buffalo, Niagara Falls, Amherst, 1969-78; assoc. Hodgson, Russ, Andrews, Woods & Goodyear, Buffalo, 1978-82, ptnr., 1983—; mem. N.Y. Gov.'s Task Force on Rec. and Filing. Pres. Ch. Mission of Help Inc., Buffalo, 1984-85, Buffalo Fedn. Neighborhood Ctrs. Inc., 1988-89, Benedict House of Western N.Y. Inc., Buffalo, 1991-92; co-chair AIDS Task Force, 1991-92, trustee, 1994—, Presbytery of Western N.Y. Mem. ABA, N.Y. State Bar Assn. (real estate sect., spl. com. on access to pub. records), Erie County Bar Assn. Presbyterian. Home: 12 Saint James Pl Buffalo NY 14222-1411 Office: Hodgson Russ Andrews Woods & Goodyear 1800 One M & T Plaza Buffalo NY 14203-2391*

GRAY, GAVIN CAMPBELL, II, computer information engineer, computer consultant; b. Levittown, N.Y., Sept. 16, 1948; s. Gavin Campbell Gray and Pauline Louise (Bauerschmidt) Gowen; m. Catherine Ann West, Aug. 23, 1969; children: Jeffrey William, Tamara Pauline. Student, U. Wis., Milw., 1966-71. Programmer, analyst Equitable Variable Life Ins., Farmingdale, N.Y., 1975-77; analyst, programmer Atty.'s Title Svcs., Orlando, Fla., 1977-78; systems analyst Cert. Grocers, Ocala, Fla., 1978-80; supr. R & D, Clay Electric Coop., Keystone Heights, Fla., 1980-86; mgr. info. svcs. Coldwell Banker Relocation Svcs., Mission Viejo, Calif., 1986-96; knowledge mgr. Oracle Corp., San Diego, 1996—; mem. Guide Internat. Bus. Rules Stds. Project, 1994—, Am. Nat. Stds. Inst. Accredited Stds. Com. X12, 1994-96, Asymetrix Corp. Adv. Coun. Author: IBM GIS Usage for IMS/DLI, 1979; developer software Map-Paint for CICS, methodology Path Evaluation Method (PEM), TRANS-FLOW Programming, Tier Diagramming Method; contbr. articles to profl. jours. Mem. IEEE, Project Mgmt. Inst., Assn. Computing Machinery, Data Adminstrn. Mgmt. Assn. Internat., Data Warehousing Inst., Software Program Mgrs. Network, Math. Assn. Am., Internat. Platform Assn., IEEE Computer Soc., IEEE Engring. Mgmt. Soc., N.Y. Acad. Scis., Am. Mus. Natural History, Zool. Soc. San Diego, Am. Mensa Ltd., Nat. Eagle Scout Assn., Intertel. Office: Oracle Corp 12230 El Camino Real San Diego CA 92130-2090

GRAY, GEORGE, mural painter; b. Harrisburg, Pa., Dec. 23, 1907; s. George Zacharias and Anna Margaret (Barger) G. Ed., Harrisburg Tech. H.S., Phila., 1927-30, Acad. Fine Arts, Wilmington, Del., 1931-33, Art Students League, N.Y.C., Howard Pyle Sch. Illustration, Wilmington. Designer stage scenery, N.Y.C., 1926; invited to sketch scenes of army life in various forts and camps; tchr. anatomy and figure constrn. while attending art classes, Phila., Wilmington, later staff artist, U.S. Inf. Jour., U.S. Cav. Jour., Washington, N.Y. Nat. Guardsmen, Pa. N.G. Mag., mural painter patron, Gen. J. Leslie Kincaid, pres., Am. Hotels Corp., N.Y.C., 1934—; murals exhibited in hotels throughout U.S., including MacArthur of Battan, Hotel Jefferson-Clinton, Syracuse, N.Y.; Gen. George Rogers Clark, Louisville; 3 murals Hist. L.I, Suffolk County Savs. and Loan Bank, Babylon, L.I., Pony Express Nat. Meml. Mus., St. Joseph, Mo.; mural painting Brooklyn Bridge, Seamen's Ch. Inst., N.Y.C.; hist. picture map, Hotel Huntington, L.I., portraits and paintings in pvt. collections, U.S. and abroad; mil. artist, Engring. Bd., Ft. Belvoir, Va., combat artist, U.S. Coast Guard Hdqrs., Washington, originator, chmn., Navy Art Cooperation and Liaison Com. of Salmagundi Club. Founder, chmn. Coast Guard Art Program Salmagundi Club. Recipient Meritorious Pub. Svc. citation Dept. Navy, 1964; Louis E. Seley NACAL award, 1970; medal of honor Salmagundi Club, 1973; George Gray award U.S. Coast Guard, 1983. Life fellow Royal Soc. Arts (London); mem. Soc. Illustrators, Am. Mil. Inst., Am. Soc. Marine Artists, Co. Mil. Collectors and Historians, Nat. Soc. Mural Painters, Am. Vets. Soc. Artists, Am. Artists Profl. League, Nat. Hist. Soc. (founding mem.), Assn. Mil. Surgeons U.S., Navy League U.S. (Commodore Club), U.S. Naval Inst., Armed Forces Mgmt. Inst., Artists Fellowship, Arts Club (Washington), Salmagundi Club of N.Y. (originator, chmn. COGAP, Coast Guard art program of club). Address: Salmagundi Club 47 5th Ave New York NY 10003-4303

GRAY, GLENN OLIVER, lawyer; b. Charleston, S.C., Jan. 23, 1963; s. James Oliver and Julie (Frazier) G.; m. Glenda Faye Coleman, Aug. 26, 1989. BS, U. S.C., 1985, JD, 1989. Bar: S.C. 1989, N.J. 1990, N.Y. 1990, U.S. Dist. Ct. N.J. 1990, U.S. Dist. Ct. (so. and ea. dists.) N.Y. 1991, U.S. Ct. Appeals (2d and 3d cir.) 1993, U.S. Supreme Ct. 1995. Assoc. Dreisman & Gross, N.Y.C., 1989-91, Bower & Gardner, N.Y.C., 1991-94, Aaronson Rappeport Feinstein & Deutsch, N.Y.C., 1994-95; sr. atty. Jones Hirsch Connors & Bull, LLP, N.Y.C., 1995—. Bd. dirs., mem. Fund for City of N.Y., 1992-96; mem. U.S. Supreme Ct. Hist. Found., S.C. Bar Found. Mem. Am. Hosp. Assn., Nat. Bar Assn., Am. Corp. Counsel Assn., N.Y. State Bar Assn., S.C. Bar Assn., N.J. Bar Assn., N.Y. Med. Def. Bar Assn., N.Y. County Lawyers Assn., Charleston County Bar Assn., Masons (King Solomon Grand Lodge), Alpha Phi Alpha. Baptist. Avocations: golf, tennis, basketball, reading, travel. Office: Jones Hirsch Connors & Bull 101 E 52nd St Fl 22 New York NY 10022-6061

GRAY, GORDON L., communications educator; b. Hampton, Iowa, May 18, 1924; s. Leroy Ernest and Arianna (Oldham) G.; m. Barbara Ann Smith, Feb. 5, 1949; children: David Gordon, Jonathan William. B.A., Cornell Coll., 1948; M.A., Northwestern U., 1951, Ph.D., 1957. Radio announcer and newsman, 1948-50; broadcast coordinator NBC-TV, Chgo, 1951; instr. to asso. prof. television and radio Mich. State U., 1953-67; prof. communications Temple U., Phila., 1967-96, prof. emeritus, 1996—, chmn. dept. radio, TV, and Film, 1967-74, 78-82, 1994-95; program assoc. Ednl. TV and Radio Ctr., Ann Arbor, Mich., 1956-57. Served to staff sgt. AUS, 1943-46. Fulbright scholar Inst. Edn. U. Leeds, U.K., 1965-66.

GRAY, GWEN CASH, real estate broker; b. Cowpens, S.C., Oct. 24, 1943; d. Woodrow C. and Marie (Hamrick) Cash; m. Charles H. Gray, Oct. 24, 1987 ; children: Dianne Marie Young, Teena Michele Bulman. BS, Limestone Coll., Gaffney, S.C., 1984. Real estate sales rep., owner and broker-in-charge Southers Real Estate, Spartanburg, S.C.; bd. dirs. Nations Bank Gaffney; lectr. in field. Contbr. articles to profl. jours. Advisor S.C. Peach Festival, Gaffney, 1977—, Clemson U. Extension Svc., 1987—. Named Woman of Yr. Bus. and Profl. Women, 1979, Woman of Yr. S.C. Rural Electric Coop., 1984, Career Woman of Yr. Breakfast Club Spartanburg Bus. and Profl. Club, 1997. Mem. Am. Farm Bur., Nat. Bd. Realtors, S.C. Farm Bur., S.C. Bd. Realtors, Spartanburg Bd. Realtors (pres. 1998, Realtor of Yr. 1997), S.C. Hort. Soc. (bd. dirs.), S.C. Assn. Agr. Agts. (Friend of Extension award 1986), Spartanburg Multiple Listing Svc. (bd. dirs.). Baptist. Democrat. Avocations: reading, tech. coll. teaching. Office: Southers Real Estate 223 E Blackstock Rd Spartanburg SC 29301-2633

GRAY, HANNA HOLBORN, history educator; b. Heidelberg, Germany, Oct. 25, 1930; d. Hajo and Annemarie (Bettmann) Holborn; m. Charles Montgomery Gray, June 19, 1954. AB, Bryn Mawr Coll., 1950; PhD, Harvard U., 1957; MA, Yale U., 1971, LLD, 1978; LittD (hon.), St. Lawrence U., 1974, Oxford (Eng.) U., 1979; LLD (hon.), Dickinson Coll., 1979, U. Notre Dame, 1980, Marquette U., 1984; LittD (hon.), Washington U., 1985; HHD (hon.), St. Mary's Coll., 1974; LHD (hon.), Grinnell (Iowa) Coll., 1974, Lawrence U., 1974, Denison U., 1974, Wheaton Coll., 1976, Marlboro Coll., 1979, Rikkyo (Japan) U., 1979, Roosevelt U., 1980, Knox Coll., 1980, Coe Coll., 1981, Thomas Jefferson U., 1981, Duke U., 1982, New Sch. for Social Research, 1982, Clark U., 1982, Brandeis U., 1983, Colgate U., 1983, Wayne State U., 1984, Miami U., Oxford, Ohio, 1984, So. Meth. U., 1984, CUNY, 1985, U. Denver, 1985, Am. Coll. Greece, 1986, Muskingum Coll., 1987, Rush Presbyn. St. Lukes Med. Ctr., 1987, NYU, 1988, Rosemont Coll., 1988, Claremont U. Ctr. Grad Sch., 1989, Moravian Coll., 1991, Rensselaer Poly. Inst., 1991, Coll. William and Mary, 1991, Centre Coll., 1991, Macalester Coll., 1993, McGill U., 1993, Ind. U., 1994, Med. U. of S.C., 1994; LLD (hon.), Union Coll., 1975, Regis Coll., 1976, Dartmouth Coll., 1978, Trinity Coll., 1978, U. Bridgeport, 1978, Dickinson Coll., 1979, Brown U., 1979, Wittenburg U., 1979, Dickinson Coll., 1979, U. Rochester, 1980, U. Notre Dame, 1980, U. So. Calif., 1980, U. Mich., 1981, Princeton U., 1982, Georgetown U., 1983, Marquette U., 1984, W.Va. Wesleyan U., 1985, Hamilton Coll., 1985, Smith Coll., 1986, U. Miami, 1986, Columbia U., 1987, NYU, 1988, Rosemont Coll., 1988, U. Toronto, Can., 1991; LDH, U. Del., 1994, Haverford Coll., 1995, Tulane U., 1995; LLD, Harvard U., 1995; LHD, McGill U., 1993, Macalester Coll., 1993, Ind. U., 1994, Med. U. S.C., 1994, Haverford Coll., 1995, Tulane U., 1995; LLD, Harvard U., 1995, U. Chgo., 1996. Instr. Bryn Mawr Coll., 1953-54; teaching fellow Harvard, 1955-57, instr., 1957-59, asst. prof., 1959-60, vis. lectr., 1963-64; asst. prof. U. Chgo., 1961-64, asso. prof., 1964-72; dean, prof. Northwestern U., Evanston, Ill., 1972-74; provost, prof. history Yale U., 1974-78, acting pres., 1977-78; pres. U. Chgo., Ill., 1978-93; prof. dept. history U. Chgo., 1978—, Harry Pratt Judson disting. svc. prof. history, 1994—; bd. dirs. Cummins Engine Co., J.P. Morgan & Co., Morgan Guaranty Trust Co., Ameritech; fellow Center for Advanced Study in Behavioral Scis., 1966-67, vis. scholar, 1970-71; vis. prof. U. Calif., Berkeley, 1970-71. Editor: (with Charles Gray) Jour. Modern History, 1965-70; contbr. articles to profl. jours. Mem. Nat. Coun. on Humanities, 1972-78; trustee Yale Corp., 1971-74; fellow Harvard Corp.; chmn. bd. Howard Hughes Med. Inst., Marlboro Sch. Music; chmn. bd. dirs. Andrew W. Mellon Found.; mem. bd. regents The Smithsonian Instn. Decorated Grosse Verdienstkreuz (Germany); fellow Newberry Libr., 1960-61, hon. fellow St. Anne's Coll., Oxford (Eng.) U., 1978—; Fulbright scholar, 1950-51; recipient Grad. medal Radcliffe Coll., 1976, Yale medal, 1978, Medal of Liberty award, 1986, Medal of Freedom, 1991, Frontrunner award Sara Lee, 1991, Laureate Lincoln Acad. Ill., 1988, Charles Frankel prize, 1993, Centennial medal Harvard U., 1994; Disting. Svc. award in edn. Inst. Internat. Edn., 1994. Fellow Am. Acad. Arts and Scis.; mem. Renaissance Soc. Am., Am. Philos. Soc. (Jefferson medal 1993), Nat. Acad. Edn., Coun. Fgn. Rels. Chgo., Coun. on Fgn. Rels. N.Y. (bd. dirs.), Phi Beta Kappa (vis. scholar 1971-72). Office: U Chgo Dept History 1126 E 59th St Chicago IL 60637-1580

GRAY, HARRY BARKUS, chemistry educator; b. Woodburn, Ky., Nov. 14, 1935; s. Barkus and Ruby (Hopper) G.; m. Shirley Barnes, June 2, 1957; children: Victoria Lynn, Andrew Thomas, Noah Harry Barkus. BS, Western Ky. U., 1957; PhD, Northwestern U., 1960, DSc (hon.), 1984; DSc (hon.), U. Chgo., 1987, U. Rochester, 1987, U. Paul Sabatier, 1991, U. Göteborg, 1991, U. Firenze, 1993, Columbia U., 1994, Bowling Green State U., 1994, Ill. Wesleyan, 1995, Oberlin Coll., 1996, U. Ariz., 1997. Postdoctoral fellow U. Copenhagen, 1960-61; faculty Columbia U., 1961-66, prof., 1965-66; prof. chemistry Calif. Inst. Tech., Pasadena, 1966—; now Arnold O. Beckman prof. chemistry and dir. Beckman Inst. Calif. Inst. Tech.; vis. prof. Rockefeller U., Harvard U., U. Iowa, Pa. State U., Yeshiva U., U. Copenhagen, U. Witwatersrand, Johannesburg, South Africa, U. Canterbury, Christchurch, New Zealand; George Eastman prof. Oxford U., U.K., 1997-98; cons. govt., industry; Kistiakowsky lectr. Harvard U., 1999. Author: Electrons and Chemical Bonding, 1965, Molecular Orbital Theory, 1965, Ligand Substitution Processes, 1966, Basic Principles of Chemistry, 1967, Chemical Dynamics, 1968, Chemical Principles, 1970, Models in Chemical Science, 1971, Chemical Bonds, 1973, Chemical Structure and Bonding, 1980, Molecular Electronic Structures, 1980, Braving the Elements, 1995. Recipient Franklin Meml. award Stanford U., 1967, Fresenius award Phi Lambda Upsilon, 1970, Shoemaker award U. Louisville, 1970, award for excellence in teaching Mfg. Chemists Assn., 1972, Centenary medal of Royal Soc. Chemistry, 1985, Nat. Medal of Sci., 1986, Alfred Bader Bioinorganic Chemistry award, 1990, Gold medal Am. Inst. Chemists, 1990, Linderstrom-Lang Prize, 1992, Priestley award Dickinson Coll., 1991, Chandler medal Columbia U., 1999; named Calif. Scientist of Yr., 1988, Achievement Rewards for Coll. Scis. Man of Sci., 1990; Guggenheim fellow, 1972-73; Phi Beta Kappa scholar, 1973-74. Fellow AAAS; mem. NAS, Am. Chem. Soc. (award pure chemistry 1970, award inorganic chemistry 1978, award for disting. service in advancement of inorganic chemistry 1984, Harrison Howe award 1972, Remsen Meml. award 1979, Tolman medal 1979, Pauling medal 1986, Priestley medal 1991, Willard Gibbs medal 1992), Royal Danish Acad. Scis. and Letters, Alpha Chi Sigma, Phi Lambda Upsilon. Home: 1415 E California Blvd Pasadena CA 91106-4101 Office: Calif Inst Tech Chemistry 127-72 1201 E California Blvd Pasadena CA 91125-0001

GRAY, HARRY JOSHUA, electrical engineer, educator; b. St. Louis, June 24, 1924; s. Harry Joshua and Mary Margaret (Davis) G.; m. Cecilia M. McNulty, Apr. 23, 1949; children—Margaret, Cecilia, Kathleen (dec.), Mary. Student, Lehigh U., 1941-43; B.S.E.E., U. Pa., 1944, Ph.D., 1953. Registered profl. engr., Pa. Instr. The Moore Sch. Elec. Engring., U. Pa., Phila., 1947-51, assoc., 1951-53, asst. prof., 1953-54, assoc. prof., 1957-64, prof. elec. engring. and computer and info. sci., 1964-89, prof. emeritus elec. engring., 1989—; mem. ENIAC staff, 1947; with Remington Rand Univac, Phila., 1954-57; cons. in field; bd. dirs. Pa. Research Assocs., Inc., 1963. Contbr. articles to profl. jours.; author: Digital Computer Engineering, 1963, High Speed Digital Circuits and Memories, 1976. Served with USN, 1943-46. Grantee U.S. Army Electronics Command, 1966-69, NSF, 1966-68, NIMH, 1971-73, Burroughs Corp., 1973-75; medalist ENIAC, 50th Anniv., 1997. Mem. IEEE (IEEE Profl. Groups, life mem. EMC group), Sigma Xi, Tau Beta Pi, Eta Kappa Nu, Pi Mu Epsilon, Phi Eta Sigma. Patentee in field.

GRAY, HELEN THERESA GOTT, religion editor; b. Jersey City, July 2, 1942; d. William E. and Cynthia B. (Williams) Gott; m. David L. Gray, Aug. 15, 1976; 1 child, David Lee Jr. BA, Syracuse U., 1963; M in Internat. Affairs, Columbia U., 1965. Editor religion sect. The Kansas City (Mo.) Star, 1971—; owner Pub. Co. and Christian Bookstore; tchr. Bible sch. Pleasant Green Bapt. Ch., Kansas City, Kans., 1975—, counselor, 1978—. Co-author, editor several books; contbr. articles. Recipient writing award Valley Forge Freedom Found., 1967-97; John Hay Whitney Found. grantee, 1963-64; named 100 Most Influential African Ams. in Greater Kansas City. Mem. Religion Newswriters Assn., Kansas City Assn. Black Journalists (life achievement award 1998). Office: The Kansas City Star 1729 Grand Blvd Kansas City MO 64108-1458

GRAY, HERBERT ESER, Canadian government official; b. Windsor, Ont., Can., May 25, 1931; s. Harry and Fannie G.; ed. Kennedy Coll. Inst., Windsor, McGill U. Grad. Sch. Commerce, Montreal, Que., Can., Osgoode Hall Law Sch., Toronto, Ont.; m. Sharon Sholzberg, July 23, 1967; children: Jonathan, Elizabeth Anne. Mem. Ho. of Commons for Windsor W., Ottawa, Ont., 1962—, chmn. standing com. on fin., trade and econ. affairs, 1966-68, served as Parliamentary sec. to Min. of Fin., 1968-69, named min. without portfolio, 1969, min. of nat. revenue, 1970-72, min. of consumer and corp. affairs, 1972-74, min. of industry, trade and commerce, 1980-82, min. regional econ. expansion, 1982-84, pres. of Treasury Bd., 1982-84, opposition ho. leader, 1984-90, dep. leader opposition, 1989-90, leader opposition, 1990, fin. critic off. opposition, 1979, 91-93, leader gov. Ho. Commons, solicitor gen. of Can., 1993-97, dep. prime min., 1997—; min. Millennium Bur. Can., 1998—; has served as mem. Can. dels. to various internat. confs. on econ. and other matters; del. IMF and World Bank meetings, 1967, 69, 70; co-chmn. Can. Del. to OECD Ministerial meeting, 1970; leader Can. Del. to Commonwealth Fin. Mins. meeting, 1970. Windsor pres. Jaycees, 1961-62. Club: Richelieu. Lodge: B'nai Brith. Office: House of Commons, Rm 209-S Centre Block, Ottawa, ON Canada K1A 0A6

GRAY, INA TURNER, fraternal organization administrator; b. Eagleville, Mo., July 25, 1926; d. Farris T. and Teloir (Anderson) Turner; m. Wallace G. Gray Jr., Dec. 18, 1948; children: Toni Jo, Tara Joy. BS with high honors, Cen. Meth. Coll., 1948; MA, Scarritt Coll., 1952; postgrad., U. Hawaii, 1969. Tchr. Rutherford-Met. Sch. Bus., Dallas, 1948-49; dir. Christian edn. 1st Meth. Ch., Lawton, Okla., 1953-54, Winfield, Kans., 1957-58; dir. religious life Southwestern Coll., Winfield, 1958-59; dir. commn. on archives and history Kans. West Conf., Winfield, 1960-78; exec. dir. Pi Gamma Mu, Winfield, 1976-96; English tchr. JoGakuin Jr. High, Hiroshima, Japan, 1971-72, Kitakyushu U., Japan, 1997-98. Mem. editorial bd. Fire on the Prairie, 1961-69; mem. editorial and pub. coms. The Lure of Kansas, 1990. Mem. Assn. Coll. Honor Socs. (del. 1986-96), Commn. Archives and History (local Ch. History award 1982—), Kans. State Assn. Parliamentarians (v.p. Walnut Valley unit 1991-92, 99—), Faculty Dames (pres. 1981-82). Republican. Avocations: travel, hist. research. Home: 1701 Winfield Ave Winfield KS 67156-1919

GRAY, J. CHARLES, lawyer, cattle rancher; b. Leesburg, Fla., Mar. 26, 1932; s. G. Wayne and Mary Evelyn (Albright) G.; m. Saundra Hagood, Aug. 18, 1955; children: Terese Ren, John Charles Jr., Lee Jerome. BA, U. Fla., 1955, JD, 1958. Bar: Fla. 1958. County atty. Orange County (Fla.), 1978-85; chmn. Gray, Harris & Robinson, P.A.; chmn. Fla. Turnpike Authority, 1965-67; city solicitor City of Orlando (Fla.), 1960-61; pres. Santa Gertrudis Breeders Internat., 1981-83. Chmn. Pres.'s Council Advisors, U. Central Fla., 1978-84; pres. U. Cen. Fla. Found., 1990-91; pres. Orange County U. Fla. Alumni Assn., Pi Kappa Alpha Alumni Assn.; past dist. v.p. U. Fla. Alumni Assn.; mem. U. Fla. Pres.'s Council; mem. Com. of 100; founding bd. dirs. Fla. Epilepsy Found.; chmn. Econ. Devel. Commn. Mid. Fla., 1987-89; mem. Fla. Econ. Devel. Adv. Coun. Mem. U. Fla. Hall of Fame. Mem. ABA, Orange County Bar Assn., Fla. Bar Assn., Fla. Blue Key, Phi Alpha Delta, Pi Kappa Alpha. Republican. Episcopalian. Clubs: University (past dir.), Citrus Club of Orlando (dir.), U. Club of Orlando. Home: PO Box 3068 Orlando FL 32802-3068 Office: 201 E Pine St Ste 1200 Orlando FL 32801-2725

GRAY, JAMES, English literature educator; b. Montrose, Scotland, May 11, 1923; s. James and Matilda (Smythe) G.; m. Pamela Doris Knight, July 26, 1947; 1 child, Caroline Gordon. M.A., U. Aberdeen, 1946; B.A. with honours, U. Oxford, Eng., 1948, M.A., 1951; Ph.D., U. Montreal, 1970. Prof. English Bishops U., Lennoxville, Que., Can., 1948-72, chmn. humanities div., 1971-72; prof., chmn. dept. English Dalhousie U., Halifax, N.S., 1972-75, dean Faculty Arts and Sci., 1975-80, Thomas McCulloch prof. English, 1980-88, prof. emeritus, 1988—; mem. Humanities Resch. Coun. Can.; vis. prof. Queen's U., Kingston, Ont., 1955, 70, U. B.C., 1958, Acadia U., 1991. Author: The Sermons of Samuel Johnson: A Study, 1972; co-editor: The Religious Writings of Samuel Johnson, 1978; mem. editorial bd.; Yale U. Press edit. Works of Samuel Johnson; contbr. articles to profl. jours. Served with Brit. and Indian Armies, 1942-46. Recipient Queen Elizabeth II Coronation medal, Jubilee medal. Fellow Royal Soc. Arts, Royal Soc. Can.; mem. Can. Inst. Internat. Affairs (br. pres.), MLA, English Inst., Am. Assn. for Eighteenth Century Studies, Can. Assn. for Eighteenth Century Studies, Internat. Assn. for Eighteenth Century Studies, Assn. Can. Univ. Tchrs. English (pres. 1982-84), Humanities Assn. Can. (past pres.). Mem. Liberal Party. Presbyterian. Club: University Faculty. Home: Ward MTN RR 2, 3856 Prospect Rd, Kentville, NS Canada B4N 3V8 Office: Dalhousie U, Dept English, Halifax, NS Canada B3H 3J5

GRAY, JAMES GORDON, JR., speech educator; b. Bedford, Va., Oct. 3, 1945; s. James and Cova Iris (Dooley) G. BA, U. Richmond, 1969; MA, Am. U., 1976. Prof. speech comm. Montgomery Coll., Germantown, Md., 1986—. Author: Technical Presentations, 1986, Managing Corporate Image, 1986, The Winning Image, 1993. Republican. Episcopalian. Avocations: astronomy, writing. Home: 7510 Old Chester Rd Bethesda MD 20817-6163

GRAY, JAMES LARRY, metals company executive; b. Southmayd, Tex., Dec. 17, 1932; s. Cecil Lawray and Coquese Adeline (Coe) G.; student Tex. Tech. U., 1954, So. Meth. U., 1956; MBA, Pepperdine U., 1978. Sales engr. Simplex Wire & Cable, Cambridge, Mass., 1958-63; pres. Integral Corp., Dallas, 1963-97; pres. Cern Internat. Corp., 1997—. Served with U.S. Army, 1956-58. Mem. IEEE, Sigma Alpha Epsilon. Republican. Club: Toastmasters (pres. 1966-67), Jaycees (v.p. 1969-70). Home: 5323 Rock Cliff Pl Dallas TX 75205 Office: 3878 Oak Lawn Ave # 100b-325 Dallas TX 75219-4460

GRAY, JAMES PATRICK, business executive, consultant, educator; b. Yonkers, N.Y., Oct. 27, 1958; s. James and Joan Frances (Saverese) G.; m. Lucy Marie Simoncic, July 26, 1985. BIE, Cleve. State U., 1982; MBA, Case Western Reserve U., 1987. Indsl. engr., project mgr. TRW, Inc., Cleve., 1980-87; gen. mgr. Ajax Mfg., Cleve., 1988-92; prin. J. P. Gray & Assocs., Chesterland, Ohio, 1991—; v.p. bus. devel. The Mentor Group, Mentor, Ohio, 1993-94; dir. SMR Bus. Svcs., Mayfield Village, Ohio, 1996—; advisor Cleve. Coun. Smaller Enterprises, 1987—; contbr. Penton Pub., Cleve., 1992; adj. quality instr. Lakeland C.C., Kirtland, 1993—. Mem. Inst. Indsl. Engr. (sr.), Am. Soc. for Quality (cert.), Inst. Mgmt. Cons., Turn-around Mgmt. Assn., Cleve. Tech. Socs. Coun. Office: 6685 Beta Dr Cleveland OH 44143-2320

GRAY, JAN CHARLES, lawyer, business owner; b. Des Moines, June 15, 1947; s. Charles Donald and Mary C. Gray; 1 child, Charles Jan. BA in Econs., U. Calif., Berkeley, 1969; MBA, Pepperdine U., 1986; JD, Harvard U., 1972. Bar: Calif. 1972, D.C. 1974, Wyo. 1992. Law clk. Kindel & Anderson, L.A., 1971-72; assoc. Halstead, Baker & Sterling, L.A., 1972-75; sr. v.p., gen. counsel and sec. Ralphs Grocery Co., L.A., 1975-97; pres. Am. Presidents Resorts, Custer, S.D., Casper/Glenrock, Wyo., 1983—; owner Big Bear (Calif.) Cabins-Lakeside, 1988—; pres. Mt. Rushmore Broadcasting, Inc., 1991—; owner Sta. KGOS/KERM, Torrington, Wyo., 1993—, Sta. KRAL/KIQZ, Rawlins, Wyo., 1993—, Sta. KZMX, Hot Springs, S.D., 1993—, Sta. KFCR, Custer, S.D., 1992—, Sta. KQLT-FM, Casper, Wyo., 1994—, Sta. KASS-FM, Casper, 1995—, Sta. KVOC-AM, Casper, 1997—, KAWK-FM, Rapid City, S.D., 1997—, KHOC, Casper, Wyo., 1998—; judge pro tem L.A. Mcpl. Ct., 1977-85; instr. bus. UCLA, 1976-85, Pepperdine MBA Program, 1983-85; arbitrator Am. Arbitration Assn., 1977-97; media spokesman So. Calif. Grocers Assn., 1979-90, Calif. Grocers Assn., 1979-97, Calif. Retailers Assn., 1979-97; real estate broker, Calif., 1973—. Contbg. author: Life or Death, Who Controls?, 1976; contbr. articles to profl. jours. Trustee South Bay U. Coll. Law, 1978-79; mem. bd. visitors Southwestern U. Sch. Law, 1983—; mem. L.A. County Pvt. Industry Coun., 1982-96, exec. com. 1984-88, chmn. econ. devel. task force, 1986-89, chmn. mktg. com. 1991-93; mem. L.A. County Martin Luther King, Jr. Gen. Hosp. Authority, 1984—; mem. L.A. County Aviation Commn, 1986-92, chmn., 1990-91; L.A. Police Crime Prevention Adv. Coun., 1986—; Angelus Plaza Adv. Bd., 1983-85; bd. dirs. RecyCAL of So. Calif., 1983-89; trustee Santa Monica Hosp. Found., 1986-91, adv. bd., 1991—; mem. L.A. County Dem. Cen. Com., 1980-90, L.A. City Employees' Retirement System Comsn., 1993—; del. Dem. Nat. Conv., 1980. Recipient So. Calif. Grocers Assn. award for outstanding contbns. to food industry, 1982, appreciation award for No on 11 Campaign, Calif./Nev. Soft Drink Assn., 1983; Tyler Price Meml. award Mex.-Am. Grocers Assn., 1995, Radio Affiliate of Yr.-Classic Rock ABC, 1998. Mem. ABA, Calif. Bar Assn., L.A. County Bar Assn. (exec. com. corp. law depts. sect. 1974-76, 79—, chmn. 1989-90, exec. com. barristers sect. 1974-75, 79-81, trustee 1991-93, jud. evaluation com. 1993—, nominating com. 1994), San Fernando Valley Bar Assn. (chmn. real property sect. 1975-77, L.A. Pub. Affairs Officers Assn., L.A. World Affairs Coun., Calif. Retailers Assn. (supermarket com.), Food Mktg. Inst. (govt. rels. com. 1977-97, benefits coun. 1993-97, chmn. lawyers and economists 1993-95), So. Calif. Bus. Assn. (bd. dirs. 1981—, mem. exec. com. 1982—, sec. 1986-91, chair 1991—), Town Hall L.A., U. Calif. Alumni Assn., Ephebian Soc. L.A., Harvard Club of So. Calif., L.A. Athletic Club, Petroleum Club, Casper Country Club, Phi Beta Kappa. Home: 2793 Creston Dr Los Angeles CA 90068-2209 Office: PO Box 2515 Casper WY 82602-2515 also: PO Box 3328 Hollywood CA 90078

GRAY, JOHN DELTON, retired manufacturing company executive; b. Ontario, Oreg., July 29, 1919; s. Elmer R. and Mabel (Ridgley) G.; m. Elizabeth Neuner, Jan. 4, 1946; children: Anne, Joan, Janet, John Richard, Laurie. B.Secretarial Sci., Oreg. State Coll., 1940; M.B.A., Harvard U., 1947; LL.D., Lewis and Clark Coll., 1967. Asst. to pres. Pointer-Willamette Co., Portland, 1947; asst. gen. mgr. Oreg. Saw Chain Corp. (now Omark Industries, Inc.), Portland, 1948-50; gen. mgr. Oreg. Saw Chain Corp. (now Omark Industries, Inc.), 1950-53, pres., gen. mgr., 1953-67, chmn. bd., 1961-83, vice chmn. bd., 1983-85; chmn. Textronix, Inc., 1985-87, ret., 1987; chmn. Grayco Resources, Inc.; bd. dirs. Precision Castparts Corp., Standard Ins. Co. Past pres. Portland area coun. Boy Scouts Am., 1959-61; past mem. exec., past pres. Columbia-Pacific Coun.; Trustee Com. Econ. Devel., 1967-81; pres. Oreg. Community Found., 1990; mem. Oreg. Progress Bd., 1989-91; mem. Chief Execs. Orgn., 1969—; trustee Reed Coll., Portland, 1961—, chmn., 1968-82; chmn. steering com. Capital Campaign, 1983-88; trustee Oreg. Grad. Inst. Lt. col. AUS, 1941-46. Decorated Bronze Star medal; recipient Silver Beaver award Portland Area council Boy Scouts Am. Republican. Episcopalian. Lodge: Rotary. Office: Grayco Resources Inc 5331 SW Macadam Ave Ste 200 Portland OR 97201-3889

GRAY, JOHN LATHROP, III, retired advertising agency executive; b. N.Y.C., Apr. 9, 1931; s. John L. and Eleanor R. (Snow) G.; m. Cynthia Hunt, June 13, 1953; children: Lisa L., Phyllis H.; m. Frances W. Pratt, Sept. 22, 1967; stepchildren: Robert T., Duncan P., Theodore P. Hennes. B.S., Yale U., 1953. Media planner J. Walter Thompson, N.Y.C., 1956-60, media supr., 1961-66, v.p., assoc. media dir., 1966-77, v.p., group media dir., 1978-80, sr. v.p., dir. media planning, 1980-90, sr. v.p., media dir., 1991-93; ret., 1993. Served with U.S. Army, 1953-56. Mem. Am. Assn. Advt. Agencies. Republican. Episcopalian. Club: Apawamis (Rye, N.Y.).

GRAY, JOHN WALKER, mathematician, educator; b. St. Paul, Oct. 3, 1931; s. Clarence Walker and Helen (Ewald) G.; m. Eva Maria Wirth, Dec. 30, 1957; children—Stephen, Theodore, Elisabeth. BA, Swarthmore Coll., 1953; PhD, Stanford U., 1957. Temp. mem. Inst. for Advanced Study, Princeton, N.J., 1957-59; Ritt instr. Columbia U., 1959-62; asst. prof. math. U. Ill., Urbana, 1962-64; asso. prof. U. Ill., 1964-66, prof., 1966—, dir. grad. studies, 1995—; organizer Category Theory Session, Oberwolfach, Germany, 1971, 72, 73, 75, 77, 79. Contbr. to: Springer Lecture Notes in Mathematics, 1974. NSF sr. fellow, 1966-67; Fulbright-Hays sr. lectr., 1975-76. Mem. Am. Math. Soc., AAAS. Home: 303 W Michigan Ave Urbana IL 61801-4945 Office: U Ill Dept Math Urbana IL 61801

GRAY, JOHNNY, track and field athlete, Olympic athlete; b. L.A., June 19, 1960. Student, L.A. C.C., 1979, Santa Monica (Calif.) C.C., 1980. Olympic track and field participant Barcelona, Spain, 1992; track and field athlete Goodwill Games, 1996, 98. Recipient 800m Track and Field Bronze medal Olympics, Barcelona, 1992. Office: US Track and Field 1 Rca Dome Ste 140 Indianapolis IN 46225-1023*

GRAY, JONI NADINE, state agency administrator; b. St. Joseph, Mo., Mar. 24, 1959; d. Albert Benjamin and M. Nadine (Harris) G.; children: John Charles, Haley Brooke, Jordan Roselle Gray-DeKraai. BA in Psychology, U. Nebr., 1982, JD, MA in Psychology, 1990. Rsch. policy analyst Gov.'s Policy Rsch. Office, Lincoln, 1985-86; dir. trainee Lancaster Comty. Mental Health Ctr., Lincoln, 1987-88; policy analyst Ea. Nebr. Comty. Office of Mental Health, Omaha, 1989; sys. developer Ctr. for Children, Families and the Law, Lincoln, 1989-90; law and psychology instr. U. Nebr., Lincoln, 1987, 90-91; rschr., analyst Nebr. Advocacy Svcs., Lincoln, 1993-94; policy analyst Ctr. for Children, Families and the Law, Lincoln, 1993-94; mental health program specialist Dept. Pub. Instns., Lincoln, 1995-96; exec. dir. Nebr. Commn. on Status of Women, Lincoln, 1996—; mem. adv. bd. Child Care and Early Childhood Edn. Coord. Com., Lincoln, 1996—, Nebr. Ctr. for Women, York, 1996—, Nebr. chpt. Nat. Mgr.'s Assn., Lincoln, 1996—. 1st author: Ethical and Legal Issues in AIDS Research, 1995; contbr. chpt. to book. Recipient Nat. Rsch. Svc. award NIMH, 1984-87, 92-93, Am. Jurisprudence award, 1989. Mem. Am. Psychology-Law Soc. (newsletter columnist 1984-85), Alpha Lambda Delta, Phi Eta Sigma. Office: Nebr Commn on Status of Women PO Box 94985 301 Centennial Mall S Lincoln NE 68508-2529

GRAY, JUDITH LYNN, adult nurse practitioner, rehabilitation nurse; b. Kansas City, Mo., Jan. 13, 1947; d. Claude Lynford and Opal Virginia (Giesler) Richardson; m. Michael Scott, Sept. 7, 1969; 1 child, Douglas Matthew. Student, U. Guam; AS, County Coll. Morris, 1976; MSN, George Mason U., 1993, George Mason U., 1993. RN, Va.; cert. adult nurse practitioner. Head nurse SCI unit N.J. Rehab., Orange, 1991-94; clin. asst. Sch. Nursing, U. Guam, Mangilao, 1981-85; clin. nurse III neuro. rehab. CVA, TBI, SCI Mt. Vernon Hosp., Alexandria, Va., 1985-87, 91-93, rehab. liaison, 1988-91. Mem. People to People Citizens Ambassador Program, Russia, Poland, Yugoslavia. Mem. ARN, VARN, George Mason U. Alumni Assn., Sigma Theta Tau. Home: 5500 De Soto St Burke VA 22015-2055 Office: Nat Rehab Hosp Stroke Recovery Unit 102 Irving St NW Washington DC 20010-2949

GRAY, KARLA MARIE, state supreme court justice. BA, Western Mich. U., MA in African History; JD, Hastings Coll. of Law, San Francisco, 1976. Bar: Mont. 1976, Calif. 1977. Law clk. to Hon. W. D. Murray U.S. Dist. Ct., 1976-77; staff atty. Atlantic Richfield Co., 1977-81; pvt. practice law Butte, Mont., 1981-84; staff atty., legis. lobbyist Mont. Power Co., Butte, 1984-91; justice Supreme Ct. Mont., Helena, 1991—. Mem. Mont. Supreme Ct. Gender Fairness Task Force. Fellow Am. Bar Found., Am. Judicature Soc., Internat. Women's Forum; mem. State Bar Mont., Silver Bow County Bar Assn. (past pres.), Nat. Assn. Women Judges. Avocations: travel, reading, piano, family genealogy, cross-country skiing. Office: Supreme Ct Mont Justice Bldg 215 N Sanders St Helena MT 59620

GRAY, KATHERINE, marriage and family counselor and support therapist, writer, educator; b. L.A., July 6, 1941; d. Edward David and Marjorie Ross; m. Daniel C. Gray, Feb. 5, 1965; children: Michael, Lisa. BA, Calif. State U., Sacramento, 1983; MS in Ednl. Cons. and Counseling, Calif. State U., 1987, MS in Sch. Counseling. Instr. Shasta Coll., Redding, Calif., 1965-69; owner Water Ojai (Calif.) Valley Chapel, 1971-77, Lipp & Sullivan, Marysville, Calif., 1978—; instr. Yuba Coll., 1988—; pres. Interagy. Coun., 1988—; cons. and organizer various cmty. outreach programs in edn. Contbr. articles to profl. jours. and newspapers. County coord., bd. dirs. Am. Cancer Soc., Marysville, 1980—; mem. exec. com., bd. dirs., com. chairperson Gateway Projects, Yuba City, Calif., 1980—; bd. dirs. Mercy Guild, Yuba City, 1980—, Easter Seals; past bd. dirs., com. chairperson Campfire, Inc., Yuba City and Morro Bay, Calif., 1979-80; past pres. Ojai Valley-Oxnard Symphony Orch. Assn., Ventura County, Calif., 1975; Sacramento focus program coord. 4-H, Yuba and Sutter Counties, 1985—; exec. officer, bd. dirs. Gateway Projects, 1985-87; pres. Interagy. Coun. of Yuba and Sutter Counties, 1988—. Recipient, Presdl. Awd. for Outstanding Performance and Contribution of Svc., awds. granted for svc. on bd. and as an ofcr. on grad. stud. counc. and numerous univ. coms., Lipp & Sullivan. Mem. Calif. Funeral Dirs. Assn. (mem. legis. bd. com., edn., ethics and mem. bd. com.), Calif. Assn. for Counseling and Devel., Sacramento Area Gifted Assn., Children's Home Soc. (chpt. bd. sec.), Soroptimists (officer, bd. dirs.), Rainbow for Girls (pres., bd. dirs. 1985-87). Avocations: music, art, travel, historical studies. Home: PO Box 611 Yuba City CA 95992-0611 Office: PO Box 148 629 D St Marysville CA 95901-5527

GRAY, KIRK LAMOND, social investment firm executive, anthropologist; b. Keene, N.H., Mar. 9, 1948; s. Norman Hamblin and Ann Elaine (Lamond) G. BA in Anthropology, Prescott Coll., 1969; MA in Anthropology, We. Mich. U., 1974. Site monitor The Rand Corp., Green Bay, Wis. and Santa Monica, Calif., 1973-78; regional dir. Common Cause, Washington, 1978-79; sr. adv. Quadel Consulting Corp., Bethesda, Md., 1980-81; dep. dir. housing and cmty. devel. divsn. Advanced Tech., Inc., Reston, Va., 1982-83; dir., founder Howland & Assocs., Ltd., McLean, Va., 1983-84; regional dir. US Dept. Housing and Urban Devel., Phila., 1984-89; program adv. office of asst. sec. US Dept. Housing and Urban Devel., Washington, 1988-89; founder, pres., CEO The Gray Group, Inc., Columbia, Md., 1990; chmn., CEO Cornerstone Housing, LLC, Columbia, Md., 1996—. Contbr. chpt. to book, articles to profl. jours. Mem. Chesapeake Bay Found., Annapolis, Md., 1992—; sustaining mem. Rep. Nat. Com., Washington, 1995. Recipient White House Commendation Office of Pres., Washington, 1989, Disting. Svc. award HUD, 1988, Disting. Alumnae award We. Mich. U., 1986. Fellow Soc. Applied Anthropology (mem. exec. com. 1984-87, 86—); mem. Washington Assn. Profl. Anthropologists (pres. 1982-84), Nat. Assn. Housing and Redevelopment Officials, Pa. Assn. Housing and Redevelopment Officials (Partnership award). Office: The Gray Group 7188 Cradlerock Way Ste 106 Columbia MD 21045-5066 also: Cornerstone Housing LLC 9841 Brokenland Pkwy Ste 208 Columbia MD 21046-3067

GRAY, LAMAN A., JR., thoracic surgeon, educator; b. Louisville, May 28, 1940; m. Julie Gray; children: Juliet, Alice, Virginia. B.A. with distinction in Chemistry, Wesleyan U., Middletown, Conn., 1963; M.D., Johns Hopkins U., 1967. Diplomate Am. Bd. Surgery, Am. Bd. Thoracic Surgery. Intern U. Mich. Hosp., Ann Arbor, 1967-68; resident in gen. surgery, 1968-72, resident in thoracic and cardiovascular surgery, 1972-74; practice medicine specializing in thoracic and cardiovascular surgery, Louisville, 1974—; asst. prof. surgery, div. thoracic and cardiovascular surgery U. Louisville, 1974-78, assoc. prof., 1978-84, prof., 1984—, dir. thoracic and cardiovascular surgery, 1976—; mem. staff Univ. Hosp., Norton's Children's Hosp., Ky. Bapt. Hosps., Meth. Hosp., Jewish Hosp., VA Hosp., Suburban Hosp.; presenter at profl. confs. Pioneer in heart transplant and use of ventricular assist devices in Ky. Contbr. numerous articles, abstracts to profl. publs., chpts. to books. Grantee Humana Inc., 1984-87. Mem. Am. Assn. Thoracic Surgery, Am. Coll. Cardiology (gov. Ky. chpt. 1992-95), Am. Coll. Chest Physicians (com. on cardiovascular surgery, pres. Ky. chpt. 1978-79), ACS, Am. Thoracic Soc., Am. Soc. Artificial Internal Organs, Innominate Soc. Med. History, Jefferson County Med. Soc., John Alexander Soc. (exec. com.), Ky. Surg. Soc., Ky. Thoracic Soc., Louisville Heart Assn. (pres. 1983-85), Louisville Medico-Chirurgical Soc., Louisville Surg. Soc., Med. Forum (v.p. 1976-77), Societe Internationale de Chirurgie, Soc. Thoracic Surgeons, So. Surg. Assn., So. Thoracic Surg. Assn. (exec. council 1983-84, chmn. membership com. 1983-84), Ky. Heart Assn. (research rev. com. 1975-79), Sigma Xi. Office: U Louisville Sch of Med Dept Surgery/Ste 1200 201 Abraham Flexner Way Louisville KY 40202*

GRAY, LAURA, human resources specialist. BA in Psychology, Cornell U., MA in in Edn.; postgrad., Pace U. Cert. neurolinguistic practitioner. V.p. Client Svcs. Consulting/Right Mgmt. Conss., Woodland Hills, Calif.; past dir. human resources Camino Healthcare, Mountainview, Calif.; past v.p. edn. Hosp. Coun. No. & Ctrl. Calif.; past dir. tng. & devel. Age Wave, Inc.; past mgmt. devel. dir. Am. Mgmt. Assn. Mellon Found. scholar; named Outstanding Performer of Yr., Tng. Dirs. Forum. Mem. ASTD, Soc. Human Resources Mgmt., Cornell Alumni Assn., Cornell Women's Networking Assn. Office: Client Svcs Consulting Ste 600 21031 Ventura Blvd Woodland Hills CA 91364

GRAY, LONNA IRENE, indemnity fund executive; b. Forsyth, Mont., Nov. 10, 1944; d. John Jr. and Inga (Hill) Gray; m. James Dodd, Nov. 26, 1964 (div. Oct. 1988); children: Sheri Dodd, James Dodd, Thaddeus Dodd. BS, Mont. State U., 1967; MPA, Boise State U., 1997. Workers compensation claims monitor Idaho State Ins. Fund, Boise, 1990-92; workers compensation claims examiner Indsl. Spl. Indemnity Fund, Boise, 1992-94, acting mgr., 1994-95, mgr., 1995—; mem. Gov.'s Adv. Com. on Workers Compensation, Boise, 1995—. Mem. Boise City Comprehensive Plan Com., 1993-96; founding mem. Log Cabin Lit. Ctr., Boise, 1996—; mem. Beaux

Arts Soc./Boise Art Mus., 1976—; mem. Boise City Planning and Zoning Commn., 1985—. Mem. Workers Compensation Surety Group (sec. 1994-95, pres. 1995-96), Bosie Adjusters Assn. (treas. 1995-96, v.p. 1996-97, pres. 1997—), City Club, Idaho Women's Network. Avocations: skiing, landscape design. Office: Indsl Spl Indemnity Fund 650 W State St Boise ID 83702-7701

GRAY, MARCIA LANETTE, health, physical education and recreation educator; b. Hampton, Va., Dec. 22, 1957; d. Henry Russell and Mildred Ann (Wilson) G. BS in Edn., Longwood Coll., 1980; MEd in Counseling, Coll. of William and Mary, 1990. Cert. health, phys. edn. and recreation tchr., Va. Health, phys. edn. and recreation tchr. Forest Glen H.S., Suffolk, Va., 1980-81, Booker T. Washington Intermediate Sch., Suffolk, Va., 1981-90, John F. Kennedy Mid. Sch., Suffolk, Va., 1990-92, Kilby Shores Elem. Sch., Suffolk, Va., 1992—; head dept. Booker T. Washington Intermediate Sch., 1982-90, John F. Kennedy Mid. Sch., 1990-93, Kilby Shores Elem. Sch., 1993—. Author: Kilby's Quest, 1994, Kilby's Quest II, 1995. Coord. for sch. Jump Rope for Heart, Tidewater, Va., 1982—. Tchr. of the Yr., Kilby Shores Elementary, 1992. Mem. Va. Assn. Health, Phys. Edn. and Recreation, Delta Psi Kappa, Kappa Delta Pi. Avocations: poetry, wood working, gardening, music. Office: Kilby Shores Elem 111 Kilby Shores Dr Suffolk VA 23434-6499

GRAY, MARVIN LEE, JR., lawyer; b. Pitts., May 9, 1945; s. Marvin L. and Frances (Stringfellow) G.; m. Jill Miller, Aug. 14, 1971; children: Elizabeth Ann, Carolyn Jill. AB, Princeton U., 1966; JD magna cum laude, Harvard U., 1969. Bar: Wash. 1973, U.S. Supreme Ct. 1977, Alaska 1984. Law clk. to judge U.S. Ct. Appeals, N.Y.C., 1969-70; law clk. to justice U.S. Supreme Ct., Washington, 1970-71; asst. U.S. atty. U.S. Dept. Justice, Seattle, 1973-76; ptnr. Davis Wright Tremaine, Seattle, 1976—; mng. ptnr., 1985-88; staff counsel Rockefeller Commn. on CIA Activities in U.S., Washington, 1974; lectr. trial practice U. Wash. Law Sch., Seattle, 1979-80. Lay reader Episcopal Ch. of Ascension, Seattle, 1982-94. Capt. USAF, 1971-73. Fellow Am. Coll. Trial Lawyers; mem. ABA, Am. Law Inst. Office: Davis Wright Tremaine 1501 4th Ave Ste 2600 Seattle WA 98101-1688*

GRAY, MARY WHEAT, statistician, lawyer; b. Hastings, Nebr., 1939; d. Neil C. and Lillie W. (Alves) Wheat; m. Alfred Gray, Aug. 20, 1964. AB summa cum laude, Hastings Coll., 1959; postgrad., J.W. Goethe U., Frankfurt, Fed. Republic Germany, 1959-60; M.A., U. Kans., 1962, Ph.D., 1964; J.D. summa cum laude, Am. U., 1979; LLD (hon.), U. Nebr., 1993; LHD (hon.), Hastings Coll., 1996. Bar: D.C. 1979, U.S. Supreme Ct. 1983, U.S. Dist. Ct., D.C. 1980. Physicist Nat. Bur. Standards, Washington, summers 1959-63; asst. instr. U. Kans., Lawrence, 1963-64; instr. dept. math. U. Calif., Berkeley, 1965; asst. prof. Calif. State U., Hayward, 1965-67; assoc. prof. Calif. State U., 1967-68; assoc. prof. dept. math., stats. and computer sci. Am. U., 1968-71, prof., 1971—, chmn. dept., 1977-79, 80-81, 83—; statis. cons. for govt. agys., univs. and pvt. firms, 1976—. Author: A Radical Approach to Algebra, 1970; Calculus with Finite Mathematics for Social Sciences, 1972; contbr. numerous articles to profl. jours. Nat. treas. dir. Women's Equity Action League, from 1981, pres., from 1982; bd. dirs. treas. ACLU, Montgomery County, Md.; mem. adv. com. D.C. Dept. Employment Services, 1983—; dir. Amnesty Internat. USA, 1985—, treas., 1988-93, chair, 1993—; mem. Commn. on Coll. Retirement, 1984-86; dir. Am.-Middle East Edn. Found., 1983—. Fulbright grantee, 1959-60; NSF fellow, 1963-64, NDEA fellow, 1960-63. Fellow AAAS (chmn. com. on women, com. on investments, com. on sci. freedom and responsibility); mem. AAUP (regional counsel 1984—, com. on acad. freedom 1978—, dir. Legal Def. Fund 1974-78, bd. dirs. Exxon Project on Salary Discrimination 1974-76, com. on status of women 1972-78, Georgina Smith award), Am. Math. Soc. (v.p. 1976-78, council 1973-78), Conf. Bd. Math. Scis. (chmn. com. on affirmative action 1977-78), Math. Assn. Am. (chmn. com. on sch. lectrs. 1973-75, vis. lectr. 1974—), Assn. for Women in Math (founding pres. 1971-74, exec. com. 1974-80, gen. counsel 1980—), D.C. Bar Assn. ABA, Am. Soc. Internat. Law, London Math. Soc., Societe de Mathematique de France, Brit. Soc. History of Math., Can. Soc. History of Math., Assn. Computing Machinery, N.Y. Acad. Scis., Am. Statis. Assn., Phi Beta Kappa, Sigma Xi, Phi Kappa Phi, Alpha Chi, Pi Mu Epsilon. Home: 6807 Connecticut Ave Chevy Chase MD 20815-4937 Office: Am U Math & Stats Dept Washington DC 20016

GRAY, MILTON HEFTER, lawyer; b. Chgo., Dec. 2, 1910; s. Jacob S. and Fannie (Hefter) G.; m. Florence Adele Subin, Apr. 12, 1937 (dec. Oct. 1991); children: Roberta (Mrs. Paul L. Katz), James. AB, Northwestern U., 1931, JD, 1934. Bar: Ill. 1934. Assoc., then ptnr. Gardner, Carton & Douglas, 1934-43; sole practice Chgo., 1943-60; sr. ptnr. Altheimer & Gray, Chgo. 1960—; co-drafter Ill. Not-for-Profit Corp. Act, 1945, Ill. Securities Law, 1953; spl. master City Savs. Assn., U.S. Dist. Ctr., 1973-78, Milw. R.R. reorgn., 1979-85; commr. Supreme Ct. Ill., 1957-62, 66-68, 70-73; corp. officer, dir.; lectr. Inst. Banking, 1943-45, U. Ill. Law Sch., 1953, Northwestern U. Law Sch., 1956, Harvard Law Sch., 1967; mem. legal adv. com.; bd. dirs. N.Y. Stock Exch., 1984-88; vice chmn. Ill. Jud. Inquiry Bd., 1992—. Mem. editorial bd. Ill. Bus. Corp. Act Annotated, 1947; contbr. articles to legal publs. Pres. N.E. Ill. council Boy Scouts Am., 1957-59, hon. pres., 1977—; exec. bd. region VII, 1959-73, vice chmn., 1966-68, chmn., 1968-70, mem. nat. exec. bd., 1968-70, mem. nat. adv. council, 1970—; mem. vis. com. Northwestern U. Sch. Law, 1982-85; pres. John Henry Wigmore Club, 1981-83. Recipient Silver Beaver, Silver Antelope, Silver Buffalo, Disting. Eagle Scout Citizens, Mortimer Shiff awards Boy Scouts Am.; merit award Northwestern U., 1973; Baden Powell fellow World Scout Orgn. Mem. ABA (com. state regulation securities 1961—, com. fed. regulation securities 1963—, com. corp. law and acctg. 1973—, adv. to commrs. on uniform laws 1980-88), Ill. Bar Assn. (past chmn. corp. and securities laws sect.), Chgo. Bar Assn. (past chmn. corp. law com., past chmn. securities law com., bd. mgrs. 1966-68, 1st v.p. 1970-71, pres. 1971-72, chmn. past pres. com. 1979—), Am. Judicature Soc., Internat., World assns. lawyers, Standard Club, Northmoor Country Club, Order of Coif. Home: 420 Lakeside Pl Highland Park IL 60035-5003 Office: Altheimer & Gray 10 S Wacker Dr Ste 4000 Chicago IL 60606-7407

GRAY, MONROE, JR., councilman; m. Teresa; children: Kevin M., Courtney Cross. Student, L.A. City Coll., 1962-64. Capt. Indpls. Fire Dept.; city councilman City of Indpls., 1992—. With U.S. Army, 1965-67. Mem. Indpls. Press Club, Marion County Dem. Club, Brickyard Crossing Men's Golf Club, Versatily Eleven Club, Skyline Club. Home: 4811 Seville Dr Indianapolis IN 46228-2174 Office: City-County Coun Office 200 E Washington St Ste 241 Indianapolis IN 46204-3310*

GRAY, MYLES MCCLURE, retired insurance company executive; b. Lansing, Mich., Aug. 28, 1932; s. Carlyle Avery and Lucile (Meitz) G.; m. Marilyn Ida Osberg, Feb. 14, 1953; children: Kathleen (Mrs. Mark Abraham), David, Patricia. BBA with distinction, U. Mich., 1954. Div. mgr. Nat. Life & Accident Ins. Co., Nashville, 1954-58; from asst. actuary to exec. v.p., actuary United Benefit Life Ins. Co., Omaha, 1958-67; v.p., actuary Gen. Reins. Life Corp., N.Y.C., 1967-69; Cal. Western States Life Ins. Co., Sacramento, 1969-74; v.p. Alexander & Alexander, N.Y.C., 1974-75, Nat. Life & Accident Ins. Co., Nashville, 1975-81, NLT Corp., Nashville, 1981-83; sr. v.p., chief actuary Life Investors, Inc., Cedar Rapids, Iowa, 1983-86; v.p. Cal Farm Life Ins. Co., Sacramento, 1986-96; ret., 1996; cons. in field. Docent Calif. State Railroad Mus., 1996—. Fellow Soc. Actuaries (sec., mem. exec. com. 1977-80, bd. govs. 1977-83); mem. Am. Acad. Actuaries (bd. dirs. 1986-87), Alpha Kappa Psi, Phi Kappa Phi, Beta Gamma Sigma. Republican. Home: 11454 Mother Lode Cir Gold River CA 95670-3042

GRAY, NANCY ANN OLIVER, college administrator; b. Dallas, Apr. 23, 1951; d. Howard Ross and Joan (Dawkins) Oliver; m. Doyle P. Gray, Nov. 24, 1973 (div. Jan. 1985); children: Paul, Jeff, Scott; m. David Nelson Maxson, Oct. 5, 1985. BA, Vanderbilt U., 1973; MEd, North Tex. State U., 1975; postgrad., Vanderbilt U., 1976-79. Cert. fund raising exec. Tchr. Highland Park High Sch., Dallas, 1973-75; dmin. drama dept. Harpeth Hall Sch., Nashville, 1975-77; assoc. dir. devel. Vanderbilt U., Nashville, 1977-78, assist. dean students, 1978-80; dir. spl. gifts U. Louisville, 1982-86; dir. major gifts Oberlin (Ohio) Coll., 1986-90; dir. capital programs The Lawrenceville (N.J.) Sch., 1990-91; v.p. devel. and univ. rels. Rider U., Lawrenceville, 1991-98; v.p. sem. rels. Princeton (N.J.) Theol. Sem., 1998-99;

pres. Converse Coll., Spartanburg. S.C., 1999—; bd. dirs. Jr. Achievement Ctrl. N.J.; cons. United Way, Cleve., 1988-90, Oberlin Coll., 1990, Princeton Project '55, 1992-93; guest lectr. Vanderbilt U., Nashville, 1987-88. Trustee Oberlin Libr., 1989, Oberlin Sch. Endowment Bd., 1988-90, Oberlin Early Childhood Ctr., 1986-88, Vanderbilt U., Nashville, 1973-77; bd. dirs. Vanderbilt U. Alumni Assn., Nashville, 1984-85, George Washington coun. Boy Scouts Am., 1996—; mem. Jr. League, 1984-89, various coms. Named Outstanding Young Woman of Am., 1982, Outstanding Woman Achievement, Lorain County (Ohio) YWCA, 1988. Mem. Nat. Soc. Fund-Raising Execs. (pres. Louisville chpt. 1985-86), Coun. for Advancement Support to Edn. (conf. presenter). Home: 488 Connecticut Ave Spartanburg SC 93202 Office: Converse Coll 580 E Main St Spartanburg SC 92302

GRAY, OSCAR SHALOM, lawyer; b. N.Y.C., Oct. 18, 1926. BA, Yale U., 1948, JD, 1951. Bar: Md. 1951, D.C. 1952, U.S. Supreme Ct. 1952. Atty.-adviser legal adviser's office U.S. Dept. State, Washington, 1951-57; sec. Nuclear Materials and Equipment Corp., Apollo, Pa., 1957-64, treas., 1957-67, v.p., 1964-71, dir., 1964-67; spl. counsel Presdl. Task Force on Communications Policy, Washington, 1967-68; cons. U.S. Dept. Transp., Washington, 1967-68, acting dir. office environ. impact, 1968-70; sole practice Washington, 1970—, Balt., 1971—; adj. prof., professorial lectr. Law Ctr. Georgetown U., Washington, 1970-71; lectr. Cath. U. Am., Washington, 1970-71; assoc. prof. U. Md., Balt., 1971-74, prof., 1974-93, Jacob A. France prof. of torts, 1993-96, prof. emeritus, 1996—; vis. prof. U. Tenn., 1977. Author: Cases and Materials on Environmental Law, 1970, 2d edit., 1973, supplements, 1974, 75, 77; (with F. Harper and F. James Jr.) The Law of Torts, 2d edit., 1986, semi-ann. supplements, 1987-97, 3d edit., vol. 1, 1996; (with H. Shulman and F. James Jr.) Cases and Materials on the Law of Torts, 3d edit., 1976; contbr. articles to legal jours. Mem. ABA, Am. Law Inst. (adviser Restatement of the Law, Third, Torts: Products Liability), D.C. Bar Assn., D.C. Fedn. of Civic Assns. (parliamentarian 1991-94), Selden Soc. (state correspondent Md.), Order of Coif, Phi Beta Kappa. Office: 500 W Baltimore St Baltimore MD 21201-1701

GRAY, PAUL CLELL, secondary school educator; b. Pikeville, Ky., July 11, 1955; s. John Paul and Patty Jean (Hall) G.; m. Charlotte Lynn Justice, July 13, 1974; children: Erin, Holly. AA in Mgmt. Sci., El Paso (Tex.) C.C., 1988; BA in History, U. Louisville, 1996. Cert. mil. sci. tchr., Ky. Served to sgt. major U.S. Army, 1973-93; tchr. Jr. ROTC North Hardin H.S., Radcliff, Ky., 1993—. Recipient Golden Apple award Ashland, Ky., 1996. Mem. VFW, Am. Legion, Ret. Sergeants Maj. Assn. Democrat. Baptist. Avocations: gardening, hunting, genealogy. Home: 490 Rabbit Run Rd Vine Grove KY 40175-6147

GRAY, PAUL EDWARD, academic official; b. Newark, Feb. 7, 1932; s. Kenneth Frank and Florence (Gilleo) G.; m. Priscilla Wilson King, June 18, 1955; children: Virginia Wilson, Amy Brewer, Andrew King, Louise Meyer. SB, MIT, 1954, SM, 1955; Sc.D., Mass. Inst. Tech., 1960. Mem. faculty MIT, 1960-71, 90—, Class of 1922 prof. elec. engring., 1968-71, dean Sch. Engring., 1970-71, chancellor, 1971-80, pres., 1980-90; mem. MIT Corp., 1971—, chmn., 1990-97; dir. A.D. Little Inc., Cambridge, Boeing Co., Seattle, Eastman Kodak Co., Rochester; dir. NVest, L.P. Trustee Wheaton Coll., Norton, Mass., 1971-97, trustee emeritus 1997—, chmn. bd. trustees, 1976-87. 1st lt. AUS, 1955-57. Fellow IEEE (life, publs. bd. 1969-70), Am. Acad. Arts and Scis.; mem. NAE (treas. 1994—), AAAS, Mex. Nat. Acad. Engring. (corr.), Sigma Xi, Eta Kappa Nu, Tau Beta Pi, Phi Sigma Kappa. Mem. United Ch. Christ. Office: MIT Dept Elec Engring 77 Massachusetts Ave Cambridge MA 02139-4307

GRAY, PAUL RUSSELL, electrical engineering educator; b. Jonesboro, Ark., Dec. 8, 1942. BS, U. Ariz., 1963, MS, 1965, PhD, 1969. Prof. dept. elec. engring. and computer sci. U. Calif., Berkeley, dean Coll. Engring., 1996—. Recipient Solid-State Circuits award IEEE, 1994. Fellow IEEE (Baker prize 1980, Morris N. Liebmann Meml. award 1983); mem. NAE. Office: U Calif Coll Engring 320 Mclaughlin Hall Berkeley CA 94720-1700

GRAY, PHILIP HOWARD, retired psychologist, educator; b. Cape Rosier, Maine, July 4, 1926; s. Asa and Bernice (Lawrence) G.; m. Iris McKinney, Dec. 31, 1954; children: Cindelyn Gray Eberts, Howard. M.A., U. Chgo., 1958; Ph.D., U. Wash., 1960. Asst. prof. dept. psychology Mont. State U. Bozeman, 1960-65; assoc. prof. Mont. State U., 1965-75, prof., 1975-92; ret., 1992; vis. prof. U. Man., Winnipeg, Can., 1968-70, U. N.H., 1965, U. Mont., 1967, 74, Tufts U., 1968, U. Conn., 1971; pres. Mont. Psychol. Assn., 1968-70 (helped write Mont. licensing law for psychologists); chmn. Mont. Bd. Psychologist Examiners, 1972-74; spkr. sci. and geneal. meetings on ancestry of U.S. presidents; presenter, instr. grad. course on serial killers and the psychopathology of murder. Organizer folk art exhbns. Mont. and Maine, 1972-79; author: The Comparative Analysis of Behavior, 1966, (with F.L. Ruch and N. Warren) Working with Psychology, 1963, A Directory of Eskimo Artists in Sculpture and Prints, 1974, The Science That Lost Its Mind, 1985, Penobscot Pioneers vol. 1, 1992, vol. 2, 1992, vol. 3, 1993, vol. 4, 1994, vol. 5, 1995, vol. 6, 1996, Mean Streets and Dark Deeds: The He-Man's Guide to Mysteries, 1998, Ghoulies and Ghosties and Long-Leggety Beasties, 1998, Ghoulies and Ghosties and Long-leggety Beasties: Imprinting Theory Linking Serial Killer, Child Assassins, Molester, Homosexuality, Feminism and DayCare, 1998; contbr. numerous articles on behavior to psychol. jours.; contbr. poetry to lit. jours. With U.S. Army, 1944-46. Recipient Am. and Can. research grants. Fellow AAAS, APA, Am. Psychol. Soc., Internat. Soc. Rsch. on Aggression; mem. NRA (life), SAR (v.p. Sourdough chpt. 1990, pres. 1991-99, trustee 1989, v.p-gen. intermountain dist. 1997-98, pres. state soc. 1996-98), Nat. Geneal. Soc., New Eng. Hist. Geneal. Soc., Gallatin County Geneal. Soc. (charter, pres. 1991-93), Deer Isle-Stonington Hist. Soc., Internat. Soc. Human Ethology, Descs. Illegitimate Sons and Daus. of Kings of Britain, Piscataque Pioneers, Order Desc. Colonial Physicians and Chirugiens, Flagon and Trencher, Order of the Crown of Charlemagne, Bozeman Rifle and Pistol Club. Republican. Avocations: collecting folk art, first and signed editions of novels, pistol shooting. Home: 1207 S Black Ave Bozeman MT 59715-5633 *We are human to the extent that we have bondings and the more bondings we have the more human we are. These attachments include familial bonding (imprinting), friendship bonding, marital bonding, ethnic-religious bonding, possession and goal bondings, and bonding to the land and ocean. My life's work is the study of these bondings and I am thereby more firmly connected to the human race.*

GRAY, PHYLLIS ANNE, librarian; b. Boston, Jan. 2, 1926; d. George Joseph and Eleanor (Morrison) G. PhB, Barry Coll., 1947, MBA, 1979; MS in LS, Cath. U. Am., 1950. Librarian U.S. Air Force Base, Miami, Fla., 1952-53; asst. librarian Brockway Meml. Library, Miami Shores, Fla., 1953-55; head librarian North Miami Pub. Library, 1955-59; supervising librarian Santa Clara County Library, San Jose, Calif., 1959-61; library dir. City of Commerce (Calif.) Pub. Library, 1961-68; adminstrv. librarian Miami Dade Pub. Library, 1969-76; library dir. Miami Beach (Fla.) Pub. Library, 1978-86; dir. Surf-Bal Bay Pub. Library, Surfside, Fla., 1987-91; Democrat. Roman Catholic. Councilwoman Bal Harbour Village, 1979-83; treas. Women in Govt. Service, 1981-86, pres., 1988-89. Mem. ALA, Barry U. Alumni Assn., Fla. Pub. Library Assn. Democrat. Roman Catholic. Club: Pilot (rec. sec. 1981-82, pres. 1982-83). Home: 575 Oakmount Pl # 2529 Las Vegas NV 89109-1472

GRAY, RALPH, editor, writer; b. Nevada, Mo., Feb. 24, 1915; s. Chester Harold and Pearl Iola (Welch) G.; m. Jean Grace Hamilton, Aug. 9, 1938; children—Judith, Mary Ellen, William, Donna. A.B., U. Md., 1937. Travel counselor, writer Am. Auto Assn., Washington, 1937-43; writer, editor Nat. Geographic Soc., Washington, 1943-52, chief of sch. service, 1952-75; editor Nat. Geographic World Mag., Washington, 1975-85, Books for World Explorers, Washington, 1979-85; editor emeritus World Mag., Books for World Explorers, Washington, 1985-90; nat. adv. bd. The Foxfire Fund, Rabun Gap, Ga., 1967—; editorial cons. Grand Canyon Pub., Salt Lake City, 1978-85, Nutrition Today Soc., Annapolis, Md., 1983-85, Bittersweet Mag., Inc., Lebanon, Mo., 1973-83. Editor: Geographic School Bull., 1952-75; contbr. articles to profl. jours. Founder, Green Meadows Boys Club, Hyattsville, Md., 1942; pres. Green Meadows Citizens Assn., Hyattsville, 1948. Ancient Oak Citizens Assn., Darnestown, Md., 1967. Recipient George Washington medal Freedoms Found., 1952; Golden Lamp award Ednl. Press Assn. of Am., 1975. Mem. Ednl. Press Assn. of Am. (pres. Washington chpt. 1957-

58, regional dir. 1971-72), Assn. Am. Geographers, AAAS, Explorers Club (bd. dirs. 1970-73), Transylvania Writers Alliance (steering com. 1998—). Republican. Presbyterian. Club: Cosmos (Washington) (mem. bd. mgmt. 1977-80). Home: 1 College Row Apt 240 Brevard NC 28712-3155 Office: Nat Geographic Soc 1145 17th St NW Washington DC 20036-4701

GRAY, RICHARD, art dealer, consultant, holding company executive; b. Chgo., Dec. 30, 1928; s. Edward and Pearl B. Gray; m. Mary Kay Lackritz, Mar. 28, 1953; children—Paul, Jennifer, Harry. Student, U. Ill., 1951. Pres. The Grayline Co., 1952-63; sec.-treas. The Edward Gray Corp., 1952-63; prin., dir. GrayCor, 1963—; dir. The Richard Gray Gallery, Chgo., 1963—; lectr., juror, panelist Guggenheim Mus., N.Y.C., Art. Inst. Chgo., Harvard U., U. Ill., Mich. State U., Milw. Art Mus., New Sch. for Social Research, N.Y., Met. Mus., N.Y.C., Colloquium-The Getty Mus., U. Chgo., Seattle Art Mus.; mem. art adv. panel U.S. Internal Revenue Svc. Contbr. articles to Chgo. Tribune, Chgo. Daily News, Crain's Chgo. Bus., Chgo. Mag., Collector Investor Mag. Bd. dirs. Sta. WFMT-FM, 1992-98, Ill. Humanities Coun.; trustee WTTW Channel 11—Chgo. Pub. TV; bd. dirs. Goodman Theatre, Chgo.; trustee Chgo. Symphony Orch.; former chair bd. Chgo. Internat. Theater Festival; adv. com. Smithsonian Inst.; bd. dirs. Old Masters Soc., Art Inst. Chgo.; mem. steering com. Friends of the Libraries, Art Inst Chgo.; mem. capital devel. bd. State of Ill., pub. arts adv. com., former mem. selection com. Gov.'s Awards for Arts; mem. nat. adv. bd. Ohio State U. Wexner Ctr. for Visual Arts; pres. Art Dealers Assn. Am.; former pres. Chgo. Art Dealers Assn.; former chmn. Navy Pier Task Force, City of Chgo., 1986-88; mem. vis. com. U. Chgo. Humanities Div., chmn., bd. govs. Alfred Smart Mus. U. Chgo. Mem. Chgo. Pub. Schs. Alumni Assn. (former chmn. bd. dirs.), Chgo. Coun. Fgn. Rels. (Chgo. com.), Chgo. Club, Quadrangle Club, Arts Club of Chgo. Specialist in contemporary, modern and impressionist masters. Office: Richard Gray Gallery 875 N Michigan Ave Ste 2503 Chicago IL 60611-1876*

GRAY, RICHARD ALEXANDER, JR., retired chemical company executive; b. Pitts., Apr. 28, 1927; s. Richard Alexander and Margaret Katheryn Gray; m. Lucia I. Long, Sept. 8, 1956; children: Richard Alexander III, James W. Midshipman, U.S. Mcht. Marine Acad., 1945-47; B.A., Princeton U., 1950: LL.B., Harvard U., 1954; postgrad., Univ. Coll., Southampton, Eng., 1949. Bar: Pa. bar 1955, U.S. Supreme Ct. bar 1975. Asso. firm Reed Smith Shaw & McClay, Pitts., 1954-62; with Air Products and Chems., Inc., Allentown, Pa., 1962-90; asst. gen. counsel Air Products and Chems., Inc., 1976-78, corp. sec., 1978-90, assoc. gen. counsel, 1980-84, v.p., 1984-90; trustee Kutztown (Pa.) U., 1988-96, chmn., 1995-96; mem. bd. regents Mercersburg (Pa.) Acad., 1968-82. Trustee First Presbyn. Ch. of Allentown. Served to lt. (j.g.) USNR, 1950-51. Mem. ABA, Am. Corp. Secs. (bd. dirs. 1985-89), Lehigh Country Club (bd. govs. 1993-96).

GRAY, ROBERT BECKWITH, electrical engineer, consultant; b. Johnstown, Pa., Apr. 9, 1912; s. Edward Townsend and Sarah Jean (Lomison) G.; m. Mary Elizabeth Ann Lynch, Jan. 17, 1942; children: William E., Rebecca Jean Fluegel, Robert F., Thomas O., Barry J. Student, Cornell U., 1934; EE, U. Pitts., 1941. Registered profl. engr., N.Y. Lab asst. Westinghouse Rsch. Magnetics, 1935-38; chief physicist Erie (Pa.) Resistor Corp., 1941-46; supr. rsch. Am. Meter Co., Erie, 1946-54; rsch. engr. Erie Resistor/Erie Tech. Products, Erie, 1954-65, Acme Electric Corp., Cuba, N.Y., 1965-67; engr. Hartman Metal Fabricators/Hartman Material Handling Systems, Victor, N.Y., 1967-81; cons. Tech. Svcs., Erie, 1981—. Editor Erie IEEE newsletter, 1988-95; patentee in field; contbr. articles to profl. jours. Initiator, sec. textbook com. Erie Engring. Socs. Coun., 1957-58. Mem. IEEE, Am. Assn. of Physics Tchrs., Pa. Inventors Assn. (sec. 1989-95), Sigma Xi, Sigma Pi Sigma. Office: Tech Svcs 1256 W 10th St Erie PA 16502-1015

GRAY, ROBERT DONALD, retired mayor; b. Quincy, Ill. May 6, 1924; s. James Arthur and Katherine Elnora (Moore) G.; m. Marie Dolores Albert, July 15, 1951; children: Michael S., Sheilah C. Student, Washington & Jefferson Coll., 1945-47; BSEE, Okla. State U., 1949; postgrad., Northwestern U. Electrolysis engr. Sinclair Refining Co., 1949-50; North Atlantic field mgr. navigation/communication systems USAF, 1950-51; cons. Lockheed Aircraft Ga. Co., 1951-52; sr. devel. engr. Harris Corp., 1952-54; dir. Gen. Telephone Electronics, Mountain View, Calif., 1954-66; dir. reliability and quality control Gen. Dynamics/Electronics, Rochester, N.Y., 1961-62; v.p. rsch./devel. Lockheed Missiles/Space Co., Sunnyvale, Calif., 1966-79; pres. Gray Assocs., Internat. Air Traffic Control System, Los Altos, Calif., 1980-87; mem. Los Altos City Coun., 1993-97; mayor City of Los Altos, Calif., 1994-95. With USN, 1941-45; ETO. Mem. IEEE (sr.), Phi Kappa Psi. Republican. Avocations: golf, amateur radio, electronics, aircraft. Home: 7307 Lost Lake Ln Roseville CA 95747-8312

GRAY, ROBERT M(OLTEN), electrical engineering educator; b. San Diego, Nov. 1, 1943; s. Augustine Heard and Elizabeth DuBois (Jordan) G.; m. Arlene Frances Ericson; children: Timothy M., Lori A. BS, MIT, 1966, MS, 1966; PhD, U. So. Calif., 1969. Elec. engr. U.S. Naval Ordinance Lab., White Oak, Md., 1963-65, Jet Propulsion Lab., Pasadena, Calif., summers 1966, 67; asst. prof. elec. engring. Stanford (Calif.) U., 1969-75, assoc. prof., 1975-80, prof., 1980—, dir. Info. Systems Lab., 1984-87, vice chair dept. elec. engring., 1993—. Author: Probability, Random Processes and Ergodic Properties, 1988, Source Coding Theory, 1990, Entropy and Information Theory, 1990; co-author: Random Processes, 1986, Vector Quantization and Signal Compression, 1992, Fourier Transforms, 1995; assoc. editor Math. of Control and System Sci. jour., 1987—; contbr. articles to profl. jours. Fireman La Honda (Calif.) Vol. Fire Brigade, 1970-80, pres., 1971-72; coach Am. Youth Soccer Orgn., La Honda, 1971-78, commr., 1976-78. Japan Soc. for Promotion Sci. fellow, 1981, Guggenheim fellow, 1982, NATO/CNR fellow, 1990. Fellow IEEE (Centennial medal 1984), Inst. Math. Stats.; mem. Info. Theory Soc. IEEE (assoc. editor Trans. 1977-80, editor in chief 1980-83, paper prize 1976, Golden Jubilee award for technol. achievement 1998), Signal Processing Soc. IEEE (sr. award 1983, sec. award 1993, program co-chmn. 1997 Internat. Conf. on Image Processing, Tech. Achievement award 1998), Soc. des Ingenieurs et Scientifiques de France. Avocations: maritime and Gilded Age history, hiking, computers, amateur radio. Home: PO Box 160 La Honda CA 94020-0160 Office: Stanford U Dept Elec Engring Stanford CA 94305

GRAY, ROBERT STEELE, publishing executive, editor; b. Beaumont, Tex., Oct. 6, 1923; s. Fred and Ruth Louise (Lewelling) G.; m. Nellie Frances McGuinness, July 3, 1945; children: Robert Steele, Laura, Ruth Ellen (Mrs. Robert Ham). BS, U. Houston, 1954. Newcaster Sta. KPRC-AM, Houston, 1947; news dir. Sta. KNUZ, Houston, 1948-49; reporter Citizens Papers, Houston, 1950; newsfilm dir. Sta. KPRC-TV, 1951-56; writer Houston Post, 1956-60; founder, pub. editor Cordovan Corp., Houston, 1960—; chmn. bd. Cordovan Corp., 1982—; pub. Cordovan Bus. Jours., Houston, 1971; co-founder Golfer Mags., Inc., 1984—. Author: Survivor, 1998, also author and co-author 5 books on horses and horse tng. 2nd lt. USMCR, 1942-46, to 1st lt. 1951-52, Korea. Mem. Soc. Profl. Journalists. Home: 14730 River Forest Dr Houston TX 77079-6423 Office: 9182 Old Katy Rd Ste 212 Houston TX 77055-7444

GRAY, RONALD W., business executive. V.p., mgr. missle and sensor sys. divsn. Automated Sci. Group, Huntsville, Ala. Office: Automated Sci Group 1555 The Boardwalk Huntsville AL 35816-1821*

GRAY, RYAN CHRISTOPHER, writer, editor, graphic artist; b. Orange, Calif., July 12, 1974; s. Robert Joseph and Ruth Ann Gray. BA in Journalism, U. Ariz., 1996. Sportswriter, editor The Ariz. Daily Star, Tucson, 1994-96; copywriter, editor Envision Group, Torrance, Calif., 1997; corp. comm. staff Trident Data Sys., L.A., 1997—. Participant, corp. contact Multiple Sclerosis Soc. Am., L.A., 1998. Mem. Pub. Rels. Soc. Am., Soc. Profl. Journalists (profl.). Roman Catholic. Avocations: music, sports. E-mail: ryanugray@tds.com. Office: Trident Data Sys Ste 700 5933 W Century Blvd Los Angeles CA 90045

GRAY, SEYMOUR, medical educator, author; b. Rochester, N.Y., Nov. 30, 1911; s. H. Louis and Eva (Bobry) G.; m. Ruth Helen Hart, July 2, 1935; children: Alfred, Roger. BA, U. Rochester, 1933; MD, U. Rochester, 1936; PhD, U. Chgo., 1944. Diplomate Am. Bd. Internal Medicine. Asst. prof. medicine U. Chgo., 1941-44; asst. prof. medicine Harvard U., Boston, 1946-

51, assoc. prof. medicine, 1951-63; vis. prof. nutrition MIT, Cambridge, 1963-67; chmn. dept. medicine King Faisal Specialist Hosp., Riyadh, Saudi Arabia, 1975-78; lectr. Harvard U., Cambridge, Mass., 1967—; lectr. cultural exchange program U.S. State Dept., Washington, 1956-60, chmn. task force on med. edn. in Latin Am., 1961-62; cons. Nat. Adv. Council, USPHS, Washington, 1955-60, USDA, Washington, 1964-67; mem. panel South Am. Health Programs, Presdl. Service Adv. Com., 1961. Author: Beyond the Veil, Harper and Row, 1983; contbr. over 160 articles to profl. jours. Founder Found. for Molecular Medicine, U. Pa., 1989. Lt. comdr. USN, 1944-46. Decorated Order of Hipolito Unanue (Peru), Comendador al Merito Bernardo (Chile); Seymour Gray Found. for Molecular Medicine at U. Pa. Sch. Medicine named in his honor, 1989. Fellow ACP; mem. AMA, Am. Physiol. Soc., Soc. Exptl. Biology and Medicine, Am. Soc. Clin. Investigation, U. Chile (hon.), Nat. Acad. Medicine Peru (hon.), Sigma Xi. Clubs: Harvard, Royal Poinciana. Home: 282 Warren St Brookline MA 02445*

GRAY, SHEILA HAFTER, psychiatrist, psychoanalyst; b. N.Y.C., Oct. 19, 1930. MD, Harvard U., 1958. cert. Washington Psychoanalytic Inst., 1969. Intern St. Elizabeths Hosp., Washington, 1958-59; resident McLean Hosp., Belmont, Mass., 1959-61; clin. and rsch. fellow Mass. Gen. Hosp., Boston, Mass., 1961-62; staff psychiatrist Chestnut Lodge, Inc., Rockville, Md., 1962-64; practice medicine, specializing in psychiatry and psychoanalysis Washington, 1964—; clin. asst. prof. psychiatry U. Md. Sch. Medicine, Balt., 1968-75, clin. assoc. prof., 1975-83, clin. prof., 1983-96; instr. Washington Psychoanalytic Inst., 1971-75, tchg. analyst, 1975-96; tchg. analyst Balt.-Washington Inst. for Psychoanalysis, 1996—; clin. prof. psychiatry Uniformed Svcs. U. Health Scis., 1997—; mem. staff U. Md. Hosp., Balt., 1970-96; physician mem. Commn. on Mental Health, Superior Ct. of D.C., 1972-98; bd. govs. Nat. Capital Reciprocal Ins. Co., 1981-98; dir. NCRIC Group, Inc., 1999—; treas. NCRIC Physicians Orgn., 1994-97; cons. Walter Reed Army Med. Ctr., Washington, 1983—. Mem. Mayor's Adv. Com. on Mental Health Svcs. Reorgn., Washington, 1984; mem. adv. panel for Mayor's Environ. Design Awards Program, 1988-89; mem. exec. com. D.C. Fedn. Civic Assns., 1984—, asst. rec. sec., 1985, rec. sec., 1986-88, 2d v.p., 1989-90, pres., 1991-92, del.-at-large, 1993—; v.p. programs Women's Equity Action League Met. D.C., 1986; commr. D.C. Adv. Neighborhood Commn., 1986-88; mem. Met. Washington Coun. of Govt.'s Partnership for Regional Excellence, 1992—. Fellow Am. Psychiat. Assn. (chair com. quality assurance and improvement, Coun. on Econ. Affairs, 1996-97); mem. Am. Psychoanalytic Assn. (diplomate Bd. Profl. Stds.), Am. Acad. Psychoanalysis (trustee 1996-99, pres.-elect 1999—), Washington Psychiatric Soc. (councillor 1981-83), Med. Soc. D.C. (exec. bd. 1982, ho. dels. 1992—), Washington Psychoanalytic Soc. (chmn. bd. dirs. psychoanalytic clinic and councillor ex officio 1987-90), Palisades Citizens Assn. (bd. dirs. 1980—, treas. 1983-84, pres. 1984-86). Office: PO Box 40612 Palisades Sta Washington DC 20016

GRAY, SUSANNE MARIE HARTMAN, ambulatory care nurse; b. Plainfield, N.J., Dec. 11, 1948; d. Wallace Harry Hartman and Gwendolyn (Pridmore) Hartman Riebeling. ASN, Essex County Coll., 1981; BSN, Bloomfield Coll., 1989. Charge nurse East Orange (N.J.) Nursing Home, 1977-81; instr. trainer in HIV/AIDS ARC, East Orange, 1988-96; med.-surg. nurse United Hosp. Med. Ctr., Newark, 1981-97; infectious disease staff nurse East Orange (N.J.) Gen. Hosp., 1983-95; ambulatory care nurse Essex Valley Healthcare, East Orange, 1997—. Mem. ANA, N.J. State Nurses Assn., Assn. Nurses in AIDS Care, Alpha Chi.

GRAY, TAMMI TERRELL, federal agency analyst, writer; b. Accomac, Va., Feb. 7, 1968; d. Clyde Daniel and Nancy Mae (Matthews) Burroughs; divorced; children: NeCole Latriese, David Leroy III. AS, No. Va. C.C., 1994. Clerk typist FBI, Washington, 1986-87; sec. CIA, Washington, 1987-94, analyst, 1994—. Author: And They Said... The Collection, 1994; mem. Secretarial Newsletter, Washington, 1988-94. Mem. Black Affairs Steering Com., Washington, 1992—. Mem. Black Profl. Secs. Assn. (v.p. 1994-95). Home: 11970 Calico Woods Pl Waldorf MD 20601

GRAY, THOMAS STEPHEN, newspaper editor; b. Burbank, Calif., Aug. 22, 1950; s. Thomas Edgar and Lily Irene (Ax) G.; m. Barbara Ellen Bronson, Aug. 27, 1977; children: Jonathan Thomas, Katherine Marie. BA, Stanford U., 1972; MA in English, UCLA, 1976. Teaching assoc. UCLA, 1976-77; reporter L.A. Daily News, 1977-79, editorial writer, 1979-84, editorial page editor, 1984-95; sr. editor Investor's Bus. Daily, L.A., 1995-98. Recipient 1st Place award Editorial Writing Greater L.A. Press Club, 1988, Inland Daily Press Association, 1993.

GRAY, VICKI LOU PHARR, music educator; b. Orange, Calif., July 11, 1944; d. Kenneth E. and Louis Pauline (Wright) Pharr; m. Haskell H. Gray, Nov. 26, 1966; children: Jennifer, Justin, Juliette. B in Music Edn., Tex. Tech. U., 1966; MusM with high honors, So. Meth. U., 1989. Permanent profl. cert. Nat. Music Tchrs. Assn. Gen. music tchr. Richardson (Tex.) Ind. Sch. Dist., 1966-68; pvt. piano tchr. Gray Piano Studios, Dallas, 1968—; owner, dir. Childrens Opera Workshop, Dallas, 1992—; owner Gray Piano Studios, Dallas, 1993—. Author: Music for Minors, 1989; writer, prodr. (childrens operas) Come Fly With Me, Mirror-Mirror, Dancing Princesses, H & G Go to Hollywood, Beauty. Mem. Tex. Music Tchrs. Assn., North Dallas Music Tchrs. Assn. (pres. 1995-97), Dallas Music Tchrs. Assn. (pres. 1995—), Jr. Pianist Guild (pres. 1994). Republican. Methodist. Avocations: raising suishis, gourmet cooking, traveling.

GRAY, VIRGINIA HICKMAN, political science educator; b. Camden, Ark., June 10, 1945; d. George Leonard and Ethel Massengale (Bell) Hickman; m. Charles Melvin Gray, Oct. 16, 1944; 1 child, Brian Charles. BA with honors, Hendrix Coll., 1967; MA, Washington U., St. Louis, 1969, PhD, 1972. Asst. prof. polit. sci. U. Ky., Lexington, 1971-73; from asst. prof. to assoc. prof. U. Minn., Mpls., 1973-83, prof., 1983—, chairperson dept. polit. sci., 1985-88; guest scholar Brookings Inst., Washington, 1977-78; vis. prof. U. Oslo, 1985, Nankai U., 1988, U. B.C., 1992, U. N.C., 1993-94; NSF vis. prof. for women, 1993-94. Co-author: The Organizational Politics of Criminal Justice, 1980, Feminism and the New Right, 1983, Politics in the American States, 1983, 7th edit., 1999, American States and Cities, 1991, 2d edit., 1997, The Population Ecology of Interest Representation, 1996. Bd. dirs. Health Ptnrs. Inc., 1992-99. Fellow Woodrow Wilson Found., 1970, NDEA, 1969-70; grantee Swedish Bicentennial Found., 1985; recipient rsch. assistantship NSF, 1968-69, rsch. grant NSF, 1997—; scholar in residence Rockefeller Ctr., Bellagio, Italy. Mem. Am. Polit. Sci. Assn. (coun. 1990-92), Midwest Polit. Sci. Assn. (coun. 1984-86, v.p. 1997-99), Policy Studies Orgn. (coun. 1977-79). Democrat. Unitarian. Home: 1776 Pinehurst Ave Saint Paul MN 55116-2117 Office: U Minn Dept Polit Sci 1414 Soc Sci Bldg Minneapolis MN 55455

GRAY, WALTER FRANKLIN, retired banker; b. Denver, Sept. 25, 1929; s. Walter Franklin and Alice (Fassig) G.; m. Susan Amy Mair, Mar. 26, 1955; children: Constance G. Newhall, Stuart Franklin. BS, Northwestern U., 1951; JD, Loyola U., 1957. V.p. First Nat. Bank of Chgo., 1953-69; exec. v.p. Merc. Safe Deposit Corp., Balt., 1969-77; vice chmn. Merc. Bank, St. Louis, 1977-93; chmn. Mercantile Trust Co., St. Louis, 1993-94, ret., 1994. Bd. dirs. St. Louis Symphony, Open Space Fedn., Mo. Hist. Soc. Mem. ABA, Am. Bankers Assn., Elkridge Club (Balt.), Boulders Club (Ariz.), St. Louis Country Club. Home: 7544 E Club Villa Cir Scottsdale AZ 85262-1506

GRAY, WALTER P., III, archivist, consultant; b. San Francisco, Aug. 8, 1952; s. Walter Patton II and Elsie Josephine (Stroop) G.; m. Mary Amanda Helmich, May 23, 1980. BA in History, Calif. State U., Sacramento, 1976. Rschr. Calif. State R.R. Mus., Sacramento, 1977-80, curator, 1980-81, 85-90, asst. dir., 1981-85, mus. dir., 1990-98; Calif. state archivist, 1998—; cons. in field, 1976—. Contbr. articles to profl. jours. Democrat. Buddhist. Avocations: woodworking, antique automobiles, photography. Office: California State Archives 1020 O St Sacramento CA 95814-5704

GRAY, WILLIAM GUERIN, civil engineering educator; b. San Francisco, Jan. 9, 1948. BS, U. Calif., 1969; MA, Princeton U., 1971, PhD, 1974. Asst. prof. dept. civil engring. Princeton U., N.J., 1975-80, dir. grad. studies dept. civil engring., 1977-84, assoc. prof. dept. civil engring., 1980-84; prof. dept. civil engring. U. Notre Dame, Ind., 1984-88, chmn. civil engring., geol. scis., 1984-95, Massman prof. civil engring. and geol. scis., 1988—. Office: U Notre Dame Dept Civil Engring Sc Notre Dame IN 46556

GRAY, WILLIAM H., III, association executive, former congressman; b. Baton Rouge, Aug. 20, 1941; m. Andrea Dash, Apr. 17, 1971; children—William H. IV, Justin Yates, Andrew Dash. B.A., Franklin and Marshall Coll., 1963; M.Div., Drew Theol. Sem., Madison, N.J., 1966; Th.M., Princeton Theol. Sem., 1970; postgrad., U. Pa., 1965, Temple U., 1966, Oxford U., 1967. Ordained to ministry Baptist Ch.; asst. minister Bright Hope Baptist Ch., Phila., 1963-64; dir. 1st Baptist Ch., Montclair, N.J., 1964-65; co-pastor, sr. minister Union Baptist Ch., Montclair, 1966-72; asst. prof., dir. St. Peter's Coll., Jersey City, 1970-74; sr. minister Bright Hope Baptist Ch., 1972—; lectr. Jersey City State Coll., 1968, Rutgers U., 1971, Montclair State Coll., 1970-72; mem. 96th-101st Congresses from 2d Dist. Pa.; House Majority Whip; pres., CEO United Negro Coll. Fund, N.Y.C., 1991—; chmn. house budget com., 1985; mem. house appropriations com. Congl. Black Caucus, Nat. Economic Commn.; vice chmn. Dem. Leadership Coun.; envoy to Haiti, 1994. Trexler Found. scholar, 1962; Rockefeller Protestant fellow, 1965. Mem. Phila. Pastor's Conf., Phila. Baptist Assn., Progressive Nat. Baptist Assn., Am. Baptist Conv., Alpha Phi Alpha. Democrat. Club: Frontier Internat. Lodges: Masons, Elks. Office: United Negro Coll Fund PO Box 10444 8260 Willow Oaks Corporate Dr Fairfax VA 22031-4513*

GRAY, WILLIAM R., lawyer; b. Peoria, Ill., Aug. 25, 1941; s. John J. and Alverna K. (Kennedy) G.; m. Tiana M. Yeager, June 12, 1982; children: Ann Katherine, Thomas William. BA, U. Colo., 1963, JD, 1966. Bar: Colo. 1966; U.S. Dist. Ct. Colo. 1966; U.S. Ct. Appeals (10th cir.) 1976. Dep. dist. atty. Dist. Atty.'s Office/10th Jud. Dist., Pueblo, Colo., 1967-69, Dist. Atty.'s Office/20th Jud. Dist., Boulder, Colo., 1969-70; dep. state pub. defender Colo. State Pub. Defender, Boulder, 1970-72; ptnr. Miller & Gray, Boulder, 1973-85, Purvis, Gray & Gordon, LLP, Boulder, 1985—; mem./vice chair, chmn., Colo. Supreme Ct. grievance com., 1983-88, mem. criminal rules com., 1982-84; adj. prof. law U. Colo. Sch. of Law, Boulder, 1984. Bd. dirs. Mental Health Ctr. of Boulder County, 1972-78. Fellow Am. Coll. Trial Lawyers (Courageous Advocacy award 1985), Internat. Soc. Barristers, Am. Bar Found., Colo. Bar Foun., Colo. Bar Assn. (Professionalism award 1995), Am. Bd. Trial Advocates. Democrat. Office: Purvis Gray & Gordon LLP 1050 Walnut St Ste 501 Boulder CO 80302-5144

GRAYBEAL, BARBARA, editor, writer; b. Mountain City, Tenn., Sept. 21, 1935; d. Claude Harold and Ruby Lucille (Hodge) G.; m. Lewis N. Kremer, June 7, 1958 (div.); m. Charles L. Ring, May 8, 1982. BA magna cum laude, Marietta Coll., 1957; grad. Pub. Procedures Course, Radcliffe Coll., 1957. With New Yorker mag., N.Y.C., 1957-58; assoc. editor Saturday Evening Post, Phila., 1958-62, Episc. mag., Phila., 1962-69; asst. editor Luth. mag., Phila., 1971-72; instr. journalism Temple U., Phila., 1972-81; founding editor CGA World mag., 1980-82, sr. editor, 1982-83. Editor, writer: Fast and Fresh (by Julie Dannenbaum), 1981, The CGA Cookbook, 1984; editorial cons.: Good Ideas for Decorating; contbr. articles, photographs and poetry to various publs. Mem. com. interpretation and promotion, dept. overseas missions Nat. Council Chs., 1966-68; mem. Phila. Dem. Com., 1968; bd. dirs., sec. Friends of Free Library Phila.; bd. dirs. N.C. Sch. Arts, The Assocs. of N.C. Sch. of the Arts, 1983-86; lay reader Episc. Ch. Mem. Women in Communications (v.p. chpt.), Marietta Coll. Alumni Assn., AAUW (pres. br.), Internat. Platform Assn., Phi Beta Kappa, Sigma Delta Chi, Alpha Xi Delta. Address: 1525 Woods Rd Apt 106 Winston Salem NC 27106-3135

GRAYBEAL, JACK DANIEL, chemist, educator; b. Detroit, May 16, 1930; s. Paul Herman and Polly Dale (McClintic) G.; m. Evelyn Alice Nicolai, June 13, 1954; children: Daniel Lee, David Eugene, Dale Kevin. BS in Chemistry, W.Va. U., 1951; MS in Chemistry, U. Wis., 1953, PhD in Chemistry, 1955. Mem. tech. staff Bell Telephone Labs., Holmdel, N.J., 1955-57; asst. prof. chemistry W.Va. U., Morgantown, 1957-63, assoc. prof., 1963-68; assoc. prof. chemistry Va. Poly. Inst. and State U., Blacksburg, 1968-69, prof., 1969-97, assoc. head dept., 1975-95, prof. emeritus, 1997—. Author: Molecular Spectroscopy, 1988; contbr. articles to profl. jours. Mem. Am. Chem. Soc., Am. Phys. Soc., Sigma Xi, Phi Lambda Upsilon (editor 1981-87, nat. sec. 1987-96, nat. pres. 1996—). Home: 312 Apperson Dr Blacksburg VA 24060-3641 Office: Va Poly Inst and State U Dept Chemistry Blacksburg VA 24061-0212

GRAYBILL, DAVID WESLEY, chamber of commerce executive; b. Council Bluffs, Iowa, Apr. 8, 1949; s. John Donald and Dorothy Lorraine (King) G.; m. Kortney Loraine Steinbeck, Aug. 17, 1974; 1 child, Darcy Lorraine. BA in Journalism, U. Iowa, 1971; MA in Mgmt. and Leadership Studies, City U., 1999. Cert. econ. developer, Chamber exec. Adminstrv. asst. Iowa City C. of C., 1972-74; exec. v.p. Brighton (Colo.) C. of C., 1974-77; pres. Fremont (Nebr.) C. of C., 1977-83; pres., chief exec. officer Tacoma-Pierce County C. of C., 1983—; pres. Nebr. C. of C. Execs., 1981-82; treas. NE Nebr. Econ. Devel. Dist., 1980-83. Charter mem. Gov.'s Small Bus. Improvement Com., Wash., 1984-86; presiding elder Tacoma (Wash.) Reorganized LDS Ch. Mem. Am. Econ. Devel. Coun. (bd. dirs. 1985-87), Am. C. of C. (bd. dirs. 1990-94), Wash. C. of C. Execs. (pres. 1988-89, bd. dirs. 1988-90), Rotary (bd. dirs. Tacoma 1985-87). Office: Tacoma-Pierce County C of C PO Box 1933 Tacoma WA 98401-1933

GRAYBILL, GUY OLDT, writer; b. Paxtonville, Pa., Apr. 6, 1934. BA in History, Gettysburg Coll.; MEd, Pa. Dept. of Edn. Social studies tchr. Contbr. numerous articles to mags. Chmn. Snyder County Rep. com.; pres. County Hist. Soc.; former chmn. Snyder County Young Reps.; former pres. county unit Am. Cancer Soc.; chmn. Cancer Crusade; former chmn. county bd. commn.; Sunday sch. tchr. Salem Luth. Ch. Recipient Kodak Spl. Merit award, 1995. Avocations: photography.

GRAY-BUSSARD, DOLLY H., energy company executive; b. Wilmington, Del., July 29, 1943; d. Henry Odell and Dorothy (Knotts) Gray; m. Robert William Bussard, Mar. 17, 1981; stepchildren: Elise Bright Chisholm, William Bussard, Robert L. Bussard, Virginia B. Barausky. BA in History and English Lit., U. Calif., San Diego, 1984; MA in History, Georgetown U., 1990. Coord. Orgn. Human Devel., San Diego, 1977-78; owner, prin. Hello Dolly, La Jolla, Calif., 1978-80; ptnr. Linda Chester Lit. Agy., La Jolla, 1978-80; owner, pres. Unicorn Literary Agy., La Jolla, 1980-85; pres., chmn. bd. Energy/Matter Conversion Corp., San Diego, Calif., 1988—; vis. lectr. writers' confs. U. Calif., San Diego, 1979-81. Co-author: The Best of San Diego, 1981. Mem. Artists Cir., Santa Fe Chamber Music Festival. Mem. NAFE, Am. Hist. Assn., Phi Alpha Theta. Episcopalian. Avocations: book collecting, skiing, sailing. Office: EMC2 Ste 103 9705 Carroll Center Rd San Diego CA 92126

GRAYCK, MARCUS DANIEL, lawyer; b. N.Y.C., Aug. 28, 1927; s. Jack and Gertrude (Seeman) G.; children from previous marriage—Howard Alexander, Amelia Beth, Joshua Avram, David Louis. AB, Bklyn. Coll., 1948; LLB, Harvard U., 1951; LLM, NYU, 1958. Bar: N.Y., Ill., U.S. Supreme Ct. Partner firm Baker & McKenzie, Chgo., 1973-88, ret., 1988; mem. adj. faculty, grad. tax program N.Y. U. Law Sch., 1959-75; adj. prof. law Loyola U. Law Sch., 1976-88. Past editor: Compensation and fringe benefits column Jour. Corp. Taxation; contbr. articles to profl. jours. Served with USN, 1945-46. Office: Baker & McKenzie Prudential Plz # 2800 Chicago IL 60601 *I was blessed to have parents who cared and taught—two essentials for a youth in his formative years. I also had the good fortune of being born in a country where, and at a time when, freedom and opportunity were available. I was able to learn early on from others that effort unstinted was to be my contribution to life. Having learned this, I still marvel at Browning's statement in Andrea del Sarto that "...man's reach should exceed his grasp, or what's a heaven for?".*

GRAYDON, FRANK DRAKE, retired accounting educator, university administrator; b. Ovalo, Tex., Feb. 11, 1921; s. Alonzo Otis and Jennie Lewis (Drake) G.; m. Mary Elizabeth Galt, June 16, 1943; children: Geoffrey Galt, David Drake. BBA, Tex. Tech. Coll., 1941; MBA, Northwestern U., 1943. CPA, Tex. Pub. acct. David Himmelblau & Co., Chgo., 1942-44; lectr. in acctg. Northwestern U., Chgo., 1942-44; instr. acctg. Tex. Tech. Coll., 1944-45; chief acct. U. Houston, 1945-46; asst. prof. acctg. U. Tex., 1946-50; with fin. statement sect. Cen. Controllers Office Ford Motor Co., Dearborn, Mich., 1950-51; budget examiner Agencies of Higher Edn., Legis. Budget Bd., Austin, Tex., 1951-55; fin. planning staff Temp. Commn. on Higher Edn., Austin, Tex., 1954-55; budget dir. and prof. acctg. U. Tex. System, Austin, 1955-90, spl. counsel budget and fin., Office of the Chancellor, 1990-93; budget dir. emeritus U. Tex. System, 1993—; prof. acctg. emeritus U. Tex., Austin, 1993—. Mem. AICPAs. Home: 8158 Ceberry Dr Austin TX 78759-8743 Office: Univ of Tex System 601 Colorado St Austin TX 78701-2904

GRAYESKI, MARY LYNN, chemist, foundation administrator. BS in Chemistry, Kings Coll., 1974; PhD in Analytical Chemistry, U. N.H., 1982. Tchg., rsch. asst. U. N.H., Durham, 1979-82; asst. prof. Seton Hall U., S. Orange, N.J., 1982-87, assoc. prof., 1987-93, chair chemistry dept., 1991-93; program officer Rsch. Corp., Tucson, 1993—; mem. govning. bd. Ea. Analytical Symposium, N.J., 1985-93. Contbr. over 30 articles to profl. jours. Vol. ACTION/VISTA, Midland, Tex., 1975; vol. recruiter ACTION, San Francisco, 1976; vol. ACTION/Peach Corps, Ghana, 1977-78; judge Internat. Sci. and Engring. Fair, 1996. Mem. Am. Chem. Soc., Delta Epsilon Sigma. Office: Rsch Corp 101 N Wilmot Rd Ste 250 Tucson AZ 85711-3361

GRAY-FUSON, JOAN LORRAINE, lawyer; b. Glendale, Calif., Mar. 25, 1938; d. Stanley Wayne Brune and Maxine Lorraine (Falconer) Talkin; m. Darrell Herbert Gray, June 26, 1959 (div. 1972); children: Michael Herbert Gray, Thomas Edward Gray; m. Arnold Max Fuson, Dec. 18, 1977; children: Marie Fuson Hudson, Karen Fuson, Gregory J. Fuson. BA in Edn., Calif. State U., 1960; JD, U. of the Pacific, 1978. Bar: Calif. 1978, U.S. Dist. Ct. (ea. dist.) Calif. 1978. Tchr. Rio Linda Union Sch. Dist., Sacramento, Calif., 1960-65; pvt. practice Sacramento, 1978-81; staff counsel State of Calif. Water Resources Control Bd., Sacramento, 1982-91; sr. staff counsel State of Calif. Dept. of Conservation, Sacramento, 1991—. Elder on session Fremont Presbyn. Ch., Sacramento, 1995-97. Avocations: gardening, folk dancing, fitness. Office: Dept of Conservation 801 K St # Ms24-3 Sacramento CA 95814-3500

GRAYHACK, JOHN THOMAS, urologist, educator; b. Kankakee, Ill., Aug. 21, 1923; s. John and Marie (Keckich) G.; m. Elizabeth Houlehin, June 3, 1950; children: Elizabeth, Anne Marie, Linda Jean, John, William. B.S., U. Chgo., 1945, M.D., 1947. Diplomate Am. Bd. Urology. Intern medicine Billings Hosp., Chgo., 1947; intern gen. surgery Johns Hopkins Hosp., 1947-48, asst. resident, 1948-49, fellow urology, 1949-50, asst. resident, 1950-52; resident urology, 1952-53; dir. Kretschmer Lab., Northwestern U. Med. Sch., 1956-75, prof. urology, 1963—, chmn. dept., 1961-90; cons. VA Rsch. Hosp. Editor Year Book of Urology, 1963-78; editor Jour. Urology, 1985-94. Served to capt. USAF, 1954-56. Recipient Outstanding Achievement award USAF, Ferdinand C. Valentine award N.Y. Acad. Medicine, Disting. Svc. award U. Chgo., 1978, Pioneer award Internat. Symposium Biology Prostate Growth, 1998; fellow Am. Cancer Soc., 1949-50, Damon Runyon Fund, 1953-54, Johns Hopkins Soc. Scholars. Mem. AMA, Ill., Chgo. med. socs., Am. Assn. Genitourinary Surgeons (Barringer medal), Am. Urology Assn. (Hugh H. Young award, Fuller award, Mary Hugh and Russell Scott award, Ramon Guiteras award 1994), Chgo. Urology Soc., Endocrine Soc., Clin. Soc. Genitourinary Surgeons, Am. Surg. Assn., Soc. Univ. Urologists, Nephrology Soc., Phi Beta Kappa, Alpha Omega Alpha. Home: 95 N Park Rd La Grange IL 60525-5938 Office: Northwestern Meml Hosp Superior St Fairbanks Ct Chicago IL 60611

GRAYSHAW, JAMES RAYMOND, judge; b. Cleve., Apr. 3, 1948; s. Thomas J. and Bettie Lee (Griffith) G.; m. Susan Hancher, Oct. 15, 1980; 1 child, John H. BA, L.I. U., Bklyn., 1970; JD, Bklyn. Law Sch., 1975. Legal asst. Cadwalader, Wickersham & Taft, N.Y.C., 1975-77; law asst. Civil Ct. City N.Y., 1977-80; sr. law asst. Supreme Ct., State N.Y., 1980-82; judge housing part Civil Ct., City N.Y., 1983—; judge advocate Cmty. Advocacy Ctr., N.Y.C., 1996. Sgt. U.S. Army, 1970-72. Mem. Queens Bar Assn., Protestant Lawyers N.Y.C. (dir. 1980—), Vietnam Vets. Am., 16th Inf. Reg. Assn., Masons. Democrat. Lutheran. Home: 21107 28th Ave Bayside NY 11360-2508 Office: Civil Ct City NY 89-17 Sutphin Blvd Jamaica NY 11435

GRAYSMITH, ROBERT, political cartoonist, author; b. Pensacola, Fla., Sept. 17, 1942; s. Robert Gray and Frances Jane (Scott) Smith; m. Melanie Krakower, Oct. 15, 1975 (div. Sept. 1980); children—David Martin, Aaron Vincent, Margot Alexandra. B.A., Calif. Coll. Arts and Crafts, 1965. Polit. cartoonist: Oakland (Calif.) Tribune, 1964-65, Stockton (Calif.) Record, 1965-68, San Francisco Chronicle, 1968-83 ; author: (non-fiction) Zodiac, 1986,Trailside, 1986, The Sleeping Lady, 1990, The Murder of Bob Crane, 1993, Unabomber: A Desire to Kill, 1997, The Bell-Tower, A True Detective Story of Gas-lit SanFrancisco, 1998, Ghost Fleet, 1999; illustrator (children's book by Penny Wallace) I Didn't Know What to Get You, 1993. Recipient 2d place Fgn. Press Awards 1973, World Population Contest 1976. Democrat. Presbyterian. Office: San Francisco Chronicle 901 Mission St San Francisco CA 94103-2905

GRAYSON, ALBERT KIRK, Near Eastern studies educator; b. Windsor, Ont., Can., Apr. 1, 1935; s. Albert Kirk and Helen (Smith) Grayson'; m. Eunice Marie Service, Aug. 3, 1956; children: Vera Lorraine, Sally Frances. B.A., U. Toronto, Ont., 1955; M.A., U. Toronto, 1958; postgrad., U. Vienna, Austria, 1959-60; Ph.D., Johns Hopkins U., 1962. Research asst. Chgo. Assyrian Dictionary Oriental Inst., Chgo., 1962-63; asst. prof. history Temple U., Phila., 1963-64; asst. prof. Near Eastern studies U. Toronto, 1964-67, assoc. prof., 1967-72, prof., 1972—; dir. Royal Inscriptions of Mesopotamia project, 1981—; vis. lectr. U. Pa., Phila., 1963-64; spl. asst. dept. Western Asiatic Antiquities Brit. Mus., London, intermittently, 1967-76; invited lectr. various univs., mus., U.S., Germany, Iraq, Eng., Austria, Italy. Author: Assyrian Royal Inscriptions vol. I, 1972, Assyrian Royal Inscriptions vol. II, 1976, Assyrian and Babylonian Chronicles, 1975, Babylonian Historical-Literary Texts, 1975, Assyrian Rulers of the Third and Second Millennia, B.C. 1987, Assyrian Rulers of the Early First Millennium BC I-II, 1991-96; contbr. chpts. to books. Can. Council fellow, 1959-61; Samuel S. Fels Fund fellow, 1961-62; Social Scis. and Humanities Research Council Can. editorial grantee, 1981—. Fellow Royal Soc. Can. (hon. sec. 1989-92); mem. Soc. Mesopotamian Studies (pres. 1980-92), Fondation Assyriologique Georges Dossin (Belgium), Oriental Club Toronto (sec. 1969-70, pres. 1979-80), Rencontre Assyriologique Internationale (sessional chmn. Berlin 1978, Vienna 1980, Leiden, Netherlands 1983), Am. Oriental Soc. (sec. Midwest br. 1965-68). Mem. Anglican Ch. of Canada. Office: U Toronto Dept Near Ea Studies, 4 Bancroft Ave, Toronto, ON Canada M5S 1A1

GRAYSON, BETTE RITA, lawyer; b. Newark, July 10, 1947; d. Sidney and Joan (Rosenman) G.; m. Stanley Noah Kruzweil, Aug. 17, 1975; children: Jeremy, Cynthia. BA, NYU, 1969; JD, Bklyn. Law Sch., 1977. Bar: N.J. 1977. Lawyer sole practice Union and Springfield, N.J., 1977—; former real estate counsel City of Plainfield, N.J.; former spl. real estate counsel City of Orange; former rev. atty. for State Bank South Orange, N.J.; chairperson Fee Arbitration Com. Union County, N.J.; mem. adv. bd. Crown Bank. V.p. Millburn (N.J.) Hadassah, 1985-87, mem. steering com. for planned gifts; trustee Internat. Youth Orgn., 1997-98; treas. Millburn Hoopsters, 1997—. Recipient Trust Bklyn. Law Sch., 1974, Woman of Excellence award Union County, 1998. Mem. Women Lawyers Union County (pres. 1990-92, v.p. 1988-90, sec. 1983-84, treas. 1986-88). Democrat. Office: 140 Mountain Ave Springfield NJ 07081-1725

GRAYSON, EDWARD DAVIS, lawyer, manufacturing company executive; b. Davenport, Iowa, June 20, 1938; s. Charles E. and Isabelle (Davis) G.; m. Alice Ann McLaughlin; children: Alice Anne, Maureen Isabelle, Edward Davis Jr. B.A., U. Iowa, 1960, LLB, 1964. Bar: Iowa 1964, Mass. 1967. Atty. Goodwin, Procter & Hoar, Boston, 1967-74; sr. v.p., gen. counsel Wang Labs., Inc., Lowell, Mass., 1974-92; v.p., gen. counsel Honeywell, Inc., Mpls., 1992—. Trustee U. Lowell, Mass., 1981-87, chmn. bd. trustees, 1982-85, 87; dir. Bus. Econs. Edn. Found., 1992—. Capt. USAF, 1964-67. Mem. ABA (com. corp. law depts.), Mass. Bar Assn. (bd. dels. 1977-80), Greater Mpls. C. of C. (dir. 1992—). Office: Honeywell Inc Honeywell Plz PO Box 524 Minneapolis MN 55440-0524*

GRAYSON, ELLISON CAPERS, JR., human resources executive; b. St. Paul, Sept. 7, 1928; s. Ellison Capers and Inez (Santos) G.; m. Jean Mason, Dec. 26, 1953; children: Darby, William. BA, U. Minn., 1950; LHD (hon.),

Nat. U., San Diego, 1984. CLU. Gen. agt. Home Life Ins. Co. N.Y., San Francisco, 1955-81; prin. dep., asst. sec. USN, Washington, 1981-84; dir. mktg. and devel. Pvt. Sector Coun., 1985; cons. Washington, 1985-86; sr. v.p. Boyden Internat., San Francisco, 1987-90; ptnr. Spencer Stuart, San Francisco, 1990—; bd. dirs. StellarNet, Inc., San Francisco; advisory bd. Clark/Bardes, Inc., Dallas. Commr. City and County of San Francisco, 1978-81; pres. bd. dirs. St. Mary's Hosp. and Med. Ctr., San Francisco, 1972-75; co-chmn. nat. finance com. Bush for Pres; bd. regents St. Ignatius Coll. Preparatory, San Francisco. Capt. USN, 1952-55. Named Eagle Scout Boy Scouts Am., 1944; recipient Nat. Brotherhood award Nat. Assn. Christians and Jews, San Diego, 1984. Mem. Sovereign Mil. (knight 1978), Order of St. John of Jerusalem, Knights of Malta, Bohemian Club, Met. Club (Washington), Villa Taverna Club (San Francisco), St. Francis Yacht Club, Army Navy Club, Alfalfa Club (Washington), Corinthian Yacht Club. Republican. Roman Catholic. Home: 95 Sea Cliff Ave San Francisco CA 94121 Office: Spencer Stuart # 3700 525 Market St Ste 3700 San Francisco CA 94105-2745

GRAYSON, JOHN ALLAN, lawyer; b. Lowell, Ind., Oct. 14, 1930; s. Cecil Alaric and May (Modesitt) G.; m. Barbara Burroughs Merrill, Aug. 28, 1954; children: Merrill Ellis, Heather Hartwell Grayson Blalock. BSS, Northwestern U., 1952; JD, U. Mich., 1955. Bar: Mich. 1955, Ind. 1955, U.S. Dist. Ct. (no. dist., so. dist.) Ind. 1955. Assoc. Ross McCord Ice & Miller, Indpls., 1955-65; ptnr. Ice Miller Donadio & Ryan, Indpls., 1966-96; ind. civil mediator, 1996—; vis. asst. prof. Ind. U., Bloomington, 1957-58, adj. instr. real estate law, Indpls., 1959-66; author, lectr., conductor seminars in field; mem. Comparative Law Study delegation to Japan, People's Republic China, 1986. Contbr. numerous articles to profl. jours. Bd. dirs. Greater Indpls. Progress Com., 1981-86, Ind. Repertory Theatre, Inc., 1979-85, Indpls. Arts Chorale, 1982-87, Bosma Industries for Blind, Inc., 1988—, chmn. bd. dirs. 1988-89, Crossroads Rehab. Ctr., 1972-82, pres. 1974-77; mem. First Congregational Ch. Mem. ABA (ho. of dels. 1988-90, nat. conf. lawyers and realtors 1989-92, pres. nat. conf. bar 1988-98), Ind. State Bar Assn. (sr. lawyers divsn., v.p. 1988, pres. 1989-90), Indpls. Bar Assn. (bd. mgrs. 1985-87), Met. Indpls. Bd. Realtors (affiliate), Indpls. Legal Aid Soc., Am. Coll. Real Estate Lawyers (bd. govs. 1987-90), Am. Bar Found., Ind. Bar Foun., Indpls. Bar Found., Ind. Land Title Assn. (hon. life), Kiwanis Club Indpls. (pres. 1994), Internat. Wine and Food Soc., Confrerie de la Chaine des Rotisseurs, Confrerie des Chevaliers du Tastevin, Ind. Repertory Soc. Avocations: travel, golf. Home: 8540 Olde Mill Run Indianapolis IN 46260-5305 Office: 1 American Sq #82001 Indianapolis IN 46282-0002

GRAYSON, RICHARD ANDREW, aerospace engineer; b. Silver Spring, Md., Aug. 5, 1966; s. Benson Lee and Helen Marie (Donovan) G. BS in Aerospace Engring., U. Va., 1988; MBA, U. Ga., 1995, postgrad. Engr. Army Rsch. Lab., Aberdeen Proving Ground, Md., 1989-95; engr., rschr. Terry Coll. Bus./U. Ga., Athens, 1995-99; vis. prof. fin. U. Del., Newark, 1999—; mem. Joint Tech. Coordinating Group Air Sys., Wright-Patterson AFB, Ohio, 1990-95; leader PATRIOT Assessment Team, Riyadh, Saudi Arabia, 1991-92. Advisor youth group Episcopal Ch., McLean, Va., 1988-94. Recipient comdr.'s award for civilian svc. Dept. Army, 1991. Mem. Am. Helicopter Soc., Internat. Platform Assn., Source Selection Evaluation bd., Army LHX helicopter. Achievements include leader of on-site investigations in Saudi Arabia and at Ballistic Rsch. Lab. to assist in evaluating PATRIOT lethality against SCUD-B tactical ballistic missiles fired in Operation Desert Storm; performed AH-64 and UH-60 crew station vulnerability tests. Home: 131 E Broad St Apt 705 Athens GA 30601-2851 Office: U of Del Dept Fin Newark DE 19716

GRAYSON, RICHARD STEVEN (LORD OF MURSLEY), foreign correspondent, international legal and political management consultant, educator; b. Harlingen, Eng., June 21, 1944; came to the U.S., 1985; s. Bernard Lewis and Lucille Ruth (Kliston) G.; m. Katherine Lilian Hunston, June 4, 1971; children: Karyn Elizabeth, Lindsey Anne. BA, BS, Cambridge U., 1965; MA, Sch. Internat. Svc., 1968; PhD, Oxford (Eng.) U., 1974. Research and lectr. in internat. law and politics Oxford (Eng.) U., 1970-74; adviser, negotiator 2d Diplomatic Conf., Geneva; mem. secretariat and sec. Round Table Diplomatic Conf., Italy; also research fellow, writer and editor Inst. Henry Dunant, Geneva, 1974; internat. legal and polit. adviser Geneva, 1974; asso. dir. Inst. World Affairs, 1975, exec. dir., 1976-77; internat. legal and polit. mgmt. cons. N.Y.C., and Washington, 1975; internat. legal and polit. cons., univ. lectr., speaker in field and adviser various internat. and orgns., TV and radio programs on fgn. policy, 1976—; pres. Grayson Assos. Internat., Inc., 1978—; adj. assoc. prof. NYU. Author: Basic Background Study of Southeast Asia, 3 vols, 1968, Political and International Legal Implications of the Problems of Civil War. Bd. dirs. Royal Buckingham Theatre, Fgn. Press Assn., UNESCO Assn. USA, Center for Farm and Food Research, Am. Ibsen Theatre, Ibsen Soc. Am.; bd. dirs., corp. mem. Assn. for World Univ.; trustee InterFuture; del. Fed. Trust Edn. and Research Conf., Eng., 1969; mem. legis. adv. com. N.Y. State Legislature. Avalon fellow, 1966-68; grantee Inst. Henry Dunant, 1971-73. Mem. Internat. Inst. Strategic Studies, Inst. Hist. Research, Inst. Advanced Legal Studies, Inst. U.S. Studies, Mensa, Am. Soc. Internat. Law, Am. Polit. Sci. Assn., Internat. Law Assn., Internat. Polit. Sci. Assn., Am. Acad. Polit. and Social Sci., Oxford Soc., Brit. and Commonwealth Inst. (charter), Brit. Inst. Internat. and Comparative Law, Brit. Acad. of Film and TV Arts, Internat. Inst. Humanitarian Law, Cambridge U. Grad. Soc. (pres. 1969-70), U.S. Polo Assn., Oxford and Cambridge Soc., Fgn. Press Assn., Fgn. Press Ctr., UN Corrs. Assn., St. George's Soc., English-Speaking Union, Westchester Council for the Arts, Am. Film Inst., Nat. Acad. Television Arts and Scis., Radio and Television News Directors Assn., Pi Sigma Alpha, Pi Gamma Mu. Clubs: University (N.Y.C.); United Oxford and Cambridge Univ. (London), Savage (London); Pilgrims (N.Y.C. and London).

GRAYSON, ROBERT ALLEN, marketing executive, educator; b. N.Y.C., Oct. 8, 1927; s. Julius and Lillian (Davidson) G.; m. Suzanne B. Bomse, June 18, 1960; children: Peter, Jocelyn, Andrea. B.S., U. Ill., 1948; M.B.A., NYU, 1962, Ph.D., 1968. Vice pres. Henry S. Harris Assos. (mgmt. cons.), 1952-58; v.p. mktg. I. Rokeach & Sons, 1958-62; new products mgr. Lever Bros., 1962-68; sr. v.p., mem. exec. com. Daniel & Charles, Inc., N.Y.C., 1968-71; chmn. Grayson Assos., Inc., mgmt. cons. and trade show producers, Santa Barbara, Calif., 1971—; prof. bus. adminstrn. NYU Grad. Sch., 1966-85; prof. bus. policy Fordham U., 1972-75; bd. dirs. Durand Comm.; trustee Bankers Trust Variable Life Ins. Co., 1992-95, Equitable of Iowa, 1995—. Author: Introduction to Marketing, 1971, Resumes that Get Interviews, Interviews that Get Jobs, 1973; editor: Marketing and the Computer, 1967; pub. Jour. Consumer Mktg., Jour. Bus. and Indsl. Mktg., Jour. Svcs. Mktg., 1983-92. Mem. Am. Marketing Assn. (pres. 1969-70), Inst. Mgmt. Sci., AAUP, Acad. Mgmt. Office: 30482 Via Andalusia San Juan Capistrano CA 92675

GRAYSON, WALTON GEORGE, III, retired lawyer; b. Shreveport, La., Aug. 18, 1928; s. Walton George and Mary Alice (Lowrey) G.; m. Bennetta McEwen Purse, May 20, 1955; children: Walton Grayson IV, Mark C., Bennett P., Dwight P. AB, Princeton U., 1949; LLB, Harvard U., 1952. Bar: Tex. 1952, Dallas. Asst. counsel Gt. Nat. Life Ins. Co., Dallas, 1954-69; ptnr. Atwell Grayson & Atwell, Dallas, 1961-69, Grayson & Simon, Dallas, 1969-72; bd. dirs. Southland Corp., Dallas, 1962-87, v.p., gen. counsel, 1965-72; exec. v.p. Southland Corp., 1972-93; of counsel Simon & Twombly, 1972-84; chmn. Cityplace Devel. Corp., Dallas, 1987-93. Bd. dirs. American Trust Co., Dallas, 1995—. Served with USN, 1952-54. Mem. Tex. Bar Assn., Dallas Bar Assn., Petroleum Club, Masons. Mem. Christian Ch. Home: 10525 Strait Ln Dallas TX 75229-5424 Office: Southland Corp 2711 N Haskell Ave Ste 2800 Dallas TX 75204-2940

GRAYSTON, J. THOMAS, medical and public health educator; b. Wichita, Kans., Sept. 6, 1924; s. Jesse T. and Luzia B. (Thomas) G.; children: Susan, Jesse, David; m. M. Nan Bryant, June 7, 1980. Student, Carleton Coll., 1942-43; B.S., U. Chgo., 1947, M.D., 1948, M.S., 1952. Diplomate: Am. Bd. Internal Medicine, Am. Bd. Preventive Medicine. Intern Albany (N.Y.) Med. Sch., 1948-49; Seymour Coman fellow preventive medicine U. Chgo., 1949-50, asst. resident medicine, 1950-51; epidemiologist epidemic intelligence service USPHS, U. Kans. Med. Center, 1951-53; chief resident medicine U. Chgo., 1953-54, instr. medicine, 1953-55; fellow Nat. Found. Infantile Paralysis, 1954-56; asst. prof. medicine U. Chgo., 1955-60, asso. prof., 1960; chief div. microbiology and epidemiology U.S. Naval Med. Research Unit 2, Taipei, Taiwan, 1957-60; cons. U.S. Naval Med. Research Unit 2, 1960-79; prof. preventive medicine, chmn. dept. Sch. Medicine, U. Wash., 1960-70, founding dean Sch. Pub. Health and Community Medicine, 1970-71, v.p. for health scis., 1971-83, prof. dept. epidemiology, 1970—, adj. prof. pathobiology, 1982—; mem. exec. com. Regional Primate Research Center, 1964-70, research affiliate, 1967-70; attending physician medicine Univ. Hosp., Seattle, 1960-70; asso. mem. commn. acute respiratory diseases Armed Forces Epidemiol. Bd., 1962-65, mem., 1965-73; mem. research and engrng. adv. panel biology and medicine Dept. Def., 1963-67; sci. group trachoma research WHO, 1963; virology and rickettsiology study sect. NIH, 1963-67; mem. internat. centers com. Nat. Inst. Allergy and Infectious Diseases, 1967-71; mem. expert adv. panel on Trachoma, WHO, 1970-88; chmn. exec. com., mem. nat. adv. council on health professions edn. NIH, 1972-75. Contbr. numerous articles to profl. jours. Fellow Am. Coll. Preventive Medicine (v.p. gen. preventive medicine 1970-71, regent 1971-74), Am. Pub. Health Assn. (governing bd. 1978-80); mem. Am. Assn. Immunologists, Am. Assn. Physicians, Am. Epidemiol. Soc. (pres. 1982-83), Am. Fedn. Clin. Research, Am. soc. Microbiology, Am. Soc. Clin. Investigation, Am. Soc. Tropical Medicine and Hygiene, Assn. Acad. Health Centers (dir. 1975-80, pres. 1978-79), Assn. Tchrs. Preventive Medicine, Infectious Diseases Soc., Internat. Epidemiol. Assn., Soc. Exptl. Biology and Medicine, Inst. Medicine of Nat. Acad. Scis., Western Assn. Physicians, Western Soc. Clin. Rsch. Office: U Washington Dept Epidemiology MS 357236 Seattle WA 98195-7236

GRAZE, PETER ROBERT, physician; b. Washington, Sept. 13, 1946; s. Stanley I. and Mildred G.; m. Patricia Reichelderfer. BS in biology, Tufts U., 1967; MD, Harvard U., 1971. Intern, resident in internal medicine Mass. Gen. Hosp., Boston, 1971-73; rsch. assoc. divsn. virology Bur. of Biologics, FDA, 1973-75; fellow in hematology and oncology UCLA Ctr. for Health Scis., 1975-77; asst. prof. medicine UCLA Sch. Medicine, L.A., 1977-78; assoc. prof. medicine U. Nev. Sch. Medicine, Reno, 1979-90, prof. medicine, 1990-92; sr. ptnr. Cancer Cons., Las Vegas, 1981-92; ptnr. Annapolis (Md.) Med. Specialists, 1993—; co-dir. Hospice of the Chesapeake, Md., 1997—; mem. adv. bd. Nathan Anderson Hospice, Las Vegas, 1986-91. Co-author: Coal Mining Health and Safety, 1971; contbr. articles to profl. jours. Fellow ACP; mem. Am. Soc. Clin. Oncology, Am. Soc. Hematology, Am. Acad. Hospice and Palliative Medicine, Md. Soc. Clin. Oncology (pres. 1996—). Office: Annapolis Med Specialists 900 Bestgate Rd Ste 300 Annapolis MD 21401-7957

GRAZER, BRIAN, film company executive. Co-chair Imagine Films Entertainment. Prodr. films including: Night Shift, 1982, Splash, 1984, Real Genius, 1985, Spies Like Us (with George Folsey Jr.), 1985, Armed & Dangerous (with James Keach), 1986, Like Father, Like Son (with David Valdes, 1987, Parenthood, 1989, Cry Baby (with Jim Abrahams, 1990, Kindergarten Cop (with Ivan Reitman), 1990, Closet Land (with Ron Howard), 1991, The Doors (with Nicholas Clainos & Mario Kassar), 1991, Backdraft (with Raffaella DeLaurentiis), 1991, My Girl, 1991, Far and Away (with Ron Howard), 1992, Boomerang (with Warrington Hudlin), 1992, Housesitter, 1992, CB4 (with Sean Daniel), 1993, For Love or Money, 1993, The Paper (with Frederick Zollo), 1994, My Girl 2, 1994, Greedy, 1994, The Cowboy Way, 1994, Apollo 13 (with Ron Howard), 1995 (Acad. Award Nom. Best Picture, 1996), Sgt. Bilko, 1996, Ransom, 1996. Office: Imagine Films Entertainment 9465 Wilshire Blvd 7th Fl Beverly Hills CA 90212*

GRAZIANI, LEONARD JOSEPH, pediatric neurologist, researcher; b. Phila., Nov. 17, 1929; s. Annibale and Norina (Ditomasi) G.; m. Amelia Honeyford, June 29, 1956; children: Paul, Amy, Virginia, David. BA, LaSalle Coll., Phila., 1951; MD, Jefferson Med. Coll., Phila., 1955. Diplomate Am. Bd. Pediatrics, Am. Bd. Psychiatry and Neurology. Intern Valley Forge Army Hosp., Pa., 1956; resident Brooke Army Hosp., San Antonio, 1959; chief pediatric svc. Ireland Army Hosp., Ft. Knox, Ky., 1960-61; neurology fellow Bronx Mcpl. Hosp. Ctr., N.Y., 1961-64; interdisciplinary fellow Albert Einstein Coll. Medicine, Bronx, N.Y., 1964-66, asst. prof. pediatrics and neurology, 1964-68; career scientist Health Rsch. Coun., N.Y.C., 1967-68; attending pediatrician, neurologist Thomas Jefferson U. Hosp., Phila., 1968—; chief div. pediatric neurology dept. pediatrics Jefferson Med. Coll., Thomas Jefferson U., Phila., 1974-99, vice chair dept. pediatrics, 1988-96, prof. pediatrics, neurology, 1968—; cons. neurologist The Woods Schs., Langhorne, Pa., 1968—, Children's Rehab. Hosp., Phila.; cons. pediatrician Wills Eye Hosp., Phila.; staff cons. Wilmington (Del.) Med. Ctr.; staff E.I. duPont Inst., Wilmington, 1984—. Contbr. articles to profl. jours. Capt. U.S. Army, 1955-61. Fellow Am. Acad. Neurology, Am. Acad. Pediatrics; mem. Am. Pediatric Soc., Soc. Pediatric Rsch., Child Neurology Soc., Alpha Omega Alpha, Sigma Xi. Office: Jefferson Med Coll 1025 Walnut St Rm 706D Philadelphia PA 19107-5001

GRAZIANI, LINDA ANN, secondary education educator; b. Erie, Pa., Aug. 16, 1951; d. Edward and Christine (Karsznia) Grzelak; m. Richard Martin Graziani, Aug. 4, 1973; 1 child, Kristen Lynn. BS, Pa. State U., 1973; MBA, Gannon U., 1978. Asst. twsp. sec. Lawrence Park Twsp., Erie, Pa., 1968-73; bus. edn. tchr. Millcreek Sch. Dist., Erie, 1973-74, Fairview (Pa.) Sch. Dist., 1974-76, 83—, Girard (Pa.) Sch. Dist., 1976; adult edn. instr. Erie (Pa.) County Tech. Sch., 1978-85; active Bus. Adv. Coun., Millcreek, Pa., 1994—. Bd. dirs. Lake Erie Jr. Women's Club, Erie, 1977-83, St. Stephen's Preschool, Fairview, 1982-83; eucharistic min. Holy Cross Ch., Fairview, 1982—. Mem. Nat. Bus. Edn. Assn., Pa. State Edn. Assn., Pa. Bus. Edn. Assn., Erie County Bus. Edn. Assn., Inst. Mgmt. Accts., Phi Chi Theta. Democrat. Roman Catholic. Avocations: aerobics, tennis, golf, cross country skiing, reading, cooking. Home: 680 Hawthorne Trce Fairview PA 16415-1723 Office: Fairview HS 7460 Mccray Rd Fairview PA 16415-2401

GRAZIANI, N. JANE, communications executive, publisher; b. Pensacola, Fla., Apr. 25, 1958; d. Hamlet and Dolly (Fields) G. BA, La. State U., 1980, M in Journalism, 1984. Asst. editor Daily Reveille, Baton Rouge, 1978-79; with Cath. Commentator, Baton Rouge, 1979-80; bur. chief Capitol News Svc., Baton Rouge, 1981-83; adminstrv. asst. Common Cause, Baton Rouge, 1983-84; reporter Sanford (Fla.) Evening Herald, 1985; assoc. editor Inst. Internal Auditors, Altamonte Springs, Fla., 1985-86; dir. publs. Fla. Soc. Assn. Execs., Winter Park, 1986-88; dir. communications Orange County Med. Soc., Orlando, Fla., 1988-91; pub. King Publs., Orlando, Fla., 1991-92; editor Assn. Source, Casselberry, Fla., 1992-93, Car & Travel/Fla., Heathrow, 1993-96; equipment editor Golf for Women, Lake Mary, Fla., 1996-97; freelance writer on golf, travel, health, bus., 1997—; mgr. pub. rels. Am. Automobile Assn., 1998—. author, editor on golf, travel, pub. rels., mktg. Team capt. March of Dimes Walk Am., Orlando, 1989. Recipient Med. Journalism award Sandoz Pharms., 1989. Mem. Soc. Profl. Journalists, Fla. Mag. Assn. (program com. 1987-89, trade show com. 1990, 91, bd. dirs. 1990-94, treas. 1991, pres. elect 1992, pres. 1993, past pres. 1994, Bronze award for Gen. Excellence 1989, Bronze award for Best Spl. Issue 1990, Bronze award for Gen. Excellence, 1994, First Place for Best Regular Editl. 1994, First Place for Best Feature, 1996), Ctrl. Fla. Soc. Assn. Execs. (comms. com. 1988-91), Fla. Soc. Assn. Execs., South Atlantic Karate Assn. (1st Kyu 1985—), Internat. Shotokan Karate Fedn. Republican. Presbyterian. Avocations: scuba diving, fishing, boating, traveling, martial arts.

GRAZIANO, CATHERINE ELIZABETH, retired nursing educator; b. Providence, Dec. 2, 1931; d. William J. and Catherine E. (Keegan) Hawkins; m. Louis W. Graziano, Oct. 9, 1954; children—Mary Lou, William F., Catherine E., Paul, Carol. B.S., Salve Regina Coll., Newport, R.I., 1949-53, M.S., Salve Regina Coll., 1984; M.S., Boston Coll., 1965; PhD, Pacific Western U., 1988. Instr. nursing Salve Regina U., 1953-66, asst. prof., 1966-74, assoc. prof., 1974-82, prof., 1982-97, chair dept. nursing, 1974-93; ret., 1997; staff-charge nurse St. Joseph's Hosp., Providence, 1953-93, part-time faculty, 1960, 65; mem. R.I. Bd. Nurse Registration and Edn., 1970-79, pres., 1977-79; charter mem., sec. R.I. Health, Sci. and Edn. Council, 1972-78; adj. asst. prof. Coll. Nursing U. R.I., 1986—; mem. R.I. Senate, Providence, 1992—. Active local and nat. senatorial campaigns. Recipient Regina medal Salve Regina U., 1997. Mem. ANA, R.I. Nurses Assn. (pres. 1969-71, 73-75), Women Educators (charter), Nursing Leadership Council R.I. (charter; chair 1981-82, sec. 1982—), Nat. League Nursing (accreditation site visitor 1990-96), Sigma Theta Tau. Roman Catholic. Home: 42 Rowley St Providence RI 02909-5521 Office: RI Senate RI State House Rm 308 Smith St Providence RI 02903

GRAZIANO, CRAIG FRANK, lawyer; b. Des Moines, Dec. 7, 1950; s. Charles Dominic and Corrine Rose (Comito) G. BA summa cum laude, Macalester Coll., 1973; JD with honors, Drake U., 1975. Bar: Iowa 1976, U.S. Dist. Ct. (no. and so. dists.) Iowa 1978, U.S. Ct. Appeals (8th cir.) 1977, U.S. Supreme Ct. 1988. Law clk. to Hon. M. D. Van Oosterhout U.S. Ct. Appeals (8th cir.), Sioux City, Iowa, 1976-78; assoc. Dickinson, Mackaman, Tyler & Hagen, P.C., Des Moines, 1978-82, ptnr., 1982-98; with Office of Consumer Advocate Iowa Dept. Justice, Des Moines, 1999—. Mem. ABA, Iowa Bar Assn. (chair specialization com. 1993-96, chair adminstrv. law sect. 1996-99), Polk County Bar Assn., Order of Coif, Phi Beta Kappa. Home: 500 44th St Des Moines IA 50312-2408 Office: 310 Maple St Des Moines IA 50319-0063

GRAZIANO, FRANK MICHAEL, medical educator, researcher; b. Easton, Pa., June 5, 1942; s. Michael and Grace (Farace) G.; m. Mary Helen Ashton, Feb. 4, 1967; children: Teresa Ann, Frank Jr., Alicia Grace. BS, St. Joseph's Coll., 1964; MS, Villanova Univ., 1967; PhD, Univ. Va., 1970, MD, 1973. Diplomate Am. Bd. of Internal Medicine, Am. Bd. of Allergy and Clinical Immunology. Internship Univ. Wis. Hosp., Madison, 1973-74; residency in medicine Univ. Wis., Madison, 1974-76, asst. prof., 1978-84, assoc. prof., 1984-89, prof. medicine, 1989—, chief section of Rheumatology, 1989—. Author numerous books, articles, papers in field. Admissions com. Univ. Wis. Medical Sch., 1983-86, Minority subcom. chmn., 1985-86; medical and scientific com. Wis. Arthritis Found., 1979-80, Univ. Wis. Madison AIDS Task Force Com., 1986-89; Bd. dirs. Wis. Arthritis Found., 1990—, Wis. Com. Based Rsch. Consortium, 1990—. Recipient Am. Acad. Travel grant, 1978, NIH Young Investigator award, 1980, NIH Allergic Disease Acad. award, 1985. Fellow Am. Acad. Allergy/Immunology, Am. Coll. Physicians; mem. Am. Assn. Immunologists, Am. Assn. Advancement of Sci., Am. Thoracic Soc., Am. Coll. Pheumatology, Clinical Immunology Soc., Wis. Allergy Soc., Wis. Rheumatism Assn., Sigma Xi. Home: 853 Tipperary Rd Oregon WI 53575-2641 Office: Univ Wis Hosp & Clinics 600 Highland Ave # H6 367 Madison WI 53792-0001*

GRAZIN, IGOR NIKOLAI, law educator, state official; b. Tartu, Estonia, June 27, 1952; came to U.S., 1990; s. Nikolai V. and Dagmar R. (Kibe) G.; m. Elena E. Rozina, May 10, 1984; 1 child, Anton. Jurist degree, U. Tartu, Estonia, 1975; candidate of sci. in law, Moscow Inst. Law, 1979; DSc in Law, Inst. State and Law, Moscow, 1986. Cert. jurist, USSR. Lectr., prof. U. Tartu, Estonia, 1977-86, prof., 1986-89; assoc. dean Law Sch. U. Tartu, Estonia, 1986-89; mem. of the coun. Popular Front of Estonia, Tallinn, 1988-90; prof. U. Notre Dame, Ind., 1990—; faculty fellow Kellogg Inst. for Internat. Studies, Notre Dame, 1994—; adj. fellow Hudson Inst., 1994—; dir. Estonian Privatization Trust Fund; prof. law Am.-Estonian Concordia U. Author: Law as Text, 1983, Jeremy Bentham, 1990, Anglo-American Philosophy of Law, 1983, Right Course, 1994; editor: Studia Juridica, 1988-90; contbr. articles to profl. jours. Dep., Congress of Peoples Deps. of USSR, 1989-91; mem. Supreme Soviet, Moscow, 1989-91; counsellor to Pres. of Republic of Estonia, 1993—; mem. Nat. Parliament of Estonia, 1995—. Mem. AAUP, Estonian Bar Assn., Federalist Soc. U.S.A., Acad. Soc. of Estonian Lawyers (co-founder, vice chmn. 1989-90), Acad. Arts (Estonia, bd. dirs.), Rotary. Republican. Lutheran. Office: U Notre Dame Law Sch Notre Dame IN 46556

GRAZZINI, GREGORY PAUL, construction company executive; b. Edina, Minn., May 1, 1968; s. Eugene Francis Jr. and Rosalie Ann (Morrissette) G.; m. Maureen Ann Weber, Aug. 6, 1994; 1 child, Adam Weber Grazzini. BA, U. St. Thomas, St. Paul, 1991. Proj. mgr. Grazzini Bros. & Co., Mpls., 1988—, dir., 1997—. Mem. Am. Soc. Profl. Estimators (dir. 1992-93), Associated Gen. Contractors, Ducks Unlimited, Inc. (nat. trustee, chmn. Barnesville chpt. 1993-94, state of Minn. trustee, sec. 1996-98, zone chmn. 1996—, Disting. Svc. award 1995). Republican. Roman Catholic. Avocations: hunting, fishing, target shooting, dog training, golfing. Home: 7230 Tartan Curv Eden Prairie MN 55346-3902 Office: Grazzini Bros and Co 1200 W 79th St Minneapolis MN 55420-1024

GREANEY, JOHN M., state supreme court justice; b. Westfield, Mass., Apr. 8, 1939; s. Patrick Joseph and Margaret Irene (Fitzgerald) G.; m. Susan H. Greaney, Nov. 23, 1967. 1 child, Jessica S. BA summa cum laude, Holly Cross Coll., 1960; JD, NYU, 1963; LLD (hon.), Westfield State Coll., 1967, Western New England Coll., 1969; LLD, New England Law Sch., 1991. Bar: Mass., Supreme Judicial Ct., U.S. Dist. Ct., U.S. Supreme Ct. Ptnr. Ely & King, Springfield, Mass., 1963-73; presiding judge Hampden County Housing Ct., Springfield, Mass., 1973-75; assoc. judge Mass. Superior Ct., Boston, 1975-76; assoc. justice Mass. Appeals Ct., Boston, 1976-84, 1976-84, chief justice, 1984-89; assoc. justice Mass. Supreme Judicial Ct., Boston, 1989—; former faculty mem. Western New England Law Sch., Westfield State Coll.; co-chair. Supreme Judicial Ct's Gender Bias Study Commn; mem. bd. Tribunes WGBY-Channel #57. Former assoc. editor Mass. Law Review. Trustee, dir. Westfield Atheneum, participant Child and Family Svcs. Program. Fellow Am. Bar Found.; mem. ABA (litigation, judicial adminstrn. section), Hampden County Bar Assn.(former mem. exec. com., grievance com., treas.), Mass. Bar Assn.(former chmn. Young Lawyers section, bd. delegates, exec. com., grievance com., legal svc. to the poor com., (current) civil litigation, criminal law sections), Am. Law Inst. Avocations: competitive running, reading. Office: Mass Supreme Jud Court Pemberton Sq 1300 New Courthouse Boston MA 02108*

GREASER, MARION LEWIS, science educator; b. Vinton, Iowa, Feb. 10, 1942; s. Lewis Levi and Elisabeth (Sage) G.; m. Marilyn Sue Pfister, June 12, 1965; children—Suzanne, Scott. B.S., Iowa State U., 1964; M.S., U. Wis., 1967, Ph.D., 1969. Postdoctoral fellow Boston Biomed. Research Inst., 1968-71; asst. prof. sci. U. Wis., Madison, 1971-73, assoc. prof., 1973-77, prof., 1977—. Contbr. articles to profl. jours. Recipient Outstanding Researcher award Am. Heart Assn.-Wis., 1985. Mem. Am. Soc. Biochem. Molecular Biology, Biophys. Soc., Inst. Food Technologists, Am. Meat Sci. Assn. (Disting. Research award 1981), AAAS. Home: 2374 Branch St Middleton WI 53562-2809 Office: U Wis Muscle Biology Lab 1805 Linden Dr W Madison WI 53706-1110

GREASON, ARTHUR LEROY, JR., university administrator; b. Newport, R.I., Sept. 13, 1922; s. Arthur LeRoy and Pauline (Brown) G.; m. Pauline Schaaf, Dec. 29, 1945; children—Randall Mark, Katherine, Douglas Bradford. BA, Wesleyan U., Middletown, Conn., 1945; MA, Harvard U., 1947, PhD, 1954; LittD (hon.), Wesleyan U., 1987; LHD (hon.), Colby Coll., 1989, Bowdoin Coll., 1990, Bates Coll., 1990, U. Maine, 1992. Asst. to dean Wesleyan U., 1945-46; teaching fellow English Harvard, 1948-52; mem. faculty Bowdoin Coll., 1952-90, assoc. prof. English, 1961-66, prof., 1966-90, dean students, 1962-66, dean of coll., 1966-75, acting pres., 1981, pres., 1981-90. Trustee Portland Stage Co., 1991-97, Westbrook Coll., 1992-96, Maine Hist. Soc., 1994-97, U. New England, 1996—, Maine Bd. Bar Examiners, 1997—, DLF Charitable Found., 1997—. Kent fellow Soc. Religion Higher Edn., 1946. Mem. Maine Bar Assn. (fee arbitration commn. 1997—), Phi Beta Kappa. Conglist. Home: 6 Longfellow Ave Brunswick ME 04011-2534

GREASON, MURRAY CROSSLEY, JR., lawyer; b. Wake Forest, N.C., Dec. 12, 1936; s. Murray Crossley and Evelyn Elizabeth (Hackney) G.; m. Joan millicent Wilder, Elizabeth Hillary. BS magna cum laude, Wake Forest U., 1959, JD magna cum laude, 1962. Bar: N.C. 1962. Assoc. firm Womble Carlyle Sandridge & Rice, Winston-Salem, N.C., 1965-70, mem., 1970—, mng. p tnr., 1988—; vis. lectr. Wake Forest U., 1972-74. Pres. Winston-Salem Estate Planning Coun., 1973; trustee Denmarl Loan Fund, scholarships to Wake Forest U.; bd. visitors Wake Forest Law Sch., 1983—, chmn., 1994—; trustee Wake Forest U., 1990, vice chmn., 1997—; chmn. N.W. N.C. chpt. ARC, 1996; chmn. bd. United Way Dorsyth County, 1995; mem. Commn. on Ministry Episcopalian Diocese N.C., 1983-93. Capt. JAG, AUS, 1962-65. Fellow Am. Coll. Tax Coun.; mem. ABA, N.C. Bar Assn., Dorsyth County Bar Assn. (pres. 1986-87), Winston-Salem C. of C. (bd. dirs.), Wake Forest U. Alumni Assn. (prs. 1973), Forsyth Country Club, Phi Beta Kappa, Omicron Delta Kappa. Episcopalian. Home: 745 Arbor Rd Winston Salem NC 27104-2209 Office: Womble Carlyle Sandridge PLLC 1600 BB&T PO Box 84 Winston Salem NC 27102-0084

GREATBATCH, WILSON, biomedical engineer; b. Buffalo, Sept. 6, 1919; married; 5 children. BEE, Cornell U., 1950; MSEE, U. Buffalo, 1957; ScD (hon.), Houghton Coll., 1971, SUNY, Buffalo, 1984, Clarkson U., 1987,

Roberts Wesleyan Coll., 1988. Project engr. Cornell Aeronaut Lab. Inc., 1950-52; asst. prof. elec. engring. U. Buffalo, 1952-57; mgr. electronics div. Taber Instrument Corp., 1957-60; v.p. Mennen Greatbatch Electronics Inc., 1962-78; adj. prof. elec. engring. SUNY, Buffalo, 1981—; adj. prof. engring. Cornell U., Ithaca, N.Y., 1989—; adj. prof. physical scis. Houghton (N.Y.) Coll., 1978—. *Wilson Greatbatch expressed an interest in science and invention from childhood. In his teens he built short-wave radio transmitters and receivers for his own amateur radio station (WZQBI). He served in the Navy from 1939 through 1945, advancing to the rank of Chief Petty Officer (ACRM). His assignments ranged from navy radioman on merchant ships, to teaching radar in a Navy school, to flying as rear gunner in carrier-based dive bombers. He has been elected to Fellow Grade in nine professional societies and to four National Halls of Fame. He is most noted for his invention of the implant ankle cardiac pacemaker.* Contbr. over 100 articles to sci. jours; holder over 150 U.S. and fgn. patents. Recipient Holley medal ASME, 1986, Chancellor Morton medal U. Buffalo, 1990, disting. svc. award NSPE, 1984, Pacemaker award Prince Rainier of Monaco, 1988, Nat. Medal of Tech. Pres. Bush, 1990, Vladimir Karapetoff award Eta Kappa Nu, 1992, Washington award Western Engring. Soc., Chgo., 1995, Lemelson/MIT Career Achievement award, 1996; named to Am. Inventors Hall of Fame, 1986, U.S. Space Tech. Hall of Fame, 1993, Sci. and Engring. Hall of Fame, 1997; Paul Harris fellow Rotary Internat., 1993. Fellow AAAS, IEEE, ASME, Am. Coll. Cardiology, Royal Soc. Health, Am. Soc. Angiology, Am. Inst. Med. and Biol. Engring. (founder), N.Y. Acad. Scis.; mem. NAE, Assn. Advancement Med. Instrumentation (Laufman award 1982), Sigma Xi, Tau Beta Pi, Eta Kappa Nu. Achievements include invention of implantable cardiac pacemaker; rsch. in implantable power supplies for medical uses, biomass energy, genetic engring. Office: Greatbatch Gen Aid Ltd 5935 Davison Rd Akron NY 14001-9457 Home: 5935 Davison Rd Akron NY 14001-9457

GREATHOUSE, PATRICIA DODD, retired psychometrist, counselor; b. Columbus, Ga., Apr. 26, 1935; d. John Allen and Patricia Ottis (Murphy) Dodd; m. Robert Otis Greathouse; children: Mark Andrew, Perry Allen. BS in Edn., Auburn (Ala.) U., 1959, M in Edn., 1966, AA in Counselor Edn., 1975. Cert. secondary tchr., Ala., Ga. Tchr. Columbus High Sch., 1959-61, Phenix City Bd. Edn., 1957-58; tchr. pub. schs. Russell County (Ala.) Bd. Edn., Phenix City and Seale, 1961-69, 71-80, 82-83, counselor pub. schs., 1969-82, 83-93; psychometrist Russell County (Ala.) Bd. Edn., Seale, 1980-82; county psychometrist Russell County (Ala.) Bd. Edn., Phenix City, 1983-93. Editor: (ann.) Tiger Tales, 1973 (award 1980). Treas. Ladonia PTA, Phenix City, 1966-68, parliamentarian, 1987-88; leader Ladonia chpt. 4-H Club, Phenix City, 1961-80; active March of Dimes, Am. Heart Assn.; rep. Mardi Gras; tchr. Sunday Sch., Vacation Bible Sch. N. Phenix Bapt. Ch.; vol. Reach to Recovery Am. Cancer Soc., 1980—; mem., sec. Ctrl. Activity Sr. Ctr., 1994—; chmn. Russell County Heritage Book Com., 1999—. Named Mardi Gras Queen Phenix City Moose Club, 1987, hon. life mem. Ladonia PTA, 1967, Outstanding Tchr. of Yr., 1972; recipient Silver Clover award 4-H Club, 1966, Outstanding PTA Performance award 1986-87; nominated to Tchr. Hall of Fame, 1980-81, 81-82, 82-83. Mem. NEA, AARP, Russell County Edn. Assn. (pres.-elect 1973), Ala. Edn. Assn., Ala. Pers. and Guidance Assn., Ala. Assn. Counseling and Devel., Coun. Exceptional Children, Am. Bus. Women's Assn. (pres. Phenix City charter chpt. 1986-87, Woman of Yr. 1987, Perfect Attendance award, treas. 1990-95, sec. 1995—, tri-county coun.), Daus. of Nile (pres. Phenix City club 1980-81, 83-84, Outstanding Svc. award, sec. 1994—), Ret. Tchrs. Assn. (ctrl. sr. activities ctr. 1993, sr. citizens' sec. 1993), East Ala. Geneal. Soc., Pike County Geneal. Soc., Muscogee County Geneal. Soc., Phenix City Arts Coun., Jetettes (v.p. Phenix City club 1976, 80), Jaycettes, Order of Eastern Star (worthy matron 1981-82), Riverview Sr. Citizens, Delta Kappa Gamma (sec. 1979-80, pres. 1990-94), Kappa Iota. Democrat. Baptist. Avocations: stamp collecting, genealogy, painting, quilting, ceramics. Home: 1502 Nottingham Dr Phenix City AL 36867-1941

GREAUX, CHERYL PREJEAN, federal agency administrator; b. Houston, July 30, 1949; m. Robert Bruce Greaux. BA, Tex. So. U., 1967; MA, U. Tex., 1973. Mgr. compliance programs Dept. Labor, N.Y.C., 1973-80; corp. human resources mgr. Allied Signal Inc., Morristown, N.J., 1980-85; account exec., sourcing specialist Dean Witter Reynolds, N.Y.C., 1986-88; dir. civil rights staff USDA Rural Devel., Washington, 1994—; cons. Gen. Foods, White Plains, N.Y., 1985, Seagrams, N.Y.C., 1984. Author: Struggling Within or Success from Within? 1973. Lectr. Nat. Urban League, 1980—; cons. Nat. Urban Affairs Coun., N.Y., 1981-86; bd. dirs. Ednl. Opportunity Fund, N.J., 1985-87. Mem. Edges Group, Delta Sigma Theta. Baptist. Office: Dept Agr 14th and Independence SW Washington DC 20250

GREAVER, HARRY, artist; b. L.A., Oct. 30, 1929; s. Harry Jones and Lucy Catherine (Coons) G.; m. Hanne Synnestvedt Nielsen, Nov. 30, 1955; children—Peter, Paul, Lotte. BFA, U. Kans., 1951, MFA, 1952. Assoc. prof. art U. Maine, Orono, 1955-66; exec. dir. Kalamazoo Inst. Arts, 1966-78; dir. Greaver Gallery, Cannon Beach, Oreg., 1978—; mem. visual com. Mich. Coun. Arts, 1976-78. One-man exhbns. include Baker U., Baldwin, Kans., 1955, U. Maine, Orono, 1958, 59, Pacific U., 1985; group exhbns. include U. Utah Mus. Fine Arts, 1972-73, Purdue U., 1977, Drawings/U.S.A, St. Paul, 1963, San Diego Mus., 1971, Rathbun Gallery, Portland, Oreg., 1988; 10-yr. print retrospective Cannon Beach Arts Assn., 1989, 20-yr. retrospective, 1998. Mem. adv. bd. Haystack Ctr. for the Arts, Cannon Beach, 1988-91. Recipient Purchase award Nat. Endowment Arts, 1971; grantee U. Maine, 1962-64. Mem. Cannon Beach Arts Assn., 1986-88. Address: PO Box 120 Cannon Beach OR 97110-0120

GREAVER, JOANNE HUTCHINS, mathematics educator, author; b. Louisville, Aug. 9, 1939; d. Alphonso Victor and Mary Louise (Sage) Hutchins; 1 child, Mary Elizabeth. BS in Chemistry, U. Louisville, 1961, MEd, 1971; MAT in Math., Purdue U., 1973. Cert. tch. secondary edn. Specialist math. Jefferson County (Ky.) Pub. Schs.; pres. Math Mentors Inc., 1962—; part-time faculty Bellarmine Coll., Louisville, 1982—, U. Louisville, 1985—; project reviewer NSF, 1983—; advisor Council on Higher Edn., Frankfort, Ky., 1983-86; active regional and nat. summit on assessment in math., 1991, state task force on math., assessment adv. com., Nat. Assessment Ednl. Progress standards com.; charter mem. Commonwealth Tchrs. Inst., 1984—; mem. Nat. Forum for Excellence in Edn., Indpls., 1983; metric edn. leader Fed. Metric Project, Louisville, 1979-82; mem. Ky. Ednl. Reform Task Force, Assessment Com., Nat. Framework, Nat. Assessment Ednl. Progress Rev. Com.; lectr. in field. Author: (workbook) Down Algebra Alley, 1984; co-author curriculum guides. Recipient Presdl. award for excellence in math. tchg., 1983; named Outstanding Citizen, SAR, 1984; named to Hon. Order Ky. Cols.; grantee NSF, 1983, Louisville Cmty. Found., 1984-86. Mem. Greater Louisville Coun. Tchrs. of Math. (pres. 1977-78, 94—, Outstanding Educator award 1987), Nat. Coun. Tchrs. of Math. (reviewer 1981—), Ky. Coun. Tchrs. of Math. (pres. 1990-91, Jefferson County Tchr. of Yr. award 1985), Math. Assn. Am., Kappa Delta Pi, Delta Kappa Gamma, Zeta Tau Alpha. Republican. Presbyterian. Avocations: tropical fish, gardening, handicrafts, travel, tennis. Home: 11513 Tazwell Dr Louisville KY 40241

GREAVES, JAMES LOUIS, art conservator; b. Middletown, Conn., Jan. 25, 1943; s. Wellington North and Mabel (Frazer) G.; divorced; 1 child, Stephen Frazer. BS in Biology, Coll. William and Mary, 1965; MA in Art History, NYU; Diploma in Art Conservation, Inst. Fine Arts, 1970. Conservation intern Los Angeles County Mus., 1968-70, conservator, 1970, asst. head conservator, 1977-79, acting head conservator, 1979-81, sr. paintings conservator, 1981-85; owner, cons. Conservation Svcs., Santa Monica, Calif., 1985—; chief conservator Detroit Inst. Arts, 1970-77; cons. conservator Art Gallery of Huntington Library, San Marino, Calif., 1979-91; part-time instr. art conservation for sr. and grad. level art historians, UCLA and Calif. State U., Fullerton, 1979-83. Fellow Internat. Inst. Conservation, Am. Inst. Conservation; mem. Western Assn. Art Conservators (past pres.). *

GREAVES, WILLIAM WEBSTER, chemist, patent analyst; b. Queenstown, Md., Jan. 10, 1951; s. William Emory and Mary Elizabeth (Wood) G. BS in Chemistry, Bucknell U., 1973; PhD in Inorganic Chemistry, Iowa State U., 1978. Tech. publ. editor Standard Oil of Ind., Naperville, Ill., 1978-81, rsch. info. scientist, 1981-84; assoc. editor Science mag., Washington, 1984-86; supr. chem. data systems SK&F Labs., Upper Merion, Pa., 1986-88; sr. patent searcher Abbott Labs., Abbott Park, Ill., 1988-90; patent analyst Amoco Corp., Chgo., 1990—. Contbr. articles to profl. publs.; contbr. revs. to Lambda Book Report. Active Frontrunners Chgo., 1988—, sec., 1991, v.p., 1992, pres., 1993, past pres., 1994, Proud to Run com., 1996—; active D.C. Front Runners, 1984—; mem. Chgo. Adv. Coun. on Gay and Lesbian Issues, 1994—; Chgo. coord. track & field and marathon events Gay Games, N.Y.C., 1994. Mem. AAAS, Am. Chem. Soc. (sec. chem. info. divsn. 1994-96, edn. com. Chgo. chpt. 1981-84, mgr. Chgo. chpt. student symposium 1982), Soc. Tech. Comm. (sr., sec. Chgo. chpt. 1983), USA Track & Field, Chgo. Area Runners Assn., Sigma Xi. Republican. Roman Catholic.

GREBB, MICHAEL D., systems analyst; b. Webster, Mass., Feb. 20, 1950; s. Max G. and Jean A. (Ansorge) G.; m. Janet Meiburger, June 27, 1981 (div. 1997); children: Kevin, David. BS, USAF Acad., 1972; MA, Ind. U., 1973; JD, Georgetown U., 1985. Commd. 2d lt. USAF, 1972, advanced through grades to maj., 1984; systems analyst, asst. program mgr., program mgr. Betac Corp., Alexandria, Va., 1986—, dir. ISR architectures. Col. USAFR, 1994—. Mem. Air Force Assn. (v.p. scholarships Steele chpt. 1994—), D.C. Bar Assn., Nat. Mil. Intelligence Assn. (v.p. reserve affairs).

GREBE, MICHAEL W., lawyer; b. Peoria, Ill., Oct. 25, 1940. BS, U.S. Mil. Acad., 1962; JD magna cum laude, U. Mich., 1970. Bar: Wis. 1970. Ptnr. Foley & Lardner, Milw. Note and comment editor U. Mich. Law Review, 1969-70. Mem. State Bar Wis., Milw. Bar Assn., Order of Coif. Office: Foley & Lardner Firstar Ctr 777 E Wisconsin Ave Ste 3800 Milwaukee WI 53202-5367*

GREBER, ROBERT MARTIN, financial investments executive; b. Phila., Mar. 15, 1938; s. Joseph and Golda (Rubin) G.; m. Judith Ann Pearlstein, Dec. 23, 1962; children: Matthew, Jonathan. B.S. in Fin., Temple U., 1962; grad., Sch. Mgmt. and Strategic Studies, 1982-84. Account exec. Merrill Lynch, Phila., 1962-68; portfolio mgr. v.p. Afuture Funds Inc., Lima, Pa., 1968-70; instl. account exec. Merrill Lynch, Phila., 1970-75; officer, mgr.-v.p. Merrill Lynch, Los Angeles, 1975-79; chief fin. officer Lucasfilm Ltd., Los Angeles, 1979-80; pres., CEO Lucasfilm Ltd., San Rafael, Calif., 1980-84, Diagnostic Networks, Inc., San Francisco, 1984-87; ptnr. Leon A. Farley Assocs., San Francisco, 1988-90; pres., COO The Pacific Stock Exch., 1990-95, chmn., CEO, 1996—; bd. dirs. Bay View Capital Group. Bd. dirs. KQED Pub. Broadcasting Sys., San Francisco, 1983, chmn. bd., 1988; bd. dirs. Film Inst. No. Calif., Marin Symphony Orch., 1981-83, Sonic Solutions, 1993—; trustee Western Behavior Scis. Inst., La JOlla, 1982-89; vice chmn. Assn. Am. Pub. TV, 1992-94; trustee Beryl Buck Inst. for Edn., 1990-93. With Army NG, 1959-60. Office: Pacific Stock Exchange Inc 301 Pine St San Francisco CA 94104-3601*

GREBOW, EDWARD, television company executive; b. Lakewood, N.J., July 17, 1949; s. Benjamin and Ruth (Blume) G.; m. Cynthia Miller, Feb. 23, 1985. BBA, George Washington U., 1971; postgrad., George Washington, 1972. V.p. Morgan Guaranty Trust Co., N.Y.C., 1972-80, J.P. Morgan & Co., Inc., N.Y.C., 1980-85; exec. v.p. Bowery Savs. Bank, N.Y.C., 1985-88; sr. v.p. CBS, Inc., N.Y.C., 1988-94, exec. v.p., 1994-95; pres. Tele-TV Sys., Reston, Va., 1995-97; pres., CEO, Chyron Corp., Melville, N.Y., 1997—; chmn. Morgan Data Svcs. Inc., Wilmington, Del., 1981-84; pres. J.P. Morgan Lease Funding Corp., N.Y.C., 1982-84; bd. dirs. CBS Studio Ctr. Inc. Bd. dirs., treas. Theater Devel. Fund, George Washington U., Ave of Americas Assn., Delaware Valley Opera ; mem. N.Y. Hosp. Rev. and Planning Coun. Mem. Nat. Assn. Bank Cost and Mgmt. Acctg. (chmn. Ea. region 1979-80, bd. dirs. 1979-82). Avocations: deep sea fishing, computer programming. Home: 1136 Fifth Ave New York NY 10128-0122 Office: Chryon Corp 5 Hub Dr Ste 3 Melville NY 11747-3591

GREBSTEIN, SHELDON NORMAN, university administrator; b. Providence, Feb. 1, 1928; s. Sigmund and Sylvia (Skotkin) G.; m. Phyllis Strumar, Sept. 6, 1953; children: Jason Lyle, Gary Wade. BA cum laude, U. So. Calif., 1949; MA, Columbia U., 1950; PhD, Mich. State U., 1954. Instr. then asst. prof. English U. Ky., 1953-62; asst. prof. U. South Fla., 1962-63; mem. faculty SUNY, Binghamton, 1963-81; prof. English SUNY, 1968-81, asst. to pres., 1974-75; dean arts and scis. Harpur Coll., 1975-81; pres. SUNY, Purchase, 1981-93, univ. prof. of lit., 1993-95; dir. edn. Westchester Holocaust Commn., 1995—; Fulbright-Hays lectr. U. Rouen, France, 1968-69; vis. lectr. Caen U., Hull U., and Edinburgh U., 1969. Author: Sinclair Lewis, 1962, John O'Hara, 1966, Hemingway's Craft, 1973; Editor: Monkey Trial, 1960, Perspectives in Contemporary Criticism, 1968, Studies in For Whom The Bell Tolls, 1971; editorial cons. univ. presses, publishers.; Contbr. articles to profl. jours.

GRECICH, DARYL GEORGE, marketing communications executive; b. Beaver Falls, Pa., Mar. 26, 1966; s. George William and Patricia Joan (Scassa) G. BA, U. Pitts., 1988, MA Public and Internat. Affairs, 1991. Dir. publs. and mktg. Inst. for the Study of Diplomacy, Georgetown U., Washington, 1992-95; dir. comm. Inst. for a Drug-Free Workplace, Washington, 1995-98; mktg. comm. mgr. Data Warehousing Inst., Washington, 1998—; dir. Coun. on Croatian-Am. Rels., Washington, 1998—. Mem. Holy Trinity Roman Cath. Ch., Washington. Recipient Wolves Club scholar, 1984. Mem. Am. Fgn. Svc. Assn., World Affairs Coun. of Washington, D.C., Delta Tau Delta Fraternity. Republican. Avocations: skiing, golf, raquetball, running, history. E-Mail: dgrecich@dw-institute.com. Home: Ste 214 3901 Connecticut Ave NW Washington DC 20008-2413 Office: Data Warehousing Inst 849 Quince Orchard Blvd Ste J Gaithersburg MD 20878-1685

GRECO, ALBERT NICHOLAS, communications educator; b. Trenton, N.J., June 15, 1945; s. Albert Charles and Nellie Marie G.; m. Elaine Anne Rovegno, Aug. 10, 1968; children: Albert, Timothy, John, Robert. BA, Duquesne U., 1967, MA, 1969; EdD, NYU, 1982. Teaching grad. asst. Duquesne U., 1967-68; tchr. Dwight-Englewood (N.J.) Sch., 1968-79, chmn. dept., 1970-73, dir. testing, 1973-75, prin. summer sch., 1970-78, prin. H.S., 1975-78, dir. devel., 1978-79; exec. dir. Met. Lithographers Assn., N.Y.C., 1979-83; dir. Ctr. for Graphic Communications Mgmt. and Tech. NYU, 1982-85; assoc. prof., assoc. dean Gallatin Sch. of Individualized Study, 1985-92, dir. pub. studies, 1992-95; clin. assoc. prof. NYU Mgmt. Inst. and Ctr. for Pub., 1995-96; assoc. prof. comm. & media mgmt., grad. sch. bus. adminstrn. Fordham U., 1996—; adj. instr. Bergen C.C., 1970-78, NYU, 1980-83; clin. assoc. prof. NYU Sch. Edn., 1982-85; exec. dir. Lithographic Industry Scholarship, Edn. and Devel. Fund., 1982-83. Author: Business Journalism: Management Notes and Cases, 1988, Advertising Management and the Business Publishing Industry, 1991, The Book Publishing Industry, 1997; editor: NYU Press Bus. mag. pub. series; editor-in-chief Allyn & Bacon Series in Mass Communications, 10 vols., The Media and Entertainment Industry, 1999; co-editor: Editorial Excellence; editl. bd. Pub. Rsch. Quar., 1994-97; contbr. articles to profl. jours. Bd. dirs. Book Industry Study Group, 1990-92. Recipient Cert. of Recognition Edn. Coun. of Graphic Arts Industry, 1985, Friedmman award N.Y.C. H.S. Graphic Comm. Arts, 1998, Svc. to Industry award The Navigators, 1998. Mem. Book Industry Study Group, Assn. Edn. in Journalism and Mass Comm., Phi Alpha Theta. Roman Catholic. Home: 183 S Queen St Bergenfield NJ 07621-2636 Office: Fordham U Dept Comm and Media Mgmt 113 W 60th St New York NY 10023-7484

GRECO, BARBARA RUTH GOMEZ, literacy organization administrator; b. Farifield, Calif., May 27, 1938; d. William Joseph and Ruth Marie (Fernandes) Gomez; m. Edward Fairfax Greco, Aug. 27, 1966 (div. Jan. 1995); children: Michelle, William. Assoc. degree cum laude, Lord Fairfax Community Coll., 1985; B, James Madison U., 1987. Commr. Warren County Crime Commn., 1988; dir. mktg. and pub. rels. Wayside of Va. Inc., Strasburg, 1988; pres. Literacy Vols. Am., Warren, Va., 1988-95; dir. Literacy Vols. Am., Warren, 1988—; bd. dirs. Region 4 Literacy Coordinating Com., Harrisonburg, Va., 1989-95, Va. Literacy Coalition, Richmond, 1990; owner Moving Forward Bus. and Personal Devel. Seminars, 1995—; regional coord. World Heritage, 1996; bus. cons. Echo Ridge Nursery, Winchester, 1990; owner Barbara Greco & Assocs., writing, editing and mktg., 1993—. Contbg. writer North Valley Bus. Jour., Winchester, 1989-93. PTA chair County of Warren, 1974-78, mem. founding bd. coun. on domestic violence, 1984-88, vice-chair dem. com., 1981, pres. coun. on domestic violence, 1985-88; mem. textbook adoption com. Warren County High Sch., 1985; bd. dirs. Va. chpt. Am. Lung Assn., 1980-82; bd. dirs. United Way, 1984; Warren County coord. Patterson for State Senate, 1979; campaign coord. William A. Hall for Clk. of Ct., 1981; supr. phone bank Charles Robb Campaign, 1981; campaign treas. Michael Kitts for Town Coun., 1984; campaign vol. Gerald Lee Baliles for Gov., 1986; troop leader Girl Scouts U.S., 1970-71, area coord., 1971-72; com. mem. Warren County Strategic Planning Partnership, 1993; pres. Warren County Home for Mentally Handicapped, 1996-98). Mem. Shenandoah Valley Writer's Guild (past pres.), Washington Soc. of Jungion Psychology (bd. dirs. 1997—). Unitarian Universalist. Home: PO Box 2085 Front Royal VA 22630-1952

GRECO, DICK A., mayor, hardware company executive; b. Tampa, Fla.. Student, U. Fla.; BS in Social Studies, U. Tampa. V.p. King-Greco Hardware Co., Ybor City, Fla.; councilman City of Tampa, Ybor City, 1963; mayor City of Tampa, 1967, 1971; resigned, 1973; v.p. devel. and govtl. rels. Edward J. DeBartolo Corp., 1973-95; resigned, 1995; mayor City of Tampa, 1995—; Bd. dirs. Tampa Aviation Authority, Tampa Expressway Atuhority, Tampa Port Authority's Bd. Commrs., Tampa Bay Regional Planning Coun., Nat. League of Cities; pres. Fla. League of Cities. Travelers' Aid Soc., Palma Ceia Optimist Club. Office: Office of the Mayor 306 E Jackson St Tampa FL 33602-5208

GRECO, JANICE TERESA, psychology educator; b. N.Y.C., May 14, 1948; d. Joseph Ralph and Harriett May (McArdle) G.; m. Forlano, July 29, 1969 (div. Feb. 1993); children: Christopher, Jason, Jennifer. BS, U. Houston, 1975, MEd, 1975; PhD, U. Tex., 1992. Ins. clk. John Hancock Life Ins. Co., West Islip, N.Y., 1965-69; instr. San Jacinto Jr. Coll., Houston, 1976-77; with assessment & referral divsn. Employee Assistance Program, U. Tex., Houston, 1987-88; instr. psychology Houston C.C., 1977—, head behavioral stats. Vol. Huppotherapy Group, Galveston, Tex., 1990-91, fellowshp., Automated Lectr., Instrl. Computing, 1998, web access to statistics course, 1998. Fellow Instructional Computing, 1998, Coll. Computer Program. Mem. ACA, Tex. Assn. Counseling and Devel., Tex. Jr. Coll. Tchr. Assn., Stats. for Behavioral Scis. (rsch. com.). Avocations: horse-back riding, travel, reading, billiards, Lionel collector. Home: 12219 Monticeto Ln Meadows Place TX 77477-1430

GRECO, JOSE, choreographer; b. Montorio nei Frentani, Italy, Dec. 23, 1918; came to U.S., 1928, naturalized, 1928; s. Paolo Emilio and Carmela (Bucci) G. Student, Leonardo da Vinci Art Sch., N.Y.C.; studied dancing with Helene Veola. Tchr. dancing, hotels and resorts, 1936-45; artistic dir. Jose Greco Co., 1949—; founder Jose Greco Found. for Hispanic Dance, Inc., N.Y.C., 1971; vis. prof. dance Franklin & Marshall Coll., Lancaster, Pa., 1992—. First profl. appearance as dancer in Carmen, N.Y. Hippodrome Opera Co., 1937; joined Gloria Belmonte in engagement at La Conga, N.Y.C. (profl. name Ramon Serrano), 1938; appeared with Argentinita, 1943; toured U.S., 1943-45; guest appearances Ballet Theater at Met. Opera House; dancer ballets including Carmen; Spanish debut with Ballet Espanol, Madrid, 1946; choreographer: Caña y Farruca, 1946, Triana, 1946, Polo, 1946, Le Tricorne, 1947, Sentimentes, 1948, Pictures of Goya, 1950, Old Madrid, 1951, Ricon Flamenco, 1951, Cante Jondo, 1951, Juerga, 1951, El Cortijo, 1951, Peteneras, 1952, Suite of Traditional Dances, 1952-53, Anda Jaleo, 1956, Masaico Sevillano, 1956, Tres Morillas, 1956, Castellana, 1956, Fantasia, 1956, Tango y Sequidilla, 1957, Los Amantes de Sierra Morena, 1957, Los Trobadores en las Calles de Cadiz, 1958, Verdiales de Valle Verde, 1958, Bulerias de Juañene, 1959, Fantasia de Valencia y Aragon, 1958, Barcelona Suite, 1964; composer: (with Roger Machado) Là Molinera Caprichosa and Other Works; dancer: (film) Manolete, 1948; organized ballet co. Ballets y Bailes de Espana, 1948; appeared in Barcelona, Paris, Norway, Sweden, Denmark, other European countries; toured Argentina, Uruguay, Chile, Peru, 1950, 45 consecutive U.S. tours, 6 world tours; appeared Sadler's Wells Theater, London, 1951, North Am. debut with, Spanish Ballet, Shubert Theater, N.Y.C., 1951; movies include Around the World in 80 Days, Ship of Fools, Holiday For Lovers, Sombrero; appeared in role of Count Dracula in Passion of Dracula, U.S. tour, 1979; role of Jonathan in Arsenic and Old Lace, 1981; author: (with Harvey Ardman) Gypsy in My Soul, 1978. Comdr. Caballero de la Cruz del Merito Civil Spain; recipient Silver Bowl award Internat. Platform Assn., 1971, hon. doctorates Fairfield U., Northwood Inst., Midland Inst., Franklin & Marshall Coll., Nosotros Golden Eagle, 1985, El Angel award Bilingual Found. of Arts, 1992, Lifetime Achievement award Internat. Spanish Dance Soc. Fellow Nat. Endowment for the Arts, 1993—; mem. Sigma Delta Pi (disting. mem. 1986). Office: care of José Greco Found 866 United Nations Plz New York NY 10017-1822

GRECO, RALPH STEVEN, surgeon, researcher, medical educator; b. N.Y.C., May 25, 1942; s. Charles Mario and Lydia Antoinette (Barone) G.; m. Irene Leonor Wapnir, Feb. 23, 1991; children: Justin Michael, Eric Matthew, Ilana Rose. BS, Fordham U., 1964; MD, Yale U., 1968. Instr. Yale U., New Haven, 1972-73; asst. prof. Rutgers Med. Sch., Piscataway, N.J., 1975-79; assoc. prof. Med. Sch. Rutgers U., Piscataway, N.J., 1979-83; chief of gen. surgery Robert Wood Johnson Med. Sch. U. Medicine & Dentistry of N.J., New Brunswick, 1982—, prof. Robert Wood Johnson Med. Sch., 1983—, chief of surgery Robert Wood Johnson Univ. Hosp., 1997—; cons. Nat. Heart, Lung and Blood Inst.-NSF, Bethesda, Md., 1991. Contbr. articles to profl. jours. Maj. U.S. Army, 1973-75. NHLBI grantee, 1980-84. Fellow Am. Surg. Assn.; mem. Soc. Univ. Surgeons. Achievements include research in antibiotic bonding, treatment of prosthetic infection, drug delivery; patents in field. Home: 2 Quail Run Warren NJ 07059-7134 Office: U Medicine & Dentistry NJ Robert Wood Johnson Med Sch 1 Robert Wood Johnson Pl # 19cn New Brunswick NJ 08901-1928

GRECO, RICHARD JUDE, plastic and reconstructive surgeon; b. Hazleton, Pa., Jan. 8, 1960; s. Victor Frank and Mary Jean Greco; m. Robin Emma Robinson, Jan. 30, 1981; children: Richard, Blake, Apryl, Dean. BS in Biology summa cum laude, Ursinus Coll., Collegeville, 1979; MD magna cum laude, Thomas Jefferson U., 1983. Diplomate Am. Bd. Plastic Surgery, Am. Bd. Gen. Surgery. Resident in gen. surgery Thomas Jefferson U. Hosp., Phila., 1983-88; resident in plastic surgery U. Pitts., 1988-91, asst. prof. surgery, 1991-93; dir. Telfair Breast Ctr. Candler Hosp., Savannah, Ga., 1993-97; CEO, pvt. practice Ga. Inst. for Plastic Surgery, Savannah, 1998—. Editor: Emergency Plastic Surgery, 1993; patentee for robotic liposuction device, pulse irrigation bag. Polit. adv. People for Pub. Edn., Savannah, 1997. Burroughs Welcome-AMA fellow, 1991. Fellow ACS; mem. AMA, Am. Soc. Plastic Surgery, Am. Soc. Aesthetic Surgery, Lipoplasty Soc. Republican. Roman Catholic. Avocations: golf, tennis, jet skiing. Home: 29 Heron's Nest Savannah GA 31410 Office: Ga Inst Plastic Surgery 5361 Reynolds St Savannah GA 31405

GRECSEK, MATTHEW THOMAS, software developer; b. Staten Island, N.Y., Nov. 17, 1963; s. Ernest Edward and Theresa Joan (Lakemann) G. Student, Rensselaer Poly. Inst., 1982-83. Software engr. IBM Corp., Boca Raton, Fla., 1983; pres., chief exec. officer Result Focused Systems Corp., Orlando, Fla., 1984-90; cons. bus. Result Focused Systems Corp., Charlotte, N.C., 1984-86, cons. software start-up, 1986-87; pres., chmn. Vi-Stat Inc. (formerly Result Focused Systems Corp.), 1990—, 1990-93; co-founder ProSkins Internat., Orlando, Fla., 1991-93; chmn. Forefront Tech. Ptnrs., Orlando, 1993—; co-founder Global Innovations Mktg., Inc., Orlando, 1990; com. chmn. Oasis Internat., 1994-95; founder, chmn. Agenetics, Inc., 1996—. Author computer software Cypher, 1984, Admissions Exec., 1985, STAR, 1986, Relocation Manager, 1988, EEO Compliance Manager, 1989, Embassy, ProCreator, ProGenitor, 1996, A-LIVE, 1996; developer Agent City (electronic workforce cmty.). Mem. Assn. for Sys. Mgmt., Better Bus. Bur., Fla. High Tech. Coun., Fla. Assn. Nomad Developers (exec. dir. 1994-95). Achievements include invention of Dynamic Energy System, biomedical consumer product, of polymorphic agent technology. Office: Forefront Tech Ptnrs Inc 4630 S Kirkman Rd Ste 183 Orlando FL 32811-2873

GREDEN, JOHN FRANCIS, psychiatrist, educator; b. Winona, Minn., July 24, 1942; m. Renee Mary Kalmes; children: Daniel John, Sarah Renee, Leigh Raymond. BS, U. Minn., 1965, MD, 1967. Diplomate Am. Bd. Psychiatry and Neurology. Assoc. dir. psychiat. research Walter Reed Army Med. Ctr., Washington, 1972-74; asst. prof. Dept. Psychiatry U. Mich., Ann Arbor, 1974-77, assoc. prof., 1977-81, dir. clin. studies unit for affective disorders, 1980-85, prof., 1981—, chmn., research scientist, 1985—; chmn. faculty group practice U. Mich. Contbr. 188 articles to profl. jours., 28 chpts. to books. Served to maj. U.S. Army, 1969-74. Recipient A.E.

Bennett research award Cen. Neuropsychiat. Found., 1974, Ralph Patterson Meml. award Ohio State U., 1980, Nolan D.C. Lewis Vis. Scholar award Carrier Found., 1982. Fellow Am. Psychiat. Assn.; mem. AAAS, Soc. Biol. Psychiatry (past pres.), Am. Coll. Neuropsychopharmacology, Psychiat. Rsch. Soc. (past pres.). Office: U Mich Med Ctr Dept Psychiatry 1500 E Medical Center Dr Ann Arbor MI 48109-0005*

GREEFF, ADELE MONTGOMERY BURCHER, artist; b. Bklyn., Dec. 10, 1911; d. Reginald Hilliard and Evelyn Eglington (Andrews) Burcher; m. Charles Alfred Greeff, Dec. 23, 1933 (dec. Feb. 1961); 1 child, Pieter. BA, Barnard Coll., 1933. V.p. Granbery, Marache-Blair & Co., N.Y.C., 1961-70; mgmt. com. N.Y. City Ctr. Gallery, N.Y.C., 1954-60. Author: (poetry) Love's Argument, 1952 (foreword by Mark Van Doren); represented in permanent collections Nat. Mus. of Women in Arts, Washington, Guild Hall Mus., East Hampton, N.Y., Schenectady (N.Y.) Mus. and Planetarium, Nott Terrace Heights. Active Dem. Nat. Com., Washington. Mem. LWV, N.Y. Artists Equity Assn. Inc., Poetry Soc. Am., Authors League/Authors Guild, Cosmopolitan Club, Barnard Coll. Club. Democrat.

GREEHEY, WILLIAM EUGENE, energy company executive; b. Ft. Dodge, Iowa, 1936; married. BBA, St. Mary's U., 1960. Auditor Price Waterhouse & Co., 1960-61; sr. auditor Humble Oil and Refining Co., 1961-63; sr. v.p. fin. Coastal Corp. (and predecessor), 1963-74; with Valero Energy Corp. (formerly LoVaca Gas Producing Co.), San Antonio, 1974—; pres., chief exec. officer Valero Energy Corp. (formerly Coastal States Gas Producing Co.), San Antonio, 1979-83, chmn. bd., 1983—, now also chief of exec. officer, dir., also chmn., chief exec. officer numerous subsidiaries, chmn., CEO; pres., chief exec. officer LoVaca Gathering Co. subs., San Antonio, 1974-79. Office: Valero Energy Corp PO Box 500 San Antonio TX 78292-0500*

GREEK, DAROLD I., lawyer; b. Kunkle, Ohio, Mar. 30, 1909; s. Albert F. and Iva (Shaffer) G.; m. Catherine Johnson, Oct. 12, 1935 (dec. 1962); 1 child, Darold I (dec.); m. Elizabeth Tracy Ridgley, Sept. 18, 1970 (dec. May 1972); stepchildren—Thomas B., David Ridgley; m. Nadine Berry Weisheimer Bivens, Dec. 23, 1976; stepchildren—Richard A. Weisheimer, Jon B. Weisheimer. Student, Bowling Green State U., 1926-28; LL.B., Ohio State U., 1932. Bar: Ohio 1932. Treas. Williams County, Ohio, 1932-33; atty. Ohio Dept. Taxation, 1934-36; practiced in Columbus, 1937-89; ptnr. George, Greek, King, McMahon & McConnaughey (and predecessors), 1937-79; of counsel Baker & Hostetler, 1979-89. Mem. Ohio Bar Assn., Columbus Bar Assn. (pres. 1966-67), Columbus Country Club, The Golf Club, Naples Yacht Club, Hole in the Wall Golf Club. Presbyterian. Home: 6635 Lake of Woods Pt Galena OH 43021 also: 2901 Gulf Shore Blvd N Naples FL 34103-3937 Office: 65 E State St Columbus OH 43215-4213

GREELEY, ANDREW MORAN, sociologist, author; b. Oak Park, Ill., Feb. 5, 1928; s. Andrew T. and Grace (McNichols) G. A.B., St. Mary of Lake Sem., 1950, S.T.L., 1954; M.A., U. Chgo., 1961, Ph.D., 1962; LHD (hon.), Bowling Green State U., 1986, No. Mich., 1993; HHD (hon.), St. Louis U., 1991; LHD (hon.), Ariz. State U., 1998. Ordained priest Roman Cath. Ch., 1954. Asst. pastor Ch. of Christ the King, Chgo., 1954-64; sr. study dir. Nat. Opinion Rsch. Ctr., Chgo., 1962-68; dir. Ctr. for Study Am. Pluralism, from 1973; lectr. sociology U. Chgo., 1963-72; prof. sociology U. Ariz., Tucson, from 1978, now adj. prof.; prof. social sci. U. Chgo., 1991—; cons. Hazen Found. Commn. Syndicated columnist People and Values, N.Y. Times Religious News Svc.; columnist Daily Southtown; guest columnist Chgo. Sun Times, 1985—; Author: The Church and the Suburbs, 1959, Strangers in the House, 1961, Religion and Career, 1963, (with Peter H. Rossi) Education of Catholic Americans, 1966, Changing Catholic College, 1967, Come Blow Your Mind With Me, 1971, Life for a Wanderer: A New Look at Christian Spirituality, 1971, The Denominational Society: A Sociological Approach to Religion in America, 1972, Priests in the United States: Reflections on A Survey, 1972, That Most Distressful Nation, 1972, New Agenda, 1973, Jesus Myth, 1971, Unsecular Man, 1974, Ethnicity in the United States: A Preliminary Reconnaissance, 1974, Ecstasy: A Way of Knowing, 1974, Building Coalitions: American Politics in the 1970's, 1974, Sexual Intimacy, 1975, Denomination Society, 1975, The Great Mysteries: An Essential Catechism, 1976, The Communal Catholic: A Personal Manifesto, 1976, Death and Beyond, 1976, The American Catholic: A Social Portrait, 1977, The Making of the Popes, 1978, 79, The Magic Cup: An Irish Legend, 1979, Women I've Met, 1979, Why Can't They Be Like Us?, 1980, Death In April, 1980, The Cardinal Sins, 1981, Religion: A Secular Theory, 1982, Thy Brother's Wife, 1982, Ascent Into Hell, 1983, Lord of the Dance, 1984, Virgin & Martyr, 1985, Piece of My Mind on Just About Everything, 1985, Happy are the Meek, 1985, The Magic Cup, 1985, God Game, 1986, Happy Are the Clean of Heart, 1986, Confessions of a Parish Priest, 1986, Patience of a Saint, 1987, Rite of Spring, 1987, Angels of September, 1986, Happy Are Those Who Thirst For Justice, 1987, The Final Planet, 1987, Angel Fire, 1988, (photography) Andrew Greeley's Chicago, 1989, Love Song, 1989, St. Valentine's Night, 1989, The Bible and Us, 1990, The short stories All About Women, 1990, (photography) The Irish, 1990, The Catholic Myth: The Behavior and Beliefs of American Catholics, 1990, The Cardinal Virtues, 1990, Faithful Attraction: Discovering Intimacy, Love, and Fidelity in American Marriage, 1991, The Search for Maggie Ward, 1991, An Occasion of Sin, 1991, Happy Are the Merciful, 1992, Wages of Sin, 1992, Fall from Grace, 1993, Sacraments of Love: A Prayer Journal, 1994, Irish Gold, 1994, Happy are the Poor Spirit, 1994, Happy are Those Who Mourn, 1995, Angel Light: An Old-Fashioned Love Story, 1995, Windows: A Prayer Journal, 1995, Religion as Poetry, 1995, Sociology and Religion, 1995, White Smoke, 1996, Irish Lace, 1996, Happy Are The Oppressed, 1996, Summer at the Lake, 1997, Star Bright!, 1997, The Bishop at Sea, 1997, I Hope You're Listening, God: A Prayer Jounal, 1997, Irish Whiskey, 1998, Contract with an Angel, 1998, The Bishop and the Three Kings, 1998, Mid-Winter's Tale, 1998; (with J. Neusner) Common Ground: A Priest and a Rabbi Read Scripture Together, 1996, others; (with Chilton, Green, and Neusner) Forging a Common Future, 1996; contbr. articles to profl. jours. Recipient Cath. Press Assn. award for best book for young people, 1965, Thomas Alva Edison award for radio broadcast, 1962, C. Albert Kobb award Nat. Cath. Edn. Assn., 1977, Mark Twain award Soc. Study Midwestern Lit., 1987, Popular Culture award Ctr. Study of Popular Culture, 1988, Freedom to Read award Friends Chgo. Pub. Libr., 1989, U.S. Cath. award, 1993, Ill. Outstanding Citizen award Coll. Lake County, 1993, Quigley Disting. Alumni award, 1997. Mem. Am. Sociol. Assn., Soc. for Sci. Study Religion, Religious Research Assn. Address: Rosner & Walsh 650 N Dearborn Chicago IL 60610

GREELEY, SEAN MCGOVERN, trust company executive; b. New Brunswick, N.J., Nov. 8, 1961; s. Horace James Jr. and Patricia Louise (McGovern) G.; m. Kristin Lindefjeld; children: Elisabeth Lindefjeld, Anna Barlinn, John Lindefjeld. BSBA, Monmouth U., 1983, MBA, 1994. With Dean Witter Reynolds, N.Y.C., 1983-85; acct. exec. U.S. Trust Co., N.Y.C., 1985-87, fin. officer, 1987-90, asst. v.p., 1990-95; v.p. global ins. Chase Manhattan Bank, N.Y.C., 1995—. Mem. Tau Kappa Epsilon (pres., bd. dirs. 1984-90, cons. bd. fin. 1986-90). Republican. Avocations: reading, running, U.S. history, golf. Home: 14 North St Rumson NJ 07760-1610 Office: Chase Manhattan Bank 4 New York Plz Fl 4 New York NY 10004-2413

GREELEY, TIMOTHY P., federal judge. BS, Western Mich. U., 1976; JD magna cum laude, Wayne State U., 1980. Bar: Mich. 1982, U.S. Dist. Ct. (we. Mich.) 1982. Law clk. to Hon. Phillip Pratt U.S. Dist. Ct. (e. dist.) Mich., Marquette, 1980-82; atty. Foster, Swift, Collins & Coey, P.C., Lansing, Mich., 1982-87; magistrate judge U.S. Dist. Ct. (we. dist.) Mich., Marquette, 1988—. Fax: (906) 226-6231. Office: US Dist Ct We Dist Mich 330 Fed Bldg 202 W Washington St Marquette MI 49855

GREEN, ADAM MITCHELL, investment banker; b. N.Y.C., June 22, 1967; s. Carl Jay Green and Judith (Slomoff) Green-Loose. BA, Harvard U., 1989; MBA, U. Va., 1993. V.p. J.P. Morgan, N.Y.C., 1993-98; prin. Nations Bank, N.Y.C., 1998—. Mem. Harvard CLub N.Y.C. Office: Nations Bank 9 W 57th St New York NY 10019-2701

GREEN, ALAN IVAN, psychiatrist; b. Norwalk, Conn., Nov. 7, 1943; s. H. Howard and Irene (Wouk) G.; m. Frances S. Cohen, Oct. 9, 1983; children: Isobel Wouk, Henry Streit. AB, Columbia Coll., 1965; MD, Johns Hopkins U., 1969. Intern Beth Israel Hosp., Boston, 1969-70; staff assoc. Nat. Inst. Mental Health, Washington, 1970-72; dir. biomed. rsch. Spl. Action Office for Drug Abuse Prevention Exec. Office of Pres., Washington, 1972-73, cons., 1973-75; resident in psychiatry Mass. Mental Health Ctr., Boston, 1973-75, 81-82, assoc. dir. psychopharmacology, 1982-93; adminstrv. dir. Commonwealth Rsch. Ctr., Mass. Mental Health Ctr., Boston, 1986-94; dir. Commonwealth Rsch. Ctr., 1994—; asst. prof. psychiatry Harvard Med. Sch., Boston, 1984-94; assoc. prof. Harvard Med. Sch., 1994—. Contbr. sci. articles to profl. jours. Recipient Milton Fund award Harvard Med. Sch., 1988, NARSAD Ind. Investigator award, 1998. Mem. Am. Psychiat. Assn., Mass. Psychiat. Soc. (Outstanding Psychiatrist award for rsch. 1998), Mass. Med. Soc. Office: Mass Mental Health Ctr 74 Fenwood Rd Boston MA 02115-6196

GREEN, ALVIN, lawyer, consultant; b. Elgin, Ill., Mar. 13, 1931; s. Samuel and Rose (Brustein) G.; m. Miriam E. Blau, June 13, 1954; children: Andrew, Marie, Jennifer. BA, U. Mich., 1953, MA, 1954; LLB, Harvard U., 1957. Bar: N.Y., Ill. Atty. Eastern Air Lines, Inc., N.Y.C., 1957-65; asst. to gen. counsel C.I.T. Corp., N.Y.C., 1965-70; gen. counsel C.I.T. Corp., 1970-72; v.p. Condren, Walker & Co., N.Y.C., 1972-75; v.p., gen. counsel, sec. Seatrain Lines, Inc., N.Y.C., 1975-81; exec. v.p., co-chief exec. officer, sr. counsel Seatrain Lines, Inc., 1981-90; exec. v.p. Seatrain Tankers Inc., 1987-90; exec. v.p., prin. Bay Tankers Inc., 1981-90; prin., exec. v.p. Bay Ocean Mgmt. Inc., Englewood Cliffs, N.J., 1990-95; NASD arbitrator; ptnr. Seham, Seham Meltz & Petersen; pres. Universal Drug Testing Svcs., Inc.; cons. in field. Woodrow Wilson fellow, 1953-54. Mem. ABA, Assn. of Bar of City of N.Y. (mem. com. on aeronautics), Am. Bur. Shipping, Phi Beta Kappa, Phi Kappa Phi. Club: Harvard (N.Y.C.). Home: 22 Arleigh Rd Great Neck NY 11021-1338 Office: Seham Seham Meltz et al 380 Madison Ave Ste 17 New York NY 10017-2513

GREEN, AMY ELIZABETH, administrator; b. Mt. Kisco, N.Y., Aug. 29, 1963; d. Philip Josiah and Joan Margaret Green; m. Kenneth M. Deutsch, May 26, 1990. BA cum laude, NYU, 1985; attended, U. Md., 1981-83. Project coord. N.Y. Pub. Interest Rsch. Group, 1986-88, reg. coord., 1988-89; cmty. liaison N.Y. State Assembly Mem. Jerrold Nadler, N.Y.C., 1989-92; adminstrv. asst. U.S. Rep. Jerrold Nadler, Washington, 1992-96; gen. cons. Julia Carson for Congress, Indpls., 1996—; chief of staff U.S. Rep. Jenla Nader, 1997-99; staff Emily's List, Washington, 1999—; co-campaign mgr. Nadler for Congress '94, N.Y.C., 1994, dep. campaign mgr., 1992. Exec. dir. Cmty. Free Dems., N.Y.C., 1992, exec. bd. dirs., 1991-92; mem. N.Y. Dem. County Com., N.Y.C., 1992. Recipient Founders Day award for acad. achievement, NYU, 1985. Office: Emily's List 805 15th St NW Washington DC 20515*

GREEN, ANDREW WILSON, economist, lawyer, educator; b. Harrisburg, Pa., May 17, 1923; s. M. Edwin and Gladys (Wilson) G.; m. Betty M. Wilson, Nov. 23, 1977. Student, Princeton U., 1940-43; BS, NYU, 1944; JD, Dickinson Law Sch., 1948; MBA, U. Pa., 1963, PhD, 1968; diploma, U. Amsterdam, 1967. Bar: Pa. 1950, D.C. 1950. Legal asst. Pa. Utility Commn., 1949-51; pvt. practice Harrisburg, 1951-61; asst. atty. gen. State of Pa., 1965-66; research assoc. Inst. Strategic and Internat. Studies, Belgium, 1968-70; prof. bus. adminstrn. West Chester U., Pa., 1970-92; prof. Del. Law Sch., Wilmington, 1973-81; pvt. practice West Chester, Pa., 1987—; solicitor Coatesville (Pa.) Sch. Dist., 1988-91; mem. Reagan Transition Team, 1980-81. Author: Political Integration by Jurisprudence, 1969. Served as capt. USAAF, 1943-46. Pennfield fellow, 1966-67. Mem. Cercle Galouis (Brussels), Gremio Literario (Lisbon). Home: 6 Ivy Rock Rd West Chester PA 19382-8148 Office: PO Box 654 West Chester PA 19381-0654

GREEN, ARTHUR E., media strategist; b. Bklyn., Feb. 10, 1949; s. Harry and Anne (Knaster) G.; m. Margo Green, June 6, 1991; children: Joshua Joseph, Jessica Raizel. BA in Am. Diplomatic History, Bklyn. Coll., 1970. Holds rank of counselor Sr. Fgn. Svc. Asst. field program officer Am. Embassy, Bonn, West Germany, 1971-73; br. pub. affairs officer, exec. dir. Colombian-Am. Cultural Ctr., Barranquilla, 1973-75; asst. cultural attache, exec. dir. Costa-Rican-N.Am. Ctr. Am. Embassy, San Jose, 1975-78; asst. cultural attache, dir. Am. Cultural Ctr. Am. Embassy, Tel Aviv, Israel, 1978-80; sr. Middle East press officer Washington Fgn. PressCtr., 1980-84; dir. Info. Ctr., Jerusalem, Israel, 1984-88; dep. exec. sec., exec. secretariat USIA, 1988-89, exec. sec., 1989-92; dir. USIA Fgn. Press Ctr., Washington, 1992-97; dir. internat. events USIA, Washington, 1997-99; CEO, founder Arthur E. Green & Assocs., Washington, 1999—; CEO, founder Arthur E. Green & Assocs., North Potomac, Md., 1997—. Mem. adult edn. com. Jewish Cmty. Ctr., Rockville, Md., 1996. Mem. Pub. Rels. Soc. Am., Nat. Press Club (vice chair internat. com.), Internat. Spl. Events Soc., Phi Beta Kappa. Jewish. Avocations: tennis, bicycle riding. E-mail: aegreenassoc@epols.com. Home: 12317 Turley Dr North Potomac MD 20878-4751 Office: Arthur E Green & Assocs Nat Press Bldg Ste 2066 Washington DC 20045

GREEN, ASA NORMAN, university president; b. Mars Hill, Maine, July 22, 1929; s. Clayton John and Annie Glenna (Shaw) G.; m. Elizabeth Jean Zirkelbach Ross, May 27, 1965; 1 son, Stephen Richard Ross. A.B. cum laude, Bates Coll., Lewiston, Maine, 1951; M.A., U. Ala., 1955; LL.D., Jacksonville (Ala.) U., 1975. Research dir. Ala. League Municipalities, Montgomery, 1955-57; city mgr. Mountain Brook, Ala., 1957-65; exec. sec. Ala. Assn. Ins. Agts., 1965-66; dir. devel. Birmingham-So. Coll., 1966-71; dir. devel. and communications Dickinson Coll., Carlisle, Pa., 1971-73; pres. Livingston (Ala.) U., 1973-93; pres. emeritus Livingston U., 1993—; con. NCAA Pres.'s Commn., 1993—; instr. polit. sci. U. Ala. Ext. Ctr., Montgomery and Birmingham, 1955-57, 58-60. Author: Revenue for Alabama Cities, 1956. Dir. U. South Ala. Found., 1998—. Served with CIC U.S. Army, 1952-54. Grad. fellow So. Regional Tng. Program in Pub. Adminstrn., 1951. Mem. Newcomen Soc. N. Am., Phi Beta Kappa. Democrat. Methodist. Office: PO Box 1620 Livingston AL 35470-1620

GREEN, BARBARA BUCKSTEIN, political scientist, educator; b. N.Y.C., Dec. 30, 1932; d. Jacob and Estelle (Schwartz) Buckstein; children: Nancy Gilreath, Richard J. AB, Wellesley Coll., 1954; MA, Radcliffe Coll., 1957; PhD, Harvard U., 1960. Tchg. fellow Harvard U., Cambridge, Mass., 1956-59, assoc. Russian Rsch. Ctr., 1967-68; from instr. to assoc. prof. Wellesley (Mass.) Coll., 1957-68; fellow Radcliffe Inst., Cambridge, 1967-68; prof. Cleve. State U., 1968—, vice provost acad. affairs, 1979-88, acting provost, 1988-89. Author: The Dynamics of Russian Politics, 1994; contbr. chpts. to books and articles to profl. jours. Trustee Wellesley Coll, 1970-76, Cleve. Bar Assn., 1989-93. Ford Found. fellow, 1955-56. Home: 13900 Shaker Blvd Cleveland OH 44120-1587 Office: Cleve State U 22nd and Euclid Cleveland OH 44115

GREEN, BARBARA-MARIE, publisher, journalist, poet; b. N.Y.C., Mar. 21, 1928; d. James Matthew and Mae (McCarter) G. BA, CCNY, 1951, MA, 1955; ABD, NYU, 1978. Adminstr., tchr. English, 1952-82; tchr. English Newtown High Sch., Elmhurst, Queens, N.Y., 1961; asst. prin. Jr. High Sch. 142, Queens, N.Y., 1963; founder, pub. The "Creative" Record, Virginia Beach, Va., 1988-92; keynote speaker; pres. Bar 'JaMae Comm. Inc. Founder, publisher The Good News, East Elmhurst, N.Y., 1985-88; author: (book of poetry) Love Pain Hope, 1990, More Poetic Thoughts, 1993, Dreams and Memories, 1996, Spirit, 1997; contbr. poetry to publs. Ch. and cmty. reporter N.Y. Voice; mem. libr. action com. Corona (N.Y.)-East Elmhurst, Inc.; mem. Langston Hughes Cmty. Libr. and Cultural Ctr., Corona, Harpers Ferry Hist. Assn., Va. Symphony League; mem. Crispus Attucks Theater Restoration Com., Norfolk. Recipient Profl. award Nat. Assn. Negro Bus. and Profl. Women's Club Inc., 1964, Trophy "Career Woman of Yr.", County Line Guild of Career Women, 1967, Cert. of Appreciation Women's Equality Action League, 1978, First Lynnhaven Bapt. Ch., Virginia Beach, Va., 1982, Cert. of merit City of N.Y., 1982, Community Svc. award Arlene of N.Y., 1990, N.Y. State Resolution commemorating the "Good" News, 1985, participation award Coalition of 100 Black Women, Valuable Service citation Phi Delta Kappa, cert. of appreciation Houston C.C., 1998, plaque U.S. Army and USAF N.G. Bur., Ageless Hero for Creativity award Blue Cross/Blue Shield, 1998; named Star Among Stars, 1991, Keeper of the Flame, 1997; named to African-Am. Biographies Hall of Fame, Atlanta, 1994; elected to Hunter Coll. Alumni Hall of Fame, 1997; poet laureate-in-residence First Lynnhaven Bapt. Ch., Virginia Beach, Va., 1996—. Mem. Am. Bus. Women's Assn. (Elizabeth River Charter chpt.), Nat. Assn. Negro Musicians (life; bd. dirs. Chgo. 1984-91, ea. region dir. 1990-91), Harpers Ferry Hist. Assn., Poetry Soc. Va., Nat. Assn. Black Journalists, Zonta Internat., Va. Fedn. Bus. and Profl. Women's Clubs (corr. sec. 1992, 1st v.p. 1993, pres. 1993, chair coastal region pub. rels. com. state level 1994-95), N.Y.C. Ret. Suprs. Assn., Chesapeake C. of C., Phi Delta Kappa, Alpha Kappa Alpha. Baptist. E-mail: barbara-marie@worldnet.att.net. Office: Bar JaMae Enterprises Inc PO Box 15442 Chesapeake VA 23328

GREEN, BARTLEY CROCKER, advertising executive; m. Nancy Green; 4 children. Grad., U. Utah, 1981. Various positions, including maj. accounts mgr. San Mateo Times Newspaper Group; retail sales rep. San Francisco Newspaper Agy., 1986, advt. dir., then retail advt. mgr., v.p. for advt., 1996—. Featured as one of 20 Under 40 salute to newspaper profls. Presstime Mag. Mem. Newspaper Assn. Am. (com. mem.), Calif. Newspaper Advt. Execs. Assn. (past pres.), San Francisco Rotary Club. Office: San Francisco Examiner 110 5th St San Francisco CA 94103

GREEN, BENNETT DONALD, biotechnologist; b. N.Y.C., Nov. 24, 1950; s. John Jerome and Leona Pearl (Gillman) G.; m. Deborah Lynn Stephen, Dec. 23, 1972; children: Rebecca Lynn, John Stephen, Sara Elizabeth. BS, Rensselear Poly. Inst., 1972, MS, 1974; Exec. MBA, Claremont Grad. Sch., 1988. Cert. quality engr. Am. Soc. Quality Control. Sr. mfg. analyst internat. div. Bristol Myers, Syracuse, N.Y., 1974-77; sect. mgr. sterilization Baxter-Travenol Labs., Deerfield, Ill., 1977-78, quality control supr., 1978-82, quality assurance plant mgr. Hyland Therapeutics div., 1982-85; dir. quality assurance NeoRx Corp., Seattle, 1985-87; dir. Genzyme Corp., Cambridge, Mass., 1987-91, v.p. quality, 1991-95, v.p. quality affairs and tech. svcs., 1996-97, sr. v.p., 1997—. Referee U.S. Soccer Fedn., Mass., 1992—. Mem. Am. Soc. for Quality Control, Parenteral Drug Assn. Avocation: golf.

GREEN, BERT FRANKLIN, JR., psychologist; b. Honesdale, Pa., Nov. 5, 1927; s. Bert Franklin and Emily May (Brown) G.; m. Hasseltine Beck Robinson, Apr. 29, 1961 (div. 1974); children: Malcolm, Edward. AB, Yale, 1949; MA, Princeton, 1950, PhD, 1951. Mem. psychology group Lincoln Lab., Mass. Inst. Tech., 1951-62, leader, 1958-62; cons. RAND Corp., 1961; prof. psychology Carnegie Inst. Tech., Pitts., 1962-69; head psychology dept. Carnegie Inst. Tech., 1962-67; prof. psychology Johns Hopkins, Balt., 1969—. Author: Digital Computers in Research, 1963. Mem. Am. Psychol. Assn., Am. Statis. Assn., Psychometric Soc., Am. Edn. Rsch. Assn. Home: 311 Eastway Ct Baltimore MD 21212-4710

GREEN, BETH INGBER, intuitive practitioner, counselor, musician, composer; b. N.Y.C., Feb. 28, 1945; d. Frank and Lillian Ingber. BA, Bklyn. Coll., 1970; MA, UCLA, 1978. Cert. in intuitive consulting, counseling, tchg. and learning, body and kinetic intervention. Spiritual dir. and founder The Stream, L.A., 1980-86, 1999—; ptnr., co-founder The Healing Partnership, L.A. and Ramona, 1986-90; spiritual dir. and founder The Triple Eye Found., Escondido, Calif., 1990-93; intuitive practitioner, counselor, cons. and tchr., founder The Stream Spiritual Orgn., Talent, Oreg., 1980—; owner The Stream, Talent; spiritual activist, co-founder Rising Mountains Setting Suns, Ramona, 1993-95; co-founder Spiritual Activist Movement, L.A. and Ramona, 1993-95; owner Treehouse Music. Author: The Autobiography of Mary Magdalene, 1988; spoken tapes include: The Healing of God, The Alienation of Love, Spirituality: The Last Block to Freedom; music tapes include Beyond the Mystery, Sara in the Clouds; videotapes include Breaking the "I" Barrier. West Coast coord. Wages for Housework Campaign, L.A., 1974-78; co-founder The Looseleaf Directory: Linking Bodies, Minds and Spirits in the Healing Arts, 1994-95.

GREEN, BONNIE JEAN, early childhood administrator; b. Crookston, Minn., Oct. 23, 1950; d. Francis Romain and Dorothy Marion (Boatman) Bagne; m. Steven Douglas Wedger, July 21, 1973 (div. Feb. 1985); m. Charles Edward Green Jr., June 15, 1985; stepchildren: Andrew Green, Russell Green. BS in Edn. magna cum laude, U. N.D., 1972; cert. human rels., Minn. State U., 1973; postgrad., U. Minn., 1975-83. Cert. elem./early childhood edn. adminstr. Math/reading tutor bilingual students U. N.D., Grand Forks, 1969-71; 1st grade tchr. Park Rapids (Minn.) Ind. Sch. Dist., 1972-73; asst. dir./curriculum writer, tchr. Child Devel. and Learning Ctr., Burnsville, Minn., 1973-75, dir., 1975-87; caring ministry outreach Luth. Ch. of Incarnation, Davis, Calif., 1990—; facilitator-parent edn. program Dakato County Vo-Tech, 1973-78; advisor, cons. Dakota County Childcare Coun., 1977-83; advisor, tchr. cert. program Augsburg Coll., Mpls., 1977-78; supr. student tchrs. Coll. of St. Catherine, Augsburg, St. Paul, 1977-87; cons. Minn. Edn. for Young Children, 1978, State of Minn., 1979-81, Am. Luth. Ch., Mpls., 1981-83; cons., kindergarten curriculum Burnsville Sch. Dist., 1983; liaison coord. Head Start Program, Burnsville, 1985-87. Vol. Prince of Peace Luth. Ch., Burnsville, 1975-87 facilitator parents of divorce, 1984-87; vol. Yolo Wayfare Ctr., Woodland, Calif., 1992; bd. dirs. Riverwoods Homeowners Assn. Arch. Control, 1978-85; mem., vol. Holy Cross Luth., Wheaton, Ill., 1987-89, Luth. Ch. of Incarnation, Davis, 1989—, curriculum planner, 1989; publicity chair, bd. dirs. U. Calif. Farm Circle, Davis, 1989—; fundraiser Wheaton (Ill.) Newcomers, 1987-89; fraternal communicator Luth. Brotherhood, 1994—. Mem. Nat. Assn. for Edn. Young Children, PEO (guard, treas., sec., v.p., pres.), Pi Lambda Theta. Avocations: gardening, interior decorating, gourmet cooking, travel. Home and Office: 39648 Lupine Ct Davis CA 95616-9756

GREEN, BRIAN GERALD, marketing executive; b. Missoula, Mont., Sept. 5, 1954; s. Gerald Jay and Ruth Anne (Althaus) G.; m. Robin Lee McIntyre, May 10, 1980; 1 child, Sean Brian. ASEE, Clark Coll., 1976; BS in Electronics Engring. Tech., Oreg. Inst. Tech., Klamath Falls, 1978; MBA, U. Hartford, 1988. Cert. electronic technician. Field engr. Triad Systems Corp., Hartford, Conn., 1978-79; midwest regional mgr. Triad Systems Corp., Chgo., 1979-81; Northwest regional mgr. Triad Systems Corp., Portland, Oreg., 1981-83; northeast area mgr. Triad Systems Corp., Bristol, Conn., 1983-88, Canadian svc. mgr., 1987-88; western area mgr. Triad Systems Corp., Tracy, Calif., 1988-89; world wide svc. mgr. Sysgen, Inc., Milpitas, Calif., 1989-91; svc. mktg. mgr. Sony Corp. Am., San Jose, 1991-93; self employed cons., 1993; bus. mgr. REPAC, Inc., Forest Park, Ga., 1993-94; dir. authentication AirTouch Cellular, Walnut Creek, Calif., 1994—. Mem. Assn. for Svcs. Mgmt. Internat., Masons (Southington, Conn. and Vancouver, Wash. chpts.), Scottish Rite (Hartford), Sphinx Shrine (Hartford). Republican. Methodist. Avocations: skiing, camping, family. Home: 12140 Carnegie Dr Tracy CA 95376-9149

GREEN, BRUCE, lawyer; b. Sallisaw, Okla.; s. J. Fred and Bulah G.; m. Barbara Ann Green; children: Robert Bruce Green Jr., Catherine A. Green Watson. Grad., Northeastern State Coll., 1955; JD, U. Okla., 1957. With Green, Green, & Green, 1958-61; asst. U.S. atty. U.S. Dist. Ct. (ea. dist.) Okla., 1961, U.S. atty., 1965-69; pvt. practice Muskogee, Okla., 1969-91; asst. U.S. atty. U.S. Dist. Ct. (ea. dist.) Okla., 1991, sr. litig. counsel, 1992-96, civil chief, 1996—; U.S. atty. U.S. Dist. Ct. (ea. dist.) Okla.atty, 1997—. With USAR. Fax: 918-684-5130. Office: US Atty's Office 1200 W Okmulgee St Muskogee OK 74401-6848*

GREEN, CAROL H., lawyer, educator, journalist; b. Seattle, Feb. 18, 1944. BA in History/Journalism summa cum laude, La. Tech. U., 1965; MSL, Yale U., 1977; JD, U. Denver, 1979. Reporter Shreveport (La.) Times, 1965-66, Guam Daily News, 1966-67; city editor Pacific Jour., Agana, Guam, 1967-68, reporter, editl. writer, 1968-76, legal affairs reporter, 1977-79; asst. editor editl. page Denver Post, 1979-81, house counsel, 1980-83, labor rels. mgr., 1981-83; assoc. Holme Roberts & Owen, 1983-85; v.p. human resources and legal affairs Denver Post, 1985-87, mgr. circulation, 1988-90; gen. mgr. Distbn. Systems Am., Inc., 1990-92; dir. labor rels. Newsday, 1992-95, dir. comm. & labor rels., 1996-97; v.p. Weber Mgmt. Cons., 1997-98; v.p. human resources Denver Post, 1998—; 1985 speaker for USIA, India, Egypt; mem. Mailers Tech. Adv. Com. to Postmaster Gen., 1991-92. Recipient McWilliams award for juvenile justice, Denver, 1971, award for interpretive reporting Denver Newspaper Guild, 1979. Mem. ABA (forum on comm. law), Colo. Bar Assn. (bd. govs. 1985-87, chair BAR-press com. 1980), Newspaper Assn. Am. (mem. human resources and labor rels. com.), Denver Bar Assn. (co-chiar jud. sel. and benefits com. 1982-85, 2st v.p. 1986), Colo. and Internat. Women's Dorum, Leadership Denver, Human Resources Planning Soc., Soc. Human Resources Mgmt., Indsl. Rels. Rsch.

Assn., Colo. Assn. Human Resources Assn., Huntington Camera Club. Episcopalian. *

GREEN, CATHERINE C., foreign language educator; b. Inchon, Korea, Feb. 13, 1962; parents Am. citizens; d. Ronald J. and Jean S. Carson; m. Nathaniel C. Green, June 16, 1985 (div. Dec. 1995). BS in French, Murray (Ky.) State U., 1985; MA in Fgn. Lang. Edn., U. Louisville, 1988, postgrad., 1991. Tchr. ESL, French and German Jefferson County Pub. Schs., Louisville, 1985—; mem. Atherton budget Com., Louisville, 1991—. Vol. adult and continuing edn., Louisville, 1996-98. Recipient Ashland Oil Tchrs. Achievement award, 1995, 97, 98; JCPS/U. Louisville Collaborative Ventures grantee, 1996-98. Mem. TESOL, Ky. TESOL, Nat. Coun. Tchrs. of English. Avocations: snorkeling, reading, travel. Email: cgreen1@jefferson.k12.ky.us. Home: 3906 Longview Rd Louisville KY 40299 Office: Atherton HS 3000 Dundee Rd Louisville KY 40205

GREEN, CECIL HOWARD, geophysicist, consultant, educator; b. Manchester, Eng., Aug. 6, 1900; s. Charles Henry and Maggie (Howard) G.; m. Ida M. Flansburgh, Feb. 6, 1926. Student, U. B.C.; BSEE, MIT, 1923, SM, 1924; DEng., Colo. Sch. Mines, 1953; DSc, U. Tulsa, 1961, U. Sydney, Australia, 1961, U. B.C., 1964, So. Meth. U., 1967, U. Mass., 1974, Tex. Christian U., 1974; D.Sc., Oxford U., 1986; LLD, Austin Coll., 1966; D Civil Jurisprudence, U. Dallas, 1976; D Comml. Sci. (hon.), Suffolk U., 1978; D Philanthropy (hon.), Hawthorne Coll., 1987; LHD (hon.), U. So. Calif., L.A., 1990. Rsch. engr. A.C. engring. dept. GE, Schenectady, 1924-26; rsch. engr. Raytheon Mfg. Co., Cambridge, Mass., 1926-28, Fed. Telegraph Co., Palo Alto, Calif., also Newark, 1928-30; party chief Geophys. Svc. Inc., Dallas, 1930-36; supr. Geophys. Svc. Inc., 1936-41, v.p., 1941-50, pres., 1950-56, chmn. bd., 1956-59, hon. chmn., 1959—; founder dir. Tex. Instruments, Inc.; hon. lectr. earth and planetary scis. MIT, 1973—; cons. prof. earth scis. Stanford U., hon. lectr. earth scis., 1983; hon. lectr. geophysics U. B.C., 1984; founder Green Coll. Oxford U., 1979, Green Ctr. Study Sci. and Soc. U. Tex. Dallas 1992, Green Coll. U. B.C., 1993. Trustee Scripps Clinic and Rsch. Found., Woods Hole Oceanographic Inst., SW Med. Found.; trustee So. Meth. U. Found. for Sci. and Engring., pres., 1964-66; trustee, past pres. St. Mark's Sch. Tex.; trustee Tex. Christian U.; trustee, mem. exec. com. Austin Coll.; membership com., life mem. corp., mem. vis. com. dept. physics, vis. com. earth and planetary scis. MIT; mem. com. earth scis. Stanford; chmn. Excellence in Edn. Found. Decorated Knight of Brit. Empire, 1991; recipient Santa Rita award U. Tex. System; with Ida Green, Linz award City of Dallas, 1974, (with Ida Green) Internat. Ednl. and Research Tribute, Nat. Acad. Scis., 1978, (with Ida Green) Pub. Welfare medal Nat. Acad. Scis., 1979, award for excellence in humanities North Dallas C. of C., 1978, citation So. Meth. U. Inst. for Study Earth and Man, 1979, Gt. Trekker award U. B.C., 1983, Hon. Lay award for disting. service AMA, 1984, Gold Plate award Am. Acad. Achievement, 1984, Freedom of City award Vancouver, B.C., Can., 1987, Philanthropist of Year awards City of Dallas, 1987, City of San Diego, 1988, (with Ida Green) Uncommon Man award Stanford U., 1988, Scientist of Year award City of San Diego, 1989, Lifetime Achievement award Reginald S. Lourie Ctr. Infants and Young Children, 1993, Nat. Philanthropist of Yr. award Nat. Assn. Fund Raising Execs., 1994, Waldo E. Smith medal Am. Geophysical Union, 1995, Lifetime Achievement award U. British Columbia, 1998; inducted into Industry Pioneer Offshore Energy Ctr. Hall of Fame, 1998. Fellow Am. Acad. Arts and Scis.; mem. AIA (hon. mem.), IEEE (hon. mem.), NAS (hon. mem.), MIT Alumni Assn. (pres. 1968-69, hon. chmn. San Diego sect. 1995), Am. Assn. Petroleum Geologists (hon. 1993), Soc. Exploration Geophysicists (hon. life mem., past pres., Kaufman medal 1966, Maurice Ewing medal 1978), Am. Assn. Petroleum Geologists (Human Needs medal 1974, hon. mem. 1993), European Assn. Exploration Geophysicists, Mex. Assn. Petroleum Geologists, Am. Geophys. Union (hon., Waldo E. Smith Medal, 1995), Tex. Assn. Grad. Edn. and Rsch. (hon. chmn.), Dallas Geol. Soc. (hon. life), Dallas Geophys. Soc. (hon. life), Knight of the Brit. Empire (hon. 1991), Explorers Club. Clubs: Dallas Country, Dallas Petroleum; La Jolla (Calif.) Country. Home and Office: 3525 Turtle Creek Blvd Apt 20A Dallas TX 75219-5514

GREEN, CECILIA ANNE, humanities educator; b. Sept. 23, 1951. BA, U. West Indies, Jamaica, 1973; MA, U. Toronto, 1980, PhD, 1998. Lectr. U. Mich., Ann Arbor, 1989-92, vis. asst. prof., 1995-97; King-Chavez-Parks scholar Wayne State U., Detroit, 1994-95; asst. prof. Bowling Green (Ohio) State U., 1998—. E-mail: cagreen@bgnet.bgsu.edu. Home: 1624 Juniper Dr Apt 85 Bowling Green OH 43402-3437 Office: Dept of Ethnic Studies Bowling Green State U 239 Shatzel Hall Bowling Green OH 43403

GREEN, CLIFFORD SCOTT, federal judge; b. Phila., Apr. 2, 1923; s. Robert Lewis and Alice (Robinson) G.; m. Mabel Wood, June 20, 1959. B.S., Temple U., 1948, J.D., 1951. Bar: Pa. 1952. Practiced law Phila., 1952-64; dep. atty. gen. State of Pa., 1954; judge County Ct., Phila., 1964-68, Ct. Common Pleas, 1968-71; judge U.S. Dist. Ct. for Eastern Dist. Pa., Phila., 1971-88, sr. judge, 1988—; former lectr. in law Temple U. Former bd. dirs. Children's Aid Soc. of Pa.; former bd. mgrs. Children's Hosp., Phila.; trustee Temple U. Served with USAAF, 1943-46. Recipient Judge William Hastie award NAACP Legal Def. Fund, 1985, awards for community service Women's Christian Alliance, awards for community service Health and Welfare Council, awards for community service Opportunities Industrialization Center, J. Austin Norris Barrister's award, 1988, Temple Law Alumni Assn. award 1994, Justice Thurgood Marshall Meml. award Nat. Bar Assn., 1994. Mem. Sigma Pi Phi. Presbyterian. Office: US Courthouse Independence Mall W #15613 601 Market St Philadelphia PA 19106-1713

GREEN, DALE MONTE, retired judge; b. Outlook, Wash., Apr. 27, 1922; s. Carey W. and Minnie M. (Gunness) G.; m. Maxine Spencer, June 30, 1946; children—Judith Louise, Frederick William. B.A. in Econs. and Bus. U. Wash., 1948, B.S. in Law, 1949, J.D., 1950. Bar: Wash. 1950. Pvt. practice Spokane, 1950-54; asst. U.S. dist. atty. Eastern Dist. Wash., 1954-56; trial atty. civil div. Dept. Justice, Washington, 1956-58; U.S. dist. atty. Eastern Dist. Wash., 1958-60; mem. firm Sherwood, Tugman & Green, Walla Walla, Wash., 1960-69; judge Wash. Ct. Appeals Div. III, Spokane, 1969-91; chief judge Wash. Ct. Appeals Div. III, 1972-74, 78-80, 84-86, 90-91; presiding chief judge Wash. Ct. Appeals, 1985; chmn. state adv. com. on judicial ethics; mem. Wash. Pattern Jury Instrn. Com., 1971-86, State Adv. Bd. Jud. Edn., 1974-77, Wash. State Jud. Council, 1972-75. Editorial bd.: Wash. Law Rev, 1949-50. Served with AUS, 1943-46. Mem. ABA, Fed. Bar Assn., Wash. Bar Assn., Am. Judicature Soc., Rotary. United Methodist. Home: 3914 S Cook St Spokane WA 99223-4423

GREEN, DAN, publishing company executive; b. Passaic, N.J., Sept. 28, 1935; s. Harold and Bessie (Roslow) G.; m. Jane Oliphant, Sept. 20, 1959; children—Matthew Kenan, Simon Pom. BA, Syracuse (N.Y.) U., 1956. Publicity dir. Dover Press, 1957-58, Sta. WNAC-TV, 1958-59, Bobbs-Merrill Co., 1959-62; with Simon & Schuster Inc., 1962-85, assoc. publisher, 1976-80, v.p., pub., 1980-84, pres. trade pub. group, 1984-85; founder, pub. Kenan Press, 1979-80; chief exec. officer Wheatland Pub., N.Y.C., 1985-89; pub. Weidenfeld & Nicolson N.Y., 1985-89; chief exec. officer Grove Press, Inc., N.Y.C., 1985-89; pres. Kenan Books, N.Y.C., 1989—; pres. Pom Literary Agy., 1989. Office: Pom Inc 611 Broadway Rm 907B New York NY 10012-2608

GREEN, DAPHNE KELLY, mental health nurse; b. Bronx, N.Y., Sept. 26, 1952; d. Quincy and Clarice (Perry) K.; children: Kimberly, Quentin. AA, Community Coll. of Balt., 1973; BA in Social Sci., Coppin State Coll., Balt., 1975; BS, Coppin State Coll., 1983, MEd in Rehab. Counseling, 1993. RN, Md.; cert. rehab. counseling. Rsch. nurse Francis Scott Key Hosp., Balt., 1984-87; night supr. Spring Grove State Hosp., Balt., 1987-89; assoc. dir. nursing Community Care Nursing and Geriatric Ctr., Balt,, 1989-91; psychiat. nurse, adult and geriatric Md. Gen. Hosp., 1991; psychiat. nurse supr. Clifton T. Perkins State Hosp., 1992-94; mgr. mental health and substance abuse svcs. Blue Cross/Blue Shield, Columbia, 1994—. Mem. ANA, Black Nurses Assn., Herbert M. Frisby Hist. Soc.

GREEN, DARLENE, comptroller, municipal official; b. St. Louis. Grad., Washington U. Budget dir. City of St. Louis, comptroller, 1995. Mem. Antioch Bapt. Ch.; vol. St. Louis Pub. Schs., St. Louis Crisis Nursery, Big Bros. & Big Sisters, YWCA Gtr. St. Louis. Mem. Nat. Assn. Black Accts., NAACP, Govt. Fin. Officers Assn., Zeta Phi Beta. Fax: (314) 622-4026. Office: City of St Louis 1200 Market St Rm 212 Saint Louis MO 63103-2805*

GREEN, DARRELL, professional football player; b. Houston, Feb. 15, 1960. Student, Tex. A&I. Cornerback Washington Redskins, 1983—. Named NFL All-Pro Team Cornerback by Sporting News, 1991. Played in Pro Bowl, 1984, 86, 87, 90, 91, Super Bowl XVIII, 1983, XXII, 1987, XXVI, 1991. Office: Washington Redskins Dulles Internat Airport PO Box 17247 Washington DC 20041-7247 also: 21300 Redskin Park Dr Ashburn VA 20147-6100*

GREEN, DAVID, manufacturing company executive; b. Chgo., Mar. 22, 1922; s. Harry B. and Carrie (Scheinbaum) G.; m. Mary I. Winton, June 15, 1951; children: Sara Edmond, Howard Benjamin, Jonathan Winton. BA in Econs., U. Chgo., 1942, MA in Social Scis., 1949. Mgr. Toy Co., Chgo., 1946-54; founder, chmn., pres. Quartet Mfg. Co., Skokie, Ill., 1954-90, chmn., prin. officer, 1990-97; pres. Colleague, Inc., Booneville, Miss., 1967-87; chmn. bd. and cons. DG Group, Chgo., 1977—; chmn. Quartet Ovonics, 1986-97. Spl. cons. to White House-Trade Expansion Act, Washington, 1962; chmn. Winnetka Caucus (Ill.), 1971; chmn. Ill. state Dan Walker for Gov., 1972, 76; spl. asst. to Gov. for intergovtl. relations, Ill., 1973-77; mem. U. Chgo. pres.'s coun., pres.'s circle Chgo. Botanic Garden, playwright's circle Stratford Festival; founder dir. circle Steppenwolf Theatre Co.; governing mem. Chgo. Symphony Orch., Art Inst. Chgo. Served with U.S. Army, 1942-45, PTO. Recipient 1st Non-Smoking Office Bldg. award Skokie Clean Air Coalition, 1987; named Office Products Divsn. Man of Yr., Richard Karasik Humanitarian award, UJA, 1997. Mem. Bus. Products Industry Assn., Office Products Wholesale Assn. (Office Product Mfr. of Yr. award 1989, 93, 94), Chgo. Soc. of Clubs, Metropolitan (Chgo.), Bay Colony (Naples, Fla.). Home: 969 Tower Manor Dr Winnetka IL 60093-1937 Office: 650 Dundee Rd Ste 456 Northbrook IL 60062-2747

GREEN, DAVID EDWARD, librarian, priest, translator; b. Adrian, Mich., June 22, 1937; s. Edward Robert Alexander and Fannie Amelia (Nadler) G.; m. Sharon Weiner, June 1, 1961; children: Alexis Ann, Philip DeWitt. BA, Harvard U., 1960; BD, Ch. Div. Sch. of Pacific, Berkeley, Calif., 1963; MLS, U. Calif., Berkeley, 1970. Ordained priest Episc. Ch., 1964. Assoc. librarian Grad. Theol. Union, Berkeley, 1970-82; libr. dir. Gen. Theol. Sem., N.Y.C., 1982—. Translator many German theol. works. Mem. Am. Theol. Libr. Assn., N.Y. Area Theol. Libr. Assn., Beta Phi Mu. Avocation: English country dancing. Home and Office: Gen Theol Sem St Mark's Libr 175 9th Ave New York NY 10011-4924

GREEN, DAVID FERRELL, law enforcement official; b. Sioux Falls, S.D., Nov. 13, 1935; s. John C. and Mary A. (Meyer) G.; m. Renata M. Kappenman, Apr. 15, 1961; children: Tobin L., Anthony F., Thomas D. BA summa cum laude, Augustana Coll., Sioux Falls, 1980; MPA Univ. S.D., 1992; grad. FBI Nat. Acad., 1972; Juvenile Officers Inst., 1966. with Sioux Falls Police Dept., 1958-88, chief, 1982-88; exec. dir. Mid-State Organized Crime Info. Ctr., Springfield, Mo., 1988—; mem. NCIC Policy Bd. Justice Dept., Washington, 1976-78; mem. NCIC North Central Group, 1978-88, State Juvenile Task Force; vice chmn. Gov.'s Police Task Force S.D., 1979-81. Bd. dirs. Vol. Nat. Ctr. for Citizen Involvement, Washington, 1978-81, St. Therese Sch. Bd., Sioux Falls, pres., 1973-74; pres. Vol. Action Ctr., Sioux Falls, 1979-80; treas. found. bd. Little Flower Sch. Served with USNR, 1953-61. Recipient J. Edgar Hoover award Justice Dept., 1972; Jaycees Officer Yr. award Sioux Falls Jaycees, 1972; named to Augustana Coll. Honor Soc., 1980. Mem. Fraternal Order of Police (trustee 1971-83, chmn. bd. trustees 1979-83, Outstanding Service award 1983). Republican, Am. Legion., Elks, K.C. Roman Catholic. Office: Mid States Orgn Crime Info Ctr 1610 E Sunshine Ste 100 Springfield MO 65804

GREEN, DAVID HENRY, manufacturing company executive; b. Worcester, Mass., Feb. 8, 1921; s. Herbert H. and Florence (Knapp) G.; m. Betty Jeppson, June 23, 1951; children: Anne L., Susan E., David Henry, Charles J., Sarah C. B.A., Wesleyan U., Middletown, Conn., 1942; M.B.A., Harvard, 1943. Asst. treas. Valley Bank & Trust Co., Springfield, Mass., 1946-51; sr. v.p. Worcester County Nat. bank, 1952-65, New Eng. Mchts. Nat. Bank (now Fleet Bank), Boston, 1965-73; chmn. L.G. Balfour Co., Attleboro, Mass., 1973-87; dir. L.G. Balfour Co. Trustee New Eng. Aquarium, Worcester Found. Exptl. Biology; hon. trustee Concord Acad.; bd. dirs. Bristol County Devel. Council, Attleboro Scholarship Found.; bd. assos. Wheaton Coll. Served as capt. AUS, 1943-46. Home: 207 Old Concord Rd Lincoln MA 01773-3602

GREEN, DAVID O., accounting educator, educational administrator; b. Chgo., Feb. 14, 1923; s. David and Gertrude (Strauss) G.; m. Nova Muir, Sept. 12, 1948 (div. 1971); children: Katherine, Nova. B.S., DePaul, U., 1947; M.B.A., U. Chgo., 1948, Ph.D., 1956. C.P.A., Ill., 1951. Mem. faculty U. Chgo., 1949-81, prof. acctg., 1963-81; dir. U. Chgo. (Inst. Profl. Acctg.), 1974-78; v.p. adminstrn. Bernard Baruch Coll., CUNY, 1979-90, prof. acctg., 1990—; vis. prof. acctg. Fla. State U., 1963-64, 70, Middle East Tech U., 1967-68, U. Birmingham, 1968, London Grad. Sch. Bus. Studies, 1971-72, U. Canterbury, N.Z., 1973, Fla. Internat. U., 1977-78; fiscal and accounting cons. City of Chgo., 1957-63; lectr. Western acctg. Guandong Culture Exch. Ctr., Guangzhou, China, 1993. Editor: Jour. Accounting Research, 1963-67; mem. editorial bd., 1968-82. Served with AUS, 1943-45. Home: 30 Waterside Plz New York NY 10010-2622 Office: Baruch Coll Sch Bus Box E0725 17 Lexington Ave New York NY 10010-5518

GREEN, DAVID WILLIAM, chemist, educator; b. Hudson, Mich., Nov. 19, 1942; s. Francis Harger and Dorotha Louise (Onweller) G.; m. Mary Sarah McCullough, July 8, 1967; children: Laura, Brenda, Mark, Brian, William. BA, Albion Coll., 1964; PhD, U. Calif., Berkeley, 1968; MBA, U. Chgo., 1985. Instr. U. Calif., Berkeley, 1968; rsch. assoc. U. Chgo., 1968-71; asst. prof. Albion (Mich.) Coll., 1971-75; chemist Argonne (Ill.) Nat. Lab., 1975-82, mgr. analytical chemistry, 1982—; prof. chemistry Coll. DuPage, Glen Ellyn, Ill., 1991-93. Editor Mng. the Modern Lab, 1995—, mem. editl. bd., 1994—. Pres. Dist. 58 Bd. Edn., Downers Grove, Ill., 1976-79. Mem. Analytical Lab. Mgrs. Assn. (pres. 1986-87, treas. 1989). Home: 5625 Carpenter St Downers Grove IL 60516-1356 Office: Argonne Nat Lab 9700 Cass Ave Argonne IL 60439-4803

GREEN, DENNIS, professional football coach; b. Harrisburg, Pa., Feb. 17, 1949. BS, U. Iowa, 1971. Asst. coach U. Iowa, 1972, 74-76, U. Dayton, 1973, Stanford U., 1977-78, 80, San Francisco 49ers, 1979; head coach Northwestern U., 1981-85; asst. coach San Francisco 49ers, 1986-88; head coach Stanford U., 1989-91, Minn. Vikings, 1992—. Office: Minnesota Vikings 9520 Viking Dr Eden Prairie MN 55344-3898*

GREEN, DENNIS G., federal judge; b. 1944. BA, Cen. State U., 1966; JD, South Tex. U., 1970. Asst. dist. atty. Harris County, Tex., 1972-75; asst. U.S. atty. we. dist. U.S. Dist. Ct. Tex., 1975-76; 1st asst. dist. atty. McLennan County, Tex.; trial counsel Shell Oil Co., 1979-82, Watson & Green, 1984-85; apptd. magistrate judge we. dist. U.S. Dist. Ct. Tex., 1985. Fax: (817) 750-1547. Office: 800 Franklin Ave Waco TX 76701-1936

GREEN, DENNIS JOSEPH, lawyer; b. Milw., Sept. 28, 1941; m. Janet McQueen; children: Karla Green Pope, Cheryl Green Ashley, Deborah. BS in Mgmt., U. Ill., 1963, JD, 1968. Bar: Ill. 1968, Mo. 1968. Atty. Monsanto Co., St. Louis, 1968-75, asst. co. counsel, 1975-76, counsel, 1976-79; gen. counsel, sec. Fisher Controls Internat. Inc., Clayton, Mo., 1979-85, v.p., gen. counsel, sec., 1985-93; v.p., assoc. gen. counsel Emerson Electric Co., St. Louis, 1992—. 1st lt. U.S. Army, 1963-65. Office: Emerson Electric Co PO Box 4100 8000 W Florissant Ave Saint Louis MO 63136-1415

GREEN, DON WESLEY, chemical and petroleum engineering educator; b. Tulsa, July 8, 1932; s. Earl Leslie and Erma Pansy (Brackins) G.; m. Patricia Louise Polston, Nov. 26, 1954; children: Guy Leslie, Don Michael, Charles Patrick. BS in Petroleum Engring., U. Tulsa, 1955; MSChemE, U. Okla., 1959, PhD in Chem. Engring., 1963. Rsch. scientist Continental Oil Co., Ponca City, Okla., 1962-64; asst. to assoc. prof. U. Kans., Lawrence, 1964-71, prof. chem. and petroleum engring., 1971-82, chmn. dept. chem. and petroleum engring., 1970-74, 96—, co-dir. Tertiary Oil Recovery project, 1974—, Conger-Gabel Disting. prof., 1982-95, Deane E. Ackers Disting. prof., 1995—; faculty rep. to NCAA. Editor: Perry's Chemical Engineers' Handbook, 1984, 97; contbr. articles to profl. jours. 1st lt. USAF, 1955-57. Fellow Am. Inst. Chem. Engrs.; mem. Soc. Petroleum Engrs. (Disting. Achievement award 1983, chmn. edn. and accreditation com. 1980-81, Disting. mem. 1986, Disting. lectr. 1986). Democrat. Avocations: handball, baseball, mountain hiking. Home: 1020 Sunset Dr Lawrence KS 66044-4546 Office: U Kans Dept Chem & Petroleum Engrg 4008 Learned Hall Lawrence KS 66044-7526*

GREEN, DONALD HUGH, lawyer; b. Elizabeth, N.J., May 16, 1929; s. Mortimer Jordan and Edna (Reinherz) G.; m. Carol Margaret Medsger, Sept. 20, 1960; children: Michael, Margaret, Matthew, Mark. AB, Syracuse U., 1951; LLB, Harvard U., 1954. Bar: Fla. 1956, N.Y. 1957, D.C. 1960. Atty. Office of Legal Counsel, U.S. Dept. Justice, Washington, 1958-60, atty. civil div., 1960-61; assoc. Bergson & Borkland, Washington, 1961-65; ptnr. Fisher, Sharlitt, Gelband & Green, Washington, 1965-66, Wald, Harkrader & Ross, Washington, 1966-87; vice chmn. exec. com. mng. ptnr. Pepper, Hamilton LLP, Washington, 1987—; mem. faculty curriculum com. Legal Edn. Inst., U.S. Dept. Justice, Washington, 1985-92; lectr. Georgetown Law Ctr., Washington, 1981—, various symposia D.C. Bar; adj. prof. Georgetown Law Ctr., 1992—. Contbr. articles to profl. jours. Mem., chmn. trustees Cedar Ln. Unitarian Ch., Bethesda, 1972-75. Col. USMCR, 1954-85. Decorated Legion of Merit. Mem. ABA, Fed. Bar Assn., Am. Arbitration Assn., Dev. Rsch. Inst., Joint Svcs. Com. on Profl. Ethics, Nat. Panel Arbitrators, Fed. Am. Inn of Ct. (pres. 1994-95). Democrat. Avocations: painting, sailing, tennis. Home: 5610 Wisconsin Ave Apt 18A Chevy Chase MD 20815-4415 Office: Pepper Hamilton LLP Hamilton Sq 600 14th St NW Washington DC 20005

GREEN, EDWARD ANTHONY, museum director; b. Milw., Apr. 20, 1922; s. Edward Eli and Elizabeth Mary (Hofmeister) G.; m. Dorinne May Traulsen, June 20, 1953; children: Erika Linden, Jeremy Jonathon. BS in Art Edn., U. Wis., 1951, MS in Applied Art, 1951; MFA in Fine Arts with honors, U. Wis., Milw., 1966; student, Layton Sch. Art, 1953. Archtl. designer Wilbur Lumber Co., West Allis, Wis., 1940-42; playground dir. Milw. Recreation Dept., 1947-49; art dir. Milw. Pub. Mus., 1951-84; landmarks commr. City of Milw., 1959-80, art commr., 1959-84; dir. mus. Mitchell Gallery Flight, Milw., 1984—; art instr. U. Wis., Milw., 1955-69, 84, Whitnall Park, Greendale, Wis., 1966-79, Cardinal Stritch U., Fox Point, Wis., 1975-90, Mt. Mary Coll., 1997; art instr., lectr. Alverno Coll., 1998; mus. cons. Roger Williams Park Nat. Hist. Mus., Providence, 1982, Mus. Architecture, Quincy, Ill., 1984, Milw. Children's Mus., 1991—, Great Lakes Naval Tng. Ctr., North Chicago, Ill., 1991—, USCG Mus., New London, Conn., 1993—, others; careers lectr. Kiwanis, Milw., 1969—, Alverno Coll., 1980; lectr. U. Wis., Milw., 1992—; bd. dirs. Great Lakes Future Resource Ctr., U. Wis. Milw. Alumni Trustees, 1995—. Designer: Bapt. Mission Ch., Bamenda, Cameroon, (books) Masks of the Northwest Coast, 1966, Iroquois Masks, 1969, Mambila, 1972; co-author: Popular Culture in Museums, 1981; works included in state and nat. exhbns., also pvt. and pub. collections. Bd. dirs. Retired Sr. Vol. Program, 1996. With USCG, 1942-46; served convoy duty in North Atlantic. Recipient European Mus. Study award U. Wis., 1959, Urban Planning award Ford Found., 1969, One of 85 Outstanding Milwaukeens Milw. Mag., 1984, Lifework award Milw. Art Commn., 1985. Mem. USCG Aux. (life, comdr. 1976), Milw. Art Mus., Wis. Painters and Sculptors (pres. 1951-54), Jackson Park Assn., Longfield Shores Assn. (pres. 1976), Phi Kappa Phi. Roman Catholic. Avocations: collecting toy trains and Britain's toy soldiers, softball, sailing, painting. Home: 3173 S 31st St Milwaukee WI 53215-4319 Office: Mitchell Gallery of Flight 5300 S Howell Ave Milwaukee WI 53207-6156

GREEN, EDWARD THOMAS, JR., education educator; b. Oxford, N.J., Apr. 19, 1921; s. Edward Thomas and Euphemia (Lanterman) G.; BS cum laude, Ithaca Coll., 1942; MS, Syracuse U., 1947, EdD, 1965; m. Margaret Evelyn Tuttle, Jan. 30, 1944; children: Marsha, Margaret, Barbara. Music instr. high sch., Palmyra, N.Y., 1942-50, dir. guidance, vice-prin., 1946-50; prin. Palmyra-Macedon Central Sch., 1950-54; supervising prin. New Berlin (N.Y.) Central Sch., 1954-58, Rondout Valley Central Sch., Accord, N.Y., also supt. schs., 1958-66; supt. schs., Oneida, N.Y., 1966-77; prof. edn. Ga. So. U., Statesboro, 1977-87, prof. emeritus, 1987—. Pres., Mid-Hudson Sch. Study Council, New Paltz, N.Y., 1960; vice chmn. CHE-MAD-HER-ON, Inc.; area sec. Cen. Sch. Study; mem. exec. com. Catskill Study on Small Sch. Design; v.p. N.Y. State Tchrs. Retirement Bd. V.p. Rip Van Winkle council Boy Scouts Am., 1964-66, v.p., then pres. Madison County council, chmn. Madison Dist., pres. Iroquois council; pres. Palmyra Betterment Club 1952; mem. Ulster County Community Action Program; past pres. Ithaca Coll. Alumni Council. Served with USN, 1942-46, ETO. Mem. N.Y. State Sch. Dist. Adminstrs. (pres.), Am. Assn. Sch. Adminstrs., Assn. for Supervision and Curriculum Devel., Nat. Sch. Pub. Relations Assn., Nat. Assn. Secondary Sch. Prins., Nat. Assn. Elem. Sch. Prins., Ga. Assn. Elem. Prins., Ga. Assn. Sch. Supts., Ga. Assn. Ednl. Leaders, So. Assn. Colls. and Schs. (Ga. sec. com. 1991-95), Nat. Orgn. for Legal Problems in Edn., Masons, Shriners, Rotary Internat., Lions Club, Phi Delta Kappa (chpt. pres., area coordinator), Phi Mu Alpha. Republican. Presbyterian. Home: 409 Cardinal Dr Statesboro GA 30461-6972

GREEN, ELBERT P., retired university official; b. Laneview, Va., June 9, 1935; s. James H. and Levallia C. (DeLeaver) G.; m. Mary M. Green, July 6, 1961; children: Mark B., Marsha B. BS, Va. State Coll., 1957; BD, Felix Adler Meml. U., Chapel Hill, N.C., 1969; MS in Edn., Troy State U., Montgomery, Ala., 1988; MBph, Am. Bible Sch., Kansas City, Kans., 1968; PhD, S.W. U., New Orleans, 1991. Cert. tchr., Ala., cert. hypnotherapist; ordained minister. 2d lt. U.S. Army, 1958, advanced through grades to maj.; ret., 1979; dir. jr. ROTC, Indianola (Miss.) City Schs., Macon County (Ala.) Schs.; dir. residence hall Tuskegee (Ala.) U. Author: Poetry Is Soul, 1988, Poetry Is Gold, 1982, The Light of the World Is Poetry, 1995; contbr. articles to newspapers. Inductee Internat. Poetry Hall of Fame, 1997, Who Is Who of Contemporary Achievers Hall of Fame, 1997. Mem. Internat. Soc. of Poets, Profl. Educators Orgn., Am. Legion, Lions Internat., Scabbard and Blade, Phi Beta Sigma, Phi Delta Kappa, Gamma Beta Phi. Home: 2910 W Martin L King Hwy Tuskegee AL 36083

GREEN, ELEANOR MYERS, veterinarian, educator; b. Phila., Feb. 10, 1948; d. Wade Cooper and Eleanor Ruth (McWherter) Myers; m. George Ashby Green, Dec. 19, 1970; children: George Ashby Jr., Stacy Elizabeth, William Wade. Student, U. South Fla., 1965-67, U. Fla., 1967-69; DVM, Auburn U., 1973. Diplomate Am. Coll. Vet. Internal Medicine, Am. Bd. Vet. Practitioners (pres. 1993-95, past pres. 1995-96). Ptnrship, owner Guntown (Miss.) Vet. Clinic, 1973-76; asst. prof. Miss. State U., Starkville, 1976-84; assoc. prof. U. Mo., Columbia, 1984-91; prof. U. Tenn., Knoxville, 1991-96; prof., chair dept. U. Fla., Gainesville, 1996—. Named Disting. Practitioner Nat. Acads. of Practice. Mem. Am. Assn. Equine Practitioners (bd. dirs. 1997—), Fla. Vet. Med. Assn., Am. Vet. Med. Assn., Internat. Soc. Vet. Perinatology, Am. Assn. Vet. Clinicians (pres.-elect 1994-95, pres. 1995-96, past pres. 1996-97), Nat. Acad.'s Practice (Disting. Practitioner 1998—), Fla. Thoroughbred Owners and Breeders Assn., Rotary Internat. Presbyterian. Avocations: horseback riding, tennis, painting. Office: U Fla Coll Vet Medicine Dept Large Animal Clin Scis Gainesville FL 32610-0136

GREEN, ERIC HOWARD, lawyer; b. N.Y.C., Jan. 5, 1950; s. Bernard and Edith Green; m. Mona M. Green, July 10, 1982; children: Zachary Samuel, Shawn Alexander. BA, SUNY, Buffalo, 1972, JD, 1976. Bar: N.Y. 1977, U.S. Dist. Ct. (so. and ea. dist.) N.Y. 1979, U.S. Supreme Ct. 1985. Assoc. Pops & Estrin, N.Y.C., 1976-77, Karp & Silver, Queens, N.Y., 1977-81, Edward Leshaw, Esq., N.Y.C., 1981-82; mng. ptnr. Eric H. Green, Esq., N.Y.C., 1982—; instr. Nat. Inst. of Trial Advocacy, Cardoza Law Sch., N.Y.C., 1987—, U. Buffalo, coll. of Urban Studies, 1974-76; lectr. NYU, Sch. Continuing Edn., N.Y.C., 1986-90; arbitrator Am. Arbitration Assn., 1987—. Mem. N.Y. Dem. Judicial Screening Panel, N.Y.C., 1989; advisor, vol. N.Y.C. Open Doors Edn. Program, 1985-89. Mem. ATLA, N.Y. County Lawyers Assn., N.Y. State Bar Assn., N.Y. State Trial Lawyers Assn. (bd. dirs., speaker cmty. speakers bur. 1988—), N.Y. County Lawyers Assn. (fee dispute com., Supreme Ct. com.), Assn. Bar City N.Y. (tort litigation com., chmn. mediation subcom.). Avocations: sports, theatre, antiques. Office: 295 Madison Ave New York NY 10017-6304

GREEN, FRANK WALTER, industrial engineer; b. Springfield, Mass., Apr. 14, 1916; s. Walter L. and Mildred (Kennedy) G.; m. Kathleen M. Green, June 12, 1944 (dec. Oct. 1979), 1 child, Sandra F. Green Burns; m. patricia Van Zant Chamberlain, July 18, 1981. BS in Bus. Adminstrn., Boston U., 1938; postgrad., Armed Forces Sch. Packaging, Madison, Wis., 1944, Indsl. Coll. Armed Forces, Washington, 1952. Registered prof. engr., Mass.; cert. profl. mgmt. cons. Indsl. engr. Robert Gair Co., N.Y.C., N.E. and Can., 1938-40; asst. divsn. mgr. Bird & Sons, East Walpole, Mass., 1940-41; regional mgr. Bird & Sons, N.J., Pa. Va., 1941; ind. profl. cons. engr. Springfield, Mass., 1946-52, 53—; chmn., instr. package engrng. Columbia Grad. Sch. Engring.; spkr. package engring. U. Ill., U. Conn., Mich. State U., Temple U., MIT, others; spkr. packaging Am. Mcht. Marine Conf., Propeller Club, TAPPI; instr. Armed Forces Packaging Sch., Indsl. Tng. Package Engring.; instr. package course Am. Internat. Coll.; cons. ITT, Veeder-Root, Picker Internat., Westvaco, Am. Optical, U.S. Envelope, Royal, Digital, Honeywell, B.F. Goodrich, Breck Shampoo, Maritime Assn., Polaroid, Keystone Camera, Sohio, Jones & Lamson Machine Tool, Corning Glass Works, Yoder Bros., ATT Internat., Am. Airlines, Western Electric, marine underwriters, carriers, mags., colls., govt., trade assns., paper mfrs. and prodrs. of packaging materials, other Am. and European cos. and groups. Contbr. articles to profl. jours and encys.; editor, author: Glossary of Packaging Technical, Closing and Sealing Corrugated Boxes; author cassette aaudio and workbook tng. program in export packaging engring., packaging specifications and manuals as an Army officer, packaging specifications for major indsl. contractors. Organizer, chmn. packaging exhibit and esminar Springfield Mus. Fine Arts. Lt. col. U.S. Army, 1941-46, 52-53. Fellow Inst. Packaging Profls. (life hon., nat. chmn. packaging competition, nat. chmn. competition judges, ea. regional dir., regional v.p., v.p. N.Y./N.J. chpt., nat. bd. dirs., nat. parliamentarian, nat. chmn. packaging cons. divsn.); mem. The Packaging Inst. (mem. tech. packaging bd., mgr. distbn. packaging divsn., chmn. nat. and regional seminars), Am. Mgmt. Assn. (spkr. packaging seminars), Am. Mgmt. Assn. (spkr. packaging seminars), Packaging Assn. Can. (spkr. nat. and chpt. programs), Am. Nat. Stds. Inst. (mem. materials handling bd.), Containerization Inst. (dir. emeritus, founder, nat. pres./dir., chmn. nat. and regional forums), Soc. Profl. Mgmt. Cons. (accredited profl. mem., nat. dir., nat. officer, spkr. chpt. programs, spkr. nat. seminars), Package Engring. Soc. New England (organizer, pres., program chmn.), San Diego Cons. Round Table, Nat. Bur. Profl. Mgmt. Cons. (bd. dirs.), Soc. Profl. Engrs. Avocations: tennis, swimming, sailing, gardening, writing. Home and Office: Point O'View E 156 Pleasant St East Longmeadow MA 01028-2409 also: 504 Glorietta Blvd Cornado CA 92118

GREEN, GARETH MONTRAVILLE, physician, educator, scientist; b. Boston, Apr. 16, 1931; s. Robert Montraville and Dorothy Bradford G.; m. Joan Allison Erskine, Sept. 5, 1953; children: Jennifer Joy, Geoffrey Ware, Alan Bradford. AB cum laude, Harvard U., 1953, MD, 1957, Program for Health Sys. Mgmt., 1976. Resident U. Wash., Seattle, 1957-58, intern, 1958-60; rsch. and tng. fellow in infectious/pulmonary disease Harvard, Channing and Thorndike Labs. Boston City Hosp., Med. Research Council U.K., 1960-64; instr. bacteriology and immunology, assoc. medicine Harvard U., Cambridge, Mass., 1964-68; assoc. prof. Coll. Medicine, U. Vt., 1968-70, prof., 1970-76; practice pulmonary medicine Burlington, Vt.; dir. pulmonary unit U. Vt. Med. Sch., 1968-76; assoc. attending physician Med. Ctr. Hosp. Vt., Burlington, 1970-72, attending physician, 1972-76; founding dir. Specialized Ctr. Rsch. in Fibrotic Lung Disease and Nat. Rsch. and Demonstration Ctr. in Lung Disease, 1970-76; prof., chmn. dept. environ. health scis. Sch. Hygiene and Pub. Health Johns Hopkins U., Balt., 1976-90, founding dir. Edn. Resource Ctr. in Occupational Safety and Health, 1978-80, dir. pulmonary medicine Sch. Medicine, 1983-86, Anna M. Baetjer prof., founding dir. Environ. Health Scis. Ctr., 1985-90; assoc. dean for profl. edn., prof. environ. health scis., dir. MPH program Harvard Sch. Pub. Health, Boston, 1990—; mem. Nat. Adv. Health Svc. Coun., 1970-74, Nat. Heart, Lung and Blood Adv. Coun., 1975-79, Nat. Environ. Health Sci. Adv. Coun., 1981-84, rsch. rev. com. Health Effects Inst., 1983-95; 1st chmn. health effects rsch. rev. com. EPA, 1979-82; mem. vis. com. Brookhaven Nat. Lab., 1975-79; mem. com. on infrastructure performance, bldg. rsch. bd. NAS-NRC, 1993; mem. adv. panel on manned space flights NAS, 1969-74; vice chmn. Md. Coun. Toxic Substances, 1978-82, Md. Devel. Coun., 1981-85; mem. sci. adv. panel Ctr. for Indoor Air Rsch., 1988-92, chmn., 1991-92; mem. adv. com. to Environ. Health Sci. Ctr. Harvard U., Rutgers U., 1990—; mem. U.S./CDC team to advise Indian govt. on methyl isocyanate release in Bhopal, 1984; chmn. NIH tech. adv. panel on Persian Gulf experience and health, 1994, mem. sci. group on methods for safety evaluation chems., 1988—. Co-author: Work, Health and Productivity, 1991; editor Am. Rev. Respiratory Diseases, 1979-84, Yearbook of Pulmonary Disease, 1985-91; co-editor: Methods for Assessing and Reducing Injury from Chemical Accidents, 1989; contbr.over 100 articles to profl. jours. Trustee Vt. Lung Assn., 1969-76; bd. dirs. Am. Lung Assn., 1973-76; mem. Md. Gov.'s com. on Three Mile Island, 1980-89. NIH grantee. Mem. Am. Thoracic Soc. (J. Burns Amberson lectr. 1970, pres. 1974-75), Am. Pub. Health Assn., Infectious Diseases Soc. Am., Am. Soc. Clin. Investigation, AAAS. Research includes concepts of lung defense mechanisms against environmental agents, risk factors for health effects of air pollutants, strengthening professional education in medicine and public health, analyzing relationships of health and productivity in the workplace. Office: Harvard Sch Pub Health Kresge Bldg # 506 677 Huntington Ave Boston MA 02115-6096 *Life is a long term investment in people; create and respond to opportunity; pursue quality and excellence in yourself and others.*•

GREEN, GENE, congressman; b. Houston, Oct. 17, 1947; s. Garland B. and Evelyn (Clark) G.; m. Helen Lois Albers; children: Angela, Christopher. BS in Bus. Adminstrn., U. Houston, 1971; student, Bates Coll., Sch. of Law. Mgr. printing co.; atty.; mem. Tex. Ho. of Reps., 1973-85, Tex. Senate, 1985-92; mem. 103d-105th Congresses from 29th Tex. dist., 1993—, mem. econ. and ednl. opportunity com., mem. govt. reform and oversight com., mem. criminal justice bd., mem. commerce com.; house commerce com, subcom. of Health and Environ., Telecommunications, Trade and Consumer Protection, Oversight and Investigations. Recipient Outstanding Legis. award Houston Park Police Assn., Appreciation award Dem. Nat. Com., Appreciation award Harris County Sheriff's Deputy Assn., Legis. Support award AFL-CIO, Support award Tex. Dem. Party. Mem. Baytown C. of C., Tex. Hist. Soc., Coastal Conservation Assn. Democrat. Methodist. Office: 256 N Sam Houston Pkwy E Ste 29 Houston TX 77060-2006 also: US House of Reps 2429 Rayburn Bldg Washington DC 20515-4329 also: 11811 1-10 East Ste 430 Houston TX 77029

GREEN, GEORGE EDWARD, surgeon; b. N.Y.C., Jan. 18, 1932; s. Robert and Hannah Augusta (Berkowitz) G.; m. Sheila Ellen Greenwald, Feb. 18, 1960; children: Samuel, Benjamin. Student, Yale Coll., 1952, MD, 1956. Diplomate Am. Bd. Thoracic Cardiovascular Surgery, Am. Bd. Surgery. Asst. attending surgeon NYU Hosp., N.Y.C., 1968-70; attending surgeon St. Lukes Roosevelt Hosp., 1970-94, Columbia Presbyn. Hosp., N.Y.C., 1992-94; attending surgeon, chief cardiothoracic surgery L.I. Jewish Hosp., N.Y.C., 1982-83; prof. clin. surgery Columbia U., N.Y.C., 1992-94. Author, editor: Surgical Revascularization of the Heart, 1991; contbr. articles to profl. jours. Lt. comdr. USN, 1962-63. Rsch. grantee Nat. Heart and Lung Inst. NIH, 1966-68. Mem. Am. Assn. Thoracic Surgery, Soc. Thoracic Surgeons, Soc. Vascular Surgery, Internat. Cardiovascular Soc. Democrat. Jewish. Avocations: wine making, skiing, windboarding. Home and Office: PO Box 364 Millerton NY 12546

GREEN, GEORGE JOSEPH, publishing executive; b. N.Y.C., May 6, 1938; s. Monroe and Ruth (Gast) G.; m. Wilma H. Jordan. BA, Yale U., 1960. Trainee advt. dept. Burlington Industries, N.Y.C., 1961-62; with The New Yorker Mag., 1962-84, salesman retail advt. N.Y.C. div., 1962-64, salesman advt. Atlanta div., 1964-66, salesman advt. N.Y.C. div., 1966-67, asst. treas., 1967-71, dir. circulation, v.p., 1971-75, pres., 1975-84; exec. v.p. Hearst Mags., N.Y.C., 1984—; pres. Hearst Mags. Internat., N.Y.C., 1989—; bd. dirs. Nat. Magazine Co. Served with USAR, 1960-65. Mem. Mag. Publs. Assn. (bd. dirs.). Office: Hearst Mags 959 8th Ave New York NY 10019-3795

GREEN, GERALD B., state legislator. Freeholder Union County; assemblyman dist. 17 N.J. State Assembly; chmn. fin. Union County Freehold, 1991, chair bd. dirs., 1990. Pvt. industry coun. Union County Coll. Bd. Sch. Estimate. Mem. Union County Police Chiefs Assn. Address: 7-9 Watchung Ave Plainfield NJ 07060-1228

GREEN, GERARD LEO, priest, educator; b. Batavia, N.Y., July 27, 1928; s. George Leo and Marian (Powers) G. BS, Mt. St. Mary's Coll., 1952; MA, St. Bonaventure U., 1958; postgrad., U. Notre Dame, summers 1961-62, U. Buffalo, 1965-66; EdM, SUNY, 1968. ordained priest Roman Catholic Ch., 1956;. Lab technician Eastman Kodak Co., 1947-48; chemist Xerox Co., 1952; parish asst. Diocese Buffalo, 1956-59; instr. chemistry Bishop Turner H.S., Buffalo, 1959-74, dir. sci., 1959-70, 72-74; adminstr. Our Lady of the Rosary Parish, Wilson, N.Y., 1968; adminstr. St. Barnabas Parish and Sch. Depew, N.Y., 1973-75, pastor, 1976-90; prelate of honor, 1984, mem., supr., leader tng. team, 1979-90; pastor Sts. Peter and Paul Parrish, Hamburg, N.Y., 1990-99; mem. sci. curriculum com. Dept. Edn. Diocese Buffalo, 1960-70, chmn. diocesan chemistry textbook evaluation com., 1961-70, mem. diocesan pastoral coun. for handicapped, 1976-82, sec. 1978-79, diocesan regional coord., 1979-80, mem. diocesan fin. com., 1984-94, diocesan priests coun., 1990—, mem. diocesan coll. of consultors, 1994—; active Diocesan Cons. Parish Computers, 1983-98, Diocesan Bd. Priests Retirement, 1985-91, Diocesan Cemetary Rd., 1994—, Sch. Bd. St. Francis H.S., 1992-98; diocesan bd. dirs. for TV prodn. 1986-94; chaplain Hyview Fire Co., 1976-81, Cheektowaga Police PBA, 1976-90, West End Fire Co., 1977-90, Depew Village Fire Co., 1980-88. Contbr. articles to profl. publs. Mem. Western N.Y. Sci. Congress Com., 1960-74, sec., 1968, co-chmn. 1969, chmn. 1972-73, state chmn. 1970; mem. gen. chemistry exam. com. N.Y. State Edn. Dept., 1970-73; mem. Maryvale Schs. Planning Bd., 1977-79; cons. sci. facilities in secondary schs.; mem. local IUE-AFL-CIO Scholarship Fund Com., 1968-71; mem. dist. com. Boy Scouts Am., Buffalo, 1957-74; bd. dirs. Tifft (Conservation) Farm, 1978-82, Hamburg Meals on Wheels, 1999—; active Nat. Cath. Cemetary Conf., N.Y. State Fire Chaplains. With AUS, 1946-47. Recipient Disting. Svc. award in sci. edn., 1975, Justice and Charity award First Cath. Charities, 1999, Cure of ARS award Outstanding Priest, 1999. Mem. Sci. Tchrs. Assn., N.Y. (dir. 1971-73), Nat. Cath. Edn. Assn., Order of Arrow, KC. Address: 9686 Oak Grove Dr Angola NY 14006

GREEN, HAROLD DANIEL, dentist; b. Scranton, Pa., Feb. 4, 1934; s. Harold Charles and Viola Mildred (Brown) G.; m. Cornelia Ann Ellis, Aug. 1, 1959; children: Scott Alan, Mary Ann. *Wife Dr. Cornelia Ann Green, former teacher of language arts and social studies, also school psychologist. She received her Masters Degree and PhD; she has been a Clinical Psychologist, Child, Adolescent and Family Practice for eighteen years. Son is a graduate of Southern Illinois University Dental Laboratory Technology Program. He is the owner of a five person Green Dental Lab. Daughter, BA, St. Olaf, BS, MAT, Beloit College. She teaches biology, chemistry and genetics. She taught three years in Cali, Columbia, two years in Bahrain, and four years in Istanbul, Turkey. She coaches basketball, soccer and volleyball.* BA, Beloit Coll. (Wis.), 1956; DDS, Northwestern U., 1960. Gen. practice dentistry Beloit, Wis., 1964—; dir. Beloit Savs. Bank, chmn. trust com., 1989—; mem loan com. Blackhawk State Bank, mem. fin. com., 1993. *Harold Daniel Green has been a strong supporter of city manager form of local government. He has been a chairman three times, 1984, 1989, and 1998 successfully retaining the professional city manager government from mayor referendums.He has been active in school, college and area technical school boards. He is active in church and on the board of Blackhawk State Bank, as well as, Lions and many community activities. He is still active in professional dental organizations.* Contbr. articles to profl. jours. Active Wis. div. Am. Cancer Soc., 1964-75; 1st pres., co-organizer Citizen's Council Against Crime, Beloit; past officer, chmn. membership Beloit YMCA; pres. Beloit Brewers, chmn. bd., 1988-91, class A midwest league affiliate of Milw. Brewers baseball team, 1986-87; chmn. Student Achievers Program, Wis., No. Ill.; mem. adv. bd. Salvation Army; chmn. Beloiters for Coun.-Mgr., 1989; stateline chmn. Student Achiever Program, 1988, 93; bd. dirs. Greater Beloit Found., 1989—; chmating com. Greater Beloit Community Trust, Inc., 1991,93; chmn. adminstrv. bd., chmn. Council of Ministries, First United Methodist Ch., Beloit, pastor parish rels., 1995—; chmn. ann. dinner, bd. dirs., nominating com., fundraising, pub. speakers Beloit Crime Stoppers, 1993—, chmn., 1995-96; chmn. facilities study com. Sch. Dist. Beloit, 1991—; chmn. Eagle Scout bd. rev. Sinnisippi coun. Boy Scouts Am., 1995-96; vice chair spkrs. bur. Beloit Sports Hall of Fame, 1998-99, chmn., 1999. Recipient award for creativity in dentistry Johnson & Johnson Co., 1970; 3 citations for Community Service United Givers Fund, 1970-75; Disting. Service citation Greater Beloit Assn. Commerce. Fellow Acad. Gen. Dentistry, Internat. Coll. Dentists. (Wis. editor), Am. Acad. Dental Practice Adminstrn. (past chmn. profl. liaison; mem. ADA (chmn. council on dental practice 1982-84), Wis. Dental Assn. (pres. 1979-80, trustee 1968-74), Wis. Dental Assn. Found., Rock County Dental Soc. (pres. 1976), Wis. Council of Professions (bd. dirs. 1974-80, pres. 1973-75), Chgo. Dental Soc., Greater Milw. Dental Assn., Fedn. Dentaire Internationale, Pierre Fauchard Acad., Am. Acad. History of Dentistry, Lions (beloit programs, 1993—, past pres.), Delta Sigma Delta. Avocations: cycling, golf, basketball, running, fishing. Home: 2207 Collingswood Dr Beloit WI 53511-2332 Office: 419 Pleasant St Beloit WI 53511-6249

GREEN, HARRY WESTERN, II, geology-geophysics educator, university official; b. Orange, N.J., Mar. 13, 1940; s. Harry Buetel and Mabel (Hendrickson) G.; children from previous marriage: Mark, Stephen, Carolyn, Jennifer; m. Maria Manuela Marques Martins, May 15, 1975; children: Alice, Miguel, Maria. AB in Geology with honors, UCLA, 1963, MS in Geology and Geophysics, 1967, PhD in Geology and Geophysics with distinction, 1968. Postdoctoral research assoc. materials sci. Case Western Res. U., Cleve., 1968-70; asst. prof. geology U. Calif., Davis, 1970-74, assoc. prof., 1974-80, prof., 1980-92, dept. chmn., 1984-88; prof. geology and geophysics U. Calif., Riverside, 1993—, dir. Inst. Geophysics and Planetary Physics, 1993-95, dir. analytical electron microscopy facility, 1994—, vice chancellor for rsch., 1995—; exch. scientist U. Nantes, France, 1973, vis. prof., 1978-79; vis. prof. Monash U., Melbourne, Australia, 1984; specialist advisor World Bank Program, China U. of Geoscis., Wuhan, 1988; adj. sr. rsch. scientist Lamont-Doherty Earth Obs., Columbia U., 1989—, Vetlesen vis. prof., 1991-92; expert advisor geophysics rev. panel NSF, 1991-94; co-founder Gordon Conf. on Rock Deformation, 1995, chmn. 2d conf., 1997; hon. faculty China U. Geoscis., Wuhan, 1998. Contbr. articles to books and profl. jours. Grantee NSF, 1969—, Dept. Energy, 1988-94. Fellow AAAS, Mineral Soc. Am., Am. Geophys. Union (N.L. Bowen award 1994, Francis Birch lectr. 1995); mem. Materials Rsch. Soc., Sigma Xi. Achievements include discovery of a new mechanism of deep earthquakes and exhumation of rocks from great depth in subduction zones. Avocations: travel, hiking. Office: U Calif Inst Geophysics and Planetary Physics Riverside CA 92521 also: U Calif Office Vice Chancellor Rsch Riverside CA 92521

GREEN, HARVEY, history educator; b. Buffalo, Sept. 15, 1946; s. Herman and Bessie Green; m. Susan Reynolds Williams, June 21, 1980. BA, U. Rochester, 1968; MA, Rutgers U., 1970, PhD, 1976. Historian Strong Mus., Rochester, N.Y., 1976-83; v.p. interpretation Strong Mus., Rochester, 1983-89; assoc. prof. history Northeastern U., Boston, 1989-93, prof. history, 1993—; Fulbright bicentennial prof. Am. studies Helsinki, Finland, 1999—. Author: Light of the Home, 1983, Fit for America, 1986, The Uncertainty of Everyday Life 1915-1945, 1992; mem. editorial bd. Northeastern U. Press, 1990-96; contbr. articles to profl. jours. Trustee Landmark Soc. Western N.Y., Rochester, 1985-89; bd. overseers Strawbery Banke Mus., 1991-96; bd. corporators Canterbury Shaker Mus., 1994—. Univ. fellow Rutgers U., 1973; NEH grantee, Washington, 1982, 83, 85; Fulbright award to Turku, Finland, 1995. Fellow Am. Antiquarian Soc., Winterthur Mus.; mem. Orgn. Am. Historians, Am. Studies Assn., Am. Hist. Assn., Am. Assn. State and Local History (coun. mem., cons. various museums 1987—). Avocations: woodworking, golf, gardening, conservation. Office: Northeastern U 249 Meserve Hall Boston MA 02115

GREEN, HENRY LEONARD, physician; b. Detroit, Apr. 9, 1931; s. Albert and Fanya (Newman) G.; m. Loretta Laurie Teplitz; children: Toby, Jennifer, Cheryl, Joseph. BA with distinction, U. Mich., 1951, MD, 1955. Cert. Am. Bd. Internal Medicine in internal medicine and cardiology. Intern Detroit Receiving Hosp., 1955-56; resident internal medicine Henry Ford Hosp., Detroit, 1956-59, resident cardiology, 1959-61; pvt. practice Southfield, Mich., 1963—; dir. cardiac care unit surveillance project, 1969-74; attending physician Sinai Hosp. of Detroit, 1963—, Providence Hosp., Southfield, 1963—; clin. assoc. prof. Wayne State U. Sch. Medicine, Detroit; attending physician William Beaumont Hosp., 1995; dir. pacemaker clinic Providence Hosp.; mem. adv. and exec. coms. Inter-Soc. Commn. for Heart Disease Resources, N.Y.C., 1968-84. Author various med. software programs; contbr. articles to med. jours.; author various oral presentations nat. and local med. meetings. Lt. comdr. USN, 1961-63. Recipient Grand award Mich. Hosp. Assn., Detroit, 1973. Fellow ACP, Am. Coll. Cardiology; mem. AMA, Am. Heart Assn., Mich. Heart Assn. (assoc. coun. on clin. cardiology), Phi Beta Kappa, Alpha Omega Alpha. Avocations: computers, photography, electronics, swimming. Office: 22250 Providence Dr Ste 204 Southfield MI 48075-6210

GREEN, HOLCOMBE TUCKER, JR., investment executive; b. Atlanta, Sept. 29, 1939; s. Holcombe Tucker and Mary Katharine (Woltz) G.; AB, Yale U., 1961; LLB, U. Va., 1967; D of Bus. Adminstrn. (hon.), Piedmont Coll., 1995; m. Nancy Reade Hall, June 18, 1966. Admitted to Ga. 1967; assoc. firm Hansell & Post, Atlanta, 1967-70, mem. firm, 1970-87, mgmt. com. 1980-87; gen. ptnr. Green Capital Investors L.P., Atlanta, 1987—; chmn., CEO WestPoint Stevens, Inc., 1992—; bd. dirs. Ga. Gulf Corp., Vytech Industries, Inc.; bd. dirs., chmn. Rhodes, Inc., 1988-96, chmn. HBO & Co., 1990-98. Trustee Atlanta Bot. Garden, 1976-92, pres. 1982-84, The Taft Sch., 1987—, Woodruff Arts Ctr., 1990-98;, vice chmn. Investments, 1992-98, Atlanta Hist. Soc., 1993-96; bd. dirs. Child Svc. and Family Counseling Center, 1972-85, pres. 1982-84; bd. dirs., mem. exec. com. High Mus. of Art, 1982-96, Atlanta Ballet, 1987-89; mem. devel. bd. Yale U., 1989—, bd. dirs. Yale U. art gallery, 1992—; active Leadership Atlanta, 1974-75; hon. Swedish consul, State of Ga., 1988-96. Served to lt. (j.g.) U.S. Navy, 1961-64. Mem. State Bar Ga., Raven Soc. of U. Va., Order of Coif, Royal Order of Polar Star. Democrat. Presbyterian. Clubs: Piedmont Driving, Capital City, Nine O'Clocks, Wade Hampton, Homosassa Fishing, The Chatooga, The Honors, Doubles, River, Ocean Forest Golf, East Lake Golf. Home: 3655 Tuxedo Rd NW Atlanta GA 30305-1015 Office: Green Capital Investors 3343 Peachtree Rd NE Ste 1420 Atlanta GA 30326-1427

GREEN, HOWARD, cellular physiologist, educator, administrator; b. Toronto, Ont., Can., Sept. 10, 1925. M.D., U. Toronto, 1947; M.S. in Physiology, Northwestern U., 1950. Research asst. dept. physiology Northwestern U., Evanston, Ill., 1948-50; research assoc., instr. biochemistry U. Chgo., 1951-53; instr. pharmacology NYU Sch. Medicine, 1954-55, asst. prof. chem. pathology, 1956-59, assoc. prof. pathology, 1959-65, prof., 1965-68, prof., chmn. cell biology dept., 1968-70; prof. cell biology MIT, Cambridge, 1970-80; Higgins prof. cellular physiology Harvard U. Med. Sch., Boston, 1980-86; George Higginson prof. physiology Harvard U. Med. Sch., 1986—, chmn. dept. physiology and biophysics, 1986-88, chmn. dept. cellular and molecular physiology, 1988-93, Higginson Prof. cell biology, 1993—; lectr. in field. Served to capt. M.C. USAR, 1955-56. Recipient Mr. And Mrs. J. N. Taub Internat. Meml. award, 1977; recipient Selman A. Waksman award, 1978, Lewis S. Rosenstiel award, 1980, Lila Gruber Research award Am. Acad. Dermatology, 1980, Passano award, 1985. Mem. NAS, Am. Acad. Arts and Scis., Am. Soc. Cellular Biology. Home: 82 Williston Rd Brookline MA 02445-2141 Office: Harvard Med Sch Dept Cell Biology 240 Longwood Ave Boston MA 02115-5701

GREEN, JACK ALLEN, lawyer; b. Detroit, Dec. 15, 1945; s. Martin and Frieda Francis (Freeman) G.; m. Pamela Arlene Stern, Aug. 20, 1967; children: Marla Elizabeth, Carrie Lynn. B.B.A., U. Mich., 1967, J.D., 1970. Bar: Ohio 1970, Mass. 1984. Assoc. Schwartz & Schwartz, Columbus, Ohio, 1970-72; gen. counsel Prestolite Co., Toledo, 1972-83; sr. v.p. adminstrn., gen. counsel, sec. Converse, Inc., North Reading, Mass., 1983—; bd. dirs. Arrow Mut. Liability Ins. Co.; adj. prof. Emmanuel Coll., Boston. Bd. dirs. Middlesex County chpt. Am. Lung Assn., Boston Olympic Organizing Com.; policyholder adv. com. to the bd. dirs. of The New England Mut. Life Ins. Co. Mem. ABA, Ohio State Bar Assn., Mass. Bar Assn., Corp. Counsel Assn. Avocations: skiing; tennis; running. Office: Converse Inc 1 Fordham Rd North Reading MA 01864-2619

GREEN, JACK PETER, pharmacology educator, medical scientist; b. N.Y.C., Oct. 4, 1925; s. Maurice and Tillie (Herman) G.; m. Arlyne Genevieve Frank, Oct. 25, 1958. B.S., Pa. State U., 1947, M.S., 1949; Ph.D., Yale, 1951, M.D., 1957; postgrad., Poly. Inst., Copenhagen, 1953-55, Inst. de Biologie Physico-Chimique, Paris, 1964-65. Vis. scientist Poly. Inst., Copenhagen, 1953-55, Inst. de Biologie Physico-Chimique, Paris, 1964-65; asst. prof. Yale, 1957-61, asso. prof., 1961-66; asso. prof. Cornell U. Med. Coll., 1966-68; prof., chmn. dept. pharmacology Mt. Sinai Sch. Medicine, 1968—; Mem. research grant rev. com. USPHS; mem. N.Y.C. Health Research Council, Dysautonomia Found., Irma T. Hirsch Trust. Contbr. articles profl. jours.; Mem. editorial bds. profl. jours. Recipient Claude Bernard Vis. Professorship U. Montreal, 1966. Mem. N.Y. Acad. Sci., Am. Chem. Soc., Am. Soc. Biol. Chemists, Soc. Drug Research, N.Y. Acad. Medicine, Harvey Soc., A.A.A.S., Am. Soc. Pharmacology and Exptl. Therapeutics, Internat. Soc. Quantum Biology, Am. Coll. Neuropsychopharmacology, Am. Soc. Neurochemistry, Soc. for Neurosci., Sigma Xi, Alpha Omega Alpha, Phi Lambda Upsilon, Gamma Sigma Delta. Home: 1212 5th Ave New York NY 10029-5210 Office: Mt Sinai Sch Medicine Dept Pharmacology Fifth Ave at 100th St New York NY 10029

GREEN, JAMES MATTHEW, anesthesiologist; b. Pitts., Dec. 7, 1960; m. Evelyn Angela Payne, July 6, 1985; children: Nicole, Kaitlin, Nathaniel. BS in Biochemistry, U. Pitts., 1983, MD, 1987. Diplomate Am. Bd. Anesthesiology with subspecialty in pain mgmt. Intern in internal medicine Allegheny Gen. Hosp., Pitts., 1987-88; resident in anesthesiology, critical care medicine Univ. Health Ctr. Pitts., 1988-91; asst. prof. anesthesia and critical care U. Pitts., 1991-95; staff anesthesiologist, dir. pain mgmt. VA Med. Ctr., Pitts., 1991-95; dir. pain svcs., coord. med. and dental student anesthesia VA Med. Ctr., Pitts., Pa., 1992-95; staff anesthesiologist Assoc. Anesthesiologists of Johnstown, Pa., 1995—. Contbr. articles to profl. jours. Recipient Dr. Leroy Harris award Dept. Anesthesiology, Pitts., 1995. Mem. Am. Soc. Anesthesiology, Pa. Soc. Anesthesiology, Pa. Med. Soc., Cambria County Med. Soc. Office: Assoc Anesthesiologists of Johnstown 1086 Franklin St Johnstown PA 15905-4305

GREEN, JAMES SAMUEL, lawyer; b. Berwick, Pa., May 24, 1947; m. Carla Eyer; children: Jennifer, Emily, James Samuel Jr., Jared. AB, Princeton U., 1969; JD, Villanova U., 1972. Bar: Del. 1972, Pa. 1973, U.S. Dist. Ct. Del. 1973, U.S. Ct. Appeals (3d cir.) 1981, U.S. Supreme Ct. 1990. Assoc. Connolly, Bove, Lodge & Hutz, Wilmington, Del., 1972-74, ptnr., 1977-90; dep. atty. gen. State of Del., Wilmington, 1975-76; ptnr. Duane Morris & Heckscher, Wilmington, 1990-99, Seitz, Van Ostrop & Green, P.A., Wilmington, 1000—. Mem. Del. Bd. Unauthorized Practice of Law, chmn., 1994-99; bd. dirs. Blue-White, Inc., David Wellborn Found. Mem. ABA, ATLA, Am. Bd. Trial Advocates (nat. bd. dirs. 1991—), Del. State Bar Assn. (treas. 1980-81, chmn. litigation sect. 1988-91), Ivy Club (Princeton), Wilmington Country Club. Home: 2603 W 17th St Wilmington DE 19806-1108 Office: Seits Van Ostrop & Green PA 222 Delaware Ave Ste 1500 Wilmington DE 19801

GREEN, JEFFREY C., lawyer; b. Newark, July 6, 1941; s. Albert and Mildred (Rosenberg) G.; m. Iris Landow, Aug. 23, 1964; children: Michelle, Marlene. BA, Rutgers U., 1963, JD, 1966; postgrad., Nat. Coll. State Judiciary, Reno, 1974-75. Bar: N.J. 1966, U.S. Dist. Ct. N.J. 1966. Law clk. to judge N.J. Superior Ct., Middlesex County Ct., New Brunswick, 1966-67; assoc. Toolan, Romond & Burgess, Perth Amboy, N.J., 1967-68; ptnr. Green & Green and predecessors, Somerset, N.J., 1968—; prosecutor Franklin Twp. Mcpl. Ct., Somerset, 1969-70, mcpl. judge, 1970-76, 97—; judge Millstone (N.J.) Mcpl. Ct., 1970-76, Manville (N.J.) Mcpl. Ct., 1972-73; atty. Cranbury (N.J.) Bd. Adjustment, 1978—. Legal counsel Temple Beth El, Somerset, 1974—; bd. dirs. Middlesex County Legal Svcs. Corp., New Brunswick, 1983—. Named Man of Yr., Temple Beth El, 1984; recipient Pro Bono Achievement award Middlesex County Legal Svcs. Corp., 1985, 87. Mem. N.J. State Bar Assn. (trustee 1997—, Gen. Practitioner of Yr. award 1997), Middlesex County Bar Assn. (pres. 1985-86), Middlesex County Bar Found. (trustee 1990—, pres. 1994-95), Franklin Twp. Jaycees (pres. 1970-71), Lions Club. Democrat. Home: 3 Denise Ct Somerset NJ 08873-2834 Office: Green & Green 838 Easton Ave PO Box 5321 Somerset NJ 08875

GREEN, JEROME GEORGE, federal government official; b. Bklyn., June 20, 1929; s. Samuel N. and Esther (Deiber) G.; m. Marie Charlotte Roder, Aug. 2, 1952; children—Karen Ann, Paul Jonathan. B.S. magna cum laude, Bklyn. Coll., 1950; M.D., Albany Med. Coll., 1954. Intern Albany (N.Y.)

Hosp., 1954-55; mem. staff br. grants and tng. Nat. Heart Inst., NIH, Bethesda, Md., 1955-57; asso. dir. extramural research and tng. Nat. Heart Inst., NIH, 1965-72; resident USPHS Hosp., San Francisco, 1957-59; spl. fellow in cardiopulmonary research Cardiovascular Research Inst., U. Calif., San Francisco, 1959-60; research div. Cleve. Clinic, 1960-65; dir. div. extramural affairs Nat. Heart, Lung and Blood Inst., 1972-85; dir. div. research grants NIH, Bethesda, 1986-95; asst. surgeon gen. USPHS, 1988-95. Fellow Am. Coll. Cardiology, Am. Heart Assn.; mem. Phi Beta Kappa, Alpha Omega Alpha. Home: 8304 Loring Dr Bethesda MD 20817-3150

GREEN, JERRY HOWARD, investment banker; b. Kansas City, Mo., June 10, 1930; s. Howard Jay and Selma (Stein) G.; BA, Yale U., 1952. m. Betsy Bozarth, July 18, 1981. Pres., Union Chevrolet, 1955-69, Union Securities, Inc., Kansas City, 1969—, Union Bancshares, Inc., Kansas City, 1969-76; chmn. Union Bank, Kansas City, 1976—, Budget Rent-A-Car Mo., Inc., 1961—, Budget Rent-A-Car Memphis, Inc., Budget Rent-A-Car Wichita, Kans.; pres. Pembroke Bancshares, Kansas City, 1983—; chmn. Union Broadcasting, Inc., Union Sports Broadcasting, Inc.; bd. dirs. Century City Artists Corp., L.A. Bd. dirs. Jackson County Pension Plan Com.; bd. dirs., chmn. bd. Mo. Higher Education Loan Authority, 1987—; chmn. bd. Mo. Valley Bancshares, Mountain Grove, Mo.; chmn. Yale Class of 1952 Reunion Gift. 1st lt. USAF, 1952-55. Mem. Am. Bankers Assn., Yale Alumni Assn. (bd. dirs.). Republican. Clubs: Kansas City, Oakwood Country, Saddle and Sirloin, University. Home: Greenleigh Farm Stilwell KS 66085 Office: Union Bank 12th And Wyandotte Kansas City MO 64105

GREEN, JILL I., dance educator, researcher; b. Bklyn., June 19, 1954; d. Charles M. and Selma Z. (Stein) Green. BS summa cum laude, Bklyn. Coll., 1976; MA, NYU, 1981; PhD, Ohio State U., 1993. Lic. tchr. dance K-12, N.C., tchr. Kinetic Awareness. Dance instr. NYU, N.Y.C., 1981; dance tchr. Pub. Sch. 46, Bronx, N.Y., 1981-83; dance and movement instr. Lee Strasberg Theatre Inst., N.Y.C., 1983-86; dance tchr. Sheepshead Bay H.S., Bklyn., 1985-89; movement and relaxation specialist Columbus (Ohio) Psychol. Ctr., 1989-92; tchg. assoc. Ohio State U., Columbus, 1989-92, lectr., 1992-93; movement and body awareness educator Columbus Somatics Ctr., 1992-93; asst. prof. dance U. N.C., Greensboro, 1993—, coord. dance edn. program, 1993—; cons. for dance curriculum N.C. State Dept. Instrn., Raleigh, 1995-96; editl. cons. Ind. U. Press, 1995-96. Contbr. chpt. to book, articles to profl. jours. Vol. tchr. Very Spl. Arts Festival, Greensboro, 1994—, N.C. 4-H Coun., Greensboro, 1993—; demonstration classes N.C. Pub. Schs., 1993—; ednl. facilitator for homeless women WINGS Ctr. for SelfDiscovery, Columbus, 1992-93. New Faculty grantee, 1993-95; Dance Connections grantee Cmty. Found. Greater Greensboro, 1997; Ctr. for Study of Social Issues grantee, 1997—, U. N.C. Tchg. Excellence award, Sch. of Health and Human Performance, 1998. Mem. Nat. Dance Assn., N.C. Dance Alliance (bd. dirs. 1996-98), Congress on Rsch. in Dance (bd. dirs. 1998—), The Somatics Soc., Am. Dance Guild, Am. Ednl. Rsch. Assn. Office: U NC at Greensboro Dept Dance 220E HHP Bldg Greensboro NC 27412

GREEN, JOAL FEKETE STAFFORD, library media specialist; b. Geissen, Germany, June 20, 1948; d. Alfred Emery and Joanna Plowden Fekete; m. Carl Andrew Stafford, Aug. 1, 1970 (div. 1980); children: Drew, Sarah; m. Earl Alexander Green, July 31, 1992; children: Earl III, Staci. BA, U. Ctrl. Fla., 1970, MEd, 1974. Reference libr. Fla. Technol. U., Orlando, 1970; English tchr. Orange County Pub. Schs., Orlando, 1970-71, media specialist, 1970-80, 82—. Mem. NEA, Fla. Edn. Assn., Classroom Tchrs. Assn., Fla. Assn. Media Educators, Orange County Assn. Ednl. Media, Phi Delta Kappa. Roman Catholic. Avocations: reading, going to the beach, traveling, antique shopping. Home: 3331 Carla St Orlando FL 32806-7405 Office: Evans HS 4949 Silver Star Rd Orlando FL 32808-4539

GREEN, JOHN ALDEN, university director study abroad program; b. Cardston, Alta., Can., Nov. 4, 1925; came to U.S., 1952, naturalized, 1961; s. John H.F. and Olivia (Thornhill) G.; m. Michele Therese Jugant, Aug. 27, 1954; children: John Scott, Jeffrey Paul (dec.), Evan Curtis, Alan Merrill, Kerry Anne, Cammie Suzanne, Nicole Renée, Brent Eric, Richard Derrin. B.A., Brigham Young U., 1954, M.A., 1955; Ph.D., U. Wash., 1960. Spl. instr. French Boeing Aircraft Co., Renton, Wash., 1958-59; asst. prof. U. N.D., 1960-63; dir. Summer NDEA Inst., 1962; assoc. prof., chmn. dept. U. Wichita, 1963-64; assoc. prof. Brigham Young U., Provo, Utah, 1964-68; prof. Brigham Young U., 1968—, chmn. dept., 1969-71, dir. semester abroad program, 1979. Appeared in (also translator) The Miser (Moliere), 1974, 76, 79, The Would-be Gentleman (Moliere), 1977; author: French Reaction to Shakespeare, 1972, Albert Roustit, 1974, Liberty vs. Authority: The Gallant Assault in France, 1975, Drama in Viet Nam, 1977, At the Top, 1977, Together, 1977, A Remarkable Discovery, 1977, Chroniques de Marcel Schwob, Droz, 1981, Marcel Schwob: Correspondence Inédite, Droz, 1985; author: (play) That's the Spirit, 1969; translator: L'Avare (Moliere), 1973, 76, 79, (play) Le Bourgeois Gentilhomme (Moliere), 19974, 77, Prophecy in Music (Albert Roustit), 1975, Tartuffe (Moliere), 1978, 2d edit., 1989, Knocking at Heaven's Door, 1982, The Imaginary Invalid (Moliere), 1985; dir., actor film, 1982; contbr. to Research on Language Teaching: annotated International Bibliography for 1945-1961 (H.L. Nostrand), 1962; spl. contbr. to libr., 1964-98; Marcel Schwob: L'Affaire Dreyfus, 10 vols. Holocaust (6,000,000 Jews) and Stalin (20,000 Jews, Gypsies) 1988-98; contbr. 60 articles and revs. to profl. jours. Apptd. judge pro tem Third Cir. Ct., Salt Lake dept., Salt Lake City, 1988—. Served with RCAF, 1944-46. Recipient David O. McKay award Brigham Young U., 1986, Disting. Faculty award Coll. Humanities Brigham Young U., 1980, Outstanding Example Brigham Young U., 1990; The Jewish Mus. grantee, N.Y.C.; Sem. of Theol. Studies grantee, N.Y.C., 1988. Home: 623 S 590 E Orem UT 84097-6501*

GREEN, JOHN DAVID, engineering executive; b. Newark, Ohio, July 20, 1948; s. John Robert and Ruth Ella (Lugenbeal) G.; m. Clare Marie McHenry, Dec. 22, 1970; children: Jennifer L., David E. BSEE, Case Inst. of Tech., 1970; MBA, Ohio U., 1983. Registered profl. engr., Ohio; cert. lighting efficiency profl.; lighting cert. Engrin. mgr., sr. rsch. engr. Holophane Corp., Newark, 1970—. Sgt. USAF, 1970-73. Recipient A award Manville Corp., 1979. Mem. Illuminating Engring. Soc. (vice chmn. 1989-91, chmn. 1991-93, author publ. 1980), Nat. Soc. Profl. Engrs. (Top 10 Achievement award 1975), Assn. Energy Engring. Achievements include patents in Method and Assembly for Measuring Equivalent Sphere Illumination, Optical Design for Poster Panel Luminaire, Electrical Design of Power Inverter Systems. Office: Holophane Corp PO Box 3004 Newark OH 43058-3004

GREEN, JOHN LAFAYETTE, JR., education executive; b. Trenton, N.J., Apr. 3, 1929; m. Harriet Hardin Hill, Nov. 8, 1962; 1 child, John Lafayette III. BA, Miss. State U., 1955; MEd, Wayne State U., 1971; PhD, Rensselaer Poly. Inst., 1974. Asst. to treas. Internat. Paper Co., 1955-57; mem. faculty U. Calif., Berkeley, 1957-65; v.p. U. Ga., Athens, 1965-71, Rensselaer Poly. Inst., Troy, N.Y., 1971-76; exec. v.p. U. Miami, 1976-80; sr. v.p. U. Houston, 1980-81; pres. Washburn U., Topeka, Kans., 1981-88; exec. dir. Assn. Collegiate Bus. Schs. and Programs, Overland Park, 1988-95; pres., chmn. bd. dirs. Strategic Planning/Mgmt. Assocs., Inc., Overland Park, Kans., 1981—; chmn. bd., CEO, Internat. Assembly for Collegiate Bus. Edn., Overland Park, 1997—; past pres. Kansas City and Topeka chpts. Planning Forum. Author: Budgeting, 1967, (with others) Cost Accounting, 1969, Administrative Data Processing, 1970, Strategic Planning, 1980, Strategic Planning: A System for Businesses, 1986, A Strategic Planning System for Higher Education, 1987, Strategy Development and Implementation for Banks, 1988, co-author: Outcomes Assessment in Higher Education Linked to Strategic Planning and Budgeting, 1997. Bd. dirs. Boy Scouts Am., Topeka, 1983-85. With U.S. Army 1951-53. Recipient Disting. Kansan of Yr. in Pub. Administrn. award Topeka Capital Jour., 1984, Kans. Pub. Adminstr. of Yr. award Am. Soc. Pub. Administrn., 1984, Disting. Exec. award Mktg. Exec. Kans., 1984, Edn. Leader's Hall of Fame award, 1995. Mem. AAUP, Conf. Bd., Am. Mgmt. Assn., Fin. Execs. Inst., Demographics Inst., Masons, Shriners, Royal Order of Jesters, Phi Delta Kappa, Beta Alpha Psi, Phi Kappa Phi, Pi Kappa Alpha, Delta Sigma Pi. Republican. Presbyterian. (elder, deacon). Avocations: golf, tennis. Home: 12018 Connell Dr Overland Park KS 66213-2526 Office: PO Box 27033 Shawnee Mission KS 66225-7033

GREEN, JONATHAN WILLIAM, museum administrator and educator, artist, author; b. Troy, N.Y., Sept. 26, 1939; s. Alan Singer and Frances (Katz) G.; m. Louise Lockshin, Sept. 16, 1962 (div. 1985); children: Raphael, Benjamin; m. Wendy Hughes Brown, Aug. 12, 1988. Student, MIT, 1958-60, Hebrew U., 1960-61; BA, Brandeis U., 1963, postgrad., 1964-67; MA, Harvard U., 1967. Photographer Jonathan Green, Photography, Boston, 1966-76, Ezra Stoller Assocs., Mamaroneck, N.Y., 1967-68; prof. MIT, Cambridge, Mass., 1968-76; dir. Creative Photography Lab MIT, Cambridge, 1974-76; editor Aperture Books and Periodical, N.Y.C., 1972-76; prof. Ohio State U., Columbus, 1976-90; dir. Univ. Gallery Fine Arts, Columbus, 1981-90; founding dir. Wexner Ctr. for the Arts, Columbus, 1981-90; dir. Calif. Mus. Photography, U. Calif., Riverside, 1990—, prof., 1990—; cons. Nat. Endowment for Arts, Washington, 1975-76, 85, 88, 94, Harry N. Abrams, Pubs., N.Y.C., 1982-84, Oxford U. Press, N.Y.C., 1977-82, Polaroid Corp., Cambridge, 1976; co-founder Visible Lang. Workshop, MIT Media Lab., 1973. Author: American Photography, 1984 (Nikon Book of Yr. award 1984, Benjamin Citation 1986), The Snapshot, 1974 (N.Y. Type Dirs. Club award 1974), Camera Work: A Critical Anthology, 1973 (Best Art Book award 1973), Continuous Replay: The Photographs of Arnie Zane, 1999; editor, essayist Re-framing History in Jean Ruiter Photo Works, 1985-1995, 1996, The Garden of Earthly Delights: Photographs by Edward Weston and Robert Mapplethorpe, 1995, New Photographs by Pedro Meyer: Truths & Fictions, An Interactive CD-ROM, 1993, 5 Celebrations of Leslie J. Payne in Leslie Payne: Visions of Flight, 1991, Algorithms for Discovery, 1989, Pink Noise: Three Conversations concerning a Collaborative acoustic Installation with Philip Glass, Richard Serra, Kurt Munacsi, 1987, Rudolf Baranik Elegies: Sleep Napalm Night Sky, 1987, Straight Shooting in America, 1985, James Friedman: Rephotographing the History of the World in James Friedman, Color Photographs 1979-1982, 1982, Aperture in the 50's: The Word and the Way, in Afterimage, 1979, others; represented in permanent collections Mus. Fine Arts, Boston, Mus. Fine Art, Houston, Cleve. Mus. Art, Va. Mus. Fine Art, Richmond, Princeton U. Art Mus., Bell System Collection, Moderna Museet, Stockholm, Ctr. for Creative Photography, Tucson, De Saisset Art Gallery and Mus., Internat. Ctr. Photography, N.Y.C., MIT, Mpls. Inst. Arts; photographs pub.: American Images: New Work by Twenty Contemporary Photographers, 1979, Aperture, 1972, 73, 74, 25 Years of Record Houses, 1981, Architectural Record, Architecture and Urbanism, Progressive Architecture, A Field Guide to Modern American Architecture. Danforth fellow, 1963-67, NEA Photographer fellow, 1978, AT & T fellow, 1979. Office: UCR/California Museum Of Photography Downtown Hist Pedestrian Mall 3824 Main St Riverside CA 92501-3624

GREEN, JOSEPH BARNET, neurologist, educator; b. Phila., Aug. 2, 1928; s. Charles and Bella (Hurwitz) B.; married; children—Charna Alice Green Evans, Robert I. B.S., St. Joseph's Coll., Phila., 1950; M.D., Jefferson Med. Coll., Phila., 1954. Intern Wilkes-Barre (Pa.) Gen. Hosp., 1954-55; resident in neurology Georgetown U. Med. Center, 1955-58; asst. neurologist Pa. Hosp., Phila., 1960-64; asst. prof., then prof. neurology Ind. U. Med. Sch., 1964-72; prof. neurology and pediatrics, chmn. dept. neurology Med. Coll. Ga., Augusta, 1972-82; prof., chmn. dept. psychiatry and neurology Tulane U. Sch. Medicine, New Orleans, 1982-87, prof. neurology, clin. prof. pediatrics, 1986-87; dir. neurology VA Cen. Office, Washington, 1987-88; chmn. dept. med. and surg. neurology Tex. Tech U. Health Scis. Ctr., Lubbock, 1988-94; prof. neurology Tex. Tech U Health Scis. Ctr., Lubbock, 1993-94; dir. rehab. rsch. Hines (Ill.) VA Med. Ctr., 1994-98; prof. neurology Loyola U. Stritch Sch. Medicine, Maywood, Ill., 1994-98; attending staff physician, rsch. investigator Spinal Cord Injury Unit, Memphis VA Med. Ctr., 1998—; chmn. profl. adv. bd. Epilepsy Assn.; mem. profl. adv. bd. Assn. Children with Learning Disabilities, Ga. chpt. Nat. Multiple Sclerosis Soc.; dir. NIH project Ga. Comprehensive Epilepsy Program, 1976; Fulbright lectr., Denmark, 1969; cons. VA Med. Ctr., Augusta. Author articles in field. Served with M.C. USNR, 1958-60. Fogarty Internat. Research fellow Israel, 1981. Mem. AMA, Am. Acad. Neurology, Child Neurology Soc., Am. Neurol. Assn., Am. EEG Soc., Am. Epilepsy Soc. (sec. 1972), Assn. U. Profs. Neurology (v.p. 1981). Democrat. Jewish. Club: B'nai B'rith. Office: Memphis VA Med Center 1030 Jefferson Ave Memphis TN 38104

GREEN, JOSHUA, III, banker; b. Seattle, June 30, 1936; s. Joshua, Jr. and Elaine (Brygger) G.; m. Pamela K. Pemberton, Nov. 1, 1974; children: Joshua IV, Jennifer Elaine, Paige Courtney. B.A. in English, Harvard U., 1958. With Peoples Nat. Bank Wash., Seattle, 1960-88; exec. v.p. Peoples Nat. Bank Wash., 1972-75, pres., 1975—, chief exec. officer, 1977-78, chmn. bd., 1979-88; chmn. bd. U.S. Bank Washington (merger PeoplesBank and Old Nat. Bank), 1988-96; chmn., CEO Joshua Green Corp., Seattle, 1996—; bd. dirs., chmn., CEO, Joshua Green Corp., U.S. Bancorp, Safeco, Port Blakely Tree Farms. Pres. Joshua Green Found.; trustee Seattle Found., Downtown Seattle Assn., Corp.Coun. for the Arts. Mem. Seattle C. of C., (dir., v.p. 1980—), U. Club, Rainier Club, Seattle Tennis Club, Wash. Athletic Club. Home: 1932 Blenheim Dr E Seattle WA 98112-2308 Office: Joshua Green Corp 1425 4th Ave Ste 420 Seattle WA 98101-2218*

GREEN, JOYCE, book publishing company executive; b. Taylorville, Ill., Oct. 22, 1928; d. Lynn and Vivian Coke (Richardson) Reinerd; m. Warren H. Green, Oct. 8, 1960. AA, Christian Coll., 1946; BS, MacMurray Coll., 1948. Pres. Warren H. Green, Inc., St. Louis, 1992—; editor Affirmative Action Register, 1977—; pres. InterContinental Industries, Inc., 1980—; chief exec. officer Pubs. Svc. Ctr. Mem. St. Louis C. of C., Jr. League Club, Media Club, Mo. Athletic Club, Media Club. Democrat. Methodist. Home: 12120 Hibler Rd Saint Louis MO 63141-6615 Office: 8356 Olive Blvd Saint Louis MO 63132-2814

GREEN, JOYCE HENS, federal judge; b. N.Y.C., Nov. 13, 1928; d. James S. and Hedy (Bucher) Hens; m. Samuel Green, Sept. 25, 1965 (dec.); children: Michael Timothy, June Heather, James Harry. BA, U. Md., 1949; JD, George Washington U., 1951, LLD, 1994. Practice law Washington, 1951-68, Arlington, Va., 1956-68; ptnr. Green & Green, 1966-68; assoc. judge Superior Ct., D.C., 1968-79; judge U.S. Dist. Ct. for D.C., 1979—; judge presiding U.S. Fgn. Intelligence Surveillance Ct., 1988-95; bd. advisors George Washington U. Law Sch. Co-author: Dissolution of Marriage, 1986, supplements, 1987-89; contbr. supplements Marriage and Family Law Agreements, 1985-89. Chair Task Force on Gender, Race and Ethnic Bias for the D.C. Cir. Recipient Alumni Achievement award George Washington U., 1975, Profl. Achievement award, 1978, Outstanding Contbn. to Equal Rights award Women's Legal Def. Fund, 1976, hon. doctor of Laws George Washington U., 1994, U.S. Dept. Justice Edmund J. Randolph award Jud. Conf. of U.S., 1995. Fellow Am. Bar Found.; ABA (jud. adminstrn. divsn., chair nat. conf. fed. trial judges), Fed. Judges Assn., Nat. Assn. Women Judges, Va. Bar Assn., Bar Assn. D.C. (jud. honoree of Yr. 1994), D.C. Bar, D.C. Women's Bar Assn., (pres. 1960-62, women lawyer of yr. 1979), Exec. Women in Govt. (chmn. 1977), Lawyers Club of Washington, Woman's Forum of Washington D.C. Office: US Dist Barrett Prettyman US Courthouse 333 Constitution Ave NW Washington DC 20001-2802

GREEN, JUDSON C., marketing agency executive. Pres. Attractions Divsn. Walt Disney Co., Burbank, Calif. Office: Walt Disney Attractions Team Disney 531 500 S Buena Vista St Burbank CA 91521-0004

GREEN, JUNE LAZENBY, federal judge; b. Arnold, Md., Jan. 23, 1914; d. Eugene H. and Jessie T. (Briggs) Lazenby; m. John Cawley Green, Sept. 5, 1936. JD, Am. U., 1941. Bar: Md. 1943, D.C. 1945. Claims adjuster Lumbermans Mut. Casualty Co., Washington, 1942-43, claims atty., 1943-47; pvt. practice Washington Bldg., Washington, 1947-68; pvt. practice Annapolis (Md.) & Washington Bldg., 1950-68; judge U.S. Dist. Ct. D.C., 1968-84, sr. judge, 1984—; mem. spl. ct. Regional Reorganization Railroad Act, 1987-97; examiner bar, Washington, 1963-68. Named Woman Lawyer of Yr., 1965; recipient Lifetime Achievement award Alumni Assn. of Am. U., 1986. Mem. ABA, Md. Bar Assn., Bar Assn. D.C. (bd. dirs. 1966-68, award 1984), Women's Bar Assn. D.C. (pres. 1955-57), Federal Judges Assn., Am. Jud. Soc. Home: 464 W Joyce Ln Arnold MD 21012-2207 also: 550 N St SW Washington DC 20024-4643 Office: US Dist Ct US Courthouse 333 Constitution Ave NW Washington DC 20001-2802

GREEN, KAREN DANIELLE, psychotherapist; b. Springfield, Ohio, May 3, 1953; d. Daniel and Loretta Louise (Parsons) G.; children: Hadley Louise, Anapoorva Gandhi. BA, Hiram (Ohio) Coll., 1975; MA, W. Ga. Coll., 1981; MDir, Starr King Sch. Ministry, 1987; postgrad. in Analytical Psychology, Union Inst., 1998—. Cert. individual, marriage and family therapist, clinical hypnotherapist; diplomate logotherapy; ordained Unitarian Universalist minister, 1989. Child care worker Clark County Children's Home, Springfield, 1975-76; juvenile probation and parole counselor Health and Rehab. Svcs., Sarasota, Fla., 1977-78; exec. dir. Safe Place and Rape Crisis Ctr., Sarasota, Fla., 1978-79; psychotherapist New Coll., Sarasota, Fla., 1980-81, Stanford Rsch. Inst., Menlo Park, Calif., 1985-86; pvt. practice Berkeley, Calif., 1985-93, Sarasota, Fla., 1980-83, 94—, Berkeley, Calif., 1980-83, 94—, St. John, V.I., 1994, London, 1995—; cons. Safe Place and Rape Crisis Ctr., Sarasota, 1980-81, St. Vincent de Paul, San Francisco, 1991; bd. dirs. Sarasota Help and Referral Svc., 1981-83, Mental Health Assn., Sarasota, 1981-83. Playwright: Conversations With Mama, 1984. Vol. therapist Children of War, San Francisco, 1985; bd. dirs. NOW, Sarasota, 1981-89, pres., NOW, Berkeley, 1989-91; ministerial vol. Pastors for Peace, Mpls., 1990. Mem. Unitarian Universalist Ministerial Assn. (bd. dirs. Pacific Ctrl. Dist., Berkeley, 1991-92), Am. Assn. Marriage and Family Therapy. Avocations: travel, swimming, yoga, writing.

GREEN, KENNETH NORTON, law educator; b. Chgo., Mar. 18, 1938; s. Martin and Sarah (Owens) G.; m. Joan Nemer, Oct. 17, 1968 (div. July 1974); 1 child, Joey. AA, Wright Jr. Coll., 1960; BA, Calif. State U., Los Angeles, 1963; postgrad. Southwestern U., 1965-67; JD, U. San Fernando Valley, 1968; Cert. (hon. teaching) Los Angeles Unified Sch. Dist., 1979. Bar: Calif. 1970, U.S. Dist. Ct. (cen. dist.) Calif. 1970, U.S. Supreme Ct. 1973. Tchr. Los Angeles, Calif., 1964-70; dep. pub. defender Los Angeles County, Calif., 1970-73, 75—; ptnr. Green & Pirosh, Los Angeles, 1973-75; chief pub. defender, 1989; instr. Paralegal dept. U. Calif., Los Angeles, 1975—; judge pro tem Los Angeles Mcpl. Ct., 1978. Contbr. articles to legal publs. Ex officio mem. Prison Preventers, Calif. Dept. of Parole; mayor's com. Project Heavy; bd. dirs. City of Hope; Vista Del Mar; legal adv. panel Jewish Family Service; vol. atty. for indigents UCLA Law Sch.; vol. in Parole Program, com. chmn. Research Prejudice-Pvt. Clubs (Disting. Service award 1971). Served with U.S. Army, 1957-58, Korea. Mem. Pub. Defender Assn. (dir. 1971-74, chief wage negotiator 1973-75) ABA, Los Angeles County Bar Assn. (vice chmn. drug abuse 1975, exec. com. criminal justice 1977). Democrat. Jewish. Lodge: Justice (bd. dirs. 1971-72). Office: Pub Defender Los Angeles County 210 W Temple St Los Angeles CA 90012-3210

GREEN, KEVIN PATRICK, career officer; m. Kate; 3 children. Grad., U.S. Naval Acad., 1971; MS, Naval Postgrad. Sch., 1977; Grad., Nat. War Coll., 1992. Ensign USN, 1971; advanced through grades to rear admiral, 1997—, assigned to frigate USS Voge (DE 1047), weapons officer USS Richard L. Page (FFG 5), ops. officer USS Preble (DDG 46), exec. officer USS Dahlgren (DDG 43), comdr. USS Taylor (FFG 50), comdr. destroyer squadron twenty-three, duty in spl. ops. br. Atlantic fleet hqrs.; instr. combat sys., tactics prospective comdg. officer course; mil. asst. office of Sec. of Def., dir. surface officer disbn. divsn. bur. naval personnel; comdr. Naval Tng. Ctr. Great Lakes, Ill., 1996—. Decorated Legion of Merit. Office: Cruiser & Destroyer Group 3 Unit 25065 San Diego CA*

GREEN, LARRY ALTON, physician, educator; b. Ardmore, Okla., Mar. 27, 1948; s. Thomas Alton and Mary Lou (Gauntt) G.; m. Margaret Joyce Ball, Mar. 27, 1971; children: Nathaniel, Katherine. BA, U. Okla., 1969; MD, Baylor Coll. Medicine, Houston, 1973. Diplomate Am. Bd. Family Practice. Intern then resident U. Rochester, Highland Hosp., N.Y., 1973-76; asst. prof. U. Colo., Denver, 1977-82, assoc. prof., 1982-85, prof., 1985—, chmn. dept., 1985-99, Woodward-Chisholm chair, 1989-99, dir. AAFP Ctr. for Policy Studies in Family Practice and Primary Care, 1998—; vis. prof. various univs., U.S., New Zealand, U.K., Republic of South Africa, 1982—; dir. residency Mercy Med. Ctr., Denver, 1980-85; found. pres. Ambulatory Sentinel Practice Network, Denver. Contbr. articles to profl. jours. Elder Presbyn. Ch., Denver, With USPHS, 1976-77. Grantee USPHS, 1978—, Kellogg Found., 1982-87. Mem. Assn. Depts. Family Medicine (pres. 1987-89), N.Am. Primary Care Rsch. Group (bd. dirs. 1989-93, pres. 1997—), Am. Acad. Family Physicians, Soc. Tchrs. Family Medicine, Inst. Medicine. Avocation: fly fishing. Office: U Colo Health Scis Ctr Dept of Family Medicine 1180 Clermont St Denver CO 80220-6216

GREEN, LAWRENCE, neurologist, educator; b. Atlantic City, N.J., Oct. 23, 1938; s. Martin and Lillian (Spector) G.; m. Ann Buchberg, Aug. 21, 1970; 1 child, Louis Aaron; stepson, Jonathan Rapkin. BS in Chemistry cum laude, Dickinson Coll., 1960; MD, Jefferson Med. Coll., 1964. Diplomate Am. Bd. Psychiatry and Neurology, Am. Bd. Clin. Neurophysiology; cert. in neurology with added qualifications in clin. neurophysiology. Intern Lankenau Hosp., Phila., 1964-65; resident in neurology Jefferson Med. Coll. Hosp., Phila., 1965-68; fellow in clin. neurophysiology Boston Va. Hosp., 1970-71; attending neurologist Phila. Gen. Hosp., 1971-72; chief, div. neurology and clin. neurophysiology Crozer-Chester (Pa.) Med. Ctr., 1971—, med. dir., Sch. of EEG Tech., 1974—; chief EEG Lab. Hahnemann U. Hosp., Phila., 1972-78, 87-91, electroencephalographer, 1978-87; asst. prof. neurology to clin. prof. neurology MCP/Hahnemann U., Phila., 1971—; instr. in neurology Boston U. Sch. Medicine, 1970-71; adj. prof. bioengring. Widener Coll., Chester, Pa., 1975-77; cons. in neurology and EEG Taylor Hosp., Ridley Pk., Pa., 1971—, St. Agnes Med. Ctr., Phila., 1971—, Hahnemann U. Hosp., 1972—; assoc. examiner Am. Bd. Clin. Neurophysiology, Am. Bd. Registered EEG Tech. Contbr. articles to Neurology, Experientia, Electroencephalography and Clin. Neurophysiology, Low Back Pain, Annals of Neurology. Lt. comdr. USNR, 1968-70. Fellow Am. EEG Soc. (coun., lab. accreditation bd., rep. 1988-92, cons. to com. on allied helath accreditation 1988-94, commr. to com. for accreditation allied health edn. programs 1994—, program com. 1991); mem. AMA, ACP, Am. Acad. Neurology (clin. practice expert panel 10, misc. internal medicine 1995—, rep.), Am. Epilepsy Soc., Am. Assn. EMG & ED, Pa. Med. Soc., Alpers Soc. for Clin. Neurology (past pres., sec., treas.), Alpha Omega Alpha. Office: Clin Neurophysiology Lab Crozer Chester Med Ctr Med Ctr Blvd Upland PA 19013

GREEN, LEON, JR., mechanical engineer; b. Austin, Tex., Aug. 13, 1922; s. Leon and Notra (Anderson) G.; m. Eleanor Broome Samuels, Apr. 14, 1951; children: John Anderson, Emily Broome, Charles Leon. B.S. in Physics, Calif. Inst. Tech., 1944, M.S. in Mech. Engring, 1947, Ph.D., 1950. With N.Am. Aviation, Inc., 1949-51, Aerojet-Gen. Corp., 1951-59, Aeronutronic div. Ford Motor Co., 1959-62; chief scientist Lockheed Propulsion Co., 1962-64; sci. dir. research and tech. div. Air Force Systems Command, Washington; 1964-67; dir. planning Washington area Lockheed Aircraft Corp., 1967-70; exec. sec. Def. Sci. Bd., Dept. Def., 1970-73; sr. staff engr. applied physics lab. Johns Hopkins U.; also cons. AEC, 1973-74; mem. tech. staff Mitre Corp., McLean, Va., 1974-77; cons. Gen. Atomic Co., 1977-80; pres. Energy Conversion Alternatives, Ltd., Washington, 1980-88, cons., 1988-93; v.p. Clean Coal Coalition, Inc., 1983-86; adj. prof. mech. and aerospace engring. W.Va. U., 1989-93. Contbr. articles to profl. jours. Mem. ASME, AAAS, Climate Inst. Home: 24055 Paseo Del Lago Laguna Hills CA 92653-2678

GREEN, LISA CANNON, business editor; b. Marshall, Ky., May 7, 1962; d. Walter L. and Phyllis (Jones) Cannon; m. Bob Dale Green, May 31, 1980; children: Emily, Ethan. BA in Journalism and English, Murray State U., 1983. With The Post-Intelligencer, Paris, Tenn., 1983-84, The Jackson (Tenn.) Sun, 1984-90, The Tennessean, Nashville, 1990—. Office: The Tennessean 1100 Broadway Nashville TN 37203-3134

GREEN, LISA R., journalist; b. Evanston, Ill., Nov. 2, 1964; d. Albert W. and Elease (Wesbrooks) G. BJ, Eastern Ill. U., Charleston, 1986. Rochelle bur. chief Register Star, 1986-88, regional reporter, 1988-90, asst. metro editor, 1990-91, city editor, 1991-93; loaner USA Today, Arlington, Va., 1995; asst. bus. editor Rockford (Ill.) Register Star, 1993—. Editor New Zion Gazette. Chair Black Achievers Steering Com., 1997-98; active New Zion Missionary Bapt. Ch. Mem. Nat. Assn. Black Journalists. Baptist. Avocation: reading. Home: 4504 Trevor Cir Rockford IL 61109-5505 Office: Rockford Register Star 99 E State St Rockford IL 61104-1004

GREEN, LORA MURRAY, immunologist, researcher, educator; b. Redfield, S.D., Feb. 8, 1955; d. Everett k. and Marlene Y. (Palm) Murray; m. Timothy W. Green, Jan. 24, 1976; 1 child, Keigm W. BS in Biochemistry, U. Calif., Riverside, 1981, MS in Biochemsitry, 1982, PhD in Immunology, 1987. Fellow in immunology U. Calif., Riverside; fellow in cell biology Loma Linda (Calif.) U.; rsch. immunologist JL Pettis VA Med. Ctr., Loma Linda, 1991—; assoc. prof. medicine Loma Linda Med. Ctr., 1996—; bd. dirs. Dept. Micro and Molecular Genetics, Loma Linda. Contbr. articles to profl. jours. Grantee VA, 1991-94, Loma Linda, 1995-96. Fellow Am. Assn. Immunology, Assn. Cell Biologists. Achievements include research in the role of the target tissue in autoimmune disease. Office: JL Pettis Vets Hosp 11201 Benton St Loma Linda CA 92357-1000

GREEN, MAE MAERA, artist; b. N.Y.C., Sept. 14, 1930; d. Phillip and Clara (Donnenfeld) Rabach; m. Sam Green, Feb. 1, 1953; children: Michelle, Tracy, Dori, Marshall. Student, Art Student League, 1947, Pratt Inst., 1951. Exhibited at Perspective Gallery, N.Y.C., 1949, State Mus. Art Gallery, Santa Fe, N.Mex., 1958, 59, 60, 72 (award), U. N.Mex. Jonson Gallery, 1972 (award), Malvina Miller Gallery, San Francisco, 1972, Meridian Gallery, Albuquerque, 1979; represented in permanent collections at Mus. of Albuquerque, City Albuquerque 1% for the Arts, Aetna Life Ins. Co., Mass., Temple Albert, Albuquerque. Recipient award Nat. Design Wallpaper/Fabric, 1950. Avocations: reading, travel, walking, gardening. Home: 1521 Sagebrush Trl SE Albuquerque NM 87123-4489

GREEN, MARGARET MILDRED, English language educator; b. Kansas City, Mo., Apr. 18, 1951; d. Edwin Franklin and Mildred Harriet (Maize) Weast; m. Michael Kent Green, Aug. 4, 1973; 1 child, Megan. BSE, U. Kans., 1973; MSE, SUNY, Oneonta, 1986. Permanent cert. tchr. English 7-12, N.Y. Tchr. English Holmes Jr. H.S., Wheeling, Ill., 1977-79, Zion (Ill.) Benton Twp. H.S., 1979-81; tchr. h.s. English Schenevus (N.Y.) Cen. Sch., 1981—; editl. asst. Acta Cytologica, U. Chgo., 1973-77, dir. drama club Schenevus Cen. H.S., 1983-98. Recipient Artie award for best TV documentary RSEC-TV, 1990. Mem. NYSUT, Nat. Coun. Tchrs. English, Catskill Area Tchrs. English, Schenevus United Tchrs. (sec. 1998, co-pres. 1999). Office: Schenevus Cen Sch 100 Main St Schenevus NY 12155-2010

GREEN, MARJORIE, automotive distribution, import and manufacturing company executive; b. N.Y.C., Sept. 27, 1943; d. Benjamin Maxon and Harriet (Weslock) Gruzen; m. Thomas Henry Green, May 31, 1964. Student Antioch Coll., 1961-63, CCNY, 1964-65. Adminstrv. asst. ednl. research U. Calif.-Berkeley, 1965-76; v.p., co-owner Automotion, Santa Clara, Calif., 1973—. Adv. bd. Import Car mag. Mem. Am. Fedn. State, County and Mcpl. Employees (pres. U. Calif. chpt. 1967), Porsche Club Am (v.p. Golden Gate region 1974, treas. region 1975). Home: 10666 W Loyola Dr Los Altos CA 94024-6513 Office: Automotion 193 Commercial St Sunnyvale CA 94086-5202

GREEN, MARK ANDREW, congressman, lawyer; b. Boston, June 1, 1960; s. Jeremy Raleigh and Elizabeth Pamela (Roome) G.; m. Susan Keske, Aug. 5, 1985; children: Rachel Eve Libinu, Anna Faith Kitali, Alexander Mark Amutavi. BA, U. Wis., Eau Claire, 1983; JD, U. Wis., Madison, 1987. Bar: Wis. 1987. Tchr., intern World Teach Project, Kakamega, Kenya, 1987-88; of counsel Godfrey & Kahn, S.C., Green Bay, Wis., 1989-98; mem. Wis. Assembly, Madison, 1992-98; chmn. assembly majority caucus, chmn. assembly jud. com., 1994-1998; state chmn. Am. Legis. Exch. Coun.; mem. 106th Congress from 8th Wis. dist., 1999—; mem. ho. budget com., 1999—, mem. ho. banking and fin. svcs. com., mem. ho. sci. com., 1999—, mem. Rep. policy com., 1999—, asst. majority whip, 1999—; legal counsel Rep. Assembly Campaign Com., Madison, 1993—. Chmn. mcpl. affairs Brown County Taxpayers Assn., Green Bay, 1990-92; chmn. Brown County Rep. Party, 1991-92; bd. dirs. Nat. R.R. Mus., Green Bay, 1992—; chmn. resolutions com. Wis. Rep. Conv., Milw., 1993. Recipient Wis. award Ind. Bus. Assn., 1996; named Wis. Outstanding Legislator of 1995, Wis. Builders Assn., Healthcare Leader of Wis., State Med. Soc., 1996; scholar U. Wis., Eau Claire, 1982. Mem. ABA, Wis. Bar Assn., Am. Legis. Exch. Coun., Nat. Conf. State Legislators, Brown County Home Builders Assn., Kiwanis. Office: Ho of Reps 1218 Longworth HOB Washington DC 20515*

GREEN, MARK JOSEPH, lawyer, author; b. Bklyn., Mar. 15, 1945; s. Irving Arthur and Anna Constance (Suna) G.; m. Denisse Michele Frand, Aug. 13, 1977; children—Jenya Frand Green, Jonah Frand Green. B.A. magna cum laude, Cornell U., 1967; J.D. cum laude, Harvard U., 1970. Bar: D.C. 1971, N.Y. 1988. Dir. Corp. Accountability Research Group, Washington, 1970-76, Public Citizen's Congress Watch, Washington, 1977-80; founding pres. Democracy Project, N.Y.C., 1981-90, now hon. chmn.; commr. consumer affairs City of N.Y., 1990-93; pub. advocate for N.Y.C., 1994—. Author: (with others) The Closed Enterprise System, 1972, The Other Government: The Unseen Power of Washington Lawyers, 1975, (with R. Nader and J. Seligman) Taming the Giant Corporation, 1976, Who Runs Congress?, 1972, 4th edit., 1984, (with Gail MacColl) Reagan's Reign of Error, 1983, (with J. Berry) The Challenge of Hidden Profits, 1985, America's Transition: Blueprints for the 1990s, 1989, The Consumer Bible, 1995, 2d edit., 1999. Dem. nominee for U.S. Senate, N.Y., 1986. Democrat. Jewish.

GREEN, MARTIN LINCOLN, author, educator, publisher, consultant; b. Des Plaines, Ill., Feb. 22, 1940; s. Martin Lincoln and Madelyne Mae (Larson) G.; m. Carolyn Elizabeth Johnson, Jan. 19, 1968; children: Peter Cranston, Edward Reavy. BA in Econs., Lawrence U., 1963; MBA, U. Chgo., 1977. News asst. N.Y. Times, N.Y.C., 1963-64; reporter Sheffield (England) Telegraph, 1964-66, Ball. Sun, 1966-67; sales rep. 3M Co., Chgo., 1967-70; stockbroker Bache & Co., Chgo., 1970-71; sales mgr. Xerox Corp., Chgo., 1971-77; mgr. strategic planning Xerox Corp., Rochester, N.Y., 1977-81; dir. sales, mktg. Bausch & Lomb, Inc., Rochester, N.Y., 1981-84, v.p. sales, mktg., 1984-87; v.p. strategic planning Cambridge Instruments, Buffalo, 1987-88, pres. ophthalmic inst. divsn., 1988-90; pres. ophthalmic inst. divsn. Leica, Inc., Buffalo, 1990-97; pres. The Thornell Inst., Pittsford, N.Y., 1998—; cons. in field. Republican. Avocations: investing, walking, reading, weight lifting, writing. Fax: (716) 218-0984. Home: 16 Forest Knl Pittsford NY 14534-3602 Office: Thornell Inst 16 Forest Knl Ste 204 Pittsford NY 14534-3602

GREEN, MAURICE, molecular biologist, virologist, educator; b. N.Y.C., May 5, 1926; s. David and Bessie (Lipschitz) G.; m. Marilyn Glick, Aug. 20, 1950; children—Michael Richard, Wendy Allison Green Lee, Eric Douglas. B.S. in Chemistry, U. Mich., 1949; M.S. in Biochemistry and Chemistry, U. Wis.-Madison, 1952, Ph.D. in Biochemistry and Chemistry, 1954. Instr. biochemistry U. Pa. Med. Sch., Phila., 1955-56; asst. prof. St. Louis U. Health Scis. Ctr., 1956-60, assoc. prof., 1960-63, prof. microbiology, 1963-77; prof., chmn. Inst. for Molecular Virology, 1964—. Office: St Louis U Health Sci Ctr Inst for Molecular Virology 3681 Park Ave Saint Louis MO 63110-2511

GREEN, MELVIN MARTIN, geneticist; b. Mpls., Aug. 24, 1916; m. 1946. BA, U. Minn., 1938, MA, 1940, PhD in Zoology, 1942; D. U. Umea, Sweden, 1972. Asst. prof. zool. U. Mo., 1946-50, from asst. prof. to prof., 1950-82, geneticist, 1969-82; emeritus prof. genetics U. Calif., Davis, 1982—. Mem. Nat. Acad. Sci., Genetics Soc. Am. (pres. 1973), Am. Soc. Naturalists. Office: U. Calif. Davis CA 95616*

GREEN, MICHAEL SCOTT, history educator, columnist; b. Santa Monica, Calif., Mar. 27, 1965; s. Robert W. and Marsha (Greene) H. BA with honors, U. Nev., Las Vegas, 1986, MA, 1988; MPhil, Columbia U., 1990. Tchg. asst. U. Nev., Las Vegas, 1986-88, adj. instr., 1988-91; adj. instr. C.C. So. Nev., N. Las Vegas, Nev., 1987-95; tchg. asst. Columbia U., 1989-90; instr. C.C. So. Nev., N. Las Vegas, Nev., 1995-99, prof., 1999—; columnist Nev.'s Washington Watch, Washington, 1996—, Sr. Press, 1998—. Editor: (with Gary E. Elliott) Nevada: Readings and Perspectives, 1997; contbr. articles to various publs. including City Life, 1997—, Las Vegas Life, 1998—; contbr. chpts. to books. Spkr. Leadership Las Vegas, 1994—; spkr., exhibit author Clark County Heritage Mus., Henderson, Nev., 1990—. Rsch. fellow The Huntington Libr., 1992, 93, Ball Bros. Found., 1992, Pres.'s fellow Columbia U., 1988. Mem. Am. Hist. Assn., Orgn. Am. Historians, We. History Assn., Nev. Hist. Soc., Far West Popular Am. Culture Assn., Phi Kappa Phi, Phi Alpha Theta. Democrat. Avocations: baseball, animation, film, music. Office: C C So Nev 3200 E Cheyenne Ave North Las Vegas NV 89030-4228

GREEN, MIRIAM BLAU, psychologist; b. New Castle, Pa., Sept. 21, 1932; d. Jacob Mont and Anne (Levine) Blau; m. Alvin Green, June 13, 1954; children: Andrew, Marie, Jennifer. BA with high honors, U. Mich., 1954; EdM, Harvard U., 1955; EdD, Columbia U., 1960. Lic. psychologist, N.Y.; diplomate Am. Bd. Profl. Psychology. Tchr. history Maimonides Sch., Boston, 1955-57; sch. psychologist Bur. Child Guidance, N.Y.C., 1960-67, Great Neck (N.Y.) Pub. Schs., 1967-81; instr. State U. Coll. Old Wesbury, Westbury, N.Y., 1982-85; fellow child psychoanalysis Postgrad. Ctr. Mental Health, N.Y.C., 1983-86, fellow family therapy, 1982-84, asst. coord. family program, 1985-89, dir. family and couples tng. program, 1989-91; mem. faculty, supr. Inst. for Child, Adolescent and Family Studies, 1991—; supr. child psychology CUNY, N.Y.C., 1997—; pvt. practice Great Neck and N.Y.C., 1983—; NIMH trainee Columbia U., 1958-60; lectr., instr. Queens Coll., CUNY, 1962-63; cons. Jewish Family Svc. of Bergen County, N.J., 1991-92; faculty supr. Postgrad. Ctr. Mental Health, 1991—. Mem. APA (sec. Divsn 39, 1991-97, Sect. II, 1991—), N.Y. State Psychol. Assn., Nassau County Psychol. Assn., Psychol. Practioners L.I. (bd. dirs. 1987-89), Phi Beta Kappa. Jewish. Home: 22 Arleigh Rd Great Neck NY 11021-1338 Office: 145 E 48th St New York NY 10017-1254

GREEN, MORRIS, physician, educator; b. Indpls., May 27, 1922; s. Coleman and Rebecca (Oleinick) G.; m. Janice Barber Gorton, Mar. 11, 1955; children: David Schuster, Alan Coleman, Carolyn Ann, Susan Elaine, Marcia Ruth, Sylvia Rebecca. A.B., Ind. U., 1942, M.D., 1944. Intern Ind. U. Med. Center, 1945; resident pediatrics U. Ill. Research and Ednl. Hosps., 1947-49; instr. pediatrics U. Ill. Coll. Medicine, 1949-52; asst. prof. Yale Sch. Medicine, 1952-57; faculty Ind. U. Sch. Medicine, Indpls., 1957—, Perry W. Lesh prof. pediatrics, 1963—; chmn. dept. pediatrics, physician-in-chief James Whitcomb Riley Hosp. for Children, Indpls., 1967-88; commr. health State of Ind., 1990-91. Author: Pediatric Diagnosis, 6th edit., 1998; co-editor: Ambulatory Pediatrics, 1968, 5th edit., 1999; mem. editl. bd. Pediat. Rev., Contemporary Pediat., Current Problems Pediat., Jour. Devel. Behavioral Pediat., Jour. Ambulatory Pediat. Assn., Social Work in Health Care; nat. adviser Children Today. Served to capt. M.C. AUS, 1945-47. Recipient George Armstrong award in ambulatory pediats., 1971, C. Anderson Aldrich award in child devel., 1982, Irving S. Cutter award Phi Rho Sigma, 1984, Ross award for pediat. edn., 1985, Simon Wile award Am. Acad. Child and Adolescent Psychiatry, 1990, Joseph W. St. Geme award Fedn. Pediat. Orgns., 1992, Disting. Career award Ambulatory Pediat. Assn., 1996. Mem. AMA (Abraham Jacobi award 1990), Am. Pediatric Soc., Soc. Pediatric Research, Am. Fedn. Clin. Research, Am. Acad. Pediatrics (Abraham Jacobi award 1990), Am. Orthopsychiat. Assn., Inst. Medicine, Soc. Research Child Devel., Phi Beta Kappa, Sigma Xi, Alpha Omega Alpha. Home: 1840 Brewster Rd Indianapolis IN 46260-1561 Office: 702 Barnhill Dr Indianapolis IN 46202-5128

GREEN, NANCY LOUGHRIDGE, academic administrator; b. Lexington, Ky.; d. William S. and Nancy O. (Green) Loughridge; BA in Journalism, U. Ky., 1964; MA in Journalism, Ball State U., 1971; postgrad. U. Ky., 1968, U. Minn., 1968. Tchr. English and publs. adv. Clark County High Sch., Winchester, Ky., 1965-66, Pleasure Ridge Park High Sch., Louisville, 1966-67, Clarksville (Ind.) High Sch., 1967-68, Charleston (W.Va.) High Sch., 1968-69; asst. publs. and pub. info. specialist W.Va. Dept. Edn., Charleston, 1969-70; tchr. journalism and publs. dir. Elmhurst High Sch., Ft. Wayne, Ind., 1970-71; adviser student publs. U. Ky., Lexington, 1971-82; gen. mgr. student publs. U. Tex., Austin, 1982-85; pres., pub. Palladium-Item, Richmond, Ind., 1985-89, News-Leader, Springfield, Mo., 1989-92; asst. to the pres., Newspaper Divsn. Gannett Co., Inc., Washington, 1992-94; exec. dir. coll. advancement Clayton State Coll., Morrow, Ga., 1994-96; v.p. for advancement Clayton Coll. & State U., 1996—; dir. Harte-Hanks urban journalism program, 1984; pres. Media Cons., Inc., Lexington, 1980; dir. urban journalism workshop program Louisville and Lexington newspaper pubs., 1976-82; sec. Kernel Press, Inc., 1971-82. Contbr. articles to profl. jours. Bd. dirs. Jr. League, Lexington, 1980-82, Manchester Ctr., 1978-82, pres., 1979-82; chmn. Greater Richmond Progress Com., 1986-87, bd. dirs. 1986-89; pres. Leadership Wayne County, 1986-87, bd. dirs., 1985-89; bd. dirs. Richmond Community Devel. Corp., 1987-89, United Way of the Ozarks, 1990-92, ARC, 1990-92, Springfield Arts Coun., 1990-91, Bus. Devel. Corp., 1991-92, Bus. Education Alliance, 1991-92, Caring Found., 1991-92, Cox Hosp. Bd., 1990-92, Springfield Schs. Found., 1991-92; mem. adv. bd. Ind. U. East, 1985-89, Richmond C. of C., 1987-89, Ind. Humanities Coun., 1988-89, Youth Communications Bd., 1988-92, Opera Theatre No. Va., 1992-94, Atlanta chpt. AIWF, 1995—, Clayton County C. of C., 1995—. Recipient Coll. Media Advisers First Amendment award, 1987, Carl Towley award Journalism Edn. Assn., 1988, Disting. Svc. award Assn. Edn. Journalism and Mass Comm., 1989; named to Ball State Journalism Hall of Fame, 1988, Coll. Media Advisers Hall of Fame, 1994. Mem. Student Press Law Ctr. (bd. dirs. 1975—, pres. 1985-87, 94-96, v.p. 1992-94), Assoc. Collegiate Press, Journalism Edn. Assn., Nat. Council Coll. Publs. Advs. (pres. 1979-83), Disting. Newspaper Adv. 1976, Disting. Bus. Adviser, 1984), Columbia Scholastic Press Assn. (Gold Key 1980), So. Interscholastic Press Assn. (Disting. Service award 1983), Nat. Scholastic Press Assn. (Pioneer award 1982), Soc. Profl. Journalists, Clayton County C. of C. (internat. com. chmn. 1996—). *An opportunity each day to make the best of every situation to help others, your community, your profession and employees to be successful.*

GREEN, NORMAN KENNETH, retired oil industry executive, former naval officer; b. Columbus, Ind., July 1, 1924; s. Otto and Bernice Escalene (Snyder) G.; m. Mary Ann McCarthy, Mar. 12, 1949; children: David Bruce, Norman K., Penny Ann, Michael Anthony, Patricia Elizabeth. B.S., U.S. Naval Acad., 1947; M.S., Naval Postgrad. Sch., 1959. Joined U.S. Navy, 1943, advanced through grades to rear adm., 1974; comdg. officer USS St. Louis, 1970-72, comdg. officer USS Ticonderoga, 1972-73; capt. aviation assignment officer Bur. Naval Personnel Washington, 1973-74; comdr. Sea Based ASW Wings Atlantic Fleet, 1974-77; comdr. Carrier Group 6 and Carrier Strike Force Mayport, Fla., 1977-79; dep. dir. command and control Office Chief Naval Ops., Navy Dept. Washington, 1979-80; ret., 1980; sr. v.p. Charter Co., Jacksonville, Fla., 1980-87. Mem. Com. of 100, Jacksonville, Fla., 1974-77; mem. exec. bd. United Way, 1974-77. Decorated Def. Superior Service medal, Legion of Merit.; recipient Brotherhood award NCCJ, 1979. Mem. Jacksonville C. of C. (bd. govs. 1974-77, 83-86). Methodist. Clubs: Army-Navy, Ponte Vedra, Marsh Landing Country. Home: 550 Granada Ter Ponte Vedra Beach FL 32082-2304

GREEN, PATRICIA PATAKY, school system administrator, consultant; b. N.Y.C., June 18, 1949; d. William J. and Theresa M. (DiGianni) P.; m. Stephen I. Green, Dec. 7, 1975. BS, U. Md., 1971, MEd, 1977, PhD, 1994. Tchr. Prince George's County (Md.) Pub. Schs., 1971-83; elem. instrnl. adminstrv. specialist Thomas Stone Sch., Mt. Ranier, Md., 1984-85, Glenridge Sch., Lanham, Md., 1984, Greenbelt (Md.) Ctr. Sch., 1983-84, Prince George's County Pub. Schs., 1985-91; prin. Columbia Park Sch., Landover, Md., 1985-91; asst. supt. Prince George's County Pub. Schs., 1991-95, assoc. supt./chief divsnl. adminstr. for pupil svcs., 1995—; cons. nationwide sch. systems, 1987—; seminar/workshop presenter in field. Editor, writer (newsletter) Tooth or Consequences, 1980—; featured in numerous mags. and on TV shows; contbr. articles to profl. jours. Apptd. commr. Prince George's Commn. for Children, Youth, and Families. Recipient Nat. Sch. Recognition award U.S. Dept. Edn., 1988, Outstanding Adminstr. award Prince George's County C. of C., 1990, Outstanding Rsch. award Md. Assn. Supervision and Curriculum Devel., 1995, Outstanding Educator award Prince George's County, 1983, Spotlight on Prevention award Md. State Atty. Gen., 1998. Mem. NAESP (Excellence of Achievement award 1988), ASCD, NEA, Nat. Sch. Bds. Assn., Nat. Assn. Secondary Sch. Prins., Am. Ednl. Rsch. Assn., Phi Kappa Phi. Kappa Delta Pi. Avocations: landscape gardening, photography, reading, writing. Office: 7501 Greenway Center Dr Ste 260 Greenbelt MD 20770-3548

GREEN, PAUL ELIOT, JR., communications scientist; b. Durham, N.C., Jan. 14, 1924; s. Paul Eliot and Elizabeth Atkinson (Lay) G.; m. Dorrit L. Gegan, Oct. 30, 1948; children: Dorrit Green Rodemeyer, Nancy E., Judith Green Godin, Paul M., Gordon M. AB, U. N.C., 1943; MS, N.C. State U., 1948; ScD, MIT, 1953. Group leader MIT Lincoln Lab., Lexington, 1951-69; sr. mgr. rsch. divsn. IBM, Yorktown Heights, N.Y., 1969-97; dir. optical networking tech. Tellabs, Hawthorne, N.Y., 1997—; mem. radio engring. adv. com. USIA, 1984-93; panel on survivable communications NRC, 1982-89. Author: Fiber Optic Networks, 1992; co-editor: Computer Communications, 1974; editor: Computer Network Architectures and Protocols, 1982, Network Interconnection and Protocol Conversion, 1988. Served to lt. comdr. USNR, 1943-60; ret. Named Disting. Engring. Alumnus N.C. State U., 1983; recipient Data Comm. award Assn. Computing Machinery, SIGCOM, 1994. Fellow IEEE (chmn. info. theory group 1960, pres. Comm. Soc. 1992-93, Aerospace Pioneer award 1981, E.H. Armstrong award 1989, Simon Ramo medal 1991); mem. NAE. Home: 35 Roseholm Pl Mount Kisco NY 10549-4619 Office: Tellabs Optical Networking Group 15 Skyline Dr Hawthorne NY 10532-2152

GREEN, PAUL JOHN, independent critic; b. Seattle, July 27, 1936; s. Howard William and Ruth Yeo G. BA in French, Seattle Pacific Coll., 1957; MA in English Lit., U. Wash., 1958; M of Libr. Sci., U. Calif., Berkeley, 1968; PhD in Libr. Studies, Wash. State U., 1981. Teaching asst. English U. Wash., Seattle, 1963-66; instr. English Ctrl. Wash. U., Ellensburg, 1966-67; rsch. asst. U. Calif., Berkeley, 1967-68; asst. serial libr. U. Oreg., Eugene, 1968-69; teaching asst. English Wash. State U., Pullman, 1974-76; ind. critic Spokane, Seattle, Pullman, 1981—. Author: The Life of Jack Gray: An Education in Living and in Love, 1991; contbr. articles to profl. jours. With USNR, 1953-65. Mem. AAUP, Am. Comp. Lit. Assn. Modern Lang. Assn., Internat. Platform Assn. Avocations: reading, writing, research. Home: 630 NE Maiden Ln #10 Pullman WA 99163

GREEN, PETER MORRIS, classics educator, writer, translator; b. London, Dec. 22, 1924; came to U.S., 1971; s. Arthur and Olive Emily (Slaughter) G.; m. Lalage Isobel Pulvertaft, July 28, 1951 (div.); children: Timothy Michael Bourke, Nicholas Paul, Sarah Francesca; m. Carin Margreta Christensen, July 18, 1975. BA, Cambridge U., 1950, MA, 1954, PhD, 1954. Dir. studies in classics Selwyn Coll., Cambridge, Eng., 1952-53; freelance writer, journalist, translator, London, 1954-63; lectr. Greek history and lit. Coll. Yr. in Athens, 1966-71; prof. classics U. Tex., Austin, 1971-97, James R. Dougherty Centennial prof., 1982-97, prof. emeritus, 1997—; vis. prof. classics UCLA, 1976; vis. prof. history U. Iowa, 1997-98, adj. prof. classics, 1998—; vis. prof. history Athens Coll., 1999; Mellon chair in humanities Tulane U., 1986. Fiction critic: Daily Telegraph, London, 1954-63; sr. cons. editor: Hodder & Stoughton Ltd., London, 1959-63; cons.: (Odyssey project) Nat. Radio Theatre, Chgo., 1980-81; author: The Sword of Pleasure, 1957 (Heinemann award for Lit. 1957), The Shadow of the Parthenon, 1972, Alexander of Macedon 356-323 BC: A Historical Biography, 1974, 2d edit., 1991, Classical Bearings, 1989, ed edit., 1998, Alexander to Actium: The Historical Evolution of the Hellenistic Age, 1990, rev. edit., 1993, The Greco-Persian Wars, 1996; translator, editor: Juvenal, The Sixteen Satires, 1967, 3d edit., 1998, Ovid: The Erotic Poems, 1982, Yannis Ritsos: The Fourth Dimension, 1993, Hellenistic History and Culture, 1993, Ovid: The Poems of Exile, 1994, Apollonios Rhodios, The Argonautika, 1997. Served to sgt. RAF, 1943-47. NEH fellow, 1983-84; Craven scholar Cambridge U., 1950; Obermann Ctr. for Advanced Rsch. fellow U. Iowa, 1997; recipient 1st prize Nat. Poetry Libr., 1997. Fellow Royal Soc. Lit. (council 1959-63); mem. Soc. for Promotion of Hellenic Studies (U.K.), Classical Assn. (U.K.), Am. Philol. Assn., Archaeol. Inst. Am., Mem. Liberal Party. Club: Savile (London). Office: Dept Classics U Iowa Iowa City IA 52242 *Prime aims, then, now always: to have maximum possible time for writing, travel, sport, relationships: to avoid any job that threatens my solitude or independence; to shun mature opinions: to go on, forever if possible, finding every day exciting, new, a fresh challenge, mentally and physically; to love and be loved always, to write all the books I have in me, and be healthy in mind and body until I die, preferably at well over the century, in Greece.*

GREEN, RAYMOND FERGUSON ST. JOHN, marketing and advertising executive; b. Phila., Aug. 15, 1950; Raymond Silvernail and Rose Dorathea (Basile) G.; BA in Psychology, Lafayette Coll., 1972; postgrad. Temple U., 1972-75; m. Lisa Rose Wardzinski, June 24, 1972; children: Katharine Amanda, Ian Ferguson Paul. Prodn. asst. Franklin Broadcasting Co., Phila., 1972-73, asst. sec., 1973-75, v.p. corp. affairs, 1975-78, exec. v.p., 1978-84; pres., gen. mgr., COO Franklin Broadcasting Co., 1983-88, pres. Magnetik Prodns., Inc., 1982-88; pres. Greenrose Corp., 1988—, also bd. dirs.; pres. Greenrose Broadcasting Svcs., WWPR Bradenton, Fla., 1996—; sec./treas. Liebert & Co.; bd. dirs. Young Audiences Eastern Pa., co-chmn., 1989-90. Associated Bio-Med. Svcs.; dir. Northwestern Corp., 1988-93; v.p. Amica Co., 1985-93; treas. NW Ctr. MH/MR, 1986-93. Mem. adv. bd. Phila. Boys Choir & Chorale, 1986—, Musical Fund Soc. of Phila. Mem. Northwest Center; mem. Musical Fund Soc. Phila., Phila. Art Alliance; dir. choral Arts Soc. of Phila., 1991-98, v.p., 1995-97, pres., 1997-98. Mem. Internat. Soc. Bacchus (trustee, chmn. Phila. chpt. 1988-91), Center Internat. Gastronomic Studies (trustee), Union League Club, Commonwealth Club, Rotary. Roman Catholic. Office: 308 Manor Rd Lafayette Hill PA 19444-1722

GREEN, RICHARD ALAN, lawyer; b. Springfield, Mass., Apr. 25, 1926; s. Herman and Emma (Rudnick) G.; m. Lorna H. Paul, Sept. 6, 1957; children: Charles C., Thomas F. A.B. cum laude, Harvard U., 1947, LL.B., 1952. Bar: N.Y. 1954, D.C. 1975, Md. 1987. Assoc. Steinberg & Patterson, N.Y.C., 1954-57; asst. U.S. atty. So. Dist. N.Y., 1957-59; 1st asst. counsel N.Y. State Commn. Investigation, 1960; individual practice law N.Y.C., 1961-64; dir. ABA Project on Standards for Criminal Justice, 1964-73; dep. dir. Nat. Commn. on Reform of Fed. Criminal Laws, 1967-71; lectr. U. Va. Sch. Law, 1971; dep. dir. Fed. Jud. Center, Washington, 1971-74; partner Rowley and Green, Washington, 1974-80, Stohlman, Beuchert, Egan & Smith, Washington, 1981—. Served with USN, 1944-46. Mem. ABA, Am. Law Inst., D.C. Bar Assn., Assn. of Bar of City of N.Y., Harvard (N.Y.C.) Club. Home: 2725 N St NW Washington DC 20007-3324

GREEN, RICHARD BERTRAM, sculptor; b. Barrie, Ont., Can., Apr. 18, 1946; s. Lawrence Bertram and Vera Valdee (Bell) G.; m. Hilary Joan McDougall, July 27, 1979. Assoc., Ont. Coll. Art, 1969. Dir. Richard Green Gallery, Barrie, 1972-76; sculptor Ricahrd Green, Barrie, Bracebridge, 1972—; originator, benevolent dictator Muskoka Autumn Studio Tour, Bracebridge, 1979-83; pres. Richard Green Design Ltd., Lanexa, Va., 1991—. Works in permanent collections of Coldwell Banker and numerous pvt. collections. Bd. dirs. Visual Arts Ont., Toronto, 1978-80. Mem. Sculptor Soc. of Can. (exec. 1974-84), Internat. Sculpture Ctr., Lions. Republican. Avocations: boating, motorcycling. Home and Office: 1019 Colony Trl Lanexa VA 23089-6019

GREEN, RICHARD CALVIN, JR., utility company executive; b. Kansas City, Mo., May 6, 1954; s. Richard Calvin and Ann (Gableman) G.; m. Nancy Jean Risk, Aug. 6, 1977; children—Allison Thompt, Ashley Jean, Richard Calvin III. BSBA, So. Methodist U., 1976. With Mo. Pub. Service, Kansas City, 1976-85, exec. v.p., 1982-85; pres., chief exec. officer UtiliCorp United Inc., Kansas City, 1985-89, pres., chmn. bd., from 1989, now CEO, chmn. bd.; bd. dirs. Commerce Bank Kansas City. Trustee Ctr. for Strategic and Internat. Studies, Washington, Urban Inst., Washington; chmn. Civic Coun. of Greater Kansas City; bd. dirs. Midwest Rsch. Inst., Greater Kansas City C. of C. *

GREEN, RICHARD E., real estate company executive; married; two children. BS in Acctg. and Fin., San Jose State U. With Price Waterhouse & Co.; with May Ctrs., Inc., 1968-80, exec. v.p.; co-pres. Westfield Group, L.A., 1980—. Bd. dirs. UCLA Armand Hammer Mus. of Art and Cultural Ctr. Office: 11601 Wilshire Blvd 12th Fl Los Angeles CA 90025

GREEN, RICHARD FREDERICK, astronomer; b. Omaha, Feb. 13, 1949; m. Joan Auerbach; children: Alexander Simon, Nathaniel Martin. AB in Astronomy magna cum laude, Harvard U., 1971; PhD in Astronomy, Calif. Inst. Tech., 1977. Physics lab instr. Harvard U., Cambridge, 1970-71; NSF trainee Calif. Inst. Tech., Pasadena, 1971-72, grad. teaching asst. in astronomy, 1972-74, grad. rsch. asst. in astronomy, 1974-77, rsch. fellow in astronomy, 1977-79; asst. astronomer Steward Observatory, U. Ariz., Tucson, 1979-83; asst. astronomer Kitt Peak Nat. Observatory, Tucson, 1983-85, assoc. astronomer, 1986-90, astronomer, 1990—, dir., 1997—; acting dir. Nat. Optical Astronomy Observatories, Tucson, 1992-93, acting dep. dir., 1993-94, dep. dir., 1994—; rsch. asst. Smithsonian Astrophys. Observatory, 1970-71; adj. asst. prof. Steward Observatory, U. Ariz., 1983-85, adj. assoc. astronomer and prof., 1986-90, adj. astronomer, 1990—; mem. users' com. Internat. Ultraviolet Explorer Satellite, NASA, 1979-81, chair proposal rev. panel, 1986-88, 93, final sci. program com., 1993, mem. sci. team Far Ultraviolet Spectroscopic Explorer Satellite, 1981—, Space Telescope Imaging

Spectrograph, 1982—, guest observer working group Extreme Ultraviolet Explorer Satellite, 1988-92, chair proposal rev. panel ROSAT Guest Observer Program, 1989, 92, ROSAT Users' Coms., 1990-93, chair HST Cycle 2 Porposal Rev. Panel, mem. time allocation com., 1991, STSDAS users' com., 1991-92, Hubble Space Telescope Program Rev., 1997; mem. panel ultraviolet and optical astronomy from space, astronomy survey com. Nat. Acad. Scis., 1989-90; mem. panel HST and Beyond AURA, 1994-95; mem. proposal rev. panels NSF, 1996-97; instrument scientist Gemini 8-m Telescopes Project, 1991-92; mem. U.S. Gemini sci. adv. com., Gemini (Internat.) sci. com. U.S. Gemini Project Office, 1991-93, acting U.S. Gemini Project scientist, 1992-93, mem. instrument forum, optical instrumentation sci. working group, chair multi-object spectrograph critical design rev., 1997. Nat. Merit scholar; Hon. scholar Harvard U. Mem. AAAS (astronomy divsn. nominating com. 1992, coun. astronomy rep. com. coun. affairs 1995-97), Am. Astronomical Soc., Internat. Astronomical Union, Astronomical Soc. of the Pacific, Phi Beta Kappa. Office: Kitt Peak Nat Observatory 950 N Cherry Ave PO Box 26732 Tucson AZ 85726-6732*

GREEN, RICHARD JOHN, architect; b. Painesville, Ohio, Mar. 14, 1944; s. Robert Franklin and Hazel (Ruble) G.; m. Judith Marie Ellen Niemi, Aug. 25, 1965 (div. 1985); children: Kevin Ward, Tyler Andrew. BArch with honors, N.C. State U., 1968; Loeb fellow, Harvard U., 1978-79. Registered architect, Mass., Calif., Pa., Ill., Ind., R.I., N.H., N.C., Nev., Conn., Minn., Tenn., S.C., Singapore. Project designer The Stubbins Assocs., Inc., Cambridge, Mass., 1968-74, assoc., 1974-77, v.p. design, 1977-83, pres., COO, 1983-92, chmn., CEO, 1992—; vis. instr. Calif. State Poly. U., Pomona, 1980-84; vis. lectr. Nat. U. Mex., Mexico City, 1981; instr. Boston Archtl. Ctr., 1971-72, 1975-76; thesis advisor Harvard U., Cambridge, 1981-82; part-time adj. faculty dept. arch. N.C. State U., 1998. Drawings, projects and photographs pub. in books. Bd. dirs. Sch. Design Found., N.C. State U. Fellow AIA (internat. com., corr. mem., com. on Design and Urban Design and Planning, Cert. of Merit 1968, Rotch Travelling scholar 1972); mem. Boston Soc. Architects, AIA Mass., Nat. Council Archtl. Registration Bds., Archtl. League N.Y. Clubs: Corinthian Yacht. Avocations: athletics, travel, sailing, Tae Kwon Do. Home: 22 Oak St Marblehead MA 01945-1947 Office: The Stubbins Assocs Inc 1033 Massachusetts Ave Cambridge MA 02138-5319

GREEN, RICHARD LANCELYN (GORDON), editor, writer; b. Bebington, Eng., July 10, 1953; s. Roger Lancelyn and June Lancelyn (Burdett) G. Student, Bradfield Coll., Eng., 1966-71; M.A., Oxford U., 1975. Former surveyor's asst., editor, freelance writer and researcher; chmn. Sherlock Holmes Soc. London. Editor: (with J.M. Gibson) My Evening with Sherlock Holmes, 1981, Arthur Conan Doyle on Sherlock Holmes, 1981, Sheerluck Jones, 1982, (with J.M. Gibson) The Unknown Conan Doyle, Uncollected Stories, 1982, Essays on Photography, 1982, Letters to the Press, 1986, The Uncollected Sherlock Holmes, 1983, The Further Adventures of Sherlock Holmes, 1985, Letters to Sherlock Holmes, 1985, The Sherlock Holmes Letters, 1986; author: (with J.M. Gibson) A Bibliography of A. Conan Doyle, 1983, The Adventures of Sherlock Holmes, The Return of Sherlock Holmes (The Oxford Sherlock Holmes, 1993); contbr. articles and revs. to The Sherlock Holmes Jour., Baker Street Miscellanea, others. Recipient award Mystery Writers Am., 1984. Avocations: book collecting; travel; theatre. Home: 39 Scarsdale Villas, London England W8 9PU

GREEN, RICKI KUTCHER, producer; b. Sioux City, Iowa, Sept. 20, 1943; d. Louis Jacob Kutcher and Annabelle (Emlein) Shapiro; m. Thomas C. Green, Nov. 1976 (div.); children: Joshua, Marisa; m. Jeffrey Graham Spragens, May 18, 1984 (div. Oct 1996). Student, Newcomb Coll., 1961-63; BA in Polit. Sci., U. Calif., Berkeley, 1965; postgrad., Stanford U., 1990-91. Sec. U.S. Mission to UN, N.Y.C., 1965-67; publs. coord. Nat. Urban Coalition, Washington, 1968-70; press officer Presdl. Commn. on Population Growth, Washington, 1970-72; mng. editor legis. newsletter Women's Equity Action League, Washington, 1972-74; writer, film producer Md. Pub. TV, Owings Mills, 1975-78; assoc. producer WETA TV, Washington, 1978-79, producer, 1979-83, exec. producer, 1983-92, v.p. news and pub. affairs, 1984-92; pres. Ever Green Communications Co., 1992-97. Producer TV specials The Power and the Glory, 1982 (Emmy 1983), Summer of Judgment: Watergate Hearings, 1983 (ABA award 1984); exec. producer TV series Making Sense of the 60's, 1991; producer, exec. producer TV series Washington Week in Review, 1980-90 (several awards); series producer Religion and Ethics News Weekly, PBS, 1997—. Bd. dirs. Women in Film and Video, Washington, 1979; mem. exec. bd. Women's Equity Action League, Washington, 1973-76. John S. Knight Profl. Journalism fellow, 1990-91. Mem. Soc. Profl. Journalists, Radio-TV Corrs. Assn., Women in Film & Video. Avocations: hiking, photography. Office: 1000 Potomac St NW Ste 202 Washington DC 20007

GREEN, ROBERT EDWARD, JR., physicist, educator; b. Clifton Forge, Va., Jan. 17, 1932; s. Robert Edward and Hazle Hall (Smith) G.; m. Sydney Sue Truitt, Feb. 1, 1962; children: Kirsten Adair, Heather Scott. BS, Coll. William and Mary, 1953; PhD, Brown U., 1959; postgrad., Aachen (Germany) Technische Hochschule, 1959-60. Physicist underwater explosions rsch. divsn. Norfolk Naval Shipyard, Va., 1959; asst. prof. mechanics Johns Hopkins U., Balt., 1960-65, assoc. prof., 1965-70, prof., 1970—, chmn. mechanics dept., 1970-72, chmn. mechanics and materials sci. dept., 1972-73, chmn. civil engring./materials sci. and engring. dept., 1979-82, chmn. materials sci. and engring. dept., 1982-85, 91-93, dir. ctr. for nondestructive evaluation, 1985—; Ford Found. resident sr. engr. RCA, Lancaster, Pa., 1966-67; cons. U.S. Army Ballistic Research Labs., Aberdeen Proving Ground, Md., 1973-74; physicist Ctr. for Materials Sci., U.S. Nat. Bur. Standards, Washington, 1974-81; program mgr. Def. Advanced Research Projects Agy., 1981-82; mem. nat. materials adv. bd. Author: Ultrasonic Investigation of Mechanical Properties (Treatise on Materials Science and Technology, vol. 3), 1973; co-editor 8 books; also articles. Fulbright grantee. Mem. ASM Internat., Am. Phys. Soc., Acoustical Soc. Am., Met. Soc. AIME, Am. Soc. Nondestructive Testing, Soc. for the Advancement of Material and Process Engring., Materials Rsch. Soc., Sigma Xi, Tau Beta Pi, Alpha Sigma Mu, Sigma Nu. Methodist. Achievements include research in recovery, recrystallization, elasticity, plasticity, crystal growth and orientation, X-ray diffraction, electro-optical systems, linear and non-linear elastic wave propagation, light-sound interactions, high-power ultrasonics, ultrasonic attenuation, dislocation damping, fatigue, acoustic emission, nondestructive testing, polymers, biomaterials, synchrotron radiation, composites, sensors and process control. Home: 936 Ellendale Dr Baltimore MD 21286-1510 Office: Johns Hopkins U Ctr Nondestructive Evaluation 3400 N Charles St Baltimore MD 21218-2680

GREEN, ROBERT LEONARD, hospital management company executive; b. Los Angeles, Mar. 20, 1931; s. Leonard H. and Helene (Rains) G.; m. Susan Wolf, June 9, 1957; children—Wendy, Julie. B.A., Stanford U., 1952, LL.B., 1956. C.P.A., Calif. Acct. John F. Grieder, San Francisco, 1957-59; assoc. Heller, Ehrman, White & McAuliffe, San Francisco, 1959-61; pres. Sutter Capital Co., San Francisco, 1961-69; chmn. bd. Community Psychiat. Ctrs., San Francisco, 1969-89; chmn. bd. VIVRA, 1989-94, pres., 1989-92; chmn. Edn. Ptnrs., San Francisco, 1994—. Trustee Sta. KQED-Pub. TV, San Francisco, 1981-91, Mus. Modern Art, 1984-89, Mt. Zion Hosp., 1985-86. 1st lt. U.S. Army, 1954-56. Avocations: bicycling, golf. Office: 2601 Mariposa St San Francisco CA 94110-1426

GREEN, ROBERT S., lawyer; b. Newark, Feb. 9, 1927; s. Mortimer J. and Edna Vera (Reinherz) G.; m. Estelle Rothenberg, Jan. 29, 1961; children—Peter, Sara. A.B., Cornell U., 1948; J.D., Columbia U., 1953. Bars: N.Y. 1954, Fla. 1957, D.C. 1959. Law clk. Cir. Judge Harold R. Medina, 1953-54; ptnr. Brennan, London & Buttenweiser, N.Y.C., 1963-70, Green, Sharpless & Greenstein, N.Y.C., 1971-80, Nixon, Hargrave, Devans & Doyle, N.Y.C., 1981-94; counsel Pepper Hamilton LLP, N.Y.C., 1995—. Contbr. articles to profl. jours. Founder, trustee Citizens for Clean Air, 1964-68; trustee William Alanson White Inst., N.Y.C., 1968-89 ; advisor U.S. Senator Robert F. Kennedy, 1966-68. Served with USNR, 1945-46, PTO. Mem. Am. Law Inst. Democrat. Jewish. Avocations: sailing, travel. Home: 90 Riverside Dr New York NY 10024-5306

GREEN, ROBERT SCOTT, biotechnology company executive; b. N.Y.C., Aug. 7, 1953; s. Morris and Sophie (Weinstock) G.; m. Jill Susan Bolhack, June 24, 1979; children: Melissa, Meredith. BA, CUNY, 1974; JD, Fordham U., N.Y.C., 1977. Bar: N.Y. 1978, D.C. 1979. Assoc. Paul, Weiss, Rifkind, Wharton & Garrison, N.Y.C., 1979-87; v.p. Kaplan Capital Mgmt. Inc., N.Y.C., 1987-89; pres. Vega Biotechs., Inc., Tucson, 1989-92; pres., bd. dirs. Integrated Biomolecule Corp., Tucson, 1992—; mng. dir. Fusion Assocs., Ltd., Tucson, 1990-92; bd. dirs. Hearing Innovations Inc., Tucson, 1990—. Contbr. articles to profl. jours. Mem. N.Y. State Bar Assn. Office: Integrated Biomolecule Corp 9030 S Rita Rd Ste 100 Tucson AZ 85747-9108

GREEN, RONALD MICHAEL, ethics and religious studies educator; b. N.Y.C., Dec. 16, 1942; s. Daniel David and Beatrice (Friedlander) G.; m. Mary Jean Matthews, June 25, 1965; children—Julie Elisabeth, Matthew Daniel. A.B., Brown U., 1964; Ph.D., Harvard U., 1973. Instr. Dartmouth Coll., Hanover, N.H., 1969-73, asst. prof., 1973-79, assoc. prof., 1979-85, John Phillips prof. of religion, 1985-98, chmn. dept. religion, 1980-83, 85, adj. prof. Amos Tuck Sch. Bus. Adminstrn., 1985-92; Cohen prof. Dartmouth Coll., Hanover, 1998—; vis. assoc. prof. Stanford U., Calif., 1984-85; adj. prof. dept. community medicine Dartmouth Med. Sch., 1980—; dir. Dartmouth Ethics Inst., 1993—, Office of Genome Ethics Nat. Human Genome Rsch. Inst. NIH, 1996-97; mem. Human Embryo Rsch. Panel NIH, 1994. Author: Population Growth and Justice, 1975, Religious Reason, 1978, Religion and Moral Reason, 1988, Kierkegaard and Kant, 1992, The Ethical Manager, 1994; assoc. editor Jour. Religious Ethics, 1973-91, mem. editorial bd., 1991—; mem. editorial bd. Jour. Am. Acad. Religion, 1985-91. Kent fellow, 1965-69; recipient Fulbright award, 1964-65, Dartmouth Distng. Teaching award, 1978. Mem. Am. Acad. Religion (sec. 1995—), Soc. Christian Ethics (bd. dirs., v.p. 1997-98, pres. 1998-99), Soc. Bus. Ethics, Am. Soc. for Study Religion. Jewish. Office: Dartmouth Coll Dept Religion Hanover NH 03755 *I continue to believe in the ideals of the enlightenment: that human beings can use their reason to expand opportunity, freedom and community.*

GREEN, RUTHANN, marketing and management consultant; b. Streator, Ill., July 14, 1935; d. John Joseph and Edna Marie (Peters) G. BS in Edn., U. Ill., 1957. Elem. tchr. Jefferson Sch., Davenport, Iowa, 1957-59; tchr. Hinsdale (Ill.) Jr. High Sch., 1959-62; ednl. cons. Harcourt Brace & World, Chgo., 1962-63; exec. sec. Everpure, Inc., Oakbrook, Ill., 1963-68; ednl. cons. Houghton Mifflin Co., Europe, 1968-69, Palo Alto, Calif., 1969-77; sr. mktg. mgr. Houghton Mifflin Co., Boston, 1977-87; v.p., nat. sales mgr. Riverside Pub. Co., Chgo., 1987-89; v.p., dir. mktg. McDougal, Littell & Co., Evanston, Ill., 1990-92; v.p., gen. mgr. Open Court Pub. Co., Chgo., 1992-94; pres. Peters & Green, Inc. Seminars & Bus. Devel., Chgo., 1994—. Author: WSIL: Why Should I Listen, 1987, 93, A Garfield Memoir, 1995. Bd. dirs. Ritchie Tower Condo Assn. Recipient Svc. award Am. Arbitration Assn., 1987, Golden Reel of Excellence Internat. TV Assn., 1983. Mem. Am. Mktg. Assn., Nat. Assn. Women Bus. Owners, Internat. Reading Assn., People for Am. Way, Common Cause, Am. Arbitration Assn., Chicagoland Radio Info. Svc., Inc., Urban Gateways (bd. dirs.), The Monroe Club (Chgo., bd. dirs.). Avocations: reading, fitness activities, travel, art. Home and Office: 1310 N Ritchie Ct Apt 21A Chicago IL 60610-8405

GREEN, SANDRA STAAP, mortgage broker, real estate appraiser; b. Washington, July 12, 1944; d. Bernard Franklin and Mary Frances (Latham) Staap; m. Charles Palmeter Martin, Nov. 4, 1978 (dec. Feb. 1980); m. Phillip Lee Green; 1 child, Mary Candace Todd. BA in Math., Randolph-Macon Woman's Coll., 1965; MBA, George Washington U., 1975. Mathematician Army Map Svc., Washington, 1965-74, Def. Mapping Agy., Washington, 1974-82; v.p., bd. dirs. Cloverleaf Corp., Warrenton, Va., 1981-86; pres., bd. dirs. Bacchus Corp., Warrenton, 1981—; real estate appraiser Appraisal Co. Key West (Fla.), Inc., 1988-91; pres. bd. dirs. Keys Mortgage Co., Key West, 1991—; treas. Wesley House, Key West, 1992-96; Lic. mortgage broker, Fla. Treas. 1st United Meth. Ch., Key West, 1990-91. Recipient Spl. Act award Army Map Svc., 1967, Def. Mapping Agy., 1974. Mem. AAUW (pres. Key West-Lower Keys chpt. 1994-96), Nat. Assn. Realtors, Fla. Assn. Realtors, Fla. Assn. Mortgage Brokers, Key West Art and Hist. Soc., Key West Woman's Club. Avocations: travel, computer programming, investing. Home: Apt 208N 1901 S Roosevelt Blvd Key West FL 33040-5258

GREEN, SAUL A., prosecutor. U.S. atty. Ea. Dist. Mich., Detroit. Office: US Atty for Ea Dist Mich 211 W Fort St Ste 2000 Detroit MI 48226-3202*

GREEN, SHIRLEY MOORE, public affairs and communications executive; b. Graham, Tex., Dec. 21, 1933; d. N. Edgar and Cora Day (Morrow) Moore; m. Paul M. Green, Aug. 26, 1967 (div. 1981); children: Ruth Lynn, Tracy Moore. Student, Midwestern U., Wichita Falls, Tex., 1952; BBA, U. Tex., 1956. Staff asst. Rep. Party, Austin, Tex., 1965-67; press asst. Bob Price U.S. Rep., Washington, 1967; coordinator Tex. and Ark. Bush for Pres. Campaign, Houston, 1979-80; dep. press sec. V.p. Bush, Washington, 1980-85, acting press sec., 1983; dir. pub. affairs NASA, Washington, 1985-86, dep. assoc. adminstr. communications, 1987-89; spl. asst. to the Pres. White House, Washington, 1989-92, dep. asst. to Pres., 1992; dir. Pres. Bush Transition Office, Washington, 1993; dir. program support Internat. Rep. Inst., Washington, 1993-96; dir. corr. and constituent svcs. Gov. George W. Bush, Austin, 1996—. Local chmn. Jim Baker for Atty. Gen., 1978, Pres. Ford Com., San Antonio, 1976; trustee S.W. Found. Forum, San Antonio, 1974-78; bd. dirs. Child Welfare Bd. Bexar County, 1975-79. Recipient Exceptional Svc. medal NASA, 1989. Mem. Women in Communications, NAFE, Am. Newswomen's Club, Tex. Fedn. Rep. Women (editor Partyline mag. 1969-72, one of 10 Outstanding Rep. Women Tex. 1979). Presbyterian. Avocations: reading, traveling. Home: 1513 W 30th St Austin TX 78703-1403

GREEN, THEREASA ELLEN, elementary education educator; b. Wichita, Kans., Nov. 22, 1945; d. Ralph Elwood and Wilma Arleen (Ambler) Becker; m. Gary Joseph Fox, May 27, 1964 (dec. Dec. 1975); children: Angela Ellen, Tamara Jo; m. Bruce Green, Aug. 21, 1977 (div. 1993); 1 child, Christian Todd. BS Edn., McPherson Coll., 1968; M Elem. Edn., Wichita State U., 1987, Reading Specialist, 1990. Cert. tchr. elem. edn., Kans. Elem. tchr. Unified Sch Dist. 308, Hutchinson, Kans., 1969-70, Hutchinson, 1970-72, 1972-78, 1978—; lead tchr. Unified Sch. Dist. Allen Elem., Hutchinson, 1994-98; McCandless reading specialist, 1998—; cons./presenter Attention Deficit Disorder Orgn. for Parents of ADHD Children, 1994, 99; tchr. summer sch., Hutchinson, mem. curriculum coms, other coms.; ct. apptd. spl. child advocate, Reno County Kans. Cts. Author curriculum for Farm Skills for City Kids, 1986. Asst. chmn. Christian Bus. Women, Hutchinson, 1970-71; Christian edn. dir. First Christian Ch., Hutchinson, 1972-78; dir. children's ministries First Ch. of Nazarene, Hutchinson, 1993-94; Kans. self-propelled camping dir. Nat. Camper/Hikers Assn., 1978-90. Excellence grantee Southwestern Bell Telephone Co., Topeka, Kans., 1991-94; recipient scholarship Performance Learning Systems Project TEACH, 1993, others. Mem. ASCD, AAUW, Kans. Assn. Tchrs. Math., Internat. Reading Assn., Performance Learning Systems, Kans. Reading Assn. (sec. Reno county chpt. 1996-98), Ark Valley Reading Assn. (sec. 1996-97, 97-98, v.p. 1999—). Democrat. Nazarene. Avocations: skiing, collecting cows and foxes, travel, working with children. Home: 602 Eldorado Dr Hutchinson KS 67502-8416 Office: USD 308 700 N Baker Hutchinson KS 67501-4419

GREEN, THOMAS JAMES, archaeologist; b. Lynwood, Calif., Apr. 5, 1946; s. Virgil Vance Green and Barbara Clarice (Hiatt) Phelps; m. Carol Jeanette Deregibus, Sept. 10, 1966 (div. 1978); children: Kelley Jeanette, Anthony Eugene; m. Stacy Gay Ericson, Dec. 18, 1981; children: Vance Stacy, Samuel Francis, Joseph Spike. BA in Anthropology, U. So. Calif., 1968; PhD, Ind. U., 1977. Instr. Iowa State U., Ames, 1975-76; state archaeologist Idaho State Hist. Soc., Boise, 1976-92, dep. state historic preservation officer, 1986-92; dir. Ark. Archaeol. Survey U. Ark., Fayetteville, 1992—; mem. environ. adv. bd. U.S. Army Corps Engrs., Washington, 1992-96; mem. exec. bd. Nat. Conf. State Historic Preservation Officers, Washington, 1987-91; instr. divsn. profl. devel. U. Ala., 1987-96, divsn. continuing edn. U. Nev.-Reno, 1990—; adj. prof. anthropology Boise State U., 1980-92; vis. instr. Iowa State U., 1975-76; coord. rsch. Buhl Burial Site, Twin Falls, Idaho, 1989—; dir. archaeol. rsch. Snake River Plain, Owyhee Mountains, Idaho, 1977-95; dir excavations DeMoss Site, Idaho. Contbr. articles to profl. jours. Named Idaho Preservationist of Yr. Idaho Historic Preservation Coun., 1992. Mem. Soc. for Am. Archaeology, S.E. Archaeol. Conf., Plains Anthrop. Soc. Office: Ark Archaeol Soc PO Box 1249 Fayetteville AR 72702-1249

GREEN, TYLER SCOTT, professional baseball player; b. Springfield, Ohio, Feb. 18, 1970. Grad. high sch., Denver; student, Wichita State U. Pitcher Phila. Phillies, 1993, 1995—. Selected to N.L. All-Star Team, 1995. Office: Philadelphia Phillies Veterans Stadium 3501 S Broad St Philadelphia PA 19101-7575*

GREEN, VERNA S., broadcast executive. Pres., gen. mgr. Sta. WJLB-AM-FM, Detroit, 1982—. Office: WJLB Radio 645 Griswold St Ste 633 Detroit MI 48226-4014*

GREEN, VICKIE LEE, gifted and talented educator, music educator; b. Sterling, Colo., Sept. 28, 1954; d. Victor Eugene and Beth Arlene (Hunter) Hanson; m. James Harvey Green, Aug. 6, 1976; 1 child, Erich Alan. B in Music Edn., U. Denver, 1976, MA in Gifted and Talented Edn., 1988. Cert. music edn. tchr., Colo. Elem. vocal tchr. East Otero R-1 Sch. Dist., La Junta, Colo., 1976-83; tchr. music Morgan C.C., Ft. Morgan, Colo., 1983-84; mid. sch. band and vocal tchr. Sch. Dist. RE-3, Ft. Morgan, 1984-89, elem. vocal tchr., 1989-91; elem. music and vocal tchr. Weld 6, Greeley, Colo., 1991—; cons. gifted edn. Colo. Dept. Edn., Denver, 1989-91; mem. artist-in-residence program Colo. Coun. Arts and Humanities, Denver, 1984. Mem. NEA, Nat. Assn. for Gifted Children, Colo. Assn. for Gifted and Talented, Colo. Music Educators Assn., Colo. Edn. Assn., Music Educators Nat. Conf., Greeley Edn. Assn. Avocations: piano, flute, clarinet, reading. Home: 2318 Sunset Ln Greeley CO 80634-7608 Office: Meeker Elem Sch 2221 28th Ave Greeley CO 80634

GREEN, WILLIAM, archaeologist; b. Chgo., May 30, 1953; s. David and Lillian (Kerdeman) G. AB, Grinnell Coll., 1974; MA, U. Wis., 1977, PhD, 1987. Staff archaeologist State Hist. Soc. of Wis., Madison, 1978-86; asst. prof. archaeology Western Ill. U., Macomb, 1980, 81; state archaeologist U. Iowa, Iowa City, 1988—, adj. asst. prof. anthropology, 1988-94, adj. assoc. prof. anthropology, 1994—. Editor jour. The Wis. Archaeologist, 1983-88; editor: Midcontinental Jour. Archaeology, 1998—; contbr. articles and revs. to profl. jours. Chair Johnson County Hist. Preservation Commn., Iowa, 1991-93. Grantee NSF, 1990-91, State Hist. Soc. Iowa, Leopold Ctr. for Sustainable Agr., Iowa Acad. Sci., 1988-91, 95. Fellow Am. Anthropol. Assn. Jewish. Office: U Iowa Office State Archaeologist Iowa City IA 52242

GREEN, WILLIAM PORTER, lawyer; b. Jacksonville, Ill., Mar. 19, 1920; s. Hugh Parker and Clara Belle (Hopper) G.; m. Rose Marie Hall, Oct. 1, 1944; children: Hugh Michael, Robert Alan, Richard William. BA, Ill. Coll., 1941; JD, Northwestern U., Evanston, Ill., 1947. Bar: Ill. 1947, Calif. 1948, U.S. Dist. Ct. (so. dist.) Tex. 1986, U.S. Ct. Customs and Patent Appeals, U.S. Patent and Trademark Office 1948, U.S. Ct. Appeals (fed. cir.) 1982, U.S. Ct. Appeals (5th and 9th cir.), U.S. Supreme Ct. 1948, U.S. Dist. Ct. (cen. dist.) Calif. 1949, (so. dist.) Tex.1986. Pvt. practice L.A., 1947—; mem. Wills, Green & Mueth, L.A., 1974-83; of counsel Nilsson, Robbins, Dalgarn, Berliner, Carson & Wurst, L.A., 1984-91; of counsel Nilsson, Wurst & Green L.A., 1992—; del. Calif. State Bar Conv., 1982—, chmn., 1986. Bd. editors Ill. Law Rev., 1946; patentee in field. Mem. L.A. world Affairs Coun., 1975—; deacon local Presbyn. Ch., 1961-63. Mem. ABA, Calif. State Bar, Am. Intellectual Property Law Assn., L.A. Patent Law Assn. (past. sec.-treas., mem. bd. govs.), Lawyers Club L.A. (past treas., past sec., mem. bd. govs., pres. 1985-86), Los Angeles County Bar Assn. (trustee 1986-87), Am. Legion (past post comdr.), Northwestern U. Alumni Club So. Calif., Big Ten Club So. Calif., Town Hall Calif. Club, PGA West Golf Club (La Quinta, Calif.); Phi Beta Kappa, Phi Delta Phi, Phi Alpha. Republican. Home: 3570 Lombardy Rd Pasadena CA 91107-5627 Office: 707 Wilshire Blvd Ste 3200 Los Angeles CA 90017-3514

GREENAGEL, DEBRA, travel agency executive; b. Beach, N.D., Aug. 13; d. Robert W. and Lucille (Booke) Taylor; m. David K. Greenagel, Sept. 11, 1976; children: Jessica, Jack. BA, Moorhead State U., 1972. Hostess Braniff Airlines, Dallas, 1973-82; acct. mgr. Talent Tree, Englewood, Colo., 1983-88; v.p. sales Corp. Travel Svcs., Englewood, 1988-91, Camelot Travel Svcs., Englewood, 1991-98; v.p. travel sales T6 Worldwide, Englewood, 1998—; mem. adv. bd. Nat. Car Rental, Mpls., 1996—, United Airlines Career Sch., Denver, 1996—. Vol. Kerpe Ctr. for Battered and Abused Children, 1993-95. Mem. Nat. Bus. Execs. (pres. 1990-91), Am. Soc. Assn. Execs., Jr. League Denver, South Metro C. of C., Rocky Mountain Bus. Travel (bd. dirs. 1995—), Gamma Phi Beta. Avocations: golf, reading, cooking, walking, travel. Office: T6 Worldwide 9200 E Mineral Ave Ste 120 Englewood CO 80112-3413

GREENAN, THOMAS J., lawyer; b. Great Falls, Mont., July 13, 1933; s. Phil G. and Ada E. (Collins) G.; m. Helen Louise Shepard, June 1, 1957; children: Gregory, Kathleen, Timothy, Maureen, Daniel. Grad., Gonzaga U., 1955, JD, 1957. Bar: Wash. 1957, U.S. Dist. Ct. (we. dist.) Wash. 1959, U.S. Ct. Appeals (9th cir.) 1961, U.S. Supreme Ct. 1970. Asst. atty. gen. State of Washington, 1957-60, 62-63; assoc. Ferguson & Burdell, Seattle, 1963-68, ptnr., 1968-95; ptnr. Gordon, Thomas, Honeywell, Malanca, Peterson & Daheim, Seattle, 1995—; lectr. on antitrust and civil practice and procedure. Trustee Gonzaga U., Spokane, Wash., 1984—, chmn., 1991-92. Fellow Am. Coll. Trial Lawyers (regent 1990-93, sec. 1993-95); mem. ABA, Wash. State Bar Assn. (chmn. antitrust sect. 1980-81, chmn. disciplinary bd. 1983-84, chmn. character and fitness com. 1991-92), Seattle-King County Bar Assn., Fed. Bar Assn. (pres. we. dist. Wash. 1982-83), Am. Judicature Soc., Wash. Athletic Club, Broadmoor Golf Club (Seattle; pres. 1988-89), KC. Democrat. Roman Catholic. Office: Gordon Thomas Honeywell Malanca Peterson & Daheim 600 University St Ste 210o Seattle WA 98101-4185

GREENAWALT, ROBERT KENT, lawyer, law educator; b. Bklyn., June 25, 1936; s. Kenneth William and Martha (Sloan) G.; m. Sanja Milic, July 14, 1968 (dec. Nov. 1988); children: Robert Milic, Alexander Kent Anton, Andrei Milenko Kenneth; m. Elaine Pagels, June 1995; children: Sarah Pagels, David Greenwalt. A.B. with honors, Swarthmore Coll., 1958; Ph.B.; Keasbey fellow, Oxford (Eng.) U., 1960; LL.B.; Kent scholar, Columbia U., 1963. Bar: N.Y. 1963. Law clk. to Justice Harlan, U.S. Supreme Ct., 1963-64; spl. asst. AID, Washington, 1964-65; mem. faculty Columbia U. Law Sch., 1965—, prof. law, 1969—, Cardozo prof., 1979—, Univ. prof., 1990—; dep. solicitor gen. U.S., 1971-72; assoc. dir. N.Y. Inst. Legal Edn., 1969; vis. prof. Stanford U. Law Sch., 1970, Northwestern U. Law Sch., 1983, Marshall-Wythe Sch. Law, 1985, N.Y.U. Law Sch., 1989-90; atty. Lawyers Com. Civil Rights, 1965, trustee, 1992; mem. staff Task Force Law Enforcement N.Y.C., 1965; vis. fellow All Souls Coll. Oxford (Eng.) U., 1979. Co-author: The Sectarian College and The Public Purse, 1970; author: Legal Protections of Privacy, 1976, Discrimination and Reverse Discrimination, 1983, Conflicts of Law and Morality, 1987, Religious Convictions and Political Choice, 1988, Speech, Crime and the Uses of Language, 1989, Law and Objectivity, 1992, Private Consciences and Public Reasons, 1995, Fighting Words, 1995; editor in chief Columbia U. Law Rev., 1962-63; contbr. articles to legal jours. Recipient Ivy award Swarthmore Coll., 1958; fellow Am. Council Learned Soc., 1972-73. Fellow Am. Acad. Arts and Scis.; mem. Am. Philos. Soc., Am. Law Inst., Am. Soc. Polit. and Legal Philosophy (pres. 1992-93). Office: Columbia U Law Sch 435 W 116th St New York NY 10027-7201

GREENAWALT, WILLIAM SLOAN, lawyer; b. Bklyn., Mar. 4, 1934; s. Kenneth William and Martha Frances (Sloan) G.; m. Jane DeLano Plunkett, Aug. 17, 1957 (div. May 1986); m. Peggy Ellen Freed Tomarkin, Oct. 31, 1987; children: John DeLano, David Sloan, Katherine Downs. AB, Cornell U., 1956; LLB, Yale U., 1961. Bar: N.Y. 1962, U.S. Dist. Ct. (so. and ea. dists.) N.Y. 1962, U.S. Ct. Apls. (2d cir.) 1962, U.S. Supreme Ct. 1966. Assoc. Sullivan & Cromwell, N.Y.C., 1961-65; N.E. regional legal svcs. dir. U.S. Office Econ. Opportunity, N.Y.C., 1965-68; assoc. Rogers & Wells, N.Y.C., 1968-69, ptnr., 1969-77, sr. ptnr., 1977-81; sr. ptnr. Halperin, Shivitz, Eisenberg, Schneider & Greenawalt, N.Y.C., 1981-86, Eisenberg Honig Fogler Greenawalt & Davis, N.Y.C., 1986-91, Bangser Klein Rocca & Blum, N.Y.C., 1991-93, Loselle Greenawalt Kaplan Blair & Adler, N.Y.C., 1993-97, Loselle Greenawalt Kaplan & Blair, N.Y.C., 1997—, Meyer Greenawalt Taub & Wild, LLP, N.Y.C., 1999—; lectr. in field. Bd. editors: Yale Law Jour., 1959-61; contbr. articles in field to profl. jours. Chmn. bd. dirs. Applied Resources, Inc., N.Y.C., 1968-70; chmn. Cmty. Aid Employment of Ex-Offenders, Westchester, N.Y., 1971; pres. Westchester Legal Svcs., 1971-74, bd. dirs., 1975-91; mem. N.Y. State Gov.'s Task Force on

Elem. and Secondary Edn., 1974-75; mem. Pres. Carter's Task Force on Criminal Justice, 1976; mem. adv. coun. N.Y. State Senate Dems., 1978—; asst. and acting treas. N.Y. State Dem. Party, 1990-96, vice chair, 1996—; chair Greenburgh Dem. Party, 1997—; mem. Greenburgh Recreation Commn., 1976-83, Dem. Statewide Spl. Commn. on Polit. Ethics, 1986-87, Statewide Spl. Commn. on Election Law and Campaign Spending Reform, 1989-95; pres. Westchester Crime Victims Assistance Agy., 1981-82; commr. Taconic State Pks., Recreation and Hist. Preservation Commn., 1984-96, chmn., 1989-96; vice chmn. N.Y. State Coun. on Pks., Recreation and Hist. Preservation, 1989-94; moderator Scarsdale Congl. Ch., 1988-90; mem. Westchester County Parks, Recreation and Conservation Bd., 1998—; mem. Westchester County Execs. Transition Team on Planning, 1997. Lt. comdr. USN, 1956-58, with Res., 1961-68. Fellow N.Y. Bar Found.; mem. ABA, Am. Arbitration Assn. (mem. panel comml. arbitrators 1977—), N.Y. State Bar Assn. (chmn. com. on availability of legal svcs. 1968-70, chmn. action unit 3 1979-81, chmn. spl. commn. on alternatives to jud. resolution of disputes 1981-85), Assn. of Bar of City of N.Y., Nat. Legal Aid and Defenders Assn., Sphinx Head, Aleph Samach, County Tennis Club Westchester (Scarsdale, N.Y., pres. 1979-80), Yale Club. Phi Alpha Delta, Chi Psi. Democrat. Congregationalist. Office: Meyer Greenawalt Et Al 230 Park Ave Ste 2525 New York NY 10017

GREENAWAY, JOSEPH ANTHONY, JR., judge; b. London, Nov. 16, 1957; came to U.S., 1959; s. Joseph Anthony Sr. and Brucel May (Lynch) G.; m. Veronica Blake, May 24, 1981; children: Joseph Anthony III, Samantha Blake. BA in History, Columbia U., 1978; JD, Harvard U., 1981. Law clk. to Hon. Vincent L. Broderick U.S. Dist. Ct. (so. dist.) N.Y., N.Y.C., 1982-83; lawyer Kramer, Levin, Nessen, Kamin & Frankel, N.Y.C., 1981-82, 83-85; chief narcotics divsn., asst. U.S. atty. Dept. Justice, Newark, 1985-90; in-house counsel Johnson & Johnson, New Brunswick, N.J., 1990-96; dist. judge U.S. Dist. Ct., Newark, 1996—; Weintraub lectr. Rutgers U. Law Sch., 1998. Presenter in field. Past sec. Columbia U. Alumni Assn. bd. dirs., N.Y.C.; bd. dirs. Columbia U. Nat. Coun. Named Minority Achiever of Yr. East Orange YMCA, 1997; recipient proclamation Newark City Coun., 1990, medal of excellence Columbia U., 1997; Earl Warren Legal scholar. Mem. ABA, Nat. Bar Assn., Garden State Bar Assn., Fed. Judges Assn., Am. Corp. Counsel Assn. (Disting. Svc. award 1997), Columbia Coll. Alumni Assn. Avocation: golf. Office: Martin Luther King Jr Fed Bldg PO Box 999 Newark NJ 07101-0999

GREENBACKER, JOHN EVERETT, retired lawyer; b. Meriden, Conn., Oct. 4, 1917; s. Charles and Isabel Alice Francis G.; m. Carolyn Robertson Perrow, July 25, 1942; children: Susan Oller, John E. Jr., Florence Linn, Christopher F. Student, U. Conn., 1935-36; BS, U.S. Naval Acad., 1940; JD, Georgetown U., 1949, LLM, 1969; MA, George Washington U., 1964, U.S. Naval War Coll., 1964. Bar: D.C. 1949, Md. 1970, Va. 1976, U.S. Dist. Ct. (we. dist.) Va. 1979. Commd. ensign U.S. Navy, 1940, advanced through grades to capt., 1960, comdg. officer subchaser, 1942-43, comdg. officer destroyer escorts, 1943-46, comdg. officer destroyer, 1955-57, comdg. officer attack transport, 1962-63, comdr. destroyer div. 262, 1961-62, comdr. destroyer squadron 6, 1965-66, ret., 1969; sr. atty. legal dept. Balt. Gas & Electric Co., 1969-72, mem. finance dept., 1972-74, treas., 1974-76; practice law Halifax, Va., 1976-94; estate planning cons., 1994—. Home: 4185 Grubby Rd Halifax VA 24558-2425 Office: 15 S Main St PO Box 488 Halifax VA 24558-0488

GREENBAUM, JAMES RICHARD, liquor distributing company executive, real estate developer; b. Cleve., July 3, 1933; s. Harold and Miriam (Lion) G.; m. Peggy Strauss, Jan. 29, 1955; children: Robert Strauss, James R., Clifford Harold. B.A., Tulane U., 1955. V.p. Strauss Distbrs., Ark., 1961—; bd. dirs. S&D Realty, Little Rock. Bd. dirs. Palm Springs Desert Mus., Jewish Fedn. Palm Springs. Lt. U.S. Army, 1955-57. Mem. Beaver Creek Club (Colo.), Tamarisk Club (Rancho Mirage, Calif.), Country Club of Rockies (Vail, Colo.), Club at Morningside (Rancho Mirage), Zeta Beta Tau. Jewish (past pres., bd. dirs. temple). Office: 1 Hawkeye Pk 69844 Us Highway 111 Ste H Rancho Mirage CA 92270-2849

GREENBAUM, MAURICE COLEMAN, lawyer; b. Detroit, Apr. 3, 1918; s. Henry and Eva (Klayman) G.; m. Beatrice Wiener, May 31, 1919. BA, Wayne State U., 1938; JD, U. Mich., 1941; LLM, NYU, 1948. Bar: Mich. 1941, N.Y. 1947, Conn. 1948. Assoc. Herman H. Copelon, New Haven, Conn., 1948-50; assoc. Greenbaum, Wolff & Ernst, N.Y.C., 1950-54; ptnr. Rosenman & Colin, N.Y.C., 1955-82; counsel, 1991—; bd. dirs. Scrambler, Inc.; mem. vis. com. U. Miami Sch. Marine and Atmospheric Sci.; mem. adv. com. Great Neck Sr. Citizen Ctr. Co-author: Estate Tax Techniques; grad. editor, tax law reviewer, 1946-47. Village Justice, Kings Point, N.Y., 1985—; assoc. trustee North Shore U. Hosp., Manhasset, N.Y., Humanity in Action, Rosenstiel Found., Mandeville Found., World Rehab. Fund.; bd. trustees N.Y. Found., 1967-83. Served to maj. U.S. Army, 1941-45. Democrat. Jewish. Home: 24 Cow Ln Kings Point NY 11024-1517 Office: Rosenman & Colin LLP 575 Madison Ave Fl 26 New York NY 10022-2585

GREENBAUM, STUART I., economist, educator; b. N.Y.C., Oct. 7, 1936; s. Sam and Bertha (Freimark) G.; m. Margaret E. Wache, July 29, 1964; children—Regina Gail, Nathan Carl. BS, NYU, 1959; Ph.D., Johns Hopkins U., 1964. Fin. economist Fed. Res. Bank of Kansas City, Mo., 1962-66; sr. economist Office of the Comptroller of the Currency, Washington, 1966-67; assoc. prof. econs. U. Ky., Lexington, 1968-74, prof., 1974-76, chmn. dept. econs., 1975-76; vis. prof. fin. Kellogg Grad. Sch. Mgmt., Northwestern U., Evanston, Ill., 1974-75, prof. fin., 1976-78, Harold L. Stuart prof. banking and fin., 1978-83, Norman Strunk disting. prof. fin. instns., 1983-95, dir. Banking Research Ctr., 1976-95, assoc. dean for acad. affairs, 1988-92; dean John M. Olin Sch. of Bus. Washington U., St. Louis, 1995—; cons. Fed. Res. Bank Chgo., 1994-95; mem. Fed. Savs. and Loan Adv. Coun., 1986-89; vis. prof. banking and fin. Leon Recanati Grad. Sch. Bus. Adminstrn., Tel Aviv (Israel) U., 1980-81. Assoc. editor Nat. Banking Rev., 1966-67, So. Econ. Jour., 1977-79, Jour. Fin., 1977-83, Jour. Banking and Fin., 1980-92, Jour. Fin. Rsch., 1981-87, Fin. Rev., 1985-89, Managerial and Decision Econs., 1989-94, Jour. Econs., Mgmt. and Strategy, 1991-95; founding and mng. editor Jour. Fin. Intermediation, 1989-96. With U.S. Army, 1958-64. Mem. Am. Econ. Assn., Am. Fin. Assn. Office: Washington U Campus Box 1133 One Brookings Dr Saint Louis MO 63130-4899

GREENBERG, AARON ROSMARIN, public relations executive; b. Bklyn., July 5, 1932; s. J. George and Etta (Rosmarin) G.; m. Felice Barmash, June 29, 1958; children: Beth Susan, Marc David. BA in Journalism, Emory U., 1954; MS in Journalism, Columbia U., 1955; postgrad., NYU, 1964-65. Editor Fairchild Pubs., N.Y.C., 1955-56; account exec. Ruder & Finn, Inc., N.Y.C., 1958-61, dir. research, 1963-72; dir. pub. Yeshiva U., N.Y.C., 1961-62; dir. research Am. Stock Exchange, N.Y.C., 1972; v.p. William G. Hetherington & Co., Newark, 1973-78; pres. Livingston (N.J.) Pub. Relations, Inc., 1978—; instr. Fairleigh-Dickinson U., Madison, N.J., 1980-81; sports corr. West Essex Tribune, Livington, N.J., 1981-92. Contbg. editor Book of Knowledge, Ency. Britannica. Mem. adv. commn. on Cable TV, Livingston, 1978-81, adv. commn. on energy, Livingston, 1981-83, adv. commn. transp., Livingston, 1983-85; chmn. adv. council parks & recreation, Livingston, 1985—. Served to sgt. U.S. Army, 1956-58. Mem. Livingston C. of C. (dir.). Jewish. Avocation: high school and amateur sports officiating. Office: Livingston Pub Rels Inc PO Box 82 Livingston NJ 07039-0082

GREENBERG, ALAN COURTNEY (ACE GREENBERG), stockbroker; b. Wichita, Kans., Sept. 3, 1927; s. Theodore H. and Esther (Zeligson) G.; m. Kathryn Olson, June 27, 1987; children: Lynn, Theodore. Student, U. Mo., 1949. With Bear Stearns & Co., N.Y.C., 1949—, gen. ptnr., 1958—, chmn. bd., CEO, 1978-93, chmn. exec. com., sr. mng. dir., 1993—. Winner Nat. Bridge Championship, 1977; recipient Horatio Alger award, 1997. Mem. Soc. Am. Magicians, Harmonie Club, Bond Club, Deep Dale Club. Office: Bear Stearns Co. 245 Park Ave New York NY 10017-2500

GREENBERG, ALBERT, art director; b. N.Y.C., Mar. 15, 1924; s. Samuel David and Mary (Miller) G.; m. Marilyn Hoffner, May 29, 1949; children: Doren Roe, Peter Cooper. BFA, Cooper Union, 1958. Art editor Gentry, Am. Fabric Mags., N.Y.C., 1951-56; art dir. Gentlemen's Quar. Mag., Esquire, Inc., N.Y.C., 1956-70; sales promotion art dir. Lampert Agy., N.Y.C., 1970-71; v.p., sales promotion art dir. Wells Rich Greene Inc., N.Y.C., 1971-83; chmn. dept. comms. design Parsons Sch. Design, N.Y.C., 1983-94; tchr. Pratt Inst., 1964-65, 73-74, Cooper Union, 1967-68, Finch Coll., 1973-75, Manhattanville Coll., 1974-75, Parsons Sch. Design, 1975-82. Contbg. editor: Typographic Directions, 1964, Advertising Directions, Photography, 1962, Advertising Directions, Visual Advertising, 1961. Trustee Cooper Union, 1979-82. Served with USAAF, 1943-45, ETO. Decorated air medal with silver oak leaf cluster; recipient more than 100 profl. awards, including Gold Medal, Art Dirs. Club, 1979, Pres.'s citation for profl. achievement Cooper Union, 1982; named Alumnus of Yr., Cooper Union, 1968. Mem. Art Dirs. Club N.Y. (designer 43d ann.), Cooper Union Alumni Coun. (1st v.p. 1970-71, pres. 1971-73).

GREENBERG, ALLAN, advertising and marketing research consultant; b. N.Y.C., Dec. 8, 1917; s. Solomon and Rose (Honik) G.; m. Rosalie Katz, Nov. 7, 1943; children—Barbara L. Gutman, Roy J. B.S., CCNY, 1942; postgrad., U. Wis., 1944, New Sch. for Social Research, 1946-54. Assoc. Psychol. Corp., N.Y.C., 1937-38; research analyst Serutan, Inc., Jersey City, 1939-41; research mgr./asst. dir. research Grey Advt., Inc., N.Y.C., 1948-55; sr. v.p., dir. research and planning Doyle Dane Bernbach, Inc., N.Y.C., 1955-74; research cons. to advt. agys. and mfrs., 1974—; former chmn. tech. rsch. com. Advt. Rsch. Found.; former pres. joint coun. Empire Blue Cross/Blue Shield-HMO. Author: (with Mary Joan Glynn) A Study of Young People; booklet, 1966; contbr. articles to profl. jours. Former pres. mems. coun. Cmty. Health Program Queens-Nassau; mem. Profls. and Execs. in Retirement Group at Hofstra U. With AUS, 1942-45. Lodge: B'nai Zion (past mem. nat. exec. bd.; past pres. L.I. region). Home and Office: 5333 Zelzah Ave Apt 140 Encino CA 91316-2207

GREENBERG, ARLINE FRANCINE, artist, photographer; b. N.Y.C.; m. Sidney Greenberg. BA, Hunter Coll.; postgrad., NYU; AS, Parson Sch. Design, Pratt Inst. Ind. practice cons. firm in jewelry and design; v.p. Reliable Textile Co., N.Y.C.; fashion dir. Burlington Klopman Fabrics, N.Y.C., 1988-92; guest lectr. AWED and F.I.T. Contbr. fashion articles to newspapers. Recipient Medal in Fine Arts; scholar NYU. Mem. AATT, AWARE, Fashion Group, Fashion News Workship, The Info. Exch.. Avocations: travel, art, architecture, opera, music. Home: 555 Kappock St Apt 15D Riverdale NY 10463-6458

GREENBERG, ARNOLD ELIHU, water quality specialist; b. Bklyn., Apr. 13, 1926; s. Samuel and Minnie (Gurevitz) G.; m. Shirley E. Singer, Aug. 2, 1952; children: Noah J., Seth M. BS, CCNY, 1947; MS, U. Wis., 1948; SM, MIT, 1950; postgrad., U. Calif., Berkeley, 1970-75. Rsch. engr., biologist U. Calif., Berkeley, 1950-54; asst. chief labs. Calif. Dept. Health Svcs., Berkeley, 1954-82; lab. mgr. East Bay Mcpl. Utility Dist., Oakland, Calif., 1982-91; cons., 1991—; instr. in engring. extension U. Calif., 1963—; instr. Contra Costa Coll., San Pablo, Calif., 1968-82; cons. Lawrence Berkeley Lab., 1973-84; vis. fellow Israel Inst. Tech., Haifa, 1981. Editor: Standard Methods for the Examination of Water and Wastewater, 1971, 75, 81, 85, 89, 92, 95, 98, Laboratory Procedures for the Examination of Seawater & Shellfish, 1985. Col. USPHS, 1955—. Recipient APHA award for excellence, 1993. Mem. APHA, Am. Acad. Microbiology, Am. Water Works Assn. (hon.).

GREENBERG, BARRY MICHAEL, talent executive; b. Bklyn., Nov. 9, 1951; s. Aaron Herbert and Alice Rhoda (Strauss) G.; m. Susan Kay Greenberg, Feb. 19, 1990; 1 child, Samuel Jacob; 1 child by previous marriage: Seth Grahame-Smith. BA, Antioch U. Dir. B'nai B'rith, Phila., 1976-80; acting dir. Jewish Nat. Fund, L.A., 1980-81; chmn. Celebrity Connection, Beverly Hills, Calif., 1981—; co-founder Beverly Hills Air Force Co.; ptnr. U.S. Film Force Co. Emeritus mem. Air Force adv. bd. USAF; mem. Wilshire cmty. police adv. bd. L.A. Police Dept.; fin. co-chair, past chair Cmty.-Police Adv. Bd. Summit; mem. 50th Anniversary of WWII com. U.S. Dept. Def.; mem. pub. safety steering com. L.A. 4th Councilmanic Dist.; mem. exec. bd. CDC Bus. Responds to AIDS program; co-founder Windsor Watch; adv. bd. Windsor Sq. Assn.; charter past pres. entertainment industry unit B'nai B'rith. With USAF, 1969-75. Recipient Chief of Chaplains Meritorious Svc. award, USAF. Mem. Def. Orientation Conf. Assn., Air Force Pub. Affairs Alumni Assn. Jewish. Avocations: pilot, music. Office: Celebrity Connection 4311 Wilshire Blvd # 300 Los Angeles CA 90010-3713

GREENBERG, BERNARD, entomologist, educator; b. N.Y.C., Apr. 24, 1922; s. Isidore and Rose (Gordon) G.; m. Barbara Muriel Dickler, Sept. 1, 1949; children: Gary, Linda, Deborah, Daniel. B.A., Bklyn. Coll., 1944; M.A., U. Kans., 1951, Ph.D., 1954. Asst. prof. biology U. Ill. Med. Center, Chgo., 1954-61; asso. prof. U. Ill. Med. Center, 1961-66, prof., 1966-90, prof. emeritus, 1990—; vis. sci. Istituto Superiore di Sanitá, Rome, 1960-61, Fulbright-Hays sr. research scholar, 1967-68; vis. sci. Instituto de Salubridad y Enfermedades Tropicales, Mexico City, 1962, 63; cons. in field; cons., expert witness in forensic entomology; pres. Bioconcern; nat. lectr. Sigma Xi Hon. Sci. Rsch. Soc., 1996—. Author: Flies and Disease, vol. 1, 1971, vol. 2, 1973; contbr. articles to profl. jours. Served with USAF, 1944-46. NSF grantee, 1959-60, 79-81; NIH grantee, 1960-67; U.S. Army Med. Research and Devel. Command grantee, 1966-72, 85; Electric Power Research Inst. grantee, 1976-85; Office Naval Research grantee, 1977-78. Fellow AAAS; mem. Entomol. Soc. Am., AAAS, Chgo. Acad. Sci. (sci. gov. 1981—),. Home: 1463 E 55th Pl Chicago IL 60637-1875 Office: Dept Biol Scis M/C 066 U Ill Chgo Chicago IL 60607

GREENBERG, BONNIE LYNN, music industry executive; b. Roslyn Heights, N.Y., May 22, 1956; d. Morris U. Greenberg and Rozlyn (Wilner) Sadkin. BA, U. Denver, 1975; JD, Southwestern U., 1978. Bar: Calif. 1979, N.Y. 1980. Lawyer ABC Records, Inc., L.A., 1977-79; dir. bus. affairs MCA Records, Inc., Universal City, Calif., 1980-83, Paramount Pictures, 1984; co-chmn. Media MusiCons., L.A., 1988-93; CEO Ocean Cities Entertainment, Inc., Santa Monica, Calif., 1993—; judge anti-drug video contest N.Y. Dept. Edn., 1988; prof. UCLA. Author: Negotiating Contracts in the Entertainment Industry, 1987, Music Volume; theatre prodr.: Getting Through the Night, 1985; music. supr. motion pictures include Hairspray, Book of Love, Menace II Society, The Mask, Corrina, Corrina, The Santa Clause, Flirting with Disaster, Dead Presidents, The Truth about Cats and Dogs, The Long Kiss Goodnight, My Best Friend's Wedding, Pleasantville, Parent Trap, The Muse, EdTV, The Grinch That Stole Christmas. Atty. Bet Tzedek, L.A., 1987. Recipient Gov's. plaque N.Y., 1988. Democrat. Avocations: photography, sports, writing, languages, music.

GREENBERG, BRADLEY SANDER, communications educator; b. Toledo, Aug. 3, 1934; s. Abraham and Florence (Cohen) G.; m. Delight Thompson, June 7, 1959; children: Beth, Shawn, Debra. B.A. in Journalism; Univ. scholar, Bowling Green State U., 1956; M.S. in Journalism; Univ. fellow, U. Wis., 1957, Ph.D. in Mass Communication, 1961. Postdoctoral fellow Mass. Comms. Rsch. Ctr., 1960-61; research asso. Inst. Communication Research, Stanford U., 1961-64; asst. prof. Mich. State U., East Lansing, 1964-66; assoc. prof. Mich. State U., 1966-71, prof. dept. communication, 1971—, Univ. Disting. prof., 1990, chmn. dept., 1977-84, prof. telecommunication, 1975—, chmn. dept., 1984-90; vis. prof. U. Calif., Berkeley, 1992; sr. fellow East-West Ctr., Comms. Inst., Honolulu, 1978-79, 81; rsch. fellow Ind. Broadcasting Authority, London, 1985-86; cons. Pres.'s Commn. on Causes and Prevention Violence, 1968-69, Surgeon Gen.'s Sci. Adv. Com. on TV and Social Behavior, 1970-72, 82. Author: The Kennedy Assassination and the American Public: Social Communication in Crisis, 1965, Use of Mass Media by the Urban Poor, 1970, Life on Television, 1980, Mexican Americans and the Mass Media, 1983, Cableviewing, 1988, Teletext in the U.K., 1988, Mass Media, Sex and the Adolescent,1993, Desert Storm and the Mass Media, 1993. Served to maj. U.S. Army Res., 1973. Recipient Chancellors award for disting. svc. in journalism U. Wis., 1978, disting. faculty award Mich. State U., 1979; named to Journalism Hall of Fame Bowling Green State U., 1980; rsch. grantee NIH, NSF, USPHS, Carnegie Corp., Hoso Bunka Found., Nat. Assn. Broadcasters. Fellow Internat. Comm. Assn. (pres. 1994-95); mem. Assn. for Edn. in Journalism, Phi Kappa Phi (pres. 1993-94). Home: 2049 Ashland Ave Okemos MI 48864-3603 Office: Mich State U Dept Telecommunication 477 Communication Arts Sci East Lansing MI 48824-1212

GREENBERG, BRUCE LOREN, health facility administrator; b. Youngstown, Ohio, Dec. 22, 1956; s. Milton and Frances (Yoffee) G. BA, Miami U., Oxford, Ohio, 1978; MPA, Pa. State U., 1979. Health care mgr. Cin. Group Health Assocs., 1980-84; gen. mgr. Health Am. of Ohio, Cin., 1984-85; v.p. ops. Metlife Healthcare, Cin., 1986-87; exec. dir. Lincoln Nat. Health Plan, Portland, Maine, 1987-92; regional v.p. Am. Biodyne, Indpls., 1992-93; sr. v.p. Gemini Cons. Group, Chgo., 1993-94; pres., CEO Ptnrs. Health Plan, South Bend, Ind., 1994—. Office: Ptnrs Nat Health Plans Ind Inc 100 E Wayne St Ste 502 South Bend IN 46601-2354*

GREENBERG, BYRON STANLEY, newspaper and business executive, consultant; b. Bklyn., June 17, 1919; s. Albert and Bertha (Getleson) G.; m. Helena Marks, Feb. 10, 1946; children: David, Eric, Randy. Student, Bklyn. Coll., 1936-41. Circulation mgr. N.Y. Post, 1956-62, circulation dir., 1962-63, bus. mgr., 1963-72, gen. mgr., dir., 1973-79; sec., dir. N.Y.. Post Corp., 1966-75, treas., dir., 1975-76, v.p., 1976-81; v.p., dir. Leisure Systems, Inc., 1978-80; pres., chief exec. officer, dir. Games Mgmt. Services, Inc., 1979-80. Bd. dirs. 92d St YMHA, 1970-71, Friars Nat. Found., 1981-82. Served with AUS, 1942-45. Mem. Friars Club. Home and Office: 2560 S Grade Rd Alpine CA 91901-3612

GREENBERG, CAROLYN PHYLLIS, anesthesiologist, educator; b. San Francisco, July 7, 1941. AB, Stanford U., 1962; MD, U. Calif., San Francisco, 1966. Diplomate Am. Bd. Anesthesiology. Rotating intern L.A. County Hosp., 1966-67; resident in anesthesiology Presbyn. Hosp., N.Y.C., 1967-69, vis. fellow in anesthesiology, 1969-70, asst. attending anesthesiologist, 1971-90, assoc. attending anesthesiologist, 1990-99, med. dir. ambulatory surgery, 1986-96, attending anesthesiologist, 1999—; asst. attending anesthesiologist N.Y. Hosp., 1970-71; instr. anesthesiology Cornell Med. Sch., 1970-71; assoc. anesthesiology Columbia U., N.Y.C., 1971-74, asst. prof. clin. anesthesiology, 1974-90, assoc. prof. clin. anesthesiology, 1990-99, dir. ambulatory anesthesia, 1996—, prof. clin. anesthesiology, 1999—. Contbr. book chpts., articles to profl. jours. Mem. Am. Soc. Anesthesiologists, N.Y. State Soc. Anesthesiologists (Media award 1992), Med. Soc. N.Y., Soc. Ambulatory Anesthesia (treas. 1994-98, 2nd v.p. 1998-99, 1st v.p. 1999—, Ambulatory Anesthesia Rsch. Found. award 1992), Malignant Hyperthermia Assn. of U.S. (hotline cons. 1983—, partnership award 1996). Jewish. Avocations: swimming, reading, piano, travel. Office: Presbyn Hosp Dept Anesthesiology 622 W 168th St New York NY 10032-3720

GREENBERG, DANIEL HERBERT, lawyer; b. N.Y.C., Dec. 30, 1919; s. Moses Bernard and Sadye (Saltzman) G.; m. Jane Marian Frank, Jan. 22, 1943 (div. Apr. 1964); 1 child, Stanley Frank (dec.); m. Patricia Joy Williams, Aug. 29, 1964 (div. Jan. 1975); children: Dale Jeremy, Jason Bernard, Andrea Elizabeth, Nicole Victoria. BA, U. Wis., 1941; JD, Columbia U., 1947. Bar: N.Y. 1947, U.S. Supreme Ct. 1953, D.C. 1957. Asst. U.S. atty. U.S. Dept. Justice, N.Y.C., 1949-53; pvt. practice, N.Y.C., 1953—; spl. commr. in admiralty U.S. Dist. Ct. (so. dist.) N.Y., 1959-64; guest lectr. in trial practice Columbia Law Sch., 1965-66. Lt. col. USAF and Res., 1941-79, World War II, Korea. Decorated Disting. Flying Cross, Air medal with three clusters, eight battle stars, Disting. Unit citation with one cluster, Cert. of Valor, 15th Air Force, Italy, 1944. Democrat. Jewish. Home: 77 Renchy St Fairfield CT 06430-4129 Office: 36 W 44th St Ste 1206 New York NY 10036-8102

GREENBERG, DANIEL JEREMY, computer game producer; b. Staten Island, N.Y., Jan. 1, 1962; s. David L. and Anne N. Greenberg. BFA in Theatre, George Mason U., 1985. Art dir. Unlimited, Ltd., Virginia Beach, Va., 1979-81; game designer Fairfax, Va., Washington, 1982-88; pres. Paradyme Prodns., Washington, 1988—; tech. writer The Washington Post, 1995—; lectr. in field. Computer game designer: (CD-ROM) Star Control 3, 1996, Jumanji, 1996, Earth Explorer, 1994; multimedia producer: (CD-ROM) Cousteau's World, 1995; interactive script writer: (CD-ROM) Star Trek: Starfleet Academy, 1997, Vampire: The Masquerade Redemption, 1999. Mem. Computer Game Developers Assn. (corr. govt. affairs 1993—), Sci. Fiction Writers Am., Game Mfrs. Assn. Office: Paradyme Prodns 1325 Corcoran St NW Washington DC 20009-4310

GREENBERG, DANIEL LAWRENCE, lawyer; b. Bklyn., Oct. 14, 1945; s. Irving and Beatrice (Rabinowitz) G.; m. Karen R. Nelson, Apr. 4, 1987; children: Ilana Nelson-Greenberg, Mara Nelson-Greenberg. BA, Bklyn. Coll., 1966; JD, Columbia U., 1969; Hon. Fellow, U. Pa. Law Sch., 1996. Elem. tchr. N.Y.C. Pub. Sch. 208, 1969-71; atty. MFY Legal Svcs., N.Y.C., 1971-73, mng. atty., 1973-87; dir. clin. edn. Harvard U. Law Sch., Cambridge, Mass., 1987-94; pres./atty.-in-chief The Legal Aid Soc., N.Y.C., 1994—; bd. visitors CUNY Law Sch., Queens, 1989—, Columbia Law Sch., 1995—, Boston Coll. Law Sch., 1996—. Contbr. guest editls. N.Y. Times, Daily News, 1989-97. Bd. advs. The Workplace Project, Hempstead, N.Y., 1995—, programs on the legal profession of the Open Soc. Inst., 1997—, Stein ethics program, Fordham Law Sch., 1996—; mem. selection panel Root-Tilden Project NYU Law Sch., 1997. Recipient First Ann. Pub. Interest Honoree award Columbia U. Law Sch., 1991; Disting. Pub. Interest Lawyer in Residence award Touro Coll. Sch. of Law, 1998. Mem. Nat. Lawyers Guild (pres. NYC chpt. 1985-87), Assn. of the Bar of the City of N.Y., N.Y. County Lawyers, N.Y. State Bar Assn. Dem. Jewish. Home: 38 Montgomery Pl Brooklyn NY 11215-2324 Office: Legal Aid Soc 90 Church St New York NY 10007-2919

GREENBERG, DAVID BERNARD, chemical engineering educator; b. Norfolk, Va., Nov. 2, 1928; s. Abraham David and Ida (Frenkil) G.; m. Helen Muriel Levine, Aug. 15, 1959 (div. Aug. 1980); children—Lisa, Jan, Jill. BS in Chem. Engring., Carnegie Inst. Tech., 1952; MS in Chem. Engring., Johns Hopkins U., 1959; PhD, La. State U., 1964. Registered profl. engr., La. Process engr. U.S. Indsl. Chem. Co., Balt., 1952-55; project engr. FMC Corp., Balt., 1955-56; asst. prof. U.S. Naval Acad., Annapolis, Md., 1958-61; from instr. to prof. La. State U., Baton Rouge, 1961-74; prof. chem. engring. U. Cin., 1974—, head dept., 1974-81; program dir. engring. divsn. NSF, Washington, 1972-73, chem. and thermal scis. divsn., 1989-90; sr. scientist Chem. Sys. Lab., Dept. Army, Edgewood, Md., 1981-83; cons. Burk & Assocs., New Orleans, 1970-78. Contbr. numerous articles on chem. engring. to profl. jours. Mem. Cin. Mayor's Energy Task Force, 1981—. Served to lt. USNR, 1947-52. Esso research fellow, 1964-65, NSF fellow, 1961. Fellow Am. Soc. for Laser Medicine and Surgery; mem. Am. Inst. Chem. Engrs., Am. Chem. Soc., Am. Soc. for Engring. Edn., Sigma Xi, Tau Beta Pi, Phi Lambda Upsilon. Jewish. Home: 8547 Wyoming Club Dr Cincinnati OH 45215-4243 Office: Univ Cin Dept Chem Engring PO Box 210171 Cincinnati OH 45221-0171

GREENBERG, DAVID ETHAN, communications consultant; b. N.Y.C., Oct. 8, 1949; s. Abraham M. and Norma B. (Jacovitz) G.; m. Kerri Shwayder, Apr. 24, 1983; children: Alison Leigh, Zachary Scott. BA cum laude, Columbia U., 1971; JD, Harvard U., 1975. Bar: Colo. 1975. Speechwriter Gov. Richard D. Lamm, Denver, 1977-78, legal counsel, 1978-79; dir. mktg. Colo. Ski Country U.S.A., Denver, 1979-82; sr. ptnr. GBSM, Denver, 1982—; adj. assoc. prof. U. of Colo., Denver, 1984-89. Columnist, The Denver Post, 1985-88. Spl. asst. to adminstr. for communications EPA, Washington, 1989; pres. Children's Mus. Denver, 1988; vice chair Colo. Ocean Journey Aquarium, 1994—; mem. Colo. Commn. Higher Edn., 1993—; trustee Clayton Coll. Found. Nat. Merit Scholar, N.Y.C., 1967; White House fellow, 1988-89. Office: GBSM Inc 535 16th St Denver CO 80202-4235*

GREENBERG, DONALD P., engineering educator. B of Computer Sci., Cornell U., 1958, PhD in Structural Engring., 1968. Cons. engr. Severud Assocs., 1960-65; Jacob Gould Schurman prof. computer graphics Cornell U., Ithaca, N.Y., 1968—, dir. computer graphics program, 1968—; guest prof. ETH, Zurich, 1970-71; vis. prof. Yale U.; dir. Nat. Sci. and Tech. Ctr. for Computer Graphics and Sci. Visualization. Mem. IEEE, NAE (NCSA educator award), Assn. Computing Machinery (Steven A. Coons award 1987), Internat. Assn. Med. and Biol. Environment. Fax: 607-255-0806. Office: Cornell U 580 Rhodes Hall Ithaca NY 14853-3801*

GREENBERG, DOUGLAS STUART, educator; b. Jersey City, Jan. 11, 1947; s. Charles and Birdy (Neuman) G.; m. Margee G. Michaels, June 21, 1970. BA, Rutgers U., 1969; MA, Cornell U., 1971, PhD, 1974. Asst. prof. history Lawrence U., 1973-78; lectr. Princeton U., 1978-82, assoc. dean faculty, 1982—, prof. history, 1978-86; vis. prof. Rutgers U., 1987-93; v.p. Am. Council Learned Socs., N.Y.C., 1986-93; pres. and dir. Chgo. Hist. Soc., 1993—. Guggenheim fellow, 1979; Nat. Endowment Humanities fellow, 1976; Huntington Library fellow, 1980; recipient N.Y. State Hist. Assn.

Manuscript award, 1974. Mem. Am. Soc. Legal History, Am. Hist. Assn., Orgn. Am. Historians, ACLU, Am. Assn. Mus., Nat. Coun. Pub. History, Am. Assn. State and Local History. Author: Crime and Law Enforcement in Colony of New York, 1691-1776, 1976; Co-author; The American People: A History, 1981; co-editor: Colonial America: Essays Political and Social Development, 1993, Constitutionalism and Democracy, 1993, The Life of Learning, 1994; contbr. articles to profl. jours., chpts. to books. Home: 1454 Asbury Ave Evanston IL 60201-4171

GREENBERG, EDWARD SEYMOUR, political science educator, writer; b. Phila., July 1, 1942; s. Samuel and Yetta (Kaplan) G.; m. Martha Ann Baker, Dec. 24, 1964; children: Joshua, Nathaniel. BA, Miami (Ohio) U., 1964, MA, 1965; PhD, U. Wis., 1969. Asst. prof. polit. sci. Stanford (Calif.) U., 1968-72; assoc. prof. Ind. U., Bloomington, 1972-73; prof. U. Colo., Boulder, 1973—, dir. research program polit. and econ. change Inst. Behavioral Sci., 1980—, chair dept. polit. sci., 1985-88. Author: Serving the Few, 1974, Understanding Modern Government, 1979, Capitalism and the American Political Ideal, 1985, The American Political System, 1989, Workplace Democracy, 1986 (Dean's Writing award Social Scis. 1987), The Struggle for Democracy, 1993, 95, 97, 99, brief edit., 1996, 99; contbr. articles to profl. jours. Recipient fellowship In Recognition of Disting. Tchg., 1968, Jeffrey Pressman award Policy Studies Assn.; grantee Russell Sage Found., 1968, U. Wis., 1968, NSF, 1976, 82, 85, NIH, 1991-94, 96-2000. Mem. Internat. Polit. Sci. Assn., Am. Polit. Sci. Assn., Western Polit. Sci. Assn. (mem. exec. bd. 1986-89). Avocations: skiing, reading, bicycling, travel. E-mail: edward.greenberg@colorado.edu. Home: 755 11th St Boulder CO 80302-7512 Office: U Colo Inst Behavioral Sci PO Box 487 Boulder CO 80309-0487

GREENBERG, ELINOR MILLER, college official, consultant; b. Bklyn., Nov. 13, 1932; d. Ray and Susan (Weiss) Miller; m. Manuel Greenberg, Dec. 26, 1955; children: Andrea, Julie, Michael. BA, Mt. Holyoke Coll., 1953; MA, U. Wis.-Madison, 1954; EdD, U. No. Colo., 1981; LittD (hon.), St. Mary-of-the-Woods, Ind., 1983; LHD (hon.), Profl. Sch. Psychology, Calif., 1987. Exec. dir. Arapahao Inst. for Community Devel., Littleton, Colo., 1969-71; founding dir. Univ. without Walls, Loretto Heights Coll., Denver, 1971-79, asst. acad. dean, 1982-84, asst. to pres., 1984-85; regional exec. officer Coun. for Adult and Experiential Learning, Chgo., 1979-91; founding exec. dir. U.S. West Comm. CWA, Pathways to the Future, 1986-91; rsch. assoc. Inst. for Rsch. on Adults in Higher Edn., U. Md., U. College, 1991; exec. dir. project leadership, 1986—; pres., chief exec. officer EMG and Assocs.; sr. cons. U.S. West Found., No. Telecom, Rose Found., Cogeoinfo., 1992-96; cons. in field. Co-editor, contbr.: Educating Learners of All Ages, 1980; co-author: Designing Undergraduate Education, 1981, Widening Ripples, 1986, Leading Effectively, 1987, In Our Fifties: Voices of Men and Women Reinventing Their Lives, 1993; editor, contbr.: New Partnerships: Higher Education and the Nonprofit Sector, 1982, Enhancing Leadership, 1989, Liberal Education Journal, 1992; author: Weaving: The Fabric of a Woman's Life, 1991; guest editor Liberal Edn., 1992; feature writer Colo. Woman News, 1993-96, Women's Bus. News, 1995-96; contbr. Sculpting The Learning Organization, 1993; contbr. articles to profl. jours. Bd. dirs., exec. com. Anti Defamation League of B'nai B'rith, Denver, 1981, chair women's leadership com., 1991-93, bd. dirs., 1985-95, emeritus, 1995-99; mem. Colo. State Bd. for Community Colls. and Occupational Edn., 1981-86, vice chair, 1984-85; bd. dirs. Internat. Women's Forum, 1986-88, Internat. Women's Forum Leadership Found., 1991-95, Griffith Ctr., Golden, Colo., 1982-86, Colo. Bd. Continuing Legal and Jud. Edn., 1984-96; pres. Women's Forum of Colo., 1986; v.p. Women's Forum Colo. Found., 1987; mem. adv. bd. Anchor Ctr. Blind Child, Colo. Coalition Prevention Nuclear War, Mile Hi Girl Scouts, Nat. Conf. on Edn. for Women's Devel., Community Adv. Bd. Colo. Woman News, adv. com. Colo. Pvt. Occupational Sch., 1990-98; co-chair Gov.'s Women's Econ. Devel. Taskforce, Women's Econ. Devel. Coun., 1988-96; mem. bd. visitors U. Hosp., U. Colo., 1990-91, gov. apptd. Colo. Math., Sci. and Tech. Commn., chair, 1991-93, co-telecom. adv. commn. TAC 14, chair, 1993-95; founding steering com. Colo. Women's Leadership Coalition, 1988-96; U.S. Dept. of Edn., mem. Tech. Panels, 1991—, mem. Expert Panel on Lifelong Learning, 1999—, Western AHEC Reg. Learning System, chair, coursework com. Named Citizen of Yr., Omega Psi Phi, Denver, 1966, Woman of Decade Littleton Ind. Newspapers, 1970; grantee W. K. Kellogg Found., 1982, Weyerhaeuser Found., 1986, Fund for Improvement of Post Secondary Edn., 1977, 80; recipient Sesquicentennial award Mt. Holyoke Coll. Alumni Assn., 1987, Minoru Yasui Cmty. Vol. award, 1991, Women of Excellence award Colo. Women's Leadership Coalition, 1996, Founding Mothers award, 1997, Woman of Dist., Mile High Girl Scouts, 1997. Mem. Am. Assn. for Higher Edn., Assn. for Experiential Edn. (editorial bd. 1978-80), Nat. Conf. Women's Devel. Edn., Kappa Delta Pi. Democrat. Jewish. Home: 6725 S Adams Way Littleton CO 80122-1801

GREENBERG, GARY HOWARD, lawyer; b. N.Y.C., Mar. 2, 1948; s. Leo and Elizabeth P. (Weissman) G.; m. Sherri Snyder, June 21, 1987; children: Benjamin, Laura, Nicholas. BA, Johns Hopkins U., 1970; JD, N.Y.U., 1974. Bar: N.Y. 1975, U.S. Dist. Ct. (so. dist.) N.Y. 1975, U.S. Dist. Ct. (ea. dist.) N.Y. 1975, U.S. Ct. Appeals (2nd cir.) 1984. Assoc. Orans, Elsen & Lupert, N.Y.C., 1975-83, ptnr., 1983—; instr. trial acad. direct and cross exam. skills N.Y. County Lawyers' Assn.-Nat. Inst. of Trial Advocacy, 1995. Mem. ABA, Assn. of Bar of City of N.Y. (mem. com. on fed. legis. 1983-86), N.Y. State Bar Assn., N.Y. County Lawyers' Assn. (chair appellate cts. com. 1996-99). Office: Orans Elsen & Lupert 1 Rockefeller Plz New York NY 10020-2102

GREENBERG, GERALD STEPHEN, lawyer; b. Phila., July 27, 1951; s. Bernard and Elaine Alice (Shapiro) G.; m. Pamela Sue Meyers, Aug. 24, 1975; children: David Stuart, Allison Brooke. BA, Dickinson Coll., 1973; JD, Harvard U., 1976. Bar: N.Y. 1977, U.S. Dist. Ct. (so. dist.) N.Y. 1977, Ohio 1988. Assoc. Kaye, Scholer, Fierman, Hays & Handler, N.Y.C., 1976-86; atty. Exxon Corp., N.Y.C., 1986-87; assoc. Taft, Stettinius & Hollister LLP, Cin., 1987-89; ptnr. Taft, Stettinius & Hollister, Cin., 1990—. Mem. ABA, Assn. of Bar of City of N.Y., Cin. Bar Assn. Office: 1800 Firstar Tower 425 Walnut St Cincinnati OH 45202-3923

GREENBERG, HINDA FEIGE, library director; b. Bayreuth, Germany, Feb. 26, 1947; came to U.S., 1951; d. Samuel Leon and Sima (Schampagnere) F.; m. Joseph Lawrence, July 6, 1968; children: David Micah, Jacob Alexander. BA, Temple U., 1969; MLS, Rutgers U., 1981; PhD, Drexel U., 1999. Assoc. librarian Ednl. Testing Svc., Princeton, N.J., 1981-86; dir. info. ctr. Carnegie Found., Princeton, 1986-97; dir. info. svcs. Robert Wood Johnson Found., Princeton, 1997—. Assoc. editor Jour. Reading, Writing and Learning Disabilities, 1984-86. Mem. Princeton/Trenton Spl. Librs. Assn. (pres. 1985-86). Avocation: travel.

GREENBERG, INA FLORENCE, retired elementary education educator; b. N.Y.C., May 1, 1933; d. David Samuel and Nettie (Schapiro) Grossman; m. Ira Greenberg, Dec. 24, 1966 (dec. Dec. 1991); 1 child, Charles Joseph. BS in Edn., CCNY, 1955, MS in Edn., 1958. Cert. elem. tchr., N.Y. Tchr. elem. Pub. Sch. 2 Bronx, N.Y.C., 1955-69; tchr. writing Pub. Sch. 46 Bronx, N.Y.C., 1983-95; retired, 1995. Mem. Hadassh (Bay Club chpt., pres. Orah group Yonkers chpt. 1992-93), B'nai B'rith (Bay Club unit, pres. Lincoln Pk. chpt. 1977-79), Sigma Tau Delta. Avocation: creative writing.

GREENBERG, IRA ARTHUR, psychologist; b. Bklyn., June 26, 1924; s. Philip and Minnie (S.) G.; m. Martha Estella Cantrell, 1949 (div. 1950); m. Judith Linda Burgard-Rials, 1952 (div. 1954); m. Monita Ruth Niborod, 1961 (div. 1965). BA in Journalism, U. Okla., 1949; MA in English, U. So. Calif., 1962; MS in Counseling, Calif. State U. L.A., 1963; PhD in Psychology, Claremont (Calif.) Grad Sch., 1967; Grad. Marine Corps Inst.'s Command and Staff Coll., 1992. Editor, Ft. Riley (Kans.) Guidon, 1950-51; copy editor, reporter Columbus (Ga.) Enquirer, 1951-55; reporter Louisville Courier-Jour., 1955-56, L.A. Times, 1956-62; free-lance writer, L.A., Montclair, Camarillo, Calif., 1960-69, 76—; counselor Claremont Coll. Psychol. Clinic and Counseling Ctr., 1964-65; lectr. psychology Chapman Coll., Orange, Calif., 1965-66; psychologist Camarillo State Hosp., 1967-69, supervising psychologist, 1969-73, part-time clin. psychologist, 1973-93; part-time asst. prof. edn. San Fernando Valley State Coll., Northridge, Calif., 1967-69, lectr. psychodrama, social welfare U. Calif. Extension Div., Santa Barbara, 1968-69; vis. prof. edn. U. Nev., Reno, 1977—; vol. psychologist Free Clinic, L.A., 1968-70; staff dir. Calif. Inst. Psychodrama, 1969-71; tng. cons. Topanga Ctr. for Human Devel., 1970-75, bd. dirs., 1971-74, faculty Calif. Sch. Profl. Psychology, 1970-80; founder, exec. dir. Behavioral Studies Inst., mgmt. cons., L.A., 1970—; pvt. practice cons. in psychology, psychodrama, hypnosis, 1970—; founder, exec. dir. Psychodrama Ctr. for L.A., Inc., 1971—, Group Hypnosis Ctr., L.A., 1976—; producer, host TV talk show Crime and Pub. Safety, Century Comm., Channel 77, 1983—. Vol. humane officer State of Calif., 1979-89; res. officer L.A. Police Dept., 1980-86; bd. dirs. Humane Educators Coun., 1982-86, ; mem. Nat. Coun. Employer Support of Guard and Res., 1998—. With AUS 11th engr. combat bn., XXI Corps, Seventh Army, ETO, 1943-46; USAR, 1950-51; capt. Calif. State Mil. Res., 1986-93, maj. 1993—. Fellow Am. Soc. Clin. Hypnosis, Am. Soc. Group Psychotherapy and Psychodrama; mem. Am. Psychol. Assn., Calif. Psychol. Assn., L.A. County Psychol. Assn., So. Calif. Soc. Clin. Hypnosis (pres. 1977-78), Group Psychotherapy Assn. So. Calif. (pres. 1987-88), So. Calif. Psychotherapy Affiliation (dir. 1976-85), Am. Soc. Psychical Rsch., Assn. Rsch. and Enlightenment. Peace Officers Assn., L.A. County, Acad. TV Arts and Scis., Nat. Acad. Cable Programming, Fraternal Order of UDT/SEAL, Navy Amphibious Scouts and Raiders Assn., 11th Engr. Combat Battalion Assn., 78th Infantry Divsn. Assn., VFW, Am. Legion, Jewish War Vets., State Def. Forces Assn. Am., State Def. Forces Assn. Calif., Mensa, Am. Zionist Fedn., NRA, Calif. Rifle and Pistol Assn., SW Pistol League, Animal Protection Inst. Am., L.A. SPCA, Hebrew Nat. Orphan Home Alumni Assn., Sigma Delta Chi. Clubs: Sierra, Greater L.A. Press; B'nai B'rith; Beverly Hills Gun. Author: Psychodrama and Audience Attitude Change, 1968. Editor, author: Psychodrama: Theory and Therapy, 1974; Group Hypnotherapy and Hypnodrama, 1977. Office: BSI & Group Hypnosis Ctr 8939 S Sepulveda Blvd Ste 318 Los Angeles CA 90045-3605

GREENBERG, IRA GEORGE, lawyer; b. N.Y.C., May 8, 1946; s. Julius M. and Florence Greenberg; m. Linda Sharon Padell, Apr. 29, 1979; children: Amanda, Glenn. AB, Harvard U., 1968, JD, 1971. Bar: N.Y. 1972, D.C. 1980. Asst. to gen. counsel Office of Sec. of Army, Washington, 1971-74; assoc. Dewey Ballantine, N.Y.C., 1974-81; assoc. Summit Solomon & Feldesman and predecessor firms, N.Y.C., 1981-83, ptnr., 1983-92; ptnr. Edwards & Angell LLP, N.Y.C., 1992—. Capt. U.S. Army, 1971-74. Mem. ABA, Assn. Bar City N.Y. Democrat. Office: Edwards & Angell LLP 750 Lexington Ave Fl 12 New York NY 10022-1253

GREENBERG, IRVING, rabbi; b. Bklyn., May 16, 1933; s. Elias and Sonya G.; m. Blu Genauer, June 23, 1952; children: Jeremy, David, Deborah, Jonathan, Judith. BA summa cum laude, Bklyn. Coll., 1953; MA, Harvard U., 1954, PhD, 1960; PhD, Brandeis U., 1986. Ordained rabbi, 1953. Rabbi Riverdale Jewish Ctr., Riverdale, N.Y., 1965-72; assoc. prof. history Yeshiva U., N.Y.C., 1964-72, asst. prof. history, 1959-64; prof. dept. Jewish studies CUNY, 1972-79; pres. The Nat. Jewish Ctr. for Learning and Leadership, N.Y.C., 1974—; bd. dirs. Student Struggle for Soviet Jewry, SAR Acad., Riverdale, N.Y.C. Holocaust Meml. Commn., Mazon: A Jewish Response to Hunger, Fedn. Jewish Philanthropies, United Jewish Appeal of N.Y., CLAL - The Nat. Jewish Ctr. for Learning and Leadership, Am. Jewish World Svc., Am. Jewish Joint Distbn. Committed, Am. Assn. for Ethiopian Jewry, others. Author: The Jewish Way: Living the Holidays, 1988, Theodore Roosevelt and Labor: 1900-1918, 1988; co-editor: Confronting the Holocaust: The Impact of Elie Wiesel, 1978; contbr. articles to profl. jours. Recipient Rothberg award, Hebrew U., 1990, Smolar award, 1983, Akiba award, 1991. Mem. Am. Acad. Religion, Am. Jewish Hist. Soc., Assn. for Jewish Studies, Religious Edn. Assn., Religious Rsch. Assn., Rabbinical Coun. of Am. Office: CLAL 99 Park Ave # C300 New York NY 10016-1601

GREENBERG, JACK, lawyer, law educator; b. N.Y.C., Dec. 22, 1924; s. Max and Bertha (Rosenberg) G.; m. Sema Ann Tanzer, 1950 (div. 1970); children: Josiah, David, Sarah, Ezra; m. Deborah M. Cole, 1970; children: Suzanne, William Cole. AB, Columbia U., 1945, LLB, 1948, LLD, 1984; LLD, Morgan State Coll., Central State Coll., 1965, Lincoln U., 1977, John Jay Coll. Criminal Justice, 1983, De Paul U., 1994. Bar: N.Y. 1949. Rsch. asst. N.Y. State Law Revision Commn., 1949; asst. counsel NAACP Legal Def. and Ednl. Fund, 1949-61, dir.-counsel, 1961-84; argued in sch. segregation, sit-in, employment discrimination, poverty, capital punishment, other cases before U.S. Supreme Ct.; adj. prof. Columbia U. Law Sch., 1970-84, prof., vice dean, 1984-89; dean Columbia Coll., 1989-93; prof. Columbia U. Law Sch., 1993—; cons. Ctr. Applied Legal Studies, U. Witwatersrand, 1978; vis. lectr. Yale U. Law Sch., 1971; vis. prof. CCNY, 1977, Tokyo U., 1993-94, 99, St. Louis U. Law Sch., 1994, Lewis and Clark Law Sch., 1994-98, Princeton U., 1995, U. Munich, 1998; lectr. Harvard U. Law Sch., 1983, Shikes fellow, 1981; Disting. lectr. humanities Columbia Coll. Phys. and Surg., 1998. Author: (with H. Hill) Citizens Guide to Desegregation, 1955, Race Relations and American Law, 1959, Judicial Process and Social Change, 1976, (with James Vorenberg) Dean Cuisine or the Liberated Man's Guide to Fine Cooking, 1990, Crusaders in the Courts, 1994; contbg. author: Race, Sex and Religious Discrimination in International Law, 1981; contbr. articles to legal jours. Bd. dirs. N.Y.C. Legal Aid Soc., Internat. League for Human Rights, Mex.-Am. Legal Def. Fund, 1968-75, Asian Am. Legal Def. Fund, 1980—, Human Rights Watch, 1978-98, NAACP Legal Def. and Ednl. Fund. Co-recipient Grenville Clark prize, 1978; hon. fellow U. Pa. Law Sch., 1975. Fellow Am. Coll. Trial Lawyers; mem. ABA (commn. to study FTC, adv. com. to spl. com. on crime prevention, sect. on individual rights and responsibilities, Silver Gavel award, Thurgood Marshall prize), N.Y. State Bar Assn. (exec. dir. spl. com. study state antitrust laws 1956), Am. Law Inst., Bar Assn. City N.Y. (Cardozo lectr. 1973) Adminstrv. Conf. U.S. Home: 118 Riverside Dr New York NY 10024-3708 Office: Columbia Law Sch 435 W 116th St New York NY 10027-7297

GREENBERG, JACK M., food products executive; b. 1942; s. Edith S. Scher; m. Donna; children: David, Ilyse, Allison. BSc in Acctg., DePaul U., Chgo., 1964, JD, 1968. Bar: Ill; CPA, Ill. With Arthur Young & Co., 1964-82; chief fin. officer, exec. v.p. McDonald's Corp., Oakbrook, Ill., 1982—; vice chmn., chief fin. officer McDonald's Corp., Oak Brook, Ill., CFO, exec. v.p., 1982, vice chmn., CFO, 1992, bd. dirs., pres & ceo, 1997—, chmn & ceo, 1999—; bd. dirs. Arthur J. Gallagher & Co., Chgo., Harcourt Gen., Boston. Bd. dirs. DePaul U., IIT, Kent Coll. Law. Mem. AICPA, Ill. Inst. Cert. Pub. Accts. Office: McDonald's Corp 1 Mcdonalds Plz Oak Brook IL 60523-1928*

GREENBERG, JACOB, biochemist, educator, consultant; b. Haifa, Israel, Mar. 10, 1929; came to U.S., 1961; s. Shlomo and Temima (Angelovitch) G.; m. Esther Kahana, May 19, 1957; children: Abraham, Daphne. PhD, Hebrew U., Jerusalem, 1958. Assoc. rsch. biochemist biochem. dept. NYU, 1962-67, assoc. rsch. scientist Sch. Medicine, 1969-71; assoc. rsch. scientist Mt. Sinai Med. Sch., N.Y.C., 1967-68; asst. prof. N.Y. Med. Coll., 1972-76; dir. R&D quality assurance Advanced Biofactures, N.Y.C., 1971-83; dir. R&D Protos, N.Y.C., 1983—; cons. Columbia U., N.Y.C., 1965-67. Contbr. articles to profl. jours. Mem. White House Inner Cir., Washington, 1984-93, Autistic Soc. NIH fellow, 1961-62, grantee, 1972-76. Mem. AAUP, Internat. Congress Biochemistry, Am. Chem. Soc. (grantee 1967), N.Y. Acad. Scis. Avocations: swimming, chess, writing. Office: Protos Co 13016 Francis Lewis Blvd Jamaica NY 11413-1841

GREENBERG, JERROLD SELIG, health education educator; b. N.Y.C., Jan. 19, 1942; s. David and Bess G.; m. Karen Lider, Aug. 29, 1970; children: Todd, Keri. BS, CCNY, 1964, MS, 1965; EdD, Syracuse U., 1969. Tchr. N.Y.C. and Syracuse Pub. Sch. Dists., 1964-67; instr. Syracuse U., 1968-69; asst. prof. Boston U., 1969-71; prof. health edn. SUNY, Buffalo, 1971-79, U. Md., 1979—; presenter in field. Author: Student Centered Health Instruction: A Humanistic Approach, 1978, Health Through Discovery, 1980, 83, 86, 89, Sexuality Education: Theory and Practice, 1981, 88, 94, Comprehensive Stress Management, 1983, 6th edit., 1999, Sexuality: Insights and Issues, 1986, 89, 93, Physical Fitness: A Wellness Approach, 1986, 89, Stress and Sexuality, 1987, Health Education: Learner-Centered Instructional Strategies, 1989, 95, 98, Coping with Stress: A Personal Guide, 1990, The College Student's Health Self-Care Diary, 1991, Exploring Health, 1992, Your Personal Stress Profile and Activity Workbook, 1992, 96, The Health Education Ethics Book, 1992, The Caregiver's Guide, 1992, Holt Health, 1994, 2d edit., 1999, Physical Fitness and Wellness, 1995, 98, Wellness: Creating a Life of Health and Fitness, 1997, Exploring the Dimensions of Human Sexuality, 2000; assoc. editor Jour. of Sch. Health, 1978-80, Jour. Health Edn., 1991-94; contbg. editor Health Education, 1974-76; exec. prodr. stress mgmt. videotapes and synchronized audiotapes/slides, 1985; author: (software) Stress Management: Taking Control of Your Life, 1990; contbr. articles to profl. jours. With U.S. Army, 1967. Grantee Western N.Y. chpt. Am. Heart Assn., 1977-78; Research Found. of SUNY, 1979-80, Met. Life Found., 1985-86. Fellow AAHPERD (alliance scholar), Am. Sch. Health Assn. (Disting. Svc. award), mem. APHA, Assn. Advancement Health Edn. (presdl. citation, Profl. Svc. to Health Edn. award, Scholar award, Thomas Ehrlich Faculty award, Vol. of Yr. award), Soc. Pub. Health Edn., Eta Sigma Gamma. Jewish. Home: 9412 Reach Rd Rockville MD 20854-2852 Office: U Md College Park MD 20742

GREENBERG, JOSEPH H., anthropologist, linguist; b. Bklyn., May 28, 1915; s. Jacob and Florence (Pilzer) G.; m. Selma Berkowitz, Nov. 23, 1940. AB, Columbia, 1936; PhD in Anthropology, Northwestern U., 1940, DSc (hon.), 1982. Faculty U. Minn., 1946-48; asst. prof. Columbia, 1948-53, asso. prof., 1953-57, prof. anthropology, 1957-62; prof. Stanford, 1962-85, Ray Lyman Wilbur prof. social scis. in anthropology, 1971; dir. Nat. Def. Edn. Act. African Lang. and Area Center, 1967-78; Vis. prof. Summer Linguistic Inst., Mich. U., 1957, U. Minn., 1960; mem. panel anthropology and philosophy and history of sci. NSF, 1959-61; vis. prof. summer inst. U. Colo., 1961; dir. West African Langs. Survey, 1959-66; Linguistic Soc. Am. prof. Summer Linguistic Inst., Oswego, N.Y., 1976; Collitz prof. Summer Linguistic Inst., Stanford, 1987, coord. Stanford Project on Language Universals. Author: Languages of Africa, 1963, Essays in Linguistics, 1957, Universals of Language, 1963, Influence of Islam on a Sudanese Religion, 1946, Anthropological Linguistics: An Introduction, 1968, Language, Culture and Communication: Essays by Joseph H. Greenberg, 1971, Language Typology, 1974, A New Invitation to Linguistics, 1977, Universals of Human Language, 4 vols, 1978, Language in the Americas, 1987, On Language: The Selected Writings of Joseph H. Greenberg, 1990; co-editor: Word, 1950-54. Served with Signal Intelligence Corp. AUS, 1940-45. Social Sci. Rsch. Coun. fellow Northwestern U., 1940; Stanford humanities fellow, 1982-83; Ford Found. grantee, 1952, 57-62; fellow Ctr. Advanced Study in Behavioral Scis., Stanford U., 1959-60, 65-66; recipient Demobilization award Social Sci. Rsch. Coun., 1945-46; Guggenheim award, 1954-55, 58-59, 82-83; Haile Selassie award for African rsch., 1967; award in behavioral scis. N.Y. Acad. Scis., 1980. Mem. Am. Anthrop. Assn. (rep. to gov. bd. Internat. Inst. 1955—, 1st distinguished lectr. 1970), Linguistic Soc. Am. (exec. com. 1953-55, v.p. 1976, pres. 1977), West African Linguistics Soc. (chmn. 1965-66), African Studies Assn. (exec. com., also com. on langs. and linguistics 1959—, pres. 1964-65), Nat. Acad. Scis., Am. Acad. Arts and Scis. (Talcott Parsons prize for social sci. 1997), Am. Philos. Soc., Phi Beta Kappa. Home: 860 Mayfield Ave Stanford CA 94305-1051

GREENBERG, JOSHUA F., lawyer, educator; b. Bklyn., Feb. 27, 1933; s. Emil and Betty (Fierer) G.; m. Reva Frances Messeloff, June 28, 1959; children: Elizabeth, James, Anne. BA, Columbia U., 1954, LLB, 1956. Bar: N.Y. 1956. Assoc. firm Kaye, Scholer, Fierman, Hays & Handler, N.Y.C., 1956-65; ptnr. Kaye, Scholer, Fierman, Hays & Handler, 1966-96; chmn. advanced antitrust workshop Practising Law Inst., N.Y.C., 1969-98; adj. prof. in residence Sch. Law Pace U., White Plains, N.Y., 1997—; adj. prof. NYU Law Sch., N.Y.C., 1970-87. Pres. Camp Ella Fohs, N.Y.C., 1965-85; trustee Beth Israel Med. Ctr., N.Y.C., 1986—; chmn. Mapplethorpe Residential Treatment Facility, 1995—. Recipient Disting. Trustee award United Hosp. Fund, 1998. Mem. ABA (council antitrust law sect. 1981-85), N.Y. State Bar Assn. (chmn. antitrust law sect. 1971). Jewish.

GREENBERG, LENORE, public relations professional; b. Flushing, N.Y.; d. Jack and Frances Orenstein. BA, Hofstra U.; MS, SUNY. Dir .pub. rels. Bloomingdale's, Short Hills, N.J., 1977-78; dir. comms. N.J. Sch. Bds. Assn., Trenton, 1978-82; dir pub. info. N.J. State Dept. Edn., Trenton, 1982-90; assoc. exec. dir. Nat. Sch. Pub. Rels. Assn., Arlington, Va., 1990-91; pres. Lenore Greenberg & Assocs., Inc., 1991—; adj. prof. pub. rels. Rutgers U. Freelance feature writer N.Y. Times. Mem. bd. assocs. McCarter Theatre, Princeton, N.J.; mem. Franklin Twp. Zoning Bd. Adjustment; mem. Franklin Twp. Human Rels. Commn.; chair Somerset County LWV; instr. Bus. Vols. for the Arts. Recipient award Am. Soc. Assn. Execs., award Women in Comms., award Internat. Assn. Bus. Communicators; Gold Medallion awrd Nat. Sch. Pub. Rels. Assn. Mem. Pub. Rels. Soc. Am. (accredited; pres. N.J. State chpt., nat. nominating and accreditation coms., Silver Anvil award), Nat. Health/Edn. Consortium. Home and Office: 30971 Carrara Rd Laguna Niguel CA 92677-2757

GREENBERG, LON RICHARD, energy company executive, lawyer; b. N.Y.C., Sept. 4, 1950; s. Ralph Austin and Miriam (Kenner) G.; m. Bonnie Small, June 25, 1972; children: Jody B. Scott B., Daniel A. BS, U. Pa., 1972; JD, Villanova U., 1975; postgrad., Harvard U., Boston, 1994. Bar: Pa. 1975. Law clk. to Hon. J. Sydney Hoffman, Superior Ct. Pa., Phila., 1975-76; assoc. Morgan, Lewis & Bockius, Phila., 1976-80; corp. devel. counsel UGI Corp., Valley Forge, Pa., 1980-82, corp. sec., 1982-87, v.p., gen. counsel, 1983-87, v.p. legal and corp. devel., 1987-89, sr. v.p. legal and corp. devel., 1989-94, pres., 1994-95, pres., CEO, 1995-96, chmn., pres., CEO, 1996—, also bd. dirs.; bd. dirs. AmeriGas Propane, Inc., chmn., CEO 1996—; bd. dirs. Valley Forge, Mellon PSFS, Phila. Bd. dirs., mem. audit com. Reading Is Fundamental, Washington, 1995—; mem. policy com. Pa. Bus. Roundtable, Harrisburg, 1995—; bd. trustees Chestnut Hill Healthcare; mem. nat. indsl. adv. coun. Industrialization Ctrs. Am.; former mem. task force com. United Way Leadership Giving Southeastern Pa., Phila.; mem. and coach Chestnut Hill Fathers Club, Phila.; adv. bd. Ea. Pa. chpt. Arthritis Found. Recipient Good Samaritan award N.W. Victim Svcs., 1994, Disting. Svc. award Chestnut Hill Cmty. Assn., 1994. Mem. ABA, Pa. Bar Assn. Avocations: swimming, tennis, golf, family activities. Office: UGI Corp 460 N Gulph Rd King Of Prussia PA 19406

GREENBERG, MARC L., education educator; b. L.A., Nov. 9, 1961; s. Howard A. and Suzanne (Blau) G.; m. Marta Pirnat-Greenberg, July 6, 1988; children: Benjamin C., Lea H. BA, UCLA, 1983; MA, U. Chgo., 1984; PhD, U. Calif., L.A., 1990. Asst. prof. U. Kans., Lawrence, 1990-95, assoc. prof., 1995—. N.Am. editor Slovenski jezik/Slovene Linguistic Studies jour., Ljubljana, Slovenia, Lawrence, Kans., 1994—; contbr. articles to profl. jours. Humanities Rsch. fellow Hall Ctr., U. Kans., Lawrence, 1994; Univ. Tchrs.' fellow NEH, Washington, 1993; Tchg. fellow Am. Coun. Learned Soc., Washington, 1990; rsch. fellow Fulbright-Hayes, Washington, 1988-89; Zahvala/Gratitude award Govt. of Rep. Slovenia, Ljubljana, 1992. Mem. Soc. Slovene Studies (exec. coun. 1994-97), Am. Assn. Advancement of Slavic Studies, Am. Assn. Tchrs. of Slavic and East European Langs., East European Anthropology Group, Assn. Croatian Studies, Phi Beta Kappa. E-mail: m-greenberg@ukans.edu. Home: 4209 Wheat State St Lawrence KS 66049-3585 Office: U Kans Slavic Dept 2134 Wescoe Hall Lawrence KS 66045-2174

GREENBERG, MARTIN JAY, lawyer, educator, author; b. Milw., Aug. 5, 1945; s. Sol and Phyllis (Schunder) G.; m. Beverly L. Young, Apr. 29, 1969; children: Kari, Steven. BS, U. Wis., 1967; JD, Marquette U., 1971. Bar: Wis. 1971. Assoc. Hoyt, Greene & Meissner, Milw., 1971-74, Weiss, Steuer, Berzowski & Kriger, Milw., 1974-76; ptnr. Greenberg & Boxer, Milw., 1976-78; pvt. practice, Milw., 1978—; asst. prof. law Marquette U., Milw., 1976-79, adj. prof., 1979—; vis. prof. Anglia Law Sch., Chelmsford, Eng., 1996; bd. dirs., pres. Law Projects, Inc.; mem. book revisions com. Wis. Real Estate Examining Bd., 1978—. Author: Real Estate Practice, 1976, rev. edit., 1977, Wisconsin Real Estate, 1982, Mortgages and Real Estate Financing, 1982, Real Estate Tax Guide, 1988, 90, Sports Biz, 1989, Sports Law Practice, 1993, Stadium Game, 1996; editor: Marquette Law Rev., 1969-71. Mem. brotherhood bd. Congregation Emanu-El B'ne Jeshurun, Milw., 1976-78, treas., 1979—; Water trustee Village of Bayside, 1995; bd. dirs. Community Coordinated Child Care, Milw., 1976-77, Project Re-Unite, Am. Jewish com., Jewish Nat. Fund, 1988—, v.p.; sec. Project Re-Unite; mem. Shorewood (Wis.) Bd. Rev., 1977-81; sec. Wis. Sports Authority, Inc.; dir. Nat. Sports Law Inst. Marquette U., Badger States Games; bd. mem. Wis. Sports Corp., Milw. Symphony Orchestra; athletic bd. dirs. Marquette U. With Wis. N.G., 1968-74. Morris Guten Vets. scholar, 1965, I.E. Goldberg scholar, 1966; Carnegie grantee, 1966; Wis. Student Assn. scholar, 1967, Thomas More scholar, 1969, Francis X. Swietlik scholar, 1971. Mem. ABA, Wis. Bar Assn., Milw. Bar Assn. (named Lawyer of Yr.-Legal Scholar 1988), Wis. Bar Found. (lectr. Project Inquiry 1980-81, Lawyer's Pro Bono

Publico award 1978, sec. Marquette U. athletic bd. 1990-93), Marquette U. Law Alumni Assn. (trustee), Jewish Vocat. Svc. (corp.), Woolsack Soc., Scribes, Tau Epsilon Rho (chancellor grad. chpt. 1972-73), Masons, Alpha Sigma Nu (Woolsack Soc. award, 1971). Home: 9429 N Broadmoor Rd Milwaukee WI 53217-1310

GREENBERG, MARVIN, retired music educator; b. N.Y.C., June 24, 1936; s. Samuel and Rae (Sherry) G.; B.S. cum laude, N.Y. U., 1957; M.A., Columbia U., 1958, Ed.D., 1962. Tchr. elem. schs., N.Y.C., 1957-63; prof. music edn. U. Hawaii, Honolulu, 1963-93, prof. emeritus, 1993, ret., 1993, rsch. cons. Ctr. for Early Childhood Rsch., 1969-71; edn. adminstr. Model Cities project for disadvantaged children Family Svcs. Ctr., Honolulu, 1971-72. Cons. western region Volt Tech. Svcs., Head Start program, 1969-71; Head Start worker, 1972-75; Child Devel. Assoc. Consortium rep., 1975—. Recipient several fed. and state grants for ednl. rsch. and curriculum projects. Mem. Hawaii Music Educators Assn., Music Educators Nat. Conf., Soc. for Rsch. in Music Edn., Coun. for Rsch. in Music Edn. Author: Teaching Music in the Elementary School: Guide for ETV Programs, 1966; Preschool Music Curriculum, 1970; Music Handbook for the Elementary School, 1972; Staff Training in Child Care in Hawaii, 1975; Your Child Needs Music, 1979, Teachers' Guides Honolulu Symphony Children's Concerts, 1980-93; also over 100 articles. Home: 2575 Kuhio Ave # 19-2 Honolulu HI 96815-3971

GREENBERG, MAURICE RAYMOND, insurance company executive; b. N.Y.C., May 4, 1925; s. Jacob and Ada (Rheingold) G.; m. Corinne Phyllis Zuckerman, Nov. 12, 1950; children: Jeffrey W., Evan G., L. Scott, Cathleen J. Pre-law cert., U. Miami, Fla., 1948; LLB, N.Y. Law Sch., 1950, also JD (hon.); JD (hon.), New Eng. Sch. Law, 1970, Bryant Coll., Middlebury Coll., Brown U., Pace U. Bar: N.Y. 1953. With Continental Casualty Co., 1952-60; joined Am. Internat. Group Inc., N.Y.C., 1960—, pres. subs. Am. Home Assurance Co., 1962-67, pres., CEO, 1967—, chmn. bd., CEO, 1989—; mem. Bus. Roundtable, pres.'s adv. com. Trade Policy and Negotiations; vice-chmn. Ctr. for Strategic and Internat. Studies; chmn. U.S.-China Bus. Coun.; vice-chmn. Coun. on Fgn. Rels.; founding chmn. U.S.-Philippine Bus. Com.; chmn. emeritus NYH, 1995; bd. govs. N.Y. Hosp. Bd. govs. N.Y. Hosp.; mem. Pres.'s adv. com. on trade negotiations Ctr. for Strategic and Internat. Studies, mem. bus. roundtable. Capt. U.S. Army, ETO, Korea. Decorated Bronze Star. Mem. N.Y. Bar Assn., The Asia Soc. (chmn.), Police Athletic League, City Athletic Club, Sky Club, India House, Lotos Club, Harmonie Club, Georgetown Club (washington). Office: Am Internat Group Inc 70 Pine St New York NY 10270-0002

GREENBERG, MICHAEL JOHN, biologist, editor; b. N.Y.C., Sept. 28, 1931; s. Abraham S. and Lena (Kirsch) G.; m. Rima Robbins, June 10, 1954; children: Peter A. (dec.), John K., Karl P. AB, Cornell U., 1953; MA, Fla. State U., 1955; PhD, Harvard U., 1958. Instr. zoology U. Ill., Urbana, 1958-60, asst. prof., 1960-64; assoc. prof. biol. scis. Fla. State U., Tallahassee, 1965-73, prof., 1973-81, dir. marine lab., 1978-80; dir. Whitney Lab. U. Fla., St. Augustine, 1981-96, prof. pharmacology Coll. Medicine, 1981—; vis. prof. Hiroshima (Japan) U. Med. Sch., 1978; vis. prof. zoology U. Hong Kong, 1981; instr. exptl. invertebrate zoology Marine Biol. Lab., Woods Hole, Mass., summers 1969-73, course dir., 1975-77; mem. adv. screening com. Internat. Exch. Scholars, 1976-78; mem. regulatory biology panel NSF, 1983-85; chmn. com. on opportunities for advancement of marine biotech. in U.S., NRC, 1994-99; mem. internat. organizing com. Internat. Marine Biotech. Conf. 2000, 1998—. Mem. editl. bd. Jour. Exptl. Zoology, 1974-77, 83-85, Comparative Gen. Pharmacology, 1970, Physiol. Zoology, 1975-85, Molecular and Cellular Neurobiology, 1979-84, Marine Biology Letters, 1979-84, Comparative Biochemistry and Physiology C, 1992-96; mem. editl. bd. Biol. Bull., 1986-89, editor-in-chief, 1989—. Grantee Nat. Heart and Lung Inst., NIH, 1960-97, NSF, 1987-90; NSF sr. postdoctoral fellow U. Melbourne, Australia, 1964-65, Misaki Marine Lab., Japan, 1965; recipient MERIT award Nat. Heart, Lung & Blood Inst., 1987. Fellow AAAS (mem.-at-large sect. G com. 1979-83); mem. Am. Soc. Zoologists (divsn. program officer 1969-70, divsn. chmn. 1976-77, co-chmn. joint task force with Am. Physiol. Soc. 1977-78), Am. Soc. Pharmacology and Exptl. Therapeutics, Soc. Gen. Physiologists, Marine Biol. Lab., Woods Hole, Tallahassee, Sopchoppy and Gulf Coast Marine Biol. Assn. (pres. 1967—). Home: 2 St Andrews Ct Saint Augustine FL 32084-3620 Office: Whiney Lab Univ Fla 9505 Ocean Shore Blvd Saint Augustine FL 32086-8610

GREENBERG, MILTON, corporation executive; b. Carteret, N.J., Apr. 21, 1918; s. David and Eva (Salzer) G.; m. Maxine Carol Baer, June 30, 1948; children: Eve Diane, David Max, Alan Baer. Student, CCNY, 1934-40; B.A., NYU, 1943; M.P.A., Harvard U., 1954; Sc.D. (hon.), Canaan Coll., 1961, Merrimack Coll., North Andover, Mass., 1981; D.H.L. (hon.), U. Lowell, 1985. Research and devel. planner Air Force Cambridge Research Center, 1947-49, dep. dir. operations and planning Geophysics Research div., 1947-54, dir. Geophysics Research Directorate, 1954-58; pres. GCA Corp., 1958-84, chmn., chief exec. officer, 1958-86; First chmn. tech. mgmt. council Air Research and Devel. Command, 1957-58; U.S. del. to XIth Gen. Assembly, Internat. Union Geodesy & Geophysics, 1957; mem. Upper-Air Rocket & Satellite Research Panel; mem. central radio propagation lab. adv. panel of NAS, 1963-1968; mem. exec. com. Mass. Tech. Park Corp., 1982-88, also bd. dirs. Editor-in-chief Planetary and Space Science, 1957-62; mem. editorial adv. bd. 1962-75. Bd. dirs. Mass. High Tech. Council, 1978-87, mem. exec. com., 1981-86, Tucson Temple Emanu-El, 1989-97, pres., 1991-95; bd. dirs. SAGE Soc., U. Ariz., 1997—; Selectman Town of Andover, Mass., 1971-77; trustee Canaan (N.H.) Coll., 1960-72, Merrimack Coll., 1983-90. Served from cadet to maj. USAAF, 1943-47; geophysicist. Recipient Exceptional Civilian Service medal USAF, 1957. Fellow AIAA (assoc.), AAAS; mem. Sigma Xi, Mu Chi Sigma, Beta Lambda Sigma.

GREENBERG, MILTON, political scientist, educator; b. Bklyn., Feb. 20, 1927; s. Samuel and Fannie (Schnell) G.; m. Sonia B. Brown, June 20, 1948; children: Anne Greenberg Bookin, Nancy R. BA, Bklyn. Coll., 1949; MA, U. Wis., 1950, PhD (univ. scholar), 1955; LLD (hon.), Am. U., 1993. Instr. polit. sci. U. Tenn., Knoxville, 1952-55; from asst. prof. to prof. Western Mich. U., Kalamazoo, 1955-64; chmn. polit. sci. dept. Western Mich. U., 1965-69; dean Coll. Arts and Scis., Ill. State U., Normal, 1969-72; v.p. acad. affairs, dean faculties Roosevelt U., Chgo., 1972-80; provost, v.p. acad. affairs Am. U., Washington, 1980-93, prof. govt., 1980-97, interim pres., provost, 1990-91, prof. emeritus, 1997—; rsch. assoc. Cleve. Met. Svcs. Commn., 1957; cons. Citizens for Mich. (constl. reform movement), 1960; cons. Supreme Ct. Hist. Soc., 1997—, Coun. for Higher Edn. Accreditation, 1997—. Author: (companion book to PBS show) The GI Bill: The Law That Changed America, 1997, (with J.C. Plano) The American Political Dictionary, 1962, 10th edit., 1997; (with others) The Poltical Science Dictionary, 1973; contbr. to Collier's Yearbook, 1959-93; mem. editl. bd. Ednl. Record, 1985-97, guest editor, 1994; cons. editor ASHE-ERIC Higher Edn. Reports, 1986-90; contbr. articles to profl. jours. Mem. Mich. Gov.'s Commn. on Legis. Apportionment, 1962, Kalamazoo Community Rels. Bd., 1964-65; mem. bd. dirs. Combined Health Appeal of Nat. Capital Area, 1982-93, v.p., 1983-85, pres., 1986-88. Social Sci. Rsch. Coun. grantee, 1959, 61. Mem. Am. Polit. Sci. Assn., Midwest Polit. Sci. Assn. (exec. coun. 1972-75), Mid. States Assn. Colls. and Schs. (cons.-evaluator 1983-97), Law and Soc. Assn., AAUP, Am. Assn. Higher Edn. (vis. scholar 1994), North Ctrl. Assn. Colls. and Schs. (commn. on instns. higher edn. 1975-80, exec. bd. 1979-80, cons.-evaluator 1975-80), Nat. Coun. Chief Acad. Officers, Am. Coun. on Edn. (exec.com. 1983-85, chmn. 1985). Office: Am U 4400 Massachusetts Ave NW Washington DC 20016-8022

GREENBERG, MORTON IRA, federal judge; b. Philadelphia, Pa., Mar. 20, 1933; s. Harry Arnold and Pauline (Hofkin) G.; m. Barbara-Ann Kissel, May 29, 1987; children from first marriage: Elizabeth, Suzanne, Lawrence. AB, U. Pa., 1954; LLB, Yale U., 1957. Bar: N.J. 1958, U.S. Dist. Ct. N.J. 1958, U.S. Ct. Appeals (3d cir.) 1972, U.S. Supreme Ct. 1973. Law clk.office of atty. gen. State of N.J., Trenton, 1957-58, dep. atty. gen., 1958-60, asst. atty. gen., 1971-73; pvt. practice, Cape May, N.J., 1960-71; judge law div. Superior Ct. N.J., New Brunswick, 1973-76; judge chancery and gen. equity divs. Superior Ct. N.J., Trenton, 1976-80, judge appellate div., 1980-87; judge U.S. Ct. Appeals (3d cir.), Trenton and Phila., 1987—. Office: US Ct Appeals US Courthouse 402 E State St Ste 7050 Trenton NJ 08608-1598*

GREENBERG, MORTON PAUL, lawyer, consultant, insurance broker, underwriter; b. Fall River, Mass., June 2, 1946; s. Harry and Sylvia Shirley (Davis) G.; m. Louise Beryl Schindler, Jan. 24, 1970; 1 child, Alexis Lynn. BSBA, NYU, 1968; JD, Bklyn. Law Sch., 1971. Bar: N.Y. 1972; CLU Am. Coll., 1975. Atty. Hanner, Fitzmaurice & Onorato, N.Y.C., 1971-72; dir., counsel, cons. on advanced underwriting The Mfrs. Life Ins. Co., Toronto, Ont., Can., 1972-98; mng. gen. agt. Viaticus, Inc., Chgo., 1999—, Coventry Fin., Ft. Washington, Pa., 1999—; mem. sales ideas com. Million Dollar Roundtable, Chgo., 1982-83; 4th ann. George M. Graves meml. lectr., 1991; speaker on law, tax, lifetime settlements, and advanced underwriting to various profl. groups, U.S., Can. Author: (tech. jour.) ManuBriefs. Mem. ABA, N.Y. State Bar Assn., Assn. for Advanced Life Underwriting (mem. bus. ins. and estate planning steering com. 1989-93), Internat. Platform Assn., Nat. Assn. Life Underwriters, Soc. of Fin. Svcs. Profls., NYU Alumni Assn., Stern Sch. Bus. Alumni Assn. Office: PO Box 183 7617 E Sunrise Trail Parker CO 80134-6915

GREENBERG, MYRON SILVER, lawyer; b. L.A., Oct. 17, 1945; s. Earl W. and Geri (Silver) G.; m. Shlomit Gross; children: David, Amy, Sophie, Benjamin. BSBA, UCLA, 1967; JD, 1970. Bar: Calif., 1971, U.S. Dist. Ct. (middle dist.) Calif. 1971, U.S. Tax Ct. 1977; cert. splst. in taxation law bd. legal specialization State Bar Calif.; CPA, Calif. Staff acct. Touche Ross & Co., L.A., 1970-71; assoc. Kaplan, Livingston, Goodwin, Berkowitz, & Selvin, Beverly Hills, Calif., 1971-74; ptnr. Myron S. Greenberg, a Profl. Corp., Larkspur, Calif., 1982—; professorial lectr. tax. Golden Gate U.; instr. U. Calif., Berkeley, 1989—; mem. taxation law adv. commn. Calif. Bd. Legal Specialization, 1998—. Author: California Attorney's Guide to Professional Corporations, 1977, 79; bd. editors UCLA Law Rev., 1969-70. Mem. San Anselmo Planning Commn., 1976-77; mem. adv. bd. cert. program personal fin. planning U. Calif., Berkeley, 1991—. Mem. AHA (bd. dirs. Marin county chpt. 1984-90, pres. 1988-89), ABA, AICPAs, L.A. County Bar Assn., Marin County (Calif.) Bar Assn. (bd. dirs. 1994—, pres. 1999), Real Estate Tax Inst. Calif. Cont. Edn. Bar (planning com.), Larkspur C. of C. (bd. dirs. 1985-87). Democrat. Jewish. Office: # 205 700 Larkspur Landing Cir Larkspur CA 94939-1715

GREENBERG, NANCY WARD, school health consultant; b. Albuquerque, Mar. 8, 1942; d. John and Virginia (Williams) Ward; m. Paul M. Greenberg, Oct. 11, 1958; children: Lyle Jon, David Alan. BSN, U. N.Mex., 1966, MS, 1974. Cert. sch. nurse. Coord. health and nursing svcs. Albuquerque Pub. Schs., 1978-95; sch. health cons. Albuquerque, 1995—. Contbr. articles to profl. jours. Recipeint Ella Mae Small award, Student Nurse of Yr. award, Disting. Svc. award N.Mex. Sch. Nurses Assn. Mem. N.Mex. Sch. Health Assn. (sec., treas.), ANA, N.Mex. Nursing Assn., NASN (exec. bd.), Sigma Theta Tau (sec.), Phi Delta Phi.

GREENBERG, NAT, orchestra administrator; b. Warsaw, Poland, May 25, 1918; came to U.S., 1928; s. Henry and Polly (Lui) G.; m. Anne Goodhart, July 19, 1941; 1 child, Betty Jeanne. BS, CCNY, 1940. Pers. mgr. Kansas City (Mo.) Philharm., 1949-59; gen. mgr. Ft. Wayne (Ind.) Philharm., 1959-66, Rochester (N.Y.) Philharm., 1966-68; mgr. Columbus (Ohio) Symphony, 1968-76; mng. dir. San Antonio Symphony, 1976-82; mgr., producer Rio Grande Music Festival, 1976-82; mgr. Kansas City (Mo.) Symphony, 1982-85; symphony mgmt. cons., 1985—; cons. Nat. Endowment for Arts, N.Y. State Arts Coun., Ohio Arts Coun.; producer host, narrator of 4 weekly radio shows Adventures in the Arts. Bass player Pitts., Buffalo, Kansas City and N.Y. symphonies, 1940-59; author: (autobiography) Once More, Without Feeling, 1983; appeared in film Carnegie Hall. Mem. Internat. Soc. Performing Arts Adminstrs., Assn. Coll., Univ. and Community Arts Adminstrs., Am. Symphony Orch. League (bd. dirs.). Democrat. Jewish. Lodge: Rotary. Avocation: photography. Home and Office: 418 Forrest Hill Dr San Antonio TX 78209-3056

GREENBERG, NATHAN, accountant; b. Worcester, Mass., May 17, 1919; s. Samuel and Ida (Katz) G.; m. Mimi Aaron, Mar. 12, 1950 (dec.); children: Henry Aaron, Ruthanne; m. Barbara Rudnick, Feb. 9, 1979. B.S. in Bus. Adminstrn, Boston U., 1942. CPA, Mass. With IRS, 1945-47; v.p. finance, dir. Gt. Am. Plastics Co., Worcester, Mass., 1948-68, Gt. Am. Chem. Corp., Fitchburg, Mass., 1968-80; founder Greenberg, Rosenblatt, Kull & Bitsoli, P.C., Worcester, 1958—; bd. dirs. Xsirius, Inc., Kleinert's, Inc. Trustee Nathan and Barbara Greenberg Charitable Trust, Jewish Home for Aged, Jewish Community Center, Jewish Fedn. Served with AUS, 1942-45, ETO. Decorated Bronze Star. Fellow AICPA, Mass. Soc. CPA's, Fla. Soc. CPA's, Controllers Inst. Am.; mem. Mu Sigma. Home: 85 Aylesbury Rd Worcester MA 01609-1217 Office: The Day Bldg 306 Main St Worcester MA 01608-1550

GREENBERG, OSCAR WALLACE, physicist, educator; b. N.Y.C., Feb. 18, 1932; s. Joseph Jacob and Betty Greenberg; m. Yael Shapiro, May 27, 1969 (div. Apr. 1997); children: Joshua Daniel, Jeremy Hillel, Benjamin Gideon. B.S., Rutgers U., 1952; A.M., Princeton U., 1954, Ph.D., 1957. Instr. Brandeis U., 1956-57; NSF postdoctoral fellow MIT, 1959-61; mem. faculty U. Md., College Park, 1961—, prof. physics, 1967—; mem. Inst. Advanced Study, 1964-65; vis. assoc. prof. Rockefeller U., 1965-66; vis. prof. Tel-Aviv U., 1968-69, Johns Hopkins U., fall, 1977, NASA/Goddard Space Flight Center, spring 1978; vis. scientist Fermilab, 1984-85; vis. scholar U. Chgo., 1984-85. Divisional assoc. editor: Phys. Rev. Letters, 1976-78. Served to 1st lt. USAF, 1957-59. Recipient award in phys. scis. Washington Acad. Scis., 1971; Sloan research fellow, 1964-66; Guggenheim fellow, 1968-69. Fellow Am. Phys. Soc. Home: 9013 Breezewood Ter Apt 103 Greenbelt MD 20770-1076 Office: Univ Md Dept Physics College Park MD 20742-4111

GREENBERG, PAMELA THAYER, public policy specialist; b. Denver, May 16, 1959; d. Paul Burton and Betty Mae (Clint) Thayer; m. Alan Greenberg, Aug. 7, 1988. BA, U. Colo., 1981, MS, 1994. Rsch. asst. Nat. Assessment of Ednl. Progress, Denver, 1982-83; rsch. coord. Regis Coll., Denver, 1983-86; program prin. Nat. Conf. State Legislatures, Denver, 1986—. Author: Guide to Legislative Information Technology, 1995; contbr. articles to profl. jours. Named one of Outstanding Young Women of Am., 1984. Mem. LWV (bd. dirs. 1990-91). Office: Nat Conf State Legislatures 1560 Broadway Ste 700 Denver CO 80202-5176

GREENBERG, PAUL, newspaperman; b. Shreveport, La., Jan. 21, 1937; s. Ben and Sarah (Ackerman) G.; m. Carolyn Levy, Dec. 6, 1964; children: Daniel, Ruth Elizabeth. B. Journalism, U. Mo., 1958, M.A. in History, 1959; student, Columbia Grad. Sch., 1960-62; LittD, Rhodes Coll., 1995. Lectr. Am. history Hunter Coll., 1962; editorial page editor Pine Bluff (Ark.) Comml., 1962-66, 67-92; syndicated columnist, 1970—; editorial page editor Ark. Dem. Gazette, Little Rock, 1992—; editorial writer Chgo. Daily News, 1966-67; adj. faculty in history U. Ark., Pine Bluff, 1978-82, vis. Fulbright fellow, 1985, mem. faculty in journalism, U. Ark., 1991. Author: Resonant Lives, 1991, Entirely Personal, 1992, No Surprises, 1996. Served to capt. U.S. Army, 1969. Recipient Grenville Clark award for best editorial, 1964, Pulitzer prize editorial writing, 1969, award Nat. Newspaper Assn., 1968, U. Mo. Sch. Journalism award, 1983, Walker Stone award for editorial writing, 1985, 86; Pulitzer Prize finalist for editorial writing, 1986; H.L. Mencken Writing award, 1987; William Allen White Journalism award U. Kans., 1988, Green Eyeshade award, 1997. Jewish. Office: Arkansas Democrat Gazette Capitol at Scott Little Rock AR 72202

GREENBERG, PHILIP ALAN, lawyer; b. Bklyn., Aug. 2, 1948; s. Harry and Jeannette (Nataf) G. BA cum laude, Bklyn. Coll., 1970; JD, N.Y.U., 1973. Bar: N.Y. 1974, U.S. Dist. Ct. (ea. and so. dists.) N.Y. 1975, U.S. Ct. Appeals (2d cir.) 1975, U.S. Supreme Ct. 1977 N.J. 1988. Assoc. Kamerman & Kamerman, N.Y.C., 1973-78, ptnr., 1978-82; ptnr. Segal, Liling, Erlitz & Greenberg, N.Y.C., 1982, Segal, Liling & Greenberg, N.Y.C., 1982-84, Segal & Greenberg, N.Y.C., 1984; mng. ptnr. Segal, Post, DeMott & Crow, N.Y.C., 1985, Segal, Greenberg, McDonald & Maher, N.Y.C., 1985-86, Segal, Greenberg & McDonald, N.Y.C., 1986-87, Segal & Greenberg, N.Y.C., 1987-93, Bizar & Martin, N.Y.C., 1993-95; ptnr. Wallman Greenberg Gasman & McKnight, N.Y.C., 1995—; mem. faculty para legal Sobelsohn Sch. Trustee Congregation Emunath Israel, 1984—, chmn. law and ins. com., 1987—. Mem. ABA (com. mem., lit. mem.), N.Y. Bar Assn., Assn. of Bar of City of N.Y., Mason (Maimonides-Marshall #739, master), Masters & Wardens Assn. (past pres. 6th Manhattan 1990-91), Internat. Assoc. Tribune, Phi Alpha Delta. Democrat. Jewish. Home: 7 Francisco Ave Little Falls NJ 07424 Office: Wallman Greenberg Gasman & McKnight 350 5th Ave Ste 3000 New York NY 10118-3022

GREENBERG, PHILIP B., symphony orchestra conductor and music director. Asst. condr. Detroit Symphony, 4 yrs.; resident condr. Phoenix Symphony; music dir., condr. Fresno (Calif.) Philharm., Savannah (Ga.) Symphony, 1984—; founder Kuhlman Changer Orch., Wachovia Chamber Orch., Branigar Chamber Orch. series, Black Heritage concert, Pops series. Gave first pub. violin concert at age 15; numerous appearances as guest condr. throughout world, including New Zealand Symphony, Spain and Portugal, Moscow State Orch., Danish Radio Orch., Austin, El Paso and Va. symphonys, Colo. Music Festival, N.H. Music Festival; made Asian debut with Beijing Broadcasting Symphony. Recipient 1st prize and orch. prize Nicolas Malko Conducting Competition, Copenhagen. Fax: 912-234-1450. Office: Savannah Symphony Orch PO Box 9505 225 Abercorn St Savannah GA 31412*

GREENBERG, RAYMOND SETH, academic administrator, educator; b. Chapel Hill, N.C., Aug. 10, 1955; s. Bernard George and Ruth Esther (Marck) G.; m. Leah Daniella Dacus, Oct. 23, 1988. BA with highest honors, U. N.C., 1976, PhD, 1983; MD, Duke U., 1979; MPH, Harvard U., 1980. Asst. prof. sch. medicine Emory U., Atlanta, 1983-86, assoc. prof., 1986-90, dep. dir. Winship Cancer Ctr., 1985-90, chair epidemiology/ biostat., 1988-90, prof., dean sch. pub. health, 1990-95; v.p. for acad. affairs, provost Med. U. S.C., Charleston, 1995—; chair preventive medicine Nat. Bd. Med. Examiners, Phila., 1991-93; chair epidemiology study sect. NIH, Bethesda, Md., 1992-94; bd. sci. counselors Nat. Inst. for Dental and Craniofacial Rsch., Bethesda, 1994-99, mem. blue ribbon panel on rsch. tng. and career devel., 1999; chair adv. coun. Prudential Ctr. for Health Care Rsch., Atlanta, 1994-96; chair Harvard Adv. Com. on Electromagnetic Fields and Human Health, Boston, 1994—; adv. com. on rsch. and med. grants, Am. Cancer Soc., Atlanta, 1994-96; breast and cervical cancer early detection and control adv. com., Ctrs. for Disease Control and Prevention, Atlanta, 1996—; adv. com. on agrl. health risks, Harvard Ctr. for Risk Analysis, Boston, 1996—; clin. adv. bd. Deloitte and Touche Healthcare Consulting Group, 1997-99. Author: Medical Epidemiology, 1993, 2d edit., 1995, Epidemiologia Medica, 1995, 2nd edit., 1998; contbr. articles to profl. jours. Bd. dirs. Am. Cancer Soc. Ga. Divsn., 1987-93. Fellow Am. Coll. Epidemiology (pres. 1990-91); mem. APHA, Am. Statis. Assn., Am. Epidemiology Soc., Soc. Epidemiol. Rsch. Democrat. Jewish. Office: Med Univ SC Rm 200 H Admin Bldg 171 Ashley Ave Charleston SC 29425-0001*

GREENBERG, ROBERT E., lawyer; b. N.Y.C., Jan. 10, 1949, AB, CUNY, 1970; JD, U. Fla., 1972; LLM, Georgetown U., 1975. Bar: Fla. 1972, D.C. 1973, Md. 1978. Of counsel Friedlander, Misler, Friedlander, Sloan & Herz, Washington. Mem. D.C. Bar, Md. Bar, Fla. Bar. Office: Friedlander Misler Friedlander Sloan & Herz 1101 17th St NW Ste 700 Washington DC 20036-4711*

GREENBERG, ROBERT MILTON, retired psychiatrist; b. Silver Spring, Md., Oct. 24, 1916; s. Joseph and Rae (Levin) G.; m. Johanna Falletti, July 30, 1942 (dec. 1970); children: Roberta Rae, Harold Ellis; m. Jean Mildred Halpern, June 18, 1972; children: Susan, Elaine, Jill. AB, George Washington U., 1937, MD, 1941. Diplomate Am. Bd. Psychiatry and Neurology, Nat. Bd. Med. Examiners. Intern Sibley Meml. Hosp., Washington, 1941-42; resident, staff physician VA Hosp., Coatesville, Pa., 1946-51; pvt. practice psychiatry Chevy Chase, Md., 1951-93; faculty to assoc. clin. prof. psychiatry George Washington U., 1951-87; chief psychiatric cons. Hebrew Home of Greater Washington, 1951-81. Contbr. articles to medico-legal jour. Trauma. Lt. comdr. USNR, 1942-46. Fellow Am. Soc. Psychoanalytic Physicians (pres. 1968-69), Am. Psychiat. Assn. (life); mem. AMA, Wash. Psychiat. Soc., Am. Coll. Psychiatrists (emeritus), Jewish War Vets. (founder and trustee Silver Spring chpt.). Democrat. Jewish. Avocations: travel, reading, antiques. Home: 5600 Wisconsin Ave Apt 405 Chevy Chase MD 20815-4409

GREENBERG, SHELDON BURT, plastic and reconstructive surgeon; b. Bklyn., July 8, 1948; s. Morris and Lillian (Liss) G.; m. Andrea R. Levy, Feb. 10, 1991; children: Matthew, Joshua. BS, Muhlenberg Coll., 1970; MD, Chgo. Med. Sch., 1974. Diplomate Am. Bd. Otolaryngology, Plastic Surgery. Resident in surgery Lenox Hill Hosp., N.Y.C., 1974-75; resident in otolaryngology Met. Hosp., Manhattan Eye and Ear Hosp., N.Y.C., 1978; resident in plastic surgery Akron (Ohio) City Hosp., 1978-80, fellow in hand surgery, 1980; pvt. practice Norwalk, Conn., 1981—; chief, plastic surgery Norwalk Hosp., 1996—. Fellow Am. Coll. Surgeons, Am. Soc. Plastic and Reconstructive Surgeons; mem. Conn. Med. Soc., Fairfield County Med. Soc., Fairfield Men's Club. Republican. Jewish. Avocations: tennis, American history, gardening. Office: 40 Cross St Norwalk CT 06851-4647

GREENBERG, STEPHEN BARUCH, physician, educator; b. May 24, 1944. BA, Johns Hopkins U., 1966; MD, U. Md., 1970. Herman Brown tchg. prof. Baylor Coll. Medicine, Houston, 1990—, vice-chmn. dept. medicine, 1990—; chief medicine svc. Ben Taub Gen. Hosp., Houston, 1990—, assoc. chief staff, 1990—. E-mail: stepheng@bcm.tmc.edu. Office: One Baylor Plaza 559E Houston TX 77030

GREENBERG, STEPHEN MICHAEL, lawyer, businesss executive; b. Passaic, N.J., July 27, 1944; s. Joseph Louis and Bess S. (Stein) G.; m. Sandra Lafer, Sept. 1, 1967; children: Seth, Sindy, Scott. BA, Washington (Pa.) Jefferson Coll., 1965; JD with honors, George Washington U., 1968. Bar: U.S. Dist. Ct. N.J. 1968, U.S. Ct. Appeals (3d cir.) 1968, U.S. Dist. Ct. (no. dist.) Ind. 1972, N.Y. 1983. Exec. asst. U.S. atty. N.J. Justice Dept., Newark, 1970-71; ptnr. Robinson, Wayne & Greenberg, Newark, 1971-82; gen. ptnr. Lafer Mgmt. Corp., N.Y.C., 1989—; ptnr. Hellring, Lindeman, Goldstein, Siegel, Stern & Greenberg, Newark, 1983-90; chmn. bd. dirs., sec. Flex Holding Co., N.Y.C., 1985-88; chmn. bd. dirs., acting chief exec. officer Graphic Scanning Corp., Teaneck, N.J., 1986-88; ptnr. Stern & Greenberg, Roseland, N.J., 1990—; bd. dirs. Switchco, Inc., Teaneck, Israel Investors Corp., N.Y.C.; chmn. bd. dirs. Time and Space Processing Inc., Santa Clara, Calif. Nat. vice chmn. United Jewish Appeal, N.Y.C., 1986—; v.p. Am. Friends of Hebrew U., N.Y.C., 1986-89; apptd. to Op. Independence by Prime Minister of Israel, Jerusalem and N.Y., 1986—. Recipient Lehman Leadership award United Jewish Appeal, 1984. Mem. ABA, N.J. Bar Assn. (Outstanding Profl. Achievement award 1986). Democrat. Home: 616 S Orange Ave Maplewood NJ 07040-1047 Office: Stern & Greenberg 75 Livingston Ave Roseland NJ 07068-3701

GREENBERG, STEPHEN S., publishing executive; b. Catskill, N.Y., Mar. 16, 1956; s. Robert and Joan (Lerner) G.; m. Sarah Price, Feb. 14, 1987; children: Anne, Rachel. BA, Kent State U., 1979. Sports editor York (Pa.) Daily Record, 1980-83; asst. sports editor Columbus (Ohio) Citizen-Jour., 1983-85, Wichita Eagle-Beacon, 1985-86, Indpls. News, 1986-89; asst. mng. editor Gary (Ind.) Post-Tribune, 1993-95; sports editor Lafayette (Ind.) Jour. & Courier, 1989-93, Poughkeepsie (N.Y.) Jour., 1993; asst. mng. editor Indpls. Newspapers Inc., 1995-97, mgr. Star/News Direct Publs., 1997-99; v.p. product devel. Sales Cons. Internat., Roswell, Ga., 1999—; co-founder The Dreaming Dog Group lit. agy. Author: The Minor League Road Trip, 1990, 101 Little Known Facts about Troy Aikman, 1997, I Remember Woody, 1997, Ohio State '68: All the Way to the Top, 1998. Mem. Inland Daily Press Assn., Nat. Spl. Sect. Network. Office: Indpls Newspapers Inc 307 N Pennsylvania St Indianapolis IN 46204-1811

GREENBERG, STEVE, brokerage house executive. Pres. Alaron Trading Corp., Chgo. Office: Alaron Trading Corp 822 W Washington St Chicago IL 60607-2302*

GREENBERG, STEVEN MOREY, lawyer; b. Jersey City, Apr. 9, 1949; s. Joseph and Rhoda (Weisenfeld) G. AB cum laude, Syracuse U., 1971; JD, U. Pa., 1974. Bar: N.J. 1974, U.S. Dist. Ct. N.J. 1974, N.Y. 1980, U.S. Dist. Ct. (so. dist.) N.Y. 1986, U.S. Dist. Ct. (ea. dist.) N.Y. 1986, U.S. Ct. Appeals (3d cir.) 1987, U.S. Ct. Fed. Claims 1989. Assoc. Carpenter, Bennett & Morrissey, Newark, N.J., 1974-77, Cole, Berman & Belsky, Rochelle Park, N.J., 1977-79; pvt. practice Hackensack, N.J., 1979-94; atty. Bergenfield (N.J.) Rent Leveling Bd., 1985-89, 92-93, 1985-89, 92-93,

1999—; atty. Bergenfield Planning Bd., 1993-96; ptnr. Greenberg & Marmorstein, Hackensack, N.J., 1994-97, Greenberg & Lanz, Hackensack, N.J., 1997—. Trustee, past chmn. youth activities com. Jewish Ctr. of Teaneck, N.J., 1978—, mem. exec. com., 1992-97, v.p., 1992-94, pres., 1994-97; pres. Jewish Inst. of Bioethics, N.Y.C., 1998—; trustee, chmn., com. campus youth svcs., sub-com. planning and allocations United Jewish Appeal Fedn. Bergen County and N. Hudson, 1997—; dir., v.p. JH & RC Sr. Housing, Inc., Jersey City, 1991-94; past v.p., past sec. Sam Gorovoy Group Care Home for Sr. Adults, Bergenfield, N.J., trustee, 1983-96, pres., 1986-90; mem. adv. bd. dirs. Jewish Home and Rehab. Ctr., Jersey City and River Vale, N.J., 1982-90, chmn. pers. com., 1986—, governing body, 1986—, exec. com., 1987—, v.p., 1990—; trustee Jewish Family Svc., Inc., Bergen County, 1986-96, exec. com., 1990-96, treas., 1990-92, v.p., 1992-96; trustee The Solomon Schechter Day Sch. of Bergen County, 1986-87, Bergenfield Mus. Soc., 1989—; trustee Teaneck Jewish Meml. Assn., 1989—, v.p., 1990-92, pres., 1992—; mem. Jewish Community Rels. Coun. No. N.J., 1986-93, 99—; mem. N.J. regional adv. bd. Anti-Defamation League of B'nai B'rith, 1989—, exec. com., 1989—; mem. Jewish Community Coun. Teaneck, 1989-93; mem. cmty. advocacy program UJA (United Jewish Appeal) Fedn. of Bergen County and North Hudson Resource Coun., 1991—, dir., 1995—; dir. Union for Traditional Judaism, 1993-97. Recipient Second Century award Jewish Theol. Sem. Am., 1988. Mem. ABA, N.J. Bar Assn., Bergen County Bar Assn., N.Y. State Bar Assn., Assn. Transp. Practitioners, Phi Kappa Phi, Pi Sigma Alpha. Home: 96 Westminster Ave Bergenfield NJ 07621-3916 Office: 2 University Plaza Hackensack NJ 07601-6202

GREENBERG, WILLIAM MICHAEL, psychiatrist; b. Bklyn., Oct. 19, 1946; s. Benjamin Greenberg and Marilyn (Berger) Hamberg; m. Wendy Faith Megerman, June 14, 1992. BA, Queens Coll., 1968; postgrad., U. Medicine & Dentistry N.J., 1974-76; MD, Albert Einstein Coll. Medicine, 1978. Diplomate Am. Bd. Psychiatry and Neurology and bd. cert. in geriatic psychiatry, forensic psychiatry and addiction psychiatry; cert. clin. psychopharmacology. Computer programmer Western Electric Co., N.Y.C., 1970-73; rsch. asst. Bklyn. Jewish Hosp., 1973-74; resident in psychiatry Bronx (N.Y.) Mcpl. Hosp. Ctr., 1978-83, house staff pres., 1981-82; acting med. dir. Met. Ctr. for Mental Health, N.Y.C., 1983; staff psychiatrist Bronx Psychiat. Ctr., 1983-84; dir. psychiatry clinic North Cen. Bronx Hosp., 1984-88; psychiatrist, cons. Montefiore Mental Health Svcs. at Rikers Island, East Elmhurst, N.Y., 1985-86; pvt. practice Bronx, 1985-88; chief psychiatrist, attending staff mem. Bergen Pines County Hosp. (now Bergen Regional Med. Ctr.), Paramus, N.J., 1988-96, dir. of psychiat. rsch., 1993—, interim med. dir. psychiatry, 1996-98, dir. psychiatry residency tng. program, 1997—, mem. spkr.'s bur., 1988—, chmn. instnl. rev. bd., 1996—; pvt. practice, N.J., 1997—; asst. clin. prof. Albert Einstein Coll. Medicine, Bronx, 1988-90; vis. asst. prof. Med. Coll. Pa., 1990-94; adj. asst. prof. Med. Coll. Pa. and Hahnemann U., 1994—; prin. investigator for clin. drug trials. Asst. editor Community Psychiatrist, 1985-89; mem. editorial bd. Einstein Quar. Jour. Biology and Medicine, 1987—; contbr. articles to profl. jours.; reviewer profl. jours., books. Union rep. Com. Interns and Residents, N.Y.C., 1979-81; speaker's bur. Physicians for Social Responsibility, N.Y.C., 1982-84. Rock Sleyster Meml. scholar AMA, 1977; recipient Bergen Pines Psychiatry Residency Teaching award, 1991, Psychiatrist Recognition award N.J. Alliance for the Mentally Ill, 1996. Mem. AAAS, APHA, Am. Psychiat. Assn., Am. Assn. Cmty. Psychiatrists, Assn. for Advancement of Philosophy and Psychiatry, North Jersey Psychiat. Soc. (pres. 1998-99). Avocations: analytic philosophy, meditation, computers, photography. Office: Bergen Regional Med Ctr Divsn Psychiatry Paramus NJ 07652

GREENBERGER, ELLEN, psychologist, educator; b. N.Y.C., Nov. 19, 1935; d. Edward Michael and Vera (Brisk) Silver; m. Michael Burton, Aug. 26, 1979; children by previous marriage—Kari Edwards, David Silver. BA, Vassar Coll., 1956; MA, Harvard U., 1959, PhD, 1961. Instr. Wellesley (Mass.) Coll., 1961-63, asst. prof., 1963-67; sr. research scientist Johns Hopkins U., Balt., 1967-76; prof. psychology and social behavior U. Calif., Irvine, 1976—. Author: (with others) When Teenagers Work, 1986; contbr. articles to profl. jours. USPHS fellow, 1956-59; Margaret Floy Washburn fellow, 1956-58; Ford Found. grantee, 1979-81; Spencer Found. grantee, 1979-81, 87, 88-91. Fellow APA, Am. Psychol. Soc.; mem. Soc. Rsch. in Child Devel., Soc. Rsch. on Adolescent Devel. Office: U Calif 3340 Social Ecology II Irvine CA 92697-7085

GREENBERGER, ERNEST, lawyer; b. Sarospatak, Hungary, Mar. 16, 1923; came to U.S., 1939, naturalized, 1944; s. Solomon and Esther (Weinberger) G.; m. Stacia Pleva, May 17, 1956; children—James J., Daniel A. B.A., Roosevelt U., 1945; J.D., U. Chgo., 1947. Bar: Ill. 1948, U.S. Supreme Ct. 1959. Assoc. firm Lawrence, Goldberg, Lawrence & Lewin, Chgo., 1947-55; ptnr. Antonow & Fink, Chgo., 1955-62; mem. firm Greenberger, Krauss & Tenenbaum (now Schwartz, Cooper, Greenberger & Krauss), Chgo., 1962—; lectr. law U. Chgo. Downtown Center, 1960-61. Editor: U. Chgo. Law Rev, 1946-47. Bd. dirs. Am. Found. for Continuing Edn., 1953-65; bd. dirs. Jewish Community Centers Chgo., 1959-81, v.p., 1964-81; mem. Evanston Econ. Devel. Com., 1975-76. Mem. Am., Ill., Chgo. bar assns., Am. Arbitration Assn. (mem. nat. panel arbitrators 1962-75), Am. Coll. Real Estate Lawyers, Order of Coif. Democrat. Jewish. Club: Standard (Chgo.). Office: Schwartz Cooper Greenberger Krauss 180 N La Salle St Ste 2700 Chicago IL 60601-2757

GREENBERGER, HOWARD LEROY, lawyer, educator; b. Pitts., July 16, 1929; s. Abraham Harry and Alice (Levine) G.; m. Bette Jo Bergad, June 15, 1959. BS magna cum laude, U. Pitts., 1951; JD cum laude, NYU, 1954; diploma in law (Fulbright scholar), Oxford (Eng.) U., 1955. Bar: Pa. 1955, D.C. 1954, N.Y. 1969, U.S. Supreme Ct. 1964. Law clk. U.S. Ct. Appeals (3d cir.), 1958-60; assoc. Kaufman & Kaufman, Pitts., 1960-61; assoc. prof. law NYU, 1961-65, prof., 1965—; assoc. dean NYU Sch. Law, 1968-72; dean and dir. Practising Law Inst., 1972-75; senior NYU, 1994—; cons. in field.; v.p. Nat. Ctr. Para-Legal Tng.; pres. Early Am. Industries Assn., 1979-82; chmn. Commn. on Fgn. Grad. Study, AALS. Author: (with G. Cole) The Meriden Experiment, 1973; Study of the Quality of Continuing Legal Education in the U.S, 1980; contbr. articles to legal publs.; chmn. editorial bd. Jour. Legal Edn, 1974-77. Pres. N.Y.C. chpt. Am. Jewish Com., 1977-79, nat. bd. govs., 1979-85; vice chmn., gen. counsel Coalition to Free Soviet Jews, 1977—; trustee Law Ctr. Found., 1973-91, Am. Friends of Hebrew U. Jerusalem, 1986—; chair New Amsterdam dist. Boy Scouts Am., 1990—, Ctr. on Social Welfare Policy and Law, 1991—, Blaustein Inst. on Human Rights, 1992—. Capt. JAGC, U.S. Army, 1955-58. Recipient Alumni Meritorious Svc. award NYU, 1977, Stanley Isaacs award Am. Jewish Com., 1982, Gt. Tchr. award NYU, 1993, Friendship award Govt. of Germany, 1988, Robert B. McKay Disting. Svc. award N.Y.U. Sch. of Law, 1997, Great Tchr. award 1999; Root-Tilden grantee NYU, 1954. Fellow Am. Bar Found.; mem. ABA, Assn. of Bar of City of N.Y., N.Y. County Lawyers Assn. (bd. dirs. 1990—), Am. Law Inst., Assn. Am. Law Schs., NYU Club (pres. 1981-83, Masons, Sojourners, Order of Coif, Phi Epsilon Pi. Democrat. Jewish. Home: 4 Washington Square Vlg Apt 16 New York NY 10012-1936 Office: NYU Sch Law Vand Hall 40 Washington Sq S New York NY 10012-1005

GREENBERGER, I. MICHAEL, lawyer; b. Scranton, Pa., Oct. 30, 1945; s. David and Betty (Kabatchnick) G.; m. Marcia Devins, July 19, 1969; children: Sarah Devins, Anne Devins. AB, Lafayette Coll., 1967; JD, U. Pa., 1970. Bar: D.C. 1971, U.S. Dist. Ct. D.C. 1971, U.S. Ct. Appeals (D.C. cir.) 1971, U.S. Supreme Ct. 1975. Law clk. to Judge Carl McGowan U.S. Ct. Appeals for D.C. Circuit, Washington, 1970-71; legis. asst. to U.S. Congresswoman Elizabeth Holtzman, 1972-73; atty., advisor Office of Criminal Justice, Office U.S. Atty. Gen., 1973; assoc. Shea & Gardner, Washington, 1973-77, ptnr., 1977-97; dir. divsn. of trading and markets U.S. Commodity Futures Trading Commn., 1997—; bd. govs. D.C. Bar 1995-98, com. on legal ethics, 1993-95; mem. D.C. Cir. Adv. Com. on Procedures, 1983-89; mem. steering com. D.C. Pro Bono Partnership, 1994-97, Lafayette Coll. Leadership Coun., 1994-99; mediator office of cir. exec. U.S. Cts. for D.C., 1989—; mem. D.C. Cir. Jud. Conf., 1983—; legal cons. Software Engring. Inst., Carnegie-Mellon U., 1986-87; mem. steering com. Pres.'s Working Group on Fin. Mkts., 1997—; mem. hedge fund task force Internat. Orgn. of Secs. Commrs., 1999—. Editor-in-chief U. Pa. Law Rev., 1969-70; contbr. articles to profl. jours. Bd. dirs. Washington Legal Clinic for the Homeless, 1993-98, Am. Rivers, 1993-98, sec., 1995-98; bd. dirs. MIT Enterprise Forum Washington, 1984-87, Advanced Tech. Assn. Md., 1985-87, D.C. Prisoners' Legal Svc. Project, 1997-98; mem. steering com. Pres.'s Working Group on Fin. Markets, 1997—; mem. Hedge Fund task force Internat. Orgn. Security Commrs., 1999—. Mem. Am. Law Inst., Phi Beta Kappa. Address: 2757 Brandywine St NW Washington DC 20008-1041

GREENBERGER, MARTIN, computer and information scientist, educator; b. Elizabeth, N.J., Nov. 30, 1931; s. David and Sidelle (Jonas) G.; A.B., Harvard, 1955, A.M., 1956, Ph.D., 1958; m. Ellen Danica Silver, Feb. 2, 1959 (div. June 1974); children: Kari Edwards, David Silver; m. Liz Attardo, Dec. 11, 1982; children: Beth Jonit, Jonah Ben, Jilly Sal. Teaching fellow, resident adviser, staff mem. Computation Lab., Harvard, Cambridge, 1954-58; mgr. applied sci. IBM, Cambridge, 1956-58; asst. prof. mgmt. Mass. Inst. Tech., Cambridge, 1958-61, assoc. prof., 1961-67; prof., chmn. computer sci., dir. info. processing Johns Hopkins U., Balt., 1967-72, prof. math. scis., sr. research asso. Center for Met. Planning and Research, 1972-75, prof. math. scis., 1978-82; IBM chair in tech. and policy UCLA Anderson Grad. Sch. Mgmt., 1982—; dir. UCLA Ctr. Digital Media, 1995—; pres. Council for Tech. and the Individual, 1985—; mgr. systems program Electric Power Research Inst., Palo Alto, Calif., 1976-77; Isaac Taylor vis. prof. Technion-Israel Inst. Tech., Haifa, 1978-79; vis. prof. Internat. Energy Program, Grad. Sch. Bus., Stanford U., 1980; vis. prof. policy and analysis MIT Media Lab., 1988-89; mem. computer sci. and engring. bd. NAS, 1970-72; chmn. COSATI rev. group NSF, 1971-72; mem. evaluation com. Internat. Inst. for Applied Systems Analysis, Laxenburg, Austria, 1980; mem. adv. panels, Office Tech. Assessment, GAO, U.S. Congress; mem. adv. com. Getty Info. Inst.; cons. IBM, A.T.&T., CBS, Rand Corp., Morgan Guaranty, Arthur D. Little, TRW, Bolt, Beranek & Newman, Brookings Inst., Resources for Future, Electric Power Rsch. Inst., Atlantic Richfield, Rockwell Internat., Security Pacific Corp, John F. Kennedy Sch. of Govt. Harvard U, Bell Atlantic Corp., Sony Corp. Mem. overseers' vis. com. Harvard U., 1975-81; founder and mem. working groups Energy Modeling Forum, Stanford U., 1978-81; mem. adv. com. Nat. Center Analysis of Energy Systems Brookhaven Nat. Lab., 1976-80, chmn., 1977; mem. rev. com. Energy and Environment div. Lawrence Berkeley Lab., 1983, applied sci. div., 1986-88; chmn. forum on electronic pub., Washington program Annenberg, 1983-84; co-founder ICC Forum, 1985; chmn. CTI Roundtable, 1990—; trustee Educom, Princeton, N.J., 1969-73, chmn. council, 1969-70. With USAF, 1952-54, USAFR, 1954-60. NSF fellow, 1955-56; Guggenheim fellow U. Calif., Berkeley, 1965-66. Fellow AAAS (v.p., chmn. sect. T 1973-75); mem. Phi Beta Kappa, Sigma Xi. Author: (with Orcutt, Korbel and Rivlin) Microanalysis of Socioeconomic Systems: A Simulation Study, 1961; (with Jones, Morris and Ness) On-Line Computation and Simulation: The OPS-3 System, 1965; (with Crenson and Crissey) Models in the Policy Process: Public Decision Making in the Computer Era, 1976; (with Brewer, Hogan and Russell) Caught Unawares: The Energy Decade in Retrospect, 1983. Editor: Management and The Computer of the Future, 1962, republished as Computers and the World of the Future, 1964; Computers, Communications, and the Public Interest, 1971; (with Aronofsky, McKenney and Massy) Networks for Research and Education, 1973; Electronic Publishing Plus: Media for a Technological Future, 1985, Technologies for the 21st Century, Vol. 1, On Multimedia, 1990, Vol. 3, Multimedia in Review, 1992, Vol. 5, Content and Communication, 1994, Vol. 7, Scaling Up., 1996. Office: UCLA Anderson Grad Sch Mgmt Los Angeles CA 90095-1481

GREENBERGER, NORTON JERALD, physician; b. Cleve., Sept. 13, 1933; s. Sam and Lillian (Frank) G.; m. Joan Narcus, Aug. 10, 1964; children: Sharon, Rachel, Wendy. A.B., Yale U., 1955; M.D., Western Res. U., 1959. Diplomate: Am. Bd. Internal Medicine (sec.-treas. 1980-82). Intern Univ. Hosps., Cleve., 1959-60, resident internal medicine, 1960-62; USPHS fellow in gastroenterology Harvard U., 1962-65, Mass. Gen. Hosp., Boston, 1962-65; with Ohio State U., Columbus, 1965-72, dir. div. gastroenterology, 1967-72, prof., 1971-72; prof., chmn. dept. medicine U. Kans., Kansas City, 1972—; mem. Nat. Bd. Med. Examiners, 1971-75; mem. gen. medicine study sect. A, NIH, 1973-76. Author: Gastrointestinal Disorders: A Pathophysiologic Approach, 1976, 4th rev. edit., 1989, Medical Book of Lists, 4th rev. edit., 1994, History Taking and Physical Examination: Essentials and Clinical Correlates, 1992; co-editor gastroent. sect. Yearbook of Medicine, 1969-98; editor Yearbook of Digestive Diseases, 1984-98; contbr. articles to med. jours. Recipient Outstanding Teaching award House Staff Dept. Medicine Ohio State U., 1970-71, Outstanding Teaching award Kans. U. Med. Sch. Class of 1978, Outstanding Med. Educator, 1984, 85, 90, 91, 98. Fellow ACP (editorial com. gastoenterology sect. 1975-77, regent 1984-92, chmn. bd. regents 1988-89, pres. 1990-91); mem. Am. Fedn. Clin. Rsch. (pres. Midwestern sect. 1973-74), Ctrl. Soc. Clin. Rsch. (councillor 1975, pres. 1979-80), N.Y. Acad. Scis., Midwestern Gut Club, Am. Gastroent. Assn. (pres.-elect 1983-84, pres. 1984-85, Disting. Educator award 1995), Am. Soc. Clin. Investigation, Am. Soc. Pharmacology and Exptl. Therapeutics, Assn. Am. Physicians, Assn. Profs. Medicine (pres. 1986-87), Phi Beta Kappa, Sigma Xi, Alpha Omega Alpha. Home: 2611 W 70th Ter Shawnee Mission KS 66208-2745 Office: U Kans Med Ctr 3901 Rainbow Blvd Kansas City KS 66160-0001

GREENBERGER, SHELDON LEE, newspaper advertising executive; b. Cleve., Jan. 15, 1941; s. Leonard S. and Frances Fern (Fertel) G.; m. Judith Anne Shenker, Sept. 8, 1963; children: Leonard, Edward. BA, Ohio State U., 1963, MA, 1964. Asst. promotion and rsch. mgr. Cleve. Press., 1964-68, promotion and rsch. mgr., 1968-72, asst. retail advt. mgr., 1972-77, retail advt. mgr., 1977-78; retail advt. mgr. Sun-Sentinel, Ft. Lauderdale, Fla., 1978-80, v.p., advt. dir., 1980—. Campaign cabinet mem. United Way, Ft. Lauderdale, 1987-91; bd. mem. Partners in Excellence, Ft. Lauderdale, 1984-90, Ft. Lauderdale C. of C., 1984-90. Mem. Newspaper Assn. of Am. (nat. com. mem. 1992—), Fla. Newspaper Advt. and Mktg. Execs., Metro Sunday Newspapers (sales adv. com.). Jewish. Avocations: reading, records, jogging. Office: Sun-Sentinel Co 200 E Las Olas Blvd Ste 1000 Fort Lauderdale FL 33301-2293*

GREENBLATT, DAVID J., pharmacologist, educator; b. Boston, Apr. 8, 1945; s. Milton and Gertrude A. (Rogers) G.; m. Lisa L. von Moltke, Nov. 29, 1991. BA, Amherst Coll., 1966; MD, Harvard Med. Sch., 1970. Diplomate Am. Bd. Clin. Pharmacology. Intern in medicine Montefiore Hosp., Bronx, N.Y., 1970-71; resident in medicine Harvard Med. Svc. Boston City Hosp., 1971-72; fellow clin. pharmacology Mass. Gen. Hosp., Boston, 1972-74, mem. staff clin. pharmacology unit, 1974-76, chief clin. pharmacology unit, 1976-79; dir. clin. pharmacology program Tufts-New England Med. Ctr., Boston, 1979—; prof. pharmacology/exptl. therapeutics, psychiatry, anesthesia Sch. Medicine, Tufts U., Boston, 1979—; chmn. dept. pharmacology and exptl. therapeutics Sch. Medicine, Tufts U., Boston, 1994—, Louis Lasagna chair in pharmacology and exptl. therapeutics, 1997—. Author, co-author 11 books; contbr. over 600 articles to profl. jours. Recipient T. George Bidder award UCLA, 1988. Fellow Am. Coll. Clin. Pharmacology (bd. regents 1987-91, McKeen-Cattell award 1985, pres.-elect 1994-96, pres. 1996-98); mem. Am. Soc. Clin. Pharmacology and Therapeutics (bd. dirs. 1983-85, Rawls-Palmer award 1980), Am. Soc. Clin. Investigation, Am. Coll. Neuropsychopharmacology. Avocation: baseball. Office: Tufts U Sch Medicine 136 Harrison Ave Boston MA 02111-1817

GREENBLATT, DEANA CHARLENE, elementary education educator; b. Chgo., Mar. 13, 1948; d. Walter and Betty (Lamasky) Beisel; BEd., Chgo. State U., 1969; MA in Guidance and Counseling, Roosevelt U., 1973; m. Mark Greenblatt, June 22, 1975. Tchr., counselor Chgo. Pub. Schs., 1969-75, City Colls. of Chgo. GED-TV, 1976; tchr. Columbus (Ohio) Pub. Schs., 1976-86; tchr. Chgo. Pub. Schs., 1993—; participant learning exchange, Chgo. Active B'nai B'rith; vol. Right-to-Read, Columbus; mem. Community Learning Exchange, Acad. Yr. in U.S.A. Com. Counselor, 1989—. Columbus. Cert. tchr. K-9, Ill., Ohio; cert. personnel guidance, Ill., Ohio; cert. Chgo. Bd. Edn. Mem. Am. Personnel and Guidance Assn., Internat. Platform Assn., B'nai B'rith Women Club (chpt. v.p.). Democrat. Home: 3820 W Touhy Ave Lincolnwood IL 60645-1026

GREENBLATT, EDWARD LANDE, lawyer; b. Augusta, Ga., Mar. 16, 1939; s. Robert B. and Gwendolyn (Lande) G.; m. Sherry Agoos, June 1, 1967; 1 dau., Susan. Student Duke U.; B.A., Birmingham So. Coll., 1961; LL.B., Emory U., 1964; LL.M., NYU, 1965. Bar: Ga. 1963, D.C. 1966, U.S. Supreme Ct. 1971. Atty., U.S. Dept. Treasury, Washington, 1965-66; assoc. Lipshutz, Greenblatt, & King, and predecessors, Atlanta, 1967-71, ptnr., 1971—. Bd. dirs. Atlanta Legal Aid Soc., Atlanta Community Ctr., Paces Battle Assn.; bd. dirs., chmn. Atlanta B'nai B'rith Youth Orgn., 1973-75; pres. The Temple, 1985-87; chmn. Southeastern Med. Rsch. Found., 1987—; pres. coun. Case Western Res. U., 1990-91. Fellow Royal Soc. Arts; mem. ABA, State Bar Ga., Atlanta Bar Assn., Lawyers Club Atlanta, Am. Judicature Soc. Jewish. Home: 3257 Teton Dr NW Atlanta GA 30339-4341 Office: Lipshutz Greenblatt & King Attys at Law 2300 Harris Tower Peachtree Ctr 233 Peachtree St NE Atlanta GA 30303-1504

GREENBLATT, FRED HAROLD, data processing consultant; b. N.Y.C., Aug. 24, 1938; s. Harry Joseph and Rose (Rosen) G.; m. Marsha R. Mechaneck, Nov. 30, 1963; 1 child, Jay S. BS in Edn., CCNY, 1960; postgrad. Baruch Sch. Bus., 1961-63. Sr. analyst Grosset & Dunlap, N.Y.C., 1969-73; asst. v.p. info. systems GNY Ins., East Brunswick, N.J., 1973-79; cons. J.P. Sedlak Assocs., N.Y.C., 1979-80; adminstr. stds. and data ITT, N.Y.C., 1980-81; dir. systems programs Reed, Roberts Assocs., Mitchell Field, N.Y., 1981-83; pres. Data Design, Holliswood, N.Y., 1983—; affiliated cons. ADR, Princeton, N.J., 1985—; affiliated software cons. Software A.G., Reston, Va., 1986—. Served with U.S. Army, 1960-61. Mem. Data Processing Mgmt. Assn. (reviewer 1984, 85, cert. achievement 1984), IEEE (assoc.), N.Y. Personal Computer Club, Soc. Profl. Mgmt. Cons. (assoc.), Assn. Computing Machinery, Personal Engring. Computer Users Soc., Internat. Platform Assn., B'nai B'rith. Republican. Avocations: golf, tennis, microprocessors, gardening. Home and Office: 19814 Epsom Crse Jamaica NY 11423-1302

GREENBLATT, MAURICE THEODORE, transportation executive; b. Vineland, N.J., Oct. 2, 1928; s. Benjamin and Emma (Pollock) G.; m. Joan Tobye Bailinger, Apr. 8, 1951; children: David, Daniel. Student, Bucknell U., 1945-48. Pres. Ware's Van and Storage Co., Inc., Vineland, 1958—; chmn., chief exec. officer United Van Lines, Inc., Fenton, Mo., 1984—; vice chmn. Security Savs. and Loan, Vineland, 1977—, also bd. dirs.; bd. dirs. United Van Lines Ltd., Toronto, Can., Am. Movers Conf., Household Goods Carriers Bur. Republican. Jewish. Office: Unigroup Inc 1 United Dr Fenton MO 63026-2535*

GREENBLATT, MIRIAM, author, editor, educator; b. Berlin; d. Gregory and Shifra (Zemach) Baraks; m. Howard Greenblatt (div. 1978). BA magna cum laude, Hunter Coll.; postgrad., U. Chgo., Spertus Coll., Spertus Coll. Editor Am. People's Ency., Chgo., 1957-58, Scott Foresman & Co., Chgo., 1958-62; pres. Creative Textbooks, Chgo., 1972—, 1972—; tchr. New Trier H.S., Ill., 1978-81. Author: (with Chu) The Story of China, 1968, (with Cuban) Japan, 1971, The History of Itasca, 1976, (with others) The American People, 1986, James Knox Polk, 1988, Franklin Delano Roosevelt, 1989, John Quincy Adams, 1990, (with Welty) The Human Expression, 1992, The War of 1812, 1994, (with Jordan and Bowes) The Americans, 1996, (with Lemmo) Human Heritage, 1999, Hatshepsut and Ancient Egypt, 1999, Alexander the Great and Ancient Greece, 1999, Augustus and Imperial Rome, 1999, Peter the Great and Tsarist Russia, 1999; edit. cons. Peoples and Cultures Series, 1976-78; subject area cons. World Georgraphy and Cultures, 1994; contbg. editor A World History, 1979. V.p. Chgo. Chpt. Am. Jewish Com., 1977-79, mem. nat. exec. coun., 1980-84; treas. Glencoe Youth Svcs., 1981-83. Mem. Nat. Coun. Social Studies, Ill. Coun. Social Studies, Am. Hist. Assn., Nat. Coun. History Edn. Jewish. Address: 2754 Roslyn Ln Highland Park IL 60035-1408

GREENBLATT, RAY HARRIS, lawyer; b. Milw., June 29, 1931; s. Charles and Ethel (Harris) G.; m. Betty Goldsmith, July 11, 1955 (dec. Mar. 1967); children: Walter, Robert, Edward; m. Helen Judith Pick, Mar. 29, 1969 (div. Dec. 1969). BS in Econs., U. Pa., 1953; JD magna cum laude, Harvard U., 1956. Bar: Ill. 1956. Assoc. Mayer, Brown & Platt, 1956-64, ptnr., 1965-94; arbitrator, mediator Am. Arbitration Assn., 1970-96; hearing officer Ill. State Banking Bd., 1989; lectr. Sch. for Bankers U. Wis., Madison, 1964, 73, Ill. Inst. Continuing Legal Edn., 1973. Contbr. articles to profl. jours. Pres. Winnetka (Ill.) Bd. Edn., 1974-75, mem. 1969-74; vol. tchr. economics, poetry and debate, Providence-St. Mel Sch., Chgo., 1994-98. Mem. ABA, Chgo. Bar Assn., Union League, Chgo. Literary Club, Econ. Club, Cliff Dwellers Club, Lake Shore Country Club. Jewish. Home: 1003 Westmoor Rd Winnetka IL 60093-1855

GREENBLATT, STEPHEN J., English language educator; b. Cambridge, Mass., Nov. 7, 1943; s. Harry J. and Mollie (Brown) G.; m. Ramie Targoff; children: Joshua, Aaron. BA, Yale U., 1964, M. in Philosophy, 1968, PhD, 1969; BA, Cambridge U., England, 1966. Prof. English U. Calif., Berkeley, 1969-97, Harvard U., 1997—; vis. prof. Peking U., Beijing, 1982, Oxford (Eng.) U., 1988, U. Bologna, Italy, 1988, 96, U. Chgo., 1989, U. Trieste, 1991, U. Florence, 1992, 96, Ecole des Hautes Etudes, Paris, 1989, 99, Harvard U., Cambridge, Mass., 1990-94, Instituto Italiano per gli Studi Filosofici, Naples, 1994, U. Ala., 1994, Wissenschaftskolleg zu Berlin, 1996-97. Author: Three Modern Satirists: Waugh, Orwell, and Huxley, 1965 (Lloyd Mifflin prize 1964), Sir Walter Raleigh, 1970, Renaissance Self-Fashioning, 1980, Shakespearean Negotiations, 1988, Learning to Curse, 1990, Marvelous Possessions, 1991; editor: Allegory and Representation, 1981, Power of Forms, 1982, Representing the English Renaissance, 1988, Redrawing the Boundaries of Literary Study in English, 1992, New World Encounters, 1992, The Norton Shakespeare, 1997; gen. editor: The Norton Anthology of English Literature. Recipient Porter prize, 1969, Brit. Coun. prize, 1982, James Russell Lowell prize MLA, 1989; Fulbright scholar, 1964-66, Woodrow Wilson scholar, 1966; Guggenheim fellow, 1975, 83. Fellow Am. Acad. Arts and Scis. Office: Harvard U Dept of English Cambridge MA 02138

GREENBURG, DAN, author; b. Chgo., June 20, 1936; s. Samuel and Leah (Rozalsky) G.; m. Nora Ephron, Apr. 9, 1967 (div.); m. Suzanne O'Malley, June 28, 1980 (div.); m. Judith Wilson, Oct. 17, 1998. BFA, U. Ill., 1958; MA, UCLA, 1960. Copywriter Lansdale Co., Los Angeles, 1960-61, Carson Roberts Advt., Los Angeles, 1961-62; mng. editor Eros mag., N.Y.C., 1962-63; copywriter Papert, Koenig, Lois (advt.), N.Y.C., 1963-65; freelance writer N.Y.C., 1965—. Author: How to Be a Jewish Mother, 1964, Kiss My Firm but Pliant Lips, 1965, How to Make Yourself Miserable, 1966, Chewsday: A Sex Novel, 1968, Jumbo the Boy and Arnold the Elephant, 1969, 89, Philly, 1969, Porno-Graphics, 1969, Scoring: A Sexual Memoir, 1972, Something's There: My Adventures in the Occult, 1976, Love Kills, 1978, What Do Women Want?, 1982; (with Suzanne O'Malley) How to Avoid Love and Marriage, 1983, True Adventures, 1985, Confessions of a Pregnant Father, 1986, How to Make Yourself Miserable for the Rest of the Century, 1987, The Nanny, 1987, Exes, 1990, The Guardian, 1990, The Bed Who Ran Away From Home, 1991, Young Santa, 1991, Great Grandpa's in the Litter Box, 1996, A Ghost Named Wanda, 1996, Through the Medicine Cabinet, 1996, Zap! I'm a Mind-Reader, 1996, Moses Supposes, 1997, Dr. Jekyll, Orthodontist, 1997, I'm Out of My Body, Please Leave a Message, 1997, My Son, the Time Traveler, 1997, Never Trust a Cat Who Wears Earrings, 1997, The Volcano Goddess Will See You Now, 1997, Bozo the Clone, 1997, How to Speak Dolphin in Three Easy Lessons, 1997, Now You See Me, Now You Don't, 1998, The Misfortune Cookie, 1998, Elvis the Turnip and Me, 1998; (films) I Could Never Have Sex with Any Man Who Has So Little Regard for My Husband, 1973, Private Lessons, 1981; (with Suzanne O'Malley) Private School, 1983, The Guardian, 1990; (plays) Arf, 1969, The Great Airplane Snatch, 1969; contbr. to Broadway revue Oh, Calcutta, 1969. Recipient Silver Key award Advt. Writers Assn., N.Y.C., 1964, Playboy Humor award, 1964, 72, 76. Mem. Dramatists Guild, Authors Guild Am., AFTRA, Screen Actors Guild, Writers Guild Am., Mystery Writers Am.

GREENDYKE, WILLIAM R., federal judge. Student, Coll. of William and Mary, 1972-74; BS, Baylor U., 1976, JD cum laude, 1979. Ptnr. Shannon, Porter, Johnson, Sutton & Greendyke, San Angelo, Tex., 1979-87; bankruptcy judge U.S. Dist. Ct. (so. dist.) Tex., Houston, 1987—. Fax: (713) 250-5550. Office: US Dist Ct So Dist Tex 515 Rusk Ave Rm 4202 Houston TX 77002

GREENE, ADDISON KENT, lawyer, accountant; b. Cardston, Alta., Can., Dec. 23, 1941; s. Addison Allen and Amy (Shipley) G.; m. Janice Hanks, Aug. 30, 1967; children: Lisa, Tiffany, Tyler, Darin. BS in Acctg., Brigham Young U., 1968; JD, U. Utah, 1973. Bar: Utah 1973, Nev. 1974, U.S. Tax Ct. 1979. Staff acct. Seidman and Seidman, Las Vegas, Nev., 1968-69, Peat Marwick Mitchell, Los Angeles, 1969-70; atty. Clark Greene & Assocs., Ltd., Las Vegas, 1973—; instr. Nev. Bar Rev., Las Vegas, 1975-78; bd. dirs. Cumorah Credit Union. Mem. Citizen's for Responsible Gov't, Las Vegas,

1979—; asst. dist. com. mem. Boy Scouts Am., Las Vegas, 1985—. Mem. ABA, Utah Bar Assn., Nev. Bar Assn., Nev. Soc. CPA's (assoc.), Am. Assn., Pension Actuaries (assoc.). Republican. Mormon. Avocations: golf, snow skiing. Office: Clark Greene & Assocs Ltd 3770 Howard Hughes Pkwy Ste 195 Las Vegas NV 89109-0976

GREENE, ADELE S., management consultant; b. Newark; d. Adolph and Sara (Schubert) Shuminer; m. Alan Greene (div.); 1 child, Joshua. Student, Juilliard Sch. Music, 1942-44, NYU, 1942-44, New Sch. Social Research, 1944-47; diploma in mgmt., Harvard Bus. Sch., 1978. Account exec. Ruder and Finn Inc., N.Y.C., 1964-66, sr. assoc., 1966-68, v.p., 1968-72, sr. v.p., 1972-76; v.p. pub. affairs Corp. Pub. Broadcasting, Washington, 1976-78; pres., CEO TV Program Group, Washington, 1978-80; pres. Greene and Assocs., N.Y.C., 1981—; exec. dir. Am. Friends of Brit. Mus., 1994—; instr. pub. relations and community affairs, NYU 1974-76; bd. dirs. Sci. Program Group, Washington 1976-81; treas., bd. dirs. Coliseum Park Apts. Co-author: Teen-Age Leadership, 1971. Advisor The Acting Co., Understudies, N.Y.C., 1987—; pres., CEO Am. Craft Coun., 1980-81, trustee, 1976-81; bd. dirs. Union Settlement, N.Y.C., 1987-90; trustee Duke Ellington Sch. Arts, Washington, 1977-81. Mem. Pub. Relations Soc. Am. (silver anvil award 1971), Nat. Assn. Edn. Broadcasters, Am. Women Radio and TV. Home and Office: 30 W 60th St New York NY 10023-7902

GREENE, ALBERT LAWRENCE, hospital administrator; b. N.Y.C., Dec. 10, 1949; s. Leonard and Anne (Birnbaum) G.; m. Jo Linda Anderson, Sept. 3, 1972; children: Stacy, Jeremy. BA, Ithaca Coll., 1971; MHA, U. Mich., 1973. Adminstrv. asst. Harper Hosp., Detroit, 1973-74, asst. adminstr., 1974-77, assoc. adminstr., 1977-80; adminstr. Grace Hosp., Detroit, 1980-84, Harper Hosp., Detroit, 1984-87; pres., CEO Sinai Samaritan Med. Ctr., Milw., 1988-90, Alta Bates Med. Ctr., Berkeley, Calif., 1990-98; CEO Sutter Health East Bay Svc. Area, Berkeley, Calif., 1998-99, HealthCtrl., Emeryville, Calif., 1999—; bd. dirs. Acuson Corp., QuadraMed Corp., Calif. Assn. Hosps. and Health Sys. Trustee Huron Valley Hosp., Milford, Mich., 1984-87. Mem. Am. Coll. Healthcare Execs., Young Pres. Orgn., Blackhawk Country Club, Lakeview Club. Avocations: tennis, golf. Home: 3819 Cottonwood Dr Danville CA 94506-6007 Office: HealthCtrl 6001 Shellmound Rd Ste 800 Emeryville CA 94705-2067

GREENE, ALVIN, service company executive, management consultant; b. Pitts., Aug. 26, 1932; s. Samuel David and Yetta (Kroff) G.; BA, Stanford U., 1954, MBA, 1959; m. M. Louise Sokol, Nov. 11, 1977; children: Sharon, Ami, Ann, Daniel. Asst. to pres. Narmco Industries, Inc., San Diego, 1959-62; adminstrv. mgr., mgr. mktg. Whittaker Corp., L.A., 1962-67; sr. v.p. Cordura Corp., L.A., 1967-75; chmn. bd. Sharon-Sage, Inc., L.A., 1975-79; exec. v.p., chief operating officer Republic Distbrs., Inc., Carson, Calif., 1979-81, also dir.; chief operating officer Memel, Jacobs & Ellsworth, 1981-87, 87—; pres. SCI Cons., Inc.; dir. Sharon-Sage, Inc., True Data Corp.; vis. prof. Am. Grad. Sch. Bus., Phoenix, 1977-81. Chmn. bd. commrs. Housing Authority City of L.A., 1983-88 . Served to 1st lt., U.S. Army, 1955-57. Mem. Direct Mail Assn., Safety Helmet Mfrs. Assn., Bradley Group. Office: 11990 San Vicente Blvd Ste 300 Los Angeles CA 90049-6608

GREENE, A(LVIN) C(ARL), author; b. Abilene, Tex., Nov. 4, 1923; s. Alvin Carl and Marie (Cole) G.; m. Betty Dozier, 1950 (dec.); children: Geoffrey, Mark, Eliot, Meredith Elizabeth; m. Judy Dalton Hyland, 1990. BA, Abilene Christian U., 1948; HLD (hon.), Austin Coll., 1992. Mem. staff Abilene Reporter-News, 1948-52, 58-60; book editor Dallas Times Herald, 1960-68, editor editorial page, 1963-65; staff U. Tex., Austin, 1968-69, 73; exec. editor Southwestern Hist. Quar., 1968-69; exec. producer Sta. KERA-TV, Dallas, 1970-71; editorial bd. KAAM, KAFM, 1979-81; narrator A.C. Greene's Historic Moments Sta. WFAA, 1982-83; commentator MacNeil/Lehrer News Hour, 1983-89; columnist Dallas Morning News, 1983—. Author: A Personal Country, 1969, new paperback edit., 1998, Living Texas, 1969, The Last Captive, 1972, Santa Claus Bank Robbery, 1972, illustrated edit., 1999, Dallas: The Deciding Years, 1973, A Christmas Tree, 1973, Views in Texas, 1974, A Place Called Dallas, 1975; (with Roger Horchow) Elephants in Your Mailbox, 1980; 50 Best Books on Texas, 1982, 2d edit., 1998, The Highland Park Woman, 1983, Dallas USA, 1984, Texas Sketches, 1985, Taking Heart, 1990, 900 Miles on the Butterfield Trail, 1994, Joy to the World, 1995, Christmas Memories, 1996, They are Ruining Ibiza, 1998, Sketches From the 5 States of Texas, 1998, (short stories) Divine Discontent, 1999, (poems) The Memory of Snow, 1999. Emeritus dir. Ctr. for Tex. Studies U. North Tex., 1993-96. With USNR, 1943-46, PTO, CBI. Recipient award NCCJ, 1964; Dobie-Paisano fellow, 1968, Tex. State Hist. Com., 1994. Fellow Tex. Inst. Letters (pres. 1969-71, award 1964, 73, 88), Tex. State Hist. Assn.; mem. Writers Guild Am., Nat. Rlwy. Hist. Assn., Salado L.R. Theater. Presbyn. Home and Office: PO Box 1170 Salado TX 76571-1170

GREENE, AURELIA, state legislator; b. N.Y.C., Oct. 26, 1934; d. Edward Henry and Sybil Elaine (Russell) Holley; children: Rhonda, Russell; m. 2d, Jerome Alexander Greene, Apr. 18, 1975. B.A., Rutgers U., 1974. Dep. exec. dir. Morrisania Community Corp., N.Y.C., 1969-76; exec. dir. Bronx Area Policy Bd. No. 6, N.Y.C., 1980-82; mem. N.Y. State Assembly, 1982—, 77th assembly dist. chair Assembly Standing Com. on Banking. Dist. leader 76th Assembly Dist., Bronx, 1990-92; sec. Bronx County Dem. Party, 1980—, mem. exec. com.; exec. mem. Bronx Unity Democratic Club; del. Dem. Nat. Conv., 1984; mem. credentials com. Dem. Nat. Conv., Atlanta, 1988, N.Y.C., 1992, Chgo., 1996. Mem. Bronx NAACP (Woman of Yr. award 1974). Democrat. also: Legis Office Bldg Rm 424 Albany NY 12248

GREENE, BARNETT ALAN, anesthesiologist; b. N.Y.C., July 30, 1907; s. Harris and Sarah (Frischman) G.; m. Lee Adelman, Dec. 24, 1932; children: Stuart A., William H. BSc cum laude, CCNY, 1929; MD cum laude, NYU, 1934. Diplomate Am. Bd. Anesthesiology. Intern, house officer Lincoln City Hosp., Bronx, N.Y., 1934-36, resident in anesthesiology, 1936-39; anesthesiologist Bklyn. Cancer Inst., Dept. Hosps. of N.Y.C., 1939-47; dir. dept. anesthesiology Prospect Heights Hosp., Bklyn., 1939-46, Unity Hosp., Bklyn., 1940-75, Bklyn. Hebrew Home and Hosp. for Aged, 1939-75, Adelphi Hosp., Bklyn., 1939-74, Bklyn. Women's Hosp., 1946-75, Cumberland Hosp. of Dept. of Hosps. City of N.Y., 1955-70, Luth. Hosp., Bklyn., 1963-78; pres. Greene, Berkowitz and Goffen, Physicians, P.C., 1971-81, Barnett A. Greene, M.D. P.C., 1978-92; Greene Family Svcs. Corp., 1992—; clin. assoc. prof. anesthesiology SUNY Downstate Med. Ctr., 1958-75; clin. practice examiner Am. Bd. Anesthesiology, 1946-52; vis. anesthesiologist Kings County Hosp., 1951-55, acting dir. dept. anesthesiology, 1951-55; attending anesthesiologist Bklyn.-Cumberland Hosp. Med. Ctr., 1970-75, emeritus, 1975—; chmn. bd. trustees Bklyn. Women's Hosp. Clinic, 1975-78; mem. malpractice mediation panel Kings County Supreme Ct., 1978-90. Contbr. articles to profl. publs. Maj. Med. Corps, U.S. Army, 1943-46. Decorated Bronze Star. Fellow Am. Anesthesiologists, N.Y. Acad. Medicine; mem. AMA, N.Y. State Med. Soc. (mem. com. on peer rev. 1981, com. on operating rm. safety 1981-83), Kings County Med. Soc. (McAteer prize 1940, mem. continuing edn. com. 1977-80), Phi Beta Kappa, Alpha Omega Alpha. Jewish. Avocation: ballroom dancing.

GREENE, BERNARD HAROLD, lawyer; b. Bklyn., Sept. 21, 1925; s. Max and Clara (Pasweg) G.; m. Magda C. Schwartz, Sept. 19, 1948; children: Michael, Edith, Susan, Jonathan, David. BBA magna cum laude, CCNY, 1948; LLB cum laude, Yale U., 1951. Bar: N.Y. 1952. Assoc. Paul, Weiss, Rifkind, Wharton & Garrison, N.Y.C., 1951-60, ptnr., 1960-94, of counsel, 1995—; vis. lectr. Yale Law Sch., New Haven, 1972-78, 81-83; adj. prof. N.Y. Law Sch., N.Y.C., 1985-88. Chmn. deferred giving and estate planning com. Community Svc. Soc., N.Y.C., 1975-82. 1st lt. U.S. Army, 1943-47. Mem. Assn. Bar City N.Y. (mem. surrogate's ct. com. 1958-61). Home: 153 Union St Montclair NJ 07042-2102 Office: Paul Weiss Rifkind Wharton & Garrison Fl 30 Rm 202 1285 Avenue of the Americas New York NY 10019-6028

GREENE, BEVERLY ANN, clinical psychologist; b. Orange, N.J., Aug. 14, 1950; d. Samuel and Thelma G. BA, NYU, 1973; postgrad. Marquette U., 1973-74; MA, Adelphi U., 1977, PhD, 1983. Lic. psychologist, N.Y., N.J.; diplomate Am. Bd. Profl. Psychology. Fellow in psychology Mental Retardation Inst., N.Y. Med. Coll., Valhalla, N.Y., 1974-76; psychol. cons. Williamsburg Child Devel. Ctr., Bklyn., 1976-78; psychology intern East Orange VA Med. Ctr., 1978-79; rsch. asst. dept. neurosci. N.J. Coll. Medicine and Dentistry, Vet.'s Hosp., 1979-80; psychology trainee, Children's Partial Hospitalization Unit, Brookdale Hosp. and Med. Ctr., 1980; cert. sch. psychologist N.Y.C. Bd. Edn., 1980-82, staff psychologist, 1982-84; sr. psychologist, dir. inpatient child and adolescent psychol. svcs. King's County Psychiat. Hosp., 1984-89; supervising psychologist Community Mental Health Ctr., U. Medicine and Dentistry N.J., Newark, 1989-91; clin. instr. in psychiatry Downstate Med. Sch., 1982-85, clin. asst. prof., 1985-89, acting dir. Children's Inpatient Unit, 1985-86; clin.asst. prof. dept. psychiatry U. Medicine and Dentistry of N.J., Newark, 1989-91; assoc. clin. prof. dept. psychology St. Johns U., N.Y., 1991-93, assoc. prof. dept. psychology, 1993-95, prof., 1995—. Contbr. articles to profl. jours.; co-author books. Recipient Disting. Humanitarian award Am. Assn. Applied & Preventive Psychology, 1994; Martin Luther King scholar, 1968-72, NIMH fellow, 1976-77. Fellow APA (soc. for the psychol. study of ethnic minority issues, co-chair continuing edn. Women's div. 1991-93, diversity in clin. psychology task force, fellow clin. psychology, psychotherapy, psychology of women, lesbian and gay issues and ethnic minority issues divsn., co-editor divsn. 44 ann. pub., Dist. Profl. Contbns. to Ethnic Minority Issues award divsn. 44, 1992, Soc. for the Psychol. Study Lesbian and Gay Issues, Psychotherapy with Women Rsch. award 1995, 96, Outstanding Achievement award Com. Lesbian and Gay Concerns 1996), Am. Orthopsychiat. Assn., Acad. Clin. Psychology; mem. Internat. Neuropsychol. Soc., Nat. Assn. Black Psychologists, N.Y. Assn. Black Psychologists, Nat. Assn. Women in Psychology (Women of Color Psychologies Publ. award, 1991, 95, Disting. Publ. award 1995), N.Y. Assn. Women in Psychology, N.Y. Coalition of Hosp. and Instnl. Psychologists.

GREENE, BOB See **GREENE, ROBERT BERNARD, JR.**

GREENE, C. MICHAEL, art association administrator. Pres., CEO NARAS, Santa Monica, Calif. Office: NARAS 3402 Pico Blvd Santa Monica CA 90405-2118

GREENE, CARL WILLIAM, financial consultant, former utility company executive; b. N.Y.C., July 29, 1935; BS, U. Pa., 1957; MBA, N.Y.U., 1960; m. Gloria Nissman, June 29, 1958; children: Andrew, Stephen, Suzanne, Nancy. With, Consol. Edison Co., N.Y.C., 1958-96, acct., 1966-67, asst. mgr., 1967-68, asst. controller, 1968-74, sr. asst. controller, 1974-75, asst. v.p., 1975-76, controller, 1976-92, v.p., contr., chief acctg. officer, 1982-92, sr. v.p. acctg. and treasury, chief acctg. officer, 1992-94, sr. v.p. fin. and regulatory matters, 1994-96. Mem. fin. acctg. standards adv. coun. FASB, 1993-96; fin., acctg. and energy cons., 1996—; with TBG Fin., L.A., Newport, Balt., N.Y.C., 1996—, cons., 1996, sr. v.p., 1997—. With U.S. Army, 1957. Mem. Am. Gas Assn. (chmn. fin. and adminstrv. sect. 1986-87, vice chmn. 1985-86, chmn. fin. div. 1983-84, vice chmn. 1990-91, chmn. 1991-92, chmn. acctg. divsn. 1990-93, mng. com. of fin. and adminstrv. sect., v. chmn. acctg. divsn. and acctg. adv. coun., 1990-91), Am. Acctg. Assn., Am. Inst. Corp. Controllers, Fin. Execs. Inst., Planning Execs. Inst., Am. Fin. Assn., Edison Electric Inst. (acctg. exec. adv. com., chmn EEI FERC Liason Group 1982-85), Eastern Fin. Assn., So. Fin. Assn., NYU Sch. Bus. Grad. Sch. Alumni Assn. (pres. 1990-93). Avocations: symphonic music, ballet, opera, fgn. travel. Office: TBG Fin 400 E 52nd St New York NY 10022

GREENE, DAVID LEE, physical anthropologist, educator; b. Denver, Aug. 23, 1938; s. Ralph Francis and Dorothy Elizabeth (Allen) G.; m. Kathleen Ann Kerger, Sept. 4, 1962; 1 son, Andrew David. BA, U. Colo., 1960, MA, 1962, PhD in Anthropology (NSF fellow). Asst. prof. anthropology and orthodontics SUNY, Buffalo, 1964-65; asst. prof., head dept. anthropology U. Wyo., 1965-67; asst. prof. U. Colo., Boulder, 1967-69; asso. prof. U. Colo., 1969-71, prof., 1971—, chmn. dept. anthropology, 1974-77, 81-83, 1990-91; dir. NSF Summer Inst. in Anthropology, 1970-71; outside grad. examiner U. Toronto, 1974, field rsch. in Sudan, 1963-64, Micronesia, 1969, Brazil, 1986, 88. Author: Genetics, Dentition and Taxonomy, 1967, (with G.J. Armelagos) The Wadi Halfa Mesolithic Population, 1972; contbr. articles to profl. jours. NSF grantee, 1978-80. Fellow Am. Anthrop. Assn.; mem. Am. Assn. Phys. Anthropologists, AAAS, Sigma Xi. Office: U Colo Dept Anthropology Boulder CO 80309

GREENE, DOUGLAS A., internist, educator. AB in Biol. Scis., Princeton U., 1966; MD, Johns Hopkins U., 1970. Intern Johns Hopkins U. Hosp., Balt., 1970-71, asst. resident, 1971-72; postdoctoral rsch. fellow George S. Cox Med. Rsch. Inst. U. Pa. Hosp., Phila., 1972-75; asst. prof. medicine U. Pa., Phila., 1975-80; assoc. prof. medicine, dir. clin. rsch. unit and diabetes rsch. labs. U. Pitts., 1980-86; prof. internal medicine, dir. Mich. Diabetes Rsch. and Tng. Ctr. U. Mich., Ann Arbor, 1986—, mem. faculty neuroscience, 1988—, chief divsn. endocrinology and metabolism, 1991—, prof. internal medicine, dir. clin. investigation and therapeutics; dir. Mich. Diabetes Rsch. Tng. Ctr.; chmn. endocrinologic and metabolic adv. com. U.S. FDA, 1991-94. Contbr. over 116 articles to Jour. Clin. Investigation, Frontiers in Diabetes, Diabetic Neuropathy, Diabetes, Diabetes Care, Am. Jour. Physiology, others. Office: U Mich Hosp-Diabetes Rsch & Tng Inst 3920 Taubman Ctr 1500 E Medical Center Dr Ann Arbor MI 48109-0354

GREENE, DOUGLAS EDWARD, hotel executive. BA, U. Maine, 1973. Pres. Ocean Hospitalities, Inc., Portsmouth, N.H. Office: Ocean Hospitalities Inc Bldg 1 Ste 300 1000 Market St Unit 1 Portsmouth NH 03801-3358

GREENE, DOUGLAS GEORGE, humanities educator, author, publisher; b. Middletown, Conn., Sept. 24, 1944; s. George Louis and Margaret Elsie (Chindahl) G.; m. Sandra Virginia Stangland, Aug. 13, 1966; children: Eric, Katherine. BA, U. South Fla., 1966; AM, U. Chgo., 1967, PhD, 1972. Instr. history U. Mont., Missoula, 1970-71; prof. history Old Dominion U., Norfolk, Va., 1971-83, 99—; dir. Inst. Humanities Old Dominion U., Norfolk, 1983-99; pub. Crippen & Landru Books, 1994—. Author: W.W. Denslow, 1976, Bibliographia Oziana, 1976, enlarged edit., 1988, St. Paul's Church, Norfolk, Virginia, 1989, John Dickson Carr: The Man Who Explained Miracles, 1995; editor: Diaries of Popish Plot, 1977, Meditations of Lady Elizabeth Delaval, 1978, The Door to Doom, 1980, enlarged edit., 1991, The Dead Sleep Lightly, 1983, The Wizard of Way Up, 1985, Death Locked in, 1987, rev. edit., 1994, Collected Short Fiction of Ngaio Marsh, 1989, enlarged edit., 1991, Fell and Foul Play, 1991, Merrivale, March and Murder, 1991, Detection by Gaslight, 1997, The Detections of Miss Cusack, 1998, The Dead Hand and Other Uncollected Stories, 1999; contbg. editor Espionage, 1987; contbr. articles and book revs. to profl. jours. and mags. Mem. Mystery Writers Am. Democrat. Episcopalian. Avocation: book collecting. Home: 627 New Hampshire Ave Norfolk VA 23508-2132 Office: Inst Humanities Old Dominion U Norfolk VA 23529-0084

GREENE, EDWARD FORBES, chemistry educator; b. N.Y.C., Dec. 29, 1922; s. Roger Sherman and Kate (Brown) G.; m. Hildegarde Forbes, June 11, 1949; children: Susan Curtis, Judith Elizabeth, David Forbes, Roger Cobb. A.B., Harvard U., 1943, A.M., 1947, Ph.D., 1949. Jr. research chemist Shell Oil Co., Wood River, Ill., 1943-44; mem. staff Los Alamos Sci. Lab., 1949; research assoc. Brown U., Providence, 1949-51, instr., 1952-53, asst. prof. chemistry, 1953-57, assoc. prof., 1957-63, prof., 1963-92, dept. chmn., 1980-83, Jesse H. and Louisa D. Sharpe Metcalf prof. chemistry, 1985-92; prof. emeritus, 1993—; vis. prof. Tougaloo (Miss.) Coll., 1965; resident visitor Bell Labs., Murray Hill, N.J., 1976-77. Co-author: (with J.P. Toennies) Chemical Reactions in Shock Waves, 1964. Served with USN, 1944-46. NSF fellow, 1959-60, 66-67. Fellow Am. Phys. Soc.; mem. Am. Chem. Soc. Home: 10 Paterson St Providence RI 02906-5502

GREENE, ELINORE ASCHAH, speech and drama professional, writer; b. Springfield, Mass., Oct. 14, 1928; d. Harry Joshua and Esther Gertrude (Cohen) Ziff; m. Kermit Greene, June 29, 1947; children: Clifford M., Laura L., William L. B Lit. Interpretation, Emerson Coll., Boston, 1949. Dramatic interpreter Margaret E. Richardson Lect. Agy., Boston, 1950s; dramatic interpreter Flora Frame Lect. Bureau, Boston, 1960s; speech tchr. Academie Moderne, Boston, early 1970s, pvt. practice, Newton, MA, 1975-87; speech cons. pvt. practice, Newton, 1985-89; writer, dir. Newton, 1989—; presenter seminars; voice-overs radio, TV, indsl. Author: children's stories, AIM, Lolli Pops, Happiness, The Communique, Players, 1970-80; poetry, Creative Urge, Dark Starr, Dreams; reviewer books; contbr. voice-overs. Life mem. Orgn. for Rehab. through Tng., Hadassah, Brandeis Women's Com. & Aid to Speech Therapy of Emerson Coll. Mem. Aid to Speech Therapy Found. (pres. 1970s, bd. dirs. 1960s, Advocate Rose award 1975), Mass. Comm. of Boston, Am. Fedn. Theatre-Radio-TV Assns., Nat. Writers Orgn. (sr. mem.), ORT (life). Avocations: music, composing greeting cards, reading, theatre, family.

GREENE, ENID, former congresswoman; b. San Rafael, Calif., Oct. 5, 1958. BS in Pol. Sci., U. Utah, 1980; JD, Brigham Young U., 1983. Caseworker, rsch. asst. U.S. Rep. Dan Marriott, R., 1980; atty. Ray, Quinney & Nebeker, 1983-90; dep. chief of staff Gov. Norman H. Bangerter, 1990-92; corp. counsel Novell, Inc., 1993-94; mem. 104th Congress from 2nd Utah dist., Washington, 1995-97; atty. Smith & Glauser, Salt Lake City, 1998—. Office: Smith & Glauser 2180 S 1300 E Salt Lake City UT 84106

GREENE, FRANK SULLIVAN, JR., investment management executive; b. Washington, Oct. 19, 1938; s. Frank S. Sr. and Irma O. Greene; m. Phyllis Davison, Jan. 1958 (dec. 1984); children: Angela, Frank, Ronald; m. Carolyn W. Greene, Sept. 1990. BS, Washington U., St. Louis, 1961; MS, Purdue U., 1962; PhD, U. Santa Clara, Calif., 1970. Part-time lectr. Washington U., Howard U., Am. U., 1959-65; pres., dir. Tech. Devel. Corp., Arlington, Tex., 1985-92; pres. Zero One Systems Inc. (formerly Tech. Devel. of Calif.), Santa Clara, Calif., 1971-87, Zero One Systems Group subs. Sterling Software Inc., 1987-89; asst. chmn., lectr. Stanford U., 1972-74; bd. dirs. ZNYX Corp., Epicentric, Inc.; bd. dirs. Networked Picture Systems Inc., 1986-94, pres. 1989-91, chmn. 1991-94; mng. mem. New Vista Capital, LLC, Palo Alto, Calif., 1993—. Author two indsl. textbooks; also articles; patentee in field. Bd. dirs. NCCJ, Santa Clara, 1980—, NAACP, San Jose chpt., 1986-89, Am. Musical Theatre of San Jose, 1995—; bd. regents Santa Clara U., 1983-90, trustee, 1990—; mem. adv. bd. Urban League, Santa Clara County, 1986-89, East Side Union High Sch., 1985-88. Capt. USAF, 1961-65. Mem. IEEE, IEEE Computer Soc. (governing bd. 1973-75), Assn. Black Mfrs. (bd. dirs. 1974-80), Am. Electric Assn. (indsl. adv. bd. 1975-76), Fairchild Rsch. and Devel. (tech. staff 1965-71), Bay Area Purchasing Coun. (bd. dirs. 1978-84), Security Affairs Support Assn. (bd. dirs. 1980-83), Sigma Xi, Eta Kappa Nu, Sigma Pi Phi.

GREENE, FREDERICK D., II, chemistry educator; b. Glen Ridge, N.J., July 9, 1927; s. Phillips Foster and Ruth (Altman) G.; m. Theodora Elizabeth Whatmough, June 5, 1953; children—Alan, Carol, Elizabeth, Phillips. Grad., Phillips Andover Acad., 1944; B.A., Amherst Coll., 1949, D.Sc. (hon.), 1969; Ph.D., Harvard, 1952. Research assoc. U. Calif., Los Angeles, 1952-53; instr. dept. chemistry Mass. Inst. Tech., Cambridge, 1953-55; asst. prof. Mass. Inst. Tech., 1955-58; assoc. prof. MIT, 1958-62, prof., 1962-95; prof. emeritus, 1995—. Editor-in-chief: Jour. Organic Chemistry, 1962-88; contbr. articles to sci. jours. Served with USNR, 1945-46. Alfred P. Sloan fellow, 1958-62; NSF Sr. Postdoctoral fellow, 1965-66. Mem. Am. Chem. Soc., Chem. Soc. (London), Am. Acad. Arts and Scis., Phi Beta Kappa. Office: Mass Inst Tech Dept Chemistry 77 Massachusetts Ave Cambridge MA 02139-4301

GREENE, GLEN LEE, secondary school educator; b. Alexandria, La., Sept. 28, 1939; s. Glen Lee and Grace Lois (Prince) G. BA, La. Coll., 1960, U. N.E. La., 1967; MLIS, La. State U., 1994. Tchr. Destrehan (La.) H.S., 1964—, social studies chair, 1980-99; mem. St. Charles Parish Profl. Improvement Program Com., Luling, La., 1981-85. Mem. ALA, ASCD, Nat. Coun. for the Social Studies, Phi Kappa Phi. Democrat. Baptist. Home: PO Box 203 Oak Ridge LA 71264-0203 Office: Destrehan HS 1 Wildcat Ln Destrehan LA 70047-4001

GREENE, HAROLD H., federal judge; b. 1923. B.S., George Washington U., 1949, J.D., 1952; LLD (hon.), Bridgeport U., George Washington U. Asst. U.S. Atty. D.C., 1953-57; with Office Legal Counsel and Civil Rights Div. (Chief of Appeals) Dept. Justice, 1957-65; judge D.C. Ct. Gen. Sessions, 1965-66, chief judge, 1966-71; chief judge Superior Ct. of D.C., 1971-78; judge U.S. Dist. Ct. (D.C. dist.), 1978—; now sr. judge. Mem. ABA, Bar Assn. D.C., Am. Judicature Soc., World Assn. Trial Judges (chmn. 1975-77). Office: US Dist Ct US Courthouse 333 Constitution Ave NW Washington DC 20001-2802*

GREENE, HERBERT BRUCE, lawyer, investor; b. N.Y.C., Apr. 13, 1934; s. Joseph Lester and Shirley (Kasen) G.; m. Judith Jean Metricks, Dec. 31, 1958; children: Pamela S., Scott L. AB, Harvard U., 1955; JD, Columbia U., 1958. Bar: N.Y. 1959, Conn. 1975. Asst. U.S. atty So. Dist. N.Y., Dept. Justice, N.Y.C., 1958-61; assoc. Kaye, Scholer, Fierman, Hays & Handler, N.Y.C., 1961-66; asst. to gen. counsel CIT Fin. Corp., N.Y.C., 1966-67; group gen. counsel Xerox Corp., Rochester, N.Y., 1967-68, v.p. adminstrn., 1968-71; sr. v.p. Xerox Edn. Group, Stamford, Conn., 1971-75; v.p., gen. counsel, sec. Lone Star Industries, Inc., Greenwich, Conn., 1976-79, sr. v.p., asst. to chmn., 1979-82; chmn., CEO Earle and Greene & Co., Westport, 1982-96, Portland, Oreg., 1997—; chmn. Charter Oak of Va. Corp., 1985—; bd. dirs. Centurion Holdings Ltd., Greenmor Internat. Corp. Mem. Phi Delta Phi. Republican. Home: 4233 SW Redondo Ave Portland OR 97201-1380 Office: Herbert B Greene & Co 4233 W Redondo Ave Portland OR 97201-1380

GREENE, HOWARD ROGER, educational consultant; b. New Haven, Conn., July 26, 1937; s. Charles and Freda (Miller) G.; m. Donna Gurian (div.); m. Laurie Ann Sheldon, Apr. 16, 1975; children: Adam Scott, Matthew West, Katharine Amanda, Andrew Charles. BA, Dartmouth Coll., 1959; MA, NYU, 1961; MEd, Harvard U., 1964. Tchr. Hopkins Grammar Sch., New Haven, 1961-63; teaching fellow Harvard U., Cambridge, Mass., 1963-64; admissions dean Princeton (N.J.) U., 1964-69; ednl. cons., 1969—; also trustee AIFS Scholarship Found., Greenwich, Conn., 1989—. Author: Scaling the Ivy Wall, 1987, Beyond the Ivy Wall, 1990, Scaling the Ivy Wall in the 90's, 1995, The Select, 1998. Elder 1st Presbyn. Ch. New Canaan, Conn., 1992—; trustee New Canaan Country Sch., 1989-98, Choate Rosemary Hall Sch., 1998—; class officer Dartmouth Coll., 1990—; nat. bd. advisors Woodrow Wilson NAt. Fellow Found., 1997—. Mem. Am. Acad. Dramatic Arts (trustee 1984-90), Harvard Club N.Y. Avocations: athletics, reading, travel. Home: Wildwood Dr Wilton CT 06897

GREENE, IRA S., lawyer; b. N.Y.C., Nov. 21, 1946; s. Melvin and Syd (Semmelman) G.; m. Robin Colin, Dec. 29, 1973; children: Jessica, Alexander. BA, Syracuse U., 1968; postgrad., U. Buffalo, 1968-69; JD, N.Y. U., 1971. Bar: N.Y. 1972, U.S. Dist. Ct. (ea. dist.) N.Y. 1972, U.S. Ct. Appeals (2d cir.) 1974. Counsel Gainsburg, Gottlieb, Levitan & Cole, N.Y.C., 1982-84; ptnr. Gainsburg, Gottlieb, Levitan, Greene & Cole, N.Y.C., 1984-86, Gainsburg, Greene & Hirsch, Purchase, N.Y., 1986-91, Squadron, Ellenoff, Plesent & Sheinfeld, N.Y.C., 1991—; lectr. in field. Mem. Assn. Comml. Fin. Attys., Bank Lawyers Conf., Bankruptcy Lawyers Bar Assn., Assn. of Bar of City of N.Y. Office: Squadron Ellenoff Plesent & Sheinfeld 551 5th Ave New York NY 10176

GREENE, JAMES S., III, school administrator; b. Harlan, Ky., Nov. 10, 1943; s. James S. Jr. and Elizabeth (Howard) G.; m. Glenda Hollors, Feb. 2, 1968; children: Laurel Elizabeth, Amy Janine, James McKeehan. Postgrad., U. N.C., 1961-62; BS in Edn. French and History, U. Wis., 1965; MA in Edn., Union Coll., Barbourville, Ky., 1973; PhD in Edn., Ohio State U., 1982. Cert. tchr. secondary edn., sch. adminstrn. and supervision, Ky. Tchr. French and History Harlan H.S., 1965-83; supr. instrn. Harlan Ind. Sch. Dist., 1983—; adj. instr. history S.E. Cmty. Coll., Cumberland, Ky., 1977-83; humanities scholar multimedia project The Lynch Legacy Project, 1987. Reviewer The History Tchr., 1973-83; contbr. (book): The Kentucky Ency., 1992. Bd. dirs. Southeastern Ky. Spl. Edn. Coop., Harlan, 1983-88; mem. adv. coun. Stokely Inst. for Liberal Arts Edn., U. Tenn., Knoxville, 1982-89; trustee Pine Mountain (Ky.) Settlement Sch., 1989—; coord. Harlan Christian Arts Festival, 1973, 76; mem. Ky. Bicentennial Commn., Frankfort, 1988-93; pres. bd. dirs. Romance of the Hills Corp., Harlan, 1992-93; elder First Presbyn. Ch., Harlan, 1968-73, 80-83, 90-95, 97—, organist, 1982—; mem. Ky. State Hist. Records Adv. Bd., 1996—. Recipient Award for Outstanding Contbns. to Math. Edn., Ky. Coun. Tchrs. Math., 1992. Avocations: composing and choral arranging. Office: Harlan Ind Sch Dist 420 E Central St Harlan KY 40831-2372

GREENE, JOE (CHARLES EDWARD GREENE), former professional football player, professional football coach; b. Temple, Tex., Sept. 24,

1946. Student, North Tex. State U. Defensive tackle Pitts. Steelers, 1969-81; commentator CBS-NFL Today, 1983; owner pvt. bus., 1983—; now def. coach Miami Dolphins, 1992-95. Named to Sporting News NFL Eastern Conf. All-Star Team, 1969, Sporting News AFC All-Star Team, 1970-74, 79, Football Hall of Fame, 1987; played in Pro Bowl 1970-76, 78, 79, Super Bowl IX, 1974, X, 1975, XIII, 1978, XIV, 1979. Office: care Pro Football Hall of Fame 2121 George Halas Dr NW Canton OH 44708-2630*

GREENE, JOE, Olympic athlete, track and field; b. Dayton, Ohio, Feb. 19, 1967. Grad., Ohio State U., 1990. Olympic track and field participant Barcelona, Spain, 1992; track and field athlete Good Will Games, 1996. Recipient Long Jump Bronze medal Olympics, Barcelona, 1992. Office: US Track & Field 1 Rca Dome Ste 140 Indianapolis IN 46225-1023*

GREENE, JOHN BURKLAND, lawyer; b. Spokane, Wash., May 15, 1939; s. Philip Burkland and Marjorie (Wilcoxson) G.; m. Karen Adele Levin, Dec. 17, 1977; 1 child, Philip Aaron; children from previous marriage—Kristin L. Daly, Kathleen L. J.D., Gonzaga U., 1967; LL.M. in Taxation, NYU, 1968. Bar: Wash. 1967, Idaho 1969. Assoc. Davis, Wright, Todd Riese & Jones, Seattle, 1968-69; assoc., gen. counsel, asst. sec. Boise (Idaho) Cascade Corp, 1969-81; sr. v.p., gen. counsel, sec. Southwest Forest Industries, Inc., Phoenix, 1981-85; ptnr. Wickwire, Goldmark & Schorr, Seattle, 1986-88, Heller, Ehrman, White & McAuliffe (successor by merger to Wickwire, Goldmark & Schorr), Seattle, 1988-89, Wickwire Greene Crosby Brewer & Seward PC, 1989—. Served with USMC, 1957-58. Recipient Dean's medal Gonzaga U., Spokane, 1967; Kenneston Found. fellow, NYU, 1967. Mem. Wash. State Bar Assn., ABA. Office: Wickwire Greene Crosby Brewer & Seward 821 2nd Ave Ste 2000 Seattle WA 98104-1506

GREENE, JOHN CLIFFORD, dentist, former university dean; b. Ashland, Ky., July 19, 1926; s. G. Norman and Ella R. G.; m. Gwen Rustin, Nov. 17, 1957; children: Alan, Lisa, Laura. A.A., Ashland Jr. Coll., 1947; student, Marshall Coll., 1948; D.M.D., U. Louisville, 1952, Sc.D. (hon.), 1980; M.P.H., U. Calif., Berkeley, 1961; Sc.D. (hon.), U. Ky., 1972, Boston U., 1975. Diplomate: Am. Bd. Dental Public Health (pres.). Intern USPHS Hosp., Chgo., 1952-53; staff USPHS Hosp., San Francisco, 1953-54; asst. regional dental cons. Region IX, San Francisco, 1954-56; asst. to chief dental officer USPHS, Washington, 1958-60; chief epidemiology program Dental Health Center, 1961-66; dep. dir. Div. Dental Health, 1966-70, acting dir., 1970, dir., 1970-73; acting dir. Bur. Health Resources Devel., 1973-74, dir., 1974-75; chief dental officer USPHS, 1974-81, dep. surgeon gen., 1978-81; with Epidemic Intelligence Service, Communicable Disease Center, Altanta and Kansas City, Mo., 1956-57; epidemiology and biometry br. Nat. Inst. Dental Research, NIH, Bethesda, Md., 1957-58; prof. and dean sch. dentistry U. Calif., San Francisco, 1981-94; prof. and dean emeritus, 1994—; spl. cons. WHO, India, 1957; faculty Calif., U. Mich., U. Pa.; cons. Am. Dental Assn. Council, Nat. Health Professions Placement Network; mem. adv. com. rsch. women's health NIH, 1995-97. Contbr. writings to profl. publs. Served with USN, 1945-46. Recipient citation Sch. Grad. Dentistry Boston U., 1971, citation U. of the Pacific, 1977, Meritorious and Disting. Service awards HEW, 1972, 75, Outstanding Alumnus award U. Louisville, 1980, award of merit FDI, 1978, Alumnus of Yr. award U. Calif. Sch. Pub. Health, Berkeley, 1984, John W. Knutson award Am. Pub. Health Assn., 1997. Fellow Internat. Coll. Dentists, Am. Coll. Dentists; mem. ADA, Calif. Dental Assn., San Francisco Dental Soc., Internat. Assn. Dental Research (pres.), Am. Assn. Dental Rsch. (pres.), Am. Assn. Pub. Health Dentists, Am. Acad. Periodontology, Am. Assn. Dental Schs. (v.p., chair coun. of deans.), Am. Assn. Pub. Health Dentistry (Disting. Svc. award 1996), Inst. of Medicine of Nat. Acad. Sci. (gov. coun.), Federation Dentaire Internationale (chmn. commn. on public dental health, mem. WHO panel of experts on dental health), U.S. Preventive Svcs., Omicron Kappa Upsilon, Delta Omega. Home: 103 Peacock Dr San Rafael CA 94901-1551 Office: U Calif Sch Dentistry 513 Parnassus Ave Rm 630S San Francisco CA 94122-2722

GREENE, JOHN COLTON, retired history educator; b. Indpls., Mar. 5, 1917; s. Edward Martin and Helen (Carter) G.; m. Ellen Wiemann Greene, Nov. 3, 1945; children: Ruth, Ned, John David. BA, U. S.D., 1938, DHL (hon.), 1986; MA, Harvard U., 1939, PhD, 1952. Instr. U. Chgo., 1948-52; asst. prof. U. Wis., Madison, 1952-56; from assoc. prof. to prof. Iowa State U., Ames, 1956-62; vis. prof. U. Calif., Berkeley, 1962-63; prof. U. Kans., Lawrence, 1963-67; prof. U. Conn., Storrs, 1967-87, prof. emeritus, 1987—. Author: The Death of Adam, 1959, Darwin and the Modern World View, 1961, Science, Ideology and World View, 1981, American Science in Age of Jefferson, 1984, Debating Darwin: Adventures of a Scholar, 1999. Capt. U.S. Army, 1942-46. Jr. fellow Harvard U., 1941-42, 46-48, Guggenheim fellow, 1966-67, Am. Antiquarian Soc. fellow, 1983—; vis. scholar Cambridge U., 1974. Mem. AAUP, History of Sci. Soc. (sec. 1960-70, pres. 1975-77), Midwest Junto History of Sci. (pres. 1961-62), Internat. Acad. History of Sci. (corr.). Democrat. Episcopalian. Avocation: singing.

GREENE, JOHN JOSEPH, lawyer; b. Marshall, Tex., Jan. 19, 1946; William Henry and Camille Anne (Riley) G.; BA, U. Houston, 1969, MA, 1974; JD, South Tex. Coll., 1978. Bar: Tex. 1978, U.S. Supreme Ct., 1982. Asst. atty. City of Amarillo, Tex., 1978-79; asst. atty. Harris County, Tex., 1979-83; pvt. practice, 1983—; city atty. City of Conroe (Tex.), 1983-89, sr. asst. city atty. City of Austin (Tex.), 1990—. Capt. USAR, 1969-76. Decorated Bronze Star, Air Medal. Roman Catholic. Office: 114 W 7th St Ste 400 Austin TX 78701-3008

GREENE, JOHN M., physicist; b. Pitts., Sept. 22, 1928; s. John W. and Frances M. Greene; m. Alice Andrews; 1 child, Emily. BS, Calif. Inst. Tech., 1950; PhD, U. Rochester, 1956. Physicist Princeton (N.J.) Plasma Physics Lab., 1956-82, Gen. Atomics Co., San Diego, 1982—. Recipient James Clerk Maxwell prize Am. Phys. Soc., 1992, Plasma Physics Rsch. Excellence award Am. Phys. Soc., 1992. Office: General Atomics Co PO Box 85608 San Diego CA 92186-5608*

GREENE, JOHN THOMAS, judge; b. Salt Lake City, Nov. 28, 1929; s. John Thomas and Mary Agnes (Hindley) G.; m. Dorothy Kay Buchanan, Mar. 31, 1955; children: Thomas Buchanan Greene, John Buchanan Greene, Mary Kay Greene Platt. BA in Polit. Sci., U. Utah, 1952, JD, 1955. Bar: Utah 1955, U.S. Dist. Ct. (10th cir.) 1955, U.S. Supreme Ct. 1966. Pvt. practice Salt Lake City, 1955-57, asst. U.S. attys., 1957-59; ptnr. Marr, Wilkins & Cannon (and successor firms), Salt Lake City, 1959-75; ptnr., pres., chmn. bd. dirs. Greene, Callister & Nebeker, Salt Lake City, 1975-85; judge U.S. Dist. Ct., Salt Lake City, 1985—. Author: (manual) American Mining Law, 1960; contbr. articles to profl. jours. Chmn. Salt Lake City Cmty. Coun., 1970-75, Utah State Bldg. Authority, Salt Lake City, 1980-85; Regent Utah State Bd. Higher Edn., Salt Lake City, 1982-86. Recipient Order of Coif U. Utah, 1955, Merit of Honor award, 1994, Utah Fed. Bar Disting. Svc. award, 1997. Fellow ABA Found. (life); ABA ho. of dels. 1972-92, bd. govs. 1987-91; mem. Dist. Judges Assn. (pres. 10th cir. 1998—); Utah Bar Assn. (pres. 1971-72, Judge of Yr. award 1995), Am. Law Inst. (life, panelist and lectr. 1980-85, advisor 1986-98); Phi Beta Kappa. Mormon. Avocations: travel, reading, tennis. Office: US Dist Ct 350 S Main St Ste 150 Salt Lake City UT 84101-2180

GREENE, JULE BLOUNTE, lawyer; b. Dublin, Ga., Aug. 15, 1922; s. Jule B. and Bette (O'Neal) G.; m. George Williams, Aug. 22, 1952; children: James Herschel, Bradley O'Neal. A.B., Mercer U., 1949, LL.B., 1950. Bar: Ga. 1950, U.S. Supreme Ct. 1960. Atty. SEC, Atlanta, 1950-53, Washington, 1956-58; atty.-in-charge SEC, Miami, Fla., 1958-69; regional adminstr. SEC, Atlanta, 1969-82; regional counsel Nat. Assn. Securities Dealers, Atlanta, 1982-90; pvt. practice law Macon and Waycross, Ga., 1953-56, Dublin, Ga., 1990—; former mem. Atlanta Fed. Exec. Bd., Interagy. Bd. U.S. Civil Service Examiners; former v.p., dir. Peachtree Fed. Credit Union.; former treas., dir. Mental Health Assn. Met. Atlanta. Served with A.C. AUS, 1942-46. Recipient award for exemplary achievement in pub. adminstrn. William A. Jump Meml. Found., 1958. Mem. Fed. Bar Assn. (pres. South Fla. chpt. 1961), Ga. Bar Assn., Rotary, Kappa Alpha. Methodist. Home: 507 Woods Ave Dublin GA 31021-3542 Office: 210 W Jackson St Dublin GA 31021-6118

GREENE, KAY C., psychologist, author; b. Yankton, S.D., July 10, 1939; d. Fred Orin and Evelyn Irene (Sundy) Green. B.Mus. in Edn., U. Nebr., 1962; MA in Psychology, New Sch. Social Rsch., 1980, PhD in Clin. Psychology, 1983. Lic. psychologist, Md., N.Y., D.C.; ordained deacon Fifth Ave. Presbyn. Ch., N.Y.C., 1997. With Gulf States Utilities, Beaumont, Tex., 1963-64, Tatham, Laird & Kudner, N.Y.C., 1965-66; mgmt. cons. John Wiersma Cons., Washington, 1966; advt. coord. Sullivan Stauffer Colwell & Bayles, N.Y.C., 1966-67; acting supr., ticket agt., svc. rep. Am. Airlines, N.Y.C., 1967; exec. sec. to v.p./chief engr. WPIX-TV, N.Y.C., 1967-71, adminstrv. asst. to news chief, 1971-72; office mgr. Lawrence Letter Svc., N.Y.C., 1973-78; clin. psychologist in pvt. practice N.Y.C., 1985—; regional trainer APA HOPE (HIV) Project, 1992—; tchr. music, English, spl. edn. MacArthur Jr. H.S., Beaumont, 1964-65; student music tchr. U. Nebr. Exptl. H.S., Lincoln, 1961-62; lectr. in field; condr. seminars in field; appeared on Donahue, Good Morning New York, Kelly and Co., Survival into the 21st Century, Turning Inward; radio shows include The Alan Colmes Show, WABC, N.Y., Alan Colmes, WPIX, N.Y., Open Session, Ben Reese, WNYE, N.Y., From Head to Heart, WXLO, N.Y., Foundation Focus, WNEW, N.Y., Wellness Workshop, WNWK FM, N.Y., others; pres. Bridge of Change; sr. rep. UN Hdqrs. for World Fedn. Mental Health, 1990-95, organizer various confs., keynote spkr. various internat. confs. past staff therapist/sr. staff psychologist Fifth Ave. Ctr. for Counseling and Psychotherapy, N.Y.C.; rep. UN Hdqrs. for Internat. Coun. of Psychologists, 1996—; adj. asst. prof. St. Francis Coll., Bklyn. Coll., 1997-98; vis. assoc. prof. Lincoln Ctr. Fordham U., N.Y.C., 1997-98, adj. assoc. prof., 1998; adj. assoc. prof. Pace U., N.Y.C., 1999—; vice chair NGO/DPI exec. com. UN Hdqs., 1998—; exec. dir. Millennium NGO Forum UN Hdqrs., 1998-2000. Contbr. articles to profl. jours. Named Internat. Woman of the Yr. in recognition of svcs. to mental health Internat. Biog. Centre, 1993-94; recipient Disting. Leadership award Internat. Directory of Disting. Leadership. Mem. APA (Nat. AIDS task force 1988—, fellow internat. divsn. 52 1999), Am. Fedn. TV and Radio Artists, Authors Guild, Authors League, Internat. Coun. of Psychologists (sec.-gen. 1997—, rep. UN hdqrs. 1996—), Internat. Platform Assn., C.G. Jung Found. for Analytical Psychology, N.Y. Acad. Sci., N.Y. State Psychol. Assn., Screen Actors Guild, Soc. for Psychol. Study of Social Issues, World Assn. for Psychosocial Rehab. (rep. UN Hdqs. 1998—), World Fedn. Mental Health, Sigma Alpha Iota (Kappa chpt.), Pi Kappa Lambda, Psi Chi. Avocations: piano, photography, pets, painting, cooking. Home and Office: 30 Waterside Plz Apt 13E New York NY 10010-2630

GREENE, KEVIN DARWIN, professional football player; b. N.Y.C., July 31, 1962. Student, Auburn U. With L.A. Rams, 1985-92; linebacker Pitts. Steelers, 1993-95, Carolina Panthers, 1996-98, San Francisco 49ers, 1998, Carolina Panthers, 1998—. Named The Sporting News NFL All-Pro Team, 1989, 94; selected to Pro Bowl, 1989, 94. Achievements: led NFL in sacks, 1994. Address: Carolina Panthers 800 S Mint St Charlotte NC 28202-1518*

GREENE, LAURA HELEN, physicist; b. Cleve., June 12, 1952; d. Sam and Frances (Kain) G.; children: Max Greene Giannetta, Leo Greene Giannetta. BS cum laude in Physics, Ohio State U., 1974, MS in Physics, 1978; MS in Exptl. Physics, Cornell U., 1980, PhD in Physics, 1984. Mem. tech. staff Hughes Aircraft Co., Torrance, Calif., 1974-75; teaching asst. Ohio State U., Columbus, 1975-76, rsch. asst., 1976-77; teaching asst. Cornell U., Ithaca, N.Y., 1977-79, rsch. asst., 1979-83; postdoctoral mem. tech. staff Bellcore (formerly Bell Labs.), Red Bank, N.J., 1983-85, Murray Hill, N.J., 1983-85; mem. tech. staff Bellcore (formerly Bell Labs.), Red Bank, N.J., 1985-92; prof. dept. physics U. Ill., Urbana, 1992—; Beckman assoc. Ctr. Advanced Study U Ill. at Urbana-Champaign, 1996-97; mem. McMillan award com. 1994-96, chair, 1995-97; chair Gordon Rsch. Conf., 1998, co-chair, 1996; mem. various rev. panels and workshops NSF and Dept. Energy; presenter in field. Contbr. over 150 articles to profl. jours.; presenter over 150 domestic and internat. invited talks. Interim and founding trustee Inst. for Complex and Adaptive Materials, Los Alamos and U. Calif. Recipient Beckman award U. Ill. Campus Rsch. Bd., 1993, E.O. Lawrence award in materials rsch. Dept. Energy, 1999; rsch. grantee NSF, 1991—, ONR, 1995—, Dept. Energy, 1995—. Fellow AAAS, Am. Acad. Arts and Scis., Am. Phys. Soc. (gen. councilor 1992—, congl. fellow screening com. 1993, exec. bd. 1995—, com. on coms. 1995—, chair 1997, search com. The Phys. Rev. 1996, nominating com. divsn. condensed matter physics 1998—, Maria Goeppert-Mayer award 1994, Centennial Spkr. 1997); mem. Materials Rsch. Soc. (symposium chair 1992), Am. Assn. Physics Tchrs., Internat. Union Pure and Applied Physicists (commr., U.S. liaison com. 1996—, U.S. del. to Low-Temperature Physics Commn. 1996—). Avocations: children, physics, working out, music. Office: U Ill Loomis Lab Physics 1110 W Green St Urbana IL 61801-3003

GREENE, LAURENCE WHITRIDGE, JR., surgical educator; b. Denver, Jan. 18, 1924; s. Laurence Whitridge Sr. and Freda (Schmitt) G.; m. Frances Stewart, Sept. 16, 1950 (dec. Dec. 1977); children: Charlotte Greene Kerr, Mary Whitridge Greene, Laurence Whitridge III; m. Nancy Kay Bennett, Dec. 7, 1984. BA, Colo. Coll., 1945; MD, U. Colo., 1947; postgrad., U. Chgo., 1948-50. Diplomate Am. Bd. of Surgery. Intern St. Lukes Hosp., Denver, 1947-48; sr. intern in ob./gyn. U. Chgo. Lying-In Hosp., 1948-49; surg. resident U. Cin. Gen. Hosp., 1952-55, sr. surg. resident, 1955-57, chief surgery resident, 1957-58; clin. surgery asst. Sch. of Medicine U. Colo., Denver, 1958-61, clin. instr. Sch. of Medicine, 1961-67, asst. clin. prof. Sch. of Medicine, 1967-75, assoc. clin. prof. Sch. of Medicine, 1975-87, clin. prof. Sch. of Medicine, 1987—; adj. prof. zoology and physiology U. Wyo., Laramie, 1970-80; mem. staff Ivinson Meml. Hosp., Laramie, 1958—; chmn. Wyo chpt. Com. on Trauma, 1973-89; tchr., mem. adv. staff U. Colo. Med. Sch., Denver, 1958-83; mem. advisor, surgeon U. Wyo. Athletics, Laramie, 1975-80, Wyo. Hwy. Patrol, 1950—. Contbr. numerous articles to profl. jours. Lt. M.C. (s.g.) USN, 1950-52, Korea. Fellow ACS; mem. Am. Assn. for Surgery of Trauma, Southwestern Surgery Congress, Western Surg. Assn., Mont Reed Soc., Masons, Shriners, Sigma Xi. Republican. Episcopalian. Avocations: golf, sports, hunting, fishing.

GREENE, LEONARD MICHAEL, aerospace manufacturing executive, institute executive; b. N.Y.C., June 8, 1918; s. Max and Lyn (Furman) G.; m. Beverly Kaufman, June 27, 1943 (div. 1957); children: Randall Ashley, Bonnie LeVar, Laurie Baldwin; m. Phyllis Saks, June 8, 1958 (dec. Oct. 1965); children: Douglas, Charles, Donald, Stephen, Terry; m. Joyce Teck, Jan. 2, 1967; stepchildren: Jeffrey Meller, William Meller, Gary Meller, Amy Meller Gerbe. BS in Engring., CCNY, 1937, MS in Engring., 1939; postgrad., Guggenheim Sch. Aeronautics, NYU; D in Civil Law (hon.), Pace U., 1977. Rsch. chemist Rubber & Asbestos Corp., New Jersey, 1938-41; aerodynamicist, engring. test pilot Grumman Aircraft Corp., L.I., N.Y., 1941-45; pres. Safe Flight Instrument Corp., White Plains, N.Y., 1946—; pres., founder SoundTitles, Inc., 1989; bd. dirs. Nationwide Ins. Author: (book) Free Enterprise Without Poverty, 1981, The National Tax Rebate: A New America With Less Government, 1998, (monographs) A Plan for a Nat. Demogrant Financed by a Value-Added Tax, The Medical Costs Recovery Program; patentee aircraft stall warning indicator, wind shear monitor and more than 60 others. Mem. adv. bd. Martha's Vineyard Hosp.; pres., founder Inst. for Socioecon. Studies, 1970; v.p., co-founder Corp. Angel Network, White Plains, 1981—; mem. spl. com. on income maintenance and council on trends and perspectives U.S. C. of C., 1975-76; bd. dirs. Blythedale Children's Hosp., Urban League Westchester Inc., Nationwide Ins.; chmn. Income Assistance/Community Devel. Program of Westchester Council of Social Agys.; pres., founder Fair Share Found., Inc.; mem. income maintenance com. Community Svc. Soc.; mem. work group on welfare reform Task Force on N.Y.C. Fiscal Crisis; mem. Westchester Coordinating Coun. on Handicapped; mem. Conf. Bd.'s Econ. Forum, 1979. Recipient Air Safety award Flight Safety Found., 1949, 81, Pilot Safety award Nat. Bus. Aircraft Assn., 1961, Employer Merit award Pres.'s Com. on Employment of Handicapped, Albert Gallatin award for Civic Leadership, Flight Safety Found award for Meritorious Svc., Disting. Svc. award Human Rights Commn. of White Plains, 1976, Medallion award Found. for Westchester C.C., 1988, U.S. EPA, Region I Spl. Act award, 1989;, Meritorious Svc. to Aviation award Nat. Bus. Aircraft Assn., 1996 nominated N.Y. State Employer of Yr; cited by N.Y. Gov.'s Com. to Employ Handicapped, 1966; commendation from sec. dept. HEW, private sector initiative commendation Pres. of U.S.; inducted into Nat. Inventors Hall of Fame, 1991. Fellow AIAA (assoc.); mem. Soc. Exptl. Test Pilots (life), Nat. Aviation Assn., Internat. 12 Meter Assn. (voting), Edgartown Yacht Club, N.Y. Yacht Club, Sheldrake Yacht Club (Mamaroneck, N.Y.), Royal Hamilton Amateur Dinghy Club (Bermuda), Quaker Ridge Golf Club (Scarsdale, N.Y.), Alpha Beta Gamma. Co-founder Courageous Sailing Ctr., Inc., Boston, to which donated 12-meter yacht Courageous IV, winner America's Cup, 1974, 77. Home: 6 Hickory Rd Scarsdale NY 10583-3016 Office: Safe Flight Instrument Corp 20 New King St White Plains NY 10604-1204

GREENE, LILIANE, French educator, editor; b. Salonica, Greece, Oct. 10, 1928; came to U.S., 1941; d. Maurice and Daisy (Kohn) Massarano; m. Thomas McLernon Greene, May 20, 1950; children: Philip James, Christopher George, Francis Richard. BA, Hunter Coll., 1948; MA, Columbia U., 1949; PhD, Yale U., 1969. Asst. in instrn. French Yale U., New Haven, 1964-65, instr., 1967-68, lectr., mng. editor Yale French Studies, 1980-94 (ret.); instr. Conn. Coll., New London, 1968-69, asst. prof., 1970-75. Contbr. articles to profl. jours. Fullbright fellow, 1949-50. Mem. MLA, Am. Assn. Tchrs. French, Ctr. Ind. Study (founding mem., pres. 1978-79, bd. dirs. 1977-89), Conn. Acad. of Arts and Scis. Democrat. Avocations: travel, theater. Home: 125 Livingston St New Haven CT 06511-2428

GREENE, LYDIA ABBI JWUAN, elementary education educator; b. La Fayette, Tenn., Sept. 20, 1963; d. Thomas and Icy (Daniel) G. BSBA, Tenn. State U., 1985, M in Elem. Edn., 1993. Customer svc. rep. JC Penney Telemarketing Ctr., Nashville, 1986-93; tchr. Paragon Mills Elem. Sch., Nashville, 1993—; tchr. Youth Hobby Shop Camp, Nashville, 1981-83, Met. Nashville Edn. Assn., 1994—; mem. Faculty Adv. Com.; sci. facilitator Paragon Mills Elem. Mem. NEA, Nat. Sci. Tchrs.' Assn., Tenn. Edn. Assn., Fed. Aviation Assn. (educator 1995—), Tenn. Reading Assn., Nashville Inst. Arts, Libr. Congress. Mem. Ch. Christ. Avocations: personal computing, reading, travel. Office: Paragon Mills Elem Sch 260 Paragon Mills Rd Nashville TN 37211-4075

GREENE, MARTIN LEE, internist; b. Omaha, Nov. 5, 1939; s. Irving and Nioma I. Greene; m. Beth Weisberg, June 24, 1962 (div. Dec. 1986); m. Toby Saks, Nov. 1, 1987. BA, Harvard Coll., 1961, MD, 1965. Diplomate Am. Bd. Internal Medicine. Resident in medicine Mass. Gen. Hosp., Boston, 1965-67; clin. assoc. NIH, Bethesda, Md., 1967-69; sr. fellow Sch. Medicine U. Wash., Seattle, 1969-71, clin. prof., 1984—; physician Minor and James Med., Seattle, 1971-95, med. dir., 1995—; chmn. gastroenterology Swedish Med. Ctr., Seattle, 1976—. Contbr. articles to profl. jours. Pres. King County Health Planning Coun., Seattle, 1974-76; bd. dirs. Seattle Youth Symphony, 1987-96. Lt. comdr. USPHS, 1967-69. Named Disting. Physician, Crohns Colitis Assn. Am., 1995. Fellow Am. Coll. Physicians; mem. Am. Gastroent. Assn. (treas. 1991-96), Am. Soc. Internal Medicine (del.), Wash. State Med. Assn. (del.), Physicians Ins. Assn. (bd. dirs. 1995—). Avocations: mountain climbing, music. Home: 2412 40th Ave E Seattle WA 98112-2540 Office: Minor and James Med 515 Minor Ave Ste 200 Seattle WA 98104-2138

GREENE, MELANIE ANITA WARD, education educator; b. Banner Elk, N.C., Jan. 14, 1956; d. Ray Floyd and Virginia (Cook) Ward; m. Ronald C. Greene; children: Erin Diana, Kevin Taylor. BS, Appalachian State U., 1976, MA, 1977; EdD (hon.), East Tenn. State U., 1983. Tchr. Watauga County Schs., Boone, N.C., 1977-87; adj. asst. prof. Appalachian State U., Boone, N.C., 1988-96, asst. prof., 1996—; advisor Collegiate Mid. Level Assn., Appalachian State U., 1996—. Contbr. articles to profl. jours. Mem. PTO, Hardin Park, Boone, 1988-97. Mem. Am. Assn. Colls. of Tchr. Edn., Nat. Mid. Sch. Assn., Assn. Advancement of Computing in Edn., N.C. Mid. Sch. Assn., Alpha Delta Kappa (pres. 1995-97). Avocations: reading, golf. Office: Appalachian State Univ Duncan Hall Boone NC 28608

GREENE, NATALIE CONSTANCE, protective services official; b. Ft. Benning, Ga., Nov. 26, 1960; d. Wilbur Murray and Vernel Jeanette (Smalls) G. BS in Phys. Edn., East Stroudsburg U., 1983; AAS in Gen. Bus., Mercer County C.C., 1989, AS in Criminal Justice, 1998; AS in Allied Health Sci., Coll. of Air Force, 1997. Mil. pay clk. Dept. Def.-U.S. Army, Trenton, N.J., 1984-85, Dept. Def.-USAF, McGuire AFB, N.J., 1985-86; spl. police officer Willingboro (N.J.) Police Dept., 1986-90; budget asst. Dept. Def., West Trenton, N.J., 1986-88; edn. planner, budget officer Dept. Edn., Edison, N.J., 1988-89; mcht. svcs. clk. Chem. Bank, Cherry Hill, N.J., 1989-90; transit police officer Southeastern Pa. Transp. Authority, Phila., 1990-97; victim support adv. and investigator dept. pub. safety. Drexel U., Phila., 1997—. Master sgt. USAFR, 1980—. Recipient Desert Shield/Storm award, 1992, Cert. of Appreciation, CAP, 1991, Willingboro Twp., 1991, Morton Elem. Sch., 1991, Outstanding Young Women of N.J., 1989. Mem. NAFE, VFW, Air Force Sgts. Assn., Fraternal Order Police, Noncommd. Officers Acad. Grad. Assn. Baptist. Avocations: volleyball, tennis, track, swimming, piano. Home: 132 Crestview Dr Willingboro NJ 08046-3538

GREENE, PAUL W., federal judge. Magistrate judge Huntsville, Ala. Fax: 205-536-0446. Office: 103 US Post Office Ct House 101 Holmes Ave NE Huntsville AL 35801

GREENE, RICHARD H., journalist; b. Milford, Conn., Aug. 12, 1955; s. Eugene Harold and Bebe (Bender) G.; m. Katherine Barrett, Feb. 21, 1982; children: Benjamin, Sandra. BS in Journalism, Northwestern U., 1977. Rschr. Forbes mag., N.Y.C., 1977-79, reporter, 1979-81, staff writer, 1981-82, assoc. editor, 1982-84, contbg. editor, 1984-89; freelance writer N.Y.C., 1984—; spkr. on state and mcpl. mgmt.; cons. Maxwell Sch. Syracuse U.; mem. adv. bd. Urban Inst., Govtl. Acctg. Stds. Bd. Author (with Katherine Barrett): The Man Behind the Magic, 1991, Frankly My Dear..., 1996; spl. projects editor Governing mag.; co-prodr. Walt Disney biographical CD-ROM; contbr. articles to mags., including Fin. World, Glamour, Ladies' Home Jour., Reader's Digest, Redbook, Working Woman, others. Curator Walt Disney Family On-line Mus. Recipient Amos Tuck award Dartmouth Coll., 1978, award for excellence in fin. journalism N.Y. Soc. CPAs, 1984, 91, cert. of merit, 1987, Washington Monthly Journalism award, 1999; named author of one of ten best articles of yr. Forbes' Media Guide, 1993. Home and Office: 25 Waterside Plz Apt GG New York NY 10010-2621

GREENE, ROBERT ALLAN, former university administrator; b. Boston, Nov. 6, 1931; s. Merrill Francis and Alice Josephine (Anderson) G.; m. Mary E. Mahoney, July 20, 1957; children—Robert, Merrill, Helen, Priscilla. B.A., Boston Coll., 1953, M.A., 1954; Ph.D., Harvard U., 1961. Lectr. dept. English Univ. Coll., U. Toronto, Ont., Can., 1958-61; asst. prof. Univ. Coll., U. Toronto, 1962-65, assoc. prof., 1966-69, prof., 1969-80; dean U. Toronto Faculty of Arts and Sci., 1972-77; Leverhulme vis. lectr. Durham (Eng.) U., 1962-63; vice-chancellor for acad. affairs, provost U. Mass., Boston, 1980-87. Editor: (With H.R. MacCallum) Nathaniel Culverwell's Discourse of the Light of Nature, 1652, 1971. Home: 19 Centre St Apt 5 Cambridge MA 02139-2112 Office: U Mass Harbor Campus Boston MA 02125

GREENE, ROBERT BERNARD, JR. (BOB GREENE), broadcast television correspondent, columnist, author; b. Columbus, Ohio, Mar. 10, 1947; s. Robert Bernard and Phyllis Ann (Harmon) G.; m. Susan Bonnet Koebel, Feb. 13, 1971; 1 dau., Amanda Sue. B.S., Northwestern U., 1969. Reporter Chgo. Sun-Times, 1969-71, columnist, 1971-78; syndicated columnist Field Newspaper Syndicate, Irvine, Calif., 1976-81, Tribune Co. Syndicate, N.Y.C., 1981—; contbg. corr. ABC News Nightline, from 1981; columnist Chgo. Tribune, 1978—; lectr. fine arts U. Chgo. Contbg. editor: Esquire Mag., 1980—; books include We Didn't Have None of Them Fat Funky Angels on the Wall of Heartbreak Hotel and Other Reports from America, 1971; Running: A Nixon-McGovern Campaign Journal, 1973, Billion Dollar Baby, 1974, Johnny Deadline, Reporter: The Best of Bob Greene, 1976, (with Paul Galloway) Bagtime, 1977, American Beat, 1983, Good Morning, Merry Sunshine, 1984, Cheeseburgers, The Best of Bob Greene, 1985, Be True to Your School, 1987, Homecoming: When the Soldiers Returned From Vietnam, 1989, Hang Time: Days and Dreams With Michael Jordan, 1992. Recipient Nat. Headliner award for best newspaper column in U.S., 1977, Peter Lisagor award, 1981. Office: Chgo Tribune 435 N Michigan Ave Chicago IL 60611-4066*

GREENE, ROBERT WILLIAM, journalism educator, media consultant; b. Jamaica, N.Y., July 12, 1929; s. Francis McLaughlin and Mary Virginia (Clancy) G.; m. Kathleen A. Greene, Jan. 28, 1951; children: Robert William, Lea Marie (dec.). Student, Fordham U., 1947-50. Reporter Jersey Jour., 1949-50; sr. investigator N.Y.C. Anti-Crime Com., 1950-55; reporter Newsday, Garden City, N.Y., 1955; leader investigative team Newsday,

1967-73, sr. editor, 1970-92, Long Island editor, 1972-78, asst. mng. editor, 1978-93; ret., 1993; Disting. Stessin prof. journalism & mass media studies Hofstra U.; staff investigator U.S. Senate Select Com. on Unfair Practices in Labor/Mgmt. Field, 1957; dir. Ariz. Project, 1976-77; pres., CEO Greene Assocs.; lectr. in field; journalism program coord. SUNY, Stony Brook, 1986-95. Author: Naked Came the Stranger, 1969, The Heroin Trail, 1973, The Sting Man, 1981. Chmn. publicity Smithtown Tercentenary, 1967; founding mem., bd. dirs. Suffolk County Happy Landings Fund; bd. visitors Inst. on Polit. Journalism Georgetown U.; bd. dirs. Smithtown Hist. Soc., Mus. at Stony Brook, Cleary Sch. for Deaf; founder, former pres. L.I. Press Club; founder St. Anthony's Gridiron Club; mem. Pres.' Coun. Xavier H.S.; chmn. Mollenhoff Journalism Award Comn. Recipient George Polk award L.I. U.; Peter Zenger award U. Ariz.; James Wright Brown award, Gold Medal Pulitzer prize, 1970, 74, Mo. medal for disting. service to Am. journalism, 1979; Front Page award, 1982, Edgar award Mystery Writers Am., 1982, Disting. Achievement award Fordham U. Grad. Sch. Journalism, 1994; named to L.I. Hall of Fame, 1991, hon. mem. Class 1996 U. Md. Coll. Journalism; hon. pres. Norwegian Investigative Reporters, Oslo, Norway, 1991. Fellow Soc. Profl. Journalists; mem. Investigative Reporters and Editors Group (pres. 1976-77, chmn. exec. bd.), Assn. Edn. Journalism & Mass Comms., Radio & TV News Dirs.'s Assn. Republican. Roman Catholic. Club: Hofstra Univ. Club, L.I. Press (pres. 1976). Office: 4 Ardmore Pl Kings Park NY 11754-4002 also: Hofstra U Dept Journalism Rm 121 Dempster Hall 111 Hofstra U Hempstead NY 11550-1090

GREENE, RONALD D., advertising executive; b. 1943. With Commentary Mag., N.Y.C., 1965-75, Franklin Mint, Franklin Center, Pa., 1975-83; prin., pres. Devon Direct Mktg. and Advt., Berwyn, Pa., 1983—. Office: Devon Direct Mktg and Advt 200 Berwyn Park Berwyn PA 19312-1178*

GREENE, STEPHEN, painter; b. N.Y.C., Sept. 19, 1917; s. William and Augusta (Lasky) G.; m. Sigrid de Lima, 1953; 1 dau., Alison de Lima. Art student, Nat. Acad. Design, 1936-37, Art Student's League, 1937-38; BFA, U. Iowa, 1942, MA, 1942. Instr. art Ind. U., 1945-46, Washington U., St. Louis, 1946-47, Parsons Sch. Design, N.Y.C., 1947-56, Pratt Inst., N.Y.U., Art Students League; artist in residence Princeton U., 1956-59; guest critic Columbia U., 1961-64, asst. prof., 1964-67; assoc. prof., then prof. Tyler Sch. Art, Temple Univ., 1968-85. One-man shows include Durlacher Bros., N.Y.C., 1947, 49, 52, Grace Borgenicht Gallery, 1955, 58, 59, Staempfli Gallery, 1961, 64, 66, 69, William Zierler Gallery, N.Y.C., 1971, 72, 73, 75, Marilyn Pearl Gallery, N.Y.C., 1977, 78, 79, 80, 82-85, 87, 88, Galeria Ponce, Mexico City, 1977, 79, 82, Ruth Bachofner Gallery, L. A., 1985, 87, 88, 90, Rosenthal Fine Arts, Chgo., 1987, Marilyn Pearl Gallery, 1989, St. Louis Art Mus., 1989, Meredith Long Gallery, Houston, 1989, Marilyn Pearl Gallery, N.Y.C., 1989, St. Louis Mus., 1989, Neilson Gallery, Boston, 1998, Bachofner Gallery, Santa Monica, Calif., 1998, David Betzel Gallery, N.Y.C., 1998; retrospectives, Dana and De Cordova Mus., 1953, Princeton, 1956, The Corcoran Gallery of Am. Art, 1963, Akron Art Inst., 1978, Columbus Gallery Fine Arts, Ohio, 1978, N.C. Mus. Art, Raleigh, 1978, Currier Gallery Art, Manchester, N.H., 1978, exhbns., Whitney Mus., Art Inst. Chgo., Nat. Acad. Design, Milw. Art Inst., Va. Mus. Fine Arts, Met. Mus., Bklyn. Mus., Mus. Modern Art, Carnegie Internat., Musee d'Art Moderne of Paris, Found., Maeght, France, Am., São Paolo Biennial, (Brazil), 1961, Painters in, Europe, Prato, Italy, 1973, Marilyn Pearl Gallery, N.Y.C., 1987, Ruth Bachofner Gallery, Los Angeles, 1987, Rosenthal Fine Arts Inc., Chgo., 1987; represented in permanent collections, Bklyn. Mus., Carnegie Inst., Inst. Contemporary Art, Chgo., Newberry Mus., Wadsworth Athenaeum, Hartford, Conn., St. Louis City Art Mus., Neuberger Mus., Purchase, N.Y., Pasadena (Calif.) Art Mus., Va. Mus. Fine Arts, Rockhill Nelson Gallery, Detroit Inst. Art, Whitney Mus., Met. Mus., Corcoran Gallery, Washington, San Francisco Art Mus., Art. Inst. Chgo., Fogg Art Inst., Addison Gallery, Mus. Modern Art, Tate Gallery, London, Guggenheim Mus., High Art Mus., Atlanta, Chase Manhattan Bank, Tenn. Fine Arts Center, Rose Art Mus. Brandeis U., others, also in pvt. collections. Recipient purchase prize Va. Mus. Fine Arts, 5th biennial contemporary Am. painting, 1946, 2d prize Kearney Meml., Milw. Art Inst., 1964, bd. dirs. award John Herron Art Mus., 1946, 1st prize ann. contemporary Am. painting Calif. Palace Legion of Honor, 1947, Prix de Rome, 1949, purchase prize Contemporary Am. Painting Exhibit, Isaac Delgado Mus., New Orleans, 1958, Corcoran Fourth prize, 1965, 2,500 award Nat. Inst. Arts and Letters, 1967, 5,000 grant Coun. of the Arts, 1967, Andrew Carnegie prize Nat. Acad. Design, 1971, Purchase award Acad. of Arts and Letters, N.Y.C., 1995, 96. Home: 407 Storms Rd Valley Cottage NY 10989-1214

GREENE, STEPHEN CRAIG, lawyer; b. Watertown, N.Y., Apr. 27, 1946; s. Harold Adelbert and Mildred Esther (Baker) G. A.B., Syracuse U., 1967, J.D., 1970; m. Nancy Jean Adams, Mar. 28, 1965; children: Kathryn, Stephen, Hilary. Bar: N.Y., 1971, U.S. Tax Ct., 1977. Asst. to pres. SUNY, Oswego, 1970-73; assoc. firm Leyden E. Brown, Oswego, 1973-75; ptnr. Brown and Greene, 1976-81; pvt. practice law, 1981—; bd. dirs. Found. Corp. Legal Studies, Inc., 1968-70; town atty. Oswego, 1972—; counsel Oswego County Bd. Realtors, 1978—. Mem. Oswego County Rep. Com., 1974-85, counsel, 1980-83; bd. dirs. Oswego Hosp., 1981—, mem. exec. com., 1985—, pres., 1996-98; pres. Oswego Health, Inc., 1997—; bd. dirs. Oswego Health, Inc., 1997—, pres., 1997—; bd. dirs. United Way of Oswego County, Inc., 1985-88; bd. dirs. Campbell's Point Assn., 1994-96; gen counsel Express Abstract Co., 1992-95. Recipient Ins. Counsel Jour. award Internat. Assn. Ins. Counsel, 1970. Mem. ABA, N.Y. Bar Assn., Oswego County Bar Assns., Greater Oswego C. of C. (bd. dir. 1980-87), Phi Delta Phi. Episcopalian. Clubs: Oswego Country (counsel 1977-81). Lodges: Masons, Shriners. Home: 611 W 1st St Oswego NY 13126-4137 Office: 85 W Bridge St Oswego NY 13126-2011

GREENE, TERRY J., legislative staff member; m. Tricia; children: Patrick, Brady, Douglas, Teddy. Student, Ariz. State U.; BA in Speech Comm., Drury Coll. Press sec. Congressman Thomas Ewing, Washington, 1991-95, dist. adminstr., 1995-96, chief of staff, chief advisor pub. policy, legis. matters, 1996—. Baseball scholar Ariz. State U. Office: Office of Congressman Thomas W Ewing 102 E Main # 307 Urbana IL 61801*

GREENE, THOMASINA TALLEY, concert pianist, educator; b. Nashville, June 29, 1913; d. Thomas Washington and Ellen Elizabeth (Roberts) Talley; m. Lorenzo Johnston, Dec. 19, 1942 (dec. 1988); 1 child, Lorenzo Thomas. BA, Fisk U., 1929; diploma in music, Julliard Sch. of Music, 1932; EdD, Columbia U., 1942. Head music dept. St. Phillips Jr. Coll., San Antonio, 1933-34; supr. music dept. Columbia (Mo.) Pub. Schs., 1932-33, Sam Houston Coll., Austin, Tex., summer 1934; head music dept. N.C. State U., Durham, 1934-39; part-time dir. art dept. Lincoln U., Jefferson City, Mo., summer 1942, part-time prof. music, 1943-45; dir. Greene Sch. of Music, Jefferson City, 1942-89; with music program Sta. KRCG-TV, Jefferson City, 1966-81. Mem. exec. bd. Jefferson City Community Concert Assn., 1967-71; dir. project upbeat grant Md. Coun. Arts, 1978-79. Named Woman of Achievement for Jefferson City, 1963; recipient Disting. Svc. award 2d Bapt. Ch., Jefferson City, 1978, 89; fellow Julliard Sch. Music, 1929-32, Rockefeller Found., 1939-42. Mem. Nat. Soc. Lit. and Arts, Nat. Music Tchrs. Assn., Mo. Music Tchrs. Assn., Area Music Tchrs. Assn., Modern Priscilla Art and Charity Club, AAUW (bd. dirs. Jefferson City chpt., Woman of Yr. award 1963), Alpha Kappa Alpha (Regional Disting. Svc. award 1965), Kappa Delta Pi, Pi Lambda Theta. Episcopalian. Avocations: painting, china, card games, exercise. Home and Office: 3608 Mall Ridge St Jefferson City MO 65109-4977

GREENE, TIMOTHY GEDDES, lawyer; b. Lewiston, Idaho, May 12, 1939; s. George and Norma (Geddes) G.; m. Patricia Apcar, Sept. 13, 1969; children: Andrew Apcar, Jonathan Apcar. BA cum laude, U. Idaho, 1961; LLB, George Washington U., 1965. Bar: D.C., 1966, Tex., 1990. Exec v.p., gen. counsel Sallie Mae SEC, Washington, 1965-69, exec. asst. to the chmn., 1969-71; spl. asst. to gen. counsel U.S. Treasury Dept., Washington, 1971-73; sec. U.S. Emergency Loan Guarantee Bd., Washington, 1971-73; exec. v.p., gen. counsel Student Loan Mktg. Assn. Sallie Mae, Washington, 1973-79; prin. Eggers & Greene, Dallas, 1979-90, Stuart Mill Capital, Inc., Arlington, Va., 1997—. Bd. dirs. Wolf Trap Found. for the Performing Arts, Vienna, Va., 1991-97, NCCJ, 1993—. Ford Found. fellow Brown U. Grad. Sch. Econs., 1961-62. Republican. Mem. LDS Ch. Avocations: sports, golf, tennis. Home: 1006 Bellview Rd Mc Lean VA 22102-1102

GREENE, WARREN W., anesthesiologist; b. Santa Monica, Calif., Sept. 12, 1912. BA, U. So. Calif., 1935; MD, U. Health Scis., L.A., 1941; MB, Chgo. Med. Sch., 1940. Diplomate Am. Bd. Anesthesiology. Intern Elmhurst Meml. Hosp., 1940-41; resident Wadsworth VA Hosp., L.A., 1949-50; mem. hon. staff St. John's Hosp., Santa Monica, Calif., 1972—. Fellow Am. Coll. Anesthesiologists; mem. AMA, Calif. Med. Assn., Calif. Soc. Anesthesiology, L.A. County Med. Assn. Home: 800 Greentree Rd Pacific Palisades CA 90272-3911

GREENE, WENDY SEGAL, special education educator; b. New Rochelle, N.Y., Jan. 9, 1929; d. Louis Peter and Anne Henrietta (Kahan) Segal; m. Charles Edward Smith (div. 1952); m. Richard M. Greene Jr. (div. 1967); children: Christopher S., Kerry William, Karen Beth Greene Olson; m. Richard M. Greene Sr., Aug. 29, 1985 (dec. 1986). Student, Olivet Coll., 1946-48, Santa Monica Coll., 1967-70; BA in Child Devel., Calif. State U., Los Angeles, 1973, MA in Elem. Edn., 1975. Cert. tchr., Calif. Counselor Camp Watitoh, Becket, Mass., 1946-49; asst. tchr. Outdoor Play Group, New Rochelle, 1946-58; edn. sec. pediatrics Syracuse (N.Y.) Meml. Hosp., 1952-53; with St. John's Hosp., Santa Monica, Calif., 1962-63; head tchr. Head Start, L.A., 1966-77; tchr. spl. edn. L.A. Unified Sch. Dist., 1977—, Salvin Spl. Edn. Ctr., L.A., 1977-85, Perez Spl. Edn. Ctr., L.A., 1986-; instr. mktg. rsch. for motivational rsch. Anderson-McConnell Agy., 1966; mentor tchr. L.A. Unified Sch. Dist., 1992—. Contbr. to house organ of St. John's Hosp.; co-editor of newspaper for Salvin Sch., L.A.; contbg. reporter El Aguiler (The Eagle), Perez. Mem. LEARN Coun., Perez, 1996—, cmty. adv. com. spl. edn. Tustin Unified Sch. Dist., 1994—; vol. Hospice of St. Joseph Hosp., Orange, Calif., 1985—; bd. dirs. Richland Ave. Youth House, L.A., 1960-63, Emotional Health Assn., L.A., 1961-66, Richland Ave. Sch. PTA, 1959-63. Mem. AAUW, Coun. Exceptional Children, Olivet Coll. Alumni Assn., United Tchrs. L.A., Westside Singers (L.A.), Celebration of Life Singers, Kappa Delta Pi. Jewish. Avocations: music, writing, theater, travel. Home: 14291 Prospect Ave Tustin CA 92780-2316

GREENE, WILLIAM HENRY L'VEL, academic administrator; b. Richburg, S.C., July 28, 1943; s. Malachi and Mattie Greene; m. Ruth Lipscomb; children—Omari, Jamila. B.A., Johnson C. Smith U., 1966; M.A., Mich. State U., 1970, Ph.D., 1972. Asst. prof. U. Mass., Amherst, 1972-76; dir. in-service tchr. edn. Ctr. for Urban Edn., 1974-76; asst. to chancellor, dir. devel. and univ. relations Fayetteville State U., N.C., 1976-79; dir. career counseling and placement Johnson C. Smith U., Charlotte, N.C., 1979-83; pres. Livingstone Coll., Salisbury, N.C., 1983-88; assoc. dean of curriculum and faculty devel. Gaston Coll., Dallas, N.C., 1989-91, dean, instr., 1991-92; assoc. v.p. curriculum & instrn., dean liberal arts & scis., 1992—; mem. Gov.'s N.C. Internship Council, Gov.'s Task Force on Racial, Religious and Ethnic Violence and Intimidation; dir. First Union Nat Bank, Salisbury. Bd. dirs. Salisbury Rowan Symphony, Salisbury Rowan YMCA, Salisbury Rowan United Way Found., Gov.'s Task Force on Racial, Religious, and Ethnic Violence and Intimidation, Gaston County YMCA, Gastonia, N.C., Mint Mus., Charlotte; chmn. Gaston County Art and History Mus.; mem. Gaston County United Arts Coun.; mem. planning com. U. N.C. State Bd. Cmty. Colls. Recipient Community Service award Delta Zeta chpt. Zeta Phi Beta, 1984, Advisor of Yr. award Fayetteville State U., 1978-79, Achievement Recognition award Am. Heart Assn., 1984; named Outstanding Black Educator, Black Caucus, 1976, one of Outstanding Young Men Am. Mem. ASCD (bd. dirs., exec. bd. Mass. chpt., chmn. of Black Caucus), Fayetteville Bus. League (exec. bd.), Salisbury C. of C. (bd. dirs.), N.C. Am. Heart Assn., Salisbury-Rowan C. of C., Rotary Club of Gastonia, William Upton Lodge, Edward Evans Consistory, Phi Delta Kappa, Omega Psi Phi, Sigma Pi Phi. Home: 1000 Clifton St Charlotte NC 28216-5404

GREENE, WILLIAM JOSHUA, III, investment executive and consultant; b. Gray, Ga., Apr. 20, 1940; s. William Joshua Greene Jr. and Charity Inez (Mercer) Barron; m. Ruth Anne Frye (div.); 1 child, William Joshua IV. BA, Union U., Jackson, Tenn., 1962; AB, Oxford (Eng.) U., 1964; MBA, Yale U., 1966. CPA, CFA; cert. in real estate. Asst. prof. fin. Vanderbilt U., Nashville, 1967-71; chmn., CEO Global Investments, NV, Atlanta and New Orleans, 1971—; founder, chmn. B&G Gourmet Candy, Albany and Atlanta, Ga., 1993—; chmn., CEO GreenePoint, Inc., Gainesville, Ga., 1999—; investment cons. Citizens & So. Nat. Bank, Atlanta, 1983-87; underwriting cons. Franklin Nat. Bank, New Orleans, 1984-88; bd. dirs. Societe de la Bourse de Luxembourg. Author monographs and articles. Capt. USAF, 1962-65, Eng. Mem. Nat. Assn. Realtors, Am. Banking Assn., Nat. Assn. Securities Dealers. Republican. Episcopalian. Avocations: classical music, pipe organ, painting, sailing. Office: Global Investments NV 705 Avalon Forest Dr Lawrenceville GA 30044-3532

GREENEBAUM, LEONARD CHARLES, lawyer; b. Langgoens, Germany, Feb. 6, 1934; came to U.S. 1937, naturalized, 1952; s. Norbert and Henny Lisa (Greenbaum) G.; m. Barbara Rosendorf, Feb. 10, 1957; children: Beth Lynn, Cathy Sue, Steven I. BS cum laude in Commerce, Washington and Lee U., 1956, JD cum laude, 1959. Bar: D.C. 1959, Va. 1959., Md. 1965. Atty. Sachs, Greenebaum & Tayler and predecessor firms, Washington, 1959-64, ptnr., 1964-75, mng. ptnr., 1975-90; ptnr., D.C. coord. litigation Baker & Hostetler, Washington, 1990-95, firmwide litigation group chair, 1996—; arbitrator Am. Arbitration Assn., Washington, 1975—; mem. Washington and Lee U. Law Coun. Chmn. bd. Davis Meml. Goodwill Industries, Washington, 1979-82; bd. dirs. Coun. for Ct. Excellence. Capt. U.S. Army, 1957. Recipient Svc. to Handicapped People award Davis Meml. Goodwill Industries, 1982. Fellow Am. Bar Found. (life); mem. Am. Bd. Trial Advocates, D.C. Bar Assn., Md. Bar Assn., Internat. Platform Assn., Jud. Conf. D.C. Cir., Supreme Ct. Hist. Soc. (hon.), Univ. Club (Washington), Bethesda (Md.) Country Club, Wild Dunes Club (Isle of Palms S.C.), Dunes West Club (Charleston, S.C.), George Town Club (Washington), Order of Coif, Phi Delta Phi. Jewish. Home: 6121 Shady Oak Ln Bethesda MD 20817-6027 Office: Baker & Hostetler 1050 Connecticut Ave NW Washington DC 20036-5304

GREENE LLOYD, NANCY ELLEN, infosystems specialist, physicist; b. Worcester, Mass., Nov. 4, 1947; d. William Arthur II and Dorothy Goddard (Fuller) Green; children: Ellen Dorothy, Gwyneth Tegan; m. Stephen C. Lloyd, July 25, 1992. BS in Physics, Ohio State U., 1969, MS in Physics, 1971. Instr. physics U. Colo., Colorado Springs, 1971-73; physics programmer U. N.Mex., Albuquerque, 1973-76; data analyst Los Alamos (N.Mex.) Nat. Lab., 1975-77, programmer, 1977-78, mem. tech. staff controlled thermonuclear reaction divsn., 1978-81, mem. tech. staff Accelerator Tech. div., 1981-84, mem. tech. staff adminstrv. data processing divsn., 1984-85, mem. tech. staff dynamic experimentation divsn., 1985-94, staff mem. supr., 1989-90, acting sect. leader, 1990-91, acting dep. divsn. leader, 1992, chief ops. explosives tech. and applications divsn., 1992-94, mem. tech. staff environ., safety, and health divsn. Instl. Affairs Office, 1994-97, with Environ., Safety and Health Divsn. Office, 1997-98, leader info. mgmt. team, 1997-98, mem. tech. staff info. mgmt. program, 1998—; speaker in field. Vol. Los Alamos Schs., 1980-88, Fountain Valley Sch., Colo., 1990-91; coord. nursery Chrstian Ch. Los Alamos, 1997—; foster parent State of N.Mex., 1998—; co-mgr. God's Pantry food bank, 1998—; ch. liaison Hope Pregnancy Ctr., 1999—. Nat. Merit scholar, Mich. State U., 1965, Nat. Defense Edn. Act Title IV fellow, Ohio State U., 1969. Mem. N.Mex. Digital Equipment Computer Users Soc. (exec. com. 1984-87, 88-90, registration chair computer conf. 1984-87, vice-chair 1988-89, publicity 1989-90), N.Mex. Network for Women in Sci. and Engring., VAX Computer Local Users Group (chmn. 1981-82, sec. 1989-92), N.Mex. Square and Round Dance Assn. (dist. co-chair 1996-97), Toastmasters. Avocations: reading, aerobics, dancing, personal computers. Office: Los Alamos Nat Lab PO Box 1663 MS K491 Los Alamos NM 87545-0600

GREENEMEIER, CHERYL S., women's health nurse; b. Washington, Dec. 7, 1957; d. William Gibson and Jeanette Irene (Miller) Stafford; m. Gregory M. Greenemeier; Mar. 10, 1979; children: Heather Lyn, Michael Stafford, Matthew Steven, Krista Marie. Diploma, Jackson Meml. Hosp., 1979; AS in Nursing, Miami-Dade Community Coll., 1980. RN, Ala., N.Mex. Obstetrics, pediatrics nurse ARC, Heilbronn, Fed. Republic Germany; staff nurse orthopedics Huntsville (Ala.) Hosp.; relief, staff nurse maternal-infant unit Meml. Gen. Hosp., Las Cruces, N.Mex.; ob-gyn. office supr. for pvt. physician Huntsville; K-8 sch. medication and procedure nurse.

GREENER, ANTHONY, food and beverage company executive; b. 1940. Chmn. Diageo plc; dir. Reed Internat., 1990-98, Reed Elsevier, 1993-98. Office: Diageo plc, 8 Henrietta Pl, London W1M 9AG, England

GREENER, RALPH BERTRAM, lawyer; b. Rahway, N.J., Sept. 23, 1940; s. Ralph Bertram and Mary Ellen (Esch) G.; m. Jean Elizabeth Wilson, Mar. 21, 1964; children: Eric Wilson, Erin Hope, Nicholas Christian. BA, Wheaton Coll., 1962; JD, Duke U., 1968. Bar: Minn. 1969, U.S. Dist. Ct. 1969, U.S. Tax Ct. 1988. With Fredrikson & Byron P.A., Mpls., 1969—; chmn. Minn. Lawyers Mutual Ins. Co., Mpls. 1981—; pres. Nat. Assn. of Bar-Related Ins. Cos., 1989-90. 1st Lt. USMCR, 1962-65. Recipient award of profl. excellence Minn. State Bar Assn., 1993. Mem. Rotary Club. Home: 1018 W Minnehaha Pky Minneapolis MN 55419-1161 Office: Fredrikson & Byron PA 1100 International Ctr 900 2nd Ave S Minneapolis MN 55402-3314

GREENFIELD, BRUCE HAROLD, lawyer, banker; b. Phila., Mar. 12, 1917; s. William I. and Bertha (Kauffman) G.; m. Adele Gersh, Sept. 18, 1955; children: Gregory Richard, Elizabeth Susan, Margaret Alison. B.A., Duke U., 1938; J.D., Yale U., 1941. Bar: Pa. 1941. Atty. Office Tax Legis. Counsel, Treasury Dept., 1941-48; partner firm Folz, Bard, Kamsler, Goodis & Greenfield, Phila., 1949-53; v.p. Bankers Securities Corp., Phila., 1953-59; exec. v.p. Bankers Securities Corp., 1959-70, pres., 1970-82; v.p., treas., dir. Sta. WSMB, Inc., New Orleans, 1957-82; pres., bd. dirs. Albert M. Greenfield & Co., Inc., until, 1982; lectr. NYU, Tulane U., Am. U. Tax Insts. Contbg. author: Taxes mag. Trustee Albert M. Greenfield Found.; bd. dirs., Phila., Am. Jewish Com., Girl Scouts U.S.A., 1978-87. Served to maj. USAAF, 1942-46. Mem. Phi Beta Kappa. Democrat. Clubs: Yale (N.Y.C.). Home: 1598 Landings Terrace Sarasota FL 34231-3215 Office: 1845 Walnut St Ste 800 Philadelphia PA 19103-4709

GREENFIELD, DAVID W., zoology educator; b. Carmel, Calif., Apr. 21, 1940; s. E. Wayne and Dorothy M. Greenfield; m. Teresa Arambula, Aug. 9, 1971. AB, Calif. State U., 1962; PhD, U. Wash., 1966. Asst. prof. biology Calif. State U.-Fullerton, 1966-70; prof. biology No. Ill. U., DeKalb, 1970-84, assoc. dean grad. sch., 1982-84, assoc. provost research, 1984; assoc. vice chancellor U. Colo., Denver, 1984-87, acting vice chancellor, 1986-87; dean grad. div. U. Hawaii, Honolulu, 1987-95, prof. zoology, 1987—. Contbr. articles to profl. jours. NSF grantee, 1975, 80, 85, 98. Mem. Am. Soc. Ichthyologists and Herpetologists (gov. 1973-78, 80-85, 87-92, pres. 1995), Soc. Study of Evolution, Soc. Systematic Biology, Biol. Soc. Wash., We. Assn. Grad. Schs. (pres. 1993-94), Sigma Xi. Democrat. Roman Catholic. Avocations: scuba diving, swimming, sailing, skiing. Office: U Hawaii Dept Zoology 2538 The Mall Honolulu HI 96822-2200

GREENFIELD, GEORGE B., radiologist; b. N.Y.C., May 4, 1928; s. Jacob and Rose (Wolf) G.; m. Barbara Anne O'Driscoll, Mar. 3, 1956; children: Edward James, Sheelagh Anne. B.A., NYU, 1949; M.D., State U. Utrecht, Netherlands, 1956. Diplomate: Am. Bd. Radiology, Am. Bd. Nuclear Medicine. Intern Bridgeport (Conn.) Hosp., 1956-57; resident radiology Presbyn.-St. Lukes Hosp., Chgo., 1957-60; practice medicine, specializing in radiology Chgo., 1960—; radiologist Cook County Hosp., 1961-66, asst. dir. diagnostic radiology, 1966-69; assoc. prof. radiology U. Ill., 1966-69; prof., chmn. dept. radiology Chgo. Med. Sch., 1969-74; prof., chmn. dept. radiology Mt. Sinai Hosp. Med. Center, 1969-89, pres. med. staff, 1983-85; prof. diagnostic radiology Rush Med. Coll., 1975-87; prof. radiology Cook County Grad. Sch. Medicine.; prof. radiology Chgo. Med. Sch., 1987-89, vice chmn. dept. radiology, 1988-89; prof. radiology U. S.Fla., Tampa, 1989—; attending radiologist H. Lee Moffitt Cancer Ctr. and Rsch. Inst., Tampa; cons. radiologist Shriner's Hosp. for Crippled Children, Tampa, 1989. Author: Radiology of Bone Diseases, 5th edit., 1990; sr. author: A Manual of Radiographic Positioning, 1973, Computers in Radiology, 1985, Imaging of Bone Tumors, 1995; contbr. articles to profl. jours. Trustee Mt. Sinai Hosp., 1986-89. Served with U.S. Army, 1951. Fellow Am. Coll. Radiology; mem. AMA, AAAS, Chgo. Med. Soc., Chgo. Roentgen Soc., Am. Roentgen Ray Soc., Radiol. Soc. N.Am., Inst. Medicine Chgo., Assn. Univ. Radiologists, Internat. Skeletal Soc., Soc. Skeletal Radiologists, Connective Tissue Oncology Soc., Sigma Xi. Office: Moffitt Cancer Ctr & Rsch Inst 12901 N 30th St PO Box 17 Tampa FL 33601-0017

GREENFIELD, GORDON KRAUS, software company executive; b. Phila., June 16, 1915; s. Albert Monroe and Edna Kraus (Paine) G.; m. Harriet F. Copelin, Feb. 6, 1945; children: Juliet Greenfield Six, Gordon Kraus, Faith Greenfield Lewis, Hope, James Donald. A.B., Princeton U., 1937; D in Musical Arts (hon.), Manhattan Sch. Music, 1994. Pres., dir. City Splty. Stores, N.Y.C., 1953-60, Am. Corp., N.Y.C., 1960-64, Franchard Corp., N.Y.C., 1965-68; pres. Autocue, Inc., N.Y.C., 1968—. Trustee Manhattan Sch. Music; bd. dirs. Opera Orch. of N.Y., Young Concert Artists. Lt. USNR, 1940-45. Mem. Met. Opera Club. Club: University (N.Y.C.). Home: 320 E 72nd St New York NY 10021-4769 also: Cobb Hill Rd Hartland VT 05048 Office: Autocue Inc 104 E 25th St New York NY 10010-2917

GREENFIELD, JAMES M., fund raiser; b. Hornell, N.Y., Feb. 12, 1936; s. James M. and Vera E. (Alger) G.; m. Diane Roberts, Aug., 1962 (div. 1973); children: Eryn J., Janine L.; m. Karen G. Gabrielson, Nov. 24, 1984. BA, U. Calif., Riverside, 1958. Exec. dir. U. Calif. Alumni Assn., Riverside, 1962-67; dir. corp. rels. Calif. Inst. Tech., Pasadena, 1967-72; dir. devel. Claremont (Calif.) U. Ctr., 1972-73; dir. spl. projects Childrens Hosp. Med. Ctr., Boston, 1973-76; dir. devel. Univ. Hosp., Boston, 1976-81, New Eng. Bapt. Hosp., Boston, 1981-85; dir. fund devel. Cleve. Clinic Found., 1985-87; sr. v.p. resource devel. Hoag Meml. Hosp. Presbyn., Newport Beach, Calif., 1987—. Author: Fund-Raising: Evaluating and Managing the Fund Development Process, 1991, 2nd edit., 1999, Fund-Raising Fundamentals: A Guide to Annual Giving for Professionals and Volunteers, 1994, Fund-Raising Cost Effectiveness: A Self-Assessment Workbook, 1996; editor: The Nonprofit Handbook: Fund Raising, 2d edit., 1997. With USNR, 1959-62. Mem. Assn for Healthcare Philanthropy (bd. dirs., Harold J. Seymour award 1993), Nat. Soc. Fund Raising Execs. (bd. dirs. 1979-88, bd. dirs. Found. 1982—, Profl. Fund-Raiser of Yr. award Orange County chpt. 1994). Democrat. Avocations: backpacking, fly fishing. Office: Hoag Meml Hosp Presbyn PO Box 6100 Newport Beach CA 92658-6100

GREENFIELD, JAMES ROBERT, lawyer; b. Phila., Mar. 31, 1926; s. Milton and Katherine E. (Rosenberg) G.; m. Phyllis Chaplowe, Aug. 17, 1947 (dec. May 1978); m. Joyce MacDonald Koehler, Mar. 22, 1980. B.S., Bates Coll., 1947; J.D., Yale U., 1950. Bar: Conn. 1950, U.S. Dist. Ct. Conn. 1951, U.S. Ct. Appeals (2d cir.) 1966, U.S. Supreme Ct. 1959. Atty. Chaplowe & Greenfield, 1950-54, Markle & Greenfield, New Haven, 1954-58; sr. ptnr. Lander, Greenfield & Krick, New Haven, 1958-80, Greenfield, Krick & Jacobs, New Haven, 1980-90, Greenfield & Murphy, New Haven, 1990-98; of counsel Tyler Cooper & Alcorn, New Haven, 1998—; lectr. U. Conn., 1966-67, 71-72, 75-76. Mem. editorial bd. Conn. Bar Jour, 1963-77. Pres. New Haven Symphony, 1976-78, Conn. Bar Found., 1976-77; bd. dirs. Nat. Jud. Coll., 1978-84. With USNR, 1944-46. Fellow Am. Bar Found. (state chmn. 1985-90); mem. ABA (state del. 1975-78, bd. govs. 1978-81, ho. of dels. 1972-83, spl. com. on goverance 1983-84, chmn. various coms.), Conn. Bar Assn. (pres. 1973-74, Disting. Profl. Svc. award 1989), Judicature Soc. (bd. dirs. 1983-87), Am. Acad. Matrimonial Lawyers (pres. Conn. chpt. 1993-94), Internat. Acad. Matrimonial Lawyers, New Haven County Bar Assn. (pres. 1969-70, Lifetime Achievment award 1993), Yale Law Sch. Assn. (sec. 1977-80), Quinnipiack Club. Office: Tyler Cooper & Alcorn 205 Church St New Haven CT 06510-1805

GREENFIELD, (HENRY) JEFF, news analyst; b. N.Y.C., June 10, 1943; s. Benjamin and Helen Evelyn (Greenwald) G.; m. Carrie Carmichael, May 11, 1968 (div. 1993); children: Casey Carmichael, David Carmichael; m. Karen Gannett, 1993 (div. 1997). BA with honors, U. Wis., 1964; LLB cum laude, Yale U., 1967. Legis. aide to Senator Robert F. Kennedy Washington, 1967-68; speechwriter to Mayor John V. Lindsay, N.Y.C., 1968-70; polit. cons. Garth Assocs., Inc., N.Y.C., 1970-76; media critic CBS News, N.Y.C., 1979-83; polit. media analyst ABC News, N.Y.C., 1983-97; sr. analyst CNN, N.Y.C., 1998—; lectr. Royce-Carlton Agency, N.Y.C., 1980; columnist Universal Press Syndicate, 1981-96, Time Mag., 1996—. Co-author: The Advance Man, 1971, A Populist Manifesto, 1972; author: No Peace, No Place, 1973, The World's Greatest Team, 1975, TV--The First 50 Years,

1977, Playing to Win, 1980, The Real Campaign, 1982, The People's Choice 1995. Recipient Emmy award NATAS, 1986, 91, 93. Office: CNN 5 Penn Plz Fl 21 New York NY 10001-1878

GREENFIELD, JOHN CHARLES, bio-organic chemist; b. Dayton, Ohio, 1945; s. Ivan Ralph and Mildred Louise (House) G.; m. Liga Miervaldis, aug. 2, 1980; children: John Hollen, Mark Richard. BS cum laude, Ohio U., 1967; PhD, U. Ill., 1974. Instr. sci. area h.s. Dayton, 1968-71; grad. rsch. asst. U. Ill., 1971-74; postdoctoral rsch. fellow Swiss Fed. Inst. Tech., Zurich, 1975-76; rsch. chemist infectious diseases rsch. Upjohn Co., Kalamazoo, 1976-82, sr. rsch. scientist drug metabolism rsch., 1982-93; sr. project mgr. Upjohn Labs., Kalamazoo, 1993-95, Pharmacia & Upjohn Inc., Kalamazoo, 1995-96; acquisitions review specialist, bus. devel. Pharmacia and Upjohn, Inc., Kalamazoo, 1996-98, clin. monitor, U.S. market co. med. affairs, 1998—. Contbr. articles to sci. jours.; patentee in field. Adult leader Boy Scouts Am. Am.-Swiss Found. for Sci. Exchange fellow, 1975; NSF-NATO postdoctoral fellow, 1975-76. Mem. AAAS, Am. Chem. Soc. (chmn. Kalamazoo sect. 1994, Disting. Svc. award 1996), N.Y. Acad. Scis., Am. Assn. Pharm. Scientists, Am. Assn. Microbiology, Sigma Xi, Phi Eta Sigma, Blue Key, Phi Lambda Upsilon, Delta Tau Delta. Achievements include identification, evaluation, and management of worldwide research and development projects for new pharmaceutical agents. Home: 6695 E E Ave Richland MI 49083-9729 Office: Pharmacia & Upjohn 7000 Portage Rd Kalamazoo MI 49001-0103

GREENFIELD, JOSEPH CHOLMONDELEY, JR., physician, educator; b. Atlanta, July 20, 1931; s. Joseph Cholmondeley and Agnes (Game) G.; m. Mary Ruth Fordham, Aug. 13, 1955; children—Mary Agnes, Ruth Ann, Susan Lee. A.B. in History, Emory U., 1954, M.D., 1956. Intern, resident in medicine Duke Med. Center, Durham, N.C., 1956-59; asst. prof. medicine Duke Med. Center, 1962-65, assoc. prof. medicine, 1965-70, prof. medicine, 1970—, James B. Duke disting. prof., 1981—; clin. assoc. NIH, USPHS, 1959-62, mem. cardiovascular and pulmonary study sect., 1974-78, chmn. sect., 1975-78, cardiovascular rev. com., 1980-84, chmn. cardiovascular rev. com., 1983-84; mem. staff Duke Med. Center, 1962—, chief cardiovascular div., 1981-89, chmn. dept. medicine, 1983-95; dir. heart sta. VA, Durham, N.C., 1962—. Contbr. numerous articles profl. jours. Fellow ACP, Am. Coll. Cardiology (disting. sci.l award 1985); mem. NRA (life), Am. Heart Assn. (fellow coun. clin. cardiology), Am. Soc. Clin. Investigation, Am. Physiol. Soc., Assn. Am. Physicians, Inst. Medicine, Sons Confederate Vets., Safari Club Internat., Phi Beta Kappa, Alpha Omega Alpha, Kappa Alpha. Methodist. Home: 1212 Virginia Ave Durham NC 27705-3264 Office: Duke U Med Ctr PO Box 3246 Durham NC 27715-3246*

GREENFIELD, LAZAR JOHN, surgeon, educator; b. Houston, Dec. 14, 1934; s. Robert G. and Betty B. (Greenfield) Heath; m. Sharon Dee Bishkin, Aug. 29, 1956; children: John, Julie, Jeff. Student, Rice U., 1951-54; M.D., Baylor U., 1958. Diplomate: Am. Bd. Surgery (dir. 1976-82), Am. Bd. Thoracic Surgery, cert. gen. vascular surgery, 1991. Intern Johns Hopkins Hosp., Balt., 1958-59; resident Johns Hopkins Hosp., 1961-66; chief surgery VA Hosp., Oklahoma City, 1966-74; prof. dept. surgery U. Okla. Med. Center, 1971-74; Stuart McGuire prof., chmn. dept. surgery Med. Coll. Va., Richmond, 1974-87; F.A. coller prof., chmn. dept of surgery U. Mich., 1987—; mem. surgery A study sect. NIH. Author: Surgery in the Aged, 1975; editor-in-chief Surgery, Scientific Principles and Practice, 1993; editor Complications in Surgery and Trauma, 1983, 2d edit., 1990; contbr. to profl. publs. Served with USPHS, 1959-61. Thomas R. Franklin scholar, 1952; John and Mary Markle scholar in med. sci., 1968-73. Mem. Inst. of Medicine of NAS, Am. Surg. Assn., Am. Assn. Thoracic Surgery, Assn. Acad. Surgery, Soc. Univ. Surgeons, Phi Delta Epsilon. Home: 505 E Huron St Ann Arbor MI 48104-1573 Office: U Mich Med Sch 2101 Taubman Ctr Ann Arbor MI 48109-0346*

GREENFIELD, LEE, state legislator; b. Bklyn., July 29, 1941; s. Solomen and Edith (Herschman) G.; m. Marcia Greenfield, Nov. 25, 1965. BS in Physics, Purdue U., West Lafayette, Ind., 1963; postgrad., U. Minn., 1963-73. Instr. applied math. U. Minn., Mpls., 1964-73; prin. asst. Hennepin County Bd. Commrs., Mpls., 1975-77; mgmt. analyst Office of Planning & Devel., Hennepin County, Mpls., 1977; rep. Minn. Ho. of Reps., St. Paul, 1979—; mem. steering com. Reforming State Group, N.Y.C., 1993, chmn., 1994-96. Bd. dirs. Twin City Cmty. Program for Affordable Health Care, Mpls., 1982-84, Arthritis Found., Mpls., 1988-90, Freeport West, Mpls., 1982—, Ams. for Dem. Action, Mpls., 1979—, v.p., 1976-78. Recipient Dwight V. Dixon award Mental Health Assn. Minn., 1994. Mem. Mental Health Assn. Minn. (Disting. Svc. award 1987), Planned Parenthood of Minn. (Pub. Svc. award 1993). Mem. Democratic-Farmer-Labor Party. Jewish. Office: Minnesota House of Reps State Capitol Saint Paul MN 55155

GREENFIELD, MICHAEL C., lawyer; b. Chgo., May 4, 1934. BA, U. Ill., 1955; JD, Northwestern U., 1957. Bar: Ill. 1957, U.S. Supreme Ct. 1974, Ind. 1982. Asst. states atty. Cook County (Ill.), 1957-59; ptnr. Asher, Gittler & Greenfield, Ltd., Chgo., 1959—, Asher, Gittler, Greenfield & D'Alba, Ltd., Chgo.; mem. inquiry bd. Ill. Supreme Ct. Disciplinary Commn., 1973-77, mem. hearing bd., 1978-94, 97—, vice chmn., 1984, chmn., 1985, mem. oversight comm., 1995-96. Mem. ABA, Internat. Found. Employee Benefit Plans (bd. dirs. 1977-80, 85-88, 92-94), Ill. Bar Assn., Chgo. Bar Assn. Office: Asher Gittler Greenfield Cohen & D'Alba Ltd 125 S Wacker Dr Ste 1100 Chicago IL 60606-4397

GREENFIELD, NORMAN SAMUEL, psychologist, educator; b. N.Y.C., June 2, 1923; s. Max and Dorothy (Hertz) G.; m. Marjorie Hanson Klein, May 17, 1969; children—Ellen Beth, Jennifer Ann, Susan Emery. BA, NYU, 1948; MA, U. Calif., Berkeley, 1951, PhD, 1953. Fellow med. psychology Langley Porter Clinic, U. Calif. Med. Center, 1949-50; VA Mental Health Clinic trainee San Francisco, 1950-53; instr. clin. psychology U. Oreg. Med. Sch., 1953-54; from asst. prof. to prof. psychiatry U. Wis. Med. Sch. at, Madison, 1954—; assoc. dir. Wis. Psychiat. Inst., U. Wis. Center for Health Scis., 1961-74; emeritus prof. psychiatry, 1991—. Co-editor: The New Hospital Psychiatry, Handbook of Psychophysiology, Psychoanalysis and Current Biological Thought; contbr. articles to profl. jours. Served with USAAF, 1943-46. Mem. AAUP, Am. Psychol. Assn., Soc. Psychophysiol. Rsch., Am. Psychosomatic Soc. Office: U Wis Psychiat Inst 6001 Research Park Blvd Madison WI 53719-1176

GREENFIELD, ROBERT KAUFFMAN, lawyer; b. Phila., Mar. 30, 1915; s. William I. and Bertha (Kauffman) G.; m. Louise Rose Stern, June 20, 1937; children: Linda Greenfield Baldwin, Mary Greenfield Davenport, William Stern, James Robert. AB, Swarthmore Coll., 1936; JD, Harvard U., 1939; LHD (hon.), Pa. Coll. Podiatric Medicine, 1990. Bar: Pa. 1939. Pvt. practice Phila., 1939-87; with firm Goodis, Greenfield, Henry & Edelstein (and predecessors), 1939-77; of counsel Montgomery, McCracken, Walker & Rhoads, 1977-87; ret.; chmn. bd. Phila. Co., 1983-85. Bd. dirs. Conv. and Tourist Bur., Phila., 1942-84; commr., v.p. Phila. Fellowship Commn., 1965-74; pres. Jewish Comty. Rels. Coun., 1962-65; chmn. bd. Moss Rehab. Hosp., 1974-77; pres. Alexis Rosenberg Found., 1983-91; fin. chmn. Inst. Contemporary Art, 1974-83; exec. com. Coun. Performing Arts, 1964-70; v.p. Nat. Comty. Rels. Adv. Coun., 1965-68; pres. Phila. chpt. Am. Jewish Com., 1966-68; trustee Pa. Coll. Podiatric Medicine, 1967-91, chmn., 1989-90; pres. Goldsmith-Greenfield Found., 1991—; dir. Asolo Ctr. Performing Arts, 1997—. Mem. Landings Racquet Club (pres. 1994-96), Phi Beta Kappa. Home: 1650 Landings Blvd Sarasota FL 34231-3223

GREENFIELD, SANFORD RAYMOND, architect; b. N.Y.C., Feb. 3, 1926; s. Harry Leon and Dorothy (Shaefer) G.; m. Stella Berger, Oct. 12, 1952; children—Lise, Daniel, Stefanie. Student, Mich. State Coll. Liberal Arts, 1946-48; B.Arch., M.I.T., 1952, M.Arch., 1954; postgrad., New Sch. Social Research, N.Y.C., 1953, L'Inst. d'Urbanisme, Paris, 1954-55; Ed.M., Harvard U., 1975. Faculty Sch. Architecture and Planning, M.I.T., 1955-57; with Samuel Glaser, Boston, 1958-60; ptnr. Carroll & Greenfield (architects), Boston, 1960-73; dir. edn. Boston Archtl. Ctr. Sch. Architecture, 1967-75; research mgr. AIA Research Corp., 1975-76; cons. Sanford R. Greenfield & Asso., Boston; chmn. dept. architecture Iowa State U., Ames, 1976-81; dean Sch. Architecture, N.J. Inst. Tech., 1981-91; lectr. Inst. Urban Design, Krakow (Poland) Politechnika, 1978; dir. edn. Boston Archtl. Center; cons. ednl. planning; lectr. Mass. Coll. Art; mem. task force on edn. and tng. for internat. constrn. Bldg. Rsch. Bd. NRC, 1987; examiner archtl. registration exam. in design, 1984, 85, 86, 87, 90. Editor: Architecture and the Computer, 1964, Forces Shaping the Role of The Architect, 1966, Systems, 1968; contbr. articles to profl. jours.; Important works include Library St. John's Sem. Mem. 5-Presidents' Task Force on Edn., 1972-73; chmn. Nat. Adv. Council Continuing Edn., 1972-73; mem. adv. bd. Ctr. for Study of Profl. Edn., U. Cin., 1992—. Served with USNR, 1944-46. Recipient Centennial Educator award Boston Archtl. Ctr., 1989; Fulbright scholar, 1954-55; Nat. Endowment for Arts grantee, 1978; Sch. of Architecture Libr. Coll. named in his honor, N.J. Inst. Tech., 1996. Fellow AIA (bd. dirs. AIA/ACSA rsch. coun. 1989-91); mem. Iowa Assn. Architects, Assn. Collegiate Schs. Architecture (v.p. 1972-73, pres. 1973-74, also dir.), N.J. Soc. Architects (bd. dirs. 1982-91).

GREENFIELD, SCOTT H., lawyer; b. Perth Amboy, N.J., Feb. 9, 1958; s. Edwin S. and Phyllis Joy Greenfield; m. Theresa Anne Amigo, Sept. 16, 1984; children: Rebecca Catherine, Jack Alexander. BS, Cornell U., 1979; JD, N.Y. Law Sch., 1982. Bar: N.Y. 1983, U.S. Dist. Ct. (so. and ea. dists.) N.Y. 1983, U.S. Ct. Appeals (2d cir.) 1985, (3d cir.) 1990, U.S. Supreme Ct. 1987. Ptnr. Meyer & Greenfield, N.Y.C., 1983-93; pvt. practice N.Y.C., 1994—; arbitrator N.Y.C. Civil Ct., 1991—. Mem. Nat. Assn. Criminal Def. Lawyers, N.Y. State Assn. Criminal Def. Lawyers (chair amicus com. 1995, bd. dirs. 1999—), N.Y. State Bar Assn., N.Y. Criminal Bar Assn. Office: 233 Broadway 51st Fl New York NY 10279-0001

GREENFIELD, SEYMOUR STEPHEN, mechanical engineer; b. Bklyn., July 9, 1922; s. Herman and Yetta (Silfen) G.; m. Eleanor Levy, Oct. 30, 1949 (dec. 1987); children: Meryl Joy, Bruce Howard; m. Judith A. Abrams, 1990. Student, N.Y. U., 1939-40; B.Mech. Engring., Poly. Inst. N.Y., 1943. Registered profl. engr., Calif., Conn., Mass., N.J., N.Y., La., Tex., Ohio. Engr. Percival R. Moses Assos., N.Y.C., 1946-47; sr. engr. and assoc. Parsons, Brinckerhoff, Quade & Douglas, N.Y.C., 1947-64, ptnr., 1964—, chmn. bd., 1979-90, chmn. emeritus, 1990—; Adviser Manhattan Coll., N.Y.C., 1974—mem. devel. council Tex. A&M Sch. Architecture, 1981; chmn. transp. adv. com. to Pres. of Poly. Inst. N.Y., 1985. Bd. dirs. N.Y. chpt. March of Dimes, 1989. Served to lt. USNR, 1944-46. Recipient Engring. News Record Citation for Outstanding Contbns. to Constrn. Industry, 1982, Moles award, 1993, Golden Eagle award Soc. Am. Mil. Engrs., 1997; named Transp. Man of Yr., March of Dimes, 1982. Fellow Poltechnic Univ. of N.Y.; mem. Soc. Am. Mil. Engrs. (nat. pres. 1977, dir. 1975—, pres. N.Y.C. post 1974-75), Nat. Acad. Engring. Bldg. Research (mem. adv. bd. 1972—), N.Y. C. of C. and Industry (vice chmn. Transp. Council 1973—), N.Y. State Soc. Profl. Engrs., ASME, Am. Soc. Heating, Refrigerating and Air Conditioning Engrs., Moles (pres. 1986, trustee). Home: 1600 Parker Ave Fort Lee NJ 07024-7050 Office: Parsons Brinckerhoff Inc 250 E 34th St New York NY 10016-4873

GREENFIELD, SHELDON, epidimiologist; b. Cin., Apr. 22, 1938. AB, Harvard U., 1960; MD, U. Cin., 1964. Epidemic intelligence svc. officer USPHS, N.Y., 1966-68; fel. Dept. Preventive Med. State U., N.Y., 1966-68; sr. asst. resident Med. Beth Israel Hosp. Harvard Med. Sch., Boston, 1968-69; fellow in Infectious Diseases Beth Israel Hosp. Harvard Med. Sch., 1969-71, chief resident, 1971-72, staff, Ambulatory Care project, 1971-76; principal investigator U.C.L.A., 1974-76, from asst. prof. to prof. Med. and Pub. Health, 1972-88, dir. Master Sci. Pub. Health track, 1980-88, dir. rsch. and devel., 1982-88; sr. scientist Health Inst., 1988-93; dir. Primary Care Outcomes Rsch. Inst. New England Med. Ctr. Hosps., Boston, 1993—; mem. first Pub. Health delegation to Cuba, 1974; Nat. Com. Quality Assurance, 1996—; vis. prof. Ben Gurion U., Negev, Israel, 1981, Mario Negri Inst., Milan, Italy, 1993; med. dir. Nat. Study Med. Outcomes, 1984—; prof. med. and chief Divsn. Health Svcs. Rsch., Dept. Med. Tufts U. Sch. Med., 1988—; adj. prof. Harvard Sch. Pub. Health, 1988; principal investigator Diabetes Patient Outcome Rsch. team, 1990—; Spinoza chair visiting prof. U. Amsterdam, 1992; Anglo-Am. visiting prof., Royal Soc. Med., England, 1994; acad. dir. Tufts Managed Care Inst., 1995—;mem. Robert Wood Johnson Found. Patient-Provider Relationship Under Managed Care Initiative, 1996. Named Blanchard lectr., Soc. Tchrs. Family Med., 1993; Yules lectr., Dept. Med., Tufts U. Med., 1993, Ann Evans Day Dist. Colin lectr., Boston U., 1994, George Silver lectr., U. Miami, 1994; recipient Primary Care Lifetime Achievement award, Pew Health Professions Commn., 1994, Glaser award, Soc. Gen. Internat. Med., 1997. Fellow Am. Col. Physicians; mem. Inst. Med. Nat. Acad. Sci., Am. Fedn. Clin. Rsch., Soc. Rsch. and Edn. Primary Care Internal Med. (pres. elect, 1983-84, pres. 1984-85), Primary Care Outcomes Rsch. Inst. Office: New England Med Ctrs Hosps 750 Washington St # Boston MA 02111-1526*

GREENFIELD, VAL SHEA, ophthalmologist; b. N.Y.C., Apr. 20, 1932; s. Frank Lynne and Helen (Meyers) G. Student, Brown U., 1948-49, 50-51, St. John's U., 1949; BA cum laude, Bklyn. Coll., 1952; MD, Yale U., 1956. Diplomate Am. Bd. Ophthalmology; lic. physician, pa., N.Y., N.J. Intern Walter Reed Army Hosp., Washington, 1956-57; asst. chief U.S. Army Dispensary, Phila., 1957-59, chief, 1959-60; postgrad. preceptorship in ophthal. under co-chief ophthal. Presbyn.-U. Pa. Med. Ctr., Phila., 1963-66; practice medicine specializing in obstetrics Phila., Riveride, N.J., 1960-63; practice medicine specializing in ophthalmology Phila., 1966—; assoc. dir., lectr. in neuro-ophthalmology Hahnemann U., Phila., 1978—, from asst. prof. to assoc. prof. ophthalmology Sch. Medicine, 1977-88; assoc. clin. prof. Robert Wood Johnson Med. Sch.-N.J. U. Medicine and Dentistry, 1988—; attending surgeon in ophthalmology Frankford and Rolling Hills Hosps., Phila., 1970—; lectr. Bibl. topics U.S., Israel, Europe, New Zealand, USSR; guest speaker TV stas. and clubs. Contbr. articles to profl. jours., chpts. to textbooks. Mem. bd. deacons Cmty. Ch., Mt. Laurel Chapel and Fellowship, 1970—; bd. dirs. Hebrew Christian Outreach of Ch. of Our Lord Jesus Christ, 1958—. Served to capt. M.C., U.S. Army, 1955-60. Inducted into Chapel of 4 Chaplains, Temple U., 1981; inducted Hon. Brave Cherokee Indians by Chief Rising Sun, Chief and High Priest of N.Am. and S.Am. Indian Tribes and Couns., 1947; recipient AMA Physicians Recognition award in med. edn., tri-annually, 1974—. Fellow ACS, Phila. Coll. Physicians; mem. AMA, Pa. Med. Soc., Phila. County Med. Soc., Am. Acad. Ophthalmology, N.Y. State Ophthal. Soc., Pa. Acad. Ophthalmology, Pan-Am. Soc. Ophthalmology, Soc. Contemporary Ophthalmology, Christian Med. Soc., Am. Soc. Cataract and Refracture Surgery, Internat. Platform Soc., Am. Judeo-Christian Fellowship, Alpha Kappa Kappa. Avocation: book collecting, Bible lectures and writings. Home: 623 S Church St Mount Laurel NJ 08054-1343 Office: David B Soll MD Eye Assocs 5001 Frankford Ave Philadelphia PA 19124-2619 *In over forty years of studying and applying the principles of medicine to my patients, I have seen the devastating toll that anger, hatred, fear, doubt, anguish, inordinate lust and jealousy have taken on men's and women's bodies and souls. I continually advise my patients that conventional medicines and therapies alone cannot heal or cure these "spiritual diseases". I add to my therapeutic armamentarium the concepts of the Ten Commandments and the Sermon on the Mount, which I suggest that my patients apply to their daily lives. The happiest moments in my professional life have been when I observe the salubrious effects that faith, hope and love have upon my patients' afflictions. Jesus, the Annointed One of God, prophetically called "The Mighty God, the Everlasting Father, the Prince of Peace", summed up His whole religion, which I heartily recommend to my patients, colleagues, friends, as well as to myself, as follows: "Thou shalt love The Lord thy God with all thy heart and with all thy soul and with all thy mind. Thou shalt love thy neighbor as thyself. On these two commandments hang all the law and Prophets." Unless mankind in general, and each and every man and woman in particular, appropriate and follow these commandments, then we will face the dire consequences that are already evolving worldwide: the scourges of war, pestilence and famine.*

GREENFIELD-MOORE, WILMA LOUISE, social worker, educator; b. Boston. BA in Social Sci., Bennington Coll., 1958; MSW, U. Calif., Berkeley; PhD Social Welfare, U. Calif., 1978; cert. in departmental leadership, Fla. State U., 1983. Lic. clin. social worker, Fla.; diplomate Am. Bd. Clin. Social Work. Teaching asst. U. Calif., Berkeley, 1964-69, teaching assoc., 1970-71; asst. prof. social svc. Calif. State Poly. U., Pomona, 1971-75, U. New Hampshire, 1976-80; asst. prof. community svcs. Fla. Atlantic U., Boca Raton, 1980-85, assoc. prof. social work, 1985—, chair Dept. Social Work, 1989-94, 97-98, prof., 1996—, dir. social work student internship, 1995-98; adj. prof. Barry U., 1984-88, Sylvester Inst. Aging Coll. Boca Raton, 1985-87; vis. prof. U. Wis., Green Bay, 1994-95; cons., psychotherapist, Fla., 1987—; mem. Gov.'s Task Force on Reorgn. of Social Svcs., 1996; presenter World Congress Social Work, Jerusalem, 1998; bd. dirs. health and human svcs. bd. Dept. Health and Rehab. Svcs., Dist. IX. Contbr. chpts. to books, articles to profl. jours. Coord., mem. state adv. bd. Palm county Campaign Dukakis for Pres., 1987-88; mem. Psychol. Svcs. Coalition, Coalition Mental Health Providers State of Fla., 1985-88; bd. dirs. May Volen Sr. Ctr., Boca Raton, 1986-90, Florence Fuller Child Devel. Ctr., Boca Raton, 1986-90, Fla. Consumer Action Network, 1988-90, South Palm Beach County Migrant Coord. Coun., 1982-87, The Children's Place Home Safe, 1997—; at-large del. Dem. Nat. Conv., 1988; mem. planning com. United Way Boca Raton. Grantee Fla. Atlantic U., 1981, 83, 89-91, 90-95. Mem. NASW (pres. Fla. chpt. 1986-88, Social Worker of Yr. Fla. chpt. 1983, chmn. bd. trustees PACE, 1990-94), Internat. Social Welfare Conf. Inter-univ. Consortium Internat. Social Devel., Coun. Social Work Edn. Fla. Assn. Social Work Edn. Adminstrs. Home: 1400 NW 9th Ave Apt 12 Boca Raton FL 33486-1325 Office: Fla Atlantic U Social Work Dept Coll Archtl Urban & Pub Aff 777 Glades Rd Boca Raton FL 33431-6424

GREENGARD, PAUL, neuroscientist; b. N.Y.C., Dec. 11, 1925; married; 3 children. AB, Hamilton Coll., 1948; PhD, Johns Hopkins U., 1953. NSF fellow in neurochemistry U. London (Eng.)Inst. Psychiatry, 1953-54; Nat. Found. Infantile Paralysis fellow U. Cambridge (Eng.) Molteno Inst., 1954-55; Paraplegia Found. fellow Nat. Inst. Med. Rsch., Eng., 1955-56; fellow Nat. Inst. Neurological Diseases and Blindness, 1956-58; dir. biochemistry dept. Ciba-Geigy Rsch. Labs., 1958-67; prof. pharmacology and psychiatry Yale U. Sch. Medicine, New Haven, 1968-83; Andrew D. White prof.-at-large Cornell U., Ithaca, N.Y., 1981-87; prof. Rockefeller U., N.Y.C., 1983—; vis. scientist Nat. Heart Inst., 1959-68; vis. assoc. prof. Albert Einstein Coll. Medicine, 1961-68, vis. prof., 1968-83; vis. prof. Vanderbilt U., 1967-68. Recipient Ciba-Geigy Drew award, 1979, Biol. and Med. Scis. award N.Y. Acad. Scis., 1980, 3M Life Scis. award Fedn. Am. Socs. Exptl. Biology, 1987, Bristol-Myers award for disting. achievement in neurosci. rsch., 1989, Goodman and Gilman award in receptor pharmacology, 1992, Karl Spencer Lashley prize Am. Philos. Soc., 1993, Charles A. Dana Found. award for pioneering achievements in health, 1997. Mem. NAS (award in neuroscis. 1991), Am. Acad. Arts and Scis., Soc. for Neurosci. (Grass lectr. 1986, Gerard prize 1994), Nat. Alliance for Rsch. on Schizophrenia and Depression (Lieber prize Outstanding Achievement Schizophrenia Rsch. 1996). Office: Rockefeller U 1230 York Ave New York NY 10021-6399*

GREENGUS, SAMUEL, academic administrator, religion educator; b. Chgo., Mar. 11, 1936; s. Eugene and Thelma (Romirowsky) G.; m. Lesha Bellows, Apr. 30, 1957; children: Deana, Rachel, Judith. Student, Hebrew Theol. Coll., Chgo., 1950-58; MA, U. Chgo., 1959, PhD, 1963. Prof. semitic langs. Hebrew Union Coll.-Jewish Inst. Religion, Cin., 1963-89, Julian Morgenstern prof. bible and near eastern lit., 1989—, dean rabbinic sch., 1979-84, dean Cin. campus, 1985-87, dean sch. grad. studies, 1985-90, dean faculty, 1987-98, v.p. for Acad. affairs, 1990-96; vis. lectr. U. of Dayton, Ohio, 1964-69, Leo Baeck Coll., London, 1976-77; area supr. Tel Gezer Excavation, Israel, 1966-67; mem. bd. editors Hebrew Union Coll. Ann. Author: Old Babylonian Tablets from Ishchali and Vicinity, 1979, Studies in Ishchali Documents, 1986; mem. bd. editors Zeitschrift fur Altorientalische und Biblische Rechtsgeschichte; contbr. articles to profl. jours. Mem. Cin. Community Hebrew Schs. Bd., 1970-75; mem. vis. com. Sch. for Creative and Performing Arts, Cin., 1980-82; chmn. acad. officers, Greater Cin. Consortium Colls. and Univs., 1984-85, mem. exec. com., 1989-96. Am. Council Learned Socs. fellow, 1970-71, Am. Assn. Theol. Schs. fellow, 1976-77. Mem. Am. Oriental Soc., Assn. Jewish Studies, Soc. Bibl. Lit., Phi Beta Kappa. Jewish. Office: Hebrew Union Coll Jewish Inst Religion 3101 Clifton Ave Cincinnati OH 45220-2404

GREENHALGH, TERRY LAMONT, marketing executive; b. Cin., Sept. 29, 1950; s. Frederick Olsen and Julia Ann (Gamble) G.; m. Erin J. Morgan, May 1992 (div. Feb. 1997); 1 child, Shannon Ann. AS in TV Prodn., Hillsborough Community Coll., Tampa, Fla., 1975; AA in Liberal Arts, Hillsborough Community Coll., 1978; BA in Pub. Rels., U. South Fla., 1981. Sports writer, reporter The Tampa (Fla.) Tribune Co., 1979-81; promotion dir. Palmer Communications, Inc., Naples, Fla., 1981-84; pres., chief exec. officer Grand Mktg. & Pub. Relations, Tampa, 1984-88; mktg. mgr. Modern Talking Picture Svc., Inc., St. Petersburg, 1988-91; gen. mgr. Europa Cruise Corp., Ft. Myers Beach, Fla., 1991-93; sales and mktg. rep. Continental Airlines, Tampa, Fla., 1993-94; v.p. mktg. and devel. Fla. Spl. Olympics, Inc., Tampa, 1994-96; mktg. specialist CBS Radio, St. Petersburg, Fla., 1997; dir. devel. The Astronauts Meml. Found., Kennedy Space Ctr., Fla., 1997—. Author: (history trivia game) Tampa Tycoon, 1985 (Addy 1986), (wine trivia game) The Wine Connoisseur, 1986 (Addy award 1987). With U.S. Army, 1970-72. Avocations: reading, fitness, snow skiing, water sports, travel writing. Home: PO Box 261616 Tampa FL 33685-1616

GREENHILL, H. GAYLON, academic administrator. Chancellor U. Wis., Whitewater. Office: U Wis-Whitewater Office of Chancellor 800 W Main St Whitewater WI 53190-1705

GREENHILL, JOE ROBERT, former chief justice state supreme court, lawyer; b. Houston, July 14, 1914; s. Joe R. Jr. and Violet (Stanuell) G.; m. Martha Shuford, June 15, 1940; children: Joe IV, William D. BBA, U. Tex., 1936, BA, 1936, LLB, 1939; LLD (hon.), So. Meth. U., 1977. Briefing atty. for chief justice Alexander Tex. Supreme Ct., Austin, 1941, 46; 1st asst. atty. gen. Tex. Austin, 1947-50; co-founder Graves, Dougherty & Greenhill, Austin, 1950-57; justice Supreme Ct. of Tex., Austin, 1957-72, chief justice, 1972-82; of counsel Baker & Botts, Austin, 1982—; co-incorporator Tex. Ctr. for Professionalism and Ethics, Austin, 1991—; pres. elect Conf. Chief Justices and Nat. Ctr. for State Courts, Williamsburg, Va., 1982. Editor Tex. Law Rev., 1937-39 (Outstanding Ex-Editor 1975). Lt. USNR, 1942-46, PTO. Named Disting. Alumnus U. Tex., 1974, Disting. Alumnus U. Tex. Law Sch., 1977, Disting. Alumnus U. Tex. Coll. Bus. Adminstrn., 1974. Fellow Tex. Bar Found. (life, Outstanding 50 yr. lawyer 1989, exec. dir. 1984—), Am. Bar Found. (life); mem. Masons (33 degree). Office: Baker & Botts 98 San Jacinto Blvd Ste 1600 Austin TX 78701-4078

GREENHOUGH, JOHN HARDMAN, business forms company executive; b. London, Aug. 6, 1939; arrived to Can., 1949; s. Thomas Chaplin and Rena (Pilling) G.; married, 1962; children: Peter, Jennifer. BA in English and Econs., Wilfrid Laurier U., Waterloo, Ont., Can., 1962. With Maclean Hunter Ltd., Toronto, Ont., 1962-72, 81-82, various sales and mktg. positions, bus. publs. div., 1962-69, group pub., 1970-72, v.p. printing, 1980-81; group pres. printing Maclean Hunter Ltd., 1990-95; v.p., gen. mgr. Data Bus. Forms Ltd., Brampton, Ont., 1972-79; pres., COO, 1979-92; chmn., CEO Data Bus. Forms Ltd., Brampton, Ont., 1992-95, chmn., 1995—; dir., treas. Internat. Bus. Forms Industries, 1995—. Mem. Can. Bus. Forms Assn. (past v.p., bd. dirs. 1982-88). Office: Data Bus Forms Ltd, 2 Shaftsbury Ln, Brampton, ON Canada L6T 3X7

GREENHOUSE, CAROL JOAN, editor, writer, educator; b. Washington, Feb. 8, 1963; d. Samuel Michael and Eleanore Press G. BA, Bennington Coll., 1984, MFA, 1998. Staff writer Denver Mag. and Denver Bus., 1985-87; assoc. editor This Week mags., 1987-89; columnist Hawaii Tribune-Herald, 1994; editor Deadsnake Apotheosis, 1997—; tchr. creative writing S. Kona Edn. Assn., 1995; tchr. intro. and advanced courses fiction and non-fiction Writing Workshops, 1993—; tchr. dept. English U. Hawaii at Kealakekua, 1996—. Editor: Maverick Guide to Hawaii, Birnbaum Guide to Hawaii, ACCESS Hawaii, 1989—. Program coord. Island Crisis Help, Kona, Hawaii, 1993-97; chair Marriage Project, Honolulu, 1994—. Recipient 1st Pl. award in travel writing Hawaii Visitor's Bur., 1995; grantee Vt. Studio Ctr., 1998. Mem. Associated Writing Programs. Democrat. Avocations: adventure travel, backpacking, pottery, running. E-mail: catmilan@aol.com.

GREENHOUSE, LINDA JOYCE, journalist; b. N.Y.C., Jan. 9, 1947; d. Herman Robert and Dorothy Eleanor (Greenlick) G.; m. Eugene R. Fidell, Jan. 1, 1981; 1 child, Hannah Margalit Fidell. BA, Radcliffe Coll., 1968; M of Studies in Law, Yale U., 1978; D.H.L. (hon.), Brown U., 1991; LLD (hon.), Colgate U., 1993, Northeastern U., 1997, City U. of N.Y., 1997. Asst. to James Reston The N.Y. Times, N.Y.C., 1968-69, met. reporter, 1970-74, state polit. reporter, 1974-77; supreme ct. corr. The N.Y. Times, Washington, 1978-85, 88—, congl. corr., 1986-88. Bd. dirs. Yale Law Sch.

Fund, New Haven, 1984-91; adv. com. Schlesinger Lib. on the History of Women in Am. Radcliffe Coll., 1995—. Recipient Pulitzer prize in journalism for beat reporting, 1998. Fellow Am. Acad. Arts and Scis.; mem. Yale Law Assn. (exec. com. 1993-97), Harvard Club Washington (bd. dirs. 1989-92). Office: The NY Times 1627 I St NW Washington DC 20006-4007

GREENHUT, MELVIN LEONARD, economist, educator; b. N.Y.C., Mar. 10, 1921; s. Ab and Lillian (Frudman) G.; m. Elmara Margaret Griffith, Mar. 24, 1944; children: Margaret Lee, Pamela Jo, John Griffith, Patricia Lynn. *Dr. Greenhut's wife is a great mother and spouse, active in charitable work, an excellent flutist and was substitute church organist for her mother. Our descendants, including spouses and grandchildren, number nineteen. Three young grandsons are very active in sports; two granddaughters are in theater. The fourteen adults now hold 16 university degrees, including two Masters, a Juris Doctor, and a Doctor of Philosophy. Professionally, Dr. Greenhut's family includes two CPAs, two custom home builders, two in sales, an attorney, teacher, golf pro, newspaper columnist, interior designer, operations director for a major company, aspiring novelist, and a university professor.* PhD, Washington U., 1951. Asst. prof. econs. Auburn (Ala.) U., 1948-52; assoc. prof. econs. Miss. State U., 1952-53; prof. bus. and econs., chmn. social relations div. Rollins Coll., 1953-57; prof. econs. Fla. State U., 1957-59, 62-66; assoc. dean Sch. Bus., U. Richmond, 1959-62; prof., head dept. econs. Tex. A&M U., College Station, 1966-69; disting. prof. econs. Tex. A&M U., 1969—, alumni disting. prof. econs., 1980-85, Abell Prof. Liberal Arts, disting. prof. econs., 1986—, Abell Prof. Liberal Arts, disting. prof. econs. emeritus, 1992—, chmn. disting. profs., 1988-89; adj. disting. prof. econs. U. Okla., 1986-91; vis. prof. Mich. State U., 1963, U. Cape Town, 1971, univs. Mannheim, Karlsruhe, Münster, 1972, 73, U. Pitts., 1976; cons. Rountree Assos., Richmond, Va., 1959, AT&T (risk and uncertainty com.), 1961-62, Atlantic Research Corp., 1962; cons. to pres. Amerad Corp., 1962-64; cons. So. Conf. Council State Govts., 1964-66, Bur. Bus. Research, Memphis State U., 1965-66. Author: Plant Location in Theory and in Practice, 1956 (transl. into Japanese, 2 vols., 1973), Full Employment, Inflation and Common Stocks, 1961, Microeconomics and the Space Economy, 1963, A Theory of the Firm in Economic Space, 1970, Location Economics: Theory and Applications, 1995, Spatial Microeconomics: Theory and Applications, 1995, (with Frank Jackson) Intermediate Income and Growth Theory, 1961, (with Marshall R. Colberg) Factors in the Location of Florida Industry, 1962, (with H. Ohta) A Theory of Spatial Prices and Market Areas, 1975, (with Charles Stewart) Economics for the Voter, 1981, From Basic Economics to Supply Side Economics, 1983, (with G. Norman and C.S. Hung) Economics of Imperfect Competition, 1987, (with Bruce Benson) The American Anti-Trust Laws in Theory and in Practice, 1989, Does Economic Space Really Matter: Essays in Honor of Melvin L. Greenhut, 1993, Biography in Exemplary Economists One: Twentieth Century America, 1999; editor: (with Tate Whitman) Essays on Southern Economic Development, 1964, (with G. Norman) The Economics of Location, 3 vols., 1994; editor So. Econ. Jour, 1966-68; cons. editor: Indsl. Devel, 1959-62; contbr. articles to profl. jours. Mem. nat. econ. policy com. and econ. adv. coun. U.S. C. of C., 1960-63. Maj. U.S. Army. Mem. Am. Econ. Assn., So. Econ. Assn. (past v.p.), Regional Sci. Assn. (councillor), Royal Econ. Soc., Econometric Soc., Delta Chi, Omicron Delta Gamma. Lutheran. Home: 5814 Constellation Cir Rockwall TX 75032-5770 Office: Tex A&M U Dept Econs College Station TX 77843

GREENKORN, ROBERT ALBERT, chemical engineering educator; b. Oshkosh, Wis., Oct. 12, 1928; s. Frederick John and Sophie (Phillips) G.; m. Rosemary Drexler, Aug. 16, 1952; children: David Michael, Eileen Anne, Susan Marie, Nancy Joanne. Student, Oshkosh State Coll., 1951-52; BS, U. Wis., 1954, MS, 1955, PhD, 1957. Postdoctoral fellow Norwegian Tech. Inst., 1957-58; rsch. engr. Jersey Prodn. Rsch. Co., Tulsa, 1958-63; lectr. U. Tulsa, 1958-63; assoc. prof. theoretical and applied mechanics Marquette U., Milw., 1963-65; assoc. prof. chem. engring. Purdue U., Lafayette, Ind., 1965-67, prof., head chem. engring. dept., 1967-72, asst. dean engring., 1972-76, assoc. dean engring., dir. engring. expt. sta., 1976-80, v.p., assoc. provost, 1980-86; v.p. programs Purdue Rsch. Found., 1980-94, v.p. rsch., 1986-92, v.p. rsch., dean grad. sch., 1993-94, spl. asst. to the pres., 1994—, v.p. spl. programs, 1994; R. Games Slayter disting. prof. chem. engring., 1995—; rsch. coord. Ind. Clean Mfg. and Safe Materials Inst., 1994—; dir. Tech. Assistance Program, 1996—. Author: (with D.P. Kessler) Transfer Operations, 1972, (with K.C. Chao) Thermodynamics of Fluids: An Introduction to Equilibrium Theory, 1975, (with D.P. Kessler) Modeling and Data Analysis for Engineers and Scientists, 1980, Flow Phenomena in Porous Media, 1983, Momentum, Heat and Mass Transfer Fundamentals (with D.P. Kessler), 1999; contbr. articles to profl. jours. Served with USN, 1946-51. Decorated D.F.C., Air medal with two oak leaf clusters; recipient Fellow Members awd., Am. Soc. for Engineering Education, 1992. Fellow AIChE, Am. Soc. Engring. Edn.; mem. AASS, Soc. Petroleum Engrs., Am. Chem. Soc., Am. Geophys. Union, Sigma Xi, Phi Eta Sigma, Tau Beta Pi, Phi Gamma Delta. Roman Catholic. Achievements include patents in field. Home: 151 Knox Dr West Lafayette IN 47906-2147

GREENLAND, LEO, advertising executive; b. N.Y.C., Mar. 4, 1920; s. Jack and Ida (Abrams) G.; m. Rita Levine, June 29, 1955; children—Seth, Andrew. Student, New Sch. for Social Research, 1945-47. Pres. Sherwood Prodns., 1949-52; exec. various advt. agys., 1952-59; pres. Smith/Greenland Co., Inc., N.Y.C., 1959—; chmn., chief exec. officer Smith/Greenland Co., Inc., 1974—; guest lectr. Fordham U. Sch. Communication Arts, 1967—, Cornell Sch. Hotel Mgmt., NYU. Nat. commr. Anti-Defamation League, chmn. radio-TV dept.; bd. dirs., pres. Friars Found.; trustee ADL Found.; hon. chief N.Y.C. Fire Dept.; mem. adv. bd. bus. coun. UN; mem. Am. Forces Info. Svc. Task Force. Served with AUS, 1943-46. Mem. Am. Advt. Agys. (bd. govs. N.Y.), Nat. Advt. Rev. Bd., Am. Mgmt. Assn. (lectr. 1969—), Am. Arbitration Assn., Nat. Businessmen's Coun., Fgn. Policy Assn. Interracial Businessmen's Coun., Ea. Frosted Foods Assn. (pres. 1965-67, bd. dirs.), Chief Execs. Orgn., Met. Pres. Orgn., Sales Execs. Club N.Y., Newcomer Soc. N.Am., Def. Orientation Conf. Assn., Am. Forces Info. Svc. Task Force, Sierra Club, Econs. Club, Gilda's Club (founding mem.), Rockrimmon Country Club, Friars Club (pres. found.), Palm Beach Round Table. Home: PO Box 806 Bedford NY 10506-0806 Office: Smith/Greenland Inc 3 E 54th St New York NY 10022-3108

GREENLAW, ROGER LEE, interior designer; b. New London, Conn., Oct. 12, 1936; s. Kenneth Nelson and Lyndell Lee (Stinson) G; children: Carol Jennifer, Roger Lee. BFA, Syracuse U., 1958. Interior designer Cannell & Chaffin, 1958-59, William C. Wagner, Arch., L.A., 1959-60, Gen. Fireproofing Co., L.A., 1960-62, K-S Wilshire, Inc., L.A., 1963-64; dir. interior design Calif. Desk Co., L.A., 1964-67; sr. interior designer Bechtel Corp., L.A., 1967-70; sr. interior designer, project mgr. Daniel, Mann, Johnson & Mendehall, L.A., 1970-72, Morganelli-Heumann & Assocs., L.A., 1972-73; owner, prin. Greenlaw Design Assocs., Glendale, Calif., 1973-76, Greenlaw Interiro Planning & Design, 1996—; lectr. UCLA; mem. adv. curriculum com. Mt. San Antonio Coll., Walnut, Calif., Fashion Inst. Design, L.A.; bd. dirs. Calif. Legis. Conf. Interior Design, treas., 1992-94, v.p., 1990-92, pres., 1997-98. Past schoutmaster Verdugo coun. Boy Scouts Am.; pres. bd. dirs. Unity Ch., La Crescenta, Calif., 1989-91. Mem. ASID (treas. Pasadena chpt. 1983-84, 1st v.p. 1985, pres. 1986-87, chmn. So. Calif. regional conf. 1985, nat. dir. 1987-89, nat. com. legis., nat com. jury for catalog award, spkr. ho. dels., nat. bd. dirs., medallist award, regional v.p., nat. chair ethics com., nat. exec. com., v.p., treas. 1992 Calif. legis. conf. interior design, chmn. stds. task force, pres. 1994-98), Glendale C. of C. (bd. dirs. 1998), Adm. Farragut Acad. Alumni Assn., Kiwanis (bd. dirs.), Delta Upsilon. Republican. Home: 2100 Valderas Dr Apt F Glendale CA 91208-1340 Office: 2155 Verdugo Blvd Montrose CA 91020-1628

GREENLEAF, DOUGLAS A., information specialist; b. July 7, 1943. Ptnr.-in-charge consulting Touche Ross, Milw., 1980-88; nat. dir. Advanced Systems Devel., Touche Ross, N.Y.C., 1988-89; chief info. officer Deloitte & Touche, Nashville, 1990—. E-mail: dgreenleaf@dttus.com. Office: Deloitte and Touche 4022 Sells Dr Hermitage TN 37076

GREENLEAF, JANET ELIZABETH, principal; b. Hazleton, Pa., May 30, 1942; d. Edgar Henry and Mary Elizabeth (Rabenold) Bohstedt; m. James Albert Greenleaf, Nov. 19, 1966; children: John Edward, Jean Marie. BS, Bloomsburg (Pa.) U., 1964; MEd, Lehigh U., 1966. Cert. tchr., Pa., NJ. Tchr. Allentown (Pa.) Sch. Dist., 1964-67; remedial reading tchr. East Orange (N.J.) Sch. Dist., 1967-70; tchr. Lehigh Valley Luth. Sch., Northampton, Pa., 1984-89, prin., 1989—; adj. prof. edn. Cedar Crest Coll., Allentown, 1989-90; mem. adv. bd. Safe Drug Free Schs. and Cmty's., 1992—. Author, presenter workshops; facilitator seminars. Bd. dirs. Bethlehem (Pa.) Pub. Libr., 1992—, treas. 1994—; bd. dirs. Sayre Child Ctr., Bethlehem, 1979-85, Ea. Pa. Luth. Camp Corp., 1993-99, v.p., 1996-99; sch. bd. pres. Lehigh Valley Luth. Sch., Northampton, 1982-85; pres. Jr. League of Lehigh Valley, Bethlehem, 1980-81; nominating chmn. Assn. Jr. Leagues, Washington, 1981-83; dir. Christian edn. St. Lukes Luth. Ch., Allentown, 1989-98, mem. ch. coun., 1981-83, 87-92, v.p. 1982-83; chmn. Luth. schs. and early childhood ctrs. com. N.E. Penn Synod, 1995-99. Recipient Vol. award Jr. League of Lehigh Valley, 1979. Mem. ASCD, Evang. Luth. Edn. Assn. Democrat. Avocations: reading, gardening, golf, working with youth. E-mail: jeg@iu20.dniu20.k12.pa.us. Home: 309 Pine Top Trl Bethlehem PA 18017-1731 Office: Lehigh Valley Luth Sch 1335 Old Carriage Rd Northampton PA 18067-8969

GREENLEAF, JOHN EDWARD, research physiologist; b. Joliet, Ill., Sept. 18, 1932; s. John Simon and Julia Clara (Flint) G.; m. Carol Lou Johnson, Aug. 28, 1960. MA, N.Mex. Highlands U., 1956; BA in Phys. Edn., U. Ill., 1955, MS, 1962, PhD in Physiol., 1963. Tchg. asst. N.Mex. Highlands U., Las Vegas, Nev., 1955-56; engring. draftsman Allis-Chalmers Mfg. Co., Springfield, Ill., 1956-57; tchg. asst. in phys. edn. U. Ill., Urbana, 1957-58, rsch. asst. in phys. edn., 1958-59, tchg. asst. in human anatomy and physiology, 1959-62; summer fellow NSF, 1962; pre-doctoral fellow NIH, 1962-63; rsch. physiologist Space Scis. Directorate, NASA, Ames Rsch. Ctr., Moffett Field, Calif., 1963-66, 67—; postdoctoral fellowship Karolinska Inst., Stockholm, 1966-67; adj. prof. biology dept. San Francisco State U., 1988—; adj. prof. dept. exercise sci. U. Calif., Davis, 1996—; Japan Soc. for Promotion of Sci. vis. prof. Kyoto Prefectural U. Medicine, 1997; mem. internat. adv. bd. Medicina Sportiva. Mem. editorial bd. Jour. Applied Physiology, 1989—; contbr. articles to profl. jours. Recipient George Huff award for Scholarship, U. Ill. 1954-55, NASA Spl. Achievement award, 1973. Served with U.S. Army, 1952-53. Recipient Disting. Alumni award N.Mex. Highlands U., 1990, Disting. Alumni award dept. molecular and integrative physiology U. Ill., 1998, Am. Coll. Sports Medicine Citation award, 1999; exch. fellow NAS, 1973-74, 77, 89, NIH, 1980. Fellow Am. Coll. Sports Medicine (trustee 1984-87), Aerospace Med. Assn. (Harold Ellingson award 1981-82, Eric Liljencrantz award 1990); mem. Am. Physiol. Soc. (mem. com. on coms. 1984-87, long range planning com. 1987-90, internat. physiol. com. 1997—), Shooting Sports Rsch. Coun. (internat. shooters devel. fund 1984), Sigma Xi. Achievements include patents in field. Home: 12391 Farr Ranch Ct Saratoga CA 95070-6527 Office: NASA Ames Rsch Ctr Life Sci Div MS 239-11 Moffett Field CA 94035-1000

GREENLEAF, WALTER FRANKLIN, lawyer; b. Griffin, Ga., Sept. 21, 1946; s. Walter Helmuth and Vida Mildred (Goheen) G. B.A., Mich. State U., 1968; M.A., U. N.C., 1970, J.D., U. Ala., 1973. Bar: Ala. 1973, Fla. 1974, U.S. Dist. Ct. (no. dist.) Ala. 1973, U.S. Ct. Appeals (5th cir.) 1974, U.S. Dist. Ct. (so. dist.) Fla. 1977, U.S. Ct. Appeals (11th cir) 1981. Law clk. U.S. Dist. Ct., Birmingham, Ala., 1973-74; assoc. Sirote, Permutt, et al., Birmingham, Ala., 1975-76; assoc., then ptnr. Welbaum Guernsey, Hingston, Greenleaf, & Gregory, LLP, Miami, Fla., 1976—. Editor, Ala. Law Rev., 1972-73. Mem. ABA, Dade County Bar Assn., Am. Arbitration Assn. (panel of arbitrators), Order Coif, Phi Beta Kappa, Phi Kappa Phi, Phi Delta Phi, Omicron Delta Kappa. Home: 417 Madeira Ave Miami FL 33134-4234 Office: Welbaum Guernsey Hingston Greenleaf & Gregory LLP 901 Ponce De Leon Blvd Miami FL 33134-3073

GREENLER, ROBERT GEORGE, physics educator, researcher; b. Kenton, Ohio, Oct. 24, 1929; s. Dallas George and Ruth Edna (Mallett) G.; m. Barbara Stacy, May 30, 1954; children: Leland S., Karen R., Robin A. BS in Physics, U. Rochester, 1951; PhD in Physics, Johns Hopkins U., 1957. Research scientist Allis-Chalmers Mfg. Co., Milw., 1957-62; assoc. prof. physics U. Wis., Milw., 1962-67, prof., 1967-91, adj. prof., 1991-98, prof. emeritus, 1998—; sr. vis. fellow U. East Anglia, Norwich, Eng., 1971-72; traveling lectr. Optical Soc. Am., 1973-74; lectr. Coop. Edn. Program, Malaysia, 1990-91; organizer pub. outreach program Sci. Bag; prodr. 25 ednl. videos; did field rsch. on optical atmospheric effects at U.S. Antarctic Rsch. Station, South Pole, 1976-77, 97-98, 98-99. Author: Rainbows, Halos and Glories, 1980; contbr. 80 articles to profl. jours. Sr. Fulbright scholar Fritz Haber Inst. of Max Planck Soc., West Berlin, 1983; grantee NSF, Petroleum Research Fund, Am. Chem. Soc. Fellow AAAS, Optical Soc. Am. (v.p. 1985, pres.-elect 1986, pres. 1987, 1st Esther Hoffman Beller award 1993); mem. Am. Assn. Physics Tchrs. (Milikan Lectr. award 1988). Research in surface science, infrared spectroscopy of adsorbed molecules, meteorological optics, iridescent colors in biological systems. Home: 1901 W Pioneer Rd Mequon WI 53097-1737 Office: U Wis Milw Dept Physics PO Box 413 Milwaukee WI 53201-0413

GREENLICK, MERWYN RONALD, health services researcher; b. Detroit, Mar. 12, 1935; s. Emanuel and Fay G.; m. Harriet, Aug. 19, 1956; children—Phyllis, Michael, Vicki. B.S., Wayne State U., 1957; M.S., U. Mich., 1961, Ph.D., 1967. Pharmacist Detroit, 1957-60; spl. instr., instr. pharmacy adminstrn. Coll. Pharmacy Wayne State U., 1958-62; dir. of research n.w. region Kaiser-Permanente, Portland, 1964-95; v.p. (research) Kaiser Found. Hosps., 1981-95; sr. fellow Ctr. for Advanced Study in the Behavioral Scis., Stanford, Calif., 1995-96; adj. prof. sociology and social work Portland State U., 1965—; clin. prof. preventive medicine and pub. health Oreg. Health Scis. U., 1971-89, prof., acting chair preventive medicine and pub. health, 1990-93, prof., chair preventive medicine and pub. health, 1993—; mem. Gov.'s Commn. on Health Care, 1988; cons. Gov.'s Health Manpower Coun. Bd. dirs. Washington County Community Action Orgn., 1966-70; pres. Jewish Edn. Assn., Portland, 1976-78; bd. dirs. Jewish Fedn., 1975-79. USPHS trainee, 1962-63, 63-64. Fellow APHA, NAS, Inst. Medicine; mem. AAAS, Assn. Health Svcs. Rsch. (Disting. Fellow, Pres.'s award 1995), N.W. Health Found. (bd. dirs. 1997—). Jewish. Home: 712 NW Spring Ave Portland OR 97229-6913 Office: Oreg Health Svcs U CB 669 3181 SW Sam Jackson Park Rd Portland OR 97201-3011

GREENLY, COLIN, artist; b. London, Jan. 21, 1928; came to U.S., 1939, naturalized, 1948; s. Arthur John and Caroline Matilda (Fantini) G.; m. Laurie Ann Zadek, May 8, 1976; 1 child, Katharine Lydia Caro Herman. AB, Harvard Coll., 1948; student, Columbia U. Sch. Painting and Sculpture, 1951-53; attended Grad. Sch. Fine Arts, Am. U., 1956. dir. art Madeira Sch., Greenway, Va., 1955-68; Dana prof. fine arts Colgate U., 1972-73; vis. artist numerous colls., univs. One-man shows Corcoran Gallery of Art, Washington, 1968, Royal Marks Gallery, N.Y.C., 1968, 70, Everson Mus., Syracuse, N.Y., 1971, Andrew Dickson White Mus., Cornell U., 1972, Picker Gallery, Colgate U., 1973, Finch Coll. Mus., N.Y.C., 1974; group shows include Mus. Modern Art, N.Y.C., 1953, 73, De Cordova Mus., Lincoln, Mass., 1965, Des Moines Art Ctr., 1967, Nat. Collection Fine Arts, Washington, 1968, Krannert Art Mus., Champaign, Ill., 1969, 74, Emmerich Gallery Downtown, N.Y.C., 1972, John Weber Gallery, N.Y.C., 1975, Whitney Mus. Am. Art, N.Y.C., 1978, N.Y. State Mus., Albany, 1981; represented in permanent collections Albright Knox Art Gallery, Buffalo, Corcoran Gallery Art, Des Moines Art Ctr., Everson Mus., High Mus. Art, Atlanta, Mus. Modern Art, N.Y.C., Phila. Mus. Art, Nat. Gallery Art, Washington, Nat. Collection Fine Arts, Washington, Herbert F. Johnson Mus., Ithaca, N.Y.; restoration and contemporary adaptation of Hulse Barn, Campbell Hall, N.Y.; contbr. works of art, videos, photographs to CDROM Images of the Whole, 1998. Grantee Nat. Endowment for Arts, 1967, Com. for Visual Arts, 1974, Creative Artists Pub. Svc. Program, 1972, 78, N.Y. State Coun. on Arts, 1993. Mem. Media Alliance N.Y.C., Nat. Audobon Soc., Nature Conservancy, Wilderness Soc., Nat. Trust for Hist. Preservation, Sierra Club. Incorporated the characteristics of a circle and a square into a single image, thereby discovering an effective visual symbol for the concepts of transition and change, 1964; Intangible Sculpture; patentee in field of playground sculpture. Address: 487 Hulsetown Rd Campbell Hall NY 10916-3201 *Developing one's abilities may require a measure of commitment and excellence, but committing excellence to indiscriminate ends is artless. The synthesis of life and art is art.*

GREEN MACIAS, ROSARIO, United Nations official. Sec. fgn. rels. Govt. Mex., Mexico City. Office: Ricardo Flores Magon, Num 19 Piso, Mexico City 06995, Mexico*

GREENMAN, DAVID LEWIS, consultant physiologist and toxicologist; b. Williamston, Mich., Jan. 19, 1934; s. Asa J. and Lucy B. (Hoover) G.; m. Jessie E. Blackman, Aug. 10, 1956; children: Karen, Martha. BA, Asbury Coll., 1956; MS, Purdue U., 1959, PhD, 1962. Asst. prof., rsch. assoc. Johns Hopkins U., Balt., 1964-70; pharmacologist FDA, Washington, 1970, EPA, Washington, 1970-72; rsch. pharmacologist Nat. Ctr. for Toxicol. Rsch., FDA, Jefferson, Ark., 1972-76, rsch. physiologist, 1976-94; cons. in toxicology and physiology, North Little Rock, Ark., 1994—; chmn. precautionary labelling com. Assn. Am. Pest Control Operators, Washington, 1971-72; mem. adv. bd. Handbook Endocrinology, CRC Press, Inc., Boca Raton, Fla., 1981; FDA cons. Nigerian FDA, Lagos, 1982; chmn. Institutional Animal Care and Use Com., 1990-92. Contbr. articles to Steroids, Endocrinology, Lab. Animal Sci., Jour. Nat. Cancer Inst., Jour. Toxicological Environ. Health. Chmn. Old York Community Coun., Balt., 1967-68; del. NE Community Orgn., Balt., 1969-70; vol. mission svc. corps South Bapt. Conv., Ark. Bapt. State vol. prayer coord., 1995—. Recipient Group FDA award Merit, 1980, Spl. Svc. award FDA, 1988, FDA Disting. Career Svc. award, 1994; fellow NSF, 1959-62, Nat. Cancer Inst., 1963-64; rsch. grantee NIH, 1965-70. Baptist. Achievements include demonstration of importance of kinetics of RNA precursor distribution in interpreting the effect of hormones on radiolabeling of RNA, of impact that rack shelf level has on body weight gain, food consumption, retinal degeneration and neoplasm frequency in laboratory mice; first identification of a mouse strain that develops thyroid neoplasm in response to diethystilbestrol and has a tendency toward a higher frequency in females than males as is true in humans.

GREENMAN, JANE FRIEDLIEB, lawyer; b. N.Y.C., Sept. 9, 1950; d. Morton Jerome and Isabelle Irene (Bisgyer) F.; m. Charles P. Greenman, Nov. 23, 1975; children: Margot, Jaclyn, Danielle. BS, Cornell U., 1972; JD, NYU, 1975, LLM in Labor Law, 1981. Bar: N.Y. 1976. Assoc. Wolf Haldenstein, N.Y.C., 1975-79; faculty NYU Law Sch., 1979-81; full time faculty Bklyn. Law Sch., 1981-82; assoc., counsel Hughes Hubbard & Reed, N.Y.C., 1982-91, ptnr., chair employee benefits dept., 1991-96; dep. gen. coun. human resources labor & benefits AlliedSignal Inc., Morristown, N.J., 1996—; bd. dirs. Corinthian Comm., N.Y.C., East Williston Ednl. Found.; adj. prof. Bklyn. Law Sch., 1982-92, Law Sch. Hofstra U. Mem. Temple Sinai of Summit; founder L.I. Assn. to Save Our Neighborhoods/Playing It Safe. Mem. ABA, N.Y.C. Bar Assn., N.Y. State Bar Assn. Jewish. Office: AlliedSignal Inc 101 Columbia Rd Morristown NJ 07960-4640*

GREENOUGH, WILLIAM BATES, III, medical educator; b. Providence, Jan. 3, 1932; s. William Bates Jr. and Dorothy Garrison (Rand) G.; m. Jane Cheney Woodruff, Aug. 14, 1954 (dec. 1964); children: William Beckley, Kate, Thomas Clark, Elisabeth Bates; m. Quaneta Ahmed, 1965; 1 child, Zarin Farah Naz. BA magna cum laude, Amherst Coll., 1953; MD cum laude, Harvard U., 1957. Intern, asst. resident Columbia U. Coll. Physicians and Surgeons, N.Y.C., 1952-59; sr. rsch. fellow Mary Imogene Bassett Hosp., Cooperstown, N.Y., 1959-61; sr. resident Peter Bent Brigham Hosp., Boston, 1961-62; staff assoc. Nat. Heart Inst. Cholera Rsch. Lab., Dhaka, Bangladesh, 1962-65; chief infectious diseases div. Johns Hopkins U. Sch. Medicine, Balt., 1970-76, dir. Robert Wood Johnson Clin. Scholars Program, 1974-77, prof. medicine, 1983—, prof. internat. health sch. pub. health, 1985—; dir. Internat. Ctr. for Diarrhoeal Disease Rsch., Dhaka, Bangladesh, 1979-85; mem. geriatric medicine div. Johns Hopkins U., 1985—; cons. infectious diseases Perry Point VA Hosp., 1972-77, Internat. Rescue Com., N.Y.C., 1971-72; mem. bacteriology and mycology study sect. NIH, 1972-76, chmn., 1974-76; mem. ad hoc study group on enteric disease Walter Reed Army Inst. Rsch., 1975-77; pres. Bangladesh Info. Ctr., Washington, 1971-84; mem. adv. coun. Bangladesh Found., Chgo., 1972; active Md. Gov.'s Commn. on Phys. Fitness and Marathon Commn., 1971-77; pres., chmn. bd., trustee Internat. Child Health Found., Columbia, Md., 1985-95, pres., 1998—; chmn. Internat. Ctr. for Diarrhoeal Disease Rsch. Endowment Fund, Bangladesh, 1997—; cons. Cera Products, 1993—. Editor Infection and Immunity, 1975-78, Topics in Infectious Disease, 1976—, Jour. Diarrheal Disease Rsch., 1983-85, 93—; internat. advisor Kuwait Med. Jour.; author monographs; contbr. articles and revs. to med. jours., chpts. to books; patentee in field. Sr. surgeon USPHS, 1962-67. Recipient Internat. Prize in Medicine, King Faisal Found., 1984; Maurice Pate prize UNICEF, 1984, recognized for svc. to children, 1983. Fellow AAAS, ACP; mem. Assn. Am. Physicians, Am. Soc. for Clin. Investigation, Infectious Diseases Soc. Am., Am. Geriatric Soc., Bangladesh Assn. for Advancement Scis., Am. Fedn. Clin. Rsch., Am. Soc. Microbiology, Internat. Epidemiol. Assn., Bangladesh Med. Soc. Islam. Home: 1300 Hollins Ln Baltimore MD 21209-2237 Office: Johns Hopkins Geriatrics Ctr. 5505 Hopkins Bayview Cir Baltimore MD 21224-6822 *"Assuredly The Creation of The Heavens And The earth Is a greater matter Than The creation of man: Yet most men understand not."*

GREENOUGH, WILLIAM TALLANT, psychobiologist, educator; b. Seattle, Oct. 11, 1944; s. Harrison and Maryon C. (Whitten) G.; 1 dau., Jennifer Anne. B.A., U. Oreg., 1964; M.A., UCLA, 1966, Ph.D., 1969. Instr. U. Ill., Urbana-Champaign, 1968-69; asst. prof. U. Ill., 1969-73, assoc. prof., 1973-77, chair neural and behavioral biology program, 1977-87, prof. psychology, psychiatry, cell and structural biology, 1978—; assoc. dir. Beckman Inst. for Advanced Sci. and Tech., 1987-91; prof. U. Ill. Ctr. Advanced Study, 1997—, Swanlund prof. psychology, psychiatry, cell biology, 1998—; vis. prof. psychobiology U. Calif., Irvine, 1972; vis. prof. psychology U. Wash., 1975-76; program chmn. Winter Conf. on Brain Rsch., 1984-85, conf. chair, 1994-95; panel mem. integrative neural sys. NSF, 1987-91; dir. NSF Ctr. of Neurobiology of Learning and Memory, 1989-94; v.p., exec. com. Forum on Rsch. Mgmt., Fed. Behavioral, Psychol. and Cognitive Scis., 1991-93; mem. sci. adv. bd. Am. Psychol. Assn. Sci. Directorate; mem. NSF Biol. Sci. Directorate Adv. Com. Editor: (with R.N. Walsh) Environments as Therapy for Brain Dysfunction, 1976, (with J.M. Juraska) Developmental Neuropsychobiology, 1987; co-editor jour. Neurobiol. Learning and Memory, 1984—; contbr. numerous articles to profl. jours. Recipient William Rosen award for rsch. Nat. Fragile X Found., 1998; Cattell Found. fellow, 1975-76; USPHS and NSF grantee, 1969—; U. Ill. sr. scholar, 1985-88. Fellow AAAS, APA (Disting. Sci. Contbn. award 1999), Am. Psychol. Soc. (William James Fellow award), Soc. Exptl. Psychology; mem. NAS, Soc. Neurosci. (councilor 1990-94), Soc. Devel. Neurosci., Soc. Devel. Psychobiology (bd. dirs. 1977-80), Sigma Xi. Research interests include morphological plasticity of cerebellum, experience and learning-based synapse formation, molecular mechanisms of mental retardation, and plasticity of glial cells. Home: 1002 S Busey Ave Urbana IL 61801-4029 Office: U Ill Beckman Inst 405 N Mathews Ave Urbana IL 61801-2325

GREENSLADE, KATHRYN ELIZABETH, art director; b. Hinsdale, Ill., Oct. 21, 1966; d. Forrest Charles and Carol Ann (Walker) G.; m. Stephen Armstrong, June 26, 1993. BFA, Parsons Sch. of Design, N.Y.C., 1989. Designer Gower Med. Pub., N.Y.C., 1989-91, art dir., 1991-93; assoc. art dir. Prevention Mag. (Rodale Press, Inc.), Emmaus, Pa., 1993-95; art dir. premiums Rodale Press, Inc., Emmaus, 1995-97, mgr. creative premiums, 1997—; art dir., cons. Intercare, Chapel Hill, N.C., 1990-97. Avocations: gardening, decorating, web design. Office: Rodale Press 33 E Minor St Emmaus PA 18098-0099

GREENSPAHN, BARBARA, university administrator, law educator, librarian; b. Portland, Oreg., Aug. 1, 1947; d. Bernard Philip and Gloria (Mink) Nirenberg; m. Frederick Edward Greenspahn, June 16, 1969 (div.); children: Rachel, Daniel. BA, UCLA, 1969; MS, Simmons Coll., 1974; JD, Boston U., 1979. Bar: Colo. 1980. Asst. to libr. Harvard Law Sch. Libr., Boston, 1974-76; reference libr. Boston U. Law Sch. Libr., 1978-79; law and libr. cons. Libr. Svcs. Profls., Denver, 1980-84; mgr. info. resources Davis, Graham & Stubbs, Denver, 1984-88; dir. libr. U. Denver Coll. Law, 1989-93, assoc. dean for planning, 1994-95; project mgr. U. Denver, 1995—. Bd. dirs. Four Mile Hist. Park, Denver, 1979-81, Herzl Jewish Day Sch., Denver, 1990-92, v.p., 1990-92, Congregation Rodef Shalom, 1998—. Jewish. Office: U Denver Facilities Mgmt 2400 S Race St Denver CO 80210-5151*

GREENSPAN, ALAN, central banker, economist; b. N.Y.C., Mar. 6, 1926; s. Herman Herbert and Rose (Goldsmith) G. BS summa cum laude, NYU, 1948, MA, 1950, PhD, 1977. Pres., CEO Townsend-Greenspan and Co., Inc., N.Y.C., 1954-74, 77-87; mem. Council Econ. Advisers, 1970-74, chmn.,

1974-77; cons. Congressional Budget Office, 1977-87; mem. Pres.'s Econ. Policy Adv. Bd., 1981-87; chmn. Nat. Commn. on Social Security Reform, 1981-83; mem. Task Force on Econ. Growth, 1969, Pres.'s Fgn. Intelligence Adv. Bd., 1983-85; commn. on an All-Vol. Armed Force, 1969-70; commn. on Fin. Structure and Regulation, 1970-71; sr. adviser panel on econ. activity Brookings Instn., 1970-74, 77-87; chmn. bd. govs. Fed. Res. System, 1987—; mem. bd. economists Time mag., 1971-74, 77-87. Bd. overseers Hoover Instn. on War, Revolution and Peace, 1973-74, 77-87. Recipient John P. Madden medal, 1975, Pub. Svc. Achievement award, 1976, William Butler Meml. award, 1977. Fellow Nat. Assn. Bus. Economists (past pres.), Hillcrest County Club, Met. Club, Century County Club, Harmonie Club. Office: Federal Reserve System Office of Chmn 20th & C Sts NW Washington DC 20551-0001*

GREENSPAN, DEBORAH, oral medicine educator. 2nd BDS, U. London, 1960, BDS, 1964, DSc, 1991; fellow in Dental Surgery (hon.), Royal Coll. Surgeons, Edinburgh, 1994; LDS, Royal Coll. Surgeons, Eng., 1964; ScD (hon.), Georgetown U., 1990. Registered dental practioner, U.K.; diplomate Am. Bd. Oral Medicine. Vis. lectr. oral medicine U. Calif., San Francisco, 1976-83, asst. clin. prof., 1983-85, assoc. clin. prof., 1985-89, clin. prof., 1989-96, prof. clin. oral medicine, 1996—; lectr. in oral biology, U. Calif., San Francisco, 1972, clin. dir. Oral AIDS Ctr., 1987—, active Sch. Dentistry coms. including admissions com., 1985—, chair task force on infection control, 1987—; cons. Joint FDI/WHO Working Group on AIDS, 1989—, EEC, 1990, WHO, 1990, 91, Dept. Health State Calif., 1991, others; ad hoc reviews Epidemiology and Disease Control Sect. Div. Rsch. Grants NIH, 1987—; mem. programs adv. com. Nat. Inst. Dental Rsch., 1989—, mem. spl. ad hoc tech. rev. panel, 1991, mem. panel Fed. Drug Adminstrn., 1991-94; other svc. to govtl. agys.; participant numerous sci. and profl. workshops, meetings, and continuing edn. courses, numerous radio, TV, and press interviews concerning AIDS and infection control in dentistry. Author: (with J.S. Greenspan, Pindborg, and Schiødt), AIDS and the Dental Team, 1986 (transl. German, French, Italian, Spanish, Japanese), AIDS and the Mouth, 1990, (with others) San Francisco General Hospital AIDS Knowledge Base, 1986, Dermatologic Clinics, 5th edit., 1987, Infectious Disease Clinics of North America, 2nd. edit., 1988, Oral Manifestations of AIDS, 1988, Contemporary Periodontics, 1989, Opportunistic Infections in AIDS Patients, 1990, AIDS Clinical Review, 1990, Oral Manifestations of Systemic Disease, 1990, others; mem. editorial bd. rev. Jour. Am. Coll. Dentists, 1991; ad hoc referee Jour. Oral Pathology, 1983—, Cancer, 1985—, Jour. Acad. Gen. Dentistry, 1986—, European Jour. Cancer & Clin. Oncology, 1986, Archives of Dermatology, 1988—, Jour. AMA, 1988—, AIDS, 1991; contbr. numerous articles to profl. jours. Mem. dental subcom. of profl. edn. com. Calif. div. Am. Cancer Soc., 1982-90, profl. health care providers task force, 1991. Nat. Cancer Inst. fellow, 1978-79, Am. Coll. Dentists fellow, 1988; recipient Woman of Distinction award, London, 1986, Commendation cert. Asst. Sec. for Health, 1989; named Seymour J. Kreshover lectr. Nat. Inst. Dental Rsch., 1989, Hon. Lectr. United Med. and Dental Schs. of Guys and St. Thomas Hosps., U. London, 1991. Fellow Royal Soc. Medicine, Royal Coll. Surgeons; mem. AAAS, ADA (vis. lectr. speaker's bur. 1988—, cons. coun. on dental therapeutics 1988—), Am. Assn. Dental Rsch. (session chair 1986-87, constitution com. 1988-91, chair 1990-91, pres. San Francisco sect. 1990—, treas. 1992—), Am. Acad. Oral Pathology, Am. Soc. Microbiology, Am. Assn. Women Dentists, Am. Acad. Oral Medicine, Am. Assn. Dental Schs., Internat. Assn. Dental Rsch. (pres. exptl. pathology group 1989-90, other coms. and offices), Internat. Assn. Oral Pathologists, Calif. Dental Assn., San Francisco Dental Soc., Internat. AIDS Soc. Achievements include rsch. on oral candidiasis in HIV infection, on HIV-associated salivary gland disease, on oral hairy leukoplakia, and on the prevalence of HIV-associated gingivitis and periodontitis in HIV-infected patients. Office: U Calif Sch Dentistry Dept Stomatology S 612 PO Box 0422 San Francisco CA 94143-0422

GREENSPAN, DONALD, mathematician, educator; b. N.Y.C., Jan. 24, 1928. B.S., NYU, 1948; M.S., U. Wis., 1949; Ph.D., U. Md., 1956. Instr. U. Md., 1948-56; research engr. Hughes Aircraft Co., 1956-57; asst. prof. Purdue U., 1957-61, asso. prof., 1961-62; permanent mem. U. Wis. Math. Research Center, Madison, 1962-68; prof. computer scis., cons. to U. Wis. Computing Center, 1965-78; prof. math. U. Tex., 1978—; lectr. Am. Math. Assn., 1963-64, U. Mich. Summer Conf., 1964; referee NRC, NSF. Author: Theory and Solution of Ordinary Differential Equations, 1960, Introduction to Partial Differential Equations, 1961, Introductory Numerical Analysis of Elliptic Boundary Value Problems, 1965, Introduction to Calculus, 1968, Lectures on the Numerical Solutions of Linear, Singular, and Nonlinear Differential Equations, 1968, Introduction to Numerical Analysis and Application, 1970, Discrete Models, 1973, Discrete Numerical Methods in Physics and Engineering, 1974, Arithmetic Applied Mathematics, 1980, Computer-Oriented Mathematical Physics, 1981, (with U. Bulgarelli and V. Casulli) Pressure Methods for the Numerical Solution of Free Surface Fluid Flow, 1984, (with V. Casulli) Numerical Analysis for Applied Mathematics, Science and Engineering, 1988, Quasimolecular Modelling, 1991, Particle Modeling, 1997; editor: Numerical Solutions of Nonlinear Differential Equations, 1966, (with Pal Rosza) Numerical Methods, 1988, 2d rev. edit., 1991; editl. bd. Jour. Computers and Math. with Applications, Systems Analysis-Modelling-Simulation, CDC Handbook of Fluid Dynamics; contbr. articles to profl. jours. Active Common Cause, NAACP. Mem. ACLU, Am. Math. Soc., Am. Phys. Soc., Assn. Computing Machinery, Ams. for Dem. Action. Office: U Tex Math Dept Arlington TX 76019

GREENSPAN, FRANCIS S., physician; b. Perth Amboy, N.J., Mar. 16, 1920; s. Philip and Francis (Davidson) G.; m. Bonnie Jean Fisher, Oct. 25, 1945; children: Richard L., Robert H., Susan L. B.A., Cornell U., 1940, M.D., 1943. Diplomate: Am. Bd. Internal Medicine. Mem. endocrinology staff U. Calif.-San Francisco; chief endocrinology Stanford (Calif.) Hosp., 1949-59; chief thyroid clinic U. Calif. Med. Ctr., San Francisco, 1959—; practice medicine specializing in endocrinology San Francisco; now clin. prof. medicine and radiology U. Calif. Med. Ctr.; chief staff U. Calif. Hosps. and Clinics, San Francisco, 1976-78. Editor: Textbook of Endocrinology; contbr. articles to med. jours. Served with USNR, 1944-45. Mem. San Francisco Med. Soc., Calif. Med. Assn., AMA, Endocrine Soc., Am. Thyroid Assn., Western Soc. Clin. Research, Western Assn. Physicians, Calif. Acad. Medicine. Office: U Calif Med Ctr 350 Parnassus Ave Ste 609 San Francisco CA 94117-3608

GREENSPAN, HARVEY PHILIP, applied mathematician, educator; b. N.Y.C., Feb. 22, 1933; s. Louis and Jessie (Scholnick) G.; m. Mirian Gordon, Sept. 6, 1953; children—Elizabeth, Judith. BS, CCNY, 1953; MS, Harvard U., 1954, PhD, 1956; D Tech. (hon.), Royal Inst. Tech., Stockholm, 1991. Asst. prof. applied math. Harvard, 1956-60; faculty MIT, Cambridge, 1960—; prof. applied math. MIT, 1964—. Author: Theory of Rotating Fluids, 1968, Calculus: An Introduction to Applied Mathematics, 1973; editor: Studies in Applied Mathematics, 1969; patentee centrifugal spectrometer. Home: 15 Chatham Cir Brookline MA 02446-5410 Office: Mass Inst Tech 77 Massachusetts Ave Cambridge MA 02139-4301

GREENSPAN, JAY SCOTT See ALEXANDER, JASON

GREENSPAN, JEFFREY DOV, lawyer; b. Chgo., July 19, 1954; s. Philip and Sylvia (Haberman) G.; m. Eleanor Helen Goldman, Aug. 28, 1983. BS in Econs., U. Ill., Urbana, 1976; JD, Ill. Inst. Tech., 1979. Bar: Ill. 1979, U.S. Dist. Ct. (no. dist.) Ill. 1979, U.S. Ct. Appeals (7th cir.) 1979. Atty. Govs. Office Consumer Services, Chgo., 1978-80; asst. pub. defender Cook County Pub. Defenders Office, Chgo., 1980-81; asst. corp. counsel Village of Skokie, Ill., 1981-91; of counsel Fioretti & Des Jardins, 1990-91; with Ancel, Glink, Diamond, Cope & Bush, P.C., 1991—; sec., treas. Polit. Cons., Inc., Skokie, 1984—. Author polit. computer software Master Campaigner, 1984. Mem. Niles (Ill.) Twp. Dem. Orgn., 1976—; chmn. Niles Twp. Com. on Youth, 1982-85, TRY-Citizens for Drug Awareness, Niles, 1983-84; mem. Centereast Bd. Authority, 1998—; bd. dirs. Niles Twp. H.S., 1999—. Mem. Chgo. Bar Assn. (chmn. devel. of law com. 1990-91, chmn. local govt. law com. 1992-93). Home: 9445 Keeler Ave Skokie IL 60076-1442

GREENSPAN, JOHN S., dentistry educator, scientist, administrator; b. London, Jan. 7, 1938; came to U.S., 1976; s. Nathan and Jessie (Dion) G.; m. Deborah, Dec. 1962; children: Nicholas J., Louise C. BSC in Anatomy with 1st class honors, U. London, 1959, B in Dental Surgery, 1962, PhD in Exptl. Pathology, 1967; ScD (hon.), Georgetown U., 1990. Licentiate in dental surgery Royal Coll. of Surgeons of Eng. Asst. house surgeon in conservation and periodontology Royal Dental Hosp. London, 1962; asst. lectr. oral pathology Sch. of Dental Surgery Royal Dental Hosp. of London, U. London, 1963-65, lectr. oral pathology Sch. of Dental Surgery, 1965-68, sr. lectr. oral pathology Sch. of Dental Surgery, 1968-75; prof. oral biology and oral pathology Sch. of Dentisty, U. Calif., San Francisco, 1976—, vice chmn. dept. oral medicine and hosp. dentistry, 1977-82, chmn. div. oral biology, 1981-89, coord. basic scis. Sch. of Dentistry, 1982-96; chmn. dept. stomatology U. Calif., San Francisco, 1989—; cons. oral pathology St. John's Hosp. and Inst. of Dermatology, London, 1973-76; cons. dental surgeon St. George's Hosp., 1972-76; prof. dept. pathology Sch. Medicine U. Calif., San Francisco, 1976—; dir. U. Calif. AIDS Specimen Bank, San Francisco, 1982—, U. Calif. Oral AIDS Ctr., San Francisco, 1987—; assoc. dir. dental clin. epidemiology program U. Calif., San Francisco, 1987—; dir. U. Calif. AIDS Clin. Rsch. Ctr., San Francisco, 1992—; Burroughs Wellcome vis. prof. Royal Soc. Medicine, U.K., 1996-97; presenter, lectr. Author: (with others) Opportunistic Infections in Patients with the Acquired Immunodeficiency Syndrome, 1989, Contemporary Periodontics, 1989, Gastroenterology Clinics of North America, 1988, Perspectives on Oral Manifestations of AIDS, 1988, AIDS: Pathogenesis and Treatment, 1988, others; contbr. articles to profl. jours.; editorial cons. Achives of Oral Biology, 1968—, Jour. of Calif. Dental Assn., 1980—; editoral adv. bd. Jour. of Dental Rsch., 1977—; editorial bd. AIDS Alert, 1987-89, Brit. Dental Jour., 1998—; sr. editor Oral Diseases, 1994-98. Rsch. grantee NIH-Nat. Inst. Dental Rsch., 1978-82, 86—, U. Calif. Task Force on AIDS, 1983—, rsch. com. Royal Dental Hosp., London, 1964-76, Med. Rsch. Coun. of U.K., 1974-77, chmn. U. Calif. San Francisco Acad. Senate, 1983-85; Nuffield dental scholar, 1958-59; fellow Am. Coll. Dentists, 1982—, AAAS, 1985—; recipient Seymour J. Kreshover Lecture award Nat. Inst. Dental Rsch., NIH, 1989, Rsch. in Oral Biology award Internat. Assn. Dental Rsch., 1992. Fellow Royal Coll. Pathologists, Royal Coll. Surgeons Faculty of Dental Surgery, Inst. Medicine of Nat. Acad. Scis.; mem. ADA, AAAS, Am. Assn. Dental Rsch. (pres. 1988-89), Internat. Assn. Dental Rsch. (pres. 1996-97), Royal Soc. Medicine (U.K.), Pathological Soc. (U.K.), Oral Pathology Soc. (U.K.), Am. Acad. Oral Pathology, Bay Area Tchrs. Oral Pathology, Internat . Assn. Oral Pathologists, San Francisco Dental Soc., Calif. Dental Assn., Calif. Soc. Oral Pathologists Histochem. Soc., Am. Assn. Pathologists. Avocations: skiing, gardening, travel, wine. Office: U Calif Dept Stomatology Box 0422 Sch Dentistry San Francisco CA 94143

GREENSPAN, LEON JOSEPH, lawyer; b. Phila., Feb. 10, 1932; s. Joseph and Minerva (Podolsky) G.; m. Irene Gordon, Nov. 2, 1958; children: Marjorie, David, Michael, Lisa. AB, Temple U., 1955, JD, 1958. Bar: N.Y. 1959, U.S. Supreme Ct., 1969, N.J. 1985, Fla. 1985, Pa. 1986, Conn., 1991. Pvt. practice law, White Plains, N.Y., 1959-64; ptnr. Greenspan & Aurnou, White Plains, 1964-77; ptnr. Greenspan & Jaffe, White Plains, 1978-87; ptnr. Greenspan, Jaffe & Rosenblatt, Whiteplains, 1987-91; ptnr. Greenspan & Rosenblatt, 1992, Greenspan & Greenspan, White Plains, 1992—; counsel Brown, Boston; lectr. Fla. Bar CLER Program, 1991, 92, 97; atty. Tarrytown (N.Y.) Housing Authority. Pres. Hebrew Inst., White Plains; vice chmn. ann. dinner NCCJ. Recipient Pres.'s award Union Orthodox Synagogues, 1982; honoree Hebrew Inst., White Plains, 1983. Mem. ABA, Westchester County Bar Assn., White Plains Bar Assn., N.Y. State Trial Lawyers Assn., Criminal Cts. Bar Assn. Westchester County. Home: 14 Pinebrook Dr White Plains NY 10605-4713 Office: Greenspan & Greenspan 34 S Broadway Fl 6 White Plains NY 10601-4400

GREENSPAN, MICHAEL ALAN, lawyer; b. Bklyn., Dec. 16, 1940; s. Abe and Leona (Peckerar) G.; m. Heather Gold, Aug. 2, 1964; children: Lisa, David. BA, Cornell U., 1962; LLB, Columbia U., 1965. Bar: N.Y. 1965, D.C. 1968. Assoc. Melrod Redman & Gartlan, Washington, 1969; asst. sec., sr. atty. Bd. Govs. Fed. Res. System, Washington, 1969-73; ptnr. Metzger, Noble, Schwarz & Kempler, Washington, 1973-78, Noble, Greenspan & Austin, Washington, 1978-82, Thompson Mitchell, Washington, 1982-96, Thompson Coburn, Washington, 1996—; adj. prof. U. Balt. Law Sch., 1998—. Author: (with others) Direct Investment and Development in the U.S., 1978; contbr. articles to profl. jours. Trustee Temple Emanuel, Kensington, Md., 1986-88; prin. Coun. for Excellence in Govt., Washington, 1990—. With U.S. Army, 1966-68. Mem. ABA (chmn. com. on fin. markets & instns. sect. antitrust law), Fed. Bar Assn. (bd. dirs.), The Federalist Soc. (chmn. mergers and acquisition subcom. of banking com.). Republican. Jewish. Avocations: chess, sign lang., photography, performing. Office: Thompson Coburn 700 14th St NW Ste 900 Washington DC 20005-2024

GREENSPAN, RALPH JAY, biologist; b. Phila., Mar. 23, 1950; s. Benjamin and Frances (Tebet) G.; m. Dani Suzanne Grady, Feb. 18, 1994. BA in Biology, Brandeis U., 1974, PhD, 1979. Postdoctoral fellow U. Calif., San Francisco, 1979-82; asst. prof. Princeton (N.J.) U., 1982-87; assoc. mem. Roche Inst. Molecular Biology, Nutley, N.J., 1987-92; prof. biology and neural sci. NYU, 1992-97; instr. The New Sch., N.Y.C., 1992-97; sr. fellow The Neuroscis. Inst., San Diego, 1997—. Author: Fly Pushing: The Theory and Practice of Drosophila Genetics, 1997; co-author: Genetic Neurobiology, 1982; contbr. articles to profl. jours. Dir. pub. edn. Thrivers' Network for Cancer Survivors, San Diego, 1994—. Fellow Helen Hay Whitney Found., 1979, Searle Scholars Program, 1982, Esther A. and Joseph Klingenstein Fund, 1984, 93. Achievements include research in genetics of behavior in the fruit fly Drosophila. Office: The Neurosciences Inst 10640 John Jay Hopkins Dr San Diego CA 92121*

GREENSPAN, STEPHEN HOWARD, retired psychology educator; b. N.Y.C., Apr. 4, 1941; s. Leonard and Rose Tell Greenspan; m. Helen Apthorp, June 10, 1988; children: Alex, Eli. BA, Johns Hopkins U., 1962; MA, Northwestern U., 1962; PhD, U. Rochester, 1976; postdoctoral cert., UCLA, 1977. Lic. psychologist, Tenn., Nebr. Asst. prof. George Peabody Coll. for Tchrs., Nashville, 1977-79; scientist Boys Town Ctr. for Study of Youth Devel., Omaha, 1979-85; from assoc. prof. to prof. U. Conn., Storrs, 1985-98, prof. emeritus, 1998—; pres. Acad. on Mental Retardation, Washington, 1995-97. Author: (book) Does Mental Retardation Exist?, 1999; editor: (book) What Is Mental Retardation?, 1999. Chairperson adv. com. State Office of Protection and Advocacy for Persons with Disabilities, Hartford, Conn., 1996-98. With U.S. Army, 1965-66. Avocation: watching sports on TV. Home: 9424 S Erin Ln Littleton CO 80127-5134

GREENSPON, ROBERT ALAN, lawyer; b. Hartford, Conn., Apr. 17, 1947; s. George Arthur and Shirley Jean (Shelton) G.; m. Claire Alice Stone, Aug. 21, 1971; children: Colin Haynes, Alison Shelton. AB, Franklin and Marshall, 1969; JD, Columbia U., 1972. Bar: Conn. 1973, N.Y. 1998, U.S. Dist. Conn. 1973, U.S. Ct. Appeals (2d cir.) 1983. Assoc. Robinson & Cole, Hartford, Conn., 1972-78; ptnr. Robinson & Cole, Hartford, 1978-81, Stamford, Conn., 1981-86; sr. v.p., gen. counsel Guinness Peat Aviation Corp., Stamford, N.Y.C., N.Y.C., Shannon, Ireland, 1985-92; ptnr. Latham & Watkins, N.Y.C., 1992—. Contbr. articles to profl. jours. Mem. ABA (comml. fin. services, aircraft fin.), Conn. Bar Assn., N.Y. State Bar Assn., Internat. Bar Assn., Southwestern Legal Found. (bd. advisors internat. and comparative law ctr.). Home: 49 Old Farm Rd Darien CT 06820-6119 Office: Latham & Watkins 885 3rd Ave Fl 10 New York NY 10022-4874

GREENSTEIN, ABRAHAM JACOB, mortgage company executive, accountant; b. Munich, Fed. Republic of Germany, May 5, 1949; came to U.S., 1950; s. Morris and Bella (Yeger) G.; m. Ruth Sanik, June 5, 1974; children: Pinchus, Yisroel, Shlomo. BS in Acctg., Bklyn. Coll., 1972. Sr. auditor State Comptrollers Office, N.Y.C., 1972-75; asst. dir. Office of Spl. Dep. Comptroller, N.Y.C., 1978-82; sr. v.p. fin. N.Y.C. Housing Devel. Corp., 1983-88, exec. v.p., 1988-98; treas. Housing Assistance Corp., N.Y.C., 1985-98, Residential Mortgage Ins. Co., N.Y.C., 1993-98; exec. v.p., chief oper. officer Housing for N.Y. Corp., N.Y.C., 1986-93, pres., 1993-98; v.p. Greystone & Co., N.Y.C., 1998—. Trustee Congregation Chasdi Gur, Bklyn., 1982-87. Mem. Am. Mgmt. Assn., Govt. Fin. Officers Assn., Council of State Housing Agys., Mortgage Bankers Assn. Jewish. Avocations: swimming, tennis. Office: Greystone & Co 60th Fl 152 W 57th St New York NY 10019

GREENSTEIN, FRED IRWIN, political science educator; b. N.Y.C., Sept. 1, 1930; s. Arthur Aaron and Rose (Goldstein) G.; m. Barbara Elferink, July 14, 1957; children: Michael, Amy, Jessica. B.A., Antioch Coll., 1953; M.A., Yale U., 1956, Ph.D., 1960. Instr. Yale U., New Haven, 1959-62, vis. prof., 1965-68; mem. faculty Wesleyan U., Middletown, Conn., 1963-73, prof. polit. sci., 1966-73; Henry Luce prof. politics, law and society Princeton U., 1973-81, prof. politics, 1973—; vis. prof. U. Essex, Eng., 1968-69, 91. Author: The American Party System and the American People, 1970, Children and Politics, 2d edit., 1969, Personality and Politics, 2d edit., 1975; co-author: (with R.E. Lane and J.D. Barber) Introduction to Political Analysis, 2 edit., 1965, (with M. Lerner) A Source Book for the Study of Personality and Politics, 1971, (with N.W. Polsby) The Handbook of Political Science, 8 vols., (with R. Wolfinger and M. Shapiro) Dynamics and American Politics, 1976, (with L. Berman and A. Felzenberg) The Evolution of the Modern Presidency: A Bibliographical Review, 1977; author: The Hidden-Hand Presidency: Eisenhower as Leader, 1982, The Reagan Presidency: An Early Appraisal, 1983, Leadership in the Modern Presidency, 1988, How Presidents Test Reality: Decisions on Vietnam, 1954 and 1965, 1989. Served with AUS, 1953-55. Fellow Ctr. Advanced Study Behavioral Scis., 1964-65; NSF sr. postdoctoral fellow, 1968-69. Fellow Am. Acad. Arts And Scis.; mem. Am. Polit. Sci. Assn. (editorial bd. 1968-72, sec. 1976-77), Internat. Soc. Polit. Psychology (pres. 1996-97). Home: 340 Jefferson Rd Princeton NJ 08540-3475 Office: Princeton Univ Dept Politics Princeton NJ 08544

GREENSTEIN, JEFFREY IAN, neurologist; b. Durban, South Africa, July 27, 1947; s. Joseph and Miriam (Shamos) G. MD, U. Cape Town, S. Africa, 1971. Diplomate Am. Bd. Neurology and Psychiatry. Asst. to assoc. prof. neurology Temple U. Sch. Med., Phila., 1983-89, prof. and chmn. neurology, 1989—. Mem. AAAS, Am. Acad. Neurology, N.Y. Acad. Sci., Nat. Multiple Sclerosis Soc. (chmn. profl. adv. com. Phila. 1992-95). Office: Temple Univ Sch Med 3401 N Broad St Ste 558 Philadelphia PA 19140-5103

GREENSTEIN, JESSE LEONARD, astronomer, educator; b. N.Y.C., Oct. 15, 1909; s. Maurice and Leah (Feingold) G.; m. Naomi Kitay, Jan. 7, 1934; children: George Samuel, Peter Daniel. AB, Harvard U., 1929, AM, 1930, PhD, 1937; DSc (hon.), U. Ariz., 1987. Engaged in real estate and investments, 1930-34, Nat. Research fellow, 1937-39; assoc. prof. Yerkes Obs., U. Chgo., 1939-48; research assoc. McDonald Obs., U. Tex., 1939-48; mil. research under OSRD (optical design), Yerkes Obs., 1942-45; prof. Calif. Inst. Tech., 1948-70, Lee A. DuBridge prof. astrophysics, 1971-81, prof. emeritus, 1981—; also staff mem. Hale Obs., 1949-79, Palomar Obs., 1979—, exec. officer for astronomy, 1949-72; chmn. of faculty of inst., 1965-67; mem. obs. com. Hale Observatories; mem. staff Owens Valley Radio Obs.; cons., also com. mem. NASA and NSF on astronomy and radio astronomy; chmn. astronomy survey Nat. Acad. Scis., 1969-72; spl. cons. NASA, 1978-83; vis. prof. Princeton, 1955, Inst. for Advanced Studies, 1964, 68-69, U. Hawaii, 1979, Niels Bohr Inst., 1979, NORDITA, Copenhagen, 1972, U. Del., 1981; lectr. in field; cons. Sci. Adv. Bd. USAF; former dir. Itek Corp., Hycon Corp.; chmn. bd. dirs. Assoc. Univs. Rsch. in Astronomy, 1974-77; bd. overseers Harvard, 1965-71; life trustee Pacific Asia Mus. Author sects. of treatises, 440 tech. papers; editor: Stellar Atmospheres, 1960; contbr. sci. articles to profl. jours.; author govt. reports. Named Calif. Scientist of Yr., 1964; recipient Apollo award, Disting. Public Service medal NASA, 1974, Centennial medal Harvard Grad. Sch., 1989. Mem. Royal Astron. Soc. (assoc.; Gold medal 1975), Astron. Soc. Pacific (Bruce medalist 1971), Am. Astron. Soc. (councillor 1947-50, v.p. 1955-57, Russell lectr. 1970), Internat Astron. Union (pres. commn. on spectroscopy 1952-58, chmn. U.S. delegation 1969-72), Nat. Acad. Scis. (councillor, sect. chmn. com. on sci. and pub. policy), Am. Philos. Soc., Am. Acad. Arts and Scis., Athenaeum (Pasadena), Phi Beta Kappa. Home: 1763 Royal Oaks Dr Apt B5 Bradbury CA 91010-1979 *A long and happy life, in which scientific discovery was like breath. With age one faces the question—was it worth doing? Were the uncomfortable thousand nights at the large telescopes drudgery or drama? Was the blood in the committee-room necessary? Yes, Yes, Yes.*

GREENSTEIN, MARTIN RICHARD, lawyer; b. Boston, Dec. 29, 1944; s. Paul and Sarah Greenstein; children: Stacey, Marc, Seth, Andrew. BSEE magna cum laude, Tufts U., 1965; MSEE, Princeton U., 1966; JD with highest honors, John Marshall Law Sch., 1971. Bar: Ill. 1971, N.Y. 1982, Calif. 1982, U.S. Patent Office 1971, U.S. Supreme Ct. 1981. Mem. tech. staff Bell Telephone Labs., Naperville, Ill., 1965-70, mem. patent staff, 1970-71; assoc. firm Baker & McKenzie, Chgo., 1971-78, ptnr., 1978-89; ptnr. Baker & McKenzie, Palo Alto, Calif., 1989-93, TechMark, Trademark and Intellectual Property Law, San Jose, Calif., 1993—; instr. John Marshall Law Sch., Chgo., 1972-76. Editorial bd. The Trademark Reporter, 1976-92. Trustee Village of Lisle, 1980-83; bd. dirs. Ill. Software Assn. and Ctr., 1984-87. Mem. ABA, State Bar Calif., Internat. Trademark Assn., Am. Intellectual Property Law Assn., Tau Beta Pi, Eta Kappa Nu. Home: 1709 Whitham Ave PO Box 179 Los Altos CA 94024 Office: TechMark 55 S Market St Ste 1630 San Jose CA 95113-2324*

GREENSTEIN, ROBERT M., non-profit organization director; b. Phila., Feb. 17, 1946; s. Daniel S. and Ruth H. (Halpren) G. BA magna cum laude, Harvard U., 1967; postgrad., U. Calif., Berkeley, 1968-69; D Pub. Svc. (hon.), Tufts U., 1992. Tchr. Newton (Mass.) South High Sch., 1969-72; staff mem., project dir. Community Nutrition Inst., Washington, 1972-77; spl. asst. to sec. USDA, Washington, 1977-79; adminstr. Food and Nutrition Service, USDA, Washington, 1979-81; dir. Project on Food Assistance and Poverty, Washington, 1981; exec. dir. Ctr. on Budget and Policy Priorities, Washington, 1981—; appointed by Pres. to Nat. Commn. on Entitlement Reform, 1994; bd. dirs. Nat. Low Income Housing Coalition, Washington, 1984-94, Coalition on Human Needs, Washington, 1982-94; mem. program rev. bd. U.S.A. for Africa/Hands Across Am., L.A., 1986-88. Contbr. articles on poverty-related issues to New Republic, Washington Post, N.Y. Times, L.A. Times, Boston Globe, other newspapers and mags. Danforth fellow, 1967, Woodrow Wilson fellow, 1967. Mem. Am. Pub. Welfare Assn. (bd. dirs. 1984-86). Jewish. Office: Ctr of Budget & Policy 820 1st St NE Ste 510 Washington DC 20002-4243*

GREENSTEIN, RUTH LOUISE, research institute executive, lawyer; b. N.Y.C., Mar. 28, 1946; d. Milton and Beatrice (Zutty) G.; m. David Seidman, May 19, 1972. BA, Harvard U., 1966; MA, Yale U., 1968; JD, George Washington U., 1980. Bar: D.C. 1980. Fgn. service info. officer USIA, Washington and Tehran, Iran, 1968-70; adminstrv. asst. Export-Import Bank U.S., Washington, 1971-72; asst. dean Woodrow Wilson Sch. Pub. and Internat. Affairs, Princeton U., 1972-75; budget examiner U.S. Office Mgmt. and Budget, Washington, 1975-79; budget coordinator U.S. Internat. Devel. Coop. Agy., 1979-81; dep. gen. counsel NSF, 1981-84; treas., then v.p. and gen. counsel Genex Corp., Gaithersburg, Md., 1984-90; v.p. adminstrn. and fin., gen. counsel Inst. for Def. Analyses, Alexandria, Va., 1990—; mem. acad. adv. panel to tech. transfer intelligence com. CIA, 1983-90; mem. def. trade adv. group U.S. Dept. State, 1994-96; mem. com. for protection of human subjects ARC, 1996—; dir. Very Spl. Arts, 1998—. Mem. NAS (panel on future design and implementation of nat. security export controls 1989-91), AAAS (com. on sci. freedom and responsibility 1987-93), D.C. Bar Assn. Home: 2737 Devonshire Pl NW Apt 511 Washington DC 20008-3458 Office: Inst for Def Analyses 1801 N Beauregard St Alexandria VA 22311-1733

GREENSTONE, ADAM FRANKLIN, lawyer; b. Washington, Dec. 1, 1963; s. James Paul and Elaine Beatrice (Hurwitz) G. BA, Gettsburg Coll., 1985; MSc, London Sch. Econs., 1986; JD, George Washington U., 1990. Bar: Pa. 1991, D.C. 1993. Law clk. to Hon. Eugene R. Sullivan, U.S. Ct. Mil. Appeals (now Ct. Appeals for Armed Forces), Washington, 1990-92; atty.-advisor Office Gen. Counsel, NASA, Washington, 1992-97; dep. gen. counsel Office Adminstrn., Exec. Office of Pres., Washington, 1997—. Mem. ABA, Am. Soc. Internat. Law, Eisenhower World Affairs Inst. Jewish. Office: Exec Office of Pres Office Adminstrn 725 17th St NW Washington DC 20503-0009

GREENSTONE, JAMES LYNN, psychotherapist, police psychologist, mediator, consultant, author, educator; b. Dallas, Mar. 30, 1943; s. Carl Bunk and Fifi (Horn) G.; m. Cynthia Beth, Pamela Celeste, David Carl. BA in Psychology, U. Okla., 1965; MS in Clin. Psychology, North Tex. State U., 1966, EdD in Edn. and Psychology, 1974; JD, Northwestern Calif. U., 1991. Lic. marriage and family therapist, profl. counselor. Psychologist Beverly Hills Hosp., Dallas, 1966-67; therapist Family Guidance Service, Dallas, 1967-68; instr. Dallas County Community Coll.

Dist., 1967-72, 78-79, 87-89; asst. prof. Tex. Women's U., 1979; assoc. prof. psychology and criminal justice Tarrant County Jr. Coll., 1987-89; tng. faculty Am. Acad. Crisis Interveners, Louisville, 1972-78; tng. dir. Southwestern Acad. Crisis Interveners, Dallas, 1977—; police instr. Dallas Sheriff's Acad., 1979-86; hostage negotiator and trainer Lancaster Police Dept., Tex., 1986-92; pvt. practice psychotherapy, 1966-96; dir. psychol. svcs. unit Ft. Worth Police Dept., 1992—; cons. Dallas County Jails, 1979-82, 89-90; dir. res. tng. Dallas Sheriff's Res., 1983-84; panel arbitrators Am. Arbitration Assn.; adj. prof. psychology Columbia Coll., Northwood Inst., 1987-89; adj. faculty dispute mediation North Tex. State U., 1987-88; instr. hostage negotiations North Cen. Tex. Council Govts. Regional Police Acad., 1987—; assoc. prof. psychology, criminal justice; adj. prof. law Tex. Wesleyan U. Sch. Law, 1991—; dir. psychol. svcs. unit Ft. Worth Police Dept. Author: Crisis Intervener's Handbook, Vol. 1, 1980; Crisis Intervener's Handbook, Vol. II, 1982; Hotline: Crisis Intervention Directory, 1981; Crisis Management: Handbook for Interveners, 1983; Winning Through Accommodation: Handbook for Mediators, 1984, Elements of Crisis Intervention, 1993; cassette tapes: Crisis Management and Intervener Survival, 1981; Stress Reduction: Personal Energy Management, 1982; Training the Trainer, 1983; contbr. chpts. to books, articles to profl. jours.; sr. editor: Crisis Intervener's Newsletter; editor-in-chief Emotional First Aid: A Jour. of Crisis Intervention, The Jour. of Crisis Negotiations, 1994-96; and others. Trustee Southeastern U., New Orleans; bd. dirs. Jewish Community Ctr., Jewish Family Service, Temple Shalom, Congregation Shearith Israel, 1975-80; active Dallas Sheriff's Res., 1978-86; v.p. Jewish Nat. Fund Dallas; adv. bd. Parents Without Ptnrs.; founder Carl B. Greenstone Meml. Library; past dir. Carrollton Rotary Club, Nat. Jewish Com., Scouting, Circle 10 Council Boy Scouts Am. With USNR, 1961-65, USMCR, 1965-67, USAR, 1967-69. Recipient Disting. Service award Southeastern Acad. Crisis Interveners, 1981; Disting. Service award Res. Law Officers Assn. Am., 1982. Mem. Am. Assn. Marriage and Family Therapy, Soc. Profls. in Dispute Resolution, Acad. Family Mediators, Am. Bd. Examiners in Crisis Intervention (diplomate), Am. Acad. Crisis Intervention, Southwestern Acad. Crisis Interveners, Acad. Criminal Justice Scis., Am. Acad. Psychotherapists, Am. Assn. Profl. Hypnotherapists, Assn. Mil. Surgeons U.S., Soc. of Police and Crim. Psychology (diplomate in police psychology), Dallas Assn. Marriage and Family Therapists. Democrat. Lodges: Masons, Scottish Rite. Office: 2222 E 4th St # 212 Fort Worth TX 76102-4209

GREENSTREET, ROBERT CHARLES, architect, educator; b. London, June 8, 1952; s. Joseph Philip Henry and Joan (Dean) G.; m. Karen Eloise Holland, Sept. 6, 1975. Diploma in architecture, Oxford Brookes U., 1976, PhD in Architecture, 1983. Registered architect, Eng. Vis. asst. prof. Kans. State U., 1978-79; asst. prof. U. Kans., 1979-80; vis. prof. Ball State U., Muncie, 1980-81; prof. U. Wis., 1981—, asst. vice chancellor, 1985-86, chmn. dept. architecture, 1986-90, dean Sch. Architecture and Urban Planning, 1990—. Author, co-author 7 books; contbr. more than 125 articles to profl. jours. Fellow Royal Soc. Arts; mem. AIA (assoc.), Royal Inst. Brit. Architects, Wis. Soc. Architects, Chartered Inst. Arbitrators, Faculty, Architects and Surveyors; mem. Am. Arbitration Assn., Assn. Collegiate Schs. of Architecture (pres. 1995-96). Anglican. Office: U Wis Dept Architecture PO Box 413 Milwaukee WI 53201-0413

GREENUP, MARION TERESA, not-for-profit health organization administrator; b. Baton Rouge, Nov. 28, 1947. BA, H. Sophie Newcomb, 1969; MEd, Tulane U., 1970; MPH, Columbia U., 1996. Urban policy specialist New Orleans Govt., 1973-75; dep. dir. human rels. com. New Orleans Mayor's Office, 1975-78; dep. dir., bus. mgr. Audubon Commn., New Orleans, 1978-81; mgr. of ops. Columbia U. Devel., N.Y.C., 1981-83; departmental adminstr. Columbia U. Pediats., N.Y.C., 1983-95; program chief of staff March of Dimes, White Plains, N.Y., 1995—. Sec., bd. dirs. Amsterdam Nursing Home, N.Y.C., 1989—; pres. Babies Prep, Inc., N.Y.C., 1990—. Mem. Nat. Perinatal Assn. (bd. dirs. 1996—), New Orleans Jazz & Heritage Found., Inc. (bd. dirs. 1975-77, v.p. 1977-79, pres. 1979-81, past pres. 1981—). Office: March of Dimes 1275 Mamaroneck Ave White Plains NY 10605-5298

GREENWALD, ANDREW ERIC, lawyer; b. N.Y.C., May 31, 1942; s. Harold and Lillian G.; m. Paula S., Aug. 20, 1967; children: Brooke Ellen, Karen Michelle. BS, U. Wis., 1964; JD, Georgetown U., 1967. Bar: D.C. 1968, Md. 1969, U.S. Ct. Appeals Md. 1969. Lawyer Nat. Labor Rels. Bd., Washington, 1967-68; asst. corp. counsel D.C. Govt., 1968-69; shareholder Joseph, Greenwald & Laake PA, Greenbelt, Md., 1969—; past mem. dept. family and cmty. devel. U. Md. *Author of articles in Trial Magazine: Deposing medical Experts, May, 1990; In the Beginning: Examples of Opening Statements, May, 1989; Shattered Dreams: A Look at the Seriously Injured Child, May, 1985; Let Me Ask You This-Some Thoughts on Cross-Examination, June, 1983; Oh, Didn't I Tell You? A Look at Informed Consent, June, 1982; Medical Malpractice Litigation: A Modest Settlement Proposal, May, 1980; Effective Pre-Trial Discovery in Medical Negligence Cases/What You Don't Know Might Hurt You, July, 1979; Contributor to Best of Trial, ATLA, 1990; The Profoundly Injured Child, ATLA, 1986; How to Recognize and Handle Recreational Liability Cases: Sports Torts, ATLA, 1980.* Contbr. articles to profl. jours. Active adv. com. Georgetown U. Continuing Legal Edn., 1991, Georgetown U. Law Ctr. Alumni Bd., 1995. Mem. ATLA (chmn. tort sect. 1985), ABA, Nat. Inst. Trial Advocacy, Am. Bd. Profl. Liability Attys., Am. Bd. Trial Advocates, William B. Bryant Inn, Am. Inns of Ct. Office: Joseph Greenwald & Laake PA 6404 Ivy Ln Ste 400 Greenbelt MD 20770-1407

GREENWALD, ARTHUR M., federal judge; b. 1936. BBA, UCLA; JD, Southwestern Sch. Law. Asst. U.S. atty. L.A., 1964-87; apptd. bankruptcy judge cen. dist. U.S. Dist. Ct. Calif., 1987. Mem. ABA, FBA, Am. Judicature Soc., Am. Inst. CPAs, Calif. Soc. CPAs, L.A. County Bar Assn., L.A. County Mus., KCET Pub. Broadcasting Sys. Fax: (818) 587-2949. Office: 21041 Burbank Blvd Ste 324 Woodland Hills CA 91367-6606

GREENWALD, CAROL SCHIRO, professional services marketing research executive; b. Phila., Mar. 2, 1939; d. Sidney L. and Adele R. (Rosenheim) Schiro; children: David Bruce, William Michael. B.A. cum laude, Smith Coll., 1961; M.A., Hunter Coll., 1965; Ph.D. in Polit. Sci., CUNY, 1972. Instr. polit. sci. Queen's Coll., CUNY, 1970-73; asst. dir. Evaluation N.Y.C. Adminstrv. Decentralization Project, 1971-73; asst. prof. Richmond Coll., CUNY, 1973-76, Bklyn. Coll., CUNY, 1976-77; research assoc. Bunting Inst., Radcliffe Coll., 1977-79; project dir. Jobs in the 1980s Pub. Agenda Found., N.Y.C., 1979-81; assoc. dir. Grant Thornton acctg. firm, 1984-86; sr. mgr. Seidman and Seidman, 1986-87; market research mgr. KPMG Peat Marwick, 1988-90; cons., 1990-91; mktg. dir. Haight, Gardner, Poor & Havens, 1991-92; dir. comm. Richard A. Eisner & Co., LLP, 1993-97; dir. mktg. Hamilton, HMC divsn. Kurt Salmon Assoc., 1997—, Whitman Breed Abbott & Morgan LLP, 1998—. Author: Group Power: Lobbying and Public Policy, 1977; mem. editl. bd. Mktg. Rev., 1997—; contbr. articles on polit. sci. to profl. jours. Lilly Found. fellow. Mem. Am. Mktg. Assn. (chair profl. devel. leadership coun. 1995—, mem. edtl. bd. 1996—), Common Cause (chmn. N.Y. 1981-83, nat. dir. 1978-84), Westchester Women in Comm. (treas. 1993-95). Home: 688 Forest Ave Larchmont NY 10538-1535

GREENWALD, CAROLINE MEYER, artist; b. Madison, Wis., Jan. 30, 1936; d. Frank Gustave and Lina Doris (Logemann) Meyer; children: Elaine Kathryn Napp, Geraldine Lynn Bodley. B.S., U. Wis., 1957, M.A. in Arts, 1975, M.F.A., 1977; student, U. Notre Dame Art Workshop, 1976. vis. artist, lectr. univs. and seminars in U.S., Korea and Japan; artist studio in Tokyo, 1983, 84, studio in Paris, 1986, 88. Exhibitor one-person shows: U. Wis.-Madison, 1975, 77, Source Gallery, San Francisco, 1977, Cin. Acad. Art, 1977, Galeria Kin, Mexico City, 1979, Loyola U.-Chgo., 1979, Getler-Pall Gallery, N.Y.C., 1980, 82, Evanston (Ill.) Art Ctr, 1980, Fendrick Gallery, Washington, 1981, Carleton Coll., Northfield, Minn., 1982, American Ctr., Tokyo, 1983, Ina Gallery, Tokyo, 1984, Nagoya Jr. Coll., Japan, 1984, Squibb Gallery, Princeton, N.J., 1984, Sakura Gallery, Nagoya, 1985, Edgewood Coll., Madison, 1988, De Ricci Gallery, Edgewood Coll., Madison, 1998; group shows include: Nat. Collection Fine Arts, Washington, 1977, Pratt Graphics Ctr., N.Y.C., 1978, Detroit Inst. Arts, 1979, Visual Arts Ctr., Beer-Sheva, Israel, 1979, Seibu Mus Art, Toyko, 1979, Alice Simsar Gallery, Ann Arbor, Mich., 1979, Rockland Ctr. for Arts, West Nyack, N.Y., 1980, New Eng. Found. Arts touring exhbn., 1980-81, Printmaking Council N.J. touring exhbn., 1981, Centre International de la Tapisserie Ancienne et Modern Lausanne (Switzerland), 1981, Mus. Applied Arts, Belgrade, Yugoslavia, 1981, New American Paperworks internat. travelling exhbn., 1982-86, Am. Craft Mus., N.Y.C., 1982, Arts Council Gt. Britain touring exhbn., 1982, Australian Nat. Gallery, Canberra, 1982, Fine Arts Mus. L.I., Hempstead, 1982-83, Eve Mannes Gallery, Atlanta, 1983, Gallery Beni, Kyoto, Japan, 1983, Bibliotheque Publiqued' Information, Centre Georges Pompidou, Paris, 1985, Nat. Mus. Am. Art, Washington, 1985, Cleve. Mus. Art, 1986, Leopold-Hoesch Mus., Fed. Republic Germany, 1986, Livres d'Artistes traveling exhbn. Aubes 3935 Gallery, Montreal, Ctr. for Book Arts, N.Y.C., and Galerie Caroline Corre, Paris, 1987, Palais de Justice, Aix en Provence, France, 1988, Leopold-Hoesch Mus., Fed. Republic Germany, 1988, Phila. Mus. Art, 1988, INAX Gallery, Tokyo, 1990, Textile Art Internat., Inc., Mpls., 1992, Salle des Fetes de la Mairie de Gentilly, Paris, 1992, Studio Galleria, Budapest, Hungary, 1992, Documenta Galeria de Arte, Sao Paulo, Brazil, 1994, Water Street Gallery, Prairie du Sac, Wis., 1995, Labyrinth Creatives, Blues Mounds, Wis., 1996; represented in permanent collections: Art Inst. Chgo., Australian Nat. Gallery, Elvehjem Mus. Art, U. Wis.-Madison, Indpls. Mus. Art, Jessie Besser Mus., Alpena, Mich., Madison Art Ctr., Mpls. Inst. Arts, Mus. Modern Arts, N.Y.C., Phila. Mus. Art, USEPA, Washington, Bibliotheque National, Paris, Nat. Mus. Am. Art, Washington, Brunswick Corp., Chgo., Ctr. Book Arts, N.Y.C., Container Corp. Am., Chgo., Davison Art Ctr. Wesleyan U., Middletown, Conn., Internat. Paper Co., N.Y.C., Libr. Congress U.S., Washington, Maseo Árte Moderno, Mexico City, St. Edwards U., Austin, Tex., Wis. Union Art Collection U. Wis., Madison. Grantee Nat. Endowment Arts, 1983; Am. Ctr. Paris residency, 1987-88. Address: 2514 Van Hise Ave Madison WI 53705-3850*

GREENWALD, GERALD, air transportation executive; b. St. Louis, Sept. 11, 1935; s. Frank and Bertha G.; m. Glenda Lee Gerstein, June 29, 1958; children: Scott, Stacey, Bradley, Joshua. BA Cumlaude (Univ. scholar), Princeton U., 1957; MA, Wayne State U., 1962. With Ford Motor Co., 1957-79; pres. Ford Venezuela; dir. non-automotive ops. Europe; vice chmn. Chrysler Corp., Highland Park, Mich., 1979-85; chmn. Chrysler Motors, 1985-88; vice chmn. Chrysler Corp., 1988-90; chief exec. officer United Employee Acquisition Corp., 1990; pres., mng. dir. Dillon, Read & Co. Inc., N.Y.C., 1991-92; pres., co. CEO Olympia & York, Toronto, 1992-93; chmn. Tatra, 1993-94; chmn., CEO, UAL Corp., Elk Grove Township, Ill., 1994—; bd. dirs. Aetna and Princeton. Civic Com. of Chgo., USAF, 1957-60. Mem. Econ. Club Chgo., Princeton (trustee). *

GREENWALD, GERALD BERNARD, lawyer; b. Chgo., May 11, 1929; s. Richard Bernard Greenwald and Frieda (Shapiro) Padnick; m. Corinne Edwards, May 29, 1955; children: David, Edward, Greig. BA, U. Chgo., 1948, JD, 1951. Bar: Ill. 1951, D.C. 1954, U.S. Supreme Ct. 1956. Ptnr. Becker & Greenwald, Washington, 1961-64, Mudge, Rose, Guthrie & Alexander, N.Y.C., Washington & Paris, 1966-75, Arent, Fox, Kintner, Plotkin & Kahn, Washington, 1975-93; energy cons., 1994—; hon. assoc. Ctr. for Petroleum and Mineral Law and Policy, U. Dundee, Scotland, 1994—. Co-author: Energy Law, 1981, The International Maritime Organization, 1984, International Energy Law, 1984, The World Gas Trade, 1986, Energy Law, 1988, Petroleum Investment Policies in the Developing Countries, 1989, Energy Law and Transactions, 1990; editor and co-author: Liquefied Natural Gas: Developing and Financing International Energy Projects, 1998; contbr. articles to profl. jours. Chmn. Arlington County, Va., Adv. Commn. on Health and Welfare, 1966-67, Arlington County Com. on Human Resources, 1968-71; pres. Nat. Health Coun., N.Y.C., 1976-77, bd. dirs.; pres. Temple Rodef Shalom, Falls Church, Va., 1988-90. Served to 1st lt. U.S. Army, 1952-54. Mem. Internat. Bar Assn. (chmn. oil and gas com. 1984-88, sec. sect. on energy and natural resources 1988-90), Cosmos Club (Washington). Democrat. Office: Washington Sq 1050 Connecticut Ave NW Washington DC 20036-5303

GREENWALD, GILBERT SAUL, physiologist; b. N.Y.C., June 24, 1927; s. Morris M. and Celia G.; m. Pola Gorsky, Sept. 9, 1950; children: Susan Greenwald Waxman, Elizabeth Greenwald Jordan, Douglas. AB with honors, U. Calif., Berkeley, 1949, PhD in Zoology, 1954. Postdoctoral fellow dept. embryology USPHS Carnegie Inst. Washington, 1954-56; instr., then asst. prof. anatomy U. Wash. Med. Sch., Seattle, 1956-61; mem. faculty U. Kans. Med. Ctr., Kansas City, 1961-96, disting. prof. physiology, 1977-96, univ. disting. prof., 1995, disting. prof. emeritus, 1996—, chmn. dept. physiology, 1977-93, prof. ob-gyn., 1977-93, prof. anatomy, ob-gyn., 1965-77, rsch. prof. in human reprodn., 1961-77; mem. reproductive biology study sect. NIH, 1966-70, mem. population rsch. adv. com., 1967-71; mem. regulatory biol. panel NSF, 1984-86. Editor Biology of Reprodn., 1974-77. With USNR, 1944-45. Recipient Higuchi Biomed. Sci. award U. Kans., 1984; USPHS fellow Carnegie Instn., 1954-56. Mem. AAAS, Soc. Study of Reprodn. (pres. 1971, Disting. Svc. award 1988, Carl Hartman award 1993), Endocrine Soc., Brit. Soc. Study Fertility, Am. Physiol. Soc., Soc. Exptl. Biology and Medicine (councillor 1991-95), Sigma Xi. Office: U Kans Med Ctr 39th and Rainbow Blvd Kansas City KS 66103

GREENWALD, HAROLD, lawyer; b. Yonkers, N.Y., Apr. 2, 1907; s. Louis and Rose (Schwartz) G.; m. Dorothy Nass, June 26, 1943 (dec.). LLB, NYU, 1928. Assoc. Law Office Waldo G. Morse, N.Y.C., 1928-34; counsel Coop. Grange League Fedn., 1934-64; ptnr. Greenwald, Kovner, Goldsmith, N.Y.C., 1944-60, Danziger, Bangser, Klipstein, Goldsmith & Greenwald, N.Y.C., 1960-77; of counsel Bangser, Klein, Rocca & Blum, N.Y.C., 1977—; counsel, N.Y.State Prisoners of War Programs, 1943-44; gen. counsel Agway Inc., 1964, Quality Bakers Am. Coop., N.Y.c., 1943-86; me. conf. N.Y. Legis. Com. for Revision of Coop. Corp. Law, 1965. Counsel to Ams. for Energy Independence, Washington, 1975-76; trustee Wall St. Synagogue, 1965—. Mem. ABA, Assn. Bar City of N.Y., Internat. Assn. Jewish Lawyers and Jurists, Zionisi Orgn. Am. (bd. dirs. 1943—, chmn. fin. com. 1945-93). Office: Bangser Klein Rocca & Blum 230 Park Ave New York NY 10169

GREENWALD, JOHN EDWARD, newspaper and magazine executive; b. N.Y.C., Oct. 28, 1942; s. Herbert and Carrie (Weisberg) G.; m. Rita Lynn Lipman, May 16, 1987. B.A., Syracuse U., 1963. Copy boy N.Y. Post, N.Y.C., 1963-64; assoc. editor Air Force Times, Washington, 1967-70; editor The Times Mag., Washington, 1970-80; editorial dir. Jour. Newspapers, Inc. (Fairfax Jour., Arlington Jour., Alexandria Jour., Prince George's Jour., Prince William Jour., Montgomery Jour.), Springfield, Va., 1980-90; editor Am. Legion Mag., Indpls., 1991-94; asst. mng. editor/Sunday & Spl. Projects The Sun, Lowell, Mass., 1994-98; asst. mng. editor Features Waterbury (Conn.) Republican-Am., 1998; free-lance writer, 1999—; film reviewer Times Jour. Co., Springfield, Va., 1967-85. Served with U.S. Army, 1964-67. Avocations: painting; drawing.

GREENWALD, MARTIN, publishing company executive; b. Bronx, N.Y., Apr. 25, 1942; s. David and Jean (Kaufman) G.; m. Irma Heldman; children: Karen Sue, Craig Mitchell. AB, Lafayette Coll., 1963; MBA, Columbia U., 1965. Mgr. acquisition planning, fin. analyst Macmillan Inc., N.Y.C., 1965-69; bus. mgr., trade div. Macmillan Inc., 1970-72; new bus. devel. analyst Holt div. CBS, N.Y.C., 1969-70; v.p., gen. mgr. Hagstrom Co. Inc., N.Y.C., 1972-76; pres. Paddington Press, N.Y.C., 1976-80; dir. mktg. Facts On File, Inc., 1980-82, v.p. mktg., 1982-88, sr. v.p., 1988-90, pub., exec. v.p., 1990-95; pres. Martin Greenwald Assocs., Inc., N.Y.C., 1995-96; exec. dir. The Pub. Strategists, Bronxville, N.Y., 1996—, Open Soc. Encyclopedia, Moscow, Russia, 1996—. Author: Maps on File, 1981, Historical Maps on File, 1984. Mem. Nassau County (N.Y.) Republican Com., 1973-80; v.p. Green Acres Libr. Bd., Hempstead, N.Y., 1976-80, Green Acres Civic Assn., 1976-89. Mem. Assn. Am. Pubs., Canadian Booksellers Assn., N.Y. Road Runners Club. Jewish. Home: 275 Central Park W New York NY 10024-3015 Office: The Publishing Strategists 22 Bronxville Glen Dr Bronxville NY 10708-6874

GREENWALD, PETER, physician, government medical research director; b. Newburgh, N.Y., Nov. 7, 1936; s. Louis and Pearl (Reingold) G.; m. Harriet Reif, Sept. 6, 1968; children—Rebecca, Laura, Daniel. BA, Colgate U., 1957; MD, SUNY Coll. Medicine, 1961; MPH, Harvard U., 1967, DrPH, 1974. Intern Los Angeles County Hosp., 1961-62; resident in internal medicine Boston City Hosp., 1964-66; asst. in medicine Peter Bent Brigham Hosp., 1967-68; mem. epidemiology and disease control study sect. NIH, 1974-78; mem. N.Y. State Gov.'s Breast Task Force, 1976-78; with N.Y. State Dept. Health, Albany, 1968-81; dir. N.Y. State Dept. Health, 1968-76, dir. epidemiology, 1976-81; prof. medicine Albany Med. Coll., 1976-81; attending physician Albany Med. Ctr. Hosp., 1968-81; adj. prof. biomed. engring. Rensselaer Poly. Inst., Troy, N.Y., 1976-81; assoc. scientist Sloan-Kettering Inst. for Cancer Research, N.Y.C., 1977-81; dir. div. cancer prevention Nat. Cancer Inst., NIH, Bethesda, Md., 1981-97, 98—; mem. VA Merit Rev. Bd. Med. Oncology, Washington, 1972-74. Editor-in-chief Jour. Nat. Cancer Inst., NIH, 1981-87; contbr. articles to profl. jours. Rear adm. USPHS, 1962-64, 81—. Recipient Disting. Svc. award N.Y. State Dept. Health, 1975; Redway medal and award for med. writing N.Y. State Jour. Medicine, 1977, N.Y. State Gov.'s Citationfor pub. health achievement, 1981, PHS commendation 1983, 88, Disting. Svc. medal, 1993, Disting. Svc. award, Am. Cancer Soc., 1997, Outstanding Rsch. award Am. Inst. Cancer Rsch., 1997, Pub. Svc. award Cancer Treatment and Rsch. Found., 1997 ; named to SUNY Honor Roll of Disting. Grads., 1997. Fellow ACP, Am. Coll. Preventive Medicine, APHA (epidemiology sect. chmn. 1981);mem. AMA, Am. Assn. Cancer Rsch. (DeWitt Goodman lectr. 1998), Am. Soc. Clin. Oncology, Am. Coll. Epidemiology (bd. dirs. 1981-82), Am. Soc. Preventive Oncology (Disting. Achievement award 1998), Am. Inst. Nutrition, Internat. Cancer Registry Assn., Internat. Epidemiology Soc., Nat. Acad. Scis. (food and nutrition bd. 1982-88). Office: NIH Cancer Prevention Rm 10A52 Bethesda MD 20892-2440

GREENWALD, ROBERT, public relations executive; b. N.Y.C., Jan. 14, 1927; s. Louis and Rebecca (Shapiro) G.; m. Genevieve Kushnir, Apr. 15, 1957 (div. 1960); m. Dorothy Pearl Brand, Apr. 19, 1963; children: Liza, Mark. BA, NYU, 1949, postgrad., 1951-54; postgrad, Columbia U., 1950, New Sch., 1950-51. Account exec. Ruder & Finn, Inc., N.Y.C., 1954—, sr. assoc., 1955-56, v.p., 1957-65; sr. v.p. Ruder, Finn & Rotman, Inc., N.Y.C., 1965-79; exec. v.p. Ruder, Finn & Rotman Inc., N.Y.C., 1980-83, sr. counsel, 1983-85; vice-chmn. Makovsky & Co. Inc., N.Y.C., 1987-93; pvt. quality control cons. N.Y.C., 1994—. Author: (with Dorothy Brand) Learning To Live with The Love of Your Life, 1979. Chmn. pub. relations com. UNICEF, N.Y.C., 1976-82, dir., 1976-82, mem. nat. adv. com., 1983-97, mem. nominating com., 1983-87; bd. dirs. Jewish Family Services, N.Y.C., 1972-75. Served with U.S. Army, 1945-46, ETO. Recipient Silver Anvil award Pub. Relations Soc. Am., 1955, 73, 81; recipient Paul B. Zucker award Ruder & Finn Inc., 1976, 82. Democrat. Jewish. Home: 88 Fairview Ave Verona NJ 07044-1315

GREENWALD, SHEILA ELLEN, writer, illustrator; b. N.Y.C., May 26, 1934; d. Julius and Florence (Friedman) G.; m. George E. Green, Feb. 18, 1960; children: Samuel, Benjamin. BA, Sarah Lawrence Coll., 1956. Author over 24 children's books, including Give Us a Great Big Smile Rosy Cole, 1980, Valentine Rosy, 1984, Rosy Cole's Great American Guilt Club, 1987, Write on Rosy, 1988, Rosy's Romance, 1989, Here's Hermione, 1991, The Mariah Delary Author of the Month Club, 1990, Rosy Cole Discovers America, 1992, My Fabulous NewLife, 1993, Rosy Cole, She Walks in Beauty, 1994, Rosy Cole: She Grows and Graduates, 1997. Mem. PEN, Authors League. Jewish. Office: Little Brown 34 Beacon St Boston MA 02108-1415 and: Orchard Books 95 Madison Ave New York NY 10016-7801

GREENWALD, THERESA MCGOWAN, medical administrator, nurse; b. Scranton, Pa., Feb. 8, 1950; d. Robert Bell and Agnes (Butler) McGowan; m. David Jeffrey Greenwald, Oct. 26, 1996; 1 child, Jennifer Emilie Nicole Drescher. Diploma in nursing, Hosp. U. Pa., Phila., 1970. Cert. Rehab. R.N., Case Mgr. Staff nurse, asst. head nurse Riddle Meml. Hosp., Media, Pa., 1971-80; rehab. nurse, mgr. Upjohn Rehab. Scvs., Phila. and Cin., 1980-85; cons., life care planner Occupl. Health Resources, Cin., 1985-87, Springfield, Va., 1987-88; dir. life care planning Rehab. Experts, Vienna, Va., 1988-89; program mgr., account exec. Comprehensive Rehab. Assocs., Cin., 1989-93; dir. managed care case mgmt. Sheakley Med. Mgmt. Sys., Cin., 1993-95; clin. program coord. Mayfield Clinic and Spine Inst., Cin., 1996—; dir. Nat. Bd. Certification Continuity of Care, 1998—; mem. cmty. adv. bd. Drake Ctr., Inc., 1998—. Mem. Nurse Case Mgrs. of S.W. ohio (membership chair). Office: Mayfield Spine Inst 506 Oak St Cincinnati OH 45219-2507

GREENWALT, MARY SUSAN, counselor; b. St. Louis, Dec. 26, 1946; d. LeGrand West and Susan Frances (Frier) Wheeler; m. Allen Duane Greenwalt, Apr. 11, 1992; stepchildren: Scott Harrison, Emily Megan. BS, So. Ill. U., 1968, MS, 1972; MBA, St. Louis U., 1982. Tchr. Lindbergh Sch. Dist., St. Louis, 1968-79, counselor, 1979—. Stage mgr. V-P Fair, St. Louis, 1984-93; vol. St. Louis Nursery Found. Book Fair, 1985-93. Recipient Tuition grant for women MBA students IBM, 1977. Mem. NEA, Mo. Edn. Assn., Lindbergh Edn. Assn. (pres. 1982-83), Am. Counseling Assn., Mo. Sch. Counselors Assn., St. Louis Suburban Sch. Counselors Assn. (Elem. Counselor of Yr. 1993), Jr. League St. Louis, Alpha Gamma Delta (St. Louis Alumnae Club). Republican. Methodist. Avocations: bridge, gardening, ballet, reading. Home: 14 Girard Dr Saint Louis MO 63119-4802 Office: Crestwood Elem Sch 1020 S Sappington Rd Saint Louis MO 63126-1005

GREENWALT, TIBOR JACK, physician, educator; b. Budapest, Hungary, Jan. 23, 1914; came to U.S., 1920, naturalized, 1943; s. Bela and Irene (Foldes) G.; m. Shirley Johnson, Aug. 6, 1960 (dec. Sept. 1970); 1 child, Peter H.; m. Pia Glas, Feb. 27, 1971 (dec. July 1996). BA summa cum laude, NYU, 1937, MD, 1937. Diplomate Am. Bd. Internal Medicine. Intern pathology and bacteriology Mt. Sinai Hosp., N.Y.C., 1937-38; rotating intern Kings County Hosp., Bklyn., 1938-40; resident medicine Montefiore Hosp., N.Y.C., 1940-41; research asso. New Eng. Med. Center, Boston, 1941-42; med. dir. Milw. Blood Center, 1947-66; faculty medicine Marquette U. Sch. Medicine, 1948-66, prof. medicine, 1963-66; cons. hematology VA Hosp., Wood, Wis., 1946-66, Milw. County Gen. Hosp., 1948-66; dir. blood program ARC, 1967-78, sr. sci. adviser blood program, 1978-79; clin. prof. medicine George Washington U. Sch. Medicine, 1967-79; prof. medicine U. Cin. Med. Center, 1979-84, prof. emeritus medicine and pathology, 1984—; dir. Hoxworth Blood Center, 1979-87, dir. research, 1987—; chmn. com. blood and transfusion problems NAS-NRC, 1963-66; mem. hematology study sect. NIH, 1960-63, chmn., 1970-72; vis. prof., speaker throughout, U.S., 1960—; mem. Med. Rsch. Srv. Merit Rev. Bd. for Hematology, VA, 1981-83; mem. blood diseases and resources adv. com. Nat. Heart, Lung and Blood Inst., 1983-87, adv. coun. 1986-90, coordinating com., Nat. Blood Resources Edn. Program, adv. com. Office of Prevention Edn. and Control, 1987-91. Author: (with others) Hemolytic Syndromes, 1942, (with Shirley Greenwalt) Coagulation and Transfusion in Clinical Medicine, 1965; editor: (with Graham A. Jamieson) The Red Cell Membrane, 1969, Formation and Destruction of Blood Cells, 1970, Glycoproteins of Plasma and Membranes, 1971, The Human Red Cell in Vitro, 1974, Transmissible Disease and Blood Transfusion, 1974, Trace Proteins of Plasma, 1976, The Granuloctye, 1977, Blood Substitutes and Plasma Expanders, 1978, The Blood Platelet in Transfusion Therapy, 1978, Methods in Hematology: Blood Transfusion, 1988; editor, contbr. Immunogenetics, 1967; editor-in-chief Transfusion, 1960-66, assoc. editor, 1966-86; editorial bd. Gen. Principles of Blood Transfusion, 1962-83, Vox Sanguinis, 1956-76, Haematologia, 1968-90, Blood, 1979-84; contbr. articles to profl. lit. Served to maj. M.C., AUS, 1942-46. Recipient Gold medal Caduceus Soc., NYU, 1933, Jr. Achievement award for outstanding contbn. sci., 1958, 1st Charles R. Drew award ARC, Washington, 1981, Disting. Citizen's award Allied Vets. Coun., 1963, award pioneer blood group rsch. Ctr. for Immunology, SUNY, Buffalo, 1976, Witebsky lectureship, 1994, Albion O. Bernstein award Med. Soc. State N.Y., 1997. Fellow AAAS, N.Y. Acad. Scis.; mem. NAS, Inst. Medicine (sr.), Am. Assn. Blood Banks (v.p. 1959-60, med. dir. central file rare donors 1960-66, 50th anniversary com., John Elliot award 1966, Grove-Rasmussen award 1988, Bernard Fantus medal 1993), Internat. Soc. Hematology, ACP, Internat. Soc. Blood Transfusion (pres. 1966-72, historian 1975-96), Am. Soc. Clin. Pathologists, Central Soc. Clin. Research, Ohio Sci. Roundtable, Am. Soc. Hematology (treas. 1963-67), Am. Assn. Immunologists, Soc. Exptl. Biology and Medicine, Am. Soc. Human Genetics, Sigma Xi, Alpha Omega Alpha. Club: Cosmos. Home: 2444 Madison Rd #1501 Cincinnati OH 45208-1228 Office: Hoxworth Blood Ctr 3130 Highland Ave Cincinnati OH 45267-0055

GREENWAY, HUGH DAVIDS SCOTT, journalist; b. Boston, May 8, 1935; s. James Cowen and Helen Livingston (Scott) G.; m. Joy Beverly Brooks, June 11, 1960; children—Julia Livingston, Alice Lauder, Sarah

Davids. B.A., Yale U., 1958; postgrad., Oxford U., Eng., 1960-62. Corr. Time mag., London, 1962-63, Washington, 1963-64, Boston, 1964-66, Saigon, 1967-68, Bangkok, 1968-70; Corr. UN, N.Y.C., 1970-72; corr. Washington Post, Hong Kong, 1973-76, Jerusalem, 1976-78; assoc. editor for nat. and fgn. news Boston Globe, 1978-91, sr. assoc. editor, 1991-93, editorial page editor, 1994—. Bd. dirs. Internat. Press Inst., Vienna. Served with USNR, 1958-60. Nieman fellow Harvard U., 1971-72. Mem. Am. Soc. Newspaper Editors. Home: 634 Charles River St Needham MA 02492-1031 Office: Globe Newspapers Co 135 Morrissey Blvd Dorchester MA 02125-3310

GREENWAY, WILLIAM CHARLES, electronics executive, design engineer; b. Worcester, Mass., Feb. 28, 1958; s. Christopher W. and Beatrice C. (Masitis) G.; m. Joy Ann Montgomery, May 5, 1984; children: Ariel, Ann, Christopher. BSEE, U. Mass., 1982; MS in Mech. Engring., Syracuse (N.Y.) U., 1987, MBA, 1990. Registered profl. engr., N.Y. Mem. mfg. mgmt. program GE, Somersworth, N.H., 1982-84; supr. assembly start GE, Syracuse, 1984-85, systems analyst, 1985-86, sr. systems engr., 1986-87; mfg. mgr. Leybold Inficon, East Syracuse, N.Y., 1987-88; v.p. ops. S&S Inficon, Liverpool, N.Y., 1988-90, exec. v.p., 1990-92, pres., 1992—. Patentee therapy imaging system, DSA exposure control. Mem. IEEE, Am. Soc. Quality Control, Am. Prodn. and Inventory Control Soc., Soc. Photo-Optical Instrumentation Engr. Avocations: reading, skiing, scuba diving. Home: 5726 Bobwhite Ln Tully NY 13159-2420 Office: Infimed Inc 121 Metropolitan Dr Liverpool NY 13088-5335*

GREENWELL, RONALD EVERETT, communications executive; b. Louisville, Oct. 28, 1938; s. Woodrow M. and Christine (Comer) Gossett G.; m. Diane J. Greenwell, Mar. 18, 1967; children: Wendy, Robin. With Motorola Inc., Schaumburg, Ill., 1962-94, sr. v.p., gen. mgr. communications internat. group, 1986-94; pres. Motorola Communications Internat. Inc., Schaumburg, Ill., 1986-94, ret., 1994; bd. dirs. Entranosa Water Co., TiJeras, N.Mex. Former bd. dirs. N.C. Ctr. for World Langs. and Culture. Home: 30 Canyon Ridge Dr Sandia Park NM 87047-8506

GREENWOOD, COLLETTE P., municipal official, finance officer; b. Summit, Ill.. BA, Ea. Wash. U., 1980. With acctg. dept. Montgomerty Ward, Spokane, Wash., 1976-90; acctg. clk. water, hydro City of Spokane, 1979-93, budget acctg., 1993-96, dir. of office of mgmt. & bufget, 1996—. Recipient Class of 1998 award Leadership Spokane Spokane C. of C. Mem. Nat. Mgmt. Assn. (elected dir. 1999), Govt. Fin. Officers Assn., Wash. Fin. Officers Assn. Office: City of Spokane 808 W Spokane Falls Blvd Spokane WA 99201-3333*

GREENWOOD, HARRIET LOIS, environmental banker, researcher; b. Detroit, Oct. 4, 1950; d. Samuel H. and Elizabeth Ann (Bode) G.; m. Michael E. Carlson, Aug. 23, 1981 (div. Sept. 1986); m. Eric J. Halbeisen, Sept. 5, 1987; 1 child, Robin Faith. BA in Biology, Antioch Coll., 1972; MS in Tchg., Antioch Coll. New Eng., 1975; postgrad., U. Mich., 1985-87. Dir. environ. studies Swanson Environ., Southfield, Mich., 1978-80; project mgr. ESEI, Ecol. Scis., Detroit, 1981-82; pres. Greenwood & Assocs., Detroit, 1982-83; mgr. environ. studies Environ. Rsch. Group, Ann Arbor, Mich., 1983-85; environ. policy specialist Clayton Environ., Southfield, 1985-91; pres. Environ. Tng. Svcs., Detroit, 1991-93; asst. v.p. Comerica Bank, 1993—; part-time instr. Wayne State U., 1992—; rec. clk. Detroit Friends Meeting, 1985-88; bd. dirs. Friends Sch. Detroit, 1987-89. U. Mich. fellow, 1985-86. Mem. Nat. Assn. Environ. Profls. (ASTM com. E-50 on environ. assessment S.W. Detroit environ. vision project, Detroit-Wayne county roundtable on sustainable redevel.), Nat. Trust Real Estate Assn., Environ. Bankers Assn., East Mich. Environ. Acton Coun., Mich. Assn. Environ. Profls., Mich. Bankers Assn. (environ. com.),. Quaker. Avocations: English country dancing, cross country skiing. Office: Comerica Bank Trust Real Estate-3228 PO Box 75000 Detroit MI 48275-0001

GREENWOOD, JAMES CHARLES, congressman; b. Philadelphia, Pa., May 4, 1951; s. James Charles and Alice Mary (Gibson) G.; m. Jane Christina Paugh, Oct. 6, 1984; children: Robert, Andrew (dec.), Laura, Kathryn. BA, Dickinson Coll., 1973. Head house parent The Woods Schs., Langhorne, Pa., 1974-76; campaign mgr. Renninger for Congress, Doylestown, Pa., 1976; caseworker Bucks County Children and Youth Agy., Doylestown, 1977-80; mem. Pa. Ho. Reps., Harrisburg, 1981-86, Pa. Senate, Harrisburg, 1987-92, 103rd-106th Congress from 8th Pa. dist., Washington, D.C., 1993—; com. mem. Commerce; subcom. on Fin. and Hazardous Materials, Health and the Environ.; mem. Com. on Edn. and Workforce, Early Childhood, Youth and Families subcom., Postsecondary Edn., Tng. and Life-Long Learning. Bd. dirs. Bucks County Coun. on Alcoholism, The Woods Sch., Parents Anonymous Pa.; hon. bd. dirs. Bucks County Assn. for Retarded Citizens, Big Bros./Big Sisters Bucks County, Friends of the Farmstead, Inc.; mem. adv. bd. Today, Inc., About Face U.S.A. Mem. League Women Voters, Sierra Club, Lions Club, Libertae (adv. com.). Republican. Home: 785 River Rd Erwinna PA 18920-9254 Office: US House of Reps 2436 Rayburn Washington DC 20515

GREENWOOD, JANET KAE DALY, psychologist, educational administrator; b. Goldsboro, N.C., Dec. 9, 1943; d. Fulton Benton and Kelminy Ethel Esther (Ball) Daly; 1 child, Gerald Thompson. AA, Peace Coll., 1963; BS in English and Psychology, East Carolina U., 1965, MEd in Counseling, 1967; postgrad., N.C. State U., 1967-69, U. London, 1969; PhD in Counseling and Higher Ednl. Adminstrn., Fla. State U., 1972. Tchr. English Kinston (N.C.) City Schs., 1965-66, Goldsboro City Schs., 1966-67; counselor and psychometrist primary and secondary schs. County of Wake, N.C., 1967-69; coord. Am. Inst. for Fgn. Study, 1969; supr. student tours in Eng., France, Switzerland, Italy, and Capri, 1969; counselor Fla. State U., Tallahassee, 1969-72; asst. dir. counseling Rutgers U., New Brunswick, N.J., 1972-73; cons. to v.p. for student svcs. Rutgers U., New Brunswick, 1973-74, lectr. in counseling psychology, 1972-74; coord. and assoc. prof. counselor edn. U. Cin., 1974-77, adviser to grad. students, 1974-77, vice provost student affairs, 1977-81; pres. Longwood Coll., Farmville, Va., 1981-87, U. Bridgeport, Conn., 1987-92; cons., ptnr., dir. Heidrick & Struggles, Washington, 1992—; guidance cons. South Plainfield Pub. Schs., 1973-76; adviser Parents without Ptnrs., 1976; bd. dirs. Hydraulic Co.; mem. Gov.'s Partnership To Prevent Substance Abuse in the Workforce, mem. audit com. and cmty. and govt. rels. com. Contbr. articles to profl. jours. Mem. Gov.'s Ad Hoc Edn. Com. on Tchr. Edn. and Counselor Edn., State of Ohio, 1975; mem. state planning comm. Nat. Identification of Women Project; chair Twin Rivers Tenants Rights Assn., 1972-74; bd. dirs. Bridgeport Hosp., Bridgeport Bus. Coun.; mem. adv. com. Bridgeport Pub. Edn. Fund; bd. dirs. Conn. Ballet Theatre, chair South End streeting com; mem. mgmt. adv. com. City of Bridgeport; mem. adv. com. United Way Tri-State; chair South End Partnership Com; mem. The Schiavone Steering Com./Downtown Bridgeport Project, YWCA Bd., Champion/United Way, United Way Community Human Svcs. Planning Coun., Bridgeport Symphony Bd., Bridgeport Opera Bd., Bridgeport Area Coll./Univ. Consortium, Conn. Conf. Ind. Colls., The Newcomen Soc. of U.S., The United Way Ea. Fairfield County; mem. adv. bd. Sacred Heart/St. Anthony Sch., Roosevelt Sch; mem. ct. com. Regional Plan Assn. Fairfield 2000; bd. dirs. Conn. Ballet Theatre; chair The Bridgeport Regional Bus. Coun. Brass Ring Task Force on Leadership; bd. govs. Fairfield County Study; mem. hon. bd. dirs. Conn. Earth Day 20, Inc.; chair L.I. Sound Western Regional Coun.; founding mem. L.I. Sound Assembly; mem. membership com., campus partnership subcom. Drugs Don't Work program, 1989-91. Recipient Spl. award Black Arts Festival, Meritorious Svc. award Am. Assn. State Colls. and Univs. Mem. AAUP, Am. Coll. Pers. Assn. (editor and chair media bd. 1975—), Am. Pers. and Guidance Assn., Cin. Pers. and Guidance Assn., Ohio Psychol. Assn., Cin. Psychol. Assn., Organizational Behavior Assn., Am. Sch. Counselors Assn., Ohio Sch. Counselors Assn., Assn. for Women Faculty, Ohio Counselor Edn. and Supervision Assn., Kappa Delta Pi.

GREENWOOD, JANET KINGHAM, sanitarian, county official; b. Houston, Sept. 29, 1939; d. Harold Lloyd and Angelina (Mann) Kingham; m. James Richard Greenwood, June 13, 1959; children: Cynthia Anne, Patricia. BA in Sociology cum laude, U. Houston, 1975. Registered sanitarian, Tex. Sanitarian-in-tng. Galveston County Health Dist., LaMarque, Tex., 1975-76, sanitarian II, 1976-79, sanitarian III, 1979-81, sr. sanitarian, 1981-88, sanitarian supr., 1988-90, chief sanitarian, 1990-93, dir. environ. and consumer health, 1993-97; ret., $, 1997; contract worker USDA, 1998—; mem. Sanitarian's adv. Com., Austin, Tex., 1984, vice chmn., 1985. Vol. St. Joseph's Hosp., Houston, 1951-53; mem. recycling com. City of Galveston, 1990-96; trustee Pub. Health Mus., 1997—. Fellow Tex. Pub. Health Assn. (governing council, 1980-81, 94-99, legis. com. 1981-83, scholarship com. 1988-90, exhibit procurement com. 1992-93, chmn. exhibit procurement com. 1993-96, benefits com. 1991-95, sect. chmn. 1980-81, fund raising com. 1992-96, 2d v.p. 1994, 1st v.p. 1995, pres. elect, 1996, pres. 1997, past pres. 1998, bd. dirs. 1998, pub. health mus. com. 1992-96, exec. bd. 1994-99, Pres.'s award 1985, 90, 94-96, 98, edn. and tng. grantee 1978); mem. Nat. Environ. Health Assn. (governing coun. 1988-89, merit award 1988), Internat. Milk, Food and Environ. Sanitarians, Tex. Environ. Health Assn. (pres. 1987-89, I.E. Scott award 1998), Gulf Coast Tex. Environ. Health Assn. (pres. 1981, President's award 1986), Tex. Assn. Mcpl. Health Ofcls. (charter, regional v.p. 1997, bd. dirs. 1997—), Rotary (LaMarque chpt., Paul Harris fellow 1998). Democrat. Roman Catholic. Avocations: yoga, reading mysteries, cooking, travel.

GREENWOOD, JOEN ELIZABETH, economist, consultant; b. Mineral Point, Wis., Aug. 29, 1934; d. John Edward and Lillian Laile (Rohr) G. BS, MA, U. Wis., 1956, 57; postgrad., Newnham Coll. Cambridge U., Eng., 1961-62; diploma in advanced mgmt. program, Harvard Bus. Sch., 1983. Instr. econs. Wellesley (Mass.) Coll., 1962-68; sr. assoc. Charles River Assocs., Boston, 1968-79, v.p., 1979—; mem. bd. editors Energy Jour., 1979-83. Co-author: Folded, Spindled and Mutilated: Economic Analysis and U.S. v. IBM, 1983; contbr. to profl. publs. Mem. Commonwealth of Mass. Pub. Health Coun., Boston, 1973-79. Earhart fellow U. Calif.-Berkeley, 1960-61; Fulbright scholar U.K., 1961-62. Mem. Internat. Assn. Energy Economists (v.p. 1978-84, exec. v.p. 1981-84), Nat. Coal Coun., U. Wis. Alumni Assn. (bd. dirs. 1987-93), Wis. Alumni Assn. Greater Boston (pres. 1987-89), Boston Club, Harvard Club, Phi Beta Kappa. Home: 11 Ellery Sq Cambridge MA 02138 Office: Charles River Assocs 200 Clarendon St Fl 33 Boston MA 02116-5092

GREENWOOD, JOHN EDWARD DOUGLAS, investment banker, lawyer; b. Blundell Sands, Lancashire, Eng., Mar. 4, 1923; came to U.S., 1948; s. Arthur and Mabel (Hunt) G.; m. Charlotte Elizabeth Sabey, May, 25, 1946; children: Marcia Barbara Hunt, Douglas Charles William. B in Econs. with 1st class honors, McGill U., 1948; JD, Yale U., 1951. Bar: N.Y. 1952. Jr. legal assoc. Milbank, Tweed, Hope & Hadley, N.Y.C., 1951-52, Chadbourne, Hunt, Jaeckel & Brown, N.Y.C., 1952-54; with legal dept. Creole Petroleum Corp., N.Y.C., 1954-55; assoc. corp. fin. Bacon Stevenson & Co., N.Y.C., 1955-59; v.p. E.F. Hutton & Co., N.Y.C., 1959-60; pres., founder Can. Alpha Lessors Ltd., Mont., Can., 1960-63; ptnr., sr. v.p. Eastman Dillon Union Securities, N.Y.C., 1963-72; prin. Blyth Eastman Dillon & Co., N.Y., 1972-78; pvt. investor, 1978—; bd. dirs. Ubiq Comm., Inc. Mahwah, N.J., Windsor/Bermuda Corp.; fin. advisor Esprit Telecom (Jersey) Ltd. Hdqrs., Reading, U.K.; chmn., pres. Greenwood Corpfin, Inc.; fin. advisor DNS Technologies, Inc., San Francisco. Mem. Rep. Boosters Club, N.Y., 1965—; patron Winslow Therapeutic Riding, Inc., warwick, 1982—, Warwick Hist. Soc., 1984—; sec., dir. Friends of McGill, Inc., N.Y., 1952-60; treas., trustee Tuxedo Park (N.Y.) Sch., 1961-63; U.S. rep. (fin.) Intertnat. Atomic Energy Agy. World Confs., Copenhagen and Paris, 1975, Stockholm, 1976, Salzberg, 1977; charter mem. Global Telecomm. Soc., Washington. With Royal Can. Navy, 1941-45, Comms. Intelligence. Mem. Am. Nuclear Energy Coun. (bd. dirs. Washington 1976-78), Atomic Indsl. Forum, Global Telecomms. Soc. (charter), Links Club of N.Y., Univ. Club. of Montreal, Racquet and Tennis Club of N.Y., Tuxedo Club of Tuxedo Park, N.Y., Capitol Hill Club of Wahsington, Bond Club of N.Y. Episcopalian. Avocations: opera, shooting, riding, skiing, golf. Office: 19 Park Ave Warwick NY 10990-1702

GREENWOOD, LAWRENCE GEORGE, banker; b. Briercrest, Sask., Can., June 16, 1921; s. Goerge Tuckfield and Mildred Jane (Clifford) G.; m. Margaret Purser, June 28, 1947 (dec.). Grad., Regina Central Collegiate, 1938; LLD (hon.), Queens U., Ont., 1980. With Cn. Bank Commerce, Regina, Sask., 1938—, merged to form Can. Imperial Bank Commerce, 1961; pres. Can. Imperial Bank Commerce, Toronto, 1968-71, vice chmn., Toronto and Montreal, 1971-76; dir. emeritus Can. Imperial Bank of Commerce, Toronto. Mem. Nat. Trust for Scotland; hon. trustee Hosp. for Sick Children, Toronto. Served with RCAF, 1941-45. Club: York. Home: 7 Tudor Gate, Willowdale, ON Canada M2L 1N3 Office: PO Box 63, Commerce Ct N Ste 2601, Toronto, ON Canada M5L 1B9

GREENWOOD, M. R. C., college dean, biologist, nutrition educator; b. Gainesville, Fla., Apr. 11, 1943; d. Stanley James and Mary Rita (Schmeltz) Cooke; m. (div. 1968); 1 child, James Robert. AB summa cum laude, Vassar Coll., 1968; PhD, Rockefeller U., 1973; LHD (hon.), Mt. St. Mary Coll., 1989. Rsch. assoc. Inst. of Human Nutrition, Columbia U., N.Y.C., 1974-75, adj. asst. prof., 1975-76, asst. prof., 1976-78; assoc. prof. dept. biology Vassar Coll., Poughkeepsie, N.Y., 1978-81, prof. biology, 1981-86, dir. animal model, CORE Lab. of Obesity Rsch. Ctr., 1985-89, dir. undergrad. rsch. summer inst., 1986-88, dir. Howard Hughes biol. scis. network program, 1988, chmn. of biology dept., John Guy Vassar prof. natural scis., 1986-89; prof. nutrition and internal medicine, dean grad. studies U. Calif., Davis, 1989-96; chancellor U. Calif., Santa Cruz, 1996—; mem. nutrition study sect. NIH, 1983-87; mem. NRC; assoc. dir. for sci. White House Office Sci. and Tech., 1993-95. Editor: Obesity, Vol. 4, 1983; contbr. over 250 articles and abstracts to profl. jours., 1974-89. Recipient Rsch. Career Devel. award NIH, 1978-83; Mellon scholar-in-residence St. Olaf Coll., Northfield, Minn., 1978; N.Y. State Regents fellow, 1968. Mem. Inst. Medicine of Nat. Acad. Scis. (chair food and nutrition bd., diet and health subcom. 1986—), N.Am. Soc. for Study of Obesity (pres. 1987-88), Am. Inst. Nutrition (BioServ 1982), Am. Physiol. Soc., The Harvey Soc., Am. Diabetes Assn., Internat. Assn. for Study of Obesity (treas. 1991—). Home: University House Santa Cruz CA 95064 Office: U Calif Chancellor Office 296 McHenry Libr Santa Cruz CA 95064-1077*

GREENWOOD, P. NICHOLAS, lawyer; b. Birmingham, Ala., Aug. 9, 1945. BS, U. N.C., 1967; JD, Vanderbilt U., 1971. Bar: Ala. 1972. Atty. Bradley Arant Rose & White LLP, Birmingham, Ala. Mem. editl. bd. Vanderbilt Law Rev., 1971. Mem. ABA, Ala. State Bar, Birmingham Bar Assn., Order of Coif. Office: Bradley Arant Rose & White LLP PO Box 830709 2001 Park Pl Ste 1400 Birmingham AL 35283*

GREENWOOD, RICHARD A., protective services official; m. Dessa Rae Greenwood; 4 children. BS in Criminal Justice, Weber State U.; grad., FBI Nat. Acad., 1992. Trooper Metro-Dade Police Dept., Miami, 1972-76; with Utah Hwy. Patrol, 1976—, trooper, 1976-86, sgt., accident reconstrn. specialist, adminstrv. asst. to supt., 1990-91, lt., comdr. protective svcs. at the state capitol, comdr. exec. protection, 1992, supt., 1993—. Office: Utah Hwy Patrol Box 141100 4501 S 2700 W Salt Lake City UT 84114

GREENWOOD, VIRGINIA MAXINE MCLEOD, real estate executive, broker; b. Ballinger, Tex., Mar. 3, 1930; d. Vernie L. and Alma (Simpson) McLeod; m. Lester Greenwood, Apr. 21, 1951 (div. May 1985), children: Virginia Leslie Pattison, Randal Lester, Sheree Lou Stiles. Student, Draughn's Bus. Sch., Wichita Falls, 1948-49; completed real estate courses, Grad. Realtors Inst., 1972. Cert. residential specialist; cert. buyer rep. Real estate agt. C. V. Perry Co., Columbus, Ohio, 1967-69, Montague, Miller and Co., Charlottesville, Va., 1970-74; sales mgr. Great Eastern Mgmt. Corp., Charlottesville, 1974-75; real estate broker Greenwood Realty Ltd., Charlottesville, 1975-93; sr. assoc. broker Coldwell Banker-Bailey Realty Co., Charlottesville, 1993-98; assoc. broker Real Estate III, Charlottesville, 1998—. Mem. Monticello Area Cmty. Action Agy. adv. bd., 1988-92, Albemarle (Va.) County Rep. com., 1974-76; Albemarle County Housing adv. com., 1991-92, 94—, Thomas Jefferson Planning Dist. Housing adv. com., 1991-92. Mem. Nat. Assn. Realtors, Va. Assn. Realtors (bd. dirs. 1985-92), Charlottesville Area Assn. of Realtors (sec. 1983-84, bd. dirs. 1983-91, 2d v.p. 1988, 1st v.p. 1989, pres. 1990), Albemarle Housing Coalition. Avocations: reading, gardening, genealogy. Office: Real Estate III PO Box 8186 Charlottesville VA 22906-8186

GREENWOOD, W. R., III, investment banker; b. Albany, N.Y., Apr. 21, 1941; s. Wilbur R. Jr. and Jean (McOrmond) G.; m. Pamela Sheridan Sutton, Nov. 8, 1974; children: Jennifer, Trevor. BA, Yale U., 1963; MBA, Cornell U., 1968. Investment banker Smith Barney, N.Y.C., 1968-75, Foster & Marshall, Seattle, 1976-82, Dain Bosworth, Seattle, 1982-86; pres., CEO Spider Staging Corp., Seattle, 1986-93, chmn. bd. dirs.; pres., CEO, Windswept Capital, Seattle, 1996—; bd. dirs. Foster & Marshall, Seattle, Advanced Imput Devices, Flow Internat., Foster & Marshall, Advanced Input Devices, Output Tech., Skyland Sci. Svcs., Port Townsend Paper. Lt. USNR, 1963-65. Mem. Wash. Athletic Club, Overlake Golf Club, Rainier Club. Home: 4915 84th Ave SE Mercer Island WA 98040-4616 Office: Windswept Capital LLC 1001 4th Ave Ste 3000 Seattle WA 98154-1101

GREENWOOD, WILLIAM WARREN, journalist; b. Richmond, Va., Mar. 28, 1942; s. William Rogers and Gloria Vivian (Brown) Warren; m. Marsha Ann Sheppard, Dec. 21, 1968; 1 child, Kelly. Student, Fla. State U., 1960-63; B.A., Am. U., 1970. Announcer Sta. WZRO, Jacksonville Beach, Fla., 1956-60; newscaster Sta. WMBR, Jacksonville, Fla., 1960-64, Sta. WPDQ, Jacksonville, 1964-66, Sta. WWDC, Washington, 1966-67; dir. pub. affairs Nat. Ednl. Radio, Washington, 1967-68; news corr. U.P.I., Washington, 1968-70; corr. MBS, Washington, 1970-74, v.p. news, 1974-76; news corr. Sta. WCBS-TV, N.Y.C., 1976-79, ABC News, N.Y.C., 1979; White House corr. ABC News, Washington, 1980-81; Washington corr. ABC News, 1981—; guest lectr. NYU, 1975, 76; chmn. Congl. Radio-TV Galleries, Washington, 1975; guest lectr. Am. U., 1967; v.p. Nat. Press Bldg. Corp., 1974, Nat. Press Club, 1974. Recipient award of merit ARC, 1960, 61; Emmy award, 1978; Emmy nomination, 1979; N.Y.C. Firefighters award, 1979; Am. Bankers Assn. award, 1981. Mem. Radio and TV Corrs. Assn. (pres. 1975), White House Corrs. Assn., Fla. State U. Alumni Assn. (v.p. Washington chpt. 1974-75), ARC Lifeguard Alumni Assn. Episcopalian. Office: ABC Washington Bur 1717 Desales St NW Washington DC 20036-4407

GREER, ALAN GRAHAM, lawyer; b. El Dorado, Ark., May 31, 1939; s. Arthur W. and Marie (Ross) G.; m. Patricia A. Seitz, Aug. 14, 1981. BS, U.S. Naval Acad., 1961; JD, U. Fla., 1969. Ptnr., Richman, Greer Weil Brumbaugh, Miami, Fla., 1969—; chmn. emeritus WLRN Pub. Radio and TV Sta. Past chmn. Dade County Coun. Arts and Scis.; past mem. Fla. State Task Force on Water Issues, Gov.'s Bus. Adv. Coun. on Edn; co-chmn. site selection com. Dem. Nat. Com., 1992, also trustee. With USN, 1961-67. Fellow Internat. Soc. Barristers, Am. Coll. Trial Lawyers; mem. ABA, Fla. Bar Assn. (cert., past chmn. internat. law com.). Home: 224 Ridgewood Rd Miami FL 33133-6614 Office: Richman Greer Weil Brumbaugh Miami Ctr 10th Fl 201 S Biscayne Blvd Miami FL 33131-4332

GREER, ALLEN CURTIS, II, lawyer; b. New Rochelle, N.Y., Dec. 6, 1951; s. Allen Wilkinson and Nancy (Carroll) G.; children: Katharine Burrage, Constance Carroll, Genevieve Forbes. AB, Harvard U., 1972, JD, 1975. Assoc. Cadwalader, Wickersham & Taft, N.Y.C., 1975-79, Palmer & Dodge, Boston, 1979-82; ptnr. Gaston & Snow, Boston and N.Y.C., 1982-91, Rogers & Wells, 1991-97, Cadwalader, Wickersham & Taft, N.Y.C., 1997—. Office: 100 Maiden Ln New York NY 10038-4818

GREER, BERNARD LEWIS, JR., lawyer; b. Knoxville, Tenn., Sept. 11, 1940; s. Bernard Lewis and Margaret Strickland (Vinsinger) G.; m. Lynda Lea Kidd, June 11, 1966; children: Andrew Scott, William Vinsinger. BA magna cum laude, U. Tenn., 1962, postgrad., 1964-65; JD, Emory U., 1968. Bar: N.Y. 1969, Ga. 1975; conseil juridique France, 1971. Assoc. Willkie Farr & Gallagher, N.Y.C., 1968-71, 73-74, Willke, Farr & Gallagher, Paris, 1971-73, Shoob, McLain, Merritt & Lyle, Atlanta, 1974-77, O'Callaghan, Saunders & Stumm, 1977-85; ptnr. Alston & Bird, Atlanta, 1985—; mem. adv. bd. Internat. and Comparative Law Ctr., Southwestern Legal Found., 1978—; participant various seminars; lectr. on European bus. instns. and practice Emory U. Law Sch., Atlanta, 1975—, Ga. State U. Law Sch., 1975—. Mem. Emory U. Law Rev., 1967-68; contbr. to legal publs. Counsel, trustee, mem. exec. com. Atlanta Bot. Garden, Inc.; mem. exec. com., bd. dirs. Ga. Coun. for Internat. Visitors, 1986-93, pres., 1989-90; bd. visitors U. Tenn. Coll. Liberal Arts, Knoxville, 1988-91. 1st lt. U.S. Army, 1962-64. Internat. bus. fellow S.E. region, 1988. Mem. ABA, Internat. Bar Assn. (coun. bus. law sect. 1990-94), State Bar Ga. (chmn. internat. law sect. 1982-83, chmn. com. on internationalization of practice of law 1989—), State Bar N.Y., Atlanta Bar Assn., Assn. Bar City N.Y., Soc. Internat. Bus. Fellows, Am. Arbitration Assn. (panel of arbitrators 1987—), Scabbard and Blade, Omicron Delta Kappa, Pi Sigma Alpha, Pi Delta Phi, Phi Eta Sigma. Office: Alston & Bird 1 Atlantic Ctr 1201 W Peachtree St NW Ste 4200 Atlanta GA 30309-3424

GREER, BRIAN R., commercial photographer, futurist; b. Oshawa, Ont., Can., Jan. 16, 1952; s. Robert William and Joan (Gorman) G.; m. Zita Patricia Dunne, July 1, 1972 (div. Dec. 1996); children: Ariana, Brian. Owner Corp. Photography, Ottawa, 1982-95; photographer, futurist self employed, Lake Worth, Fla., 1995—; apptd. mem. consultative com. for copyright amendments Govt. of Can., 1992-96; mem. by appt., Consultative Comm. for Copyright Amendments, Govt. of Canada, advisor, mem. adv. bd. Algonquin Coll., Nepean, Can., 1992-94; mem. Photog. Copyright Coalition, Toronto, 1995; nat. rep. Pacific Rim Photography Coun., 1996—. Author: Not Another Photo Book, 1996; columnist Studio Probe, 1992-94, The Jour., 1993-96. Vice chair Ottawa Dist. Hockey Assn., 1991-92; v.p. Ottawa West Hockey Assn., 1988-90. Recipient 1st in Category award Printing House Craftsmen, 1989. Mem. Internat. Electronic Picture Exch. Coun., Internat. Indsl. Photographers Assn., Internatl. Elec. Picture Exchange Counc. (EPIX, by invitation), 1997—, Can. Assn. Photographers and Illustrators in Comms. (v.p. 1990-94, pres. 1995-96, internat. affairs liaison 1996—, Outstanding Contbn. award 1997). Avocations: cycling, military history, film. Home: #6 106 S O St Lake Worth FL 33460-4278

GREER, CARL CRAWFORD, petroleum company executive; b. Pitts., June 12, 1940; s. Joseph Moss and Gene (Crawford) G.; m. Jerrine Ehlers, June 16, 1962 (div.); children: Caryn, Michael, Janet; m. Patricia Taylor, Feb. 4, 1989. B.S., Lehigh U., 1962; Ph.D., Columbia U., 1966; PsyD, Ill. Sch. Profl. Psychology, Chgo., 1993. Assoc. in bus. Columbia U., 1964-66, asst. prof. banking and finance, 1966-67; retail mktg. mgr. Martin Oil Service Inc., Alsip, Ill., 1967-68; exec. v.p. Martin Oil Service Inc., 1968, pres., dir., 1968-76, chmn. bd., pres., 1976—; pres., dir. Martin Mktg. Corp. GP Martin Oil Mktg. Ltd., 1982, MEMCO Mgmt. Corp. GP Martin Exploration Mgmt. Co., 1985; bd. dirs. Fin. Assocs., Inc. Mem. Beta Theta Pi, Tau Beta Pi, Beta Gamma Sigma, Omicron Delta Kappa. Presbyterian.

GREER, CAROLE KILBY, reading specialist; b. Anawalt, W.Va., Jan. 11, 1950; d. Mark W. Kilby and Helen S. (Shepherd) Byrd; m. Jackie D. Greer Sr., July 3, 1965; children: Jackie D. Jr., Sara, Tara. BA in Edn., Emory & Henry Coll., 1979; MEd, U. Va., 1990. Tchrs. aide Head Start, Marion, Va.; tchr. Sugar Grove (Va.) Sch., 1979—. presenter in field. Vol. Falling Water Bapt. Ch., Marion, 1980-97; sec. Sugar Grove PTO, 1979-80. Mem. Va. Reading Assn., S.W. Va. Reading Coun., Internat. Reading Assn., Delta Kappa Gamma. Home: 445 Wassona Dr Marion VA 24354-4425 Office: Smuth County Sch System 242 Teas Rd Sugar Grove VA 24375-3047

GREER, CHARLES EUGENE, company executive, lawyer; b. Columbus, Ohio, Mar. 28, 1945; s. Earl E. Greer and Margaret I. Cavanass; 1 child, Erin Elizabeth. BS, Ind. U., 1972, JD, 1976. Bar: Ind. 1976. Pres. Willoughby Industries, Inc., Indpls., 1976-91, pres., CEO, 1991-93; ptnr. Ice Miller Donadio & Ryan, 1976-91; pres. ECM Corp., Indpls., 1993—; pres. Loggins, Inc., Indpls., 1995—, bus. turnaround specialist, 1995—. Served to sgt. USAF, 1965-68, Vietnam. Mem. Ind. Bar Assn., Order of Coif, Phi Eta Sigma, Beta Gamma Sigma. Office: 5581 Sunset Ln Indianapolis IN 46228-1468

GREER, DAVID S., university dean, physician, educator; b. Bklyn., Oct. 12, 1925; s. Jacob and Mary (Zaslawsky) G.; m. Marion Clarich, June 25, 1950; children—Jeffrey, Linda. B.S., U. Notre Dame, 1948; M.D., U. Chgo., 1953; M.A. (hon.), Brown U., 1975; L.H.D. (hon.), Southeastern Mass. U., 1981. Diplomate: Am. Bd. Internal Medicine. Intern Yale-New Haven Med. Center, 1953-54; resident in medicine U. Chgo. Clinics, 1954-57; instr. endocrinology and medicine U. Chgo., 1957; practice medicine specializing in internal medicine Fall River, Mass., 1957-74; chief staff dept. medicine Fall River Gen. Hosp., 1959-62; med. dir. Earle E. Hussey Hosp., Fall River, 1962-75; chief staff dept. medicine Truesdale Clinic and Truesdale Hosp., Fall River, 1971-74; pres. med. staff Truesdale Clinic and Truesdale Hosp., 1968-70; sr. clin. instr. medicine Tufts U. Coll. Medicine, 1969-71, asst. clin.

prof., 1971-78; clin. asso. prof. community health Brown U., 1973-75, dir. family practice residency program, 1975-78, prof. community health, 1975-93, prof. emeritus, 1993—, assoc. dean medicine, 1974-81, dean medicine, 1981-92, dean emeritus, 1992—, chmn. sect. community health, 1978-81; mem. Gov.'s Task Force on Quality of Care, Medicaid Program, Commonwealth of Mass., 1969-70; del. White House Conf. Aging, 1971, 81; Pres. Ind. Living Authority, State of R.I., 1975-81; mem. exec. com. Cancer Control Bd. R.I., 1975-80; mem. R.I. Gov.'s Task Force for Inst. of Mental Health, 1976-81; bd. dirs. Health Planning Council, Inc., Providence, 1976-78; chmn. com. on aging Jewish Fedn. R.I., 1978-80; chmn. Gov.'s Commn. on Provision of Comprehensive Mental Health Services in R.I., 1980-81; trustee Southeastern Mass. U., 1970-81, chmn., 1973-74; chmn. Providence Mayor's Sr. Citizens Task Force, 1975; bd. dirs. Assn. Home Health Agys. R.I., 1975-80; founding dir. Internat. Physicians for Prevention of Nuclear War, Inc., 1980-85; vis. prof. dept medicine Georgetown U., 1992-93; scholar-in-residence Assn. Am. Med. Colls., 1992-93. Contbr. articles to profl. jours. Fellow in health Kellogg Found. Internat., 1986-89; vis. fellow Green Coll. Oxford U., 1985; recipient Outstanding service award Mass. Easter Seal Soc., 1970; Outstanding Citizens award Jewish War Vets. Aux., 1973; Disting. Service award U. Chgo. Med. Alumni Assn.; Cutting Found. medal Andover Newton Theol. Sem., 1976; Professor of the Yr., Brown U., 1992. Master ACP; mem. Inst. Medicine, Gerontol. Soc., Am. Congress Rehab. Medicine, Internat. Soc. Rehab. Medicine, R.I. Med. Soc. Jewish. Office: Brown U Box G Providence RI 02912

GREER, GERMAINE, author; b. Melbourne, Australia, Jan. 29, 1939; d. Eric Reginald and Margaret May Mary (Lafrank) G. B.A. with honors in English and French Lit, U. Melbourne, 1959; M.A. with honors in English, U. Sydney, Australia, 1961; Ph.D. (Commonwealth scholar), Newnham Coll. of Cambridge U., Eng., 1967; Doctorate (hon.), U. Griffith, 1996. Sr. tutor U. Sydney, 1963-64; lectr. English U. Warwick, Eng., 1967-72; prof. modern letters U. Tulsa, 1980-83; dir. Tulsa Ctr. for Study of Woman's Lit.; vis. prof. grad. faculty modern letters U. Tulsa, fall 1979; founder-dir. Tulsa Centre for the Study of Women's Lit.; founder, editor Tulsa Studies in Women's Lit., 1981; dir. Stump Cross Books, 1988—; spl. lectr. and unofcl. fellow Newnham Coll., Cambridge, 1989—; lectr. in N.Am. Am. Program Bur., 1973-78. Author: The Female Eunuch, 1969, The Obstacle Race: The Fortunes of Women Painters and their Work, 1979, Sex and Destiny: The Politics of Human Fertility, 1984, Shakespeare, 1986, The Madwoman's Underclothes, 1986, Daddy, We Hardly Knew You, 1989 (J.R. Ackerly Prize, Premio Internazionale Mondello), The Change: Women, Aging and the Menopause, 1991, Slip-Shod Sibyls: Recognition, Rejection and the Woman Poet, 1995; editor: (with Susan Hastings, Jeslyn Medoff, Melinda Sansone) Kissing the Rod: An Anthology of Seventeenth Century Women's Verse, 1988, The Uncollected Verse of Aphra Behn, 1989, The Change: Women, Aging and the Menopause, 1991, Slip-Shod Sibyls: Recognition, Rejection and the Woman Poet, 1995, The Whole Woman, 1999; selected journalism published as The Madwoman's Clothes, 1986, columnist Sunday Times, London, 1971-73, broadcaster/journalist/reviewer various publs. 1972-79. Jr. Govt. scholar, 1952, Diocesan scholar, 1956, Sr. Govt. scholar, 1956, Commonwealth scholar, 1964, Teacher's Coll. Studentship, 1956, Hon. Doctorate Univ. of Griffith, 1996.

GREER, GORDON BRUCE, lawyer; b. Butler, Pa., Feb. 17, 1932; s. Samuel Walker and Winifred (Fletcher) G.; m. Nancy Linda Hannaford, June 14, 1959; children: Gordon Bruce, Alison Clark. BA, Harvard U., 1953, JD cum laude, 1959. Bar: Wis. 1959, Mass. 1961. Assoc. Foley, Sammond & Lardner, Milw., 1959-61; assoc. Bingham Dana LLP, Boston, 1961-67, ptnr., 1967-97, of counsel, 1997—; lectr. Boston U. Sch. Law. Editor Harvard Law Rev. Vos. 71, 72. Maj. USAFR. Mem. Mass. Bar Assn., Boston Bar Assn., Brae Burn Country Club, Harvard Club (Boston). Republican. Home: 45 Fieldmont Rd Belmont MA 02478-2606 Office: Bingham Dana LLP 150 Federal St Boston MA 02110-1709

GREER, HAROLD EVERETT, retired basketball player; b. Huntington, W.Va., June 26, 1936. Basketball player Syracuse Nationals, N.Y., 1958-63; basketball player Phila. 76ers, 1963-73, coach, 1980-81. Named to Basketball Hall of Fame, 1981; mem. NBA Chamionship Team, 1967; selected All-NBA 2d Team, 1963, 64, 65, 66, 67, 68, 69, NBA All-Star Most Valuable Player, 1968; Phila 76ers all-time leading scorer. Office: c/o Basketball Hall Fame 1150 W Columbus Ave Springfield MA 01105-2532*

GREER, HERSCHEL LYNN, JR., real estate broker; b. Nashville, June 28, 1941; s. Herschel Lynn and Mary Martha (Bradley) G.; children: Kathy, Lynn III, Bradley, Houston, Karen. AA, Martin Coll., Pulaski, Tenn., 1961; BS, Middle Tenn. State U., 1963. Pres., chmn. Guaranty Mortgage Co., Nashville, 1960-75; v.p., then pres. Greer Investment Co. (formerly Guaranty Realty Co.), Nashville, 1963-96; chmn. Tenn. Regulatory Authority, 1996—. Vice chmn., chmn. Tenn. Bd. Edn., 1971-84; fin. chmn. Tenn. Rep. Com., Nashville, 1977; chmn. bd. trustees Martin Meth. Coll., Pulaski, Tenn., 1992-98; trustee Calvary United Meth. Ch.; trustee Mid. Tenn. State U. Found., pres., 1970-71; chmn. Tenn. Housing Devel. Agy., 1985-88; bd. dirs. Nashville Ballet, (pres. 1996-98). Named Disting. Alumnus Middle Tenn. State U., 1987. Mem. Nashville Bd. Realtors (pres. 1975, Realtor of Yr. 1971), Tenn. Assn. Realtors (pres. 1986, Realtor of Yr. 1972), Nat. Assn. Realtors (v.p. region IV 1989), Kappa Alpha (exec. coun.). Republican. Methodist. Avocation: running. Home: 5137 Boxroft Nashville TN 37205

GREER, JOSEPH EPPS, architect; b. Seattle, Feb. 13, 1923; s. Joseph and Gertrude (Greene) G.; m. Francoise Aubert, Sept. 15, 1957; children: Christine, Eric, Alan. BA in Bldg. and Contracting, U. Wash., 1948, BArch, 1950. Registered architect, D.C., Md. Pvt. practice offices in Paris, Washington, Madrid, Geneva, Switzerland and Karachi, Pakistan, 1951—. Prin. works in N. Africa, Europe, Middle East, Iran, Pakistan. With USMCR, 1942-46. Fellow ASCE (life); mem. Soc. Am. Mil. Engrs. (life), Soc. des Amis des Chateaux de la Loire (life), La Confrérie des Chevaliers du Tastevin, Am. C. of C. France (hon. dir.), Delta Kappa Epsilon, Tau Sigma Delta. Home: 1 Ave du Bijou de Florian, Ferney-Voltaire 01210, France

GREER, K. GORDON, banker; b. Tulsa, Oct. 28, 1936; s. H.K. and Afton (Goodman) G.; m. Nancy Lang, Nov. 22, 1958; children—Keith G., Scott A. BS in Banking and Fin., Okla. State U., 1958; postgrad. Grad. Sch. Banking, U. Wis.-Madison, 1964-67. Pres. Liberty Nat. Bank, Oklahoma City, 1958-84; CEO The First Nat. Bank and Trust Co., Tulsa, 1984-94, pres., 1984-94, now also chmn., dir.; vice chmn. BancFirst Corp., Tulsa. With Air Force N.G., 1958-64. Named to Hall of Fame, Bus. Adminstrn. Sch. Okla. State U., 1984. Mem. Am. Bankers Assn., Okla. Bankers Assn. (pres. 1983-84), Assn. Res. City Bankers. Democrat. Methodist. Clubs: So. Hills Country, Tulsa (Tulsa). Avocation: golf. *

GREER, KATHLEEN E., college registrar; b. Apr. 29, 1949. B in Religious Edn., Life Bible Coll., San Dimas, Calif., 1970; MA, Azusa Pacific U., 1995. Mem. faculty Life Bible Coll., 1983—, registrar, adminstr., 1994—; fgn. student advisor, VA rep. Life Bible Coll., 1994—. Missionary, Papua New Guinea, 1983-93.

GREER, MELVIN, medical educator; b. N.Y.C., Oct. 14, 1929; s. Aaron and Ceil (Cohen) Jefkel; m. Arline Ebert, Dec. 16, 1951; children: Jonathan, Richard, Alison, David. B.A. magna cum laude, NYU, 1950, M.D., 1954. Intern, resident Bellevue Hosp., N.Y.C., 1954-56; fellow N.Y. Neurol. Inst., Columbia, 1958-61; prof., chmn. dept. neurology U. Fla. Coll. Medicine, Gainesville, 1963—; cons. NIH, 1971—, Fla. Div. Corrections, 1971—; lectr., cons. Navy Dept.; chmn. med. adv. com. Community Clinic, Gainesville, 1971-73; endowed professorship neurology U. Fla. Coll. Medicine, Gainesville, 1991—. Author: Mass Spectrometry of Biologically Important Aromatic Acids, 1969, Differential Diagnosis of Neurological Diseases, 1977; also articles.; Editorial bd.: Neurology, Geriatics, 1968—. Served to lt. comdr. USNR, 1956-58. Recipient Medallion award Columbia U., 1968, Hippocratic award U. Fla., 1970, Outstanding Clin. Tchr. award, 1975, 79; NIH grantee, 1962-71. Fellow Am. Acad. Neurology (councillor, sec.-treas. 1977-81, pres.-elect 1983-85, pres. 1985-87), Am. Acad. Pediatrics; mem. Am. Neurol. Assn. (councillor), Soc. Pediatric Research, Am. Pediatric Soc., Phi Beta Kappa, Alpha Omega Alpha. Home: 2058 NW 14th Ave Gainesville FL 32605-5245

GREER, MONTE ARNOLD, physician, educator; b. Portland, Oreg., Oct. 26, 1922; s. William Wallace and Rose (Rasmussen) G.; m. Peggy Johnson, Dec. 31, 1943; children: Susan Elizabeth, Richard Arnold. Student, Oreg. State U., 1940-43; AB, Stanford U., 1944, MD, 1947. Intern San Francisco Gen. Hosp., 1946-47; rsch. fellow endocrinology New England Med. Ctr., Boston, 1947-49; resident internal medicine Mass. Meml. Hosp., Boston, 1949-50; rsch. assoc. in endocrinology New England Med. Ctr. Hosp., 1950-51; sr. investigator, sr. asst. surgeon USPHS, Nat. Cancer Inst., NIH, Bethesda, Md., 1951-55; chief radioisotope unit D.C. Gen. Hosp., Washington, 1951-55; clin. asst. prof. medicine UCLA, 1955-56; chief radioisotope svc. VA Hosp., Long Beach, Calif., 1955-56; head div. endocrinology Oreg. Health Scis. U. (formerly U. Oreg. Med. Sch.), Portland, 1956-80, assoc. prof., 1956-62, prof. medicine, 1962—, prof. physiology, 1992—, head divsn. endocrinology, metabolism and clin. nutrition, 1980-84, head sect. endocrinology, 1984-90. Author: (with H. Studer) The Regulation of Thyroid Function in Iodine Deficiency, 1968, (with P. Langer) Antithyroid Drugs and Naturally Occurring Goitrogens, 1977; editor: The Thyroid Gland, 1990, (with D.H. Solomon) The Thyroid, 1974; mem. editorial bd. Endocrinology, 1960-72, Neuroendocrinology, 1965-76, Endocrine Regulations, 1971—; contbr. articles to profl. jours. Mem. Thyroid Task Force NIH Com. for Evaluation of Endocrinology and Metabolic Diseases, 1977-80, Endocrinology Study Sect., NIH, 1977-80. Pharmacol. and Endocrinology fellowship study sect. NIH, 1968-72; recipient Oppenheimer award Endocrine Soc., 1958, Rsch. Career award NIH, 1962-81, Discovery award Med. Rsch. Found. Oreg., 1985, DeMolay Legion of Honor award, 1988. Mem. AAAS, Am. Fedn. for Clin. Rsch. (chmn. Western sect. 1958-59), Western Soc. for Clin. Rsch. (v.p. 1963-64, pres. 1967-68), Endocrine Soc. (mem. council 1965-68, v.p. 1976-77), Am. Thyroid Assn. (v.p., dir. 1974-77, pres. 1980, Disting. Service award 1985), Am. Soc. Clin. Investigation, Soc. Exptl. Biology and Medicine, Western Assn. Physicians (sec.-treas. 1974-77), Assn. Am. Physicians, Internat. Brain Rsch. Orgn., Internat. Soc. Neuroendocrinology, European Thyroid Assn., Japan Endocrine Soc. (hon.), Czechoslovak Endocrine Soc. (hon.), Rotary, Sigma Chi. Office: Oreg Health Scis U Portland OR 97201

GREER, NORRIS E., lawyer; b. San Francisco, June 21, 1945. BA, U. Mo., Kansas City, 1967, JD, 1974. Bar: Mo. 1974. Atty. Shughart Thomson & Kilroy, Kansas City, Mo. Mem. ABA, Nat. Assn. Coll. and Univ. Attys., The Mo. Bar, Kansas City Met. Bar Assn., Lawyers Assn. Kansas City. Office: Shughart Thomson & Kilroy 12 Wyandotte Plz 120 W 12th St Ste 1500 Kansas City MO 64105-1929

GREER, ROBERT BRUCE, III, orthopedic surgeon, educator; b. Butler, Pa., 1934. BA, Haverford Coll., 1956; MD, Harvard U., 1960. Diplomate Am. Bd. Orthopaedic Surgery (bd. dirs. 1985-94, pres. 1990-91). Intern Mich. Med. Ctr., 1960-61, resident in surgery, 1961-62; resident in orthopaedic surgery Pitts. Med. Ctr., 1964-67; fellow orthopaedic surgery NIH, Bethesda, Md., 1967-69; orthopaedist MS Hershey Med. Ctr., Pa.; prof., chief orthopaedic surgery Pa. State U., 1971-91; med. dir. Howmedica, Inc., 1997-99. Mem. ACS, Am. Acad. Orthopaedic Surgeons, Am. Orthopaedic Assn., Ea. Orthopaedic Assn., Alpha Omega Alpha. Home: 166 Lake Meade Dr East Berlin PA 17316-9388

GREER, ROBERT STEPHENSON, insurance company executive; b. Apr. 2, 1920; s. Fred Jones and Nannie (Stephenson) G.; m. Patrica Pettry, Oct. 1, 1944; children: Robert S., John P. BS, La. State U., 1941. Ins. agt. Union Nat. Life Ins. Co., Baton Rouge, 1941-42, dist. mgr., 1945-48, v.p., 1948-56, exec. v.p., 1956-70, pres., CEO, 1970-85, chmn. bd., CEO, 1985-90; pres., CEO Union Nat. Fire Ins. Co., Baton Rouge, 1970-85, chmn. bd., CEO, 1985-90; dir. Premier Regional Bank. Chmn. United Way, 1977, pres., 1980-81; bd. dirs. Salvation Army, Our Lady of the Lake Found., Hospice Found., NCCJ, Pennington Biomed. Rsch. Ctr., Woman's Hosp., Baton Rouge, 1976-80, Baton Rouge Area Found., 1978-82, 87—; chmn. bd. trustees 1st United Meth. Ch., 1970—; past bd. dirs., past pres. YMCA. Lt. USN, WWII. Named Alumni Endowed Chair of Bus. Adminstrn., La. State U., 1989, Disting. Citizen of Yr., Boy Scouts Am., 1989, Alumnus of Yr., La. State U. Alumni Assn., 1990; recipient YMCA Lifetime Achievement award, 1999. Mem. Baton Rouge C. of C. (past pres.), BBB Baton Rouge (past pres.), La. State U. Coll. Bus. Alumni (past pres.), La. State U. Alumni Fedn. (past pres., Hall of Distinction 1987), Life Insurers Conf. (past chmn. Disting. Svc. award 1991), Life Insurers Conf., Coun. for a Better La. (past pres.), Country Club (past pres.), City Club (bd. dirs. 1968-70), Rotary (past pres., Free Enterpriser of Yr. 1985, Exec. of Yr. 1986), Kappa Sigma (Disting. Alumnus award 1996), Beta Gamma Sigma. Home: 3075 Gilbert Dr Baton Rouge LA 70809-1570 Office: Union Nat Life Ins Co 8282 Goodwood Blvd Baton Rouge LA 70806-7738

GREER, SCOTT L., economist; b. June 10, 1967. BA, U. N.C., 1989, MPA, 1998. Bus. analyst Md. Casualty Co., Balt., 1990-93; claim rep. Md. Casualty Co., Charlotte, N.C., 1993; workers' compensation specialist City of Charlotte, 1993-97, economist, 1997—. E-mail: fnslg@mail.charmeck.nc.us. Office: 8725 Digital Dr # 106 Charlotte NC 28262

GREER, THOMAS H., newspaper executive; b. Nashville, July 24, 1942; s. Thomas H. and Eliza (Scruggs) G.; children: Kasey Lynn, Janna Whitney. BA in Polit. Sci., Dillard U., 1963. News/sports reporter Trenton (N.J.) Evening Times, 1965-73; news reporter The Plain Dealer, Cleve., 1973-75, sports editor, 1983-86, mng. editor, 1986-89, exec. editor, 1989-92; v.p., sr. editor The Plain Dealer, 1992—; sports writer, columnist Phila. Daily News, 1977-80; sports columnist N.Y. Daily News, 1980-83; judge Scripps-Howard Founds. Walker Stone/Editl. Writing award, 1993; nominating jury mem. Pulitzer Prize, 1989-90. Bd. dirs. Greater Cleve. Roundtable, Cleve., Bus. Volunteerism Coun., ARC, Cleve., Cuyahoga Plan, Plain Dealer Credit Union, Am. Cancer Soc. Named Paul Miller Disting. Journalism Lectr., Oklahoma State U., 1993. Mem. Am. Press Inst., Nat. Assn. Minority Media Execs. (bd. dirs.), Freedom Forum's Adv. Coun. for Sports Journalism, Am. Soc. Newspaper Editors, Nat. Assn. Black Journalists, AP Mng. Editors Assn., AP Sports Editors' Assn., Cleve. Zool. Soc., Cleve. Press Club, Omega Psi Phi. Office: Plain Dealer 1801 Superior Ave E Cleveland OH 44114-2198

GREER, WILLIS ROSWELL, JR., accounting educator; b. Memphis, Nov. 16, 1938; s. Willis Roswell and Myra Bell (Bridges) G.; m. Melinda S. Scott, June 28, 1963; children: Howard Willis, Catherine Irene Grubbs, Charles Walker. BS, Cornell U., 1961, MBA with distinction, 1966; PhD in Acctg., U. Mich., 1971. Cert. Mgmt. Acct., Cert. Bus. Appraiser. Lectr. acctg. and stats. U. West Indies, Trinidad, 1966-67; teaching asst., Paton fellow U. Mich., 1967-71; asst. prof. acctg. U. Oreg., 1971-75, assoc. prof., 1975-76; vis. prof. acctg. Dartmouth Coll., Amos Tuck Sch., 1976-77, assoc. prof., 1976-82; vis. scholar Manchester (Eng.) Bus. Sch., 1981; prof. acctg. Naval Postgrad. Sch., 1982-88, acad. assoc. fin. mgmt., 1983-84, chmn. dept. adminstrv. scis., 1984-87; prof. acctg. U. Iowa, Iowa City, 1988-96, assoc. dean grad. programs, 1989-92, head dept. acctg., 1992-95; lectr. acctg. and fin. analysis Tohoku U., Japan, 1993-94; dean Coll. Bus. Adminstrn. U. No. Iowa, Cedar Falls, 1996—; cons. U.S. Small Bus. Adminstrn. Minority Bus. Devel. Program, several large firms in various mfg. and svc. industries; presenter numerous seminars and workshops. Co-author: (with Paul Wasserman) Consultants and Consulting Organizations, 1966, (with J. Peter Williamson) Interim Inventory Estimation Error, 1979, (with Shu Liao) Cost Analysis for Dual Source Weapon Procurement, 1983, Cost Analysis for Competitive Major Weapon Systems Procurement: Further Refinement and Extension, 1984; author: A Method for Estimating and Controlling the Cost of Extending Technology, 1988; editor: (with Dan Nussbaum) Cost Analysis and Estimating: Tools and Techniques, 1990; contbr. articles to profl. jours. Treas. Oaknoll Retirement Cmty., 1993—. Mem. Inst. Mgmt. Accts. (dir. Cedar Rapids chpt. 1990—), Am. Acctg. Assn., Decision Scis. Inst., Inst. Bus. Appraisers, Inc. Republican. Achievements include research on conditions under which dual source procurement of major weapon systems is beneficial to goverment; building an accurate model for forecasting research and development costs for specified technology advancement; avocations: travel, photography. Home: 421 Olive St Cedar Falls IA 50613-2520

GREESON, JENNIFER, press secretary. BA in Mktg., Coll. William and Mary, 1994. With various pub. rels. and mktg. firms, 1994-96; comm. dir. Bedford for Senate '96, Montgomery, Ala., 1996; dep. press sec. Office of Senator Chris Dodd, Washington, 1996-98, comm. dir., 1998; press sec. minority staff Spl. Senate Com. Y2K Problem, Washington, 1998-99, Office of Senator Blanche L. Lincoln, Washington, 1999—. Office: Dirksen Senate Office Bldg Washington DC 20510-0401

GREEVER, MARGARET QUARLES, retired mathematics educator; b. Wilkensburg, Pa., Feb. 7, 1931; d. Lawrence Reginald and Ella Mae (LeSueur) Quarles; m. John Greever, Aug. 29, 1953; children: Catherine Patricia, Richard George, Cynthia Diane. Cert. costume design, Richmond Profl. Inst., 1952; student, U. Va., 1953-56; BA in Math., Calif. State U., L.A., 1963; MA in Math., Claremont Grad. Sch., 1968. Cert. tchr. specializing in Jr. Coll. math., Calif. Tchr. math. Chaffey Unified H.S. Dist., Alta Loma, Calif., 1963-64, L.A. Unified Sch. Dist., 1964-65, Chino (Calif.) Unified Sch. Dist., 1965-81; from asst. prof. to prof. Chaffey Coll., Rancho Cucamonga, 1981-96; phys. sci. divsn. chmn. Chaffey Coll., Alta Loma, 1985-92, dean, phys., life, health sci., 1992-96. Mem. AAUW (pres. local chpt. 1998—), Orcas Island Garden Club (treas. 1997—), Orcas Island Yacht Club, Pi Lambda Theta. Avocations: quilting, cooking, sewing, gardening.

GREEVER, WILLIAM ST. CLAIR, educator, historian; b. Lexington, Va., July 22, 1916; s. Gustavus Garland and May St. Clair (Stocking) G.; m. Janet Elizabeth Groff, Aug. 24, 1951; 1 dau., Barbara Clair. B.A., Pomona Coll., 1938; M.A., Harvard U., 1940, Ph.D., 1949. Instr. bus. history Northwestern U., 1947-49; mem. faculty U. Idaho, 1949—, chmn. dept. history, 1956-82, prof. history, 1958-82, prof. emeritus, 1982—. Author: Arid Domain: The Santa Fe Railway and Its Western Land Grant, 1954 (prize Pacific history Pacific Coast br. Am. Hist. Assn. 1954), The Bonanza West: The Story of the Western Mining Rushes, 1963 (Spur award best nonfiction Western, Western Writers Am. 1963); bd. editors: Pacific Hist. Rev., 1956-58; Bd. editors: Idaho Yesterdays, 1976-86; Contbr. articles to profl. jours. Served with AUS, 1942-46. Guggenheim fellow, 1958-59. Mem. Am. Hist. Assn. (council Pacific Coast br. 1957-59), Western Hist. Assn. (council 1980-83, Award of Merit 1987), Orgn. Am. Historians, AAUP (pres. local chpt. 1955-56), Mining Hist. Assn. (Paul award 1990), Phi Beta Kappa. Home: 315 S Hayes St Moscow ID 83843-3419

GREFE, BRUCE PAUL, art educator, artist; b. Longbranch, N.J., Apr. 17, 1946; s. William Francis and Margaret Barbara (Toth) G.; m. Victoria Maria Theresa Valdes-Dapena, Feb. 14, 1970 (div. Oct. 1986); children: Julian-Alexander, Christiana Morgan. BA, Temple U., 1968. Cert. tchr., N.J. Tchr. art Camden (N.J.) City Schs., 1968—; mem. State Bd. on Art Stds. for Secondary Schs., 1991; art cons. Bureat Co., Haddon Heights, N.J., 1992-94. Mem. NEA, N.J. Edn. Assn., Camden City Edn. Assn., Camden County Edn. Assn. Democrat. Avocation: collecting illustrated texts from 1880-1940. Home: 304 3rd Ave Hammonton NJ 08037-9531

GREFÉ, RICHARD, graphic design executive; b. Buffalo, May 21, 1945; s. Richard W. and Marjorie Louise (Sine) G.; m. Karen Lee Vogel, Oct. 8, 1978; children: Justin Sine, Gillian Scarborough. AB, Dartmouth Coll., 1967; MBA, Stanford U., 1973. Book designer Stinehour Press, Lunenburg, Vt., 1967; writer Time Mag., N.Y.C., 1972; pres. Richard Grefé Assocs., San Francisco and Washington, 1973-83; dir. policy devel. and planning Corp. Pub. Broadcasting, Washington, 1983-88; exec. v.p. Am.'s Pub. TV Stas., Washington, 1989-95; exec. dir. Am. Inst. of Graphic Arts, 1995—. Trustee Phillips Collection, Washington, 1993-95; bd. dirs. Silvermine Guild Art Ctr., 1995-98, Friends of Thirteen, 1995-97, Darien Environ. Protection Commn., 1996—. Lt. USN, 1967-71. Home: 19 Raymond St Darien CT 06820-4923 Office: 164 5th Ave New York NY 10010-5901

GREFE, ROLLAND EUGENE, lawyer; b. Ida County, Iowa, June 27, 1920; s. Alfred William and Zoma Corrine (Lasher) G.; m. Mary Arlene Cruikshank, June 12, 1943; 1 son, Roger Frederick. B.A., Morningside Coll., 1941; J.D., State U. Iowa, 1946. Bar: Iowa 1946. Assoc. Schaetzle, Williams & Stewart, Des Moines, 1946-48, Schaetzle, Swift, Austin & Stewart, Des Moines, 1948-52; ptnr. Schaetzle, Austin & Grefe (and related firms), Des Moines, 1952-60, Austin, Grefe & Sidney, Des Moines, 1960-71; sr. ptnr. Grefe & Sidney, Des Moines, 1971-95; mem. Grefe & Sidney P.L.C., 1995—; dir. Freeman Decorating Co., 1969—, Cowles Syndicate, Inc., 1982-86; mem. bd. mgrs. Lawyers Com. Network, L.L.C., 1997—, chair, 1998—. Bd. dirs. Des Moines Area C.C., 1966-76, pres., 1967-76; bd. dirs. Westminster Presbyn. Ch. Found., 1975-89, Iowa State Bar Found., 1979-91; trustee Des Moines Water Works, 1984-99, pres., 1987, 91, 96. Lt. USNR, 1942-45. Fellow Am. Bar Found., Am. Coll. Trust and Estate Counsel; mem. ABA (ho. of dels. 1982-96, Iowa state del. 1992-93, bd. govs. 1993-96), Assn. Endowment Found. Coll. (mem. pension plan adminstrn. com. 1994—), Polk County Bar Assn. (pres. 1971-72), Iowa State Bar Assn. (bd. govs. 1972-76, pres. 1978-79, chmn. com. on long-range planning 1979-81, Award of Merit 1982), Des Moines Estate Planning Coun., Lincoln Inne. Republican. Presbyterian. Clubs: Sertoma (Des Moines), Des Moines (Des Moines), Wakonda (Des Moines). Home: 3524 Grand AveApt 803 Des Moines IA 50312-4344 Office: PO Box 10434 2222 Grand Ave Des Moines IA 50312-5306

GREGAN, EDMUND ROBERT, landscape architect; b. New Haven, Feb. 4, 1936; s. Edmund Arthur and Elizabeth (Kochiss) G.; m. Janet Lamson Shaw, Aug. 22, 1959; children: Edmund Robert, Darianne Lee, Christyn Elizabeth. BS in Landscape Architecture, R.I. Sch. Design, 1960. Lic. landscape architect, Conn. Landscape architect and site planner Morton S. Fine & Assocs., Hartford, Conn., 1960-62; landscape architect New Haven Redevel. Agy., 1962-66, chief landscape architect, 1966-78; landscape architect, cons., lectr. E. Robert Gregan Landscape Architect, North Branford, Conn., 1965—; chief landscape architect New Haven City Plan Dept., 1978-91; instr. landscape architecture Guilford/Madison (Conn.) Adult Edn. Programs, 1979-88; tchr., critic Yale, R.I. Sch. Design, U. Conn. Conway Sch. Landscape Design, So. Conn. State U.; tchr. environ. design Yale Sch. of Forestry and Environtl. Studies Elem. Schs. New Haven, 1992; tchr. Federated Garden Clubs Conn. Sch. Landscape Design, 1979—; lectr. various orgns. and clubs. Contbr. numerous profl. jours. Bd. dirs. North Branford Land Conservation Trust, 1968-72, v.p., 1973—; mem. North Branford Conservation Commn., 1969-73, chmn., 1971-72, assoc. mem., 1973-92; cons. North Branford Ctr. Improvement Com., 1991-95; mem. North Branford-Northford Town Design Dists. Adv. Com., 1995—; bd. dirs. New Haven Urban Resources Initiative, 1991-96; mem. steering com. Long Wharf Nature Preserve, 1995—; landscape arch., vice chair spl. events 1995 Spl. Olympics World Games, 1994-95. Recipient Cert. of Achievement award Federated Garden Clubs. Conn., 1981, Bronze medal Federated Garden Clubs Conn., 1991, Cert. of Merit for Excellence in Study of Landscape Architecture, RISD, 1960. Fellow Am. Soc. Landscape Architects; mem. Conn. Soc. Landscape Architects (bd. dirs. 1981-86, hist. and landscape preservation com. 1987—, George A. Yarwood Cert. Svc. award 1987, numerous profl. design awards), Totoket Hist. Soc. (mem. design cons. 1972—), Garden Club New Haven (hon. mem.), Federated Garden Clubs of Conn., Inc. (hon. mem. landscape design critics coun. 1993). Episcopalian. Avocations: design, gardening, photography, travel. Home and Office: 34 Edgewood Rd North Branford CT 06471-1466

GREGAN, JOHN PATRICK, finance executive, small business owner; b. Sigourney, Iowa, Nov. 24, 1947; s. Raymond Stephen and Ellen Mary (O'Brien) G.; m. Rhonda Mason Weissberg, Nov. 19, 1977; children: Brien Geoffrey, Audrey Jane. BA in Acctg., St. Ambrose Coll., Davenport, Iowa, 1970. Profl. lic. enrolled agt. Internal revenue agt. IRS, Davenport, Iowa, 1970-71; computer audit specialist OIO (office of internal ops.), Washington, 1971-79; tax acct. SMATAX Corp., Waldorf, Md., 1979—; Md. del. to Internat. Soc. Pub. Accts. Conv., 1987, 92. Diplomate, Rome, 1973; bd. dirs. The Home Inc., Alexandria, Va., 1992-96. Mem. Nat. Soc. Pub. Accts., Md. Soc. Pub. Accts., Nat. Assn. Enrolled Agts., Md. Soc. Enrolled Agts., Nat. Soc. Tax Profls. Democrat. Catholic. Home: 13210 Breezy Ct Waldorf MD 20601-2000 Office: TS SMATAX Ste 106 11865 Federal Sq Waldorf MD 20602-3662

GREGANTI, MAC ANDREW, physician, medical educator; b. Cleveland, Miss., Apr. 13, 1947; s. Mack Americo and Grace Margaret (Barbati) G.; m. Susan Taylor, Aug. 8, 1971; children: Paul Andrew, Mack Taylor, Mary Catherine. BS summa cum laude, Millsaps Coll., 1969; MD summa cum laude, U. Miss., 1972. Diplomate Am. Bd. Internal Medicine and cert. in geriatric medicine. Intern U. Rochester, N.Y., 1972-73, resident, 1973-75; instr. dept. medicine U. Miss. Sch. Medicine, Jackson, 1975-76, asst. prof., 1976-77; asst. prof. U. N.C. Sch. Medicine, Chapel Hill, 1977-83, assoc. prof., 1983-90, prof., 1990—, chief div. gen. medicine, 1986-91, assoc. chair for clin. affairs, 1991—; dir. med./pediatric residency U. N.C. Dept. Medicine, Chapel Hill, 1980-86, dir. medicine residency, 1981-86. Contbr. articles on med. edn. and patient care to profl. jours. Fellow ACP; mem. Am. Geriatrics Soc., Alpha Oemga Alpha. Roman Catholic. Avocations: computers, tennis, golf. Office: Univ NC Chapel Hill Dept of Medicine 3029 Old Clinic Bldg CB 7005 Chapel Hill NC 27599-7005

GREGG, BILLY RAY, seed industry executive, consultant; b. Taylorsville, Miss., Aug. 31, 1930; s. Hinds and Lillie Mae (Moore) G.; m. Mary Frances Barber, Aug. 12, 1950 (div. Jan. 1987); children: Kathryn, Patricia, Lisa; m. Orawan Chonlavorn, Dec. 20, 1988; 1 child, Nathan Paul. AA, Perkinston (Miss.) Jr. Coll., 1950; BS, Miss. State U., 1954, MS, 1956, PhD, 1968; postgrad., Wash. State U., 1957-63. Asst. prof. Wash. State U., Pullman, 1956-63; mgr. Ala. Crop Improvement Assn., Auburn, Ala., 1964-66; seed technologist Miss. State U., 1966-68; chief party/processing specialist seed improvement project U.S. AID, New Delhi, India, 1968-72; chief party and seed specialist seed project U.S. AID, Brasilia, Brazil, 1972-74; chief, seed industry devel. specialist U.S. AID, Bangkok, 1977-87; seed industry devel. specialist U.S. AID, Cairo, 1987-93; chief party and seed industry specialist IDB and GOB Agiplan Project, Brasilia, 1974-76; seed industry specialist Internat. Plant Breeders, Maringa, Parana, Brazil, 1976, Interam. Agrl. Sci. Inst., Brasilia, 1976-77; seed industry devel. specialist internat. programs Miss. State U., 1993—; cons./advisor on seed tech. matters, mgmt., quality control and industry devel. nat. govts., pvt. cos., World Bank, Interam. Devel. Bank, FAO, GTZ, U.S. AID in more than 80 countries, 1960-95. Contbr. over 480 articles to profl. jours.; author 2 books. With U.S. Army, 1950-52; ETO. Indian Soc. Seed Technologists fellow, 1987. Mem. Kiwanis Internat. (dir., Kiwanian of the Yr. 1968), Agrl. Sci. Soc. Thailand (hon.), Wash. State Crop Improvement Assn. (hon. life), Phi Kappa Phi, Sigma Xi, Phi Theta Kappa. Buddhist. Avocations: vegetable and flower gardening, writing, travel. Home: PO Box 1756 Starkville MS 39760-1756

GREGG, CHARLES THORNTON, research company executive; b. Billings, Mont., July 27, 1927; s. Charles Thornton and Gertrude (Hurst) G.; m. Elizabeth Whitaker, Dec. 20, 1947; children: Paul, Diane, Brian, Elaine. BS in Physics, Oreg. State U., 1952, MS in Organic Chemistry, 1955, PhD in Biochemistry, 1959. Postdoctoral fellow Nat. Cancer Inst., Johns Hopkins Sch. Med., Balt., 1959-63; mem. staff Los Alamos (N.Mex.) Nat. Lab., 1963-85; sr. scientist Mesa Diagnostics, Los Alamos, 1985-86; v.p. rsch. Los Alamos Diagnostics, 1986-90; pres. Innovative Surg. Tech. Inc., 1991—; pres. Bethco, Inc., 1972—; vis. prof. The Free U., Berlin, 1973-74; cons. internat. tech. div. Los Alamos Nat. Lab., 1985-90. Author: Plague, 1978, The Virus of Love, 1983, Tarawa, 1985; patentee bacterial identification apparatus, safe surg. knife. Bd. dirs. Friends of Mesa Pub. Libr., Los Alamos, 1981-83, County Libr. Los Alamos, 1983-85, Los Alamos Arts Coun., 1985-87, bd. dir., Lukens Med. Corp., 1996-97. Served in U.S. Navy, 1944-46. Fellow AAAS; mem. Am. Soc. Biochemistry and Molecular Biology, Am. Soc. Microbiology, Sigma Xi, Sigma Pi Sigma, Phi Lambda Upsilon. Democrat. Unitarian. Avocation: hiking. Office: 901 18th St Los Alamos NM 87544-3009

GREGG, DAVID, III, investment banker; b. N.Y.C., Jan. 29, 1933; s. David Gregg and Virginia (Wyckoff) Macgregor; m. May Foster Bowers, Dec. 21, 1963 (div. Apr. 1984); children: Justine Simms Barkstrom, David; m. Sarah Choate Massengale, Dec. 8, 1984. Assoc., Eastman Dillon Union Securities & Co., N.Y.C., 1959-67, ptnr., 1967-69; v.p. Blyth & Co., Inc., N.Y.C., 1969-72; 1st v.p. Blyth, Eastman Dillon & Co., N.Y.C., 1972-73; exec. v.p. Overseas Pvt. Investment Corp., Washington, 1973-77; mng. dir. Pierce Internat., Ltd., Washington, 1978-85; mng. dir. Pierce Investment Banking Corp., 1985-97, Pierce Fin. Corp., Arlington, Va., 1986—; chmn. bd. dirs. Gator Broadcasting Corp., Del., 1986—; trustee Calvert Tax Free Res. Fund, 1978-83; dir. No. Ireland and Border Counties Trade and Investment Coun., 1994-98. Served with U.S. Army, 1955-57. Republican. Episcopalian. Clubs: Onteora (dir. 1969-72) (Tannersville, N.Y.); Chesapeake Bay Yacht (Easton, Md.); Amateur Ski of N.Y. Office: Pierce Fin Corp 2200 Clarendon Blvd Ste 1410 Arlington VA 22201-3331

GREGG, DAVID PAUL, information storage media specialist; b. Los Angeles, Mar. 11, 1923; s. David D. and Ferol Adelle (Bozardt) G.; m. Donna M. Ostrom, Aug., 1959 (div. 1979); children: Daniel P., Debora N., Alicia L., Wade A. K., Thomas R., Connie J. Student, Kans. State U., 1945-47; BSEE, U. So. Calif., 1950, postgrad., 1960; postgrad., Case Inst. Tech., 1956. Video engr. Ampex Corp., Redwood City, Calif., 1955-56; optical and disk sys. engr. Westrex subs. AT&T, Hollywood, Calif., 1956-60; digital magnetic tape and videodisk cons. Mincom divsn. 3M Co., West Los Angeles, Calif., 1960-61; v.p., co-founder digital magnetic tape and video disk sys. Winston Rsch. Corp., Culver City, Calif., 1961-62; pres., founder ultra high speed music tape duplicators and video disk Gauss Electrophysics, Inc., Santa Monica, Calif., 1964-67, also chmn. bd.; video disk cons. MCA/DiscoVision, Inc., Universal City, Calif., 1968-71; sys. cons. ITT Laboratorios de España, Madrid, 1969-73; cons. Del Mar Avionics, Culver City, 1973-75, cons. laser stripchart recorder, recordable CD, 1986-91; cons. Model 757 design Boeing Comml. Aircraft, Renton, Wash., 1979-81; cons., lic. info. storage media specialist DiscoVision Assocs., Irvine, Calif., 1982—; cons. satellite infrared optics Hughes Aircraft, Culver City, 1976-78. Contbr. articles to profl. jours.; basic patentee in videodisk, optical ribbon and XUV fields. With USN, 1940-43. Mem. AAAS, Soc. Motion Picture and TV Engrs. (life), Optical Soc. Am. (sr.), European Optical Soc., Soc. Photo-Instrumentation Engrs. (sr.), Audio Engring. Soc. (sr.), Tech. Coun. of Motion Picture-TV Industry (sr.). Avocations: collecting video disks, reading classics in original language. Fax: (310) 202-6325. E-mail: eclectic@opticaldisk.com. Home and Office: 3650 Helms Ave Culver City CA 90232-2417

GREGG, ERIC EUGENE, umpire; b. Phila., May 8, 1951; m. Romona Camilo, Dec. 31, 1974; children: Eric, Kevin, Ashley, Jamie. Umpire N.Y.-Pa. League, Fla. State League, Ea. League, Dominican Republic League, Pacific Coast League, Nat. League, 1975—. Office: Nat League 350 Park Ave New York NY 10022 Office: Umpires Union 1735 Market St Philadelphia PA 19103

GREGG, HUGH, former cabinet manufacturing company executive, former governor New Hampshire; b. Nashua, N.H., Nov. 22, 1917; s. Harry A. and Margaret R. (Richardson) G.; m. Catherine M. Warner, July 24, 1940; children: Cyrus Warner, Judd Alan. Grad., Phillips Exeter Acad., 1935; AB, Yale U., 1939; LLB, Harvard U., 1942; LLD, U. N.H., 1953; MA, Dartmouth Coll., 1953; DCL, New England Coll., 1954. Bar: N.H. 1942, Mass 1948. Mem. Sullivan & Gregg, Nashua; former pres., treas. Gregg & Son, Inc., Nashua; gov. of N.H., 1953-55; chmn. bd. dirs., treas. Gregg Cabinets Ltd., Chambly, Que., Can.; former owner Greggs Greenhouse Restaurant, Sarasota, Fla.; clk., former co-pub. N.H. Profiles; v.p. Forum on N.H.'s Future, 1977-81; pres. Resources of N.H., Inc., Nashua; bd. dirs. Saphikon Inc., 1988. Author: The Candidates: See How They Run, 1990, A Tall State Revisited, 1993, Birth of the Republican Party, 1995. Mem. Nat. Exec. Res.; alderman-at-large, City of Nashua, 1948-50, mayor, 1950; bd. dirs. New England Coun., 1952-55, pres., 1955-57; Rep. nat. committeeman from N.H., 1988; law commr. N.H. Ballot, 1992—; chmn. N.H. Polit. Libr., 1997—. Spl. agt. CIC, U.S. Army, 1942-46, 50-52. Mem. Can. Kitchen Cabinet Assn. (bd. dirs.), VFW, Amos Tuck Soc. (founder 1994). Home: 17 Gregg Rd Nashua NH 03062-1002

GREGG, JAMES D., federal judge. BS, Mich. State U., 1969; MA, Ctrl. Mich. U., 1973; JD magna cum laude, Wayne State U., 1977. With Schmidt, Howlett, Van't Hoff, Snell & Vana, Grand Rapids, Mich.; assoc. Varnum, Schmidt & Howlett, Grand Rapids, 1977-87; bankruptcy judge U.S. Bank Ct. (we. dist.) Mich., Grand Rapids, 1987—; adj. prof. Grand Valley State Coll., 1981-82, Thomas Cooley Law Sch., 1990, 94-97. Fax: (616) 456-2425. Office: US Bank Ct We Dist Mich 780 Fed bldg 110 Michigan St NW Grand Rapids MI 49503

GREGG, JOHN PENNYPACKER, lawyer; b. Phila., May 25, 1947; s. William Pemberton and Sarah E. (High) G. AB, Trinity Coll., 1969; JD, Villanova U., 1974. Bar: Pa. 1974, U.S. Dist. Ct. (ea. dist.) Pa. 1974. Tchr., dir. student activities The Pennington (N.J.) Sch., 1969-71; atty. Pub. Defenders Office, Norristown, Pa., 1974—, High, Swartz, Roberts & Seidel, Norristown, 1975—; bd. dirs. Rittenhouse Book Distbr. Inc., King of Prussia, Pa. Bd. dirs. Phila. Toboggan Co., Lansdale, 1987-91, Lower Merion Shared Housing Corp., Ardmore, Pa., 1991-95, Lower Merion Affordable Housing, Narberth, Pa., 1995—, The Episcopal Acad., Merion, Pa., 1986-89; ann. giving com. Inglis House, Phila., 1991-92. Recipient Legion of Honor Chapel of the Four Chaplains, Phila., 1980, Harry L. Green Svc. award, 1990, Disting. Svc. award Episcopal Acad., 1990. Mem. Pa. Bar Assn., Montgomery Bar Assn. (com. chmn. 1991-94). Home: 635 Walnut Ln Haverford PA 19041-1225 Office: High Swartz Roberts & Seidel 40 E Airy St Norristown PA 19401-4803

GREGG, JUDD, senator, former governor; b. Nashua, N.H., Feb. 14, 1947; m. Kathleen MacLellan, 1973; children—Molly, Sarah, Joshua. A.B., Columbia U., 1969; J.D., Boston U., 1972, LL.M., 1975. Bar: N.H. 1972. Ptnr. Sullivan, Gregg and Horton, Nashua, N.H.; mem. 97th-100th Congresses from 2d N.H. dist., Washington, 1981-89; governor of N.H., Concord, 1989-93; U.S. Senator from N.H., 1993—; mem. Budget/Appropriations Com.; chmn. Appropriations Subcom. on Commerce, Justice, State, Judiciary; chmn. Labor and Human Resources Subcom. on Children & Families; mem. N.H. Gov.'s Exec. Coun., 1978-80. Pres. Crotched Mountain Rehab. Found. Mem. ABA, N.H. BAr Assn., Nashua Bar Assn. Office: US Senate 393 Senate Russell Bldg Washington DC 20510-2904

GREGG, LAUREN, women's soccer coach; b. Rochester, Minn., July 20, 1960. BS in Psychology, U. N.C.; MS in Counseling and Consulting Psychology, Harvard U. Asst. soccer coach U. N.C., 1983; asst. coach Harvard U., Cambridge, Mass.; head coach U. Va., 1987-95; asst. coach U.S. Women's Nat. Soccer Team. Named Coach of Yr. Nat. Soccer Coaches Assn. Am., 1990; recipient Gold medal Atlanta Olympics, 1996; Marie Jane postgrad. scholar. Office: US Soccer Fedn US Soccer House 1801 S Prairie Ave Chicago IL 60616-1357*

GREGG, LAWRENCE J., physician; b. Shawnee, Okla., July 29, 1944; s. L.J. and Annell (Criswell) G.; m. Lynda Antoinette Lawrence, May 15, 1985; children: Laura K., Kimberly B. Rogers, Lawrence James. BS, U. Okla., 1967, MD, 1970. Diplomate Am. Bd. Dermatology. Intern St. Francis Hosp., Wichita, 1970-71; resident in dermatology U. Okla., Oklahoma City, 1973-76; dermatologist Tulsa Dermatol. Clinic, 1976—; clin. prof. U. Okla., Tulsa. Capt., flight surgeon USAF, 1971-73. Fellow Am. Acad. Dermatology; mem. Dermatol. Surg. Soc., Okla. State Dermatol. Soc. (pres. 1981-82), Tulsa City Dermatol. Soc. (sec.). Avocations: photography, travel. Office: Tulsa Dermatol Clinic PO Box 52588 2121 E 21st St Tulsa OK 74114-1409

GREGG, LUCIUS PERRY, JR., aerospace executive; b. Henderson, N.C., Jan. 16, 1933; s. Lucius Perry and Rachel (Jackson) G.; m. Doris Marie Jefferson, May 30, 1959 (dec. Nov. 1980); 1 child, Lucius Perry III; m. Beverly E.E. Ward, Jan. 3, 1994. BSEE, U.S. Naval Acad., 1955; MS in Aero and Astronautics, MIT, 1961; AMP Program, Harvard U., 1975; D of Sci. (hon.), Grinnell Coll., 1973. Pilot, aircraft commdr. mil. air command USAF, 1956-59; project scientist Air Force Office Scientific Rsch., Washington, 1961-65; dir., rsch. coord., assoc. dean sci. Northwestern U., Evanston, Ill., 1965-69; program officer Alfred P. Sloan Found., N.Y.C., 1969-72; pres. First Chgo. U. Finance Corp., Chgo., 1972-79; v.p. First Nat. Bank Chgo., 1972-79; v.p. corp. planning Bristol-Myers Co., N.Y.C., 1979-83; dir. nat. pub. rels., v.p. gov. rels. Citibank/Citicorp, N.Y.C., 1983-87; v.p. pub. affairs N.Y. Daily News, N.Y.C., 1987-89; v.p. corp. communications Hughes Electronics Corp., L.A., 1989—; vis. com. on aero and astronautics MIT, Cambridge, 1971-79; vis. com. on physics Harvard U., Cambridge, 1973-79; mem. commn. on human resources Nat. Acad. Sci., Washington, 1973-78; vice chmn., bd. dirs. Corp. for Pub. Broadcasting, Washington, 1975-81; bd. trustees W Net Pub. TV, N.Y.C., 1981-89; bd. dirs. Chgo. Coun. on Fgn. Rels., Chgo., 1975-79; mem. academic bd. U.S. Naval Acad., Annapolis, Md., 1971-81; mem. NASA U. Rels., Washington, 1968-72; chmn. bd. Tulane U., New Orleans, 1972-82; trustee Roosevelt U., Chgo., 1976-79, Loyola Marymount U., L.A., 1994—, Freeman Hosps. Found., L.A., 1994—; mem. Ill. Commn. on Urban Gov., Chgo., 1976-79, Chgo. Mayor's Coun. Econ. Advisors, Chgo., 1976-79; intelligence rev. com. Chgo. Police Depart., 1977-79. Maj. USAF, 1965-85. Named Engr. of Yr. Washington Acad. Sci., 1964, One of 10 Outstanding Young Men Chgo. Jr. Assn. Commerce and Industry, 1966. Office: Hughes Electronics Corp PO Box 956 200 N Sepulveda Blvd El Segundo CA 90245-0956

GREGG, MARIE BYRD, retired farmer; b. Mount Olive, N.C., Jan. 12, 1930; d. Arnold Wesley and Martha (Reaves) Byrd; m. Robert Allen Gregg, July 11, 1953; children: Martha Susan, Kathryn Elizabeth, Kenneth Allen. BA in Elem. Edn., Furman U., 1951. Tchr. 3rd grade Greenville (S.C.) City Schs., 1951-53; med. social worker Ctrl. Carolina Rehab. Hosp., Greensboro, N.C., 1959-61; window display designer Kerr Rexall Drugs, Durham, N.C., 1960's; shop owner Something Else Antiques, Lima, Ohio, 1979-81; farm owner Mt. Olive, 1978-92. Democrat. Methodist. Avocations: antique collecting, traveling, reading, interior decorating. Home and Office: 212 Baucom Park Dr Greer SC 29650-2972

GREGG, MICHAEL B., health science association administrator, epidemiologist; b. Paris, Jan. 6, 1930; married; three children. BA, Stanford U., 1952; MD, Western Reserve U. Sch. Medicine, 1956. Diplomate Am. Bd. Med. Examiners, Am. Bd. Preventive Medicine. Intern in internal medicine Presbyn. Hosp., N.Y.C., 1956-57, jr. asst. resident in internal medicine, 1957-58, sr. asst. resident in internal medicine, 1958-59; sr. asst. surgeon USPHS, NIH, Rocky Mountain Lab., 1959-61, surgeon, 1962; research assoc. div. infectious diseases U. Md. Sch. Medicine, 1962-63; research assoc. Inst. Internat. Medicine U. Md., 1963-64, asst. prof., 1964-66; acting assoc. dir. Pakistan Med. Research Ctr., Lahore, 1964, dir. dept. malariology, 1964, dir. dept. serology and immunology, 1964-65; chief epidemic intelligence service, epidemiology program Ctr. for Disease Control, 1966-68; dir. viral diseases div. Bur. Epidemiology, Ctrs. Disease Control, 1968-76, dep. dir., 1970-81; dep. dir. epidemiology program office Ctrs. for Disease Control, 1981-88, dir. epidemiology program office, 1988-89; pvt. practice specializing in epidemiology and disease control, 1989—; editor Ctrs. for Disease Control Morbidity and Mortality Weekly Report, 1967-88; cons. on poliomyelitis WHO, Geneva, 1969; cons. to govt. of Indonesia for WHO, 1969, 70, 72, 74, 78; internat. cons. to various countries for WHO, 1969-81; mem. com. on Viral Hepatitis div. Med. Scis., NRC, Washington, 1970-74; mem. Ctrs. for Disease Control Study Sect. Office Rsch. Grants, 1970-72; mem. Data Registry Com. Nat. Cystic Fibrosis Found., Atlanta, 1972-78; mem. U.S. Influenza Del. to the USSR, 1973. Fellow Am. Coll. Epidemiology; mem. AAAS, Am. Pub. Health Assn., Am. Epidemiol. Soc., Alpha Omega Alpha. Home and Office: 855 Stony Hill Rd Brattleboro VT 05301

GREGG, PAULA ANN, middle school educator; b. Corpus Christi, Tex., Feb. 26, 1956; d. Roy Paul and Mary Faye (Smith) G. BS, Coll. of Charleston, 1978; MEd, U. S.C., 1987, postgrad.; PhD, Clemson U., 1998. Cert. elem. and mid. sch. math. tchr., S.C. Tchr. Bells Elem. Sch., Ruffin, S.C., 1979-80; tchr. math. Hanberry Mid. Sch., Blythewood, S.C., 1980-86, Northside Mid. Sch., West Columbia, S.C., 1986-92, Irmo Mid. Sch., Columbia, S.C., 1992-98; with Converse Coll., Spartanburg, S.C., 1998—. Pres. Walterboro (S.C.) Jaycee-ettes, 1979. Named Tchr. of Yr., Northside Mid. Sch., 1992. Mem. NEA, S.C. Edn. Assn., Nat. Coun. Tchrs. Math. (v.p. mid. schs. 1985), S.C. Coun. Tchrs. Math., Daus. of Nile. Baptist. Avocations: singing, pianist, bowling, reading, walking. Home: 1070J Hunt Club Ln Spartanburg SC 29301 Office: Converse Coll 580 E Main St Spartanburg SC 29302

GREGG, WALTER EMMOR, JR., financial corporation executive, accountant, lawyer; b. Utica, N.Y., Sept. 24, 1941; s. Walter Emmor Sr. and Anne (Roberson) G.; m. Pamela Greco, Oct. 25, 1969; children—Ashlee Anne, Marguerite Tadman. B.S. in Psychology, U. Pitts., 1968, J.D., 1973. CPA, Pa. Bar: Pa. 1973. Asst. dist. atty. Allegheny County Dist. Atty. Office, Pitts., 1972-74; resident counsel, asst. sec. PNC Fin. Corp., Pitts., 1975-77, asst. gen. counsel, asst. sec., 1978-83, sr. v.p., treas., chief regulatory counsel, 1983-87, sr. v.p., chief regulatory counsel, 1987, exec. v.p., 1987-89, exec. v.p. fin. and adminstrn., 1989—; vice chmn. Banc Corp., Pitts., 1999—; bd. dirs. PNC Venture Corp., PNC Bridge Capital Inc., Pitts. Nat. Leasing Corp. Bd. dirs. D.T. Watson Rehab. Hosp., Sewickley, Pa., 1985, Watson Healthcare, Inc., Sewickley, 1988, Sewickley YMCA, 1985—. Mem. ABA, Pa. Bar Assn., Allegheny County Bar Assn., Am. Soc. Corporate Secs., Nat. Assn. Accts., Am. Inst. CPA's, Pa. Inst. CPA's. Republican. Episcopalian. Club: The Duquesne (Pitts.). *

GREGG-MULLINGS, LINDA, educator; b. N.Y.C., Nov. 8, 1949; d. Eldredge Payne and Ruth Barrymore Gregg; m. Paul Anthony Mullings, Apr. 25, 1970 (div. Apr. 1974); 1 child, Andre. BBA, Baruch Coll., 1972, MPA, 1997; postgrad., Rutgers U., 1997—. Full charge bookkeeper Nat. Assn. Supply Coop., N.Y.C., 1966-72; sr. analyst Trans World Airlines, N.Y.C., 1974-85; asst. mgr. Don Travel-UN, N.Y.C., 1983-85; pres., CEO SFASS, Inc., N.Y.C., 1979-96; graphics operator Custom, N.Y.C., 1989-98; instr. Baruch Coll., N.Y.C., 1998—. Treas. LeFrak City Tenants Assn., N.Y.C., 1984. Mem. Am. Soc. Pub. Adminstrn., Baruch Coll. Alumni Assn., Pi Alpha Alpha. Avocation: travel. Home: PO Box 737697 Elmhurst NY 11373

GREGOIRE, CHRISTINE O., state attorney general; b. Auburn, Wash.; m. Michael Gregoire; 2 children. BA, U. Wash.; JD cum laude, Gonzaga U., 1977. Clerk, typist Wash. State Adult Probation/ Parole Office, Seattle, 1969; caseworker Wash. Dept. Social and Health Scis., Everett, 1974; asst. atty. gen. State of Wash., Spokane, 1977-81, sr. asst. atty. gen., 1981-82; dep. atty. gen. State of Wash., Olympia, 1982-88; dir. Wash. State Dept. Ecology, 1988-92; atty. gen. State of Wash., 1992—; dir. Wash. State Dept. Ecology, 1988-92. chair Puget Sound Water Quality Authority, 1990-92, Nat. Com. State Environ. Dirs., 1991-92, States/B.C. Oil Spill Task Force, 1989-92. Mem. Nat. Assn. Attys. Gen. (consumer protection and environment com., energy com., children and the law subcom.). *

GREGOR, DOROTHY DEBORAH, librarian; b. Dobbs Ferry, N.Y., Aug. 15, 1939; d. Richard Garrett Heckman and Marion Allen (Richmond) Stewart; m. A. James Gregor, June 22, 1963 (div. 1974). BA, Occidental Coll., 1961; MA, U. Hawaii, 1963; MLS, U. Tex., 1968; cert. in Library Mgmt., U. Calif., Berkeley, 1976. Reference libr. U. Calif., San Francisco, 1968-69; dept. libr. Pub. Health Libr. U. Calif., Berkeley, 1969-71, tech. services libr., 1973-76; reference libr. Hamilton Libr., Honolulu, 1971-72; head serials dept. U. Calif., Berkeley, 1976-80, assoc. univ. libr. tech. svcs. dept., 1980-84, univ. libr., 1992-94; ret., 1994; chief Shared Cataloging div. Libr. of Congress, Washington, 1984-85; univ. libr. U. Calif.-San Diego, La Jolla, 1985-92, OCLC asst. to pres. for acad. and rsch. libr. rels., 1995-98; instr. sch. libr. and info. studies U. Calif., Berkeley, 1975, 76, 83; cons. Nat. Libr. of Medicine, Bethesda, Md., 1985, Ohio Bd. Regents, Columbus, 1987; trustee Online Computer Libr. Ctr., 1988-96; dir. Nat. Coordinating Com. on Japanese Libr. Resources, 1995-98. Mem. ALA, Libr. Info. Tech. Assn., Program Com. Ctr. for Rsch. Librs. (bd. chair 1992-93, Hugh Atkinson award 1994).

GREGOR, TIBOR PHILIP, management consultant; b. Levoca, Czechoslovakia, Apr. 25, 1919; s. Philip and Emma (Aufricht) G.; m. Helen Frances Lorenz, Sept. 15, 1942 (dec. 1989); children: Jan Michael, Charlotte Anne; m. Valma Costa, Dec. 17, 1994. Student, U. London, 1938-41. Gen. sales mgr. Eastern Steel Products Ltd., Toronto, Ont., Can., 1952-57; pres., gen. mgr. Roneo Co. Ltd., Toronto, 1957-63, also Roneo, Inc., Phila.; pres. Mcpl. Sand & Gravel Co., Kingston, Ont., 1964-71; exec. dir. Can. Soft Drink Assn., Toronto, 1972-86; pres. T.P. Gregor Assocs., Toronto, 1986—. Author: On the Employment of Mentally Handicapped, 1971. Pres. Met. Toronto Assn. for Mentally Retarded, 1961-64; past pres. Can. Assn. for Mentally Retarded, 1969-71, life mem.; vice chmn. Toronto Centennial Com., 1964-67; founder, chmn. Friends of Royal Can. Acad. Arts, 1985-89; chmn. Can. Fund for Czech and Slovak Univs. With Czechoslovak Armoured Brigade Group, Brit. Forces, 1940-45; lt. col. ret. Decorated Medal of Merit; Paul Harris fellow, 1980. Mem. Toronto Bd. Trade, Can. Soc. Assn. Execs., Am. Soc. Assn. Execs., Royal Can. Mil. Inst. Club, Toronto Law Tennis Club, Rotary (past treas., bd. dirs. Rotary Internat., past trustee, v.p. Rotary Found. (Can.) Ltd.), Masons. Mem. United Ch. Home and Office: 218 Glen Rd, Toronto, ON Canada M4W 2X3

GREGORI, MARIA ISABEL, critical care nurse; b. N.Y.C., Dec. 1, 1955; d. Jose and Maria (Perez) Gonzalez; m. Jose M. Gregori, Nov. 7, 1981; children: Danielle Elizabeth, Michael Alexander. BSN cum laude, Molloy Coll., 1980. RN, N.Y.; cert. post anesthesia nurse. Clin. nurse neorology ICU Meml. Sloan Kettering Hosp., 1980-83, clin. nurse post anesthesia care unit, 1983—. Mem. STT, ASPAN, N.Y. State Post Anesthesia Nurses Assn. Office: Meml Sloan Kettering Hosp 1275 York Ave New York NY 10021-6007

GREGORIAN, VARTAN, academic administrator; b. Tabriz, Iran, Apr. 8, 1934; came to U.S., 1956; s. Samuel B. and Shushanik G. (Mirzaian) G.; m. Clare Russell, Mar. 25, 1960; children: Vahe, Raffi, Dareh. Grad., Coll. Armenian, 1955; BA, Stanford U., 1958, PhD, 1964; hon. degree, Boston U., 1983, Brown U., 1984, Jewish Theol. Seminary, 1984, SUNY, 1985, Johns Hopkins U., 1987, NYU, 1987, U. Pa., 1988, Dartmouth Coll., 1989, Rutgers U., 1989, CUNY, 1990, Tufts U., 1994. From instr. to assoc. prof. history San Francisco State Coll., 1962-68; assoc. prof. UCLA, 1968; from assoc. prof. to prof. U. Tex., 1968-72, dir. spl. programs, 1970-72; Tarzian prof. Armenian and Caucasian history U. Pa., Phila., 1972-80; dean U. Pa. (Faculty Arts and Scis.), 1974-78, provost, 1978-80; pres. N.Y. Pub. Libr., 1981-89; prof. New Sch. Social Rsch., N.Y.C., 1984-89; prof. History and Near Eastern studies NYU, 1984-89; pres., prof. History Brown U., Providence, 1989-97; pres. Carnegie Corp., N.Y.C., 1997—. Author: The Emergence of Modern Afghanistan, 1880-1946, 1969. Bd. dirs. Aaron Diamond Found., 1990-97, Brookings Instns., 1994—, Inst. for Internat. Edn., 1989—, Internat. League of Human Rights, 1984-97, Inst. for Advanced Study, 1987—, J. Paul Getty Trust, 1988—; chmn. bd. visitors Grad. Sch. and Univ. Ctr., CUNY, 1984-90; bd. trustees Mus. Modern Art, 1994—. Decorated Officier de l'Ordre des Arts et Lettres (France), Grand Official Ordem Infante D. Henrique Portuguese Govt., 1995; recipient Danforth E.H. Harbison Teaching award 1969, Cactus Teaching award 1971, award of distinction Phi Lambda Theta and Phi Delta Kappa, 1980, Silver Cultural medal Italian Ministry Fgn. Affairs, 1977, Gold medal of honor City and Province of Vienna, Austria, 1976, 1st Disting. Humanist award Pa. Humanities Coun., 1983, Nat. Fellowship award Fellowship Commn., Phila., 1984, Gold medal Nat. Inst. Social Scis., 1985; fellow Social Sci. Rsch. Coun., 1960, Ford Found. Fgn. Area Tng., 1960-62, Am. Coun. Learned Socs.-Social Sci. Rsch. Coun., 1965, John Simon Guggenheim Found., 1971-72, Social Sci. Rsch. Coun., 1971-72, Am. Coun. Edn., 1973. Fellow Acad. Arts Scis., Am. Philos. Soc.; mem. Am. Antiquarian Soc., Am. Hist. Assn. (program chmn. 1972), Am. Philos. Soc. (grantee 1965, 66), Internat. Fedn. Libr. Assns. (co-chmn. program com. 1985), Assn. Advancement Slavic Studies (program chmn. Western Slavic Conf. 1967), Mid-East Studies Assn., Coun. Fgn. Rels., Grolier Club, Round Table, Century Club, Econ. Club, Phi Beta Kappa. Office: Carnegie Corp Office of the Pres 437 Madison Ave 27th Fl New York NY 10022*

GREGORICH, PENNY DENISE, purchasing agent; b. Newark, Ohio, May 27, 1968; d. William Raymond and Ethel Faye (Wineman) G. AS in Office Adminstrn., Ctrl. Ohio Tech. Coll., 1989, AS in Bus. Mgmt., 1991; postgrad., Otterbein Coll., 1991—. Accts. receivable clk. Rockwell Automotive, Newark, 1987-89, purchasing trainee, 1989-92, inventory control specialist, 1992—; bookkeeper's asst. Spenley Newspapers/Fostoria Times Rev., Newark, 1986-87. Licking County Joint Vocat.-Tech. Sch./Coop. Office Edn. historian, 1985-86. Mem. NAFE, Pinnacle Non-traditional Honor Soc., Licking County Humane Soc., Phi Theta Kappa, Tau Pi Phi. Avocations: classic cars, auto racing, coin collecting, photography, taekwondo (purple belt). Office: Rockwell Internat Rt 79 Heath OH 43056-1440

GREGORIE, CORAZON ARZALEM, operations supervisor; b. Bethesda, Md., Aug. 6, 1947; d. Faustino and Rosalina Arzalem. AA in Bus. Adminstrn., Palm Beach Coll., 1967; postgrad., Fla. Atlantic U., 1967; BA in Bus. Adminstrn., U. Fla., 1969. Mgmt. trainee Burdines Dept. Store, West Palm Beach, Fla., 1969; adminstrv. asst. divsn. econs. Nat. Food Processors Assn., Washington, 1970-71, statis. analyst divsn. econs. and stats., 1972-77, acting dir. divsn. econs. and stats., 1978; asst. editor Airfare Pub. Co., Washington, 1979-81; product specialist Arbitron Co., Beltsville, Md., 1982-83; tng. supr. Arbitron Co., Laurel, Md., 1984-87; night shift ops.

supr. Arbitron Co., Columbia, Md., 1988—; collective mem., bd. dirs. Glut Food, Mt. Rainier, Md., 1973-78. Force vol. Nat. Park Svc., Washington, 1973-76; coord. College Park Food Coop., Md., 1970-72. Mem. Lotus Ltd. (bd. dirs. 1974—, treas., parts and tech. chmn., membership dir., corr. sec.). Avocations: photography, sports cars. Office: Arbitron Co 9705 Patuxent Woods Dr Columbia MD 21046-1572

GREGORY, ANN YOUNG, editor, publisher; b. Apr. 28, 1935; d. David Marion and Pauline (Adams) Young; m. Allen Gregory, Jan. 29, 1957; children: David Young, Mary Peyton. BA with high distinction, U. Ky., 1956. Sec. Ky. Edit. TV Guide, Louisville, summer 1956; traffic mgr. Sta. WVLK, Lexington, 1956-61; part-time tchr. adult basic edn. Wise County (Va.) Sch. Bd., St. Paul, 1966-72; adminstrv. asst. Appalachian Field Svcs., Children's TV Workshop, St. Paul, 1971-74; editor, co-pub. Clinch Valley Times, 1974—; pres. Clinch Valley Pub. Co., Inc., St. Paul, 1974—; mem. mktg. com. Mountain Empire TechPrep Consortium, 1993—. Editor, text writer: The Flood of '77 in the St. Paul Area, 1977; weekly newspaper columnist: Of Shoes...and Ships...and Sealing Wax, 1974—. V.p. St. Paul PTA, 1970-73; trustee Lonesome Pine Regional Libr. Bd., 1972-80, chmn., 1978-80; chmn. com. to establish br. libr. in St. Paul, opened 1975; mem. adv. bd. Pro-Art, Wise County chpt. Va. Mus. Fine Arts, 1979-86; co-leader Brownie troop Girl Scouts U.S.A., 1971-76, bd. dirs. Appalachian coun., 1983-95, 1st v.p., 1985-91; mem. adv. bd. Wise County YMCA, 1977-80; mem. Wise County Bd. Edn., 1975—, vice-chmn., 1981-99; pres. So. Region Sch. Bds. Assn., 1987-88; mem. Va. Edn. Block Grants Adv. Com., 1981-86, Region I State Literacy Coun., 1989-91; mem. Local Vocat. Adv. Coun., 1980—, chmn., 1981—; mem. statewide planning coun. Va. Dept. Edn.; mem. Va. Coun. on Vocat. Edn., 1987-95, chmn., 1989-91; mem. exec. com. Va. H.S. League, 1984-88; past pres. Wise County Humane Soc., Inc.; bd. dirs. Va. Sch. Bds. Assn., 1979-89, pres., 1985-86; bd. dirs. Va. Literacy Found., 1987-89, Appalachian Ednl. Lab., 1995—; sec., treas. S.W. Va. Pub. Edn. Found. Bd., 1993—; mem. Mountain Empire C.C. Found. Bd., 1994—; mem. adv. com. Va. State Supt. Pub. Instrn., 1993-96; mem. devel. and comty. rels. com., mem. music adv. com. Clinch Valley Coll.; mem. adv. bd. Wise Appalachian Regional Hosp., 1995-98; mem. Wise County Info. Tech. Task Force, 1998—, St. Paul Tomorrow Steering Com., 1998—. Named Outstanding Clubwoman of Yr., St. Paul Jr. Women's Club, 1964, 66, Outstanding Citizen, S.W. Va. dist. Va. Fedn. Women's Clubs, 1968, Woman of Yr. Wise County/Norton Dem. Women's Club, 1986, Citizen of Yr., Wise County C. of C., 1990; recipient Rufus Beamer award Va. Poly. Inst., 1989, William P Kanto Meml. award for contbns. to edn. Clinch Valley Coll., Mountain Empire C.C. and Wise County and Norton Pub. Schs., 1990, Literacy award S.W. Reading Coun., 1994; Ky. Broadcasters Assn. scholar, 1956. Mem. Va. Press Assn. (1st pl. award for editl. writing 1976), Nat. Press Women, Va. Press Women, Nat. Newspaper Assn., Women in Comms., Nat. Sch. Bds. Assn. (pub. rels. com., nominating com. 1987), Mortar Bd., Delta Kappa Gamma (hon. mem. Alpha Psi chpt.), Phi Beta Kappa, Alpha Delta Pi, Chi Delta Phi, Alpha Epsilon Rho, Alpha Lambda Delta, Theta Sigma Phi. Democrat. Methodist. Home: PO Box 303 Saint Paul VA 24283-0303 Office: PO Box 817 Saint Paul VA 24283-0817

GREGORY, BETTINA LOUISE, journalist; b. N.Y.C., June 4, 1946; d. George Alexander and V. Elizabeth Friedman; m. John P. Flannery, II, 1981; 1 child, Diana Elizabeth. Student, Smith Coll., 1964-65; diploma in acting, Webber-Douglas Sch. Dramatic Art, London, 1968; BA in Psychology, Pierce Coll., Athens, Greece, 1972; LittD (hon.), Susquehanna U., 1988, St. Thomas Aquinas U., 1992; LLD (hon.), Wilmington Coll., 1989; D in Journalism (hon.), U. Findlay, 1990. Reporter Sta. WVBR-FM, Ithaca, N.Y., 1972-73, Sta. WCIC-TV, Ithaca, 1972; reporter, anchorwoman Sta. WGBB, Freeport, N.Y., 1973, Sta. WCBS, N.Y.; freelance reporter, writer AP, N.Y.C., 1973-74; freelance reporter N.Y. Times, 1973-74; with ABC News, 1974—; corr. ABC News, Washington, 1977-79; White House corr. ABC News, 1979—, sr. gen. assignment corr., 1980—; elected rep. for corr.'s ABC News Women's Adv. Bd. Reporter TV spl. Flaws in the Shield, 1989 (1st pl. Headliner award), A&E's Biography of Hillary Rodham Clinton, 1994 (Best Documentary ACE award 1994), Murder Trial O.J. Simpson (Edward R. Murrow award Best News Series 1996). Recipient 1st Place award Nat. Feature News, Odyssey Inst., N.Y., 1978, Clarion award Women in Communications, Inc., 1979, hon. mention Nat. Commn. on Working Women, 1979, Media award for Am. Agenda segment on homeless World Hunger Found., 1990, Cable Ace Best Documentary award, 1995, Edward R. Murrow award for coverage of O.J. Simpson Murder trial, 1996; named one of top 10 investigative reporters, TV Guide, 1983. Mem. Radio TV Corrs. Assn., White House Corrs. Assn. Clubs: Newswomen's N.Y. (recipient Front Page award 1976); Nat. Press; Washington Press. Office: ABC News Washington Bur 1717 Desales St NW Washington DC 20036-4407

GREGORY, CALVIN, insurance service executive; b. Bronx, N.Y., Jan. 11, 1942; s. Jacob and Ruth (Cherchian) G.; m. Rachel Anna Carver, Feb. 14, 1970 (div. Apr. 1977); children—Debby Lynn, Trisy Sue; m. 2d, Carla Deane Deaver, June 30, 1979. AA, L.A. City Coll., 1962; BA, Calif. State U.-L.A., 1964; MDiv, Fuller Theol. Sem., 1968; MRS, Southwestern Sem., Ft. Worth, 1969; PhD in Religion, Universal Life Ch., Modesto, Calif., 1982; DDiv (hon.), Otay Mesa Coll., 1982. Notary pub., real estate lic., casualty lic., Calif.; ordained to ministry Am. Baptist Conv., 1970. Youth minister First Bapt. Ch., Delano, Calif., 1964-65, 69-70; youth dir. St. Luke's United Meth. Ch., Highland Park, Calif., 1969-70; tchr. polit. sci. Maranatha High Sch., Rosemead, Calif., 1969-70; aux. chaplain U.S. Air Force 750th Radar Squadron, Edwards AFB, Calif., 1970-72; pastor First Bapt. Ch., Boron, Calif., 1971-72; ins. agt. Prudential Ins. Co., Ventura, Calif., 1972-73, sales mgr., 1973-74; casualty ins. agt. Allstate Ins. Co., Thousand Oaks, Calif., 1974-75; pres. Ins. Agy. Placement Svs., Thousand Oaks, 1975—; head youth minister Emanuel Presbyn. Ch., L.A., 1973-74; owner, investor real estate, U.S., Wales, Eng., Can., Australia. Counselor YMCA, Hollywood, Calif., 1964, Soul Clinic-Universal Life Ch., Inc., Modesto, Calif., 1982. Mem. Apt. Assn. L.A., Life Underwriter Tng. Coun., Forensic Club (L.A.), X32 Club (Ventura, Calif.), Kiwanis (club spkr. 1971). Republican. Office: Ins Agy Placement Svc PO Box 4407 Thousand Oaks CA 91359-1407

GREGORY, DEIRDRE DIANNE, secondary educator; b. Fairview Park, Ohio, Feb. 12, 1958; d. Richard Whiting and Ruth Elizabeth (Moody) Mason; m. Thomas Bradford Gregory, July 15, 1995. BS, Ashland U., 1981; MS, Ohio State U., 1986; MEd, Ashland U., 1989, U. Dayton, 1993. Cert. tchr., Ohio; cert. vocat. family and consumer sci. sch. guidance counselorand supr. Tchr. home econs. Mansfield (Ohio) City Schs., 1981-93, coord. GRADS, 1993—; mem. adv. bd. Mansfield (Ohio) City Schs. Parents as Tchrs., 1993—, Pioneer Career and Tech. Ctr. GRADS Adv. Bd., Shelby, Ohio, 1993—; chair Children Family Health Svcs. Consortium, Mansfield, 1996-98. Named one of Tw Thousand Notable Am. Women, 1993, Outstanding Young Woman, 1987-88, 88-89, 97-98. Mem. AAUW (pres. 1997-99), Mansfield Sch. Employee Assn. (pres. 1994-95), Am. Assn. Family and Consumer Sci., Order of Eastern Star, Kappa Omicron Phi, Phi Delta Kappa (pres. 1994-96, historian 1996-98). Republican. Presbyterian. Avocations: reading, singing, music, cross stitch, walking. Home: 411 Overlook Rd Mansfield OH 44907-1533 Office: Mansfield Sr H S 145 W Park Blvd Mansfield OH 44906-2621

GREGORY, DICK, comedian, civil rights activist; b. St. Louis, Oct. 12, 1932; m. Lillian Smith, 1959; children: Michele, Lynne, Paula, Pamela, Stephanie, Gregory, Christian, Ayanna, Miss, Yohance. Student, So. Ill. U., 1951-53, 55-56. Lectr. univs. throughout U.S.; nutritionist world-heavyweight boxing champion Riddick Bowe, 1992. Entertainer, Esquire Club, Chgo., opened night club, Apex, Robbins, Ill., master ceremonies, Roberts Show Club, Chgo., 1959-60, night club appearances, Akron, Milw., Chgo., 1960, San Francisco, Hollywood, numerous other cities, 1961—, comedy act, Playboy Club, Chgo., 1961; TV guest appearances Jack Paar show, others; record albums Dick Gregory: The Light Side-Dark Side; others; Author: The Back of the Bus, 1962, Nigger, 1964, What's Happening, 1965, The Shadow That Scares Me, Write Me In, No More Lies, 1971, Dick Gregory's Political Primer, 1971, Dick Gregory's Natural Diet for Folks Who Eat, Cookin' With Mother Nature, 1973, Dick Gregory's Bible Tales, with Commentary, 1974, Up From Nigger, 1976, (with Mark Lane) Code Name Zorro: The Murder of Martin Luther King, Jr, 1977, Murder in Memphis, 1993. Peace and Freedom party presdl. candidate, 1968. Served with AUS, 1953-55. Winner Mo. mile championship, 1951, 52; named Outstanding Athlete So. Ill. U., 1953; recipient Ebony-Topaz Heritage and Freedom award, 1978. Creator Dick Gregory's Bahamian Diet Drink, 1984. Office: Dick Gregory Hlth Enterprises PO Box 3270 Plymouth MA 02361-3270

GREGORY, FREDERICK D., career officer, space agency administrator; b. Washington, Jan. 7, 1941; s. Francis Anderson and Nora Drew Gregory; m. Barbara Ann Archer, June 3, 1964; children: Frederick D. Jr., Heather Lynn Gregory Skeens. BS in Aerospace Engring., USAF Acad., 1964; MS in Info. Systems, George Washington U., 1977; DSc, U. D.C., 1986. Cert. astronaut shuttle comdr. Commd. 2nd lt. USAF, 1964, advanced through grades to col., 1983, helicopter pilot, 1964-69, fighter pilot, 1969-70; exptl. test pilot NASA and USAF, 1971-78; astronaut NASA, Houston, 1978-93; assoc. adminstr. NASA, Washington, 1992—; sr. advisor Reliability and Maintainability Symposium, Washington, 1992—; active Aerospace Safety and Adv. Panel, Washington, 1992—. Bd. dirs. Young Astronaut Coun., Washington, 1988—, Kaiser Permanente Mid-Atlantic States, 1994—, Nat. Capital Area coun. Boy Scouts Am., 1996—; bd. visitors Air Force Inst. Tech., Maxwell AFB, Ala., 1993—. With USAF, 1970-74. Decorated Legion of Merit, Air medal (16), Disting. Flying Cross (2); recipient Air Force Meritorious Svc. medal USAF, Def. Superior Svc. medal Dept. Defense, Nat. Intelligence Achievement medal CIA, Black Sci. award Nat. Tech. Assn., Pres. award Black Enterprise Mag., George Washington U. Outstanding Alumni award. Mem. AMVET, Am. Helicopter Soc., Daedalians, The Naval Order, Soc. Experimental Test Pilots, Assn. Space Explorers. Avocations: power boating, audio/video equipment, automobiles, reading, world travel. Office: NASA Safety & Mission Assurance 300 E St SW Washington DC 20546-0005

GREGORY, GEORGE ANN, writer, Native American educator; b. Ft. Smith, Ark., Aug. 17, 1945; d. George Eugene Miller and Maxine (Manuel) Eggensperger; m. Gavino Sanchez, June 21, 1995; children: Matthew Gregory, James Smiley. BA, U. Ark., 1969; MA, U. N.Mex., 1987, PhD, 1993. Ordained min., 1977. Grad. asst. U. N.Mex., Albuquerque, 1984-89, 92-93; instr. Oglala Lakota Coll., Kyle, S.D., 1989-90; lectr. No. Ariz. U., Flagstaff, 1990-92; dir. Ho Anumpoli!, Albuquerque, 1995—; adj. prof. U. N.Mex., 1993—; cons., evaluator Indian Edn. Albuquerque, 1988-96; cons. emergency med. svcs. acad. U. N.Mex., 1994-95; cons. Okla. Native Am. Langs. Devel. Inst., 1990. Author: (short story) People Before Columbus, 1993, (poetry) Neon Pow Wow, 1993, (juvenile) Mr. Finnegan and the Bear, 1990 (Honorable Mention), (textbook) Native American Holocaust for Beginners, 1997; editor: Nizhoni mag., 1985; guest poet Writer's Alive, Corrales, N.Mex., 1995, 96. Ednl. task force Commn. on Indian Affairs, 1994-99; mem. Multicultural Task Force, Albuquerque, 1995; mem. ops. com. Women Studies U. N.Mex., 1994-95; mem. pres.'s ad hoc com. Native Am. Student Concerns U. N.Mex., 1986-87, Dept. Justice Seed com.; treas. Albuquerque Indian Ctr., 1999. Emma Mae Olson scholar Native Am. Coll. Edn. U. N.Mex., 1986; named Top Ten Native Am. Scholars Cornell U., Ithaca, N.Y., 1993. Mem. Native Am. Tchrs. Assn., Native Writer's Circle of Ams., Soc. Study Indigenous Langs. Scientology. Avocations: Aztec dancing, costuming, painting. Home: PO Box 40184 Albuquerque NM 87196-0184 Office: Ho Anumpoli! 137 Manzano St NE Apt C Albuquerque NM 87108-1362

GREGORY, HEROLD LA MAR, chemical company administrator; b. Farmington, Utah, Nov. 9, 1923; s. Elijah B. and Julia Ellen (Tree) G.; m. Mary Ethel Eccles, Aug. 15, 1951; children—Vicki McGregor, Walter E., Suellen Winegar. B.A., U. Utah, 1949. Exec. dir. Utah Symphony, Salt Lake City, 1957-86; asst. to chmn. Huntsman Corp., 1986—; pres. East German mission Ch. of Jesus Christ of Latter-day Saints, Berlin, 1953-57, mission sec., 1949-51; assoc. prof. arts adminstrn. U. Utah, 1976-85. Mem. Mormon Tabernacle Choir, 1978-85, adminstrv. asst. 1987—; mem. Utah Symohony Chorus, 1985—; sec. Utah Symphony Bd., 1957—, Tanner Gift of Music Trust, 1983—; bd. dirs. Utah chpt. Freedoms Found. Valley Forge. With AUS, 1943-45. Home: 3215 Skycrest Cir Salt Lake City UT 84108-1611 Office: 500 Huntsman Way Salt Lake City UT 84108-1235 *The guiding light in my life has been an abiding faith in the eternal destiny of man and a never ending quest to determine or identify my earthly mission and achieve it, thus reaching my full human potential.*

GREGORY, JAMES, retired actor; b. N.Y.C., Dec. 23, 1911; s. James Gillen and Axemia Theresa (Ekdahl) G.; m. Ann Catherine Miltner, May 25, 1944. Grad. high sch. Actor, 1936—. Actor: (summer stock prodns.) Deer Lake, Pa., 1936-37, 39, Millbrook, N.Y., 1938, Braddock Heights, Md., 1940, Buck's County Playhouse, New Hope, Pa., 1941, Ivy Tower Playhouse, Spring Lake, N.J., 1951, (Broadway shows) Key Largo, 1939, Journey to Jerusalem, 1940, In Time to Come, 1941, Dream Girl, 1945, All My Sons, 1947, Death of a Salesman, 1948-49 (played Biff on Broadway with 5 Willy Lomans), Dead Pigeon, 1954, Fragile Fox, 1955, Desperate Hours, 1956-57, (films) The Young Strangers, 1955, Al Capone Story, 1955, Gun Glory, 1956, Nightfall, 1956, The Big Caper, 1956, A Distant Trumpet, 1961, Underwater Warrior, 1962, PT-109, 1965, The Sons of Katie Elder, 1967, The Manchurian Candidate, 1967, Captain Newman, M.D. 1967, Million Dollar Duck, 1968, Clam Bake, 1967, Secret War of Harry Frigg, 1968, Beneath the Planet of the Apes, 1970, The Hawaiians, 1970, Shoot Out, 1971, The Late Liz, 1971, $1,000,000. Duck, 1971, The Strongest Man in the World, 1974, The Main Event, 1979, Wait Til Your Mother Gets Home, 1982, X-15, Death of a Salesman, also 5 Matt Helm pictures, (TV shows) Big Valley, Bonanza, Gunsmoke, Rawhide, Playhouse 90, Climax, Alfred Hitchcock Presents, Twilight Zone, Quincy, as Inspector Luger in Barney Miller, Mr. Belvedere, 1986. Served with USNR, USMCR, 1942-45, PTO. Mem. Soc. Preservation and Encouragement Barber Shop Quartet Singing Am. Club: Hollywood Hackers, Golf. Home: 55 Cathedral Rock Dr Unit 33 Sedona AZ 86351-8624

GREGORY, JERRY, real estate agent; b. London, Ky., Jan. 8, 1956; s. Chester and Gladys Gregory. BS, Union Coll., 1978. Ins. salesman Woodmen of the World, Omaha, 1981-82; advt. salesman Wilderness Road Advt., London, 1983—; real estate salesman Robinson Realty, London, 1987—. Editor: History of Laurel County Churches, 1988; author: Touching the Past, 1996. Capt. Rep. Party, Bush, Ky., 1988—. Mem. Laurel County Kiwanis. Mem. Assembly of God Ch. Avocation: photography. Home: 11201 E Laurel Rd London KY 40741-7119

GREGORY, JOHN C., artist, sculptor; b. Phila., Jan. 13, 1930; s. John Charles and Emilie G.; m. Jacqueline Helene Theis, Aug. 14, 1954; children: Elizabeth Lee, Mindy Emilie. Student, Kenyon Coll., 1947-51, Phila. Mus. Sch. Art, 1949-53. Sculptor, painter Gregory Studio, Phila., 1956-94, Natick, Mass., 1994—. Represented in permanent collections including Nat. Portrait Gallery, Washington, Silkeborg Mus., Denmark, Container Corp. Am., Chgo., Am. Psychiatric Assn., Washington, Pa. Hosp., Phila., Temple U., Phila., U. Pa., Phila.; private collections. Home and Studio: 75 Park Ave Natick MA 01760-2038

GREGORY, JOHN FORREST, information technology consultant, writer; b. Springfield, Mass., Apr. 3, 1950; s. Howard Burdett and Mary Augustine (Reilly) G. BS of Fgn. Svc., Georgetown U., 1972; MSLS, Simmons Coll., 1974. Libr. Libr. of Congress, Washington, 1974-78, Sino-Soviet Inst., George Washington U., Washington, 1978-80, The Heritage Found., Washington, 1981-96; market rsch. and analysis staff U.S. Postal Svcs. Hdqrs., Washington, 1997—, market rsch. specialist, 1998—, mkt. rsch. specialist, 1998—; cons. 1997-98. Author: Climber's Guide to Carderock, 1980, Rocksport! Tools Training and Technique for Climbers, 1989. Democrat. Roman Catholic. Home: 4114 Davis Pl NW Apt 105 Washington DC 20007-3948 Office: US Postal Svc HQ 475 Lenfant Plz SW Washington DC 20260-0004

GREGORY, KARL DWIGHT, economist, educator, consultant; b. Detroit, Mar. 26, 1931; s. Bertram and Sybil (Wynter) G.; m. Tenicia Ann Banks, June 7, 1959; children: Karin Diane, Sheila Therese, Kurt David. BA, Wayne State U., 1952, MA, 1957; PhD, U. Mich., 1962. Fiscal economist Office of Mgmt. and Budget, Washington, 1961-64; prof. Wayne State U., Detroit, 1960-61, 64-68; prof. Oakland U., Rochester, Mich., 1968-96, disting. prof. emeritus, 1996—, ret.; chmn. bd., interim CEO Greater Detroit Bidco, Inc., 1996; mem. coun. econ. advisors Gov. Engler of Mich., 1992-96; cons. UN Devel. Program, Beijing, People's Republic of China, 1991; chief organizer, dir. First Ind. Nat. Bank Detroit, 1968-81, interim pres., 1980-81; vis. prof. SUNY, Buffalo, 1975; vis. scholar, mem. exec. staff U.S. Congl. Budget Office, Washington, 1975-76; chmn. bd., chief exec. officer Accord, Inc., Detroit, 1969-71. Author (with others) State of Black Michigan, 1984-87, 91; contbr. articles to pubns. Trustee Episcopal Diocese of Mich., Detroit, 1981-83, 84-87, 90-92; mem. Gov.'s Entrepreneurial Commn., Lansing, Mich., 1984-88, Regional Devel. Initiative S.E. Mich. Coun. Govts., 1990-91, Gov.'s Task Force on Tourism, Lansing, 1986-89; bd. dirs., v.p. United Way S.E. Mich., Mich. Ctr. High Tech., 1991-95. 1st lt. U.S. Army, 1953-56. Recipient rsch. award Detroit chpt. NAACP, 1987, entrepreneurial awards Small Bus. Adminstrn., 1989, Mich. Dept. Commerce, 1992. Mem. Nat. Econ. Assn. Avocations: reading, music, photography, travel. Home: 18495 Adrian St Southfield MI 48075-1803

GREGORY, LEWIS DEAN, trust company executive; b. Wichita, Kans., May 13, 1953; s. Harry Samuel III and Virginia Dorothy (Womer) G.; m. Laura Lorraine Davis, March 4, 1978; children: Paul Lewis, Erin Elizabeth. BA in Communications, U. Kans., Lawrence, 1975; MS in Journalism, U. Kans., 1976; JD, Washburn U., 1983. Bar: Kans. 1984, U.S. Dist. Ct. Kans. 1984. Cons. Delta Upsilon Frat., Inc., Indpls., 1975-76; mktg. rep. IBM, Kansas City, Mo., 1976-80; assoc. Hershberger, Patterson, Jones & Roth, Wichita, 1983-84; trust mktg. mgr. Bank IV Wichita, 1984-86; v.p., trust officer, sales mgr. BancOklahoma Trust Co., Tulsa, 1986-88, Boatmen's Trust Co., Kansas City, 1988-97; dist. trust mgr. Merrill Lynch Trust Co., 1997—. Dir. Am. Heart Assn., Wichita, Kans., 1985-86; pres. YMCA Men's Club, Tulsa, 1987-88; del. Rep. Party, Tulsa, 1988; trustee Leukemia Soc., 1992-96. Mem. ABA, Kans. Bar Assn., Johnson County Bar Assn., Kansas City Met. Bar Assn., Estate Planning Soc., Kiwanis, Kans. Univ. Alumni Assn. (pres. Greater Kansas City chpt. 1994-96, nat. bd. dirs. 1997—), Delta Upsilon (Indpls. dir. 1987-90, dir. Kans. chpt. 1977-90). Republican. Methodist. Avocation: running. Home: 12205 Aberdeen Rd Shawnee Mission KS 66209-1208

GREGORY, MARY SHARON, educator; b. Washington, June 24, 1947; d. John Lynn and Dolores Katherine (Monahan) Sullivan; m. Brent E. Gregory, Aug. 16, 1969; children: Kathleen, Jean, Anne. BA, U.Ill., 1969; MA, Chgo. State U., 1973. Tchr. English Homewood/Flossmoor (Ill.) Jr. High Sch., 1969-72, U. Chgo. Lab. Schs., 1972-75, Dominican High Sch., Whitefish Bay, Wis., 1978-90, Homestead High Sch., Mequon, Wis., 1990—. Recipient Sen. Herb Kohl Tchr. award, 1990. Mem. Nat. Coun. Tchrs. English, Wis. Coun. Tchrs. English, Milw. Alliance English Tchrs. (planning com. 1987-99). Avocations: reading, travel.

GREGORY, MEL HYATT, JR., retired insurance company executive; b. Frankfort, Ky., Mar. 28, 1936; s. Mel Hyatt and Audrey (Fraley) G.; m. Joyce Klein, Sept. 9, 1955; children: Susan Gregory Lawson, Scott, Lisbeth Gregory Olesky. BS, Stetson U., 1958. Mgr., agt. Equitable Life Ins. Co., Louisville, 1959-66; agy., mgr. Equitable Life Ins. Co., Dayton, Ohio, 1966-70, Atlanta, 1970-73; v.p. Equitable Life Ins. Co., Cin., 1974-77; sr. v.p. Equitable Life Ins. Co., N.Y.C., 1978-85; pres. so. ops. Equitable Life Ins. Co., Atlanta, 1985-90; exec. v.p. Equitable Life Ins. Co., N.Y.C., 1990-93; ret., 1993; bd. dirs. Ga. Blue Cross, Greater Ga. Life Ins. Co. Bd. dirs. Stetson U. Sch. Bus. Capt. U.S Army, 1958-62. Mem. Gen. Agts. and Mgrs. (pres. 1966-74), Canoe Brook Country Club, Cherokee Country Club. Republican. Home: 4570 Jett Rd NW Atlanta GA 30327-4562

GREGORY, MYRA MAY, religious organization administrator, educator; b. N.Y.C., Sept. 21, 1912; d. Thomas and Anna (Collins) G. *Father Thomas Gregory, a deacon, and mother Anna (nee Collins) were members of the Berean Baptist Church, which was the first church in New York built by a Negro Congregation from foundation to belfry. The same distinction is afforded the parsonage built during the pastorate of Dr. Schuyler Thomas Eldridge. Sister Beatrice (diploma Maxwell Teacher Training, 1930; BS in Edn. Bklyn. Coll., 1939, MS City College, 1952) was a New York City teacher and acting principal. She was honored by the Berean Baptist Church for 60 years of service as an administrator, educator, and musician. Aunt Bessie Collins was a Berean Baptist Church teacher, honored for decades of outstanding service. Grandfather Nicholas E. Collins, ordained pastor of the African Methodist Episcopal (AME) Zion Church, was a Navy veteran in the Spanish American War.* Diploma, Maxwell Tchrs. Tng. Sch., Bklyn., 1933; BS in Edn., Bklyn. Coll., 1940, MA in History, 1952. Cert. music tchr. Tchr. N.Y.C. Bd. Edn., Bklyn., 1943-75; social worker Berean Bapt. Ch., Bklyn., 1932-48, supr., 1932-94, fin. sec. Sunday sch., 1935-94; bd. dirs. Berean-Vacation Bible Sch., Bklyn., 1935-86; tchr. Protestant Coun., N.Y.C., 1940-81; bd. dirs. Recreation Bedford-Stuyvesant Area Project, Bklyn.; dir. seminar Christian Teaching, Bklyn., 1974-86, 1990—. *Myra Gregory served her community through the borough presidential project, Aiding Children's Education (ACE), which promoted pre-school parent involvement. The Berean Baptist Church (the first church in the history of the United States to be built by an African American congregation from foundation to belfry) afforded enriching experiences through varying tenures of service involving administrative, educational, and editorial responsibilities which maintained lines of communication with the community. She held the challenging position of executive secretary/educator of the Bedford-Stuyvesant Area Project, Inc., through which juvenile delinquents were guided to discover their talent and potential for noble creativity. Under the separate aegis of the Brooklyn Church and Mission Federation and the New York City Board of Education, her service as a demonstration teacher affected the professional growth of student teachers. She also served as an orchestra director and a music appreciation educator.* Bd. mgrs. Bklyn. Sun. Sch. Union, 1974—; bd. dirs. Bklyn. Divsn. Coun. of Chs. 1974—; pres. Bklyn. divsn. Coun. of Ch. N.Y.C., 1984-86. Named Tchr. of Yr. Cmty. Sch. Bd. Dist. 14, Bklyn., 1973, Outstanding Tchr., Stuyvesand divsn., Bklyn. Sunday Sch. Union, 1977, Educator/Leader Berean Bapt. Ch., 1977; recipient Ecumenism citation Borough Pres.'s Office, Bklyn., 1985, Religious Educator citation Bklyn. Ch. Women United, Inc., 1993, Cmty. Svc. awrd Mayors Office, N.Y.C., 1993, Ecumenical Svc./Educator Honors Office the Coun. City of N.Y., 1994, Lifetime Achievement award Bklyn. Coll., 1995, Outstanding Svc. award Coun. Chs. the City of N.Y., 1995, Leadership/Educator Citation Borough Pres. Office, Bklyn., 1999. Mem. ASCD, Am. String Tchrs. Assn., Am. Viola Soc., Assn. Childhood Edn. Internat., Orgn. Am. Historians, Ctr. Study of Presidency, Assn. Bible Tchrs. Democrat. Avocations: string ensemble, drama, writing. *When one reverently and humbly acknowledges that each individual is created by God to be his "temple", then life becomes a journey exemplifying the ideals and commands of His Son. Love's banner is seen regardless of challenging self-sacrifice.*

GREGORY, NORMAN WAYNE, chemistry educator, researcher; b. Albany, Oreg., June 23, 1920; s. Arthur Donald and Edith Florence (Self) G.; m. Lillian Virginia Larson, May 21, 1943; children: Norman Wayne Jr., Martha Jean, Brian Neil. Student, Lower Columbia Jr. Coll., 1936-38; B.S., U. Wash., Seattle, 1940, M.S., 1941; Ph.D., Ohio State U., 1943. Research chemist Radiation Lab., U. Calif., Berkeley, 1944-46; instr. U. Wash., Seattle, 1946-47, asst. prof., 1947-53, assoc. prof., 1953-57, prof. chemistry, 1957-89, prof. emeritus, 1989—, chmn. dept., 1970-75. Author: Physical Chemistry, 1964; contbr. articles to profl. jours. Mem. Am. Chem. Soc. (chmn. Puget Sound sect. 1964, treas. 1962), Sigma Xi. Office: U Wash PO Box 351700 Seattle WA 98195-1700

GREGORY, RICHARD JOSEPH, youth services professional; b. Syracuse, N.Y., Feb. 13, 1952; s. Joseph Howard Gregory and Marian Louise (Illenberg) Soper; m. Virginia Ruth McKean, July 31, 1976; children: Melissa, Jonathan. BA, Ind. U., 1974. Dist. exec. Illowa Coun. Boy Scouts Am., Davenport, Iowa, 1974-81; dist. dir. Two Rivers Coun. Boy Scouts Am., St. Charles, Ill., 1981-84; program dir. Rainbow Coun. Boy Scouts Am., Morris, Ill., 1984-88; asst. coun. exec. Lake Huron Area Coun. Boy Scouts Am., Auburn, Mich., 1988—; program instr. Nat. Camp Sch. Boy Scouts Am., Oconomowoc, Wis., 1987; asst. dir. activities mobilization, 1997 Nat. Jamboree Boy Scouts, Fredericksburg, Va.; dir. Nat. Cub Scout Camp Sch., Kellogg Ctr., Mich., 1999. Mem. bicentennial planning commn. C. of C. Davenport, Iowa, 1975; youth activities chmn. Kiwanis Club, Muscatine, Iowa, 1978-80; dir. youth activities Optimist Club, Aurora, Ill., 1982-84. Mem. Michigoning Lodge- Order of the Arrow (asst. chief of the fire 1988-99). Office: Lake Huron Area Coun Boy Scouts Am PO Box 129 5001 11 Mile Rd Auburn MI 48611

GREGORY, ROBERT GRANVILLE, historian; b. Denver, May 16, 1924; s. Robert Lloyd and Mina Clare (Williams) G.; m. Patricia Dolores Rio, Apr. 16, 1932; children: Robert Joseph, Theresa Mina. BA, UCLA, 1948, MA, 1950, PhD, 1956. Civilian historian SAC, March AFB, Calif., 1956; asst. prof. Wake Forest Coll., Winston-Salem, N.C., 1956-66; asst. prof. history Syracuse (N.Y.) U., 1966-71, assoc. prof., 1971-80, prof., 1971-95, prof. emeritus, 1995—; chair Assn. African Studies Program, Syracuse, 1974-77. Author: Sidney Webb and East Africa, 1962, India and East Africa, 1971, Rise and Fall of Philanthropy in East Africa, 1993, South Asians in East Africa, 1994, Quest for Equality: Asian Politics in East Africa, 1994. Pvt. U.S. Army, 1941-42. Mem. African Studies Assn. Avocation: farming. Home: 3479 Watervale Rd Manlius NY 13104-8600 Office: Syracuse U Dept History Syracuse NY 13244

GREGORY, SHARON E., neonatal clinical nurse specialist; b. San Francisco, Aug. 26, 1955; d. Donald J. and Nadalie S. Goldstein; m. John Karl Gregory, Aug. 31, 1986; 1 chld, Leah Nicole. BSN, U. Fla., 1977; MSN, Emory U., 1985. Cert. CNNP. Staff RN Children's Med. Ctr., Dallas, St. Paul's Hosp., Dallas, Meth. Hosp., Dallas; clin. nurse specialist DeKalb Med. Ctr. ICN, Decatur, Ga. Contbr. articles to profl. jours. Mem. NANN (newsletter editor), GANN (pres.). Home: 603 Collingwood Dr Decatur GA 30032-1721

GREGORY, THOMAS BRADFORD, mathematics educator; b. Traverse City, Mich., Dec. 13, 1944; s. Philip Henry and Rhoda Winslow (Hathaway) G.; m. Deirdre Dianne Mason, July 15, 1995. BA, Oberlin (Ohio) Coll., 1967; MA, Yale U., 1969, M of Philosophy, 1975, PhD, 1977. Lectr. Ohio State U., Mansfield, 1977-78, asst. prof. math., 1978-84, assoc. prof. math., 1984—. Reviewer: Math. Revs., 1984—; contbr. articles to profl. jours. Active Mansfield (Ohio) Symphony Chorus, 1977—, Presbytery Youth Ministries Com., New Philadelphia, Ohio, 1980-87, Ohio State U. Community Singers, Mansfield, 1985—; mem. Presbytery Biblical Authority task force, 1994-95; bd. dirs. Lay Acad. Religion, Wooster (Ohio) Coll., 1997—; commd. lay min. Presbytery of Muskingum Valley, New Philadelphia, Ohio, 1998—. Comdr. USNR, 1969-96. Fellow NSF, Washington, 1967; hon. fellow U. Wis., Madison, 1987-88, 92. Mem. Am. Math. Soc. (translator 1974-82), Ohio Coun. Tchrs. Math., Am. Soc. Naval Engrs., Res. Officers Assn., Naval Res. Assn., Navy League, Phi Beta Kappa (elected assoc. 1997), Sigma Xi, Phi Delta Kappa. Republican. Avocations: classical piano, singing. Home: 411 Overlook Rd Mansfield OH 44907-1533 Office: Ohio State U 1680 University Dr # O-15 Mansfield OH 44906-1547

GREGORY, THOMAS RAYMOND, management consultant; b. N.Y.C., Aug. 15, 1951; s. Thomas Henry and Dorothy Lorraine (Crowe) G.; m. Mary Jo McCormick, June 9, 1973; children: Sean, Brian, Keith. BBA in Mktg., Pace U., 1973; MBA in Food Mktg., St. Joseph's U., 1979. Dist. mgr. Nabisco Brands Inc., N.Y.C., 1973-78; brand mgr. R.J. Reynolds Industries-Del Monte Corp., San Francisco, 1978-84; v.p. mktg. Iroquois Brands Ltd., Stamford, Conn., 1984-85; Ea. sales mgr. Borden Inc., Ft. Lee, N.J., 1985-87; sr. v.p., gen. mgr. Food Enterprises, Inc., Fairfield, N.J., 1987-89; prin. The Apogee Group, Inc., Tequesta, Fla., 1989—. Mem. Am. Mktg Club, Innis Arden (Old Greenwich, Conn.). Roman Catholic. Avocations: sailing, autoracing, golf. Home: 59 Algonquian Dr Natick MA 01760-6094

GREGORY, WILLIAM STANLEY, lawyer; b. Greenwood, Miss., Mar. 12, 1949; s. Carlyle and Charlotte Ruby (Richardson) G.; m. Vicki Sue Lovelady, Aug. 15, 1970. BS in Commerce and Bus. Adminstrn., U. Ala., 1971, MBA, 1973, JD, 1974. Bar: Ala. 1974, U.S. Dist. Ct. (mid. dist.) Ala. 1979, U.S. Ct. Appeals (5th cir.) 1979, U.S. Ct. Appeals (11th cir.) 1980, U.S. Tax Ct. 1979, U.S. Dist. Ct. (no. dist.) Ala. 1991. Assoc. Johnson, Thorington, North, Haskell & Slaughter, Montgomery, Ala., 1974-78; jr. ptnr. Johnson & Thorington, Montgomery, Ala., 1979-90; sr. ptnr. Thorington & Gregory, Montgomery, Ala., 1990—; spl. asst. atty. gen. State of Ala., Montgomery, 1978-82; mem. taxpayer bill of rights drafting com. tax sect. Ala. State Bar, Montgomery, 1990-91. Pres. Montgomery Symphony Assn., 1980, 92, Highland Ave. Adult & Sr. Citizens Ctr., Montgomery, 1986-99; mem. Montgomery Estate Planning Coun. Capt. USAR, 1971-75. Mem. SAR, Kiwanis (v.p. 1989-90). Presbyterian. Avocation: music. Home: 8218 Wynlakes Blvd Montgomery AL 36117-5101 Office: Thorington & Gregory 504 S Perry St Montgomery AL 36104-4616

GREGORY, WILTON D., bishop; b. Chgo., Dec. 7, 1947; s. Wilton and Ethel Duncan G. Student, Niles Coll., Loyola U., Chgo., St. Mary of Lake Sem., Mundelein, Ill., Pontifical Liturgical Inst., Sant'Anselmo, Rome; D in Sacred Liturgy, Pontifical Liturgical Inst., Sant'Anselmo, Rome, 1980. Ordained priest Roman Cath. Ch., 1973, ordained bishop, 1983. Aux. bishop, Chgo., 1983-93; Bishop of Belleville, 1994—; spkr. in field. Author in field. Avocations: travel, music, racquetball, golf. Address: Chancery Office 222 S 3rd St Belleville IL 62220-1916*

GREGSON, GARRY EVAN, network administrator, information consultant; b. Murray, Utah, Dec. 17, 1965; s. Garry Wilbur and Patricia Joan (Rolfson) G.; m. Bonnie Kay Secrist, June 10, 1989; children: Samantha Nishell, Garry William, Maddison Marie, Parker Douglas. BS in Psychology, BS in Health Adminstrn, Weber State U., Ogden, Utah, 1993. Microsoft Cert. Sys. Eng., (MCSE). Pesticide applicator Pest Control, Kelonna, B.C., Can., 1987; personal computer functional test operator IOMEGA, Roy, Utah, 1988; statis. engr. Matrixx Mktg., Ogden, 1988—; habilitation technician North Side Ctr., Ogden, 1989; cons., ptnr. Prestige Mktg., Ogden, 1995—; cons. Estate Mgmt., Ogden, 1995. Co-author: Mount Olympus Power System, 1995. Scoutmaster Boy Scouts Am., Ogden, 1995—; missionary LDS Ch., Des Moines, 1985-87. Recipient Chief Scout award Boy Scouts Can., Calgary, 1979, Duty to God award LDS Ch., Calgary, 1980. Mem. Psi Chi. Avocations: fencing, photography, camping, hiking, fishing. Home and Office: 959 E 325 S Layton UT 84041-4478

GREGWARE, JAMES MURRAY, financial planner; b. Plattsburgh, N.Y., Dec. 17, 1956; s. John William and Patricia Ann (Murray) G.; m. Kathleen Mary Stanley, June 23, 1979; children: Ryan James, Kailee Michelle. BA in Bus. and Psychology, SUNY, Potsdam, 1979. Cert. investment advisor, stockbroker, fin. planner. Commodities trader The Exch., Plattsburgh, 1979-82; stockbroker, collections supr., loan officer Champlain Valley Fed. Savs., Plattsburgh, 1982-84; fin. planner, securities instr. New Life Fin. Services, Waterville, Maine, 1984-87; stockbroker Investacorp, Inc., Waterville and Pittsfield, Mass., 1985-89; pres. Fin. Designs & Mgmt., Inc., Manchester, N.H., 1985—; pres. Eastern Fin. Group, Waterville, 1984-87, Pittsfield, 1987—; stockbroker, fin. planner Investment Ctr. Inc., 1989—; investment mgr. Comfed Savs. Bank, Pittsfield, Mass., 1990-91; pres. Comtrust, Pittsfield, Mass., 1991—. Mem. Nat. Assn. Security Dealers, Coll. Fin. Planning. Republican. Roman Catholic. Avocations: golf, football, baseball, weight-lifting. Home: 11 Riverwind Dr Rexford NY 12148-1223 Office: Comtrust 1450 East St Pittsfield MA 01201-5319 also: Eastern Fin Group NY The Investment Bank Rexford NY 12148

GREIDANUS, IDA, biology educator; b. Mykirk, The Netherlands, July 24, 1945; came to U.S., 1945; d. Emil and Jessie Greidanus; m. Michael Patrick Ley, Jan. 27, 1997. BA, Calvin Coll., 1967; MS, Wayne State U., 1969; EdD, Columbia U., 1984. Prof.biology Passaic County C.C., Paterson, N.J., 1972—, chair sci. dept., 1986-91, 96—. Bd. dirs. N.J. Fed. Credit Union, Totowa, 1976—, North Jersey 4 C's, Paterson, 1972—; founding mem. Paterson Habitat for Humanity, 1984-89. Democrat. Avocations: gardening, art, community service, nature studies, natural history. Office: Passaic County C C 1 College Blvd Paterson NJ 07505-1102

GREIDER, JOHN CALHOUN, English educator; b. Atlanta, Dec. 26, 1928; s. William Fredrick Greider and Nadine Calhoun; m. Marilyn Joanna Muench, Aug. 1, 1964; children: Wendel Calhoun Greider, Courtney Ann Greider. BA, U. Ga., 1953; MA, Peabody Coll. of Vanderbilt, 1956; BD, New Orleans Bapt. Theol. Sem., 1955; PhD, U. Liverpool, Eng., 1966; postgrad., U. Heidelberg, 1959-61, U. Chgo., 1961-63. Instr. English, DePaul U., Chgo., 1961-63; prof. English, U. Thessaloniki, Greece, 1963-64; assoc. prof. English, Kennesaw (Ga.) State U., 1966-72, prof., 1973-97, prof. emeritus, 1997—; chmn. divsn. humanities Kennesaw State U., Marietta, Ga., 1966-83, chmn. dept. English, 1984-85. Author: The Teaching of English, 1964, American Literature: A Critical Bibliography, 1966; editor: Ednl. Studies Jour., 1964. Bd. dirs. Cobb County Youth Mus., Marietta, 1968-70, March of Dimes, Marietta, 1970-75. Mcht. seaman, 1948-49; Lt. USN, 1958-59. Fulbright scholar U.S. Govt., Greece, 1963-64; classical studies grantee Fed. Rep. of Germany, 1960. Mem. MLA, Medieval Assn., Ga. Classical Assn., South Atlantic Modern Lang. Assn., Civitan Internat. (pres. 1978-79, chaplain 1987-99, Outstanding Citizenship award 1975, Civitan of Yr. 1990). Southern Baptist. Avocations: photography, gardening.

GREIF, JOSEPH, lawyer; b. N.Y.C., June 25, 1943; s. Jacob J. and Dorothy (Harrison) G.; m. Aline Bohm, Jan. 1, 1966; children: Jeffrey, Julie. BBA, U. Pitts., 1964; JD, NYU, 1967. Bar: N.Y. 1967, D.C. 1968, U.S. Tax Ct. 1986; CPA, Md., D.C. Instr. No. Va. C.C., Annandale, 1967-68; mgmt. cons. Computer Sci. Corp., Silver Spring, Md., 1967-70; tax mgr. Arthur Andersen & Co., Washington, 1970-75; sr. assoc. Ginsberg, Feldman & Bress, Washington, 1975-77; ptnr. Touche Ross & Co., Washington, 1977-84, McGuffie, Greif, Whitney & Handal, Washington, 1984-90; of counsel McNeily, Rosenfeld & Rubenstein, Washington, 1991-98, Neimark & Nadel, Washington-Ft. Lauderdale, Fla., 1998—; lectr. George Washington U. Grad. Sch. Bus., Washington, 1993-95. Co-author, editor: Managing Membership Societies, 1979; contbr. articles on taxation, comml. leasing, computer systems contracting, exec. compensation, exec. contracts to profl. jours. Bd. dirs. Nat. Assn. for Mental Health, Washington, 1973-75, Combined Health Appeal, Washington, 1980-81, Assn. Devel. Coun., Washington, 1987-89; task force mem. White House Task Force on Charitable Giving, Washington, 1979-80. Mem. AICPA (chmn. fed. tax divsn. task force on exempt orgns. 1983-86), ABA, D.C. Bar Assn., Am. Soc. Assn. Execs. (mem. govt. affairs and long range planning coms., Outstanding Svc. award, tech. sect. coun. 1996—), D.C. Inst. CPAs, Greater Washington Soc. Assn. Execs. (mem. tech. task force 1994—), Computer Law Assn. Avocations: boating, squash. Home: 6108 Wayside Dr North Bethesda MD 20852-3534 Office: Neimark & Nadel Ste 360 5335 Wisconsin Ave NW Washington DC 20015-2032 also: Neimark & Nadel 800 Corporate Dr Ste 420 Fort Lauderdale FL 33334

GREIF, ROBERT, mechanical engineering educator; b. N.Y.C., Jan. 17, 1938; s. Harry and Anne (Reiter) G.; m. Joyce Ambrose; children: Jessica, Andrew. BSME, NYU, 1958; SM, Harvard U., 1959, PhD, 1963. Registered profl. engr., Mass. Staff scientist Missile Systems div., Avco Corp., Wilmington, Mass., 1963-65, sr. staff scientist, 1965-67; asst. prof. mech. engring. Tufts U., Medford, Mass., 1967-70, assoc. prof., 1970-78, prof., 1978—, chmn. dept. mech. engring., 1981-89; cons. Stone & Webster, Boston, 1971-78, U.S. Dept. Transp., Cambridge, Mass., 1977—; vis. scholar Harvard U., Cambridge, 1981; vis. research fellow U. Sussex, Eng., 1974; sr. rsch. assoc. NASA Langley Rsch. Ctr., 1988. Fellow AIAA (assoc.), ASME; mem. AAUP. Office: Tufts U Dept Mech Engring Medford MA 02155*

GREIG, BRIAN STROTHER, lawyer; b. Austin, Tex., Apr. 10, 1950; s. Ben Wayne Greig and Virginia Ann (Strother) Higgins; m. Jane Ann Sentilles, June 17, 1972; children: Travis Darden, Grace Hanna. BA, Washington and Lee U., 1972; JD, U. Tex., 1975. Bar: Tex. 1975, U.S. Dist. Ct. (ea. dist.) Tex. 1976, U.S. Ct. Appeals (5th cir.) 1976, U.S. Dist. Ct. (so. dist.) Tex. 1977, U.S. Dist. Ct. (we. dist.) Tex. 1980, U.S. Supreme Ct. 1980, U.S. DIst. Ct. (no. dist.) Tex. 1984, U.S. Ct. Appeals (11th cir.) 1984. Law clk. to chief judge U.S. Dist. Ct., Beaumont, Tex., 1975-76; ptnr. Fulbright & Jaworski L.L.P., Austin, 1976—; mem. Austin Tomorrow On-Going Goals Assembly Com., 1981; pres. Austin Mgmt. Lawyers Forum, 1987, 93. Editor-in-chief Tex. Assn. Bus. Employment Law Handbook; editorial bd. Tex. Labor Letter. Pres. Austin Lawyers and Accts. for Arts, 1981; trustee Laguna Gloria Art Mus., Austin, 1983-91, pres., 1989-90, chmn., 1990-91; bd. dirs. Zachary Scott Theater Ctr., Austin, 1981; mem. devel. bd. Inst. Texan Cultures, 1991-98; trustee Westminster Manor Health Facilities Corp. of Travis County, Tex., 1991-96, sec., 1995-96; trustee St. Stephen's Episcopal Sch., 1995—; pres. Austin Mus. Art, 1991-92, trustee, 1991-93. Fellow Tex. Bar Found. (life), Am. Coll. Labor and Employment Lawyers; mem. ABA, Am. Arbitration Assn. (employment adv. coun. 1995—), Tex. Bar Assn., Travis County Bar Assn., Tex. Commn. on Human Rights Task Force, Tarry House Club, Headliners Club (trustee 1998—), Met. Club, Admirals Club. Methodist. Avocations: hunting, fishing. Office: Fulbright & Jaworski LLP 600 Congress Ave Ste 2400 Austin TX 78701-3271

GREIG, ROBERT THOMSON, lawyer; b. N.Y., Nov. 23, 1945; s. Robert George and Marion Ethel (Thomson) G.; m. Susan Mary Abrams, Sept. 1, 1973; children—James Andrew, Katherine Helen, Fiona Elizabeth, Robert Charles. A.B., Cornell U., 1967; J.D., U. Mich., 1970, postgrad. (Humphrey fellow), 1971. Bars: Mich. 1971, N.Y. 1972, U.S. Dist. Ct. (so. dist.) N.Y. 1974, U.S. Dist. Ct. (ea. dist.) N.Y. 1974, U.S. Ct. Appeals, 2nd circuit 1975. Law clk. Chief Judge Charles D. Breitel, N.Y. Ct. Appeals, 1971-73; assoc. Cleary, Gottlieb, Steen & Hamilton, N.Y.C., 1973-78, ptnr., 1979—; mem. council Hong Kong Internat. Arbitration Centre. Fellow Chartered Inst. Arbitrators; mem. Am. Law Inst., Am. Soc. Internat. Law, Internat. Bar Assn., ABA, N.Y. Bar Assn., Order of the Coif. Clubs: American, Hong Kong, Royal Hong Kong Yacht, Heights Casino. Contbr. articles to profl. jours. Office: Cleary Gottlieb Steen & Hamilton One Liberty Plz New York NY 10006*

GREIG, THOMAS CURRIE, retired financial executive; b. Edinburgh, Scotland, Dec. 16, 1931; s. Thomas Currie and Elsie E. (Bell) G. M.A., U. Edinburgh, 1953. Chartered accountant. With Peat, Marwick, Mitchell & Co., Toronto, Can., 1956-62; acting mgr. Peat, Marwick, Mitchell & Co., 1961-62; with M. Loeb Ltd., Ottawa, 1962—; v.p., treas. M. Loeb Ltd., 1965-67, sr. v.p., treas., 1967-71, exec. v.p. finance, 1971-72; asst. dep. minister finance Canadian Dept. Nat. Def., Ottawa, 1972-77; asst. dep. minister customs program Canadian Dept. Nat. Revenue, Ottawa, 1977-87; ptnr. Price Waterhouse, Toronto, 1987-90; ret., 1990. Served to lt. Royal Navy, 1953-56. Home: 304-4 Lowther Ave. Toronto, ON Canada M5R 1C6

GREIGG, RONALD EDWIN, lawyer; b. Washington, June 29, 1946; s. Edwin E. and Helen Marie (Marcy) G.; m. Patricia Anne Crowe, June 5, 1968; children: Elizabeth, Rebecca. BBA, Am. U., 1969, MBA in Fin., 1971; JD, Stetson U., 1976. Registered patent atty.; bar: Fla. 1976, D.C. 1978, Va. 1985, U.S. Dist. Ct. (mid. dist.) Fla. 1976, U.S. Dist. Ct. (ea. dist.) Va. 1988, U.S. Ct. Appeals (D.C. cir.) 1979, U.S. Ct. Appeals (fed. cir.) 1982, U.S. Supreme Ct. 1980. Assoc. David E. De Serio, St. Petersburg, Fla., 1977-78, Edwin E. Greigg, Washington, 1979-82, Harris, Barrett & Dew, St. Petersburg, Fla., 1982-84; ptnr. Greigg & Greigg, Arlington, Va., 1984—. Author: A Guide to the FTC Franchise Disclosure Rule, 1979, Patent Infringement Damages, 1988. Mem. ABA, Am. Intellectual property Law Assn., Assn. Internationale pour la Protection de la Propriete Industrielle, Soc. Automotive Engrs., D.C. Bar Assn., Fla. Bar Assn., Va. Bar Assn., Washington Area Lawyers for the Arts, Inst. of Trademark Agts. (London), Internat. Trademark Assn., Phi Alpha Delta. Republican. Episcopalian. Avocations: sailing, classic cars. Office: Greigg & Greigg 5203 Leesburg Pike Ste 600 Falls Church VA 22041-3401

GREILSHEIMER, JAMES GANS, lawyer; b. N.Y.C., Oct. 14, 1937; s. Jerome J. and Lillian (Gans) G.; m. Louise B. Steiner, Aug. 11, 1974; children: Lauren, Julie, Michael, Jeremy. AB cum laude, Princeton U., 1959; LLB, Harvard U., 1962. Bar: N.Y. 1963, D.C. 1969. Asst. U.S. atty. So. Dist. N.Y., 1963-68; litigating asst. corp. counsel City of N.Y., 1974-77, 1st asst. corp. counsel, 1978-80; ptnr. Tenzer, Greenblatt LLP, N.Y.C., 1993—; mediator mediation program U.S. Dist. Ct. (so. dist.) N.Y., 1993—. Mem., sec. N.Y.C. Charter Rev. Commn., 1982-83; pres. N.Y. chpt. Am. Jewish Com., 1981-84; v.p. Jewish Cmty. Rels. Coun. N.Y., 1981-85, bd. dirs., 1995—; bd. dirs. Com. on Decent Unbiased Campaign Tactics, 1983—, Nonprofit Coordinating Com., N.Y., 1985—, Vol. Cons. Group, Inc., 1986—; v.p., bd. dirs. Fund for Pub. Schs., Inc., 1986-91, pres., 1992—; mem. Citizens Budget Commn., Inc., 1991-93. Mem. N.Y. State Bar Assn. (spl. com. on cts. and cmty. 1975-81), New York County Lawyers Assn. (bd. dirs. 1981-87, chmn. fed. cts. com. 1977-80, mem. spl. com. on condemnation 1990—), Assn. Bar of City of N.Y. (mcpl. affairs com. 1979-81, govt. ethics com. 1990—, com. on condemnation and tax certiorari 1993-95). Office: Tenzer Greenblatt LLP 405 Lexington Ave New York NY 10174-0002

GREIN, RICHARD FRANK, bishop, pastoral theology educator; b. Bemidji, Minn., Nov. 29, 1932; s. Lester Edward and LaVina Minnie (Frost) G.; m. Joan Dunwody Atkinson, Nov. 25, 1961; children: David, Margaret, Mary Leslie, Sara. BA in Geology, Carleton Coll., 1955; MDiv, Nashotah House Sem., Wis., 1959; STM, Nashotah House Sem., 1970, DDiv., 1982; DDiv., Gen. Theol. Sem., 1989. Ordained priest Episcopal Ch., 1959; priest-in-charge Elk River mission field, Minn., 1959-63; rector St. Matthew's Ch., Mpls., 1964-69, St. David's Ch., Minnetonka, Minn., 1969-73; prof. pastoral theology Nashotah House Theol. Sem., 1973-74; rector St. Michael and All Angels Ch., Mission, Kans., 1974-81; bishop The Episcopal Ch., Topeka, Kans., 1981-88; bishop co-adjutor The Episcopal Ch., N.Y.C., 1988-89; bishop of N.Y., 1989—; prelate of priory in U.S., Most Venerable Order of Hosp. of St. John of Jerusalem, 1996—. Co-author: Preparing Younger Children for First Communion, 1972. Priest assoc. Order Holy Cross; pres. Guardian Angels Found., Elk River, 1963-64. Hon. Metropolitan, Ecumenical Throne of Ecumenical Patriarch in Istanbul, 1994—. Fellow Coll. Preachers, 1970; mem. Coun. Assoc. Parishes. Office: 1047 Amsterdam Ave New York NY 10025-1747

GREINER, JACK VOLKER, ophthalmologist, physician, surgeon, research scientist; b. Fountain Hill, Pa., Aug. 25, 1949; s. Harry Sandt and Vera Lilian G.; m. Cynthia Ann Mis., May 17, 1980; children: Ashley Lauren, Logan Nicholas Jack, Jordan Dean Jack. AA, Valley Forge Mil. Coll., 1969; BA, U. Vt., 1971; MS in Anatomy, Purdue U., 1974, PhD, U. Toledo, 1975; DO, Midwe. Univ., 1982. Rsch. fellow in ophthalmology Howe Lab. of Ophthalmology, Harvard U. Med. Sch. and Mass. Eye and Ear Infirmary, Boston, 1974-76; rsch. fellow in ophthalmology Harvard U. Med. Sch., Boston, 1975-78, instr. ophthalmology, 1988-90, clin. instr., 1991—; rsch. fellow in corneal and external diseases of eye Schepens Eye Rsch. Inst., Retina Found., 1976-78, clin. assoc. scientist, 1991—; rsch. assoc. in ophthalmology U. Ill. Eye and Ear Infirmary, Chgo., 1979-81, rsch. asst. prof. ophthalmology, 1981-83; med. intern Cook County Hosp., Chgo., 1982-83; resident in ophthalmology Georgetown U. Med. Ctr., 1983-86; adj. asst. scientist Eye Rsch. Inst., Retina Found., Boston, 1978; adj. asst. prof. ophthalmic pathology Midwe. Univ., 1979-82, asst. prof. dept. pathology, 1982-83, assoc. prof., 1983-87; co-dir. Eye Rsch. Lab., Chgo. Osteo. Hosp., 1980-87; clin. fellow in opthalmology Harvard Med. Sch./Mass. Eye and Ear Infirmary, 1986-88; mem. med. staff Beth Israel Hosp., Boston, Winchester Hosp., Lawrence Meml. Hosp., Medford, Melrose-Wakefield Hosp., Boston Regional Med. Ctr., Stoneham, Spaulding Rehab. Hosp., Boston. Patentee in field. Contbr. chpts. to books, over 120 articles to profl. publs. Served to capt. C.E. USAR, 1971-78. Fight For Sight grantee, 1980-82; Nat. Soc. to Prevent Blindness grantee, 1981-82; NIH Nat. Eye Inst. grantee, 1982-85, 92-97. Fellow Am. Acad. Osteopathic Surgeons (pres. 1995-96); mem. AMA, Mass. Soc. Eye Physicians and Surgeons, Am. Assn. Osteo. Specialists, Am. Assn. Osteo. Specialists (bd. cert. in surgery-ophthalmology), Disting. Practioner, Nat. Acads. of Practice (editl. bd.), Am. Bd. of Cert. Surgery, 1994—, Nat. Soc. Prevent Blindness (bd. dirs. Prevent Blindness Mass.), Contact Lens Assn. Ophthalmologists, Assn. Rsch. in Vision and Ophthalmology, Mass. Med. Soc., Am. Acad. Ophthalmology, Sigma Xi, Phi Kappa Phi, Sigma Sigma Phi. Office: Harvard Med Sch 20 Staniford St Boston MA 02114-2508

GREINER, PETER CHARLES, mathematics educator, researcher; b. Budapest, Hungary, Nov. 1, 1938; came to Can., 1957; s. Anthony Charles and Ildiko (Willner) G.; m. Kathryn Susanne Dewald, July 3, 1965; children—Michael Anthony, Melissa Susanne. B.Sc., U. B.C., 1960; M.A., Yale U., 1962, Ph.D., 1964. Instr. math. Princeton U., N.J., 1964-65; asst. prof. math. U. Toronto, Ont., Can., 1965-70, assoc. prof., 1970-77, prof., 1977—; mem. Inst. for Advanced Study, Princeton, N.J., 1973-74; vis. prof. U. Paris VI, 1980-81. Contbr. articles to profl. jours.; editor-in-chief Canadian Jour. Mathematics, 1981—; mem. editorial bd.: Com. Partial Differential Equations, 1976—. Recipient Steacie prize in nat. sci., Can., 1977. Fellow Royal Soc. Can.; mem. Am. Math. Soc., Canadian Math. Soc. Home: 86 Gloucester St #1407, Toronto, ON Canada M4Y 2S2 Office: Univ Toronto, Dept Math, 100 St George St, Toronto, ON Canada M5S 1A1

GREINER, WILLIAM ROBERT, university administrator, educator, lawyer; b. Meriden, Conn., June 9, 1934; s. William Robert and Dolores (Quinn) G.; m. Carol A. Morrissey, Aug. 24, 1957; children: Kevin Thomas, Terrence Alan, Daniel Robert, Susan Lynn. BA, Wesleyan U., Conn., 1956; MA in Econs., Yale U., 1959, JD, 1960, LLM, 1966. Bar: Conn. 1961, N.Y. 1973. Asst. prof. Sch. Bus., U. Wash., 1960-64, assoc. prof., 1964-67; assoc. prof. Sch. Law, SUNY, Buffalo, 1967-69, prof., 1969—, assoc. provost, 1970-74, assoc. dean, 1975-80; assoc. v.p. acad. affairs SUNY, Buffalo, 1980-83; interim v.p. acad. affairs Sch. Law, SUNY, Buffalo, 1983-84, provost, 1984-91, pres., 1991—; cons. in field. Author: (with Harold J. Berman) Nature and Functions of Law, 1966, 72, 80, 96; contbr. articles to profl. jours. Home: 889 Lebrun Rd Amherst NY 14226-4224 Office: U at Buffalo SUNY Box 601600 506 Capen Hall Buffalo NY 14260-1600

GREINKE, EVERETT DONALD, corporate executive, international programs consultant; b. Elmhurst, Ill., Oct. 31, 1929; s. Herman and Marie Barbara (Kline) G.; m. Clara Joan Plasil, Sept. 29, 1951; children: Donald James, David Carl, Mark Andrew. BS with honors, No. Ill. U., 1951, MS with honors, 1956; postgrad., U. Wis., 1956, George Washington U., 1957. Project officer Bur. Aeronautics USN, Washington, 1956-60, asst. br. head Bur. Aeronautics, 1960-61, tech. advisor Automatic Data Processing Office Chief Naval Ops., 1961-65, asst. dir. command/control Office Chief Naval Ops., 1965-67; sr. staff specialist reconnaissance Office Dir. Def. Research and Engring., Washington, 1967-73, sr. staff specialist tactical command, control and intelligence, 1973-76, asst. dir. combat support, 1976-77, dir. combat support, 1977-80, dir. NATO/Europe affairs, 1980-82; acting dep. undersec. internat. programs and tech. Office UnderSec. Def. Research & Engring., Washington, 1982; scientific advisor to Supreme Comdr. NATO/Supreme Hdqrs. Allied Powers Europe, Casteau, Belgium, 1982-86; dep. undersec. internat. programs and tech. Office Undersec. Def. (Acquisition), Washington, 1986-88; internat. programs cons., 1988-90; v.p. corp. devel. Internat. Partnerships Group (Interpar), 1990-93; cons. Def. Sci. Bd. and U.S. industry on internat. cooperation and high tech. programs, 1988—; v.p. Internat. Planning and Analysis Ctr., 1993-96, Global Mktg. Devel. Solutions, 1996—; lectr. on armaments cooperation various orgns., 1977—. Contbr. articles to profl. jours. Pres. Chapel Sq. Sch. PTA, Annandale, Va., 1966-67, v.p. 1965; pres. W.T. Woodson High Sch. PTA, 1972-73; pres. Hope Luth. Ch. Coun., Annandale, 1970-71, mem. ch. coun., 1987-89, mem. bd. elders, 1974-82, mem. planning com., 1986-87, chmn. bldg. com., 1987-92, trustee, 1993—; com. chmn. Boy Scouts Am., Annandale, 1966-68, chmn. Explorer Post, Annandale, 1972-73, scoutmaster, 1968-78; Santa Claus for local civic orgns., Annandale, 1961-94. Comdr. USNR, 1951-55. Decorated Def. D.S.M. (3), Def. Meritorious Service Medal; Comdr.'s Cross (Austria); recipient Def. Outstanding Pub. Service award, Service plaque W.T. Woodson High Sch. PTA, 1973, Service award Boy Scouts Am., 1975, Disting. Alumni award No. Ill. U., 1987. Mem. Nat. Def. Indsl. Assn., Armed Forces Com. Elec. Assn. Lutheran. Avocations: gardening, fishing. Home: 8315 Toll House Rd Annandale VA 22003-4630

GREISEN, KENNETH INGVARD, physicist, emeritus educator; b. Perth Amboy, N.J., Jan. 24, 1918; s. Ingvard C. and Signa (Nielsen) G.; m. Elizabeth C. Chase, Apr. 12, 1941 (dec.); children: Eric Winslow, Kathryn Elise; m. Helen A. Leeds, Mar. 27, 1976 (dec. 1996). Student, Wagner Coll., 1934-35; BS, Franklin and Marshall Coll., 1938; PhD, Cornell U., 1942. Instr. Cornell U., 1942-43, asst. prof., 1946-48, assoc. prof., 1948-50, prof. physics, 1950-84, prof. emeritus, 1984—, chmn. dept. astronomy, 1976-79, univ. ombudsman, 1975-77, dean faculty, 1978-83; scientist Manhattan Project, Los Alamos, 1943-46. Fellow Am Phys. Soc.; mem. Am. Astron. Soc., Internat. Astron. Union, Nat. Acad. Sci., AAUP. Rsch. cosmic rays. Home: 379 Savage Farm Dr Ithaca NY 14850-6505

GREISLER, DAVID SCOTT, healthcare executive; b. McKeesport, Pa., Mar. 12, 1956; s. Roy Sylvester and Dorothy Lorraine (Turney) G.; m. Stephanie Josanna Rouse, Jan. 17, 1981. BA, Johns Hopkins U., 1978; M Health Svc. Adminstrn., George Washington U., 1981; MPA, U. So. Calif., 1995, DPA, 1997. Assoc. adminstr. Lewistown (Pa.) Hosp., 1981-85, sr. v.p., 1985-88; assoc. adminstr. York (Pa.) Yosp., 1988-93; cardiovascular adminstr. York Hosp. and Health Sys., 1993—. Contbr. articles to profl. jours. Bd. dirs. York County Blind Ctr., 1995—, exec. com., 1996—. Sr. acad. fellow Mt. Vernon Coll., 1996-97. Mem. Am. Coll. Healthcare Execs., Am. Coll. Cardiovascular Adminstrs. (mem. strategic focus com. 1997—). Avocations: running, weightlifting, church, family, home. Home: 180 Lynbrook Dr N York PA 17402-3238 Office: York Health Sys 1001 S George St York PA 17403-3676*

GREIST, MARY COFFEY, dermatologist; b. Ft. Wayne, Ind., Jan. 31, 1947; d. George Alma and Irene Katherine (Zollinger) Coffey; m. Timothy William Greist, June 10, 1972; children: Heather Maria, Thomas Coffey, Timothy Michael. BA, Valparaiso (Ind.) U., 1969; MD, Ind. U., 1973. Intern in family medicine Duke U., Durham, N.C., 1973-74, resident in dermatology, 1974-77; asst. prof. dermatology sch. medicine Ind. U., Indpls., 1977-82, clin. asst. prof. dermatology sch. medicine, 1982—; pvt. practice Indpls., 1982—; dermatology cons. Eli Lilly and Co., Indpls., 1977-86, Elizabeth Arden and Co., Indpls., 1978-88, Medicare-Blue Cross/Blue Shield, Indpls., 1989—. Mem. Ind. State Dermatological Soc. (sec. 1985, v.p. 1986, pres. 1987-88). Democrat. Avocation: gardening. Office: Greist & Ozols Dermatology 6820 Parkdale Pl Ste 211 Indianapolis IN 46254-4670

GREITZER, EDWARD MARC, aeronautical engineering educator, consultant; b. N.Y.C., May 8, 1941; s. Arthur O. and Harriet G.; m. Helen Moulton, Nov. 24, 1966; children: Mary Lee, Jennifer Elizabeth. BA, Harvard U., 1962, MS, 1964, PhD, 1970. Asst. project engr. Pratt & Whitney divsn. United Techs., East Hartford, Conn., 1969-76; indsl. fellow commoner Churchill Coll., Cambridge U., Eng., 1975-76; asst. prof. MIT, Cambridge, 1977-79, assoc. prof., 1979-84, prof., dir. Gas Turbine Lab., 1984-96, H.N. Slater prof. aero. and astronautics, 1988—, assoc. head dept., 1996—; sr. rsch. engr. United Techs. Rsch. Ctr., East Hartford, 1976-77, dir. aeromech., chem. & fluid sys., 1996-98; Royal Soc. guest fellow, SERC vis. fellow, overseas fellow Churchill Coll., Cambridge U., 1983-84; vis. fellow Japan Soc. for Promotion of Sci., 1987, Peterhouse, Cambridge U., 1990-91; mem. aeronautics adv. com. NASA, 1990-94; mem. sci. adv. bd. USAF, 1992-96. Contbr. articles to profl. jours., handbooks. Recipient T. Bernard Hall prize Instn. Mech. Engrs., London, 1978, Exceptional Civilian Svc. award USAF, 1996. Fellow AIAA (Air Breathing Propulsion Best Paper award 1987), Nat. Acad. Engring., ASME (gas turbine award 1977, 79, 96, Freeman scholar in fluids engring. 1980, bd. dirs. Internat. Gas Turbine Inst. 1993-98, chmn. 1996-97, chmn. turbomachinery com. 1989-91, chmn. gas turbine scholar selection com. 1989-93, turbomachinery com., Best Paper award 1991, 92, 95, Aircraft Engine Tech. award 1995, Controls and Diagnostics com. Best Paper award 1998). Avocations: jogging, photography, rock climbing. Home: 77 Woodridge Rd Wayland MA 01778-3611 Office: MIT Dept Aeronautics & Astronautics Bldg 31-264 Cambridge MA 02139

GREJTAK, GENA RENEE, critical care nurse; b. Litchfield, Ill., Oct. 15, 1962; d. George Vincent and Beulah Jean (Duvall) G.; 1 child, Corey Grejtak-Heaps. Diploma, Deaconess Coll. Nursing, 1986; BSN, Webster U., 1991. RN, Mo.; cert. ACLS, BLS instr., IV therapist, chemotherapist. Staff nurse emergency dept. Deaconess Hosp., St. Louis, 1985-86; clin. nurse surg. floor Barnes Hosp., St. Louis, 1986-88, charge nurse surg. ICU, 1988-91; clin. cons. IVAC Corp., 1991; head nurse IV therapy/ nutritional support Deaconess Hosp., St. Louis, 1991; charge nurse, staff nurse cardiac cath/E.P. lab Barnes Hosp., 1991-94; dir. edn. and infection control Integrated Health Svcs. St. Louis at Gravois, 1994-96; newborn & spl. care nursery nurse Deaconess Hosp., St. Louis, 1996—. Mem. AACN.

GREMBOWSKI, EUGENE, retired leasing company executive; b. Bay City, Mich., July 21, 1938; s. Barney Thomas and Mary (Senkowski) G.; m. Teresa Ann Frasik, June 27, 1959; children: Bruce Allen, Debora Ann. AA, Allan Hancock U., 1963; BA, Mich. State U., 1967; MBA, George Washington U., 1972. Lifetime cert. profl. contracts mgr.; CLU. Enlisted USAF, 1955, commd. 2d lt., 1968, advanced through grades to capt., 1971; pers. officer USAF, Goldsboro, N.C., 1968-70; chief of procurement USAF, Cheyenne, Wyo., 1971-73; contract analyst USAF, Omaha, 1973-76; chief of contracting USAF, Atwater, Calif., 1976-79; ret. USAF, 1979; office supr. Farmers Ins. Group of Cos., Merced, Calif., 1980-85, office mgr., 1985-86; corp. fleet mgr. L.A., 1986-95; corp. transp. mgr., v.p. Fig Leasing Co., L.A., 1995-96; ret., 1996. Author: Governmental Purchasing: Its Progression Toward Professional Status, 1972. Cubmaster Boy Scouts Am., Goldsboro, 1968; com. chmn. Am. Heart Assn., Merced-Mariposa, Calif., 1985, sec.-treas., 1986. Decorated Commendation medals, 1965, 70, 79; recipient Meritorious Svc. medals Office of the Pres., 1973, 76. Mem. Nat. Contract Mgmt. Assn., Nat. Assn. Fleet Adminstrs., Am. Legion (life), Air Force Assn. (life), Ret. Officers Assn. (life). Avocations: travel, stamp collecting, amateur golf, financial planning and investing. Home: 1988 Antelope Hill Ct Henderson NV 89012-2182

GREMILLION, DAVID H(ENRY), internist, educator; b. L.A., Sept. 30, 1946; s. Tellisma James and Arvillia Belle (Crichton) G.; m. Charlotte Matthews, Aug. 17, 1968; children: Christy, Elizabeth, Laura, Scott. BS, La. State U., 1968, MD, 1972. Diplomate Am. Bd. Internal Medicine. Commd. 2d lt. USAF, 1968, advanced through ranks to col., 1984, ret., 1988; intern, resident David Grant Med. Ctr., Fairfield, Calif., 1972-75; chief infectious disease Wilford Hall Med. Ctr., San Antonio, Tex., 1977-84; chmn. dept. medicine David Grant Med. Ctr., Fairfield, Calif., 1984-88; prof. U. N.C. Sch. of Medicine, Chapel Hill, 1988—; infectious disease cons. U.S.A.F. Surgeon Gen., Bolling AFB, Md., 1977-80; mem. Gov.'s Crime Commn. State N.C., Raleigh, 1994—. Editor: (book) Problems in Critical Care, 1990; contbr. articles to various profl. jours., 1977—. Fellow ACP, Infectious Diseases Soc. Am.; mem. AMA, N.C. Med. Soc., Wake County Med. Soc. (mem. exec. com., chair ann. delegation). Avocations: wood working, hiking, photography. Home: 2016 Prescott Pl Raleigh NC 27615-5554 Office: 2024 New Bern Ave Raleigh NC 27610-2429

GREMMEL, GILBERT CARL, family physician; b. Robstown, Tex., Nov. 29, 1922; s. Albert Henry and Tennie Elizabeth Gremmel; m. Helen Kistler, 1949 (div. 1965); children: Gilbert Jr., Shirley, Rebecca, Susan, Curtis, James; m. Ilse Elizabeth Schreiber Bell, Apr. 23, 1969; children: Erika Barbara, Albert Henry, Heidi. MD, U. Tex., Galveston, 1951; BA, U. Tex., San Antonio, 1978, BBA in Fin., 1982. Diplomate Am. Bd. Family Practice. Intern U.S. Army, San Antonio, 1951-52; pvt. practice Boerne, Tex., 1955-64, San Antonio, 1964-82, Sonora, Tex., 1982-86, Halletsville, Tex., 1986-88; family physician Med. Networks, Houston, 1988, Med. Clinic, Mabank, Tex., 1988-90; pvt. practice Shamrock, Tex., 1990-92, Seminole, Tex., 1992—; chief of staff Meml. Hosp., Seminole, Tex., 1995—; emergency physician S.W. Med. Assocs., Rockport, Tex., 1990—. Trustee Boerne County Line Ind. Sch. Dist., 1959-62; pres. San Antonio Community Dept. of Family Practitioners, 1980. With U.S. Army, 1943-46, 51-53. Mem. Am. Assn. Family Practitioners, Five-County Med. Soc. (v.p. 1993, pres. 1994). Republican. Avocations: classical music, books on history, archeology, the Civil War. Office: 912 E Winkler St Kermit TX 79745-3644

GRENALD, RAYMOND, architectural lighting designer; b. Louisville, Feb. 10, 1928; s. Samuel Solomon and Bertha (Borgenicht) Greenwald; m. Arlene Rubin, Nov. 21, 1961 (div. Nov. 1985); children: Seth Jonathan, Bethany Leigh; m. Elizabeth Pfaelzer Kapnek, Dec. 10, 1989. Student, U. Cin., 1945-46; BS in Engring., Wash. State U., 1951, BArch, 1954; postgrad., U. Wash., 1952-53. Registered architect, Pa., Md., Calif., Nat. Coun. Archtl. Registration Bds. Liaison engr. Boeing Airplane Co., Seattle, 1952-53; staff architect Thalheimer & Weitz, Architects, Phila., 1955-56, Nolen & Swinbourne, Architects, Phila., 1957-59; pvt. practice Phila., 1959-61; architect Vincent Kling, Architect, Phila., 1962-63, Wolfgang Rapp, Architect, Phila., 1963-64; asst. city architect Phila., 1964-66; archtl. lighting designer, assoc. Sylvan Shemitz & Assocs., New Haven, 1966-68; archtl. lighting cons. Phila., 1969—; chmn. Grenald Waldron Assocs., Narberth, Pa., 1968—; instr. U. Pa., 1974-75, Drexel U., 1972-74, Temple U., 1964-67, U. Cin., 1977-80, UCLA, 1982-86, U. Conn., 1967; adj. assoc. prof. U. Soc. Calif., 1984-86; vis. lectr. Harvard U., Yale U., Moore Coll. Art, 1973-76. Designer archtl. lighting Carlsbad Cavern Nat. Park, 1976, Pennsylvania Avenue Devel. Corp., Washington, 1976-96, Boat House Row, Phila., 1978, Monumental Fed. Core, Washington, 1987—, motion picture Gremlins 2, Franklin Ct., Independence Mall Nat. Park, N.Mex. State Capitol, Puerto Cuervo, Sardinia, Hilton Hawaiian Village, Honolulu, Conn. Gen. Life Ins. Hdqrs., U.S. Supreme Ct., The Mall and Federal Triangle, Washington, West Wing White House, Washington, Balt. Bus. Dist., Phila. Bus. Dist., Akmerkaz Istanbul Beijing Fin. Ctr., China, Cempaka Mas, Jakarta, Inha Hosp., Inchon, Korea, Eastgate, Harare, Zimbabwe, U. Pa. Lighting Master Plan and Implementation, Naval Acad. Chapel, Annapolis, Md. With USAF, 1946-47; 2d lt. U.S. Army, 1950-51. Recipient Presdl. Design Award of Excellence, Nat. Endowment Arts and AIA, 1984, 88, Waterbury citation IIDA, 1996, Award of Excellence, GE, 1997, Eight Schuylkill River Bridges, Memlyon Park Pretoria South Africa Dreamand (Resort, Mixed Use) Cairo, Egypt, Cocoa Walk, Bogata, Columbia; Fels fellow U. Pa., 1966. Fellow AIA, Internat. Assn. Lighting Designers (v.p. 1971-72, pres. 1973-74), Illuminating Engring. Soc. N.Am. (com. chmn. Nat. Mus. Lighting 1985-92, bd. dirs. EPRI Lighting Rsch. Orgn., Goddard trophy 1963, 97, Guth award of excellence 1984), Waterbury citation of excellence, 1996. Avocations: skiing, writing, traveling, photography. Office: Grenald Assocs Ltd PO Box 525 260 Haverford Ave Narberth PA 19072-2343

GRENANDER, ULF, mathematics educator; b. Våstervik, Sweden, July 23, 1923; came to U.S., 1966; s. Sven and Maria (Persson) G.; m. Emma-Stina Hallquist, Dec. 22, 1946; children: Sven, Angela, Charlotte. Fil. Dr., U. Stockholm, Sweden, 1950; DSc (hon.), U. Chgo. Prof. U. Stockholm, 1958-66, Brown U., Providence, R.I., 1966—. Author: General Pattern Theory, 1993. Fellow Inst. Math. Stats., Am. Acad. Arts and Scis.; mem. Royal Swedish Acad. Sci., Royal Statis. Soc. (hon.), Nat. Acad. Sci.

GRENDLER, PAUL FREDERICK, history educator; b. Armstrong, Iowa, May 24, 1936; s. August Paul and Josephine Lucy (Girres) G.; m. Marcella T. McCann, June 16, 1962; children: Peter, Jean. BA, Oberlin Coll., 1959; MA, U. Wis., 1961, PhD, 1964. Lectr. history U. Pitts., 1963-64; lectr. history U. Toronto, Ont., Can., 1964-65, asst. prof., 1965-69, assoc. prof., 1969-73, prof., 1973-98; prof. emeritus, 1998; postdoctoral fellow Inst. for Research in Humanities, U. Wis., 1967-68. Author: Critics of the Italian World, 1530-1560, 1969, The Roman Inquisition and the Venetian Press, 1540-1605, 1977, rev. Italian transl., 1983, Culture and Censorship in Late Renaissance Italy and France, 1981, Schooling in Renaissance Italy, 1989, paperback, 1991, Italian transl., 1991, Books and Schools in the Italian Renaissance, 1995; editor: An Italian Renaissance Reader, 1987, 2d edit., 1992, Roman and German Humanism 1450-1550, 1993; editor-in-chief: Encyclopedia of the Renaissance, 1996—; mem. editl. bd., exec. com.: Collected Works of Erasmus, from 1976; contbr. articles to profl. jours. Fulbright fellow Italy, 1962-63; Can. Council fellow, 1970-71; Am. Council Learned Socs. fellow, 1971-72; I Tatti fellow Harvard U. Ctr. for Italian Renassance Studies, Florence, Italy, 1970-72; sr. fellow Soc. for Humanities Cornell U., 1973-74; Guggenheim Meml. fellow, 1978-79; Social Scis. and Humanities Research Council Can. fellow, 1979-80, 85-86; Woodrow Wilson Internat. Ctr. for Scholars fellow, 1982-83; Nat. Humanities Ctr. fellow, 1988-90; grantee NEH, 1989-92; Connaught fellowship, 1997. Mem. Renaissance Soc. Am. (v.p. 1991-92, pres. 1992-94), Am. Hist. Assn. (Marraro prize 1989), Am. Cath. Hist. Assn. (pres. 1984, Marraro prize 1978), Soc. Italian Hist. Studies (sr. scholar citation 1998). Address: 110 Fern Ln Chapel Hill NC 27514-4206

GRENDYS, EDWARD CHARLES, obstetrician-gynecologist, gynecologic oncologist; b. Chgo., Oct. 12, 1957; s. Edward Charles Sr. and Loretta Marie (Koziel) G.; m. Mary Jo Kaminsky, Apr. 22, 1989. BS, DePaul U., 1979; MD, Northwestern U., 1987. Diplomate Nat. Bd. Med. Examiners, Am. Bd. Ob-gyn. Instr. medicine Georgetown U., Washington, 1987-94; asst. prof. gynecology Tufts U., Boston, 1994-97; asst. prof. Moffitt Cancer Ctr. U. South Fla., Tampa, 1997—. Contbr. articles to profl. jours. Fellow ACS, Soc. Gyne Oncology. Avocation: golf. Office: Moffitt Cancer Ctr Dept Gynecology Oncology 12902 Magnolia Dr Tampa FL 33612-9416

GRENELL, JAMES HENRY, retired manufacturing company executive; b. Mpls., Feb. 19, 1924; s. Harrison Morton and Harriet Elizabeth (Kuch) G.; m. Naomi Betty Callerstrom, Sept. 15, 1945; children—Bonita (Mrs. Michael Wolfe), Suzanne Naomi, Andrea (Mrs. Edward Mendes). BBA, U. Minn., 1947; postgrad. Advanced Mgmt. Program, Harvard U., 1974. With Honeywell Inc., Mpls., 1951-86; accountant Honeywell Inc., 1951-56, div. controller, 1956-68, group controller, 1968-71, asst. corp. controller, 1971-74, v.p., controller, 1974-82, v.p., staff exec., 1982-86; Instr. Mgmt. Inst. U. Wis.-Madison, 1960-69, Inst. Tech. U. Minn., Mpls., 1963-65; asso. dir. Mgmt. Center U. St. Thomas, 1959-69. Contbr. articles to profl. jours. Bd. dirs. Mpls. Soc. for Blind, 1963-71, pres., 1970-71; bd. dirs. U. Minn. Coll. Bus. Alumni Bd., 1975-82; mem. Acctg. Adv. Coun. U. Minn., 1977-83. Served to 1st lt. 1943-46, ETO. Decorated 4 Battle Stars, U.S. Army. Mem. Fin. Execs. Inst., Alpha Kappa Psi, Harvard Club of Ariz., Harvard Club of Minn., Ariz. Club. Republican. Home: 10056 E Calle De Cielo Scottsdale AZ 85258-5652 also: 1201 Skyview Flagstaff AZ 86004-8718

GRENFELL, GLORIA ROSS, freelance journalist; b. Redwood City, Calif., Nov. 14, 1926; d. Edward William and Blanch (Ross) G.; m. June 19, 1948 (div. Nov. 15, 1983); children: Jane, Barbara, Robert, Mary. BS, U. Oreg., 1948, postgrad., 1983-85. Coll. bd., retail sales Meier & Frank Co., Portland, Oreg., 1945; book sales retailer J.K. Gill & Co., Portland, Oreg., 1948-50; advisor Mt. Hood Meadows Women's Ski Program, Oreg., 1968-78; corp. v.p. OK Delivery System, Inc., Oreg., 1977-82; ski instr. Willamette Pass, Oreg., 1983-85, Mt. Shasta, 1986; Campfire girls leader Portland, 1958-72; freelance journalist Marina, Calif., 1986—. Mem. Assn. Jr. League Internat., 1957-87; mem. Monterey County Mental Health Commn., 1994—, So. Poverty Law Ctr., No. Mariposa County History Ctr., Calif. Recipient Golden Poles award Mt. Hood Meadows, 1975. Mem. Soc. Profl. Journalists, Profl. Ski Instrs. Am., U.S. Ski Assn., Calif. State Sheriffs' Assn. (assoc.), Monterey History and Art Assn., Monterey Sports Ctr., Carmel Women's Club, Mariposa County C. of C., Monterey Bay Area Nat. Alumnae Panhellenic (Woman of Yr. award 1999), Order Ea. Star, DAR (Commodore Sloat chpt.), Citizens for Law and Order, Mortar Bd., Kappa Alpha Theta. Democrat. Episcopalian. Home and Office: 3128 Crescent Ave Lot 9 Marina CA 93933-3131

GRENIER, EDWARD JOSEPH, JR., lawyer; b. N.Y.C., Nov. 26, 1933; s. Edward Joseph and Jane Veronica (Farrell) G.; m. Patricia J. Cederle, June 22, 1957; children: Victoria-Anne, Edward Joseph III, Peter C. BA summa cum laude, Manhattan Coll., N.Y.C., 1954; LLB magna cum laude, Harvard U., 1959. Bar: D.C. 1959, N.Y. 1983, U.S. Ct. Appeals (D.C. cir.) 1959, U.S. Ct. Mil. Appeals 1960, U.S. Ct. Appeals (3d cir.) 1966, U.S. Supreme Ct. 1966, U.S. Ct. Appeals (9th cir.) 1973, U.S. Ct. Appeals (10th cir.) 1977, U.S. Ct. Appeals (5th cir., 11th cir.) 1982. Law clk. U.S. Ct. Appeals (D.C. cir.), 1959-60; assoc. Covington & Burling, Washington, 1960-68; ptnr. Sutherland, Asbill & Brennan, Washington, 1968—; speaker in field of energy related issues to profl. orgns.; bd. dirs. Found. of Energy Law Jour., 1990-91, 97-98. Contbr. articles in field to legal jours. Chmn. bd. trustees, mem. exec. com. Connelly Sch. Holy Child, Potomac, Md., 1976-85, trustee, 1976-88; bd. dirs. D.C. Recording for the Blind, Washington, 1977-89. 1st lt. USAF, 1954-56. Fellow Am. Bar Found.; mem. ABA (chmn. sec. adminstrv. law 1986-87, sec., del. Ho. of Dels. 1991-97), FBA, D.C. Bar Assn., Fed. Energy Bar Assn. (bd. dirs. 1986-89, 95-99, v.p. 1995-96, pres.-elect 1996-97, pres. 1997-98), Am. Inns of Ct. (master of bench Prettyman-Leventhal Inn of Ct. 1988—, pres. 1991-92, counselor 1997-98), Met. Club, Congl. Country Club. Office: Sutherland Asbill & Brennan 1275 Pennsylvania Ave NW Ste 1 Washington DC 20004-2415

GRENQUIST, PETER CARL, consultant; b. East Orange, N.J., Feb. 15, 1931; s. Ernst Alexander and Carmela (Anastasia) G.; m. Barbara Ross Krone, Dec. 20, 1967; children: Carl Robert (dec.), Louisa Beatrice. B.A., Dartmouth Coll., 1953; M.A., Columbia U., 1957, Ph.D., 1963. Vice pres. Am. Assembly, Columbia U., 1957-62; dir. Spectrum Books, Prentice-Hall, Inc., 1962-70; v.p. coll. divsn. Prentice-Hall, Inc., 1970-72, pres. Trade Book divsn., 1972-80; CEO Arco Pub., Inc. (subs.), 1981-85; gen. mgr. gen. books divsn. McGraw-Hill Book Co., 1986-89; exec. dir. Assn. Am. Univ. Presses, Inc., N.Y.C., 1990-97; sr. assoc. Moseley Assocs. Inc., 1997—. Served to lt. (j.g.) USNR, 1953-56. Woodrow Wilson fellow, 1956-57. Mem. Devon Yacht Club, Phi Beta Kappa. Office: Moseley Assocs Inc 342 Madison Ave Rm 1414 New York NY 10173-1423

GRENZ, LINDA L., Episcopal priest; b. Eureka, S.D., Apr. 9, 1950; d. Milbert A. and Frieda (Junker) G.; m. Delbert C. Glover, Dec. 27, 1992. BA, Westmar Coll., 1972; M Theol. Studies, Harvard U., 1974; MDiv, Episcopal Div. Sch., 1977. Rector St. Paul's Episcopal Ch., Camden, Del., 1977-83; mgmt. and tng. cons. Wilmington, Del., 1983-89; assoc. dir. overseas devel. Episcopal Ch. Ctr., N.Y.C., 1990-92, coord. adult edn. and leadership devel., 1992-94; pres. LeaderResources, Wilmington, 1994—. Author: (tng. manuals) Discipleship Groups, 1994, (booklet) Covenant of Trust, 1994; editor, contbr. In Dialogue With Scripture, 1992 (Polly Bond award 1992), Ministry in Daily Life, 1994. Office: LeaderResources 38 Mulberry St PO Box 302 Leeds MA 01053-0302*

GREPPIN, JOHN AIRD COUTTS, philologist, editor, educator; b. Rochester, N.Y., Apr. 2, 1937; s. Ernest Haquette and Edna Barbara (Kill) G.; m. Mary Elizabeth Cleland Hannan, Sept. 30, 1961; children: Sally Cleland Coutts, Carl Hannan Haquette. AB in Greek, U. Rochester, N.Y., 1961; MA in Classics, U. Wash., 1966; PhD in Indo-European Studies, UCLA, 1972. Tchr. Greek, Latin Stowe (Vt.) Prep. Sch., 1961-62; tchr. Woodstock (Vt.) Country Sch., 1962-65, admissions dir., 1968-69; interim asst. prof. U. Fla., Gainesville, 1971-72; tchr. Isidore Newman Sch., New Orleans, 1972-74; rsch. instr. Yerevan State U., USSR, 1974-75; from asst. to assoc. to prof. linguistics Cleve. State U., 1975—, dir. program in linguistics, 1979-83, 99—; vis. prof. linguistics Philipps U., Marburg, Germany, 1993. Author: Initial Vowel and Aspiration in Classical Armenian, 1973, Classical Armenian Nominal Stiffixes, 1975, Classical and Middle Armenian Bird Names: A Taxonomic and Mythological Study, 1978, An Entymological Dictionary of the Indo-European Components of Classical Armenian, 1984, Bark Galianosi: The Greek Armenian Dictionary to Galen, 1985, A Handbook of Armenian Dialectology, 1986, An Arabic-Armenian Pharmaceutical Dictionary, 1997, The Diffusion of Greek Medicine in the Middle East and the Caucasus, 1999; editor: Proc. of 1st Internat. Conf. on Armenian Linguistics, Phila., 1979, (with others) Interrogativity: A Colloquium of the Grammar, Typology and Pragmatics of Questions in Seven Diverse Languages, 1984, When Worlds Collide: The Indo-Europeans and the Pre-Indo-Europeans: The Bellagio Papers, 1990, Studies in Classical Armenian Literature, 1994, Studies in Honor of Jean Phuvel, Part One: Ancient Languages and Philogy, 1997, Part Two: Mythology and Religion, 1997; editor Ann. Armenian Linguistics, 1980—, Armenian and Anatolian Studies, 1979—, Proc. 4th Internat. Conf. on Armenian Linguistics, 1992, Classical Armenian Literature: Studies in Early Armenian Authors; mng. editor Raft, A Jour. of Armenian Poetry and Criticism, 1987—; contbr. over 190 articles to Am., European and Soviet jours., over 210 revs. to Times Lit. Supplement, N.Y. Times Book Rev., others. Recipient Silver medal Congregazione Mekhitarista, Venice, Italy, 1978; fellow Am. Coun. Learned Socs., 1965, NEH, 1978-79, NIH, 1984, Internat. Rsch. and Exchs. Bd., 1974, grantee, 1979-81, 84-87, 89, 92, 94; grantee AGBU Manoogian Fund, 1977, 79-94, Gulbenkian Found., 1982, 85, 96, Rockefeller Found., 1987, Am. Coun. Learned Socs., 1987. Mem. Assn. Internat. des Études Arméniennes, Soc. for Study of the Caucasus, Am. Philol. Soc., Linguistic Soc. Am., Soc. for Armenian Studies (mem. exec. bd. 1982-86, sec. 1983-85), Am. Oriental Soc., Soc. Caucasologia Europaea. Avocations: pianist, chamber music assns., bird watching. Home: 3349 Fairmount Blvd Cleveland OH 44118-4262 Office: Cleve State U Dept Linguistics Cleveland OH 44115

GRESHAM, ANN ELIZABETH, retailer, horticulturist executive, consultant; b. Richmond, Va., Oct. 11, 1933; d. Allwin Stagg and Ruby Scott (Faber) Gresham. Student, Peace Coll., Raleigh, N.C., 1950-52, East Carolina U., 1952-53, Penland Sch., N.C., 1953-54, Va. Commonwealth U., 1960-64. Owner, prin. Ann Gresham's Gift Shop, Richmond, 1953-56; pres., treas. Gresham's Garden Ctr., Inc., Richmond, 1955-79; v.p. Gresham's Nursery, Inc., Richmond, 1959-73, pres., treas., 1973-84; pres., treas. Gresham's Country Store, Richmond, 1964-92; tchr., 1982—. Bd. dirs. Bainbridge Community Ministry, 1979, Handworkshop, 1984-89; class agt. Peace Coll., Raleigh, 1987-88, mem. alumnae council, 1987, 88—, bd. visitors, 1987-93; focus group mem. Hand Workshop, Richmond, 1983, bd. dirs., 1984-87. Mem. Midlothian Antique Dealers (treas. 1975-79), Richmond Quilt Guild (chpt. v.p. 1983-84), Nat. Needlework Assn., Quilt Inst., Am. Hort. Soc. Episcopalian. Clubs: Chesmond Women's (v.p. 1979-80), James River Woman's (Richmond) (tres. 1990-92). Home and Office: Gresham's Inc 2324 Logan St Richmond VA 23235-3462

GRESHAM, DOROTHY ANN, operating room nurse, educator; b. Washington, Ga., Oct. 5, 1954; d. Daniel Webster Sr. and Mary Lee (Smith) Dunn; m. Roy Lee Gresham, July 5, 1975; children: Isaac Patrick, Jillian Jeanine, Phillip Michael. Diploma in Nursing, Ga. Bapt. Sch. Nursing, Atlanta, 1975; BSN, Creighton U., 1987; MS in Cmty. Health Adminstrn., Calif. Coll. Health Scis., 1997. RN, Nebr., Ga., Ala., Mo.; cert. nurse operating rm., HIV/AIDS instr., ARC nurse, BLS, ACLS. Staff nurse recovery rm., eye, ears and throat nurse Ga. Bapt. Hosp., Atlanta, 1975-76; gen. duty nurse Wills Meml. Hosp., Washington, Ga., 1976; staff nurse recovery rm. and emergency rm. Southeastern Bapt. Hosp., San Antonio, 1977-78; staff nurse med.-surgery, oper. and recovery rm. Johnson County Hosp., Warrensburg, Mo., 1979-81; mem. operating rm. staff, asst. supr. Whiteham AFB (Mo.) Hosp., 1982-83; med.-surg. and oper. rm. staff nurse Barksdale AFB (La.) Hosp., 1983-85; staff nurse operating rm. Erlingh Bergquist Regional Hosp., Offutt AFB, Nebr., 1986-88; staff nurse telemetry unit, crital care and on-call nurse St. Joseph Hosp., Omaha, 1987-88; staff nurse, charge nurse ICU West Ala. Gen. Hosp., Northport, Ala., 1988-90; mem. oper. rm. staff Air Univ. Hosp., Maxwell AFB, Ala., 1989-90; staff nurse operating rm. Langley AFB (Va.) Hosp., 1990-91, 502d Med. Group, Maxwell AFB, 1991-94; HIV/AIDS instr. ARC, Ramstein and Landstuhl, Germany, 1994—; cmty. health nurse, early interventionist Incirlik AFB, 1996-98; part-time clin. instr. Capstone Coll. Nursing, Tuscaloosa, Ala., 1989-90; substitute tchr., nurse Dept. Def. Dependent Schs., Kaiserslautern Mil. Cmty., Germany, 1994-95; instr. Emet Ctrl. Tex. Coll. Europe Campus, 1994—; oper. rm. staff nurse Landstuhl 2d Gen. Hosp., 1995-96. Maj. USAF, 1991-94. Decorated Nat. Def. Svc. medal; recipient Recognition for Outstanding Svc. cert. 1st Med. Group Langley AFB, 1991, Appreciation cert. USAF, 1991, numerous others. Mem. AACN, ANA, Nat. League for Nursing, Assn. Operating Rm. Nurses, Sigma Theta Tau, Phi Delta Kappa. Baptist. Avocations: aerobics, sewing, cooking, ceramics, cross stitch. Home: 8698 Young Ct Springfield VA 22153-2253

GRESHAM, GLEN EDWARD, physician; b. Ft. Worth, Dec. 1, 1931; s. Perry Epler and Elsie Inez (Stanbrough) G.; m. Phyllis Elaine Kilmer, Nov. 9, 1957; children: Stephen Deane, David Epler, Elizabeth Anne Kilmer, Jennifer Gordon. B.A., Harvard Coll., 1953; M.D., Columbia U., 1958. Intern, then resident in internal medicine Univ. Hosps., Cleve., 1958-60, 62-64; asst. prof. preventive medicine Ohio State U., Columbus, 1964-69; asst. prof. medicine Yale U., New Haven, 1969-70; assoc. prof. rehab. medicine, medicine and cmty. medicine Tufts U., Boston, 1970-78; prof., chmn. dept. rehab. medicine SUNY, Buffalo, 1978-98, prof. emeritus, 1998—, Gresham vis. prof., 1989, med. dir. Erie County Med. Ctr., 1990-92. Served with USPHS, 1960-62. Nat. Found. fellow rehab., 1962-64; recipient Disting. Service award Mass. Council Orgns. Handicapped, 1972. Fellow ACP, Am. Coll. Rheumatology (emeritus); mem. Assn. Acad. Physiatrists, Am. Acad. Phys. Medicine and Rehab. (hon.), Harvard Club (Boston), Gross Med. Club. Rsch. epidemiology chronic disease, functional assessment. Office: Erie County Med Ctr SUNY/Buffalo Dept Rehab Medicine 462 Grider St Dept Rehab Buffalo NY 14215-3021 Office: Dept Rehab Medicine SUNY Buffalo 232 Parker Hall 3435 Main St Buffalo NY 14214

GRESHAM, JAMES STEVE, health service administrator; b. Greenville, S.C., Oct. 13, 1951; s. James William and Ruby Etta (Ayers) G.; m. Sharon Dee Barfield, Nov. 15, 1975 (dec. 1989); children: Ashley Lynn, David Bruce; m. Kathleen Perry Jennings, Sept. 8, 1990; 1 child, James Steven Jennings. BS, Clemson U., 1973; MBA, Pacific Western U., 1984. Mgmt. assoc. Citizens & So. Nat. Bank, Greenville, 1973-75; dir. spl. svcs. USAF, Nellis AFB, Nev., 1975-77; med. squadron cmdr. USAF Hosp., Columbus AFB, Miss., 1977-80; cmdr. 70th Aeromed. Evacuation Squadron, Niagara Falls, N.Y., 1980-82; dir. ops. 72d Aeromed. Evacuation Squadron, McGuire AFB, N.J., 1982-85; dir. health svcs. Headquarters 14th Air Force, Marietta, Ga., 1985-90; adminstr. cancer ctr. Greenville Hosp. Sys., 1990—. Author: Disaster Casualty Management, 1979. Mem. Res. Officers Assn., Am. Acad. Med. Adminstrs., Assn. Cancer Execs., Am. Coll. Oncology Adminstrs., So. Air Force Res. Med. Svc. Corps Officers, Assn. Mil. Surgeons U.S. Republican. Methodist. Office: Cancer Treatment Ctr 701 Grove Rd Greenville SC 29605-5601*

GRESHAM, JAMES THOMAS, foundation executive; b. Griffin, Ga., Dec. 6, 1937; m. Marcine Miller, June 12, 1960; children: Deborah G. Lynn, Elizabeth G.Harlin, James T. Gresham, Jr. BS in Textiles, Ga. Tech, 1960. With Callaway Found., Inc., La Grange, Ga., 1969—, now pres., gen. mgr., and treas.; bd. trustees Ga. Tech Rsch. Corp., Ga. Heart Clin., Inc.; past pres., bd. trustees Ga. Tech Found., Inc.; pres., bd. trustees Med. Park Found., Inc.; pres., bd. trustees Enoch Callaway Cancer Clin. Past pres. LaGrange Rotary Club; former campaign chmn. United Way; deacon First Bapt. Church, LaGrange; mem. Highland Country Club. Mem. Sigma Chi; hon. mem. Tau Beta Pi, Phi Kappa Phi. Office: Callaway Found Inc PO Box 790 Lagrange GA 30241-0014

GRESHAM, ZANE OLIVER, lawyer; b. Mobile, Ala., Dec. 16, 1948; S. Charles Brandon and Lillian Ann (Oliver) G.; m. Marian Gan, Mar. 3, 1988. BA cum laude, Johns Hopkins U., 1970; JD magna cum laude, Northwestern U., 1973. Bar: Calif. 1973. Assoc. Morrison & Foerster, San Francisco, 1973-79, ptnr., 1980—, co-chair land use and environ. law group, 1987-97, co-chair airports and aviation law group, 1996—; chair Latin Am. Group, 1998—; dir., v.p. (Latin Am.) Internat. Private Water Assn., 1999—. Cons. editor: Environ. Compliance and Litigation Strategy. Pres. San Francisco Forward, 1980-85; bd. dirs. Regional Inst. Bay Area, Richmond, Calif., 1989-95, Regional Parks Found., Oakland, Calif., 1992—, pres., 1995; spl. counsel Grace Cathedral, San Francisco, 1991—; dir., exec. v.p. Pan Am. Soc. Calif., 1995-97, pres. 1998—; vice chmn. Nat. Youth Sci. Found., 1997. Mem. State Bar Calif., Urban Land Inst. (devel. regulation coun.), Lambda Alpha. Avocations: opera, sketching. Office: Morrison & Foerster 425 Market St Ste 3100 San Francisco CA 94105-2482

GRESS, ALLEN E., newspaper editor; b. Zanesville, Ohio, Dec. 18, 1939; s. Carl Edward and Aura Leon (Bell) G.; m. Leslie Kay Marsh, June 4, 1960 (dec. Mar. 17, 1989); children: Julia Lynn, Jeffrey Michael, James Nelson, Jennifer Elizabeth; m. Gail Aiken, Aug. 28, 1993. BA, Otterbein Coll., 1961; MA, Syracuse U., 1965. Reporter Morrow County Sentinel, Mt. Gilead, Ohio, 1991-94, editor, 1994—. Planning commn. Village of Mt. Gilead, 1986—, Rep. ctrl. com., 1992-94; trustee Rivercliff Cemetery, Mt. Gilead, 1990-95; councilman Village of Mt. Gilead, 1990-95. Mem. Soc. Profl. Journalists. Avocation: writing. Home: 290 N Cherry St Mount Gilead OH 43338-1143

GRESSAK, ANTHONY RAYMOND, JR., sales executive; b. Honolulu, Jan. 22, 1947; s. Anthony Raymond and Anne Tavares (Ferreira) G.; m. Catherine Streb, Apr. 11, 1981; children: Danielle Kirsten, Anthony Raymond III, Christina Michelle. A.A., Utah State U., 1967; postgrad., U.S. Army Inf. Officers Candidate Sch., 1968. Restaurant mgr. Ala Moana Hotel, Honolulu, 1970-72; gen. mgr. Fred Harvey, Inc., Ontario, Calif., 1972-73; regional mgr. So. Calif., 1972-73, regional mgr. tollway ops., 1973; divisional mgr. Normandy Lane, 1973; resident mgr. Royal Inns of Am., San Diego, 1974; food and beverage dir. Asso. Inns & Restaurant Co. of Am. (Aircoa), Big Sky, Mont., 1974-75; condominium mgr. Big Sky, 1975; asst. gen. mgr. Naples (Fla.) Bath and Tennis Club, 1975-76; food and beverage dir. Nat. Parks, Grand Canyon, Ariz., 1976-77; gen. mgr. Grand Canyon Nat. Park Lodges, 1977-79; divisional v.p. food services The Broadway, Carter Hawley Hale, Inc., Los Angeles, 1979-82; exec. v.p. Silco Corp., Los Angeles, 1982-84; mktg. mgr. Interstate Restaurant Supply, 1984-85; dir. mktg. and merchandising S.E. Rykoff & Co., Los Angeles, 1986-91; nat. accounts sales mgr. healthcare and hospitality Rykoff-Sexton, Inc., L.A., 1991-93; v.p. distbr. sales The Cheesecake Factory, Calabasas, Calif., 1993—; maitre de table Chaine des Rotisseurs-Los Angeles; mem. edn. culinary steering com. Los Angeles Trade Tech. Coll.; mem. City of Hope Food Svc. Exec. Com. So. Calif. Asst. leader troop 92 Boy Scouts Am., Northridge, Calif. With U.S. Army, 1967-70. Decorated Silver Star, Bronze Star, Purple Heart; South Vietnamese Cross of Gallantry. Mem. Nat. Restaurant Assn. (assoc.), Internat. Order DeMolay (life, chevalier), Smithsonian Assocs., Am. Culinary Fedn. (assoc., Presdl. Medallion award 1991), Calif. Restaurant Assn. (assoc.), Les Toques Blanches Internat. Roman Catholic. Home: 20301 Minnehaha St Chatsworth CA 91311-2540 Office: The Cheesecake Factory 26950 Agoura Rd Agoura Hills CA 91301-5335 *Common sense isn't so common. Self discipline and respect for yourself will achieve success. Strive for perfection and you will attain it. Never give up. You never get a second chance to make a first impression.*

GRESSEL, GARY LEE, telecommunications professional; b. Columbus, Ind., Oct. 6, 1968; s. Daryl Lee and Jeanie Ramona (Willis) G.; m. Jeanne Williams Reynolds, June 1, 1996. BS in Computer Sci., Ball State U., 1991, MS in Info. and Communication Scis., 1992; cert. bus. contingency planner, Disaster Recovery Inst. Internat. Cons. Cummins Engine Co., Columbus, 1991-92, Kamdon Interactive, Muncie, Ind., 1991-92; rsch. fellow Ctr. for Info. and Comm. Scis., Muncie, 1991-92; supr. AT&T, Kansas City, Mo., 1992-96; tech. staff AT&T, Kansas City, 1996-98; corp. info. officer Bus. Ptnrs., Inc., Overland Park, Kans., 1997—; cons. Maxim Group, Overland Park, 1998—, H & R Block, Kansas City, Mo., 1999. Bd. dirs. East Columbus United Meth. Ch., 1984-85; bd. dirs. Ctrl. Comm. Credit Union, Kansas City, 1993—, chmn. bd. dirs., 1995—; volleyball coach Holy Cross Luth. Sch., Gladstone, Mo., 1993-94; active The Wilderness Soc., Nat. Pks. and Conservation Assn., Libr. Congress Assocs. (charter mem.). Mem. Electronic Frontier Found., Good Sam's Club. Methodist. Avocations: volleyball, model trains, golf, tennis. Home: 16528 W 80th Ter Lenexa KS 66219-2804

GRESSETTE, LAWRENCE M., JR., utilities executive; b. St. Matthews, S.C., Feb. 23, 1932; s. Lawrence Marion and Florence Beech (Howell) G.; m. Felicia Arrington Gold, June 19, 1954; children: Felicia Ann Ruf, Virginia G. Spencer, L. Marion III. BS with honors, Clemson U., 1954; LLB with honors, U. S.C., 1959. Ptnr. Gressette & Prickett, St. Matthews, 1959-82; sr. v.p. S.C. Electric and Gas Co. subs. SCANA Corp., Columbia, 1983—, exec. v.p., 1983-87, vice chmn., 1987; chmn., pres., CEO SCANA Corp., Columbia, 1990-97; chmn., CEO S.C. Electric & Gas Co. and other SCANA subs.; chmn. exec. com. SCANA, 1997—; bd. dirs. Watchovia Corp., SCANA Corp., Powertel, Palmetto Bus. Forum. Bd. dirs. Columbia C. of C., S.C. Bus. & Industry Edn. Com. Adv. Coun., S.C. Orch. Assn., S.C. Found. Ednl. and Econ. Excellence, S.C. Commn. on Higher Edn.; chmn. bd. trustee Clemson U., 1995—, Columbia Art Assn., U. S.C. Bus. Partnership Found., Children's Trust Fund Adv. Bd.; chmn. ETV Endowment of S.C., Columbia Mus. Art, Midlands Tech. Coll. Found.; campaign chmn. United Way of Midlands, 1992, group chmn., 1984, v.p. planning, 1985, 86; chmn. Midlands March of Dimes WalkAm./Teamwalk, 1985, Coun. College Pres. Blue Ribbon Com. on Higher Edn.; mem. Gov. Restructuring Com.; steering com. S.C Gov. Sch. Arts. 1st lt. inf. U.S. Army, 1954-56. Mem. ABA, S.C. Bar Assn., Edison Electric Inst., Southeastern Electric Exch., Palmetto Soc. (Columbia), Newcomen Soc. Baptist. Avocations: golf, reading, travel. Office: SCANA Corp 1400 Lady St Columbia SC 29201-2834

GRESSMAN, EUGENE, lawyer; b. Lansing, Mich., Apr. 18, 1917; s. William Albert and Bess Beulah (Nagle) G.; m. Nan Alice Kirby, Aug. 6, 1944; children: William, Margot and Nancy (twins), Eric. AB, U. Mich., 1938, JD with distinction, 1940; LLD, Seton Hall U., 1994. Bar: Mich. 1940, D.C. 1948, Md. 1959, U.S. Supreme Ct. 1945. Atty. SEC, Washington, 1940-43; law clk. to Justice Frank Murphy, U.S. Supreme Ct., 1943-48; ptnr. firm Van Arkel, Kaiser, Gressman, Rosenberg & Driesen, Washington, 1948-77; of counsel Van Arkel, Kaiser, Gressman, Rosenberg & Driesen, 1977-81, Bredhoff & Kaiser, Washington, 1981-84, Brand, Lowell & Ryan, Washington, 1984—; spl. counsel U.S. Ho. of Reps., 1976-84; William Rand Kenan Jr. prof. law U. N.C., Chapel Hill, 1977-87, prof. emeritus, 1987—; disting. vis. prof. Fordham U. Law Sch., 1982-83, 1987-88; Disting. vis. prof. Seton Hall U. Law Sch., 1987-94; vis. prof. law Ohio State U., 1967, Mich. Law Sch., 1969, George Washington U., 1971-77, Ind. U., 1976, Cath. U. Am., 1977; judge Appeals Tax Ct. Montgomery County, Md., 1959-62; chmn. rules com. U.S. Ct. Appeals for 4th Cir., 1984-89. Author: (with Robert L. Stern, Stephen M. Shapiro and Kenneth Geller) Supreme Court Practice, 7th edit., 1993, (with Charles A. Wright and others) Federal Practice and Procedure, vol. 16, 1977, (with David Crump and David Day) Cases and Materials on Constitutional Law, 1989, 3d edit., 1998; contbr. articles to legal jours. Fellow Am. Acad. Appellate Lawyers (hon.); mem. ABA, Fed. Bar Assn., D.C. Bar, Am. Law Inst., Am. Judicature Soc., Order of the Coif, Order of Barristers, Phi Beta Kappa, Delta Theta Pi (lifetime achievement award). Home: 325 Glendale Dr Chapel Hill NC 27514-5915 Office: U NC Sch Law Chapel Hill NC 27599-3380

GRETCH, PAUL, federal agency administrator; b. Bklyn., Dec. 8, 1941. BA, Bklyn. Coll., 1963; JD, Harvard U., 1966; LLM, NYU, 1967. With Civil Aeronautics Bd. U.S. Dept. Transp., Washington, 1974-85, dir. ops. Aviation Office, 1985-87, dir. internat. aviation, 1987—. Office: Dept Transp Internat Aviation 400 7th St SW Washington DC 20590-0003*

GRETENCORD, DAVID C., tax consultant. BS, Ind. U., 1971. CPA, Ind., Ky. Sr. auditor Ind. Revenue, St. Louis, 1971-84; specialist state taxes GE Co., Louisville, 1984-89; mgr. state taxes Emerson Elec. Co., St. Louis, 1989-97; sr. mgr. state taxes Ernst & Young LLP, Ft. Wayne, Ind., 1997—. Home: Ernst & Young LLP 110 W Berry St Ste 2300 Fort Wayne IN 46802

GRETHEN, CHERYL ANN, artist; b. Emmetsburg, Iowa, Apr. 1, 1953; d. Norman D. and Emilie M. (Kruml) Clark; m. David J. Grethen, Sept. 2, 1972; 1 child, Christopher J. Artist Elegant Expressions, Mallard, Iowa; mem. Assn. Crafts and Creative Industries. Mem. Am. Craft Coun. Roman Catholic. Office: Elegant Expressions PO Box 237 Mallard IA 50562-0237

GRETSER, GEORGE WESTFALL, publisher; b. Frankfurt, Germany, Mar. 16, 1947; came to U.S., 1948; s. George Rushmore and Edythe (Westfall) G.; m. Linda J. Goff, Jan. 25, 1969; 1 child, Jennifer L. BJ, U. Tex., 1969; MBA, Keller Grad. Sch. Mgmt., Chgo., 1982. Advt. dir. Comms. Pub Corp., Denver, 1970-76; pub. Profl. Remodeling mag. Harcourt Brace Jovanovich Publs., Chgo., 1976-82; with Restaurants & Instns. mag. Cahners Pub. Co., Des Plaines, Ill., 1982-86; COO, pub. Brighton Sq. Pub., Austin, Tex., 1986-87; pub. East/West Network, N.Y.C., 1987-88; pres. ACPI pub. div. ClubCorp, pub. Pvt. Clubs mag. Assoc. Club Publs., Inc., Dallas, 1988-96; mag. mgr. L.A. Times Mag., 1996; advt. dir. Chgo. Mag., 1996—. Avocations: running, marathons, cycling, diving, golf, tennis.

GRETZINGER, RALPH EDWIN, III, management consultant; b. Louisville, Sept. 7, 1948; s. Ralph Edwin Jr. and Martha Irene (Jennings) G.; m. Jewel Jean Rocker, Mar. 21, 1970; children: Ralph Edwin IV, Sarah Elizabeth. BS in Applied Math., Ga. Inst. Tech., 1970; MBA, U. Utah, 1974. Group mgr. Prudential Ins. Co., Cin., 1974-76; owner, regional office mgr. Hewitt Assocs., Lincolnshire, Ill., 1976-78, Dayton, Ohio, 1978-81, Dallas, 1981—. Trustee Child Care Partnership of Dallas, 1985-90. Served with U.S. Army, 1971-74. Mem. S.W. Pension Conf., Ga. Tech. Club of North Tex. (pres. 1986-88), Beta Gamma Sigma. Roman Catholic. Avocation: golf. Office: Hewitt Assocs 600 Las Colinas Blvd E Ste 2100 Irving TX 75039-5628

GRETZKY, WAYNE DOUGLAS, retired professional hockey player; b. Brantford, Ont., Can., Jan. 26, 1961; s. Walter and Phyllis G.; m. Janet Jones, July 16, 1988; 3 children: Paulina, Ty Robert, Trevor Douglas. Center Peterborough Petes, Jr. Ont. Hockey Assn., 1977-78, Sault Ste. Marie Greyhounds, 1977-78, Indpls. Racers, World Hockey Assn., 1978, Edmonton Oilers (Alta., Can.), NHL, 1988, Los Angeles Kings, NHL, 1988-96, Saint Louis Blues, NHL, 1996; center N.Y. Rangers, NHL, 1996-99, ret., 1999; player NHL All-Star game, 1980-86, 1988-94; mem. Stanley Cup championship teams, 1984, 85, 87, 88. Player NHL All-Star first team, 1980-92, 1990-91; named Rookie of Yr. World Hockey Assn., 1978-79, Sportsman of Yr. Sports Illus., 1982, Sporting News NHL Player of the Year, 1980-81, 86-87, Sporting News All-Star team, 1980-81, 86-87, 90-91, Sporting News Man of the Year, 1981, All-Star game MVP, 1983, 89, Canadian Athlete of the Year, 1985, Dodge Performer of the Year, 1984-85, 1986-87; recipient Art Ross Meml. trophy NHL, 1981-87, 89-90, 90-91, 93-94, Conn Smythe trophy, 1985, 88, William Hanley trophy, 1977-78, Lemms Family award, 1977-78, Hart Meml. trophy, 1974-80, Lady Byng Meml. tropy, 1979-80, 90-91, 91-92, 93-94, Lester B. Pearson award, 1982-82, 84-85, 86-87, Emery Edge award, 1983-84, 84-85, 86-87, Lester Patrick trophy, 1993-94; holder NHL career scoring record. Record holder for points, goals, assists, overtime assists and others. Office: care NY Rangers Madison Square Garden 2 Penn Plz New York NY 10121-2819*

GREULICH, RICHARD CURTICE, anatomist, gerontologist; b. Denver, Mar. 22, 1928; s. William Walter and Mildred Almena (Libby) G.; m. Betty Brent Mitchell, Dec. 19, 1948 (div. 1955); children: Christopher, Robert; m. Leonora Faye Colleasure, Dec. 27, 1958 (dec. 1993); children: Jeffrey, Hilary; m. Bertha Margaret Voelker, Aug. 12, 1994. A.B., Stanford U., 1949; Ph.D. (AEC fellow), McGill U. (Can.), 1953. Instr. Sch. Medicine, UCLA, 1953-55, asst. prof. anatomy, 1955-61, asso. prof. anatomy, 1961-64, prof. anatomy, 1964-66, asso. prof. oral biology Sch. Dentistry, 1961-64, prof. oral biology, 1964-66; sci. dir. Nat. Inst. Dental Research, NIH, Bethesda, Md., 1966-74; acting dir. Nat. Inst. Aging, Bethesda, 1975-76; dir. Gerontology Research Center and sci. dir. Nat. Inst. Aging, Balt., 1976-88; exec. officer Am. Assn. Anatomists, 1994-95; staff dir. U.S. Pres.'s Biomed. Research Panel, 1974-75; vis. investigator Karolinska Inst., Stockholm, 1955-57, U. London, 1962-63, McGill U., 1963; vis. prof. anatomy U. Va., 1966-73. Served with F.A., U.S. Army, 1946-48. Recipient award for basic research in oral sci. Internat. Assn. Dental Research, 1963, Superior Service award HEW, 1971; Bank of Am.-Giannini Found. fellow, 1955-57; USPHS spl. fellow, 1962-63. Mem. Am. Assn. Anatomists, Gerontol. Soc., Am. Inst. Biol. Scis., AAAS, Am. Soc. Cell Biology, Sigma Xi. Club: Cosmos (Washington). Rsch., publs. on growth, differentiation and aging at cellular and organismic level. Home: 137 St Andrews Rd Severna Park MD 21146-1539

GREULICH, ROBERT CHARLES, insurance company marketing executive; b. Milw., July 1, 1958; s. Richard Paul and Shirley Ann (Knapp) G.; m. Kathleen Ann Olsen, Sept. 19, 1981; children: Stephanie Rae, Christopher Ryan. Asst. mgr. Toy Fair, Des Moines, 1973-77; mgr., buyer Gen. Novelty, Des Moines, 1977-80; agt. The Equitable, Des Moines, 1980-88, asst. dist. mgr., 1981-83, dist. mgr., 1983-84, registered rep., 1984—; regional mktg. dir. The Equitable, Chgo., 1988-90; nat. mktg. mgr. The Equitable, N.Y.C., 1990-91; pres. Diversified Retirement Svcs., Des Moines, 1986-89, Midwestern Flexible Benefits, Des Moines, Ill., 1986-89; dist. mgr. The Equitable, Rotter & Assocs., Chgo., Ill., 1992-98; br. office mgr., regional dir., profl. advisors group The Equitable, Rotter & Assocs., Chgo., 1998—; cons. Flexsoft 401(k) Inc., N.Y.C., 1980—; bd. dirs. Rotter and Assocs. Found., bd. dirs. and exec., devel., spl. benefits com., Thresholds, Chgo. Mem. Nat. Assn. Life Underwriters, Nat. Assn. CLUs. Republican. Roman Catholic. Home: 105135 Madison Ave Burr Ridge IL 60521

GREVE, DIANA LEE, community health nurse; b. Lima, Ohio, Feb. 10, 1949; d. Lee and Betty (Hedrick) Kinstle; m. Lawrence J. Greve, Feb. 1, 1969; children: Brian, Scott, Matthew, Bradley. ADN, Lima Tech. Coll., 1983; BSN, Bowling Green State U., 1989; MSN, Med. Coll. Ohio, Toledo, 1993; family nurse practitioner postgrad cert., Ind. Wesleyan Coll., 1995. Cert. in cmty. health nursing, family nurse practitioner. Staff nurse ob.-gyn. Van Wert (Ohio) County Hosp.; hospice coord. Van Wert Area Vis. Nurse Assn.; instr. Luth. Coll. of Health Professions, Ft. Wayne, Ind.; Wright State U., dayton, Ohio; clin. nurse specialist Joint Twp. Dist. Meml. Hosp., St. Marys, Ohio; adj. faculty Med. Coll. Ohio and Wright State U.; family nurse practitioner Caylor-Nickel Med. Ctr., Bluffton, Ind. Mem. Am. Coll. Nurse Practitioners, Ohio Nurses Assn., Van Wert Area Nurses Assn., Sigma Theta Tau. Home: 1056 Mockingbird Ln Van Wert OH 45891-2642

GREVE, GUY ROBERT, lawyer; b. Bay City, Mich., Oct. 25, 1947; m. Nancy Lisbeth Mueller, Sept. 21, 1991; 1 child, Tyler James. BA, U. Mich., 1970; postgrad., U. Kent, Canterbury, Eng., 1974; JD, Detroit Coll., 1975. Bar: Mich. 1975, U.S. Dist. Ct. (ea. dist.) Mich. 1975. Ptnr. Patterson & Greve, Bay City, 1975-78; asst. atty. City of Bay City, 1975-76, atty., 1976-78; pvt. practice Bay City, 1978—. One-man photography exhbn. Bd. dirs. Bay Arts Coun., 1999—, Women's Crisis Ctr., Bay City, 1977-79, Am. Cancer Soc., 1975—, pres. 1982-83; pres. Muse-Hopper Mobile Mus., Eastern Mich., 1980-82. Named Disting. Alumnus Handy H.S., 1985; recipient Disting. Svc. award Bay City Jaycees, 1981. Mem. ABA, ATLA, Mich. Bar Assn., Bay County Bar Assn. (bd. dirs. 1994-98, Liberty Bell chmn. 1994-98, pres. elect 1997-98, pres. 1998-99), Mich. Trial Lawyers Assn., Bay Area C. of C., Studio 23 (hon. life), U. Mich. Alumni Club (Bay City chpt. pres. 1994-97), Saginaw Bay Yacht Club, Optimists (pres. Bay City 1979-80, lt. gov. Mich. 1985-86, chmn. new club bldg. 1986-87, chmn. club svcs. 1989-90, asst. gov. Mich. 1996-97, internat. conv. com. 1997, founder, chair travel series 1993—). Home: 2300 Nurmi Dr Bay City MI 48708-6872 Office: PO Box 851 919 Washington Ave Bay City MI 48707

GREVE, JOHN HENRY, veterinary parasitologist, educator; b. Pitts., Aug. 11, 1934; s. John Welch and Edna Viola (Thuenen) G.; m. Sally Jeanette Doane, June 21, 1956; children—John Haven, Suzanne Carol, Pamela Jean. B.S., Mich. State U., East Lansing, 1956, D.V.M., 1958, M.S., 1959; Ph.D., Purdue U., West Lafayette, Ind., 1963. Assoc. instr. Mich. State U., East Lansing, 1958-59; instr. Purdue U., West Lafayette, 1959-63; asst. prof. Iowa State U., Ames, 1963-64, assoc. prof., 1964-68, prof. dept. vet. pathology, 1968-99, interim chair dept. vet. pathology, 1992-95, counselor acad. and student affairs, 1991-92; cons. parasitologist various zoos. Mem. editl. bd. Lab. Animal Sci., 1971-83, Vet. Rsch. Comm., 1977-84, Vet. Parasitology, 1984-98; contbr. articles to sci. jours., chpts. to books. Dist. chmn. Broken Arrow Dist., Boy Scouts Am., Ames, Iowa, 1975-77. Named Disting. Tchr. Norden Labs., 1965, 99, Outstanding Tchr. Amoco Oil, Iowa State U., 1972, Faculty Mem. of Yr., Coll. Vet. Medicine, 1999; recipient Faculty Citation Iowa State U. Alumni Assn., 1978. Mem. AVMA (mem. editl. bd. jour. 1975-98, Excellence in Teaching award student chpt. 1990), Iowa Vet. Med. Assn., Am. Soc. Parasitologists, Midwestern Conf. Parasitologists (sec.-treas. 1967-75, presiding officer 1975-76), Am. Assn. Vet. Parasitologists (pres. 1968-70), Helminthological Soc. Washington, World Assn. for Advancement Vet. Parasitology, Am. Assn. Vet. Med. Colls., Izaak Walton League (bd. dirs. Iowa 1968-70), Honor Soc. Cardinal Key, Gamma Sigma Delta, Phi Eta Sigma, Phi Kappa Phi, Phi Zeta. Republican. Lodges: Kiwanis (Town and Country-Ames pres. 1967, Nebr.-Iowa lt. gov. 1972-73). Avocations: philately, camping, gardening. Office: Iowa State U Dept Vet Pathology Ames IA 50011

GREVE, LUCIUS, II, metals company executive; b. St. Paul, July 23, 1915; s. Joseph and Lillian (King) G.; m. Marguerita Philippa Buller Colthurst, Aug. 31, 1940; children: Lucius Richard, Guy Robert. Salesman Electric Auto-Lite Co., Detroit, 1934-42; methods engr. Electric Auto-Lite Co., Bay City, Mich., 1944-45; project engr. Electric Auto-Lite Co., Bay City, 1944-45, with sales dept., 1946-49; pres. L. Greve Sales Co., Bay City, 1949—; exec. v.p. Graphic Metals Co., 1962—, dir., chmn. fin. com., 1962—; pres. Montezuma Mining Co., 1963—. Mem. Soc. Sites Com., 1952, Sch. Citizens Com., 1957; sec. Saginaw Bay Assn., 1957. Mem. U.S. Power Squadron, Saginaw Bay Yacht Club (dir. 1961, comdr. 1965, 66, chmn. nom. com. 97), Bay City Country Club, Great Lakes Crusing Club. Home: 194 Athlone Bch Bay City MI 48706-1179 Office: PO Box 331 Bay City MI 48707-0331 also: # 7 Blvd de Belgique, Monte Carlo Monaco

GREVE, SALLY DOANE, English educator; b. Detroit, June 2, 1934; d. Haven Frazelle and Keitha Maxine (Littler) Doane; m. John Henry Greve, June 21, 1956; children: John Haven, Suzanne Carol, Pamela Jean. BA, Mich. State U., 1956; MA in Tchg. English as Second Lang., Iowa State U., 1989. Adj. instr. ESL off-campus Des Moines Area C.C., Ankeny, Iowa, 1975—, ESL cons., 1975—. Vol. tutor trainer Iowa Refugee Svc. Ctr., Des Moines, 1979-82; chmn. bldg. com. Episcopal Parish Ames, Iowa, 1972-74, supt. ch. sch., jr. warden, 1963-64, newsletter editor, mem. choir, 1991—. Mem. TESOL, Mid-Am. TESOL (bd. dirs. 1985-91, pres. 1989-90), Missouri Valley Adult Edn. Assn., Iowa Assn. for Lifelong Learning, AVMA Aux., Internat. Hon. for Leadership in Univ. Apt. Cmtys. (hon.), Omega Tau Sigma (hon.). Avocation: church activities.

GREW, PRISCILLA CROSWELL, university official, geology educator; b. Glens Falls, N.Y., Oct. 26, 1940; d. James Croswell and Evangeline Pearl (Beougher) Perkins; m. Edward Sturgis Grew, June 14, 1975. *Great-grandfather Charles Miller Croswell was governor of Michigan 1876-1880. Great-grandfather Samuel Perkins sailed from Maine around Cape Horn to California in the 1849 Gold Rush. Grandfather James Coffin Perkins (University of California-Berkeley class of 1874) served as a missionary in Kodaikanal, South India for 30 years. Father James Croswell Perkins (Princeton class of 1929) was a Congregational minister and Professor of Religion and Philosophy at Huston-Tillotson College in Austin, Texas. Mother Evangeline Pearl Beougher Perkins attended the Oberlin Conservatory of Music, led church choirs, and taught private piano lessons.* BA magna cum laude, Bryn Mawr Coll., 1962; PhD, U. Calif., Berkeley, 1967. Instr. dept. geology Boston Coll., 1967-68, asst. prof., 1968-72; asst. rsch. geologist UCLA, 1972-77, adj. asst. prof. environ. sci. and engring., 1975-76; dir. Calif. Dept. Conservation, 1977-81; commr. Calif. Pub. Utilities Commn., San Francisco, 1981-86; dir. Minn. Geol. Survey, St. Paul, 1986-93; prof. dept. geology U. Minn., Mpls., 1986-93; vice chancellor for rsch. U. Nebr., Lincoln, 1993—, prof. dept. geoscis., 1993—, prof. conservation/survey divsn. Inst. Agr., 1993—; vis. asst. prof. geology U. Calif., Davis, 1973-74; chmn. Calif. State Mining and Geology Bd., Sacramento, 1976-77; exec. sec., editor Lake Powell Rsch. Project, 1971-77; cons., mem. vis. staff Los Alamos (N.Mex.) Nat. Lab., 1972-77; mem. com. on minority participation in earth sci. and mineral engring. Dept. Interior, 1972-75; chmn. Calif. Geothermal Resource Task Force, 1977, Calif. Geothermal Resources Bd., 1977-81; mem. earthquake studies adv. panel U.S. Geol. Survey, 1979-83, mem. adv. com., 1982-86; mem. adv. coun. Gas Rsch. Inst., 1982-86, mem. rsch. coord. coun., 1987—, vice chmn., 1994—, chmn., 1996-98; mem. bd. on global change rsch., 1995—, mem. subcom. on earthquake rsch., 1985-88, mem. bd. on earth scis. and resources, 1986-91; mem. bd. on mineral and energy resources NAS, 1982-88, Minn. Minerals Coord. Com., 1986-93; mem. adv. bd. Stanford U., 1989—, Sec. of Energy Adv. Bd., 1995-97; mem. com. on equal opportunities in sci. and tech. NSF, 1985-86, mem. adv. com. on earth scis., 1987-91, mem. adv. com. on sci. and tech. ctrs. devel., 1987-91, mem., adv. com. on sci. and tech. ctrs., 1996, adv. com. on geoscis., 1994-97; mem., bd. of trustees, Amer. geo. inst. found., 1988; mem. State-Fed. Tech. Partnership Task Force, 1995—, Fed. Coun. for Continental Sci. Drilling, 1992—, Gt. Plains Partnership Coun., 1995—, mem. brd. trustees, Amer. Geological Found., 1998—. Contbr. articles to profl. jours. Bd. dirs. Abendmusik:Lincoln, 1995-97; trustee 1st Plymouth Congl. Ch., Lincoln, 1997—; coord. Native Am. Graves Protection and Repatriation Act, 1998—. Fellow NSF, 1962-66. Fellow AAAS (chmn. electorate nominating com. sect. E 1980-84, mem.-at-large 1987-91, chmn.-elect 1994, chmn. 1995, coun. del. 1997-98), Geol. Soc. Am. (nominations com. 1974, chmn. com. on geology and pub. policy 1981-84, audit com. 1988-90, chair 1990, com. on coms. 1986-87, 91-92, chmn. com. on coms. 1995, chair Day medal com. 1990, councilor 1987-91), Mineral. Soc. Am., Geol. Assn. Can.; mem. Am. Geophys. Union (chmn. com. pub. affairs 1984-89), Soc. Mayflower Descs., Nat. Parks and Conservation Assn. (trustee 1982-86), Nat. Assn. Regulatory Utility Commrs. (com. on gas 1982-86, exec. com. 1984-86, com. on energy conservation 1983-84), U.S. Nat. Com. on Geology (at-large 1985-93), Cosmos Club. Congregational. Office: U Nebr Vice Chancellor for Rsch 302 Canfield Adminstrn Bldg Lincoln NE 68588-0433

GREW, ROBERT RALPH, lawyer; b. Metamora, Ohio, Mar. 25, 1931; m. Anne Gano Bailey, Aug. 2, 1958. AB in Letters and Law, U. Mich., 1953, JD, 1955. Bar: Mich. 1955, N.Y. 1958. Assoc. Carter, Ledyard & Milburn, N.Y.C., 1957-68, ptnr., 1968-98, of counsel, 1999—; lectr. legal problems in banking and in venture capital investments Practising Law Inst. Mem. Pilgrims of U.S., English Speaking Union (nat. v.p. 1989-93), Union Club, Lansdowne Club (London). Republican. E-mail grew@clm.com. Office: Carter Ledyard & Milburn 2 Wall St New York NY 10005-2001 also: 1350 I St NW Washington DC 20005-3305

GREWAL, PARWINDER S., biologist, researcher; b. Dharour, Punjab, India, May 26, 1961; came to U.S., 1991; s. Joginder S. and Amarjit K. (Sekhon) G.; m. Sukhbir K. Battu, Feb. 22, 1987; children: Parbir, Sharanbir. BS with honors, Punjab Agrl. U., Ludhiana, India, 1981, MS in Nematology, 1983; PhD in Zoology, U. London, 1990; DIC Nematology, Imperial Coll., London, 1990. Scientist Indian Coun. Agrl. Rsch., Solan, 1984-87; higher sci. officer Horticulture Rsch. Internat., Littlehampton, Eng., 1987-91; postdoctoral rsch. assoc. Rutgers U., New Brunswick, N.J., 1991-93; mgr. nematode rsch. Biosys, Inc., Palo Alto, Calif., 1993-95; rsch. leader Biosys, Inc., Columbia, Md., 1995-97; asst. prof. Ohio State U., Wooster, 1997—; mem. Mich. State Legislature Task Force, 1995. Contbr. chpts. to books, numerous articles to profl. jours. Recipient Team award for Environ. Achievement, Her Majesty the Queen, 1993, Young Scientist of Yr. award U.K. Mushroom Growers Assn., 1991. Mem. Soc. Nematologists, European Soc. Nematologists, Entomol. Soc. Am., Assn. Applied Biologists, Afro-Asian Soc. Nematologists (exec. bd. 1990—, editorial bd. 1990—). Avocations: running, travel, gardening. Office: Dept Entomology Ohio State U 1680 Madison Ave Wooster OH 44691-4114

GREWELL, JUDITH LYNN, computer services executive; b. New Orleans, Aug. 27, 1945; d. Raymond Walter and Dorothy Marie (Reymann) Potratz; m. John Nolting Grewell, Aug. 28, 1964; children: Patricia Lynn, Amy Elizabeth. BA with honors, Wayne State U., 1972; MA with honors, Oakland U., 1976. Cert. prodn. and inventory mgmt. Am. Prodn. and Inventory Control Soc. Supr. mfg. Chevrolet-Pontiac-GM of Can. div., Pontiac, Mich., 1978-80, purchasing agt., 1980-82, trainer, organizational cons., 1982-84; supr. systems tng. Electronic Data Systems Div., Troy, Mich., 1985-86, supr. tech. tng. devel., 1986-88, supr. tng. and communications, 1988-89, prin. sr. cons. divsn., 1989-95, client server program dir., 1995—. Co-author: Capacity Measurement and Improvement, 1996. Mem. Midwest Soc. Orgnl. Learning, Pi Lambda, Phi Upsilon Omicron. Republican. Evangelical Presbyterian. Avocations: art, cross country skiing, fitness, reading, investing. Home: 1711 Ferris Ave Royal Oak MI 48067-3687 Office: 5555 New King Dr Troy MI 48098-2616

GREWELLE, LARRY ALLAN, travel agency owner; b. Longview, Wash., Sept. 10, 1937; s. John Vincent and Ruth (Hansicky) G.; m. Marjorie Anne McGee, Aug. 31, 1964; 1 child, John Lawrence. AA, City Coll. San Francisco, 1961; BA, San Francisco State U., 1963; MPA, Golden Gate U., 1970. Personnel mgr. Spain Area Exch., Madrid, 1965-66, Turkey Area Exch., Izmir, 1966-68; personnel specialist Golden Gate Exch. Region, San Francisco, 1968-70, Hdqrs. U.S. Army, USAF, Dallas, 1970-72; personnel mgr. Philippine Exch., Clark AFB, 1972-74; personnel specialist Alamo Exch. Region, San Antonio, 1974-78; chief personnel Western Distbn. Region, Oakland, Calif., 1978-82; chief human resources S.E. Exch. Region, Montgomery, Ala., 1982-89; travel agy. mgr. Barry's Travel Ctr., Montgomery, 1988—. Pres. Capitol City Civitan, Montgomery, 1989-90; bd. dirs. Montgomery Area Food Bank, 1989-95, One Montgomery, 1992-96, Capri Cmty. Film Soc., 1983—, pres., 1984-85; mem. Untied Way Cmty. Coun., 1993-95; bd. dirs. Internat. Assistance Project Ala., Ala. Prison Project, Friends of the Theatre Ala. State U. Sgt. U.S. Army, 1957-60. Democrat. Presbyterian. Avocations: skiing, photography, sailing. Home: 1220 Westmoreland Ave Montgomery AL 36106-2018 Office: Barrys Travel Ctr Inc 514 Cloverdale Rd Montgomery AL 36106-1855

GREY, BRAD, producer, agent. Mgr., prodr. Brillstein-Grey Entertainment, Beverly Hills, Calif., now chmn. prodr. (films) The Burning, 1981; del. prodr. Opportunity Knocks, 1990; exec. prodr. (films) The Celluloid Closet, 1995, Cat and Mouse, 1995, Happy Gilmore, 1996, The Cable Guy, 1996, Bulletproof, 1996, The Replacement Killers, 1998, Dirty Work, 1998, (TV movie) Don't Try This at Home!, 1990, (TV series) The Larry Sanders Show, 1992, Mr. Show, 1995, The Naked Truth, 1995, The Steve Harvey Show, 1996, Just Shoot Me!, 1997, Alright Already, 1997, C-16: FBI, 1997. Office: Brillstein-Grey Entertainment Ste 350 9150 Wilshire Blvd Beverly Hills CA 90212-3427*

GREY, DEBORAH CLELAND, Canadian government official; b. Vancouver, B.C., Can., July 1, 1952; d. Mansell Caverhill Grey and Lilian Joyce (Russell) Levy; m. Lewis Larson, Aug. 7, 1993. BA, U. Alta., Edmonton, Can., 1978, B of Edn., 1979. Tchr. Frog Lake (Alta.) Indian Res., 1979-80, Dewberry (Alta.) Sch., 1980-89; M.P. Ho. of Commons, Ottawa, Ont., Can., 1989—. Caucus chmn. Reform Party, 1993—, apptd. dep. parliamentary leader, 1995—. Recipient Can. 125 medal, 1993, Alumni award of distinction Trinity Western U., 1996. Avocations: kayaking, gospel singing, motorcycles. Office: Ho of Commons, House of Commons, Parliament Bldgs, Ottawa, ON Canada K1A 0A6

GREY, ELIZABETH K., critical care nurse, retired; b. Lansdowne, Pa., Feb. 18, 1951; d. Charles Knight and Marian Swope (Wing) Morgan; m. James Tracy Grey III, Dec. 27, 1980; children: Michael, James Tracy IV, Joshua. AA, Elmira (N.Y.) Coll., 1976; grad., Upper Bucks Voc-Tech, Perkasie, Pa., 1979; AA in Nursing, Bucks County Community Coll., Newtown, Pa., 1989; student, LaSalle U., 1992-96. Cert. health profl. paramedic, Pa.; cert. CPR, ACLS, TNCC. Paramedic Warminster (Pa.) Ambulance; staff practical nurse Warminster Gen. Hosp.; ICU/CCU staff nurse Nazareth Hosp., Phila.; mem. Warrington Ambulance Corps. Mem. AACN.

GREY, JENNIFER, actress; b. N.Y., Mar. 26, 1960; d. Joel and Jo (Wilder) G. appearances include: (stage) Album, 1980, The Twilight of the Golds, 1993, (film) Reckless, 1984, Red Dawn, 1984, The Cotton Club, 1984, Reckless, 1984, American Flyers, 1985, Ferris Beuller's Day Off, 1986, Dirty Dancing, 1987 (Golden Globe award nom. for best actress 1988), (voice) Light Years, 1988, Bloodhounds of Broadway, 1989, Stroke of Midnight, 1991, Wind, 1992, (T.V. movies) Murder in Mississippi, 1990, Criminal Justice, 1990, Eyes of a Witness, 1991, A Case for Murder, 1993, The West Side Waltz, 1995, Outrage, 1998, Since You've Been Gone, 1998; films include: Portraits of a Killer, 1996, Lover's Knot, 1996, Red Meat, 1997; other TV appearances include Friends, 1995.

GREY, JOEL, actor; b. Cleve., Apr. 11, 1932; s. Mickey and Grace Katz; m. Jo Wilder, June 29, 1958; children: Jennifer, Jimmy. Litt.D. (hon.), Cleve. State U., 1974. Began stage career in childhood, traveling with father as song and dance man, played Chez Paris, Chgo., at age 18; N.Y. stage debut in The Littlest Revue, 1956; appeared with nat. touring co. of Stop the World on Broadway, 1963, Come Blow Your Horn, 1961, Half a Sixpence, 1965, George M, 1969, Harry, Noon and Night, 1965, Marco Polo Sings a Solo, 1977; appeared on stage in Goodtime Charley, 1975, The Grand Tour, 1979, Silverlake, 1981, Pal Joey, 1983, 1988-89, (off-Broadway), The Normal Heart, 1986, When We Dead Awaken, 1991; starring role (Broadway prodn.) Cabaret, 1966-67, (Tony award 1967) (revival 1987-88, nat. tour 1988—), also motion picture, 1972 (Acad. award 1972); TV appearances include Evening at Pops, 1979, Dallas, 1991, others; (TV spls.) George M, 1970, Twas the Night Before Christmas, 1974, Jubilee!, 1976; Night of 100 Stars, 1982, The Yeoman of the Guard, 1984; (TV movie) The Wizard of Oz in Concert, 1995; (TV miniseries) Queenie, 1987, Marilyn and Me, 1991, The Dangerous, 1995; (films) About Face, 1952, Calypso Heat Wave, 1957, Come September, 1961, Man on a Swing, 1974, Buffalo Bill and the Indians, 1975, The Seven Percent Solution, 1976, Remo Williams: The Adventure Begins, 1985, Kafka, 1992, The Music of Chance, 1993, Venus Rising, 1995, The Fantasticks, 1995, The Empty Mirror, 1996, My Friend Joe, 1996. Address: Innovative Artists Talent and Literary Agy 1999 Ave Of Stars Ste 2850 Los Angeles CA 90067-4612*

GREY, JOSEPH EDWARD, II, artist; b. Lancaster, Ohio, May 20, 1927; s. Joseph E. and Lyla Belle (Goodwin) G.; m. Mary Gargiulo, Aug. 15, 1957; children: Catherine Alexandra, Anthony Joseph. CFA, Columbus Coll. of Art & Design, 1950, M Visual Arts, 1986. Graphic designer N.Y.C. Housing Authority, 1953-57; illustrator Chas Bracket Studio, N.Y.C., 1957-56; designer M&M Studio, N.Y.C., 1958-60, Paul Klemptner, N.Y.C., 1960-61; art dir. Hockaday Assocs., N.Y.C., 1961-65, Sullivan, Stoffer, Cowell & Bayles, N.Y.C., 1965-69; creative dir. McCann Erickson, Jamaica, W.I., 1969-72; art dir. McCann Erickson, N.Y.C., 1972-76, Troy, Mich., 1976-80; art dir. Campbell Ewald, Warren, Mich., 1980-90, McCann SAS, Troy, 1990-92; fine art painter Beverly Hills, Mich., 1992—. Pub. in: The Best of Watercolor 1996, Best of Watercolor Painting Composition, 1997, New Art Internat., 1997, Portrait Inspirations, 1997. Recipient Chevrolet-One Car Co. award Am. Film Festival, N.Y., 1986, Caddy/Gold award, Detroit, 1978, N.Y. Ad Club/Gold, N.Y., 1975, Am. Film Festival/Gold, N.Y., 1968. Mem. Tex. Watercolor Soc., Ariz. Watercolor Soc., Ft. Worth Watercolor Soc., Art Birmingham, Houston Watercolor Art Soc., Emily Lowe Nat. Watercolor Competition. Roman Catholic. Avocations: tennis, classical and jazz music. Home: 19100 Beverly Rd Beverly Hills MI 48025-3901

GREY, ROBERT DEAN, academic administrator, biology educator; b. Liberal, Kans., Sept. 5, 1939; s. McHenry Wesley and Kathryn (Brown) G.; m. Alice Kathleen Archer, June 11, 1961; children: Erin Kathleen, Joel Michael. BA, Phillips U., 1961; PhD, Washington U., 1966. Asst. prof. Washington U., St. Louis, 1966-67; from asst. prof. to full prof. zoology U. Calif., Davis, 1967—, chmn. dept., 1979-83, dean biol. scis., 1985—, interim exec. vice chancellor, 1993-95, provost, exec. vice chancellor, 1995—. Author: (with others) A Laboratory Text for Developmental Biology, 1980; contbr. articles to profl. jours. Recipient Disting. Tchg. awrd Acad. Senate U. Calif., Davis, 1977, Magnar Ronning award for tchg. Associated Students U. Calif., Davis, 1978, Disting. Alumnus award Phillips U., 1991. Mem. Am. Soc. Cell Biology, Soc. Developmental Biology, Phi Sigma. Avocations: music, hiking, gardening. Office: U Calif Office of the Provost 5th Flr Mrat Hall 1 Shields Ave Davis CA 95616

GREY, RUTHANN E., management consultant; b. Buffalo, N.Y., May 13, 1945; d. Wilson Campbell and Rosalie (Briggs) Evege; m. Daine A. Grey, Aug. 25, 1990; children: Daine, Jr., Keenan, Nichole. BS, SUNY, Buffalo, 1966, MS, 1970, PhD, 1980; postgrad., Harvard U., 1988. Tchr. Bennett High Sch., Buffalo, 1966-69; prof. Erie C.C., Buffalo, 1970-73; adminstr. No. Va. Community Coll., Annandale, 1975-76, Wayne State U., Detroit, 1978-80; dir. pub. affairs Burroughs Corp., Detroit, 1981-86; exec. asst. to chmn. bd. dirs. The Equitable, N.Y.C., 1986-89; mgr. pub. affairs N.Y. Times, N.Y.C., 1989-90; mgr. divsn. corp. rels. Pub. Svc. Corp. Colo., Denver, 1990-93; v.p. comm. and pub. affairs Hoechst Celanese, Bridgewater, N.J., 1993—; v.p. global media and external rels. Hoechst Marion Roussel, Bridgewater, 1996—; cons. A+ For Kids, Newark, 1989-90, Rockefeller Found., N.Y.C., 1989-90. Bd. dirs. Citizens Scholarship Found., Minn., 1990-94. Mem. Pub. Rels. Seminar, Arthur Page Soc., The Wisemen, Pub. Rels. Rsch. Found. Avocations: gardening, walking. E-mail: regrey@lx.netcom.com. Home: 28 Stonegate Dr Watchung NJ 07060-5471 Office: The Caunos Group 28 Stonegate Dr WE Watchung NJ 07060

GREYSER, LINDA LORRAINE, education educator; b. Lynn, Mass., Oct. 8, 1942; d. Paul and Minnie E. (Sogoloff) Segel; m. Stephen A. Greyser, June 30, 1968; 1 child, Naomi Judith. BA, Lake Erie Coll., 1964; MA, Middlebury Coll., 1965; EdM, Harvard U., 1990, EdD, 1994. Tchr. Beverly (Mass.) Pub. Schs., 1965-67, Wayland (Mass.) Pub. Schs., 1967-73; cons. Edn. Coop., Wellesley, Mass., 1991-94; assoc. dir. programs in profl. edn. Grad. Sch. Edn. Harvard U., Cambridge, Mass., 1994—; mem. Comm. for Common Core of Learning, Mass. Dept. Edn., 1993-94. Mem. sch. bd. Wayland Pub. Schs., 1981-90; mem. learning svcs. com. Pub. Broadcasting Svc., 1994—. Democrat. Home: 46 Campbell Rd Wayland MA 01778-1024 Office: Harvard U Grad Sch Edn PPE Gutman 339 Cambridge MA 02138

GREYSON, CLIFFORD RUSSELL, internist; b. N.Y.C., 1958. AB, Harvard Coll., 1980; MSEE, Stanford U., 1985, MD, 1987. Cert. internal medicine and cardiovascular diseases, critical care medicine. Resident in internal medicine Stanford U. Hosp., 1987-90, fellow in critical care, 1990-91; fellow in cardiovasc. disease U. Calif., San Francisco, 1991-95, faculty cardiology divsn., 1995—; co-dir. med. intensive care unit San Francisco VA Med. Ctr., 1998—. Elected to city coun. Town of Woodside, Calif., 1995. Recipient Clinician Scientist award Am. Heart Assn., 1995-96, Clin. Investigator Devel. award NIH, 1996—. Fellow Am. Coll. Cardiology; mem. ACP. Office: San Francisco VA Med Ctr Cardiology 111C 4150 Clement St San Francisco CA 94121-1545

GREYTAK, LEE JOSEPH, financial services and real estate development company executive; b. Bridgeport, Conn., Sept. 14, 1949; s. Eugene E. and Dorothy B. Greytak; BA in Acctg., Calif. State U., Fullerton, 1973; m. Judy C. Welch, Aug. 31, 1974; children: Marzette Rachelle, Melissa Renee, Joseph Scott. Sr. acct. Collins Foods Internat., Los Angeles, 1974-75; asst. controller Jack La Lanne European Health Spas, Los Angeles, 1975-77; controller Trammell Crow Co., Los Angeles, 1977-83, corp. sec., 1981-83; exec. v.p., chief fin. officer T.D. Service Fin. 1983-98, also bd. dirs., 1983-98; pres., Territory Devel., 1983-90. Mem. Nat. Assn. Accts., Am. Mgmt. Assn., Nat. Cash Mgmt. Assn., So. Calif. Cash Mgmt. Assn., Builders, Owners, and Mgrs. Assn., Aircraft Owners and Pilots Assn., C. of C. of U.S., Young Execs. of So. Calif., Forum of Corp. Dirs., Christian Businessmens Com. of USA, Forum of Corp. Dirs. and Internat. Devel. Rsch. Coun. Home: 2918 Shamrock Ave Brea CA 92821-4748

GRIBBEN, ALAN, English language educator, research consultant; b. Parsons, Kans., Nov. 21, 1941; s. J.S. and Ruth E. (North) G.; m. Irene Wong, Feb. 14, 1974; children: Walter Blake, Valerie Janet. BA in English, U. Kans., 1964; MA, U. Oreg., 1966; PhD, U. Calif., Berkeley, 1974. Rsrch. editor Mark Twain Papers, Bancroft Libr. U. Calif., Berkeley, 1967-74, instr. dept. English, 1972-73; asst. prof. dept. English, U. Tex., Austin, 1974-80, assoc. prof., 1980-88, prof., 1988-91, chmn. grad. studies dept. English, 1984-88; head dept. English and philosophy Auburn U., Montgomery, Ala., 1991—; disting. rsch. prof. Auburn U., Montgomery, 1998—; mem. State Graduation Requirements Task Force, 1995-96; spl. cons. Mark Twain Libr. Assn., 1981; co-chair nat. conf. The State of Mark Twain Studies, 1993, nat. conf. Cotton: The Fiber, The Land, The People, 1994. Author: Mark Twain's Library: A Reconstruction, 1980; editor: Mark Twain's Rubaiyat, 1983; co-editor: Overland with Mark Twain: James B. Pond's Photographs and Jour. of the North American Lecture Tour of 1895, 1992; mem. editl. bd. Studies in Am. Fiction, 1988-97, U. Miss. Studies in English, 1986-96, Studies in Am. Humor, 1982—, Western Am. Lit., 1991-98; nat. panel juror NEH, 1990-94; assoc. editor Librs. and Culture, 1980-91; contbr. articles to profl. jours. Recipient President's Assocs. Tchg. Excellence award U. Tex., 1983, Henry Nash Smith fellow Ctr. for Mark Twain Studies, Elmira Coll., 1997, Jervis Langdon Jr. fellow Ctr. for Mark Twain Studies, Elmira Coll., 1990. Mem. South Atlantic MLA, Mark Twain Cir. of Am. (hon. life, pres. 1987-89), Am. Lit. Assn. (exec. bd. 1989-96), Am. Humor Studies Assn., Western Am. Lit. Assn., Phi Kappa Phi. Avocations: bicycling, tennis, record and CD collecting (bands of 1930s and 1940s), rare book collecting, gardening. Home: 308 Arrowhead Dr Montgomery AL 36117-4108 Office: Auburn U at Montgomery Dept English and Philosophy PO Box 244023 Montgomery AL 36124-4023 *Libraries constitute the heart of higher education and the essence of civilization itself, whether in modern-day San Francisco or ancient Alexandria. To befriend a library collection, then, is to contribute tangibly to general human knowledge, intellectual freedom, and aspirations for humanity.*

GRIBBIN, ROBERT E., III, former ambassador; b. Durham, N.C., Feb. 5, 1946; m. Connie Chapman; children: Matt, Mark. BA, U. of the South, 1968; MA, Sch. Advanced Internat. Studies, 1973. Vol. Peace Corps., Kenya, 1968-70; econ. and comml. officer Bangui, 1974-76; prin. officer U.S. Consulate, Mombasa, Kenya, 1981-84; congl. fellow to Rep. Stephen J. Solarz, N.Y., 1984-85; dep. dir. Office of East African and Ctrl. African Affairs Dept. State, 1985-88; dep. chief of mission Am. Embassy, Kampala, Uganda, 1988-91, Kigali, Rwanda, 1979-81; sr. advisor for Africa UN; amb. to Ctrl. African Rep. Bangui, 1993-95; amb. to Rwanda, 1996-98. Recipient Superior Honor awards for combating famine in horn of Africa and for mgmt. of crisis in Rwanda. Office: Blvd De la Revolution, Kigali Rwanda*

GRIBBLE, CHARLES EDWARD, editor, Slavic language educator; b. Lansing, Mich., Nov. 10, 1936; s. Charles P. and Elizabeth K. G. B.A., U. Mich., 1957; A.M., Harvard U., 1958, Ph.D., 1967; postgrad. Moscow State U., 1960-61. Instr., asst. prof. Russian, Brandeis U., Waltham, Mass., 1961-68; asst. prof. Slavic langs. Ind. U., Bloomington, 1968-75; assoc. prof. Slavic langs. Ohio State U., Columbus, 1975-89, prof. Slavic lang., 1989—, chairperson of dept., 1990-96; pres., editor Slavica Pubs., Inc., Columbus, 1966-97; vis. assoc. prof. Slavic langs. U. Va., 1977. Woodrow Wilson fellow, 1957-58, Am. Council Learned Socs. fellow, 1972; Internat. Rsch. and Exchanges Bd. grantee, 1960-61, 72, 80, Fulbright grantee, 1987. Mem. Am. Assn. Advancement of Slavic Studies, Am. Assn. Tchr. of Slavic and E. European Langs. (Disting. Contribution to the Profession award 1992), Linguistic Soc. Am., MLA, Linguistic Soc. Europe, S.E. European Studies Assn., Phi Beta Kappa. Author: Russian Root List, 1973, A Short Dictionary of 18th-Century Russian, 1976; editor-in-chief Folia Slavica, 1977-88; editor: Studies Presented to Professor Roman Jakobson by His Students, 1968, Medieval Slavic Texts, vol. 1, 1973; contbr. articles to scholarly jours. Office: Ohio State U Slavic Lang 1841 Millikin Rd Rm 232 Columbus OH 43210-1229 also: PO Box 14388 Columbus OH 43214-0388

GRIBBON, DANIEL MCNAMARA, lawyer; b. Youngstown, Ohio, Jan. 27, 1917; s. James Edward and Loretta (Hogan) G.; m. Jane Retzler, Sept. 13, 1941; children: Diana Jane Gribbon Motz, Deborah Ann Gribbon Alt. AB, Case Western Res. U., 1938; JD, Harvard U., 1941. Bar: N.Y. 1942, D.C. 1946, U.S. Supreme Ct. 1950. Clk. Judge Learned Hand, N.Y.C., 1941-42; assoc. Covington & Burling, Washington, 1946-50, ptnr., 1950—; chmn. adv. com. on procedures U.S. Ct. Appeals (D.C. cir.), 1983-88. Served with USNR, 1942-46. Fellow Am. Bar Found.; mem. Am. Coll. Trial Lawyers, D.C. Bar Assn. (chmn. bd. profl. responsibility 1976-79). Roman Catholic. Clubs: Met. (Washington) (pres. 1981-82); Chevy Chase (Md.). Office: Covington & Burling 1201 Pennsylvania Ave NW Washington DC 20004-2401

GRIDER, JOHN ANTHONY, child and family therapist, consultant; b. Altus, Okla., Aug. 12, 1955; s. Johnny Wilson and Betty Lou (Hall) G.; m. Carolyn Rebecca Callahan, June 9, 1979; children: Christopher Stuart, Callan Rebecca. BA, U. Okla., 1977; MEd, U. Ctrl. Okla., 1981. Cert. counselor, Nat. Bd. Cert. Counselors. Domiciliary facility inspector Okla. State Dept. Health, Altus, 1977-78; psychol. asst. Okla. State Dept. Health, Moore, 1989—; social worker Okla. Dept. Human Svcs., Norman, 1978-89; cons., founder The Enthesis Group, Norman, 1997. Contbr. articles to profl. publs. Analyst State of Okla. Gov.'s Performance Team, Oklahoma City, 1995. Mem. Okla. State Workers Union (sec.-treas. 1993-95), Okla. Inst. for a Viable Future, World Future Soc., Ctrl. Okla. Futures Soc. Presbyterian. Home: 3604 Chatham Ct Norman OK 73072-4228 Office: State of Okla Dept Health 224 S Chestnut Ave Moore OK 73160-5223

GRIECO, PAUL ANTHONY, chemistry educator; b. Framingham, Mass., Oct. 27, 1944; married; 4 children. BA, Boston U., 1966; MA, Columbia U., 1967, PhD in Organic Chemistry, 1970. NSF fellow Harvard U., 1970-71; from asst. prof. to prof. chemistry U. Pitts., 1971-80; prof. chemistry Ind. U., Bloomington, 1980-85, Earl Blough prof. chemistry, 1985—, chmn. dept., 1988-97; head of chemistry and biochemistry dept. Mont. State U., 1999—; William P. Timmie lectr. Emory U., 1977; Abbott lectr. Yale U., 1984; H.C. Brown lectr. Purdue U., 1984; Disting. lectr. U. Wyo., 1986; Conv. Intercantonale Romande pour L'Enseignement du Troisième Cycle en Chimie, Switzerland, 1987; Centennial lectr. Abbott Labs., Chgo., 1988; H. Martin Friedman lectr. Rutgers U., 1988; Centennial Anniversary lectr. 1st Internat. Conf. on Organic Chem. Nomenclature, Geneva, 1992. Fellow Alfred P. Sloan Found., 1974-76, Japan Soc. Promising Scientists, 1978-79; recipient Ernest Guenther award, 1982, NIH-Nat. Cancer Inst. Merit award, 1988. Mem. Am. Chem. Soc. (Akron sect. award 1982, Arthur C. Cope Scholar award 1990, award for creative work in synthetic organic chemistry 1991, lectr. French.-Am. socs. meeting in France 1992), Royal Soc. Chemistry, Chem. Soc. Japan, Swiss Chem. Soc. Rsch. in the devel. of new synthetic methods for constrn. of complex natural products. Office: Mont State U Dept Biochemistry & Chem 108 Gains Hall Bozeman MT 59717

GRIEFEN, JOHN ADAMS, artist, educator; b. Worcester, Mass., Nov. 24, 1942; s. Robert John and Faith (Adams) G.; m. Paulette Joy Hunsicker, Sept. 27, 1970; 1 child, Katherine Abigail Jacqueline. Student, Chgo. Art Inst., 1964-65, Bennington Coll., 1965-66; B.A., Williams Coll., 1966; postgrad., Hunter Coll., 1966-68. Instr. Bennington Coll., 1968-69, Great Neck Adult Edn., N.Y., 1971-76. One-man shows Kornblee Gallery, 1969, 70, 73, Deitcher O'Reilly Gallery, N.Y.C., shows, William Edward O'Reilly Inc., N.Y.C., Martha Jackson Gallery, N.Y.C., Frank Watters Gallery, Sydney, Australia, 1979, Salander O'Reilly Galleries, N.Y.C., 1981, 82, 84, 85, 91, 93, Harcus-Hrakow Gallery, Boston, Phyllis Kind Galley, Chgo., B.R. Kornblatt Gallery, Balt., Diane Brown Gallery, Washington, 1978, Sunne Savage Gallery, Boston, 1979, Williams Coll. Mus. Art, Williamstown, Mass., 1980, Martin Gerard Gallery, Edmonton, Alta., Can., 1981, Gallery Moos Ltd., Toronto and Calgary, 1981, Edmonton Art Gallery, 1984, Hirondelle Gallery, N.Y.C., 1986, Salander O'Reilly Galleries, L.A., 1991, Edmonton Art Gallery, Alberta, Can., 1993, Swift Current Art Gallery, Sask., 1993, S.C. Schultz Gallery, N.J., 1994; exhibited group shows Indpls. Mus. Art, Phoenix Mus., Sydney Mus., Whitney Mus. Purdue U., N.Y. Mus. Modern Art, Santa Barbara Mus., Boston Mus. Fine Arts; represented in pub. collections Larry Aldrich Mus. Contemporary Art, Allen Art Mus., Arthur A. Anderson Co., Bank of Ill., Calgary (Can.), Boston Mus. Fine Arts, Bklyn. Mus., Carnegie Inst. Mus. Art, Chase Manhattan Bank, Continental Resources Inc., Hines Indsl., Boston, N.Y.C., Washington, Dallas, Hirshhorn Mus. and Sculpture Garden, Washington, Met. Mus. Art, Michner Collections-U. Tex., Musnson-William-Proctor Art Inst., Mus. Modern Art, Newark Mus. Fine Arts, Reader's Digest Assn. Inc., Rose Art Mus., Brandeis U., Rothmans Art Gallery, St. Lawrence U., Sydney Mus., Australia, Whitney Mus., Williams Coll. Art Mus., Worcester Mus. Art, Mass., Met. Mus. Art, N.Y.C., Vassar Coll. Mus. Art, Poughkeepsie, N.Y., Lowcart Gallery, Miami. Recipient Esther Forbes award Bancroft Sch., Worcester, Mass., 1996. Home: 57 Laight St New York NY 10013-2042 Office: care Salander O'Reilly Galleries 20 E 79th St New York NY 10021-0106 *For the love of art and the kindness of strangers.*

GRIEGO, ELIZABETH BROWNLEE, college dean; b. Lincoln, Nebr., Nov. 9, 1949; d. John Templeton and Elizabeth (Waugh) B.; m. Robert Frederick Griego, Aug. 19, 1972; children: Ann Elizabeth Brownlee, Paul Christopher. BS Speech, Hearing Pathology/Audiology, U. Nebr., 1971; MS, Ohio State U., 1972; PhD in Higher Edn. Adminstrn., U. Calif., Berkeley, 1983. Residence dir. U. Nebr., Lincoln, 1972-73, summer conf. mgr., 1973, 74, complex program dir. office of univ. housing, 1973-75; dir. student activities for residence halls San Francisco State U., 1975-76; asst. dean students/dir. residential life Mills Coll., 1976-80, assoc. dean students/dir. student activities, 1980-81, dir. planning and rsch., sec. to bd. trustees, 1981-86, dir. planning and rsch./spl. asst. to pres., 1986-89; dean student affairs and rsch. Samuel Merritt Coll., Oakland, Calif., 1989—; condr. numerous workshops in field; evaluator various orgns./instns.; lectr. in field. Contbr. articles to profl. jours.; author: Samuel Merritt College Factbook, 1992, 3d edit. 1994, (monograph) Samuel Merritt College Alumni Profile, 1992. Bd. dirs. Inst. for Hist. Study of Bay Area, 1983-85; organizer Habitat for Humanity, Oakland, 1994—; organizer, mem. cmty. svc. tchr. aide and tutoring program Lakeview Elem. Sch., Oakland, 1995-96; organizer, mem. after-sch. tutoring program santa Fe Elem. Sch., Oakland, 1993—; deacon Piedmont Cmty. Ch., liaison to Oakland Coalition of Cmty. chs. and cmty. organizing chair, 1993-96; bd. dirs. Citizens Highly Interested in Music Edn., Piedmont, 1988-89; prodr. original children's opera The Pillow of Kantan, Piedmont Choirs, 1990; 1st v.p. bd. dirs., chair long range planning com. Camp Fire Internat., Alameda, Contra Costa Coun., 1987-90; bd. dirs. Ctr. for Edn. of the Infant Deaf, 1987-89, Mothers Club of Wildwood Sch., 1987-89; adv. com. Mercy H.S. Project 2000, San Francisco, 1985-86; adv. bd. Displaced Homemakers Assn., 1983-85; pres. Claremont Hills Neighborhood Assn., 1983-85. Recipient Blue Bird award for outstanding leadership Alameda-Contra Costa Coun. of Camp Fire Boys and Girls, 1990, Award of the Wolf for greatest ann. achievement and svc. to multicultural group Samuel Merritt Coll., 1994; Student Body Assn. Yearbook dedication for Educator Who Had Greatest Impact on Students, 1990. Mem. Nat. Assn. Student Pers. Adminstrs. (chair exec. com. for no. Calif. 1994-96), Western Assn. Schs. and Colls. (mem. accreditation team 1991-95), Calif. Assn. Instl. Rsch. (exec. com. 1992-93, pres. 1991-92, mem. reorganizing com. 1986-87, Award recognition for serving on 1st exec. bd. 1989, Pres.'s Award for Leadership 1992, Outstanding Svc. award 1993), Western Assn. Women Historians (bd. dirs., chair com. grad. scholarship award 1986-87). Home: 7 Abbott Way Piedmont CA 94618-2609 Office: Samuel Merritt College 370 Hawthorne Ave Oakland CA 94609-3108

GRIEM, HANS RUDOLF, physicist, educator; b. Kiel, Schleswig-Holstein, Germany, Oct. 7, 1928; came to U.S., 1954; s. Rudolf H. and Paula D. (Schwarz) G.; m. Irmgard H. Höhling, May 11, 1957; children: Jens, Torsten, Rowena, Bridget. Abitur, Max-Planck Sch. Kiel, 1949; PhD, U. Kiel, 1954; PhD (hon.), Ruhr U., Bochum, Fed. Republic Germany, 1990. Rsch. asst. U. Md., College Park, 1954-55, asst. prof., 1957-61, assoc. prof., 1961-63, prof., 1963-94; prof. emeritus, sr. rsch. scientist, 1994—; Wissenschaftlicher asst. U. Kiel, 1955-57; dir. Lab. for Plasma Rsch. U. Md., 1980-87; cons. Naval Rsch. Lab., Washington, 1957-96, Lawrence Livermore (Calif.) Nat. Lab., 1979—. Author: Plasma Spectroscopy, 1964, Spectral Line Broadening by Plasmas, 1974, Principles of Plasma Spectroscopy, 1997; editor: Methods of Experimental Physics, Vol. 9A, 1970; contbr. articles to sci. jours., chpts. to books. NSF sr. postdoctoral fellow, 1963; Guggenheim Found. fellow, 1968; European Space Rsch. Orgn. fellow, 1971; recipient Humboldt prize, 1978, William F. Meggers award Optical Soc. Am., 1987. Fellow Am. Phys. Soc. (councilor 1983-87, J.C. Maxwell prize 1991). Achievements include devel. of quantitative spectroscopic methods for high temperature plasma diagnostics. Office: Univ of Md Inst for Plasma Rsch College Park MD 20742-3511

GRIEMAN, JOHN JOSEPH, communications executive; b. St. Paul, Minn., Sept. 7, 1944; s. Roy and Agnes (Thell) G.; m. Joan Schultz, Sept. 12,

1964; children: Nancy, Amy, Angie, Ginette. BS in Acctg., Coll. of St. Thomas, St. Paul, 1966. Supr. Coopers & Lybrand, Mpls., 1966-72; treas. 1st Midwest Corp., Mpls., 1972-75; pvt. practice fin. cons. Mpls., 1975-76; dir. corp. planning and systems, asst. controller constrn. equipment, group mgr. corp. acctg. Am. Hoist & Derrick Co., St. Paul, 1976-82; controller Cowles Media Co., Mpls., 1982, v.p., 1983; controller Mpls. Star and Tribune Co., 1983-96; v.p., CFO Mpls. Star and Tribune, 1983-96; cons. bus. improvement New Brighton, Minn., 1996—. Bd. dirs. Jr. Achievement Upper Midwest, 1987-97, Project for Pride in Living, Mpls., 1994—. Mem. Am. Inst. CPA's (chmn. mems. in industry com. 1979-81), Minn. Soc. CPA's (bd. dirs., treas. 1980-81, mem. of month 1977). Home and Office: 1410 18th St NW New Brighton MN 55112-5407*

GRIEP, ANN MARIE, education association education coordinator; b. Grand Rapids, Mich., Jan. 2, 1964; d. John Arthur Griep and Hope Ann DeJonge; m. Philippe Ferdinand Backeljauw, Dec. 1, 1985; children: Barynia, Nathalia. BA magna cum laude, Hope Coll., 1985; MA in Romance Lang. & Lit., U. Chgo., 1988, PhD in Romance Lang. & Lit. with honors, 1994. Instr. French Ctrl. Piedmont C.C., Charlotte, N.C., 1996-97; edn. coord. Lang. Masters, Inc., Charlotte, N.C., 1997-98; French tchr. Smith Acad. Internat. Languages, Charlotte, N.C., 1998—. Mem. MLA, Am. Assn. Tchrs. French, South Atlantic MLA, Phi Beta Kappa, Pi Delta Phi. Avocations: family, creative writing. Office: Smith Acad of International Languages 1600 Tyvola Rd Charlotte NC 28210-3509

GRIEP, DAVID MICHAEL, astronomical scientist, researcher; b. Mpls., Oct. 13, 1957; s. Richard Arthur Sr. and Carole Elaine (Bengal) G.; m. Carolina May Von Gnechten, Nov. 19, 1994. BS in Astrophysics, U. Minn. Inst. Tech., 1979; MS in Astronomy, U. Minn., 1981. Rsch. assoc. Inst. Astronomy U. Hawaii, Hilo, 1982—. Office: Univ Hawaii Inst Astronomy PO Box 4729 Hilo HI 96720-0729

GRIER, DAVID ALAN, actor. Grad., U. Mich., Yale U. Actor (Broadway plays) The First (Tony award nomination, Theatre World award), Dreamgirls, A Funny Thing Happened on the Way to the Forum, (off-Broadway plays) A Soldier's Play, various other stage credits; appeared in tv series All is Forgiven, 1986, In Living Color, 1990, The Preston Episodes, 1995, Damon, 1998, appeared in films Streamers, 1983, A Soldier's Story, 1984, Beer, 1985, Ich und Er, 1987, From the Hip, 1987, Amazon Women on the Moon, 1987, I'm Gonna Git You Sucka, 1998, Off Limits, 1988, Almost an Angel, 1990, Loose Cannons, 1990, The Player, 1992, Boomerang, 1992, In the Army Now, 1994, Blankman, 1994, Tales from the Hood, 1995, Jumanji, 1995, Top of the World, 1997, McHale's Navy, 1997, also TV movies. Office: c/o St James Theatre 246 W 44th St New York NY 10036-3910*

GRIER, DOROTHY ANN PRIDGEN, secondary education specialist; b. Pitts., Jan. 14, 1936; d. Jay Lawrence and Myra (Morgan) Pridgen; m. Robert Warren Grier, Mar. 27, 1959; children: Cassandra Ann, Robert Warren Jr. BS, U. Pitts., 1959, MEd, 1981, PhD, 1989. Tchr. Pitts. Pub. Schs., 1960-63, 72-75, reading specialist, 1975-84, program specialist, 1984-85, supervisory instructional specialist, 1985—; state evaluator Dept. Edn. State of Pa., Harrisburg, 1988—; mem. tech. com. strategic plan Pitts. Pub. Schs., 1995—; invited speaker 4th No. Am. Conf. on Adolescent/Adult Literacy, Washington, 1996. Mem. Strategic Planning Com. for Sewickley (Pa.) Acad., 1988-91; trustee Pine Richland Sch. Dist. Opportunities, Inc., 1994—. Mem. Internat. Reading Assn. (exec. com. Pitts.-Three Rivers coun. 1990-93), Internat. Assn. Secondary Reading Interest Group (pres.-elect 1992, pres. 1994-96, com. media awards for broadcast and print 1998—), Secondary Reading Interest Group (chmn. 1990-94, v.p. Pa. Keystone State coun. 1991—), Pitts. Women's Missionary Circle, Harty Bible Sch. Alumni Assn. (pres. 1992—), No. Allegheny County C. of C. (tchr. excellence award selection com. 1996). Avocations: walking, knitting, reading.

GRIER, JAMES EDWARD, hotel company executive, lawyer; b. Ottumwa, Iowa, Sept. 7, 1935; s. Edward J. and Corinne (Bailey) G.; m. Virginia Clinker, July 4, 1959; children: Michael, Susan, James, John, Thomas. BSc, U. Iowa, 1956, JD, 1959. Bar: Iowa 1959, Mo. 1959. Mng. ptnr. Hillix, Brewer, Hoffhaus & Grier, Kansas City, Mo., 1964-77, Grier & Swartzman, Kansas City, 1977-89; pres. Doubletree Hotels Corp., Phoenix, 1989-94; chmn. Sonoran Hotel Capital, Inc., Phoenix, 1994-96; mng. ptnr. Copa Investments, 1996—, Gainey Hotel Co., 1996—; bd. dirs. Iowa Law Sch. Found., Iowa City, St. Joseph Healthcare Ariz., Phoenix, Homeward Bound, Phoenix. Home: 3500 E Lincoln Dr Phoenix AZ 85018-1010 Office: Copa Investments Ste 169 7300 E Gainey Suites Dr Scottsdale AZ 85258

GRIER, JOSEPH WILLIAMSON, JR., lawyer; b. Charlotte, N.C., Aug. 5, 1915; s. Joseph Williamson and Beulah Mae (Wallace) G.; m. Catherine Langdon Smart, Oct. 28, 1949; children: Joseph Williamson, III, Catherine Grier Kelly, Susan Grier Bennett, Roy Smart, Bruce Taliaferro, Robin Wallace. AB in Econs, U. N.C., Chapel Hill, 1937; JD, Harvard U., 1940. Bar: N.C. 1940, U.S. Supreme Ct. 1947. Sr. ptnr. Grier, Parker, Poe, Thompson, Bernstein, Gage & Preston, Charlotte, 1946-83; ptnr. Grier & Grier, P.A., Charlotte, 1984-97; of counsel Grier & Furr, P.A., Charlotte, 1998—. Mem. N.C. Bd. Higher Edn., 1964-65; chmn. bd. trustees Queens Coll., Charlotte, 1974—, chmn., 1974-82, chmn. emeritus, 1982—; chmn. permanent jud. commn. Presbyn. Ch., 1966-71; trustee Presbyn. Found., 1972-78, v.p., 1973-76, pres., 1977-78; chmn. Charlotte Pks. and Recreation Commn., 1959-63, Presbyn. Hosp. Found., 1980—; pres. Charlotte-Mecklenburg YMCA, 1968-70, trustee, 1986—; bd. dirs. Cmty. Sch. Arts, Ginter Found.; bd. visitors U. N.C., Charlotte, 1987—, Lineberger Comprehensive Cancer Ctr., 1994—; mem. Nalle Clinic Found., 1988; vice chair Commn. to Present Charter of Consolidation of City and County Govt. With U.S. Army, 1942-45. Decorated Bronze Star; recipient Man of Yr. award Civitan Club of Charlotte, 1967, Algernon Sydney Sullivan award Queens Coll., 1984, Disting. Alumni award Darlington Sch., 1996, John R. Mott award YMCA of Greater Charlotte, 1996. Fellow Am. Bar Found., Am. Law Inst., Presbyn. Hosp. Found.; mem. ABA, N.C. Bar Assn. (bd. govs., v.p. 1983, inducted Gen. Practice Hall of Fame 1989), Am. Judicature Soc., 26th Jud. Dist. Bar Assn. (pres. 1956), Am. Legion (dept. comdr. N.C. 1948-49), Charlotte Country Club, Charlotte City Club, Phi Delta Theta. Democrat. Home: 1869 Queens Rd W Charlotte NC 28207-2456 Office: Grier & Furr PA Ste 1240 1 Independence Ctr Charlotte NC 28246

GRIER, PAMELA, actress, writer, singer; b. Winston-Salem, N.C., May 26, 1949; d. Clarence Ransom Grier and Gwendolyn (Sylvia) Samuels. Appeared in films Bill and Teds Bogus Adventure, The Package, Class of 1991, Rocket Gibraltar, Above the Law, Something Wicked This Way Comes, Fort Apache: The Bronx, Tough Enough, Greased Lightening, Posse, 1993, Serial Killer, 1995, Original Gangstas, 1996, Escape from L.A., 1996, Mars Attacks!, 1996, Strip Search, 1997, Fakin' Da Funk, 1997, Jackie Brown, 1997, Holy Smoke, 1999, (on stage) Fool For Love, Frankie and Johnnie, In the Claire De Lune. Named Best Actress NAACP, 1986. Mem. Acad. Motion Picture Arts and Scis., Amnesty Internat. Methodist. Avocations: skiing, scuba diving, western and English horseback riding, tennis.

GRIER, PHILIP TODD, philosophy educator; b. Greenville, S.C., Nov. 3, 1942; s. Rufus Todd and Ernestine (Carty) G.; m. Eleonora Feodorovna Veremeitchik, Feb. 22, 1969; children: Andrew Todd, Alexandra Elaine. BA, Swarthmore Coll., 1964, Oxford (Eng.) U., 1966; cert. in Russian and Soviet studies, U. Mich., 1968, U. Mich., 1968; PhD, U. Mich., 1973. Lectr. in Russian studies U. Keele, North Staffordshire, Eng., 1969-73; asst. prof. philosophy Northwestern U., Evanston, Ill., 1973-80; assoc. prof. Dickinson Coll., Carlisle, Pa., 1980-94, prof., 1994—, Thomas Bowman prof. philosophy, 1997—. Author: Marxist Ethical Theory in the Soviet Union, 1978; editor: Dialectic and Contemporary Science, 1989; editl. cons. The Owl of Minerva, 1991—; mem. editl. bd. Studies in East European Thought, 1980—, Sovietica Series of Monographs, 1980—; mem. adv. bd. Russian Studies in Philosophy, 1988—. U.S./USSR Cultural Exch. scholar, 1968-69; Ford Fgn. Area fellow, 1969; NEH grantee, 1993. Mem. Am. Philos. Assn., Hegel Soc. Am. (councillor 1994-98). Avocations: skiing, flying. Office: Dickinson Coll Philosophy Dept Carlisle PA 17013

GRIER, PHILLIP MICHAEL, lawyer, former association executive; b. Quitman, Ga., Aug. 31, 1941; s. Phillip Moore and Helen Dale Parrish (Cottingham) G. BA, Furman U., 1963; JD, U. S.C., 1969. Bar: S.C. 1969, U.S. Dist. Ct. S.C. 1969, U.S. Ct. Appeals (4th cir.) 1972, U.S. Supreme Ct. 1978, U.S. Ct. Appeals (fed. cir.) 1985. Assoc. Haynsworth, Perry, Bryant, Marion & Johnstone, Greenville, S.C., 1969-70; asst. to pres. U. S.C., Columbia, 1969, staff counsel, 1970-74, gen. counsel, 1974-79; exec. dir., CEO Nat. Assn. Coll. and Univ. Attys., Washington, 1979-96; cons. Fulbright & Jaworski, Washington, 1996—; bd. dirs. Am. Coun. Edn., 1992-94; mem. adv. bd. Ctr. for Constl. Studies, U. Notre Dame and Mercer U., 1981-92; mem. secretariat of nat. higher edn. orgns. Nat. Ctr. for Higher Edn., Washington, 1979-96. Author: (with Joseph P. O'Neill) Financing in a Period of Retrenchment: A Primer for Small Private Colleges, 1984. Editor: The Corporate Counsellors Deskbook (Non-Profit Organizations Supplement), 1983; editor, contbg. author: Legal Deskbook for Administrators of Independent Colleges and Universities, 1982, 83, 84; editor Coll. Law Digest, 1980-96; mem. editorial adv. com. West Pub. Co., St. Paul, 1980-96; editorial bd. Jour. Coll. and Univ. Law, U. Notre Dame, Ind., 1979-96. With U.S. Army, 1963-66, USAR, 1966-74. Mem. ABA, Nat. Assn. Bar Execs., S.C. Bar Assn., Furman U. Alumni Assn. (bd. govs. 1970-74), Entomol. Soc. Am., U.S. Supreme Ct. Hist. Soc., Assn. Bar City of N.Y., Bar Assn. D.C., Order of St. John, Soc. Colonial Wars, St. Nicholas Soc. of N.Y., Mil. Order Fgn. Wars, Ancient and Honorable Artillery Co., City Tavern Club (bd. govs. 1992—, sec. 1994, v.p. 1996—), Cosmos Club (legal affairs com. 1986-90, com. reciprocity 1988-90, house com. 1990-95, chmn. 1992-95), Omicron Delta Kappa, Phi Delta Phi. Home: 801 Pennsylvania Ave NW Washington DC 20004-2615 Office: 5th Fl 801 Pennsylvania Ave NW Washington DC 20004-2615

GRIER, RUTH, environmentalist; b. Dublin, Ireland, Oct. 2, 1936; arrived in Can., 1956; d. Alexander Earls and Gertrude (Sykes) Dowds; m. Terence Wyly Grier, Dec. 5, 1958; children: David, Timothy, Patrick. Diploma in pub. adminstrn., Trinity Coll., Dublin, 1956; BA in Polit. Sci., Econs. with honors, U. Toronto, Ont., Can., 1958. Min. of the environment Ontario, 1990-93; min. of health Toronto, 1993-95; vis. environmentalist Innis Coll. U. Toronto, 1996-98. Alderman City of Etobicoke, Ont., 1970-85; mem. provincial parliament Etobicoke-Lakeshore, 1985-95. Anglican. Home: 74 Arcadian Circle, Toronto, ON Canada M8W 2Y9

GRIESA, THOMAS POOLE, federal judge; b. Kansas City, Mo., Oct. 11, 1930; s. Charles Henry and Stella Lusk (Bedell) G.; m. Christine Pollard Meyer, Jan. 5, 1963. A.B. cum laude, Harvard U., 1952; LL.B., Stanford U., 1958. Bar: Wash. 1958, N.Y. 1961. Atty. Justice Dept., 1958-60; with firm Symmers, Fish & Warner, N.Y.C., 1960-61, Davis Polk & Wardwell, N.Y.C., 1961-72; partner Davis Polk & Wardwell, 1970-72; judge U.S. Dist. Ct. So. Dist. N.Y., 1972—, chief judge, 1993—. Mem.: Stanford Law Rev., 1956-58. Bd. visitors Stanford Law Sch., 1982-84. Served to lt. (j.g.) USCGR, 1952-54. Mem. Bar Assn. City N.Y., Union Club N.Y.C. Christian Scientist. Office: US Dist Ct US Courthouse 500 Pearl St New York NY 10007-1316

GRIESBAUER, MICHELE ELAINE, newspaper official; b. Balt., July 29, 1964; d. Stanley Raymond and Leni Elfreide (Bischoff) Siminski; m. Melvin B. Griesbauer, Sept. 8, 1984 (div. June 1988). AS, SUNY, Albany, 1988; AA, Dundalk C.C., Balt., 1995; student, Towson U., 1995—. Photoengraver Balt. Sun, 1988-96, classified advt. rep., 1996—. Contbr. articles to various mags. and poetry to various publs. With USN, 1983-88. Mem. Soc. Profl. Journalists, Am. Legion, Nat. Honor Soc., Golden Key, Moose. Roman Catholic. Avocations: reading, arts and crafts, photography, music journalist and critic.

GRIESCHE, ROBERT PRICE, hospital purchasing executive; b. Berkeley, Calif., July 21, 1953; s. Robert Bowen and Lillian (Price) G.; m. Susan Dawn Albers, June 8, 1985 (div. Apr. 1989); 1 child, Sara Christine. AA, Coll. of the Canyons, Valencia, Calif., 1984. Warehouse supr. John Muir Hosp., Walnut Creek, Calif., 1973-82; purchasing mgr. Henry Mayo Newhall Hosp., Valencia, 1982-85; materials mgr. Foothill Presbyn. Hosp., Glendora, Calif., 1985-87; materials mgmt. dir. Huntington Meml. Hosp., Pasadena, Calif., 1987-96; sys. dir. purchasing So. Calif. Healthcare Sys., Pasadena, 1996—; chmn. Huntington Employee Campaign, 1990-92. V.p. Coll. of Canyons Found., Valencia, 1985-90. Named to Outstanding Young Men of Am., 1988. Mem. Am. Soc. Healthcare Materials Mgmt., Calif. Cen. Svc. Assn. (charter). Republican. Presbyterian. Avocations: swimming, gardening, photography. Home: 3651 Cosmos Ct Palmdale CA 93550-5748 Office: So Calif Healthcare Sys 1300 E Green St Pasadena CA 91106-2606

GRIESÉ, JOHN WILLIAM, III, astronomer, mental health advocate; b. Norwalk, Conn., Sept. 27, 1955; s. John William Jr. and Celia (Bolté) G. Student, Franklin and Marshall Coll., 1974-77, U. Bridgeport, 1977-78; diploma, Morse Sch. Bus., Hartford, 1986; student, U. Conn., 1991-95, Trinity Coll., Hartford, 1995-97, Wesleyan U., Middletown, Conn., 1995-96. Observer Stamford (Conn.) Obs., 1973, asst. dir., 1978—; observer Van Vleck Obs., Middletown, Conn., 1986, asst. astrometry program, 1992—; user Perkin-Elmer PDS, Yale U., New Haven, 1992—, rsch. asst., 1993—; rsch. asst. astrometry-photometry group Wesleyan U., Middletown, 1997—; asst. editor Hartford Lit. mag. U. Conn., 1991-95; founder Morse Tutoring Svc., 1985; tutor Math. Ctr., Trinity Coll., 1995-96; lectr. Stamford Mus., 1985—; presenter and lectr. in field, 1996—; adj. instr. Middlesex Cmty. Tech. Coll., Conn., 1996—; course asst. Wesleyan U., 1998—, instr., adult edn., 1998—; alternate consumer rep. Nat. Alliance for Mentally Ill-CT (NAMI-CT), 1998-99. Contbr. articles to Jour. Am. Assn. Variable Star Obs., Deep Sky Mag., The Astronomical Jour.: observations of variable stars pub. on circulars of Cen. Bur. for Astron. Telegrams, Internat. Astron. Union, Smithsonian Astrophys. Obs., The Astron. Jour. Mem. consumer support coun. Conn. Alliance for Mentally Ill., Hartford, 1997-98. Named one of Outstanding Young Man of Am., 1987. Mem. Am. Assn. Variable Star Observers (coun. 1985-90, liaison and rep. to mems. in Hungary, contbr. Variable Star Atlas, edits. I and II, preliminary charts com., supernova search com., telescopes com., Observer award 1994), Am. Aston. Soc., Royal Astron. Soc. Can., Hungarian Astron. Assn., Astron. Soc. Pacific, Mt. Wilson Obs. Assn., Western Observatorium (bd. dirs. 1994—), Western Amateur Astronomers (pub. info. coord. 1989-90, Caroline Herschel Astronomy project award 1988, v.p., acting pres. 1992, v.p. 1992-94), L.A. Astron. Soc., Fairfield County Astron. Soc. (treas. 1985-88, 99—, pres. 1988-94, v.p. 1994-96, pres. 1996-99, acting treas. 1996-97, 98—), Astron. Soc. Greater Hartford (pres. 1992-93), Astron. League (long range planning com. 1992-94), Westport Astron. Soc., Riverside Astron. Soc., Astron. Soc. Coonabarabran (NSW, Australia), Mental Health Assn. Conn. (facilitator self-help support groups and adv. com. 1998—), Nat. Alliance for Mentally Ill-Conn., Golden Key, Phi Beta Lambda (pres. 1985). Democrat. Home: 965 Elms Common Dr Rocky Hill CT 06067-1833

GRIESEMER, ALLAN DAVID, retired museum director; b. Mayville, Wis., Aug. 13, 1935; s. Raymond John and Leone Emma (Fisher) G.; m. Nancy Jean Sternberg, June 6, 1959; children: David, Paul, Steven. A.B., Augustana Coll., 1959; M.S., U. Wis., 1963; Ph.D., U. Nebr., 1970. Curator; coordinator ednl. services U. Nebr., Lincoln State Museum, 1965-77, assoc. prof., assoc. dir., 1977-79, acting dir., 1980-81, assoc. dir. and coordinator, 1981-82, interim dir., 1982-84; dir. San Bernardino County Mus., Calif., 1984-97, dir. emeritus, 1997—; mem. faculty dept. geology U. Nebr., Lincoln, 1968-80; lectr. geology U. Nebr., Lincoln State Mus., 1968-80; CEO, dir., curator Mousley Mus. Natural History, San Bernardino County Mus., Yucaipa, Calif.; adj. prof. Calif. State U., San Bernardino, 1986. Contbr. articles to sci. jours., mus. publs., 1965—. Bd. dirs. Redland Music Assn., Prospect Pk., Boys and Girls Club, Inland Harvest, Calif. Desert Studies Consortium, Redlands Cmty. Hosp. Found.; mem. adv. bd. Redlands Cmty. Hosp., brd. mem., Habitat Humanity San Bernardino, adv. mem., Montessori in Red Lands. Recipient Hon. award Sigma Gamma Epsilon, 1958. Mem. Paleontol. Soc., Nebr. Mus. Conf. (pres. 1976-79), Nebr. Geol. Soc., Nebr. Acad. Scis., Mountain Plains Conf., Mountain Plains Mus. Assn. (pres. 1979), Am. Assn. Museums (v.p. 1983), Am. Assn. State and Local History, Western Museums Conf., Rotary. Lutheran. Home: 306 La Colina Dr Redlands CA 92374-8247

GRIEVE, PIERSON MACDONALD, retired specialty chemicals and services company executive; b. Flint, Mich., Dec. 5, 1927; s. P.M. and Margaret (Leamy) G.; m. Florence R. Brogan, July 29, 1950; children: Margaret, Scott, Bruce. BSBA, Northwestern U., 1950; postgrad., U. Minn., 1955-56. Staff engr. Caterpillar Tractor Co., Peoria, Ill., 1950-52; mgmt. cons. A.T. Kearney & Co., Chgo., 1952-55; pres. Rap-in-Wax, Mpls., 1955-62; exec. AP Parts Corp., Toledo, 1962-67; pres., CEO Questor Corp., Toledo, 1967-82; CEO Ecolab Inc., St. Paul, 1983-96; ret.; bd. dirs. St. Paul Cos. Inc., Media One Group Inc.; chmn. Minnegasco; ptnr. Paladium Equity Ptnrs. LLC. Chmn. Met. Airport Commn., State of Minn.; mem. adv. coun. J.L. Kellogg Grad. Sch. Mgmt., Northwestern U.; chmn. bd. overseers Carlson Sch. Mgmt., U. Minn.; bd. dirs. Guthrie Theatre; bd. trustees St. Thomas U. With USNR, 1945-46. Mem. Chevaliers du Tastevin, Mpls. Club, Beta Gamma Sigma (dirs. table). Episcopalian.

GRIEVE, WILLIAM ROY, psychologist, educator, educational administrator, researcher,; b. N.Y.C., Mar. 15, 1917; s. Walter Stuart and Grace (Buttendorf) G.; m. Harriet Bush, Mar. 30, 1978; children: Leslie Lynne Grieve Bainbridge, Davelyn Anne Grieve Sandhowe. Student, SUNY, Oswego, 1934-35; BS, NYU, 1937, MA, 1938; EdD, Rutgers U., 1954. Tchr. secondary edn. N.Y.C., 1938-48; rsch. fellow Ohio State U., 1942; ind. arts editor High Point Mag. N.Y.C. Bd. Edn., 1948-65, textbook and instnl. materials com., 1954-65, curriculum specialist Bur. Curriculum Rsch., 1948-50, supr., adminstr. secondary edn., 1950-65; prof. NYU, 1965-72, ombudsman Sch. Edn., 1969-71; prof. grad. program Rio Piedras, NYU/U. P.R., P.R., 1966-67; rsch. predictive testing specialist in vocat./tech. edn. Rio Piedras; ESSA and ESAA evaluation studies in reading, math., ESL, 1970-83; assoc. dir. evaluation studies divsn. Psychol. Corp., 1972-75; dir. Ednl. Planning and Rsch. Inc., Boston, 1975-83; pres. Ednl. Planning and Rsch. Inc., Glencove, N.Y. and Stuart, Fla., 1983—; asst. examiner ind., supervision, guidance lics., N.Y.C. Bd. Edn., 1950-72; chmn. ind. edn. standing com. Bd. Supts., N.Y.C., 1960-65; adj. prof. psychology L.I. U., Bklyn., 1965-70; adj. prof. edn. N.Y. Inst. Tech., Westbury, N.Y., 1981-86, SUNY, Westbury, 1986-89; cons. N.Y. C.C. orthodontics and prosthetics, 1966, N.C. State U., 1968, Pub. Edn. Assn./Nat. Alliance Businessmen, N.Y., 1968-72, Citibank, P.R., 1970, Met. Mus. Art, N.Y.C., The Art of Black Africa, 1970, Sta. UFT-TV, N.Y., 1970, Young and Rubicam, N.Y., 1974, Cautaulds Internat., Mobile, Ala., 1975, Rheem Mfg., Chgo., 1975, Bankers Trust, N.Y.C.,1 975, Republic Steel, Akron and Canton, Ohio, 1977, S.W. Regional Lab., Calif., 1980, N.Y. State Dept. Edn., 1985—, spl. cons. lat. edn. progress, coop. edn., work study, career edn. tng. and devel., 1990—. *His pioneering work in field of predictive testing has been used to establish specific procedures to determine occupational characteristics necessary for success in business, industrial, and food service job titles. He has continued to develop innovative progressive measurement scales, and "hands-on" tests in actual job settings to determine strengths and weaknesses of employment applicants, candidates for promotion, and workers in various industrial occupations. These tests have been and are used in upgrading of employees through training and development in large corporations and in industrial/technical education. Procedures he had developed are also applied in major cities in implementation and operation of alternative education programs in inner-city schools.* Author rsch. and evaluation reports, curriculum, testing programs and other publs., 1985—; contbr. articles to profl. publs. Bd. mgrs. Prospect Park YMCA, Bklyn., 1960-65; adviser desegregation measures Boston Pub. Schs., 1976-81. With U.S. Army, 1944-45. Mem. Am. Vocat. Edn. Rsch. Assn. (charter), Am. Vocat. Assn., Am. Assn. Tchr. Educators, Am. Psychol. and Guidance Assn., Masons, N.Y. Schoolmasters Club, Phi Delta Kappa, Epsilon Pi Tau, Kappa Phi Kappa, Kappa Delta Pi. Home: Frost Mill Rd Mill Neck NY 11765 Office: Ednl Planning and Research Co 18 Frost Mill Rd Mill Neck NY 11765-1101

GRIEVE-CARLSON, GARY ROBERT, secondary education educator; b. Bristol, Conn., Feb. 5, 1955; s. Robert Walfrid and Betty Ruth (Peterson) C.; m. Bridget Marie Grieve, Aug. 20, 1983; children: Timothy, Jessye, Grace. BA, Bates Coll., 1977; MA, SUNY-Binghamton, 1980; PhD, Boston U., 1988. Instr. English Va. Polytechnic Inst., Blacksburg, Va., 1985-87; Fulbright jr. lectr. Carolo-Wilhelmina Tech. U., Braunschweig, Germany, 1987-88; instr. English U. Tenn., Knoxville, 1988-90; prof., dept. chmn. English Lebanon Valley Coll., Annville, Pa., 1990—. Home: 1433 E Walnut St Annville PA 17003-2022 Office: Lebanon Valley Coll 101 N College Ave Annville PA 17003-1404

GRIEVES, ROBERT BELANGER, engineering educator; b. Evanston, Ill., Oct. 15, 1935; s. Roy and Marie (Belanger) G.; m. Sandra Lee Artman, Dec. 10, 1966; children: Christopher Robert, Jaime Robert. B.A. in Russian, Northwestern U., 1956, M.S. in Chem. Engring, 1959, Ph.D. in Chem. Engring, 1961. Asst. prof. civil engring. Northwestern U., Evanston, 1961-63; from asst. prof. to assoc. prof. civil and environ. engring. Ill. Inst. Tech., Chgo., 1963-67; prof., chmn. chem. engring. dept. U. Ky., Lexington, 1967-79, dir. Ky. Water Resources Rsch. Inst., 1973-82, assoc. dean adminstrn., grad. programs and rsch. Coll. Engring., 1976-82; dean Coll. Engring., prof. civil engring. U. Tex.-El Paso, 1982-89, prof. civil engring., instr. Slavic langs., 1989-94; cons. to industry in air and water pollution control; spl. employee and mem. ESWQIA Com., U.S. EPA, 1975-79. Author articles on phys.-chem. separations, indsl. waste treatment. Mem. Phi Beta Kappa, Tau Beta Pi. Home: 705 Cresta Mira Dr El Paso TX 79912-2622

GRIFEL, STUART SAMUEL, management engineer, consultant; b. Bklyn., May 21, 1947; s. Harry Grifel and Selma (Goldblatt) Spitalnik; m. Barbara Palermo, Nov. 27, 1977. BA with distinction, Ariz. State U., 1969; MPA, Bernard Baruch Coll. CUNY, 1978; MBA, Suffolk U., 1986. Mgmt. intern City of Kansas City, Mo., 1978; mgmt. auditor State of Mass., Boston, 1980-82; sr. methods analyst Shawmut Bank, Boston, 1983-87; mgmt. engr. A.T. Hudson & Co., Inc., Paramus, N.J., 1987-88; mgmt./indsl. engr. City of Tampa, Fla., 1988-91; sr. cons. KPMG Peat Marwick, LLP, Tampa, Fla., 1995-97; assoc. dir. Nat. Ctr. for Pub. Productivity Rutgers U., Newark, N.J., 1997-99; auditor City of Austin, 1999—. Author: Performance Measurement and Budgetary Decision Making, 1993, Organizational Culture: Its Importance in Performance Management, 1994. Reader, Radio Reading Svcs. for the Blind, Tampa, 1993—. Mem. Am. Soc. Pub. Adminstrn. (exec. com. sect. on mgmt. sci. and policy analysis 1990—), Nat. Ctr. Pub. Productivity (staff assoc. 1992—), Fla. Govt. Fin. Officer's Assn. (com. mem. 1992—). Avocations: golf, skiing, reading. Home: 12342 Hunters Chase Dr Austin TX 78729 Office: 2 Commodore Plz Austin TX 78701 also: Rutgers U Nat Ctr for Pub Productivity 360 King Blvd Newark NJ 07102-1801

GRIFFEN, AGNES MARTHE, library administrator; b. Ft. Dauphin, Madagascar, Aug. 25, 1935; d. Frederick Stang and Alvilde Margrethe (Torvik) Hallanger; m. Thomas Michael Griffen (div. Nov. 1969); children: Shaun Helen Griffen D'Antoni, Christopher Patrick, Adam Andrew; m. John H.P. Hall, Aug. 26, 1980. BA cum laude in English, Pacific Luth. U., 1957; MLS, U. Wash., 1965; Urban Exec. cert., MIT, 1976; postgrad., Harvard U., 1993. Cert. librarian, Wash., Md. Area children's libr. King County Libr. Sys., Seattle, 1965-68, coord. instl. librs., 1968-71, dep. libr. for staff and program devel., 1971-74; dep. libr. dir. Tucson Pub. Libr., 1974-80; dir. Montgomery County Dept. Pub. Librs., Rockville, Md., 1980-96; libr. dir. Tucson-Pima Pub. Libr., 1997—; lectr. Grad. Libr. Sch., U. Ariz., Tucson, 1976-77, 79; vis. lectr. Sch. Librarianship, U. Wash., Seattle, 1983. Contbr. articles to library periodicals and profl. jours. Active Md. Humanities Coun., Balt., 1986-92, Ariz. Humanities Coun., Phoenix, 1977-80; charter mem. Exec. Women's Coun. of So. Ariz., Tucson, 1979-80; mem. coun. Nat. Capital Area Pub. Access Network, 1992-94, pres. bd., 1993-94. Recipient Helping Hand award Md. Assn. of the Deaf, 1985, Cert. Recognition Montgomery County Hispanic Employees Assn., 1985; Henry scholar U. Washington Sch. Librarianship, 1965. Mem. ALA (exec. bd. 1989-93, divsn. pres. pub. libr. assn. bd. 1981-82, councilor-at-large 1972-76, 86-93, chmn. com. on program evaluation and support 1987-88, legis. com. 1998—), Md. Libr. Assn., Ariz. Libr. Assn. Democrat. Home: 1951 N El Moraga Dr Tucson AZ 85745-9070 Office: Tucson-Pima Public Library PO Box 27470 Tucson AZ 85726-7470*

GRIFFEN, CLYDE CHESTERMAN, retired history educator; b. Sioux City, Iowa, July 29, 1929; s. Clyde Rumbaugh and Rosanna Susan (Chesterman) G.; m. Sarah Goldsborough Donoho, Feb. 14, 1959; children: John Winslow, Sarah Bolling, Robert Henry. BA, State U. Iowa, 1952; MA, Columbia U., 1953, PhD, 1960. Lectr. Columbia U., N.Y.C., 1954-57; instr. history Vassar Coll, Poughkeepsie, N.Y., 1957-61; asst. prof. Vassar Coll. 1961-67, assoc. prof., 1967-75, Lucy Maynard Salmon prof. Am. history, 1975-92, chmn. dept. history, 1982-85, dir. Am. culture program, 1977-79. Author: (with Sally Griffen) Natives and Newcomers: The Ordering of Opportunity in Mid-Nineteenth-Century Poughkeepsie, 1978; editor: New Perspectives on Poughkeepsie's Past, 1988; co-editor: Meanings for Manhood: Constructions of Masculinity in Victorian America, 1990. NSF grantee, 1973-74; Nat. Humanities Inst. fellow, 1976-77; Fulbright rsch. scholar N.Z., 1984. Mem. Am. Hist. Assn., Orgn. Am. Historians, Social Sci. History Assn. (editorial bd. 1976-89). Home: 9 MacCracken Ln Poughkeepsie NY 12604

GRIFFEN, JULIET E., federal judge; b. 1948. BA, Oberlin U., 1971; JD, U. Tenn., 1978. Law clk. to Hon. Thomas A. Wiseman, Jr., U.S. Dist. Ct. (mid. dist.), Tenn., 1978-80; staff atty. Legal Svcs. Mid. Tenn., 1980-85; clk. U.S. Dist. Ct. (mid. dist.), Tenn., 1985-95, magistrate judge, 1995—. Mem. Lawyers Assn. for Women, Nashville Bar Assn. Office: US Courthouse 801 Broadway Ste 756 Nashville TN 37203-3874

GRIFFEN, WARD O., JR., surgeon, educator, medical board executive; b. New Orleans, July 21, 1928; s. Ward O. and Dorothea (Rosenberg) G.; m. Margaret Mary Taylor, Dec. 27, 1952; children—Peter, Mary Ellen, Steven, Colleen, Timothy, Margaret Mary, Leah. AB, Princeton U., 1948; MD, Cornell U., 1953; PhD, U. Minn., 1963. Diplomate Am. Bd. Surgery, Am. Bd. Thoracic Surgery. Asst. prof. dept. surgery U. Minn, Mpls., 1962-65; assoc. prof. U. Ky. Coll. Medicine, Lexington, 1965-67, prof., chmn. dept. surgery, 1967-84; exec. dir., sec.-treas. Am. Bd. Surgery, Phila., 1984-94; prof. surgery U. Ky. Coll. Medicine, Lexington, 1994—. Contbr. articles to profl. jours. Served to comdr. USNR, 1955-67. John R. Markle Found. scholar, 1962-67. Fellow ACS (bd. govs. 1972-78, 2d v.p. 1995-96); mem. Am. Surg. Assn., So. Surg. Assn. (1st v.p. 1995-96, pres. 1997-98), Assn. Acad. Surgery (pres. 1971), Ctrl. Surg. Assn. (sec. 1980-82, pres. 1984), Soc. Surgery Alimentary Tract (v.p. 1984-85), Halsted Soc. (sec. 1983-85, pres. 1986). Republican. Roman Catholic. Avocations: cooking; gardening; fishing. Office: U Ky Med Ctr Dept Surgery 800 Rose St Rm C243 Lexington KY 40536-0001

GRIFFENHAGEN, GEORGE BERNARD, trade association executive; b. Portland, Oreg., June 9, 1924; s. Richard Bernard and Clara (Schoenian) G.; m. Joan Helen Houston, June 21, 1946; children: Gary Bernard, Gordon Wesley, Barbara Clare. BS in Pharmacy, U. So. Calif., 1949, MS, 1950; student, Fresno State Coll., 1946, U. London, 1948. Dir. research Nion Corp., Hollywood, Calif., 1950-52; curator div. med. scis. Smithsonian Instn., Washington, 1952-59; sec. sect. history of pharmacy Am. Pharm. Assn., Washington, 1952-59, pres. local chpt., 1958-59, assoc. exec. dir., 1959-89, hon. pres., 1990-91; trustee Am. Pharm. Assn. Found., Washington, 1989-94; editor Jour. Am. Pharm. Assn., Washington, 1960-76; sec.-gen. 4th Pan Am. Congress Pharmacy and Biochemistry, Washington, 1957; sec. organizing com. 31st Internat. Congress Pharm. Scis., Washington, 1971; sec.-gen. Internat. Congress History of Pharmacy, Washington, 1983, Japan-U.S. Congress of Pharm. Scis., Honolulu, 1987; v.p. Pan Am. Pharm. and Biochem. Fedn., 1963-82, 85-91, Pharmacy World Congress, Washington, 1991; U.S. del. Internat. Pharm. Fedn. Gen. Assemblies, London, 1955, Brussels, 1958, Copenhagen, 1960, Vienna, 1962, Amsterdam, 1964, Hamburg, 1968, Geneva, 1970, Lisbon, 1972, Rome, 1974, Warsaw, 1976, Cannes, 1978; U.S. del. FIP Coun., Bucharest, 1969, Dublin, 1975, Montreal, 1985, Helsinki, 1986, Amsterdam, 1987, Sydney, 1988, Munich, 1989, Istanbul, 1990, Lyon, 1992, Tokyo, 1993, Lisbon, 1994, Jerusalem, 1996, Vancouver, 1997, The Hague, 1998; congress coord., The Hague, 1977; U.S. del. Pan Am. Fedn. Pharmacy Congress, Mexico City, 1963, Buenos Aires, 1966, Caracas, 1969, Panama, 1972, Guatemala City, 1985, Santo Domingo, 1988, Buenos Aires, 1994, San Jose, Costa Rica, 1997; U.S. del. Internat. Congress History of Pharmacy, Budapest, Hungary, 1981, Fedn. Asian Pharm. Assns. Congress, Seoul, Korea, 1982; mem. Nat. Action Com. on Drug Edn., Office of Edn., 1970-71, Va. Gov.'s Coun. on Narcotic and Drug Abuse Control, 1970-72. Editor: Scalpel and Tongs, 1972-73; Contbr. articles to profl. jours. Mem. Fairfax County (Va.) Rep. Com., 1962-97; adminstrv. asst. to chmn. Va. State Rep. Com., 1969-71; life mem. Rep. Nat. Com., 1979—; founding pres. Nat. Coordinating Coun. on Drug Edn., 1968-69. Served with C.E. AUS, World War II, ETO. Recipient Pfizer Merit award U.S. CD Coun., 1964, U. So. Calif. Alumnus award, 1969; Hugo H. Schaefer award Am. Pharm. Assn., 1984; Disting. Svc. award Pharmacy Guild of Australia, 1988, Internat. Pharmacy Jour. Editor's prize, 1989, 95, Remington Honor medal Am. Pharm. Assn., 1991; named to Nat. Philatelic Writers Hall of Fame, 1990. Mem. Am. Inst. History of Pharmacy (pres. 1960-61, Edward Kremers award 1969, sec. 1991—), Friends of Hist. Pharmacy (pres. 1957-58), Pharm. Wholesalers Assn. (Distinguished Service award 1971), Am. Topical Assn. (1st v.p. 1972-75, pres. 1976-79, pres. med. subjects unit 1969-72, Distinguished Topical Philatelist award 1970, Myrtle Watt Med. Philately Topicalist award 1980, editor Topical Time 1992—), Am. Philatelic Congress (Jere Hess Barr award 1969), Am. Philatelic Soc. (sec.-treas. Writers Unit 1982—; U.S. commr. to Internat. Exhbn. Thematic Philately, Basel, Switzerland 1983), Am. Revenue Assn. (named to Sterling Meml. Roll of Disting. Fiscalists 1979), Council Philatelic Orgns. (treas. 1983-91), Philatelic Lit. Assn., Academie Internationale d'Histoire de la Pharmacie (treas. 1971-81, 1989-97), Pharm. Soc. Gt. Britain (hon.), Sigma Xi, Rho Chi, Phi Kappa Psi. Home: 2501 Drexel St Vienna VA 22180-6906 Office: Am Pharm Assn 2215 Constitution Ave NW Washington DC 20037-2907

GRIFFEY, KEN, JR. (GEORGE KENNETH GRIFFEY, JR.), professional baseball player; b. Donora, Pa., Nov. 21, 1969. Grad. high sch., Cin. Outfielder Seattle Mariners, 1987—. Recipient Gold Glove award, 1990-96; named to All-Star team, 1990-95, All-Star game MVP, 1992, , Sporting News Am. League Silver Slugger team, 1991, 93-94, 96 Sporting News All-Star team, 1991, 93-94. Office: Seattle Mariners/The Kingdome PO Box 4100 83 King St Seattle WA 98104-2860*

GRIFFEY, LINDA BOYD, lawyer; b. Keokuk, Iowa, Aug. 6, 1949; d. Marshall Coulter and Geraldine Vivian (White) Boyd; m. John Jay Griffey, June 24, 1972. BS in Pharmacy, U. Iowa, 1972; JD, Duke U., 1980. Bar: Calif. 1980; lic. pharmacist, Iowa, N.C. Pharmacist Davenport (Iowa) Osteo. Hosp., 1972-75, Wagner Pharmacy, Clinton, Iowa, 1975-77, Durham (N.C.) County Gen. Hosp., 1977-80; assoc. O'Melveny & Myers, L.A., 1980-88, ptnr., 1988—; spkr., writer in field of employee benefits and exec. compensation; pres. L.A. chpt. Western Pension and Benefits Conf., 1998-99. Active L.A. Philharm. Bus. & Profl. Assn.; bd. dirs. Hillsides Home for Children, Pasadena Playhouse. Mem. ABA (employee benefits com. tax sect.), Am. Law Inst., L.A. County Bar Assn. (former chair employee benefits com. 1994-95), L.A. Duke Bar Assn. (pres. 1987-90, 91-92), Rotary (L.A. chpt. bd. dirs. 1995-97). Avocations: golf, reading, swimming. Office: O'Melveny & Myers 400 S Hope St Los Angeles CA 90071-2899

GRIFFIE, GAYLE G., retired principal; b. York Springs, Pa., Mar. 27, 1941; d. Lawrence W. and Elsie M. Gulden; m. Harold Leon Griffie, Aug. 8, 1964. BSEd, Shippensburg State Coll., 1962, MEd, 1966; Prin.'s Cert., We. Md. Coll., 1979. Tchr. Spring Grove (Pa.) Area Sch. Dist., 1962-63; tchr. grade four to tchr. grade five Upper Adams Sch. Dist., Biglerville, Pa., 1963-82, prin. grades K-6, 1983-98; adv. coun. mem. Adams County Children and Youth Svc., Gettysburg, Pa., 1979-82. Artist-in-edn. grantee Pa. Coun. for the Arts, 1987-88. Mem. ASCD, Pa. Assn. Elem. Sch. Prins., Pa. Assn. Fed. Program Coords., Delta Kappa Gamma.

GRIFFIN, ANITA JANE, elementary education educator; b. East Chicago, Ind., Dec. 16, 1945; d. John Tatu and Alfreda (Kaspick) Granger; m. Joseph Raymond Griffin, June 14, 1969; children: Jason David, Jennifer Sue. BA, Purdue U., Hammond, Ind., 1969, MS, 1972. Tchr. 2d grade Dist. 158, Lansing, Ill., 1969-73; tchr. 6th grade sci. Lake Cen. Sch. Corp., St. John, Ind., 1983, tchr. 6th grade English, 1984, tchr. 5th grade, 1985—; advisor, coach Sci. Club, 1992-94; mem. core team Integrated Learning System Computer Tech., 1992—; faculty advisor Star Lab. Program, 1988—; coord. Artist in Residency Program, 1993; mem. Peifer Sch. Parent's Adv. Com., 1991-94, prin.'s selection com., 1993, performance bd. accreditation team, 1993-94; advt. mgr. Lake Ctrl. Hockey Club, 1991-92; staff devel. com. Lake Ctrl. Sch. Corp., 1996-98. Editor newspaper on staff devel. Success Connection, 1988—. Mem. pastoral adminstrv. bd. Meth. Ch., Dyer, Ind., 1988-90; chmn. pastoral comm. bd. Griffith Meth. Ch., 1996—. Named Tchr. of the Yr., Ind. Aux. Law Related Edn., 1997, Am. Aux. Law Related Edn., 1997. Mem. AAUW, NEA, ASCD (conv. presenter 1988), Ind. Tchrs. Assn., Peifer Home and Sch. Assn. (treas. 1990-91), Kappa Kappa Kappa (chpt. pres. 1990-91). Avocations: water skiing, snow skiing, snowmobiling, jogging, travel. Office: Lake Cen Sch Corp Peifer Sch 1824 Cline Ave Schererville IN 46375-2260

GRIFFIN, ANNETTE L., critical care nurse, educator; b. Fall River, Mass., Oct. 21, 1959; d. Robert F. and Annette (Berard) Couture; m. Michael P. Griffin, Oct. 28, 1983; children: Brendan Patrick, Kate Elizabeth, Allison Ann, Trevor John. BSN, U. Mass., Dartmouth, 1981, MSN, 1990; MBA, Providence Coll., 1997. Ops. mgr. HMO R.I., Providence, 1985-87; clin. coord. Charlton Meml. Hosp., Fall River, 1989-90; staff nurse CCU R.I. Hosp., Providence, 1987-90, clin. educator, 1990-98, asst. dir. adult patient svcs., 1998—. Mem. AACN, Sigma Theta Tau (Kappa Theta chpt., chpt. v.p. 1991-95, chairperson program com. 1991-95).

GRIFFIN, BARBARA CONLEY, kindergarten and adult educator, antique store owner, retailer; b. Valdosta, Ga., Mar. 29, 1955; d. Paul and Sarah Elizabeth (Ganas) Conley; children: Stephanie E., Paul E. AA in Art, Middle Ga. Coll., Cochran, 1975; EdB, Mercer U., 1977, MEd in Early Childhood, 1986. Cert. early childhood and middle grades edn. tchr., Ga. Kindergarten tchr. Houston County Bd. Edn., Perry, Ga., 1978-80; 1st grade tchr. Houston County Bd. Edn., Bonaire, Ga., 1980-87, kindergarten tchr., 1987—, faculty advisor student coun. and tchr. empowerment com., 1991-95, tchr. empowerment chmn., 1992-94; devel. reading tchr. Middle Ga. Tech., 1998—; owner Timeless Treasures Antiques and Collectibles, Bonaire, Ga.; assoc. mgr. Eddie Bauer, Macon Mall. Mem. PTO, 1980—, Parents Assisting With Students, 1989—; tchr. Shirley Hills Bapt. Ch.-Tng. Union, Warner Robins, Ga., 1987-91; summer missionary Inst. Caribbean Missions, Jamaica, 1992; mem. Shirley Hills Baptist Church. Recipient Exemplary Svc. award Pilot Club of Houston County, Warner Robins, Ga., 1990, Tchr. of Yr. award Bonaire Elem. Sch., 1990. Mem. PAGE (state and local chpts.), Internat. Reading Assn. (state and local chpts., v.p. and pres. HOPE reading coun. 1993-95), Bonaire/Kathleen Jaycettes (sec. 1979-81, Outstanding Young Woman of the Year award 1981), Warner Robins Jr. Womens Club (co-chair spl. projects 1991, corr. sec. 1993, presenter 1993 conf. children's lit., Athens). Democrat. Mem. Southern Baptist Ch. Avocations: swimming, entertaining, traveling, walking, gardening. Home: 202 Williams Dr Bonaire GA 31005-3825 Office: Bonaire Elem Sch PO Box 729 Bonaire GA 31005-0729

GRIFFIN, BENJAMIN S., military career officer; b. Emporia, Va., Aug. 11, 1946; m. Carolyn Noel Elliott; children: Elizabeth, Jennifer, Jason. BS in Bus. Mgmt., Old Dominion U., 1969; MBA, Mercer U., 1981; grad., Officer Candidate Sch., 1970, Command and Gen. Staff Coll., Indsl. Coll. Armed Forces, Nat. Def. U. Commd. officer U.S. Army, 1970, advanced through grades to brig. gen., various positions; sec. gen. staff 8th Inf. Divsn. U.S. Army, Germany, bn. exec. officer 2d Bn. (Mechanized), 87th Inf.; comdr. 3d Bn. (Mechanized), 8th Inf. Divsn. U.S. Army, 1988-90; comdr. 2d Brigade, 6th Inf. Divsn. (Light) U.S. Army, Alaska, 1992-94; U.S. Army Europe staff Office of Dep. Chief of Staff Ops. U.S. Army, U.S. Army Forces Command in the Office of Dep. Chief Staff, staff officer Dept. of the Army, Ops. Divsn. Readiness; spl. asst. to chief of staff Office Chief of Staff of Army, exec. officer to commdg. gen. U.S. Army Forces Command, 1994-95; comdr. Joint Task Force Six Ft. Bliss, Tex., 1995-96; asst. divsn. comdr. Support of 1st Cavalry Divsn. Ft. Hood, Tex., 1996-97; dir. Force Programs, Office Dep. Chief Staff Ops. and Plans U.S. Pentagon, U.S. Army, Washington, 1997—. Decorated Def. Superior Svc. medal, Legion of Merit with two oak leaf clusters, Meritorious Svc. medal with four oak leaf clusters, Army Commendation medal, Army Achievement medal. Office: Office of Dep Chief of Staff for Ops & Plans US Army 460 Army Pentagon Washington DC 20310-0460

GRIFFIN, BETTY JO, elementary school educator; b. Monroe, La., Jan. 12, 1947; d. Julia Odell (Foster) Calhoun; divorced; 1 child, James Odell Griffin, Jr. BA, So. U., 1969; MA, San Francisco State U., 1975. Cert. elem. tchr., Calif. Tchr. lang. arts Oakland (Calif.) Unified Sch. Dist., 1970-73, Garfield Elem. Sch., 1973-77; Garfield Elem. Sch., Stonehurst Elem. Schs., 1977-96; splty. prep. libr. and lang. arts tchr. Webster Acad., 1996—. Trustee Allen Temple Bapt. Ch., Oakland, Calif., 1987—; lit. tutor Delta Sigma Theta, Oakland, 1990—; chairperson African Am. Chain Read In, 1995—. Recipient Libr. Protection Fund award State Dept. Edn., 1997, Leadership award Dem. Nat. Com., 1997. Mem. NAACP, NEA, Oakland Edn. Assn. (bd. dirs.), Calif. Tchrs. Assn. (coun. of edn. 1996), Nat. Alliance Black Sch. Educators, Delta Sigma Theta, Phi Delta Kappa. Democrat. Avocations: reading, helping others, public speaking. Home: 2559 Oliver Ave Oakland CA 94605-4820

GRIFFIN, CAMPBELL ARTHUR, JR., lawyer; b. Joplin, Mo., July 17, 1929; s. Campbell Arthur and Clara M. (Smith) G.; m. Margaret Ann Adams, Oct. 19, 1958; children: Campbell A., Laura Ann. BA, U. Mo., 1951, MA in Acctg., 1952; JD, U. Tex., 1957. Bar: Tex. 1957. Assoc. Vinson & Elkins, L.L.P., Houston, 1957-67, ptnr., 1968-92; mem. mgmt. com. Vinson & Elkins, L.L.P., 1981-90, mng. ptnr. Dallas office, 1986-89; adj. prof. adminstrv. sci. Jones Grad. Sch. Adminstrn., Rice U., 1992-94. Mem. ofcl. bd. Bethany Christian Ch., Houston, 1962-65, 66-69, chmn. bd. elders, 1968; bd. dirs. Houston Pops Orch., 1982-87; councilman City of Hunters Creek Village, Tex., 1993-95; pres. Windcliff Property Owners Assn., Estes Park, Colo., 1995-96; dir. Cornell Corrections, Inc., 1996—; mem. St. Martin's Episcopal Ch., Houston. Mem. ABA, Houston Bar Assn., State Bar Tex. (bus. law sect. chmn. 1974-75), Tex. Bus Law Found. (chmn. 1988-89, dir. 1988—), Houston Racquet Club (dir. 1992-94).

GRIFFIN, CARLETON HADLOCK, accountant, educator; b. Richmond Heights, Mo., Oct. 30, 1928; s. Merle Leroy and Bernice Hilder Edwards (Nelson) G.; m. Mary Lou Goodrich, Dec. 26, 1953; children: Julia, Anne. B.B.A., U. Mich., 1950, J.D., 1953, M.B.A., 1953. Mem. audit and tax staff Touche Ross & Co., Detroit, 1955-59; adminstrv. partner Touche Ross & Co., Denver, 1959-71; nat. tax dir. Touche Ross & Co., N.Y.C., 1971-72; nat. dir. ops. and adminstrn. Touche Ross & Co., 1972-74, chmn. bd., 1974-82, sr. ptnr., 1982-85, regional ptnr., 1983-85; prof. acctg. U. Mich., 1985-95; dir. Paton Acctg. Ctr., U. Mich., 1997—. Contbr. articles to profl. jours. Sr. warden St. Paul's Episcopal Ch., Darien, Conn., 1979-81; trustee Siena Heights Coll., Adrian, Mich., 1988—. Served with Fin. Corps AUS, 1953-55. Mem. AICPA, Colo. Soc. CPAs (pres. 1970-71), N.Y. Soc. CPAs, Mich. Soc. CPAs. Republican.

GRIFFIN, CAROLYN LEIGH, English educator, genealogist; b. Ypsilanti, Mich., Nov. 2, 1945; d. William Beckwith Fuqua and Hazel Marie (Gray) Lucado; m. Earnest Ellsworth Griffin, June 17, 1967; 1 child, Michael Allen. BA, Eastern Mich. U., 1967, MA, 1972. Cert. thcr. English and history, Mich. Substitute English tchr. Ypsilanti, Lincoln, Willow Run, Ypsilanti, Mich., 1967-68; English tchr. Ypsilanti H.S., 1968—; spkr. in field. Author: (genealogy/family history) Lucadou, Lookadoo, Luckado, and Lucado Family History, 1986, supplements, 1987, 91. Recipient 1st and 2d place awards for The Palladian creative arts mag. for Ypsilanti H.S., Am. Scholastic Press, 1993, 94, 95, 96, 97. Mem. Mich. Coun. Tchrs. English, Mich. Secondary Reading Interest Coun., Geneal. Soc. Washtenaw County (edn. dir., spkr.). Baptist. Avocation: genealogy. Home: 1200 S Harris Rd Ypsilanti MI 48198-6513 Office: Ypsilanti HS 2095 Packard Rd Ypsilanti MI 48197-1833

GRIFFIN, CHRISTOPHER OAKLEY, hospital professional, humanities educator; b. Memphis, Apr. 27, 1970; s. Charles Ray Griffin and Gladys Lee (Oakley) Slappey. BA in English, Miss. Coll., 1992; MA in English, Baylor U., 1996; M in Humanities, U. Dallas, 1998. Tchg. asst. dept. English Baylor U., Waco, Tex., 1993-95; hosp. worker Baylor Med. Ctr. at Irving, Tex., 1996-98; project devel. coord. White Coat Med., Inc., Austin, Tex., 1999—; mem. ethics com. Baylor Med. Ctr., Irving, 1997-98; adj. faculty mem. Brookhaven Coll., Dallas, 1998. Author of poetry, criticism, philosophy. Presdl. scholar Miss. Coll., Clinton, 1988-92. Avocation: guitar.

GRIFFIN, CLAYTON HOUSTOUN, retired power company engineer, lecturer; b. Atlanta, June 14, 1925; s. George Clayton and Eugenia (Johnston) G.; m. Gloria Giegel Handley; 1 child, Clayton Houstoun; m. Lela Lounsbery Griffin, June 6, 1953; children—Lela Griffin Lofgren, George Duncan Bryan, Phillips Lounsbery. B.E.E., Ga. Inst. Tech., 1945, M.S. in E.E., 1950. Registered profl. engr., Ga. Tester Ga. Power Co., Atlanta, 1949-51, test engr., 1953-58, protection engr., 1958-63, chief protection engr., 1963-79, mgr. system protection and control, 1979-89. Contbr. tech. papers to profl. publs. Trustee Ga. Tech Nat. Alumni Assn., Atlanta, 1977-80. Served to lt. comdr. USNR, 1943-47, 51-53. Named Engr. of Yr., Ga. Power Engring. Soc., Atlanta, 1966, Ga. Soc. Profl. Engrs., Atlanta, 1984. Fellow IEEE (chmn. Atlanta chpt. 1974, chmn. standards com. on dispersed generation 1982-89, chmn. power systems relaying com. 1987-89, Disting. Svc. award power systems relaying com. 1990, Charles Proteus Steinmetz Major Contributions to Devel. Elec. Engring. Standards award 1994). Republican. Episcopalian. Club: Cherokee Town and Country (Atlanta). Avocations: stamp collecting, golfing. Home: 221 The South Chace NE Atlanta GA 30328-4262

GRIFFIN, DAVID, mycologist; b. Buffalo, Mar. 13, 1937; s. R. Gardner and Edwina Macomber Griffin; m. Barbara Ruth Nelson, Dec. 23, 1960; children: Laureen Barbara, Kathleen Marie, Karen Sue. BS, SUNY, Syracuse, 1959; MA, U. Calif., Berkeley, 1960, PhD, 1963. Rsch. fellow Calif. Inst. Tech., Pasadena, Calif., 1963-64; asst. prof. U. Iowa, Iowa City, 1964-68, SUNY Coll. of Environ. Sci. and Foresty, Syracuse, 1968—; rsch. fellow U. Louis Pasteur, Strasburg, France, 1974-75. Author: Fungal Physiology, 1981, 2d edit., 1994; assoc. editor Mycologia, 1995-96, editor-in-chief, 1996—; assoc. editor Experimental Mycology, 1983-95. Fellowship Nat. Acad. Scis., Calif. Inst. Tech., 1963-64. Mem. Mycological Soc. of Am. (editor-in-chief 1996—). Unitarian-Universalist. Avocations: ornithology, travel, singing. E-mail: griffin@mailbox.syr.edu. Office: SUNY 350 Illick Hall 1 Forestry Dr Syracuse NY 13210-2788

GRIFFIN, DENNIS JOSEPH, middle school principal; b. Chgo., Feb. 4, 1943; s. Dennis Joseph and Ruth G.; m. Janet A. Maender; children: Nathan, Jonathan. BA, Western Mich. U., 1969; MA, Portland State U., 1980; postgrad., U. South Fla. Counselor U.S. Job Corps, Ft. Custer, Mich.; tchr. Kalamazoo (Mich.) Ctrl. H.S., Charlotte Amalie H.S., St. Thomas, U.S. Virgin Islands; tchr., head basketball coach Eudora Kean H.S., St. Thomas; program coord. CATCH Program Portland (Oreg.) Pub. Schs.; counselor Blanton Elem., St. Petersburg, Fla.; asst. prin. Southside Fundamental Mid. Sch., St. Petersburg; prin. Bay Point Mid. Sch., St. Petersburg. Bd. dirs. Ctr. Against Spouse Abuse, St. Petersburg; vol. Boy Scouts Am., 1988; mem. Leadership St. Petersburg, 1987—, mem. planning com., 1989-91; commr. Southside Youth Soccer, 1988. Mem. Nat. Assn. Secondary Sch. Prins., Mid. Sch. Prin. Assn. (pres. Largo, Fla. chpt.), Rotary (leadership com. St. Petersburg, 1987, planning com., 1989-91). Office: Bay Point Mid Sch 2161 62d Ave S Saint Petersburg FL 33705

GRIFFIN, DIANE EDMUND, research physician, virologist, educator; b. Iowa City, Ia., May 12, 1940; d. Rudolph William and Doris Irene (Swanson) Edmund; m. John Wesley Griffin, June 13, 1965; children: Christopher Todd, Erik Edmund. BA, Augustana Coll., Rock Island, Ill., 1962; MD, Stanford U., 1968, PhD, 1970. Diplomate Am. Bd. Internal Medicine, Am. Bd. Infectious Diseases. Resident in medicine Stanford (Calif.) U. Hosp., 1968-70; fellow Johns Hopkins U. Sch. Medicine, Balt., 1970-73, asst. prof., 1973-79, assoc. prof., 1979-86, prof., 1986—; prof., chair molecular microbiol. immunology Johns Hopkins U. Sch. Pub. Health, 1994—; investigator Howard Hughes Med. Inst., Balt., 1973-79; mem. virology study sect. NIH, 1982-86; mem. adv. com. Nat. Multiple Sclerosis Soc., 1986-92; mem. microbiology and infectious diseases rsch. adv. com. NIH, 1989-92, chair, 1992-94. Author films and tapes; contbr. chpts. to books, articles to profl. jours. Grantee NIH, 1983—, Nat. Multiple Sclerosis Soc., 1986—, WHO, 1993—, Muscular Dystrophy Assn., 1996—. Fellow Infectious Diseases Soc. Am., AAAS; mem. Am. Soc. for Clin. Investigation, Am. Soc. for Virology (council 1987-89), Interurban Clin. Club. Democrat. Lutheran. Avocation: gardening. Office: Johns Hopkins Sch Pub Health 615 N Wolfe St Baltimore MD 21205-2103

GRIFFIN, DONALD R(EDFIELD), zoology educator; b. Southampton, N.Y., Aug. 3, 1915; s. Henry Farrand and Mary Whitney (Redfield) G.; m. Ruth M. Castle, Sept. 6, 1941 (div. Aug. 1965); children: Nancy Griffin Jackson, Janet Griffin Abbott, Margaret, John H.; m. Jocelyn Crane, Dec. 16, 1965. B.S., Harvard U., 1938, M.A., 1940, Ph.D., 1942. Jr. fellow Harvard U., Cambridge, Mass., 1940-41, 46; rsch. assoc. Harvard U., Cambridge, 1942-45, prof., 1953-65, assoc. Mus. of Comparative Zoology, 1989—; asst. prof. Cornell U., Ithaca, N.Y., 1946-47; assoc. prof. Cornell U., Ithaca, 1947-52, prof., 1952-53; prof. Rockefeller U., N.Y.C., 1965-86, prof. emeritus, 1986—, trustee, 1973-76; vis. lectr. Princeton U., N.J., 1987-89; pres. Harry Frank Guggenheim Found., N.Y., 1979-83. Author: Listening in the Dark, 1958 (Nat. Acad. Scis. Elliot medal 1961), Echoes of Bats and Men, 1959, Animal Structure and Function, 1962, Bird Migration, 1964 (Phi Beta Kappa prize 1966), The Question of Animal Awareness, 1976, Animal Thinking, 1984, Animal Minds, 1992. Mem. Am. Ornithologists Union, Am. Soc. Zoologists, Am. Physiol. Soc., Ecol. Soc. Am., Am. Acad. Arts and Scis., Nat. Acad. Scis., Am. Philos. Soc., Animal Behavior Soc., Phi Beta Kappa, Sigma Xi. Office: Harvard U Concord Field Sta Old Causeway Rd Bedford MA 01730

GRIFFIN, DONALD SPRAY, mechanical engineer, consultant. BME, Cornell U., 1952; MS in Engring. Mechanics, Stanford U., 1953, PhD in Engring. Mechanics, 1959. From sr. engr. to mgr. structural mechanics Bettis Atomic Lab. Westinghouse, Pitts., 1959-72, with advance energy systems divsn., 1974-91; ind. cons. Pitts., 1972-74, 91—; ad hoc visitor Accreditation Bd. Engring. and Tech., 1977-85. Assoc. editor Jour. Applied Mechanics, 1973-80; former mem. editl. bd. Internat. Jour. Computers and Structures, Jour. Structural Mechanics Software; contbr. articles, papers to profl. jours. Officer Civil Engring. Corps, USN, 1953-56. Recipient Literature award PVP, 1987. Fellow ASME (life, divsn. applied mechanics, chmn. divsn. pressure vessels ane piping, publs. com., mem. com. computer tech., com. computing in applied mechanics, op. bd. materials and structures, subcom. boiler and pressure vessel code, com. solar energy standards codes, policy bds. comm. and rsch., Pressure Vessel and Piping award 1992), Nat. Rsch. Coun. (computational math. com.), Welding Rsch. Coun. (pressure vessel rsch. com.). Achievements include research in design methods, design criteria and software for structural analysis and computer operations for design of advanced energy systems. Home: 208 Oakcrest Ln Pittsburgh PA 15236-4208

GRIFFIN, DONALD WAYNE, diversified chemical company executive; b. Evansville, Ind., Mar. 1, 1937; s. Pauline Marie (Rahm) G.; m. Kristanya Johnson; children: Kristanya Anne, Kirstin Alyson. Student, Ind. U., 1954-57; BSBA, Evansville Coll., 1961. Sales rep. organics and explosives Olin Corp., Knoxville, Tenn., 1961-62; sales rep., dist. sales mgr. brass sales dept. Olin Corp., Indpls., 1964-69; dist. sales mgr. Milw., 1969-73; asst. to dir. field sales, s.w. region sales mgr. East Alton, Ill., 1973-77, dir. field sales, 1977-80, dir. internat. bus. devel., 1980-81; v.p. mktg. brass group Olin Corp., East Alton, 1981-83, pres. brass group, 1983-85, pres. Winchester group, 1985-86, pres. def. systems group, 1986-87, exec. v.p., pres. def. systems, 1987-93, vice chmn. bd. ops., 1993-94; pres., CEO, chmn. Olin Corp., Norwalk, Conn., 1996—; bd. dirs. Riverbend Bancshares, Inc., Ill. State Bank, East Alton, Olin Corp., Rayonier, Inc., Rayonier Forst Resources Co. Bd. dirs. Leadership Coun. S.W. Ill., Edwardsville, 1984—, Alton Meml. Hosp., Ill., 1983-89, St. Louis Regional Growth Assn., 1986-89. Mem. Assn. U.S. Army, Am. Def. Preparedness Assn., Navy League U.S. (life), Am. Soc. Metals, Small Arms Ammunition Mfrs. (bd. dirs. 1985—), S.W. Ill. Indsl. Assn. (bd. dirs. 1985—), Ill. C. of C. (bd. dirs. 1985-89), Wildlife Mgmt. Inst. (bd. dirs. 1986—), Nat. Shooting Sports Found. (bd. dirs. 1985—, trustee Buffalo Bill Hist. Ctr. 1991—), Chem. Mfrs. Assn. (bd. dirs. 1994—). Office: Olin Corp 501 Merritt 7 Ste 1 Norwalk CT 06851-6261*

GRIFFIN, ELAINE B., educator; b. Westfield, N.Y.; m. Ned Griffin; 3 adopted daughters: Vera, Marie, Marjeena. BA in Am. studies, Barnard Coll., 1969; MLS, U. Calif., Berkeley, 1971. Cert. tchr., Ariz. Head tchr. Chiniak Sch., Alaska. Recipient Coun. of Chief State Sch. Officers Tchr. of Yr. award, 1995. Office: Chiniak Sch PO Box 5529 Chiniak AK 99615-5657*

GRIFFIN, ELEANOR, magazine editor. Exec. editor Southern Living, Birmingham, 1993—. Office: Southern Living 2100 Lakeshore Dr Birmingham AL 35209-6721*

GRIFFIN, EREN G., retired nursing educator; b. Antigua, West Indies, Jan. 30; d. John and Hilda Griffin. Diploma in nursing, Radcliffe Sch. Nursing, Oxford, Eng., 1966; diploma in dietetics, No. Poly., London, 1968; BA in Vocat. Edn., Coll. V.I., St. Croix, 1986. Nurse Radcliffe Infirmary, Oxford; therapeutic dietitian Western Meml. Hosp., Corner Brook, NF, Can.; nurse Dept. Health, Christiansted, V.I.; health occupations educator, vocat. dept. Dept. Edn., Christiansted, ret. With Women's Royal Army Corps, 1960-63. Mem. Brit. Dietetic Assn., Am. Fedn. Tchrs. Baha'i faith.

GRIFFIN, GARY ARTHUR, technological products executive; b. Yonkers, N.Y., Nov. 23, 1937; s. William Edmund and Madeline (Lane) G.; student Manhattan Coll., 1956-57, Westchester Community Coll., 1957-62; diploma LaSalle Extension U., 1968; m. Jacqueline Cahill, June 21, 1958; children: Lynn, Elizabeth, Margaret. Engring. cons. IBM Corp., Yorktown, N.Y., 1960-61; engring. cons. Perkin Elmer Corp., Norwalk, Conn., 1961-63; product devel. mgr. Technicon Corp., Tarrytown, N.Y., 1963-69; chmn., pres. Dynacon Research Corp., Rockland, N.Y., 1969-72; with Nat. Patent Devel. Corp., New Brunswick, N.J., 1973-82, corp. group v.p. new technologies, 1977-82, pres. Hydromed Scis. div., 1978-82, pres. NDP Dental Systems, Inc., 1979-82, pres. NPD Epic Systems, Inc., 1979-82, pres., dir. Amalgamated Fin. Services, Inc., 1979-82, v.p., dir. NPD Productos Médicos, S.A., 1979-82, Washburn Ltd., 1979-82; pres., dir. Applied Genetics, Inc., 1981-82; dir. FCS Industries, Inc., Flemington, N.J., 1982-98, sr. v.p., 1982-87, treas., 1984-87; chmn. chief operating officer, pres. Circuitech Inc., Eatontown, N.J., 1982-85, dir., 1985-87; chmn., pres., treas. Executrex Internat. Inc., New Brunswick, N.J., 1985—. Patentee in field. With USNR, 1954-62. Mem. Am. Prodn. and Inventory Control Soc., Am. Mgmt. Assn., IEEE, Am. Assn. Advancement of Med. Instrumentation, Am. Entrepreneurs Assn., Internat. Entrepreneurs Assn., Turnaround Mgmt. Assn., Smithsonian Assocs., N.Y. Vet. Police Assn. Republican. Roman Catholic. Office: Executrex 100 Jersey Ave Ste D-9 New Brunswick NJ 08901-3200

GRIFFIN, JAMES ANTHONY, bishop; b. Fairview Park, Ohio, June 13, 1934; s. Thomas Antohny and Margaret Mary (Hanousek) G. BA, Borromeo Coll., 1956; JCL magna cum laude, Pontifical Lateran U., Rome, 1963; JD summa cum laude, Cleve. State U., 1972; DHL (hon.), Ohio Dominican Coll., 1994. Ordained priest Roman Catholic Ch., 1960, bishop, 1979; asso. pastor St. Jerome Ch., Cleve., 1960-61; sec.-notary Cleve. Diocesan Tribunal, 1963-65; asst. chancellor Diocese of Cleve., 1965-68, vice chancellor, 1968-73, chancellor, 1973-78, vicar gen., 1978-79; pastor St. William Ch., Euclid, Ohio, 1978-79; aux. bishop Diocese of Cleve.; vicar of western region Diocese of Cleve., Lorain, Ohio, 1979-83; bishop Diocese of Columbus (Ohio), 1983—; mem. clergy relations bd. Diocese of Cleve., 1972-75, mem. clergy retirement bd., 1973-78, mem. clergy personnel bd., 1979-83. Author: (with A.J. Quinn) Thoughts for Our Times, 1969, Thoughts for Sowing, 1970, (with others) Ashes from the Cathedral, 1974, Sackcloth and Ashes, 1976, The Priestly Heart, 1983, Reflections on the Law of Love, 1991, Summary of the New Catholic Catechism, 1994. Bd. dirs. Holy Family Cancer Home, 1973-78; trustee St. Mary Sem., 1976-78; bd. dirs., mem. pension com. Cath. Cemeteries Assn., 1978-83; bd. dirs. Meals on Wheels, Euclid, 1978-79; vice-chancellor Pontifical Coll. Josephinum, 1983—; bd. dirs. Franklin County United Way, 1984-90; chmn. bd. govs. N.Am. Coll., Rome, Italy, 1984-88; chmn. Mayor's Coun. on Youth, 1986-90; treas. Cath. Relief Svc. Bd., 1988-91, pres., 1991-96; co-chair Columbus Cmty. Rels. Commn., 1992-95; mem. America's Promise, Columbus, 1997—. Decorated Knight of the Holy Sepulchre, 1993; recipient Human Rights award Anti-Defamation League B'nai B'rith, 1987, Gov.'s award State of Ohio, 1994, Jessing award Pontifical Coll., 1993, Don Bosco medal, 1997. Mem. Am. Canon Law Soc., Columbus Bar Assn. (chmn. jud. advt. com. 1987-91, Liberty Bell award 1989).

GRIFFIN, JAMES V., artist; b. Kitchener, Ont., Can., July 22, 1949; s. Vincent Oswald and Gibson Aureola (Beatty) G.; m. Virginia Sing, 1972 (div. 1978); m. Tabita Freimanis, Nov. 27, 1981. BFA, Pratt Inst., 1972. Artist Lagrangeville, N.Y., 1976—. Prin. works include World War Two, a Remembrance, 1994-95, Battles of the Civil War, 1995-96, book covers, 1976—, Royal Doulton series of figurines based on his romance paintings, 1998—, Princess Diana-A Woman of Style, 1998, The Titanic, 1999. Mem. Sierra Club, Common Cause, Nature Conservancy. Avocation: landscape gardening. Home: 385 Andrews Rd Lagrangeville NY 12540-6124

GRIFFIN, (ALVA) JEAN, entertainer; b. Detroit, June 1, 1931; d. Henry Bethel White and Ruth Madelyn (Gowen) Durham; m. Francis Jay Griffin, July 8, 1958 (dec.); stepchildren: Patra, Rodney; 1 adopted child, Donald; children: Rhonda Jean, Sherree Lee. Student, Anderson Coll., 1952-53; DD (hon.), Ministry of Salvation, Chula Vista, Calif., 1990, Ministry of Salvation, 1990. Ordained minister, 1990. Supr. Woolworth's, Detroit, 1945-46; operator, supr. Atlantic Bell Tel. Co., Detroit, 1947-51, Anderson, Ind., 1952-56; sec. to div. mgr. Food Basket-Lucky Stores, San Diego, 1957-58; owner, mgr. Jay's Country Boy Markets, Riverside, Calif., 1962-87; entertainer, prodr., dir., singer Mae West & Co., 1980—; past owner The Final Touch, Colorado Springs; owner Omega Communique Co., 1997—; tchr. art Grant Sch., Riverside, 1964-65; tchr., adviser Mental Retarded Sch., Riverside, 1976-77; instr. Touch for Health Found., Pasadena, Calif., 1975-79; cons., hypnotist, nutritionist, Riverside, 1976-79; mem., tchr. Psi field parapsychology. Writer children's stories and short stories. Mem. Rep. Presdl. Task Force, 1983. Recipient svc. award Rep. Presdl. Task Force, 1986. Mem. Parapsychology Assn. Riverside (pres. 1981-82). Mem. Ch. of Religious Science New Thought. Avocations: arts and crafts, photography, hiking, horseback riding, travel. Home: 201 W Chapel Rd Sedona AZ 86336-7031

GRIFFIN, JEAN LATZ, writer, political strategist, small business owner; b. Joliet, Ill., Mar. 6, 1943; d. Carl Joseph and Helene Monica (Bradshaw) Latz; m. Dennis Joseph Griffin, Sept. 16, 1967; children: Joseph, Timothy, Peter. BS in Chemistry, Coll. St. Francis, Joliet, 1965; MS in Comm., U. Wis., 1967. Clin. investigation coord. Baxter Labs., 1967-68; reporter Joliet Herald News, 1968-70, Raleigh (N.C.) Times, 1974-75; reporter Suburban Trib, Hinsdale, Ill., 1976-78, regional edn. reporter, 1978-82; gen. assignment reporter Chgo. Tribune, 1982-84, edn. writer, 1984-88, pub. health writer, 1988-94, govt., politics, and pub. policy reporter, 1994-97, econ. devel. reporter, 1997; strategist The Strategy Group, Chgo., 1998—; owner CyberINK, 1998—. Bd. dirs. Residents for Emergency Shelter, Chgo., 1978-82, Genesis House, Chgo., 1995-98, vol. cook, 1994-98; devel. com. mem. Hope Now, Inc., 1998—. Recipient Writing award Am. Dental Assn., 1969, Alumna Profl. Achievement award Coll. St. Francis, Joliet, 1985, First Prize in ednl. writing Edn. Writers Am., 1986, Grand prize, 1988, Benjamin Fine award Nat. Assn. Secondary Sch. Prins., 1988, Edward Scott Beck award for reporting Chgo. Tribune, 1988, Peter Lisagor award for pub. svc. Soc. Profl. Journalists, Chgo. chpt., 1988, Mark of Excellence Chgo. Assn. Black Journalists, 1992, Cushing award for Journalistic Excellence, Chgo. Dental Soc., 1992, Human First award Horizon Cmty. Svcs., Chgo., 1993, Robert F. Kennedy Grand Prize in Journalism, 1994, Editl. Excellence award Ill. Merchandising Coun., 1994; finalist Pulitzer Prize, 1994. Mem. Emily's List, Women's Leadership Coun., Victory Fund. Office: CyberINK 621 N Belmont Ave Arlington Heights IL 60004 Office: The Strategy Group 730 N Franklin St Chicago IL 60610-3563 *Keep climbing mountains. Invent challenges if you have to. Love all life--amoeba to stars. Dive into the flow of the universe. And wash your dishes when you're done.**

GRIFFIN, JERRY J., chaplain; b. Wauseon, Ohio, Feb. 13, 1938; s. Peter Clair Griffin and Sadie Irene (Stratton) Behnke; m. Jean Ann Sutherland, June 25, 1961 (div. Dec. 15, 1988); children: Anne Marie Kapral, John William; m. Ruth Emma Shook, Dec. 30, 1988; stepchildren: Michael J. Kapral Jr., MaryLynn Kapral Ahart, Mark D. Kapral. BA, Hiram Coll., 1961; MDiv, Drake U., 1965; ThM, Tex. Christian U., 1966. Cert. chaplain, Assn. Profl. Chaplains, Inc. Staff chaplain Iowa Meth. Hosp., Des Moines, 1966-68; pastor First Christian Ch., Coon Rapids, Iowa, 1968-70; chaplain Bethel Deaconess Hosp. & Home for Aged, Newton, Kans., 1970-79; chaplain, counselor Dorothy Love Retirement Cmty., Sidney, Ohio, 1979-83; chaplain Corning (N.Y) Hosp. & Founders Pavilion, 1983-93; sys. dir. spiritual svcs. Lee Meml. Health Sys., Ft. Myers, 1993—; pres. bd. dirs. Midwest Area Alcohol Edn. & Tng. Program, Chgo., 1972-75. Bd. edn. Hesston (Kans.) Pub. Schs., 1978-79; bd. dirs. Fla. Bioethics Network, 1994-98. Mem. Assn. Clin. Pastoral Edn., Internat. Critical Incident Stress Found., Coll. of Chaplains, Inc. (pres. 1989-91), Samaritan Counseling Ctr. Southwest Fla. (bd. dirs. 1996-98). Avocations: reading, gardening. Home: 9100 Lady Bug Ct Fort Myers FL 33919-8342 Office: Lee Meml Health Sys 2776 Cleveland Ave # Fort Myers FL 33901-5864

GRIFFIN, JO ANN THOMAS, retired financial planner, tax specialist; b. Dallas, July 20, 1933; d. John Baxton and Joan Marion (Ament) Thomas; m. John Barrett Brown, June 29, 1963 (div. 1972); children: John Barrett Jr., Daniel Thomas; m. Thomas Reese Griffin, Jan. 25, 1976; stepchildren: Gregory Crawford, Kevin Bradley. BA, U. Miss., 1955; BS magna cum laude, Lamar U., 1964; MEd, U. Del., 1972. Cert. fin. planner; enrolled agt. U.S. Treas. Dept. SSite mgr. Motivational Ctr., Inc., Wilmington, Del., 1976-78; asst. dir. Indochinese social svcs. Assoc. Cath. Charities, New Orleans, 1978-79; dir. continuing edn. St. Mary's Dominican Coll., New Orleans, 1979-80; with fin. mgmt. U.S. Dept. Agr., New Orleans, 1981; tax auditor IRS, New Orleans, Phila., Del., 1981-86; revenue agt. IRS, Wilmington, Del., 1987-92; tax specialist Horty & Horty, CPA's, Wilmington, 1986-87; quality control H&R Block, Wilmington, 1992-94; counselor Svc. Corps Ret. Execs., Wilmington, 1994-96; dir. Wilmington River-City Com., 1997—. Docent Winterthur, New Orleans Mus. Art, Wilmington and New Orleans, 1966-85; sustaining mem., advisor Jr. League Wilmington, 1989-92; lay reader, mem. oureach com. Episc. Ch. Diocese of Del., Wilmington, 1971—; counselor Svc. Corps. Ret. Execs., Wilmington, 1992; regent Vieux Carre chpt. DAR, New Orleans, 1984; bd. dirs. Neighborhood Watch, New Orleans, 1983-85, Waterfront Coalition, Inc., 1998—. Recipient Grad. Scholarship award AAUW, 1971, Sustained Superior Performance award IRS, New Orleans, 1984, Spl. Achievement award IRS, Wilmington, 1988, 89, Customer Svc. awards, 1989, 90. Mem. Am. Soc. Women Accts. (sec. 1986-89), Del. Valley Soc. Cert. Fin. Planners, Wilmington Tax Group, Estate Planning Coun. Del., Wilmington Women in Bus., Rotary, Blue and Gold Club, Mortar Bd., Phi Kappa Phi. Democrat. Episcopalian. Home: 900 N Broom St Apt 16 Wilmington DE 19806-4546

GRIFFIN, JOHN HENRY, medical researcher; b. Seattle, June 26, 1943; s. John Henry and Lillian Louise (O'Connell) G.; m. Antonia Lastreto, 1965 (div. 1984); children: John, Deanna, Paul. BS, U. Santa Clara, 1965; PhD, U. Calif., Davis, 1969. Tchg. asst. U. Calif., 1967-69; guest worker NIH, 1971-73; with staff Svc. Biochimie Ctr. Etudes Nucleaires, Saclay, France, 1973-74; asst. dept. immunopathology Scripps Clinic Rsch. Found., La Jolla, Calif., 1974-75; assoc. depts. immunopthology, molecular immunology Scripps Clinic Rsch. Found., La Jolla, 1975-80; prof. dept. molecular exptl. medicine Scripps Rsch. Inst., La Jolla, 1994—; peer rev. com. NIH, 1979. Contbr. articles to profl. jours. Treas. San Diego Assn. Gifte Children, 1978-81; active Pub. Sch. Cluster Com., University City, S.D., 1984-85; mem. adv. com. High Sch. Cmty., University City, 1979-82, 86-88. Recipient Rsch. Career Devel. award NIH, 1976-81, fellow, 1966-69, 72-73; RCA physics scholar 1961-64; Harvard Med. Sch. fellow, 1969-71, Helen Hay Whitney Found. fellow, 1969-72. Mem. Internat. Soc. Thrombosis Hemostasis, Am. Soc. Clin. Investigators, Am. Soc. Hematology, Am. Chem. Soc., Am. Soc. Biochem. Molecular Biologists, Am. Assn. Pathologists, Am. Heart Assn., Sigma Xi, Alpha Sigma Nu, Phi Kappa Phi.

GRIFFIN, JOHN JOSEPH, JR., chemist, video producer; b. Chgo., Sept. 11, 1946; s. John Joseph, Sr. and Louise (Griswold) G.; m. Ramona Rodriguez, Apr. 19, 1969; 1 child, Marcus. BS, Tex. A&M U., 1972, MS, 1974. Lab. technician Johns-Manville, Chgo., 1964-66; chemist, rsch. chemist Dow Chemical USA, Tex. Divsn., Freeport, 1974-78; sr. chemist Soltex Polymers, Deer Pk., Tex., 1978-80; plant chemist Air Products & Chemicals, Pasadena, Tex., 1980-84; quality assurance supr. Core Lab., Chromaspec Divsn., Houston, 1984-88; plant chemist and quality assurance supr. Ga. Gulf Corp., Pasadena, Tex., 1988-95; synthesis chemist KMCO, Inc., Crosby, Tex., 1995—; propr. Petro-Star, Houston, 1995-96, owner, 1996-97; propr. and owner JJ's Quality Custom Video, Houston, 1986-88; propr., prodr. Pro-Star Video Prodns., Houston, 1988—; video prodr. J. Frank Dobie and So. Houston H.S. Graduation, U. Houston Graduation, also weddings and seminars, v.p. 1996—. Pres. Kirkwood Civic Club, Houston, 1991-96, v.p. 1996—; bd. dirs. Southbelt Security Alliance, Houston, 1988—, Houston Better Bus. Bur., 1996. With USAF, 1966-70. Mem. ASTM (D-16 com. aromatic compounds and D-2 petro products and lubricants, D-2 petroleum products and lubricants), Am. Chem. Soc. Office: KMCO Inc Crosby TX 77532

GRIFFIN, KEITH BROADWELL, economics educator; b. Colon, Republic of Panama, Nov. 6, 1938; came to U.S., 1988; s. Marcus Samuel Griffin and Elaine Ann (Broadwell) Fabick; m. Dixie Beth, Apr. 2, 1956; children: Janice, Kimberley. BA, Williams Coll., 1960, DLitt (hon.), 1980; PhB, Oxford U., Eng., 1962, PhD, 1965. Fellow and tutor in econs. Magdalen Coll. Oxford (Eng.) U., 1965-76, fellow Magdalen Coll., 1977-79, pres., 1979-88, hon. fellow, 1988; acting warden, dir. Queen Elizabeth House, Inst. Commonwealth Studies, 1973, 77-78, warden, dir., 1978-79; prof. U. Calif., Riverside, 1988—, chmn. dept. econs., 1988-93, Presdl. prof., 1988-90, Disting. prof., 1997—; vis. prof. Inst. Econs. and Planning U. Chile, 1962-63, 64-65; chmn. bd. UN Rsch. Inst. for Social Devel., 1988-95, sr. cons., 1971-72; mem. UN com. for devel. planning, 1987-94; mem. coun. UN Univ., 1986-92, chmn. fin. and budget com., 1988-90; mem. Marshall Aid Commemoration Commn., 1984-88; mem. World Commn. on culture and Devel., 1994-95; chief ILO Employment Adv. Mission to Ethiopia, 1982; econ. advisor Govt. of Bolivia, 1989-91; pres. Devel. Studies Assn., U.K., 1978-80; chief rural and urban employment policies br. ILO, 1975-76; cons. ILO on rurual devel. in Ecuador, 1974; sr. adviser OECD Devel. Centre, Paris, 1986-91; adviser to Inter-Am. Com. for Alliance for Progress on copper expansion programme in Chile, 1968, to FAO/ICO, IBRD World Coffee Study in Guatemala, El Salvador and Colombia, 1967; rsch. advisor Pakistan Inst. Devel. Econs., Karachi, 1965, 70; expert on agrl. planning to Govt. of Algeria, acting chief FAO Mission, Algiers, 1963-64; cons. IBRD on land reform on Morocco, 1973; head UN Devel. Program Poverty Alleviation Mission to Mongolia, 1994; head ILO Social Policy Review Mission to Uzbekis, 1995; cons. on econ. reform in Vietnam, UNDP, 1997; head ILO Employment and Social Protection Mission to Kazakstan, 1997. Author: Underdevelopment in Spanish America, 1969, 2d edit., 1971, Spanish edit., 1972, The Green Revolution: An Economic Analysis, 1972, The Political Economy of Agrarian Change, 1974, 2d edit., 1979, Spanish edit., 1982, Hindi edit., 1983, Land Concentration and Rural Poverty, 1976, 2d edit., 1981, Spanish edit., 1983, International Inequality and National Poverty, 1978, Spanish edit., 1984, World Hunger and the World Economy, 1987, Alternative Strategies for Economic Development, 1989, Chinese edit., 1992, Studies in Globalization and Economic Transitions, 1996; co-author: Comercio Internacional y Politicas de Desarrollo Economico, 1967, Planning Development, 1970, Spanish edit., 1975, The Transition to Egalitarian Development, 1981, Globalization and the Developing World, 1992, Implementing a Human Development Strategy, 1994; editor: Financing Development in Latin America, 1971, Institutional Reform and Economic Development in the Chinese Countryside, 1984, The Economy of Ethiopia, 1992, Poverty and the Transition to a Market Economy in Mongolia, 1995, Social Policy and Economic Transformation in Uzbakistan, 1996, Economic Reform in Vietnam, 1998; co-editor: Ensayos Sobre Planificacion, 1967, Growth and Inequality in Pakistan, 1972, The Economic Development of Bangladesh, 1974, Human Development and the International Development Strategy for the 1990s, 1990, The Distribution of Income in China, 1993, also numerous articles. Vis. fellow Oxford Ctr. Islamic Studies, 1998. Fellow AAAS; mem. Royal Econ. Soc., Am. Econ. Assn. Avocation: travel. Office: Univ Calif Dept Econs Riverside CA 92521-4198

GRIFFIN, KEITH E., legislative administrator; b. Evanston, Ill., Jan. 28, 1972. BA, Albright Coll., Readington, Pa., 1995. Legis. dir. to Rep. Albert R. Wynn U.S. Ho. of Reps., Washington, 1998—. Office: US Ho of Reps 407 CHOB Washington DC 20515

GRIFFIN, KELLY ANN, public relations executive, consultant; b. Buffalo, May 20, 1964; d. Michael Gerald and Patricia Frances (Lippert) G.; m. Thomas Richard Kleinberger, Oct. 11, 1992. B in Polit. Sci., SUNY, Geneseo, 1986; postgrad., CUNY, Bklyn., 1994—. Legis. asst. to N.Y. State Assembly Spkrs. Stanley Fink and Mel Miller Buffalo, 1986-87; acct. exec. Griffin Media Group, N.Y.C., 1987-88, acct. supr., v.p., 1988-90, pres., CEO, 1990-94; pub. rels. cons. N.Y.C., 1994—; assoc. dir. N.Y. State Funeral Dirs. Assn., N.Y.C., 1992-94, Met. Funeral Dirs. Assn., N.Y.C., 1992-94, County Execs. of Am., N.Y.C. and Washington, 1993—; instr. remedial reading Cornell U. Sch. Industry/Lab. Rels., Buffalo, 1987; v.p. Fairfield Owners Cooperative, Riverdale, 1996—. Editor N.Y. State AFL-CIO Unity, 1988-90, County Execs. News, 1993—, N.Y. State Funeral Dirs. Assn./Met. Funeral Dirs. Assn. News, 1992-94, Amalgamated Transit Union News, 1988-90. cons. Interfaith Assembly on Homelessness, N.Y.C., 1994—, Voter Assistance Commn., N.Y.C., 1990-92; participant, cons. Erie County Dem. Party, Buffalo, 1985-87; mem. assocs. steering com. Children's Health Fund, N.Y.C., 1991—. Recipient Acad. award DAR, 1978. Mem. Pub. Rels. Soc. N.Y.C. Roman Catholic. Avocations: reading, swimming, bike riding. Home: 640 W 231st St Apt 7B Bronx NY 10463-3258 Office: Griffin Media Group 640 W 231st St Apt 7B Bronx NY 10463-3258

GRIFFIN, LARRY ALLEN, minister, evangelist; b. Clark AFB, The Philippines, Dec. 22, 1949; s. Richard Eugene and Lilia (Nepomuceno) G.; m. Mary-Jane Stewart, Dec. 11, 1977; children: Lilia Adah, Leslie Ann, Caleb Andrew, Arvin Alcantara. BS in Secondary Edn., U. Maine, Presque Isle, 1973; MDiv, Meth. Theol. Sch., Delaware, Ohio, 1978. Ordained to ministry United Meth. Ch., 1974, Am. Bapt. Chs. in U.S.A., 1986; cert. secondary tchr., Maine, Ohio. Pastor Monticello (Maine) United Meth. Ch., 1972-73; pastor youth Sixth Ave. United Meth. Ch., Lancaster, Ohio, 1973-75; pastor Beulah United Meth. Ch., Baltimore, Ohio, 1975-76, Meadow Farm United Meth. Ch., Zanesville, Ohio, 1977-78; asst. pastor Broad St. United Meth. Ch., Columbus, Ohio, 1978-79; pastor Duncan Falls (Ohio) Bapt. Ch., 1984-86, 1st Bapt. Ch., Sunbury, Ohio, 1986—; chmn. state adv. com. for ordination Am. Bapt. Chs. Ohio, 1986, campus ministry task force, 1989, Commn. on Profl. Ministry, Commn. for Town/Country Ministries, 1988-91, staff coord. for evangelism and ch. growth, Am. Bapt. Ch., Ohio, 1988-93; pastor, counselor Am. Bapt. Men of Ohio, 1987-91; chmn. fin. Judson Hills Camp Bd., Loudonville, Ohio, 1988-90; pres. Big Walnut Ministerial Assn., Sunbury, Ohio, 1987-88. Mem. Rep. Presdl. Task Force, 1983—, Nat. Right to Life, 1983—, Am. Bapt. Friends of Life, 1986—. Recipient Harry Manning award Town/Country Commn., Am. Bapt. Chs. Ohio, 1989. Mem. Nat. Assn. Evangelicals, Am. Bapt. Evangelism Team (steering com. 1990-93), Am. Bapt. Chs./USA (bd. dirs. 1994—, bd. nat. ministries 1994, minister's coun. senate 1998—), Am. Bapt. Chs./Ohio (bd. regional ministries 1994—, pers. com. 1997—, treas. minister's coun. 1995-97). Home: 3324 Carters Corner Rd Sunbury OH 43074-9626 Office: 1st Bapt Ch PO Box 394 89 E Cherry St Sunbury OH 43074-8393 *Having been raised in a Christian home, I have always known that God loved me and had a purpose for my life. Since committing my life to Christ, my quest in life has been and shall continue to be to seek His will and strive to be faithful to His calling. I receive the advice of Colossians 3:17 and 3:23 and claim the promise of Proverbs 16:3.*

GRIFFIN, LAWRENCE JOSEPH, lawyer; b. Chgo., Dec. 11, 1965; s. Eugen Leo and Elena Rachel (Bruno) G.; m. Elizabeth Griffin, Mar. 18, 1995. BA, Cornell U., 1988; JD, DePaul U., 1991. Bar: Ill. 1991, Calif. 1997, Wis. 1997, U.S. Dist. Ct. (no. dist.) Ill. 1991, U.S. Ct. Appeals (7th cir.) 1992. Assoc. Eugene L. Griffin & Assocs., Ltd., Chgo., 1991—; arbitrator Cook County Manditory Arbitration, Chgo., 1994—. Mem. ATLA, ABA, Ill. Bar Assn., Chgo. Bar Assn. (profl. reponsibility com. 1994—, tort law com. 1994—), Calif. Bar Assn., Wis. Bar Assn., Ill. Trial Lawyers Assn. Office: Eugene L Griffin & Assocs 29 N Wacker Dr Ste 650 Chicago IL 60606-3203

GRIFFIN, LESLIE DEE, educational administrator; b. Velasco, Tex., Feb. 18, 1945; d. Charles Richard and Emma-Lee (Baker) Brown; m. Larry Carter Walrath, June 15, 1964 (div. Apr. 1973); children: Helen, Cassandra, Ray; m. Robert Barry Griffin, Aug. 29, 1981; 1 child, John-David. Student, Cornell Coll., Mt. Vernon, Iowa, 1963-64; BS in Exptl. Psychology, Ea. Wash. U., 1974, BA in Elem. Edn., MEd in Spl. Edn., 1977, postgrad., 1980—; postgrad., Wash. State U. Cert. elem. and secondary tchr., Wash.; advanced exceptional child cert., Wash., tchr., Pa., Mont. Master tchr., program dir. Brazoria County Infant Devel. Ctr., Galveston, Tex., 1974-75; tchr. learning disabled Mead (Wash.) Sch. Dist., 1977-78, Spokane (Wash.) Ednl. Therapy Assocs., Inc., 1978; tchr. dist. devel. ctr. Coeur d'Alene (Idaho) Sch. Dist. 271, 1978-79, tchr. learning disability resource room elem. sch., 1979-81; tchr. spl. edn. Priest River Elem. Sch., Bonner County Sch. Dist. 82, Sandpoint, Idaho, 1981-84; tchr. semi-self contained resource room Moscow (Idaho) Jr. High Sch., 1985-87; coord. VISTA, Havre, Mont., 1989-92; vis. instr. dept. applied psychology Ea. Wash. U., Cheney, spring 1978; part-time asst. prof. edn. dept. No. Mont. Coll., Havre, 1988-91; cons. 1st Luth. Pre-Kindergarten, Havre, 1990; chmn. bd. dirs. Project Vols. for Adult Literacy, 1987-88; presenter in field; advisor on mental health worker curriculum adv. com. Brazosport Coll., Lake Jackson, Tex., 1975. Community rep. Havre Head Start Bd. Mem. Coun. for Exceptional Children, Mont. Bus. and Profl. Women (pres.), AAUW. Home: 1010 E Court PO Box 1583 Deer Park WA 99006-1583

GRIFFIN, LUANNE MARIE, automotive corporation executive; b. Pitts., Dec. 19, 1961; d. Louis F. and Bernadette (Piekarski) Chapman; m. James E. Griffin, July 19, 1997. BA, Thiel Coll., 1983; MA, George Washington U., 1987. Sr. legis. asst. U.S. Rep. Thomas Ridge, Washington, 1983-87; English instr. Japan Min. Edn., Kagoshima, 1987-88; congrl. liaison Embassy of Japan, Washington, 1989-93; trade policy analyst Powell, Goldstein, Frazer & Murphy, Washington, 1993-95; mgr. govt. affairs Nissan N.Am., Inc., Washington, 1995—. Mem. Women in Internat. Trade., Washington Internat. Trade Assn., Tenn. State Soc. (bd. dirs.). Republican. Roman Catholic. Office: Nissan N Am 750 17th St NW Ste 900 Washington DC 20006-4607

GRIFFIN, MARTIN EDWARD, music educator; b. Dover, N.J., Aug. 3, 1967; s. Edward Martin and Barbara Catherine (Boyd) G.; m. Alison Beth Cichy, Apr. 22, 1995; children: Chelsea Lynne, Edward Martin. B in Music, William Paterson U., 1990. Cert. elem. and secondary tchr., N.J. Dir. band and choir Bergen County Vocat. H.S., Hackensack, N.J., 1990-91, Pt. Pleasant Beach (N.J.) H.S., 1991-93; dir. band Sayreville War Meml. H.S., Parlin, N.J., 1993—; percussion arranger Morris Hills H.S., Rockaway, N.J., 1987—, Ramsey (N.J.) H.S., 1991—; drum corps. adjudicator E. Coast Judges Guild, Belleville, N.J., 1997—. Assembly resolution N.J. Gen. Assembly, 1993; resolution Sayreville Mayor and Borough Coun., 1996. Mem. Internat. Assn. Jazz Educators, Music Educators Nat. Conf., Ctrl. Jersey Music Educators. Roman Catholic. Office: Sayreville War Meml HS 820 Washington Rd Parlin NJ 08859-1050

GRIFFIN, MARVIN ANTHONY, industrial engineer, educator; b. Pine Apple, Ala., Mar. 28, 1923; s. Randolph Simpson and Linnie (Barrett) G.; m. Jane Pearle A. L'Herisson, Sept. 4, 1949 (dec. Dec. 1992); children: Margaret Lynn, John Marvin, Barbara Lee, Elizabeth Ann. B.S., Auburn U., 1949; M.S. Engring, U. Ala., 1952; D.Eng., Johns Hopkins, 1960. Registered profl. engr., Ala. Chief ops. analysis Anniston Ordnance Depot, Ala., 1949-51; sr. mfg. engr. Western Electric Co., Winston-Salem, N.C., 1952-55; chief engring. Cumberland Mfg. Co., Chattanooga, 1955-57; instr. Johns Hopkins, 1957-60; chief indsl. engr. Matson Navigation Co., San Francisco, 1960-61; v.p. corporate devel. Matson Navigation Co., 1977-78, group v.p., 1978-79; prof. indsl. engring. U. Ala., 1961-76, chmn. dept., 1965-71, chmn. dept. computer sci. and ops. research, 1971-76, dir. computer sci., 1969-76, prof. indsl. engring. and computer sci., 1980—, prof. emeritus indsl. engring., 1987—, chmn. dept., 1983—; mem. maritime transp. research bd., maritime info. com. Nat. Acad. Sci., 1976—; mgmt. cons. to industry, govt.; labor arbitrator Fed. Mediation and Conciliation Service, Am. Arbitration Assn.; cons. indsl. engring., ops. rsch., arbitration, mediation svcs., 1987-92. Contbr. articles to profl. jours. Served to comdr. USNR, 1943-47, PTO. Sr. postdoctoral fellow Johns Hopkins U., 1969. Mem. Operations Research Soc. Am., Am. Inst. Indsl. Engrs. (dir. 1954-55, chpt. pres. 1959-60), Am. Soc. Engring. Edn., Inst. Mgmt. Sci., Assn. Computing Machinery, Johns Hopkins Soc. Scholars. Home and Office: 2640 Claymont Cir Tuscaloosa AL 35404-4261

GRIFFIN, MARY FRANCES, retired library media consultant; b. Cross Hill, S.C., Aug. 24, 1925; d. James and Rosa Lee (Carter) G. BA, Benedict Coll., 1947; postgrad., S.C. State Coll., 1948-51, Atlanta U., 1953, Va. State Coll., 1961; MLS, Ind. U., 1957. Tchr., libr. Johnston (S.C.) Tng. Sch., Edgefield County Sch. Dist., 1947-51; libr. Lee County Sch. Dist., Dennis High, Bishopville, S.C., 1951-52, Greenville County (S.C.) Sch. Dist., 1952-66; libr. cons. S.C. Dept. Edn., Columbia, 1966-87; vis. tchr. U. S.C., 1977.

bd. dirs. Greater Columbia Lit. Coun.; mem. Richland County unit Assault on Illiteracy. Recipient Cert. of Living the Legacy award Nat. Coun. Negro Women, 1980. Mem. ALA, Assn. Ednl. Comms. and Tech., S.C. Assn. Curriculum Devel., AAUW (pres. Columbia br. 1978-80), Southeastern Libr. Assn. (sec. 1979-80), S.C. Libr. Assn. (sec. 1979), S.C. Assn. Sch. Librarians, Nat. Assn. State Ednl. and Media Pers. Baptist. Home: PO Box 1652 Columbia SC 29202-1652 also: 1100 Skyland Dr Columbia SC 29210-8127

GRIFFIN, MARY JANE RAGSDALE, educational consultant, writer, small business owner; b. Crawfordsville, Ind., Aug. 15, 1927; d. Ira Vincent and Sophronia Burdetti (Thompson) Ragsdale; m. Walter Wanzel Griffin, Jan. 20, 1951; children: Walter Vincent, Glenn Edwin, Edwin Wanzel. BS, U. Tenn., 1949, MS, 1970, EdS, 1976, EdD, 1980. Cert. math., sci., physics, chemistry, computer programming, elem. tchr., secondary and elem. adminstr., Tenn. Instr. physics lab., pianist, accompanist modern dance class U. Chattanooga (Tenn.), 1945-47; pvt. tchr. piano and violin, Knoxville, Tenn., 1947-50; asst. dir. Sunshine Schoolette, Knoxville, 1954-69; tchr. sci. and math. Knox County Schs., Knoxville, 1970-74; tchr. math. methods U. Tenn., Knoxville, 1975-76; tchr. math. and computer programming Knox County Schs., Knoxville, 1977-88; freelance writer Knoxville, 1970—, real estate investor and mgr., 1975—; owner, pres. MJRG Enterprises, Knoxville, 1976—; freelance edn. cons. Knoxville, 1988—. Contbr. articles to various publs.; writer curriculum guides. Violinist Chattanooga Symphony, 1944-47; officer bd. dirs. Ossoli Circle, Knoxville, 1954-64, 89-90; poetry contest chmn. Fontinalis, 1993-96, fine arts chair, 1995-96; officer, bd. dirs. Girls Club Knoxville, Inc., 1962-70, charter signer, 1962; mem. Fountain City Town Hall, 1985—, Knoxville Symphony League, 1990—; tchr. adult Sunday sch., 1988-92; mem. chancel choir 1st Christian Ch., Knoxville, 1949-85, bd. dirs., 1982-85; mem. chancel choir Fountain City United Meth. Ch., Knoxville, 1985-91, bd. dirs., 1993-97, cert. 50 yr. mem.; pres. United Meth. Women, 1993-97, v.p. Knoxville Dist., 1996-98; mem. steering com. Just Older Youth, Fountain City, Tenn., 1998—. U. Chattanooga scholar, 1947; U. Tenn. fellow, 1968-70. Mem. NEA, ASCD, AAUW, DAR, Nat. Coun. Tchrs. Math. (life), Tenn. Edn. Assn. (workshop presenter 1980-88), East Tenn. Edn. Assn., Knox County Edn. Assn. (rep. 1980-85), East Tenn. Hist. Soc. (life), Ind. Hist. Soc. (life), Ky. Hist. Soc. (life), Va. Hist. Soc., Montgomery County (Ind.) Hist. Soc., Boone County (Ind.) Hist. Soc., Union County (Tenn.) Hist. Soc., Gen. Fedn. Womens Clubs, Tenn. Fedn. Womens Clubs, Appalachian Zool. Soc. (life), Soc. for Preservation Tenn. Antiquities (life), First Families of Tenn., U. Tenn. President's Club (life), Smoky Mountain Z-Car Club, Optimists Internat. (life, local bd. dirs. 1990-92, Tenn. dist. essay contest chmn. 1990-91, 1992-93, 1993-94, Tenn. dist. 1st lady 1990-91), Optimists Internat., Sigma Phi Sigma (life, chpt. pres. U. Chattanooga 1945-47), Delta Kappa Gamma (fin. com. 1980-91), Phi Delta Theta, Kappa Delta Pi (internat. voting del. 1982, 84, 86, conf. presenter 1982), Kappa Delta (life). Avocations: nature walks and study, travel, photography, reading, public speaking. Home: 5213 Haynes Sterchi Rd Knoxville TN 37912-2816

GRIFFIN, MERV EDWARD, former entertainer, television producer, entrepreneur; b. San Mateo, Calif., July 6, 1925; s. Mervyn Edward and Rita (Robinson) G.; m. Julann Elizabeth Wright, May 18, 1958 (div. June 1976); 1 son, Anthony Patrick. Student, San Mateo Coll., 1942-44; L.H.D., Emerson Coll., 1981. Owner Teleview Racing Patrol Inc., Miami, Fla., Video Racing Patrol Inc., Seattle, Beverly Hilton Hotel, Beverly Hills, Calif., The Scottsdale (Ariz.) Hilton, Wickenburg (Ariz.) Inn; chmn. bd. Griffin Group, Inc., Beverly Hills, Givenchy Hotel and Spa, Palm Springs, Calif., Merv Griffin Prodns., Beverly Hills; owner Merv Griffin Entertainment, Beverly Hills, 1996—. Performer Merv Griffin Show radio sta. KFRC, San Francisco, 1945-48, vocalist Freddy Martin's Orch., 1948-52; contract player, star So This is Love, Warner Bros., 1953-55; TV master ceremonies, 1958—, Merv Griffin Show, NBC-TV, 1962-63, Westinghouse Broadcasting Co., 1965-69, CBS-TV, 1969-72, syndication, 1972-86; currently exec. producing: Wheel of Fortune, Jeopardy. Club: Bohemian (San Francisco). Office: Merv Griffin Enterprises 3000 31 St Santa Monica CA 90405 also: The Griffin Group 780 3rd Ave New York NY 10017-2024

GRIFFIN, MYRNA MCINTOSH, critical care nurse; b. Carrollton, Ga., May 30, 1948; d. Clifford H. and Vertie Maude (Potts) McIntosh; m. John Thomas Griffin II, June 20, 1981. Diploma, Floyd Sch. Nursing, Berry Coll., 1972. Staff nurse neonatal ICU Kennestone Hosp., Marietta, Ga.; staff nurse neonatal ICU Floyd Med. Ctr., Rome, Ga., charge nurse spl. care nursery; staff nurse neonatal ICU Gwinnett Med. Ctr., Lawrenceville, Ga. Mem. Nat. Assn. Neonatal Nurses.

GRIFFIN, OSCAR O'NEAL, JR., writer, former oil company executive; b. Daisetta, Tex., Apr. 28, 1933; s. Oscar O'Neal and Myrtle Ellen (Edgar) G.; m. Patricia Lamb, July 28, 1955; children: Gwendolyn Ann, Amanda Karen, Gregory O'Neal, Marguerite Ellen. B. Journalism, U. Tex., 1958; grad., Harvard U. Sch. Bus., 1982. Editor Canyon (Tex.) News, 1959-60, Pecos (Tex.) Ind., 1960-62; reporter Houston Chronicle, 1962-66, White House corr., 1966-69; asst. dir. pub. affairs U.S. Dept. Transp., Washington, 1969-74; pres. Griffin Well Service, Inc., El Campo, Tex., 1974-88; sr. v.p. 395 Enterprises, Inc., 1986-88; free-lance writer Houston, Tex., 1988—. Served with AUS, 1953-55. Recipient award for investigative reporting Southwest Journalism Forum, 1963; Pulitzer prize for local reporting not under pressure of edit. time, 1963. Mem. Houston Livestock Show and Rodeo (life), U. Tex. Alumni Assn. (life), Harvard Bus Sch. Club of Houston, Soc. Profl. Journalists (Disting. Svc. in Journalism award Ft. Worth chpt. 1962, Courage in Journalism award Des Moines chapt. 1963, award for gen. reporting nat. orgn. 1963). Club: National Press. Home and Office: 9850 Meadowglen Ln Apt 123 Houston TX 77042-4357

GRIFFIN, PEGGY, university administrator; b. Marshalltown, Iowa, Nov. 25, 1947; d. LaVern L. Eckhart; m. James M. Griffin, Jan. 16, 1971; children: Bridgette, Sean. AA, Marshalltown C.C., 1969. Ops. supr. Nat. Sch. Bus, Mundelein, Ill.; distbn. clk. Lake Forest (Ill.) Post Office; material control asst. Altec Industries, St. Joseph, Mo.; fair and recruiting coord. U. No. Colo., Greeley. Constrn. asst. Habitat for Humanity, Greeley. Home: 2313 42nd Ave Greeley CO 80634-3815 Office: U No Colo University Ctr Greeley CO 80639

GRIFFIN, RICHARD J., federal agency administrator; b. Chgo., Oct. 9, 1949; m. Mary Jean Lang; three children. B in Econs., Xavier U., 1971; grad., Nat. War Coll., 1983; MBA, Marymount U., 1984. Agt. U.S. Secret Svc., Chgo., 1971; agt. in charge U.S. Secret Svc., L.A.; dep. asst. dir. Office of Investigations U.S. Secret Svc., asst. dir. protective ops., dep. dir.; inspector gen. Dept. Vets. Affairs, Washington, 1997—. Office: Dept Vets Affairs 810 Vermont Ave NW Washington DC 20420

GRIFFIN, RICHARD RAY, minister; b. Topeka, Sept. 1, 1945; s. Walter O. and Ruth Marie (Gordon) G.; m. Barbara June Van DoDoeselaar, Aug. 3, 1968; children: Robert Ray, Sherilyn Sue. BA, Bob Jones U., 1968; M in Ministry, Internat. Sem., 1983, LittD, 1984; DD, Heritage Bapt. U., 1984; ThM, Fundamental Bapt. Theol. Sem., 1987. Ordained to ministry Bapt. Ch., 1970. Pastor First So. Meth. Ch., Savannah, Ga., 1968-70; assoc. pastor Faith Missionary Bapt. Ch., Easley, S.C., 1970-71; pastor First Bapt. Ch., Brown City, Mich., 1971-78; pastor, sch. adminstr. Grace Missionary Bapt. Ch., Kinston, N.C., 1978-81; pastor Calvary Bapt. Ch., Sterling, Kans., 1981-86; pastor, sch. adminstr. Grace Tabernacle Bapt. Ch., Centerville, Iowa, 1986-93; pastor Ocqueoc Bapt. Ch., Millersburg, Mich., 1993—; former trustee Bapt. Bible Fellowship, N.C., 1981; former v.p. Iowa Bapt. Bible Fellowship, 1986-89. Mem. Gospel Fellowship Assn., Alumni Assn. Bob Jones U., Alumni Assn. Heritage Bapt. U. Republican. Home: 4226 Millersburg Rd Millersburg MI 49759-9701 Office: Ocqueoc Bapt Ch M68 Millersburg Rd Millersburg MI 49759 *Life is what one makes of it. It is exciting or dull, fulfilling or devastating, depending on our outlook. Thankfully in Christ and with His help, we can enjoy life "abundantly."*

GRIFFIN, ROBERT DOUGLAS, publishing executive, genealogist; b. Ventura, Calif., Sept. 3, 1943; s. Clarence Herbert and Mary Evelyn (Davis) G.; m. Nikki Ann Worski, Jan. 26, 1964 (div. Sept. 1980); children: Patrick Stephen, Wendy Michelle; m. Judith Ann Lane, Jan. 10, 1983. BA, U. Colo., 1967; MS, Columbia U., 1981. Asst. cashier Equitable Life Assurance U.S., Cheyenne, Wyo., 1970-72; sr. supr. Equitable Life Assurance U.S., Chgo., 1972-74; mgr. Equitable Life Assurance U.S., N.Y.C., 1974-76, asst. v.p., 1977-85; founding ptnr. R.J. Peters Assocs., Leonia, N.J., 1985-91; prof. genealogist pvt. practice, Englewood, N.J., 1985—; owner, publisher Bergen Historic Books, Englewood, N.J., 1991—; adj. prof. Bergen C.C., Paramus, N.J., 1993. Contbr. articles to profl. jours. Historian Twp. Teaneck, N.J., 1989—; chmn. Bergen County Historic Sites Adv. Bd., Hackensack, 1992-97; trustee Flat Rock Brook Nature Ctr., Englewood, 1995—; vice chmn. Historic Preservation Commn., Teaneck, 1991-95; chmn. Historic New Bridge Landing State Park Commn., River Edge, N.J, 1996. Congrl. fellow Brookings Inst., Washington. 1976-77. Mem. N.Y. Geneal. and Biog. Soc., N.J. Geneal. Soc., N.J. Hist. Soc., Bergen County Geneal. Soc., Bergen County Hist. Soc. (pres. 1997—), Friends Historic New Bridge Landing (chmn., vice-chmn.), Assn. Profl. Genealogists (trustee 1996—). Democrat. Avocations: public speaking, teaching adult education. Office: Bergen Historic Books PO Box 244 Englewood NJ 07631-0244

GRIFFIN, ROBERT F., military career officer; b. Ft. Pierce, Fla., Dec. 21, 1944; m. Ann Griffin; children: Carolyn, Laura, Thomas; children from previous marriage: James, Daniel, Robert Jr. Grad., U.S. Mil. Acad., 1967; MD, Emory U., 1974; grad., U.S. Army War Coll. Diplomate Am. Bd. Surgery. Commd. officer U.S. Army Infantry, advanced through grades to brig. gen.; intern and resident Letterman Army Med. Ctr., San Francisco; chief gen. surgery U.S. Army, Ft. Sill, Okla.; brigade surgeon 193d Inf. Brigade Panama Canal Zone U.S. Army; divsn. surgeon 8th Inf. Divsn. (Mechanized) U.S. Army, Bad Kreuznach, Germany; comdr. 3d Med. Bn., 3d Inf. Divsn. (Mechanized) U.S. Army, Wuerzburg, Germany; chief dept. surgery, dep. comdr. 34th Gen. Hosp. U.S. Army, Augsburg, Germany; comdr. USA Med. Dept. Activity and 98th Gen. Hosp. U.S. Army, Nuernberg, Germany; corps surgeon VII (US) Corps U.S. Army, Stuttgart, Germany, Saudi Arabia; dep. comdr. 332d Med. Brigade U.S. Army, Saudi Arabia; comdr. USA Med. Dept. Activity, 45th Surgeon U.S. Mil. Acad. U.S. Army, West Point, N.Y.; command surgeon U.S. Army Forces Command; dep. comdr. Health Care Ops., chief Med. Corps Affairs U.S. Army Med. Command; commdg. gen. Dwight David Eisenhower Army Med. Ctr. S.E. Regional Med. Command. Decorated Silver Star, Legion of Merit with three oak leaf clusters, Bronze Star with oak leaf cluster, Purple Heart, Meritorious Svc. medal with four oak leaf clusters, Air medal, Army Commendation medal. Fellow ACS. Office: Dwight D Eisenhower Army Med Ctr SE Region Med Command DOD/TRICARE Region 3 Fort Gordon GA 30905

GRIFFIN, ROBERT H., army officer; b. Atlanta, Oct. 4, 1947. BS in Mech. Engring., Auburn U.; MS in Geotech. Engring.; MBA, Long Island U.; grad., U.S. Army War Coll., Army Command/Gen. Staff Coll. Registered profl. engr., Va. Commd. 2d lt. U.S. Army, advanced through grades to brig. gen.; served in Dharan, Saudi Arabia; chief of staff Hdqrs., U.S. Army C.E., Washington, to 1996; comdr. and divsn. engr. U.S. Army C.E. Northwestern Divsn., Portland, Oreg., 1996—. Decorated Legion of Merit with oak lead cluster, Bronze Star medal, others. Office: US Army Engr Northwestern Divsn PO Box 2870 Portland OR 97208-2870

GRIFFIN, ROBERT PAUL, former United States senator, state supreme court justice; b. Detroit, Nov. 6, 1923; s. J.A. and Beulah M. G.; m. Marjorie J. Anderson, 1947; children—Paul Robert, Richard Allen, James Anderson, Martha Jill. AB, BS, Central Mich. U., 1947, LLD, 1963; JD, U. Mich., 1950, LLD, 1973; LL.D., Eastern Mich. U., 1969, Albion Coll., 1970, Western Mich. U., 1971, Grand Valley State Coll., 1971, Detroit Coll. Bus., 1972, Detroit Coll. Law, 1973; L.H.D., Hillsdale (Mich.) Coll., 1970; J.C.D., Rollins Coll., 1970; Ed.D., No. Mich. U., 1970; D. Pub. Service, Detroit Inst. Tech., 1971. Bar: Mich. 1950. Pvt. practice Traverse City, Mich., 1950-56; mem. 85th-89th congresses from 9th Dist. Mich., Washington, 1957-66; mem. U.S. Senate from Mich., Washington, 1966-79; counsel Miller, Canfield, Paddock & Stone, Traverse City, 1979-86; assoc. justice Mich. Supreme Ct., Lansing, 1987-95. Trustee Gerald R. Ford Found. Served with inf. AUS, World War II, ETO. Named 1 of 10 Outstanding Young Men of Nation U.S. Jaycees, 1959. Mem. ABA, Mich. Bar Assn., D.C. Bar Assn., Kiwanis.

GRIFFIN, ROBERT THOMAS, automotive company executive; b. Somerville, Mass., July 3, 1917; s. Michael and Cecelia (Rourke) G.; m. Mary Ellen Mulcahy, Sept. 10, 1960; children: Mary Catherine, Christiane Marie, Justine Dufresne, Joseph Michael. B.S., Boston Coll., 1939; M.A. in Pub. Adminstrn, Boston U., 1954; postgrad., Harvard U. Grad. Sch. Pub. Adminstrn., 1954-55. Regional mgr. War Assets Adminstrn., 1946-49; with GSA, Washington, 1950-56, 58-80; spl. asst. to adminstr. GSA, 1961-62, asst. adminstr., 1962-70, asst. commr. property mgmt., 1970-73; spl. asst. to adminstr. for coordination John F. Kennedy Library, 1973-77, acting adminstr., 1977—; dep. adminstr. GSA, 1977-78; sr. advisor Pres.'s Spl. Trade Rep., White House, 1977-78; sr. advisor to Personal Rep. of Pres. to Middle East Negotiations, White House, 1978-80; staff exec. to pres. Chrysler Corp., 1980—; dir. Van Pool Services, Inc.; mem. Pres.'s Inflation Task Force, 1978-79; conferee White House Conf. Natural Beauty, 1964, Pres.'s Fed. Agy. Task Force on Cost Reduction, 1965; adminstrv. cons. Govt. of Iran, 1956-58; mem. Pres.'s Com. Minority Enterprise. Bd. dirs. Hamlet Citizens Assn., Chevy Chase, Md., 1981—, John F. Kennedy Libr., 1991— (dir. emeritus). Served with USCGR, 1943-46. Mem. Am. Soc. Pub. Adminstrn., DAV. Clubs: Washington Athletic, Columbia Country. Office: 1100 Connecticut Ave NW Washington DC 20036-4101

GRIFFIN, STANLEY RAY, machinist; b. Little Rock, Apr. 22, 1940; s. Stanley Earl and Era Mae (Overton) G.; m. Vicki Diane Harris, Aug. 3, 1958 (div. Apr. 1992); children: Kit Wade, Scott Allen, Diana Lee, Donna Sue; m. Thelma Alice Roberts, Sept. 4, 1993. Tech. asst. Tex. A&M Experiment Sta., Angleton, Tex., 1959-61; utility, chemist asst. Dow Chem. Co., Freeport, Tex., 1961-75; mgr. city parks City of Angleton, 1975-76; water dept. asst. South Tex. Farms, Rosharon, 1976-77; foreman body shop Scott Chevrolet, Oldsmobile, Angleton, 1977-78; material handler Collins Instrument Co., Angleton, 1978—. Author numerous poems. Mem. Brazosport Soc. Avocations: writing poetry, poetry recitals and public readings. Home: 33 Deerfield Dr Sweeny TX 77480-9700

GRIFFIN, T. DAVID, family physician, pharmacist; b. Baldwyn, Miss., May 16, 1950; s. George Troy and Jewel Catherine (Towery) G.; m. Ingrid Lavonne Voyles, Dec. 28, 1980; children: Michelle Renee, Jessica Anne. AA, Northeast C.C., Booneville, Miss., 1970; BS in Pharmacy, U. Miss., 1973; DO, U. Health Scis. Kansas City, 1983. Lic. pharmacist, Miss., 1973, Dr. of Pharmacy, Tenn., 1976; MD, Miss., 1984. Cmty. pharmacist Med. Arts Pharmacy, Baldwyn, 1973-79; intern U. Health Scis. Hosp., Kansas City, Mo., 1983-84; staff physician Family Med. Ctr., Vardaman, Miss., 1984-86, Calhoun City, Miss., 1986-90; staff physician, med. dir. Rural Health Clinic, Houston, Miss., 1990—; vice-chief of staff Trace Regional Hosp., Houston, Miss., 1995—. Active Rep. Com. Miss., 1996—. Fellow Am. Acad. Family Practice; mem. Am. Osteo. Assn., Miss. Osteo. Assn., Psi Sigma Alpha. Methodist. Avocations: Civil War studies, hunting, fishing. Home: 115 Highland Rd Houston MS 38851-2424 Office: Houston Rural Health Clinic 105 Hillcrest Dr Houston MS 38851-2404

GRIFFIN, THOMAS LEE, JR., industrial and federal government specialist; b. Sumter, S.C., Feb. 10, 1929; s. Thomas Lee and Gladys (Moore) G.; m. Aileen Casey; children: Elizabeth, Leigh. BS in Engr., U.S. Naval Acad., 1952; MA, George Washington U., 1965; grad., U.S. Naval War Coll., Newport, R.I., 1965, U.S. Army War Coll., Carlisle, Pa., 1972. Commd. 2d lt. USMC, 1952, advanced through grades to col., ret., 1979; with Electronic Data Systems, Dallas, 1979-83; dir. computerized automotive maintenance systems and caterpillar accounts Electronic Data Systems, 1984-90; v.p. complex systems and govt. svcs. divsn. Electronic Data Systems, Washington, 1990-92; ret., 1993; v.p. CACI Aviation Industry and Mfg., Arlington, Va., 1993-96; corp. cons. aviation industry and mfg., 1996; sr. v.p. ops. Joseph Del Balzo Assoc., Washington, 1996—; chief of staff Second Marine Aircraft Wing, 1977, U.S. Marine Forces West Pacific, 1978, Marine Corps Air Base East, 1979. Chmn. pastoral rels. Franklin Community Ch., Mich. 1988-90; pres. Raceway Farms Assn., Lorton, Va., 1980-83; area dir. Boy Scouts Am., New Bern, N.C., 1979. Decorated Legion of Merit Combat V, 1966, 1969, 1979, Disting. Flying Cross, 1969. Mem. Soc. Mfg. Engrs., Automation Forum (chmn. bd. dirs.), Air Traffic Contr. Assn., U.S. Naval Acad. Alumni Assn., Assn. U.S. Army, Armed Forces Comm. and Electronic Assn., Marine Corps. Assn., Marine Corps Aviation Assn., Hancock Yacht Club, Bogue Banks Country Club. Republican. Methodist. Avocations: running, sailing, fishing, racquetball, antiques, golf. Home: PO Box 2763 Pine Knoll Shores NC 28512

GRIFFIN, THOMAS MCLEAN, retired lawyer; b. Lake Placid, N.Y., Sept. 12, 1922; s. Nathaniel Edward and Anne (McLean) G.; m. Hope Wiswall, July 16, 1949; children: Richard Wiswall, Anne McLean, Thomas McLean, David Coggin. AB, Harvard Coll., 1943; LLB, Harvard U., 1949. Bar: Mass. 1950, U.S. Supreme Ct. 1976. Atty. State Mutual Life Assurance Co. Am., Worcester, Mass., 1949-58; assoc. counsel Old Colony Trust Co., Boston, 1958-67; sec., bd. dirs. 1st Nat. Bank Boston, 1967-87, gen. counsel, 1971-87, ret., 1987; gen. counsel Bank of Boston Corp., 1973-87, sec. bd. dirs., 1970-87, ret., 1987. Trustee Marlboro (Vt.) Coll., 1986-95, House of Seven Gables Settlement Assn., Salem, Mass., 1987-95, Harmony Grove Cemetery, Salem. Lt. (j.g.) USNR, 1943-46. Mem. Ea. Yacht Club, White Mountain Ski Runners, Whiting Club. Democrat. Avocations: bridge, skiing, sailing, hiking, sketching. Home: 14 Beckford St Salem MA 01970-3206*

GRIFFIN, VILLARD STUART, JR., geology educator; b. Birmingham, Ala., May 19, 1937; s. Villard Stuart and Myra (Justice) G.; m. Raija Tuulikki Nikander, June 12, 1966; children: Victoria Sirkka, Elizabeth Roosa-Maria, Anna Kristina, Ester Kaarina. B.A., U. Va., 1959, M.S., 1961; Ph.D., Mich. State U., 1965. Grad. asst. U. Va., Charlottesville, 1960-61, Mich. State U., East Lansing, 1961-63; geologist Little Bob Mining Co., Marietta, Ga., summer 1960; geologic aide Roland F. Beers, Inc., Alexandria, Va., summer 1960, Va. Div. Mineral Resources, Charlottesville, summers, 1961, 62, 64; mem. faculty Clemson U., S.C., 1964-94; prof. geology Clemson U., 1975-94, prof. emeritus, 1994—, acting head dept. earth scis., 1990-92; vis. research investigator Geol. Survey Finland, Helsinki, 1975; project geologist S.C. Geol. Survey, Columbia, 1965-86; cons. Bechtel Corp., 1966, John Wiley & Sons., 1971, C. D'Appolonia Engrs., Inc., 1973, S.C. Electric and Gas Co., 1973-76, Chevron Corp., 1976; cons. dept. energy E.I. duPont de Nemours Co., 1978; cons. Fulton Nat. Bank, 1980, Ga. Geol. Survey, 1980; lectr. Geologisk-Mineralogisk Mus. and Inst., Oslo, Norway, 1975, Mineral. Soc. Stockholm, 1975, Geologiska-Mineralogika Inst. Uppsala, Sweden, 1975, Turku U. Geol. and Mineral. Inst., 1975, others; assoc. investigator U.S. Office Water Resources Research, 1965-66; chmn. S.C. State Mapping Adv. Com., 1984-85. Cons. editor: Rocks and Minerals, 1976-79; mem. editorial bd. Geologic Notes, 1976-80, S.C. Geology, 1980-88; contbr. articles to profl. jours. Recipient W.A. Tarr award Sigma Gamma Epsilon, 1960, J.K. Roberts Geology dept. award U. Va., 1961; Mich. State U. scholar, 1961-63; Phillip Francis du Pont fellow, 1960-61; NSF grantee, 1968, 70, 72. Home: PO Box 1204 Clemson SC 29633-1204

GRIFFIN, WALTER ROLAND, college president, educator, historian; b. Carbondale, Pa., Nov. 20, 1942; s. Walter Joseph and Maud Loftus (Boland) G.; m. Mary Eleanor Armstrong, Aug. 16, 1961 (div. 1980); children: Rebecca, Kathleen, Shawn; m. Penni Susan Oncken, Dec. 6, 1980; 1 child, Megan. BA, Loyola Coll., Balt., 1963; MA, U. Cin., 1964, PhD, 1988. Lectr. history Xavier U., Cin., 1965-66; asst. prof. history Mt. St. Mary's Coll., Emmitsburg, Md., 1967-68; asst. prof. history Upper Iowa U., Fayette, 1966-67, 68-84, chmn. dept., chmn. div. social sci. and bus. adminstrn., 1969-78, assoc. acad. dean, 1977-78, assoc. prof., 1984-89, head coach men's and women's tennis, 1979-88, dir. off-campus programs, 1981-89; assoc. dean Union Inst., Cin., 1989-92; pres. Limestone Coll., Gaffney, S.C., 1992—. Contbr. articles to profl. jours. Councilman City of Fayette, 1971-76; chmn. Fayette County (Iowa) Dems., West Union, 1972-77, 79-80; mem. Iowa State Dem. Ctrl. Com., Des Moines, 1974-78; del. Dem. Nat. Conv., N.Y.C., 1976; Dem. candidate for Iowa Sec. of State, 1978; mem. S.C. Higher Edn. Tuition Grants Commn., 1992-95, 99—, Crustbreakers, 1997—; bd. dirs. Cherokee County Boys and Girls Club, 1993-98. Recipient Community Svc. award Fayette Jaycees, 1973, Appreciation award Iowa Democratic Party, 1974, 78, Cert. Appreciation, Iowa N.G., Camp Dodge, 1985; named Coach of Yr. in Men's Tennis, Iowa Intercollegiate Athletic Conf., Waverly, 1985; Taft Teaching fellow U. Cin., 1963-64. Mem. Phi Alpha Theta, Pi Gamma Mu, Rotary. Avocations: tennis, traveling. Home: 1008 College Dr Gaffney SC 29340-3708 Office: Limestone Coll 1115 College Dr Gaffney SC 29340-3778

GRIFFIN, WILLIAM ARTHUR, clergyman, religious organization executive; b. Cococonk, Ont., Can., July 29, 1936; s. Arthur Campbell and Anne (Bradamore) G.; m. Patricia Rose Russell, Aug. 18, 1956; children: Kent, Wendy, Mark, Patti, Becky. Diploma, Ea. Pentecostal Bible Coll., Peterborough, Ont., 1957; BA, U. Toronto, Ont., 1960; MDiv, Luth. Theol. Sem., Saskatoon, Sask., Can., 1970; MA, U. Sask., Saskatoon, 1973. Ordained to ministry Pentecostal Assemblies Can., 1962. Pastor Pentecostal Ch., Fergus, Ont., 1960-62; dean of students Cen. Pentecostal Coll., Saskatoon, 1963-69; lectr. U. Sask., 1970-72; acad. dean Ea. Pentecostal Bible Coll., 1973-79; exec. dir. Pentecostal Assemblies Can., Mississauga, Ont., 1980-92; gen. sec. Pentecostal Assemblies Can., Mississauga, 1992-94, exec. asst. gen. supt., 1995-98, stewardship/pub. rels. profl., 1998—; estab. Can. Pentecostal Sem., 1996. Exec. editor Resource, 1980-92, Youth Profile, 1980-92, Family Talk, 1988-92; editor: Canadian Pentecostals: A History of the Pentecostal Assemblies of Canada, 1994. Mem. Soc. for Pentecostal Studies. Office: Pentecostal Assemblies Can, 6745 Century Ave, Mississauga, ON Canada L5N 6P7*

GRIFFIN, WILLIAM R., consulting company executive; b. S.D., June 11, 1949. Cert. sr. carpet insp., hard & resilient wood floor care specialist. Pres. Cleaning Cons. Svcs. Inc., Seattle, 1975—. Mem. ISSA (com. mem.). Office: Cleaning Cons Svcs Inc PO Box 1273 Seattle WA 98111-1273

GRIFFIN-BURRILL, KATHLEEN R. F. See BURRILL, KATHLEEN R. F.

GRIFFIN-THOMPSON, MELANIE, accounting firm executive; b. San Antonio, Tex., Oct. 25, 1949; d. Roy Albert and Ola Emma (Hunt) G.; m. Robert Thompson; children: Maurice Dale, Donald Dwight, Merideth Thompson Ferguson, Laura Thompson. BBA summa cum laude, Corpus Christi State U., 1977; MBA, Tex. A&M U., 1994. CPA, Tex.; cert. fin. planner. Sec.-treas. Roy Hunt, Inc., Corpus Christi, 1970-78, dir., 1970-82; v.p. White, Sluyter & Co., Corpus Christi, 1978-80; pres. Whittington & Griffin, Corpus Christi, 1980-82, also dir.; sec.-treas., dir. Sand Express, Inc., Corpus Christi, 1975-82; prin. Melanie Hunt Griffin & Assocs., CPAs, Corpus Christi, 1982-84; v.p. Fields, Nemec & Co., P.C., Corpus Christi, 1984-97; ptnr. Arthur Andersen, LLP, San Antonio, Tex., 1997—; mem. edn. and tng. task force White Ho. Conf. Small Bus., 1993; adj. prof. Tex. A&M, Corpus Christi. Contbr. articles to profl. jours. Devel. chair Am. Heart Assn., chmn. bd. 1989-90, Leadership Corpus Christi Alumni, 1982—; mem. adv. coun. Tex. A&M U., Corpus Christi. Recipient Women in Careers award YWCA, 1989. Mem. AICPA (personal fin. planning dir. small bus. taxation com. 1990-93), Tex. Soc. CPAs (bd. dirs. 1987—, v.p. 1988-89, 93-94, treas. 1995-96, pres. elect 1996-97, pres. 1997-98, pres. Corpus Christi chpt. 1987-88, chmn. devel. new legis. leaders 1990-93, vice chair CPAs Helping Schs. 1994-95, Outstanding Svc. award 1990-91, Presdl. citation, pres. elect, 1996-97, Outstanding Svc. award Corpus Christi chpt. 1990-93, hon. fellow award 1998), Corpus Christi State U. Alumni Assn. (bd. dirs. 1987-90), Tex. State CPAs Ednl. Found. (trustee 1990-93), Exec. Women Internat. (chmn. philanthropy com. 1986-87), San Antonio Rotary. Home: 268 Eden Ranch Dr New Braunfels TX 78133 Office: Arthur Andersen LLP 70 NE Loop 410 Ste 1100 San Antonio TX 78216-5893

GRIFFITH, ALAN RICHARD, banker; b. Mineola, N.Y., Dec. 17, 1941; s. Charles Ernest and Amalia (Guenther) G.; m. Elizabeth Ferguson, Nov. 28, 1964; children: Timothy, Elizabeth. BA, Lafayette Coll., Easton, Pa., 1964; MBA, CUNY, 1971. Asst. credit officer The Bank of N.Y., N.Y.C., 1968-72, asst. v.p., 1972-74, v.p., 1974-82, sr. v.p., 1982-85, exec. v.p., 1985-88, sr. exec. v.p., 1988-90, pres., 1990-94, vice chmn., 1994—. Trustee Amyothrophic Lateral Sclerosis Assn., Sherman Oaks, Calif., Lafayette Col., Chesapeake Bay Found., Annapolis, Md. Mem. Univ. Club, (N.Y.C.), Marco Polo Club. Office: Bank of NY One Wall St New York NY 10286

GRIFFITH, ANDY (ANDREW SAMUEL GRIFFITH), actor; b. Mt. Airy, N.C., June 1, 1926; s. Carl Lee and Geneva (Nunn) G.; m. Barbara Edwards, 1949 (div.); children: Sam, Dixie Nan; m. Cindi Knight, Apr. 2, 1983. BA in Music, U. N.C., 1949. Performed for civic clubs, night clubs; TV debut as monologuist: Ed Sullivan show, 1954; Broadway debut as illiterate hillbilly draftee in: No Time for Sergeants, 1955, also in TV prodn., also in motion picture, 1958; motion pictures include A Face in the Crowd, Onionhead, 1958, Second Time Around, Savages, 1974, Adams of Eagle Lake, 1975, The Treasure Chest Murder, 1975, Hearts of the West, 1975, Six Characters in Search of an Author, Hollywood TV Theatre, 1976, The Girl in the Empty Grave, 1977, Rustler's Rhapsody, 1985, Spy Hard, 1996, Daddy and Them, 1999; role: Broadway mus. comedy Destry Rides Again, 1959; rec. What It Was Was Football; TV star: Andy Griffith Show, 1960-68; series Headmaster, 1970-71, The New Andy Griffith Show, 1970, Matlock, 1986-95; TV movies Winter Kill, Abel, Go Ask Alice, Under the Influence, From Here to Eternity, Salvage, 1978, Return to Mayberry, 1986, The Gift of Love, 1994, Gramps, 1995; TV mini series Washington Behind Closed Doors, 1977, Centennial, Murder in Texas (Emmy award), Murder in Coweta County, Fatal Vision, Scattering Dad, 1998; also numerous TV appearances including Hotel; TV spls. include The Andy Griffith-Don Knotts-Jim Nabors Show; exec. producer Mayberry, R.F.D.; appeared in TV comml. for Ritz Crackers and AT&T. Recipient Tarheel award, 1961, Disting. Salesman's award, 1962; named Outstanding TV Personality of Yr., Advt. Club of Balt., 1968. Avocations: swimming, skeet and trap shooting. Office: William Morris Agy care Jerry Katzman 151 S El Camino Dr Beverly Hills CA 90212-2775*

GRIFFITH, BARBARA E., social worker, political activist; b. Bklyn., Feb. 17, 1943; d. Carl and Ruth (Cramer) Horowitz; m. Richard Michael Griffith, Feb. 12, 1942; children: Kim Griffith McFadden, David Wark. BSW, Ohio State U., 1965; postgrad., Adelphi U., 1965-66. Social worker Columbus Home for Mentally Disturbed Children, Columbus, Ohio, 1965; case worker Nassau County Social Svcs., L.I., N.Y., 1965-66, Red Bank (N.J.) Dept. Social Svcs., 1966-67, Dept. Social Svcs. Honolulu, 1967-69; asst. dir. nursery sch. Cleve., 1975-78; advt. mgr. mags. Toronto, Ont., Can., 1979-84; substitute tchr. West Windsor (N.J.) Plainsboro H.S., 1987-90; polit. activist Bus. & Profl. Women's Assn., N.J., 1989-93; owner R.M.G. Assocs., Inc., Princeton Junction, N.J., 1993—; v.p. mktg. and sales Thornhill Month Mag. Pub., 1985; real estate devel. cons., 1991—; owner Lady Limo of N.J., 1996—. Counselor for homeless people; active Clinton Presdl. Campaign, N.J.; dir. Hughes Congl. Campaign for U.S. Congress, 1992, N.J.; local town councilwoman, Can., 1982; participant Lobby Day, Washington, 1990-94. Mem. NOW, LWV (Princeton chpt. 1988—), N.J. Bus. & Profl. Women Assn. (chmn. N.J. legis. chpt. 1992-93), Women's Agenda (com. mem. N.J. law sect.). Avocations: traveling, working with children, video projects, working with homeless. Home: 14 Zeloof Dr Lawrenceville NJ 08648-5409

GRIFFITH, B(EZALEEL) HEROLD, physician, educator, plastic surgeon; b. N.Y.C., Aug. 24, 1925; s. Bezaleel Davies and Henrietta (Herold) G.; m. Jeanne B. Lethbridge, 1948; children: Susan, Tristan. BA, Johns Hopkins U., 1992; M.D., Yale U., 1948. Diplomate: Am. Bd. Plastic Surgery (dir. 1976-82, chmn. 1981-82). Intern Grace New Haven Community Hosp.-Yale U., 1948-49; resident in surgery VA Hosp., Newington, Conn., 1949-50; asst. resident in surgery 2d (Cornell) Surg. Div., Bellevue Hosp., N.Y.C., 1952-53; resident in plastic surgery VA Hosp., Bronx, 1953-55, U. Glasgow, Scotland, 1955, N.Y. Hosp. Cornell Med. Center, N.Y.C., 1956; rsch. fellow in plastic surgery Cornell U. Med. Coll., 1956-57; pvt. practice specializing in plastic surgery Chgo., 1957-96; attending plastic surgeon Northwestern Meml., Children's Meml., VA Lakeside hosps., Rehab. Inst. Chgo.; instr. surgery Northwestern U., 1957-59, assoc. in surgery, 1959-62, asst. prof. surgery, 1962-67, assoc. prof., 1967-71, prof., 1971-96, prof. emeritus, 1996, chief div. plastic surgery, 1970-91; chief plastic surgery Shriner's Hosp. for Crippled Children, Chgo., 1994-96; retired. Assoc. editor: Plastic and Reconstructive Surgery, 1972-78; contbr. articles to profl. jours. Lt. M.C., USNR, 1950-52. Fellow ACS, Am. Assn. Plastic Surgeons, Chgo. Surg. Soc., Royal Soc. Medicine; mem. AAAS, AMA, Am. Soc. Plastic and Reconstructive Surgeons (sec. 1972-74), Brit. Assn. Plastic Surgeons, Plastic Surgery Rsch. Coun. (chmn. 1969), Am. Cleft Palate Assn., N.Y. Acad. Scis., Ill., Chgo. Med. Socs., Midwestern Assn. Plastic Surgeons, Soc. Head and Neck Surgeons, Ill., Chgo. Hist. Socs., Civil War Round Table, Evanston Hist. Soc. (trustee 1974-78), Sigma Xi (pres. Northwestern U. 1986-87, 94-95). Club: Yale (Chgo.). Lodge: Masons. Achievements include research in transplantation, skin tumors, cleft palate, paraplegia.

GRIFFITH, CARL LESLIE, protective services official; b. Mullins, S.C., Sept. 12, 1956; s. William R. and Julia A. (Willis) G.; m. Nona E. Hunt, Jan. 12, 1980 (div. June 1986); children: Carl L. Jr., James R.; m. Lisa D. Anderson, July 20, 1987; 1 child, Charles R. AAS, U. S.C., 1976, BA, 1977; MA, Webster U., 1981. Dep. sheriff Lexington (S.C.) County Sheriff's Dept., 1978; patrolman Horry County Police Dept., Conway, S.C., 1979-81; spl. investigator S.C. Tax Commn., Columbia, 1981-83; spl. agt. U.S. Naval Intelligence, Cherry Point, N.C., 1983—, Drug Enforcement Adminstrn., Miami, Fla., 1986—; assoc. prof. Horry-Georgetown Tech. Coll., Conway, 1981-82. Mem. Rep. Nat. Task Force, Washington, 1984. Officer USNR, 1985-92. Mem. Internat. Narcotic Officers Assn., Dade County Police Benevolent Assn., Fed. Law Enforcement Officers Assn. Avocations: rugby, skydiving, weightlifting.

GRIFFITH, CHARLES DEE, JR., state official. BA in Philosophy, Elon Coll., 1978; JD, Washington & Lee U., 1982. Bar: Va., 1982. Asst. commonwealth atty. Commonwealth of Va., Norfolk, 1983-87; commonwealth Commonwealth of Va., 1992—; asst. U.S. atty. Ea. Dist. Va., 1987-92. Bd. dirs. Southampton Rds. YMCA. Mem. Va. Bar Assn., Va. Assn. Commonwealth Attys. Office: Office of the Commonwealth Atty Commonwealth of Va 800 E City Hall Ave Norfolk VA 23510-2723

GRIFFITH, CLARK DEXTER, consultant; b. Suffern, N.Y., Dec. 21, 1965; s. William Fredrick Jr. and Lillian Griffith. BA in Econs. and Japanese, San Diego State U., 1991; postgrad., Columbia U., 1997—. Realtor Elegado Realty & Prudential Calif. Realty, San Diego, 1988-92; coord. import housing projects Sotetsu Real Estate Co., Ltd., Yokohama, Japan, 1991-97; regional mgr. Intradex Corp., Pearl River, N.Y., 1995—; customer svc. rep. Wells Fargo Bank, San Diego, 1988-90; cons. Kirin Breweries, Inc., Yokohama, 1989, Nichiei Co., Ltd. Yokohama, 1990, Perillo-Griffith Travel Svc., Pearl River, N.Y., 1976-86. Contbr. articles to profl. jours. Mem. Am. C. of C. in Japan (vice chmn. trade expansion com. 1992-97, chmn. import housing sub-com. 1995-97), Japan Studies Assn. (founder, pres. 1989-91). Avocations: scuba diving, golfing, jet skiing, snow skiing, reading. Home: 992 Route 9W S Nyack NY 10960-4916 Office: Intradex Corp 59 E Central Ave Pearl River NY 10965-2306

GRIFFITH, DAVID L., protective services official. AS, Monroe C.C., 1974. Corp. chief City of Rochester (N.Y.) Fire Dept., 1984-93, exec. dep. chief, 1993-94, chief, 1994-98; retired. Mem. NFPA, Internat. Assn. Fire Chiefs, N.Y. State Fire Chiefs, N.Y. State Career Chiefs. *

GRIFFITH, DEWEY MAURICE, mechanical engineer, investor; b. Conway, S.C., Feb. 13, 1938; s. Edwin Dewey and Addie Lee (Pittman) G.; m. Margaret Louise Taylor, Aug. 18, 1963 (div.); 1 child, Jeffrey Scott. BSME, N.C. State Coll. Agr. & Engr., 1959. Mfg. engr. Westinghouse Electric Corp., Richmond, Ky., 1960-63; design adminstrv. engr. Westinghouse Electric Corp., Bloomfield, N.J., 1963-70; project mech. engr. PPG Industries, Shelby, N.C., 1970-71, GE, Lexington, Ky., 1971-72, E.D. Griffith Renaissance, Greenville, N.C., 1972-74, Catalytic Inc., Charlotte, N.C., 1974-75; profl. engr. D.M. Griffith Design and Rsch., Charlotte, N.C., 1975-79; The Delta Error-Sq. investor The Master E. with Accent Entity, Charlotte, N.C., 1979—. *His personal entity symbol, drawn to perfection in 1975, represents the statistical one-ratio, the price variance ratio, displays God-is-love and the one-ratio of the universe. His in-depth research of four years resulted in 1979 in his nobel prize-level discovery of the universal measure of change, the delta error-square. His impersonal entity symbol, drawn to perfection in 1991, displays the essential two error-squares and the delta error-square within the five-pointed star area. His three-dimension geometric model of the delta error-square, generated in 1994, exhibits his mathematics formula and each fusion of time and space. His one-ratio and zero-difference decide.* Inventor flashing miniature lamp. Mem. Math. Assn. Am. Republican. Methodist. Avocations: art, design, finance, geometry, mathematics.

GRIFFITH, DONALD KENDALL, lawyer; b. Aurora, Ill., Feb. 4, 1933; s. Walter George and Mary Elizabeth Griffith; m. Susan Smykal, Aug. 4, 1962; children: Kay, Kendall. Grad. in History with honors, Culver Mil. Acad., 1951, BA, U. Ill., 1955, JD, 1958. Bar: Ill. 1958, U.S. Supreme Ct. 1973. Assoc. Hinshaw & Culbertson, Chgo., 1959-65, ptnr., 1965-98, of counsel, 1999—; spl. asst. atty. gen. Ill., 1970-72; lectr. Ill. Inst. Continuing Legal Edn., 1970—. Trustee, Lawrence Hall Youth Svcs., 1967—, v.p. for program, 1969-74; bd. dirs. Child Care Assn. Ill., 1970-73; mem. Lake Forest High Sch. Bd. Edn., 1983-84. 2d lt. USAF, 1956. Fellow Am. Acad. Appellate Lawyers; mem. ABA (chmn. appellate advocacy com., tort and ins. practice sect. 1983-84), Ill. Bar Assn., Chgo. Bar Assn., Appellate Lawyers Assn. Ill. (pres. 1973-74), Def. Rsch. Inst., Ill. Def. Counsel, Chgo. Trial Lawyers Club, Alpha Chi Rho (chpt. pres.), Phi Delta Phi. Club: University of Chgo., Knollwood. Mem. editorial bd. Ill. Civil Practice After Trial, 1970; co-editor The Brief, 1975-83; contbg. author Civil Practice After Trial, 1984, 89; contbr. article to legal jour. Office: Hinshaw & Culbertson 222 N La Salle St Ste 300 Chicago IL 60601-1081

GRIFFITH, DOTTY (DOROTHY GRIFFITH STEPHENSON), journalist, speaker, author; b. Terrell, Tex., Nov. 4, 1949; d. Edward Morrill and Dorothy (Koch) Griffith; children: Kelly Griffith, Caitlin Lee. BJ, U. Tex., 1972; MLA, So. Methodist U., 1980. Gen. assignment reporter Dallas Morning News, 1972-73, edn. writer, 1973-74, gen. assignment reporter, 1974-76, polit. writer, 1976-78, food editor, 1978-95; host "In the Kitchen with Dotty" KRLD Radio, 1992-94; lifestyles editor, food columnist Design and Production, 1995-97; dining editor, restaurant critic, 1997—; guest host Warner-Amex, Qube Cable TV, Dallas, 1982-83. Mem. nutrition task force Am. Heart Assn., Dallas, 1981-87. Author: Wild about Chili, 1985, Wild About Manchies, 1989, Gourmet Grains, Beans and Rices, 1992; editor: The Mansion On Turtle Creek Cookbook (Dean Fearing), 1987, Dallas Cuisine, 1994, The Texas Holiday Cookbook, 1997, Cooking with Days of Our Lives, 1997. Mem. Newspaper Food Editor's and Writer's Assn. (v.p. 1984-86, pres. 1986-88), Les Dames d'Escoffier (founding mem. Dallas chpt.). Office: The Dallas Morning News Communications Ctr PO Box 655237 Dallas TX 75265-5237*

GRIFFITH, EDWARD, II, lawyer; b. Wilkes-Barre, Pa., Feb. 9, 1948; s. Edward Meredith Griffith and Jane (Randall) Griffith Jones; m. Linda Christine Scribner, Aug. 9, 1969 (div. July 1982); children: Trevor Scribner, Stewart Randall; m. Katherine Greybill, Oct. 24, 1987. BA, Lehigh U., 1970; JD, Dickinson Sch. Law, 1973. Bar: Pa. 1973, U.S. Dist. Ct. (ea. dist.) Pa. 1973, U.S. Ct. Appeal (3rd cir.) 1973, U.S. Supreme Ct. 1978. Ptnr. Duane, Morris & Heckscher, Phila., 1973—; cons. Pa. State Bd. Law Examiners, Phila, 1974-77. Master John E. Stively Inn of Ct.; mem. ABA, Pa. Bar Assn., Chester County Bar Assn., Def. Rsch. Inst., Pa. Def. Inst. Republican. Presbyterian. Avocations: hunting, fishing, gardening. Office: Duane Morris & Heckscher 735 Chesterbrook Blvd Ste 300 Wayne PA 19087-5638

GRIFFITH, ELWIN JABEZ, lawyer, university administrator; b. Barbados, W.I., Mar. 2, 1938; came to U.S., 1956, naturalized, 1963; s. Vincent and Ermie G.; m. Norma Joyce Rollins, June 9, 1962; 1 child, Traci. BA, L.I. U., 1960; JD, Bklyn. Law Sch., 1963; LLM, NYU, 1964. Bar: N.Y. 1963. Asst. counsel Chase Manhattan Bank, N.Y.C., 1964-68, 68-71; asst. prof. law Cleveland Marshall Law Sch., Cleve. State U., 1968; asst. counsel Tchrs. Ins. and Annuity Assn., N.Y.C., 1971-72; asst. dean Drake U. Law Sch., 1972-73; assoc. prof. U. Cin., 1973-76, prof., 1976-78, assoc. dean, 1974-78; dean DePaul U. Law Sch., 1978-85; prof. Fla. State U. Coll. Law, Tallahassee, 1986—; legal counsel Bedford-Stuyvesant Jaycees, 1968-71; vis. prof. colls.; vis. prof. Black Exch. program Nat. Urban League, 1970-75. Contbr. articles to law revs. Mem. ABA, N.Y. State Bar Assn. Office: Fla State U Coll Law Tallahassee FL 32306

GRIFFITH, EMLYN IRVING, lawyer; b. Utica, N.Y., May 13, 1923; s. William A. and Maud A. (Charles) G.; m. Mary L. Kilpatrick, Aug. 13, 1946; children: William L., James R. AB, Colgate U., 1942; JD, Cornell U., 1950; 9 hon. doctorates. Bar: N.Y. 1950, U.S. Supreme Ct. 1954. Pvt. practice law Lockport, N.Y., 1950-52, Rome, N.Y., 1952—; bd. dirs. various corps. and founds.; treas. N.Y. State Photonics Devel. Corp., 1989—. Contbr. articles to profl. jours. in U.S. and U.K. Mem. N.Y. State Bd. Regents, 1973-96, Gov.'s Com. on Librs., 1976-78; co-chmn. State Conf. Professions, 1974-77, 85-90; mem. U.S. Forum Edn. Orgn. Leaders, 1978-80, Intergovtl. Adv. Coun. on Edn., 1982-86; del. to China-U.S. Joint Session on Trade and Law, Beijing, 1987, Soviet-Am. Conf. on Comparative Edn., Moscow, 1988, N.Y. State-USSR Lawyers Conf., Moscow, 1990; pres. Nat. Assn. State Bds. Edn., 1979-80, Nat. Assn. State Bds. Edn. Found., 1997-99; pres. Nat. Welsh-Am. Found., 1981-83; v.p. Hon. Soc. Cymmrodorion, London, 1988—; trustee, bd. pensions United Presbyn. Ch., 1966-72, Aerospace Edn. Found., 1979-96, Erie Canal Mus., 1996—, Cazenovia Coll., 1996—. Maj. USAAC, 1942-46. Recipient Disting. Svc. to Am. Edn. award Nat. Assn. State Bds. Edn., 1995, Conspicuous Svc. award State of N.Y., 1992, Exceptional Svc. citation Air Force Assn., 1980; Doolittle fellow Aerospace Edn. Found., 1988, Welsh Heritage award Nat. Welsh Am. Found., 1997. Fellow Am. Bar Found., N.Y. Bar Found. (recipient Root-Stimson award for pub. svc. 1986, bd. dirs. 1989—); mem. ABA (com. pub. edn. 1974—), N.Y. State Bar assn. (ho. dels. 1974-76, com. lawyer competency 1986-89, co-chmn. com. atty. professionalism, 1989-92, mem. bd. editors Bar Jour. 1986-97), Oneida County Bar Assn. (pres. 1974-75), State Conf. County Bar Officers (chmn. 1974-76), Osgoode Soc. Can., Selden Soc., Eng., Rome Club, Colgate Club N.Y.C., Cornell Club of N.Y., Phi Gamma Delta Internat. (pres. bd. trustees 1982-86, pres. edn. found. 1992-94). Office: 225 N Washington St Rome NY 13440-5724

GRIFFITH, EZRA EDWARD HOLMAN, health facility administrator, educator; b. Barbados, W.I., Feb. 18, 1942; came to the U.S., 1956; s. Vincent Edward and Ermie (Morris) G.; m. Brigitte Jung; children: Veronique, Pierre. BA, Harvard U., 1963; MD, U. Strasbourg, France, 1973, diploma tropical medicine, 1973. Diplomate Am. Bd. Psychiatry and Neurology, Am. Bd. Forensic Psychiatry. Internship French and Polyclinic Health Ctr., N.Y., 1973-74; residency in psychiatry Albert Einstein Coll. of Medicine, Bronx, N.Y., 1974-77; asst. prof. psychiatry Sch. Medicine Yale U., New Haven, 1977-82, assoc. prof. psychiatry Sch. Medicine, 1982-91; prof. psychiatry Sch. Medicine, 1991—; lectr. dept. Afro-Am. studies Yale U., New Haven, 1979-84, assoc. prof. dept. Afro-Am. studies, 1986-91; prof. Afro-Am. studies, 1991—; assoc. dir. Conn. Mental Health Ctr., New Haven, 1986-89, acting dir., 1987-88, dir., 1989-96; dep. chmn. dept. psychiatry Sch. Medicine Yale U., New Haven, 1996—; cons. Pan Am. Health Orgn., Jamaica, W.I., 1983—, Antigua and St. Kitts, 1985—, Project HOPE Mental Health Program, Grenada, 1986-89, Comm. on Security and Cooperation in Europe, U.S. Congress; apptd. Conn. Psychiat. Security Rev. Bd., Hartford, 1988-94; external examiner dept. psychiatry, U. W.I., 1986, 95. Editor: Clinical Guidelines in Cross-Cultural Mental Health, 1988, Suicide and Ethnicity in the United States, 1989. Mem. Black Psychiatrists of Am. (pres. 1982-84), Am. Acad. Psychiatry and Law (v.p. 1993-94, pres. 1996-97), Am. Psychiat. Assn. (mem. coun. psychiatry and law 1985-91), Conn. Psychiatry Soc. (mem. ethics com. 1983—, pres. 1991-92), Am. Orthopsychiat. Assn. (pres.-elect 1996-97, pres. 1997-98), Group for the Advancement of Psychiatry. Office: Yale Sch Medicine Dept Psych 25 Park St New Haven CT 06519

GRIFFITH, G. LARRY, lawyer; b. Keokuk, Iowa, Mar. 6, 1937; s. Charles Floyd and Lillian Mae (McClinton) G.; m. Jean Whitford, Oct. 29, 1961; children: Randall Dale, Kristin Lin, Barry Wynn. BA, DePauw U., 1959; JD, U. Iowa, 1962. Bar: Iowa 1962, Minn. 1963. Ptnr. Dorsey & Whitney, Mpls., 1962—, chair real estate dept., 1991-95; instr. modern real estate transactions U. Minn., Mpls., 1970-71; bd. dirs. Brock-White Co. Comment editor U. Iowa Law Rev., 1961-62. Scout master Boy Scouts Am., Mpls., 1965-69; bd. dirs. Jr. Achievement, 1991—. Rector scholar De Pauw U., 1955-59. Mem. ABA, Minn. Bar Assn., Hennepin County Bar Assn., U.S. Ski Assn. (alpine competition com. cen. div. 1981-87, chmn. region I 1984-86), Mpls. Athletic Club, Burnsville Athletic Club (bd. dirs., legal advisor 1980-92), Phi Alpha Delta. Avocations: skiing, tennis, hunting, scuba diving, golf. Home: 1414 Laurel Ave Minneapolis MN 55403-1218 Office: Dorsey & Whitney 220 S 6th St Minneapolis MN 55402-1498*

GRIFFITH, JAMES LEIGH, lawyer; b. Knoxville, Tenn., May 25, 1951; s. James M. and Margurite B. Griffith; m. Catherine West; children: Catherine Leigh, James Leigh. BA, U. Va., 1973; JD, Vanderbilt U., 1976; LLM, NYU, 1977. Bar: Tenn. 1977, N.Y. 1977, D.C. 1978; CPA, Tenn., Miss. Sr. tax acct. Ernst & Whinney, Nashville, 1977-81; mem. Waller, Lansden, Dortch & Davis PLLC, Nashville. Contbr. articles to profl. jours. Past bd. dirs. Grace Eaton Day Home, Nashville, Sneed Forest Homeowners Assn., Franklin, Tenn.; past pres., chmn. bd. Versailes Homeowners Assn., Nashville. Fellow Am. Coll. Tax Counsel; mem. ABA (tax sect., various coms.), Tenn. Bar Assn., Nashville Bar Assn., D.C. Bar Assn., Tenn. Soc. CPA's (coun. mem.), Am. Tax Policy Inst. (life), Phi Beta Kappa. Office: Waller Lansden Dortch & Davis PLLC 511 Union St Ste 2100 Nashville TN 37219-1760

GRIFFITH, JAMES LEWIS, lawyer; b. Phila., Sept. 13, 1940; s. Lewis Kenneth and Mary G. (Connors) G.; m. Eleanor May Hazlin, Feb. 27, 1965; children: Mary Eleanor, James Lewis, Anne Elisabeth; m. Linda Lee Ramsey, Sept. 16, 1978. BA, St. Francis Coll., Loretto, Pa., 1962; JD, Villanova U., 1965. Bar: Pa. 1965, D.C. 1974, N.J. 1987, N.Y. 1990, U.S. Supreme Ct. 1976. Assoc. Liebert, Short, Fitzpatrick & Lavin, Phila., 1965-69, Obermayer, Rebmann, Maxwell & Hippel, Phila., 1969-79; pres., prin. trial counsel Griffith & Hemsley, P.C., Phila., 1979-92; ptnr. Mannino Griffith P.C., Phila., 1992-95, Wolf Block Schorr & Solis-Cohen, Phila., 1995-98, Klett Lieber Rooney & Schorling P.C., 1998—; lectr. Villanova U., 1969-73; mem. com. standard jury trial instrns. for Commonwealth of Pa., Pa. Supreme Ct.; lectr. conf. on civil litigation Phila. Ct. Common Pleas.; judge pro tem Ct. of Common Pleas of Phila. County, Pa., 1992—. Author: Hospital Peer Review; editor-cons. Medical Economic. 1st lt. USAR, 1966-72. Mem. ATLA, Pa. Bar Assn., Phila. Bar Assn., Pa. Trial Lawyers Assn., Def. Rsch. Inst., Internat. Assn. Ins. Counsel.

GRIFFITH, JAMES WILLIAM, engineer, consultant; b. Waco, Tex., Apr. 11, 1922; s. Paul Isaac and Willie Elizabeth (Rawlin) G.; m. Dorothy Louise Cannon., Oct. 17, 1949; children: Pamela D. (Mrs. John Fletcher Freeman), James William. Student, Tex. Tech U., 1940-41, U. Utah, 1943-44; B.S., So. Meth. U., 1949, M.S., 1956. Dir. engrng. grad. div. So. Meth. U., 1960-67, chmn. dept. indsl. engrng., 1965-67, prof., chmn. dept. systems engring., 1967-69; ptnr. K-G Assocs., 1970-80; prin. James W. Griffith Inc., Dallas, 1980—; U.S. expert in daylighting Commn. Internat. Eclairage, 1957—; cons. to govt. agys. including HUD, HEW, NAS; tech. cons. Nat. Fenestration Coun., 1984-87, LBL Windows and Daylighting, 1980-85; tech. cons. profl. devel. program AIA, 1982-86, instr., 1982-86, now cons.; mem. AIA Found. Contbr. articles to profl. jours. Served with USAAF, 1942-46. Named to Engrs. of Distinction Engrs. Joint Council, 1970. Fellow Illuminating Engrs. Soc. (nat. pres.); mem. ASHRAE, NSPE, Illuminating Engring. Rsch. Inst., Bldg. Environment and Thermal Envelope Coun., Nat. Fenestration Rating Coun., Bldg. Rsch. Inst. (bd. dirs. 1965-67, 73-75), Tex. Soc. Profl. Engrs., Soc. Mayflower Descs., Sigma Tau, Eta Kappa Nu. Achievements include a patent on the method of and assembly for measuring equivalent sphere illumniation. Home and Office: 751 Sunset Hill Dr Rockwall TX 75087-3236

GRIFFITH, JERRY LYNN, physical education educator; b. Chattanooga, July 24, 1954; s. Marvin Joy and Nerine (Greer) G.; m. Dianne Gooslby, June 11, 1977; children: Matthew, Coleman. AS, Cleveland (Tenn.) State U., 1974; BS, David Lipscomb Coll., Nashville, 1976; MS, Mid. Tenn. State U., Murfreesboro, 1980, D of Arts, 1990. Tchr., basketball coach Boyd-Buchanan H.S., Chattanooga, 1977, Ezell-Harding H.S., Antioch, Tenn., 1977-80; coll. tchr., coach David Lipscomb U., Nashville, 1980—; dir. tennis camp David Lipscomb U., Nashville, 1984-93; adj. tchr. Free Will Bible Coll., Nashville, 1994; profl. tennis tchr. West Meade Club, Nashville, 1983-84, Sequoia Club, Nashville, 1980-82. Author: Tennis Manual, 1991, also articles. Youth baseball coach Crieve Hall Youth Athletic Assn., Nashville, 1987—, Jr. Pro, Nashville, 1988, 94. Named Tennis Coach of Yr., Tenn. Collegiate Athletic Conf., 1981, 82, 84, 85, 91; named to Outstanding Young Men of Am., 1982. Mem. Internat. Sport Sci. Assn., Nat. Strength and Conditioning Assn., Am. Coll. Sports Medicine, Intercollegiate Tennis Assn., Am. Fitness Profls. and Assocs., Tenn. Alliance of Health, Phys. Edn., Recreation and Dance. Mem. Ch. of Christ. Avocations: biking, tennis, swimming, strength training. Home: 4029 Outer Dr Nashville TN 37204-4025 Office: David Lipscomb U 3901 Granny White Pike Nashville TN 37204-3903

GRIFFITH, JOHN RANDALL, health services administrator, educator; b. Balt., Mar. 22, 1934; s. Richard Robinson and Eleanor (Bond) G.; m. Helen Klenner, Sept. 17, 1955; children: Julia, Alison, Richard. BS Indsl. Engring., The Johns Hopkins U., 1955; MBA Hospital Adminstrn., U. Chgo., 1957. From asst. prof. to prof. U. Mich. Sch. Pub. Health Dept. Health Mgmt. Policy, Ann Arbor, 1960—, interim dept. chair, 1987-88, dept. chair, 1988-91, Andrew Pattullo Collegiate prof. Hosp. Adminstrn., 1982—; dir. program, chmn. dept. Bur. Hosp. Adminstrn., Ann Arbor, Mich., 1970-82; bd. dirs. Allegiance Corp., Ann Arbor, Mich., 1992—; examiner Baldridge Nat. Quality Award, 1997-98. Author: Quantitative Techniques for Hospital Planning and Control, 1972, Measuring Hospital Performance, 1978, The Well Managed Community Hospital, 1987 (award 1991), Moral Challenges of Health Care Management, 1993, The Well-Managed Health Care Organization, 1995, 4th edit., 1999, (with others) Re-Engineering Health Care: Building on Continuous Quality Improvement, 1995, Designing 21st Century Healthcare: Leadership in Hospitals and Health Systems, 1998. Bd. dirs., pres., Assn. Univ. Programs Health Adminstrn., 1974-75, Pattallo lectr., 1999; bd. dirs. Accredation Commn., 1977-83. Fellow Am. Coll. Health Care Execs. (gold medal 1992, James A. Hamilton award), Tau Beta Pi, Omicron Delta Kappa. Home: 333 Rock Creek Ct Ann Arbor MI 48104-1857 Office: U Mich SPH II 109 Observatory St Ann Arbor MI 48109-2029

GRIFFITH, JOHN VINCENT, academic official; b. Oneida, N.Y., Dec. 24, 1947; s. William F. and Dorothy (Roberts) G.; m. Nancy E. Snell, Jan. 25, 1969; children: Matthew, Christopher. BA cum laude, Dickinson Coll., 1969; MDiv magna cum laude, Harvard U., 1972; PhD, Syracuse U., 1980. Dean admissions Davidson Coll., N.C., 1979-85, v.p. inst. advancement, 1985-89; pres. Lyon Coll., Batesville, Ark., 1989-97, Presbyn. Coll., Clinton, S.C., 1998—. Mem. Omicron Delta Kappa, Sigma Alpha Epsilon, Phi Mu Alpha Sinfonia. Office: Presbyn Coll Office of Pres PO Box 975 Clinton SC 29325-0975

GRIFFITH, KATHERINE SCOTT, communications executive; b. Atlanta, Jan. 16, 1942; d. Robert Sherrill and Emily Howell (Reynolds) G.; m. Henry Armand Terjen, Sept. 4, 1970 (div. Nov. 1979); 1 child, Henry Foster Terjen; m. Michael Christopher Healy, May 20, 1995. AB, Sweet Briar Coll., 1964; Masters, Emory U., 1968. Editor South Today, So. Regional Coun., Atlanta, 1969-72; editor Phoenix, Bklyn., 1972-73; dir. communications N.Y. C. of C. and Industry, N.Y.C., 1978-79; dir. pub. liaison N.Y.C. Dept. Ports and Terminals, 1979-80; sr. pub. affairs officer Citicorp/Citibank, N.Y.C., 1981-83; asst. v.p., pub. rels. mgr. Citicorp Diners Club Media Svcs., N.Y.C., 1983-84; asst. v.p., pub. rels. dir. Citicorp Pub., N.Y.C., 1985-86, asst. v.p. corp. human resources, 1986-87; v.p. First Atlanta Corp., Atlanta, 1984; sr. mgr. Can. Imperial Bank of Commerce, N.Y.C., 1987-88, v.p. USA corp. communications, 1989-95; dir. mktg. and comm. Can. Imperial Bank Commerce Wood Gundy divsn. of Can. Imperial Bank Commerce, N.Y.C., 1995-97; v.p., dir. corp. comm. Signet Banking Corp., Richmond, Va., 1997; comm. cons. Greenwich, Conn., 1998—; pres. 150 Joralemon Street Corp., Bklyn., 1987-89. Pres. 78th Precinct Cmty. Coun., Bklyn., 1977-78; mem. com. Cmty. Bd. 6, Bklyn., 1978-80; mem. coun. So. Regional Coun., Atlanta, 1984-98; bd. dirs. Atlanta Chamber Players, 1984. Mem. Coun. Comm. Mgmt., Internat. Assn. Bus. Comm., Fin. Women's Assn. N.Y. (bd. dirs. 1995-96), Women Execs. in Pub. Rels., Jr. League, Beta Phi Mu. Democrat. Episcopalian.

GRIFFITH, LADD RAY, retired chemical research manager; b. Cory, Colo., Nov. 21, 1930; s. William Roy and Ida Geneva G.; m. Jeanne Maryly Hoffman, Feb. 6, 1955; children—Dina Jane, Julie Lynne, David Ladd. A.B., U. Colo., 1952, Ph.D., U.Calif.-Berkeley, 1957. Research chemist Calif. Research Corp., Richmond, 1956-62; research supr. Chevron Research Corp., Richmond, 1963-67; product mgr. Chevron Chem. Co., San Francisco, 1967-72, research mgr., Richmond, 1972-77, devel. mgr., San Francisco, 1978-79, planning, analytical mgr., 1979-84; mgr. inventive research Ortho Research Co., Richmond, 1984-86, dir. research 1986-90; ret., 1990. Mem. Phi Beta Kappa, Sigma Xi. Democrat. Unitarian. Home: 852 Gelston Pl El Cerrito CA 94530-3047

GRIFFITH, LAWRENCE STACEY CAMERON, cardiologist; b. Washington, Sept. 16, 1937; s. Ernest Stacey and Margaret Dyckman (Davenport) G.; m. Anne Gorman Young, June 20, 1959; children: Lawrence, John, Melinda, Gordon. BA, Haverford Coll., 1959; MD with honors, U. Rochester, 1963. Diplomate Am. Bd. Internal Medicine, Am. Bd. Cardiovascular Disease. Intern in medicine and surgery Strong Meml. Hosp., Rochester, N.Y., 1963-64, asst. resident in surgery, 1964-65, asst. and assoc. resident in medicine, 1967-69; rsch. fellow in cardiology Johns Hopkins U., Balt., 1969-71, asst. prof. medicine Sch. Medicine, 1971-76, asst. prof. radiology, 1974-80, assoc. prof. medicine, 1976-88, prof. medicine, 1988—; cons. VA Coop. Study Surgery for Coronary Artery Disease, Program on Surg. Control of Hyperlipidemias, U. Minn. Contbr. numerous articles to profl. jours. Bd. dirs. Julia Dychman Andrus Meml., Inc., Yonkers, N.Y., 1971—, chmn., pres., 1976—; bd. dirs. John E. Andrus Meml. Home for Aged, Hastings-on-Hudson, N.Y., 1974-97; bd. dirs. Surdna Found., N.Y.C., 1976—, v.p., 1988-94; chmn. adv. bd. Balt. Pastoral Counseling Svc., 1971-80. With USPHS, 1965-67. Fellow ACP, Coun. Clin. Cardiology of Am. Heart Assn., Am. Coll. Cardiology; mem. Alpha Omega Alpha. Democrat. Methodist. Home: 802 W Saint Georges Rd Baltimore MD 21210-1409 Office: Johns Hopkins Hosp Carnegie 530 600 N Wolfe St Baltimore MD 21287-0005

GRIFFITH, MADLYNNE VEIL, controller; b. Johnstown, Pa., Jan. 2, 1951; d. J. Donald and Mary Jane (Veil) G.; 1 child, Philip Bryce. BA, St. Mary's Coll., 1973; MBA, U. Notre Dame, 1975; DEd, Pa. State U., 1996. Cost and budget analyst U. Mich., Ann Arbor, 1980-81; acct. U. N.C., Wilmington, 1981, Johnstown Med. Devel. Corp., 1982-83; controller Mt. Aloysius Coll., Cresson, Pa., 1983—. Republican. Roman Catholic. Avocations: swimming, reading. Office: Mt Aloysius Coll Cresson PA 16630

GRIFFITH, MELANIE, actress; b. N.Y.C., Aug. 9, 1957; d. Tippi Hedren; m. Steven Bauer (div.); 1 child, Alexander; m. Don Johnson, 1989 (div.); 1 child, Dakota; m. Antonio Banderas, 1996; 1 child, Stella. Student, Hollywood Profl. Sch., 1981; studied acting with, Stella Adler. Acting debut in Night Moves, 1975, other films include The Drowning Pool, 1975, Smile, 1975, One on One, 1977, Roar, Joyride, 1977, Underground Aces, Body Double, 1984, Fear City, Something Wild, 1986, Cherry 2000, 1988, The Milagro Beanfield War, 1988, Stormy Monday, 1987, Working Girl, 1988 (Acad. Award nominee), In the Spirit, The Grifters, Pacific Heights, 1990, Bonfire of the Vanities, Shining Through, Paradise, 1991, A Stranger Among Us, 1992, Born Yesterday, 1993, Milk Money, 1994, Nobody's Fool, 1994, Two Much, 1996, Mulholland Falls, 1996, Now and Then, 1996, Shadow of Doubt, Another Day in Paradise, Lolita, 1996, Celebrity, Crazy in Alabama; TV appearances include (series) Carter Country, (mini-series) Once an Eagle, Buffalo Girls, 1995, (movies) Hills Like White Elephants, Celebrity, Daddy, I Don't Like This, Steel Cowboy, The Star Marker, (pilots) Golden Gate; guest in Alfred Hitcock Presents. Recipient Golden Globe award, 1989.

GRIFFITH, MELVIN EUGENE, entomologist, public health official; b. Lawrence, Kans., Mar. 24, 1912; s. George Thomas and Estella (Shaw) G.; m. Pauline Sophia Bogart, June 23, 1941. AB, U. Kans., 1934, AM, 1935, PhD, 1938; postgrad., U. Mich., summers 1937-40. Instr. zoology N.D. Agrl. Coll., Fargo, 1938-39, asst. prof., 1939-41, assoc. prof., 1941-42; commd. officer USPHS, 1943-71, malaria control entomologist State Dept. Health, Oklahoma City, 1943-46, communicable disease ctr. entomolgist, 1946-51; chief malaria adviser ICA, Bangkok, Thailand, 1951-60, assoc. dir. Malaria Eradication Tng. Ctr., Kingston, Jamaica, 1960, regional malaria advisor SE Asia, AID, New Delhi, 1960-62, Near East and So. Asia, 1962-64, dep. chief malaria eradication br., Washington, 1964-67, chief, 1967-71, ret. as capt., 1971; assoc. prof. zool. scis. U. Okla., Norman, 1946-52, prof., 1952-56; cons. Office of Health, AID, Washington, 1971-75. Contbr. articles and monographs on entomology, malaria control and pub. health. Recipient citation for disting. service U. Kans., 1962. Mem. Am. Pub. Health Assn., Am. Soc. Tropical Medicine and Hygiene, Am. Soc. Limnology and Oceanography, Entomol. Soc. Am., Explorers Club, N.Y. Acad. Scis., Siam Soc., Phi Beta Kappa, Sigma Xi. *Over 30 years in combating malaria began in World War II military and war supply areas in Oklahoma. Subsequent USPHS, State Health Department and University positions were held concurrently in developing malaria eradication, vector-borne disease control and medical entomology. Overseas and Washington posts thereafter were linked with the WHO-initiated worldwide malaria eradication program in which major U.S. technical and economic support was provided by AID and USPHS. Intensive multinational operations achieved early widespread success. Later, as problems emerged, U.S. support turned to research in new and improved methods in prevention and control, including potential malaria vaccination.* Address: PO Box DG Williamsburg VA 23187-3550

GRIFFITH, OSBIE HAYES, chemistry educator; b. Torrance, Calif., Sept. 14, 1938; s. Osbie and Mary Belle (Neathery) G.; m. Karen Hedberg; 2 sons; B.A., U. Calif.-Riverside, 1960; Ph.D., Calif. Inst. Tech., 1964. NAS-NRC postdoctoral Stanford U., 1965; asst. prof. chemistry U. Oreg., Eugene, 1966-69, assoc. prof., 1969-72, prof. chem. Inst. Molecular Biology, 1972—. Co-editor: Lipid-Protein Interactions, 1982; mem. editl. bd. Biophysical Jour., 1974-78, Chemistry & Physics of Lipids, 1974-95, Microscopy and Microanalysis, 1995—; contbr. articles to profl. jours. Scholar Camille and Henry Dreyfus Found., 1970; Career Devel. award Nat. Cancer Inst., 1972-76; fellow Sloan Found., 1967-69, Guggenheim Found., 1972-76; Faculty Achievement award for Teaching Excellence, Burlington No. Found., 1987, Dean's Devel. award, 1991, Creativity Extension NSF, 1992. Mem. Am. Chem. Soc., Biophys. Soc., Microscopy Soc. Am. Home: 2550 Charnelton St Eugene OR 97405-3216 Office: U Oreg Inst Molecular Biology Eugene OR 97403

GRIFFITH, OWEN WENDELL, biochemistry educator; b. Oakland, Calif., June 19, 1946; s. Charles H. and Gladys C. (Farrar) G. BA, U. Calif., Berkeley, 1968; PhD, Rockefeller U., 1975. Asst. prof. Cornell U. Med. Coll., N.Y.C., 1978-81, assoc. prof., 1981-87, prof., 1987-92; prof., chmn. biochemistry Med. Coll. of Wis., Milw., 1992—; mem., chmn. med. biochemistry study sect. NIH, Bethesda, Md., 1988-92. Contbr. more than 140 articles to profl. jours. Grantee NIH. Mem. Am. Chem. Soc., Am. Soc. Biochemistry and Molecular Biology, Am. Soc. Pharmacology and Exptl. Therapeutics. Achievements include more than 35 patents and patent applications in biomedical research. Office: Med Coll Wis Dept Biochemistry 8701 W Watertown Plank Rd Milwaukee WI 53226-3548

GRIFFITH, PATRICIA BROWNING, writer, educator; b. Ft. Worth; d. Robert Browning and Alonza Lee Johnston; m. William Byron Griffith; 1 child, Ellen Flannery. BA, Baylor U. Asst. prof. creative writing and playwriting George Washington U., 1991—; pres. PEN/Faulkner Found. Award for fiction, Folger Libr., Washington. Author: The Future is Not What it Used to Be, Tennessee Blue, The World Around Midnight, 1992, (One of Notable Books of 1992, ALA), Supporting the Sky, 1996; contbr.: Skin Deep, Black Women and White Women Write About Race, 1995, paperback edit., 1996; playwright Outside Waco, 1984, Safety, 1987, Risky Games, 1992; screenwriter. Mem. PEN, Author's Guild, Dramatist's Guild, Tex. Inst. Letters.

GRIFFITH, PATRICIA KING, journalist; b. San Francisco, Jan. 20, 1934; d. Earl Beardsley and Frankie Mae (Kelly) King; m. Winthrop Gold Griffith, Oct. 4, 1958 (div. Jan. 1986); children: Kevin Winthrop, Christina Suzanne. BA, Stanford U., 1955. Copy asst., reporter Washington Post, 1956-57, 60-64; reporter San Francisco Examiner, 1957-59; Washington bureau chief Monterey Herald and Toledo Blade, Washington, 1979-81; investigative reporter Monterey (Calif.) Peninsula Herald, 1973-79, city editor, 1981-83, mng. editor, 1983-88; Washington bureau chief, White House corr. Toledo Blade and Pitts. Post-Gazette, Washington, 1988—. Bd. dirs. Lyceum of Monterey Peninsula, 1977-79, All Sts. Episcopal Day Sch., Carmel, Calif., 1977-79, Monterey Coll. Law, 1978-79; sr. warden St. Dunstan's Episcopal Ch., Carmel Valley, Calif., 1983-84. Recipient Silver Gavel award ABA, 1978. Mem. Stanford Alumni Assn., Nat. Press Club, Gridiron Club, Stanford Club Washington, Stanford Cap and Gown Soc. Home: 3001 Veazey Ter NW Washington DC 20008-5454 Office: Blade Comm 955 National Press Building Washington DC 20045-1901

GRIFFITH, PHILIP ARTHUR, elementary school educator; b. N.Y.C., Nov. 13, 1934; s. Jesse Lloyd and Anna (McGovern) G.; m. Nancy Sullivan, June 18, 1960; children: Philip, Margaret. BA, Hunter Coll., 1960; MS, CUNY, 1963. Cert. edn. Tchr. 6th grade N.Y.C. Pub. Schs., 1960-64; tchr. Central Islip (N.Y.) Pub. Schs., 1964—; instr. Dowling Coll., Oakdale, N.Y., 1970-75; supr. N.Y.C. (N.Y.) Bureau of Cmty. Edn., 1970-80. Contbr. articles to profl. publs. Hockey coach Cath. Youth Orgn., Central Islip, 1976-82, St. Anthony's H.S., 1986-87; baseball coach Police Athletic League, Central Islip, 1976-86; del. L.I. Fedn. Labor, Mineola, N.Y., 1976-90; N.Y. state del. N.Y. State AFL-CIO, Albany, 1976-95, N.Y. Com. Health and Safety, N.Y.C., 1988-95; N.Y. State Tenure Hearing Panelist, Albany, 1978-99; mem. parents coun. Boston Coll., Chestnut Hill, Mass., 1990-92. Cpl. U.S. Army, 1954-56. Recipient N.Y. State PTA Jenkins award Charles Mulligan Sch. PTA, Central Islip, 1978, Leadership award United Way, L.I., 1978, Pride in the Union award Am. Fedn. Tchrs., 1990, 92, Influential Tchr. award MIT, Cambridge, 1980. Mem. Am. Fedn. Tchrs. (del. 1972-95), Ctrl. Islip Tchrs. Assn. (pres. 1976-95), N.Y. State United Tchrs. (del. 1970-95), N.Y. State Tchrs. Retirement Sys. (del. 1974-95), U.S. Golf Assn., Port Jefferson Country Club, Port Jefferson Hist. Soc., Nat. Geographic Soc., L.I. Pres. Coun. (dist. dir.), Indsl. Rels. Rsch. Assn., Smithsonian Inst. Democrat. Roman Catholic. Avocations: golf, folk art, Irish history, theatre, travel. Home: 14 Cove Ln Prt Jefferson NY 11777-1103 Office: Central Islip Tchrs Assn Central Islip NY 11722

GRIFFITH, RACHEL, neonatologist; b. LaJunta, Colo., Dec. 14, 1951; s. Charles Wayne Hampton and Billie Jean (Blackburn) Boosahda; 1 child, Keri. BS in Biology, Dallas Bapt. U., 1973; MD, U. Tex. Med. Br., Galveston, 1977. Diplomate Am. Bd. Pediatrics, Am. Bd. Neonatal-Perinatal Medicine. Resident in pediatrics U. Tex. Med. Br., fellow in neonatology; staff neonatologist Presbyn. Hosp., Dallas, 1982-83; neonatal ICU physician Med. City Dallas Hosp., 1983—, med. dir., pediatric sect. chief, chmn. perinatal com., 1983; pres. Upper Trinity Valley Perinatal Assn., 1983-85. Pres., bd. dirs. Chaplaincy Ministry, Inc., Dallas, 1990-93; bd. dirs. Journeys/Cmty. Based Counseling/Ministry, 1989-98. Mem. Am. Acad.; mem. Christian Med./Dental Assn. Republican. Episcopalian. Avocations: snow skiing, golf, exercise, baseball, reading. Office: Magella Med Assocs NICU Med City Dallas Hosp 7777 Forest Ln Dallas TX 75230-2505*

GRIFFITH, REGINALD W., federal agency administrator. Masters Degree, MIT, 1959. Exec. dir. Nat. Capital Planning Commn., Washington, 1979—. Office: Nat Capital Planning Commn 801 Pennsylvania Ave NW Washington DC 20576

GRIFFITH, ROBERT CHARLES, allergist, educator, planter; b. Shreveport, La., Jan. 9, 1939; s. Charles Parsons and Madelon (Jenkins) G.; m. Loretta Dean Secrist, July 15, 1969; children: Charles Randall, Cameron Stuart, Ann Marie. BS, Centenary Coll., 1961; MD, La. State U., 1965. Intern, Confederate Meml. Med. Ctr., Shreveport, 1965-66, resident in internal medicine, 1966-68; fellow in allergy and chest disease, instr. U. Va. Med. Sch. Hosp., Charlottesville, 1968-70; practice medicine specializing in allergies, Alexandria, La., 1970-72, The Allergy Clinic, Shreveport, 1972; pres. Griffith Allergy Clinic, Shreveport, 1973—; faculty internal medicine La. State U., 1972—; owner, planter Riverpoint Plantation, Caddo Parish, La. and Miller and Lafayette Counties, Ark. Bd. dirs. Caddo-Bossier Assn. Retarded Citizens, 1977-84, Access (formerly Child Devel. Ctr.), Shreveport, 1979-85; mem. med. adv. com., spl. edn. adv. com. Caddo Parish Sch. Bd., 1977—; mem. commission on missions and social concerns First Methodist Ch., 1981-84, mem. adminstrv. bd., 1981-84; mem. med. panel for transfer Caddo Parish Sch. Bd., 1974-94; mem. adopt a flag program Confederate Meml. Mus. New Orleans; co-chair Loyola Fund Drive, 1994-95. Served to maj. M.C., U.S. Army, 1965-71. Recipient Physician of the Yr. award Shreveport-Bossier Med. Assts., 1984. Fellow Am. Coll. Asthma, Allergy and Immunology, Am. Coll. Chest Physicians (assoc.), Am. Thoracic Soc.; mem. AMA, SAR (chpt. surgeon 1994—), Am. Acad. Allergy, Asthma and Immunology, Am. Legion, Jamestowne Soc., So. Med. Assn., La. Med. Soc., Shreveport Med. Soc. (allergy spokesman 1984—), La. Allergy Soc. (charter; past pres.), U. Va. Med. Alumni Assn. (life), Pace Soc. Am., La. State U. Med. Alumni Assn., Conferderate Soc. Am., Heritage Preservation Assn., So. League (charter, sustainer), So. League La. (bd. dirs.), Legion South, Am. Legion (Viet Nam), Mil. Order Stars and Bars, Order of So. Cross, Shreveport C. of C., Kappa Alpha, Methodist. Lodges: Masons (32 degree). Clubs: Shreveport Country, Petroleum of Shreveport, Shreveport, Ambs., Cotillion, Royal, Plantation, Shriners (El Kahruba Temple), Jesters, Les Bon Temps., Demoiselle Club. Home: 7112 E Ridge Dr Shreveport LA 71106-4749 also: Riverpoint Plantation Ida LA 71044

GRIFFITH, ROBERT DEAN, military careerman, registered nurse; b. McAllen, Tex., Jan. 6, 1962; s. Roger Leroy and Susan Lynn (Disney) G.; m. Dianne Mary Clark, July 6, 1995; children: Lee Austin, Jayna Lynn. BSN magna cum laude, Old Dominion U., 1996, Degree in Biology and Chemistry, 1990. Enlisted E-1 USN, 1980; commd. ensign USN Naval Nurse Corps, 1996; student US Naval Schs., Gt. Lakes, Ill., 1980-81; profl. USS Monongahela, Norfolk, Va., 1981-82, Naval Spl. Warfare, Norfolk, 1982-93; RN Nat. Naval Med. Ctr., Bethesda, Md., 1996—, mem. staff edn. com. surg. ward, 1996-98; mem. staff ICU Nat. Naval Med. Ctr., Bethesda, 1998—. Mem. AACN, Emergency Nurses Assn., Old Dominion U. Alumni Assn., Sigma Theta Tau, Phi Kappa Phi. Avocations: family time, reading, running, bicycling, camping. Office: Nat Naval Med Ctr 8901 Wisconsin Ave Bethesda MD 20889

GRIFFITH, STEPHEN RAY, philosophy educator; b. Williamsport, Pa., July 1, 1943; s. James Stephen and Margaret Adelaide (Henninger) G.; m. Erica Preston Fischer, Sept. 4, 1965; children: Maureen, Todd, Jennifer, Meghan. AB, Cornell U., 1966; MA in Philosophy, U. Pitts., 1968, PhD in Philosophy, 1973. Prof. philosophy Lycoming Coll., Williamsport, Pa., 1970—. Bd. dirs. Williamsport Area Schs., 1982-91, v.p. bd. dirs., 1990. Vis. fellow Ctr. Philosophy of Religion, Notre Dame, Ind., 1996, Andrew Mellon Found. fellow, 1969, Woodrow Wilson Found. fellow, 1969. Mem. Am. Philos. Assn., Soc. Christian Philosophers, Phi Beta Kappa, Phi Kappa Phi, Phi Sigma Tau. Office: Lycoming Coll PO Box 2 Williamsport PA 17703-0002

GRIFFITH, STEVEN FRANKLIN, SR., lawyer, real estate title insurance agent and investor; b. New Orleans, July 14, 1948; s. Hugh Franklin and Rose Marie (Teutone) G.; m. Mary Elizabeth McMillan Frank, Dec. 9, 1972; children: Steven Franklin Jr., Jason Franklin. BBA, Loyola U., New Orleans, 1970, JD, 1972. Bar: La. 1972, U.S. Dist. Ct. (ea. dist.) La. 1975, U.S. Ct. Appeals (5th cir.) 1975, U.S. Supreme Ct. 1976. With Law Offices of Senator George T. Oubre, Norco, La., 1971-75; sole practice Destrehan, La., 1975—. Served to 1st lt. U.S. Army, 1970-72. Fellow La. State Bar Found.; mem. ABA, ATLA, La. State Bar Assn. (ho. of dels. 1987—), La. Trial Lawyers Assn., New Orleans Trial Lawyers Assn., Fed. Bar Assn., Lions. Democrat.

GRIFFITH, WILLIAM ALEXANDER, former mining company executive; b. Sioux Falls, S.D., Mar. 28, 1922; s. James William and Adeline Mae (Reid) G.; m. Gratia Frances Hannan, Jan. 27, 1949; children—Georgeanne Reid, James William, Wade Andrew. B.S. in Metall. Engring., S.D. Sch. Mines and Tech., 1947; M.S. in Metallurgy, M.I.T., 1950; Mineral Dressing Engr. (hon.), Mont. Coll. Mineral Sci. and Tech., 1971; D in Bus. Adminstrn. (hon.), S.D. Sch. Mines & Tech., 1986; D in Sci. (hon.), U. Idaho, 1990. With N.J. Zinc Co., 1949-57, chief milling and maintenance Bertha minerals divsn., 1956-57; metallurgist Rare Metals Corp. Am., Tuba City, Ariz., 1957-58; dir. rsch. Phelps Dodge Corp., Morenci, Ariz., 1958-68; with Hecla Mining Co., Coeur d'Alene, Idaho, 1968-87, exec. v.p., 1978, pres., chief exec. officer, 1979-86, chmn., chief exec. officer, 1986-87; pres. Granduc Mines Ltd., 1987-88; chmn. Inland N.W. Bancorp., Inc., 1989-96; bd. dirs. The Coeur d'Alenes Co. With USNR, 1943-46. Mem. AIME (Gaudin award 1977, Richards award 1981, Disting. mem. 1977, Hon. 1987), NAE, Am. Mining Congress (past dir.), Idaho Mining Assn. (past pres.), Idaho Assn. Commerce and Industry (past bd. dirs.), Western Regional Coun. (chmn. 1986-87), Nat. Strategic Materials and Minerals Adv. Com. to Sec. Interior, Silver Inst. (past pres., past chmn.), Nat. Acad. of Engring., Sigma Tau, Theta Tau. Republican. Lodge: Rotary. Home: 630 S 14th St Coeur D Alene ID 83814-3820

GRIFFITHE, TODD ALLEN, television associate director; b. Lakewood, Calif., Aug. 24, 1966; s. Thomas Delano and Rosemary Pearl (Lowery) G.; m. Lisa Jill Mandarino, June 8, 1991. BA in Comms., Calif. State U., Fullerton, 1992. Prodn. staff mem. Comcast Cablevision, Seal Beach, Calif., 1988-92; ENG camera/editor Sta. KDOC-TV, Anaheim, Calif., 1988-91; prodn. staff mem. Fin. News Network, L.A., 1990-91; videotape oper. Johnson Controls, San Bernardino, Calif., 1991-94; assoc. dir., dir. Sta. KTLA-TV, L.A., 1992—, E! Entertainment Tel., L.A., 1994-97; assoc. dir. Sta. KTTV-TV (Fox), L.A., 1996. Mem. Serrano Hills Cmty. Ch., Tustin, Calif., 1994—. Recipient ACE award Cable ACE Awards, 1989, 90, Best ENG Feature Story award Orange County Press Club, 1990. Mem. Nat. Assn. Broadcast Employees and Technicians. Office: KTLA-TV 5800 W Sunset Blvd Los Angeles CA 90028-6607

GRIFFITH FRIES, MARTHA, controller; b. Brockton, Mass., Sept. 9, 1945; d. Ishmael Hayes and Jettie L. (Dudley) Davis; m. Jack C. Griffith, May 29, 1965 (dec. June 1984); Michael S., David M.; m. Dan H. Fries, Nov. 5, 1994. Student, U. Ark., 1962-64; BA, Ball State U., 1967. Prin. Griffith Acctg. Co., Indpls., 1968-70; probate adminstr. Johnson & Weaver, Indpls., 1970-74; personnel adminstr. Hercules Inc., Houston, 1974-76; adminstr. Lapin Totz & Mayer, Houston, 1976-80; bus. mgr. Pasadena (Tex.) Citizen, 1980-84; contr. Houston Community Newspapers, 1984-88, DCI Pub., Alexandria, Va., 1989-90, Telescan Inc., Houston, 1990-93, Advolink, Inc., 1993—. *Martha has over 20 years' experience providing formulation and implementation oflong-term strategic planning in the communications industry. She is a specialist in analyzing problems, troubleshooting and creating solutions. She designed and implemented policies and procedures to cut costs, increase productivity, improve cash flow, and increase profits. While at Telescan, Martha established credit policies that reduced losses by 85%. She established central purchasing system at DCI Publishing, generating $100K annual savings: she developed a system to increase cash flow by 30%. At Houston Community News, she downsized staff by 36% while maintaining productivity and successfully negotiated appeal hearing with state resulting in savings of $120K.* Commr. Houston council Boy Scouts Am., 1983. Recipient Dist. Merit awards Boy Scouts Am., Houston, 1983. Mem. Internat. Newspaper Fin. Execs. (com. mem. 1986-89), Collier Jackson Users Group (moderator 1986-89), Nat. Assn. Female Execs. Democrat. Baptist. Avocations: dancing, boating, traveling. Address: 14911 Walters Rd Houston TX 77068-2501

GRIFFITHS, BARBARA LORRAINE, psychologist, writer; b. Glendale, Calif., July 15, 1927; d. David William and Mabel Augusta (Gaarder) G.; m. Dale Elmo Rumbaugh, Mar. 28, 1948; 1 child, David Wynn. AA in Journalism, Valley C.C., 1958; BA in Psychology, U. Calif. Riverside, 1972; BS in Rehab. Counseling, Calif. State U., 1976; PhD in Clin. Psychology, Calif. Grad. Inst., 1984. Cert. addiction specialist. Alcoholism counselor Kaiser Permanente, L.A., 1976-82; pvt. practice Hollywood, L.A., 1979-89, Glendale, Burbank, Calif., 1989-97, L.A., 1997—; mem. State of Calif. Med. Divsn. Eval. Com., 1998—;. Editor: (child abuse newsletter) Directions, 1976-86; contbr. short stories, feature articles, columns to various mags. and newspapers. Mem. Glendale Rotary, 1990-95, Verdugo BPW, 1988-91; Nat. Ski Patrolwoman #122, 1952-56. Recipient Editor's Choice award for poetry, 1997. Mem. APA, L.A. County Psychol. Assn. Avocations: script writing, tennis, skiing, swimming and water sports, reading. Home & Office: 3002 Hyperion Ave Los Angeles CA 90027-2564

GRIFFITHS, DANIEL EDWARD, dean emeritus; b. Bridgeport, Conn., May 8, 1917; s. Frederick George and Helen (Quist) G.; m. Priscilla Tomlinson, June 22, 1946; children: Priscilla Ann Griffiths Russel, Michael Edward. EdB, Central Conn. State Coll., 1940; MEd, U. N.H., 1949; PhD, Yale, 1952. Asst. prof. edn. Colgate U., 1949-52; prof. State Coll. Tchrs., Albany, N.Y., 1952-55; dir. coop. devel. pub. sch. adminstrn., asso. coordinator ednl. research N.Y. State Dept. Edn., 1955-56; assoc. prof., then prof. edn. Columbia Tchrs. Coll., 1956-61; assoc. dean Sch. Edn. NYU, N.Y.C., 1961-65; dean Sch. Edn., Health, Nursing and Arts Professions NYU, 1965-83, spl. asst. to chancellor, 1983-86, dean emeritus, 1986—, prof. emeritus, 1988—; dir. devel. criteria of success in sch. adminstrn. project, coop. research br. U.S. Office Edn., 1957-61, dir. devel. taxonomies of orgnl. behavior in edn. project, 1964; dir. N.Y.C. Study Tchr. Mobility, 1963; pres. N.Y. State Tchr. Edn. Conf. Bd., 1973-83; chmn. Nat. Commn. on Excellence in Ednl. Adminstrn., 1986-88. Author: Human Relations in School Administration, 1956, Administrative Theory, 1959, Organizing Schools for Effective Education, 1962, Administrative Performance and Personality, 1962, The School Superintendent, 1967; editor: Behavioral Science and Educational Administration, 1964, Developing Taxonomies of Organizational Behavior in Education, 1969, The Dilemma of the Deanship, 1980, Administrative Theory in Transition, 1985; co-editor: Leaders for America's Schools: The Report and Papers of the National Commission on Excellence in Education Administration, 1988; chmn. editorial bd. NYU Edn. Quar., 1968-83; editor: Ednl. Adminstrn. Quar, 1975-79; editor spl. issue Ednl. Adminstrn. Quar., summer 1991; mem. editorial bd. Libr. of Edn., 1961-67, chmn., 1964-67; contbn. author or editor of over 300 articles, pamphlets and books. Pres. Sch. Bd. Greenburgh, N.Y., 1961-64. Served with USAAF, 1943-46. Recipient 1st Roald F. Campbell Lifetime Achievement award in ednl. adminstrv., 1992. Mem. Am. Ednl. Rsch. Assn., Nat. Conf. Profs. Ednl. Adminstrn., Am. Assn. Colls. Tchr. Edn. (dir. 1975-78), Assn. Colls. and Schs. of Edn. in State Univs. and Land Grant Colls. and Affiliated Pvt. Units. (exec. bd. 1972-83), Assn. Deans of Edn. in Pvt. Univs. (chmn. 1972-83), Univ. Coun. Ednl. Adminstrn., Ea. Srs. Golf Assn. (pres. 1992-94), Scarsdale Golf Club (pres. 1980), Westchester Srs. Golf Assn. (pres. 1978-80), Westchester Golf Assn. (mem. exec. com. 1993—), Kappa Delta Pi, Phi Delta Kappa. Home: 54 Clarendon Rd Scarsdale NY 10583-2420*

GRIFFITHS, DAVID NEAL, utility executive; b. Oxford, Ind., Sept. 11, 1935; s. David Scifres and Lorene Francis Griffiths; m. Alice Anne Goodpasture, Aug. 9, 1959 (div. 1972); children—Beth Anne, David Douglas; m. Barbette Suzanne Goetsch, June 7, 1975; children—Michael, Megan. BS in Indsl. Econs., Purdue U., 1957. Various positions Delco Remy div. Gen. Motors Corp., Anderson, Ind., 1957-69; dep. commr. revenue State of Ind., Indpls., 1969-71, adminstrv. asst. to gov., 1971-72; exec. dir. Environ. Quality Control, Inc., Indpls., 1972-75; project mgr. EDP Corp., Sarasota, Fla., 1975-76, v.p. adminstrn., 1977-78; asst. to pres. Citizens Gas and Coke Utility, Indpls., 1978-80, v.p. pub. affairs, 1980-82, sr. v.p. adminstrn., 1982-92, exec. v.p., 1995-98, exec. v.p., COO,, 1998—, pres., CEO, 1999—; mem. ind. Energy Devel. Bd., Indpls., 1980-92, Midwest Govs.' Energy Task Force, 1972-75; chmn. Fed. Home Loan Bank of Indpls., 1990-93; bd. dirs. Ind. Farmers Mut. Ins. Co., Midwest Energy Assn., Meth. Med. Group, Rose-Hulman Inst. Tech. Author: Implementing Quality with a Customer Focus, Management in a Quality Environment. Pres. Indsl. Mgmt. Club, Anderson and Madison County, Inc., 1961; Cen. Coun. Indsl. Mgmt. Clubs 1966; bd. dirs., chmn. Environ. Quality Conrol, Inc., Indpls., 1983-98, Life/Ledership Devel., Inc.; bd.dirs. Greater Indpls. Progress Com., Goodwill Industries Found., Indpls. Econ. Devel. Corp. Recipient Exchange Industrialist with USSR award YMCA, 1963; named Sagamore of Wabash, Gov. of Ind., 1971, 75. Mem. Govtl. Affairs Soc. Ind. (past pres.), Ind. Gas Assn. (bd. dirs.), Indpls. C. of C. (bd. dirs.). Republican. Methodist. Clubs: Columbia (Indpls.), Downtown Kiwanis (Indpls.). Avocations: golf, swimming. Home: 8158 Brent Ave Indianapolis IN 46240-2725 Office: Citizens Gas & Coke Utility 2020 N Meridian St Indianapolis IN 46202-1393

GRIFFITHS, PHILLIP A., mathematician, academic administrator; b. Raleigh, N.C., Oct. 18, 1938; s. Phillip and Jeanette (Field) G.; m. Ann Lane Crittenden, 1958-67; children: Jan Kirsten, David; m. Marian Folsom Jones, 1968; children: Sarah, Rebecca. BS, Wake Forest U., 1959; PhD, Princeton U., 1962; D (hon.), Angers U., France, 1979; DSc (hon.), Wake Forest U., 1973, U. Peking, China, 1983. Prof. math. Princeton (N.J.) U., 1968-72; prof. Harvard U., Cambridge, Mass., 1972-83, Dwight Parker Robinson prof. math., 1983; provost, James B. Duke prof. math. Duke U., Durham, N.C., 1983-91; dir. Inst. for Advanced Study, Princeton, N.J., 1991—; bd. dirs. Bankers Trust N.Y. Corp., Oppenheimer Funds; mem. faculty U. Calif., Berkeley, 1964-67; vis. prof. Princeton U., 1967-68, mem. Inst. Advanced Study, 1968-70; chmn. bd. on math. scis. NRC, 1986-91, chmn. commn. on phys. scis., math. and applications, 1992, chmn. com. on sci., engring. and pub. policy, 1992-99; mem. Nat. Sci. Bd., 1991-96; sec. Internat. Math. Union, 1999—; convenor Sci. Insts. Group, 1999—. Editor Jour. Differential Geometry, 1980-90, Compositio Mathematica, 1980-92, Duke Math. Jour., 1983—, Selecta Mathematica, 1994—, Annals of Math., 1997—. Bd. dirs. Rsch. Triangle Inst., 1983-91; trustee Woodward Acad., N.C. Sch. Sci. and Math. Recipient LeRoy P. Steel prize Am. Math. Soc., 1971, Dannie Heineman Preis, Acad. Scis. Gottingen, 1979; Miller fellow U. Calif. Berkeley, 1962-64, 1975-76, Guggenheim fellow, 1980-82. Mem. NAS (mem. Coord. Coun. Edn. 1992-93), Am. Philos. Soc., Am. Acad. Arts and Scis., Internat. Math. Union (sec. 1999—). Office: Inst Advanced Study Office of Dir Olden Ln Princeton NJ 08540

GRIFFITHS, RACHEL, actress; b. Melbourne, Australia, 1968. Motion picture actress. Films include Muriel's Wedding, 1994, Jude, 1996, Cosi, 1996, Th Have and to Hold, 1997, My Best Friend's Wedding, 1997, Hilary and Jackie, 1998 (nominee Best Supporting Actress Oscar 1999), My Son the Fanatic, 1998, Among Giants, 1998, Amy, 1998, Me Myself I, 1999; T.V. series include Secrets, 1993, Jimeoin, 1994. Office: c/o SAG 5757 Wilshire Blvd Los Angeles CA 90036*

GRIFFITHS, ROBERT PENNELL, banker; b. Chgo., May 6, 1949; s. George Findley and Marion E. (Winterrowd) G.; m. Susan Hillman, Jan. 31, 1976. BA, Amherst Coll., 1972; MS in Mgmt., Northwestern U., 1974. Comml. banking officer No. Trust Co., Chgo., 1978-80, 2d v.p., 1980-83, v.p., 1983-85; sr. v.p. comml. lending UnibancTrust Co., Chgo., 1985-88; pres., chief exec. officer Old Kent Bank (formerly Ill. Regional Bank of Naperville, Ill.), 1988-90; sr. v.p. Old Kent Bank-Chgo., 1991-92; sr. v.p. UnibancTrust/Hawthorne (merged into Old Kent Bank of Naperville), 1987-89; pres., CEO, Uptown Nat. Bank of Chgo., 1993—. Mem. Univ. Club (Chgo.), Onwentsia Club. Home: 691 Rockefeller Rd Lake Forest IL 60045-3141 Office: Uptown Nat Bank 4753 N Broadway St Chicago IL 60640-4993

GRIFFITHS, SYLVIA PRESTON, physician; b. London, Dec. 25, 1924; d. Wheeler Bate and Dorothy (Hartley) Preston; m. Raymond B. Griffiths; 1 dau., Wendy Elizabeth. B.A., Hunter Coll., 1944; M.D., Yale U., 1948. Intern Grace-New Haven Community Hosp., 1948-49, resident, 1949-52; fellow in pediatric cardiology Yale U., 1952-54; asst. to prof. clin. pediatrics Columbia U., N.Y.C., 1955; prof. clin. pediatrics Columbia U., 1977-90, prof. emeritus, 1990—. Recipient career scientist award Health Research Council, City of N.Y., 1963-69. Mem. N.Y. Heart Assn. (dir. 1977-83), Am. Acad. Pediatrics, Am. Pediatric Soc., Am. Heart Assn., Am. Coll. Cardiology, Babies Hosp. Alumni Assn. (pres. 1991-92). Office: Columbia Presbyterian Med Ctr 622 W 168th St New York NY 10032-3784

GRIFFITH-THOMPSON, SARA LYNN, resource reading educator; b. Kansas City, Mo., July 27, 1965; d. Hugh Wallace and Mary Elizabeth (Mullinix) Griffith; m. Joey Lee Thompson, May 30, 1992. BS in Edn., Ctrl. Mo. State U., 1986, MS in Reading, 1992. Tchr. grade 4 East Lynne (Mo.) Sch. Dist., 1987-88, Pleasant Lea Elem., Lee's Summit, Mo., 1988-93; tchr. grade 4 resource reading K-6 Trailridge Elem., Lee's Summit, 1993—; asst. After Sch. Group, Lee's Summit, 1993-94; mem. Tchr. Expectation Student Achievement, Lee's Summit, 1992, sponsor Student Coun., Lee's Summit, 1994-96, supr. Student Tchrs., Lee's Summit, spring 1992; v.p. elect reading coun. Lee's Summit. Recipient Excellence in Tchg. award Lee's Summit C. of C., 1992. Mem. Internat. Reading Assn. (bldg. rep. 1994-98, presenter Plains regional 1995, state conf. 1996), Mo. State Tchr. Assn., PEO, Grand Cross, Optimist Club (super friends), Phi Delta Kappa. Office: Trailridge Elem 3651 SW Windemere Dr Lees Summit MO 64082-4412

GRIFFITTS, KEITH LOYD, oil industry executive; b. Wichita Falls, Tex., July 10, 1942; s. Loyd and Fannie (Moore) G. BS, Hardin-Simmons U., 1964; MEd, North Tex. State U., 1965. Counselor, adminstr. Dist. #6 Schs., Littleton, Colo., 1965-69; div. mgr. Westamerica Securities, Inc., Denver, 1969-71; project sales mgr. U.S. Home Corp., Denver, 1971-74; comml. real estate salesperson Wilton O. Davis & Co., Dallas, 1974-75; dir. mktg. Schneider Bakery Co., Longview, Tex., 1975-77; nat. account mktg. White Swan, Inc., Dallas, 1977-79; pres. Vantage Petroleum Resources, Inc., Dallas, 1979-82; pres., owner Western Petroleum Resources, Inc., Dallas, 1982—; v.p., mgr. corp. trust devel. 1st City Tex.-Dallas, 1984-91; lectr. North Tex. State U., 1982-86. Author, editor, pub. periodical Oil Patch, 1980-84; editor periodical Trust Trends, 1984-90. Trustee Hardin-Simmons U., Abilene, Tex., 1991—, vice chmn., chmn. bd. devel., 1987-90. Mem. Soc. Ind. Profl. Earth Scientists (assoc.), North Tex. Oil and Gas Assn., Dallas and Midland Exploration Fin. Group, Soc. of Ind. Profl. Earth Scientists, Dallas Wildcatters Club. Baptist. Avocations: water and snow skiing, hunting. Home: 1089 Edith Cir Richardson TX 75080-2924 Office: Ste 290 15441 Knoll Trail LB # 2 Dallas TX 75248-7066

GRIFFY, THOMAS ALAN, physics educator; b. Oklahoma City, Dec. 16, 1936; s. Judson H. and Dicie (Johnston) G.; m. Peggy Lynn Walker, June 6, 1958; children—David, Alan, Marjorie. BA, Rice U., 1959, MA, 1960, PhD, 1961. Asst. prof. physics Duke U., Durham, N.C., 1961-62; research assoc. High Energy Physics Lab., Stanford U., Calif., 1962-65; assoc. prof. physics U. Tex., Austin, 1965-68, prof., 1968—, chmn. dept., 1974-84, assoc. dean grad. sch., 1970-73, 96—. Contbr. articles to profl. jours. Fellow Am. Phys. Soc. Methodist. Office: U Tex Dept Physics Austin TX 78712

GRIGG, EDDIE GARMAN, minister, educator; b. Shelby, N.C., Feb. 20, 1957; s. Gaston Theodore and Sylvia Evlyn (Davis) G.; m. Susan Wanda Ray, May 28, 1977; children: Mark Zolton, Jamie Ray, Steven Russell. BA, Gardner-Webb Coll., 1980; MDiv, Southeastern Bapt. Theol. Sem., 1985; D Ministry, Emmanuel Bapt. U., 1994, DRE, 1995; DD (hon.), New Life U., 1998. Ordained to ministry So. Bapt. Conv., 1976. Pastor Victory Bapt. Ch., Kings Mountain, N.C., 1975-79, Christian Freedom Bapt. Ch., Kings Mountain, 1979-81, Sanford Meml. Bapt. Ch., Brodnax, Va., 1981-85, Pleasant Hill Bapt. Ch., Shelby, N.C., 1985-89; sr. min. Wilson Grove Bapt. Ch., Charlotte, N.C., 1989-93; founder, pastor New Life Bapt. Ch., Charlotte, 1993—; co-founder, pres. New Life Theological Seminary, 1996—. Mem. Bapt. Metrolina Ministries Pastor's Conf. (pres. 1995-97), Bapt. Metrolina Ministries Assn. (evangelism com. 1990-93, urban ch. com. 1990-94). Republican. Office: New Life Bapt Ch 10132 Harrisburg Rd Charlotte NC 28215-7305

GRIGG, NEIL S., civil engineering educator. Grad., U.S. Mil. Acad., 1961; MS in Civil Engring., Auburn U., 1965; PhD in Civil Engring., Colo. State U., 1969. Dir. Colo. Water Resources Rsch. Inst., Internat. Sch. Water Resources, Colo. State U., 1988-91; asst. sec. natural resources State of N.C., 1979-81, dir. environ. mgmt., 1980-81; dir. U. N.C. Water Resources Rsch. Inst., 1979-82; co-founder Sellards & Grigg, Inc., Denver; prof., head dept. civil engring. Colo. State U., Fort Collins, 1991—; organizer confs.; advocate pub. works edn. and rsch.;mem. working groups Nat. Coun. on Pub. Works Improvement; mem. Edn. Found. Com. on Govt. Affairs, 1992 U.S.-Japan Infrastructure Delegation, Top Ten Selection Panel, Coun. on Internat. Collaboration; pres. Ft. Collins Water Bd., 1991—. Contbr. articles to profl. jours. Fellow ASCE (chair exec. com., water resources planning and mgmt. divsn. 1995, chmn. water pricing task com. 1990-92, founding chair WP&M Divsn. Urban Water Com. 1986-88, chair tech. coun. on rsch. 1983-85, chmn. urban water resources rsch. coun. 1978-79, nat. water policy com. 1981, chmn. nat. environ. systems policy com. 1983), Am. Pub. Works Assn. (bd. dirs., chair mgmt. practices evaluation com.), Am. Water Works Assn., Ft. Collins C. of C. (chmn. water com. 1989—). Office: Colo State U Dept Civil Engring Fort Collins CO 80523-1372*

GRIGG, WILLIAM CLYDE, electrical engineer; b. Chester, Pa., Mar. 12, 1952; s. Carl C. and Joan K. (Kaufman) G. BS in Engring., Widener Coll., 1974, M of Engring. in Engring. Mgmt., 1979. Registered profl. engr., Pa. Test engr. Phila. Electric Co., 1974-77, project engr., 1977-88; engr. supr. Phila. Electric Co., Wayne, Pa., 1988-93; sr. info. systems analyst PECO Energy Co., Wayne, Pa., 1993—. Mem. NSPE, IEEE, IEEE Comm. Soc., IEEE Computer Soc., Delaware County Soc. Profl. Engrs., Pa. Soc. Profl. Engrs., Project Mgmt. Inst. (cert. project mgmt. profl., pres. Keystone chpt. 1997), Keystone AAA Club, Widener U. Alumni Assn. Republican. Presbyterian. Avocations: bowling, fishing, music, swimming. Home: 110 Linda Ln Media PA 19063-5038 Office: PECO Energy Co Mail Stop 62B-1 965 Chesterbrook Blvd Wayne PA 19087-5635

GRIGG, WILLIAM HUMPHREY, utility executive; b. Shelby, N.C., Nov. 5, 1932; s. Claud and Margy (Humphrey) G.; m. Margaret Anne Ford, Aug. 11, 1956; children: Anne Ford, John Humphrey, Mary Lynne. A.B., Duke U., 1954, LL.B., 1958. Bar: N.C. 1958. Gen. practice Charlotte, 1958-63; with Duke Power Co., 1963-97, v.p. finance, 1970-71, v.p., gen. counsel, 1971-75; sr. v.p. legal and finance Duke Power Co., Charlotte, 1975-82, exec. v.p., 1982-90, vice chmn., 1990-94, chmn., pres., CEO, 1994-97; also dir. Duke Power Co., 1997; chmn. emeritus Duke Energy Corp., Charlotte, 1997—; bd. dirs. NationsFunds, Inc., Aegis Ins. Svcs., Koltec Industries, Shaw Group, Inc. Editor-in-chief Duke Law Jour, 1957-58; contbr. articles to profl. jours. Bd. dirs. Carolinas Med. Ctr., Found. for the Carolinas. Capt. USMCR, 1954-56. Mem. AMA, N.C. Bar Assn., Charlotte Country Club. Methodist. Office: Duke Power Co 422 S Church St Charlotte NC 28242-0001

GRIGGS, BOBBIE JUNE, civic worker; b. Oklahoma City, Feb. 14, 1938; d. Robert Jefferson and Nora May (Green) Fish; m. Peter Harvey Griggs, Apr. 16, 1955; children: Diana (dec.), Terry, James. Grad. high sch., Salina, Kans. Commissary rep. Family Mag., Charleston AFB, S.C., 1976—; rep. Avon Corp., Charleston, S.C., 1976—; freelance demonstrator to USAF and USN orgns. Charleston, 1976—; rep. Salute Mag., Charleston AFB, 1986—; consumer edn. counselor Air Force-Navy exchs. Oster Kitchen Appliances, Charleston, 1987-90. Contbr. World's Largest Poem for Peace, 1991, Selected Works of our Best Poets, 1992, In A Different Light, 1992. Youth advisor, Charleston AFB, 1966-78; vol. doll distbn. program Salvation Army; clinic vol. ARC, Charleston AFB, 1967-75, chmn. family svcs. publicity and spl. projects, 1989; clinic vol. Clara Barton award, 1972; vol. Spoleto Festival, 1989—, Twin Oaks Retirement Ctr., 1992—, Chapel SUMMOM program, 1991—; asst. coord., publicity chmn. Family Svcs., 1967-83, named vol. of quarter, 1970, 72, 74, 76, named vol. of yr., 1970; active various scouting orgns., 1967—; asst. kindergarten Sunday sch. supt. Chapel I, 1966-68; active North Charleston (S.C.) Christian Women's Club, 1988—, hosp. chmn., mem. Charleston AFB Protestant Women's Club., 1965—; tchr. Bible sch., 1984-89; vol. tutor Lambs Elem., 1992, Trident Literacy Assn. (Laubach Literacy Action cert. 1992); coun. rep. Charleston AFB parish coun., 1988—; mem. Rocketeers Actors Group, Goals 2000 com. 1993—, Barnabas Outreach program, 1991—, Clown Ministry Charleston AFB, 1993—; chairperson Helping Hands Charleston AFB, 1991—, Voyagers Sunday Sch. Class Project, Summerville Homeless Shelter Charleston AFB, 1993—, Publicity Protestant Women, 1993—; vol. Lambs Elem., 1992—, Twin Oaks Retirement Ctr., 1992—, Barnabas Outreach Com., 1991—, Military Retirees, 1994—; counselor Jr. Achievement Program, 1994; mem. Charleston Raptor Ctr., 1996, S.C. Homeless Shelter Planning com., 1995-96, Am. Indian Heritage Coun., 1996; vol. tutor Lambs Elem., Charleston County, S.C., 1990—, jr. achievement counselor, 1992—, career day spkr., 1998. Recipient 1,000 Hours award Air Force Times, 1971, 1st Pl. award Designer Craftsman show, 1967-71, Dedicated Svc. award Charleston AFB, 1981, Hurricane Hugo Hero award, 1989, 1st Pl. award Bake-Off Contest YMCA, 1981, Hist. Charleston Trail Hike award Cub Scouts, 1988, Family Svcs. Vol. of Quar. award, 1990, Family Svcs. 6,000 Hour award, 1990, Golden Poet award, 1991, 1992, In a Different Light award Libr. Congress, 1991; named Enlisted Wife of Yr., Charleston AFB, 1974, Family Svcs. Vol. of Quarter Charleston AFB, 1990, Family Svcs. 6000 Hour award, 1991, Outstanding Vol. Svc. award Operation Desert Shield/Storm, 1991, Family Svcs. Spl. Recognition award, 1991, Appreciation acknowledgement Pres. of U.S., 1991, 98-99, First Lady Barbara Bush, 1992, Pres. of U.S., 1994, First Lady Hillary Clinton, 1994, Disting. Vol. award Charleston County Sch. Dist., 1995, Retiree Volunteer of the Quarter Charleston AFB, 1995, Vol. of Month Lambs Elem. Sch., 1995, Voting Slogan award Sec. Def., 1995, Family Svcs. Vol. of Quarter, 1996, Disting. Vol. award Lambs Elem., 1995-98, Family Mag. Poster/Display award Charleston Air Force Base, 1998, Disting. Vol. award Charleston County Sch. Bd., 1995-99, Vol. of Month Lambs Elem., 1998. Mem. Nat. Trust Hist. Preservation, Smithsonian Inst., Charleston AFB Non-Commd. Officers' Wives Club (pres. 1971-73, publicity chmn. 1969-70, wife of month 1967, wife of quarter 1973), Rocketeers Actors Group, Friends of Dock St.-Ushers. Avocations: cooking, sewing, collecting antiques, writing, decorating.

GRIGGS, CATHERINE M., educator; b. N.Y.C., Apr. 26, 1947; d. Laurence S. and Catherine A. Thorp; m. Clifford F. Griggs. MA, George Washington U., PhD. Prof. Exkerd Coll., St. Petersburg, Fla., 1994—. Mem. AAUP, AAUW, Phi Beta Kappa. Avocation: growing orchids. Office: Eckerd Coll 4200 54th Ave N Saint Petersburg FL 33711

GRIGGS, EMMA, management executive; b. Cleveland, Ark., Feb. 8, 1928; d. James and Frazier (Byers) Wallace; m. Augusta Griggs, Mar. 20, 1954 (dec.); children: Judy A., Terri V. *My two professional daughters, Judy A. Griggs and Terri V. Griggs have been and are still extremely influential in my professional career success. We, my daughters and I, have influenced one another's respective careers and in one another's personal lives.* Grad. H.S., Chgo. Pres., CEO Burlington No. Inc., Inglewood, Calif., 1986—. *I am privileged to be President and C.E.O of a successful company, "Burlington Northern, Inc.". My career began at BNI in January of 1986. Because of my contribution to the Republican Presidential Task Force in 1996, my name will be permanently enshrined on the National Republican Victory Monument, Ronald Reagan Republican Center, 425 Second Street N.E., Washington, D.C. I received the 1998 National Republican Victory Campaign Certificate of Valor for my outstanding devotion and loyalty to the Republican party. In 1997, I received from the Speaker of the House, the honorable Newt Gingrich, The Speaker's Citizen Task Force Certificate of Merit.* Republican. Avocations: reading, gardening, housekeeping.

GRIGGS, GAIL, marketing executive; b. 1937. Grad., U. Oreg., U. Chgo. Instr. Chgo. Art Inst., Roosevelt U., Chgo., Evergreen State U., Olympia, Wash.; with Griggs-Anderson, Inc., 1979—; now pres. Griggs-Anderson, Inc./Gartner Group. Office: Griggs-Anderson Inc/Gartner Group 308 SW 1st Ave Fl 4 Portland OR 97204-3400

GRIGGS, GARY BRUCE, earth sciences educator, oceanographer, geologist, consultant; b. Pasadena, Calif., Sept. 25, 1943; s. Dean Brayton and Barbara Jayne (Farmer) G.; m. Venetia Gina Bradfield, Jan. 11, 1980; children: Joel, Amy, Shannon, Callie, Cody. BA in Geology, U. Calif., Santa Barbara, 1965; PhD in Oceanography, Oreg. State U., 1968. Registered geologist, Calif.; cert. engr. geologist, Calif. Rsch. asst., NSF grad. fellow in oceanography Oreg. State U., 1965-68; from asst. prof. to prof. earth scis. U. Calif., Santa Cruz, 1969—; Fulbright fellow Inst. for Ocean & Fishing Rsch., Athens, Greece, 1974-75; oceanographer Joint U.S.A.-N.Z. Rsch. Program, 1980-81; chair earth scis. U. Calif., Santa Cruz, 1981-84; assoc. dean natural scis. U. Calif., 1992-95; from acting dir. to dir. Inst. of Marine Scis., 1991-99; vis. prof. semester at sea program U. Pitts., 1984-96; guest lectr. World Explorer Cruises, 1987. Author: (with others) Geologic Hazards, Resources and Environmental Planning, 1983, Living with the California Coast, 1985, Coastal Protection Structures, 1986, California's Coastal Hazards, 1992; mem. editl. bd. Jour. of Coastal Rsch., Shore and Beach, Geology; contbr. numerous articles to profl. jours. Fellow Geol. Soc. Am.; mem. Am. Geophys. Union, Am. Geol. Inst., Coastal Found., Am. Shore and Beach Preservation Assn. (bd. dirs. 1991—). Achievements include research in coastal processes; coastal erosion and protection; coastal engineering and hazards; sediment yield, transport and dispersal; geologic hazards and land use. Office: U Calif Inst Marine Scis Santa Cruz CA 95064

GRIGGS, JOHN BRONSON, technology executive; b. Houston, Feb. 18, 1972; s. Wade Garney and Janita (Frye) G.; m. Carolyn Ruth Naftzger, Aug. 3, 1996. BA, U. Tex., 1994. Analyst Southwest Bancorp, Houston, 1994-95, Simmons & Co. Internat., Houston, 1995-98; assoc. McKinsey & Co., Houston, 1998; dir. bus. devel. Campus Pipeline, Inc., Salt Lake City, 1998—. Founder, Houston Involvement Project, 1995-98; cons. Jr. Achievement, Houston and Salt Lake City, 1994—. Mem. U. Tex. Exes. Republican. Methodist. Avocations: mountain climbing, skiing, hunting, golf, reading. Email: jgriggs@campuspipeline.com. Home: 900 W Bitner Rd # E27 Salt Lake City UT 84098

GRIGGS, JOHN ROBERT, financial and consumer credit services executive; b. Franklin, N.J., Oct. 19, 1949; s. Frank E. and Verna L. (Geddes) G.; m. Sally Shutt, June 15, 1974; children: Brian, Dan, Carole. BS in Acctg., U. Tulsa, 1971, MBA, 1973. Cert. fin. and ops. prin. Nat. Assn. Securities Dealers, consumer credit exec. Fin. analyst Citicorp Person to Person, St. Louis, 1974, dir. fin. planning and analysis and various positions, 1975-78, chief of staff, 1978-79; sr. area mgr. Citicorp Person to Person, Seattle, 1979; area v.p. Citicorp Acceptance Co., Seattle, 1979-82; v.p., chief fin. officer, treas. Citicorp Acceptance Co., St. Louis, 1982-85; v.p. ops. Citicorp Acceptance Co., Atlanta, 1985-86; v.p., gen. mgr. Household Fin. Svcs., Chgo., 1986-91, sr. v.p., 1991-93; exec. v.p., CFO, treas., dir. Hamilton Investments, subs. Household Internat., Chgo., 1993-94; v.p. Household Internat., Prospect Heights, Ill., 1994-96; sr. v.p. nat. ops. mgr. Banc One Credit Corp., Columbus, Ohio, 1996-97; exec. v.p., COO First Merchant's Acceptance Corp., Deerfield, Ill., 1997, mgmt. cons., 1997-98; divsn. pres. First Plus Fin., Dallas, 1998-99; chmn., bd. dirs. Consumer Credit Counseling Svc. Greater Chgo. (cert. consumer credit exec.). Coach Little League baseball, St. Louis, Atlanta, Chgo.; advisor Cub Scouts, Atlanta; trustee, treas. Homeowner's Assn., St. Louis; mem., bd. dirs., treas. Barrington (Ill.) Youth Baseball. Mem. Am. Fin. Svcs. Assn. (bd. dirs., exec. com.), Nat. Second Mortgage Assn. (bd. dirs., exec. com.), Internat. Credit Assn., Alpha Phi Omega, Omicron Delta Kappa, Beta Gamma Sigma. Avocations: softball, racquetball.

GRIGGS, LEONARD LEROY, JR., federal agency administrator; b. Norfolk, Va., Oct. 13, 1931; s. Leonard LeRoy and Mary (Blair) G.; m. Denise Ziegler, Mar. 18, 1977; children: Margaret Rosalyn, Virginia Lorraine Williams, Julia Blair Havey, Deborah Branham Taylor. BS, U.S. Mil. Acad., 1954; MS in Aero. Engring., Air Force Inst. Tech., 1960; MS in Internat. Affairs, George Washington U., 1967; disting. grad., Naval War Coll., 1967, Army War Coll., 1971. Registered profl. engr., Mo. Commd. 2d lt. U.S. Army, 1954; advanced through grades to col. USAF, 1970; served in Vietnam, ret., 1977; dir. Lambert St. Louis Internat. Airport, 1977-87; v.p. Ross & Baruzzini, Inc., 1987-89, Bangert Bros. Constrn. Co., St. Louis and Denver, 1989—; asst. adminstr. for airports FAA, Washington, 1990-93; airport dir. St. Louis Internat. Airport, 1993—; adj. prof. St. Louis U.; apptd. to Nat. Civil Aviation Rev. Commn., 1997. Bd. dirs. USO, St. Louis/Lambert, Airports Coun. Internat., 1997-98. Decorated Silver Star, D.F.C. with 4 oak leaf clusters, Bronze Star, Meritorious Service medal, Air medal with 22 oak leaf clusters, Purple Heart, Air Force Commendation medal with 2 oak leaf clusters, Army Commendation medal; Medal of Honor; Medal of Gallantry (Vietnam); recipient Aviation Engring. Safety award FAA, 1979. Mem. Airport Operators Coun. Internat., Am. Assn. Airport Execs., Profl. Engring. Soc. St. Louis, Order of Dadelians, St. Louis Air Force Assn., Engr. Club, Mo. Athletic Club, Army Navy Club, Univ. Club., Order DeMolay. Home: 4400 Lindell Blvd Apt 17M Saint Louis MO 63108-2427 Office: Lambert-St Louis Intl Airport PO Box 10212 Lambert Airport MO 63145

GRIGGS, ROBERT CHARLES, physician; b. Wilmington, Del., Jan. 8, 1939; s. Albert Bertin and Virginia (Robertson) G.; m. Rosalyne Hoggard, June 16, 1964; children—Jennifer, Heather. A.B., U. Del., 1960; M.D., U. Pa., 1964. Intern Case Western Reserve U., Cleve., 1964-65; resident Case Western Reserve U., 1965-66, Nat. Inst. Neurol. Disease and Blindness, Bethesda, Md., 1966-68; resident in medicine, neurology U. Rochester, N.Y., 1968-71; prof. neurology, medicine, pathology, pediatrics, co-dir. neuromuscular disease ctr. U. Rochester, 1972—, chmn. dept. neurology, 1986; practice medicine specializing in neurology Rochester, 1971—; hon. cons. Univ. Coll. Hosp., London, 1981-82. Author: Evaluation and Treatment of Myopathies; editor in chief Neurology, 1997—. Served to lt. comdr. USPHS, 1966-68. ACP Rsch. and Teaching grantee, 1971-74. Office: Strong Meml Hosp Dept Neurology 601 Elmwood Ave Dept Rochester NY 14642-0002

GRIGGS, RUTH MARIE, retired journalism educator, writer, publications consultant; b. Linton, Ind., Aug. 11, 1911; d. Roy Evans Price and Mary Blanche (Hays) P.; m. Paul Philip Griggs, Aug. 4, 1940. BS, Butler U., 1933; postgrad. U. So. Calif., 1938, Northwestern U., 1939; MA, U. Wyo., 1944. Cert. tchr. journalism, English, speech, bus. edn. Travel writer Indpls. Star, 1927-37; summer reporter Worthington Times, Ind., 1928-33; journalism, speech tchr. Warren Cen. High Sch., Indpls., 1937-37; tchr. bus. edn., journalism Greene Twp. High Sch., South Bend, Ind., 1937-38; tchr. journalism, English, bus. edn. Howe High Sch., Indpls., 1938-46; tchr. journalism Butler U., Indpls., 1946-48, evenings 1972-76; dir. publs. Broad Ripple High Sch., Indpls., 1948-77; summer journalism workshop instr. numerous univs. 1949-80. Author: History of Broad Ripple, 1968; co-author: Handbook for High School Journalism, 1951; Teacher's Guide to High School Journalism, 1965, Marquette Memoirs, 1996. Dow Jones Newspaper Fund fellow U. Minn., 1967; named Nat. Journalism Tchr. of Yr. Wall Street Jour., 1968, Woman of Achievement Woman's Press Club of Ind., 1984; recipient Rabb award Women's Press Club of Ind., 1988, Disting. Alumni award Butler U. Alumni Bd., 1989. Mem. Journalism Edn. Assn. (v.p., pres. 1963-69, Towley award 1965), Women in Communications (pres. Indpls. 1969-70, Wright award 1969, Kleinhenz award 1978), Nat. Fed. Press Women (youth projects bd. 1979-87, Recognition award 1991), Columbia Scholastic Press Assn. (Gold Key award 1964, Golden Crown 1975, life mem. 1977), Ind. High Sch. Advisers Assn. (pres. 1972, Sengenberger award 1965), Delta Zeta (Ind. Woman of Yr. 1984). Republican. Presbyterian. Home: 8140 Township Line Rd Apt 3405 Indianapolis IN 46260-5863

GRIGGS, STEPHEN LAYNG, management consultant; b. Morristown, N.J., Nov. 30, 1947; s. Paul and Frances G.; m. Margaret Anne Hastings, Nov. 27, 1970; children: Jocelyn Hastings, Diana Hastings. BSME, Villanova (Pa.) U., 1969; MS, MIT, 1971; MBA, Harvard U., 1974. Mem. tech. staff Bell Telephone Labs., Holmdel, N.J., 1969-72; div. mgr. Norlin Industries, Carlisle, Pa., 1974-77, contr., chief fin. officer, 1977-79; sr. assoc. Booz Allen & Hamilton, N.Y.C., 1979-82; v.p. ops., chief fin. officer Phys. Acoustics Corp., Princeton, N.J., 1982-83; sr. ptrn. KSM Group Inc., Short Hills, N.J., 1983-88; pres. The Tewksbury Group Inc., Oldwick, N.J., 1988—. Mem. IEEE, Am. Inst. Ultrasound Medicine, Am. Assn. Clin. Chemists, Soc. Competitive Intelligence Profls., Parenteral Drug Assn., Med. Mktg. Assn., Am. Soc. Materials, Soc. for Advancement of Materials and Process Engring., Am. Soc. for Microbiology, Am. Soc. Echocardiography, Hunterdon County Hist. Soc., Geneal. Soc. N.J., Nat. Geneal. Soc., New Eng. Hist. Geneal. Soc., Controlled Release Soc., Sigma Xi, Tau Beta Pi, Pi Tau Sigma. Republican. Episcopalian. Avocations: trout fishing, architecture. Office: Tewksbury Group Inc PO Box 48 Oldwick NJ 08858-0048

GRIGONIS, RICHARD WILLIAM, technical editor; b. Passaic, N.J., Sept. 24, 1956; s. William Vincent and Louise Medla (DiServio) G. BA in Journalism, Rowan U., 1978. Prodn. asst. Sesame Street prodn. dept. Children's TV Workshop, N.Y.C., 1980-85; Wang office info. sys. technician Peat, Marwick, N.Y.C., 1985-86; MIS dir. Squadron, Ellenoff, Plesent & Sheinfeld, N.Y.C., 1987-94; tech. editor Computer Tel. Mag., N.Y.C., 1994-98, chief tech., editor, 1998—; pres. Grigonis Rsch., Harrison, N.J., 1992—; cons., multimedia programmer AT&T Bell Labs., Holmdel, N.J., 1992—. Author: Fault Resilient PCs, 1996, Encyclopedia of Computer Telephony, 1999. Avocations: writing, photography. Office: Miller Freeman 12 W 21st St New York NY 10010-6902

GRIGORIAN, MARCOS, artist, art gallery director; b. Krapotkin, Krasnadar, Russia, Dec. 25, 1924; came to U.S., 1962; d. Bagrat and Shoushanik (Aloyan) G. BA, Acad. Fine Arts, Rome, 1954. Founder, executor Iranian First Biennial, Tehran, Iran, 1957; del. Iranian Pavilion to Venice (Italy) Biennial, 1958; dir. Universal Gallery, Mpls., 1963-64; prof. arts Minnetonka Ctr. of Arts, Wayzata, Minn., 1963-64; guest prof. arts Tehran U., 1970-78; dir. Gorky Gallery, N.Y.C., 1980-98; lectr. Iranian Folk Art, Tehran, 1958-78; founder Near East Mus. Nat. Instn., Yerevan, Armenia, 1993. One-man shows in N.Y.C., rome, Paris, Tehran, Iran, Mpls., Yerevan, Bochum; exhibited in group shows at Walter Art Ctr., 1963, Johnson Mus., Ithaca, N.Y., 1981, Near East Mus., Tehran, Gorky Gallery, N.Y.C., 1988, Mus. Modern Art N.Y., others. Recipient Hon. Citizen award Mayor of Yerevan, 1994. Dem. Home: 70-33 Manse St Forest Hills NY 11375

GRIGSBY, HENRY JEFFERSON, JR., editor; b. Denver, Dec. 29, 1930; s. Henry Jefferson and Thelma Pearl (Nispel) G.; m. Joan Shirley Rinker, Sept. 6, 1953 (div. 1973); children: Kevin, Lisa, Lincoln. B.A., U. Colo., 1954. Reporter Sterling (Colo.) Jour.-Advocate, 1954-55; reporter, Sunday editor Lewiston (Idaho) Morning Tribune, 1955-57; reporter Denver bur. UPI, 1958-59, mgr., 1961-66; bur. mgr. UPI, Cheyenne, Wyo., 1959-61; S.W.

div. news editor Dallas bur. UPI, 1966-69, mgr. San Francisco bur., 1969-72; night mng. editor UPI, N.Y.C., 1972-74; mng. editor for news UPI, 1974-75; assoc. editor Forbes mag., N.Y.C., 1976-77, sr. editor, 1977-81, exec. editor, 1981-86; sr. editor Fin. World mag., N.Y.C., 1988-90. Pres. Dallas chpt. Nat. Soc. Autistic Children, 1967-69. Served with USAF, 1950-52. Mem. N.Y. Fin. Writers Assn., Sigma Delta Chi, Phi Delta Theta. Home: 160 W 16th St Apt 1E New York NY 10011-6267

GRIGSBY, PERRY WAYNE, physician; b. Cadiz, Ky., Aug. 11, 1952; s. Oscar McAtee and Irene Grigsby; m. Susan; children: Allison, Amy, James, Thomas, Isabella, Barbara, David, Susan. BS in Zoology, U. Ky., 1974, MS in Physics, 1978, MD, 1982; MBA, Washington U., 1990. Intern, then resident Barnes Hosp., St. Louis, 1982-84; asst. chief resident Barnes Hosp., 1984-85, chief resident in radiology, 1985-86; prof. radiology Washington U./Barnes Hosp., 1986—; cons. in field to hosps. Contbr. articles to profl. jours. Vol. Am. Cancer Soc., St. Louis, 1983—. Recipient Am. Cancer Soc. Clin. Oncology award, 1987—; Am. Radium Soc. grantee, 1986, others. Mem. AMA (Physicians Recognition award 1985), Am. Assn. of Physicists in Medicine, Am. Coll. Radiology, Am. Soc. Clin. Oncology, Am. Soc. Therapeutic Radiology and Oncology. Avocations: reading, investing, woodwork, music. Home: 3 Elm Ave Saint Louis MO 63122-4836 Office: Barnes Hosp 510 S Kingshighway Blvd Saint Louis MO 63110-1016

GRIGSBY, R. KEVIN, social work and psychiatry educator; b. Pitts., June 27, 1954; s. Herbert and Mary Ann (Potter) G.; m. Martha Ann Wilcox, June 20, 1987; children: Samuel Wilcox, Emily Jean. BA in Philosophy, U. Ga., 1976; MSW, Fla. State U., 1981; D Social Work, U. Pa., 1990. Lic. clin. social worker, Ga. Forensic counselor, program supr. Peace River Ctr., Bartow, Fla., 1981-83; rsch. asst. U. Pa., Phila., 1983-84, counselor, evaluator, 1984-85; clin. instr. Yale U., New Haven, 1985-88, asst. clin. prof., 1988-91; asst. prof. U. Ga., Athens, 1991-93; dir. R&D Med. Coll. Ga. Telemedicine Ctr., Augusta, 1993—; prof. psychiatry and health behavior Med. Coll. Ga., Augusta, 1995—; bd. dirs. Child Enrichment, Inc., Augusta, 1995—; cons. Newton County Dept. Family and Child Svcs., Covington, Ga., 1993-96. Editor: Advancing Family Preservation Practice, 1993; book rev. editor Telemedicine Jour., 1995-99. Mem. NASW (Ga. chpt., Social Worker of Yr. Augusta chpt. 1997), Soc. for Social Work And Rsch. Office: Med Coll Ga Telemedicine Ctr 100 E Ct Augusta GA 30904-3047

GRIGSBY-STEPHENS, KLARON, corporate executive; b. East Prairie, Mo., Feb. 15, 1952; d. Claron Grigsby and Sylvia (Grigery) Oliver; m. Richard Earl Stephens, Aug. 13, 1986. Exec. asst. Quasar Petroleum Corp., Ft. Worth, 1974-80; sales mgr. ITT Life Ins. Corp., Ft. Worth, 1980-83; media buyer Boca Blue Star, Boca Raton, Fla., 1983-84; video editor Video Workshop, Pompano Beach, Fla., 1984-85; pres. Stephens Alfa Corp., Pompano Beach, 1985—. Contbr. articles to profl. jours., also numerous poems. Sgt. USAF, 1970-74. Mem. Alfa Romeo Owners Club, Challenger Ctr. (Washington, hon.). Avocations: collecting antiques, classic automobiles, gardening, flutist, poetry. Office: 1321 S Dixie Hwy W Pompano Beach FL 33060-8520

GRIJALVA, J. R., police chief. Profl. designation, Law Enforce. Mgmt. Inst. Tex., 1998. Acting police chief El Paso Police Dept., 1998—. Office: 911 Rayner St El Paso TX 79903

GRIJNS, LAINE, investment company executive. Chmn. bd. Internat. Nederlanden, N.Y.C.; CEO Patricof & Co. Capital Corp. N.Y.C.; sr. adv. BNY Capital Mkts., Inc., N.Y.C., 1998—. Office: BNY Capital Mkts Inc 445 Park Ave 12th fl New York NY 10022-2606*

GRILICHES, ZVI, economist, educator; b. Kaunas, Lithuania, Sept. 12, 1930; came to U.S., 1951, naturalized, 1959; m. Diane Asseo, Apr. 26, 1953; children: Eve, Marc. Student, Hebrew U., Jerusalem, 1950-51; BS, U. Calif., Berkeley, 1953, MS, 1954; MA, U. Chgo., 1955, PhD, 1957; PhD (hon.), Hebrew U., 1991. From asst. prof. to assoc. prof. econs. U. Chgo., 1956-64, prof., 1964-69; prof. Harvard U., 1969-78, Nathaniel Ropes prof. polit. economy, 1979-87, chmn. dept. econs., 1980-83, Paul M. Warburg prof. of econs., 1987—; rsch. assoc. Nat. Bur. Econ. Rsch., 1959-60, 78—; vis. prof. Econometric Inst., The Netherlands Sch. Econs., Rotterdam, 1963-64, Hebrew U., 1964, 72, 77, 84, 87, Ecole des Hautes Etudes en Sciences Sociales, Paris, 1984, Tel Aviv U., 1991, 95, New Economic Sch., Moscow, 1995, also adv. bd. 1991—; trustee Falk Inst. Econ. Rsch., Israel, 1975—; mem. internat. adv. com. Patinkin Sch. Econs., Hebrew U., Israel, 1996—, Econ. Edn. & Rsch. Consortium on Russia, 1996—; cons. Rand Corp., Brookings Instn.; bd. govs. Fed Res. System, Ford Found., NSF; mem. Pres. Sci. Adv. Coun. Panel on Youth, 1970-73; mem. selection com. for Frank E. Seidman Disting. Award in Polit. Economy, 1992-93; mem. com. U.S./U.S.S.R. Exchanges, 1988-90; appointed mem. adv. com to study consumer price index U.S. Senate Finance Com., 1995-97. Co-author: Economics of Scale and the Form of the Production Function, 1971; author: Technology, Education and Productivity: Early Papers with Notes to Subsequent Literature, 1988, R&D and Productivity: The Econometric Evidence, 1998, Practicing Econometrics: Essays in Method and Application, 1998; editor: Price Indexes and Quality Change, 1972, Income Distribution and Economic Inequality, 1978, Handbook of Econometrics, 1983, 3d edit., 1986, R&D, Patents, and Productivity, 1984, Output Measurement in the Service Sectors, 1992, Productivity Issues in Services at the Micro Level, 1993; co-editor Econometrica, 1969-77; adv. bd. Jour. Applied Econometrics, 1985—; contbr. numerous articles to profl. jours. With Israeli Army, 1948-49. Fellow AAAS, Am. Acad. Arts and Scis., Econometric Soc. (pres. 1975), Am. Statis. Assn., Am. Farm Econ. Assn. (award of merit 1958-60, 65, Disting. fellow 1991), Am. Agrl. Econ. Assn.; mem. NAS (com. on ability testing 1979-81, com. on nat. stats. 1980-82, com. on sci. engring. and pub. policy 1983-88), Am. Econ. Assn. (mem. exec. com. 1979-81, 92-95, v.p. 1984, J.B. Clark medal 1965, pres. 1993, Disting. fellow 1995). Home: 62 Shepard St Cambridge MA 02138-1523 Office: Harvard U Dept Econ Cambridge MA 02138

GRILL, LAWRENCE J., lawyer, accountant, corporate/banking executive; b. Chgo., Nov. 5, 1936; s. Samuel S. and Evelyn (Wollack) G.; m. Joan V. Krimston, Dec. 16, 1961; children: Steven Eric, Elizabeth Anne. B.S. with honors, U. Ill., 1958; postgrad., U. Chgo., 1959-60; LL.B., Northwestern U., 1963. Bar: Ill. 1963, Calif. 1965; C.P.A., Ill. Audit and tax mgr. Arthur Anderson & Co., Chgo., 1958-60; with firm Aaron, Aaron, Schimberg & Hess, Chgo., 1963-64, Gendel, Raskoff, Shapiro & Quittner, Los Angeles, 1964-66; sec., gen. counsel Traid Corp., Los Angeles, 1966-69; v.p., sec., gen. counsel Kaufman & Broad, Inc., Los Angeles, 1969-78; pres. Kaufman & Broad Asset Mgmt., dir. subs.; v.p., sec., gen. counsel AM Internat., Inc., Century City, 1979-82, dir. subs.; sr. v.p., group ops. officer, dir. subs. Wickes Cos., Inc., Santa Monica, 1982-85; acting chief exec. officer, chief operating officer, mem. exec. com. Barco of Calif., Gardena, 1985-86; pres. Lawrence J. Grill & Assocs., L.A., Calif., 1985-94; pres., CEO and dir. Pan Am. Bank and United Pan Am. Fin. Corp., San Mateo, Calif., 1994—; chmn., pres., CEO Universal Savs. Bank, Orange, Calif., 1988-90; cons. bd. dirs. World Trade Bank, N.A., 1992, Marathon Nat. Bank, 1992-93; spl. advisor to Fed. Home Loan Bank Bd. San Francisco, Fed. Deposit Ins. Co. for Distressed Savs. Instns., 1986-88; arbitrator Am. Arbitration Assn. Served with AUS, 1958-59. Home: 790 Bromfield Rd San Mateo CA 94402-1115 Office: 1300 S El Camino Real San Mateo CA 94402-2963

GRILL, STEPHEN ELLIOTT, neuroscientist, neurologist, educator; b. N.Y.C., May 23, 1957; s. Bernard Grill and Annette Spector; m. Marcie Karen Weil, Sept. 1, 1991; children: Gabriella, Benjamin. BS cum laude, Union Coll., 1979; PhD, Northwestern U., 1986, MD, 1987. Bd. cert. neurology. Resident neurology Washington U., St. Louis, 1988-91; fellow NIH, Bethesda, Md., 1991-93; sr. clin. investigator NIH, Bethesda, 1993-95; neurologist, neuroscientist Neurology Specialists, Columbia, Md., 1995—; instr. Johns Hopkins U., Balt., 1996—. Contbr. articles to profl. jours. Med. advisor Greater Washington Dystonia Support Group, 1995—, Howard County Ataxia Support Group, Columbia, 1998—. Comdr. USPHS, 1991-95. Mem. Soc. for Neurosci., Movement Disorder Soc. Democrat. E-mail: sgrill@pol.net. Office: Neurology Specialists DA 10770 Hickory Ridge Rd Columbia MD 21044

GRILLER, DAVID, economics and technology consultant; b. London, England, May 29, 1948; came to Can., 1977; s. Lewis and Renee (Kellinger) G.; m. Alexis Myers, Aug. 22, 1971; children: Hannah, Mark, Nadia. BS, U. Coll. London, 1969, PhD, 1972. Salters Co. fellow London, 1973; postdoctoral fellow NRC of Can., Ottawa, 1973-75, head organic chemistry, 1977-91; mgmt. cons. Deloitte, Haskins and Sells, London, 1975-77; sr. ptnr. Secor Inc., Ottawa, Ont., Can.; 1991—. Author over 180 sci. papers and books. Recipient CNC-Iupac award Internat. Union Pure and Applied Chemists, 1984, Rutherford medal Royal Soc. Can., 1986, Organic Reaction Mechanisms award Royal Soc. of Chemistry, 1986. Fellow Royal Soc. Can., Can. Inst. Chemistry (Merck Sharp and Dohme award 1985). Avocations: squash, skiing. Home: 2026 Delmar Ct, Ottawa, ON Canada K1H 5R6 Office: Groupe Secor, 155 Queen St 8th Fl, Ottawa, ON Canada K1P 6L1

GRILLER, GORDON MOORE, court administrator; b. Sioux City, Iowa, Feb. 3, 1944; s.Joseph Edwards and Arlene (Searles) G. m. Helen Mary Friederichs, aug. 20, 1966; children: Heather, Chad. BA in Political Sci., U. Minn., 1966, MA in Pub. Affairs, 1969. Mgnt. analyst Hennepin County Adminstr., Mpls., 1968-72; asst. court adminstr. Hennepin County Municipal Ct., Mpls., 1972-77, ct. adminstr., 1977-78; judicial dist. adminstr. 2nd Dist. Ct. Minn., St. Paul, 1978-87; ct. adminstr. Superior Ct. Ariz., Phoenix, Ariz., 1987—; bd. dirs. Nat. Ctr. State Cts., 1997—. Vice-chmn. Bloomington Sch. Bd., Minn., 1981-87. Sgt. USAAF, 1968-74 Res. Recipient Warren E. Burger award Inst. Ct. Mgnt.,1988, Leadership Fellows award Bush Leadership Program, 1974. Mem. Nat. Assn. Trial Ct. Adminstrs.(pres. 1983-84), Ariz. Ct. Assn., Nat. Assn Ct. Mgmt., Am. Judicature Soc., (bd. dirs. 1997—). Lutheran. Avocations: running, kyaking, racquetball, scuba diving. Home: 8507 E San Jacinto Dr Scottsdale AZ 85258-2576 Office: Superior Ct Ariz 201 W Jefferson St Fl 4 Phoenix AZ 85003-2243

GRILLI, CYNTHIA DYAN, artist, educator; b. Point Pleasant, N.J., June 29, 1970; d. Donald Anthony and Lesley-Ann (Carpenter) G. BFA in Illustration, R.I. Sch. Design, Providence, 1992; MFA in Painting, N.Y. Acad. Art, 1994. Adj. asst. prof. art St. John's U., Jamaica, N.Y., 1994—; dir. Gallery On 2nd, N.Y.C., 1996-97. Grantee Elizabeth Greenshields Found., Montreal, Que., Can., 1994, 96. Office: St John's Univ 8000 Utopia Pkwy Jamaica NY 11432-1343

GRILLY, EDWARD ROGERS, physicist; b. Cleve., Dec. 30, 1917; s. Charles B. and Julia (Varady) G.; m. Mary Witholter, Dec. 14, 1942 (dec. 1971); children: David, Janice; m. Juliamarie Andreen Langham, Feb. 1, 1973. BA, Ohio State U., 1940, PhD, 1944. Rsch. scientist Carbide & Carbon Chemicals Corp., Oak Ridge, Tenn., 1944-45; asst. prof. Chemistry U. N.H., Durham, 1946-47; mem. staff U. Calif. Nat. Lab., Los Alamos, N.Mex., 1947-80, cons., 1980—. Contbr. articles to books and profl. jours. Mem. N.Mex. House of Reps., Santa Fe, 1967-70, Los Alamos County Coun., Los Alamos, 1976-78. Mem. Am. Physical Soc., Kiwanis Club, Los Alamos Golf Club (pres. 1974-75). Republican. Avocation: golf. Home: 705 43rd St Los Alamos NM 87544-1807 *The key to my life is discovery. It always amazes me how learning can be so fascinating. Of course, the ultimate is discovery in my own vocation-physics-whether it is of my own doing or learning of a colleague's work. But, I also found that intense involvement in community work can lead to surprising results.*

GRIM, PATRICIA ANN, banker; b. Everett, Pa., Sept. 7, 1940; d. Harry Grant and Nellie Elizabeth (Koontz) Foor; m. James Woodrow Grim, Feb. 21, 1970. Student, Am. Inst. Banking, Rolling Meadows, Ill., Bank Adminstrn. Inst., The Bus. Women's Tng. Inst. Sec. William H. Snyder, Atty. at Law, Bedford, Pa., 1958-60; sec., loan teller First Nat. Bank of Everett, Pa., 1960-70; teller Orrstown (Pa.) Bank, 1970-81, asst. cashier, asst. sec., 1981-82, v.p., asst. sec., 1982-94; mgr. Mellon Bank, Shippensburg, Pa., 1994—. Recipient Family Tng. Hour Leader of Yr. award Ch. of God State of Pa., Layman of Yr. award, 1979; nat. nominee Layperson of Yr., 1984. Mem. Ch. of God. Office: Mellon Bank 153 W Orange St Shippensburg PA 17257-1750

GRIM, SAMUEL ORAM, chemistry educator; b. Landisburg, Pa., Mar. 11, 1935; s. Oram Michael and Esther Blanche (Gable) G.; m. Faith H. Rojahn, June 8, 1957 (div. 1982); children: Stephen W., Amy R., Lucy G.; m. Caren L. Klarman, Mar. 11, 1983 (div. 1993); 1 child, Christina K. B.S., Franklin and Marshall Coll., 1956; Ph.D., MIT, 1960. Faculty U. Md., College Park, 1960—; prof. chemistry U. Md., 1968—, chmn. inorganic chemistry div., 1970-77, 80-86, chmn. Inorganic Divsn., 1995-96, assoc. chmn., chemistry dept., 1996-98; program officer in inorganic chemistry NSF, 1988-90. Contbr. articles to profl. jours. Union Carbide Co. scholar, 1954-56; NSF fellow, 1958-60; summer teaching fellow, 1960; research fellow Imperial Coll., London, 1961-62; Sir John Cass's Found. sr. research fellow City of London Poly., 1979-80. Fellow Am. Inst. Chemists, Royal Soc. Chemistry (London); mem. Am. Chem. Soc., AAAS, N.Y. Acad. Scis., Internat. Union Pure and Applied Chemistry, Internat. Coun. Main Group Chemistry, Chem. Soc. Washington, Phi Beta Kappa, Sigma Xi (Sci. Achievement award 1983), Phi Lambda Upsilon, Alpha Chi Sigma. Republican. Clubs: Mason, Terrapin (College Park). Home: 4816 Broad Brook Dr Bethesda MD 20814-3906 Office: U Md Dept Chemistry College Park MD 20742-2021

GRIMALDI, JAMES THOMAS, investment fund executive; b. Elizabeth, N.J., Dec. 8, 1928; s. Anthony and Helen (Bernatt) G.; m. Norma Miriello, June 17, 1951; children: Patricia Ann, Pamela Gay, Donna Lynne. BS in Econs., U. Pa., 1951; MBA, Columbia U., 1955. CLU, 1964. Br. acct. Watson-Flagg Engring. Co., Paterson, N.J., 1953-56; from agt. to sr. asst. dist. mgr. Met. Life Ins. Co., Paterson, Ridgewood, N.J., 1956-61; reg. agy. dir., asst. v.p. Am. Amicable Life Ins. Co., Ft. Lauderdale, Fla., 1961-66; v.p. mktg. Inland Life Ins. Co., Chgo., 1966-69; exec. v.p. Peoples Home Life Ins. Co. Ind., 1969-71, Fed. Life & Casualty Co., Battle Creek, 1970-71; pres., chief exec. officer, also dir. Peoples Home Life Ins. Co. of Ind., 1971-74; pres., CEO, bd. dirs. Fed. Life & Casualty Co., 1971-74, Keystone Co., Boston, 1974-76, Cornerstone Fin. Svcs., Inc., Boston, 1974-76; exec. v.p. sales Keystone Custodian Funds, Inc., Boston, 1974-76; engaged in pvt. investments, 1976—; mem. faculty De Paul U., Chgo., 1969. 1st lt. USAF, 1951-53. Recipient Spl. Tribute as Outstanding Citizen, State of Mich., 1974. Mem. Sales Mktg. Execs. Internat., Am. Soc. CLU, Nat. Assn. Life Underwriters, Am. Mktg. Assn., Assn. Individual Investors, Life Assn. Mich. (pres. 1973, exec. com.), Nat. Assn. Security Dealers, Acad. Polit. Sci., U. Pa. Alumni Assn., Columbia U. Alumni Assn. Home: 4904 Sentinel Post Rd Charlotte NC 28226-7445

GRIMALDI, NICHOLAS LAWRENCE, social services administrator; b. Stamford, Conn., Mar. 15, 1950; s. Dominick Lawrence and Marion Theresa (Colucci) G. Student, Manhattan Coll., 1967-70, Fordham U., 1999—. Bus. mgr. DeBare Saunders, Ltd., N.Y.C., 1973; account exec. The Haas Group, N.Y.C., 1973-76; registrar Am. Ballet Theatre Sch., N.Y.C., 1976-79; exec. assoc. Nat. Assn. Regional Ballet, N.Y.C., 1979-87; exec. dir. Nikolais/Louis Found. for Dance, Inc., N.Y.C., 1987-89; dir. devel. Hartley House, N.Y.C., 1989-93; dir. ann. campaigns Fountain House, Inc., N.Y.C., 1993—; cons. mgmt. and fund raising; mem. steering com./pastoral coun. Ch. of St. Francis Xavier, N.Y.C., 1993-97. Office: Fountain House Inc 425 W 47th St New York NY 10036-2397

GRIMALDI, VINCE, artist; b. N.Y.C., July 21, 1929; s. Vincenzo and Sebastiana Grimaldi. Student, Art Students League, N.Y.C., 1947-50, New Sch. Social Rsch., N.Y.C., 1952-55. One-man shows at Falmouth (Mass.) Art Guild, 1968, Michael's Gallery, N.Y.C., 1976, Soho Photo Gallery, N.Y.C., 1977, Cin. Art Acad., 1984, Claire Dunphy Studio, N.Y.C., 1986, 89, Ednl. Alliance, N.Y.C., 1989, 92, Monaco Studio, Providence, 1995, Café La France, Providence, 1996, Providence Art Club, 1998, Central Congregational Ch., 1998; exhibited in group shows at East Hampton Gallery, N.Y.C., 1967, Feiner Gallery, N.Y.C., 1967, Cape Cod Assn., Hyannis, Mass., 1967, Falmouth Art Guild, 1967, Soho Photo Gallery, N.Y.C., 1975-76, Floating Found. Photography, N.Y.C., 1982, Donnell Libr., N.Y.C., 1985, Kenkeleba Gallery, N.Y.C., 1985, N.Y. State Mus., N.Y.C., 1986, New Rochelle (Conn.) Mus., 1986, Ctrl. Pk. Gallery, N.Y.C., 1986, Silvermine Gallery, Conn., 1987, Window Box Gallery, N.Y.C., 1987, 89, Ch. Ctr., N.Y.C., 1988, Claire Dunphy Studio, N.Y.C., 1988, AMMO Gallery, Bklyn., 1989, Vasarely Mus., Budapest, Hungary, 1991, Forum Gallery, Jamestown Coll., N.Y., 1992, Madrid, 1993, Sarajevo, Bosnia, 1993, Glasgow (Scotland) Gallery, 1994, West Broadway Gallery, N.Y.C., 1994, Sarah Doyle Gallery, Providence, 1995, 97, Providence Art Club, 1996, 97, others; represented in permanent collections at Bklyn. Mus. Art, N.Y.C., Butler Inst. Am. Art, Hambidge Ctr. Arts, Tate Gallery, London, Met. Mus. Art, UCLA, N.Y. Pub. Libr., Newark Pub. Libr., Mus. Modern Art, N.Y.C., Musee Antibes France, Louis Held Collections, pvt. collections; illustrator: 2,000 Years in Rome, 1967, Celebrating the Statue of Libery, 1986, (slide talks) Galapagos Islands, 1993; commn. photographic portraits of writer, musicians & actors. With U.S. Army, 1951-53, Korea. Avocations: swimming, mail art, slide talks. Home: 532 Charles St Providence RI 02904-2237

GRIMBALL, CAROLINE GORDON, sales professional; b. Columbia, S.C., Dec. 21, 1946; d. John and Caroline Grimball. B.A. in Polit. Sci., Converse Coll., 1968; postgrad., S.C. Law Sch., 1968-69. Asst. buyer, buyer Rich's, Inc., Atlanta, 1971-78, spl. events fashion coordinator, Columbia, S.C., 1978-83; gen. mdse. mgr. Rackes, Inc., Columbia, 1983-84, Parasol Boutique, Columbia, 1984-86; retail cons. Retail Mdsg. Service Automation, Columbia, 1986-88; sales rep. Palmetto Promotions, 1989-93; retail mdse. supr. Riverbanks Zoo & Garden, 1993-94; retail mgr., buyer Riverbanks Zoo & Garden, 1994—. Pres. Columbia Action Coun., 1990-92; bd. dirs. Palmetto Leadership Coun., 1991-92, Palmetto State Orch. Assn., Columbia, 1979-89, Women's Symphony Assn., Columbia, 1985; com. chmn. Columbia Action Coun., 1984-85, exec. com., 1989-92; Piedmont Found. S.C., Columbia Classical Ballet. Named one of Outstanding Young Women Am., 1979, 80; recipient Community Service award Rich's, Inc., 1981. Mem. Nat. So. Colonial Dames Am., Columbia Jr. League. Democrat. Episcopalian. Club: Columbia Drama. Avocations: bridge, reading, needlepoint, tennis. Home: 109 Walden Ct Columbia SC 29204-4043

GRIMBALL, WILLIAM HEYWARD, retired lawyer; b. Charleston, S.C., Feb. 6, 1917; s. William Heyward and Panchita (Heyward) G.; m. Frances Lucas Ellerbe, Aug. 9, 1944; children—William Heyward, Henry E., Arthur, Francis E. A.B., Coll. of Charleston, 1938; LL.B., U. Va., 1941. Bar: S.C. bar 1941. Practiced in Charleston, 1941-97. Pres. Preservation Soc., Charleston, 1974-75; mem. S.C. Legislature, 1951-57; chmn. Charleston County del., 1955-57; alderman City of Charleston, 1960-72, mayor pro tem, 1969; mem. Charleston County Election Commn., 1978-81. Served with USNR, 1942-46; to lt. comdr. 1962. Fellow Am. Coll. Trial Lawyers, Am. Bar Found., S.C. Bar Found. (v.p. 1984); mem. Am. Law Inst., Am. Bar Assn., S.C. Bar Assn., Charleston County Bar Assn. (past pres.), Alumni Assn. Coll. of Charleston (pres. 1953), Soc. of Cin., S.C. Soc., St. Andrews Soc., St. Cecilia Soc., Carolina Yacht Club, Masons (past grand master S.C.). Republican. Episcopalian. Home: 107 Chadwick Dr Charleston SC 29407-7425

GRIMBLATOV, VALENTIN, physicist, biomedical engineer; b. Ivano-Frankovsk, Ukraine, Mar. 24, 1940; came to U.S., 1996; s. Michael and Berta (Vorcel) G.; m. Larisa Kalinichenko, Mar. 7, 1977 (div. May 1993); 1 child, Veniamin; m. Galina Tatarik, Apr. 28, 1997. MS in Physics, All USSR State U., Rostov-on-Don, 1967, PhD in Physics, 1973. Rschr., sr. rsch. engr. All USSR Rsch. Inst. Plasma, Moscow, 1968-78; sr. rsch. fellow, assoc. prof. Mechnikov State U., Odessa, Ukraine, 1979-89; head dept. quantum electronics Mechnikov State U., Odessa, 1992-96; invited prof., cons. Electromedikale, Cremona, Italy, 1990-91; sci. cons. Reliant Techs. Inc., Foster City, Calif., 1996; sr. laser biomed spec. Columbia Presbyn. Med. Ctr., N.Y.C., 1997—; assoc. prof. B.C. Occidental Inst., 1992-94; v.p. R & D Next Day Inc., Odessa, 1994-95. Author: Cold Lasers for Medical Application, 1989. Served with Ukrainian Navy, 1957-61. Recipient Best Young Rschr. award USSR Ministry of Sci., 1973; named Inventor of USSR, Ministry of Sci., 1978; grantee Am. Phys. Soc., 1993. Mem. Internat. Soc. Optical Engring., N.Y. Acad. Scis. Jewish. Achievements include development of theoretical foundation of noninvasive optical diagnostics in medicine, description of mechanism of laser oscillation in optical resonators with aberrations, formulation of basic principles and invention of bioresonance feedback for real time dose individualization in laser medicine, invention of new technologies for laser parameter measurements. Avocations: volleyball, music, computers. Home: 3000 Ocean Pkwy Apt 22L Brooklyn NY 11235-8350

GRIMES, CALVIN M., JR., oil industry executive; b. Boston, Jan. 12, 1940. Pres., CEO Grimes Oil Co. Inc., Boston, 1940—. Mem. adv. bd. Boys and Girls Clubs Boston; mem. Gov.'s Com. Bus.; bd. dirs. Dimock Cmty. Health Ctr. Found.; mem. corp. Northeastern U. Recipient Disting. Svc. award Union Meth. Ch.; named Outstanding Citizen of Yr., Prince Hall Mason, Contractor of Yr., U.S. Small Bus. Adminstrn. Mem. Am. Assn. Blacks Energy, Black Bus. Coun., New England Fuel Inst. Office: 50 Redfield St Boston MA 02122

GRIMES, CRAIG ALAN, electrical engineering educator; b. Ann Arbor, Mich., Nov. 6, 1956; s. Dale Mills and Janet LaVonne (Moore) G.; m. Elizabeth Carol Dickey, 1998. BS in Physics, Pa. State U., 1984, BSEE, 1984; MS, U. Tex., 1985, PhD, 1990. Engr. Applied Rsch. Labs., Austin, Tex., 1981-83; pres. Crale, Inc., Austin, 1985-90; rsch. scientist Lockeed Rsch. Labs., Palo Alto, Calif., 1990-92; dir. advanced materials lab. Southwall Techs., Palo Alto, Calif., 1992-94; asst. prof. dept. elec. engring. U. Ky., Lexington, 1994-98, assoc. prof., 1998—; rsch. asst. U. Tex., Austin, 1985-88, teaching asst., 1987-90; cons. Eastman Kodak, San Diego, 1989, Storage Tech., Boulder, Colo., 1989, Read-Rite, Fremont, Calif., 1994, AT&T Bell Labs., Murray Hill, N.J., 1995; mem. Clark County Rural Electric Coop. Co-author: Essays on the Formal Aspects of E&M Theory, 1992, Advanced Electromagnetism: Foundation, Theory and Applications, 1995; contbr. articles to profl. jours. Active Nature Conservancy, 1988-95, Austin Triathletes, 1987-90. Mem. AAAS, IEEE, Bluegrass Masters. Achievements include 6 patents, 2 pending in field; development and manufacture of permeameters, magnetic measurement tools for high frequency permeability measurements; development of size independent antennae. E-mail: grimes@engr.uky.edu. Home: 525 Mccalls Mill Rd Lexington KY 40515-9719 Office: U Ky Dept Elec Engring 453 Anderson Hall Lexington KY 40506

GRIMES, DALE MILLS, physics and electrical engineering educator; b. Marshall County, Iowa, Sept. 7, 1926; s. LeRoy and Helen (Mills) G.; m. Janet LaVonne Moore, Mar. 22, 1947; children: Prudence Rae, Craig Alan. B.S. in Physics, Math. and Chemistry, Iowa State U., 1950, M.S. in Physics and Math, 1951; Ph.D. in Elec. Engring, U. Mich., Ann Arbor, 1956. From rsch. assoc. to assoc. prof. elec. engring. U. Mich., 1951-61, prof. elec. engring., 1961-76; chief scientist Conductron Corp., Ann Arbor, 1960-63; prof. elec. engring., chmn. dept. U. Tex., El Paso, 1976-79; prof. elec. and computer engring. Pa. State U., 1979-91, prof. emeritus, 1992—, chmn. dept., 1979-86; adj. prof. physics U. Ky., 1996—; cons. Environ. Rsch. Inst. Mich., U.S. Dept. Transp., GM Corp., 1968-91; vis. prof. elec. and computer engring. U. Tex.-Austin, 1985-86; chief scientist Crale, Inc., 1985—. Author: Electromagnetism and Quantum Theory, 1969, Automotive Electronics, 1974, Advanced Electromagnetics: Foundations, Theory, Applications, 1995; also articles on automotive radar, biconical antennas, quantum theory, electromagnetic radiation; patentee in field. Served with USNR, 1943-46. Fellow AAAS, IEEE; mem. IEEE, Am. Phys. Soc., Lexington Acad. Sr. Profls. Home: 1204 Sheffield Pl Lexington KY 40509-2034

GRIMES, DAPHNE BUCHANAN, priest, artist; b. Tulsa, Apr. 12, 1929; d. George Sidney and Dorothy Elnora (Dodds) Buchanan; m. Thomas Edward Grimes, Nov. 6, 1964 (dec. Oct., 1986). BFA, U. Houston, 1952; MA, Columbia U., 1954; MA in Religion, Episcopal Seminary of the Southwest, 1985. Ordained deacon Episcopalian Ch., 1982, priest, 1986. Tchr. history Rockland County Day Sch., Nyack, N.Y., 1959-61; dir. Am. Sch., Tunis, Tunisia, 1962-64; priest vicar St. Andrew's Ch., Meeteetse, Wyo., 1987-90; dir. Thomas the Apostle Ctr., Cody, Wyo., 1990—; stewardship chmn. Diocese Wyo., 1979-85, mem. bd. diocesan coun., 1987-90, chmn. social svcs., 1987-91; mem. N. Am. regional com. St. George's. Author of poems. Chaplain West Park County Hosp., Cody, Wyo., 1981-84, West Park County Long Term Care Ctr., Cody, 1982—; bd. dirs. Park County Arts Coun., 1995-98. Mem. Cody Country Arts League, Cmty. of Celebration (spiritual adv. 1990—), Order of Julian of Norwich (assoc.), St. Andrew's Cmty. (assoc.), Compass Rose Soc., NARC of St. George Coll. Jerusalem. Avocations: reading science, theology, fiction, journaling, travel, skindiving, animals. Home and Office: Thomas the Apostle Ctr 45 Road 3cx S Cody WY 82414-9601

GRIMES, DAVID LYNN, communications company executive; b. Oklahoma City, June 9, 1947; s. Glenn Ross and Kathleen Sue G.; m. Sandra Kay Belt, Mar. 6, 1970; children: David Edwin, Emily Kathleen. BBA in Mktg., Cen. State U., Edmond, Okla., 1979; grad. internat. sr. mgrs. program, Harvard U. Grad. Sch. Bus., 1988. With Southwestern Bell Telephone, 1970-83; rates and tariff Southwestern Bell Telephone, Oklahoma City, 1975-77, industry mgr., 1977-79; dist. mgr. sales ops. Southwestern Bell Telephone, St. Louis, 1979-80; mktg. mgr. Southwestern Bell Telephone, Kansas City, Mo., 1980-82, Houston, 1982-83; div. mgr. Am. Bell, Houston, 1983-84; br. mgr. nat. accts. AT&T, Houston, 1984-85; v.p. sales AT&T, Dallas, 1986-98; chief operating officer Sharetech, Parsippany, N.J., 1985-86; pres. and CEO Sykes Enterprises, 1998—. Mem. Nat. Bd. of Visitors Tex. Christian U., 1990-96; mem. adv. coun. Sch. Nat. Sci., U. Tex., Austin, 1988-93; bd. dirs. Tex. Bus. Hall of Fame Found., Dallas, 1988-93. Mem. Dallas C. of C. (mem. exec. com. econ. devel. 1991-93), Harvard Bus. Club Dallas, Univ. Club (Dallas), Prestonwood Country Club (Dallas). Republican. Methodist. Avocations: golf, tennis, fishing, hunting. Home: 1303 Bayshore Blvd Tampa FL 33606 Office: Sykes Enterprises Ste 400 100 N Tampa St Ste 3900 Tampa FL 33602-6813

GRIMES, HEILAN YVETTE, publishing executive; b. Hamilton, Ohio, Sept. 16, 1949; d. J and Claudette (Hinkle) G. Grad., New Eng. Sch. Photography, 1987. Founder, pres. Dot & Line Graphics, 1975—, Color Computer Weekly, 1982—, Hollow Earth Pub., 1983—. Author: Norse Mythology, 1984, Legend of Niebelungenlied, 1984, Using QuarkXPress 3.3, 1994, Beginning Internet, 1994, Filemaker Pro Developer's Guide, 1997; founder Byte Mag., 1974, Macpower Mag., 1993. Recipient various photographic awards and grants. Democrat. Avocations: magic, juggling, hiking, traveling. E-mail: HEP2@aol.com. Office: PO Box 1355 Boston MA 02205-1355

GRIMES, HOWARD RAY, management consultant; b. Manilla, Iowa, July 24, 1918; s. Ray Herb and Sarah Alice (Saunders) G.; m. Nancy Palmer, Nov. 17, 1993; children from previous marriage: Patricia, Susan, Nancy, Sarah, Laura. Student, U. Wis., 1939; B.A., Grinnell Coll., 1940. With Aetna Life & Casualty Co., 1940-82; field supr., regional mgr. Aetna Life & Casualty Co., Boston, 1950-74; regional dir., v.p. field Aetna Life & Casualty Co., 1974-82; mgmt. cons., 1983-95; chmn. Benefit Svcs. Inc., 1968-93; bd. dirs. Waterville Co. Inc. Served with USAAF, 1942-45. Sports-Illustrated Silver Anniversary All-Am. Mem. Down Town Club (Boston), Weston Golf Club (Mass.), Bald Peak Colony Club (N.H.). Home: PO Box 513 10 W Branch Rd Waterville Valley NH 03215-0513 Office: Benefit Svcs Inc 36 Washington St Wellesley Hills MA 02481-1904 also: Benefit Svcs Inc Waterville Valley NH 03215-0513

GRIMES, HUGH GAVIN, physician; b. Chgo., Aug. 19, 1929; s. Andrew Thomas and Anna (Gavin) G.; m. Rose Anne Leahy, Aug. 21, 1954; children—Hugh Gavin, Paula Anne, Daniel Joseph, Sarah Louise, Nancy Marie, Jennifer Diane. Student, Loyola U., 1947-50; B.S., U. Ill., 1952, M.D., 1954. Diplomate Am. Bd. Ob-Gyn. Intern St. Joseph Hosp., Chgo., 1954-55; resident in ob-gyn St. Joseph Hosp., 1955-58; practice medicine specializing in ob-gyn Chgo., 1960—; lectr., asst. clin. prof. Stritch Sch. Medicine, Loyola U., Chgo.; active staff St. Joseph Hosp., Chgo., also v.p. med. staff, 1977-78, pres. staff, 1979-80; asst. prof. clin. ob-gyn Northwestern U. Med. Sch., 1980—. Contbr. articles to profl. jours. Trustee Regina Dominican High Sch. Served to capt. M.C., AUS, 1958-60. Recipient nat. faculty award Coun. on Resident Edn. in Ob-gyn., Am. Bd. Ob-Gyn. Fellow Am. Coll. Ob-Gyn., Chgo. Gynecol. Soc.; mem. Am. Cancer Soc. (mem. profl. edn. com. Chgo. unit), Am. Soc. Reproductive Medicine, Cath. Physicians Guild, Assn. Am. Physicians and Surgeons, Am. Soc. Colposcopy and Colpomicroscopy, Am. Assn. Gynecologic Laparoscopists, Assn. Art Inst. Chgo., Assn. Field Mus., Assocs. Smithsonian Instn., Pi Kappa Epsilon.

GRIMES, JAMES CAHILL, retired publishing executive, advertising executive; b. Oklahoma City, July 20, 1918; s. James Arthur Grimes and Kathryn Shanahan; m. Roma Ellison, Oct. 18, 1958; children: Joseph Edward, Jill. BA in Journalism, U. Okla., 1940. With J.C. Grimes & Assocs., Oklahoma City, 1946-49, 56-97; fundraiser Girl Scouts U.S.A., Kansas City, Mo., 1963-70; ptnr. Grimes-Valentine, Arlington, Tex., 1972-75; co-publ., S.W. Travel & Recreation Quarterly, Ariz., 1983-97; publ. Cochise County Mag., 1988-96, Nogales/Santa Cruz County Mag., 1990-96, Okla. Home Builder Mag., 1946-49; co-publ. Ariz...Discover It! mag., 1992-94. Officer-in-charge Beachhead News, 1944-45; publ. League of Young Dem. Newspaper, Oklahoma City, 1946-49; pres. O'Odham Tash (Indian Days), 1996-97; chmn. Mining Days, Silver City, N. Mex., 1985; chmn. Winter Art Festival, Sierra Vista, Ariz., 1990; dist. commr. Boy Scouts Am., Phoenix, 1982-86. Maj. U.S. Army, 1942-46. Decorated Bronze Star; named Tourism Citizen of Yr. C. of C., Silver City, N.M., 1985, Sierra Vista, 94. Mem. Rotary Internat., Masons, Tex. Rabbit Breeders Assn., N. Mex. Rabbit Breeders Assn. (pres.), Ariz. Rabbit Breeders Assn., Sigma Delta Chi, Delta Upsilon Fraternity (gen. sec. 1949-56). Republican. Mem. LDS Ch. Home and Office: #3109 3245 S Wilmot Rd Apt 3109 Tucson AZ 85730-2286

GRIMES, LARRY BRUCE, lawyer; b. Salt Lake City, Apr. 26, 1940; s. Eugene J. and Gean (Bruce) G.; m. AnneMarie Vandendriessche, June 9, 1967; children: Bruce Remi, Eric Charles; m. Margaret Regina Prophet, Aug. 20, 1976; children: Richard Charles, Russell Eugene, Mitchell James. BA in Econs., U. Idaho, 1965, JD, 1967. Bar: Idaho 1967, D.C. 1974, U.S. Dist. Ct. Idaho 1967, U.S. Dist. Ct. (cen. dist.) Calif. 1970, U.S. Dist. Ct. (ea. dist.) Pa. 1973, U.S. Dist. Ct. (so. dist.) Fla. 1974, U.S. Dist. Ct. (ea. dist.) N.Y. 1972, U.S. Dist. Ct. D.C. 1984. City magistrate City of Moscow (Idaho), 1967; trial atty., br. chief, asst. chief trial atty./enforcement SEC, Washington, 1967-75; sr. chief counsel Westinghouse Electric, Pitts., 1975-81; pvt. practice Washington, 1981-83; ptnr. McGuire Woods Battle & Boothe, Washington, 1984-97; of counsel Tighe, Patton, Tabackman & Babbin, Washington, 1997—; bd. dirs., gen. counsel Lor-West Ltd. Westinghouse JV (now Northrop Grumman JV), Bermuda, 1982—; alternate dir., gen. counsel Lorad-Boeing Ltd., Bermuda, 1988-91; gen. counsel Nat. Coal Coun., Arlington, Va., 1986—; mem. adv. coun. U. Idaho; mem. U. Idaho Found.; spkr. on corp. counseling and countertrade, U.S., Can., Europe, Latin Am., Asia. Mem. nat. adv. bd. Mountain West Ctr. for Regional Studies, Utah State U., Logan, 1988-96; coach Little League Baseball, Great Falls, Va., 1983-88; sr. mem. synthesis group NASA, 1991. Fellow Am. Bar Found.; mem. ABA, River Bend Golf & Country Club, Army & Navy Club (Washington), Nat. Eagle Scout Assn. Mormon. Avocations: golf, skiing, music. Office: Tighe Patton Tabackman & Babbin 1747 Pennsylvania Ave NW Washington DC 20006-4604

GRIMES, RICHARD ALLEN, economics educator; b. Toledo, Ohio, Apr. 24, 1929; s. Robert Howell and Mary Mildred (Hatcher) G.; m. Helen Ann Schaeffer, Aug. 25, 1951; children: Gregory Allen, Julianne, Frank Edwin, Mary Ann. BS in Chemistry, U. Ga., 1951; MS in Indsl. Mgmt., Ga. Inst. Tech., 1959; postgrad., Ga. State U., 1979. Commd. lt. U.S. Army, 1951, advanced through grades to lt. col., ret. 1971; asst. prof. econs. Clayton State Univ., Morrow, Ga., 1971-74; assoc. prof. econs. DeKalb Coll., Decatur, Ga., 1974-97; adj. prof. Jacksonville State U., 1959-63, Va. Commonwealth U., 1964-67, Ga. Mil. Coll., 1979-91, Ctrl. Tex. Coll., 1997—, Gordon Coll., 1998—; ednl. cons.; real estate broker and instr. Reviewer: (textbook) Economics, 1979, 93, 95, 97. Umpire, Atlanta Area Football Ofcls. Assn., treas., 1971-95; evaluator Ga. H.S. Football Ofcls., 1996—; active Spl. Olympics, Atlanta, 1971—; founding pres. Rex Civic Assn., 1973; sec.-treas. Villages Homeowners Assn., 1994-95. Decorated Solider's medal for valor, Vietnam, 1963; named Rotarian of Yr. 1976, Football Ofcl. of Yr., Atlanta area, 1980; recipient Eagle Scout award. Mem. AAUP (pres. DeKalb chpt. 1987-97), VFW (life), Am. Legion, So. Econ. Assn., Am. Acctg. Assn., Ga. Assn. Econs. and Fin. (pres. 1992-93), Ga. Assn. Acctg. Profls. (past pres.), Nat. Soc. Pub. Accts., So. Metro Ga. Tech. Alumni Club, Atlanta U. Ga. Alumni Club (scholarship chmn.), U. Ga. Varsity Letterman, The Retired Officers Assn., Delta Pi Epsilon. Republican. Presbyterian (elder). Avocations: football, golfing, camping, swimming. Home: Eagles Landing 118 Carron Ln Stockbridge GA 30281-6302

GRIMES, RICHARD STUART, editor, writer; b. Wheeling, W.Va., June 28, 1939; s. Harold George and Sarah (Rebic) G.; m. Katheryn Perrine Johnson, Nov. 7, 1964; children: Sara Jane, Richard Harold, Stephen Ross. Grad., W.Va. U., 1961. Reporter Charleston (W.Va.) Daily Mail, 1964—, polit. editor, 1985—, also regular columnist; master of ceremonies TV show Underfire, Pub. TV, 1989—. Author: Old Money, New Politics, 1984; syndicated columnist in some 40 newspapers. Chmn. of bd. Meth. Ch., 1990. Sgt. U.S. Army, 1961-64. Mem. Southridge Lions Club (pres. 1994—). Republican. Avocations: woodworking, furniture building, music. Home: 679 Gordon Dr Charleston WV 25314-1751

GRIMES, RUSSELL NEWELL, chemistry educator, inorganic chemist; b. Meridian, Miss., Dec. 10, 1935; s. Newell Cleveland and Marion Esther (Zehner) G.; m. Nancy Farrow Hall, Sept. 21, 1962; children—Susan, David. B.S. in Chemistry, Lafayette Coll., 1957; Ph.D. in Chemistry, U. Minn., 1962; postdoctoral, Harvard U., 1962, U. Calif., Riverside, 1962-63. Asst. prof. chemistry U. Va., Charlottesville, 1963-68, assoc. prof. chemistry, 1968-73, prof. chemistry, 1973—, chmn. dept. chemistry, 1981-84; guest prof. U. Canterbury, N.Z., 1974-75, U. Heidelberg, Fed. Republic of Germany, 1986, 1997-98. Author: Carboranes, 1970; editor: Metal Interactions with Boron Clusters, 1982, Inorganic Syntheses Vol. 29, 1992; contbr. over 200 articles to profl. jours. Grantee Office Naval Rsch., 1965-83, Army Rsch. Office, 1983—, NSF, 1976—; Fulbright sr. rsch. scholar, New Zealand, 1974-75; recipient Alexander von Humboldt Sr. Rsch. prize, 1996. Fellow AAAS; mem. Am. Chem. Soc. (sec.-treas. inorganic divsn. 1981-84, grantee 1965—), Corp. Inorganic Syntheses, Sigma Xi (President's and Visitors' rsch. prize 1981, 85, 96). Office: U Va Dept Chemistry McCormick Rd Charlottesville VA 22904

GRIMES, RUTH ELAINE, city planner; b. Palo Alto, Calif., Mar. 4, 1949; d. Herbert George and Irene (Williams) Baker; m. Charles A. Grimes, July 19, 1969 (div. 1981); 1 child, Michael; m. Roger L. Sharpe, Mar. 20, 1984; 1 child, Teresa. AB summa cum laude, U. Calif., Berkeley, 1970, M in City Planning, 1972. Rsch. and evaluation coord. Ctr. Ind. Living, Berkeley, 1972-74; planner City of Berkeley, 1974-76, sr. planner, 1983—, analyst, 1976-83; bd. dirs. Vets. Asssistance Ctr., Berkeley, pres., 1978-93; bd. dirs. Berkeley Design Advocates, treas., 1987-94. Author: Berkeley Downtown Plan, 1988; contbr. numerous articles to profl. jours. and other publs. Bd. dirs. Berkeley-Sakai Sister City Assn., 1994—, pres., 1995-97, Ctr. Ind. Living. Honored by Calif. State Assembly Resolution, 1988; Edwin Frank Kraft scholar, 1966. Mem. Am. Inst. Cert. Planners, Am. Planning Assn., Mensa, Lake Merrit Joggers and Striders (sec. 1986-89, pres. 1991-93), Lions Internat. (bd. dirs. Berkeley club 1992-94, v.p. 1997-98, pres. 1998-99, chair membership com. 1999—), U. Calif. Coll. Environ. Design Alumni Assn. (bd. dirs. 1992-98, treas. 1994-96). Avocation: long distance running. Home: 1330 Bonita Ave Berkeley CA 94709-1925 Office: City of Berkeley 2121 Mckinley Ave Berkeley CA 94703-1519

GRIMES, STEPHEN HENRY, retired state supreme court justice; b. Peoria, Ill., Nov. 17, 1927; s. Henry Holbrook and June (Kellar) G.; m. Mary Fay Fulghum, Dec. 29, 1951; children: Gay Diane, Mary June, Sue Anne, Sheri Lynn. Student, Fla. So. Coll., 1946-47; BS in Bus. Adminstrn. with honors, U. Fla., 1951, LLB with honors, 1954; LLD (hon.), Stetson U., 1980. Bar: Fla. 1954, U.S. Dist. Ct. (no. and so. dists.) 1954, U.S. Ct. Appeals (5th cir.) 1965, U.S. Supreme Ct. 1972. Since practiced in Bartow, Fla.; ptnr. Holland and Knight and predecessor firm, Tallahassee, 1954-73, 98—; judge Ct. Appeal 2d Dist. Fla., Lakeland, Fla., 1973-87; chief judge Ct. Appeal 2d Dist. Fla., 1978-80; chmn. Conf. Fla. Dist. Cts. Appeal, 1978-80; justice Fla. Supreme Ct., Tallahassee, 1987-97, chief justice, 1994-96; chair Article V Task Force, 1994-96; mem. Fla. Jud. Qualification Commn., 1982-86, vice chmn., 1985-86; chmn. Fla. Jud. Coun., 1989-94. Contbr. articles U. Fla. Law Rev., 1951, 54. Bd. dirs. Bartow Meml. Hosp., 1958-61, Bartow Library, 1968-78; trustee Polk Community Coll., Winter Haven, Fla., 1967-70, chmn., 1969-70; bd. govs. Polk Pub. Mus., 1976—; bd. dirs. Fla. History Assocs. Lt. (j.g.) USN, 1951-53. Fellow Am. Coll. Trial Lawyers; mem. ABA, Fla. Bar Assn. (bd. govs. jr. bar 1956-58, bd. dirs. trial lawyers sect. 1967-69, sec. 1969, vice chmn. appellate rules com. 1976-77, vice chmn. tort litigation rev. commn. 1985-86), 10th Cir. Bar Assn. (pres. 1966), Am. Judicature Soc., Bartow C. of C. (pres. 1964), Rotary (dist. gov. 1960-61). Episcopalian (sr. warden 1964-65, 77). Office: Holland & Knight LLP 315 S Calhoun St Tallahassee FL 32301-1807

GRIMES, WILLIAM ALVAN, retired state supreme court chief justice; b. Dover, N.H., July 4, 1911; s. Frank J. and Annie (Ash) G.; m. Barbara Terry Parsons, June 22, 1940; children: Gail Terry, Gordon Francis. BS, U. N.H., 1934, LLD, 1969; JD, Boston U., 1937; LLD, William Mitchell Coll. Law, 1979, Calif. Western Sch. Law, 1981. Bar: N.H. 1937. Assoc. Cooper & Hall, Rochester, N.H., 1937-41; ptnr. Cooper, Hall & Grimes, Rochester, 1941-47; solicitor City of Dover, 1946-47; justice N.H. Superior Ct., Concord, 1947-66; justice Supreme Ct. of N.H., 1966-79, chief justice, 1979-81; mem. faculty Nat. Jud. Coll.; disting. vis. prof. Calif. Western Sch. Law, 1982-85, U. San Diego Sch. Law, 1986, U. Okla. Coll. of Law, 1987—; adj. prof. U. Nev.; mem. exec. com., past chmn. Appellate Judges Conf.; chmn. N.H. Vocat. Rehab. Planning Commn., N.H. Gov.'s Commn. on Crime and Delinquency; mem. council judges Nat. Council Crime and Delinquency; chmn. edn. com. Appellate Judges Conf.; mem. adv. council Nat. Center for State Cts.; mem. Gov.'s Commn. on Laws Affecting Children, Gov.'s Com. on Correctional Tng.; mem. adv. council for Appellate Justice; mem. planning com. Nat. Conf. Standards for Adminstrn. Criminal Justice; del. to White House Conf. on Children, Nat. Conf. on Correctional Manpower and Tng. Author: Criminal Law Outline, annually, 1974—. Mem. N.H. Ho. of Reps., 1933-35, 37-39; mem. adv. council Lincoln Filene Ctr. for Citizenship and Pub. Affairs. Lt. USNR, World War II. Recipient Silver Shingle award, Centennial award Boston U. Sch. Law, Meritorious Svc. award Nat. Rehab. Assn., Archie award N.H. Easter Seal Soc., Irwin Griswold award for teaching excellence Nat. Jud. Coll., 1988, Appellate Judges Conf. Recognition award, 1996, Lifetime Achievement award Student Bar Assn., U. Okla. Coll. Law, 1998; William A. Grimes Fund for Jud. Edn. created by Nation's Appellate Judges; Civil Libertarian award created in his name U. Okla. Coll. Law. Mem. ABA (past chmn. div. jud. adminstrn., chmn. drug abuse com. criminal law sect., pres.'s task force on appellate advocacy, com. to investigate fed. law enforcement agys., Spl. Merit award jud. adminstrn. div.), Stafford County Bar Assn., N.H. Bar Assn. (gavel award, disting. service award, Lifetime Achievement award 1996, William A. Grimes award for jud. professionalism 1999), Am. Judicature Soc. (Herbert Harley award 1988), N.H. Judges Assn. (William A. Grimes lecture fund). Democrat.

GRIMES-FREDERICK, DOROTHEA D., communications executive; b. New Orleans; d. Morris and Rosemary (Birch) Grimes; m. John H. Frederick. BS in Physics, So. U., Baton Rouge; EDD, Rutgers U., 1980. Mem. tech. staff. AT&T Bell Labs., 1980-85; tech. supr. small system devel. lab. AT&T Bell Labs., Middletown, N.J., 1985-88; tech. supr. quality system devel. AT&T Bell Labs., Parsippany, N.J., 1988-89; dept. head communications systems devel. lab. AT&T Bell Labs, Middletown, 1989-94; dir. technology planning AT&T Bell Labs, Basking Ridge, N.J., 1994-95; sr. dir. ops. and logistics Lucent Techs. (an AT&T Co.), Basking Ridge, N.J., 1995—. Contbr. articles to profl. jours. Mem. YWCA Mgmt. Forum, Summit, N.J., 1988, bd. dirs., 1989-93. Mem. NAACP, Nat. Platform Assn., C. of C. Office: Lucent Techs 211 Mount Airy Rd Rm 2e110 Basking Ridge NJ 07920-2311

GRIMLEY, JANET ELIZABETH, newspaper editor; b. Oelwein, Iowa, Dec. 3, 1946; d. Harold E. and Ida Mae (Anderson) Teague; m. Terry L. Grimley, June 15, 1968; 1 child, Brynn Sara Mae Grimley. BA, U. Iowa, Iowa City, 1969; attended, U. Wash., Seattle, 1979-82. Asst. mng. editor Seattle Post-Intelligencer; publs. dir. Marycrest Coll., Davenport, Iowa, 1969-70; reporter Quad-Cities Times, Davenport, Iowa, 1970-74; reporter Seattle Post-Intelligence, Seattle, 1974-76, feature editor, 1976-95, asst. mng. editor, 1995—; past pres. Am. Assn. Sunday and Feature Editors; mem. Newspaper Features Coun. Mem. Shoreline Strategic Planning Com., Seattle, 1993, Shorewood Site Coun., 1997—, Shorewood Boosters; co-chair Shoreline Capitol/Bond Com., Seattle, 1994, Einstein Site Coun., Seattle, 1994-96. Mem. Junior League of Seattle (bd. dirs. 1989-90, exec. bd. 1991-92), City Club Seattle. Avocations: sailing, skiing, gardening. Office: Seattle Post Intelligencer 101 Elliott Ave W Ste 200 Seattle WA 98119-4295

GRIMLEY, JEFFREY MICHAEL, dentist; b. Alton, Ill., Feb. 3, 1957; s. John Richard and Joyce Imogene (Mallin) G.; m. Julie Ellen Gardner, Aug. 2, 1980; children: Joel Michael, Christopher Mark, Benjamin Jeffrey. BS, U. Iowa, 1979, DDS, 1983; cert., Miami Valley Hosp, Dayton, Ohio, 1984. Gen. practice dentistry Naperville, Ill., 1984—. Mem. ADA, Acad. Gen. Dentistry, Ill. Dental Soc., Chgo. Dental Soc. Methodist. Avocations: sports, photography. Office: 14 S Main St Naperville IL 60540-5365

GRIMLEY, ROBERT THOMAS, chemistry educator; b. North Attleboro, Mass., Jan. 3, 1930; s. John Thomas and Ivy (Frost) G.; m. Margaret Rockwood, June 21, 1952; children: Mark, Maureen, Kevin, Terrence, Peter. BS, U. Mass., 1951; PhD, U. Wis., 1958. Rsch. chemist Corning (N.Y.) Glass, Inc., 1957-59; fellow U. Chgo., 1959-61; prof. chemistry Purdue U., West Lafayette, Ind., 1961-94, prof. emeritus, 1995—; vis. prof. Calif. Inst. Tech., Pasadena, 1992-96. 1st lt. USAF, 1951-53. Mem. Am. Chem. Soc. (chmn. Purdue U. sect.), Am. Phys. Soc., Sigma Xi, Alpha Chi Sigma. Home: 3368 Peppermill Dr West Lafayette IN 47906-1079 Office: Purdue U Dept Chemistry West Lafayette IN 47907

GRIMM, BEN EMMET, former library director and consultant; b. Jersey City, Sept. 27, 1924; s. Benjamin Harrison and Eunice Blanche (Whitenack) G.; m. Jean Kay Bohrer, Aug. 19, 1950 (div. 1982); children: Jeffrey, Kevin, Mark, Wendy; m. Lucy Ann Taylor, Jan. 21, 1989. BA, Washington and Lee U., 1949; MS, Columbia U., 1950. Librarian youth services Detroit Public Library, 1950-52; sr. librarian Fair Lawn (N.J.) Public Library, 1952-54; reference and reading librarian Montclair (N.J.) Public Library, 1955-56, asst. dir., 1956-61; dir. Belleville (N.J.) Public Library, 1961-72, Jersey City Public Library, 1973-85; prin. Grimm/McPherson Assocs., Montclair, N.J., 1988-92; ind. libr. cons., 1992-93; chmn. Hudson County Audio-Visual Aids Commn., 1975-85; cons. libr. bldgs., svcs. and adminstrn., 1966-93; cons., mem. state aid constrn. adv. bd. N.J. State Libr., 1985-88, chmn. adv. coun. Libr. Svcs. and Constrn. Act, 1979-83. Mng. editor Libr. Trustee Newsletter, 1978-80. Bd. dirs. Orange County (Va.) Hist. Soc., 1994-96, pres., 1995; bd. dirs. Orange County Libr. Found., 1995-98, v.p., 1997-98. With USAAF, 1942-45. Decorated D.F.C., Air medal with oak leaf clusters. Mem. N.J. Libr. Assn. (pres. 1968-69). Home and Office: PO Box 145 Rapidan VA 22733-0145

GRIMM, DONALD LEE, executive; b. Uniontown, Pa., Feb. 19, 1954; s. James Richard and Edna Arlene (Savage) G.; m. Linda Diane Ferris, Oct. 6, 1979; children: Patrick Ryan, Jason Thomas. Grad. high sch., Clarion (Pa.) State Coll., Washington, Pa. Sales Budd Baer Buick/Pontiac Inc., Washington, Pa., 1976-78; svc. mgr., asst. mgr. Uniroyal, Pleasant Hills, Pa., 1978; store mgr. Uniroyal, Kendalville, Ind., 1978-79, Am. Automotive, Morgantown, W.Va., 1979-80; owner, CEO Car Care Ctr., Washington, Pa., 1981—. Deacon, elder Presbyn. Ch. Mem. NRA, Elks, Dormont Mt. Lebanon Sportsmens Assn., Jaycees (bd. dirs. 1984-85). Republican. Avocations: boating, target shooting, historical research. Office: Car Care Ctr 887 Henderson Ave Washington PA 15301-1361

GRIMM, JAMES R. (RONALD GRIMM), multi-industry executive; b. Monroe, Mich., Nov. 5, 1935; s. Carl S. and Annie B. (Platt) G.; m. Carol Ann Forman, Aug. 24, 1957; children: James R., Phillip H. BS in Bus. Adminstrn, Ariz. State U., 1958. Dir. internal audit Motorola, Inc., Phoenix, 1961-68; bus. and fin. mgr. Europe Motorola Semicondr. Co., Geneva, 1968-70; dir. internat. fin. Fairchild Camera & Instrument Co., Mountain View, Calif., 1970-71; v.p. internat. fin. Computer Scis. Corp., Los Angeles, 1971-74; sr. v.p., chief fin. exec. Pertec Computer Corp., Los Angeles, 1974-80; exec. v.p. fin. and adminstrn. MAPCO, Inc., Tulsa, 1980-84; v.p., chief fin. officer Greyhound Corp., Phoenix, 1984-88, now chmn.; chmn. Security Products Co. Inc., Phoenix, 1989—; pres. Internat. Bus. Cons., Phoenix, 1988—; bd. dirs. Petro Star Inc., Fairbanks, Alaska. Contbr. articles to Inst. Internal Auditors publs., 1964-68. Inducted into Ariz. State U. Hall of Fame, 1982. Mem. Inst. Internal Auditors (founder and 1st pres. Phoenix chpt. 1963), Fin. Exec. Inst. Clubs: Southern Hills, Okla., Tulsa. Home: 6500 E Caron Dr Paradise Valley AZ 85253

GRIMM, JOHN LLOYD, business executive, marketing professional; b. N.Y.C., Oct. 21, 1945; s. Judson Lloyd and Nanette (Locke) G.; m. Stephanie L. Cassagne, Dec. 23, 1969; children: Samantha, Jonathan. BBA, Tulane U., 1967, MBA, 1969. Asst. prof. Dillard U., New Orleans, 1969-82; pres. Multi-Quest Internat. Inc., New Orleans, 1966—, Analytical Studies Inc., New Orleans, 1966—, Response Behavior Corp., New Orleans, 1966—. Author: Interviewer's Handbook & Training Manual, 1970. Chmn. Rsch. Com. United Way, New Orleans, 1988-89, 94—; mem. Mktg. Com. United Way, New Orleans, 1986-88, Mktg. Com. YMCA, New Orleans, 1985-98, Pub. Rels. Com. Goodwill Industries, New Orleans, 1986-89. Named Prof. of the Yr., Dillard U., 1981. Mem. Am. Mktg. Assn. (New Orleans chpt. pres. 1985-87, 94-95, treas. 1984-85, sec. 1983-84), Market Rsch. Assn. Avocation: stamp collecting. Office: Multi-Quest Internat Inc 708 Rosa Ave Metairie LA 70005-2126

GRIMM, LOUIS JOHN, mathematician, educator; b. St. Louis, Nov. 30, 1933; s. Louis and Florence Agnes (Hammond) G.; m. Barbara Ann Mitko, May 6, 1967; children: Thomas, Mary. BS, St. Louis U., 1954; MS, Ga. Inst. Tech., 1960; PhD, U. Minn., 1965. Chemist USPHS, Savannah, Ga., 1958-61; asst. prof. U. Utah, Salt Lake City, 1965-69; assoc. prof. U. Mo., Rolla, 1969-74, prof., 1974—, chmn. dept. math. and stats., 1981-87, dir. Inst. Applied Math., 1983-87; vis. asst. prof. U. Minn., Mpls., 1966; vis. prof. U. Nebr., Lincoln, 1978-79, U. So. Calif., L.A., 1987-88; exch. scientist Polish Acad. Scis., Warsaw, Poland, 1981. Contbr. articles to profl. jours. With Med. Svc. Corps, AUS, 1956-58. Jefferson Smurfit fellow Univ. Coll. Dublin (Ireland), 1984; NSF rsch. grantee. Mem. AAUP, Soc. for Indsl. and Applied Math., Polish Math. Soc., Gesellschaft für angewandte Mathematik und Mechanik, Math. Assn. Am., Sigma Xi. Office: U Mo Dept Math & Stats Rolla MO 65409-0020

GRIMM, PHILLIP HENRY, electronic security company executive; b. Arcadia, Calif., Sept. 9, 1959; s. James Ronald and Carol Ann (Forman) G.; m. Cynthia Hunt, Feb. 17, 1983; children: Stephanie, Katelyn. BS in Fin. and Acctg., Brigham Young U., 1984. Intern 1st Tulsa (Okla.) Nat. Bank, 1982; corp. auditor Motorola, Inc., Phoenix, 1983-85; corp. contr. Bowmar Instrument Corp., Phoenix, 1985-90; CFO, gen. mgr. DOD Electronics Corp., Salt Lake City, 1990-94; U.S. contr. Bull HN Info. Systems, Phoenix, 1994-95; CEO U.S. Currency Protection, Scottsdale, Ariz., 1995—. Bd. dirs. Utah Transp. Planning, Salt Lake City, 1991-92. Mem. IAA. Republican. Mem. LDS Ch. Avocations: golf, skiing, boating, flying. Office: US Currency Protection Corp PO Box 6021 Scottsdale AZ 85261

GRIMM, ROBERTA PAULINE JOHNSON, performing arts company director; b. Kansas City, Mo., Aug. 12, 1921; d. Howard Russell and Ethel Mae (Dickinson) Johnson; m. Robert E. Grimm, Sept. 24, 1943; children: Carole Barnes, Michael, Leslie Archer, Marcia Grimm-Buck, Nancy Grimm-Fisher, Mark. BA, Denison U., 1943; postgrad., Colgate-Rochester Div. Sch., 1946-48, Canisius Coll., 1977-78. Jr. high sch. tchr. Cleveland Heights (Ohio) schs., 1943-44; workshop leader for chs. Syracuse, N.Y., 1950-76; dir. children's theater Erie (Pa.) Playhouse, 1963-65; religious edn. dir. Plymouth United Ch. of Christ, Syracuse, 1966-68; dir. The Celebrants Liturgical Dance Choir, Buffalo, 1977—; movement and dance instr. to nursing homes, Buffalo area, 1988—. Storyteller United Ch. Home, Buffalo; vol. clown at ch. schs. and nursing homes; workshop leader Alternatives to Violence, 1992—; bd. dirs. Pastoral Counseling/VIVE, Western N.Y. Peace Ctr.; local and state pres. Ch. Women United of Buffalo and Erie County, 1997—; mem. exec. coun. Ch. Women United U.S., 1978-92. Recipient Valiant Woman award Ch. Women United, 1987, Outstanding Lay Woman award Nat. Synod United Ch. of Christ, 1985, Jr. League Mentor award, Buffalo, 1999. Democrat.

GRIMMET, ALEX J., clergyman, school administrator, elementary and secondary education educator; b. McVeigh, Ky., July 17, 1928; s. Alex A. and Edna Mae (Boyd) G.; m. Lois Jean Carter, June 24, 1949; children: Larry Bruce, Raven Alexis. A.B., Ky. Christian Coll., 1949; M.Ed., U. Cin., 1964; postgrad. in math. Washburn U., 1967, U. Cin., 1968-69, Georgetown U., 1968. Ordained to ministry Ch. of Christ, 1948. Elem. tchr. Highland County schs., Hillsboro, Ohio, 1957-62; tchr. math. Warren County, Morrow, Ohio, 1964-67; tchr. math. Lebanon High Sch., Ohio, 1967-85, head dept., 1969-84; student minister Olympia Christian Ch., Owensville, Ky.; minister Choatville Christian Ch., Frankfort, Ky., 1949-51, Evang. Mountains Ky. and W.Va., Pike County, Ky., Mingo County, W.Va., 1951-52, Jefferson and Capella Chs. of Christ near Winston Salem, N.C., 1952-57;

Danville Ch. of Christ, Hillsboro, Ohio, 1957-62, Loveland (Ohio) Ch. of Christ, 1962-66, Lerado Ch. of Christ, 1966—; adminstr. Christian Schs. of Greater Cin., 1991-96; chmn. math. curriculum revision com. Lebanon City Schs., 1969-70, 82-85, chmn. competency based edn. program for math., 1982-85; with IRS, 1986-89; sub. tchr. Cin. Hills Ch. Sch., 1996—. Vol. math instr. GED program Loveland Lit. Program, 1986—, Adult Literacy Program, 1996, Sub. Teacher at Cincinnati Hills Cristian Acad., Loveland; precinct exec. Democrats Hamilton County, Loveland, 1980—. Mem. NEA, Ohio Edn. Assn., Ohio Council Tchrs. Math. (dist. dir. 1981-84, v.p. 1984-87, conv. program chmn. 1986), Lebanon Tchrs. Assn. (mem. liaison com.), Kiwanis (sec. local chpt., sec.-treas. 8th Ohio divsn.). Home: 848 Kenmar Dr Loveland OH 45140-2819 *My life has been centered around helping my fellow man. I believe in the Bible as the inspired Word of God and accept it without change and compromise. I believe in and try to follow Matthew 6:33, "Seek you first the Kingdom of God and His Righteousness and all these things shall be added unto you." If we put Him and His church first in our lives I believe the necessities of life will be provided by our loving heavenly Father.*

GRIMMETTE, MARK, olympic athlete; b. Ann Arbor, Mich., Jan. 23, 1971. Olympic athlete, Luge, men's doubles, front man, named to Devel. Team, 1989. Winner 1998 Bronze Medal in Luge in Men's Doubles, Nagano; named 1996 U.S. Nat. Champion in doubles; winner 6 World Cup medals, winner bronze medal, 1996 (Lillehammer), All-Japan Championships, Nagano; World Cup champion, 1998, Bell Atlantic Nat. champion, 1998. Office: US Luge Assn PO Box 651 Lake Placid NY 12946-0651*

GRIMSBO, RAYMOND ALLEN, forensic scientist; b. Portland, Oreg., Apr. 25, 1948; s. LeRoy Allen and Irene Bernice (Surgen) G.; m. Barbara Suzanne Favreau, Apr. 26, 1969 (div. 1979); children: John Allen, Kimberly Suzanne; m. Charlotte Alice Miller, July 25, 1981 (div. 1994); children: Sarah Marie, Benjamin Allen. BS, Portland State U., 1972; D of Philosophy, Union for Experimenting Colls. & Univs., Cin., 1987. Diplomate Am. Bd. Criminalistics; cert. profl. competency in criminalistics DEA Rschr. Registration. Med. technician United Med. Labs., Inc., Portland, 1969-74; criminalist Oreg. State Police Crime Lab., Portland, 1975-85; pvt. practice forensic science Portland, 1985-87; pres. Intermountain Forensic Labs., Inc., Portland, 1987—; adj. instr. Oreg. Health Scis. U., Portland, 1987-95; adj. prof. Portland State U., 1986-88, adj. asst. prof., 1988—; clin. dir. Intermountain Forensic Labs., Inc., 1988-92, Western Health Lab., Portland; adj. faculty Union Inst.; mem. substance abuse methods panel Oreg. Health Divsn. Contbr. articles to profl. jours. Fellow Am. Acad. Forensic Scientists; mem. ASTM, STM, Soc. Forensic Haemogenetics, N.W. Assn. Forensic Scientists, Internat. Assn. Bloodstain Pattern Analysis, Electrophoresis Soc., Internat. Assn. Identification, internat. Assn. Forensic Toxicologists, Pacific N.W. Forensic Study, New Horizons Investment Club. Avocations: gardening, camping, photography, forensic science, study of ritualistic crime. Home: 16936 NE Davis St Portland OR 97230-6239 Office: Intermountain Forensic Labs Inc 11715 NE Glisan St Portland OR 97220-2141

GRIMSLEY, BESSIE BELLE GATES, special education educator; b. Iola, Kans., Feb. 22, 1938; d. Dwight Leonard and Ruth Bebee (Colwell) Gates; m. Dale Dee Grimsley, Feb. 14, 1959; 1 child, Lendi Lea Grimsley Bland. BS in Edn., Emporia State U., 1962, MS in Edn., 1970. Music tchr. Hamilton, Kans., 1957-58; music tchr. Belle Plaine, Kans., 1958-59; 3rd grade tchr. Johnson, Kans., 1959-61; mid. sch. tchr. Kendall, Kans., 1961-63-68; kindergarten tchr. Alma, Kans., 1968-69; music, reading, phys. edn., math. tchr. Council Grove, Kans., 1969-94; chpt. I reading, math. tchr. Council Grove, 1994—; polit. chmn. USD #417 Tchr.'s Orgn., Council Grove, 1992-94, pres., 1987-89, uniserve rep., 1987-93, sec., 1997—. Vice chmn. Lyon County Dem. com., 1988-94; mem. planning bd. Americus, Kans. zoning commn., 1985-97; mem. Americus Fall Festival com., parade chmn., 1992-94, 97; pres. WKDC, 1997-98; chmn. Americus Days, 1997-99. Mem. Americus C. of C. (pres. 1993-95, 97-99), Emporia Antique Auto Club (sec.-treas. 1993-94), 4-H Alumni, VFW Aux., Am. Legion Aux., Woman's Kans. Day Club (2d v.p. 1994, state pres. 1997—), Delta Kappa Gamma. Presbyterian. Avocations: tap dancing, running, softball, bowling. Home: PO Box 147 Americus KS 66835-0147 Office: Council Grove Elem Sch 706 E Main St Council Grove KS 66846-1126

GRIMSTAD, KIRSTEN JULIA, educator; b. Milw., Nov. 17, 1944; d. James Marion and Elsie Koch G. BA, Barnard Coll., 1968; MA, Columbia U., 1970; PhD, The Union Inst., 1997. Preceptor dept. German Columbia U., N.Y.C., 1969-73; exec. editor Chrysalis Mag., L.A., 1976-80; acquisitions editor J.P. Tarcher, L.A., 1980-81; ind. pub. cons. L.A., 1986-93; core faculty advisor Norwich U., Northfield, Vt., 1988—; pub. cons. Internat. Coun. Mus., Paris, 1986-93, Getty Conservation Inst., L.A., 1986-93. Author: Ancient Heresy in Modern Lit.; co-author: New Woman's Survival Catalog, 1973, New Woman's Survival Sourcebook, 1975. Mem. MLA, AAUW (Am. fellow 1996-97), Kafka Soc. Am., Thomas Mann Gesellschaft, German Studies Assn. Avocations: travel, poodles, art, opera. E-mail: grimstad@primenet.com. Home: 14709 Beston Blvd Pacific Palisades CA 90272 Office: Norwich U Regional Office 15237 Sunset Blvd Pacific Palisades CA 90272

GRIMWADE, RICHARD LLEWELLYN, lawyer; b. Chgo., Apr. 26, 1945; s. Eric Illingworth and Pauline J. (Crandall) G.; m. Alexandra M. Galbraith, Feb. 22, 1981; children: Eric Montgomery, Sarah Elizabeth. BA, Lawrence U., 1967; JD cum laude, U. Wis., 1971. Bar: Wis. 1971, N.Y. 1971, Ill. 1978, Calif. 1981, U.S. Dist. Ct. (so. dist., ea. dist.) N.Y., 1971, U.S. Dist. Ct. (no. dist.) Wis., 1971, U.S. Dist. Ct. (no. dist.) Ill., 1978, U.S. Dist. Ct. (ctrl. dist.) Calif., 1981, U.S. Ct. Appeals (2d cir.) 1971, U.S. Ct. Appeals (7th cir.) 1978, U.S. Ct. Appeals (9th cir.) 1981. Atty. Davis Polk, N.Y.C., 1971-75; ptnr. Barton Klugman, L.A., 1983-93; pvt. practice L.A., 1993—. Mem. U. Wis. Law Rev., 1969-71. Bd. mgrs. Ketchum Downtown YMCA, L.A., 1991-97; trustee Reform L.A. Pub. Schs. (LEARN). Recipient 3 Am. Jurisprudence awards for evidence, legis., and acctg. and law Bancroft-Whitney, 1970. Mem. State Bar Calif., State Bar Wis., State Bar N.Y., State Bar Ill., Rotary L.A. (bd. dirs. 1991-93, sec. 1994), Toastmasters (Best Spkr. award, Best Performer award 1996, Best Table Topics award 1997), Order of Coif. Avocations: gardening, poetry, running, public speaking. Office: MCI Center 700 S Flower St Ste 1100 Los Angeles CA 90017-4113

GRIN, LEONID, conductor; b. Dniepropetrovsk, Ukraine, June 19, 1947; came to U.S., 1981; s. Gavriil and Ita (Sklar) Grinshpun; m. Marina Gusak, Apr. 25, 1970; children: Radmila, Daniel. BMus, Dniepropetrovsk Music Coll., 1966; MusM, Onesin's Music Inst., 1971; MusM in Conducting, Moscow State Conservatory, 1975, DMus, 1977. Assoc. condr. Moscow Philharm. Symphony Orch., 1977-79; prof. conducting U. Houston, 1983-86; prin. guest condr. Tampere (Finland) Philharm Orch., 1988-90, music dir., condr., 1990-94; music dir., condr. San Jose (Calif.) Symphony Orch., 1992—; guest condr. various orchs. in Denmark, Sweden, Norway, Finland, Eng., Scotland, Israel, Germany, The Netherlands, Italy, Belgium, Spain, Portugal, New Zealand, USA, Can., many others. Recs. include music by Tchaikovsky, Procofrev, Shostakovitch, all 6 symphonies by Erkki Mellartin. Office: San Jose Symphony Orchestra 495 Almaden Blvd San Jose CA 95110*

GRIN, OLIVER DANIEL WOODHOUSE, neurosurgeon; b. Buffalo, Apr. 30, 1942; married; 3 children. Assoc. degree, Delta Coll., 1962; BS with honors, Mich. State U., 1964; MD, U. Mich., 1968; postgrad., Davenport Coll. Bd. cert. neurol. surgeon Am. Bd. Neurol. Surgery; lic. multiengine instrument pilot FAA. Rotating intern Blodgett Meml. Med. Ctr., 1968-69, surg. resident, 1969-71; resident in neurol. surgery U. Iowa Hosp. and Clinics, Iowa City, 1970-74, resident in neuropathy, 1972; chief resident in neurosurgery Iowa City VA Hosp., Iowa City, 1972-73; chief resident in neurol. surgery U. Iowa Hosp. and Clinic, Iowa City, 1973-74; pvt. practice neurol. surgery Neurosurg. Assocs. Western Mich., P.C., Grand Rapids, 1974-89, Grand Rapids, 1989—; chief divsn. neurosurgery, active staff mem. Blodgett Meml. Med. Ctr., Grand Rapids; mem. consulting staff neurosurgery Gerber Meml. Hosp., Fremont, Mich., North Ottawa Comty. Hosp., Grand Haven, Mich., Holland (Mich.) Comty. Hosp.; mem. courtesy staff Mary Free Bed Hosp. and Rehab. Ctr., Grand Rapids, St. Mary's Hosp., Grand Rapids, Butterworth Hosp., Grand Rapids; assoc. clin. prof. Coll. Human Medicine, Mich. State U., East Lansing; key person mem. Joint Washington Com., Am. Assn. Neurol. Surgeons and Congress of Neurol. Surgeons; CEO, co-founder Ludann Edn. Svcs., Grand Rapids; chief neurosurgery, co-founder Neurologic-Orthopaedic Inst. for Spinal Rehab. and Sports Medicine, Grand Rapids; presenter in field. Contbr. articles to med. jours. Fellow ACS; mem. AMA, Am. Assn. Neurol. Surgeons (past mem. publs. com.), Congress Neurol. Surgeons, N.Am. Skull Base Soc., Mich. State Med. Soc. (chmn. legis. subcom. on pub. affairs workshops legis. com.), Mich. Assn. Neurol. Surgeons (past pres.), Western Mich. Neurol. Soc. (past pres.), Kent County Med. Soc., Phi Kappa. Fax: (616-949-6096). E-mail: ollcar@aol.com. Home and Office: Ste 212 3230 Eagle Park Dr NE Grand Rapids MI 49525

GRINBERG, MEYER STEWART, educational institute executive; b. New Brunswick, N.J., Aug. 31, 1944; s. Allen Lewis and Edith (Bart) G.; children: David, Lee, Benjamin. BA, Franklin and Marshall Coll., 1965; JD, U. Pa., 1968; MBA, George Washington U., 1973. Bar: Pa., U.S. Ct. Claims, U.S. Customs Ct., U.S. Ct. Internat. Trade, U.S. Ct. Mil. Appeals, U.S. Supreme Ct.; CPA, Pa. Tax acct. Arthur Andersen & Co., Pitts., 1973-77; v.p., co-owner Buy-Wise, Inc., Pitts., 1977-91; exec. dir. Jewish Edn. Inst. Pitts., 1991—; chmn. Maccabi Culture and Edn. com., JCCA. Exec. v.p. Cong. B'nai Israel, Pitts., 1982—; v.p. western Pa. region United Synagogues Am., Pitts., 1984—, mem. nat. adv. bd., 1986—; v.p. Sch. Advanced Studies, Pitts., 1983—; pres. Community Day Sch., 1988—, past v.p.; bd. dirs. Solomon Schechter Nat. Day Sch. Assn.; co-founder Solomon Schechter Day Sch., Pitts.; bd. dirs. Forward-Shady Housing Project, United Synagogue of Conservative Judaism-Israel Affairs Com.; chmn. Pitts. delegation to the Maccabi Games of Israel; mem. Israel Bond Cabinet, Jewish Com. Ctr. (Rogal-Ruslander award, Pitts. 1990), coach Little League; chmn. health and phys. edn. com. Jewish Community Ctr.; gen. chmn. Invitational Maccabi Youth Games, 1989; mem. N.Am. YouthMaccabar Games Com.; bd. dirs. Hebrew Inst. of Pitts.; mem. wish com. Make-A-Wish Found., Pitts.; chair Nat. Maccabi Culture and Edn. Com. Lt. USCG, 1968-73. Recipient Latterman Vol. Mitzuah award, 1988, JWB New Leadership award, 1990, Rogal-Ruslander Leadership award Jewish Community Ctr., 1990; named Outstanding Citizen of Pitts., Sta. WQEX, Pitts. Post-Gazette, 1989. Mem. Am. Inst. CPA's, Pa. Inst. CPA's, Pa. Bar Assn., Commn. on Jewish Edn. Democrat. Lodge: Kiwanis. Avocations: jogging, photography. Address: Jewish Education Institute 6424 Forward Ave Pittsburgh PA 15217-2521

GRINDAL, MARY ANN, former sales professional; b. Michigan City, Ind., Sept. 9, 1942; d. James Paxton and Helen Evelyn (Koivisto) Gleason; m. Bruce Theodore Grindal, June 12, 1965 (div. Sept. 1974); 1 child, Matthew Bruce. BSBA, Ind. U., 1965. Sec. African studies program Ind. U., Bloomington, 1965-66; rsch. aide Ghana, West Africa, 1966-68; exec. sec. divsn. biol. scis. Ind. U., Bloomington, 1968-69; office asst. Dean of Students office Middlebury (Vt.) Coll., 1969-70; exec. sec. Remo, Inc., North Hollywood, Calif., 1974-76; sec., asst. to product mgrs. in cosmetic and skin care Redken Labs., Canoga Park, Calif., 1976-79; various sec. and exec. sec. positions L.A., 1979-81, 85-89; exec. sec. Sargent Industries, Burbank, Calif., 1981-85; sales asst. Chyron Graphics, Burbank, Calif., 1989-97; adminstrv. sec. divsn. instructional svcs. Burbank Unified Sch. Dist., 1998—. Author of poems and essays. Mem. U.S. Navy Meml. Found. Mem. DAR (chpt. registrar 1988-91, chpt. regent 1991-94, chpt. chmn. pub. rels. and pub. 1994—, chpt. chaplain 1994—, mem. spkrs. staff 1995—, state chmn. Am. Heritage 1994-96, state chmn. Calif. DAR scholarship com. 1996-98), Daus. of Union Vets. of Civil War, 1861-65, Inc., Nat. Soc. Dames of the Ct. of Honor (state chaplain 1997—). Episcopalian. Avocations: travel, writing, genealogy.

GRINDEA, DANIEL, international economist; b. Galatz, Romania, Feb. 23, 1924; came to U.S., 1975; s. Samy and Liza (Kaufman) Grünberg; m. Lidia Bunaciu; 1 child, Sorin. MS in Econs., Inst. Econ Scis., Bucharest, Romania, 1948; MLaw, Faculty of Law, Bucharest, 1948; PhD in Econs., Inst. Fin. and Planning, St. Petersburg, Russia, 1953. Assoc. prof. econs. various univs., Bucharest, 1953-69, prof. econs., 1969-75; cons. State Planning Com., 1953-56, Ministry of Fin., 1956-68; mem. Sci. Coun. of Ctrl. Statis. Office, 1956-68; internat. economist Republic Nat. Bank of N.Y., N.Y.C., 1976-78, sr. internat. economist, dept. head, 1978-79, v.p., sr. internat. economist, 1979-84, sr. v.p., chief economist, 1984-89, sr. cons., 1990-95; pres. Romanian-Am. C. of C., N.Y.C., 1990-92; sr. advisor U.S. Congl. Adv. Bd., 1988; prof., elected mem. sci. coun. l'Ecole Supérieur des Scis. Commls. d'Angers, France, 1989; mem. econ. adv. bd. Inst. Internat. Fin., Washington, 1988; invited vis. prof. l'Institut Internat. de la Planification de l'Edn., UNESCO, Paris, 1973; mem. adv. group Com. on Asian Econ. Studies, 1983. Contbr. articles on forecasts in field to U.S. and internat. publs.; papers presented to profl. confs. in U.S., France, Sweden, Ireland, Bulgaria, Romania. Recipient 1st prize in econ. rsch. Ministry of Edn., Romania, 1969, Book award Am. Romanian Acad. Art and Scis., 1995, 98, emeritus mem., 1998. Achievements include correct predictions on world economy and individual countries; special research regarding the transition period to a free market economy in the ex-communist European countries.

GRINDLAY, JONATHAN ELLIS, astrophysics educator; b. Richmond, Va., Nov. 9, 1944; s. John Happer and Elizabeth (Ellis) G.; m. Sandra Kay Smyrski, Oct. 10, 1970; children: Graham Charles, Kathryn Jane. A.B., Dartmouth Coll., 1966; M.A., Harvard U., 1969, Ph.D., 1971. Jr. fellow Harvard U., Cambridge, Mass., 1971-74, asst. prof., 1976-81, prof. astronomy, 1981—; chmn. dept. astronomy Harvard U., 1985-90; astrophysicist Smithsonian Obs., 1974-76; cons. MIT Lincoln Lab., Bedford, Mass., 1982—; mem. vis. com. astronomy U. Chgo., 1983, Astrophys. Lab. Saclay, France, 1988—, NASA/Goddard Space Flt. Ctr., 1995-96, chmn., 1997; mem. vis. com. dept. physics Columbia U., 1998; vis. com. Naval Rsch. Lab., 1998; mem. users com. Cerro Tololo Interam. Obs., La Serena, Chile, 1981-84; mem. Aspen Ctr. for Physics, Colo., 1991—, trustee, 1989-90, mem. astrophysics program com., 1983—; chmn. high energy astrophysics mgmt. ops. group NASA, 1986-88, Compton Gamma Ray Obs. users com., 1992-94; mem. Space Sci. Bd., NAS, 1986-89; mem. com. Astronomy and Astrophysics NRC, 1992-98; mem. com. on internat. programs NRC, 1996-98; mem. High Energy Astronomy From Space Panel, NRC, 1998—; mem. Space Telescope Inst. Coun., 1993-96, Space Telescope Ind. Sci. Rev. com. 1996-97; chmn. Binary Panel, Space Telescope Cycle 7 Time Allocation Commn.; chmn. Space Sci. Working Group AAU, 1990-92; mem. sci. orgn. com. for numerous internat. mtgs. Contbr. articles to profl. jours. and books. Recipient Bart J. Bok prize dept. astronomy Harvard U., 1976; NSF and NASA rsch. grantee, 1978—; Guggenheim fellow, 1991-93, Sloan fellow, 1981-84. Fellow AAAS, Am. Phys. Soc. (nat. chair divsn. astrophysics 1998-99), Am. Astron. Soc. (councilor, nat. sec.-treas. high energy astrophysics div. 1982-84, v.p. 1994-97); mem. Internat. Astron. Union (pres. commn. 6 1991-94). Home: 195 Lincoln Rd Lincoln MA 01773-4102 Office: Harvard Coll Obs 60 Garden St Cambridge MA 02138-1516

GRINE, FLORENCE MAY, secondary education educator; b. Sycamore, Ohio, Apr. 21, 1927; d. Murray J. and Ethel (Kingseed) G. BS, Bowling Green State U., 1949, MEd, 1966. Cert. tchr., Ohio. Bus. tchr. McCutchenville (Ohio) Sch., 1949-51, Fostoria (Ohio) High Sch., 1951-60, Tiffin (Ohio)-Columbian High Sch., 1960-90. Mem. NEA, AAUW, Nat. Bus. Edn. Assn., Ohio Edn. Assn., N.W. Ohio Edn. Assn., Ohio Vocat. Assn., Ohio Bus. Tchrs. Assn., Tiffin Edn. Assn. (pres. 1965-66), Tiffin Bus. and Profl. Women (pres. 1955, 63, Woman of Yr. award 1987), Delta Kappa Gamma (chpt. pres. 1970-72, state pres. 1989-91). Republican. Presbyterian. Avocations: travel, gardening.

GRINELL, SHEILA, museum director; b. N.Y.C., July 15, 1945; d. Richard N. and Martha (Mimiless) G.; m. Thomas E. Johnson, July 15, 1980; 1 child, Michael; stepchildren: Kathleen, Thomas. BA, Radcliffe Coll., 1966; MA, U. Calif., Berkeley, 1968. Co-dir. exhibits and programs The Exploratorium, San Francisco, 1969-74; promotion dir. Kodansha Internat., Tokyo, 1974-77; traveling exhbn. coord. Assn. Sci. Tech. Ctrs., Washington, 1978-80, exec. dir., 1980-82, project dir. traveling exhbn. Chips and Changes, 1982-84; assoc. dir. N.Y. Hall of Sci., 1984-87; exec. dir. Ariz. Sci. Ctr., Phoenix, 1993—; cons. Optical Soc. Am., 1987, Nat. Sci. Ctr. Found., 1988, Interactive Video Sci. Consortium, 1988, Assn. Sci. Tech. Ctrs., 1988-89, Found. for Creative Am., 1989-90, Am. Assn. for World Health, 1990, Children's TV Workshop, 1991, Sciencenter, 1991, SciencePort, 1991, The Invention Factory, 1992, N.Y. Bot. Garden, 1992-93. Author: Light, Sight, Sound, Hearing: Exploratorium '74, 1974; editor A Stage for Science, 1979, A New Place for Learning Science: Starting and Running A Science Center, 1992, (with Mark St. John) Vision to Reality: Critical Dimensions in Science Center Development, Vol. I, 1993, II, 1994. Fulbright teaching asst., 1966; hon. Woodrow Wilson fellow, 1967. Fellow AAAS; mem. Am. Assn. Mus., Phi Beta Kappa. Office: Ariz Sci Ctr 600 E Washington St Phoenix AZ 85004-2303

GRINER, PAUL FRANCIS, physician; b. Phila., Jan. 1, 1933; s. John and Josepha (Snyder) G.; m. Miriam Millard; children: Laura, Paul Jr. BA, Harvard U., 1954; MD with honors, U. Rochester, 1959. Diplomate Am. Bd. Internal Medicine, Nat. Bd. Med. Examiners. Intern in medicine Mass. Gen. Hosp., Boston, 1959-60, asst. resident, 1960-61, sr. resident, 1963-64; chief resident in medicine Strong Meml. Hosp., Rochester, N.Y., 1964-65; fellow in pathology U. Rochester Sch. Medicine & Dentistry, 1956-57, instr. medicine, fellow in hematology, 1964-65, clin. instr., 1965-66, clin. sr. instr., 1966-67, asst. prof. medicine, 1967-69, assoc. prof., 1969-73, Samuel E. Durand prof. medicine, 1973-95, head. gen. medicine unit, 1976-84, acting chmn. dept. medicine, 1977-79, chmn. dept. health svcs., 1985-94; gen. dir. Strong Meml. Hosp., 1984-94; v.p. dir. Assn. Am. Med. Colls., Washington, 1995—; dir. med. edn. Rochester Gen. Hosp., 1965-67, cons. 1969-95; cons. Genesee Hosp., 1969-95, Highland Hosp., 1969-95; chmn., bd. dirs. Acad. Med. Ctr. Consortium, 1991-92. Contbr. numerous articles to profl. jours., chpts. to books. Mem. N.Y. Gov.'s Health Care Adv. Bd., 1990-94, Mayoral Commn. on Health and Hosps. Corp. of City of N.Y., 1991-92. Capt. USAF, 1961-63. Recipient Doran Stephens prize U. Rochester, 1959. Master ACP (mem. health and pub. policy com. 1981-84, 87-88, chmn. 1988-90; chmn bd. regents 1991-92, chmn. clin. efficacy assessment subcom. 1986-88, pres. 1993-94), Venezuelan Soc. Internal Medicine (hon.); mem. AAAS, Am. Clin. and Climatol. Assn., Assn. Am. Physicians, Internat. Soc. Tech. Assessment in Health Care,Soc. Med. Decision Making, So. Gen. Internal Medicine, Soc. Med. Adminstrs., Inst. Medicine Nat. Acad. Scis. (com. quality rev. and assurance in Medicare 1987-90, mem. bd. healthcare svcs. 1987—, mem. com. on future primary care 1994-95), Alpha Omega Alpha. Avocations: skiing, tennis, surf fishing, zither. Office: Assn Am Med Colls 2450 N St NW Washington DC 20037-1167*

GRING, DAVID M., academic administrator; b. Reading, Pa., May 19, 1945; s. Carl Willard and Kathryne Flora (Abele) G.; m. Susan Marie Dietrich, June 3, 1967; children: Lisa, Christian. AB, Franklin and Marshall Coll., 1967; MA, Ind. U., 1970, PhD, 1971. Asst. prof. Lebanon Valley Coll., Annville, Pa., 1971-76; asst. dean of coll. Concordia Coll., Moorhead, Minn., 1976-78, assoc. dean of coll., 1978-79, v.p. acad. affairs, 1979-89; pres. Roanoke Coll., Salem, Va., 1989—; acad. adminstrn. fellow Am. Coun. Edn., Washington, 1975-76; participant Inst. Ednl. Mgmt., Harvard U, 1986. Trustee North Cross Sch., Roanoke; dir. Roanoke Regional Chamber. Recipient J.L.K. Preus Leadership award Am. Luth. Ch., 1986; Bush Found. summer fellow, 1986. Fellow Soc. Values in Higher Edn.; mem. Am. Assn. Higher Edn., Coun. Coll. Pres. Evangel. Luth. Ch. Am. (mem. exec. com., pres.), Hastings Ctr., Sigma Xi (assoc.), Phi Beta Kappa. Avocations: hiking, tennis. Office: Roanoke Coll 221 College Ln Salem VA 24153-3747*

GRINNELL, ALAN DALE, neurobiologist, educator, researcher; b. Mpls., Nov. 11, 1936; s. John Erle and Swanhild Constance (Friswold) G.; m. Verity Rich, Sept. 30, 1962 (div. 1975); m. Feelie Lee, Dec. 23, 1996. BA, Harvard U., 1958, PhD, 1962. Jr. fellow Harvard U., 1959-62; research assoc. biophysics dept. Univ. Coll. London, 1962-64; asst. research zoologist UCLA, 1964-65, from asst. prof. to prof. dept. biology, 1965-78, prof. physiology, 1972—; dir. Jerry Lewis Neuromuscular Research Ctr. UCLA Sch. Medicine, 1978—; head Ahmanson Lab. Cellular Neurobiology UCLA Brain Research Inst, 1977—; dir. tng. grant in cellular neurobiology UCLA, 1968—, rsch. assoc. Fowler Mus. Cultural History, 1990—, chmn. dept. physiol. sci., 1997—. Author: Calcium and Ion Channel Modulation, 1988, Physiology of Excitable Cells, 1983, Regulation of Muscle Contraction, 1981, Introduction to Nervous Systems, 1977, others; contbr. editorial revs. to profl. jours., pub. houses, fed. granting agys. Guggenheim fellow, 1986; recipient Sr. Scientist award Alexander von Humboldt Stiftung, 1975, 79, Jacob Javits award NIH, 1986. Mem. AAAS (mem.-at-large neurosci. steering group 1998—), Muscular Dystrophy Assn. (mem. med. adv. com. L.A. chpt. 1980-92), Soc. for Neurosci. (councilor 1982-86), Am. Physiol. Soc. (mem. neurophysiol. steering com. 1981-84), Soc. Fellow, Phi Beta Kappa, Sigma Xi, others. Avocations: music, anthropology, archaeology, travel. Home: 510 E Rustic Rd Santa Monica CA 90402-1116 Office: UCLA Sch Medicine Jerry Lewis Neuromuscu Los Angeles CA 90095

GRINNELL, HELEN DUNN, musicologist, arts administrator; b. N.Y.C., Nov. 22, 1936; d. Kempton and Susan Barret (Gill) D.; children: Taylor, James Bodman; m. Alexander Grinnell, July 6, 1991. New Eng. Conservatory, 1957-60; BMus in Music Theory, San Francisco Conservatory of Music, 1968; MA in Musicology, Am. U., 1982. Dir. Opera and Symphony Previews, San Francisco, 1966-67; Congressional Aide U.S. House of Reps., Washington, 1973; arts. coord. Del. State Arts Coun., 1977-78; music libr. Am. U., Washington, 1981-84; pres. Arts Info. Specialists, 1984—, dir. Discovering Music, 1984—; dir. Rsch. Ctr. for Chinese Mus. Iconography, 1984—; cons. Young Artist program Boys Clubs of Am., 1985-90, dept. musical instruments Met. Mus. Art, 1996—, China Inst. in Am., 1999—. Author: Chinese Musical Iconography: A History of Musical Instruments Depicted in Chinese Art, 1987, National Symphony Orchestra Discography, 1988, Yayue Depicted on Ancient Chinese Bronzes, 1994; program annotator Dumbarton Concert Series, Smithsonian Institution, Kennedy Ctr. Stagebill, Handel Festival Orch., Nat. Chamber Orch.; editor: American Women Composers' Forum; steering com. Friends of Music Smithsonian Instn. Bd. dirs. Spring Opera of San Francisco, 1967-71, Jr. League of San Francisco, 1967-71, Wilmington Music Sch., 1973-78, Washington Performing Arts Soc., 1980-90, Nat. Symphony Orch., Washington, 1979-82, Bargemusic Ltd., 1992—, Nat. Orchestral Assn., 1993—, Shelter Island Hist. Soc., 1993-95, New Eng. Conservatory Alumni Assn., 1995—; chmn. acad. policy com., trustee San Francisco Conservatory of Music, 1967-71; bd. overseers New Eng. Conservatory, 1985-90; chmn. archl. rev. bd. Village of Dering Harbor, N.Y., 1991-95. Mem. Am. Musical Instruments Soc., Am. Musicol. Soc., Amateur Ski Club N.Y., Shelter Island Yacht Club, Cosmopolitan Club.

GRINSPUN, RICARDO, economist, educator. BA in Econs., Hebrew U., 1976, MA in Econs., 1983; PhD, U. Mich., 1990. Economist Govt. of Israel, 1975-81; instr. econs. Tel Aviv U., 1982-83; prof. econs. York U., Toronto, Ont., Can., 1989—, dir. Ctr. for Rsch. on L.Am. and Caribbean, 1995—; cons. in field. Contbr. articles to profl. jours. Mem. Can. Assn. L.Am. and CaribbeanStudies (v.p., pres.-elect 1996—). Office: York U CERLAC, 240 York Lanes 4700 Keele St, Toronto, ON Canada M3J 1P3*

GRINSTEAD, PAUL LEE, materials company official; b. Chilhowie, Va., May 3, 1951; s. Fred Love Grinstead and Anna (Lee) Eller; m. Barbara Ann Sturgill, Aug. 5, 1972; children: Paul Jeremy, Justin Ross. AS, Va. Highlands C.C., 1994; BS, U. Va., 1996; cert. in Bible, Belle Meadows Bible Coll., Va., 1998. Prodn. coord. Brunswick Corp., Marion, Va., 1976-81, material specialist, 1982-86, program specialist II, 1987-96; estimator Marion Composites, TPG, 1996-97, program coord. II, 1998—; mem. gov.'s adv. com. Commonwealth of Va., Richmond, 1998—. Dir. children's ch. and youth Bapt. chs., Smyth and Tazewell Counties, Va., 1976—; chmn. 5th Legis. and 39th Senatorial dists. Smyth County Rep. Com., 1994—; vice chmn. Smyth County Planning Commn., 1994—; mem. Smyth County Sch. Sys. Sch. Bd., 1998—. Mem. Masons (worshipful master 1988-89). Avocations: hunting, fishing, camping, hiking. E-mail: pgrinstead@smyth.net. Home: 323 Greystone Rd Marion VA 24354

GRINSTEIN, GERALD, transportation executive; b. 1932; married. B.A., Yale U., 1954; LL.B., Harvard U., 1957. Bar: D.C., Wash. Counsel to merchant marine and transp. subcoms., chief counsel U.S. Senate Commerce Com., Washington, D.C., 1958-67; adminstrv. asst. U.S. Senator Warren G. Magnuson, Washington, D.C., 1967-69; ptnr. Preston Thorgrimson Ellis & Holman, 1969-83; chmn. bd. Western Air Lines Inc., Los Angeles, 1983-84, pres., COO, 1984-85, CEO, 1985-86, chmn., CEO, 1986-87; vice chmn. Burlington Northern Inc., Ft. Worth, 1987-88; pres., CEO Burlington Northern, Inc., Ft. Worth, 1989-90, chmn., CEO, 1990-95; pres., CEO, Burlington No. R.R. Co., 1989-90; chmn., CEO Burlington Northern R.R. Co., 1990-95; chmn. Delta Air Lines, Inc., 1997—; chmn. Delta Air Lines, Inc.; bd. dirs. Browning-Ferris Industries, Inc., Sundstrand Corp., Imperial

Holly Corp., Paccar, Inc. Office: 1000 2nd Ave Ste 3700 Seattle WA 98104-1053*

GRIPE, ALAN GORDON, minister; b. Indpls., Sept. 8, 1920; s. Otto Herman and Bertha (Anderson) G.; m. Elizabeth Howell, Sept. 29, 1951 (div. 1972); children: Stephen, David. BA, Lake Forest (Ill.) Coll., 1942; BD, Princeton Theol. Sem., 1946; STM, Union Theol. Sem., N.Y.C., 1953. Ordained to ministry, Presbyn. Ch. (U.S.A.), 1946. Asst. prof. Silliman U., Dumaguete City, Philippines, 1946-50; chaplain Davidson (N.C.) Coll., 1951-52; asst. chaplain U.S. Mil. Acad., West Point, 1952-55; pastor First Presbyn. Ch., Westfield, N.Y., 1955-65; exec. coord. Personnel Svcs., United Presbyn. Ch. USA, 1965-88; interim pastor Genesee Valley Presbytery, Rochester, N.Y., 1991—. Author: The Interim Pastor's Manual, 2d edit., 1997. Treas. John Milton Soc. for Blind, N.Y.C., 1988-90. Mem. Assn. of Presbyn. Interim Ministry Specialists (coun. mem. 1987-90). Home: 95 Penarrow Rd Rochester NY 14618-1721

GRIPPI, SALVATORE WILLIAM, artist; b. Buffalo, Sept. 30, 1921; s. Leonardo and Josephine (Orlando) G.; m. Rosalind Ratzenberg, Apr. 14, 1945. Student, Mus. Modern Art, N.Y.C., 1944-45, Art Students' League, N.Y.C., 1945-48, Atelier 17, N.Y.C., 1951-53; student (Fulbright grantee), Istituto Statale d'Arte, Florence, Italy, 1953-55. Instr. Atelier 17, summer 1953, Cooper Union Art Sch., 1956-59, Sch. Visual Arts, N.Y.C., 1961-62; asso. prof. art Claremont Grad. Sch., 1962-68, Pomona Coll., 1962-68; prof., founder art dept. Ithaca Coll., 1968—; invited participant Ford Found. Conf. Visual Artists, 1961. One-man shows include, N.Y. U., N.Y.C., 1958, Zabriskie Gallery, N.Y.C., 1956, 59, Krasner Gallery, N.Y.C., 1962, 64, 79, 81, Feingarten Galleries, 1967, 70, Everson, Mus., Syracuse, N.Y., 1978, Handwerker Gallery, Ithaca Coll., 1978, group shows include, Met. Mus. Art, N.Y.C., 1952, Schneider Gallery, Rome, 1954, Galleria La Fontanella, Rome, 1955, Whitney Mus. and Smithsonian Inst. Traveling show, 1958-59, Corcoran Gallery Art, Washington, 1959, 63, Whitney Mus., N.Y.C., 1960, Mus. Modern Art, N.Y.C., 1962, 1994-95, Hunter Coll. Leubsdorf Gallery, N.Y.C., 1995; represented in permanent collections, Whitney Mus., Met. Mus. Art, N.Y. Pub. Library, N.Y.C., Joseph Hirshorn Collection, Washington, Milw.-Downer Coll., Ithaca Coll., St. Lawrence U., Everson Mus. Served with USNR, 1942-45. Mem. Art Students' League (life, treas. 1961-62, bd. control 1961-64), Coll. Art Assn. Home: PO Box 234 Ithaca NY 14851-0234 Office: Ithaca Coll Art Dept Ithaca NY 14850

GRIPPO, JAMES JOSEPH, writer, educator; b. Ridgway, Pa., Oct. 18, 1947; s. William and Marie (Pyne) G.; m. Susan Bell Williams, Dec. 21, 1971; children: James D., Daniel A., Ryan J. BS, W.Va. U., 1972; MS, Mich. State U., 1980. Ext. agt. Pa. State U., University Park, 1973—, instr., 1981-94; mem. adv. bd. Clearfield (Pa.) Vo-tech Sch., 1979—; employers adv. com. Employment Security Office, Clearfield, 1987—. Editor: Trout Unlimited, 1978-80. With USN, 1965-68, Vietnam. Recipient Citation for Leadership Pa. Ho. of Reps., 1975. Mem. Pa. Outdoor Writers Assn. Republican. Roman Catholic. Avocations: fly fishing, hiking. Home: 415 Spruce St Clearfield PA 16830-1940 Office: Pa State U 650 Leonard St Clearfield PA 16830-3243

GRISCHKOWSKY, DANIEL RICHARD, research scientist, educator; b. St. Helens, Oreg., Apr. 17, 1940; s. Oscar Edward and Christine Hazel (Olsen) G.; m. Frieda Rosa Bachmann; children: Timothy and Stephanie (twins), Daniela. BS, Oreg. State U., 1962; AM in Physics, Columbia U., 1965, PhD in Physics, 1968. Postdoctoral studies Columbia U., N.Y.C., 1968-69; mem. rsch. staff IBM Watson Rsch. Ctr., Yorktown Heights, N.Y., 1969-77; sci. advisor to dir. rsch. div. IBM, Yorktown Heights, 1978; mgr. atomic physics with lasers group IBM Watson Rsch. Ctr., Yorktown Heights, 1979-83, mgr. ultra-fast sci. with lasers group, 1983-93; Bellmon chair optoelectronics Sch. Elec. and Computer Engring. Okla. State U., Stillwater, 1993—; chmn. Internat. Coun. on Quantum Electronics, 1989-93, Am. Phys. Soc./Optical Soc. Am./IEEE Joint Coun. on Quantum Electronics, 1989-93. Contbr. articles to profl. jours.; patentee in field. Recipient Boris Pregel award N.Y. Acad. of Sci., 1985. Fellow IEEE, Am. Phys. Soc. (chmn. laser sci. topical group 1993-94), Optical Soc. Am. (R.W. Wood prize 1989). Office: Okla State U Sch Elec Computer Engring Stillwater OK 74078-0321

GRISHAM, GEORGE ROBERT, mathematics educator; b. Wheeler, Miss., Nov. 30, 1930; s. George B. and Maggie (Oakley) G.; m. Garnette S. Swinney, May 28, 1955; children: Deborah K. Grisham O'Neal, Jennifer L. Grisham Rochford. BS, Miss. State U., 1952, MEd, 1956. Cert math. tchr., K-14 gen. supervision, Ill.; cert. math. tchr., Tex. Tchr. Streator (Ill.) Twp. High Sch., 1956-68; prof. math. Ill. Cen. Coll., East Peoria, Ill., 1968-86, chmn. dept., 1981-86; tchr. N.E. Ind. Sch. Dist., San Antonio, 1986-87; asst. prof. Bradley U., Peoria, Ill., 1987-92; ret., 1992. Author algebra study guides; editor The Math Connexion, 1972-75. Bd. dirs. Am. Field Svc., Morton, Ill., 1972. With USN, 1952-54, Korea, comdr. USNR, ret. Named Tchr. of Yr., Peoria Savs. and Loan Assn., 1972. Mem. Math. Assn. Am., Nat. Coun. Tchrs. Math. (conv. chmn. Peoria 1980), Ill. Coun. Tchrs. Math. (pres. 1976, co-chmn. conv. 1989), Ill. Math. Assn. C.C.'s (life, pres. 1981), Res. Officers Assn. (life), Moose, Elks. Democrat. Presbyterian. Avocations: reading, gardening, ballroom dancing. Home: 22 Maple Ridge Dr Morton IL 61550-1152

GRISHAM, JOE WHEELER, pathologist, educator; b. Smith County, Tenn., Dec. 5, 1931; s. William Wince and Grace (Allen) G.; m. Jean Evelyn Malone, July 2, 1955. B.A., Vanderbilt U., 1953, M.D., 1957. Intern Washington U.-Barnes Hosp., St. Louis, 1957-58; resident in pathology Washington U.-Barnes Hosp., 1958-60; mem. faculty Washington U., Med. Sch., 1960-73, prof. pathology and anatomy, 1969-73; assoc. pathologist Barnes Hosp., 1969-73; vis. instr. Makerere Med. Coll., Kampala, Uganda, 1961; prof. pathology, chmn. dept. U. N.C. Med. Sch., Chapel Hill, 1973-99, Kenan prof., 1992—; also pathologist-in-chief U. N.C. Hosp., 1973-99; mem. pathology study sect. A NIH, 1969-73, chmn., 1970-73, chmn. pathology study sect. B, 1979-83; Norma Berryhill disting. lectr. U. N.C., 1998—; bd. sci. counsellors Nat. Inst. Environ. Health Scis., 1974-78; mem. sci. advisory panel Chem. Industry Inst. Toxicology, 1977-88, chmn., 1980-88; adv. bd. Given Inst. Pathobiology, 1983-87; Berryhill lectr. U. N.C., 1998. Contbr. articles to med. jours. Served to lt. comdr. USNR, 1961-63. John and Mary R. Markle scholar acad. medicine, 1964-69; fellow Life Ins. Med. Rsch. Fund, 1959-61, Nat. Cancer Inst., 1958-59; Brindley prof. U. Tex. Med. Br., 1993; named Disting. Med. Alumnus Vanderbilt U., 1994. Mem. Am. Assn. Pathologists (pres. 1984-85), Am. Assn. Cancer Research, Fedn. Am. Soc. Exptl. Biology (pres., chmn. bd. 1984-85), Am. Assn. Study Liver Diseases, Am. Soc. Cell Biology, Univ. Assn. Research and Edn. in Pathology (v.p. 1985-86), Tissue Culture Assn., Internat. Acad. Pathology, Cell Kinetics Soc., AMA, AAAS. Home: 1703 Curtis Rd Chapel Hill NC 27514-7614 Office: Univ NC Med Sch Dept Pathology CB # 7525 Chapel Hill NC 27599

GRISHAM, JOHN, writer; b. Jonesboro, Ark., Feb. 8, 1955; m. Renee Jones; children: Ty, Shea. BS, Miss. State U., 1977; JD, U. Miss., 1981. Bar: Miss. 1981. Practiced law Southaven, Miss., 1981-91; mem. Miss. Ho. Reps., 1984-90. Author: A Time to Kill, 1989, The Firm, 1991, The Pelican Brief, 1992, The Client, 1993, The Chamber, 1994, The Rainmaker, 1995, The Runaway Jury, 1996, The Partner, 1997, The Street Lawyer, 1998, The Testament, 1999. Office: Doubleday Pub 1540 Broadway New York NY 10036-4039*

GRISHAM, LARRY RICHARD, physicist; b. Henderson, Tex., Feb. 2, 1949; s. James Marion and Eva Fay (Powell) G.; m. Jacqueline Lea Criswell, June 24, 1972; children: Austin Nathanial, Rachel Nicole, Hilary Jane. BS in Physics, U. Tex., 1971; PhD in Physics, Oxford (Eng.) U., 1974. Postdoctoral fellow Princeton (N.J.) U., Plasma Physics Lab., 1974-75, staff rsch. physicist, 1975-82, rsch. physicist, 1982-89, prin. rsch. physicist, 1989—, head beam physics, 1988—; cons. Northrop Corp., L.A., 1985, Phys. Dynamics, La Jolla, Calif., 1986-88, Teledyne Brown Engring., Huntsville, Ala., 1989—; mem. and chmn. various rev. panels U.S. Army Strategic Def. Command, 1986—. Contbr. numerous articles to profl. jours. Mem. N.J. Rhodes Scholar Selection Com., Morristown, 1986—. Recipient Tex. Exes Centennial Honored Alumnus award U. Tex., Austin, 1985, Wolfson Grad. award, 1972; winner Westinghouse Sci. Talent Search, Washington, 1967; Rhodes scholar, 1971; Woodrow Wilson fellow, 1971, invited rsch. fellow Japan Atomic Energy Rsch. Inst., 1996. Mem. AAAS, Am. Phys. Soc., Phi Beta Kappa. Methodist. Achievements include research in energy confinement properties of tokamak plasmas as a fuction of major and minor radius; physics and technology of high power neutral beam systems physics of excited nuclear states. Avocation: hiking. Home: 2 Dennick Ct Princeton NJ 08540-2202 Office: Princeton Univ Plasma Physics Lab PO Box 451 Princeton NJ 08543-0451

GRISKEY, RICHARD GEORGE, chemical engineering educator; b. Pitts., Jan. 9, 1931; s. George and Emma (Maskell) G.; m. Pauline Anne Becker, June 11, 1955; children: Paula Louise, David Richard. B.Ch.E., Carnegie-Mellon U., 1951, M.Ch.E., 1955, Ph.D., 1958. Registered profl. engr., Wis. Sr. engr. E. I. duPont Co., Seaford, Del., 1958-60; asst. prof. U. Cin., 1960-62; assoc. prof. Va. Poly. Inst., 1962-64, prof., 1964-66; prof., head chem. engring. dept. U. Denver, 1966-68; dir. research and found. research prof. Newark Coll. Engring., 1968-71; prof. chem. engring., dean U. Wis.-Milw., 1971-82; prof. chem. engring., dean engring. U. Ala.-Huntsville, 1982-85; v.p., provost Stevens Inst. Tech., 1985-86, exec. v.p., provost, 1986-88, The Institute prof. chemistry and chem. engring., 1988—; vis. scientist Polish Acad. Sci.-NAS, 1971; OAS vis. prof. Multi Nat. Food Project, Brazil, 1973; vis. prof. Monash U., Australia, 1974, Algerian Inst. Petroleum, 1975, 76; chem. engring. cons. Editor, Marcel Dekker Inc., 1974—; referee, reviewer: Canadian Jour. Chem. Engring., Am. Inst. Chem. Engrs. Jour., Jour. Polymer Sci., Jour. Fluid Mechanics, Jour. Heat Transfer; author: Chemical Engineering for Chemists; author: Polymer Process Engineering, 1995, 97; contbr. numerous articles to sci. jours. Served with AUS, 1951-53. Fellow ASME, Am. Inst. Chemists, Am. Inst. Chem. Engrs.; mem. Soc. Rheology, Am. Soc. Engring. Edn., Am. Assn. Higher Edn., Plastics Inst. Am. (bd. dirs. 1986—), Soc. Plastics Engrs., Am. Chem. Soc. (congl. counselor, exceptional achievement award 1991), Tau Beta Pi, Sigma Xi, Triangle, Scabbard and Blade. Office: Stevens Inst Tech Dept Chem & Chem Engring Hoboken NJ 07030

GRISMORE, ROGER, physics educator, researcher; b. Ann Arbor, Mich., July 12, 1924; s. Grover Cleveland and May Aileen (White) G.; m. Marilynn Ann McNinch, Sept. 15, 1950; 1 child, Carol Ann. BS, U. Mich., 1947, MS, 1948, PhD, 1957; BS in Computer Sci., Coleman Coll., 1979. From asst. to assoc. physicist Argonne (Ill.) Nat. Lab., 1956-62; assoc. prof. physics Lehigh U., Bethlehem, Pa., 1962-67; specialist in physics Scripps Inst. Oceanography, La Jolla, Calif., 1967-71, 75-78; prof. physics Ind. State U., Terre Haute, 1971-74; from mem. staff to sr. scientist JAYCOR, San Diego, 1979-84; lectr. Calif. Poly. State U., San Luis Obispo, 1984-92, rsch. prof., 1992—, lunar sample investigator, 1994—. *Experimental research scientist and educator specializing in measurements of natural and manmade gamma radioactivities in environmental and lunar samples. Codiscoverer of the radioisotope Silver-108m in the general marine environment. Developed the technique of radiosilver dating.* Contbr. numerous articles to profl. jours. Served as ensign USNR, 1945-46, PTO. Mem. Am. Phys. Soc., Am. Geophys. Union, N.Y. Acad. Scis., Sigma Xi. Home: 535 Cameo Way Arroyo Grande CA 93420-5574 Office: Calif Poly State U Dept Physics San Luis Obispo CA 93407

GRISSINO-MAYER, HENRI DEE, research scientist; b. Monterrey, Calif., Dec. 24, 1954; s. Keith Alva and Sigrid Leota (Mayer) Summers. BS, U. Ga., 1985, MS, 1988; PhD, U. Ariz., 1995. Tchg. asst. U. Ga., Athens, 1985-88, rsch. asst., 1986, map rm. asst., 1988; grad. rsch. assoc. U. Ariz., Tucson, 1988-95, rsch. assoc. Lab. Tree-Ring Rsch., 1995—; mem. com. Internat. Tree-Ring Data Bank, Boulder, Colo., 1988—, internet list mgr., 1988—; group leader N.Am. Dendroecological Fieldweek, Ft. Collins, Colo., 1991—; internet list mgr. Biogeography Speciality Group, Tucson, 1992—. Contbr. articles to profl. publs., chpt. to book.; programmer software in field. Sci. grantee USDA Forest Svc., 1990-94, Nat. Park Svc., 1991-95, NOAA, 1992—, SWCA, Inc., 1996—, NSF, 1998—. Mem. Assn. Am. Geographers, Assn. Pacific Coast Geographers, Ariz./Nev. Acad. Sci., Ariz. Archeol. and Hist. Soc., Assn. Southwestern Naturalists, Tree-Ring Soc. Avocations: camping, hiking, rare books. Office: Dept Phys Astro Geos Valdosta State Univ Valdosta GA 31690

GRISSOM, GARTH CLYDE, lawyer; b. Syracuse, Kans., Jan. 24, 1930; s. Clyde and Bernice Minnie (Eddy) G.; m. Elena Joyce Kerst, Aug. 17, 1958; children: Colin, Grady, Cole, Kent. B.S., Kans. State U., 1951; LL.B., Harvard U., 1957. Bar: Colo. 1957, U.S. Dist. Ct. (fed. dist.) Colo., 1957, U.S. Ct. Appeals (10th crct.) 1957, U.S. Supreme Ct. 1989. Ptnr., mem., counsel Sherman & Howard, L.L.C., Denver, 1963—. Sec., counsel, trustee Mile High United Way, Denver, 1985-88; trustee Kans. State U. Found., Manhattan, 1962-89; mem. Colo. Gov.'s Commn. on Life and the Law, 1990—, chmn., 1996—. Mem. ABA, Colo. Bar Assn., Denver Bar Assn. (pres. 1985-86, award of merit 1994), Rotary (sec. Denver 1983-84, bd. dirs. 1983-86, pres. 1989-90), Pi Kappa Alpha (pres. 1968-70). Home: 1777 Larimer St Apt 1610 Denver CO 80202-1548 Office: Sherman & Howard LLC 633 17th St Ste 3000 Denver CO 80202-3665

GRISSOM, GERALD HOMER, lawyer, mediator, arbitrator; b. Waco, Tex., Jan. 4, 1951; s. Joe Bryan Jr. and Mary Elizabeth (Askins) G.; m. Susan Downs Parks, June 3, 1978; children: Gillian, Andrew. BA in Polit. Sci., Baylor U., 1973; JD, Harvard U., 1976; postgrad., Oxford U., 1977. Bar: Tex. 1976, U.S. Dist. Ct. (no. dist.) Tex. 1978, U.S. Ct. Appeals (5th cir.) 1978, U.S. Supreme Ct. 1981, U.S. Dist. Ct. (ea. dist.) Tex. 1989. Sr. shareholder Thompson & Knight, P.C., Dallas, 1977-97; mediator, arbitrator JAMS/ENDISPUTE, Dallas, 1997—; adj. prof. So. Meth. U. Sch. Law, 1981-84, 97. Mem. cmty. adv. bd. Sta. KERA-TV, Dallas, 1990-95; bd. dirs. North Tex. Pub. Broadcasting, 1995—; elder 1st Presbyn. Ch., Dallas, 1987-90, 93-96, vice moderator, 1995. Rotary fellow Oxford U., 1976-77. Mem. ABA, Assn. Atty.-Mediators, Am. Arbitration Assn. (panel arbitrators and mediators), Dallas Bar Assn. (chmn. CLE com.). Office: JAMS/ENDISPUTE 2323 Bryan St Ste 2100 Dallas TX 75201-2638

GRISSOM, JOSEPH CAROL, retired leasing and investments business executive; b. Lufkin, Tex., Apr. 29, 1931; s. B. R. and Carolyn (Riley) G.; m. Audrey Pedarre, Dec. 23, 1952; children—Joseph Carol, David Scott. B.S., La. State U., 1952. Asst. store mgr. Western Auto Supply Co., Kansas City, Mo., 1954-55, territorial sales mgr., store mgr., 1955-59, wholesale sales mgr., 1959-60, retail sales mgr., 1960-64, regional promotions mgr., 1964-65, div. mgr., 1965-67, regional v.p., 1967-73, corp. v.p. ops., 1973-76, exec. v.p., 1976, pres., 1976-78, chief exec. officer, 1977-80, chmn. bd., 1978-80, also bd. dir.; owner, pres. dir. Sight Leasing Co., 1981-92; owner, v.p., sec., dir. Beach Investment Group, Inc., 1988-91. Former exec. dir. Heart of Am. council Boy Scouts Am.; former bd. govs. Am. Royal, Starlight Theatre, United Fund. Served with USAF, 1952-54. Mem. Placida Harbour Club, Riverwood Golf Club. Republican. Methodist. Home: 11000 Placida Rd Apt 2103 Placida FL 33946-2103

GRISSOM, MARQUIS DEAN, professional baseball player; b. Atlanta, Apr. 17, 1967. Student, Fla. A & M. Outfielder Montreal Expos, 1988-94; with Atlanta Braves, 1994-97, Milwaukee Brewers, 97-. Named to Nat. League All-Star team, 1993, 94; recipient Golden Glove award, 1993-96. Leader Nat. League stolen bases, 1991-92. Office: Milwaukee Brewers County Stadium P.O.Box 3099 Milwaukee WI 53201-3099

GRIST, JOHN, retired government official, engineering consultant; b. Havana, Cuba, Nov. 17, 1928 (father Am. citizen); s. John Rivers and Raphaela Matilda (Santiesteban) G.; came to U.S., 1945; B.S., Ga. Inst. Tech., 1958; m. Ana Dolores D'Almonte, Nov. 22, 1961; children—Ana Cecilia, John Alexander, Paul Steven. Aircraft indsl. engring. cons. Parr Engring., Atlanta, 1958; food mfg. indsl. engring. cons. U.S. Dept. Agr., Washington, 1958-60; postal mechanization indsl. engr. U.S. Post Office Dept., Washington, 1960-62; hosp. indsl. engr. cons. VA, Washington, 1962-64; bldgs. mgmt. indsl. engr. cons. GSA, Washington, 1964-65; parks mgmt. sr. mgmt. analysis cons. Nat. Park Service, Washington, 1965-71; sr. indsl. engring. cons. U.S. Postal Service, N.Y.C., 1971-74, sr. indsl. engring. cons. Western Mass., Springfield, Mass., 1974-89; internat. bilingual export-import tech. cons., 1958—. Pres. parents council Arlington (Va.) Pub. Schs. Deaf Edn. Program, 1970-71; mem. Parents' Council, Lexington Sch. for Deaf, Queens, N.Y., 1972-74; mem. fund raising com. Clarke Sch. for Deaf, Northampton, Mass., 1975-76. Served with USAF, 1951-55. Mem. Ga. Inst. Tech. Nat. Alumni Assn. Roman Catholic. Home: 8A Duncan Dr South Deerfield MA 01373-9771

GRISWOLD, DAVID JAMES, therapist and physician's assistant; b. Morrisville, Vt., Aug. 6, 1940; s. Floyd Jerry and Gladys Nellie (Dowing) G.; m. Carol Ann Locke, Dec. 29, 1962; children: Gary Alan, Dana Scott. AS, Community Coll. of Vt., 1975. Lic. physician's asst., Vt. Psychiat. aide Vt. State Hosp., Waterbury, 1963-66, psychiat. technician, 1966-67, psychiat. charge, 1967-69, psychiat. ward coord., 1968-69, psychiat. team specialist, 1969-75; day hosp. therapist Washington County Mental Health, Montpelier, Vt., 1975-93, physician's asst., 1976—; asst. dir. Washington County Day Hosp., 1980-93. With U.S. Army, 1959-62. Methodist. Avocation: amateur radio. Home: RR 2 Box 845 Waterbury VT 05676-9715 Office: 9 Heaton St Montpelier VT 05602-2489

GRISWOLD, FRANK TRACY, III, bishop; b. Bryn Mawr, Pa., Sept. 18, 1937; s. Frank Tracy Jr. and Louisa Johnson (Whitney) G.; m. Phoebe Wetzel, Nov. 27, 1965; 2 children. AB, Harvard U., 1959; student, Gen. Theol. Sem., 1959-60; BA, Oxford U., 1962, MA, 1966. Ordained to ministry Episcopal Ch. as deacon, 1962, as priest, 1963. Bishop Coadjutor Diocese of Chgo., 1985-87, Bishop, 1987-97; Presiding Bishop Episcopal Ch. of USA, N.Y.C., 1998—; dep. to Gen. Conv.; former chmn. Pa. Liturgical Commn. Former chair Standing Liturgical Commn., Episcopal Ch. U.S.; former co-chair Anglican-Roman Catholic Dialogue U.S.; co-chair Anglican-Roman Cath. Internat. Consultation. Office: Episcopal Ch Ctr 815 2d Ave New York NY 10017

GRISWOLD, GARY NORRIS, engineering company executive; b. Fairbanks, Feb. 12, 1947; s. Norris Rockwell and Margaret Moore (Kennedy) G.; m. Lois Ruth Brinkman, June 17, 1967; children: Mark David, Melissa Robin. BS, U. Wash., 1970; MS, Union Coll., 1980. Cert. in data processing. Computer programmer Knolls Atomic Power Lab., Schenectady, N.Y., 1972-75; sr. systems analyst State of N.Y., Albany, 1975-79; mgr. mgmt. info. systems devel. Phoenix Data Systems, Inc., Albany, 1979-85; pres. InfoLogic Software, Inc., Boston, 1985—; adj. asst. prof. Union Coll., 1980-83; cons. on mgmt. info. systems. Mem. IEEE, Assn. Computing Machinery.

GRISWOLD, GEORGE, marketing, advertising and public relations executive; b. N.Y.C., Mar. 5, 1919; s. George and Isabel (Bridgman) G.; student Ecole des Beaux Arts, Fontainebleau, France, 1939; B.A., Yale U., 1941; postgrad. N.Y. U., 1947; m. Tracy Haight, May 15, 1942 (div. 1985); children: Tracy Griswold Glass, Mariana Van Rensselaer Griswold Geer, Alice Bradford Griswold Stetson; m. Joan Loosley McNamara, Mar. 11, 1986; m. Nancy Cox Holbrook, Apr. 3, 1993. Editor, Fairchild Publs., N.Y.C., 1945-46; pub. relations, operating positions long lines dept. AT&T, 1946-49, pub. relations exec., N.Y.C., 1962-79; exec. Newsweek mag., N.Y.C., 1950-55; exec. dir. pub. rels. and publs. divsn. Bell Labs., Inc., N.Y., N.J., 1955-62; pres. Litchfield Distbrs., Inc. (Conn.), 1949-52; tchr. Fairleigh Dickinson U. Grad. Sch., 1961; sr. v.p. Sheldon Satin Assocs., Inc., N.Y., 1979-83; pres. Griswold Comm. Hilton Head, S.C., 1983-89; v.p. mktg. and pub. rels., Environ. Am. Inc., Hilton Head, 1989-92. Comdr. USNR, 1941-45. Mem. AAAS, SAR, Soc. Mayflower Descs., Soc. Colonial Wars, Huguenot Soc. Am., Piedmont Club. Pres. Norfolk (Conn.) Library, 1965-75. Mem. Pub. Relations Soc. Am. (accredited), Nat. Assn. Sci. Writers, AAAS, SAR, Soc. Mayflower Descs., Soc. Colonial Wars, Huguenot Soc. of S.C., Huguenot Soc. Am., Soc. of First Families of S.C., Yale Club (N.Y.C.), S.C. Yacht Club. Home: 509 Claridge Cir Winston Salem NC 27106-6301

GRISWOLD, JOHN A., hotel executive. Pres. Tishman Hotel Corp., Fla. Office: Tishman Hotel Corp Lake Buena Vista FL 32830

GRISWOLD, MARTHA KERFOOT, social worker; b. Oklahoma City, Mar. 22, 1930; d. John Samuel III and Frances (Mann) Kerfoot; m. George Littlefield Griswold, Jan. 28, 1967. AB, Occidental Coll., 1951; MRE, U. So. Calif., 1956, postgrad., 1962. Cert. social worker. Teen dir. Toberman Settlement, San Pedro, Calif., 1954-56; social worker County of L.A., 1956-62; cons. community orgn. L.A., 1962-84; dir. LIV Disability Resources Ctr., Altadena, Calif., 1984—; instr. Calif. State U., L.A., 1966-68, 1983-84; chair Childrens' Adv. Com. L.A. County Dept. Mental Health, 1985-86; coordinator So. Calif. Conf. on Living Long Term with Disability, 1985-87. Co-host, prodr. radio program on disability Access Unlimited, Sta. KPFK-FM, 1987—, host. prodr. cable TV program on disability issues LIVstyles, 1992—. Mem. Pasadena (Calif.) City Cisability Issues Com., 1984-86, Pasadena Strategic Planning Task Force, 1985-86, commn. disability access City of Pasedena, 1990-97, commn. on diversity, 1997—; com. on aging and long-term care Region 2 United Way, L.A., chairperson, 1989-90, Pasadena Awareness: A Cmty. Effort for Disabled (PACED v.p.), 1983—. Recipient award So. Calif. Rehab. Assn., 1986, Disting. Alumna award Claremont Sch. Theology, 1996. Mem. AAUW, NASW, Californians for Disability Rights, Acad. Cert. Social Workers, Health and Social Svc. Workers with Disabilities. Congregationalist (UCC). Office: LIV Ctr 943 E Altadena Dr Altadena CA 91001-2033

GRISWOLD, PAUL MICHAEL, clinical psychologist, consultant; b. Milw., Sept. 26, 1945; s. Willard Matthew and Evelyn (Haerle) G.; m. AnnMari Gerardine La Valle, Aug. 2, 1969; children: Matthew Paul, Jennifer Jean. BA, Marquette U., 1967, MS, 1969; PhD, Kent State U., 1972. Sr. staff psychologist Wis. Div. Corrections, Milw., 1972-83; pvt. practice clin. and cons. psychology Menomonee Falls, Wis., 1973—; lectr. Mount Mary Coll., Milw., 1973-78; faculty Wis. Sch. of Profl. Psychology, Milw., 1981—; cons. Ethan Allen Sch. Wis. Div. Corrections, Wales, Wis., 1984—. Contbr. articles to profl. jours. Mem. Am. Psychol. Assn., Wis. Psychol. Assn., Milw. Area Psychol. Assn. Avocations: old cars, sailing, ice boating. Home: 1366 County Hwy J Hubertus WI 53033-9426 Office: Clin Psychology Assocs W156 N8327 Pilgrim Rd Menomonee Falls WI 53051-3776

GRITSCH, RUTH CHRISTINE LISA, editor; b. Duisburg, Germany, July 18, 1931; came to the U.S., 1941; d. Carl and Maria Augusta (Janssen) Sandman; m. Eric Walter Gritsch, June 4, 1955 (div. 1993); children: Deborah, Erika. BA, NYU, 1953. Assoc. Inst. for Internat. Edn., N.Y.C., 1953-55; sec. Zeigler Bros., Inc., Gardners, Pa., 1993—. Translator: (books) Hildrich Zwingli, 1983, I Am a Palestinian Christian, 1995, Violence, 1996; co-translator: Luther's Works, Vols. 39, 41, 1966, 67; editor: Roly, 1988. Active So. Poverty Law Ctr. Mem. LWV (bd. dirs., v.p. 1969-90). Democrat. Lutheran. Avocation: reading. Home: 1 West St Gettysburg PA 17325-2130

GRITTON, EUGENE CHARLES, nuclear engineer; b. Santa Monica, Calif., Jan. 13, 1941; s. Everett Mason and Matilda (Benne) G.; children from previous marriage: Dennis Mason, Kathleen Wanda; m. Gwendolyn O. Gritton. BS, UCLA, 1963, MS, 1965, PhD, 1966. Research engr., def. systems analyst RAND, Santa Monica, Calif., 1966-73, project leader advanced undersea tech. program, 1973-76, program dir. marine tech., 1974-76, program dir. applied sci. and tech., 1976-94, head dept. phys. scis., 1975-77, head engring. and applied scis. dept., 1977-86, RAND resident scholar for tech., 1990-93, dep. v.p. Nat. Security Rsch. Divsn., 1986-93, dep. v.p. Rsch. Ops. Group, 1986-90, dir. Acquisition and Tech. Policy Ctr., 1994—; acting dir. Nat. Security Rsch. Divsn., 1997-98; vis. lectr. dept. mech. engring. U. So. Calif., L.A., 1967-72; vis. lectr. dept. energy and kinetics UCLA, 1971, 73; mem. Def. Sci. Bd. Study, 1996, 98. Recipient Engring. Alumnus of Yr. award UCLA Sch. Engring. and Applied Sci., 1985-86; AEC fellow, 1963, NSF Coop. Grad. fellow, 1964-66. Mem. Am. Nuclear Soc. (mem. exec. com. aerospace and hydrospace div. 1974-75), AIAA. E-mail: geneugritton@rand.org. Home: 3616 The Strand # C Manhattan Beach CA 90266-3276 Office: Rand PO Box 2138 1700 Main St Santa Monica CA 90401-3297

GRIZANTI, ANTHONY J., lawyer; b. Cin., Jan. 27, 1949; s. Anthony Joseph and Mary Emma (Schroeder) G.; m. Judith L. Grizanti, July 26, 1969; children: Virginia A. Madonna, Christina E., Anthony J. III, Michael F. BA, Canisius Coll., 1971; MBA, SUNY, Buffalo, 1980; JD, Syracuse U., 1984. Bar: N.Y. 1985, Pa. 1990, U.S. Dist. Ct. (no. dist.) N.Y. 1986, U.S. Ct. Claims 1985, U.S. Supreme Ct. 1991. V.p. Grizanti Music Co., Inc., Niagara Falls, N.Y., 1972—; atty. advisor U.S. Tax Ct., Washington, 1984-

85; ptnr. Scolaro, Shulman, Cohen, Lawler & Burstein, P.C., Syracuse, N.Y., 1985—. Dir. Syracuse Symphony Orch., 1993-98. Mem. Estate Planning Coun. Ctrl. N.Y. (pres. 1996-97), Performing Arts Medicine Assn. (pres. 1994-97). Office: Scolaro Shulman Cohen Lawler & Burstein PC 90 Presidential Plz Ste 500 Syracuse NY 13202-2200

GRIZZARD, GEORGE, actor; b. Roanoke Rapids, N.C., Apr. 1, 1928; s. George Cooper and Mary Winifred (Albritton) G. BA, U. N.C., 1949. Appeared at Arena Stage, Washington, 1950, 52-54; Broadway appearances include The Desperate Hours, 1955, The Happiest Millionaire, 1956-57, The Disenchanted, 1958-59 (nominee Tony award), Face of a Hero, 1960, Big Fish, Little Fish, 1961 (nominee Tony award), Mary, Mary, 1962, Who's Afraid of Virginia Woolf?, 1962, The Glass Menagerie, 1965, You Know I Can't Hear You When the Water's Running, 1967, Sweet Potato, 1968, The Gingham Dog, 1969, Inquest, 1970, The Country Girl, 1972, The Creation of the World and Other Business, 1972, Crown Matrimonial, 1973, The Royal Family, 1975, California Suite, 1976, Man and Superman, 1978, A Delicate Balance, 1996 (Best Leading Actor Tony award 1996); also appeared with Assn. of Producing Artists, N.Y.C., 1961-62, Tyrone Guthrie Theatre, Mpls., 1963-65, Show Boat, Toronto, 1995, London, 1998; film appearances include From the Terrace, 1960, Advise and Consent, 1961, Warning Shot, 1967, Happy Birthday, Wanda June, 1971, Comes a Horseman, 1978, Firepower, 1979, Seems Like Old Times, 1980, Wrong is Right, 1981, Bachelor Party, 1983; TV appearances include Twilight Zone, The Adams Chronicles (nominated Emmy award), 1976, The Oldest Living Graduate (recipient Emmy award 1980), Caroline?, 1988, Simple Justice, 1993, Breaking the Silence, 1993, Queen, 1993, Scarlett, 1994, Suspicion of Innocence, 1997. Mem. Kappa Alpha. Office: PO Box 2275 New Preston CT 06777-0275

GRIZZARD-BARHAM, BARBARA LEE, artist; b. Roanoke, Va., Apr. 4, 1935; d. Alton Lee and Mable (Jewell) Grizzard; m. Charles Thomas Barham, Sr., June 25, 1955; children: Charles Thomas, Christopher. *Great, great, great, great grandfather, Ambrose Grisard (French), came to the English colony of Virginia in the early 1700s. Grandfather, Robert Lee Grizzard, continued farming vocation. His four children each earned Masters Degrees. Father, Alton Lee Grizzard, earned PhD-Agronomy and Agriculture and was a Professor at Virginia Tech. Brother, Wm. Samuel Grizzard is an OB/GYN. Maternal grandmother, Grace Farmer, very creative. Daughter of Issac Newton Farmer, MD. Her mother was a professional church singer. Son Charles T. Barham Jr. is Lt. Colonel, U.S. Army. Son Christopher Alton Grizzard Barham work at Dupont and is an inventor, artist, professional musician. He and his wife have one child, Samantha.* BS, Va. Commonwealth U., 1971. Educator Colonial Heights (Va.) Sch. Sys., 1971-88. Exhibited in solo shows at Wakefield (Va.) Ctr. for Aarts, 1993, 94, Petersburg (Va.) Area Art League, 1993, 95, Rappahannock Westminster-Canterberry Gallery, 1995, Assn. for Visual Artists Gallery, Chattanooga, 1999, Rappahanock Westminster Canterberry Gallery, Va., 1999, Williamsburg Regional Libr./Gallery/Theater Complex, Va., 1999; group shows include Richmond Jewish Cmty. Ctr., 1991, 93, Rappahannoc Art League Show, 1995, Assoc. Artists of Winston-Salem, 1991, 92, 96, Hoyt Inst. Fine Arts, Pa., 1998. Recipient awards for art. Mem. Petersburg Area Art League, Shockoe Bottom Art League, 1708 Art Gallery, Va. Mus. Art, Whitney Mus. Art, Mus. Modern Art. Republican. Episcopal. Avocations: investing, amateur genealogist, breeding Am. Cocker Spaniels champions, piano, Civil War tours. Home: 701 Forestview Dr Colonial Heights VA 23834-1116

GRMEK, DOROTHY ANTONIA, accountant; b. Cleve., July 7, 1930; d. Louis and Antonia (Korosec) Lipanye; m. M. Charles Stelmach, June 13, 1953 (div. May 1977); children: Monica Doran Meade, Dwayne Alan Stelmach, Dale Richard Stelmach; m. William Edward Grmek, Aug. 18, 1978. BBA in Acctg., Fenn Coll., 1953. Chief acct. Pyromatics, Inc., Willoughby, Ohio, 1975-87; acct., exec. sec. Auctor Assocs., Inc., Cleveland Heights, 1972-96; ptnr., tax cons. Diversified Bus. Svc., Rocky River, Ohio, 1980—; contr., human rels. specialist Telefast Industries, Inc., Berea, Ohio, 1988—; treas., buyer River Toy Box, Inc., Rocky River, 1990—. Mem. Slovene Nat. Benefit Soc. (ins. agt. 1982—, charter mem., fin. sec. lodge 781 1982—, Cleve. Fedn. Lodges rec. sec. 1968-72, fin. sec. 1972-82). Home: 3645 Kings Post Pky Rocky River OH 44116-3816 also: River Toy Box Inc 20130 Center Ridge Rd Rocky River OH 44116-3500

GROAH, LINDA KAY, nursing administrator, educator; b. Cedar Rapids, Iowa, Oct. 5, 1942; d. Joseph David and Irma Josephine (Zitek) Rozek; m. Patrick Andrew Groah, Mar. 20, 1975; 1 child, Kimberly; stepchildren: Nadine, Maureen, Patrick, Marcus. Diploma, St. Luke's Sch. Nursing, Cedar Rapids, 1963; student, San Francisco City Coll., 1976-77; BA, St. Mary's Coll., Moraga, Calif., 1978; BSN, Calif. State U.; MSN, U. Calif. Staff nurse to head nurse U. Iowa, 1963-67; clin. supr., dir. oper. and recovery rm. Michael Reese Hosp., Chgo., 1967-73; dir. oper. rms. Med. Ctr. Ctrl. Ga., Macon, 1973-74; dir. oper. and recovery rms. U. Calif. Hosps. and Clinics, San Francisco, 1974-90, asst. dir. hosps. and clinics, 1982-86; patient care leader, dir. hosp. ops. Kaiser Found. Hosp., San Francisco, 1990—; asst. clin. prof. U. Calif. Sch. Nursing, San Francisco, 1975—; cons. to oper. room suprs., to div. ednl. resources and programs Assn. Am. Med. Colls., 1976—; condr. seminars. Author: Perioperative Nursing Practice, 1983, 3d edit., 1996; contbr. articles to project jours. and textbooks; author, prodr. audio-visual presentations; author computer software. Mem. ANA (vice chmn. oper. rm. conf. group 1974-76), Assn. Oper. Rm. Nurses (com. on nominations 1979-84, treas. 1985-87, 93-95, bd. dirs. 1991-93, pres.-elect 1995-96, pres. 1996-97, found. bd. trustees 1995-97, pres. found. 1992-95, Excellence award in Preoperative Nursing 1989), Nat. League for Nurses, Ctr. for Study Dem. Instns. Home: 5 Mateo Dr Belvedere Tiburon CA 94920-1071 Office: 3020 Bridgeway Ste 399 Sausalito CA 94965-2839

GROAT, CHARLES, geologist. PhD, U. Tex. Faculty mem. U. Tex., Austin, mem. rsch. staff Bur. Econ. Geology; prof. geology and geophysics La. State U., exec. dir. Ctr. Coastal, Energy, and Environ. Resources; state geologist, dir. La. Geol. Survey; exec. dir. Am. Geol. Inst., Washington; dir. Ctr. Environ. Resource Mgmt., UTEP; dir. environ. sci. and engring. PhD program La. State U. Contbr. articles to profl. jours. E-mail: groat@utep.edu. FAX: 703-648-4454. Office: US Geol Survey Dept of Interior 12201 Sunrise Valley Dr Reston VA 20192-0002

GROAT, PAMELA FERNE, school media specialist; b. Kalamazoo, Mich., Sept. 17, 1949; d. Jay J and Margaret Ann (Jones) G. BA, Western Mich. U., 1971, MS in Librarianship, 1973. Substitute media specialist St. Charles (Mich.) Cmty. Schs., 1974; dist. libr. Baldwin (Mich.) Cmty. Sch., 1974—; del. Pre-White House Conf. on Librs., Lansing, Mich., 1990; advisor Lake County Regional Ednl. Materials Ctr. II, Traverse Bay Area Intermediate Sch. Dist., Traverse City, Mich., 1974. Mem. NEA, AAUW, Mich. Edn. Assn. (rep. to regional coms. 1974), Baldwin Edn. Assn. (pres., v.p., sec., bldg. rep.), Mich. Assn. for Media in Edn. (regional chair, bd. dirs.), Lake County Hist. Soc. (charter mem.). Democrat. Methodist. Avocations: reading, history, family genealogy, classic movies.

GROB, GEORGE FREDERICK, health, social services association administrator. M in Math., Georgetown U., 1969. Comptroller Office of Asst. Sec. Def.; ops. rsch. analyst Office of Asst. Sec. Navy for Fin. Mgmt.; dir. planning and policy coordination Office of Asst. Sec. Planning and Evaluation, USHHS, 1976-88; dep. insp. gen. evaluation and inspections USHHS, Washington, 1988—; co-chair Evaluation and Inspections Round Table adj. Pres.'s Coun. Integrity and Efficiency. Mem. Am. Evaluation Assn. (co-chair Evaluation Mgrs. and Suprs. Group). Home: 38386 Millstone Dr Purcellville VA 20132-3739 Office: USHHS 330 Independence Ave SW Rm 5660 Washington DC 20547-0008

GROB, GERALD N., historian, educator; b. N.Y.C., Apr. 25, 1931; s. Sidney and Sylvia G.; m. Lila Kronick, Dec. 25, 1954; children: Bradford S., Evan D., Seth A. B.S., CCNY, 1951; M.A., Columbia U., 1952; Ph.D., Northwestern U., 1958. Instr. history Clark U., Worcester, Mass., 1957-59; asst. prof. Clark U., 1959-61, assoc. prof., 1961-66, prof., 1966-69, chmn. dept. history, 1967-69; Henry E. Sigerist prof. of the history of medicine Rutgers U., New Brunswick, N.J., 1969—, chmn. dept., 1969-71, 73-74, 81-84; mem. fellowship adv. com. NEH, 1975-76; chmn. study sect. history of medicine NIH, 1975-77, 87-89, 93-98. Author: books including Ed Jarvis and the Medical World of 19th Century America, 1978, Workers and Utopia, 1961, The State and the Mentally Ill, 1966 (ann. prize Am. Assn. for State and Local History 1965), Mental Institutions in America, 1973, Mental Illness and America Society, 1875-1940, 1983, The Inner World of American Psychiatry, 1890-1940, 1985, From Asylum to Community, 1991, The Mad Among Us, 1994; contbr. articles to profl. jours. Elected to Inst. Medicine NAS. With C.E. U.S. Army, 1955-57. NIH grantee, 1960-65, 67-81, 84-92; NEH fellow, 1972-73, 89-90; Am. Council Learned Socs. fellow, 1976-77; Guggenheim fellow, 1980-81; fellow Davis Ctr., Princeton U., 1985-86. Mem. Am. Assn. for History of Medicine (coun. 1978-81, William H. Welch medal 1986, v.p. 1994-96, pres. 1996-98), Am. Antiquarian Soc., Orgn. Am. Historians. Jewish. Home: 821 Star View Way Bridgewater NJ 08807-1824 Office: Rutgers U Inst Health Care 30 College Ave New Brunswick NJ 08901-1293 *My philosophy of history is essentially a tragic one; a study of the past, if undertaken in as honest and objective a manner as is humanly possible, should render us less certain about our omniscience and ability to control the future.*

GROBAN, LEE DAVID, artist; b. Chgo., Mar. 20, 1947; s. Milton Lenard and Elinor Lucille (Mendelsohn) G. BA in Russian Lang. and Area studies, U. Ill., 1970; MA in Libr. Sci., No. Ill. U., 1972. Author: (book) Higher Than the Ground, 1988; artwork pub. in: One, Chgo. Lerner Newspaper, 1973, Triad Radio Guide, 1973, Oyez Rev., 1974, Chgo. Observer, 1974, The Paper Gallery, 1979, Midway Rev., 1984, Lucky Star, 1984, others; exhibited in one man show at Glencoe Pub. Libr., 1974; exhibited in group shows at The Quiet Knight, 1975-78, Artifacts, 3 Forms Art Gallery, 1974, Design Alliance, 1974, Glencoe Art Fair, 1974-85, Chgo. Lawn Art Fair, 1974, Bernard-Horwich Ctr. Art Fair, 1974, Andersonville Art Fair, 1974, Custer St. Art Fair, Evanston, 1975—, 82-83, 86, Monroe Gallery, Chgo., 1979, Freebird Gallery, 1982-83, WPA Gallery, 1985, First Contacts Gallery, 1978, Lake Shore Art Fair, Evanston, 1985, Two Plane Feet Studio, 1985, Holsum-Roc Gallery, 1987, others; works in permanent collections at Imagination Gallery, Sieber-McIntyre, Inc., Lake Forest Coll. Radio Sta., others.; appeared in film The Cure for Insomnia; contbr. numerous articles to profl. jours.; poetry, stories, broadcast or read various locations. Recipient First prize in art Glencoe (Ill.) Art Fair Com., 1981. Avocations: foreign languages, genealogy, history, geography, anthropology.

GROBAN, ROBERT SIDNEY, JR., lawyer; b. N.Y.C., June 8, 1948; s. Robert Sidney and Irene (Schiff) G.; m. Nora Solomon, July 1, 1973; children: Eli Solomon, Matthew Solomon. BA, Williams Coll., 1970; JD, N.Y.U., 1973. Bar: Mass. 1973, N.Y. 1975, U.S. Dist. Ct. (so. and ea. dists.) N.Y. 1977, U.S. Ct. Appeals 2d cir.) 1977, U.S. Ct. Appeals (6th cir.) 1986, U.S. Supreme Ct. 1986, U.S. Ct. Appeals (1st cir.) 1992. Assoc. Law Office Joel S. Greenberg, Pittsfield, Mass., 1973-74, Law Office Robert S. Groban, N.Y.C., 1974-76; spl. asst. U.S. atty. U.S. Atty's. Office, southern dist. N.Y., N.Y.C., 1976-81; assoc. Skadden, Arps, Slate, Meagher & Flom, N.Y.C., 1982-84; of counsel Friedman & Shaftan P.C., N.Y.C., 1984-86; ptnr. Fink Weinberger p.c., N.Y.C., 1986-92, Epstein, Becker & Green, P.C., N.Y.C., 1992—. Chmn. Town Club Edn. Com., Scarsdale, N.Y., 1986-89; asst. sec. Town & Village Civic Club, Scarsdale, 1988-93. Mem. N.Y. State Bar Assn., Assn. of the Bar of the City of N.Y., Am. Immigration Lawyers' Assn., Fed. Bar Coun. Office: Epstein Becker & Green PC 250 Park Ave New York NY 10177

GROBE, CHARLES STEPHEN, lawyer, accountant; b. Columbus, Ohio, May 5, 1935; s. Harry A. and Bertha S. (Swartz) G.; m. Ila Silverman, Aug. 30, 1964; children—Eileen, Kenneth. B.S., U. Calif. at Los Angeles, 1957; J.D., Stanford, 1961. Bar: Calif. 1962; CPA, Calif. Tax accountant Beverly Hills, Calif., 1961-63; tax atty. Los Angeles, 1963—. Author: Guide to Investing Pension and Profit-Sharing Trust Funds, 1973, Guardianship, Conservatorship and Trusts on Behalf of Persons Who Are Mentally Retarded—An Assessment of Current Applicable Laws in the State of California, 1974, Using an Individual Retirement Savings Plan and the Related Rollover Provisions of the Pension Reform Act of 1974, 1975, Guide to Setting Up a Group Term Life Insurance Program Under IRC Section 79, 1976, Practical Estate Planning, 1988, Planning for Incapacity, 1989, Planning to Reduce the Generation Skipping Tax, 1989, Estate Planning Considerations for Community Property Interests, 1990, Legal and Tax Problems of Joint Tennancy as a Form of Ownership, 1990, The Tax Economics of Using the Generating Skipping Tax Exemptions, 1992, The Tax Economics of Gifting Property, 1992, Saving Estate Taxes with Life Insurance and a Life Insurance Trust, 1992, Family Wealth Transfer Planning, The Tax Economics of a Qualified Personal Residence Trust, also articles. Capt. AUS, 1957-64. Mem. ABA, State Bar Calif., L.A. County Bar Assn., Beverly Hills Bar Assn., Calif. Soc. CPAs. Home: 501 N Cliffwood Ave Los Angeles CA 90049-2621 Office: 12110 Wilshire Blvd Los Angeles CA 90025-1104

GROBEL, MICHAEL LAWRENCE, writer, editor; b. Feb. 10, 1947. BA, UCLA, 1968. Instr. Ghana Inst. Journalism Peace Corps, Accra, 1968-71; dir. MFA in Profl. Writing Antioch U., L.A., 1976-80; contbg. editor Playboy mag., Movieline mag., L.A., 1980—. Author: Conversations with Capote, 1985, The Hustons, 1989, Conversations with Brando, 1990, Talking with Michener, 1999.

GROBERG, JAMES JAY, information sciences company executive; b. Bklyn., May 29, 1928; s. David and Anna (Gross) G.; m. Marcia J. Black, June 25, 1950 (div. June 1986); children: Neil H., Richard L., Eric L.; m. Carol Ann De Barros, Sept. 4, 1986. BS in Econs., U. Pa., 1951. Asst. v.p. Economy Fin. Corp., Indpls., 1959-62; v.p. Rosenthal & Rosenthal, Inc., N.Y.C., 1962-68, Brandon Applied Systems, Inc., N.Y.C., 1970-71; fin. v.p. Telco Mktg. Svcs., Inc., Chgo., 1971-73; exec. v.p. Volt Info. Scis., Inc., N.Y.C., 1973-81, sr. v.p., CFO,, 1985—, bd. dirs.; chmn., chief exec. officer Multivest, Inc., Ft. Lauderdale, Fla., 1981-82; chmn., chief exec. officer Mego Corp., N.Y.C., 1982-85, also bd. dirs.; chmn. bd. dirs. Am. Community Pubs. Inc., 1989-91; bd. dirs. Autologic Info. Internat., Inc. Capt. USAFR, 1950-66. Mem. Fin. Execs. Inst. Office: Volt Info Scis Inc 1221 Ave of Americas New York NY 10020-1001

GROBMAN, ARNOLD BRAMS, retired biology educator and academic administrator; b. Newark, Apr. 28, 1918; s. Samuel H. and Sophia (Brams) G.; m. Hulda Gross, Feb. 20, 1944; children: Marc Ross, Beth Burruss. BS, U. Mich., 1939; MS, U. Rochester, 1941, PhD, 1943. Instr. zoology U. Rochester, 1943-44; research asso. Manhattan project, 1944-46; from asst. prof. to asso. prof. biology U. Fla., 1946-59; research participant Oak Ridge Inst. Nuclear Studies, summer 1950, research specialist, med. center study, 1951-52; dir. Fla. State Mus., 1952-59; dir. biol. scis. curriculum study U. Colo., 1959-65; dean (Coll. Arts and Scis.); prof. zoology Rutgers U., New Brunswick, N.J., 1965-72; dean Rutgers Coll. Rutgers U., 1966-72; vice chancellor for acad. affairs, prof. biol. scis. U. Ill., Chgo., 1973-74; spl. asst. to pres. U. Ill., 1974-75; chancellor U. Mo.-St. Louis, 1975-85, chancellor emeritus, 1985—, prof. biology, 1975—, research prof., 1986—; adj. curator Fla. Mus. Natural History, 1982—; vis. lectr. Utah State U., U. Ind./Purdue U., U. So. Ill., Nat. Taiwan Normal U., U. Campinas, Brazil, U. New Delhi, India, U. No. Sumatra, Indonesia, U. Sind, Pakistan, Chulalongkorn U., Bangkok, Thailand, U. Singapore, Sophia U., Japan, Internat. Christian U., Japan, Chiang Mia U., Thailand; cons. to govt., industry, founds. and ednl. instns., 1954—; Mem. div. biology and agr. NRC-Nat. Acad. Scis., 1954-58, com. adult edn., 1956-58; sec. U.S. nat. com. Internat. Union Biol. Scis., 1966-69; Chmn. Ednl. Opportunity Center of Met. St. Louis, 1976-78; mem. advisory team sci. soc., Thailand, 1971; fgn. observer Treaty Plebiscite, Gov. Panama, 1977-78; mem. Commn. on Adult Learner. Author: (with others) Island Life: A Study of the Land Vertebrates of Eastern Lake Michigan, 1948, Our Atomic Heritage, 1951, Genetics Effects of Chronic X-irradiation Exposure in Mice, 1960; author: BSCS Biology Implementation in the Schools, 1964, The Changing Classroom, 1969, Urban State Universities, 1988; editor: Social Implications of Biological Education, 1970; also articles to profl. jours., encys. and newspapers. Bd. dirs. in St. Louis United Way, Laumeier Sculpture Park, Narcotics Service Council, Regional Commerce and Growth Assn., St. Louis Higher Edn. Ctr., St. Louis Pub. Library; v.p. St. Louis Conf. on Edn., 1980-82; adv. bd. Indian River County Pub. Libr., 1997—. Recipient Fred H. Stoye prize Am. Soc. Ichthyologists and Herpetologists, 1941; A Cressy Morrison prize N.Y. Acad. Scis., 1943; Macalaster award Nat. Assn. Biology Tchrs., 1966; award of merit Urban League, 1984; Commanders Cross, Order of Merit, Fed. Republic Ger., 1985. Mem. Acad. Zoology in India (exec. com. 1967-69), Am. Assn. Higher Edn., AAAS (council 1961-65), Am. Assn. Museums (mus. tng. com. 1960-63), Am. Assn. State Colls. and Univs. (urban affairs com. 1977-85), Am. Ednl. Research Assn., Am. Inst. Biol. Scis. (exec. com. 1958-61, Disting. Service award 1984), Am. Soc. Ichthyologists and Herpetologists (bd. govs. 1952—, pres. 1964), Am. Soc. Naturalists, Am. Soc. Zoologists, Assn. Am. Med. Colls., Assn. Southeastern Biologists, Assn. Supervision and Curriculum Devel., Assn. Tropical Biology, Asian Assn. Biol. Edn., Biol. Scis. Curriculum Study (chmn. steering com. 1965-69), Biol. Soc. China, Biol. Soc. Washington, Council on Fgn. Relations, NEA, Edn. Programs Improvement Corp. (trustee 1970-74), Colo.-Wyo. Acad. Sci., AAUP, Explorers Club, Fla. Acad. Sci., Fla. Found. Future Scientists (chmn. 1957-59), Herpetologists League, Mo. Council Pub. Higher Edn. (exec. com. 1977-82, v.p. 1978, pres. 1979), Mo. Bot. Garden, Nat. Council Accreditation Tchr. Edn. (chmn. 1970-71), Genetics Soc., Herpetologists League, Philippine Assn. Sci. Tchrs., Nat. Assn. Biology Tchrs. (pres. 1966, editorial bd. 1974-77, dir. 1978-80), Nat. Assn. Research Sci. Teaching, Nat. Assn. State Univs. and Land Grant Colls. (exec. com. 1979-80, council on acad. affairs 1974-76, chmn. div. urban affairs 1978-79), Nat. Sci. Tchrs. Assn., Nature Conservancy, Newcomen Soc., N.J. Acad. Scis., Orgn. Tropical Studies, Sci. Soc. Thailand, Soc. Study Amphibians and Reptiles, Soc. Study Evolution, Soc. Systematic Zoology, Soc. Vertebrate Paleontology, Southeastern Museums Conf. (pres. 1955-57), Phi Beta Kappa, Sigma Xi, Phi Kappa Phi, Phi Sigma, Alpha Sigma Lambda, Alpha Epsilon Delta. Home: 855 Live Oak Ln Vero Beach FL 32963-2926

GROBMAN, HULDA GROSS (MRS. ARNOLD B. GROBMAN), retired health sciences educator; b. Phila., Aug. 2, 1920; d. Joseph and Dora (Abrahams) Gross; m. Arnold B. Grobman, Feb. 20, 1944; children—Marc Ross, Beth Alison. AB, U. Pa., 1940; MPA, U. Mich., 1941; EdD, U. Fla., 1958. Rsch. asso. Western Interstate Commn. on Higher Edn., Boulder, Colo., 1959-60; staff cons. Biol. Scis. Curriculum Study, Boulder, 1960-65, Joint Council on Econ. Edn., N.Y., 1965-66; prof. edn. N.Y. U., 1966-72, Bklyn. Coll., City U. N.Y., 1972-73; sr. rsch. assoc. ADA, Chgo., 1973-74; dir. edn./career mobility, area health edn. system, prof. med. edn. U. Ill. Med. Center, 1973-75; prof. health scis. edn. St. Louis U. Med. Ctr., 1975-88; prof. emeritus St. Louis U. Med. Center, 1988—; cons. Sci. Edn. Center, U. Sao Paulo, Brazil; vis. prof. Asian Assn. Biol. Edn., Hebrew U. Jerusalem Inst. on Test Writing, 1972; cons. Fundacao Carlos Chagos, Sao Paulo, Brazil. Author: Developmental Curriculum Projects, 1970, Evaluation Activities of curriculum Projects, 1968, also articles; cons. editor Jour. Ednl. Rsch., 1973-80, Am. Ednl. Rsch. Jour.; mng. editor Serin Press. Mem. bd. League Women Voters Fla., 1950-55; candidate for City Commn., Gainesville, Fla., 1955. Recipient A-Individual Achievement award 3d Army Res. Command, 1956. Fellow AAAS (council 1967-73); mem. Asian Assn. Biology Edn. (charter hon. mem.), Am. Ednl. Research Assn. (sec. div. I 1979-81). Home: 855 Live Oak Ln Vero Beach FL 32963-2926

GROCE, EWIN PETTY, lawyer; b. Ft. Worth, Dec. 19, 1953; s. Charles Tillman and Mary Elizabeth (Hill) G.; m. Elisita Bernis Groce, Oct. 29, 1982; children: Tamara Roxanne, Jonathan Paul, Meghan Elizabeth. BA cum laude, U. Tex., 1979; postgrad., Golden Gate Seminary, 1982; JD, Whitter Law Sch., 1989; postgrad., Fuller Seminary. Bar: Kans. Supreme Ct. 1990, Mo. Supreme Ct. 1991, U.S. Dist. Ct. (ea. dist.) Kans. 1990, U.S. Dist. Ct. (we. dist.) Mo. 1991. Paralegal Groce & Groce Law Offices, Ft. Worth, 1979-81, Abraham Liao Law Offices, Monterey Park, Calif., 1987-88; paralegal litigation dept. Charles M. Finkel Law Offices, Beverly Hills, Calif., 1988-90; lawyer Ewin Groce Law Offices, Overland Park, Kans., 1990—; lectr. continuing legal edn. Consiliators Training Workshop, Kansas City, Mo., 1991—. Author numerous poems. Worked with immigrant Chinese for Evang. Formosan Ch., L.A., 1983-90; vol. mediatorChristian Conciliation Svc., L.A., 1989-90, Kansas City, 1990—, bd. dirs., 1990—; First Amendment law advisor Metro Vineyard Fellowship, Kansas City, 1990-92; cons. immigration law Grace Training Ctr., Kansas City, 1991-92. Mem. ABA, Assn. Trial Lawyers Am., Christian Legal Soc., Christian Conciliation Svc, Kansas City (mediators panel). Republican. Avocations: music (drums and orchestral percussion) karate/kung fu, poetry, chinese language. Office: Law Offices Abraham C Liao 300 S Garfield Ave Monterey Park CA 91754-3336

GROCE, JAMES FREELAN, financial consultant; b. Lubbock, Tex., Nov. 24, 1948; s. Wayne Dee and Betty Jo (Rice) G.; m. Patricia Kay Rogers; 1 child, Jason Eric. BS cum laude, Tex. Tech U., 1971. Registered profl. engr., Tex. Petroleum engr. Texaco, Inc., Sweetwater, Tex., 1971-74; drilling and prodn. engr. Texaco, Inc., Wichita Falls, Tex., 1974-77; asst. dist. engr. Texaco, Inc., Midland, Tex., 1977-78; sr. prodn. engr. Bass Enterprises Prodn., Midland, 1978-81; petroleum engr. Murphy H. Baxter Co., Midland, 1981-82, Henry Engring., Midland, 1982-87; petroleum engr. Fasken Oil and Ranch Interests, Midland, 1987, mgr. engring./ops., 1987-95; fin. cons. Smith Barney, Midland, 1996—. Scoutmaster Boy Scouts Am., Midland, 1980-83, merit badge counselor, 1987; mem. Community Bible Study, Midland, 1987-93. Mem. Soc. Petroleum Engrs. (local sect. chmn. 1987, 25 Yr. Mem.), Soc. Petroleum Evaluation Engrs. (local sect. chmn. 1996), Mensa, Toastmasters Internat., Tex. Tech. Ex-Student Assn., Century Club, Tau Beta Pi. Presbyterian. Avocations: individual investments, real estate, gardening. Home: 2117 Bradford Ct Midland TX 79705-1726

GROCE, WILLIAM HENRY, III, environmental engineer, consultant; b. Greer, S.C., Feb. 9, 1940; s. William Henry Jr. and Mary Alvis (Williams) G.; 1 child, William H. IV. BS in Chemistry, Newberry Coll., 1964. Registered profl. engr., S.C.; diplomate environ. engring.; master hazardous material mgmt. Chemist FDA, Atlanta, 1966-68; chemist, engr. Celanese Corp., Greer, 1968-74; prin. engr. Groce Labs., Greer, 1974-86; dir. rsch. Aqua-Tech Corp., Port Washington, Wis., 1986-89; cons. Chemotech Corp., Greer, 1989-90; sr. scientist Savannah River Site U.S. Dept. of Energy, Aiken, S.C., 1990—; cons. Environ. Resource Tech., Greer, 1990. Recipient Silver Beaver award Boy Scouts Am., 1990. Fellow Am. Inst. Chemists; mem. NSPE, Am. Inst. Chem. Engrs. Achievements include research in process and treatment methods for hazardous waste including reclamation, detoxification, in situ treatment, and deactivation of highly reactive materials. Office: Savannah River Site Bldg 730-1B Aiken SC 29801

GROCHMAL, DAVID, municipal government official; b. Norfolk, Va., Nov. 17, 1947. BA, Wake Forest U., 1977; MA in Pub. Adminstrn., Old Dominion U., 1977. Right of way agent City of Virginia Beach, Va., 1971-75; asst. to city mgr. City of Virginia Beach, 1976-84, dir. gen. svcs., 1985—. With USAR, 1970. Office: City of Virginia Beach Mcpl Ctr Bldg 18 Rm 228 Virginia Beach VA 23456*

GROCHOWSKI, JELSIA, music educator; b. Bklyn., Oct. 4, 1936; d. Frank and Maria (Pollifrone) Artuso; m. Anthony Joseph Grochowski, Oct. 6, 1956; children: Robert, Thomas, Maria. Student, NYU, Manhattan Sch. Music; cert. program ch. music, Lebanon Valley Coll. Choir dir. P.S. 127, Bklyn., 1975-80; tchr. music Our Lady of Angels Sch. (formerly St. Peter Sch.), Columbia, Pa., 1990—; dir. sr. citizens choir YMCA, Lancaster, Pa., 1982-84; accompaniest St. John Neumann Folk Group, Lancaster, 1982-87; dir. St. John Neumann Youth Choir, 1988—; organ tchr. Dominican Nuns, Lancaster, 1996—. Mem. Nat. Guild Piano Tchrs., Pa. Music Tchrs. Assn., Am. Organist Guild, Music Edn. Nat. Conf., Choristers Guild, Pastoral Musicians-Music Edn. Republican. Roman Catholic. Avocations: reading, walking, stitchery. Home: 2627 Pinewood Rd Lancaster PA 17601-4865

GROCHOWSKI, MARY ANN, psychotherapist; b. Milw., Oct. 8, 1944; d. Leonard Edward and Mary (Hitti) Rebatzke; m. James Allen Grochowski, Jan. 27, 1968; children: Bradley, Brandon. BA, Marquette U., 1966; MSW, U. Wis., Milw., 1968. Cert. social worker; lic. ind. clin. social worker. Psychotherapist L.A. Child Guidance Clinic, 1968-70, Milw. Children's Hosp., 1970-74; psychotherapist Family Social & Psychotherapy Svcs., Milw., 1972-74, 79-93, clinic dir., 1986-93; psychotherapist Apogee-Winston Clinic, Inc., Milw., 1993—; chair adv. coun. Family Social & Psychotherapy Svcs., Milw., 1987-90; mem. bd. Children's Legal Action Fund, Milw., 1989; active Nat. Clin. Adv. Bd. Apogee, 1994—. Contbr. articles to jours. Mem. NASW, Am. Profl. Soc. on Abuse of Children, Internat. Soc. Study of Dissociation, Eye Movement Desensitization and Reprocessing Internat. Assn. (charter). Roman Catholic. Avocations: pub. speaking, writing. Office: Apogee Winston Clinics Inc 7330 W Layton Ave Milwaukee WI 53220-3849

GRODEN, GERALD, psychologist; b. Cambridge, Mass., Apr. 11, 1931; s. Eugene and Ruth (Patten) G.; A.B., U. Vt., 1957, M.A., 1960; Ph.D., Purdue U., 1963; m. June Handwerger, Mar. 28, 1975; 1 son, John. Instr., then asst. prof. dept. neurology Ind. U. Med. Sch., Indpls., 1963-66, asso. faculty mem. dept. psychology, 1964-66, U. R.I. extension, Providence, 1966—, clin. assoc. prof., Kingston, 1969—; instr. dept. pediatrics Brown U., Providence, 1969; dir. psychology dept. R.I. Hosp. Child Devel. Center, Providence, 1966-78; dir. Groden Ctr., Providence, 1976—; dir. Behavioral Assocs., Providence, 1980-88; cons. in field; bd. dirs. Sophia Little Home, R.I. Protective and Advocacy System, Providence, 1975-84; mem. R.I. Gov.'s Adv. Commn. on Mental Retardation, R.I. Gov.'s Adv. Commn. on Children and Youth, R.I. Senate Adv. Commn. on Early Intervention. Served with USNR, 1952-54. State of R.I. grantee, 1972. Mem. APA, Eastern Psychol. Assn., R.I. Psychol. Assn. (dir.), Assn. for Advancement of Behavior Therapy, Assn. for Behavioral Analysis, Sigma Xi. Contbr. articles to profl. jours. Home: 99 Fosdyke St Providence RI 02906-3537 Office: 86 Mount Hope Ave Providence RI 02906-1648

GRODEN, MICHAEL LEWIS, English literature educator; b. Buffalo, May 30, 1947; s. Sheldon Robert and Maxine (Helper) G.; m. Molly Peacock, 1992. BA, Dartmouth Coll., 1969; MA, Princeton U., 1972, PhD, 1975. Vis. asst. prof. English U. Western Ont., London, Can., 1975-77, asst. prof. English, 1977-78, assoc. prof., 1978-83, prof., 1983—. Author: Ulysses in Progress, 1977, James Joyce's Manuscripts: An Index, 1980; gen. editor: James Joyce Archive, 63 vols., 1977-79; co-editor: Johns Hopkins Guide to Literary Theory and Criticism, 1994; contbr. articles to profl. jours. Fellow John Simon Guggenheim Meml. Found., 1979-80, Social Scis. and Humanities Rsch. Coun. of Can., 1983-84, 91-94, 95-98. Mem. MLA, James Joyce Found., Assn. Can Coll. and Univ. Tchrs. of English, Soc. for Textual Scholarship, Assn. for Computers and Humanities. Home: 229 Emery St E, London, ON Canada N6C 2E3 Office: Univ Western Ontario, Dept English, London, ON Canada N6A 3K7

GRODNICK, SCOTT RANDALL, internet executive, music company executive; b. Mpls., Dec. 16, 1949; s. Armil Harold Grodnick and Naomi (Rosen) Chanen; m. Susan A. Frank, Aug. 4, 1974; children: Zoe, Max. BS in Econs., U. Pa., 1971. CPA, N.Y. Asst. to asst. to the mayor N.Y.C., 1972-73; mgr. Coopers & Lybrand, N.Y.C., 1974-82; v.p. Citibank, N.Y.C., 1982-83; v.p., CFO Equitable Variable Life, N.Y.C., 1983-88; v.p., CFO Integrity Life Ins. Co., N.Y.C., 1984-92, pres., CEO, 1992-93; pres. First Variable Life Ins. Co., Boston, 1994-95; sr. v.p., CFO, COO Paradigm Music Entertainment Co., N.Y.C., 1996-98; COO, CFO SonicNet, N.Y.C., 1998—. Author: (with others) Montgomery's Auditing, 1983. Dir. Hamilton-Madison House, N.Y.C., 1989—. Office: SonicNet 67 Irving Pl New York NY 10003-2202

GRODSKY, GEROLD MORTON, biochemistry educator; b. St. Louis, Jan. 18, 1927; s. Louis and Goldie B.; m. Kayla Deane Wolfe, Dec. 6, 1952; children: Andrea, Jamie. BS, U. Ill., 1946, MS, 1947; PhD, U. Calif., Berkeley, 1954; postgrad., Cambridge (Eng.) U., 1954-55. Prof. biochemistry U. Calif. Med. Sch., 1961-92, prof. emeritus (active status), 1992—; vis. prof. U. Geneva, 1968-69, U. paris VII, 1989; Somogyi Meml. lectr., 1972, Helen Martin lectr., 1976, Herman Rosenthal lectr., 1986; cons. various pharm. houses; cons. UCSF Diabetes Program Project, 1993—. Mem. editl. bd. Diabetes, 1965-73, 86-90, Am. Jour. Physiology, 1977-94, Diabetologia, 1990-92, Endocrinology, 1992-96; founding adv. editor: Diabetes Tech. and Therapy, 1998—, Diabetes New World (China); contbr. chpts. to books; contbr. over 200 articles on diabetes and storage, secretion of insulin to profl. jours. Mem. med. adv. bd. Juvenile Diabetes Found., 1974-77, 80-85; program dir. NIH Diabetic Animal Program, 1978-82, chmn. diabetes rsch. adv. bd. to Sec. Health, 1982-87. Lt. (s.g.) USNR, 1944-54. Recipient David Rumbough Internat. award Juvenile Diabetes Found., 1984, Williams-Levine award, 1990, NIH Merit award, 1987, Juvenile Diabetes Found. endowed Grodsky award for basic rsch. in diabetes, 1994—; named as one of 1000 most cited world scientists. Mem. Internat. Diabetes Found., Am. Soc. Biol. Chemists, Soc. Exptl. Biology, Am. Fedn. Clin. Rsch., European Diabetes Assn., Endocrine Soc., Am. Diabetes Assn. (rsch. bd. 1974-77, chmn. rsch. policy com. 1977, bd. dirs. Calif. chpt. 1989-91, nat. grant rev. com. 1992-96), Calif. Tennis Club, Harborpoint Club. Home: 3969 Washington St San Francisco CA 94118-1613 Office: U Calif Sch Medicine Metabolic Unit Box 0540 San Francisco CA 94143

GRODSKY, JAMIE ANNE, lawyer; b. San Francisco; d. Gerold Morton and Kayla Deane (Wolfe) G. BA in Human Biology/Natural Scis. and History with distinction, Stanford U., 1977; MA in Econ. Geography, U. Calif., Berkeley, 1986; JD, Stanford Law Sch., 1992. Ednl. dir. Oceanic Soc., San Francisco, 1979-81; rsch. asst. Woods Hole (Mass.) Oceanog. Inst., 1983; analyst Office Tech. Assessment U.S. Congress, Washington, 1984-89; counsel Com. Natural Resources, U.S. Ho. of Reps., Washington, 1993-94; counsel to Com. on Judiciary U.S. Senate, Washington, 1995-97; jud. clk. with chief judge U.S. Ct. Appeals (9th cir.), 1997-98; sr. adv. to gen. couns. US Environmental Protection Agency, Washington, DC, 1999—. Articles editor Stanford Law Rev.; contbr. articles to profl. jours. Mem. Calif. Bar Assn., D.C. Bar Assn.

GRODY, DONALD, actor, judge, lawyer, arbitrator; b. N.Y.C., Dec. 18, 1927; s. Charles E. and Jeannette (Kessler) G.; m. Judith Anderson Weston, Oct. 21, 1989; children by previous marriage: Dion, Gordon, James, Jeremy. Student, Royal Acad. Dramatic Art, 1949-50; BA cum laude, Hunter Coll., 1951; LLB, N.Y. Law Sch., 1959. Bar: N.Y. State bar 1959. Profl. actor, singer, 1950-58; atty. U.S. Dept. Labor, Washington, 1959-60; labor union atty. N.Y.C., 1960-65; atty.-advisor Nat. Labor Relations Bd., Washington, 1965-67; asst. gen. counsel Retail Clerks Internat. Assn., Washington, 1967-69; gen. counsel dist. 65 Distributive Workers Am., N.Y.C., 1970-73; exec. sec. Actors Equity Assn., N.Y.C., 1973-80; asst. exec. dir. NFL Players Assn., Washington, 1980-81, arbitrator, mediator, 1984-93; sole practice law N.Y.C., 1981-89; supervising adminstrv. law judge N.Y.C. Parking Violations Bur., 1989-93; Mem. theatre adv. panel Nat. Endowment for the Arts; mem. exec. bd., dept. profl. employees AFL-CIO.; Chmn. Equity-League Pension and Welfare Trust Funds, 1973-80. Appeared: (pre-Broadway tour) Yiddle with a Fiddle, 1994-95, Little Shop of Horrors, Tenn. Repertory Theatre, 1995, Sweeney Todd, Pitts. Pub. Playhouse, 1995-96, Let's Do It, Long Wharf Theatre, 1996, Jekyll & Hyde, Broadway, N.Y.C., 1997-98, Gypsy, Paper Mill Playhouse, 1998, Golf With Alan Shepard, Buffalo Studio Arena Theatre, 1998, (returned to theatre) Nat. Co. Guys & Dolls, 1993-94, (TV show) Law & Order, 1999. Served with AUS, 1945-47. Mem. AFTRA, Actors Equity Assn., Dramatists Guild.

GRODY, MARK STEPHEN, public relations executive; b. Milw., Jan. 1, 1938; s. Ray and Betty (Rothstein) G.; m. Karen Goldstein, Mar. 6, 1965 (div. 1972); 1 child, Laura; m. Susan Tellem, Mar. 25, 1979 (div. 1989); 1 child, Daniel. BS, U. Wis., 1960. Pub. rels. exec. GM, Detroit, 1961-74; v.p. pub. affairs Nat. Alliance of Businessmen, Washington, 1973-74; v.p. Carl Terzian & Assocs., L.A., 1974-75; chmn. Mark Grody Assocs. and Grody Tellem Comm., Inc. (now The Rowland Co.), L.A., 1975-90; pres. Mark Grody Assocs., L.A., 1990-93; exec. v.p., gen. mgr. Ogilvy Adams & Rinehart, L.A., 1993-96; pres. Mark Grody Assocs., L.A., 1996—; ptnr. Mktg. Golf Resources, L.A., 1996—, thegolfspot.com, 1998. Co-author: Corporate Golf: How to Play the Game for Business Success, 1996. Capt. U.S. Army, 1960. Mem. Internat. Network Golf (bd. dirs.), Nat. Golf Found., Pub. Rels. Soc. Am., Industry Edn. Coun. of Calif. (bd. dirs.), Nat. Alliance of Bus./West (bd. dirs.), Mountain Gate Country Club, L.A. Sports Club . Avocations: golf, bridge.

GROEBLI, WERNER FRITZ (MR. FRICK), professional ice skater, realtor; b. Basel, Switzerland, Apr. 21, 1915; s. Fritz and Gertrud (Landerer) G.; m. Yvonne Baumgartner, Dec. 30, 1954. Student architecture, Swiss Fed. Inst. Tech., 1934-35. Lic. realtor, Calif. Chmn. pub. relations com. Profl. Skaters Guild Am., 1972—. Performed in ice shows, Patria, Brighton, Eng., 1937; command performance in, Marina, London, 1937, Symphony on Ice, Royal Opera House, 1937; mem. Ice Follies, 1939-81, partner (with Hans Mauch) in comedy team Frick & Frack, 1939-53; solo act as Mr. Frick (assisted by comedy team), 1955-81; numerous TV appearances including Snoopy on Ice, 1973, Snoopy's Musical on Ice, 1978, Sportsworld, NBC-TV, 1978, Donnie and Marie Osmond Show, 1978, Mike Douglas Show, 1978, Dinah Shore Show, 1978; films include Silver Skates, 1942, Lady Let's Dance, 1943, Jinxed, 1981; interviewed by Barbara Walters NBC Today, 1974; appeared in Christmas Classics on Ice at Blue Jay Ice Castle, 1991. Served with Swiss Army, 1934-37. Named Swiss jr. skating champion, 1934; named to Madison Sq. Garden Hall of Fame for 10,000 performances in Ice Follies, 1967, U.S. Figure Skating Assn. World Hall of Fame, 1984; recipient Hall of Fame Ann. award Ice Skating Inst. Am. Mem. SAG, Profl. Skaters Guild Am., Swiss Club of San Francisco (hon.). Lasted 15,000 performances in Ice Follies; originator of "Frick" cantilever spread-eagle skating movement; comedic choreography consultant. Address: PO Box 7886 Incline Village NV 89452

GROENEVELD, DAVID PAUL, plant ecologist, hydrologist; b. Harvey, Ill., Mar. 20, 1952; s. Robert D. and Ruth M. (Terranova) G. BA, U. Colo., 1975, MA, 1977; PhD, Colo. State U., 1985. Rsch. asst. Inst. Arctic and Alpine Rsch., Boulder, Colo., 1972-76; cons., pres. GEOS, Inc., Telluride, Colo., 1977-81; plant ecologist Inyo County Water Dept., Bishop, Calif., 1981-96; cons. Resource Mgmt. Cons., Bishop, 1983-98; mem. tech. group Inyo City/City of L.A., 1983-95; tech. advisor Great Basin Air Pollution Control Dist., Bishop, 1985-96; mem. mined land reclamation expert's panel, Denver, 1980. Contbr. articles to profl. jours. Mem. Ecol. Soc. Am., Range Soc. Am. (life), Am. Water Res. Assoc., Soc. of Wetland Scientists. Achievements include development of management tools to monitor and protect vegetation from effects of groundwater pumping; research in physiology and evapotranspiration of Owens Valley floor vegetation that requires shallow groundwater. Home and Office: Resource Mgmt Cons PO Box 3296 Telluride CO 81435-3296

GROENHEIM, HENRI ARNOLD, psychologist, consultant; b. Bklyn., Oct. 18, 1927; s. Herman and Suzanna May (Bierman) G.; m. Gail Thacker, June 29, 1957; children: Lisa Gail, Gary Thomas. BA in Psychology, Pa. State U., 1950; MA in Counseling, George Washington U., 1954; PhD in Counselor Edn., Fla. State U., 1968. Lic. psychologist Md. State Bd. Examiners of Psychologists. Sch. counselor Brookville (Pa.) Jr.-Sr. H.S., 1950-51; dean of boys Derry Twp. Jr.-Sr. H.S., Hershey, Pa., 1951-52; sch. counselor Frederick (Md.) H.S., 1952-54; counselor Nurnberg Am. H.S., Germany, 1954-55; sch. counselor Kenwood Sr. H.S., Balt., 1955-61; sch. counselor, guidance dept. chair Overlea Sr. H.S., Balt., 1961-66; coll. counselor Catonsville C.C., Balt., 1968-69; assoc. prof. Johns Hopkins U., Balt., 1970-74; assoc. prof. psychology Towson State U., Balt., 1969-94; cons. psycholog. testing Divsn. Rehab. Svcs., Balt., 1973—, Disability Determination Svcs., Balt., 1973—, Kennedy Inst., Balt., 1985-86, Balt. City Pub. Schs., 1990-98; sr. counseling profl. mentor dept. counseling George Washington U., 1996—; med. staff allied health profl. Harford Meml. Hosp., Harford County, Md. Contbr. articles to profl. jours.; moderator TV program, 1987. Bd. dirs. Cmty. Counseling & Resource Ctr., Cockeysville, Md., 1985-90; com. mem. State Democratic Election Com., Balt., 1994. Recipient Sparks medal for outstanding scholarship Pa. State U., 1948. Fellow APA; mem. Md. Psychol. Assn. (mem. ins. com.), Balt. Psychol. Assn., Johns Hopkins Club, Rotary Club Aberdeen, Md. Avocations: swimming, travel, golf. Home and Office: 526 St Francis Rd Baltimore MD 21286-1325

GROENING, MATTHEW, writer, cartoonist; b. Portland, Oreg., Feb. 15, 1954; s. Homer Philip and Margaret Ruth (Wiggum) G.; m. Deborah Lee Caplan; 2 children. BA, Evergreen State Coll., 1977. Cartoonist Life in Hell weekly comic strip (syndicated by Acme Features Syndicate), Sheridan, Oreg., 1980—; pres. Matt Groening Prodns., Inc., L.A., 1988—, Bongo Entertainment, Inc., L.A., 1993—. Cartoonist for tv cartoon Futurama, 1999. Named New Pub. of Yr. Diamond Distbn. Gem awards, 1993. *

GROESCH, JOHN WILLIAM, JR., marketing research consultant; b. Seattle, Nov. 22, 1923; s. John William and Jeanette Morrison (Gilmur) G.; BSChemE, U. Wash., 1944; m. Joyce Eugenia Schauble, Apr. 25, 1948; children—Sara, Mary, Andrew. Engr., Union Oil Co., L.A., 1944-48, corp. economist, L.A., 1948-56, chief statistician, 1956-62, mgr., 1962-68, mgr., Schaumburg, Ill., 1968-90; exec. v.p. Performance Systems, Inc., Barrington, Ill., 1990—. Bd. dirs. Mt. Prospect (Ill.) Boy Scouts Am., 1977-88, 94-95, adv. bd., 1989-94, 96—, v.p., 1979, 82-85; commr. 1980-81, mem. OakBrook (Ill.) East Cen. Region, 1984-88; treas. Scout Cabin Found., Barrington, 1977—. Served with USN, 1944-47. Mem. West Coast Mktg. Rsch. Coun. (chmn. 1969), Am. Petroleum Inst. (chmn. com. 1970-72), Am. Mktg. Assn. (emeritus). Lodge: Mason. Home and Office: 17 Shady Ln Barrington IL 60010-3634

GROETHE, REED, lawyer; b. Indpls., Mar. 21, 1952; s. Alfred Philip and Kathryn (Skerik) G.; m. Nancy Jayne Radefeld, June 2, 1974; children: Jacob Peter, Eric Alfred. BA, St. Olaf Coll., 1974; JD, U. Chgo., 1977. Bar: Wis. 1977. Law clk. to judge U.S. Ct. Appeals (5th cir.), Montgomery, Ala., 1977-78; assoc. Foley & Lardner, Milw., 1978-86, ptnr., 1986—. Pres. Bay Shore Luth. Ch., Whitefish Bay, Wis., 1985-89. Mem. ABA (tax sect.), Nat. Asn. Bond Lawyers, Wis. Bar Assn. Lutheran. Office: Foley & Lardner 777 E Wisconsin Ave Ste 3800 Milwaukee WI 53202-5367*

GROETZINGER, JON, JR., lawyer, consumer products executive; b. N.Y.C., Feb. 12, 1949; s. Jon M. and Elinor Groetzinger; m. Carol Marie O'Connor, Jan. 24, 1981; 3 children. AB magna cum laude, Middlebury Coll., 1971; JD in Internat. Legal Affairs, Cornell U., 1974. Bar: N.H. 1974, N.Y. 1980, Mass. 1980, Fla. 1982, Md. 1985, Ohio 1991, U.S. Supreme Ct. 1980. Assoc. McLane, Graf, Greene, Raulerson and Middleton, P.A., Manchester, N.H., 1974-76; atty. John A. Gray Law Offices, Boston, 1978-81; pvt. practice N.H., Boston, 1977-81; chief internat. counsel Martin Marietta Corp., Bethesda, Md., 1981-88; pres., exec. v.p. Martin Marietta Overseas Corp., Bethesda, 1984-88; sr. v.p., gen. counsel, corp. sec. Am. Greetings Corp., Cleve., 1988—; chmn. internat. adv. bd. Case Western Res. U. Law Sch., 1995—. Disting. vis. lectr., 1997—. Trustee Middlebury (Vt.) Coll., 1974-76, mem. bd. overseers, 1977—; mem. exec. com., bd. dirs. Cleve. Coun. on World Affairs, 1991-98, 99—; bd. dirs. Can.-U.S. Law Inst.; mem. exec. com. The Conf. Bds. Coun. Chief Legal Officers, 1996—, membership chmn., 1997-98, program chair, 1999—. Mem. ABA, N.H. Bar Assn., Fla. Bar Assn., Ohio Bar Assn., Cleve. Bar Assn., Md. Bar Assn., Am. Soc. Corp. Secs. (sec. Ohio chpt. 1995—, v.p. 1996-97, pres. 1997-98), Phi Beta Kappa. E-mail: jgroetzi@yahoo.com. Office: Am Greetings Corp 1 American Rd Cleveland OH 44144-2301

GROEZINGER, LELAND BECKER, JR., investment professional; b. San Francisco, Dec. 6, 1941; s. Leland Becker Sr. and Clara Catherine (Hudson) G. BS and BA, U. Ariz., 1964, MS in Fin., 1967. Asst. legis. adv. Leland B. Groezinger Sr., Sacramento, 1970-78; personal investor Sacramento, 1978—. Mem. Episcopal Cmty. Svcs. for the Diocese of No. Calif., Sacramento, 1983-91, bd. dirs., 1984-91, treas., 1985-91; mem. Sacramento Traditional Jazz Soc., Sacramento, 1985—, bd. dirs., 1992—, treas., 1994-95, v.p., 1996-97, pres. 1998—. Republican.

GROFF, CHARLOTTE VIRGINIA, elementary education educator; b. Hinsdale, Ill., Aug. 9, 1932; d. Robert Earle and Virginia Fairchild (Boone) G. BA with hons., Emmanuel Missionary Coll., 1954; MA summa cum laude, Andrews U., 1965, PhD, 1986. Cert. elem educator (permanent), Mich. Elem. educator Coloma (Mich.) Cmty. Schs., 1956-68, head bldg., 1968-74, reading specialist, 1975—, summer migrant tchr., 1968-85, summer migrant resource tchr., 1986—. Author: (short story) in Youth's Instr. Mag., 1954 (Grand prize 1954); editor: (units of study) Coloma Career Units K-6, 1975. Asst. head deaconess Pioneer Meml. Seventh Day Adventist Ch., 1989—. Mem. Mich. Reading Assn., Internat. Reading Assn., Tri County Reading Coun. (past treas. 1974—), Alden Kindred of American, Colonial Dames SVII Century, Soc. Mayflower Descendants in Mich., Algonquin chpt. DAR (chair Am. History 1974—, three nat. winners, 1992, 93, 99), Phi Delta Kappa, Phi Kappa Phi Hon. Frat. Seventh Day Adventist. Avocation: genealogist. Home: 624 N Cass Berrien Springs MI 49103-1024 Office: Coloma Elem Sch 262 S West St Coloma MI 49038-9511

GROFF, DAVID CLARK, JR., lawyer; b. Detroit, June 16, 1946; s. David Clark and Marguerite (Lowrie) G.; children: Eric W., Paul D. BA in Polit. Sci., U. Mich., 1968, JD, 1972. Bar: Wash. 1972, U.S. Dist. Ct. (we. dist.) Wash. 1972, U.S. Ct. Appeals (9th cir.) 1972. Assoc. Davis, Wright & Jones, Seattle, 1972-78; ptnr. Davis Wright Tremaine (previously Davis, Wright & Jones), Seattle, 1978-92, Groff & Murphy, Seattle, 1992—. Author: Washington Constrn. Law, 1980-91; mem. editorial bd. Mich. Law Rev., 1971-72; contbr. articles to legal jours. Bd. govs. Wash. Spl. Olympics, 1990-96; trustee Seattle Repertory Theatre, 1992—. Mem. ABA (steering com. on Constrn. Forum 1987-90), Wash. State Bar Assn. (bd. dirs., sect. pub. contracts and pvt. constrn. law 1987-90), Order of Coif. Avocations: bicycling, sailing. Home: 1700 36th Ave Seattle WA 98122-3419 Office: Groff & Murphy 1191 2nd Ave Ste 1900 Seattle WA 98101-2994

GROFF, JAMES EDWARD, education educator, academic administrator; b. Wellman, Iowa, July 11, 1946; s. Milford W. and Virginia A. Groff; m. Patricia E. Johnson, Dec. 19, 1970; children: Christian, Anna, Ruth. BA, U. Iowa, 1969, PhD, 1984; MBA, Stetson U., 1974. Cert. mgmt. acct. Asst. prof. Okla. State U., Stillwater, 1983-88; assoc. prof. U. Tex., San Antonio, 1988-94, assoc. dean Coll. Bus., 1994-99; cons. TIEC, Austin, 1998. Contbr. articles to profl. jours. Mem. Am. Acctg. Assn., Assn. Govt. Acct., Inst. Mgmt. Accts., S.W. Am. Acctg. Assn., Phi Beta Kappa. E-mail: jgroff@utsa.edu. Office: U Tex Coll Bus 6900 W Loop 1604 N San Antonio TX 78249

GROFF, JOANN, organization director; b. Ft. Leonardwood, Mo., Oct. 10, 1956; d. Barry T. Groff and Ann (Ferry) Ragsdale. Student Georgetown U., 1974-76; B.S. in Bus. Adminstrn., Babson Coll., Wellesley, Mass., 1978. Office mgr. Morgan Smith for Congress, Northglenn, Colo., 1978; fair and rodeo asst. Adams County Commrs., Brighton, Colo., 1979; mktg. devel. officer Columbine Title Co., Lakewood, Colo., 1979-80; express agt., loan officer Wells Fargo Credit Corp., Englewood, Colo., 1981-84; pub. banking rep. Cen. Bank of Denver, 1985-89; mem. Colo. Ho. of Reps., Denver, 1983-89, chmn. audit com., 1989, fin. com.; dir. Leadership Giving Mile High United Way, 1991-92; pres. Colo. Retail Coun. 1992—. Past pres. Westminster Community Artist Series; mem. bd. Pub. Svc. Credit Union, Mem. Colo. State Dem. Com., 1980-93, Colo. State Exec. Com., 1983-93, del. Nat. Conv., 1980, 84, alternate del., 1976. Bd. dirs. Westminster (Colo.), Cmty. Artist Series, Marycrest High Sch. Roman Catholic. Office: Colo Retail Coun 451 E 58th Ave Denver CO 80216-1404

GROFF, STANLEY ALLEN, human services administration executive, educator; b. Madison, Minn., Oct. 24, 1942; s. Sherwood Allen and Rosella Belinda (Hanson) G.; m. Margaret Louise Parsons, May 5, 1990; children: Beth Ann, Steve; stepchild, Marco Parsons. BA in Sociology, U. Minn., Morris, 1965; MSW, Fla. State U., 1971. Dir. McLeod County Welfare Dept., Glencoe, Minn., 1967-69; supr. Stearns County Social Svcs., St. Cloud, Minn., 1971-72; dir. Faribault County Social Svcs., Blue Earth, Minn., 1972-75; mgmt. analyst Gov.'s Office Human Svcs., St. Paul, 1975-77; supr. Dakota County Social Svc., South St. Paul, Minn., 1977-80; dir. Steele County Human Svcs., Owatonna, Minn., 1980—, Steele County Transit Authority, Owatonna, 1997—; founder, leader Steele County Coun. of Dirs., 1982—; grad. adj. asst. prof. St. Mary's U. Minn., Mpls., 1989—; vice chair Region 6 Health Coordinating Bd., S.E. Minn., 1994—. Author: Minnesota Public Social Welfare Administrators in Times of Change, 1994. Founder, bd. dirs. Exch. Club Ctr. for Family Unity, Owatonna, 1982-94; mem. Healthy Owatonna 2000, 1993-98; trustee Owatonna Hosp. Bd., 1995—; founder, bd. dirs. Steele County Clothesline, Inc., 1997, Crossroads Youth Shelter of Owatonna, 1990. Mem. NASW, Minn. Social Svcs. Assn. (pres. 1996), Minn. Assn. County Social Svcs. Adminstrs. (pres. 1983), Owatonna Rotary Club, Owatonna C. of C. Avocations: flying, motorcycling, classic cars, boating, reading. Office: Box 890 630 Florence Ave Owatonna MN 55060-4704

GROGAN, DAVID R., company executive. Pres., chmn., CEO Toter, Inc., Statesville, N.C. Office: Toter Inc 841 Meacham Rd Statesville NC 28677-2983*

GROGAN, DEBBY ELAINE, geriatric and intensive care nurse; b. Roanoke, Va., Sept. 8, 1955; d. Jauquin B. and Hope Thomas (Smith) Holton; div.; children: Tina Nicole, Christopher J. (dec.). AD, South Ga. Coll., 1985. RN, Ga. Nurse's asst. Jeff Davis Hosp., Hazlehurst, Ga., 1984; staff nurse med. Coffee Regional Hosp., Douglas, Ga., 1984-89, head nurse 2 North Med., 1989-91; ICU day charge nurse Appling Gen Hosp., Baxley, Ga., 1991-95; asst. clin. team leader/field RN Care One Home Health, Baxley, 1994-96; clin. team leader Care One Home Health, Alma, Ga., 1996-98; field staff nurse Care One Home Health, Hazlehurst, 1998-99; intensive care unit staff nurse Appling Healthcare System, Baxley, 1999—.

GROGAN, JAMES J., real estate company executive. Grad. cum laude, Coll. of the Holy Cross, 1976; grad., U. Cin., 1979. Mng. atty. Gallagher and Kennedy, Phoenix; sr. exec. v.p. UDC Homes; pres., CEO Samoth Capital Corp. and Samoth USA Inc., Scottsdale, Ariz., 1998—; bd. dirs. AMERCO. Bd. trustees Coll. of the Holy Cross. Office: Samoth USA Inc 6900 E 2d St Scottsdale AZ 85251

GROGAN, PAULA CATALDI, newspaper editor; b. Syracuse, N.Y., May 8, 1950; d. Peter Paul and Gilda Sarah (Ingano) Cataldi; m. John Patrick Grogan, June 24, 1978. B.A., Syracuse U., 1972. Reporter, Syracuse (N.Y.) Post-Standard, 1972-75; feature writer Ft. Lauderdale (Fla.) News, 1975-78; successively copy editor, lifestyle editor, assoc. features editor, exec. features editor Dayton (Ohio) Daily News and Jour. Herald, from 1978; v.p., bus. mgr. Atlanta Jour.-Constn., now pub. Atlanta Jour.-Constn.; author column Paula Cataldi Grogan. Dir. Dayton YWCA. Mem. Ohio Newspaper Women's Assn. (2d place award 1983), Women in Communication. Office: Atlanta Journal-Constitution PO Box 4689 Atlanta GA 30302-4689

GROGAN, STANLEY JOSEPH, educational and security consultant; b. N.Y.C., Jan. 14, 1925; s. Stanley Joseph and Marie (Di Giorgio) G.; m. Mary Margaret Skroch, Sept. 20, 1954; 1 child, Mary Maureen. AA, Am. U., 1949, BS, 1950, MA, 1955; grad., Fed. Emergency Mgmt. Agy. Staff Coll., 1970; degree, Indsl. Coll. Armed Forces Air War Coll., 1972; MS, Calif. State Coll., Hayward, 1973; EdD, Nat. Christian U., 1974. Personal asst., recruitment asst. CIA, Washington, 1954-56; disting. grad. acad. instr., allied officer course Maxwell AFB, Ala., 1962; asst. prof. air sci. U. Calif., Berkeley, 1963-64, Chabot Coll., 1964-70, Oakland Unified Sch. Dist., 1962-83, Hayward Unified Sch. Dist., 1965-68; instr. ednl. methods, edn. rsch. methods of instrn. Nat. Christian U., 1975—, Nat. U. Grad. Studies, Belize, 1975—; pres. SJG Enterprises, Inc., cons., 1963—; cons. pub. rels., 1963—; bd. dirs. We T.I.P., Inc., 1974. Contbr. articles to profl. jours. and newspapers. Asst. dir. Nat. Ednl. Film Festival, 1971. With AUS, 1945; lt. col. USAFR, 1948-76; col. Calif. State Mil. Res. Decorated Air medal with oak leaf cluster; recipient citation Korea, 1963; RCVP Korean Vets. Assn. medal, 1994; named to Hon. Order Ky. Cols. Commonwealth of Ky., 1970, Outstanding Secondary Educators of Am., 1972. Fellow Internat. Inst. of Security and Safety Mgmt.; mem. NRA (life), VFW (life), DAV (life), Am. Def. Preparedness Assn. (life), Internat. Inst. Security and Safety Mgmt. (v.p. 1998), Assn. Nat. Def. and Emergency Resources (bd. dirs. 1995-98), Night Fighter Assn. (nat. publicity chmn. 1967), Air Force Assn. (life), Res. Officers Assn. (life), Phi Delta Kappa, Am. Soc. Indsl. Security (cert. protection profl.), Nat. Def. Exec. Res./FEMA, Marines Meml. Home: 2585 Moraga Dr Pinole CA 94564-1236

GROGAN, TIMOTHY JAMES, information technology executive; b. Hillsboro, Oreg., Aug. 5, 1940; s. James John and Joan Louise (Harper) G.; m. Jean Louise Egbert, Aug. 3, 1963 (div. June 1984); children: Susan, Erin; m. Kathryn Stetson, Aug. 9, 1985; children: Stephanie, Katherine. BS, U.S. Mil. Acad., 1963; MA in English, Columbia U., 1971; postgrad., U.S. Army War Coll., 1980-81, Royal Coll. Def. Studies, London, 1986. Commd. 2d lt. U.S. Army, 1963, advanced through grades to gen., 1987; asst. div. comdr. 8th Inf. Div. U.S. Army, Europe, 1987-88; chief of staff Hdqrs. U.S. V Corps, Frankfurt, Germany, 1988-89; asst. dep. chief staff for concepts and doctrine Hdqrs. Training and Doctrine Commd., Ft. Monroe, Va., 1989-93; ret., 1993; exec. Perot Sys. Corp., Dallas, 1993-98. Decorated DSC, Silver Star, Legion of Merit, Purple Heart. Republican. Roman Catholic. Avocations: golf, basketball, skiing, scuba, guitar. Home: 3501 Lakebluff Way Plano TX 75093-7522

GROGAN, WILLIAM ROBERT, university dean; b. Pittsfield, Mass., Aug. 2, 1924; s. William Patrick and Irene A. (Finch) G.; m. Mae Jean Kafer, Jan. 26, 1966. B.S., Worcester Poly. Inst., 1945, M.S., 1949, DEng (hon.), 1990.

Instr. elec. engring. Worcester Poly. Inst., Mass., 1946-49; asst. prof. Worcester Poly. Inst., 1949-56, assoc. prof., 1956-62; prof. WorcesterPoly. Inst., 1962—; dean undergrad. studies Worcester Poly. Inst., 1970-90, dean emeritus, 1990—; engring. cons. Gen. Electric Co., Pittsfield, Mass., 1953-61; cons. U.S. Navy, Washington, 1963-66, Bell Telephone Labs., Holmdeli, N.J., 1964-65; trustee Bay State Savs. Bank, Worcester, 1973—. Patentee in field. Chmn. Diocese of Worcester bd. edn., 1974-76; mem. adv. bd. Worcester br. Arthritis Found., 1987. Served to lt. USN, 1942-46, 51-52. Recipient Outstanding Teaching award Worcester Poly. Inst. Trustees, 1969; recipient Sci. Achievement award Worcester Engring. Soc., 1979, Chester F. Carlson award Am. Soc. Engring. Edn., 1979, William Wickenden award, 1980, IEEE/EAB Major Ednl. Innovation award, 1986, Trustees award for Outstanding Svc., 1989. Fellow IEEE; mem. Worcester Econ. Club, Sigma Xi, Tau Beta Pi, Eta Kappa Nu; Phi Kappa Theta nat. pres. (1960-64). Roman Catholic. Home: 10 Laconia Rd Worcester MA 01609-1508 Office: Worcester Poly Inst Off of the Dean Off of Undergrad Studies Worcester MA 01609

GROGG, TERRIE LYNN, factory assembler; b. Ft. Wayne, Ind., Feb. 27, 1956; d. Robert Emor and Margaret Berneice Foreman; m. Randy Ray Grogg (div. 1985); 1 child, Justin Robert. Cert. advanced model and finishing, Charmaine Finishing, Ft. Wayne, 1973; student, Ind. U., Ft. Wayne, 1979; cert. solder elec. contractor, ITT Industries, Ft. Wayne, 1989; student, Ivy Tech. State Coll., Ft. Wayne, 1997, 98, 99. Instr. English riding Lomond Farms, Ossian, Ind., 1972; factory worker Tony's Pizza Co., Salina, Kans., 1974-76; clk. N.Am. Vanlines, Ft. Wayne, 1976-79; factory worker Ft. Wayne Wire & Die, 1979-80; clk. Temp. Agys., Ft. Wayne, 1981-84; policy change clk. Mut. Security Ins., Ft. Wayne, 1984-87; die maker AJAX Industries, Ft. Wayne, 1987-88; inspector Ind. Coatings Corp., Ft. Wayne, 1988-89; assembler ITT Industries, Ft. Wayne, 1989—; mem. adv. bd. edn. ITT Industries, 1995. Contbg. poet The World of Poetry, 1990, The Sound of Poetry, 1994. Recipient Golden Poets award Nat. Libr. Poetry, Owings Mills., Md., 1990, 91, 92, Editors Choice award, 1994, named to Internat. Poetry Hall of Fame, 1996. Mem. Acad. Am. Poets, Ind. Poets (Mack chpt.), Am. Health and Fitness (life). Religious Scientist. Avocations: music, sewing, art, camping. Home: 1314 Ludwig Park Dr Fort Wayne IN 46825-4028

GROGINS, JACK LAWRENCE, state judge; b. Norwalk, Conn., Feb. 27, 1931; s. Abraham Robert Grogins; m. Marilyn Jean Leichtman, Mar 16, 1958; 1 child, Auden. BA, U. Conn., 1952; JD, U. Conn., Hartford, 1955. Bar: Conn. 1955. Asst. prosecuting atty. State of Conn. Cir. Ct., Bridgeport, 1963-74; superior ct. judge State of Conn., Danbury, 1994—; pres. Fairfield (Conn.) Bar Assn., 1980-82. Mem. bd. student editors U. Conn. Law Sch., 153-55. Mem. Fairfield Dem. Town Com., 1961-63; chmn. bd. of recreation City of Fairfield, Conn., 1970s. With U.S. Navy, 1956-57. Mem. Conn. Judges' Assn. Avocations: tennis, book collecting, travel. Office: Conn Superior Ct 14 W River St Milford CT 06460-3396

GROH, JENNIFER CALFA, law librarian; b. Patchogue, N.Y., Mar. 28, 1970; d. Anthony Bernard and Mary (Fogerty) C.; m. William Matthew Groh, May 10, 1997. BA in Social Sci., St. Joseph's Coll., 1992; MA in Internat. Edn., NYU, 1993; MSLS, Pratt Inst., Bklyn., 1996. Reference page Patchogue (N.Y.)-Medford Libr., 1986-93; from libr. asst. to asst. libr. Morgan & Finnegan, N.Y.C., 1994—. NYU grad. scholar, 1992, Law Libr. Assn. scholar, N.Y. 1995, Am. Assn. Law Librs. scholar, 1996. Mem. ALA, Spl. Librs. Assn., Law Libr. Assn. Greater N.Y. Home: 2750 Sawmill Rd N Bellmore NY 11710-2330 Office: Morgan & Finnegan 345 Park Ave New York NY 10154-0053

GROH, SUSAN LAUREL, public relations consultant; b. Escondido, Calif., May 4, 1960; d. Clarence Gary and Ann Sheyl (Litzenberger) Howard; m. Arthur J. Groh, Jr., Oct. 19, 1985; children: Sarah Ann, John Arthur, James Michael. AA, Spokane (Wash.) Falls C.C., 1980; BS magna cum laude, Ea. Wash. U., 1982. Prodr. King Broadcasting, Spokane, 1980-84, reporter, 1984-88; sr. account exec. FitzGerald & Co., Cranston, R.I., 1988-94; exec. v.p. Groh Assocs., Warwick, R.I., 1992—; v.p. Soc. Profl. Journalists, Spokane, 1986-87; pub. rels. cons. New Eng. Inst. Tech., Warwick, 1990—, R.I. State Dem. Party, Providence, 1992. Prodr. (tv documentary) Kaiser Aluminum Corp., 1983; author of poetry; contbr. articles to jour. Writing instr. Warwick Pub. Schs., 1996—. Recipient Excellence in Journalism, Soc. Profl. Journalists, Spokane, 1984, Bell Ringer award Pub. Rels. Soc. Am., Boston, 1992. Office: Groh Assocs PO Box 6044 Warwick RI 02887-6044

GROISS, FRED GEORGE, lawyer; b. Glen Cove, N.Y., Mar. 12, 1936; s. Frederick F.W. and Dorothy C. (Roberts) G.; m. Jacqueline C. Grosse; children—Frederick C., Katherine E., Jennifer L. A.B., Cornell U., 1958, LL.B., 1961. Bar: N.Y. 1961, Wis. 1963, U.S. Dist. Ct. (ea. dist.) Wis., 1963, U.S. Ct. Appeals (7th cir.) 1965. Assoc. Sage, Gray, Todd & Sims, N.Y.C., 1961-63; assoc. Porter, Quale, Porter & Zirbel, Milw., 1963-65, Brady, Tyrrell, Cotter & Cutler, Milw., 1965-70; ptnr. Quarles & Brady, Milw., 1970—; lectr. various labor law confs. Mem. Gov.'s Commn. on Civil Service Reform, Madison, Wis., 1977-78. Mem. ABA, Wis. Bar Assn. (bd. dirs. labor law sect. 1975-77), Milw. Bar Assn. Republican. Club: Milw. Athletic. Avocation: sports. Home: 144 Washington Dr West Bend WI 53095-9764 Office: Quarles & Brady 411 E Wisconsin Ave Ste 2550 Milwaukee WI 53202-4497

GROLLMAN, JULIUS HARRY, JR., cardiovascular and interventional radiologist; b. L.A., Nov. 26, 1934; s. Julius Harry and Alice Carolyn (Greenlee) G.; m. Alexa Jule Silverman, May 20, 1959; children: Carolyn, David, Elizabeth. BA, Occidental Coll., 1956; MD, UCLA, 1960. Diplomate in radiology and vascular and interventional radiology Am. Bd. Radiology. Intern L.A. VA Hosp., 1960-61; resident in radiology UCLA Med. Ctr., 1961-64; chief cardiovascular radiology Walter Reed Gen. Hosp., 1965-67, UCLA Ctr. Hlth Srvcs, 1967-78; chief cardiovascular and interventional radiology Little Company of Mary Hosp., Torrance, Calif., 1978—; clin. prof. radiol. sci. UCLA, 1978—. Contbr. over 120 articles and papers to profl. jours., and 9 chpts. to books. Fellow Soc. for Cardiac Angiography and Interventions (trustee 1992-95), Am. Coll. Radiology, Coun. Cardiovascular Radiology, Am. Heart Assn., Soc. Cardiovascular and Interventions Radiology; mem. AMA, Am. Roentgen Ray Soc., Radiol. Soc. N.Am., Western Angiographic and Interventional Soc. (pres.), N.Am. Soc. for Cardiac Imaging (pres.). Republican. Presbyterian. Office: Little Company of Mary Hosp Dept Radiology 4101 Torrance Blvd Dept Torrance CA 90503-4664 also: RPM 100 Oceangate Ste 1000 Long Beach CA 90802-4347

GROLLMAN, SIGMUND SIDNEY, physiology educator; b. Stevensville, Md., Feb. 12, 1923; s. Ellis Phillip and Rachel Naomi (Krystal) G. BS, U. Md., 1947, MS, 1949, PhD, 1952. Cert. biochem. physiology. Teaching asst. U. Md. Zoology Dept., College Park, 1947-49, instr., 1949-51, asst. prof., 1952-55, assoc. prof., 1955-58, prof., 1958-84, chair div. physiology, 1966-73, dir. grad. studies, 1973-83, prof. emeritus, 1984; pres. Sigmund Grollman Ltd., Balt., 1970—. Author: (textbook) The Human Body--Its Structure and Function, 1964, 4th rev. edit., 1984, (manual) Anatomy and Physiology, 1960-84, Experimental Mammilian Physiology, 1971-83; contbr. articles to profl. jours. Sgt. U.S. Army, 1940-43, ETO. Fellow Am. Coll. Sports Medicine; mem. Soc. Exptl. Biology and Medicine, N.Y. Acad. Sci., Sigma Xi. Home: 4001 N Charles St Baltimore MD 21218-1749

GROMACK, ALEXANDER JOSEPH, state legislator; b. East Patterson, Dec. 30, 1953; s. Alexander and Camelia (Marchesio) G.; m. Joan Nurra, June 15, 1991; 1 child, Jenna. BS, St. John's U., 1977. Sr. recreation leader Town of Clarkstown, New City, N.Y., 1977-90; mem. N.Y. State Assembly, Albany, 1990—, also mem. aging, transp., local govt., corps., authorities and commns., real property coms., mem. subcom. on vol., chmn. transp. safety com., chmn. racing and wagering com. Bd. dirs. People to People, Jr. Achievement; mem. adv. bd. CANDLES; mem. coun. Girl Scouts U.S.A.; mem. adv. com. Rockland Coun. for Young Children; mem. Rockland County Legislature, 1984-90, also vice chmn., majority leader, chmn. ways and means com., vice chmn. budget and fin. com., chmn. rules and confirmation com.; active Venture Bd., United Italian-Am. Civic Assn., Very Spl. Arts Festival, Rockland Conservation Assn., Rockland YMCA; also others. Recipient awards United Jewish Appeal, Very Spl. Arts Festival, Nathan Kline Inst., Carpenter Local 964, Office Rockland County Dist. Atty., Rockland Police Athletic League, Rockland County Vol. Fire Svcs. Mus., Good Apple award Rockland Srs. Mem. Rotary, Lions. Democrat. Roman Catholic. Avocations: golf, jogging, water skiing. Home: 23 Reginald Dr Congers NY 10920-2160 Office: 67 N Main St New City NY 10956-3700

GROMADA, THADDEUS V., historian, administrator; b. Passaic, N.J., July 30, 1929; s. John W. and Aniela (Pudzisz) G.; m. Theresa M. Michalski, Aug. 25, 1951; children: Joseph, John, Ann. BS magna cum laude, Seton Hall U., 1951; MA, Fordham U., 1953, PhD, 1966. From asst. prof. history to prof. European history N.J. City U., 1959-92; v.p., exec. dir. Polish Inst. Arts and Scis., N.Y.C., 1991—; chmn. Gov.'s Commn. Ea. European History, Trenton, N.J., 1985-89; vice chmn., trustee Kosciusko Found., N.Y.C., 1981—; cons. ethnic heritage Dept. Edn., Washington, 1977; cons. NEA, 1975—, N.J. Edn. Assn., 1975—. Author, editor: Essays on Poland's Foreign Policy 1918-1939, 1969; editor: Jadwiga of Anjou & Rise of East Central Europe, 1991; co-editor: Polonia Amerykanska, 1988; founder, co-editor The Tatra Eagle, 1947—. Awards com. Korczak Literary Prize, N.Y.C., 1980-85; dialog com. Polish-Am.-Jewish Am. Task Force, N.Y.C., 1981-86; co-organizer Conf. Germany, Poland & Europe, 1992. Sgt. U.S. Army, 1953-55. Recipient Haiman medal Polish Am. Hist. Assn., 1985, cross of merit Pres. Poland, 1993, L'Ordre du Merite Culturel, Poland's Minister of Culture and Arts, 1996. Mem. Am. Assn. for Advancement of Slavic Studies, Am. Hist. Assn., Polish Am. Hist. Assn. (pres. 1995-96). Roman Catholic. Avocations: classical music, violin, Polish Highlander folklore, hiking. Home: 2722 Old Oak Walk Johns Island SC 29455-6213 Office: Polish Inst Arts & Scis 208 E 30th St New York NY 10016-8202

GROMAN, NEAL BENJAMIN, microbiology educator; b. Chisholm, Minn., May 21, 1921; s. Raphael Simon and Jenny Rebecca (Levine) G.; m. Elaine Ruth Spigle, Nov. 19, 1943; children: Jo Ann Tamarin, Nancy Sheffer, Richard, Ellen Groman Fair. BS, U. Chgo., 1947, PhD, 1950. Instr. U. Wash., Seattle, 1950-53, asst. prof., 1953-58, assoc. prof., 1958-63, prof. microbiology, 1963-89, prof. emeritus, 1989—, dir. office of biol. edn., 1971-75, acting chmn. dept. microbiology, 1981-82. Contbr. articles to profl. pubs. Served with AUS, 1942-46. John and Mary Markle Found. scholar, 1955-60; John Simon Guggenheim fellow, 1958-59; USPHS fellow, 1966-67. Fellow Am. Acad. Microbiology; mem. Am. Soc. Microbiology (chmn. virology sect. 1963-64), Acad. Am. Poets, Sigma Xi. Home: 4805 NE 40th St Seattle WA 98105-5216 Office: U Wash Dept Microbiology Seattle WA 98195

GROMEN, RICHARD JOHN, historian, educator; b. Cleve., Dec. 3, 1930; s. John Rudolph and Rena Marie (Calcagni) G.; m. Joyce Margaret Pawlak, Jan. 27, 1951; children: Margot Lynn, Doreen Rae, Richard John. *Wife Joyce, BA 1983, MA 1985 Edinboro, taught dance and communication for Allegheny College and Penn State Erie. Daughter Margot, BSED 1976, MED 1981 Edinboro, has co-authored several conference presentations on science teaching and is president of Richmond Area Speleological Society. Daughter Doreen, BS 1977 Indiana University of Pennsylvania, MED 1984 Cleveland State, is an administrator at Olmstead Falls High School. Son Richard, BA 1983 Wittenberg, JD 1986 Akron, is practicing law in the Lancaster/Harrisburg Pennsylvania area.* BA, Adelbert Coll., 1953; MA, Western Res. U., 1961; PhD, 1969. Salesman Beck Shoe Store, Parma, Ohio, 1946-48; cowboy Minor Cattle Ranch, Hyannis, Nebr., 1949; with classified advt. dept. Cleve. News, 1949-50; office mgr. Parma Cut Stone, 1950-60; part-time bookkeeper Cleve., 1960-64; acct., bookkeeper Broadview Savs. and Loan, Cleve., 1960-64; tchr., summer sch. dir. Brunswick (Ohio) High Sch., 1960-64; mem. faculty Edinboro U. of Pa., 1964-98, prof., dean faculty arts and scis. Author: British Historians and Their View of the British Policy of Appeasement, 1931-39, 1969; contrb. to Hist. Abstracts, 1972-98. Treas. Edinboro Found.; bd. dirs. Edinboro State Coll. United Cerebral Palsy Joint Coun.; past pres. Ams. for Competitive Enterprise System; pres. Tri-Boro Little League, 1979-89. Tuition scholar, 1949-55. Mem. NEA (life), AAUP, Am. Hist. Assn., N.Am. Conf. Brit. Studies, Phi Alpha Theta. Lutheran. *The standards one sets should be for oneself and not for others. Nor should one express a view on a controversial issue until one can understand why someone as sincere and honest as oneself can hold the opposite view.*

GROMOSIAK, PAUL, historian, consultant, science and math educator; b. Niagara Falls, N.Y., Aug. 21, 1942; s. John and Anna (Rimanosky) G. BS in Chemistry, Niagara U., 1964. Chemist Eastman Kodak, Rochester, N.Y., 1965, Durez Plastics div. Occidental, North Tonawanda, N.Y., 1966-68; tchr. Niagara Falls Bd. Edn., 1969-89; author Western N.Y. Wares, Inc., Buffalo, 1990—; guest lectr. Ctr. of Renewal, Stella Niagara, N.Y., 1991—; curator Mus. Niagara. Author: Soaring Gulls and Bowing Trees, 1990, Answers to the 100 Most Common Questions About Niagara Falls, 1990, Zany Niagara, 1992, Sensing the Wonders of Niagara, 1994, Water Over the Falls, 1996, Daring Niagara, 1998. Vol. historian Schoellkopf Geol. Mus., Niagara Falls, 1984-90; cons. to Niagara Falls Mus., Mus. of Niagara. Mem. Old Fort Niagara Assn. (life), Friends of Local History. Avocations: public speaking, gardening, hiking. Home: 5819 Grauer Rd Niagara Falls NY 14305-1455

GROMOV, MIKHAEL, mathematician; b. Boksitogorsk, USSR, Dec. 23, 1943. MS, U. Leningrad, USSR, 1965, PhD, 1969, DSc, 1973. Asst. prof. U. Leningrad, 1967-74; prof. SUNY, Stony Brook, 1974-81, U. Paris VI, 1981-82; permanent fellow, chmn. math dept. Inst. Hautes Etudes Scientifiques, Bures-sur-Yvette, France, 1982—; lectr. ICM Nice, France, 1970, Helsinki, Finland, 1978, Warsaw, Poland, 1982, Berkeley, Calif., 1986. Author: Structures Métriques Pour Les Variétés Riemanniennes (Paris), 1981, Partial Differential Relations (Springer), 1986. Recipient prize Moscow Math. Soc., 1971, prix Elie Cartan Académie des Scis. Paris, 1984, prix sci. Union Assurances Paris, 1989, Wolf Prize in Mathematics, 1993. Mem. Am. Math. Soc. (Oswald Veblen Prize Geometry 1981, Leroy P. Steele prize 1997), Nat. Acad. Scis. U.S.A. (fgn. assoc.), Associé Étranger de l'Académie Scis. Office: IHES Le Bois-Marie, 35 Route de Chartres, F-91440 Bures-sur-Yvette France

GROMULTS, JOSEPH MICHAEL, JR., internist; b. Ansonia, Conn., Nov. 8, 1932; s. Joseph Michael and Mary Margaret (Marcelynas) G.; m. Paula Ruth Beeler Casella, July 6, 1967; 1 stepchild, Stephen. BA in History, Yale U., 1954; MD, NYU, 1958. Diplomate Am. Bd. Internal Medicine. Intern in medicine Bellevue Hosp., N.Y.C., 1958-59, resident in medicine, 1959-61; rsch. fellow NYU Sch. Medicine, N.Y. Heart Assn., 1961-62; pvt. practice Stamford, Conn., 1965—; attending physician St. Joseph Hosp., Stamford, 1966—, Stamford Hosp., 1965—; clin. instr. medicine N.Y. Med. Coll., Valhalla, N.Y., 1970-97; clin. instr. medicine Columbia Med. Sch., 1997—. Capt. USAF, 1962-65. Mem. ACP, Am. Legion, Conn. State Med. Soc. (del. 1980—). Republican. Roman Catholic. Avocations: gardening, handyman, music appreciation, travel. Office: 95 Morgan St Ste 1-c Stamford CT 06905-5435

GRONDIN, JERRY RENE, marriage and family therapist; b. Portland, Maine, Feb. 23, 1946; s. Robert J. and Laurance (Giguere) G.; m. Betsy Grondin, Aug. 3, 1996; children: Maggie, Jerry, Duncan, Justin. M of Religious Edn., Mary Knoll Theol. Sem., 1971. Supr. Am. Assn. of Marriage and Family Therapy, 1989—; dir. Greater Portland Counseling Ctr., 1986—; co-facilitator Batterer's Intervention Program, Portland, 1986—. Mem. Men's Movement, Portland, 1986—. Mem. Maine Counselor Assn., Maine Assn. of Batter's Intervention Programs. Home: 125 Harriet St S Portland ME 04106-2001 Office: Greater Portland Counseling Ctr 21 Northbook Dr Falmouth ME 04106

GRONER, SAMUEL BRIAN, lawyer; b. Buffalo, Dec. 27, 1916; s. Louis and Lena (Blinkoff) G.; m. Beverly Anne Groner; children: Jonathan B. (dec. 1962), Morri Lou Morell, Lewis A. Davis, Laurence M., Andrew G. Davis. AB, Cornell U., 1937, JD, 1939; MA in Econs., Am. U., 1950. Bar: N.Y. 1939, D.C. 1952, Md. 1953, U.S. Supreme Ct. 1944. Pvt. practice law Buffalo, 1939-40; atty. U.S. Dept. War and Office Price Adminstrn., 1940-43; atty.-adviser U.S. Dept. Justice, Washington, 1946-53; pvt. practice law Md. and Washington, 1953-63; ptnr. Groner, Stone & Greiger, Washington, 1955-57, Groner & Groner, Silver Spring and Bethesda, Md., 1962—; asst. counsel Naval Ship Systems Command, Washington, 1963-73; trial atty. Office Gen. Counsel, Dept. Navy, Washington, 1973-74, assoc. chief trial atty., 1974-79; adminstrv. law judge and mem. Bd. Contract Appeals U.S. Dept. Labor, Washington, 1979—, acting chmn., 1987, mem. Bd. Alien Labor Certification Appeals, 1990—, acting adminstrv. appeals judge Benefits Rev. Bd., 1988-89; instr. Terrell Law Sch., Washington, 1948; mem. faculty USDA Grad. Sch., 1972—; reporter Md. Gov.'s Commn. on Domestic Rels. Laws, 1977-87; participant in continuing legal and jud. edn. Author: Modern Business Law, 1983, (with others) The Improvement of the Administration of Justice, 6th edit., 1981; assoc. editor Fed. Bar Jour., 1948-55; contbr. articles to profl. jours. Active PTA, civic assns., Jewish Community Coun., Community Chest; mem. Montgomery County Commn. on Handicapped Individuals, 1977-85, vice chmn., 1980-81. 1st lt. inf. and M.I.S., U.S. Army, 1943-46, ETO. Recipient Navy Superior Civilian Service award, 1979. Mem. ABA (liaison commn. on professionalism 1985—, advisor to standing com. on lawyer competence 1986—, family law sect., jud. adminstrn. div., vice chmn. pub. contract law sect., com. on adminstrv. claims and remedies 1976-79, chmn. 1979-80), Fed. Bar Assn., Montgomery County Bar Assn. and Bar Found., Bar Assn. of D.C., Bar Assn. Met. St. Louis, Cornell Law Assn. (pres. D.C. chpt. 1947-54), Am. Law Inst., Inst. for Jud. Adminstrn., Am. Judicature Soc., Supreme Ct. Hist. Soc., Govt. Adminstrv. Trial Lawyers Assn., Nat. Lawyers Club, Cosmos Club, Cornell Club N.Y.C., Officers and Faculty Club (U.S. Naval Acad., Annapolis), Phi Beta Kappa. Home: 5600 Wisconsin Ave Apt 1602 Chevy Chase MD 20815-4413 Office: 800 K St NW Ste 400 Washington DC 20001-8000

GRONKA, M(ARTIN) STEVEN, educational association executive, film and television producer; b. Westchester, Pa., Apr. 30, 1952; s. Martin Joseph and Dorothy Elizabeth (Snyder) G.' BA in Arts and Scis., U. Del., 1974, MBA, 1982, postgrad. in econs., 1982; postgrad. in div., Westminster Theol. Sem., 1976. Prodr., dir. Synthetic Imagery, Princeton, N.J., 1987-90, Masterworks Prodns., Newark, Del., 1989—; vice chmn., CEO Found. Against Smoking & Tobacco, Newark, 1988—; exec. dir. Americape, 1988—; chmn., pres. Advance Am. Found., Cape May Court House, N.J., 1989—; U.S. nat. sales rep. Natural Environment Recovery, Inc., Toronto, Ont., Can., 1993—; exec. dir. Americape, 1988—; U.S. nat. sales cons. Earth Care Systems, Inc., Lincoln, Ark., 1993—; v.p. Sail U.S.A. Inc., 1993—; cons. pub. rels. Cape May (N.J.) Harbor Marine & Resort, 1990-93; bd. dirs. Reggie Brown, Inc., Couture Womens Apparel, Unusual Villas and Islands; chmn., prodr., dir. Hobie 16 Open Nat. Sailing Championships, U.S.A., 1986, Hobie 16 Women's World Championships, 1986; fo-founder, prodr., dir., mgr. 1st all women's sailing team allowed into an all men's sailing event The Hog's Breath 1,000 Internat. Sailing Challenge, 1987; chmn., prodr., dir. Hobie 17 Nat. Sailing Championship, U.S.A., 1988; prodr., dir. largest exhibit of Magna Charta on Am. Express; tour for Bicentennial Commn., 1988; dir. advt. and promotions Domino's World Pizza Record, Wildwood, N.J., 1988; author 1st Rap radio comml. Domino's Pizza World Record Rap, 1988; founder See Kids in Action family of programs, Sea Quest Kids Boat Bldg., Fish Tales Anglers Club, Sea Post Times and Mighty Mates Safety Club, 1998—; pres., bd. dirs. Heartlight Ministries Ch. Without Walls, Children's Outreach for Jesus Christ, 1998—; chief adminstr. Hearts of Fire Christ Fest, Internat. Christian Family Conf., 1997—; founder, adminstr. Latino Migrant Farm Workers MIssions, 1998—; founder See Kids In Action Family of Programs, Sea Quest Kids Boat Bldg., Fish Tales Anglers Club, Sea Post Times, Mighty Mites Safety Club, 1998—. Prodr., art dir. 3-D computer-animated opening Am.'s Cup Opening, 1988; co-prodr. SUSA Cup and TV show, 1993; (music video, film) Please Save Us the World, UN Global Youth Forum, 1992; exec. prodr. (ednl. children's shows) Chessie Kids, Chessie Build a Boat and Water Safety Program, Huckleberry Finn Fishing and Water Safety Program, 1993—, Water Safety Primer, 1994; author rap radio comml. Domino's Pizza World Record Rap, 1988; restorer Civil War Battleship model Merrimack for Valentine Mus., Richmond, Va., 1993; exec. prodr., dir. (video) How to Build a Chessie Boat, 1996. Bd. dirs. Cape May Ctr. Pub. Policy, 1989-97; com. 100 to Honor Law Enforcement Officers, Cape May, 1991; pres., chmn. Advance Am. Found.; dir. TV and video prodn. Faith City Family Ch., 1996-97; bd. dirs., pres. Heartlight Ministries, Children's Outreach for Jesus Christ, 1998—; chief adminstr. Heart of Fire Christ Fest, Internat. Christian Family Conf., 1997—; founder Latino Migrant Farm Workers Missions, 1998—; dir. Boat Bldg. for Spl. Olympics Athletes, Spl. Olympics World Games, 1995, 99—; prodr. Advance Am., Am.'s Cup Campaign, 1984-91. Mem. U. Del. Bus. and Econ. Alumni Assn. (founding 1000), Stone Harbor Hobie Cat Sailors Assn. (commodore), Internat. Platform Assn., Les Ami Du Vin Internation Wine Club (life). Presbyterian. Avocations: sailing, physical fitness, gemology, the arts, engineering. Home: 6 S Dillwyn Rd Newark DE 19711-5544

GRONLUND, ROBERT B., art collector, fund raising consultant; b. Duluth, Minn., May 2, 1926; s. Bernard S. and Lena J. (Manske) G.; m. Dorothy M. Dahlstrom, June 2, 1951; children: Gaye, Robin, Gregg, Jamie. BA, Wartburg Coll., Waverly, Iowa, 1949; MDiv, Wartburg Sem., Dubuque, 1953; LittD, Thiel Coll., Greenville, Pa., 1973. Ordained Luth. Ch., 1953. Pastor Newport Harbor Luth. Ch., Newport Beach, Calif., 1953-56; exec. dir. Inter Ch. Fellowship, L.A., 1956-59; asst. to pres. Calif. Luth. U., Thousand Oaks, Calif., 1959-62; exec. dir. Am. Luth. Ch. Found., Mpls., 1962-63; v.p. devel. Capital U., Columbus, Ohio, 1963-69, U. Tampa, Fla., 1969-76; pres. Gronlund Assocs., West Palm Beach, Fla., 1976—, Northwood U., West Palm Beach, 1981-83; mem. works of art com. Norton Mus., West Palm Beach, 1993-96; chair PBCC Art Gallery, Palm Beach Gardens, Fla., 1995-96; chair Tampa Bay Art Ctr., Tampa, 1973-74; chair Vision for Mission Com., Evang. Luth. Ch. Am., Chgo., 1995-99. Exhibited works at Norton Mus., Pensacola Mus., Tampa Mus., Wartburg Coll., Lighthouse Gallery, Tequesta, Fla., Ctr. for Arts, Vero Beach, Fla., others. Sr. warden Bethesda By Sea Episcopal Ch., 1995; chair Fla. Repertory Theater, West Palm Beach, 1990-92; founding pres. Planned Giving Coun., West Palm Beach, 1982-84; chair S.E. Diocese Episcopal Found., 1999—. Cpl. U.S. Army, 1943-46, ETO. Republican. Episcopalian. Avocations: golf, travel, grandchildren. Home: 2330 Saratoga Bay Dr West Palm Beach FL 33409-7222

GRONSETH, DANIEL EDWARD, park ranger; b. Oak Park, Ill., Feb. 4, 1962; s. Ralph Sverre and Doris Arlene Gronseth; m. Karen Renae Bleeker, July 28, 1990; children: Erik, Jakob. BS in Math., Calvin Coll., 1984; MPA, Ariz. State U., 1996. Park ranger City of Phoenix, 1988—. Editor (newsletter) Outdoor Program Press; designer interpretive trail signs; designer, leader environ. edn. programs. Recipient City Mgr.'s Excellence award City of Phoenix, 1995, 97, Teamwork award South Dist. Phoenix Parks, Recreation, and Libr. Dept., 1989. Mem. ASPA, Nat. Recreation and Parks Assn., Nat. Assn. for Interpretation, Ariz. Parks and Recreation Assn. Avocations: drawing, hiking, bicycling, photography. E-mail: rangerdg@juno.com. Office: South Mountain Park 10919 S Central Ave Phoenix AZ 85040

GROOM, DALE, physician, educator; b. Tulsa, Nov. 6, 1912; s. Fernando Hooker and Mary (Dale) G.; m. Marjorie Ruth Tweed, Jan. 26, 1944; children: Shelley Ann, Lincoln Dale, Randall Tweed. A.B., Hiram Coll., 1936; M.D., Med. Coll. Va., 1943; M.S. in Medicine, U. Minn., 1948. Diplomate: Am. Bd. Internal Medicine (subsplty. cardiovascular disease). Intern Northwestern U. Passavant Hosp., Chgo., 1943; fellow in medicine Mayo Clinic, 1945-49; pvt. practice internal medicine Miami, Fla., 1949-53; assoc. prof. medicine, asst. dean Med. Coll. S.C., 1953-68; prof. medicine, assoc. dean continuing edn. U. Okla. Med. Center, Oklahoma City, 1968-78; prof. emeritus U. Okla. Med. Center, 1978—; mem. staff Univ. Hosp.; cons. Oklahoma City VA, Presbyn. Hosp., Mercy Hosp.; nat. cons. cardiology USAF, 1965-75, FAA, 1970-74; vis. prof. medicine U. Saigon, Vietnam, 1974. Author: Clinics in Electrocardiography, 1961; editorial bd. Am. Heart Jour., 1977-85; contbr. articles on coronary heart disease, EKG and cardiovascular sounds to profl. jours. Trustee Ednl. Resources Found., 1964-92. Lt. M.C. USNR, 1944-45, Invasion of Normandy. Fellow ACP (regent 1969-75, chmn. bd. govs. 1968, 69), Am. Coll. Cardiology, Am. Heart Assn. Coun. Clin. Cardiology; mem. AMA (coun. on Sci. Assembly 1965-74), Mayo Cardiovascular Soc. (pres. 1971-73), Mayo Alumni Assn. (pres. 1969-71, mem. adv. bd. 1971—), The Doctors Mayo Soc., Sigma Xi, Alpha Omega Alpha. Home: Ste A-730 4600 Middleton Park Cir Jacksonville FL 32224

GROOM, GARY LEE, recreational vehicle manufacturing executive; b. Rensselaer, Ind., Jan. 3, 1946; s. Robert D. and Margery Ellen (Spain) G.; divorced; children: Richard L., Angela K. B.S.I.M., Purdue U., 1969; M.B.A. (valedictorian), U. Notre Dame, 1971. C.P.A., Fla., Ind. Auditor Arthur Young & Co., Tampa, Fla., 1971-72; exec. v.p. fin., sec. Coachmen Industries, Inc., Elkhart, Ind., 1972—; dir. Coachmen Industries, Inc., Elkhart, 1981—. Mem. Am. Inst. C.P.A.s, Inst. Mgmt. Accts. Republican.

Methodist. Home: 51007 Beach Dr Elkhart IN 46514-8101 Office: Coachmen Industries Inc 601 E Beardsley PO Box 3300 Elkhart IN 46515-3300

GROOME, KIMBERLY VONGONTEN, administrative assistant; b. Coral Gables, Fla., Mar. 11, 1966; d. Kenneth M. and Ernestine (Freeman) VonGonten; m. Thomas Steven Groome, Dec. 2, 1989. AA in Broadcasting, Miami (Fla.)-Dade C.C., 1987; B in Pub. Adminstrn., Fla. Internat. U., 1993; MPA, U. Miami, 1999. Sec. Nautilus Investigations, Miami, 1988-90; sec. occupl. therapy dept. Fla. Internat. U., 1990-94; adminstrv. asst. City of Coral Gables Planning Dept., Miami, 1994—. Mem. Am. Soc. Pub. Adminstrs. (bd. dirs.), Sigma Sigma Sigma (pres. South Fla. alumnae chpt. 1996—). Lutheran. Avocations: dance, piano, football, basketball, gardening. Home: 9824 SW 195th St Miami FL 33157-8660 Office: City Coral Gables Planning Dept 405 Biltmore Way Coral Gables FL 33134-5717

GROOME, REGINALD KEHNROTH, company executive, consultant; b. Montreal, Que., Can., Dec. 18, 1927; s. Cyril T. and Muriel H. (Forbes-Toby) G.; m. Christina M. Walker, June 20, 1953; children: Reginald A., Roderick, Richard. Ed., McGill U., Cornell U. With Montreal Pub. Co., 1945-53; broadcaster CBC Internat. Svc.; also overseas corr. Can. daily newspapers, 1951; dir. advt. and pub. rels., then pers. mgr. hotel chain Montreal, 1953-57; with Hilton Can., 1957, v.p., then exec. v.p., 1965-72, pres., 1972, chmn. bd. dirs., 1978; pres., dir., also gen. mgr. Queen Elizabeth Hotel, Montreal, 1972-83; v.p. Hilton Internat., N.Y.C., 1982-90; chmn. Hotel Assn. Can., Ottawa, Ont., 1991-93; spl. advisor to pres. C.P. Hotels & Resorts, 1991-96; past pres. Montreal Bd. Trade; bd. dirs. Voyageur Ins. Co., Arctic Group Inc. Hon. v.p. nat. Coun. Boy Scouts Can.; life gov., Montreal Gen. Hosp.; chmn., bd. govs. Concordia U. Decorated officer Order of Can.; recipient Silver Wolf award Boy Scouts Can.; Outstanding Citizenship award Montreal Citizenship Coun., 1976.

GROOMS, HENRY RANDALL, civil engineer; b. Cleve., Feb. 10, 1944; s. Leonard Day and Lois (Pickell) G.; m. Tonie Marie Joseph; children: Catherine, Zayne, Nina, Ivan, Ian, Athesis, Shaneya, Yaphet, Rahsan, Dax, Jevay, Xava. BSCE, Howard U., 1965; MSCE, Carnegie-Mellon U., 1967, PhD, 1969. Hwy. engr. D.C. Hwy. Dept., Washington, 1965; structural engr. Peter F. Loftus Corp., Pitts., 1966; structural engr., engring. mgr. Rockwell Internat. (now Boeing), Downey, Calif., 1969—. Contbr. articles to profl. jours. Scoutmaster Boy Scouts Am., Granada Hills, Calif., 1982-87; basketball coach Valley Conf., Granada Hills, 1984—; coach Am. Youth Soccer Orgn., Granada Hills, 1985-90, 94—; tutor Watts Friendship Sports League, 1989—; co-founder Project Reach, 1993. Recipient Alumni Merit award Carnegie-Mellon U., 1985; named Honoree Black History Project Western Res. Hist. Soc., 1989. Fellow Inst. Advancement Engring. (Outstanding Engring. Vol. award, 1999); mem. ASCE, Tau Beta Pi, Sigma Xi. Office: Boeing Mail Code AD 69 12214 Lakewood Blvd Downey CA 90242-2693

GROOMS, RED, artist; b. Nashville, June 2, 1937. Student, Peabody Coll., Chgo. Art Inst., New Sch. Social Research, Hans Hofmann Sch., Provincetown, Mass. One-man exhbns. include, Sun Gallery, Provincetown, 1958, Reuben Gallery, N.Y.C., 1960, Tibor de Nagy Gallery, 1963, 65-67, 69-70, Artists Guild, Nashville, 1962, Allan Frumkin Gallery, Chgo., 1967, John Bernard Myers Gallery Discount Store, 1971, Happenings: A Play Called Fire, Sun Gallery, 1958, Burning Bldgs, N.Y.C., 1958, Rutgers Gallery Art, New Brunswick, N.J., 1973, N.Y. Cultural Center, 1973, Mus. de Arte Contemporaneo, Caracas, Venezuela, 1973, Brooke Alexander Gallery, N.Y.C., 1975, Ft. Worth Art Mus., 1976, Stanford Mus., 1976, SUNY-Purchase, 1978, Hudson River Mus., Yonkers, N.Y., 1979, Lowe Art Mus., U. Miami, 1980, Aspen Ctr. Visual Arts, 1981, Seibu Mus., Tokyo, 1982, Marlborough Gallery N.Y.C., 1984, 86, 87, 89, 90, 92, 95, 96, Marlborough Fine Art, London, 1985, Hokin/Kaufman Gallery, Chgo., 1985, Benjamin Mangel Gallery, Phila., 1985, Circulo de Bellas Artes, Madrid, 1985, Sette Pub. Co., Tempe, Ariz., 1985, Pa. Acad. Fine Arts, 1985-86, Stanton Gallery Denver Art Mus., 1986, Mus. Contemporary Art, Los Angeles, 1986, Tenn. State Mus., Nashville, 1986, Cumberland Gallery, Nashville, 1985-86, 1986, Marlborough Fine Art, Tokyo, 1986, Fine Arts Ctr., Cheekwood, Nashville, 1986—, Muscarelle Mus. Art Coll. William and Mary, Williamsburg, Va., 1986—, Ruth Eckerd Hall, Clearwater, Fla., 1986—, Erie (Pa.) Art Mus., 1986—, William Benton Mus. Art U. Conn., Storrs, 1986—, S.D. Meml. Art Ctr., Brookings, 1986—, The Nelson-Atkins Mus. Art, Kansas City, Mo., 1986—, Arvada (Colo.) Ctr. Arts and Humanities, 1986—, Carpenter Ctr. Visual Arts Harvard U., Cambridge, Mass., 1986, Whitney Mus., N.Y.C., 1973, 87, Marlborough Gallery, Paris, 1990, Arvada Ctr. for Arts and Humanities, Colo., 1992, Cabaret Voltaire, Turin, Italy, 1992, Grand Ctrl. Terminal, N.Y.C., 1993, Nagoya City Mus., Japan, 1993, others; group exhbns. include, Chgo. Art Inst., 1964, Delancey St. Mus., N.Y.C., 1959, 60, also, Provincetown/Chrysler Mus., Tibor de Nagy Gallery, N.Y.C., 1969, Walker Art Center, Mpls., 1970, , 88-89, Guggenheim Mus., N.Y.C., 1972, Ruckus Manhattan, N.Y.C., 1975-76, 81, SUNY, Purchase, 1978, Lowe Art Mus. U., Miami (Fla.), 1980, The New Gallery, Cleve., 1982, ICA, Phila., 1982, Allen Frumkin Gallery, N.Y.C., 1985, Open Air Mus. Sculpture, Middelheim, Antwerp, Belgium, 1985, Sewell Art Gallery Rice U., Houston, 1985, Artists' Choice Mus., N.Y.C., 1986, Mus. Art, Ft. Lauderdale, Fla., 1986, Wilson Art Ctr., Rochester, N.Y., 1986, Allentown (Pa.) Art Mus., 1986, N.Y. Acad. Art, 1986, Whitney Mus. Am. Art at Philip Morris, N.Y.C., 1986-87, Nat. Mus. Am. History Smithsonian Instn., Washington, 1986—, Saxon Lee Gallery, L.A., 1988, Baruch Coll., N.Y.C., 1988, Lockport Gallery, Ill., 1988-89, Bucknell U., Lewisburg, Pa., 1989, others; (with Rudy Burckhardt) movie Shoot the Moon, 1962, Big Sneeze, 1965, Before'n After, 1966, Washington's Wig Whammed!, 1966, Fat Feet, 1966, (with Rudi Burckhardt) Meow, Meow!, 1967, Small Fry Gangster, 1985; represented in permanent collections, Mint Mus. Art, Charlotte, N.C., Chgo. Art Inst., Mus. Modern Art, N.Y.C., Chrysler Mus. Art, Provincetown, Mass., Cheekwood Fine Arts Mus., Nashville, Met. Mus. Art, N.Y.C., Moderna Mus., Stockholm, Agrl. Bldg. Des Moines Art Ctr.; (theatre) set design The Mysteries and What's So Funny, 1991; commd. (with Lysiane Luong) for Am. Mus. of Moving Image, N.Y., for movie theater titled Tuts Fever. Recipient Pres.'s award R.I. Sch. Design, 1985, Ten Best Illustrated Childrens' Books award N.Y. Times, 1986, Gov.'s award in Art, State of Tenn., 1986, Nat. Arts Club award, 1986, N.Y.C. Mayor's award of Honor, 1988, Founders medal Pa. Acad. Arts, 1990. Address: 85 Walker St New York NY 10013-3523

GROOS, ARTHUR BERNHARD, JR., German literature educator; b. Fullerton, Calif., Feb. 5, 1943; s. Arthur Bernhard and Nancy Elizabeth (Stowe) G.; m. Bonnie Cleo Buettner, May 16, 1979; children: Peter, Jan. AB magna cum laude, Princeton U., 1964; MA, Cornell U., Ithaca, N.Y., 1966; PhD, Cornell U., 1970; postgrad., Freie Universitat Berlin, 1966-67. Asst. prof. UCLA, 1969-73; asst. prof. German lit. Cornell U., 1973-76, assoc. prof., 1976-82, prof., 1982—, dir. medieval studies, 1974-86, chmn. dept. German studies, 1986-91, 96—; chmn. German dept. adv. coun. Princeton U., N.J., 1981-85; vis. prof. U. Paderborn, W.Ger., 1982; bd. dirs. Centro Studi Giacomo Puccini (Lucca). Author: Puccini: La Boheme, 1986, Romancing the Grail, 1995; co-author: Medieval Christian Literary Imagery, 1988; editor: Dichtkunst und Lebenkunst, 1981, Magister Regis, 1986, Reading Opera, 1988, Cambridge Opera Jour., 1988-98, Studi pucciniani, 1998—; gen. editor: Cambridge Opera Monographs. Fulbright fellow Berlin, 1966, Fulbright sr. fellow Munich, 1979, Guggenheim fellow Munich, 1979; recipient ASCAP-Deems Taylor prize, 1993. Mem. MLA, Internat. Arthurian Soc., Medieval Acad. Am., Wolfram v. Eschenbach Gesellschaft, Internat. Courtly Lit. Soc., Am. Musicol. Soc., Phi Beta Kappa. Home: 492 Valley Rd Brooktondale NY 14817-9701 Office: Cornell U Dept German Studies 185 Goldwin Smith Hall Ithaca NY 14853-3201

GROOVER, SANDRA MAE, business executive; b. Ft. Ord, Calif., Sept. 10, 1955; d. Ralph Hillis Jr. and Joanne (Hodges) G.; m. L. Scott Butterfield, Mar. 16, 1985 (div. July 1991). AS in Bus. Adminstrn., No. Va. C.C., Alexandria, 1983; BS in Behavioral Sci., Nat. Louis U., 1990; MBA in Mgmt. Policy and Orgnl. Behavior, Case Western Res. U., 1992—. Mgr. credit, collection Kay Jewelers Inc. (acquired by Sterling, Inc.), Alexandria, 1976-80, mgr. accounts payable, 1980-84, exec. asst. to sr. v.p., 1984-86, dir. inventory control, 1986-87, div. v.p. mdse. ops., 1987-90; v.p. distbn. Sterling, Inc., Akron, Ohio, 1990-96; v.p. mdse. support ops. Mayor's Jewelers, Inc., Coral Gables, Fla., 1996-97; v.p. distbr. Aurafin Corp., Sunrise, Fla., 1997—. Mem. Gemological Inst. Am. (grad. gemologist), Case Western Res. U. Alumni Assn. (pres. South Fla. chpt. 1997—), Mensa. Republican. Avocations: reading, art application, gemology, scuba diving. Home: 20425 NE 10th Court Rd N Miami Beach FL 33179-2523 Office: Aurafin 14001 NW 4th St Sunrise FL 33325-6228

GROPP, LOUIS OLIVER, editor in chief; b. LaPorte, Ind., June 6, 1935; s. Hosea Howard and Carol Gladys (Pagel) G.; m. Jane Margaret Goodwin, Aug. 15, 1965; children—Amy Alison, Lauren Elizabeth Forbes. B.A. in Communication Arts, Mich. State U., 1957. Design editor Home Furnishings Daily, Chgo. and N.Y.C., 1960-67; v.p. Milo Baughman Design, Wellesley, Mass., 1967; exec. editor House and Garden Guides, Conde Nast Co., N.Y.C., 1968-72, editor-in-chief, 1973-80; editor-in-chief House and Garden mag., N.Y.C., 1981-88; v.p. design and creative svcs., consumer products div. Westpoint-Pepperell, N.Y.C., 1988-89; editor in chief Elle Decor, Hachette Pub. co., N.Y.C., 1990-91; editor-in-chief House Beautiful, Hearst Mags. Div., N.Y.C., 1991—. Author: Solar Houses, 1978. Chmn. bd. deacons Riverside Ch., N.Y.C., 1973-75; pres. Bd. Christianity and Crisis, 1988-90. Mem. Am. Soc. Mag. Editors (bd. dirs. 1990-94). Home: 140 Riverside Dr Apt 6G New York NY 10024-2605 also: 44 Old Depot Rd Quogue NY 11959 Office: Hearst Mags House Beautiful 1700 Broadway New York NY 10019-5905

GROPPER, ALLAN LOUIS, lawyer; b. N.Y.C., Jan. 25, 1944; s. Jerome F. and Susan M. (Weingarten) G.; m. Jane Evangelist, Aug. 10, 1968 (dec. Feb. 1999); 1 child, Andrew. BA, Yale U., 1965; JD, Harvard U., 1969. Bar: N.Y. 1969, U.S. Dist. Ct. (so. and ea. dists.) N.Y. 1971, U.S. Ct. Appeals (2d cir.) 1971, U.S. Supreme Ct. 1974. Atty. Civil Appeals Bur., Legal Aid Soc., N.Y.C., 1969-71; assoc. White & Case, N.Y.C., 1972-77, ptnr., 1978—. Bd. dirs. Browning Sch., 1990—, pres., 1997—; bd. dirs. Legal Aid Soc., 1990—, v.p., 1996—; bd. dirs. N.Y. Lawyers for Pub. Interest, 1990—. Mem. ABA (bus. bankruptcy com.), Assn. of Bar of City of N.Y. (v.p. 1995-96, mem. exec. com. 1991-96, chmn. 1994-95), N.Y. State Bar Assn. (bankruptcy law com. 1984—). Home: 115 Central Park W New York NY 10023-4153 Office: White & Case Bldg Ll 1155 Avenue Of The Americas New York NY 10036-2787

GROS, FRANCISCO ROBERTO ANDRÉ, banker; b. Rio de Janeiro, Apr. 21, 1942; s. André and Dulce (Simões Corrêa) G.; m. Sandra Mattmann, June 8, 1968 (div. 1989); children: Francisco H., Carlos R., Alexandra M.; m. Isabel Teixeira Mendes, Dec. 12, 1994. BA, Princeton U., 1964; postgrad., Columbia U., 1965-67. Exec. dir. Metropolitana Fin. Group, Rio de Janeiro, 1967-72; assoc. Kidder, Peabody and Co., Inc., N.Y.C., 1972-75; exec. dir. Corretora Multiplic, brokerage house, Rio de Janeiro, 1975-77, Brazilian SEC (CVM), Rio de Janeiro, 1977-81, Unibanco, São Paulo, 1981-85; exec. dir., v.p. BNDES-Nat. Devel. Bank, Rio de Janeiro, 1985-87; pres., CEO, Aracruz Celulose S.A., Rio de Janeiro, 1987-89, BFC Banco S.A., Rio de Janeiro, 1989-91, 93; pres. Ctrl. Bank Brazil, Brasilia, 1987, 91-92; mng. dir. Morgan Stanley & Co., N.Y.C., 1993—. Decorated officier French Legion of Honor, comdr. Brazilian Navy, Brazilian Air Force, Govt. of Minas Gerais State, Brazilian Army; recipient O Equilibrista award Brazilian Inst. Fin. Execs. Roman Catholic.

GROS, JEFFREY, ecumenical theologian; b. Memphis, Jan. 7, 1938; s. C. Jefferson and Faye Elizabeth (Dickenson) G. BA, St. Mary's Coll., 1959, MEd, 1962; MA, Marquette U., 1965; PhD, Fordham U., 1973. Tchr. various high schs. and coll., Chgo., St. Louis, Memphis, 1959-81, Christian Bros. U., Memphis, 1972-81, Memphis Sem., 1976-81; dir. faith and order Nat. Coun. Chs. of Christ in U.S.A., N.Y.C., 1981-91; assoc. dir. Secretariat for Ecumenical and Interreligious Affairs, Nat. Conf. Cath. Bishops, Washington, 1991—. Editor: The Search for Visible Unity, 1984, (with J. Burgess) Building Unity, Growing Consensus, 1994, (with E. Wondra R. Elder) Common Witness to the Gospel, 1997, (with W. Rusch) Deepening Communion, 1998; author: (with A. Riggs, E. McManus) Introduction to Ecumenism, 1998; contbr. articles to profl. jours. NSF fellow, 1961-64; Hebrew Union Coll. travel grantee, 1968. Mem. Cath. Theology Soc., Coll. Theology Soc. (bd. dirs. 1996-98), Nat. Assn. Ecumenical Officers (bd. dirs. (1979-81), Nat. Assn. Evangs. Office: Nat Conf Cath Bishops 3211 4th St NE Washington DC 20017-1106*

GROSE, ANDREW PETER, foundation executive; b. Washington, July 16, 1940; s. Peter Andrew and Mildred (Holston) G.; m. Jacqueline Stamm, Aug. 17, 1963; children: Peter Andrew II, Tracey Christine. BS with high honors, U. Md., 1962, MA, 1964. Mem. legis. staff Fla. Ho. of Reps., Tallahassee, 1972-74; rsch. dir. Nev. Legislature, Carson City, 1974-83; chief of staff Office of Gov. Nev., Carson City, 1983-84, dir. econ. devel., 1984-90; dir. Western region Coun. of State Govt., San Francisco, 1990-95; pres. Westrends, 1990-95; CFO Pub. Policy Inst. Calif., 1995—; mem. exec. com. Nat. Conf. State Legislatures, Denver, 1982-83. Author: Florida Model City Charter, 1974; mem. editl. bd. Nev. Rev. of Bus. and Econs., Reno, 1976-90. Chair trustees Temple United Meth. Ch., San Francisco, 1998—; active Habitat for Humanity. Capt. USAF, 1964-70, to brig. gen., Res. Recipient Spl. citation Nev. Libr. Assn., Carson City, 1981. Mem. Air Force Assn., Res. Officers Assn., Nat. Assn. State Devel. Agys. (1st v.p.), Western Govt. Rsch. Assn. (pres. 1993-95), Kiwanis (pres. 1981-82, bd. dirs. 1994-97, treas. 1997—). Democrat. Home: 405 Hazelwood Ave San Francisco CA 94127-2129 Office: Public Policy Inst of California 500 Washington St Ste 800 San Francisco CA 94111-2934

GROSE, CHARLES FREDERICK, pediatrician, infectious disease specialist; b. Faribault, Minn., Apr. 15, 1942; s. Frederick G. and Marie A. (Swelland) G. BA, Beloit Coll., 1963; MD, U. Chgo., 1967. Bd. cert. in pediatric infectious disease. Resident Albert Einstein Coll. Medicine, Bronx, N.Y., 1967-68, fellow, 1970-71; fellow U. Calif., San Francisco, 1975-76; asst. prof. Health Sci. Ctr. U. Tex., San Antonio, 1976-84; prof. pediatrics U. Iowa Hosp., Iowa City, 1985—; cons. NIH, Bethesda, Md., 1988—. Mem. editorial bd. Pediatric Infectious Disease Jour., 1991—, Virology Jour.; contbr. articles to profl. and sci. jours. Capt. U.S. Army Med. Corps., Vietnam, 1968-70. Grantee NIH, 1978—. Fellow Infectious Disease Soc. Am., Pediatric Infectious Disease Soc., Am. Acad. Pediatrics, Am. Soc. Virology. Achievements include research on diagnosis and treatment of chickenpox and shingles, and on the etiologic agent which is varicella virus. Office: U Iowa Hosp Pediatrics 200 Hawkins Dr Iowa City IA 52242-1009

GROSE, ELINOR RUTH, retired elementary education educator; b. Honolulu, Apr. 23, 1928; d. Dwight Hatsuichi and Edith (Yamamoto) Uyeno; m. George Benedict Grose, Oct. 19, 1951; children: Heidi Diane Hill, Mary Porter, John Tracy, Nina Evangeline. AA, Briarcliff Jr. Coll., 1948; postgrad., Long Beach State U., 1954-55; BS in Edn., Wheelock Coll., Boston, 1956; MA in Edn., Whittier Coll., 1976. Cert. tchr., Mass., N.Y., Calif. Reading tchr. Cumberland Head Sch., Plattsburgh, N.Y., 1968-70; master tchr. Broadoaks Sch., Whittier (Calif.) Coll., 1971; reading tchr. Phelan/Washington Schs., Whittier, 1971-73; elem. tchr. Christian Sorensen Sch., Whittier, 1977-94, ret., 1994; cons. Nat. Writing Projet, 1987—, South Basin Writing Project, Long Beach, 1987—; team tchr. first Young Writers' Camp, Long Beach State U., 1988. Author: Primarily Yours, 1987, Angel Orchid Watercolor, 1994. First v.p. Women's League of Physicians Hosp., Plattsburgh, 1970; asst. to Christian, Jewish and Muslim pres., v.p.s of Acad. Judaic, Christian and Islamic Studies 6th Assembly World Coun. Chs., Vancouver, 1983. Mem. AAUW (assoc. in dialogue 1996—), NEA, Calif. Tchrs. Assn., Whittier Elem. Tchrs. Assn., English Coun. of Long Beach, Acad. Judaic, Christian and Islamic Studies (named companion Order of Abraham 1987), Orange County Soc. Calligraphy. Presbyterian. Avocations: travel, painting, gardening, gym. Home: Museum Hgts 171 N Church Ln Condo 619 Los Angeles CA 90049-2068

GROSE, IVAN, member of parliament; b. North Toronto, ON, Canada, Jan. 8, 1928; m. Beverley Grose, 1981; children: Steven, Randy, Chris, Monty, Jeff. Line installer Bell Can.; salesman in various cos.; owner Ajax Portable Svcs., Ltd., 1964; M.P. for Oshawa House of Commons, 1993—, vice chmn. standing com. on pub. accounts, past mem. standing com. on transp., past mem. standing com. on justice and human rights, past mem. standing com. on the status of disabled people. Past chmn. Greater Toronto Area Liberal Caucus; exec. mem. Ratepayers Assn. North York; bd. dirs. Cmty. Coun., Umbrella of the Ratepayers Assn.; former bd. dirs. fundraising com. Courtice Cmty. Complex Fund, mem. project com., mem. citizens planning com.; dir. Air Cadet League Can., Ont. Provincial Com. With RCAF, 1947-52. Mem. Optimist Club (pres. North York chpt.), Portable Sanitation Assn. (past dir.), Victorian Order Nurses (past dir. Durham region), Royal Can. Air Force Assn. (past bd. dirs.), Royal Can. Legion (charter pres. br. 637), Can. Warplane Heritage, Durham Region Can. Club (past pres.), Can. Corps Commrs. (adv. bd. Durham region). Office: House of Commons, Rm 313 Confederation Bldg, Ottawa, ON Canada K1A 0A6

GROSE, ROBERT FREEMAN, psychology educator; b. Norwood, Mass., July 12, 1924; s. Arthur Dexter and Alice Buck (Littlefield) G.; m. Ann Bawden Huntington, Aug. 9, 1947; children: Peter Huntington, Catherine Littlefield, Margaret Susan, Amy Tarrant. B.A., Yale U., 1944, M.S., 1947, Ph.D., 1953; M.A. hon., Amherst Coll., Mass., 1970. From instr. to prof. psychology Amherst Coll., 1950-92, prof. psych. emeritus, 1992, registrar, 1956-78, dir. instl. research, 1974-92, affirmative action officer, 1980-83; adj. prof. Grad. Sch. Edn. U. Mass., Amherst, 1975-92; ret., 1992; cons. Silliman U., Dumaguete City, Philippines, 1963-64. Co-author: Data Book I, 1978, Data Book II, 1983, Data Book III, 1987, Ethics and Standards in Institutional Research, 1992; co-editor: Transfer of Learning, 1963. Vice chmn. Town Amherst Zoning Bd., 1975-82, Town of Amherst Planning Bd., 1997—; town meeting rep. Town of Amherst, 1964—; mem. planning group Five Coll. Learning in Retirement Program, 1988-90, pres., 1997—trustee Amherst Hist. Soc., 1990-96, Pioneer Valley Living Care Ctr., Applewood, Amherst, 1985-96, sec./clk., 1985-96. Lt. (j.g.) USNR, 1944-46. Mem. Am. Assn. Coll. Registrars, New Eng. Assn. Coll. Registrars (pres. 1972), Assn. Instl. Rsch. (Outstanding Svc. award 1989), N.E. Assn. Instl. Research (pres. 1979-80), Am. Psychol. Assn., Am. Ednl. Research Assn., Am. Assn. for Higher Edn., Amherst Club, Rotary (chmn. internat. found. 1978-81, 85-88), Sigma Xi. Democrat. Mem. United Ch. of Christ. Home: 132 Farmington Rd Amherst MA 01002-3251*

GROSE, WILLIAM RUSH, publishing executive; b. Charleston, W.Va., Jan. 29, 1939; s. William Ellis and Mary W. (Morrison) G. Grad., Haverford Coll., 1961. With Prentice-Hall, Inc., Englewood Cliffs, N.J., 1962-70, Warner Communications, Inc., N.Y.C., 1970-72; editor-in-chief Dell Pub. Co., Inc., N.Y.C., 1972-79; v.p., pub. Jove Publs., Inc., N.Y.C., 1979-81; v.p., editorial dir. Berkeley/Jove Pub. Group, 1981-82; v.p., editor-in-chief New Am. Library Inc., 1982-83; exec. v.p., editorial dir. Pocket Books, 1983—. Democrat. Episcopalian. Clubs: Knickerbocker; Groucho (London). Home: 929 Park Ave New York NY 10028-0211 also: 128 Blackville Rd Washington CT 06794-1209 Office: Simon and Schuster Ste 383 1230 Avenue Of The Americas Fl Concl New York NY 10020-1586

GROSECLOSE, EVERETT HARRISON, retired editor; b. Childress, Tex., June 25, 1938; s. Everett Jackson and Eula Margaret (Snider) G.; m. Edna Kathryn Hunter, Dec. 24, 1962 (div. 1986); children: Kirsten Lee, Megan Margaret; m. Susan Kahne Greer, Dec. 22, 1990. B.A. in Journalism, Tex. Tech. U., Lubbock, 1961. Reporter Wall St. Jour., Dallas and N.Y.C., 1965-70; asst. mng. editor Cleve., 1970-76; dir. pub. affairs Dow Jones & Co., N.Y.C., 1976-80; mng. editor Dow Jones News Services, N.Y.C., 1980-88; exec. editor Dow Jones Profl. Investor Report, N.Y.C., 1988-92; dir. product devel. Dow Jones Info. Services, N.Y.C., 1988-92; dir. internat. mktg., news and database svcs. Telerate, Inc. subs. Dow Jones, N.Y.C., 1992-94; mng. editor Dow Jones Emerging Markets Report, N.Y.C., 1994-97, Servicio Dow Jones Americas, N.Y.C., 1996-97. Served with AUS, 1961-64. Decorated Army Commendation medal. Unitarian. Home: 57 Goodnight Trl E Santa Fe NM 87501-7925

GROSFELD, JAY LAZAR, pediatric surgeon, educator; b. N.Y.C., May 30, 1935; m. Margie Faulkner; children: Lisa, Denise, Janice, Jeffrey, Mark. A.B. cum laude, NYU, 1957, M.D., 1961. Diplomate: Am. Bd. Surgery (spl. qualification Pediatric Surgery). Intern in gen. surgery dept. surgery Bellevue and Univ Hosps. NYU, N.Y.C., 1961-62; resident in gen. surgery Bellevue and Univ. Hosps. NYU, N.Y.C., 1962-66; resident in pediatric surgery Ohio State U. Coll. Medicine, Children's Hosp., 1968-70; clin. instr. surgery NYU Sch. Medicine, N.Y.C., 1965-66, asst. prof. surgery and pediatrics, 1970-72; instr. surgery Ohio State U. Coll. Medicine, 1968-70; prof., dir. pediatric surgery Ind. U. Sch. Medicine, Indpls., 1972—, Lafayette F. Page prof., 1981—, chmn. Dept. Surgery, 1985—; surgeon-in-chief James Whitcomb Riley Hosp. Children. Author: Common Problems in Pediatric Surgery, 1991, Central Surgical Association: The First 50 Years, 1991, Progress in Pediatric Trauma, 1992, Essentials of Pediatric Surgery, 1995, Pediatric Surgery, 5th edit., 1998; contbr. over 500 papers, reports, book chpts., articles for med. jours.; editor-in-chief Jour. Pediat. Surgery; editor Seminars in Pediat. Surgery. Served to capt. M.C. U.S. Army, 1966-68. Decorated Commendation medal; recipient numerous fellowships, grants, teaching awards. Fellow ACS (bd. govs. 1985-91), Am. Acad. Pediats. (exec. com. surg. sect. 1989-95, sec. surg. sect., chmn. surg. sect. 1994-95), Royal Coll. Physicians and Surgeons Glasgow; mem. AMA, Assn. Acad. Surgery, N.Y. Cancer Soc., Am. Pediat. Surg. Assn. (bd. govs., pres.-elect, pres. 1994-95), Am. Surg. Assn., Soc. Univ. Surgeons, Marion County Med. Soc., Ind. State Med. Assn., Pediat. Surgery Biology Club, Am. Trauma Soc., Soc. Surgery Alimentary Tract, Ctrl. Surg. Assn. (sec. 1987—, pres.-elect 1988, pres. 1990), Brit. Assn. Pediat. Surgeons (exec. coun. 1990-93, Denis Browne Gold medal 1998), Soc. Surg. Oncology, Western Surg. Assn. (pres. 1997-98), Internat. Soc. Surgery, Am. Pediatric Surg. Assn. Found. (chmn. bd. dirs.), Am. Bd. Surgery (bd. dirs. 1989—, vice chair 1995, chmn.-elect, chmn. 1996-97), World Fedn. Assns. Pediat. Surgeons (v.p., pres. 1998—), Am. Bd. Med. Specialities, Halsted Soc. (v.p. 1995-96, pres. 1996-97), Phi Beta Kappa, Alpha Omega Alpha. Office: J W Riley Childrens Hosp 702 Barnhill Dr Rm 2500 Indianapolis IN 46202-5128 also: Ind U Med Ctr Dept Surgery 545 Barnhill Dr Dept Surgery Indianapolis IN 46202-5112*

GROSHART, CAROLINE KING, technical writer, editor; b. Orlando, Fla., June 27, 1947; d. Willard Van Orsdel and Leila Esther King; m. Larry Robert Groshart, May 29, 1971; 1 child, Terra Soluna. BA in English, Fla. Atlantic U., 1969, BA in Computer Sci., 1983; MA in English Edn., U. Fla., 1970. Prof. English Broward C.C., Davie, Fla., 1973-82; tech. writer, editor IBM, Boca Raton, Fla., 1983-97, Ft. Lauderdale, Fla., 1997—. Contbr. article to profl. jour. mem. Internat. Gamefish Assn., Harbour Beach Surf Club (v.p. 1991-93, sec. 1994—), Soc. Tech. Comm. (Excellence award 1985, 88). Republican. Mem. Ch. Scientology. Avocations: fishing, fiction writing, photography. Home: 1336 Seabreeze Blvd Fort Lauderdale FL 33316-2430 Office: IBM 6301 NW 5th Way Fort Lauderdale FL 33309-6186

GROSHOLZ, EMILY ROLFE, philosophy educator, poet; b. Phila., Oct. 17, 1950; d. Edwin DeHaven and Frances Skerrett Grosholz; m. Robert Roy Eddwards, Jan. 2, 1987; children: Benjamin, Robert, William, Mary-Frances. BA, U. Chgo., 1972; PhD in Philosophy, Yale U., 1979. Fellow Nat. Humanities Ctr., Research Triangle Park, N.C., 1985-86; sr. rsch. fellow Inst. History & Philosophy of Sci. & Tech. U. Toronto, Can., 1988-89; assoc. Ctr. for Philosophy of Sci. U. Pitts., 1992—; adj. assoc. prof. dept. philosophy U. Pa., Phila., 1992; prof. philosophy Pa. State U., University Park, 1993—, fellow Inst. for the Arts and Humanistic Studies, 1995—; mem. poets' prize com. Nicholas Rsch. Mus., N.Y.C., 1993—. Author: Shores and Headlands, 1988, Cartesian Method and the Problem of Reduction, 1991, Eden, 1992; co-author: Leibniz's Science of the Rational, 1998; adv. editor The Hudson Rev., 1984—; mem. editl. bd. Jour. History of Ideas, 1998—. Fellow NEH and Nat. Humanities Ctr., 1985-86, Guggenheim Found., 1988-89, Am. Coun. Learned Socs., 1997; Transatlantic Cooperation Rsch. grantee Alexander von Humboldt Found., 1994-97. Mem. Am. Philos. Assn., Leibniz Soc. N.Am., Leibniz Gesellschaft, Clare Hall U. Cambridge (life). Democrat. Episopalian. E-mail: ergz@psu.edu. Home: 116 Kennedy St State College PA 16801 Office: Pa State Univ Dept Philosophy Sparks Bldg University Park PA 16802

GROSKIN, SHEILA MARIE LESSEN, primary school educator; b. Syracuse, N.Y., Sept. 18, 1946; d. Saul and Juliette (Port) Lessen; m. Lawrence J. Groskin, Nov. 23, 1967; children: Stefanie, Elissa, David. BA, SUNY, Buffalo, 1968, MA, 1971. 3d grade tchr. Maryvale East Elem. Sch., Cheektowaga, N.Y., 1968-71; pre-sch. tchr. ABC Nursery Group, Spring Valley, N.Y., 1972-74; pres., ceo Ambrosia, Tuxedo Park, N.Y., 1979-83; tchr. Monroe (N.Y.) Sch. Dist., 1983-87; 2d grade tchr. Tuxedo Park Sch., 1987—; pres. bd. edn. Reform Temple of Suffern, N.Y., 1984-94, trustee, 1984-94. Mem. panel of educators assessing sch. accreditation for the N.Y. State Assn. Ind. Schs., 1995, 99. Recipient Reform Temple of Suffern annual award of Appreciation for Commitment, 1990. Mem. Internat. Reading Assn., Orton Dyslexia Soc. Avocations: cross-country skiing, knitting, reading, travel. Office: Tuxedo Park Sch Mountain Farm Rd Tuxedo Park NY 10987

GROSKOPF, AUBREY BUD, motion picture television executive, lawyer; b. Milw.; s. George Norman and Rose (Becker) G.; m. Nancy Lee, Dec. 31, 1983; 1 son, James E. Fields. B.S., U. Wis.-Madison, 1952, LL.B, 1956. Bar: Wis. 1957. Dir. bus. affairs CBS-TV Network, N.Y.C., 1958-73; exec. v.p. Four Star Internat., Los Angeles, 1973-76; pres. Republic Pictures Corp., Los Angeles, 1976-87; ind. motion picture and TV prodr., 1987—. Prodr. (motion picture) Boys of Paul St., 1969 (Best Fgn. Film 1969); writer, prodr., dir. (TV spl. and video) A Norman Rockwell Christmas, 1994; creator Tales of Edgar Allan Poe, 1998. Served to 1st lt. U.S. Army, 1952-54, Korea. Decorated Bronze Star. Mem. Nat. Acad. TV Arts and Scis., Acad. Motion Picture Arts and Scis.

GROSLAND, EMERY LAYTON, banker; b. Holden, Alta., Can., July 19, 1929; s. Arne and Lillie Olivetta (Jacobson) G.; m. Margaret Grace Woodward, Sept. 3, 1952; 1 child, Roberta Jayne. Student pub. schs., Holden; student Amos Tuck Sch. Exec Program, Dartmouth Coll., 1980. With The Royal Bank of Can., 1949—; sr. v.p. The Royal Bank of Can., Toronto, Ont., 1983—, ret., 1987; cons. in field. Clubs: N. Halton Golf and Country. Avocation: golf.

GROS LOUIS, KENNETH RICHARD RUSSELL, university chancellor; b. Nashua, N.H., Dec. 18, 1936; s. Albert W. and Jeannette Evelyn (Richards) Gros L.; m. Dolores K. Winandy, Aug. 28, 1965; children: Amy Katherine, Julie Jeannette. BA, Columbia U., 1959, MA, 1960; Ph.D. (Knapp fellow), U. Wis., 1964. Asst. prof. Ind. U., Bloomington, 1964-67, assoc. prof. English and comparative lit., 1967-73, prof., 1973—, assoc. chmn. comparative lit. dept., 1967-69, assoc. dean arts and scis., 1970-73, chmn. dept. English, 1973-78, dean arts and scis., 1978-80, v.p., 1980-88, chancellor, 1988—; v.p. acad. affairs, 1994—; bd. dirs. Anthem, Inc.; exec. coun. acad. affairs Nat. Assn. Univ. and Land Grant Colls., 1986-97—, bd. dirs. Bd. dirs. Editor Yearbook of Comparative and Gen. Lit., 1968—, Vol. I: Literary Interpretations of Biblical Narratives, 1974, Vol. II, 1982; contbr. articles to profl. jours. Bd. dirs. Assoc. Group, 1983-95, Anthem Blue Cross and Blue Shield, 1995—; mem. Ind. Com. Humanities, chmn., 1980-81; chmn. Com. on Instnl. Coop., 1986—; mem. Nat. Commn. on Libr. Preservation and Access, 1986-93; vice chmn., bd. dirs. Ctr. for Rsch. Librs., 1986—, chmn. bd. dirs., 1987-88. Recipient Disting. Teaching award Ind. U., 1970. Mem. MLA, Nat. Coun. Tchrs. English, AAUP, Phi Beta Kappa. Home: 4965 E Heritage Woods Rd Bloomington IN 47401-9313 Office: Ind U Bryan Hall Rm 100 Bloomington IN 47405

GROSMAN, ALAN M., lawyer; b. Mar. 13, 1935; s. Charles M. and Grace (Fishman) G.; m. Bette Bloomenthal, Dec. 27, 1967; children, Ellen, Carol. BA, Wesleyan U., 1956; MA, Yale U., 1957; JD, N.Y. Law Sch., 1965. Bar: N.J. 1965, U.S. Dist. Ct. N.J. 1965, U.S. Supreme Ct. 1969. Ptnr. Grosman & Grosman and predecessors, Millburn, N.J., 1965—; asst. prosecutor Essex County, N.J., 1968-69; prosecutor Millburn, 1981—; mem. family part practice com. N.J. Supreme Ct., 1984-88, mem. dispute resolution task force, 1987-88, com. on women in the cts., 1991-93; chmn. N.J. World Trade Coun., 1975-77, dir., 1978—; lectr. in field. Reporter New Haven Jour., 1959-60, Newark Evening News, 1961-62; author: New Jersey Family Law, 1999; contbr. articles to profl. jours. Mem. ABA (chmn. alimony, maintenance and support com. family law sect. 1983-87, editor ABA Family Law Quar. 1993—), N.J. State Bar Assn. (exec. editor N.J. Family Lawyer 1980-91, mem. exec. com. family law sect. 1980—, chmn. sect. 1987-88, appellate practice com. 1995—), Am. Acad. Matrimonial Lawyers (pres. N.J. chpt. 1983-85, nat. bd. govs. 1984-88, editor Jour. AAML 1980-90), Essex County Bar Assn. (chmn. family law com. 1970-72), N.Y. Law Sch. Alumni Assn. (bd. dirs. 1988-98), Millburn-Short Hills Rep. Club, Inc. (counsel 1988—), Phi Beta Kappa. Address: 75 Main St Ste 304 Millburn NJ 07041-1322

GROSS, ABRAHAM, rabbi, educator; b. Bklyn., June 29, 1928; s. Joseph and Tillie (Lauer) G.; m. Hannah Leah Stern, Dec. 18, 1952; children—Israel Meyer, Elijah Moses, Vitel, Adel Binah, Hilda Mindy, Solomon Abel. Rabbi, Ch'san Sofer Rabbinical Sem., 1952; B.B.A., Coll. City N.Y., 1951; M.S. Edn, Yeshiva U., 1959; 6th yr. profl. certificate, Hunter Coll., 1968. Rabbi Young Israel of Coll. Av., Bronx, N.Y., 1953-63, Congregation Adath Jeshurum, Bronx, 1963-68, Young Israel of Vanderveer Park, Bklyn., 1968-72, Congregation Shaare Hatikvah, N.Y.C., 1972-98; asst. prin. pub. schs. N.Y.C., 1966-73; prin., 1973-84; Jewish Chaplain Columbia-Presbyn. Med. Ctr., N.Y.C., 1987-97. Mem. Community Planning Bd. 4, Bronx, 1966-69; active Bonds for Israel, Yeshiva, Beth Jacob movements.; Treas. Charles and Ana Elenberg Found. Mem. Rabbinical Alliance Am. (pres. 1969-71), Met. Bd. Orthodox Rabbis (treas. 1965-69). Home: 2720 Avenue J Brooklyn NY 11210-3734

GROSS, AL, electrical engineer, consultant; b. Toronto, Ont., Can., Feb. 22, 1918; came to U.S., 1919; m. Ethel Marie Stanka, May 29, 1982. BSEE, Case Sch. Applied Sci., 1939. Chief engr. Gilmore Industries, Cleve., 1974-76; staff engr. Hickok Elec. Instrument Co., Cleve., 1976; sr. engr. controls Parson-Peebles Electric Products, Cleve., 1979-82; specialist product design ITT Cannon Electric, Phoenix, 1983-85; aerospace and marine group Sperry Corp., Phoenix, 1985-86; fellow engr. Westinghouse Electric Corp., Pitts., 1986-87; mem. tech. staff GTE Comm. Sys. Corp., Phoenix, 1987-88; staff engr. AG Comm. Sys. Corp., Phoenix, 1988-90; sr. staff engr. Orbital Scis. Corp., Chandler, Ariz., 1990—. Contbr. articles to profl. jours.; patentee antenna, high frequency transmitter and receiver, radio tuning apparatus, radio frequency oscillator, digital radio paging, others. Recipient Presdl. commendation for affirmative contbns. in telecom. field, commendation U.S. Dept. Def., 1969, honor award Japan Electronics Assn., 1987, First Centennial Series award Va. Poly. and State U., 1992; inducted in Mayfield Alumni Hall of Fame, 1997. Fellow IEEE (life, exec. com. Phoenix sect. 1988—, Century of Honors award 1984, U.S. activities bd. Profl. Leadership award 1992); mem. Vehicular Tech. Soc. of IEEE (Avant Garde award 1990), European Radio Fedn., Fedn. Personal Radio, Nat. Personal Radio Coun. Ireland, U.K. Personal Radio Fedn. (hon.), Electromagnetics Acad. MIT (hon.), Internat. Telecom. Union (hon.), Veterans Wireless Operators Assn. (Marconi Meml. gold medal of achievement 1996), Personal Comm. Industry Assn. (Pioneer award 1996), Eta Kappa Nu (Vladimir Karapetoff Eminent Mem.'s award). Office: 12219 N 112th Ln Youngtown AZ 85363-1205

GROSS, ALLEN JEFFREY, lawyer; b. Wheeling, W.Va., May 2, 1948; s. Arthur and Bertyl (Kahn) G.; m. Carol n McGuire, May 2, 1982; children: Alexander, Lindsey. BS, Ohio State U., 1970; JD, Georgetown U., 1974. Bar: Pa. 1974, U.S. Dist. Ct. (ctrl. and we. dists.) Pa., Calif. 1989, U.S. Dist. Ct. (no., so. and ctrl. dists.) Calif. 1989, U.S. Ct. Appeals (3d and 6th cirs.). Ptnr. Morgan, Lewis & Bockius, Phila., 1974-89, Orrick, Harrington & Sutcliffe, L.A., 1989-93; now with Mitchell, Silberberg & Knupp, L.A.; mem. corp. counsel inst. adv. bd. Georgetown U. Law Ctr. Author: Survey of Wrongful Discharge Cases in the United States, 1979, Employee Dismissal Laws, Forms, Procedures, 1986, 2d edit. 1992. Mem. ABA (chair trial advocacy supcom. 1989-93, employee rights and responsibilities com. 1991—, co-chair Nat. Advocacy Inst. 1992), Calif. Bar Assn., Pa. Bar Assn. (mgmt. chair employee rights responsibilities com., sect. insts. spl. programs subcom.), L.A. County Bar Assn. Office: Mitchell Silberberg & Knupp 11377 W Olympic Blvd Los Angeles CA 90064-1625

GROSS, CATHERINE MARY (KATE GROSS), writer, educator; b. Seattle, Jan. 21, 1931; d. Daniel Bergin Hutchings and Eleanor Paris (Miller) Bold. Student, Northwestern U., Evanston, Ill., 1958; BA, U. Wash., 1962, postgrad, 1984, cert. fiction grad., 1996. Cert. vocat. tchr. Copywriter Pacific Nat. Advt., Seattle, 1963; prodn. coord. Sta KRON-TV, San Francisco, 1963-65, acting program mgr., 1965; chief copywriter, TV and radio producer Teawell-Shoemaker Advt., San Diego, 1966-68; asst. pub. rels. dir. San Diego Zoo, 1968-70; pub. relations dir. Univ. Village, Seattle, 1975-77; pub. rels. dir. Seattle/King County Bd. Realtors, 1978; adj. instr. bus. Seattle Pacific U., 1980-89; instr. ASUW Exptl. Coll., 1980—; instr. humanities Heritage Inst. Antioch U., 1991—; instr. humanities Bellevue C.C., 1992-96; instr. U. Wash. Exptl. Coll., 1985—; instr. Wonder Sch. Art, 1998; cons. in field. Author: Advertising for a Small Business, 1984, Fund Raising Magic, 1984, Conversations With Writers, 1993, Sunshine the Magician's Rabbit, 1996 (juvenile fiction award Wash. Press Assn. 1996, 2d place best book Rocky Mountain Outdoor Writers 1996, creative nonfiction award Klondike Centennial Anthology 1997), Mary, The Mouse and the coal Mine, 1999; editor: Hiking and Bushwalking in Papua, New Guinea, 1987; tech. editor oceanography and medicine U. Wash., 1974-75; contbr. short stories to Compass and Sea Classics, 1982. Vol. sponsor Big Sisters of Puget Sound, Seattle, 1978-87, Seattle Parks; vol. coordinator World Affairs Council, Seattle, 1986; bd. dirs. Seattle Aquarium, 1985-87. Recipient Non-Fiction Book award Pacific Northwest Writers' Conf., 1979, Juvenile Story award Pacific Northwest Writers' Conf., 1984, Short Story award Fictioneers, 1993, Juv. Fiction award Washington Press Assn., 1997. Mem. AAUW (internat. rep. 1988), Seattle Freelance Writers Assn., Wash. Press Assn., Wash. Ornithol. Soc., Rocky Mountain Outdoor Writers, Mountaineers, Issaquah Alps Trails Club, Audubon Soc. Republican. Avocation: hiking. Office: Kate Finegan Books Box 381 117 E Louisa St Seattle WA 98102-3203

GROSS, CHARLES GORDON, psychology educator, neuroscientist; b. N.Y.C., Feb. 29, 1936; s. Frank and Sara (Gordon) G.; m. Gaby Ellen Peierls, Sept. 23, 1961 (div. Mar. 1985); children: Melanie, Monica (dec.), Derek, Rowena; m. Greta Berman, May 1, 1988. BA, Harvard U., 1957; PhD, Cambridge U., Eng., 1961. From postdoctoral fellow to asst. prof. psychology MIT, 1961-65; vis. lectr., asst. prof., then lectr. Harvard U., 1963-70; prof. psychology Princeton U., 1970—; vis. prof. U. Calif., Berkeley, 1970-71, MIT, 1975-76, Beijing U., 1986; vis. scientist Tokyo Met. Inst. Neurosci., 1988-89, Nencki Inst. Exptl. Biology, Warsaw, Poland, 1961; Fulbright lectr. Inst. Biophysics, Fed. U. Rio de Janeiro, 1986; U.S. Nat. Program vis. scientist Shanghai Inst. Physiology, 1987; vis. fellow Magdalen Coll., Oxford U., 1990, vis. scholar Wolfson Coll., 1995, McDonnell-Pew vis. fellow Med. Rsch. Coun. Ctr. in Brain and Behaviour, 1995. Author books and papers on brain, visual function and history of science. Grantee NIH, NSF, Spencer Found., Sloan Found., McDonald-Pew Found., Office Naval Rsch. Fellow APA, AAAS, Soc. Exptl. Psychologists, Brazilian Acad. Scis. (fgn.), Nat. Acad. Sci., am. Acad. Arts and Scis. Home: 45 Woodside Ln Princeton NJ 08540-5417 Office: Princeton Univ Green Hall Princeton NJ 08544 also: 106 Glasco Tpke Woodstock NY 12498-1006

GROSS, CHARLES ROBERT, personnel executive, legislator, appraiser; b. St. Charles, Mo., Aug. 20, 1958; s. Jack Robert and Margaret Ellen (Stumberg) G.; m. Leslie Ann Goralczyk, May 27, 1984; children: Megan Marie, Madelynn Ann. BS in Pub. Adminstrn., U. Mo., 1981, MPA, 1982. Pers. mgr. Army and Air Force Exch. Svc., various cities, 1983-89; pers., safety dir. Ever-Green Lawns Corp., St. Charles, 1989-92; state rep. Mo. Legislature, Jefferson City, 1993—; real estate appraiser, 1994—. Pres. St. Charles County Young Reps., 1990-92; active Youth in Need, Bridgeway Counseling. Mem. St. Charles DARE, Kiwanis, Pacaderms, Alpha Kappa Psi (life). Lutheran. Avocations: golf, scuba diving, ice hockey. Home: 3019 Westborough Ct Saint Charles MO 63301-4550

GROSS, CYNTHIA SUE, patreochemicals maintenance manager; b. Palmyra, Mo., Aug. 14, 1959; d. Floyd Raymond and Carolyn Elizabeth (Howell) Mette; m. Edward Lee Gross, June 8, 1985; 1 child, Ray E.; stepchildren: Troy A., Christina M. BS in Metall. Engring., U. Mo., Rolla, 1980. Metallurgist Bryon Jackson Pump, Tulsa, Okla., 1981-82; metall. engr. Conoco, Inc., Ponca City, Okla., 1982-84, Vista Chem., Houston, 1984-89; staff maintenance engr. Hoechst Celanese, Clear Lake, Tex., 1989-92; instr. of welding metallurgy San Jacinto Coll., 1992; sect. leader maintenance engring. Hoechst Celanese, Bishop, Tex., 1992-93; sect. leader maintenance Hoechst Celanese, Bishop, 1993-95; prodn. supt. for polyester Hoechst Celanese, Trevira, Spartanburg, S.C., 1995-97; process hazards prevention leader Celanese, Clear Lake, 1997-98, methanol and maintenance mgr., 1999—; spkr. symposium Nat. Petroleum Refiners Assn., San Antonio, 1993; instr. welding metallurgy San Jacinto Coll., Houston, 1992. Mem. quality mgmt. com. Houston Bus. Roundtable, 1990-92, chmn. Quality Day '91. Mem. Alpha Chi Sigma. Avocations: youth baseball, piano. Office: Celanese Clear Lake Plant 9502 Bayport Blvd Pasadena TX 77507-1402

GROSS, DAVID LEE, geologist; b. Springfield, Ill., Nov. 20, 1943; s. Carl David and Shirley Marie (Northcutt) G.; m. Claudia Cole, June 11, 1966; children: Oliver David, Alexander Lee. AB, Knox Coll., 1965; MS, U. Ill., 1967, PhD, 1969. Registered profl. geologist, Ill., Calif. Asst. geologist Ill. State Geol. Survey, Champaign, 1969-73, assoc. geologist, 1973-80, geologist, 1980—, coord. environ. geology, 1979-84, head environ. studies, 1984-89, asst. chief, 1991—; exec. dir. Gov.'s Sci. Adv. Com., Chgo., 1989-91; bd. dirs. First State Bank, Beardstown, Ill. Contbr. numerous articles to profl. jours. Bd. govs. Channing-Murray Found., 1973-76, pres., 1976; trustee Unitarian Universalist Ch., Urbana, 1977-80, chmn., 1977-79; bd. dirs. Vol. Action Ctr., 1981-85, chmn., 1984-85; bd. dirs. United Way Champaign County, 1984-89, exec. com., 1984-85, chmn. United Way Campaign, U. Ill., 1986; bd. dirs. Vol. Ctr., 1994-97; mem. Gov.'s Sci. Adv. Com., 1989-97; vol. summer camp counselor for teenage youth, 1984-96, 97, 98; bd. dirs. Ill. Prairie chpt. ARC, 1997—. NDEA fellow, 1969. Fellow Geol. Soc. Am., AAAS; mem. Internat. Union Quaternary Rsch., Am. Quaternary Assn., Internat. Assn. Gt. Lakes Rsch., Am. Inst. Profl. Geologists (pres. Ill.-Ind. sect. 1980), Ill. State Acad. Sci., Rotary (pres. Urbana, Ill. chpt. 1986-87), Sigma Xi. Home: 3 Flora Ct Champaign IL 61821-3216 Office: Ill State Geol Survey 615 E Peabody Dr Champaign IL 61820-6918 *Strive for reasonable balance among family, volunteer and professional responsibilities. All are essential for a healthy life.*

GROSS, DOROTHY-ELLEN, library director, dean; b. Buffalo, June 13, 1949; d. William Paul and Elizabeth Grace (Hough) G. BA, Westminster Coll., 1971; MLS, Rosary Grad. Sch. Libr. Sci., 1975; MDiv, McCormick Theol. Sem., 1975. Jr. cataloger McCormick Theol. Sem., Chgo., 1972-75; head tech. svcs. Barat Coll., Lake Forest, Ill., 1975-79, head libr., 1980-82; dir. coll. libr. North Park Coll. and Theol. Sem., Chgo., 1982-87, dir. coll. and sem. librs., 1987-96, assoc. dean, 1990-96, prof., 1991—; cons. acad. librs.; spkr. various profl. meetings and confs. Author (with Karsten) From Real Life to Reel Life, 1993, also book chpt.; editor: Libras Handbook and Directory, 1982-96, co-editor North Park Faculty Publs. and Creative Works, 1992, Pvt. Acad. Librs. in Ill. newsletter; contbr. articles, book reviews to profl. jours. Dir. rsch. United Way, Chgo., 1996—. Mem. ALA, LIBRAS (pres. 1983-85), Assn. Coll. and Rsch. Librs., Pvt. Acad. Librs. Ill. (pres. 1981-83, 91-95. Presbyterian. Home: 14 Pequod Ln Eastham MA 02642

GROSS, EDWARD, retired sociologist, educator, lawyer; b. Nagy Genez, Romania; s. Samuel and Dora (Levi) G.; m. Florence Rebecca Goldman, Feb. 18, 1943; children—David P., Deborah L. BA, U. B.C., Can., 1942; MA, U. Toronto, Ont., Can., 1945; PhD, U. Chgo., 1949; JD, U. Wash., 1991. Prof. Wash. State U., Pullman, 1947-51, 53-60; prof. U. Wash., Seattle, 1951-53, 65-89, prof. emeritus, 1990—; prof. sociology U. Minn., Mpls., 1960-65; vis. prof. Australian Nat. U., Canberra, 1971, U. Queensland, U. New South Wales, Australia, 1977; invited lectr. Cen. China Poly. Inst., 1987. Author: Work and Society, 1958, University Goals and Academic Power, 1968, Changes in University Organization, 1964-71, The End of a Golden Age: Higher Education in a Steady State, 1981, Organizations in Society, 1985, Embarrassment in Everyday Life, 1994; contbg. author: Handbook of Sociology and Encyclopedia of Sociology, 2d edit.; former assoc. editor Social Problems, Symbolic Interaction, Can. Jour. Sociology; contbr. numerous articles to profl. jours. Trustee Temple Beth Am, Seattle, 1993-97. Fulbright scholar Australia, 1977, 87. Mem. Am. Sociol. Assn., Pacific Sociol. Assn. (pres. 1971, coun. 1983-85). Office: U Wash Dept Sociology Seattle WA 98195

GROSS, FELIKS, sociologist, educator, author; b. Cracow, Poland, June 17, 1906; came to U.S., 1941; s. Adolf and Augusta (Alexander) G.; m. Priva Baidaff, July 25, 1937; 1 child, Eva Helena Gross Friedman. LLM, Jagiellonian U., 1930; LLD, Jagiellanian U., 1931. Bar: Poland 1937. Sec., gen. Cen. Ea. European Planning Bd., 1941-45; editor New Europe and World Reconstrn. jour., N.Y.C., 1942-45; prof. sociology and anthropology grad. ctr. Bklyn. Coll., N.Y.C., 1946-77, prof. emeritus, 1977—, resident prof. CUNY grad. ctr., 1988—; vis. prof. NYU, 1945-68; vis. prof., dir. Inst. Internat. Affairs, U. Wyo., Laramie, summers 1945-52; vis. prof. Woodrow Wilson Sch. Fgn. Affairs, U. Va., Charlottesville, 1951, 54-56, U. Vt., Burlington, 1957; sr. Fulbright sr. lectr. U. Rome, 1957-58, 64-65, 74; lectr. other European, Am. univs.; mem. rsch. coun. Fgn. Policy Rsch. Inst., Phila., 1966—; vis. prof. Columbia U., N.Y.C., 1973; lectr. U. Florence, 1977, Italian Fgn. Office, Rome; cons. Nat. Com. on Causes and Prevention of Violence, 1968. Pres., Taraknath Das Found., N.Y., 1965; hon. pres. CUNY Acad. Humanities and Scis., 1985; co-founder, bd. dirs. Non-Profit Coordinating Com. N.Y., 1984-86. Author: Nomadism, 1936; Polish Worker, 1945; Foreign Policy Analysis, 1954; Seizure of Political Power, 1957; Valori Sociali e Struttura, 1967; World Politics and Tension Areas, 1967; Violence in Politics, 1973; Il Paese, Values and Social Change in an Italian Village, 1974; The Revolutionary Party, 1974; Ethnics in the Borderland, 1979; Ideologies, Goals and Values, 1986; Working Class and Culture (in Polish), 1986, Toleration and Pluralism (in Polish), 1992, European Federation & Confederations, Origin and Visions (in Polish), 1994, The Civic and the Tribal State, 1998, others; contbr. numerous articles to profl. jours. Decorated Golden Cross of Phoenix (Greece); Order Polonia Restituta (Poland); Carnegie scholar, Paris, 1931, Pub. Affairs Found. NYU, 1962-63; recipient Ethnic New Yorker award N.Y.C., 1987, Alfred Jurzykowski Price award for scholarship contbn., Polish Nat. Archives award, 1995, award Polish Ministry Culture and Art, 1995, N.Y.C. commendation for serving the Polish-Am. Cmty., 1998; ILO/League of Nations scholar, Geneva, 1930, Carnegie Scholarship, 1931; grantee Sloan Found., 1963, City U. Rsch. Found., 1971-74, NSF, 1972, Rockefeller Found., 1974; Fulbright grantee, 1956-57, 64-65, 74. Fellow Polish Inst Arts and Scis. (pres. 1988); mem. Internat. League Rights of Man (dir. 1960), Am. Sociol. Assn., Acad. Polit. Sci., N.Y. Acad. Scis., Polish Acad. Scis. (fgn.), Sigma Xi. Home: 310 W 85th St New York NY 10024-3819 Office: Polish Inst Arts and Scis of Am 208 E 30th St New York NY 10016-8202

GROSS, GARY NEIL, allergist, physician; b. Fort Lewis, Wash., July 25, 1944; s. Norman Harold and Dorothy Naomi (Bercie) G.; m. Elaina Wee, Mar. 23, 1974; children: Risa, Lara. BA, U. Tex., 1967; MD, Southwestern Med. Sch., Dallas, 1969; MBA, Southern Methodist U., Dallas, 1987. Diplomate Am. Bd. Internal Medicine, Am. Bd. Allergy and Clin. Immunology. Intern U. Utah Med. Ctr. Hosp., Salt Lake City, 1969-70; resident U. Utah Med. Ctr. Hosp., 1970-71; fellow Nat. Jewish Hosp., Denver, 1971-74; founding physician Dallas Allergy and Asthma Ctr., Tex., 1979—; med. dir. Pharm. Rsch. and Cons., Dallas, 1992—; clin. prof. internal medicine Southwestern Med. Sch., Dallas, 1994—. Contbr to profl. jours. Bd. dirs. Am. Jewish Com., Dallas, 1990-94, Am. Lung Assn., 1978-88, Temple Emanuel Brotherhood, 1978-80. Fellow Am. Coll. Physicians, Am. Acad. Allergy Immunology (chmn. seminars com., 1987-88, chmn. pub. edn. com., 1989-90); mem. Fedn. Regional State Local Allergy Socs. (gov. reg. 5, 1992—, chmn. 1993-94), Joint Coun. Allergy Clin. Immunology (sec. bd. dirs. 1992-96, exec. v.p. 1998—). Jewish. Avocations: cycling, skiing, photography. Office: 5499 Glen Lakes Dr Ste 100 Dallas TX 75231-4383

GROSS, GIL, radio talk show host, columnist; b. Kew Gardens, N.Y., Apr. 11, 1948; s. William and Ruth (Rose) G.; m. Rhoda Gail Bodzin, Oct. 5, 1980; 1 child, Spencer Darrow. Anchor, reporter NBC News, N.Y.C., 1975-78, WCBS, N.Y.C., 1978-81, RKO, N.Y.C., 1981-84, ABC News, N.Y.C., 1985-87; host The Gil Gross Show WABC, N.Y.C., 1987-89, WOR, N.Y.C., 1989-91, CBS, N.Y.C., 1992-98; morning drive host WWDB-Radio, Phila., 1999—. Exec. prodr. The Bob Berkowitz Show; syndicated columnist Gross Point. Bd. dirs. Cmty. Access, N.Y.C., 1985-91. Jewish.

GROSS, HAL RAYMOND, bishop; b. Walla Walla, Wash., Jan. 15, 1914; s. John J. and Millie (Hale) G.; m. Evelyn Blythe Kerr, July 22, 1933; 1 dau., Patricia Ann Gross Simmons. Student, Oreg. State U., 1931-36; J.D., Willamette U., 1939; student, Ch. Div. Sch. of Pacific, 1946, D.D., 1965. Bar: Oreg. bar 1939. Pvt. practice in Corvallis, 1939-42; atty. Oreg. Unemployment Compensation Commn., 1942-44; ordained to ministry Episcopal Ch., 1946; pastor U. Oreg., 1946-47; rector St. Paul's Ch., Oregon City, 1947-61; archdeacon Episcopal Diocese Oreg., 1961-65; suffragan bishop Oreg., 1965-79; ret., 1979; mem. exec. council Episcopal Ch., 1975-79; vice chmn. Ho. of Bishops, 1976-79. Trustee Ch. Div. Sch. of Pacific, 1950-55, 72-73. Mem. Oreg. Bar Assn., Phi Delta Theta. Democrat. Club: Rotary (hon.). Home: 8255 SW Fairway Dr Wilsonville OR 97070-9419

GROSS, HANNS, history educator; b. Stockerau, Austria, June 20, 1928; came to U.S., 1961; s. Arthur and Gabriele (Schneider) G.; m. Bonnie Jean Rotter, July 20, 1991. BA with honors, U. London, 1950; AM, U. Chgo., 1963, PhD, 1966. Tchr. Emmanuel Grammar Sch., Swansea, Wales, 1950-61; tutor Bible Coll. Wales, Swansea, 1950-61; asst. prof. So. Ill. U., Carbondale, 1966-67; asst. prof., assoc. prof. history Loyola U., Chgo., 1967-78, prof., 1978-99, emeritus, 1999—. Author: Empire and Sovereignty, 1973, Rome in the Age of Enlightenment, 1990. Elder Moody Ch. Mem. Am. Hist. Assn., Am. Soc. for Legal History, Am. Soc. for 18th Century Studies, Conf. on Faith and History, 16th Studies Conf., Soc. Italian Hist. Studies. Avocations: travel, walking, conversation. Office: Loyola U Dept History 6525 N Sheridan Rd Chicago IL 60626-5344

GROSS, HARRIET P. MARCUS, religion and writing educator; b. Pitts., July 15, 1934; d. Joseph William and Rose (Roth) Pincus; children: Sol Benjamin, Devra Lynn. AB magna cum laude, U. Pitts., 1954; cert. in religious teaching, Spertus Coll. of Judaica, Chgo., 1962; MA, U. Tex., Dallas, 1990. Assoc. editor Jewish Criterion of Pitts., 1955-56; publs. writer B'nai B'rith Vocat. Svc., 1956-57; group leader Jewish Community Ctrs. of Met. Chgo., 1958-63; columnist Star Publs., Chicago Heights, Ill., 1964-80; pub. info. specialist Operation ABLE, Chgo., 1980-81; dir. religious sch. Temple Emanu-El, Dallas, 1983-86; freelance writer, 1986—; columnist Dallas Jewish Life Monthly, 1992—; lectr. U. Tex., Dallas, 1994—; tchr. writing Homewood-Flossmoor (Il.) Park Dist., Brookhaven Jr. Coll., Dallas; advisor journalism program Prairie State Coll., Chicago Heights, 1978-80; adv. bd. The Creative Woman quar. publ. Governors State U., Governors Park, Ill., The Mercury U. Tex., Dallas. Bd. dirs., sec. Family Svc. and Mental Health Ctr. of South Cook County, Ill., 1965-71; active Park Forest (Ill.) Commn. on Human Rels., 1969-80, chmn., 1974-76; bd. dirs. Ill. Theatre Ctr., 1977-80, Jewish Family Svc. of Dallas, 1982-95; mem. Dallas Jewish Edn. Com., 1992-95; bd. dirs. Dallas Jewish Historical Soc., 1995—. Recipient Humanitarian Achievements award Fellowship for Action, 1974; Honor award Anti-Defamation League of B'nai B'rith, 1978; Community Service award Dr. Charles E. Gavin Found., 1978, 1st Ann. Leadership award Jewish Family Svc., 1990, Katie award Dallas Press Club, 1995. Mem. Nat. Fedn. Press Women, Tex. Press Women, Ill. Woman's Press Assn. (named Woman of Yr. 1978), Intertel (pres. Gateway Forum of Dallas 1984-85), Nat. Assn. Temple Educators, Mensa, Soc. Profl. Journalists, Phi Sigma Sigma. Jewish. Developed 1st community newspaper action line column, 1966. Office: 8560 Park Ln Apt 23 Dallas TX 75231-6312

GROSS, IAN, academic pediatrician, neonatologist; b. Pretoria, Republic of South Africa, Oct. 15, 1943; came to U.S., 1971; s. Kenneth and Gladys Bakst (Cooper) G.; m. Melanie Belman, Dec. 3, 1967; children: David Anthony, Adam Charles. BS, U. Witwatersrand, Johannesburg, Republic of South Africa, 1963, MBBCh, 1967. Diplomate Am. Bd. Pediatrics, Am. Bd. Neonatal-Perinatal Medicine. Rotating intern Johannesburg Gen. Hosp., 1968; pediatric resident U. Witwatersrand Hosps., Johannesburg, 1970-71, Children's Hosp. Harvard Med. Sch., Boston, 1971-72; postdoctoral fellow in pediatrics Harvard Med. Sch., Boston, 1972-73, Yale U., New Haven, Conn., 1973-74; asst. prof. Yale U. Sch. Medicine, New Haven, 1974-78, assoc. prof., 1978-85, prof., 1985—; dir. newborn spl. care unit Yale-New Haven Hosp., 1982—; mem. study sect. NIH, Bethesda, Md., 1981-85; mem. adv. bd. Hood Found., Boston, 1988-94. Editor Pediat. Rsch., 1992-98, Seminars in Perinatology, 1997—; contbr. chpts. to books, numerous articles to profl. jours. Named Most Disting. Med. Grad. U. Witwatersrand, Johannesburg, 1967; James Hudson Brown fellow, Yale U., 1973; rsch. grantee NIH and Am. Heart Assn. Fellow Am. Acad. Pediatrics; mem. Soc. Pediatric Rsch., Am. Physiol. Soc., Am. Thoracic Soc., Am. Pediatric Soc. Avocations: cycling, photography. Office: Yale Sch Medicine 333 Cedar St New Haven CT 06510-3289

GROSS, IRIS LEE, association executive; b. Bklyn., Aug. 11, 1941; d. Frank and Anne (Schecter) Goodman; children: Michael, Henry. m. William E. Fullington. BA, Am. U., 1963. Cert. assn. exec. Field rep. mid-Atlantic region B'Nai Brith Women, Rockville, Md., 1973-76, dir. mid-Atlantic region, 1976-81; cen. svcs. dir. Nat. Coun. Jewish Women, N.Y.C., 1981-90, exec. dir., 1990—; exec. dir. Birmingham (Ala.) Internat. Festival, 1994—; pres. Nonprofit Resource Ctr. Ala., 1997-99. Leadership, Birmingham - Class of 98; Commr. Montgomery County Commn. for Women, 1980-81. Recipient Achievement Cert. City of Rockville, 1975, Cert. of Appreciation March of Dimes, 1980. Mem. Am. Soc. Assn. Execs., N.Y. Soc. Assn. Execs. (bd. dirs. 1987-90, Outstanding Com. Chair 1986), Soc. Non-Profit Orgns. Democrat. Avocations: reading, antiques, art history, archeology. Home: 1050 Highland Dr Birmingham AL 35244-3363 Office: Birmingham Internat Festival Frank Nelson Bldg Ste 423 205 20th St N Birmingham AL 35203-3609*

GROSS, JAMES DEHNERT, pathologist; b. Harvey, Ill., Nov. 15, 1929; s. Max A. and Marion (Dehnert) G.; m. Marilyn Agnes Robertson, Jan. 9, 1960; children: Kathleen Ann, Terrence Michael, Brian Andrew, Kevin Matthew. B.S. in Biology, U. Chattanooga, 1951; M.D., Vanderbilt U., 1955. Diplomate Am. Bd. Pathology, Am. Bd. Med. Mgmt. Rotating intern U.S. Naval Hosp., St. Albans, N.Y., 1955-56; resident in anatomic and clin. pathology Nat. Naval Med. Ctr., Bethesda, Md., 1956-59; dir. labs. U.S. Naval Hosp., Memphis, 1959-62; dir. labs. St. Mary's Hosp., Streator, Ill., 1962—, pres. med. staff, 1972-73; instr. pathology and microbiology U. Tenn. Med. Sch., 1960-62; bd. dirs. La Salle County bd. Am. Cancer Soc., 1966-68. Mem. parish council St. Anthony's Roman Catholic Ch., Streator, 1969-72. Served to lt. comdr. M.C., USNR, 1955-68. Fellow Am. Soc. Clin. Pathologists, Coll. Am. Pathologists, Assn. Clin. Scientists (founder); mem. AMA, Ill. Med. Soc., Sigma Chi, Alpha Kappa Kappa. Republican. Lodges: K.C., Rotary (past bd. dirs.). Home and Office: 374 MacEwen Dr Osprey FL 34229-9233

GROSS, JAMES HOWARD, lawyer; b. Springfield, Ohio, Sept. 21, 1941; s. Cyril James and Virginia (Stieg) G.; m. Gail Sue Helmick, July 13, 1968; children: Karin G. Cramer, David James. BA, Ohio State U., 1963; LLB, Harvard U., 1966. Bar: Ohio 1966, D.C. 1975. Assoc. Vorys, Sater, Seymour and Pease, Columbus, Ohio, 1966-75; resident ptnr. Vorys, Sater, Seymour and Pease, Washington, 1975-77; ptnr. Vorys, Sater, Seymour and Pease LLP, Columbus, 1975—; White House fellow, spl. asst. to sec. HUD, Washington, 1972-73; city atty. City of Bexley, Ohio, 1985—. Mem. Franklin County Rep. Cen. Com., 1973-75, Bexley City Coun., 1981-85. Lt. comdr. USNR, 1968-74. Mem. ABA, Ohio Bar Assn. (corp. law com.), Columbus Bar Assn. (securities law com.), D.C. Bar Assn. Lutheran. Home: 5 Sessions Dr Bexley OH 43209-1440 Office: Vorys Sater Seymour and Pease LLP 52 E Gay St # 1008 Columbus OH 43215-3161

GROSS, JEFFREY, software engineer; b. Chgo., Feb. 23, 1963; s. Mickey and Evelyn (Udwin) G. BSEE, Ill. Inst. Tech., Chgo., 1985. Software engr. Gen. Dynamics, San Diego, 1986-91; sci. programmer Biosym Technologies, San Diego, 1991-94; sr. software engr. Qualcomm, San Diego, 1994-99; ind. software engring. cons. San Diego, 1999—. Ill. State scholar; recipient Gen. Dynamics Excel award. Mem. Assn. Computing Machinery, San Diego Macintosh Users Group, Mensa. Home: 11224 Sirias Rd San Diego CA 92126

GROSS, JEROME, physician, biologist, educator; b. N.Y.C., Feb. 25, 1917; married 1947; 3 children. B.S., MIT, 1939; M.D., NYU, 1943. Rsch. fellow in medicine Harvard U. Med. Sch., 1948-50, rsch. assoc., 1950-54, assoc., 1954-57, asst. prof., 1957—, assoc. prof., to 1969, prof. medicine, 1969-87, prof. medicine emeritus, 1987; clin. and rsch. fellow Mass. Gen. Hosp., Boston, 1948-51, assoc. biologist, 1951-66, biologist, 1966—; acting assoc. dir. Cutaneous Biology Rsch. Ctr., Dept. Dermatology Mass. Gen. Hosp, 1989-91; sr. investigator cutaneous Biology Research Ctr. Dept. Dermatology Mass. Gen, Hisp., 1992—; rsch. assoc. MIT, 1946-55; mem. subcom. skeletal system NRC, 1955-62; mem. sci. adv. com. Helen Hay Whitney Found., 1956-91; established investigator Am. Heart Assn., 1956-61; mem. adv. panel molecular biology NSF, 1959-62; chmn. Bd. Sci. Counselors Nat. Inst. Dental Rsch., 1963-66; mem. molecular biology study sect. NIH, 1966-70, mem. breast cancer task force, 1975-78; bd. dirs. Med. Found., Inc., 1974-80. Adv. editor. Jour. Exptl. Medicine, 1963; cons. editor Devel. Biology, 1965. Trustee, Helen Hay Whitney Found., 1985—; bd. dirs. sci. affairs com. W. Alton Jones Sci. Ctr., 1986-96. Recipient CIBA award, 1959, Kappa Delta award Am. Acad. Orthopedic Surgery, 1965, Klemperer award N.Y. Acad. Medicine, 1988. Mem. Nat. Acad. Sci., Am. Acad. Arts and Sci., Am. Soc. Cell Biology, Am. Soc. Biol. Chemistry, Inst. Medicine, Histochem. Soc. (sec. 1956-60). Office: Mass Gen Hosp Cutaneous Biology Rsch Ctr Rm 3006 13th St # 149 Charlestown MA 02129-2000*

GROSS, JONATHAN LIGHT, computer scientist, mathematician, educator; b. Phila., June 11, 1941; s. Nathan K. and Henrietta E. (Light) G.; m. Susan Fay Kodner, Aug. 29, 1976; children: Aaron, Jessica, Joshua, Rena Lea, Alisa Sharon. B.S., M.I.T., 1964; M.A., Dartmouth Coll., 1966, Ph.D., 1968. Instr. math. Princeton (N.J.) U., 1968-69; asst. prof. math. stats. Columbia U., N.Y.C., 1969-72, assoc. prof., 1973-78, prof. computer sci., math. and stats., 1978—, vice-chmn. dept. computer sci., 1982-89; dir. edn. Ctr. for Advanced Tech., 1989-93; cons. Russell Sage Found., Inst. Def. Analyses., AT&T Bell Labs., Alfred P. Sloan Found., IBM, Oak Ridge Nat. Lab.; vis. scientist Carnegie-Mellon U., Pitts., 1984-85. Co-author: Fundamental Programming Concepts, 1972, FORTRAN 77 Programming, 1978, Introduction to Computer Programming, 1979, Pascal Programming, 1982, Measuring Culture, 1985, PASCAL, 1984 FORTRAN 77 Fundamentals and Style, 1985, Topological Graph Theory, 1987, WATFIV-S Fundamental Style, 1986, Graph Theory and Its Applications, 1999; adv. editor: Columbia U. Press, Jour. Graph Theory, Computers and Electronics, CRC Press; Contbr. Jour. Graph Theory; articles to profl. jours. IBM postdoctoral fellow, 1972-73; Sloan fellow in math., 1973-75; rsch. grantee NSF, Office of Naval Rsch., Exxon Found., ARCO Found., Mellon Found., Russell Sage Found., N.Y. State Sci. and Tech. Found., Citicorp. Mem. Am. Math. Soc., Assn. Computing Machinery, Soc. Indsl. and Applied Math. (sec. discrete math. 1994-96), Jewish Ctr. of Princeton (v.p. 1997—). Jewish. Home: 3 Stuart Ln W Princeton Junction NJ 08550-1844 Office: Columbia U Dept Computer Sci New York NY 10027 *The essence of acquiring an education is internalizing an acute awareness of the distinctions among feeling, conjecturing, doing, and actually knowing.*

GROSS, KATHLEEN ALBRIGHT, interventional radiology nurse, educator; b. Mechanicsburg, Pa., June 10, 1951; d. Clyde Nelson and Louise Aldine (Swigert) Albright; m. Richard Joseph Gross, Oct. 15, 1972; children: David, Jonathan. Diploma, Harrisburg Hosp. Sch. Nursing, 1972; BS summa cum laude, Pa. State U., Harrisburg, 1977; BSN summa cum laude, Coll. Notre Dame Md., 1982. Cert. med.-surg. nurse, ACLS. Staff nurse ICU M.S. Hershey (Pa.) Med. Ctr., 1972-74; rsch. asst. in dermatology Johns Hopkins Bayview Med. Ctr. (formerly Balt. City Hosps.), 1977; rsch. asst. dept. health svcs. rsch. Johns Hopkins Sch. Hygiene and Pub. Health, Balt., 1978; staff nurse crit. care unit, ICU, med.-surg. Upjohn Healthcare, Balt., 1978-81; camp nurse Friends Sch., Balt., 1985; office nurse Balt., 1982-94; instr. Greater Balt. Med. Ctr. Sch. Radiologic Tech., Balt., 1991—; staff nurse interventional radiology Greater Balt. Med. Ctr., 1988—; staff nurse Patient First, 1994—; cons. Edumed, 1996—. Instr. BCLS, Am. Heart Assn., Balt., 1983—, vol. fundraiser, 1985, 87, 88, author, 1999; vol. Gilman Sch., Balt., 1981—; vol. naturalist Irvine Natural Sci. Ctr., Stevenson, Md., 1987-91; vol. fundraiser Leukemia Soc. Am., Balt., 1989; aux. membership chairperson Balt. City Hosps., 1976, 77. Mem. Am. Radiol. Nurses Assn. (sec. 1997—, mem. exec. com. 1994-96, ANA-nursing orgn. liaison forum, sec. 1997—), Md. Radiol. Nurses Assn. (v.p. 1991-92, pres. 1993-94, bd. dirs. 1995-96, rep. to 1st nursing summit 1991, sec. 1997-98), Soc. for Vascular Nursing, Balt. Interventional Radiol. Technologists Assn., Delta Tau Kappa, Sigma Theta Tau. Avocations: gardening, reading. Home: 1243 Berans Rd Owings Mills MD 21117-1641 Office: Greater Balt Med Ctr Interventional Radiology 6701 N Charles St Baltimore MD 21204-6808

GROSS, KATHLEEN FRANCES, parochial school mathematics educator; b. Phila., Nov. 16, 1945; d. John Paul and Margaret Regina (Moore) G. BS in Edn., St. Joseph's U., 1968; postgrad. various instns., 1968-96. Cert. tchr., N.J. Tchr. St. Edmond's Grade Sch., Phila., 1964-68; tchr. math. St. Maria Goretti High Sch., Phila., 1968-71; tchr. math. Holy Spirit High Sch., Absecon, N.J., 1971—, chair dept. math., 1973-86, 91-94; adj. tchr. math. Atlantic C.C., Mays Landing, N.J., 1989-96. Mem. AAUW, Nat. Coun. Tchrs. Math., Assn. Math. Tchrs. N.J., Nat. Cath. Edn. Assn., South Jersey Cath. Sch. Tchrs. Orgn. Avocations: needlepoint, gardening. Home: 332 Asbury Ave Ocean City NJ 08226-4022

GROSS, LARRY PAUL, communications educator; b. Washington, Nov. 22, 1942; s. Bertram Myron and Nora (Faine) G. B.A., Brandeis U., 1964; Ph.D., Columbia U., 1968; M.A. (hon.), U. Pa., 1973. Asst. prof. U. Pa., Phila., 1968-73; assoc. prof. U. Pa., 1973-82, prof., 1982—, Sol Worth prof., 1998—, assoc. dean for grad. studies, 1989-93. Author: Contested Closets: The Politics and Ethics of Outing, 1993; editor: Communications Technology and Social Policy, 1973, Between Men-Between Women book series, 1991—, Studying Visual Communication, 1981, Image Ethics, 1988, Studies in Visual Communications, 1977-85, On the Margins of Art Worlds, 1995, The Columbia Reader on Lesbians and Gay Men in media, Society and Politics, 1999; assoc. editor Internat. Ency. Comm., 1989; contbr. articles to profl. jours. Chair Phila. Lesbian and Gay Task Force, 1981—; mem. Pa. Humanities Coun., 1985-90. Guggenheim fellow, 1998-99. Fellow Am. Anthrop. Assn. (co-chmn. rsch. group on homosexuality 1981-84); mem. Internat. Comm. Assn. (chair task force on diversity 1992—, lesbian and gay studies interest group 1993-96), Nat. Comm. Assn., Phi Beta Kappa, Sigma Xi. Home: 1916 Lombard St Philadelphia PA 19146-1411 Office: U Pa Annenberg Sch Philadelphia PA 19104

GROSS, LAURA ANN, marketing and communications professional, acupuncturist, herbalist; b. Kew Gardens, N.Y., July 11, 1948; d. Melvin Fredericks and Harriette (Levy) G. BA, Boston U., 1970; MA, Columbia U., 1974. Staff writer Am. Banker, N.Y.C., 1974-82, assoc. editor, 1982-88; dir. fin. svcs., instns., communications Am. Express Travel/Related Svcs. Co., N.Y.C., 1988-89; dir. sales promotion and pub. rels. Am. Express Travelers Cheque Group/Am. Express Travel Svcs., N.Y.C., 1989-92; dir. strategic bus. comm. Am. Express Travel Related Svcs., N.Y.C., 1992-93; pres. Strategic Comm. Cons., N.Y.C., 1993—. Author, editor consumer surveys and articles; speaker in field. Recipient editorial awards Pannell Kerr Forster, 1984, N.E. Bus. Press Editors, 1986, N.Y. Bus. Press. Editors, 1987, first Boston U. Coll. of Liberal Arts Young Alumni award, 1985. Mem. Bank Mktg. Assn., Promotion Mktg. Assn. (Spire award 1991), Pub. Rels. Soc. Am. (Silver Anvil award 1990, Big Apple award 1992, Creativity in Pub. Rels. award 1993). Avocations: fiction writing, travel, snorkeling.

GROSS, LEROY, sugar company executive; b. N.Y.C., Aug. 11, 1926; s. Morris and Sarah (Leichter) G.; m. Betty Koch, Aug. 28, 1949; children: Michael Stephen, Kenneth Richard, Emily Jayne Gross Eider. BS in Acctg., NYU, 1948; postgrad., Fordham U., 1951-53; MBA in Acctg., NYU, 1955. With SuCrest Corp., N.Y.C., 1948-77, internal audit mgr., 1962-65, corp. acctg. mgr., 1965-69, contr., 1969-75, asst. sec., 1971-77; v.p. N.Y.C., 1975-77; v.p., contr. Revere Sugar Corp., 1977-86; lectr. NYU, 1968-71; cons. in field. With USAAF, 1946-47. Mem. Inst. Internal Auditors, Nat. Assn. Accountants, Fin. Execs. Inst. Home and Office: 118 Winder Rd Yorktown VA 23693

GROSS, LESLIE JAY, lawyer; b. Coral Gables, Fla., July 24, 1944; s. Bernard Charles and Lillian (Adler) G.; m. Frances L. Londow, June 16, 1968; children: Jonathan Eric, Jason Marc. BA magna cum laude, Harvard U., 1965, JD, 1968. Bar: Fla. 1971, U.S. Dist. Ct. (so. dist.) Fla. 1971, U.S. Ct. Appeals (5th cir.) 1971, U.S. Tax Ct. 1971, U.S. Supreme Ct. 1971; registered real estate broker, registered mortgage broker, registered securities broker. Rsch. aide Fla. 3d Dist. Ct. Appeal, Miami, Fla., 1968-69; prof. social sci. Miami-Dade Community Coll., 1969-70; assoc. Greenberg, Traurig, et al., Miami, 1969-70, Patton, Kanner, et al., Miami, 1970-71, Fromberg, Fromberg, Roth, Miami, 1971-72; ptnr. Fromberg, Fromberg, Gross, et al., Miami, 1973-88; assoc. Thornton, David, Murray, et al., Miami, 1988-94; atty. agt. Atty.'s Title Ins. Fund, First Am. Title, Miami, 1971-94; adj. prof. U. Miami Sch. Law, 1984; lectr. seminar Nat. Aircraft Fin. Assn., 1990. Contbr. articles to profl. jours. Mem. transp. com. Greater Miami C. of C., 1984-85; v.p., pres., bd. dirs. Kendale Homeowners Assn., Miami, 1970-81; vol. Dem. candidates in state and nat. elections, Miami, 1968, 70, 72, 87, 88; mem. Vision Coun. Land Use Task Force, Miami, 1988-89; judge Silver Knight awards Miami Herald, 1987, 92, 93, 94, 95, judge spelling bee, 1987; bd. dirs. Internat. Assn. Fin. Planning, 1983-84; founding mem., bd. dirs. The Actors Playhouse, 1987—, sec., 1990—. Mem. Harvard Law Sch. Assn., Harvard Club of Miami (v.p. 1985-90, pres. 1990-94, dir. 1985—). Democrat. Jewish. Avocations: gardening, humorous creative writing, photography, aerobics, travel. Home: 10471 SW 126th St Miami FL 33176-4749

GROSS, LILLIAN, psychiatrist; b. N.Y.C., Aug. 18, 1932; d. Herman and Sarah (Widelitz) Gross. BA, Barnard Coll., 1953; postgrad. U. Lausanne (Switzerland), 1954-56; MD, Duke U., 1959. Diplomate Bd. Pediatrics, Am. Bd. Psychiatry and Neurology, Am. Bd. Child Psychiatry; m. Harold Ratner, Feb. 4, 1961; children: Sanford Miles, Marcia Ellen. Intern Kings County Hosp., Bklyn., 1959-60, resident, 1967-70, fellow in child psychiatry, 1969-70, psychiatrist devel. evaluation clinic, 1970-72; resident Jewish Hosp. Bklyn., 1960-62, fellow in pediatric psychiatry, 1962-63; physician in charge pediatric psychiat. clinic Greenpoint (N.Y.) Hosp., 1964-67; pvt. practice psychiatry, Great Neck, N.Y., 1970—; clin. instr. psychiatry Downstate Med. Ctr., Bklyn., 1970-74, clin. asst. prof., 1974—; lectr. in psychiatry Columbia U., 1974—; psychiat. cons. N.Y.C. Bd. Edn., 1972-75, Queens Children's Hosp., 1975-96; mem. med. bd. Camp Sussex (N.J.), 1963—, Saras Ctr., Great Neck, N.Y., 1977—. Fellow Am. Acad. Pediatrics, Am. Acad. Psychiatry, Am. Acad. Child Psychiatry, Am. Soc. Clin. and Experiential Hypnosis, N.Y. Soc. Clinical Hypnosis (past pres.); mem. AMA, Am. Psychiat. Assn., Nassau Psychiat. Assn., Bklyn. Psychiat. Assn., Bklyn. Pediatric Soc. (sr. mem.), Nassau Pediatric Socs., Soc. Adolescent Psychiatry, N.Y. Coun. Child Psychiatry, Soc. Clin. and Exptl. Hypnosis, Am. Med. Women's Assn. (Nassau, pres. 1985-86, 95-96), N.Y., Kings County med. socs., N.Y. Soc. Clin. Hypnosis (past pres.), Internat. Soc. for Study of Multiple Personality and Dissociation (founder, pres. L.I. component study group). Home and Office: 55 Blue Bird Dr Great Neck NY 11023-1001

GROSS, MATT G., executive; b. L.A., July 20, 1964; s. Edgar Fleischer and Marcellina Perry G.; m. Hedi Lynn, July 1, 1995. BS in Econs., UCLA, 1986; MFA, Am. Film Inst., 1990. V.p. devel. Paramount Television, L.A., 1990-96; v.p. prodn. Kopelson Entertainment, L.A., 1997—. Producer (film) Bronx Cheers, 1990. Mem. Screen Actors Guild, Brentwood Country Club. Office: Kopelson Entertainment 2121 Ave of the Stars #1400 Los Angeles CA 90067

GROSS, MICHAEL FRED, biologist, educator, researcher; b. Carlisle, Pa., June 6, 1960; s. Fred Norman and Judith Louise (Martin) G. BS in Biology and Acctg., Lebanon Valley Coll., Annville, Pa., 1982; PhD in Marine Studies, U. Del., 1987. Postdoctoral fellow U.Del., Newark, 1987-88; asst. prof. biology Georgian Court Coll., Lakewood, N.J., 1992-96, assoc. prof., chair dept. biology, 1996—. Editor: (booklet) Common Pinelands Plants for Lake Carasaljo Park, 1997; author: (website) Plants of the New Jersey Pinelands, 1996; contbr. articles to profl. jours. Mem. Bot. Soc. Am., Ecol. Soc. Am., Estuarine Rsch. Fedn., Am. Inst. Biol. Scis., Am. Fern Soc., Soc. Wetland Scientists. Avocations: photography, running, travel, horticulture. Office: Georgian Court Coll 900 Lakewood Ave Lakewood NJ 08701-2600

GROSS, MICHAEL ROBERT, writer, editor; b. N.Y.C., July 16, 1952; s. Milton and Estelle (Murov) G.; m. Barbara Hodes, June 21, 1986. BA, Vassar Coll., Poughkeepsie, N.Y., 1974. Music columnist Andy Warhol's Interview, N.Y.C., 1973-74; contbg. editor Circus Mag., N.Y.C., 1973-76; editor-in-chief Rock Mag., N.Y.C., 1976-78, Fire Island News, N.Y.C., 1978; sr. copywriter Bantam Books, N.Y.C., 1978-80; columnist Photo Dist. News, N.Y.C., 1981-83; contbg. editor East Side Express, N.Y.C., 1983-84; contbg. editor, columnist Manhattan, Inc., N.Y.C., 1984-85; reporter, columnist N.Y. Times, N.Y.C., 1985-88; contbg. editor N.Y. Mag., N.Y.C., 1988-94; commentator CBS This Morning, N.Y.C., 1992-93; sr. writer Esquire Mag., N.Y.C., 1994-95; contbg. editor Tatler mag., London, 1994—; writer at large GQ Mag., N.Y.C., 1996—; contbg. editor N.Y. Mag., N.Y.C., 1997—, Travel and Leisure mag., N.Y.C., 1997—. Author: Robert Plant, 1975, Bob Dylan, 1978, Model: The Ugly Business of Beautiful Women, 1995; co-author: The Rock Yearbook, 1980, Temple Kent, 1982, Shattered Mask, 1983, Precious Objects, 1984; contbr. articles to profl. jours. Mem. Am. Soc. Journalists and Authors, Authors Guild. Office: Ellen Levine Lit Agy 15 E 26th St New York NY 10010-1505

GROSS, PATRICK WALTER, business executive, management consultant; b. Ithaca, N.Y., May 15, 1944; s. Eric T. B. and Catharine B. (Rohrer) G.; m. Sheila Eve Proby, Apr. 12, 1969; children: Geoffrey Philipp, Stephanie Lovell. Student, Cornell U., 1962-63; B in Engring. Sci., Rensselaer Poly. Inst., 1965; MSE in Applied Math., U. Mich., 1966; MBA, Stanford U., 1968. Cons. info. mgmt. operation Gen. Electric Co., Schnectady, 1965-67; sr. staff mem. Office Sec. Def., Washington, 1968-69, spl. asst., 1969-70; founder, prin. exec. officer, chmn. exec. com. Am. Mgmt. Systems, Inc., Arlington, Va., 1970—, also bd. dirs.; also bd. dirs.; chmn. bd. dirs. Medlantic Enterprises, Inc., 1988-94, Baker and Taylor Holdings, Inc., 1994—, dir., 1992—, Medlantic Healthcare Group, Capital One Fin. Corp., Landmark Sys. Corp., Powersim Corp., Computer Network Tech. Corp.; adv. coun. Stanford Grad. Sch. of Bus., 1999—, Ctr. for Strategic and Internat. Statis., 1998—. Trustee Washington Hosp. Ctr., 1977-87, Sidwell Friends Sch., 1980-88, 92—, Wolf Trap Found. Performing Arts, 1997—, Com. for Econ. Devel.; mem. exec. com., treas. Youth for Understanding, 1984-90, 93—, vice chmn., 1996—, Youth for Understanding Found., Germany, 1989—; mem. Econ. Policy Coun. UNA-USA, mem. Coun. on Competitiveness, Fed. City Coun., Washington, 1992—; bd. dirs. Wolf Trap Fund. for the Performing Arts, 1997—; mem. adv. bd. Ctr. Strategic Internat. Studies; adv. coun. Stanford Grad. Sch. Bus.; adv. bd. Stanford Inst. for Econ. Policy Rsch. Mem. Fgn. Policy Assn. (bd. govs., bd. dirs., mem. exec. com. 1977-86, 87—), World Affairs Coun. Washington (bd. dirs., founding vice chmn. 1980-91, chmn. 1991—), Coun. Excellence in Govt. (bd. dirs. 1996—), Jamestown Found. (bd. dirs. 1997—), Coun. Fgn. Rels., Washington Inst. Fgn. Affairs, Internat. Inst. Strategic Studies (London), World Econ. Forum (Geneva), Econ. Club Washington, Nat. Economists Club, Aspen Inst. Soc. Fellows, Pilgrims of U.S., Smithsonian Luncheon Group, Met. Club Washington, Chevy Chase Club, Univ. Club N.Y.C., Useless Bay Country Club (Wash.), Sigma Xi, Tau Beta Pi. Home: 7401 Glenbrook Rd Bethesda MD 20814-1327 Office: Am Mgmt Sys Inc 4050 Legato Rd Fairfax VA 22033-4087

GROSS, PAUL ALLAN, health service executive; b. Va., VA, Oct. 1, 1937; s. Albert and Cynthia (Saxe) G.; m. Gail Byrd, Nov. 19, 1966; children: Lorri, Garry, Randy. Student, U. Richmond, 1956-59; B.A., U. Ga., 1961; M.H.A., Va. Commonwealth U., 1964; cert. in hosp. adminstrn., U. Miami. Adminstrv. resident in hosp. adminstrn. Tampa Gen. Hosp., Fla., 1964; adminstrv. asst. Dallas County Hosp. Dist., 1964-66, asst. adminstr., 1966-69, sr. asst. adminstr., 1969-70, assoc. adminstr., 1971-72; clin. assoc. prof. hosp. med. care U. Tex. Southwestern Med. Sch., 1964-72, Sch. Allied Health Scis., Dallas, 1964-72; exec. dir. Humana Inc. Suburban Hosp., Louisville, 1972-76; v.p. Fla. region Humana Inc., Miami, 1976-81; sr. v.p. Pacific Region Humana Inc., Newport Beach, Calif., 1981-84, exec. v.p., pres. hosp. div., 1984-92; ret. Humana Inc., 1992; prof., health adminstr. Va. Commonwealth U./Med. Coll. Va., 1992-95, prof. emeritus, 1996—; nat. cons. emeritus Surgeon Gen. USAF, 1987—; vice chmn. bd. trustees MedEcon, Inc., Louisville, 1993-96, also bd. dirs.; bd. dirs. St. Anthony Pub. Co., Washington, 1993-96; advisor, bd. chmn., dir. KBL Healthcare Inc.; advisor Comprehensive Med. Mgmt., Inc. Contbr. articles to profl. jours. Mem. health adv. com. Senator Paul Carpenter, Cypress, Calif., 1983; mem., asst. chmn. U.S. Selective Svc. System Local Bd. 154, Newport Beach, 1983, Bd. 113, Louisville; bd. assocs. U. Richmond, Va., 1990-96; bd. dirs. St. Francis High Sch., Louisville, 1989-92, Louisville Zool. Found. Bd., 1989-96, chmn. investment com., 1992; mem. adv. bd. Sch. Nursing Spalding U., Louisville, 1992-97; chmn. devel. bd. Jefferson County Community Coll., Kentuckiana Edn. and Work Force Com.; preceptor Fellowship Program-Education with Industry, USAF, 1986-92. With USNR, 1955-63; bd. dirs. Spaulding U., 1996—. Recipient Humana Club award Suburban Hosp. Central Region, Louisville, 1974, 75, 76; named Outstanding Adminstr. Cen. Region Humana Inc., 1975, 76. Fellow Am. Coll. Health Care Execs. (ethics com., chmn. inv. droped sect. 1993—); mem. Tex. Hosp. Assn., Hosp. Coun. So. Calif. (chmn. multi-instnl. corp. liaison com. 1983—), United Hosp. Assn. Calif., Fedn. Am. Healthcare Sys. & Am. Hosp. Assn. (hon. life). Home: 2576 Fox Point Rd Quinlan TX 75474-9047

GROSS, RICHARD ALAN, lawyer; b. Chgo., Jan. 6, 1949; s. Jacob N. and Rita (Berliant) G.; m. Roberta Lee Laschever, May 16, 1971; children: Edward, Eric. BA, Wesleyan U., 1970; JD, Harvard U., 1973. Bar: Mass. 1973, U.S. Dist. Ct. Mass. 1974, U.S. Ct. Appeals (1st cir.) 1978, D.C. 1980, U.S. Dist. Ct. D.C. 1981, U.S. Ct. Appeals (D.C. cir.) 1982, U.S. Supreme Ct. 1988, U.S. Ct. Appeals (4th cir.) 1995. Mng. atty. Greater Boston Legal Svcs., 1973-75; dep. chief, then chief consumer protection divsn. Dept. Atty. Gen., Boston, 1975-79; exec. dir. U.S. Consumer Product Safety Commn., Washington, 1979-81; v.p., gen. coun. Nat. Consumer Coop. Bank, Washington, 1981-83; ptnr. Wald, Harkrader & Ross, Washington, 1983-85, Foley, Hoag & Eliot, Washington, 1985-93, Rosenman & Colin, Washington, 1994—. Trustee Dem. Nat. Com., 1986-92, U. D.C., 1990-94; pres. Sinai Assisted Housing Found., Inc., 1994-96, bd. dirs, 1993—. Jewish. Office: Rosenman & Colin 805 15th St NW 9th Flr Washington DC 20036-1652

GROSS, RICHARD BENJAMIN, lawyer; b. Santa Monica, Calif., Sept. 26, 1947; s. Edward L. and Adele P. Gross; m. Pamela McGovern, June 1, 1985; 1 child, Hannah McGovern. Student, UCLA, 1965-68; BA, U. Calif., Berkeley, 1970; JD, Harvard U., 1973; postgrad., Cambridge (Eng.) U., 1973-74. Bar: N.Y. 1975, U.S. Dist. Ct. (so. dist.) N.Y. 1975, U.S. Ct. Appeals (2d cir.) 1975, Ill. 1987. Assoc. White & Case, N.Y.C., 1974-77; assoc. counsel Am. Express Co., N.Y.C., 1977-82; sr. v.p., gen. counsel and sec. Citicorp Diners Club, Inc., Chgo., 1982-90; sr. v.p., gen. counsel Citicorp Ins. Group, Inc., N.Y.C., 1990-91; sr. v.p., gen. counsel, sec. Ambac Fin. Group, Inc., N.Y.C., 1991-98; mng. dir., gen. counsel U.S. Trust Corp., N.Y.C., 1998—; bd. dirs. Randall's Island Sports Found. Bd. dirs. Randall's Island Sports Found., 1999—. Mem. ABA (com. of corp. gen. counsel, com. on fed. regulation of securities, com. on banking), N.Y. State Bar Assn., Assn. of the Bar of the City of N.Y., Am. Soc. Internat. Law, Am. Soc. Corp. Secs., Am. Corp. Counsel Assn., Fin. Svcs. Roundtable (mem. lawyers coun.). Fax: (212) 852-1310. Office: US Trust Corp 114 W 47th St New York NY 10036-1532

GROSS, RICHARD EDMUND, education educator; b. Chgo., May 25, 1920; s. Edmund Nicholas and Florence (Gallistel) G.; m. Jane Clare Hartl, May 25, 1943; children: Kathryn Ann, Elaine Clare, Edmund Ralph, John Richard. BS, U. Wis., 1942, MS, 1946; EdD, Stanford U., 1951. Jr. personnel officer FSA, Milw., 1942-43; tchr. Central High Sch., Madison, Wis., 1943-48; instr. Menlo Sch. and Coll., Menlo Park, Calif., 1948-51; asso. prof. Fla. State U., 1951-55; mem. faculty Sch. Edn., Stanford U., 1955—, prof., 1965—, chmn. curriculum and tchr. edn., 1977-90; chief cons. central com. social studies Calif. Dept. Edn., 1958-60; Fulbright lectr. tchr. edn. U. Wales, Swansea, 1961-62; guest prof. Am. Inst., U. Frankfurt, Germany, 1968-69; ednl. adviser World Bank Pilot Center project U. Santiago, Spain, 1973; vis. prof. Monash U., Melbourne, Australia, 1976; curriculum cons. to schs., 1952—; guest lectr. Taiwan Tchrs. Inst., Taipei, 1990, Seoul Nat. U., Republic of Korea, 1995; Bicentennial lectr. U. Alaska, Anchorage, 1987; adv. bd. Edn. Policy Com., 1958-68; chmn. nat. advisory bd. E.R.I.C. Social Sci. Center, U. Colo., 1969-71; dir. social studies, adviser Addison-Wesley Publs., 1970-83; bd. dirs. Calif. Inst. Internat. Studies, Inst. Devel. Human Resources; co-dir. nat. citizenship edn. study, 1985-93. Author: How to Handle Controversial Issues, 1952, The Problems Approach and the Social Studies, 1955, The Sociology of the School, 1957, The United States Congress, 1957, Educating Citizens for Democracy, 1958, The Heritage of American Education, 1962, British Secondary Education, 1965, Civics in Action, 1966, Man's World: A Physical Geography, 1966, The History of Education: A Timeline, 1967, Teaching the Social Studies, 1969, Profile of America, 1971, Quest for Liberty, 1971, Teaching Social Studies Skills, 1973, The Human Experience, 1974, Social Studies for Our Times, 1978, American Citizenship: How We Govern, 1979, Learning to Live in Society, 1980, What Should We Be Teaching in the Social Studies, 1983, Ciencias Sociales, 1983, What Chinese Children Have Learned about the United States, 1990, Social Science Perspectives on Citizenship, 1990, Designing Effective Instruction for Secondary Social Studies, 1998; editor: Phi Delta Kappa Bi-centennial Fast-Backs, 1976, Calif. Social Sci. Rev, 1962-68; contbr. articles to encys., profl. jours.; creator Scholastic World-Affairs Multitext Publs, 1963; K. and E. overhead viewer transparencies for U.S. History, 1964. Mem. ASCD, AAUP, NEA, Nat. Coun. Social Studies (pres. 1967, Career Rsch. award 1990), Nat. Soc. Study Edn., Am. Acad. Polit. and Social Sci., History of Edn. Soc., World Assn. Civic Edn. (exec. com.), Phi Alpha Theta, Kappa Delta Tau, Phi Delta Kappa (Hilda Taba hon. award, 1988). Home: 26304

Esperanza Dr Los Altos CA 94022-2653 Office: Stanford Univ Cubberley Hall Stanford CA 94305

GROSS, ROBERT ALAN, history educator; b. New Haven, Feb. 17, 1945; s. Samuel and Roslyn (Chadys) G.; m. Ann Leslie Goldman, May 22, 1966; children: Matthew Benjamin, Stephen Alexander, Eleanor Elizabeth. B.A., U. Pa., 1966; M.A. (Woodrow Wilson nat. fellow), Columbia U., 1968, Ph.D., 1976; M.A. (hon.), Amherst Coll., 1986. Gen. sec. U.S. Student Press Assn., Washington, 1966-67; asst. editor Newsweek, N.Y.C., 1966-70; NIMH trainee in social history Columbia U., 1970-72; adj. asst. prof. Worcester Poly. Inst., 1973-76; asst. prof. history and Am. studies Amherst Coll., 1976-80, assoc. prof., 1980-86, prof., 1986-88; prof. Am. studies and history, dir. Am. studies Coll. of William and Mary, 1988-98, Forrest D. Murden prof. Am. studies, 1992—; prof. Am. studies U. Sussex, Brighton, England, 1982-83; vis. prof., dir. studies Ecoles des Hautes Etudes en Sciences Sociales, Paris, 1985; vis. assoc. prof. Brandeis U., 1985; core scholar New England and the Constitution, 1986-88; Am. Studies specialist U.S. Info. Agy., 1991-92; dir. NEH Summer Inst., 1993; Fulbright chair of Am. studies Odense (Denmark) U., 1998—. Author: The Minutemen and Their World, 1976 (Nat. Hist. Soc. Book award, Bancroft prize), Books and Libraries in Thoreau's Concord, 1988, In Debt to Shays: The Bicentennial of an Agrarian Rebellion, 1993; mem. editorial bd. Jour. Am. History, 1995-98. Guggenheim fellow, 1979-80, Charles Warren fellow Harvard U., 1979-80, Amherst Coll. Trustees faculty fellow, 1979-80, Bibliog. Soc. Am. fellow, 1984, Kate and Hall Peterson fellow Am. Antiquarian Soc., 1984, Howard Found. fellow, 1988-89, Old Sturbridge Village Rsch. fellow, 1991, NEH fellow, 1994; residency Rockefeller Found.'s Study and Conf. Ctr., Bellagio, Italy, 1994. Fellow Soc. Am. Historians; mem. Am. Hist. Assn., Orgn. Am. Historians, Am. Studies Assn., Am. Antiquarian Soc. (chair program in the history of the book in Am. culture 1993—), Colonial Soc. Mass., Mass. Hist. Soc., New Eng. History Tchrs. Assn. (Kidger award 1987), Phi Beta Kappa. Democrat. Jewish. Home: 133 Little John Rd Williamsburg VA 23185-4907 Office: Am Studies Program Coll William and Mary Williamsburg VA 23187-8795*

GROSS, ROBERT EMANUEL, collateral loan broker; b. N.Y.C., May 13, 1920; s. Solomon Sidney and Estelle (Prager) G.; m. Gloria Polansky, Dec. 30, 1942 (dec. Feb. 1986); children: Gary, Kenneth. BA, Franklin and Marshall Coll., 1942. Sec. Sol S. Gross Co. Inc., N.Y.C., 1943-71; pres. S&G Gross Co. Inc., N.Y.C., 1971—. Mem. Collateral Loan Brokers Assn. (sec.-treas. 1982—). Avocations: piano, tennis. Office: S&G Gross Co Inc 486 8th Ave New York NY 10001-1806

GROSS, ROBERTA LEE, inspector general; b. Dayton, Ohio, Mar. 11, 1947; m. Richard A. Gross; children: Edward, Eric. BA cum laude, Vassar Coll., 1969; MA in English, U. Mich., 1970; JD, Northeastern U., 1978. Tchr. Sharon, Newton (Mass.) jr. high sch. system, 1971-75; asst. district attorney Office of the District Attorney, Cambridge, Mass., 1978-79; from staff attorney to chief civil litigation section Office of the Corp. Counsel D.C., Washington, 1982-89; sr. dir. investigations, counsel Amtrak, Washington, 1990-95; insp. gen. NASA, Washington, 1995—. Office: NASA Office of the Inspector Gen 300 E St SW Washington DC 20546-0005*

GROSS, RONALD MARTIN, forest products executive. BA, Ohio State U., 1955; MBA, Harvard U., 1960. With Battelle Meml. Inst., Columbus, Ohio, 1957-58, Champion Internat., 1960-68; with Can. Cellulose Co. Ltd., Vancouver, B.C., 1968-78, pres., CEO, dir., 1973-78; pres., COO ITT Rayonier, Inc., Stamford, Conn., 1978-81, pres., CEO, 1981-84, chmn., pres., CEO, 1984-96; chmn., CEO, 1996-98, chmn. emeritus, 1999—; bd. dirs. Rayonier Inc., Pittston Co., Corn Products Internat. Office: 6 Landmark Sq Ste 400 Stamford CT 06901-2792

GROSS, RUTH TAUBENHAUS, physician; b. Bryan, Tex., June 24, 1920; d. Jacob and Esther (Hirshenson) Taubenhaus; m. Reuben H. Gross, Jr., Aug. 22, 1942; (div. June 1952); 1 son, Gary E. BA, Barnard Coll., 1941; MD, Columbi U., 1944. Intern, Charity Hosp., New Orleans, 1944; resident in pediatrics Tulane U., New Orleans, 1945, Columbia U., N.Y.C., 1946, 47; instr. Radcliffe Infirmary, Oxford, Eng., 1949-50; instr. pediatrics Stanford (Calif.) U., 1950-53, asst. prof., 1953-56, assoc. prof., 1956-60, prof., 1973-92, prof. emerita, 1992; acting exec. pediatrics, 1957-59, assoc. dean student affairs, 1973-75, dir. div. gen. and ambulatory pediatrics, 1975-85, dir. Stanford-Children's Ambulatory Care Ctr., 1980-85, nat. study dir. Infant Health and Devel. Program, 1983-92; assoc. prof. pediatrics, co-dir. div. human genetics Albert Einstein Coll. Medicine, Yeshiva U., N.Y.C., 1960-64, prof. pediatrics, 1964-66; clin. prof. pediatrics U. Calif. Med. Ctr., San Francisco, 1966-73; dir. dept. pediatrics Mt. Zion Hosp. and Med. Ctr., San Francisco, 1966-73. Commonwealth fellow human genetics Instituto de Genetica, Pavia, Italy, 1959-60. Mem. Inst. Medicine, NAS, Am. Fedn. Clin. Rsch., Am. Pediatric Soc., Soc. Pediatric Rsch., Am. Acad. Pediatrics, Ambulatory Pediatric Assn., Soc. Rsch. in Child Devel., Phi Beta Kappa, Alpha Omega Alpha, Sigma Xi. Contbr. articles to profl. jours.

GROSS, SAMSON RICHARD, geneticist, biochemist, educator; b. N.Y.C., July 27, 1926; s. Isidor and Ethel (Mermelestein) G.; m. Helen Hudi Steinmetz, Sept. 16, 1952; children—Deborah Ann, Michael Robert, Eva Elizabeth. B.A., NYU, 1949; A.M., Columbia, 1951, Ph.D. (USPHS fellow), 1953. Asst. prof. genetics Stanford U., 1956-57; asst. prof. genetics Rockefeller U., N.Y.C., 1957-60; assoc. prof. dept. microbiology and immunology Duke, Durham, N.C., 1960-65, prof. genetics and biochemistry, 1965-91, prof. emeritus genetics and biochemistry, 1991—; dir. div. genetics dept. biochemistry Duke, 1965-77, dir. univ. program in genetics, 1967-77; bd. dirs. Cold Spring Harbor Lab. Quantitative Biology, N.Y., 1967-72. USPHS Spl. fellow Weizmann Inst., 1969-70; Josiah Macy Found. fellow Hebrew U., 1977-78; John Simon Guggenheim fellow Hebrew U., 1985-86. Mem. Genetic Soc. Am., AAAS, Am. Soc. Microbiology, Am. Soc. Biol. Chemists, Phi Beta Kappa. Home: PO Box 498 Little Switzerland NC 28749-0498 also: 2411 Prince St Durham NC 27707-1432

GROSS, SHARON RUTH, forensic psychologist, researcher; b. L.A., Mar. 21, 1940; d. Louis and Sylvia Marion (Freedman) Lackman; m. Zoltan Gross, Mar. 1969 (div.); 1 child, Andrew Ryan; m. Ira Chroman, June 1994. BA, UCLA, 1983; MA, U. So. Calif., L.A., 1985, PhD, 1991. Diplomate Am. Bd. Psychol. Spltys.; cert. Am. Coll. Forensic Examiners. Tech. Rytron, Van Nuys, Calif., 1958-60; computress on tetrahedral satellite Space Tech. Labs., Redondo Beach, Calif., 1960-62; owner Wayfarer Yacht Corp., Costa Mesa, Calif., 1962-64; electronics draftsperson, designer strokewriter characters Tasker Industries, Van Nuys, 1964-65; pvt. practice cons. Sherman Oaks, Calif., 1965-75, 77-80; printed circuit bd. designer Systron-Donner, Van Nuys, Calif., 1975-76; design checker, tech. writer Vector Gen., Woodland Hills, Calif., 1976-77; undergrad. adv. U. So. Calif., L.A., 1987-89, rsch. asst. prof., rsch. assoc. social psychology, 1991—; owner Attitude Rsch. Litigation and Orgn. Cons. Contbr. articles to profl. jours., chpts. to books. Recipient Haynes Found. Dissertation fellowship U. So. Calif., 1990. Mem. APA, AAAS, Computer Graphics Pioneers, Am. Psychol. Soc., Western Psychol. Assn. Democrat. Jewish. Office: Ste 124 16350 Ventura Blvd Encino CA 91436

GROSS, SHIRLEY MARIE, artist, farm manager; b. Beardstown, Ill., Apr. 4, 1917; d. Robert Lee and Marie Elizabeth (Ellrich) Northcutt; m. Carl David Gross, Oct. 4, 1941; children: David Lee, Susan Jean Gross Conner. BA, Ill. Coll., 1938. Med. technologist St. John's Hosp., Springfield, Ill., 1938-41, Schmidt Meml. Hosp., Beardstown, 1957-64; libr. Beardstown Pub. Libr., 1970-76; farm mgr., 1958—; bd. dirs. 1st State Bank Beardstown, Heart of Ill. Investment Clubs. Co-author: Beardstown Ladies Commonsense Investment Guide, 1994, Beardstown Ladies, Stitch-in-Time Guide to Growing Your Nest Egg, 1996, Beardstown Ladies Guide To Smart Spending for Big Savings, 1997, The Beardstown Ladies Little Book of Investment Wisdom, 1997, Beardstown Ladies Pocketbook Guide To Picking Stock, 1998; exhibited in various art shows, Ill., 1969—. Bd. dirs., mem. aux. Beardstown Hosp.; bd. dirs. Head Start; trustee 1st Congl. Ch., Beardstown. Recipient awards from various art shows. Mem. Am. Soc. Clin. Pathologists (cert. med. technologist), Beardstown Bus. and Profl. Women's Investment Club, Cass County Hist. Soc., Beardstown Restoration Soc., Jacksonville Area Artists League, Beardstown Woman's Club, Cass County Coun. for Arts Club, Beardstown Bus. and Profl. Womens Club (pres. 1968-70), Supreme Emblem Club. Democrat. Home: 15 Boulevard Rd Beardstown IL 62618-8105

GROSS, STANISLAW, environmental sciences educator, activist; b. Lodz, Poland, Nov. 27, 1924; came to U.S., 1960; s. Oskar and Janina (Gundelach) G.; children: Krzysztof, Zbigniew, Richard. BChemE, Tech. U., Lodz, 1947, MChemE, 1949; PhD in Organic Chemistry, U. London, 1961. Dep. mgr. organic dyestuffs Boruta, Zgierz, Poland, 1946-50; assoc. prof. Inst. for Indsl. Medicine, Lodz, 1950-58; biochemical cancer rschr. Chester Beatty Rsch. Inst., London, 1958-62; sr. scientist plant tumor rsch. Boyce Thompson Inst., Yonkers, N.Y., 1962-66; assoc. mem., head molecular biology divsn. Inst. for Muscle Diseases, N.Y.C., 1966-74; rsch. assoc. prof. biochemistry N.Y. Med. Coll., Valhalla, 1973-78; vis. prof. biochemistry Lódź (Poland) Med. Sch., 1979-81; founder, first dir. environ. health scis. program N.Y. Med. Coll. Grad. Sch. Health Scis., Valhalla, 1982-93, adj. prof., 1982-95. Contbr. over 45 articles to profl. jours. Tech. advisor to Congressman from N.Y., 1985—. Mem. N.Y. Acad. Scis. (founding mem. Lyceum Club), Biophys. Soc., Polish Inst. of Arts and Scis. of Am, Radiation Rsch. Soc. Home: PO Box 422 Tarrytown NY 10591-0422

GROSS, STEPHEN MARK, pharmacist, academic dean; b. Bklyn., July 31, 1938; s. Arthur S. and Hazel F. (Marks) G.; m. Susan S. Farber, Nov. 5, 1961; 1 child, Julie S. BS, Columbia U., 1960, MA, 1969, EdD, 1975. Pharmacist/mgr. C.O. Bigelow Chemists Inc., N.Y.C., 1960-65, Bigelow-Americana Chemists Inc., N.Y.C., 1963-65; asst. to dean Coll. Pharm. Scis., Columbia U., 1965-68, asst. dean, 1968-71, assoc. dean, 1971-72, acting dean, 1972-74, dean, 1974-76; dean grad. studies Arnold & Marie Schwartz Coll. Pharmacy and Health Scis. L.I. U., 1976-79; dean Sch. Bys. and Pub. Adminstrn., Bklyn. Ctr. L.I. U., 1983-84; dean grad. studies and research Conolly Coll. L.I.U., 1979-83, dean Faculties Pharmacy and Health Professions, 1984-88; dean Schwartz Coll. Pharmacy L.I. U., 1985—, dean Sch. of Health Professions, 1990—; dir. Arden House Confs. on Indsl. Pharmacy, 1976-79; v.p. Pond Assn., 1972, pres., 1976-78; mem. N.Y. State Bd. Pharmacy, 1991—, chmn., 1997-98; mem. health care quality improvement steering com. Island Profl. Rev. Orgn., 1995—. Mem. editl. Bd. U.S. Pharmacist, 1978-80, Am. Druggist, 1989-92, For the Pharmacist, 1997—; contbr. articles to profl. publs. Recipient numerous grants instnl. improvement. Mem. Am. Pharm. Assn., Am. Assn. Colls. Pharmacy (chmn. sect. continuing edn. 1979-80), Pharm. Soc. State N.Y., Nat. Cmty. Pharmacists Assn., Am. Soc. Health-System Pharmacists, Soc. Am. Magicians (v.p. N.Y. Assembly 1981-83, pres. 1983-84). Home: 43 Knott Dr Glen Cove NY 11542-4116 Office: LI U 1 University Plz Brooklyn NY 11201-8423

GROSS, STEPHEN RANDOLPH, accountant; b. Newark, Oct. 8, 1947; s. Edward Thomas and Frances (Randolph) G.; m. Barbara Louise Schutz, June 14, 1969 (div. Jan. 1981); children: David Randolph, Matthew Jeffrey. AB, Duke U., 1970. CPA, Ga.; cert. fraud examiner, Ga.; cert. valuation analyst, Ga. From staff acct. to ptnr. Lester Witte & Co., Atlanta, 1970-74; ptnr. Lester Witte & Co., Chgo., 1974-79, nat. dir. tng., 1978-79, exec. com.; founder, mng. ptnr. Gross, Collins & Cress, P.C., Atlanta, 1979—; trustee Saloman Smith Barney Concert Investment Series Mutual Funds; bd. dirs. Ikon Ventures, Inc., MZ Direct, Inc., Lifestyles Beverages of N.A., Inc., Exec. Lodging, Inc., Atlanta, Commerce Bank, Atlanta, Anderson Calhoun, Ltd., Super Corp., Inc., United Telesis, Inc., MfgDirect.com., Careerfair.com.; treas. Henry Aaron Enterprises, Inc., Milw.; v.p. Coventry Holding Group, Inc., Decatur, Ga.; sec. Carint of NA, Milan. Active Atlanta Symphony Orch., 1975—, High Mus. Art, Atlanta, 1985—, Ga. Pub. Policy Found., 1991—. Mem. AICPA, Ga. Soc. CPAs, Nat. Assn. Cert. Valuation Analysis, Assn. Cert. Fraud Examiners, Inst. Bus. Appraisers, Cherokee Town amd Country Club, Chaine des Rotisseurs (Paris), Ravinia Club. Episcopalian. Home: 175 River North Dr NW Atlanta GA 30328-1111 also: SE Corner Carmello St and 11th Ave Carmel CA 93923 Office: Gross Collins & Cress PC 2625 Cumberland Pkwy SE Ste 400 Atlanta GA 30339-3993

GROSS, STEVEN, medical marketing communications and device company executive; b. Jersey City, Aug. 12, 1946; s. Milton and Mildred G.; m. Janice Gross; children: Meredith Paige, Sharlee Beth. With Merck Sharp and Dohme, 1969-79; dir. mktg. food and pharm. divsn. FMC Corp., 1980-81; sr. v.p. acct. svcs. Dorland and Sweeney, 1981-82; CEO, founder DevCom, Princeton, N.J., 1982—; founder MDDM Inc., 1986, SymCom, 1989. Patentee in field; inventor numerous med. devices for measuring therapeutic progress of disease and other devices, including one to measure body surface and one to measure edema. Founder Pregnant Physicians for DHA; bd. dirs. Am. Heart Assn. Heritage Affiliate; mem. Joint Mayor's Citizens Adv. Task Force for Kingston, N.J. Mem. AMA, Am. Med. Writers Assn., Healthcare Mktg. and Comms. Coun., Healthcare Exhibitors Assn., Creative Media Coun. (pres.), Princeton Music Club (v.p.), Princeton C. of C. Avocations: music, violin, music history, photography, automobiles. E-mail: sg@devcom-adv.com. Office: DevCom 114 Main St Kingston NJ 08528

GROSS, STEVEN JAY, education educator; b. July 2, 1951. BA magna cum laude, Temple U., 1973; student Chinese lang., Chinese U. Hong Kong, 1973; MA in Chinese History, U. Wis., 1978; EdD in Ednl. Adminstrn., U. Pa., 1980. Ednl. cons., 1980-81; dir. Continental Import, Inc., 1981-86; dir. curriculum staff devel. Rutland N.E. Supervisory Union, Brandon, Vt., 1986-90; chief curriculum and instrn. Vt. Dept. Edn., Montpelier, 1990-93; assoc. prof. edn. Trinity Coll., Burlington, Vt., 1993-99; assoc. prof. ednl. adminstrn. Temple U., Phila., 1999—. Author: Staying Centered: Curriculum Leadership in a Turbulent ERA, 1998; contbr. articles to jour. Ednl. Leadership. Exec. dir. The China Project, Burlington, Vt., 1988-93. Klingensten fellow, 1979-80. E-mail: gross@charity.trinity.vt.edu.

GROSS, STEVEN ROSS, lawyer; b. N.Y.C., June 15, 1946; s. Alexander and Lola (Mandelbaum) G.; m. Georgette Francine Kleinhaus, Dec. 14, 1968; children: Amy, Jillian. BA, Columbia U., 1968, MA, 1969; LLB, Cambridge U., 1971; JD, Yale U., 1973. Bar: U.S. Dist. Ct. (ea. and so. dists.) N.Y. 1974. Assoc. Debevoise & Plimpton, N.Y.C., 1973-80, ptnr., 1981—. Co-author: Collier Business Workout Guide; contbr. articles to profl. jours. Mem. ABA, Assn. of Bar of City of N.Y. Jewish. Home: 145 E 74th St New York NY 10021-3225 Office: Debevoise & Plimpton 875 3rd Ave Fl 23 New York NY 10022-6256

GROSS, TERRY R., radio producer, host; b. Bklyn., Feb. 14, 1951; s. Irving and Anne (Abrams) G.; m. Francis Davis, 1996. BA, SUNY, Buffalo, 1972, MEd, 1974; DLitt (hon.), Drexel U., 1989; LittD (hon.), Haverford Coll., 1998. Exec. prodr., host Fresh Air Sta. WHYY Radio, Phila., 1975—. Recipient Best Live Program award Corp. for Pub. Broadcasting, 1981, award Ohio State, 1987, Disting. Alumni award SUNY, Buffalo, 1993, Peabody award, 1994, Fi st Amendment award Ford Hall Forum, 1997, Gracie award Nat. Radio Personality, Am. Women in Radio & Television, 1999.

GROSS, THEODORE LAWRENCE, university administrator, author; b. Bklyn., Dec. 4, 1930; s. David and Anna (Weisbrod) G.; m. Selma Bell, Aug. 27, 1955 (dec. 1991); children: Donna, Jonathan; m. Marion Simon, 1992. BA, U. Maine, 1952; MA, Columbia U., 1957, PhD, 1960. Prof. English CCNY, 1958-78, chmn. dept., 1970-72, assoc. dean and dean humanities, 1972-78, v.p. instl. advancement, 1976-77; provost Capitol Campus, Pa. State U., Middletown, 1979-83; dean Sch. Letters and Sci. SUNY Coll., Purchase, 1983-88; chmn. SUNY-Purchase Westchester Sch. Partnership, 1984-88; pres. Roosevelt U., Chgo., 1988—; vis. prof., Fulbright scholar, Nancy, France, 1964-65, 68-69, Dept. State lectr., Nigeria, Israel, Japan, Austria. Author: Albion W. Tourgée, 1964, Thomas Nelson Page, 1967, Hawthorne, Melville, Crane: A Critical Bibliography, 1971, The Heroic Ideal in American Literature, 1971, Academic Turmoil: The Reality and Promise of Open Education, 1980, Partners in Education: How Colleges Can Work with Schools to Improve Teaching and Learning, 1988; also essays, revs.; editor: Fiction, 1967, Dark Symphony: Negro Literature in America, 1968, Representative Men, 1969, A Nation of Nations, 1971, The Literature of American Jews, 1973; gen. editor: Studies in Language and Literature, 1974, America in Literature, 1978. With AUS, 1952-54. Grantee, Rockefeller Found., 1976-77, Am. Coun. Learned Socs. Mem. MLA, PEN, Nat. Coun. Tchrs. of English (chmn. lit. com.), Century Assn., Univ. Club, Chgo. Club. Home: 1515 N Astor St Chicago IL 60610-1627

GROSS, THOMAS LESTER, obstetrician, gynecologist, researcher; b. Decatur, Ill., Aug. 17, 1945; s. Gilbert Wayne and Anna (Graham) G.; m. Judy Beth Osborn, Dec. 30, 1967; children: Elizabeth, Matthew, Joshua. BA in Chemistry, Bluffton (Ohio) Coll., 1967; MD, U. Ill., 1971. Diplomate Am. Bd. Ob-Gyn., subsplty. maternal/fetal medicine. Intern, resident Akron (Ohio) Gen. Med. Ctr., 1973-77; fellow maternal/fetal medicine Case Western Res. U., Cleve., 1977-79; asst. to dir perinatal clin. rsch. ctr. Cleve. Met. Gen. Hosp., 1982-85; acting dir. Perinatal Clin. Rsch. Ctr., 1985-86; asst. prof. ob-gyn. Case Western Res. U., Cleve., 1977-85, assoc. prof., 1985-86; assoc. prof. ob-gyn. U. Ill. Coll. Medicine, Peoria, 1986—, chmn. dept., 1986-97; dir. perinatology St. Francis Med. Ctr., Peoria, 1987—; instr. Internat. Symposium Fetal Evaluation, Lima, Peru, 1983. Contbr. numerous articles to sci. jours. Mem. Physicians for Social Responsibility, Am. Coll. Obstetricians and Gynecologists (1st prize rsch. 1984), Ctrl. Assn. Obstetricians and Gynecologists (Cmty. Hosp. Rsch. award 1981, Ann. prize award for rsch. 1982), Soc. Perinatal Obstetricians, Soc. Gynecologic Investigation, Perinatal Rsch. Soc., Peoria Ob-Gyn. Soc. Office: St Francis Hosp 530 NE Glen Oak Ave Peoria IL 61637-0001

GROSS, WILLIAM ALLEN, mechanical engineer; b. L.A., Nov. 17, 1924; s. William Allen and Margaret Florence (Hill) G.; m. Shirley Mae Jackson, Aug. 10, 1948 (dec. 1968); children: Constance, Ellen, Mark, David; m. Sharon Carol Philbrick, Aug. 22, 1970. BS, USCG Acad., New London, Conn., 1945; MS, U. Calif., Berkeley, 1949, PhD, 1951. Registered profl. engr., N.Mex. Lectr. to asst. prof. U. Calif., Berkeley, 1949-52; asst. prof. Iowa State U., Ames, 1952-55; mem. tech. staff Bell Telephone Labs., Murray Hill, N.J., 1955-56; mem. rsch. staff, mgr. applied mechanics dept. IBM, San Jose, 1956-61; v.p. adv. tech. div., dir. rsch. AMPEX, Redwood City, Calif., 1961-72; vis. lectr. U. Calif., Berkeley, 1973-74; dean engring. U. N.Mex., Albuquerque, 1974-80, prof. mech. engring., elec. and computer engring., 1974-93; prof., dean emeritus, 1993—; dir. new techs. Tejas Power Corp., 1993-97; vis. prof. Poly. U. Bucharest, 1991,93; dir. Lovelace Inhalation Toxicology Rsch. Inst., Albuquerque, 1976-97, U. N.Mex. Tech. Innovative Prog., 1978-87, Renewable Energy Program, Vols. in Tech. Assistance, 1980-81; cons. in field. Editor, author: Fluid Film Lubrication, 1961; author: Gas Film Lubrication, 1962; editor/author: Fluid Film Lubrication, 1982; patentee in field; contbr. articles to profl. jours. Bd. dirs. Am. Friends Svc. Com., 1970-72, Inhalation Toxicology Rsch. Inst., 1974-97, Futures for Children, Albuquerque, 1982-88, Trinity Forum, 1989-92. Recipient Chief Manuelito award, Navajo Tribe, 1982; named N.Mex. Engr. of Yr., 1991, Disting. Alumnus U. Calif. Berkeley Coll. Engring., 1995, Disting. Alumnus, USCG Acad., 1997. Fellow ASME (Centennial award 1978), IEEE; mem. Nat. Acad. Engrs., Profl. Engrs. N.Mex. Soc. Democrat. Soc. of Friends. E-mail: wgross@unm.edu. Home: 1401 Las Lomas Rd NE Albuquerque NM 87106-4529 Office: U NMex Dept Mech Engring Albuquerque NM 87131

GROSSBERG, DAVID BURTON, cardiologist; b. Bronx, N.Y., Oct. 28, 1956; s. Jules Harold and Florence (Greenbaum) G.; m. Karen Leslie Sonin, Apr. 17, 1988; children: Samuel Benjamin, Hannah Rachel. BA, SUNY, Binghamton, 1977; MD, SUNY, Syracuse, 1981. Diplomate Am. Bd. Internal Medicine, Am. Bd. Cardiology. Resident in internal medicine Overlook Hosp., Coll. Physicians and Surgeons, Columbia U., Summit, N.J., 1981-84; asst. clin. prof. medicine George Washington U., Washington; adj. asst. prof. medicine Baylor U. Sch. Medicine; staff physician St. Mary's Hosp., East Orange, N.J., 1982; internist Sumter County Pub. Health, Wildwood, Fla., 1984-86; cardiology fellow Albany (N.Y.) Med. Ctr. Hosp., 1986-88; cardiologist Md. Cardiology Assoc., Silver Spring, 1988-91; pvt. practice Silver Spring, Rockville, Md., 1991-97; ptnr. Assocs. in Cardiology, Silver Spring, Md., 1997—; mem., dir. Cen. Fla. Ambulance Svcs., Sumterville, 1984-85; active attending staff Washington Adventist Hosp., Shady Grove Adventist Hosp., Holy Cross Hosp., Suburban Hosp., Laurel Hosp., Montgomery Gen. Hosp.; co-investigator gusto trial-thrombolytic therapy post myocardial infarction. Recipient Elsbeth Kroeber Meml. award N.Y. Biology Tchrs. Assn., 1973, Regents scholar, 1973. Fellow Am. Coll. Cardiology, Am. Coll. Chest Physicians; mem. ACP, Physicians for Social Responsibility, Md. Med. Soc. (alt. del. 1992-95, del. 1995—), Sierra Club (vol. physician Wilderness Project 1982), Audubon Soc., Md. Soc. Cardiology, Montgomery County Med. Soc. Avocations: karate, hiking, philately, numismatics. Office: 2415 Musgrove Rd Ste 307 Silver Spring MD 20904-5200

GROSSBERG, GEORGE THOMAS, psychiatrist, educator; b. Hungary, Aug. 20, 1948; came to the U.S., 1957; s. Henry and Barbara (Rothman) G.; m. Darla Jean Brown, June 13, 1976; children: Jonathan, Anna-Leah, Aviva, Aliza Becky, Jeremy. BA, Yeshiva U., 1971; MD, St. Louis U., 1975. Diplomate Am. Bd. Psychiatry and Neurology. Chief resident in psychiatry St. Louis U., 1978-79, instr., 1979-81, asst. prof., 1982-86, assoc. prof., 1986-90, prof., 1990—, Samuel W. Fordyce prof. and chmn. dept. psychiatry, 1995-98, Samuel w. Fordyce prof., dir. divsn. geriat. psychiatry, 1998—; cons. on aging U.S. VA Hosps. Assn., Washington, 1990—. Contbr. articles to profl. jours. Adv. bd. St. Louis Alzheimers Assn., 1983—. Recipient Pub. Svc. award St. Louis Alzheimers Assn., 1989. Mem. Am. Assn. Geriat. Psychiatry (pres. 1989-90), Am. Psychiat. Assn. (cons. on aging 1990—, Falk fellow 1977-79), Am. Geriat. Soc., Gerontol. Soc. Am., Internat. Psychogeriat. Assn. (treas. 1997—). Avocations: collectibles, art, skiing. Office: Saint Louis U Med Ctr 1221 S Grand Blvd Saint Louis MO 63104-1016

GROSSBERG, MARC ELIAS, lawyer; b. Houston, Dec. 26, 1940; s. Sylvester and Leah (Hochman) G.; m. Eva M. Wolski, Jan. 3, 1981; 1 child, Nicole; children from previous marriage: Lee Ann Krishnan, Toni. BS in Polit. Sci., U. Houston, 1961; JD with honors, U. Tex., 1965. Bar: Tex. 1965, Calif. 1966, Fla. 1980, U.S. Supreme Ct. 1980; bd. cert. fed. income taxation, Tex. Acct. Brochstein Toomin & Co CPAs (now Deloitte Touche), Houston, 1961-62; law clk. hon. Walter Ely U.S. Ct. Appeals (9th cir.), L.A., 1965-66; assoc. Fulbright & Jaworski, Houston, 1966-71; ptnr. Schlanger Mills Mayer & Grossberg, LLP, Houston, 1974—. Advanceman, speech writer 1968 Hubert Humphry Presdl. Campaign; pres. Tex. Bill of Rights Found., Houston, 1971-72, Jewish Family Svc., Houston, 1986-87, U. Tex. Law Rev. Assn.; commr. Housing Authority City of Houston, 1974-78. Mem. ABA (tax sect. and litig. sects.). Democrat. Jewish. Avocations: computers, racquetball. Home: 9127 Briar Forest Dr Houston TX 77024-7213 Office: Schlanger Mills Mayer & Grossberg 5847 San Felipe St Ste 1700 Houston TX 77057-3009

GROSSBERG, MICHAEL LEE, theater critic, writer; b. Houston, Sept. 7, 1952; s. Fred Samuel and Esther R. (Rosenstein) G. BA, U. Tex., 1979, BS in Journalism, 1983. Film, theater critic, reporter Victor Valley Daily News, Victorville, Calif., 1983-85; film, theater critic Columbus (Ohio) Dispatch, 1985-87, theater critic, 1987—; co-founder Free Press Assn., Mencken awards for outstanding journalism, dir., 1981-94. Contbr. Otis Guernsey/Burns Mantle Theater Yearbook: Best Plays, 1993-94, 94-95, 95-96, 96-97, 97-98, 98-99; regional report columnist Backstage, 1997—. Mem. Outer Critics Cir., Am. Theatre Critics Assn. (chmn. awards new plays com. 1993-99, exec. com. 1996—), Libertarian Futurist Soc. (chmn. Prometheus award judges com. 1997—). Avocations: reading, traveling, meditation, public speaking. Home: 3164 Plymouth Pl Columbus OH 43213-4236 Office: Columbus Dispatch 34 S 3rd St Columbus OH 43215-4241

GROSSEN, BONNIE JOY, education research scientist; b. Hillsboro, Oreg., Aug. 25, 1947; d. Elmer John and Lillie Maud (Wagner) G. BA in German, Lewis and Clark Coll., 1969; MA in German Lit., U. Wash., 1970; MA in Spl. Edn., U. of Oreg., 1977, PhD in Spl. Edn., 1988. Tchr. McAllen (Tex.) H.S., 1970-73; instr. Gymnasium Damme, Lower Saxony, Germany, 1973-74; tchr., dir. of cultural curriculum devel. project Coeur d'Alene Indian Tribal Sch., DeSmet, Idaho, 1975-76; secondary spl. edn. tchr. Junction City (Oreg.) H.S., 1977-85, talented and gifted tchr., 1982, ESL instr., 1979-82; instr. U. Oreg., Eugene, 1985-89; head English dept. Hoxani Coll., South Africa, 1989-90; instrnl. designer Systems Impact, Eugene, 1990-93; rsch. assoc. U. Oreg., Eugene, 1990—. Editor (sch. quarterly) Effective School Practices, 1993—; contbr. articles to profl. jours.; presenter over 20 nat. workshops. Home: 2450 Jefferson St Eugene OR 97405-2411

GROSSER, BERNARD IRVING, psychiatry educator; b. Boston, Apr. 19, 1929; s. John and Katherine (Russman) G.; children: Steven, Mark, Minda; m. Karen Grosser. BA, U. Mass., 1950; MS, U. Mich., 1953; MD, Case-

Western Res. U., 1959. Diplomate Am. Bd. Psychiatry and Neurology. Intern U. Utah, 1959-60, resident in psychiatry, 1960-65; asst. prof. psychiatry U. Utah Sch. Medicine, Salt Lake City, 1967-71, assoc. prof., 1971-75, prof., 1975—, chmn. dept., 1978—; mem. pre-clin. and clin. psychopharm. rev. com. NIMH, Washington, 1974-79, 80-84, mem. sci. adv. bd., 1984-88; mem. merit rev. bd. VA, Washington, 1988-91; sr. sci. advisor Alcohol, Drug Abuse and Mental Health Adminstrn., Washington, 1987-88; ad hoc mem. Mental Health Clin. Rsch. Ctr. rev. com. NIMH, 1997, ad hoc mem. mental health clin. contracts rev. com., 1998. Contbr. chpts. to books, articles to profl. jours. Capt. USAF, 1965-67. Grantee NIMH, 1959-84, FDA, 1985-88; recipient Exemplary psychiatrist award Nat. Alliance for Mentally Ill, 1997. Fellow Am. Psychiat. Assn. (life); mem. Internat. Soc. Psychoneuroendocrinology (treas. 1974-88), Utah Psychiat. Assn. (pres. 1995-96), Psychiat. Rsch. Soc. (pres. 1986-87), Am. Coll. Neuropsychopharmacology, Soc. Neurosci., N.Y. Acad. Scis., Collegium Internat. Neuro-psychopharmacologicum, Am. Assn. Psychiatry Dept. Chairmen (coun. 1997-2000). Republican. Jewish. Home: 511 Perrys Hollow Rd Salt Lake City UT 84103-4245 Office: U Utah Sch Medicine Dept Psychiatry 50 N Medical Dr Salt Lake City UT 84132-0001

GROSSER, T.J., administrator, developer, fundraiser; b. Milw., Oct. 17, 1938; s. Owen Henry and Ethel Clare (Hathazy) G.; m. Mary Janet McClanahan, Apr. 3, 1976; children: Paul Howard, Julie Anne, Philip Owen, Peter John, Elizabeth Michelle. BA, U. Wis., 1958, MA, 1962, EdD, 1971; DD (hon.), Union Theol. Sem., Richmond,Va., 1972. Min. edn. Cross Luth. Ch., Milw., 1957-62; assoc. Christ Luth. Ch., Oshkosh, Wis., 1962-65; preacher/tchr. Trinity Luth. Ch., Santa Barbara, Calif., 1966-71; pres. Amigos de las Ams., Houston, 1972-79, Vols. in Internat. Svc. & Awareness, L.A., 1980-84; v.p. Pacific Clinics, Pasadena, Calif., 1985-87; pres., chief exec. officer Children's Aid Internat., San Diego, 1987-97; pres., CEO Angelcare, 1998—; bd. dirs. Am. Devel. Found., Washington, 1981-95; bd. dirs., pres. End Hunger Network, L.A., 1983-87; bd. dirs., v.p. Ind. Charities of Am., San Francisco, pres., 1988—; bd. dirs. Children's Charities Am.; advisor numerous internat. and religious agys. Contbr. 200 articles to profl. jours. Advisor African Refugee Ctr., L.A., 1989—; worker priest Hope Luth. Ch., Hollywood, Calif., 1983—, 1st Luth., San Diego, 1991—. Named Educator of Yr. Am. Luth. Ch., Mpls., 1966, exec. of Yr. Coun. Internat. Vol. Orgn., Geneva, 1975, 76; recipient Papal medal Pope John Paul II, Rome, 1979. Mem. Fund Raising Execs., Rotary (Paul Harris fellow) 1987). Democrat. Avocations: reading, speaking, travel, promoting internat. adoptions. Home: 8295 Churchill Dr El Cajon CA 92021-1151 Office: Anglecare PO Box 600370 San Diego CA 92160-0370

GROSSET, ANNE MARIE, biophysicist, researcher; b. Pitts., June 26, 1957; d. Serge Philippe and Helen Mary (Walton) G.;m. Denis Louis Pilloud, Mar. 23, 1991; children: Hélène Marie, Aurélie Véronique. BSCE, MIT, 1980; MS in Colloids, Polymers and Surfaces, Carnegie-Mellon U., 1988, MSCE, 1989; postgrad. in Biophysics, U. Pa., 1989—. Sr. rsch. engr. Westinghouse Elec. Corp. R&D Ctr., Pitts., 1980-85; asst. in phys. chemistry Swiss Fed. Inst. Tech., Lausanne, 1989; asst. in biochemistry U. Fribourg, Switzerland, 1992-93; doctoral candidate in biophysics U. Pa., Phila., 1989-92, 93—. Contbr. articles to profl. jours. Mem. Am. Inst. Chemists, Am. Peptide Soc., Biophys. Soc., Protein Soc. Achievements include research in ultraviolet light curable paints; peptide design and assembly, synthesis of maquettes of biological redox proteins, molecular switches, electrochemistry.

GROSSET, JESSICA ARIANE, computer analyst; b. Paris, Aug. 31, 1952; came to U.S., 1970; d. Raymond Louis and Barbara Ann (Byrne) G.; m. Bruce Edward Kaskubar, May 23, 1986. AA, Berkshire Community Coll., Pittsfield, Mass., 1972; BS, SUNY, Potsdam, 1979; postgrad., Ariz. State U., 1980, U. Minn., 1980-81. Computer programmer Kay-Bee Toy and Hobby Shops, Lee, Mass., 1974-78; computer analyst Mayo Clinic, Rochester, Minn., 1981—; voting staff Mayo Clinic, Rochester, 1996. Mem. Nat. Assn. Female Execs. Avocations: reading, sailing, travel, horseback riding, skiing. Office: Mayo Clinic 200 1st St SW Rochester MN 55905-0002

GROSSETETE, GINGER LEE, retired gerontology administrator, consultant; b. Riverside, Calif., Feb. 9, 1936; d. Lee Roy Taylor and Bonita (Beryl) Williams; m. Alec Paul Grossetete, June 8, 1954; children: Elizabeth Gay Blech, Teri Lee Zeni. BA in Recreation cum laude, U. N.Mex., 1974, M in Pub. Adminstrn., 1978. Sr. ctr. supr., Office of Sr. Affairs, City of Albuquerque, 1974-77, asst. dir. Office of Sr. Affairs, 1977-96; conf. coord. Nat. Consumers Assn., Albuquerque, 1978-79; region 6 del. Nat. Coun. on Aging, Washington, 1977-84; conf. chmn. Western Gerontol. Soc., Albuquerque, 1983; N.Mex. del. White House Conf. on Aging, 1995; mem. adv. coun. N.Mex. Agy. on Aging, 1996-99. Contbr. articles to mags. Campaign dir. March of Dimes N.Mex., 1966-67; pres. Albuquerque Symphony Women's Assn., 1972; mem. exec. com. Jr. League Albuquerque, 1976; mem. Gov.'s Coun. on Phys. Fitness, 1987-91, chmn. 1990-91; mem. bd. dirs. N.Mex. Sr. Olympics, 1995—. Recipient N.Mex. Disting. Pub. Service award N.Mex. Gov.'s Office, 1983, Disting. Woman on the Move award YWCA, 1986, Outstanding Profl. award N.Mex. State Conf. on Aging, 1995, Presdl. citation S.W. Soc. on Aging, 1995; inductee Albuquerque Sr. Citizens Hall of Fame, 1998. Fellow Nat. Recreation and Pk. Assn. (bd. dirs. S.W. regional coun. rep., bd. dirs. leisure and aging sect., pres. N.Mex. chpt. 1983-84, 97-98, bd. dirs. N.Mex. Sr. Olympics, 1994—, pres. leisure and aging sect. 1997-98, Outstanding profl. award 1982); mem. ASPA (pres. N.Mex. coun. 1987-88), S.W. Soc. on Aging (pres. 1984-85, bd. dirs., Outstanding Profl. award 1991, Presdl. citation 1996), U. N.Mex. Alumni Assn. (bd. dirs. 1978-80, Disting. Alumni award 1985), Las Amapolas Garden Club (pres. 1964), Phi Alpha Alpha, Chi Omega (pres. alumni 1959-60). Avocations: tennis, water skiing, snow skiing, racewalking, arts and crafts. Home: 517 La Veta Dr NE Albuquerque NM 87108-1403

GROSSETT, DEBORAH LOU, psychologist, behavior analyst, consultant; b. Alma, Mich., Feb. 16, 1957; d. Charles M. and Margaret A. (Roethlisberger) G. BS, Alma Coll., 1979; MA, Western Mich. U., 1981, PhD, 1984. Lic. psychologist, Tex.; cert. in diagnostic evaluation, Tex.; registered behavior analyst, Tex. Grad. rsch. and teaching asst. Western Mich. U., Kalamazoo, 1979-84; asst. group home supr., community outreach Residential Opportunities, Kalamazoo, 1982-84; psychologist Richmond (Tex.) State Sch., 1984-87, Shapiro Devel. Ctr., Kankakee, Ill., 1987-88; clin. coord. Monroe Devel. Ctr., Rochester, N.Y., 1988; chief psychologist Denton (Tex.) State Sch., 1989-90; dir. psychol./behavioral svcs. Ctr. for the Retarded, Houston, 1990—; behavioral cons. Ctr. for Developmentally Disabled Adults, Kalamazoo, 1984, Goodman-Wade Enterprises, Houston, 1987; instr. psychology Houston Community Coll., 1985-86, U. Houston-Clear Lake, 1987, 92, 95—. Contbr. chpt. to book, articles to profl. jours. Western Mich. U. fellow, 1984. Mem. Am. Psychol. Assn., Am. Assn. on Mental Retardation, Assn. for Behavior Analysis (chair Outreach Bd. 1989-91), Tex. Assn. for Behavior Analysis (bd. dirs. 1989-91, program chair 1996, pres. 1997). Democrat. Presbyterian. Avocations: golf, camping, jogging. Home: 9750 Ravensworth Dr Houston TX 77031-3130 Office: Ctr for the Retarded Inc 3550 W Dallas St Houston TX 77019-1795

GROSSFELD, STAN, newspaper photography executive, author; b. Bronx, N.Y., Dec. 20, 1951. B.S. in Profl. Photography, Rochester Inst. Tech., 1973; M. Journalism, Boston U., 1980. Staff photographer Newark Star-Ledger, 1973-75; staff photographer The Boston Globe, 1975-82, chief photographer, 1983-85, dir. photography, 1985-86, assoc. editor, 1986—. Co-author: Two on the River, 1986, The Whisper of Stars, 1988 (Lowell Thomas award best travel book 1988); author, photographer: Nantucket: The Other Season, 1982; editor: Eyes of The Globe, 1985. Nieman fellow Harvard U., 1991-92; recipient Pulitzer prize for news photography Columbia U., 1984, Gold medal for photography Soc. Newspaper Designers, 1985, Pultizer prize for feature photography Columbia U., 1985, Humanitarian award Overseas Press Club, 1985, 94, Best Reporting from abroad citation Overseas Press Club, 1984, 89, Canon Photo Essayist award U. Mo., 1985, World Hunger Media award, 1986, NASA journalist in space finalist, 1986; named New Eng. Photographer of Yr. by Boston Press Photographers Assn., 1979, 80, 81, 84, 85. Office: The Boston Globe 135 Morrissey Blvd Boston MA 02125-3338*

GROSSI, FRANCIS XAVIER, JR., lawyer, educator; b. Somerville, Mass., May 8, 1943; s. Francis Xavier and Angela Mary (LoGiudice) G.; m. Betty Morene Ballenger, May 12, 1962 (div. 1987); children: Francis Xavier III, Gina Maria, Andrea Mary, Cynthia Marie; m. Milada Dvorak, Dec. 31, 1987; children: Lukas Paolo, Anna Milada. BS, U. Mo., 1964; JD, U. Mich., 1967. Bar: D.C. 1968, U.S. Ct. Appeals (7th and 9th crcts.) 1969, U.S. Tax Ct. 1970, U.S. Ct. Appeals (4th crct.) 1972, U.S. Ct. Appeals (2d crct.) 1973, Ill. 1977. Appellate atty. U.S. Dept. Justice, Washington, 1967-69; assoc. Williams & Connolly, Washington, 1970-76; ptnr., chmn. litigation dept. Katten Muchin & Zavis, Chgo., 1977-95; ptnr. Bates, Meckler, Bulger & Tilson, Chgo., 1995—; adj. prof. Loyola U. Law Sch., Chgo., 1979-81, DePaul Law Sch., Chgo., 1981-94; faculty Nat. Inst. Trial Advocacy, Chgo., 1989—; chmn. com. Chgo. Coun. Lawyers, 1991-92. Contbg. author: Survey Bankruptcy Law, 1981; author, editor (legal publ.) Evidence Practice Guide. Mem. Joint Civic com. Italian Ams., 1988; bd. dirs. Italian Am. Polit. Coalition, 1995-96; pres. Univ. Village Assn., Chgo., 1992-95. With USMCR, 1960. Fellow Am. Coll. Trial Lawyers; mem. Chgo. Bar Assn., Justinian Soc. Democrat. Roman Catholic. Avocations: writing, camping, workshop. Office: Bates Meckler Bulger & Tilson 8300 Sears Tower Chicago IL 60606

GROSSI, OLINDO, architect, educator; b. N.Y.C., July 17, 1909; s. Alexander and Ferdinanda (Bartalini) G.; m. Martha Seymour, Sept. 26, 1940; childrenSusan, John, Thomas. AB, Columbia U., 1930, BArch, 1932, MArch, 1933; postgrad., Am. Acad. Rome; student (fellow), 1933-36. Assoc. architecture and fine arts Bard Coll., 1938-42, Columbia, 1944-45; dean sch. architecture Pratt Inst., 1946-69, dir. internat. programs, 1969; dean architecture and arts N.Y. Inst. Tech., 1971-83; dir. N.Y. Inst. Tech. (Center for Architecture), 1979; pvt. practice architecture N.Y.C., 1945—; cons. N.Y.C. Planning Commn., Office of Information, U.S. Govt., L.I.U., N.Y.U.; adviser on tropical architecture and archtl. edn. in S.E. Asia for Asia Found. Author: Downtown Brooklyn Civic Center, 1963; Contbr. articles and designs in miscellaneous publs. Chmn. Goals for Nassau Com.; Mem. Mayor's Panel of Architects, N.Y.C. Recipient Brunner scholarship, 1949, Rome prize in Architecture, 1933; Carnegie scholarship to Paris, 1930; first prize Residential Design at Conv. N.Y. Assos. Architects, 1950; first prize beach house design Archtl. League; Strauss Meml. award for contbn. to profession, 1954. Fellow A.I.A., Beaux Arts Inst. Design (trustee), Am. Acad. Rome Alumni (pres.), Assn. N.Y. State Architects (dir.), Archtl. Historians, N.Y. Soc. Architects, Assn. Collegiate Schs. Architecture (pres.), Archtl. League N.Y. (pres.), Municipal Art Soc., Fine Arts Fedn. Home and Office: 234 Manhasset Ave Manhasset NY 11030-2220

GROSSI, RALPH EDWARD, agricultural conservation organization executive, farmer, rancher; b. San Rafael, Calif., Feb. 16, 1949; s. James Joseph and Rose Marie (Halter) G.; m. Judy Arlene Lamb, Sept. 9, 1972; children: Amy, Erin, Kathryn. BS, Calif. Poly. State U., San Luis Obispo, 1971. Mng. ptnr. Marindale Dairy, Novato, Calif., 1971-87, Marindale Ranch, Novato, 1987—; pres. Am. Farmland Trust, Washington, 1985—, also bd. dirs.; founder, bd. dirs. Marin Agrl. Land Trust, Marin County, Calif., 1980-84, chmn., 1980-82; pres. Marin County Farm Bur., 1979-81; mem. water adv. com. Calif. Agrl., Sacramento, 1979-81, U.S. Implementation Bd. of N.Am. Waterfowl Mgmt. Plan, Washington, 1988-94. Mem. adv. com. Calif. Poly. State U. Sch. Agr., 1988—; bd. dirs. Wildlife Habitat Enhancement, Washington, 1989-94; v.p. Alpha Gamma Rho Found., Kansas City, Mo., 1991-94. Recipient Feinstone Environ. award Sol Feinstone Awards Com., 1985. Mem. Soil and Water Conservation Soc., Calif. Farm Bur. Fedn. (Outstanding Young Farmer and Rancher award 1976), Inst. for Alternative Agr. (pres.' coun. 1990—). Presbyterian. Avocations: golf, hunting, fishing. Office: Am Farmland Trust 1200 18th St NW Ste #800 Washington DC 20036

GROSSMAN, ALLEN NEIL, publishing executive; b. Bklyn., May 14, 1946; s. William Lester and Shirley Miriam (Jacobson) G.; m. Pamela Jean Pearson, June 8, 1969; children: Steven Mueller, Elizabeth Jane. AB, Princeton U., 1968; JD, Harvard U., 1971. Bar: Pa. 1971, N.J. 1973. Assoc. Dechert Price & Rhoads, Phila., 1971-73, Smith Stratton Wise & Heher, Princeton, N.J., 1973-75; ptnr. Smith Stratton Wise & Heher, 1975-81; dir. bus. devel. Dow Jones Info. Svcs. Group, Princeton, 1981-91, exec. dir. bus. ops. and devel., 1991-92; exec. dir. prodn. mktg. and devel. Dow Jones Bus. Info. Svcs. Group, Princeton, 1992-93, exec. dir. corp. products, 1993-94, exec. dir. content and distbn., 1994-96; exec. dir. content and distbn. Dow Jones Interactive Pub., Princeton, 1997—. Dir. Princeton Area United Way, 1978-79; mem. Princeton Regional Bd. Edn., 1980-84, 86-91, Coun. of Princeton U. Community, 1990-92; coach Princeton Youth Soccer Assn., 1984-91. Democrat. Jewish. Avocations: running, photography. Home: 39 Tyson Ln Princeton NJ 08540-4141 Office: Dow Jones Bus Info Svcs Group PO Box 300 Princeton NJ 08543-0300

GROSSMAN, ANN, professional tennis player; b. Columbus, Ohio, Oct. 13, 1970. Grad., Am. Sch., Chgo., 1989. Profl. tennis player, advanced to 2d round French Open, 1998. MVP U.S. Jr. Wightman Cup team, 1987; rep. U.S. on Maureen Connolly Brinker team and Nat. team, 1988, Ohio H.S. AAA State and Regl. champion, 1985; co-ranked No. 1 in U.S. 18 singles in 1987, winner Nat. Singles Title, 1987. Office: USTA 70 W Red Oak Ln White Plains NY 10604-3602*

GROSSMAN, ARNOLD JOSEPH, writer, producer; b. Jersey City, May 10, 1934; s. Alex and Pearl (Dynkine) G.; m. Katherine Chorley, Dec. 28, 1958 (div. Aug. 1980); children: Alex, Rachel, Daniel. BA, U. Denver, 1959. Asst. editor Redbook Mag., N.Y.C., 1960-62, Good Housekeeping, N.Y.C., 1962-63; pres. Grossman & Bartholomew, Denver, 1969-76; owner Grossman Prodns., Denver, L.A., 1976—; cons. Patricia Schroeder for Congress, Colo., 1972-74, Richard Lamm for Gov., Colo., 1976-84, Gary Hart for U.S. Senate, 1974-80, Timothy Wirth for U.S. Senate, 1986. Author: 1988, 1985, California Conspiracy, 1988; prodr.: (movie) Cries Unheard, 1993; contbr. articles to profl. jours. Chmn. bd. dirs. Denver Internat. Film Festival, 1980-82; bd. dirs. Hist. Denver, Inc., 1979-81; commr. Colo. Film Commn., Denver, 1984-85, bd. dirs., Planned Parenthood 1992—. With USN, 1952-56. Democrat. Jewish. Avocations: skiing, long distance running, scuba diving, sailing. Home and Office: 1177 Race St #507 Denver CO 80206

GROSSMAN, DAN STEVEN, lawyer; b. N.Y.C., Apr. 6, 1953; s. George M. and Jeanne L. (Stickle) G.; m. Patrice Irene Michaelson, June 27, 1976; children: Deborah, Andrea. BA, SUNY, Albany, 1975; JD, Albany Law Sch., 1978; LLM, Georgetown Law Ctr., 1980. Bar: D.C. 1978, N.Y. 1979. Law clk. to judge U.S. Tax Ct., Washington, 1978-80; assoc. Webster and Sheffield, N.Y.C., 1980-84, Finley Kumble Wagner, N.Y.C., 1984-87; assoc. Willkie Farr and Gallagher, N.Y.C., 1987-90, ptnr., 1991—. Mem. ABA (tax sect.), N.Y. State Bar Assn. (tax sect.), Assn. of Bar of City of N.Y., D.C. Bar Assn. Office: Willkie Farr and Gallagher 787 7th Ave New York NY 10019-6099

GROSSMAN, DEBRA A., lawyer, real estate manager, radio talk show host; b. Cleve., July 29, 1951; d. Morris M. and Idelle R. (Bialosky) G. BA, Syracuse U., 1973; JD, Suffolk U., 1976. Bar: Mass. 1977, U.S. Dist. Ct. Mass. 1977. Sole practice Lexington, Mass., 1977-79; ptnr. Kurland & Grossman, P.C., Lowell, Mass., 1979-94; property mgr. KD Mgmt. Co., Lowell, 1983—, Chelmsford, Mass., 1994-98; talk show host "Legal Briefs" WCCM Radio, Lawrence, Mass., 1989-97. Bd. dirs. Downtown Lowell Bus. Assn., 1987; lectr. Greater Lowell Alzheimers Assn., 1987; vice chair Lowell Hist. Bd., 1995-97, chair, 1997—. Mem. Mass. Assn. Women Lawyers (asst. treas. 1981-82, bd. dirs. 1979-81), Mass. Bar Assn. (mem. family law sect.), Mass. Acad. Trial Lawyers, Greater Lowel Bar Assn. (bd. dirs. 1993-96, Lawyer for the Day program dir. 1990-92), Syracuse U. Alumni Club, Greater Boston Club, Assn. Trial Lawyers Am., Mass. Family and Probate Am. Inn Ct. Office: Kurland & Grossman PC 34 Chelmsford St Chelmsford MA 01824-3060

GROSSMAN, DOROTHEA G., consulting services administrator, poet; b. Phila., Aug. 27, 1937; d. Nathan Theodore and Shirley (Gerson) Dwartzin; m. Richard Grossman, June 29, 1958 (dec. Oct. 1992). BA in English Lit., Temple U., 1959. Registrar So. Calif. Inst. Architecture, Santa Monica, 1987-91; office mgr. Gerontological Svcs., Inc., Santa Monica, 1993—. Author: (books of poetry) Cuttings, 1988, Poems from Cave 17, 1996. Performance grantee Meet the Composer, Calif., 1996. Avocation: music. Home: 2414 S Barrington Ave Apt 302 Los Angeles CA 90064-2934

GROSSMAN, ELMER ROY, pediatrician; b. L.A., Jan. 30, 1929; s. Harry and Reta (Frankel) G.; m. Rosalind Nagin, June 24, 1951 (div. 1976); children—Deena, Marianna; m. Pamela Canfield Antoncich, July 29, 1976; stepchildren: Camilla Sutter, Michael A. Antoncich. A.B., U. Calif.-Berkeley, 1949; M.D., U. Calif. Sch. Medicine, San Francisco, 1953. Intern Orange County Gen. Hosp., Orange, Calif., 1953-54; resident U. Calif. Hosps., San Francisco, 1957-59; practice medicine specializing in pediatrics Berkeley Pediatric Med. Group, Calif, 1959-92; assoc. clin. prof. health and med. scis. U. Calif.-Berkeley, 1978-80; clin. prof. pediatrics emeritus U. Calif. Sch. Medicine, San Francisco; chmn. dept. pediatrics Alta Bates Hosp., Berkeley, 1972-74, chmn. infant care ethics com., 1984-90. Author: Everyday Pediatrics, 1993, Everyday Pediatrics for Parents, 1996; columnist The Everyday Pediatrician; contbr. articles to profl. jours. Mem. Berkeley Schs. Master Plan Com., 1966-68, Berkeley Schs. Child Care Com., 1968-70; pres. Temple Beth El, Berkeley, 1970-72. Served to capt. USAF, 1954-56. Fellow Am. Acad. Pediatrics; mem. Alameda-Contra Costa Med. Assn., Physicians for Social Responsibility, Physicians for a Nat. Health Program. Democrat. Jewish. Avocations: wine making; gardening. Home and Office: 899 Euclid Ave Berkeley CA 94708-1305

GROSSMAN, GEORGE STEFAN, library director, law eductor; b. Poltar, Czechoslovakia, May 31, 1938; m. Suzi Herczeg, 1960; 1 child, Zoltan. B.A., U. Chgo., 1960; LL.B., Stanford U., 1966; M.A. in Library Sci., Brigham Young U., 1971. Bar: Calif. 1966, Minn. 1974. Tech. processes law librarian U. Pa., 1966-68; assoc. prof. law, law librarian U. Utah, 1968-70, prof., law librarian, 1970-73; prof., dir. law library U. Minn., 1973-79, Northwestern U., Chgo., 1979-93; prof., dir. law libr. U. Calif., Davis, 1993—; cons. to univs. Author: Legal Research: Historical Foundations of the Electronic Age, 1994; contbr. articles to legal jours. Mem. Indian rights com. ACLU, 1973-92, pres. Utah affiliate, 1972-73, bd. dirs. Ill. affiliate, 1982-87. Mem. Am. Assn. Law Libraries, Internat. Assn. Law Libraries. Office: U Calif Sch Law Libr King Hall Davis CA 95616*

GROSSMAN, HERBERT BARTON, urologist, researcher; b. Tampa, Fla., June 25, 1945; s. Benjamin and Pauline (Mattis) G.; m. Amy C. Becker, Aug. 24, 1969; children: Beth, Sara, Rebecca. BA, La Salle Coll., Phila., 1966; MD, Temple U., 1970. Diplomate Am. Bd. Urology. Surg. intern U. Mich. Med. Ctr., Ann Arbor, 1970-71; surg. resident St. Joseph Mercy Hosp., Ann Arbor, 1973-74; urology resident U. Mich. Med. Ctr., Ann Arbor, 1974-77; instr. U. Mich. Med. Sch., Ann Arbor, 1977-78; rsch. and clin. fellow Meml. Sloan-Kettering Cancer Ctr., N.Y.C., 1978-80; asst. prof. U. Mich. Med. Sch., Ann Arbor, 1980-85, assoc. prof., 1985-90, prof., 1990-94; dir., urologic oncology U. Mich. Cancer Ctr., Ann Arbor, 1986-94; prof. U. Tex. M.D. Anderson Cancer Ctr., Houston, 1994—; dep. chair Dept. Urology U. Tex. M.D. Anderson Cancer Ctr., 1998—; cons. Taubman Med. Libr., 1985-94, The Med. Letter, 1991, Jour. Vascular Surgery, 1991; reviewer VA Merit Rev. Bd. for Surgery, 1986, NIH Pathology B Ad Hoc (SI) Study Sect., 1988, NIDDK Ad Hoc Rev. Groups 12 and 13, 1992; spl. reviewer NIH Exptl. Therapeutics Study Sect., 1986, reviewer spl. study sect., 1995, reviewer cancer ctr. support grant, 1996; reviewer NGI Rev. Group/subcom. 4, 1997; external reviewer Alberta Cancer Bd., 1998; mem. surg. quality control and edn. com. S.W. Oncology Group, 1980-90, GU com., 1980—, organ site chmn. for local bladder cancer, 1991—; mem. surg. oncology adv. com. dept. surgery U. Mich. Med. Ctr., Ann Arbor, 1981-82, dept. surgery computer sys. adv. com., 1983-88, cancer ctr. clin. rsch. com., 1987-94, laser safety com., 1987-94, med. sch. admissions com., 1988-94, patient care com., 1989-90, hosps. quality mgmt. com., 1990-94, rsch. coord. sect. urology, 1991, fin. adv. com., adv. promotion com. for primary rsch. staff dept. surgery, 1993-94; med. practice subcom. U. Tex. M.D. Anderson Cancer Ctr., Houston, 1994—, grad. med. edn. com., 1994—, surveillance com., 1994-95, dir. clin. rsch., 1994—, dep. chmn. dept. urology 1998—; prostate cancer adv. com. Mich. Dept. Pub. Health, 1993-94, clin. rsch. com. mem. 1994—, chmn. 1997—, dir. bladder cancer multidisciplinary rsch. program, 1999—; mem. scientific adv. bd. Anthra Pharms., Inc., 1994—. Contbr. 137 articles to profl. jours.; authored 21 book chpts. Capt. USAF, 1971-73. Recipient 2d prize Ferdinand C. Valentine Urology Essay Contest, 1980, also numerous rsch. grants; named to W.A. "Tex" and Deborah Moncrief, Jr. Disting. Chair in Urology, 1994; Ferdinand C. Valentine fellow N.Y. Acad. Medicine, 1979-80, clin. fellow Am. Cancer Soc., 1979-80. Office: U T MD Anderson Cancer Ctr 1515 Holcombe Blvd # 110 Houston TX 77030-4009

GROSSMAN, HERSCHEL I., economics educator; b. Phila., Mar. 6, 1939. BA with highest honors, U. Va., 1960; BPhil, U. Oxford, Eng., 1962; PhD, Johns Hopkins U., 1965. Asst. prof. econs. Brown U., Providence, R.I., 1964-69, assoc. prof. econs., 1969-73, prof. econs., 1973—, Merton P. Stoltz prof. social scis., 1980—, chmn. dept. econs., 1982-85, 86-91; rsch. assoc. Nat. Bur. Econ. Rsch., 1979—; faculty rep. NCAA, 1985-90. Author: Money, Employment and Inflation, 1976, Chinese translation, 1981, Japanese translation, 1982, Italian translation, 1982; mem. editorial bd. Jour. Monetary Econs., 1977-83, rev. editor, 1984-91; bd. editors Am. Econ. Rev., 1980-83; contbr. numerous articles to profl. jours. John Simon Guggenheim Meml. Found. fellow, 1979-80; grantee NSF, 1969, 72, 76, 78, 82, 84, U.S. Dept. Labor, 1974, 80, Social Sci. Rsch. Coun., 1982; IRIS scholar, 1991. Office: Brown U Dept Econs Box B Providence RI 02912-9079

GROSSMAN, JACK, advertising agency executive; b. N.Y.C., Mar. 22, 1925; s. Benjamin Robert and Sarah Dora (Bender) G.; m. Esther Arline Goldman, Nov. 23, 1949; children—Barbara Ruth, Neil David. B.Sc., NYU, 1950, M.B.A., 1952. With Biow Co., Inc., N.Y.C., 1952-56; mgr. sales research Biow Co., Inc., 1954-56; with William Esty Co., Inc., N.Y.C., 1956-87; mgr. research dept., then v.p. research William Esty Co., Inc., 1964-73, sr. v.p., dir. research, 1973-87; pres. MBN Research Assocs., N.Y.C., 1987—; adj. asso. prof. mktg. Pace U., 1962-74, adj. prof., 1988; adj. prof. mktg. Parsons Sch. Design, 1988; lectr. Baruch Coll., CUNY, 1990. Bd. dirs. L.I. Cons. Center, 1979—. Served with AUS, 1943-47. Decorated Bronze Star with oak leaf cluster, Purple Heart. Jewish. Home: 1025 Fifth Ave New York NY 10028-0134 Office: MBN Rsch Assocs 1025 5th Ave New York NY 10028-0134

GROSSMAN, JANICE, magazine publishing company executive; b. Montreal, Que., Can., Nov. 3, 1949; m. Daniel Rubinstein, July 11, 1978; 1 child, Lauren Alexandra. MA, NYU, 1970; BA, New Sch. Social Research, 1971. Advt. sr. exec. recruiter Merrill, Lynch, Pierce, Fenner & Smith Inc., N.Y.C., 1976-78; advt. sales rep. Ms. mag., N.Y.C., 1978-80; N.Y. advt. mgr. Ms. Mag., N.Y.C., 1980-82, advt. dir., 1982-84; advt. dir. New Woman Mag., N.Y.C., 1984-86, assoc. pub., 1986-88, became pub., 1989; became pub. In Fashion Mag., N.Y.C., 1988, N.Y. Mag., 1991; pub. Seventeen mag., N.Y.C., 1992-96; v.p., group pub. PRIMEDIA Mags., N.Y.C., 1992-96; pres. Advt. & Mktg., N.Y.C., 1996—; exec. v.p. Primedia Consumer mags., N.Y.C., 1997—; exec. v.p. of Primedia Primedia, N.Y.C., 1997; pres. advt. and mktg. Primedia Consumer mags., N.Y.C., 1996-97; mem. Am. Mag. Conf. Com. Mem. adv. bd. Strang-Cornell Breast Ctr. Mem. Fragrance Found., Fashion Group, Advt. Women N.Y., Cosmetic Exec. Women, Advt. Club N.Y. Home: 12 Colvin Rd Scarsdale NY 10583-1408 Office: Seventeen Mag 850 3d Ave New York NY 10022-6222*

GROSSMAN, JEROME BARNETT, retired service firm executive; b. Kansas City, Kans., Sept. 9, 1919; m. Marian Navran, Sept. 19, 1945; children: Jean Zeldin, Janet Zwillenberg. AB, U. Mich., 1941. Exec. v.p., gen. mgr. Helzberg's Diamond Shop Inc., 1941-66; dir. mktg. H & R Block, Inc., Kansas City, Mo., 1966-69, asst. to pres., 1969-71, exec. v.p., chief oper. officer, 1971-88, sr. exec. v.p., chief oper., 1988-89, vice chmn. of the bd., 1989-92, vice chmn. emeritus, 1992—; bd. dirs. Interim Svcs., Inc. Served to maj. USAF, 1941-45. Office: H & R Block Inc 4400 Main St Kansas City MO 64111-1812

GROSSMAN, JEROME KENT, lawyer, accountant; b. St. Louis, Apr. 15, 1953; s. Marvin and Myra Lee (Barnholtz) G.; m. Debbie Ada Kogan, Aug. 7, 1977; children: Hannah Felicia, Marni Celeste. AB cum laude, Georgetown U., 1974, JD, 1977. Bar: Mo. 1977, D.C. 1978, U.S. Ct. Claims 1979, U.S. Tax Ct. 1979, Del. 1980, U.S. Dist. Ct. Del. 1982; CPA, Mo. Acct., controller U.S. Dept. State, Washington, 1974-77; acct. Arthur Andersen & Co., St. Louis, 1977-79; mem. firm Bayard, Handelman and Murdoch, P.A., Wilmington, Del., 1979-88; ptnr. Young Conaway Stargatt & Taylor LLP, Wilmington, 1988—. Co-author: ALI-ABA Course of Study on the Reform Act of 1984, 86. V.p. Jewish Cmty. Ctr., Wilmington, 1986-

88, 89-90, treas., 1989-90, Congregation Beth Shalom, Wilmington, 1988-90, pres., 1990-92; co-chmn. Del. State Com., State of Israel Bonds, 1992-95, chmn., 1995—; treas. Jewish Fedn. Del., 1989-90; pres. Del. Gratz Hebrew H.S., 1997—; trustee Jewish Com. of Del. Endowment Fund, 1988-95; bd. dirs., trustee Del. Symphony Assn., 1998—. Fellow Am. Coll. Tax Counsel; mem. ABA (tax sect., chmn. inventories subcom. 1982-86, vice chmn. 1986-88, chmn. 1988-90, com. on tax acctg.), Del. Bar Assn. (chair sect. of taxation 1996-97), Del. Tax Inst. (planning com. 1985-86, 94—), Del. Soc. CPAs (chmn. tax com. 1980-85, com. 1985-87, 93—, ethics com. 1989-92, pres. elect 1999—), Alpha Sigma Nu. Democrat. Avocations: choir, opera, bridge. Home: 803 Westover Rd Wilmington DE 19807-2978 Office: Young Conaway Stargatt & Taylor LLP PO Box 391 Wilmington DE 19899-0391

GROSSMAN, JERROLD B., pharmaceutical executive; b. N.Y.C., Oct. 23, 1947. BA, Fairleigh Dickinson U., 1969, MBA, 1973; D of Profl. Studies in Bus. Mgmt., Pace U., 1989. Gen. mgr. Nomis Svc. Stores, Bklyn., 1969-72; fin. analyst Irving Trust Co., N.Y.C., 1972-74; sr. adminstr. Greater N.Y. blood program ARC, N.Y.C., 1974-79; dir. mktg., sales and biologic resources N.Y. Blood Ctr., 1979-85; v.p., dir. mktg. N.Am. Immuno-U.S., Inc., N.Y.C., 1985-90; pres. Genesis Bio-Pharm., Inc., Tenafly, N.J., 1990—; bd. dirs. Govan, Inc.; cons. Can. Red Cross, 1996. Author: Overview of Plasma Derivatives, 1984 (ency. sect.) Impact of Technology on the Plasma Derivative Industry, 1989, Blood and Plasma Industry, 1992-94. Bd. dirs. Temple Sinai Bergen County; mem. fin. com. Congressman Robert Torricelli, 1995-96. Sgt. N.Y. Nat. Guard, 1969-75. Mem. Am. Assn. Blood Banks.

GROSSMAN, JOEL B(ARRY), political science educator; b. N.Y.C., June 19, 1936; s. Joseph and Selma G.; m. Mary Hengstenberg, Aug. 23, 1964; children: Alison, Joanna, Daniel. BA, Queens Coll., 1957; MA, U. Iowa, 1960, PhD, 1963. Faculty dept. polit. sci. U. Wis., Madison, 1963-96; prof. U. Wis., 1971-96, chmn. dept., 1975-78; prof. Johns Hopkins U., 1996—; fellow in law and polit. sci. Harvard Law Sch., Cambridge, Mass., 1965-66; Fulbright lectr. U. Strathclyde, Glasgow, 1968-69; vis. prof. law U. Stockholm, 1973, John Hopkins U., 1995-96. Editor: Law and Soc. Review, 1978-82; author: Lawyers and Judges, 1965, Frontiers of Judicial Research, 1969, Law and Change in Modern America, 1971, Constitutional Law and Judicial Policy Making, 1972, 80, 88; contbr. articles to profl. jours. Chmn. Wis. Jud. Commn. 1985-87. Served with USAR, 1960-66. Mem. Wis. Civil Liberties Union (vice chmn. 1970-72), Am. Polit. Sci. Assn., Midwest Polit. Sci. Assn. (v.p. 1988-90), So. Polit. Sci. Assn., Law and Soc. Assn. Democrat. Home: 6606 Walnutwood Cir Baltimore MD 21212-1213

GROSSMAN, JOHN HENRY, III, obstetrician, gynecologist, educator; b. New Haven, Aug. 10, 1945; s. John Henry and Marya (Fryczynski) G.; m. Georgette Mary Czekanski, Aug. 23, 1969; children: Lisa Michelle, John Henry IV. AB, U. Rochester, 1967, MD, 1971; PhD, George Washington U., 1981, MPH, 1995. Diplomate Am. Bd. Ob-Gyn (examiner 1984—). Intern in medicine and surgery Strong Meml Hosp., U. Rochester (N.Y.), 1971-72; resident in ob-gyn. Yale U. Sch. Medicine, New Haven, 1972-75; instr. Yale U., New Haven, 1975-76; asst. prof. ob-gyn. George Washington U., Washington, 1976-81, assoc. prof., 1981-86, prof., 1986—, dir. div. maternal-fetal medicine, 1982—, prof., 1986—, chief of obstetrics, 1992—, acting chmn. microbiology and immunology, 1995—, acting dean Sch. Medicine and Health Scis., 1998—; chmn. microbiology panel div. clin. lab. devices FDA, Silver Spring, Md., 1984-87. Author: Handbook of Perinatal Infections, 1979, 2d edit., 1989. Capt. U.S. Army, 1971-77. Recipient Meade-Johnson award Meade-Johnson Inc., 1975; Rochester scholar, 1963. Fellow Am. Coll. Ob-Gyns. (chmn. course coordination com. 1986-89), Am. Bd. Obstetrics and Gynecology (examiner 1985—); mem. Soc. Prenatal Obstetricians, Infectious Disease Soc. for Ob-Gyn., Assn. Profs. of Gynecology and Obstetrics, Potomac Unit Club, Herb. Soc. Am., Phi Beta Kappa, Sigma Xi, Alpha Omega Alpha. Methodist. Avocations: gardening, military strategy, collecting bubble gum trading cards. Office: George Washington U Deans Snite Ross 713 W 2300 Eye St NW Washington DC 20037-3201

GROSSMAN, JONATHAN HAMILTON, English literature educator, researcher; b. Oxford, Eng., Apr. 17, 1967; s. Marc Winston and Penny Hemilton (Lobo) G. BA, Brown U., 1989; MA, U. Pa., 1993, PhD, 1996. Asst. prof. U. Del., Newark, 1997—. Contbr. articles to profl. jours. Mellon Dissertation fellow, 1995. Mem. MLA, Phi Beta Kappa. Office: U Del Dept English 127 Memorial Hall Newark DE 19716

GROSSMAN, LAWRENCE, biochemist, educator; b. Bklyn., Jan. 23, 1924; s. Isidor Harry and Anna (Lipkin) G.; m. Barbara Meta Mishen, June 24, 1949; children—Jon David, Carl Henry, Ilene Rebecca. Student, Coll. City N.Y., 1946-47; B.A., Hofstra U., 1949; Ph.D., U. So. Calif., 1954; postdoc., Johns Hopkins U., 1954-56. Scientist NIH, Bethesda, Md., 1956-57; asst. prof. biochemistry Brandeis U., Waltham, Mass., 1957-62; assoc. prof. Brandeis U., 1962-67, prof., 1967-75; E.V. McCollum prof. and chmn. dept. biochemistry Johns Hopkins Sch. Hygiene and Pub. Health, Balt., 1975-89, Univ. Disting. Svc. prof., 1989—; mem. sci. adv. com. Am. Cancer Soc.; adviser in biochemistry NIH; U.s. rep. to Internat. Union of Biochemistry, NAS. Author: Method in Nucleic Acids, 12 vols., since 1968; assoc. editor Cancer Rsch.; mem. editorial bd. Jour. Biol. Chemistry, Mutation Rsch.-DNA Repair, cancer rsch.; contbr. articles to profl. jours. Trustee Brandeis U. Lt. USNR, 1942-45. Decorated DFC (2), Air medal; recipient USPHS Career Devel. award, 1964-76, Merit award NIH, 1989—, Stebbins medal Pub. Health Edn.; named M. Katz lectr. in atmospheric chemistry, 1994; Dept. Energy rsch. grantee; Commonwealth fellow, 1963, Guggenheim fellow, 1973, Burroughs-Wellcome fellow, 1989. Mem. AAAS (program com.), Am. Soc. Biol. Chemistry and Molecular Biology, Am. Chem. Soc., Am. Soc. Photobiology, Environ. Mutagen Soc. Home: 5828 Pimlico Rd Baltimore MD 21209-4203 Office: 615 N Wolfe St Baltimore MD 21205-2103

GROSSMAN, LAWRENCE MORTON, nuclear engineering educator; b. N.Y.C., Aug. 2, 1922; married; 1 child. B.Chem. Engring., City Coll. N.Y., 1942, M.Sc. (Standard Oil Co. Calif. fellow), 1944; Ph.D. in Engring. Sci., U. Calif. at Berkeley, 1948. Chem. engr. E.I. du Pont de Nemours & Co., Niagara Falls, N.Y., 1942-43; instr. mech. engring. U. Calif., Berkeley, 1944-46, lectr., 1946-48, asst. prof., 1948-54, assoc. prof. mech. engring., 1954-59, prof., 1959—, chmn. dept. nuclear engring., 1969-74; Fulbright lectr. U. Delft, 1952-53; NSF Sr. research fellow Saclay Nuclear Research Center, France, 1961-62; NATO sr. fellow, 1974. Recipient Berkeley Citation, 1991. Mem. A.A.A.S., Am. Nuclear Soc. Office: U Calif Etcheverry Hall Berkeley CA 94720

GROSSMAN, LISA ROBBIN, clinical psychologist, lawyer; b. Jan. 22, 1952; d. Samuel R. and Sarah (Kruger) G. BA with highest distinction & honors, Northwestern U., 1974, JD cum laude, 1979, PhD, 1982. Bar: Ill. 1981; registered psychologist, Ill. Jud. intern U.S. Supreme Ct., Washington, 1975; pre-doctoral psychology intern Michael Reese Hosp. and Med. Ctr., Chgo., 1979-80; therapist Homes for Children, Chgo., 1980-83; psychologist Psychiat. Inst. Cir. Ct. Cook County, Chgo., 1981-87; pvt. practice Chgo., 1984—; invited participant workshop HHS, Rockville, Md., 1981. Contbr. articles to profl. jours. Mem. ABA, APA (com. on legal issues 1992-95, com. on profl. practice and stds. 1996-99, chair 1998, state leadership organizing com. 1996-98), Ill. Psychol. Assn. (pres. 1995-96), Chgo. Assn. for Psychoanalytic Psychologists (parliamentarian 1982), Ill. State Bar Assn., Chgo. Bar Assn., Soc. Personality Assessment, Mortar Bd., Phi Beta Kappa, Shi-Ai, Alpha Lambda Delta. Office: 500 N Michigan Ave Ste 1520 Chicago IL 60611-3758

GROSSMAN, MARC, diplomat; b. L.A., Sept. 23, 1951; s. Melvin and Estelle Grossman; m. Mildred Patterson, May 29, 1982; 1 child, Anne. BA, U. Calif., Santa Barbara, 1973; MSc in Internat. Rels., London Sch. Econs./Polit. Sci., 1974. Polit. officer U.S. Embassy, Islamabad, Pakistan, 1977-79; staff asst. Bur. Near Eastern and South Asian Affairs U.S. Dept. State, 1979-80; dep. spl. adviser to Pres. Carter The White House, Washington, 1980; chief profl. staff State Dept. Transition Team, 1980; country officer for Jordan Dept. of State, 1981-83; polit. officer U.S. Mission to NATO, 1983; dep. dir. pvt. office of sec. gen. NATO, 1984-86; exec. asst. to dep. sec. Dept. State, 1986-89; dep. chief U.S. Mission in Turkey, 1989-92; exec. sec., spl. asst. to sec. Dept. of State, Washington, 1993-94; U.S. amb. to Turkey Dept. of State, Ankara, 1995-97; asst. sec. for Europe and Can. affairs Dept. of State, Washington, 1997—. Mem. Am. Friends of the London Sch. of Econs., Army and Navy Club (Washington). Avocations: reading, travel, sports. *

GROSSMAN, MARC RICHARD, media consultant; b. L.A., Sept. 11, 1949; s. Morris Grossman and Esther Beatrice (Wishnow) Goldstein; m. Maria Luisa Lopez, Sept. 23, 1987; children: Joshua, Aaron, Matthew. BA, U. Calif., Irvine, 1972; M of Journalism, UCLA, 1973. Press sec., personal aide to Pres. Cesar Chavez, United Farm Workers, 1975-81; legis. cons. to Spkr. Willie Brown, Calif. Assembly, Sacramento, 1981-87; media cons. Words in Public, Sacramento, 1987—; comms. dir., spokeswoman United Farm Workers, 1993—. Ghostwriter speeches, columns and pieces for dozens of pub. figures; contbr. articles to daily newspapers and mags. Democrat. Jewish. Office: Words in Public 1700 L St Sacramento CA 95814-4024

GROSSMAN, MARY MARGARET, elementary education educator; b. East Cleveland, Ohio, Sept. 26, 1946; d. Frank Anthony and Margaret Mary (Buda) G. Student, Kent State Univ., 1965-67; BS in Elem. Edn. cum laude, Cleveland State Univ., 1971; postgrad, Lake Erie Coll., 1974-77, John Carroll Univ., 1978, 81, 82, 83, 85, Cleveland State Univ., 1985. Cert. elem. sch. tchr. grades 1 to 8, Ohio; cert. data processing, Ohio. Tchr. Cleve. Catholic Diocese, Cleve., Ohio, 1971-72, Willoughby-Eastlake Sch. Dist., Willoughby, Ohio, 1972—; participant Nat. Econ. Edn. Conf., Richmond, Va., 1995. Eucharistic min. St. Christine's Ch., Euclid, 1988—, mem. parish pastoral coun., 1995—. Recipient Samuel H. Elliott Econ. Leadership award, 1986-87, Consumer Educator award N.E. Ohio Region, 1986, 1st pl. award for excellence in tchg. Tchrs. in Am. Enterprise, 1984-85, 89-90; Martha Holden Jennings scholar, 1984-85. Mem. Edn. Computer Consortium Ohio, Nat. Edn. Assn., Ohio Edn. Assn. (human rels. award 1986-87, cert. merit 1987-88), Northeast Ohio Edn. Assn. (Positive Tchr. Image award 1988). Roman Catholic. Avocations: racquetball, softball, walking, tennis, bicycling. Home: 944 E 225th St Cleveland OH 44123-3308 Office: McKinley Elem Sch 1200 Lost Nation Rd Willoughby OH 44094-7324

GROSSMAN, NANCY, artist; b. N.Y.C.; d. Murray and Josephine G. BFA, Pratt Inst., 1962. mem. jury sculpture N.Y. State Council on Arts, 1973, Prix de Rome fellowships Am. Acad. in Rome, 1974. Exhibited in one-woman shows, Krasner Gallery, N.Y.C., 1964, 65, 65, 67, Cordier & Ekstrom, N.Y.C., 1968, 69, 71, 73, 75, 76, Church Fine Arts Gallery, U. Nev., Reno, 1978, Barbara Gladstone Gallery, N.Y.C., 1980, 82, Heath Gallery, Atlanta, 1981, 86, Terry Dintenfass Gallery, 1984, Exit Art, N.Y.C., 1991, Sculpture Ctr., N.Y.C., 1991, Hillwood Art Mus., Brookville, N.Y., 1991, Exit Art, N.Y.C., 1991, Hillwood Art Mus., Brookville, N.Y., 1991, Sculpture Ctr., N.Y.C., 1991, Artemisia, Chgo., 1992, Beacon St. Gallery, Chgo., 1992, Ark. Art Ctr., Little Rock, 1992, Contemporary Mus., Honolulu, 1992, Binghamton U. Art Gallery, 1992, Hooks-Epstein Galleries, Houston, 1993, 95, LedisFlam, N.Y.C., 1994, Weatherspoon Art Gallery, Greensboro, N.C., 1994; exhibited in numerous group shows, including, Whitney Mus. Am. Art, N.Y.C., 1968, 69, 73, 80, 81, 93, 95, Fogg Art Mus., Cambridge, Mass., 1972, Am. Acad. Arts and Letters/Nat. Inst. Arts and Letters invitational, N.Y.C., 1974, 1987, New Mus. New American Painting exhbn., Hungary, Czechoslovakia, Poland, 1978, Betté Stoler, 1983, Whitney Mus. at Phillip Morris, 1984, Exit Art, N.Y.C., 1991, Michael Rosenfeld Gallery, N.Y.C., 1996, Nat. Acad., N.Y.C., 1996; represented in permanent collections, Whitney Mus. Am. Art, Hirshhorn Mus., Washington, Smithsonian Inst., Dallas Mus. Fine Arts, Balt. Mus., Mus. Boymans Van Beuningen, Rotterdam, Netherlands, U. Calif., Berkeley, Princeton U. Art Mus., N.J., Contemporary Arts Mus., Houston, Met. Mus. Art, N.Y.C., Va. Mus. Fine Arts, Richmond, Weatherspoon Art Gallery, Greensboro, N.C., Contemporary Mus., Honolulu. Recipient Inaugural Contemporary Achievement award Pratt Inst., 1966, award AAAL and Nat. Inst. Arts and Letters, 1974, Hassam, Speicher, Betts and Symons purchase award Am. Acad. and Inst. Arts and Letters, 1989, Alumni Achievement award Pratt Inst., 1995, Joan Mitchell Found. fellowship, 1996; Ida C. Haskell scholar, 1962; Guggenheim fellow, 1965, fellow for sculpture Nat. Endowment for Arts, 1991; grantee Nat. Endowment for Arts, 1984. Mem. Nat. Acad. Address: 105 Eldridge St New York NY 10002-4405 Office: Michael Rosenfeld Gallery 24 W 57th St New York NY 10019-3918

GROSSMAN, ROBERT ALLEN, transportation executive; b. Port Jervis, N.Y., July 24, 1941; s. George and Helen (Garson) G.; m. Joan Ward, June 15, 1962 (div.); children: Jeffrey, Wendy; m. Gloria Schswartz, Nov. 22, 1987. Student, Cornell U., 1959-60, U. Pa., 1960-62. fin. divsn. North Shore Packing Co., Inc., North Bellmore, N.Y., 1962-64; mgr. refin. and legal dept. Coburn Corp. Am., Rockville Centre, N.Y., 1964-67; stockbroker Weis, Volson & Cannon, Inc., N.Y.C., 1967-69, Nadel & Co., N.Y.C., 1969-70; chmn. bd., CEO, pres. Emons Industries, Inc., York, Pa., 1970—; chmn., CEO Emons Transp. Group, 1986—; mem. exec. com., legis. policy com. Am. Assn. Shortline and Regional Railroad Assn., 1998—. Bd. dirs. Better York, Inc., 1996—. Mem. York Area C. of C. (dir. 1978-83), Pa. Chamher of Bus. and Industry (transp. com. 1991), Pa. Rail Freight (adv. com. 1993—), Keystone State Railroad Assn. (pres. 1996—). Office: 96 S George St York PA 17401-1434

GROSSMAN, ROBERT GEORGE, physician, educator; b. N.Y.C., Jan. 24, 1933; s. Ferenc and Vivian (Isenberg) G.; m. Ellin Friedman, June 26, 1955; children—Amy, Kate, Ruth. B.A., Swarthmore Coll., 1953; M.D., Columbia U., 1957. Diplomate Am. Bd. Neurosurgery. Intern Strong Meml. Hosp., Rochester, N.Y., 1957-58; resident Presbyn. Hosp., Columbia U., N.Y.C., 1960-63; acad. practice medicine, specializing in neurol. surgery Houston, 1973—; instr., assoc. prof. neurol. surgery U. Tex. SW Med. Sch., 1963-68; assoc. prof., prof. neurol. surgery Albert Einstein Coll. Medicine, 1969-73; prof., chmn. div. neurol. surgery U. Tex. Med. Br., Galveston, 1973-80; prof., chmn. dept. neurol. surgery Baylor Coll. Medicine, 1980—; chief neurosurg. service Meth. Hosp., Houston, 1980—; chmn. neurology B study sect. USPHS, NIH, 1972-74; mem. bd. sci. counsellors Nat. Inst. Neurol. Diseases and Stroke, NIH, 1989-93; mem. nat. adv. coun. Nat. Inst. Neurol. Diseases and Stroke, NIH, 1993-96. Author: (with W. D. Willis) Medical Neurobiology, 3d edit, 1981; chmn. editorial bd. Jour. Neurosurgery, 1987. Served with AUS, 1958-60. Mem. Am. Assn. Neurol. Surgeons, ACS, Soc. Univ. Surgeons, Am. Bd. Neurol. Surgery (chmn. bd. 1989-90), Am. Acad. Neurol. Surgery (v.p.), Soc. Neurol. Surgeons (pres. 1995). Home: 1821 South Blvd Houston TX 77098-5421 Office: Tex Med Ctr 6565 Fannin St Houston TX 77030-2704

GROSSMAN, ROBERT JAMES, architect; b. Spokane, Wash., Feb. 3, 1936; s. George Christian and Corinne (Shelton) G.; m. Shirley Rozelle, Aug. 7, 1956; children: Kevin James, Heidi Rozelle. B Archtl. Engring. with highest honors, Wash. State U., 1959. Lic. architect, Wash. Architect Heylman-Trogdon, Spokane, 1962-64, Trogdon-Smith, Architects, Spokane, 1964-72; prin. architect Trogdon-Smith-Grossman, TSG Architects, Spokane, 1973-83; mng. prin. N.W. Archtl. Co. (A Joint Venture), Spokane, 1979-83; pres., prin. N.W. Archtl. Co., P.S., Seattle, 1983-85, 98—, mng. prin., 1986—; coord. architect for site planning and devel. Expo'74 World's Fair, Spokane, 1971-74; mem. adv. coun. Sch. Architecture Wash. State U., Pullman, 1986-93, mem. adv. bd. Coll. Engring. and Architecture, 1991—. Prin. works include 15 elem. schs., Spokane, sch. projects, pvt. and pub. projects. Bd. dirs., pres. Salvation Army-Booth Care Ctr., Spokane, 1972-85; bd. dirs. Med. Svc. Corp., Spokane, 1984-86; mem. state adv. bd. Lien Law Reform, 1990; founding pres. Downtown Exch. Club of Seattle Found., 1990—; mem. adv. bd. for master planning Children's Hosp., Seattle, 1991-94; chair Wash. State Archs. and Engrs. Legis. Coun., 1994-97. 1st lt. C.E., U.S. Army, 1960-62. Recipient Disting. Svc. award Govt. State of Wash. and State Commn. for Expo '74, 1974. Mem. AIA (pres. Spokane chpt. 1976), Wash. State Coun. Architects (bd. dirs. 1975-78), Wash. State U. Alumni Assn. (Alumni Achievement award 1990), Exch. Club (bd. dirs. 1988-91). Avocations: travel, music. Office: NW Archtl Co 2201 6th Ave Ste 1405 Seattle WA 98121-1847

GROSSMAN, ROBERT LOUIS, lawyer; b. Cleve., Dec. 20, 1954; s. Sidney and Lillian Belle (Davis) G.; m. Rochelle Carol Shear, Nov. 7, 1987; children: Zachary, Jonathan, David, Andrew. BA with honors, Ohio State U., 1975, JD with Honors, 1978, MA with honors, 1979. Bar: Ohio 1978, U.S. Ct. Appeals (5th cir.) 1979, Fla. 1982. Law clk. U.S. Dist. Ct. (so. dist.) Ohio, Columbus, 1977-78; sr. atty. U.S. Govt. EEOC, Houston, 1979-82; shareholder Greenberg, Traurig, Hoffman, Lipoff, Rosen & Quentel, P.A., Miami, 1982—. Editor: Florida Corporate Practice, 2d edit., 1991. Chmn. South Dade Jewish Leadership Coun., 1997-99; bd. dirs. Greater Miami Jewish Fedn. South Dade, Miami, 1987—, campaign chmn., 1995-97; bd. dirs. Greater Miami Jewish Fedn., 1995—, exec. com., 1997-99, Alper Jewish Comm. Ctr., 1997-99, exec. com., 1998—. Donald Becker Meml. scholar Ohio State U., 1975, 76, fellow, 1978. Mem. ABA (corp. securities sect.), Fla. Bar Assn., Dade County Bar Assn., Order of Coif. Avocations: sports, reading, travel. Office: Greenberg Traurig 1221 Brickell Ave Miami FL 33131-3224

GROSSMAN, ROBERT MAYER, lawyer; b. Chgo., Oct. 16, 1934; s. Raymond Mandel and Frances Ruth (Krucoff) G.; m. Frances Ann Rosenbacher, Mar. 17, 1963; children—Theodore, Anthony, Kate. A.B., Dartmouth Coll., 1956; LL.B., Yale U., 1961. Bar: Ill, 1961. Law clk. U.S. Dist. Ct. Judge Hubert L. Will, 1961-63; assoc. Schiff, Hardin, Waite, Dorschel & Britton, 1963-66; exec. dir. Ill. Legis. Commn. Low Income Housing, 1966-67; ptnr. Grossman, Kasakoff, Magid & Silverman, 1968-70; mng. ptnr. Roan & Grossman, Chgo., 1970-83; sr. ptnr. Keck, Mahin & Cate, Chgo., 1983-95, of counsel, 1995-97; counsel to Gardner, Carton & Douglas, Chgo., 1997—; prin. draftsman Ill. Housing Devel. Act, 1967; gen. counsel Dermatology Found., 1979—; gen. counsel Ill. Housing Devel. Authority, 1967-69, 73-77; adj. prof. Chgo. Theol. Sem., 1996—. Author: Jeshua, Our Brother, 1989, Opening the Door, 1991, Widening the Path, 1997. V.p., bd. dirs. Hyde Park Coop Soc., 1977-81; chmn. by mayoral appointment Hyde Park-Kenwood Conservation Community Coun., 1991—; bd. dirs. Chgo. Theol. Sem., 1989—, No. Ill. region NCCJ, 1989—; chmn. Coun. for Jewish-Christian Studies Ctr., 1991—. Lt. (j.g.) USNR, 1956-58. Mem. Chgo. Bar Assn., Law Club, Standard Club, Quadrangle Club. Jewish. Home: 5529 S Kimbark Ave Chicago IL 60637-1618

GROSSMAN, RUTH KOSTIK, medical education company executive; b. N.Y.C., June 15, 1949; d. Nathan and Hannah (Klein) Kostik; m. Andrew Jay Grossman, July 8, 1977; 1 child, Dane Nolan. BS, Hunter Coll., 1983. Assoc. editor Sci. and Medicine Pub. Co., N.Y.C., 1972-76; sr. editor Medcom Inc., N.Y.C., 1976-77; prin. Ruth Grossman & Assoc., N.Y.C., 1977-86; copywriter William Douglas McAdams, N.Y.C., 1986-88; v.p., group project dir. Health Sci. Comms., N.Y.C., 1989-93; pres. Signa Programs, N.Y.C., 1993-96; assoc. pub. Elsevier Sci. Inc., N.Y.C., 1996-97; pres. ACG Signa, N.Y.C., 1997—. Mem. Nat. Assn. Sci. Writers, Healthcare Businesswomens Assn., Healthcare Marketers Coun. Office: ACG Signa 375 Hudson St New York NY 10014-3658

GROSSMAN, SANFORD, retired lawyer; b. N.Y.C., July 4, 1929; s. Philip and Irene (Hare) G.; m. Barbara Rothman, May 23, 1951; children: Daniel J., Donna A. Student, NYU, 1947-49; LL.B., Bklyn. Law Sch., 1952. Bar: N.Y. 1953, U.S. Supreme Ct. 1964. Pvt. practice law N.Y.C., 1954-79; ptnr. Simpson Thacher & Bartlett, N.Y.C., 1979-90, of counsel, 1991-93, retired, 1993. Served with U.S. Army, 1952-54. Mem. Assn. Bar City N.Y., N.Y. County Lawyers Assn., Westchester Bar Assn., Am. Coll. Real Estate Lawyers, Princeton Club (N.Y.C.). Office: Simpson Thacher & Bartlett 425 Lexington Ave Fl 14 New York NY 10017-3954

GROSSMAN, SANFORD JAY, economics educator; b. Bklyn., July 21, 1953; s. Sloane and Florence G.; m. Naava. B.A. in Econs. with honors, U. Chgo., 1973, M.A. in Econs., 1974, Ph.D. in Econs., 1975. Asst. prof. econs. Stanford U., Calif., 1975-77; economist Bd. Govs. Fed. Res., 1977-78; assoc. prof. econs. U. Pa., Phila., 1978-79, prof. econs., 1979-81; prof. econs. U. Chgo., 1981-85; John L. Weinberg prof. econs. Princeton U., N.J., 1985-89; Steinberg trustee prof. fin. U. Pa., Phila., 1989—; dir. Wharton Ctr. Quantitative Finance, 1994—; pub. dir., bd. dirs. Chgo. Bd. Trade, 1992-95. Mem. editl. bd. Finance India, 1994—; mem. adv. bd. Math. Finance, 1994—; contbr. articles to profl. jours. Recipient Irving Fisher grad. monograph award; award for best article Graham and Dodd Scroll, Fin. Analyst Jour., 1988, Q Group, Roger F. Murray 1st Prize award, 1988; Guggenheim Meml. fellow, Sloan Found. fellow, Am. Econometric Soc. fellow, 1980. Fellow AAAS, Econometric Soc.; mem. Am. Fin. Assn. (v.p. 1992, pres.-elect 1993, pres. 1994, bd. dirs.), Am. Econ. Assn. (John Bates Clark medal). Office: U Pa Dept Fin 3620 Locust Walk Philadelphia PA 19104-6302*

GROSSMAN, STEVEN, company executive, political party executive; m. Barbara Wallace; children: David, Benjamin, Joshua. AB cum laude, Princeton U., 1967; MBA with distinction, Harvard U., 1969. Pres. Mass. Envelope Co. Mem. Dem. Nat. Com., 1989-92, chmn., 1997-99; chmn. Mass. State Dem. Party, 1991-92; mem. Dem. Platform Com. and Drafting Com., 1992; past pres. Am. Israel Pub. Affairs Com.; trustee Brandeis U., Beth Israel Hosp.; overseer Mus. Fine Arts, Boston; bd. dirs. Combined Jewish Philanthropies of Greater Boston; mem. exec. com. Anti-Defamation League, New Eng. Baker scholar. Jewish. E-mail: grossman@www.democrats.org. Home: 30 Cobble Hill Rd Somerville MA 02143-4412 Office: 430 S Capitol St SE Washington DC 20003-4024

GROSSMAN, THEODORE MARTIN, lawyer; b. N.Y.C., Dec. 31, 1949; s. Albert and Sylvia Pia (Greenstein) G.; m. Linda Gail Steinbook, Dec. 5, 1976; children: Andrew Scott, Michael Steven. AB, Cornell U., 1971, JD, 1974. Bar: N.Y. 1975, U.S. Ct. Appeals (D.C. cir.) 1981, U.S. Ct. Appeals (2nd cir.) 1982, U.S. Ct. Appeals (5th cir.) 1984, U.S. Dist. Ct. (no. dist.) Ohio 1986, Ohio 1987, U.S. Dist. Ct. (so. dist.) N.Y. 1988, U.S. Dist. Ct. (ea. dist.) N.Y. 1988, U.S. Ct. Appeals (6th cir.) 1988. Assoc. Debevoise, Plimpton, Lyons & Gates, N.Y.C., 1974-77, Rosenman Colin Freund Lewis & Cohen, N.Y.C., 1977-80; trial and appellate counsel fed. programs br. of civil div. U.S. Dept. Justice, Washington, 1980-84; assoc. Jones, Day, Reavis & Pogue, Cleve., 1984-86, ptnr., 1987—. Editor Cornell U. Law Rev., 1974. Trustee Cleve. Ctr. for Contemporary Art, 1992-96, treas., 1992-94. Mem. ABA. Home: 2979 Broxton Rd Cleveland OH 44120-1819 Office: Jones Day Reavis & Pogue 901 Lakeside Ave E Cleveland OH 44114-1116*

GROSSMAN, WILLIAM, medical researcher, educator; b. N.Y.C., 1940. MD, Yale U., 1965. Intern Peter Bent Brigham Hosp., Boston, 1965-66, resident in medicine, 1968-69, rsch. fellow in cardiology, 1969-71; dir. cardiac catheterization labs. N.C. Meml. Hosp., Chapel Hill, 1971-75, Peter Bent Brigham Hosp., Boston, 1975-81; chief cardiovasc. divsn. Beth Israel Hosp., Boston, 1981-94; tchg. fellow in medicine Harvard U., Boston, 1968-71, assoc. prof., 1975-81, prof., 1981-84, Herman Dana prof. medicine, 1984-94; exec. dir. cardiovasc. rsch. Merck & Co., West Point, Pa., 1994-95, v.p., 1996-97; prof. medicine U. Calif., San Francisco, 1997—; chief cardiology U. Calif. San Francisco Med. Ctr., 1997—; adj. prof. U. Pa., 1995-97. Served as sr. asst. surgeon USPHS, 1966-68. Fellow Am. Coll. Cardiology, Am. Heart Assn., Assn. Am. Physicians, Am. Physiol. Soc., Am. Soc. Clin. Investigation. Office: UCSF Med Ctr Dept Cardiology 505 Parnassus Ave San Francisco CA 94143-0124

GROSSMANN, IGNACIO EMILIO, chemical engineering educator; b. Mexico City, Nov. 12, 1949; s. Donat and Marie-Louise (Epper) G.; m. Ignacio E. Blanca Espinal, Nov. 26, 1977; children: Claudia, Andrew, Thomas. BSc ChemE, U. Iberoamericana, 1974; MSc ChemE, Imperial Coll., 1975, hon. diploma, 1975, PhD ChemE, 1977. Research and devel. engr. Inst. Mexicano del Petroleo, Mexico City, 1978; asst. prof. chem. engring. Carnegie Mellon U., Pitts., 1979-83, assoc. prof., 1983-86, prof., 1986-90, Rudolph R. and Florence Dean prof. chem. engring., 1990—, head dept. chem. engring., 1994—; Robert W. Vaughan lectr. Calif. Inst. Tech., Pasadena, 1986; Mary Upson vis. prof. engring. Cornell U., Ithaca, N.Y., 1986-87; acad. trustee Computer Aids for Chem. Engring. Edn. (CACHE), Austin, Tex., 1983—; mem. governing bd. Coun. for Chem. Rsch. Editor: CACHE Design Case Studies; mem. editorial bd. Computers and Chem. Engring. Jour., 1987—, Jour. Global Optimization, 1991—; author more than 170 tech publs. Recipient Presdl. Young Investigator award NSF, Washington, 1984. Mem. AIChE (chmn. computing and systems tech. div. 1992, Computing in Chem. Engring. award 1994, William H. Walker award 1997), Am. Chem. Soc., Mex. Acad. Engring., Sigma Xi. Roman Catholic. Avocations: classical music. Home: 6385 Douglas St Pittsburgh PA 15217-1821 Office: Carnegie Mellon Univ Dept of Chem Engring Pittsburgh PA 15213

GROSSNICKLE, TED RICHARD, non-profit consulting company executive; b. Wabash, Ind., Feb. 10, 1951; s. Harry L. and Helen Edith (Hirshy)

G.; m. Marcia L. Kessler, July 12, 1975; children: Douglas, Lee. BA, Wabash Coll., 1973; MA in Pub. Adminstrn., No. Ill. U., 1983. With field offices divsn. Proctor and Gamble, Cin., 1973-74; admissions officer Wabash Coll., Crawfordsville, Ind., 1974-76; dir. spl. giving No. Ill. U., DeKalb, 1976-83; v.p. devel. and pub. affairs Franklin (Ind.) Coll., 1983-94, acting exec. v.p., 1993; mng. ptnr. Johnson, Grossnickle & Assoc., Franklin, 1994-95, pres., 1995—; cons. in field, 1989-94. Bd. dirs. Presdl. Classroom for Young Americans, 1995—, Leadership Johnson County. Named Sagamore of the Wabash, Gov. of Ind., 1994, Hon. Alumnus, Franklin Coll., 1994, Fundraising Exec. of Yr., Ind./Nat. Soc. Fund Raising Execs., 1994; USIS exch. fellow Republic of Italy, 1997, 98. Mem. Lambda Chi Alpha (bd. dirs. 1996—). Presbyterian. Avocations: reading, water sports, Civil War history, biking. Office: Johnson Grossnickle and Assocs PO Box 576 Franklin IN 46131-0576

GROSSO, JAMES ALAN, information technology executive; b. Chgo., Aug. 29, 1948; s. George Alfred and Adrienne Cecelia (Ryan) G.; m. Mary Kathryn Prodehl, July 4, 1970; children: Gabriel James, Adam George, Michael Francis. BA, Loyola U., 1972. Estimator Fel-Pro, Inc., Skokie, Ill., 1972-76, indsl. engr., 1976-80, dept. mgr., 1980-92, fin. projects mgr., 1992-95; sales and mktg. mgr. electronic commerce Kanbay, Inc., Chgo., 1996-98, sr. project mgr., 1998—; project team chair Automotive Industry Action Group, Southfield, Mich., 1991-96, chmn. supplier support group Chgo. chpt., 1988-95. Contbr. articles to profl. jours. 2d lt. USAR, 1972. Recipient Outstanding Achievement award Automotive Industry Action Group, 1990, 94. Mem. Soc. Mfg. Engrs. (sr.), Project Mgmt. Inst., Am. Mensa Ltd. Avocations: acoustic string instruments, long distance running. Office: Kanbay Inc 6666 N Western Ave Chicago IL 60645

GROSSWEINER, LEONARD IRWIN, physicist, educator; b. Atlantic City, Aug. 16, 1924; s. Jules H. and Rae (Goldberger) G.; m. Bess Tornheim, Sept. 9, 1951; children-Karen Ann, Jane (dec.), James Benjamin, Eric William. B.S., Coll. City N.Y., 1947; M.S., Ill. Inst. Tech., 1950, Ph.D., 1955. Asst. chemist Argonne Nat. Lab., Ill., 1947-50; assoc. physicist Argonne Nat. Lab., 1950-57; assoc. prof. physics Ill. Inst. Tech., Chgo., 1957-62; prof. physics Ill. Inst. Tech., 1962-95, rsch. prof. physics, 1995-96, emeritus prof., 1996—, chmn. dept. physics, 1970-81, Sang Exchange lectr., 1972-73; rsch. dir. Wenske Laser Ctr. Ravenswood Hosp. Med. Ctr., Chgo., 1986—; vis. prof. radiology Stanford U. Sch. Medicine, 1979; vis. prof. physics U. Ill. Coll. Medicine, 1983-88; adj. prof. biomed. engring. Northwestern U. Tech. Inst., Evanston, Ill., 1987—; cons. Donner Lab. U. Calif., Berkeley, Chgo. Med. Sch., North Chicago, Ill., Hines VA Hosp., Ill., Michael Reese Med. Ctr., Chgo., U.S. Com. on Interagy. Radiation Research and Policy Coordination; mem. U.S. Nat. Com. Photobiology, 1977-81, chmn., 1980-81; trustee Midwest Bio-Laser Inst., 1983—, sec., 1986-97, v.p., 1997—. Author: Organic Photoconductors in Electrophotography, 1970, The Science of Phototherapy, 1994; contbr. articles to profl. jours.; mem. editl. bd. Jour. Irreproducible Results, 1995—. Served with AUS, 1944-46. Fellow Am. Phys. Soc. (sec.-treas. div. biol. physics 1972-76, vice chmn. 1976-77, chmn. 1977-78), Am. Soc. Laser Medicine and Surgery, N.Y. Acad. Scis.; mem. AAAS, Am. Chem. Soc., Radiation Rsch. Soc., Midwest Bio-Laser Inst. (exec. com. 1985-86, sec. 1986-96, v.p. 1997—), Am. Soc. Photobiology (coun. 1977-80, sec.-treas. 1981-86, pres.-elect 1986-87, pres. 1987-88, past pres. 1988-89), Biophys. Soc., Inter-Am. Photochem. Soc. (exec. com. 1976-78), Sigma Xi (disting. faculty lectr. 1970). Home: 231 Wentworth Ave Glencoe IL 60022-1931

GROSVENOR, GILBERT MELVILLE, journalist, educator, business executive; b. Washington, May 5, 1931; s. Melville Bell and Helen (Rowland) G.; m. Donna C. Kerkam, June 16, 1961 (div.); children: Gilbert Hovey II, Alexandra Rowland; m. Wiley Jarman, June 1, 1979; 1 child, Graham Dabney. BA, Yale U., 1954; D in Pub. Svc. (hon.), George Washington U., 1983; LHD (hon.), U. Colo., 1983, Curry Coll., 1984; LLD (hon.), Coll. of Wooster, Ohio, 1983; LHD (hon.), Coll. William and Mary, 1987, Miami U., Oxford, Ohio, 1988, Syracuse U., 1989, R.I. Coll., 1991, Old Dominion U., 1993, Longwood Coll., Worcester, Mass., 1997. With Nat. Geog. Soc., 1954—, trustee, 1966—, v.p., 1966-80, assoc. editor, 1967-70, editor, 1970-80, pres., 1980-96, chmn. bd. dirs., 1987—; bd. dirs. Chevy Chase Bank, FSB, Marriott Internat., Inc., Saul Ctrs., Inc., Ethyl Corp.; former fellow Yale Corp. Trustee Nat. Wildflower Rsch. Ctr., Fed. City Coun., B.F. Saul Real Estate Trust, Saul Ctrs., Inc., Wildlife Conservation Soc.; past vice chmn. Pres.'s Commn. Ams. Outdoors; chmn. emeritus, found. bd. Alexander Graham Bell Assn. for Deaf; bd. dirs. Conservation Fund, Environments Project, Dian Fossey Gorilla Fund Internat.; bd. visitors Duke U. Nicholas Sch. Environ.; former bd. visitors Coll. William and Mary; ann. corp. mem. Children's Hosp.; former mem. Pres.'s Commn. Environ. Quality; mem. Washington Cathedral Bldg. Com. Recipient Editor of Year award Nat. Press Photographers Assn., 1975, Disting. Achievement award U. So. Calif. Sch. Journalism and Alumni Assn., 1977, Pres. medal George Washington U., 1993, Golden Plate award Am. Acad. Achievement, 1996. Mem. Assn. Am. Geographers, Explorers Club (citation of merit 1997), Newcomen Soc., Alfalfa Club, Alibi Club, Cosmos Club, Chevy Chase Club (Md.). Office: Nat Geog Soc 1145 17th St NW Washington DC 20036-4701

GROSZ, BARBARA JEAN, computer science educator; b. Phila., July 21, 1948; d. Joseph Eugene and Judith Phyllis (Zander) Gross. AB in Math., Cornell U., 1969; MA in Computer Sci., U. Calif., Berkeley, 1971, PhD in Computer Sci., 1977. Rsch. mathematician Artificial Intelligence Ctr., SRI Internat., Stanford, Calif., 1973-77, computer scientist, 1981-82, sr. computer scientist, 1981-82, program dir. nat. lang. and representation, 1982-83, sr. staff scientist, 1983-86; co-founder, mem. exec. com., prin. researcher Ctr. for Study of Lang. and Info. Stanford U. and SRI Internat., 1983-86; Gordon McKay prof. computer sci. divsn. engring. and applied scis. Harvard U., Cambridge, Mass., 1986—, interim assoc. dean for affirmative action, 1993-94; vis. faculty dept. computer sci. Stanford U., fall 1982, cons. assoc. prof. computer sci. and linguistics, 1984-85, computer sci., 1985-87; vis. scholar dept. computer and info. sci. U. Pa., Jan.-June 1982; conf. chair Internat. Joint Conf. on Artificial Intelligence (IJCAI-91), chair bd. trustees IJCAI Inc., 1989-91, mem. bd. trustees, 1987-97, program com. 1982; Harold Perlman vis. prof. faculty sci. Hebrew U., Jerusalem, 1992; invited spkr. numerous nat. and internat. profl. assns., confs., symposia; reviewer program proposals NSF; participant adv. meetings for rsch. and funding various govtl. agys. Author: (with others) Elements of Discourse Understanding, 1982, Understanding Spoken Language, 1982, Foundations of Cognitive Science, 1988, Intentions in Communications, 1988; editor: (with Sparck Jones, Webber) Readings in Natural Language Processing, 1986; assoc. editor: Ann. Rev. Computer Sci.; editl. bd.: Artificial Intelligence, Am. Jour. Computational Linguistics, 1981-83; contbr. articles and papers to profl. jours., workshops and conf. procs. Recipient Disting. Alumna award Computer Sci. & Engring., U. Calif., Berkeley, 1997. Fellow AAAS, Am. Assn. Artificial Intelligence (exec. coun. 1981-84, 86-89, pres.-elect 1991-93, pres. 1993-95, past pres. 1995-97); mem. NRC (computer sci. & telecom. bd. 1994-98), Assn. Computational Linguistics (exec. com. 1986-88), Assn. Computing Machinery (vice chair 1979-81, chair 1981-83). Avocations: hiking, wildflower photography, snorkeling. Office: Harvard U Div Engring and Applied Sci 40 Oxford St Cambridge MA 02138-1903

GROSZ, EDWARD M., bishop; b. Buffalo, N.Y., Feb. 16, 1945. Student, St. John Vianney Sem., Notre Dame U. Ordained priest Roman Catholic Ch., 1971. Titular bishop Morosbisdus and aux. bishop Buffalo, N.Y., 1990—. Office: Chancery Office 795 Main St Buffalo NY 14203-1215

GROSZ, PHILIP J., lawyer; b. Oshkosh, Wis., Feb. 1, 1952; s. Joseph Otto and Marjorie (Berkhoel) G.; m. Linda Marie Ondrejka, Dec. 29, 1973. BA with honors, U. Wis., 1973; JD, Yale Law Sch., 1977. Bar: Calif. Ptnr. Loeb & Loeb, L.A., 1983-92, mng. ptnr., 1992-96, founder, bd. dirs. Love is Feeding Everyone, L.A., 1983-94. Mem. Calif. Bar Assn. Democrat. Office: Loeb & Loeb 10100 Santa Monica Blvd Ste 2200 Los Angeles CA 90067-4164

GROTE, RICHARD CHARLES, management consultant, educator, radio commentator; b. N.Y.C., Dec. 14, 1941; s. Charles Henry and Muriel (Steele) G.; m. Jacqueline Center, May 11, 1991. BA, Colgate U., 1959; M Liberal Arts, So. Meth. U., 1992. Pers. mgr. GE, Schenectady, 1964-67; mgr. mgmt. devel. United Air Lines, Chgo., 1967-72; mgr. tng. and devel. Frito-Lay, Inc., Dallas, 1972-77; pres. Performance Systems Corp., Dallas, 1977-87; prin. Grote Cons., Dallas, 1987—; adj. prof. U. Dallas Grad. Sch. Mgmt., 1977—; commentator NPR, 1993—; reviewer Inst. Mus. Svcs., 1974-77. Author: Positive Discipline, 1985, Discipline Without Punishment, 1995, The Complete Guide to Performance Appraisal, 1996; host (film series) Respect and Responsibility, The Complete Guide to Performance Appraisal, 1996; also articles. Trustee, pres. Schaumburg (Ill.) Pub. Libr., 1969-72; bd. dirs. Shakespeare Festival Dallas, 1981-84, Dallas Opera, 1981-88; chmn. So. Meth. U. Conservatory Soc., 1988—; bd. councillors U. Dallas, 1989—. Recipient Torch award ASTD, 1979, Disting. Svc. award Malaysian Soc. for Tng. and Devel., 1984, Bapindo award Govt. of Indonesia, 1984. Republican. Office: The Madison 15851 Dallas Pkwy Ste 600 Addison TX 75001-3369

GROTEN, BARNET, energy company executive; b. Bklyn., Oct. 25, 1933; s. Irving and Pearl G.; m. Iris Diane Brand, Aug. 1955; children: Eric Allen, Kurt David, Jessica Amy. BS, Bklyn. Coll., 1954; PhD, Purdue U., 1961. Joined Exxon Co., various locations, 1961; dir. research and bus. devel. Tex. Eastern Corp., Houston, 1977-87; exec. v.p. Tex. Eastern Devel., Inc., 1980-87; sec. Gulf Univs. Research Consortium, 1980-81, chmn. bd., 1982-83; exec. dir. Energy Ctr. U. Okla., Norman, 1987-91; v.p. Energy Internat., Inc., Bellevue, Wash., 1991-99, Grait Techs., LLC, Bellevue, 1999—. Contbr. articles to profl. jours. Mem. Gov.'s Energy Adv. Coun.; chmn. Natural Gas Vehicle Task Force. Office: Grait Techs LLC 13706 NE 36 Pl Bellevue WA 98005-1413

GROTH, ALEXANDER JACOB, political science educator; b. Warsaw, Poland, Mar. 7, 1932; came to U.S., 1947; s. Jacob and Maria (Hazenfuss) Goldwasser; m. Marilyn Ann Wineburg, Dec. 15, 1961; children: Stevin James, Warren Adrian. BA magna cum laude, CCNY, 1954; MA, Columbia U., 1955, PhD, 1960. Instr. polit. sci. Trinity Coll., Hartford, Conn., 1957-58, CUNY, 1960-61; asst. prof. Harpur Coll., Binghamton, N.Y., 1961-62, U. Calif., Davis, 1962—; cons. Ency. Am., Danbury, Conn., 1966—. Author: Comparative Politics, 1971, Major Ideologies, 1971, 2d rev. edit., 1983, People's Poland, 1972, Progress and Chaos, 1984, Lincoln: Authoritarian Savior, 1995, Democracies Against Hitler, 1999; co-author: Contemporary Politics: Europe, 1976, Comparative Resource allocation, 1984, Public Policy Across Nations, 1985; editor: Revolution and Political Change, 1996; contbr. numerous articles to encys., scholarly jours. Recipient Ward medal dept. govt. CCNY, 1954; grantee Am. Co. Learned Socs. and Social Sci. Research Council, 1965-66. Mem. Western Polit. Sci. Assn., Policy Studies Assn., Far West Slavic Assn., Jewish Fellowship of Davis, Phi Beta Kappa. Republican. Avocations: baseball, baseball history, research and writing. Home: 1848 Rushmore Ln Davis CA 95616-6654 Office: U Calif Dept Polit Sci Davis CA 95616

GROTH, JON QUENTIN, management consultant; b. Washington, Aug. 29, 1941; s. Quentin Neil and Rena Gladys (Lund) G.; m. Karrell Sue Keeney, Sept. 5, 1985; children: Jennifer, Kristen, Kendall. Student, Ohio U., 1959-60, 62-63, Baldwin-Wallace Coll., 1964. Asst. mgr. Ins. Co. of N. Am., Phila., 1966-72; regional mgr. Ryan Ins. Group, Chgo., 1972-79; asst. sec. Cin. Ins. Co., 1979-85; exec. v.p., chief ops. officer Cin. Equitable Ins. Co., 1985-90; chmn., CEO Metanoia Assocs., Inc., Cin., 1991—; COO, CEO Concept 3 Ins. Agy., Inc., 1996—; COO Concept 3 Fin. Svcs., Inc., 1996—. Chmn., CEO Metanoia Ministries. Avocation: amateur radio. Home: 9968 Arbor Montgomery Ln Cincinnati OH 45249-8018

GROTH, MARK ADAM, audio visual specialist, photographer; b. Evanston, Ill., Aug. 5, 1950; s. Carl Adam and Marjorie Dreyer G.; m. Kathy Hackwith, Sept. 30, 1973; children: Christian Galen, Jessie Addis. BA, Rockford Coll., 1972. Photographer Philmont Scout Ranch, Cimarron, N.Mex., 1972; audio/visual producer and dir. U. Colo. Health Scis. Ctr., Colo. Psychiat. Hosp., Denver, 1976—. Photographer (book) Philmont, Where Spirits Soar, 1989; prodr., dir. (videotape) Depression...Navajo, 1994 (Bronze award 1994), others. Scoutmaster troop 630 Boy Scouts Am., Aurora, Colo., 1998—; vol. videographer, photographer Ponderosa Elem. Sch., Aurora, 1990—. With U.S. Army. Mem. Internat. TV Assn. Democrat. Avocations: skiing, photography, guitar, reading. E-mail: mark.groth@uchsc.edu. Home: 2108 S Joliet Ct Aurora CO 80014 Office: U Colo Health Scis Ctr Colo Psychiat Hosp 4200 E 9th Ave Denver CO 80262

GROTHAUS, PAMELA SUE, marketing professional; b. Alameda, Calif., Mar. 25, 1958; d. Michael James and Patricia Ann (Owsley) Spillers; m. David Michael Grothaus, June 3, 1977; children: Shannon Marie, Matthew David. Student, Webster U., Webster Groves, Mo., 1984-86, Cen. Mo. State U., 1976-77, St. Louis Community Coll., 1981-83. With U.S. Civil Svc., K.I. Sawyer AFB, Mich., 1979-80; adminstrv. asst. Mo. Dept. Consumer Affairs, Jefferson City, Mo., 1980-81; adminstrv. coord. Baur Properties, Inc., St. Louis, 1981-82; account exec. Atkinson Group Inc., St. Louis, 1982-87; advt. coord. Eveready Battery Co., St. Louis, 1987; advt. officer Mercantile Bancorporation, Inc., St. Louis, 1987-88; copywriter, sr. account exec. Wilson Sculley Assoc. Inc., 1989-91; mktg. mgr., copywriter Nehmen-Kodner, Inc., St. Louis, 1991-92; dir. mktg. and creative svcs. AdSell, St. Louis, 1993-94; account supr. Wilson Sculley Assocs., St. Louis, 1994-95, Clarion Direct, St. Louis, 1995-97; exec. dir. Direct Mktg. Assn. St. Louis, 1998—. Fitness instr. YMCA, Webster Grove, 1988-89. Mem. Direct Mktg. Assn. St. Louis (pres., bd. dirs. 1995). Republican. Roman Catholic. Avocations: aerobics, reading, music. Home and Office: 3921 Carey Ave Cheyenne WY 82001

GROTTA, SANDRA BROWN, interior designer; m. Louis William Grotta. Pres. S.G. Interiors, New Vernon, N.J., 1964—. Mem. Am. Soc. Interior Designers.

GROTTEROD, KNUT, retired paper company executive; b. Sarpsborg, Norway, Feb. 12, 1922; emigrated to Can., 1945, naturalized, 1954; s. Klaus and Maria Magdalena (Thoresen) G.; m. Isabel Edwina MacMaster, Feb. 25, 1950; children: Ingrid, Christopher, Karen. Grad., Tech. Coll., Horten, Norway, 1945; BME, McGill U., Can., 1949, postgrad, 1951; DSc (hon.), U. Maine, 1987; Exec. in Residence (hon.), U. New Brunswick, 1989. With Consol. Bathurst Ltd. Que., 1951-70; v.p. prodn., gen. mgr. N.S. Forest Industries, Port Hawkesbury, 1970-73; v.p. mfg. Fraser Cos. Ltd., Edmundston, N.B., Can., 1973-75, sr. v.p. ops., 1975-80; exec. v.p. Fraser Inc., Edmundston, 1980-85, pres., chief operating officer, 1985-87, chmn., chief exec. officer; chmn. bd. Atlantic Waferboard, Chatam, N.B., 1985-87, Island Paper Mills, Vancouver, B.C., 1985-87, Alta. Newsprint Co. Ltd., Whitecourt, 1988-90, Rsch. and Productivcity Coun., Fredericton, N.B., 1986—, Incutech Brunswick, 1988-94, Potato Devel. and Mktg. Coun., Fredericton, 1989-90. Bd. dirs. Canadian-Scandinavian Found., Montreal, 1974-75, v.p., 1975-77, pres., 1978-94; mem. bd. govs. U. New Brunswick. With Norwegian Underground Army, 1941-45. Mem. N.B. Forest Products Assn. (dir. 1983-88, pres. 1985-88), Can. Pulp and Paper Assn., Corp. Profl. Engrs. of Province of Que. and N.B., Rotary Internat. (dist. gov. 1996-97). Home: 67 Castleton Ct, Fredericton, NB Canada E3B 6H3 Office: Rsch & Productivity Coun, 921 College Hill Rd, Fredericton, NB Canada E3B 5H1

GROTZINGER, LAUREL ANN, university librarian; b. Truman, Minn., Apr. 15, 1935; d. Edward F. and Marian Gertrude (Greeley) G. BA, Carleton Coll., 1957; MS, U. Ill., 1958, PhD, 1964. Instr., asst. libr. Ill. State U., 1958-62; asst. prof. Western Mich. U., Kalamazoo, 1964-66; assoc. prof. Western Mich. U., 1966-68, prof., 1968—, asst. dir. Sch. Librarianship, 1965-72, chief rsch. officer, 1979-86, interim dir. Sch. Libr. and Info. Sci., 1982-86, dean grad. coll., 1979-92, prof. univ. libr., 1993—. Author: The Power and the Dignity, 1966; mem. editl. bd. Jour. Edn. for Librarianship, 1973-77, Dictionary Am. Libr. Biography, 1975-77, Mich. Academician, 1990—; contbr. articles to profl. jours. Trustee Kalamazoo Pub. Libr., 1991-93, v.p., 1991-92, pres., 1992-93; pres. Kalamazoo Bach Festival, 1996-97, bd. dirs. 1992-98, exec. com. 1996-98. Mem. ALA (sec.-treas. Libr. History Round Table 1973-74, vice chmn., chmn-elect 1983-84, chmn. 1984-85, mem.-at-large 1991-93), Spl. Librs. Assn., Assn. Libr. Info. Sci. Edn., Mich. acad. Sci., Arts and Letters (mem.-at-large, exec. com. 1980-86, pres. 1983-85, exec. com. 1990-94, pres. 1991-93, vice chmn. libr./info. scis. 1996-97, chair 1997-98), Internat. Assn. Torch Clubs (v.p. Kalamazoo chpt. 1992-93, pres. 1993-94, exec. com. 1989-95), Soc. Collegiate Journalists, Phi Beta Kappa (pres. S.W. Mich. chpt. 1977-78, sec. 1994-97, pres. 1997—), Beta Phi Mu, Alpha Beta Alpha, Delta Kappa Gamma (pres. Alpha Psi chpt. 1988-92), Phi Kappa Phi. Home: 2729 Mockingbird Dr Kalamazoo MI 49008-1626

GROUNDS, VERNON CARL, seminary administrator; b. Jersey City, July 19, 1914; s. John and Bertha Barbara (Heimburg) G.; m. Ann Barton, June 17, 1939; 1 child, Barbara Ann Grounds Owen. BA, Rutgers U., 1937; BD, Faith Theol. Sem., 1940; PhD, Drew U., 1960; DD (hon.), Wheaton Coll., 1954; LHD (hon.), Gordon Coll., 1977. Pastor Paterson (N.J.) Gospel Tabernacle, 1935-45; dean, prof. theology Bapt. Bible Sem., Johnson City, N.Y., 1945-51; dean Denver Conservative Bapt. Sem., 1951-55, pres., 1955-79, chancellor, 1979—. Author: Yes, But How?, Emotional Problems and the Gospel, Evangelicalism and Social Responsibility, The Reason for Our Hope, Revolution and the Christian Faith; contbg. editor Christianity Today, 1980—. Sec. Evangelical Theol. Soc., Lynchburg, Va., 1963-76; bd. dirs. Radio Bible Class Ministries. Home: 3455 S Corona St Apt 513 Englewood CO 80110-2878 Office: Denver Sem PO Box 10,000 Denver CO 80250

GROVE, ANDREW S., electronics company executive; b. Budapest, Hungary, 1936; married; 2 children. B.S., CCNY, 1960, DSc (hon.), 1985; Ph.D., U. Calif.-Berkeley, 1963; DEng (hon.), Worcester Poly. Inst., 1989. With Fairchild Camera and Instrument Co., 1963-67; pres., COO, Intel Corp., Santa Clara, Calif., 1967-87, pres., CEO, 1987—, also bd. dirs. Recipient medal Am. Inst. Chemists, 1960, Merit cert. Franklin Inst., 1975, Townsend Harris medal CCNY, 1980, Enterprise award Profl. Advt. Assn., 1987, George Washington award Am. Hungarian Found., 1990, Citizen of Yr. award World Forum Silicon Valley, 1993, Exec. of Yr. award U. Ariz., 1993, Achievement medal Am. Electronics Assn., 1993, Heinz Family Found. award for tech. and economy, 1995, John von Neumann medal Am. Hungarian Assn., 1995, Steinman medal City Coll. N.Y., 1995, Statesman of the Yr. award Harvard Bus. Sch., 1996, Internat. Achievement award World Trade Club, 1997, Cinema Digital Technols. award Internat. Film Festival, 1997, Cinema Digital Tech. award Cannes Film Festival, 1997, Tech. Leader of Yr. award Industry Week, 1997, Man of Yr. award Time mag., 1997; named CEO of Yr. CEO mag., 1997. Fellow IEEE (Achievement award 1969, J.J. Ebers award 1974, Engring. Leadership Recognition award 1987, Computer Entrepreneur award 1997), Acad. Arts and Scis.; mem. Nat. Acad. Engring. Office: Intel Corp PO Box 58119 2200 Mission College Blvd Santa Clara CA 95054-1549

GROVE, BRANDON HAMBRIGHT, JR., diplomat, public and international affairs consultant; b. Chgo., Apr. 8, 1929; s. Brandon Hambright and Helen Julia (Gasparska) G.; m. Marie Cheremeteff, 1959 (div. 1983); children: John C., Catherine C.G. Jones, Paul C., Mark C.; m. Mariana Alfaro Moran, 1988; 1 step child, Michele Parsons Shotts. A.B., Bard Coll., 1950; M.P.A., Princeton U., 1952. Joined U.S. Fgn. Svc., 1959; vice consul Abidjan, Ivory Coast, also Upper Volta, Niger, and Dahomey, 1959-61; staff asst. to undersec. state, 1961-62, spl. asst. to dep. undersec. state for adminstrn., 1962-63; spl. asst. to Am. ambassador New Delhi, India, 1963-65; U.S. liaison officer to city govt. Berlin, 1965-69; dir. Office Panamanian Affairs, State Dept., 1969-71; mem. Sr. Seminar in Fgn. Policy, 1971-72; dep. dir. State Dept. policy planning staff, Washington; also staff dir. Under Secretaries Com. of NSC, 1972-74; chargé d' affaires, then dep. chief of mission Am. Embassy to German Dem. Republic, Berlin, 1974-76; fgn. svc. sr. insp. Dept. State, 1976-78; dep. asst. sec. state for Inter-Am. affairs, 1978-80; consul gen. Jerusalem, 1980-83; Capstone fellow Nat. Def. U., Fort McNair, Washington, 1984; ambassador to Zaire, Kinshasa, 1984-87; coord. State Dept. Budget Rev., Washington, 1987-88; dir. Fgn. Service Inst., Washington, 1988-92; diplomat-in-residence Georgetown U., Washington, 1992-93; sr. advisor State Dept. Policy Planning Staff, Washington, 1993-94; retired U.S. Fgn. Svc., 1994; asst. instr. Princeton U., 1953; sr. cons. APCO Assocs., Inc., Washington, 1996—. Editorial bd. chmn. Fgn. Svc. Jour., 1992-94. Served to lt. USNR, 1954-57. Recipient Pres.'s Meritorious Service award, 1985, 90, 92, John Dewey medal for disting. pub. svc. Bard Coll., 1990. Mem. Am. Acad. Diplomacy (bd. dirs.), Am. Fgn. Svc. Assn., Washington Inst. Fgn. Affairs, Coun. on Fgn. Rels., Georgetown U. Inst. for Study of Diplomacy (bd. dirs.), Assn. for Diplomatic Studies and Tng. (bd. dirs.), Atlantic Coun. of U.S. (bd. dirs.), Diplomatic and Consular Officers Ret., Met. Club of Washington. Home: 2029 Connecticut Ave NW Washington DC 20008-6141 Office: APCO Assocs Inc 1615 L St NW Washington DC 20036-5610

GROVE, DAVID LAVAN, lawyer; b. Johnstown, Pa., Nov. 4, 1937; s. William Morgan and Edith Elizabeth (Boyd) G.; m. Barbara Pearson Fogg, Aug. 26, 1961; children: Jonathan Morgan, Amy Pearson. BA in Polit. Sci. with honors, Dickinson Coll., 1959; LLB, Yale U., 1962. Bar: Pa. 1965, U.S. Dist. Ct. (ea. dist.) Pa. 1966, U.S. Ct. Appeals (3d cir.) 1972, U.S. Supreme Ct. 1976, U.S. Ct. Internat. Trade 1977, U.S. Dist. Ct. (mid. dist.) Pa. 1990. Vol. U.S. Peace Corps, Nigeria, West Africa, 1962-64; atty-advisor U.S. Peace Corps, Washington, 1967-69; assoc. Montgomery, McCracken, Walker & Rhoads, Phila., 1964-67, 69-72, ptnr., 1972—; asst. lectr. law faculty U. Lagos, Nigeria, 1962-64, Office of Peace Corps Gen. Counsel, Washington, 1967-69; advisor on fed. law and regulations Peace Corps ofcls.; U.S. del. to Coun. Internat. Secretariat for Vol. Svc., Washington, 1968, Geneva, 1969. Bd. sch. dirs. Wallingford (Pa.)-Swarthmore Sch. Dist., 1975-87, bd. pres., 1977-79, 82-84; mem. Wallingford-Swarthmore Sch. Authority, 1988—, pres., 1995—; bd. dirs. Recordings for the Blind and Dyslexic, Phila., 1994—. Fellow Am. Coll. Trial Lawyers; mem. ABA, Pa. Bar Assn., Phila. Bar Assn., Delta Phi Alpha, Pi Gamma Mu, Omicron Delta Kappa, Theta Chi. Democrat. Mem. Soc. of Friends. Avocations: tennis, golf, snorkeling, scuba diving. Home: 80 Yale Ave Swarthmore PA 19081-1607 Office: Montgomery McCracken Walker & Rhoads 123 S Broad St Fl 24 Philadelphia PA 19109-1099

GROVE, DOUGLAS DAVID, insurance company executive; b. Corona, Calif., Aug. 6, 1957; s. David Malley and Kathleen Lillian (Hogan) G.; m. Gail DeBenedictis, Sept. 12, 1992. BS in Bus. Adminstrn., U. Pacific, Stockton, Calif., 1980. CPCU, ARM. Package underwriter Kemper Group, San Francisco, 1980-85; comml. account underwriter Northbrook Property & Casualty Co., San Francisco, 1985-86, Chubb Ins. Cos., San Francisco, 1986-87; sr. underwriter nat. accounts Fireman's Fund Ins. Cos., San Rafael, Calif., 1987-88, exec. underwriter nat. accounts, 1989-93; exec. underwriter nat. brokerage unit Fireman's Fund, Novato, Calif., 1993-96; comml. lines product mgr. product mgmt. dept. Home Office Product Devel. Dept., 1996-97; underwriter Am. Internat. Group, San Francisco, 1997—. Mem. Underwriters Forum of San Francisco (sec. 1987, v.p. 1988, pres. 1989), Nat. Assn. Clock and Watch Collectors, Commonwealth Club of San Francisco, Alpha Kappa Lambda (chpt. sec., v.p., pres.). Avocations: boating, antique collection, real estate, travel, car collection. Office: Am Internat Group Nat Accts 2 Viver Plzstries 1 Spear St San Francisco CA 94105-1504

GROVE, JEFFREY SCOTT, family practice physician; b. Paxton, Ill., Sept. 21, 1964; s. Ronald Edwin and Delores Ann (Martensen) G.; m. Karen Beth Hanlon, June 17, 1989; 1 child, Garrett Jeffrey. *Dr. Grove is a third generation osteopathic family physician. His grandfather, Dr. Edwin T. Grove, graduated from Des Moines Still College of Osteopathy on May 26, 1927. He practiced medicine in Paxton, Illinois, until his death on April 4, 1964. Dr. Ronald E. Grove, Jeffrey Grove's father, graduated from the Chicago College of Osteopathic Medicine on June 4, 1962. Father and son practice together as SunCoast Family Medical Associates with two locations in Pinellas County, Florida.* BS in Biology, Fla. So. Coll., 1986; DO, Southeastern Coll. Osteo Med., North Miami Beach, Fla., 1990. Diplomate Am. Bd. Quality Assurance and Utilization Rev. Physicians; bd. cert. family practice in geriatrics. Intern Suncoast Hosp., Largo, Fla., 1990-91, resident in family practice, 1991-93; pvt. practice SunCoast Family Med. Assocs., Largo, 1993—; med. dir. Barrington Properties, Largo, 1994-97, Oak Manor Nursing Ctr., Largo, 1993—, Drew Village Nursing Ctr., Clearwater, Fla., 1996—; rep.-at-large exec. com. Suncoast Hosp., 1995—, chief adminstrv. resident, 1992-93, family practice teaching staff, geriatrics program dir., 1993-96, faculty devel. com., 1994—, legal compliance com., 1998—; mem. quality assurance/utilization rev. com., 1993—, med. dir. of quality assurance/utilization rev. dept., 1995—, legal compliance com., 1998—; bd. dirs. Suncoast Cmty. Care PHO, Largo, 1994-98, med. dir., 1998; clin. asst. prof. family medicine Nova Southeastern U. Coll. Osteo. Medicine, North Miami Beach, 1994—; clin. instr. Kirksville Coll. Osteo. Medicine, 1993—; bd. trustees SunCoast Hosp. Found., 1996—, SunCoast Hosp., 1998—; regional med. dir. Tampa Bay for Elder Health. *Dr. Jeffrey S. Grove practices* *primarily through SunCoast Hospital, located in Largo, Florida. SunCoast Hospital is the West Coast Academic Center for Nova Southeastern University, College of Osteopathic Medicine. He also has staff privileges at Morton Plant Hospital in Clearwater, Florida.* Vice-chmn. bd. trustees SCH Found., 1997-98, chmn. bd. trustees SCH Found., 1998—. Named to Outstanding Young Men of Am. Mem. Am. Osteo. Assn., Fla. Osteo. Med. Assn., Am. Coll. Osteo. Family Physicians (trustee 1997—, chair membership com. 1997—), Pinellas County Osteo. Med. Soc. (bd. govs. 1995—, treas. 1996—), Nat. Eagle Scout Assn. (life), Scouting Res. Republican. Methodist. Avocations: golf, stamp collecting, travel, snow skiing. Home: 301 Osceola Rd Clearwater FL 33756-1453 Office: SunCoast Family Med Assocs 360 Clearwater Largo Rd N Largo FL 33770-2335

GROVE, MYRNA JEAN, elementary education educator; b. Bryan, Ohio, Oct. 24, 1949; d. Kedric Durward and N. Florence (Stombaugh) G. Student, Bowling Green State U., 1970-71; BA in Edn., Manchester Coll., 1971; postgrad., U. No. Colo., 1974-76, Purdue U., 1977, St. Francis Coll., Ft. Wayne, Ind., 1986, Coll. Mount St. Joseph, Ohio, 1986; MLS, Kent State U., 1999. Cert. elem. tchr., Ohio. Tchr. elem. sch. Bryan City Schs., 1972—. Author: Asbestos Cancer: One Man's Experience, 1995; editor newspaper column Education Today, 1975-82, newsletter N.W. Ohio Emphasis, 1981-83 (award 1981). Dir., violinist Bryan String Ensemble, 1981—; organist Trinity Episc. Ch., Bryan, 1979-89; active Lancaster Mennonite Hist. Soc., Hans Herr Found.; trustee Bryan Area Cultural Assn., 1984-89; bd. dirs. William County Cmty. Concerts. Jennings scholar Martha Holden Jennings Found., Bowling Green State U., 1982-83. Mem. ALA, NEA (Ohio del., state contact 1986-87), Am. Booksellers Assn. (assoc. mem.), Ohio Edn. Assn. (presenter 1984, del. global issues 1986, sec. N.W. Ohio Tchrs. Uniserv. 1975-78), Ohio Assn. Gifted Children, Bus. and Profl. Women Ohio (individual devel. com. 1986-90, speaking skills cert. 1987), Ohio Libr. Coun., Ohioana Libr. Assn., N.W. Ohio Manchester Coll. Alumni Assn. (past pres.), Bryan Edn. Assn. (exec. com., pres. 1985-86), Williams County Geneal. Soc., Williams County Hist. Assn., P. Buckley Moss Soc., Trees of Life (v.p. 1994-99, region moss docent), Alpha Delta Kappa (pres. 1996-98), Alpha Mu. Avocations: collecting dolls, playing piano, organ and violin, reading, travel.

GROVE, NANCY CAROL, academic administrator; b. Johnstown, Pa.; d. Henry and Marie (Boerstler) Frambach; m. William M. Grove; children: Eric William, Carol Ann. BS in Nursing, U. Pitts., 1968, MEd, 1972, PhD, 1988; MS in Nursing, Duquesne U., 1980. Staff nurse Conemaugh Valley Meml. Hosp., Johnstown, 1963-66, head nurse, 1967, 70, nursing care supr., 1968-71, instr., course dir. Sch. Nursing, 1971-79, dir. Sch. Nursing, 1979-91; assoc. prof. RN-BSN program, dir. Sch. Nursing U. Pitts., Johnstown, 1990—; instr. refresher course Votech. Sch., Johnstown, 1973-76; adj. assoc. prof. U. Pitts., 1979-91; site visitor Nat. League for Nursing, N.Y.C.; chair Cambria/Somerset Coun. for Health Profls., Inc., Johnstown, 1984-89, Cambria/Somerset Mgmt. Com., 1994-96. Mem. rehab. com. Am. Cancer Soc., Johnstown, 1988-94, bd. dirs., 1992—; sec., bd. dirs. Victim Svcs., Inc., Johnstown; chmn. YWCA Tribute to Women, 1991; active task force Am. Heart Assn., 1991-94. Recipient Tribute to Women award for excellence in edn. YWCA, 1988. Mem. Soroptimist Internat. (pres. 1994-96), Sigma Theta Tau. Lutheran. Avocations: calligraphy, art. Home: 810 Linden Ave Johnstown PA 15902-2856 Office: U Pitts 141 Biddle Hall Johnstown PA 15904

GROVE, RICHARD CHARLES, power tool company executive; b. Bethlehem, Pa., Aug. 13, 1940; s. Dale Addison and Mary Elizabeth (Ripple) G.; m. Cynthia Ann Dimmick, Dec. 7, 1963; 1 child, Jeffrey. BEE, Cornell U., 1962; MBA, U. Pitts., 1967. Mgmt. cons. Touche Ross & Co., Detroit, 1967-72; mgr. bus. planning Amstar Corp., N.Y.C., 1972-75; treas. Spreckels Sugar div. Amstar Corp., San Francisco, 1975-82; treas. Amstar Corp., N.Y.C., 1983-84; v.p., controller Amstar Corp., Stamford, Conn., 1985-88, v.p., chief fin. officer, 1988-89; sr. v.p. Esstar Inc., New Haven, 1989, exec. v.p., dir., 1995; exec. v.p. Milw. Electric Tool Corp., 1990-91, pres., chief exec. officer, 1991—. Mem., bd. regents Milw. Sch. Engring. Served to 1st lt. U.S. Army, 1964-66. Mem. Blue Mound Golf and Country Club. Republican. Avocations: golf, skiing. Office: Milw Electric Tool Corp 13135 W Lisbon Rd Brookfield WI 53005-2551

GROVE, TIMOTHY LYNN, geology educator; b. York, Pa., July 15, 1949; s. Arthur Leib and Ruby Janette (Finger) G.; m. Madeline Scadden, June 15, 1971; m. Ann Marie Reilly, June 19, 1979; children: Matthew Brian, Michael Thomas. BA, U. Colo., 1971; AM, Harvard U., 1975, PhD, 1976. Rsch. asst. SUNY, Stony Brook, 1975-79; from asst. prof. to assoc. prof. dept. earth, atmospheric and planet sci. MIT, Cambridge, Mass., 1979-91, prof. dept. earth, atmospheric and planet sci., 1991—; vis. prof. divsn. geology and sci. Caltech, Pasadena, Calif., 1979. Editor Contbns. to Mineralogy and Petrology, 1985—. Fellow Mineral. Soc. Am.; mem. Am. Geophys. Union (Bowen award 1993), Geol. Soc. Am., Geochem. Soc. Home: 87 Menotomy Rd Arlington MA 02476-6111 Office: MIT Earth Atmospheric & Planet Sci 77 Massachusetts Ave # 541220 Cambridge MA 02139-4307

GROVE, WILLIAM JOHNSON, physician, surgery educator; b. Ottawa, Ill., Mar. 23, 1920; s. Joseph Roy and Florence (Johnson) G.; m. Betty Pedigo, Mar. 23, 1944; children: William Johnson, Pamela J. Holly Lynn. B.S., U. Ill., 1941, M.D., 1943, M.S. in Surgery, 1949. Intern U. Ill. Research and Ednl. Hosps., 1944, asst. resident surgery, 1949-50, chief resident surgery, 1951-52; asst. resident surgery Hines VA Hosp., 1950-51; mem. faculty U. Ill. Coll. Medicine, 1951—, prof. surgery, 1964-81, prof. emeritus, 1981—, dean, 1968-70, exec. dean, 1970-76; vice chancellor for acad. affairs U. Ill. Coll. Medicine (U. Ill. Med. Center), 1976-80, vice chancellor emeritus, 1981—; acting dir. U. Ill. Coll. Medicine (Center for Study of Patient Care), 1980-81; attending surgeon U. Ill. Hosp.; cons. W.K. Kellogg Found., 1981-86; prof. med. edn. U. Ill., Chgo., 1981-86. Author numerous articles in field. Served to capt. AUS, 1944-46. Fellow ACS; mem. Assn. Am. Med. Colls., Central, Chgo. Surg. Socs., Soc. Univ. Surgeons, Warren H. Cole Soc., Soc. Clin. Surgery, Am. Surg. Assn., Sigma Xi, Alpha Omega Alpha, Phi Delta Epsilon. Home: 2221 Viewpoint Dr Naples FL 34110-7949

GROVER, CAROLE LEE, mathematics educator, translator; b. Seattle, Nov. 25, 1948; d. Charles L. and Peggy D. (Reilly) Hardin; m. Sushil Kumar Grover (div. 1976); 1 child, Vikram; m. Charles Vernon Coffman; 1 child, Valerie. B.S., U. Wash., 1970, M.A., 1971; Ph.D., Carnegie-Mellon U., 1977. NSF trainee U. Wash., Seattle, 1970-71; NSF trainee Carnegie-Mellon U., Pitts., 1971-72, grad. instr., 1972-76, lectr. in math., 1976-77; asst. prof., U. Pitts., 1977-78; asst. prof. Carlow Coll., Pitts., 1981-85, assoc. prof., 1985—. Translator Russian math. jours., Allerton Press, N.Y.C., 1976—. Bd. dirs. Collegiate YMCA, Pitts., 1984—. Participant Advanced Study Inst. NATO, Istanbul, Turkey, 1977; dir. curriculum devel. project Council Independent Colls., Washington, 1984—. Mem. Am. Math. Soc., Assn. for Women in Math., Three Rivers Osborne Group (sec. 1984—), Phi Beta Kappa, Sigma Xi, Pi Mu Epsilon. Office: Carlow Coll Dept Math and Computer Sci 3333 5th Ave Pittsburgh PA 15213

GROVER, JAMES ROBB, chemist, editor; b. Klamath Falls, Oreg., Sept. 16, 1928; s. James Richard and Marjorie Alida (van Groos) G.; m. Barbara Jean Ton, Apr. 14, 1957; children: Jonathan Robb, Patricia Jean. BS summa cum laude, valedictorian, U. Wash., Seattle, 1952; PhD, U. Calif., Berkeley, 1958. Rsch. assoc. Brookhaven Nat. Lab., Upton, N.Y., 1957-59, assoc. chemist, 1959-63, chemist, 1963-67, chemist with tenure, 1967-77, sr. chemist, 1978-93, rsch. collaborator, 1993—; cons. Lawrence Livermore (Calif.) Nat. Lab., 1962; assoc. editor Ann. Rev. of Nuclear Sci., Ann. Revs., Inc., Palo Alto, Calif., 1967-77; vis. prof. Inst. for Molecular Sci., Okazaki, Japan, 1986-87; vis. scientist Max-Planck Inst. für Strömungsforschung, Göttingen, Fed. Republic Germany, 1975-76. Contbr. numerous articles to profl. jours. With USN, 1946-48. Mem. Am. Chem. Soc. (chmn. nuclear chemistry and tech. 1989), Am. Phys. Soc., Triple Nine Soc., Sigma Xi, Phi Beta Kappa, Phi Lambda Upsilon, Zeta Mu Tau, Pi Mu Epsilon. Libertarian. Presbyterian. Achievements include naming of the nuclear yrast levels and discovery of their importance in nuclear reactions; invention of use of short-lived radioactivity in molecular beams; first to successfully use radioactivity for detection in chemically reactive scattering experiments; invention of threshold photoionization method for measuring the dissociation energies of neutral weak complexes in molecular beams. Home and Office: 1536 Pinecrest Ter Ashland OR 97520-3427

GROVER, MARK DONALD, computer scientist; b. Augusta, Maine, July 12, 1955; s. Donald William and Aletha D. (Wells) G. BA, U. Fla., 1976; MS, Northwestern U., 1978, PhD, 1982. Cert. EMT. Instr. Northwestern U., Evanston, Ill., 1978-81; mem. tech. staff TRW Def. Sys., Redondo Beach, Calif., Fairfax, Va., 1981-85; sr. computer scientist Advanced Decision Sys., Arlington, Va., 1985-89; prin. software engr. Oberon Software Inc., Cambridge, Mass., 1990-94; software design engr. DeLorme Mapping, Yarmouth, Maine, 1995—; program chmn. Nat. Symbolics User Group Conf., Washington, 1986; presenter to confs. in field. Contbr. articles to sci. jours. Vol. EMT; instr. CPR; trustee 1st Congl. Ch. Gray, Maine. Mem. NRA (life), Phi Beta Kappa, Tau Beta Pi. Avocations: travel, rare books, drama, marksmanship, history. Office: DeLorme Mapping PO Box 298 Yarmouth ME 04096-0298

GROVER, NORMAN LAMOTTE, theologian, philosopher; b. Topeka, Feb. 9, 1928; s. LaMotte and Virginia Grace (Alspach) G.; m. Anne Stottler, June 24, 1950; children: Jennifer Jean, Peter Neal, Rebecca Louise Grover Verna, Sandra Christine Grover Lloyd. B. Mech. Engring., Rensselaer Poly. Inst., 1948; B.D., Yale, 1951, S.T.M., 1952, Ph.D., 1957. Mem. faculty, chaplain Hollins (Va.) Coll., 1954-57, asst. prof. religion, 1956-57; ordained to ministry Presbyn. Ch., 1952; head dept. philosophy and religion Va. Poly. Inst. and State U., 1957-75, prof. philosophy and religion, 1961-83, prof. religion, 1983-91, prof. emeritus, 1991—; adj. prof. Ctr. for Study Sci. in Soc., 1983-86; mem. supervising com. So. leadership tng. project Fund for Republic, 1955-56; assoc. Danforth Found., 1958—, sr. assoc., 1962—, chmn. Va., N.C. and S.C. conf., 1962; psychotherapeutic counsellor Blacksburg Community Counselling Center, 1962-65. Bd. dirs. United Campus Ministries of Blacksburg, 1986-95; mem. Amnesty Internat., Blacksburg Master Chorale and Va. Tech. Concert Choir Concert Tour in Berlin, Poland, Czech Republic, Salzburg, 1992, Germany, Austria, Czech Republic, 1995; study trip to Costa Rica, Nicaragua, El Salvador and Guatemala Presbyn. Ch. U.S.A. Presbytery of Peaks Partnership with CEDEPCA, 1989, 91. Mem. AAUP (pres. Va. Poly. Inst. and State U. chpt. 1961-62, 81-82, sec.-treas. chpt. 1959-60, 77-80, v.p. chpt. 1960-61, 80-81, 92-94), NAACP (exec. bd. Montgomery, Floyd, Radford chapt., 1999), ACLU, Amnesty Internat., Va. Philos. Assn. (pres. 1969), So. Soc. Philosophy and Psychology, Am. Acad. Religion (chmn. S.E. region theology/philosophy religion sect. 1983-85, mem. citizen amb. team to Ukraine and Russia 1993, China 1994), Coalition for Justice in Ctrl. Am. (bd. dirs., v.p. 1990-94), Bread for the World, Sierra Club, Smithsonian Assocs., Wilderness Soc., Am. Assn. Retired Persons, People to People Internat. (Am. People amb. del. to India, Nepal and Tibet 1996). E-mail: ngrover@vt.edu. Home: 705 Burruss Dr Blacksburg VA 24060-3205 Office: Va Poly Inst and State U Ctr for Interdiscipl Study Blacksburg VA 24061-0135

GROVER, PETER DUN, cultural organization administrator; m. Julia Gamble; children: Peter Dun Jr., Edward Douglass, Katheryn Gamble. BA in Econs., Washington and Lee U., 1973; MA in Art History, Va. Commonwealth U., 1978; MBA, Coll. William and Mary, 1981. Rschr. Catalog of Am. Portraits Nat. Portrait Gallery, Smithsonian Instn., Washington, 1978-79; student intern Abby Aldrich Rockefeller Folk Art Ctr./Colonial Williamsburg, Va., 1980; dir./appraiser mus. and estate svcs. C.G. Sloan & Co., Inc., Washington, 1981-86; adminstrv. dir. Belmont, the Carl Melchers Meml. Gallery, Fredericksburg, Va., 1986-90; exec. dir. The Assn. for Preservation of Va. Antiquities, Richmond, 1990—; past assoc. prof. Mary Washington Coll., Fredericksburg. Former bd. dirs. Fredericksburg Ctr. for Creative Arts; past mem. pres.'s house com. Coll. of William & Mary, Williamsburg, Va., past sec.-treas. alumni bd. grad. sch. bus. adminstrn.; mem. Celebration 2007 Adv. Com., Jamestown; mem. State Hist. Records Adv. Bd., Va. Mem. Va. Assn. Mus. (past bd. dirs.). Avocation: swimming. Office: APVA 204 W Franklin St Richmond VA 23220-5012*

GROVER, ROBERT LAVERN, retired auto worker; b. Mpls., May 21, 1938; s. La Vern Wilber and Opal Elizabeth (Thompson) G.; m. Carolyn Sue Donavant, Oct. 6, 1962; children: Denise Marie, David Scott, Kevin Robert, Richard Thomas. Grad., Graphic Arts Tech. Sch., Mpls., 1963, Am. Computer Sch., Kansas City, Mo., 1971. Printer Raytown (Mo.) News, 1963, Phoenix Box & Label, Kansas City, Mo., 1963-65, Gustion Bacon, Kansas City, Mo., 1965; utility relief man Claycomo (Mo.) plant Ford Motor Co., 1965-97. Author: Compendium of Microfilm and Census in Missouri and Kansas, 1980, Missouri Genealogical Periodical Index A County Guide 1960-1982, 1983, others. Served with USN, 1957-61. Mem. MOSSAR SAR (registrar 1992-94, v.p. 1995-97, exec. v.p., 1998, pres., 1999, comdr. color guard 1995, 97-2000, pres., treas., sec. and v.p. Harry S Truman chpt. 1989-93, Color Guardsman of Yr. 1996, 98, Vietnam War Svc. medal 1993, Bronze Good Citizenship medal 1993, 96, Cert. of Disting. Svc. 1993, 97, 98, Meritorious medal 1994, Liberty medal 1994, 98, Centennial medal, others), Jackson County Genealogy Soc. (v.p. 1979-81, 98—, pres. 1999—), Heart of Am. Geneal. Soc. (publ. coord. 1975-79), Mo. State Geneal. Soc. (founder). Avocations: genealogy, muskie fishing, blues music. Home: 3929 S Milton Dr Independence MO 64055-4043

GROVER, ROSALIND REDFERN, oil and gas company executive; b. Midland, Tex., Sept. 5, 1941; d. John Joseph and Rosalind (Kapps) Redfern;m. Arden Roy Grover, Apr. 10, 1982; 1 child, Rosson. BA in Edn. magna cum laude, U. Ariz., 1966, MA in History, 1982; postgrad. in law, So. Methodist U., Dallas. Libr. Gahr H.S., Cerritos, Calif., 1969; pres. The Redfern Found., Midland, 1982—; ptnr. Redfern & Grover, Midland, 1986—; pres. Redfern Enterprises Inc., Midland, 1989—; chmn. bd. dirs. Flag-Redfern Oil Co., Midland. Sec. park and recreation commn. City of Midland, 1969-71, del. Objectives for Convocation, 1980; mem., past pres. women's aux. Midland Cmty. Theatre, 1970; chmn. challenge grant bldg. fund, 1980, chmn. Tex. Yucca Hist. Landmark Renovation Project, 1983, trustee, 1983-88; chmn. publicity com. Midland Jr. League, Midland, Inc., 1972, chmn. edn. com., 1976, corr. sec., 1978; 1st v.p. Midland Symphony Assn., 1975; chmn. Midland Charity Horse Show, 1975-76; mem. Midland Am. Revolution Bicentennial Commn., 1976; trustee Mus. S.W., 1977-80, pres. bd. dirs., 1979-80; co-chmn. Gov. Clements Fin. Com., Midland, 1978; mem. dist. com. State Bd. Law Examiners; trustee Midland Meml. Hosp., 1978-80, Permian Basin Petroleum Mus., Libr. and Hall of Fame, 1989—. Recipient HamHock award Midland Cmty. Theatre, 1978. Mem. Ind. Petroleum Assn. Am., Tex. Ind. Producers and Royalty Owners Assn., Petroleum Club, Racquet Club (Midland), Horseshoe Bay (Tex.) Country Club, Phi Kappa Phi, Pi Lambda Theta. Republican. Office: PO Box 2127 Midland TX 79702-2127

GROVER, WILLIAM HERBERT, architect; b. Phila., Feb. 10, 1938; s. William Oliver Grover and Lucy Gertrude (Whetzel) Grover Lott; m. Dora Bradford Apted, Feb. 24, 1962; children: Virginia Lucy, Amy Ellen. Student in mech. engring., Cornell U., 1955-58; B in Profl. Art, Art Ctr. Coll., Pasadena, Calif., 1962; MArch, Yale U., 1969. Registered architect, N.Y., N.H., Conn., Mass., Ohio, Md. Designer Gen. Motors Corp., Warren, Mich., 1962-65; draftsman MLTW/Moore Turnbull, New Haven, 1969-70; architect, mgr. Charles W. Moore Assocs., Essex, Conn., 1970-75; architect, pres. Moore Grover Harper P.C., Essex, Conn., 1975-84; architect, ptnr. Centerbrook Architects, Essex, Conn., 1984—; pres. Centerbrook, Inc., Essex, 1984—, bd. dirs.; pres. Mainstream, Inc., 1984—. Prin. works include Jones Lab., 1973 (AIA Honor award 1981), Grace Auditorium, 1986, Neurosci. Ctr., Cold Spring Harbor Lab., 1991, DeKalb Discovery Rsch. Ctr., 1992; designer (light fixtures) Slice of Light, 1981 (Progressive Architecture award 1982, 85, Eidolon 1984). Member Essex Zoning Commn., 1972-77, Essex Rep. Town Com., 1973-74; bd. dirs. Essex Art Assn., 1989—, Community Music Sch., 1991—. Recipient Builders' Choice award Nat. Home Builders, 1987, Sportmanship award U.S. Sailing Assn., 1990; named to Domino's Top 30 Architects, 1991, Architectural Digest's Top 100 Architects, 1991. Fellow AIA (Honor award 1981, N.Eng. honor award 1994, 95, Firm award 1998); mem. Conn. Soc. Architects (Honor awards 1980, 85, 92, 93, 94, 95), Pettipaug Yacht Club (Commodore Essex chpt. 1984-86), Essex Yacht Club. '. Avocations: yacht racing, jazz musician, watercolor artist. Home: 69 Main St Ivoryton CT 06442-1032 Office: Centerbrook Architects PO Box 955 Essex CT 06426-0955

GROVES, BERNICE ANN, educator; b. Bklyn., Feb. 5, 1928; d. Charles and Mary (Silverman) Lichtenstein; m. Stuart Weiss, June 5, 1949 (div. June 1978); children: Joel Weiss, Patricia Weiss Levy; m. Sidney Groves, July 30, 1978. MA, Adelphi U., 1971; MS in Edn., Coll. of New Rochelle, 1975. Cert. adminstr., supr., N.Y. K-6th grade tchr., reading tchr. Ossining (N.Y.) Schs., Byram Hills Schs., Armonk, N.Y., Bedford (N.Y.) Schs., 1964-84; reading specialist The Hallen Sch., Mamaroneck, N.Y., 1984-88; coord. testing and curriculum The Hallen Sch., New Rochelle, N.Y., 1988—; mgr. nutrition ctr. GNC, Scarsdale, N.Y., 1981-82; mem. curriculum adv. coun. Lower Westchester BOCES, 1988—. Pres. Mineola (N.Y.) Elem. Sch. PTA, 1962-63. Mem. ASCD, Lower Hudson Coun. Adminstrv. Women in Edn., Westchester Reading Coun., Orton Dyslexia Soc., Am. Mensa Ltd. Avocations: tennis, U.S.T.A., gourmet cooking, nutrition.

GROVES, DOROTHY FRANCES, nursing education specialist; b. Camden, N.J., Oct. 8, 1946; d. George William and Dorothy Frances (Shaw) G. Diploma in Nursing, Methodist Hosp., 1970; BS in Nursing, La Salle U., 1988, MS in Nursing, 1992. Cert. EMT instr., N.J.; CPR inst., Am. Heart Assn. Staff nurse Methodist Hosp., Phila., 1970-73, head nurse, 1973-75, night coord. and staff devel. instr., 1975-77, staff devel. instr., 1977-96; edn. splst. Methodist Hosp. divsn. Thomas Jefferson U. Hosp., Phila., 1996—. Mem. Haddon Hts. (N.J.) Ambulance Corps, 1964—, pres. 1981-84, 1996—. Mem. N.J. State First Aid Coun. (del. 1964—), Meth. Hosp. Sch. of Nursing Alumnae (pres. 1990—). United Methodist. Avocations: ballroom dancing, reading, sewing, travel. Office: Meth Hosp 2301 S Broad St Philadelphia PA 19148-3594

GROVES, HURST KOHLER, lawyer, oil company executive; b. Indpls., Mar. 30, 1941; s. John Hurst and Mary Ellen (Sisco) G.; m. Marilyn Anne Woislaw, Nov. 18, 1967; children: Jennifer, Catherine. AB, Princeton U., 1963; JD, U. Mich., 1967. Bar: Ind. 1967, N.Y. 1968. Assoc. Cravath, Swaine & Moore, N.Y.C. and Paris, 1967-77; with Mobil Corp. and subs. cos., 1977—; sr. counsel Mobil Oil Corp., N.Y.C., 1977-80; gen. counsel Mobil Sekiyu K.K., Tokyo, 1980-84; sr. counsel Mobil South Inc., N.Y.C., 1984-88; v.p. Mobil Sales & Supply Corp., N.Y.C., 1988-90, Fairfax, Va., 1990-91; asst. gen. counsel internat. sales and supply Mobil Oil Corp., N.Y.C., 1988-90, Fairfax, Va., 1990-91; asst. gen. counsel exploration and producing div. Mobil Oil Corp., Fairfax, 1991-94, gen. counsel exploration and producing divsn., 1994-95; mng. counsel Mobil Bus. Resources Corp., Fairfax, Va., 1996-98, Mobil Corp., Fairfax, Va., 1999—. Vice chmn., treas. U.S.-Japan Trade Study Group, Tokyo, 1983-84. Fellow Am. Bar Found.; mem. ABA, Assn. of Bar of City of N.Y., Internat. Bar Assn., Am. C. of C. in Japan (chmn. investments com. 1982, bd. govs. 1984), Tokyo Am. Club, Cosmos Club. Episcopalian. Avocations: amateur radio, flying, sailing. Office: Mobil Corp 3225 Gallows Rd Fairfax VA 22037-0002

GROVES, JOHN TAYLOR, III, chemist, educator; b. New Rochelle, N.Y., Mar. 27, 1943; s. John Taylor and Frances (Gaylor) G.; m. Karen Joan Morrison, Apr. 15, 1967; children—Jay, Kevin. B.S., M.I.T., 1965; Ph.D., Columbia U., 1969. Asst. prof. U. Mich., Ann Arbor, 1969-76, assoc. prof., 1976-79, prof. organic chemistry, 1979-85; prof. organic and inorganic chemistry Princeton (N.J.) U., 1985—, chmn. dept. chemistry, 1988-93, Hugh Stott Taylor prof. chemistry, 1991—; Morris S. Kharasch Vis. Prof. U. Chgo., 1993; cons. in field; dir. Mich. Center for Catalytic and Surface Scis., Ann Arbor, 1981-85. Bd. editors: Bioorganic Chemistry, 1984—, Bioorganic and Medicinal Chemistry, 1994—, Bioorganic and Medicinal Chemistry Letters, 1994—; mem. editl. bd.: Reaction Kinetics and Catalysis Letters, 1989—, Jour. of Biol. Inorganic Chemistry, 1995—; contbr. articles to profl. jours.; mem. adv. bd. Inorganic Chemistry, 1995-97. Recipient Phi Lambda Upsilon award for outstanding teaching and leadership, 1978, NSF Extension award, 1990-92. Fellow AAAS, Am. Acad. Arts and Scis.; mem. Am. Chem. Soc. (Arthur C. Cope Scholar award 1991, Alfred Bader award in bioorganic and bioinorganic chemistry 1996), N.Y. Acad. Sci., Sigma Xi. Office: Princeton U Dept Chemistry 203 Hoyt Lab Princeton NJ 08544

GROVES, MARTHA, newspaper writer. Computer writer L.A. Times, 1992-93, staff writer, 1985—. Office: LA Times Times Mirror Sq Los Angeles CA 90053

GROVES, MICHAEL, banker; b. London, Jan. 2, 1936; came to U.S., 1969; s. Percy Reginald and Lily Sarah (Bentley) G.; m. Monica Rosario, June 8, 1963; children: Christopher, Carolyn, Jonathan. Grad., Inst. Chartered Accts., London, 1958; licentiate and tchg. cert., Royal Acad. Music, 1959; grad., Sch. Bank Adminstrn., U. Madison, Wis., 1976. Chief acct. Malaysian Estate Agys. Group Ltd., Kuala Lumpur, Malaysia, 1959-61; chief acct. Flour Mills Nigeria, Ltd., Lagos, 1961-62; asst. fin. mgr. Fábrica de Tejidos La Union Ltda, Lima, Peru, 1963-69; asst. to comptr. internat. Firstar, Milw., 1969-70; asst. auditor Firstar, 1970-72; loan rev. officer First Wis. Corp., 1972-79; sr. v.p. AmSouth Bancorp., Birmingham, 1979-82; v.p., mgr. credit rev. Merc. Bancorp, St. Louis, 1982-84; sr. v.p. internat. banking, sr. v.p. risk mgmt. Merc. Trust Co., St. Louis, 1985-87, chief credit policy officer, 1988-90; dir. risk mgmt. Integra Fin. Corp., Pitts., 1990-96; mem. faculty Sch. Bank Adminstrn., U. Madison, 1979-92. Author: Loan Review: A Guide, 1978, 2d edit., 1987, Management of Problem Loans, 1989, mus. compositions, arrangements. Mus. dir., com. mem. Selangor Philharm. Soc., Kuala Lumpur, 1959-61, Brit. Coun. Activities, Lima, 1963-69. Fellow Inst. Chartered Accts. Eng. and Wales; mem. Robert Morris Assocs. (mem. faculty loan rev. seminars 1977-80, chmn. 1978-79), Bank Adminstrn. Inst. (faculty, audit course 1970-74 Sch. for Bank Adminstrn. 1977-90).

GROVES, RAY JOHN, accountant; b. Cleve., Sept. 7, 1935; m. Anne Keating, Aug. 18, 1962; children: David, Philip, Matthew. BS summa cum laude, Ohio State U., 1957. CPA, Conn., N.Y., Ohio. With Ernst & Whinney, Cleve. and N.Y.C., 1957-94; ptnr. Ernst & Whinney, 1966-71, nat. ptnr., 1971-77; chmn., chief exec. officer Ernst & Whinney, N.Y.C., 1977-89; co-CEO, Ernst & Young, N.Y.C., 1989-91, chmn., CEO, 1991-94; chmn. Legg Mason Merchant Banking, Inc., 1995—; bd. govs. Am. Stock Exch., 1987-93; bd. dirs. Alleghany Teledyne Inc., Am. Water Works Co., Inc., Boston Sci. Corp., RJR Nabisco, Inc., Marsh & McLennan Cos., Inc., Consol. Natural Gas Co., EDS. Bd. overseers Wharton Sch. U. Pa., 1986-95; vice chmn. bd. trustees Ursuline Coll., Cleve., 1970-86; mng. dir., treas. Met. Opera Assn., 1988—; trustee Pub. Policy Inst. N.Y. State, 1988—, Bus. Coun UN, 1993—; vice chair bd. dirs. Ohio State U. Found., 1994—. Mem. AICPA (chmn. bd. dirs. 1984-85), Nat. Assn. Securities Dealers (bd. govs. 1981-84), Union Club, Pepper Pike Club, Links Club, Met. Club, Blind Brook Club. Republican. Home: 1566 Ponus Rdg New Canaan CT 06840-3430 also: 15 W 53rd St Apt 20A New York NY 10019-5401 Office: 787 7th Ave Fl 26 New York NY 10019-6018 also: 100 Light St Fl 34 Baltimore MD 21202-1036

GROVES, SHARON SUE, elementary education educator; b. Springfield, Mo., Apr. 25, 1944; d. William Orin Jr. and Ruth M. (Jones) Hodge; m. Donald L. Groves, July 20, 1963. BA, Drury Coll., 1966, MEd, 1969. Cert. life elem. tchg.; Psychol. Examiners Cert. Adminstrn. Elem. tchr. Springfield Pub. Schs., 1966-96; asst. instr. individual testing Drury Coll., Springfield, 1969-76; asst. instr. enhancing math. S.W. Mo. State U., Springfield, 1991-94; parent resource educator Springfield Pub. Schs.; sr. leader MAP 2000 (Mo. Assessment Project) Class I. Author: Modeling Effective Practices: Geometry and Computation. Active Springfield's Curriculum Coun.; mem. Tchg. Cadre, Strategic Planning Team; hon. life mem. PTA; chmn. adminstrv. coun. Hood United Meth. Ch.; children's coord., math. workshops.; sr. leader Mo. Assessment Project, 1993—. Recipient Extra Mile award, 1989; named Fremont Tchr. of the Yr., 1988, 93. Mem. ASCD, Internat. Reading Assn., Assn. for Childhood Edn., Nat. Coun. Tchrs. Math., Mo. Coun. Tchrs. Math., Mo. State Tchrs. Assn. (pres. S.W. dist. 1994-95, Educator of Yr. 1989), Springfield Edn. Assn. (pres. 1989-90, 93-96, Leader of Yr. 1990, pres. Scholarship corp. 1998—), Delta Kappa Gamma (1st v.p.). Home: 8076 W Farm Road 144 Springfield MO 65802-8782

GROVES, SHERIDON HALE, orthopedic surgeon; b. Denver, Mar. 5, 1947; s. Harry Edward Groves and Dolores Ruth (Hale) Finley; m. Deborah Rita Threadgill, Mar. 29, 1970 (div. Apr. 1980); children: Jason, Tiffany; m. Nanely Marie Lamont, July 1, 1980 (div. Dec. 1987); 1 child, Dolores; m. Elaine Robbins, Feb. 7, 1991. BS, U.S. Mil. Acad., 1969; MD, U. Va., Charlottesville, 1976. Commd. 2nd lt. U.S. Army, 1969, advanced through grades to maj., 1979, ret., 1992; surg. intern U.S. Army, El Paso, Tex., 1976-77, resident in orthop. surgery, 1977-80; staff orthop. surgeon U.S. Army, Killeen, Tex., 1980-83; ret. U.S. Army, 1992; staff emergency physician various emergency depts. State of Tex., 1983-84, 87; emergency dept. dir. Victoria (Tex.) Regional Med. Ctr., 1984-86; med. dir. First Walk-In Clinic Victoria, 1986-87; tchr. U. Tex. Med. Br., Galveston, 1986-90; emergency dept. dir. Gulf Coast Med. Ctr., 1988-89; with Amerimed Corp., 1990-92, Primedex Corp., 1992-93; clinic med. dir, staff orthop. surgeon Pain Relief Network, 1993—; lectr. Spkrs. Bur., Victoria, 1984-86, Cato Inst., Ludwig Von Mises Inst. Contbr. articles to profl. jours. Mem. Victoria Interagy. Coun. Sexual Abuse, 1984-86; treas. bd. dirs. Youth Home Victoria, 1986-90. Recipient Physician's Recognition award, AMA, 1980, 83, 86, 89, 92, 95. Fellow Am. Acad. Neurologic and Orthop. Surgeons; mem. Soc. Mil. Orthop. Surgeons, Am. Coll. Emergency Physicians, Tex. Med. Found., Assn. Grads. of U.S. Mil. Acad. (life), Am. Assn. Disability Evaluation Physicians, Coalition of Med. Providers, Am. Coll. Sports Medicine, Am. Running and Fitness Assn. (cert. of recognition 1987), Internat. Coll. Surgeons (pres., vice regent), Internat. Martial Arts Assn., Hurricane Sports Club of Houston, Smithsonian Assocs., So. Calif. Striders Track Club. Avocations: track and field masters (3-time nat. champion), martial arts.

GROVES, WILLIAM ARTHUR, industrial hygiene educator; b. Butler, Pa., Mar. 7, 1962; s. William Theodore and Alice Love (Kinzer) G.; m. Lisa Carol Fuqua, Sept. 5, 1993; 1 child, Andrew William. BA, Edinboro U. Pa., 1985; BS in Chem. Engring., Case Western Res. U., 1985; MPH in Indsl. Health, U. Mich., 1993, PhD in Indsl. Health, 1997. Cert. indsl. hygienist, cert. safety profl. Loss control engr. Aetna Life & Casualty, Harrisburg, Pa., 1986-87; indsl. hygienist Aetna Life & Casualty, Hartford, Conn., 1987-90, Newport News (Va.) Shipbldg., 1990-91, Dow Chem. Co., Midland, Mich., 1992; rsch. asst. U. Mich., Ann Arbor, 1993-97, tchg. asst., 1993-96; asst. prof. indsl. hygiene U. Iowa, Iowa City, 1997—. Contbr. articles to profl. jours. Dow fellow U. Mich., 1991-93, Rackham fellow, 1996. Fellow Am. Acad. Indsl. Hygienists; mem. Am. Indsl. Hygiene Assn. (sec., vice-chair gas and vapor detection sys. com. 1996-99). Home: 63 Durango Pl Iowa City IA 52246-8620 Office: U Iowa Dept Preventive Medicine 100 Oakdale Campus 136 IREH Iowa City IA 52242

GROW, ROBERT THEODORE, economist, association executive; b. Newton, Mass., Aug. 14, 1948; s. William and Lempi (Kangas) G.; m. Anita L. Capps, Nov. 20, 1982; 1 child, Margaret Celia. BS magna cum laude, U. Mass., 1970, MS, 1973. Regional economist Southeastern Va. Planning Dist. Commn., Norfolk, 1973-80; dir. met. coord. Met. Washington (D.C.) Coun. Govts., 1980-85; exec. dir. Washington/Balt. Regional Assn., Washington, 1985-94; dir. transportation The Greater Washington Bd. Trade, 1994—; chmn. met. com. Capital Area chpt. Am. Planning Assn., Washington, 1988-89. Fellow Am. Ctr. for Internat. Leadership; mem. Am. Soc. Assn. Execs., Va. Econs. Devel. Assn., Phi Kappa Phi. Avocations: sailing, golf.

GROWE, JOAN ANDERSON, former state official; b. Mpls., Sept. 28, 1935; d. Lucille M. (Brown) Johnson; children: Michael, Colleen, David, Patrick. B.S., St. Cloud State U., 1956; cert. in spl. edn., U. Minn., 1964; exec. mgmt. program State and local govt., Harvard U., 1979. Tchr. elem. pub. schs. Bloomington, Minn., 1956-58; tchr. for exceptional children elem. pub. schs. St. Paul, 1964-65; spl. edn. tchr. St. Anthony Pub. Schs., Minn., 1965-66; mem. Minn. Ho. of Reps., 1973-74; sec. of state State of Minn., St. Paul, 1975-98; mem. exec. coun. Minn. State Bd. Investment. Mem. Women Execs. in State Govt., Women's Polit. Caucus, Minn. Women's Econ. Roundtable; candidate U.S. Senate, 1984; bd. dirs. Minn. Internat. Ctr.; mem. Nat. Commn. for the Renewal of Am. Democracy (Project Democracy); bd. dirs. Nat. Dem. Inst. for Internat. Affairs, Riohard Green Inst.; mem. adv. bd. Hubert H. Humphrey Inst. for Pub. Affairs. Recipient Minn. Sch. Bell award, 1977, YMCA Outstanding Achievement award, 1978, Disting. Alumni award St. Cloud State U., 1979, Charlotte Striebel Long Distance Runner award Minn. NOW, 1985, The Woman Who Makes a Difference award Internat. Women's Forum, 1991, Esther V. Crosby Leadership award Greater Mpls. Girl Scout Coun., 1992, Pathfinder award for Innovative Solutions, Ctr. for Policy Alternatives, 1996, Breaking the Glass Ceiling award Women Execs. in State Govt., 1998. Mem. Nat. Assn. Secs. of State (pres. 1979-80), Internat. Womens Forum. Roman Catholic.

GROZINGER, KARL GEORG, chemist, researcher; b. Galmuthöfen/Biberach, Germany, Sept. 3, 1940; s. Karl and Frida (Gloeckle) G.; m. Monika Theresia Schuetze, Dec. 21, 1963; children: Thomas, Stephan, Christina. BSc, Concordia U., Montreal, Que., Can., 1973; PhD, McGill U., Montreal, 1976. Chemist Wyeth-Ayerst, Montreal, 1961-64, Pharma Rsch. Can. Ltd., Montreal, 1964-73, 76-78; chemist, assoc. dir. chem. devel. Boehringer Ingelheim, Ridgefield, Conn., 1978—. Patentee in field. Mem. Order Que. Chemists, Am. Chem. Soc., Chem. Inst. Can. Achievements include co-invention of Ciclosidimine (CAS 66564-16-7), Setazindol-process (CAS 56481-43-7), Nevirapine (Viramune), others. Home: 171 High Ridge Ave Ridgefield CT 06877-4418 Office: Boehringer Ingelheim 900 Ridgebury Rd Ridgefield CT 06877-1030

GRUB, PHILLIP DONALD, business educator; b. Medical Lake, Wash., Aug. 8, 1931; s. Carl Dryer and Barbara Rosalie (Johnson) G. BA in Econs. and Bus. Edn. with honors, Eastern Wash. State U., 1953; MBA (Scottish Rite Found. fellow), George Washington U., 1960, DBA (Am. Security and Trust scholar), 1964; DBus (hon.), U. Internat. Bus. and Econs., Beijing, 1986. Pres. Phillip D. Grub, Inc., Spokane, Wash., 1953-54; pvt. practice, 1956-62; co-owner, co-mgr. 7G Ranch, Medical Lake, 1962-70; assoc. prof., dir. programs in internat. bus. George Washington U., Washington, 1964-70, chmn. dept. bus. adminstrn., 1968-70, prof. bus. adminstrn., 1971-73, Aryamehr prof. multinat. mgmt., 1974-94, Aryamehr prof. emeritus, 1994—, spl. asst. to pres., 1974-80; mng. ptnr. Phillip Grub and Assocs., 1994—; disting. exec. in residence Ea. Washington U., Cheney, 1997—; cons. Summa Group, Jakarta, Indonesia, 1991-92; mgmt. cons. to industry and govts.; ptnr. C & P Investments, Medical Lake, Wash., 1988—; mem. Md.-D.C. Export Expansion Coun., 1968-89; vis. prof. internat. bus. adminstrn., acting dir. Ohio World Trade Edn. Ctr., Cleve. State U., 1972-73; dir., chmn. exec. com. Diplomat Nat. Bank, 1978-80; mem. bd. adv. Donaldson, Luftkin & Jenrette, 1980-83; bd. dirs. U.S.-Japan Culture Ctr.; dir. Washington World Trade Inst., 1983-91, pres., 1983-86; dir. U.S. Vietnam Ednl. Found., 1990—; sr. advisor Shanghi Ctr. Internat. Studies, 1987—. Author: A Guide to Personnel Development, 1966, A Handbook for Term Papers, Theses and Dissertations, 1967, American-East European Trade: Controversy, Progress, Prospects, 1968; (with Norma M. Loeser) Executive Leadership: The Art of Successfully Managing Resources, 1969, Management U.S.A., 1968; (with Mika S. Kaskimies) International Marketing in Perspective, 1971; (with Ashok Kapoor) The Multinational Enterprise in Transition, 1972, 3d edit., 1986; (with Ghadar and Khambata) Asia Dimensions of International Business, 1982, Foreign Investment Analysis: Cases and Country Studies, 1986, Global Business Management in the 1990's, 1990, Foreign Direct Investment in China, 1991, The Re-Emerging Securities Market in China, 1992, Vietnam, The New Investment Frontier in Southeast Asia, 1992, (with Dara Khambata) The Multinational Enterprise: Strategies for Global Competitiveness, 1993, Global Business Strategies for the Year 2000, 1995; contbr. articles to profl. jours. Bd. dirs. U.S. Forestry, 1987-90; sr. advisor Shanghai Ctr. Internat. Studies, 1987—. With U.S. Army, 1954-56. Named a Univ. Prof. in Peoples Republic of China, 1986. Mem. Acad. Internat. Bus. (pres. 1975-77), Acad. Mgmt., Am. Mgmt. Assn., U.S.-Japan Culture Soc. (bd. dirs., exec. sec.), Fellows Acad. Internat. Bus., Masons, Alpha Kappa Psi, Beta Gamma Sigma. Home: 4810 S St Andrews Ln Spokane WA 99223-4304 Office: C & P Investments PO Box 220 Medical Lake WA 99022-0220

GRUBB, DAVID H., construction company executive; b. 1936; married. BSCE, Princeton U.; MSCE, Stanford U. With Swinerton and Walberg Co., San Francisco, 1964—, then exec. v.p. Structural divsn., exec. v.p. ops., pres., also bd. dirs.; pres. Swinerton Incorp., 1993-96, CEO and chmn. bd.; chmn. bd. Swinerton & Walberg Co., SW Indsl., Inc., Westwood Swinerton Constrn., Swinerton & Walberg Property Svcs., Inc., chmn. William P. Young Construction, Inc., Bud Bailey Constrn., Inc. Office: Swinerton Incorp 580 California St Ste 1200 San Francisco CA 94104-1045

GRUBB, DONALD HARTMAN, paper industry company executive; b. West Chester, Pa., Oct. 22, 1924; s. Donald C. and Bessie (Hanthorne) G.; m. Jean Louise Flounders, Sept. 7, 1946; children: Donna Jean (Mrs. Robert Kanich), Deborah Anne (Mrs. James R. Jackson), Donald Philip. BA, U. Pa., 1949; MA, Am. U., 1954; postgrad., NYU, 1963-64. With U.S. Treasury Dept., Washington, 1949-57; recruitment officer U.S. Treasury Dept., 1951-53, dir. personnel, 1953-57; mgr. personnel Westvaco Corp., N.Y.C., 1957-59; regional adminstrv. mgr. Westvaco Corp., Hoboken, N.J., 1959-61; mgr. sales Westvaco Corp., 1961-64; asst. to v.p. Huyck Corp., Stamford, Conn., 1964; v.p. adminstrn. and mktg. Huyck Corp., 1969-70, exec. v.p., 1970-73, pres., dir., chief exec. officer, 1973-81; chmn. BTR Paper Group, 1981-82; pres. Gedon Enterprises, 1982—; v.p., gen. mgr. Formex Co. of Can., Kentville, N.S., 1965-67; also dir.; v.p., gen. mgr. Huyck Formex Co. of U.S., Greeneville, Tenn., 1967-69; bd. dirs. Goodberry Creamery Inc.; mgr. Grubb Assocs., LLC dba Fasteners Supply of Goldsboro. Bd. dirs. Blanchard-Fraser Meml. Hosp., Kentville, N.S., Can., 1966-67, Wake County Hosp. System, Raleigh, 1983-87, N.C. State U. Pulp and Paper Found. Served with AUS, 1943-46. Mem. Raleigh C. of C. (dir. 1976-78), Phi Beta Kappa. Presbyterian. Office: 6713 Foxfire Pl Raleigh NC 27615-7011

GRUBB, L(EWIS) CRAIG, investment company executive, consultant; b. Canton, Ohio, June 1, 1954; s. Lewis G. and Janet M. (Hornback) G.; m. Carol Elizabeth Norvell, Dec. 19, 1981; children: Carie Lynne, Chelsea Michelle. Student, W.Va. Wesleyan Coll., 1972-74. Regional rep. IDS/Am. Express Corp., Tucson, 1982-84; v.p. Mut. Benefit Fin. Group, Tucson, 1984-86, Am. Fin. Cos. (formerly Estate Fin. Services Ltd.), Tucson, 1986-88; also bd. dirs. Estate Fin. Svcs. Ltd., Tucson; fin. cons. Merrill Lynch, Tucson, 1989-94; investment advisor Dain Rauscher (formerly Rauscher, Pierce, Refsnes), Tucson, 1994—; governing bd. pres. Tanque Veroe Unified Sch. Dist. # 13, 1999; gov. bd. Tanque Verde Unified Sch. Dist. #13, 1997—. Trustee, treas. Carondelet Found., Tucson, 1995, chmn. investment and fin. com., 1995—, v.p., 1997-98, pres., 1998—; bd. dirs. Desert Survivors Inc., Tucson, 1984-86, Carondele t Health Care Sys., 1995—, mem. fin. com., 1995—. Mem. Masons. Republican. Avocations: basketball, body building, photography, American motorcycles. Home: 10621 E Sundance Cir Tucson AZ 85749-9540 Office: Dain Rauscher 3430 E Sunrise Dr Ste 250 Tucson AZ 85718-3226

GRUBB, RICK, secondary education educator. Formerly tchr. Carter High Sch., Strawberry Plains, Tenn.; transp. facilitator Dept. Transp., Knosville, Tenn., 1997—. Recipient Tchr. Excellence award Internat. Tech. Edn. Assn., 1992. Office: Dept Transp PO Box 2188 Knoxville TN 37901-2188*

GRUBB, ROBERT L., JR., neurosurgeon; b. Charlotte, N.C., May 9, 1940. MD, U. N.C., 1965. Intern Barnes Hosp., St. Louis, 1965-66, resident in gen. surgery, 1966-67, resident in neurosurgery, 1969-73; fellow NIH, Bethesda, Md., 1968-69; mem. staff Barnes-Jewish Hosp., St. Louis, Jewish Hosp., St. Louis, St. Louis Children's Hosp.; prof. neurosurgery Washington U., St. Louis. Fellow ACS; mem. Am. Acad. Neurol. Surgery, AANS, CNS, SNS. Office: Washington U Sch Medicine 660 S Euclid Ave # 8057 Saint Louis MO 63110-1010*

GRUBB, WILLIAM FRANCIS X., consumer software executive, marketing executive; b. N.Y.C., Aug. 11, 1944; s. William Martin and Eileen F. (Donnelly) G.; m. Eileen B. O'Leary, Apr. 4, 1964; children: Catherine E., William M., Kerri A., Christopher M. BA in Econs., Fordham U., 1966; MBA in Mktg. and Fin., Seton Hall U., 1972. bd. dirs. several privately-held cos. Mktg. and sales exec. Black & Decker, Towson, Md., 1968-79; v.p. mktg. Atari, Sunnyvale, Calif., 1979-81; chmn., pres. New West Mktg., Mountain View, Calif., 1981; pres., chief exec. officer, chmn. Imagic, Los Gatos, Calif., 1981-84; exec. v.p. Dataspeed, 1984-85; pres. Axlon Inc., 1985-86; exec. v.p., gen. mgr. Worlds of Wonder, Inc., Freemont, Calif., 1986-87; pres., chief exec. The Complete PC, San Jose, Calif., 1987-93; CEO, ICTV Inc., Los Gatos, Calif., 1994-96; CEO Millenia Software Inc., Saratoga, Calif., 1996—; pres. Toolz Ltd., Palo Alto, Calif., 1998—. Bd. regetns Holy Names Coll. Home: 12421 Fredericksburg Dr Saratoga CA 95070-3828 Office: Toolz Ltd 555 Bryant St # 355 Palo Alto CA 94301-1704

GRUBBS, CHRISTOPHER ANDREW, electronics company executive; b. Dallas, Jan. 9, 1948; s. Otis Henry Grubbs and Geraldine (Williams) Mudry; m. Gayla Jo Ruhmann, Oct. 5, 1983; children: Joseph Allen, Jorden Christopher, Jonah Ruhmann, Jakob Emil. BA in Bus., U. Houston, 1977. Regional mgr. Guardian Technologies, Cin., 1987-90; v.p. Electronic Surveillance, Inc., Dallas, 1990-93; CEO, pres. ProTell System, Inc., New Braunfels, Tex., 1993—; bd. dirs. CGHM, Inc., New Braunfels, Protell Systems, Inc., New Braunfels, PSI Futures Trading Co., New Braunfels, MX Imports, New Braunfels. Patentee Tamper Detect Monitoring Device, 1997. With USNR, 1967-72, Vietnam. Mem. Masons, Shriners, Lions. Republican. Roman Catholic. Avocations: pilot, numismatic, sailboating.

GRUBBS, CONWAY E., marine company executive; b. Tribbey, Okla., Mar. 26, 1918; s. Harvey Kendrick and Ida Irene (Wright) G.; m. Clyde Laverne Mason, Aug. 23, 1941; children: Jimmy Conway, Barri Lynn. Student, Northeastern Okla. A&M Coll., 1937-38. Mgr. ops., mgr. mktg., gen. mgr, v.p., dir. Caribbean, Ctrl. and So. Am. Chgo. Bridge & Iron Co., Oakbrook, Ill., 1955-69, asst. mgr. marine ops., dir. underwater welding rsch., 1969-76; mgr. worldwide underwater constrn. Chgo. Bridge & Iron Co., Prairieville, La., 1976-79; pres., owner D&W Underwater Welding Svc., Inc., Baton Rouge, 1979-84; dir. underwater welding R & D Global Divers and Contractors, Inc., Lafayette, La., 1984—; cons. U.S. Nat. Rsch. Coun., U.S. Dept. Interior; chmn. exec. com. Joint Industry Underwater Welding Devel. Program. Contbr. articles to profl. jours. With USAAF, 1941-44. Mem. Am. Welding Soc. (chmn. coms., tech. rep., Meritorious Award for Outstanding Achievements in the Science of Welding 1987), Internat. Inst. Welding (chmn., del.). Achievements include patents for Method of Underwater Welding Using Pressurized Welding Electrode Transfer Capsule and Dry Welding Electrode Insitu Storage, Viewing Scope for Turbid Environment and Use in Underwater Welding, and Method of Underwater Welding Using Viewing Scope; major advancements in underwater 'wet' welding. Office: Global Divers & Contractors PO Box 10840 New Iberia LA 70562-0840 Address: 7411 Prarie Greenwell Springs LA 70739

GRUBBS, DONALD SHAW, JR., retired actuary; b. Bellvue, Pa., Dec. 15, 1929; s. Donald Shaw and Zora Fay (Craven) G.; m. Margaret Helen Crooke, Dec. 27, 1969; children: David, Deborah, Daniel, Dawson, Dwight, Douglas. AB, Tex. A&M U., 1951; postgrad., L.A. State Coll., 1953-54, Fresno State Coll., 1954-55, Boston U., 1955-57, Princeton Theol. Sem., 1959-60, Westminster Theol. Sem., 1960-61; JD, Georgetown U., 1979. Bar: D.C. 1979. Actuarial asst. New Eng. Mut. Life Ins. Co., Boston, 1955-58, Warner Watson, Inc., Boston, 1958-59; cons. actuary John B. St. John, Penllyn, Pa., 1959-65, Grubbs & Co., Phila., 1965-72; v.p. actuary Nat. Health and Welfare Retirement Assn., N.Y.C., 1972-74; dir. actuarial div. IRS, Washington, 1974-76; cons. actuary Buck Cons., Inc., Washington, 1976-86; pres. Grubbs and Co., Inc., Silver Spring, Md., 1986-95, retired, 1995—; chmn. Joint Bd. for Enrollment Actuaries, Washington, 1975-76. Author: (with G.E. Johnson) The Variable Annuity, 1967, (with D.M. McGill) Fundamentals of Private Pensions, 6th edit., 1989. V.p. NAACP, Ambler, Pa., 1961-62; chmn. Warminster (Pa.) Child Day Care Assn., 1962-64. 1st lt. U.S. Army, 1951-53, Korea. Decorated Bronze Star with V U.S. Army, 1953; recipient Employee Benefits Outstanding Achievement award Pension World, 1986. Fellow Soc. of Actuaries (sec. 1983-84), Conf. Consulting Actuaries; mem. ABA, Middle Atlantic Actuarial Club (pres. 1981-82), UN Assn. (v.p. nat. capital area divsn. 1996-98). Democrat. Unitarian. Home: 10216 Royal Rd Silver Spring MD 20903-1613

GRUBBS, ELVEN JUDSON, retired newspaper publisher; b. Taylor County, Fla., Dec. 26, 1930; s. Judson Omer and Nancy Lourainie (Lundy) G.; m. Loretta Caruthers, June 4, 1950; 1 son, Russell Elven. Student public schs., Ocala, Fla. With Ocala Star-Banner, 1947-77, advt. dir., 1964-77, gen. mgr., 1968-77; v.p., publisher The Ledger, Lakeland, Fla., 1977-82; pub. Sarasota (Fla.) Herald-Tribune, 1982-91, ret., 1991. Former trustee John and Mable Ringling Mus. Art, Sarasota. Republican. Baptist. Home: PO Box 962 Steinhatchee FL 32359-0962

GRUBBS, J. PERRY, church administrator. Pres. Bd. of Ch. Ext. and Home Missions of the Ch. of God, Anderson, Ind., 1987—. Office: Church of God PO Box 2069 Anderson IN 46018-2069*

GRUBBS, JUDITH EVANS, classical studies educator; b. Atlanta, Nov. 30, 1956; d. Trevor and Ellen Enid (Lovell) Evans; m. Charles Thompson Grubbs, Aug. 18, 1979; 1 child, Charlotte. BA with highest honors, Emory U., 1978; postgrad., Am. Sch. Classical Studies, Athens, Greece, 1978-79; PhD in Classics, Stanford U., 1987. Lectr. Intercollegiate Ctr. Classical Studies, Rome, 1984-85; tchg. fellow classics Stanford (Calif.) U., 1983-84, 85-87; asst. prof. Sweet Briar (Va.) Coll., 1987-93, dir. honors program, 1995-96, assoc. prof. classical studies, 1993—. Author: Law and Family in Late Antiquity: The Emperor Constantine's Marriage Legislation, 1995; contbr. articles and book revs. to profl. jours. Recipient ITT internat. fellowship, Greece, 1978-79, grad. fellowship Stanford U., 1979-83, Mednick grant Va. Found. Ind. Colls., 1988, Jessie Ball Dupont fellowship Nat. Humanities Ctrs., N.C., 1993-94, fellowship for coll. tchrs. NEH, 1997-98. Mem. Am. Philol. Assn. (edn. com. 1997—), Assn. Ancient Historians, Classical Assn. Mid. West and South, Classical Assn. Va., Women's Classical Caucus, N.Am. Patristics Soc. Episcopalian. Home: PO Box 52 Sweet Briar VA 24595-0052 Office: Sweet Briar Coll Dept Classical Studies Sweet Briar VA 24595

GRUBBS, ROBERT HOWARD, chemistry educator; b. Calvert City, Ky., Feb. 27, 1942; s. Henry Howard and Faye (Atwood) G.; m. Helen Matilda O'Kane; children—Robert B., Brendan H., Kathleen M. B.S., U. Fla., 1963, M.S., 1965; Ph.D., Columbia U., 1968. NIH postdoctoral fellow Stanford U., Calif., 1968-69; asst. prof. Mich. State U., East Lansing, 1969-73, assoc. prof., 1973-78; prof. chemistry Calif. Inst. Tech., Pasadena, 1978—, Victor and Elizabeth Atkins prof., 1989. Contbr. articles to profl. publs.; patentee in field. Fellow Sloan Found., 1974-76, Alexander von Humboldt Found., 1975; Dreyfus Found. scholar, 1975-78; recipient award in Polymer Chem. Am. Chem. Soc., 1995. Mem. AAAS, NAS, Am. Chem. Soc. (Organic Chemistry award 1989, Polymer Chemistry award 1995). Democrat. Home: 1700 Spruce St South Pasadena CA 91030-4721 Office: Calif Inst Tech Dept Chemistry 164-30 Pasadena CA 91125

GRUBE, BRUCE F., academic official. Assoc. v.p. adminstrn. Calif. State Poly. U., Pomona, until 1987, provost, acad. v.p., 1987-95; pres. St. Cloud (Minn.) U., 1995—. Office: Saint Cloud Univ Office of the President Stearns County Saint Cloud MN 56301-4498

GRUBE, JAMES R., federal judge; b. 1942. BA, U. Santa Clara, 1964; JD, U. Calif., 1967. Asst. dist. atty. City and County of San Francisco, 1970-75; with Murray & Grube, Palo Alto, Calif., 1975-79, Campeau & Grube, San Jose, Calif., 1980-88; apptd. bankruptcy judge no. dist. U.S. Dist. Ct. Calif., 1988. With U.S. Army, 1968-69. Mem. ABA, Am. Bankruptcy Inst., Nat. Conf. Bankruptcy Judges, U.S. Dist. Ct. for State Bar of Calif., No. Dist. of Calif. Histo. Soc., Santa Clara County Bar Assn., Bay Area Bankruptcy Forum, Bench and Bar Hist. Soc. of Santa Clara County. Office: US Bankruptcy Ct Rm 3035 280 S 1st St San Jose CA 95113-3002

GRUBE, KARL BERTRAM, judge; b. Elmhurst, Ill., Jan. 13, 1946; s. Karl Ludwig and Gerturde (Bertram) G.; m. Mary B. Harr, May 4, 1974 (div. Aug. 1991). BSBA, Elmhurst Coll., 1967; JD, Stetson U., 1970; M in Judicial Studies, U. Nev., 1992. Asst. pub. defender State of Fla., Clearwater, 1970-73; county ct. judge State of Fla., St. Petersburg, 1977—; pvt. practice Seminole, Fla., 1973-76; city atty. City of Redington Beach, Fla., 1975-76; asst. dean Fla. Jud. Coll., Tallahassee, 1984-85; faculty mem., course coord., mem. faculty coun. Nat. Jud. Coll.; mem. Nat. Hwy. Traffic Safety Jud. Tng. Implementation Bd. Contbr. articles to profl. jours. Dir. Pinellas Comprehensive Addiction Svcs., Clearwater, 1982-88. Jud. fellow U.S. Dept. Transp., 1998, Nat. Hwy. Traffice Safety Adminstn., 1999. Mem. ABA (conf. chmn. divsn. jud. adminstrn. 1992, del. to jud. divsn. coun. 1997—, Dedicated Svc. award 1991), Fla. Bar Assn. (civil rule com.), Colo. Bar Assn., Fla. Conf. County Ct. Judges (pers. com. 1984-85), Rolls Royce Owner's Club (editor 1982-84). Lutheran. Avocations: collecting fountain pens, collecting antique watches, auto restoration. Office: Pinellas County Ct 150 5th St N Ste 304 Saint Petersburg FL 33701-3700

GRUBER, FREDRIC FRANCIS, financial planning and investment research executive; b. Pekin, Ill., July 16, 1931; s. Louis Simon and Lillian Frances (Klein) G.; m. Dolores Rae Hanson, Aug. 15, 1960; children: Darrell Grant, Eric Tyson. B.S. in Acctg., Bradley U., 1956; postgrad., Northwestern U. C.P.A. Audit mgr. Arthur Young & Co., Chgo., 1956-63; controller Associated Coca-Cola Bottling Co., Inc., Daytona Beach, Fla., 1963-66; asst. treas. Associated Coca-Cola Bottling Co., Inc., 1964-66, treas., 1966-83, v.p., 1976-83; exec. v.p. Rich-United Corp., 1983-84; pres. Aquaculture Food Farms Inc., 1984-85; fin. cons., 1985-86; exec.v.p. G.A. Repple Fin. Group, Inc., Maitland, Fla., 1986-87; registered rep. Mut. Svc. Corp., 1987-93; CFP Investment Mgmt. and Rsch., Inc., 1993-96; CFP, CEP G.A. Repple & Co., 1996—; reg. repr. NASD. Served with USCG, 1950-53. Mem. AICPA, Fin. Execs. Inst., Fla. Inst. CPA's, Inst. CFP's (registry practitioners), Nat. Coun. Cert. Estate Planners.

GRUBER, GEORGE MICHAEL, accountant, financial systems consultant; b. Euclid, Ohio, Sept. 9, 1951; s. George and Cecilia Marie (Cantwell) G.; m. Alice Armas Peralta, June 22, 1985; 1 child, Christian Alexander. BS in Acctg. and Fin., San Francisco State U., 1983, MBA in Fin., 1991. Letterpress printer Custom Printing Assocs., San Francisco, 1973-78; voucher examiner U.S. Dept. Labor, San Francisco, 1980-81; teamster United Courier, Inc., San Francisco, 1979-81; bookkeeper, tile setter Curry Tile, Albany, Calif., 1982; sr. staff acct., fin. analyst Marriott Corp. divsn. Farrells Restaurants Inc., San Francisco, 1983-85; asst. contr. Bay Area Seating Svc., Oakland, Calif., 1985-87; mgr. acctg. and fin. divsn. Grand Met. Plc (Pillsbury) The Häagen Dazs Co. Inc., Hayward, Calif., 1987-90; corp. contr. Andronico's Park & Shop Inc., Albany, Calif., 1991; div. contr. Core-Mark Internat., Hayward, 1991-93; founder, owner Gruber Fin. Svcs. (GFS), 1993—; mid-Pacific regional fin. acctg. contr. DFS, L.P., Tamuning, Guam, 1993-95; guest lectr. fin. San Francisco State U., 1990-91. With USMC, 1969-72, Vietnam. Mem. Inst. Mgmt. Accts. (v.p. edn. 1991-92, pres. 1992-93, cert. of appreciation 1992-93), Nat. Soc. Pub. Accts., VFW, 3d Marine Divsn. Assn., Am. Legion. Avocations: cycling, archery, pistol, reading, martial arts (Tang Soo Do). Email: GGruber@PacBell.net. Home and Office: Gruber Fin Svcs Co 432 Congo St San Francisco CA 94131-3111

GRUBER, IRA DEMPSEY, historian, educator; b. Phila., Jan. 6, 1934; married; 3 children. AB, Duke U., 1955, AM, 1959, PhD, 1961. Instr. history Duke U., 1961-62; fellow Inst. Early Am. History and Culture, 1962-65; asst. prof. Occidental Coll., 1965-66; from asst. prof. to assoc. prof., 1966-74; prof. Rice U., Houston, from 1974, now Harris Masterson prof. history, chmn. dept. history, 1983-87; master Hanszen Coll., Rice U., 1968-73; John F. Morrison prof. U.S. Army Command and Gen. Staff Coll., 1979-80; vis. prof. mil. history U.S. Mil. Acad., 1984-85, 92-93; mem. hist. adv. com. USAF, 1987-91, Dept. Army, 1992-95; trustee Soc. for Mil. History, 1987-95. Author: Lord Howe and Lord George Germain, 1965, The American Revolution as a Conspiracy: The British View, 1969, The Howe Brothers and the American Revolution, 1972, The Education of Sir Henry Clinton, 1990; co-author: Classical Traditions in Early America, 1976, Reconsiderations on the Revolutionary War, 1978, Limits of Loyalty, 1980, Arms and Independence, 1984, Against All Enemies, 1986, America's First Battles, 1986, Warfare in the Western World, 1996; editor: John Peebles American War, 1998; mem. editl. bd. Jour. of Mil. History, 1995—, chair editl. bd., 1999—. Office: Rice Univ Dept History 6100 Main St Houston TX 77005-1892

GRUBER, JACK, medical virologist, biomedical research administrator; b. Bklyn., Apr. 18, 1931; s. Harry and Rose (Kramer) G.; m. Patricia Ann Mason, June 28, 1964; 1 child, Harry Mason. BS, CUNY, Bklyn., 1954; PhD, U. Ky., 1963. Rsch. asst., lab. instr. dept. microbiology U. Ky., Lexington, 1955-61; rsch. bacteriologist U.S. Army Biol. Labs., Ft. Detrick, Frederick, Md., 1962-63; bacterial immunology microbiologist Med. Scis. Lab., Ft. Detrick, 1963-67, viral immunology microbiologist, 1967-70; microbiologist, rsch. program adminstr. viral biology br. Nat. Cancer Inst., NIH, 1970-72, chief office of program resources and logistics, viral oncology program, 1972-78, asst. chief biol. carcinogenesis br., divsn. cancer etiology, 1978-80; dep. chief biol. carcinogenesis br., divsn. cancer biology Nat. Cancer Inst., Bethesda, Md., 1980-84, chief, 1984—. Editor: (with others) Primates and Human Cancer, 1979; contbr. articles to profl. jours. Achievements include research and publications on rheumatic fever and in vitro leukocytic hypersensitivity with group A streptococci; purification, concentration and inacivation of Venezuelan equine encephalitis virus; the relationship of DNA viruses and cervical carcinoma; the biology of SV40 and polyomavirus transformations; prospects for viral vaccine development; pathogenic diversity of Epstein-Barr virus; viral T-antigen interactions with cellular proto-oncogenes and anti-oncogene products; the role of human viruses in malignancies associated with AIDS; progress and prospects for human cancer vaccines; viral interactions with the P53 gene; vaccines for human cancers of viral etiology; Helicobacter and human cancer; development of Epstein-Barr virus vaccines. Office: National Cancer Institute NIH Exec Plz N # 540 Bethesda MD 20892

GRUBER, JOHN BALSBAUGH, physics educator, university administrator; b. Hershey, Pa., Feb. 10, 1935; s. Irvin John and Erla R. (Balsbaugh) G.; m. Judith Anne Higer, June 20, 1961; children: David Powell, Karen Leigh, Mark Balsbaugh. B.S., Haverford (Pa.) Coll., 1957; Ph.D., U. Calif. at Berkeley, 1961. NATO postdoctoral fellow Inst. Tech. Physics, Tech. U. Darmstadt, Germany, 1961-62; gastdozent Inst. Tech. Physics, Tech. U. Darmstadt, 1961-62; asst. prof. physics U. Calif. at Los Angeles, 1962-66; asso. prof. physics Wash. State U., Pullman, 1966-71; prof. chem. physics Wash. State U., 1971-75; asst. dean Wash. State U. (Grad. Sch.), 1968-70, assoc. dean, 1970-72; prof. physics, dean Coll. Sci. and Math., N.D. State U., Fargo, 1975-80; prof. physics and chemistry, v.p. for acad. affairs Portland (Oreg.) State U., 1980-84; prof. physics San Jose State U., 1984—, acad. v.p., 1984-86, v.p. devel., 1986, dir. Inst. for Modern Optics, 1992—; vis. prof. Joint Ctr. Grad. Study, Richland, Wash., 1964, 65, 66, Ames Lab., Dept. of Energy, Iowa State U., 1976-80; Disting. vis. prof. U.S. Navy Naval Weapons Ctr., China Lake, Calif., 1984-93, Stanford U., 1993—; invited lectr., U.S., Can., Europe, 1966—; cons. in laser physics and spectroscopy Aerospace Corp., El Segundo, Calif., 1962-65, Douglas Aircraft and McDonnell Douglas Astronautics Co., Santa Monica, Calif., 1963-69, N.Am. Aviation, Space and Info. Systems, Downey, Calif., 1964-66, Battelle-Northwest, Richland, Wash., 1964-69, Los Alamos (N.Mex.) Sci. Lab., 1969-71, 73-74; mem. task force lunar exploration sci. Apollo, NASA, 1964-69, 71-73; cons. Harry Diamond Labs. U.S. Army, 1981—, U.S. Army Rsch. Lab., IBM, 1985-90, GTE, 1986-89, Lasergenics, 1986—, Night Vision Lab. U.S. Army, Ft. Belvoir, 1988—, Deltron, 1990-91, Rey Tech Corp., 1998—, Laser Sci. and Tech., 1999—; mem. Rare Earth Rsch. Conf. Com., 1976-83, exec. com., 1977-83, sec. bd. dirs., 1979-84; gen. conf. chmn. XIV Internat. Rare Earth Rsch. Conf., 1979, Novel Laser Sources and Materials, 1982; exec. sec. Internat. Frank H. Spedding Award, 1979, 83, Willig award, 1986, Internat. Spencer prize for outstanding contbrn. to sci., 1987, Pres.'s Scholar, 1994-95, Outstanding Achievement awards U.S. Dept. Def., 1995, 96, 98, Nom. U.S. Asst. Sec. Def. (Spl. Ops.), 1986-87; chmn. U.S. Navy/ASEE Postdoctoral Selection Bd., 1988—, U.S. Nat. Inst. Sci. and Tech. Postdoctoral Selection Bd., 1989-91; mem. rev. panel U.S. Navy/ASEE Grad. Fellowship Program, 1990—; chmn., mem. NASA/ASEE program rev. bd., 1994—; chmn. Internat. Conf. on Novel Laser Sources and Applications, San Jose, Calif., 1993, chmn. Battelle U.S. Dept. Def. Scholarship Prgram, 1994—; mem. Battelle Sci. Bd. for selection of grad. scholarship fellows, 1998—; vis. scholar Stanford U., 1993—. Contbr. articles to profl. jours., chpts. to books; holder numerous patents in laser sci. and tech. Trustee Symphony Bd. Fargo-Moorhead Symphony Orch., 1978-80; pres. Franklin Elementary Sch. PTA, Pullman, 1973-74; pres. elect PTA coordinating council, City of Pullman, 1974-75; v.p. Horace Mann Elementary Sch. PTA, Fargo, 1975-76, pres., 1976-77; mem. PTA coordinating council, City of Fargo, 1976-77, N.D. State Bd. PTA; chmn. Univ., Coll. and Pub. Sch. Relations Bd., 1979-80; active Boy Scouts Am.; trustee Pullman Pub. Library, 1973-75, N.D. Symphony Orchestras Assn., 1978-80; mem. planning commn. City of Pullman, 1972-75; bd. dirs. Westminster Found., 1982-84. Recipient Outstanding Merit and Performance award San Jose State U., 1990, San Jose State Pres.'s Scholar award, 1994-95, Dist. Tchr./scholar award, 1996, 97, 99, Disting. Performance award in the field of lasers and electro-optics U. Chgo., 1995, Citation for Svc. and Achievement Dept. of Def., 1996, Award for Rsch. into night vision devices U.S. Army, 1997, Outstanding World Leadership in Sci. award Acad. Scis., Poland, 1998; grantee AEC-ERDA, 1963-75, NSF, 1966-72; 76-78, 92—, U.S. Army Rsch. Office, Durham, 1979-80, Am. Chem. Soc. Petroleum Rsch. Funds, 1979-80, Dept. Energy, 1979-84, Dept. Def., 1984—, Office Naval Rsch., 1987—, Office Naval Tech., 1988-93, Dept. Def., DARPA, 1998—; fellow NASA Ames Lab., 1993-95; vis. scholar Stanford U., 1993—. Fellow Am. Soc. Engring. Edn. (disting.), Am. Phys. Soc. (chmn. nat. mtg. sessions), Am. Acad. Spectral Scis.; mem. AAAS, IEEE (sec. lasers and electro-optics 1995-96), NSF (reviewer and panel mem. divsn. material sci. 1994—), N.Y. Acad. Scis., N.D. Acad. Sci., Oreg. Acad. Sci., Acad. Scis. of Ukraine, Nat. Acad. Scis. (com. on lasers and electro-optics), Coun. Colls. Arts and Scis., Optical Soc. No. Calif. (v.p. 1992, pres. 1993), Lasers and Electro-optics Soc. (mem. program com. nat. meeting 1995), Internat. Soc. Optical Engring. (bd. dirs. 1993), Phi Beta Kappa, Sigma Xi, Phi Kappa Phi, Sigma Pi Sigma, Phi Sigma Iota. Presbyterian (ruling elder). Clubs: Mason (Shriner), Kiwanian. E-mail: jbgruber@email.sjsu.edu. Home: 5870 Meander Dr San Jose CA 95120-3839

GRUBER, JOHN EDWARD, editor, railroad historian, photographer; b. Chgo., May 18, 1936; s. Edward David and Leah Elizabeth (Diehl) G.; m. Bonnie Jean Barstow, May 12, 1962; children: Richard J., Timothy J. BA in Journalism, U. Wis., 1959, postgrad., 1981-84. Editor, writer U. Wis., Madison, 1960-95; editor Vintage Rails, Waukesha, Wis., 1995—. Author: Focus on Rails, 1989, (pamphlet) Madison's Pioneer Buildings, 1987; acting editor Rail News, 1999—; also articles; contbr. photographs to Trains mag., 1960—. Dir. Historic Madison, Inc., 1981-89. Recipient Nat. Award in R.R. History for photography Rwy. and Locomotive Hist. Soc., 1994; James J. Hill rsch. grantee Hill Reference Libr., 1986. Mem. Mid-Continent Railway Hist. Soc. (bd. dirs. 1984-87, 88-97, pres. 1988-89, sec. 1990-95, v.p. 1995-97, editor Mid-Continent Railway Gazette 1982-99), Ctr. for R.R. Photography and Art (pres. 1997—). Home: 1430 Drake St Madison WI 53711-2211 Office: Pentrex Pub Waukesha WI 53187-0379

GRUBER, WILLIAM PAUL, journalist; b. Chgo., May 2, 1932; s. Frank and Gisella (Rudelitch) G. B.S. in Journalism, U. Ill., 1954. Asst. editor Community News, Woodstock, Ill., 1954-55; reporter, markets editor UPI, 1958-63; mem. staff Chicago's Am., 1963—; fin. editor Chgo. Today, 1968-74; fin. writer, columnist Chgo. Tribune, 1974-98; ret., 1998. Served with AUS, 1955-57. Mem. Soc. Am. Bus. Editors and Writers, Chgo. Press Vets. Assn., Soc. Profl. Journalists. Home: 5901 N Sheridan Rd Chicago IL 60660-3616

GRUBERG, MARTIN, political science educator; b. N.Y.C., Jan. 28, 1935; s. Benjamin and Mollie (Stolnitz) G.; m. Rosaline Kurfirst, Mar. 25, 1967 (dec. 1980); m. Humaira Sayeed, Aug. 15, 1983. BA, CCNY, 1955; PhD, Columbia U., 1963. Agt.-adjudicator Passport Agy., Dept. State, N.Y.C, 1960-61; tchr. social studies Pelham (N.Y.) High Sch., 1961-62; instr. polit. sci. CUNY-Hunter Coll., 1961-62; tchr. social studies James Monroe and Seward Park High Schs., N.Y.C., 1962-63; asst. prof. polit. sci. U. Wis., Oshkosh, 1963-66, assoc. prof., 1966-69, prof., chmn. dept., 1969-72, dir. pre-law program, 1966-69, 83—, coord. criminal justice program, 1983-87. Author: Women in American Politics, 1968, A Case Study in U.S. Urban Leadership: The Incumbency of Milwaukee Mayor Henry Maier, 1996, A History of Winnebago County Government, 1998; newspaper column: Women: Our Largest Minority, The Paper for Ctrl. Wiso., 1970-71, Spotlight on Women for Oshkosh Northwestern, 1971-73; Broadcast 16 weeks Civil Rights Revolution, Wis. State FM Network, 1974; editor: Wis. Polit. Scientist, 1986-91; contbr. articles to encys., profl. jours. Pres. Oshkosh Human Rights Coun., 1966-68; v.p. Winnebago chpt. NOW, 1970-71, sec. Oshkosh chpt., 1980-81, pres., 1981-83; pres. Women's Caucus of Midwest Polit. Scientists, 1980-81; pres. Fox Valley ACLU, 1985—. Recipient Am. Legion Aux. Americanism award, 1949, Buckvar award, 1955, Steigman award, 1955; N.Y. State scholar, 1952; Columbia grantee, 1961, 62, Wis. Regents' rsch. grantee, 1964-70, 73-75. Mem. AAUP (state sec. 1975-81, pres.-elect 1981-82, 91-92, pres. 1982-83, 92-93), Am. Polit. Sci. Assn., Midwest Polit. Sci. Assn., Wis. Polit. Sci. Assn. (pres. 1974-75), Law and Soc. Assn., Acad. Criminal Justice Scis., Candlelight Club, Optimists. Home: 2121 Oregon St Oshkosh WI 54901-7058 Office: U Wis Clow Hall Oshkosh WI 54901

GRUBIC, ADRIANNE, journalist; b. Morristown, N.J., Mar. 2, 1975; d. Roger Allen and Janice Faye Grubic. BA, Auburn U., 1997; M Mass comms., U. S.C., 1998. Grad. asst. S.C. Press Assn., Columbia, 1997-98; intern WGNX-TV, Atlanta, 1998; assoc. editor HockeyInsider.com, 1998—. Mem. Soc. Profl. Journalists (publs. chmn. 1997), Assn. Women in Sports Media, Omega Phi Alpha (comms. dir. 1997—). Avocations: running, basketball, web design, volunteering, rollerblading. E-mail: krinklefish@mindspring.com. Home: 2255 Lenox Rd NE Apt A24 Atlanta GA 30324

GRUBIN, SHARON E., federal judge; b. Newark, Feb. 9, 1949; d. Harold and Blanche (Dultz) G. AB with honors, Smith Coll., 1970; JD with honors in Legal Writing and Analysis, Boston U., 1973. Bar: N.Y. 1974, U.S. Dist. Ct. (so. and ea. dists.) N.Y. 1974, U.S. Ct. Appeals (2nd cir.) 1974. Litigator White & Case, N.Y.C., 1973-84; judge U.S. Dist. Ct. (so. dist.) N.Y., N.Y.C., 1984—; chair 2d Cir. Task Force on Gender, Racial and Ethnic Fairness in the Cts.; lectr. NYU Sch. Law, Yale Law Sch., Bklyn. Law Sch., N.Y. Law Sch.; dir., sec., exec. com. Lawyers' Com. on Violence, Inc. Author: (with others) Advocacy-The Art of Pleading a Cause, 1985, Removal, Federal Civil Practice, 1989, and supplement, 1993; spkr. seminars in field. Mem. ABA (chair spl. projects com. 1996-97, nat. conf. fed. trial judges, jud. adminstrn. divsn.), Nat. Assn. Women Judges (chair fed. gender bias com., publicity and pub. affairs com., newsletter com.), Fed. Bar Coun. (trustee, exec. com., chair nominating com. 1994, v.p. 1990-94, award com. 1988-94, com. on 2d cir. cts. 1982-96, long-range planning com. 1992-96), N.Y. State Bar Assn. (exec. com., nominations com., fed. cts. task force, comml. and fed. litig. sect.), N.Y. Sttate Assn. Women Judges (bd. dirs.), Assn. of Bar of City of N.Y. (long-range planning com., chair nominating com. 1995—, chair spl. com. on legal history 1994-96, chair spl. com. on Orison S. Marden Meml. lectrs., chair 1994-96, exec. com. 1990-94, spl. com. on gender bias in fed. cts. 1991-94, coun. on jud. adminstrn. 1986-90, prof. and jud. ethics com. 1986-89, nominating com. 1984-85, 95-96, com. on jud. 1982-83, chair young lawyers com. 1979-81), Am. Judicature Soc. (editl. com. 1994-97). Office: US Dist Ct US Courthouse 500 Pearl St Rm 1360 New York NY 10007-1316

GRUBMAN, WALLACE KARL, chemical company executive; b. N.Y.C., Sept. 12, 1928; s. Samuel and Mildred G.;/ m. Ruth R. Winer, July 29, 1950; children: James (dec.), Steven L., Eric P. BSChemE, Columbia U., 1950; MS, NYU, 1954. With Nat. Starch and Chem. Corp., 1950-93; corp. v.p., gen. mgr. adhesive div. Nat. Starch and Chem. Corp., Bridgewater, N.J., 1972-77; group v.p. Nat. Starch and Chem. Corp., 1977-78, pres., chief operating officer, dir., 1978-83, pres., chief exec. officer, 1983-84, chmn., chief exec. officer, 1984-85, also bd. dirs.; group head chems. Unilever PLC and Unilever NV, 1986-91; pres. Ridge Assocs. Mgmt. Cons.; bd. dirs. Jorin Ltd., U.K.; cons. bd. dirs. United Nat. Bancorp, Bridgewater, N.J., dir. Jorin Corp. Ltd., 1998—. Fellow London Inst. Dirs., Instn. Chem. Engrs. London; mem. Chem. Mfrs. Assn., Soc. Chem. Industry, Am. Inst. Chem. Engrs., Princeton Club, Sky Club (N.Y.C.), Roxiticus Golf Club (Mendham, N.J.), Mid-Ocean (Bermuda) Club, Wentworth Golf (Eng.) Club, Chmns. Club (London). Office: PO Box 977, Ascot Berkshire SL5 ORD, England

GRUCA, PAWEL PIOTR, neuroradiologist; b. Warsaw, Poland, Oct. 13, 1959; came to U.S., 1977, naturalized, 1996; s. Jerzy and Stefania Maria (Swigon) G.; m. Renata Maria Olejnik, June 15, 1989 (div. May 1993). *Father, Jerzy Gruca, was born in 1931 in Warsaw, Poland. He studied Polish language, literature, and philosphy at the University of Warsaw. He completed theological studies at the Academy of Catholic Theology in Warsaw in 1966. He was a contributing editor to the Catholic Weekly, Kierunki (Directions), and assistant editor of the Catholic monthly, Zycie i Mysl (Life and Thought). He was an accredited correspondent to the Holy See and to the Republic of Italy with the office in Rome, 1982-86. His daily correspondences from Rome and Vatican City were published on pages of the Polish Catholic daily, Slowo Powszechne (Popular Word). His memoirs and observations from the Vatican were compiled in the book titled Watykan znany i nieznany (Vatican Known and Unknown), published by Oficyna Wydawniczo-Poligraficzna ADAM, Warszawa, 1993.* BS in Radiologic Tech. cum laude, St. Mary's Coll., Orchard Lake, Mich., 1981; DO, Coll. Osteo. Medicine, 1987. Diplomate Am. Osteo. Bd. Radiology. Intern Muskegon (Mich.) Gen. Hosp., 1987-88; instr., resident Mich. State U., East Lansing, 1988-92; fellow in neuroradiology Henry Ford Hosp., Detroit, 1992-94; pvt. practice radiology and neuroradiology, Pottsville, Pa., 1994-95, Aberdeen, S.D., 1995—; asst. med. dir. dept. radiology Avera St. Luke's, 1995—; med. dir. health sci. program in radiologic tech. Presentation Coll., Aberdeen, 1998—; vis. lectr. neuroradiology Temple U., Phila., 1994; lectr. diagnostic radiology S.D. State U., 1996; lectr. ultrasound S.D. Soc. Radiologic Technologists Conv., 1997. Mem. AMA, Am. Coll. Radiology, Am. Osteo. Coll. Radiology, Radiol. Soc. N.Am., Am. Soc. Neuroradiology, Am. Soc. Spine Radiology, Am. Soc. Pediat. Neuroradiology, S.D. State Med. Assn. Republican. Roman Catholic. Home: 1006 N 2d St Apt 5 Aberdeen SD 57401-2316 Office: St Luke's Midland Radiology 305 S State St Aberdeen SD 57401-4527

GRUCHACZ, CRAIG M., financial executive; b. Glen Ridge, N.J., Nov. 13, 1954; s. Thaddeus Adam and Edith (Wilby) G.; m. Rita Maria Maltino, May 25, 1980; children: Christina Maria, Gabrielle Lyn. BS in BA, Montclair (N.J.) State Coll., 1978; MBA in Fin., Seton Hall U., 1983. With Inspiration Copper Consol. Co., Morristown, N.J., 1978-79, Westinghouse Elec. Co., Bloomfield, N.J., 1979-83; with Philips Lighting Co., Bloomfield, 1983-84, corp. cost mgr., 1984-86; group contr. Philips Electronics, N.Y.C., 1986-90; v.p., CFO Philips Electronic Instruments, Mahwah, N.J., 1990-92; sr. v.p., CFO Philips Credit Corp., N.Y.C., 1992-95; v.p., CFO Philips Lighting Co., Somerset, N.J., 1995—; chmn. SAP steering com. Republican. Roman Catholic. Avocations: politics, financial markets, gardening, children. Home: 7 Vale Rd Whippany NJ 07981-2317 Office: Philips Lighting Co 200 Franklin Square Dr Somerset NJ 08873-4186

GRUCHACZ, ROBERT S., real estate executive; b. Bloomfield, N.J., May 15, 1929; s. Stanley A. and Mae (Zalenski) G.; m. LaVerne T. Stein, Mar. 2, 1957; children—Robert S., Thomas A., Christopher J. B.S., Seton Hall U., 1950; M.B.A., NYU, 1971; student, Advanced Mgmt. Program, Harvard U., 1973. C.P.A., N.J. With Arthur Young & Co., C.P.A.'s, 1955-58, Sterling Drug Inc., N.Y.C., 1958-65; controller Nabisco Inc., 1965-72, asst. to pres., 1973-74, 76—, v.p., 1979-84; broker Dunes Mktg. Group and Sea Pines Realty, 1985-94; exec. v.p. Aurora Products, 1974-76. Served as 1st lt. USAF, 1952-54. Mem. Am. Inst. CPAs. Home: 11 Timbermarsh Ln Hilton Head Island SC 29926-2790 Office: 6 Queens Folly Rd Hilton Head Island SC 29928-5110

GRUCHALLA, MICHAEL EMERIC, electronics engineer; b. Houston, Feb. 2, 1946; s. Emeric Edwin and Myrtle (Priebe) G.; m. Elizabeth Tyson, June 14, 1969; children: Kenny, Katie. BSEE, U. Houston, 1968; MSEE, U. N.Mex., 1980. Registered profl. engr., Tex. Project engr. Tex. Instruments Corp., Houston, 1967-68; group leader EG&G Washington Analytical Services Ctr., Albuquerque, 1974-88; sr. staff engr. EG&G Energy Measurements Inc., Albuquerque, 1988-94; engring. specialist Allied Signal FM&T, Albuquerque, 1994—; cons. engring., Albuquerque; lectr. in field, 1978—; expert witness in field; presenter sci. testimony before Ho. of Reps. Sci. Com., 1996. Contbr. articles to tech. jours.; patentee in field. Judge local sci. fairs, Albuquerque, 1983—. Served to capt. USAF, 1968-74. Recipient R&D 100 award, 1991, Gen. Mgr.'s Vision award Dept. Energy, 1994. Mem. IEEE, Instrumentation Soc. Am., Planetary Soc., N.Mex. Tex. Instruments Computer Group (pres. 1984-85), Electric Auto Assn. (v.p. Albuquerque chpt. 1994—), Sigma Xi, Tau Beta Pi, Eta Kappa Nu. Avocations: electro-optics, photography, woodworking. Office: Allied Signal KCD PO Box 5250 Albuquerque NM 87185-5250

GRUDEN, JON, professional football coach; b. Sandusky, Ohio, Aug. 17, 1963. Student, U. Dayton. Asst. coach U. Tenn., 1986-87, U. Southeast Mo., 1988-89, San Francisco 49ers, 1990, U. Pitts., 1991, Green Bay Packers, 1992-94; offensive coord. Phila. Eagles, 1994-97; head coach Oakland Raiders, 1998—. Office: Oakland Raiders 1220 Harbor Bay Pky Alameda CA 94502

GRUDENS, RICHARD WILLIAM, retail executive, writer; b. Bklyn., May 3, 1932; s. Walter Joseph and Elizabeth Grudzinski; m. Joan Harrington, May 23, 1953 (div. May 1970); children: Donna, Nancy, Richard, Kenneth; m. Jeannette Snyder, Feb. 10, 1971; children: Peter, James, William, Robert. Student, La Salle Ext. U., 1970-73. Tickets mgr., newswriter NBC Studios, N.Y.C., 1951-55; sales mgr. Tomkins Bros., Jamaica, N.Y., 1955-67; owner, operator, pres. Alamo Art Corp., Selden and L.I., N.Y., 1967-75, St. James Gen. Store, N.Y., 1975-79, Edison & Kellogg Stores, St. James, 1979—; freelance writer, 1960—. Author: The Best Damn Trumpet Player, 1996, The Song Stars, 1997, The Music, Men, 1998, Jukebox Saturday Night, 1999, Snootie Little Cutie, 1999. Prse. Depot Hills Joint Coun. Civic Assn., Huntington, N.Y., 1960-67. With USN, 1950-58. Mem. Am. Soc. Portrait Artists, Assoc. Locksmiths Am., Soc. Singers, Pub. Mktg. Assn., L.I. Salesmens Assn. (sec. 1958-67), Lions (v.p. 1960-65). Roman Catholic. Avocations: portrait painting, writing magazine articles, gardening. Home: 553 N Country Rd Saint James NY 11780 Office: Celebrity Profiles Pub Box 344 Main St Stony Brook NY 11790

GRUDZIELANEK, MARK JAMES, professional baseball player; b. Milw., June 30, 1970. Student, Trinidad (Colo.) Jr. Coll. Selected 11th round free-agt. draft Montreal Expos, 1994, shortstop, 3d baseman, 2d baseman, 1995-99; infielder L.A. Dodgers, 1999—; selected Nat. League All-Star Team, 1996. Office: LA Dodgers Dodger Stadium 1000 Elysian Park Ave Los Angeles CA 90012*

GRUEBELE, MARTIN, chemistry educator; b. Stuttgart, Federal Republic of Germany, Jan. 10, 1964; came to U.S., 1980; s. Helmut and Edith Victoria (Berner) G.; m. Nancy Makri, July 10, 1992; 2 children. BS in Chemistry, U. Calif., Berkeley, 1984, PhD in Chemistry, 1988. Rsch. fellow Calif. Inst. Tech., Pasadena, 1989-92; asst. prof. dept. chemistry U. Ill., Urbana, 1992-98, assoc. prof., 1998-99, prof., 1999—. Sr. editor Jour. Phys. Chemistry; mem. editl. bd. Jour. Chem. Physics. Recipient New Faculty award Dreyfus Found., 1992, Nat. Young Investigator award NSF, 1994; fellow IBM, 1986-87, Dow Chem. Co., 1987-88, David and Lucile Packard Found., 1994, Sloan fellow, 1997; Cottrell scholar, 1995, Camille and Henry Dreyfus scholar, 1998, Alfred P. Sloan fellow, 1998; Univ. scholar U. Ill., 1998. Mem. Am. Phys. Soc., Am. Chem. Soc., Biophys. Soc., Sigma Xi. Achievements include theoretical and experimental studies of novel transient molecular species, studies in laser-control of chemical reactions and molecular vibrational relaxation, as well as fast time-resolved protein folding dynamics. Office: U Ill Dept Chemistry Box 5-6 600 S Mathews Ave Urbana IL 61801-3602

GRUEN, DAVID HENRY, financial executive, consultant; b. Buffalo, Aug. 12, 1929; s. Edward Charles and Florence (Knoche) G.; m. Joan Willard, Jan. 3, 1976; children by previous marriage: David E., Stephen P., Cathryn E., Edward Charles II, William A. B.A., Cornell U., 1951, M.B.A., 1954. C.P.A., N.Y. Sr. accountant Arthur Andersen & Co., N.Y.C., 1954-59; asst. treas. Marine Midland Banks, Inc., 1959-60, asst. v.p., 1960-63, v.p., treas., 1963-69; sr. v.p. Marine Midland Bank-Western, 1969-74; sr. v.p., treas. Marine Midland Banks, Inc., Buffalo, 1974-80; sr. v.p., gen. auditor, 1980-85; cons. Gruen Assocs., Buffalo, 1986—; v.p., chief fin. officer Niagara Envelope Group Inc., Buffalo, N.Y., 1986-89. Served from 2d lt. to 1st lt. USAF, 1951-53. Mem. Am. Inst. C.P.A.s, Tax Execs. Inst., N.Y. Soc. C.P.A.s, Am. Accounting Assn., Financial Execs. Inst. Home: 34 Middlesex Rd Buffalo NY 14216-3616

GRUEN, GERALD ELMER, psychologist, educator; b. Granite City, Ill., July 19, 1937; s. Elmer George and Velma Pearl G.; m. Karol Jane Selvidge, Mar. 20, 1960; children—Tami Jane, Christy Lynn. B.A., So. Ill. U., 1959; M.A., U. Ill., 1963, Ph.D., 1964. Postdoctoral fellow Heinz Werner Inst. of Developmental Psychology, Clark U. and Worcester (Mass.) State Hosp., 1964-66; asst. prof. dept. psychol. scis. Purdue U., West Lafayette, Ind., 1966-69; assoc. prof. Purdue U., 1969-74, prof., 1974—, head dept. psychol. scis., 1985-97. Author: (with T. Wachs) Early Experience and Human Development; contbr. chpt. to The Structuring of Experience, 1977; contbr. articles to profl. jours. Deacon Calvary Baptist Ch., West Lafayette. Recipient USPHS research awards, 1968-71, Nat. Research Service award NIMH, 1976-80, Research award Nat. Insts. Child Health and Human Devel., 1981-83. Fellow Am. Psychol. Assn., Am. Psychol. Soc. (charter mem.); mem. Midwestern Psychol. Assn., Soc. for Research in Child Devel., Sigma Xi. Home: 1001 Eton St West Lafayette IN 47906-1323 Office: Purdue U Psychology Dept West Lafayette IN 47907

GRUEN, MICHAEL STEPHAN, lawyer; b. L.A., Mar. 25, 1942; s. Victor and Elsie Caroline (Krummeck) G.; m. Susanna Lloyd, July 18, 1964; m. Vanessa Elisabeth Ahlfors, Jan. 3, 1976; children: Madeleine, Alexis, Viveca; stepchildren: Stefan, Sebastian. BA cum laude, Harvard U., 1963; LLB, UCLA, 1966. Bar: Calif. 1966, N.Y. 1967, U.S. Ct. Appeals (2d cir.) 1976, U.S. Supreme Ct. 1975, U.S. Dist. Ct. (so. and ea. dists.) N.Y. 1986. Assoc. Paul, Weiss, Rifkind, Wharton & Garrison, N.Y.C., 1966-69, Gilinsky, Stillman & Mishkin, N.Y.C., 1969-70, Wolf, Popper, Ross, Wolf & Jones, N.Y.C., 1970-74; gen. counsel Bio-Med. Scis., Inc., Fairfield, N.J., 1974-75; pvt. practice N.Y.C., 1975-80; mem. Gruen & Muskin, N.Y.C., 1980, Gruen, Muskin & Thau, N.Y.C., 1981-88, Gruen, Gilliatt & Livingston, N.Y.C., 1989-90, Gruen & Livingston, N.Y.C., 1990-97, Gruen & Farrelly LLP, N.Y.C., 1998—. Contbr. articles to legal and gen. publs. Bd. dirs. Boys' Athletic League, 1966-82, Columbia Land Conservancy, 1986—, pres., 1988-91; dir. N.Y. Landmarks Conservancy, 1972-94, adv. coun., 1994-97; chmn. Historic Dists. Coun., 1974-79; bd. advisors Prep. Divsn. Bklyn. Coll. Ctr. for Performing Arts, 1980-83; mem. law com. Mcpl. Art Soc., 1987—; pres. Riverside Dems., N.Y.C., 1971-72. Mem. ABA (litig. sect.), N.Y. State Bar Assn., Assn. of Bar of City of N.Y. Office: 500 5th Ave Ste 5225 New York NY 10110-5299

GRUENBERG, ALAN MARK, psychiatrist; b. Knoxville, Apr. 12, 1952; s. Julius and Maria (Wilner) G.; m. Patricia Sewel, June 6, 1976; children: Matthew, Eva. BA, U. Pa., 1973; MD, U. Tenn., 1976. Diplomate Am. Bd. Psychiatry and Neurology (examiner 1984—); lic. physician, Conn., Pa. Intern Yale U. Affiliated Hosps., New Haven, 1976-77, resident in psychiatry and postdoctoral fellow, 1977-80; asst. resident in psychiatry Conn. Mental Health Ctr., New Haven, 1977-78; asst. resident/chief resident psychiatry Yale-New Haven Hosp., 1979-80; assoc. unit chief Hill-West Haven Divsn. Conn. Mental Health Ctr., New Haven, 1980-82; dir. admission and evaluation divsn. Yale Psychiat. Inst., New Haven, 1982-85; attending psychiatrist Inst. of Pa. Hosp., Phila., 1985-91, dir. evaluation unit, 1985-89, sr. cons. evaluation svcs., 1989—; mng. ptnr. Psychiatry Assocs., Phila., 1987—; med. cons. Yale Psychiat. Inst. Day Hosp., 1982-85; dir. Dave Garroway Lab. for Study of Depression, Pa. Hosp., Phila., 1989—; sr. attending psychiatrist Inst. of Pa. Hosp., 1991—; asst. prof. psychiatry Yale U., New Haven, 1980-85, lectr. dept. psychiatry, 1985—; clin. assoc. prof. psychiatry U. Pa. Sch. Medicine, 1987—; lectr. in field. Contbr. numerous articles to profl. jours. Named Outstanding Grad. in Psychiatry, U. Tenn. Coll. Medicine, 1976, Excellence in teaching award Inst. of Pa. Hosp., 1989, Outstanding Preceptor, 1991; named among "Best Doctors", Phila. Mag., 1991; Van Amerigen Found. grantee; NIMH grantee. Mem. AMA, Am. Psychiat. Assn., Phila. Psychiat. Soc., Psychiat. Physicians of Pa., Assn. for Rsch. in Nervous and Mental Diseases, Coll. of Physicians of Phila., Am. Coll. Psychiatrists, Soc. of Biol. Psychiatry, Phila. Psychoanalytic Soc., Am. Psychoanalytic Assn., Assn. for Clin. Psychosocial Rsch., Group for Advancement of Psychiatry (com. on therapeutic care). Office: Inst of Pa Hosp 950 E Haverford Rd Ste 302 Bryn Mawr PA 19010-3851

GRUENBERG, ELLIOT LEWIS, electronics engineer and company executive; b. N.Y.C., Mar. 16, 1918; s. Lewis and Sadie (Schoenbrun) G.; m. Ruth Frankel, Apr. 19, 1947. BEE, CCNY, 1938. Engr., inspector U.S. Signal Corps Line Inspection, Newark, N.J., 1939-43; quality control mgr. Tech. Devices, Roseland, N.J., 1943-48; sr. engr. J.H. Bunnell, Bklyn., 1948-51, Freed Radio, N.Y.C., 1951; sr. engr., mgr. W.L. Maxson, N.Y.C., 1951-58; sr. engring. mgr. Fed. Systems div. IBM, Bethesda, Md., 1958-73; cons. West New York, N.J., 1974-79; chmn. BroadCom, Inc., Secaucus, N.J., 1979-88, also bd. dirs.; chmn., pres. CompFax Corp., West N.Y., N.J., 1988-92; pres. Digital Compression Tech., L.P., N.Y.C., 1993—. Editor: Handbook of Telemetry and Remote Control, 1967; inventor SYNAPZ Microwave Comm., radar, electronic telecomm., telemetry, BGET Secure Comm., DTIC Digital Transmission Bandwidth Compression, Superresonant Digital Modulation and Filtering; patentee in field; contbr. articles to profl. jours. Fellow Am. Inst. Aeronautics and Astronautics (assoc.); mem. IEEE (sr. life mem. 1940—). Democrat. Mem. Ethical Culture. Avocations: puzzles, astronomy, art collecting, artificial intelligence. Home: 6040 Boulevard E Apt 30G West New York NJ 07093-3825

GRUENWALD, GEORGE HENRY, new products development management consultant, writer; b. Chgo., Apr. 23, 1922; s. Arthur Frank and Helen (Duke) G.; m. Corrine Rae Linn, Aug. 16, 1947; children: Helen Marie Gruenwald Orlando, Paul Arthur. BS in Journalism, Northwestern U., 1947; student, Evanston Acad. Fine Arts, 1937-38, Chgo. Acad. Fine Arts, 1938-39, Grinnell Coll., 1940-41. Asst. to pres. UARCO, Inc., Chgo., 1947-49; creative dir., mgr. mdse. Willy-Overland Motors Inc., Toledo, 1949-51; new products, brand and advt. mgr. Toni Co./Gillette, Chgo., 1951-53; v.p., creative dir., account supr. E.H. Weiss Agy., Chgo., 1953-55; exec. v.p., mgmt. supr. North Advt., Chgo., 1955-71; pres., treas., dir. Pilot Products, Chgo., 1963-71; pres., dir. Advance Brands, Inc., Chgo., 1963-71; owner Venture Group, 1971—; exec. v.p., dir. Campbell Mithun Inc., Mpls. and Chgo., 1971-72; pres., dir. Campbell Mithun Inc., 1972-79, chmn., dir., 1979-81, CEO, dir., 1981-83, chief creative officer, dir., 1983-84; vice-chmn., dir. Ted Bates Worldwide, N.Y.C., 1979-80, mgmt. cons. new product devel., 1984—. Author: New Product Development-What Really Works, 1985, 2d edit., New Product Development-Responding to Market Demand, 1992, How to Create Profitable New Products, 1997, Creative Choices-How to Make Them, 1999, (workbook) New Product Development Checklists: From Mission to Market, 1991, (videos) New Products Seven Steps to Success, 1988, New Product Development, 1989; editor-in-chief Oldsmobile Rocket Cir. mag., 1955-65, Hudson Family mag., 1953-56; feature writer Mktg. News, 1988—; contbr. articles to profl. jours. Trustee Chgo. Pub. TV Assn., 1969-73, Mpls. Soc. Fine Arts, 1975-83, Linus Pauling Inst. Sci. and Medicine, Palo Alto, 1984-92, 95-96; advisor Linus Pauling Inst., Oreg. State U., Corvallis, 1996—; chmn., v.p., chmn. class reps. Northwestern U. Alumni Fund Coun., Chgo., 1965-68; trustee, chmn., chmn. exec. com. Twin Cities Pub. TV Corp., 1971-84; trustee Minn. Pub. Radio Inc., 1973-77, vice chmn., 1974-75; bd. dirs., mem. exec. com. PBS, Alexandria, Va., 1978-86, 88-94, mem. comm. adv. com., 1993-95, vice chmn. task force on funding, 1991-92; chmn. task force on tech. applications, lay rep., 1971—; del. Am.'s Pub. TV Stas., Washington, 1971—; bd. dirs. St. Paul Chamber Orch., 1982-84, San Diego Chamber Orch., 1986-88; mem. adv. bd. San Diego State U. Pub. Broadcasting Comty., 1986—, pub. rels. specialist, editor. With USAAF, 1943-45, MTO. Recipient Hermes award Chgo. Federated Advt. Clubs, 1963, Ednl. TV awards, 1969, 71, 86, Best of the Best award San Diego Book Awards, 1997; charter mem. Medill Sch. Journalism Hall of Achievement, 1997. Mem. Am. Mktg. Assn., Am. Assn. Advt. Agys. (mgmt. com. 1976-84), Nat. Soc. Profl. Journalists, Am. Inst. Wine and Food (bd. dirs. 1985-92), So. Calif. Advt. Media Soc., Rancho Santa Fe Art Guild. Office: PO Box 1696 Rancho Santa Fe CA 92067-1696 *To learn. To teach. To make a difference.*

GRUENWALD, JAMES HOWARD, association executive, consultant; b. Cin., Aug. 30, 1949; s. Howard Francis and Geraldine Emma (Mueller) G. BS, Xavier U., 1971. Cert. profl. in recreation and leisure svc., Ill. Rep. pub. rels. Cath. Youth Orgn., Cin., 1969-72; advtransp. sales rep. Spade Trucking Co., Cin., 1972-73; field rep. Ohio Dept. Transport, Columbus, 1973-76; editorial, sales rep. Cin. Suburban Newspaper, 1976-77; asst. devel. dir. Cin. Art Acad., 1977-79; nat. exec. dir. Say Soccer USA, Cin., 1979-93; co-founder, exec. dir. U.S. Indoor Soccer Orgn., 1985-90; bd. dirs. Buckeye Men's Baseball, Cin., 1982-90, chmn. 1982-86, 89-90; dir. Amateur Athletic Union, Indpls., 1983-85; assoc. mgr. of devel., Am. Youth Soccer Organization, L.A., 1993—. cert. trainer Am. Coaches Effectiveness Program, Champaign, Ill., 1983-92. Contbr. articles to profl. jours including Jour. Nat. Recreation and Parks, 1983, Jour. Ohio Parks and Attractions, 1985, Jour. Mich. Leisure, 1986, Strategies, AAPHER, 1989. Editor: jour. Touchline, 1980-92, Parents Guide to Soccer, 1985-92. Candidate for city coun. City of St. Bernard, Ohio, 1977; mem. adv. bd. Church Parish, Cin., 1974-76. Recipient Exec. Dir. Svc. award Say Soccer USA, 1979; State of Mich. Community Svc. award, 1986. Mem. Nat. Council Youth Sports Dirs., Nat. Recreation and Parks Assn., Mich. Recreation and Parks Assn. (Community Service award 1986), Soc. for Non Profits. Avocations: hiking, reading, writing, teaching, conducting workshops. Home: 11986 Cedarcreek Dr Cincinnati OH 45240-1550 Office: 12501 S Isis Ave Hawthorne CA 90250-4149

GRUENWALD, RENEE, special education educator; b. Bklyn., Oct. 8, 1948; d. Isidor and Monia (Kaczanowska) Oshinsky; m. Laurence David Gruenwald, June 22, 1969; children: Kate, Sara. BA, Brandeis U., 1969; MA, Kean Coll., 1983. Cert. elem., spl. edn., learning disabilities tchr., cons. supervision and adminstrn. Tchr. Marlboro (Mass.) Pub. Schs., 1969-71, Colegio Anglo-Mexicano, Guadalajara, Mex., 1971-73, So. Orange/Maplewood (N.J.) Pub. Schs., 1981—. Mem. N.J. Edn. Assn. (negotiations cons. 1993-97), South Orange-Maplewood Edn. Assn. (v.p. 1984-86, pres. 1986-88, negotiations chair 1991-94, grievance chair 1994-96), N.J. Assn. Learning Cons., Kappa Delta Pi. Home: 364 Redmond Rd South Orange NJ 07079-1505 Office: South Orange Middle Sch 70 N Ridgewood Rd South Orange NJ 07079-1518

GRUGGEL, JOHN STUART, JR., judge; b. Portsmouth, Va., Jan. 19, 1944; s. John Stuart and Ann (Lashe) G.; m. Jeanne Anne Garaux, Aug. 16, 1969; children: Erin, Kristin. BA, Middlebury Coll., 1965; JD, U. Va., 1971. Assoc. chief trial atty. Office of Gen. Counsel U.S. Navy, 1974-87; judge Armed Svcs. Bd. Contract Appeals, Falls Church, Va., 1987—. Col., USMCR, 1962-94. Decorated Purple Heart, 1966-67. Mem. VFW, Mil. Order of Caribao. Lutheran. Avocations: bowling, fishing, golf. Office: Armed Svcs Bd Contract Appeals 5109 Leesburg Pike Ste 700 Falls Church VA 22041-3208*

GRUHL, ANDREA MORRIS, librarian; b. Ponca City, Okla., Dec. 9, 1939; d. Luther Oscar and Hazel Evangeline (Anderson) Morris; m. Werner Mann Gruhl, July 10, 1965; children: Sonja Krista, Diana Krista. BA, Wesleyan Coll., 1961; MLS, U. Md., 1968; postgrad., Johns Hopkins U., 1970-71, U. Md., 1968, 71-73, Oxford U., 1996. Tchr. Broward County, Fla., Dept. Def. Montgomery County, Md., 1961-66; libr. Prince Georges County (Md.) Pub. Libr., 1966-68, 81-83, U. Md., College Park, 1970-72; art. history rschr. Joseph Alsop, Washington, 1972-74; libr. Howard County Pub. Libr., Columbia, Md., 1969-70, 74-79; European exch. staff Libr. of Congress, Washington, 1982-86; cataloger fed. documents GPO, Washington, 1986-93, supervisory libr., 1993—; women's program adv. com., processing dept. rep. Libr. of Congress, 1983-86, mem. ofcl. Libr. of Congress delegation to Internat. Fedn. Libr. Assn. ann. conf., Munich, 1983, Chgo., 1985; state del. White House Conf. on Librs., 1978, 90. Indexer, editor: Learning Vacations, 3d edit., 1980; editor: Federal Librarian, 1994—; LCPA Index to Libr. of Congress Info. Bull., 1984. Trustee Howard County (Md.) C.C., 1989-95, Howard County Pub. Libr., Columbia, Md., 1979-87; publ. chmn. LWV Howard County, 1974, bd. dirs., 1996-97; citizens rep. Howard County, exec. bd. Balt. Regional Planning Coun. Libr. com., 1976-79; Friends of Libr., Howard County, pres., 1976; vol. Nat. Gallery Art Libr., Washington, 1978-80. Mem. ALA (Councilor 1997—, fed. libr. round table 1988—, v.p. 1997-98, pres. 1998-99, editor 1994—, IFLA rep. 1996—, govt. documents roundtable 1986—, internat. rels. roundtable 1988—, map and geography roundtable 1996—), Assn. Libr. Collections and Tech. Svcs., Libr. Info. Tech. Assn., Libr. Adminstrn. and Mgmt. Assn. (planning and evaluation libr. svcs. 1996-97), D.C. Libr. Assn. (co-chair mgmt. interest group 1996-97), Assn. Coll. and Rsch. Librs., Internat. Fedn. Libr. Assns. and Institutions, UN Assn. (Nat. Capitol area chpt., membership com., Md. telephone chair 1992-94), Art Librs. Soc. N.Am. (coord. mems.' publ. exhbn. 1980-82). Libr. Congress Profl. Assn. (coord. ann. staff art shows 1982-83, chmn. libr. sci interest group 1985-87), Libr. Congress Am. Fedn. State County and Mcpl. Employees Union (program chair 1984-86), Oxford Soc. Washington, Md. Libr. Assn. (pres. trustee divsn. 1982-83), Assn. C.C. Trustees, Md. Assn. C.C. Trustees (sec. 1991-92, bd. dirs. 1992-93), Md. Assn. C.C. (bd. dirs. 1992-95), Beta Phi Mu. Democrat. Lutheran. Home: 5990 Jacobs Ladder Columbia MD 21045-3817 Office: Govt Printing Office Washington DC 20401

GRUHL, JAMES, energy scientist; b. Milw., Apr. 9, 1945; s. Alfred and Helen (Vandervеer) G.; m. Nancy Lee Huston, July 4, 1974; children: Amanda Natalie, Steven Christopher. BS, MIT, 1968, MS, 1968, PhD, 1973. Lectr. MIT, 1969-83; rsch. scientist MIT Energy Lab., Cambridge, 1973-83, program mgr., 1978-83, rsch. affiliate, 1984; sci. adv. bd. U.S. EPA, 1986-93; energy cons. U.S. Congress, rsch. insts., internat. energy industries, 1973—. Ednl. counselor MIT, 1978—. Recipient Silver Beaver award Boy Scouts Am., 1986, numerous art awards, 1990—; NSF grantee. Mem. IEEE, AAAS, Math. Programming Soc., MIT Alumni Assn. (officer 1978—), Tau Beta Pi, Eta Kappa Nu. Achievements include research on uncertainties and validity of analytic models, validity of government and industry energy policy models, and climate change models. Office: Gruhl Assocs PO Box 36524 Tucson AZ 85740-6524

GRUHL, SUZANNE SWIDERSKI, accountant; b. Monroe, Mich., May 20, 1946; d. John Joseph and Grace Kathryn (Kautz) Swiderski; m. Robert H. Gruhl, Aug. 2, 1968; children: Jonathan, Jason. BA, Rosary Coll., River Forest, Ill., 1968; MA, U. Mich., 1969; MBA, Boston U., 1982. CPA, Mass. Staff acct. Peter H. Dinsmore, CPA, Marblehead, Mass., 1981-84; ptnr. Stevens & Gruhl, CPA's, Marblehead, 1984-86, Dinsmore Gruhl & Co., P.C., Salem, Mass., 1986—. Bd. dirs. Citizens Scholarship Found. Marblehead, 1988-91, The Salem Partnership, 1989-92; treas. Marblehead YMCA, 1990-94; corporator Salem Hosp., 1991-93, Home for Aged Women, Inc., 1989—; trustee Abbott Pub. Libr. 2d Century Fund, 1992-96, Salem Hosp., 1993—. Mem. AICPA, Mass. Soc. CPAs, Am. Women's Soc. CPAs, Essex Estate Planning and Bus. Coun. (bd. dirs. 1989-91, treas. 1991-97). Avocations: tennis, sailing, skiing. Office: 265 Essex St Salem MA 01970-3400

GRUHN, ROBERT STEPHEN, parole officer; b. N.Y.C., Dec. 9, 1938; s. Jerome and Beatrice (Fuchs) G.; m. Shirley Darlene Brayfield, Sept. 14, 1984. BS, NYU, 1961; MA in Criminology, Sam Houston State U., 1975; AB in Legal Studies, Drury Coll., 1987. Cert. criminal investigator, gang crime specialist, State of Ill. Collection mgr. Sears, Roebuck & Co., Albuquerque, 1961-64; adjuster Gen. Adjustment Bur., Albuquerque, 1964-65; indsl. engr. LTV Aerospace Corp., Dallas, 1965-66; agy. sec. Am. Nat. Ins., Dallas, 1966-72; parole officer Tex. Bd. Parole, Dallas and Houston, 1974-80, Mo. Bd. Parole, Springfield, 1980-99; investigator Greene County (Mo.) Prosecuting Atty. Office, 1999—; with Springfield Police Dept. Tng. Acad. Facility, 1984—; presenter Gang Awareness Program, S.W. Mo., 1992—. Author Collision Course, 1984. Bd. dirs. Wayback Halfway House, Dallas, 1977-80; chmn. Gang Task Force, Springfield, 1996-97, So. Mo. Fugitive Task Force, Springfield, 1992—; bd. dirs. youth svcs. Mo. Dept. Corrections, 1993—; sr. v.p. One Missing Link, Children Non-Profit Orgn., 1994—, active P.E.A.C.E. Project, Springfield, 1994-95. Recipient commendation cert. N.Y. Police Dept., 1961, Cert. of Achievement in Extremism and Terrorism, Mo. Dept. Corrections, 1986, Cert. of Achievement in Satanism and the Occult, Mo. Dept. Corrections, 1989, Cert. of Achievement in Dangerous Gangs, 1989, Cert. Achievement, Mid States Organized Crime Info. Ctr., 1990, Cert. of Appreciation, U.S. Treasury Dept., 1992. Mem. Am. Mgmt. Assn. (internat. v.p. 1971-74), Soc. for Advt. Mgmt. (sec. 1968-71, pres. 1971-72), Soc. for Advancement of Mgmt. (Profl. Achievement award 1972), Mo. Corrections Assn., Midwest Gang Investigations Assn., Mu Gamma Tau. Avocation: writing. Home: 2214 E Nora St Springfield MO 65803-4952 Office: 1010 Boonville Springfield MO 65806

GRUITZA, MICHAEL, state legislator, lawyer; b. Sharon, Pa., May 2, 1951; s. John and Aurelia Gruitza; m. Joan Shaw; children: Rebecca Jean, William John, David Michael. BA, Gannon U., 1973; JD, Ohio No. U., 1977. Bar: Pa. 1977. Pvt. practice Sharon, Pa., 1977—; state legislator Pa. Ho. of Reps., Harrisburg, 1981—; mem. judiciary com., appropriations com., consumer affairs com., task force on decedents estate laws Pa. Ho. of Reps.; apptd. chmn. Dem. Game and Fisheries Com., 1995; chmn. Dem. Ho. State Gov. Com. Named one of Outstanding Young Men Am. Mem. Pa. Bar Assn., Mercer County Bar Assn. Office: 401 State Office PO Box 202020 Harrisburg PA 17120-2020

GRULIOW, REBECCA AGNES LINDSAY, editor, translator, artist; b. N.Y.C., Jan. 28, 1956; d. Leo and Agnes (Forrest) G.; m. Michael Barnhart, Jan. 1977 (div. 1982). BA in Russian studies and lit., Bryn Mawr Coll., 1979; BFA in glass and ceramics with honors, Temple U., 1989. Prodn. editor J.B. Lippincott Co., Phila., 1980-83; project editor Saunders Coll. Pub., Phila., 1983, 1987-88; prodn. editor Extracorporeal, Inc., 1983-84, W.B. Saunders Co., Phila., 1984-85; free-lance, 1985—; devel. editor Mosby Yearbook, Phila., 1996, 97—; tchg. asst. The Pilchuck Sch., Seattle, 1986, Tyler Sch. Art, Phila., 1986; demonstrator Paley Design Ctr., Phila., 1992. One-person shows include The Hunterdon Art Ctr., Clinton, N.J., 1991, The Clay Studio, Phila, 1995, Abington Art Ctr. Gallery Store, Jenkintown, Pa., 1997; exhibited at group shows at Temple Gallery, 1987, Franklin Plaza, 1987, The Armory, 1987, del Mano Gallery, 1988, Gallery 479, 1990, The Clay Studio, 1990, 95, 96, 97, 98, Luckenbach Mill Gallery, 1990, Hunterdon Art Ctr., 1991, Noyes Mus., 1991, Nat. Mus. Ceramic Art, 1991, Paley Design Ctr., 1992, Long Beach Island Found Arts & Scis., 1992, 93, 98, Gallery Am. Craft at Wheaton Village, 1994, 95, 96, 97, Abington Art Ctr., 1996; co-translator: Lysenko and the Tragedy of Soviet Science, 1994; contbr. articles to profl. jours. Mem. Am. Craft Coun., Clay Studio. Home: 114 S 43rd St Philadelphia PA 19104-2927 Office: 510 Walnut St Ste 1050 Philadelphia PA 19106-3601

GRUM, CLIFFORD J., manufacturing company executive; b. Davenport, Iowa, Dec. 12, 1934; s. Allen F. and Nathalie (Cate) G.; m. Janelle Lewis, May 1, 1965; 1 son, Christopher J. B.A., Austin Coll., 1956; M.B.A., U. Pa., 1958. Formerly with Republic Nat. Bank, Dallas; former v.p. fin. Temple Industries, Diboll, Tex.; with Time, Inc., N.Y.C., treas., 1973-75, v.p., 1975-80, exec. v.p., 1980-83, also bd. dirs.; pub. Fortune, 1975-79; chief exec. officer Temple-Inland, Inc., Diboll, 1983—, chmn. bd., 1991—; dir. Cooper Industries, Inc., Tupperware Corp., Inc., Trinity Industries, Inc. Trustee Austin Coll. Office: Temple Inland Inc PO Drawer N 303 S Temple Dr Diboll TX 75941-2419*

GRUMAN, ROBERT RICHARD, energy management consultant; b. Calgary, Alta., Can., Mar. 21, 1967; came to U.S., 1976; s. William Paul and Pauline Adams Gruman; m. Olga Vladimirovna Bordanova, Jan. 27, 1996. BS summa cum laude, Ariz. State U., 1989. Fin. analyst Conoco, Inc., Casper, Wyo., 1989; staff supr. Conoco, Inc., Lafayette, La., 1990-91, fin. analyst, 1991-93; sr. fin. analyst Conoco, Inc., Moscow, 1993, material and logistics supr., 1993-95, sr. staff fin. analyst, 1995-96; region fin. analyst Conoco, Inc., Lafayette, 1996; mgmt. cons. Price Waterhouse Coopers LLP, Houston, 1996—. Contbr. papers to profl. jours. Mem. Houston Prodrs.' Forum, Beta Gamma Sigma, Phi Kappa Phi, Alpha Lambda Delta. Republican. Roman Catholic. Avocations: golf, reading, exercise, running, traveling. e-mail: bob.gruman@us.pwcglobal.com. Home: 8610 Malardcrest Dr Humble TX 77346

GRUMBACH, DORIS, novelist, editor, critic, educator, bookseller; b. N.Y.C., July 12, 1918; d. Leonard and Helen Isaac; divorced; children: Barbara Wheeler, Jane Emerson, Elizabeth Cale, Kathryn Grumbach-Yarowsky. BA, NYU, 1939; MA, Cornell U., 1940; DHL (hon.), Russell Sage Coll., 1980. Title writer MGM, N.Y.C., 1940-41; asso. editor Archtl. Forum, Time, Inc., 1941-43; prof. English Coll. St. Rose, Albany, N.Y., 1952-72; vis. prof. Empire State Coll., State U. N.Y., Saratoga Springs, 1972-73; contbg. editor The New Republic, Washington, 1971-73; literary editor The New Republic, 1973-75; prof. Am. lit. Am. U., Washington, 1975-85; adj. prof. English U. Md., 1974-75; vis. prof. Iowa Writers' Workshop, 1980, 83, 85, 86, Johns Hopkins U. (writing seminars), 1983, 85, 86; writer-in-residence SUNY Writers Inst., Albany. Freelance critic: Washington Star, Washington Post, L.A. Times, Chgo. Tribune, Fine Print; nonfiction columnist: N.Y. Times Book Rev., 1976-81; fiction columnist: Chronicle Higher Edn., 1979-81; columnist: Fine Print, Sat. Rev., 1977-78; author: The Spoil of the Flowers, 1962, The Short Throat, The Tender Mouth, 1964, The Company She Kept, 1967, Chamber Music, 1979, The Missing Person, 1981, The Ladies, 1984, The Magician's Girl, 1989, Coming Into the End Zone, 1992, Extra Innings, 1993, 50 Days of Solitude, 1994, The Book of Knowledge, 1995, Life In a Day, 1996, The Presence of Absence, 1998; contbg. author: Book Reviewing, 1978, Writer's Choice, 1978; book critic: Nat. Pub. Radio, 1985-90, MacNeil/Lehrer News Hour, PBS, 1988-89. Bd. dirs. Atlantic Ctr. for the Arts, Nat. Book Critics Circle, 1980-91, Lit. Landmarks, 1987-89; Lit. Lion N.Y. Pub. Libr., 1988. Recipient Lifetime Achievement award New Eng. Booksellers Assn., 1996. Mem. PEN/Faulkner (bd. dirs. 1984-89, exec. bd. 1985-91), Phi Beta Kappa (senator 1988-94). Office: care Timothy Seldes Russell & Volkening 50 W 29th St New York NY 10001-4227

GRUMBACH, MELVIN MALCOLM, physician, educator; b. N.Y.C., Dec. 21, 1925; s. Emanuel and Adele (Weil) G.; m. Madeleine F. Butt, Dec. 1, 1951; children: Ethan Malcolm, Kevin Lawrence, Anthony Havemeyer. Student, Columbia Coll., MD, 1948; DM (hon.), U. Geneva, 1991. Diplomate Am. Bd. Pediatrics, Am. Bd. Pediatric Endocrinology (com. mem. 1975-79). Resident in pediatrics Babies Hosp., Presbyn. Hosp., N.Y.C., 1949-51; vis. fellow Oak Ridge Inst. Nuclear Studies, 1952; postdoctoral fellow, asst. pediatrics Johns Hopkins Sch. Medicine, 1953-55; mem. faculty Columbia U. Coll. Physicians and Surgeons, N.Y.C., 1955-65; assoc. prof. pediatrics Columbia U. Coll. Physicians and Surgeons, 1961-65; asst. attending pediatrician to assoc. attending pediatrician, head pediatric endocrine div. and postdoctoral tng. program pediatric endocrinology Babies Hosp. and Vanderbilt Clin., Columbia-Presbyn. Med. Ctr., 1955-65; prof. pediatrics, chmn. dept. U. Calif. Sch. Medicine, San Francisco, 1966-86, Edward B. Shaw prof. pediatrics, 1983-94, Edward B. Shaw prof. emeritus pediatrics (active), 1994—, acting dir. Lab. Molecular Endocrinology, 1987-89; dir. pediatric svc. U. Calif. Hosps., 1966-86; vis. prof. Vanderbilt U., 1961, Emory U., 1962, U. Western Ont., 1962, U. N.C., 1963; Alpha Omega Alpha lectr. State U. N.Y. Downstate Med. Ctr., 1961, U. Calif. at San Francisco, 1966; univ. lectr. U. Zurich, 1971; Clausen vis. prof. U. Rochester, 1972; Richard E. Weitzman vis. prof. UCLA, 1981; Culpepper vis. prof. U. N.C., 1982; Frederick Moll lectr. U. Wash., 1979; Kenneth C. Haltalin vis. prof. U. Tex.-Dallas, 1983; Eley lectr. Harvard U. Med. Sch., Children's Med. Ctr., Boston, 1979; domestic lectr. Jour. Pediatrics Edn. Found., 1962, 79; Mali Dittman lectr. U. Chgo., 1980; Frederick M. Kenny lectr. Children's Hosp. Pitts., 1981; Winthrop award lectr. Am. Fertility Soc., 1981; Grover Powers lectr. Yale U., 1981; univ. lectr. Assembly of Profs., Coll. de France, Paris, 1979; Meredith Campbell lectr. Am. Urol. Assn., 1982; Prader lectr. Tel Aviv U. Med. Sch., 1982; Hopkins-Maryland lectr., 1983; Felton Bequests prof. Royal Childrens Hosp., Melbourne, 1983; Sandoz lectr. Can. Soc. Clin. Investigation, 1983; vis. prof. U. Minn., 1984, Royal Soc. Medicine, London, 1985, Joint Endocrine Societies of Great Britain, Oxford; John Lind lectr. Karolinska Inst., Stockholm, 1984; Bilderback lectr. Oreg. Health Scis. U., 1986; Mathew Steiner lectr. Northwestern U., Children's Meml. Hosp., 1989, Gurson lectr. U. Istanbul, 1991, Maranon Symposium lectr. Universidad Autonoma de Madrid, Spain, 1991, Judson Van Wyk lectr. U. N.C., 1993, James Etteldorf lectr. La Bonheur Children's Hosp. U. Tenn., 1994; U.S. Plenary lect. X Asia Oceania Congress Endocrinology, Beijing, 1994, VIII Asia Oceania Congress of Endocrinology, Bangkok, 1986; Robert N. Ganz lectr. Mass. Gen. Hosp., 1996; cons. Letterman Gen. Hosp., 1966-94, Children's Hosp., San Francisco, U.S. Naval Hosp., Oakland, Calif., 1966-94, HEW, NIH, Nat. Bd. Med. Examiners, 1964-68; mem. human embryology and devel. study sect. NIH, 1962-66, endocrinology study sect., 1967-71; bd. sci. counselors Nat. Inst. Child Health and Human Devel., 1971-75; mem. gen. clin. rsch. ctrs. com., div. rsch. resources NIH, 1976-80; mem. com. for rev. NIH Clin. Ctr., 1984-85, nat. adv. coun. Nat. Inst. Child Health and Human Devel., NIH, 1991-96; mem. sci. adv. com., clin. rsch. adv. com. Nat. Found.-March of Dimes, 1969-94, chmn. clin. rsch. adv. com., 1974-82, Basil O'Connor starter scholar rsch. award comm., 1995—; mem. awards com. Lita Annenberg Hazen Award for Excellence in Clin. Rsch., 1981-86; mem. sci. adv. bd. Scripps Clinic and Rsch. Found., 1977-78; mem. sci. adv. bd. Princesse Marie Christine Found., Brussels, 1981-91, U. Mich. Ctr. for Human Growth and Devel., 1982-89; mem. adv. bd. Nat. Pituitary Agy., 1965-69, NIH Evaluation of Endocrinology and Metabolic Diseases, 1977-79; mem. sci. adv. bd. U. Colo. Health Scis. Barbara Davis Ctr., 1986-93; Dean's Bd. of Vis., Mt. Sinai Sch. of Medicine, 1986-87; mem. sci. adv. bd. Hosp. for Sick Children, Toronto, 1984-88, Children's Hosp. of Los Angeles, 1987-92; sci. and med. adv. bd. Whittier Inst. Diabetes and Endocrinology, 1987-92; mem. sci. adv. coun. Cin. Children's Hosp. Rsch. Found., 1997-98; pres. bd. trustees Internat. Pediatric Rsch. Found., Inc., 1984-89; mem. sci. coun. Aid Pour la Recherche Medicale a l'enfance, Paris, 1981-89; del. to Chinese Acad. of Med. Scis., 1986; vis. prof. Peking Union Med. Coll. and Hosp., 1986; vis. prof. U. Hong Kong, 1986. Assoc. editor, mem. editorial bd. Jour. Clin. Endocrinology, 1957-70; adv. editor Jour. Pediatrics, 1966-73; editorial bd., 1973-79; assoc. editor Pediatric Rsch., 1970-84, Barnett Pediatrics, 14th-15th edits., Rudolph Pediatrics, 16th-21st edits., Current Topics in Experimental Endocrinology; mem. internat. editorial bd. pediatrics and pediatric surgery: Excerpta Medica, 1974—; editorial bd. Biology of Reproduction, 1968-70; editorial com. Endocrinologic Clinica Metabolismo, 1981—; editorial bd. Pediatrics in Rev., 1982-84, Jour. Endocrinol. Investigation, 1982-90, Endocrine Revs., 1984-88, Jour. Pediatric Endocrinology, 1984—, Trends in Endocrinology, 1989—, Monographs on Endocrinology, Springer-Verlag, 1975-90, Clinical Pediatric Endocrinology (Jour. of the Japanese Soc. for Pediatric Endocrinology), 1992—; contbr. articles to med. and sci. books and jours. Served to capt. M.C. USAF, 1951-53. Postdoctoral fellow Nat. Found. Infantile Paralysis, 1953-55; recipient Joseph M. Smith prize Columbia U., 1962; Career Scientist award Health Research Coun. City N.Y., 1961-66; Silver medal Bicentennial Columbia Coll. Physicians and Surgeons, 1967, Gold medal, 1988; Clin. Endocrinology Trust medal (U.K.), 1985, Centennial Medallist award Babies Hosp., Columbia-Presbyn. Med. Ctr., 1987, Borden award, Am. Acad. Pediatrics, 1971, Collège de France medal, 1979, Robert H. Williams Disting. Leadership award, Endocrine Soc., 1980, Winthrop award, Am. Fertility Soc., 1981, Fred Conrad Koch award Endocrine Soc., 1992, Lifetime Achievement award Am. Acad. Pediatrics, 1996, John Howland award Am. Pediatric Soc., 1997. Fellow Am. Acad. Arts & Scis., Am. Acad. Pediatrics, N.Y. Acad. Scis., AAAS; mem. NAS, Am. Pediatric Soc. (pres.-elect 1988-89, pres. 1989-90), Inst. Medicine of Nat. Acad. Scis. (com. on the Future of Pub. Health, 1985-87, com. to study AIDS rsch. program of NIH, 1989-91), Assn. Med. Sch. Pediatric Dept. Chairmen (exec. coun. 1967-72, pres. 1973-75, task force on Pediatric Scientist Tng. Program, 1984-91, chmn. selection com. 1986-91), Am. Soc. Clin. Investigation, Assn. Am. Physicians, Am. Soc. Human Genetics, Harvey Soc., Lawson Wilkins Pediatric Endocrine Soc. (pres. 1975-76), Western Soc. Pediatric Rsch. (pres. 1978-79), Soc. Pediatric Rsch., Teratology Soc., Endocrine Soc. (coun. 1968-71, 80-83, pres. elect 1980-81, pres. 1981-82, Internat. Endocrine Soc. (del. to central com. 1976-92; exec. com. 1984-92), Soc. Study Reprodn., European Soc. Pediatric Endocrinology (corr.), Société Française de Pediatrie (corr.), Internat. Neuroendocrinology Soc., Argentine Soc. Endocrinology and Metabolism (hon.), Can. Soc. Endocrinology and Metabolism (hon.), Japanese Soc. Pediatric Endocrinology (hon.), Western Assn. Physicians, Calif. Acad. Medicine, Western Soc. Clin. Rsch., Pacific Coast Fertility Soc. (hon.), Israeli Endocrine Soc. (hon.), Sigma Xi, Alpha Omega Alpha. Club: University (N.Y.C.). Office: U Calif Sch Medicine Dept Pediatrics San Francisco CA 94143-0434

GRUMBINE, FRANCIS, gynecologic oncologist, educator; b. Waynesboro, Pa., Nov. 3, 1945; s. Francis Levine and Emma Jane (Kercheval) G.; m. Caroline Neville Mauck, June 1, 1974; children: Caroline Neville, Francis Lawson, Anne Brooke. BA, Washington & Lee U., 1970; MS, MD, U. Va., 1974. Diplomate Am. Bd. Ob-Gyn., Am. Bd. Gynecologic Oncology. Asst. prof. ob-gyn. Johns Hopkins Hosp., Balt., 1980—; chief divsn. gynecologic oncology Greater Balt. Med. Ctr., 1983—. Bd. dirs. Roland Pk. Country Sch., Balt., 1991-97. With U.S. Coast Guard, 1966-68. Fellow ACOG; mem. Soc. Gynecologic Oncology, L'Hirondelle Club, Green Sprain Valley Hunt Club. Avocations: tennis, golf. Home: 305 Golf Course Rd Owings Mills MD 21117-4113 Office: Physician Pavillion West 6569 N Center St Baltimore MD 21204

GRUMET, PRISCILLA HECHT, fashion specialist, consultant, writer; b. Detroit, May 11, 1943; d. Lewis Maxwell and Helen Ruth (Miller) Hecht; m. Ross Frederick Grumet, Feb. 24, 1968; 1 child, Auden Lewis. AA, Stephens Coll., 1963; student, Ga. State Coll., 1983-85. Buyer Rich's Dept. Store, Atlanta, 1963-68; instr. fashion retail Fashion Inst. Am., Atlanta, 1968-71; pres., lectr., cons. Personally Priscilla Personal Shopping Svc., Atlanta, 1971—; retail and customer svc. cons. By Priscilla Grumet, Atlanta, 1989—; instr. Cont. Edn. Program Emory U., Atlanta, 1976—; fashion merch. coord. Park Pl. Shopping Ctr., Atlanta, 1979-83; writer Atlanta Bus. Mag., 1984—; cons., buyer Greers-Regensteins Store, Atlanta, 1986-87; writer Atlanta Mag., 1994—; guest lectr. Fashion Group of Am., Rancho La Puerta Resort, Tecate, Mex., 1985—; bus. cons. Atlanta Apparel Mart, 1992—; adv. bd. Bauder Fashion Col., 1986—, Atlanta Apparel Mart, 1992—; fashion panel judge Weight Watchers Internat., 1981; columnist Marquee mag., Atlanta, 1992—; lectr. on customer svc. Rhodes Furniture, Marriott Corp., So. Bell, Lady Love Cosmetics, Atlanta Retail Stores, others, 1994—; presenter profl. seminars on bus. etiquette, 1996—; lectr. on profl. etiquette corps., Emory U. Continuing Edn. program, 1996—. Author: How to Dress Well, 1981; reporter Women's Wear Daily, 1976-90; columnist Atlanta Scene Mag.; contbr. articles to mags. and publs. including Atlanta, Seventeen, Nat. Jeweler's (Editor's Choice award The Nat. Libr. of Poetry 1995), The Old

Farmer's Almanac, Bus. Seminars Profl. Etiquette, Performance Plus, 1996—. Pub. rels. dir., Atlanta Jewish Home Aux., 1986-89; admissions advisor, Stephens Coll., 1979—. Mem. Fashion Group, Inc., Women in Comm., Nat. Coun. Jewish Women, Atlanta Press Club, Buckhead Bus. Assn., Temple Sisterhood (spkr., spl. events com. 1983—). Avocations: antiques, aerobics. Home and Office: 2863 Careygate NW Atlanta GA 30305-2821

GRUMMER, EUGENE MERRILL, commodity futures market development executive; b. Luzerne, Iowa, Aug. 12, 1924; s. William Henry and Louise Wilhamena (Schroeder) G.; m. Priscilla Ann Storrs, Sept. 17, 1955; children: James Hollister, Nancy Louise, Sarah Storrs. BA, Brown U., 1947. Sr. v.p. Merrill Lynch, N.Y.C., 1950-80, ptnr., 1974—; chmn. N.Y. Cotton Exch., N.Y. Citrus Exch., N.Y.C., 1970-74; dir. N.Y. Commodity Exch., N.Y.C., 1969-72, N.Y. Wool Futures Exch., N.Y.C., 1954-60; originated N.Y. market for frozen concentrated orange juice future market; helped develop futures market in crude oil, live cattle and lumber; tchr. Merrill Lynch Commodity Tng. Sch.; lectr. to U.S. and internat. industry groups on hedging use of future markets, 1951-74; chmn. Internat. Futures Exch., Bermuda, 1981-85. Mem. Anglers Yacht Club. Republican. Avocations: hunting, fishing, snowmobiling, cross country skiing, golf. Home: Ste 1108 5275 S Atlantic Ave Apt 1108 New Smyrna Beach FL 32169-4564

GRUNBAUM, ADOLF, philosophy educator, author; b. Cologne, Germany, May 15, 1923; came to U.S., 1938, naturalized, 1944; s. Benjamin and Hannah (Freiwillig) G.; m. Thelma Braverman, June 26, 1949; 1 child, Barbara Susan. B.A., Wesleyan U., Middletown, Conn., 1943; M.S. in Physics, Yale U., 1948, Ph.D in Philosophy, 1951; Dr. Honoris Causa, U. Konstanz. Mem. faculty Lehigh U., 1950-60, prof. philosophy, 1955-56, Selfridge prof. philosophy, 1956-60; vis. rsch. prof. Minn. Ctr. Philosophy of Sci., 1956, 59; Andrew Mellon prof. philosophy U. Pitts., 1960—, rsch. prof. psychiatry, 1979—, dir. Ctr. Philosophy of Sci., 1960-78; now chmn. U. Pitts. (Ctr. Philosophy of Sci.); Chmn. sect. philosophy of phys. scis. Internat. Congress for Logic and Philosophy of Sci., Jerusalem, Israel, 1964, Bucharest, Rumania, 1971, Salzburg, Austria, 1983; physicist div. war research Columbia U., World War II; Werner Heisenberg lectr. Bavarian Acad. Scis., 1985; Gifford lectr., Scotland, 1985; vis. Mellon prof. Calif. Inst. Tech., 1990. Author: Philosophical Problems of Space and Time, 1963, 2d edit., 1973, Russian edit., 1969, Modern Science and Zeno's Paradoxes, 2d edit, 1968, Geometry and Chronometry in Philosophical Perspective, 1968, The Foundations of Psychoanalysis: A Philosophical Critique, 1984, German, Italian, French, Hungarian, Japanese edits., 1988, Psicoanalisi: Obiezioni E Risposte, 1988, Validation in the Clinical Theory of Psychoanalysis, 1993, La Psychanalyse à L'Épreuve, 1993; also over 335 articles; mem. editorial bd.: Ency. Philosophy, 1961—; bd. editors Philosophy Sci., 1959—, Am. Philos. Quar., Psychoanalysis and Contemporary Thought, Studies in History and Philosophy of Science, The Philosopher's Index; co-editor Pitts. Series in Philosophy and History of Sci.; assoc. editor Behavioral and Brain Scis. Served with M.I.S. U.S. Army, 1944-46. Recipient J. Walker Tomb prize Princeton U., 1958, honor citation Wesleyan U., 1959, U.S. sr. scientist award Alexander von Humboldt Found., 1985, Fregene Prize in Sci., Italian Parliament, 1989, Wilbur Lucius Cross medal Yale U., 1990. Fellow AAAS (v.p. sect. L 1963); mem. Acad. Internat. de Philosophie des Scis., Am. Philos. Assn. (pres. Ea. divsn. 1982-83), Philosophy of Sci. Assn. (pres. 1965-70), Am. Acad. Arts and Scis., Acad. Humanism (laureate 1985), Phi Beta Kappa, Sigma Xi. Subjects of books. Home: 7141 Roycrest Pl Pittsburgh PA 15208-2737 Office: U Pitts 2510 Cathedral Of Learning Pittsburgh PA 15260-6125

GRUNBAUM, MARIANNE HETTNER, artist; b. Freiberg, Germany, Nov. 6, 1894; came to U.S., 1937; d. Franz and Anna (Stuebel) Hettner; m. Franz Victor Grunbaum, Oct. 27, 1919 (dec. Dec. 31, 1980; children: Elizabeth Lord, Werner Grunbaum. *Mrs. Grunbaum's husband, daughter, and seven-year-old son had to leave their home in Germany in 1937, 4 years after Hitler came to power. Their choice to live in Houston, Texas, proved a happy one. They saw the city grow from a "lowtown" to a fascinating metropolis, with the arts blooming. She has been most fortunate also to have seen a great deal of this beautiful country. She spent many years in Washington state, where her married daughter, Dr. Elizabeth Lord, lives. Vacations in former French territory, Lake Pend'oreille (Earringlake), North Idaho, are unforgettable.* Student, U. Heidelberg, 1918-19, U. Houston, 1950-51. Exhbns. include New Accessions U.S.A., Colorado Springs, Colo., 1954 (Smith Coll. acquired oil painting for permanent collection), Tex. Fine Arts Assn., Laguna Gloria Art Mus., Austin, Tex., 1955, Nat. Exhbn. of Painters Casein, Nat. Arts Club, N.Y.C., 1967, 20th Century Women Artists in Tex. Laguna Gloria Art Mus., 1974, DuBose Gallery, Houston, 1971, Roberto Molina Gallery, Houston, 1980-92, Wash. State U. Fine Arts Dept., 1984, Retrospective A Study in Color, Cheney Cowles Meml. Mus., Spokane, 1986. *Ms. Grunbaum's art teacher, Robert Preusser from the new Bauhaus, Chicago. An excellent instructor, he had profound influence in her painting.* Paintings Let There Be Apathy Under the Stars, Smith Coll. Mus. of Art, Crossed Sqares Cheney Cowles Meml. Mus., Spokane, Wash., several pvt. collections including De Menil collection, Houston; contbr. book The Best of Acryllic Painting, 1996.

GRUNBERG, ROBERT LEON WILLY, nephrologist; b. Bucharest, Romania, July 23, 1940; came to U.S., 1972, naturalized, 1977; s. William A. and Isabelle L. (Rosen) G.; m. Donna M. Fishman, Oct. 19, 1975; children: Wendie I., Andrea B. MD, U. Orleans-Tours, France, 1969. Diplomate Am. Bd. Internal Medicine, Am. Bd. Nephrology. Intern, then resident in cardiology Vichy (France) Hosp., 1968-72; resident in internal medicine Albert Einstein Med. Ctr., Phila., 1972-74; fellow in nephrology-hypertension Hahnemann Univ. Hosp., Phila., 1974-76, sr. clin. instr. then asst. clin. prof. div. nephrology, 1976; pvt. practice medicine specializing in nephrology Allentown, Pa., 1976—; attending physician St. Luke's Hosp., Bethlehem, Pa., Lehigh Valley Ctr. (now Lehigh Valley Hosp.), Allentown; attending charge divsn. nephrology Easton (Pa.) Hosp.; courtesy staff Hahnemann Univ. Hosp.; dir. Renal Dialysis Ctr. at Easton (Pa.) Hosp., 1989. Fellow ACP; mem. AMA (Physician's Recognition award 1975, 79, 82, 85, 88, 89-92, 92-95, 95-98), Pa. Med. Soc., Am. Soc. Nephrology, Am. Soc. Artificial Internal Organs, Internat. Soc. Hypertension, Am. Soc. for Parenteral and Enteral Nutrition, Internat. Soc. for Artificial Organs, Internat. Soc. Nephrology, Assn. for Advancement of Med. Instrumentation, Internat. Soc. for Peritoneal Dialysis, Nat. Kidney Found., N.Y. Acad. Scis. Office: 50 S 18th St Easton PA 18042-3912 also: 401 N 17th St Allentown PA 18104-5034

GRUNBERG, SLAWOMIR, film and television producer and director, director of photography; b. Lublin, Poland, Apr. 6, 1951; came to the U.S., 1981; s. Karol Nathan and Danuta Czosnowska (Ostrowska) G.; m. Wanda Turek, Aug. 15, 1976; children: Karolina, Sarah, Joanna. MA, SGGW, Warsaw, 1974; cert. film and TV dir., Polish Film Sch., Lodz, 1981. Vis. scholar MIT, Boston, 1982; asst. prof. U. Cin., 1982-84, Govs. State U., Chgo., 1984-85; vis. prof. Webster U., St. Louis, 1985-86; asst. prof. Ithaca (N.Y.) Coll., 1986-90; TV and film prodr., cameraman, editor Log In Enterprises, Spencer, N.Y., 1987—. Prodr., dir.: School Prayer: A Community At War, 1998 (Sch. Prayer selected by PBS Broadcast 1999), From Chechnya To Chernobyl, 1996, Chelyabinsk: The Most Contaminated Spot, 1994; co-prodr.: Messenger to Poland, 1989; second unit prodr.: Shtetl, 1996, 97; Guggenheim fellow in documentary film making, 1997. Prodn. grantee Ind. TV Svc., 1997, Soros Documentary Fund, 1996; recipient Silver Apple award, Grand Prix Best in Prague, 1998, Golden Cine award, Grand Prix award Internat. Environ. Film Fest, 1996, Best Journalistic award Okomedia Film Festival, 1995. Mem. Assn. Ind. Video and Filmmakers, Internat. Documentary Assn. Avocation: nature. Office: Log In Prodns 4 Larue Rd Spencer NY 14883-9657

GRUNBERGER, DEZIDER, biochemist, researcher; b. Kosice, Czechoslovakia, May 29, 1922; came to U.S., 1968; s. Louis and Janka (Gluck) G.; m. Marta Herman, Dec. 23, 1948; children—George, Ivan. M.Sc., U. Prague, 1950; Ph.D., Acad. Sci., Prague, 1956, D.Sc., 1968. Head dept. Acad. Sci., Prague, Czechoslovakia, 1956-64, head dept., 1965-68; asst. prof. George Washington U., Washington, 1964-65; prof. biochemistry and biophysics Columbia U., N.Y.C., 1968-92, prof. emeritus biochem./molecular biophysics and pub. health, 1993—; E. and J. Michaels prof. Weizmann Inst., Rehovot, Israel, 1983. Author: Molecular Biology of Mutagens and Carcinogens, 1983; editor: Mechanisms of Cellular Transformations by Carcinogenic Agents, 1987; assoc. editor: Oncology Rsch.; contbr. 180 articles to profl. jours.; U.S. patent for preparation and use of caffeic acid phenethyl ester. Leukemia Soc. U.S.A. scholar, 1972-77, Rockefeller Found. scholar, 1981; grantee NIH, EPA, Am. Cancer Soc. Mem. AAAS, Am. Soc. Biol. Chemists, Am. Assn. Cancer Rsch., N.Y. Acad. Sci. Achievements include patent for preparation and use of caffeic acid phenethyl ester. Office: Columbia U 701 W 168th St New York NY 10032-2704

GRUND, DAVID IRA, lawyer; b. Feb. 5, 1947; s. Julian and Ethel (Brudner) G.; m. Rachel Reifer, Dec. 16, 1972; 1 child, Melissa. BS, DePaul U., 1968, JD, 1972. Bar: Ill. 1973, U.S. Dist. Ct. (no. dist.) Ill. 1973. Prin. ptnr. Grund & Starkopf, Chgo.; lectr. in field. Bd. dirs. Ill. Holocaust Meml. Found., Skokie, 1989—, U.C.P., Ill. Chgo., 1988—; bd. dirs. Glencoe Social Svcs. Mem. Am. Acad. Matrimonial Lawyers (bd. mgrs. Ill. chpt. 1987—, chmn. admissions com. 1992-97), Ill. Bar Assn., Chgo. Bar Assn. (matrimonial law sect., cts. and legis. subcom.), Ill. Trial Lawyers Assn., Ill. Leading Lawyers, Decalogue Soc. Lawyers, Standard Club (Chgo.). Jewish. Avocations: golf, running, photography. Office: Grund & Starkopf 111 E Wacker Dr Chicago IL 60601-3713

GRUNDBERG, BETTY, state legislator, property manager; b. Woden, Iowa, Feb. 16, 1938; d. Edwin and Eva Ruth Meyer; m. Arnie Grundberg, Dec. 31, 1960; children: Christine, Julie, Michael, Susan. BA, Wartburg Coll., 1959; MA, U. Iowa, 1969; postgrad., Drake U. Cert. tchr. Property mgr. and renovator Des Moines, 1973—; with Des Moines Sch. Bd., 1975-90; legis. State of Iowa, Des Moines, 1993—; chmn. edn. com.; mem. human resources com., labor com. Active LWV, Des Moines, 1972—. Republican. Home and Office: 224 Foster Dr Des Moines IA 50312-2540

GRUNDER, FRED IRWIN, program administrator, industrial hygienist; b. Detroit, Aug. 17, 1940; s. Fritz and Mary Kathrine (Irwin) G.; m. Barbara Ann Ward, May 7, 1966; children: John Frederick, Robert William. BS in Engr. Physics, U. Mich., 1963, MS in Physics, 1967. Diplomte Am. Bd. Indsl. Hygiene; cert. indsl. hygienist. Rsch. assoc. U. Mich., Ann Arbor, 1960-69; chemist G.D. Clayton & Assocs., Southfield, Mich., 1969-72; lab. dir. Bethlehem (Pa.) Steel Corp., 1972-85; dir. indsl. hygiene Am. Med. Labs., Fairfax, Va., 1985-92; mgr. lab. accreditation programs Am. Indsl. Hygiene Assn., Fairfax, 1992—. Sect. editor: Methods for Biological Monitoring, 1988. Scoutmaster Boy Scouts Am., Bethlehem, 1972-84; pres. U. Mich. Club, Lehigh Valley, 1980-84; mem. toxic planning and oversight panel Chesapeake Rsch. Consortium, Solomons Island, Md., 1990-91, site visitor AIHA Lab., 1992; bd. dirs., vice-chair Nat. Coop. Lab. Accreditation, 1997-98, pres., 1998—. Fellow Am. Indsl. Hygiene Assn.; mem. ASTM, Coun. Engring. and Sci. Soc. Execs., Am. Chem. Soc., Am. Acad. Indsl. Hygiene. Democrat. Methodist. Avocations: reading, stamp and coin collecting, gardening. Office: Am Indsl Hygiene Assn 2700 Prosperity Ave Ste 250 Fairfax VA 22031-4320

GRUNDFAST, KENNETH MARTIN, otolaryngologist; b. Bklyn., Mar. 12, 1944; s. Theodore Harvey and Anne Gertrude (Goldberg) G.; m. Ruthanne Blatt Grundfast, May 26, 1974; children: Rena Brett, Dara Beth. BA, Johns Hopkins U., 1965; MD, SUNY, Syracuse, 1969. Clin. instr. dept. of community medicine Georgetown U. Sch. of Medicine, Washington, 1972-74, prof. depts. otolaryngology and pediat., 1996—; interim chmn. dept. otolaryngology Georgetown U. Sch. of Medicine; resident otolaryngology Boston U. Hosp., 1974-77; fellow in pediatric otolaryngology Childrens Hosp. of Pitts., 1977-78, staff otolaryngologist, 1978-79, asst. prof. of otolaryngology, 1978-79; prof. dept. otolaryngology, 1980-96; chmn. dept. otolaryngology Children's Nat. Med. Ctr., Washington, 1980-94, vice-chmn., 1994-96; lectr. in field. Author: (with others) Ear Infections in Your Child, 1987, Pediatric Otology/Neurotology, 1997; contbr. articles to profl. jours. Lt. comdr. USPHS, 1971-73. Fellow ACS, Am. Acad. Pediat.; mem. AMA (Humanitarian award 1973), Soc. for Ear, Nose and Throat Advancement in Children (bd. dirs. 1985, v.p. 1988, pres. 1989), Am. Bronchoesophagologic Soc., Montgomery-Prince George's County Pediatric Soc., Soc. of U. Otolaryngologists, Am. Neurotology Soc., Trilogical Soc. (hon. mention clin. rsch. thesis), Am. Soc. Pediatric Otolaryngology (pres. 1993-94), Am. Acad. Otolaryngology (v.p. 1994-96, Presdl. Citation award 1996). Avocations: swimming, bicycling. Office: Georgetown U Med Ctr 3800 Reservoir Rd NW Washington DC 20007-2113*

GRUNDHOFER, JOHN F., banking executive; b. L.A., 1939. Student, Loyola U., 1960, U. So. Calif., 1964. Formerly with Wells Fargo & Co., San Francisco, also vice chmn.; now chmn., pres., chief exec. officer First Bank System, Inc. (now named U.S. Bancorp), Mpls., 1990—; also dir. First Bank System, Inc., Mpls. Office: US Bancorp 601 2nd Ave S Minneapolis MN 55402-4303*

GRUNDLEHNER, CONRAD ERNEST, information company executive, economic consultant; b. N.Y.C., Mar. 12, 1942; s. Ernest and Elise Louise (Eicks) G.; m. Marietta Ferebee Guidon, Feb. 19, 1977; children: Marietta Ferebee Karen, Guidon Steven. BS, MIT, 1964; MA, U. Pa., 1968. V.p. Simumatics, Inc., Haddonfield, N.J., 1969-72; mgr. Hay Assocs., Phila., 1973-79, Strategic Planning Assocs., Washington, 1980-82; chief economist Donoghue Orgn. Inc., Holliston, Mass., 1982-84; pres. Conrad Grundlehner Inc., McLean, Va., 1984—; bd. dirs. Conrad Grundlehner Inc., McLean, 1984—, bd. dirs., cons. economist W.E. Donoghue & Co., Inc., Holliston, Mass., 1986—. Editor: Donoghue's Mutual Funds Alamanac, 1984-86, contbg. editor: Donoghue's Mutual Funds Alamanac, 1987. 1st lt. U.S. Army, 1971. Mem. MIT Enterprise Forum, Am. Econ. Assn., Nat. Assn. Bus. Econs., MIT Club Washington. Republican. Episcopalian. Avocation: photography.

GRUNDSTEIN, NATHAN DAVID, lawyer, management science educator, management consultant; b. Ashland, Ohio, Sept. 19, 1913; s. Samuel Lewis and Rose J. (Kolinsky) G.; m. Dorothy Deborah Davis, Nov. 12, 1938; children: Miriam R. (Mrs. Bruce R. Levin), Margaret Judith, Leon D., Robert H. BA, Ohio State U., 1935, MSc, 1936; PhD, Syracuse U., 1943; LLB, George Washington U., 1951. Bar: Mich. 1954, Ohio 1981, U.S. Dist. Ct. Ohio, U.S. Dist. Ct. (ea. dist.) Mich. Legal research asst. Office Head Atty., Dept. Agr., 1939-40; adminstrv. asst. to asst. commr. FDA, 1940-41; adminstrv. officer, exec. asst. to vice chmn. for labor prodn. WPB, 1941-47; prof. pub. law and adminstrn. Wayne State U., 1947-58; prof. adminstrn. Grad. Sch. Pub. and Internat. Affairs, U. Pitts., 1958-64; prof. mgmt. policy, dir. grad. program pub. mgmt. sci. Case Western Res. U., 1964-84; prin. Enterprise Achievement Assocs., Ohio, 1982—; prof. emeritus Case Western Res. U., 1984—; mgmt. cons. Van Dresser Corp. and Ctr. for Minority Entrepreneurs, Inc., 1984-87; gen. counsel Luminal Inc., Ohio, 1984-87; sr. vis. scholar, Canberra, Australia, 1979; cons. Digital Equipment Corp., 1991-92, Paul Cox Assocs., 1992-97, Knowledge Project, Monash U., Australia, 1993-96, Korea Langtek, Seoul, 1994-96; also to govt. and industry; prin. Enterprise Achievement Assn., 1987—; founding mem. Urban Knowledge Group World Wide Web, 1996; lectr. in field. Author: Adminstrative Practice and Procedure Under the Federal Plant Quarantine Act, 1940, Administrative Practice and Procedure Under the Federal Food, Drug and Cosmetic Act, 1941, Industrial Mobilization for War, Vol. I, Part III, 1947, Cases and Readings on Administrative Law, (with J.F. Davison), 1952, Administrative Law and the Regulatory System, 1966, Presidential Delegation of Authority in Wartime, 1961, Ethical Concerns and the City Managers Code of Ethics, 1967, Administrative Law and the Regulatory System, rev. edit, 1968, The Managerial Kant, 1982, Futures of Prudence, 1984, The Knowledge of Strategy, 1993; donor book collection to Memphis State U.; donor Judaica Collection to U. Memphis, 1997. Chmn. Citizens Com. for Cleveland Heights Progress, 1979-81, 83-84; donor book collection Goddard Coll. Bus. Inst., 2,000 vol. book collection U. Canberra, 1999. Mem. Inst. Mgmt. Sci. (exec. com. Coll. Philosophy 1980-84), Mich. Bar Assn., Ohio Bar Assn., Order of Coif, Phi Beta Kappa, Beta Gamma Sigma. Jewish. Donated book collections to U. Canberra, Australia, 1990, 93, 2000 volume library, 1999. Office: Case Western Res U Sch Mgmnt Enterprise Hall Cleveland OH 44106

GRUNDY, KENNETH WILLIAM, political science educator; b. Phila., Aug. 6, 1936; s. William and Alma (Hahn) G.; m. Martha Jonet Paxson, June 25, 1960; children: William MacIntyre, Thomas Paxson, Anne Edmunds. BA with honors, Ursinus Coll., 1958; MA, Pa. State U., 1961, PhD, 1963. Asst. prof. polit. sci. San Fernando Valley State Coll., Northridge, Calif., 1963-66; assoc. prof. Case Western Res. U., Cleve., 1966-74, prof., 1974-88, Marcus A. Hanna prof., 1988—, chmn. dept. polit. sci., 1974-76, dir. Ctr. for Policy Studies, 1998—; vis. sr. lectr. Makerere U. Coll., Kampala, Uganda, 1967-68; vis. scholar Inst. Social Studies, The Hague, The Netherlands, 1972-73, U. Pretoria, 1998; vis. Fulbright prof. U. Zambia, Lusaka, 1977, Nat. U. Ireland, Galway, 1979-80; vis. adj. prof. Cleve. State U., 1992—; editl. adv. bd. Ctr. Internat. Race Rels., 1968—. Author: Conflicting Images of the Military in Africa, 1968, Guerrilla Struggle in Africa, 1971, Confrontation and Accommodation in Southern Africa, 1973, (with Weinstein) The Ideologies of Violence, 1974, We're Against Apartheid, But, 1974, Defense Legislation and Communal Politics, 1978, (with V. McHale and B. Hughes) Evaluating Transnational Programs in Government and Business, 1980, Soldiers Without Politics, 1983, The Militarization of South African Politics, 1986, rev. edit., 1988, South Africa: Domestic Crisis and Global Challenge, 1991, The Politics of the National Arts Festival, 1993; also articles; book rev. editor Internat. Jour. Comparative Sociology, 1973-83; assoc. editor Jour. African Policy Studies, 1991—; contbg. editor Current History, 1982—; mem. editl. adv. bd. African Affairs, 1983-93; mem. editl. bd. Jour. Third World Studies, 1988—, South African Jour. Internat. Affairs, 1993—. Fellow NDEA, 1959-62, Rhodes U., Grahamstown, South Africa, 1989-90, Ctr. Internat. Race Rels., 1969-70; 1st Bradlow fellow South African Inst. Internat. Rels., 1982; grantee Rockefeller Found., 1967-68, Social Sci. Rsch. Coun., 1972, 79-80, Earhart Found, 1979. Mem. African Studies Assn. (mem. exec. coun.), Inter-Univ. Seminar on Armed Forces and Soc., Internat. Studies Assn. Home: 2602 Exeter Rd Cleveland OH 44118-4246 Office: Case Western Res U Dept Polit Sci Cleveland OH 44106

GRUNDY, ROY RAWSTHORNE, marketing educator; b. Hackensack, N.J., Feb. 4, 1930; s. Albert Victor Rawsthorne and Ann Beatrice (Nelson) G.; m. Priscilla Ann Noble, June 17, 1961; children: John, Christopher, William. BS, Ill. Inst. Technology, 1952; MBA, Roosevelt U., 1965; EdD, No. Ill. U., 1989. Lab. technician Container Labs., Chgo., 1955-57; advt. rep. Miller Freeman Pubs., Chgo., 1957-59; sales mgr. Celanese Corp. Am., Chgo., 1959-65; gen. mgr. Intec Inc., Chgo., 1965-70; prof. mktg. Coll. DuPage, Glen Ellyn, Ill., 1970—; vis. prof. Brit. Inst. Mgmt., Oxford U., 1972, Queensland U. Tech., Brisbane, Australia, 1990, Park Lane Coll., Leeds, Eng., 1992, Inst. for Entrepreneurship, Zholtye Vody, Ukraine, 1994, WSI-Inst. Mgmt. and Mktg., Koszalin, Poland, 1995, Ctr. for Citizens Initiatives, Voronezh, Russian Fedn., 1996, Zhengzhou (China) Inst. Tech., 1997, Rural Enterprise Adaptation Program, Siberia, 1997, Kazak State Nat. U., Almaty, Kazakhstan, 1998, Vols. Overseas Coop. Assn.; pres. Rawsthorne Rsch. and Assocs., Naperville, 1970—. Contbr. articles to profl. jours. Mem. Sch. Bd. Dist. 203, Naperville, 1976-79, Transp. Adv. Bd., 1970-75, Cable TV Com., 1970-76, Zoning Bd. Appeals, 1982-84, 1997 Historic Sites Commn.; mem. secondary edn. adv. com. Congressman Fawell's 13th Congl. Dist.; mem. local draft bd. # 051. Fellow Dept. Energy, Solar Energy Rsch. Inst., 1979. Mem. Ill. Community Coll. Faculty Assn. (rep. 1987-88), Am. Mktg. Assn., Mktg. Educators Group Eng., Rotary (sec. 1985-87), Delta Sigma Phi. Republican. Mem. United Ch. Christ. Avocation: local history-Willard Scott (Naperville's first settler). Home: 512 Bayberry Ln Naperville IL 60563-2826 Office: Coll DuPage Dept Mktg Glen Ellyn IL 60137

GRUNDY, SCOTT MONTGOMERY, physician, medical educator; b. Memphis, July 10, 1933. BS, Tex. Tech. Coll., 1955; MD, MS, Baylor U., 1960; PhD, Rockefeller U., 1966. Biochemistry instr. Baylor U., 1960-61; asst. prof. Rockefeller U., 1968-70; chief Phoenix Indian Med. Ctr. Nat. Inst. Arthritis, 1971-73; prof. medicine-in-residence U. Calif., San Diego, 1974-81; prof. biochemistry, prof. internal medicine U. Tex. Health Sci. Ctr., Dallas, 1981-95, dir. Ctr. Human Nutrition, 1981—, chmn. dept. clin. nutrition, 1981—; chief med. svcs. metabolism sect. VA Hosp., San Diego, 1974-81. Mem. NAS, Assn. Am. Physicians, Am. Soc. Clin. Investigation. Office: U Tex SW Med Ctr 5323 Harry Hines Blvd Dallas TX 75235-7208

GRUNE, GEORGE VINCENT, publishing company executive; b. White Plains, N.Y., July 18, 1929; m. Betty Lu Albert, Aug. 9, 1952; children: George, Robert, Steven. AB, Duke U., 1952; postgrad., U. Fla., 1955-56. Dir. exec. recruitment Continental Corp., N.Y.C., 1957-60; sales rep. Reader's Digest Assn., Inc., N.Y.C., 1960-63; advt. sales mgr. Reader's Digest Assn., Inc., Pitts., 1963-66; advt. sales mgr. Reader's Digest Assn., Inc., N.Y.C., 1966-69, mktg. dir. advt. sales ops., 1969-71, v.p., dir. advt. sales worldwide, 1971-74, dep. dir. internat. ops., 1974-76, dep. dir. books and records divsn., 1975-76, v.p., dir. books and home entertainment divsn., 1976-83, v.p. and pub., 1984, chmn.; pres., CEO Source Telecomputing Co. subs. Reader's Digest Assn., 1983-84, chmn., CEO, 1984-94; chmn. bd. Reader's Digest Assn., 1984-95; bd. dirs. Avon Products, Inc., CPC Internat., Chase Manhattan Corp., Federated Dept. Stores, Inc. Chmn. emeritus Boys and Girls Clubs Am., Atlanta; Met. Mus. Art, N.Y.C.; chmn. DeWitt Wallace, Lila Wallace Reader's Digest Funds; bd. overseers, bd. mgrs. Meml. Sloan-Kettering Cancer Ctr.; mem. Inst. de France Acad. des Beaux-Arts; mng. dir. Met. Opera Assn. Recipient Henry Johnson Fisher award, 1987; Nat. Leader's fellow YMCA. Mem. Blind Brook Club (Purchase, N.Y.), Ponte Vedra Club (Fla.), Sawgrass Club (Ponte Vedra Beach, Fla.), Union League, Sky Club N.Y.C., Augusta Nat. Golf Club. Republican. Home: 1001 Ponte Vedra Blvd Ponte Vedra Beach FL 32082-4016 Office: DeWitt Wallace-Reader's Digest Fund Lila Wallace-Digest Fund 2 Park Ave Fl 23 New York NY 10016-9301

GRUNEBAUM, ERNEST MICHAEL, investment banker; b. London, Dec. 26, 1934; came to U.S., 1941; naturalized, 1947; s. Erich Otto and Gabrielle (Neumann) G.; m. Marjorie Bleetstein, Aug. 20, 1957; children: Edward, Lauren, David. BA, Dartmouth Coll., 1956; MA, Brown U., 1958. With N.Y. Hanseatic Corp., investment bankers, N.Y.C., 1956-74, pres., 1973-74; gen. ptnr., mgr. Hanseatic divsn. Stuart Bros., N.Y.C., 1974-81; exec. v.p., mgr. Hanseatic divsn. The Securities Groups, N.Y.C., 1981-85; sr. exec. v.p. Yamaichi Internat. (Am.) Inc., N.Y.C., 1985-87; mng. dir. Hanseatic Hirschland Ptnrs. Inc, Dobbs Ferry, N.Y., 1987—. Mem. exec. com. Self-Help Cmty. Svcs. Inc.; pres., exec. bd. Greater N.Y. Coun. of Reform Synagogues; trustee, mem. exec. com. Union of Am. Hebrew Congregations, 1989—; mem. exec. com. Am. Fedn. Jews from Ctrl. Europe, 1992; dir. United Help, Inc., 1996—. Mem. Money Marketeers (bd. govs., pres.). Jewish (pres., trustee temple). Home: 31 Austin Hill Rd Pound Ridge NY 10576-1811 Office: Hanseatic Hirschland Ptnrs Inc 267 Clinton Ave Dobbs Ferry NY 10522-3003

GRUNER, GEORGE RICHARD, retired secondary education educator; b. Springfield, Mo., Apr. 6, 1940; s. George Fredrick and Elsie Rachel (Souders) G.; m. Grayce Anne Hartman, Mar. 29, 1957 (div. June 1977); children: Mark Randall, Stephen Eric; m. Rita Marie Torres, May 31, 1982; children: Gregory Lee, Dawn Marie. BA in History, Lincoln U. of Mo., 1961; tchg. credentials, U. Puget Sound, 1965; MS in Edn., Calif. State U., Fullerton, 1972; postgrad., U.S. Army War Coll., Carlisle, Pa., 1986. Cert. tchr. Calif. History tchr. Huntington Beach (Calif.) High Sch., 1965-69; tchr., coord. for gifted/talented edn. Edison High Sch., Huntington Beach, 1969-81, English tchr., 1983-90, chmn. English dept., 1991-98, chmn. site restructuring com., 1992-97, cross-curricular integration mentor, 1993-95; commandant Calif. Mil. Acad., Sacramento, Calif., 1986-90; dep. dir. Nat. Interagy. Counterdrug Inst., San Luis Obispo, Calif., 1991; acad. bd. dirs. Calif. Mil. Acad., Sacramento, 1986-91; mem., nat. rep. State Mil. Acad. Adv. Coun., Region VII, Calif., Nev., Utah, Ariz., Hawaii, 1986-90; cons. Calif. Army Nat. Guard, L.A., 1992—; mem. Orange County Vital Link Assessment Com., 1993-98; adminstrv. coord. Ctr. for Internat. Bus. and Comm. Studies, 1994-99. Contbr. articles to regional and nat. jours., author publs. in field. Exec. bd. PTA Edison High Sch., 1971-75; adult leader, cubmaster Boy Scouts Am., Huntington Beach, 1967-74; mem. Huntington Beach Dist. Tech. Coun., 1994-95, Action Planning Com., 1993-95; steering com. CIBACS Found., 1995-99. Col. U.S. Army, 1962-92. Decorated Legion of Merit, Order of Calif., 1992; grantee AST Rsch. Corp., 1993, Calif. Dept. Edn., 1994-98; recipient Hon. Svc. award Calif. Congress of Parents, Tchrs. and Students, 1995. Mem. Dist. Educators Assn. (faculty rep.), Calif. Tchrs. Assn., NEA, Nat. Coun. Tchrs. English, Nat. Guard Assn. U.S. and Calif., Am. Legion. Avocations: hiking, camping, nature study. Home: 2161 Big Buck Ln Paso Robles CA 93446

GRUNES, DAVID LEON, research soil scientist, educator, editor; b. Paterson, N.J., June 29, 1921; s. Jacob and Gussie (Griggs) G.; m. Willa Freeman Grunes, June 26, 1949; children—Lee Alan, Mitchell Ray, Rima

Louise. B.S., Rutgers U., 1944; Ph.D., U. Calif., 1951. With USDA, 1950-96, tech. assistance expert to Internat. Atomic Energy Agy., UN, 1963-64; research soil scientist USDA, Ithaca, N.Y., 1964-96; assoc. prof. soil, crop and atmospheric sci. dept. Cornell U., Ithaca, 1967-76, prof., 1976-97; collaborator USDA, Ithaca, N.Y., 1996—; cons. editor soils, agr. McGraw-Hill Ency., Sci. and Tech., 1965-88. Contbr. chpts. to books, articles to profl. jours. Served with U.S. Army, 1944-45. Recipient Rsch. award USDA, 1959, 82, 89, 92, Am. Soc. Agronomy (Northeastern chpt.), 1988. Fellow AAAS, Am. Inst. Chemists, Am. Soc. Agronomy, Soil Sci. Soc. Am.; mem. Internat. Soc. Soil Sci., Council for Agrl. Sci. and Tech., Sigma Xi. Home: 307 Salem Dr Ithaca NY 14850-1915 Office: US Plant Soil and Nutrition Lab Tower Rd Ithaca NY 14853-2901

GRUNEWALD, DONALD, former college president, educator; b. N.Y.C., Feb. 9, 1934; s. Harry A. and Tina (Gegner) G.; m. Barbara Susan Frees, Feb. 7, 1981; children: Donald Frees, Susan Christina Irene. AB, Union Coll., 1954; MA, Harvard U., 1955, MBA, 1959, DBA, 1962; LLD, Emerson Coll., 1973; LittD, Suffolk U., 1974; DSc, Far East U., 1979, Medaille Coll., 1983; D of Polit. Sci., Kyung Hee U., 1983; LHD, Mercy Coll., 1984; PhD honoris causa, U. Mindanao, 1981. Cert. profl. mgr. Instr. U. Kans. Sch. Bus., 1959-60; lectr. Boston U. Coll. Bus. Adminstrn., 1961-62; research agt. Harvard U. Grad. Sch. Bus., 1962; asst. prof. Rutgers U. Grad. Sch. Bus., 1962-65, assoc. prof., 1965-67; dean, prof. Coll. Bus. Adminstrn., Grad. Sch. Adminstrn. Suffolk U., 1967-69, v.p., dean Coll. Liberal Arts and Scis., Coll. Journalism, 1969-72; pres. Mercy Coll., Dobbs Ferry, N.Y., 1972-84, disting. prof., 1984-86; prof. Iona Coll., 1986—; ednl. cons., propr. Boston Athenaeum; life gov. Manchester Coll., Oxford, Eng.; former trustee Trinity Coll., Washington, chmn. bd., 1984-87. Author: Cases in Business Policy, 1962, (with Moranian and Reidenbach) Business Policy and Its Environment, 1964, (with H. Bass) Public Policy and the Modern Corporation, 1966, Small Business Management, 1966, (with Fenn and Katz) Business Decision Making and Government Policy, 1966, (with Flink) Managerial Finance, 1969, I Am Honored to Be Here Today, 1985, (with Shaviro and Baron) Cases in Strategic Management, 1989, 2d. edit., 1993, (with Andersson, Baron & Shaviro) Readings in Business Policy and its Environment, 1991, Cases in Strategic Management and Policy, 1997, (with Shaviro) The Complete Book of Management, 1998. Trustee Dobbs Ferry Hosp., Heidelberg Coll., Lab. Inst. Merchandising. Lt. USAF, 1955-57. Decorated knight Sovereign Order St. John of Jerusalem, Comdr., Order of St. Lazarus, Knight Grand Cross with Collar, Order of St. Gregory the Illuminator, 5 other knighthoods. Fellow Royal Soc. Arts, Inst. Commerce, Coll. Preceptors; mem. Internat. Assn. Mgmt., Internat. Assn. Univ. Pres.'s (exec. com.), Harvard Club, Cosmos Club. Home: 5 River Rd # 307 Wilton CT 06897-4069 *I have always relied on the old motto: "Never rest until you have made the good better and the better best."*

GRUNIG, JAMES ELMER, communications educator, researcher, public relations consultant; b. Storm Lake, Iowa, Apr. 18, 1942; s. Roy Albert and Gladys Erma (Harjes) G.; m. Juretta Ann Weisgerber, Sept. 11, 1965 (dec. May, 1984); children: Andrew, John, Neil; m. Larissa Ann Johnson, May 11, 1985; 1 stepchild, Lara Schneider. BS, Iowa State U., 1964; MS, U. Wis., 1966, PhD, 1968. Asst. prof. Land Tenure Ctr. U. Wis., Madison, 1968-69; asst. prof. communications Coll. Journalism, U. Md., College Park, 1969-72, assoc. prof., 1972-78, prof., 1978-99, prof. dept. comm., 1999—; pub. rels. cons. numerous orgns. Author: Decline of the Global Village, 1976, Managing Public Relations, 1984, Excellence in Public Relations and Communication Management, 1992, Public Relations Techniques, 1993, Manager's Guide to Excellence in Public Relations and Communication Management, 1995; co-editor Pub. Rels. Rsch. Ann., 1989-91, Jour. Pub. Rels. Rsch., 1992-94; contbr. articles to profl. jours. Scoutmaster Boy Scouts Am., Hyattsville, Md., 1985-90; tchr. Rockville (Md.) United Ch. of Christ, 1980-92. Recipient Pathfinder award for rsch. Inst. for Pub. Rels. Rsch. and Edn., N.Y., 1984; Internat. Assn. Bus. Communicators Found. grantee, 1986-95. Mem. Assn. for Edn. in Journalism and Mass Comm., Internat. Comm. Assn., Pub. Rels. Soc. Am. (Outstanding Educator award 1989, Jackson, Jackson and Wagner award for behavioral sci. rsch. 1992), Internat. Assn. Bus. Communicators, Nat. Comm. Assn., Assn. Advancement Policy, Rsch. and Devel. in Third World, Internat. Pub. Rels. Assn. Democrat. Avocations: sports, camping. Home: 41 Brinkwood Rd Brookeville MD 20833-2300 Office: U Md Coll Journalism 41 Brinkwood Rd College Park MD 20472

GRUNNET, MARGARET LOUISE, pathology educator; b. Mpls., Feb. 20, 1936; d. Leslie Nels and Grace Harriet (Thomson) Grunnet; m. Irving Noel Einhorn, Mar. 10, 1972; stepchildren: Jeffrey Allan, Franne Ruth, Eric Carl, Stanley Glenn. BA summa cum laude, U. Minn., Mpls., 1958; MD, U. Minn., 1962; MS, Ohio State U., 1969. Resident in psychiatry U. Pa. Sch. Medicine, Phila., 1963-64; resident anatomic pathology Presbyn.-U. Pa. Med. Ctr., Phila., 1965-66; fellow neuropathology Phila. Gen. Hosp., 1967, Ohio State U. Hosp., Columbus, 1968-69; instr. Ohio State U., 1969; asst. prof. U. Utah Sch. Medicine, Salt Lake City, 1970-76, assoc. prof., 1976-80; assoc. prof. pathology U. Conn. Sch. Medicine, Farmington, 1980-90, prof., 1990—. Contbr. articles to profl. jours. Mem. Am. Med. Women's Assn., Internat. Soc. Neuropathology, Conn. Soc. Pathologists, World Muscle Soc., Am. Assn. Neuropathologists, Phi Beta Kappa, Alpha Omega Alpha. Mem. Ch. of Christ. Avocations: reading, music, travel. Home: 1550 Asylum Ave West Hartford CT 06117-2805 Office: U Conn Health Ctr Dept Pathology Farmington CT 06032

GRUNSFELD, ERNEST ALTON, III, architect; b. Chgo., June 5, 1929; s. Ernest Alton Jr. and Mary Jane (Loeb) G.; m. Sally Riblett, July 10, 1954; children: Marcia Grunsfeld Henner, John Mace. Student, Inst. Design, Chgo., 1945, Art Inst. Chgo., 1946; BArch, MIT, 1952. Registered architect, Ill., Conn., Ind., Mich., N.C., Ohio, Mo., Tex., Wis. Ptnr. Yerkes & Grunsfeld, Chgo., 1956-65; owner Grunsfeld & Assocs., Architects, Chgo., 1965-75, sr. ptnr., 1975-84, owner, 1984—; corp. mem. Woodlawn Hosp., Chgo., 1968-70; mem. Highland Park (Ill.) Planning Commn., 1969-75; pres. Grunsfeld Meml. Fund, Chgo., 1970—. Contbr. articles to profl. jours. Bd. dirs. Urban Gateways, Chgo., 1968-89, mem. adv. bd., 1989—; life mem. Field Mus. Natural History, Chgo., 1970—, Chgo. Symphony Orch. Assn., 1975—, governing mem., 1995—; mem. exec. com. Coun. for Arts MIT, Cambridge, 1977-89, bd. dirs., 1977—; governing mem. Chgo. Hort. Soc., 1995—; benefactor, hon. governing mem. Art Inst. Chgo., 1980—. Recipient 1st Honor award Burlington Mills, 1968. Fellow AIA (corp. mem. Chgo. chpt., Honor award 1962, citation of merit 1969); mem. Tavern Club, Lake Shore Country Club, Arts Club of Chgo. Office: Grunsfeld & Assocs Architects 211 E Ontario St Chicago IL 60611-3219

GRUNSKA, GERALD P(AUL), former secondary educator, sports official; b. Appleton, Wis., Sept. 14, 1930; s. Raymond Gerald and Etna Anna Rohde Grunska; m. Carol Dawn Wehrs, June 2, 1952; children: Jane, Vicki, Gerald R., Randall, Timothy. BS, U. Wis., 1952; MA, Northern Colo. U., 1959; PhD, Northwestern U., 1978. Phys. edn., English, coach Oostburg (Wis.) H.S., 1953-56, Clintonville (Wis.) H.S., 1956-60; English chmn. Highland Park (Ill.) H.S., 1960-88; dir., supr. Tri-County Offcls., Lake Park, Ill., 1971-78. Author: (biography) Hack, 1978, Mechanics, 1982, Goal to Go, 1988, The Ball is Ready, 1994; contbr. articles on sport officiating to profl. publs. Advisor Key Club, Highland Park, 1976-88. Mem. Nat. Assn. Sports Offcls. (spkr., presenter 1986-99). Avocations: reading, travel, sports officiating. Home: 2221 Baldy Ln Evergreen CO 80439

GRUNSTEIN, LEONARD, lawyer; b. Milw., July 18, 1952; s. Morris and Ida (Gutheric) G.; m. Chana Tambor, Sept. 30, 1973; children: Eli, Michal, Rachel. BA magna cum laude, CUNY, 1972; JD, Bklyn. Coll., 1975. Bar: N.Y. 1976, U.S. Dist. Ct. (so. and ea. dists.) N.Y. 1978, U.S. Ct. Appeals (2d cir.) 1978. Assoc. Walter Handelman, N.Y.C., 1975-76; atty. corp. counsel City of N.Y., 1977-78; counsel to the mayor's Midtown Office of Devel.; assoc. Herrick, Feinstein, N.Y.C., 1978-80, ptnr., 1980—; adj. prof. Cardoza Law Sch., N.Y.C., 1988; bd dirs. N.Y. Fed. Savs. Bank, N.Y.C. Bd. dirs. RJJ Sch., N.Y.C., 1987-89, Jewish Found. Sch., S.I., 1985-88. Mem. ABA, N.Y. State Bar Assn., Phi Beta Kappa. Avocations: photography, carpentry. Office: Herrick Feinstein 2 Park Ave New York NY 10016-5675

GRUNTHAL, DONNA MARIE, art gallery executive, artist; b. Spokane, Aug. 12, 1942; d. Thomas M. and Margie Retzel. Degree in fine arts, Wash. State U., 1970. Cert. ski instr. Mgr. Waterfront Gallery, Lahaina, Hawaii, 1993-96; pres. Treasures of Taos (N.Mex.) Art Gallery, 1996—. Exhibited in juried shows Nat. Soc. Caesin and Acrylics, N.Y.C., Audubon Soc., N.Y.c., Salmagundi Soc., N.Y.C. Mem. Nat. League Am. PEN Women (chmn. hdqs.), Salmagundi Club. Avocations: tennis, golf. Office: Treasures of Taos—The Grunthal Gallery 104-5 Plz Taos NM 87571

GRUNWALD, HENRY ANATOLE, ambassador, editor, writer; b. Vienna, Austria, Dec. 3, 1922; came to U.S., 1940, naturalized, 1948; s. Alfred and Mila (Loewenstein) G.; m. Beverly Suser, Jan. 7, 1953 (dec. 1981); children: Peter, Madeleine, Lisa; m. Louise Melhado, May 1, 1987. AB, N.Y.U., 1944; LHD, NYU, 1975; LLD, Iona Coll., 1981; LHD, Bennett Coll., 1983; LittD (hon.), Webster U., Vienna, 1989. Editorial staff Time mag., 1945-87, sr. editor, 1951-61, fgn. editor, 1961-66, asst. mng. editor, 1966-68, mng. editor, 1968-77; corp. editor Time Inc., 1977-79, editor-in-chief, 1979-87; amb. to Austria, 1988-90. Author: Salinger, a Critical and Personal Portrait, 1962, Churchill, The Life Triumphant, 1965, One Man's America, 1997; contbr. to Time, Life, New Yorker, Fgn. Affairs and Wall St. Jour. Trustee Am. Austrian Found.; adv. bd. Ctr. for Comm., Nat. Press Inst. Russia; vice chmn. World Press Freedom Com.; bd. dirs. Internat. Rescue Com., Met. Opera Guild; bd. overseers faculty arts and scis. NYU. Named sr. fellow Salzburg Seminar. Fellow Royal Soc. Arts, Coun. Fgn. Rels. (adj. sr.); mem. ASCAP, Am. Coun. on Germa, Coun. Am. Ambassadors, Met. Opera Assn., Internat. Press Inst., Century Assn., Knickerbocker Club, Phi Beta Kappa. Office: 654 Madison Ave New York NY 10021-8404

GRUPE, ROBERT CHARLES, corporate training consultant; b. Alice, Tex., Sept. 3, 1948; m. Dorothy E. Cleveland, Nov. 22, 1975; children: Amber, Robert, Elisabeth, Jonathan. BA, MBA, Calif. Coast U., 1977, PhD, 1992. Announcer Stein Broadcasting Co., Sweetwater, Tex., 1966-68; news announcer Ea. Okla. TV Co., Ada, 1969-72; announcer Anadarko (Okla.) Broadcasting Co., 1972-74; news dir. Cleveland County Broadcasting Co., Norman, Okla., 1974-75; instr. Elkins Inst., Oklahoma City, 1975-77; mng. editor Okla. World Media, Oklahoma City, 1977-78; pres., owner Quality Prodns. Inc., Oklahoma City, 1978—; job skills cons. Okla. Pvt. Industry Coun., Oklahoma City, 1989; vol. trainer U.S. Olympic Festival, Oklahoma City, 1989; mem. Total Quality Mgmt. Faculty Okla. State U., 1990-95; TV prodr./host Cox Cable Pub. Programming, Oklahoma City, 1990-96; syndicated radio commentator, 1993—. Author: The Miracle of Speech, 1981, The Change, 1993, Creating The Future, 1994; contbr. articles to profl. jours. Vol. media devel. Vol. Action Com. Oklahoma City, 1991. Mem. ASTD (v.p. 1992), Internat. Assn. Bus. Communicators (v.p. 1996-97), Neuro Linguistic Programming Assocs. (v.p. 1991-92). Avocation: historical research. Office: Quality Prodns Inc 4230 NW 36th St Oklahoma City OK 73112-2910

GRUPP, CARL ALF, art educator, artist; b. Moorhead, Minn., Sept. 11, 1939; s. Carl Martin and Solveig Marie (Johnson) G.; m. Diane DeVito, Jan. 27, 1968 (div. 1985); children: Carl Michael, Sarah Ann Elizabeth, Saskia Marie. Student, Augustana Coll., 1957-58, Sch. Assoc. Arts, 1958-59; BFA, Mpls. Sch. Art, 1964; MFA, Ind. U., 1969. Art prof. Augustana Coll., Sioux Falls, S.D., 1969—, chmn. art dept., 1987—. Art shows include M. Perleman Gallery, Chgo., 1986, S.D. Meml. Art Mus., 1989, No. State U., 1991. Ind. U. fellow, 1968; Emerging Artist grantee S.D. Arts Coun., 1979, Artist Fellowship grantee S.D. Arts Coun., 1988. Office: Augustana Coll 29th & S Summit Sioux Falls SD 57197*

GRUSH, OWEN CHARLES, psychiatry educator; b. Beverly, Mass., Jan. 7, 1940; s. Maurice and Martha (Weisholz) G.; m. Susan Ann Naman, Apr. 5, 1972 (div. Aug. 1990); children: Eric Nathan, Emily Beth; m. Ellen Margaret Wenz, Jan. 18, 1992; stepchildren: Ivy, Jonathan Benjamin. BA, Columbia U., 1960; MD, U. Rochester, 1964. Diplomate Am. Bd. Pediats., Am. Bd. Pediat. Hematology, Am. Bd. Psychiatry and Neurology. Intern in pediats. Children's Hosp., Boston, 1964-65, resident in pediats., 1965-66; sr. resident in pediats. Children's Hosp., Cin., 1966-67; fellow in pediat. hematology-oncology Children's Rsch. Found., Cin., 1967-69; asst. prof. pediats. Emory U., Atlanta, 1969-72; assoc. prof. pediats., chief hematologist, oncologist Emory U., 1972-74; assoc. prof. Med. U. S.C., Charleston, 1974-90; resident in psychiatry Med. U. S.C., 1991-94, clin. asst. prof. psychiatry, 1994—; fellow in med. ethics Inst. Med. Humanities, Galveston, Tex., 1985-86; attending psychiatrist Inst. Psychiatry, Charleston, 1994—, clin. assoc. prof. psychiatry, 1998—; attending psychiatrist VA Hosp., Charleston, 1995—; clin. investigator Pdiat. Oncology Group, St. Louis, Mo., 1974-90. Contbr. articles to profl. jours., chpts. to books. Pres. Synagogue Emanu-El, Charleston, S.C., 1988-90; mem. med. missions team St. Philip's Episcopal Ch., Charleston, 1989-95; med. advisor Camp Happy Days for Children With Cancer, Charleston, 1982-91; mem. Jewish Fedn. Bd., Charleston, 1987-91; bd. dirs. Grief and Loss Ctr. of s.C., 1997—. Fellow Am. Acad. Pediats., Am. Psychiat. Assn., Hypnosis Soc. S.C.; mem. Chamber Music Soc. Charleston, Grief and Loss Ctr. S.C. Jewish. Avocations: gardening, theology, ethics. Office: 1064 Gardner Rd Ste 101 Charleston SC 29407-5711

GRUSHOW, SANDY, broadcast executive. BA in Communication, UCLA, 1983. Former v.p. creative advtg. 20th Century Fox Film Corp.; sr. v.p. advtg. and promotion Fox Broadcasting Co., 1988-90, exec. v.p. programming and scheduling, 1990-91; exec. v.p. Fox Entertainment Group, 1991-92, pres., 1992-95; pres. Tele-TV Media, 1995-97, Twentieth Century Fox TV, LA, 1997—. Office: Twentieth Century Fox TV PO Box 900 Beverly Hills CA 90213*

GRUSKY, ROBERT R., investor; b. N.Y.C., Aug. 19, 1957; s. Burton and Barbara (Rudoy) G.; m. Hope Holmes Eiseman, Feb. 25, 1989; children: Robert R. Jr., Katherine Elizabeth, Alexandra Rose. BA in History cum laude, Union Coll., 1979; MBA with distinction, Harvard U., 1985. Banking assoc. to banking officer to 2nd v.p. U.S. Banking Dept. Continental Ill. Nat. Bank and Trust Co., Chgo., 1979-83; assoc. to v.p. investment banking divsn. Goldman Sachs & Co., N.Y.C., 1985-93, v.p., prin. investment, 1993-97; asst. to the sec. of def. for spl. projects The Pentagon, Washington, 1990-91; sr. advisor Hon. Ronald S. Lauder, N.Y.C., 1997—; pres. RSL Investments Corp., N.Y.C.; bd. dirs. Ctrl. European Media Enterprises, Ltd., Multiple Myeloma Found. Trustee Hackley Sch., Tarrytown, N.Y., 1992—. White House fellow, 1990-91. Mem. Harvard Club N.Y.C. Presbyterian. Office: 767 5th Ave Ste 4200 New York NY 10153-0023

GRUSON, MICHAEL, lawyer; b. Berlin, Sept. 17, 1936; came to U.S., 1962; s. Rudolf and Barbara (Nauhaus) G.; m. Hiroko Tsubota, July 11, 1964; children; Rudolf, Andreas, Sebastian, Matthias, Florian, Konrad. LLB, U. Mainz, Fed. Republic of Germany, 1962; M in Comparative Law, Columbia U., 1963, LLB, 1965; Dr. iur, Freie Univ., Berlin, 1966. Bar: N.Y. 1969, U.S. Ct. Appeals (2d cir.) 1969, U.S. Dist. Ct. (so. dist.) N.Y. 1971, U.S. Supreme Ct. 1977. Assoc. Shearman & Sterling, N.Y.C., 1966-73, ptnr., 1973—; bd. dirs. Fuji Bank and Trust Co., U.S. subs. of Adolf Ahlers, Zumtobel Lighting, Inc. Author: Die Bedurfniskompetenz, 1967; co-author: Sovereing Lending: Managing Legal Risk, 1984, Legal Opinions in International Transactions, 3d edit., 1997, Regulation of Foreign Banks, 2 vols., 2d edition, 1995, Acquisition of Shares in a Foreign Country, 1993; contbr. articles to profl. jours. Mem. Internat. Bar Assn. (past vice chmn. com. banking law, past chmn. subcom. on legal opinions), N.Y. State Bar Assn. (com. internat. banking, securities and fin. transaction, internat. law and practice sect., gen. practice div., mem. com. on internat. monetary law of the internat. law assn.). Home: 850 Park Ave New York NY 10021-1845 Office: Shearman & Sterling 599 Lexington Ave Fl C2 New York NY 10022-6069

GRUTMAN, JEWEL HUMPHREY, lawyer, writer; b. N.Y.C., Mar. 13, 1931; d. Robert and Gladys Humphrey; m. Robert W. Bjork, June 26, 1954 (div. Apr. 22, 1975); 1 child, Bruce Bjork; m. Roy Grutman, Oct. 30, 1975 (wid. 1994); m. Fredrick Yonkman, July 4, 1998. BA magna cum laude, Mt. Holyoke Coll., 1952; LLB, Columbia U., 1955. Bar: N.Y., U.S. Dist. Ct. (So. Dist.) N.Y. 1971, U.S. Dist. Ct. (ea. dist.) N.Y. 1974, U.S. Dist. Ct. Conn. 1984, U.S. Supreme Ct. 1984. Atty. Debevoise & Plimpton, N.Y.C., 1954-60; ptnr. Eaton Van Winkle, N.Y.C., 1976-79, Grutman Greene & Humphrey, N.Y.C., 1979—. Co-author: (with CD-ROM) The Ledgerbook of Thomas Blue Eagle, 1994 (Christopher award 1995, Internat. Reading Assn. award), (CD-ROM) The Journey of Thomas Blue Eagle, 1995 (Best Project award Intermedia, Asia, 1995, Creative NGee ANN Disting. award 1995, EMMA award best visual content 1996), The Journal of Julia Singing Bear, 1995; asst. prodr., editor (ednl. film on art) Where Time is a River (1st prize Women's Film Festival); contbr. photograph illustrations: The Reforming Power of the Scriptures, 1996; developer series of designs based on Native Am. art; contbr. articles to mags. and newspapers. Dir. Inwood Ho., N.Y.C., 1970-80; past mem. various coms. Mt. Holyoke Coll.; mem. com. sr. advisors N.Y. Commn. for Internat. Bus. and UN, 1997; past chmn. com. to establish Barbara Black Fellowship at Columbia U. Law Sch.; past pres. 85th St. Playground Assn., N.Y.C.; active supporter The Children's Storefront, Harlem, N.Y.C.; active fundraiser N.Y. Jr. League. Mem. Assn. Bar of City of N.Y. (past mem. young lawyers com., admissions com., post-admission edn. com. in field of securities), The River Club (N.Y.C.), The Stanwich Club (Greenwich, Conn.), Sombrero Golf Club (Marathon, Fla.). Avocations: opera, golf, tennis, poetry.

GRUVER, WILLIAM ROLFE, investment banker; b. Denver, May 31, 1944; s. John and Marion Jean (Plummer) G. AB with distinction, Dartmouth Coll., 1966; MBA, Columbia U., 1968. Ltd. ptnr. Goldman, Sachs & Co., N.Y.C., 1972—; disting. exec. in residence, prof. Bucknell U., 1993—; mem. adv. bd. Geisinger Med. Ctr., Danville, Pa., 1994—, Hirtle, Callaghan & Co., Wayne, Pa., 1996—; arbitrator NASD. Mem. adv. bd. The Lymphoma Found., N.Y.C., 1985—; chmn. bd. trustees Woodbridge (N.J.) Devel. Ctr., 1982-87; vol. Big Bros., Morristown, N.J., 1981-84; trustee Eagles Mere (Pa.) Cmty. Ch., 1993—, Berea Coll., 1995—, Eagles Mere Lake Assn., 1993—, Eagles Mere Found., 1998—; mayor Eagles Mere Borough, 1994—; founder Bucknell Harvest, 1997—. Lt. USN, 1968-72. Mem. Am. Legion. Home: PO Box 359 Eagles Mere PA 17731-0359 Office: Goldman Sachs & Co 85 Broad St New York NY 10004-2456

GRUZINSKA, ALEKSANDRA, language educator. BA, SUNY, Buffalo, 1964, MA, 1966; PhD, Pa. State U., 1973. Instr. French Sweet Briar (Va.) Coll., 1971-73; asst. prof. French Ariz. State U., 1973—. Contbr. articles to profl. jours. Fulbright scholar, Paris, 1968-69. Mem. Phi Beta Kappa. E-mail: gruzinska@asu.edu. Home: 1929 W Javelina Ave Mesa AZ 85202-5724 Office: Dept Langs & Lits Ariz State U PO Box 870202 Tempe AZ 85202

GRYC, STEPHEN MICHAEL, composer, music educator; b. St. Paul, June 26, 1949; s. George and Jean (Funk) G.; m. Judith Drake King, May 7, 1977; 1 child, William Edward. MusB, U. Mich., 1971, MusM, 1978, D of Musical Arts, 1983. Prof. music composition U. Hartford, Conn., 1980—. Composer: Wind Machine for Organ and Orch., 1978 (ASCAP grant to Young Composers 1979), 3 Fantasies for Orch., 1983 (Rudolph Nissim prize 1986), Dance Concerto for Clarinet & Orch., 1989 (Conn. Commn. on Arts grant 1988), Fantasy Variations for Oboe and String Quartet, 1992 (New Music Del. prize 1996). Official town composer Town of Farmington, Conn., 1995. MacDowell Colony fellow, Peterborough, N.H., 1985, 88; recipient citation of merit Gen. Assembly State of Conn., 1995, Ucross (Wyo.) Found. residency, 1996; Meet the Composer grantee, 1997. Mem. ASCAP, Am. Composers Forum, Am. Music Ctr., Soc. Composers, Inc., Conn. Composers, Inc., Pi Kappa Lambda. Avocations: geyser study and observation, regional U.S. cuisine. Home: 19 Tanglewood Rd Farmington CT 06032-1162 Office: U Hartford The Hartt Sch 200 Bloomfield Ave West Hartford CT 06117-1545

GRYSON, JOSEPH ANTHONY, orthodontist; b. Rahway, N.J., Feb. 11, 1932; s. Elmer Joseph Anthony and Joyce Asher (Toms) G.; m. Patricia Ann Huddleston, Nov. 22, 1961; children—Karen Ann, David Joseph. B.Chem. Engring., Cornell U., 1954; D.D.S., U. Calif., San Francisco, 1964. Diplomate: Am. Bd. Orthodontics. Engr. div. refinery tech. service Standard Oil of Calif., Richmond, 1954, 58-60; individual practice dentistry specializing in orthodontics San Rafael, Calif., 1964-96; clin. instr. orthodontics U. Calif., San Francisco, 1965-87, assoc. clin. prof. orthodontics, 1987—; referee Am. Jour. Orthodontics and Dentofacial Orthopedics. Contbr. articles to profl. jours. Treas., pres., dir. Hmeowners Assn., San Rafael, 1970-74. Served as carrier pilot USN, 1954-58. Mem. ADA, Pacific Coast Soc. Orthodontists (dir. 1980-85, pres. 1985-86, award of merit 1992), Am. Assn. Orthodontists (ho. of dels. 1982-87, 94-95, spkr. ho. of dels. 1988-91, James E. Brophy Disting. Svc. award 1996), Calif. Dental Assn. (Disting. Svc. award 1994), E.H. Angle Soc. (sec. No. Calif. component 1992-96). E-mail: jagryson@aol.com. Home: 1060 Lea Dr San Rafael CA 94903-3726

GRZANKA, LEONARD GERALD, writer, consultant; b. Ludlow, Mass., Dec. 11, 1947; s. Stanley Simon and Claire Genevive Grzanka; m. Christine Duncan Pearson, May 15, 1997. BA, U. Mass., 1972; MA, Harvard U., 1974. Asst. prof. Gakushiun U., Tokyo, 1975-78; pub. rels. specialist Pacific Gas and Electric Co., San Francisco, 1978-80; sales promotion writer Tymshare Transaction Svcs., Fremont, Calif., 1980-81; account exec. The Strayton Co., Santa Clara, Calif., 1981-82; mng. editor Portable Computer Mag., San Francisco, 1982-84; prin. Grzanka Assocs., San Francisco, 1984-86; San Francisco bur. chief Digital News, 1986-91; battery program cons. Bevilacqua Knight Inc., Oakland, Calif., 1991-97; freelance writer, cons., 1997—; staff asst. Electric Power Rsch. Inst./U.S. Advanced Battery Consortium, Palo Alto, Calif., 1991-96; lectr. Golden Gate U., San Francisco, 1985-87. Author: Neither Heaven Nor Hell, 1978; translator, editor: (art catalog) Masterworks of Japanese Crafts, 1977; translator: (book chpt.) Manajo: The Chinese Preface to the Kokinwakashu, 1984 (Literary Transl. award 1984), Spanish translation, 1994. Sgt. USAF, 1965-69. Fellow Danforth Found., 1974. Mem. United Anglers Calif., Harvard Club of San Francisco (bd. dirs. 1984-88, Cert. Appreciation 1986, 88), Phi Beta Kappa, Phi Kappa Phi. Avocations: writing, fishing. Home: 2909 Madison St Alameda CA 94501-5426

GRZEBIENIAK, JOHN FRANCIS, psychologist; b. New Castle, Pa., Jan. 9, 1949; s. John and Helen (Mielcuszny) G.; married; children: Anna Helen, Sarah Mary, Andrew John. BA, Youngstown (Ohio) State U., 1970, MS in Edn., 1974; PhD, U. Pitts., 1982. Lic. psychologist, Ohio, Pa.; cert. chem. dependency counselor. Substance abuse counselor, mental health counselor Columbiana County Mental Health Counseling Ctr., 1974-82, intern in psychology, 1982-84; cons. psychologist Diagnostic and Evaluation Clinic, Youngstown, 1985—; dir. diagnostic assessment Columbiana County Mental Health Ctr., 1984-95, sr. psychologist, 1995—, dir. diagnostic svcs., 1997—; cons. psychologist Beaver (Pa.) Valley Psychol. Svcs., 1988-90; adj. prof. dept. psychology Kent (Ohio) State U., 1989—; mem. consulting staff Salem (Ohio) Cmty. Hosp., 1996—. Contbr. articles to Salem (Ohio) News. Mem. APA. Roman Catholic. Avocations: woodworking, gardening, fishing, sausage making. Office: Psychological Svcs 128 Leeper Dr New Castle PA 16102-2716

GRZESIAK, KATHERINE ANN, primary educator. BS, Ctrl. Mich. U., 1968; MA in Tchg., Saginaw Valley State U., 1975; postgrad., various univs., 1975—. 6th grade tchr. Buena Vista Sch. Dist., Saginaw, Mich., 1968-69, 70-71; tchr. Carrollton Pub. Schs., Saginaw, 1972-80, St. Peter and Paul Elem. Sch., Saginaw, 1981-84, Sch. Dist. of City of Saginaw, 1984-90; instr. Ctr. for Innovation in Edn., Saratoga, Calif., 1989—; tchr. Midland (Mich.) Pub. Schs., 1991—; 5th grade tchr. Eastlawn Elem., Midland; adj. faculty Saginaw Valley State U., University Center, Mich., 1976-80, 88-90; presenter in field. Contbr. articles to profl. jours. Recipient Presdl. award for Excellence and Math. Tchg., 1994, Top Tchr. in Mich. Met. Woman mag., 1997, Nat. Educator award Milken Family Found., 1998; named Mich. Tchr. of Yr., 1998. E-mail: grzesiak@mindnet.org. Home: 3115 McGill St Midland MI 48642 Office: Eastlawn Elem Sch 115 Eastlawn Dr Midland MI 48640

GSCHNEIDNER, KARL ALBERT, JR., metallurgist, educator, editor, consultant; b. Detroit, Nov. 16, 1930; s. Karl and Eugenie (Zehetmair) Gschneidner; m. Melba E. Pickenpaugh, Nov. 4, 1957; children: Thomas, David, Edward, Kathryn. BS, U. Detroit, 1952; PhD, Iowa State U., 1957. Mem. staff Los Alamos Sci. Lab., 1957-62, sec. chief, 1961-62; vis. asst. prof. U. Ill., Urbana, 1962-63; assoc. prof. materials sci. and engring. Iowa State U., Ames, 1963-67, prof., 1967-79, Disting. prof., 1979—, metallurgist, 1963-67, sr. metallurgist, 1967—, dir. Rare-earth Info. Ctr., 1966-96; vis. prof. U. Calif.-San Diego, La Jolla, 1979-80; cons. Los Alamos Nat. Lab., 1981-86, Teltech, 1987—. Author: Rare Earth Alloys, 1961, Scandium, 1975, others; editor: (26 vol. book) Handbook on the Physics and Chemistry of Rare Earths, 1978-99, Industrial Applications of Rare Earth Elements, 1981; contbr. numerous chpts. in books and articles to profl. publs. Recipient

William Hume-Rothery award AIME, Warrendale, Pa., 1978, Burlington No. award for Excellence in Rsch., Iowa State U., 1989, Significant Implication for Energy Related Techs. in Metallurgy and Ceramics award Dept. Energy, 1997; co-recipient Outstanding Sci. Accomplishment in Metallurgy and Ceramics award Dept. Energy, Washington, 1982, Frank H. Spedding award Rare Earth Rsch. Confs., 1991, Russell B. Scott Meml. award Cryogenic Engr. Conf., 1995, David R. Boyland Eminent Faculty award in Rsch. Coll. Engring., Iowa State U., 1997. Fellow Minerals, Metals and Materials Soc., Am. Soc. for Materials Internat.; mem. AAAS, Am. Chem. Soc., Am. Crystallographic Assn., Materials Rsch. Soc., Am. Phys. Soc., Iowa Acad. Sci., Materials Rsch. Soc. India (hon.), Cryogenic Soc. Am. Roman Catholic. Office: Iowa State U Ames Lab Ames IA 50011-3020

GSCHWIND, DONALD, management and engineering consultant; b. Youngstown, Ohio, July 3, 1933; s. Mark Leon and Esther Lillian (Wauschek) G.; s. Eleanor Ann Tyken, May 27, 1961; children: Sandra J., Kurt L. BSME, Case Western Res. U., 1955; MS in Auto Engring., Chrysler Inst. Engring., 1957; MBA, Mich. State U., 1975. With Chrysler Corp., Detroit, 1955-58, mgr. steering and suspension engring., 1968-72, mgr. product engring., 1972-74, mgr. quality control, 1974-76, dir. chassis engring., 1976-80, v.p. product planning, 1980-84, v.p. program mgmt., 1984-88; dir., master automotive engring. Lawrence Tech. U., 1994-96. Served to 1st lt. USAF, 1957-59. Mem. Soc. Auto Engrs., Tau Beta Pi.

GSTALDER, HERBERT WILLIAM, publisher; b. New Rochelle, N.Y., Dec. 27, 1942; s. HerbertHerbert Charles and Mary Jane (McDonald) G.; m. Barbara Elizabeth Kraus, Sept. 11, 1965; children—Karen Elizabeth, Steven Herbert, Ellen Catherine. BA, Georgetown U., 1965; MBA, NYU, 1968. With Kraus Periodicals, Millwood, N.Y., 1965—; mgr. Kraus Reprint Co., Millwood, 1970—; v.p. Kraus-Thomson Orgn., Millwood, 1974; pres. Kraus Orgn., Ltd., 1976—; also dir. Kraus Orgn.; pres. Humanas, 1984—. Bd. dirs. Georgetown U. Libr. Assocs., 1982—; pres., trustee Chappaqua Pub. Libr. Roman Catholic. Home: 20 Haights Cross Rd Chappaqua NY 10514-2907

GUADAGNO, MARY ANN NOECKER, social scientist, consultant; b. Springville, N.Y., Sept. 21, 1952; d. Francis Casimer and Josephine Lucille (Fricano) Noecker; m. Robert George Guadagno, Aug. 29, 1970 (div. Mar. 1981). BS in Edn. cum laude, SUNY, Buffalo, 1974; MS, Ohio State U., 1977, PhD, 1978. Grad. teaching assoc. Ohio State U., Columbus, 1974-77, grad. rsch. assoc., 1977-78; asst. prof. U. Minn., St. Paul, 1978-83; cons. Nationwide Ins. Co., Columbus, 1982-83, rsch. assoc. Corp. Rsch., 1983-86, product devel. assoc., Office of Mktg., 1986-89; adjunct prof. Coll. Bus. & Pub. Adminstrn. Franklin U., Columbus, Ohio, 1985-89; lectr. Coll. Bus. Adminstrn. and Econ. Ohio Dominican Coll., Columbus, 1986-89; scientist family econ. rsch. group USDA, Washington, 1989-93; survey statistician Nat. Ctr. for Health Stats., HHS, Washington, 1993—; chair Women's Coun., DHHS, Hyattsville, Md., 1993-96; mem. women in sci., 1991-93; health scientist adminstr. Nat Inst. Health, Nat. Inst. Aging DDHS, Washington. Author: Family Inventory of Money Management, 1982, Family Inventory, 1982; contbr. articles to profl. jours., 1978—. Com. mem. United Way, Mkt. Rsch. Info. Exchange, Columbus, Ohio. Recipient Spl. Recognition award Ohio House Reps., 1987, Cert. Grad. award Columbus Area Leadership Program, 1987, Cert. Appreciation award Am. Mktg. Assn., 1987, Cert. Merit award U.S. Dept. Agr., 1991. Mem. Columbus Area Leadership Program, Ohio State U. Coll. Human Ecology Alumni. Republican. Roman Catholic. Avocations: horseback riding, classical music, eastern philosophy, gardening. Home: 4853 Cordell Ave Apt 921 Bethesda MD 20814-3024 Office: Nat Inst Health, Nat Inst Aging 7201 Wisconsin Ave Bethesda MD 20814-4810

GUAJARDO, ELISA, counselor, educator; b. Roswell, N. Mex., Nov. 13, 1932; d. Alejo Najar and Hortensia (Jiminez) Garcia; m. David Roberto Guajardo, Oct. 15, 1950; 1 child, Elsie Edith. BS, Our Lady of the Lake U., 1962, MEd, 1971; MA, Chapman U., 1977. Cert. tchr., adminstr., counselor, Calif. Elem. tchr. San Antonio (Tex.) Sch. Dist., 1962-63; tchr. social sci. Newport Mesa Sch. Dist., Costa Mesa, Calif., 1963-67; tchr. social sci. Orange (Calif.) Unified Sch. Dist., 1967-70, project dir., 1970-71, tchr. English, 1972-73, counselor, 1973—; pres. Bilingual, Bicultural Parent Adv. Bd., Orange, Calif., 1971-72; reader bilingual projects Calif. State Dept. Edn., Orange, 1971-72; vis. lectr. We. Wash. Univ., Bellingham, 1972-73; mem. curriuculum and placement couns., Orange Unified Sch. Dist., 1973-78, 95-96. Author: (Able)Adaptations of Bilingual/Bicultural Edn, Fed. Project Proposal. Mem. NEA, AAUW, Calif. Tchrs. Assn., Orange Unified Edn. Assn, Hon., Alpha Chi, Our Lady of Lake U., Tex. chpt. Democrat. Mem. Assemblies of God Church. Avocations: choir and solo singing, piano, marimba, organ. Home: 335 E Jackson Ave Orange CA 92867-5743 Office: Canyon HS 220 S Imperial Hwy Anaheim CA 92807-3945

GUALTIERI, JOSEPH PETER, museum director; b. Royalton, Ill., Dec. 25, 1916; s. Simone and Teresa (Toracca) G.; m. Marie E. MacDonald, Nov. 21, 1939; children: Ricardo Simone, Renee Marie; m. Angeline Lanzetta, Sept. 19, 1987. Diploma, Art Inst. Chgo., 1939; postgrad. study in, Italy, 1969-70, Mex., 1939-40. Tchr. art Hull House, Chgo., 1942, Lyman Allyn Mus., New London, Conn., 1945-46, Eastern Conn. State U., Willimantic, Conn., summers 1950-52, Hillyer Coll., Hartford, Conn., 1957-58, Norwich (Conn.) Art Sch., 1943-79; tchr. Norwich Free Acad.; dir. Slater Meml. Mus., Norwich, 1962—. One-man exhbns. include Chgo. Art Inst., 1941, Contemporary Art Gallery, N.Y.C., 1951, Nexus Gallery, Boston, 1965, Parnassus Gallery, Chgo., 1941-42, Cummings Art Ctr., New London, Conn., 1979; retrospective exhbn. Slater Mus., 1992. Bd. dirs. Otis Library, Norwich, 1975-81; mem. Norwich Charter Revision Com. Recipient 1st prize Chgo. Art Inst., 1941, Logan medal, 1941; purchase prize Pa. Acad. Fine Arts, 1948, 51; prize Eastern States Exposition Conn. Artists, 1951. Mem. Conn. Acad. Fine Arts, United Italian Soc. (chmn.). Democrat. Roman Catholic. Home: 179 Liberty St Pawcatuck CT 06379-1335 Office: Slater Meml Mus 108 Crescent St Norwich CT 06360-3556

GUARE, JOHN, playwright; b. N.Y.C., Feb. 5, 1938; s. John Edward and Helen Clare (Grady) G.; m. Adele Chatfield-Taylor, 1981. AB, Georgetown U., 1961; MFA, Yale U., 1963; PhD (Hon.), Georgetown U., 1991. Seminar in writing fellow Saybrook Coll., Yale U., New Haven, 1977-78, adj. prof., 1978-81; fellow Juilliard Sch., 1993-94; lectr. NYU, CCNY; vis. artist Harvard U., 1990-91. Author: (plays) Universe, 1949, Thirties' Girl, 1959, The Toadstool Boy, 1960, The Golden Cherub, 1962, Did You Write My Name in the Snow, 1962, To Wally Pantoni, We Leave a Credenza, 1964, The Loveliest Afternoon of the Year, 1966, Something I'll Tell You Tuesday, 1966, Muzeeka, 1967 (Obie award 1968), Cop-out, 1968 (N.Y. Drama Critics' award 1969), A Play by Brecht, 1969, Home Fires, 1969, Kissing Sweet, 1969, The House of Blue Leaves, 1971 (N.Y. Drama Critics' Circle award 1971, Outer Critics' Circle award 1971, Obie award 1971, Tony award 1986), (musical) Two Gentlemen of Verona, 1971 (N.Y. Drama Critics' Circle award 1972, 2 Tony awards 1972, 2 Drama Desk awards 1972), A Day for Surprises, 1971, Un Pape a New York, 1972, Marco Polo Sings a Solo, 1973, Optimism, or the Adventures of Candide, 1973, Rich and Famous, 1974, Landscape of the Body, 1977 (Joseph Jefferson award 1977), Take a Dream, 1978, Bosoms and Neglect, 1979, In Fireworks Lie Secret Codes, 1981, Lydie Breeze, 1982, Gardenia, 1982, Hey, Stay a While, 1984, Women and Water, 1984, Gluttony, 1985, The Talking Dog, 1985, Moon Over Miami, 1989, Six Degrees of Separation, Broadway, 1990 (N.Y. Drama Critics' Circle award 1991), London, 1993 (Olivier Best Play award 1993), Four Baboons Adoring the Sun, 1992 (Tony award nomination Best Play 1992), Moon Under Miami, 1995, The General of Hot Desire, 1997; co-adapter, lyricist: (plays) Two Gentlemen of Verona, 1971; (screenplays) Taking Off, 1970, Atlantic City, 1981 (Academy award nomination Best Original Screenplay 1981, N.Y. Film Critics' award 1981, L.A. Film Critics' award 1981, Nat. Soc. Film Critics' award 1981, Venice Film Festival Grand prize 1981), Six Degrees of Separation, 1993, Chuck Close: Life and Work 1988-1995, 1996, War Against the Kitchen Sink, 1996; playwright-in-residence N.Y. Shakespeare Festival, 1976-77; co-editor Lincoln Ctr. Rev. Recipient Award of Merit, Am. Acad. Arts and Letters, 1981; named Lit. Lion, N.Y. Pub. Libr., 1986; Rockefeller grantee. Mem. Dramatist Guild Council, Am. Acad. Arts and Letters. Address: Kay Collyer & Boose LLP 1 Dag Hammarskjold Plz New York NY 10017-2201*

GUARINO, ANTHONY MICHAEL, pharmacologist, educator, consultant, counselor; b. Framingham, Mass., Dec. 11, 1934; s. Alfred V. and Nellie L. (Beatrice) G.; m. Aida Iris Gerena, Nov. 9, 1957; children: Theresa, Elizabeth, Barbara, Cathy, Tom, Gregory, Paula, Phil, Richard, Paul. BS in Chemistry, Boston Coll., 1956; MS in Chemistry, U. R.I., 1963, PhD in Pharmacology and Toxicology, 1966; MA in Counseling, Liberty U., 1993. Lic. profl. counselor. Lt. comdr. USPHS, 1966, advanced through grades to capt., 1979; staff fellow pharmacology-toxicology rsch. assoc. program Nat. Heart Inst., NIH, Bethesda, Md., 1966-68; rsch. pharmacologist NCI Nat. Cancer Inst., NIH, Bethesda, Md., 1968-73, chief lab. toxicology, 1973-80; regulatory pharmacologist Ctr. for Drugs and Biologics-FDA, Md., 1980-84; lab. dir. fishery rsch. br. FDA, Dauphin Island, Ala., 1984-93; adj. prof. U. South Ala. Coll. Medicine, Mobile, 1984—, U. South Ala. Coll. Allied Health Professions, Mobile, 1996—; marriage and family counselor Cath. Social Svcs., Mobile, 1993—; vice chmn. com. on animals as monitors in environ. hazards NAS. Contbg. author: Handbook of Experimental Pharmacology—Concepts in Biochemical Pharmacology, 1971, Handbook of Experimental Pharmacology, Antineoplastic and Immunosuppressive Agents, 1974, Methods in Cancer Research, 1979, Pesticides and Xenobiotics Metabolism in Aquatic Organisms, 1979, Pesticides and Xenobiotics Metabolism in Aquatic Organisms, 1979, Cisplatin—Current Status and New Developments, 1980, Modern Pharmacology, 1982; contbr. 106 articles to profl. jours. Mem. Am. Soc. Pharmacology and Exptl. Therapeutics, Soc. Toxicology, Am. Chem. Soc., Am. Assn. Christian Counselors. Roman Catholic. Home: 968 Westbury Dr Mobile AL 36609-3332 Office: U S Ala Coll Medicine Dept Pharmacology MSB 3130 Mobile AL 36688

GUARINO, LOUIS JOSEPH, mechanical engineer, consultant; b. N.Y.C., June 21, 1917; s. Joseph J. and Marie (Ferrara) G.; m. Iris Cooper, May 13, 1950; 1 child, Victoria Anne. BME, NYU, 1943. Registered profl. engr., N.Y. Consulting engr. Frank J. Guarino and Assoc., N.Y.C., 1948-61; project engr. Port Authority of N.Y. and N.J., N.Y.C., 1961-86; consulting engr. Louis J. Guarino, P.E., Washingtonville, N.Y., 1986—; rsch. assoc. VA Hosp., Boise, Idaho, 1986-87. Co-inventor diagnostic apparatus utilizing low frequency vibration. Mem. NYU Alumni. Achievements include pioneer in the development of the artificial kidney; co-inventor diagnostic apparatus utilizing low frequency vibration. Avocations: research, skiing, boating. Home: PO Box 164 Washingtonville NY 10992-0164

GUASTAFERRO, ANGELO, company executive; b. Hoboken, N.J., June 4, 1932; s. Carlo and Rafaela Nancy (Gioffi) G.; m. Eleanor Lago, Sept. 12, 1954; children: Carl, Mark, John Brian. B.S. in Mech. Engring, N.J. Inst. Tech., 1954; M.B.A., Fla. State U., 1963; A.M.P., Harvard U., 1984. With NASA, 1963-85; dep. project mgr. NASA (Viking Project), 1974-76; dir. planetary programs NASA Hdqs., Washington, 1979-81; dep. dir. Ames Research Center, Moffett Field, Calif., 1981-85; v.p., program dir. Lockheed Missiles & Space Co., 1985-96, exec. dir., 1994-96; CEO, pres., chmn. bd. N View Corp., Newport News, Va., 1996—; bd. trustees Internat. Space U., 1993-96; chmn. bd. dirs. View Corp., 1995—; mem. sci. adv. com. NJIT. Chair bd. dirs. Hampton Rds. Tech. Coun. Served with USAF, 1955-58. Recipient Langley Spl. Achievement award NASA, 1974, 77, 78, Outstanding Leadership medal, 1977, Superior Performance award, 1980, Exceptional Service medal, 1981, Presdl. Meritorious rank, 1982; Disting. Alumnus NJIT, 1997. Fellow AIAA (Space Systems medal 1982), Am. Astronautics Soc.; mem. Mars First Landing Soc. (pres. 1978-79), Internat. Astronautics Fedn. (bd. dirs.), Tau Beta Pi (eminent engr. 1989). Roman Catholic. Office: N View Corp 860 Omni Blvd Newport News VA 23606-4213

GUASTAFESTE, ROBERTA HARRISON, cellist; b. N.Y.C., Feb. 20, 1929; d. Michael and Rena (Fish) Harrison; m. Joseph R. Guastafeste, June 21, 1953 (div. 1982); children: Camille Avellano, Manon Spadaro. Student, L.A. City Coll., 1946-49, UCLA, 1949-51. Cellist Dallas Symphony Orch., 1950-60; instr. So. Meth. U., Dallas, 1951-60; prin. cellist Arie Crown Theatre, Chgo., 1966-86, Auditorium and Schubert Theaters, Chgo., 1986-89; instr. North Park Coll., Chgo., 1975-89; sole propr. A440 String Instrument Shop, Chgo., 1982—; pvt. cello instr. Mem. ACLU, Nat. Mus. for Women in Arts, U.S. Holocaust Mus., Art Inst. Chgo., Chgo. Mus. Contemporary Art, Chamber Music Am., Greenpeace, Arts Club Chgo., Sierra Club. Democrat. Jewish. Avocations: painting, writing, theater, travel. Home: 2031 N Halsted St Chicago IL 60614-4371

GUAY, GORDON HAY, postal service executive, marketing educator, consultant; b. Hong Kong, Aug. 1, 1948; came to U.S., 1956; s. Daniel Bock and Ping Gin (Ong) G. AA, Sacramento City Coll., 1974; BS, Calif. State U., Sacramento, 1976, MBA, 1977; PhD, U. So. Calif., 1981. Mgmt. assoc. U.S. Postal Svc., Sacramento, 1980-82, br. mgr., 1982-83, fin. mgr., 1983-84, mgr. quality control, 1984-86, mgr. tech. sales and svcs. divsn., 1986-91, dir. mktg. and comm., 1991-95, postmaster, 1996—; assoc. prof. bus. adminstrn., mktg. and mgmt. Calif. State U., Sacramento, 1981-85; prof. mktg. Nat. U., San Diego, 1984—; pres. Gordon Guay and Assocs., Sacramento, 1979—; cons. Mgmt. Cons. Assocs., Sacramento, 1977-79. Author: Marketing: Issues and Perspectives, 1983; also articles to profl. jours. With U.S. Army, 1968-70. Recipient Patriotic Svc. award U.S. Treasury Dept., San Francisco, 1985. Fellow Acad. Mktg. Sci.; mem. NEA, AAUP, Am. Mgmt. Assn., Am. Mktg. Assn. (Outstanding Mktg. Educator award 1989), Am. Soc. Pub. Adminstrn., Soc. Advancement Mgmt. (Outstanding Mem. 1976), Assn. MBA Execs. Democrat. Avocations: photography, golf, tennis, fishing, camping. Office: US Postal Svc 4131 S Shingle Rd Shingle Springs CA 95682

GUBER, PETER, producer; b. Syracuse, 1942; m. Linda Gellis. BA, Syracuse U.; SSP, U. Florence, Italy, JD, LLM; postgrad., NYU. Bar: N.Y., Calif., D.C. Exec. asst. Columbia Pictures, studio chief, co-chmn., 1989-94; prin. Peter Guber's Filmworks; co-prin., chmn. bd. Casablanca Record and Filmworks (merger Peter Guber's Filmworks and Casablanca Records), 1976-80; prin. Polygram Pictures, 1980-83, Guber-Peters, 1983-88; co-chmn., mng. dir. Guber-Peters-Barris Entertainment Co, 1988-89, chmn., 1989; chmn., chief exec. officer Sony Pictures Entertainment, 1989-94; vis. prof., chmn. producer's dept. UCLA Sch. Theatre Arts. Author: Inside the Deep, Above the Title; prodr.: (films) The Deep, 1977; (with Jon Peters) Vision Quest, 1985, Batman, 1989, Tango & Cash, 1989; (with Peters and Neil Canton) The Witches of Eastwick, 1987, Caddyshack II, 1988; (television) Stand By Your Man, 1981, Brotherhood of Justice, 1986, Bay Coven, 1987, Nightmare at Bitter Creek, 1988, Finish Line, 1989; exec. prodr.: Midnight Express, 1978; (with Peters) An American Werewolf in London, 1981, Six Weeks, 1982, Missing, 1982 (Academy award nomination for best picture 1982), Flashdance, 1983, D.C. Cab, 1983, Head Office, 1985, The Legend of Billie Jean, 1985, The Color Purple, 1985 (Academy award nomination for best picture 1985), Youngblood, 1986, Gorillas in the Mist, 1988, Rain Man, 1988 (Academy award for best picture 1988), Missing Link, 1989, The Bonfire of the Vanities, 1990, This Boy's Life, 1993, With Honors, 1994; (with Peters, George Folsey, Jr., and John Landis) Clue, 1985; (with Peters, Mark Damon, John Hyde, and Sydney Kimmel) The Clan of the Cave Bear, 1986; (with Peters, Kathleen Kennedy, Frank Marshall, and Steven Spielberg) Innerspace, 1987; (with Peters and Roger Birnbaum) Who's That Girl?, 1987; (with Peters, Benjamin Melniker, and Michael E. Uslan) Batman Returns, 1992; (television) The Toughest Man in the World, 1984; (with Peters) Television and the Presidency, 1983 (Emmy award nomination 1984); asst. prodr.: High Spirits, 1988. Named Producer of Yr., NATO, 1979; Albert Gallatin fellow NYU. Office: Mandalay Entertainment Astaire Bldg 10202 W Washington Blvd Culver City CA 90232-3119*

GUBERMAN, SIDNEY THOMAS, painter, writer; b. Greenville, S.C., Aug. 24, 1936; s. Morris and Louise (Cook) G.; m. Jennifer Glidden, June 5, 1965 (div. 1977); children: Maxwell, Angus; m. Rebecca Wilson, July 31, 1977; children: Elizabeth Tindall, Dore Hopkins Brooks. BA, Princeton U., 1958; MArch, U. Pa., 1967. Asst. prof. Ecole Polytechnique, Lausanne, Switzerland, 1973-75; vis. artist U. S.C., Columbia, 1981-82, Atlanta Coll. Art, 1989, 91; vis. lectr. Princeton (N.J.) U., 1981; artist invité Federale de Lausanne Ecole des Beaux-Arts, Switzerland, 1971-73; chmn. bd. dirs. New Visions Gallery, Atlanta, 1987-93; bd. dirs. Atlanta Arts Festival, 1986-88. Solo exhbns. include Henri Gallery, Washington, 1970, 73, 75, Galerie R-B, Fribourg, Switzerland, 1975, 79, Image South Gallery, Atlanta, 1976, Harcus/Krakow/Rosen/Sonnabend, Boston, 1976, Fraser's Stable Gallery, Washington, 1978, Heath Gallery, Atlanta, 1979, Leah Levy Gallery, San Francisco, 1979, Diane Brown Gallery, Washington, 1980, Galerie Jonas, Cortaillod, Switzerland, 1980, Barbara Fiedler Gallery, Washington, 1981, Fay Gold Gallery, Atlanta, 1981, 82, 83, 85, Gertrude Herbert Gallery, Augusta, Ga., 1985, Gibbes Art Mus., Charleston, S.C., 1988, Galerie von der Milwe, Aachen, Germany, 1990, Hodges-Taylor, Charlotte, N.C., 1990, Louisa McIntosh Gallery, Atlanta, 1991, Susan Conway Carroll Gallery, Washington, 1991; group exhbns. include Prix de peinture, Vevey, Switzerland, 1974, City Gallery Contemporary Art, Raleigh, N.C., 1987, SECCA, Winston-Salem, N.C., 1988, Birmingham (Ala.) Mus. Art, 1988-89; permanent collections include The High Mus., Atlanta, The Hunter Mus., Chattanooga, Tenn., The Nat. Mus. Am. Art, Washington, Princeton (N.J.) U. Mus., Colo. Springs Fine Arts Ctr.; author: Frank Stella: An Illustrated Biography, 1995. Mem. alumni coun. Phillips Exeter (N.H.) Acad., 1993. Individual Artist's grantee NEA, 1980; Guggenheim fellow, 1988-89. Mem. Coll. Art Assn., The Ivy Club. Democrat. Presbyterian. Avocations: films, tennis, opera. Home: 131 Montgomery Ferry Dr NE Atlanta GA 30309-2712 Office: 1174 Zonolite Pl NE # C Atlanta GA 30306-2002

GUBERNATIS, THOMAS FRANK, SR., electrical buyer; b. Balt., Sept. 16, 1947; s. Elmer Charles and Agnes Elizabeth (Haupt) G.; m. Susan Marie Furst, Apr. 4, 1970; children: Thomas F. Jr., Marie E., Elaine K. BS, U. Balt., 1971. Project mgr. H.A. Harris Co., Towson, Md., 1971-79; estimator, purchasing Blumenthal-Kahn Elec. Co., Owings Mills, Md., 1979-88; prof. buyer Brown & Heim Inc., Lansdowne, Md., 1988—. Coord. South Carroll Alcohol and Drug Awareness Team, Sykesville, Md., 1980—, Concerned Citizens/Carroll County, 1981-83; treas. Carroll County Crime Solvers, 1983-91; 3d v.p. No. MADD, Balt., 1986-87. With USNR, 1966-72. Recipient Good Citizen award Md. State Police, 1982, Bro. Kenneth award Mt. St. Joseph, Balt., 1965. Mem. KC. Democrat. Roman Catholic. Avocations: trains, videos, computers. Home: 5915 Forest Ct Sykesville MD 21784-6714

GUBITOSI, MICHAEL See BLAKE, ROBERT

GUBLER, DUANE J., research scientist, administrator; b. Santa Clara, Utah, June 4, 1939; s. June and Thelma (Whipple) G.; m. Bobbie J. Carroll, Mar. 1, 1958; children: Justin Chase, Stuart Jefferson. BS, Utah State U., 1963; MS, U. Hawaii, 1965; ScD, Johns Hopkins U., 1969; AS, So. Utah State U., 1962, DSc (hon.), 1988. Asst. prof. pathobiology Sch. Hygiene Johns Hopkins U., Balt. and Calcutta, 1969-71; assoc. prof. tropical medicine Sch. Medicine U. Hawaii, Honolulu, 1971-75; head virology dept. Naval Med. Rsch. Unit Number 2, Jakarta, Indonesia, 1975-78; assoc. prof. entomology and microbiology U. Ill., Urbana, 1978-79; rsch. microbiologist divsn. vector-borne viral diseases Ctrs. for Disease Control and Prevention, Fort Collins, Colo., 1980-81; dir. San Juan (P.R.) Labs. Ctrs. for Disease Control and Prevention, 1981-89; dir. divsn. vector-borne infectious diseases Ctrs. for Disease Control and Prevention, Ft. Collins, Colo., 1989—; cons. NRC, 1972, South Pacific Commn., 1972-76, WHO, Geneva, 1974—, AID, Washington, 1977—, Pan Am. Health Orgn., 1981—, Internat. Devel. Rsch. Ctr., Ottawa, Can., 1977—, Rockefeller Found., N.Y.C., 1987—, numerous nat. ministries of health, 1972—; Bailey K. Ashford meml. lectr. U. P.R. Sch. Medicine, 1999. Contbr. numerous articles to profl. jours. Lt. USN, 1975-77; capt. USPHS. Recipient Commendation medal, 1984, Outstanding Svc. medal, 1988, Meritorious Svc. medal, 1991, Outstanding Unit citation, 1995, Outstanding Alumni award for sci. and rsch. Johns Hopkins U. Sch. Pub. Health, 1997, Chuck Alexander Operational award La. Mosquito Control Assn., 1998; selected as one of 90 Illustrious Alumni in celebration of U. Hawaii's 90th year, 1997. Mem. AAAS, Am. Soc. Tropical Medicine (Charles Franklin Craig lectr. 1988, pres.-elect 1998, pres. 2000), Am. Soc. Parasitologists, Am. Mosquito Control Assn., Entomol. Soc. Am. (highlights in med. entomology lecture 1979, 95), Soc. Vector Ecologists, Infectious Disease Soc. Am., Rotary (Rotarian of Yr. San Juan chpt. 1986, Meritorious Svc. award Rotary Found., Evanston, Ill. 1990). Home: 717 Dartmouth Trl Fort Collins CO 80525-1522 Office: Ctrs for Disease Control and Prevention USPHS PO Box 2087 Fort Collins CO 80522-2087

GUBLER, JOHN GRAY, lawyer; b. Las Vegas, June 16, 1942; s. V. Gray and Loreta N. (Newton) G.; m. Mollie Boyle, Jan. 10, 1987; 1 child, J. Gray; children from previous marriage: Laura, Matthew. BA, U. Calif.-Berkeley, 1964; JD, U. Utah, 1971; LLM in Taxation, NYU, 1973. Bar: Nev. 1971, U.S. Dist. Ct. Nev. 1973, U.S. Tax Ct. 1974, U.S. Ct. Appeals (9th cir.) 1978. Dep. pub. defender Clark County, Nev., 1973-74; ptnr. Gubler & Gubler, Las Vegas, 1974-88, ptnr. Gubler and Peters, Las Vegas, 1989—; instr. continuing edn. community coll. Served with U.S. Army, 1966-68. Mem. Clark County Bar Assn., ABA, State Bar of Nev. (disciplinary com. 1979-88), Las Vegas-Paradise Rotary (pres. 1981-82), Knife & Fork Club (pres. 1978-80). Ch of Jesus Christ of Latter Day Saints. Office: Gubler & Peters 302 E Carson Ave Ste 601 Las Vegas NV 89101-5989

GUBSER, PETER ANTON, political scientist, writer, educator; b. Tulsa, May 9, 1941; s. Eugene Herbert and Mary (Douglass) G.; m. Annie Yeni-Komshian, Aug. 15, 1969; children: Sasha Mary-Helen, Christi Valerie. BA, Yale U., 1964; MA, Am. U. Beirut, 1966; PhD, Oxford (Eng.) U., 1970. Rsch. fellow U. Manchester, Eng., 1970-72; assoc. rsch. scientist Am. Insts. for Rsch., Washington, 1972-74; asst. rep. Ford Found., Beirut, 1974-77; pres. Am. Near East Refugee Aid, Washington, 1977—; bd. dirs. Internat. Svc. Agys., Washington, Am. Coun. Vol. Internat. Action, Internat. Coll., Beirut, Nat. Coun. on U.S.-Arab Rels., Washington, Found. for Mid. East Peace, Washington, Global Devel. Forum, Amman, Jordan; adj. prof. Georgetown U., Washington, 1990—; lectr. various govt. and non-govt. instns., 1977—. Author: Politics and Change at Karak, Jordan, 1973, Jordan: Crossroads of Middle East Events, 1983, Historical Dictionary of Hashemite Kingdom of Jordan, 1991. Mem. Somerset (Md.) Town Coun. Mem. Am. Polit. Sci. Assn., Mid. East Inst., Mid. East Studies Assn., Washington Inst. Fgn. Affairs. Democrat. Mem. Christian Ch. Avocations: hiking, reading, travel. Office: Am Near East Refugee Aid 1522 K St NW Ste 202 Washington DC 20005-1202

GUCCIONE, ROBERT CHARLES JOSEPH EDWARD SABATINI, publisher; b. Bklyn., Dec. 17, 1930; s. Anthony and Nina G.; children: Tonia, Bob, Jr., Nina, Tony, Nick; m. Kathy Keeton, Jan. 17, 1988. Mng. editor London Daily American; pub. Forum mag., Variations mag., Viva mag. Omni mag., Four Wheeler mag., Saturday Review, Longevity mag.; chmn. Gen. Media Internat. Inc., 1988—. Artist, 1948-55, 92—; several gallery exhibits and museum shows, 1992-93; formerly cartoonist and greeting card designer; producer film Caligula, 1979; exec. producer TV shows Omni: The New Frontier, Omni: Visions of Tomorrow; pub. Omni, Longevity, Compute, Four Wheeler, Variations, Penthouse Letters, Saturdy Rev., Hot Talk, Girls of Penthouse, Open Wheel, Superstock and Drag, Stock Car Racing, Forum; contbr. articles to profl. jours. Avocation: collecting art, mostly Impressionist, some Old Masters. Office: General Media Internat 1100 Penn Plz New York NY 10001*

GUDANEK, LOIS BASSOLINO, clinical social worker; b. N.Y.C., Jan. 28, 1944; d. Frank and Anna (Scarlata) Bassolino; m. Richard Stanley Gudanek, Sept. 3, 1977. BA in Anthropology and Sociology, Queens Coll., 1973; postgrad., Hunter Coll., 1973-76, JRW Inst. Alcohol Studies, 1988-89; attended Eating Disorders Inst., Rollins Coll., 1991; MSW, Fordham U., 1994. Credentialed alcohol and substance abuse counselor, cert. social worker, HIV counselor, N.Y. Student intern Arms Acres, Carmel, N.Y., 1988-89; adult therapist Arms Acres, Carmel, 1989-91; vocat. counselor Westchester County Med. Ctr.-Alcoholism Treatment Svcs., Yonkers, 1991-94, Westchester County Med. Ctr.-WEST-PREP, Valhalla, N.Y., 1994-96; pvt. practice White Plains, N.Y., 1994—; social worker The Week-End Ctr., Mt. Kisco, N.Y., 1996—; lectr. JRW Inst. on Alcohol Studies, Yonkers, N.Y., 1991, St. Thomas Aquinas Coll., 1994; presenter in field. Mem. NASW (chair chem. dependency com. Westchester divsn. 1996-97), Internat. Assn. Eating Disorders Profls. (sec. tri-state region 1989-91, vice-chmn. 1991-96, ednl. coord. 1992-96), N.Y. Womens Coalition on Chem. Dependency (treas. 1991-92, bd. dirs. 1994-96), Adoptees' Liberty Movement Assn. Avocation: anthropology. E-mail: socialworker@rocketmail.com. Office: The Week-End Ctr 24 Smith Ave Mount Kisco NY 10549-2814 also: 200 Bloomingdale Rd Ste 1 White Plains NY 10605-1514

GUDAS, LORRAINE JEAN, biochemist, molecular biologist, educator; b. Syracuse, N.Y., May 12, 1949; d. Albert Joseph and Eleanor (Bogden) G.; 1

child, Gregory Paul Wagner. BA, Smith Coll., 1970; PhD, Princeton U., 1975. Postdoctoral fellow U. Calif., San Francisco, 1975-80; mem. faculty Harvard Med. Sch., Boston, 1980—; prof., chmn dept of pharmacology Cornell Med Coll, New York. Home: 431 E 85th St New York NY 10028-6301 Office: Weill-Med Coll of Cornell U 1300 York Ave New York NY 10021-4805*

GUDE, GILBERT, former state and federal legislator, nurseryman, writer; b. Washington, Mar. 9, 1923; s. Adolph Elbert and Inez Elinor (Gilbert) G.; m. Jane Wheeler Callaghan, June 19, 1948; children: Sharon, Gilbert Jr., Gregory, Daniel, Adrienne. BS, Cornell U., 1948; MA, George Washington U., 1958; DSc (hon.), Georgetown U., 1977. Del. Md. Gen. Assembly, Annapolis, 1953-58; senator Md. Gen. Assembly, 1962-66; mem. U.S. Congress from Md. dist., 1967-76; dir. Congl. rsch. svc. Library of Congress, Washington, 1977-86; ind. cons. Bethesda, Md., 1987—; mem., past chmn. consultative com. Ctr. Parliamentary Documentation Inter-Parliamentary Union, Geneva, 1984-89; mem. exec. com. Environ. and Energy Study Inst., Washington, 1986-89; exec. dir. Potomac River Basin Consortium, Bethesda. Author: Where the Potomac Begins, 1984, Small Town Destiny, 1989; contbr. articles on rsch. and info. systems in support of legis. bodies to various publs. Mem. pres.'s coun. St. Mary's (Md.) Coll.; trustee Montgomery County Hist. Soc., Rockville, Md., Md. Hist. Trust. With U.S. Army, 1943-46, PTO. Mem. Nat. Acad. Pub. Adminstrn., Chevy Chase Club, Capitol Hill Club. Republican. Roman Catholic. Home and Office: 5411 Duvall Dr Bethesda MD 20816-1871

GUDE, NANCY CARLSON, computer consultant; b. Kane, Pa., Aug. 5, 1948; d. Edward Walter and Theo Alberta (Herzog) Carlson. BA in History, Pa. State U., 1969; MS in Computer Sci., U. Central Fla., 1981; postgrad., Thomas M. Cooley Law Sch., 1998—. Programmer Group Hospitalization, Inc., Washington, 1969-70; programmer analyst Space Age Computer Sys., Washington, 1970-73, Ky. Fried Chicken, Louisville, 1973-75; sys. analyst Sentinel Comm. Co., Orlando, Fla., 1975-77, programming supr., 1977-78; sys. and programming mgr. Sentinel Comm. Co., Orlando, 1978-80, asst. dir. data processing, 1980, mgr. staff devel., 1981-82; mgmt. info. svcs. mgr. Sun-Sentinel Co., Ft. Lauderdale, Fla., 1982-83; v.p., dir. info. sys. Sun-Sentinel Co., Ft. Lauderdale, 1983-94, sys. cons., 1994-98; adj. instr. U. Central Fla., Orlando, 1981-82. Participant Leadership Broward X, chair LBX Artserve Intervention Group. Mem. IEEE, Am. Mgmt. Assn., Assn. Sys. Mgmt., Penn State Club Greater Ft. Lauderdale (treas. 1990-92, v.p. 1992-93, prs. 1993-95). Presbyterian. Home: 1101 River Reach Dr Apt 216 Fort Lauderdale FL 33315-1177

GUDEA, DARLENE, publishing company executive. V.p., pub., editor-in-chief Tradeshow Week, L.A. Office: Tradeshow Week 5700 Wilshire Blvd Ste 120 Los Angeles CA 90036-3644*

GUDEMAN, STEPHEN FREDERICK, anthropology educator; b. Chgo., June 29, 1939; s. Edward and Frances (Alschuler) G.; m. Roxane Harvey, Sept. 20, 1965; children: Rebecca, Elise, Keren. AB, Harvard U., 1961, MBA, 1965; MA, Cambridge U., Eng., 1963, PhD, 1970. Asst. prof. anthropology U. Minn.-Mpls., 1969-74, assoc. prof. anthropology, 1974-78, prof. anthropology, 1978—, chmn. dept., 1984-89, 96—; mem. Inst. Advanced Study, Princeton, N.J., 1978-79; fellow Ctr. for Advanced Study, Palo Alto, Calif., 1995-96; sr. fellowship NEH, 1983-84; mem. selection com. Marshall Scholarships, 1983-86; Benedict Disting. vis. prof. Carleton Coll., 1981; Hardy Chair lecture Hartwick Coll., 1985. Author: Relationships, Residence and the Individual, 1976, Demise of a Rural Economy, 1978, Economics As Culture, 1986, Conversations in Colombia, 1990; editor Cambridge Studies in Anthropology, 1989-96; contbr. numerous articles to profl. jours. Marshall scholar, 1961-63. Fellow Am. Anthropol. Assn. (bd. dirs. 1987-91), Am. Ethnological Soc. (pres. 1989-91, bd. dirs. 1987-91, assoc. editor 1981-84), Royal Anthropol. Inst. (sec., chmn. N.Am. com. 1983-88, Curl Bequest Essay prize 1971), Soc. Econ. Anthropology. Avocations: tennis, jogging, music. Home: 1650 Dupont Ave S Minneapolis MN 55403-1101

GUDENBERG, HARRY RICHARD, arbitrator, mediator; b. Frankfurt, Germany, May 20, 1933; s. Albert and Erna (Bacharach) G.; m. Sharon Rickey, Nov. 23, 1978; children—Lori, Bruce. B.S., N.Y. U., 1960, M.B.A., 1964; J.D., Seton Hall U., 1970. Bar: N.J. bar 1970, U.S. Supreme Ct 1973. With ITT, N.Y.C., 1970-88, v.p., dir. indsl. and employee relations, employment and labor law, 1978-88; cons. on benefits, compensation and employment law William M. Mercer Inc., N.Y.C., 1988-93; arbitrator, mediator fact finder, dispute resolution, employment and labor law, panel mem. Am. Arbitration Assn., Fed. Mediation and Conciliation Svc., N.J. State Bd. Mediation, N.J. Pub. Employment Rels. Commn., 1994—. Served with U.S. Army, 1953-55. Mem. ABA, N.J. Bar Assn., Indsl. Res. Rsch. Assn.

GUDEON, ARTHUR, podiatrist; b. N.Y.C., Feb. 27, 1935; s. Samuel and Mina (Kaminsky) G.; m. Loretta Bachrach, June 16, 1957 (div. 1976); children: Karla, Marilyn, Adam; m. Susan Steinmetz, Apr. 8, 1979; 1 child, Andrea. BA, NYU, 1956; D Podiatric Medicine, N.Y. Coll. Podiatric Medicine, 1960. Diplomate Am. Bd. Podiatric Surgery, Am. Bd. Foot and Ankle Surgery. Pvt. practice podiatry Family Podiatry of Rego Park, N.Y., 1960—; sr. faculty, mem. residency selection com. St. Joseph's Hosp. Catholic Med. Ctr., N.Y.C., 1980—; clin. assoc. prof. surgery, external faculty N.Y. Coll. Podiatric Medicine, 1989—; dep. examiner N.Y. State Bd. Podiatry, 1981; podiatry chmn., mem. adv. coun. for occupational edn. N.Y.C. Bd. Edn., 1980—; cons. utilization and peer rev. coms. Vol. local health fairs, sch. programs, sports events, N.Y., 1965—. Fellow Am. Coll. Foot and Ankle Surgeons (pres. N.Y. divsn. 1990-93), Am. Assn. Hosp. Podiatrists; mem. N.Y. State Podiatric Med. Assn. (chmn. sci. affairs com. Queens divsn. 1984—, chmn. N.Y. state sci. affairs com. 1986-90, Podiatrist of Yr. 1969, 74), Am. Soc. Podiatric Med. Assts. (hon., bd. dirs. 1983-87, Podiatrist of Yr. 1989), Am. Podiatric Med. Assn., Am. Podiatric Sports Medicine Acad. Democrat. Jewish. Avocations: tennis, art, music, travel. Office: Family Podiatry of Rego Pk 91-35 63rd Dr Rego Park NY 11374-3849

GUDMUNDSON, BARBARA ROHRKE, ecologist; b. Chgo.; d. Lloyd Ernest and Helen (Bullard) Rohrke; m. Valtyr Emil Gudmundson, June 14, 1951 (dec. Dec. 1982); children: Holly Mekkin Leighton, Martha Rannveig. BA, U. Tenn., 1950; MA, Minn. State U., 1965; PhD, Iowa State U., 1969. Microbiologist Hektoen Inst. & Ill. Ctr. Hosp., Chgo., 1950-52; immunologist Jackson Meml. Lab., Bar Harbor, Maine, 1952-54; dist. ecologist Corps of Engrs., St. Paul, 1971-72; sr. ecologist North Star Rsch. Inst., Mpls., 1972-76; staff engr. Met. Waste Control Commn., St. Paul, 1976-77; pres., prin. ecologist Ecosystem Rsch. Svc./Upper Midwest, Mpls., 1978-99; pvt. practice as cons. ecologist, Des Moines and Mpls., 1968-70; mem. Citizens League Task Force on the Mississippi Riverfront, 1973-74; mem. adv. com. Mpls. Lakes Water Quality, Mpls., 1974-75; river ecologist Mississippi River Canoe Expdn., Coll. of the Atlantic, Bar Harbor, 1979. Author: V. Emil Gudmundson: Icelandic Canadian Unitarian, A Personal Biography, 1991; editor-in-chief The Icelandic Unitarian Connection, 1984; contbr. articles to profl. jours. Mem. from 61st dist. Dem.-Farmer-Labor Ctr. Com., Minn., 1978-80; mgr. Minnehaha Creek Watershed Dist., 1979-83, sec., 1982-83; mem. Capital Long-Range Improvements Com., Mpls., 1981; mem. steering com. Nokomis East Neighborhood Assn., 1995-97, bd. dirs. 1997—. Recipient Leadership award Izaak Walton League, 1982; River Basin Ecology grantee Iowa Acad. Scis., Cedar Falls, 1976, Mississippi River Ecology grantee Freshwater Biol. Rsch. Found., Navarre, Minn., 1979; Fulbright Sr. Rsch. grantee USA/Iceland Fulbright Commns., Washington, Reykjavik, 1986, 92. Mem. NOW (Minn. state bd. 1989-96, Anita Hill Courage and Justice award Twin Cities chpt. 1994, Minn.-NOW's Charlotte Striebel Long Distance Runner award 1998), Ecol. Soc. Am. (pres. Minn. chpt. 1971-75), Geol. Soc. Minn. (pres. 1981), Phycological Soc. Am., Internat. Assn. Diatom Rsch., Icelandic Assn. Minn., Hekla Icelandic Club (pres. 1977), Fulbright Assn., Sigma Xi, Phi Kappa Phi, Sigma Delta Epsilon-Grad. Women in Sci. (nat. mem. com. 1990-93, chmn. 1991-93). Unitarian Universalist. Achievements include discovery of diatom genus Biddulphia in the state of Iowa; establishment of Diatom Herbarium of Iceland. Home: 5505 28th Ave South Minneapolis MN 55417-1957

GUDNITZ, ORA M. COFEY, secondary education educator; b. Crawforddsville, Ark., Jan. 24, 1934; d. Daniel S. and Mary (Oglesby) Cofey; children: Ingrid M. Hunt, Carl Erik, Katrina Beatrice. BA, Lane Coll., Jackson, Tenn., 1955; MEd, Temple U., 1969; student, U. Copenhagen, 1957; MA in Theol. Studies, Ea. Bapt. Theol. Sem., Pa., 1995, Eastern Bapt. Theol. Sem., Pa., 1995. Cert. permanent English, social studies and French tchr., Pa. Tchr. English, chmn. dept. Sayre Jr. High Sch., Phila.; tchr. English, Overbrook High Sch., Phila.; founder, exec. dir. Young Communicators Workshop, Inc.; lectr., Denmark. Contbr. articles to newspapers, poetry to anthologies. Recipient award Chapel of Four Chaplains, 1976, Women in Edn. award, 1988; grantee Haas Found., 1977, also others. Mem. Nat. Coun. Tchrs. English, Assn. for Ednl. Communication and Tech., Phi Delta Kappa, Delta Sigma Theta.

GUDORF, KENNETH FRANCIS, business executive; b. Minster, Ohio, Mar. 3, 1939; s. Norbert Herman and Freda Elizabeth (Moorman) G.; m. Evelyn Margaret Sommer, Aug. 31, 1962; children: Eric, Craig, Caroline. AB, U. Dayton, 1961; MBA, U. Mich., 1967. Dep. treas. Gulf Oil Corp., London, 1970-74; fin. rep. Gulf Corp., Washington, 1974-76; v.p. planning Gulf Oil Corp., Reston, Va., 1976-78; sr. dir. mergers, acquisitions and divestments Gulf Oil Corp., Pitts., 1978-81; sr. v.p. fin., CFO Diversified Energies Inc., Mpls., 1981-85; v.p., CFO Carlson Cos., Inc., 1985-90; pres. KFG Ventures, Mpls., 1990—; vice chmn. Gage Mktg. Inc., 1991—, BOD Gage Mktg.; pres., CEO AGIO Capital Magmt. LLC; mem. coun. Minn. State Bd. Investments Adv. Coun., St. Paul, 1983—; bd. dirs. Global Tool Dallas, Nat. Flood Svcs. Inc., Kalispell, Mont., Electro Source LLC, L.A., Engineered Products Inc., Waterloo, Iowa, Endres Processing LLC, St. Paul. Served to capt. U.S. Army, 1962-65. Mem. Fin. Execs. Inst. (bd. dirs. Twin Cities). Clubs: Minneapolis; Interlachen Country (Mpls.). Office: Agio Capital LLC 4600 First Bank Pl 601 2nd Ave S Minneapolis MN 55402-4303

GUEDRY, JAMES WALTER, lawyer, paper corporation executive; b. Morgan City, La., Jan. 7, 1941; s. J. Walter and P. Marie (McNulty) G. A.B. magna cum laude, Georgetown U., 1962; postgrad., U. Brussels, 1962-63; LL.B., U. Va., 1966. Bar: N.Y. 1967. Assoc. Lord, Day & Lord, N.Y.C., 1966-76; v.p., corp. sec./assoc. gen. counsel Internat. Paper Co., N.Y.C., 1976—. Mem. Assn. Bar City N.Y. Home: 79 Charles St New York NY 10014-2638 Office: Internat Paper Co 2 Manhattanville Rd Purchase NY 10577-2118

GUELICH, ROBERT VERNON, retired management consultant; b. Dayton, Ohio, Oct. 30, 1917; m. Jane E. Schory, Dec. 6, 1941; children: Susan MacKenzie, Robert V. Jr., Helen Jane. B.A., Ohio Wesleyan U., 1938; M.B.A., Harvard U., 1940. Reporter Dayton Jour., 1935-37; overseas corr., staff editor Air Force mag., 1942-46; asst. dir. public relations Firestone Co., Akron, Ohio, 1946-57; sr. v.p. pub. relations Montgomery Ward & Co., Chgo., 1957-81; sr. mgmt. cons. Hill & Knowlton, Chgo., 1981-83; asst. to chmn. Nat. Fitness Found., 1981-90; pres. Robert V. Guelich & Assocs., Inc., 1981—; pub. rels. cons. Exec. Svc. Corp. of Chgo., 1983-89; chmn. Nat. Pub. Rels. Seminar, 1981. Bd. dirs. Nat. 4-H Coun., 1972-81; pres. bd. edn. New Trier Twp. High Sch., 1965-70. Maj. USAF, 1941-46. Recipient George Washington Honor medal Freedoms Found., 1977. Mem. Pub. Rels. Soc. Am. (bd. dirs. 1976-79, 3 Silver Anvil awards, 4 Presdl. Citations 1976, Outstanding Film award 1977), Chgo. Yacht Club, Mich. Shores Club, Phi Beta Kappa, Phi Gamma Delta, Sigma Delta Chi. Presbyterian. Home and Office: 380 Sterling Rd Kenilworth IL 60043-1048

GUENIN, LOUIS MAURICE, ethics scholar; b. Saginaw, Mich., Sept. 13, 1950; s. Louis Joseph and Bernadette Lourdes (King) G. AB, U. Mich., 1972; JD, Harvard U., 1975. Assoc. Cravath, Swaine & Moore, N.Y.C., 1975-76, Hanson, Bridgett & Marcus, San Francisco, 1976-77, Boyd, MacCrellish & Wheeler, Boston, 1978-82; mng. ptnr. Boyd, MacCrellist & Wheeler, Boston, 1982-94; lectr. on ethics Harvard Med. Sch., Boston, 1994—; dir. Shipley Inst. Medicine, Boston, 1978—. James B. Angell scholar U. Mich., 1968-72. Mem. Am. Philos. Assn., Phi Beta Kappa. Office: Harvard Med Sch Dept Microbio and Molecular Genetics 641 Huntington Ave Boston MA 02115-6019

GUENTHER, GEORGE CARPENTER, travel company executive, retired; b. Reading, Pa., Aug. 27, 1931; s. John H. and Eleanor (Carpenter) G.; m. Kathleen Lance Coyle, Oct. 20, 1962; children: George Carpenter, Todd C., John E., Gregory C. A.B. in Psychology, Amherst Coll., 1952. Pres. John H. Guenther Hosiery Co., Reading, 1955-67; dep. sec. Pa. Dept. Labor and Industry, 1967-69; dir. Bur. Labor Standards, Dept. Labor, 1969-71, asst. sec. labor for occupational safety and health, 1971-73; sr. v.p. Ins. Co. N. Am., Phila., 1973-75; v.p. Talmage Tours, Inc., Phila., 1975-77, pres., 1977-96; ret., 1996; bd. dirs., exec. com. Phila. Convention and Visitors Bureau, 1979-96. Served with USNR, 1952-55. Mem. Nat. Tour Assn. (bd. dirs., exec. com. 1982-90, pres. 1990). Home: 44 Overlook Cir Berwyn PA 19312-2531

GUENTHER, GORDON P., mechanical engineer; b. La Cross, Wis., July 11, 1934. BS, U. Mich., 1968; MA, La. Tech. U., 1978, MBA, 1983. Registered profl. engr., La. Instr. navigation 2 Bomb Wing, Barksdale AFB, La., 1974-75; chief design engr. 2 Civil Engring. Squadron, Barksdale AFB, La., 1975-76; product engr. Riley Beard, Inc., Shreveport, 1976-77; sr. product engr. WKM Wellhead Sys., Shreveport, 1977-83; chief energy mgmt. sys. 2 Civil Engring. Squadron, 1983-86; chief engr. 1 Electronic Combat Range Group, Barksdale AFB, 1986-95; chief contracts 2 Civil Engring. Squadron, 1995-99; adj. instr. Embry-Riddle Aero. U., Barksdale AFB, 1998—. Mem. ASME (chmn. 1998-99), So. Am. Mil. Engrs. (pres. 1976-77). Home: 1200 Cove St Bossier City LA 71112-4002

GUENTHER, JACK DONALD, banker; b. Little Rock, Jan. 21, 1929; s. Gottlob and Josephine Margaret (Presley) G.; m. Margaret Adah Beltz, June 11, 1956; children—Elizabeth, Katherine, John. BA, Yale U., 1950; postgrad., King's Coll., Cambridge U., Eng., 1952-53; MA, Harvard U., 1957, PhD, 1959. Various staff positions IMF, Washington, 1960-79; sr. v.p., sr. advisor internat. ops. Citibank, N.Y.C., 1979-95; cons. MBIA, N.Y.C., 1995-98. Served as sgt. U.S. Army, 1953-55. Home: 4231 42d St Washington DC 20016

GUENTHER, JACK EGON, lawyer; b. San Antonio, Dec. 14, 1934; s. Egon E. and Camilla (Mallepell) G.; m. Valerie Urschel, Feb. 1, 1964; children: Abigail Guenther Kampmann, Jack Egon. BBA, U. Tex.-Austin, 1956; LLB magna cum laude, St. Mary's U., 1959; LLM in Taxation, NYU, 1960. Bar: Tex. 1959; C.P.A., Tex. Practice pub. acctg. San Antonio, 1957-59, pvt. practice, 1960—; assoc. Cox & Smith (and predecessor firm), 1961-65, ptnr., 1965—, of counsel, 1986—; chmn. bd. BMW Ctr., Ltd., 1965—, Rivergate Toyota, Inc., 1983—, Performance Toyota, Inc., 1984—, Performance Honda, Isuzu and Jeep, 1987, Lexus of Nasville, 1989—, Volvo and Porsche Ctr., 1990—, Performance Toyota of Plano, 1990—, U.S. Enercorp LLC, 1994—, Performance Ford, L.P., 1995—; adj. prof. law St. Mary's U.; lectr. various tax insts. Served to capt., JAG Corps AUS, 1957. Mem. ABA, Tex. Bar Assn., Tex. Soc. CPA's, Sigma Chi, Phi Delta Phi. Episcopalian. Office: 1777 NE Loop 410 San Antonio TX 78217-5209

GUENTHER, PAUL BERNARD, volunteer; b. N.Y.C., May 1, 1940; s. Bernard and Elsie G.; m. Diane Erceg, July 31, 1965; children—Matthew, Elizabeth, Christopher. BS in Econs., Fordham U., 1962; MBA in Fin., Columbia U., 1964. Credit analyst Mfrs. Hanover Trust, N.Y.C., 1964-66; various positions Paine Webber Inc., N.Y.C., 1966-80, exec. asst. to chief exec. officer, 1981, sr. v.p., dir. adminstrn. div., 1981-82, exec. v.p., dir. adminstrv. div., 1982-84, exec. v.p., chief adminstrv. officer, 1984-87, exec. v.p., adminstrn., ops., systems and consumer markets, 1987-88, pres., 1988-95; cons., 1995, retired, 1995; bd. dirs. Consol. Freightways, Frontier Ins.; mem. adv. com. Walden Capital Ptnrs. L.P. Trustee, chmn. Fordham U.; mem. bd. overseers grad. sch. bus. Columbia U.; chmn. N.Y. Philharm., Frost Valley YMCA; trustee Gov.'s Com. on Scholastic Achievement, Mary Flagler Cary Charitable Trust, Lincoln Ctr. for Performing Arts, Lenox Hill Hosp. Mem. Inst. Chartered Fin. Analysts. Democrat. Lutheran. Office: Walden Ptnrs 150 E 58th St Fl 34 New York NY 10155-0002

GUENTHER, ROBERT STANLEY, II, investment and property executive; b. Orange, Calif., Sept. 29, 1950; s. Robert Stanley and Fanny Newman (Shaw) G. BA in Psychology, U. Calif., Santa Barbara, 1975; BA in Sociology, U. Calif., 1975. Cert. radio telephone 3rd class operator. Pvt. practice Templeton, Calif., 1975—. Mem. Templeton Hist. Soc. (life), Space Explorers Network, Internat. Platform Soc. Assn., The Planetary Soc., Nat. Geog. Soc., Canine Companions for Independence, U. Calif. Santa Barbara Alumni Assn., San Francisco Soc. for Prevention of Cruelty to Animals (life). Home and Office: 5340 El Pomar Dr Templeton CA 93465-8628

GUENTHER, SHEILA WALSH, sales and promotion executive; b. Hamilton, Mont., Sept. 19, 1933; d. Leo Frederick and Edith Frances (Leonard) W.; James William Guenther, June 29, 1957; children: Kurt Dennis, Kelly David, Gayla Koleen. BA cum laude, Wash. State Coll., 1955. Layout artist The Bon Marche, Spokane, Wash., 1955-56; sales promotion mgr. The Bon Marche (formally The Paris), Great Falls, Mont., 1956-57; faculty staff artist info. and pub. rels. Mont. State Coll., Bozeman, 1958-61; sales promotion mgr. David's House Name Brands, Wichita, Kans., 1961-65; writer, graphic artist Warren Printing, Chamberlain Graphics, Olympia, Wash., 1965-73; art instr. Wichita State U.; writer, graphics freelancer Prescott Co. Advt. Pub. RelS., Olympia, Wash., 1970-77; instr. Clark Coll., Vancouver, Wash., 1979-81; sales promotion dir. Vancouver Furniture, 1974-94; pres. Walsh Guenther & Assocs., Inc., Vancouver, 1982—; Printer's Ink juror; mem. adv. coun. Columbian newspaper, 1996—. Co-author: Vancouver on the Columbia Business History, 1986. Columbian People in Need Adv. Com., Ellen Goodman Project for YWCA Emergency Shelter, Hands Across Clark County Stop Hunger Campaign; co-founder Swift Charity Auction, 1977. Recipient Spokane and Wichita Newspaper and TV Advt. award, Sertoma, Benjamin Franklin Svc. award, 1984, Woman of Achievement award YWCA, 1988. Mem. Wichita Press Women, Advt. Fedn., Oreg. Women in Comms., Retail Advt./Mktg. Assn., Columbian Newspaper Adv. Coun., Delta Phi Delta. Democrat. Office: PO Box 61628 Vancouver WA 98666-1628

GUEQUIERRE, JOHN PHILLIP, manufacturing company executive; b. Milw., Sept. 10, 1946; s. Gerald Herbert and Louise Ann (Fenske) G.; m. Mary Rowlands Speer, Aug. 17, 1968; children: William Edward, Robert John, Elizabeth Louise. BA, U. Wis., 1968; MBA, U. Chgo., 1972. Systems analyst Inland Steel Co., East Chgo., Ind., 1968-72; analyst inventory INRYCO, Milw., 1972-73, supr. material planning, 1973-74, mgr. contract adminstrn., 1974-76; mgr. fin. Inland Steel Devel. Corp., Washington, 1976-78; mgr. fin. analysis Inland Steel Urban Devel. Corp., Chgo., 1978-80; v.p. adminstrn. Scholz Homes Inc., Tol., 1980-83; sr. v.p. adminstrn., dir. Schult Homes Corp., Middlebury, Ind., 1983-92, sr. v.p. ops., dir., 1992-95, pres. manufactured housing group, 1995—. Chmn. budget subcom. United Way, Elkhart, Ind., 1983-89, bd. dirs. 1989—, treas., 1990-92, chmn. 1992; adult leader 4H, Elkhart County, 1983—; bd. dirs. Elkhart Chamber Found., 1993—; bd. dirs. Ind. Assn. United Ways, 1993—, vice chmn., 1995-97, chmn., 1997. Mem. Phi Beta Kappa, Phi Kappa Phi, Beta Gamma Sigma. Republican. Presbyterian. Office: Schult Homes Corp 221 US 20 W PO Box 151 Middlebury IN 46540-0151

GUERARD, ALBERT JOSEPH, retired modern literature educator, author; b. Houston, Nov. 2, 1914; s. Albert Leon and Wilhelmina (McCartney) G.; m. Mary Maclin Bocock, July 11, 1941; children: Catherine Collot, Mary Maclin, Lucy Lundie. AB, Stanford U., 1934, PhD, 1938; AM, Harvard U., 1936. Instr. Amherst (Mass.) Coll., 1935-36; mem. faculty Harvard U., Cambridge, Mass., 1938-61, successively instr. English, asst. prof., assoc. prof., 1948-54, prof., 1954-61; prof. Stanford (Calif.) U., 1961-85, Albert L. Guerard prof. lit., 1965-85. Author: The Past Must Alter, 1937, Robert Bridges, 1942, The Hunted, 1944, Maquisard, 1945, Joseph Conrad, 1947, Thomas Hardy, 1949, Night Journey, 1950, Andre Gide, 1951, Conrad the Novelist, 1958, The Bystander, 1958, The Exiles, 1963, The Triumph of the Novel: Dickens, Dostoevsky, Faulkner, 1976, The Touch of Time: Myth, Memory and the Self, 1980, Christine/Annette, 1985, Gabrielle, 1992, The Hotel in the Jungle, 1996, Suspended Sentences, 1999; co-editor: The Personal Voice, 1964. Served as tech. sgt. psychol. warfare br. AUS, World War II. Recipient Paris Rev. Fiction prize, 1963, Lit. award Am. Acad. Arts and Letters, 1998; Rockefeller fellow, 1946-47; Fulbright fellow, 1950-51; Guggenheim fellow, 1956-57; Ford fellow, 1959-60; Nat. Found. Arts fellow, 1967-68; Nat. Found. Humanities fellow, 1974-75. Mem. Am. Acad. Arts and Scis., Pen Ctr. West, Phi Beta Kappa. Home: 635 Gerona Rd Stanford CA 94305-8452

GUERBER, HOWARD P., retired electrical engineer; b. Rifle, Colo., July 29, 1926; s. Arnold and Mary G.; s. Marion Bretherton, Feb. 24, 1962; children: Jeffrey, Eric. BSEE, U. Colo., 1947, MSEE, 1955. Engr. Westinghouse Elec., East Pittsburgh, Pa., 1948-50; from engr. to engring. supervisor RCA, Camden, N.J., 1950-72; tech. staff MITRE Corp., McLean, Va., 1972-91; engring. cons. LISAN Corp., Washington, 1992-94, PSS Inc., Washington, 1995-97. Mem. IEEE, Assn. Computing Machinery.

GUERIN, DEAN PATRICK, executive; b. St. Paul, Feb. 21, 1922; s. Joseph Henry and Della (Booth) G.; m. Jo Alice Maryman, Sept. 3, 1959; children: Dean William, Stephen Patrick, Mark Joseph. BSBA, Boston U., 1949. With Sperry Gyroscope Co., N.Y.C., 1940-42; registered rep. Chas. A. Day & Son, Boston, 1946-49, Dallas Rupe & Son, 1949-51; from exec. v.p. to chmn. bd. dirs. Eppler, Guerin & Turner, Inc., Dallas, 1951-89; CEO, chmn. bd. dirs. Berry Barnet Food Dist. Co., Mexia, Tex., 1990-94; ind. dir. cos., 1994—; bd. dirs. Lone Star Tech., Seagull Energy Corp., Trinity Industries, Components Corp., Macklanburg-Duncan Co., Gen. Aluminum Corp., chmn.; chmn. Alpha Environ. Biosys., Inc. Past trustee Marine Mil. Acad. With USMCR, 1942-46, PTO. Mem. Dallas Country Club, Dallas Petroleum Club. Republican. Episcopalian. Home: 9400 Rockbrook Dr Dallas TX 75220-3948

GUERIN, DIDIER, magazine executive; b. Neuilly/Seine, France, Aug. 2, 1950; came to U.S. 1973; s. Jacques Guerin and Jeanine (Vaesken) Florange; m. Margaret Moray, Dec. 31, 1982; 1 son, Didier Guy Jr. BA in Pub. Law, U. Paris, 1973, BA in Comm., 1973; MA in Journalism, Mich. State U., 1975. Editor Soc. Gen. de Presse, Paris, 1976-79; asst. pub. Look mag., N.Y.C., 1979-81; mng. dir. Hachette Comm. Ltd., London, 1982-93; exec. v.p., dir. Hachette Publs., Inc., N.Y.C., 1983-86, Publs. Filipacchi, N.Y.C., 1983-86; pub. ELLE Mag., 1984-85; pres., CEO, dir. Hachette Publs., Inc., N.Y.C., 1987-91; pres., CEO Publs. Filipacchi, N.Y.C., 1987-91, Interdeco Inc., N.Y.C., 1989-91, Hachette-Filipacchi Asia-Pacific, Sydney, 1991-95; pres. Conde Nast Asia-Pacific, Sydney, 1995—; chmn. The Conde Nast Publs. Pty. Ltd. (VOGUE Australia), Sydney, 1995—, The Conde Nast Publs. Pte. Ltd. (VOGUE Singapore), Singapore, 1995-97, The Conde Nast China (VOGUE, GQ Taiwan), Taipei, 1996—, Nikkei-Conde Nast (VOGUE Nippon), Tokyo, 1997—, Interculture Comm. Ltd., Taipei, 1996—; chmn. bd. Toyo Fashion Kaihatsu, Tokyo, 1984-92, Hachette-Consol. Press. (ELLE Australia), Sydney, 1990-95, Hachette Filipacchi Australia, Sydney, 1990-95, Hachette-Interculture, (ELLE Taiwan), Taipei, 1992-95, Hachette Mags. Ltd., Hong Kong, 1993-95, ELLE Mag. Ltd. (ELLE Hong Kong), 1993-95, Hachette Filipacchi-Post, Bangkok (ELLE Thailand), 1994-95, Hachette Filipacchi Japan Ltd., Tokyo (Elle Japan); fgn. trade advisor French Govt., 1988—. Office: Conde Nast Asia-Pacific, 170 Pacific Hwy, Greenwich NSW 2065 Sydney Australia

GUERIN, JOHN WILLIAM, artist; b. Houghton, Mich., Aug. 29, 1920; s. Omer Francis and Mildred Montague (Miller) G.; m. Anne Walden Dewey, Dec. 28, 1948 (dec. 1979); m. Martha McAshan, Apr. 10, 1982. Student, Am. Acad. Art, Chgo., Art Students League, N.Y.C., Escuela de Bellas Artes, San Miguel, Mexico. Prof. art U. Tex., 1953-80, prof. emeritus, 1980—. Artist in residence, Skowhegan (Maine) Sch. Painting and Sculpture, 1960; one-man shows, Kraushaar Galleries, N.Y.C., 1960, 63, 68, Ft. Worth Art Center, 1956, 64, 65, Marion Kooglar McNay Art Inst., San Antonio, 1961, 65, Centennial Mus., Corpus Christi, Tex., 1963, Carlin Galleries, Ft. Worth, 1962, 64, 67, 70, 77, 81, 87, Nat. Acad. Design, N.Y.C., 1987; one-man retrospective show, Nave Mus., Victoria, Tex., 1982, group exhbns. include, Met. Mus. Art, Whitney Mus. Art, Art Inst. Chgo., Corcoran Mus. Art, Carnegie Inst.; represented in permanent collections, Chrysler Mus., Provincetown, Mass., Joslyn Mus., Omaha, New Britain (Conn.) Mus., Houston Mus., Dallas Mus., U. Notre Dame Art Gallery, Colorado Springs (Colo.) Fine Art Center., Archives Am. Art, Smithsonian Instn., Washington. Served with USAAF, 1942-45. Grantee Am. Acad Arts, Nat. Inst. Arts & Letters, 1960, Ford Found., 1978; recipient Henry Ward Ranger Fund Purchase prize NAD, 1958; Research Inst. grant U.

Tex., 1960, 66. Mem. Art Students League N.Y.C. (life), Nat. Acad. Design (academician). Episcopalian. Home: 3400 Stoneridge Rd Austin TX 78746-7716

GUERNSEY, LOUIS HAROLD, retired oral and maxillofacial surgeon, educator; b. Port Chester, N.Y., Sept. 22, 1923; s. Harold Allen and Odette Marcelle (Caillat) G.; m. Isabelle Margaret Napoli, Mar. 15, 1946; children: John Allen, Nancy Jean, Paula, Louis Harold. B.S., N.Y. U., 1959; D.D.S., U. Pa., 1947, M.Sc. in Dentistry, 1956. Diplomate Am. Bd. Oral and Maxillofacial Surgery. Gen. practice dentistry Gooding, Idaho, 1947-52; commd. 1st lt. Dental Corps U.S. Army, 1953, advanced through grades to col., 1967; service in W. Ger.; ret., 1974; prof. oral surgery, chmn. dept. oral and maxillofacial surgery U. Pa. Sch. Dental Medicine, 1974-80, prof. oral and maxillofacial surgery, from 1980, dir. postgrad. oral surgery programs, 1974-86; dir. oral surgery U. Pa. Hosp., 1974-90, prof., chief oral surgery, 1980-86, prof. emeritus oral and maxillofacial surgery, 1986—; prof. emeritus, attending oral maxillofacial surgery Hosp. U. of Pa., 1986-90; ret., 1990; mem. staff U. Pa. Med. Ctr. Editor: Reconstructive Implant Surgery/Implant Prosthodontics Dental Clinics of North America, 2 edits., 1986; contbr. articles profl. jours. Decorated Legion of Merit; recipient Harold Krogh Oral Cancer award Washington chpt. Am. Cancer Soc., 1974. Fellow Internat. Coll. Dentists, Am. Coll. Dentists, Am. Dental Soc. Anesthesiology; mem. ADA, Am. Soc. Oral and Maxillofacial Surgeons, Brit. Assn. Oral Surgeons, Internat. Assn. Oral Surgeons, Am. Assn. Hosp. Dentists, Pa. Soc. Oral and Maxillofacial Surgeons. Republican. Roman Catholic. Home: 14 Highfield Ln Wayne PA 19087-2760

GUERNSEY, THOMAS FRANKLIN, law educator; b. Battle Creek, Mich., Nov. 3, 1951; s. Richard L. and Ruth F. (Davis) G.; m. Kathe A. Klare, June 22, 1974; children: Alison, Adam. BA with distinction, U. Mich, 1973; JD cum laude, Wayne State U., 1976; LLM, Temple U., 1980. Bar: N.H. 1976, Va. 1983, U.S. Supreme Ct. Instr. law Vt. Law Sch., Royalton, 1976-78; asst. gen. counsel Temple Legal Aid Office, Phila., 1978-80; asst. prof. law T.C. Williams Sch. Law, U. Richmond (Va.), 1980-83, assoc. prof., 1983-86, assoc. dean, 1992-95, prof., 1986-96; dean, prof. law So. Ill. U., Carbondale, 1996—, interim vice chancellor acad. affairs, provost, 1999—; mediator Offender Aid and Restoration Community Mediation Project, 1984—; cons. Calif. Bd. Bar Examiners, San Francisco, 1984—, Nat. Conf. of Bar Examiner, Chgo., 1992—; master Am. Inns of Ct., Ill., 1996—. Author: Admissibility of Evidence in Virginia, 1990, Problems and Simulations in Evidence, 1991, 2d edit. 1995, Trial Practice, 1991, Special Education Law, 1993, A Practical Guide to Negotiation, 1996; sr. assoc. editor Wayne Law Rev., 1974-76; also articles. Mem. ABA (chmn. competition com. 1983—). Avocations: scuba diving, water skiing. Home: 2914 W Alveria Dr Carbondale IL 62901-5227 Office: So Ill U Sch of Law Carbondale IL 62901-6804

GUERRA, ARMANDO J., corporate professional; b. St. Clara, Las Villas, Cuba, Nov. 3, 1951; came to U.S., 1961; s. Armando and Ofelia (Bolanos) G.; m. Maria Cata, Sept. 7, 1974; children: Adrianne, Corinne, Eric. BS in Pharmacy, U. Fla., 1974. Staff pharmacist Eckerd Drugs, Miami, 1975-77; pres. Sedano's Pharmacy & Discount, Miami, 1977—; also CEO 13 brs. Sedano's Pharmacies, Miami; Fla. Region bd. dirs. Union Planters Bank; vice chmn., Century Ptnrs. Ltd.; bd. dirs., v.p. Sedano's Supermarkets, Inc., Miami. Bd. dirs. South Fla. Cmty. Blood Bank, Latin Bldrs. Assn.; mem. Met. Dade County Econ. Devel. Program Com. Recipient City of Hialeah Proclamation, Mayor, City of Hialeah, 1982, 86, The Merck award U. Fla., Gainesville, 1975, Dade County Proclamation, Dade County Mayor, Miami, 1986. Mem. Nat. Assn. Retail Druggists, Am. Pharm. Assn., Fla. Pharmacy Assn., Dade County Pharm. Assn., Secops Pharmacy Assn., Century 100 Club (U. Fla.). Republican. Roman Catholic. Avocations: automobile driving clubs, tennis, racquetball.

GUERRA, CHARLES ALBERT, financial consultant and executive; b. Hialeah, Fla., Dec. 4, 1960; s. Charles M. and Elsa Guerra; m. Alicia E. Martell. AA, Miami-Dade Community Coll., 1980; BBA, Fla. Internat. U., 1982; grad., Coll. for Fin. Planning, 1986, Dale Carnegie course, 1989. CPA, Fla.; cert. fin. planner, Fla., pension plan cons.; lic. real estate agt., investment securities, life ins., health ins., disability ins. Tax auditor IRS, Miami, Fla., 1982; acct. Arthur Young & Co., Miami, 1983-85, Peat, Marwick, Mitchell & Co., Miami, 1985; fin. planner H.M. Barth & Co., Miami, 1985-86, Moring-Armstrong & Co., Miami, 1986-88; fin. svcs. cons. The New Eng. and Integrated Resources Equity Corp., Miami, 1986-89; pres., fin. cons. The Fin. Strategies Group, Miami, 1989—. Mem. AICPA, Fla. Inst. CPAs (mem. personal fin. planning com. 1988-89), Inst. Cert. Fin. Planners, Internal Assn. for Fin. Planning, Leaders Assn. of The New England. Avocations: running, weight training, racquetball, scuba diving, cycling. Office: The Fin Strategies Group 4001 NW 97th Ave Miami FL 33178-2384

GUERRA, JOHN MICHAEL, optical engineer. Registered profl. engr., Mass., N.H. Program mgr. near-field optics tech. Polaroid Corp., Cambridge, Mass.; George Eastman lectr. Rocky Mountain Optical Soc. Am., 1991. Recipient Engring. Excellence award for invention and devel. of photon tunneling microscope Optical Soc. Am., 1994, Photonics Cir. of Excellence award, 1993, R & D 100 award, 1992. Mem. Internat. Soc. Optical Engring., Optical Soc. Am. Achievements include 18 patents in applications of near-field optics in microscopy, optical data storage and metrology. Office: Polaroid Optical Engring Dept 38 Henry St # 2A Cambridge MA 02139-4894

GUERRA, ROLAND, regional property manager; b. N.Y.C., Aug. 4, 1961; s. Rolando and Migdalia (Morin) G.; m. Ellen Mary De Rogatis, Oct. 20, 1979; children: Patrick James, Leslie Anne. AS, AA, Miami Dade Community Coll., 1982; student, Barry U., 1982-83; BS in Constrn. Mgmt. with highest honors, Fla. Internat. U., 1991; postgrad., Duke U., 1998—. Lic. real estate agt., Fla; cert. gen. contractor (inactive), Fla. Property mgr. Hasco Homes, Inc., Hollywood, Fla., 1978-83; mgr. India House Inc. Wholesale Clothier, Miami, Fla., 1982-84; adminstrv. asst. Lennar Corp., Miami, 1984-87, dir. customer svc., 1987-88, asst. project supt., 1988-89, rental properties adminstr., 1989-93, regional property mgr., 1993—; mem. student honors mentor program Fla. Internat. U., 1988. Mem. Internat. Platform Soc., Phi Kappa Phi, Sigma Lamda Chi. Avocations: real estate analysis, computers, bicycling, hiking, swimming. Home: 1050 NE 107th St Miami FL 33161-7374

GUERRANT, DAVID EDWARD, retired food company executive; b. Elizaville, Ky., Sept. 27, 1919; s. William Upton and Claire (Jordan) G.; m. Charlotte L. Lander, Feb. 6, 1942; children: Stephen, Jeffrey. B.S., Kans. State U., 1941. With Potts-Turnbull Agy., Kansas City, Mo., 1941-48; creative dir. Campbell-Ewald Co., Chgo., 1948-51; with John W. Shaw Advt., Inc., Chgo., 1951-61; pres. John W. Shaw Advt., Inc., 1959-61, MacFarland, Aveyard & Co., Chgo., 1961-64; v.p. marketing Libby, McNeill & Libby, Chgo., 1964-68; pres., chief exec. officer Libby, McNeill & Libby, 1968-73, chmn. bd., 1971-77; chmn., pres., CEO Nestlé Co., Inc., White Plains, N.Y., 1973-81, Nestlé Enterprises Inc. (holding co. for Nestlé Co. Inc., Libby, McNeill & Libby and Stouffers Inc.), 1977-83; ret., 1983. Presbyn. Clubs: Island Country (Marco Island, Fla.); Cullasaja Club (Highlands, N.C.). Home: 591 Hammock Ct Marco Island FL 34145-5848

GUERRERI, CARL NATALE, electronic company executive; b. Bronx, N.Y., Dec. 24, 1940; s. James Vincent and Ida (Dettori) G.; m. Elizabeth Ann Boerker, June 27, 1964; children: Cynthia Lee, Lisa Ann, Linda Ann, Christopher Alan. BSEE, Norwich U., 1962; OPM, Harvard Bus. Sch., 1982. Registered profl. engr., Vt. Engr. Raytheon Co., Wayland, Mass., 1965-67; sr. engr. HRB Singer, Inc., Reston, Va., 1967-68; project engr. Scope Inc., Reston, 1968-70; prin. engr. Amecom divsn. Litton Industries, College Park, Md., 1970; sect. leader SWL Labs., Herndon, Va., 1970-77; pres., CEO Electronic Warfare Assocs., Inc., Herndon, 1977—. Mem. Manassas (Va.)-Prince William Rep. Com., 1970—, chmn., 1977-78; instr. trainer ARC, Fairfax, Va., 1975-93; trustee Norwich U., 1996—. 1st lt. Signal Corps, U.S. Army, 1963-65. Mem. IEEE, Am. Electronics Assn. (Potomac coun., mem. exec. com.), Airplane Owners and Pilots Assn., Conf. Bd. Roman Catholic. Achievements include patents for System for Distinguishing between Friendly Ground Targets and a Foe; for Remote Detonation of Explosive Charges. Avocations: flying, skiing. Home: 10102 Holland Ct Manassas VA 20110-6059 Office: Electronic Warfare Assocs Inc 13873 Park Center Rd Herndon VA 20171-3223*

GUERRERO, DEBRA ANN, council woman; b. San Antonio, Sept. 14, 1966; d. Moses and Emma (Oliva) G. BA in Polit. Sci., St. Mary's U., 1988; JD, M in Pub. Affairs, U. Tex., 1994. Legal intern Am. Fedn. of State, County and Mcpl. Employees, Austin, Tex., 1989-90; planning coord. Alamo Area Coun. of Govt., San Antonio, 1992-96; planning/resource devel. cons. San Antonio, 1997—; coun. woman City of San Antonio, 1997—; chmn. City of San Antonio Mission Trails Oversight, 1995—, mil. com. San Antonio, 1997—; mem. Housing Task Force, San Antonio, 1997—, state initiatives com., 1997—. Active Highland Hills Neighborhood Assn., San Antonio, 1984—, Sunny Slope Neighborhood Assn., San Antonio, 1988—, South SA C. of C., San Antonio, 1994—, San Antonio Conservation Soc., 1994—. Fellow Patricia Harris Found., Austin, 1988-94. Dem. Roman Catholic. Avocations: theatre, reading. Home: 4001 Skylark Ave San Antonio TX 78210-5746 Office: City of San Antonio PO Box 839966 San Antonio TX 78283-3966

GUERRERO, LILIA, school nurse; b. McAllen, Tex., Aug. 5, 1953; d. Manuel C. and Olivia (Garza) G. BSN, Tex. Woman's U., 1975; postgrad., Calif. Coll. Health Scis., 1994—. RN, Tex.; cert. sch. nurse. Emergency rm. supr. McAllen (Tex.) Med. Ctr., 1975-80; staff nurse Mission (Tex.) Hosp., 1980-85; nurse Mission Cen. Ind. Sch. Dist., 1980—; tchr., insvc. trainer Am. Cancer Soc., 1991-92. Editor newsletter Mission Pediatric Ctr., 1990-92. Past dist. pub. edn. chmn. Am. Cancer Soc.; mem. Super Saturday Asthma Day Planning Com., 1990, planning com. Epilpsy Conf., 1991; mem. adv. com. Mission Hosp. Asthma Support Group; chmn. adv. bd. Mission CISD Wellness, 1994-95. Recipient Achievement award Am. Cancer Soc. Mem. Nat. Assn. Sch. Nurses, Tex. Assn. Sch. Nurses (pres. region 1, bd. dirs. ann. conv. 1991, regional pres. 1989-91).

GUERRERO, VLADIMIR, professional baseball player; b. Nizao Bani, Dominican Rep., Feb. 9, 1976. Outfielder Montreal Expos, 1996—. Holder Expo franchise records including most extra base hits, 1996, RBIs by a right fielder, 1996, total bases, others. Officec: c/o Montreal Expos, 4549 Pierre-de-Coubertin, Montreal, PQ Canada H1V 3N7*

GUERRI, WILLIAM GRANT, lawyer; b. Higbee, Mo., Mar. 30, 1921; s. Grant and Pearl (Zambelli) G.; m. Millicent K. Branding; children: Paula Ann Guerri Baker, Glenda Kay, William Grant. AB, Central Meth. Coll., 1943; LLB, Columbia, 1946. Bar: N.Y. 1946, Mo. 1947. Ptnr. Thompson Coburn, St. Louis, 1956—. Mem. bd. editors: Columbia Law Rev, 1945-46. Hon. mem. bd. dirs. St. Louis Heart Assn., chmn., 1972-73; bd. dirs. United Way Greater St. Louis, 1976-94; curator Ctrl. Meth. Coll., 1981-97. Fellow The Fellows of Am. Bar; mem. ABA, Mo. Bar Assn. (trustee 1984-92), Bar Assn. Met. St. Louis, Assn. of Bar of City of N.Y., Am. Law Inst., Am. Judicature Soc., Noonday Club, Round Table Club, Phi Delta Phi. Home: 1993 Windmoor Pl Saint Louis MO 63131-3005 Office: Thompson Coburn Ste 3000 1 Mercantile Ctr Saint Louis MO 63101-1643

GUERTIN, ROBERT POWELL, physics educator, university dean; b. Trenton, N.J., July 5, 1939; s. Alfred N. and Rhoda (Thomas) G.; m. Margaret Eipper, Aug. 13, 1966; children: Lynn Frances, Laura Thomas. BS, Trinity Coll., 1961; MA, Wesleyan U., 1963; PhD, U. Rochester, 1969. Asst. prof. physics Tufts U., Medford, Mass., 1968-75, assoc. prof., 1975-83, prof., 1983—, dean Grad. Sch. Arts and Scis., 1985-96, dean Grad. Sch. Rsch. and Profl. Edn., 1994-96; bd. govs. Univ. Press New England, Hanover, N.H., 1985-96, chmn., 1986-87, 93-94; vis. scientist Nat. High Magnetic Field Lab., Fla., 1996—. Editor books on crystalline electric fields and anomalous rare earth magnetic effects, 1980, 83, 90, 94; contbr. articles to profl. jours. Mem. Lucretia Crocker adv. council Commonwealth Mass., 1986—; bd. dirs. N.E. Assn. Grad. Schs. NSF and NIH rsch. award, 1972-90. Mem. Am. Phys. Soc. (mem. various coms. 1968—). Unitarian. Avocations: piano, swimming. Home: 478 Beacon St Apt 3 Boston MA 02115-1021

GUESON, EMERITA TORRES, obstetrician, gynecologist; b. Angeles City, Philippines, Jan. 4, 1942; came to U.S., 1964; d. Lina (Torres) Gueson. AA, U. Sto. Tomas, Manila, Philippines, 1958, MD, 1963. Resident in ob-gyn. Phila. Gen. Hosp., 1966-71; attending physician Nazareth Hosp., Phila., 1973—, Holy Redeemer Hosp., Meadowbrook, Pa., 1983—; bd. dirs. Physicians Who Care; lectr. healthcare issues to consumer groups, Phila. Author: Doctors Under Fire, 1989, Scales of Justice: Exploring the Wilderness of Health Care and Society's Moral Conscience, 1992, Do HMO's Cut Costs...and Lives, 1997, Survival Guide for HMO Patients, 1997, Survival Guide for HMO Patients, 1997; pub. ThereseVision Publs.; also med. writer, screenplay writer, line dir., prodr. Fellow ACOG, ACP; mem. AMA, Pa. Med. Soc., Philadelphia County Med. Soc., Pro-Life Ob.-Gynecologists (charter). Avocations: writing, painting, refinishing furniture. Office: 3336 Aldine St Philadelphia PA 19136-3802 also: Holy Redeemer Med Ctr Med Bldg Ste 309 Meadowbrook PA 19046

GUESS, JAMES DAVID, lawyer; b. Lampasas, Tex., Jan. 21, 1941; s. David Ira and Lila Blanch (Reagan) G.; m. Susan Lawyer, Dec. 19, 1981; children: Corey, Stephanie, Casey, Chris. BS in Edn., Southwestern U., 1963; JD, St. Mary's U., 1968. Bar: Tex. 1968, U.S. Dist. Ct. (we. dist.) Tex. 1974, U.S. Ct. Appeals (5th cir.) 1974, U.S. Dist. Ct. (so. dist.) Tex. 1978, U.S. Dist. Ct. (no. dist.) Tex. 1982. Assoc. Groce Locke & Hebdon, San Antonio, 1968-74, ptnr., 1975-86; shareholder Groce Locke & Hebdon P.C., San Antonio, 1986-96, Jenkens & Gilchrist, San Antonio, 1996-99, Law Offices of James D. Guess, San Antonio, 1999—; sustaining mem. Products Liability Adv. Coun.; mem. Am. Bd. Trial Advs. With USN, 1961-67, Vietnam. Mem. Tex. Assn. Def. Coun. (past pres.), Def. Rsch. Inst. (bd. dirs. 1998—), Internat. Assn. Def. Counsel. Avocations: sports, golf, hunting. Home: 13318 Southwalk St San Antonio TX 78232-4843 Office: Law Offices of James D Guess Ste 310 8620 N New Braunfels San Antonio TX 78217

GUEST, BARBARA, author, poet; b. Wilmington, N.C., Sept. 6, 1920; d. James Harvey and Ann (Hetzel) Pinson; m. Lord Stephen Haden-Guest, 1948 (div. 1954); 1 child, Hon. Hadley; m. Trumbull Higgins, 1954 (dec.); 1 child, Jonathan van Lennep. AB, U. Calif., Berkeley, 1943. Editorial assoc. Art News, 1951-59. Author: (plays) The Ladies Choice, 1953, The Office, 1961, Port, 1965; (poems) The Location of Things, 1960, Poems, 1963, The Blue Stairs, 1968, Moscow Mansions, 1973; (with Sheila Isham) I Ching: Poems and Lithographs, 1969, The Countess from Minneapolis, 1976, The Türler Losses, 1980, Biography, 1981, Quilts, 1981, Fair Realism, 1989; (with June Felter) Musicality, 1989; (with Richard Tuttle) The Altos, 1991, Defensive Rapture, 1993, Selected Poems, 1995, Stripped Tales, 1995; Rocks on a Platter, an Essay on Poetry, 1999; (novel) Seeking Air, 1978 (reprint 1997), (biography) Herself Defined: The Poet H.D. and Her World, 1984, (poems) Quill Solitary Apparition, 1996, The Confetti Trees: Motion Picture Stories, 1999. Recipient Longview award Longview Found., 1960, Laurence Lipton prize in lit., 1990, San Francisco State U. award for poetry, 1994, Fund for Poetry award, 1995, The America award, 1996, Pen West Josephine Miles award, 1996, Robert Frost medal Poetry Soc. Am., 1999; Yaddo fellow, 1958; Nat. Endowment for the Arts grantee, 1978. Address: 1301 Milvia St Berkeley CA 94709-1934

GUEST, CHRISTOPHER, actor, director, screenwriter; b. New York City, Feb. 5, 1948; m. Jamie Lee Curtis; 1 child. Grad., High Sch. Music and Art, N.Y.C.; student, Bard Coll., NYU. Appeared in Broadway plays include Room Service (debut) 1970, Moonchildren, 1972; Off-Broadway plays include National Lampoon's Lemmings (also writer), 1973, East Lynne, 1975; films (actor) The Hospital, 1971, The Hot Rock, 1972, Death Wish, 1974, The Fortune, 1975, La Honte de la Jungle, 1975, Girlfriends, 1978, The Last Word, 1979, The Long Riders, 1980, The Missing Link, 1980, Heartbeeps, 1981, This is Spinal Tap, (also writer), 1984, Little Shop of Horrors, 1986, Beyond Therapy, 1987, The Princess Bride, 1987, Sticky Fingers, 1988, A Few Good Men, 1992, Small Soldiers (voice), 1998; film dir.: The Big Picture, 1989, Edwards and Hunt, 1997, Almost Heroes, 1998; dir. tv movie: D.O.A., 1999; TV series: Saturday Night Live with Howard Cosell, 1975, Saturday Night Live, 1984-85; TV movies: It Happened One Christmas, 1977, Haywire, 1980, Million Dollar Infield, 1982, A Piano for Mrs. Cimino, 1982; TV specials: The Lily Tomlin Special (also writer, Emmy award 1976), 1975, Billion Dollar Bubble, 1977, How to Survive the 70's and Maybe even Bump into Happiness, 1978, Close Ties, 1983, Martin Short Concert for the North Americas, 1985, Billy Crystal-Don't Get me Started, 1986; TV director of Johnny Appleseed segment Tall Tales and Legends, The Attack of the 50 Foot Woman, 1993; actor, dir., composer, writer (film) Waiting for Guffman, 1996; albums: Six albums with National Lampoon, This is Spinal Tap, 1984, Break like the Wind (with Spinal Tap), 1992. Office: CAA c/o Jane Berliner 9830 Wilshire Blvd Beverly Hills CA 90212-1804*

GUEST, LARRY SAMUEL, newspaper columnist; b. Waycross, Ga., Mar. 27, 1942; s. Lawton Samuel and Lillian Synthia (Fussell) Taylor; m. Mary Nell Boyd, Apr. 5, 1963; children: Christa, Dorrie, Gina. BS, U. So. Miss., 1963. Dir. recreation dept. City of Brookhaven, Miss., 1963-65; advt. mgr., sports columnist Daily Leader, Brookhaven, 1965-70; sports editor, columnist Clarion-Ledger, Jackson, Miss., 1970-73; sr. sports columnist Orlando (Fla.) Sentinel, 1973—; mem. Sports Journalism Bd., Stetson U., Deland, Fla., 1994; radio sports commentator WGT-Radio, Orlando, 1992-94. Co-author: Making Magic, 1989, Confessions of a Coach, 1991; author: Arnie-Inside the Legend, 1993. Chmn. selection com. Butkus award Downtown Athletic Club of Orlando, 1984-90. With USNG, 1961-67. Named Fla. Sportswriter of Yr., Nat. Sportswriters and Sportscasters Assn., 1982, 83, 85; named to Fla. Citrus Bowl Hall of Fame, 1986. Mem. Football Writers Assn. Am., Golf Writers Assn. Am. Baptist. Avocations: golf, tennis. Office: Orlando Sentinel 633 N Orange Ave Orlando FL 32801-1349*

GUEST, LINDA SAND, education educator; b. Ft. Morgan, Colo., Sept. 9, 1945; d. Robert E. and Leona Mae (Prettyman) Sand; m. Richard E. Guest, June 5, 1966; children: Elise M., Gregory D. BA, Colo. State U., 1967, MEd, 1983; EdD, Harvard U., 1990. Ednl. cons. Nat. Office for Rural Edn., Ft. Collins, Colo.; tchr. Denver Pub. Schs., East Maine Sch. Dist. 63, Niles, Ill., Poudre R-1 Sch. Dist., Ft. Collins, 1979-91; asst. prof. curriculum and instrn. U. Denver Sch. Edn., 1991-94; project coord. Rocky Mountain Tchr. Edn. Collaborative, Greeley, Colo., 1994-98; dir. curriculum Am. Honda Eagle Rock Sch. and Profl. Devel. Ctr., Estes Park, Colo., 1998—; adj. faculty mem. Sch. Edn. Colo. State U., 1997—. Mem. ASCD, Am. Ednl. Rsch. Assn., Phi Delta Kappa. Home: PO Box 1770 Estes Park CO 80517-1770 Office: Eagle Rock Sch PO Box 1770 Estes Park CO 80517-1770

GUEST, RICHARD EUGENE, psychologist; b. LaJunta, Colo., Mar. 16, 1944; s. John William and Lorraine Alice (Smith) G.; m. Linda Jeanne Sand, June 5, 1966; children: Elise Michelle, Gregory Douglas. BS, Colo. State U., 1966, postgrad., 1966-67; MDiv, Iliff Sch. Theology, Denver, 1970; PhD, Northwestern U., Evanston, Ill., 1979. Lic. psychologist, Colo. Resident supr. Ft. Logan Mental Health Ctr., Denver, 1968-70; interim Protestant chaplain Denver Gen. Hosp., 1970; dir. Winnetka (Ill.) Youth Orgn., 1973-74; prin. chaplaincy rschr. McGaw Med. Ctr., Chgo., 1974-76; adminstr. dir. Des Moines Pastoral Counseling Ctr., 1976-79, co-dir., co-founder grief clinic, 1977-79; dir. Interfaith Ctr. for Edn. in Marriage and Family Living, Ft. Collins, Colo., 1979-81; EAP mgr. EAP Sys., Woburn, Mass., 1987-88; asst. prof. Colo. State U., Ft. Collins, 1988-90, faculty affiliate, 1990—; pvt. practice Ft. Collins, 1981—; found. and pres. GCS Consulting, Ft. Collins, CO; dir. Ctr. Human Relationships, Ft. Collins, 1990-97; psychol. cons. Iowa Conf. United Meth. Ch., Des Moines, 1977-79; cons. Iowa Children's Family Svcs., Des Moines, 1977-79; v.p., dir. tng. Transitions Mediation Svcs., Ft. Collins, 1982-86; allied health staff Poudre Valley Hosp., 1984-87 and Mountain Crest Hosp., Ft. Collins, 1990-99; presenter workshops and presentations; psychologist New Beginnings, Ft. Collins, 1991-93. Co-author: Organization and Administration of Pastoral Counseling Centers, 1981; contbr. articles to profl. jours. Adv. coun. Resource Assistance Ctr. for Non-Profits, Ft. Collins, 1980-82; pres., bd. dirs. Crossroads Safehouse for Battered Women, Ft. Collins, 1981-84; psychol. advisor Hospice of Larimer County, Ft. Collins, 1984-86; co-founder, bd. dirs. Children and Family Ctr., Ft. Collins, 1994-97; chmn. Mental Health Blue Ribbon Panel, Larimer County, 1999. Named Outstanding Young Man of Sterling, Jaycees, 1972. Mem. APA, Am. Assn. for Marriage and Family Therapy (clin. mem.), Larimer County Mental Health Profls. Network, Ft. Collins Ind. Practice Assn., No. Colo. Mental Health Profls., Inc. (stds. com.), Beta Beta Beta, Alpha Kappa Delta. Avocations: reading, painting, photography, camping, folk guitar. Office: 181 Boardwalk Dr Unit 10 Fort Collins CO 80525-3033

GUEST, RITA CARSON, interior designer; b. Atlanta, Aug. 17, 1950; d. Walter Harold and Doris Rebecca Carson; m. John Franklin Guest Jr., Jan. 20, 1979. BVA, Ga. State U., 1973. Registered interior designer, Ga., Fla., Washington, D.C., Ala. Pres., dir. design Carson Guest, Inc., Atlanta, 1984—; lectr. in field. Recipient 5 1st place awards Gwinnett Home Show and Interior Design Expo, 1991. Fellow ASID (dir. 1984, treas. 1985-86, nominating com. 1987, chmn. interprofl. devel. com. Ga. chpt. 1988-90, pres.-elect Ga. chpt. 1991-92, pres. 1992-93, coun. of pres.'s steering com. 1993-94, nat. dir. for region 14 1995-96, legis. adv. coun. 1997-98, mem. coun. fellows 1998, Comml. Design Project award 1983, Presdl. citation Ga. chpt. 1984, Residential Design award 1987, 1st Pl. Office Design award Ga. chpt. 19987, Comml. Offices 1st Pl. Project award 1989, Profl. Office Design award 1989, 1st Pl. Libr. Design/1st Pl. Comml. Offices award 1991, Pres. citation 1991, Designer of Yr. 1992, 1st Pl. Nat. award 1993, 2 Comml. Project awards 1992), 1st Pl. Instnl. Design award 1994, 1st Pl. Instnl. Design award Ga. chpt. 1994, 1st Pl. Healthcare Project award 1995), Ga. Bd. Archs., Ga. Alliance Interior Design Profls. (pres. 1991-92, bd. advisor), Atlanta C. of C., Midtown Bus. Alliance. Presbyterian. Avocation: painting. Office: Carson Guest Inc 1720 Peachtree St NW Ste 1001 Atlanta GA 30309-2459

GUEST, ROBERT HENRY, state legislator, management educator; b. East Orange, N.J., May 3, 1916; s. James Henry and Charlotte (Newbould) G.; m. Kate Hay, Dec. 18, 1942; children: David Hartley, Gregory Alan, John Hay, Peter Staples. AB cum laude, Amherst Coll., 1939, LHD, 1974; MA, Columbia U., 1941, PhD, 1960; MA (hon.), Dartmouth Coll., 1963. Dir. indsl. relations Limerick Yarn Mills, Me., 1941-42; sr. field examiner NLRB, 1946-47; mem. field research staff Labor and Mgmt. Center Yale, 1948-52; assoc. dir. research tech. project, 1952-60; ptnr. Charles R. Walker Assocs. (mgmt. cons.), New Haven, 1952-61; prof. organizational behavior Amos Tuck Sch. Dartmouth, 1960-81; mng. dir. Health Mgmt. Assocs. (mgmt. cons.), 1975; Mediator Conn. Labor-Mgmt. Com. Econ. Devel., 1960; mem. N.H. Gov's. Mental Health Com., 1964, N.H. Aeros. Commn., 1968; mem. mgmt. adv. panel NASA, 1969; disting. lectr. U. Leeds, U.K. 1959, U. Strathclyde, U.K. 1969, U. Canterbury, New Zealand, 1981, U. Sapporo, Japan, 1982. Author: (with C. R. Walker) The Man on the Assembly Line, 1952, (with C. R. Walker and A. N. Turner) The Foreman on the Assembly Line, 1957, Organizational Change: The Effect of Successful Leadership, 1962, (with others) Hospital Policy: Process and Action; contbg. editor: Changing Forces In American Society, 1964, Organizational Research in Health Institutions, 1973, IL Mutamento Della Organizzazione Aziendale, 1976, (with Paul Hersey and Kenneth H. Blanchard) Organizational Change Through Effective Leadership, 1977, rev. edit., 1986, Innovative Work Practices, 1981, Robotics: The Human Dimension, 1984, Work Teams and Team Building, 1986, As Good Luck Would Have it: An Autobiography on the Light Side, 1987. Exec. com. N.H. Dem. Party; ofcl. U.S. Winter Olympics, Lake Placid, N.Y., 1980; rep. N.H. State Legislature, 1988—; prime sponsor First Physician-Assisted Suicide Legis. in USA, 1991. With USNR, 1942-45. Reicpient Book of Yr. award Nat. Orgn. Devel. Coun., 1963, Article of Yr. awards Can. Assn. Mgmt., 1967, Am. Coll. Hosp. Adminstrs., 1974, Disting. Svc. medal Amherst Coll., 1986; marshal Brit. Open Golf Championship, 1990. Mem. Alpha Delta Phi. Club: Royal and Ancient Golf (St Andrews, Scotland). Home: 8 Barrett Rd Hanover NH 03755-2421

GUETHLEIN, WILLIAM O., lawyer; b. Cin., May 4, 1927; s. William O. and Catherine (Sandmann) G.; m. Bette Mivelaz, Aug. 4, 1961 (dec. 1974). LLD, U. Louisville, 1950. Bar: Ky. 1950, U.S. Dist. Ct. Ky. 1954, U.S. Ct. Appeals (6th cir.) 1954. Assoc. Boehl Stopher and Graves, Louisville, 1950-60, sr. ptnr., 1960—. Lt. USAR, 1952-60. Fellow Am. Acad. Trial Lawyers; mem. ABA, Jefferson County Bar Assn., Ky. Bar Assn., Am. Assn. Hosp. Attys. Avocation: tennis. Office: Boehl Stopher & Graves Aegon Ctr 400 W Market St Ste 2300 Louisville KY 40202-3354

GUETTEL, HENRY ARTHUR, retired arts executive; b. Kansas City, Mo., Jan. 8, 1928; s. Arthur Abraham and Sylva (Hershfield) G.; 1 dau. by previous marriage, Laurie C. (dec.); m. Mary Rodgers, Oct. 14, 1961; children: Matthew Rodgers (dec.), Adam Arthur, Alexander Burton. Student, Wharton Sch. of U. Pa., 1944-47, U. Kansas City, 1947-48. Stage mgr. on Broadway and TV, also stock cos., 1949-60; gen. mgr. Royal Ballet, Can., 1953-54; producer nat. touring cos. The Best Man, Sound of Music, Camelot, Oliver; then also gen. mgr. Music Theatre of Lincoln Center; touring cos. The Merry Widow, Kismet, Carousel, Annie Get Your Gun, Show Boat, 1964-67; mng. dir., then v.p. Am. Nat. Opera Co., 1967-68; prodn. supr. exploratory music theatre prodns., forum Vivian Beaumont Theater and theatre concerts Philharmonic Hall, N.Y. State Theatre, 1966-69; assoc. Kaplan Veidt, Ltd., 1970-72; v.p., prodn. assoc. Cinema 5, Ltd., 1972-78; v.p. creative affairs Columbia Pictures, 1978-80; sr. v.p. East Coast Prodn. Twentieth Century-Fox, 1980-82; exec. dir. Theatre Devel. Fund, 1982-92; mem. theatrical adv. panel N.Y. State Coun. of Arts, 1965-70; cons. theatre to SUNY, 1969-70; bd. dirs. Chelsea Theatre Ctr., N.Y.C., 1966-72, Performing Arts Repertory Theatre, N.Y.C., 1971-82, Theatre Devel. Fund, 1980-93, AFS Internat., 1987-89, Alliance for Arts, The Actor's Fund of Am., 1980—, Lit. Vols. N.Y.C., 1995-97, The New 42nd St., 1995—, Young Concert Artists, 1998—. Mem. Century Assn., Quogue Field Club, Quogue Beach Club. Address: 211 Central Park W New York NY 10024-6020

GUEVARA, A.P., network consultant; b. Mar. 29, 1958. AA, C.C. San Francisco, 1993. Comm. support analyst Chevron Overseas Petroleum, Inc., Angola, West Africa, 1989-93; sr. network analyst Chevron Info. Tech. Co., San Ramon, Calif., 1994-97; sr. network engr. Sprint Paranet, San Francisco, 1997-98; sr. network cons. Realtime Consulting Svcs., Hercules, Calif., 1998—. E-mail: apgu@rtconsult.com. Home: 367 Grenadine Way Hercules CA 94547

GUFFEY, MARSHA KIDD, grant writer, consultant; b. Jan. 6, 1958. BS, U. Ctrl. Ark., 1978; MPA, U. Ala., 1979; PhD, Tex. Tech U., 1996. Grant writer, acting facility mgr., pres. bd. dirs. Bethlehem House, Conway, Ark., 1991-94; temp. asst. prof. polit. sci. Ark. State U., Jonesboro, 1996-98; grant writer, cons. Therapeutic Strategies, Jonesboro, Ark., 1998—. Office: Therapeutic Strategies 2712 Harrisburg Rd Jonesboro AR 72401

GUGEL, CRAIG THOMAS, advertising and new media executive; b. Detroit, Jan. 18, 1954; s. Paul Walter and Patricia Angela (Sullivan) G. BA, U. Windsor, Ont., Can., 1976. Asst. br. mgr. Mich. Nat. Bank, Livonia, 1975-77; analyst media research Kenyon & Eckhardt, Inc., Birmingham, Mich. and N.Y.C., 1977-81; supr. media rsch. Kenyon & Eckhardt, Inc., N.Y.C., 1981-82; v.p., asst. dir. media rsch. McCann-Erickson, Inc., N.Y.C., 1982-84; v.p., dir. media rsch. Foote, Cone & Belding, Inc., N.Y.C., 1984-86; sr. v.p., corp. dir. media resources Bozell, Jacobs, Kenyon & Eckhardt, Inc., N.Y.C., 1986-88; sr. v.p., dir. media research Bates Worldwide, Inc., N.Y.C., 1988-91, sr. v.p., exec. dir. media rsch. and tech., 1991-94, sr. v.p., exec. dir. interactive media and rsch., 1994-95, exec. v.p. new media and interactive rsch., 1995-97, exec. v.p., dir. media resources and rsch., 1997; pres., CEO Manhattan-Pacific Multimedia Inc., N.Y.C., 1997—; chief rsch. svcs. officer Organic, Inc., N.Y.C., 1997-98. Mem. Advt. Rsch. Found. (chmn. interactive media com.), Assn. for Interactive Media, CTAM, Advt. Rsch. Found. (bd. dirs. 1995—). Avocations: reading, theatre, computers.

GUGELOT, PIET CORNELIS, physics educator; b. Bussum, The Netherlands, Feb. 24, 1918; came to U.S., 1947, naturalized, 1954; s. Pieter Cornelis and Anna (Arnold) G.; m. Ursula Federspiel, June 27, 1944; 1 son, Oliver C. Physics degree, Fed. Sch. Tech., Zurich, Switzerland, 1940, Ph.D., 1945. Research asso. Phys. Inst., Fed. Sch. Tech., Zurich, 1940-47; research asso. Princeton, 1947-49, asst. prof., 1949-56; dir. Inst. for Nuclear Research, Amsterdam, The Netherlands; prof. nuclear physics U. Amsterdam, 1956-66; prof. physics U. Va., Charlottesville, 1966-92, prof. emeritus, 1992—; vis. prof. U. Wash., 1954; vis. scientist Oak Ridge Nat. Lab., 1959, U. Calif., Livermore, 1960; vis. prof. Stanford, 1963-64, Fermi Inst., U. Chgo., 1970; dir. NASA Space-Radiation Lab., 1966; cons. NASA Langley Research Center, Los Alamos Sci. Lab.; vis. scientist dept. nuclear physics Saclay CERN, 1975-76; vis. prof. U. Lyon, France, 1977; invited lectr. Japan Soc. Promotion Sci., U. Tokyo, 1984. Contbr. articles to profl. jours. Recipient Alexander von Humboldt award. Fellow Am. Phys. Soc.; mem. Swiss, European phys. socs., Gesellschaft Ehemaliger Polytechn., Sigma Xi, Sigma Pi Sigma (hon.). Office: U Va Dept Physics Mccormick Rd Charlottesville VA 22904

GUGGENHEIM, CHARLES E., motion picture and television producer; b. Cin., Mar. 31, 1924; s. Jack Albert and Ruth Elizabeth (Stix) G.; m. Marion Davis Streett, June 29, 1957; children: Grace Stix, Jonathan Streett, Philip Davis. BA, U. Iowa, 1948; HHD (hon.), Washington U., St. Louis, 1978, Am. U., 1995. Prodr. Louis G. Cowan, Inc., N.Y.C., 1948-51; prodr., dir. Fund for Adult Edn., Ames, Iowa, 1951-52; acting dir. KETC Ednl. TV Commn., St. Louis, 1952-54; pres. Guggenheim Prodns., Inc., Washington, 1955—. Prodr.: (TV series) Sunday at the Zoo, 1950 (George Foster Peabody award); prodr., dir.: (films) Nine from Little Rock, 1964 (Acad. award 1964), Robert Kennedy Remembered, 1968 (Acad. award 1968), Monument to the Dream, 1967 (Acad. award nomination 1968), Children Without, 1964 (Acad. award nomination 1964), The Klan: A Legacy of Hate in America, 1982 (Acad. award nomination 1983), High Schools, 1983 (Acad. award nomination 1984), The Johnstown Flood, 1989 (Acad. award 1990), A Time for Justice, 1994 (Acad. award 1995), D-Day, 1994 (Acad. awrad nomination 1995), The Shadow of Hate, 1995 (Acad. award nomination 1996), A Place in the Land, 1998 (Acad. award nomination 1999). Trustee Danforth Found., St. Louis, 1968—, Found. for the Nat. Archives, 1994—, White House Hist. Assn., 1998—; media dir. Stevenson Presdl. Com., 1956, Kennedy Presdl. Com., 1968, McGovern Presdl. Com., 1972, Kennedy for Pres. Com., 1980, 75 U.S. senator and gov.'s campaigns, 1955-85. Sgt. U.S. Army, 1943-46. Recipient Disting. Achievement award U. Iowa, Conservation Svc. award U.S. Dept. Interior, 1968, Inst. Honors, AIA, 1987, Eartwatch award, 1991, 99. Mem. Acad. Motion Picture Arts and Scis., Writer's Guild of Am., Cosmos Club, Univ. Club (N.Y.). Home: 4343 Cathedral Ave NW Washington DC 20016-3560 Office: Guggenheim Prodns Inc 3121 South St NW Washington DC 20007-4419

GUGGENHEIM, FREDERICK GIBSON, psychiatry educator; b. Chgo., July 8, 1935; s. Melvin Elias and Marjorie Stone (Gibson) G.; m. Bethany Reed (div. Apr. 1976); m. Olivia Bishop Rogers, Nov. 23, 1984; children: Jennifer, Hannah, Russell Alderson, Rhoades Alderson. BA, Yale U., 1957; MD, Columbia U., 1961. Resident in medicine Bellevue Hosp., N.Y.C., 1961-63, Columbia Presbyn. Med. Ctr., N.Y.C., 1963-64; clin. assoc. NIMH, Bethesda, Md., 1964-66; resident in psychiatry Strong Meml. Hosp., Rochester, N.Y., 1966-69; asst. prof. Harvard Med. Sch., Boston, 1970-79; from asst. in psychiatry to assoc. psychiatrist Mass. Gen. Hosp., Boston, 1969-79; assoc. prof. Southwestern Med. Sch. in Tex., Dallas, 1979-85; Marie Wilson Howells prof. and chair dept. psychiatry U. Ark. for Med. Scis., Little Rock, 1985—; mem. nat. adv. com. clin. scholars program Robert Wood Johnson Found., Princeton, N.J., 1988-94; mem. com. on career devel. awards VA, Washington, 1990-95; mem. nat. adv. coun. Substance Abuse and Mental Health Svcs. Adminstrn., 1993-96; chief of staff U. Hosp., 1992-94. Recipient Allison travel fellowship Yale U., 1956, 57, Saybrook Fellows prize, 1957. Fellow Am. Psychiat. Assn., Am. Coll. Psychiatrists, Acad. Psychosomatic Medicine; mem. So. Assn. Rsch. in Psychiatry (pres. 1991-92), Am. Assn. Chairmen of Depts. Psychiatry (pres. 1995-96), Ark. Psychiat. Soc. (pres. 1988-89), Assn. Acad. Psychiatry (pres. 1992-93), Cosmos Club of Washington, Alpha Omega Alpha (faculty). Home: 2 River Oaks Cir Little Rock AR 72207-1702 Office: U Ark Med Scis Dept Psychiatry Slot 554 4301 W Markham St Little Rock AR 72205-7101

GUGGENHEIM, MARTIN FRANKLIN, law educator, lawyer; b. N.Y.C., May 29, 1946; s. Werner and Fanny (Monatt) G.; m. Denise Silverman, May 29, 1969; children—Jamie, Courtney, Lesley. BA, SUNY-Buffalo, 1968; JD, NYU, 1971. Bar: N.Y. 1972, U.S. Dist. Ct. (so. dist. and ea. dist.) N.Y. 1973, U.S. Ct. Appeals (2d cir.) 1974, U.S. Ct. Appeals (3d cir.) 1979, U.S. Ct. Appeals (6th cir.) 1977, U.S. Supreme Ct. 1976. Staff atty. Legal Aid Soc., N.Y.C., 1971-72, dir. spl. litigation unit, juvenile rights div., 1972-73; clin. instr. NYU Sch. Law, N.Y.C., 1973-75; staff atty. juvenile rights project ACLU, N.Y.C., 1975-79, acting dir., 1976-77; asst. prof. clin. law NYU, N.Y.C., 1975-77, assoc. prof. clin. law, 1977-79, prof. clin. law, 1980—; exec. dir. Washington Sq. Legal Services, Inc., N.Y.C., 1986—; pres., founding dir. Family Def. Law Project, Inc., N.Y.C., 1992—; advisor program for children Edna McConnell Clark Found., 1993—; dir. clin. and advocacy programs, NYU, 1989—; cons. juvenile justice standards project ABA/Inst. Jud. Adminstrn., 1979-81; acting dir. Clin. Advocacy Programs, Sch. of Law N.Y.U., 1988-89. Author: (with Alan Sussman) The Rights of Parents, 1980; Abuse and Neglect Volume, 1982; The Rights of Young People, 2d edit., 1985, (with Anthony G. Amsterdam and Randy Hertz) Trial Manual for Defense Attorneys in Juvenile Court, 1991, (with Alexandra Lowe and Diane Curtis) The Rights of Families, 1996. Dir. William J. Brennan Ctr., NYU, 1995—, adv. bd. N.Y.C. Adminstrn. Children, 1997—. Arthur Garfield Hays Civil Liberties fellow, 1970-71, Criminal Law Edn. and Research fellow, 1969-70. Mem. ABA (juvenile justice sect.), Am. Assn. Law Schs. (clin. legal edn. sect.). Office: NYU Sch Law 249 Sullivan St New York NY 10012-1079

GUGGENHEIMER, HEINRICH WALTER, mathematician, educator; b. Nurnberg, Germany, July 21, 1924; came to U.S., 1959; s. Siegfried and Marguerite Erna (Bloch) G.; m. Eva Auguste Horovicz, June 6, 1947; children: S. Michael, Esther H., Tobias I.S., Hanna Y. Diploma in math., Swiss Fed. Inst. Tech., Zurich, 1947, DSc in Math., 1950. Lectr. Hebrew U., Jerusalem, 1954-56; prof. Bar Ilan (Israel) U., 1956-59; assoc. prof. Wash. State U., Pullman, 1959-60; assoc. prof. U. Minn., Mpls., 1960-62, prof., 1962-67; prof. Poly U. (formerly Poly. Inst. Bklyn.), 1967-89; prof. emeritus Poly. U. N.Y. (formerly Poly. Inst. Bklyn.), 1989—. Author: Differential Geometry, 2d edit., 1977, Plane Geometry and Its Groups, 1967, Mathematics for Engineering and Science, 1976, Applicable Geometry, 1977, BASIC mathematical Programs for Engineers and Scientists, 1987, (with Eva H. Guggenheimer) Jewish Family Names and Their Origins: An Etymological Dictionary, 1992, German edit., 1996, The Scholar's Haggadah, 1995, Seder Olam: A Translation and Commentary, 1998 (bilingual edit.), The Jerusalem Talmuo, part I, vol. 1 (bilingual edit.), 2000; contbr. articles to profl. jours. With Swiss Army, 1944-54. Mem. Swiss Math. Soc. (life), Math. Assn. Am., Soc. Indsl. Applied Math., Assn. Computing Machinery, Am. Mathematical Soc. Home: PO Box 401 West Hempstead NY 11552-0401

GUGGENHEIMER, TOBIAS IMMANUEL SIMON, architect; b. Basel, Switzerland, Jan. 30, 1953; s. Heinrich Walter and Eva Augusta (Horowicz) G.; m. Lisa Ann Shapiro, June 27, 1976 (div. 1999); children: Anna Bella, Leanora Margaret. BA in Lit., SUNY, Binghamton, 1975; MArch, U. Colo., 1985. Registered architect, N.Y. Pres. Tobias Guggenheimer Architects, Dobbs Ferry, N.Y., 1991—; educator Pratt Inst. Sch. of Architecture, Bklyn., 1987—; lectr. various univs., mus. Author: (books) A Taliesin Legacy: The Architecture of Frank Lloyd Wright's Apprentices, 1995, Architectural Competitions: Their Significance in the Practice of Architecture, 1999; contbg. editor: Jour. of Taliesin Fellows, 1996-97; architect: (restorations) Frank Lloyd Wright's Serlin Residence, 1996-97, Yannuzzi Residence, Tuxedo Park, N.Y., 1997-99, (bldgs.) Mittman Residence, Spearfish, S.D., 1999. Mem. Nat. Coun. Archtl. Registration Bds. Home: 445 Broadway Apt 2cc Hastings Hdsn NY 10706-2318 Office: Tobias Guggenheimer Archs 145 Palisade St Dobbs Ferry NY 10522-1617

GUGGENHIME, RICHARD JOHNSON, lawyer; b. San Francisco, Mar. 6, 1940; s Richard E. and Charlotte G.; m. Emlen Hall, June 5, 1965 (div.); children: Andrew, Lisa, Molly; m. Judith Perry Swift, Oct. 3, 1992. AB in Polit. Sci. with distinction, Stanford U., 1961; JD, Harvard U., 1964. Bar: Calif. 1965, U.S. Dist. Ct. (no. dist.) Calif. 1965, U.S. Ct. Appeals (9th cir.) 1965. Assoc. Heller, Ehrman, White & McAuliffe, 1965-71, ptnr., 1972—; spl. asst. to U.S. Senator Hugh Scott, 1964; bd. dirs. Comml. Bank of San Francisco, 1980-81, Global Savs. Bank, San Francisco, 1984-86, North Am. Trust Co., 1996-99. Mem. San Francisco Bd. Permit Appeals, 1978-86; bd. dirs. Marine World Africa USA, 1980-86; mem. San Francisco Fire Commn., 1986-88, Recreation and Parks Commn., 1988-92; chmn. bd. trustees San Francisco Univ. High Sch., 1987-90; trustee St. Ignatius Prep. Sch., San Francisco, 1987-96. Mem. Am. Coll. Probate Counsel, San Francisco Opera Assn. (bd. dir.), Bohemian Club, Wine and Food Soc. Club, Olympic Club, Chevaliers du Tastevin Club (San Francisco), Thunderbird Country Club (Rancho Mirage, Calif.). Home: 2621 Larkin St San Francisco CA 94109-1512 Office: Heller Ehrman White & McAuliffe 333 Bush St San Francisco CA 94104-2806

GUGINO, CARL FRANK, orthodontist, educator; b. Buffalo, Nov. 7, 1928; s. Anthony Samuel and EmoiJane (Ursitti) G.; divorced; children: Megan Eileen Schapp, Carla Neill, Carl Anthony; m. Linda Barrett, Nov. 19, 1995. DDS, SUNY, Buffalo, 1956. Gen. practice dentistry Buffalo, 1955-59; tng. in orthodontics SUNY, 1964; pvt. practice orthodontics Buffalo, 1961—, Sarasota, Fla.; world lectr. on orthodontics, 1964—; vis. prof. Howard U., Washington, 1983—; hon. pres., hon. chmn., advisor to ZeroBase Bioprogressive Therapy Groups, Italy, France, Japan; former mem. bd. dirs. and rsch. dir. Found. for Orthodontic Rsch. Lt. comdr. USN, 1953-55. Named hon. citizen, Paris and Monte Carlo; recipient honors Assoc. Orthodontic Jour. Europe. Fellow Am. Coll. Dentists, Internat. Coll. Dentists; mem. ADA, Am. Assn. Orthodontists, Northeastern Soc. Orthodontists, Erie County Dental Soc., 8th Dist. Dental Soc., Soc. Francaise Orthopedic Dento-Faciale, Bioprogressive Study Club Japan (chmn.), Ricketts Club France (hon. pres.). Avocations: skiing, walking, homeopathic studies, travel, golf. Office: 1648 Bonita Ln Sarasota FL 34239-6812

GUGINO, LAWRENCE JAMES, medical educator; b. Buffalo, June 17, 1957; s. Joseph James and Carol (Matteson) G.; m. Mary Elizabeth Eppink, May 9, 1987; children: Nicholas, Thomas, Joseph. BS, Mich. State U., 1979; MD, U. Tex., 1986. Diplomate Am. Bd. Ob-Gyn. Clin. asst. prof. SUNY, Buffalo, 1990-96, clin. assoc. prof., 1996—. Co-author: (chpts.) Practical Guide to the Care of Gyn and OB Patient, 1997. Bd. trustees Hospice Assn. N.Y., Buffalo, 1996—. Fellow Am. Coll. Ob-Gyn.; mem. Am. Soc. Colposurgery and Cervical Pathology, Buffalo Gynecologic and Obstetric Soc., Soc. Laparoendoscopic Surgeons, Assn. Reproductive Health Profls., Assn. Profs. Gynecology and Obstetrics. Avocations: skiing, water skiing, hiking, gardening. Office: SUNT 219 Bryant St Buffalo NY 14222-2006

GUGLIELMINO, LUCY MARGARET MADSEN, education educator, researcher, consultant; b. Charleston, S.C., Feb. 20, 1944; d. Robert Allen and Margaret Webb (Rodgers) Madsen; m. Paul Joseph Guglielmino, July 31, 1965; children: Joseph Allen, Margaret Rose. BA in English magna cum laude, Furman U., 1965; MEd in English and Edn., Savannah Grad. Ctr., 1973; EdD in Adult Edn., U. Ga., 1977. Tchr. English various pub. schs., Mass., N.J., S.C., Ga., 1965-72; vis. asst. prof. adult and cmty. edn. Fla. Atlantic U., Boca Raton, 1978-87, asst. prof., 1987-88, assoc. prof., 1988-90, prof., 1991—, chmn. dept. ednl. leadership, 1991-94, dir. Melby Cmty. Edn. Ctr., 1994—; cons. AT&T, Motorola, Westvaco, S.E. banks, 1979—; bd. dirs. South Fla. Ctr. for Ednl. Leaders. Author: Adult ESL Instruction: A Sourcebook, 1991, Community Education and Florida's Future: Proceedings of the Commissioner's Summit, 1997; co-author: Administering Programs for Adults, 1997; author (adult form) Self-Directed Learning Readiness Scale, 1978, 3 other forms and translations into 10 other langs., 1979-94, Learning Preference Assessment (self-scoring format for business), 1991; contbr. over 80 articles to profl. jours., chpts. to books. Mem. Fla. Literacy Coalition, 1990—, Riviera Civic Assn., 1979—, Commn. on Status of Women. Recipient Tchr. of Yr. award Coll. Edn., Fla. Atlantic U., 1990, Outstanding Achievement award 1991, Presdl. Merit award, 1993, Profl. Excellence award, 1998; named to Fla. Adult and Cmty. Edn. Hall of Fame, Fla. Adminstrs. Adult and Cmty. Edn., 1992; numerous grants, 1979—. Mem. AAUW, Nat. Cmty. Edn. Assn., Am. Assn. for Adult and Continuing Edn., Commn. Profs. Adult Edn. (chmn. self-directed learning task force 1987-88, 90-91), Fla. Adult Edn. Assn. (bd. dirs. 1989-90), Phi Kappa Phi, Phi Delta Kappa. Episcopalian. Avocations: reading, swimming, biking, flower arranging, gardening. Home: 734 Marble Way Boca Raton FL 33432-3007 Office: Fla Atlantic U ED251 777 Glades Rd Boca Raton FL 33431-6424

GUGLIELMO, EUGENE JOSEPH, software engineer, consultant; b. Bklyn., Nov. 23, 1958; s. Anthony and Carlotta Sylvia (Grossi) G.; m. Nancy Eleanor Booth, Aug. 13, 1983; children: Tiffany, Trevyn, Kyle, Quentyn. BS in Computer Sci., St. John's U., 1979; MS in Computer Sci., Calif. State U., Chico, 1987; PhD in Computer Sci., Naval Postgrad. Sch., 1992. Computer asst. St. John's U., Jamaica, N.Y., 1977-79; mem. tech. staff Bell Telephone Labs., Whippany, N.J., 1979-80; sys. designer AT&T Comm., Piscataway, N.J., 1980-85; computer scientist Naval Air Warfare Ctr., China Lake, Calif., 1985-94; sr. cons. IBM Cons. Group, Boulder, Colo., 1994; prin. investigator Monterey Bay Aquarium Rsch. Inst., Moss Landing, Calif., 1994-96; prin. cons. BEA Systems, San Jose, Calif., 1996-99; v.p. Media Knowledge Decisions, Inc., San Jose, Calif., 1999; pres. William Enterprises Inc., Carson City, Nev., 1998—; tech. dir. Object Stream, Inc., Pleasanton, Calif., 1999—. Contbr. articles to profl. jours. Mem. IEEE, IEEE Computer Soc., Assn. Computing Machinery (Info. Retrieval, Artificial Intelligence), N.Y. Acad. Scis. Roman Catholic. Avocations: model building, baseball, basketball, reading, coaching. Home: 35 Bayview Rd Castroville CA 95012-9725 also: William Enterprises Inc 675 Fairview Dr #246 Carson City NV 89701

GUI, JAMES EDMUND, architect; b. Wooster, Ohio, Aug. 13, 1928; s. Harry Ludwig and Mabel Josephine (Olson) G.; B.Arch., Ohio State U., 1954; m. Anne Louise Outram, Oct. 15, 1955; children—Linda Anne, Jeffrey Allen. Asso. firm Charles F. McKirahan & Assocs., Architects, Ft. Lauderdale, Fla., 1958-63; chief specifications Architects Collaborative, Cambridge, Mass., 1963-67; propr. James E. Gui, Archtl. and Specifications Cons., Belmont, Mass., 1967—; cons. to Architects Collaborative, Benjamin Thompson & Assocs., Cambridge Seven Assocs., Archtl. Resources Cambridge, Inc., Harvard, MIT, Juilliard Sch. Music, Lincoln Center, N.Y.C., U.S. Pavillion Expo 67, Montreal, New Eng. Aquarium, Children's Hosp. Med. Ctr.; Harvard U. Law Sch. Complex (2d award Constrn. Specifications Inst.), Harvard Gutman Library, Harvard Obs., Kirkland Coll., Berkshire Community Coll., Tufts U. Dental Health Center, Independence Nat. Hist. Park Visitors Center; Wilmington Jewish Community Center (1st award Constrn. Specifications Inst.), Faneuil Hall Marketplace, Boston; Harborplace, Balt., Seaport Market, N.Y.C., Harvard Kennedy Sch. Govt., Cambridge, Ordway Music Theater, Mpls., Union Sta. Restoration, Washington. Mem. Constrn. Specifications Inst. Address: 50 Starfish Dr Unit 307 Hilton Head Island SC 29928-6901

GUIBBORY, ACHSAH, English educator, writer; b. Norwalk, Conn., June 30, 1945; d. Moses and Bathyah (Rasmussen) Guibbory; m. Anthony D. Kaufman, June 11, 1972; 1 child, Gabriel Benjamin. BA, Ind. U., 1966; MA, UCLA, 1967, PhD, 1970. Asst. prof. U. Ill., Urbana, 1970-76, assoc. prof., 1976-89, prof. English, 1989—. Author: The Map of Time, 1986, Ceremony and Community from Herbert to Milton, 1998; editor Jour. English and Germanic Philology, 1976-95, mng. editor, 1995—. Mem. MLA, Milton Soc. Am. (exec. com. 1988-90), John Donne Soc. (exec. com. 1991-93, pres. 1996-97, Disting. Publ. award 1992, 94). Jewish. Office: U Ill Dept English 608 S Wright St Urbana IL 61801-3613

GUICE, JOHN THOMPSON, retired career officer; b. Kosciusko, Miss., Nov. 5, 1923; s. Gustave Nathaniel and Anne Mae (McCool) G.; m. Charlotte Webb, Mar. 8, 1949; children—John Thompson, James G., Steven L., Thomas A., Joseph D. B.S. in Engring, U.S. Mil. Acad., 1947; M.S. in Internat. Relations, George Washington U., 1966; disting. grad., Air Command and Staff Coll., 1962, Air War Coll., 1966. Commd. 2d lt. U.S. Army, 1947; advanced through grades to maj. gen. USAF, 1974; tactical and interceptor pilot, 1947-55; officer Air N.G. and N.G., 1956—; dep. dir. Air N.G., 1974-77, dir., 1977-81, ret., 1981. Decorated Legion of Merit, Air Force D.S.M. Mem. Air Force Assn., N.G. Assn., Sigma Chi. Home: 4901 N Calle Luisa Tucson AZ 85718-4925

GUIDA, PAT, information broker, literature chemist; b. Highland Park, Mich.; d. Wilfred Bernard and Patricia Mary (Kelly) Graham; m. Edward Silvio Guida, Aug. 29, 1965; children: Niels Bohr, Eric Bohr. Student, Regis Coll., 1946-48, Rutgers U., 1952-55; BS cum laude, Fairleigh Dickinson U., 1961. Asst. librarian Warner-Lambert Research Inst., Morris Plains, N.J., 1961-64; librarian Reaction Motors Div. Thiokol, Denville, N.J., 1964-69; mgr., info. ctr. Foster D. Snell Div., Booz Allen & Hamilton Inc., Florham Park, N.J., 1969-80; pres. Pat Guida Assocs., Fairfield, N.J.; mem. Sci. Adv. Bd. EPA, Washington, 1978-82, Library Com. Chemists Club, N.Y.C., 1983-89. Editor: Chemical Digest, 1971-74. Pres. PTA, Sparta, N.J., 1959-60. Mem. Inst. Food Technologists (profl.). Avocations: theatre, West Highland white terriers, music, travel. Office: 24 Spielman Rd Fairfield NJ 07004-3412

GUIDA, PETER MATTHEW, surgeon, educator; b. N.Y.C., July 18, 1927; s. Santo and Anna (Tamburri) G.; m. Bernadette Castro, Mar. 10, 1979; children—Patricia, Peter M. B.S., L.I. U., 1949; M.D., Albany Med. Coll., 1954. Diplomate Am. Bd. Surgery, Am. Bd. Thoracic Surgery. Intern N.Y. Hosp., N.Y.C., 1954-55, resident in surgery, 1955-60; prof. surgery Cornell U., N.Y.C., 1968—; attending surgeon N.Y. Hosp., N.Y.C., 1968—; sr. aviation med. examiner FAA. Served to lt. comdr. USNR, 1943-46; PTO. Recipient Horatio Alger award Horatio Alger Soc., 1981; named Knight of the Order of the Holy Sepulchre of the Roman Cath. Ch., 1982, Knight of the Order of Merit of the Republic of Italy, 1982, Knight of Malta, 1989. Fellow ACS, Internat. Coll. Surgeons, Am. Coll. Cardiology, Am. Coll. Chest Physicians, Am. Coll. Angiology, Aerospace Med. Assn., AIAA. Roman Catholic. Office: N Y Hosp-Cornell U Med Ctr 525 E 68th St New York NY 10021-4885

GUIDO, MICHAEL ANTHONY, evangelist; b. Lorain, Ohio, Jan. 30, 1915; s. Mike and Julia (DePalma) G.; m. Audrey Forehand, Nov. 25, 1943. Student, Moody Bible Inst., Chgo., 1933-35. Ordained to ministry So. Bapt. Conv., 1939. Min. youth and music lst Presbyn. Ch., Sebring, Fla., 1936-38, lst Bapt. Ch., Lake Charles, La., 1939; evangelist Moody Bible Inst., 1940-50; founder, pres., speaker Guido Evangelistic Assn., Metter, Ga., 1950—; writer, speaker daily telecast A Seed from the Sower, 1972—, daily broadcaster The Sower, A Seed from the Sower, Seeds from the Sower, Your Favorite Ten, 1957—. Author: (autobiography) Seeds from the Sower, 1990; editor Sowing and Reaping mag., 1957—; daily newspaper columnist Seeds from the Sower, 1957—. Named Alumnus of Yr., Moody Bible Inst., 1982, Citizen of Yr., Kiwanis Club, Metter, 1982. Home: PO Box 508 Metter GA 30439-0508 Office: 600 N Lewis St Metter GA 30439-1428 *Life to me is loving God and serving Him by finding a need and supplying it, and searching for a lost soul and bringing that one home to God.*

GUIDRY, RODNEY-LEE JOSEPH, small business owner; b. Jennings, La., Nov. 20, 1935; s. Claude and Eda (Richard) G.; m. Haruko Komatsuzaki, Oct. 23, 1958; children: Emme Marie Stansbury, Emma Marie Pool. AAS, Community Coll. USAF, Lackland AFB, Tex., 1977, 79; BA, Northwestern State U., Natchitoches, La., 1978; MA, Pepperdine U., 1980. Commd. USAF, 1955; advanced through grades to sr. master sgt., 1976; ret. USAF, 1979; asst. personnel mgr. Seahorse, Inc., Morgan City, La., 1980-81; pers. dir. Acadian Marine, New Orleans, 1981; owner, cons. Rod Guidry Cons., Lafayette, La., 1980—; owner, operator Rod Guidry Ins. Ctr., Lafayette, 1982—. Editor: USAF Retiree Newsletter, 1989-91. Sec. Retirees Activities Office, England AFB, La., 1986-88, bd. dirs., 1983—. Mem. Am. Soc. Safety Engrs. (sec. 1985-86, chmn. scholarships 1984—, Plaque 1986), VFW (life), Vietnam Vets. Am. (life, treas. 1984-88), Air Force Assn. (life), Air Commando Assn. (life), Civitan Internat. (pres. Lafayette chpt. 1989-91, sec. 1987-89), French Toastmasters. Republican. Roman Catholic. Avocations: archery, photography, canoeing. Home: 215 Fendler Pky Pineville LA 71360-4729 Office: 2229 Moss St Lafayette LA 70501-2123

GUIHER, JAMES MORFORD, JR., publisher, writer; b. Clarksburg, W.Va., Feb. 21, 1927; s. James Morford and Ruth Holt (Souders) G.; m. Elizabeth Ewing Hart, Aug. 20, 1954; children: Catharine Brownfield, Deborah Hart. B.A., Princeton U., 1951; postgrad., Harvard U., 1951-52, Boston Mus. Sch. Fine Arts, 1953-54. Editor coll. textbooks Prentice-Hall, Inc., Englewood Cliffs, N.J., 1954-66; exec. editor Ednl. Book div. Prentice-Hall, Inc., 1966-68, editor-in-chief, 1968-74, v.p., gen. mgr., 1974-76; publishing cons. Author: (play) Aphrodite, 1999. Served with AUS, 1945-47. Home: 4 E 88th St New York NY 10128-0509

GUILARTE, PEDRO MANUEL, holding company executive; b. Cuba, May 19, 1952; s. Miguel G. and Emma G.; m. Zulima Piedra, May 26, 1979. BS in Indsl. Engring., Northwestern U., 1975; MBA, Washington U., St. Louis, 1977; cert. systems dynamics MIT, 1978; m. Zulima Piedra, May 26, 1979. Market analyst Cummins Engine Co., Columbus, Ind., 1976; corp. devel. exec. FPL Group, North Palm Beach, 1977-94; pres. Cable LPI, 1989-93; internat. project mgr. ESI Energy, 1993-94, internat. power devel. cons.,

1994—. Consortium for Grad. Study in Bus. fellow, 1975-77; scholar Northwestern U., 1975. Mem. Planning Execs. Inst. Republican. Methodist. Home: 6464 Woodlake Rd Jupiter FL 33458-2447

GUILBEAU, BRIAN GERALD, sportswriter; b. Lafayette, la., Nov. 2, 1971; s. Gerald William Guilbeau and Virginia Alice Newell. BA, U. Southwestern La., 1996. Sportswriter The Daily Iberian, New Iberia, La., 1996-98, Lake Charles (La.) Am. Press, 1998—. Mem. Soc. Profl. Journalists. Home: 901 Hampton Ln #B Iowa LA 70647

GUILBEAUX, WILSON, JR., military officer; b. Lafayette, La., Dec. 28, 1952. BS in Engring., Wayland Bapt. U., 1977; M in Internat. Rels., U. Okla., 1990; grad., Squadron Officer Sch., 1984, Air Command and Staff Coll., 1992, U. Ill., 1995. Commd. 2d lt. USAF, 1971, advanced through grades to col.; computer maintenance technician Clark Air Base, The Philippines, 1974-78; air surveillance officer 552d Air Control Wing, Tinker AFB, Okla., 1978; chief 28th Air Divsn. Exercise Br., 1982; chief command and control, comms., computers/intell. br. Hdqs. Air Force ops. directorate, 1988-91; spl. asst. to ops. group comdr. Tinker AFB, 1992; comdr. 654th Comms. Computer Sys. Group, Tinker AFB, 1993; sr. exercise planner, CINC initiatives fund program mgr. Joint Staff, Directorate of Operational Plans/Interoperabil., 1995-98; dep. dir. Air Force Mgmt. Reform Office, Sec. of Air Force, 1998—. Decorated D.F.C., Def. Meritorious Svc. medal, Meritorious Svc. medal with 2 oak leaf clusters; Nat. Def. Fellow U. Ill., 1995. Office: HA USAF/XP Rm 4E128 1070 Air Force Pentagon Washington DC 20330-1070

GUILD, ALDEN, retired lawyer; b. Boston, July 3, 1929; s. Howard Redwood and Frances Allen (Warren) G.; m. Ruth Ineta Creighton, Sept. 14, 1957; 1 child, Heather Louise. BA, Dartmouth Coll., 1952; JD, U. Chgo., 1957; LLD (hon.), Norwich/Vt. Coll., 1977. Bar: Vt. 1958, U.S. Dist. Ct. Vt. 1958. With law dept. Nat. Life Ins. Co., Montpelier, Vt., 1957-90, asst. v.p., counsel, corp. sec., 1974-83, v.p., gen. counsel, 1983-89, sr. v.p., gen. counsel, 1989-90; ret. McKee, Giuliani & Cleveland, Montpelier, of counsel, 1990-97. Author: Stock-Purchase Agreements, 1960, Professional-Partnership Purchase Agreements, 1961, Business-Partnership Purchase Agreements, 1962; contbr. articles to legal jours. Trustee Norwich U., 1972-96, Vt. Coll., 1967-72, Kimball U. Acad., 1972-74, Wood Art Gallery, 1961-72; mem. Dartmouth Coll. Alumni Council, 1975-78. Served with USAF, 1950-53, Korea. Recipient Disting. Service award Montpelier Jr. C. of C., 1962. Mem. Vt. Bar Assn., Assn. Life Ins. Counsel, Am. Coun. Life Ins., VFW, Am. Legion, Order of Coif, Lake Mansfield Trout Club (Stowe, Vt.), Masons, Elks, Phi Beta Kappa, Theta Chi. Republican. Home: 63 Murray Rd Montpelier VT 05602-8514

GUILD, CLARK JOSEPH, JR., lawyer; b. Yerington, Nev., May 14, 1921; s. Clark Joseph and Virginia Ellen (Carroll) G.; m. Elizabeth Ann Ashley, July 20, 1945 (div. 1977); children: Clark J. III, Jeffrey S., Daniel E. (dec.), Jann Cademartori. BA, U. Nev., 1943; JD, Georgetown U., 1948. Bar: Nev. 1948, D.C. 1948, U.S. Dist. Ct. (no. dist.) Nev. 1948, U.S. Ct. Appeals (D.C. cir.) 1948, U.S. Supreme Ct. 1959, U.S. Ct. Appeals (9th cir.) 1984. Ptnr. Guild, Hagen & Clark, Ltd., Reno, Nev., 1953-88, Guild, Russell, Gallgher & Fuller Ltd., Reno (formerly Guild, Hagen & Clark Ltd.), 1988—. Pres. YMCA, Reno, 1954, 64; regent U. Nev. System, 1972. Capt. inf. U.S. Army, 1942-46. Recipient Disting. Nevadan award U. Nev., 1989. Fellow Am. Coll. Trial Lawyers; mem. ABA, State Bar Nev., Clark County Bar Assn., Washoe County Bar Assn. (pres. 1959-60), Masons, Elks. Democrat. Episcopalian. Office: Guild Russell Gallagher & Fuller Ltd 100 W Liberty St Reno NV 89501-1962

GUILD, NELSON PRESCOTT, retired state education official; b. Keene, N.H., Nov. 20, 1928; s. Louis F. and Hope (Mason) G.; m. Margaret Adele Graf, June 24, 1950; children: Douglas, Matthew. B.A., U. N.H., 1953; M.A., Pa. State U., 1955, Ph.D., 1958. Asst. prof. govt. Hamilton Coll., Clinton, N.Y., 1958-64, assoc. prof., 1964-66; dean Frostburg (Md.) State Coll., 1966-69, pres., 1969-85; interim exec. dir. bd. trustees Md. State Univs. and Colls., 1985-87. Author: (with Kenneth T. Palmer) Introduction to Politics: Essays and Readings, 1968. Served with USAF, 1946-49.

GUILD, RICHARD SAMUEL, trade association management company executive; b. Boston, Nov. 5, 1925; s. Walter Rayford and Anna (Hollander) G.; BS, Boston U., 1949; m. Susan Jane Coughlin, July 3, 1965; children: Laura Ann, Linda Jean. With Guild Assocs., Inc., Boston, 1949—, mng. dir., 1960-65, pres., 1965—; owner Copypro, 1975-92; treas. Resource Matching System, Inc., 1982-83; exec. sec. New Eng. Marine Trade Assn., 1963, Liquified Petroleum Gas Assn. New Eng., 1972-1985; mng. dir. Shoe Pattern Mfrs. Assn., 1951-94 , Mass. Automatic Merchandising Coun., 1964—, Tel. Answering Assn. New Eng., 1983; exec. v.p. Am. Boat Builders and Repairers Assn., 1979-90; treas. Wet Ground MICA Assn., 1983-87. With USNR, 1944-45. Cert. assn. exec. Mem. Multiple Assn. Mgmt. Inst. (past pres.), Am. Soc. Assn. Execs. (past bd. dirs.), N.Am. Paddlesports Assn. (exec. v.p. 1987-90), Boston Soc. Assn. Execs. (past pres.), Def. Orientation Conf. Assn., Soc. Mgmt. of Profl. Computing (exec. sec. 1985-94), New Eng. Honda Automobile Dealers Assn. (exec. sec. 1985-95), Acura Dealers of N.E. (exec. sec. 1989-93, 96—). Home: 5 Glengarry Rd Winchester MA 01890-2511 Office: 100 Boylston St Boston MA 02116-4610

GUILFOYLE, JAMES JOSEPH, financial executive, accountant; b. Trenton, N.J., Mar. 11, 1956; s. James Clarence and Eleanor Josephine (Zientek) G.; m. LuAnn Calabro, Sept. 18, 1982. BS, Fordham U., 1978; MBA, U. Detroit Mercy, 1999. CPA, N.J. Cost acct. Triangle Industries, New Brunswick, N.J., 1978-79; consolidations acct. Wheelabrator-Frye Inc., Belle Mead, N.J., 1979-81, cost acct., 1981-82; asst. controller Wheelbrator subs. Airpol, Englewood, N.J., 1982-83; gen. acctg. mgr. U.S. Lines, Cranford, N.J., 1983-84; controller PRC Mgmt. Co. Inc., West Long Branch, N.J., 1984-86; asst. v.p., chief fin. officer Tryon Equities Corp., Charlotte, N.C., 1987-88; sr. staff asst. fin. acctg. and reporting GM, Detroit, 1988-95, employment cost analysis and health care initiatives team, 1995—. Mem. AICPA, Mich. Assn. CPA's, N.J. Soc. CPA's, Inst. Mgmt. Accts., Beta Gamma Sigma. Roman Catholic. Avocations: basketball, reading. Home: 2563 Wenona Dr Wixom MI 48393-2157 Office: GM 3044 W Grand Blvd Ste 13115 Detroit MI 48202-3037

GUILIANI, MARILYN KAY, educator; b. Missoula, Mont., Mar. 16, 1948; d. Joseph Pedrotti and Elvira Mary Deloris G. BA in Edn., U. Mont., 1970, MA in Edn., 1997. Tchr. Helena, Mont., 1971—. Author of poems. Mem. NEA, Mont. Edn. Assn., Helena Edn. Assn. Roman Catholic. Home: PO Box 493 Helena MT 59601

GUILIANO, FRANCIS JAMES, office products manufacturing company executive; b. Feb. 1, 1932; s. James V. and Mary C. Guiliano; m. Mary Beth Eberly, Jan. 9, 1957; children: Barbara Jean, James Francis, Janet Marie, John Alden. BBA in Fin., U. Mass., 1959; MBA, U. Pa., 1978. Salesman Continental Can Co., 1959-63; sales mgr. State of Mich., 1964-65; plant gen. mgr. Internat. Paper Co., Greensburg, Pa., 1966-67; gen. mktg. mgr. container divsn. Internat. Paper Co., Greensburg, 1967-69, world-wide gen. mktg. mgr., 1969-72; v.p., gen. mgr. Folding Carton divsn. Internat. Paper Co., N.Y.C., 1972-76; exec. v.p. Simkins Industries, New Haven, 1977; chmn., CEO, pres. Ampad Corp., Holyoke, Mass., 1979-90; owner, CEO Rite-Now Container Corp., East Longmeadow, Mass., 1990—; CEO 4M Corp., 1987—; dir. Shawmut First Bank & Trust; CEO and pres. PCL Industries, 1990-93. Bd. dirs. United Way, 1981-82; chmn. bus. adv. coun., mem. exec. com. U. Mass. Sch. Bus., 1980-82; bd. govs. Holyoke Libr. Served with USN, 1951-55. Mem. Am. Mgmt. Assn., Ind. Box Makers Assn., Paper Converters Assn., Nat. Office Products Assn., Wholesale Stationers Assn., Colony Club (Springfield, Mass.), Longmeadow Country Club.

GUILL, MARGARET FRANK, pediatrics educator, medical researcher; b. Atlanta, Jan. 18, 1948; d. Vernon Rhinehart and Margaret N. (Tichenor) Frank; m. Marshall Anderson Guill III, July 6, 1974; children: Daniel Marshall, Laura Elizabeth. BA, Agnes Scott Coll., 1969; MD, Med. Coll. Ga., 1972. Diplomate Am. Bd. Pediatrics, Am. Bd. Pediatrics subbd. pulmonology, Am. Bd. Allergy and Immunology, Nat. Bd. Med. Examiners. Resident in pediatrics Kaiser Found. Hosp., San Francisco, 1976-78, fellow in allergy, 1978-79; staff physician Waipahu (Hawaii) Clinic, 1973-76; intern in internal medicine Med. Coll. Ga., Augusta, 1973, resident in pediatrics, 1974, fellow in allergy and immunology, 1979-80, from asst. prof. to prof. pediatrics, 1981—, also chief sect. pediatric pulmonology and dir. Asthma Ctr., dir. Cystic Fibrosis Ctr., 1990—; spkr. in field. Host Healthwatch weekly program WJBF-TV, 1982-83; contbr. articles to profl. jours. Active Reid Meml. Presbyn. Ch.; vol. tchr. Episcopal Day Sch., 1982-85; career day participant Acad. Richmond County, 1982, 83; med. advisor Augusta Area Allergy and Asthma Support Group, 1984-86; adv. bd. East Cen. br. Am. Lung Assn. Ga., 1985—, program of work com., 1987—, bd. dirs., 1987—, program coordinating com., 1990-91, exec. bd., 1989-91; med. staff Camp Breathe Easy, 1985—, med. dir., 1996-98. Recipient Mosby Book award, 1973; rsch. grantee BRSG, 1981-86, Del Labs., 1982, Merrell-Dow, 1983, 84, Elan Pharms., 1986, Am. Lung Assn. Ga., 1986, 87, Hollister-Stier, 1986, Fisons Corp., 1989, 91-93, 95, Med. Coll. Ga., 1989, Am. Heart Assn., 1991, Genentech, 1991-96, Miles, 1992, Clintrials, 1990-95, PathoGenesis, 1995, SmithKline Beecham, 1996. Fellow Am. Acad. Pediat., Am. Coll. Chest Physicians, Am. Acad. Allergy, Asthma and Immunology, Am. Coll. Allergy, Asthma and Immunology, Am. Assn. Cert. Allergists; mem. Med. Assn. Ga., Richmond County Med. Soc., Allergy and Immunology Soc. Ga., S.E. Allergy Assn. (Hal Davison award 1985), Am. Assn. Clin. Immunologists and Allergists, Ga. Thoracic Soc. (Med. Profl. of Yr. 1998), Am. Thoracic Soc., Assn. for Care Asthma, Alpha Omega Alpha. Home: 2247 Pickens Rd Augusta GA 30904-4462 Office: Med Coll Ga Dept Pediatrics Augusta GA 30912

GUILLAMA-ALVAREZ, NOEL JESUS, healthcare company executive; b. Havana, Cuba, Nov. 30, 1959; came to U.S., 1966; s. Jesus Mario Guillama and Rosa Maria Alvarez Guillama; m. Elayne Z. Cueto, Oct. 30, 1967; 1 child, Jahziel Mikhail Guillama. Student, Palm Beach C.C., Lake Worth, Fla., 1978-80; BS in Bus. Adminstrn., Pacific We. U., L.A., 1992. Cert. bldg. contractor, Fla.; lic. real estate broker, mortgage broker, gen. ins. agt. Dir. programing Teleprompter Corp., West Palm Beach, Fla., 1976-79; pres., CEO JMG Holdings Inc, Palm Beach, Fla., 1980-90; v.p. ops. Quality Care Networks, Boca Raton, Fla., 1990-95; v.p. devel. Medpartners, Inc., Birmingham, 1995; pres., CEO Met. Health Networks, Boca Raton, 1995—; chmn., mng. ptnr. Millenium Capital Ptnrs., Boca Raton, 1997—; vice chair Palm Beach County Adv. Bd., West Palm Beach, 1990-92; co-founder, vice chair Lake Worth Cmty. Devel. Corp., 1990-92; co-founder, dir. Project Lake Worth, 1989-92; chair, mng. ptnr. Millenium Capital Group, Inc., Boca Raton, Fla., 1997—. Writer weekly column Palm Beach Latino Newspaper, 1991-92. Recipient award Leukemia Soc. Am., 1979, Chin de Plata award Todo Mag., Miami, Fla., 1978. Mem. Am. Fin. Assn., Am. Coll. Healthcare Execs. (assoc.), Med. Group Practice Assn. Avocations: scuba diving, tennis, golf, fishing. Office: 5100 Town Center Cir Ste 560 Boca Raton FL 33486-1070

GUILLAUME, JUANITA CONNOR, account clerk, minister; b. N.Y.C., Feb. 3, 1957; d. Zinnie Pickett and Queen Esther Lipscomb; m. Odner Guillaume, June 12, 1976; children: Gary Andre, Natasha Nichelle. AA, Bethel Bible Inst., Jamaica, N.Y., 1977; DD (hon.), World Christianship, Fresno, Calif., 1994; B of Theology in Religious Edn., Open Bible Faith Ministries, Bklyn., 1998. Ordained min. Fireside Ch. Claims devel. clerk Human Resource Adm., 1970-82; account clerk U. Hosp., Bklyn., 1983—. Author: Express of the Heart, 1997. Assoc. min. Fireside Pentacostal Ch., 1970—, supt. Sunday sch., 1995—; pres. Promises Faith Ministry, 1996—. Mem. Am. Assn. Christian Counselors Calif. Democrat. Home: 661 E 80th St 2nd Fl Brooklyn NY 11236 Office: Fireside Pentecostal Assembly 69-71 Thayer St New York NY 10040

GUILLAUME, RAYMOND KENDRICK, banker; b. June 19, 1943; s. William Raymond and Marguerite (Lyons) G.; m. Ann Greenwell, June 26, 1965; children—Lee Kendrick, Jill Lyons Kissel. BS, Western Ky. U., 1965. Asst. cashier Liberty Nat. Bank, Louisville, 1968, asst. v.p., 1969-70, v.p., 1970-72, sr. v.p., 1973-78, exec. v.p., 1978-92; pres. Liberty Nat. Bank, 1993-95, also bd. dirs.; vice chmn., CEO Bank of Louisville, 1995—. Chmn., bd. dirs. ARC, Louisville, 1985; treas., bd. dirs. Met. United Way, Louisville, 1984-92, 93—, St. Anthony's Hosp., Louisville, 1985; trustee Christ Ch. United Meth., Louisville, 1984; chmn. Leadership Louisville, 1992-95; chmn. bd. dirs. Metro United Way, Western Ky. Univ. Found., Ky. Ctr. for the Arts Endowment Fund. Mem. Western Ky. U. Nat. Alumni Assn. (pres. 1985), Ky. Bar Assn. (bd. dirs.), Pendennis Club, Louisville Boat Club, Jefferson Club, Kentuckians of N.Y. Home: 415 Rolling Ln Louisville KY 40207-1807 Office: Bank of Louisville PO Box 1101 Louisville KY 40201-1101

GUILLEMETTE, GLORIA VIVIAN, dressmaker, designer; b. North Attleboro, Mass., June 27, 1929; d. Wilfred Anthony Roy and Sylviana (Bonnoyer) King; student Nat. Sch. Dress Design, 1976; m. Thomas William Guillemette, Mar. 24, 1963; children: Sylvia Marie, Katherine Anne, John Thomas. Machine operator dress mfg. cos., 1945-60; asst. to dressmaker and designer, Windsor, Conn., 1960-63; owner Mrs. G's Studio, Enfield, Conn., 1963-87; dir. Fashion Show, 1973, 76. Cub Scout commr. Boy Scouts Am., 1979-85; mem. Enfield Fair Rent Commn., 1979-87; justice of peace Conn., 1979—; mem. Republican Town Com., 1976-91; sec. United Meth. Women, 1977-82; mem. Enfield Fair Rent Commn., 1979-87, Presdl. Task Force, 1982-83. Club: Republican Women (pres. 1995-97).

GUILLEMETTE, MARK EDGAR, textile technologist; b. Fall River, Mass., Sept. 13, 1956; m. Elaine Marie Sylvain, Oct. 5, 1996. BS, U. Mass., Dartmouth, 1978; MS, Inst. Textile Tech., Charlottesville, Va., 1980. Tech. svc. mgr. Globe Mfg. Co., Fall River, 1980—. Recipient Hrary Riemer Vets. award No. Textile Vets. Assn., 1978. Mem. Am. Chem. Soc. (sr.), Am. Assn. Textile Chemists and Colorists (sr.; pub. spkr.). Avocation: golf. Office: Globe Mfg Co 456 Bedford St Fall River MA 02720-4894

GUILLEMIN, ROGER C. L., physiologist; b. Dijon, France, Jan. 11, 1924; came to U.S., 1953, naturalized, 1963; s. Raymond and Blanche (Rigollot) G.; m. Lucienne Jeanne Billard, Mar. 22, 1951; children: Chantal, Francois, Claire, Helene, Elizabeth, Cecile. B.A., U. Dijon, 1941, B.Sc., 1942; M.D., Faculty of Medicine, Lyons, France, 1949; Ph.D., U. Montreal, 1953; Ph.D. (hon.), U. Rochester, 1976, U. Chgo., 1977, Baylor Coll. Medicine, 1978, U. Ulm, Germany, 1978, U. Dijon, France, 1978, Free U. Brussels, 1979, U. Montreal, 1979, U. Man., Can, 1984, U. Turin, Italy, 1985, Kyung Hee U., Korea, 1986, U. Paris, Paris, 1986, U. Barcelona, Spain, 1988, U. Madrid, 1988, McGill U., Montreal, Can., 1988, U. Claude Bernard, Lyon, France, 1989, Laval U., Quebec, Can., 1996, Sherbrooke U., Quebec, 1997. Intern, resident univs. hosps. Dijon, 1949-51; asso. dir., asst. prof. Inst. Exptl. Medicine and Surgery, U. Montreal, 1951-53; asso. dir. dept. exptl. endocrinology Coll. de France, Paris, 1960-63; asst. prof. physiology Baylor Coll. Medicine, 1953-57, assoc. prof., 1957-63, prof., dir. labs. neuroendocrinology, 1963-70, adj. prof., 1970—; resident fellow, chmn. labs. neuroendocrinology Salk Inst., La Jolla, Calif., 1970-89, adj. rsch. prof., 1989-94; Disting. Scientist Whittier Inst., 1989-97, med. and sci. dir., 1993-94; adj. prof. medicine U. Calif., San Diego, 1995-97; disting. prof. Salk Inst., La Jolla, Calif., 1997—. Decorated chevalier Legion d'Honneur (France), 1974, officer, 1984; recipient Gairdner Internat. award, 1974; U.S. Nat. Medal of Sci., 1977; co-recipient Nobel prize for medicine, 1977; recipient Lasker Found. award, 1975; Dickson prize in medicine, 1976; Passano award sci., 1976; Schmitt medal neurosci., 1977; Barren Gold medal, 1979; Dale medal Soc. for Endocrinology U.K., 1980, Ellen Browning Scripps Soc. medal Scripps Meml. Hosps. Found., 1988, Disting. Scientist award Nat. Diabetes Rsch. Coalition. Fellow AAAS; mem. NAS, Am. Physiol. Soc., Am. Peptide Soc. (hon.), Assn. Am.Physicians, Endocrine Soc. (pres. 1986), Soc. Exptl. Biology and Medicine, Internat. Brain Rsch. Orgn., Internat. Soc. Rsch. Biology Reprodn., Soc. Neuro-scis., Am. Acad. Arts and Scis., French Acad. Scis. (fgn. assoc.), Academie Internationale de Medecine (fgn. assoc.), Swedish Soc. Med. Scis. (hon.), Academie des Scis. (fgn. assoc.), Academie Royale de Medecine de Belgique (corr. fgn.), Internat. Soc. Neurosci. (charter), Western Soc. Clin. Rsch., Can. Soc. Endocrinal Metabolism, (hon.), Club of Rome. Office: The Salk Inst 10010 N Torrey Pines Rd La Jolla CA 92037-1099

GUILLEN, MICHAEL ARTHUR, mathematical physicist, educator, writer, television journalist; b. L.A.; s. Marin Arthur and Betty Guillen; m. Laurel Lucas, Sept. 7, 1991. BS in Physics with distinction, UCLA; MS in Physics, Math. and Astronomy, Cornell U., PhD in Physics, Math. and Astronomy, 1982. Tchr. physics and math. Core Curriculum Program Harvard U., Cambridge, Mass., 1985—; sci. editor Sta. WCVB-TV, Boston, 1985—; sci. editor, Good Morning Am. ABC-TV, N.Y.C., 1988—; sci. correspondent ABC News, N.Y.C., 1990—; tech. advisor Metro Goldwyn Mayer; participant numerous ednl. improvement programs; sci. cons. MGM/VA; adv. bd. AIP. Author: Bridges to Infinity: The Human Side of Mathematics, 1984, Five Equations that Changed the World: The Power and Poetry of Mathematics, 1995; contbr. articles to numerous newspapers and mags. including N.Y. Times, Washington Post, Sci. Digest, Sci. News., Psychology Today, Esquire; chief cons. NOVA TV show A Mathematical Mystery Tour; host/writer (TV spls.) Time, Tides and Tuning Forks (Emmy award, Ohio State award), To Be or Not to Be: Endangered Species of New England (Ohio State award), Heads or Tails: Predicting the Unpredictable, 1987, Greenland Polar Ice Cap, 1991 (Ohio State award), War in the Gulf: Answering Children's Questions, 1991 (ACT award, Nat. TV Critics award, Dupont-Columbia U. award), Monteverde Cloud Forest, 1991 (TEDDY award), What Are the Differences Between Men and Women?, 1991 (EMMA award), U.S. Disabled Ski Team, 1992 (EDI award), Russian Space Program-ABC News Nightline, 1992 (Aviation/Space Writers Assn. award); formerly sci., tech. contbr. CBS Morning News; TV spls. include Laetrile: The Last Chance. Recipient Danforth award for disting. teaching Harvard U., 1989, 90, Broadcast Media award for overall excellence AIAA, 1987. Mem. AAAS (chmn. sci. and math. edn. symposium), NAS (chmn. scis. and humanities conf., com. rsch. in math., sci. and tech. edn.), Leonardo Da Vinci Soc. (founder), Phi Eta Sigma, Sigma Pi Sigma, Pi Mu Epsilon. Achievements include research in theoretical plasma physics, liquid physics and astrophysics. Office: Good Morning AM 147 Columbus Ave Flr 63 New York NY 10023-5900*

GUILLERY, RAINER WALTER, anatomy educator; b. Greifswald, Germany, Aug. 28, 1929; came to U.S., 1964; s. Hermann and Eva (Hackel) G.; m. Margot Cunningham Pepper, Dec. 21, 1954; children: Peter, Edward, Philip, Jane. B.Sc. in Anatomy, U. Coll., London, Eng., 1951; Ph.D., 1954. Asst. lectr. Univ. Coll., London, Eng., 1953-57; lectr. Univ. Coll., 1957-63, reader, 1963-64; asso. prof. U. Wis. at Madison, 1964-68, prof. anatomy, 1968-77; prof. dept. pharm. and physiol. Scis. U. Chgo., 1977-84; Dr. Lee's prof. anatomy Oxford U., Eng., 1984-96; vis. prof. dept. anatomy U. Wis., Madison, 1996—. Mem. editorial bd.: Jour. Comparative Neurology, 1971—, Jour. Neurocytology, 1972-76, Jour. Neurophysiology, 1975-81, Neurosci., 1979—, Jour. Neurosci., 1980-90; editor-in-chief European Jour. Neurosci., 1987-92. Fellow U. Coll. London, 1987. Fellow Royal Soc.; mem. Soc. Neurosci., Physiol. Soc., Anatomical Soc. G.B., Ireland (pres. 1994-96). Rsch. on central nervous system, synapses, degeneration, devel. visual pathways. Offices: U Wis Dept Anatomy Sch Medicine 1300 University Ave Madison WI 53706-1510

GUILLIOUMA, LARRY JAY, JR., performing arts administrator, music educator; b. Massillon, Ohio, Apr. 23, 1950; s. Larry Jay and Molly (Galob) G. BS, U. North Ala., 1972, MA, 1975; postgrad., U. Miss., 1976-78. Cert. tchr., Tex. Band dir. Phil Campbell (Ala.) H. S., 1972-76; grad. asst. U. Miss. Band, Oxford, 1976-78; asst. dir. Victoria (Tex.) H. S., 1978-81; dir. bands Harlingen (Tex.) H. S., 1981-87, McAllen (Tex.) Pub. Schs., 1991—; musician Huntsville (Ala.) Symphony Orchestra, 1970-76, Victoria (Tex.) Symphony Orchestra, 1978-81. Named Outstanding Dir. Alamo Tournament of Bands, San Antonio, 1985, Best in Class, World of Music Festival, Dallas, 1986; named to Nata. Band Dirs. Hall of Fame, Daytona Beach, Fla.; Harlingen High Sch. Big Red Cardinal Band marched in Pasadena Tournament of Roses Parade, 1987. Mem. Nat. Band Assn., Tex. Music Educators Assn. (bd. dirs, region vice chmn., region band chmn.), Tex. Band Masters Assn., Phi Beta Mu. Avocations: bicycling, travel, computers, telecommunications. Home: 8951 S Gessner Apt 141 Houston TX 77074-2835

GUILLORY, CURTIS J., bishop; b. Mallet, La., Sept. 1, 1943. Student, Divine Word Coll., Chgo. Theol. Union, Creighton U. ordained priest Roman Cath. Ch., Dec. 16, 1972. Appointed titular bishop of Stagno and Aux. Bishop of Galveston-Houston, 1988. Office: Chancery Office 1700 San Jacinto St Houston TX 77002-8291*

GUILLORY, JEFFERY MICHAEL, lawyer; b. Kansas City, Mo., July 26, 1966; s. Glenford Lee and Brenda Charlene (Thomas) G.; m. Leanna Carol Rainbolt, Aug. 10, 1991. Student, Mo. So. State Coll., Joplin, 1984-86; BA in Polit. Sci., Ctrl. Meth. Coll., Fayette, Mo., 1988; JD, U. Ark., 1991. Bar: Mo. 1991, U.S. Dist. Ct. (we. dist.) Mo. 1991, U.S. Supreme Ct. 1994. Law clk. Hall, Wright & Baker, P.A., Fayetteville, Ark., 1989-91; assoc. atty. Law Office of Allan C. Wilcox, Joplin, 1991-92; ptnr. Wilcox & Guillory, Joplin, 1992-95; assoc. atty. Roberts, Fleischaker, Williams, Wilson & Powell, Joplin, 1995-97; pvt. practice Law Office Jeffery M. Guillory, Joplin, 1997—; adj. prof. Mo. So. State Coll., 1995—. Bd. dirs., v.p. Habitat for Humanity, 1996—; property trustee United Meth. Ch. Mo. West Conf., 1996—; asst. scoutmaster Boy Scouts Am., Joplin, 1991—; chmn. bd. Discovery Presch., 1996-98. Mem. ABA, ATLA, Am. Immigration Lawyers Assn., Mo. Bar Assn., Mo. Assn. Trial Lawyers, Jasper County Bar Assn., Kiwanis. Avocations: camping, travel, skiing, volleyball, arts and crafts. Office: PO Box 1613 Joplin MO 64802-1613

GUILLOT, CYRIL ETIENNE, international organization administrator; b. Paris, Sept. 24, 1962; s. Jacques Rene and Ann Patricia (Lawrence) G. Cert., U. de Belgrano, Buenos Aires, 1984, U. de Los Andes, Bogota, Colombia, 1984; BA, Johns Hopkins U., 1984, MA, 1985. Field implementation officer UN Capital Devel. Fund, N'Djamena, Chad, 1987-89; assoc., project mgmt. officer UN Office for Project Svcs., N.Y.C., 1989-93; country officer UN Capital Devel. Fund, N.Y.C., 1993—. Study grantee Orgn. of Am. States, 1984. Mem. Fgn. Policy Assn. Avocation: travel. Home: 17 Birch Ln Larchmont NY 10538-3817 Office: UN Capital Devel Fund 1 UN Plz # Dc2-2623 New York NY 10017-3515

GUIMBELLOT, BOBBY E., hotel executive; b. La., July 27, 1941. Pres. Southern Scottish Inns, 1976-94, CEO; prin. shareholder, chmn. bd. Western Wireline Svcs., Inc., Belle Chasse, La.; chmn. Red Carpet Inns Internat., Inc., pres., 1992; CEO Hospitality Internat. subsidiary Southern Scottish Inn, Inc., 1995—. Office: Hospitality Internat Inc 1726 Montreal Circle Tucker GA 30084-6809

GUIMOND, JOHN PATRICK, retired financial consultant; b. Green Bay, Wis., June 5, 1927; s. Herbert A. and Elizabeth M. Guimond; m. Avyce L. Veek, Aug. 20, 1949 (dec. Sept. 1981); children: John Patrick, James T., Cheryl L., Lisa M., Leanne M.; m. Marilyn L. Lippitt, Oct. 23, 1985. B.B.A., U. Wis., 1951. Controller Rayovac div. ESB Inc., Madison, Wis.; v.p. adminstrn. Rayovac div. ESB Inc., 1974-77; treas. ESB Inc., Phila., 1977-79; sr. v.p. Rayovac Corp., Madison, Wis., 1979-83; prin. Guimond Fin. Services, Madison, 1983-93, Tucson, 1994-96. With USAF, 1945-47.

GUIN, JEFFERY KEITH, graphic designer; b. Natchitoches, La., July 9, 1971; s. Jacky Lee and Jeannie Carolyn (Thompson) G. BA, N.W. State U., 1995. News editor, sales Wal-Mart Stores, Natchitoches, La., 1988-95; comm. coord. so. region Willamette Industries, Ruston, La., 1995—; graphic designer Want Ads of Shreveport, La., 1996—; pub. rels. cons. Red River Mill, Campti, La., 1994—; editor Current Sauce Newspaper, Natchitoches, 1994-95. Vol. Christian Coalition. Mem. Soc. Profl. Journalists. Rep. Bapt. Avocations: photography, novel writing, oil painting. Home: 166 Ezell Rd Dubach LA 71235-3430

GUIN, JUNIUS FOY, JR., federal judge; b. Russellville, Ala., Feb. 2, 1924; s. Junius Foy and Ruby (Pace) G.; m. Dorace Jean Caldwell, July 18, 1945; children: Janet Elizabeth Smith, Judith Ann Mullican, Junius Foy III, David Jonathan. Student, Ga. Inst. Tech., 1940-41; AB magna cum laude, U. Ala., JD, 1947; LLD, Magic Valley Christian Coll., 1963. Bar: Ala. 1948. Pvt. practice law Russellville; sr. ptnr. Guin, Bouldin & Porch, 1948-73; fed. dist. judge U.S. Dist. Ct. (no. dist.) Ala., Birmingham, from 1973, now sr. judge; commr. Ala. Bar, 1965-73, 2d v.p., 1969-70; Pres. Abstract Trust Co., Inc., 1958-73; sec. Iuka TV Cable Co., Inc., Haleyville TV Cable Co., Inc., 1963-73; former dir., gen. counsel First Nat. Bank of Russellville, Franklin Fed. Savs. & Loan Assn. of Russellville.; Lectr. Cumberland-Samford Sch. Law, 1974—, U. Ala. Sch. Law, 1977—. Chmn. Russellville City Planning Com., 1954-57; 1st chmn. Jud. Commn. Ala., 1972-73; mem.

Ala. Supreme Ct. Adv. Com. (rules civil procedure), 1971-73; mem. adv. com. on standards of conduct U.S. Jud. Conf., 1980-87, mem. com. on Fed.-State Jurisdiction, 1982-88, mem. ad hoc com. on cameras in the courtroom, 1982-83; Rep. county chmn., 1954-58, 71-72, Rep. state fin. chmn., 1972-73; candidate for U.S. Senator from, Ala., 1954; Ala. Lawyers' Finance chmn. Com. to Re-elect Pres., 1972; former trustee Ala. Christian Coll., Faulkner U., Magic Valley Christian Coll., Childhaven Children's Home; elder Ch. of Christ. Served to 1st lt., inf. AUS, 1943-46. Named Russellville Citizen of Year, 1973; recipient Dean's award U. Ala. Law Sch., 1977. Mem. ABA (mem. spl. com. on resdl. real estate transactions 917-73), Am. Radio Relay League, Ala. Bar Assn. (com. chmn. 1965-73, Award of Merit 1973), Jefferson County Bar Assn., Fed. Bar Assn., Am. Law Inst., Ala. Law Inst. (dir. 1969-73, 76—), Am. Judicature Soc., Farrah Law Soc., Farrah Order Jurisprudence (now Order of Coif), Phi Beta Kappa, Omicron Delta Kappa, Delta Chi. Office: US Dist Ct 619 US Courthouse 1729 5th Ave N Birmingham AL 35203-2000

GUINDON, YVAN, science administrator, research scientist; b. Montreal, Que., Can., Nov. 7, 1951; s. Fernand and Gilberte (Fortin) G.; children: Marie-Eve, Veronique, Vincent, Nicolas. BSc in Chemistry, U. Montreal, 1974, PhD in Organic Chemistry, 1981; Diploma in Adminstrv. Scis., H.E.C. Sch. Bus. Adminstrn., Montreal, 1983. Sr. rsch. chemist Merck Frosst Can., Inc., Montreal, 1979-82, group leader, rsch. fellow, 1982-83, assoc. dir. medicinal chemistry, then dir. and sr. dir., 1983-87; sci. dir. Bio-Mega/Boehringer Ingelheim Rsch. Inc., Laval, Que., 1987-88; v.p. R&D Bio-Mega/Boehringer Ingelheim Rsch. Inc., Laval, 1988-94; also bd. dirs. Bio-Mega/Boehringer Ingelheim Rsch. Inc., 1991-94; CEO and sci. dir. Inst. Rsch. Cliniques de Montreal, 1994—; mem. com. on targeted rsch. Natural Scis. and Engring. Rsch. Coun. Can., 1988, 95-97, Fonds pour la Formation de chercheurs et l'Aide à la Rsch. Que., 1991; spkr. in field. Contbr. articles to profl. jours., chpts. to books; holder 48 patents. Natural Scis. and Engring. Rsch. Coun. Can. scholar, 1976-78. Fellow Chem. Inst. Can.; mem. AAAS, Royal Soc. Can., Can. Acad. Scis., Am. Chem. Soc., Ordre des Chimistes du Que., Assn. Canadienne-Francaise pour l'Avancement des Scis., Pharm. Soc. Can., N.Y. Acad. Scis. Office: Inst Rsch Cliniques de Montréal, 110 Pine Ave W, Montreal, PQ Canada H2W 1R7

GUINEY, MORTIMER MARTIN, French educator; b. Phila., June 23, 1959; s. Mortimer Martin and Louise (Purves) G.; m. Amy Kathleen Mock, July 16, 1995. BA, U. Mass., 1980; PhD, Yale U., 1987. Asst. prof. French Kenyon Coll., Gambier, Ohio, 1987-94; assoc. prof. French Kenyon Coll., Gambier, 1994—. Contbr. articles to jours. in field. Mem. MLA, Am. Assn. Tchrs. French, Am. Comparative Lit. Assn., Soc. Study Narrative Lit. Office: Kenyon Coll Gambier OH 43022

GUINN, JANET MARTIN, psychologist, consultant; b. Rapid City, S.D., Aug. 16, 1942; d. Verne Oliver and Carolyn Yetta (Clark) Martin; m. David Lee Guinn, Oct. 27, 1962 (div. June 1988); children: Cynthia Gail, Kevin Scott, Garrett Lee. BS in Psychology, U. Alaska, 1980, MS in Counseling Psychology, 1983; PhD in Clin. Psychology, Calif. Sch. Profl. Psychology, 1988. Lic. psychologist, Alaska, Nev. Pvt. practice Anchorage, 1988-93, Carson City and Reno, Nev., 1993—; clinician Behavior Medicine Cons., 1983-84; pvt. practice clinician, 1983-84; supr. Southcentral Counseling Ctr., Anchorage, 1984-85; cons. City/Borough of Juneau, Alaska, 1988; psychologist youth treatment program Alaska Psychiat. Inst., Anchorage, 1989-90; psychologist Nev. Mental Health Inst., Sparks, 1994-97; cons. in field; cons. Alaska Small Bus. Coalition, Anchorage, 1990-92; reviewer Blors Corp. Contbr. articles to profl. jours. Active in politics. Mem. APA, Am. Coll. Forensic Examiners, Nev. Psychol. Assn., Internat. Neuropsychol. Soc., Rotary, Psi Chi. Republican. Avocations: skiing, gourmet cooking, dancing. Office: 2470 Wrondel Way # 102 Reno NV 89502-3701

GUINN, KENNY C., governor; b. Garland, Ark., Aug. 24, 1936; married. BA, Calif. State U., Fresno, MA; EdD, Utah State U. Supt. Clark County Sch. Dist.; v.p. adminstrn. Nev. Savs. and Loan Assn. (PriMerit Bank), 1978-80, pres., chief operating officer, 1980-85, chief exec. officer, 1985-92, now chmn. bd.; pres. Southwest Gas Corp., 1987-88, chmn., chief exec. officer, 1988-93; chmn. bd. S.W. Gas Corp.; gov. State of Nev., Carson City, 1999—. Office: Office of the Governor Capitol Bldg 101 N Carson St Carson City NV 89710

GUINN, STANLEY WILLIS, lawyer; b. Detroit, June 9, 1953; s. Willis Hampton and Virginia Mae (Pierson) G.; m. Patricia Shirley Newgord, June 13, 1981; children: Terri Lanae, Scott Stanley. BBA with high distinction, U. Mich., 1979, MBA with distinction, 1981; MS in Taxation with distinction, Walsh Coll., 1987; JD cum laude, U. Mich., 1992. CPA, Mich.; cert. mgmt. acct., Mich. Tax mgr. Coopers & Lybrand, Detroit, 1981-87; tax cons. Upjohn Co., Kalamazoo, 1987-89; litigation atty. Brobeck, Phleger & Harrison, 1992-94, Coughlan, Semmer & Lipman, San Diego, 1994-95; consumer fin. atty. Bank Am. NT & SA, San Francisco, 1995-98, Green Point Credit Corp., San Diego, 1998—. Served with USN, 1974-77. Mem. AICPA, ABA, Calif. State Bar Assn., Inst. Cert. Mgmt. Acctg., Phi Kappa Phi, Beta Gamma Sigma, Beta Alpha Psi, Delta Mu Delta. Republican. Presbyterian. Avocations: tennis, racquetball, running. E-mail: sguinn@gp-credit.com. Home: 3125 Crystal Ct Escondido CA 92025-7763 Office: Green Pt Credit Corp 10089 Willow Creek Rd San Diego CA 92131-1603

GUINNESS, SIR ALEC, actor; b. London, Apr. 2, 1914; m. Merula Salaman; 1 child, Matthew. Student, Pembroke Lodge, Eng., Roborough Sch., Eng., Fay Compton Studio Dramatic Art; DFA (hon.), Boston Coll., 1962; DLitt (hon.), Oxford U., Eng., 1977; LittD (hon.), Cambridge (Eng.) U., 1991. Copywriter, Arks Publicity, 1933. Debut with walk-on role in Libel!, 1934; Shakespearean debut in Hamlet, 1934; appeared with Old Vic Co., 1936-37; toured Europe and Egypt, 1938-39; with John Gielgud's Co., 1937-38; appeared in own adaptation of The Brothers Karamazov, 1946; in Vicious Circle, 1946; with Old Vic Co., 1946-48; dir.: Twelfth Night, 1948; appeared in: The Human Touch, 1949, The Cocktail Party, N.Y.C. and Edinburgh, Scotland, 1949-50; Richard III and All's Well That Ends Well, Stratford Shakespeare Festival, Ont., Can., 1953, The Prisoner, 1954, Hotel Paradiso, 1956, Ross, 1960 (London Evening Standard award), Exit the King, 1963, Dylan, N.Y.C., 1964 (Tony award), Time Out of Mind, 1970, A Voyage Round My Father, 1971, Habeas Corpus, 1973, Yahoo, 1976, The Old Country, 1977-78, The Merchant of Venice, 1983, A Walk in the Woods, 1988; actor, dir.: The Cocktail Party, 1968; film appearances include Great Expectations, 1945, Oliver Twist, 1948, Mudlark, 1950, Kind Hearts and Coronets, 1951, The Lavender Hill Mob, 1951 (Acad. award nomination), The Man in the White Suit, 1951, Captain's Paradise, 1953, The Prisoner, 1956, The Bridge on the River Kwai (Acad. award, Golden Globe award, Brit. Film Acad. award 1957), The Horse's Mouth, 1958 (Venice Film Festival award, Acad. award nomination for script), Our Man in Havana, 1960, Tunes of Glory, 1960, Lawrence of Arabia, 1962, Dr. Zhivago, 1965, The Comedians, 1967, Cromwell, 1970, Murder by Death, 1976, Star Wars, 1977 (Acad. award nomination), Lovesick, 1982, Passage to India, 1984, Little Dorritt, 1986 (Acad. award nomination), A Handful of Dust, 1987, Kafka, 1990; Am. TV debut in The Wicked Scheme of Jebal Deeks, 1959; Brit. TV appearances include Tinker Tailor Soldier Spy, 1979 (Brit. Film Acad. TV award), Little Lord Fauntleroy, 1980, Smiley's People, 1981 (Brit. Film Acad. TV award), Edwin, 1983, Monsignor Quixote, 1985, Tales from Hollywood, 1991, A Foreign Field, 1992; author: Blessings in Disguise, 1985, My Name Escapes Me, 1996, A Positively Final Appearance, 1999, Eskimo Day, 1996. Served in Vol. Res., Royal Navy, 1941-45; commd. lt. 1942. Decorated comdr. Order Brit. Empire, 1955 (U.K.); knight bachelor, 1959 (U.K.); recipient Acad. award for svcs. to cinema, 1980, Swet/Olivier Spl. award for lifetimes's contbn. to theatre, 1989; Film Soc. of Lincoln Ctr. Tribute, 1987; Berlin Film Festival Golden Bear Tribute, 1988. Fellow Brit. Acad. Film and TV Arts, Brit. Film Inst., Companion of Honour.

GUINOUARD, DONALD EDGAR, psychologist; b. Bozeman, Mont., Mar. 31, 1929; s. Edgar Arthur and Venabell (Ford) G.; m. Irene M. Egeler, Mar. 30, 1951; children: Grant M., Philip A., Donna I. BS, Mont. State U., Bozeman, 1954; MS, Mont. State U., 1955; EdD, Wash. State U., Pullman, 1960; postdoctoral, Stanford U., 1965; grad., Indsl. Coll. of the Armed Forces, 1964, Air War Coll., 1976. Lic. psychologist, Ariz., counselor, Wash., Mont.; cert. secondary tchr. and sch. adminstr., Wash., Mont.; diplomate Am. Psychotherapy Assn. Advanced through grades to col. USAFR, 1946-84, ret., 1984; dir. counseling Consol. Sch. Dist., Pullman, Wash., 1955-60; assoc. prof. Mont. State U., Bozeman, 1960-66; field selection officer Peace Corps, U.S., S.Am., 1962-68; prof. counseling, counseling psychologist Ariz. State U., Tempe, 1966-90; prof. emeritus, 1990; co-owner Forensic Cons. Assocs., Tempe, 1970—; pvt. practice, 1990—; admissions liaison officer USAF Acad., Colo. Springs, 1967-84; assessment officer Fundamental Edn. Ctr. for the Devel. of the Latin American Community, Patzcuaro, Mex., 1963-64; expert witness on vocat. and psychol. disability for fed. and state cts. Contbr. articles to profl. jours. Mem. Ariz. Psychol. Assn., Am. Assn. Counseling & Devel., Reserve Officers Assn. Democrat. Methodist. Avocations: photography, woodworking, camping, fishing, silversmithing. Home and Office: 112 E Cairo Dr Tempe AZ 85282-3606

GUINOUARD, PHILIP ANDRE, restaurant executive; b. Pullman, Wash., Apr. 9, 1960; s. Donald Edgar and Irene (Egeler) G.; m. Miquela Teresa Padilla, Feb. 16, 1988; childern: Mia, Angela. Student, Mesa (Ariz.) Community Coll. Dir. quality Garcia's, Phoenix, 1978-84; area spr. El Pollo Asado Inc., Phoenix, 1985-89; gen. mgr. Quinto Patio, Evergreen, Colo., 1989-90, Garcia's, Littleton, Colo., 1990—, Quila's Fresh Mexican Cantina, 1993-94; field tng. mgr. Internat. House of Pancakes, 1994-95; pres., CEO Sub & Munch, 1995—; pres. S.W. Automated Payment Svc., 1997—. Mem. Colo. Restaurant Assn. Avocations: sports, photography. Home: 1714 W Manor St Chandler AZ 85224-5105 Office: 230 W Baseline Rd Ste 103B Tempe AZ 85283-1261

GUINSBURG, PHILIP FRIED, alcohol and substance abuse counselor; b. N.Y.C., Sept. 13, 1946; s. Theodore and Elena (Fried) G.; m. Debrah Josias Guinsburg, June 15, 1968; children: Mark, Michael. BA, Columbia Coll., 1968; MA, U. N.D., 1970, PhD, 1973. Diplomate Am. Bd. Med. Psychotherapy; lic. alcohol and drug abuse counselor. Clin. dir. Nashville Drug Treatment Ctr., Dede Wallace Ctr., 1973-78; pvt. practice Nashville, 1974—; asst. clin. prof. psychiatry Vanderbilt U., Nashville, 1987-93; cons. Crisis Intervention Ctr., 1974—; pres. Dreammakers, Inc., Nashville, 1989-91. Baseball coach Brentwood (Tenn.) Civitan Little League, 1982-92. Mem. Am. Counseling Assn., Am. Group Psychotherapy Assn., Am. Acad. Psychoterhapists (chair continuing edn., treas.), Assn. for Spiritual, Ethical and Religious Values in Counseling, Nat. Assn. Alcoholism and Drug Abuse Counselors, Tenn. Assn. Alcohol and Drug Abuse Counselors (pres.-elect). Jewish. Avocations: gardening, sports, gourmet foods. Home: 8121 Maryland Ln Brentwood TN 37027-7341 Office: 2313 21st Ave S Nashville TN 37212-4908

GUION, ROBERT MORGAN, psychologist, educator; b. Indpls., Sept. 14, 1924; s. Leroy Herbert and Carolyn (Morgan) G.; m. Mary Emily Firestone, June 8, 1947; children: David Michael, Diana Lynn, Keith Douglas, Pamela Sue, Judith Elaine. BA, State U. Iowa, 1948; MS, Purdue U., 1950, PhD, 1952. Vocat. counselor Purdue U., 1948-51, research fellow, 1951-52; mem. faculty Bowling Green (Ohio) State U., 1952—, prof. psychology, 1964—, univ. prof., 1983-85, univ. prof. emeritus, 1985—, chmn. dept., 1966-71; vis. prof. U. Calif. at Berkeley, 1963-64, U. N.Mex., summer 1965; tech. adviser Dept. Personnel Services, State Hawaii, summer 1970; vis. research psychologist Ednl. Testing Service, 1971-72; cons. in field, 1954—. Author: Personnel Testing, 1965, Assessment, Measurement and Prediction for Personnel Decisions, 1998; editor Jour. Applied Psychology, 1983-88. Served with AUS, 1943-46. Mem. Am. Psychol. Assn. (pres. div. 14 1972-73, pres. div. 5 1982-83, James McKeen Cattell award div. 14 1965, 81, Disting. Sci. Contbn. award div. 14 1987, Disting. Svc. award div. 14 1993, Lifetime Contbrn. award divsn. 5 1997), Internat. Assn. Applied Psychology, Am. Edn. Rsch. Assn., Nat. Coun. on Measurement in Edn., Am. Psychol. Soc. Methodist. Home: 632 Haskins Rd Bowling Green OH 43402-1615

GUIRGUIS, RAOUF ALBERT, health science executive; b. Cairo, Egypt, Aug. 25, 1953; came to U.S., 1983; s. Albert Amin Guirguis and Georgette Dahabi; m. Dana Lynn Lebo, Aug. 26, 1982 (div. June 1988); 1 child, Sandra Gene; m. Loretta Elisabeth Moschetti, July 14, 1989; 2 children. MD, Alexandria U., Alexandria, Arab Republic of Egypt, 1978; MS, Georgetown U., 1986, PhD, 1988. Intern Alexandria U. Sch. Medicine, 1979-80, navy fellow, 1980-83; rsch. assoc. Lombardi Cancer Ctr., Washington, 1983-84; rsch. fellow Nat. Cancer Inst., NIH, Bethesda, Md., 1984-89; chmn. of the bd. Antibody Resources Inc., Gaithersburg, Md., 1989-93; pres., CEO Cancer Diagnostics Inc., Rockville, Md., 1989-94; chmn. of the bd. Fingerprint Biotek Inc., Rockville, 1989-94; chmn., CEO Lamina Ltd., Wilmington, Del., 1991—; chmn. Comprehensive Cancer Care Ctrs. LLP, 1994—, Cancer Diagnostics Holding Co., Fairfax, Va., 1995—; co-founder, chmn., CEO Point of Care Techs. Inc., Fairfax, Va., 1996-97; pres., CEO MonoGen, Inc., Fairfax, Va., 1996—; cons. Nephrology Cancer Ctr., Mansura, Arab Rep. of Egypt, 1988-94; adj. assoc. prof. dept. physiology and biophysics Georgetown U. Med. Sch., Washington, 1988-94. Contbr. articles to profl. jours. Assoc. Smithsonian, Washington, 1990; mem. Kennedy Ctr., Washington, 1990, Georgetown Club, Washington, 1989; mem. Balt. Coun. on Fgn. Affairs; bd. dirs. U.S. Israel Biotech. Coun. Georgetown U. scholar, 1984-88, Saudi Minister of Health scholar, 1986-88; Nat. Coun. of Churches Rsch. grantee, 1986, Hoffmann-LaRoche Innovation Rsch. grantee, 1986. Mem. AMA (chief exec. divsn.), AAAS, Am. Math. Assn., Am. Assn. for Clin. Chemistry, Am. Soc. for Microbiology, Am. Chem. Soc., Am. Mgmt. Assn., N.Y. Acad. Sci., Soc. for Computer Simulation, IEEE Computer Soc., Sigma Xi. Republican. Coptic Orthodox. Achievements include patents and trademarks for CDI Shuttle System, a cancer screening and laboratory testing device, a method for CytoShuttle a monolayer cytology device, a method for LC-Shuttle a chromatography device for multiple marker panels, for Assay-Shuttle a bead based immuno-assay, a Cell Chamber for chemotaxis assay, a Modular Multiple Fluid Sample Preparation Assembly, a Blood Withdrawing Apparatus and a Antigen Testing Method, a Enviromental Sample Collection and Testing Device, a Blood Testing and Fingerprint Identification Method; patents pending for Preparation and Isolation of Intact Pseudopodia Fragments, a Urine Testing Apparatus with Urinary Sediment Device, a Intact and Isolated Pseudopodia Fragments/A Model SYstem for Cell Migration, a Possible Role for Membrane Fusion in Tumor Cell Invasion and Metastasis, and a New Method and Device for the Early Detection of Cancer Using Body Fluids (mainly urine). Office: MonoGen Inc 2190 Fox Mill Rd Herndon VA 20171-3017

GUIROLA, LOUIS, JR., federal judge; b. 1951. BA, William Carrey Coll., 1973; JD, U. Miss., 1979. Assoc. Holleman & Assocs., 1979-80; asst. dist. atty. Miss., 1980-84; county bd. atty. Jackson County Port Authority, 1984-86; ptnr. Guirola & Jackson, 1986-90; dep. chief criminal divsn., lead Crime and Drug Envorcement Task Force, 1990-93; magistrate judge U.S. Dist. Ct. (we. dist.) Tex., 1993-96, U.S. Dist. Ct. (so. dist.) Miss., 1996—; adj. prof. William Carey Coll., 1979-81, U. So. Miss., 1981-85. Fax: (601) 554-9177. Office: US Dist Ct (so dist) Miss 701 Main St Ste 216 Hattiesburg MS 39401

GUISE, DAVID EARL, architect, educator; b. N.Y.C., Dec. 29, 1931; s. Jack I. and Frances (Haberman) G.; m. Gretchen Grunenfelder, Nov. 21, 1962; children: Gabrielle Ann, John George, Jacqueline Alexis, Ursula Claire. BArch with honors, U. Pa., 1957. Job capt. Kahn & Jacobs, Architects N.Y.C., 1957-60; designer draftsman E.J. Robin, Architect, N.Y.C., 1961; architect David Guise, Architect, N.Y.C., 1962—; asst. prof. Sch. Architecture, CCNY, 1966-70, assoc. prof., 1970-76, prof., 1976-91; prof. emeritus CCNY, 1991—; adj. prof. Columbia U., 1983-85, CCNY, 1993—; vis. prof. U. Pa., 1990. Author: Design and Technology in Architecture, 1985, rev. edit., 1991; contbr. articles to profl. jours., Ency. Britannica yearbook; architect numerous comml. and residential bldgs. Mem. panel Am. Arbitration Assn., 1967—; sec. Irvington Planning Bd., N.Y., 1974-88. Mem. Bldg. Rsch. Inst. Home: PO Box 132 Georgetown ME 04548-0132 Office: 250 W 57th St New York NY 10107

GUITTAR, LEE JOHN, retired newspaper executive; b. St. Louis, May 4, 1931; s. LeRoy and Edna Mae (Johnston) G.; m. Elizabeth Madden Shedrick, Aug. 23, 1980; children—David Lee, Stephen Joseph, Mitchell John, Jeanne Marie, Richard Laughran; step-children: Elisabeth F. Shedrick, Kathryn S. Shedrick, Daniel C. Shedrick. AB, Columbia U., 1953; postgrad., U. Mass., 1962; MA, Columbia U., 1993. With Gen. Electric Co., 1955-65; mgr. community and govt. relations programs Gen. Electric Co., N.Y.C., 1963-65; mgr. employee and pub. relations Tidewater Oil Co., N.Y.C., 1965-66; from personnel dir. to circulation dir. Miami (Fla.) Herald, 1967-71; v.p., bus. mgr. Detroit Free Press, 1972-74, v.p., gen. mgr., 1974-75, pres., dir., 1975-77; pub. Dallas Times Herald, 1977-80; Publisher The Denver Post, 1980-83; chmn. Denver Post, 1983; pres. U.S.A. Today, 1984-86; v.p. group exec. newspapers The Hearst Corp., N.Y.C., 1986-98; editor, pub. San Francisco Examiner, 1995-98, ret., 1998. Lt. (j.g.) USNR, 1953-55, Korea. Mem. Am. Newspaper Pubs. Assn., Am. Press Inst., Farm Neck Golf Club (Martha's Vineyard, Mass.), Phi Beta Kappa. Republican. Roman Catholic.

GUIVENS, NORMAN ROY, JR., mathematician, engineer; b. Brockton, Mass., May 8, 1957; s. Norman Roy and Lula Elizabeth (Wager) G. SB in Math., MIT, 1979, SM in Meteorology, 1979; MTS in Pastoral Ministry, St. Meinrad Sch. Theology, 1992. Teaching asst. MIT Dept. Ocean Engring., Cambridge, Mass., 1979; cons. to Lincoln Lab. Mass. Tech. Lab., West Newton, 1984; sr. engr. SPARTA, Inc., Lexington, Mass., 1984—. Contbr. over 15 articles to profl. jours. Lt. USN, 1979-84. Mem. IEEE (chpt. chmn. 1990-93), Soc. Photo-Optical Instrumentation Engrs., U.S. Naval Inst. Roman Catholic. Achievements include devel. of first successful simulation of coherent laser radars, comprehensive model for optical detection system, defense laser/target signatures (DELTAS) code, application of genetic algorithms to design of unconventional imaging systems, modular software architecture for control of robots and peripheral equipment, devel. of scene description language compiler for 3-D solid models, devel. of adaptive topographic model with automatic resolution matching capability. Office: SPARTA Inc 24 Hartwell Ave Lexington MA 02421-3157

GULATI, SUNIL, sports association administrator; b. Allahabad, India, 1959; m. Marcela Gulati; 1 child, Emilio. BA magna cum laude, Bucknell U.; MA, MPhil in Econs., Columbia U. Asst. prof. econs. Columbia U., 1986-90; with World Bank, 1991; dep. commr. Major League Soccer, 1993—; mng. dir. nat. teams, chmn. internat. games com., nat. teams com., U.S. Cup 1992 and 1993 U.S. Soccer Fedn., 1987-94; exec. v.p., chief internat. officer, mem. mgmt. com. World Cup USA, 1994; bd. dirs. 1999 Women's World Cup, U.S. Soccer, U.S. Soccer Found. Mem. Phi Beta Kappa. Office: c/o Major League Soccer 110 E 42nd St 10th Fl New York NY 10017-5611*

GULATI, VIPIN, accountant; b. New Delhi, India, Nov. 3, 1953; came to U.S., 1982; s. Har Kishan Lal and Shakuntalarani (Sachdeva) G.; m. Raman Bais, July 24, 1986; children: Sheena, Shawn. Diploma hotel mgmt., Inst. Hotel Mgmt., Bombay, India, 1976; BA, U. Delhi, 1979; MBA, U. Rajasthan, Jaipur, India, 1981. CPA, Mich. Gen. mgr. Hotel Kandhari, Vijayawada, India, 1979-81; mgr. food and beverage Holiday Inn, Agra, India, 1981-82; acct. Irving Kaplan, Farmington Hills, Mich., 1983-87, S.B. Malerman P.C., Southfield, Mich., 1987-88; chief fin. officer Heidi's Salon, Birmingham, Mich., 1989-90; pres. Vipin Gulati, CPA, P.C., Bingham Farms, Mich., 1990—. Fellow AICPA, Mich. Assn. CPAs, Sports Club (West Bloomfield, Mich.). Avocations: tennis, golf, traveling. Home: 1961 Golf Ridge Dr Bloomfield Hills MI 48302-1724

GULBRANDSEN, NATALIE WEBBER, religious association administrator; b. Beverly, Mass., July 7, 1919; d. Arthur Hammond and Kathryn Mary (Doherty) Webber; m. Melvin H. Gulbrandsen, June 19, 1943 (dec. Feb. 23, 1991); children: Karen Ann Bean, Linda Jean Goldsmith, Eric Christian, Ellen Dale Williams, Kristin Jane Morgan. BA, Bates Coll., 1942, LLD (hon.), 1996; LHD (hon.), Meadville/Lombard Theol. Sch., Chgo., 1991. Social worker Bur. Child Welfare, Bangor, Maine. Exec. dir. Girl Scouts U.S., Belmont, Mass., 1943-45, leader 1941-44, 52-65, leadership trainer 1946-63, bd. dirs., Wellesley, Mass., 1950-63, pres. 1960-63; mem. permanent sch. accomodations com., Wellesley, 1970-76, Wellesley Youth Commn., 1968-70, Wellesley town meeting, 1967-91; trustee Wellesley Human Rels. Svc., 1964-76, pres. 1973-76; bd. dirs. Newton Wellesley Weston Needham Area Mental Health Assn., 1975-78, Am. Field Svc., 1964-70; co-chairperson METCO Program of Wellesley, 1965-69; trustee Unitarian Universalist Women's Fedn., 1971-81, pres. 1977-81, mem. commn. on appraisal, 1981-85; moderator Unitarian Universalist Assn., Boston, 1985-93; bd. dirs. Unitarian Universalist Ch. of the Larger Fellowship, 1992-98, chairperson bd. dirs., 1996-98, bd. dirs. Unitarian Universalist Women's Heritage Soc., 1994—. Recipient Wellesley Ctr. Cmty. award, 1981. Mem. AAUW, Boston Bates Alumnae Assn. (pres. 1966-69), Internat. Assn. Religious Freedom (mem. coun. 1981-90, v.p. 1990-93, pres. 1993-96, co-pres. U.S. and states chpt. 1997—). Home: 35 Riverdale Rd Wellesley MA 02481-1625 Office: Internat Assn for Religious Freedom, 2 Market St, Oxford 0X1 3EF, England

GULBRANDSEN, PATRICIA HUGHES, physician; b. May 9, 1940; d. Patrick Boland and Anne Hughes; m. Jon Alf Gulbrandsen, Mar. 6, 1972 (dec. Oct. 1984). BA, Cornell U., 1962; MD, U. Pa., 1967; MPH, Johns Hopkins U., 1980. Cert. Am. Bd. Disability Analysts; diplomate Am. Bd. Phys. Medicine and Rehab., Am. Bd. Occupl. Medicine; cert. med. rev. officer. Rotating intern Chgo. Wesley Meml. Hosp., 1967-68; resident in neurology Pa. Hosp., Phila., 1968-69, Georgetown U. Hosp., Washington, 1972-74; fellow in gynecologic endocrinology Chelsea Hosp. for Women, London, 1969-71; resident in phys. medicine and rehab. Good Samaritan Hosp., Phoenix, 1974-76; commd. maj. U.S. Army, 1979, advanced through grades to lt. col., 1982; with Walter Reed Army Med. Ctr., Washington, 1979-81; occupational medicine officer U.S. Army/Army Environ. Hygiene Agy., Aberdeen Proving Ground, Md., 1981-83; resigned U.S. Army, 1983; med. dir. USN/Naval Surface Warfare Ctr., Silver Spring, Md., 1984-89, Silver Spring, 1994; med. dir. NASA Hdqs., Washington, 1990-93; acting chief med. officer Hdqs. FBI, Washington, 1995; chief med. officer Hdqs. Drug Enforcement Adminstrn., Arlington, Va., 1996; dir. occupational medicine Profl. Occupational Health Svcs., 1997-98; staff physiatrist, head consultation svc. New Eng. Med. Ctr. Hosps., Boston, 1977-78; instr. neurology and phys. medicine and rehab. Tufts U. Sch. Medicine, Boston, 1977-78; med. cons. Fairfax County (Va.) Health Dept., 1990, Hummer and Assocs., Cleve., 1990-93, Allied Med. Cons., Inc., Washington, 1994-95, Hunter Med. Inc., Vienna, Va., 1995-96, Occu Save, Inc., Lanham, Md., 1996, staff proviledges Drs. Cmty. Hosp., Lanham, Md., 1996—, Hummer Whole Health Mgmt., 1998—. Mem. Montgomery County Med. Soc., Med. and Chirurgical Faculty of Md., Med. Soc. D.C., Am. Pub. Health Assn., Am. Coll. Occupational and Environ. Medicine. Republican. Avocations: phys. fitness, noetic scis., computer applications. Fax: 301-585-6519. Office: 9412 Hale Pl Silver Spring MD 20910-1307

GULCHER, ROBERT HARRY, aircraft company executive; b. Columbus, Ohio, Aug. 26, 1925; s. Alban H. and Beatrice (Plohr) G.; m. Barbara Witherspoon, June, 1949 (div.); 1 child, Robert; m. Anne Cummings, Dec. 14, 1959 (dec.); children: Jeffrey, Donald; m. Suzanne K. Kane, Apr. 12, 1969; children: Andrew, Kristin. B.S., U.S. Marine Acad., 1945; B.E.E., Ohio State U., 1950. Third asst. engr. Am. Petroleum Transp. Co., N.Y.C., 1945-46; engr. Capital Elevator & Mfg. Co., Columbus, Ohio, 1949-51; engr. Columbus div. N. Am. Aviation, 1951-53, various mgmt. engring. positions, 1953-66; chief engr. Columbus div. Rockwell Internat., 1966-79; v.p. rsch. and engring. N.Am. aircraft ops. Rockwell Internat., El Segundo, Calif., 1979-85, v.p. advanced programs N.Am. aircraft ops., 1985-87; v.p., program mgr. nat. aerospace plane Rockwell Internat., 1987-90; v.p. hypersonic programs Rockwell Internat., Downey, Calif., 1990-91; retired, 1991, aerospace cons., 1992—. Trustee Little Co. of Mary Hosp. Found., 1992—, chmn. bd. trustees, 1996-97; trustee coun. LCMH Hosp., 1997—. Fellow AIAA, IEEE (sr. mem.); mem. Rotary Internat. Republican. Lutheran.

GULDA, EDWARD JAMES, automotive executive; b. Detroit, Oct. 28, 1945; s. Alfred and Lucy Irene (Ball) G.; m. Nancy Mary Greenlee, Nov. 28, 1964; children: Kimberly Sue Marsh, Nicholas Edward. BS in Aerospace Engring., U. Mich., 1968, MBA, 1979. Systems engr. LTV Aerospace Corp., Sterling Heights, Mich., 1966-72; mgr. systems engring. Ford Motor Co., Dearborn, Mich., 1972-78; mgr., prodn. plan. Rockwell Internat. Corp., Dearborn, Mich., 1978-79; dir. prod. plan. Rockwell Internat. Corp., Troy, Mich., 1979-80, dir. mkt. electronics, 1980-81, gen. mgr. auto electronics, 1981-84, v.p. rsch. and engring., 1984-85; pres. ITT Teves Am., Troy, 1985-87; group v.p. engring. ITT Auto, Inc., Troy, 1987-88; pres., chief exec. officer Dayton Walther (Varity) Corp., Dayton, Ohio, 1988-89; pres. Varity Brake Group Kelsey-Hayes Brake Group N.Am., Romulus, Mich., 1989-94; pres. Kelsey-Hayes Co., Romulus, Mich., 1994-95; chief exec. Kelsey-Hayes Co., Livonia, Mich., 1995; chmn. and CEO Peregrine Inc., Southfield, Mich., 1996-98; pres. Kinnick Group LLC, 1998—. Mem. Soc. Automotive Engrs., Engring. Soc. Detroit, MENSA, Birmingham Country Club. Avocations:

hunting, golf. Office: Pergrine Inc 27777 Franklin Rd Ste 300 Southfield MI 48034-8254

GULDAN, JANICE MARIE, librarian; b. Roseboro, N.C., Sept. 19, 1949; d. Harold and Lillie Mae Faircloth; m. Robert Gene Guldon Sr., Jan. 8, 1968; children: Anjonette, Jenifer, Robert Jr., Matthew. BRE, Heritage Bible Coll., 1995; MLS, NCCU, 1998. Registrar Wang Lags., Inc., Rosslyn, Va., 1986-89; adminstrv. asst. Sears Operation Ctr., Millersville, Md., 1989-90; libr. Heritage Bible Coll., Dunn, N.C., 1990—. Avocations: reading, walking, gardening, church activities, sewing. Home: 919 Gremic Dr Linden NC 28356 Office: Heritage Bible Coll PO Box 1628 Dunn NC 28335

GULDEN, SIMON, lawyer, investment company executive; b. Montreal, Que., Can., Jan. 7, 1938; s. David and Zelda (Long) G.; m. Ellen Lee Barbour, June 12, 1977. B.A., McGill U., Montreal, 1959; cert., U. Rennes, 1961; LL.L., U. Montreal, 1962; cert., Wharton Sch., 1979. P. Adminstrn. Inst. Chartered Secs. and Adminstrs., 1982; Bar: Que. Ptnr. Genser, Philips, Friedman & Gulden, Montreal, 1963-68; sec., legal counsel Pl. Bonaventure, Inc., 1969-72; legal counsel real estate Steinberg Inc., Montreal, 1972-74; solicitor, prime atty. Bell Can., Montreal, 1975-76; v.p., gen. counsel, sec., dir. Nabisco Ltd, Toronto, 1975-98; pres., dir. Interlude Capital Corp., Unionville, Ont., Can., 1997—. Mem. ABA, Internat. Assn. Lawyers and Jurists, Internat. Fiscal Assn., Am. Corp. Counsel Assn., Am. Mgmt. Assn., Can. Mfrs. Assn., Can. Bar Assn., Internat. Bar Assn., Lord Reading Law Soc. Que., Osgoode Law Soc., Toronto Bd. Trade, Am. Mgmt. Assn., Inst. Chartered Secs. and Adminstrs. (cert.), Bar of Que., Island Yacht Club, Canadian Club, Cambridge Club (Toronto). Home: 23 Danbury Ct, Unionville, ON Canada L3R 7S1 Office: Interlude Capital Corp, 23 Danbury Ct, Unionville, ON Canada L3R 7S1

GULDNER, JOEL RAYMOND, librarian; b. Jan. 27, 1959. BA in German cum laude, U. Iowa, 1982, MA in Libr. and Info. Scis., 1990. Session libr. Legis. Counsel Bur., Carson City, Nev., 1990-91; asst. legis. libr., 1996—; bibliographic instrn. libr. Cornell Coll., Mt. Vernon, Iowa, 1991-92; mgr. Mich. Newspaper Project Libr. of Mich., Lansing, 1993-95. E-mail: guldner@lcb.state.nv.us.

GULGOWSKI, PAUL WILLIAM, German language, social science, and history educator; b. Oberhausen, Germany, July 4, 1940; s. Paul and Katharina (van Look) G.; m. Heide Anna Maria Hegenscheidt, July 6, 1989; children: Audrey-Annette, Paul William. BSc. U. Tex., El Paso, 1970; MA, Marquette U., 1992; PhD, U. Bremen, Germany, 1981. Cert. tchr., social sci., German and history. Commd. 2d lt. U.S. Army, 1970, advanced through grades to maj., 1981; gen. staff officer, comdr. combat and support forces U.S. Army, worldwide, 1970-80; polit. advisor, forces comdr. U.S. Army, Germany, 1980-82; prof. German U.S. Mil. Acad., West Point, N.Y., 1982-85; personal rep. of NATO Land Forces comdr., Heidelberg, Germany, 1985-87; ret. U.S. Army, 1987; lectr. German and fgn. lang. study methodology U. Wis., Whitewater, 1993—. Author: U.S. Military Government in Germany, 1983, Flucht aus Ostpreussen, 1986; author articles. Chief historian USCG Aux., Washington, 1992-94; comdr. Great Lakes Flotilla, 1994—; v.p. Wis. Profl. Edn. & Info. Coun., 1997—. Decorated D.S.M. with four oak leaf clusters; comdr.'s cross German Order of Merit. Mem. Phi Kappa Phi. Roman Catholic. Avocations: classical music, literature, skiing, boating, travel. Home: PO Box 180 347 Delafield WI 53018 Office: Heide Hall 800 W Main St Whitewater WI 53190-1705

GULICK, DONNA MARIE, accountant; b. N.Y.C., Jan. 25, 1956; d. H.R. and M.G. Gulick. MBA, Fairleigh Dickinson U., 1981, MS, 1986. Programmer Wash. State U., Pullman, 1983; acctg. analyst IBM, Tarrytown, N.Y., 1983-89, program mgr., 1989-91; program mgr. long-term disability plan IBM, Purchase, N.Y., 1991-92; staff acctg. analyst labor charges IBM, Tarrytown, N.Y., 1992-94; project mgr. IBM, Somers, N.Y., 1994—. Mem. Assn. MBA Execs., ACM, Inst. of IEEE, Nat. Assn. Unknown Players, Delta Mu Delta. Roman Catholic. Avocations: flying, skiing. Home: 395 State Route 28 Bridgewater NJ 08807-2471 Office: IBM Rt 100 Somers NY 10589

GULICK, PETER VANDYKE, lawyer; b. Honolulu, Feb. 15, 1930; s. Willard Clark and Harriet (Winch) G.; m. Kathryn Christen, June 23, 1952 (div. Mar. 1987); children: Willard, Sarah, Scott. AB, Princeton U., 1952; postgrad. Stanford U., 1952-53; LLB, U. Wash., 1956. Bar: Wash. 1956, U.S. Dist. Ct. (we. dist.) Wash. 1956, U.S. Ct. Appeals (9th cir.) 1957. Mem. Foster, Pepper & Riviera, Seattle, 1956-78; pvt. practice, Bellevue, Wash., 1979—. Scoutmaster, dist. Round Table commr., chief Seattle coun. Boy Scouts Am., 1971-77; pres. Lake Heights Community Club, 1960; commr. Newport Hills Sewer Dist., 1966-72. Recipient dist. merit award Boy Scouts Am., 1976. Mem. Wash. State Bar Assn., Seattle-King County Bar Assn. Office: 1380 112th NE Ste 202 Bellevue WA 98004-3759

GULICK, WALTER LAWRENCE, psychologist, former college president; b. Summit, N.J., July 4, 1927; s. Walter Lawrence and Carol (Dewey) G.; m. Winifred Bourn Frazee, Oct. 18, 1952; children—Hans, Tod, Kristina. A.B., Hamilton Coll., Clinton, N.Y., 1952; M.A. (Theta Delta Chi fellow), U. Del., 1955; M.A. (hon.), Dartmouth, 1968; Ph.D. (psychology scholar 1955-57), Princeton U., 1957; LHD (hon.), St. Lawrence U., 1989. Mem. faculty U. Del., 1957-65, prof. psychology, 1963-65, chmn. dept., 1964-65; prof. psychology Dartmouth, Hanover, N.H., 1965-74, chmn. dept., 1970-73; 74-75, Distinguished Class of 1925 prof., 1973-75; dean of coll. Hamilton Coll., 1975-79, prof. psychology, 1975-81, William R. Kenan prof., 1979-81; pres. St. Lawrence U., 1981-87, Gulick Assocs., 1987—; vis. prof. U. Vt., summer 1977; resident scholar U. Del., 1988—; cons. Presbyn. Hosp., Phila., 1961-63; editl. cons. Oxford U. Press, 1963—, McGraw-Hill Pub. Co., 1966-67, Harper & Row, 1971-73, Cambridge U. Press, 1979—; dir. Key Bank, N.A., 1981-87, NGM Ins. Co., 1981-86. Author: Hearing: Physiology and Psychophysics, 1971, Human Stereopsis: Psychophysical Analysis, 1976, Hearing: Physiological Acoustics, Neural Coding and Psychoacoustics, 1989; contbr. to Encyclopedia of Human Behavior, 1994; contbr. articles to profl. jours. Mem. Hanover Sch. Bd., 1972-75, Dresden Bd. Sch. Dirs., 1972-75; Mem. grad. council Princeton U., 1972-75; mem. adv. council Nat. Inst. for Humanities, 1975—; mem. teaching evaluation project HEW. Served with AUS, 1946-48. Recipient nat. svc. award 1955, 81; Dale prize music Hamilton Coll., 1952, alumni achievement medal Hamilton Coll., 1995. Mem. N.Y. Acad. Scis., Ea. Psychol. Assn., Psychonomic Soc., Phi Beta Kappa, Omicron Delta Kappa, Sigma Xi (pres. Dartmouth chpt. 1967-68, Gold Medal Lifetime Achievement award 1995), Psi Chi (pres. U. Del. chpt. 1954-55). Rsch. vision and hearing. Home: 205 Winslow Rd Newark DE 19711-4531 Office: Gulick Assocs Inc PO Box 1036 Newark DE 19715-1036

GULKIN, HARRY, arts administrator, film producer; b. Montreal, Que., Can., Nov. 14, 1927; s. Peter Oliver and Raya (Shinderman) G. Portrait photographer, 1942-44, mcht. seaman, trade union organizer, 1944-49, labour journalist, critic, trade union organizer, 1950-56, market researcher, cons., 1956-71, ind. film producer, 1971—; exec. and artistic dir. Saidye Bronfman Ctr., 1983-87; dir. projects Soc. Developpement Entrerises Culturelles, 1987; producer BAYO, 1985; challenger Nat. Film Bd., Can., 1979; adv. coun. film dept. Concordia U. Producer: Penny and Ann (2d prize Film Festival Internat. Congress Rehab. Centres 1976, award Amtec Media Festival 1977), 1974 (Red Ribbon Am. Film Festival 1977), Lies My Father Told Me (Hollywood Fgn. Critics award as best fgn. film 1975, Canadian Film award 1976, Grand prize V.I. Internat. Festival 1975, Christopher awards 1975, Assn. Can. TV and Radio Artists award 1976, Can. Motion Picture Distbrs. Assn. award 1976), Jacob Two Meets The Hooded Fang, 1976 (Gold medallion spl. jury award Miami Internat. Film Festival 1978, Spl. Jury award 8th Internat. Children's Film Festival, Los Angeles 1979), Two Solitudes, 1977; editor: The Marketer Jour., 1966. Mem. Motion Picture Inst. Can. (pres. 1977), Can. Film Inst. (past pres., chmn.), Assn. Que. Film Producers, Cinematheque Québecoise (v.p. 1995-99), Am. Mktg. Assn. (past chpt. pres.), Acad. Can. Cinema, Quebec Soc. for Promotion of English Lang. Lit. (mem. adv. coun.). Home: 111 St Joseph Blvd W, Montreal, PQ Canada H2T 2P7 Office: Soc Generale des Industries Culturelles, 1755 Blvd Rene-Levesque E, Bur 2006, Montreal, PQ Canada H2K 4P6

GULKO, EDWARD, health care executive, consultant; b. Paterson, N.J., Nov. 22, 1950; s. Benjamin and Anita (Yankelevsky) G.; m. Judith Ilene Lee, May 29, 1977. BS in Indsl. Engring., N.J. Inst. Tech., 1972; MBA, Temple U., 1974. Cert. healthcare exec., med. practice exec. Health program analyst Morrisania Hosp., Bronx, N.Y., 1974-75; assoc. dir. Mission Health Ctr., San Francisco, 1976; supervising systems analyst Health and Hosp. Corp., N.Y.C., 1977-78; dep. exec. dir. Greenpoint Hosp., Bklyn., 1978-82; assoc. exec. dir. Woodhull Med. Ctr., Bklyn., 1982-84; adminstr. Montclair (N.J.) Med. Group, 1984-87; asst. adminstr. Summit (N.J.) Med. Group, Summit, N.J., 1987-91; adminstr. Wooster (Ohio) Clinic, Inc., 1991-96; COO Grove Hill Med. Ctr., New Britain, Conn., 1996-99; exec. dir. Old Bridge-Sayreville Med. Group, Old Bridge, N.J., 1999—. Trustee Society Hill Townhouse Assn., 1986-90, v.p., 1987-88, pres., 1988-89; bd. dirs. Residential Support Svcs., 1993-96, v.p. 1993-96. Lt. cmdr. Med. Svcs. Corp. USNR, 1982-96. Mem. Am. Coll. Healthcare Execs., Assn. Mil. Surgeons U.S. (exec. com. N.J. chpt. 1985-87, pres. 1988-89), Med. Group Mgmt. Assn. (nat. comm. com. 1993-95), Naval Res. Assn. (dist. v.p. 1987-91), Am. Acad. Med. Adminstrs., Naval Inst., Am. Coll. Med. Practive Execs. Democrat. Home: 230 Seton Hall Dr Freehold NJ 07728 Office: Old Bridge-Sayreville Med Group 26 Throckmorton Ln Old Bridge NJ 08857

GULL, PAULA MAE, renal transplant coordinator, nephrology nurse, medical-surgical nurse; b. L.A., Mar. 7, 1955; d. Gerald Henry and Artemis (Cubillas) Balzer; m. Randell Jay Gull, July 10, 1976. AA, Cypress (Calif.) Coll., 1976; AS with high honors, Rancho Santiago Coll., Santa Ana, Calif., 1985; BSN with high honors, Calif. State U., Fullerton, 1993; MSN, Calif. State U., Long Beach, 1996. Cert. med. surg. nurse, nephrology nurse, nurse practitioner, clin. transplant coord. Staff RN U. Calif. Irvine Med. Ctr., Orange, Calif., 1986-87, asst. nurse mgr., 1987-88, nurse mgr., 1988; med.-surg. nurse N000, 1990—; coord. renal transplant U. Calif.-Irvine Med. Ctr., Orange, 1992—, St. Joseph Hosp., Orange. Mem. Am. Nephrology Nurses Assn., N.Am. Transplant Coord. Orgn., Calif. Coalition Nurse Practitioners. Mormon. Home: 24974 Enchanted Way Moreno Valley CA 92557-6410

GULLACE, MARLENE FRANCES, information engineer, systems analyst, consultant; b. Ft. Belvoir, Va., Jan. 12, 1952; d. Amerigo Francis and Martha Arlene (Wise) Guy; m. Gerald Lynn Tolley, June 26, 1970 (div. Nov. 1974); 1 child, Gerald Lynn Tolley Jr.; m. Salvatore Gullace, Nov. 19, 1976 (div. Apr. 1991). AA in Pre-Law, Cochise Coll., 1979; BA in Polit. Sci., U. Ariz., 1982; AA in Computer Sci., Bus., Chaparral Coll., 1985. Realtor, entrepreneur, inventor Sierra Vista, Ariz., 1977-84; ADP instr. Chaparral Coll., Tucson, 1985; model Barbizon, Tucson, 1986-87; clk. HUD/FHA, Tucson, 1987-88; computer programmer DOD Inspector Gen., Arlington, 1988-89; programmer analyst U.S. Army Corps of Engrs., USAF, Washington, 1989-91, Calibre Systems Inc., Falls Church, Va., 1991; cons., systems analyst/programmer EDP, Vienna, Va., 1991-93; info. engr. Ogden/Anteon Corp., Vienna, 1993-96, Orkand Corp., 1996, SRA Internat., Inc., 1997—. Patented toy, registered trademark. Realtor assoc. Cochise County Bd. Realtors, 1977-84. Mem. IEEE, Fed. Women's Program at SBA (sec. 1976), Internat. Council of System Engrs. Methodist. Avocations: art, design, crafts, sewing. Home: 7829 Piccadilly Dr Warrenton VA 20186-8623

GULLAND, EUGENE D., lawyer; b. Endicott, N.Y., Aug. 27, 1947; s. George Raymond and Virginia (Fisher) G.; m. Kristin Spearing, Aug. 29, 1970; children: Michael Spearing, Molly Spearing, Samuel Spearing. AB, Princeton U., 1969; JD, Yale U., 1972. Bar: D.C., Va., U.S. Supreme Ct., U.S. Ct. Appeals (1st, 2d, 3d, 4th, 6th, 9th, D.C., Fed. cirs.), U.S. Dist. Ct. D.C., (ea. dist.) Va., Md., Ariz., Ind. Assoc. Covington & Burling, Washington, 1973-80, ptnr., 1980—; practitioner before London Ct. Internat. Arbitration, Internat. C. or C., Am. Arbitration Assn., also other arbitral tribunals; mem. faculty Nat. Inst. for Trial Advocacy. Trustee Loudoun Day Sch., Leesburg, Va., 1986-98; vestryman, treas. Our Redeemer Ch., 1987-97; mem. alumni schs. com. Princeton U. Capt. U.S. Army, 1972-73. Woodrow Wilson scholar Princeton U., Princeton U. scholar. Mem. Nat. Assn. Coll. and Univ. Attys., Phi Beta Kappa. Home: Little River Farm Aldie VA 22001 Office: Covington & Burling PO Box 7566 1201 Pennsylvania Ave NW Washington DC 20004-2401

GULLANDER, WERNER PAUL, retired consultant, retired corporate executive; b. Big Rapids, Mich., July 19, 1908; s. Paul and Elvira Esther (Werner) G.; m. Dorothy Mae Becker, July 12, 1930 (div. 1971); children: Barbara Louise Gullander Weinberger, Judith Maria; m. Elizabeth B. Famme, Sept. 16, 1971. B.S., U. Minn., 1930; LL.D. (hon.), U. Puget Sound, 1966. Acctg. trainee Gen. Electric Co., 1930-33, traveling auditor, 1933-38, supervising auditor, 1938-44; sec., treas. Gen. Electric Supply Corp., 1945-48, dist. mgr., 1948-51; fin. v.p. Weyerhauser Co., Tacoma, 1952-60; exec. v.p., dir. Gen. Dynamics Corp., 1960-62; pres. NAM, N.Y.C., 1962-72; now bd. dirs. NAM; pres., bd. dirs. Columbia & Cowlitz RR Co., 1952-60; pres. Weyerhaeuser Found., 1952-60, Wash. State Rsch. Coun., 1957-58. Mem. Washington Athletic Club (Seattle), Marrakesh Country Club, Tau Kappa Epsilon. Home: 47085 Marrakesh Dr Palm Desert CA 92260 also: 47085 Marrakesh Dr Palm Desert CA 92260-5845

GULLEDGE, KAREN STONE, educational administrator; b. Fayetteville, N.C., Feb. 3, 1941; d. Malcolm Clarence and Clara (Davis) Stone; m. Parker Lee Gulledge Jr, Oct. 17, 1964. BA, St. Andrews Presbyn. Coll., Laurinburg, N.C., 1963; MA, East Carolina U., 1979; EdD, Nova U., 1986. Social worker Lee County, Sanford, N.C., 1963-64; tchr. Asheboro (N.C.) City Schs., 1964-67, Winston-Salem (N.C.)/Forsyth County Schs., 1967-70; research analyst N.C. Dept. Pub. Instrn., Raleigh, 1971-76, sch. planning cons., 1976-89, dir. sch. planning, 1989-95; dir. ednl. svcs. Peterson Assocs., Raleigh, 1995-98, The Roberts Group, PA, Raleigh, 1998—; chmn. N.C. Elem. Commn. of So. Assn. Colls. and Schs., 1995; leader profl. seminars; spkr. in field. Trustee St. Andrews Coll. Recipient Outstanding Educator award East Carolina U., 1992. Mem. Am. Biographical Assn., So. Assn. Colls. and Schs. (Distinguished Educator award 1994), Coun. Ednl. Facility Planners (pres., chmn. 1995, Disting. Ednl. Achievement award 1994, Disting. Svc. award 1996, 98), The Order of the Long Leaf Pine, Five Hundred Leaders of Infullerence, Delta Kappa Gamma. Democrat. Avocations: reading, needlework, entertaining, travel. Home: 9119 Carrington Ridge Dr Raleigh NC 27615-1000 Office: The Roberts Group 4011 W Chase Blvd Ste 100 Raleigh NC 27609

GULLEN, CHRISTOPHER ROY, lawyer; b. Detroit, Feb. 17, 1950; s. George Edgar and Mary Ruth Gullen; m. Sheila Rae Collins, Aug. 25, 1973; children: Brian Christopher, Katelyn Elizabeth. BA, U. Mich., 1972; JD, Ohio Northern U., 1975. Bar: Mich. 1975, U.S. Dist. Ct. (ea. dist.) Mich. 1975, U.S. Ct. Appeals (6th cir.) 1978. Law clk. Mich. Ct. Appeals, Lansing, 1975-77; ptnr. Gullen & Fitzsimmons, Rochester, Mich., 1977-82, Sarvis, Gullen & Herrmann, Birmingham, Mich., 1982-86; pub. liability atty. Kmart Corp., Troy, Mich., 1986-90; pub. liability counsel Kmart Corp., Troy, 1990—; mediator Oakland County Cir. Ct., 1986—. Author: Rules and Regulations of the Science Court, 1980. Mem. ABA, Mich. Bar Assn. Office: K Mart Corp 3100 W Big Beaver Rd Troy MI 48084-3163

GULLEY, JAMES CLARENCE, JR., television producer, marketing specialist, internet consultant; b. Detroit, Apr. 2, 1948; s. James Clarence Sr. and Mildred Lee (Griffin) G.; m. Anita Oliver; m. Jeanola Jackson; m. Phyllis Antoinette Hill, May 25, 1991; children: Marc, Darnell, James, Melanie, Delano. Pres. Big G Prodns., Detroit, 1972-94; v.p. ATAC Internat., Detroit, 1994-95, P.J. Internat., Detroit, 1995; pres. Gulley Group, Detroit, 1995—. Co-pub. King Kong Souvenir Book, 1976 (Movie Industry Champ award 1978); co-prodr. (music video) The Real Side TV Show, 1973-74. Mem. bd. United Citizens of Detroit, 1990-; bd. dirs. 15th Congrl. Dist. Dems., Detroit; Dem. precinct del., Detroit; mem. Barton-Mcfarlane Neighborhood Assn., Detroit. With USMC, 1966-69, Vietnam. Recipient Wayne County (Mich.) cert. of appreciation, 1994, Assn. Govt. Accts. cert. achievement, 1984, Black United Fund of Mich. cert. appreciation, 1990. Mem. Detroit Million Man March Orgn., Adults Asserting Themselves, Internat. Masons. Democrat. Home: 10367 Beechdale St Detroit MI 48204-2564

GULLEY, WILBUR PAUL, JR., former savings and loan executive; b. Little Rock, Aug. 8, 1923; s. Wilbur Paul and JaJa Douglas (Ashburn) G.; m. Mary Elizabeth Bragg Hunt, Mar. 13, 1971; children by previous marriage: Wilbur Paul III and William H. (twins), James Ransom, Michael Pierce. *Great Grandfather John G. Gulley was born in 1783 in Johnston County, North Carolina. Grandfather Ransom was born in 1839 in Raleigh, North Carolina; later moving to Batesville, Arkansas in 1859. He enlisted in the Confederate Army, becoming a colonel; eventually serving as a delegate at the Constitutional Convention in 1874, and as Treasurer of Arkansas. He fathered twelve children; the youngest Wilbur Paul Sr. Twin sons graduated from Duke University in 1970. Wilbur Paul III served as mayor of Durham, and currently as State Senator for Durham County. William H. heads the small business division of Durham Community College.* A.B. in Bus. Adminstrn., Duke U., 1947. With Gulley Ins. Agy., Little Rock, 1947; ptnr., mng. officer Gulley Ins. Agy., 1947-58; with Savers Fed. Savs. & Loan Assn., Little Rock, 1947-89; sec. Savers Fed. Savs. & Loan Assn., 1948-52, v.p., 1952-58, pres., 1959-83, chmn. bd., 1983-89, also dir.; bd. dirs. Little Rock br. Fed. Res. Bank St. Louis, 1983-87. Pres. BBB, Ark., 1962; gen. campaign chmn. United Fund, Pulaski County, Ark., 1963-64; v.p. Little Rock Boys Club, 1970-71, pres. 1971-72; trustee George W. Donaghey Found., 1958—, pres., 1969-72, 81-83, 95-96; commr. Metroctr. Improvement Dist., 1977-81, chmn. 1981; trustee Ark. State U., 1968-73, sec.-treas., 1971-72, chmn. 1972-73; trustee Savs. & Loan Found., 1977-81, Hendrix Coll., Conway, Ark., 1980-92, Roselawn Meml. Park, 1975—, v.p. trustees, 94—; bd. stewards First United Meth. Ch. of Little Rock, 1960-90, fin. chmn., 1989. With USNR 1943-46. Mem. Southwestern Savs. and Loan Conf. (pres. 1960-61), Fin. Instns. Retirement Fund (trustee 1960-65), U.S. League Savs. Instns. (mem. exec. com. 1963-66), Pulaski County Savs. and Loan League, pres. 1964), Ark. Savs. and Loan League (pres. 1965-66), Little Rock C. of C. (pres. 1968), Phi Beta Kappa, Sigma Alpha Epsilon, Beta Omega Sigma. Club: Little Rock Country. Home: Unit 3 South 3500 Cedar Hill Rd Little Rock AR 72202-1914 Office: PO Box 3573 Little Rock AR 72203-3573

GULLICKSON, GLENN, JR., physician, educator; b. Mpls., July 9, 1919; s. Glenn and Grace (Stellwagen) G.; m. Glenna A. Swore, May 18, 1957; children: Mary, Glenn III. B.A., U. Minn., 1942, M.D., 1945, Ph.D., 1961. Diplomate: Am. Bd. Phys. Medicine and Rehab. Intern Gallinger Municipal Hosp., Washington, 1944-45; faculty U. Minn. Med. Sch., Mpls., 1946—; assoc. prof. phys. medicine and rehab. U. Minn. Med. Sch., 1961-66, prof. phys. medicine and rehab., 1966-86, prof. emeritus, 1986—, acting head dept., 1974-75, interim head, 1982-85, asst. dir. Rehab. Center, 1954-61, dir. Rehab. Center, 1961-86; exec. dir. Am. Congress Phys. Medicine and Rehab., 1960-66; mem. exam. com. phys. therapists Minn. Bd. Med. Examiners, 1961-71, pres., 1968-71; mem. med. adv. com. Minn. Soc. for Crippled Children and Adults, 1967-72; fellow stroke council Am. Heart Assn., mem. exec. com., 1971-74; mem. neurol. scis. research tng. com. Nat. Inst. Neurol. Diseases and Blindness, 1965-69; exec. com. Joint Com. Stroke Facilities, 1969-78. Served to lt. (s.g.), M.C. USNR, 1945-46, 53-54. Mem. AMA (prin. rep. interspity. com. 1968-72, mem. residency review com. phys. medicine, rehab. 1971-79), AAUP, Minn. Med. Soc., Hennepin County Med. Soc., Minn. Med. Found., Am. Acad. Phys. Medicine and Rehab. (gov., v.p. 1968-69, pres. 1970-71), Am. Bd. Phys. Medicine and Rehab. (chmn. 1976-81, asst. to exec. dir. 1987-90), Am. Congress Rehab. Medicine (v.p. 1978-84, pres. 1984-85), Assn. Acad. Physiatrists, Sigma Xi. Home: # 225 9550 Collegeview Rd Bloomington MN 55437-2175 Office: Health Scis Ctr Univ Minn Minneapolis MN 55455

GULLIVER, EDWARD QUENTIN, marine consultant, writer; b. Needham, Mass., July 30, 1919; s. Everett Lee and Fanny Maude (Pullen) G.; m. Kathryn Ellen, Jan. 4, 1957 (div. Jan. 1974); children: Willard, Priscilla, Timothy Lee, Jonathan Edward, Christopher Alan, Susan Kay. Grad., Bishop-Lee Coll., 1937-40. Announcer WNAC, Boston, 1941-43, Answer Man feature program, WOR, N.Y.C., 1943-53; dist. supr. Crown Life Ins. Co., L.A., 1954-64; yacht dealer Gulliver's Sea Travels, St. Thomas, V.I., 1965-79; bus. broker Calif. Bus. Brokers, San Diego, 1980-86; cons. San Diego, 1987—. Author: Puretic Power Block; contbr. articles to profl. jours. Mem. Larchmont Yacht Club, Royal Hong Kong Yacht Club, St. Thomas Yacht Club, Virgin Islands Charter Boat League. Presbyterian. Avocation: sailing. Office: Business Ventures 3707 5th Ave Ste 415 San Diego CA 92103-4221

GULMAN, RICHARD BRUCE, tax accountant; b. Boston, Oct. 28, 1957; s. Philip and Barbara Lois (Wasserman) G.; m. Susan Joan Mann, Oct. 2, 1983; children: Jonathan, Kerry. BBA, U. Mass., 1979; MS in Taxation with high distinction, Bentley Coll., 1988. CPA. Prin. Laventhol & Horwath, Boston, 1979-90, Tofias, Fleishman & Shapiro, Cambridge, Mass., 1990-92; ptnr. Shapiro, Weiss & Co., Boston, 1992-94; founder Richard B. Gulman CPA, Boston, 1994-95, DiCicco, Gulman & Co., Boston, 1995—; dir. tech. tax tng. Laventhol & Horwath, 1987-90; speaker to local and nat. audiences on various tax topics. Contbr. articles to profl. jours. Mem. AICPA, Mass. Soc. CPAs, Helvering Soc., Beta Kappa Phi (dir. 1988—), Beta Kappa Phi Scholarship Found. (trustee 1992—). Avocations: basketball, fitness, coaching Little League baseball, reading. Office: DiCicco Gulman & Co 50 Congress St Boston MA 02109-4002

GULMI, JAMES SINGLETON, apparel manufacturing company executive; b. Schenectady, Mar. 16, 1946; s. Henry Charles and June (Singleton) G.; m. Claire Ann Moody, Jan. 16, 1988; children by previous marriage: Bradford Charles, Leah Cole. B.A., Baldwin Wallace Coll., 1968; M.B.A., Emory U., 1971. With Genesco, Inc., Nashville, 1971—, asst. treas., 1974-79, dir. fin. ops., 1978-79, treas., 1979-83, v.p., treas., 1983—, v.p. fin., chief fin. officer, 1986—, sr. v.p. fin., CFO, 1996—; mem. young exec. council Nashville City Bank. Chmn. allocations com. United Way, Nashville, 1987-88. Mem. Fin. Execs. Inst. (chpt. dir. 1979-80), Leadership of Nashville (treas.). Episcopalian. Office: Genesco Inc Genesco Rm 490 Nashville TN 37209-1396

GULYA, AINA JULIANNA, neurotologist, surgeon, educator; b. Syracuse, N.Y., Feb. 3, 1953; d. Aladar and Sylvia E. Gulya; m. William R. Wilson, May 21, 1983. AB cum laude, Yale Coll., 1974; MD with distinction in rsch., U. Rochester, 1978. Diplomate Am. Bd. Otolaryngology. Intern, jr. resident in gen. surgery Beth Israel Hosp., Boston, 1978-80; resident in otolaryngology Mass. Eye & Ear Infirmary, Boston, 1980-83; fellow in otology/neurotology Bapt. Hosp. Ear Found., Nashville, 1983-84; asst. prof. surgery George Washington U., Washington, 1984-87, assoc. prof. surgery, 1987-90; assoc. prof. otolaryngology and head and neck surgery Georgetown U., Washington, 1990-94, prof. otolaryngology and head and neck surgery, 1994-96; chief clin. trials br. Nat. Inst. on Deafness and other Comm. Disorders, Bethesda, Md., 1996—; clin. prof. surgery, otolaryngology, head and neck surgery George Washington U., Washington, 1998—; assoc. examiner Am. Bd. Otolaryngology, 1993-97, bd. dirs., 1997—. Co-author: Anatomy of the Temporal Bone With Surgical Implications, 1986, 95; assoc. editor Am. Jour. Otology, 1989-99. Bd. dirs. Deafness Rsch. Found., 1994—. Recipient Libr. award Rochester Acad. Medicine, 1975, Honor award Am. Acad. Otolaryngology-Head and Neck Surgery, 1991, Presdl. Citation, Am. Otol., Rhinol. and Laryngol. Soc., 1999. Mem. Am. Otological Soc. (coun. 1993—, editor-libr. 1995—, trustee rsch. fund 1993—, pres.-elect 1999), Am. Neurotology Soc. (coord. for continuing med. edn. 1990-95), Am. Acad. Otolaryngology, Head and Neck Surgery Inc. (bd. dirs. 1995-97). Avocation: water skiing. Office: EPS 400D-7 6120 Executive Blvd Rockville MD 20852-4909

GUMBEL, BRYANT CHARLES, broadcaster; b. New Orleans, Sept. 29, 1948; s. Richard Dunbar and Rhea Alice (LeCesne) G.; m. June Carlyn Baranco, Dec. 1, 1973; children: Bradley Christopher, Jillian Beth. BA, Bates Coll., 1970. Writer Black Sports mag., N.Y.C., 1971; editor Black Sports mag, N.Y.C., 1972; sportscaster KNBC-TV, Burbank, Calif., 1972-76, sports dir., 1976-81; sports host NBC Sports, N.Y.C., 1975-82; co-host Today Show NBC, N.Y.C., 1982-97; host Public Eye CBS, N.Y.C., 1997—. Recipient Emmy award, 1976, 77, Golden Mike award, Los Angeles Press Club, 1978, 79, Edward R. Murrow award Overseas Press Club, 1988. Mem. AFTRA. *

GUMBEL, GREG, sportscaster; b. New Orleans, May 3, 1946; s. Richard Dunbar and Rhea Alice (LeCesne) G.; m. Marcy; 1 child, Michelle. B, Loras Coll., Dubuque, Iowa, 1967. Sales rep. Am. Hosp. Supply Corp., Detroit; broadcaster L.A., 1973; with WMAQ-TV, Chgo., 1973-81; sportscaster SportsCenter (ESPN), Bristol, Conn., 1981-86, Madison Square Garden Network, N.Y.C., 1986-88, CBS Sports, 1988-90; host The NFL Today, 1990-94, NFL on NBC, 1994, NFL on CBS, 1998—. Anchor Sports Forum, H.S. Sportweek, Jets Jour., 1981-87; host WFAN; sports commentator CBS This Morning, 1990; CBS Morning co-anchor Winter Olympic Games, Albertville, France, 1992, anchor, Lillehammer, Norway, 1994; daytime anchor Summer Olympic Games, Altanta, 1996. Office: care CBS Sports 51 W 52d St New York NY 10019*

GUMBINER, KENNETH JAY, lawyer; b. Chgo., Sept. 2, 1946; s. Bernard and Sylvia (Oguss) G.; m. Christy Habecost, June 11, 1972; children: Rebecca, Benjamin, Sara. BS in Indsl. Engring., Purdue U., 1968; JD, U. Ill., 1971. Bar: Ill. 1971, Mass. 1981, N.C. 1985, U.S. Supreme Ct. 1985; cert. mediator, N.C. Assoc. Neuman, Williams, Anderson & Olson, Chgo., 1971-72; asst. atty. gen. environ. div. Ill. Atty. Gen.'s Office, Chgo., 1972-74; ptnr. Pedersen & Houpt, Chgo., 1974-81; v.p., gen. counsel Riley Stoker Corp., Worcester, Mass., 1981-84; ptnr. Patton Boggs, L.L.P., Greensboro, N.C., 1984—. Author: Construction Law Digest, 1986—, Construction Industry Forms, 1988. Mem. ABA (litigation, dispute resolution and constrn. sects.), N.C. Bar Assn. (sec. coun. dispute resolution sect.), Ill. Bar Assn., Mass. Bar Assn. Office: Patton Boggs LLP 101 W Friendly Ave Greensboro NC 27401-2532

GUMBLETON, THOMAS J., bishop; b. Detroit, Jan. 26, 1930. Student, St. John Provincial Sem., Mich., Pontifical Lateran U., Rome. Ordained priest Roman Cath. Ch. 1956. Apptd. titular bishop Ululi and aux. bishop Roman Catholic Arch Diocese, Detroit, 1968—. Office: Chancery Office 1234 Washington Blvd Detroit MI 48226-1808*

GUMEN, MURAD, artist, writer, film director and producer; b. N.Y.C., May 29, 1956; s. Sururi and Makbule Gumen. Student, NYU, 1975-76; BA cum laude, Queens Coll., N.Y.C., 1977. Artist The Walt Disney Co., N.Y.C., 1983-89; film dir. and prodr. Take Twelve Prodns., N.Y.C., 1990—. Artist/writer humor mags.: Crazy Cracked, N.Y.C., 1975-82; writer/animator short film: Erased Off, 1976 (ASIFA award 1977); writer, dir., prodr.: (cable TV show) Renald Rap's Rambling with Renald Rap, 1983-87, (feature film) Wonderguy, 1992, Eve's Preyer, 1999; writer graphic novel: Wonderguy, 1992. Mem. Assn. of Ind. Video and Filmmakers.

GUMERSON, JEAN GILDERHUS, health foundation executive; b. Hayfield, Minn., Mar. 19, 1923; d. Nordeen Palmer and Mable Jeannette (Scharberg) Gilderhus; m. William Dow Gumerson Sr., Mar. 5, 1943 (dec. Jan. 1978); children: William Dow Jr., Ted Lee, Jon David. Student, U. Minn., 1941-42, U. Okla., 1961-62. Adminstrv. asst. to Rep. state party chmn. Oklahoma City, 1976-77; campaign coord. 1st dist. Paula Unruh for Congress, Tulsa, 1978; dir. pub. rels. C.R. Anthony Co., Oklahoma City, 1979-87; dir. human rels. Wilson Agy., Mass. Mut. Ins. Co., Oklahoma City, 1987; adminstrv. dir. Okla. Art Ctr., Oklahoma City, 1988-89; exec. dir. Children's Med. Rsch., Inc., Oklahoma City, 1989—. Presbyn. Health Found., Oklahoma City, 1989—. Active exec. com. Pres.'s Com. on Mental Retardation, Washington, 1986-91; So. Govs. Conf. on Infant Mortality, Washington, 1987-92; chmn. City-County Health Dept. Bd., Oklahoma City, 1980-93; gov. appointee steering com. Healthy Futures, Oklahoma City, 1988-92; bd. dirs. Children's Med. Rsch. Inc., Okla. City 1982—; nat. bd. Contact U.S.A., Okla. City, 1992—. Recipient Gov.'s Arts award for community svc. Okla. Arts Coun., Woman of Yr. award Okla. Mental Health Assn., Humanitarian award Opportunities Indsl. Ctr., Outstanding Vol. Fund Raiser award Okla. chpt. Nat. Soc. Fund Raising Execs., 1988, Humanitarian award Nat. Conf. for Comty. and Justice, 1999; inducted to Okla. Hall of Fame, 1999; Jean Gumerson Endowed Chair in Pediat. Psychology established in his honor, 1999. Mem. AIA (hon.), Exec. Women in Govt., Charter 35, Econ. Club. Okla., Oklahoma City C. of C., Theta Sigma Phi. Presbyterian. Home: 6206 Waterford Blvd Apt 50 Oklahoma City OK 73118-1109

GUMM, JAY PAUL, association executive; b. Durant, Okla., Nov. 29, 1963; s. Jay William and Harlene (Taylor) G. BA in Polit. Sci., Southeastern Okla. State U., 1986. LBJ Congl. intern Hon. Wes Watkins, U.S. Congressman, Washington, summer 1984; gov., chmn. bd. Okla. Intercollegiate Legislature, Inc., Oklahoma City, 1987-88; rsch. asst. Okla. Ho. of Reps., Oklahoma City, 1986-87, staff asst., 1987-90, sr. media specialist, 1990-99; exec. dir. Durant (Okla.) Area C. of C., 1999—. Recipient Presdl. scholarship Southeastern Okla. State U., 1985; named Outstanding Young Dem. in Okla., Okla. Fedn. Dem. Women, 1983, Outstanding Young Men of Am., 1986, 87, 92. Mem. Pub. Rels. Soc. Am. (bd. dirs. Oklahoma City chpt., awards of merit 1992, 93, 95, 96, Upper Case awards 1993, 94, 95, 96), Am. Soc. Legis. Clks. and Secs. (elected nat. exec. com. 1997-98), Nat. Conf. State Legislatures (media rels. sect.). Avocations: golf, bowling, parliamentary procedure, politics, Star Trek. Home: 523 N 5th Ave Durant OK 74701-4009 Office: Durant Area Chamber of Commerce 215 N Fourth Ave Durant OK 74701

GUMMEL, HERMANN KARL, retired physicist, laboratory administrator; b. Hannover, Germany, July 6, 1923; came to U.S., 1953; s. Johannes and Charlotte (Elgeti) G.; m. Erika Ilse Reich, Aug. 31, 1952; children—Monica Ruth, Margaret Grace. MS, Syracuse U., 1952, PhD, 1957; diploma in Physics, Philipps U., Marburg-Lahn, 1952. Mem. tech. staff Bell Telephone Labs, Murray Hill, N.J., 1957-62, supr., 1962-67, dept. head, 1967-82, asst. dir., 1982-84; dir. AT&T Bell Labs, Murray Hill, N.J., 1984-86, ret., cons. Contbr. articles to profl. jours.; patentee in field. Recipient Phil Kaufman award Electronic Design Automation Co., 1994. Fellow IEEE (David Sarnoff award 1983, Guillemin-Cauer prize paper award Circuits and Systems Soc. 1977, Tech. Achievement award Circuit and Systems Soc. 1990); mem. Am. Phys. Soc., Nat. Acad. Engring., Sigma Xi. Presbyterian.

GUMMERE, JOHN, insurance company executive; b. Mt. Holly, N.J., Feb. 12, 1928; s. John Westcott and Ruth (Clark) G.; m. Eleanor Frances Greene, Oct. 9, 1954; children: Cynthia Clark, John Greene. BA, Yale U., 1948. With Phoenix Mut. Life Ins. Co., Hartford, Conn., 1949-92, sec. charge underwriting dept., 1961-64, v.p., 1965-72, sr. v.p., 1972-78, exec. v.p., 1978-81, dir., pres., COO, 1981-83; pres., CEO Phoenix Mut. Life Ins. Co., Hartford, 1983-87, chmn. bd., CEO, 1987-92; chmn. bd., CEO Phoenix Home Life Mut. Ins. Co., Hartford, 1992-94. Mem. exec. com. Med. Info. Bur., 1972-77, chmn., 1977; past bd. dirs. Hartford Grad. Ctr., Old State House, Am. Coun. Life Ins. and Health Ins. Assn. Am. Fellow Soc. Actuaries; mem. Greater Hartford C. of C. (past chmn., bd. dirs.), Sigma Xi.

GUMMERE, WALTER COOPER, educator, consultant; b. Columbus, Ohio, Apr. 24, 1917; s. Walter Cooper and Glenn (Becker) G.; m. Virginia Lee Jeffries, Jan. 10, 1942; children: Virginia Glenn Gummere Stewart, Deborah Gummere Lilgendahl (dec.), Rebecca Jane Gummere Pivetta. A.B., Brown U., 1940; M.B.A., U. Louisville, 1953. Chief indsl. engr. Colgate Palmolive Co., 1947-53; gen. supt., dir. Rich's Inc., Atlanta, 1953-57; personnel adminstr. Montgomery Ward & Co., Chgo., 1957-60; v.p., gen. mgr. Plasti-Line Inc., Knoxville, Tenn., 1960-62; mgmt. cons., 1962-63; with Tappan Co., 1963-73, exec. v.p., 1966-72, pres., chief exec. officer, 1972-73; also dir.; chmn., chief exec. officer The Vendo Co., 1974-78; pres. Square Pegs Assocs., Inc., 1978—; exec.-in-residence U. Central Fla., 1982-83, Centre Coll. Ky., winter 1983, Am. Coll., London, spring and summer 1984; Goodyear exec. prof. Sch. Bus., U. Akron, 1984-85; vis. prof. Clemson U., 1986, Lander Coll., 1987, Am. Coll., London, 1988, Centre Coll. Ky., 1990, U. Louisville, 1990—. Served to capt. AUS, 1942-46. Mem. Newcomen Soc., Acad. Mgmt., Delta Upsilon, Phi Beta Kappa, Delta Sigma Pi, Sigma Iota Epsilon, Omicron Delta Kappa. Republican. Presbyterian. Home and Office: 202 Meadowvista Ln Sun City Center FL 33573-5562

GUMP, BARRY HEMPHILL, chemistry and food science educator; b. Columbus, Ohio, Nov. 12, 1940. BS, Ohio State Univ., 1962; PhD, Univ. Calif., 1966. Rsch. assoc. Bureau Sci., Food & Drug Adminstrn., Washington, 1966-67; asst. prof. to assoc. prof. Calif. State Univ., 1967-74, prof. chemistry, 1974—, prof. enol. and food sci., 1981—; vis. scientist Bioorg. Standards Sec. Analysis Divsn., Nat. Inst. Sci. and Tech., 1974-76; Fulbright lectr. U. Repub. Montivideo, Uruguay, 1983; assoc. referee for sulfur dioxide in wine, AOAC, 1986. Mem. Am. Chem. Soc., Am. Soc. Enology and Viticulture, Sigma Xi. Achievements include research separation methods in chemistry, especially chromatographic methods; analytical methods development, trace components in foods and wine; hydrocardon analysis in marine sediment, water and tissue samples. Office: Calif State U Fresno Viticulture & Rsch Ctr Fresno CA 93740-8003*

GUMPEL, GLENN J., association executive. Pres. internat. and global bus. affairs Universal Studios Recreation Group, Universal City, Calif.; pres. Internat. Global Affairs. Mem. Dirs. Guild Am. Office: Universal Studios Recreation Group Universal City Plaza LRW 11 Universal City CA 91608

GUMPEL, LISELOTTE, German language educator; b. Berlin; d. Karl and Gretchen (Philipps) G. BA summa cum laude, State U. of San Francisco, 1964; MA, Stanford (Calif.) U., 1966, PhD, 1971. Asst. prof. U. Minn., Morris, 1968-72, assoc. prof., 1972-80, prof. in German, 1980—; lectr. in field. Author: (books) Concrete Poetry from East and West Germany: The Language of Exemplarism and Experimentalism, 1976, Metaphor Reexamined: A non-Aristotelian Perspective, 1985; contbr. articles to profl. jours. Nat. Endowment fellow, 1972, Helen Cam fellow Girton Coll., Cambridge, Eng., 1977. Mem. MLA, Am. Assn. of Tchrs. of German, Women in German, Soc. for Internat. Germanistics, Internat. Union of Germanic Lang. and Lit. Democrat. Jewish. Avocations: reading, visiting museums, libraries, theatres, concerts.

GUMPERT, GUNTHER, artist; b. Krefeld, Germany, Apr. 17, 1919; came to U.S., 1967, naturalized, 1971; s. Karl and Erna (Cordes) G.; m. Anita Von Kahler, Nov. 28, 1967. Grad., Human. Gymnasium, Krefeld, 1937, Sch. Fine Arts, Krefeld, 1938, Sch. Fine Arts, Wuppertal, 1939. Numerous one-man shows in, Europe and U.S. including: Zurich, 1955, Winterthur, 1959, Paris, 1960, Vienna, 1961, Rome, 1962, N.Y.C., 1963, 96, 98, Chgo., 1963-64, London, 1963, Pforzheim, 1964, Seattle, 1965, 68, 70, 73, 76, Denver, 1972, Washington, 1966, 68, 69, 72, 75, 79, 82, 85, 87, 88, 90, 93, Cleve., 1971, Santo Domingo, 1978, group shows include, Suermondt Mus., Aachen, Ger., 1948, Kaiser-Wilhelm Mus., Krefeld, 1949, 50, 51, Internat. Exhibit Abstract Art, Pistoia, Italy, 1961, Salon Realites Nouvelles, Paris, 1959, 60, 61, Salon De Mai, Paris, 1962, Gruppe Z, Wuppertal, 1960, Internat. Exhbn. Contemporary Art, London, 1964; represented in permanent collections, Met. Mus. Art, N.Y.C., Victoria and Albert Mus., London, Albertina, Vienna, The Phillips Collection, Washington, Kaiser-Wilhelm Mus., Krefeld, Museo Nacional de Bellas Artes, Santiago, Chile, Sch. Design, Providence, R.I., Princeton U. Art Mus., Mus. Fine Arts, Dallas, Denver Art Mus., Finch Coll. Mus., N.Y.C., Wesleyan U., Middletown Conn., Ohio U. Mus. Am. Art, Athens, Roosevelt House, New Delhi, India, Museo de Arte Moderno, Santo Domingo, George Washington U., Washington, and others; TV film Gumpert At Work, 1963. Address: 3752 Mckinley St NW Washington DC 20015-2510

GUMPERT, LYNN, gallery director. Student, Sorbonne, Paris, 1971-72; cert. completion first year, Ecole du Louvre, Paris, 1971-72; BA in History of Art with honors, U. Calif., Berkeley, 1974; MA in History of Art, U. Mich., 1977. Curatorial asst. The Jewish Mus., N.Y.C., 1978-80; curator The New Mus. Contemporary Art, N.Y.C., 1980-84, sr. curator, 1984-88; adj. curator Mus. Contemporary Art, L.A., 1988-89, We. States Arts Fedn., Santa Fe, 1988-89; coord. Eighth Biennale of Sydney Art Gallery N.S.W., Sydney, Australia, 1989-90; guest curator, adminstrv. dir. Amway (Japan) Ltd. and Setagaya Art Mus., Tokyo, 1989-91, Nat. Mus. Art, Osaka, Japan, 1989-91; cons. curator Gallery at Takashimaya, Inc., N.Y.C., 1992-95; guest curator, U.S. coord. ARC/Musée d'Art Moderne de la Ville de Paris, 1994-95; guest curator Grey Art Gallery, N.Y.C., 1996-97, dir., 1997—; lectr. in field; juror in field; panelist in field; ind. curator/cons., 1988-97. Exhbns. include The New Mus. Contemporary Art, 1980, 81, 82, 84, 86, 89, Pitts. Ctr. Arts, 1983, Mus. Contemporary Art, Chgo., 1988, Galerie Ghislaine Hussenot, Paris, 1992, The Gallery at Takashimaya, N.Y.C., 1994, 95, numerous others; author: Christian Boltanski, 1993, 94, reprint, 1996. Univ. fellow U. Mich., 1975. Mem. Internat. Assn. Art Critics (bd. dirs. U.S. divsn.), Etant Donnés, The French-Am. Fund Contemporary Art (bd. dirs.), ArtTable (N.Y.). Fax: 212-995-4024. E-mail: greygallery@nyu.edu. Office: Grey Art Gallery NYU 100 Washington Sq East New York NY 10003

GUMPERTZ, WERNER HERBERT, structural engineering company executive; b. Berlin, Dec. 26, 1917; s. Richard and Olga H. (Prenzlau) G.; m. Elizabeth Mildred Lewit, Nov. 25, 1949; children: Richard H., Ruth O. Gumpertz Moses. BCE, Swiss Fed. Inst. Tech., 1939; SBCE, MIT, 1948, SM in Bldg. Engring. and Constrn., 1950, advanced profl. degree in bldg. engring. and constrn., 1954. Registered profl. engr., Mass., Pa., Calif., Colo., Okla., Md., Kans., Tex., Ga., La. Constrn. supr., expeditor, draftsman Homes & Gardens Inc., N.Y.C., 1940; engring. draftsman, surveyor Lockwood Kessler & Bartlett, Bklyn., 1940-41; office engr., estimator, constrn. supr. M Shapiro & Sons Constrn. Co., N.Y.C. and Newport News, Va., 1941-43; engring. asst. to head Kaiser Co. Inc. Shipyard, Vancouver, Wash., 1943; structural engr. U.S. Army C.E., ETO, 1946-47; office and field engr. United Engrs. & Constructors Inc., Phila. and Devon, Conn., 1948-49; prof. civil engring. MIT, Cambridge, Mass., 1949-57; sr. prin. Simpson Gumpertz & Heger Inc., Arlington, Mass., 1956—; part-time instr. structural engring. Bridgeport Engring. Inst., 1948-49, U. Mass. Extension, 1953-62; cons. bldg. constrn. and material tech., bldg. systems and assemblies of materials; lectr. Harvard Grad. Sch. Design, 1985, 87. Contbr. articles to profl. jours. Mem. Adv. Com. on Pub. Bldg. Constrn., City of Newton, Mass., 1956-68; guidance lectr. Cambridge Pub. Sch. System, 1955-57. Served to cpl. U.S. Army, 1943-46, ETO. Fellow ASCE (nat. com. on stds., sec.-treas., joint com. on profl. conduct Mass. sect.), ASTM (chmn. com. D-8 on roofing, waterproofing and bituminous materials 1981-85, real estate com. 1988-95, Award of Merit 1986, Walter C. Voss award to Engr. for Outstanding Contbn. to Advancement of Bldg. Tech. 1987); mem. Am. Concrete Inst. (com. on residential concrete slabs, cellular concrete com.), U.S. Metric Assn. (cert. advanced metrication specialist), Am. Soc. Engring. Edn. (chmn. archtl. engring. divsn.), Am. Arbitration Assn. (nat. panel arbitrators), Nat. Fire Protection Assn., Midwest Roofing Contractors Assn. (assoc.), Nat. Roofing Contractors Assn. (assoc.), Sigma Xi. Office: Simpson Gumpertz & Heger Inc 297 Broadway Arlington MA 02474-5310

GUMPPERT, KARELLA ANN, federal government official; b. N.Y.C., Oct. 16, 1942; d. Leonard Lewis and Florence M. Gumppert. AB in Polit. Sci., George Washington U., 1963, postgrad., 1963-65. Lic. in real estate sales, Md., 1984. Jr. editor to Bd. Govs. Fed. Res. Sys., Washington, 1966-67; editl. asst. Jour. of Maritime Law and Commerce, N.Y.C., 1969-71; adminstr. NYU Law Sch., N.Y.C., 1968-73; law asst. White & Case and other firms, N.Y.C., Boston, Hartford, 1974-80; vol. asst. U.S. Presdl. Inaugural Com., Washington, 1981; confidential asst. The White House Staff, Washington, 1981; publs. asst. Congressional Budget Office, Washington, 1982-84; credit summarizer Xerox Corp., Arlington, Va., 1985-86; asst. in govtl. affairs Mut. Omaha, Washngton, 1988; land law adjudicator U.S. Dept. Interior, Anchorage, 1991—. Author, illustrator: (children's book) An Adventure, 1949; founding editor lit. mag. Springboard, 1959; mem. editorial bd. newspaper Amicus Curiae, 1964-65. Charity asst. Girl Scouts U.S.A., N.Y.C., 1952-54, Christian Assn., N.Y.C., 1959-61, Wesley Found., Washington, 1962-63; vol. asst. N.Y. Rep. County Com., 1959-62, Conn. Reps. State Com., Hartford, 1979-80. Recipient numerous scholarships, 1957-60. Mem. NAFE, Nat. Trust for Hist. Preservation, Nat. Audubon Soc., Women's Nat. Rep. Club, Anchorage Opera Assn., Library of Cong. Assocs. (founding mem.). Avocations: music, nostalgia, travel, theatre, sports.

GUNASEKERA, THILAK WIJENAYAKA, mathematician, educator; b. Colombo, Sri Lanka, Jan. 14, 1939; came to U.S., 1989; s. James and Sisiliya Stella (Wijesinghe) G.; m. Padmini Senaratna, June 8, 1964; children: Prasad, Pradeep, Prabath, Kumudini, Geethani, Indira, Prasanna. BS in Math. with honors, U. Ceylon, Peradeniya, Sri Lanka, 1962; MEd in Math. Edn., Wayne State U., 1992, PhD in Ednl. Evaluation and Rsch., 1997. Tchr. math. Ananda Coll., Colombo, 1962-81, Sokoto (Nigeria) Tchrs. Coll., 1981-89, Highland Park (Mich.) Schs., 1990-92; worksite edn. specialist UAW/Ford Rouge Acad., Dearborn, Mich., 1992—; faculty math. Wayne County C.C., Detroit, 1993—; faculty math. Detroit Coll. Bus., Warren, 1993—, faculty adv. com., 1997; mem. math. faculty Henry Ford C.C., Dearborn, 1998—. Wilmer Menge Meml. scholar for leadership in math. edn. Wayne State U., 1993. Mem. Nat. Coun. Tchrs. Math., Mich. Coun. Tchrs. Math. Avocations: tennis, film, photography. Office: Eastern Mich Univ Dept Bus Ypsilanti MI 48197

GUND, GEORGE, III, financier, professional sports team executive; b. Cleve., May 7, 1937; s. George and Jessica (Roesler) G.; m. Mary Theo Feld, Aug. 13, 1966; children: George, Gregory. Student, Western Res. U., Menlo (Calif.) Sch. Bus. Engaged in personal investments San Francisco, 1967—; cattle ranching Lee, Nev., 1967—; partner Calif. Seals, San Francisco, 1976-77; pres. Ohio Barons, Inc., Richfield, 1977-78; chmn. bd. Northstar Fin. Corp., Bloomington, Minn., from 1978; formerly chmn. bd. Minn. North Stars, Bloomington; chmn., co-owner San Jose Sharks, NHL, San Jose, CA, 1991—; co-owner Cleve. Cavaliers; film prodr. Caipirinha Prodns., San Francisco; dir. Ameritrust Cleve.; vice-chmn. Gund Investment Corp., Princeton, N.J.; chmn. North Stars Met Center Mgmt. Corp., Bloomington; v.p. hockey Sun Valley Ice Skating, Inc., Idaho. Chmn. San Francisco Internat. Film Festival, 1973—; mem. sponsors council Project for Population Action; adv. council Sierra Club Found.; mem. internat. council Mus. Modern Art, N.Y.C.; collectors com. Nat. Gallery Art; bd. dirs. Calif. Theatre Found., Bay Area Ednl. TV Assn., San Francisco Mus. Art, Cleve. Health Museum, George Gund Found., Cleve. Internat. Film Festival, Sun Valley Center Arts and Humanities, U. Nev. Reno Found., Sundance Inst. Served with USMCR, 1955-58. Clubs: Calif. Tennis (San Francisco), University (San Francisco), Olympic (San Francisco); Union (Cleve.), Cleve. Athletic (Cleve.), Kirkland Country (Cleve.), Rowfant (Cleve.); Ranier (Seattle). Office: 1821 Union St San Francisco CA 94123-4307

GUND, GORDON, advertising executive, sports team executive; b. Cleve., Oct. 15, 1939; s. George and Jessica (Roesler) G.; m. Llura Liggett; children: Grant Ambler, Gordon Zachary. BA, Harvard U., 1961; DPubSvc (hon.), U. Maryland, 1980; DHL, Whittier Coll., 1993; LLD (hon.), U. Vt., 1994. Pres., chmn., CEO Gund Investment Corp., Princeton, N.J.; gen. ptnr. GUS Enterprises; prin. owner Cleve. Cavaliers, NBA, 1983—; chmn. Nationwide Advt. Svc. Inc.; co-owner San Jose Sharks, NHL, 1990—; mem. bd. govs. NHL, NBA; bd. dirs. Kellogg Co., Corning Inc. Co-founder The Found. Fighting Blindness, 1971, also chmn.; pres., trustee Gund Collection of Western Art; mem. Nat. Adv. Eye Coun., 1980-84. Office: Nationwide Advt Svc 1228 Euclid Ave Ste 600 Cleveland OH 44115-1845*

GUNDERSEN, ALLISON MAUREEN, management consultant; b. Syracuse, N.Y., Oct. 14, 1959; d. Jerrold Paul and Rosemarie Noël (Harvey) G. AB, Cornell U., 1981; postgrad., NYU, 1982-83, Swedish Inst., 1991; MA in Intercultural Rels., Lesley Coll., 1996. Assoc. Morgan Stanley & Co., N.Y.C., 1981-84, sr. assoc., 1985-86; project mgr. Morgan Stanley Internat., Tokyo, 1987-88; cons. Computech Cons. Svcs., Winchester, N.J., 1989-90; pres. Woman About Globe, Ltd., N.Y.C., 1990-93; assoc. Cambridge (Mass.) Myotherapy, 1992-95; intern UN Indsl. Devel. Orgn., Vienna, 1996; prin. cons. Data Dimensions, 1997-98; cons. Culpeper Consulting Group, N.Y.C., 1998—. Mem. NOW (dir. membership processing N.Y.C. 1990), Internat. Feminists Japan (coord. 1987-88), Am. Massage Therapists Assn., City Island Yacht Club, Cornell Club N.Y. Democrat. Avocations: travel, languages, photography, sailing.

GUNDERSEN, MARY LISA KRANITZKY, finance company executive; b. Schenectady, N.Y., July 20, 1955; d. Charles William Kranitzky and Shirley Ann (Thomas) Ballou. BS in Fin., U. Ala., 1982. Fin. specialist GE Co., Birmingham, Ala., 1981-83; supv. acctg. adminstrn. GE Co., Atlanta, 1984-85; corp. auditor GE Co., Schenectady, 1985-87; mgr. fin. analysis and auditing GE Constrn. Svcs., Burkville, Ala., 1988-90; mgr. fin. Manheim Auctions Inc., Atlanta, 1990-92; program fin. mgr. Latin Am. Sales Gen. Elec. Indsl. and Power Systems, Schenectady, 1992-94; dir. fin. GE Capital/PT Astra Sedaya Fin., Jakarta, Indonesia, 1995-97, GE Capital Asia Pacific, Hong Kong, 1997—. Bd. dirs. Birmingham Opera Theater, 1980—. Recipient Acad. Excellence medal Fin. Execs. Inst., 1982. Mem. Beta Gamma Sigma, Phi Kappa Phi, Omicron Delta Epsilon. Episcopalian. Avocations: music, water skiing, reading, travel. Home: care GEII Distbn PO Box 6027 Schenectady NY 12301-6027 Office: GE Capital Asia Pacific, 16/F 3 Exch Sq 8 Connaught Pl, Hong Kong China

GUNDERSEN, WAYNE CAMPBELL, management consultant, oil and gas consultant; b. Elgin, Ill., May 27, 1936; s. LeRoy Arthur and Jean Ellen (Campbell) G.; m. Gail Andrews, Mar. 21, 1959; children—Thomas Dexter, Lori Ann, Kathy Lee. B.S., U. Nebr., 1959, M.S., 1961. Advisor fgn. ops. Standard Oil of Calif., San Francisco, 1974-76; asst. to v.p. Chevron Overseas Petroleum, San Francisco, 1976-80; dir. oil and gas Kaiser Aluminum & Chem. Corp., Oakland, Calif., 1980-81; v.p., gen. mgr. Kaiser Energy, Inc., Oakland, 1983-85, pres., 1985-87; v.p. Kaiser Aluminum and Chem. Corp., Oakland, 1983-87; pres. Kaiser Aluminum Exploration Co., Oakland, Kaiser Exploration and Mining Co., Oakland, 1985-87; cons. in oil and gas, 1987—; chmn. bd., chief exec. officer The Petroleum Synergy Group, Inc., 1988—; mem. geology adv. bd. U. Nebr., Lincoln, 1984-87. Co-author articles in field. Pres. Parents Club Foothill Sch., Walnut Creek, Calif., 1978-79. Named Man-of-Yr., New Orleans Jaycees, 1973; Sinclair fellow, 1960-61. Mem. Am. Assn. Petroleum Geologists. Republican. Methodist.

GUNDERSON, BERNICE BLOWER, retired nurse, genealogy researcher; b. Kelseyville, Calif., Jan. 8, 1925; d. Richard Marion and Ruth Emily (Flint) Blower; m. Bill Dean Neff, Apr. 10, 1949 (div. Nov. 1960); children: Brenda Elaine, Beverly Ellen, Bruce Elbert; m. Gilbert M. Gunderson, Aug. 8, 1965 (dec.). BS, Loma Linda U., 1960. RN, Calif. Nurse White Meml. Hosp., L.A., 1948-49, Vancouver (B.C.) Gen. Hosp., Can., 1950, Avenal (Calif.) Dist. Hosp., 1952-53, Long Beach (Calif.) Cmty. Hosp., 1953-55, 86-96; nursing supr. Rancho Los Amigos County Hosp., Downey, Calif., 1955-80, St. Frances Hosp., Lynwood, Calif., 1982-86; spkr. in field. Contbg. author The Searcher, 1980-96; editor Durkee Family History newsletter, 1982-99; co-author article to profl. nursing jour. Singer Sweet Adelines, Downey, 1960-65. Mem. So. Calif. Geneal. Soc. (bd. mem.), Native Daughters of Golden West (2d v.p. 1960-65, officer), Solbakken Lodge Sons of Norway, (libr. 1987-90, sec. 1990-93, treas. 1993-95, found. chmn. 1995-96, circulation mgr. 1997-98, pres. 1999—), Freya Club (pres. 1997-98). Republican. Avocations: stamp collecting, handicrafts, gardening. Home: 4100 E Theresa St Long Beach CA 90814-1758

GUNDERSON, CLARK ALAN, orthopedic surgeon; b. Watertown, S.D., Aug. 27, 1948; s. Harvey Alfred and Eugenie (Tulson) G.; m. Robbie Gunderson; children: Ashley, Camille. Student, U. Minn., 1966-69; BS, U. S.D., 1971; MD, Baylor Coll. of Medicine, 1973. Diplomate Am. Bd. of Orthopaedic Surgery, 1979. Intern in gen. surgery Charity Hosp., New Orleans, 1973-74, resident in orthopedic surgery, 1974-78; chief of surgery Lake Charles (La.) Meml. Hosp., 1980-83, 90-91, sec., treas. med. staff, 1983-87, pres. med. staff, 1992-93, also trustee, 90-94, chief of surgery, 1998-99; clin. assoc. prof. La. State U. Sch. of Medicine, New Orleans, 1987-90. Bd. dirs. Arthritic Found. La., 1987. Mem. AMA, ACS, Am. Acad. Orthopaedic Surgeons, La. Orthopaedic Assn. (pres. 1995-96), Calcasieu Parish Med. Soc., La. State Med. Soc., N.Am. Spine Assn., Mid Am. Orthopaedic Assn., Lake Charles Country Club (pres. 1987-89), Clin. Orthopedic Rsch. Soc., Sigma Chi. Avocation: golf. Office: 2615 Enterprise Blvd Lake Charles LA 70601-7675

GUNDERSON, CLEON HENRY, management consultant corporation executive; b. Great Falls, Mont., June 5, 1932; s. Leon H. and Mona (Emmett) G.; m. Virginia Ellen Hudson, Aug. 26, 1972; children: Craig H., Robert S., Laura E. BS, Inst. Tech., Dayton, Ohio, 1971, Mont. State U., 1957; MAPA, U. Okla., 1975. Communications engr. Mountain States Tel & Tel, Helena, Mont., 1953-54; aerospace engr. Boeing Co., Seattle, 1957-58; commd. 2nd lt. USAF, 1958, advanced to col., 1974, ret., 1976; pres. Precision Prodn. & Engring., Walla Walla, Wash., 1976-79, Western Skies Energy Systems, Spokane, Wash., 1979-88, Computer Central, Olympia, Wash., 1988-90, C.H. Gunderson & Assocs., Littlerock, Wash., 1990—; Mem. Am. Inst. Elec. Engrs., Seattle, 1957-60, Am. Inst. Indsl. Engrs., Spokane, 1982-85. Inventor heatexchange solar panels, comml. solar panels. V.p. Tumwater Lions Club. Decorated Silver Stars, Disting. Flying Crosses, Purple Heart, Air medals. Mem. Soc. Mfg. Engrs. (sr. mem.), Soc. Mil. Engrs., Nat. Assn. Small Businesses, Toastmasters Internat., Walla Walla C. of C., Canto Blanco Gun Club (Madrid, v.p. 1973-75, Scott Air Force Base Gun Club (v.p. 1975-76), Spokane Gun Club, Evergreen Gun Club (Littlerock). Republican. Avocations: hunting, fishing, competitive shooting. Home: 13001 Littlerock Rd PO Box 246 Littlerock WA 98556-0246 Office: C H Gunderson & Assocs PO Box 246 Littlerock WA 98556-0246

GUNDERSON, ELMER MILLARD, state supreme court justice, law educator; b. Mpls., Aug. 9, 1929; s. Elmer Peter and Carmaleta (Oliver) G.; m. Lupe Gomez, Dec. 29, 1967; 1 son, John Randolph. Student, U. Minn., U. Omaha, 1948-53; LL.B., Creighton U., 1956; LL.M., U. Va., 1982; LL.D.,

Calif. Western Sch. Law; student appellate judges seminar, N.Y. U., 1971; LL.D., U. Pacific. Bar: Nebr. 1956, Nev. 1958. Atty.-adviser FTC, 1956-57; pvt. practice Las Vegas, 1958-71; justice Nev. Supreme Ct., 1971-89, now sr. justice; instr. bus. law So. regional div. U. Nev.; lectr., author bulls. felony crimes for Clark County Sheriff's Dept.; counsel Sheriff's Protective Assn.; mem. legal staff Clark Council Civil Def. Agy.; legal counsel Nev. Jaycees. Compiler, annotator: Omaha Home Rule Charter; project coordinator: Jud. Orientation Manual, 1974. Chmn. Clark County Child Welfare Bd., Nev. central chpt. Nat. Multiple Sclerosis Soc.; hon. dir. Spring Mountain Youth Camp. Served with U.S. Army. Recipient A.J.S. Herbert Harley award. Mem. Am., Nebr., Nev. bar assns.; Mem. Inst. Jud. Adminstrn., Am. Law Inst., Am. Trial Lawyers Assn., Am. Judicature Soc., Phi Alpha Delta, Alpha Sigma Nu. Office: Nev Supreme Ct 100 N Carson St Carson City NV 89701-4717

GUNDERSON, GERALD AXEL, economics educator, administrator; b. Seattle, May 24, 1940; s. Marian A. and Ethel Ann (Hamon) G.; m. Margaret Jean Overway, Sept. 10, 1965; children: David Eric, Laura Lynn. B.A. in Econs., U. Wash., 1962, M.A. in Econs., 1965, Ph.D. in Econs., 1967. Asst. prof. econs. U. Mass., Amherst, 1967-74; vis. assoc. prof. econs. Mt. Holyoke Coll., South Hadley, Mass., 1974-75; spl. lectr. econs. N.C. State U., Raleigh, 1975-78; prof. econs. Trinity Coll., Hartford, Conn., 1978-82; Shelby Cullom Davis prof. Am. bus. and econ. enterprise Trinity Coll., Hartford, 1982—, dir. S.C. Davis Endowment, 1982—; bd. dirs. exec. com. Yankee Inst. for Pub. Policy Studies; acad. adv. com. Inst. on Research on Econs. of Taxation. Author: A New Economic History of America, 1976, The Wealth Creators: An Entrpenurial History of the United States, 1989; contbg. author: Explorations in Econs. History, 1973—, Jour. Econ. History, 1974, Social Sci. History, 1977, Wall Stree Jour.; editor Jour. Pvt. Enterprise. Grantee Freedom Found. at Valley Forge, 1980. Mem. Assn. Pvt. Enterprise Edn. (pres. 1984-85), Econ. History Assn. Home: 6 Andrew Dr Weatogue CT 06089-9725 Office: Trinity Coll 300 Summit St Hartford CT 06106-3100

GUNDERSON, JUDITH KEEFER, golf association executive; b. Charleroi, Pa., May 25, 1939; d. John R. and Irene G. (Gaskill) Keefer; m. Jerry L. Gunderson, mar. 19, 1971; children: Jamie L., Jeff S.; stepchildren: Todd G. (dec.), Marc W. Student pub. schs., Uniontown, Pa. Bookkeeper Fayette Nat. Bank, 1957-59, gen. leader bookkeeper, 1960-63; head bookkeeper 1st Nat. Bank, Broward, Fla., 1963-64; bookkeeper Ruthenberg Homes, Inc., 1966-69; bookkeeper, asst. sec.-treas. Peninsular Properties, Inc. subs. Investors Diversified, Mpls., 1969-72; conptr., pres. Am. Golf Fla., Inc. (doing bus. as Golf and Tennis World), Deerfield Beach, Fla., 1972-89, stockholder, 1972-92; sales assoc. Realty Brokers Internat., Inc., 1990; sec.-treas. Internat. Golf, Inc., 1974-89, stockholder, 1989-94; dir. Mary Kay Cosmetics, 1993-97; ind. distbr. Nikken, Deerfield Beach, 1997—.

GUNDERSON, KEITH ROBERT, philosophy educator; b. New Ulm, Aug. 29, 1935; s. Luverne Robert G. and Rosalyn Emma Swark; m. Donna Mae Beernink, Dec. 29, 1959 (div. July 1979); children: Christopher, Jonathan, Nathaniel; m. Sandra Jean Reikki, July 28, 1979. BA, Macalester Coll., 1957, Oxford U., England, 1959; PhD, Princeton U., 1962. Author: Mentality and Machine, 1971, 3d edit., 1985, A Continual Interest in the Sun and Sea, 1971, 3142 Lyndale Avenue South, 1976, To See a Thing, 1976. Minn. State Arts Bd. grantee, 1979; Fulbright fellow, 1957-59.

GUNDERSON, ROBERT VERNON, JR., lawyer; b. Memphis, Dec. 4, 1951; s. Robert V. and Suzanne (McCarthy) G.; m. Anne Durkheimer, May 15, 1982; children: Katherine Paige, Robert Graham. BA with distinction, U. Kans., 1973; MBA, U. Pa., 1974; MA, Stanford U., 1976; JD, U. Chgo., 1979. Bar: Calif. 1979, U.S. Dist. Ct. (no. dist.) Calif. 1979. Assoc. Cooley, Godward, Castro, Huddleson & Tatum, San Francisco and Palo Alto, Calif., 1979-84, ptnr., 1984-88; ptnr. Brobeck, Phleger & Harrison, Palo Alto, 1988-95, mem. exec. com., 1991-95, chmn. bus. and tech. practice, 1992-95; founder, ptnr. Gunderson Dettmer Stough Villeneuve Franklin & Hachigian, Menlo Park, Calif., 1995—; panelist Venture Capital and Pub. Offering Negotiation, San Francisco and N.Y.C., 1981, 83, 85, 92, Practicing Law Inst., N.Y.C. and San Francisco, 1986; moderator, panelist Third Ann. Securities Law Inst., 1985; dir. Heartport, Inc., Redwood City, Calif.; sec. Dionex Corp., Sunnyvale, Calif., 1983-88, Southwall Techs., Inc., Palo Alto, 1985-88, Conductus, Inc., Sunnyvale, 1992—, Remedy Corp., Mountain View, Calif., 1995-97; vis. lectr. U. Santa Clara Law Sch., 1985, 89. Exec. editor U. Chgo. Law Rev., 1978-79; contbr. articles to profl. jours. Mem. ABA (bus. law sect., various coms.), State Bar Calif. (panelist continuing legal edn. 1984), San Francisco Bar Assn., Am. Fin. Assn., Am. Soc. Corporate Secs., Wharton Club (San Francisco Bay area). Avocations: contemporary art, music, travel. Home: 243 Polhemus Ave Menlo Park CA 94027-5442 Office: Gunderson Dettmer Franklin & Hachigian 155 Constitution Dr Menlo Park CA 94025-1106

GUNDERSON, SCOTT LEE, state legislator; b. Oct. 24, 1956; m. Lisa Gunderson, Oct. 17, 1981; children: Joshua, Hannah, Rebecca. Grad. H.S., Waterford, Wis. Former supr. Town of Waterford, Wis.; assemblyman Wis. State Dist. 83; owner Gundy's Sport. dir. Racine County Fair Bd. Mem. Wind Lake C. of C. (past pres.), Waterford Lions, Wings Over Wis. Commn. Address: PO Box 7 Waterford WI 53185-0007

GUNDERSON, STEVE CRAIG, consultant, former congressman; b. Eau Claire, Wis., May 10, 1951; s. Arthur E. and Adeline C. G. BA, U. Wis., 1973. Mem. Wis. Assembly, 1974-79; legis. dir. Rep. Toby Roth, 1979; mem. 97th-104th Congresses from 3d Wis. dist., 1981-96; chmn. agrl. subcom. on livestock, dairy and poultry, mem. econ. and ednl. opportunity com.; sr. cons. The Greystone Co., Arlington, Va., 1996—; Dir. spl. projects Gov. Dreyfus of Wis. campaign, 1978. Mem. Lions (Pleasantville chpt.). Republican. Lutheran. Office: The Greystone Co Ste 1003 1601 N Kent St Arlington VA 22209-2105*

GUNDERSON, TED LEE, security consultant; b. Colorado Springs, Colo., Nov. 7, 1928. BBA, U. Nebr. Sales rep. George A. Hormel Co., Austin, Minn., 1950-51; spl. agt. in charge U.S. Dept. Justice FBI, Los Angeles, Dallas, Memphis, Phila., 1951-79; internat. security cons. Ted L. Gunderson & Assocs., Santa Monica, Calif., 1979—; cons. Calif. Narcotic Authority. Author: How to Locate Anyone Anywhere, 1989, Be Smart, Be Safe, 1994; appeared on numerous nat. and local TV and radio talk shows; prodr. TV documentary on Satanism. Mem. Bel Air U.S. Navy League, Internat. Assn. Chiefs of Police, Internat. Footprinters Assn., Philanthropic Found. (Los Angeles chpt.), Royal Soc. Encouragement of Arts, Mfrs. and Commerce, Sigma Alpha Epsilon. Avocations: golf, racquetball.

GUNDLACH, HEINZ LUDWIG, investment banker, lawyer; b. Dusseldorf, Germany, July 6, 1937; came to U.S., 1969, naturalized, 1980; s. Heinrich Otto and Ilse (Schuster) G.; m. Cornelia T. Gundlach; children: Andrew, Annabelle, Julia Olivia. ML, U. Heidelberg, 1962, LLD, 1962. V.p. Thyssen A.G. Dusseldorf, 1964-68; v.p., partner Loeb, Rhoades & Co., N.Y.C., 1969-75; vice-chmn., CEO Fed-Mart Corp., San Diego, 1975-81; vice chmn., chief exec. officer successor cos. Sunbelt Investment Holdings, Inc., 1981-88; chmn. successor cos. Trucolor Foto Inc., 1981-88, Clearfoto, Inc., 1981-88; mng. dir. Dean Witter Reynolds, Inc., N.Y.C. and London, 1988-91; prin., chmn. Cardinal Capital Corp., Cardinal Realty Corp., Palm Beach, Fla., 1991—. Served with W. Ger. Army, 1958-59. Mem. St. James's Club (London). Republican. Home: 150 Algoma Rd Palm Beach FL 33480-4902 Office: Cardinal Capital Corp 217 Peruvian Ave Palm Beach FL 33480-4635

GUNDLACH, ROBERT WILLIAM, retired physicist; b. Buffalo, Sept. 7, 1926; s. Emanuel G. and Helen (Fuchs) G.; m. Audrey Jean Baker, Jan. 27, 1928; children: Gregory E., Eric R., Kurt B. BA in Physics, U. Buffalo, 1949, postgrad., 1949-51. Teaching asst. physics U. Buffalo, 1949-51; physicist Durez Plastics & Chems., North Tonawanda, N.Y., 1951-52; project leader Xerox Corp. (then Haloid Co.), Rochester, N.Y., 1952-55, sr. project leader, 1955-57, rsch. assoc., 1957-59; sr. rsch. assoc. Haloid-Xerox Corp., Rochester, 1959-61; sr. scientist Xerox Corp., Rochester, 1961-63, prin. scientist, 1963-66, rsch. fellow, 1966-78, sr. rsch. fellow, 1978-95; cons. Xerox Corp., 1995—. Contbr.: Xerography and Related Processes, 1965, Inventors at Work; 156 patents related to xerographic copying and printing, 1957—; contbr. articles to profl. jours. Recipient Inventor of Yr. award Rochester Patent Law Assn., 1974, C.F. Furnas Meml. award U. Buffalo, 1992, Johann Gutenberg prize Soc. Info. Display, 1993. Mem. Electrostats. Soc. Am. (pres., sr. advisor 1971-94), Imaging Sci. and Tech. (Kosar Meml. award 1976, Vis. Lectr. award 1985, Carlson Meml. award 1986, Fellowship award 1991), elected to Nat. Acad. of Engring., 1994. Mem. Soc. of Friends. Avocations: skiing, canoe camping, birding, windsurfing, inventing.

GUNDY, JEFFREY GENE, English educator; b. Bloomington, Ill., Aug. 7, 1952; s. Roger Eugene and Arlene (Ringenberg) G.; m. Marlyce Martens, Oct. 27, 1973; children: Nathan, Ben, Joel. BA, Goshen Coll., 1975; MA, Ind. U., 1978, PhD, 1983. Instr. Hesston (Kans.) Coll., 1980-84; prof. English, Bluffton (Ohio) Coll., 1984—; C. Henry Smith peace lectr. C. Henry Smith Trust, 1989, 99. Author: Inquiries: Poems, 1992, Flatlands: Poems, 1995, A Community of Memory: My Days with George and Clara, 1996. Creative writing fellow Ohio Arts Coun., 1988, 91, 96, 99. Mem. MLA, Nat. Coun. Tchrs. English. Mennonite. Avocations: guitar, soccer. Office: Bluffton Coll English Dept Bluffton OH 45817

GUNHUS, GAYLORD T., military career officer; b. Enderlin, N.D., May 22, 1940; m. Ann Broten; children: Kevin, Michael, Holly. BS, Seattle Pacific U., 1962; MDiv, Luth. Brethren Sem., 1967; ThM, Princeton Theol. Sem., 1976; grad., Armed Forces Staff Coll., 1980, Army War Coll., 1989. Ordained clergyman Luth. Ch., Ch. Luth. Brethren of Am. Synod, 1967. Army chaplain U.S. Army, 1967, advanced through grades to brig. gen.; asst. brigade chaplain Arty. Officer Candidate Sch. U.S. Army, Ft. Sill, Okla., 1967-68; bn. chaplain 520th Transp. Bn. U.S. Army, Phu Loi, Vietnam, 1968-69; asst. ctr. chaplain U.S. Army Pers. Ctr. U.S. Army, Ft. Lewis, Wash., 1969-72; group chaplain 164th Aviation Group U.S. Army, Can Tho, Vietnam, 1972-73; cmty. chaplain Stanley R. Mikkelson Safeguard Complex U.S. Army, Nekoma, N.D., 1973-75; asst. cmty. chaplain U.S. Army, Heidelberg, Germany, 1976-79; chief Concepts and Studies Divsn., chief Concepts Divsn. U.S. Army, Ft. Benjamin Harrison, Ind., 1980-85; divsn. chaplain 9th Inf. Divsn. U.S. Army, Ft. Lewis, Wash., 1985-87; I Corps and Installation chaplain U.S. Army, Ft. Lewis, 1987-88; USAREUR chaplain U.S. Army, 1989-92; TRADOC chaplain U.S. Army, Ft. Monroe, Va., 1992-94; dep. chief of chaplains U.S. Army, Washington, 1994—. Decorated Legion of Merit with oak leaf cluster, Bronze Star medal with oak leaf cluster, Meritorious Svc. medal with two oak leaf clusters, Air medal, Army Commendation medal with oak leaf cluster. Office: US Army 2700 Army Pentagon Washington DC 20310-2700

GUNN, ALAN, law educator; b. Syracuse, N.Y., Apr. 8, 1940; s. Albert Dale and Helen Sherwood (Whitnall) G.; m. Bertha Ann Buchwald, 1975; 1 child, William. BS, Rensselaer Poly. Inst., 1961; JD, Cornell U., 1970. Bar: D.C. 1970. Assoc. Hogan & Hartson, Washington, 1970-72; asst. prof. law Washington U., St. Louis, 1972-75, assoc. prof., 1975-76; assoc. prof. law Cornell U., Ithaca, N.Y., 1977-79, prof., 1979-84, J. duPratt White prof., 1984-89; prof. law U. Notre Dame, Ind., 1989-96, John N. Matthews prof., 1996—. Author: Partnership Income Taxation, 1991, 2d edit., 1995; (with Larry D. Ward) Cases, Text and Problems on Federal Income Taxation, 4th edit., 1998; (with Vincent R. Johnson) Studies in American Tort Law, 1994. Methodist. Office: U Notre Dame Law Sch Notre Dame IN 46556

GUNN, ALBERT EDWARD, JR., internist, educator, lawyer, administrator; b. Port Washington, N.Y., Oct. 31, 1933; s. Albert Edward and Esther Frances (Williams) G.; m. Joan Marie Jacoby, May 18, 1968; children: Albert Edward III, Emily Williams Gunn Hebert, Andrew Robert, Clare Margaret, Catherine Ann, Philip David. *Albert E. Gunn Sr. was born on September 16, 1891, in Port Washington, New York,where he later died on October 14, 1952. His son Edward Mott Gunn was married toSarah Olivia (Nelson) G. and was valedictorian, at the Port Washington High School in 1910. He received a LL.B. from the Brooklyn Law School of St. Lawrence University in 1912, and passed the New York Bar in 1914. He had a law practice in New York City until 1919, and then relocated to Port Washington with the firm Gunn and Gunn and Gunn, and then Neier and Gunn until 1952. He was the president of the Chamber of Commerce in 1932. He was a Regiment Sergeant Major with the Judge Advocate Generals Department form 1918-19. He married Esther Frances (Williams) G., daughter of Edward Williams and Ellen (Bevan) W. on April 27, 1924. She was born on October 22, 1898 in New York, and died April 30, 1969 in Stuart Florida.* BS, Fordham Coll., 1955, LLB, 1958; MB BCh BAO, Nat. U. Ireland, Galway, 1967. Bar: N.Y. 1958, D.C. 1972; diplomate Am. Bd. Internal Medicine. Owner, agt. Albert E. Gunn Ins. Agy., Port Washington, 1953-65; intern Montefiore Hosp., N.Y.C., 1967-68; resident in medicine Roosevelt Hosp., N.Y.C., 1968-70; USPHS trainee in neurology U. Rochester, N.Y., 1970-72; asst. dir. govtl. rels. AMA, Washington, 1972-74; med. dir. Geriat. Svcs. Suffolk County, Hauppauge, N.Y., 1974-75; med. dir. Rehab. Ctr., U. Tex./M.D. Anderson Cancer Ctr., 1975-88, chief rehab. sect., 1988-93, chief geriat. sect., 1993—, dep. chmn. dept. internal med. spltys., 1998—; asst. prof. medicine U. Tex. Med. Sch., Houston, 1976-80, assoc. prof., 1980—, also assoc. dean for admissions; med. dir. Region IV, Tex. Med. Found., 1986-93; del.-at-large White House conf. on Handicapped Individuals, 1977; pres. Mus. Med. Sci., 1990; cons. CDC, Legal Svcs. Corp., Nat. Libr. Medicine. Co-author: Rehabilitation of the Cancer Patient, 1976, AIDS in Africa, 1988; editor, contbg. author: Cancer Rehabilitation, 1984; mem. editl. bd. Cancer Bull., 1977-90, Gerontology and Geriatrics Edn., Linacre Quar.; contbr. articles to profl. jours. Mem. nat. adv. health coun. HEW, 1974-75; mem. adv. com. Nat. Inst. Law Enforcement and Criminal Justice, Law Enforcement Assistance Adminstrn., U.S. Dept. Justice, 1974-76; mem. bd. regents Nat. Libr. Medicine, NIH, 1983-87, chmn., 1986-87, chmn. lit. selection tech. adv. com., 1988-91; bd. dirs. Right to Life Advs., 1977-78, Tex. Med. Ctr. Libr., 1990. With USAF, 1958-61, capt., 1961-75. Fellow ACP; mem. Tex. Med. Assn. (trustee ins. trust, chmn. bd. trustees 1997-99), Harris County Med. Soc. (exec. bd. 1986-90, v.p. 1998), Royal Coll. Physicians London (licentiate), Royal Coll. Surgeons Eng., Houston Acad. Medicine (bd. dirs. 1986-90, pres. 1990), Houston Bar Assn., D.C. Bar, Cath. Med. Assn. (regional bd. dirs. 1992—, Thomas Linacre award 1997), Sons of Union Vets. of Civil War, Am. Legion, Army and Navy Club, Cosmos Club, Drs. Club (Houston). Roman Catholic. Home: 2329 Watts St Houston TX 77030-1139 Office: U Tex MD Anderson Cancer Ctr 1515 Holcombe Blvd Houston TX 77030-4009

GUNN, CLARE ALWARD, travel consultant, writer, retired educator; b. Grandville, Mich., Oct. 28, 1916; s. Fred Melvin and Lila Barton (Alward) G.; married; children: Thomas, Bruce, Richard, William. BS, Mich. State U., 1940, MS in Land and Water Conservation, 1952; PhD in Landscape Architecture, U. Mich., 1965. Lic. landscape architect. Prof. dept. tourism-recreation devel. Mich. State U., East Lansing, 1945-66; vis. prof. tourism Sch. Travel Industry Mgmt. U. Hawaii, 1966-67; prof. tourism-recreation devel. Tex. A&M U., College Station, 1967-74, prof. dept. recreation, park and tourism scis., 1975-85, prof. emeritus, 1985—; prof. resources recreation Oreg. State U., summer 1974; prof. Sch. Landscape Arthitecture, U. Guelph, Ont., Can., 1974-75; vis. prof. Clemson U., 1989; cons. state tourism plans N.Y., 1986, Okla., 1987, Wash., 1988, Del., 1990, Ill., 1993; cons. analysis tourism potential Whiteman Park, Perth, Australia, 1989; cons. South African Tourism Bd., 1988, natural resource potential for Tourism in Del., 1991; mem. task force Moorea & Tourism, French Polynesia, 1990, tourism potential Finger Lakes Region, N.Y., 1989-91, resort devel. plan Chun-Cheon Lake Area, Korea, 1991; tourism plan Newfoundland, Labrador, Can., 1994; prepared Agenda Item 13 World Tourism Conf., The Pilippines, 1980, major destination zone study for Can., 1982. Author: A Concept for the Design of a Tourism-Recreation Region, 1965, An Annotated Bibliography of Resource Use of the Texas Gulf Coast, 1969, Vacationscape: Designing Tourist Regions, 3d edit., 1997, Chinese edit., 1998, Tourism Planning, 3d edit., 1994, others; contbr. articles to profl. jours. Mem. George Bush Libr. Com., College Station, 1994; chair adv. com. CVB of Bryan, College Station, 1992-93; mem. sch. bd. Okemos (Mich.) Dist., 1958-64. Recipient Tex. Gov. award, 1984, Disting. Alumni award Landscape Architecture Program, Mich. State U., 1999. Fellow Am. Soc. Landscape Architects (Spl. award 1973); mem. Travel and Tourism Rsch. Assn. (bd. dirs.), Rotary Internat. (chmn. dist. group study exch. com. 1992-93, chair dist. exch. com. 1992-94, Role of Fame award 1990), Gamma Sigma Delta, Epsilon Sigma Phi, Beta Gamma Sigma, Phi Kappa Phi, Sigma Lambda Alpha (Disting. Mem. award 1991). Republican. Methodist. Avocations: photography, travel, sketching. Home: 1602 Glade St College Station TX 77840-4365 Office: Tex A&M U Dept Park Recreation T College Station TX 77843

GUNN, G. GREG, insurance executive; b. Washington, Sept. 10, 1958; s. W. Guy and Emily (Hamby) G. BS, Pa. State U., 1980. Cert. ins. counselor. Account exec. Byerly Ins. Agts. & Brokers, Inc., Lemoyne, Pa., 1980-83, v.p., 1983-88; pres. Gunn-Mowery Ins. Group, Lemoyne, 1988—; pres. Am. Subcontractors Assn. Central Pa., 1988-89, exec. com. 1985-89, 98-99; chmn. Central Pa. Ins. Com., Harrisburg, 1988; mem. bd. dirs. Big Brothers/Big Sisters, Harrisburg Cmty. Theater, Capital Area Ind. Agts. Assn., Associated Pa. Constructors, AMS Users Group. Contbr. articles to profl. jours. Mem. Profl. Ins. Agts. Assn., Shriners. Republican. Methodist. Avocation: finisher 1987 N.Y.C. marathon. Home: 22 Paddock Ln Camp Hill PA 17011-1268 Office: Gunn-Mowery Ins Group Inc PO Box 900 Camp Hill PA 17001-0900

GUNN, GILES BUCKINGHAM, English educator, religion educator; b. Evanston, Ill., Jan. 9, 1938; s. Buckingham Willcox and Janet (Fargo) G.; m. Janet Mears Varner, Dec. 29, 1969 (div. July 1983); 1 child, Adam Buckingham; m. Deborah Rose Sills, July 9, 1983; 1 child, Abigail Rose. BA, Amherst Coll., 1959; student, Episc. Theol. Sch., Cambridge, Mass., 1959-60; MA, U. Chgo., 1963, PhD, 1967. Prof. religion and lit. U. Chgo., 1966-74; prof. religion and Am. studies U. N.C., Chapel Hill, 1974-85; prof. English and Religion U. Fla., 1984-85; prof. English U. Calif., Santa Barbara, 1985—, chmn. English dept., 1993-97, chmn. global and internat. studies, 1998—; vis. asst. prof. religion Stanford U., Palo Alto, Calif., 1973; Benedict Disting. vis. prof. religion Carleton Coll., Northfield, Minn., 1977; William R. Kenan Disting. vis. prof. humanities Coll. William and Mary, Williamsburg, Va., 1983-84; Humanities Disting. vis. prof. U. Colo., 1989; Eric Yoegelin Disting. prof. Am. Studies, U. Munich, 1994-95; dir. NEH summer sems. for coll. and univ. tchrs., 1979, 81, 85, 94, for sch. tchrs., 1987, 88, 89, 91; cons. Libr. of Am. Author: F.O. Matthiessen, The Critical Achievement, 1975, The Interpretation of Otherness: Literature, Religion and the American Imagination, 1979, The Culture of Criticism and The Criticism of Culture, 1987, Thinking Across the American Grain: Ideology, Intellect, and the New Pragmatism, 1992; editor: Literature and Religion, 1971, Henry James, Senior: A Selection of His Writings, 1974, New World Metaphysics: Readings on the Religious Meaning of the American Experience, 1981, The Bible and American Arts and Letters, 1983, Church, State, and American Culture, 1984, Early American Writing, 1994; co-editor: Redrawing the Boundaries: The Transformation of English and American Literary Studies, 1992; contbr. numerous articles to profl. jours. Bd. dirs. Fund for Santa Barbara. Edward John Noble Leadership grantee, 1959-63; Amherst-Doshisha fellow, Kyoto, Japan, 1960-61, Kent fellow, Danforth Found., 1963-65, Guggenheim fellow, 1978-79, Nat. Endowment for Humanities fellow, 1990, U. Calif. Pres.'s Rsch. fellow, 1990. Mem. MLA, Am. Acad. Religion (dir. research and pubs. 1974-77), Am. Studies Assn., Soc. Religion, Arts and Contemporary Culture, Soc. Am. Phil., Nat. Critics Book Circle. Democrat. Avocations: walking, motorcycling. Home: 2744 Macadamia Ln Montecito CA 93108-1658 Office: U Calif Dept English Santa Barbara CA 93106

GUNN, JAMES E., English language educator; b. Kansas City, Mo., July 12, 1923; s. J. Wayne and Elsie M. (Hutchison) G.; m. Jane Frances Anderson, Feb. 6, 1947; children: Christopher Wayne, Kevin Robert. BS, U. Kans., 1947, MA, 1951. Editor Western Printing and Litho, Racine, Wis., 1951-52; asst. dir. Civil Def., Kansas City, Mo., 1953; instr. U. Kans., Lawrence, 1955, mng. editor Alumni Assn., 1956-58, adminstrv. asst. to the chancellor for univ. rels., 1958-70, lectr. English, 1970-74, prof., 1974-93, emeritus prof., 1993—; cons. Easton Press, Norwalk, Conn., 1985—; lectr. in field. Author over 22 books including Station in Space, 1958, The Immortals, 1962, The End of the Dreams, 1975, Alternate Worlds: The Illustrated History of Science Fiction (World Sci. Fiction Conv. Spl. award 1976, Pilgrim award Sci. Fiction Rsch. Assn. 1976), The Listeners, 1972, Isaac Asimov: the Foundations of Science Fiction, 1982 (Hugo award World Sci. Fiction Conv. 1983), numerous plays, screenplays, radio scripts; editor The Road to Sci. Fiction, 6 vols., 1977-98, 8 other books; contbr. 90 stories to mags.; contbr. articles to profl. jours. Dir. Ctr. for Study Sci. Fiction, Lawrence, 1984—. Lt. (j.g.) USN, 1943-46, PTO. Recipient Eaton award Eaton Conf., 1992, Hugo award, 1983; Mellon fellow U. Kans., 1981, 84. Mem. Author's Guild, Sci. Fiction and Fantasy Writers Am. (pres. 1971-72), Sci. Fiction Rsch. Assn. (pres. 1981-82, Pilgrim award 1976).. Avocations: golf, bridge. Home: 2215 Orchard Ln Lawrence KS 66049-2707 Office: U Kans English Dept Lawrence KS 66045

GUNN, JOAN MARIE, health care administrator; b. Binghamton, N.Y., Jan. 29, 1943; d. Andrew and Ruth Antoinette (Butler) Jacoby; m. Albert E. Gunn, Jr., May 18, 1968; children: Albert E. III, Emily W. Hebert, Andrew R., Clare M., Catherine A.B., Philip D. Diploma, Binghamton State Hosp., 1966; BS summa cum laude, Tex. Woman's U., 1983; MSN, U. Tex., Houston, 1989. RN, N.Y., Tex., Va., Gt. Britain. Staff nurse Columbia/Presbyn. Med. Ctr., N.Y.C., 1966-67; head nurse, ICU Montefiore Hosp. and Med. Ctr., N.Y.C., Va., 1967-68; staff nurse Nat. Orthopedic and Rehab. Hosp., Arlington, Va., 1972-73, Woman's Hosp. of Tex., Houston, 1976-80; staff nurse geriatrics St. Anthony's Ctr., Houston, 1985-86; charge nurse gero psychiatry Bellaire Gen. Hosp., Houston, 1986; head nurse gero psychiat. unit U. Tex./Harris County Psychiat. Ctr., Houston, 1986-88, asst. dir. nursing adult svcs., 1988-90, DON adult svcs., 1990-93, nurse exec., 1991-93, DON, 1993-98, asst. adminstr., 1994—. Mem. Nat. Soc. Colonial Dames of the XVII Century, Daus. of Union Vets. of Civil War, Sigma Theta Tau. Roman Catholic. Avocation: reading history. Home: 2329 Watts St Houston TX 77030-1139 Office: U Tex Harris County Psychiat Ctr 2800 S Macgregor Way Houston TX 77021-1032

GUNN, MOREY WALKER, JR., secondary school educator, choir director, organist; b. Orangeburg, S.C., June 23, 1939; s. Morey Walker Sr. and Marjorie (Dusek) G.; m. Sheila Diane Taylor, Nov. 26, 1994; 1 child, Andrew Walker. BA in Music, Furman U., 1961, MA, 1967. Cert. music edn. tchr., S.C. Band dir. Holly Hill (S.C.) High Sch., 1961-65, Orangeburg High Sch., 1965-71, Greer (S.C.) High Sch., 1971-73, Ft. Johnson High Sch., Charleston, S.C., 1973-77, Berkeley County Schs., Goose Creek, S.C., 1978—. Mem. Nat. Rep. Senatorial Com. 1978-97; deacon 1st Presbyn, Ch., 1965-71; elder James Island Presbyn. Ch., 1974-76, 78-80, choir dir., organist, 1980-94; organist St. Andrews United Meth. Ch., Orangburg, S.C., 1994—; bd. dirs. excellence in teaching award com. Charleston County Youth Symphony, 1975; bd. dirs. Charles Towne Landing Band Festival Com., 1988-89. Mem. NEA, Music Educators Nat. Conf., Am. Guild Organists, S.C. Music Educators Assn., Sertoma Club (bd. dirs. 1989-90), Kiwanis Club (bd. dirs. 1997—, sec. 1998—, Disting. Kiwanian award 1998), Elks, Phi Mu Alpha (hon. life). Avocations: dancing, reading, church work, table tennis, collecting seascape prints. Home: 980 Anchor Dr Charleston SC 29412-4930

GUNN, ROBERT BURNS, physiology educator; b. Washington, July 12, 1939; s. Ross and Gladys J. (Rowley) G.; m. Sharon McClellan, Aug. 24, 1963; children: Lora, Heather, Molly, Ian. BS, U. Mich., 1961; MD, Harvard U., 1966. Spl. fellow U.S. Pub. Health Svc., 1969-71; rsch. assoc. dept. physiology and pharmacology Duke U. Med. Ctr., Durham, N.C., 1969-71, asst. prof. dept. physiology and pharmacology, 1971-75; assoc. prof. dept. pharmacol. and physiol. scis. Pritzer Sch. Medicine, U. Chgo., 1975-81; prof., chmn. dept. physiology Emory U. Sch. Med., Atlanta, 1981—; vis. researcher Inst. for Biophysics, U. Copenhagen, Denmark, 1971-72. Lt. commdr. USPHS, 1967-69. NATO fellow NSF, 1971. Mem. Biophysical Soc. (treas. 1987-95, Kenneth S. Cole award 1987), Soc. Gen. Physiologists (treas. 1981-84, pres. 1989-90), Assn. Chmn. Depts. of Physiology (pres. 1989-90), Am. Physiol. Soc. (edn. com., chmn. cell and gen. sect. 1998—). Methodist. Office: Emory U Sch Medicine Dept Physiology Atlanta GA 30322-3110*

GUNN, S. JEANNE, writer, artist, Reiki educator; b. Janesville, Wis., Feb. 28, 1939; d. David J. Nehls and Shirley Mara Nehls Popanz; m. Harold David Gunn, Sept. 13, 1957 (div. 1982); children: Daryl Andrew, Dennis Alan, Jennifer Gunn Link. Grad. H.S., Evansville, Wis. Cert. Reiki master, massage therapy, aromatherapy, Ayurveda; ordained minister. Office mgr. constrn. co., 10 yrs.; developer Bodywork & Co., Virginia Beach, Va., 1992, Sacred Earth Ctr., Virginia Beach, 1994. Author: Reiki and Beyond Healing Manual, 1994, also Reiki instrn. booklets, 1994, Natural Healing-Alternative Resources for Total Health, 1999, poems; editor several newsletters; contbr. articles to newspapers and tng. manuals interior designer, painter greeting cards; designer southwestern wall hangings; developer tng. manuals for Reiki edn. chmn. book fair PTA; troop leader Girl Scouts U.S.A.; den mother Boy Scouts Am.; softball coach; hosp. vol.; seminar developer Teen Imagines; founder Talk of Towne, Emergency Mgmt. Team. Recipient award for outstanding media person in cmty. Talk of the Towne. Mem. Internat. Toastmistresses (past pres.). Avocations: writing poetry, gardening, walking, painting, quilting. E-mail: wddancer@pilot.infi.net. Office: Sacred Earth Ctr PO Box 1734 Virginia Beach VA 23451-9734

GUNN, SANDRA JOYCE, musician and church lay leader; b. Allentown, Pa., Oct. 30, 1951; d. Hilbert Guy and Joyce Marie (Mantz) Snyder; m. Bruce Myron Gunn, Oct. 17, 1981. BS in Music Edn., Lebanon Valley Coll, 1973. Cert. instrumental and vocal music tchr. Handbell dir. Calvary Presbyn. Ch., Riverton, N.J., 1983-87; dir. music (choir and instruments) Broad St. United Meth. Ch., Burlington, N.J., 1987—; part-time bookkeeper Lippincott Fuel Co., Delanco, N.J., 1985-92; ch. auditor Calvary Presbyn. Ch., Riverton, 1988, 91; chmn. Christian edn., elder Calvary Presbyn. Ch., Riverton, 1979-82, 96—, chmn. worship com., 1996—; youth advisor Broad St. United Meth. Ch., 1987, chmn. Ann. Choir Festival, 1990—; chmn. worship com. Broad St. United Meth. Ch., Burlington, 1991-93, coord. youth Sunday and Christmas Eve svcs., 1989-94; asst. dir. N.J. Meth. Chorale for Gr. Britain concert tour, 1991. Treas. Porch Club, Riverton, 1983-85; sec. Riverton Rep. Club, 1985-86; mem. Riverton Improvement Com., 1989: pres. N.J. Women's Clubs, Riverton, 1985-90, dir. chorus, 1992—: instr. music appreciation course Burlington County Continuing Edn. Program, 1991. Home: 808 Main St Riverton NJ 08077-1707 Office: Broad St United Meth Ch 36 E Broad St Burlington NJ 08016-1631

GUNN, THOM(SON) (WILLIAM), poet; b. Gravesend, Eng., Aug. 29, 1929; came to U.S., 1954; s. Herbert Smith and Ann Charlotte (Thomson) G. BA, Trinity Coll., Cambridge (Eng.) U., 1953. Tchr. English, sr. lectr. U. Calif., Berkeley, 1958-66, 73-99. Author: Fighting Terms, 1954, The Sense of Movement, 1957, My Sad Captains, 1961, Touch, 1967, Moly, 1971, Jack Straw's Castle and Other Poems, 1976, Selected Poems, 1979, The Passages of Joy, 1982, The Occasions of Poetry, 1982, expanded edit., 1985, The Man with Night Sweats, 1992, Shelf Life, 1993, Collected Poems, 1993. Recipient Robert Kirsch award L.A. Times, 1988, Shelley Meml. award Poetry Soc. Am., 1990, Forward 1st prize, 1992, Bay Area Book Reviewers award for poetry, 1973, 93, PEN USA West Poetry award, 1973, 93, Lenore Marshall Poetry prize, 1993, Medal of Merit for poetry Am. Acad. Arts and Letters, 1998; Lila Wallace Reader's Digest grantee, 1991; MacArthur fellow, 1993;. Fellow Am. Acad. Arts and Sci. Address: 1216 Cole St San Francisco CA 94117-4322

GUNNELS, LEE O., retired finance and management educator, manufacturing company executive; b. Huntington Park, Calif., Sept. 11, 1933; s. LeRoy O. and Marrion W. Gunnels; m. Laura Gunnels, Nov. 7, 1958; children: Cornelia, Amelia, Sarah. BA in Math./Physics, U. Hawaii, 1960; MBA, Xavier U., Cin., 1970. Nuclear physicist Bettelle Meml. Inst., Columbus, Ohio; ret. assoc. prof. fin. and mgmt. Muskingum Tech. Coll., Zanesville, Ohio; past chmn. faculty senate Muskingum Tech. Coll., Zanesville; chmn. bd. dirs. Pallet Systems and Mgmt. Corp., Inc., Zanesville (Ohio) Pallet, Inc. Contbr. articles to various publs. Home: 1849 Drugan Ct SW Reynoldsburg OH 43068-8181 also: Stoney Meadow Farms Zanesville OH 43702-0382

GUNNELS, MARY DAHLGREN, trauma coordinator; b. San Antonio, Apr. 24, 1958; d. John Howard and Lucile Ruth (Yarborough) Dahlgren; m. Mark Dale Gunnels, Aug. 27, 1991. BA, Trinity U., San Antonio, 1979, Trinity U., San Antonio, 1982; BS, Tex. Woman's U., 1991, MS, 1994. RN, Tex., Oreg.; cert. ACLS instr.; cert. emergency nurse. Mgmt. positions San Antonio, 1980-87; nurse intern critical care program Parkland Hosp., Dallas, 1991-92, assoc. unit mgr., weekend night supr., emergency svcs. nurse, 1992-95; trauma coord., instr. Oreg. Health Scis. U., Portland, 1995—. Cons. editor Jour. Emergency Nursing; contbr. articles to profl. jours. and books. Vol. Jr. League, Dallas, San Antonio, Portland, Oreg., 1983—, ARC, Dallas, 1992-95; bd. dirs. San Antonio Downtown Merchants Assn., 1984-85, Young Art Patrons of San Antonio Mus. of Art, 1984-85. Recipient Five Star Spirit award Baylor Med. Ctr., 1990. Mem. APHA (injury control sect.), Assn. for Advancement of Automotive Medicine, Oreg. Emergency Nurses Assn., Emergency Nurses Assn. (nat. del. 1994, 95, 97, nat. trauma com.), Dallas County Emergency Nurses Assn. (pres.-elect 1995), Phi Kappa Phi, Eta Sigma Gamma. Avocations: film, theater, travel, cooking. Office: Oreg Health Scis U Trauma Program 3181 SW Sam Jackson Park Rd Portland OR 97201-3011

GUNNERSON, ROBERT MARK, manufacturing company executive, accountant, lawyer; b. Washington Island, Wis., Apr. 6, 1949; s. Roger William and Ester Victoria (Rosengren) G.; m. Mary Beth Fischer, Oct. 28, 1978; children: Carl Robert, Karen Jane. B.B.A., U. Wis. at Milw., 1971; J.D., Marquette U., 1974. Bar: Wis. 1974; CPA, Wis. Staff atty. Modine Mfg. Co., Racine, Wis., 1974-77; asst. sec. Modine Mfg. Co., 1977, sec., 1977-79, sec., asst. treas., 1979-80, treas., 1980-98; sec., treas., exec. com., dir. MEI, Inc., Racine, 1990—, v.p. strategic planning, 1995—. Treas. Racine Environ. Com., 1980-81, pres., 1982-85, bd. dirs., 1980-91; trustee, dir., treas. Racine Edn. Coun., 1991—, v.p. Mem. Wis. Bar Assn., Midwest Bus. Group on Health (Racine chpt.), Chgo. Internat. Fin. Assn. Home: 4704 White Oak Ln Racine WI 53403-4448 Office: MEI Inc Ste 110 1100 Commerce Dr Racine WI 53406

GUNNESS, ROBERT CHARLES, chemical engineer; b. Fargo, N.D., July 28, 1911; s. Christian I. and Elizabeth (Rice) G.; m. Beverly Osterberger, June 18, 1936; children: Robert Charles, Donald Austin, Beverly Anne. B.S., U. Mass., Amherst, 1932; M.S., MIT, 1934, D.Sc., 1936. Asst. prof. chem. engring. MIT, 1936-38; research dept. Standard Oil Co. Ind., 1938-47, mgr. research, 1947-51, asst. gen. mgr. mfg., gen. mgr. supply and transp., 1952-56, exec. v.p., 1956-65, pres., 1965-74, vice chmn., 1974-75, dir., 1953-75; vice chmn. research and devel. bd. Dept. Def., 1951. Trustee U. Chgo., Rush-Presbyn.-St. Lukes Hosp.; life mem. Mass. Inst. Tech. Corp.; past chmn. Nat. Merit Scholarship Corp.; past pres., trustee John Crerar Library. Fellow Am. Inst. Chem. Engrs. (council 1951); mem. Nat. Acad. Engring., Am. Chem. Soc., Am. Acad. Arts and Scis., Crystal Downs Club, Augusta Nat. club, Sigma Xi, Phi Kappa Phi, Kappa Sigma. Home: 807 Morningside Dr Fullerton CA 92835

GUNNING, FRANCIS PATRICK, lawyer, insurance association executive; b. Scranton, Pa., Dec. 10, 1923; s. Frank Peter and Mary Loretta (Kelly) G.; m. Nancy C. Hill, Aug. 10, 1951; 1 son, Brian F. Student, City Coll. N.Y., 1941-43; LLB, St. John's U., 1950. Bar: N.Y. 1950. Legal editor Prentice Hall Pub. Co., N.Y.C., 1950-51; legal specialist Tchrs. Ins. & Annuity Assn. Am., Coll. Retirement Equities Fund, N.Y.C., 1951-53, asst. counsel, 1953-57, assoc. counsel, 1957-60, counsel, 1960-65, asst. gen. counsel, 1965-67, assoc. gen. counsel, 1967, v.p., assoc. gen. counsel, 1967-73, sr. v.p., gen. counsel, 1973-74, exec. v.p., gen. counsel, 1974-88, ret., 1988; trustee, mem. exec. and audit coms. Mortgage Growth Investors (now MGI Properties). Contbr. articles on mortgage financing to profl. jours. With USAAF, 1943-46. Mem. ABA, N.Y. State Bar Assn., Am. Land Title Assn., Am. Law Inst., Assn. of Bar of City of N.Y., Assn. Life Ins. Counsel, Nat. Assn. Coll. Univ. Attys., Am. Coll. Real Estate Lawyers. Republican. Roman Catholic. Home and Office: 32 Kewanee Rd New Rochelle NY 10804-1324

GUNNING, ROBERT CLIFFORD, mathematician, educator; b. Longmont, Colo., Nov. 27, 1931; s. Clifford Henry and Inez (Wilhelm) G.; m. Wanda S. Holtzinger, July 9, 1966. A.B., U. Colo., 1952; M.A., Princeton U., 1953, Ph.D., 1955. NSF fellow U. Chgo., 1955-56; mem. faculty Princeton U., 1956—, prof. math., 1966—, chmn. dept., 1976-79, dean of faculty, 1989-95; vis. prof. U. São Paulo, Brazil, 1957, U. Munich, 1967, ULCA, 1972, Oxford (Eng.) U., spring 1968, fall, 1980, 88, 95; Sloan fellow, 1958-61; asst. dir. studies, math. St. Catharines Coll., Cambridge (Eng.) U., 1959-60; mem. editl. bd. Princeton (N.J.) U. Press, 1969-73. Author: Lectures on Modular Forms, 1962, (with H. Rossi) Analytic Functions of Several Complex Variables, 1965, Lectures on Riemann Surfaces, Vol. I, 1966, Vol. II, 1967, Vol. III, 1972, Complex Analytic Varieties, Vol. I, 1970, Vol. II, 1974, Generalized Theta Functions, 1976, Uniformization of Complex Manifolds, 1978, Introduction to Holomorphic Functions of Several Variables, 3 vols., 1990; editor: Problems in Analysis, 1970, Theta Functions, 1989, Collected Papers of Salomon Bochner, 4 vols., 1991; contbr. articles to profl. jours. Fellow AAAS; mem. Am. Math. Soc., Princeton Club (N.Y.C.), Nassau Club (Princeton), Phi Beta Kappa, Sigma Xi. Episcopalian. Office: Fine Hall Washington Rd Princeton NJ 08544-1000

GUNNING, TOM, art educator. PhD in Cinema Studies, NYU. Prof. dept. art history U. Chgo. Author: D.W. Griffith and the Origins of American Narrative Film: The Early Years, 1991; contbr. articles to profl. jours. Guggenheim fellow, 1998. Fax: (773) 702-5901. E-mail: tgunning@midway.uchicago.edu. Office: Dept Art History U Chgo 5540 South Greenwood Ave Chicago IL 60637

GUNNOE, NANCY LAVENIA, food executive, artist; b. Southside, Tenn., Jan. 7, 1921; d. Edgar Hatton and Clara Sharp (McCurdy) Thompson; m. Raymond Glen Gunnoe, Dec. 6, 1941; children: Lynn Thompson Gunnoe Sheets, Paul Randall (dec.), Joy Virginia Gunnoe Woodrum. Student, Austin Peay Coll., 1939, U. Charleston, 1973-87, 91. Cashier Kroger Co., Charleston, W.V., 1939-40; with Superior Laundry & Cleaning, Charleston, 1940-41; file clk. Hancock Oil Co., Oakland, Calif., 1942; office clk. Office Price Adminstrn., Stockton, Calif., 1943; sec.-treas. R.G. Gunnoe Farms Inc., Charleston, 1947—. Exhibited at local orgns. Mem. Nat. League Am. Pen Women, Inc., Allied Artists W.Va., Univ. Charleston Builders, Kanawha Valley Hist. and Preservation Soc., Charleston Woman's Club, Sunrise Mus. Republican. Avocations: china painting, porcelain sculpture. Home: 2040 Oakridge Dr Charleston WV 25311-1112 Office: 2115 Oakridge Dr Charleston WV 25311-1409

GUNSUL, BROOKS R. W., architect; b. Seattle, Aug. 7, 1928; s. Frank Justus and Phyllis (Webster) G.; m. Marilyn Thompson, Aug. 26, 1950; children: Robin, Karen, David, Jana. B.S. in Archtl. Engring., Wash. State U., 1952. Registered architect, Oreg., Wash., Ill., N.Y. Architect Stewart & Richardson architect, Portland, 1952-57, Scott & Payne, Portland, 1957-59, Wolff & Zimmer, 1959-65; ptnr. Wolff, Zimmer Gunsul. Frasca, Portland, 1966-77; ptnr. Zimmer Gunsul Frasca, Portland, 1977—, Seattle, 1987—, L.A., 1988—; mem. adv. com. Wash. State U. Dept. Architecture, Pullman, 1983-93, found. adv. bd., 1994-96; dir., founder Architecture Found., Portland, 1980-88; trustee Wash. State U. Found. Contbr. articles to profl. jours. Chmn. adv. com. Oreg. Maritime Ctr. and Mus.; trustee Wash. State U. Found. With U.S. Army, 1946-47. Recipient Wash. State U. Achievement award, 1991. Fellow AIA (Firm of Yr. award 1991), Portland Yacht Club, Multnomah Athletic Club. Office: Zimmer Gunsul Frasca Partnership 320 SW Oak St Ste 500 Portland OR 97204-2737*

GUNTER, BRADLEY HUNT, capital management executive; b. Norfolk, Va., Dec. 8, 1940; s. J.A. and Virginia (Whalen) G.; m. Susan Mason Hart, Dec. 27, 1962 (div. 1977); children: Bradley Hunt, Valerie Mason; m. Anne A. Macon, Nov. 7, 1985 (dec. 1994); 1 child, Bradford Macon Gunter; m. Meredith Laura Strohm, Dec. 16, 1994. BA, U. Richmond, 1962; MA, U. Va., 1963, PhD, 1969. Instr. Washington and Lee U., Lexington, Va., 1967-69; asst. prof. Boston Coll., 1969-71; corp. sec. Fed. Res. Bank, Richmond, Va., 1971-80; pres. Bartleby's Inc., Richmond, 1980-85; dir. found. rels. U. Va., Charlottesville, 1985-86; investment broker Scott and String fellow, Richmond, 1987-89; mng. dir. Scott & Stringfellow Capital Mgmt., Richmond, 1989-97, pres., CEO,, 1997—; cons. NEH, Washington, 1975-80. Author: Studies in The Waste Land, 1971, Guide to T.S. Eliot, 1970, Checklist of T.S. Eliot, 1969; contbr. articles to profl. jours. Vestryman St. Paul's Ch., Richmond, 1975-78; chmn. fund drive United Way, Richmond, 1980; mem. arts and scis. alumni coun. U. Va., also mem. Emeritus Soc.; bd. dirs. St. Christopher's Sch. Found., Richmond, 1981-85, Richmond Ballet, Big Bros. Richmond Inc., Va. Found. for Humanities and Pub. Policy, Elk Hill Farm; trustee St. Paul's Endowment Fund, Inc., United Way Greater Richmond; pres. Arts Coun. Richmond, Hist. Richmond Found., Poe Found.; bd. dirs., chmn. U. Va. Cancer Ctr., U. Va. Health Scis. Coun., U. Va. Libr. Bd. Mem. Richmond Assn. Bus. Economists, Investment Mgmt. Cons. Assn., Assn. for Investment Mgmt. and Rsch., U. Va. Alumni Assn. (chpt. pres. Richmond 1981), Va. Soc. Mayflower Descs. (bd. dirs.), Country Club Va., Colonnade Club, Focus Club, Univ. Club, Farmington Country Club, Phi Beta Kappa, Omicron Delta Kappa. Episcopalian. Avocation: tennis. Office: Scott & Stringfellow Capital Mgmt 103 E Water St Ste 201 Charlottesville VA 22902-5293 also: Scott & Stringfellow Capital Mgmt 909 E Main St Richmond VA 23219-3002

GUNTER, EDWIN DALE, JR., pilot; b. Randolph AFB, Tex., Jan. 8, 1946; s. Edwin Dale and Gloria Mae (Ludwig) G.; m. Rita Carla, Aug. 1967 (div. July 1971); children: Edwin D. III, Lisa Michelle; m. Elleen Winn, Nov. 17, 1972. BS in Engring. Mgmt., USAF Acad., 1967; PhD in Flight Instrn. (hon.), Air Tng. Command, 1975; MS in Counseling, Vanderbilt U., 1976. Lic. comml. pilot, flight instr., FAA, pvt. investigator, Tex. Commd. 2d lt. USAF, 1967, advanced through grades to col., 1988; flight instrn., chief pilot instr. tng. USAF, Peterson Field, Colo., 1970-72; instr. pilot, asst. flight comdr., air ops. officer USAF, Laughlin AFB, Tex., 1972-75; shift comdr., chief ops. br. 48th Security Police Squadron USAF, RAF Lakenheath, Eng., 1975-78; chief wing aircrew tng. br. USAF, England AFB, La., 1978-81; asst. ops. officer 89th Flying Tng. Squadron USAF, Sheppard AFB, Tex., 1981-84; with HQ ATC/IG, Randolph AFB, 1984; chief ops. and safety br., comdr. 557th Tng. Squadron USAF Acad., Colorado Springs, Colo., 1984-86; chief readiness dir. HQ ATC/IG, Randolph AFB, Tex., 1986-90; vice comdr. 3300th Tech. Tng. Wing, Keesler AFB, Miss., 1990-92, HQ CAP-USAF, Maxwell AFB, Ala., 1992-94; ret. USAF, 1994; investigator Profl. Ins. Investigating, Inc., Seguin, Tex., 1994—; chief pilot Petra Aviation, Seguin, 1995-97. Chmn. Biloxi (Miss.)-Keesler 50th Anniversary Com., 1991; presiding judge Guadalupe County Elections Office, Seguin, 1996-98; pres. Treasure Island Homes Assn., Lake McQueeney, Tex., 1987-89; cert. water quality monitor, team leader Tex. Natural Resources Conservation Commn., Austin, Tex., 1994-98; pres., bd. dirs. Friends of Guadalupe River State Park/Honey Creek State Natural Area, 1997-98. Decorated Vietnamese Cross of Gallantry, Republic of Vietnam, 1969, Legion of Merit. Mem. Am. Legion, Air Commando Assn., Friends of Lake McQueeney (bd. dirs. 1994-96). Republican. Avocations: camping, hunting, fishing, flying, classic cars. Home: 132 Trelawney St Mc Queeney TX 78123-3423

GUNTER, EMILY DIANE, communications executive, marketing professional, real estate developer, author, educator; b. Atlantic City, N.J., Apr. 5, 1948; d. Fay Gaffney and Verlee (Wright) G.; children: Saliha, Kadir, Amin, Shedia. BA in Math. Stats., Am. U., 1970, postgrad. computer sci., 1971; postgrad. mktg., San Diego C.C., 1986. Cert. Qualtec Total Quality mgmt. trainer. Traffic engr. C&P Bell, Washington, 1970-71; market analyst Market Towers Inc., Atlantic City, N.J., 1978-79; outside plant engr. N.J. Bell, Atlantic City, 1979-81; market analyst Empcor Group, Atlantic City, 1981-83; outside plant engr. Pacific Bell, San Diego, 1983-91, account exec., 1991-93; v.p. Black Am. of Achievement, Inc., San Diego, 1994-95; founder Women's Wholistic Enpowerment Ctr., 1996-97; pres. Gunter Devel. Enterprises, 1987—; lectr. women and minorities in engring. and math. Princeton (N.J.) U., 1979-81, Atlantic C.C., Atlantic City, 1979-81; customer coord. Pacific Bell-Telsam, San Diego, 1983-85; prof. math. Grossmont Coll., 1992-94, instr. super learning skills seminar, 1992—; motivational spkr. Author: Superlearning 2000: The New Technologies of Self-Empowerment, 1993, Supermath 2000: How to Learn Math Without Fear, 1993, Achieve Goals 2000: A Personal Handbook for the Lifelong Learner, 1995, Living, Learning & Healing Through The Right Use of Your Mind, 1996, SL2000 Learning Made Easy-Everybody Can Learn, 1997. Bd. dirs. Lead, San Diego, Atlantic City Transp. Authority, 1981-82, San Diego Urban Math. Collaborative; trustee Reuben H. Fleet Sci. Found., 1989, San Diego Sci. Found., 1989-97, 1990 class Lead-Leadership Edn. Awareness Devel., San Diego; mem. steering com. United Negro Coll. Fund, San Diego; mem. Atlantic City Urban Area Transp. Commn., 1982-83; mem. Am. Humanics Bd. U. San Deigo, 1991-94; pres. bd. World Beat Cultural Ctr., Balboa Park, Calif., 1992-93; nat. exec. dir. Rites of Passage Youth Empowerment Programs of Am., 1997—; youth advocate, chmn., founder and CEO Rites of Passage Youth Empowerment Found., 1998; chmn. and CEO Heart of Africa Holding Corp., 1998—. Mem. African Am. Womens Conf., Women on Tour (exec. bd. 1992—), Coalition Women's Groups (bd. dirs. 1996-97). Democrat. Avocations: chess, painting, aerobics, walking, piano. Home: PO Box 72372 Durham NC 27722-2372 also: Gunter Devel Enterprises PO Box 72372 Durham NC 27722-2372 also: Rites of Passage Youth Empowerment Found PO Box 72372 Durham NC 27722-2372 also: Heart of Africa Holding Corp PO Box 72372 Durham NC 27722-2372

GUNTER, JOHN EDWARD, dean. BS in Forestry, So. Ill. U., 1966; MS in Forest Mgmt., Mich. State U., 1967, MBA, 1973, PhD in Forest Mgmt. & Econs., 1974. Forestry aide U.S. Forest Svc., Salem, Mo., 1965; rsch. asst. forestry So. Ill. U., Carbondale, 1965-66; from asst. dist. forester to asst. forester tech. forestry Ga.-Pacific Corp., Crossett, Ark., 1967-71; asst. prof. dept. forestry and forest products Va. Poly. Inst., Blacksburg, 1974-75; from forest fin. taxation specialist to forest economist USDA Forest Svc., Atlanta, 1975-79; assoc. prof. forestry Mich. State U., East Lansing, 1979-83; prof., head extension forest resources dept. U. Ga., Athens, 1983-93; dean sch. forest resources, dir. Ark. Forest Resources Ctr. U. Ark., Monticello, 1993-94; dean coll. forest resources, dir. Forest Rsch. Ctr. Miss. State U., 1995—. Recipient Wise Owl award Ga. Forestry Assn., Pres.'s award, award for timber tax reform; Excellence award So. Extension Forest Resource Specialists; grantee Kellogg Found., Ctr. for Integrated Forest Mgmt. Strategies, USDA Forest Svc., Ga. Forestry Commn. Fellow Soc. Am. Foresters; mem. Soc. Am. Foresters (chmn. hall of fame com. Ark. divsn., chmn.-elect, chmn. Ga. divsn., sec., chmn.-elect, chair econs., policy and law working group, vice-chmn. lower Mich. chpt., forester of yr. 1994), Alpha Zeta, Beta Gamma Sigma, Epsilon Sigma Phi, Sigma Xi, Xi Sigma Pi, Phi Kappa Phi. Office: Miss State U Coll Forest Resources PO Box 9680 Mississippi State MS 39762-9680*

GUNTER, LAURIE M., retired nurse educator. BS, Tenn A&I State U., 1948; MA, Fisk U., 1952; PhD in Human Devel., U. Chgo., 1959. Staff nurse George W. Hubbard Hosp., Nashville, 1943-44, 46-47, head nurse, 1945-46, supr., 1947-48; instr. Sch. Nursing, Meharry Med. Coll., Nashville, 1950-55, asst. prof., 1955-57, project dir. mental health tng., 1957-58, acting dean, 1957-58, dean, 1958-61; asst. prof. nursing UCLA, 1961-63, assoc. prof., 1963-65; prof. nursing Ind. U. Med. Ctr., Indpls., 1965-66; assoc. prof. U. Wash., Seattle, 1966-69, prof., 1969-71; head dept. nursing Pa. State U., 1971-75, prof., 1971-87, prof. emeritus, 1987. Contbr. articles to profl. jours. Mem. ANA. Home: 4008 47th Ave S Seattle WA 98118-1218

GUNTER, RUSSELL ALLEN, lawyer; b. Amarillo, Tex., Feb. 21, 1950; s. J.B. and Shirley Ann (Russell) G.; children: Kim, Sarah, Laura, Rachel, Lindsay. BS in Polit. Sci., So. Ark U., 1972; JD, Tex. Tech U., 1975. Bar: Ark., 1975, Tex, 1975, U.S. Dist. Ct. (ea. and we dists.) Ark. 1975, U.S. Supreme Ct. (8th cir.) 1975, U.S. Dist. Ct. (no. dist.) Tex. 1976, U.S. Ct. Appeals (5th cir.), 1980, U.S. Supreme Ct. 1986. Assoc. Gaines N. Houston, Little Rock, 1975-79, Wallace, Dover & Dixon, P.A., Little Rock, 1979-90, McGlinchey Stafford Lang P.L.L.C., Little Rock, 1990-97; Cross, Gunter, Witherspoon & Galchus P.C., Little Rock, 1997—. Mem. ABA (com. on practice and procedure before NLRB labor sect.), Soc. for Human Resource Mgmt. (cert. sr. profl. in human resources), Ark. Bar Assn., Tex. Bar Assn. Office: 500 E Markham St Ste 200 Little Rock AR 72201-1747

GUNTER, SUE, women's basketball coach; b. Walnut Grove, Miss., May 22, 1941. BA, Peabody Coll., 1962, MA, 1962. Head coach women's basketball Mid. Tenn. State U., Murfreesboro, 1969-71, Stephen F. Austin State U., Nacogdoches, Tex., 1971-83, La. State U., Baton Rouge, 1983—. Recipient Silver medal Olympic Com., 1976, Carol Eckman award, 1994; named Coach of Yr., Converse Region 4 Athletic Commn., 1983, SCC, 1997, La. State Collegiate Athletics Commn., 1997. Office: La State U Women's Athletic Dept PO Box 25095 Baton Rouge LA 70894-5095*

GUNTER, WILLIAM DAWSON, JR. (BILL GUNTER), insurance company executive; b. Jacksonville, Fla., July 16, 1934; s. William Dawson and Tillie G.; m. Teresa Arbaugh, June 26, 1971; children—Bart, Joel, Rachel, Rebecca. B.S.A. with high honors, U. Fla., 1956. Tchr. pub. schs. Live Oak and Orlando, Fla., 1956, 58; ins. agt., agy. mgr. Central Fla., 1959-72; mem. Fla. State Senate, 1966-72, U.S. Congress from 5th Fla. dist., 1973-74; treas., ins. commr. State of Fla., Tallahassee, 1976-88; CEO, chmn. Rogers-Atkins-Gunter & Assocs. Ins., Inc., Tallahassee, 1997—; chief exec. officer Bill Gunter & Assocs. (govt. cons.), Tallahassee, 1989—; sr. v.p. Southland Equity Corp., Orlando, Fla.; pres. Southland Capital Investors, Inc., Orlando, 1975-76. Deacon Baptist Ch.; bd. dirs. Central Fla. Fair Assn. Served with U.S. Army. Recipient good govt. award Fla. State Jaycees, 1972. Mem. U. Fla. Nat. Alumni Assn. (pres. 1985-86), Orlando Area C. of C. (past dir.). Democrat. Clubs: Jaycees, Kiwanis, Masons. Office: 1117 Thomasville Rd Tallahassee FL 32303-6223

GUNTER, WILLIAM DAYLE, JR., physicist; b. Mitchell, S.D., Jan. 10, 1932; s. William Dayle and Lamerta Berniece (Hockensmith) G.; m. Shirley Marie Teshera, Oct. 24, 1955; children: Maria Jo, Robert Paul. BS in Physics with distinction, Stanford U., 1957, MS, 1959. Physicist Ames Rsch. Ctr. NASA, Moffett Field, Calif., 1960-81, asst. br. chief electronic optical engring., 1981-85; pvt. practice cons. Photon Applications, San Jose, Calif., 1985-98, Modesto, Calif., 1998—. Patentee in field; contbr. articles to profl. jours. With U.S. Army, 1953-55. Recipient Westinghouse Sci. Talent Search award, 1950; Stanford U. scholar, 1950. Mem. IEEE (sr.), Am. Phys. Soc., Optical Soc. Am., Soc. Photo-Optical Instrumentation Engrs., Planetary Soc., Nat. Space Soc., NASA Alumni League. Office: Photon Applications 3701 Rosanne Ln Modesto CA 95356-9416

GUNTHER, BARBARA, artist, educator; b. Bklyn., Nov. 10, 1930; d. Benjamin and Rose (Lev) Kelsky; m. Gerald Gunther, June 22, 1949; children: Daniel Jay, Andrew James. BA, Bklyn. Coll., 1949; MA, San Jose State U., 1975. Instr. printmaking, drawing, painting Cabrillo Coll., Aptos, Calif., 1976-93; instr. lithography Calif. State U., Hayward, 1978-79; instr. studio arts Calif. State U., San Jose, summer 1977, 78, 80; co-founder San Jose Print Workshop, 1975. One-woman shows include Palo Alto (Calif.) Cultural Ctr., 1981, Miriam Perlman, Inc., Chgo., 1984, D.P. Fong & Spratt Galleries, San Jose, 1991, 93, Branner/Spangenburg Gallery, Palo Alto, U. Calif., Santa Cruz, 1991, Frederick Spratt Galleries, San Jose, 1996, Cabrilto Coll., 1997; exhibited in numerous group shows; represented in permanent collections at San Jose Art in Pub. Places Program, Hilton Towers Hotel, GM, Found. Press, Inc. Recipient Purchase award Palo Alto Cultural Ctr., 1975, Judges' Merit award Haggin Mus., 1988. Mem. Calif. Printmakers Soc., San Jose Inst. of Contemporary Art. Studio: 199 Martha St Ste 22 San Jose CA 95112-5878

GUNTHER, GEORGE LACKMAN, state senator, natureopathic physician, retired; b. Bridgeport, Conn., Nov. 22, 1919; s. George and Gwendolyn (Cliff) G. ; m. Priscilla A. Staples, June 5, 1941; children: Pattie K., Karla Gwen (Mrs. R. Mazzey), Lance Inder. Grad., Nat. Coll. Drugless Physicians, Chgo., 1942. Intern Chgo. Gen. Health Svc., 1940-41, pvt. practice natureopathic medicine, 1943-89; mem. Conn. Senate, Stratford, Conn., 1967—; dep. minority leader Conn. Senate, Stratford, 1971-72, 75-76, 78-80, 87-94, 1973-74, asst. minority leader, 1977-80, minority leader, 1981-82, dep. minority leader, 1987-92, sr. majority leader, 1995-96, dep. minority leader, 1997-98, dep. minority leader-at-large, 1999—; mem. Conn. Bd. Natureopathic Examiners, 1946-49; mem. Capitol Restoration Commn.; mem. L.I. Sound Study Com. of New Eng. River Basins Commn.; mem. Coun. of State Govts.; commrd. Atlantic State Marine Fisheries commn. co-chmn., BiState L.I. Sound Marine Resources com.; mem., state chmn., bd. dirs. Am. Legis. Exch. Coun. Recipient Am. Motors Conservation award Am. Motors Corp., 1966, Outstanding Civic Leader of Am., 1967, Nat. Wildlife Fedn. and Sears and Roebuck Found., 1969, Conservation award SHAME, Inc., 1974, Legislator of Yr. award NRA, Environ. conservations award L.I. sound Am., 1986, Comdr.'s Cross of the Order of Merit Fed. Republic of Germany, 1987, numerous others; named Water Conservationist of Yr. for Conn., Conn. State League of Sportsmens and Conservation Clubs, Nat. Wildlife Fedn. and Sears and Roebuck Found., 1966; Nat. water Conservationist of Yr., Nat. Wildlife Fedn. and Sears and Roebuck Found., 1966. Mem. Stratford Antique Gun Collectors Assn. (organizer, 1st pres.). Office: Conn State Senate State Capital Bldg Hartford CT 06106-1591

GUNTHER, GERALD, lawyer, educator; b. Usingen, Germany, May 26, 1927; came to U.S., 1938, naturalized, 1944; s. Otto and Minna (Floersheim) Gutenstein; m. Barbara Kelsky, June 22, 1949; children: Daniel Jay, Andrew James. BA, Bklyn. Coll., 1949; MA, Columbia, 1950; LLB, Harvard, 1953; LLD (hon.), Ill. Inst. Tech., 1987, Bklyn. Law Sch., 1990, Bklyn. Coll. of CUNY, 1990, Duquesne U., 1995, Valparaiso U., 1996. Bar: N.Y. 1955.

Law clk. Judge Learned Hand, 1953-54, Chief Justice Earl Warren, 1954-55; asso. firm Cleary, Gottlieb, Friendly & Hamilton, N.Y.C., 1955-56; asso. prof. law Columbia U., N.Y.C., 1956-59, prof., 1959-62; prof. law Stanford U., 1962-72, Wm. Nelson Cromwell prof., 1972-95, prof. emeritus, 1995—; lectr. polit. sci. Bklyn. Coll., 1949-50. Author: John Marshall's Defense of McCulloch versus Maryland, 1969, (with K.M. Sullivan) Constitutional Law, 13th edit., 1997, Learned Hand: The Man and the Judge, 1994, 95, (with K.M. Sullivan) First Amendment Law, 1999; mem. editl. bd. Found. Press, 1972—, Stanford Univ. Press, 1983-86; mem., Overseas Com. to visit The Harvard Law Sch., 1974-80, 1995—; mem. adv. bd. and editl. bd. Ency. of Am. Constn., 1983-86; contbr. articles to profl. jours. Recipient Disting. Alumnus award Bklyn. Coll., 1961, Learned Hand medal for excellence in fed. jurisprudence Fed. Bar Coun., 1988, Richard J. Maloney prize for disting. contbns. to legal edn. Bklyn. Law Sch., 1990, Erwin N. Griswold Triennial prize Supreme Ct. Hist. Soc., 1995, Bernard Witkin medal State Bar Calif., 1995, Triennial award (for Hand biography) Order of the Coif, 1999; Guggenheim fellow, 1962-63; Ctr. Advanced Study in Behavioral Scis. fellow, 1969-70; Fulbright-Hays lectr. Ghana, 1970; NEH fellow, 1980-81, 85-86. Fellow AAAS; mem. Am. Philos. Soc., Am. Law Inst., Am. Hist. Assn. (mem. com. Littleton-Griswold Fund, 1968-73). Office: Stanford U Law Sch Nathan Abbott Way Stanford CA 94305

GUNTHER, JACK DISBROW, JR., lawyer; b. Wilmington, Del., Mar. 15, 1941; s. Jack D. and Geraldyne (Beyea) G. Grad., Phillips Exeter Acad., 1959; AB, Princeton U., 1963; LLB, Columbia U., 1966. Assoc. Shearman & Sterling, N.Y.C., 1967-85, sr. atty., 1985-97, counsel, 1997—; bd. dirs. Kirk/Acorn Inc., N.Y.C., Doherty Found., N.Y.C., Stony Creek Fund, N.Y.C. Mem. The Pilgrims, The Links, Racquet and Tennis Club, Rockaway Hunting Club. Republican. Episcopalian. Home: 1225 Park Ave New York NY 10128-1758 Office: 599 Lexington Ave Fl C2 New York NY 10022-6030

GUNTHER, LEON, physicist; b. Bklyn., Aug. 22, 1939; s. Joseph and Esther Gunther; m. Harriet S. Gamrin, Oct. 10, 1962; children: David Michael, Benjamin Gene, Rachel Leah; m. Johanna Ellen Cotter, Nov. 11, 1979; 1 stepchild, Erika Rae Brown; 1 child, Avi Yosef. BS, CCNY, 1960; PhD, MIT, 1964. Asst. prof. Tufts U., Medford, Mass., 1965-72, assoc. prof., 1972-78, prof., 1978—; cons. in field; vis. prof. Technion, Tel-Aviv U., Louis Néel Lab. of Magnetism, Grenoble, France. Contbr. numerous articles to profl. jours. Prin. 2d violinist Newton Symphony Orch., Mass., 1974-83; founder, dir. Mak'haylah chorus Temple Emunah, Lexington, Mass. NATO Postdoctoral fellow NSF, 1965-66, Research grantee. Mem. AAUP, Am. Phys. Soc. Office: Tufts Univ Dept Of Physics Medford MA 02155

GUNTHER, WILLIAM DAVID, university administrator, economics educator; b. Balt., Oct. 11, 1940; s. Geneva (Gee) G.; m. Irene Leveja Reineks, Jan. 8, 1966; children: William B., Kristine A., Jennifer R. BS, Kent State U., 1962, MA, 1965; PhD, U. Ky., 1969. Asst. prof. econs. U. Ala., Tuscaloosa, 1968-72, assoc. prof. econs., 1972-76, prof. econs., 1976—, assoc. dean for rsch., 1988-98; dean sch. bus. U. So. Miss., Hattiesburg, 1998—. Contbr. articles to profl. jours. Fulbright scholar Fulbright Commn., 1972, Faculty fellow USAF, 1979. Mem. Assn. Coll. Honor Socs. (exec. coun. 1983—), Nat. Assn. Bus. Economists, Am. Econs. Assn., So. Regional Sci. Assn. Avocations: boating, coin collecting, paper money collecting. Office: U Ala PO Box 870221 Tuscaloosa AL 35487-0154

GUNTHEROTH, WARREN GADEN, physician; b. Hominy, Okla., July 27, 1927; s. Harry William and Callie (Cornett) G.; m. Ethel Haglund, July 3, 1954; children: Kurt, Karl, Sten. M.D., Harvard U., 1952. Diplomate: Am. Bd. Pediatrics, Am. Bd. Pediatric Cardiology, Nat. Bd. Med. Examiners. Intern Peter Bent Brigham Hosp., Boston, 1952-53; fellow in cardiology Children's Hosp., Boston, 1953-55; resident in pediatrics Children's Hosp., 1955-56; research fellow physiology and biophysics U. Wash. Med. Sch., Seattle, 1957-58; mem. faculty U. Wash. Med. Sch., 1958—, prof. pediatrics, 1969—, head div. pediatric cardiology, 1964-91. Author: Pediatric Electrocardiography, 1965, How to Read Pediatric ECGs, 1981, 3d edit., 1992, Crib Death (Sudden Infant Death Syndrome), 1982, 3d edit., 1995, Climbing With Sasha, a Washington Husky, 1995; also numerous articles; mem. editl. bd. Am. Heart Jour., 1977-80, Circulation, 1980-83, Am. Jour. Noninvasive Cardiology, 1985-94, Jour. Am. Coll. Cardiology, 1988-94, Am. Jour. Cardiology, Jour. Noninvasive Cardiology, 1996—; sect. editor Practice of Pediatrics, 1979-87. Served with USPHS, 1950-51. Spl. research fellow NIH, 1967. Mem. Soc. Pediatric Rsch., Biomed. Engring. Soc. (charter), Am. Heart Assn. (chmn. N.W. regional med. rsch. adv. com. 1978-80), Cardiovascular System Dynamics Soc. (charter), Am. Coll. Cardiology. Democrat. Home: 13201 42nd Ave NE Seattle WA 98125-4626 Office: U Wash Med Sch Dept Pediatrics PO Box 356320 Seattle WA 98195-6320 *My career includes medical practice, teaching and research; my hobby is mountain climbing. Both work and hobby benefit from courage. Encouraging students to ask difficult—and even embarrassing—questions, reaching a timely diagnosis, starting treatment in a dangerously ill patient, and raising challenging questions in research that may provoke anger or scorn; all require courage. Silent convictions are not enough.*

GUNTON, JAMES DOUGLAS, physics educator; b. Medford, Oreg., Mar. 28, 1937; s. Harold N. Gunton and Hazel M. Gold Scanlan; m. Margaret R. Taylor, June 24, 1962; children: Deborah, James, Michael. BA in Chemistry, Linfield Coll., McMinnville, Oreg., 1958; BA in Physics, Oxford U., Eng., 1961; PhD in Physics, Stanford U., 1966. Asst. prof. physics Temple U., Phila., 1968-73, assoc. prof. physics, 1973-76, prof. physics, 1976-88, dir. Ctr. for Advanced Computational Sci., 1985-88; provost Kenyon Coll., Gambier, Ohio, 1994-95; dean Coll. Arts and Scis., Lehigh U., Bethlehem, Pa., 1988-94, prof. physics, 1995—. Author: Dynamics of Metastable and Unstable States, 1983; contbr. articles to profl. jours. Rhodes scholar, 1958; Danforth fellow, 1962, Woodrow Wilson fellow (hon.), 1958. Fellow Am. Phys. Soc. Avocations: fishing, skiing, sailing, reading. Office: Lehigh U Dept Physics Bethlehem PA 18015*

GUNTY, CHRISTOPHER JAMES, newspaper editor; b. Hometown, Ill., Oct. 13, 1959; s. Harold Paul and Therese Agnes (Kohs) G.; m. Nancy Louise Blanton, July 10, 1982; children: William, Amy, Timothy. BA, Loyola U., Chgo., 1981. Circulation mgr. The Chgo. Catholic, 1981-83, assoc. mnging. editor, 1983, mng. editor, 1983-85; editor, mng. editor The Catholic Sun, Phoenix, 1985-96; assoc. pub. The Cath. Sun, Phoenix, 1996—. Author: He Came to Touch Us, 1987; co-author videotape script The Pope in Arizona, 1987; contbg. author: (anthologies) Mission and Future of the Catholic Press, 1998, Freedom of Journalist, 1998; contbr. articles to spl. Catholic news svcs. as well as papers where employed. Mem. Fiesta Bowl Com., Phoenix, 1987-92; bd. dirs. Catholic Journalism Scholarship Fund, 1990—, pres., 1995-96. Named Honoree Summer U. Internat. Cath. Union of the Press, Switzerland, 1988. Mem. Cath. Press Assn. (bd. dirs. 1988-99, sec. 1990-92, v.p. 1994-96, pres. 1996-98), Assoc. Ch. Press, Ariz. Newspapers Assn., Soc. Profl. Journalists. Roman Catholic. Avocations: bicycling, sci. fiction. Office: The Catholic Sun 400 E Monroe St Phoenix AZ 85004-2336

GUNZENHAUSER, GERARD RALPH, JR., management consultant, investor; b. Mt. Vernon, N.Y., Sept. 26, 1936; s. Gerard Ralph and Helen Elizabeth (Carey) G.; m. Alfa Marjorie Vendetti, Sept. 17, 1960; children: Cathy Susan, Michael Gerard, Christopher John, Eric David. BBA, Iona Coll., 1965; postgrad., NYU Sch. Bus. Adminstrn., 1967-68. Asst. mgr. fin. analysis Gen. Foods Corp., White Plains, N.Y., 1962-68; dir. fin. planning and analysis RJR Foods, Inc., Winston-Salem, N.C., 1968-76; area fin. dir. R.J. Reynolds Tobacco Internat., Winston-Salem, 1976-79; comptroller R.J. Reynolds Tobacco. Co., Winston-Salem, 1979-81; v.p., comptroller R.J. Reynolds Tobacco Co., Winston-Salem, 1981-83, v.p. fin., chief fin. officer, 1983-84; sr. v.p., chief fin. officer Del Monte Corp., San Francisco, 1984-85; sr. v.p. fin., controller RJR Nabisco, Inc., Winston-Salem, 1986-87; sr. v.p. fin. R.J. Reynolds Tobacco Co., Winston-Salem, 1987-88, exec. v.p., chief fin. officer, 1988-91, also exec. com., bd. dirs.; pres., chief exec. officer GRG Assocs., Inc., Winston-Salem, 1991—; mem. local adv. bd. Branch Banking & Trust Co., 1987—; mem. Consumer Credit Counseling Svc., 1983-84, 87-90; mem. Reynolds Carolina Credit Union Bd., 1973-83. Trustee Winston-Salem Arts Coun., 1987-94; bd. dirs. Winston-Salem Piedmont Triad Symphony, 1986—, Piedmont Opera Theatre, 1989—, Tanglewood Pk. Found., 1991—; mem. N.C. Gov.'s Bus. Coun. on Arts and Humanities, 1987-91; chmn. fund appeal Bishop McGuinness High Sch., Winston-Salem, 1982-83, mem. bd. edn., 1987-90, chmn. bd., 1988-90; chmn. St. Leo's Parish Coun., Winston-Salem, 1974-77; exec. v.p. Winston-Salem Nat. Little League, 1981-84; chmn. sch. budget task force C. of C., 1976; mem. bd. advisors Catholic Conf. Ctr., 1990-93; exec. com., bd. trustees Forsyth County Park Authority, 1992—; bd. dirs., vice chmn. Found. Roman Cath. Diocese of Charlotte. Named to Hon. Order Ky. Cols., 1983. Mem. Fin. Execs. Inst. Roman Catholic. Home: 2814 Galsworthy Dr Winston Salem NC 27106-5107 Office: GRG Assocs Inc 101 S Stratford Rd Ste 201 Winston Salem NC 27104-4224*

GUNZENHAUSER, STEPHEN CHARLES, conductor; b. N.Y.C., Apr. 8, 1942; s. M(ax) Kurt and Ruth (Sorsky) G.; m. Rochelle E. Davis, June 14, 1970; children—Marisa, Amy. MusB, Oberlin Coll., 1963; diploma, Salzburg (Austria) Mozarteum, 1962; MusM, New Eng. Conservatory Music, 1965; artist diploma, Hochschule, Cologne, Fed. Republic Germany, 1968; LittD (hon.), Widener U., 1987. Guest condr. Rhenish Chamber Orch., Cologne, 1967-69, City of Gelsenkirchen Orch., 1972, Nat. Orch. Costa Rica, 1975, Del. Pro Musica, 1974-75, Lancaster (Pa.) Symphony, 1979, Radio Orch. Ireland, Dublin, 1979, 82, Hessian State Broadcasting Network Orch., 1969, RIAS Orch. of Berlin, 1969, Knoxville (Tenn.) Symphony, 1982, Duluth-Superior (Wis.) Wymphony, 1982, Ala. Symphony, 1983, Spokane Symphony, 1983, Laredo (Tex.) Symphony, 1983, Slovak Philharm., 1988, 90, Silesia Philharm., Poland, 1988, Seoul Philharm., Republic of Korea, 1988, Innsbruck Symphony, Austria, 1989, Hagen Symphony, Germany, 1990; resident condr. Costa Verde and Sintra Festival, Portugal, 1984, Va. Symphony, 1984, Sacramento Symphony, 1985, Symphony N.S., 1986, Peoria Symphony, 1987, Okla. Symphony, 1987, 96, Charlotte Symphony, 1987, Israel Chamber Orch., 1993, Berlin Symphony Orch., 1995, 96, 97, Colo. Music Festival, 1996, Munich Symphony, 1996, Nat. Kibbutz (Israel) Chamber Orch., 1996, Hagen (Germany) Philharm., 1996; asst. condr. Monte Carlo Nat. Orch., 1968-69, Am. Symphony Orch., N.Y.C., 1969-70; music dir. Bklyn. Ctr. Chamber Orch., 1970-72, Kennett (Pa.) Symphony Orch., 1974-78, Wilmington (Del.) Chamber Orch., 1976-79, Del. Symphony, 1978—; prin. condr. Lancaster Symphony, 1978—, music dir., 1981; artistic dir. Wilmington Music Sch., 1974-82, artistic advisor, 1982-87, clarinettist, rec. artist; recs. with HNH Internat., 1985-92. Trustee Nat. Guild Community Schs. Arts, 1977-83. Recipient 1st prize Santiago (Spain) Competition, 1967, medal of distinction U. Del., 1990, Collector's Choice prize Classic CD mag.; apptd. Cultural Amb., State of Del., 1990; Fulbright grantee, 1965-68. Mem. Musicians Union, Condrs. Guild, Am. Symphony Orch. League. Home: 901 Shallcross Ave Wilmington DE 19806-3232 Office: Del Symphony Orch PO Box 1870 Wilmington DE 19899-1870 *As musician, I can neither build nor repair the tangible aspects of life. My hope is to minister successfully to the spirit.*

GUO, CHU, chemistry educator; b. Fengyang, Shanxi, China, Aug. 25, 1933; came to U.S. 1986; s. FengTian and Fengyi G.; m. Shihua Wang, July 1, 1962; 1 child, Huizhong. PhD, Moscow State U., 1962. Sr. rsch. fellow Inst. Chem. Physics, Academia Sinica, Dalian, China, 1963-75; full rsch. prof. Inst. Chemistry, Academia Sinica, Beijing, China, 1975-86; vis. prof. Royal Instn. of G.B., London, 1986; vis. prof. chemistry CCNY, 1986, CASI, Dept. Chemistry, CCNY, 1990—. Author: The Primary Process of Photosynthesis, 1986; contbr. articles to profl. jours. Mem. N.Y. Acad. Scis., Sigma Xi. Achievements include research in photoinitiated electron transfer on membranes, interplay between electron transfer and conformetional change of surrounding protein, raman spectroscopy of porphyrins and molecular aggregates. Office: CCNY Dept Chemistry W 138th St at Convent Ave New York NY 10031

GUO, PEIXUAN, molecular virology educator; b. Chaoyang, Guangdong, China, Apr. 4, 1951; came to U.S., 1983; s. Yongjian Guo and Huifang Zhang; m. Mar. 29, 1981; children: Yinyin, Sida. DVM, Foshan (Guangdong) Vet. Coll., 1978; MS in Microbiology, South China Agr. U., Guangzhou, 1981; PhD in Microbiology and Genetics, U. Minn., 1987. Guest rschr. U. Basel, Switzerland, 1985; rsch. scientist II N.Y. State Dept. Health, Albany, 1987-88; vis. scientist NIH, Bethesda, Md., 1988-89; asst. prof. Purdue U., West Lafayette, Ind., 1990-93, assoc. prof., 1994-97; prof. molecular virology Purdue U., West Lafayette, 1998—; cons. Integrated DNA Tech., Inc., 1989—, Integrated Biotech., Inc., Indpls., 1991—; ad hoc mem. study sect. on biomed. and behavioral rsch facilities, NIH, 1997; chmn. search com. for tenure-track faculty, 1994-95; chmn. workshop of 3d Asia-Pacific Congress Med. Virology, Beijing, 1994; chmn. Workshop of Vaccines and Vaccine Vectors Internat. Congress Vet. Virology, Interlake, Switzerland, 1994; chmn. workshop viral structure and assembly, Internat. Symposium Molecular Virology, Xian, China, 1996, Beijing, 1998; advisor Inst. Microbiology Chinese Acad. Scis. Contbr. over 40 articles to profl. jours. including Sci., Procs. NAS, Jour. Molecular Biology, Jour. Virology, RNA, Molecular Cell, Gene, Nuc. Acid Rsch., Virology and Viral Genes; editor seminars in virology, 1994. Recipient 1st award NIH, 1993, Pfizer Disting. Faculty award for rsch. excellence, 1995; grantee Solvay, 1991-93, Integrated Biotech. Corp., 1991-94, NIH, 1992—, NSF, 1997—; Purdue faculty scholar, 1999. Mem. AAAS, Am. Soc. Virology, Am. Soc. Microbiology, Am. Soc. Biochemistry and Molecular Biology, Soc. Chinese Bioscientists in Am., RNA Soc. Achievements include discovery of a small viral RNA novel and essential in viral DNA packaging leading to the opening of a new area of research; successful assembly of infectious double-stranded DNA virion of phage ø29 in vitro with recombinant proteins and synthetic nucleic acids; design of a novel strategy for high efficient inhibitiion of ø29 virion assembly and by the use of a mutant RNA with two functional domains and multile-copy involvement in viral DNA packaging; development of particle vaccines, subunit vaccines with multiple gene products, and recombinant vaccines of ILT virus; development of new methods for the quantification of stoichiometry for intermediate reactions; discovery of a hexameric molecular motor composed of 6 RNA molecules. Office: Purdue U Cancer Ctr S University St Purdue University IN 47907

GUO, QIZHONG, engineering educator, researcher; b. Guangdong, China, Oct. 8, 1962; came to U.S., 1984; m. Xiaolan Wang; 1 child, Lillian. B of Engring., Tianjin (China) U., 1982; MS, U. Minn., 1987, PhD, 1991. Registered profl. engr., Minn. Rsch./tchg. asst. U. Minn., Mpls., 1985-91, rsch. assoc., 1991-92; R&D engr. Lemna Corp., St. Paul, 1992; asst. prof. Rutgers U., Piscataway, N.J., 1992-98, assoc. prof., 1998—; mem. tech. adv. steering com. Barnegat Bay Nat. Estuary Program, Trenton, N.J., 1996—; mem. tech. adv. com. Whippany Watershed Project, Trenton, 1996—. Contbr. articles to profl. jours. Mem. ASCE, Am. Waterworks Assn., Am. Geophysical Union, Am. Water Resources Assn. (U. Minn. student chpt. pres. 1990-91), Water Environ. Fedn. Achievements include research in solutions to hydraulic problems in deep tunnel project for Greater Chicago; developing a numerical model for the entire river ice breakup and jamming process; revealing environmental problems that may occur as a result of processing hazardous waste derived fuel in cement kilns. Office: Rutgers Univ 623 Bowser Rd Piscataway NJ 08854-8014

GUO, SHENG MING, retired history educator; b. Zhengjiang, Jiangsu, China, Dec. 25, 1915; came to U.S., 1989, naturalized, 1996; s. Dun Xue Guo and Xiao Chun Wu; m. Hong Yi Wang, Jan. 24, 1045; children: Victor Kuo, John Kuo, Meide Guo. BA in History, Nat. Ctrl. U., Chongching, China, 1938; MA, Ctrl. Inst. Polit. Sci., Chongching, 1941; postgrad., Tulane U., 1949. Vice consul Chinese Consulate, New Orleans, 1945-47, acting consul, 1048-50; prof. history Kuangsi (China) U., 1951-53, Hunan (China) U., 1053-56, East China Normal U., Shanghai, 1957-89; advisor Chinese Assn. Medieval History, Beijing, 1976—, Shanghai Assn. Social Sci., 1983—; U.S. State Dept. vis. prof., Georgetown U., Harvard U., U. Chgo., Stanford U., also others, 1983. Author: A Survey of Western Historiography, 1983 (State prize 1985), Am Outline of World Civilization, 1989 (State prize 1991); editor-in-chief: Dictionary of World History, 1986; editor History of Foreign Countries in Ency. Sinica, 1987. Presbyterian. Avocation: gardening.

GUP, BENTON EUGENE, banking educator; b. Reading, Pa., Mar. 5, 1936; s. Abe L. and Germaine B. Gup; married; children: Lincoln, Andrew, Jeremy. BA, U. Cin., 1961, MBA, 1963, PhD, 1966. Economist Fed. Res. Bank of Cleve., 1967-70; prof. fin. U. of Tulsa, 1970-82, prof., chair banking, 1970-82; vis. prof., chair banking U. Va., Charlottesville, 1980-81; prof., chair banking U. Ala., Tuscaloosa, 1983—. Author: Guide to Strategic Planning, 1980, Financial Intermediaries, 2d editl, 1980, Principles of Financial Management, 1983, 2d edit., 1987, Management of Financial Institutions, 1984, The Basics of Investing, 5th edit., 1992, (with Charles Meiburg) Cases in Bank Management, 1986, Personal Investing: A Complete Handbook, 1987, Commercial Bank Management, 1989, Bank Mergers: Current Issues and Perspectives, 1989, Bank Fraud: Exposing the Hidden Threat to Financial Institutions, 1990, (with Robert Brooks) Interest Rate Risk Management, 1993, Targeting Fraud: Uncovering and Detering Fraud in Financial Institutions, 1995 (with Donald Fraser and James Kolari) Commercial Banking: The Management of Risk, 1995, The Bank Director's Handbook, 1996, Bank Failures in the Major Trading Countries of the World, 1998, International Banking Crises, 1999. Served with USAF, 1954-58. Mem. Fin. Mgmt. Assn. (chmn. site selection 1975-85), Midwest Fin. Assn. (pres. 1982-83), Am. Fin. Assn., Fin. Execs. Inst., Acad. Fin. Svcs. (v.p., dir. 1988-91). Home: 1124 Forest Oaks Ln Tuscaloosa AL 35406-2673 Office: U Ala Dept Fin PO Box 870224 Tuscaloosa AL 35487-0154

GUPTA, ANIL KUMAR, management educator; b. New Delhi, India, Sept. 24, 1949; came to U.S., 1975; s. Charan Dass and Chandra (Prabha) G.; m. Rekha Yeshwant Talcherkar, July 6, 1975; 1 child, Rahul. B in Tech., Indian Inst. Tech., Kanpur, India, 1970; diploma bus. adminstrn., Indian Inst. Mgmt., Ahmedabad, India, 1972; D in Bus. Adminstrn., Harvard U., 1980. Area sales mgr. Hindustan Lever Ltd., Bombay, India, 1972-73, product mgr., 1973-75; asst. prof. Boston U. Sch. Mgmt., 1980-86; assoc. prof. strategic mgmt. U. Md., College Park, 1986-92, prof. strategic mgmt., 1992—; cons. in field. Contbr. articles to profl. jours.; mem. editl. bd. Jour. High Tech. Mgmt. Rsch., Acad. Mgmt. Rev. Recipient Broderick prize for excellence in rsch. Boston U., 1984, Allen J. Krowe prize for excellence in tchg. U. Md., 1989, 98, Disting. Scholar-Tchr. award, 1997. Mem. Am. Acad. Mgmt. (Glueck Best Paper award in bus. policy and planning 1991), Inst. Mgmt. Scis., Strategic Mgmt. Soc. Avocations: tennis, travel. Home: 8000 Overhill Rd Bethesda MD 20814-1145 Office: U Md Coll Bus and Mgmt College Park MD 20742

GUPTA, ASHWANI KUMAR, mechanical engineering educator; b. Punjab, India, Oct. 23, 1948; s. Ram Nath and Vidya G. BSc, Panjab U., India, 1966; MSc, Southampton U., U.K., 1970; PhD, Sheffield (Eng.) U., 1973, DSc, 1986. Chartered engr., fuel technologist, U.K. Rsch. engr. Internat. Combustion Co., Derby, Eng., 1967-71; rsch. asst. Sheffield U., 1971-73, rsch. fellow, ind. rsch. worker, 1973-76; mem. rsch. staff MIT, Cambridge, 1977-82; prof. dept. mech. engring. U. Md., College Park, 1983—; mem. sci. adv. bd., Sonex Rsch., Annapolis, 1984—, State of Md., 1985—. Author: Swirl Flows, 1984, Flowfield Modeling and Diagnostics, 1985; editor 8 books in Energy and Engineering Science series, 1980—; founding co-editor: Environmental and Energetics series, 1990—; author over 250 tech. papers. Fellow AIAA (chmn. propellants and combustion tech. com. 1988-90, chmn. terrestrial energy systems tech. com. 1991—, Energy Systems award 1990, Propellant and Combustion award 1999), Inst. Energy U.K.; mem. ASME (chair Fuels and Combustion Tech. divsn., George Westinghouse gold medal 1998), Soc. Automotive Engrs., Combustion Inst., Am. Soc. Engring. Edn. Avocations: flying, swimming, squash, photography. Office: U Md Dept Mech Engring College Park MD 20742

GUPTA, KAUSHAL KUMAR, internist; b. Firozpur, Punjab, India, Nov. 9, 1949; came to U.S., 1975; s. Hardayal and Lilawati (Gupta) G.; m. Meena Anand, May 23, 1978; children: Ruchi, Ajay, Nishi. MBBS, MD, Christian Med. Coll., Ludhiana, India, 1975. Diplomate Am. Bd. Internal Medicine. Rotating intern Govt. Med. Coll. and Hosp., Jodhpur, India, 1974-75, Christian Med. Coll. and Hosp., Ludhiana, India, 1974-75; rsch. assoc. dept. pharmacology Baylor Coll. Medicine, Houston, 1975-76; resident in internal medicine St. John Hosp., Detroit, 1976-79; pvt. practice internal medicine Lansing, Mich., 1979-80, Houston, 1980—; chmn. dept. medicine Columbia NHMC, 1999; mem. utilization rev. com. Parkway Hosp., Houston, 1994; quality assurance com. Houston N.W. Med. Ctr., 1989-92; chmn. ER/ICU com. Doctors Hosp.-Airline, Houston, 1992-94; chmn. dept. medicine HNHMC, Houston, 1999; mem. exec. com. CNHMC, 199. Contbr. articles to profl. jours. Mem. resource allocation and funding com. United Way, 1984; vol. physician Eastwood Health Clinic, Houston, 1985, 86; Congress key contact Am. Soc. Internal Medicine, 1993-94, ACP, 1994; dir. IndoAm. Charity Found., Houston, 1996. Fellow ACP; mem. AMA, Tex. Med. Assn., Am. Soc. Internal Medicine, Am. Soc. Echocardiography, Mich. Med. Soc., Harris County Med. Soc., Indian Doctors Club of Houston (sec. 1988). Hindu. Avocations: hiking, water and mountains, basketball, football. Home: 8015 Theisswood Rd Spring TX 77379-4637 Office: 11206 Airline Dr Houston TX 77037-1116

GUPTA, KRISHNA CHANDRA, mechanical engineering educator; b. Ajmer, India, Sept. 24, 1948; s. Jagat Narain and Malti G.; m. Karuna Gupta; 1 child, Anupama. B.Tech. with distinction, Indian Inst. Tech., 1969; M.S. in M.E., Case Inst. Tech., 1971; Ph.D. in M.E., Stanford U., 1974. Grad. asst. Case Inst. Tech., Cleve., 1969-71; research asst. Stanford U., Calif., 1971-74; asst. prof. mech. engring. U. Ill., Chgo., 1974-79, assoc. prof. mech. engring., 1979-84, prof. mech. engring., 1984—, dir. grad. studies, 1982-84, 97—, acting dept. head, 1991-92. Mem. editorial adv. bd. Jour. Applied Mechanisms and Robotics; assoc. editor Mechanism and Machine Theory; contbr. articles to profl. jours. Recipient award of merit Procter & Gamble Co., 1978, South Pointing Chariot award, 1989, AM&R G.N. Sandor award, 1997; grantee in field. Fellow ASME (assoc. editor Jour. Mech. Design 1981-82, mem. editorial adv. bd. Applied Mechanics Rev. 1985-93, chmn. mechanisms com. 1989-90, gen chmn. 1990 design tech. conf., chmn. 1990 mechanisms conf., best paper computers in engring. conf. 1991, Henry Hess award 1979). Avocations: investments, speed reading. Office: Univ Ill Dept Mech Engring (M/C 251) 842 W Taylor St Chicago IL 60607-7021

GUPTA, KULDIP CHAND, electrical and computer engineering educator, researcher; b. Risalpur, India, Oct. 6, 1940; came to U.S., 1982; s. Chiranjiva Lal and Gauran (Agarwal) G.; m. Usha Agarwal, Apr. 4, 1971; children: Parul, Sandeep, Anjula. BSc, Punjab U., Chandigarh, India, 1958; BE, Indian Inst. Sci., Bangalore, India, 1961, ME, 1962; PhD, Birla Inst. Tech. Sci., Pilani, India, 1969. Asst. prof. Punjab Engring. Coll., Chandigarh, 1964-65, Birla Inst. Tech. and Sci., Pilani, 1968-69; asst. prof., then prof. Indian Inst. Tech., Kanpur, India, 1969-84; prof. U. Colo., Boulder, 1983—; vis. assoc. prof. U. Waterloo, Ont., 1975-76; vis. prof. Swiss Fed. Tech. Inst., Lausanne, 1976, Zurich, 1979, Tech. I. Denmark, Lynby, 1976-77, U. Kans., Lawrence, 1982-83, Indian Inst. Sci., 1993-94; advisor, cons. UN Devel. Programme, People's Republic of China, 1987, India, 1990, 94-95; cons. UNIDO project, India, 1993, Indian Telephone Industries, 1993-94. Author: CAD of Microwave Circuits, 1981, Chinese transl., 1986, Russian transl., 1987, Microstrip Lines and Slotlines, 1979, 2d edit., 1996, Microwaves, 1979, Spanish transl., 1983; editor, author: Microwave Integrated Circuits, 1974, Microstrip Antenna Design, 1988, Analysis and Design of Planar Microwave Components, 1994; founding editor Internat. Jour. Microwave Millimeter-Wave Computer Aided Engring., 1991—; contbr. articles to profl. jours. and chpts. to books; patentee in field. Bd. dirs. Hindu U. of Am. Fellow IEEE (guest editor spl. issue IEEE Transactions on Microwave Theory and Tech. 1988), Instn. Electronics and Telecommunication Engrs. India (guest editor jour. July 1982). Hindu. Office: U Colo PO Box 425 Boulder CO 80309-0425 *Success in profession should be judged not by how much money one makes, nor by the status one attains; but by the satisfaction we get by being useful to the society.*

GUPTA, MADHU SUDAN, electrical engineering educator; b. Lucknow, India, June 13, 1945; came to U.S., 1966; s. Manohar Lal and Premvati Gupta; m. Vijaya Lakshmi Tayal, July 9, 1970; children: Jay Mohan, Vineet Mohan; m. Manorama Vyas, May 29, 1985. BS, Lucknow U., India, 1963; MS, Allahabad U., India, 1966, Fla. State U., 1967; MA, U. Mich., 1968, PhD, 1972. Registered profl. engr., Ont. Asst. prof. elec. engring. Queen's U., Kingston, Ont., Can., 1972-73; asst. prof. elec. engring. MIT, Cambridge, 1973-78, assoc. prof. elec. engring., 1978-79; assoc. prof. elec. engring. U. Ill., Chgo., 1979-84, prof. elec. engring., 1984-87, dir. grad. studies, 1980-83; vis. prof. elec. and computer engring. U. Calif., Santa Barbara, 1985-86; sr. staff engr. Hughes Aircraft Co., 1987-95; prof. elec. engring., chmn. dept. elec. engring. Fla. State U., Tallahassee, 1995—; cons. Lincoln Lab. MIT, Lexington, 1976-79, Hughes Research Labs., Malibu, Calif., 1986-87. Editor: Electrical Noise, 1977, Teaching Engineering, 1987, Noise in Circuits and Systems, 1988; contbr. articles to profl. jours.; editor in chief IEEE

Microwave & Guided Wave Letters, 1998—. Lilly fellow, 1974-75. Fellow IEEE; mem. IEEE Microwave Soc. (vice chmn. 1984-85, chmn. 1986-87). Achievements include patents in field. Office: Florida State Univ Dept Elec Engring 2525 Pottsdamer Rd Tallahassee FL 32310-6046 *A person's level of maturity is measured by what he wants from other members of the society: something for nothing, equal return for everything, or nothing except the opportunity to put something back in the kitty.*

GUPTA, PAUL R., lawyer; b. Cambridge, Eng., Mar. 7, 1950; came to U.S., 1953; naturalized, 1963; s. Suraj Narayan Gupta and Letty J.R. Paine; m. Mary Lee Gupta, Sept. 30, 1978; children: Adam, Margaret. BA, Yale U., 1971; JD, Harvard U., 1974. Bar: Mass., N.Y. Assoc. Simpson, Thacher & Bartlett, N.Y.C., 1974-79, Cravath, Swaine & Moore, N.Y.C., 1980-83; ptnr. Sherin and Lodgen, Boston, 1983-91, Nutter, McClennen & Fish, Boston, 1991-94, Sullivan & Worcester, LLP, Boston, 1995—; dir. technology law group Sullivan & Worcester, LLP. Corres. European Intellectual Property Review; bd. editors Multimedia Strategist; contbr. articles to profl. jours.; editl. adv. bd. Elec. Banking Law and Commerce Report; mem. editl. bd. Am. Lawyer Y2K Counselor. Mem. ABA (co-chair year 2000 subcom., internat. property litigation com.), Boston Bar Assn. (chair ct. tech. com. 1994—), Boston Patent Law Assn. (co-chair anti-trust com. 1994—), Assn. of the Bar of the City of N.Y. (mem. computer law com. 1994—), Phi Beta Kappa. Office: Sullivan & Worcester One Post Office Square Boston MA 02109

GUPTA, PRATAP CHANDRA, neurologist, educator; b. Allahabad, Uttar Pradesh, India, Mar. 6, 1935; came to U.S., 1974; s. Ram Prasad and Samudri G.; m. Krishna Gupta, May 7, 1960 (dec. Mar. 1992); children: Seema, Sanjay, Priya; m. Christine A. Solka, Sept. 30, 1995. BSc, Allahabad U., India, 1954; MBBS, Lucknow U., India, 1959, MD, 1962. Diplomate Am. Bd. Clin. Neurophysiology, Am. Bd. Psychiatry and Neurology. Jr. house physician K.G. Med. Coll., Lucknow, 1959, demonstrator in pharmacology, 1960, resident in medicine, 1960-62; registrar in medicine and neurology All India Inst. Med. Scis., New Delhi, 1962-64, asst. attending neurology, 1966-74; asst. attending neurology G.B. Pant Hosp., New Delhi, 1964-65; fellow in neurology and EEG Bronx Mcpl. Hosp. Ctr., 1975, resident in neurology, 1975-77; jr. attending neurology N. Ctrl. Bronx Hosp., 1978; asst. attending neurology Montefiore Hosp. and Med. Ctr. and N. Ctrl. Bronx Hosp., Bronx, 1979-81; neurologist Elkhart (Ind.) Clinic, 1981-84, Upper Peninsula Neurologist, P.C., Marquette, Mich., 1985-92; dir. neurology and neurophysiology Marquette Gen. Hosp., 1987—; neurologist Neurology Assocs. Marquette, 1992—; lectr. neurology G.B. Pant Hosp, New Delhi, 1964-65, All India Inst. Med. Scis., 1966-68; asst. prof. neurology All India Inst. Med. Scis., 1968-74; clin. instr. neurology Albert Einstein Coll. Medicine, Bronx, N.Y., 1978-79, asst. prof. neurology, 1980-81; asst. clin. prof. dept. medicine Mich. State U., 1986—; dir. Muscular Dystrophy Assn. Clinic, Elkhart, 1983-84. Recipient Shakuntala Amir Chand prize Indian Coun. Med. Rsch., 1974. Fellow Am. Acad. Neurology. Avocations: watercolor painting, oil painting. Home: 3108 Lake Shore Blvd Marquette MI 49855 Office: Neurology Assocs Ste 138 1414 West Fair Ave Marquette MI 49855

GUPTA, RAJAT, management consultant. BA, Indian Tech; MBA, Harvard U. Pres., CEO McKinsey & Co. Inc., N.Y.C. Office: McKinsey & Co Inc 55 E 52nd St New York NY 10022-5907*

GUPTA, RAJAT KUMAR, lawyer, accountant; b. New Delhi, Apr. 22, 1960; came to U.S., 1970; s. Ravindra Kumar and Rama G. BBA, Rutgers Coll., New Brunswick, N.J., 1978-82; JD, Rutgers U., Newark, 1985-88. Bar: N.J. and Pa. 1989, U.S. Tax Ct. 1992; lic. CPA. Staff acct. Borrelli & Assoc's., Highland Park, N.J., 1983-84, S. Kirschenbaum & Co., CPA, East Brunswick, N.J., 1984-85; tax assoc. Coopers & Lybrand, Princeton, N.J., 1988-89; pvt. practice atty. New Brunswick, 1989-98; sr. assoc. Spevack & Cannan, P.A., Iselin, N.J., 1998—; vol. Acct's. for the Public Interest, N.J., 1991—; mentor Rutgers Law Sch., Seton Hall Law Sch., Asian and Pacific Law Students Assn. Prodn. editor Rutgers Computer & Technology Law Jour., 1987-88, Cannonball-One Lap of America, 1988; contbr. articles to profl. jours. Arbitrator Better Bus. Bur., Newark, 1986-87; vol. atty. Rutgers U. Off Campus Housing Ctr., 1996—; mem. com. on character N.J. Supreme Ct., 1997—. Mem. ABA, Asian and Pacific Lawyers Assn. N.J., N.J. State Bar Assn, mem. Middlesex Co. Bar Assn. Hindu. Avocations: tennis, travel, photography, astronomy. Office: Spevack & Cannan PA 525 Green St Iselin NJ 08830

GUPTA, RAJESH, industrial engineer, quality engineer; b. Calcutta, India, Oct. 27, 1961; came to U.S., 1986; s. Chandra Kumar and Indira (Karnani) G.; m. Amita Negi, Jan. 26, 1989. BSME, Bangalore (India) U., 1984; postgrad., San Jose State U., 1988. Cert. total quality mgmt. Engr. trainee Incoducts Pvt. Ltd., Bangalore, 1983-84, quality and prodn. control supr., 1984-86; quality assurance engring. supr. Gen. Signals Semiconductor Systems, Fremont, Calif., 1988-89, quality assurance engring. mgr., 1989-90; quality assurance engring. mgr. Semiconductor Systems, Inc., Fremont, 1990-93; sr. quality engr. Applied Materials Inc., Santa Clara, Calif., 1993-97, total product quality mgr. metal deposition divsn., 1997-98; quality systems mgr. Cisco Systems, San Jose, Calif., 1998-99; ASIA quality mgr. Cisco Systems, San Jose, 1999—. Mem. Soc. Mfg. Engrs., Inst. Indsl. Engrs., Am. Soc. for Quality. Office: Applied Materials Inc Mail Stop 0571 3330 Scott Blvd Santa Clara CA 95054-3101

GUPTA, RAMESH CHANDRA, geotechnical engineer, consultant; b. Khurja, India, Jan. 1, 1941; came to U.S., 1978; s. Chhitar Mal and Gunvati Devi G.; m. Radha Devi, Feb. 23, 1966; children: Vineet, Suneet, Nidhi. B in Tech. with honors, Indian Inst. Tech., Kharagpur, 1962; M Engring., U. Fla., 1980, PhD, 1983. Registered profl. engr., Fla., Md., Va., Del., D.C. Asst. engr. U.P. Irrigation Dept., Lucknow, India, 1963-74; exec. engr. U.P. Irrigation Dept., Lucknow, 1974-78; geotechnical engr. Hayward Baker Co., Odenton, Md., 1983-87; assoc. Kidde Cons., Inc., Jessup, Md., 1987-89; sr. geotechnical engr. Greiner, Inc., Timonium, Md., 1989-96; cons. Greiner, Inc., Burtonsville, Md., 1996-98; sr. transp. engr. Va. Dept. of Transp., Richmond, 1998—; mem. Hydraulic Structures com., Indian Standards Inst., New Delhi, 1975-78. Contbr. articles to profl. jours. including Jour. Geotech. Engring., Jour. Soils and Found., Jour. Instl. Engrs., Indian Geotech. Jour. Mem. ASCE, U.S. Nat. Soc., Internat. Soc. Soil Mechanics and Found. Engrs., Tau Beta Pi. Republican. Hindu. Achievements include development of new test setup for in situ shear tests, of new method for determining consolidation characteristics of saturated clays, and of new methodology for analyzing strains around cone penetrometers; derivation of formulas for finite strain components in spherical and cylindrical coordinates.

GUPTA, SANJAY, psychiatrist; b. Bombay, Sept. 24, 1959; s. Parkash Ram and Sarla Rani; m. Sadhna Kayastha, Jan. 14, 1992; 1 child, Sheila. MD, The U. Delhi, India, 1984. Diplomate Am. Bd. Psychiatry and Neurology, Am. Bd. Forensic Examiners, Am. Bd. Addiction Medicine, Am. Bd. Forensic Medicine, Am. Bd. Geriat. Psychiatry, Am. Bd. Adolescent Psychiatry. Resident in psychiatry SUNY, Syracuse, 1987-91; rsch. fellow U. Iowa Hosps. and Clinics, Iowa City, 1991-94; asst. prof. psychiatry U. Nebr., Omaha, 1994-95; clin. assoc. prof. psychiatry health scis. ctr. SUNY Health Scis. Ctr., 1996—; clin. assoc. prof. dept. psychiatry U. Buffalo, 1997—; rschr. brain imaging U. Iowa, 1991-94; examiner Am. Bd. Psychiatry & Neurology Examinations, 1993-95; bd. advisors profl. standards Am. Bd. Forensic Medicine, Springfield, Mo., 1995-96; dir. psychiatry Olean (N.Y.) Gen. Hosp., 1995—, chmn. dept. psychiatry, 1997—; spkr. in field. Contbr. articles to profl. jours. Travel fellow Am. Coll. Neuropsychopharmacology, 1992. Mem. Am. Psychiat. Assn., Am. Assn. Geriatric Psychiatrists, Am. Bd. Forensic Examiners, Internat. Soc. Neuroimaging in Psychiatry, Am. Assn. Physicians from India, U. Iowa Alumni Assn. Hindu. Achievements include involvement in trials of new drugs for schizophrenia. Office: Psychiatric Network Olean Gen Hosp W 2221 W State St Olean NY 14760-1921

GUPTA, SUBHASH CHANDRA, metallurgical engineer; b. Doggadda, Utter Prad, India, Aug. 12, 1941; came to U.S., 1967; s. Shiv Dayal and Munni Devi Gupta; m. Madhu, Apr. 28, 1967; children: Sharad, Paresh. BS, U. Rajasthan, Jaipur, India, 1962; BE in Metallurgy, Indian Inst. Sci., Bangalore, 1964, ME, 1966; MBA, Renssalaer Poly. Inst., Troy, N.Y., 1985. Lectr. dept. of metallurgy Indian Inst. Sci., Bangalore, 1966-67; metall. engr. The Bendix Corp., Utica, N.Y., 1968-70; sr. metall. engr. The Bendix Corp., Utica, 1973-74, mgr. metallurgy, 1974-76, mgr. metallurgy, reliability, 1976-82; plant metallurgist Kelsey Hayes Co., Utica, N.Y., 1970-73; mgr. engring. Allied Corp., Utica, N.Y., 1982-85; mgr. metallurgy Allied Signal, Utica, 1985-88, Lucas Aerospace Power Transmission Corp., Utica N.Y., 1988-94, AAR Engine Component Svcs., Frankfort, N.Y., 1994-96, Spl. Metals Corp., New Hartford, N.Y., 1996—. Mem. ASM Internat. (named Outstanding Young Mem., 1975), Soc. Mfg. Engrs., Am. Soc. for Quality Control, Rotary Internat. Republican. Hindu. Avocations: photography, travel, tennis, golf. Home: 50 Imperial Dr New Hartford NY 13413-3210 Office: Spl Metals Corp 4317 Middle Settlement Rd New Hartford NY 13413-5317

GUPTA, SUDHIR, immunologist, educator; b. Bijnor, India, Apr. 14, 1944; came to U.S., 1971; s. Tej S. and Jagdishwari Gupta; m. Abha, Jan. 28, 1980; children: Ankmalika Abha, Saurabh Sudhir. MD, King George's Med. Coll., Lucknow, India, 1966, PhD, 1970. Diplomate Am. Bd. Allergy and Immunology, Am. Bd. Diagnostic Lab. Immunology, Clin. Immunology Bd., Royal Coll. Physicians and Surgeons Can. Intern King George's Med. Coll., Lucknow, 1966, resident in medicine, 1967-70; teaching faculty fellow dept. medicine Tufts U. Med. Sch., Boston, 1971-72; vis. fellow in medicine Columbia U., N.Y.C., 1972-74; rsch. fellow Sloan-Kettering Inst. Cancer Rsch., N.Y.C., 1974-76, asst. prof., 1976-78, assoc. prof., 1978-82; instr. Cornell U., N.Y.C., 1976-77, asst. prof., 1977-79, assoc. prof., 1979-82; prof. medicine U. Calif., Irvine, 1982—, prof. microbiology and molecular genetics, 1984—, prof. pathology, 1986—, prof. neurology, 1988—, vice chair Dept. Medicine, 1994—; mem. adv. panel FDA, Washington, 1989—; sci. advisor Inst. Immunopathology, Kohn, Germany, 1990—; mem. allergy-immunology subcom. NIH, Bethesda, Md., 1985-89; vis. prof. Hematologic Rsch. Found., Roslyn, N.Y., 1992. Editor-in-chief Jour. Clin. Immunology, 1980—; editor: Immunology of Clinical and Experimental Diabetes, 1984, Mechanisms of Lymphocyte Activities and Immune Regulation I-VII, 1985-98, New Concepts in Immunbodeficiency Diseases, 1993, Multidrug Resistance in Cancer, 1996, Immunology of HIV Infections, 1996. Pres. Nargis Dutt Meml. Found., So. Calif., 1990; vice-chair AIDS Task Force, Orange County (Calif.) Med. Assn., 1987-95; mem. Indo-Am. Republican Club, Orange County, 1991—. Recipient Arthur Manzel Rsch. award R.A. Cooke Inst., N.Y.C., 1976, Outstanding Achievement award in med. scis. Nat. Fedn. Asian Indians in N.Am., 1986, Lifetime Achievement award Jeffrey Modell Found., N.Y.C., 1990, Disting. Scientists award Assn. Scientists Indian Origin in Am., 1994, Disting. Physician award Indian Med. Assn. Master ACP; fellow Royal Coll. Physicians and Surgeons Can., Am. Soc. Medicine (London); mem. Am. Assn. Immunologists. Achievements include description of the presence of K+ channels in human T cells, their role in T cell function and assn. with exptl. autoimmune diseases, reversal of multidrug resistance of cancer cells by cyclosporin A both in vitro and in vivo, described a new human intracisternal retrovirus associated with CD4+ cell deficiency without HIV infection; increased apoptosis in T cells in human aging. Fax: 949-824-4362. E-mail: sgupta@uci.edu. Office: U Calif Dept Medicine C240 Med Sci I Irvine CA 92697*

GUPTA, SURAJ NARAYAN, physicist, educator; b. Haryana, India, Dec. 1, 1924; came to U.S., 1953, naturalized, 1963; s. Lakshmi N. and Devi (Goyal) G.; m. Letty J.R. Paine, July 14, 1948; children: Paul, Ranee. MS, St. Stephen's Coll., India, 1946; PhD, U. Cambridge, Eng., 1951. Imperial Chem. Industries fellow U. Manchester, Eng., 1951-53; vis. prof. physics Purdue U., 1953-56; prof. physics Wayne State U., Detroit, 1956-61, Distinguished prof. physics, 1961—; researcher on high energy physics, nuclear physics, relativity and gravitation. Author: Quantum Electrodynamics, 1977. Fellow Am. Phys. Soc., Nat. Acad. Scis. of India. Achievements include quantum theory with negative probability and quantization of the electromagnetic field; flat-space interpretation of Einstein's theory of gravitation and quantization of the gravitational field; regulatization and renormalization of elementary particle interactions; development of the theory of bound states in quantum electrodynamics and quantum chromodynamics; mass matrix formulation of quark mixing and CP violation in weak interactions; investigation of phenomena at supercollider energies. Home: 30001 Hickory Ln Franklin MI 48025-1566 Office: Wayne State U Dept Physics Detroit MI 48202

GUPTA, SURENDRA KUMAR, chemical firm executive; b. Delhi, India, Apr. 5, 1938; came to U.S., 1963, naturalized, 1971; s. Bishan Chand and Devki G.; m. Karen Patricia Clarke, Oct. 12, 1968; children—Jay, Amanda. B.Sc. with honors, Delhi U., 1959, M.Sc., 1961; M.Tech., Indian Inst. Tech., Bombay, 1963; Ph.D., Wayne State U., 1968. Research assoc. Western Mich. U., Kalamazoo, 1968-73; indsl. postdoctoral fellow Starks Assocs., Buffalo, 1973-74; group leader New Eng. Nuclear Co., Boston, 1974-80, Pathfinder Labs., St. Louis, 1981-83; chmn. bd., chemist Am. Radiolabeled Chem., Inc., St. Louis, 1983—. Contbr. numerous articles to internat. sci. jours. Mem. Am. Chem. Soc. (chmn. pub. relations com. 1970-73). Hindu. Avocations: table tennis; stamp collecting; traveling. Home: 22 Muirfield Ln Saint Louis MO 63141-7380 Office: Am Radiolabeled Chems Inc 11624 Bowling Green Dr Saint Louis MO 63146-3506

GUPTA, SURESH K., pathologist; b. Nabha, Punjab, India, Aug. 14, 1951; came to U.S., 1980; s. Pyaralal and Vidyawati (Gupta) G.; m. Santosh Sharma, Dec. 12, 1976; 1 child, Nishi. MD, Govt. Med. Coll./Punjabi U., Patiala, India, 1975. Diplomate in anat. and clin. pathology Am. Bd. Pathology; lic. physician, N.J.; lic. lab. dir., N.J. Resident in orthopedic surgery and emergency medicine Govt. Med. Coll., Punjab, 1976-77; med.-surg. officer Govt. Health Svcs., Punjab, 1978-80; resident in anat. and clin. pathology U. Medicine and Dentistry N.J.-N.J. Med. Sch., 1982-86; fellow in renal pathology Barnert Hosp./U. Medicine and Dentistry N.J.-N.J. Med. Sch., 1986-88; assoc. pathologist, dir. pathology and lab.svcs. Alexian Bros. Hosp., Elizabeth, N.J., 1988-90; asst. pathologist Barnert Meml. Hosp. Ctr., Paterson, N.J., 1990; assoc. pathologist Franciscan Health System of N.J., Inc., 1990-92; clin. asst. prof. lab. medicine and pathology U. Medicine and Dentistry N.J.-N.J. Med. Sch., Newark, 1992—; med. dir. pathology and lab. svcs. Meml. Med. Ctr. at S.A., South Amboy, N.J., 1992—. Contbr. articles to profl. jours. Fellow Coll. Am. Pathologists, Am. Soc. Clin. Pathologist; mem. Pathologists Club N.Y. Hindu. Avocations: tennis, skiing. Office: Meml Med Ctr SA 540 Bordentown Ave South Amboy NJ 08879-1546

GUPTA, VIJAY KUMAR, chemistry educator; b. Ambala Cantt, Haryana, India, Apr. 27, 1941; m. Surjit Mohini Aggarwal, Sept. 5, 1968; children: Sonia, Angela, Ashish. BS in Chemistry with honors, Panjab U., Chandigarh, India, 1961, MS in Chemistry with honors, 1962, PhD in Chemistry, 1969. Asst. prof. chemistry Punjab Engring. Coll., Chandigarh, India, 1962-64, 67-68; postdoctoral rsch. assoc. Wright State U., Dayton, Ohio, 1968-69; rsch. chemist Lawrence Livermore Nat. Lab., Livermore, Calif., summer 1980; adj. faculty mem. Lebanon Correctional Inst., Ohio, fall 1977, 78, summer 1982; fellow Wright Patterson AFB, Dayton, summer 1981, with aero-propulsion lab., 1981-83, with materials lab., 1984, fellow materials lab., 1985, summers 1987, 88, 91, vis. scientist materials lab., 1985-87; adj. faculty mem. Wright State U., 1985; adj. faculty in chemistry Wilberforce U., Ohio, spring/summer 1981, 82, 83, 84, 1983-84, fall 1986-87; prof., chmn. chemistry, researcher Cen. State U., Wilberforce, Ohio, 1969-98; ret.; cons. E.G.&G. Mound Labs., summer, 1989, 90, 92, 93; researcher in environ. pollution, lubricant devel. and characterization, devel. of radioluminescent light sources, thermodynamics, electrochemistry, chem. kinetics, trace metals analysis, energy conversion and storage, for IBM Corp., Pitts. Plate Glass Fiber Glass Tech. Ctr., NASA, Johnson Johnson Controls Inc., Lawrence Livermore Nat. Lab., Wright Patterson AFB, Universal Energy Systems Inc., AF Office of Sci. Research, San Jose State U., United Tech. Systems Inc., SCEEE, Systran Corp., E.G.&G. Mound Techs., Inc., U. Dayton Rsch. Inst. Contbr. numerous articles to profl. jours. Recipient Appreciation award Ctrl. State U., 1975-76, Talmadge McKinney award, 1986, Excellence in Rsch. award, 1995, Outstanding Svc. to Cmty. award India Club of Greater Dayton, 1985, Clarence E. Bowman award for Comm. Svcs., 1991, others; Nat. Urban League fellow, IBM Corp. fellow, summer 1973, Pittsburgh Plate Glass Fiberglass Tech. Ctr., summer 1976, Johnson Johnson Control Inc. fellow, 1979, NSF summer fellow, 1979; USAF grantee, 1982-83, NASA grantee, 1976-79. Mem. Am. Chem. Soc. (chmn. Dayton sect. 1988, Outstanding Sect. award 1988), Nat. Inst. Scis., Assn. Energy Engrs., AAUP, Electrochem. Soc., Am. Soc. Lubrication Engrs., India Club (Dayton). Democrat. Hindu. Home: 2810 Dennis Ct Beavercreek OH 45434-6522

GUPTA, VIPIN K., neurologist; b. New Delhi, Nov. 22, 1954; m. Ankan Gupta, June 30, 1989; children: Rajesh, Apar. MD, All India Inst. Med. Scis., New Delhi, 1976. Bd. cert. neurology Am. Bd. Psychiatry and Neurology. Intern and resident A.I.I.M.S., New Delhi, 1977-82; resident in neurology Med. Coll. Pa., Phila., 1983-85; fellow in EMG and neuromuscular disorders U. Miss., Jackson, 1986-87; pvt. practice law Vineland, N.J., 1987—. Me. Am. Acad. Neurology, Am. Assn. Electrodiagnostic Medicine. Home: 1580 Linden Blvd Vineland NJ 08360 Office: 2848 S Delsea Dr Vineland NJ 08360

GURA, TIMOTHY JAMES, speech educator; b. Peoria, Ill., Sept. 3, 1947; s. John Thomas and Violet Edythe (Hunt) G. BS in Speech, Northwestern U., 1969; MA in English, U. Mich., 1971; PhD in Interpretation, Northwestern U., 1974. Prof. speech, chair CUNY, Bklyn. Coll., 1974—. Co-author: Oral Interpretation, 1997. Mem. Nat. Comm. Assn. Avocations: performance ofliterature, wines, culinary arts. Home: 275 W 12th St New York NY 10014-1913 Office: Bkly Coll Dept Speech Dept. Speech Commn. A&S Brooklyn NY 11210-2814

GURALNICK, SIDNEY AARON, civil engineering educator; b. Phila., Apr. 25, 1929; s. Philip and Kenia (Dudnik) G.; m. Eleanor Alban, Mar. 10, 1951; children—Sara Dian, Jeremy. BSc, Drexel Inst. Tech., Phila., 1952; MS, Cornell U., 1955, PhD, 1958. Registered profl. engr., Pa.; lic. structural engr., Ill. Instr., then asst. prof. Cornell U., 1952-58, mgr. structural research lab., 1956-58; mem. faculty Ill. Inst. Tech., Chgo., 1958—; prof. civil engring. Ill. Inst. Tech., 1967—, disting. prof. engring., 1982—, dir. structural engring. labs., 1968-71, dean Grad. Sch., 1971-75, exec. v.p., provost, 1975-82, trustee, 1976-82, dir. Advanced Bldg. Materials and Sys. Ctr., 1987—; devel. engr. Portland Cement Assn., Skokie, Ill., 1959-61; participant internat. confs.; cons. to govt. and industry. Author numerous papers in field. Trustee Inst. Gas Tech., 1976-81, Rsch. Inst. of Ill. Inst. Tech., 1976-82; commr.-at-large North Ctrl. Assn. Schs. and Colls., 1985-89, cons., evaluator, 1989-93. With C.E., U.S. Army, 1950-51. McGraw fellow, 1952-53; Faculty Rsch. fellow Ill. Inst. Tech., 1960; European travel grantee, 1961. Fellow ASCE (Lifetime Achievement award Ill. sect. 1997, Civil Engr. of Yr. award Ill. sect. 1998, Collingwood prize 1961); mem. Am. Concrete Inst., Am. Soc. for Engring. Edn., Soc. Exptl. Mechanics, Structural Engrs. Assn. Ill. (bd. dirs., pres.-elect 1989-90, pres. 1990-91, John F. Parmer award 1993), Transp. Rsch. Bd., Ill. Univs. Transp. Rsch. Consortium (adminstrv. com. 1983-93), Sigma Xi, Phi Kappa Phi, Tau Beta Pi, Chi Epsilon. Office: Ill Inst Tech 3300 S Federal St Chicago IL 60616-3793

GURASH, JOHN THOMAS, insurance company executive; b. Oakland, Calif., Nov. 25, 1910; s. Nicholas and Katherine (Restovic) G.; student Loyola U. Sch. Law, Los Angeles, 1936, 38-39; m. Katherine Mills, Feb. 4, 1934; 1 child, John N. With Am. Surety Co. N.Y., 1930-44; with Pacific Employers Ins. Co., 1944-53; pres., organizer Meritplan Ins. Co., 1953-59; exec. v.p. Pacific Employers Ins. Co., 1959-60, pres., 1960-68, chmn., bd., 1968-76; v.p. Ins. Co. N. Am., 1966-70; exec. v.p., dir. INA Corp., 1968-69, chmn., pres., CEO, 1969-74, chmn., CEO, 1974-75, chmn. bd., 1975, chmn. exec. com., 1975-79; chmn. bd. CertainTeed Corp. and Saint Gobain Corp., 1978-92, chmn. emeritus, 1992—; chmn. Horace Mann Educators Corp., Springfield, Ill., 1989-96, chmn. emeritus, 1996—; dir. St. Gobain Corp., chmn. bd. dirs., 1991-92. Trustee emeritus Occidental Coll., L.A.; former trustee Orthopaedic Hosp., Los Angeles; dir. Weingart Found. Office: 1000 Wilshire Blvd Ste 610 Los Angeles CA 90017-2463

GURASICH, STEPHEN WILLIAM, JR., advertising executive; b. Long Beach, Calif., Mar. 26, 1948; s. Stephen W. and Joan Marie (Cotter) G.; m. Nancy Ruth Hamlin, June 6, 1970; children: Amy Marie, John Hamlin. BJ, U. Tex., 1971. Chmn., chief exec. officer GSD&M Advt., Austin, Tex., 1971-86, 1986—; bd. dirs. Cornerstone Devel., Austin, 1980—, G&S Assn., Inc., 1971—. Served with Tex. N.G., 1970-76. Recipient Addy awards, 1987. Mem. Austin Advt. Club (bd. dirs.), Austin Assn. Advt. Principles (bd. dirs. 1979-80), Am. Assn. Advt. Agys. (mem. client service com. 1986-87). Roman Catholic. Avocations: reading, raquetball, hunting, fishing. Home: 16100 Chateau Ave Austin TX 78734-2631 Office: GSD&M Advt 828 W 6th St Austin TX 78703-5420*

GUREVICH, GRIGORY, visual artist, educator; b. St. Petersburg, Russia, Dec. 26, 1937; came to U.S., 1976; s. Abram Grigoryevich Gurevich and Klara Mihailovna (Olshvang) Fleitman; m. Mongita Zalmanovna Freedman, Aug. 8, 1958 (div. Feb. 1967); 1 child, Jelena Gurevich Scherbina; m. Erika Wittmann, Jan. 17, 1987; 1 child, Alexander. Diploma, Acad. Fine & Indsl. Art, St. Petersburg, 1966. Interior designer Lenprojekt, Lenzneeap, St. Petersburg; founder Grigur's Pantomime Theater, St. Petersburg, 1966-69; founder mime sch. St. Petersburg, 1969-75; founder Grigur's Pantomime Theater, N.Y.C., 1977-79; tchr. visual arts Bergen Sch., Jersey City, 1980-82; instr. sculpture Newark Sch. Fine and Indsl. Art, 1982-96; prof. St. Johns U., Jamaica, N.Y., 1994-97; conductor workshops on sculpture, U.S., Italy, Denmark; founder art workshops, 1998—. Exhibited in solo and group exhbns. U.S., Russia, France, Denmark, Germany; bronze sculpture tableau Commuters for Newark Penn Sta., 1985, bronze bust Kazuo Hashimoto, 1996; representr in numerous pvt. collections, Russia, U.S. and Europe, Hermitage Mus., N.Y. Pub.-Libr., Libr. Newark Mus., Montclair Mus., Libr. St. Bonaventure U.; pub. poetry Reflections, 1992; author: Book of Numbers 1-10, 10-1, 1993 (collection Bklyn. Mus. 1994); inventor process of wood firing, 1963, manifolding book, 1995. Recipient Grumbacher award, Marian Reitman award, others. Mem. N.Y. Artists Equity Assn., Am. Artists Profl. League (1st Place Nat. award 1993, 98), Hudson Artists (Artist of Yr. 1995, other awards). E-mail: grigur@agorou.com. Home: 282 Barrow St Jersey City NJ 07302-3502

GUREVICH, ROBERT, international development administrator; b. N.Y.C., Sept. 6, 1938; s. Aaron and Vera (Solotroff) G.; m. Adele Landsman, Oct. 23, 1971; children: Deborah Aree, Reuben Aron. BA, City Coll. N.Y., 1960; MEd, U. Hawaii, 1967; PhD, U. Pitts., 1972. Faculty edn. Khon Kaen U., Thailand, 1969-70; exec. assoc. Asia fgn. area fellowship program Social Sci. Rsch. Coun., N.Y.C., 1971-73; asst. prof. anthropology SUNY, Brockport, 1973-77; dir. Foster Parents Plan Internat., Yogyakarta, Indonesia, 1977-79; dir. Office Edn. & Tng. S.E. Consortium Internat. Devel., Chapel Hill, N.C., 1979-84; sr. assoc. Internat. Orientation Svc., Chapel Hill, 1984-87; chief party/tech. advisor Expt. In Living, Mogadishu, Somalia, 1987-89; dir. Ctr. Improving Mountain Living Western Carolina U., Cullowhee, N.C., 1990-95, dir. internat. programs, 1996-98; exec. sec. Ctr. Pvt. Vol. Orgn./Univ. Collaboration in Devel., Cullowhee, 1990-98; sr. program advisor Inst. for Ednl. Policy, Open Soc. Inst. (Soros Found.), Budapest, 1998—; exec. dir. Albanic Edn. Devel. Project, Tirana, Albania; mem. N.C. Internat. Commn., Raleigh, 1994-97; bd. dirs., chmn. Sustainable Agr. and Natural Resources Mgmt., Collaborative Rsch. Support Program, Athens, Ga., 1992-95; bd. dirs. N.C. Global Ctr. Contbr. articles to profl. jours. Vol. Peace Corps, Pitsanuloke, Thailand, 1963-65; coord. Internat. Network Western Carolina Coll., 1996-97; mem. internat. com. N.C. Bd. Sci. & Tech., Raleigh, 1996-97; mem. adv. bd. Self Help Credit Union, Asheville, N.C., 1990-97; bd. dirs. Internat. Devel. Conf., Washington, 1995-97, N.C. Govs. Sch., 1998—; mem. N.C. Coun. on the Holocaust, 1997—. NDEA fellow U. Pitts., 1967-69, East-West Ctr. fellow U. Hawaii, 1965-67, Fgn. Area Fellowship Program, Thailand, 1969-70, SUNY fellow, N.Y., 1972. Mem. Am. Anthropol. Assn., Nat. Assn. Practice Anthropology, Nat. Coun. Returned Peace Corps Vols., Assn. for Internat. Educators, Coun. Anthropology and Edn., Cmty. Devel. Soc. Office: Western Carolina U Internat Programs & Svcs Cullowhee NC 28723

GUREVITZ, BERNARD HERMAN, painter; b. Scranton, Pa., Apr. 30, 1921; s. Isaac and Tillie (Ginsberg) Gurevitz; m. Marnie Hutchinson, Apr. 30, 1966; children: Enid, Ted. Student, Corcoran Sch. Art, Washington, 1939-42, Art Students League, N.Y.C., 1945-46, Bklyn. Mus. Sch., 1947-48. Pres., owner M. Toberoff & Co., Inc., N.Y.C., 1954-89. Exhibited in one man shows at Everhart Mus., Pa., East End Arts Coun., N.Y., Clayton-Liberatore Gallery, Bridgehampton, N.Y., Cook Pony Farm Gallery, Sag Harbor, N.Y., Gallery 84, N.Y.; group show at Parrish Mus., Southampton, N.Y.; paintings in collections of Chapellier Galleries, N.Y.C., Johnson & Johnson Pharms., Irving Trust Co., East River Savs. Bank, Colt Industries, Chubb & Son, South African Marine Corp. Cpl. USAF, 1942-45. Louis Comfort Tiffany fellow, 1941. Mem. Jimmy Ernst/Artist Alliance, Audubon Artists (assoc.). Jewish. Home: PO Box 419 Shelter Island NY 11964-0419

GURFEIN, PETER J., lawyer; b. N.Y.C., Sept. 13, 1948; m. Pamela Hedin, June 23, 1976; children: Diana, William, Eva. BA, NYU, 1969; JD, George Washington U., 1973. Bar: N.Y. 1976, U.S. Supreme Ct. 1976, US. Dist. Ct. (so. and ea. dists.) N.Y. 1976, U.S. Ct. Appeals (2d cir.) 1979, Internat. Ct. Trade 1979, U.S. Ct. Appeals (9th cir.) 1986, Calif. 1986, U.S Dist. Ct. (no., ea., so. and cen. dists.) Calif. 1987, D.C. 1993. Project dir. Commn. on Correctional Facilities and Scs. ABA, Washington, 1973-76; asst. dist. atty., spl. narcotics prosecutor Dist. Atty.'s Office N.Y. County, N.Y.C., 1976-81; assoc. Zalkin, Rodin & Goodman, N.Y.C., 1981-83, Moses & Singer, N.Y.C., 1983-86; ptnr. Morrison & Foerster, San Francisco, 1986-92, Sonnenschein, Nath & Rosenthal, L.A. and San Francisco, 1993—. Editor-in-chief The Calif. Bankruptcy Jour., 1995—; contbr. articles to handbooks and profl. jours. Mem. Bar Assn. San Francisco (chmn. bankruptcy and comml. law sect. 1993), L.A. County Bar Assn. Office: Sonnenschein Nath & Rosenthal 601 S Figueroa St Los Angeles CA 90017-5704

GURFEIN, RICHARD ALAN, lawyer; b. N.Y.C., Nov. 4, 1946; s. Jack and Ruth (Kronowitz) G.; m. Erica P. Temchin, Oct. 20, 1978; children: Jared L., Amanda, Jessica M., Sarah R. BE, NYU, 1967; JD, Bklyn. Law Sch., 1971. Bar: N.Y. 1972, U.S. Dist. Ct. (so. and ea. dists.) N.Y. 1973, U.S. Supreme Ct. 1976, U.S. Ct. Appeals (2d cir.) 1990. Assoc. Mark B. Wiesen, PC, N.Y.C., 1972-78; ptnr. Wiesen & Gurfein, N.Y.C., 1978-82, Wiesen, Gurfein & Jenkins, N.Y.C., 1982—; pres. Trial1.com, Inc., 1997—; moderator, lectr. Nassau Acad. Law, 1984—, N.Y. State Trial Lawyers Inst., 1985—, treas., 1989-91, pres. 1995-96. Recipient Crown of Good Name award Inst. Jewish Humanities, 1996. Mem. Assn. Trial Lawyers Am., N.Y. State Trial Lawyers Assn. (lectr. continuing legal edn. 1985—, bd. dirs. 1986—, chmn. com. on coms. 1987-88, exec. com. 1987—, dep. treas. 1988-89, treas. 1989-91, sec. 1991-92, v.p. 1992-94, pres. elect 1994-95, pres. 1995-96, past pres. 1996—), N.Y. County Lawyers Assn., Nassau County Bar Assn. (chmn. com. on med. jurisprudence 1983-86), Million Dollar Advocates Forum. Avocations: astronomy, amateur radio, photography, golf, computing. Office: Wiesen Gurfein & Jenkins 11 Park Pl Rm 1100 New York NY 10007-2889

GURFEIN, STUART JAMES, data processing executive; b. N.Y.C., Mar. 24, 1947; s. Louis J. and Ruthe (Jacobs) G.; divorced; children: Scott Eric, Heather Gill; m. Kathryn Merine, Apr. 4, 1981; children: Kody Allana. BS, Cornell U., 1968; MBA, Columbia U., 1970. Account exec. Cunningham & Walsh Advt., N.Y.C., 1970-71; v.p. Gurfein Bros. Inc., N.Y.C., 1971-82, M. Fabrikant & Sons, N.Y.C., 1983-86; chmn. A.B.L. Jewelers Inc., N.Y.C., 1986-91, Jeffrey Stevens, Inc., N.Y.C., 1988-91; chief oper. officer ODI Famor, Long Island City, N.Y., 1992-94; pres., CEO Pvt. Source Jewelry Corp., Rye, N.Y., 1994-95; mng. dir. Pvt. Source Jewelry Ltd., Hong Kong, 1994-95, Private Source Jewelry, Thailand, 1994-95; pres. Diners' Grapevine, Ltd., Port Chester, N.Y., 1995-96, Restaurant Row Inc., Port Chester, 1997—; chmn. Coolmedia Networks, Inc., 1996—. Bd. dirs. Nat. Found. for Advancement in Arts, 1985-88; chmn. Crime Stoppers of Westchester County. Mem. Friars Club. Office: Restaurant Row Inc Coolmedia Networks Inc 56 Locust Ave Rye NY 10580

GURGANUS, ALLAN, writer, educator; b. Rocky Mount, N.C., June 11, 1947; s. Marvin F and Ethel Morris Gurganus. BA, Sarah Lawrence Coll., 1972; MFA, Iowa Writers' Workshop, 1975. Prof. writing and lit. Stanford (Calif.) U., 1976-78, Duke U., Durham, N.C., 1978-79, Sarah Lawrence Coll., Bronxville, N.Y., 1979-89, Iowa Writers' Workshop, Iowa City, 1989-90; guest Eng. lectr. Cambridge U., 1995. Author: Oldest Living Confederate Widow Tells All, 1989 (Sue Kaufman prize Am. Acad. Arts and Letters, 1989), White People, 1990 (La. Times Book prize, 1990), Plays Well With Others, 1997. With USN, 1966-70. Recipient Amb. Book award English Speaking Union, 1989, Nat. Mag. prize Nat. Mag. Assn., 1994. Mem. PEN, Soc. Values in Higher Edn., Boston Atheneum. Democrat. Avocations: painting, drawing, gardening. Office: Internat Creative Mgmt c/o Amanda Urban 40 West 57th St New York NY 10019

GURIAN, MAL, telecommunications executive; b. N.Y.C., Nov. 17, 1926; s. George Joseph and Rose (Graff) G.; m. Gloria Dickler; children: Randy Harlan, Nancy Ellen Newman. Ptnr. Mal Gurian Assocs., N.Y.C., 1946-77; v.p. Radio Telephone Corp., N.Y.C., 1960-83; sr. v.p. Aerotron, Inc., Raleigh, N.C., 1965-81; v.p. Oki Advanced Comm., Hackensack, N.J., 1981-84; pres. Oki Telecom, Fairlawn, N.J., 1984-88, Cartell, Inc., Romulus, Mich., 1988, Cellcom Cellular Corp., Fairfield, N.J., 1989-91; CEO Universal Cellular, Inc., Anaheim, Calif., 1992; chmn., CEO Global Link Comm., Inc., Irvine, Calif., 1993—; pres., CEO Authentix Network, Inc., Tucson, 1995-98, chmn., 1998—; pres. Ea. Profl. Photographers Assn., N.Y.C., 1951-53; exec. advisor TRW Wireless Commn., Sunnyvale, Calif., 1994; advisor Sims Comms., Inc., Delray Beach, Fla., 1994—; arbitrator Am. Arbitration Assn., 1994—; bd. dirs. N.E. Digital Networks, Inc., Melville, N.Y., Rangestar Internat., San Jose, Calif. Life mem. Old Tappan (N.J.) First Aid Corp., 1966—. Cpl. USMC, 1943-46. Decorated Air medal; recipient Alexander S. Popov Hon. Medal award St. Petersburg Electrotech. U., Russia, 1995. Fellow and life mem. Radio Club Am. (life mem., v.p. 1976-92, exec. v.p. 1993, pres. 1994, pres. emeritus 1995—, Spl. Svcs. award 1986, Sarnoff citation 1988, Fred Link award 1989); mem. Am. Assn. Pub. Safety Comm. Officers, Nat. Assn. Bus. and Ednl. Radio (bd. dirs. 1977-84, Chmn.'s award 1986). Home: 5245 88th St E Bradenton FL 34202-3715 *Advances in technology is rapidly moving on. Mankind must strive to utilize our developments in a positive vein and promote compatibility amongst each other.*

GURLAND, JOSEPH, engineering educator; b. Berlin, Jan. 26, 1923; came to U.S., 1940; s. Otto Rosenthal and Henny (Meyer) Gurland; m. Doris Hurwitch, 1948; children—Lisa, Johanna. B. Engring., NYU, 1944, M.E., 1947; Sc.D., MIT, 1951. Research engr. Battelle Meml. Inst., Columbus, Ohio, 1947-48; rsch. engr., mgr. basic research Firth Sterling, Inc., Pitts., 1951-55; asst. prof. engring. Brown U., Providence, R.I., 1955-57, assoc. prof., 1957-64, prof., 1964-87, prof. emeritus, 1988—; disting. vis. scientist Boston U. Mfg. Engring. Dept., 1990—. Co-editor: Science of Hard Materials, 1983; contbr. articles on materials sci. and engring. to profl. jours. Served with U.S. Army, 1944-46. Recipient Plansee medal Internat. Plansee Soc. Powder Metallurgy, 1989, Civil Libertarian of Yr. award R.I. Civil Liberties Union, 1990; NSF fellow, 1961, NATO fellow, 1970. Fellow Am. Soc. for Metals; mem. AIME, Internat. Metallographic Soc., Internat. Soc. Stereology. Jewish. Office: Brown U Divsn Engring PO Box D Providence RI 02912-9104

GURLEY, CURTIS RAYMOND, lawyer; b. Joplin, Mo., Apr. 5, 1959; s. Carl R. and Glenda (Cummins) G.; m. Rebecca Lynn Miller; 2 children: Jackson M. and Davis C. AB, U. Mo., 1986, JD, 1989. Bar: N.Mex., 1989, Mo. 1990, Colo. 1998. Ptnr. Hynes, Hale & Gurley, Farmington, N.Mex. Mem. NACDL, San Juan County Bar (pres. 1993), N.Mex. Trial Lawyers Assn. (bd. dirs.), N.Mex. Criminal Def. Attys. Assn., Elks. Republican. Presbyterian. Office: Hynes Hale & Gurley 1000 W Apache St Farmington NM 87401-3805

GURLEY, FRANKLIN LOUIS, lawyer, military historian; b. Syracuse, N.Y., Nov. 26, 1925; Swiss national, 1994 (dual nationality); s. George Bernard and Catherine Veronica (Moran) G.; m. Elizabeth Anne Ryan, June 17, 1950. A.B., Harvard U., 1949, J.D., 1952. Bar: Mass. 1952, N.Y. 1956, Ill. 1956, Mich. 1956, D.C. 1956. Fgn. service staff officer Dept. State, Washington and Germany, 1953-55; atty. N.Y. Central R.R. Co., 1955-56; asst. dist. atty. New York County, 1956-57; atty. firm Dewey, Ballantine, Bushby, Palmer & Wood, N.Y.C., 1957-63; gen. counsel, sec. IBM Europe Corp., Paris; also mng. atty. IBM Corp., Armonk, N.Y., 1963-68; sr. v.p., gen. counsel Nestle S.A., Vevey, Switzerland, 1968-83; spl. legal adv. Nestle S.A., Vevey, 1984-85; internat. legal cons., 1985—. Author: 399th in Action in World War II, 1946, (play) King Philip's War, 1952; chief editor Beachhead News (Germany), 1945-46; contbr. articles to profl. and mil. jours. Pres. Tappan Landing Assn. Tarrytown N.Y. 1958-60. Served with inf. AUS, 1944-46, ETO. Decorated Bronze Star, Combat Inf. Badge; 7th Army mile run champion, 1945; set West Point and Heptagonal 1000-yard records in track, 1948. Mem. SAR (sec., bd. mgrs. N.Y. chpt. 1957-63, founding mem. Swiss chpt. 1970), 100th Inf. Divsn. Assn. (historian 1984—). Home and Office: 1626 Romanens, Fribourg Switzerland

GURLEY, STEVEN HARRISON, sales executive; b. Macon, Ga., Apr. 22, 1957; s. Harrison Wade and Louise (Forester) G.; m. Dona Ray Skelton, July 14, 1978; children: Stephanie Ray, Jonathan Steven. AA, Macon Jr. Coll., 1977; BS, Ga. Coll., 1979; cert., Cert. Med. Rep. Inst., Roanoke, Va., 1987. Med. sales rep. Adria Labs., Columbus, Ohio, 1980-81; sr. profl. sales rep. Knoll Pharms., Macon, 1981—. Democrat. Methodist. Avocations: golf, hunting, fishing. Home and Office: 5698 Charles Dr Macon GA 31210-1104

GURLIK, PHILIP JOHN, artist; b. Beaver Dam, Wis., Sept. 26, 1958; s. Philip John and Jean Marie (Klingbile) G.; m. Janiece Lee Lesher; 1 child, Robert Graham. Student, U. Wis., Green Bay, 1976-79, Milw. Coll., 1979-80. Solo shows include L'Esprit Salon, Houston, 1992, Paradox Gallery, Houston, 1992, 1010 1/2 Loft, Houston, 1993, Stone House Gallery, Fredonia, Kans., 1995, Collin Coll., Plano, tex., 1995, Northwest Coll., Houston, 1998; exhibited in group shows at Westside Fine Art Gallery, Houston, 1992, Louisville (Colo.) Ctr. for the Arts, 1993, Nicolet Coll., Rhinelander, Wis., 1993, Houston Visual Arts Alliance, 1993, Barnwell Art Ctr., Shreveport, La., 1993, Chautaugua Art Assn. Gallery, N.Y., 1993, Cooperstown (N.Y.) Art Assn., 1993, Mich. Gallery, Detroit, 1994, Lawndale Art and Performance Ctr., Houston, 1994, U. North Tex., Ft. Worth, 1994, Haggin Mus., Stockton, Calif., 1994, Dwight Merrimon Davidson Print Exbhn., Elon College, N.C., 1994, Met. Ctr. for the Arts, Detroit, 1995, Sam Houston Meml. Mus., Huntsville, Tex., 1995, Stamford (Conn.) Mus., 1995, Miss. Mus. Art, Jackson, 1995, San Bernardino Mus., Redlands, Calif., 1995, Minot (N.D.) State U., 1996, Valdosta (Ga.) State U., 1996, Lamar U. Dishman Art Gallery, Beaumont, Tex., 1996, Dean Day Gallery, Houston, 1997, El Presidio Gallery, Tucson, 1997, others; works in permanent collectoins of Dwight Merrimon Davidson, Elon College, SAP America, Houston, Interchem Corp., Houston, JNC Design, Houston, 1997, Ark. Art Ctr., Little Rock, 1998, DeMatteis Gallery, Annapolis, Md., 1998; author: Art Picture Book, 1996, Best of Painting, 1998. Recipient Merit award Contemporary Arts Ctr./Walter Hopps, North Adams, Mass., 1995; contbr. articles to profl. jours. Avocations: sailing, music, backpacking, literature. Office: PO Box 4474 Annapolis MD 21403

GURNACK, DEAN HILTON, artist; b. East Orange, N.J., Apr. 1, 1945; s. Walter A. and Virginia (Hilton) G.; m. Elizabeth Anne Lehman, June 7, 1980. AB, Colgate U., 1967; MBA, Columbia U., 1970; AA, Am. Acad. Art, Chgo., 1981. Exhibited in group shows at Covenant Club, Chgo., 1980, Libertyville (Ill.) Arts Ctr., 1981-85, Salmagundi Club, N.Y.C., 1985, Bennett Galleries, Knoxville, Tenn., 1991, 92, 94, 96, Nashville, 1993, Bryant Galleries, Birmingham, Ala., 1992, Indpls. Mus. Art Regional Juried Exhbn., Columbus, Ind., 1998 (award of merit), Nat. Oil and Acrylic Painters' Soc. Juried Exhbn., Osage Beach, Mo., 1998, others; represented in permanent collections Knoxville Mus. Art, 1st Knoxville Bank, Suntrust Bank, Knoxville, Hyatt Rescorp., Chgo., others. 2d lt. U.S. Army N.G., 1967-68. Union League Club of Chgo. scholar, 1978, 79, 80. Avocations: flying, computers. Home: 1771 Orchard Hill Rd Nashville IN 47448

GURNETT, DONALD ALFRED, physics educator; b. Cedar Rapids, Iowa, Apr. 11, 1940; s. Alfred Foley and Velma (Trachta) G.; m. Marie Barbara Schmitz, Oct. 10, 1964; children: Suzanne, Christina. B.S. in Elec. Engring., U. Iowa, 1962, M.S. in Physics, 1963, Ph.D. in Physics, 1965. Prof. physics and astronomy U. Iowa, Iowa City, 1965-75, 76-79, 80—; rsch. scientist Max-Planck Inst., Garching, Fed. Republic Germany, 1975-76; vis. prof. UCLA, 1979-80; mem. space physics com. Nat. Acad. Sci., Washington, 1975-78, mem. com. on solar terrrestrial research, 1976-79, mem. com. on planetary and lunar exploration, 1982-85. Recipient Alexander von Humboldt Found. award, 1975, Disting. Sci. Achievement award NASA, 1981, Space Act award NASA, 1986, Sci. Achievement medal Gov. of Iowa, 1987, Disting. Iowa Scientist award Iowa Acad. Sci., 1989, Marion L. Huit award U. Iowa, 1990, Iowa Bd. Regents award for faculty excellence, 1994. Fellow Am. Geophys. Union (assoc. editor Jour. Geophys. Rsch. 1974-77, Fleming medal 1989), Am. Phys. Soc. (award for excellence in plasma physics 1989); mem. Internat. Union Radio Sci. (Dellinger gold medal 1978), Soaring Soc. Am. (Iowa State gov. 1983-86), Nat. Acad. of Sci. Home: 6 Durham Ct Iowa City IA 52240-2832 Office: U Iowa Dept Physics and Astronomy 715 Van Allen Hall Iowa City IA 52242-1403

GURNEY, ALBERT RAMSDELL, playwright, novelist, educator; b. Buffalo, Nov. 1, 1930; s. Albert Ramsdell and Marion (Spaulding) G.; m. Mary Forman Goodyear, June 8, 1957; children: George, Amy, Evelyn, Benjamin. BA, Williams Coll., 1952, DDL (hon.), 1984; MFA, Yale U., 1958; LLD (hon.), Buffalo State U., 1992. Mem. faculty MIT, 1960-96, prof. lit., 1970-96. Contbr. works to Best Short Plays, 1955-56, 57-58, 69, 70, 92; author: (plays) The Golden Fleece, 1969, Public Affairs, 1970, Scenes from American Life, 1971, Children, 1974, Richary Cory, 1976, The Middle Ages, 1977, The Wayside Motor Inn, 1977, The Golden Age, 1980, The Dining Room, 1981, What I Did Last Summer, 1982, The Perfect Party, 1985, Another Antigone, 1985, Sweet Sue, 1986, The Cocktail Hour, 1988, Love Letters, 1988, The Snow Ball, 1991, The Old Boy, 1991, The Fourth Wall, 1992, Later Life, 1993, A Cheever Evening, 1994, Sylvia, 1994, Overtime, 1995, Let's Do It!, 1996, The Guest Lecturer, 1998, Labor Day, 1998, Far East, 1999, Ancestral Voices, 1999, (teleplays) O Youth and Beauty, 1979, The Hit List, 1988, Love Letters, 1999, (novels) The Gospel According to Joe, 1974, Entertaining Strangers, 1977, The Snow Ball, 1984, (one-act opera) Strawberry Fields, 1999. Served with USNR, 1952-55. Recipient award N.Y. Drama Desk, 1971, Rockefeller Playwrights, 1977, playwriting award Nat. Endowment for Arts, 1981-82, award of merit Am. Acad. and Inst. Arts and Letters, 1987, Lucile Lortel award for body of work, 1994. Mem. Authors League Am., Writers Guild. Home: 40 Wellers Bridge Rd Roxbury CT 06783-1616

GURNEY, DANIEL SEXTON, race car manufacturing company executive, racing team executive; b. L.I., Apr. 13, 1931; s. John R. and Roma (Sexton) G.; m. Evi B., July 7, 1969; children: Justin B., Alexander R.; children by previous marriage: John, Lyndee, Danny, Jimmy. Grad., Menlo Jr. Coll., 1951. Profl. race car driver, 1955-70; pres., owner Dan Gurney's All Am. Racers, Inc. (doing bus. as); Dan Gurney Eagle Racing Cars, U.S.A., Santa Ana, Calif., 1964-65; mgr. Eagle Racing Team (Indpls. 500 winners 1968, 73, 75, U.S. Auto Club Nat. Championship winners 1968, 74), Formula A Championship winners 1968, 69); TV sports commentator; mem. Automobile Competition Com. for U.S.A.; car owner, builder Fed Ex Championship Series, Santa Ana, Calif. Served with U.S. Army, 1952-54, Korea. Recipient numerous racing awards including GTO driving championship Internat. Motor Sports Assn. (driver Chris Cord), 1987, GTO Mfrs.' championship Interrnat. Motor Sports Assn. (mfr. Toyota), 1987, Norelco Cup championship (driver Willy T. Ribbs), 1987, IMSA Camel GTP championship, 1992, 93, IMSA mfrs. championship for Toyota, 1992, 93. Mem. Screen Actors Guild, AFTRA, U.S. Auto Club, Sports Car Club Am., U.S. C. of C., Championship Auto Racing Teams, Inc., Soc. Automotive Engrs., Fedn. Internationale de L'Automobile, Internat. Motor Sports Assn. Clubs: Balboa Bay, Eagle.

GURNEY, EVALYN HARTUNG, retired secondary school educator; b. Jersey City, Oct. 19, 1931; d. Arthur Bullivant and Eva May (Ennis) Hartung; m. Charles William Gurney, June 22, 1957; children: Judith Gurney Hooper, Pamela Gurney Barnhart, Susan Gurney Martin, William Charles. BA, Montclair State Coll., Upper Montclair, N.J., 1951; MA, SUNY, Albany, 1973. Cert. pre-sch., elem., English, social studies, reading, alternative edn., remedial English tchr., N.Y. Elem. tchr. Mary C. House Sch., Exton, Pa., 1965-70, Pine Hill Union Sch., Cheektowaga, N.Y., 1954-55, Verona (N.J.) Schs., 1951-54, 55-58; organizer, prin. migrant sch. Brigham City, Utah, 1960-65; tchr. English Shenendehowa Cen. Sch., Clifton Park, N.Y., 1970-91; ret., 1995; 9th grade dean, adviser Newspaper Club, Builders Club, Jr. High Yearbook. dir. Bible Sch., Downingtown, Pa., 1964, 65; active community orgns. Facilitator Capital Dist. World of Difference Campaign; recipient Excellence in Edn. award Shenendehowa. Mem. ASCD, Nat. Coun. Tchrs. English, N.Y. State Tchrs. Assn., Shenendehowa Tchrs. Assn., Kiwanis, Holiday Rambler Recreational Vehicle Club (wagonmaster). Home: 3859 Pine Rd Pine AZ 85544-0627

GURNEY, FRANK IRVING, transportation executive; b. Tehran, Iran, Aug. 22, 1929; arrived in U.S., 1940; m. Peggy G.; 3 children. BA, Coll. of Wooster (OH), 1951; MS, Georgetown U., 1956. Mgr., area dir. Mid-East, U.S., Far East, South Asia, N.Y.C. Pan Am. Airways, 1954-91, ret., 1991; bd. sec. Sarasota Manatee (Fla.) Airport Authority, 1997-98, chmn., 1998—. Pres. U.S. C. of C. Okinawa; v.p. U.S. C. of C. Japan; bd. dirs. Indo-Am. C. of C. New Delhi, Iran-American C. of C.; mem. U.S. Fulbright Commn. for Cultural Exchange; bd. dirs. Iran-Am. Soc.; mem. Newark C. of C. Airline com.; pres. Skal Club; elected to bd. commrs. Sarasota-Manatee (Fla.) Airport Authority, 1996 (sec. 1997-98, chair 1998-99); bd. dirs. Gov.'s Tourism Coun. for State of N.J., 1980-91; mem. Coll. of Wooster Alumni Bd., 1981-84, Habitat for Humanity Venice Area Inc. (Fla.), 1993— (v.p. 1998, pres. 1999). Recipient Gov.'s Tourism Svc. award Gov. Thomas Kean, 1985. Presbyterian. Office: Sarasota Manatee Airport Authority 6000 Airport Cir Sarasota FL 34243-2105

GURNEY, MARY KATHLEEN, pharmacist; b. Chgo., Mar. 8, 1964; d. John Lewis and Sylvia Yvonne (Lopatka) G. BS in Pharmacy, Drake U., 1987. From pharmacist to pharmacy mgr. Osco Drug/Am. Drug Stores, Indpls., 1987—. Vol. Children's Mus. Indpls., Ind., 1990—. Mem. Am. Pharm. Assn. (del. 1994, 95), Ind. Pharmacists Assn. (chmn. pub. affairs 1993—, Marion Merrell Dow Disting. Young Pharmacist award for Ind. 1993), Phi Beta Phi. Avocations: ballroom dancing, figure ice skating. Home: 6610 Offshore Dr Madison WI 53705-4236

GURNEY, PAMELA KAY, social services official; b. Joliet, Ill., Sept. 25, 1948; d. Wayne Franklin and Charlotte Marie (Geissler) G. BA, Coll. St. Francis, 1971. Tchr. Joliet Pub. Schs., 1971-73; field dir. Trailways coun. Girl Scouts U.S., Joliet, 1973-76; dir. adult devel. Mich. Waterways coun. Girl Scouts U.S., Port Huron, 1976-80; dir. adult devel. Irish Hills coun. Girl Scouts U.S., Jackson, Mich., 1980-88; cmy. planner Northeastern Ill. AAOA (formerly Region Two Area Agy. on Aging), Kankakee, 1989—; adv. bd. Kankakee chpt. Alzheimer's Disease and Related Disorders. Trainer Trailways coun. Girl Scouts U.S.; chairperson child care bd. 1993-96, chmn. ch. and soc. com. 1996, tchr. Sunday sch., former leader youth group Asbury United Meth. Ch., Kankakee, chair older adult ministries; mem. svc. team Kankakee Girl Scouts. Mem. Nat. Assn. Nutrition and Aging Svcs. Programs. Avocations: outdoor activities, needlework, conf. planning, travel. e-mail: PKGurney@aol.com. Home: 1090 S Nelson Ave # 8 Kankakee IL 60901-5675 Office: Northeastern Ill AAOA PO Box 809 Kankakee IL 60901-0809

GURNIS, MICHAEL CHRISTOPHER, geological sciences educator; b. Boston, Oct. 22, 1959; s. George Albert and Barbara (Dempsey) G. BS, U. Ariz., 1982; PhD, Australian Nat. U., Canberra, 1987. Rsch. fellow in geophysics Calif. Inst. Tech., Pasadena, 1986-88, assoc. prof. geophysics, 1994-96; asst. prof. geol. scis. U. Mich., Ann Arbor, 1988-93, assoc. prof., 1993—; assoc. dir. Seismological Lab. Calif. Inst. Tech., Pasadena, 1995—, prof. geophysics, 1996—. Recipient Presdl. Young Investigator award NSF, 1989, fellowship David and Lucile Packard Found., 1991. Fellow Am. Geophys. Union (Macelwance medal 1993), Geol. Soc. Am. (sr., Donath medal 1993). Achievements include research in the linkage of sedimentary rocks deposited in the interiors of continents to geodynamic processes within the earth; global dynamics, mantle convection, plate tectonics, sea level changes, evolution of mantle and crust; computational and visual fluid mechanics. Office: Calif Inst Tech Seismol Lab Pasadena CA 91125

GURR, TED ROBERT, political science educator, author; b. Spokane, Wash., Feb. 21, 1936; s. Robert Lucas and Anne (Cook) G.; m. Erika Brigitte Klie, Feb. 20, 1960 (dec. May 1980); children: Lisa Anne, Andrea Mariel; m. Barbara Harff, Jan. 14, 1981. BA, Reed Coll., 1957; postgrad., Princeton U., 1957-58; PhD, NYU, 1965. From asst. editor to assoc. editor Am. Behavioral Scientist, 1961-64; asst. to dir. NYU Office Research Services, N.Y.C., 1962-64; research assoc. Princeton (N.J.) U., 1965-67, asst. prof., 1967-69, assoc. dir. workshop in comparative politics, 1966-69; assoc. prof. polit. sci. Northwestern U., Evanston, Ill., 1969-72, prof., 1972-74, Payson S. Wild prof. polit sci., 1974-84, chmn. dept., 1977-80; prof. polit. sci., dir. Ctr. for Comparative Politics U. Colo., Boulder, 1985-89; prof. govt. and politics U. Md., College Park, 1989—, disting. univ. prof., 1995—; co-dir. hist. and comparative task force Nat. Commn. Causes and Prevention of Violence, 1968-69; vis. fellow Inst. Criminology Cambridge (Eng.) U., 1976; dir. Minorities at Risk project Ctr. Internat. Devel. and Conflict Mgmt. U. Md., College Park, 1987—; fellow U.S. Inst. Peace, Washington, 1988-89, PIOOM fellow Leiden U., 1993, sr. cons. Task Force on State Failure, U.S. Govt., 1994—; Olof Palme vis. prof. Uppsala U., 1996-97. Author: (with A. de Grazia) American Welfare, 1961; Why Men Rebel (Woodrow Wilson Found. award 1970), 1970, Politimetrics, 1972; (with C. Ruttenberg) Cross National Studies of Civil Violence, 1969; (with H.D. Graham) Violence in America: Historical and Comparative Perspectives, 1969, rev. edit., 1979; (with H. Eckstein) Patterns of Authority, 1975; Rogues, Rebels, Reformers, 1976; (with P. Grabosky and R.C. Hula) The Politics of Urban Crime and Conflict, 1977; Handbook of Political Conflict: Theory and Research, 1980; (with D.S. King) The State and the City, 1987; Violence in America, Vol. 1: History of Crime, Vol. 2: Protest, Rebellion, Reform, 20th ann. edit., 1989, (with J.A. Goldstone and F. Moshiri) Revolutions of the Late Twentieth Century, 1991, Minorities at Risk: A Global View of Ethnopolitical Conflict, 1993, (with B. Harff) Ethnic Conflict in World Politics, 1994, (with J.L. Davies) Preventive Measures: Building Risk Assessment and Crisis Early Warning Systems, 1998; mem. editorial bd. World Politics, 1970-73, Comparative Polit. Studies, 1968—, Nationalism and Ethnic Politics, 1994—; co-editor Sage Professional Papers in Comparative Politics, 1969-73; editor: Comparative Political Studies, 1979-80. Fellow Wilson Nat., 1957, Ford Found., 1970, Guggenheim, 1972-73, German Marshall Fund., 1976, Fulbright, Australia, 1981. Mem. Am. Polit. Sci. Assn. (coun. 1989-91, Lifetime Achievement award 1991), Peace Sci. Soc., Social Sci. History Assn., Internat. Studies Assn. (chmn. profl. rights and responsibilities com. 1985-88, chmn. govtl. rels. com. 1989-91, pres. 1994-95), Phi Beta Kappa. Home: 3551 Narragansett Ave Annapolis MD 21403-4937 Office: Univ Md CIDCM Tydings Hall College Park MD 20742

GURSKY, ANDREAS, artist; b. Leipzig, Germany, Jan. 15, 1955. Student, Folkwangschule, Essen, 1978-81, Kunstakademie, Dusseldorf, 1981-87; studied with Bernd Becher, 1985. One-person shows include Flughafen Dusseldorf, 1987, Galerie Johnen & Schottle, Cologne, 1988, 91, 303 Gallery, N.Y.C., 1989, 91, 95, Mus. Haus Lange, Krefeld, 1989, P.S. 1 The Clocktower, N.Y., 1989, Ctr. Genevois de Gravure Contemporaine, Geneva, 1989, Kunstlerhaus, Stuttgart, 1991, Galerie Rudiger Schottle, Paris, 1991, Munich, 1991, Hypobank, N.Y., 1992, Galleria Lia Rumma, Naples, 1992, Victoria Miro Gallery, London, 1992, Kunsthalle, Zurich, 1992, Monika Spruth Galerie, Cologne, 1993, Deichtorhallen, Hamburg, 1994, De Appel Found., Amsterdam, 1994, Le Case D'Arte, Mailand, 1994, Portikus, Frankfurt, 1995, Tate Gallery, Liverpool, 1995, Galerie Mai 36, Zurich, 1995, Rooseum Ctr. Contemporary Art, Malmo, 1995, Galerie Ghislaine Hussenot, Paris, 1996, Matthew Marks Gallery, N.Y., 1997, Milw. Art Mus., 1998, others; exhibited in group shows at Kunstlerwerkstatt Lothringer Str., Munich, 1985, Galerie Rudiger Schottle, Munich, 1986, 88, Galerie Wittenbrink, Munich, 1987, Galerie Mosel & Tschechow, Munich, 1988, Galleria Lia Rumma, Naples, 1989, Nat. Mus. Modern Art, Tokyo, 1990, Castello di Rivoli, 1991, Musee d'art Moderne de la Ville de Paris, 1992, Hayward Gallery, London, 1992, Mus. Folkwang, 1993, Galerie des Archives, Paris, 1994, Matthew Marks Gallery, N.Y.C., 1995, Berlinische Galerie, 1997, The Photographer's Gallery, London, 1998, numerous others. Office: care Matthew Marks Gallery 523 West 24th St New York NY 10011

GURSTEL, NORMAN KEITH, lawyer; b. Mpls., Mar. 24, 1939; s. Jules and Etta (Abramowitz) G.; m. Jane Evelyn Golden, Nov. 24, 1984; children: Todd, Dana, Marc. BA, U. Minn., 1960, JD, 1962. Bar: Minn. 1962, U.S. Dist. Ct. Minn. 1963, U.S. Supreme Ct. 1980. Assoc. Robins, Davis & Lyons, Mpls., 1962-67; prin. Gurstel & Gurstel, Mpls., 1967—; arbitrator Hennepin County Dist. Ct., 1988-91; parttime referee family ct. Hennepin County Dist.; lectr. U. Minn. Family Law Seminar. Mem. ABA (corp. banking and bus. law and family law sects.), Minn. Bar Assn. (co-chmn. family ct. com. bankruptcy law sect. 1966-67, family law and bankruptcy law), Hennepin County Bar Assn. (chmn. family law com. 1964-65, vice chmn. 1981-91, fee arbitration bd., creditors remedy com.), Fed. Bar Assn., Assn. Trial Lawyers Am., Minn. Trial Lawyers Assn., Am. Acad. Matrimonial Lawyers, Nat. Council Juvenile and Family Ct. Judges, Comml. Law League Am. (recording sec. 1980-81, bd. govs. 1983-89, pres. 1987-88), Comml. Law League Fund for Pub. Edn. (sec. 1981-83, pres. 1989-92, bd.

dirs. 1989-94), Phi Delta Phi. Jewish. Club: Oak Ridge Country (Mpls.). Lodges: Shriners, Masons. Office: Marc Shawn Inc 3660 Galleria Edina MN 55435

GURTIN, MORTON EDWARD, mathematics educator; b. Jersey City, Mar. 7, 1934; s. Saul Gurtin and Irene (Hoffman) Burns; children—Amy Lynn, William Robert. B.M.E., Rensselaer Poly. Inst., 1955; Ph.D., Brown U., 1961; PhD in Civil Engring. (hon.), U. Rome, 1994. Structures engr. Douglas Aircraft Co., 1955-56, Gen. Electric Co., 1956-59; research asso. Brown U., 1961-62, asst. prof., 1962-64, assoc. prof., 1964-66; prof. math. Carnegie Mellon U., 1966—; alumni prof. math., 1992—; sr. Fulbright-Hays fellow, Guggenheim fellow U. Pisa, Italy, 1974; lectr., Europe, South Am., Japan, Can; cons. to industry. Author: (with B.D. Coleman, I Herrera, and C. Truesdell) Wave Propagation in Dissipative Media, 1965, An Introduction to Continuum Mechanics, 1981, Thermomechanics of Evolving Phase Boundaries, 1993; assoc. editor Archive for Rational Mechanics and Analysis, Jour. Elasticity; contbr. articles to profl. jours., including Handbuch der Physik. Recipient Disting. Grad. Sch. Alumnus award Brown U., 1995. Mem. Soc. Natural Philosophy, Sigma Xi. Office: Dept Math Carnegie-Mellon U Pittsburgh PA 15213

GURUSWAMY, DHARMITHRAN, urban planner; b. Colombo, Sri Lanka, Oct. 2, 1972; came to U.S., 1978; s. Lakshman D. and Vinodini (Chanmugam) G. BA, U. Md., 1994; M of City Planning, Ga. Inst. Tech., 1997, MS, 1998. Rsch. asst. Internat. Inst. Energy Conservation, Washington, 1994, 95; grad. rsch. asst. Ga. Inst. Tech., Atlanta, 1994-95, 95-97; assoc. Apogee Rsch., Bethesda, Md., 1997-98, Hagler Bailly Svcs., Arlington, Va., 1998—. Contbr. or co-contbr. articles to profl. publs. Mem. student-at-large bd. Md. Media Inc., College Park, 1993-94; newsletter editor Action Com. for Transit, Silver Spring, Md., 1997-98. Mem. Am. Planning Assn., Transp. Rsch. Bd. (mem. com. on nonmotorized transport 1997—, newsletter editor), Inst. Transp. Engrs. (assoc.), Urban Land Inst. (assoc.), Assn. Collegiate and Schs. of Planning (ind.). Democrat. Methodist. Office: Hagler Bailly Svcs 1530 Wilson Blvd Arlington VA 22204

GURVIS, SANDRA JANE, writer; b. Dayton, Ohio, Jan. 23, 1951; d. Tsadore R. and Regina Goldberg; m. Ronald Alan Gurvis, July 20, 1975; children: Amy Lynn, Alexander Bryan. BS in Sociology/Psychology, Miami U., Oxford, Ohio, 1973. Job classification specialist Def. Constrn. Supply Ctr., Columbus, 1973-78; prodn. editor Charles Merrill Pub., Columbus, 1983-84; corr. People Mag., Columbus, 1981-96; Author: 30 Great Cities to Start Out In, 1997, Way Stations to Heaven: 50 Sites Where You Can Experience the Miraculous, 1996, America's Strangest Museums, 1996, 98, The Off-the-Beaten-Path Job Book, 1995, Careers for Non-conformists, 1999; author/editor: Swords Into Ploughshares: A "Home Front" Anthology, 1991. Author: 30 Great Cities to Start Out In, 1997, Way Stations to Heaven: 50 Sites Where You Can Experience the Miraculous, 1996, America's Strangest Museums, 1996, 2d edit., 1998, The Off-the-Beaten-Path Job Book, 1995; author/editor: Swords Into Ploughshares: A "Home Front" Anthology, 1991; pub. provider written materials Gahanna-Jefferson Sch. Dist., Ohio, 1996, Pickerington (Ohio) Sch. Dist., 1990. Recipient Media award Ohio Optometric Assn., 1991. Mem. Am. Soc. Journalists and Authors, Ohioana Soc. Avocations: tennis, walking, travel, theater.

GURVITZ, MILTON SOLOMON, psychologist; b. Buffalo, Nov. 27, 1919; m. Sylvia Klein, June 20, 1948; children: Lynda Irene, Robert. BS, SUNY, Buffalo, 1941; MA, NYU, 1948, PhD, 1950. Diplomate in clin. psychology and psychoanalysis Am. Bd. Profl. Psychology. Psychologist USPHS Hosp., Lewisburg, Pa., 1942-46, Ctr. for Psychol. Services, N.Y.C., 1947-48; chief psychologist Hillside Hosp.-L.I. Jewish Med. Ctr., Glen Oaks, N.Y., 1949-55; clin. assoc. prof. Adelphi U., Garden City, N.Y., 1950-55; cons. psychologist Jewish Cmty. Svcs. L.I., 1955-61; pvt. practice psychology Great Neck, N.Y., 1950-87; dir. Great Neck Consultation Ctr., 1960-85, dir. emeritus, 1986—; cons. Conn. Commn. on Alcoholism, 1947-53; clin. prof. postdoctoral program in psychoanalysis, chmn. child and adolescent faculty Adelphi U., 1968-87; pvt. practice psychology Sarasota, Fla., 1987; cons. psychologist Sarasota Child Protection Team, 1990, Jewish Family Svc. Sarasota, 1991—; active med. staff Sarasota Meml. Hosp., 1992; cons. psychologist Fla. State U.-Asolo Film Conservatory, 1993—. Author: Dynamics of Psychological Testing, 1950. Fellow APA, Am. Acad. of Clin. Psychology, Soc. Pers. Assessment; mem. Nat. Psychol. Assn. for Psychoanalysis (sr.). Jewish. E-mail: drmiltpsyc@aol.com. Home: 1111 N Gulfstream Ave Sarasota FL 34236-5563 Office: 5 S Gulfstream Ave Sarasota FL 34236-8907

GURWITCH, ARNOLD ANDREW, communications executive; b. Hamburg, Germany, Jan. 29, 1925; came to U.S., 1946; s. Max and Bertha Ida (Schereschevsky) G.; m. Barbara Anne Guthrie, July 21, 1961; children: Laurence Andrew, Sara Anne. Student, U. Basle, Switzerland, 1943-46; LLB, Bklyn. Law Sch., 1955. Bar: N.Y. Resident atty. Leeds Music Corp., N.Y.C., 1956-60; ptnr. Rosen, Seton and Sarbin, N.Y.C., 1960-64; internat. rep. ASCAP, N.Y.C., 1964-74, head fgn. dept., 1974-78, fgn. mgr., 1978-89, dir. internat. rels., 1989-94, cons. internat. rels., 1995-96. Editor: Guide to Jazz, 1956. Mem. N.Y. State Bar Assn., Copyright Soc. U.S.A., Am. Arbitration Assn. (nat. panel arbitrators). Democrat. Unitarian.

GURWITZ, ARNOLD, city official, pediatrician; b. Worcester, Mass., Oct. 11, 1931; s. William H. and Ida (Snyder) G. BS, U. Mass., 1953, MS, 1955; MD, Tufts U., Boston, 1965. Intern St. Vincent Hosp., Worcester, Mass., 1962-63, resident, 1963-65; commr. pub. health and code enforcement City of Worcester, 1969—; pvt. practice pediatrics Worcester, 1965—. 1st lt. USAF, 1953-55. Fellow Am. Acad. Pediatrics; mem. AMA, Mass. Med. Soc., Worcester Dist. Med. Soc. Jewish. Office: Dept Pub Health and Code Enforcement 25 Meade St Worcester MA 01610-2715

GURWITZ-HALL, BARBARA ANN, artist; b. Ayer, Mass., July 7, 1942; d. Jack and Rose (Baritz) Gurwitz; m. James M. Marshall III, Mar. 12, 1966 (div. 1973); m. William D. Hall, May 3, 1991; 1 ward: Samantha Hollinger, 1994-96. Student, Boston U., 1960-61, Katherine Gibbs Sch., Boston, 1961-62. Represented by Karin Newby Gallery, Tubac, Ariz.; represented by Wilde-Meyer Gallery, Scottsdale, Ariz., Martin and Roll Gallery, Durango, Colo.; Artist-in-residence Desert House of Prayer, Tucson, 1989-91; oblate mem. Benedictine Sisters Perpetual Adoration, 1986—. One-woman show Henry Hicks Gallery, Bklyn., 1978, Misty-Mountain Gallery, Tubac, Ariz., 1987, Karin Newby Gallery, Tubac, 1989, West Ctr. Gallery, Green Valley, 1998, CCGV Artist of Month 1998, Martin and Roll Gallery, Durango, 1998; exhibited in group shows YWCA, Bklyn., 1977, Henry Hicks Gallery, 1977-79, Becket (Mass.) Art Ctr., 1978, Winter Gallery, Tucson, 1980, Johnson Gallery, Bisbee, Ariz., Hilltop Gallery, Nogales, Ariz., 1981, Scharf Gallery, Santa Fe, 1982, Data Mus., Ein Hod, Israel, 1985, C.G. Rein Gallery, Santa Fe, 1986, Tubac Ctr. for Arts Invitational, 1985, Mesquite Gallery, Patagonia, Ariz., 1986, Beth O'Donnell Gallery, Tucson, 1989, Karin Newby Gallery, 1989—, Wilde-Meyer Gallery, Scottsdale, Ariz., 1991—, Art Collector's Gallery, Tulsa, 1992, Contemporary Landscape Show Wilde-Meyer, 1996, Mountain Oyster Club, Tucson, 1994, Phoenix Mus. League, 1994, Brewster Ctr., 1994-98, Tubac Ctr. for Arts Biennial Gala, 1994, 96, Tubac Ctr. for Arts Ann. Members Show, 1980-94, 96, 97, 25th Anniversary Invitational SCV/aa, 1997, Juried Exhibit, Tucson Mus. Art, 1997, NLAPW/GV Juried Exhibit (2d prize) 1997, (hon. mention) 1998, Santa Cruz Valley Art Assn. juried show 1989-94, 96-98, 99, (Best of Show award 1989, award for excellence 1992, Hon. Mention 1990), Tucson Mus. of Art, 1998, Marathon-Milagro, 1998, Wilde-Meyer, 1998, U. Tampa juried exhibit, award of Honor, 1998, Wilde-Meyer, 1999, Courtyard Gallery, New Buffalo, Mich., 1999, Sophia Georg Gallery, Denver, 1999; represented in permanent collections Diocese of Tucson, Data Mus., Desert House of Prayer, Tucson, Ethical Culture Soc., Bklyn., St. Andrews Episcopal Ch., Nogales, Tubac Elem. Sch., Sheraton Corp., also numerous corp. and pvt. collections in U.S. and Europe. Mem. Tubac Village Coun., 1979-86; bd. dirs. Pimeria Alta Hist. Soc., Nogales, Ariz., 1982-84, Rose and Jack Baritz Gurwitz Found.; creator Children's Art Walk, Tubac Sch. Sys. and Village Coun., 1980; set designer, choreographer DeAnza Ann. Pageant, Tubac Ctr. Arts, 1982—; pastoral asst. St. Ann's Parish, Tubac, 1986-89, religious edn. com., 1996-97; team mem. R.C.I.A. Our Lady of the Valley Parish, Green Valley, Ariz., 1994—. Mem. Nat. League Am. PEN Women, Inc. (Sonoran Desert br.), Rose and Jack Baritz Gurwitz Found. (bd. dirs.), Assn. Contemplative Sisters, Tuscon Mus. Art, Santa Cruz County Art Assn., Los Angeles County Mus., Women's Mus. Washington. Avocations: golf, teaching, theater, singing, travel.

GUSBERG, SAUL BERNARD, physician, educator; b. Newark, Aug. 3, 1913; m. Dorothy Cushner, June 17, 1938; 1 son, Richard. Student, U. Mich., 1934; M.D., Harvard U., 1937; Sc.D, Columbia U., 1948; D.Sc. (hon.), U. Barcelona, 1985, U. Barcelona. Rsch. fellow Collis P. Huntington Hosp., Harvard; resident obstetrics, gynecology Sloane Hosp. for Women, Columbia-Presbyn. Med. Ctr., 1946; asst. attending obstetrician and gynecologist Sloane Hosp. for Women, Francis Delafield Hosp., Vanderbilt Clinic, 1946-53, asso. attending, 1954-62; asst. prof. clin. obstetrics and gynecology Coll. Phys. and Surg., Columbia, 1953; assoc. prof. Coll. Phys. and Surg., 1953-62, clin. prof., 1962-66; obstetrician and gynecologist-in-chief Mt. Sinai Hosp., N.Y.C.; prof., chmn. obstetrics and gynecology Mt. Sinai Sch. Medicine, CUNY, 1962-80, disting. svc. prof., 1980-84, dir. emeritus, cons., 1980—; mem. adv. com. divsn. cancer control Nat. Cancer Inst., 1976-79; bd. dirs. N.Y. divsn. Am. Cancer Soc., chmn. nat. adv. com. on rsch. and therapy, 1962, pres.-elect N.Y.C. divsn., 1977, pres., 1967-70, nat. pres., 1979-80, spl. cons. on med. affairs and rsch., 1980—. Author, editor: Gynecologic Cancer, 4th and 5th edit., Female Genital Cancer, 1988; assoc. editor: Obstetrics and Gynecology, 1963-67, Cancer, 1980-91; mem. editorial bd.: Obstetrics and Gynecological Survey; founder, editor-in-chief: Gynecologic Oncology, 1972-90, editor emeritus, 1990—; contbr. articles on pelvic surgery and cancer to profl. jours. Bd. dirs. Am. Cancer Soc. Benjamin Franklin fellow Royal Soc. Arts, 1964—. Fellow Royal Belgian Soc. Obstetrics and Gynecology (hon.), Royal Coll. Obstetricians and Gynecologists (hon., London), N.Y. Acad. Sci., N.Y. Acad. Medicine (past pres.), A.C.S. (gov. 1975-80), Am. Gynecol. Soc., Am. Radium Soc. (v.p. 1968), Am. Coll. Obstetricians and Gynecologists (chmn. com. on malignant disease 1965-70), Am. Assn. Obstetricians and Gynecologists (council 1971-74, past pres.), Ctrl. Assn. Ob.-Gyn., Soc. Gynecologic Oncologists (past pres.), Venezuelan Gynecol. Soc. (hon.), Venezuelan Cancer Soc. (hon.), Ecuadorian Cancer Soc. (hon.); mem. Am. Profs. Obstetrics and Gynecology, Soc. Gynecol. Investigation, N.Y. Obstet. Soc. (pres. 1962-63), Am. Soc. Cytology (v.p. 1962), Soc. Pelvic Surgeons (past pres.), Fedn. Oncologic Socs. (pres. 1976), Central (hon.), S.W. (hon.), Am. Gynecology Club, N.W. Assn. Obstetricians and Gynecologists (hon.), South Atlantic Assn. Obstetricians and Gynecologists (hon.), Phi Beta Kappa, Sigma Xi. Clubs: Harvard of N.Y.C., Ardsley Country. Rsch. on gynecol. cancer. Office: Am Cancer Soc 1180 Avenue Of The Americas New York NY 10036-8401*

GUSDON, JOHN PAUL, JR., obstetrics and gynecology educator, physician; b. Cleve., Feb. 13, 1931; s. John and Pauline (Malencek) G.; m. Marcelle Deiber, June 6, 1956 (dec. 1979); children: Marguerite, John Phillip, Veronique; m. R. Carolyn Gallager Aycock, July, 1989. BA, U. Va., 1952, MD, 1959. Diplomate Am. Bd. Ob-Gyn. Rotating intern U. Hosps. Cleve., 1959-60, resident, 1960-64; instr. ob-gyn. Sch. Medicine, Case Western Res. U., Cleve., 1964-66, asst. prof., 1967; asst. prof. ob-gyn. Bowman Gray Sch. Medicine, Wake Forest U., Winston-Salem, N.C., 1967-70, assoc. prof., 1970-74, prof., 1974-90, prof. emeritus, 1990—; staff IHS Hosps. Contbr. articles to sci. jours., chpts. to books. Lt. USN, 1952-55, Korea. Recipient John Horsley Meml. award U. Va., Charlottesville, 1968, Pres. award South Atlantic Assn. Ob-Gyn., 1973. Fellow ACOG (Pres. award 1970, 72), Am. Assn. Immunology; mem. Am. Soc. Immunology of Reproduction (founder, pres. 1981-84), Am. Gynecol. and Obstet. Soc. Republican. Roman Catholic. Avocations: reading, fishing, amateur boxing, cooking.

GUSEH, JAMES SAWALLA, public administration educator; b. Zenalomai, Liberia, Dec. 5, 1951; s. Abraham Massawalla and Sonie Kennedy; m. Thelma Amy Broderick, Mar. 3, 1984; children: Sawalla J., Sonie K., Nahsan S. BA in Econs., Brandeis U., 1976; MS in Econs., U. Oreg., 1977; JD, Syracuse U., 1980, MPA in Law and Pub. Adminstrn., 1980; PhD in Polit. Economy, U. Tex.-Dallas, Richardson, 1991. Counsellor-at-law, Republic of Liberia. Legal advisor, economist Ministry of Fin. Republic of Liberia, Monrovia, 1980-83, asst. atty. gen. Ministry of Justice, 1983-87; asst. prof. SUNY, Fredonia, 1991-92; asst. prof., dir. Shaw U., Raleigh, N.C., 1992-97; assoc. prof. N.C. Ctrl. U., Durham, 1997—; rsch. fellow U. Tex.-Dallas, 1990-91; cons. in field. Mem. editl. bd. African Social Sci. Rev., 1998—; contbr. articles to profl. jours. Mem. legis. com. Kannapolis (N.C.) C. of C., 1996-97; proposal reviewer Gov.'s Commn. on Nat. and Com. Svc., Raleigh, 1999—. Wien Internat. scholar, 1973-76. Mem. ASPA, Liberian Studies Assn., Conf. Minority Pub. Adminstrs., Assn. Third World Studies. Avocations: soccer, basketball, swimming, writing. E-mail: guseh@juno.com. Office: NC Ctrl U Sch Pub Adminstrn Durham NC 27707

GUSELLA, JAMES F., geneticist, educator; b. Ottawa, Ont., Dec. 9, 1952. BSc in Biology, U. Ottawa, 1974; MSc in Med. Biophysics, U. Toronto, 1976; PhD of Genetics, MIT, 1980. Rsch. asst. biology MIT, 1976-80; asst. in genetics children's svc. Mass. Gen. Hosp., Charlestown, 1980-83, asst. geneticist children's svc., 1983-87, assoc. geneticist children's svc., 1987—, geneticist children's svc., 1994—, asst. in genetics neurology svc., 1980-83, asst. geneticist neurology svc., 1983-84, assoc. geneticist neurology svc., 1984-93, geneticist neurology svc., 1992—, dir. molecular neurogenetics lab., 1984-92, dir. Huntington's Disease Ctr. Without Walls, 1989—, dir. molecular neurogenetics unit, 1992—; dir. MGH Genomics Core Facility, 1997; instr. Neurology Harvard Med. Sch., 1980-84, asst. prof., 1984-87, assoc. prof., 1987—, prof., 1992—; Mallinckrodt assoc. prof. genetics, Mass. Gen. Hosp., 1988-92; vis. scientist MIT, 1980-83; mem. DNA adv. bd. METPATH Inc., 1991-94; co-chmn. Com. Genetic Constitution of Chromosomes 3 and 4 Human Gene Mapping 8; Fifth John Flynn meml. lectr. dept. psychiatry Yale U. 1986; Andrew Mark Lippard meml. lectr. dept. neurology Columbia U., 1986; chmn. Com. on Genetic Constitution of Chromosomes 3 and 4 Human Gene Mapping 9, 1987; disting. lectr. NINCDS, 1987; Founders Day lectr. Med. Sch. U. Ottawa, Can., 1989; invited spkr. dedication of biomed. rsch. bldg. Health Scis. Ctr. U. Colo., Denver, 1991; mem. neurology C study sect. NIH, 1988-91; mem. exec. com. MGH Neurosci. Ctr., 1991-95; chmn. external adv. bd. Chromosome 22 Genome Ctr. U. Pa., 1991—; mem. Ptnr.'s Rsch. Task Force Working Group on Gene Therapy, 1994. Mem. editl. bd. DNA and Cell Biology, Reviews in the Neurosci., Molecular Brain Rsch., Molecular and Cellular Probes, Genomics, Somatic Cell and Molecular Genetics, Neuropsychiatric Genetics sect. Am. Jour. Med. Genetics, Neurobiology of Disease, Contemporary Neurology; contbr. numerous articles to profl. jours. Mem. med. adv. bd. Huntington's Disease Found. Am. Mass. chpt., 1981—, mem. nat. sci. coun., 1983-86; mem. sci. adv. bd. Hereditary Disease Found., 1984-88, 89-93; mem. rsch. adv. bd. Nat. Neurofibromatosis Found., 1986—, co-chmn. scientific adv. bd., 1993—; mem. scientific adv. bd. Familial Alzheimer's Disease Rsch. Found., 1987—, Nat. Alliance for Autism Rsch., 1994—. Recipient Pres.'s award Com. to Combat Huntington's Disease Mass. chpt., 1983, Devel. award McKnight Found., 1983, Jordi Folch Meml. award Am. Soc. Neurochemistry, 1986, U.S. Dept. Health and Human Svcs. Pub. Health Svc. award NIH, 1987, Bronze medal U. Helsinki, 1987, award for Med. Rsch. The Met. Life Found., 1987, Wadsworth awardd N.Y. State Dept. Health, 1987, A. Cressy Morrison award in natural scis. N.Y. Acad. Sci., 1987, Med. Rsch. award Met. Life Found., 1987, Bennett award lecture Am. Neurol. Assn., 1988, Nat. Health Coun. award for Med. Rsch. Huntington's Disease Collaborative Group, 1993, Med. Rsch. award Nat. Health Coun., 1993, Freidrich von Recklinghausen award Nat. Neurofibromatosis Found., CINN-ELEKTA Decade of the Brain award, 1994, J. Allyn Taylor Internat. Prize in Medicine, 1994, award of appreciation Neurofibromatosis Inc., 1997, numerous others; co-recipient King Faisal Internat. prize for Medicine, 1997, Lois Pope LIFE Internat. Rsch. Award, 1999. Fellow Nat. Huntington's Disease Assn.; mem. Am. Soc. Human Genetics, AAAS, Am. Acad. Neurology, Am. Soc. Microbiology, Internat. Mammalian Genome Soc., Genetics Soc. Am., Soc. Neurosci. (spl. lectr. annual meeting 1984), Human Genome Orgn. Office: Mass. Gen. Hosp. E Bldg 149 13th St Charlestown MA 02129 Home: 7 Woodstock Dr Framingham MA 01701*

GUSELLA, MARY MARGARET, commissioner; b. Ottawa, Ont., Can., Nov. 15, 1948; d. Frank and Helen (Noel) G. BA, U. Toronto, 1970; LLB, U. Ottawa, 1977; cert., Can. Securities Inst., 1981, Harvard Program for Lawyers/, Negotiation, 1996, 98. Bar: Ont. 1979. Dir. Internat. Women's Yr., 1974-76; sr. negotiator Native Claims, 1976-80; corp. sec. Emergency Energy Group, 1980-82; dir. Can. Oil & Gas Lands Adminstrn., 1980-82, Dept. of Fin., 1982-83, Crown Corps. Directorate, 1983-86; asst. sec. to cabinet comms., 1986-90; assoc. under sec. of state Ottawa, 1990-91; dep. minister Multiculturalism & Citizenship Can., Ottawa, 1991-93; pres. Atlantic Can. Opportunities Agy., 1993-95; commr. Pub. Svc. Commn. of Can., Ottawa, 1995—. Office: Rm 1931 L'Esplanade Laurier, West Tower 300 Laurier Ave W, Ottawa, ON Canada KIA 0M7

GUSEWELLE, CHARLES WESLEY, journalist; b. Kansas City, Kans., July 22, 1933; s. Hugh L. and Dorothy (Middleton) G.; m. Katie Jane Ingels, Apr. 17, 1966; children—Anne Elizabeth, Jennifer Sue. BA in English, Westminster Coll., 1955; LHD (hon.), Park Coll., 1990. Reporter Kansas City (Mo.) Star, 1955-66, editorial writer of fgn. affairs, 1966-76, fgn. editor, 1976-79, asso. editor, columnist, 1979—. Author: A Paris Notebook, 1985, An Africa Notebook, 1986, Quick as Shadows Passing, 1988, Far from Any Coast, 1989, A Great Current Running, 1994, Another Autumn, 1996, The Rufus Chronicle, 1998; contbr. short stories to Brit., Am. lit. quars. Served to 1st lt. AUS, 1956-58. Recipient Aga Khan prize for fiction, 1977, Thorpe Menn Lit. award, 1989. Home: 1245 Stratford Rd Kansas City MO 64113-1325 Office: 1729 Grand Ave Kansas City MO 64108-1413

GUSHEE, RICHARD BORDLEY, lawyer; b. Detroit, Aug. 25, 1926; s. Edward Tisdale and Norine Amelia (Bordley) G.; m. Marilyn Lucy Flynn, June 9, 1951; children: Jacqueline Lowe (dec. 1977), Peter Hale. BA, Williams Coll., 1947; JD, U. Mich., 1950. Bar: Mich. 1951, U.S. Supreme Ct. 1961. Assoc. Miller, Canfield, Paddock and Stone, Detroit, 1950-58, ptnr., 1959-93, of counsel, 1994—; mem. Corp. and Securities Bur. Securities Adv. Com.; chmn. Tri-county Hearing Panel #18 of Atty. Discipline Bd.; bd. dirs. Motor City Elec. Co. Former trustee United Community Svcs.; former chancellor Episc. Diocese Mich. With USAF, 1945. Mem. ABA, Detroit Met. Bar Assn. Office: Miller Canfield Paddock & Stone 150 W Jefferson Ave Ste 2500 Detroit MI 48226-4429

GUSHMAN, JOHN LOUIS, former corporation executive, lawyer; b. Lima, Ohio, May 29, 1912; s. Louis Alexis and Belle (Whitney) G.; m. Helen Louise Little, Sept. 11, 1937; children: Sally Gillespie, Susan Fetters, John Louis. B.A., Ohio State U., 1934, J.D., 1936; certificate of completion, Inst. Mgmt., Northwestern U., 1953. Bar: Ohio 1936. Practiced law with Williams, Eversman & Morgan, Toledo, 1936-47; with legal dept. and successively v.p., gen. mgr. internat. div. Owens-Ill., Inc., 1947-61; pres., chief operating officer, dir. Anchor Hocking Corp., 1961-67, pres., dir., chief exec. officer, 1967-71, chmn. bd., chief exec. officer, 1971-77, chmn. exec. com. of bd. dirs., 1977-82. Former chmn. bd. trustees Ohio State U. Served as maj. USAAF, World War II. Mem. Order of Coif, Phi Beta Kappa, Phi Delta Theta. Presbyterian. Home: 621 Bentley Dr Naples FL 34110-8097

GUSKIN, ALAN E., university president; b. Bklyn., Mar. 22, 1937; s. David N. and Frances (Midler) G.; m. Lois La Shell, 1990; children from previous marriage: Sharon, Andrea. BA with honors, Bklyn. Coll., 1958; PhD, U. Mich., 1968; LHD (hon.), Saybrook Inst., 1989, Antioch U., 1997. Instr., Peace Corps. vol. Chulalongkorn U., Thailand, 1961-64; dir. of selection VISTA, 1964-65; asst. dir. Ctr. for Research on the Utilization of Scientific Knowledge, Inst. for Social Research, 1968-69; lectr. dept. of psychology and residential coll. U. Mich., 1968-71, dir. ednl. change team, Sch. of Edn., 1969-71, assoc. prof. edn., 1971; provost Clark U., Worcester, Mass., 1971-73, acting pres., 1973-74, prof. sociology and edn., 1973-75; chancellor, prof. edn. U. Wis.-Parkside, Kenosha, 1975-85; pres., prof. Antioch Coll. and Antioch U., Yellow Springs, Ohio, 1985-94; chancellor, Disting. univ. prof. Antioch U., 1994-97, disting. prof., 1997—. Author: (with Samuel Guskin) A Social Psychology of Education, 1970; editor New Directions on Teaching and Learning, The Administrator's Role in Effective Teaching, 1981; contbr. numerous articles and reports to profl. jours. Chmn. bd. Coun. on Adult and Experiential Learning, 1993-95. Mem. Am. Assn. Higher Edn. Office: Antioch U Office of Chancellor 2326 6th Ave Seattle WA 98121*

GUSOFF, PATRICIA KEARNEY, elementary education educator; b. Phila., Jan. 25, 1951; d. William Anthony and Helen Frances (Budnik) Kearney; m. Ronald Gusoff, June 22, 1975; children: Wayne Kenneth, Howard Brandon. BS in Edn., Temple U., 1973, MEd, 1977, EdD, 1988. Cert. elem. tchr., supr., adminstr., Pa., N.J. Elem. sch. tchr. Sch. Dist. Phila., 1973—, elem. sci. tchr., 1989-90, basic skills tchr., 1990-96, tchr. remedial work primary grades, 1990-96; asst. facilitator, tutor William McKinley Elem. Sch., Phila., 1992-96. Coord. sch. recycling Phila. Pride, 1990-96. Mem. ASCD (assoc.), Pa. ASCD, Phila. Fedn. Tchrs. Home: 1119 Hedgerow Ln Philadelphia PA 19115-4808

GUSSIN, ARNOLD MARVIN, lawyer; b. Bklyn., Nov. 11, 1936; s. Albert and Beatrice (Stutman) G.; m. Leslie Ann Defren, Aug. 22, 1965; children: Randy Alan, Gerri Brooke, Ronni Bara. BA, Queens Coll., 1958; JD, Bklyn. Law Sch., 1961. Bar: N.Y. 1962. Pvt. practice N.Y.C., 1962—; arbitrator Am. Arbitration Assn., N.Y.C., 1967-87. Dir., v.p., pres. Men's Club Temple Israel of Great Neck, N.Y., 1975—, trustee, v.p., 1985-95; dir., v.p. Great Neck Estates Civic Assn., 1990—; chair pub. works adv. com. village Great Neck Estates, 1992-94. Recipient Lion of Judah award State of Israel Bonds, 1989, Chavarim Kol Yisroel award Fedn. Jewish Men's Clubs, N.Y.C., 1992, Burning Bush award Men's Club, Temple Israel, 1992. Mem. N.Y. State Bar Assn. Avocation: skiing. Office: 9 Murray St New York NY 10007-2223

GUSSOW, WILLIAM CARRUTHERS, petroleum engineer, geologist; b. London, Apr. 25, 1908; came to Can., 1909; s. H.T. and Jenny Maria (Hitzigrath) G.; m. Margaret Blackett Robinson, Sept. 24, 1936; children—Christopher H., David William, James Frederick Robinson. B.S., Queen's U., Kingston, Ont., 1933, M.S., 1935; Ph.D., MIT, 1938. Registered profl. geologist. Engring. resident engr. Shipshaw Power Devel., Shipshaw, Arvida, Que., Can., 1939-44; chief geol. exploration mgr. Shell Oil Co., Can., Okla., Tex., 1945-52; cons. geology, engring. Calgary, Can., 1953-55; sr. research assoc. Union Oil Co. of Calif., Brea, Calif., 1956-71; cons. Japan Petroleum Devel. Corp., Tokyo, 1972-74; cons. petroleum engring. Ottawa, Ont., Can., 1975—; lectr. in field. Contbr. articles to profl. jours.; patentee oil recovery techniques worldwide. Royal Soc. of Can. research fellow, 1936. Fellow Royal Soc. of Can., Geol. Assn. Can., Geol. Soc. Am.; mem. Am. Assn. Petroleum Geologists (life; Disting. Lectr. award 1955), Can. Soc. Petroleum Geologists (pres. 1959, hon. 1979), Can. Inst. Mining and Metall. (life), Soc. Econ. Geologists, Am. Inst. Profl. Geologists (charter mem., emeritus, hon. 1998). Avocations: travel; geological field work; mountain-building tectonics. Home: 322-20 Cleary Ave, Ottawa, ON Canada K2A 3Z9

GUST, DAVID R., military career officer; b. Platte City, Mo., Oct. 20, 1942; m. Peggy A. Gimbel; children: Scott, Thomas. BEE, U. Denver, 1974; M in Sys. Mgmt., U. So. Calif., 1976; grad., Command and Gen. Staff Coll., Naval War Coll. Drafted U.S. Army, 1966, commd. 2d lt. Signal Corps, 1967, advanced through grades to maj. gen., various positions; European tel. sys. and AUTOVON officer 5th Signal Command U.S. Army, Germany, 1974-77; bn. CE officer 1st Bn., 40th Field Arty. U.S. Army, Vietnam; with 74th Signal Co., 3rd Bn., 3rd Arty., 194th Brigade U.S. Army, Ft. Knox, Ky.; project officer Def. Comm. Sys. Comm. Sys. U.S. Army, sys. project leader Directorate for Sys. Mgmt., Comm., product mgr. PEO Fire Support, acting project mgr. PEO Intelligence and Electronic Warfare; fielding officer Program Exec. Office, Comm. Sys., project mgr. Mobile Subscriber Equipment PEO Comm. Sys., program exec. officer for comm. sys., 1992-95, program exec. officer for Intelligence & Electronic Warfare, 1995—. Decorated Bronze Star medal, Purple Heart, Legion of Merit, Meritorious Svc. medal with two oak leaf clusters, Army Commendation medal with two oak leaf clusters, Good Conduct medal, Vietnam Svc. medal with four campaign stars. Office: Intelligence & Electronic Warfare and Sensors Fort Monmouth NJ 07703

GUSTAFSON, ALICE FAIRLEIGH, lawyer; b. Houston, Dec. 1, 1946; d. William H. and Mary Davis (McCord) Bell; m. Charles R. Gustafson, May 30, 1971. BA in Econs., Wellesley (Mass.) Coll., 1968; JD, U. Puget Sound, 1976. Bar: Wash. 1976. Various positions U.S. Dept. HEW, various locations, 1968-75; assoc. Graham & Dunn, Seattle, 1977-83, ptnr., 1983—. Bd. dirs. King County Am. Cancer Soc., Seattle, 1983-85, Women & Bus., Inc., Seattle, 1984-87; mem. nominating com. YWCA Seattle-King County, 1985-88. Mem. ABA, Wash. State Bar Assn. (chair Bench-Bar-Press com. 1988-90), Seattle-King County Bar Assn. (trustee young lawyers divsn. 1980-83, treas. 1985-87), N.W. Comm. Lawyers, Met. Seattle Urban League (bd. dirs. 1991-93). Avocations: sailing, bicycling, skiing. Home: 13560 Riviera Pl NE

Seattle WA 98125-3845 Office: Graham & Dunn 1420 5th Ave Fl 33 Seattle WA 98101-4087

GUSTAFSON, DEBORAH LEE, educational administrator, educator; b. Boston, Dec. 17, 1948; d. Edward Michael and Patricia Frances (Curtin) Lee; m. Robert Edward Gustafson, Oct. 1, 1977; children: Lauren Elizabeth, Jared Lee. BS in Edn., Wagner Coll., 1970, MEd, 1973; cert. advanced grad. studies, Bridgewater State Coll., 1993. Tchr. Trinity Luth. Sch., Staten Island, N.Y., 1970-74; tchr. Town of Wareham, Mass., 1974—, elem. curriculum developer, 1983—; dir. after sch. program Town of Wareham, 1988-92; chmn. com. to write statement of mission and goals for Wareham Pub. Schs., 1987-89. Mem. Wareham 250th Anniversary Commn., 1987-89, Constn. Bicentennial Commn. Wareham, 1986-88; chmn. 250th Anniversary Sch. Planning Commn., Wareham, 1988-89; pres. Wareham Hist. Soc., 1989-95; tour guide Fearing Tavern, Wareham, 1988—; reader Talking Infor Ctr. for the Visually Impaired. Horace Mann grantee State of Mass., 1988-89. Mem. Mass. Tchrs. Assn. (regional rep., 1995—), Plymouth County Tchrs. Assn. (honor 1985, citation 1988), Plymouth County Edn. Assn. (bd. dirs. 1989-95), prof. recognition com. 1990-92), Wareham Edn. Assn. (sec. 1978-83, pres. 1983-89, chmn. profl. rights and responsibilities com. 1990—), People to People Student Amb. Program (tchr. leader 1995—), Delta Kappa Gamma Soc. Internat. Roman Catholic. Avocations: needlework, travel. Office: Minot Forest Sch Minot Ave Wareham MA 02571

GUSTAFSON, DENISE KRUPKA, special education educator; b. Milw., May 16, 1957; d. Kermit Roger and Dorothy June (Sustman) Krupka; m. John Ragnar Gustafson, June 22, 1985; children: Jennifer Heather, Jeremy Michael. BS in Mental Retardation, U. Wis., Eau Claire, 1979; MA in Learning Disabilities, U. No. Colo., 1983; cert. in resource specialist, Calif. State U., Sacramento, 1990. Cert. multisubject, Calif. Tchr. resource rm. Unified Sch. Dist. #294, Oberlin, Kans., 1979-82; tchr. resource Sweetwater Sch. Dist. #1, Rock Springs, Wyo., 1982-85; tchr. special day class Washington Unified Sch. Dist., West Sacramento, Calif., 1985-89, resource specialist, 1989-94; resource tchr. Clark County Sch. Dist., Las Vegas, Nev., 1994—; coach bowling and track, Special Olympics, Oberlin, Kans. 1980-82, 84; sponsor, Jr. High Student Coun., Oberlin, Kans., 1980-82. Mem. NEA, Coun. Exceptional Children. Democrat. Episcopalian. Avocations: sewing, crafts, skiing, traveling, Spanish.

GUSTAFSON, JIM, broadcast executive. Gen. mgr. Sta. WCCO-AM-FM, Mpls., 1995-98, Renda Broadcasting, Ft. Myers, 1998—. Office: Redna Broadcasting 4210 Metropark Way Ste 210 Fort Myers FL 33916*

GUSTAFSON, JOHN ALFRED, biology educator; b. Boston, Mar. 31, 1925; s. Walter Alfred and Lilly Christine (Anderson) G.; m. Nancy Gay Johnson, June 30, 1951; children: Walter A., Laura E., Daniel D., Martha E., J. Olaf. A.B., Dartmouth, 1948; Ph.D., Cornell U., 1954. Asst. prof. biology State U. N.Y. Coll., Brockport, 1954-55; asst. prof. biology State U. N.Y. Coll., Cortland, 1955-57; asso. prof. biology State U. N.Y. Coll., 1957-63, prof. biology, 1963-81, chmn. dept. biol. scis., 1965-77; project dir. NSF Grant for Outdoor Sci. Edn., 1980-82; participant NSF Inst., 1962; pres. Alliance for Environ. Edn., 1974; mem. Temporary State Commn. on Youth Edn. in Conservation, N.Y., 1969-73; owner, pub. Slingerland-Comstock Co., 1976-91. Author: (with B.A. Hall) Laboratory Studies in Botany, 1960; Editor: Nature Study, Jour. Environ. Edn. and Interpretation, 1965-79, Alliance Exchange, 1975-76. Chmn. Town of Homer (N.Y.) Zoning Bd., 1959-69, Town of Homer Planning Bd., 1969-75; vice chmn. Eastern Susquehanna Water Resources Bd., 1969-76; pres. Highvista Nature Center, Inc., 1973-92; mem. Labrador Hollow Unique Area Adv. Coun., 1978—; chmn. Cortland County Environ. Mgmt. Council, 1980-82, Cortland County Anderson-Lucey campaign, 1980; mem. bd. edn. Homer Cen. Sch. Dist., 1982-88; treas. Pocono Environ. Edn. Ctr., 1988-91, Lime Hollow Nature Ctr., 1992—; Cortland County rep. to open space com. N.Y. State, Region 7, 1996—; bd. dirs. Iroquois Assn., Am. Baptist Chs., 1986-89, 97—, moderator, 1987; pres. Cortland County Council of Chs., 1986-89; adminstr. 1st Bapt. Ch., Homer, N.Y., 1990-94, treas., 1995—; mem. steering com. N.Y. State Grazing Lands Conservation Initiative, 1997—. Served with USMCR, 1943-46, 51-53. Recipient Taft Campus award No. Ill. U., 1989, Griffith-Balcom Leadership award Am. Bapt. Chs., 1998. Fellow AAAS (coun. 1968-73); mem. Am. Nature Study Soc. (pres. 1962-63, treas. 1964-75, 79-97, Disting. Svc. award 1969, John Gustafson award for exemplary svc., 1995), Nature Conservancy (dir., treas., chmn. ctrl. N.Y. chpt., chmn. N.Y. State bd. dirs. 1983-87, vice chmn., ctrl/western N.Y. chpt. 1994-96, Oak Leaf award 1984), Phi Delta Kappa. Republican. Baptist. Home: 5881 Cold Brook Rd Homer NY 13077-9709 *As I think back over my life, I am impressed by the evidence that God, through my commitment to him, has given guidance and direction at those times when crucial decisions were made. So often what seemed at the time to be a relatively insignificant decision turned out to have been a key turning point. It is God's Spirit within me, and his love and concern, that gives meaning to what I do.*

GUSTAFSON, KIRK, performing company executive. Student, U. Colo.; D in Mus. Arts, U. Wash. Music dir. Grand Junction (Colo.) Symphony Orch., 1981—; guest condr. Rogue Valley (S.D.) Symphony, Salt Lake Symphony, Boulder Philharmonic, Arapahoe Philharmonic, Arvada Chamber Orch., Colo. Festival Orch.; soloist various orchs.; lectr. Mesa State Coll. Boeing fellow U. Wash. Office: Grand Junction Symphony Orch PO Box 3039 Grand Junction CO 81502-3039*

GUSTAFSON, LEWIS ALLAN, engineering geologist; b. Lansing, Mich., Dec. 12, 1931; s. Palmer Leonard and Erma Beryl (Washburn) G.; m. Mary Joanne Porter, Oct. 1, 1955; children: Lori, Steven, Leslie. BS in Geology, Mich. State U., 1955, MS in Geology, 1960; postgrad., U. Minn., 1974. Cert. engring. geologist, Oreg., Calif. Staff geologist Walla Walla Dist. U.S. Army Corps Engrs., 1963-68, Omaha Dist. U.S. Army Corps Engrs., Omaha, 1968-74; resident geologist RIRIE Dam U.S. Army Corps Engrs., Idaho Falls, 1974-75; chief, geology sect. Portland Dist. U.S. Army Corps Engrs., 1975-81; divsn. geologist North Pacific Divsn. U.S. Army Corps Engrs., Portland, 1981-88; chief geologist Hdqtrs. U.S. Army Corps of Engrs., Washington, 1988-92; cons. engring. geologist Bend, Oreg., 1992—. *During his government career, Mr. Gustafson was closely associated with foundation investigations and geotechnical studies for Dworshak Dam, Idaho, John Day Dam, Oregon, Chatfield Dam, Colorado, Bear Creek Dam, Colorado, Bonneville Second Powerhouse and Railroad Tunnel, Washington, Applegate Dam, Oregon, and Snettisham Second Power Tunnel, Alaska. His review responsibilities involved numerous additional construction projects throughout the United States and possessions.* Lt. U.S. Army, 1956. Mem. Soc. Am. Mil. engrs., Assn. Engring. Geologists, Am. Underground Constrn. Assn., U.S. Com. on Large Dams. Avocations: hunting, shooting, fishing, hiking, history. Home: 1275 NE Paula Dr Bend OR 97701-6058

GUSTAFSON, RANDALL LEE, city manager; b. Sidney, Nebr., Nov. 11, 1947; s. Robert John and Hilda Lydia (Sims) G.; m. Cynthia Ann Taylor, Oct. 18, 1974. Student, U. Kans., 1965-68, Rockhurst Coll., 1968-70; BS in Pub. Adminstrn., Upper Iowa U., 1992; MS in Pub. Adminstrn., Hamilton U., Jackson, Wyo., 1998, PhD in Pub. Adminstrn., 1998. City mgr. City of Bonner Springs, Kans., 1970-77; bus. owner Lambquarters, Dix, Nebr., 1977-83; city mgr. City of Aurora, Mo., 1983-85, City of Sterling, Colo., 1985—; bd. dirs. Logan Area Devel. Co., Sterling. Bd. dirs. Fire and Police Pension Assn. Colo., Denver, 1987-95, 13th Jud. Dist. Cmty. Corrections, Brush, Colo., 1988-90; mem. Colo. Mcpl. League Policy Com., Denver, 1987-89. Recipient Disting. Svc. award Jaycees, 1976. Mem. Internat. Assn. City Mgmt. (full mem.), Colo. Assn. City Mgmt., Am. Soc. for Pub. Adminstrn., Govs. Fin. Assn., Rotary, Elks, Mensa. Republican. Lutheran. Office: Centennial Sq Sterling CO 80751

GUSTAFSON, RICHARD ALRICK, college president; b. Peekskill, N.Y., May 15, 1941; s. Richard Altrick Sr. and Faye Alice (Jones) G.; m. Joanne Marie Walters, Sept. 5, 1964; children: Richard III., Peter. AB in Biology and Chemistry, Boston U., 1963, MEd in Sci. Edn., 1964; PhD in Statistics and Measurement, U. Conn., 1970; attended, Harvard Inst. Ednl. Mgmt., 1982; MEd in TESOL, Notre Dame U., 1997. Tchr. sci. Newtown (Conn.) Pub. Sch., 1964-65; tchr. chemistry Greenwich (Conn.) Pub. Schs., 1965-68; research specialist Ctr. for Planning and Evaluation, San Jose, Calif., 1970-71; dir. mgmt. services New England Resource Ctr. for Occupational Edn., Newton, 1971-73; asst. dean career studies Keene (N.H.) State Coll., 1973-78, assoc. dean acad. affairs, 1978-81, v.p. acad. affairs, 1981-87; pres. N.H. Coll., Manchester, 1987—; bd. dirs., vice chmn. N.H. Higher Edn. Savs. Trust Commn., 1997—; bd. dirs. Optima Health. Contbr. articles to profl. jours. Bd. dirs. Keene Family YMCA, 1975-80, 1st No. Bank, Keene, 1984-86, Cheshire Med. Ctr., Keene, 1986-88, Federated Arts Bd., 1989-92, Leadership Manchester Bd., 1989-91, Manchester United Way Bd., 1990-97, chmn., 1993, Hillcrest Terr. Bd., 1991-93. Augustus Howe Buck scholar, Boston U., 1960-62. Mem. Am. Assn. Higher Edn., Am. Ednl. Rsch. Assn., Am. Vocat. Assn. (Svc. award 1980), Nat. Assn. Ind. Colls. and Univs. (bd. dirs. 1991-94), N.H. Coll. and U. Coun. (bd. dirs. 1987—, chmn. 1995-97), N.H. Postsecondary Assn. (chmn. 1994-96, bd. dirs. 1987—), Greater Manchester C. of C. (bd. dirs. 1990-97, chmn. 1996), Rotary (bd. dirs. Keene 1985-87). Episcopalian. Avocations: skiing, tennis, running. E-mail: Gustafri@nhc.edu. Office: NH Coll 2500 N River Rd Hooksett NH 03106-1067

GUSTAFSON, ROBERT ERIC, artistic director; b. N.Y.C., Oct. 7, 1935; s. Eric Theodore and Ebba Marie (Johnson) G. BA, Queens Coll., 1957; MFA, Carnegie Tech., 1959. Founder, artistic dir. Apollo Muses Ctr. for the Arts, Peapack, N.J., 1983—; curator selected exhbns. Cooper-Hewitt Mus., N.Y.C., 1978, Libr. and Mus. of the Performing Arts Lincoln Ctr., 1980. Author, lectr.: Court Theatres of Europe, 1982, Cinderella is a Man, Autobiography, 1998; columnist (Gannett newspapers) Classical Notes, 1995-98; cameo performances in the N.J. Ballet, others on stage, TV and cinema. Avocations: collecting art and porcelains, hiking, international travel, creating beautiful environments. Home: Riverview Box 16 Peapack NJ 07977

GUSTAFSON, SANDRA LYNNE, secondary education educator; b. Phila., Mar. 8, 1948; d. William Henry Gustafson and Ruth Blossom (Berger) Watson. BS in Edn., Temple U., 1969. Tchr. Lincoln H.S., Phila., 1969-78, 85-88, Germantown H.S., Phila., 1978-85; tchr. Germantown-Lankenau Motivation H.S., Phila., 1988-98, dean of discipline, 1994-96; asst. to vice prin. Lincoln H.S., Phila., 1970-78; sponsor Nat. Honor Soc., Phila., 1989-92, 93-96, Peer Counselors and Peer Tutors, Phila., 1989-98, records mgr., testing coord. Germantown-Lankenau Motivation H.S., 1997-98; chaperone on choir's trip to Europe, Lincoln H.S., 1973, coord. Freshman Orientation Program, Phila., 1993-98. Sponsor Big Brother/Big Sister Program, 1994-98. Mem. MLA, Phila. Fedn. Tchrs. (del. to state conv. 1973, del. to nat. conv. 1973, 74), Phila. Area Spanish Educators, Sigma Delta Pi, Kappa Delta Epsilon. Democrat. Jewish. Avocations: theater, music, ballet, opera, reading, computer programming. Office: Germantown HS Germantown Ave and High St Philadelphia PA 19144

GUSTAFSON, WINTHROP ADOLPH, aeronautical and astronautical engineering educator; b. Moline, Ill., Oct. 14, 1928; s. Gustav A. and Katherine (Wenger) G.; m. Sarah Elizabeth Garner, Aug. 3, 1957; children: Charles Lee, Stanley Scott, John Winthrop, Richard Neil. B.S., U. Ill., 1950, M.S., 1954, Ph.D., 1956. Research scientist Lockheed Missiles & Space Co., Palo Alto, Calif., 1956-60; asso. prof. Sch. Aeros. and Astronautics, Purdue U., Lafayette, Ind., 1960-66; prof. Sch. Aeros. and Astronautics, Purdue U., 1966-98, assoc. head sch., 1980-98, acting head sch., 1984-85, 93, prof. emeritus, 1998—; vis. prof. U. Calif. at San Diego, 1968; research engr. Allison div. Gen. Motors Co., Indpls., summer 1962; mem. tech. staff Bell Telephone Labs., Whippany, N.J., summer 1966, NASA-Dryden Flight Research Center, summer 1976; cons. Goodyear Aerospace Corp., Akron, Ohio, 1964, Los Alamos Sci. Lab., 1977, U.S. Army, 1986-87. Contbr. articles to profl. jours. Served to 1st lt. USAF, 1951-53. Mem. AIAA. Home: 209 Lindberg Ave West Lafayette IN 47906-2109 Office: Purdue U Sch Aeros & Astronautics Lafayette IN 47907

GUSTAFSSON, BORJE KARL, veterinarian, educator; b. Varnamo, Sweden, Feb. 26, 1930; s. Albin Karl and Svea Gertrud (Andersson) G.; m. Gunilla A. Granzelius, July 11, 1958; children: Katarina, Charlotte, Lars. BVetSc, Royal Vet. Coll., Stockholm, 1953, DVM, 1960, PhD, 1966. From rsch. assoc. to asst. prof. Royal Vet. Coll. Stockholm, 1960-67, tchr., researcher animal reproduction, head clinics dept. Ob-Gyn, 1967-75, acting prof., chmn. dept. Ob-Gyn, 1970-73; vis. prof. U. Minn. Coll. Agr., St. Paul, 1974; prof. theriogenology Coll. Vet. Medicine, 1976-78; dir. grad. edn. in theriogenology U. Minn., 1976-78; prof., head dept. vet. clin. medicine U. Ill. Coll. Vet. Medicine, Urbana-Champaign, 1978-87; prof., chmn. dept. vet. clin. medicine and surgery Coll. Vet. Medicine Wash. State U., Pullman, 1987-88; dean Wash. State U. Coll. Vet. Medicine, Pullman, 1988-98, dean emeritus, 1998—; cons. to U.S. Army Surgeon Gen., 1993-96. Contbr. articles to profl. jours. With Swedish Vet Corps, 1952-54. Lagerlof's fellow, 1974; hon. diplomate Am. Coll. Theriogenologists, 1991; named Wash. State Veterinarian of Yr., 1998. Mem. AVMA, Nat. Acad. of Practive in Vet. Medicine, Royal Swedish Acad. Agr. and Forestry (fgn. mem.), Swedish Vet. Med. Assn., Assn. Am. Vet. Med. Colls., Am. Assn. Vet. Clinicians, Soc. for Theriogenology. Office: Wash State U Coll Vet Medicine Pullman WA 99164

GUSTAFSSON, LARS ERIK EINAR, writer, educator; b. Västerås, Sweden, May 17, 1936; came to U.S., 1983; s. Einar H. and Lotten Margaretha (Carlson) G.; m. D. Alexandra Chasnoff, Nov. 6, 1982; children: Benjamin, Karen. PhD, Uppsala (Sweden) U., 1978. Editor-in-chief Bonners Pub. House, Stockholm, 1961-72; rsch. fellow Ctr. Advanced Studies, Bielefeld, Germany, 1980-81; Aby Warburg rsch. prof. Warburg Found. U. Hamburg, Germany, 1997-98; bd. dirs. Svenska Dagbladet Found.; bd. regents Uppsala (Sweden) U., 1994-97; adj. prof. U. Tex., Austin, 1983—; Jamail Disting. prof., 1998—. Author numerous novels and poetry collections. Adv. bd. Poetry Internat., Rotterdam. John Simon Guggenheim Meml. fellow of poetry, 1993. Mem. Acad. of Arts (Berlin), Acad. Scis. and Lit. (Mainz, Germany), Royal Swedish Acad. Engring. (Stockholm). Avocation: painting. Office: U Tex Austin Dept Philosophy Austin TX 78712

GUSTAVSON, BRANDT, religious association executive. Pres. Nat. Religious Broadcasters. Address: 7839 Ashton Ave Manassas VA 20109-2883*

GUSTAVSON, CARRIE, museum director. Dir. Bisbee (Ariz.) Mining and Hist. Mus. Office: Bisbee Mining and Hist Mus PO Box 14 Bisbee AZ 85603

GUSTAVSON, CYNTHIA MARIE, social worker, writer; b. St. Paul, June 18, 1947; d. John Gustave Adolf and Dorothy Elvira (Knoblauch) Blomquist; m. Edward Ernest Gustavson, June 7, 1969; children: Britta Joy Gustavson, Kent Samuel. BS, Boston U., 1969; M in Social Work, La. State U., 1984. Lic. clin. social worker, Okla. Tchr. Plymouth River Sch., Hingham, Mass., 1969-70; dir. St. Croix Preschool, Stillwater, Minn., 1970-72; edn. dir. Mother Against Drugs, Shreveport, La., 1984-85; social worker, therapist Forest Lake (Minn.) Dr.'s Clinic, 1986-90; social worker St. Croix Family Svcs., Stillwater, 1990-94; instr., social worker La. State U. Children's Ctr., Shreveport, 1994-97; writer, 1997—; psychotherapist Ctr. for Counseling and Edn., Tulsa, Okla., 1999—. Author: Scents of Place: Seasons of the St. Croix, 1987, Re-Versing Your Life: A Poetry Workbook for Self-Discovery and Healing, 1995; conbtr. articles to profl. jours. Chair pub. rels. Child Passenger Safety Assn., Shreveport, 1982-84, ARC, Stillwater, 1986-89; pres. Am Heart Assn., Stillwater, 1988-91, v.p., program chair, nominating chair; chair environ. ctr. com. Minn. Sch. Dist. 834, Stillwater, 1991; mem. Minn. State Commn. Caregiving, St. Paul 1993-94, Shreveport Regional Arts Coun. Writers Panel, 1995-97, Caddo Cmty. Action Mental Health Task Force, Shreveport, 1995-97, Caddo Cmty. Action Head Start Adv. Commn., 1996-97; coord. River Cities Writers Conf., Shreveport, 1995-97. Fellow Acad. Cert. Social Workers; mem. Nat. Assn. Pastoral Counselors, Nat. Assn. Social Workers, Nat. Assn. Poetry Therapy, Phi Kappa Phi. Democrat. Lutheran. Avocations: reading, writing, playing guitar, bike riding. Home: 1262 E 27th St Tulsa OK 74114-3923

GUSTAVSON, MARK STEVEN, lawyer; b. Berkeley, Calif., Jan. 3, 1951; s. Dean Leonard and Barbara (Knight) G.; m. Janet Daly, Jan. 24, 1974; children: Eric Karl, Stephen Earl, Jennifer Ann. BA in Philosophy magna cum laude, U. Utah, 1973, JD, 1976. Bar: Utah 1976. Gen. counsel The Gustavson Group, Inc., Salt Lake City, 1976-91; pvt. practice Salt Lake City, 1976-82; sr. ptnr. Gustavson & Williams Attys., 1983-85, Gustavson, Hall & Williams, Salt Lake City, 1985-86, Gustavson, Schultz, Hall & Williams, Salt Lake City, 1986-93; corp. counsel, sec. Christensen Boyles Corp., Salt Lake City, 1993-96; pvt. practice Gustavson Law Assocs., 1996-98, Gustavson Law Assoc., 1999—; pres. Concours Automotive Restoration, Inc., 1981—; adj. prof. philosophy Utah C.C., 1991; mem. devel. com. Tanner Humanities Ctr., U. Utah. Columnist Scale Auto Enthusiast, Car Modeler, Model Car Jour., IPMS Jour., The Builder; contbr. articles to profl. jours. Founder Nat. Model Car Builders' Mus, GSL Internat. Model Car Championship. Faculty scholar, U. Utah, 1972-73. Mem. Utah Bar Assn., Salt Lake County Bar Assn., Sunstone Found., Owl and Key. Libertarian. Mormon. Avocations: model automotive building, gardening, restoring old cars.

GUSTER, DENNIS CHARLES, computer scientist, educator; b. Algona, Iowa, Mar. 9, 1952; s. Russell Charles and Marguerite Geraldine (Churchill) G.; m. Marilyn Helen Braun, July 16, 1976; children: Daria Anne, John Samuel. BS, Bemidji (Minn.) State U., 1973, MS, 1974; EdD, U. Mo., St. Louis, 1981. Sys. analyst St. Louis Metro Police, 1978-83; prof., chmn. Meramec C.C., St. Louis, 1983-88; prof. dir. CNRC St. Cloud (Minn.) State U., 1988—; network trainer Tech. Exch., Reading, Mass., 1989—. Contbr. articles to profl. jours., chpts. to books. Grantee Minn. Tech. Software Ctr., 1993-97, Hempac, fed. Dept. of Def., 1996-98, Fed. title III, 1990-92. Office: Saint Cloud State Univ 720 4th Ave S # Ecc254 Saint Cloud MN 56301-4498

GUSTIN, ANN WINIFRED, psychologist; b. Winchester, Mass., 1941; d. Bertram Pettingill and Ruth Lillian (Weller) G.; B.A. with honors in Psychology, U. Mass., 1963; M.S. (USPHS fellow), Syracuse U., 1966, Ph.D., 1969. Registered psychologist, Sask.; lic. psychologist, Ga.; Diplomate Am. Bd. Med. Psychotherapists, Am. Bd. Forensic Examiners . Research asst., psychology trainee U. Mass., Tufts U., Harvard U., Syracuse U., 1961-66; psychology intern VA, Canandaigua, N.Y., 1967-68; asst. prof. psychology U. Regina (Sask., Can.), 1969-74, assoc. prof. psychology, dir. counseling services, head clin. tng., 1974-78; pvt. practice psychology, Carrollton, Ga., 1978—, Atlanta, 1980—; staff tng. cons. Frobisher Bay Dept. Social Services, N.W. Territories, Can., 1979-80; cons. staff Tanner Hosp.; ancillary staff West Paces Ferry Hosp.; psychiat. cons. Social Security Adminstrn., Ga. Dept. Human Resources, 1980—. Membership chmn. Carroll County Mental Health Assn., 1979-81; mem. nat. mental health disaster response team ARC. Fellow Ga. Psychol Assn. (exec. divsn. lic. psychologists 1986-91, 92—, Nat. Red Cross disaster mental health team 1991); mem. Am. Psychol. Assn., Sask. Psychol. Assn. (mem. exec. council 1971-72, registrar 1972-73), Nat. Assn. Disability Examiners, Ga. Assn. Disability Examiners. Office: 107 College St Carrollton GA 30117-3136 also: One Decatur Town Ctr 150 E Ponce De Leon Ave Ste 220 Decatur GA 30030-2547

GUSTIN, CARL E., JR., manufacturing company executive. Sr. v.p., chief mktg. officer Eastman Kodak Co., Rochester, N.Y. Office: Eastman Kodak Co 343 State St Rochester NY 14650-0001*

GUSTIN, MARK DOUGLAS, hospital executive; b. Bklyn.. BS in Acctg., N.Y. Inst. Tech., 1969, MBA in Bus. Mgmt., 1973; M Profl. Studies, L.I. U., 1975; residency diploma in hosp. adminstrn., Kings County Hosp. Ctr., 1979; health care fin. mgmt. cert., Molloy Coll., 1993, elder care studies cert., 1994. Cert. behavioral health care executive; diplomate in healthcare adminstrn. Acct. Fass, Tuchler & Muster, N.Y.C., 1969-74; asst. adminstr. Manhattan Kidney Ctr., Nat. Nephrology Found., Inc., N.Y.C., 1974-76; adminstr. Carter Cmty. Health Ctr., Jamaica, N.Y., 1976-77; resident in hosp. adminstrn. Kings County Hosp. Ctr., N.Y.C. Health and Hosps. Corp., Bklyn., 1978-79, evening dir. (asst. dir.), 1979-80, assoc. dir., 1980-92, sr. assoc. dir., 1992—; mem. surrogate decision making program N.Y. State Commn. on Quality of Care for the Mentally Disabled, 1993—. Fellow Am. Acad. Med. Adminstrs. (bd. dirs. N.Y. State 1989—, pres. N.Y. Met. chpt. 1990—, State Dir. of Yr. award 1994), Am. Coll. Healthcare Execs., Assn. Behavioral Healthcare Mgmt. (bd. dirs. N.Y. chpt. 1993—, dep. gov. region II 1993-96, gov. 1997—, treas. 1998—), Royal Soc. Health; mem. Healthcare Execs. Club (treas. 1996-98). Home: 32 Jasmine Ln Valley Stream NY 11581-2412 Office: Kings County Hosp Ctr 451 Clarkson Ave Brooklyn NY 11203-2097

GUSTUS, STACEY A., legal secretary; b. Lakewood, Colo., Sept. 10, 1961; d. Norman Gaylord and Sandra S. (Melton) Holder; m. Wayne A. Gustus, Jr., June 14, 1980; children: Gregory K., Cynthia Jo. Student, U. North Colo., 1979-80. Cert. paralegal. County court tech Adams County DA, Brighton, Colo., 1980-83; legal sec. Peter L. Mattisson, Esq., Westminster, Colo., 1983-85, Hall & Evans, Denver, 1985-90; paralegal Machol & Machol, Denver, 1990-91; legal sec. McKenna & Cuneo, Denver, 1991—. Mem. Nat. Contract Mgmt. Assn. (Denver chpt., treas., newsletter editor, registrar 1994—, sec.). Avocations: sewing, crafts, bowling, sand court volleyball. Office: McKenna & Cuneo LLP 370 17th St Ste 4800 Denver CO 80202-5648

GUT, RAINER E., banker; b. Baar, Switzerland, Sept. 24, 1932; s. Emil Anton and Rosa (Müller) G.; m. Josephine Lorenz; 4 children. Ed., Cantonal Sch. Zug. Gen. ptnr. Lazard Freres & Co., N.Y.C., 1968-71; chmn., CEO Swiss-Am. Corp., N.Y.C., 1971-73; dep. mem. exec. bd. Credit Suisse, Zürich, 1973-75; exec. bd. mem. Credit Suisse, Zurich, 1975-77, spkr. exec. bd., 1977-82, pres. exec. bd., 1982-83, chmn., 1983—; bd. dirs. Nestlè, Vevey, Sofina, Brussels, Pechiney, Paris, Union Carbide Corp., Danbury, Conn., Daimler-Benz Holding, Zurich; chmn. Credit Suisse First Boston, 1988; chmn. CS Holding, 1986-96, Credit Suisse Group, 1997—, WATT, 1998. Office: Credit Suisse Group, PO Box 7 Paredeplatz 8, 8070 Zurich Switzerland

GUTCHË, GENE, composer; b. Berlin, July 3, 1907; came to U.S., 1925; s. Maximillian and Flora (von Zerbst) G.; m. Marion Frances Buchan, Dec. 1, 1935. M.A., U. Minn.; M.A. (creative scholar), 1950; Ph.D. (creative scholar), State U. Iowa, 1953. Guggenheim fellow, 1963-65. Contbr. articles to profl. jours.; World premieres include Piano Concerto Opus 24, Mpls. Summer Session, 1956, Third String Quartet Opus 12 No. 3, Arts Quartet, 1958, Holofernes Overture Opus 27 No. 1, Mpls. Symphony, 1959, Rondo Capriccioso Opus 21, N.Y. Chamber Orch., 1960, Concertino for Orch. Opus 28, Mpls. Summer Session, 1961, Fourth String Quartet Opus 29 No. 1, Fine Arts Quartet, 1962, Symphony IV Opus 30, Albuquerque Symphony, 1962, Timpani Concertante Opus 31, Oakland Symphony, 1962, Symphony V for Strings Opus 34, Chautauqua Festival, 1962, Bongo Divertimento Opus 35, St. Paul Chamber Orch., 1962, Raquel Opus 38, Tulsa Philharmonic, 1963, Genghis Khan Opus 37, Mpls. Symphony, 1963, Rites in Tenochtitlàn Opus 39, St. Paul Chamber Orch., 1965, Gemini Opus 41, Mpls. Summer Session, 1966, Hsiang Fei Opus 40, Cin. Symphony, 1966, Rites in Tenochtitlàn Opus 39 No. 1, New Orleans Symphony, 1967, Classic Concerto for Chamber Orch. Opus 44, St. Paul Chamber Orch., 1967, Aesop Fabler Suite Opus 43, Fargo-Moorhead Symphony, 1968, Epimetheus USA Opus 46, Detroit Symphony, 1969, Symphony VI, Opus 45, Detroit Symphony, 1971, Icarus, Opus 48, Nat. Symphony, 1976, Bi-Centurion, Opus 49, Rochester Philharmonic, 1976, Perseus & Andromeda XX, Opus 50, Cin. Symphony, 1977, Helios Kinetic, Opus 52, Fla. Philharmonic, 1978, Akhenaten, Opus 51, Milw. Symphony, 1980, Opus 51, No 2, St. Louis Symphony, 1983; European premieres include Symphony V For Strings, Opus 34, Radio-TV Luxembourg, 1968, Violin Concerto, Opus 36, Orch. Stabile Trieste, 1969, Bongo Divertimento, Opus 35, Munich Philharmoniker, 1967, Hsiang Fei, Opus 40, Oslo Philharm., 1970, Epimetheus U.S.A., Opus 46, Stockholm Philharm., 1969, Genghis Khan, Opus 37; also recs. (Recipient Minn. State Centennial prize 1958, Luria award 1959, prize Albuquerque Nat. Composition 1962, prize Oscar Esplá Internat. Composition 1962, XVI Premio Cittá di Trieste 1969, Louis Moreau Gottschalk Gold medal 1970, XIX Premio Cittá di Trieste 1972), commd. works include, St. Paul Philharmonic, 1962, St. Paul Arts and Scis., 1965, regents U. Minn., 1966, Fargo-Moorhead Symphony, 1967, St. Paul Chamber, 1967, Detroit Symphony, 1969, Nat. Symphony Orch., 1975, Rochester Philharmonic, 1976, Cin. Symphony Orch., 1977, Fla. Philharmonic, 1978,, Milw. Symphony, 1980 (nationwide broadcast of Akhenaten, Opus 51 by NPR/N/C radio 1980, by St. Louis Symphony Orch. on Nat. Pub. Radio, 1983). NEA Bicentennial grantee, 1976, 77, 78; Ford Found. rec. grantee, 1976. Address: Regus Pub 10 Birchwood Ln White Bear Lake MN 55110-1601 *I have always bent every effort to meet the public on common ground because music must involve a People. By that means only can it reflect what we are, what we do, and what culture, here in America, contributes to the World.*

GUTEKUNST, RICHARD RALPH, microbiology educator; b. Allentown, Pa., Jan. 20, 1926; s. George D. and Jennie L. (Alsop) G.; m. Anna Frances Fetterman, Dec. 27, 1946; children: Mary Jane Ellickson, Richard M., Jo Anne Loughery. BS, Phila. Coll. Pharmacy and Sci., 1951; MS, Cornell U., 1957, PhD, 1958. Commd. ensign USN, advanced through grades to comdr., 1968; mem. faculty Hahnemann Med. Coll. and Hosp., Phila., 1968-80; prof. microbiology and immunology Hahnemann Med. Coll. and Hosp., 1974-80; dir. Clin. Micro Lab., 1968-75; dean Coll. Allied Health Professions, 1975-80, Coll. Health Related Professions; prof. dept. med. tech. and microbiology U. Fla., Gainesville, 1980-95; dean emeritus, 1995—. ,.p. Lower Gwynedd (Pa.) Twp. Commrs., 1972-80; mem. coun. St. Peter's Luth. Ch., North Wales, Pa., 1972-77, pres., 1974-77; No. Ctrl. Fla. Regional Planning Coun., 1987-92; bd. dirs. Citizens' Crime Commn., Alachua County, 1984-88, vice-chmn., 1986-87; bd. dirs. United Way Alachua County, 1984-90, 98—, pres., 1988; bd. dirs. ARC of Alachua County, 1989-93; pres. Fla. Alliance of 100, Healthcare Manpower, 1988-90; mem. adv. bd. AIDS Inst., UF; mem. com. on pub. health FMA, 1986-95, mem. com. on allied health, 1991-94, mem. task force on nursing shortage, 1990-95; bd. dirs. DAYTOP Fla., 1996-98, chmn. 1998; bd. dirs. Phoenix Ho. of Fla., 1999—, chmn. 1999—. Recipient Lindback award, 1975; Faculty Achievement award Coll. Allied Health Professions; Faculty Achievement award Hahnemann Med. Coll. and Hosp., Phila., 1980. Fellow Am. Acad. Microbiology, Am. Soc. for Allied Health Professions (pres.-elect 1981-82, pres. 1982-83); mem. Assn. Practitioners Infection Control, Am. Soc. Microbiology, N.Y. Acad. Scis., Masons. Republican. Lutheran. Home: 3942 NW 25th Cir Gainesville FL 32606-7435 Office: U Health Sci Ctr PO Box 100014 Gainesville FL 32610-0014

GUTENTAG, PATRICIA RICHMAND, social worker, family counselor, occupational therapist; b. Newark, Apr. 10, 1954; d. Joseph and Joan (Miller) Leflein; m. Herbert Norman Gutentag; children: Steven, Jesse. BS in Occupational Therapy, Tufts U., 1976; MSW, Boston Coll., 1979. Lic. family and marriage counselor, lic. clin. social worker, N.J.; diplomate Am. Bd. Examiners in Clin. Social Work; registered occupational therapist, N.J. Social worker Jewish Family Svc., Salem, Mass., 1979-82; pvt. practice family and marriage counselor Westfield and Red Bank, N.J., 1982—; cons. high stress, Westfield and Red Bank, 1982—. Fellow N.J. Soc. for Clin. Social Work; mem. NASW, Am. Occupational Therapists Assn., Registered Occupational Therapists Assn., Soc. for Advancement Family Therapy in N.J., Am. Anorexia-Bulimia Assn., Am. Assn. Marriage and Family Therapy. Avocation: reading. Office: 200 Maple Ave Red Bank NJ 07701-1732

GUTERMUTH, SCOTT ALAN, accountant, pharmaceutical company executive; b. South Bend, Ind., Nov. 24, 1953; s. Richard H. and Barbara Ann (Bracey) G. BS in Bus., Ind. U., 1976. CPA, Ind. With Coopers & Lybrand, Indpls., 1976-83, supervising auditor, 1980-83, audit mgr., 1983; v.p., contr. Society Nat. Group, Indpls., 1983-89; v.p., CFO Am. Svc. Life Ins. Co., 1989-90; CFO Quad Pharms., Inc., 1990-96; CFO, treas. Lilly Ranbaxy Pharmas. LLC, 1996—; instr., nat. update analyst Becker CPA Rev. Course, 1980—. Advisor Jr. Achievement; mem. Marion County Rep. Com., 1978—, Rep. Nat. Com., 1972—. Fellow Life Mgmt. Inst.; mem. AICPA, Nat. Assn. Accts., Ins. Acctg. and Statis. Assn., Ind. Assn. CPAs (ins. com. 1984—), Life Mgmt. Inst. (assoc.). Methodist. Home: 3132 Sandpiper South Dr Indianapolis IN 46268-3229 Office: 8910 Purdue Rd Ste 230 Indianapolis IN 46268-1177

GUTFELD, NORMAN E., lawyer; b. Pitts., Dec. 8, 1911; s. Adolph and Fannie (Haupt) G.; m. Evelyn Kirtz, Aug. 9, 1938 (dec. Jan. 1989); children: Nancy Gutfeld Brown, Howard, Charles, Joan Gutfeld Miller, Rose Gutfeld Edwards, Steven. BA, Case-Western Res. U., 1933, LL.B., 1935. Bar: Ohio 1935. Individual practice law Cleve., 1935-43; atty. U.S. Regional War Labor Bd., Cleve., 1944; assoc. firm Benesch, Friedlander & Morris, Cleve., 1944-53; treas. Builders Structural Steel Corp., Cleve., 1953-59; partner Garber, Gutfeld & Jaffe, Cleve., 1959-73, Simon, Haiman, Gutfeld, Friedman and Jacobs, Cleve., 1973-80; of counsel Hertz Kates Friedman & Kammer, Cleve., 1981-93; pvt. practice Cleve., 1993-95; retired, 1995. Mem. Cleveland Heights-University Heights Bd. Edn., 1956-63, pres., 1958-59; treas. Bur. Jewish Edn. Cleve., 1974-79; trustee Cleve. Jewish Community Fedn., 1976-77. Mem. Bar Assn. Greater Cleve., Ohio State Bar Assn., Citizen's League Cleve. Club: Cleve. City. Home: 3189 Monmouth Rd Cleveland Heights OH 44118*

GUTH, ALAN HARVEY, physicist, educator; b. New Brunswick, N.J., Feb. 27, 1947; s. Hyman and Elaine (Cheiten) G.; m. Susan Tisch, Mar. 28, 1971; children: Lawrence David, Jennifer Lynn. SB and SM, MIT, 1969, PhD in Physics, 1972. Instr. Princeton U., 1971-74; research assoc. Columbia U., N.Y.C., 1974-77, Cornell U., Ithaca, N.Y., 1977-79, Stanford Linear Accelerator Ctr., Calif., 1979-80; assoc. prof. Physics MIT, Cambridge, 1980-86, prof., 1986-89, Jerrold Zacharias prof. physics, 1989-91, Victor F. Weisskopf prof. physics, 1992—; physicist Harvard-Smithsonian Ctr. for Astrophysics, 1984-89, vis. scientist, 1990-91. Alfred P. Sloan fellow, 1981; on Sci. Digest's list of America's 100 Brightest Scientists Under 40, 1984; on Esquire Mag.'s list of Men and Women Under 40 Who Are Changing the Nation, 1985; on Newsweek's list of 25 Top Am. Innovators, 1989. Fellow AAAS, Am. Phys. Soc. (mem. exec. com. astrophysics div. 1986-88, vice chmn. astrophysics div. 1988-89, chmn. div. 1989-90, recipient Lilienfeld Prize 1992), Am. Acad. Arts and Scis.; mem. NAS, Am. Astron. Soc. Achievements include being originator of inflationary model of early universe. Office: MIT Ctr Theor Physics 6209 77 Massachusetts Ave Cambridge MA 02139-4307*

GUTH, PAUL C., lawyer; b. Vienna, Austria, Nov. 8, 1922; came to U.S., 1940; s. Alfred and Margaret (Haas) G.; m. Joan Margaret Totman, Mar. 28, 1962. B.A., Columbia U., 1943, LL.B., 1947. Bar: N.Y. 1948. Assoc. Cleary Gottlieb Friendly & Cox, N.Y.C., 1947-49; assoc. Lauterstein & Lauterstein, N.Y.C., 1950-51, ptnr., 1952-81; ptnr. Kelley Drye & Warren, N.Y.C., 1981—. Mem. editorial bd. Columbia Law Rev. Bd. dirs., officer Robert Lehman Found., Inc., N.Y.C., 1969—, Philip Lehman Found., Inc., N.Y.C., 1972—; pres., bd. dirs. Lutece Found., Inc., N.Y.C., 1983—; mem. fin. adv. bd. Victoria Home for Aged Men and Women, Ossining, N.Y., 1977—; asst. prosecutor war crimes trials Dachau and Mauthausen, 1945-46, chief war crimes investigator 3d Army Intelligence Ctr., 1945. 2d lt. AUS, 1943-46, ETO. Recipient Beck prize Columbia Law Sch., 1943. Mem. Am. Coll. Trust and Estate Counsel, Am. Judicature Soc., Fed. Bar Assn. Republican. Episcopalian. Clubs: Princeton (N.Y.C.), Lake (New Canaan, Conn.), City Club (Lafayette, La.). Avocation: historical studies. Home: 136 Mariomi Rd New Canaan CT 06840-3311 also: 103 N Lemans St Lafayette LA 70503-4028 Office: Kelley Drye & Warren 101 Park Ave New York NY 10178-0002

GUTH, SHERMAN LEON (S. LEE GUTH), psychologist, educator; b. N.Y.C.; s. Arthur and Caroline (Laub) G.; children from previous marriage: Melissa, Victoria; m. Ling Zhao; 1 child, Lillian. B.S., Purdue U., 1959; M.A., U. Ill., 1961, Ph.D., 1963. Lectr. dept. psychology Ind. U., Bloomington, 1962-63; instr. Ind. U., 1963-64, asst. prof., 1964-67, assoc. prof., 1967-70, prof., 1970—; dir. research and grad. devel. Sch. Optometry, 1980-88, chmn. dept. visual scis., 1982-85; vis. assoc. prof. psychology Mich. State U., 1968-69; NIH spl. research fellow in psychology U. Calif., Berkeley, 1971-72; NSF program dir. for sensory physiology and perception, 1977-78. NIH research grantee, 1964-70, NSF research grantee, 1963-86. Fellow Optical Soc. Am.; mem. Assn. for Research in Vision and Ophthalmology. Office: Ind U Sch Optometry or Dept Psychology Bloomington IN 47405

GUTHART, LEO A., electronics executive; b. N.Y.C., Sept. 26, 1937; s. Harry and Lillian (Singer) G.; m. Laura Carrol, June 16, 1960; children:: Rebecca, Margaret. AB, Harvard U., 1958, MBA, 1960, D in Bus. Adminstrn., 1966. Rsch. assoc. Bus. Sch Harvard U., Boston, 1960-62; with Pittway Corp., 1963—; vice chmn. Pittway Corp., Chgo., 1988—, also bd. dirs., 1979—; exec. v.p. Ademco divsn., Syosset, N.Y., 1963-71; pres. Ademco divsn., Syosset, 1971-89; chmn., CEO Pittway Security Group, Syosset, 1989—; chmn. bd. trustees Hofstra U., Hempstead, N.Y., 1993-96; bd. dirs. Aptargroup, Acorn Fund, L.I. Venture Fund; chmn. Cylink Corp., Sunnyvale, Calif., 1996—; chmn. Alarm Industry Rsch. and Edn. Found., 1997—. Contbr. articles to profl. jours. Fellow Ford Found., 1961; named Baker scholar, Harvard U., 1960. Mem. Harvard Club, Racquet Club, Beta Gamma Sigma (hon.). Avocation: tennis. Office: Ademco 165 Eileen Way Syosset NY 11791-5312 also: Pittway Corp 200 S Wacker Dr Chicago IL 60606-5829*

GUTHERY, CAROLYN J., pediatrics nurse; b. Kansas City, Mo., Mar. 11, 1962; d. Gail K. and Nicolina (Servedio) Renner; m. Randy Guthery, July 30, 1988. BSN, U. Tulsa, 1985; MS, U. Kans., 1993. Staff nurse pediatrics Freeman Hosp., Joplin, Mo. Mem. Mo. Nurses Assn., Sigma Theta Tau. Home: 14940 Hwy TT Neosho MO 64850-9032

GUTHKE, KARL SIEGFRIED, foreign language educator; b. Lingen, Germany, Feb. 17, 1933; came to U.S., 1956, naturalized, 1973; s. Karl Hermann and Helene (Beekman) G.; m. Dagmar von Nostitz, Apr. 24, 1965; 1 child, Carl Ricklef. MA, U. Tex., 1953; PhD, U. Göttingen, Germany, 1956; MA (hon.), Harvard U., 1968. Faculty U. Calif., Berkeley, 1956-65; prof. German lit. U. Calif. at Berkeley, 1962-65, U. Toronto, Ont., Can., 1965-68; prof. German lit. Harvard U., 1968-78, Kuno Francke prof. German art and culture, 1978—; vis. prof. U. Colo., 1963, U. Mass., 1967; vis. fellow Sidney Sussex Coll., Cambridge U., Nat. Rsch. Ctr., Wolfenbüttel, Inst. for Adv. Studies, U. Edinburgh, Humanities Rsch. Ctr., Australian Nat. U., Canberra. Author: Englische Vorromantik und deutscher Sturm und Drang, 1958, (with Hans M. Wolff) Das Leid im Werke Gerhart Hauptmanns, 1958, Geschichte und Poetik der deutschen Tragikomödie, 1961, Gerhart Hauptmann: Weltbild im Werk, 1961, rev. edit., 1980, Haller und die Literatur, 1962, Der Stand der Lessing-Forschung: Ein Bericht über die Literatur, 1932-1962, 1965, Modern Tragicomedy: An Investigation into the Nature of the Genre, 1966, Wege zur Literatur: Studien zur deutschen Dichtungs-und Geistesgeschichte, 1967, Hallers Literaturkritik, 1970, Die Mythologie der entgötterten Welt: Ein literarisches Thema von der Aufklärung bis zur Gegenwart, 1971, Das deutsche bürgerliche Trauerspiel, 1972, 5th rev. edit., 1994, G.E. Lessing, 3d edit., 1979, Literarisches Leben im 18. Jahrhundert in Deutschland und in der Schweiz, 1975, Das Abenteuer der Literatur, 1981, Haller im Halblicht, 1981, Der Mythos der Neuzeit, 1983, Erkundungen, 1983, Das Geheimnis um B. Traven entdeckt, 1984, B. Traven: Biographie eines Rätsels, 1987, The Last Frontier: Imagining Other Worlds, 1990, Letzte Worte, 1990, B. Traven: The Life Behind the Legends, 1991, Last Words, 1992, Trails in No-Man's Land, 1993, Die Entdeckung des Ich, 1993, Schillers Dramen, 1994, Ist der Tod eine Frau, 1997, The Gender of Death, 1999, Der Blick in die Fremde, 1999, also others; transl.: Die moderne Tragikomödie: Theorie und Gestalt, 1968; editor: Haller, Die Alpen, 1987; co-editor: (Hanser) Gotthold Ephraim Lessing, Werke, 1970-72, Joh. H. Füssli, Sämtliche Gedichte, 1973, B. Traven: Briefe aus Mexiko, 1992, Lessing Yearbook, Colloquia Germanica, Twentieth Century Literature, German Quarterly. Honored in History and Literature: Essays in Honor of Karl S. Guthke, 1998. Fellow Humanities Rsch. Ctr., Canberra Australia, Inst. Advanced Studies, Edinburgh, Scotland, Rsch. Ctr., Wolfenbuttel; mem. Lessing Soc. (past pres.), Inst. Germanic Studies (London corr. fellow). Office: Harvard U Dept German Cambridge MA 02138

GUTHMAN, JACK, lawyer; b. Cologne, Germany, Apr. 19, 1938; came to U.S., 1939, naturalized, 1945; s. Albert and Selma (Cahn) G.; m. Sandra Polk, Nov. 26, 1967. B.A., Northwestern U., 1960; LL.B., Yale U., 1963. Bar: Ill. bar 1963. Law clk. to dist. judge U.S. Dist. Ct. No. Ill., 1963-65; since practiced in Chgo.; ptnr. Sidley & Austin, 1970-94, Shefsky & Froelich Ltd., Chgo., 1995—. Mem. City Chgo. Zoning Bd. Appeals, 1970-75, chmn., 1975-87. Democrat. Jewish. Club: Standard (Chgo.). Office: Shefsky & Froelich Ltd 444 N Michigan Ave Ste 2600B Chicago IL 60611-3998

GUTHMAN, SANDRA POLK, foundation executive; b. Chgo., Mar. 9, 1944; d. Samuel Henry and Thelma Amy (Bank) Polk; m. Jack Guthman, Nov. 26, 1967. BA, Wellesley (Mass.) Coll., 1965; hon. doctorate, Columbia Coll., Chgo., 1995. Sys. engr. IBM Corp., Chgo., 1965-73; mktg. mgr. IBM Corp., 1974-76; asst. to div. pres. IBM Corp., White Plains, N.Y., 1976-77; br. mgr. IBM Corp., Chgo., 1977-88; dir. mktg. IBM Corp., 1988-92, dir. bus. transformation, 1992-93; pres., CEO Polk Bros. Found., Chgo., 1993—; bd. dirs. MB Fin. Corp., No. Instnl. Funds, MBIA Ins. Corp. Ill. Chmn. Hubbard St. Dance Co., Chgo., 1989-90; prs. Polk Bros. Found., Chgo., 1988—; bd. dirs. Chgo. Ednl. TV Assn. (WTTW), 1976—; mem. svc. priorities com. United Way of Metro. Chgo., 1978-82; chair Music and Dance Theater, Chgo.; chair bd. dirs. Chgo. Network, 1998-99. Recipient Outstanding Achievement award YWCA, Chgo., 1984, Midwest Women's Ctr., Chgo., 1990. Mem. The Chgo. Network, Econ. Club of Chgo., Comml. Club of Chgo.

GUTHRIDGE, BILL, university basketball coach; b. Parsons, Kans., July 27, 1937; m. Leesie Guthridge; children: Jamie, Stuart, Megan. BS in Math., Kans. State U., MEd, 1963. Coach Scott City (Kans.) H.S; asst. football coach Kans. State U.; freshman basketball coach, co-asst. varsity coach U. N.C., Chapel Hill, from 1973, asst. coach, 1968-97, head coach, 1998—; coach Puerto Rican AAU Summer Leagues; coach Puerto Rican Olympic Team, 1968. Named Coach of Yr., Puerto Rican AAU, Nat. Coach of Yr., Nat. Assn. Basketball Coaches, Sporting News, CBS/Chevrolet, Columbus Touchdown Club, Atlantic Coast Conf., 1998; recipient Naismith award Atlanta Tipoff Club. Office: U NC Office Basketball Coach PO Box 2126 Chapel Hill NC 27515-2126*

GUTHRIE, DIANA FERN, nursing educator; b. N.Y.C., May 7, 1934; d. Floyd George and A. May (Moler) Worthington; m. Richard Alan Guthrie, Aug. 18, 1957; children: Laura, Joyce, Tammy. AA, Graceland Coll., 1953; RN, Independence (Mo.) Sanitarium, 1956; BS in Nursing, U. Mo., 1957, MS in Pub. Health, 1969; EdS, Wichita State U., 1982; PhD, Walden U., 1985. RN, Mo., Kans.; lic. profl. counselor, Kans.; cert. in stress mgmt. edn.; cert. clin. hypnosis; cert. holistic nursing; cert. healing touch; advanced RN practitioner; lic. marriage and family therapist. Instr. red cross U.S. Naval Sta., Sangley Point, Philippines, 1961-63; acting head nurse newborn nursery U. Mo., Columbia, 1963-64, birth defect nurse dept. pediat., 1964-65, nursing dir. clin. research ctr., 1965-67, research asst., 1967-73; diabetes nurse specialist Sch. Medicine U. Kans., Wichita, 1973—, asst. then assoc. prof. Sch. Medicine, 1974-85, prof. dept. pediat. and psychiatry Sch. Medicine, 1985—; prof. dept. nursing Kans. U. Med. Ctr., Wichita, 1985—; nurse cons. diabetes Mo. Regional Med. Program, Columbia, 1970-73; nat. advisor Human Diabetes Ctr. for Excellence, Lexington, Ky., 1982-90, Phoenix, 1983-92, Charlottesville, Ky., 1990-95; adj. prof. Sch. Nursing Wichita State U., 1985—; bd. trustees Graceland Coll., 1996—. Author: Nursing Management of Diabetes, 4th edit. 1997, The Diabetes Source Book, 3d edit., 1997, 4th edit., 1999; contbr. articles to profl. jours. Mem. health adv. bd. Mid-Am. All Indian Ctr., Wichita, 1978-80; bd. dirs. Wichita Urban Indian Health Clinic, 1980-82; trustee Graceland Coll., Lamoni, Iowa, 1996—. Fellow Am. Acad. Nursing; mem. ANA, APHA, Am. Diabetes Assn. (affiliate bd. dirs. 1979-83, pres. Kans. affiliate 1980-81, 90-91, Outstanding Educator award 1979), Am. Assn. Diabetes Educators (Kans. area, cert., Disting. Svc. award 1984), Am. Assn. Med. Psychotherapists (profl. adv. bd. 1985—), Sigma Theta Tau (Exemplary Recognition award Epsilon Gamma chpt. 1996, Outstanding Svc. award 1999). Democrat. Mem. Reorganized LDS Ch. Avocations: harp, piano, oil painting, crafts, reading. Office: U Kans Sch Medicine 1010 N Kansas St Wichita KS 67214-3124

GUTHRIE, FRANK ALBERT, chemistry educator; b. Madison, Ind., Feb. 16, 1927; s. Ned and Gladys (Glick) G.; m. Marcella Glee Farrar, June 12, 1955; children: Mark Alan, Bruce Bradford, Kent Andrew, Lee Farrar. AB, Hanover Coll., 1950; MS, Purdue U., 1952; PhD, Ind. U., 1962. Mem. faculty Rose-Hulman Inst. Tech., Terre Haute, Ind., 1952—, assoc. prof., 1962-67, prof. chemistry, 1967-94, prof. emeritus, 1994—, chmn. dept., 1969-72, chief health professions adviser, 1975-94; Kettering vis. lectr. U. Ill., Urbana, 1961-62; vis. prof. chemistry U.S. Mil. Acad., West Point, N.Y., 1987-88, 93-94. Mem. exec. bd. Wabash Valley council Boy Scouts Am., 1971-87, adv. bd., 1988—, v.p. for scouting, 1976; selection chmn. Leadership Terre Haute, 1978-80. Served with AUS, 1945-46. Recipient Silver Beaver award Boy Scouts Am., 1980. Fellow Ind. Acad. Sci. (pres. 1970, chmn. acad. found. trustees 1986—); mem. Am. Chem. Soc. (sec. 1973-77, editor directory 1965-77, chmn. divsn. analytical chemistry 1979-80, chmn. 1958, counselor Wabash Valley sect. 1980—, local sect. activities com. 1982-86, nominations and elections com. 1988-94, sec. 1992-94, coun. policy com. 1995, constn. and bylaws com. 1996—, steering com. for Joint Ctrl.-Gt. Lakes Regional Meetings, Indpls., 1978, 91, vis. assoc. com. profl. tng. 1984—, chmn. analytical chemistry exam. inst. std. exam. 1994), Coblentz Soc., Midwest Univs. Analytical Chemistry Conf., Hanover Coll. Alumni Assn. (pres. 1974, Alumni Achievement award 1977), Sigma Xi (treas. Wabash Valley chpt. 1994-98), Phi Lambda Upsilon, Phi Gamma Delta, Alpha Chi Sigma (E.E. Dunlap scholarship selection com. 1986—, chmn. 1990—, dir. expansion 1995-99, profl. rep. 1997—). Presbyterian. Club: Masons (32 deg.). Home: 120 Berkley Dr Terre Haute IN 47803-1708 Office: Rose Hulman Inst Tech 5500 Wabash Ave Terre Haute IN 47803-3999

GUTHRIE, GLENDA EVANS, educational company executive; b. De Funiak Springs, Fla., Aug. 10, 1945; d. Owen Clement and Vera Mae (Adams) Evans; m. Theron Asbury Guthrie Jr., June 10, 1967; children: Michael Patrick, Jennifer Leigh. BS in Elem. Edn., Samford U., 1967; MA in Elem. Edn., U. Ala., 1983; EdS in Ednl. Leadership, U. Fla., 1990. Tchr. grades 8-9 Warrington Jr. High, Pensacola, Fla., 1967; tchr. grades 4-5 Birmingham (Ala.) City Schs., 1967-69; tchr. grade 5 Faith Christian Sch., Bessemer, Ala., 1969-70; tchr. grade 4 Fairfield Highlands Christian Sch., Birmingham, 1973-74, First Bapt. Sch., Pleasant Grove, Ala., 1974-83; tchr. grade 5 Ctrl. Park Christian Sch., Birmingham, 1983-84, elem. dir., 1984-86; tchr. grades 5-6 Duval County Sch., Jacksonville, Fla., 1986-90; ednl. cons. Jostens Learning Corp., Phoenix, 1990-92; sr. ednl. cons., 1993-95; profl. devel. specialist Jostens Learning Corp., Phoenix, 1995—; co-founder Success Unlimited Learning Ctr., Birmingham, 1985-86; judge Sci. Fair, Jacksonville, 1988-90; seminar/workshop leader; mem. elem. textbook com. Duval County Schs., 1988-89. Active 1st Bapt. Ch. Franklin. Named Tchr. of Yr. Livingston Sch., Jacksonville, 1989, Ednl. Cons. of Yr., 1991-92. Mem. ASCD, Internat. Reading Assn., Nat. Coun. Tchrs. Math., Kappa Delta Pi. Republican. Baptist. Avocations: reading. Home and Office: 300 Cannonade Cir Franklin TN 37069-1826

GUTHRIE, HUGH DELMAR, chemical engineer; b. Murdo, S.D., May 11, 1919; s. John Arlington and Farol Venus (Smith) G.; m. Elizabeth Anne Harris, Mar. 4, 1950; children: Katherine Farol, Gretchen, Mary Melissa, Elizabeth Lenore, Emily Jo. BSChemE with highest distinction, State U. Iowa, 1943. Jr. engr., engr., group leader Shell Devel. Co., San Francisco, 1943-52; technologist, sr. technologist, asst. dept. mgr. Shell Oil Co., Wood River, Ill., 1952-56; staff engr., group leader Shell Oil Co., N.Y.C., 1956-60; dept. mgr. Shell Oil Co., Wood River, 1960-62; asst. mgr. to mgr. mktg. Shell Oil Co., N.Y.C., 1962-70; from dept. mgr. to sr. staff Shell Oil Co., Houston, 1970-76; div. dir. ERDA, Dept. Energy, Washington, 1976-78; dir. Energy Ctr., Stanford Rsch. Inst., Menlo Park, Calif., 1978-80; v.p. licensing, mgr. tech. assessment Occidental Rsch. Corp., Irvine, Calif., 1980-83; v.p. licensing, mgr. rsch. planning Cities Svc., Tulsa, 1983-86; dir. extraction divsn. Morgantown (W.Va.) Energy Tech. Ctr. Dept. Energy, 1987-92, gen. engr. products tech. mgmt., mgr. gas products, 1992-97, sr. mgmt., tech. advisor, 1997—; cons. Hugh D. Guthrie & Assocs., Tulsa, 1986-87; mem. adv. bd. U. Iowa, U. Calif., Berkeley, Tulsa U., U. Tex., U. Pitts., W.Va. U. Former sr. warden Episcopal chs., Conn., Ill., Tex. Fellow AIChE (pres. 1969, chair Assembly of Fellows 1990-92, chair mgmt. divsn. 1991, chair membership campaign found. 1992—, Founder's award 1974, F.J. Van Antwerpen award 1986, Robert L. Jacks Meml. award 1992); mem. AAAS, Am. Chem. Soc., Soc. Petroleum Engrs., N.Y. Acad. Scis., Sigma Xi, Tau Beta Pi, Phi Lambda Upsilon, Omicron Delta Kappa. Republican. Achievements include patents on distillation equipment. Home: 901 Stewart Pl Morgantown WV 26505-3688 Office: Dept Energy Morgantown Energy Fed Ctr 3610 Collins Ferry Rd Morgantown WV 26505-2353

GUTHRIE, JAMES RUSSELL, data system analyst; b. Lynbrook, N.Y., June 12, 1948. BBA, George Washington U., 1970; postgrad., Pa. State U., 1970-73. Gen. mgr. NBS Radio Network, Phila., 1979-85; v.p., gen. mgr. Am. Radio Network, Hollywood, 1985-91; writer, editor Newsday Electronic Pub., N.Y.C., 1991-95; transp. data systems analyst, cons. N.Y.C., 1995—. Historian N.J. Midland Railway Hist. Soc. E-mail: jguthrie@pipeline.com. Home and Office: 20 Trent Ln Smithtown NY 11787-1238 Office: 6801 Shore Rd Apt 5R Brooklyn NY 11220

GUTHRIE, JANET, professional race car driver; b. Iowa City, Mar. 7, 1938; d. William Lain and Jean Ruth (Midkiff) G. B.S. in Physics, U. Mich., 1960. Comml. pilot and flight instr., 1958-61; research and devel. engr. Republic Aviation Corp., Farmingdale, N.Y., 1960-67; publs. engr. Sperry Systems, Sperry Corp., Great Neck, N.Y., 1968-73; racing driver Sports Car Club Am. and Internat. Motor Sports Assn., 1963-86; profl. racing driver U.S. Auto Club and Nat. Assn. for Stock Car Racing, 1976-80; pres. Janet Guthrie Racing Enterprises Inc., 1978—; highway safety cons. Met. Ins. Co., 1980-87. Recipient Curtis Turner award Nat. Assn. for Stock Car Racing-Charlotte World 600, 1976; First in Class, Sebring 12-hour, 1970; North Atlantic Road Racing champion, 1973; named to Women's Sports Hall of Fame, 1980. Mem. Madison Ave. Sports Car Driving and Chowder Soc., Women's Sports Found., Les Dames d'Aspen, Internat. Wine and Food Soc., Nat. Spkrs. Assn. First woman to qualify for and race in Indpls. 500, 1977, finished 9th, 1978.

GUTHRIE, JOHN CRAVER, insurance agency owner; b. Bryan, Tex., Mar. 4, 1946; s. Claude Edward and Verle (Craver) G.; m. Miriam Florence Chapman, Apr. 29, 1969 (div.); children: Cheryl Denise, John Craver Jr.; m. Margot Elizabeth French, July 29, 1978. ASBA, St. Petersburg Jr. Coll., 1975. Gen. mgr. Pier Restaurants, Greenville, S.C., 1968-69; dept. mgr. Bellas Hess Dept. Stores, Clearwater, Fla., 1970-74; advt. rep. Clearwater Sun, 1974-76, St. Petersburg (Fla.) Times, 1976-81, Suncoast News, New Port Richey, Fla., 1981-82; inst. agt. Fergueron & Assoc., St. Petersburg, Fla., 1982-84; owner John Guthrie Agy., Inc., Largo, Fla., 1984—. Pres. Bicentennial Sertoma Club, Largo, 1987; sr. warden Holy Spirit Episcopal Ch., Safety Harbor, 1989; treas. Forestbrook Homeowners Assn., Largo, 1989; trustee St. Paul's Sch., Inc., Largo, 1990; mem. ch. sch. com. Episcopal Ch., St. Petersburg, 1990-94; bd. dirs. Lakeside Homeowner's Assn., 1994-97. Recipient award Leatherneck Mag., 1975, Challenger award Nationwide Ins. Co., Columbus, 1986, Exec. award, 1986, Life Exec. award, 1987. Fellow Life Underwriters Assn. Office: John Guthrie Agy Inc 1110 E Bay Dr Largo FL 33770-2533

GUTHRIE, JUDITH K., federal judge; b. Chgo., July 13, 1948; d. David Curtis and Kathleen McAfee G.; m. John H. Hannah, Jr., May 9, 1992. Student, Ariz. State U., 1966-68; BA, St. Mary's U., 1971; JD cum laude, U. Houston, 1980; postgrad., Harvard U., 1990. Bar: Tex. 1981, U.S. Dist. Ct. (ea. dist.) Tex. 1982, U.S. Ct. Appeals (5th cir.) 1982, U.S. Dist. Ct. (no. dist.) Tex. 1983, U.S. Dist. Ct. (we. dist.) Tex. 1984. Editor Am. Coun. Edn., Washington, 1972-73; exec. asst. Tex. Ho. Reps., Austin, 1973-75; lobbyist Bracewell & Patterson, Austin, 1975-80; assoc. Bracewell & Patterson, Houston, 1980-81; briefing atty. Tex. Ct. Appeals, Tyler, 1981-82; ptnr. Hannah & Guthrie, Tyler, Tex., 1982-86; magistrate judge U.S. Dist. Ct. (ea. dist.) Tex., Tyler, 1986—; instr. legal asst. program, Tyler Jr. Coll., 1986-87; apptd. Tex. Judicial Coun., 1991-97, gender bias task force, 1991-92; lectr. in field. Contbr. articles to profl. jours. Bd dirs. Found. Women's Resources, Leadership Am., Leadership Tex.; adv. bd. Main St. Project; former Dem. chmn. Smith County; legal asst. adv. bd. Tyler Jr. Coll., 1986—, chmn. of adv. bd. 1996—; mem. Citizens Commn. Tex. Judicial System, 1992-93. Mem. ABA (fed. trial judges legis. com. 1991-93), Am. Judges Assn., Fed. Magistrate Judges Assn., 5th Cir. Bar Assn., State Bar Tex. (dist. 2A grievance com. 1990-96, chmn. 1995-96, coun. mem. women and law sect. 1981-84, bd. dirs. lawyers' credit union 1983-84, citizens and law focused edn. com. 1984-85), Smith County Bar Assn. (chmn. law libr. com. 1985—). Office: US District Court 300 Federal Bldg & US Ct House 211 W Ferguson St Tyler TX 75702-7212

GUTHRIE, M. PHILIP, insurance company executive; b. Vicksburg, Miss., Mar. 26, 1945; s. Marion P. Jr. and Aileen (Perry) G.; m. Beverly Alice Blackmon, June 2, 1966; children: Philip Todd, Edward Tait, Stuart Trent. BS, La. Tech U., 1967; MBA, U. Mich., 1968. CPA, La., Tex. Sr. cons. Price Waterhouse & Co., Houston, 1968-72; v.p. fin. and mfg. Vicra div. Baxter Labs., Dallas, 1972-78; v.p. fin., CFO, treas. S.W. Airlines Co., Dallas, 1978-81; exec. v.p., CFO, Braniff Internat., Dallas, 1981-84; pres. Diamond Mgmt. Group, Dallas, 1984-89; mng. dir. Mason Best Co., Dallas, 1989—; chmn., CEO, Am. Eagle Group, Inc., Dallas, 1992—; CEO Aircraft Interior Resources Group Inc., 1998—; bd. dirs. Mainstream Data, Inc., Salt Lake City, Safeguard Bus. Sys., Ft. Washington, Pa., Internat. Autotech, Dallas, Westmark Sys., Inc., Austin, Tex., Sunrise Pubs., Inc., Bloomington,

Ind. Assoc. bd. dirs. So. Meth. U. Grad. Sch. Bus., Dallas, 1985—. Mem. AICPA, Fin. Execs. Inst., Nat. Assn. Casualty and Surety Execs., Tex. Soc. CPA's, Coun. of Ins. Co. Execs., Northwood Club, Phi Kappa Phi, Omicron Delta Kappa, Beta Gamma Sigma, Delta Sigma Pi, Beta Alpha Psi. Office: Am Eagle Group Inc 12801 N Ctrl Expy Ste 340 Dallas TX 75243-1795

GUTHRIE, MICHAEL STEELE, magnetic circuit design engineer; b. Murray, Ky., Nov. 22, 1954; s. Steele G. and Lunelle (Holmes) G. BS in Physics, Murray State U., 1976. Engr. quality control & mfg. Allegheny Ludlum, Princeton, Ky., 1977-79; engr. applications & design Hitachi Magnetics Corp., Edmore, Mich., 1979-86; engr. applications & design Delco Remy div. GM, Anderson, Ind., 1986-91; regional mgr. applications engring. Carbone of Am., Farmville, Va., 1991-96, Stackpole Magnetic Systems, Kane, Pa., 1991-98; mgr. application & design engring. Crumax Magnetics Inc., Elizabethtown, Ky., 1998—. Co-author: Rapidly Solidified Alloys, 1993. Mem. IEEE, Magnetics Soc., Am. Phys. Soc., Clan Guthrie, Ky. Cols. Home: 110 Cambron Dr Bardstown KY 40004-2245 Office: Crumax Magnetics Inc 101 Magnet Dr Elizabethtown KY 42701-3044

GUTHRIE, RANDOLPH HOBSON, JR., plastic surgeon, consultant; b. N.Y.C., Dec. 8, 1934; s. Randolph Hobson and Mabel Edith (Welton) G.; m. Beatrice Mills Holden, Mar. 20, 1965; children: Randolph Hobson III, Michael Phipps, Philip Holden. AB, Princeton U., 1957; MD, Harvard U., 1961. Intern N.Y. Hosp., N.Y.C., 1961-62, resident, 1962-63, 69-71, chief resident, 1971; resident St. Luke's Hosp., N.Y.C., 1963-66, chief resident, 1966-74; chief plastic & reconstructive surgery svc. Meml. Sloan-Kettering Cancer Ctr., N.Y.C., 1971-77; chief dept. plastic and reconstructive surgery N.Y. Downtown Hosp., N.Y.C., 1979—; asst. prof. Cornell U. Med. Coll., 1971-74, assoc. prof., 1974-89, prof., 1989—; asst. attending surgeon, N.Y. Hosp., 1971-74, assoc. attending surgeon, 1974-89, attending surgeon, 1989—; attending surgeon Sloan-Kettering Cancer Ctr., 1977-93, cons., 1994—. Author: The Truth About Breast Implants, 1994; co-author: Reconstruction and Esthetic Mammoplasty, 1989; contbr. articles to profl. jours., books. Pres. East River Med. Found., N.Y.C., 1970-80, Acacia Found., N.Y.C., 1980-94; alumni dir. St. Paul's Sch., Concord, N.H., 1979-83, form agt., 1983-87, term trustee, 1985-89, life trustee, 1989-94; trustee Episcopal Sch., N.Y.C., 1976-84; bd. dirs. Am.-Italian Found. Cancer Rsch., N.Y.C., 1985-94; bd. dirs., treas. Save Venice, Inc., 1985-89, pres., 1989-97, chmn., 1997—; trustee N.Y. Downtown Hosp., 1985-92, Isabella Stewart Gardner Mus., Boston, 1998—. Maj. M.C. AUS, 1966-69. Decorated Cavaliere nell 'Ordine Al Merito della Repubblic altaliana; rsch. fellow Sloan Kettering Cancer Ctr., 1971-77. Mem. ACS, Plastic Surgery Rsch. Coun., Am. Geriatrics Soc., Am. Soc. Plastic and Reconstructive Surgeons, Pan Am. Med. Soc., N.Y. Soc. Plastic and Reconstructive Surgery, N.Y. Med. Soc., Med. Soc. County N.Y., Herbert Conway Soc., Doubles Club, Century Club, Knickerbocker Club (N.Y.C.). Home and Office: 15 E 74th St New York NY 10021-2604

GUTHRIE, RICHARD ALAN, physician; b. Pleasant Hill, Ill., Nov. 13, 1935; s. Merle Pruitt and Cleona Marie (Weaver) G.; m. Diana Fern Worthington, Aug. 18, 1957; children: Laura, Joyce, Tamara. AA, Graceland Coll., 1955; MD, U. Mo., 1960. Diplomate Am. Bd. Pediatrics, Am. Bd. Pediatric Endocrinology; cert. Nat. Bd. for Diabetes Educators. Intern U.S. Naval Hosp., Camp Pendleton, Calif., 1960-61; dir. dependent svcs. U.S. Naval Hosp., Sangley Point, The Philippines, 1961-63; asst. instr., resident in pediatrics U. Mo., 1963-65, NIH fellow in endocrinology and metabolism, 1965-68, asst. prof., dir. newborn svcs., 1968-71, assoc. prof. pediat., 1971-73; prof., chmn. dept. pediatrics U. Kans. Med. Sch., Wichita, 1973-82; exec. dir. Kans. Regional Diabetes Ctr., Wichita, 1982-84; pres. Mid-Am. Diabetes Assocs., Wichita, 1984—; dir. Robert L. Jackson Diabetes Treatment, Edn. and Rsch. Ctr., 1985—. Author: Nursing Management in Diabetes Mellitus, 1976, 3rd edit., 1991, 4th edit., 1997, The Child with Diabetes, 1970, Physiologic Management of Diabetes in Children, 1986, Diabetes Source Book, 1990, 2d edit., 1994, 3rd edit., 1997; mem. editl. bd. Practical Diabetology, 1982-92, Diabetes Self-Management, 1984-97, Diabetes Educator, 1985-89; contbr. articles to profl. jours. Mem. health ministries bd. Reorganized Ch. Jesus Christ Latter-day Saints; mem. adv. bd. Kans. Action for Children, 1978—, Kans. State Diabetes, 1988-93, 95—. With USN, 1960-63. Recipient grants NIH, 1968—, Outstanding Faculty award Wichita State U., 1976, Disting. alumnus award Graceland Coll., 1984, Humanitarian award Wesley Med. Found., 1997; Dr. McIver Furman Disting. lectureship in health scis. Del Mar Coll., Corpus Christi, Tex., 1986. Fellow Am. Acad. Pediatrics, Am. Coll. Endocrinology; mem. AMA, Am. Diabetes Assn. (bd. dirs. 1972-77, Outstanding Contbn. to Camping award 1992), Kans. Diabetes Assn. (pres. 1974, chmn. bd. 1974-77, 85-87), Kans. State Med. Soc., Sedgewick County Med. Soc., Am. Pediat. Soc., Soc. Pediat. Rsch., Wichita Pediat. Soc. (bd. dirs. 1988, pres. 1990-92), Lawson Wilkins Pediat. Endocrinology Soc., Midwest Soc. Pediat. Rsch., Internat. Soc. for Pediat. and Adolescent Diabetes (edn. com. 1995—), Am. Assn. Diabetes Educators (bd. dirs. 1994-97), Am. Assn. Clin. Endocrinology 1992—), Sigma Xi, Alpha Omega Alpha. Home: 14210 SW 60th St Andover KS 67002-8237 Office: Mid-Am Diabetes Assocs 200 S Hillside St Wichita KS 67211-2127*

GUTHRIE, ROBERT VAL, retired psychologist and educator; b. Chgo., Feb. 14, 1930; s. Paul Lawrence and Lerlene Yvette (Cartwright) G.; m. Elodia S. Guthrie, Sept. 15, 1952; children: Robert S., Paul L., Michael V., Ricardo A., Sheila E., Mario A. B.S., Fla. A&M U., 1955; M.A., U. Ky., 1960; Ph.D., U.S. Internat. U., 1970. Tchr. San Diego City Schs., 1960-63; instr. psychology San Diego Mesa Coll., 1963-68, chmn. dept., 1968-70; assoc. prof. U. Pitts., 1971-73; sr. research psychologist Nat. Inst. Edn., Washington, 1973-74; asso. dir. orgnl. effectiveness and psychol. scis. Office Naval Research, Arlington, Va., 1975; supervising research psychologist Naval Pers., R & D Center, San Diego, 1975-82; pvt. practice psychology, San Diego, 1982-90; prof. psychology So. Ill. U., Carbondale, 1991-95; ret., 1995; adj. assoc. prof. George Washington U., Washington, 1975; lectr. Georgetown U., 1975; adj. assoc. prof. U. Pitts., 1977, adj. prof. San Diego State U., 1989. Author: Psychology in the World Today, 1968, 2d edit., 1971, Encounter, 1970, Black Perspectives, 1970, Man and Society, 1972, Psychology and Psychologists, 1975, Even the Rat Was White, 1976. Served with USAF, 1950-59, Korea. Mem. AAAS, Am., Western, Calif. psychol. assns., Fedn. Am. Scientists, Am. Acad. Polit. and Social Scis., Kappa Alpha Psi. Achievements include research on social psychology, organizational and personnel psychology variables in small groups.

GUTHRIE, TIMOTHY SEAN, art educator, artist; b. Omaha, Nebr., May 11, 1965; s. Robert U. and Dorothy (Booth) G.; m. Elizabeth Ann Broderick, Apr. 11, 1966. BFA cum laude, Creighton U., 1989; MFA, U. Idaho, 1996. Instr. asst. U. Idaho, Moscow, 1993-96; art instr., 1995-96; art instr. Western Nev. C.C., 1997—, U. Mont., Missoula, 1997—. One man shows include St. George Museum of Art, St. George, Utah, Art Museum, Reno; exhbns. include Boise Art Mus., 1995, Paris-Gibson Mus. Art, Great Falls, Mont., 1995 (Juror's Choice award, Mus. Biennial Purchase award 1997), Applalachian State U., Boone, N.C., 1996 (Summa Composite Purchase award), Internat. Sculpture Ctr., Washington, 1996; permanent collections Boise Art Mus., Paris-Gibson Square Mus. Art,. Named to A List of Top 25 MFA Sculptors in U.S.

GUTHRIE, WALLACE NESSLER, JR., naval officer; b. N.Y.C., Feb. 22, 1939; s. Wallace Nessler and Rena Otis (Robertson) G.; m. Virginia Dale Sargeant, June 7, 1961; children: Wallace Edward, Gail Elizabeth, Virginia Lynn. BS, U.S. Naval Acad., Annapolis, Md., 1961; MS, Rollins Coll., 1972, EdS, 1981. Commd. ensign USN, 1961, advanced through ranks to rear adm., 1987; edn. specialist Naval Tng. Systems Ctr., Orlando, Fla., 1967-89; dep. dir. Naval Res., Washington, 1989-92; dir. tng., supt. schs. Am. Forces Info. Svc., 1993-97; past head Naval Acad. Candidate Selection Com., 9th Congl. Dist., Fla. Sr. officer adv. panel Joint Mil. Intelligence Coll.; bd. dirs., trustee Navy Mut. Aid Assn. Mem. Naval Res. Assn. (life), Res. Officers Assn. (life), Surface Navy Assn. (life), Naval Submarine League. Republican. Avocations: camping, boating, fishing, hiking.

GUTHRIE, WILLIAM ANTHONY, minister; b. Bartica, Essequibo, Guyana, May 11, 1949; came to U.S., 1980; s. Charles and Lachmin (Bridjlall) G.; m. Elizabeth Ann Feidtkou, June 24, 1977; children: Tony, Pat, Carol. BA (hon.), U. West Indies, Barbados, 1972, Licentiate in Theology, 1974; Diploma in Theology, Codrington Coll., Barbados, 1974; D Ministry, Va. Theol. Sem., 1986. Ordained to ministry Episcopal Ch. as deacon, 1973, as priest, 1974. Asst. to dean St. George's Cathedral, Georgetown, Guyana, 1974-77; rector St. Patrick's Ch., Canje, Guyana, 1977-79; priest-in-charge Berbice River Missions, Berbice, Guyana, 1977-79; vicar Trinity Episcopal Ch., Charlottesville, Va., 1980-88; dean of region XV Diocese of Va., Charlottesville, 1985-88; rector St. Cyprian's Episcopal Ch., San Francisco, 1989-90, Christ Episcopal Ch., East Orange, N.J., 1992—; mem. Diocesan Commn. on Race Rels., Richmond, Va., 1982-87, Commn. on Evangelism, Diocese of Calif., 1989-90. Mem. bd. mgmt. Trinity Child Care Ctr., Charlottesville, 1980-88, sec. 4-H Club, Bartica, 1960-62; elected clergy del. nat. conv., Diocese of Va., 1987. Named one of Outstanding Young Men Am., 1985; recipient fellowship Va. Theol. Sem., 1987, Bp. Allin Fellowship, Geneva. Mem. NAACP, Nat. Orgn. Episcopalians for Life, East Orange Clergy Assn. (sec. 1995—), Black Clergy Caucus in Diocese of Newark (sec. 1995-98). Avocations: reading, swimming, travel. Home: 8 Rosemont Ct West Orange NJ 07052-2212 *Perhaps, the only thing worse than evil itself is to sit back and do nothing in the face of evil.*

GUTIERREZ, CARL T. C., governor. Gov. Govt. of Guam, Agana, 1994—. Address: Ricardo J Bordallo Gov's Complex PO Box 2950 Agana GU 96932-2950

GUTIÉRREZ, ELISA DE LEÓN, languages educator; b. Mercedes, Tex., July 30, 1931; d. Juventino and Felipa (Sanchez) de León; children: Richard, Laura, Carlos, Daniel, Emilio F. Jr., Martha. BA, U. Tex., 1952, MEd, 1972, PhD, 1985. Registered med. technologist. Chief med. technologist Dr. Rodriguez Hosp., Rio Grande City, Tex., 1953-60; biology tchr. Rio Grande City H.S., 1953-64; exec. dir. Cmty. Action Program Starr County, Tex., 1965-67; specialist divsn. dir. bilingual edn. Tex. Edn. Agy., Austin, 1972-95; planner Ark. Dept. Edn., Little Rock, 1995—. *Negotiated international research and teacher exchange programs with the Secretaría de Educación Pública for Mexico and teacher exchange programs between Texas and the University of Madrid, Spain. Has written curriculum K-12 for environmental protection education and articles on neurological aspects of memory, attention, and cognition.* Mem. Tex. Assn. Bilingual Edn. (legis. chmn. 1998-99). Roman Catholic. Avocations: reading. Home: 6309 Treadwell Blvd Austin TX 78757-4321

GUTIERREZ, GERALD ANDREW, theatrical director; b. N.Y.C., Feb. 3, 1955; s. Andrew and Obdulia A. (Concheiro) G.; m. Wendy J. Wasserstein, Dec. 3, 1983 (div. Dec. 1986); children: Ginger Joy, Phyllis Kate. BS in Theater Arts, Juilliard Sch., 1972. Resident dir. St. Nicholas Theater, Chgo., 1977-80, Playwrights Horizons, N.Y.C., 1980-84; assoc., artistic dir. Lincoln Ctr. Thea., N.Y.C., 1993—. Co-author Sunset at Camp O'Henry, 1984; co-author play for TV Latenite, 1985; author film script A Bag of Shells, 1980; dir. A Delicate Balance, 1996 (Tony award 1996). Recipient Award for best direction of a musical Conn. Drama Critics, 1991, L.A. Drama Critics Circle award Best Direction of a Musical, 1992; nominated Tony award for Abe Lincoln in Illinois, 1994; recipient Tony award for The Heiress, 1995. Democrat. Episcopalian. Avocation: gourmet chef.

GUTIERREZ, LINO, diplomat; b. Havana, Cuba, Mar. 26, 1951; s. Lino Gabriel and Maria C. (Fernandez) G.; m. Miriam A. Messina, Nov. 12, 1979; children: Alicia, Diana, Susana. Student, U. Miami, 1968-69; BA, U. Ala., 1972, MA, 1976. Tchr. social studies Urban League, Miami, 1973-75; Nicaragua desk officer ARA Dept. State, Washington, 1981-83, Portugal desk officer EUR, 1985-87; consular officer Am. Embassy, Santo Domingo, PR, 1977-79; polit. officer Am. Embassy, Lisbon, Portugal, 1979-81; polit. sect. chief Am. Embassy, Port-au-Prince, Haiti, 1983-85; polit./internal chief Am. Embassy, Paris, 1987-90; dep. chief of mission Am. Embassy, Nassau, The Bahamas, 1990-93; mem. Sr. Seminar Dept. Seminar, 1993-94; dir. policy planning Bur. Inter-Am. Affairs Dept. State, Washington, 1994-96, amb. to Nicaragua, 1996—. William P. Bloom scholar U. Ala., Tuscaloosa, 1972. Avocations: tennis, fishing, boating, reading, chess. Address: US Embassy Managua Unit 2407 Box 3 APO AA 34021

GUTIERREZ, LUIS V., congressman, elementary education educator; b. Chgo., Dec. 10, 1956. BA magna cum laude in English, Northeastern Ill. U., 1976. Social worker Ill. Dept. Children and Family Svcs.; adminstrv. asst. Mayor's Subcom. on Infrastructure, 1984-85; alderman for 26th ward Chgo., 1986-93; pres. Pro Tempore, 1992; mem. 103d-106th Congresses from 4th Ill. Dist., 1993—; mem. banking and fin. svcs. com.; chmn. Housing, Land Acquisition and Disposition com., 1989-93. Democrat. Office: US Ho of Reps 2438 Rayburn House Off Bldg Washington DC 20515-1304*

GUTIN, MYRA GAIL, communications educator; b. Paterson, N.J., Aug. 13, 1948; d. Stanley and Lillian (Edelstein) Greenberg; m. David Gutin, Sept. 5, 1971; children: Laura, Sarah, Andrew. BA, Emerson Coll., 1970, MA, 1971; PhD, U. Mich., 1983. Asst. prof. comm. Cumberland County Coll., Vineland, N.J., 1972-80; asst. prof. comm. Rider U., Lawrenceville, N.J., 1981-88, prof., 1989—; adj. instr. Essex County Coll., Newark, 1971-72, Nassau C.C., Garden City, N.Y., 1972, Trenton (N.J.) State Coll., 1981-84; adj. asst. prof. Rider U., 1981-85; vice-chmn. Harry B. Kellman Acad., 1998—; lectr. in field. Author: The President's Partner The First Lady in the 20th Century, 1989; contbr. articles to profl. jours. Officer Emerson Coll. Nat. Alumni Bd., 1994— (pres. 1998—); mem. Kellman Acad. Sch. Bd., 1996—. Recipient Alumni Achievement award Emerson Coll., Boston, 1991. Mem. Ctr. for Study of the Presidency, Nat. Comm. Assn., Ea. Comm. Assn. Avocations: travel, theatre. Home: 119 Greenvale Ct Cherry Hill NJ 08034-1701

GUTJAHR, ALLAN LEO, mathematics educator, researcher; b. Hosmer, S.D., Mar. 20, 1938; s. Christian E. Gutjahr and Emma Preszler; m. Ellen Troxel, Nov. 21, 1959 (div. 1978); children: Kurt, Eric, Kristin; m. Margaret Rae Sjostedt, Aug. 15, 1981; children: Ted, Meghan. Student, Cen. Wash. Coll., 1958-59; BS in Math., U. Wash., 1962; MSE, Johns Hopkins U., 1963; PhD in Stats., Rutgers U., 1970. Tech. staff Bell Labs., Holmdel, N.J., 1962-71; prof. math. N.Mex. Tech. U., Socorro, 1971—, chmn. dept. math., 1985-88, assoc. v.p. acad. affairs, 1990-92, v.p. rsch. and econ. devel., 1992-97; vis. rschr. Ecole Des Mines, Paris, 1978, U.S. Geol. Survey, Denver, 1978, Stanford U., fall 1989, U. Poly. Catalonia, Barcelona, fall 1997. Contbr. articles to profl. jours. Bd. dirs. V.I.A. With U.S. Army, 1956-58. Recipient Disting. Tchg. award N.Mex. Tech. U., 1987, Disting. Rsch. award Nimex Tech. U., 1999. Fellow Am. Geophys. Union; mem. Math. Assn. Am., Am. Statis. Assn., Internat. Assn. of Math. Geol., Sigma Xi. Avocations: reading, writing, jogging. Home: 445 Aquina Ct Belen NM 87002-6345

GUTKNECHT, GILBERT WILLIAM, JR., congressman, former state legislator, auctioneer; b. Cedar Falls, Iowa, Mar. 20, 1951; s. Gilbert William Sr. and Joan (Kerns) G.; m. Mary Catherine Keefe, June 3, 1972; children: Margaret, Paul, Emily. BA, U. No. Iowa, 1973. Sales rep. J. S. Latta, Cedar Falls, 1973-78, Valley Sch. Supplies, Appleton, Wis., 1978-81; auctioneer Rochester, Minn., 1978-95; state legis. State of Minn., Rochester, 1982-95; mem. 104th-105th Congresses from 1st Minn. Dist., Washington, D.C., 1995—; mem. science and budget coms. 104th-106th Congresses from 1st Minn. Dist., Washington, 1997—. Avocations: fishing, boating, baseball. Office: US House Reps 425 Cannon Bldg Ofc Bldg Washington DC 20515-2301 Office: Midway Office Plaza 1530 Greenview Dr SW Ste 108 Rochester MN 55902-1080*

GUTMAN, RICHARD EDWARD, lawyer; b. New Haven, Apr. 9, 1944; s. Samuel and Marjorie (Leo) G.; m. Jill Leslie Senft, June 8, 1969 (dec.); 1 child, Paul Senft; m. Rosann Seasonwein, Dec. 10, 1987. AB, Harvard U., 1965; JD, Columbia U., 1968. Bar: N.Y. 1969, U.S. Ct. Appeals (2d cir.) 1969, U.S. Dist. Ct. (so. and ea. dists.) N.Y. 1975, U.S. Supreme Ct. 1982, Tex. 1991. Counsel Exxon Corp., N.Y.C., 1978-90; Dallas, 1990-91; asst. gen. counsel Exxon Corp., Dallas, 1992—; pres. 570 Park Ave Apts., Inc., N.Y.C., 1984-89, past bd. dirs. Fellow Am. Bar Found. (life); mem. ABA (fed. regulation securities com., vice chmn. 1995-98), Am. Law Inst., N.Y. State Bar Assn. (exec. com. 1983-86, 93—, securities regulation com. 1980—, chmn. 1993-97, sec. bus. law sec., 1999—), Assn. of Bar of City of N.Y. (securities regulation com. 1980-81, 83-86), Dallas Bar Assn., Coll. of the State Bar of Tex., N.A.M. (corp. fin. and mgmt. com.), Harvard Club (N.Y.C., admissions com. 1983-86, chmn. 1985-86, nominating com. 1986-87, bd. dirs. 1988-91, v.p. 1990-91), Harvard Club (Dallas, bd. dirs. 1998—).

GUTMAN, ROBERT WILLIAM, retired educator; b. N.Y.C., Sept. 11, 1925; s. Theodore and Elsie G. B.A., NYU, 1945, M.A., 1948. Instr. New Sch. for Social Research, 1955-57; founder, lectr. Bayreuth Festival Master Classes, 1959-61; lectr. design history art and design div. Fashion Inst. Tech., SUNY, N.Y.C., 1957-66; asst. prof. Fashion Inst. Tech., SUNY, 1966-71, assoc. prof., 1971-76, prof., 1971-88, dean div. art and design, 1974-79, dean grad. studies, 1979-88, ret., 1988; vis. prof. Bard Coll., 1991; lectr. PBS Telecast of Bayreuth Festival, 1983. Author: Richard Wagner, The Man, His Mind, and His Music, 1968, German transl., 1970, Italian transl., 1983; editor: Volsunga Saga (transl. by William Morris), 1961. Bd. dirs. Am. Friends of Internat. Found. Mozarteum, 1991—, The Collegiate Chorale, 1990—. Biography juror Nat. Book Awards, 1973; Guggenheim fellow, 1979. Clubs: Nat. Arts (N.Y.C.), Princeton (N.Y.C.), Lotos (N.Y.C.). Home: 37 W 12th St New York NY 10011-8502

GUTMAN, ROY WILLIAM, reporter; b. N.Y.C., Mar. 5, 1944; s. Ira H. and Linda (Snyder) G.; m. Elizabeth Jane Dribben, May 17, 1979; 1 child, Caroline. BA, Haverford Coll., 1966; MS, London Sch. Econs., 1968; DLitt (hon.), Haverford Coll., 1995. Reporter UPI, Frankfurt, Federal Republic of Germany, 1968-70; corr. Reuters News Agy., Bonn, Federal Republic of Germany, 1971-72; bur. chief Reuters News Agy., Belgrade, Yugoslavia, 1973-75; Dept. State corr. Reuters News Agy., Washington, 1976-80, Capitol Hill bur. chief, 1981; nat. security reporter Newsday, Washington, 1982-89; European bur. chief Newsday, Bonn, 1990-94; pres. Overseas Writers, Washington, 1983-85. Author: Banana Diplomacy, 1988 (named one of best 200 books of 1988, New York Times, best Am. book of yr., Times Literary Supplement, London, 1988), A Witness to Genocide, 1993; contbr. articles to profl. jours. Recipient Human Rights in Media award Internat. league for Human Rights, 1992, Pulitzer Prize for internat. reporting, 1993, George Polk Foreign Reporting award, 1993, Selden Ring Investigative Reporting award U. So. Calif., 1993, Nat. Headliner Outstanding News Reporting award, 1993, Heywood Brown award Newspaper Guild, 1993, Excellence in Series/Investigation award Deadline Club, 1993, Hal Boyle award Overseas Press Club, 1993, Exemplary Community Svc. Alumni awrd Haverford Coll., 1994; named one of 10 best foreign affairs reporters in Washington, The Washingtonian, 1989. Mem. Inst. Current World Affairs. Jewish. Avocations: gardening, photography. Home: 13132 Curved Iron Rd Herndon VA 20171-2930 Office: News Day 1730 Pennsylvania Ave NW Washington DC 20006-4706 *Facts matter. And collecting them requires a readiness to get your fingernails dirty.**

GUTMAN, STEVE, professional football team executive. Pres. N.Y. Jets. Office: NY Jets 1000 Fulton Ave Hempstead NY 11550-1030*

GUTMANN, AMY, political science and philosophy educator; b. Bklyn., Nov. 19, 1949; 1 child, Abigail. BA, Radcliffe Coll.-Harvard U., 1971; MS in Polit. Sci., London Sch. Econ., 1972; PhD in Polit. Sci., Harvard U., 1976. Dir. grad. studies dept. politics Princeton (N.J.) U., 1986-88, dir. polit. philosophy program, 1987-89, dir. ethics and pub. affairs program, 1990-95, founding dir. Ctr. Human Values, 1990-95, 97-98, dean faculty, 1995-97, Laurance S. Rockefeller U. prof., 1990—; Tanner lectr., Stanford U., 1994-95. Author: Liberal Equality, 1980, Democratic Education, 1987; co-author: (with Dennis Thompson) Democracy & Disagreement, 1996, (with Anthony Appiah) Color Conscious (award N.Am. Soc. Social Philosophy 1996); editor: Democracy and the Welfare State, 1988, Multiculturalism, 1992, Freedom of Association, 1998, (with Dennis Thompson) Ethics and Politics, 3d edit., 1997. Bd. trustees Princeton U. Press, 1996—, Ctr. for Advanced Study in the Behavioral Scis., U. Calif., Stanford, 1998—; mem adv. coun. Kennedy Sch. Govt.-Harvard U., 1996—. Recipient award AAAS, 1997, Ralph J. Bunche award Am. Polit. Sci. Assn., 1997. Mem. Assn. Practical and Profl. Ethics (bd. dirs.). Office: Princeton U Louis Marx Hall Princeton NJ 08544

GUTMANN, BARBARA LANG, nurse, educator; b. Niagara Falls, N.Y.; d. Frank J. and Beryl (Tennant) Lang; m. James F. Gutmann, June 25, 1960; children: Carolyn P., Bennett J. BSN cum laude, Niagara U., 1956; cert. sch. nurse tchr., Syracuse U., 1962; MSN, SUNY, Buffalo, 1975. Cert. pub. health nurse, basic CPR instr., Calif., N.Y., aids educator, Calif. Nurses Assn., 1987. Staff nurse VA Hosp., Syracuse, N.Y., 1956-58; pub. health nurse Syracuse City Health Dept., 1958-62, County Dept. Pub. Welfare, 1961-62; sch. nurse tchr. North Syracuse Ctrl. Schs., 1962-65; vol. Peace Corps, India, 1965-66; tchr. educable retarded North Syracuse Ctrl. Schs., 1966-67; staff nurse Stanford U. Hosp., Palo Alto, Calif., 1970-71; pvt. duty nurse Buffalo, 1972-74; assst. prof. nursing Niagara County C.C., Sanborn, N.Y., 1975-77; dir. nursing svcs. Homemaker Upjohn Contract Offices, Santa Barbara County, Calif., 1977-78; project dir. Upjohn Health Care Svcs., Santa Barbara, 1978; dir. nursing Sansum Med. Clinic, Santa Barbara, 1979-81; dir. inservice edn. and staff devel. Pinecrest Hosp., Santa Barbara, 1981-82; dir. edn. Meml. Rehab. Hosp., Santa Barbara, 1982-84; instr. nursing, health tech. and adult edn. Santa Barbara City Coll., 1984-89, 96—; profl. adv. bd. upper divsn. nursing program Daemen Coll., Buffalo, 1975-77; mem. Niagara Falls Regional Hypertension Bd., 1975-77, Buffalo Quality of Life Com., 1976-77; profl. adv. com. and utilization rev. com. Niagara County Health Dept., 1976-77; home nurse multiple sclerosis patients ARC, 1978; adv. com. Upjohn Health Care Svcs., 1979-82; health occupations adv. com. med. assisting program Santa Barbara C.C., 1980; mem. Head Trauma Recovery Group, Santa Barbara, 1982-85; contbr. to core curriculum Assn. Rehab. Nurses, 1987; health care cons., 1996—. Adv. com. Friendship Ctr., Santa Barbara, 1977-79; bd. dirs. Friendship Sr. Day Care Ctr., Montecito, Calif., 1986-94, pres., 1989-91, 92-94, v.p., 1985-86, bd. dirs. emeriti, 1994—; mem. basic CPR com. Am. Heart Assn., 1982-85; bishop's com. Diocese of Syracuse, 1965; bd. dirs. Onondaga County Health Assn., 1965; edn. com. Hillbrook Detention Home, 1967-70; mem. Inner City Bd. Dirs., Syracuse, 1968-70; sec. exec. com. bd. dirs. Onondaga Pastoral Counseling Ctr., 1967-70; asst. leader Girl Scouts Am., 1981-88; bd. dirs. Jodi House, 1982-85; docent Cachuma Nature Ctr., 1996—, sec., 1997—. Roman Catholic. Home and Office: 5474 Berkeley Rd Santa Barbara CA 93111-1614

GUTMANN, DAVID LEO, psychology educator; b. N.Y.C., Sept. 17, 1925; s. Isaac and Masha (Agronsky) G.; m. Joanna Redfield, Aug. 18, 1951; children: Stephanie, Ethan. M.A., U. Chgo., 1956, Ph.D., 1958. Lectr. psychology Harvard U., Cambridge, Mass., 1960-62; prof. U. Mich., Ann Arbor, 1962-76; prof. Northwestern U., Chgo., 1976-97, prof. emeritus, 1998—, chief of psychology, 1976-81, dir. older adult program, 1978-95; vis. emeritus prof. Hebrew U., Jerusalem, 1997. Author: Reclaimed Powers: Toward a New Psychology of Men and Women in Later Life, 1987, Reclaimed Powers: Men and Women in Later Life, 1994, The Human Elder in Nature, Culture, and Society, 1997; co-author: (with Bardwick, Douvan and Horner) Feminine Personality and Conflict, 1979. Served with U.S. Mcht. Marine, 1943-46. Recipient Career Devel. award NIMH, 1964-74. Fellow Gerontol. Soc. Am.; mem. Am. Vets. of Israel, Nat. Assn. Scholars. Jewish. Office: Northwestern U Med Sch Clin Psychology 303 E Chicago Ave Chicago IL 60611-3093

GUTMANN, JOSEPH, art history educator; b. Wuerzburg, Unterfranken, Germany, Aug. 17, 1923; came to U.S., 1936; s. Henry and Selma (Eisemann) G.; m. Marilyn Tuckman, Oct. 8, 1953; children: David H., Sharon D. BS, Temple U., 1949; MA, NYU, 1952; PhD, Hebrew Union Coll., 1960, DD, 1984, DHL, 1999. Ordained Rabbi. Assoc. prof. art history Hebrew Union Coll., Cin., 1960-69; adj. prof. art. Univ. of Cin., 1961-68; vis. prof. art. Antioch Coll., Yellow Springs, Ohio, 1964; prof. art history Wayne State U., Detroit, 1969-89, prof. art history emeritus, 1989—; vis. prof. art history U. Mich., Ann Arbor, 1985, Spertus Coll. Judaica, Chgo., 1989; vis. prof. religious studies U. Windsor, Ont., Can., 1990-92, U. Ctrl. Fla., Orlando, 1998, 99, cons. Spertus Mus. Chgo., Skirball Mus., L.A., The Jewish Mus., N.Y., Yeshiva U. Mus., N.Y.; adv. bd. Internat. Survey of Jewish Monuments of CAA-SAH. Author: Juedische Zeremonialkunst, 1963, Jewish Ceremonial Art, 1964, 2d edit. 1968, Images of the Jewish Past, 1965, (with S.F. Chyet) Moses Jacob Ezekiel: Memoirs from the Baths of Diocletian, 1975, Ephraim Moses Lilien's Jerusalem, 1976, Hebrew Manuscript Painting, 1978, (with V. Mann) Danzig 1939: Treasures of a Destroyed Community, 1982, The Jewish Sanctuary, 1983, The Jewish Life Cycle, 1987, Sacred Images: Studies in Jewish Art from Antiquity to the Middle Ages, 1989; editor Beauty in Holiness: Studies in Jewish Customs and Ceremonial Art, 1970, No Graven Images: Studies in Art and the Hebrew Bible, 1971, Die Darmstaedter Pessach-Haggadah, 1972, The Dura-Europos Synagogue:

A Re-Evaluation, 1973, rev. 2d edit., 1992, The Synagogue: Studies in Origins, Archaeology and Architecture, 1975, The Temple of Solomon: Archaeological Fact and Medieval Tradition in Christian, Islamic and Jewish Art, 1976, The Image and the Word: Confrontations in Judaism, Christianity and Islam, 1977, Ancient Synagogues: The State of Research, 1981; author (monthly column) Gutmann on Art Nat. Jewish Post and Opinion. Chmn. Community Forum Midrasha, Birmingham, Mich., 1986-88. Served as cpl. USAF, 1943-46. Recipient Faculty Recognition award Wayne State U., 1980; Gershenson Disting. Faculty fellow, 1986-88, Henry Morgenthau fellow Hebrew Union Coll., 1957-58, Meml. Found. Jewish Culture grantee 1959, 72; Am. Council of Learned Socs. grantee, N.Y., 1983, Am. Philos. Soc. grantee, Phila., 1965. Mem. Cen. Conf. Am. Rabbis, Coll. Art Assn. Jewish. Avocations: reading, painting. Home: 13151 Winchester Ave Huntington Woods MI 48070-1726

GUTMANN, REINHART BRUNO, clergyman, social worker; b. Munich, Bavaria, Germany, May 1, 1916; came to U.S., 1942, naturalized, 1946; s. Franz and Berta G.; m. Vivian Carol Brunke, Oct. 7, 1944; children: Robin Peter Edward, Martin Francis. Student, History Honours Sch., Manchester U., Eng., 1936-38; MA in Social Scis, St. Andrews U., Scotland, 1939; postgrad., Coll. of Resurrection, Eng., 1939-41, Coll. Preachers, Washington, 1948, 52, U. Wis., summer, 1951, St. Augustine's Coll., Eng., 1964. Ordained deacon Ch. of Eng., 1941, ordained priest, 1942; curate St. Michael's Parish, Golders Green, London, 1941-42; rector St. Mark's Parish, Green Island, N.Y., 1944-45, St. Andrew's Parish, Milw., 1952-54; chaplain and mem. faculty Hoosac (N.Y.) Sch., 1943-45; founder, exec. dir. Neighborhood House and Episcopal City Mission, Milw., 1945-60; part-time priest-in-charge St. Peter's Mission, North Lake, Wis., 1958-60; exec. dir. Friendship House, Washington, 1960-62; cons. Indian Social welfare Exec. Council of Episcopal Ch., N.Y.C., 1962-64; exec. sec. div. community services Exec. Council of Episcopal Ch., 1964-68, exec. for social welfare and field services, 1968-71; part-time priest-in-charge St. Thomas of Alexandria, Pittstown, N.J., 1968-75; hon. asst. priest St. Martin's Ch., Pawtucket, R.I., 1980; mgr. spl. projects Human Resources Adminstrn., N.Y.C., 1971-72, spl. asst. to asst. adminstr., 1972-73, dir. mgmt. office community services, 1973, spl. asst. to dep. adminstr. social services, 1973-75; nat. exec. dir. Foster Parents Plan, Inc., Warwick, R.I., 1975-82; pres. Cedar Brook Cons., Inc., 1982-86, ret., 1987. Chmn. dept. Christian social relations Province of Midwest, Episcopal Ch., 1954-60; chmn. social edn. and action Nat. Fedn. Settlements, 1960-62; hon. canon All Saints Cathedral, Milw., 1971; founder Silver Spring Neighborhood Ctr., Milw., 1958; founder Northcott House, Milw., 1959. Mem. Acad. Cert. Social Workers, Nat. Assn. Social Workers. Democrat. *Personal success is not measured by wealth or public recognition. It is the knowledge that one has done everything possible to help people achieve dignity, security, and fulfillment; and in so doing has transmitted a sense of personal caring for the needs of others.*

GUTMANN, RONALD J., electrical engineering educator; b. Bklyn., Nov. 16, 1940; s. Ludwig G. and Dorothy (Levy) G.; m. Suzanne French, Aug. 27, 1967; children: David, Jennifer. BSEE, Rensselaer Poly. Inst., 1962, PhD in Electrophysics, 1970; MSEE, NYU, 1964. Mem. tech. staff Bell Telephone Labs., Whippany, N.J., 1962-66; sr. engr. Lockheed Electronics Co., Plainfield, N.J., 1966-67; rsch. asst. Rensselaer Poly. Inst., Troy, N.Y., 1967-70, asst. prof. elec. engring., 1970-74, assoc. prof., 1974-80, prof., 1980—; dir. Ctr. for Integrated Electronics, 1989-94; vis. mem. tech. staff Bell Labs., Whippany, 1979; program dir. NSF, Washington, 1981-83; reviewer for pub. cos. and tech. jours. Author, editor McGraw Hill series on continuing edn. in electonics; co-author: Chemical-Mechanical Planarization of Microelectronic Materials, 1997, Copper as a Microelectronics Material, 1999; contbr. numerous articles on semicondr. devices, microwave techniques and interconnect tech. to profl. jours; numerous presentations nat./internat. confs. Recipient Disting. Svc. award NSF, 1983, Alumni Faculty award Rensselaer Poly. Inst., 1990; engring. fellow NASA, 1977. Fellow IEEE (chmn. awards com. 1984-85, vice chmn. awards bd. 1987-88, mem. numerous tech. program coms., fellow award for contbns. to microwave semiconductor tech.). Avocations: jogging, tennis, reading. Office: Rensselaer Poly Inst CII 6129 15th St Troy NY 12181

GUTOW, BERNARD SIDNEY, packaging manufacturing company executive; b. Chgo., Nov. 11, 1939; s. Max and Betty (Warshawsky) G.; m. Carol Lerch, June 5, 1960; children: Jeffrey, Bryon. BS in Engring., U. Ill., 1961, MS in Engring., 1962; MBA, U. Santa Clara, 1965; JD Golden Gate U., 1997, LLM, 1998. Registered profl. engr., Ill. Sr. engr. Lockheed Missiles, Sunnyvale, Calif., 1962-65; project engr. U.S. Steel Co., Chgo., 1965-67; engr., prin. A.T. Kearney Co., Chgo., 1967-78; dir. Shaklee, San Francisco, 1978-79; v.p. H.S. Crocker, San Bruno, Calif., 1979-85; v.p., gen. mgr. First Data Resources subs. Am. Express Corp., Tustin, Calif., 1985-88; gen. ptnr., Mgmt. Resource Ptnrs., Redwood Shores, Calif., 1988-96. Editor: Plant Engineering Management, 1974; pres., CEO Bayline Ptnrs., Bayline Paper Supply, Union City, Calif., 1991—; contbr. articles to profl. jours. Pres. Morton Grove Park Dist., Ill., 1973-78; mem. Morton Grove Youth Commn., 1973-78. Recipient Plaque, Morton Grove Park Dist., 1978, cert. Soc. Mfg. Engrs., Chgo., 1975, Bronze award Internat. Film and TV Festival N.Y., N.Y.C., 1984, internat. law writing competition award N.Y. State Bar Assn., 1998. Mem. ASME (chpt. chmn. 1972-73). Home: 3263 La Mesa Dr San Carlos CA 94070-4244

GUTOWICZ, MATTHEW FRANCIS, JR., radiologist; b. Camden, N.J., Feb. 23, 1945; s. Matthew F. and A. Patricia (Walczak) G.; m. Alice Mary Bell, June 27, 1977; 1 child, Melissa. BA, Temple U., 1968; DO, Phila. Coll. Osteo. Medicine, 1972. Diplomate Am. Bd. Radiology, Am. Bd. Nuclear Medicine. Intern Mercy Hosp., Denver, 1972-73; resident in diagnostic radiology Hosp. of U. Pa., Phila., 1973-76, fellow in nuclear medicine, 1976-77; chief dept. radiology and nuclear medicine Fisher Titus Med. Ctr., Norwalk, Ohio, 1977—; pres. Firelands Radiology, Inc., Norwalk, 1977—. Republican. Roman Catholic. Avocations: photography, tennis, scuba diving. Home: 23 Patrician Dr Norwalk OH 44857-2463

GUTOWSKY, HERBERT SANDER, chemistry educator; b. Bridgman, Mich., Nov. 8, 1919; s. Otto and Hattie (Meyer) G.; m. Barbara Stuart, June 22, 1949 (div. Sept. 1981); children: Daniel Kurt (dec.), Robb Edward, Christopher Carl; m. Virginia Warner, Aug. 1, 1982. AB, Ind. U., 1940, DSc (hon.), 1983; MS, U. Calif.-Berkeley, 1946; PhD, Harvard U., 1949. Mem. faculty U. Ill., Urbana, 1948—, prof. chemistry, 1956—, head div. phys. chemistry, 1956-63, head dept. chemistry and chem. engring., 1967-70, dir. Sch. Chem. Scis., head dept. chemistry, 1970-83, mem. Ctr. for Advanced Study, 1983—; mem. chemistry panel NSF, 1963-66, chmn. panel, 1965-66, mem. adv. com. on planning, 1971-74; mem. Ill. Bd. Natural Resources and Conservation, 1973-98; G.N. Lewis Meml. lectr., 1976, G.B. Kistiakowsky lectr., 1980. Mem. adv. bd. Petroleum Research Fund, 1959-61; mem. selection and scheduling com. Gordon Research Conf., 1959-64, 68-72, trustee, 1969-72, chmn. bd. trustees, 1971-72. Served to capt., chem. warfare service AUS, 1941-45. Recipient 1966 Irving Langmuir award Am. Chem. Soc., Midwest award St. Louis sect., 1973, prize Internat. Soc. Magnetic Resonance, 1974, Peter Debye award in phys. chemistry Am. Chem. Soc., 1975, Nat. Medal of Sci., 1977, Wolf prize in Chemistry, 1983, Chem. Pioneer award Am. Inst. Chemists, 1991, Pitts. Spectroscopy award, 1992, Kuebler award Alpha Chi Sigma, 1996; Guggenheim fellow, 1954-55. Fellow AAAS, Am. Phys. Soc. (chmn. div. chem. physics 1973-74), AAAS, Am. Acad. Arts and Scis.; mem. AAUP, NAS (mem. com. sci. and pub. policy 1972-75, chmn. panel on atmospheric chemistry 1975-77, mem. com. impacts of stratospheric change 1975-77), Am. Philos. Soc., Am. Chem. Soc. (chmn. div. phys. chemistry 1966-67, com. on profl. tng. 1969-77, chmn. 1974-77), Phi Beta Kappa, Sigma Xi. Avocation: tea rose gardener. Home: 202 W Delaware Ave Urbana IL 61801-4905 Office: U Ill 177 Noyes Lab Box 25 600 S Mathews Ave Urbana IL 61801-3602

GUTREUTER, JILL STALLINGS, financial consultant, financial planner; b. Chgo., Mar. 25, 1937; d. C.G. and Ann (Subject) Stallings; m. Robert L. Gutreuter, June 5, 1971; 1 child, Julia E. BA, U. Ill., 1967; postgrad., Chgo.-Kent, 1968-69, Coll. Fin. Planning, Denver, 1994. Staff dir. ABA, Chgo., 1969-71; trust officer Peoples Trust/Summit Bank, Ft. Wayne, Ind., 1980-87; fin. cons. Merrill Lynch, Ft. Wayne, Ind., 1987—; fin. planning tchr., continuing edn. divsn. Ind. U.-Purdue U., Ft. Wayne, 1990—. Bd. dirs. Girl Scouts of the Limberlost, No. Ind., 1997—; bd. dirs., mem. fin. com. YWCA, Ft. Wayne, 1995—; trustee Episcopal Diocese of North Ind. Found., South Bend, 1995—; pres. Art League, Ft. Wayne Mus. Art, 1992-93. Recipient Women of Achievement award YWCA, Ft. Wayne, 1994. Mem. Inst. CFPs, Altrusa Internat. (pres. Ft. Wayne chpt. 1992-94). Episcopalian. Avocations: swimming, walking, painting, knitting. Home: 2312 Forest Park Blvd Fort Wayne IN 46805-3619 Office: Merrill Lynch 130 W Main St Fl 1 Fort Wayne IN 46802-1794

GUTSCH, WILLIAM ANTHONY, JR., astronomer; b. Newark, Jan. 14, 1946; s. William Anthony and Mary (Ellenback) G. B.S., St. Peter's Coll., 1967; M.S., U. Va., 1973, Ph.D., 1978; LHD, St. Peter's Coll., 1995. Staff astronomer Rochester Museum and Sci. Ctr., N.Y., 1973-82; chmn. Am. Mus.-Hayden Planetarium, N.Y.C., 1982-95; ind. cons., writer, prodr. for sci. ctrs., pubs. and TV, Computer & Multi-Media, 1995—; cons., lectr. in field; news columnist Rochester Times-Union, 1980-84; sci. reporter Sta.-WOKR-TV, Rochester, N.Y., 1976-82; sci. corr. Sta.-WABC-TV, N.Y.C., 1982-84, sci. editor., 1984-88; on-air meteorologist, spl. sci. corr. ABC Network, 1986-93; sci. columnist Gannett, 1980-90; cons. U. Santiago, Chile, 1982; sci. corr. USA Network, 1993—. Author: The Search for Extraterrestrial Life, 1991, 1001 Things Everyone Should Know About the Universe, 1998, (with Isaac Asimov) The Exploding Suns, 1996; author other books, also newspaper articles, TV news and planetarium scripts; writer, contbg. editor New Book of Knowledge, 1992—; writer Discovery Channel, 1994-95; ind. writer, prodr., cons. planetariums, sci. ctr. and TV, 1985—. Recipient award of svc. U. Santiago, 1982, City of Buenos Aires, 1983, City of San Juan, 1991, City of Jaharta, Indonesia, 1991; Emmy nominee, 1987. Mem. Am. Astron. Soc., Am. Meteorol. Soc., Am. Assn. Physics Tchrs., Internat. Planetarium Soc. (pres. 1992-94, past pres. 1994-96). E-mail: 102417.2073@compuserve.com.

GUTSCHE, CARL DAVID, chemistry educator; b. LaGrange, Ill., Mar. 21, 1921; s. Frank Carl and Vera (Mutchler) G.; m. Alice Eugenia Carr, June 4, 1944; children: Clara Jean, Betha Lynn, Christopher Glenn. BA, Oberlin Coll., 1943; PhD, U. Wis., 1947. With U.S. Dept. Agr. Office Sci. Devel., 1943-44; instr. chemistry Washington U., St. Louis, 1947-48, asst. prof., 1948-51, assoc. prof., 1951-59, prof., 1959-89, prof. emeritus, 1989—; chmn. dept. Washington U., 1970-76; emeritus prof. Washington U., St. Louis, 1989—; Robert A. Welch prof. chemistry Tex. Christian U., Fort Worth, 1989—; cons. in field; mem. adv. bd. Petroleum Rsch. Fund, 1971-74; chmn. medicinal chemistry study sect. NIH, 1978-81; Bd. dirs. St. Louis Conservatory and Schs. for Arts, 1978-82. Author: The Chemistry of Carbonyl Compounds, 1967, Carbocyclic Ring Expansion Reactions, 1968, Fundamentals of Organic Chemistry, 1975, Calixarenes, 1989, Calixarenes Revisited, 1998; mem. adv. bd.: Jour. Organic Chemistry, 1979-83; mem. editorial bd.: Organic Preparations and Procedures Internat., 1968—, Jour. Inclusion Phenomena, 1993—; contbr. articles to profl. jours. Guggenheim fellow, 1981. Fellow AAAS; mem. Am. Chem. Soc. (chmn. St. Louis sect. 1959, mem. pub. com. 1974-77, com. on coms. 1977-80, com. on profl. tng. 1980-89, cons. to com. 1990-98, councilor and dir., St. Louis sect. award 1971, Midwest award 1988, Doherty award 1998), Chem. Soc. (London), AAUP, Phi Beta Kappa (mem. qualifications com. 1992—), Sigma Xi. Home: 3521 Arborlawn Dr Fort Worth TX 76109-2533 Office: Tex Christian U Dept Chemistry Fort Worth TX 76129

GUTSTEIN, CAROL FEINHANDLER, realtor; b. Chgo., Aug. 31, 1941; d. Emanuel Joshua and Rose (Paster) Feinhandler; m. Solomon Gutstein, Sept. 3, 1961; children: Jonathan, David, Daniel, Joshua. BS in Edn., Loyola U., 1962; MA in Spl. Edn., DePaul U., 1969. Cert. comml. investment mem.; grad. residential real estate; cert. comml. real estate. Spl. cons. Mayor's Office of Sr. Citizens and Handicapped, Chgo., 1977-79; realtor C-21 Shoreline, Evanston, Ill., 1982-84, Matanky, Chgo., 1985, Hallmark & Johnston, Chgo., 1986-95, L.H. Properties, Ltd., Lincolnwood, Ill., 1996—; cons. Nursing Homes, Chgo., 1978-80. Compiler, editor Community Resources for the Disabled Person in the Chicago Metropolitan Area, 1978. Active campaigner Paul Simon for Senate campaign, 1984-85, 89-90; mgr., dir. Aldermanic campaigns, Chgo., 1975, 79, 95; del. 11th Congrl. Dist. Dem. Nat. Conv., 1980; mem. Dist. 1 Chgo. Sch. Coun., 1989-91. Fellowship Northwestern U., 1962. Mem. WCR (bd. dirs. 1997-98), CCIM (bd. dirs. 1997), Camp Ramah (bd. dirs. 1985-97), Hadassah (corr. sec. 1998, bd. mem. 1999). Democrat. Jewish.

GUTSTEIN, SOLOMON, lawyer; b. Newport, R.I., June 18, 1934; s. Morris Aaron and Goldie Leah (Nussbaum) G.; m. Carol Feinhandler, Sept. 3, 1961; children: Jon Eric, David Ethan, Daniel Ari, Joshua Aaron. AB with honors, U. Chgo., 1953, JD, 1956. Bar: Ill. 1956, U.S. Dist. Ct. (no. dist.) Ill. 1957, U.S. Ct. Appeals (7th cir.) 1958, U.S. Ct. Appeals (5th cir.) 1971, U.S. Supreme Ct. 1980; Rabbi, 1955. Assoc., Schradzke, Gould & Ratner, Chgo., 1956-60; ptnr. firm Schwartz & Gutstein, Chgo., 1961-65, Gutstein & Cope, Chgo., 1968-72, Gutstein & Schwartz, Chgo., 1980-83, Gutstein & Sherwin, Chgo., 1983-85; ptnr. Arvey, Hodes, Costello & Burman, 1991-92, Tenney & Bentley, 1992—; spl. asst. atty. gen. State of Ill., 1968-69; adj. prof. law, John Marshall Law Sch., 1993—; lectr. bus. law U. Chgo. Grad. Sch. Bus., 1973-82; lectr. in field, real estate broker. Author: Illinois Real Estate, 2 vols., 1983, rev. ann. updates, 1984-95; co-author: Construction Law in Illinois, annually 1980-84, Judaism in Art (The Windows of Shaare Tivkah), 1995, Illinois Real Estate Practice Guide, 2 vols., 1996, rev. annual edit., 1997-98; contbr. chpt. to Commercial Real Estate Transactions, 1962-76. Assoc. editor U. Chgo. Law Rev., 1954-56; editl. adviser Basic Real Estate I, also Advanced Real Estate II, 1960s-70s.; author: Analysis of the Book of Psalms, 1962; cons. Ill. Real Property Svc., Bancroft Whitney Co., 1988-89; contbr. articles to profl. publs. Mem. Cook County Citizens Fee Rev. Com., 1965; alderman from 40th ward Chgo. City Council, 1975-79; mem. govt. affairs adv. com. Jewish Fedn., 1984-94. Fuerstenberg scholar U. Chgo., 1950-56; Kosmerl fellow U. Chgo., 1953-56. Mem. Chgo. Bar Assn., Ill. State Bar Assn., Decalogue Soc. Lawyers. Lodge: B'nai B'rith. Office: Tenney & Bentley 111 W Washington St Ste 1900 Chicago IL 60602-2769

GUTTAU, MICHAEL K., state agency administrator, banker; b. Council Bluffs, Iowa, Nov. 8, 1946; s. Detlef Hugo and Ethel Evelyn (Schmidt) G.; m. Judith Ann Frazier, June 28, 1968; children: Heidi Ann, Joshua Michael. BS in Farm Operation, Iowa State U., 1969; postgrad., U. Nebr., Omaha, 1975. Administrv. asst. to dean students, asst. instr. sociology Iowa State U., Ames, 1969; trainee, asst. cashier, cashier Treynor (Iowa) State Bank, 1972-78, pres., chmn., CEO, 1978—; appt. Iowa Supt. Banking, 1995; bd. dirs. Mercy Midlands Corp., Omaha; advisor N.Y. Fed. Res. Bank, Russian Am. Bankers Forum Acad. for Advanced Studies in Banking and Fin.; presenter Internat. Russian Banking Conf. 1992-93, mem. steering com., 1992-93; mem. U.S. Dept. State-U.S./Slovakian Counterpart Team Agr. Fin. and Credit. Chmn. steering com. Pottawattamie County Riverbend Indsl. Site, Western Iowa Devel. Assn., Mercy Hosp., Council Bluffs, Treynor Cmty. Devel. Com.; bd. dirs. Deaf Missions Worldwide Christian Ministry for Deaf; mem. youth com. Pottawattamie County 4-H; founder, pres., bd. dirs. Treynor Devel. Found. Corp.; deacon, moderator, adult and H.S. Sunday sch. tchr. Zion Congl. Ch., Treynor. With U.S. Army, 1969-72, Vietnam; with Nebr. Army NG, 1972-80. Decorated DFC with oak leaf cluster, Bronze Star, Air medal with V device, 28 Air medals; Recipient Outstanding Citizen award Treynor Town and Country Club, Swords to Plowshares award Bus.-Banks Exch. Newspaper, Moscow, 1992. Mem. Am. Bankers Assn. (chmn. future of cmty. banking study, cmty. bankers adv. bd. and coun., dir. edn. coun., mem. adminstrv. com. govt. rels. com.), Iowa Bankers Assn. (pres.-elect 1994-95, chmn. legis. com., bd. dirs.), S.W. Iowa Bank Adminstrn. Inst. (pres.), Treynor Bus. Assn. (founder, past pres., bd. dirs.), Scabbard and Blade, Gamma Gamma, Theta Delta Chi. Republican. Avocation: aviation. Home: RR 2 Box 82B Council Bluffs IA 51503-9802 Office: Treynor State Bank 15 E Main St Treynor IA 51575

GUTTENBERG, ALBERT ZISKIND, planning educator; b. Chelsea, Mass., Nov. 6, 1921; s. Harry and Edith (Bernstein) G.; m. Mariella Mascardi, June 29, 1964. AB in Social Rels., Harvard U., 1948; postgrad. in sociology, U. Chgo., 1949-51; postgrad. in city planning, U. Pa., 1958-59. Planning asst. Planning Bd., City of Portland, Maine, 1954-56; planning analyst Planning Commn., City of Phila., 1956-60; chief gen. plans and programming sect. Comprehensive Planning div., 1960-61; sr. planner Nat. Capital Downtown Com., Washington, 1962-63; assoc. prof. urban planning U. Ill., 1964-69, prof. urban and regional planning, 1969-89; chair in urban and regional renewal Dept. Geodesy, Delft U. Tech., The Netherlands, 1977-78; cons. in field. Author: (with others) Explorations Into Urban Structure, 1964, New Directions in Land use Classification, 1965, (with others) Human Ecology, 1975, The Language of Planning, 1993; editor Planning and Public Policy, 1974-89; contbr. articles on land use planning to profl. pubs. Served with U.S. Army, 1942-46. Guggenheim fellow, 1970-71; Brookings Inst. guest scholar, 1970-71; Gelderman Fund grantee Delft U. Tech., 1977; German Marshall Fund Travel grantee, Holland, 1979; recipient Fulbright Travel award Italy, 1986. Mem. Am. Planning Assn., Am. Inst. Cert. Planners, Regional Sci. Assn., Soc. Am. City and Regional Planning History, Fulbright Alumni Assn., Am. Assn. Italian Studies. Home: 711 Hamilton Dr Champaign IL 61820-6811 Office: 111 Temple Hoyne Buell Hall 611 E Lorado Taft Dr Champaign IL 61820-6921

GUTTENBERG, STEVE, actor; b. Bklyn., Aug. 24, 1958; s. Jerome Stanley and Ann Iris (Newman) G. Student, Albany State U. Appeared in films: The Chicken Chronicles, 1977, Something For Joey, 1977, Rollercoaster, 1977, The Boys From Brazil, 1979, Players, 1979, Can't Stop the Music, 1980, Diner, 1982, The Man Who Wasn't There, 1983, Police Academy, 1984, Police Academy II, 1985, Cocoon, 1985, Bad Medicine, 1985, Police Academy 3, 1986, Short Circuit, 1986, The Bedroom Window, 1987, (also assoc. prodr.) Police Academy IV: Citizens on Patrol, 1987, Three Men and A Baby, 1987, Amazon Women on the Moon, 1987, Surrender, 1987, High Spirits, 1988, Cocoon: The Return, 1988, Don't Her It's Me, 1990, Three Men and a Little Lady, 1990, Tower of Terror, 1997, Airborne, 1998, Love and Fear, 1999; actor, dir.: Love Off Limits, 1992; TV films: Something For Joey, 1976, To Race the Wind, 1980, Billy, 1976, Miracle On Ice, 1980, The Day After, 1984, The Magical World of Chuck Jones, 1992, It takes Two, 1995, Home for the Holidays, 1995, The Big Green, 1995, Zeus and Roxanne, 1997, Casper: The Beginning, 1997; TV series: Billy, 1979, No Soap, Radio, 1982, Storytime, 1994; stage: Broadway debut Prelude to a Kiss, 1991. *

GUTTENPLAN, HAROLD ESAU, retired food company executive; b. Flushing, N.Y., Oct. 12, 1924; s. Adolph and Mollie (Penner) G.; m. Jeanette Harris, Apr. 17, 1948; children—Bruce David, Mark Stuart. BA, Queens Coll., 1948; MBA, NYU, 1951. Statistician printing ink div. Sun Chem. Corp., 1948-49; cost accountant, chief accountant, asst. treas. DCA Food Industries, Inc., N.Y.C., 1949-66, treas., 1966-96, asst. sec., 1972-73, sec., dir., 1973-96; ret., 1996; bd. dirs. Nisshin-DCA. Vol. spkr. Anti-Defamation League; co-chmn. Queens Coll. 50th Alumni Day Reception, 1998; cub Scout leader Nassau County Thunderbird coun. Boy Scouts Am., 1955-63. With USAAF, 1943-45, PTO. Recipient Anti-Defamation League citation award, 1968. Mem. Daus. of Jacob Relatives Assn. (pres. 1976-77), Alpha Phi Omega (pres. 1947-48), B'nai B'rith (pres. Sagamore lodge 1963-64), Am. Assn. Ret. Persons (asst. state coord. 55 Alive/Mature Driving 1998). Home: 69 Joyce Ln Woodbury NY 11797-2124

GUTTENPLAN, JOSEPH B., biochemistry researcher and educator; b. N.Y.C., May 16, 1943; s. Henry L. and Elizabeth (Phillips) G.; m. Hilde Krohn, Sept. 20, 1971; children: Nils, Alys. BS, Bklyn. Coll., 1965; MS, PhD, Brandeis U., 1970, MPH Columbia U., 1992. Postdoctoral fellow Max Planck Inst., Goettingen, W. Ger., 1969-71, U. Calif., Berkeley, 1971-73; research asst. prof. Mt. Sinai Sch. Medicine, N.Y.C., 1973-74; from asst. to assoc. prof. biochemistry NYU Dental Ctr., N.Y.C., 1974-87; full prof. biochemistry, 1987, coord. biochemistry/microbiology, 1991—, dir. rsch., 1993—; assoc. prof. environ. medicine NYU Med. Ctr., 1983-98, acting chmn., 1987-88, full prof., 1998—; cons. Mt. Sinai Med. Ctr., 1980-84; pvt. cons. Co-author: Biochemistry, 1995; editl. bd. Mutation Rsch., 1997—; contbr. articles to profl. jours. and chpt. to book. Mem. N.C.I. site visit team Eppley Inst. Grantee NIH, 1976, 79, 83, 87, 94, 98, Am. Inst. Cancer Rsch., 1996, Air Force 1996, Smokeless Tobacco Rsch. Coun., 1998; fellow Am. Inst. Chemists (study sect. to rev. superfund grants). Mem. Am. Assn. Cancer Research, Environ. Mutagen Soc., Am. Soc. Biol. Chemists. Home: 110 E Brookside Dr Larchmont NY 10538-1736

GUTTENTAG, JOSEPH HARRIS, lawyer, educator; b. Boston, Feb. 8, 1929; s. Samuel Alexander and Sara (Hurwitz) G.; m. Merna Fay Cohn, June 18, 1961; children: Steven, Adam, Alice. AB, U. Mich., 1950; LLB, Harvard U., 1953. Bar: D.C. 1953, Mich. 1954. Internat. tax counsel U.S. Treasury, Washington, 1967-68; ptnr. Surrey & Morse, Washington, 1965-67, 68-79; ptnr. Arnold & Porter, Washington, 1979-94, Japan, 1991-94; dep. asst. sec. internat. tax affairs U.S. Treasury, Washington, 1994-99, sr. advisor Office of Tax Policy, 1999—; adj. prof. Howard Law Sch., Washington, 1964-67; professorial lectr. George Washington U. Sch. Law, 1968-75. Chmn. com. fiscal affairs Orgn. Econ. Coop. and Devel., Paris; v.p. Levine Sch. Music. Capt. USAF, 1954-57. Mem. D.C. Bar Assn. (treas.), Am. Soc. Internat. Law. Democrat. Jewish.

GUTTERIDGE, THOMAS G., academic administrator, consultant and labor arbitrator; b. Flint, Mich., Oct. 31, 1942; s. George Ernest and Mary Ruth (Stewart) G.; m. Judith Kay Grubbs Gutteridge, Aug. 28, 1965; children: Theresa, Debbie, Cindy. BS in Industrial Engring., Gen. Motors Inst., 1965; MS in Ind. Admin., Purdue U., 1966, PhD, 1971. Teaching asst. Purdue U., Lafayette, Ind., 1967-70; asst., assoc. prof. SUNY, Buffalo, N.Y., 1970-83; dean, full prof. So. Ill. U., Carbondale, 1983-92; dean, dist. prof. U. Conn., Storrs, 1992—; safety engr. Buick Motors, Flint, Mich., 1964-65; corp. recruiter Industrial Nucleonics, Columbus, Ohio, 1966-67; labor arbitrator Am. Arbitration Assn., Fed. Mediation and Conciliation Svc., 1972—; arbitrator, cons. State of Conn. Career Devel., 1995—. Co-author: Organizational Career Development: Benchmarks for Building a World-Class Workforce, Organizational Career Development: State of the Practice; contbr. numerous articles to profl. jours. Recipient Career Devel. awards Am. Soc. for Tng. and Devel., 1983. Mem. Acad. of Mgmt. Human Resource Planning Soc. Democrat. Avocation: sports. Home: 9 Louise Dr Tolland CT 06084-2536 Office: U Conn Sch Bus 368 Fairfield # U-41D Storrs Mansfield CT 06269-6016

GUTTERSEN, MICHAEL, ranching and investments professional; b. San Francisco, Mar. 26, 1939; s. William L. and Grace Tooee (Smith) Vogler; m. Penny Leonora Quinn, Aug. 29, 1959; children: Michael William, Arthur Roy, Shawn Patrick. Student, U. Col., 1957-58. Foreman Crow Creek Ranch, Ault, Colo., 1960-61; owner/mgr. Flying G Ranch, Briggsdale, Colo., 1961-86; pres. Two E Ranches Inc., Greeley, Colo., 1969-86, PX Ranch, Elko, Nev., 1969-71, Indian Creek Ranch, Encampment, Wyo., 1970-83, Lake Farms Co., Eaton, Colo., 1969-86; gen. ptnr. Guttersen & Co./ Guttersen Ranch, Kersey, Colo., 1986—; mgr. ins. agy. Am. Nat. Ins. Co., Greeley, 1962-70; owner FGF Ins. Brokers, Inc., Greeley, 1962-70. Bd. dirs. United Way, Weld County, Colo., 1979-81, Greeley Philharmonic Orch., 1991-94, Nat. Cowboy Hall of Fame, Oklahoma City, 1994—. With U.S. Army, 1958-60. Mem. Nat. Cattlemens Assn., Colo. Cattlemens Assn., Colo. Cattle Feeders Assn., Tex. and S.W. Cattle Raisers Assn., Weld County Livestock Assn., Greeley Country Club. Republican. Roman Catholic. Avocations: fishing, hunting in Africa. Home: Woods Lake Farm 13696 RD 74 Eaton CO 80615 Office: Guttersen and Co PO Box 528 Kersey CO 80644-0528

GUTTMAN, ARNOLD R., chemist, educator; b. Chgo., Oct. 22, 1947; s. Joseph Reese and Sally (Meyers) G.; m. Cheryl L. Krader, Aug. 20, 1978; children: Lawrence, Mark. BA, DePaul U., 1970; BS in Chemistry, Northeastern Ill. U., 1982; MEd, Nat. Louis U., 1990. Chemist G.D. Searle & Co., Skokie, Ill., 1980-83, Abbott Labs., North Chicago, Ill., 1983-84; phys. sci. tchr. Hardey Prep Sch., Chgo., 1988-91; chemistry tchr. Waukegan (Ill.) H.S., 1991—; tchr. rsch. assoc. Argonne (Ill.) Nat. Labs., 1995; tchr. materials rsch. ctr. Northwestern U., Evanston, Ill., 1999. Contbr. articles to profl. jours. Recipient Excellence in tchg. Sci. award Ill. Jr. Acad. Sci., 1989; Am. Soc. Biochemistry and Molecular Biology fellow The Chgo. Med. Sch., 1996. Mem. Am. Chem. Soc. (chpt. h.s. com., 2001 h.s. chemistry exam. com.), Ill. Chemistry Tchrs. Assn., Ill. Sci. Tchrs. Assn. Avocations: tennis, chess, walking. Home: 701 Indian Hill Rd Deerfield IL 60015-4048

GUTTMAN, EGON, law educator; b. Neuruppin, Germany, Jan. 27, 1927; came to U.S., 1958, naturalized, 1968; s. Isaac and Blima (Liss) G.; m. Inge Weinberg, June 12, 1966; children: Geoffrey David, Leonard Jay. Student, Cambridge U., 1945-48; LLB, U. London, 1950, LLM, 1952; postgrad., Northwestern U. Sch. Law, 1958-59. Barrister: Eng. 1952. Sole practice Eng., 1952-53; faculty Univ. Coll. and U. Khartoum Sudan, 1953-58, legal advisor to chief justice, 1953-58; founder, editor Sudan Law Jour. & Reports,

1956-57; researcher, lectr. Rutgers U. Sch. Law, Newark, 1959-60; asst. prof. U. Alta., Edmonton, Can., 1960-62; prof. Howard U. Law Sch., Washington, 1962-68, vis. adj. prof., 1968-96; adj. prof. law Washington Coll. Law, Am. U., 1964-68, Levitt Meml. Trust scholar-prof., 1968—; lectr. Practicing Law Inst., 1964—; adj. prof. law Georgetown U. Law Ctr., 1972-74, Johns Hopkins U., Balt., 1973-81; vis. prof. Faculty of Law, U. Cambridge, Wolfson Coll., Eng., 1984; atty.-fellow SEC, 1976-79; cons. to various U.S. agys. and spl. commns.; U.S. rep. to UNCITRAL working groups; mem. various ALI-ABA working groups on the revision of the uniform comml. code; mem. Sec. of State's Adv. Com. on Pvt. Internat. Law. Author: (books) Crime, Cause and Treatment, 1956, (with A. Smith) Cases and Materials on Domestic Relations, 1962, Modern Securities Transfers, 1967, 3d edit. 1987, cumulative supplement, 1998, (with R.G. Vaughn) Cases and Materials on Policy and the Legal Environment, 1973, rev. 1978, 3d edit. 1980, (with R.B. Lubic) Secured Transactions- A Simplified Guide, 1996; (with L.F. Del Duca and A.M. Squilante) Problems and Materials on Secured Transactions Under the Uniform Commercial Code, Commercial Transactions, vol. 1, 1992, (with F. Miller) supplement, 1996-98, Problems and Materials on Sales Under the Uniform Commercial Code and the Convention on International Sale of Goods, Commercial Transactions, vol. 2, 1990, supplement, 1997-98, Problem and Materials on Negotiable Instruments under the Uniform Commerical Code and the U.N. Convention on International Bills of Exchange and International Promissory Notes, Commercial Transactions vol. 3, 1993, supplement, 1997-98, Securities Laws in the United States - A Primer for Foreign Lawyers, 1996-99; contbr. numerous articles, revs., briefs to profl. lit. Howard U. rep. Fund for Edn. in World Order, 1966-68; trustee Silver Spring Jewish Ctr., Md., 1976-79; mem. exec. com. Sha'are Tzedek Hosp., Washington, 1971-72, 97—. Leverhulme scholar, 1948-51; U. London studentship, 1951-52; Ford Found. grad. fellow, 1958-59, NYU summer workshop fellow, 1960, 61, 64; Levitt Meml. Trust scholar-professor 1982; recipient Outstanding Svc. award Student Bar Assn., Am. U., 1970, Law Rev. Outstanding Svc. award, 1981, Washington Coll. of Law Outstanding Contbn. to Acad. Program Devel. award, 1981. Mem. Am. Law Inst., ABA, Fed. Bar Assn. Assn. Trial Lawyers Am., Brit. Inst. Internat. and Comparative Law, Soc. Pub. Tchrs. Law (Eng.), Hon. Soc. Middle Temple, Hardwick Soc. of Inns of Ct., Sudan Philos. Soc., Assn. Can. Law Tchrs., Am. Soc. Internat. Law, Can. Assn. Comparative Law, Phi Alpha Delta (John Sherman Myers award 1972). Club: Argo. Lodge: B'nai B'rith. Fax: (202) 274-4130. E-mail: guttman@wcl.american.edu. Home: 14801 Pennfield Cir Silver Spring MD 20906-1580 Office: Am U Washington Coll Law 4801 Massachusetts Ave NW Washington DC 20016-8180

GUTTMAN, HELENE NATHAN, biomedical research consultant, transpersonal counselor, regression therapist; b. N.Y.C., July 21, 1930; d. Arthur and Mollie (Bergovoy) Nathan. BA, Bklyn. Coll., 1951; AM, Harvard U., 1956; MA, Columbia U., 1958; PhD, Rutgers U., 1960. Registered and cert. profl. past-life regression therapist; bd. cert. nutrition specialist; bd. cert. and registered hypnotherapist; registered and cert. transpersonal counselor. Rsch. technician Pub. Health Rsch. Inst., N.Y.C., 1951-52; control bacteriologist Burroughs-Wellcome, Inc., Tuckahoe, N.Y., 1952-53; vol. researcher Haskins Labs., N.Y.C., 1952-53; rsch. asst. Haskins Labs., 1953-56, rsch. assoc., 1956-60, staff microbiologist, 1960-64; lectr. dept. biology Queens Coll., N.Y.C., 1956-57; rsch. collaborator Brookhaven Nat. Labs., Upton, L.I., N.Y., 1958; guest investigator Botanisches Institut der Technisches Hochschule, Darmstadt, Germany, 1960; rsch. assoc. dept. biol. scis. Goucher Coll., Towson, Md., 1960-62; vis. asst. rsch. prof. dept. medicine Med. Coll. Va. Richmond, 1960-62; asst. prof., then assoc. prof. dept. biology NYU, 1962-67; from assoc. prof. to prof. dept. biol. scis. U. Ill.-Chgo., 1967-75, prof., 1969-75; prof. dept. microbiology U. Ill. Med. Sch., 1969-75; assoc. dir. for rsch. Urban Systems Lab. U. Ill., 1975; expert Office of Dir. Nat. Heart, Lung and Blood Inst., NIH, Bethesda, Md., 1975-77; coordinator rsch. resources Office Program Planning and Evaluation Nat. Heart, Lung and Blood Inst., NIH, 1977-79; dep. dir. Sci. Adv. Bd., Office of Adminstr., EPA, 1979-80; program coordinator, post-harvest tech., food safety and human nutrition, sci. and edn. adminstrn. USDA, 1980-83, assoc. dir. Beltsville Human Nutrition Rsch. Ctr., Agrl. Rsch. Svc., 1983-89; pres. HNG Assocs., 1983—; nat. animal care coord. Nat. Program Staff Agr. Rsch. Svc./USDA, Beltsville, Md., 1989-95; bd. advisors The Monroe Inst., 1993—. Sr. author: Experiments in Cellular Biodynamics, 1972; co-editor (procs.) First Joint USA-USSR Joint Symposium on Blood Transfusion, Moscow, 1976, DHEW Publ. No. (NIH) 78-1246, 1978; editorial bd. Jour. Protozoology, 1972-75, Jour. Am. Med. Women's Assn., 1978-81, Methods in Cell Science, 1994—; sr. editor: Science and Animals: Addressing Contemporary Issues, 1989; editor: Guidelines for Well-being of Rodents in Research, 1990, Rodents and Rabbits: Current Research Issues, 1994; (with others) Rodents and Rabbits: Addressing Current Issues, 1994; contbr. articles profl. jours. Mem. edn. com. Ill. Commn. on Status Women, 1974-75; cons. EPA, sci. adv. bd., 1974-79; bd. dirs. Du Page County Comprehensive Health Care Agy., 1974-75. Andelot fellow Harvard U., 1956, Rutgers scholar Rutgers U., 1960; recipient Thomas Jefferson Murray prize Theobald Smith Soc., 1959; spl. award for work in Germany Deutscher Forschungs Gemeinschaft, 1960; Fellow Dazian Found., 1956; research grantee. Fellow AAAS, Am. Inst. Chemists (com. chmn.), Am. Acad. Microbiology, N.Y. Acad. Scis.; mem. Soc. Am. Bacteriologists (pres.'s fellow 1957), Internat. Soc. for the Study of Subtile Energies and Energy Medicine, Assn. for Transpersonal Psychology (profl. mem.), Soc. for In Vitro Biology (chair constn. and bylaws com. 1994—, Disting. Svc. award 1995), Tissue Culture Assn. (com. chmn. Nat. Capital Area br. 1988-90), Am. Soc. Neurochemistry, Am. Soc. Biol. Chemistry and Molecular Biology, Neuroscis. Soc., Am. Soc. Microbiologists, Am. Soc. Cell Biology (past com. chmn.), Am. Soc. Clni. Nutrition, Soc. Protozoology (past mem. exec. com., past jour. editl. bd.), Assn. Women in Sci. (past mem. exec. bd., past com. chmn.), Fed. Orgn. Profl. Women (past task force chmn., past pres.), Univ. and Coll. Women Ill. (past v.p.), Am. Running and Fitness Assn. (bd. dirs., mem. editl. bd., mem. bd. advisors 1993-95), Assn. Past Life Rsch. and Therapy, Sigma Xi, Sigma Delta Epsilon (past coord. regional ctrs.). Home and Office: 5607 Mclean Dr Bethesda MD 20814-1021 *Personal philosophy: If it's worth having, it's worth fighting for.*

GUTTMAN, IRVING ALLEN, opera stage director; b. Chatham, Ont., Can., Oct. 27, 1928; s. Shea and Bernetta (Schaffer) G. Opera student, Royal Conservatory Music, Toronto, 1947-52; LittD (hon.), U. Winnipeg, 1996. Asst. to Herman Geiger Torel of Can. Opera Co., Toronto, 1948-52; dir., under Pauline Donalda Montreal (Que., Can.) Opera Guild, 1959-68; artistic dir. Edmonton Opera, Manitoba Opera; mem. adv. com. Can. Coun. Founding artistic dir., Vancouver (B.C., Can.) Opera Assn., 1960-74, artistic dir., Edmonton (Alta., Can.) Opera Assn., from 1966, Man. (Can.) Opera Assn., Winnipeg, from 1972; dir. numerous TV productions of opera, including first full-length TV opera for, CBC French Network, 1953, operatic productions for numerous U.S. opera cos., also Can. and European cos.; founding artistic dir., Opera Group, Courtenay Youth Music Camp; author: The Unlikely Pioneer-David Watmough, 1987. Decorated Centennial medal, Queen Elizabeth Jubilee medal, Order of Can., Alberta Govt. award of Excellence, 1989, Gov. Gen.'s Can.'s 125th medal for contbn. to arts in Can., Opera Am. Achievement award for 25 yrs. of disting. svc., 1996; named to Edmonton Hall of Fame, 1989, Vancouver Hall of Fame, 1994, Montreal Hall of Fame, 1996. Mem. Canadian Equity, Am. Guild Musical Artists.

GUTTMAN, STEVEN J., real estate company executive. Grad. with honors, U. Pitts.; JD with honors, George Washington U. With Fed. Realty Investment Trust, Rockville, Md., 1972—, dir. acquisitions, 1972-75, COO, 1975-79, mng. trustee, 1979-80, pres., CEO, trustee, 1980—. Bd. advisors George Washington U. Law Sch.; mem. Real Estate adv. bd., mem. exec. com., chmn. membership program com. Wharton Sch. U. Pa. Mem. Internat. Coun. Shopping Ctrs. (trustee 1991-97), Nat. Assn. Real Estate Investment Trusts (bd. govs., chmn., mem. exec. com.). Office: Fed Realty Investment Trust 1626 E Jefferson St Rockville MD 20852

GUTWIRTH, MARCEL MARC, French literature educator; b. Antwerp, Belgium, Apr. 11, 1923; s. Jacob Nahum and Frieda (Willner) G.; m. Madelyn Katz, June 20, 1948; children: Eve, Sarah, Nathanael. Student, NYU, 1941-42; AB, Columbia, 1947, MA, 1948, PhD, 1950. Mem. faculty Haverford (Pa.) Coll., 1948-87, William R. Kenan, Jr. prof. French lit., 1977-82, John Whitehead prof., 1983-87; Disting. Prof. Grad. Ctr. CUNY, 1987-94, exec. officer PhD program in French, 1987-93; vis. prof. Johns Hopkins U., 1967, Queens Coll., 1968, Bryn Mawr Coll., 1969, 76; Andrew Mellon vis. prof. humanities Tulane U., 1980. Author: Molière ou l'Invention Comique, 1966, Jean Racine: Un Itinéraire Poétique, 1970, Stendhal, 1971, Michel de Montaigne ou le Pari d'Exemplarité, 1977, Un Merveilleux sans Eclat: La Fontaine ou la Poésie Exilée, 1987, Laughing Matter, 1993. Bd. dirs. Childbirth Edn. Assn. Greater Phila., 1961-64. With AUS, 1943-46, ETO. Fulbright postdoctoral fellow Paris, 1953-54, Am. Coun. Learned Socs. fellow, 1964-65, Guggenheim fellow, 1971-72, 85, Nat. Humanities Ctr. fellow, 1985-86. Mem. ACLU, MLA (mem. editl. bd. publs. 1973-76), Am. Assn. Tchrs. of French. Jewish. Home: 640 Valley View Rd Ardmore PA 19003-1029

GUTZMAN, PHILIP CHARLES, aerospace executive, logistician; b. Salmon, Idaho, June 23, 1938; s. Lester Theodore and Mildred Cordelia (Hinchey) G.; m. Karen Diane Withington, June 17, 1957 (div. Sept. 30, 1957); m. Linda Ann Young, Aug. 28, 1960; children: Kevin Raeder, Lance. BS, U. Ariz., 1962, BA, 1962; MPA, U. Okla., 1977. Cert. Profl. Logistician. Hardrock miner Calera Mining Co., Cobalt, Idaho, 1955; enlisted U.S. Army, 1955-62, commd. 2d lt., 1962, advanced through grades to maj., 1970; supr. logistics engrng. Gen. Dynamics Land Systems, Detroit, 1983-84, chief advance systems, 1984-85; ops. mgr. Gen. Dynamics Svcs., St. Louis, 1985-87, dir. ground elec., 1987-88; dep. program mgr. Gen. Dynamics Svcs., Taif, Saudi Arabia, 1988-89; dir. logistics Gen. Dynamics Svcs., Detroit, 1989-91, program mgr. Saudi Arabian Tank program, 1992-93; sr. cons. Shipley Assocs., Boise, 1994—; adj. prof. mgmt. Boise State U., 1995. Author: Dictionary of Military Acronyms, 1990; contbr. numerous mil. articles to profl. jours., 1972—. Decorated Bronze Star (3), Purple Heart (5), Air medal, Meritorious Svc. medal (2), Cross of Gallantry with Palm. Mem. Soc. Logistics Engrs. (chpt. chmn. 1990-93, bd. dirs. 1992). Republican. Avocations: judo, fishing, reading. Office: Shipley Assocs 111 W 200 S Farmington UT 84025

GUTZWILLER, MARTIN CHARLES, theoretical physicist, research scientist; b. Basel, Switzerland, Oct. 12, 1925; married; 2 children. BS, Swiss Fed. Inst. Tech., 1947, MS, 1950; PhD in Physics, U. Kans., 1953; DSc honoris causa, U. Lausanne, Switzerland, 1995. Physicist Brown, Boveri & Co., Baden, Switzerland, 1950-51; with exploration and production divsn. Shell Devel. Co., Tex., 1953-60; with rsch. divsn. Internat. Bus. Machines, Zurich, 1960-63; IBM Corp., N.Y.C., 1963-70; rsch. sci., physicist IBM Corp., Yorktown Heights, N.Y., 1970-93, rsch. sci. emeritus, 1993—77; adj. prof. Columbia U., 1963-83, Yale U., 1993—. Fellow Am. Phys. Soc. (Dannie N. Heineman prize for math. physics 1993), Am. Acad. Arts and Sci.; mem. Nat. Acad. Sci. Achievements include research in propagation of waves, electron correlation in metals, quantum and classical mechanics, especially the chaotic phenomenon, celestial mechanics. Office: IBM TJ Watson Rsch Ctr PO Box 218 Yorktown Heights NY 10598-0218*

GUY, ANDREW A., lawyer; b. Kansas City, Mo., May 11, 1952. AB summa cum laude, Princeton U., 1974; JD, U. Va., 1979. Bar: Wash. 1979. With firm Bogle & Gates, P.L.L.C., Seattle, 1979—, ptnr., 1987—. Mem. ABA (litigation sect.), Wash. State Bar Assn. (litigation sect.), King County Bar Assn. (litigation sect., creditors' rights, real property, probate and trust sects.). Office: Bogle & Gates PLLC Two Union Sq 601 Union St Ste 4700 Seattle WA 98101-2346

GUY, ARTHUR WILLIAM, electrical engineering educator, researcher; b. Helena, Mont., Dec. 10, 1928; s. Arthur Jack and Evelyn (Hebb) G.; m. Vivian Ruth Walker, June 12, 1952; children: William, Sandra, Fred, Arla. BSEE, U. Wash., 1955, MSEE, 1957, PhDEE, 1966. Rsch. asst. elec. engrng. dept. U. Wash., Seattle, 1956-57; rsch. engr. Boeing Airplane Co., Seattle, 1957-63; cons. engr. rehab. medicine U. Wash., Seattle, 1963-65, rsch. engr. elec. engrng. dept., 1964-66, prof. elec. engrng. dept., rehab. medicine, 1966-83, prof., dir. bioelectromagnetics rsch. lab. Ctr. for Bioengineering, 1983-91, prof. emeritus, 1991—; cons. Bioelectromagnetics Cons., Seattle, 1991—; mem. telecomms. facilities adv. com. Seattle City Coun., 1991-92; mem. Sci. Adv. Group on Wireless Tech., 1993-95; active Wireless Tech. Rsch., L.L.C., 1993-97. Contbr. articles to profl. jours. Mem. Electromagnetic Field Task Force State Dept. Health, Olympia, Wash., 1991-92. Sgt. USAF, 1947-52. Recipient Achievement award Westinghouse Co., 1954, spl. award for the decade internat. Power Inst. for Med. and Biol. Rsch., 1980. Fellow AAAS, IEEE (life, vice chair SCC 28 stds. bd. 1989-94, mem. COMAR 1974-89, 92-98, chair COMAR 1987-89); mem. Nat. Coun. on Radiation Protection and Measurements (SC89 1992—), Bioelectromagnetic Soc. (charter mem., pres. 1984, d'Arsenval award 1987). Methodist. Home and Office: 18122 60th Pl NE Kenmore WA 98028-8901

GUY, BUDDY, blues guitarist; b. Lettsworth, La., July 30, 1936; m. Began to play guitar professionally in Chgo. Chgo., 1957—; toured widely, performing in internat. blues & folk festivals, concert halls, clubs; owner, Legends bar, Chgo. Legends Bar, Chgo. Recordings include Stone Crazy, 1965, With the Blues, 1965, Hoodoo Man Blues, 1966, Its My Life Baby, 1966, Coming at You, 1968, A Man and His Blues, 1968, I Left My Blues in San Francisco, 1968, This is Buddy Guy, Blues Today, 1968, In the Beginning, 1971, Hold That Plane, 1972, Buddy Guy & Junior Wells Play the Blues, 1972, Hot & Cool, 1979, I Was Walking Through the Woods, Got to Use Your Head, 1979, Dollar Done Fell, 1980, Drinkin' TNT, Smoking Dynamite, 1981, DJ Play My Blues, 1982, Buddy Guy, 1983, Damn Right, I've Got the Blues, 1991 (Grammy award Best Contemporary Blues Recording), Alone and Acoustec, 1991, Feels Like Rain, 1992 (Grammy award Best Contemporary Blues Album 1994), Live in Montreux, 1992, My Time After Awhile, 1992, Slippin' In (Grammy award Best Contemporary Blues Recording 1995), Buddy Guy Live "The Real Deal", 1996, Heavy Love, 1998, Buddy's Baddest, The Best of Buddy Guy, 1999. Recipient Century award Billboard Mag., 1993, grammay award for best contemporary blues recording "Stevie Ray Vaughan Shuffle", 1997 (with B.B. King, Bonnie Raitt, Dr. John and others). Office: The Cameron Orgn Inc 2001 W Magnolia Blvd Ste E Burbank CA 91506-1704

GUY, ELEANOR BRYENTON, writer; b. Pitts., Sept. 6, 1930; d. Lloyd Charles and Verda Eleanor (Hooper) Bryenton; m. Daniel Sowers Guy, Dec. 22, 1962; children: Stanley, Sharon. BA, Ohio Wesleyan U., 1953. Program dir. Cleve. Met. YWCA, Lakewood, Ohio, 1953-56, ctr. dir., 1956-57; residence dir., mem. faculty St. Luke's Hosp. Sch. Nursing, Shaker Heights, Ohio, 1957-59; pers. asst., counselor Acacia Mutual Life Ins. Co., Washington, 1959-62; admissions counselor Ohio No. U., Ada, 1963-64; freelance writer, photographer Kenton (Ohio) Times, 1984-88, Ada Herald, 1988-96; coord. external affairs, editor the Writ, Pettit Coll. of Law, Ohio No. U., 1995-96. Sec. bd. trustees, chmn. pub. rels. com. Ada Pub. Libr., 1982-86; mem. pub. rels. com., bd. dirs. Hardin County Alcohol and Drug Abuse Ctr., Kenton, 1989-92; chmn. publicity Town and Gown Planning Com., Ada, 1988; tchr., mem. co-chair edn. com., mem. missions com., mem. adminstrv. coun. local ch., mem. centennial com., 1985—; lay del. to West Ohio Ann. conf. Mem. AAUW (pres. local br. 1978-80), Ohio No. U. Women (parliamentarian, pub. rels. chair Christmas Arts Festival 1990-96), P.E.O. (v.p. 1994-96, sec. 1998—), Twice Ten Art Club (pres. 1984-85, 90-91, 97-98, sec. 1988-89). Methodist. Avocations: photography, travel, music.

GUY, JASMINE, actress; b. Boston. Actress TV show A Different World; film debut in School Daze, 1988, starred in films Harlem Nights, 89, Kla, 1995, American Dream, 1996, Cat's Don't Dance (voice), 1997, Perfect Crime, 1997, Lillie, 1999, Guinevere, 1999; appeared in Broadway mus. Leader of the Pack, The Wiz (revival), Grease, 1997 and Off-Broadway prodn. Beehive; TV credits include Fame, A Killer Among Us; TV Spl. Stompin at the Savoy, 1992; TV mini-series Queen, 1993, A Century of Women, 1994; writer short stories, poems; co-wrote episode of A Different World. Office: Innovative Artists Talent and Lit Agy Ste 2850 1999 Avenue Of The Stars Los Angeles CA 90067-4612*

GUY, MILDRED DOROTHY, retired secondary school educator; b. Brunswick, Ga., 1929; d. John and Mamie Paul (Smith) Floyd; m. Charles H. Guy, Aug. 18, 1956 (div. 1979); 1 child, Rhonda Lynn. *Mildred Dorothy Guy, retired secondary school educator, the fifth child of six children, was born in Brunswick, Georgia to John and Mamie Paul (Smith) Floyd. Her successful career was impacted by the teachings of her parents. Her father worked as a pile driver operator for a bridge-building construction company. Her mother, a housewife, instilled in her children high moral and ethical standards. On August 18, 1956, she married Charles H. Guy, Jr. (divorced 1979). Her only child is Rhonda Lynn, who married Brian D. Phillips. They are her two major sources of encouragement.* BA in Social Sci., Savannah State Coll., 1949; MA in Am. History, Atlanta U., 1952; postgrad., U. So. Calif., U. Colo. Tchr. social studies L.S. Ingraham H.S., Sparta, Ga.; tchr. English and social studies North Jr. H.S., Colorado Springs, 1958-84, ret., 1984; cooperating tchr. Tchr. Edn. Program, Col. Coll., 1968-72. Fund raiser for Citizens for Theatre Auditorium, Colorado Springs, 1979; bd. dirs. Urban League, 1971-75; del. to County and State Dem. Conv., 1972, 76, 80, 84, 92, 96; mem. Pike's Peak C.C. Coun., 1976-83; mem. Colo. Springs Opera Coun. of 500, 1984-88; mem. nominating com. Wagon Wheel coun. Girl Scouts U.S.A., 1985-87; active Fine Arts Ctr., Pikes Peak Hospice; mem. St. John's Bapt. Ch., former sanctuary choir mem.; mem. Svcs. of Charity (local and nat.). Recipient Viking award North Jr. H.S., 1973, Woman of Distinction award Girl Scouts Wagon Wheel Coun., 1989, 94; Outstanding Black Woman of Colorado Springs award, 1975; named Pacesetter, Atlanta U., 1980-81, Outstanding Black Educator of Yr., Black Educators of Dist. II, Colorado Springs, 1984; Outstanding Ednl. Svc. award Colo. Dept. and State Bd. Edn., 1983; Dedicated Svc. award Pikes Peak C.C., 1983, Outstanding Cmty. Leadership award Alpha Phi Alpha, 1985, Award Colo. Black Woman for Polit. Action, 1985, Sphinx award, 1986; named in recognition sect. Salute to Women, Colorado Springs Gazette Telegraph, 1986; Wall of Fame honoree Nat. Women's Hall of Fame, 1997. Mem. LWV (Colo. chpt.), Negro Hist. Assn., Women's Found. Colo., NAACP (life mem., Golden Heritage), NEA, AAUW, Colo. Coun. Social Studies Assn. Study Afro-Am. Life and History, Women's Ednl. Soc. Colo. Coll. (bd. mgrs. 1992-98), Alpha Delta Kappa, Alpha Kappa Alpha (pres. Iota Beta Omega chpt. 1984-85, Chpt. Pres. award 1985). Home: 3132 Constitution Ave Colorado Springs CO 80909-2177

GUY, RALPH B., JR., federal judge; b. Detroit, Mich., Aug. 30, 1929; s. Ralph B. and Shirley (Skladd) G. AB, U. Mich., 1950, JD, 1953. Bar: Mich. 1953. Sole practice Dearborn, Mich., 1954-55; asst. corp. counsel City of Dearborn, 1955-58, corp. counsel, 1958-69; chief asst. U.S. Atty.'s Office (ea. dist.), Detroit and Mich., 1969-70, U.S. Atty., 1970-76; judge U.S. Dist. Ct. (ea. dist.) Mich., Ann Arbor, 1976-85; judge U.S. Ct. Appeals (6th cir.), Ann Arbor, 1985-1994, sr. judge, 1994—; treas. Detroit-Wayne County Bldg. Authority, 1966-73; chmn. sch. study com. Dearborn Bd. Edn., 1973; mem. Fed. Exec. Bd., 1970—, bd. dirs., 1971-73. Recipient Civic Achievement award Dearborn Rotary, 1971; Distinguished Alumni award U. Mich., 1972. Mem. ABA (state chmn. sect. local govt. 1965-70), Fed. Bar Assn. (pres. 1974-75), State Bar Mich. (commr. 1975—), Detroit Bar Assn., Dearborn Bar Assn. (pres. 1959-60), Am. Judicature Soc., Nat. Inst. Municipal Law Officers (chmn. Mich. chpt. 1964-69), Mich. Assn. Municipal Attys. (pres. 1962-64), Mich. Municipal League, Out-County Suprs. Assn. (pres. 1965), Phi Alpha Delta, Lambda Chi Alpha. Club: U. Mich. Alumni (local pres. Dearborn 1961-62). Lodge: Rotary (local pres. 1973-74). Office: US Ct Appeals PO Box 7910 200 E Liberty St Rm 226 Ann Arbor MI 48107-7910*

GUY, RICHARD P., state supreme court justice; b. Coeur d'Alene, Idaho, Oct. 24, 1932; s. Richard H. and Charlotte M. Guy; m. Marilyn K. Guy, Nov. 16, 1963; children: Victoria, Heidi, Emily. JD, Gonzaga U., 1959. Bar: Wash. 1959, Hawaii 1988. Former judge Wash. Superior Ct., Spokane, from 1977; chiefjustice Wash. Supreme Ct., Olympia, 1998—. Capt. USAS. Mem. Wash. State Bar, Spokane County Bar Assn. Roman Catholic. Office: Wash Supreme Ct Temple of Justice PO Box 40929 Olympia WA 98504-0929

GUY, SHARON KAYE, state agency executive; b. Nashville, Apr. 5, 1958; d. Dallas Hearold and Elizabeth Jean (Towns) Gregory; 1 child, Anthony Lee. Grad. high sch., Chgo. Clk. Pub. Health dept. State of Tenn., Nashville, 1979-84, office mgr. Health Facilities commn., 1984-92; asst. Legis. Svcs., Nashville, 1992-95; rep. State Ins., Nashville, 1995-98, mem. commerce ins. contractors bd., 1998-99; commerce and ins. adminstr. permits and license State Fire Marshal's Office, 1999—; acct. Bryant Guy Constrn., Nashville, 1984—. Blood drive coord. ARC, Nashville, 1984—; campaign vol. United Way, Nashville, 1984—; vol. State Community Coll., 1990—, Nashville Tech., 1991—. Baptist. Avocations: snow and water skiing, motor bikes. Home: 121 Candle Woods Dr Hendersonville TN 37075-4452 Office: 500 James Robertson Pkwy Nashville TN 37243-1220

GUYER, BERNARD, maternal and child health educator. Assoc. prof. maternal and hild health Harvard U. Sch. Pub. Health, 1986-89, dir. MPH program, head injury prevention ctr., 1986-89; officer, med. epidemiologist Ctr. for Disease Control; prof., chmn. dept. maternal and child health Johns Hopkins U., Sch. Hygiene and Pub. Health, 1989—; dir. maternal and child health agy., State Mass. Dept. Pub. Health, 1979-86. Contbr. articles to profl. jours. Mem. Inst. Medicine Nat. Acad. Sci. *

GUYER, CHARLES GRAYSON, II, psychologist; b. High Point, N.C., May 22, 1949; s. Charles Grayson Sr. and Mildred Louise (Wrokman) G.; m. E.R. Ward, June 24, 1986; children: Charles Grayson III, Jarvis Griffith. BA, Appalachian State U., 1972, MA, 1974; EdD, Coll. William & Mary, 1978. Resident No. Wyo. Mental Health, Buffalo, 1978-80; pvt. practice pvt. practice, High Point, N.C., 1980-83, Greensboro, N.C., 1988-98; chief sch. psychologist Perquimans County Schs., Hertford, N.C., 1998—; pres. Am. Bd. Family Psychology, 1992-94. Contbr. articles to profl. jours., chpts. to books. Lt. USN, 1983-88. Fellow APA, Am. Soc. Clin. Hypnosis, Acad. Family Psychologists (pres. 1995-96), Acad. Counseling Psychology; mem. Am. Group Psychotherapy Assn., Nat. Assn. Sch. Psychologists, Va. Acad. Clin. Psychologists, Va. Psychol. Assn., N.C. Soc. Clin. Hypnosis, Guilford County Psychol. Assn. (treas. 1997-98), Soc. Clin. Exptl. Hypnosis. Methodist. Avocations: running, reading. Home: 803 Grubb St Hertford NC 27944

GUYER, HEDY-ANN KLEIN, special education educator; b. Phila., Dec. 25, 1947; d. Edward Chuck Klein and Gladys Selma (Shapiro) Sussman; m. Eugene August Guyer, Aug. 24, 1980. BS in Secondary Edn., St. Joseph's U., Phila., 1981; MEd in Spl. Edn., Beaver Coll., 1996. Cert. in social studies, elem. edn., spl. edn. of mentally and/or physically handicapped, Pa. Tchr. spl. edn. Sch. Dist. Phila., 1996—. Mem. ASCD, Women in Edn., George Washington H.S. Alumni Assn., B'nai B'rith (educators unit), Coun. Exceptional Children. Home: 1033 Bloomfield Ave Philadelphia PA 19115-4829

GUYKER, WILLIAM CHARLES, JR., electrical engineer, researcher; b. Donora, Pa., Aug. 21, 1933; s. William Charles G. and Mary Kurylak (Guyker); m. Alice Jane Burns, June 26, 1971; 1 dau., Patricia Lynn. BSEE, MIT, 1959. Registered profl. engr., Pa. Various engrng. positions, 1959-68; with Allegheny Power Service Corp., Greensburg, Pa., 1968—, prin. engr. research and devel., 1985-90, prin. engr., engrng. group, 1990-91, mgr. R&D, 1991-96, cons. R&D, 1996-99, corp. rsch. dir., 1999—; mgr. EPRI Tech. Transfer, 1982—; adj. prof. W.Va. U., Morgantown, 1970—; lectr. U. Pitts., 1970—; accreditor Accreditation Bd. for Engrng. and Tech., N.Y.C., 1977—; cons., 1996—. Contbr. in field. Served with U.S. Army, 1952-55. Fellow IEEE (life, chmn. Pitts. sect. 1973-74 Power Group award, Centennial medal 1984); mem. Am. Mgmt. Assn., AAAS. Republican. Episcopalian. Lodge: Elks. Research in pioneering developments of transmission tech., mining, power plant work, customer applications, multiple system control and comm. application; expertise in Acid Rain, Global Warming, EMF, Power Quality, and other issues developed at sites and with engineering and regulatory requirements. Office: Allegheny Power Svc Corp 800 Cabin Hill Dr Greensburg PA 15601-1689 *Education is key to understanding energy and demystifying junk science.*

GUYMON, GARY LEROY, civil engineering educator, consultant; b. Farmington, N.Mex., Nov. 5, 1935; s. Leland W. and Grace E. (Cumming) G.; m. Lucinda A. Kemmis, June 11, 1988; children by previous marriage: Gary Jr., Richard, Marisa, Michael. BS, U. Calif., Davis, 1966, MS, 1967, PhD, 1970. Asst. civil engr. Calif. Dept. Water Resources, L.A., 1955-66; asst. rsch. engr. U. Calif., Davis, 1969-71; assoc. prof. U. Alaska, Fairbanks, 1971-74; prof. U. Calif., Irvine, 1974-94, chmn. dept. civil engrng., 1984-88, prof. emeritus, 1994—; mem. coordinating bd. U. Calif. Water Resources Ctr., Berkeley, 1985-89; del. Univs. Coun. on Water Resources, Carbondale, Ill., 1980-94. Author: Unsaturate Zone Hydrology, 1994; contbr. numerous articles to profl. jours.; assoc. editor Advances in Water Resources,

Southampton, U.K., 1981-89. Fellow ASCE; mem. Am. Geophys. Union, U.S. Com. on Large Dams, Phi Beta Kappa, Tau Beta Pi, Chi Epsilon. Republican. Avocations: woodworking, skiing, physical fitness. Office: U Calif Dept Civil & Environ Engring Irvine CA 92717

GUYNES, DEMI See MOORE, DEMI

GUYNN, ROBERT WILLIAM, psychiatrist, educator; b. Streator, Ill., Oct. 27, 1942; s. William Digby and Helen Louise (Dancey) G. BA, Mich. State U., 1963; MD, Johns Hopkins U., 1967. Diplomate Am. Bd. Psychiatry and Neurology. Clin. fellow Nat. Inst. of Mental Health, Washington, 1970-73; asst. prof. Dept. of Psychiatry and Behaviorial Scis. U. Tex., Houston, 1973-76, assoc. prof., 1976-83, vice-chmn., prof. psychiatry, 1983-87, interim chmn., 1987-89, chmn., 1989—; dir. U. Tex. Mental Scis. Inst., Houston, 1987—; exec. dir. Harris County Psychiat. Ctr., 1988—; sr. examiner Am. Bd. Psychiatry and Neurology, 1997—. Contbr. articles to profl. jours. and book chpts.; mem. editl. bd. Internat. Rev. Psychiatry, 1988-93, editor-in-chief, 1989-93. Bd. dirs. Vols. of Am., Houston, 1982-88, Harris County Mental Health Assn., Houston, 1992-97. Full surgeon USPHS, 1970-73. Fellow Am. Psychiat. Assn.; mem. Am. Coll. Psychiatrists, Am. Soc. Biol. Chemistry, Tex. Rsch. Soc. on Alcoholism (pres. 1985-87), Tex. Soc. of Am. Assn. Psychiat. Adminstrs. (treas. 1990-91, pres. 1992-93), Biochem. Soc., Rsch. Soc. on Alcoholism, Houston Psychiat. Soc. (v.p. 1989-90, pres. 1991-92), Harris County Med. Soc. (bd. ethics 1989-92), Tex. Dept. Mental Health and Mental Retardation (med. adv. com., 1997—). Avocation: printmaking. Office: U Tex Health Sci Ctr PO Box 20708 Houston TX 77225-0708

GUYON, JOHN CARL, retired university administrator; b. Washington, Pa., Oct. 16, 1931; s. Carl Alexander and Sara Myrle (Bumgarner) G.; m. Elizabeth Joyce Smith, Nov. 12, 1955; children—Cynthia Joan, John Carl, II. B.A., Washington and Jefferson Coll., 1953; M.S., Toledo U., 1958; Ph.D., Purdue U., 1961. Mem. faculty U. Mo., 1961-71, prof. chemistry, chmn. dept., 1970-71; prof. chemistry, chmn. dept. Memphis State U., 1971-74; dean Coll. Sci., So. Ill. U., Carbondale, 1974-75; dean Coll. Sci., So. Ill. U. (Grad. Sch.), assoc. v.p. research, 1976-80, v.p. acad. affairs and research, from 1980; pres. So. Ill. U., 1987-95, chancellor, 1996-97; ret., 1997. Author: Aanlytical Chemistry, 1965, Qualitative Analysis, 1966, Solution Equilbria, 1969; also articles, abstracts.; Gen. editor: Instrumental Methods of Analysis. Served with AUS, 41954-56. Eli Lilly Co. fellow, 1959-61; Owens Ill. Co. fellow, 1958; Jesse W. Lazear scholar, 1953. Mem. Am. Chem. Soc., AAAS, Phi Beta Kappa, Sigma Xi, Phi, Lambda Upsilon.

GUYOT, JAMES FRANKLIN, political science educator; s. Robert P. and Lucille Eleanor (Fritsch) G.; m. Dorothy Jean Hess, Dec. 31, 1960; children: Erik Robert, Maria Khin Khin, Daniel Karl. BA in Polit. Sci., Mich. State U., 1953; AM in Polit. Sci., Yale U., 1954, PhD in Polit. Sci., 1961. Instr. in polit. sci. Swarthmore Coll., 1959-60, U. Conn., Storrs, 1960-61; rsch. student U. Rangoon, Burma, 1961-62; asst. prof. polit. sci. UCLA, 1963-68; vis. lectr. in govt. Columbia U., N.Y.C., 1968-69, assoc. prof. govt., 1969-72; assoc. prof., then prof. polit. sci. and pub. affairs Baruch Coll., CUNY, 1973—; asst. in instrn. polit. sci. Yale U., New Haven, 1956; vis. lectr. U. Malaya, 1966-67, U. Pa., 1970; rsch. assoc. So. Asian Inst., Columbia U., 1968-82; assoc. faculty mem. indsl. engring. Asian Inst. Tech., 1982-83; JFK Found. prof. Sch. Bus. & Pub. Adminstrn., Nat. Inst. Devel. Adminstrn., 1982-83, Commerce & Accountancy Human Resource Inst., Thammasat U., 1983; cons. in field. Co-author: Population, Politics, and the Future of Southern Asia, 1974; mem. editorial Jour. Comparative Adminstrn., 1969-73; referee for various manuscripts; contbr. revs., articles to profl. publs. Grantee John F. Kennedy Found.-Fulbright Found., 1982-83, U.S. Action, 1976-77, Rockefeller Found., 1968-70; Cowles grad. fellow, 1953-54, Falk grad. fellow, 1954-56, Fulbright fellow, 1961-62. Mem. AAAS, ACLU, ASPA (mem. exec. com. comparative adminstrv. group 1967-70), Am. Polit. Sci. Assn., Assn. for Asian Studies, Soc. for Values in Higher Edn., Asia Soc., Amnesty Internat., Yale Russian Chorus. Avocations: running, singing, sailing. Home: 134 Conduit St Annapolis MD 21401-2625 Office: CUNY Sch Pub Affairs 17 Lexington Ave New York NY 10010-5518

GUYTON, ARTHUR CLIFTON, physician, educator; b. Oxford, Miss., Sept. 8, 1919; s. Billy Sylvester and Mary Katherine (Smallwood) G.; m. Ruth Alice Weigle, June 12, 1943; children—David Lee, Robert Allan, John Richard, Steven William, Catherine A., Jean M., Douglas, James, Thomas, Gregory Paul. A.B., U. Miss., 1939; M.D., Harvard, 1943. Intern Mass. Gen. Hosp., 1943, asst. resident, 1946; acting asso. prof. physiology U. Tenn. Med. Sch., 1947; asso. prof. pharmacology U. Miss. Med. Sch., Oxford, 1947-48; prof. chmn. dept. physiology and biophysics U. Miss. Med. Sch., Jackson, 1948-89, prof. emeritus, 1989—; mem. cardiovascular research study sect. NIH, 1954-58, mem. physiology tng. com., 1958-64, chmn., 1961-64; mem. adv. council Nat. Heart and Lung Inst., 1971-75; mem. physiology com. Nat. Bd. Med. Examiners, 1960-64, chmn., 1962-64. Author: Function of the Human Body, 6th rev. edit., 1984, Textbook of Medical Physiology, 9th rev. edit., 1996, Circulatory Physiology: Cardiac Output and Its Regulation, rev. edit., 1973, Circulatory Physiology II: Dynamics of the Body Fluids, Circulatory Physiology III: Arterial Pressure and Hypertension, 1980; Human Physiology and Mechanisms of Disease, 6th rev. edit., 1997; contbr. articles to profl. jours.; editor Internat. Rev. Physiology. Served in med. research USN, 1944-46. Recipient commendation by Army for wartime research, One of 10 Outstanding Young Men of Am. award U.S. Jr. C. of C., 1951, Ida Gould award AAAS, 1959, Wiggers award Am. Physiol. Soc., 1972, ALZA award Biomedical Engring. Soc., 1972, Ross McIntyre award, 1972; Disting. Research award Am. Heart Assn., 1976; Einthoven award Leiden, Holland, 1979; CIBA award for hypertension research Am. Heart Assn., 1980, Merck internat. award for hypertension research, 1984, Sci. Achievement award AMA, 1990, ACP award, 1992. Fellow Am. Coll. Cardiology (v.p. 1965-66), AAAS; mem. Am. Heart Assn., Fedn. Am. Socs. Exptl. Biology (pres. 1975-76), Am. Physiol. Soc. (pres. 1974-75), Miss. Acad. Sci. (pres. 1963-64), So. Soc. for Clin. Research (pres. 1956-57), Circulation Soc. (chmn. 1970), Miss. Heart Assn. (pres. 1955-56), Russian Acad. Natural Sci., Alpha Omega Alpha, Pi Kappa Pi, Sigma Alpha Epsilon, Tau Kappa Alpha, Alpha Kappa Kappa, Phi Eta Sigma, Alpha Epsilon Delta, Omicron Delta Kappa. Home: 234 Meadow Rd Jackson MS 39206-3527 Office: Miss Med Ctr PO Box Dept Physiology Jackson MS 39216

GUYTON, SAMUEL PERCY, retired lawyer; b. Jackson, Miss., Mar. 20, 1937; s. Earl Ellington and Eulalia (Reynolds) G.; m. Jean Preston, Oct. 11, 1959; children: Tamara Reynolds, William Preston, David Sage. BA, Miss. State U., 1959; LLB, U. Va., 1965. Bar: Colo. 1965, U.S. Dist. Ct. Colo. 1965, U.S. Tax Ct. 1977, U.S. Ct. Appeals (10th cir.) 1965, U.S. Ct. Appeals (5th cir.) 1981. Ptnr. Holland & Hart, Denver, 1965-92, ret., 1992; mem. faculty Am. Law Inst. ABA, 1976-88bd. dirs. Royal St. Corp., Royal St. Utah Inc., Deer Valley Ski Resort. Co-author: Cattle Owners Tax Manual, 1984, Supplement to Federal Taxation of Agriculture, 1983, Colorado Estate Planning Desk Book, 1984, 90; contbr. articles to profl. jours., mags.; bd. advs. Agrl. Law Jour., 1978-82; mem. editl. bd. Jour. Agrl. Tax and Law, 1983-92. Sec., trustee Colo. Hist. Found., 1971-92, pres., 1983-87; trustee Music Assn. Aspen and Aspen Music Festival, 1980-88; precinct com. chmn. Dem. Party, 1968-70; mem. Gov.'s Mansion preservation com., 1989-92; bd. advisors Coll. Arts and Scis., Miss. State U., 1996-98; mem. com. govt. and legal affairs Hampshire Coll.; chmn. com. on legis. Woodmen of the World, 1972—. Fellow Am. Coll. Tax Counsel (bd. regents 1985-92, chmn., pres. 1989-91), Am. Tax Policy Inst. (trustee 1989-92, v.p. 1989-92); mem. ABA (sect. taxation 1967-92, chmn. sect.'s com. on agr. 1980-82), Colo. Bar Assn. (tax coun. 1983-86, sec. 1983, chmn. 1985-86), Colo. Bar Found., Greater Denver Tax Csls. Assn. (chmn. 1978), Law Club Denver, Little River Lectures Assn. (bd. dirs., v.p. 1985-96, pres. 1996—), Am. Alpine Club (life), Colo. Mountain Club (life, planned giving com.), Eleanore Mullen Weckbaugh Found. (trustee 1983-95), Humphreys Found. (sec., treas., trustee), Colo. Trail Found. (trustee 1987-99), Colo. Mountain Club Found. (dir.), Colo. Hist. Soc. (bd. dirs., chmn. nominating com.), Holland & Hart Found. (bd. dirs., pres.). Mem. Unity Ch. Home and Office: 12345 W 19th Pl Lakewood CO 80215-2516 *To live fully and consciously in the present is both challenge and reward.*

GUZAK, DEBRA ANN, special education educator; b. Blue Island, Ill., Jan. 11, 1963; d. Robert Joseph and Angeline (Kozak)G. BS in Edn., Ea. Ill. U., 1985; MEd, U. Ill., 1993; postgrad., U. Wis., Whitewater, U. Manosh, Frankston, Australia. Cert. tchr., early childhood spl. edn., Ill. Spl. edn. tchr. Southwest Cook County Coop., Oak Forest, Ill., 1985; early childhood specialist Sunnybrook Sch. Dist. # 171, Lansing, Ill., 1985—, intern in administrn., 1992-93; pvt. tutor, Lansing, 1985—; track coach Heritage Mid. Sch., Lansing, 1990—. Editor: Share a Story, 1992. Vol. Little City, Paletine, Ill., 1986—, Orland Park (Ill.) Spl. Recreation; fundraiser Misericordia/Heart of Mercy, Chgo., 1986—; steering com. Young Hearts Am. Heart Assn., Chgo., 1987-91; co-chmn. fashion show seating com. Ronald McDonald House, Chgo., 1994, 95, 97, 98. Grantee Ill. State Bd. Edn., 1990; recipient Educator of Yr. award Lansing Rotary, 1996, Educators Making a Difference award South Suburban Chgo. chpt. Children and Adults with Attention Deficit Disorders. Mem. Assn. Supervision and Curriculum Devel., Coun. Exceptional Children (divsn. early childhood, svc. award 1981-86), Ind. Order Foresters. Republican. Roman Catholic. Avocations: water sports, winter sports, golf, fine dining, theater. Home: 3205 186th St Lansing IL 60438-3233

GUZAK, KAREN JEAN WAHLSTROM, artist; b. Cambridge, Mass., May 21, 1939; d. Ernest E. and Kathryn E. (Kemp) Wahlstrom; m. Steven V. Guzak, Aug. 29, 1959 (div. 1983); children: Gretchen, Christopher, Lauren. BS, Univ. Colo., 1961; BFA, Cornish Sch. Allied Arts, Seattle, 1976. Pres. Karen Guzak Inc., Seattle, 1982—. One-woman shows in various exhibits including, Foster White Gallery, Seattle, 1981, 84, 87, 89, 91, 94, 96, 98, Davidson Galleries, Seattle, 1981, 84, 87, Tom Luttrell Gallery, San Francisco, 1981, Harris Gallery, Houston, 1982, Laura Russo Gallery, Portland, Oreg., 1987, 89, 91, 96, Musee Hyacinth Rigaud, Perpignan, France, 1988; group exhibitions in various exhibits including Bklyn. Mus., 1981, Brentwood Gallery, St. Louis, 1982, Seattle Art Mus., 1983, San Francisco Mus., 1983, Portland Art Mus., 1985, Davidson Gallery, 1992, Stifel Fine Arts Ctr., Wheeling, W.Va., 1993, Bellevue (Wash.) Art Mus., 1988, 90, 95, 96, DeCordova Mus., 1991, Purdue U., 1995, U. Brighton, Eng., 1997, Bronx Mus., 1987, Portland Art Mus., 1997; represented in permanent collections Portland Art Mus., Jundt Mus. Gonzaga U., Brooklyn Mus., N.Y.C. Libr. Print Collection, Pratt Inst., City of SEattle, King County Wash.; pub. commns. So. Oreg. State Coll., King County Coun. Chambers, South Seattle Cmty. Coll. Mem. bd. commrs. King County Arts Commn., Seattle, 1981-86, commr., 1984-85; mem. arts adv. com. METRO Arts Program, Seattle, 1985-91; bd. dirs. Ctr. Contemporary Art, 1987-88; mem. contemporary coun. Seattle Art Mus., 1990-96; pres., developer Sunny Arms Coop., Seattle, 1988-90; co-developer, pres. Union Arts Coop., Seattle, 1992-93; pres. bd. dirs. Artist Trust, Seattle, 1996-99. Boettcher scholar Univ. Colo., 1957-61; recipient Housing Designs that Work award, Seattle Design Commn., 1991, Home of Yr. award, Seattle Times and AIA, 1994. Democrat. Home & Office: Karen Guzak Inc 707 S Snoqualmie St Ste 5A Seattle WA 98108-1700

GUZDA, HENRY PETER, industrial relations specialist; b. Stamford, Conn., Jan. 9, 1950; s. Henry and Marion (Wujcik) G. BA in History, Alliance Coll., 1971; MA in History, Edinboro U., 1974; postgrad., Cath. U., 1986—. Historian U.S. Dept. Labor, Washington, 1976-84, indsl. rels. specialist, 1984—; hist. advisor to U.S. Dept. Labor Libr.; dir. internat. visitor program Office of Am. Workplace, Washington, 1989—; cons. Readers Digest, Pleasantville, N.Y., 1993. Contbr. articles to profl. jours. Block capt. Neighborhood Watch, Foxwood Cmty. Assn., Burke, Va., 1986-92; chief steward Office of Am. Workplace, Am. Fedn. Govt. Employees, Washington, 1993-94. Mem. Indsl. Rels. Rsch. Assn. (exec. bd. D.C. chpt. 1989-94, pres. 1992-93, award 1993). Democrat. Achievements include research in tracing origins and development of new forms of work organization/labor-mgmt. coop., research in covering origins of equal employment opportunity programs in Dept. of Labor. Home: 5654 Sutherland Ct Burke VA 22015-1850 Office: Office Asst Sec for Policy Dept Labor 200 Constitution Ave NW Washington DC 20210-0001

GUZE, PHYLLIS ARLENE, internist, educator, academic administrator. MD, U. So. Calif., 1971. Resident in internal medicine Harbor UCLA Med. Ctr., fellow; dean of edn. UCLA, 1991-95, prof. medicine, vice chair, 1985—; chief dept. medicine West L.A. VA Med. Ctr., 1985—. Contbr. numerous articles to profl. jours. Recipient Disting. Tchr. award in clin. scis. Assn. Am. Med. Colls., 1995, Sherman M. Melinkoff Faculty award UCLA Sch. Medicine, 1995, Luckman Disting. Tchg. award, 1996, Disting. Tchr. award Alpha Omega Alpha, 1995. Mem. ACP, Am. Bd. of Internal Medicine (cert. com.), Assn. of Program Dirs. in Internal Medicine, Assn. of VA Chiefs of Medicine. Office: Chief Dept Medicine West LA VA Med Ctr 11301 Wilshire Blvd Los Angeles CA 90073-1003*

GUZE, SAMUEL BARRY, psychiatrist, educator; b. N.Y.C., Oct. 18, 1923; s. Jacob and Jenny (Berry) G.; m. Joy Lawrence Campbell, June 7, 1946; children: Jonathan, Ann. Student, CCNY, 1939-41; MD, Washington U., St. Louis, 1945. Diplomate Am. Bd. Internal Medicine, Am. Bd. Psychiatry and Neurology. Mem. faculty Washington U. Sch. Medicine, 1951—, prof. psychiatry, assoc. prof. medicine, 1964—, asst. to dean, 1965-71, vice chancellor for med. affairs, 1971-89, asst. dir. Psychiatry Clinic, 1951-55, dir. Psychiatry Clinic, 1955-75, head dept. psychiatry, 1975-89, 93-97, Spencer T. Olin prof., 1974—; pres. Washington U. Med. Center, 1971-89; mem. staff Barnes Hosp., St. Louis, 1951—, psychiatrist-in-chief, 1975-89, 93-97; mem. psychiat. staff Renard Hosp., 1953—, psychiatrist-in-chief, 1975-89, 93-97. Contbr. articles to profl. jours. Fellow ACP, Am. Psychiat. Assn., Royal Coll. Psychiatry, Am. Coll. Psychiatry; mem. AMA, Am. Fedn. for Clin. Rsch., Psychiat. Rsch. Soc., Am. Psychosomatic Soc., Assn. for Rsch. in Nervous and Mental Diseases, Am. Psychopathol. Soc., Soc. Biol. Psychiatry, Soc. Neurosci., Inst. of Medicine of NAS, Sigma Xi, Alpha Omega Alpha. Home: Apt 14A 710 S Hanley Rd Saint Louis MO 63105-2654 Office: 4940 Childrens Pl Saint Louis MO 63110-1002

GUZMA'N, ANA MARGARITA, university administrator; b. Havana, Cuba, June 12, 1947; came to U.S., 1960; d. Gabriel and Margarita (Gomez) G.; children: Sean, Ryan; m. Gilberto Sosa Ocañas, May 27, 1989. BS in Edn., Stout State U., Menomonie, Wis., 1968; MA in Sociology, Tex. So. U., 1974; EdD in Edn., U. Houston, 1979. Lic. tchr., Va., Tex., supt., Va., mid-mgmt. tchr., Tex., Va. Dir. bilingual edn. Goose Creek Ind. Sch. Dist., Houston, 1981-85, dir. program devel., 1985-86; dir. staff devel. Houston Ind. Sch. Dist., 1986-88, prin., 1988-89; dir. regional program Fairfax County Pub. Schs., Fairfax, Va., 1988-89; program officer NSF, Washington, 1990-92; fellow to chancellor, assoc. prof. edn. Tex. A&M U., Kingsville, 1992—, program dir. Alliances for Minority Participation, 1995-99; exec. v.p. Austin C.C., Cedar Park, Tex., 1993—; mem. Gov.'s Commn. on Lit., Tex., 1985-87; cons. N.Y. Pub. Schs., 1990, Edn. Devel. Corp., State Systems Inst., 1992; mem. Task Force for NSF State Systemic Initiatives. Author: Questions and Answers About Bilingual Education-Quality Education for Mentors, 1991, Science Strategies for Limited English Proficient Student, 1992. Mem. Assn. for Advancement of Mexican Americans, Houston, 1986-88, Hispanic Action Com., Washington, 1992—; mem. Supt. Minority Achievement Com., Fairfax County, 1980-92; vice-chair Mexican Am. Legal Def. Edn. Fund, L.A., 1988-92; bd. dirs. ERIC Clearinghouse, N.Y., 1991—; chair Pres. Clinton's Adv. Commn. Ednl. Excellence for Hispanic Ams., 1994—. Doctoral fellow HEW, Washington, 1975-78. Mem. Am. Ednl. Rsch. Assn., Nat. Assn. Bilingual Edn., Am. Assn. Sch. Adminstrs. Democrat. Roman Catholic. Avocations: reading, aerobics, swimming, travel. Office: Austin CCEVP Adminstrn Instl Advmts & Cmty Rels 5930 Middle Fiskville Rd Austin TX 78752-4341

GUZMAN, ARMANDO, electrical research engineer; b. Mazatlan, Mexico, Jan. 15, 1958; came to U.S., 1993; s. Armando and Concepcion (Casillas) G.; m. Claudia Uribe, Dec. 5, 1992; children: Elizabeth Andrea, Armando Daniel. BSEE with honors, U. Autonoma de Guadalajara, Mexico, 1979. Product engr. Burroughs of Mexico, Guadalajara, 1979-80; regional supr. Fed. Electricity Commn., Guadalajara, 1980-84; application engr. GE, Malvern, Pa., 1984-85; regional supr. Fed. Electricity Commn., Guadalajara, 1985-93; application engr. Schweitzer Engring. Labs., Pullman, Wash., 1993-94, rsch. engr., 1994—. Co-author, editor: Extra-High Voltage Transmission Line Protection, 1990. Mem. IEEE. Achievements include patent for development of a new ground directional relay for transmission line protection, of a very economical digital relay for transformer protection. Home: 525 NW Robert St Pullman WA 99163-3691 Office: Schweitzer Engring Labs 2350 NE Hopkins Ct Pullman WA 99163-5600

GUZMAN, RONALD A., federal judge. Magistrate judge U.S. Dist. Ct. (no. dist.) ill., 1990—. Office: US Dist Ct 1828 Dirksen Bldg 219 S Dearborn St Chicago IL 60604-1702

GUZY, CAROL, photojournalist. ADN, Northampton County Area C.C., Pa.; AAS in Photography, Art Inst. Ft. Lauderdale. Staff photographer The Miami Herald, 1980-88, The Washington Post, 1988—. Recipient Best Portfolio award Atlanta Seminar Photojournalism, 1982, 85, 90, Robert F. Kennedy award, 1984, Excellence citation Overseas Press Club, 1986, Pulitzer Prize in spot news photography, 1986, 95, Leica Excellence medal, 1994; named Newspaper Photographer of Yr. Nat. Press Photographer Assn., 1989, 92, Photographer of Yr. White House News Photographers Assn., 1991, 93, 94, 96. Office: The Washington Post 1150 15th St NW Washington DC 20071-0002*

GUZZETTI, BARBARA JEAN, education educator; b. Chgo., Nov. 15, 1948; d. Louis Earnest and Viola Genevive (Russell) G. BS, No. Ill. U., 1971, MS, 1974; PhD, U. Colo., 1982. Title I reading tchr. Harlem Consolidated Sch. Dist., Loves Park, Ill., 1971-72; elem. classroom tchr. Rockford (Ill.) Pub. Schs., 1972-77; diagnostic tchr. Denver Pub. Schs., 1977-78; secondary reading tchr. Jefferson County Pub. Schs., Lakewood, Colo., 1979-81, secondary reading specialist, 1983-84; rsch. and program assoc. Mid-Continent Regional Ednl. Lab., Aurora, Colo., 1983-84; evaluation specialist N.W. Regional Ednl. Lab., Denver, 1984-85; assoc. prof. Calif. State U., Ponoma, 1985-88; prof. Ariz. State U., Tempe, 1988—; chair, tech. com. Nat. Reading Conf., 1994-96. Author: Literacy Instruction in Content Areas, 1996; editor: Perspectives on Conceptual Change; mem. editl. bd. The Reading Tchr., Jour. of Reading Behavior, Nat. Reading conf. Yearbook; contbr. articles to profl. jours. Mem. Am. Ednl. Rsch. Assn., Nat. Reading Conf., Internat. Reading Assn. (chair studies and rsch. grants com. 1992-95). Democrat. Lutheran. Avocations: reading, oenology, raising a pot-bellied pig, Piglet. Home: 2170 E Aspen Dr Tempe AZ 85282-2953 Office: Ariz State U Coll of Edn Tempe AZ 85287-0311

GUZZI, R. JAMES, JR., health care fraud consultant; b. Long Branch, N.J., Apr. 18, 1935; s. Roland James and Ruth M. G.; m. Rosemary Tellalian, Aug. 30, 1959; children: Roland James III, Kristin M. Guzzi Casey. BSBA, Monmouth U., West Long Branch, N.J., 1961. Claims adminstrn. Travelers Ins. Co., Perth Amboy and Ramsey, N.J., 1961-70; dir. security managed care and employee benefits Travelers Ins. Co., Hartford, Conn., 1970-93; pres. RJG Assocs., LLC, Glastonbury, Conn., 1993—; lectr. in field, 1992—; GAO, 1991, Office Mgmt. and Budget, 1992, FBI Hdqs., Washington, 1992, Ins. Assn. Conn., 1993, Workgroup on Electronic Data Interchange, 1993, ABA and Nat. Assn. Medicaid Fraud Control Units, 3994, Robert Wood Johnson Found., 1998, Conn. Superior Ct., 1997-98. Contbr. articles to profl. jours. Pres., v.p., other offices Glastonbury chpt. UNICO, 1977—; bd. dirs. Econ. Devel. Commn., Glastonbury, 1978-80; bd. mgrs. YMCA, Glastonbury, 1980-91. Petty officer 3d class USN, 1952-56. Mem. Assn. Cert. Fraud Examiners (cert., v.p. Conn. chpt. 1996, pres. 1997, bd. dirs. 1998), Health Ins. Assn. Am. (anti-fraud task force 1989-92), Nat. Health Care Anti-Fraud Assn. (life, bd. govs. 1985-93, sec. 1987-88, chmn. 1989-90, exec. com. 1990-93), Internat. Claim Assn. (group ins. com. 1986-89), New Eng. Anti-Fraud Assn. Avocation: golf. Office: RJG Assocs LLC 25 Heywood Dr Glastonbury CT 06033

GWADOSKY, DAN A., secretary of state; b. Fairfield, Maine, Feb. 16, 1954; m. Cheryl Norton; children: Joshua, Jessica. BS in Mgmt., Thomas Coll., LHD (hon.). Mem. Maine Ho. of Reps., Augusta, 1978-96, asst. majority floor leader, house majority leader, 1988-94; spkr. Maine Ho. Reps., 1994-96; sec. of state State of Maine, Augusta, 1997—; adminstr. Atrium Hotels Corp., 1985—. Mem. adv. bd. Kennebec Valley Vocat. Tech. Coll., State YMCA; bd. trustees Thomas Coll.; bd. dirs. State Leaders Found.; mem. exec. com. Coun. of State Govts.; co-chair Fairfield Cmty. Fest; co-chair bldg. com. Lawrence Pub. Libr.; active Lawrence HS Alumni Assn., Booster Club; coach boys and girls baseball, soccer, and basketball teams. Democrat. Home: 12 Mckenzie Ave Fairfield ME 04937-3341 Office: 148 State House Sta Augusta ME 04333-0148*

GWALTNEY, CORBIN, editor, publishing executive; b. Balt., Apr. 16, 1922; s. Howell Corbin and Margaret (Bell) G.; m. Doris Jean Kell, July 13, 1946 (dec.); children: Margaret Kell, Jean Corbin, Thomas Stewart; m. Jean Caryl Wyckoff, June 20, 1973 (dec.). B.A., Johns Hopkins U., 1943; LHD (hon.), L.I. U., 1970, Johns Hopkins U., 1998; DHL (hon.), Johns Hopkins U., 1998. Instr., English Johns Hopkins U., 1946; with indsl. relations dept. Western Electric Co. and Locke div. Gen. Electric Co., 1946-49; editor Johns Hopkins Mag., 1949-59; editor, exec. dir., pres. Editorial Projects for Edn., Inc., Balt. and Washington, 1959-78; exec. editor, pres. Chronicle Higher Edn., Washington, 1966—; editor in chief Chronicle of Philanthropy, 1988—. Served with AUS, 1943-45. Recipient Robert Sibley award Am. Alumni Council, 1951, 56, 59, Disting. Service to Higher Edn. awards Columbia U. Alumni Fedn., 1964, Disting. Service to Higher Edn. awards Am. Coll. Public Relations Assn., 1971; George Polk award for edn. reporting, 1979. Home: 5104 Brookview Dr Bethesda MD 20816-1602 also: 4755 Bayfields Rd Harwood MD 20776-9576 Office: Chronicle Higher Edn 1255 23rd St NW Ste 700 Washington DC 20037-1190

GWARTNEY, PATRICIA ANNE, sociology educator; b. Glendale, Calif., Mar. 30, 1951; d. Robert Alan and Marilyn Arline (Sanborn) G.; m. Stanley Morshead Gibbs, July 31, 1971 (div. Feb. 1994); children: Loren, Spencer; m. George Gordon Goldthwaite Jr., Apr. 29, 1995; children: Emily Eleanor, Lisa Margaret, Adam Michael. AB, U. Calif., Berkeley, 1973; MA, U. Mich., 1979, PhD, 1981. Asst. prof. U. Oreg., Eugene, 1981-88, assoc. prof., 1988-96, prof. sociology, 1996—, affiliate Ctr. for Study of Women in Soc., 1984—, founding dir. Oreg. Survey Rsch. Lab., 1992—. Contbr. articles to profl. publs.; editl. bd. Jour. Marriage and the Family, 1995-97. Cons. Task Force on Gender Fairness Oreg. Supreme Ct., 1996-98. Fulbright fellow U. Auckland, New Zealand, 1986. Mem. AAAS (sect. K nominating com.), AAUP, Am. Sociol. Assn., Pacific Sociol. Assn. (com. on coms., coun.), Population Assn. Am. Democrat. Congregationalist. Home: 2875 Spring Blvd Eugene OR 97403-2510 Office: U Oreg Dept Sociology Eugene OR 97403-1291

GWATHMEY, CHARLES, architect; b. Charlotte, N.C., June 19, 1938; s. Robert and Rosalie Dean (Hook) G.; m. Bette-Ann Damson, Dec. 15, 1974. Student, U. Pa., 1956-59; M.Arch., Yale U., 1962. Partner firm Gwathmey-Siegel and Assocs. Architects, N.Y.C., 1971—; vis. prof. archtl. design Pratt Inst., Yale U., Princeton U., Harvard U., Columbia U., Cooper Union, UCLA. Pres. bd. trustees Inst. Architecture and Urban Studies, N.Y.C., 1978; trustee Cooper Union, N.Y.C. Recipient Arnold Brunner prize AAAL, 1970; William Wirt Winchester traveling fellow, 1962-63; Fulbright grantee France, 1962-63; recipient AIA Nat. Honor awards for Straus residence, Purchase, N.Y., 1969, Whig Hall, Princeton U., 1976, Dormitory, Dining and Student Union SUNY, Purchase 1976, Taft Residence, Cin., 1984, Westover Sch., Middlebury, Conn., 1988, AIA N.Y. awards for Sch. Agr. Cornell U., 1991, Guggenheim Mus., N.Y.C., 1995, Progressive Architecture design awards for Whig Hall, Princeton U., 1973, Wick Alumni Ctr., U. Nebr., 1982, de Menil residence, East Hampton, N.Y., 1982, Yale Arts award for outstanding achievement, 1985. Fellow AIA (firm award 1982, Medal of honor 1983); mem. Am. Acad. Arts and Letters. Address: 1115 5th Ave New York NY 10128-0100 Office: Gwathmey Siegel & Assoc Arch 475 10th Ave Fl 3 New York NY 10018-1198*

GWATHMEY, JOE NEIL, JR., broadcasting executive; b. Brownwood, Tex., Jan. 4, 1941; s. Joe Neil and Grace Christine (Henry) G.; m. Linda Sue Sams, Aug. 22, 1965; children: Sara Lynn, David Alan. BA, Howard Payne Coll., 1963; postgrad., U. Denver, 1963-64, George Washington U., 1964-65. Sta. mgr. Sta. KUT-FM, Austin, 1965-71; various mgmt. positions Nat. Pub. Radio, Washington, 1971-83, v.p., 1983-88; pres. Tex. Pub. Radio, San ANtonio, 1988—. Review panel chair United Way Bexar County, San Antonio, 1994, 95, 96, 97; adv. coun. mem. Coll. Fine Arts Univ. Tex., Austin, 1990-93; trustee Tex. Student Publs., Austin, 1995-98. Recipient Edward R. Murrow award Corp. Pub. Broadcasting, 1988. Mem. Rotary. Democrat. Protestant. Avocations: singing, acting, public speaking, reading. Home: 2926 Meadow Cir San Antonio TX 78231-1720 Office: Tex Pub Radio 8401 Datapoint Dr Ste 800 San Antonio TX 78229-5903

GWERTZMAN, BERNARD, newspaper editor. Sr. editor Electronic Media Co. N.Y. Times, N.Y.C., 1995-98; editor N.Y. Times on the Web, N.Y.C., 1998—. Office: 1120 Ave of Americas 6th Fl New York NY 10036*

GWIAZDA, CAROLINE LOUISE, school system administrator; b. Cleve., Jan. 6, 1941; d. Michael Anthony and Catherine Anna (Papciak) Skutnik; m. Stanley John Gwiazda, June 30, 1962; children: Stanley, Cheryl, Catherine, Stephen. BA, Ursuline Coll., 1978; MEd, John Carroll, 1982; EdD, U. Akron, 1988. Tchr. St. Thomas More, Brooklyn, Ohio, 1961-62, 64-65, Washington Park Sch., Newburgh Heights, Ohio, 1963-64, St. Stephen Sch., Cleve., 1976-79; reading cons. Cleve. Bd. Edn., 1979-85; asst. prin. Case Sch., Cleve., 1985-87; prin. Bolton Sch., Cleve., 1987-89; curriculum cons. Lucas County Bd. Edn., Toledo, 1989-90; prin. Revere Bd. Edn., Bath, Ohio, 1990-91; curriculum dir. Diocese of Cleve., 1991-93; gen. edn. supr. Avon Lake (Ohio) Bd. Edn., 1993—; mem. exec. bd. Project Discovery Cleve., 1992—, John Carroll Ctr. Profl. Devel., University Heights, Ohio, 1992-94; mem. exec. bd. Cleve. Coun. Adminstrs. and Suprs.; chairperson, dist. rep. Ohio Assn. Elem. Adminstrs.; presenter in field. Mem. exec. bd. Coalition for Literacy, Cleve., 1992—, Jr. Achievement, Cleve., 1992-94; mem. adv. coun. Cancer Soc., Cleve., 1992-94; treas. Fire Safety Task Force, Cleve., 1992-94; active IDEA Acad. Fellows, 1998, Broadview Heights Planning Commn. Bd. Appeals. Effective Schs. grantee Ohio Dept. Edn., Columbus, 1992, Jennings grantee, 1992, Stocker Found. grantee, 1993, Continuous Improvement Plan grantee, 1999. Mem. ASCD, Ohio ASCD, Am. Assn. Adminstrs. and Suprs., Nat. Secondary, Elem. Sch. Adminstrs., Buckeye Assn. Sch. Adminstrs., Internat. Reading Assn. (initiated Greater Cleve. chpt. 1980), Ohio Reading Assn., Lillian Hinds Coun., Avon Lake Wellness Coun. (pres.), Phi Delta Kappa (pres. Cuyahoga Valley chpt., Disting. Kappan Svc. Key award, Outstanding Educator). Avocations: travel, reading, exercising, music, theatre. Home: 8595 Broadview Rd Broadview Hts OH 44147-1905 Office: Avon Lake Bd Edn 175 Avon Belden Rd Avon Lake OH 44012-1600

GWIAZDA, STANLEY JOHN, university dean; b. Phila., Feb. 14, 1922; s. Nicholas and Pauline (Stanczak) G.; m. Regina R. Grzeskowiak, Nov. 26, 1944; 1 dau., Marianne C. B.S. in Mech. Engring., Drexel Inst. Tech., 1944, M.S., 1952. Mem. faculty Drexel U., 1946-87, assoc. prof. mech. engring., 1952-87, dean evening coll., 1963-87, assoc. prof. emeritus mech. engring., dean emeritus evening coll., 1987—; bd. dirs. Phila. Govt. Tng. Inst.; mem. pres.'s coun. Holy Family Coll., 1984-89, acad. affairs com., 1989—. Author: (with J. H. Billings) Advanced Machine Design, 1958. Lt. (j.g.) USNR, 1944-46, PTO; lt. comdr. Res. ret. Stanley Gwiazda Professorship named in his honor Drexel U.; recipient Vol. Svc. award Holy Family Coll., 1994. Mem. Assn. Univ. Evening Colls. (chmn. com. on faculty devel. 1971-72), Am. Soc. Engring. Edn., Assn. Continuing Higher Edn. (dir. 1976-79, chmn. ethics com. 1979-83, pres. 1985-86, chmn. adv. com. 1986-87, Educator of Yr. award Region IV 1991), Res. Officers Assn. (pres. N.J. dept. 1973-74), Naval Res. Assn., Ret. Officers Assn., Cross Keys, Pi Tau Sigma, Alpha Sigma Lambda (assoc. dir. adult edn. found. 1984-90, bd. dirs. 1990—, Alpha Sigma Lambda Leadership award in Adult Edn. 1986). Roman Catholic. Home: 2001 Wayne Ave Haddon Heights NJ 08035-1036

GWIN, JOHN MICHAEL, marketing educator, consultant; b. Montgomery, Ala., June 21, 1949; s. Emmett Brindley Jr. and Irma Rebecca (Watkins) G.; m. Pamela Jane Blair, Sept. 7, 1970 (dec. Dec. 1998); children: Colin Blair, Connor Brindley. BBA, Auburn U., 1971; MBA, U. Ga., 1973; PhD, U. N.C., 1979. Fiscal officer U. Ga., Athens, 1971-73; ops. mgr. Bedsole & Gwin Inc., Fairhope, Ala., 1973-75; instr. Faulkner Coll., Bay Minette, Ala., 1975-76; research asst. U. N.C., Chapel Hill, 1976-78, vis. lectr., 1978-79; asst. prof. Ind. U., Bloomington, 1979-81; asst. prof. U. Va., Charlottesville, 1981-83, assoc. prof., 1983—, mktg. area coord., 1990-93, dir. Ctr. for Entrepreneurial Studies, 1992-96; Fulbright prof. Trinity Coll., Dublin, Ireland, 1986-87;, vis. prof., 1993; exec. educator numerous U.S. firms, 1981—; cons. numerous internat. and U.S. firms, 1983—; invited lectr. Sorbonne, U. Paris, Alsace Inst., Strasbourg, France, 1987. Inventor LaMaze Timer and audio text. Sesquicentennial Research Assoc., U. Va., 1986-87, 93-94; named Outstanding Young Man Am., U.S. Jr. C. of C., 1976. Mem. Am. Mktg. Assn. (conf. coord. Cen. Va. chpt. 1986), So. Mktg. Assn., Acad. Mktg. Sci., Japan-Va. Soc. Planning Forum, Colonnade Club. Episcopalian. Avocations: fiction writing, golf. Home: 824 King William Dr Charlottesville VA 22901-0618 Office: U Va 226 Monroe Hall Charlottesville VA 22903-2438

GWINN, CASEY, city attorney San Diego, California; m. Beth Gwinn; 3 children. BA in Polit. Sci. with honors, Stanford U., 1982; JD, UCLA, 1985. Bar: Calif. 1995. Dep. city atty. City of San Diego, 1985-88, head dep. city atty., 1988-95, prin. asst. to city atty., 1995-96, asst. atty., 1996, atty., 1996—; faculty Nat. Coll. Dist. Attys., Nat Judges Conf. on Domestic Violence, Nat. Navy Family Advocacy Conf., Nat. U.S. Marine Corps Love and Violence Conf., Calif. Dist. Attys. Assn. Contbr. articles to profl. jours. Adv. bd. Home Start, San Diego Ctr. for Children, Children' Edn. with Care; founder San Diego Task Force on Domestic Violence. Recipient Gov.'s Recognition award, 1990, Diogenes award Pub. Rels. Soc. Am., 1990, Recognition award Nat. Coun. Juvenile and Family Ct. Judges, 1993, State Resolution, Calif. Assembly, 1994; named 1 of Top 45 Pub. Lawyers in Am., American Lawyer. Mem. ABA, Calif. Dist. Attys. Assn., San Diego County Bar Assn., League of Calif. Cities, City Atty. Dept. Office: City Atty Office 1200 3rd Ave Ste 1620 San Diego CA 92101-4112

GWINN, MARY ANN, newspaper reporter; b. Forrest City, Ark., Dec. 29, 1951; d. Lawrence Baird and Frances Evelyn (Jones) G.; m. Richard A. King, June 3, 1973 (div. 1981); m. Stephen E. Dunnington, June 10, 1990. BA in Psychology, Hendrix Coll., 1973; MEd in Spl. Edn., Ga. State U., 1975; MA in Journalism, U. Mo., 1979. Tchrs. aide DeKalb County Schs., Decatur, Ga., 1973-74, tchr., 1975-78; reporter Columbia (Mo.) Daily Tribune, 1979-83; reporter Seattle Times, 1983—, internat. trade and workplace reporter, 1992-96, book editor, 1996-98, asst. city editor, 1996-98, book editor, 1998—; instr. ext. divsn. U. Wash., Seattle, 1990; journalism instr., Seattle U., 1994. Recipient Charles Stewart Mott Found. award for edn. reporting, 1980, C.B. Blethen award for enterprise reporting Blethen Family, Seattle, 1989, Pulitzer Prize for nat. reporting, 1990. Mem. Newspaper Guild. Avocations: writing fiction, gardening, reading, wilderness camping. Office: Seattle Times PO Box 70 1120 John St Seattle WA 98109-5321

GWINN, MARY DOLORES, business developer, philosopher, writer, speaker; b. Oakland, Calif., Sept. 16, 1946; d. Epifanio and Carolina (Lopez) Cruz; m. James Monroe Gwinn, Oct. 23, 1965; 1 child, Larry Allen. Student, Monterey Peninsula Jr. Coll., 1965. Retail store mgr. Consumer's Distbg. divsn. May Co., Hayward, Calif., 1973-78; mktg. rep. Dale Carnegie Courses, San Jose, Calif., 1978-79; founder, pres. Strategic Integrations, Ariz.'s Innovative Bus. Devel. Ctr., Scottsdale, 1985—, Gwinn Genius Inst., Scottsdale, 1998—; speaker St. John's Coll. U. Cambridge, England, 1992, INC. Mag., U.S.A., 1996, Clemson Univ., 1996, Antelope Valley Coll., Lancaster, Calif., 1998; founder, pres. Internat. Inst. for Conceptual Edn., Scottsdale, 1993—; chairperson Keble Coll., Oxford (Eng.) U., 1997. Founder new fields of study Genestics and NeuroBus.; profiled the Thought Process of Genius; conceived Whole Brain Business Theory, 1985; author: Genius Leadership Secrets from the Past for the 21st Century, 1995; writer bus. column Gwinn on Bus., IMAGE Networker, Pa., 1996; contbr. articles to profl. jours. Chairperson Keble Coll., Oxford (Eng.) U. Republican. Avocations: reading, imagination games, playing with grandchildren. Home and Office: 5836 E Angela Dr Scottsdale AZ 85254-6410

GWINN, ROBERT P., publishing executive; b. Anderson, Ind., June 30, 1907; s. Marshall and Margaret (Cather) G.; m. Nancy Flanders, Jan. 20, 1942 (dec. 1989); 1 child, Richard Herbert. PhB, U. Chgo., 1929. With Sunbeam Corp., Chgo., 1936-51, gen. sales mgr. elec. appliance div., 1951-52, v.p., dir., 1952-55, pres., chief exec. officer, 1955-71, chmn. bd., chief exec. officer, 1971-82, also bd. dirs.; chmn. bd., chief exec. officer Ency. Britannica, Inc., Chgo., 1973-93, chmn. emeritus, 1993—; chmn. bd., CEO Titan Oil Co., Riverside; bd. dirs. Continental Assurance Co., Continental Casualty Co., CNA/Fin. Corp., Inst. for Philos. Rsch., Alberto-Culver Corp. Trustee Chgo. Zool. Soc., U. Chgo.; mem. Citizens Adv. Com., Chgo.; bd. fellows Harvard Med. Sch., James Madison Coun., Libr. of Congress. Mem. Soc. Chgo., Internat. Food and Wine Soc. Chgo., Mid. Am. Club, Elec. Mfrs. Club (hon.), Comml. Club Chgo., Casino Club, Execs. Club, Bird Key Yacht Club, Riverside Golf Club, U. Chgo. Club, Alpha Sigma Phi. Office: 1 Riverside Rd Riverside IL 60546-2255

GWOZDZ, KIM ELIZABETH, interior designer; b. Spokane, Wash., June 10, 1958; d. Myron Marcus and Marilyn Kay (Alsterlund) Westerkamp; m. Edwin Eugene Gwozdz, June 14, 1981; children: Ryan Marcus, Lauren Taylor. Student, U. Florence, Italy, 1979; BFA in Graphic Design, Illustration and Art History, U. Ariz., 1980. Interior designer Pat Bacon & Assocs., 1983-88; prin. interior designer Kim E. Gwozdz/Provenance, Phoenix, 1988—. Contbr. articles to profl. jours. Active Mt. Cavalry Luth. Ch., Phoenix, 1981-96, trustee, 1993-96; active Christ Luth. Ch., Phoenix, 1996—; mem. Jr. League of Phoenix, 1989—, HIV/AIDS com., 1994—; mem. Orpheum Theater com., 1989-94, vice chmn., 1990-91, chmn., 1992-94, Gift Mart com. Design Decorations, 1991-92, chmn., 1991, exec. com. Orpheum Theatre Found., 1989-91, bd. dirs., 1992—; active annual gala com. Am. Cancer Soc., 1993-94, 94-95, 95-96, 97-98, 98—, March of Dimes Gourmet Gala, 1991, 93, 95, 97; design affiliate Nat. Trust for Hist. Preservation, 1986—. Recipient 1st place award Ann. Wool Rug Design Competition, Edward Fields, Inc., 1989, 2d place award, 1990, 3d place award, 1991; Internat. Illumination design awards, 1998, Cutler award, 1998, Lumen award, 1998. Mem. Am. Soc. Interior Designers (assoc. Ariz. North chpt., significant interiors survey com. 1975-91, chmn. 1990-91, Phoenix Home and Garden com. 1989-90, Herberger Theatre com. 1989-91, awards com. 1989, 91, chmn. 1990, competitions com. 1991, 96, chmn. 1989-90, Rosson House Christmas chmn. 1986-91, hist. preservation chmn. 1988-91, directory chmn. Designers Market 1991, project designer, 1996, 97, mem. nominating com. 1991-92, 98, mktg. com. 1995, 3d place award Ariz. North 1987, 96, 2d place award 1987, 88, 92, 95, 1st place award Nat. 1989, 94, 95, 97). Republican. Lutheran. Avocations: art, gardening, cooking. Home: 210 W Royal Palm Rd Phoenix AZ 85021-5649 Office: Kim E Gwozdz/Provenance 2425 E Camelback Rd Ste 450 Phoenix AZ 85016-4236*

GWYNN, ANTHONY KEITH (TONY GWYNN), professional baseball player; b. L.A., May 9, 1960; m. Alicia; children: Anthony, Anisha Nicole. Student, San Diego State U. Player minor league teams Walla Walla and Amarillo, Hawaii, 1981-82; with San Diego Padres, 1981—. Winner Nat. League batting title, 1984, 87, 88, 89, 95; recipient Gold Glove award, 1986-87, 89-91; mem. All-Star team, 1984-87, 89-96; named MVP N.W. League, 1981, Sporting News Nat. League Silver Slugger team, 1984, 86-87, 89, 94, Sporting News Nat. League All-Star Team, 1984, 86-87, 89, 94. Office: San Diego Padres Qualcomm Stadium PO Box 2000 San Diego CA 92112-2000*

GWYNNE, ROBERT HAROLD, minister; b. Bklyn., May 28, 1937; s. Harold and May Belle (Mott) G.; m. Jessie Ellen McGovran, May 27, 1960; children: Owen, Neil, Gail. AB, Dartmouth Coll., 1959; MA, U. Colo., 1965; MDiv, Chgo. Theol. Sem., 1997. Lic. profl. counselor, Wis. Tchr. Kanawha County Schs., Charleston, W.Va., 1962-63; tchr., counselor Aurora (Colo.) Pub. Schs., 1964-67; counselor McCoy Job Corps/RCA Svc., Sparta, Wis., 1967-68, Madison (Wis.) Area Tech. Coll., 1968-94; pastor First Congl. UCC, Steger, Ill., 1996-97, First UCC, Belleville, Wis., 1998—, First Congl. UCC, Fox Lake, Wis., 1999. Editor (newsletter) Wisperan, 1968-74. Bd. dirs. East Side YMCA, Madison, 1974-80; treas. North Side Cmty. Coun., Madison, 1969-71; del. Wis. Dem. Conv., 1990, 92. With U.S. Army, 1960-62; del. to labor coun. Local 243 WFT, AFT, Madison, 1988-94, bargaining team, 1986-92. Mem. WFT, ACLU, Am. Counseling Assn., Am. Vocational Assn., Chgo. Theol. Sem. Alumni Coun., Madison Area Ret. Educators Assn. (sec. 1999), Assn. Attending Clergy, Phi Delta Kappa. Avocations: music, travel, theatre/dance, philanthropy. Home: 1029 Spaight St Apt 3B Madison WI 53703-3562

GYANI, MOHAN, communications company executive; b. Goa, India, June 15, 1951. MBA with distinction, San Francisco State U., 1978. V.p., contr. Pacific Bell; v.p., treas. Pacific Telesis; CFO for internat. subs. AirTouch Comm., San Francisco, v.p. fin., treas., 1994-95, exec. v.p., CFO, 1995—; former lectr. San Francisco State U.; participant Pvt. Sector Coun.; bd. dirs. PCS Prime Co. Inc., Mannesman Arcor. Mem. exec. bd. Boy Scouts Am. Office: Airtouch Comm 1 California St San Francisco CA 94111-5401

GYEMANT, ROBERT ERNEST, lawyer; b. Managua, Nicaragua, Jan. 17, 1944; s. Emery and Magda (Von Rechnitz) G.; came to U.S., 1949, naturalized, 1954; A.B. magna cum laude, U. Calif. Los Angeles, 1965; J.D., U. Calif. Berkeley, 1968; children from previous marriage: Robert Ernest Jr., Anne Elizabeth; m. Sally Bartch Libhart, Oct. 17, 1992; children: Emily Bartch, Amanda Nancy, Katherine Libhart. Tax accountant Ernst & Ernst, CPAs, Oakland, Calif., 1966-68; CPA, Calif., 1967; admitted to Calif. bar, 1969, N.Y., 1981; asso. atty. Orrick, Herrington, Rowley & Sutcliffe, San Francisco, 1968-69; partner law firm Skornia, Rosenblum & Gyemant, San Francisco, 1969-74; law offices Robert Ernest Gyemant profl. corp., San Francisco, 1975; exec. v.p. finance Topps & Trowsers, San Francisco, 1977-79; cons., pvt. investor, 1979; with ComDial Corp, San Francisco; co-founder Com Vu Corp., N.Y.C., 1979-83; ptnr. Rosen, McCarthy, Gyemant & Babbits, P.C., San Francisco, 1993-97; prin. Knapp, Petersen & Clarke, P.C., Glendale, Calif., 1997—; instr. U. Calif. at Berkeley, 1968. Mem. Calif. Council Criminal Justice Jud. Process Task Force, 1971-73. Mem. Calif. State Rep. Ctrl. Com.; trustee French-Am. Bilingual Sch., San Francisco, 1978-82; hon. vice consul Republic of Costa Rica, 1981—. Mem. ABA, San Francisco Bar Assn. (co-chmn. sect. on juvenile justice 1971) State Bar Calif. (cert. specialist criminal law 1988-93, com. on unauthorized practice law 1974-76, spl. com. on juvenile justice 1974, commr. San Francisco County juvenile justice comm. 1976—), AICPA, Calif. CPA Soc. (mem. accounting prins. com. 1969), Assn. Def. Counsel, Calif. Trial Lawyers Assn., San Francisco Downtown Assn., San Francisco World Trade Club, N.Y. Athletic Club, Racquet and Tennis Club (N.Y.C.). Author publs. in field; editor: Calif. Law Rev., 1967-68. Email: rgyemant@hfbllp.com. Office: Hill Farrer & Burrill LLP 37th floor 1 California Plz 300 S Grand Ave Los Angeles CA 90071

GYLLENHAMMAR, PEHR GUSTAF, finance company executive, retired automobile company executive, writer; b. Gothenburg, Sweden, Apr. 28, 1935; s. Pehr and Aina (Kaplan) G.; M.Law, U. Lund, 1959; MD (hon.), U. Gothenburg, 1981; Tech D (hon.), Brunel U., 1987, ED (hon.), Tech. U. Nova Scotia, 1988; D Soc. Sci. (hon.), U. Helsinki, 1990; LLD (hon.) U. Vt.; m. Christina Engellau; children: Cecilia, Charlotte, Oscar, Sophie. With Ins. Co. Amphion, 1961-64; asst. adminstrv. mgr. Ins. Co. AB. Skandia, 1965-66, v.p., 1966, dep. mng. dir., 1968-70, mng. dir., chief exec., 1970; mng. dir., CEO AB Volvo, Gothenburg, 1971-83, chmn., CEO, 1983-90, exec. chmn., 1990-93, also bd. dirs.; chmn. CGU plc, 1998—; chmn. CGU Union plc; sr. advisor Lazard Freres & Co. LLC; dir. United Techs. Corp.; chmn. bd. Swedish Ships Mortgage Bank, Cofinec N.V.; supervisory bd. Lagardère SCA; trustee Reuters Founders Share Co. Ltd. Author 5 books. Office: CGU plc, St Helens 1 Undershaft, London EC3P 3DQ, England

GYLSETH, DORIS (LILLIAN) HANSON, retired librarian; b. Helena, Mont., May 26, 1934; d. Richard E. and Lillie (Paula) Hanson; m. Arlie Albeck, Dec. 26, 1955 (div. Apr. 1964); m. Hermann M. Gylseth, Apr. 29, 1983 (dec. Aug. 1985). BS in Edn., Western Mont. Coll. Edn., 1958; MLS, U. Wash., 1961. Tchr. Helena Sch. Dist., 1955-56, Dillon (Mont.) Elem. Sch., 1957-59, Eltopia (Wash.) Unified Sch. Dist., 1959-60; sch. libr. Shoreline Sch. Dist., Seattle, 1960-64, Dept. of Def., Chateauroux, France, Hanau, Fed. Republic Germany, Tachikawa, Japan, 1964-68, Long Beach (Calif.) Unified Sch. Dist., 1968-70; br. libr. Long Beach Pub. Libr., 1970-74, coord. children's svcs., 1974-85; libr. Long Beach (Calif.) Unified Sch. Dist., 1986-94; realtor Century 21, All Pacific, 1994-96. Bd. dirs. Children's Svcs. divsn. Calif. Libr. Assn., 1985, Literary Guild of Orange County, 1993—; co-chmn. Long Beach Authors Festival, 1978-86; mem. planning coun. Third Pacific Rim Conf. on Children's Lit., UCLA, 1986. Mem. So. Calif. Coun. on Lit. for Children and Young Poeple (bd. dirs. 1974-88, pres. 1982-84), Helen Fuller Cultural Carrousel (bd. dirs. 1985—), Friends of Long Beach Pub. Libr. (bd. dirs. 1988—), Zonta (pres. 1978-80). Avocations: cats, traveling. Home: 5131 Kingscross Rd Westminster CA 92683-4832

GYSBERS, NORMAN CHARLES, education educator; b. Waupun, Wis., Sept. 29, 1932; s. George S. and Mabel (Landaal) G.; m. Mary Lou Ziegler, June 23, 1954 (dec. July 1997); children—David, Debra, Daniel. A.B., Hope Coll., 1954; M.A., U. Mich., 1959, Ph.D., 1963. Lic. psychologist, Mo. Tchr. Elem. and Jr. High Sch., Muskegon Heights, Mich., 1954-56; lectr. edn. U. Mich., 1962-63; prof. counseling psychology U. Mo., Columbia, 1963—; cons. U.S. Office Edn.; mem. nat. adv. coms. ERIC Clearinghouses in Career Edn. and Counseling and Personnel Services; research and devel. com. for CEEB, Am. Insts. for Research Project on Career Decision Making, Comprehensive Career Edn. Model, TV Career Awareness Project KCET-TV, Los Angeles; dir. 10 nat. research projects and state projects in career devel.-guidance; Francqui prof. Universite Libre de Bruxelles. Editor: Vocat. Guidance Quar. 1962-70; (with L. Sunny Hansen) spl. issue Personnel and Guidance Jour., May 1975, Jour. Career Devel., 1979—, (with E. Moore and W. Miller) Developing Careers in the Elementary School, 1973, (with E. Moore and H. Drier) Career Guidance: Practices and Perspectives, 1973; author: (with E. Moore) Improving Guidance Programs, 1981, Designing Careers, 1984, (with E. Moore) Career Counseling, 1987, (with P. Henderson) Developing and Managing Your School Guidance Program, 1988, 2d edit., 1994, (with C. McDaniels) Counseling for Career Development, 1992, (with P. Henderson) Guidance Programs that Work, 1997, (with M. Heppner and J. Johnston) Career Counseling, 1998, (with P. Henderson) Leading and Managing Your School Guidance Program Staff, 1998; contbr. articles to profl. jours. and chpts. to textbooks. Elder Presbyn. Ch. Served with arty. U.S. Army, 1956-58. Recipient Am. Spirit award USAF, 1987. Mem. Am. Assn. Counseling and Devel. (pres. 1977-78, disting. profl. service award 1983), Nat. Career Devel. Assn. (pres. 1972-73, nat. merit award 1981, Eminent Career award 1989), Assn. for Counselor Edn. and Supervision, Am. Sch. Counselor Assn., Am. Vocat. Assn. (v.p. 1979-82, merit award guidance div. 1978), Mo. Guidance Assn. (outstanding service award 1978), Internat. Assn. Ednl. and Vocat. Guidance. Home: 1701 Kathy Dr Columbia MO 65202-3132 Office: U Mo Rm 305 Noyes Bldg Columbia MO 65211

HA, ANDREW KWANGHO, education educator; b. Korea, Nov. 14, 1939; s. Hyunku and Soonnam (Kim) H.; m. Jumok Lim; children: Susan, Steve, Joanna, Toby. BA, Chosun U., Kwangju, Korea, 1965; MA, Glassboro (N.J.) State Coll., 1967; EdD, Seton Hall U., 1988. Cert. elem. and secondary social studies tchr., guidance counselor, prin., supr., N.J. Tchr. Mantua (N.J.) Twp. Pub. Schs., Greenwich Twp. Pub. Schs., Gibbstown, N.J.; instr. ESL tchg. Passaic County C.C., Paterson, N.J.; adj. prof. English teaching Glassboro (N.J.) State Coll.; tchr. reading and English lang. arts methods Potsdam Coll., SUNY, 1991—. Author: The Key to Reading Comprehension, 1994, Get'em to Plunge into the Sea of English, 1995, Get'em to Swim in the Sea of English, 1996, Get'em to Rise in the Sea of English, 1997, Dr. Ha's English Grammar, 1998. Elected into the Internat. Ctr. for Ednl. Achievement, 1997. Mem. NEA, ASCD, N.J. Edn. Assn., Am. Fedn. Tchrs., Am. Ednl. Rsch. Assn., United Univ. Profession, Nat. Coun. Tchrs. English, Internat. Reading Assn., Tchrs. English to Speakers of Other Langs, Phi Delta Kappa, Kappa Delta Pi,. Home: PO Box 873 Potsdam NY 13676-0873

HA, CHANG SIK, polymer science educator; b. Pusan, Korea, Jan. 30, 1956; s. Won Do and Bong Soon (Eh) H.; m. Sun Ja Han, Jan. 13, 1983; children: Ji Won, Ji Hyun, Jae Hun. BS, Pusan Nat. U., 1978; MS, Korea Adv. Inst. Sci. & Tech., Seoul, 1980, PhD, 1987. Engr. Lucky Chem. Co. Ltd., Pusan, 1982; from instr. to asst. prof. Pusan Nat. U., 1982-89, faculty advisor univ. English newspaper, 1987, assoc. prof., 1989-94, chmn. dept., 1992-94, prof., 1994—; vis. scholar U. Cin., 1988-89, Stanford U., 1997-98; mem. editl. adv. bd. Materials Sci. Found. (Trans Tech. Publs. Switzerland). Author: Polymer Chemistry, 1990, Polymer Processing, 1991, Polymer Engineering, I, 1995, II, 1997; editor: Polymer: Structure and Properties, 1988; mem. editl. bd. Material Sci. Found., 1998—; contbr. over 200 articles to sci. jours. on polymer blends and composites or electroluminescent devices. Mem. Am. Chem. Soc., Soc. Plastics Engrs., Polymer Processing Soc., Polymer Soc. Korea (Polymer Science award 1995), Soc. Polymer Sci. Japan, Korean Inst. Rubber Industries (Best Paper of Yr. award 1989). Avocations: classical music, climbing. Fax: 82 51 514 4331. Office: Pusan Nat U, Dept Polymer Sci & Engring, Pusan 609-735, Republic of Korea

HA, DINH TRONG, retired air force officer, computer specialist; b. Nam Dinh, Vietnam, Feb. 1, 1940; came to U.S., 1975; s. Kinh Trong and Nhu (Nguyen) H.; m. Dung Thi Va; children: Nguyen, Trang, Khoi, Van, Cuong. BA, Chu Van An, Saigon, Vietnam, 1958; degree in law, Saigon U., 1974. Cert. airforce mgr., Maxwell AFB, Ala. Commd. Vietnam Air Force, advanced through grades to lt. col.; air observation pilot, observer Vietnam Air Force, Vietnam, 1961-63; master weapons contr. Vietnam Air Force, Vietnam and U.S., 1963-75; ret. Vietnam Air Force, 1975. Mem. Air Force Vets. Assn., No. and Ea. regions, U.S., 1986—, Unarmed Forces Assn., 1993—. Decorated Bronze Star, Vietnam War Medal. Home: 5756 Heming Ave Springfield VA 22151-2713

HAAC, OSCAR ALFRED, retired French educator; b. Frankfurt, Germany, Jan. 28, 1918; s. Oscar Eugen and Charlotte (Sternberg) H.; m. Clare Lytle, Dec. 1942 (dec. 1970); children: Alice Haac Vessell, Clifford; m. Gunilla Nohrlander, 1982; children: Isabelle Schaffner, Beatrice Turpin. BA, Yale U., 1939, MA, 1942, PhD, 1948; Docteur, U. Paris, 1948. Asst. prof. French Pa. State U., University Park, 1948-54; assoc. prof. French Emory U., Atlanta, 1954-65; prof. French SUNY, Stony Brook, 1965-88, NYU, N.Y.C., 1988; ret., 1988. Author: Les Principes Inspirateurs de Michelet, 1951, Jules Michelet, 1982, The Correspondence of John Stuart Mill and Auguste Comte, 1995, Lamennais Philosophie, 1996; editor: (with Paul Viallaneix and Irène Tieder) Jules Michelet, Cours au Collège de France 1838-1851, 1995, 2 vols.; contbr. over 50 articles to profl. jours; pub. 17 books. Lt. col. U.S. Army, 1941-68, ETO. Guggenheim Found. fellow, 1955; recipient Chevalier der Palmes Academiques, French Govt., 1958. Mem. Phi Sigma Iota (hon., pres. 1964-67, treas. 1967-70). Unitarian. Avocations: reading, writing. Home: 138 E 36th St Apt 9C New York NY 10016-3507

HAACK, RICHARD WILSON, retired police officer; b. Chgo., July 7, 1935; s. Arthur Frank and Mildred Ann (Meyer) H.; m. Ruth Marie Tietz, May 27, 1972; children: Laura Marie, Karl Richard. Grad., Sheriff's Police Acad., Cook County (Ill.), 1967; AS, Triton Coll., 1973; cert., Chgo. Police Acad., 1974; BA, Lewis U., 1975; MA, Northeastern Ill. U., 1979; BS in Bus. Adminstrn., Elmhurst Coll., 1982. Shipping clk. Am. Furniture Mart, Chgo., 1955-60; quality control insp. Nat. Can Co., Chgo., 1961-67; police officer Northlake (Ill.) Police Dept., 1967-92, watch comdr. patrol divsn., 1978-85, dept. chief of police, 1986-87, in-svc. tng. coord., 1991-92, retired, 1992; realtor Internat. Realty World-Norton & Assocs., 1984-87. Author Ency. Am. Judiciary; contbr. articles to profl. publs. Mem. Bill Bruce fundraising com. Aid Assn. Luths., Christ Evang. Luth. Ch., Northlake, 1981-82, mem. Gala Varsity Show, 1982, chmn. evang. bd., 1981-85, ch. rep. Internat. Luth. Laymen's League, 1984—, pub. rels. dir., usher, 1873-85; choir Apostles Luth Ch., 1985-87; membership chmn. Redeemer Luth. Ch. Men's Club, 1995—; dir., emcee German-Am. Police Assn. Oktoberfest, 1980—, chmn. entertainment, 1984—; coach Northlake Little League baseball team, 1985; trustee Northlake Police Pension Fund, 1997—; active March of Dimes-Mothers March, 1997-99. Served with USMC, 1952-55, Korea, with res. 1955-60. Recipient John Edgar Hoover Meml. Golg medal, 1987, numerous letters of commendation, competitive shooting awards. Mem. NRA, Internat. Assn. Chiefs of Police, Ill. Police Assn. (life), Fraternal Order Police (life, sec.-treas. Perri-Nagle Meml. Lodge 18 1977-85), St. Jude Police League, Nat. Police Officers Assn., Internat. Police Assn. (life), German/Am. Police Assn. (life, bd. dirs 1980—), Combined Counties Police Assn., Internat. Juvenile Officers Assn., Ill. Juvenille Officers Assn., Ill. Police Assn. (life), Emerald Soc. Ill. Irish/Am. Police Assn., Northeastern Ill. U. Alumni Assn. (bd. dirs. 1980-86), Am. Polit. Sci. Assn., Schwaben Verein, N.W. Real Estate Bd., Leyden Real Estate Bd. (inner circle 1984-87), Sharkhunters, Internat. Platform Assn., Realtors Polit. Action Com. Ill. (inner circle 1984-87). Lic. sales and Retd. and Disabled Police of Am., Kaire Ind. Distbr., Die Hard Cub Fans, Moose Lodge. Republican. Home: 244 E Palmer Ave Northlake IL 60164-1735 Office: 55 E North Ave Northlake IL 60164-2518

HAACKE, HANS CHRISTOPH CARL, artist, educator; b. Cologne, Germany, Aug. 12, 1936; s. Carl and Antonie Haacke; m. Linda Snyder, 1965; 2 sons. MFA, State Acad., Kassel, 1960; DFA (hon.), Oberlin Coll., 1991; D (hon.), Bauhaus U., Weimar, Germany, 1998. Asst. prof. Cooper Union for Advancement of Sci. and Art, N.Y.C., 1971-75, assoc. prof., 1975-79, prof., 1979—; guest prof. Hochschule für Bildende Künste, Hamburg,

1973, 94, Gesamthochschule, Essen, 1979. One-man shows include Galerie Schmela, Düsseldorf, 1965, Howard Wise Gallery, N.Y.C., 1966, 68, 69, Galerie Paul Maenz, Cologne, 1971, 74, 81, Museum Haus Lange, Krefeld, 1972, John Weber Gallery, N.Y.C., 1973, 75, 77, 79, 81, 83, 85, 88, 90, 92, 94, Kunstverein, Frankfurt, 1976, Galerie Durand-Dessert, Paris, 1977, 78, Mus. of Modern Art, Oxford, 1978, Stedelijk van Abbemuseum, Eindhoven, 1979, Renaissance Soc., Chgo., 1979, Galerie France Morin, Montreal, Que., Can., 1983, Tate Gallery, London, 1984, Neue Gesellschaft für Bildende Kunst, Berlin, 1984, Kunsthalle, Berne,, 1985, Le Consortium, Dijon, France, 1986, The New Mus. Contemporary Art, N.Y.C., 1986, Victoria Miro Gallery, London, 1987, Centre Georges Pompidou, Paris, 1989, Biennale Venice, Italy, 1993, Fundació Antoni Tàpies, Barcelona, 1995, Mus. Boijmans Van Beuningen, Rotterdam, 1996; group exhbns. Stedelijk Mus., Amsterdam, 1962, 65, 82, Mus. Modern Art, N.Y.C., 1968, 70, 88,99, Tokyo Biennale, 1970, Jewish Mus., N.Y.C., 1970, 94, Documenta Kassel, 1972, 82, 87, 97, Biennale Venice, 1976, 78, Mus. van Hedendaagse Kunst, Ghent, Belgium, 1980, Hirshhorn Mus., Washington, 1984, Palais des Beaux-Arts, Brussels, 1984, Sydney (Australia) Biennale, 1984, 90, Sao Paulo (Brazil) Biennale, 1985, Nationalgalerie, Berlin, 1984, Centre Georges Pompidou, 1987, 89, 90, 92, 96, Musee d'Art Moderne de la Ville de Paris, 1981, 89, Russian Mus., L.A. Cty. Mus., 1987, Whitney Mus., NY, 1989, St. Petersburg, 1990, Irish Mus. Modern Art, Dublin, 1992, Musee d'art contemporain, Montreal, 1992, Bundeskunsthalle, Bonn, Germany, 1992, Kunsthalle Basel, Basel, Switzerland, 1994, Mus. Contemporary Art, L.A., 1995, Mus. Contemporary Art, Tokyo, 1995; Stage set: Ernst Jünger, Volksbühne, Berlin, 1994, Skulptur Projekte Münster, Germany, 1997, Deutschlandbilder, Gropius-Bau, Berlin, 1997, Johannesburg Biennale, 1997; Chicago Cultural Ctr., 1998; author: (with Edward F. Fry) Werkmonographie, 1972, (with others) Framing and Being Framed, 1975, Nach allen Regeln der Kunst, 1984, (with others) Unfinished Business, 1987, Artfairismes, 1989, (with others) Bodenlos, 1993, (with Pierre Bourdieu) Libre-Echange, 1994, Obra Social, 1995; AnsichtsSachen/ViewingMatters, 1999, contbr. articles to profl. jours. Recipient Golden Lion Venice Biennale. Office: The Cooper Union Cooper Square New York NY 10003

HAAG, CAROL ANN GUNDERSON, marketing professional, consultant; b. Mpls.; d. Glenn Alvin and Genevieve Esther (Knudson) Gunderson; m. Lawrence S. Haag, Aug. 30, 1969; 1 child, Maren Anne. BJ, U. Mo., 1969; postgrad., Roosevelt U., Chgo., 1975—. Pub. relations writer, advt. copywriter Am. Hosp. Supply Corp., Evanston, Ill., 1969-70; asst. dir. pub. relations Rush-Presbyn. St. Luke's Med. Ctr., Chgo., 1970-71; asst. mgr. pub. and employee communications Quaker Oats Co., Chgo., 1971-72, mgr. editorial communications, 1972-74, mgr. employee communications programs, 1974-77; dir. pub. relations Shaklee Corp., San Francisco, 1978-82; pres. CH & Assocs., San Francisco, 1982-84; dir corp. communications BRAE Corp., San Francisco, 1984; dir. mktg. St. Francis Meml. Hosp., San Francisco, 1985-89, dir. mktg. and planning svcs., 1989-91; ptnr. Haag & Rohan, San Francisco, San Diego, 1991—; examiner Calif. Coun. for Quality and Svc., 1997, 98, 99; cons. in field. Bd. dirs. Calif. League Handicapped; mem. adv. bd. San Francisco Spl. Olympics; mem. pub. relations com. San Francisco Recreation and Parks Dept., San Francisco Vol. Bur. Recipient 1st place cert. Printing Industry Am., 1972, 74, 1st place spl. comm. award Internat. Assn. Bus. Communicators, 1974, 1st place citation Chgo. Assn. Bus. Communicators, 1974, gold award Healthcare Mktg. Reports, 1989, 90. Mem. NATAS, Indsl. Com. Coun., Pub. Rels. Soc. Am., San Francisco C. of C. (grad. leadership program 1991, bd. dirs. leadership coun.). Home and Office: 133 Fernwood Dr Moraga CA 94556-2315

HAAG, EVERETT KEITH, architect; b. Cuyahoga Falls, Ohio, Jan. 27, 1928; s. Arnold and Ida (Martz) H.; m. Eleanor Jean Baker, Nov. 1, 1961; children—Kurt, Paula, Pamela. B.S. in Architecture, Kent State U., 1951; B.Arch., Western Res. U., 1953. Founder, prin. firm Keith Haag & Assos. (architects), Cuyahoga Falls, 1955-72; founder, pres. Keith Haag Assos. Inc. (architecture-engring.-planning), Cuyahoga Falls, 1972-81; archtl. and planning cons. Cuyahoga Falls, 1981—; instr. Kent State U., 1952-54. Pres. Tri-County Planning Commn., 1960-61; chmn. Urban Renewal Review Commn., Cuyahoga Falls, 1971—, Regional Planning Group, Northampton Twp., 1970—; mem. Akron Regional Devel. Bd.; bd. dirs. Goodwill Industries, chmn. strategic planning com., 1988—, Akron, Stan Hywet Hall Found., Inc. (pres. 1991-92); chmn. Historic Bldgs. Com., 1988—; mem. alumni bd. Kent State U., 1970-72, co-developer Polymer Housing system, 1989. Recipient 46 archtl. design awards. Fellow AIA (past pres. Akron chpt., nat. com. on office practice); mem. Architects Soc. Ohio (exec. com., sec. 1975-76, v.p. 1977-78, pres. 1979, Gold medal 1986), Northampton C. of C. (pres. 1972), Summit County Hist. Soc. (dir. 1974—). Clubs: President's (Kent State U.), Hilltoppers (Akron U.). Home: 1007 W Steels Corners Rd Cuyahoga Falls OH 44223-3111 Office: PO Box 1147 Cuyahoga Falls OH 44223-0147

HAAG, HARVEY EUGENE, physics educator; b. DuBois, Pa., July 2, 1950; s. Harvey E. and Miriam Haag; m. Janet M. Postlewait, June 9, 1973; children: Elizabeth Ann, Christian J.W. BS in Secondary Edn. Physics, Pa. State U., 1971, MEd in Curriculum and Instruction, 1979. Instr. physics and math. Moshannon Valley Schs., Houtzdale, Pa., 1971-75; tchr. physics and math. computers Clearfield (Pa.) Area Schs., 1975-83, tchr. physics and engring., 1983—; tchr. physics and computers Pa. State U., DuBois, 1979—; owner, photographer Haag's Photography Svc., Clearfield, 1974—. Borough councilman Clearfield Borough, 1993—; Rep. precinct area chmn. Rep. Party, Clearfield County, 1976-85; dist. advancement chmn. Bucktail coun. Boy Scouts Am., DuBois, Pa., 1975-98, coun. advancement chmn., 1990-98, vigil mem. Order of Arrow. Recipient Silver Beaver award Boy Scouts Am. Mem. Nat. Sci. Tchrs. Assn., Pa. Sci. Tchrs. Assn., U.S. Power Squadron, Cen. Pa. Assn. Physics Tchrs., Western Pa. Assn. Physics Tchrs., Clearfield Edn. Assn. (past pres. 1977-78), Masons (# 314, Master 1989, ednl. chmn. Grand Lodge 1990—). Republican. Presbyterian. Avocations: sailing, woodworking, photography, camping, hunting. Home: 4 Turnpike Ave Clearfield PA 16830-1742 Office: Clearfield Area Schs PO Box 710 Clearfield PA 16830-0710

HAAG, MARK WALDO, II, director network operations; b. Bklyn., Jan. 11, 1963; s. Mark Waldo Haag and Linda (Tamblyn) Loth. BS in Telecomms., Ohio U., 1994. Prodn. dir. WVVA TV Ch. 6, Bluefield, W.Va., 1987-89; owner, operator Haag II Prodns., Bluefield, 1989-96; dir. network ops. Wisdom Network, Bluefield, 1996—. Cons. Ptrns. in Edn.; bd. dirs. Bluefield Jaycees, 1988-90. Mem. Nat. Assn. TV Programming Execs., Nat. Assn. Broadcasters, Internat. TV Assn., Soc. of Motion Picture and TV Execs. Home: PO Box 555 Bluefield WV 24701-4618 Office: Wisdom Network Southview Mall Rte 52 N Bluefield WV 24701

HAAG, WALTER M(ONROE), JR., philatelist; b. Williamsport, Pa., Apr. 25, 1940; s. Walter Monroe and Julia Maria (Halabura) H.; m. Joanne Marie Spudis, May 22 1971; 1 child, Steven Joseph. B.S.I.E., Pa. State U., 1962, M.S. in Indsl. Engring., 1968; M.P.H., U. Mich., 1971. Indsl. engr. Sylvania, Montoursville, Pa., 1962-64, supr. quality control, 1965-66; commd. lt. (j.g.) U.S. Pub. Health Services, 1966; advanced through grades to capt., 1977; mgmt. analyst NIH, Bethesda, Md., 1966-69; global community health career fellow USPHS, Washington, 1969-71; tech. officer WHO, Geneva, 1972-73; br. chief resource mgmt. Nat. Inst. Occupational Safety and Health, Rockville, Md., 1973-74, dep. dir. planning, 1974-76; dir. phys. scis. and engring. Nat. Inst. Occupational Safety and Health, Cin., 1976-87; cons. Assn. Media-Based Continuing Edn. for Engrs., Atlanta, 1979, assoc. dir. div. tng. and manpower devel., 1987-95, indsl. engr., 1995-96; philatelist Loveland, Ohio, 1997—; adminstr. research for instruments, fibrous aerosol monitor Indsl. Research 100 award, 1972. Speaker Am. Lung Assn., Las Vegas, Nev., 1979; speaker Air Pollution Control League, Cin., 1982, 87; mem. indsl. and profl. adv. council Pa. State Coll. Engring. Recipient Commendation medal USPHS, Rockville, 1976, Citation award USPHS, Cin., 1986, Unit Commendation medal USPHS, 1988, 92, Meritorius Svc. medal USPHS, 1992; named Supr. of Yr., Federally Employed Women, Cin., 1980. Mem. Inst. Indsl. Engrs. (sr. treas. chpt. 1964-65, v.p. chpt. 1966), Am. Mgmt. Assn., Am. Soc. for Tng. and Devel., Am. Conf. Govtl. Indsl. Hygienists (bd. dirs. 1986-89), Air Pollution Control League Greater Cin. (trustee 1982—). Republican. Roman Catholic.

HAAK, HAROLD HOWARD, university president; b. Madison, Wis., June 1, 1935; s. Harold J. and Laura (Kittleson) H.; m. Betty L. Steiner, June 25, 1955; children—Alison Marie, Janet Christine. B.A., U. Wis., 1957, M.A., 1958; Ph.D., Princeton U., 1963. From asst. prof. to assoc. prof. polit. sci., pub. adminstrn. and urban studies San Diego State Coll., 1962-69, dean coll. profl. studies, prof. pub. adminstrn. and urban studies, 1969-71; acad. v.p. Calif. State U., Fresno, 1971-73, pres., 1980-91, pres. emeritus, 1991—, trustee prof., 1991—, trustee, prof., vice chancellor acad. affairs, 1992-93; v.p. U. Colo., Denver, 1973, chancellor, 1974-80. Trustee William Saroyan Found., 1981-91; mem. NCAA Pres. Commn., 1987-91; bd. dirs. Fresno Econ. Devel. Corp., 1981-91, Cmty. Hosps. Ctrl. Calif., 1989-92; mem. bd. visitors Air Univ.; mem. Army adv. panel on ROTC affairs, 1988-92; vice chair Calif. Commn. on Agr. and Higher Edn., 1993-96; bd. dirs. Pacific Luth. Theol. Sem. Recipient U. Colo. medal, 1980. Mem. Phi Beta Kappa, Phi Kappa Phi. Office: Calif State U Fresno Off of Pres Fresno CA 93740-0019

HAAKE, PAUL, chemistry, biochemistry and history of science educator; b. Winona, Minn., June 28, 1932; s. Arnold Paul and Clara B. (Olson) H.; m. Janet C. Burrows (div. June 1975); children: David Arnold, Philip Carl. AB, Harvard U., 1954; postgrad., Harvard U. Med. Sch., 1954-56, Harvard U., 1956-60; PhD, Harvard U., 1961. Noyes fellow Calif. Inst. Tech., Pasadena, 1960-61; instr. UCLA, 1961-62, asst. prof., 1962-65, assoc. prof., 1965-68; prof. Wesleyan U., Middletown, Conn., 1968—. Author: Case Studies in Energy, 1988, Molecular Basis of Living Systems, 1989; contbr. over 95 articles on history and philosophy of science, edn., inorganic, organic and biochemistry to profl. jours. Mem. State Conn. Nuclear Power Evaluation Council, Hartford, 1975-78; mem. Charter Commn., Durham, Conn., 1970. Grantee NSF, NIH; Alfred P. Sloan rsch. fellow, 1964-67, NATO sr. fellow, 1970, NSF faculty fellow, 1975. Office: Wesleyan U Dept Molecular Bio & Biochem Middletown CT 06459-0175

HAAKENSON, PHILIP NIEL, pharmacist, educator; b. Hatton, N.D., Apr. 15, 1924; s. Martin Selmer and Theodora H.; m. Eldora Ida Robinson, June 18, 1950; children: Mary Kim, Martin Niel. BS in Pharmacy, N.D. State U., 1950, MS in Pharmacy, 1965; PhD in Pharmacy Adminstrn., U. Wis., 1972. Owner Portland (N.D.) Drug, 1950-60, Hatton Drug, 1956-60; asst. prof. pharmacy adminstrn. N.D. State U., Fargo, 1961-65, assoc. prof., 1965-70, prof., 1970-87, prof. emeritus, 1987—, dean sch. of pharmacy, 1970-88; dir. Pharmacy Continuing Edn., 1982-87; vis. prof. Univ. Mont. Sch. Pharmacy, 1987-88, Univ. Man. (Can.), 1988-95. Editor Nodak Pharmacist, 1962-74, 1982-87. Mgmt. counselor Svc. Corps Ret. Execs. Assn. Served with USN, 1942-45. Mem. Am. Assn. colls. of Pharmacy, N.D. Pharm. Assn. (recipient Bowl of Hygiea 1979), Am. Pharm. Assn., Kappa Psi (named Outstanding Alumni 1974, Pharmacist of Yr. 1977), Sigma Xi. Republican. Lutheran. Lodges: Lions, Masons, Shriners. Home: 210 28th Ave N Fargo ND 58102-1624 Office: ND State U Sch of Pharmacy Fargo ND 58105 also: Svc Corps of Ret Execs Assn Box 3086 Rm 225 Main PO Bldg Fargo ND 58108-3086

HAAR, ANA MARIA FERNÁNDEZ, advertising and public relations executive; b. Oriente Province, Cuba, Mar. 25, 1951; came to U.S., 1960, naturalized, 1970; d. Gilberto and Esmeralda Emiliana (Díaz) Fernández. Grad., Miami Dade Community Coll., 1971; student, Barry Coll., 1972-78. Adminstrv. asst. thru asst. v.p. nat. accounts Flagship Bank, Miami Beach, Fla., 1971-77; v.p. comml. lending Jefferson Nat. Bank, Miami Beach, 1977-78; pres. IAC Advt. Group, Miami, 1978—; instr. Miami Dade Community Coll. Women in Mgmt. Program, 1980-81; hostess Sta. WPBT Program Viva; exec. com. World Trade Ctr., Miami. Mem. Dade County Commn. on Status of Women, 1979-82; chmn. Econ. Devel. Task Force of Commn. on Status of Women, 1979-82; bd. dirs. Downtown Miami Bus. Assn., 1979-82. Recipient Gran Orden Martiana of Cuban Lyceum for excellence in community svc., 1976, Up and Comers award South Fla. Bus. Jour., 1988; named one of 100 Most Influential Hispanics Hispanic Bus. Mag. Mem. Advt. Fedn. Greater Miami, Greater Miami Advt. Fedn. (bd. dirs.), Asociación de Publicitarios Latino-Americanos (v.p.), Japan Soc. (bd. dirs.), Miami Beach C. of C. (hon. life, trustee), Greater Miami C. of C., Hispanic Heritage Festival Com., Cuban Women's Club (past pres.), Assn. Hispanic Advt. Agys. (pres. 1998-99). Office: IAC Advt Group 2725 SW 3rd Ave Miami FL 33129-2335

HAAS, CHARLIE, screenwriter; b. Bklyn., Oct. 22, 1952; s. Philip and Eunice (Dillon) H.; m. Barbara K. Moran, Dec. 21, 1981. BA, U. Calif., Santa Cruz, 1984. Editorial dir. Warner Bros. Records, Burbank, Calif., 1974-76; contbg. editor New West Mag., Beverly Hills, Calif., 1976-80; freelance writer L.A., 1976-80, Oakland, Calif., 1980—. Co-author: (movies) Over the Edge, 1979, Tex, 1982, Gremlins 2, 1990, Matinee, 1993, Runaway Daughters, 1994; contbr. articles to mags. Mem. Friends of Oakland Parks & Recreation, Friends of Oakland Pub. Libr. Avocations: fountain pens, mountain bikes.

HAAS, EILEEN MARIE, homecare advocate; b. Pitts., Feb. 27, 1948; d. Michael Joseph and Bridget Agnes (Connolly) McNulty; m. Jerry Albert Haas, July 19, 1975; 1 child, Melissa. Student, York Coll. of Pa., 1975-78, Messiah Coll., Grantsville, Pa., 1978-80. Clk. Exch. Bur. Pitts., 1966-67; debt. collector Nat. Account Sys., Pitts., 1967-71; preadoptive advocate Hershey, Pa., 1983-84, Phila., 1984-85; homecare advocate Dillsburg, Pa., 1985-88, Deer Lodge, Mont., 1988-92, Gibsonia, Pa., 1992—; interpreter svcs. St. Victors Ch., Bairdsford, Pa., 1992—; presenter Harrisburg (Pa.) Area C.C., 1985, Pa. Soc. Respiratory Therapy, Ctrl. Pa. chpt., 1985; co-presenter Coun. Exceptional Children, Salt Lake City, 1997; rschr. in pulmonary rehab. *Instrumental in developing homecare of long term, medically complex, ventilator dependent child, infancy through 16 years of age. Advocated for various therapeutic and educational services in Pennsylvania and Montana. Demanded and enforced state and federal regulations, enabling a medically fragile, technology assisted child to attempt educational endeavors in a mainstream setting. Successfully advocated and created a fully developed, resource rich, in home deaf education classroom to facilitate a "school-like" environment for this child due to health constraints. Together with husband Jerry, developed and enabled safe, national and international travel for medically complex individuals to include land, air and sea.* With USN, 1971-74. Mem. DAV, Am. Soc. Deaf Children, Coun. Exceptional Children, Assn. Severe Handicaps, Profl. Networking for Excellence in Svc. to Deaf and Hard of Hearing. Republican. Roman Catholic. Avocations: deaf education research, dysphagia research, writing, needlepoint, knitting. Home: 90 Kaufman Rd Gibsonia PA 15044-7950

HAAS, ELEANOR A. (MRS. PETER RALPH HAAS), investment banker; b. Jersey City; d. Nicholas Mark and Eleanor (Cochran) Alter de Csanytelek; m. Peter Ralph Haas. BA, Smith Coll. Account exec. Ruder & Finn, Inc., N.Y.C., 1966-68; founder, pres. The Haas Group, Inc., N.Y.C., 1968-86, MarketQuest, N.Y.C., 1986-98; v.p., dir. HMG Planning The Howard Marlboro Group, N.Y.C., 1988-91; managing dir. E-Technologies Assocs., LLC, N.Y.C., 1998—; founder, editor CyberScout, N.Y.C., 1996—; adj. assoc. prof. dept. journalism NYU, 1980-83, lectr. Sch. Continuing Edn. NYU, 1981-83; mem. adv. bd. InterTrade Techs. Corp. Bd. dirs. MIT Enterprise Forum of N.Y. Mem. Advt. Women N.Y., Advt. Club N.Y., N.Y. New Media Assn., Fin. Women's Assn. (entrepreneurs com.), Women in New Media. Office: E-Technologies Assocs LLC 611 Broadway Ste 725 New York NY 10012

HAAS, FREDERICK CARL, paper and chemical company executive; b. Buffalo, Feb. 16, 1936; s. Karl A. and Marie S. (Shilling) H.; m. Dorothy A. Wittlief, Aug. 31, 1957; children—Kenneth Karl, Lawrence Frederick, Sandra Dorothy. B.S. in Chem. Engring, Purdue U., 1957; M.S. in Nuclear Engring, Rensselaer Poly. Inst., Troy, N.Y., 1959, Ph.D. in Chem. Engring, 1960; grad., Advanced Mgmt. Program, Harvard U., 1978. Registered profl. engr., N.Y. Research engr. Cornell Aero. Lab., 1960-63; with Westvaco Corp., 1963—, corp. research dir., then v.p., 1978-81; sr. v.p. ops. Westvaco Corp., N.Y.C., 1982—; asst. prof. Potomac State Coll., 1966; mem. curriculum com., research com. U. Maine; chmn. research adv. com. Inst. Paper Chemistry; mem. president's key exec. com. Rensselaer Poly. Inst. Author papers in field. Bd. dirs. Syracuse Pulp and Paper Found. AEC fellow, 1957, Tappi fellow, 1994; recipient Disting. Engring. Alumnus award Purdue U., 1993, Outstanding Chem. Engring. award, 1993. Mem. Am. Mgmt. Assn. (research and devel. council), Am. Inst. Chem. Engrs., Am. Chem. Soc., TAPPI, Nat. Soc. Profl. Engrs., Indsl. Research Inst., Dirs. Indsl. Research, Can. Pulp and Paper Assn., Tri-State Shetland Sheep Dog Club, Sigma Xi. Methodist. Office: Westvaco Corp 299 Park Ave New York NY 10171

HAAS, GEORGE AARON, lawyer; b. N.Y.C., July 6, 1919; s. Herman Joseph and Violet (Cowen) H.; m. Miriam Durkin, Aug. 1942; children—Thomas Leonard, Karen Ann (Mrs. Michael Davenport), James G.D. A.B., Princeton U., 1940; LL.B., Yale U., 1947. Bar: Ga. 1947. Since practiced in Atlanta; partner Haas, Bridges & Kane (and predecessor firms), 1947—; Sec., dir. Lucerne Corp., East Freeway Corp., Crescent View Corp., Mountain View Corp., Lake Placid Corp. Mem. hosp. and health div. Atlanta Community Council, 1962-68; mem. tech. assistance com., del. White House Conf. on Children and Youth, 1970; state trustee from Ga. Nat. Easter Seal Soc. for Crippled Children and Adults, 1959-65, mem. exec. com., 1961-65, v.p., 1963-65, 1st v.p., 1965-66, mem. ho. of dels., 1965-73, pres. 1971-73; bd. dirs. 1965-73, chmn. formula rev. bd., mem. relations and standards rev. com., 1967-69, pres., 1969-71; trustee Ga. Easter Seal Soc. for Crippled Children and Adults, 1955-65, 78—, sec., 1957-58, pres., 1959-61, chmn. ho. of dels., 1967-69; Bd. dirs. Fulton-DeKalb chpt. Nat. Found.; mem. med. adv. bd. Ga. chpt. Am. Phys. Therapy Assn. Served to capt. F.A. AUS, World War II. Mem. ABA, Ga. Bar Assn., Atlanta Bar Assn. Club: Standard (Atlanta) (past sec., dir.). Lodge: Kiwanis. Home: 2575 Peachtree Rd NE Atlanta GA 30305-3694 Office: 2964 Peachtree Rd NW Atlanta GA 30305-2153

HAAS, HOWARD GREEN, retired bedding manufacturing company executive; b. Chgo., Apr. 14, 1924; s. Adolph and Marie (Green) H.; m. Carolyn Werbner, June 4, 1949; children: Jody, Jonathan. Student, U. Chgo., 1942; BBA, U. Mich., 1948. Promotion dir. Esquire, Inc., Chgo., 1949-50; advt. mgr. Mitchell Mfg. Co., Chgo., 1950-52; v.p. advt. Mitchell Mfg. Co., 1952-56, v.p. sales, 1956-58; sales mgr. Sealy, Inc., Chgo., 1959-60; v.p. marketing Sealy, Inc., 1960-65, exec. v.p., 1965-67, pres., treas., 1967-86, 87; bd. dirs. Morgan Products, Ingersoll Holding Co., Avora Custom Machinery, Inc., Chittenden & Eastman, Inc.; chmn. Howard Haas Assocs.; vis. prof. strategic mgmt. U. Chgo. Grad. Sch. Bus., 1990—. Author: The Leader Within, 1993. Past mem. nominating com. Glencoe Sch. Bd.; mem. print and drawing com. Art Inst. Chgo.; past chmn. parent's com. Washington U., St. Louis; past bd. dirs. Jewish Children's Bur.; mem. vis. com. Oriental Inst., U. Chgo., Northbrook Symphony, Meet the Composer. 1st lt. USAAF, 1943-45, ETO. Decorated Air medal with 3 oak leaf clusters; recipient Brotherhood award NCCJ, 1970, Human Relations award Am. Jewish Com., 1977. Mem. Nat. Assn. Bedding Mfrs. (past vice chmn., trustee), Birchwood Tennis Club (Highland Pk., Ill.), Masons. Jewish. Office: Howard Haas Assocs 208 S La Salle St Ste 1275 Chicago IL 60604-1101

HAAS, JACQUELINE CRAWFORD, lawyer; b. St. Louis, Nov. 9, 1935; d. Ernest Augustus and Nora (Fullard) Crawford; m. Karl Alan Haas, Jan. 27, 1962 (dec. Mar. 1986); children: James Andrew, Susan Jennifer, David Reid, Peter Crawford. AB, Cornell U., 1957; LLB, Harvard U., 1961. Bar: N.Y. 1962, U.S. Dist. Ct. (so. dist.) N.Y. 1963, U.S. Ct. Appeals (2d cir.) 1968, Mass. 1972. Assoc. Lord, Day & Lord, N.Y.C., 1961-63; atty. family ct. div. Legal Aid Soc., Bklyn., 1964-66; exam. atty. N.Y.C. Dept. of Investigation, 1966-68, exec. asst. to commr., 1969-71; pvt. practice Weston, Mass., 1971—; mem. Greater Boston com. Harvard U. Law Sch. Fund, Cambridge, Mass., 1976—. Del. Mass. Dem. Issues Conv., 1983, 85, 87, 89, 92, 93, 95, 97, 99, Mass. Dem. Nominating Conv., 1984, 86, 94, 96, 98; mem. platform com. Mass. Dem. Com., 1993; mem. Dem. Town Com., Weston, 1984—, vice chmn., 1984-86; chmn. bd. Roxbury-Weston Programs, Inc., 1982-84; mem. family com. METCO, 1973-75, mem. cmty. coord. coun., 1982-85; mem. Weston Housing Needs Com., 1991-93. Mem. ABA (civil practice and procedure of the antitrust sect.), Mass. Bar Assn., Assn. of Bar of N.Y.C., Harvard Law Sch. Assn. Mass. (v.p. 1991—). Democrat. Episcopalian. Avocations: skiing, sailing, literature, travel. Office: 42 Partridge Hill Rd Weston MA 02493-1750

HAAS, JAY, professional golfer; b. St. Louis, Dec. 2, 1953. Grad., Wake Forest Coll., 1971. Profl. golfer, 1976—, Ryder Cup Team, 1995. Recipient Fred Haskins award, 1975; won NCAA Championship, 1975, Andy Williams-San Diego Open, 1978, Greater Milw. Open, 1981, B.C. Open, 1981, Hall of Fame Classic, 1982, Tex. Open, 1982, Big "I" Houston Open, 1987, Bob Hope Chrysler Classic, 1988, Fed. Express St. Jude Classic, 1992, H-E-B Tex. Open, 1993; mem. U.S. Ryder Cup team, 1983. Office: PGA Am Box 109601 100 Avenue Of Champions Palm Beach Gardens FL 33410*

HAAS, JERE DOUGLAS, nutritional sciences educator, researcher; b. Lancaster, Pa., Sept. 15, 1945; s. Jacob Charles and Dorothy Louise (Graeter) H.; m. Sharon Faye Pitt, June 22, 1968; children: Jeremy Michael, Jonathan Andrew. AB, Franklin and Marshall Coll., 1967; MA, Pa. State U., 1970, PhD, 1973. Trainee in human biology USPHS, Peru, 1971-73; asst. prof. anthropology U. Mass., Amherst, 1973-75; asst. prof. nutrition Cornell U., Ithaca, N.Y., 1975-80, assoc. prof., 1980-87, prof., 1987—; Nancy Schlegel Meinig prof. maternal and child nutrition; dir. human biology program, dir. divsn. nutritional scis. Cornell U., Ithaca, N.Y.; hon. rsch. fellow anatomy dept. U. Aberdeen, Scotland, 1982; vis. prof. Food Rsch. Inst., Stanford (Calif.) U., 1988-89; mem. com. on nutrition during pregnancy and lactation Inst. Medicine, NAS, 1988-90; advisor panel on nutrition WHO, 1991—; chair subcom. on maternal anthropometry, 1991-94; tech. adv. group on food and nutrition Pan Am. Health Orgn., 1996—; dir. divsn. nutrition and health Nat. inst. Pub. Health, Cuernavaca, Mex., 1998. Mem. editorial bd. Human Biology, 1984-88, Annals Human Biology, 1985—, Am. Jour. Human Biology, 1990—; contbr. over 130 articles to profl. jours., chpts. to books. Rsch. grantee NSF, Bolivia, Peru, 1975-96, NIH, N.Y., Kans., Guatemala, 1978-94, U.S. Dept. Agr., N.Y. Fellow AAAS, Human Biology Assn. (exec. com. 1981-85); mem. Am. Assn. Phys. Anthropologists (v.p. 1992-94, pres. 1995-97), Am. Soc. Nutritional Scis., Internat. Nutrition Rsch., Am. Soc. Clin. Nutrition. Office: Cornell U #127 Savage Hall Ithaca NY 14853-6301

HAAS, JOHN C., architect; b. Columbus, Ohio, Nov. 3, 1934; s. John Clyde and Margaret (Merideth) H.; m. Jean Ann Scigliano, June 12, 1958 (dec. Apr. 10, 1986); m. Joyce Conklin, May 9, 1987; children: Jeffrey, Joel, John. BArch, Pa. State U., 1958. Registered architect Pa., Ohio, N.J., N.Y., Del., W.Va., Md., Va., Mass., Fla. Archtl. draftsman Arthur E. Tennyson, Pitts., 1959-62; archtl. designer Diehl and Stein, Architects, Princeton, N.J., 1962-63; staff architect Hankins and Hyres, Architects, Trenton, N.J., 1963-67; architect, prin. firm Mahony and Zvosec, Princeton, 1967-71; dir. archtl. planning dept. Gen. Housing Industries, State College, Pa., 1971-72; pres., chief exec. officer John C. Haas Assocs Inc. Architects Engrs. Planners, State College, 1972—. Prin. works include Nittany Apt. Housing, The Meadows Clinic, Fraser St. Parking Garage, BCH Office Bldg., Geisinger Med. Clinic, The Bryce Jordan Convocation Ctr., Pa. State U. (all State College). Active Centre County United Way Campaign Cabinet, 1994, 95, 96; county chmn. United Way Campaign, 1997; mem. bd. dirs. Chamber of Bus. and Ind. of Centre County, 1996—, Centre County United Way, 1998—. Served as capt. U.S. Army, 1958-59. Mem. Nat. Council Archtl. Registration Bds., AIA (pres. mid. Pa. chpt. 1986-87), Pa. Soc. Architects (pres. 1993), Architects Licensure Bd., Pa., 1997—, State College Area C. of C. (pres. 1990-91, bd. dirs. 1984-92). Republican. Presbyterian. Lodge: Rotary (pres. 1988-89, bd. dirs.). Home: 14 High Meadow Ln State College PA 16803-1853 Office: John C Haas Assocs Inc Architects Engrs Planners 1301 N Atherton St State College PA 16803-2932

HAAS, JOSEPH ALAN, court administrator, lawyer; b. Riverside, Calif., June 30, 1950; s. Garland August and Pauline (Anderson) H.; m. Barbara Roberts, May 27, 1978; children: Natalie C., Christina R. BA in Econs., U. Wash., 1972, MA in Econs., 1974; JD, U. Puget Sound, 1983. Bar: Wash. 1984, U.S. Dist. Ct. (we. dist.) Wash. 1984, Md. 1986, U.S. Ct. Appeals (4th cir.) 1986. Regional coord. Adminstrv. Office U.S. Cts., Washington, 1975-80; chief dep. clk. U.S. Dist. Ct. for Western Wash., Seattle, 1981-84; clk. U.S. Dist. Ct. Md., Balt., 1984-96, U.S. Dist. Ct. for S.D., Sioux Falls, 1996—. Mem. Nat. Assn. for Ct. Mgmt., Fed. Ct. Clks. Assn. (pres. 1987-88), Fed. Bar Assn. (bd. govs. 1989-96, treas. 1991-95), Wash. State Bar Assn. Office: US Dist Ct 400 S Phillips Ave Rm 128 Sioux Falls SD 57104-6851

HAAS, JOSEPH MARSHALL, petroleum consultant; b. Alexandria, La., June 21, 1927; s. Samuel and Lulu Susan (Haupt) H.; m. Mary Louise

Nance, June 4, 1949 (dec. Jan. 1950); 1 child, Samuel Douglas; m. Marion Barker, Apr. 9, 1954; children: Joseph Marshall, Suzanne M., Thomas B., Katherine L. B of Mech. Engring., Ga. Inst. Tech., 1949. With Gen. Am. Oil Co., Dallas, 1949-78; asst. v.p. prodn. and engring. Gen. Am. Oil Co., 1957-60, v.p. engring., 1960-78; petroleum cons. Haas Engring., 1978—; pres., bd. dirs. Conejo Investments Inc., 1994—. With USNR, 1945-46. Mem. Am. Inst. Mining and Metall. Engrs., Ind. Petroleum Assn. Am., Masons (32 degree, Shriner), Dallas Petroleum Club, Tau Beta Pi, Sigma Chi, Pi Tau Sigma. Methodist. Home: 1119 Challenger St Austin TX 78734-3801 Office: 1123 Challenger St Austin TX 78734-3801

HAAS, LESTER CARL, retired architect; b. Shreveport, La., Apr. 9, 1913; s. Jacob and Hanna (Kahn) H.; m. Niki Kal, Nov. 1, 1942; children: Dale Frances, Catherine Kal (Mrs. Fred Donald Youngswick). BA, Johns Hopkins U., 1933; BArch, U. Pa., 1936; postgrad., Ecole Des Beaux-Arts, N.Y.C., 1936-37; diplome, Ecole Des Beaux-Arts, Fontainebleau, France, 1939; vis. student in residence, Am. Acad., Rome, Italy, 1940. Archtl. apprentice W. Pope Barney, Phila., 1936-39; architect Robert & Co., 1940-41; prin. Lester C. Haas, Architect, Shreveport, 1946-65; ptnr. Haas Massey & Assocs. (architects), Shreveport, 1966-88; mng. partner TAG-The Archtl. Group, 1978-85; prin. Lester C. Haas, FAIA(E), CCS-Architect, 1989-98, ret., 1998. Co-author: weekly column Ark-La-Texture, 1967-71. Principal works include, Pioneer Bank and Trust Co., Shreveport main office and 9 br. banks, 1948-78, KTBS offices, radio and TV studios, Shreveport, 1948-76, Caddo Sch. Exceptional Children, Shreveport, 1956, also addition, 1977, La Sands Western Hills Motel, Bossier City, La., 1957, St. Pius X Sch., convent and sanctuary alterations, North Shreveport, 1962, Barksdale Officer Club, Barksdale AFB, La. Alteration and Addition, 1965, Northwestern State U. at Shreveport, 1966, Restoration and Renovation of the Strand Theatre, Shreveport, 1978-85, C-Barc Adult Workshop, Shreveport, 1970, additions, 1979, Adminstrv. Center, Caddo Parish Sch. Bd., Shreveport, 1971, Master Plan and Adminstrn. Bldg., Delgado Coll., New Orleans, 1979-81, Shreveport Chamber Pla., 1983, Caddo Parish Communications Dist. Number 1, Emergency Communication Ctr. E-911, 1988. Chmn. rev. com. N.W. La. Areawide Health Planning Council, 1973-75, pres., 1975-76; pres. Travelers Aid, 1951, Children's Service Bur., 1952, Courtyard Players Civic Theatre, 1954, ARC, 1963-65, NCCJ, 1965-69; nat. bd., 1970-73, St. Vincent Acad. Parents Club, 1966-67, Lyric Ball, 1967, Caddo Found. for Exceptional Children, 1972-74; v.p. Caddo-Bossier Assn. Retarded Citizens, 1957, United Fund, 1963-67, Caddo Found. Exceptional Children, 1967-72; adv. bd. Congregation Daughters of Cross, 1965-69; community adv. com. Jr. League, 1973-76, all Shreveport; mem. Shreveport Bldg. Bd., 1979-83; pres. Mental Health Assn. Caddo-Bossier, 1981-82; founding mem. Caddo-Bossier Assn. Retarded Citizens Found., 1997. Lt. USNR, 1942-45. Decorated Navy Commendation ribbon; recipient Merit award 2d Internat. Lighting Exposition, 1947; Ann. Brotherhood citation Shreveport chpt. NCCJ, 1974; John Stewardson Travelling scholar in architecture, 1939-40; honoree Martin Luther King Health Ctr. Christian Svc. Inst., 1991; recipient 5 CSI Regional Specification awards. Fellow AIA (pres. N.La. chpt. 1955, exec. com. Gulf States regional council 1956, pres. Shreveport chpt. 1984); mem. Constrn. Specifications Inst. (cert. constrn. specifier 1979, pres. Shreveport chpt. 1970-71, Nat. Jury Fellows 1974-76), La. Architects Assn. (rep. to Gov.'s Com. to Rewrite Fire Marshal's Act 1973, bd. dirs. 1984), Shreveport Jr. C. of C. (past v.p.), Shreveport C. of C. (bd. dirs., officer), Am. Legion, D.A.V., Tau Sigma Delta. Jewish (pres. congregation 1967, 68). Club: Greater Shreveport Racquet. Home: 1031 Dudley Dr Shreveport LA 71104-4732

HAAS, LU ANN, counselor; b. Waterloo, Iowa, Oct. 16, 1956; d. Leonard Edward and Naomi Lee (Binley) H.; divorced; children: Shauna Lee Haas, Nicholas William Smith. AAS, Ctrl. Tex. Coll., 1986; BA magna cum laude, Mt. mercy Coll., 1992; MA, U. Iowa, 1993. Cert. rehab. counselor. Ind. truck driver, 1982-83; night supr. Four Oaks-John Mcdonald Residential Treatment, Monticello, Iowa, 1991-92; security officer RA-CO Security Co., 1993-94; substance abuse counselor Area Substance Abuse Coun., Anamosa, Iowa, 1993-94; counseling psychologist Dept. Vets Affairs, Cin., 1994-96, Dallas, 1996-97; spkr. in field; cons. in field. Sgt. U.S. Army, 1975-81, 83-87. Leonard A. Miller scholar, 1993. Mem. ACA, Nat. Rehab. Assn., Am. Rehab. Counseling Assn., Nat. Rehab. Counseling Assn. (sec./treas. 1997, 98, bd. dirs. 1995, 96, membership chmn. 1995-97), Iowa Rehab. Counseling Assn., Disabled Am. Vets. (life), U. Iowa Alumni Assn., Kappa Gamma Pi (liaison Mt. Mercy Coll.), Am. Legion, Vietnam Vets. Am. (assoc. Miami Valley (Ohio) chpt.). Democrat. Methodist. Avocations: crocheting, reading, writing. Home: 205 Fawn Creek Cir Anamosa IA 52205-2141

HAAS, MERRILL WILBER, geologist, oil company executive; b. Albert, Kans., July 9, 1910; s. Frederick William and Ella (Keller) H.; m. Maria Lara, June 10, 1944; children: Mariella, Merrill Wilber, Maria Cecilia, Frederick Harold. Student, Kans. U., 1928-31; BA in Geology, U. Mich., 1932; postgrad., Harvard U., 1932-33. Paleontologist Exxon Co. USA, Houston, 1933-34; dist. geologist Lago Petroleum Corp., Venezuela, 1934-36, paleontologist, 1936-38; paleontologist Standard Oil. Co., Venezuela, 1938-41; div. geologist Creole Petroleum Corp., Venezuela, 1941-49; area geologist Standard Oil Co., N.Y.C., 1949-50; with Carter Oil Co., Tulsa, 1950-60, successively chief geologist exploration mgr., dir., v.p., 1957-60; v.p. for exploration Exxon Co., U.S.A., Houston, 1960-75; pvt. practice petroleum cons., 1975—; Merrill W. Haas disting. vis. prof. geology, 1973. Recipient Erasmus Haworth Disting. Alumni award U. Kans., 1961, Disting. Service Citation, 1966, Outstanding Achievement award U. Mich., 1981; named to Gallery of Outstanding Kansans, U. Kans., 1986. Fellow Geol. Soc. Am.; mem. Am. Assn. Petroleum Geologists (pres. 1974-75, Sidney Powers Meml. medal 1986, trustee 1976-91, chmn. found. 1989-91), Tulsa Geol. Soc., Paleontol. Research Inst. (pres. 1973-75), Houston Geol. Soc., The Explorers Club, Sigma Gamma Epsilon, Acacia. Methodist. Club: Petroleum. Lodge: Masons. Home: 10910 Wickwild St Houston TX 77024-7615

HAAS, PAUL RAYMOND, petroleum company executive; b. Kingston, N.Y., Mar. 10, 1915; s. Frederick J. and Amanda (Lange) H.; m. Mary F. Diedrick, Aug. 30, 1936; children: Rheta Marie, Raymond Paul, Rene Marie. A.B., Rider Coll., 1934, LL.D., 1976. C.P.A., Tex. Acct. Arthur Andersen & Co. (C.P.A.s), N.Y.C. and Houston, 1934-41; with La Gloria Oil & Gas Co., Corpus Christi, Tex., 1941-59; v.p., treas., dir. La Gloria Oil & Gas Co., 1947-59; adminstrv. v.p. Tex. Eastern Transmission Corp., Houston, 1958-59; pres., chmn. bd. Prado Oil & Gas Co., 1959-66, Wiltex Corp., 1950-65, Garland Co., 1956-65, Citronelle Oil & Gas Co., 1967-69, Corpus Christi Oil and Gas Co., 1968-90, Corpus Christi Leaseholds Inc., 1990—, Corpus Christi Exploration Co., 1976-90; ltd. partner Salomon Bros., 1973-81; ind. oil and gas operator, 1959—. Trustee Corpus Christi Ind. Sch. Dist., 1951-58, pres., 1956-58; mem. Tex. Bd. Edn., 1962-72, vice chmn., 1970-72; mem. Gov.'s Com. Edn., 1966-69; Trustee Paul and Mary Haas Found., 1954—, Robert T. Wilson Found., 1954-72, Rider Coll., 1959-67, Moody Found., 1966-73, Found. Center, 1970-75, Council on Founds., 1970-76, Commn. on Philanthropy and Pub. Needs, 1973-75, Univ. Cancer Found. M.D. Anderson Hosp. and Tumor Inst., 1975—. Presbyn. (elder). Home: 4500 Ocean Dr Apt 9A Corpus Christi TX 78412-2572 Office: Corpus Christi Holding Co PO Box 779 Corpus Christi TX 78403-0779

HAAS, PETER E., SR., company executive; b. San Francisco, Dec. 20, 1918; s. Walter A. and Elise (Stern) H.; m. Josephine Baum, Feb. 1, 1945; m. Mimi Lurie, Aug., 1981; children: Peter E., Michael Stern, Margaret Elizabeth. Student, Deerfield Acad., 1935-36; A.B., U. Calif., 1940; MBA cum laude, Harvard, 1943. With Levi Strauss & Co., San Francisco, 1945—, exec. v.p., 1958-70, pres., 1970-81, CEO, 1976-81, chmn. bd., 1981-89, chmn. exec. com., 1989—, also bd. dirs.; chmn. exec. com., bd. dirs. Levi Strauss Assocs. Inc. Holding Corp.; dir. emeritus AT&T. Trustee San Francisco Found., 1984—; assoc. Smithsonian Nat. Bd., 1988—; bd. dirs. No. Calif. Grantmakers, 1989—; former mem. exec. com. Strive for Five; former mem. Golden Gate Nat. Recreation Area Adv. Com.; Former pres. Jewish Welfare Fedn.; former trustee Stanford U.; former dir., vice chmn. San Francisco Bay Area Council; former trustee United Way of San Francisco Bay Area; former pres. Aid to Retarded Children; former bd. govs. United Way of Am. Recipient Alexis De Tocqueville Soc. award, United Way Am., 1985; named CEO of Yr., Fin. World mag., 1981, Bus. Statesman of Yr., Harvard Bus. Sch., 1982; Baker scholar, 1940. Office: Levi Strauss & Co 1155 Battery St San Francisco CA 94111

HAAS, ROBERT DOUGLAS, apparel manufacturing company executive; b. San Francisco, Apr. 3, 1942; s. Walter A. Jr. and Evelyn (Danzig) H.; m. Colleen Gershon, Jan. 27, 1974; 1 child, Elise Kimberly. BA, U. Calif., Berkeley, 1964; MBA, Harvard U., 1968. With Peace Corps, Ivory Coast, 1964-66; fellow White House, Washington, 1968-69; assoc. McKinsey & Co., 1969-72; with Levi Strauss & Co., San Francisco, 1973—, sr. v.p. corp. planning and policy, 1978-80, pres. new bus. group, 1980, pres. operating groups, 1980-81, exec. v.p., COO, 1981-84, pres., CEO, 1984-89, CEO, chmn. bd., 1989—, also bd. dirs.; pres. Levi Strauss Found., mem. global leadership team. Hon. dir. San Francisco AIDS Found.; trustee Ford Found.; bd. dirs. Bay Area Coun.; past bd. dirs. Am. Apparel Assn. White House fellow, 1968-69. Mem. Brookings Inst. (trustee), Bay Area Com., Conf. Bd., Coun. Fgn. Rels., Trilateral Commn., Calif. Bus. Roundtable, Meyer Friedman Inst. (bd. dirs.), Phi Beta Kappa. Office: Levi Strauss & Co 1155 Battery St San Francisco CA 94111-1256*

HAAS, ROBERT JOHN, aerospace engineer; b. Dayton, Ohio, Apr. 14, 1930; s. Robert J. Haas and Harriett (Longstreth) Bevan; m. Florence A. Eldred, June 6, 1952 (div. June 1984); adopted children: Jeffrey (dec.), Lisa Haas Cappuccio; m. Gayle F. Byrne, Dec. 14, 1984; stepchildren: Patrick Barton, Marissa Barton; children: Amber Haas, Robert J. Haas III. Student, U.S. Mil. Acad., 1948-51; BS in Petroleum Engring., U. Tulsa, 1954. Petroleum engr. Skelly Oil Co., Tulsa, 1953-54; propulsion engr., supr. Marquardt, Van Nuys, Calif., 1957-64; mgr. rocket programs Marquardt, Van Nuys, 1964-69, dir. test and facilities, 1969-72, gen. mgr. environ. systems, 1972-75; plant gen. mgr. Williams Internat., Ogden, Utah, 1975-79; sr. v.p. engring. Williams Internat., Walled Lake, Mich., 1979-86; sr. v.p. product planning and mktg. Williams Internat., Walled Lake, 1986-90; sr. advisor, cons. Las Vegas, Nev., 1990—; CEO Haas Enterprises, Consulting Firm, Las Vegas, 1992—; cons. Marquardt, Van Nuys, 1961-75. Author: Approach to Aerospace Plane Propulsion, 1960. Lectr. and advisor Weber State Coll., U. Utah and various high schs. and clubs., 1975-79; pres. Marquardt Mgmt. Club, 1971. 1st lt. USAF, 1954-56. Mem. AIAA, Navy League (lifetime). Republican. Roman Catholic. Achievements include contribution to devel. and prodn. of world's smallest turbofan for cruise missiles; discoveries in the field of integrated propulsion modules for missiles, economical methods of testing ramjets, turbines and rocket engines. Home and Office: Haas Enterprize PO Box 33126 Las Vegas NV 89133-3126

HAAS, SUZANNE NEWHOUSE, human resources generalist; b. Akron, Ohio, Feb. 7, 1945; d. Earl Wallace and Bernice (Pikoski) Newhouse; m. Raymond John Haas, Feb. 8, 1975; children: Monique, John, Alexander. BA in Psychology, Kent (Ohio) State U., 1984, BA in Bus. Adminstrn., 1985; MA in Indsl. Psychology, Cleve. State U., 1991. Job analyst McKinley Life Care, Canton, Ohio, 1988; mgmt. cons. Paragon Human Resource Systems, Canton, 1989—; rsch. asst. N.E. Ohio U. Coll. Medicine, Rootstown, 1990-93; site coord. Vanderbilt U. Inst. Mental Health Policy, Nashville, 1993-95; sr. human resources generalist Bioproducts Corp. Hdqs., Fairlawn, Ohio, 1997-98, program adminstr. mgmt. devel. and human resources rsch., 1998—. Mem. APA, ASTD (pres. N.E. chpt. 1998), Am. Psychol. Soc., Acad. Mgmt., Ohio Psychol. Assn. Republican. Roman Catholic. Avocations: classical music, golf, gardening. Home and Office: 9221 Corporate Blvd Rockville MD 20850

HAAS, THOMAS JOSEPH, chemistry educator; b. Staten Island, N.Y., Mar. 5, 1951; s. Joseph Walter and JoAnne (Pawloski) H.; m. Marcia Jane Knapp, Jan. 12, 1974; children: Eric, Gregory, Sarah. BS with honors, USCG Acad., New London, Conn., 1973; MS in Chemistry, U. Mich., 1976, MS in Environ. Health Sci., 1977; MS in Human Rsch. Mgmt., Rensselaer Poly. Inst., 1981; PhD, U. Conn., 1987; MLE, Harvard U., 1999. Cert. indsl. hygienist. Commd. ensign USCG, 1973, advanced through grades to capt., 1996; ops. officer USCG Cutter Acacia, Port Huron, Mich., 1973-75; mem. staff USCG Hdqrs., Washington, 1977-80, br. chief, 1980-81; advanced from asst. prof. to prof. USCG Acad., New London, 1981-96, from section chief to assoc. dean acads., 1981—; v.p. acad. and student affairs William Penn Coll., Oskaloosa, Iowa, 1996-98; dean, supervisory prof. USCG Acad., New London, Conn., 1998—; disting. vis. faculty U. Mich., Ann Arbor, 1980; mem. group experts UN, Geneva, 1980; mem. Chem. Transport Adv. Com., Washington, 1977-81, 87-92; data mgr. USCG Valdez (Alaska) Oil Spill, 1989; vis. faculty fellow Yale U., 1991-92. Editor: Descriptions of Selected Hazardous Materials, 1991; contbr. articles to profl. jours. Chair Ledyard (Conn.) Congregation Ch. Session, 1983-90, deacon, 1985; chair Scholarship Com., Ledyard, 1987-90; pres. Parsonage Hill Homeowners Assn., Ledyard, 1987-91. Yale fellow, 1991-92, Am. Coun. on Edn. fellow, 1992-93. Mem. Am. Chem. Soc., Am. Conf. Govtl. Indsl. Hygienists, USCG Officers Assn., N.Y. Acad. Scis., USCG Acad. Officers Club. Republican. Achievements include research on investigation of synthetic materials. Home: 7 North Road Niantic CT 06357-1514 Office: USCG Acad New London CT 06320

HAAS, WARD JOHN, research and development executive; b. N.Y.C., Aug. 26, 1921; s. M.A. and Pauline (Ward) H.; m. Jane Corya, Dec. 25, 1943; children: Margaret P., Jeffrey W., Elizabeth H. Anderson. BS, MIT, 1943, PhD, 1949. Biochemist E.I. duPont de Nemours & Co., 1949-51; fgn. service attache Am. Embassy, London, 1951-54; asst. to dir. Agrl. Research and Devel. Ctr., Charles Pizer & Co., Inc., Terre Haute, Ind., 1954-56; asst. to pres. Charles Pizer & Co., Inc., N.Y.C., 1957-60; dir. ops. Pfizer Labs. div., N.Y.C., 1960-64; asso. prof. mgmt., dir. Space Scis. Research Center, U. Mo., 1964-68; dir., pres. Warner-Lambert Research Inst., Morris Plains, N.J., 1968-69; v.p. research and devel. Warner-Lambert Co., 1969-72; corp. v.p. research and devel. S.C. Johnson & Son, Inc., Racine, Wis., 1972-75; v.p. research and devel. Chesebrough-Pond's, Inc., Greenwich, Conn., 1975-85; prin. Innovation Mgmt., Southport, Conn., 1986—; assoc. The Fusfeld Group, Inc., 1992—. Served with U.S. Army, 1943-46. AAAS/Sloan fellow White House Office Sci. and Tech. Policy, 1991-92. Fellow AAAS, Am. Inst. Chemists; mem. Indsl. Rsch. Inst. (dir. 1979-82), Assn. Rsch. Dirs. (pres. 1986-87), Am. Mgmt. Assn. (R & D coun. 1976-82), Conn. Acad. Sci. and Engring., Sigma Xi. Home and Office: 3909 Belle Rive Ter Alexandria VA 22309-3002

HAAS, WILLIAM PAUL, humanities educator, former college president; b. Newark, May 31, 1927; s. Joseph J. and Elizabeth (Ryan) H. A.B., Providence Coll., 1948; S.T.L., Pontifical Inst., Washington, 1954; Ph.D., U. Fribourg, Switzerland, 1962; D.B.A. (hon.), Bryant Coll., Providence, 1966; LL.D., U. R.I., 1967, Brown U., 1969; D.D., Conn. Wesleyan U., 1969; D.H.L., R.I. Coll., 1970, Salve Regina Coll., 1971. Ordained priest Roman Cath. Ch., 1953, laicized, 1973; prof. theology and philosophy Emmanuel Coll., Boston, 1954-60; prof. philosophy Providence Coll., 1962-63, 71-72, pres., 1965-71; asso. prof. U. Notre Dame, 1963-65; on leave as post-doctoral research asso. Boston U., 1972-73; vice chancellor for acad. affairs Mass. State Coll. System, 1973-79; pres. North Adams State Coll., Mass., 1979-83; prof. humanities Bryant Coll., Smithfield, R.I., 1983-96; inaugurated spl. program religious studies Purdue U., 1963-65; vis. prof. contemporary theology Wabash Coll., Crawfordsville, Ind., 1964-65; vis. distinguished prof. U. R.I., 1971-72; Mem. R.I. Council Arts, 1967-70, R.I. Adv. Council State Tech. Services Act, 1965, 1967-71; mem. commn. learning Assn. Am. Colls., 1966-69; adv. council extension and continuing edn. Dept. Health, Edn. and Welfare, 1966-70; mem. commn. humanities in schs. Nat. Found. on Arts and the Humanities, 1967-71; chmn. R.I. Higher Edn. Council, 1969-71. Author: The Conception of Law and the Unity of Peirce's Philosophy, 1964, The Contemporary Arts, 1965; Contbr. articles to profl. jours. Bd. dirs. R.I. Philharmonic Orch., 1965-68, R.I. Found. Repertory Theatre, 1966-71, R.I. Urban Coalition, 1969-71, Packard Manse (center ecumenical studies), Boston, 1965-67; trustee John F. Kennedy Meml. Fund R.I., 1966-71, New Eng. Colls. Fund, 1970-71, Rocky Hill Sch., 1971-73, Bryant Coll., 1971-79; bd. dirs. United Fund R.I., 1967-71, Howard Found., Brown U., 1969-73; chmn. R.I. com. Rhodes Scholarship Trust, 1969, mem., 1970; bd. dirs. Humanities Forum of R.I., 1989—; mem. R.I. Com. for the Humanities, 1991—. Mem. Am. Soc. Aesthetics, Nat. Cath. Edn. Assn. (exec. com. coll. and univ. dept. 1970-73). Home: 2 Vanderbilt Ave Newport RI 02840-4342

HAASE, ASHLEY THOMSON, microbiology educator, researcher; b. Chgo., Dec. 8, 1939; s. Milton Conrad and Mary Elizabeth Minter (Thomson) H.; m. Ann DeLong, 1962; children: Elizabeth, Stephanie, Harris. BA, Lawrence Coll., 1961; MD, Columbia U., 1965. Intern Johns Hopkins Hosp., Balt., 1965-67; clin. assoc. Nat. Inst. Allergy and Infectious Disease, Bethesda, Md., 1967-70; vis. scientist Nat. Inst. Med. Rsch., London, 1970-71; chief infectious disease sect. VA Med. Ctr., San Francisco, 1971-84, med. investigator, 1978-83; prof. microbiology U. Minn., Mpls., 1984—, head dept., 1984—; mem. fellowship screening com. Am. Cancer Soc., San Francisco, 1978-81; mem. UNESCO Internat. Cell Rsch. Orgn., India, 1978; mem. nat. adv. coun. Nat. Inst. Allergy and Infectious Diseases, 1986-91, mem. task force on microbiology and infectious diseases, 1991, merit investigator, 1989—, chair AIDS rsch. adv. com., 1993-96, chmn. vaccine sub-com.; Javits neurosci. investigator Nat. Inst. Neurol. and Communicative Disorders and Stroke, 1988-95; chmn. panel on AIDS, U.S.-Japan Coop. Med. Sci. Program, 1988-95; mem. OAR AIDS Rsch. Evaluation Working Group, 1995-96; mem. adv. com. for career awards in biomed. scis. Burroughs-Wellcome Fund, 1995—; trustee Lawrence U., 1997—. Editor: Microbial Pathogenesis, 1988-94; contbr. articles on AIDS pathogenesis and other topics in neurovirology to profl. jours. Recipient Lucia R. Briggs Disting. Achievement award Lawrence Coll., 1990. Mem. Am. Soc. Microbiology, Assn. Am. Physicians, Am. Soc. Clin. Investigation, Am. Soc. Virology, Assn. Med. Schs. Microbiology Chmn., Infectious Diseases Soc. Am., Nat. Multiple Sclerosis Soc. (adv. com. 1978-84), Phi Beta Kappa, Alpha Omega Alpha. Democrat. Home: 14 Buffalo Rd Saint Paul MN 55127-2136 Office: U Minn Dept Microbiology 420 Delaware St SE Minneapolis MN 55455-0374

HAASE, WILLIAM R., IV, urban planner; b. Delhi, N.Y., Oct. 27, 1955; s. William R. III and Mary Alice (Catlin) H. BA, SUNY, Binghamton, 1978; MA, Wash. State U., 1983; M Urban and Regional Planning, U. Colo., 1987. Cert. planner. Planner Ctr. Cmty. Devel. and Design, U. Colo., Denver, 1986-87; dir. planning Town of Ledyard, Conn., 1988—. Dir. Avalonia Land Conservancy, Mystic, Conn., 1991—. Mem. Am. Inst. Cert. Planners, Am. Planning Assn. Office: Town of Ledyard 741 Colonel Ledyard Hwy Ledyard CT 06339-1511

HAASS, RICHARD NATHAN, federal agency administrator, educator; b. Bklyn., July 28, 1951; s. Irving B. and Marcella (Rosenthal) H. BA, Oberlin (Ohio) Coll., 1973; M in Philosophy, Oxford U., Eng., 1975, PhD, 1982. Legis. asst. U.S. Sen. Claiborne Pell, Washington, 1975; research assoc. Internat. Inst. for Strategic Studies, London, 1977-79; spl. asst. to undersec. def. U.S. Dept. Def., Washington, 1979-80; dir. office regional security affairs U.S. Dept. State, Washington, 1981-82, dep. for policy bur. European and Can. affairs, 1982-85, spl. Cyprus coordinator, 1983-85; lectr. pub. policy John F. Kennedy Sch. govt. Harvard U., Cambridge, Mass., 1985-89; spl. asst. to pres. Nat. Security Affairs, 1989-93; sr. dir. near east and south Asia Nat. Security Coun., 1989-93; sr. assoc. Carnegie Endowment for Internat. Peace, Washington, 1993-94; dir. nat. security programs, sr. fellow Coun. on Fgn. Rels., Washington, 1994-96; vis. prof. internat. studies Hamilton Coll., 1995; cons. NBC News, 1993—; dir. fgn. policy studies, Brookings Instn., Wash., 1996—. Author: Congressional Power: Implications for American Security Policy, 1979, Beyond the INF Treaty: Arms, Arms Control and the Atlantic Alliance, 1988, Conflicts Unending: The United States and Regional Disputes, 1990, The Power to Persuade, 1994, Intervention: The Use of American Military Force in The Post-Cold War World, 1994, The Reluctant Sheriff: The United State after the Cold War, 1997, The Bureaucratic Entrepreneur, 1999; editor: Superpower Arms Control: Setting the Record Straight, 1987, Economic Sanctions and American Diplomacy, 1998, Transatlantic Tensions, 1999. Recipient Superior Honor award Dept. State, 1982, Presdl. Citizens medal, 1991; Rhodes scholar Oxford U., 1973. Mem. Internat. Inst. for Strategic Studies, Coun. on Fgn. Rels. Office: Brookings Institution 1775 MassachusettsAve NW Washington DC 20036

HAAVELMO, TRYGVE, economics educator; b. Skedsmo, Norway, Dec. 13, 1911. Grad., U. Oslo, 1933, PhD, 1946. Rsch. asst. Cowles Commn., U. Chgo., 1945-46; with Norwegian Trade Commn., Oslo; prof. econs. U. Oslo, 1948-79, prof. emeritus, 1979—. Recipient Nobel prize in econs., 1989. Mem. Am. Econ. Assn., Am. Acad. Arts and Letters. Office: U Oslo, PO Box 1095 Blindern, N-0317 Oslo Norway

HAAYEN, RICHARD JAN, university official, insurance company executive; b. Bklyn., June 30, 1924; s. Cornelius Marius and Cornelia Florence (Muskus) H.; m. Marilyn Jean Messner, Aug. 30, 1946; children—Richard Jan, Peter Wyckoff, James Carell. BS, Ohio State U., 1948; D in Pub. Svc. (hon.), Nat. Coll. Edn., Evanston, Ill. With Allstate Ins. Co., 1950—, v.p. underwriting, 1969-75; exec. v.p. Allstate Ins. Co., Northbrook, Ill., 1975-80; pres. Allstate Ins. Co., 1980-86, chmn., chief exec. officer, 1986-89; exec.-in-residence So. Meth. U., Dallas, 1989—; bd. dirs. Guaranty Fed. Savs. Bank, Dallas, R.L.I. Ins. Co., Peoria, Ill. Bd. dirs. Dallas World Salute, Communities-in-Schs., Dallas, Dallas Opera. Mem. Nat. Assn. Ind. Insurers, Am. Arbitration Assn. (arbitrator), Phi Delta Theta. Republican. Home: 9 Glenshire Ct Dallas TX 75225-2040 Office: 7557 Rambler Rd Ste 1424 Dallas TX 75231-2307

HABACHY, SUZAN SALWA SABA, development economist, non profit administrator; b. Cairo, Egypt, July 15, 1933; came to the U.S., 1952; d. Saba and Gameela (Gindy) H. BA, Bryn Mawr (Pa.) Coll., 1954; MA, Harvard U., Cambridge, Mass., 1956. Teaching fellow Ohio U., Athens, 1957-58; economist Mobil Oil Co., N.Y.C., 1959-64; reporter, editor Petroleum Intelligence Weekly, N.Y.C., 1964-65, McGraw Hill News Bur., London, England, 1965-68; program officer UN, N.Y.C., 1969-75, section chief, 1975-88; focal point for women UN Office of Pers., N.Y.C., 1988-93; exec. dir. The Trickle Up Program, N.Y.C., 1994—. Avocations: theatre, travel, reading. Home: 1056 5th Ave New York NY 10028-0112

HABECKER, EUGENE BRUBAKER, religious association executive; b. Hershey, Pa., June 17, 1946; s. Walter Eugene and Frances (Miller) H.; m. Marylou Napolitano, July 27, 1968; children: David, Matthew, Marybeth. AB, Taylor U., 1968; MA, Ball State U., 1969; JD, Temple U., 1974; PhD, U. Mich., 1981. Bar: Pa. 1974. Asst. dean Ea. Coll., St. Davids, Pa., 1970-74; dean students, asst. prof. polit. sci. George Fox Coll., Newberg, Oreg., 1974-78; exec. v.p. Huntington (Ind.) Coll., 1979-81, pres., 1981-91; pres, CEO Am. Bible Soc., N.Y.C., 1991—; evaluation cons. North Ctrl. Assn., Chgo., 1982-91; dir. Christian Coll. Coalition, Washington, 1982-88, ICUI Inc., Indpls., 1983-85; sec., mem. bd. Assoc. Colls. Inc., Indpls., 1983-85; bd. dirs. Christianity Today, Inc., United Bible Socs. internat. exec. com. Author: Affirmative Action in Independent College, 1977, The Other Side of Leadership, 1987, Leading With a Follower's Heart, 1990, Rediscovering the Soul of Leadership, 1996; contbr. articles to profl. jours. Recipient Christian Mgmt. award Christian Mgmt. Assn., 1989. Mem. Nat. Assn. Intercollegiate Athletes (coun. of pres.' 1985-90), Nat. Assn. Evangs. (bd. dirs. 1985-90), Am. Mgmt. Assn., Christian Mgmt. Assn. Republican. Presbyterian. Office: Am Bible Soc 1865 Broadway New York NY 10023-7503

HABECKER, SANDRA K., retired nurse; b. Columbia, Pa., Apr. 5, 1937; d. Ralph Marvin and Emma Hubley (Eshleman) Kilheffer; m. Charles N. Habecker, Oct. 4, 1958; children: Jean, Marianne, Lisa, Susan. AS, RN, Lancaster (Pa.) Gen. Hosp., 1958. Pediatriac nurse Montgomeryville (Pa.) Pediatrics, 1975-90; sch. nurse Calvary Bapt. Sch., Lansdale, Pa., 1988-99; ret., 1999. Republican. Baptist. Avocations: gardening, reading, cooking, playing bassoon. Home: 361 Oakland Ave Lansdale PA 19446-3225

HABEDANK, GARY L., brokerage house executive; b. Glendive, Mont., Feb. 17, 1944; s. Otto T. and Arleen T. (Miller) H.; m. Kathryn Ann Czyhold, June 18, 1967; children: Silke, Anne. BBA, Pacific Lutheran U., 1966; postgrad., U. Mont., 1966-67. CFP, 1980. Sr. v.p., asst. br. mgr. Salomon Smith Barney Inc., Tacoma, 1968—; adv. coun. John Nuveen & Co., Chgo., 1986—; adv. bd. Planned Giving & Fin. Bd. of Visitors. Trustee Tacoma Art Mus., 1984-90; trustee, pres. Tacoma Philharm., Inc., 1977-83; sec. Annie Wright Sch., 1985-91; mem. Christ Episc. Ch. (vestry, fin. chmn. 1987-91). Recipient Community Svc. award Jr. League of Tacoma, 1990, Disting. Alumnus Centennial award, Pacific Lutheran U., 1990. Mem. Tacoma Club, Tacoma Elks, Boy Scouts Am. Republican. Episcopalian. Avocations: community service, sailing, classical music, reading, gardening. Home: 3 N Rosemount Way Tacoma WA 98406-7117 Office: Tacoma Fin Ctr 1145 Broadway Ste 1400 Tacoma WA 98402-3587

HABEEB, GREGORY G., hotel executive. Dir. new mem. devel. SRS Hotels, N.Y.C. Office: SRS Hotels 33rd Fl 152 W 57th St New York NY 10019

HABEN, JOHN WILLIAM, funeral director; b. Evanston, Ill., Oct. 11, 1956; s. R. William and Barbara A. (Wilson) H.; m. Mary Anne McNulty, Nov. 28, 1981; children: John W. Jr., Peter W., Clare M., William D., Thomas E., Nicholas R. BS in Bus., Miami U., Oxford, Ohio, 1978; diploma in mortuary sci., Worsham Coll., 1979. Intern, apprentice Haben Funeral Home, Skokie, Ill., 1979-80, lic. funeral dir. and embalmer, 1980—, sec., treas., 1982-92, pres., 1992—. Mem. steering com. Skokie Centennial Celebration, 1987, 88; bd. dirs. Skokie Hist. Soc., 1988-91; active Young Families Task Force, Skokie, 1988-89; commr. zoning bd. appeals Village of Skokie, 1989-94; bd. dirs., pres., mem. steering com. 125th Anniversary St. Peter Ch. Sch., 1995—; bd. dirs. Met. Family Svcs. Evanston and Skokie Valley; pres. bd. Youth Found., Skokie, 1998—. Named One of Outstanding Young Men of Am., 1985. Mem. Nat. Funeral Dirs. Assn., Nat. Selected Morticians, Ill. Funeral Dirs. Assn., Funeral Dirs. Svcs. Assn. (bd. dirs. 1982), Skokie C. of C. (bd. dirs. 1989-93, pres. 1992), Luxembourg Brotherhood of Am. (officer 1994-96), KC, Rotary (bd. dirs. Skokie chpt. 1987-91), Evanston Golf Club (fin. com. 1990-93, house com. 1996-98, chmn. permanent planning com. 1997—). Roman Catholic. Avocations: golf, historic rehabilitation, youth baseball, volleyball, basketball, and softball. Home: 8051 Lincoln Ave Skokie IL 60077-3612 Office: Haben Funeral Home 8057 Niles Center Rd Skokie IL 60077-2599

HABER, BARBARA FRAN, psychologist; b. N.Y.C., June 5, 1951; d. Eugene and Lily (Langsner) Braude; m. Daniel Marvin Haber, Aug. 18, 1974; 1 child, Jason. BA in Speech Pathology and Audiology, CCNY, 1972; MS in Speech Pahtology, Columbia U., 1973; PD in Sch. Psychology, Fordham U., 1981, PhD in Ednl. Psychology, 1985. Lic. psychologist, N.J.; cert. sch. psychologyst, N.J., N.Y., speech/lang. specialist, N.J. Tchr. speech improvement N.Y.C. Bd. Edn., 1973-75, tchr. trainer, supr. speech and lang., 1975-76; grad. asst. Fordham U., N.Y.C., 1977-78; sch. psychology intern Bergenfield (N.J.) Pub. Schs., 1980-81, sch. psychologist, 1981-83; sch. psychologist Dumont (N.J.) Pub. Schs., 1983-84; pvt. practice cons. N.J., 1985-87; sch. psychologist, chair Englewood Cliffs (N.J.) Bd. Edn., 1987-88, sch. psychologist, 1989—; supr. interns N.Y.C. Bd. Edn., 1974-75, Fordham U., 1992-94. Vol. PTA, Ft. Lee (N.J.) Pub. Schs., 1990-96, mem. parent adv. com., 1992; mem. Ft. Lee Bd. Edn., 1998—. Baruch Termaine scholar, 1970, Easter Seals scholar, 1972. Mem. APA, Am. Speech Lang. Hearing Assn., Phi Beta Kappa. Avocations: reading, painting, tennis. Home: 21 Warwick Ave Fort Lee NJ 07024-4303 Office: Englewood Cliffs Bd Edn Charlotte Pl Englewood Cliffs NJ 07632

HABER, IRA JOEL, artist, art educator; b. N.Y.C., Feb. 24, 1947; s. Oscar and Rosalind (Tilzer) H. Student public schs. Instr. art SUNY, Stony Brook, 1981—, U. Calif.-San Diego, 1982, 84, Ohio State U. (Columbus), 1984. One-man shows include Fischbach Gallery, N.Y.C., 1971, 72, 74, Kent (Ohio) State U., 1977, Pam Adler Gallery, N.Y.C., 1978, 80, 82, Rutgers U., 1980, SUNY, Stony Brook, 1981, Phila. Art Alliance, 1984, J.N. Herlin Inc., N.Y.C., 1984, 86, 55 Mercer St. Gallery, N.Y.C., 1991; group shows include Mus. Modern Art, N.Y.C., 1970, Whitney Mus., N.Y.C., 1971, 73, Public Sch. One, L.I., N.Y., 1976, Albright-Knox Gallery, Buffalo, 1979, Ohio State U., 1984; represented in permanent collections NYU, Guggenheim Mus., N.Y.C., Hirshhorn Mus., Washington, Allen Meml. Art Mus., Oberlin (Ohio) Coll., Albright-Knox Gallery, Buffalo. NEA fellow, 1974, 77, 84; grantee Creative Artists Public Service, 1974, 77, Ariana Found., 1982, Pollock-Krasner Found., 1986-87. Address: 105 W 27th St New York NY 10001-6213

HABER, JUDITH ELLEN, nursing educator; b. N.Y.C.; d. Michael and Yetta (Frank) Adler; m. Leonard Haber, June 13, 1963; children: Laurie Beth, Andrew David. BS cum laude, Adelphi U., 1965; MA, NYU, 1967, PhD, 1984. Cert. clin. specialist in adult psychiat. nursing ANCC (mem. commn. on cert. 1995—); cert. advanced achievement in family therapy. Instr. Adelphi U., Garden City, N.Y., 1968-70; asst. prof. Norwalk (Conn.) Community Coll., 1972-81; assoc. prof. nursing, coord. acad. affairs Coll. of Mt. St. Vincent, Riverdale, N.Y., 1985-88, prof., dir. dept., 1988-92; prof., dir. master's prgm. & post master's adv. cert. prgm. div. nursing NYU, 1994—; pvt. practice family therapy, Stamford, Conn., 1976—. Editor, author: Comprehensive Psychiatric Nursing, 1978, 4th edit., 1992, 5th edit., 1997 (Book of Yr. award Am. Jour. Nursing 1978, 82), Nursing Research: Methods, Critical Appraisal and Utilization, 1986, 3d edit., 1994, 4th edit., 1998 (award Am. Jour. Nursing 1994); contbr. chpts. to books. Bd. dirs. Smith House, Stamford, 1989-95; chmn. Conn. Coun. Mental Health Providers. Recipient Disting. Alumni award Adelphi U., 1998, Nursing Media award Am. Acad. of Nursing, 1998, Award Aegis Video Industry, 1998. Fellow Am. Acad. Nursing; mem. ANA (exec. bd. coun. psychiat. mental health nursing 1991-94, ad hoc com. on credentialing in advanced practice 1992-94, exec. bd. coun. advanced practice nursing 1994, congress of nursing practice 1994—), Am. Psychiat. Nurses Assn. (editl. bd., contbg. editor Jour. 1994—, Psychiat. Nurse of Yr. award 1995, ANA Hildegard Peplau awd., 1998), N.Y. State Nurses Assn. (rsch. coun. 1991-93, chmn. 1994-95), Deans and Dirs. Greater N.Y. (chmn. legis. com. 1991-92), Am. Assn. Marriage and Family Therapists (clin.), Sigma Theta Tau (region V media award). Avocations: skiing, golf, tennis, travel. Home: 111 New England Dr Stamford CT 06903-5018 Office: 666 Glenbrook Rd Ste 2C Stamford CT 06906-1439

HABER, RALPH NORMAN, psychology consultant, researcher, educator; b. Lansing, Mich., May 15, 1932; s. William and Fannie (Gallas) H.; m. Ruth Lea Boss, 1961 (div. 1974); children—Sabrina Beth, Rebecca Ann; m. Lyn R. Roland, 1974. B.A., U. Mich., 1953; M.A., Wesleyan U., Middletown, Conn., 1954; Ph.D., Stanford U., 1957; Postdoctoral fellow, Med. Research Council, Applied Psychology Unit, Cambridge, Eng., 1970-71. Rsch. assoc. Inst. for Comm. Rsch., Stanford, 1957-58; instr. psychology San Francisco State Coll., Calif., 1957-58; asst. prof. psychology Yale, 1958-64; assoc. prof. psychology U. Rochester, N.Y., 1964-67, prof. psychology, 1967-70, prof. psychology and visual sci., 1970-79, chmn. dept. psychology, 1967-70, mem. faculty senate, 1968-70, sec., mem. steering com., 1969-70; prof. psychology U. Ill., Chgo., 1979-91, rsch. prof., 1991-94, rsch. prof. emeritus, 1994—; ptnr. Human Factors Cons., Bishop, Calif., 1988—; rsch. assoc. psychology U. Calif., Santa Cruz, 1995—; adj. prof. U. Calif., Riverside, 1997—; vis. prof. Air Force Human Resources Lab., Williams AFB, Ariz., 1981-83; ptnr. Human Factors Cons., Highland Park, Ill.; vis. scientist Med. Rsch. Coun. Applied Psychology Unit, Cambridge, Eng., 1970-71; chmn., divisional maj. III Yale, 1959-64; vis. asst. prof. New Sch. for Social Research, 1963; research cons. VA, 1967-71; adv. editor for exptl. psychology Holt, Rinehart & Winston Book Pubs., 1969-77. Author: (with Hershenson) The Psychology of Visual Perception, 1973, 2d edit., 1980, (with Fried) An Introduction to Psychology, 1975, (with others) Discovering Psychology, 1977; editor: Current Research on Motivation, 1966, Contemporary Theory and Research on Visual Perception, 1968, Information Processing Approaches to Visual Perception, 1969; Contbr. articles to profl. jours. Committeeman 18th Ward, Brighton (N.Y.) Democratic Com., 1967-70; founding mem., trustee Coll. Admission Prep. Program, Rochester, 1968-70; commr. Wheeler Crest Fire Prevention Dist., Bishop, Calif., 1995—. Recipient Outstanding Achievement award U. Mich., 1977; Behavioral Sci. fellow Ford Found., 1953-54; grantee NSF, NIH, Nat. Inst. Edn., Air Force Office Sci. Research, Dept. Army. Fellow APA, AAAS; mem. Am. Psychol. Soc., Psychonomics Soc., Midwestern Psychol. Assn., Brit. Psychol. Assn., Optical Soc. Am., Human Factors and Ergonomics Soc., Am. Contract Bridge League (dir. Bishop unit 517 1996—), Sigma Xi, Pi Lambda Phi.

HABER, WARREN H., investment company executive; b. Mar. 9, 1941; s. S. Jack and Ruth (Kalish) H.; m. Suellen Green, Nov. 3, 1964; children: Warren Jr., Kristin T. BA in Fin., CUNY, 1962. Chmn. Founders Equity, Inc., N.Y.C., 1967—, ptnr., 1969-87; chmn. Internat. Power Machines Corp., N.Y.C., 1986-93; ptnr. Founders Property Mgmt. Co., Inc., N.Y.C., 1980—; Chmn., CEO Batteries-Batteries, Inc., 1995-98, chmn., dir., 1998—; bd. dirs. Beverly Glen Med. Sys., Inc., Am. Lifecare, Inc., Realty Info. Group; chmn. Batteries Batteries, Inc., 1996. With M.C. USAR, 1962. Recipient Disting. Alumni award CUNY, 1984. Mem. City Athletic Club, University, Econ. Club.

HABERER, JOHN HENRY, JR., minister; b. Queens, N.Y., Feb. 16, 1955; s. John H. and Maureen (Hastings) H.; married; children: David, Kelly. BA magna cum laude, Roberts Wesleyan Coll., Rochester, N.Y., 1976; MDiv cum laude, Gordon-Conwell Theol. Seminary, South Hamilton, Mass., 1982; D of Ministry, Columbia Theol. Seminary, Decatur, Ga., 1989. Ordained to ministry Presbyn. Ch., 1984. Asst. mgr. Christian Ctr. Bookstore, Allendale, N.J., 1976-79; dir. of worship First United Ch., Swampscott, Mass., 1979-82; dir. of family ministries New Covenant Ch., Pompano Beach, Fla., 1982-84; sr. minister Trinity Presbyn. Ch., Satellite Beach, Fla., 1984-94, Clear Lake Presbyn. Ch., Houston, 1994—; bd. dirs., chmn. Spl. Gathering, Inc., Cocoa, Fla., 1987-93; mem. evangelism commn. Fla. Coun. Chs., Orlando, 1989-91; chmn. Brevard-Indian River Counties Presbyn. Mission Conf., Satellite Beach, 1989-92, chmn. long-range planning com. Presbytery Coordinating Coun., Cen. Fla. Presbytery, Orlando, 1985-90; bd. dirs. Aids Alliance of Bay Area, 1994—; vice moderator evangelism and ch. devel. divsn. Presbytery of New Covenant, 1995-97; moderator, chmn. bd. The Presbyn. Coalition, 1996-98. Contbr. articles to profl. jours. Vol. chaplain Brevard Pub. Schs., Satellite Beach, 1984-94; mgr. Little League Baseball, Satellite Beach, 1984-88; founder, dir. Mustard Seed Coffeehouse, Ramsey, N.J., 1971-79. Recipient Good Will award for 1990, City of Satellite Beach City Coun., 1990; named to Outstanding Young Men of Am., 1986. Mem. Presbyns. for Renewal, Evangel. Tchr. Tng. Assn. Republican. *The Indefatigable optimist's credo: "People are not God. God is God.*

HABERKORN, JOHN G., small business owner; b. Oct. 10, 1955. BA, St. John's U., 1977. Owner Venice Tool Works, Beverly Hills, Calif., 1991—, Eagle Releasing, Beverly Hills, 1993—. E-mail: johnhaberkorn@netscape.net. Office: PO Box 572245 Tarzana CA 91356-1357

HABERL, JUDY ANN, artist, educator; b. Denver, Sept. 22, 1948; d. Frank Joseph and Dorothy L. (Hotchkiss) H.; m. Donald Heiman, Nov. 23, 1995; children: Kelly Liedike, Riley Heiman. MFA, Tufts U., 1984. Assoc. prof. sculpture Mass. Coll. Art, Boston, 1988—; vis. critic R.I. Sch. Design Sculpture Dept. Reviews, Providence, 1992; juror Arts on the Line, Boston, 1992; artist cons. Artery Tunnel Project, Boston, 1993; curator Outdoor Sculpture Exhbn., Art Complex Mus., 1995; panelist Fulbright Traveling Fellowships for Students, 1995, 96; spkr. in field. One-woman shows include Inst. Contemporary Art, Boston, 1984, Stux Gallery, Boston, 1986, Rathbone Gallery, Albany, N.Y., 1987, Akin Gallery, Boston, 1988, 90, 92, Duxbury (Mass.) Art Complex Mus., 1996; group exhbns. include Berkshire Art Mus., Pittsfield, Mass., 1985, Alan Stone Gallery, N.Y.C., 1985, Stux Gallery, 1986, Rose Art Mus., Waltham, Mass., 1988, Inst. Contemporary Art, Boston, 1988, Montserrat Coll. Art, Beverly, Mass., 1989-90, Fitchburg (Mass.) Art Mus., 1991, DeCordova Mus., Lincoln, Mass., 1992, Yale U. Sch. Art and Arch. Gallery, New Haven, Conn., 1994, Snug Harbor Cultural Ctr., S.I., N.Y., 1995, AIR Gallery, N.Y., 1996. Recipient Howard Found. fellowship Brown U., 1995-96; L.E.F. Found. grantee, 1992, New Eng. Found. for the Arts grantee in sculpture, 1995.

HABERL, VALERIE ELIZABETH, physical education educator, company executive; b. N.Y.C., July 6, 1947; d. William Anthony and Rose Mary (Hoholecek) H. BS, So. Conn. State U., 1969, postgrad., 1979. Cert. elem. tchr., Conn. Tchr. phys. edn. West Haven (Conn.) Bd. Edn., 1969—; pres. Creative Studio, 1992—; inventory controll specialist, 1997—. Mem. Conn. Assn. Health, Phys. Edn., Recreation and Dance. Republican. Roman Catholic.

HABERMAN, CHARLES MORRIS, mechanical engineer, educator; b. Bakersfield, Calif., Dec. 10, 1927; s. Carl Morris and Rose Marie (Braun) H. BS, UCLA, 1951; MS in Mech. Engring., U. So. Calif., 1954, MS in Aeronautical Engring., 1960. Lead, sr. and group engr. Northrop Aircraft, Hawthorne, Calif., 1951-59, cons., 1959-61; asst. prof. to prof. mech. engring. Calif. State U., L.A., 1959-91; cons. Royal McBee Corp., 1960-61. Author: Engineering Systems Analysis, 1965, Use of Computers for Engineering Applications, 1966, Vibration Analysis, 1968, Basic Aerodynamics, 1971. Served with AUS, 1946-47. Mem. Am. Soc. Engring. Edn. Democrat. Roman Catholic.

HABERMAN, F. WILLIAM, lawyer; b. Princeton, N.J., Apr. 20, 1940; s. Frederick William and Louise (Power) H.; m. Carmen Marie Duffy, June 15, 1963; children: Frederick, Sarah. BA, U. Wis., 1962; LLB, Harvard Law Sch., 1965. Bar: Wis. 1965, Fla. 1993, U.S. Dist. Ct. (ea. dist.) Wis. 1966, U.S. Dist. Ct. (we. dist.) Wis. 1967, Fla. 1993. Ptnr. Michael, Best & Friedrich, Milw., 1965—; mem. adv. bd. Johnson Bank, 1994—. Co-author: Marital Property Law in Wisconsin, 1986. Trustee Pub. Policy Forum, Milw., 1992—; bd. dirs. Ctrl. YMCA, Milw., 1988-93, Richard and Ethel Herzfeld Found., Milw., 1985—, Wis. affiliate Am. Heart Assn., 1993-97; mem. adv. bd. Milw. Fair Housing Coun., 1989-90; mem. deferred giving adv. bd. Milw. Sch. Engring., 1989-93; bd. dirs. Milw. Children's Hosp. Found., 1994—, Milw. Repertory Theater, 1997—. Fellow Am. Coll. Trust & Estate Counsel; mem. ABA, Wis. Bar Assn. Home: 2727 E Shorewood Blvd Milwaukee WI 53211-2459 Office: Michael Best & Friedrich 100 E Wisconsin Ave Ste 3300 Milwaukee WI 53202-4108

HABERMAN, LOUISE SHELLY, consulting company executive; b. N.Y.C.; d. Harry Martin and Rebecca (Binstock) H.; m. Gordon Joel Schochet. BA, Cornell U., 1971; PhD, Princeton (N.J.) U., 1984. Mem. faculty numerous colls. and univs.], 1975-84; researcher pub. policy U.S. Dept. Commerce, 1976; prin. investigator pub. policy study State of N.J., Trenton, 1979-80; pvt. practice cons. Highland Park, N.J., 1984-86; head regional bank svcs. Multinational Strategies, Inc., N.Y.C., 1986-90; pres. Haberman Assocs., Inc., Edison, N.J., 1990—. Author: (monograph) Regional Banks: International Strategies for the Future, 1987; editor: (with Paul Sacks) Ann. Rev. of Nations, 1988; contbr. articles to profl. jours. Issues advisor selected polit. candidates and civil liberties causes. Avocations: gardening, painting. Office: Haberman Assocs Inc 315 N 8th Ave Edison NJ 08817-2914

HABERMAN, SHELBY JOEL, statistician, educator; b. Cin., May 4, 1947; s. Jack Leon and Miriam Leah (Langberg) H.; m. Elinor Penny Levine, Feb. 18, 1979 (dec. 1996); children: Shoshanah, Chasiah, Sarah, Milcah, Boaz, Devorah. AB, Princeton U., 1968; PhD, U. Chgo., 1970. Asst. prof. to prof. U. Chgo., 1970-82; prof. Hebrew U., Jerusalem, 1982-84; prof. stats. Northwestern U., Evanston, Ill., 1984—; chmn. dept. Northwestern U., Evanston, 1986-88. Author: Analysis of Frequency Data, 1974, Analysis of Qualitative Data, Vol. I, 1978, Vol. II, 1979, Advanced Statistics, Vol. I, 1996; contbr. articles to profl. jours. Guggenheim fellow, 1977-78. Fellow AAAS, Inst. Math. Stats., Am. Statis. Assn. Home: 2935 W North Shore Ave Chicago IL 60645-4225 Office: Northwestern U Dept Stats 2006 Sheridan Rd Evanston IL 60208-0852

HABERMANN, HELEN MARGARET, plant physiologist, educator; b. Bklyn., Sept. 13, 1927. AB, SUNY, Albany, 1949; MS, U. Conn., 1951; PhD, U. Minn., 1956. Asst. botanist U. Conn., Storrs, 1949-51; asst. U. Minn., Mpls., 1951-53, asst. plant physiologist, 1953-55, head residence counselor, 1955-56; rsch. assoc. U. Chgo., 1956-57; rsch. fellow Hopkins Marine Sta. Stanford (Calif.) U., 1957-58; from asst. prof. to assoc. prof. biol. scis. Goucher Coll., Towson, 1958-70, chmn. dept. biology, 1963-66, 68, 78-79, prof., 1970-92, Lilian Welsh prof. biol. scis., 1982-92; prof. emeritus, 1992—. Co-author Biology: A Full Spectrum, 1973, Mainstreams of Biology, 1977. NIH spl. rsch. fellow Rsch. Inst. Advanced Study, Balt., 1966-67. Fellow AAAS; mem. Phytochem. Soc. N.Am. (sec. 1987-93), Am. Soc. Plant Physiologists, Am. Soc. Hort. Sci., Soc. Devel. Biology, Am. Soc. Photobiology, Am. Inst. Biol. Scis., Scandinavian Soc. Plant Physiology, Internat. Soc. Plant Molecular Biology, Japanese Soc. Plant Physiology, Soc. Exptl. Biology and Medicine, Am. Camellia Soc., Pioneer Camellia Soc. (pres. 1994-95), Am. Hort. Soc., Sigma Xi. Office: Goucher Coll Dept Biol Scis 1021 Dulaney Valley Rd Baltimore MD 21204-2753

HABERMEHL, LAWRENCE LEROY, philosophy educator; b. Joplin, Mo., June 13, 1937; s. Roland William and Ruth Esther (Kelly) H.; m. Kathryn J. Barnes, June 8, 1958 (div. 1974); children: Elizabeth Anne, R. William, Edward Hale; m. Sue Ellen Lovejoy, Sept. 16, 1989 (div. 1996). AB, Phillips U., 1959; BD, Union Theol. Sem., 1961; PhD, Boston U., 1967. House mgr. Boston Seaman's Friend Soc., 1963-65; teaching fellow Boston U., 1965-66; asst. prof. philosophy Am. Internat. Coll., Springfield, Mass., 1966-73, assoc. prof., 1973—. Author: The Counterfeit Wisdom of Shallow Minds: A Critique of Some Leading Offenders of the 1980s, 1994; author/editor: Morality in the Modern World, 1976. Mem. AAUP, Am. Philos. Assn., Metaphys. Soc. Am., Common Cause, Amnesty Internat., Assn. Informal Logic and Critical Thinking. Unitarian-Universalist. Home: 7 Allen Pl Hampden MA 01036-9745 Office: Am Internat Coll Dept Philosophy Springfield MA 01109

HABERSTROH, RICHARD DAVID, insurance agent; b. St. Louis, Mar. 21, 1943; s. Richard J. and Helen M. (Jones) H.; m. Patricia Steinlage, Aug. 22, 1964; children: Michelle, Stacy, Richard David. BA, S.E. Mo. State U., Cape Girardeau, 1965. CLU. Ins. agt. Constitution Life, Chgo., 1963-70; gen. agt. Monarch Life, Springfield, Mass., 1971-78; pres. Richard D. Haberstroh, CLU, Inc., St. Louis, 1978—; bd. mem. Jefferson Bank, St. Louis, Family Physician Health Svc. Corp. of Ind., Ind. Acad. Family Physicians; cons. Purdue U. Ins. Mktg. Inst., West Lafayette, Ind., 1992, dir. Contbr. articles to profl. jours. Bd. mem., chmn. United Cerebral Palsy, 1982. Mem. St. Louis Assn. Life Underwriters (bd. mem. 1992), St. Louis Soc. CLUs (bd. dirs.), Gateway Chpt. Nat. Speakers (pres. 1987), King's Men (bd. mem. 1978—), Million Dollar Round Table (life). Republican. Roman Catholic. Avocations: golf, hunting, fishing, reading, public speaking. Office: Richard D Haberstroh CLU 1023 Executive Parkway Dr Ste 2 Saint Louis MO 63141-6323

HABGOOD, ANTHONY JOHN, corporate executive; b. Woodbastwick, Eng., Nov. 8, 1946; s. John Michael and Diana Margaret (Dalby) H.; m. Nancy Ray Atkinson, June 29, 1974; children: Elizabeth Ann, John Alan, George Michael. BA in Econs., Gonville and Caius Coll., Cambridge U., 1968; MA, Cambridge U., 1971; MS in Indsl. Adminstrn., Carnegie-Mellon U., Pitts., 1970. From staff to v.p., dir. Boston Cons. Group Inc., 1970-86, exec. com., 1983-86; dir. Tootal, PLC, London, 1986-91, CEO, 1991; dir. Geest, PLC, London, 1988-93; CEO Bunzl, PLC, London, 1991-96, chmn., 1996—; dir. Powergen, PLC, London, 1993—, Schroder Ventures Internat. Investment Trust, PLC, London, 1995—, Nat. Westminster Bank, PLC, London, 1998—. W.L. Mellon fellow, 1968-70. Mem. Ch. of Eng. Club: Royal Norfolk and Suffolk Yacht. Office: 110 Park St, London W1Y 3RB, England

HABGOOD, ROBERT P., publishing executive; b. Va., Mar. 16, 1959. BA, Boston U., 1982. Pres. Dawbert Press, Duxbury, Mass., 1984—. Office: Dawbert Press PO Box 2758 Duxbury MA 02331-2758

HABIBI, DON A., philosophy educator; b. Glendale, Calif., July 30, 1956; s. Benayahu and Adele Matorin Habibi; m. Leah Miriam Habibi, Dec. 31, 1995; children: Benjamin A., David Max. BA, UCLA; MA, Cornell U., 1982, PhD, 1985. Asst. prof. Ithaca (N.Y.) Coll., 1985-86, Calif. State U., Fresno, 1986-87, Pomona Coll., Claremont, Calif., 1987-88; rsch. fellow Hebrew U., Jerusalem, 1993-95; asst. prof. U. N.C., Wilmington, 1988-96, assoc. prof., 1996—. Author: John Stuart Mill and the Ethic of Human Growth, 1999; contbr. articles to profl. jours. Recipient Best Article of Vol. 13 award, Edit. Bd. Midwest Law Rev., 1995. Jewish. Office: U NC Dept Philosophy 601 S College Rd Wilmington NC 28403

HABICH, ELIZABETH CHAMBERLAIN, librarian; b. Boston, Mar. 23, 1955; d. Eugene Randolph and Helen Howard Chamberlain; m. Michael Paul Habich, Sept. 10, 1977. BA in English, Wellesley Coll., 1977; MS in Libr. and Info. Sci., Simmons Coll., 1980; MBA, Northeastern U., 1990. Libr. asst., page Hingham Pub. Libr., 1971-78; circulation asst. MIT, Cambridge, 1978-80; reference libr. Saugus (Mass.) Pub. Libr., 1980-82; head res. svcs. Northeastern U. Libr., Boston, 1982-87, bldg. projects officer, 1986-91, adminstrv. svcs. officer, 1991—; cons. in field. Author: Moving Library Collections: A Management Handbook, 1998; contbr. articles to profl. jours., chpts. to books. Trustee North Reading (Mass.) Pub. Libr., 1992—. Mem. ALA, Assn. Coll. Rsch. Libr., Libr. Adminstrn. Mgmt. Assn. (bldg. equipment sect. 1987—, vice-chair, chair-elect 1993-94, chair 1994-95, past chair 1995-96, program com. 1996—, chair nominating com. 1997-98), Libr. Info. Tech. Assn., Beta Phi Mu, Beta Gamma Sigma. Avocations: quilting, gardening, music. E-mail: e.habich@nunet.neu.edu.

HABICHT, CHRISTIAN HERBERT, history educator; b. Dortmund, Germany, Feb. 23, 1926; came to U.S., 1972; s. Hermann Christian and Emile Julie (Diefenbach) H.; m. Freia Renate Wilkowski, Aug. 15, 1952; children: Susanne, Christoph, Nikolaus. Dr.Phil., U. Hamburg, 1952, Habil, 1957. Asst. to assoc. prof. U. Hamburg, 1952-61; prof. ancient history U. Marburg/Lahn, 1961-65; prof. U. Heidelberg, 1965-73, dean, 1966-67; prof. Inst. Advanced Study, Princeton, N.J., 1973-98; vis. prof. Princeton U., 1973-80. Author books; contbr. articles to profl. jours. Mem. British Acad., Am. Philos. Soc., Acad. Heidelberg, German Archeol. Inst., Austrian Archeol. Inst., Am. Inst. Archeology, Assn. Ancient Historians (Reuchlin-Price award 1991, Criticos-Price award 1998). Office: Inst Advanced Study Sch Hist Studies Princeton NJ 08540

HABICHT, FRANK HENRY, retired industrial executive; b. Chgo., Sept. 4, 1920; s. Geroge Jr. and Gertrude A. (Tronc) H.; m. Jeanne Ellen Patrick, Mar. 9, 1943; children: Pamela, Patricia, Frank Henry II. BSME, Purdue U., 1942; postgrad., Cornell U., 1942, Am. U., 1944. From sales engr. to pres. Marshall & Huschart Machinery Co., Chgo., 1946-70; vice chmn. Cone-Blanchard Machine Co., Windsor, Vt. and Aldridge, Eng., 1971-74; chmn. bd., pres. United Tech. Corp., Chgo., 1970-81; pres. Steego Tech. Corp., West Palm Beach, 1981-86; chmn., pres. Corp. Assocs., Inc., 1986-97; tech. cons. U.S. Dept. Def., Washington, 1963-64; pres. UNISIG Corp., 1980-86, King & Gavaris Cons. Engrs. Inc., 1980-84; U.S. projects mgr. Boehringer GmbH, Germany, 1989-95; 1997; lectr. in field; bd. dirs. Am. SIP Corp., Botemp Corp., Switzerland. Author: Modern Machine Tools, 1964; contbr. articles to profl. jours. Mem. def. indsl. plant equipment com. Dept. Def. Lt. comdr.USN, 1942-45. Mem. ASME, Am. Machine Tool Distbrs. Assn. (dir., past pres.), Fabricating Mfrs. Assn. (dir., past pres.), Conf. Bd. (exec. coun.), Order Knights St. John of Jerusalem, Oakbrook Polo Club, Palm Beach Club, Beach Club, Palm Beach Yacht Club, Soc 4 Arts (Palm Beach, Navy League (bd. dirs.), Masons. Episcopalian. Avocations: hunting, fishing, tennis. Office: Corp Assocs Inc PO Box 746 Palm Beach FL 33480-0746

HABICHT, JEAN-PIERRE, public health researcher, educator, consultant; b. Geneva, Dec. 15, 1934; s. Max H. and Elizabeth (Peterson) Herzog; m. Pat Hinxman, Jan. 3, 1959 (div. Oct. 1990); children: Heidi, Christopher, Oliver; m. Gretel H. Pelto, June 13, 1997. MD, U. Zurich, 1962, Dr. Med., 1964; MPH, Harvard U., 1968; PhD, MIT, 1969. Cert. in clin nutrition Am. Bd. Nutrition. Biochem. rsch. asst. Merck, Sharpe & Dohme, Rahway, N.J., 1958-59; pediat. intern Children's Hosp. Med. Ctr., Boston, 1965-66; med. officer WHO, Guatemala, 1969-74; prof. maternal and child health U. San Carlos, Guatemala, 1972-74; spl. asst. Nat. Ctr. for Health Stats., Washington, 1974-77; James Jamison prof. nutritional epidemiology Cornell U., Ithaca, N.Y., 1977—; cons. pub. health issues nat. and internat. govts., profl. agys., 1975—; mem. expert com. on nutrition WHO, Geneva, 1975—, com. on epidemiology and disease prevention, 1986-89; mem. epidemiology and disease control study sect. NIH, Washington, 1980-83; mem. food and nutrition bd. NAS, Washington, 1981-84, com. evaluation of Women Infant and Child nutrition risk criteria, 1994-96, com. internat. nutrition, 1994-97; mem. com. uses dietary reference intakes Inst. Medicine Nat. Acad. Scis., 1997—; adv. group coordinating subcom. on nutrition UN, 1983-89, chmn., 1986-87; joint nutrition monitoring and evaluation com. HHS-USDA, 1982-86; chmn. expert com. phys. status: Use and Interpretation of Anthropometry, WHO, 1991-93. Contbr. articles to profl. jours., chpts. to books. Fellow Am. Coll. Epidemiology; mem. APHA, Am. Soc. Clin. Nutrition, Am. Soc. Nutritional Scis. (Kellogg prize 1994, Atwater Meml. lectr. 1998, Conrad A. Elvehjem award 1999), Soc. for Epidemiologic Rsch., Internat. Epidemiol. Assn., Internat. Soc. Rsch. on Human Milk and Lactation (mem. exec. com. 1995-96), Sigma Xi, Gamma Sigma Delta, Delta Omega. Office: Cornell U Div Nutritional Sci Savage Hall Ithaca NY 14853

HABIGER, EUGENE E., career officer; m. Barbara Habiger; children: Karl, Kurt. Grad. with honors, Officers Tng. Sch., Lackland AFB, 1963; grad., Air Intelligence Officer Course, Lowry AFB, 1964; grad. with honors, Air Command and Staff Coll., Maxwell AFB, 1975. Second lt. U.S. Army, 1959; advanced through grades to comdr. in chief, U.S. Strategic Command USAF, Offutt AFB, Nebr., 1996—. Decorations include Legion of Merit with oak leaf cluster, Air medal with four oak leaf clusters, Republic of Vietnam Gallantry Cross with Palm, others. Office: USCINCSTRAT 901 Sac Blvd Ste 2a1 Offutt A F B NE 68113-5455

HABKIRK, SUE ANN, education educator; b. Flint, Mich., July 1, 1957; d. Kenneth Albert and Dora Jean (Haley) H.; m. Vincent Guerriero, Jr., May 5, 1990; 1 child, Kent Vincent Guerriero. BS, U. Ariz., 1979, MEd, 1981, PhD, 1987, postgrad. Cert. secondary tchr., community coll. educator, Ariz. Lectr. in health edn. U. Ariz., Tucson, 1981-85, grad. asst. in student svcs., 1985-87, curriculum specialist, substance abuse prevention edn., 1987-91; sch. health specialist Ariz. Dept. of Edn., 1992-97; health resource tchr. Tucson Unified Sch. Dist., 1997—; writer, editor state curriculum in health edn.; cons. in field. Contbr. articles to profl. jours. Mem. AAHPERD, Ariz. Alliance for Health, Phys. Edn., Recreation and Dance (bd. dirs.), Ariz. Sch. Health Assn. (bd. dirs.), Am. Assn. Tchr. Educators, Am. Sch. Health Assn.

HABLE, STEVEN JAMES, recreational therapist, track coach; b. Oshkosh, Wis., Aug. 18, 1961; s. Lawrence Edgar and Ruth Alice (Hansen) H.; m. Susan Paulette Aumann, Oct. 21, 1995; children: Grace Julia, Lane Paul Hable. BS in Devel. Psychology, U. Wis., Oshkosh, 1987; BS in Recreational Therapy, U. Wis., Milw., 1990; MSE in Counseling, U. Wis., Oshkosh, 1998. Cert. therapeutic recreation specialist; nat. cert. counselor. Counselor Camp Greylock, Becket, Mass., 1984-85; asst. track coach U. Wis., Oshkosh, 1987—; recreational therapist Winnebago (Wis.) Mental Health Inst., 1990, Kettle Moraine Correctional Inst., Plymouth, Wis., 1990-91, Wis. Resource Ctr., Winnebago, 1991—. Sec. U. Wis.-Oshkosh Jaycees, 1985-86. Named All-Am. Athlete in pole vault NCAA, 1986; mem. U.S.A. Nat. Track Team, Internat. Sports Exch., 1985. Mem. ACA, Wis. Counseling Assn., Wis. Park and Recreation Assn., Wis. Therapeutic Recreation Soc. (bd. dirs. 1991-96), Midwest Masters Track Club, U. Wis.-Oshkosh Letter Winner's Club (pres. 1986-87). Avocations: pole vaulting, reading, refinishing furniture, sports, Green Bay Packers. Office: Wis Resource Ctr PO Box 16 Winnebago WI 54985-0016

HABLUTZEL, MARGO LYNN, lawyer; b. St. Louis, Dec. 16, 1961; d. Philip Norman and Nancy Carol (Zimmerman) H. AB in English Lang. and Lit., U. Chgo., 1983; JD, Ill. Inst. Tech./Chgo.-Kent, Coll. of Law, 1986; LLM, John Marshall Law Sch., 1995. Bar: Ill. 1986, U.S. Dist. Ct. (no. dist.) Ill. 1994, U.S. Ct. Appeals (7th cir.) 1995, U.S. Supreme Ct. 1995. Computer cons. various orgns., Chgo., 1984-89; legal writing instr. U. Oreg. Sch. Law, Eugene, 1986-87; project coord. ABA/net, Chgo., 1987-89; appellate brief writer, copyright cons. Whitted & Spain P.C. (now Spain, Spain & Varnet), Chgo., 1988-89; hearing officer Ill. Dept. Rehab. Svcs., Chgo., 1989-91; jud. clk. Ill. Appellate Ct., Chgo., 1989-90; pvt. practice Chgo., 1990-97; counsel tech. law Nortel Networks, Inc., Richardson, Tex., 1997—; panel atty. Chgo. Vol. Legal Svcs. Found., 1988-97; mem. juvenile protection divsn. Cir. Ct. of Cook County, 1990-97; copyright cons. to various non-profit corps., 1987—. Contbr. articles to profl. jours. Mem. ABA (chmn. com. on delivery legal svcs. to disabled, young lawyers divsn. 1989-91, new products editor Law Practice Mgmt. 1990-94, chmn. bus. law interest group, computer divsn. 1992-94, vice-chmn. transactional practice interest group, law divsn. 1993-94, chmn. employment and law subcom., small bus. com., bus. law sect.), Ill. Bar Assn. (mem. assembly 1995-97, exec. coun. intellectual property sect. 1995-97, co-chmn. computer law com. 1989-94, chmn. standing com. on legal tech. 1993-95), Chgo. Bar Assn. (bd. dirs. young lawyers sect. 1989-91, chmn. corp. law com. case law devel. 1992-96, liaison cont. legal edn. bd. program 1993-97). E-mail: margolh@nortelnetworks.com. Office: Nortel Networks Inc Mail Stop 07J/03/A10 PO Box 833858 Richardson TX 75083-3858

HABUSH, ROBERT LEE, lawyer; b. Milw., Mar. 22, 1936; s. Jesse James and Beatrice (Liebenberg) H.; m. Miriam Lee Friedman, Aug. 25, 1957; children: Sherri Ellen, William Scott, Jodi Lynn. BBA, U. Wis., 1959, JD, 1961. Bar: Wis. 1961, U.S. Dist. Ct. (ea. and we. dists.) Wis. 1961, U.S. Ct. Appeals (7th cir.) 1965, U.S. Supreme Ct. 1986. Pres. Habush, Habush, Davis & Rottier, S.C., Milw., 1961—; lectr. U. Wis. Law Sch., Marquette U. Law Sch., State Bar Wis., other legal orgns. Author: Cross Examination of Non Medical Experts, 1981. Contbr. articles to legal jours. Served to capt. U.S. Army, 1959-75. Mem. ABA, Wis. Bar Assn., Wis. Acad. Trial Lawyers (pres. 1968-69), ATLA (bd. govs. 1983-86, pres. 1986-87, mem. Nat. Coll. Advocacy), Internat. Acad. Trial Lawyers (bd. dirs. 1983-87, 91-92), Am. Bd. Trial Advocates, Internat. Soc. Barristers, Inner Circle Advocates, Am. Soc. Writers on Legal Subjects, Nat. Bd. Trial Advocates, Trial Lawyers for Pub. Justice, Roscoe Pound Found. Office: Habush Habush Davis & Rottier 777 E Wisconsin Ave Ste 2300 Milwaukee WI 53202-5381

HABZANSKY, ANDREW MELVIN, quality manager, maintenance manager, trainer; b. Hammond, Ind., Nov. 13, 1946; s. Andrew and Sophie (Zabzdar) H.; m. Jean Thomas, June 29, 1968; children: Stephen (dec.), Tanya. A in Mech. Maintenance, East Chicago (Ind.) Pub. Schs., 1977. Payroll clk. Youngstown Sheet Tube, East Chicago, 1964-66; with USAF, 1966-73; mech. apprentice Inland Steel Co., East Chicago, 1973-77, supr. maintenance, 1978-94, 97—, coord. tng., 1994-96; auditor Inland Steel Co., 1996—, trainer maintenance, 1994-98, sec. mgmt. assn., 1989-90; quality mgr. Carestone, Inc., 1998—. Staff sgt. USAF, 1966-73. Mem. Am. Soc. for Quality, Assn. Iron and Steel Engrs. (lubrication and hydraulics engring. divsn.). Roman Catholic. Avocations: karate (5th degree black belt), kobudo. Home: 4708 Torrence Ave Hammond IN 46327-1672 Office: 1646 Summer St Hammond IN 46320

HACAULT, ANTOINE JOSEPH LEON, archbishop; b. Bruxelles, Man., Can., Jan. 17, 1926; s. Francois and Irma (Mangin) H. B.A., U. Man., 1947; theol. student, St. Boniface Maj. Sem., 1947-51; S.T.D., Angelicum U., Rome, 1954; D.C.L. honoris causa, St. John's Coll., Winnipeg, Man., 1977; D.L.L. honoris causa, U. Man., 1989. Ordained priest Roman Cath. Ch., 1951; chaplain St. Boniface Sanatorium, 1954; prof. theology St Boniface Maj. Sem., 1954-64; dir. diocesan rev. Les Cloches de Saint Boniface, 1961; former personal theologian to archbishop of St. Boniface; also council expert 2d Vatican Ecumenical Council, 1962-65; bishop titular of Media; aux. bishop of St. Boniface, 1964-72; coadjutor bishop, 1972-74; archbishop St. Boniface, 1974—; rector Coll. St. Boniface, 1966-69; mem. Pontifical Coun. for Promoting Christian Unity, Rome, 1976-89; pres. Western Cath. Conf. Bishops, 1988-92. Address: Cathedrale, 151 Ave de la Cathedrale, Saint Boniface, MB Canada R2H 0H6*

HACCOUN, DAVID, electrical engineering educator; b. Bizerte, Tunisia, July 4, 1937; arrived in Can. 1957; s. Charles and Emma (Melloul) H.; m. Lyson Tobaly, Dec. 26, 1971; children—Nathalie, Laurent. B.Sc. Engring. Physics, U. Montreal, 1965; M.S., MIT, 1966; Ph.D., McGill U., 1974. Registered profl. engr., Que. Communications engr. City of Montreal, Que., Can., 1965; research asst. MIT, Cambridge, 1965-66; prof. Ecole Polytech. U., Montreal, Que., Can., 1966—; vis. research prof. Concordia U., Montreal, Que., Can., 1984-85; cons. govt. agys. univs. and industry, Can., U.S.A., France, 1974—; project leader Can. Inst. for Telecom. Rsch. under Nat. Ctrs. Excellence of Govt. Can., 1990—; vis. rsch. fellow Advanced Study Inst., U. BC, Vancouver, 1992; vis. rschr. INRIA, Paris, 1992; vis. rsch. prof. Higher Sch. Tech., Montreal, 1999, U. Victoria, B.C., Can., 1999; mem. exec. com. telecom. engring. Mgmt. Inst. Can., 1997—. Co-author: Digital Communications by Satellite, 1981, translated in Japanese, 1984, in Chinese, 1989, The Communications Handbook, 1997; contbr. articles to profl. jours. in French and English. Mem. exec. com. Can. Jewish Congress, 1996—. Commonwealth fellow London, 1965; Grass fellow MIT, 1966, scholar, MIT, 1965-66; Hydro-Que. fellow, Montreal, 1969-72. Fellow IEEE (Inst. of Elec. and Electronics Engrs., N.Y.); mem. Order of Engrs. of Que., Can. Soc. of Info. Theory (founding pres. 1986), N.Y. Acad. Scis., Sigma Xi. Avocations: photography; swimming; skiing. Office: Ecole Polytechnique, PO Box 6079 Sta Centre Ville, Montreal, PQ Canada H3C 3A7

HACHEY, THOMAS EUGENE, British and Irish history educator, consultant; b. Lewiston, Maine, June 8, 1938; s. Leo Joseph and Margaret Mary (Johnson) H.; m. Jane Beverly Whitman, June 9, 1962. B.A., St. Francis Coll., 1960; M.A., Niagara U., 1961; Ph.D., St. John's U., 1965. Asst. prof. history Marquette U., Milw., 1964-69, assoc. prof., 1969-77, prof., 1977—, chmn. dept. history, 1979-93, dean Coll. Arts and Scis., 1993—; vis. prof. history Sch. Irish Studies, Dublin, 1977-78; cons. investments in Ireland Frost & Sullivan, N.Y.C., 1978-82; pres. Am. Conf. Irish Studies, 1983-85; dir. Bradley Inst. for Democracy and Pub. Values, 1988—. Author: Problem of Partition: Peril to World Peace, 1972, Britain and Irish Separatism, 1977; co-author: The Irish Experience, 1988, expanded edit., 1996, Perspectives of Irish Nationalism, 1988; editor: Voices of Revolution, 1972, Confidential Despatches, 1975; contbr. over 100 articles and revs. to Brit., Irish and Am. jours. and newspapers. Danforth assoc., 1979-85. Fellow Anglo-Am. Assocs. Roman Catholic. Home: 663 N 75th St Wauwatosa WI 53213-3503 Office: Marquette U Coll of Arts and Scis Milwaukee WI 53201-1881

HACHTEN, WILLIAM ANDREWS, journalism educator, author; b. Wichita, Kans., Nov. 30, 1924; s. George Charles and Emma Elizabeth (Andrews) H.; m. Harva Kaaren Sprager, Apr. 5, 1952; children: Elizabeth, Marianne. BA, Stanford U., 1947; MS, UCLA, 1952; PhD, U. Minn., 1961. Profl. football player N.Y. Giants, 1947; reporter Santa Paula (Calif.) Chronicle, 1948-49, Long Beach (Calif.) Press-Telegram, 1952-54, Santa Monica (Calif.) Outlook, 1954; copy editor L.A. Examiner, 1955-56; prof. Sch. Journalism and Mass Communication U. Wis., Madison, 1959-89, asst. dir., 1973-75, dir., 1975-80; Fulbright lectr. U. Ghana, 1972-73. Author: The Supreme Court on Freedom of the Press, 1968, Muffled Drums: The News Media in Africa, 1971, Mass Communications in Africa: An Annotated Bibliography, 1971, World News Prism, 1981, 92, 96, 99, The Press and Apartheid, 1984, Growth of Media, 1993, The Troubles of Journalism, 1998; assoc. editor Journalism Quar., 1972-75. Recipient Sigma Delta Chi award for rsch. in journalism, 1968, Fulbright-Hays Rsch. award for Africa, 1968. Mem. Assn. Edn. Journalism, Internat. Press Inst., Internat. Assn. Mass Communication Rsch. Unitarian. Home: 90 Oak Creek Trl Madison WI 53717-1510

HACK, ELIZABETH, artist; b. Frankfurt, Germany, Feb. 27, 1954; d. Sidney and Eleanor Barbara (Bermak) H. BFA, U. Miami, Coral Gables, Fla., 1976; M Media Arts, U. S.C., 1979. Art instr. Berkeley, Calif., 1991-97; art instr. W. Contra Costa (Calif.) Adult Sch., 1994-96; lectr., workshops Nat. League Am. Pen Women, El Cerrito Cmty. Ctr., Albany Sr. Ctr., 1992—. Featured artist Commonwealth Club gallery, San Francisco, 1994; solo exhbns. Newall Assocs., 1997, Henry Hardy Gallery, Univ. Club, San Francisco, 1992, Gallery 57, Fullerton, Calif., 1992, AMEX, San Rafael, Informative Edge, San Francisco, 1991, Conv. Plz. Bldg., San Francisco, 1990, Heller Gallery, U. Calif. Berkeley, Sumitomo Bank, San Francisco, ASUC Studio, U. Calif. Berkeley, 1988, Musical Offering, Berkeley, Coldwell Banker, Kensington home, French Hotel Berkeley, 1987, Coffee Cantata, San Francisco, 1985; group exhbns. include Gloria Delson Fine Art, L.A., 1995, 96, Cameo Art Gallery, Columbia, S.C., 1992, 94, Ashkenazy Galleries, L.A., 1991; group shows include: Hayward Arts Coun., Nat. League of Am. Pen Women Exhibit, Hayward, Calif., 1999, Cruising the Triton, Santa Clara, Calif., 1999, Palos Verdes Cultural Ctr., 1997, Orlando Gallery, Sherman Oaks, Calif., 1997, Triton Mus. of Art, Benefit Auction, Santa Clara, Calif., 1997, Richmond Art Ctr., Holiday Acution, Calif., 1997, Newall Assocs., Santa Monica, Calif., 1997, Soolip Gallery, West Hollywood, Calif., 1997, Hayward Arts Coun., 1998, Nat. League Am. Pen Women, Hayward, 1998, Triton Mus. Art, Santa Clara, 1997, 98, 3 Com Corp., Santa Clara, Calif., 1998, Network Assoc., Menlo Park, Calif., 1998, Triton Mus. Art, Santa Clara, Calif., 1998, Mad River Post Nancy Sadler Fine Arts, Calif., 1998. Curator multiple abstractions W. Contra Costa Adult Sch., 1995, 4th ann. Gift of Life Ctr. for Visual Arts, Oakland, 1996—, AIDS auction, 1994. Recipient Critic's Choice award San Francisco Bay Guardian, 1990, award of distinction Berkeley Art Ctr., 1989. Mem. Nat. League Am. Pen Women (sec. 1994-96, v.p. 1996-98, pres. Diablo-Alameda chpt. 1998—). Avocations: skiing, music, hiking. E-mail: studio@elizabethhack.com. Home and Office: PO Box 8057 Berkeley CA 94707-8057

HACK, GARY ARTHUR, dean; b. Abernethy, Sask., Can., Apr. 8, 1942; came to U.S., 1964; s. Arthur and Marie (Banerd) H.; m. Lynda Lloy Lewis, Sept. 5, 1964 (div.); children: Andrew Arthur, Carolyn Sarah. BArch, U. Manitoba, 1964; MArch, U. Ill., 1966, M in Urban Planning, 1967; PhD, MIT, 1976. Project mgr. Gruen Assocs., N.Y.C., 1967-69; asst. prof. MIT, Cambridge, 1970-75; gen. mgr. Can. Mortgage and Housing Corp., Ottawa, Ont., 1975-79; prin. Carr Lynch Hack & Sandell, Cambridge, 1986-94; dean, Paley prof. U. Pa., Phila., 1996—; lectr. U. Ill., Urbana, 1967, Pratt Inst., Bklyn., 1968-69; assoc. prof., prof. MIT, Cambridge, 1979-96. Co-author: Site Planning, 3d edit., 1984; chief planner West Side Waterfront, N.Y.C., 1986-91, Prudential Ctr. Redevel., Boston, 1988-91. Recipient 1st award Progressive Architecture, 1975. Fellow Urban Land Inst.; mem. Am. Inst. Cert. Planners. Avocations: travel, architectural photography, collecting Yi Cheng teapots. Office: U Pa 101 Meyerson Hall/6311 Philadelphia PA 19104

HACKAM, REUBEN, electrical engineering educator; b. Baghdad, Iraq, Feb. 18, 1936; arrived in Can., 1978; s. Yechiel and Rachel (Cohen) H.; m. Estelle Malkinson, June 7, 1964; children: Judy, David, Abby, Dan. BSc, Israel Inst. Tech., Haifa, 1960; PhD, U. Liverpool, Eng., 1964, DEng, 1988. Sr. engr. GE, Stafford, Eng., 1964-69; lectr. elec. engring. U. Sheffield, Eng., 1969-73, sr. lectr., 1973-74, reader, 1974-78; prof. U. Windsor, Ont., Can., 1978—, chmn. dept., 1981-82, 84-86, Disting. prof., 1997—; vis. staff dept. math. Staffordshire Poly., Stafford, 1964-69, Sheffield Poly, 1970-78, Hong Kong Poly. U., 1990-91; cons. Brit. Rail, Derby, Eng., 1975-78, English Electric Co., Stafford, 1975-77, Windsor Star, 1981-91, Corp. City of Windsor, 1983-92, Green Shield Prepaid Svcs., Inc., 1982—, County of Essex Libr., 1986—, Can. Salt Co., 1988—, Windsor Real Estate Bd., 1996—; vis. prof. Kumamoto U., Japan, 1998-99. Contbr. articles to profl. jours. Cons. Windsor Bd. Edn., 1988, Essex Bd. Edn., Windsor, 1989-94. Fellow IEEE (gaseous dielectrics tech. com. 1985—, program com. publicity and publ. chmn., bd. dirs. conf. on elec. insulation and dielectric phenomena 1985-91, various working groups 1987—, asst. editor Digest IEEE Transactions on Dielectrics and Elec. Insulation 1990-99, assoc. editor 1999—, fellows award com. 1993-96, mem. editl. bd. IEEE Elec. Insulation Mag. 1990-98, vice-chmn. conf. on elec. insulation and dielectric phenomena 1994-95, chmn. 1996-97, sec. 1992-93, mem. permanent sci. com. int. synops. on discharges and elec. insulation in vacuum 1991—, mem. tech. program com. IEEE-CEIDP 1986-97); mem. IEEE Dielectrics and Elec. Insulation Soc. (nominating and adv. coms. 1988-91, chmn. publ. com. 1990-91, asst. treas. 1991-92, treas. 1993-94, 99—, v.p. adminstrn. 1995-96, pres. 1997-98, pub. com. 1988-96, 99—, edn. com. 1990-95), Can. Soc. Elec. and Computer Engrs. (v.p. 1990-93), Assn. Profl. Engrs. Ont. Jewish. Office: U Windsor, 401 Sunset Ave, 401 Sunset Ave, Windsor, ON Canada N9B 3P4

HACKBIRTH, DAVID WILLIAM, aluminum company executive; b. Butler, Ind., Jan. 25, 1935; s. Ernest William and Bessie Mae (Snyder) H.; m. Anna Katherine Shaffer, July 19, 1959; children: Cynthia Kay, David William. Student, Defiance Coll., 1953; B.S., Ind. U., 1959; J.D., Wayne State U., 1963, postgrad., 1965; M.B.A., U. Detroit, 1965. Bar: Mich. bar 1963. Auditor Ernst & Ernst, Indpls., 1958-59; fin. and budget analyst Ford Motor Co., Dearborn, Mich., 1959-62; legal adminstr. Chrysler Corp., Detroit, 1962-63; tax atty. Chrysler Corp., 1963-66, Glidden Co., Cleve., 1966-67; asst. to treas. Alcan Aluminum Corp., Cleve., 1967-70; asst. to group v.p. ops. Alcan Aluminum Corp., 1970-73; pres., dir. Aluminio de Colombia S.A., 1973-76; v.p. Alcan Bldg. Products div. Alcan Aluminum Corp., Warren, Ohio, 1976-78; pres. Alcan Bldg. Products div. Alcan Aluminum Corp., 1978-83, Alcan Sheet and Plate div., 1983-86, Alcan Bldg Products div., 1986-89, Alcan Extrusions USA div., 1989-90; pres., dir. Alcan Aluminum Corp., 1990-95, Bus. Concepts, Inc., 1995—; bd. dirs. Luxfer USA Ltd., Alcan-Toyo-Am., Inc., Laxide Corp., Liberty Mutual Ins. Co. Bd. dirs. ARC, NCCJ. Served with U.S. Army, 1954-56. Mem. ABA, Am. Arbitration Assn., Mich. Bar Assn., Cleve. Growth Assn. (dir.), Akron Regional Devel. Bd., Pine Lake Trout Club, Country Club of Hudson, Union Club, Cotillion Soc. Cleve., Scottish Rite, Beta Alpha Psi, Delta Theta Phi. Home: 290 Bicknell Dr Hudson OH 44236-2922 Office: 920 Key Bldg 159 S Main St Akron OH 44308-1317

HACKEL, EMANUEL, science educator; b. Bklyn., June 17, 1925; s. Henry N. and Esther (Herbstman) H.; m. Elisabeth Mackie, June 24, 1950 (dec. Apr. 1978); children: Lisa M., Meredith Anne, Janet M.; m. Rachel A. Fisher, Oct. 18, 1981; stepchildren: Daniel E., Tabitha A., and Jessica K. Harrison. Student, N.Y. U., 1941-42; B.S., U. Mich., 1948, M.S., 1949; Ph.D., Mich. State U., 1953. Fisheries biologist Mich. Dept. Conservation, 1949; mem. faculty Mich. State U., East Lansing, 1949—; prof. natural sci. Mich. State U., 1962-74, chmn. dept. natural sci., 1963-74, prof. medicine, 1974-95, prof. emeritus, 1995—, prof. zoology, 1974-95, prof. emeritus, 1995—; asst. dean coll. 1958-63; rsch. fellow Galton Lab., U. Coll., London, 1970-71, 77-78; vis. investigator blood group rsch. unit Lister Inst., London, 1956-57; cons. Mpls. War Meml. Blood Bank, 1983-95. Author: Guide to Laboratory Studies in Biological Science, 1951, Studies in Natural Science, 1953, Natural Science, 1955, Vols. 1, 2, 3, 1952-63. Editor: The Search for Explanation-Studies in Natural Science, Vols. 1, 2, 3, 1967-68, Laboratory Manual for Natural Science, Vol. 1, 2, 3, 1967-68, Human Genetics, 1974, Theoretical Aspects of HLA, 1982, Bone Marrow Transplantation, 1983, HLA Techniques for Blood Bankers, 1984, Human Genetics 1984: A Look at the Last Ten Years and the Next Ten, Transfusion Management of Some Common Heritable Blood Disorders, 1992, Advances in Transplantation, 1993, HLA Typing Section, Clinical Laboratory Medicine, 1994, Human Genetics '94: A Revolution in Full Swing, 1994; contbr. articles on genetics, human blood group immunology and chem. nature of blood group antigens, human biochem. genetics, tissue typing, human histocompatibility antigens to sci. jours. Served to lt. (j.g.) USNR, 1943-47; now lt. comdr. USNR Ret. Recipient Cooley Meml. award Am. Assn. Blood Banks, 1969, Elliott Meml. award Am. Assn. Blood Banks, 1987, alumni disting. faculty award Coll. Natural Sci. Mich. State U., 1995. Mem. Assn. Gen. and Liberal Studies (sec.-treas. 1962-65), AAUP, AAAS, Genetics Soc. Am., Am. Soc. Human Genetics, Am. Assn. Blood Banks (dir. 1983-84, chmn. sci. sect. 1983-84), Mich. Assn. Blood Banks (v.p. 1970, pres. 1975-77), Am. Inst. Biol. Sci., Biometric Soc., Transplantation Soc. Mich. (dir. 1975-84), Am. Assn. for Clin. Histocompatibility Testing, N.Y. Acad. Scis., Sigma Xi, Phi Kappa Phi. Home: 244 Oakland Dr East Lansing MI 48823-4747 Office: Mich State U Dept Pathology East Lansing MI 48824

HACKEL-SIMS, STELLA BLOOMBERG, lawyer, former government official; b. Burlington, Vt., Dec. 27, 1926; d. Hyman and Esther (Pocher) Bloomberg; m. Donald Herman Hackel, Aug. 14, 1949; children: Susan Jane, Cynthia Anne; m. Arthur Sims, Aug. 28, 1980. Student, U. Vt., 1943-45; J.D. cum laude, Boston U., 1948. Bar: Vt. 1948, Mass. 1948, D.C. 1979, Va. 1982. Individual practice law Burlington, 1948-49, Rutland, Vt., 1949-59, 73—; city prosecutor City of Rutland, 1957-63; commr. Vt. Dept. Employment Security, 1963-73; treas. State of Vt., 1975-77; dir. U.S. Mint, Dept. Treasury, Washington, 1977-81; chmn. Vt. Municipal Bond Bank, 1975-77. Mem. Vt. Adv. Com. on Mental Retardation, Interdept. Council on Aging, Commn. on Status Women, Human Resource Inter-Agency Com., Emergency Resource Priorities Bd., Info. Planning Council, Legis. Council Equal Opportunity Com., Vt. Indsl. Devel. Authority, Vt. Housing Fin. Agy., Vt. Claims Commn., Vt. Tchrs. Retirement Fund. Bd., Vt. Home Mortgage Guaranty Bd.; chmn. Vt. State Employees Retirement Fund; ex-officio mem. Nat. Manpower Adv. Com., 1971-72, Fed. Adv. Council on Unemployment Ins., 1971-72; Pres. Rutland Girl Scouts Leaders Assn., 1949-50, Rutland League Women Voters, 1951-52, Rutland Council Jewish Women, 1955-56; chmn. womens div. Rutland Community Chest Dr., 1952, Rutland County-Vt. Assn. for Blind, 1953-56; pres. Rutland County Democratic Women's Assn., 1956-63; treas. Rutland City Dem. Com., 1957-63; former rep. office women's activities Dem. Nat. Com., Regional Council I., Women's CD Councils; mem. Vt. bd. Girl Scouts U.S.A.; chmn. Arlington County Tenant-Landlord Commn., Va., 1986—. Mem. Vt. Bar Assn., Rutland County Bar Assn. (pres. 1973), Bus. and Profl. Women's Club, AAUW (pres. Rutland county br. 1961-62), Vt. Council Social Agys., League Women Voters, Am. Soc. Pub. Adminstrn., Interstate Conf. Employment Security Agencies (v.p. region I 1966-68, legis. com. 1969, sr. v.p. 1970-71, pres. 1971-72), Delta Phi Epsilon. Clubs: Emblem (dir. 1960-63), Woodmont Country; Internat. (Washington).

HACKENBERG, BARBARA JEAN COLLAR, retired advertising and public relations executive; b. Venango County, Pa., Apr. 15, 1927; d. Guy Lamont and Marion Leona (Kingsley) Collar; m. George Richardson, June 13, 1953; children: Kurt Edward, Kim Ellen, Caroline Kingsley. BA, Grove City (Pa.) Coll., 1948; ML, U. Pitts., 1949. Advt. dir. The Halle Bros. Co., Erie, Pa., 1950-52, advt. and sales promotion dir. Pa. divsn., 1952-54; exec. dir. Wyomissing (Pa.) Inst. Fine Arts, 1970-74; dir. and cmty. liason Freedman Gallery, Albright Coll., Reading, Pa., 1976-78; selling supr. Pomeroy's Children's Dept., Wyomissing, Pa., 1981-83; pub. rels. account exec. Wentworth Assocs., Lancaster, Pa., 1983-84; exec. dir. World Affairs Coun., Reading, 1987-97; owner The WRITE Place, Reading, 1979-97, ret., 1997. V.p. Harrisburg (Pa.) Foreign Policy Assn., 1964-67; various fund-raising activities, 1954-70; pub. relations chmn. Erie World Affairs Ctr., 1957-60; mem. mil. affairs com. Berks County chpt. ARC, 1998—; apptd. to Parks and Recreation Bd., Twp. of Cumru, 1998—; mem. Internat. Com. YMCA, Burks County, Pa., 1999—. Mem. Women in Communications, Inc. (pub. relations chmn. ctrl. Pa. chpt., 1984-87, sec. ctrl. Pa. chpt., 1986-87). Avocations: writing, theater, art, concerts, bicycling. Home and Office: 1334 Welsh Rd Reading PA 19607-9334

HACKENBROCK, CHARLES R., cell biologist, educator; b. Bklyn., Dec. 23, 1929; s. Arthur and Stella H.; m. Linda; children: Laura, Sheila, Sandra; m. Linda Hackenbrock, 1993. B.S., Wagner Coll., 1961; Ph.D. (univ. acad. scholar, 1961, NIH fellow, 1962-66), Columbia U., 1966. Asst. prof. anatomy Sch. Medicine, Johns Hopkins U., 1965-68, assoc. prof. anatomy, 1968-71; prof. cell biology U. Tex. Health Sci. Ctr., Dallas, 1971-77; prof., chmn. cell biology and anatomy dept. Sch. Medicine, U. N.C., Chapel Hill, 1977—; dir. Labs. for Cell Biology, Electron Microscope Labs. Editor: Jour. of Cell Biology, 1981-83; adv. editor: Electron Microscopy in Biology, 1980—; contbr.: research articles to Cell Biology and Bioenergetics, 1965—. Served with U.S. Army, 1951-53. Mem. Am. Soc. Biol. Chemists, Am. Soc. Cell Biology, Biophys. Soc., Electron Microscopy Soc., Am., N.Y. Acad. Scis., Am. Assn. Anatomists, Assn. Anatomy Chairmen, Council Nat. Soc. for Med. Research. Office: U NC Sch Medicine Chapel Hill NC 27599

HACKENMILLER, THOMAS RAYMOND, writer, publisher; b. Riceville, Iowa, May 15, 1951; s. Clarance Joseph and Angela Rose (Miller) H.; m. Joyce Marie Wingenbach, Dec. 18, 1971 (div. June 1980); children: Andrew, Timothy, Anna; m. Kathie D. Teeley, Mar. 21, 1985. AAS, Yakima (Wash.) Valley Coll., 1973; BA in Edn., Ctrl. Wash. U., 1985, MA in History, 1986. Tchr. Lake Chelan Sch. Dist., Chelan, Wash., 1986-94; author, pub. Point Pub., Manson, Wash., 1994—; adj. prof. City U., Bellevue, Wash., 1991-92. Author: Wapato Heritage: The History of the Chelan and Entiat Indians, 1995, Ladies of the Lake: Tales of Transportation, Tragedy, and Triumph on Lake Chelan, 1998. Chmn. Tech. 2000 Com. Lake Chelan Sch. Dist., Chelan, 1993-94; mem. State WEDNET Com., Office Supt. of Pub. Instns., Olympia, Wash., 1993-94; mem. exec. com. State History Day, Ellensburg, Wash., 1987-89; bd. dirs. Lake Chelan Cmty. Hosp. Found., Chelan, 1991-93. Avocations: fishing, golf, reading. Home: PO Box 355 Manson WA 98831-0355 Office: Point Pub PO Box 355 Manson WA 98831-0355

HACKER, ANDREW, political science educator; b. N.Y.C., Aug. 30, 1929; s. Louis Morton and Lilian (Lewis) H.; m. Lois Sheffield Wetherell, June 17, 1955; 1 dau., Ann. A.B., Amherst Coll., 1951; M.A., Oxford (Eng.) U., 1953; Ph.D., Princeton U., 1955. Instr. govt. Cornell U., Ithaca, N.Y., 1955-56; asst. prof. Cornell U., 1956-60, asso. prof., 1960-66, prof., 1966-71; prof. polit. sci. Queens Coll., CUNY, 1971—; cons. Conf. Bd., Brookings Instn., Rockefeller Bros. Fund, NBC, Ency. Brit. Author: Political Theory: Philosophy, Ideology, Science, 1960, Congressional Districting, 1963, The Study of Politics, 1973, The Corporation Take-Over, 1964, The End of the American Era, 1970, The New Yorkers, 1975, Free Enterprise in America, 1977, U.S.: A Statistical Portrait of the American People, 1983, Two Nations: Black and White, Separate, Hostile, Unequal, 1992, updated edit., 1995, Money: Who Has How Much and Why, 1997. Mem. AAUP, Phi Beta Kappa. Home: 20 W 64th St Apt 16K New York NY 10023-7104 Office: CUNY Queens Coll Dept Polit Sci Flushing NY 11367

HACKER, LARRY E., advertising executive; b. Balt., Mar. 11, 1943; s. Ureal Al and Norma E. (Schroeder) H.; m. Jenna L. Plunkett, Jan. 25, 1965; children: Brett L., Laura L. Student, Ariz. State Coll., 1961-63. Account exec. Philip G. Back, Advt., Little Rock, 1963-64, Ark. Dem. Newspaper, Little Rock, 1964-66; mktg. exec. Internat. Graphics, Inc., Little Rock, 1966-77, Parkin Printing Co., Little Rock, 1977-82; pres. N.Am. Advt. Agy., Little Rock, 1982-85; owner The Printery-Advt., Pub., Mabelvale, Ark., 1985—; sr. arbitrator Better Bus. Bur., Little Rock, 1980—. Author: Colt Single Action Chronology, 1982, Colt 1911 Chronology, 1983, Colt Woodsman Chronology, 1984; also articles. Republican. Methodist. Avocations: collecting antique firearms, hunting, fishing, photography, building and flying radio control aircraft. Home: 15409 Myna Dr Mabelvale AR 72103-4039

HACKER, ROBERT GORDON, educator, consultant; b. Chgo., Dec. 8, 1931; s. Robert Clarence and Emma Augusta (Schauer) H.; m. Mary Elizabeth Wolff, Oct. 17, 1959; children: Robyn Cheryl Hoyt, Robert Jonathan Hacker. BE, Chgo. Tchrs. Coll., 1960; MS, S.D. State U., 1962; PhD, U. Iowa, 1969. Asst. prof. Rochester (N.Y.) Inst. Tech., 1962-65, prof., 1969-98, Paul and Louise Miller disting. prof., 1979—; cons. New House Newspapers, Newark, 1969—, numerous others, 1969—. Contbr. articles to profl. jours. Adv. Boy Scouts Am., Fairport, N.Y., 1975; pres. Genesee Valley Ski Patrol, Rochester, 1979. Fulbright prof. U.S. Fulbright Com., Finland, 1976-77. Mem. TAGA, Am. East (bd. dirs. 1980—), Nat. Ski Patrol, Fulbright Alumni Assn., Phi Kappa Phi, Kappa Tau Alpha. Avocations: fly fishing, skiing, traveling. Office: Rochester Inst Tech Sch Printing Mgmt Scis 69 Lomb Memorial Dr Rochester NY 14623-5603

HACKER, THOMAS OWEN, architect; b. Dayton, Ohio, Nov. 4, 1941; s. Homer Owen and Lydia (McLean) H.; m. Margaret (Brooks) Stewart, Mar. 21, 1965; children: Jacob, Sarah, Alice. BA, U. Pa., 1964, MArch, 1967. Registered arch., Oreg.; registered Nat. Coun. Archtl. Registration Bds. Intern architect Office of Louis I. Kahn, Phila., 1964-70; mem. faculty architecture U. Pa., Phila., 1967-69, U. Oreg., Eugene, 1970-84; design prin. Thomas Hacker and Assocs. Architects P.C., Portland, Oreg., 1983—; vis. profl. architecture, U. Oreg., 1985—. Prin. works include Biomed. Info. Comm. Ctr., Oreg. Health Scis. U., Sch. Nursing, Oreg. Health Scis. U. (Regional Honor award AIA 1993), Portland Art Mus., High Desert Mus., Bend, Oreg.; designer crystal vase for Steuben Inc., Spokane Pub. Libr., Yellowstone Art Mus., Billings, Mont., Lewis & Clark Coll. Signature Project, Multnomah County Midland Libr., Columbia Gorge Interpretive Ctr., Portland State U. Urban Ctr., Whitman Coll. Penrose Meml. Libr., Portland 1st Unitarian Ch. Office: 34 NW 1st Ave Ste 406 Portland OR 97209-4017 Home: 2762 SW Montgomery Dr Portland OR 97201-1693

HACKERMAN, NORMAN, chemist, academic administrator; b. Balt., Mar. 2, 1912; s. Jacob and Anne (Raffel) H.; m. Gene Allison Coulbourn, Aug. 25, 1940; children: Patricia Gale, Stephen Miles, Sally Griffith, Katherine Elizabeth. AB, Johns Hopkins U., 1932, PhD, 1935. Asst. prof. Loyola Coll., Balt., 1935-39; research chemist Colloid Corp., 1936-40; asst. chemist USCG, S.I., 1939-41; asst. prof. Va. Poly. Inst., Blacksburg, 1941-43; research chemist Kellex Corp., 1944-45; asst. prof. chemistry U. Tex., 1945-46, assoc. prof., 1946-50, prof., 1950-70, chmn. dept., 1952-61, dir. corrosion research lab., 1948-61, dean research and sponsored programs, 1960-61, v.p., provost, 1961-63, vice chancellor acad. affairs, 1963-67, pres., 1967-70, prof. emeritus chem., 1985—; prof. chemistry Rice U., Houston, 1970-85, Disting. prof. emeritus, 1985—, pres., 1970-85, pres. emeritus, 1985—; chmn. Gordon Corrosion Research Conf., 1950; cons. in corrosion, 1946—; chmn. Inter Soc. Corrosion Com., 1956-58; chmn. Gordon Research Conf. on Surface Chemistry, 1959; mem. nat. sci. bd. NSF, 1968-80, chmn., 1974-80; mem. Def. Sci. Bd., 1978-85; chmn. sci. adv. bd. Welch Found., 1982—; mem. Nat. Bd. Grad. Edn., 1971-75; chmn. bd. energy studies Nat. Acad. Scis./NRC Commn. Natural Resources, 1974-77; mem. Energy Research Adv. Bd., 1980-82; mem. Tex. Gov.'s Task Force on Higher Edn., 1981-82; trustee MITRE Corp., 1980-85. Recipient Whitney award Nat. Assn. Corrosion Engrs., 1956, Joseph J. Mattiello Meml. lectr. Fedn. Socs. Paint Tech., 1964, Gold medal Am. Inst. Chemists, 1978, Mirabeau B. Lamar award Assn. Tex. Colls. and Univs., 1981, Disting. Alumnus award Johns Hopkins U., 1982, Alumni Gold medal for disting. service to Rice U., 1984, Vannevar Bush award NSF, 1993, Nat. Medal of Sci. award, 1993. Fellow AAAS (Phillip Hauge Abelson prize 1987), Am. Acad. Arts and Scis., N.Y. Acad. Scis., 1978; mem. Am. Chem. Soc. (bd. editors 1956-62, exec. com. colloid div. 1955-58, chmn. chemistry and public affairs com. 1982-88, S.W. Regional award 1965, Charles Lathrop Parsons award 1987), Electrochem. Soc. (pres. 1957-58, Palladium medal 1965, Edward Goodrich Acheson award 1984), Faraday Soc., Nat. Corrosion Engrs. (bd. dir. 1952-55, chmn. com. edn. Corrosion Research Council 1957-60), Argonne Univs. Assn. (chmn. bd. trustees 1969-73), Nat. Acad. Scis., 1971, Am. Philos. Soc., 1972, Sigma Xi, Phi Lambda Upsilon, Alpha Chi Sigma, Phi Kappa Phi. Editor Jour. Electrochem. Soc., 1969-89; mem. editorial bd., mem. adv. edn. bd. Corrosion Sci., 1965-70; mem. editorial bd. Catalysis Reviews, 1968-73. Home: 2001 Pecos St Austin TX 78703-2119 Office: The Robert A Welch Found 5555 San Felipe St Ste 1900 Houston TX 77056-2727

HACKETT, BARBARA (KLOKA), federal judge; b. 1928. B of Philosophy, U. Detroit, 1948, JD, 1950. Bar: Mich. 1951, U.S. Dist. Ct. (ea. dist.) Mich. 1951, U.S. Ct. Appeals (6th cir.) 1951, U.S. Supreme Ct. 1957. Law clk. U.S. Dist. Ct. (ea. dist.) Mich., 1951-52; chief law clk. Mich. Ct. Appeals, 1965-66; asst. pros. atty. Wayne County, Mich., 1967-72; pvt. practice Detroit, 1952-53, 72-73; assoc. Frasco, Hackett & Mills, 1984-86; U.S. magistrate U.S. Dist. Ct. (ea. dist.) Mich., Detroit, 1973-84, judge, 1986—; mem. Interstate Commerce Commn., 1964. Trustee U. Detroit, 1983-89, Mercy High Sch., Farmington Hills, Mich. 1984-86, Detroit Symphony Orch., Orch. Hall Assocs., Detroit Sci. Ctr., United Community Svcs. Recipient Pres.'s Cabinet award U. Detroit Mercy, 1991. Mem. ABA (spl. ct. judge discovery abuse com. 1978-79, com. on cts. in cmty. 1979-84), Am. Judicature Soc., Fed. Bar Assn. (sec. 1981-82), Fed. Judges Assn., Nat. Assn. Women Judges, Nat. Dist. Attys. Assn., Nat. Assn. R.R. Trial Counsel, State Bar Mich., Women Lawyers Assn. Mich. Pros. Attys. Assn. Mich. (Disting. Svc. award 1971), Oakland County Bar Assn., U. Detroit Law Alumni Assn. (officer 1970-75, pres. 1975-77, Alumni Tower award 1976), Women's Econ. Club (bd. dirs. 1975-80, pres. 1980-81, named Detroit's Dynamic Women 1992), Econ. Club Detroit (bd. dirs. 1979-85, 88—), Phi Gamma Nu. Office: US Dist Ct Federal Bldg 200 E Liberty St Ste 400 Ann Arbor MI 48107-7760

HACKETT, BUDDY, actor; b. Bklyn., Aug. 31, 1924; s. Philip and Anna (Geller) Hacker; m. Sherry Cohen, June 12, 1955; children—Sandy Zade, Ivy Julie, Lisa Jean. Ed. pub. schs., Bklyn. Theatrical appearances include: Call Me Mister, 1946, Lunatics and Lover, 1954, I Had A Ball, 1964; motion picture appearances include: Walking My Baby Back Home, 1953, Gods Little Acre, 1958, Music Man, 1962, The Wonderful World of The Brothers Grimm, 1961, All Hands on Deck, 1961, Everything's Ducky, 1961, It's a Mad, Mad, Mad, Mad World, 1962, Golden Head, 1963, Muscle Beach Party, 1964, The Love Bug, 1969, Friend to Friend, Scrooged, 1988, (voice) The Little Mermaid, 1989, Paulie, 1998; star TV series Stanley, 1956-57, Fish Police, 1992; TV, cafe and nightclub appearances throughout U.S.; recipient Donaldson award 1955, Venice Film Festival award 1961. Office: care Paul Sherman 410 Park Avenue 10th Floor New York NY 10022*

HACKETT, CAROL ANN HEDDEN, physician; b. Valdese, N.C., Dec. 18, 1939; d. Thomas Barnett and Zada Loray (Pope) Hedden; BA, Duke, 1961; MD, U. N.C., 1966; m. John Peter Hackett, July 27, 1968; children: John Hedden, Elizabeth Bentley, Susanne Rochet. Intern. Georgetown U. Hosp., Washington, 1966-67, resident, 1967-69; clinic physician DePaul Hosp., Norfolk, Va., 1969-71; chief spl. health services Arlington County Dept. Human Resources, Arlington, Va., 1971-72; gen. med. officer USPHS Hosp., Balt., 1974-75; pvt. practice family medicine, Seattle, 1975—; mem. staff, chmn. dept. family practice Overlake Hosp. Med. Ctr., 1985-86; clin. asst. prof. Sch. Medicine U. Wash. Bd. dirs. Mercer Island (Wash.) Preschool Assn., 1977-78; coordinator 13th and 20th Ann. Inter-profl. Women's Dinner, 1978, 86; trustee Northwest Chamber Orch., 1984-85. Mem. AAUW, Am. Acad. Family Practice, King County Acad. Family Practice (trustee 1993-96, pres.-elect, 1997-98, pres. 1998-99), King County Med. Soc. (chmn. com. TV violence), Wash. Acad. Family Practice, Wash. State Med. Soc., DAR, Bellevue C. of C., NW Women Physicians (v.p. 1978), Seattle Symphony League, Eastside Women Physicians (founder, pres.), Sigma Kappa. Wash. Athletic Club, Columbia Tower, Seattle Yacht Club. Episcopalian. Home: 4304 E Mercer Way Mercer Island WA 98040-3826 Office: 1414 116th Ave NE Bellevue WA 98004-3801

HACKETT, EARL RANDOLPH, neurologist; b. Moulmein, Burma, Feb. 16, 1932; s. Paul Richmond and Martha Jane (Lewis) H.; m. Shirley Jane Kanehl, May 25, 1953; children: Nancy, Raymond, Susan, Lynn, Laurie, Richard, Alicia. B.S., Drury Coll., Springfield, Mo., 1953; M.D., Western Res. U., 1957. Diplomate Am. Bd. Psychiatry and Neurology, Am. Bd. Electrodiagnostic Medicine. Intern, then resident in neurology Charity Hosp., New Orleans, 1957-62; resident in internal medicine VA Hosp., New Orleans, 1958-59; mem. faculty La. State U. Med. Sch., New Orleans, 1962—, prof. neurology, 1973-88, head dept., 1977-88; clin. prof. neurology U. Mo., Columbia, 1988—; mem. med. adv. bd. Myasthenia Gravis Found. Fellow Am. Acad. Neurology; mem. Am. Assn. Electrodiagnostic Medicine, Soc. Clin. Neurologists, Mo. Med. Assn., Greene County Med. Soc., AOA. Methodist. Home: 2517 S Brentwood Blvd Springfield MO 65804-3201 Office: 1965 S Fremont Ave Ste 2800 Springfield MO 65804-2258

HACKETT, EDWARD JOHN, sociology educator and researcher; b. New Britain, Conn., Oct. 15, 1951; s. Edward Maurice and Irene M. Hackett; m. Sharon Lee Harlan, Oct. 7, 1978; children: Jocelyn Judith, Valerie Christine. BA, Colgate U., 1973; PhD, Cornell U., 1979. Rsch. assoc. Boston U., 1979-80, 82-85; rsch. scientist Am. Insts. for Rsch., Cambridge, Mass., 1980-82; rsch. assoc. Wellesley (Mass.) Coll., 1982-83; prof. dept. sci. and tech. studies Rensselaer Poly. Inst., Troy, N.Y., 1984-97; program officer Nat. Sci. Found., 1996-98; prof. Arizona State U., 1997—. Co-author: Peerless Science, 1990; contbr. articles to Group & Orgn. Studies, Jour. Higher Edn., Jour. Applied Psychology, Monthly Labor Rev. NIMH Postdoctoral fellow; NSF rsch. grantee; recipient Acad. Mgmt. Scholarly Contbn. award, 1987. Achievements include research on social organization of science and technology, science policy, technology and work life. Office: Dept Sociology Ariz State U Box 872101 Tempe AZ 85287-2101

HACKETT, EDWARD VINCENT, investment research company executive; b. N.Y.C., Jan. 17, 1946; s. Edward Vincent and Gladys Theresa (O'Connell) H. BA, Fordham U., 1967; MBA, Columbia U., 1969. CPA, N.Y.; registered gen. securities rep. Cons. Irving Trust Co., N.Y.C., 1968; mgr. cons. svcs. Arthur Young & Co., N.Y.C., 1969-78; dir. mgmt. svcs. Insilco Corp. Group, Meriden, Conn., 1978-84; v.p. ops., COO, CFO Coatings div. Insilco Corp., Tampa, Fla., 1984-86; pres. mid-Atlantic div. Insilco Corp., Tampa, 1986-90; exec. v.p., COO Coronado Paint Co., Edgewater, Fla., 1990-92, bd. dirs.; fin. advisor Dean Witter Reynolds, Tampa, 1992-96; sr. investment officer Baybridge Fin. Group, Tampa, 1996-98; mng. dir. fin. Ned Davis Rsch. Group, Sarasota, 1998—. Editor Productivity News, 1984. Capt. U.S. Army, 1969-71. Mem. AICPA, Fla. Inst. CPAs (personal fin. planning com., acctg. show com. chair), Columbia Alumni Assn. (v.p.), Ivy League Club (treas.), Tampa Rotary Club (benefactor). Avocations: tennis, skiing, jogging. Home: Ste 914 988 Blvd of the Arts Sarasota FL 34236 Office: Ned Davis Rsch Group 600 Bird Bay Dr Venice FL 34292

HACKETT, JAMES P., manufacturing executive; b. 1955. BA, U. Mich., 1977. With Proctor and Gamble Co., 1977-81; joined Steelcase Inc., Grand Rapids, Mich., 1981—; sr. v.p. sales and mktg. Steelcase Inc., Grand Rapids, 1990, pres. Turnstone, 1993; exec. v.p. Steelcase Ventures, 1994; exec. v.p., CEO Steelcase N.Am., 1994, pres., CEO, 1995—. Office: Steelcase Inc 901 44th St SE Grand Rapids MI 49508-7594 Office: Steelcase Inc PO Box 1967 Grand Rapids MI 49501-1967*

HACKETT, JOHN BYRON, advertising agency executive, lawyer; b. N.Y.C., Dec. 28, 1933; s. John Joseph and Cecelia Elizabeth (Meehan) H.; m. Patricia P. Briordy, May 23, 1964 (div. 1980); children: Kimberly, John; m. Kathryn Meyer, Mar. 28, 1982. BBA, Iona Coll., 1956; JD, St. Johns U., 1960. Bar: N.Y. 1961. Sales adminstr. NBC, N.Y.C., 1962-65; with J. Walter Thompson Co., N.Y.C., 1965-85; v.p. legal dept. J. Walter Thompson Co., 1971-76, sr. v.p. adminstrn., 1976-80, sr. v.p., gen. mgr. entertainment div., 1980-83, sr. v.p., dir. spot broadcasting U.S.A., 1983-85; pvt. legal practice, 1985—; faculty mem. Practising Law Inst. Mem. ABA, U.S. Trademark Assn. (dir.). Home and Office: 1 Toms Point Ln Apt 10B Port Washington NY 11050-2120

HACKETT, JOHN PETER, dermatologist; b. N.Y.C., Feb. 10, 1942; s. John Thomas and Helen (Donohue) H.; m. Carol A. Hedden, July 27, 1968; children: John, Elizabeth, Susanne. AB, Holy Cross Coll., 1963; MD, Georgetown U., 1967. Diplomate Am. Bd. Internal Medicine, Am. Bd. Dermatology. Intern Georgetown U. Hosp., 1967-68, resident, 1968-69; fellow Johns Hopkins Hosp., 1972-75, chief resident, 1975; practice medicine specializing in dermatology Seattle, 1975—; chmn. bd. dirs. NW Dental Ins. Co., 1989-92; clin. asst. prof. dermatology U. Wash., 1976-88, clin. assoc. prof., 1988—; active staff Swedish Hosp., Providence Hosp.; cons. Wash. State Dept. Labor and Industries, 1992—; pres. Psoriasis Treatment Ctr., Inc., 1978-80; cons. physician Children's Orthopedic Hosp. Contbr. articles to profl. jours. Bd. dirs. Mercer Island Boys and Girls Club, 1976-81, Seattle Ctr. for Blind, 1979-80, N.W. Chamber Orch., 1983-86. Served to lt. condr. USNR, 1969-71. Mem. Am. Acad. Dermatology, Seattle Dermatol. Soc. (pres. 1981-82), Soc. Investigative Dermatology, Am. Contact Dermatitis Soc., Wash. State Med. Soc., King County Med. Soc. (chmn. media rels. com. 1977-80, grievance com. 1991—), Wash. Physicians Ins. Exch. (chmn. actuarial subcom. 1983-85, chmn. subscribers adv. com. 1986-90, audit com. 1988-92, fin. com. 1990-92), Wash. Athletic Club, Seattle Yacht Club, Columbia Tower Club, Marine Corps Meml. Club, Rotary. Office: 1500 Cabrini Tower 901 Boren Ave Seattle WA 98104-3508

HACKETT, JOHN THOMAS, economist; b. Fort Wayne, Ind., Oct. 10, 1932; s. Harry H. and Ruth (Greer) H.; m. Ann E. Thompson, July 24, 1954; children: Jane, David, Sarah, Peter. BS, Ind. U., 1954, MBA, 1958; PhD, Ohio State U., 1961. Instr. Ohio State U., 1958-61; asst. v.p., economist Fed. Res. Bank, Cleve., 1961-64; dir. planning Cummins Engine Co., Columbus, Ind., 1964-66; v.p. finance Cummins Engine Co., 1966-71, exec. v.p., 1971-88, also dir.; v.p. fin. and adminstrn. Ind. U., Bloomington, 1988-91; mng. gen. ptnr. CID Equity Ptnrs., L.P., Indpls., 1991—; bd. dirs. Irwin Fin. Corp., Meridian Mut. Ins. Co., Wabash Nat. Corp., Ball Corp., Ind. Corp. for Bus. Modernization and Tech.; chmn. Ind. Secondary Mkt. for Edn. Loans; mem. com. indsl. tech. devel. Argonne Nat. Lab. 1st lt. AUS, 1954-56. Mem.Beta Gamma Sigma. Home: PO Box 2337 Columbus IN 47202-2337

HACKETT, KEVIN JAMES, insect pathologist; b. Phila., Apr. 24, 1947; s. James Patrick and Betty Corrine (Hulsey) H.; m. Kathleen Ruth Schmitt, Mar. 22, 1969; children: Ryan Hale, Aislinn Elizabeth. BS, Rutgers U., 1969, MS, 1971; PhD, U. Calif., Berkeley, 1980. Ea. coord. John Muir Inst. Environ. Studies, Washington, 1979-83; rsch. entomologist insect biocontrol lab. USDA Agrl. Rsch. Svc., Beltsville, Md., 1983—; nat. program leader for biocontrol USDA Agrl. Rsch. Svc., Beltsville, 1983—. Author: The Mycoplasmas, 1990; contbr. articles to jour. Sci. Founder, coord. Dept. of Peace and Conflict Studies (formerly Ind. Peace Studies), U. Calif., Berkeley, 1972-74. Mem. AAAS, Internat. Orgn. Mycoplasmology (team leader spiroplasma working team 1990—, Derrick Edward award 1988), Soc. Invertebrate Pathology, Am. Soc. Microbiology, Entomology Soc. Am. Unitarian. Achievements include development of insect cell spiroplasma coculture, hypothesis for spiroplasma evolution. Office: Insect Biocontrol Lab Rm 214 Bldg 011A BARC-W Beltsville MD 20705

HACKETT, KEVIN R., lawyer; b. Atlantic City, N.J., Apr. 16, 1949. BA summa cum laude, Boston Coll., 1971; JD, Harvard U., 1974. Bar: N.Y. 1975. Ptnr. Shearman & Sterling, N.Y.C. Fellow Am. Coll. Real Estate Lawyers; mem. ABA, N.Y. State Bar Assn., Assn. Bar City of N.Y., Phi Beta Kappa. Office: 599 Lexington Ave Fl 1448 New York NY 10022-6030

HACKETT, LOUISE, personnel services company executive, consultant; b. Sheridan, Mont., Nov. 11, 1933; d. Paul Duncan and Freda A. Johnson; m. Lewis Edward Hackett, June 24, 1962; 1 child, Dell Paul. Student, U. Oreg., 1959-61; BA, Calif. State U., Sacramento, 1971. Legal sec. Samuel R. Friedman, Yreka, Calif., 1952-58, Barbara & Cottrell, Eugene, Oreg., 1958-59; paralegal Elmer Sahlstrom, Eugene, 1959-62; legis. aide Calif. Legislature, Sacramento, 1962-72; owner Legal Personnel Svcs., Sacramento, 1973-78, corp. pres., 1979—; pres. Legalstaff, Inc., 1987-99; curriculum adv. dept. bus. Am. River Coll., Sacramento, 1974-79; founder, adminstr. Pacific Coll. Legal Careers, Sacramento, 1973-85; cons. legal edn. Barclay Schs., Sacramento, 1984; active Sacramento Employees Adv. Coun.; mem. Sierra Dopstion Assn., Women Escaping a Violent Envrion. Designer, pub. Sacramento/Yolo Attys. Directory, 1974—. Author ops. manual and franchise tng. textbook; contbr. articles to profl. jours. Mem. adv. bd. San Juan Sch. Dist., 1975-84; mem. Los Amigos. Mem. Calif. Assn. Personnel Cons., Sacramento Coun. Pvt. Edn. (pres. 1976-77), Order of Rainbow, Pi Omega Pi. Avocations: skiing, sailing, gardening, horseback riding. Office: Legal Personnel Svcs 1415 21st St Sacramento CA 95814-5208 also: 2103 Landings Dr Mountain View CA 94043-0839 also: 111 W Saint John St # 724 San Jose CA 95113-1101

HACKETT, ROBERT JOHN, lawyer; b. N.Y.C., Feb. 6, 1943; s. John P. and Marie S. (Starace) H.; m. Anita Carlile, Apr. 19, 1969; children: Robert J., John Peter, Kathryn Marie. AB, Rutgers U., 1964; JD, Duke U., 1967. Bar: N.Y. 1967, Ariz. 1972. Assoc. Milbank, Tweed, Hadley, McCloy, N.Y.C., 1967-71; ptnr. Evans, Kitchel & Jenckes, Phoenix, 1971-89; dir. Fennemore Craig, Phoenix, 1989—, course dir. seminar and mergers and acquisitions, 1996, 99. Mem. editl. bd. Duke Law Jour. Bd. dirs. Xavier Coll. Prep. Mem. ABA (com. on fed. securities regulation), State Bar Ariz. (past chmn. securities regulation sect.), Maricopa County Bar Assn., Assn. Corp. Growth (past bd. dirs., past pres. Ariz. chpt.), Phoenix Duke U. Law Alumni Club (past pres.), Pi Sigma Alpha. Republican. Roman Catholic.

HACKETT, ROGER FLEMING, history educator; b. Kobe, Japan, Oct. 23, 1922; s. Harold Wallace and Anna Luena (Powell) H.; m. Caroline Betty Gray, Aug. 24, 1946; children: Anne Marilyn, David Gray, Brian Vance. B.A., Carleton Coll., 1947; M.A., Harvard U., 1949, Ph.D., 1955. Prof. history Northwestern U., Evanston, Ill., 1953-61; prof. history U. Mich., Ann Arbor, 1961-93; prof. emeritus U. Mich., 1993—, chmn. dept., 1975-77; dir. Center for Japanese Studies, 1968-71, 78, 79; cons. Office of Edn., HEW; mem. sub-com., joint com. Social Sci. Research Council. Author: Yamagata Aritomo in the Rise of Modern Japan 1838-1922, 1971; Editor: Jour. Asian Studies, 1959-62; contbr. articles and chpts to profl. jours. and books. Served with USMC, 1942-46. Social Sci. Research Council fellow; Japan Found. fellow; Fulbright-Hays fellow; fellow St. Antony's Coll. Oxford U. Mem. Japan Soc., Assn. for Asian Studies (exec. com., bd. dirs. 1966-69), Internat. House of Japan, Phi Beta Kappa. Club: Racquet (Ann Arbor). Home: 2122 Dorset Rd Ann Arbor MI 48104-2604 Office: U Mich Dept History Ann Arbor MI 48109

HACKETT, WESLEY PHELPS, JR., lawyer; b. Detroit, Jan. 3, 1939; s. Wesley P. and Helen (Decker) H.; children: Kelly D. Hackett Pell, Robin C. BA, Mich. State U., 1960; JD, Wayne State U., 1968. Bar: Mich. 1968, U.S. Dist. Ct. (we. dist.) Mich. 1971, U.S. Ct. Appeals (6th cir.) 1972, U.S. Dist. Ct. (ea. dist.) Mich. 1972, U.S. Supreme Ct. 1972, U.S. Ct. Mil. Appeals 1991. Law clk. Mich. Supreme Ct., Lansing, 1968-70; ptnr. Brown & Hackett, Lansing, 1971-73; pvt. practice Lansing, 1973-84; ptnr. Starr, Bissell & Hackett, Lansing, 1984-87; pvt. practice East Lansing, Mich., 1987-98, Saranac, Mich., 1998—; adj. prof. Thomas M. Cooley Law Sch., Lansing, 1973—; instr. Lansing C.C., 1981-99. Author: Evidence: A Trial Manual for Michigan Lawyers, 1981, Hackett's Evidence: Michigan and Federal, 2d edit., 1995; co-author: Hiring Legal Staff, 1990. Mem. City of East Lansing Planning Commn., 1969-72; bd. dirs. St. Vincent Home for Children, Lansing, 1974-82. 1st lt. USAF, 1961-65. Fellow Coll. Law Practice Mgmt.; mem. ABA (sec. gen. practice sect. 1990-91, vice-chair 1991-92, chair 1993-94, standing com. on lawyer referral and info. svcs. 1997—, sole practitioner of yr. 1994, founders award 1997), State Bar Mich. (chair legal econs. sect. 1990-91).

HACKFORD, TAYLOR, film director, producer; b. Santa Barbara, Calif., Dec. 31, 1944; s. Joseph and Mary (Taylor) H. B.A. in Internat. Relations, U. So. Calif. Vol. Peace Corps, Bolivia, 1968-69; dir., producer, reporter, writerr Sta.-KCET, Community TV of So. Calif., Los Angeles, 1970-77; dir., producer, writer Hackford Littman Films, Los Angeles, 1977-79; dir. United Artists Films, Los Angeles, 1979-80, Paramount Pictures, Los Angeles, 1981-82; producer, dir. Columbia Pictures, Los Angeles, 1983—. Producer, dir., writer short dramatic film Teenage Father, 1978 (Oscar 1979); dir. feature film The Idolmaker, 1980, An Officer and A Gentleman, 1982, Hail! Hail! Rock and Roll, 1987 (documentary); prodr., dir.: Against All Odds, 1984, White Nights, 1985, Everyone's All American, 1988, Bound by Honor (Blood In, Blood Out), 1993, Dolores Claiborne, 1994, When We Were Kings, 1996, The Devil's Advocate, 1998; prodr.: La Bamba, 1987; exec. prodr.: Rooftops, 1989, The Long Walk Home, 1990, Sweet Talker, 1991, Queens Logic, 1991, Defenseless, 1991, Mortal Thoughts, 1991. Recipient Silver Reel award San Francisco Film Festival, 1972; recipient Emmy award Acad. TV Arts and Scis., 1974, Emmy award Acad. TV Arts and Scis., 1977, Acad. award Acad. Motion Picture Arts and Scis., 1979. Mem. Dir.'s Guild Am., Writers Guild Am. Office: CAA 9830 Wilshire Blvd Beverly Hills CA 90212-1825*

HACKL, ALPHONS J., publisher; b. Warman, Can.; s. John J. and Anna (Moser) H.; m. Muriel J. Forster, Feb. 2, 1946; 1 son, John Raymond. Grad., Handelsschule, Salzburg, Austria, 1934; student, Nat. U., 1937-38, Corcoran Sch. Art, 1938-40, U. Chgo., 1941; BA, Sussex Coll. Tech., 1945; postgrad., Internat. Summer Sch., St. Peter Coll., Oxford U., 1976; JD, LaSalle U., 1991. Apprentice Funder & Mueller, printers, Salzburg, 1934-36; advt. copywriter, art dir., account exec. advt. agy. and dept. store Washington, 1936-40; founder, chmn. emeritus Colortone Press, Washington, 1946—; founder Acropolis Books, Ltd., Washington, 1959—; lectr., instr. George Washington U., 1974-78; past mem. adv. coun. SBA; mem. adv. bd. publ. specialist program George Washington U.; adv. bd. Washington Tech. Inst.; adj. prof. LaSalle U., 1992; counselor Svc. Corps Ret. Execs. (S.C.O.R.E.), chmn. chpt. Manasota #116. Contbr. articles to profl. publs. Chmn. Met. Sch. Printing, 1972-74. Capt. AUS, 1941-45. Decorated Bronze Star.; recipient George Washington Honor medal Freedoms Found., Award of Excellence Image Industry Coun. Internat. Fellow Corcoran Art Gallery; mem. Pub. Rels. Soc. Am., Assn. Am. Pubs., Nat. Press Club, Svc. Corp Ret. Execs. (chmn. chpt. # 116), Sarasota Yacht Club, Lotos Club (N.Y.C.), U.S. Power Squadron Club. Episcopalian. Patentee programmed instruction device. Home: 415 Wood Duck Dr Sarasota FL 34236-1823 *Always do more than is expected of you, and keep your promises.*

HACKL, DONALD JOHN, architect; b. Chgo., May 11, 1934; s. John Frank and Frieda Marie (Weichmann) H.; m. Bernadine Marie Becker, Sept. 29, 1962; children: Jeffrey Scott, Craig Michael, Cristina Lynn. BArch., U. Ill., 1957, MS in Architecture, 1958. With Loebl Schlossman & Hackl Architects, Chgo., 1963—, assoc., 1967-74, exec. v.p., dir., 1974, pres., dir., 1975—; prof. architecture Internat. Acad. Architecture, Sofia, Bulgaria; mem. Nat. Coun. Archtl. Registration Bds., 1986—; bd. dirs. Chgo. Bldg. Congress, 1983-94, v.p., 1985-94; design juries include: Reynolds Metals, Western Mont. Regional Design, Am. Inst. Steel Constrn., Precast Concrete Inst., Okla. Soc. Architects, UIA/UNESCO; chmn. Ariz. Soc. Architects, Midwest Design Conf., 1983; design critic dept. arch. U. Ill., 1975-76, 81; vis. critic sch. architecture U. Notre Dame, 1977, 78, 80, 82; adj. prof. Kent Coll. Law, Ill. Inst. Tech., 1983—; cons. Pub. Svcs. Adminstrn., Washington, 1974-76. Prin. works include Water Tower Place, Chgo., 1976, King Faisel Specialist Hosp. and Rsch. Ctr., Riyadh, Saudi Arabia, 1978, Household Internat. Hdqrs., Prospect Heights, Ill., 1978, Shriners Hosp. for Children, Chgo., 1979, Square D Co. Hdqrs., Palatine, Ill., 1979, West Suburban Hosp., Oak Park, Ill., 1981, Allstate Pla. West, Northbrook, Ill., 1990, Sears Roebuck & Co. stores of future concept, 1985-89, Ford City Shopping Ctr. Redevel., Chgo., 1989, Commerce Clearing House, Riverwoods, Ill., 1986, Physicians' Pavilion Greater Balt. Med. Ctr., 1987, Two Prudential Plaza, Chgo., 1990, City Place with Omni Hotel, Chgo., 1990, 350 N. LaSalle, Chgo., 1990, Infinitec, Assistive Tech. Application Ctr. for United Cerebral Palsy Assn., Chgo., 1992, Shenzhen AVIC Plaza Bldg., Shenzhen, China, 1993, Ill. State U. Biol. and Chemistry Scis. Lab. Bldg., Normal, 1995, Old Orchard Shopping Ctr. Redevel., Skokie, Ill., 1994, Sun Comml. City, Changchun, China, 1993, Shekou Harbor Bldg., Shenzhen, 1995, East Shanghai Film and TV Ctr., 1995, Luo-Hu Comml. Ctr., Shenzhen, 1994, Shenzhen Internat. Exch. Pllz., Shanghai, 1996, Shenzhen Cultural Ctr., 1997, Changchun Sun Housing Estates, China, Hdqrs. for Almacenes Paris LTDA, Santiago, Chile, 1998, Cook County Hosp. Replacement Facility, 1995—, Grand Pier Ctr., Chgo., 1998, Computer/Engrng. Bldg. U. Ill., 1999—. Mem. Met. Am. Cancer Crusade, 1973; life trustee West Suburban Hosp., 1983—, mem. exec. com., 1986-87; vice chmn. North Ctrl. Coll., 1990—; mem. Pres.'s Coun. U. Ill. Found.; mem. curricula adv. com. Dept. Architecture, U. Ill.; bd. dirs. World Trade Ctr., Chgo., 1995—. Fellow AIA (treas. Chgo. chpt. 1977-78, exec. com. 1978-81, v.p. 1981, pres. 1981, bd. dirs. Chgo. AIA Found. 1981-83, nat. v.p. 1985, 1st v.p. 1986, nat. pres. 1987, chmn. design com. 1985, exec. com. 1985-87, bd. dirs. 1981-84, documents com. 1974-79, chmn. 1980, exec. com. AIA Svc. Corp. 1983-84, chmn. internat. com. 1987—), Royal Archtl. Inst. Can. (hon.), Colegios Architectos Mexicanos (hon.), Internat. Acad. Architecture (hon.); mem. Union Internat. Archs. (bd. dirs., del. 1987—, v.p. 1990-93, 96—), Union Bulgarian Archs. (hon.), Soc. Cuban Archs., Japan Inst. Archs. (hon.), Colegio Arquitectos Cochabamba (Bolivia), Colegios Arquitectos Espana, Art Inst. Chgo., Tavern Clubs, Carlton Club, Econ. Club, Lake Zurich Club. Office: Loebl

Schlossman and Hackl Inc 130 E Randolph St Ste 3400 Chicago IL 60601-6378

HACKLIN, ALLAN, artist, art educator; b. N.Y.C., Feb. 11, 1943; m. Pamela Hacklin; children: Wendy Lehman, Ethan. BFA, Pratt Inst., 1965. Instr. Pratt Inst., N.Y.C., 1969-70; instr. Calif. Inst. Art, 1970-77, assoc. dean, 1976-77; prof. The Rhode Island Sch. Design, 1979-80, apptd. head painting dept., 1980-82; dir. The Glassell Sch. of Art Mus. of Fine Arts, Houston, 1982-89; Meadows prof. of art Southern Methodist Univ., 1987; chmn. divsn. visual arts Columbia U., 1989-97, LeRoy Neiman prof. art, 1995—; apptd. dir. LeRoy Neiman Ctr. for Print Studies, 1996—; instr. Nova Scotia Coll. of Art and Design, summers, 1973, 74, 78, 79; vis. prof. Cooper Union, N.Y.c., 1977-80. Represented in permanent collections: The Mus. of Fine Arts, Houston, The Dallas Mus. of Fine Art, The Whitney Mus., N.Y.C., Allen Mus., Oberlin Coll., Ohio, Aldrich Mus. of Am. Art, N.C. Mus. of Fine Art, Va. Mus. Fine Arts, Currier Mus., N.H., Bass Mus., Fla.; one-man shows include Alan Stone Gallery, N.Y.C., 1967, Galerie Muller, Germany, 1969, 70, Galerie Neuendorf, Germany, 1969, Betty Parsons Gallery, N.Y.C., 1969, 71, 75, Galerie Zwirner, Germany, 1970, Galerie Furneisen, Germany, 1970, Joseph LoGuidice Gallery, N.Y., 1972, 73, Truman Gallery, N.Y., 1978, David Settles Gallery, Houston, 1983, Meredith Long & Co., Houston, 1984, 86, 88, Meadows Mus., Dallas, 1987, MB Modern N.Y., 1997; numerous group exhbns. Fellow Nat. Endowment for the Arts, Drawing, 1976, Sculpture, 1980, 1984; Grantee Yaddo Foundation, 1969. Office: Columbia Univ Sch of the Arts 310 Dodge Hall New York NY 10027

HACKMAN, GENE (EUGENE ALDEN), actor; b. San Bernardino, Calif., Jan. 30, 1930; s. Eugene Ezra H.; m. Faye Maltese, 1956 (div. 1985); children: Christopher, Elizabeth, Leslie. Appeared in stage prodns. The Natural Look, Death and the Maiden, others; film roles include Lilith, 1964, Hawaii, 1966, Bonnie and Clyde, 1967, First to Fight,1967, The Split, 1968, Riot, 1969, The Gypsy Moths, 1969, Downhill Racer, 1969,I Never Sang for My Father, 1969, Marooned, 1970, Doctor's Wives, 1971, The French Connection 1971 (Acad. Best Actor award, Golden Globe award, Brit. Acad. award, N.Y. Film Critics award), Cisco Pike, 1971, Scarecrow, 1973 (Cannes Film Festival award), The Poseidon Adventure, 1972 (Brit. Acad. award), The Conversation, 1974, Zandy's Bride, 1974, The French Connection II, 1975, Bite the Bullet, 1975, Night Moves, 1975, Lucky Lady, 1975, A Bridge Too Far, 1977, The Domino Principle, 1977, March or Die, 1977, Superman, 1978, All Night Long, 1980, Superman II, 1981, Eureka, 1983, Under Fire, 1983, Uncommon Valor, 1983, Target, 1985, Twice in a Lifetime, 1985, Power, 1986, Superman IV, 1987, No Way Out, 1987, Another Woman, 1988, Bat 21, 1988, Mississippi Burning, 1988 (Best Actor award Nat. Soc. Film Critics, Acad. Award nomination), Full Moon in Blue Water, 1988, The Package, 1989, Postcards From The Edge, 1989, Class Action, 1989, Loose Cannons, 1990, Narrow Margin, 1990, Company Business, 1991, Unforgiven, 1992 (Acad. Award Best Supporting Actor, Golden Globes, N.Y., L.A., Boston Film Critics, Nat. Soc.Film Critics awards), The Firm, 1993, Geronimo, 1993, Wyatt Earp, 1994, The Quick and the Dead, 1995, Crimson Tide, 1995, Get Shorty, 1995, Extreme Measures, 1996, The Chamber, 1996, The Birdcage, 1996, The Magic Hour, 1997, Absolute Power, 1997, Enemy of the State, 1998, Antz (voice), 1998, Twilight, 1998, Under Suspicion, 1999; various TV and stage roles. Hon. chmn. Permanent Charities Com. of the Entertainment Industries. Named Star of Year, Nat. Assn. Theatre Owners, 1974. Address: care Barry Haldeman Ste 2000 1900 Avenue Of The Stars Los Angeles CA 90067-4501 also: care Fred Spector 9830 Wilshire Blvd Beverly Hills CA 90212-1804*

HACKMAN, GWENDOLYN ANN, private duty nurse; b. Phila., Mar. 22, 1932; d. Stanley Heaney and Joy Hayes (Sands) H. Diploma, Phila. Gen. Hosp. Sch. Nursing, 1953; postgrad., La. State U., Tulane U. RNC, La.; cert. gerontol. nurse. Staff nurse pediatrics Phila. Gen. Hosp., 1953; staff nurse premature ctr. Charity Hosp., New Orleans, 1953-55, head nurse premature ctr., 1955; asst. instr. fundamentals of nursing, 1956-57; asst. instr. med. surg. nursing Touro Infirmary Sch. Nursing, 1957-60; rsch. assoc. maternal and child health sect. Tulane U., New Orleans, 1965-67; pvt. duty nurse New Orleans, 1955, 60-65, 67—. Mem. ANA, Nat. League for Nursing, New Orleans Dist. Nurses Assn., Nat. Gerontol. Assn., La. State Nurses Assn. (profl. practice com. 1962-63, 2d vice chmn. pvt. duty sect. 1962-66, chmn. 1968-69, bd. dirs. 1966), New Orleans Dist. Nurses Assn. (chmn. pub. rels. com. 1962, chmn. pvt. duty sect. 1962-67, bd. dirs. 1962-67, One of Great 100 Nurses 1998), Phila. Gen. Hosp. Sch. Nursing Alumnae (life mem. 1999), DAR. Home: 1460 Henry Clay Ave New Orleans LA 70118-6062

HACKMAN, LARRY J., program director; m. Sandra McFarland, 1966; children: Alex, Kate. LHD (hon.), U. Mo., 1999. Former archivist State of N.Y., John F. Kennedy Libr., others; asst. commr. of edn. for archives and records adminstrn. N.Y. State; dir. Harry S. Truman Presdl. Libr., Independence, Mo., 1995—; lectr. in field; Mellon fellow in Modern Archives, U. Mich., Littauer fellow Sch. of Govt. at Harvard; past mem. governing bd. Rockefeller Archives Ctr.; pres. Truman Libr. Inst., 1998—. Recipient Disting. Pub. Svc. award Rockefeller Coll. of Pub. Affairs, SUNY, Albany. Office: Harry S Truman Libr 500 W Us Highway 24 Independence MO 64050-2481

HACKNEY, FRANCIS SHELDON, university president; b. Birmingham, Ala., Dec. 5, 1933; s. Cecil Fain and Elizabeth (Morris) H.; m. Lucy Judkins Durr, June 15, 1957; children: Virginia Foster, Sheldon Fain, Elizabeth Morris. BA, Vanderbilt U., 1955; MA, Yale U., 1963, PhD, 1966. Mem. faculty Princeton U., 1965-75, assoc. prof. history, 1969-72, prof. and provost, 1972-75; pres. Tulane U., New Orleans, 1975-80; pres. U. Pa., Phila., 1981—, prof. history, 1981-96; chmn. Nat. Endowment for the Humanities, Washington, 1993-97. Author: Populism to Progressivism in Alabama, 1969; editor: Populism: The Critical Issues, 1971; (with others) Understanding the American Experience, 1973. Bd. dirs. Carnegie Found. for Advancement Teaching, 1976-84, 86-93, Ednl. Testing Svc., 1977-83, Am. Coun. on Edn., 1977-78, 91-93. With USNR, 1956-61. Recipient Charles S. Sydnor award So. Hist. Assn., 1970; Bevridge prize Am. Hist. Assn., 1970. Mem. Am. Philos. Soc., Am. Hist. Assn., So. Hist. Assn., Orgn. Am. Historians. Office: U Pa Dept History 100 College Hall Philadelphia PA 19104-6380*

HACKNEY, HOWARD SMITH, retired county official; b. Clinton County, Ohio, May 20, 1910; s. Volcah Mann and Gusta Anna (Smith) H.; B.S. cum laude, Wilmington Coll., 1932; m. Lucille Morrow, June 28, 1934; children: Albert Morrow, Roderick Allen, Katherine Ann Luby. Farmer, Wilmington, Ohio; farm reporter Agrl. Adjustment Adminstrn., Wilmington, 1934-40, committeeman, 1940-52, office mgr., 1952—, county exec. dir. Agrl. Stblzn. and Conservation Service, 1961-88. Treas., dir. Clinton County Community Action Council; treas. Clinton County Council Chs.; dir. Ohio Pork Producers Coun.; trustee, mem. agrl. adv. com. Wilmington Coll.; trustee Clinton County Hist. Soc. Named to Ohio State Fair Hall of Fame, 1983, Swine Hall of Fame, 1986. Mem. Nat. Assn. Stblzn. and Conservation Service Office Employees (awards 1970, state, regional legis. cons., Agriculturist of Yr. 1987), AAAS, Soil Conservation Soc. Am., Farmers Union, Ohio Duroc Breeders Assn. (pres., dir.), Ohio Acad. Sci., Ohio Acad. History, Ohio Hist. Soc., Grange, Ohio Southdown Breeders Assn., Clinton County Farm Bur. (sec., dir.), Clinton County Agrl. Soc. (treas., dir., award 1975), Clinton County Lamb and Fleece Improvement Assn. (dir.), Clinton County Hist. Soc., Delta Theta Sigma (hon.), Masons. Republican. Quaker. Home: 2003 Inwood Rd Wilmington OH 45177-9424

HACKNEY, JACK DEAN, physician; b. Marion, Ill., Oct. 11, 1924; s. William F. and Betty (Monical) H.; m. Dorothy Anne Stublefield, Sept. 8, 1946; children: Richard W., Robert J. Student, So. Ill. Univ., 1941-43, Yale U., 1943; MD, St. Louis U. Sch. Medicine, 1948. Diplomate Am. Bd. Internal Medicine, Acad. Toxicol. Scis. Resident in internal medicine VA Hosp., St. Louis, 1949-51, White Meml. Hosp., L.A., 1953-54; rsch. assoc. Loma Linda U., L.A., 1954-57, asst. to assoc. prof., 1957-69; prof. medicine U. So. Calif., L.A., 1969-94, prof. emeritus, 1994—; dir. pulmonary lab. Rancho Los Amigos Med. Ctr., Downey, Calif., 1969-92, chief environ. health, 1970-94, emeritus, 1994—; mem. EPA Sci. Adv. Bd., Washington, 1984-86; cons., 1986-92. Editor/author: Inhalation Toxicology of Air Pollution, 1993; contbg. author: Bronchial Asthma: Mechanics and Therapeutics, 1985, 93; contbr. articles to profl. jours. Mem. air quality adv. com. Dept. Health Svcs., State of Calif., 1974-94, med. adv. panel South Coast Air Quality Mgmt. Dist., 1985-92. 1st lt. AMC, 1951-53, Korea. Recipient Calif. medal Am. Lung Assn. Calif., 1992. Fellow Am. Coll. Chest Physicians, Am. Coll. Toxicology; mem. Am. Physiol. Soc., Am. Thoracic Soc., Alpha Omega Alpha, Sigma Xi. Achievements include development of indirect method for measuring respiratory ventilation; extraction of gases from blood for Gas Chromatographic analysis; control of exposure facilities and methods to study human inhalation toxicology and use of these facilities to demonstrate ozone toxicity, adaptation to ozone, and determine exposure responses to many inhaled gas and particle pollutants. Home: 5181 Duenas Laguna Hills CA 92653-1878 Office: Environmental Health Svc RLAMC 7601 Imperial Hwy # 51 Downey CA 90242-3456

HACKNEY, JAMES ACRA, III, industrial engineer, consultant, retired manufacturing company executive; b. Washington, N.C., Sept. 27, 1939; s. James Acra Jr. and Margaret Dunston (Hodges) H.; m. Constance Garrenton, June 5, 1961; children: Kenneth Ross, Jane H. Kemsley. BSME, N.C. State U., 1961, BS in Indsl. Engring, 1962. Registered profl. engr., N.C. With Hackney Industries, Inc., Washington, N.C., 1961-95, chief engr., 1961-63, asst. gen. mgr., 1963-65, exec. v.p., gen. mgr., 1965-70, pres., chief exec. officer, 1970-90; chmn. bd. dirs. Hackney & Sons, Inc., Washington, N.C., 1990-95; mng. dir. The Hackney Group, Washington, N.C., 1995—; bd. dirs. Sprint Mid-Atlantic Telecom, Wake Forest, N.C., 1987-97, Bank of Am., North Coast region, N.C., chmn., 1995—. Chmn. Blackbeard dist. Boy Scouts Am., 1970-74, pres. East Carolina coun., 1976-77, mem. nat. exec. bd., 1987—, pres. S.E. region, 1987-89; chmn. bd. trustees Beaufort County Hosp., 1975-77; trustee N.C. State U., Raleigh, 1979-87, chmn. bd. trustees, 1985-87; mem. Interam. Scout Com., World Orgn. of Scout Movement, 1984-88, Zion Episcopal Ch., Washington. With U.S. Army, 1963-65. Recipient Disting. Service award Washington Jaycees, 1970; Silver Beaver award Boy Scouts Am., 1975, Silver Antelope award, 1982, Disting. Eagle Scout award, 1980, Silver Buffalo award, 1992; Youth of the Ams. award World Orgn. Scout Movement, 1990, John Southam Journalism award Sail Am., 1997; named N.C. Small Businessman of Yr., SBA, 1971, Young Engr. of Yr., NSPE, 1971. Mem. Inst. Indsl. Engrs. (chpt. pres. 1967-68), Profl. Engrs. N.C. (pres. Ea. Carolina chpt. 1971-72, Outstanding Young Engr. 1970-71), N.C. Engring. Found. (bd. dirs. 1977—, N.C. Citizens for Bus. and Industry (bd. dirs. 1979-86), Washington C. of C. (pres. 1972-74), N.C. State U. Alumni Assn. (bd. dirs. 1976-80, Outstanding Young Alumnus 1975, Disting. Engring. Alumnus 1984, Watauga Medal 1997), Rotary (pres. 1978-79), Pamlico Plantation Yacht Club (commodore 1993). Home and Office: PO Box 1987 117 Riverview Dr Washington NC 27889-9763

HACKNEY, ROBERT WARD, plant pathologist, nematologist, parasitologist, molecular geneticist, commercial arbitrator; b. Louisville, Dec. 11, 1942; s. Paul Arnold and Ovine (Whallen) H.; m. Cheryl Lynn Hill, June 28, 1969 (div. Dec. 1995); 1 child, Candice Colleen; m. Jacqueline Monica Eisenreich, Dec. 27, 1995. BA, Northwestern U., 1965; MS, Murray State U., 1969; PhD, Kans. State U., 1973. Postgrad. rsch. nematologist U. Calif., Riverside, 1973-75; plant nematologist Calif. Dept. Food and Agr., Sacramento, 1975-85, sr. plant nematologist, supr. 1985-89, sr. plant nematologist, specialist, 1989—; comml. arbitrator Am. Arbitration Assn., 1980—; chmn. Calif. Nematode Diagnosis Adv. Commn., Sacramento, 1981—. Contbr. articles to profl. jours. Hon. dep. Sheriff, Sacramento, 1982-83. Served with USMC, 1966. NSF grantee, 1974. Mem. Soc. Nematologists, Internat. Council Study of Viruses and Virus Diseases of the Grape, Delta Tau Delta, Sigma Xi. Democrat. Baptist. Office: Calif Dept Food & Agriculture Plant Pest Diagnostic Ctr 3294 Meadowview Rd Sacramento CA 95832-1448

HACKNEY, SHELDON, federal agency administrator, academic administrator; b. 1933. Pres. Univ. of Penn., Philadelphia, Penn., 1981-93; chmn. NEH, Washington, DC, 1993-97; prof. history U. Pa., Phila., 1997—. Address: U Pa Dept History Philadelphia PA 19104*

HACKNEY, VIRGINIA HOWITZ, lawyer; b. Phila., Jan. 11, 1945; d. Charles Rawlings and Edith Wrenn (Pope) Howitz; m. Barry Albert Hackney, Feb. 15, 1969; children: Ashby Rawlings, Roby Howison, Trevor Pope. BA in Econs., Hollins Coll., 1967; JD, U. Richmond, 1970. Bar: Va. 1970. Assoc. Hunton & Williams, Richmond, Va., 1970-77, ptnr., 1977—; pres. Am. Acad. Hosp. Attys. Chgo., 1992-93. Mem. agy. evaluation com. United Way of Greater Richmond, 1981-86; sustainer Jr. League of Richmond; mem. Am. Acad. Hosp. Attys. (pres. 1992-93, bd. dirs. 1988-94). Named Outstanding Woman in field of law, YWCA, Richmond, 1981. Mem. ABA (bus. law sect. 1984—, forum com. on health law 1982—), Va. State Bar (long range planning com. 1985-90, chmn. standing com. lawyer discipline 1986-90, exec. com. 1988-90, Bar Coun. mem. 1984-90). Avocations: tennis, skiing, reading, boating, walking. Office: Hunton & Williams Riverfront Plz East Tower 951 E Byrd St Richmond VA 23219-4074

HACKSTADT, CHIQUITA DARLEEN, medical/surgical nurse; b. Cullman, Ala., Apr. 15, 1955; d. John W. Russell; m. R. David Hackstadt, Sept. 29, 1991. AS, Jefferson State U., Birmingham, Ala., 1986. RN, Ala. Staff nurse med. unit U. Ala. Hosp., Birmingham, staff nurse cardiology unit; staff nurse neurosurgery unit Bapt. Med. Ctr. at Montclair, Birmingham; mem. nurse care neurosurgery unit Flexpool St. Joseph's Hosp., Tampa, Fla.; mem. nurse pool neurosurgery progressive trauma Tampa (Fla.) Gen. Hosp., mem. pediatric nurse pool. Mem. Am. Heart Assn. (quality assurance com., nurse recruitment and retainment com., clin. level advancement com.), Phi Theta Kappa.

HADALLER, DAVID LAWRENCE, dean; b. Chelsea, Mass., Oct. 21, 1954; s. David Lawrence I and Ruth M.; m. Mirela Mustaca, Mar. 19, 1990; 1 child, David Lawrence III. BA, Gonzaga U., 1976; MA, St. Louis U., 1979, Columbia U., 1999; PhD, Washington State U., 1993. English instr. St. Louis U., 1976-79, Washington State U., Pullman, 1980-83, 85-86; asst. prof. Mayville (N.D.) State U., 1983-84, 86-87; Fulbright prof. Iasi, Romania, 1987-88; English dept. faculty Clovis (N.Mex.) Coll., 1989-92; rschr. N.Y.C., 1993-95; coord. spl. projects Hostos C.C., CUNY, N.Y.C., 1996-98, asst. dean, 1998—; tech., mktg. writer Topaz, Inc., San Diego, 1984-85; adj. prof. Westchester C.C., Valhalla, N.Y., 1994. Author: Gynicide: Women in the Novels of William Styron, 1996. Mem. Alpha Sigma Nu, Phi Theta Kappa (hon.). Office: Hostos C C/CUNY 500 Grand Concourse Bronx NY 10451-5323

HADAS, ELIZABETH CHAMBERLAYNE, publisher; b. Washington, May 12, 1946; d. Moses and Elizabeth (Chamberlayne) H.; m. Jeremy W. Heist, Jan. 25, 1970 (div. 1976); m. Peter Eller, Mar. 21, 1984 (div. 1998). A.B., Radcliffe Coll., 1967; postgrad. Rutgers U., 1967-68; M.A., Washington U., St. Louis, 1971. Editor U. N.Mex. Press, Albuquerque, 1971-85; dir., 1985—. Mem. Assn. Am. Univ. Presses (pres. 1992-93). Democrat. Home: 2900 10th St NW Albuquerque NM 87107-1111 Office: U New Mexico Press 1720 Lomas Blvd NE Albuquerque NM 87106-3807

HADAS, JULIA ANN, social services administrator; b. Rome, Ga., May 23, 1947; d. Robert Franklin and Myrtle Julia (Patrick) Richmond; m. John R. Hadas, Apr. 22, 1967 (div.); children: Kevin, Brian. BS magna cum laude, No. Mich. U., 1972, MA, 1977. Cert. social worker; lic. profl. counselor. Placement worker adult community Mich. Family Independence Agy., Marquette, 1976-80, supr. vol. svcs., 1980-86, supr. children svcs., 1986-93; dir. Marquette Local Office Mich. Family Independence Agy., 1993—. Chair Parent Adv. Coun. Marquette Area Pub. Schs., 1984-85; pres. Upper Peninsula Children's Coalition, 1986-96; adv. bd. Student Vol. Orgn. No. Mich. U., 1984-85; sec., pers. com. Women's Ctr.; mem. Alger-Marquette Human Svcs. Coordinating Body, 1994—, treas., 1994-97. Named one of Outstanding Young Women in Am., 1982. Mem. Childbirth Edn. Assn. (pres. 1975-76), Mich. Assn. Vol. Adminstrs., Zonta (pres. Marquette chpt. 1982-83). Episcopalian. Avocations: reading, travel, interior decorating, skiing.

HADASH, BRENDAN DOUGLAS, minister; b. Windsor, Ont., Canada, Apr. 25, 1951; came to U.S., 1982; s. Eli and Madeline (Stewart) H.; life ptnr. Alan Martin Hultquist, Mar. 30, 1985. BA, U. Windsor, 1973; MDiv, Starr King Sch., Berkeley, Calif., 1981. Ordained minister Unitarian Universalist Ch., 1981. Minister Unitarian Universalist Chs., Derby Line, West Burke, Vt., North Hatley, Quebec, 1982-86; activity dir. Pine Knoll Nursing Home, Lyndonville, Vt., 1988-90, Union House Nursing Home, Glover, Vt., 1990-94; nurse aide Craftsbury (Vt.) Cmty. Care Ctr., 1994—; minister Universalist Ch., St. Johnsbury, Vt., 1997. Chair Glover (Vt.) Dem. Party, 1987—, vice chair Orleans County, Vt., 1989—. Mem. Unitarian Universalist Ministers Assn., Vt. Freedom to Marry Task Force. Avocations: singing, working towards the legalization of same sex marriages. Home: 964 Beach Hill Rd West Glover VT 05875-9136

HADDAD, ABRAHAM HERZL, electrical engineering educator, researcher; b. Baghdad, Iraq, Jan. 16, 1938; came to U.S., 1963; s. Moshe M. and Masuda (Cohen) H.; m. Carolyn Ann Kushner, Sept. 9, 1966; children: Benjamin, Judith, Jonathan. BSEE, Technion-Israel Inst. Tech., Haifa, 1960, MSEE, 1963; MA in Elec. Engring., Princeton U., 1964, PhD in Elec. Engring., 1966. Asst. prof. elec. engring. U. Ill., Urbana, 1966-70, assoc prof., 1970-75, prof., 1975-81; sr. staff cons. Dynamics Research Corp., Wilmington, Mass., 1979; program dir. NSF, Washington, 1979-83; prof. Ga. Inst. Tech., Atlanta, 1983-88; Dever prof., chmn. elec. engring and computer sci. dept. Northwestern U., 1988-98, Dever prof. dept. elec. and computer engring., 1996—; dir. Computer Integrated Mfg. Systems Program, 1987-88; advisor U.S. Army Missle Command, Huntsville, Ala., 1969-79; vis. assoc. prof. Tel Aviv U., 1972-73; cons. to Lockheed-Ga. Co., 1984-88; sec. Am. Automatic Control Coun., 1990—; gen. chair Am. Control Conf., 1993; chair policy com. Internat. Fedn. Automatic Control, 1996—. Editor: Non-linear Systems, 1975. Fellow AAAS, IEEE (editor Trans. on Automatic Control 1983-89, Centennial medal 1984); mem. Control Systems Soc. of IEEE (gen. chair 1984 Conf. on Decision and Control, Disting. mem. award 1985, v.p. fin. affairs 1989-90, pres.-elect 1991, pres. 1992). Jewish. Office: Northwestern U Dept ECE Evanston IL 60208-3118

HADDAD, DAPHNE WHARTON, education educator; b. Stoke-on-Trent, England; came to U.S., 1978; m. Roger H. Haddad. BA in Theology, Birmingham (Eng.) U., 1966, MA in Islamic Studies, 1968; MEd in Elem. Edn., Converse Coll., 1985, MEd in Gifted Edn., 1987; PhD in Founds. of Edn., U. S.C., 1995. Tchr. pub. and pvt. schs., S.C., N.H., 1992-94, Cobb County (Ga.) Schs., 1994-96; assoc. prof. edn. Covenant Coll., Lookout Mountain, Ga., 1996—; adv. bd. Dushkin/McGraw Hill Annual Editions, 1997—. Contbr. articles to profl. jours. Internat. adv. com. Greenville (S.C.) Tech. Coll., 1990-91. Francis Corder Clayton scholar Birmingham U., 1966-67, Leverhulme Rsch. scholar Lever Bros., 1967-68; George Poda Jr. scholar U. S.C., 1992, James A. Stoddrd fellow, 1993. Mem. Am. Ednl. Rsch. Assn., Nat. Assn. Multicultural Edn., Nat. Middle Sch. Assn., Phi Delta Kappa, Sigma Delta Pi (v.p. 1992-93). Presbyterian. Home: 3451 Barnwood Pl Powder Springs GA 30127-5321 Office: Covenant Coll 14049 Scenic Hwy Lookout Mountain GA 30750-4100

HADDAD, EDMONDE ALEX, public affairs executive; b. Los Angeles, July 25, 1931; s. Alexander Saleeba and Madeline Angela (Zail) H.; m. Harriet Ann Lenhart; children: Mark Edmonde, Brent Michael, John Alex. AA, Los Angeles City Coll., 1956; BA, U. Southern Calif., 1958; MA, Columbia U., 1961. Staff writer WCBS Radio News, New York, 1959-61; news commentator, editor KPOL AM/FM Radio, Los Angeles, 1961-67, dir., pub. affairs, 1967-73; exec. dir. Los Angeles World Affairs Council, 1973-84; pres. L.A. World Affairs Coun., 1984-88; deputy asst. sec. of State for Pub. Diplomacy Dept. State, U.S. Govt., Wash., 1987-88; mem. steering com., moderator Conf. environ., L.A., 1989-90; pres. Nat. Coun. World Affairs Orgns., 1981-83; pres. Radio and TV News Assn. So. Calif., 1965-66; sr. fellow Ctr. Internat. Rels., U. Calif., L.A., 1991-94; bd. dirs. Pen Ctr. USA West. Author: Look to the Rainbow, 1997; contbg. author: How Peace Came to the World,, 1985; founder, pub. World Affairs Jour. Quar., 1981. Bd. dirs. PEN Ctr. USA West, 1994—, World Affairs Coun., Ventura County, 1995-97. Recipient Am. Polit. Sci. Assn. award for Disting. Reporting of Pub. Affairs, 1967. Mem. Am. Assn. Ret. Persons (coord. 12d congrl. dist. 1999), Friends of Wilton Park (exec. com. So. Calif.), Brit. Fgn. Office Conf. Ctr. Democrat. Avocations: writing poetry, nonfiction, and oped articles for newspapers, public speaking, travel. Home: 582 Pacific Cove Dr Port Hueneme CA 93041-2175

HADDAD, ERNEST MUDARRI, lawyer; b. Boston, Oct. 30, 1938; s. Abraham and Elaine (Mudarri) H.;m. Kathleen L. Tracy; 1 child, Barton Edward; children from previous marriage: Scott Cochrane, Mark Mudarri. BA, Trinity Coll., Hartford, Conn., 1960; LLB, Boston U., 1964. Bar: Mass. 1964, U.S. Dist. Ct. Mass. 1966, U.S. Supreme Ct., 1981. Asst. dean and mem. faculty sch. law Boston U., 1966-71; asst. sec., gen. counsel Commonwealth of Mass. Exec. Office Human Svcs., Boston, 1971-76; gen. counsel Blue Cross and Blue Shield Mass. Inc., Boston, 1976-80; sec., gen. counsel The Mass. Gen. Hosp., Boston, 1981—, Ptnrs. HealthCare Sys., Inc., Boston, 1995—. Program chmn., mem. exec. com. Boston Study Group, 1979—; bd. commrs. Black Achievers Br. Greater Boston YMCA, 1995—. Recipient Trinity Coll. Alumni medal for Excellence, 1990. Mem. ABA (health law, antitrust law and legal edn.-bar admissions sects.), Am. Corp. Counsel Assn., Am. Health Lawyers Assn., Mass. Bar Assn., Boston Bar Assn. (mem. coun. 1998—, exec. com. 1999—), Boston Bar Found. (trustee, 1998—), Boston U. Law Sch. Alumni Assn. (pres., 1998—). Home: 144 Mount Vernon St Boston MA 02108-1128 Office: Office of Gen Counsel 800 Boylston St Ste 1150 Boston MA 02199-8001

HADDAD, FREDDIE DUKE, JR., hospital development administrator; b. Charleston, W.Va., Oct. 18, 1952; s. Freddie Duke Haddad Sr. and Betty Jane (Perry) Campbell; m. Cynthia Ann LaMaster, July 17, 1976; children: Freddie Duke III, Shannon Lynn. BS, W.Va. U., 1974; MPA, W.Va. Grad. Coll., 1976; EdD, W.Va. U., 1986. Grad. asst. W.Va. Grad. Coll., Charleston, 1974-75; assoc. dir. devel. U. Louisville, Ky., 1975-77; dir. alumni affairs Fla. Internat. U., Miami, 1977-79; dir. alumni/devel. U. Charleston, W.Va., 1979-81; pvt. practice bus. cons. Charleston, 1981-82; dir. alumni/devel. Butler U., Indpls., 1982-89; dir. devel. St. Vincent Hosp. Found., Indpls., 1989-98, v.p. devel., exec. dir., 1998—; exec. dir. St. Vincent Mercy Hosp. Found., Elwood, Ind., 1995—; adj. prof. Nova U., Ft. Lauderdale, Fla., 1978-79; cons. in field. Contbr. articles to profl. jours. Mem. parish coun. St. George Orthodox Ch., Indpls., 1990-93; mem. com. Red Cross Awards Program, Indpls., 1991—; sec., v.p. Lawrence Twp. Babe Ruth League, Indpls., 1991-93; bd. dirs. Lawrence Twp. Edn. Found., Indpls., 1994-98, pres., 1999. Named Ky. Col., Gov. Ky., Frankfort, 1976, Outstanding Young Men of Am., 1986, Outstanding West Virginian, Gov. W.Va., Charleston, 1994, Sagamore of Wabash, Gov. Ind., 1996. Mem. Nat. Soc. Fund Raising Execs. (cert. fund raising exec., bd. mem. 1990-95, v.p., pres.-elect Ind. chpt. 1992-94, pres. Ind. chpt. 1995, nat. NSFRE edn. curriculum com. 1996, Pres.'s award 1993), Assn. Healthcare Philanthropy (Jour. award 1993), W.Va. U. Alumni Assn. (mountaineer amb. 1991—), Daus. of Charity Nat. coun. Founds. (1st v.p. 1998, pres. 1999). Avocations: reading, writing, jogging, golfing. Office: St Vincent Hosp Found 8402 Harcourt Rd Ste 213 Indianapolis IN 46260-2051

HADDAD, GABRIEL G., physician, pediatrics educator; b. Beirut, Mar. 20, 1947; came to U.S., 1974; s. George Gabriel and Ida (Bitar) H.; m. Karen Chmielski, June 14, 1975; children: Christopher, Diana, Justin. BS in Biology and Chemistry, Am. Univ. Beirut, 1969, MD, 1973. Diplomate Am. Bd. Pediatrics. Fellow in pediatrics, pulmonary Columbia U., N.Y.C., 1975-78, asst. prof. pediatrics, 1978-84, assoc. prof. pediatrics, 1984-88, dir. sleep physiology lab., 1980-88; dir. sect. respiratory medicine Yale U. Sch. Medicine, New Haven, 1988—, prof. pediatrics, 1990—; mem. NIHD study sect. NIH, Md., 1982; mem. editorial bd. Jour. Applied Physiology, 1983-85, assoc. editor, 1989-93; NIHLB site visitor NIH Program Project, Cleve., 1985; conf. chmn. NIHLB, 1987, NICHD, 1988, NIH subcom. chmn. Contbr. over 100 chpts. and articles and abstracts to profl. jours. and books. Recipient Edward Livingston Trudeau award Am. Lung Assn., 1979-82, Pediat. Faculty Tchg. award Yale U. Sch. Medicine, 1991, Excellence in Pediat. Rsch. award Am. Acad. Pediats., 1992; Parker B. Francis fellow, 1976-79, Milton Singer fellow Columbia U. Coll. Physicians, 1977-78. Mem. AAAS, Am. Heart Assn. (established investigator 1985-90), Soc. for Pediatrics Rsch., Am. Physiol. Soc., Am. Thoracic Soc. (respiratory neurobiology & sleep sect.), Soc. for Neurosci., Alpha Omega Alpha. Home: 383 Schoolside Ln Guilford CT 06437-1854 Office: Yale U Sch Medicine 333 Cedar St Fitkin 506 New Haven CT 06520*

HADDAD, GEORGE ILYAS, engineering educator, research scientist; b. Aindara, Lebanon, Apr. 7, 1935; came to U.S., 1952, naturalized, 1961; s.

Elias Ferris and Fahima (Haddad) H.; m. Mary Louella Nixon, June 28, 1958; children—Theodore N., Susan Anne. BS in Elec. Engring, U. Mich., 1956, M.S., 1958, Ph.D., 1963. Mem. faculty U. Mich., Ann Arbor, 1963—, assoc. prof., 1965-69, prof. elec. engring., 1968—, Robert J. Hiller prof., 1991—, dir. electron physics lab., 1968-75, chmn. dept. elec. engring. and computer sci., 1975-87, 91-97, dir. ctr. for high-frequency microelectronics, 1987—; cons. to industry. Contbr. articles to profl. jours. Recipient Curtis W. McGraw research award Am. Soc. Engring. Edn., 1970, Excellence in Research award Coll. Engring., U. Mich., 1985, Disting. Faculty Achievement award U. Mich., 1985-86, S.S. Attwood award, 1991, MTT-S Disting. Educator award, 1996. Fellow IEEE (editor proc. and trans.); mem. NAE, Am. Soc. Engring. Edn., Am. Phys. Soc., Acad. Engring., Sigma Xi, Phi Kappa Phi, Eta Kappa Nu, Tau Beta Pi. Office: U Mich Dept Elec Engring & Computer Sci 3316 EECS 1301 Beal Ave Ann Arbor MI 48109-2122

HADDAD, HESKEL MARSHALL, ophthalmologist; b. Baghdad, Iraq, Sept. 26, 1930; came to U.S., 1953, naturalized, 1962; s. Moshe M. and Masuda (Cohen) H.; m. Doris I. Fatzer, July 4, 1963; children: Ava Masuda, Andreas Moshe, Michael Albert. Student, Royal Coll. Medicine, Baghdad, 1945-50; M.D., Hebrew U., Jerusalem, 1953. Diplomate Am. Bd. Pediatrics, Am. Bd. Ophthalmology; ordained rabbi, 1997. Intern Donolo Hosp., Jaffo-Tel Aviv, Israel, 1950-51; rotating intern Hadassah U. Hosp., Jerusalem, 1951-53; pediatric resident Children's Med. Center, Boston, 1953-56; fellow in pediatric endocrinology Johns Hopkins Hosp., Balt., 1956-58; fellow in clin. endocrine br. Nat. Inst. Arthritis and Metabolic Diseases, NIH, Bethesda, Md., 1958-59; pediatrician sect. clin. endocrinology NIH, 1959-60; asst. prof. pediatrics sch. medicine Howard U., Washington, 1959-60; resident, asst. dept. ophthalmology sch. medicine Washington U., St. Louis, 1960-64; leave of absence, 1962-63; fellow pediatric ophthalmology Inst. Visual Sci., San Francisco, 1962; research fellow Hôpital des Quinze-Vingts, Laboratoire de Physiologie de Vision, Ecole des Hautes Etudes, Paris, 1962-63; ophthalmologist Hôpital Beni Messous, Algiers, Algeria, 1964; asst. attending ophthalmic surgeon, also asst. prof. ophthalmology Mt. Sinai Hosp. and Sch. Medicine, N.Y.C., 1964-67; dir. dept. ophthalmology Beth Israel Med. Center, N.Y.C.; also assoc. prof. ophthalmology Mt. Sinai Sch. Medicine, 1967-71; clin. prof. ophthalmology N.Y. Med. Coll., 1971—. Author: Endocrine Exophthalmos, 1973, Metabolic Eye Diseases, 1974, Metabolic-Peditric Eye Diseases, 1979, Metabolic Ophthalmology: Diagnostic Techniques Vols. I and II, 1985, Jews of Arab and Islamic Countries: History, Problems and Solutions, 1984, (autobiography) Flight from Babylon, 1986; editor-in-chief: Metabolic Ophthalmology, 1976-79, Metabolic and Ophthalmology, 1976-79, Metabolic and Pediatric Ophthalmology, 1979-82, Metabolic, Pediatric and Systemic Ophthalmology, 1982—; contbr. numerous articles and revs. to profl. jours.; holder 7 U.S. patents. Pres. Am. Com. for Rescue and Resettlement of Iraqui Jews, World Orgn. Jews from Arab Countries, Parents' Assn. of Sch. of Performing Arts, 1980-83. Fellow ACS, Am. Inst. Chemists; mem. Am. Endocrine Soc., Am. Fedn. Clin. Research, Assn. Research Ophthalmology and Vision, AMA, New York County Med. Soc., AAAS, Am. Acad. Ophthalmology, N.Y. Acad. Medicine, N.Y. Acad. Scis., N.Y. Soc. Clin. Ophthalmology, Soc. Eye Surgeons, Société Française d' Ophthalmologie, German Ophthal. Soc., Internat. Soc. Metabolic Eye Disease (founder, sec.-treas. 1973—), World Soc. on Systemic Ophthalmology (founder, sec.-treas. 1982, chmn.), N.Y. County Med. Soc. (chmn. com. fgn. med. grads. 1985-90, del. N.Y. State Med. Soc. 1985-86). Patentee in field. Office: 1125 Park Ave New York NY 10128-1243 *The Commandment of "loving one's neighbor" should read "Thou shalt love for thy neighbor as for thy self." Whereas we cannot always control the emotion of love, we are consciously able to stop doing unto others what we do not like for ourselves.*

HADDAD, JAMIL RAOUF, physician; b. Mosul, Iraq, Aug. 18, 1923; came to U.S., 1952, naturalized, 1965; s. Raouf Sulaiman and Fadhila (Shaya) H.; m. Mary Lou Scorsone, Aug. 1, 1959; children—Ralph J., John L., James M. M.B., Ch.B., Iraqi Royal Coll. Medicine, Baghdad, Iraq, 1946. Med. officer Khanaqin (Iraq) Hosp., 1946-52; asst. resident pathology Crawford W. Long Meml. Hosp., Atlanta, 1953-54; resident Bellevue Hosp., N.Y.C., 1954-56; practice medicine specializing in pathology N.Y.C., 1963—, Passaic, N.J., 1981—; chmn. dept. anatomic and clin. pathology St. Clare's Hosp. and Health Center, N.Y.C., 1971-81; dir. pathology and clin. lab. Gen. Hosp. Ctr. at Passaic, 1981—; assoc. Sloan-Kettering Inst. for Cancer Research, N.Y.C., 1960-66; asst. prof. pathology NYU Coll. Medicine, 1959-65, asst. clin. prof. pathology, 1965-67, asso. clin. prof. pathology, 1967-70, clin. prof. pathology, 1970—; asst. prof. exptl. cell biology Mt. Sinai Grad Sch. Biol. Scis., N.Y.C., 1966-70, lectr., 1971-83, adj. asst. prof., 1983—. Mem. Coll. Am. Pathologists, Am. Soc. Clin. Pathologists, AMA, N.Y. Pathol. Soc., N.Y. State, New York County med. socs. Home: 420 E 23rd St Apt Mc New York NY 10010-5043 Office: 350 Boulevard Passaic NJ 07055-2840

HADDAD, LOUIS NICHOLAS, paralegal; b. Beggs, Okla., Sept. 3, 1923; s. Abraham and Tammam (Lelo) H.; m. Jacqueline Marie Pratali, Sept. 22, 1945 (div. 1952); children: Carole, Shirley, Charles; m. Martha Maria Laengst, Dec. 31, 1954; children: Sheila, Stephanie. Co-owner Haddad Bros. Wholesalers, Lancaster, Calif., 1955-57; regional v.p. Nulite Corp., No. Calif., 1957-60; owner, mgr. Shamrock Motors, Seaside, Calif., 1960-68, Gateway Liquors, Seaside, 1968-70, Wagontown Auto Sales, Seaside, 1971-73, Camptown West Motor Homes, Seaside, 1973-79; co-owner, mgr. Monterey (Calif.) Bay Tribune, 1983-89. Councilman City of Seaside, 1964-66, 78-80, mayor, 1966-72; charter bd. dirs. Monterey Peninsula Boys Club; bd. dirs. Alliance on Aging, Assn. Monterey Bay Area Govts., Monterey Peninsula Water Mgmt. Dist., 1993-97; chmn. Laguna Grande Agy., Seaside County Sanitation Dist., Monterey Overall Econ. Devel. Com.; chmn. adv. com. Project Aquarius; mem. Seaside Planning Comn.; vice chmn. So. Monterey Bay Water Pollution Control Agy.; chmn. tri-county bd. Calif. Coun. on Criminal Justice; former vice chmn. Monterey County Local Agys. Formation. Capt. U.S. Army, 1940-46, 50-55. Mem. VFW, NCO Assn. Am. (hon.), Am. Legion, Seaside C. of C. (bd. dirs.), K.C., Lions (past pres. Seaside chpt.), Rotary (past pres. Seaside chpt.). Republican. Roman Catholic. Home: 5 Deer Stalker Path Monterey CA 93940-6311

HADDAD, WASSIM MICHAEL, aerospace engineer, educator; b. Athens, Greece, July 14, 1961; s. Michael Sulayman and Sofia (Carinou) H.; m. Lydia Katinas, Mar. 15, 1986. BS in Mech. Engring., Fla. Inst. Tech., 1983, MS in Mech. Engring., 1984, PhD in Mech. Engring., 1987. Cons. engr. Harris Corp., Melbourne, Fla., 1987—; asst. prof. Fla. Inst. Tech., Melbourne, 1988-93, assoc. prof., 1993-94; control sys. rschr. Space Rsch. Inst., Melbourne, 1989-90; assoc. prof. Ga. Inst. Tech., Atlanta, 1994—; vis. prof. aerospace engring. dept. U. Mich., Ann Arbor, 1992-93. Author chpts. to books; contbr. articles to profl. jours. Grantee Air Force Office Sci. Rsch., 1987-89, 89-91, 91-94, Fla. Space Grant Consortium-NASA, 1990-91, 92-93, 93-94, NSF, 1991-94; recipient Rsch. Initiation award NSF, 1991, Presdl. Faculty Fellow award, 1993. Mem. IEEE, Tau Beta Pi. Roman Catholic. Avocations: travel, art, history, classical music. Home: 557 Fairway Dr Woodstock GA 30189-8143 Office: Ga Inst Tech Aerospace Engring Dept Atlanta GA 30332*

HADDAWAY, JAMES DAVID, retired insurance company official; b. Louisville, July 25, 1933; s. Charles Montgomery Jr. and Viola (Sands) H.; m. Myrna Lou Harris, June 5, 1954; children: Peggy Ann, Robert Marshall, Susan Gayle. BS in Commerce, U. Louisville, 1960; MBA, Xavier U., 1973. Cert. adminstrv. mgr. (life); cert. purchasing mgr. (life); accredited personnel mgr.; sr. profl. human resources (life). Ins. cons. Met. Life Ins., Louisville, 1955-59; supt. Byck Bros. & Co., Louisville, 1959-61; dir. purchasing Liberty Nat. Bank, Louisville, 1961-63; v.p. and mgr. gen. services adminstrn. Citizens Fidelity Bank, Louisville, 1963-79; asst. v.p. and mgr. human resources Ky. Farm Bur. Ins. Co., 1979-95. Founder, chmn. emeritus Kentuckiana Expn. of Bus. and Industry, 1973-85. Served with U.S. Army, 1953-55. Named Boss of Year, Louisville chpt. Nat. Secs. Assn., 1978, 79. Mem. Adminstrv. Mgmt. Soc. (nat. dir. 1979-81), Nat. Assn. Purchasing Mgmt. (dir. nat. affairs 1970-71), Adminstrv. Mgmt. Soc. Louisville (pres. 1975-76, bd. dirs. 1976-92), Adminstrv. Mgmt. Soc. Found. (charter), Purchasing Mgmt. Assn. Louisville (pres. 1969-70), Louisville Soc. Human Resource Mgmt. (pres. 1983-84, chmn. strategic planning com. 1989, chmn. reorganization com. 1992, Professional Excellance award 1993), Conf. Casualty Ins. Cos. (chmn. nat. personnel conf. com. 1983), Nat. Eagle Scout Assn. (life), Soc. Human Resource Mgmt. (chmn. conf. com. region 9, 1984, dist. dir. for Western Ky. 1984, v.p. region 9 1985-86, Ky. coun. chmn. 1986), Nat. Assn. Ind. Insurers (mem. personnel com. 1987-95), Ky. C. of C. (benefits com., 1987-88, chmn. banking and ins. health and welfare sub-com. project 21, 1988), Hon. Order Ky. Cols., Am. Assn. of Individual Investors (life), Am. GO Assn., Louisville Soc. for Advancement Mgmt. (charter, pres. 1993-94, dir. 1994-95). Clubs: U. Club Louisville (charter), Wally Byam Caravan Internat. (pres. Ky. unit 1993, chmn. long range planning com. 1994, 2d v.p. region 5 1996-97, 1st v.p. region 5 1998-99, Land Yacht Port O'Call (co-chmn. computer club 1998, chmn. 1999), Good Sam Recreational Vehicle (life), Bass Anglers Sportsman Soc. (life), Am. Legion. Lodges: Masons, Shriners. Baptist. Home: 974 Breckenridge Ln # 155 Louisville KY 40207-4619

HADDEN, JOHN RANDOLPH, sales and marketing executive; b. Charlotte, N.C., Oct. 4, 1961; s. James Hickman and Sylvia Elaine (Smith) H.; m. Mary Sue Van Overloop, Apr. 15, 1989; children: Lindsey Kaye, Victoria Christian. AA, St. Petersburg Jr. Coll., Clearwater, Fla., 1982; BS in Mktg., U. South Fla., Tampa, 1985, postgrad., 1999. Assoc. v.p. sales and mktg. Lab. Corp. Am., Tampa, 1985-97; v.p. sales and mktg. Horus Global HealthNet, Clearwater, 1997-99; v.p. bus. devel. group Am. Med. Labs., Tampa, 1999—; cons. Barnhill Clin. Lab., Savannah, Ga., 1988-91; mem. adv. bd. U. South Fla. Sch. Bus., Tampa., 1990-94; bd. dirs. Progressive Staffing, Horus Global Health Net. Author, speaker seminar. Bd. dirs. March of Dimes, Tampa, 1995—; v.p., bd. dirs. Make A Wish Found., Sarasota and Bradenton, Fla., 1986-89; vol. fund raiser All Children's Hosp., St. Petersburg, Fla., 1992-94; fund raiser Muscular Dystrophy, 1980-96; mktg. dir. Republican Party, Tampa and Miami, Fla., 1985-86; nat. spokesman March of Dimes, 1995—. Avocations: reading, golf, exercise, running, family activities. Home: 2257 Pinnacle Cir S Palm Harbor FL 34684-1764 Office: Am Med Labs Inc 3907 W Kennedy Blvd Tampa FL 33609

HADDEN, JOHN WINTHROP, immunopharmacology educator; b. Berkeley, Calif., Oct. 23, 1939; s. David Rodney Hadden; m. Elba Mas, July 31, 1964; children: John W. II, Paul J. BA, Yale U., 1961; MD, Columbia U., 1965. Asst. prof. pathology U. Minn., Mpls., 1972-73; assoc. prof. Cornell Grad. Sch., N.Y.C., 1973-82; assoc. mem., dir. lab. immunopharmacology Sloan-Kettering Meml. Cancer Inst., N.Y.C., 1973-82; prof. medicine, dir. div. immunopharmacology U. South Fla., Tampa, 1982—; cons. in field. Assoc. editor Internat. Jour. Immunopharmacology, 1978-86, editor, 1986-98; editor 12 textbooks; contbr. chpts. to books, more than 280 articles to profl. jours. Mem. Am. Assn. Immunologists, Am. Soc. Pharm. & Exptl. Therapy, Internat. Soc. Immunopharmacologists (v.p. 1982-85, pres. 1985-88), Tampa Yale Club (v.p. 1986-91). Achievements include 7 patents for method of imparting immunomodulating activity. Home: 2413 Bayshore Blvd Apt 2105 Tampa FL 33629-7336 Office: Univ S Fla Med Coll 12901 Bruce B Downs Blvd Tampa FL 33612-4742

HADDIX, CAROL ANN MIGHTON, journalist; b. Cedar Rapids, Iowa, Mar. 10, 1946; d. John Wallace and Mary Ellen (Ferriter) Mighton; m. James Loyal Haddix, Nov. 4, 1967 (div. 1976); 1 child, Leigh Ann. B.S. in Home Econs., Mich. State U., 1968. Asst. women's editor Midland Daily News, Mich., 1970; editorial asst. Detroit Free Press, 1971-74, food reporter, 1974-77; food reporter Chgo. Tribune, 1977-81, food guide editor, 1981—. Co-author: Cooks Marketplace, 1985; food editor: Chicago Tribune Cookbook, 1989, Chicago Tribune Desserts, Chicago Tribune Grilling, Chicago Tribune Holidays, 1993, Ethnic Chicago Cookbook, 1998; contbr. chpts. to Where to Eat in America. Mem. James Beard Found. Recipient Vesta award Chgo. Tribune, 1981. Mem. Am. Inst. Wine and Food, Chgo. Culinary Guild, James Beard Found., Les Dames d'Escoffier Chgo. (sec. 1983-85, v.p. 1985, pres. 1986-87), Les Dames D'Escoffier Internat. (v.p. 1987-88, sec. 1988-90), assoc. of Food Journalists (bd. dirs. 1977, award for Best Food Sect. 1990, 93, 95, 96), Culinary Historians Chgo. Avocations: cooking; reading; tennis. Home: 226 N Clinton St # 662 Chicago IL 60661-1185 Office: Chicago Tribune 435 N Michigan Ave Chicago IL 60611-4066

HADDOCK, FRED THEODORE, JR., astronomer, educator; b. Independence, Mo., May 31, 1919; s. Fred Theodore Sr. and Helen (Sea) H.; m. Margaret Pratt, June 24, 1941 (div. Sept. 1976); children: Thomas Frederick, Richard Marshall. SB, MIT, 1941; MS, U. Md., 1950; DSc (hon.), Rhodes Coll., 1965, Ripon Coll., 1966. Physicist U.S. Naval Rsch. Lab., Washington, 1941-56; assoc. prof. elec. engring. and astronomy U. Mich., Ann Arbor, 1956-59, prof. elec. engring., 1959-67, prof. astronomy, 1959-88, emeritus prof., 1988—; lectr. radio astronomy Jodrell Bank U. Manchester, Eng., 1962; vis. assoc. radio astronomy Calif. Inst. Tech., 1966; vis. lectr. Raman Inst., Bangalore, India, 1978; sr. cons. Nat. Radio Astron. Obs., W.Va., 1960-61; founder, dir. U. Mich. Radio Astron. Obs., 1961-84. Author: (chpts. in books) Space Age Astronomy, 1962, Radio Astronomy of the Solar System, 1966; contbr. articles to prof. jours. and publs. Mem. Union Radio Sci. Internat., nat. chmn. commn. on radio astronomy, 1954-57; trustee Associated Univs., Inc., 1964-68; prin. investigator, five Orbiting Geophys. Observatories, 1960-74, and Interplanetary Probe 9, 1964-77; co-investigator on Voyager planetary probes, 1970-86, NASA, Washington; mem. astronomy adv. panel NSF, Washington, 1957-60, 63-66. With USN, 1944-45. Fellow IEEE (life), Am. Astron. Soc. (v.p. 1961-63); mem. Internat. Astron. Union (commn. on radio astronomy 1948—), NAS (adv. panel astronomy facilities 1962-64), AIA (hon. mem. Huron Valley chpt. 1980—), Sigma Xi (past pres U. Mich. chpt. 1956—). Achievements include design and development of first submarine periscope radar antenna, 1943-44; early discoveries in microwave astronomy, gaseous nebulae in 1953 and early space detection of kilometer waves from galaxy and the sun, 1962. Home: 3935 Holden Dr Ann Arbor MI 48103-9415 Office: U Mich Astronomy Dept Ann Arbor MI 48109

HADDOCK, HAROLD, JR., retired accounting firm executive; b. Newark, July 26, 1932; s. Harold and Lilian (Smith) H.; m. Constance M. Beltz, June 23, 1962 (div. 1986); children: Anita Jane, Carolyn Jeanne; m. Margot Mahoney, Dec. 31, 1986. AA, Union Coll., 1957; BS, Rutgers U., 1959. CPA, N.J., Fla., Mich., N.C. Sr. acct. Price Waterhouse, Newark, 1959-64; exec. asst. to treas. AP, N.Y.C., 1964-68; mgr. Price Waterhouse, N.Y.C., 1969-74, ptnr., 1974; nat. dir. fin., chief fin. officer Price Waterhouse, N.Y.C. and Tampa, Fla., 1975-90; nat. dir. adminstrn. Price Waterhouse, 1990-93. Pres. Scotch Plains-Fanwood YMCA, N.J., 1979-80, bd. dirs., trustee, 1975-84, Man of Yr., 1985; pres., dir. The Westshore Alliance, Tampa, 1991-93; bd. dirs. Eastman Cmty. Assn., 1997—, pres., 1998—. With USAF, 1952-56. Fellow AICPA, Fla. Inst. CPA, N.J. Soc. CPA; mem. Rockefeller Ctr. N.Y.C. (pres. 1979). Republican. Roman Catholic. Avocations: flying, golf, spectator sports.

HADDOCK, RAYMOND EARL, career officer; b. Oklahoma City, Sept. 26, 1936; s.Clyde William and Ida Belle (Lemmon) H.; m. Brunhilde Ernestine Becker, Oct. 21, 1960; children: Ralph William, Ronald Raymond, Karen Elizabeth Haddock Fralen. BS in Chemistry, W. Tex. State U., 1958; MS in Pub. Adminstrn., Shippensburg U., 1977; grad., U.S. Army War Coll., Carlisle Barracks, Pa., 1977. Commd. 2d lt. U.S. Army, advanced through grades to maj. Gen.; bn. comdr. Pershing Missile Bn., 56th F.A. U.S. Army, Fed. Republic Germany, 1973-75, pers. staff officer (G-1) 8th Inf. Div., 1975-76; dir. internat. programs Tng. and Doctrin Command U.S. Army, Fort Monroe, Va., 1977-80; comdr 9th Div. Arty. U.S. Army, Fort Lewis, Wash., 1980-83; chief of staff Tng. Ctr. U.S. Army, Fort Dix, N.J., 1983-84; comdg. gen. Pershing Missile Command 56th F.A. U.S. Army, Fed. Republic Germany, 1984-87; U.S. comdr. U.S. Command and U.S. Army, Berlin, 1988-90; comdg. gen. Security Assistance Command U.S. Army, Alexandria, Va., 1990-92; v.p. ITT Def. Internat., McLean, Va., 1993—; participator fall of Berlin wall, reunification of Germany and U.S.-Soviet nuclear forces treaty, 1987. Decorated D.S.M. with two oak leaf clusters, Fed. Order of Merit (Fed. Republic Germany), Gold Nat. Def. medal (France). Avocations: sailing, fishing, jogging, hunting. Home: Psc 1203 Box 5019 APO AE 09803-5019 Office: ITT Def Internat 1650 Tysons Blvd Ste 1700 Mc Lean VA 22102-4827

HADDOCK, RONALD WAYNE, oil company executive; b. St. Elmo, Ill., July 29, 1940; s. Clarence and Marie (Price) H.; m. Sandra Sue Thomas, Sept. 1957; children: Roni Sue Haddock Campey, Mark Tayler, Rick Wayne. BMechE, Purdue U., 1963. With Exxon Corp., 1963-86; various tech. staff, mgmt. positions Baton Rouge Refinery, 1963-71; specialties econs. coordinator, adminstrv. mgr., planning mgr. Refining Dept. Houston hdqrs., 1971-75; ops. mgr., refinery mgr. Baytown Refinery, 1975-78; corp. planning mgr. then v.p. for refining Houston hdqrs., 1978-81; exec. asst. to chmn. Exxon Corp. Hdqrs. N.Y.C., 1981-82; v.p., dir. Esso Eastern Houston hdqrs., 1982-85; exec. v.p., COO FINA, Inc., Dallas, 1986-88; pres., CEO Fina, Inc., Dallas, 1988—; also bd. dirs. FINA, Inc., Dallas. Mem. Dallas Morning News Energy Adv. Bd.; hon. consul of Belgium in Dallas; mem. Dallas Together Forum; chmn.'s adv. bd. Dallas Arboretum; mem. Gov.'s Bus. Coun.; mem. bd., Zale Lipshy Hosp., Sci. Pl. Named Man of Yr. Belgian-Am. Chamber, Disting. Engring. Alumnus Purdue U, Humanitarian of Yr. Anti-Defamation League; recipient award Multiple Sclerosis Dinner of Champions, Chmns. award D/FW Minority Bus. Devel. Coun., Entrepreneurs award African Am. Women, Advocate of Yr. award Golden Triangle Minority Bus. Coun. Mem. Am. Petroleum Inst. (bd., com. hon. dirs., mgmt. com., Ind. Reputation Strategic Issues Grp.), Nat. Petroleum Coun. (bd., coordinating com.), Chems. Mfrs. Assn. (bd., Responsible Care Com., Fin. Com.), Ind. Petroleum Assn. Am. (regional adv. bd.), Tex. Mid-Continenta Oil and Gas Assn. (exec. com.), Petrochem. Industry Founders Club, 25 Yr. Club Petroleum Industry, Dallas Petroleum Club (adv. com. chmn., past pres.), Dallas Wildcatters (past pres.), Brook Hollow Golf Club, Bd. Dallas Citizens Counc., co-chair, Dallas Together Forum, bd., The Science Place. Methodist. Avocations: jogging, music. Office: FINA Inc 6000 Legacy Dr Plano TX 75024

HADDON, SAM ELLIS, lawyer; b. West Monroe, La., June 19, 1937; s. James Charlie and Letha (Daughtry) H.; m. Betty G. Loyd, Dec. 22, 1958; children: Elizabeth Anne Haddon Alexander, Steven Craig Haddon, Allison Lee Haddon Conover. BS, Rice U., 1959; student, Border Patrol Acad., El Paso, Tex., 1959-60, Treasury Law Enforcement Sch., Washintgon, 1961; JD with honors, U. Mont., 1965. Bar: Mont. 1965, U.S. Ct. Appeals (9th cir.) 1966, U.S. Dist. Ct. Mont. 1966, U.S. Supreme Ct. 1975. Immigration patrol insp. U.S. Border Patrol, 1959-61; agt. Fed. Bur. Narcotics, 1961-62; rsch. asst. in law U. Mont., 1964-65; law clk. to judge U.S. Dist. Ct., 1965-66; assoc. Anderson, Symmes, Forbes, Peete and Brown, Billings, Mont., 1966-69; ptnr. Boone, Karlberg, and Haddon, Missoula, Mont., 1969—; instr. U. Mont. Sch. Law, 1971-99; chmn. Mont. Supreme Ct. Commn. on Rules of Evidence, 1975—; mem. Mont. Supreme Ct. Comm. on Practice, 1986—, chmn., 1996—; judge pro tem Mont. Dist. Ct. 4th Jud. Dist., 1975; spl. master Mont. Supreme Ct., 1978; del. Jud. Conf. 9th Cir., 1975, rep., 1977-80. Editor-in-chief Mont. Law Rev., 1964-65. Fellow Am. Coll. Trial Lawyers; mem. ABA, Am. Acad. Appellate Lawyers, Am. Judicature Soc. (bd. dirs. 1976-79), Am. Bd. Trial Advocates, Am. Law Inst., Mont. Bar Assn. (chmn. sect. young lawyers 1967-68, exec. com. 1968-69), State Bar Mont. (trustee 1976-78), Western Mont. Bar Assn. Office: Boone Karlberg and Haddon 300 Central Sq 201 W Main St Missoula MT 59802-4326

HADDY, FRANCIS JOHN, physician, educator; b. Walters, Minn., Sept. 6, 1922; s. Thomas J. and Frances (Shaheen) H.; m. Theresa Eileen Brey, Sept. 21, 1946; children: Richard, Carol, Alice. *Wife Theresa Brey is a guest researcher in the Pediatric Oncology Branch of the National Cancer Institute. Son Richard Ian is professor and vice chair for clinical affairs in the Department of Family and Community Medicine at the University of Louisville. He and his wife Cheryl Mitchell have four children, Kari, Jennifer, Michael and Sarah. Daughter Carol Elaine is a nurse and artist. She and her husband Stuart Froelich have two daughters, Jessica and Rachel. Daughter Alice Elizabeth is assistant professor of physical chemistry at the University of North Caroina at Greensboro. She and her husband have a daughter, Deborah.* Student, Luther Coll., Decorah, Iowa, 1940-42; B.S., U. Minn., 1943, B.M., 1946, M.D., 1947, M.S. in Physiology, 1949, Ph.D. in Physiology (Am. Heart Assn. fellow), 1953. Diplomate: Am. Bd. Internal Medicine. Intern Mpls. Gen. Hosp., 1946-47; fellow internal medicine Mayo Found., 1949-51; asst. prof. physiology and medicine Northwestern U. Med. Sch., 1953-61; clin. investigator VA Research Hosp., Chgo., 1957-59; prof. physiology, chmn. dept., asso. prof. medicine U. Okla. Med. Center, 1961-66; prof. physiology, chmn. dept. Mich. State U., East Lansing, 1966-76; prof. physiology Uniformed Services U., Bethesda, Md., 1976-98; chmn. dept. physiology Uniformed Services U., 1976-87; mem. cardiovasc. study sect. NIH, 1963-69; tng. com. Nat. Heart and Lung Inst., NIH, 1970-73; mem. atherosclerosis and hypertension adv. com. Nat. Heart, Lung and Blood Inst., NIH, 1983-86; rsch. com. Am. Heart Assn., 1974-80; mem. life scis. adv. com. NASA, 1986-92, chmn., 1988-92, mem. aerospace med. adv. com., 1988-93, mem. NASA-NIH adv. com., 1993-95; sr. scientist NASA/Johnson Space Ctr. S.C. med. scis. divsn., Houston, 1989-90; cons., peer rev. adminstr. for cardiopulmonary, integrative physiology, and clin. areas Univs. Space Rsch. Assn., 1995—, NASA, 1995—. Mem. editorial bd. Am. Jour. Physiology, 1963-69, 80-86, Jour. Applied Physiology, 1963-69, Procs. Soc. Exptl. Biology and Medicine, 1969-72, Circulation Rsch., 1975-81, Microvascular Rsch., 1978-81, Hypertension, 1978-81, Jour. Am. Coll. Nutrition, 1993—. Recipient Med. Sci. Achievement award Am. Heart Assn., 1987. Fellow Am. Coll. Nutrition (coord. hypertension and cardiovasc. diseases 1992-98, bd. dirs. 1993-97, publs. com. 1994—, ann. award 1986); mem. Am. Physiol. Soc. (steering com. circulation group 1972-75, chmn. com. on coms. 1974-77, mem. coun. 1976-79, pres. 1981, fin. com. 1983-89, chmn. fin. com. 1985-89, select com. on animal care 1988-91, chmn. long range planning com. 1990-93, hon. mem. com. 1993-95, chmn. 1995, Carl J. Wiggers award 1966), Am. Soc. Clin. Investigation, Fedn. Am. Socs. Exptl. Biology (bd. dirs. 1980-83, treas. 1990-92, rep. to Am. Assn. Accreditation Lab. Animal Care trustees 1993-96, exec. com. 1995-96), Internat. Union Physiol. Scis. (U.S. nat. com. 1976-79, 81-84), Nat. Hypertension Assn. (trustee 1979—), NAS (basic biomed. scis. panel, com. on nat. needs for biomed. and behavioral rsch. pers. Inst. Medicine 1983-86), Assn. Chairmen Depts. Physiology (chmn. animal welfare com. 1986-87), Aerospace Med. Assn. (publ. com. 1994-95), Am. Soc. for Gravitational and Space Biology (awards com. 1994—), Montgomery County Art Assn. (pres. 1997-98). Achievements include left heart catherization, small vein and artery catherization, mechanisms of pulmonary edema, fluid flux across the capillary membrane, local regulation of blood flow, ionic action on blood vessels, and low renin hypertension. Home: 10804 Whiterim Dr Potomac MD 20854-1784

HADEN, CHARLES, jazz bassist, composer; b. Shenandoah, Iowa, Aug. 6, 1937. Formed group with Ornette Coleman, Biley Higgins and Don Cherry; performing debut N.Y.C., 1959. Performed throughout, U.S., Europe, played with: Archie Shepp, Keith Jarrett, Alice Coltrane, Pee Wee Russell, Liberation Music Orch., others; recs. include Escalator Over the Hill, (with Carla Bley) Relativity Suite, (with Don Cherry) Expectations, (with Keith Jarrett) Tribute, Ballet of the Fallen, Dream-Keeper, (with Don Cherry, Ed Blackwell) The Montreal Tapes I, 1994, Liberation Music Orchestra, 1996, Now is the Hour, 1996; appeared at, Newport Jazz Festival, 1966-67, 70-72, Monterey Jazz Festival, 1966-67. Recipient Downbeat Critic's New Star award, 1961, acoustic base award, 1989; Guggenheim Found. grantee, 1970; Nat. Endowment Arts grantee, 1973. Office: Joel Chriss & Co 300 Mercer St Apt 3J New York NY 10003-6732*

HADEN, CHARLES H., II, federal judge; b. Morgantown, W.Va., Apr. 16, 1937; s. Charles H. and Beatrice L. (Costolo) H.; m. Priscilla Ann Miller, June 2, 1956; children: Charles H., Timothy M., Amy Sue. BS, W.Va. U., 1958, JD, 1961. Ptnr. Haden & Haden, Morgantown, W.Va., 1961-69; state tax commr. W.Va., 1969-72; justice Supreme Ct. Appeals W.Va., 1972-75, chief justice, 1975; judge U.S. Dist. Ct. No. and So. Dists. W.Va., Parkersburg, 1975-82; chief judge U.S. Dist. Ct. (so. dist.) W.Va., 1982—; mem. W.Va. Ho. of Dels., 1963-64; asst. prof. Coll. Law, W.Va. U., 1967-68; mem. com. adminstrn. probation system Jud. Conf., 1979-86; mem. 4th Cir. Jud. Coun., 1986-91, 96—, U.S. Jud. Conf., 1997—; dist. ct. rep. to U.S. Jud. Conf., 1998—. Mem. Bd. Edn., Monongalia County, W.Va., 1967-68; bd. dirs. W.Va. U. Found., 1988—; past. mem. vis. coms. W.Va. U. Coll. Law & Sch. Medicine; bd. dirs. W.Va. u. Found.,; mem. U.S. Jud. Conf.; mem. 4th cir. Jud. Coun., 1986-91, 96—. Recipient Outstanding Alumnus award W.Va. U., 1986. Fellow Am. Bar Found.; mem. ABA, W.Va. Bar Assn., W.Va. State Bar Assn., Am. Judicature Soc., 4th Cir. Dist. Judges Assn. (pres. 1993-95), W.Va. U. Alumni Assn. (pres. 1982-83). Office: US Dist Ct PO Box 351 Charleston WV 25322-0351*

HADEN, CLOVIS ROLAND, university administrator, engineering educator; b. Houston, Apr. 10, 1940; s. Clovis Newton and Mary Aline (Baker) H.; m. Joyce Elaine Weathers, Aug. 8, 1956; children: Cathy, Kimberly, Clay. Student, Navarro Jr. Coll., 1958-59; BSEE, U. Tex.-Arlington, 1961; MSEE, Calif. Inst. Tech., 1962; PhD, U. Tex., 1965. Asst. prof. U. Okla.,

1965-68; dir. Sch. Elec. Engring. and Computing Scis., 1972-78; asso. prof. Tex. A&M U., College Station, 1968-71, prof., 1971-72, dir. Inst. Solid State Electronics, 1969-72; dean Coll. Engring and Applied Scis. Ariz. State U., Tempe, 1978-87, 89-91, v.p. for acad. affairs, 1987-88; provost west campus Ariz. State U., Phoenix, 1988-89; mem. Research Park bd. Ariz. State U., Tempe, 1983-91; bd. dirs. Ariz. Transp. Research Ctr., 1980-91; vice chancellor for acad. affairs La. State U., Baton Rouge, 1991-93; vice chancellor/dean engring., dir. engring. experiment sta. Tex. A&M U., 1993—; mem. Gov.'s Commn. on Sci. and Tech., 1980-82, chmn. transp. subcom., 1981-83, mem. adv. coun. for engring., 1979-91; mem. Gov.'s High Tech. Coun., 1990-91; mem. Gov.'s Coun. Sci. & Tech., 1997—; chair strategic planning La. Ednl. Quality Support Fund, 1991-93; mem. Nat. Engring. Dean's Exec. Bd., 1984-87, 95—; mem. adv. group Coun. on Competitiveness, 1994-95; chmn. bd. Ariz. R&D Co., 1983-90; bd. dirs. Inter-tel, Wave Phore; adv. bd. A.T. Kearney, 1986-90; chair Engring. Dean's Coun. of Tex., 1995-98. Exec. editor: Electric Power Systems Research jour, 1978—. Bd. mgrs. Tempe YMCA, 1982-84; mem. Ariz. Econ. Devel. Bd., 1982-85; bd. dirs. Harrington Arthritis Rsch. Ctr., 1983-87, Square D. Co., 1985-91, E-Sys., 1994-95. Recipient George Washington Honor medal Freedoms Found., 1989, Disting. Alumnus award U. Tex., Arlington, 1995; Bur. Engring. rsch. fellow, 1964. Fellow IEEE (Oklahoma City Engr. of Yr. award 1977), Am. Soc. Engring. Edn. (Marlowe award 1998); mem. NSPE, Ariz. Soc. Profl. Engrs. (Engr. of Yr. award 1983), Ariz. Assn. Indsl. Devel., Coun. Tex. Engring. Deans (chmn. 1995-98), Tex. Soc. Profl. Engrs. (bd. dirs. 1995-98), Soc. Mfg. Engrs., Sigma Xi, Phi Kappa Phi, Eta Kappa Nu, Tau beta Pi. Republican. Mem. Ch. of Christ. Office: Tex A&M Univ Coll 301 Werc Engring Program College Station TX 77843

HADERLEIN, THOMAS M., lawyer; b. Chgo., Sept. 2, 1935. BSC, DePaul U., 1957; JD, Georgetown U., 1960, LLM, 1962. Bar: Ill. 1960, D.C. 1960. With Baker & McKenzie, Washington, 1959-64; ptnr. Baker & McKenzie, Chgo. Office: Baker & McKenzie One Prudential Plz 130 E Randolph St Ste 3700 Chicago IL 60601-6342*

HADGES, THOMAS RICHARD, media consultant; b. Brockton, Mass., Mar. 13, 1948; s. Samuel Charles and Ethel Toli (Prifti) H.; m. Beth Evelyn Rastad, Oct. 22, 1988. BA in Biology magna cum laude, Tufts U., 1969; student, Harvard Sch. Dental Med., 1969-71. Announcer Sta. WOKW, Brockton, 1965-67, Sta. WTBS-FM, MIT, Cambridge, 1966-68; announcer, program dir. Sta. WTUR, Medford, Mass., 1967-69; announcer Concert Network, Sta. WBCN-FM, Boston, 1968-78, program dir., 1977-78; program dir. Sta. WCOZ-FM, Blair Broadcasting, Boston, 1978-80, Sta. KLOS-FM, ABC, L.A., 1980-85; sr. programming advisor Pollack Media Group, Pacific Palisades, Calif., 1985-89, pres., 1989—; pres. Pollack/Hadges Enterprises, Pacific Palisades, 1985-89. Named Program Dir. of Yr., L.A. Times, 1981. Mem. Phi Beta Kappa. Avocations: jogging, electronics. Office: Pollack Media Group 860 Via De La Paz Ste D2 Pacific Palisades CA 90272-3663

HADIPRIONO, FABIAN CHRISTY, engineering educator, researcher; b. Cirebon, Java, Indonesia, Oct. 6, 1947; came to U.S., 1976; s. Robertus Sudarjo and Wertriani (Yoyoh) H. BCE, MCE, Parahyangan U., 1973; MS, U. Calif., Berkeley, 1978, M of Engring., 1980, DEng, 1982. Registered profl. engr., Ohio. Project engr. various design and constrn. cos., SE Asia, 1965-75; project mgr. Phoenix Inc., Jakarta, Indonesia, 1974-75; engr., asst. bd. dirs. Mahkota Group, Indonesia, 1975-77; instr., teaching assoc. U. Calif., Berkeley, 1981-82; asst. prof. civil and constrn. engring. and mgmt. Ohio State U., Columbus, 1982-89, assoc. prof. civil engring., constrn. engring. and mgmt., 1989—, prof. civil and constrn. engring. and mgmt., 1995—; tech. cons. various attys. at law for forensic engring. cases, 1984—; advisor to numerous constrn. cos. and univs. in Indonesia, 1984—; dir. Constrn. Lab. for Automation and System Simulation, Ohio State U., 1993—. Contbr. more than 160 articles to profl. jours.; presenter in field. Recipient Dale Carnegie Human Rels. award, 1976, Rsch. award Ohio State U. Coll. Engring., 1989, Lichtenstein Meml. award 1989; Ohio State U. grantee, 1985, 86, U.S. Army C.E. grantee, 1986, USAF fellow and grantee, 1986, Newhouse Found. fellow U. Calif., Berkeley, 1978, Harry H. Hilp fellow U. Calif., Berkeley, 1981, Robert B. Rothchild Jr. fellow U. Calif., Berkeley, 1982. Fellow ASCE; mem. NSPE, ASME, Internat. Assn. Bridge and Structural Engring., Am. Concrete Inst., Archtl. and Engring. Roman Catholic. Avocations: nature, cultural arts, classical music, tennis. Home and Office: Ohio State U 2070 Neil Ave Columbus OH 43210-1226

HADLEY, JANE BYINGTON, psychotherapist; b. N.Y.C., Apr. 24, 1929; d. David and Ruth (Johnson) Millar; m. Arthur Twining Hadley, Feb. 24, 1979; children: Elisabeth Jane Wheeler, Caroline Anne Thies. BA, U. Va., 1951; MA, Columbia U., 1967; analytic tng., Met. Ctr. for Mental Health, 1970-73. Intern Queens Coll., 1969; pvt. practice psychotherapy N.Y.C., 1971—. Mem. APA, Cosmopolitan Club, Century Assn. Democrat. Episcopalian.

HADLEY, JOHN BART, financial analyst; b. Oil City, Pa., Feb. 17, 1942; s. James Edward and Genevieve A. (Rowley) H.; B.A., Hiram Coll., 1964; M.B.A., (Samuel S. Fels scholar), U. Pa., 1967. Fin. analyst Westinghouse Electric Corp., Bloomington, Ind., 1967-69, mgr. fin. planning, Pitts., Tucson, Richmond, Va., 1969-71, staff asst. corporate fin. planning, Pitts., 1971-74; bus. analyst Farah Mfg. Co., El Paso, Tex., 1974-75, fin. analyst (Treasury), 1975-76, div. controller young men's and boys' div., 1976-77; chief agy. and fin. rev. U.S. Ry. Assn., Washington, 1977-79, chief fin. analysis, 1979-80, spl. asst. to dir. fin. analysis, 1980-82; mgr. ops. budgets NJTRO, 1982-85, mgr. capital budgets, 1986—. Mem. Inst. Mgmt. Accts., Transp. Research Forum, Chi Sigma Phi. Episcopalian. Clubs: Circle K (sec. 1963), Propeller (publicity coordinator 1966-67), Wharton Sch. Home: 52 Gill Ln # 1H Iselin NJ 08830-2850 Office: NJTRO 1160 Raymond Blvd Newark NJ 07102-4168

HADLEY, LEILA ELIOTT-BURTON (MRS. HENRY LUCE, III), author; b. N.Y.C., Sept. 22, 1925; d. Frank Vincent and Beatrice Boswell Eliott Burton; m. Arthur T. Hadley, II, Mar. 2, 1944 (div. Aug. 1946); 1 child, Arthur T. III; m. Yvor H. Smitter, Jan. 24, 1953 (div. Oct. 1969); children: Victoria C. Van D. Smitter Barlow, Matthew Smitter Eliott, Caroline Allison F.S. Nicholson; m. William C. Musham, May 1976 (div. July 1979); m. Henry Luce III, Jan. 1990. MD, St. Timothy's Sch., 1943. Author: Give Me the World, 1958, How to Travel with Children in Europe, 1963, Manners for Children, 1967, Fielding's Guide to Traveling with Children in Europe,1972, rev., 1974, 84, Traveling with Children in the U.S.A., 1974, Tibet-20 Years After the Chinese Takeover, 1979, (with Theodore B. Van Itallie) The Best Spas: Where to Go for Weight Loss, Fitness Programs and Pure Pleasure in the U.S. and Around the World, 1988, rev., 1989, A Journey with Elsa Cloud, 1997, Give Me the World, 1999; assoc. editor: Diplomat mag., N.Y.C., 1964-65, Saturday Evening Post, N.Y.C., 1965-67; editorial cons. TWYCH, N.Y.C., 1985-87; book reviewer Palm Beach Life, Fla., 1967-72; consulting editor: Tricyle, The Buddhist Rev., 1991—; garden columnist Fishers Island Gazette; contbr. articles to various newspapers, mags. Mem. bd. advisors Tricycle, the Buddhist Rev., 1991—; bd. dirs. Wings Trust, Inc., Tibet House, 1995, Fishers Island Conservancy, 1995. Mem. Acad. Am. Poets, Soc. Woman Geographers (exec. council 1984—), Authors Guild, Nat. Writers Union, Nat. Press Club, PEN, Explorers Club, Central Park Conservancy, N.Y. Acad. Medicine (guest bd.), Nat. Arts Club. Home: 4 Sutton Pl New York NY 10022-3056

HADLEY, LEONARD ANSON, appliance manufacturing corporation executive; b. Earlham, Iowa, July 4, 1934; s. Willard J. and Berneice (Cook) H.; children: Philip, Christine. Student Drake U., 1952-53; BSC in Acctg., U. Iowa, 1958. Cost acct. Maytag Co., Newton, Iowa, 1959-61, sr. cost acct., 1961-63, mktg. budget supr., 1964-67, mgr. budgets, 1967-75, asst. controller, 1975-79, v.p. corp. planning, 1979-86, pres., 1986-89; exec. v.p., pres. Appliance Group Maytag Corp., 1989-90, exec. v.p., COO, 1990-91, pres., COO, 1991, pres., CEO, 1992, chmn., CEO, 1993—; bd. dirs. Maytag Corp., Deere & Co., Norwest Bank, Snap-on Inc. Bd. visitors U. Iowa Bus. Sch., U. Iowa Found.; active Newton First United Meth. Ch. Served with U.S. Army, 1954-56. Mem. Newton C. of C., Iowa Bus. Coun. (chmn. 1998—), Nat. Assn. Mfrs., Iowa Coll. Found., Des Moines Club. Republican. Office: Maytag Corp 403 W 4th St N Newton IA 50208-3034

HADLEY, MARLIN LEROY, direct sales financial consultant; b. Mankato, Kans., Jan. 5, 1931; s. Charles LeRoy and Lillian Fern (Dunn) H.; m. Clarissa Jane Payne, Sept. 17, 1949; children: Michael LeRoy, Steven Lee. B.S., U. Denver, 1953; postgrad., Harvard U., 1966. Pres. Jewel Home Shopping Service div. Jewel Cos., Inc., Barrington, Ill., 1953-72; pres., chief exec. officer, dir. Beeline Fashions, Inc., Bensenville, Ill., 1972-82; chmn. bd. HAS Originals, Blairstown, NJ, 1984—; fin., bus. cons.; pres., dir. Beeline Real Estate Corp., Act II Jewelry, Inc., Home Galleries, Inc.; dir. Goulder Co., Inc., Climax Spltys., Inc. Club: Economics (Chgo.). Home and Office: 4298 W Lake Cir Littleton CO 80123

HADLEY, NANCY LYNNE, community foundation executive; b. Valhalla, N.Y., Mar. 1, 1951; d. Joseph and Emelia (Scavnicky) Nassetta; m. J. Dwight Hadley, May 13, 1978 (div. Aug. 1995); children: Stephen, Elizabeth. BA in Sociology and Urban Studies with honors, Manhattanville Coll., Purchase, N.Y., 1972. Asst. dir. Urban Renewal Agy., Ossining, N.Y., 1971-74; dir. cmty. devel. program Mayor's Office, Stamford, Conn., 1974-84; asst. commr. housing N.Y. State Divsn. Housing, Albany, 1984-91; dept. transportation commr. Conn. Dept. of Transportation, Newington, 1991-93; commr. Conn. Dept. of Motor Vehicles, Wethersfield, 1993-95; sr. program dir. Conn. multi-cities program Local Initiatives Support Corp., Hartford, 1995-96; exec. dir. Comty. Found. for Greater New Haven, Conn., 1996—; spkr. in field. *Nancy L. Hadley is the Community Foundation of Greater New Haven's fourth director in its 70-year history and the first woman director. The foundation is a donor services philanthropic organization that serves 21 towns in Greater New Haven. With over 20 years experience in community revitalization, Nancy brings a deep understanding of economic and community development issuesand a keen appreciation of the need for grassroots and policy innovation in tackling these issues. Prior to her appointment to the foundation, Ms. Hadley served in senior positions in local government as well as Governors Mario Cuomo, Lowell Weicker, and John Rowland's administrations.* Fellow Am. Leadership Forum (sr.); mem. Nat. Assn. Housing and Redevel. Officials, Conn. Women's Coun., N.Y. State Assn. Housing and Redevel. Officials, Women Transportation Seminar (founding mem. Conn. Valley chpt.), Conn. Coun. Philanthropy (bd. mem., chair mem. comm. 1998). Office: Cmty Found Grtr New Haven 70 Audubon St New Haven CT 06510-1248

HADLEY, PAUL BURREST, JR. (TABBIT HADLEY), domestic engineer, photographer; b. Louisville, Apr. 26, 1955; s. Paul Burrest and Rose Mary (Ruckert) H. Grad. in Computer Ops. and Programming, No. Ky. Vocat. Sch., 1975. Floor mgr. reconciling dept. Cen. Trust Co., Cin., 1974-76; freelance photographer Ky., Ohio, Colo., 1975—; chef mgr. The Floradora, Telluride, Colo., 1978-96; domestic engr. Telluride Resort Accomodations, 1996—; pres. Tabbit Enterprises; freelance recipe writer, Telluride, 1978—. Author poetry (Golden Poet award 1989, Silver Poet award 1990); actor: (plays) Of Mice and Men, The Exercise, Crawling Arnold, A Thousand Clowns, The Authentic Life of Billy The Kid, others. Actor The Plunge Players, Telluride; v.p. Telluride Coun. for Arts and Humanities, 1989. Mem. Plan Internat. USA, Christian Children's Fund. Avocations: mountain climbing, hiking, photography, travel. Home: PO Box 923 Telluride CO 81435-0923

HADLEY, PAUL ERVIN, international relations educator; b. South Ovid, Mich., July 17, 1914; s. Ervin C. and Viola M. (Barnes) H.; m. Virginia Faye Last, May 15, 1945; 1 dau., Deborah Faye. A.B., Occidental Coll., Los Angeles, 1934; A.M., U. So. Calif., 1946, Ph.D. in Comparative Lit, 1955; L.H.D., Nat. U., 1980. Tchr. El Monte (Calif.) Union High Sch., 1935-42; exec. sec. Centro Cultural Paraguayo Americano, Asunción, Paraguay, 1943-44; head Cultural Insts. unit U.S. Dept. State, Washington, 1945; instr. internat. relations U. So. Calif., Los Angeles, 1945-47; asst. prof. U. So. Calif., 1947-55, assoc. prof., 1955-64, prof., 1964-81, emeritus prof., 1981—, disting. emeritus prof., 1992; dean summer session, 1960-73; dean Coll. of Continuing Edn., 1966-73, assoc. v.p. acad. adminstrn., 1973-77, interim acad. v.p., 1975-77, acad. v.p., 1977-81, dir. emeriti ctr., 1997—; exec. sec. Inst. World Affairs, 1948-73, chmn. Pacific Coast Council Latin Am. Studies, 1956-57; mem. Woodrow Wilson Fellowship selection com. Region XV, 1960-67; fgn. leader and specialist program Am. Council on Edn., 1960-62; mem. State Com. on Continuing Edn., 1966-76; mem. adv. com. Servicemembers Opportunity Colls., 1978-81; chmn. edn. sect. Town Hall of Calif., 1965-68, chmn. internat. relations sect., 1969-71; trustee Latin Am. Scholarship Program Am. Univs., 1972-74; trustee So. Calif. Presbyn. Homes(chmn. 1988-89). Mem. Assn. Univ. Summer Sessions (pres. 1970-71), Inst. Internat. Edn. (adv. bd. West Coast region), Nat. U. Extension Assn. (chmn. region VI 1970-71, pres. 1976-77), Adult Educators Greater Los Angeles (chmn. 1970-71), Bd. Life Svcs. Inc., Phi Beta Kappa, Pi Sigma Alpha, Sigma Alpha Epsilon, Phi Kappa Phi. Presbyn. (elder, stated clk. Presbytery 1983-87). Home: 1230 E Windsor Rd Apt 305 Glendale CA 91205-2642

HADLEY, ROBERT JAMES, lawyer; b. Wilmington, Ohio, Oct. 27, 1938; s. Robert Edwin and Ethel Edith (Slade) H.; m. Judith Ellen Gilbert, Aug. 11, 1962; children: Scott, Laura, Stephen. BA in History cum laude, Ohio State U., 1960; LLB, Harvard U., 1963. Bar: Ohio 1963. Assoc. Smith & Schnacke, Dayton, 1963-69, ptnr., 1970-89; ptnr. Thompson, Hine and Flory, Dayton, 1989—. Pres. Man-to-Man Assocs., 1978-84, Dayton Habitat for Humanity, 1988; v.p. COPE Halfway House, Dayton, 1982-85; dir., sec. Friendship Village of Dayton, 1985—; bd. dirs. Cmty. Blood Ctr., Dayton, 1987—; loaned exec. United Way, 1980-82; mem. Kettering Civic Band, 1968—, v.p. Parish Resource Ctr., 1996-99, pres., 1999—; bd. dirs. South Cmty. YMCA, 1996-98, Greater Dayton Youth for Christ, 1980-86, Dayton Area Peace Accords Project; mem., treas. Ministry of Money bd., 1992—. Named Kettering Man of the Yr., 1986; Rotary Found. grantee, Israel, 1974. Mem. ABA, Ohio Bar Assn., Dayton Bar Assn., Dayton Racquet Club, Rotary (pres. Kettering 1986-87, dist. gov., group rep. Dist. 667 1989-90, dist. gov. 1993-94), Phi Beta Kappa. Republican. Methodist. Avocations: music, travel, sports. Home: 4848 Glenmina Dr Dayton OH 45440-2002 Office: Thompson Hine & Flory PO Box 8801 2000 Courthouse Plz NE Dayton OH 45401-8801

HADLEY, STANTON THOMAS, international manufacturing and marketing company executive, lawyer; b. Beloit, Kans., July 3, 1936; s. Robert Campbell and Helen (Schroeder) H.; m. Charlotte June Holmes, June 9, 1962; children: Gayle Elizabeth, Robert Edward, Stanton Thomas, Steven Holmes. B.S. in Metall. Engring., Colo. Sch. Mines, 1958; LL.B., U. Colo., 1962. Bar: Colo. 1962, U.S. Dist. Ct. 1962, U.S. Patent Office 1963. Metallurgist ASARCO, Leadville, Colo., 1957; tng. engr. Allis-Chalmers Co., West Allis, Wis., 1958-61; adminstrv. engr. Ball Corp., Boulder, Colo., 1961-62; atty. Ball Corp., 1962-65; patent counsel Scott Paper Co., Phila., 1965-71; patent counsel USG Corp., Chgo., 1971-76, gen. mgr. metals div., 1976-79, group v.p. indsl. group, 1979-84, sr. v.p. adminstrn., sec., 1984, sec., 1984-87, sr. v.p. staff services, 1987-89; pres. Ansco Photo-Optical Products Corp., Chgo., 1989-93, Visador Co., Marion, Va., 1994-98; bd. dirs. Masonite Corp., WJE Assocs. Inc., USG Found. Bd. dirs. Ill. Safety Council, North Suburban YMCA, Northbrook Symphony Orch.; former mem. founders' council Field Mus.; mem. Chgo. United, Chgo. Assn. Commerce and Industry. Served with U.S. Army, 1959. Mem. Am. Soc. Metals, Licensing Execs. Soc., Assn. Corp. Patent Counsel. Republican. Clubs: Union League, Sunset Ridge Country, Executives. Home: 555 Valley Way Northfield IL 60093-1067 Office: 5th Cons Northfield IL 60093

HADLEY, THERESA IGUICO, medical/surgical and psychiatric nurse; b. Seattle, Sept. 15, 1963; d. Alfredo Ignacio and Zenaida Bascara (Vinzon) Iguico. AS in Human Biology, Mesa Coll., 1984; BSN, San Diego State U., 1988. RN Calif.; cert. BCLS, ACLS. Staff nurse U.S. Naval Hosp., Camp Pendleton, Calif., 1988-91; staff nurse ICU and critical care unit Alvarado Hosp., San Diego, 1991-92; staff RN Specialty Med. Clinic, Inc., La Jolla, Calif., 1993-98; nurse Dermatology Assocs., LaJolla, Calif., 1998—. Lt. comdr. USNR, 1988—. Home: 12846 Pinefield Rd Poway CA 92064-1502

HADLEY, WILLIAM MELVIN, college dean; b. San Antonio, June 4, 1942; s. Arthur Roosevelt and Audrey Merle (Barrett) H.; m. Dorothy J. Hadley, Jan. 21, 1967 (div. July 1989); children: Heather Marie, William Arthur; m. Jane F. Walsh, Oct. 13, 1990. BS in Pharmacy, Purdue U., West Lafayette, Ind., 1967, MS in Pharmacology, 1971, PhD in Toxicology, 1972. Registered pharmacist, Ind. Teaching and grad. asst. Purdue U., West Lafayette, 1967-72; asst. prof. U. N.Mex., Albuquerque, 1972-76, assoc. prof., 1976-82, prof., 1982—, asst. dean Coll. Pharmacy, 1984-86, acting dean Coll. Pharmacy, 1985, dean Coll. Pharmacy, 1986—; vis. scientist Lovelace Inhalation Toxicology Inst., Albuquerque, 1981, adj. scientist, 1991—; mem. adv. bd. Waste Edn. Rsch. Consortium, Las Cruces, N.Mex., 1989—; mem. NIH Proposal Rev. Panels, Bethesda, Md., 1983-84; mem. Gov.'s PCB Expert Adv. Panel, Santa Fe, 1985-86; toxicology cons. numerous law firms N.Mex.; mem. sci. adv. bd. Carlsbad Environ. Monitoring Ctr., 1992-97; mem. sci. adv. com. S.W. Regional Spaceport, Las Cruces, 1992-94. Mem. steering com. United Fund, U.N.Mex., 1987, key person, 1988-97. NIH grantee, 1974-80, 83-87. Mem. AAAS, Am. Assn. Colls. of Pharmacy, Soc. Toxicology (pres. Rocky Mt. chpt. 1990-91), Western Pharmacology Soc., Southwestern Assn. Toxicologists. Achievements include research in biotransformation of xenobiotics with special emphasis on nasal tissue; the effects of heavy metals on biotransformation with emphasis on cadmium; the toxic effects of xenobiotics on the immune system. Office: U NMex Coll Pharmacy Albuquerque NM 87131

HADLOCK, PHILIP G., French language educator; b. Watertown, N.Y., Mar. 19, 1969; s. George Robert and Cynthia Eileen (Hitsman) H.; m. Jeanine S. Alesch, Apr. 8, 1995. BA, U. Mich., 1991; MA, U. Pa., 1993, PhD, 1997. Lectr. English, U. Lumière Lyon II, Lyons, France, 1994-95; lectr. French, U. Pa., Phila., 1997—. Mem. MLA, Soc. for Study Narrative Lit., Am. Assn. Tchrs. French. Avocation: downhill skiing. Office: U Pa 521 Williams Hall Philadelphia PA 19104-6305

HAEBERLE, ROSAMOND PAULINE, retired educator; b. Clearwater, Kans., Oct. 23, 1914; d. Albert Paul and Ella (Lough) H. BS in Music Edn., Kans. State U., 1936; MusM, Northwestern U., 1948; postgrad., Wayne State U., 1965-66. Profl. registered parliamentarian. Tchr. sch. dist., Plevna, Kans., 1936-37, Esbon, Kans., 1937-41, Frankfort, Kans., 1941-43, Garden City, Kans., 1943-44; music supr. sch. dist., Waterford Twp., Mich., 1944-47; tchr. sch. dist., Pontiac, Mich., 1947-80; ret. sch. dist., Pontiac, 1980; pres. Pontiac Fedn. Tchrs., 1961-63. Bd. dirs., ho. chmn. Pontiac-Oakland Symphony; bd. dirs. Pontiac Oakland Town Hall; adv. coun. Waterford Sr. Citizens, chmn., 1990-93; pres. Oakland County Pioneer and Hist. Soc., 1992-94. Recipient Tchrs. Day award Mich. State Fair, 1963. Mem. AAUW (pres. Pontiach br. 1970-72, founds. chair Pontiac br.), Mich. Fedn. Music Clubs (state pres. 1993-95, chmn. state bylaws and citations com., pres. Tuesday musicale of Pontiac 1984-86, pres. S.E. dist. 1986-90, chmn. Nat. Music Week northeastern region), Mich. Fedn. Bus. and Profl. Womens Club (Woman of Achievement award dist. IX 1994), Mich. DARS (state parliamentarian 1985-96), DAR (Gen. Richardson chpt., regent 1983-85, libr. and parliamentarian, Excellence in Cmty Svc. award 1995), Waterford-Clarkston Bus. and Profl. Womens Club (bylaws and parliamentarian), Pontiac Area Ret. Sch. Pers. (parliamentarian, pres. 1981-84), Mich. Assn. Retired Sch. Pers (Disting. Svc. award 1994), Mich. Bus. and Profl. Women's Club,(dir. dist. 10 1965-67), Pontiac Bus. and Profl. Women (pres. 1959-61), Pontiac Area Fedn. Women's Clubs (pres. 1976-78, 81-84), Mich. Registered Parliamentarians, Louise Saks Parliamentary Unit (pres. 1990-92), Bloomfield Rep. Women's Club (parliamentarian 1999-2000), Eastern Star, Mu Phi Epsilon, Beta Sigma Phi (life), Zeta Tau Alpha. Republican. Methodist. Avocations: travel, playing piano, reading, bell ringing.

HAEBERLE, WILLIAM LEROY, corporate director, business educator, entrepreneur; b. Marion County, Ind., Mar. 19, 1922; s. Louis Leroy and Marjorie Ellen (Jared) H.; m. Yvonne Carlton, June 17, 1947; children: Patricia, William C., David C. BS, Ind. U., 1943, MBA, 1947, DBA, 1952. Mem. faculty Ind. U., Bloomington, 1946—, prof. mgmt., 1963-85, prof. emeritus, 1985—; sr. fellow Johnson Ctr. for Entrpreneurship & Innovation, Kelly Sch. Bus. Indiana U., 1989—; pres., dir. Nat. Entrepreneurship Found., 1982—; bd. dirs. Ind. Inst. for New Bus. Ventures, Inc., 1983-91, Nat. Assn. Corp. Dirs., 1983-84; with Tternat. Consortium Univ. Exec. Edn. Dirs., 1972-73; chmn. Command Corp., 1996—, Stratigent Inc., 1998—, vice chmn. Prime Tech. Inc., 1994—, Syndicate Sales Inc., 1994—, Norcote Internat. Inc., 1994—, Impact Forge Inc., 1995—; dir. Wildbirds Unltd. Inc., 1995—, St. Elmo Inc., 1996—, Command Equity Group, 1969—; dir., pres. Cambridge Aircraft Leasing Co. Inc., 1998—. Capt. U.S. Army, 1943-46; lt. col. USAFR, 1947-82. Recipient Entrepreneur of Yr. award Ernst & Young, 1989, Entrepreneur of Yr., Inst. Hall of Fame. Mem. VFW, Air Force Assn., Res. Officers Assn. Sagamore of the Wabash, Am. Legion, Met. Club N.Y., Union League Club Chgo., Columbia Club Indpls., Sigma Alpha Epsilon. Office: 320 W 8th St Ste 100 Bloomington IN 47404-3700

HAEFELE, EDWIN THEODORE, political theorist, consultant; b. Burnt Prairie, Ill., Oct. 5, 1925; s. Monroe Edwin and Lola Amanda (Coles) H.; m. Ruth Anne Woods, Dec. 23, 1948; children: Ann Katherine, Douglas Monroe, John Joseph. Student, Mich. State U., 1943, Ill. Wesleyan U., 1946-48, U. Chgo., 1948-50. Staff asst. Pub. Adminstrn. Clearing House, Chgo., 1951-54; asst. dir. Transp. Center, Northwestern U., 1954-62; mem. sr. staff Brookings Instn., Washington, 1962-67; mem. sr. research staff Resources for Future, Inc., Washington, 1967-73; prof. polit. sci. U. Pa., Phila., 1973-82, prof. emeritus, 1982-84, 88—; prof., chmn. dept. polit. sci. U. Pa., 1985-88; exec. v.p. Consortium of Govtl. Counselors Inc., 1989-96. Author: Government Controls on Transport, 1965, Representative Government and Environmental Management, 1973; editor: Transport and National Goals, 1967, The Governance of Common Property Resources, 1974, What Constitutes the American Republic?, 1993. Served with AUS, 1943-46. Decorated Purple Heart, Presdl. Unit citation. Republican. Congregationalist. Home: 1215 Box Butte Ave Alliance NE 69301-2522

HAEGELE, JOHN ERNEST, business executive; b. Phila., July 11, 1941; s. Ernest F. and Cecilia (Wheeler) H.; m. Victoria J. Brasten, July 31, 1965; children: John, Scott, Lisa. B.S. Drexel U. in Acctg. and Fin., 1964. C.P.A., N.Y. Acct. Arthur Young & Co., N.Y.C., 1964-68, mgr., 1968-71; asst. controller Indian Head Inc., N.Y.C., 1971-76, v.p., controller, 1976-82; exec. v.p. dir. Interpool, Ltd., N.Y.C., 1982-85, chmn., chief exec. officer, 1987-88; sr. v.p. fin. TBG Group, N.Y.C., 1985-87, exec. v.p., 1988-92; pres., COO TBG Group, Inc., N.Y.C., Monte Carlo, 1992-96; chmn. bd. dirs., CEO TBG Industries Inc., N.Y.C., 1997—, TriPoint Global Comm. Inc., 1998—. Mem. bus. sch. adv. bd. Drexel U. Served with U.S. Army, 1964-69. Mem. AICPA, N.Y. Soc. CPAs. Republican. Roman Catholic.

HAEGI, MARCEL, scientist, physicist; b. Geneva, Oct. 29, 1931; arrived in Italy, 1962; s. Emile and Rosa (Voegeli) H.; m. Sybilla Kool, Apr. 14, 1961; children: Vlasta, Anita, Eric, Tamara. D in Phys. Scis., U. Geneva, Switzerland, 1968. Cert. thermonuclear physicist. Scientist Univ. Geneva, Switzerland, 1960-62; scientist Euratom, Brussels, 1962-78, prin. scientist, 1978—; cons. Inst. Parliamentary Studies, Rome, 1992—. Guest editor Fusion Tech., 1994; contbr. articles to profl. jours. Pres. European Fedn. Rd. Crash Victims, Geneva, 1991—. Mem. Swiss Phys. Soc., European Phys. Soc. E-Mail: mhaegi@pelagus.it. Home: via del Piscaro No 4, I-00044 Frascati Italy Office: Euratom-ENEA, via Enrico Fermi 27, I-00044 Frascati Italy

HAEMMELMANN, KEITH ALAN, minister; b. Billings, Mont., Jan. 5, 1956; s. Herbert Carl and Edna Francis (Pfeif) H.; m. Jeanne Louise Thorman, Dec. 28, 1978; children: Kevin, Katie, Kelli. BA summa cum laude, Whitworth Coll., 1978; MDiv summa cum laude, Andover/Newton Seminary, Boston, 1982; D in Ministry cum laude, McCormick Seminary, Chgo., 1993. Ordained to ministry United Ch. of Christ, 1982; cert. clin. pastoral educator. Christian edn. dir. Congregational Ch. United Ch. of Christ, Burlington, Mass., 1979-82; minister Wiggins (Colo.) Community Ch., 1982-85; sr. minister Faith United Ch. of Christ, Windsor, Colo., 1985-92, First Congl. Ch. United Ch. of Christ, Crystal Lake, Ill., 1992—; moderator Northeast Assn. of Rocky Mountain Conf. United Ch. of Christ, 1991; del. Gen. Synod of the United Ch. of Christ, 1989-91; chmn. ch. and ministry com., pers. com. of the Rocky Mountain Conf., United Ch. of Christ, 1991; treas. Windsor (Colo.) Ministerial Alliance; mem. Evangelism bd. Ill. Conf., United Ch. Christ; adj. faculty Andover-Newton Theol. Sch., 1998-99. Bd. dirs. Weld County Referral Svc. for the Homeless, Greeley, Colo., 1989—, Good Shepherd Hosp., 1996—; founder Computers-for-Kids Program, Crystal Lake. Recipient Peace and Justice award for Parish Ministry, Office for Ch. in Soc., United Ch. of Christ, 1989. Home: 1287 Knollwood Cir Crystal Lake IL 60014-1815 Office: First Congl Ch UCC 401 Country Club Rd Crystal Lake IL 60014-5605 *The greatest challenge of the Church in the years ahead is to cease being reactive and begin to be proactive in our ministries. Only in this way will we shape our culture rather than allowing our culture to shape us!.*

HAENICKE, DIETHER HANS, university president emeritus, educator; b. Hagen, Germany, May 19, 1935; came to U.S., 1963, naturalized, 1972; s. Erwin Otto and Helene (Wildfang) H.; m. Carol Ann Colditz, Sept. 29, 1962; children: Jennifer Ruth, Kurt Robert. Student, U. Gottingen, 1955-56, U. Marburg, 1957-59; Ph.D. magna cum laude in German Lit. and Philology, U. Munich, 1962; DHL (hon.), Cen. Mich. U., 1986; DHL, We. Mich. U., 1998. Asst. prof. Wayne State U., Detroit, 1963-68; assoc. prof. Wayne State U., 1968-72, prof. German, 1972-78, resident dir. Jr. Year in Freiburg (Ger.), 1965-66, 69-70, dir. Jr. Year Abroad programs, 1970-75, chmn. dept. Romance and Germanic langs. and lits., 1971-72, assoc. dean Coll. Liberal Arts, 1972-75, provost, 1975-77, v.p., provost, 1977-78; dean Coll. Humanities Ohio State U., 1978-82, v.p. acad. affairs, provost, 1982-85; pres. Western Mich. U., Kalamazoo, 1985—; asst. prof. Colby Coll. Summer Sch. of Langs., 1964-65; lectr. Internationale Ferienkurse, U. Freiburg, summers 1961, 66, 67. Author: (with Horst S. Daemmrich) The Challenge of German Literature, 1971, Untersuchungen zum Versepos des 20. Jahrhunderts, 1962; editor: Liebesgeschichte der schonen Magelone, 1969, Der blonde Eckbert und andere Novellen, 1969, Franz Sternbalds Wanderungen, 1970; contbr. articles to acad. and lit. jours. Fulbright scholar, 1963-65. Mem. MLA, AAUP, Am. Assn. Tchrs. of German, Mich. Acad. Arts and Scis., Phi Beta Kappa. Office: Western Mich U 3019 Waldo Library Kalamazoo MI 49008-3804

HAENSEL, VLADIMIR, chemical engineering educator; b. Freiburg, Germany, Sept. 1, 1914; came to U.S., 1930; s. Paul and Nina (Tugenhold) H.; m. Mary Magraw, Aug. 28, 1939 (dec. 1979); children: Mary Ann (Mrs. Michael J. Ahlen, dec. 1982), Kathee Webster; m. Hertha Skala, Sept. 14, 1986. BS, Northwestern U., 1935, PhD, 1941, DSc, 1957; MS, MIT, 1939; DSc (hon.), U. Wis., Milw., 1979. Rsch. chemist Universal Oil Products Co. (name changed to UOP Inc.), Des Plaines, Ill., 1937-64, v.p., dir. rsch., 1964-72, v.p. sci. and tech., 1972-79, cons., 1979—; prof. U. Mass., Amherst, 1979—, now prof. emeritus. Contbg. author several sci. books; contbr. more than 120 articles to profl. jours.; patentee in field. Recipient Chgo. Jr. C. of C. award, 1944, Precision Sci. Co. award in Petrolem Chemistry, 1952, Profl. award AIChE, 1957, Indsl. and Engring. Chemistry award Esso Rsch. and Engr. Co., 1965, Modern Pioneers in Creative Industry award Nat. Assn. Mfrs., 1965, Chem. Pioneer award Am. Inst. Chemists, 1967, Perkin medal, 1967, Nat. Medal Sci., 1973, Eugene J. Houdry award in Applied Catalysis, 1977, Henry J. Albert award Internat. Precious Metal Inst., 1993. Mem. NAS (award for chemistry in svc. to soc. 1991), NAE (Charles Stark Draper prize 1997), ACS, AIChE, Catalysis Soc., Sigma Xi, Phi Lambda Upsilon, Tau Beta Pi. Home: 83 Larkspur Dr Amherst MA 01002-3438 Office: U Mass Dept Chem Engring Amherst MA 01003*

HAENSLY, PATRICIA ANASTACIA, psychology educator; b. Kronenwetter, Wis., Dec. 4, 1928; d. Paul Frank and Valeria (Woyak) Banach; m. William E. Haensly, 1954; children: Paul, Robert, Thomas, James, John, David, Mary, Katherine. BS, Lawrence U., 1950; MS in Genetics, Iowa State U., 1953; PhD in Ednl. & Devel. Psychology, Tex. A&M U., 1982. Histo technique specialist dept. vet. pathology Iowa State U., Ames, 1958-63; asst. prof. dept. ednl. psychology Tex. A&M U., College Station, 1982-97; instr. Blinn Jr. Coll., College Station; prin. Investigator Project Mustard Seed, U.S.D.O.E. Javits Grant, 1993-96; assoc. dir. programs Inst. for Gifted and Talented Tex. A&M U., College Station, dir. summer presch. program Minds Alive, 1987-95; mem. adj. faculty psychology We. Wash. U., Bellingham, 1996—. Contbd. editor Roeper Rev., 1996—; contbr. articles to profl. jours., chpts. to books; mem. editl. bd. Gifted Child Quar., 1996—, Gifted Child Today, 1997—. alt. U.S. del. World Coun. Gifted and Talented Children, 1997-99, del., 1999—; del. People to People amb. program Pacific N.W. Initiative to the People's Rep. of China., 1998. Recipient Outstanding Woman award AAUW, 1980, Govt. Rsch. Javits grante, 1993-96, Hon. Mention Hollingworth award Intertel Found., 1993. Mem. Tex. Assn. for Gifted and Talented (1st v.p. 1988, 89, editor news mag. 1988, 89), Nat. Assn. Gifted Children (co-chmn. rsch. and evaluation com. 1985-87, John Curtis Gowan Rsch. award 1981, program chair Conceptual Found. divsn. 1997—), World Coun. for Gifted and Talented Children, Inc., Soc. for Rsch. in Child Devel., Coun. for Exceptional Children, Assn. for Childhood Edn. Internat., Am. Creativity Assn. (charter), Am. Psychol. Soc., Phi Kappa Phi. Home: 3384 Northgate Rd Bellingham WA 98226-9263

HAERER, CAROL, artist; b. Salina, Kans., Jan. 23, 1933; d. Alfred Vesper and Helen Margaret (Bozarth) H.; m. Philip W. Wofford, Nov. 1962; 1 child, Sara Gwyn Haerer-Wofford. Student, Doane Coll., 1950-51; BFA cum laude, U. Nebr., 1954; student, Chgo. Art Inst., Summers 1952, 53; MA, U. Calif., Berkeley, 1958. Dir., instr. Summer Painting Workshop, Bennington Coll., 1976-80; dir. Hand Hollow Artists' Found., 1984; lectr. NYU, 1964-69; instr. art Bennington (Vt.) Coll., 1973-85, 86, U. Vt., Burlington, 1980; prof. art Fordam U., N.Y.C., 1986-90. One-person shows include Galerie Prismes, Paris, 1956, Berkeley Gallery, Calif. 1958, Albright Coll., Reading, Pa., 1964, Max Hutchinson Gallery, N.Y.C., 1971, 73, Bennington (Vt.) Coll., 1978, Landmark Gallery, N.Y.C., 1979, Oscarsson-Hood Gallery, N.Y.C., 1981, 83, Sherkat Gallery, N.Y.C., 1988, Albany Ctr. Galleries, N.Y., 1993, So. Vt. Art Ctr., Manchester, Vt., 1995, Doane Coll., Crete, Nebr., 1996, Colburn Gallery, U. Vt., Burlington, 1996, No.B.I.A.S. Gallery, North Bennington, Vt., 1996, Sheldon Meml. Art Galleries, U. Nebr., 1998, Salina (Kans.) Art Ctr, 1998, Mitchel Algus Gallery, N.Y.C., 1999; group shows include Whitney Mus. Ann., N.Y.C., 1970, 72, Syracuse (N.Y.) U. Mus., 1977, Bklyn. Mus., 1980-81, Berkshire Mus., Pittsfield, Mass., 1981, 82, 85, Artists Space, N.Y.C., 1990, SUNY-Albany, 1991, Williams Coll. Mus. Art, 1991, Gibbs Mus., Charleston, S.C., 1992, Inst. Progressive Art, Boston, 1994, Helen Cevern Gallery, N.Y.C., 1994, Boulder (Colo.) Mus. Contemporary Art, 1995, Bennington Coll., 1997, Eighth Floor Gallery, N.Y.C., 1997, Mitchell Algus Gallery, N.Y.C., 1998, Dartmouth Coll. Hanover, N.H., 1999; represented in numerous permanent pvt. and mus. collections including, Guggenheim Mus., N.Y.C., Whitney Mus., N.Y.C., Bklyn. Mus., Oakland Art Mus. (Calif.), Sheldon Art Galleries, U. Nebr., Lincoln, Williams Coll. Mus. of Art, Williamstown, Mass., U. Kans. Mus. Art, Kans. State Art Mus., Albany (N.Y.) Inst. History and Art. Fulbright scholar Paris, 1954; Woolley fellow Paris, 1955, MacDowell Colony fellow, 1969, 79, Guggenheim fellow, 1988; Yaddo resident, 1982; NEA grantee, 1985. Home: 90 Bedford St New York NY 10014-3764

HAERER, DEANE NORMAN, marketing and public relations executive; b. N.Y.C., Feb. 14, 1935; s. Frederick Sidney and Florence Agnes (Jackson) H.; m. Polly Ann Dunn, Feb. 24, 1961; children: Jennifer A., Heather J. AA, Boston U., 1955, BS, 1957, cert. achievement U. Iowa, 1979. Account exec. pub. rels. and advt. Charles Abbott Assos., Inc., N.Y.C., 1957-60; dir. alumni, community and ch. rels. Iowa Wesleyan Coll., 1960-61; tech. editor J.I. Case Co., Burlington, Iowa, 1961-64; dir. publs., asst. dir. pub. rels. Drake U., 1964-68; v.p. pub. rels. account supr. Thomas Wolff Assocs., Des Moines, 1968; dir. sch.-community rels. Des Moines Pub. Sch. System, 1968-74; dir. mktg. communications and corp. pub. rels. Stanley Cons., Inc., Muscatine, Iowa, 1974-78, dir. corp. pub. rels. and mktg. svcs., 1978-82; dir. mktg. svcs. Howard Needles Tammen & Bergendoff, Kansas City, Mo., 1982-84; vice pres., dir. corp. mktg. Robert E. McKee, Inc., 1984-88, pres., chief exec. officer Haerer, Stoltz & Assocs., Inc., Dallas, 1988-90; prin., mgmt. cons. Haerer & Assocs. Inc., Dallas, 1990-95; v.p. corp. mktg. Price Consulting, Inc., Dallas, 1995-97; sen. v.p., cons., The Arnold Price Joint Venture, guest lectr. Sch. Journalism, Drake U., 1970-74, U. Iowa, 1974-78. Bd. dirs. Heart of the Hawkeye coun. Camp Fire Girls, Des Moines, 1969-72. Recipient 1st place publ. award Univ. div. Mid-Am. Conf., Am. Coll. Pub. Rels. Assn., 1965, 66; nat. awards outstanding ednl. publs. Nations Schs. and Sch. Mgmt. mags., 1972, 73. Mem. Pub. Rels. Soc. Am. (accredited; charter mem., co-founder, past pres. and dir. Iowa chpt.; charter mem., co-founder, del. assembly, past chpt. dirand v.p. Quad Cities chpt.), Nat. Sch. Pub. Rels. Assn., Acad. Am. Educators, Soc. Mktg. Profl. Svcs., Am. Mktg. Assn., Tex. Indsl. Devel. Coun., So. Indsl. Devel. Coun., Pub. Rels. Soc. Am., Soc. Am. Mil. Engrs. Nat. Alumni Coun. of Boston U. Contbr. articles profl. publs. Home: 17 Cypress Ct Trophy Club TX 76262-5543

HAERING, EDWIN RAYMOND, chemical engineering educator, consultant; b. Columbus, Ohio, Dec. 8, 1932; s. Edwin Jacob and Mary Mildred (Kunst) H.; m. Suzanne Rowe, June 9, 1956; children: Cynthia, David Arthur, Elizabeth. BChemE, Ohio State U., 1956, MS, 1956, PhD, 1966. Mem. faculty Ohio State U., Columbus, 1959-91, assoc. prof., 1973-82, prof. chem. engring., 1982-91, prof. emeritus, 1991—, vice chmn. dept., 1974-76, chmn. dept., 1977-78; cons. in field, 1966—. Author: Laboratory Manual for Unit Operations Laboratory, 1980; also tech. articles to profl. jours. Lt. (j.g.) USNR, 1956-59. NROTC scholar, 1951-56, Dow Chem. Co. scholar, 1956; Keppers tchg. fellow, 1962. Mem. AIChE (treas. Cen. Ohio sect. 1974-79), Am. Chem. Soc., Port Clinton Power Squadron, Sigma Xi, Tau Beta Pi, Ohio State U. Faculty Club (pres. 1988-89), Bay Point, Columbus Maennerrhor Club, Yacht Club, Lake Erie Shouth Shore Hunter Sailing Assn. (treas. 1997-99). Avocations: golf, gardening, sailing. Home: 701 Stoutenberg Dr Marblehead OH 43440-2049 Office: Ohio State Univ Dept Chem Engring 701 Stoutenberg Dr Marblehead OH 43440-2049

HAERLE, PAUL RAYMOND, judge; b. Portland, Oreg., Jan. 10, 1932; s. George William and Grace (Soden) H.; m. Susan Ann Wagner, May 30, 1953 (div. Apr. 1973); children: Karen A. Haerle D'Or, David A.; m. Michele A. Monson, June 1, 1991. AB, Yale U., 1953; JD, U. Mich., 1956. Bar: Calif. 1956, U.S. Supreme Ct. 1962. Assoc. Thelen, Marrin, Johnson & Bridges, San Francisco, 1956-64, ptnr., 1965-67, 69-94, mng. ptnr., 1990-93; appointments sec. Office of Gov., State of Calif., Sacramento, 1967-69; assoc. justice Calif. Ct. Appeal (1st dist.), San Francisco, 1994—; lawyer rep. 9th Cir. Jud. Conf., 1985-88. Editor-in-chief Mich. Law Rev., 1955-56. Presdl. elector, 1972; del. Rep. Nat. Conv., 1972; vice chmn. Calif. Rep. Com., 1973-75, chmn., 1975-77; mem. Rep. Nat. Com., 1975-77; trustee World Affairs Coun. No. Calif., 1994—. Fellow Am. Coll. Trial Lawyers; mem. Tiburon Peninsula Club, Yale Club of San Francisco, Order of Coif. Avocations: tennis, travel, hiking. Office: Calif Ct Appeal 350 McAllister St San Francisco CA 94102-3600

HAERTLING, GENE HENRY, ceramic engineering educator; b. Old Appleton, Mo., Mar. 15, 1932; married, 1958; 3 children. BS, U. Mo., Rolla, 1954; MS, U. Ill., 1960, PhD in Ceramics, 1961. Rsch. ceramic engr. Ipsen Ceramics Inc., 1954-55, plant engr. ceramics devel., 1957-58; staff ceramics rsch. Sandia Corp., 1961-65, divsn. supr. elec. ceramics R&D, 1965-73; pres. Optoceram, Inc., Albuquerque, 1973-74; mgr. opto-ceramics dept. Motorola Inc., 1974-80, officer tech. staff, 1980-87; prof. ceramic engring. Clemson U., 1989-96, prof. emeritus, 1997—. Recipient R&D 100 award 1995. Fellow IEEE, Am. Ceramic Soc.; mem. NAE, Nat. Inst. Ceramic Engrs. (Pace award 1972). Achievements include research in electrooptic ceramics, oxide ceramics, ferroelectrics. Address: 9512 Layton Pl NE Albuquerque NM 87111-1368*

HAESSLE, JEAN-MARIE GEORGES, artist; b. Buhl/Haut/Rhin, France, Sept. 12, 1939; came to U.S., 1967; s. Georges and Marguerite H. Student, Ecole Nationale des Beaux Arts, Paris, France, 1965-67, Ecole de la Grande Chaumiere, Paris, 1966-67. Painter Paris, 1965-67, N.Y.C., 1967—. One man shows include Panoras Gallery, N.Y.C., 1968, West Broadway Gallery, N.Y.C., 1973, Atlantic Gallery, Washington, 1979, Nat. Acad. Sci., Washington, 1979, RR Gallery, N.Y.C., 1980, Gabrielle Bryers Gallery, N.Y.C., 1981, Kerr Gallery, N.Y.C., 1984-85, Little John-Smith Gallery, N.Y.C., 1986, Lucien Durand Galerie, Paris, 1987-91; exhibited in groups shows U.S. and abroad including Salon de la Jeune Peinture, Musee d'Art Moderne, Paris, 1968, Palace of Fine Arts, Mexico City, 1972, Aldrich Mus. Contemporary Art, Ridgefield, Conn., 1978; represented in permanent collections U.S. and abroad including So. Ill. U., Edwardsville, Bank of N.Y., N.Y.C., Atlantic-Richfield, Los Angeles, Am. Express, Fla., IBM, Los Angeles, Exxon, Fla., Chase Manhattan Bank, Los Angeles, Citibank, Los Angeles, Owen Corning Fiberglass, Toledo; works reviewed in profl. and popular publs. Roman Catholic. Home: 106112 Spring St New York NY 10012

HAFEMEISTER, DAVID WALTER, physicist; b. Chgo., July 1, 1934; s. Lester David and Alma Doris (Schmidt) H.; m. Gina Rohlander, June 10, 1961; children: Andrew, Jason, Heidi. MS in Physics, U. Ill., 1959, PhD in Physics, 1964. Asst. prof. physics Carnegie-Mellon U., Pitts., 1966-69; prof. physics Calif. Poly. State U., San Luis Obispo, 1969—; sci. advisor Sen. John Glenn U.S. Senate, Washington, 1975-77; spl. asst. to Under Sec. State Benson and Nye U.S. State Dept., Washington, 1977-79; vis. scientist U. Groningen, The Netherlands, 1971, 80, Program Sci. Tech. in Internat. Security, MIT, Cambridge, 1983-84, Ctr. for Bldg. Scis. Lawrence Berkeley (Calif.) Lab., 1985-86, Office Strategic Nuc. Policy U.S. Dept. State, 1987, Ctr. Internat. Security and Arms Control Stanford U., 1988; program on nuc. policy alternatives Princeton U., 1989; mem. profl. staff Senate Fgn. Rels. Com., 1990-92; staff Senate Gov. Affairs Com., 1992-93, Sch. Pub. Affairs, U. Md., 1996; Foster fellow Office of Strategic Negotiations, U.S. Arms Control and Disarmament Agy., 1997-98. Co-author: Physics of Modern Architecture, 1983; co-editor: Energy Sources: Conservation and Renewables, 1985, Arms Control Verification, 1986, Nuclear Arms Technologies in the 1990s, 1988, Physics and Nuclear Arms Today, 1990, Global Warning: Physics and Facts, 1991, Biological Effects of Low-Frequency Electromagnetic Fields, 1988. Grantee Levinson Found. Fellow Am. Phys. Soc. (chmn. forum on physics and soc. 1985-86, chair panel on pub. affairs 1996, Leo Szilard award for Physics in the Pub. Interest 1996); mem. AAAS (congl. fellow 1975-76, arms control fellow 1987), Fedn. Am. Scientists, Arms Control Assn., Am. Inst. Physics (co-editor books). Home: 553 Serrano Dr San Luis Obispo CA 93405-1758 Office: Calif Poly U Dept Physics San Luis Obispo CA 93407

HAFENSTEIN, NORMA LU, educator, administrator; b. Topeka, Jan. 24, 1957; d. Arnold William and Lola Frances (Barger) H.; m. Keith Douglas Holmes, Feb. 14, 1988; children: Claire Dorianne, Austin William. BS in Edn., Emporia State U., 1979; MS, Kans. State U., 1980; postgrad., U. Kans., 1981-83; PhD, U. Denver, 1986. Tchr. lang. arts and art St. George (Kans.) Jr. H.S., 1979-80; gifted facilitator Leavenworth County (Kans.) Spl. Edn. Coop., 1980-83; grad. rsch. asst. sch. edn. U. Denver, Denver, 1983-84, program dir. Univ. for Youth, 1984-86, asst. prof. edn., 1984—, dir. Ricks Ctr. for Gifted Children, 1984—; cons. on gifted edn. nationwide, 1980—; commr. math., sci. and tech. State of Colo., Denver, 1990-92; presenter regional, nat. and internat. confs. Contbr. articles to profl. jours., chpts. to books. Supporter Women's Found. of Colo., Denver, 1989—, The Safehouse, Denver, 1989—. Ctr. for Internationalization grantee U. Denver, 1992, 93, 94. Mem. ASCD, Am. Ednl. Rsch. Assn., Nat. Assn. for Gifted Children (presch./primary co-chair 1985-87, program chair 1994—, com. chair 1996-97). Office: U Denver Ricks Ctr Gifted Children 2040 S York St Denver CO 80210-4310

HAFER, BARBARA, state official; b. L.A., Aug. 1, 1943. BS, Duquesne U., Pitts., 1969; postgrad., U. Pitts., U. London. Auditor State of Pa., Harrisburg, 1992-96, auditor gen., 1996-97, 1989—. Office: State of Pennsylvania Treasury Dept 129 Finance Building Harrisburg PA 17120-0018

HAFER, FREDERICK DOUGLASS, utility executive; b. West Reading, Pa., Mar. 12, 1941; s. Charles Frederick and Irene Naugle (Renninger) H.; m. Martha Louise Gartner, Apr. 6, 1963; children: Frederick, Craig, Keith. Student, Drexel Inst. Tech., 1959-62; LHD, Alvernia Coll., 1993. With Met. Edison Co., Reading, Pa., 1962-68; with Gen. Pub. Utilities Corp., N.Y.C., 1968-78, asst. treas., 1970, treas., 1970-78; v.p. rates GPU Service Corp., 1977-86; v.p. Met. Edison Co., Pa. Electric Co., 1982-86; pres. Met. Edison Co., 1986—; pres., CEO, chmn. bd. Pa. Electric Co., 1994—, also bd. dirs.; bd. dirs. Met. Edison Co., Pa. Electric Co., GPU Service Corp., GPU Nuclear Corp., Utilities Mut. Ins. Co., Meridian Bancorp, Inc., Meridian Bank. Bd. dirs. Reading Hosp. and Med. Ctr., Leadership Pa., Found. For Drug-Free Pa., Berks Festivals, Inc., Berks Bus.-Edn. Coalition, Kutztown U. Found.; trustee Wyomissing Found., Caron Found. Mem. Berks County C. of C. (formely bd. dirs.), Mfrs. Assn. Berks County (bd. dirs.), Pa. Electric Assn. (exec. com.). Club: Berkshire Country. Office: GPU Svc 100 Interpace Pkwy Parsippany NJ 07054-1149*

HAFER, JOSEPH PAGE, lawyer; b. Harrisburg, Pa., June 28, 1941; s. George Horace and Betty (Page) H.; children: Bradford G., Susan P., David E. AB, Lafayette Coll., 1963; JD with distinction, U. Mich., 1966. Bar: Pa. 1966, U.S. Dist. Ct. (mid. dist.) Pa. 1966, U.S. Supreme Ct. 1969, U.S. Ct. Appeals (3d cir.) 1976. Assoc. Metzger, Hafer, Keefer, Thomas & Wood, Harrisburg, 1966-77; mng. ptnr. Thomas, Thomas & Hafer, Harrisburg, 1977—; adj. prof. law Dickinson Law Sch., Carlisle, Pa. Pres. Cumberland Valley Sch. Bd., Mechanicsburg, Pa., 1976-85; pres. Hampden Twp. Rep. Assn., Camp Hill, Pa. Fellow Am. Coll. Trial Lawyers; mem. ABA, Pa. Bar Assn., Assn. Trial Lawyers Am., Pa. Trial Lawyers Assn., Dauphin County Bar Assn. (ct. rels. com.). Methodist. Home: 1530 Waterford Camp Hill PA 17011-1229 Office: Thomas Thomas & Hafer PO Box 999 Harrisburg PA 17108-0999

HAFETS, RICHARD JAY, lawyer; b. N.Y.C., Apr. 23, 1951; s. Meyer Hafets and Marilyn (Glanzrock) Bell; m. Claire Margolis, June 18, 1972; children: Brooke, Amy. BS in Bus. summa cum laude, Am. U., Washington, 1973, JD magna cum laude, 1976. Bar: Md. 1976, U. S. Dist. Ct. Md. 1976, U.S. Ct. Appeals (4th cir.) 1976, U.S. Supreme Ct. 1981, D.C. 1997, U.S. Dist. Ct. (D.C.) 1997. Assoc. Piper & Marbury, Balt., 1976-84, ptnr., 1984—, chmn. labor and employment practice, 1990—, chmn. hiring and assoc. coms., 1988-91. Labor atty. Balt. Symphony Orch., 1986-93; bd. dirs., gen. counsel Am. Cancer Soc., Balt., 1983-89; bd. dirs. Md. Ballet, Balt., 1978-80. Mem. ABA, Md. Bar Assn., Balt. City Bar Assn., Order of Coif. Avocations: horses, skiing. Home: 7346 Narrow Wind Way Columbia MD 21046-1262 Office: Piper & Marbury 36 S Charles St Baltimore MD 21201-3020

HAFEY, JOSEPH MICHAEL, health association executive; b. Annapolis, Md., June 25, 1943; s. Edward Earl Joseph and Verna (Hedlund) H.; m. Mary Kay Miller, Dec. 30, 1978; children: Erin Catherine, Ryan Michael. BA, Whittier Coll., 1965; MPA, UCLA, 1967. Sr. asst. health officer HHS, Washington, 1967-69; dir. govt. relations Alliance for Regional Community Health, St. Louis, 1969-71; exec. dir. Contra Costa Comprehensive Health Assn., Richmond, Calif., 1971-74, Bay Area Comprehensive Health Planning Coun., San Francisco, 1974-76, Western Ctr. for Health Planning, San Francisco, 1976-86, Western Consortium for Pub. Health, Berkeley, 1980-95; pres., CEO Pub. Health Inst. (formerly Calif. Pub. Health Found.), 1985—; chmn. Contra Costa Pub. Health Adv. Body, Martinez, Calif., 1987-93; founder Calif. Coalition for Future of Pub. Health, Sacramento, 1988—; co-founder Calif. Healthy Cities Program, Berkeley, 1987—. Chmn. United Way Com. for the Uninsured, San Francisco, 1985-93; bd. dirs. Eugene O'Neill Found., 1980-89. With USPHS, 1967-69. Recipient fellowship WHO, Geneva, 1987. Mem. Am. Pub. Health Assn. (governing coun. 1984-87), Am. Health Planning Assn. bd. dirs., chmn. annual meeting 1982). Avocations: jogging, tennis, skiing, collecting political campaign buttons. Home: 1749 Toyon Rd Lafayette CA 94549-2111 Office: Pub Health Inst 2001 Addison St Ste 200 Berkeley CA 94704-1103

HAFFNER, ALDEN NORMAN, university official; b. Bklyn., Oct. 3, 1928; s. Irving and Irene (Gutfleisch) H. AB, Bklyn. Coll., 1948; OD, Pa. Coll. Optometry, 1952; MPA, NYU, 1960, PhD, 1964; DOS (hon.), Mass. Coll. Optometry, 1960; ScD (hon.), Pa. Coll. Optometry, 1973. Exec. dir. Optometric Center of N.Y., N.Y.C., 1957—; acting chief administrv. officer State Coll. Optometry, SUNY, N.Y.C., 1970-71; dean State Coll. Optometry, SUNY, 1971-76, pres., 1976-78; assoc. chancellor for health scis. SUNY, Albany, 1978-82, vice chancellor for research, grad. studies and profl. programs, 1982-87, pres. coll. optometry, 1987—; pub. svc. prof. health poligy Rockefeller Coll., SUNY-Albany, 1986; chmn. N.Y. State Com. on Health Personnel and Productivity, 1990—; cons. in field. Contbr. articles in field to profl. jours. Mem. adv. com. Commn. for Blind and Visually Handicapped, State Dept. Social Services, 1966-70; mem. bd. nat. study commn. on optometry Nat. Commn. on Accrediting, 1968-70; mem. health manpower planning com. Comprehensive Health Planning Agy., N.Y.C., 1969-73; project dir. Fed. Program of Identification, Counseling, Guidance and Recruitment of Minority Students in Profession of Optometry, 1968-74; mem. Mayor's Com. for Study of Aging, N.Y.C., 1958; chmn. bd. trustees Manhattan Health Plan, Inc., 1976-81. Served to 1st lt. M.C. U.S. Army, 1953-55. Recipient Albert Fitch Meml. award, 1962; Prof. Frederick A. Woll Meml. award, 1961; Distinguished Achievement award Alumni Assn., N.Y. U. Grad. Sch. Pub. Health Adminstrn., 1974. Fellow Am. Pub. Health Assn., AAAS, Am. Sch. Health Assn., Am., N.Y. Acad. Optometry; mem. N.Y. Acad. Scis., Group Health Assn. Am., Am. Pub. Welfare Assn., Am. Soc. Pub. Adminstrn., Nat. Rehab. Assn., Illuminating Engring. Soc., Am. Optometric Assn., N.Y. State Optometric Assn., Gerontol. Soc., Am. Assn. Univ. Adminstrs., Pub. Health Assn. City of N.Y. (dir. 1967—), Nat. Assn. Land Grant Colls. and State Univs. (com. health affairs 1981), Community Family Planning Coun., Am. Coun. on Edn., Assn. Cad. Health Ctrs., Hermann Biggs Soc., Beta Sigma Kappa (Gold Medal award 1974),. Home: 201 E 36th St New York NY 10016-3668 Office: SUNY Coll Optometry 100 E 24th St New York NY 10010-3676

HAFFNER, ALFRED LOVELAND, JR., lawyer; b. Bklyn., Sept. 11, 1925; s. Alfred Loveland and Mary Ellen (Myers) H.; m. Mary Dolores Hyland, July 10, 1965; children: Mary Elizabeth, Anne Dolores, Jeanne Marie, Catherine Diane. BS in Engring., U. Mich., 1950, JD, 1956. Bar: N.Y. 1958, U.S. Patent and Trademark Office, 1958, U.S. Dist. Ct. (so. and ea. dists.) N.Y. 1959, U.S. Ct. Claims 1959, U.S. Ct. Appeals (fed. cir.) 1961, U.S. Supreme Ct. 1961, U.S. Ct. Appeals (2d cir.) 1962. Draftsman-engr., indsl. engr., asst. plant engr. Owens-Ill. Glass Co., Bridgeton, N.J., 1950-53, Streator, Ill., 1953-54; since practiced N.Y.C.; assoc. Kenyon & Kenyon, N.Y.C., 1957-60, Ward, McElhannon, Brooks & Fitzpatrick, N.Y.C., 1960-61; ptnr. Ward, McElhannon, Brooks & Fitzpatrick, 1961-71, Brooks Haidt Haffner & Delahunty, N.Y.C., 1971-98, Morgan & Finnegan, LLP, N.Y.C., 1998—; chmn. Nat. Coun. Patent Law Assns., 1973-74, councilman, 1971-88; mem. founding com. Nat. Inventors Hall of Fame Found., 1972, pres., 1973-74, sec., 1980-94, exec. com. 1989-94, endowment trust com., 1991-93, chmn. exhibits com., 1992-95, legal com., 1993-95, 97-98, fin. com., 1993-94, 97—, strategic planning com., 1994-97, chmn., 1995-97, sel. com., 1996-98, bd. dirs. Served with USNR, 1943-46. Mem. ABA, N.Y. State Bar Assn., Am. Intellectual Property Law Assn., N.Y. Intellectual Property Law Assn. (sec. 1964-68, dir. 1968-70, 71-72, pres. 1970-71), Strathmore Assn. Westchester (treas. 1976-79, v.p. 1980-82, pres. 1982-83, exec. com. 1983—), Phi Gamma Delta, Phi Alpha Delta. Home: 1 Gainsborough Rd Scarsdale NY 10583-4811 Office: Morgan & Finnegan LLP 345 Park Ave New York NY 10154-0053

HAFFNER, CHARLES CHRISTIAN, III, retired printing company executive; b. Chgo., May 27, 1928; s. Charles Christian and Clarissa (Donnelley) H.; m. Anne P. Clark, June 19, 1970. BA, Yale U., 1950. With R.R. Donnelley & Sons Co., Chgo., 1951—; treas. R.R. Donnelley & Sons Co., 1962-68, v.p. and treas., 1968-83, vice-chmn. and treas., 1983-84, vice-chmn., 1984-90, ret., 1990; bd. dirs. DuKane Corp., Protection Mut. Ins. Co. Chmn. Morton Arboretum, Newberry Libr., Sprague Found.; trustee Art Inst. Chgo., Latin Sch., Chgo., 1974-84, Ill. Cancer Coun., 1984-92, Chgo. City Day Sch., Lincoln Pk. Zool. Soc., Brooks Sch., 1987-95; bd. govs. Nature Conservancy, 1973-84, chmn. Ill. chpt., 1984-87, life trustee, 1987—; mem. Chgo. Plan Commn., 1986-91. 1st lt. USAF, 1952-54. Mem. Chgo. Club, Comml. Club, Commonwealth Club, Racquet Club, Caxton Club, Casino Club. Home: 1524 N Astor St Chicago IL 60610-1610 Office: 35 E Wacker Dr Ste 2650 Chicago IL 60601-2309

HAFFNER, WILLIAM H.J., obstetrician-gynecologist; b. Jersey City, Mar. 31, 1939; s. William S. and Jean W. (Krueger) H.; m. Marlene E. Brings, Aug. 13, 1963; children: Stephanie E., Andrea J. AB, Wesleyan U., 1961; MD with distinction, George Washington U., 1965. Diplomate Am. Bd. Ob-Gyn., Nat. Bd. Med. Examiners. Intern George Washington U. Hosp., Washington, 1965-66; resident in ob-gyn. Sloan-Columbia-Presbyn. Hosps., N.Y.C., 1966-71; head ob-gyn. Gallup (N.Mex.) Indian Med. Ctr., 1971-81; staff Nat. Naval Med. Ctr., Bethesda, Md., 1981—; attending staff ob-gyn. Uniformed Svcs.-U. Health Scis., Bethesda, 1981—, resident program dir. ob-gyn., 1985-94, prof., chmn., 1992—; chief med. officer Office of Surgeon Gen. USPHS, 1990-94. Editor Obstetric Neonatal and Gynecologic Care, 1993-99. Fellow AMA, ACOG, Am. Soc. Reproductive Medicine; mem. Assn. Profs. Gynecology and Obstetrics, Coun. Univ. Chairs in Ob-Gyn., D.C. Gynecol. Soc., Alpha Omega Alpha. Office: Uniformed Svcs-U Health Sci Dept Ob-Gyn Bethesda MD 20814-4799

HAFKENSCHIEL, JOSEPH HENRY, JR., cardiologist, educator; b. Youngstown, Ohio, Apr. 2, 1916; s. Joseph Henry and Anna Marie (Conroy) H.; m. Lucinda Buchanan Thomas, July 18, 1942 (dec. 1983); children: Joseph Henry III, Benjamin A. Thomas, Mark Conroy, John Proctor; m. Carol MacDonald Smith Rush, Jan. 25, 1985. AB, Swarthmore Coll., 1937; MD, Johns Hopkins U., 1941. Diplomate Am. Bd. Internal Medicine. Intern, U. Pa. Hosp., Phila., 1941-42, resident, 1948-49, fellow in cardiology, 1949; instr. pharmacology U. Pa. Sch. Medicine, Phila., 1946-47, instr. medicine,

1949-51, assoc. medicine, 1951-66; cardiovascular disease physician in pvt. practice, Phila., 1949-65, Palo Alto, Calif., 1969-78; med. dir. West Coast Office Sandoz Pharm., San Francisco, 1965-67; staff physician Cowell Student Health Svc. Stanford U., Calif., 1967-69, clin. instr. medicine, 1966-69, asst. to assoc. prof., 1969-84, emeritus clin. assoc. prof. medicine, 1984—; staff physician Extended Care Service VA Med. Ctr., Palo Alto, 1978-84. Contbr. articles to profl. jours. Pres. Peninsula Meml. and Funeral Soc., Palo Alto, 1984. Served to maj. M.C., USAAF, 1942-46. Fellow Coll. Physicians Phila., ACP, Am. Heart Assn.; mem. Air Force Assn., Am. Irish Hist. Soc., , San Francisco Golf Club, Merion Golf Club, Gulph Mills Golf Club, Ballybunion Golf (Ireland) Club, Am. Legion (post comdr. 1960-62), Sigma Xi. Republican. Roman Catholic. Avocations: world travel, golf, gardening, art history. Home: 870 Lesley Road Villanova PA 19085-1118

HAFNER, JOSEPH A., JR., food company executive; b. San Bernadino, Calif., Oct. 9, 1944; s. Joseph Albert and Mary Florence (McGowan) H.; m. Merrill Hafner; children: John Michael, Daniel Stephen, Caroline Elizabeth. A.B. cum laude, Dartmouth Coll., 1966; M.B.A. with high distinction, Amos Tuck Sch. Bus. Adminstrn., 1967. C.P.A. Intern Latin Am. Cornell U.-Ford Found., Lima, Peru, 1967-69; sr. cons. Arthur Andersen & Co., Houston, 1969-71; controller C/A div. Riviana Internat., Inc., Guatemala City, Guatemala, 1972-73; treas., v.p. fin. Riviana Internat., Inc., Houston, 1973-77; v.p. Riviana Foods Inc., Houston, 1977-81, pres., chief operating officer, 1981-84, pres., chief exec. officer, 1984—, dir., 1985—; bd. dirs. Tex. Commerce Bank-Houston. Recipient C.P.A. Gold medal Ark. State Bd. Pub. Accountancy, 1969. Mem. AICPA, Coun. on Fgn. Rels. Office: Riviana Foods Inc 2777 Allen Pky Houston TX 77019-2141

HAFNER-EATON, CHRIS, health services researcher, educator; b. N.Y.C., Dec. 9, 1962; d. Peter Robert and Isabelle (Freda) Hafner; m. James Michael Eaton, Aug. 9, 1986; children: Kelsey James, Tristen Lee, Wesley Sean. BA, U. Calif., San Diego, 1986; MPH, UCLA, 1988, PhD in Health Svcs., 1992. Cert. health edn. specialist; internat. bd. cert. lactation cons. Cons. dental health policy UCLA Schl. Dentistry, 1989; grad. teaching asst. UCLA Sch. Pub. Health, 1987-92; health svcs. researcher UCLA, 1987-92; cons. health policy U.S. Dept. Health & Human Svcs., Washington, 1988—; analyst health policy The RAND/UCLA Ctr. Health Policy Study, Santa Monica & L.A., 1988-94; asst. prof. health care adminstrn. Oreg. State U. Dept. Pub. Health, Corvallis, 1992-95; pres. Health Improvement Svcs. Corp., 1994—; dir. rsch. rev. La Leche League Internat., 1996—; adj. faculty pub. health Linn-Benton Coll., 1995—; bd. dirs. Benton County Pub. Health Bd., Healthy Start Bd.; mem. Linn-Benton Breastfeeding Task Force, Samaritan Mother-Baby Dyad Team., Am. Public Hlth. Assn. (sect. Council Med. Care). Peer reviewer for NIH jours., others; contbr. articles to profl. jours. Rsch. grantee numerous granting bodies, 1988-97. Mem. AAUW, NOW, La Leche League Internat. (area profl. liaison for Oreg.), Am. Pub. Health Assn. (med. care sect. coun., women's caucus), Am. Assn. World Health, Oreg. Pub. Health Assn., Oreg. Health Care Assn., Assn. Health Svcs. Rsch., Soc. Pub. Health Edn., Physicians for Social Responsibility, UCLA Pub. Health Alumni Assn., Pub. Health Honor Soc., Delta Omega. Home: 1807 NW Beca Ave Corvallis OR 97330-2636

HAFT, GAIL KLEIN, pediatrician; b. N.Y.C., Mar. 5, 1938; d. Herbert and Pearl (Mittleman) Klein; m. Jacob I. Haft, Mar. 27, 1964; children: Bethanne, Ian. AB in Chemistry, Vassar Coll., 1959; MD, U. Rochester, 1963. Diplomate Nat. Bd. Med. Examiners, Am. Bd. Pediatrics. Intern Albert Einstein Coll. Medicine, N.Y.C., 1963-64, resident, 1964-65; resident Mt. Sinai Hosp., N.Y.C., 1967-68; pediatrician Dept. Health, Staten Island, N.Y., 1965-67, Head Start, Englewood, N.Y., 1969-71, Dept. Health, Hackensack, N.J., 1970-71; utilization rev. physician Hosp. Corp., N.Y.C., 1973-76; pediatrician Westchester County Health Dept., N.Y., 1974-76; sch. physician Bd. Edn., Yonkers, N.Y., 1974-76; bus. mgr. Heartronics, Newark, 1980-94; chief med. officer Bergen County Spl. Svcs., Paramus, N.J., 1984—; physician Tenafly (N.J.) Sch. Bd. Edn., 1990-94. Mem. Tenafly Bd. Edn., 1983-89, pres., 1986-88.

HAFT, ROBERT J., law educator; b. N.Y.C., 1930; m. Sarah C. Haft; 4 children. BA cum laude, CCNY, 1951; JD, Columbia U., 1954. Bar: N.Y. 1955, D.C. 1981. Law clk. to judge Irving R. Kaufman U.S. Courthouse, N.Y., 1954-55; assoc. Goldstein, Judd & Gurfein, N.Y., 1955-59; ptnr. Stamer & Haft, N.Y., 1959-73, Kronish, Lieb, Shainswit, Weiner & Hellman, N.Y., 1973-77; spl. counsel Securities and Exch. Commn., Washington, 1977-78; assoc. prof. Law Ctr. Georgetown U., Washington, 1978-82, prof., 1982—, mem. faculty senate, 1979—; spl. counsel SEC, 1978-81; vis. prof. law U. Paris, Sorbonne, U. Nice, Jesus and Darwin Colls., Cambridge U., European U., Kings Coll., London, Florence, Italy. Author: Liabilities of Attorneys and Accountants for Securities Transactions, 1998 edit., Venture Capital and Small Business Financings 1998 edit., Tax Advantaged Securities, 1998 edit., Key SEC No-Action Letters, 1998 edit., Due Diligence in Securities Transactions, 1998; editor Columbia U. Law Rev., 1953-54; contbr. articles to profl. publs. and jours. Harlan Fiske Stone scholar Columbia U. Mem. ABA (fed. regulation securities law com. 1974—), Am. Law Inst., Fed. Bar Assn. (exec. coun., securities law com. 1979—). Office: Georgetown U Law Ctr 600 New Jersey Ave NW Washington DC 20001-2022

HAGAN, CLIFFORD O., retired basketball player; b. Owensboro, Ky., Dec. 9, 1931. Grad., U. Ky., 1954; MA, Washington U., St. Louis, 1958. Basketball player St. Louis Hawks, 1956-66; player-coach Dallas Chaparrals, 1967-70. Named to Basketball Hall of Fame, 1977, Nat. H.S. Hall of Fame, 1989; mem. NBA Championship Team, 1958; selected All-Am., 1952, 54, Southeastern Conf. All-Time Team, 1974, NBA All-Star Team. Office: c/o Basketball Hall Fame 1150 W Columbus Avenue PO Box 179 Springfield MA 01101-0179

HAGAN, JOHN AUBREY, financial executive; b. Pulaski, Tenn., Sept. 30, 1936; s. Edwin Jackson and Rebecca Maria (Smith) H.; m. Nicole Emilie Thiltges, Sept. 7, 1958; children—Mark, Alex, Micheline. A.B., Harvard U., 1958, M.B.A., 1963. With R. J. Reynolds Tobacco Co. (name later changed to R. J. Reynolds Industries, then to RJR Nabisco), Winston-Salem, N.C., 1963-85, asst. controller, 1970-75, controller, chief acctg. officer internal auditing and fin. info. system, 1975-79, v.p., contr., 1979-85; chief fin. officer Embrex Inc., Research Triangle Park, N.C., 1986-95, v.p. fin. and adminstrn., 1988-95. Bd. dirs. United Way of Forsyth County, 1976-80, pres., 1979. Officer USN, 1958-61. Mem. Fin. Execs. Inst. (com. on corp. reporting 1979-85, pres. N.C. chpt. 1981-82), Common Cause, Greater Winston-Salem C. of C. (speakers bur. 1977-85), Am. Mgmt. Assn. (fin. coun. 1981-86). Home: 104 W Lochwood Dr Cary NC 27511-9744

HAGAN, JOHN CHARLES, III, ophthalmologist; b. Mexico, Mo., Oct. 7, 1943; s. John Charles Hagan II and Cleta L. (Book) Neely; m. Rebecca Jane Chapman, July 15, 1967; children: Carol Ann, Catherine Elizabeth. B.A., U. Mo., 1965; M.D., Loyola U., Chgo., 1969. Diplomate Am. Bd. Ophthalmology. Intern Med. Coll. Wis., Milw., 1969-70; resident Emory U., Atlanta, 1972-75; practice medicine specializing in ophthalmology, North Kansas City, Mo., 1975—; cons. Am. Running and Phys. Fitness Assn., Washington, 1973—. Contbr. articles to med. jours. Served to capt. USAF, 1970-72. Fellow ACS; mem. Mo. Soc. Eye Physician and Surgeons (pres. 1998), Kansas City Soc. Ophthalmology (Continuing Edn. award), AMA, Mo. Soc. Ophthalmology, Am. Intraocular Implant Soc. Avocations: marathons; triathalons; phys. fitness. Office: 2700 Clay Edwards Dr Kansas City MO 64116-3251

HAGAN, JOSEPH HENRY, university adminstrator; b. Providence, Mar. 2, 1935; s. Joseph Henry and Claire Veronica (Gorman) H.; m. Patrice O'Malley; 1 child, Kevin O'Malley. AB, Providence Coll.; EdM, Boston U.; D. Min., Grad. Theol. Found.; DCL, Salve Regina Coll.; DPA, Mount St. Joseph Coll.; MBA, Bryant Coll.; LLD, Boston U.; DPS, Providence Coll.; EdD, Assumption Coll., Rivier Coll. Tchr. Providence Public Schs., 1958-61; legis. asst. U.S. Ho. of Reps., 1961-64; staff asst. Pres.'s Com. on Juvenile Delinquency, 1964-65; spl. asst. OEO, 1965-68; dir. planning, devel. and fed. relations Bryant Coll., Smithfield, R.I., 1968-70; v.p. for public affairs Bryant Coll., 1970-73, lectr. public adminstrn., adj. prof. social scis.; asst. to chmn. Nat. Endowment for Humanities, Washington, 1973-78; pres. Assumption Coll., Worcester, Mass., 1978-98, pres. emeritus, 1998—; sr. v.p., chief operating officer Roger Williams U., 1999—. Chmn. bd. trustees John Cabot U., Rome; trustee Providence Coll.; mem. Nat. Coun. on the Humanities; dir. Fallon Cmty. Health Plan. Decorated Knight in Obedience of Malta, Knight Grand Cross, St. Gregory the Great, comdr. Palmes Academiques (France), Knight Grand Cross Jure Sanguinis of the Sacred Mil. Constantinian Order St. George, comdr. Order of Saints Maurice & Lazarus, Knights of the Holy Sepulchre, Comdr. of Order of Merit, Knights of Malta, Gentleman-in-Waiting to Pope John Paul II. Mem. Univ. Club (Providence), Sakonnet Golf Club, Circulo della Caccia (Rome), KC. Roman Catholic.

HAGAN, PHILIP EDWARD, JR., academic administrator; b. Roanoke, Va., Jan. 11, 1954; s. Philip Edward Hagan Sr. and Dorothy Murray. BS in Environ. Health, E. Carolina U., 1985; MPH, George Washington U., 1992; cert. in hazardous materials mgmt., Inst. Hazardous Materials, 1989. Cert. healthcare safety profl., 1990, hazard control mgr., 1990, indsl. hygenist, 1993. Engring. lab. tech. Wright Chem. Corp., Wilmington, N.N., 1976-79; safety officer, indsl. hygienist Wright Chem. Corp., Wilmington, N.C., 1985-87; sr. indsl. hygienist AMA, Washington, 1987-88; asst. dir. med. ctr. George Washington U., Washington, 1988-92; dir. occpl. safety and environ. health programs Georgetown U., Washington, 1992—; with lab. consortium environ. excellence EPA, Boston and Washington, 1997—; exec. dir. oversight com. IAFCA, 1992—; spkr. in field. Author: Indoor Environments and Health: The Building Owner's and Manager's Guide to Resolving Indoor Environmental Problems, 1998, Occupational Health, 1995, Environmental and Workplace Safety, 1996; mng. editor Am. Biol. Safety Assn., Mundelein, Ill., 1992—, Internat. Air Filtration Certifiers Assn., Arlington, Va., 1992—, Acad. Cert. Hazardous Material Mgrs., Rockville, Md., 1990-92; tech. editor, appearance (video) Hazard Communication in Health Care Facilities, 1992-93; contbr. articles to profl. jours. Mem. APHA, Assn. Physical Plant Officers, Am. Chem. Soc., Am. Conf. Govt. Indsl. Hygienists, Am. Indsl. Hygiene Assn., Nat. Assn. Coll. and Univ. Bus. Officers, Nat. Environ. Tng. Assn. (cert.), Nat. Inst. Bldg. Scis., Nat. Fire Protection Assn., Nat. Assn. Environ. Profls., Nat. Environ. Health Assn. (registered hazardous substances profl.), Nat. Safety Coun. (mem. editl. adv. bd. tech. pub. 1997—), Internat. Air Filtration Cert. Assn., Environ. Auditing Roundtable (mng. editor newsletter 1992-94, Acad. Cert. Hazardous Material Mgrs. (mng. editor 1990-92), Campus Safety Assn. Office: Georgetown U Dept Safety & Environ Mgmt New S Bldg M-14 3700 O St NW Washington DC 20057-0002

HAGAN, WILLIAM THOMAS, history educator; b. Huntington, W.Va., Dec. 19, 1918; s. William Fleming and Verna (Grass) H.; m. Charlotte Evangeline Nix, Jan. 31, 1943; children: Thomas M., Martha D., Daniel B., Sarah E. BA, Marshall U., 1941; PhD, U. Wis., 1950. From asst. prof. to prof. North Tex. State U., 1950-65; from prof. to Disting. prof. State Univ. Coll., Fredonia, N.Y., 1965-88, chmn. dept. history, 1965-70, acting acad. v.p., 1970-71; prof. to adj. prof. U. Okla., Norman, 1989-95; ret.; vis. disting. prof. U. Houston, 1977. Author: The Sac and Fox Indians, 1958, American Indians, 1961, Indian Police and Judges, 1966, United States-Comanche Relations, 1976, The Indian Rights Association, 1985, Quanah Parker, 1993, Theodore Roosevelt and Six Friends of the Indian, 1997; bd. editors: Western Hist. Quar., 1973-78; editorial cons. Arizona and the West, 1978-85. Mem. adv. bd. Newberry Library's Ctr. Indian History, Chgo., 1972-86. Served to 1st lt. AUS, 1942-45, PTO. Mem. Am. Hist. Assn., Orgn. Am. Historians, Western History Assn. (pres. 1979-80, council 1980-82), Am. Soc. Ethnohistory (pres. 1963). Democrat. Home: 2542 Cypress Ave Norman OK 73072-6846

HAGANS, ROBERT FRANK, industrial clothing cleaning company executive; b. Augusta, Kans., Sept. 4, 1926; s. Frank Alexander and Velma Neva (Morris) H.; m. Mary Joanne Wright, Dec. 26, 1950 (dec. 1993); children: Robin Ann Hagans Maupin, Karen Jo Hagans Steppe; m. Marcia Naughton, May 16, 1993. BS, Kans. State U., 1950. Acct. Ford, Bacon & Davis, Monroe, La., 1950-54; analyst budget Hallmark Cards, Kansas City, Mo., 1954-56; controller to pres. Payway Feed Mills, Inc., Kansas City, Mo., 1956-71; dir. planning Cen. Soya Co., Ft. Wayne, Ind., 1972-73; sr. v.p. Unitog Co., Kansas City, Mo., 1973-79, chmn. bd., 1979-91, ret., 1991. Mem. exec. com. Kans. State U. Found., Manhattan, 1985-94, chmn., 1989-91, nat. chmn. essential edge campaign, 1989-93; chmn. bd. dirs. Kansas City Pub. TV, 1985-86. With USN, 1944-46, PTO. Mem. Fin. Execs. Inst., Brookridge Country Club (pres. 1967-68), Blue Hills Country Club, Masons, Shriners, Rotary (pres. Kansas City club 1988-89). Republican. Methodist. Avocations: golf, managing golf tournaments. Home: 8327 W 102nd St Shawnee Mission KS 66212-3421

HAGANS, ROBERT REGINALD, JR., financial executive; b. Erie, Pa., Aug. 3, 1954; s. Robert Reginald and Geneva (Reid Wells) H.; m. Andrea Crittenden; children: Robert III, Alexander Charles. BA, Lake Forest Coll., 1976; MBA, U. Chgo., 1983. Lic. rep. series 7, 63 Nat. Assn. Securities Dealers. Asst. treas. Harris Bank, Chgo., 1976-81; account exec. Merrill Lynch, N.Y.C., 1983-84; cons. H & C Cons., Washington, 1984-85; treas. D.C. Govt., Washington, 1985-87; investment banker Alex. Brown & Sons Inc., Balt., 1987-89; asst. v.p. for asset mgmt., treas. Howard U., Washington, 1989-94; chief fin. officer Prince George's County Govt., Upper Marlboro, MD, 1995—. Chmn. adv. bd., chmn. fin. com. Howard U. Small Bus. Devel. Ctr.; mem. D.C. regional bd. U.S. SBA; apptd. trustee Md. Local Govt. Ins. Trust; trustee Prince George's County Police and Fire Svc. Pension Plans; chmn., County's Risk Mgmt. Com.; served on Prince George's County Task Force on Edn. Funding; pres. PTA Samuel Ogle Elem. Sch., 1998-99; mem. Leadership Md. Class of 1999. Recipient award for Excellence Demonstrated by Entrepreneurial Spirit. Mem. Washington Cash Mgrs. Assn., mem. & sec. Govt. Fin. Officers Assn., Nat. Forum for Black Pub. Adminstrs., Chgo. Athletic Assn. Home: 2003 Shadowrock Ln Mitchellville MD 20721-4100

HAGAR, JACK, mathematics and science educator; b. Marietta, Ohio, June 8, 1951; s. E. Andrew and Nora Hagar; m. Susan Burnside, June 15, 1974. BS, U. Rio Grande, 1977; MEd, Ashland U., 1981. Cert. secondary tchr., prin., Ohio. Math. team tchr. Worthington (Ohio) City Schs., 1977-78; math. and sci. tchr. Dublin (Ohio) City Schs., 1978—. Vice chmn. Zoofari Columbus Zoo, Powell, Ohio, 1990-91, gen. chmn., 1992, 93, Scrip chmn., 1985-89. Mem. ASCD, Nat. Coun. Tchrs. Math., Ohio Coun. Tchrs. Math., U. Rio Grande Alumni Assn. (bd. dirs. 1983-87, pres. 1985-87, Alumni award 1983, citation Appreciation 1987). Office: Dublin Scioto High School Ann Simpson Davis Mid Sch 4000 Hard Rd Dublin OH 43016

HAGAR, JAMES THOMAS, retail executive; b. Nashville, Jan. 11, 1950; s. Thomas Cecil and Lydia Pauline (Spicer) H. AS, Cumberland U., 1973; BA, U. Tenn., 1975; MBA, Georgetown U., 1998. Buyer Davidson's Dept. Stores, Atlanta, 1975-78; ter. mgr. DuCommon Metals, Corpus Christi, Tex., 1978-82; franchise field dir. Workbench Furniture, Inc., N.Y.C., 1982-89; dir. training Expressions Custom Furniture, New Orleans, 1990-93; dir. retail ops. and sales mgr. Rowe Furniture Corp., McLean, Va., 1993—; desktop pub.; design cons.; mgmt. lectr. U. New Orleans, 1990—. Author, editor: Professional Selling Techniques, 1990. Vol. New Orleans AIDS Task Force, 1990, Buddy Roemer for Gov., New Orleans, 1991; mem. Wyes Pub. Broadcasting, New Orleans, 1990; co-chmn. Lamar Alexander for Gov., Montgomery County, Tenn., 1978. 1st lt. USMC, 1969-72. Mem. Citizens for Airline Safety, Greenpeace, Am. Soc. Training and Devel. Republican. Avocations: bicycling, jogging, collecting contemporary fine art, video and film production and editing. Home: 6299 Walkers Croft Way Alexandria VA 22315-5212 Office: Rowe Furniture Corp 1650 Tysons Blvd Ste 710 Mc Lean VA 22102-3915

HAGAR, SUSAN MACK, school psychologist, school counselor; b. Phila., Apr. 5, 1948; d. Walter J. and Margaret Anne (Yurchisin) Mack; m. James Newton Hagar, Jan. 19, 1974; children: Kristin, Greg. *Husband Jim Hagar, Bachelor of Science, 1969 Duke University; Doctor of Dental Medicine, 1973, University of Pennsylvania School of Dental Medicine; Major United States Air Force Dental Corp, 1977. He is presently in dental practice in Bethlehem, Pennsylvania, where he focuses on dentures. Daughter Kristin Hagar, listed in Who's Who Among American High School Students 1998, is currently an undergraduate at Sarah Lawrence College majoring in art history. Son Greg Hagar is a middle school student interested in football, basketball, snowboarding and math.* BA in Spanish, Temple U., 1970, MEd in Elem. Edn., 1975; MS in Sch. Psychology with honors, Ea. Coll., St. Davids, Pa., 1997. Cert. sch. psychologist, sch. counselor, tchr., Pa. Tchr. St. Mary's Sch., Phila., 1971-72, Morton Elem. Sch., Phila., 1972-73, Monty St. Sch., Plattsburgh, N.Y., 1976-77; reading tchr. Gladwyne (Pa.) Montessori Sch., 1986-96; sch. psychologist Colonial Intermediate Unit, Easton, Pa., 1997-98, Bethlehem Area Sch. Dist., Bethlehem, Pa., 1998—. Recipient Congratulatory Letter, First Lady Barbara Bush, 1990. Mem. NASP, APA, NEA, Pa. Psychol. Assn., Pa. Sch. Counselors Assn. Avocations: reading, cooking, walking, traveling. Home: 3414 W Union St Allentown PA 18104-5947 Office: Bethlehem Area Sch Dist 1516 Sycamore St Easton PA 18017

HAGAR, WILLIAM GARDNER, III, photobiology educator; b. Chester, Pa., Aug. 14, 1940; s. William Gardner and Florence (Allcutt) H.; m. Dorothy Marie Sollinger, June 8, 1963; children: Doreen Marie, Cheryl Ann, William Robert, Jennifer Lynn. BS in Chemistry, Widener U., 1962; PhD in Biochemistry, Temple U., 1972. Teaching asst. chemistry Temple U., Phila., 1963-68; Carnegie fellow Carnegie Inst. Washington, Stanford, Calif., 1971-74; asst. prof. biology U. Mass., Boston, 1974-79, assoc. prof. biology, 1980—; sci. coord. Upward Bound Math. Sci., U. Mass., 1991-99; mem. design team Nat. TRIO Workshop Conv., Washington, 1992. Contbr. articles to Plant Physiology, Review of Scientific Instruments, other sci. publs. Com. mem. Concerned Area Residents Preservation Tinicum Marsh, 1972; organizer, coach numerous youth sports teams, Newton, Mass., 1978-84; bd. dirs. Newton Conservators, 1992-99; judge high sch. sci. fairs, Boston area, 1990-99, state finals, 1993-98. Capt. U.S. Army, 1969-71, Vietnam. Grantee NSF, 1975, 80-81, 83, 88-91, 92-94. Mem. AAAS, Am. Soc. Photobiology (charter), Am. Chem. Soc., Nat. Sci. Tchrs. Assn., Nat. Assn. Biology Teachers. Achievements include patent for cordless telephone data logger for environmental monitoring. Home: 248 Winchester St Newton MA 02461-2034 Office: U Mass Dept Biology Morrisey Bldg Quincy MA 02171

HAGARTY, EILEEN MARY, pulmonary clinical nurse specialist; b. Chgo., June 17, 1950; d. Lawrence C. and Eleanore R. (Mark) Pauls; m. Jon R. Hagarty, June 23, 1979; children: Patrick Michael, Rita Kristine. BSN, DePaul U., Chgo., 1974; MS, No. Ill. U., 1975. RN, Ill.; cert. clin. specialist in med.-surg. nursing. Staff nurse Edward Hines Jr. VA Hosp., Hines, Ill., 1971-75, pulmonary clin. nurse specialist, 1975—; chair membership com. of nursing assembly Chgo. Lung Assn., 1980-86; nat. recognized lectr. in the field of pulmonary nursing, funded prin. investigator. Contbr. articles to profl. jours. Recipient Excellence in Nursing award Dept. VA, 1992. Mem. ANA (task force), Ill. Nurses Assn., Respiratory Nursing Soc. Avocations: boating, fishing, travel. Home: 7824 Mayfair Ln Darien IL 60561-4864 Office: Edward Hines Jr Hosp 118B Dept VA Hines IL 60141

HAGBERG, CARL THOMAS, financial executive; b. S.I., N.Y., Dec. 19, 1942; s. Charles W. and Dorothy (Van Hoesen) H.; m. Patricia Rasile, Sept. 21, 1972; children: Karl, Peder, Erik. BA, NYU, 1971; MS, Columbia U., 1983. V.p. Mfrs. Hanover Trust Co., N.Y.C., 1972-92, sr. v.p., 1984-92; chmn., CEO Carl T. Hagberg and Assocs., Strategic Mktg. Cons., Jackson, N.J., 1992—; bd. dirs., chmn. audit com. Mfrs. Hanover Trust Co. of Calif., San Francisco, 1984-92; dir. The Minerva Fund, Inc.; pub. The Shareholder Svc. Optimizer. Mem. Am. Arbitration Assn., Am. Soc. Corp. Secs., Inc. (nat. treas. 1991-97, N.Y. chpt. pres. 1991-92), Nat. Assn. Securities Dealers (bd. arbitration), Nat. Investor Rels. Inst., Securities Transfer Assn., Inc., Tiro A. Segno of N.Y. Home and Office: 6 Lakeview Dr Jackson NJ 08527-2703

HAGBERG, VIOLA WILGUS, lawyer; b. Salisbury, Md., July 3, 1952; d. William E. and Jean Shelton (Barlow) Wilgus; m. Chris Eric Hagberg, Feb. 19, 1978. BA, Furman U., Greenville, S.C., 1974; JD, U. S.C., 1978, U. Tulsa, 1978; DOD Army Logistics Sch. honor grad. basic mgmt. def. acquisition, def. small purchase, advanced fed. acquisition regulation, Fort Lee, Va., 1981-82. Bar: Okla. 1978, Va. 1979, U.S. Ct. Appeals (4th cir.) 1979. With Lawyers Com. for Civil Rights, Washington, 1979; pub. utility specialist Fed. Energy Regulatory Commn., Washington, 1979-80; contract specialist U.S. Army, C.E., Ft. Shafter, Hawaii, 1980-81; contract officer/supervisory contract specialist Tripler Army Med. Ctr., Hawaii 1981-83; supervisory procurement analyst and chief policy Procurement Div. USCG, Washington, 1983; contracts officer and chief Avionics Engring Contracting Br., 1984; procurement analyst office of sec. Dept. Transp., 1984-85; contracting officer Naval Regional Contracting Ctr., Long Beach, Calif., 1985-87; chief acquisition rev. and policy, Hdqrs. Def. Mapping Agy., Washington, 1987-92, dir. acquisitions, Fairfax, Va., 1992-93, dir. acquisition policy, 1994-96; dir. acquisition polity, tech., and legis. programs Nat. Mapping and Imagery Agy., 1996-97, Office of Gen. Counsel. Mem. ABA (law student div. liaison 1977-78), Nat. Contract Mgmt. Assn., Va. State Bar Assn., Okla. Bar Assn., Phi Alpha Delta, Kappa Delta Epsilon. Home: 9810 Meadow Valley Dr Vienna VA 22181-3215 Office: Nat Imagery and Mapping Agy Office Gen Counsel 4600 Sangamore (MS-D-10) Bethesda MD 20816

HAGE, CHRISTINE LIND, library administrator; b. Detroit, Nov. 26, 1949; d. Richards I. and Letizia L. (Majorana) Lind; m. Robert M. Hage, Aug. 21, 1971; children: Paul R., Andrew M. BA in English, Oakland U., Rochester Hills, Mich., 1970; MLS, U. Mich., 1971. Cert. libr., Mich. Head of adult and circulation svcs. Troy (Mich.) Pub. Libr., 1971-77; dir. Shelby Twp. (Mich.) Libr., 1977-81; head of adult svcs. Rochester Hills Pub. Libr., 1981-88, dir., 1988-99; dir. Clinton-Macomb Pub. Libr., Mich., 1999—; chair Detroit Suburban Librs. Roundtable, 1981, 92; chair Oakland County Union List of Serials, 1989. Editor: Public Library Policy Resource Manual, 1987, Michigan Associations Directory, 1987. Bd. dirs. Greater Rochester Area Cmty. Found., 1994-98. Recipient Rose award AAUW, Utica, Mich., 1980; named Mich. Libr. of the Yr., 1997. Mem. LWV (membership chair Rochester area 1994), Pub. Libr. Assn. (bd. dirs. 1990-94, pres. 1998—), Mich. Libr. Assn. (chair numerous units 1971—), Greater Rochester C. of C., Mount Clemns Rotary, Greater Rochester Torch Club (founding mem. 1990, sec. 1990). Democrat. Lutheran. Home: 1893 Ludgate Ln Rochester Hls MI 48309-2965 Office: Clinton-Macomb Pub Libr 43245 Garfield Rd Clinton Township MI 48038-1115

HAGE, GEORGE CAMPBELL, social studies educator, minister, and counselor; b. Huntington, W.Va., Nov. 12, 1944; s. Campbell Joseph and Martha (George) H.; m. Ellen Elaine Harner, July 1, 1972; 1 child, Shauna Kristin. BA, Marshall U., 1971; BRE, Washington Bible Coll., 1971; MEd, U. N.C., Greensboro, 1984, EdD, 1990. Lic. tchr., N.C.; lic. profl. counselor, N.C.; ordained to ministry Christian Ch. (Disciples of Christ), 1982. Religious educator, 1971—; tchr. adult and continuing edn. Forsyth Tech. C.C., Winston Salem, N.C., 1979-85; min. New Hope Christian Ch., Winston Salem, N.C., 1982-88; rsch. asst. Sch. Edn. U. N.C., Greensboro, 1986-89; social studies tchr. Guilford Tech. C.C., Greensboro, 1986-88, Carver High Sch., Winston Salem, 1988-89; min. South Pk. Christian Ch., Reidsville, N.C., 1988-89; social studies tchr. Forsyth Tech. C.C., Winston Salem, 1990—; social worker/therapist Children's Home, Inc., Winston Salem, 1989-92; min. of music Trinity Christian Ch., 1990—; social worker/therapist Elon Homes for Children, 1993; youth and family therapist Host Homes of Cath. Social Svcs., Winston Salem, 1992-98; program dir. Seven Homes: A Residential Youth Devel. Alternative, Inc., Greensboro, N.C., 1999—. Author: (booklet) The Seed Within You, 1976, A Symbolic Analysis of the Dimensions of Holiness in American Culture and Curriculum: Toward a Symbolic Synthesis of Wholeness, 1990; author poems (winner of George Herbert Meml. Poetry Competition 1982); composer booklet: Rhapsodia Fantaa: A Musical Design for an Autobiographical Theory of Curriculum, 1986; art works in temperas and oils. Recipient Editor's Choice award Nat. Libr. Poetry, 1996; named Poet of Yr. Internat. Soc. Poets, 1996. Fellow Nat. Assn. Forensic Counselors (cert. criminal justice splist), Am. Acad. Forensic Counseling (diplomate), Nat. Acad. for Cert. Family Therapists, Inc. (cert. family therapist), Am. Coll. Counselors (diplomate), Nat. Coun. Social Studies (presdl. appointee adv. com. religion 1986-90), Winston-Salem Profl. Piano Tchrs. Assn.; mem. Internat. Soc. Poets (disting. mem.), Chi Alpha Omega. Avocations: writing poetry, writing music, pianist, organist, painting and drawing.

HAGE, STEPHEN JOHN, radiology administrator, consultant; b. Chgo., July 22, 1943; s. Steve and Irene (Lewandowski) H.; m. Constance Louise Simonis, June 10, 1967. AAS, YMCA C.C., Chgo., 1970. Registered radiol. tech. Staff tech. Highland Park (Ill.) Hosp., 1966-68; chief radiotherapy tech. VA Hines (Ill.) Hosp., 1968-70; chief radiology tech. Gottlieb Meml. Hosp., Melrose Park, Ill., 1970-71; radiology adminstr. S. Chgo. Cmty.

Hosp., 1971-79; adminstrv. dir. radiology Cedars-Sinai Med. Ctr., L.A., 1979-93; CEO HumiPerfect Co., Chatsworth, Calif., 1994—; cons. Computer Sci. Corp., El Segundo, Calif., 1983—. Contbr. articles to profl. jours. Served with USMC, 1961-64. Recipient 1st pl. Essay award Ill. State Soc. Radiol. Technicians, 1966. Mem. Am. Hosp. Radiology Adminstrs. (charter), Am. Soc. Radiol. Technologists, AAAS, Phi Theta Kappa. Avocations: motorcycling, Tai Chi Chuan. Home and Office: HumiPerfect 22115 Halsted St Chatsworth CA 91311-4027

HAGEDORN, DONALD JAMES, phytopathologist, educator, agricultural consultant; b. Moscow, Idaho, May 18, 1919; s. Frederick William and Elizabeth Viola (Scheyer) H.; m. Eloise Tierney, July 18, 1943; 1 child, James William. BS, U. Idaho, 1941, DSc (hon.), 1979; MS, U. Wis., 1943, PhD, 1948. Prof. agronomy and plant pathology U. Wis., Madison, 1948-64, prof. plant pathology, 1964—; courtesy prof. plant pathology Oreg. State U., Covallis, 1972-73; vis. scientist DSIR Lincoln Rsch. Ctr., Christchurch, N.Z., 1980-81; cons. Asgrow Seed Co., 1987-93; affiliate prof. plant pathology U. Idaho, 1991—. Contbr. chpts. to books, articles to profl. jours. With USAAF, 1943-46. Recipient Campbell award AAAS, 1961, CIBA-Geigy award, 1974, Meritorious Svc. award Nat. Pea Improvement Assn., 1979, Bean Improvement Coop., 1979, Forty-Niners award, 1983, Citation for Outstanding Sci. Achievement, Wis. Acad. Letters, Arts and Scis., 1986; NSF sr. fellow, 1957; named Disting. Centennial Alumnus, U. Idaho, 1989; named to U. Idaho Alumni Hall of Fame, 1990. Fellow Am. Phytopath, Soc.; mem. Kiwanis, Sigma Xi, Gamma Sigma Delta, Alpha Zeta. Methodist. Home: 927 University Bay Dr Madison WI 53705-2248 Office: U Wis 583 Russell Labs 1630 Linden Dr Madison WI 53706-1520

HAGEL, CHARLES, senator; b. North Platte, Nebr., Oct. 4, 1946; m. Lilibet Ziller; 2 children. Student, Brown Inst. Radio & TV, Minn., 1966; BA, U. Nebr., 1971. Dep. adminstr. VA, 1981-82; pres./CEO World USO, 1987-90; pres. McCarthy & Co., 1991-96; U.S. senator from Nebr., 1996—; mem. fin. svcs. & tech., housing opportunity & cmty. devel., internat. fin., fgn. rels. coms. U.S. Senate, chmn. senate global climate change observer group, mem. NATO observer group; mem. coms. banking, housing and urban affairs, 1997—, spl. com. on aging, 1997—; founder/dir. Vanguard Cellular Syss. Inc. Active Bellevue U., Red Cross, No Greater Love, World USO; chair Paralyzed Veterans of Am., 10 Anniversary Vietnam Vets. Meml. With U.S. Army, 1967-68. Mem. Am. Legion VFW, Omaha C. of C. (trustee). Office: 346 Russell Senate Office Washington DC 20510-2705*

HAGEL, RAYMOND CHARLES, publishing company executive, educator; b. Jersey City, Sept. 5, 1916; s. Morris and Theresa (Feigenbaum) H.; m. Ruth Block, May 30, 1941; children: Keith W., Wendy A. B.S. cum laude, NYU, 1937. Promotion mgr. McGraw-Hill Pub. Co., 1937-38, 41-42, 45-46; with bus. dept. N.Y. World-Telegram, 1939-40; with Asso. Mag. Contbrs., Inc., 1947-48; pres. Smith, Hagel & Knudsen, Inc., N.Y.C., 1948-59; pres. P.F. Collier & Son Corp., N.Y.C., 1959-60, chmn. bd., 1961-65; exec. v.p. Crowell-Collier Pub. Co. (name changed to Crowell Collier and Macmillan, Inc. 1965, Macmillan Inc., 1973), 1959-60, pres., 1960-76, chief exec. officer, 1963-80, chmn. bd., 1964-80, also bd. dirs.; David L. Tandy exec.-in-resident, vis. prof. M.J. Neeley Sch. Bus., Tex. Christian U., 1980-81, mem. adv. bd. dept. journalism, 1981—; prof. mgmt. Barney Sch. Bus. and Public Adminstrn., U. Hartford, 1981-90, chmn. dept. mgmt., 1983-84; mem. Rockefeller Center adv. bd. Chem. Bank, N.Y.C.; mem. Council Internat. Exec. Service Corps.; disting. adj. prof. Coll. Bus. and Pub. Adminstrn., NYU, 1972-79, mem. dean's adv. council, 1973. Trustee, Coll. of New Rochelle, 1970-76, 77-80. Served with USNR, 1942-45. Recipient John T. Madden Meml. medal NYU, 1972; Disting. Service award in investment edn. Investment Edn. Inst. of Nat. Assocs. Investment Clubs, 1973; Madden asso., Gallatin asso. NYU. Mem. Fgn. Policy Assn., Am. Assn. Higher Edn., Dirs. Table, Assn. Am. Pubs., Alpha Delta Sigma, Beta Gamma Sigma, Beta Alpha Psi, Econ. Club, Metro. Club, Pub.'s Lunch Club.

HAGELSTEIN, ROBERT PHILIP, publisher; b. N.Y.C., Dec. 15, 1942; s. H. Robert and E. Ann (Buhrow) H.; m. Ann G. Linguvic, Apr. 26, 1970; children: Christopher R., Jonathan W. B.A. in English Lit., L.I. U., 1964. Prodn. mgr. Johnson Reprint Corp., N.Y.C., 1965-68; editor-in-chief Johnson Reprint Corp., 1968-70; v.p. Greenwood Press, Inc., Westport, Conn., 1970-73; pres. Greenwood Pub. Group, 1973—; bd. dirs. Aldwych Press, London; Heinemann, Portsmouth, N.H., Reed Ednl. and Profl. Pub., Oxford. Contbr. articles to scholarly and profl. jours.; author Converticalc computer software program. Mem. Info. Industry Assn., Am. Soc. Info. Sci., Spl. Librs. Assn. (George Polk Awards com.), Scholarly Pub. Assn., Shore and Country Club, South Norwalk Boat Club. Office: Greenwood Pub Group PO Box 5007 88 Post Rd W Westport CT 06880-4208

HAGELSTON, KARMAN WEATHERLY, speech pathologist; b. Jackson, Miss., Feb. 18, 1965; d. Bobby Frank and Linda Faye (Ware) Weatherly; m. Matthew Knox Hagelston, Dec. 28, 1996; children: Steven Blake, Alexandria Weatherly. BA, U. Miss., 1987, MS, 1988. Speech-lang. pathologist New Medico Neurologic Rehab. Ctr. of Gulf Coast, Slidell, La., 1988-90, Psychology, Speech Pathology Assocs., Greenwood, Miss., 1990-91, Rosewood Med. Ctr., Houston, 1991-96; pvt. practice Franklin, 1992—; speech pathologist Robertson County Spl. Svcs. Coop., Franklin, 1996—. Contbr. articles to profl. jours. Pres. Assn. Women Students, U. Miss., 1986-87; active Delta Gamma Alumni fundraising activities; equestrian coach Spl. Olympics. Mem. Am. Speech Lang. Hearing Assn., Nat. Head Injury Found., Tex. Speech Lang., Hearing Assn., Houston Assn. for Communication Disorders (cert. Spl. Olympics coach). Avocations: walking, reading, cooking, skiing, horseback riding.

HAGEMAN, PATRICIA ANN, physical therapy educator; b. Manhattan, Kans., Dec. 24, 1957; m. Bruce E. Hageman. BS, U. Nebr., 1979, MS, 1985, PhD, 1994. Lic. phys. therapist, Nebr. Phys. therapist Luth. Hosp., Omaha, 1979-84; mem. phys. therapy faculty, dir. phys. therapy edn. U. Nebr. Med. Ctr., Omaha, 1984—. Author: (with others) Geriatric Rehabilitation, 1998; contbr. articles to profl. jours. Mem. Am. Phys. Therapy Assn. (chair nominating com., Nebr. chpt.). Office: U Nebr Med Ctr 984420 Nebr Med Ctr Omaha NE 68198-4420

HAGEMAN, RICHARD PHILIP, JR., educational administrator; b. Derby, Conn., Dec. 21, 1941; s. Richard Philip and Jane Elizabeth (Serafinowicz) H.; m. Patricia Steele; children: Margaret Anne, Sheila Marie. BS, Cen. Conn. State U., 1964; MS, U. Bridgeport, 1968, profl. diploma, 1972. Cert. counselor Nat. Bd. Cert. Counselors; cert. tchr., Conn. Tchr. Stony Brook Sch., Stratford (Conn.) Bd. Edn., 1964-69, elem. sch. guidance counselor, 1969-81, secondary sch. guidance counselor, 1981-83; asst. prin. Stratford (Conn.) Acad., 1983-90; prin. Whitney Sch., 1990-95, Ctr. Sch., 1995—; lectr. edn. Fairfield U. Grad. Sch. Edn., 1971-93; head counselor Stratford Continuing Edn. Program, 1983-91, chief examiner Gen. Ednl. Devel., 1986-91; assessor, trainer Beginning Educator Support and Tng. program Conn. State Dept. of Edn.; mem. adv. bd. counselor edn. Fairfield (Conn.) U., 1970-74; co-chmn. Stratford Juvenile Deliquency Prevention Team, 1979-81; pres. Stratford Elem. Prin. Assn., 1991-92. Mem. Youth Adv. Bd. Stratford, 1981-85, chairperson, 1984-85; radio announcer Sta. WMNR, Monroe, Conn., 1982—. Mem. ACA, ASCD, NEA (life), Stratford Edn. Assn. (pres. 1978-79), Am. Sch. Counselor Assn., New Eng. Assn. Specialists Group Work (pres. 1982-83), Nat. Assn. Elem. Sch. Prins., Phi Delta Kappa. Roman Catholic. Democrat. Office: Center Sch 55 Sutton Ave Stratford CT 06615-5916

HAGEMASTER, JULIA NELSON, nursing educator; b. Batesville, Ark., Oct. 16, 1942; d. Alvie Allen and Clevie Elaine Nelson; m. Fredrick M. Hagemaster, Mar. 1, 1964(div.); children: Allen Fredrick, Andrew Lee. RN, St. Luke's Hosp. Sch. Nursing, Kansas City, Mo., 1963; BS in Nursing summa cum laude, N.W. Mo. State U., 1980; MN in Nursing, U. Kans., 1982, PhD, 1987. Cert. advanced RN practitioner, Kans., Mo. Community health nurse Leavenworth (Kans.) City-County Health Dept., 1970-73; sch. nurse Unified Sch. Dist. 453, Leavenworth, 1975-78; asst. prof. dept. nursing St. Mary Coll., Leavenworth, 1982-87; asst. prof., dir. RN-BSN Nursing Program U. Kans. Med. Ctr., Kansas City, 1987—; site visitor for nursing sch. accreditation Nat. League Nursing; project dir. endl. tng. grant for nursing faculty devel. in alcohol and other drug abuse Nat. Inst. Alcohol Abuse and Alcoholism, Nat. Inst. Drug Abuse, Ctr. Substance Abuse Prevention. Contbr. articles to profl. jours. Mem. Am. Nurses Assn., Assn. Med. Edn. and Rsch. Substance Abuse, Kans. State Nurses Assn., Coun. Community Health Nurses, Coun. Nursing and Anthrpology, Sigma Theta Tau (outstanding nurse educator 1985), AAUP, Nat. Nurses Soc. on Addiction, Consortium of Colls. and Univs. on Drug and Alcohol Issues. Home: 11711 Mackey Overland Park KS 66210

HAGEMEIER, JUANITA ELIZABETH, human services administrator; b. Kirkwood, Mo., June 30, 1933; d. Raliegh Anless and Dollie Elizabeth (Shelby) Gray; m. Leland William Hagemeier, Nov. 18, 1950; children: Dora, Delores, Shane, Susan. Asst. ind. living Disabled Citizens Alliance for Independence, Viburnum, Mo., 1980-84, asst. dir., 1984-87, exec. dir., 1987—; mem. Crawford County Bd. for People with Devel. Disabilities, 1991—; mem. Mo. Ind. Living Coun. finance com. Recipient Nat. Disting. Svc. award Nat. Disting. Exec. Coun., 1987. Mem. Nat. Coun. for Ind. Living, Assn. Programs for Rural Ind. Living, Nat. Rehab. Assn., Mo. Rehab. Assn., Vocat. Rehab. Ind. Living Coun. (exec. com.), Viburnum C. of C. Lutheran. Avocations: travel, crafts. Home: HC 88 Box 8269 Steelville MO 65565-9307 Address: 369 Crabtree Rd Steelville MO 65565

HAGEMIER, HERMAN FREDERICK, chemist; b. Linton, Ind., Oct. 23, 1908; s. Clarence Frederick and Estella (Davidson) H.; m. Georgia Emmiline Tracy, Jan. 28, 1939 (dec. 1966); children: Evelyn Louise, Frederick Louis; m. Loueva Elizabeth Stoner Helton, Nov. 4, 1971. BS in Botany and Chemistry, Butler U., 1953. Independent researcher, 1962-98. Author: Magnetic Double Helix, 1992, Magnetic Double Helix II, 1996, Magnetic Double Helix III, 1998.

HAGEN, DANIEL RUSSELL, physiologist, educator; b. Springfield, Ill., Sept. 29, 1952; s. Robert William and Russella Mae (Lane) H.; m. Rosemary Ellen Simonetta, Mar. 25, 1978; children: Matthew, Mark, Lane, Elise. BS, U. Ill., 1974, PhD, 1978. Rsch. assoc. Cornell U., Ithaca, N.Y., 1978; asst. prof. Pa. State U., University Park, 1978-84, assoc. prof., 1984-93, prof., 1993—; vis. assoc. prof. U. Wis., Madison, 1988-89, interim dept. head, 1995-98. Mem. editl. bd. Jour. Animal Sci., 1983-86, 93-96, Biology Reprodn., 1997—; contbr. over 25 articles to profl. jours. Mem. Am. Soc. for Animal Soc., Soc. for Study of Reprodn., Soc. for Study of Fertility, Sigma Xi. Office: Pa State U 324 Henning Bldg University Park PA 16802-3503

HAGEN, DANIEL URBAN, editor, writer; b. Effingham, Ill., June 3, 1954; s. Lubert and Patricia (Schwermin) H. BA in Philosophy, Journalism, Eastern Ill. U., 1977. Reporter Effingham Daily News, 1975-76; feature writer, editor Mid-Ill. Newspapers, Charleston, 1976-92; editor News-Progress, Sullivan, Ill., 1994—; instr. journalism Eastern Ill. U., Charleston, 1985—. Recipient numerous journalism awards, 1978—. Home: 200 Harrison Ave Charleston IL 61920-2154 Office: News-Progress PO Box 290 Sullivan IL 61951-0290

HAGEN, DAVID WARNER, judge; b. 1931. BBA, U. Wis., 1956; LLB, U. San Francisco, 1959. Bar: Washoe County 1981, Nev. 1992. With Berkley, Randall & Harvey, Berkeley, Calif., 1960-62; pvt. practice Loyalton, Calif., 1962-63; with Guild, Busey & Guild (later Guild, Hagen and Clark Ltd. and Guild & Hagen Ltd.), Reno, 1963-93; judge U.S. Dist. Ct. Nev., Reno, 1993—, chmn. 9th Cir. Art. III, judge edn. com., 1998—; lectr U. Nev., 1968-72; acting dean Nev. Sch. of Law, 1981-83, adj. prof., 1981-87; mem. Nev. Bd. Bar Examiners, 1972-91, chmn., 1989-91; chmn. Nev. Continuing Legal Edn. Com., 1967-75; mem. Nev. Uniform Comml. Code Com. S/sgt. USAF, 1949-52. Fellow Am. Coll. Trial Lawyers (state chmn. 1983-85); mem. VFW, Nev. Bar Assn., Calif. Bar Assn., Washoe County Bar Assn., Am. Bd. Trial Advocates (advocate), Nat. Maritime Hist. Soc., U.S. Sailing Assn. Office: US Dist Ct Fed Bldg & US Courthouse 400 S Virginia St Reno NV 89501-2193

HAGEN, DONALD FLOYD, university administrator, former military officer; b. Ambrose, N.D., Jan. 2, 1938; s. Alvin Hagen and Edith I. (Abell) Olsen; m. Karen Pizzino, May 11, 1973; children: Dana, Lisa Amanda. BA, Concordia Coll., Moorhead, Minn., 1959; BS in Medicine, U. N.D., 1961; MD, Northwestern U., Evanston, Ill., 1963. Diplomate Am. Bd. Surgery. Commd. ensign USN, 1964, advanced through grades to rear adm., 1989; internship L.A. County Gen. Hosp., 1963-64; residency gen. surgery Portmouth (Va.) Naval Hosp., 1970-73; staff surgeon Naval Aerospace Med. Ctr., Pensacola, Fla., 1973-75; chief surgery U.S. Naval Hosp., Yokosuka, Japan, 1973-79; dir. clin. svcs. U.S. Naval Hosp., Jacksonville, Fla., 1979-81; commdg. officer U.S. Naval Hosp., Camp Pendleton, Calif., 1984-86; dir. contingency planning div. Bur. Medicine and Surgery, Washington, 1981-82; dir. med. edn. and tng. Office of Surgeon Gen., Washington, 1982-84, dir. health care ops., 1986-88; dep. comdr. health care ops. Naval Med. Command, Washington, 1988; comdr. Nat. Naval Med. Ctr., Bethesda, Md., 1988-91; surgeon gen., vice admiral USN, 1991-95, retired, 1995; exec. vice chancellor U. Kans. Med. Ctr., Kansas City, 1995—; mem. bd. regents Uniformed Svcs. U. Health Scis., Bethesda, 1988-90; asst. chief Navy Med. Corps., 1989-90. Decorated bronze star; recipient Fed. Exec. award of excellence Am. Hosp. Assn., 1989. Mem. AMA, Am. Coll. Physician Execs., Assn. Mil. Surgeons of the U.S. (Founder award 1984), Army-Navy Club (Washington). Republican. Avocations: piano playing, church choir. Office: U Kans Med Ctr 3901 Rainbow Blvd Kansas City KS 66160-0001

HAGEN, EDNA MAE, retired medical nurse; b. Jasper, Ark., Nov. 30, 1932; d. Eugene and Dovie (Combs) Keef; m. Harry Hagen, Jan. 4, 1952; children: Catherine, Harry, Jr. ADN, Santa Barbara Coll., 1973. RN, Calif. Staff nurse Cottage Hosp., Santa Barbara, Calif., 1970-74; head nurse to pvt. physician L.A. Price, M.D., Inc., Santa Barbara, 1974-95; retired, 1995. Mem. U.S. Army Med. Corps, 1951-52. Mem. ANA, CNA.

HAGEN, GLENN W(ILLIAM), lawyer; b. Detroit, July 8, 1948; s. William A. and Lilian (Abrolat) H.; m. Cynthia Winn, July 21, 1984. BS in Chemistry, U. Ala., 1970; JD, Valparaiso U., 1973. Bar: Mich. 1973, U.S. Dist. Ct. (we. dist.) Mich. 1974, Colo. 1981, U.S. Dist. Ct. Colo. 1982. Ptnr. Peters, Seyburn & Hagen, Kalamazoo, 1973-76; dep. city atty. City of Battle Creek, Mich., 1976-79; staff and regulatory counsel CF&I Steel Corp., Pueblo, Colo., 1979-81; gen. counsel Commonwealth Investment Properties Corp., Littleton, Colo., 1981-82; assoc. Berkowitz & Brady, Denver, 1982-83, Zarlengo, Mott, Zarlengo & Winbourn, Denver, 1983-87; pvt. practice Glenn W. Hagen, P.C., Denver, 1987—; lectr. law office mgmt., small bus. issues, corp. entity and formation issues. Del. Colo. Rep. Com., 1986, 90, 92, 94, 96, 98; referee property tax appeals Douglas and Jefferson Counties; chmn. 18th Jud. Dist., 1999—; small bus. cons. South Met. Denver C. of C., 1994—. Mem. ABA (young lawyers exec. com. 1978-81, chmn. small bus. enterprises 1986, regional dir. constabars 1992-94, nat. editors conf. 1995, mem. constrn. forum 1996—), Mich. Bar Assn. (young lawyers exec. coun. 1976-80), Colo. Bar Assn. (chmn. long-range planning com. 1983-86, gen. practice exec. coun. 1985—, chmn. small firm sect. 1991-96, law office mgmt. com. 1995—, constrn. law sect. 1996—, chmn. budget com. 1987-89, mem. svcs. com. 1987-89, bus. law sect. 1986-91, alt. dispute resolution com. 1990-94), Denver Bar Assn., Douglas-Elbert County Bar Assn., Colo. Lawyers for Arts, Am. Arbitration Assn. (lectr. law office mgmt.). Lutheran. Avocations: travel, photography, golf. Home: 2303 E Lansdowne Pl Highlands Ranch CO 80126 Office: Mellon Fin Ctr 1775 Sherman St Ste 2550 Denver CO 80203-4319

HAGEN, IONE CAROLYN, religion educator; b. Spring Grove, Minn., Nov. 19, 1924; d. Peter Norris and Ina Bertina (Kittelson) Wennes; m. Dean LeRoy Hagen, Oct. 16, 1954; children: Steven Dean, David Lee, Deone Marie, Susan Ilene, Daniel Paul. BA, Luther Coll., 1947. Cert. music tchr., Minn. Parish worker Glenwood (Minn.) Luth. Ch., 1947-53, Trinity Luth. Ch., LaCrosse, Wis., 1953-55; sec. Nat. ELC Hdqrs. Higher Edn., Mpls., 1955; instr. Bethel series Zion Luth., Buffalo, Minn., 1966-67; supr. Christian Sch. Rivercrest, Monticello, Minn., 1979-81, Christian Sch. New Life, Buffalo, Minn., 1981-82; adminstr. Cmty. Christian Sch., Buffalo, 1982-97; ret., 1997. Del. State Rep. Conv., Rochester, 1988; clarinetist Assembly of God Orch., Buffalo, 1974-95; choir mem. Assembly of God Choir, Buffalo, 1990-91. Mem. Nat. Parish Workers Assn. (pres. 1951-53), Internat. Choral Union (sec. 1951-55). Republican. Home: 409 Sigrid Dr Buffalo MN 55313-1259 *The greatest joy of living for me has been the knowledge that I am just a vessel—a pitcher with handle and spout—filled with the results of my choices and the choices of everyone who has touched my life, sanctified by Jesus Christ, and poured out wherever He chooses.*

HAGEN, MICHAEL DALE, family physician educator; b. St. Louis, Nov. 11, 1949; s. Hubert Dale and Gwendel (Carden) H.; m. Barbara Carroll Keifer, Aug. 21, 1971; children: Laura Carrol, Sandra Ann. BS in Biology, Denison U., 1971; MD cum laude, U. Mo., Columbia, 1975. Cert. family practice bd. Pvt. practice Family Medicine Assocs., Aurora, Mo., 1978-81; asst. prof. dept. family practice U. Ky., Lexington, 1981-87, assoc. prof. dept. family practice, 1987-92, prof. dept. family practice, 1993—, interim chmn. dept. family practice, 1992-93, assoc. chmn. dept. family practice, 1993-97, project dir., computer-based assessment, 1996—; fellow Clin. Decision Making, New Eng. Med. Ctr., Boston, 1987-89; at-large dir. Am. Bd. Family Practice, Lexington, 1991-96, pres., 1995-96; residency rev. com. family practice Accreditation Coun. for Grad. Med. Edn., Chgo., 1994-97. Author: Saunders Review Family Practice, 1992, 97; contbr. articles to profl. jours. Mem. AMA, Am. Acad. Family Practice (clin. policies task force 1994-95), Soc. for Med. Decision Making, Soc. for Tchrs. Family Medicine, Alpha Omega Alpha, Phi Kappa Phi, Omicron Delta Kappa. Presbyterian. Avocations: amateur radio, gardening. Home: 2012 Blairmore Rd Lexington KY 40502-2435 Office: Assessment Techs Inc 2224 Young Dr Lexington KY 40505-4219

HAGEN, NICHOLAS STEWART, medical educator, consultant; b. Plentywood, Mont., Aug. 6, 1942; s. William Joseph and June Janette (Reuter) H.; m. Mary Louise Edvalson, July 26, 1969; children: Brian Geoffrey, Lisa Louise, Eric Christopher, Aaron Daniel, David Michael. BS in Chemistry, Ariz. State U., 1964; MBA in Internat. Bus., George Washington U., 1969; MD, U. Ariz., 1974. Lic. physician Ariz., Utah, Idaho.; diplomate Nat. Bd. Med. Examiners. Intern., resident Good Samaritan Hosp., Phoenix, 1974-75; pvt. practice Roy, Utah, 1975-77; dir. clin. rsch. Abbott Labs., North Chicago, Ill., 1977-84; v.p. med. affairs Rorer Group, Inc., Ft. Washington, Pa., 1984-88; clin. prof. Ariz. State U., Tempe, 1988-90; pres. Southwestern Clin. Rsch., Tempe, 1987—, Travel Profl. Internat., Tempe, 1989—; mem. Ariz. Bd. Med. Student Loans, 1998—. Author: Valproic Acid: A Review of Pharmacologic Properties and Clinical Use in Pharmacologic and Biochemical Properties of Drug Substances, 1979; contbr. articles to med. jours.; patentee in field. Bishop Ch. Jesus Christ of Latter-day Saints, Gurnee, Ill., 1981-84; various positions with local couns. Boy Scouts Am., 1988—; active Rep. campaigns, Mesa, Ariz., 1988—; 2d vice chmn. Maricopa County Rep. Assembly, 1997-99; dist. republican chmn., 1996-98; mem. tech. governing bd. East Valley Inst. Tech., 1998—. Lt. comdr. USCG, 1965-69. Joan Mueller-Etter scholar Ariz. State U., 1960, Phelps-Dodge scholar Ariz. State U., 1961; NASA fellow Brigham Young U., 1964. Mem. Am. Coll. Sports Medicine, Eagle Forum, Nat. Right-to-Life Assn., Utah Hist. Soc., Nat. Geneal. Soc., Bucks County Geneal. Soc., Sons of Norway, Soc. Descendants Emigrants from Numedal, Hallingdal and Hedmark, Norway, Blue Key, Archons, Kappa Sigma, Beta Beta Beta, Alpha Epsilon Delta, Phi Eta Sigma, Sophos. Republican. Mormon. Avocations: genealogy, swimming, philately, medieval history, art collecting. Office: 2251 N 32d St Lot 20 Mesa AZ 85213-2445

HAGEN, PAUL BEO, physician, medical scientist; b. Sydney, Australia, Feb. 15, 1920; emigrated to Can., 1959, naturalized, 1965; s. Conrad and Mary (McFadzean) von H.; m. Jean Himms, Sept. 29, 1956; children—Anna, Nina. M.B., B.S., U. Sydney, 1945. Intern, resident New South Wales Dept. Health, Sydney, 1945-48; lectr. physiology U. Sydney, 1948-50; sr. lectr. physiology U. Queensland, 1950-52; research fellow Oxford U., 1952-54; asst. prof. pharmacology Yale U., 1954-56, Harvard U., 1956-59; head biochemistry dept. U. Man., 1959-64, Queens U., 1964-67; dir. NRC, Ottawa, Ont., 1967-68; dean grad. studies U. Ottawa, 1968-83, chmn. pharmacology dept., 1983-86; mem. med. bd. Muscular Dystrophy Assn. Can., 1961-87, chmn., 1976-87, nat. pres., 1980-83; vice chmn. Med. Research Council, 1967; trustee Can. Inst. Particle Physics, 1971-79. Mem. Editorial bd. Biochem. Pharmacology, 1961-66, Jour. Pharmacology and Exptl. Therapeutics, 1960-64, Can. Jour. Biochemistry, 1963-67; contbr. to books and periodicals on physiol., biochem. and pharm. subjects. Chmn. Ont. Bd. Libr. Coordination, 1971-73; trustee Ottawa Gen. Hosp., 1984-94. Recipient Lederle Faculty award Yale U., 1956, Centennial medal Govt. of Can., 1967; Jubilee medal, 1977; C.J. Martin fellow Oxford U., 1952; J.H. Brown fellow Yale U., 1954; Fulbright fellow, 1954. Fellow Chem. Inst. Can. (v.p., pres. biochem. div. 1962-64); mem. Physiol. Soc., Brit. Pharm. Soc., Am. Soc. Pharmacology. Home: 233 Todor Pl, Ottawa, ON Canada K1L 7Y1 Office: U Ottawa Med Sch, Dept Pharmacology, Ottawa, ON Canada K1H 8M5

HAGEN, THOMAS BAILEY, business owner, former state official, former insurance company executive; b. Buffalo, Sept. 19, 1935; s. Walter B. and Isabella S. (Bailey) H.; m. Susan R. Hirt, May 31, 1958; children: Jonathan, Sarah. Student, Pa. State U., Erie, 1953-55; BS in Commerce, Ohio State U., 1957; DPubSvc (hon.), Edinboro U. Pa., 1996. With Erie (Pa.) Ins. Group, 1953-93, exec. v.p., 1976-82, pres., 1982-90, chmn., CEO, 1990-93; sec. of commerce Commonwealth of Pa., 1995-96, sec. cmty. and econ. devel., 1996-97; chmn. bd. dirs. Custom Engring. Co., 1997—; chmn. Team Pa. Found., 1997—; bd. dirs. Pa. Housing Fin. Agy., GPU, Inc.; chmn. Pa. Indsl. Devel. Authority, 1995-97, Pa. Econ. Devel. Fin. Authority, 1995-97, Pa. Ben Franklin/IRC Partnership, 1995-97. Bd. dirs. Erie Philharmonic, 1962-75, pres., 1970-71; bd. dirs. Erie Coun. Navy League U.S., 1977-86; pres. Erie Tomorrow Corp., 1979-86; vice chmn., bd. dirs. Bayfront East Side Taskforce, Erie, 1978—; bd. dirs. Erie Conf. on Community Devel., 1985-93, hon. dir., 1993—; bd. dirs. Pa. Chamber Bus. and Industry, Harrisburg, 1986-95, Pa. Econ. Devel. Partnership, 1987-94, Pa. for Effective Govt., 1987-95. Capt. USNR. Alumni fellow Pa. State U., 1988; recipient Ins. Mentor award U. Ala., 1976, Golden Baton award Erie Philharmonic, 1974, Disting. Pennsylvanian award Gannon U., 1987, Phila. C. of C., 1980, Outstanding Community Service award Multiple Sclerosis Soc., 1980, Alumni Citizenship award Ohio State U., 1981, Man of the Yr. award Erie and Chautauqua Mag., 1986, Preservationist of the Yr. award Pa. Hist. and Mus. Commn., 1987, Honor award Pa. Soc. Architects, 1993. Mem. Internat. Ins. Soc. (bd. dirs. 1978—, hon. counselor award 1982), Ins. Fedn. Pa. (chmn. 1984-86), Ins. Inst. Am. (inst. for property and liability underwriters, trustee 1987-93), Griffith Found. (v.p. 1985-92, trustee 1985-95, trustee emeritus 1995—), The Pa. Soc. (pres. 1995-97, bd. dirs. 1990—). Office: 100 State St Ste 440 Erie PA 16507-1456

HAGEN, UTA THYRA, actress; b. Göttingen, Germany, June 12, 1919; came to U.S., 1926; d. Oskar F. L. and Thyra A. (Leisner) H.; m. Herbert Berghof, Jan. 25, 1957 (dec. Nov. 1990); 1 child, Leticia. DFA (hon.), Smith Coll., 1978; LHD (hon.), De Paul U., 1981, Wooster Coll., 1982; DFA (hon.). Tchr. acting Herbert Berghof Studio, N.Y.C., 1947—, now chmn. Appeared as Ophelia, Dennis, Mass., 1937, as Nina in Sea Gull, N.Y.C., 1938, Key Largo, 1939, Vicki, 1942, Othello, 1943-45, Masterbuilder, 1947, Faust, 1947, Angel Street, 1948, Street Car Named Desire, 1948, 50, Country Girl, 1950, G.B. Shaw's Saint Joan, 1951-52, Tovarich, City Center, 1952, In Any Language, 1952, The Deep Blue Sea, 1953, The Magic and the Loss, 1954, The Island of Goats, 1955, A Month in the Country, 1956, Good Woman of Setzuan, 1957, Who's Afraid of Virginia Woolf, 1962-64, The Cherry Orchard, 1968, Charlotte, 1980; also univ. tour 1981-82, Mrs. Warren's Profession, Roundabout Theatre, N.Y.C., 1985—, You Never Can Tell, Circle in the Square, 1986—, Mrs. Klein, Lortel Theatre, 1995-96, on tour, 1996-97, Collected Stories, Lortel Theatre, 1998-99; (films) The Other, 1972, The Boys from Brazil, 1978, Reversal of Fortunes, 1990; TV appearances include A Month in the Country, 1956, Out of Dust, 1959; appeared in numerous TV spls. and guest star appearances including Lou Grant, 1982, A Doctor's Story, 1984, PBS Am. Playhouse prodn. The Sunset Gang, 1991; author: Respect for Acting, 1973, Love for Cooking, 1976, Sources, a Memoire, 1983, A Challange for the Actor, 1991; appearances include numerous roles with the H.B. Playwrights Found., 1965-98. Chmn. bd. HB Playwrights Found., 1991—. Recipient Antoinette Perry award, 1951, 63, N.Y. Drama Critics award, 1951, 63, Donaldson award for best actress, 1951, London Critics award for best actress, 1963-64 season, Outer Cir. award, Mayor's Liberty medal, 1986, Drama Legend award 1986, John Houseman award for disting. svc., 1987, Campostella award for disting. svc., 1987, Living Legacy award Women's Internat. Ctr., 1994, Lucille Lortell Lifetime Achievement award, 1995, Lortell award, 1996, Drama League Lifetime Achievement award, 1996, Obie Lifetime Achievement award 1996, Jeffry award, chgo., 1997, Antoinette Perry Lifetime Achievement award,

1999; named to Theatre Hall of Fame, 1981. Office: Herbert Berghof Studio 120 Bank St New York NY 10014-2126

HAGENBECK, FRANKLIN L., army officer; b. Morocco, Nov. 25; m. Judy Vaughn; children: Kelly, Leeann. BS, U.S. Mil. Acad., 1971; MS in Exercise Physiology, Fla. State U.; MBA, Long Island U. Commd. 2d lt. U.S. Army, 1971, advanced through grades to brig. gen.; served with XVIII Airborne Corps, 1981-84; sec. of gen. staff 82d Airborne Divsn.; exch. officer, tactics instr. Royal Australian Inf. Ctr.; from exec. officer to chief inf. br. U.S. Army Pers.; chief of staff 10th Mountain Divsn. (Light); dir. office pers. mgmt. U.S. Total Army Pers. Command, to 1998; asst. divsn. comdr. ops. 101st Airborne Divsn. (Air Assault), Ft. Campbell, Ky., 1998—. Decorated Legion of Merit with 3 oak leaf clusters, Bronze Star, numerous others. Office: 101st Airborne Divsn Air Assault Fort Campbell KY 42223

HAGENBUCH, JOHN JACOB, investment banker; b. Park Forest, Ill., May 31, 1951; s. David Brown and Jean Iline (Reeves) H.; children: Henry, Hunter, Hilary. AB magna cum laude, Princeton U., 1974; MBA, Stanford U., 1978. Assoc. Salomon Bros., N.Y.C., 1978-80; v.p. Salomon Bros., San Francisco, 1980-85; gen. ptnr. Hellman & Friedman, 1985-93; owner John J. Hagenbuch & Co., San Francisco, 1993—; gen. ptnr. M&H Realty Ptnrs., L.P., 1993—. Bd. govs. Town Sch. for Boys. Mem. Burlingame Country Club, Pacific-Union Club, Calif. Tennis Club, Villa Taverna Club, Menlo Circus Club, Bohemian Club, Valley Club. Office: M&H Realty Ptnrs 353 Sacramento St Fl 21 San Francisco CA 94111-3620

HAGENBUCH, RODNEY DALE, stock brokerage house executive; b. Saxville, Wis.; s. Herbert Jenkin and Minnie Leona (Hayward) Hagenbuch; children: Kris, Beth, Patricia; m. LaVerne Julia Scoonover, Sept. 1, 1956. BS, Mich. State U., 1980. Cert. fin. mgr. Designer Olds div. Gen. Motors, Lansing, Mich., 1960-66; institutional account exec. Merrill Lynch, Lansing, 1966-75, institutional mgr., 1975-80; sales mgr. Merrill Lynch, Columbus, Ohio, 1980-82; sr. resident v.p. Merrill Lynch, Tacoma, 1982-93, L.A., 1993-98; ret., 1998; prin. Oxford Group, 1999, Securities Expert Witness Network, 1999, Quantum Leap Inst., 1999; bd. dirs. Merrill Lynch Trust Co., CommunityGate.com.; adv. bd. U. Wash. Sch. Bus., Tacoma. Mem. adv. bd. L.A. Bus. Jour. Bd. dirs. Tacoma Club, 1989-93, treas. 1990, pres. 1993, L.A. Acad. Finance, 1993-98, L.A. United Cerebral Palsey, 1994—; adv. bd. Charles Wright, 1989-93; bd. dirs. L.A. Red Cross, 1996—; mem. econ. devel. bd. City of Tacoma, 1986-93, chmn. 1987-88; pres. Downtown Tacoma Assn., 1986; chmn. Corp. Coun. for the Arts, 1986, L.A. United Way, 1993—; pres. Tacoma Symphony, 1988; chmn. Human Resources Commn., Meridian Twp., 1972-74, Meridian Planning Commn., Lansing, 1964-70, Meridian Police and Fire Com., Lansing, 1964-70; pres. adv. bd. U. Wash., Tacoma, chmn. 1992; mem. State Wash. Arts Stabilization Bd., Tacoma Art Mus. Bd., sec. 1992; legis. chmn. N.W. Securities Industry Assn.; campaign chmn. Pierce County United Way Bd., 1991-92; non-resident dir. Tacoma Art Mus., 1994—, Tacoma Urban League, 1983-93; bd. mem. New L.A. Mktg. Plan; bd. mem., dist. 2 com. NASD; bd. mem. L.A. Red Cross, 1997—; mem. bd. govs. L.A. Town Hall, 1996; mem. fraternity of friends L.A. Music Ctr. Recipient Outstanding Citizen award Mcpl. League Pierce County, 1988; named Nat. Vol. of Yr., Urban League Western Divsn., 1987. Mem. Tacoma C. of C. (bd. dirs.), Forward Washington (bd. dirs.), L.A. Children's Hosp. Rsch. Inst. (bd. govs. 1994—). Avocations: running, skiing. Home: 16826 Monte Hermoso Dr Pacific Palisades CA 90272-1910

HAGENDORN, WILLIAM, lawyer; b. Bklyn., Sept. 1, 1925; s. William V. and Florence (Hull) H.; m. Patricia Yarvote, Apr. 6, 1974; children: Katherine Florence, Patricia Ann. A.B., Princeton U., 1944; J.D., Harvard U., 1949; LL.M., NYU, 1952. Bar: N.Y. 1949. Practiced in N.Y.C., 1949—; assoc. firm Debevoise, Plimpton & McLean, N.Y.C., 1953-61, Carter, Ledyard & Milburn, N.Y.C., 1961-65; gen. counsel Am. Express Co., 1965-72, Wells Fargo & Co., 1965-68, Equitable Securities, Morton & Co., N.Y.C., 1966-72; sr. atty. Shearman & Sterling, N.Y.C., 1973-91; ptnr. Burlingham Underwood, N.Y.C., 1991—; adviser to com. Uniform consumer credit code Nat. Conf. Uniform State Laws, 1966-68; adj. prof. Rutgers Law Sch., Newark, 1991, 93. Served with inf. AUS, 1944-46. Mem. N.Y. State Bar Assn. (chmn. com. admiralty and maritime law internat. law sect. 1990-93, 98—), Assn. of Bar of City of N.Y., Univ. Club (N.Y.C.). Home: 5 Sherman Ave Bronxville NY 10708-4201 Office: 1 Battery Park Plz New York NY 10004-1405

HAGENLOCKER, EDWARD E., retired automobile company executive; b. 1939; married. BS, Ohio State U., 1962, MS, 1962, PhD, 1964; MBA, Mich. State U., 1982. With Ford Motor Co., 1964—, chief engr., 1973-77, 78-80; dir., v.p. ops. Ford Motor Co., Brazil, 1984-85, dir., pres., 1985-86; v.p., gen. mgr. truck ops. Ford Motor Co., Dearborn, Mich., 1986-92, exec. v.p. N.Am. automotive ops., 1992-94, pres. Ford automotive ops., 1994-96; vice chmn. Ford Motor Co., Dearborn, 1996-98. Office: Ford Motor Co Ste 165 1400 N Woodward Bloomfield Hills MI 48304

HAGENSTEIN, WILLIAM DAVID, forester, consultant; b. Seattle, Mar. 8, 1915; s. Charles William and Janet (Finigan) H.; m. Ruth Helen Johnson, Sept. 2, 1940 (dec. 1979); m. Jean Kraemer Edson, June 16, 1980. BS in Forestry, U. Wash., 1938; MForestry, Duke, 1941. Registered profl. engr., Wash., Oreg. Field aid in entomology U.S. Dept. Agr., Hat Creek, Calif., 1938; logging supt. and engr. Eagle Logging Co., Sedro-Woolley, Wash., 1939; tech. foreman U.S. Forest Svc., North Bend, Wash., 1940; forester West Coast Lumbermen's Assn., Seattle and Portland, Oreg., 1941-43, 45-49; sr. forester FEA, South and Central Pacific Theaters of War and Costa Rica, 1943-45; mgr. Indsl. Forestry Assn., Portland, 1949-80; exec. v.p. Indsl. Forestry Assn., 1956-80, hon. dir., 1980-87; pres. W.D. Hagenstein and Assocs., Inc., Portland, 1980—; H.R. MacMillan lectr. forestry U. B.C., 1952, 77; Benson Meml. lectr. U. Mo., 1966; S.J. Hall lectr. indsl. forestry U. Calif. at Berkeley, 1973; cons. forest engr. USN, Philippines, 1952, Coop. Housing Found., Belize, 1986; mem. U.S. Forest Products Trade Mission, Japan, 1968; del. VII World Forestry Congress, Argentina, 1972, VIII Congress, Indonesia, 1978; mem. U.S. Forestry Study Team, West Germany, 1974; mem. sec. Interior's Oreg. and Calif. Multiple Use Adv. Bd., 1975-76; trustee Wash. State Forestry Conf., 1948-92, Keep Oreg. Green Assn., 1957—, v.p., 1970-71, pres., 1972-73; adv. trustee Keep Wash. Green Assn., 1957-95; co-founder, dir. World Forestry Ctr., 1965-89, v.p., 1965-79; hon. Dir. for Life, 1990. Author: (with Wackerman and Michell) Harvesting Timber Crops, 1966; Assoc. editor: Jour. Forestry, 1946-53; columnist Wood Rev., 1978-82; contbr. numerous articles to profl. jours. Trustee Oreg. Mus. Sci. and Industry, 1968-73. Served with USNR, 1933-37. Recipient Hon. Alumnus award U. Wash. Foresters Alumni Assn., 1965, Forest Mgmt. award Nat. Forest Products Assn., 1968, Western Forestry award Western Forestry and Conservation Assn., 1972, 79, Gifford Pinchot medal for 50 yrs. Outstanding Svc., Soc. Am. Foresters, 1987, Charles W. Ralston award Duke Sch. Forestry, 1988, Lifetime Achievement award Oreg. Soc. Am. Foresters, 1995. Fellow Soc. Am. Foresters (mem. coun. 1958-63, pres. 1966-69, Golden Membership award 1989); mem. Am. Forestry Assn. (life, hon. v.p. 1966-69, 74-92, William B. Greeley Forestry award 1990), Commonwealth Forestry Assn. (life), Internat. Soc. Tropical Foresters, Portland C. of C. (forestry com. 1949-79, chmn. 1960-62), Nat. Forest Products Assn. (forestry adv. com. 1949-80, chmn. 1972-74, 78-80), West Coast Lumbermen's Assn. (v.p. 1969-79), David Douglas Soc. Western N. Am., Lang Syne Soc., Hoo Hoo Club, Xi Sigma Pi (outstanding alumnus Alpha chpt. 1973). Republican. Home: 3062 SW Fairmount Blvd Portland OR 97201-1439 Office: 921 SW Washington St Ste 803 Portland OR 97205-2826

HAGEN-STUBBING, YVONNE FORREST, writer; b. Ile Aux Moines, Morbihan, France, Aug. 14, 1920; came to U.S., 1929; d. Wilbur Studley and Floss May (Springer) Forrest; m. Karl-Victor Hagen, Sept. 15, 1940 (dec. July 1948); children: Nina, Karen, Anthony; m. N.H. Stubbing, May 10, 1983. Student, Fontainbleau Sch. of Fine Arts, Columbia U., 1940-41. Interviewer Am. Mag. Art, N.Y., 1946-48; art reviewer European edit. N.Y. Herald Tribune, 1954-61; art critic Art Aujourdhui, monthly mag., 1957, 58, 59; dir. Modern Art Munich, 1967-71; advisor to numerous galleries in Europe and Calif. Author: (autobiography) From Life to Art and Back, 1999, also monographs; contbr. forewords and articles to art mags.; editor catalogs on modern art. Mem. Lindisfarne (assoc.). Democrat. Avocations: enjoy seeing Chinese art, travel, chamber music. Home: PO Box 104 329 Sagaponack Rd Sagaponack NY 11962

HAGER, ANTHONY WOOD, mathematics educator; b. Marshfield, Wis., Dec. 16, 1939; s. Cyril Francis and Margaret Ruth (Wood) H.; 1 child, Amanda D. BS, Pa. State U., 1960, PhD, 1965. Rsch. scientist Leeds & Northrup Co., N. Wales, Pa., 1960-61; instr. U. Rochester, N.Y., 1965-67, asst. prof., 1967-68; asst. prof. Wesleyan U., Middletown, Conn., 1968-69, assoc. prof., 1969-75, prof., 1975—, chmn. dept. math., 1976-77, 88-90, 93, 95-96. Contbr. articles to profl. jours. NAS vis. rschr., Prague, 1973, 75; Italian N.C.R. vis. rschr. Padua, 1978. Mem. Am. Math. Soc. Office: Wesleyan U Math Dept Middletown CT 06459

HAGER, CHARLES READ, lawyer; b. N.Y.C., Aug. 16, 1937; s. Read and Louisa (Wilson) H.; m. Susan Detweiler, Sept. 19, 1959 (div. 1977); children: Eric, Timothy, Jonathan; m. Nancy Mould, Dec. 31, 1977; 1 child, Anne. BA, Harvard U., 1959, LLB, 1962. Bar: N.Y. 1962, U.S. Dist. Ct. (so. and ea. dists.) N.Y. 1975. Assoc. Dewey, Ballantine, Bushby, Palmer & Wood, N.Y.C., 1962-71, ptnr., 1971—. Mem. Com. on Housing and Urban Devel., Com. Bankruptcy and Corp. Reorganization; bd. dirs. Legal Aid Soc., N.Y.C., 1976-83; bd. dirs., chmn. N.Y. Lawyers for the Pub. Interest, Inc., 1994-96. Mem. ABA, N.Y. State Bar Assn., Assn. Bar City N.Y., Harvard Club. Democrat. Episcopalian. Avocations: squash, tennis. Home: 256 W 10th St New York NY 10014-6520 Office: Dewey Ballantine 1301 Avenue Of The Americas New York NY 10019-6022

HAGER, DONALD WAYNE, secondary education educator; b. Bluefield, W.Va., Jan. 4, 1935; s. Buford Jennings Hager and Cleo Cecil Day; m. Addie Mae Wright, Aug. 24, 1957; children: Melinda Susan Testerman, Karen Elizabeth Back. BS in Mus. Edn., Concord Coll., 1958; MA, James Madison U., 1962; postgrad., Mashall U. Tchr. Graham H.S., Bluefield, 1957, Lexington (Va.) Town Sch., 1958-60, Lashmeet Sch., Matoaka, W.Va., 1960-97. Mem. Masterworks Chorale, Bluefield, 1988-97. Presbyterian. Avocations: reading, music, TV movies. Home: 2023 Jefferson St Bluefield WV 24701-4705

HAGER, EDWARD PAUL, development executive; b. Pottsville, Pa., Jan. 15, 1948; s. Edward Louis and Pauline Ann (Macalush) H.; m. Kathleen C. Roseman. BA magna cum laude, St. Charles Borromeo, Phila., 1970. Dist. exec. Hawk Mountain coun. Boy Scouts Am., Reading, Pa., 1971-78, sr. dist. exec. Hawk Mountain coun., 1978-80, devel. dir. Hawk Mountain coun., 1980-83; fin. dir. Nassau county coun. Boy Scouts Am., Roslyn, N.Y., 1983-85; dir. devel. Luth. Home, Topton, Pa., 1985-94, St. Vincent Archabbey, Latrobe, Pa., 1994—. Campaign worker United Way So. Schuykill, Pottsville, Pa., 1977-79, United Way Berks County, Reading, 1982, 85-92; com. chmn. Hawk Mountain coun. Boy Scouts Am., 1986-89. Named one of Outstanding Young Men Am., 1977; recipient St. George award Nat. Cath. Com. on Scouting, 1978. Mem. Nat. Soc. Fundraising Execs. (bd. dirs. northeastern Pa. chpt. 1986-94, v.p. 1988, pres. 1989, 92, Outstanding Fund Raising Exec. 1993), Rotary (bd. dirs. West Reading Club 1980-83, Reading Club 1990-94, dist. Rotary Found. group study exch. 1991-94), Mt. View Rotary Club, Luth. Brotherhood (br. v.p. 1991-93). Roman Catholic. Avocations: aquatics, hiking, backpacking, furniture refinishing. Home: 1407 Clearview Dr Greensburg PA 15601-3703 Office: St Vincent Archabbey Latrobe PA 15650

HAGER, ELIZABETH SEARS, state legislator, social services organization administrator; b. Washington, Oct. 31, 1944; d. Hess Thatcher and Elizabeth Grace (Harper) Sears; m. Dennis Sterling Hager, Sept. 3, 1966; children: Annie Elizabeth, Lucie Caroline. BA, Wellesley Coll., 1966; MPA, U. N.H., 1979. Prin. Philbrook Ctr., Concord, N.H., 1970-71; rep. N.H. Gen. Ct., Concord, 1973-76, 85-94, 1996—; del. N.H. Constitutional Conv., Concord, 1974, 84; campaign coord. Anderson for Pres. Rep. Primary, N.H., 1980; mem. Concord City Coun., 1982-90; mayor City of Concord, 1988-90; exec. dir. United Way of Merrimack County, Concord, 1996—; bd. dirs. Jefferson Pilot Funds, Concord, Bank of NH, Soc. for Protection of N.H. Forests. Pres. Greater Concord United Way, 1980-81; campaign chair United Way of Merrimack County, Concord, 1986. Republican. Episcopalian. Home and Office: 5 Orchard St Concord NH 03301-3849 Office: 46 N Main St Concord NH 03301-4913

HAGER, JOHN HENRY, state official; b. Durham, N.C., Aug. 28, 1936; m. Margaret Dickinson Chase, Feb. 27, 1971; children: John Virgil, Henry Chase. BSME, Purdue U., 1958; MBA, Harvard U., 1960. Various positions Am. Tobacco Co., 1961-94; lt. gov. State of Va., Richmond, 1998—. Pres. of State Senate; chmn. of Disability Commission; co-chmn. com. on Public Sch. Infrastructure; trustee, Jamestown Yorktown Edul. Trust; vice pres. Jamestown-Yorktown Edul. Trust; chmn. Richmond Center Expansion; dir. Sorensen Inst. Political Leadership; dir. Partnership for Urban Va., dir. Va. State C of C; trustee, exec. com., finance com. Va. Mus. of Fine Arts; 1st vice pres., dir. Va. Pub. Safety Found., Inc.; Chldn's Hosp. (past pres., trustee, exec. com.); Met. Richmond Convention and Vis.. Bureau (past chmn., dir., founding dir.); Va. Health Care Found. (past chmn., dir., exec. com.); 7th District Rep. Party (past vice chmn. 3rd district, exec. com. mem. past precinct, ward and campaign chmn.); Rep. Party of Va. and delegate/alternate to 4 natl. conventions (past treas., past exec. com. mem., state central com. mem., numerous other pos.); ruling elder 1st Presbyn. Ch., Richmond. 2nd lt. U.S. Army, 1960-61, capt. USAR. Named one of Outstanding Young Men of Am., 1976, Man of Yr., Tobacco Internat. Mag., 1990; recipient Alumni Citizenship award Purdue U., 1987, Svc. award Richmond Rep. Com., 1992, Disting. Alumni award Durham Acad., 1992, Good Govt. award Richmond First Club, 1996, Tourism Leadership award Met. Richmond Convention and Visitors Bur., 1997, Lettie Pate Whitehead Evans award Westminster-Canterbury, 1997, Citizenship award Va. Coun. Indians, 1998. Mem. Am. Legion, Va. C. of C. (dir.), Va. Comm. on Fam. Violence Prevention; mem. Special Statewide Taskforce Investigating Organized Crime and Drug Trafficking in Va.; mem. South. Growth Policies Bd.; mem. Adv. Bd. Tobacco History Corp.; mem. Celebration, 2007; mem. Richmond Rep. Party Com., 25 yrs.; Richmond German, Richmond Hundred (past pres., dir.), City of Richmond Electoral Bd. (past chmn.) Pub. Affairs Group (past chmn.), Forum Club (past pres.), Commonwealth Club (past dir.), Custis Fishing and Hunting Club (past dir.), Country Club Va. (past pres. and CEO, past dir.). Office: State of Va Office of Lt Gov 900 E Main St Ste 1400 Richmond VA 23219-3513

HAGER, JOHN PATRICK, metallurgy engineering educator; b. Miles City, Mont., Oct. 2, 1936; s. John Herman and Agnes C. (Hart) H.; m. Mary Anna McCloskey, Aug. 26, 1961; children: Patrick, Michael, Charles, Justine, Brendan, Thomas, John Jr. BS, Mont. Sch. Mines, 1958; MS, Mo. Sch. Mines, 1960; ScD, MIT, 1969. Asst. scientist AVCO Corp., Wilmington, Mass., 1961; instr. MIT, Cambridge, 1961-64, research asst., 1964-66; asst. prof. Colo. Sch. Mines, Golden, 1966-69, assoc. prof., 1969-71, dept. head, prof., 1971-74, prof. metallurgy, 1971—, St. Joe Mineral's Corp. prof. extractive metallurgy, 1974-87, Hazen research prof. extractive metallurgy, 1988—. Mem. TMS-AIME. Republican. Roman Catholic. Home: 2054 Crestvue Cir Golden CO 80401-1763 Office: Colo Sch Mines Dept Metal and Materials Enging Golden CO 80401

HAGER, LARRY STANLEY, book editor, publishing executive; b. Elmira, N.Y., May 23, 1942; s. Howard Mark and Merle E. (Woodard) H.; m. Anita K. Liedtke; children: Larry Mark, Lori Ann. B.A., Mansfield U. Editor Internat. Textbook Co., Scranton, Pa., 1969-72; sr. editor Intext Inc., N.Y.C., 1972-74, Thomas Y. Crowell, N.Y.C., 1974-77; sr. editor Van Nostrand Reinhold, N.Y.C., 1977-82, editor in chief, 1982-83, editorial dir. profl. reference div., 1983-84; pub. Enging. and Tech., N.Y.C., 1984-85; v.p., editorial dir. TAB Profl. and Reference Books, N.Y.C., 1985-91; sr. editor profl. book group McGraw-Hill, Inc., N.Y.C., 1991—. Exec. bd., v.p. program Thomas A. Edison council Boy Scout Am., 1982-83. Served with U.S. Army, 1964-66, Vietnam. Recipient as pub. Best Tech. Book award Am. Assn. Pubs., 1980 as pub. Best Enging. Book Am. Assn. Pubs., 1981, Best Phys. Sci. Book Am. Assn. Pubs., 1982, Best Enging. Handbook Am. Assn. Pubs., 1994, Best Gen. Enging. Book Am. Assn. Pubs., 1995, Silver Beaver award Boy Scouts Am., 1986. Methodist. Home: 403 Prospect Ave Avenel NJ 07001-1133 Office: McGraw-Hill Inc Profl Book Group 11 W 19th St Fl 3 New York NY 10011-4285

HAGER, LOUISE ALGER, retired chaplain; b. Spokane, Wash., Dec. 15, 1923; d. Russel S. and Thelma Ella (Geib) Alger; m. Bernard Coe, Nov. 16, 1945 (dec. July 1965); children: Cynthia W., Marjorie L.; m. Onslow B. Hager, Jan. 16, 1970 (dec. Dec. 1983). BEd, Nat. Coll. Edn., 1946; M of Theol. Studies, St. Paul Sch. Theology, 1997. Kindergarten tchr. Edgewater Park Bd. Edn., Beverly, N.J., 1946-47, 59-83; pres. bd. mgrs. Cinnaminson (N.J.) Home, 1985-88; chaplain Rsch. Med. Ctr., Kansas City, Mo., 1986-88; assoc. chaplain John Knox Village, Lee's Summit, Mo., 1988-98; ret., 1998. Chaplain vol. Burlington County Hosp., Mt. Holly, N.J., 1987-88; lay minister. Mem. NEA, Lee's Summit Ministerial Soc., Coll. Chaplains, Am. Soc. on Aging, Mid-Am. Congress on Aging. Democrat. Quaker. Avocations: reading, piano playing, singing, sewing, walking. Home: 13801 York Rd #M-1 Cockeysville MD 21030-1899

HAGER, LOWELL PAUL, biochemistry educator; b. Girard, Kans., Aug. 30, 1926; s. Paul William and Christine (Selle) H.; m. Frances Erea, Jan. 22, 1949; children: Paul, Steven, JoAnn. AB, Valparaiso U., 1947; MA, U. Kans., 1950; PhD, U. Ill., 1953. Postdoctoral fellow Mass. Gen. Hosp., Boston, 1953-55; asst. prof. biochemistry Harvard U., Cambridge, Mass., 1955-60; mem. faculty U. Ill., Urbana, 1960—, prof. biochemistry, 1965—, head biochem. div., 1967-89, dir. Biotech. Ctr., 1987—; chmn. physiol. chemistry study sect. NIH, 1965—; vis. scientist Imperial Cancer Rsch. Fund, 1964; cons. NSF, 1976. Editor life scis. Archives Biochemistry and Biophysics, 1966—; assoc. editor Biochemistry, 1973—; mem. editorial bd. Jour. Biol. Chemistry, 1874—. With USAAF, 1945. Guggenheim fellow U. Oxford, Eng., 1959-60, Max Planck Inst. Zellchemie, 1959-60. Mem. NAS (elected), Am. Chem. Soc., Am. Soc. Biol. Chemists, Am. Soc. Microbiology (chmn. physiology divsn. 1967). Achievements include rsch. in enzyme mechanisms, intermediary metabolism, tumor virus. Home: 801 W Delaware Ave Urbana IL 61801-4808

HAGER, MARY HASTINGS, nutritionist, educator, consultant; b. Upland, Calif., Mar. 27, 1948; d. Howard Benjamin and Miriam Agnes Hastings; m. Douglas Francis Hager, Jan. 4, 1982; children: Marghet Janet, Bettina Miriam. BS in Foods and Nutrition, U. Del., 1971; MS in Nutrition and Dietetics, U. Calif., Davis, 1973, PhD in Nutrition, 1978. Registered, lic. dietitian. Nutritionist U. Calif. Sch. Medicine, Davis, 1973-74; staff scientist Procter and Gamble Co., Cin., 1978-83, devel. staff, 1986-87; asst. prof. Coll. Mount St. Joseph, Cin., 1983-85, Tex. Christian U., Ft. Worth, 1987-89; vis. lectr. Rutgers U., New Brunswick, N.J., 1989-90; assoc. prof. Coll. of St. Elizabeth, Morristown, N.J., 1991-96, prof., assoc. dean, 1996—; cons. IGA Grocers, Cin., 1984-85, Hoffman-LaRoche Corp., Nutley, N.J., 1989-90, Procter and Gamble Co., Cin., 1990—; dietetic internship site visitor. Contbr. articles and abstracts to profl. publs. Chmn. bd. dirs. Greater Cin. Nutrition Coun., 1985-86; mem. edn. task force Am. Heart Assn., Ft. Worth, 1988-89; pub. edn. com. Am. Cancer Soc., Ft. Worth, 1988-89; mem. Health Care Reform Adv. Bd., 11th Congl. Dist., 1993-94. Grad. fellow Procter and Gamble Co., 1975-78; Amy Rextrew scholar U. Del., 1970; grantee Tex. Christian U. Rsch. Fund, 1988. Fellow Am. Dietetic Assn; mem. Am. Inst. Nutrition (rsch. award 1978), Am. Soc. Enteral Parenteral Nutrition Soc. for Nutrition Edn., N.J. Dietetic Assn. (pres.-elect 1996-97, pres. 1997-98, ho. dels. 1998—), Mortar Bd., Sigma Xi. Democrat. Episcopalian. Avocations: swimming, walking, drawing. Home: 9 Jay Dr Randolph NJ 07869-4102 Office: Coll of St Elizabeth Dept Foods and Nutrition Morristown NJ 07960

HAGER, PAULA MICHELE, critical care nurse; b. Palmerton, Pa., Sept. 29, 1957; d. Edward L. and Pauline A. (Macalush) H. Diploma, Hazleton (Pa.) State Gen. Hosp, 1978. CCRN; cert. ACLS, pediatric advanced life support. Staff nurse, med./surgical Coaldale (Pa.) State Gen. Hosp., 1978-86, staff nurse ICU/CCU, 1986-92; staff nurse ICU/CCU Miners Meml. Med. Ctr., 1992—; instr. ACLS, CPR. Vol. Am. Heart Assn. Mem. Pa. Nurses Assn.

HAGER, ROBERT, journalist; b. N.Y.C.. Ed., Dartmouth Coll., 1960. Broadcaster minor league baseball Sta.-WBUY, Lexington, N.C., 1960-61; reporter on state govt. Sta.-WPTF, Raleigh, N.C., 1961-63; polit. reporter Sta.-WBTV, Charlotte, N.C., 1963-65; Corr. and local news anchorman for Sta.-WRC-TV, NBC News, Washington, 1965-69; corr. NBC Network News, Saigon, Vietnam, 1969-70, Berlin, 1970-73; corr. NBC Network News (N.E. Bur.), N.Y.C., 1973-79, NBC Network News (Washington Bur.), 1979—. Office: care NBC News 4001 Nebraska Ave NW Washington DC 20016-2733*

HAGER, ROBERT WORTH, retired aerospace company executive; b. Longview, Wash., June 20, 1928; s. Josiah Denver and Merle (Worth) H.; m. Margaret Goodnough, Aug. 25, 1950; children: Stephen M., Sandra Hager Dahl, Shane D. BS in Civil Engring, U. Wash., 1949, MS in Civil Engring, 1950; DSc (hon.), U. Ala., 1995. Rsch. fellow U. Wash., 1949-50; rsch. engr. U.S. Navy Civil Engring. Lab., Port Hueneme, Calif., 1950-53; mem. staff Sandia Corp., Albuquerque, 1953-55; with Boeing Co., Seattle, 1955-93, Minuteman program mgr., 1973-78, v.p., gen. mgr. ballistic missile and space div., 1978-80, v.p. engring., 1980-84; v.p. space sta. Boeing Co., Huntsville, Ala., 1984-89, v.p., gen. mgr. Huntsville div. Boeing Aerospace and Electronics, 1989-91, v.p., gen. mgr. Missiles and Space Div. Boeing Def. and Space Group, 1991-93. Past chmn. bd. Univ. Space Rsch. Assn.; past chmn. Bus. Coun. Ala.; vice chmn. Lower Hood Canal Watershed Com., 1996; treas. Hood Canal Salmon Enhancement Group. Fellow AIAA, Am. Astron. Soc. Methodist.

HAGERMAN, ALLEN REID, mining executive; b. Calgary, Alta., Can., May 11, 1951; s. Douglas Reid and Isobel (Allen) H.; m. Patricia Helen Race, May 11, 1974; children: Allison Margaret, Christine Patricia. B Comm, U. Alta., 1973; CA, 1975; MBA, Harvard U., 1977. Articling student, staff acct. Arthur Andersen & Co., Calgary, 1973-75; fin. analyst Hudson Bay Oil & Gas Co., Calgary, 1977-79, dir. project analysis, 1979-80, mgr. treas., 1980-82; corp. sec., exec. asst. Home Oil Co. Ltd., Calgary, 1982-84, treas., 1984-87; treas. Interhome Energy Inc., Calgary, 1987-88, v.p., treas., 1988-90, v.p. fin., 1990-91; v.p., chief fin. officer Home Oil Co. Ltd., Calgary, 1991-95; pres. Springbank Enterprises, 1995-96; v.p., CFO Fording Inc., Calgary, 1996—. Chmn. Alta. Children's Hosp. Found. Mem. Can. Inst. Chartered Accts., Inst. Chartered Accts. Alta., Fin. Execs. Inst. (bd. dirs. 1989-94). Progressive Conservative. Mem. United Ch. Home: 1275 85 St SW, Calgary, AB Canada T3H 4A4

HAGERMAN, JAMES BRIEN, speech and drama educator; b. Lincoln, Nebr., June 28, 1959; s. James Franklin Hagerman and Nadia Bailey; m. Lori Louise Kuntz, June 16, 1990; 1 child, James Alexander. BA, U. Findlay, 1983; MFA, Syracuse U., 1986. Cert. in speech and theater. Asst. artistic dir., mng. dir. U. Findlay (Ohio) Summer Stock, 1983-95; tchr. speech and theater Beechcroft H.S., Columbus, Ohio, 1988—. Bd. trustees Gahanna (Ohio) Comty. Congregational Ch., 1995-97. Ft. Findlay Playhouse scholar, 1978; Ingram grantee, 1978. Mem. NEA, Ednl. Theatre Assn., Ohio Edn. Assn., Ohio Theatre Alliance. Avocations: videography, movies. Home: 6683 Skywae Dr Columbus OH 43229-7023

HAGERMAN, MICHAEL CHARLES, lawyer, arbitrator, mediator; b. Webster City, Iowa, Aug. 20, 1951; s. Charles Arnold and Jill Hamilton (Son de Regger) H.; children: Kelly, Douglas. BA with honors, U. Iowa, 1973; MBA, U. Utah, 1978; JD, Drake U., 1981; Grad., U.S. Army Command/Gen. Staff, Coll., Ft. Leavenworth, Kans., 1988. Bar: Iowa 1981, Mass. 1995. Clk. Iowa Resources, Legal Aid of Polk County, and State of Iowa, Des Moines, 1978-81; contract atty. Fisher Controls Internat., Inc., Marshalltown, Iowa, 1981-84; contracts mgr. Emerson & Cuming, Inc., Canton, Mass., 1984-85; contract atty. GTE Govt. Sys., Taunton, Mass., 1986-90; v.p., gen. counsel, sec. ISI Sys., Inc., Andover, Mass., 1990-94; legal counsel Swan Tech. Inc., Marlboro, Mass., 1994-95; pvt. practice Franklin, Mass., 1995—; sr. contracts mgr. BankBoston, N.A., 1998—. Contbr. articles to profl. jours. Capt. U.S. Army, 1973-78, Germany; lt. col. U.S. Army Res. ret. Mem. Mass. Bar Assn., Sigma Chi (chpt. Balfour award 1973), Phi Alpha Delta (chpt. pres. 1980-81). Avocations: sailing, writing, travel.

HAGEY, WALTER REX, retired banker; b. Hatfield, Pa., July 24, 1909; s. Justus T. and Martha Mabel Hagey; m. Dorothy E. Rosenberger, Oct. 17, 1931; 1 child, Donald C. Grad., Peirce Coll., 1929; student, U. Pa., 1931-36; LLB, La Salle Extension U., 1938; STB, Temple U., 1943; grad., Stonier Grad. Sch. Banking Rutgers U., 1951; LLD, Muhlenberg Coll., 1963. With Fidelity Bank (formerly Fidelity-Phila. Trust Co.), 1929—, asst. sec., 1948—, asst. v.p., 1957-66, v.p., 1966-74. Supply pastor Eastern Pa. Synod Lutheran Ch. Am., 1950-80, treas., 1950-80, now Luth. Synod S.E. Pa.; treas. Luth.

Synod Northeastern Pa., 1969-70; pres., dir. Phila. Luth. Social Union; treas. Luth. Laymens Movement for Stewardship of United Luth. Ch., 1959-63; mem. bd., exec. com. Luth. Council in U.S., 1962-74; mem. bds., treas. home missions, inner missions, Christian edn. Eastern Pa. Synod, Luth. Ch. Am., 1950-69; vice chmn. adminstrn. and fin. Luth. Ch. in Am., 1972-78, mem. bd. pensions, 1978-84, v.p. Bd. Am. Missions, 1972-78; bd. dirs., adv. bd. Muhlenberg Med. Center; bd. dirs., chmn. Prosser Found., 1968-89; bd. dirs., treas. Luth. Retirement Homes, 1978-82; mem. com. for investments Luth. Ch. in Am., 1978-82; bd. dirs., sec. Silver Spring-Martin Luther Sch., 1976-89; treas. Bethesda House, 1950-69; treas., registrar Luth. Lay Acad., 1981-96; treas. The Auxiliary-Luth. Theol. Sem. at Phila., 1986-89, The Religious Tercentenary Com., 1982-89. Mem. Am. Inst. Banking, Phila. Estate Planning Coun., Pa. Coun. Chs. (dir. 1954-70), Pa. Soc., Luth. Hist. Soc. Ea. Pa., Men of Mt. Airy Sem. (pres. 1976-86), Pa. Bible Soc. (treas., sec., pres., dir. 1971-95), Rotary, Elm Club (sec. 1951-63), Midday Club, Anglers Club (Phila.). Home: 25 Lutheran Home Dr Telford PA 18969-1728

HAGGARD, WILLIAM HENRY, meteorologist; b. Woodbridge, Conn., Nov. 20, 1920; s. Howard Wilcox and Josephine Cecelia (Foley) H.; m. Blanche Woolard, Mar. 21, 1944 (div. May 1967); children: William Henry Jr., Robert H.; m. Martina Wadewitz, Oct. 1, 1967. BS in Physics, Yale U., 1942; cert. in profl. meteorology, MIT, 1942; MS in Meteorology, U. Chgo., 1946; postgrad., Fla. State U., 1958-59. Instr. meteorology N.C. State U., Raleigh, 1946-47; rsch. meteorologist U.S. Weather Bur., 1947-48; forecaster USWB Nat. Airport, 1949-50; instr. U.S. AID, Washington, 1950-51; staff weather rsch. project U.S. Navy, Norfolk, Va., 1951-54; chief adv. svcs. br. U.S. Weather Bur., Washington, 1954-59, asst. chief Office of Plans, 1960-61; dep. dir. Nat. Weather Records Ctr., Asheville, N.C., 1961; dir. Nat. Climatic Ctr., Asheville, 1963-75; pres. Climatol. Cons. Corp., Asheville, 1976-97, v.p., 1998; cons., 1999—; mem. weather com. U.S. Power Squadron, Raleigh, N.C., 1988-98. Contbr. articles to tech. jours., 1947-99. Bd. dirs. ARC, Asheville, 1965-70, United Way, Asheville, 1964-70. Capt. USN, 1942-45, with Res. 1951-54. Recipient Tech. Adminstr. award NOAA, Washington, 1970. Fellow Am. Meteorol. Soc. (cert. cons. meteorologist, bd. dirs. pvt. sector meteorology sect. 1989-92, mem. cert. cons. meteorologist bd. 1983-88), Nat. Coun. Indsl. Meteorologists (pres. 1988-89, bd. dirs. 1987-90, 94-96, sec., treas. 1994-99). Republican. Presbyterian. Avocations: sailing, photography. Office: William H Haggard CCM LLC 150 Shope Creek Rd Asheville NC 28805-9795

HAGGEN, DONALD E., food products executive. CEO Haggen Foods, Bellingham, Wash., co-chmn., 1996—. Office: Haggen's Inc PO Box 9704 Bellingham WA 98227-9704*

HAGGERTY, ANCER LEE, judge; b. 1944. BS, U. Oreg., 1967; JD, Hastings Coll. Law, 1973. Law clk. Metro. Pub. Defender, Portland, 1972, 73, staff atty., 1973-77; assoc. Souther, Spaulding, Kinzey, Williamson and Schwabe, 1977-82, Schwabe, Williamson & Wyatt, 1983-88; judge Multnomah County Dist. Ct., 1989-90, Multnomah County Cir. Ct., 1990-93; dist. judge U.S. Ct. Appeals (9th cir.), Portland, 1994—; Mem. Gov.'s task force evaln.Oreg. Liquor Control Commn., 1978, Jud. Conduct Com., 1989-92; coord. Multnomah County Bar Pro Bono program, 1983-88; mem. Oreg. State Bd. Bar Examiners, 1979-82. Coach, practice judge mock ct. team Jefferson H.S.; asst. coach Whitaker 7th and 8th grade Pop Warner football teams. 1st lt. USMC, 1967-70, Vietnam. Decorated Silver Star medal, Purple Heart; recipient award Alumni Assn. U. Oreg., Local Hero award Martin Luther King, Jr. Elem. Sch. Fifth Grade, 1993. Mem. ABA, Am. Bridge Assn., Oreg. State Bar Assn., Nat. Bar Assn., Lloyd Ctr. Racquet Club, Marine Corps League, Phoenix Bridge Club. Office: 9th Dist Ct Appeals Pioneer Courthouse 620 SW Main St Ste 615 Portland OR 97205-3037*

HAGGERTY, ARTHUR DANIEL, stress and chronic pain management specialist; b. Bklyn., Mar. 25, 1925; s. Arthur Daniel and Sophia Edna (Stendera) H.; m. Asta Constance Gundersen, Sept. 11, 1949 (dec. May 1993); children: Donna, Mark, Lynne, Gayle. BA, L.I. U., Bklyn., 1949; MA, NYU, 1951; PhD, Western U., San Diego, 1953. Lic. psychologist, N.Y.; lic. nursing home adminstr., N.Y. Adminstr. homes for aged and blind St. John's Episcopal Hosp., Bklyn., 1956-73; prof., dir. grad program in health care adminstrn. L.I. U., Greenvale, N.Y., 1973-77; pvt. practice psychologist Boca Raton, Fla., 1977-85; dir. edn. and rsch. Palm Beach chpt. Alzheimer's Assn., Boca Raton, 1986-89; health psychologist Psychiat. and Psychol. Assocs., Atlantis, Fla., 1985-96; CEO Stress and Chronic Pain Mgmt. Sys., East Northport, N.Y., 1996—; psychol. cons. Grace Med. Group, Bklyn., 1956-58; mem. N.Y. State Bd. Examiners Nursing Home Adminstrn., Albany, 1970-75; cons. in tng. Fla. State Commn. Criminal Justice, Tallahassee, 1982-92; cons. continuing edn. Palm Beach C.C., Lake Worth, Fla., 1982-92. Editor Long Term Care and Health Svcs. Adminstrn. Quar., 1976-80. Sgt. U.S. Army, 1944-46, PTO. Recipient Nat. Edn. award Am. Coll. Nursing Home Adminstrn., Washington, 1978. Fellow Am. Inst. Stress; mem. The Monroe Inst. (prof.), Am. Acad. Experts in Traumatic Stress. Home: 423 Clay Pitts Rd East Northport NY 11731-3801 Office: Stress & Chronic Pain Mgmt Sys 423 Clay Pitts Rd East Northport NY 11731-3801

HAGGERTY, CHARLES A., electronics executive. Student, U. St. Thomas. Pres., chief exec. officer, chmn. bd. dirs. IBM, 1964-92; pres., COO Western Digital Corp., Irvine, Calif., 1992-96. Office: Western Digital Corp 8105 Irvine Center Dr Irvine CA 92618-2937*

HAGGERTY, GRETCHEN R., accounting and finance executive. V.p. acctg. and fin. U.S. Steel Group, Pitts. Office: USX Corp 600 Grant St Ste 6100 Pittsburgh PA 15219-2805

HAGGERTY, JAMES JOSEPH, lawyer; b. Scranton, Pa., June 12, 1936; s. James J. Haggerty and Margaret W. Cummings; m. Cecelia Ellen Lynett; children: Jean Margaret McGrath, Mauri Elizabeth Collins, James Joseph Jr., Matthew Edward, Cecelia Ellen, Daniel Patrick, Kathleen Mary. BA in Econs., Holy Cross Coll., Worcester, Mass., 1957; JD, Georgetown U., 1960; LLD (hon.), U. Scranton, 1987; LHD (hon.), Villanova U., 1995. Bar: Pa. 1961, Ct. Common Pleas Lackawanna County 1961, U.S. Dist. Ct. (mid. dist.) Pa. 1961, U.S. Ct. Appeals (3d cir.) 1962, U.S. Ct. Claims 1985. Assoc. Farrell Butler Kearney & Parker, Scranton, 1961-62; law clk. to Hon. William J. Nealon U.S. Dist. Ct. (mid. dist.), Scranton, 1963-64; ptnr. Casey Haggerty and McDonnell, Scranton, 1965-70, Haggerty McDonnell O'Brien, Scranton, 1970-87; former sec. of commonwealth State of Pa., Harrisburg, 1987-89; gen. counsel to gov. Commonwealth of Pa., Harrisburg, 1989-93; ptnr. Haggerty, McDonnell & O'Brien, Scranton, 1993—; apptd. by U.S. Dist. Ct. trustee in bankruptcy of Blue Coal Corp., 1976-86; mem. hearing com. 3.03 Disciplinary Bd. Pa. Supreme Ct.; permanent mem. Jud. Conf. U.S. 3d Jud. Cir.; mem. Fed. Jud. Screening Com., 1996—; chmn. bd. dirs. Shamrock Comm. Corp.; past bd. dirs. Specialty Plastics Products Inc.; past. bd. dirs., solicitor 1st Nat. Community Bank Dunmore. Trustee U. Scranton, 1979-86, chmn. bd., 1982-86, mem. Pres.'s Cir., mem. Pres.'s Club; chmn. Real Bob Casey Com., 1985-86; former dir. Lackawanna United Way, former chmn. profl. and geog. divsn.; mem. Scranton Area Found., bd. dirs. assocs.; mem. bd. trustees Scranton Prep. Sch., 1995—, chmn. bd., 1999—. With U.S. Army and Pa. N.G. Mem. ABA, ATLA, Am. Bankers Assn., Pa. Bar Assn. (Spl. Achievement award 1988-89), Pa. Trial Lawyers Assn., Pa. Bankers Assn., Lackawanna Bar Assn. (past pres., bd. dirs.), Greater Scranton C. of C. (bd. dirs., former v.p.), Holy Cross Coll. Alumni Assn. N.E. Pa. (past pres., Outstanding Alumnus award 1982), Scranton Prep. Sch. Alumni Assn. (past mem. bd. govs., T. Donald Reinfret S.J. award Outstanding Alumnus of Yr. 1985), Friendly Sons of St. Patrick Lackawanna County (mem. exec. com., past pres.), Country Club Scranton (bd. dirs.). Roman Catholic. Office: Haggerty McDonnell & O'Brien 203 Franklin Ave Ste 1 Scranton PA 18503-1989

HAGGERTY, JOHN EDWARD, research center administrator, former army officer; b. Reading, Mass., Sept. 9, 1918; s. Timothy Steven and Kathryn Margaret (Kyle) H.; m. Elizabeth Penn Hammond, Sept. 29, 1945; children: John Edward, William S., Thomas M., David B., Richard K. LLB cum laude, Suffolk U., 1941; postgrad., N.C. State U., 1972; grad., Command and Gen. Staff Coll., Ft. Leavenworth, Kans., 1954, Army War Coll., Carlisle Barracks, Pa., 1961; postgrad. in advanced mgmt., Harvard U., 1964; BS, U. Md., 1971. Enlisted U.S. Army, 1941-42, commd. 2d lt., 1942, advanced through grades to brig. gen., 1973; troop comdr. U.S. Army, ETO, 1942-45; instr. health care Baylor U., Ft. Sam Houston, Tex., 1945-50; congl. liaison officer Dept. Army gen. Staff, Washington, 1950-54; dir. med. personnel Dept. Army Gen. Staff (European Command), 1954-57; dir. spl. projects and med. legis. Dept. Army Gen. Staff, Washington, 1957-60; exec. officer, chief adminstr. Med. Rsch. and Devel. Command, Washington, 1961-63; exec. officer, chief adminstrv. svcs. U.S. Army Hosp., Ft. Knox, Ky., 1963-66; exec. asst., dir. med. plans and ops. Pacific Command, Hawaii, 1966-69; U.S. med. rep. SEATO, Bangkok, 1966-69; exec. officer, chief adminstrv. svcs. U.S. Army Hosp., Airborne Ctr., Ft. Bragg, N.C., 1969-72; dir. civilian health and med. program of uniformed svcs. Office Sec. Def., Washington, 1972-73; dir. resource mgmt. Army Med. Dept., Washington, 1973-77; chief Med. Svc. Corps, Washington, 1973-77; ret. U.S. Army, 1977; assoc. dir. New Eng. Regional Primate Rsch. Ctr., Harvard U. Med. Sch., Southborough, Mass., 1978-90. Decorated Disting. Svc. medal; decorated Legion of Merit medal, Meritorious Svc. medal, Joint Commendation medal, Army Commendation medal; decorated Army Med. Dept. medallion; recipient Presdl. citation Baylor U., 1977, Ray Brown award Assn. Mil. Surgeons U.S., 1978; named hon. alumni Harvard U. Med. Sch., 1981. Mem. U.S. Army War Coll. Alumni Assn., Fed. Health Care Exec. Inst., Baylor U. Alumni Assn., Harvard Bus. Sch. Alumni Assn., Am. Coll. Hosp. Adminstrs. Home: 9 North St Grafton MA 01519-1215

HAGGERTY, MICHAEL, advertising executive. Exec. v.p. media dir. Wells, Rich, Greene BDDP Advertising, N.Y.C. Office: Wells Rich Greene BDDP Advertising 11 Madison Ave New York NY 10010-3629*

HAGGERTY, ROBERT JOHNS, physician, educator; b. Saranac Lake, N.Y., Oct. 20, 1925; s. Gordon Abbott and Nina (Johns) H.; m. Muriel Ethel Protzmann, Oct. 29, 1949; children: Robert, Janet, Richard, John. AB, Cornell U., 1946, MD, 1949; AM (hon.), Harvard U., 1975; DSc (hon.), Ind. U., 1990. Diplomate Am. Bd. Pediatrics. Intern Strong Meml. Hosp., Rochester, N.Y., 1949-51; from resident to chief resident pediatrics Children's Hosp. Med. Ctr., Boston, 1953-55; med. dir. family health care program Harvard Med. Sch., also asst. prof. pediatrics, 1953-64; prof. pediatrics, chmn. dept. U. Rochester Sch. Medicine, 1964-75; Roger I. Lee prof. health services, chmn. dept. health services Harvard Sch. Pub. Health, 1975-78; prof. pediatrics Harvard Med. Sch., Boston, 1975-78; clin. prof. Harvard Med. Sch., 1978-80; pres. Wm. T. Grant Found., N.Y.C., 1980-92; clin. prof. pediatrics Cornell U. Med. Sch., N.Y.C., 1980-92; prof. pediatrics emeritus U. Rochester Sch. Medicine, 1992—; exec. dir. Internat. Pediatric Assoc., 1993-98; dir. gen. pediatrics acad. devel. program Robert Wood Johnson Found., 1978-88; mem. health svcs. rsch. sect. USPHS, 1964-70, 82-84, chmn., 1968-70, 82-84; mem. N.Y. State Health Planning Adv. Coun., Carnegie Coun. on Children, 1972-77; chmn. panel health scis. rsch., com. on nat. needs for biomed. and behavioral rsch. per. NRC, 1975-78; mem. bd. U.S. Com. on UNICEF, 1981-87; mem. Gov.'s Coun. on Grad. Med. Edn., N.Y. State, 1989-93. Editor: (with M. Green) Ambulatory Pediatrics, 1968, 5th edit., 1999, (with J. Lucey) Pediatrics, 1973-80, Pediatrics in Rev., 1978—, Bull. N.Y. Acad. Medicine, 1992-99; assoc. editor New Eng. Jour. Medicine, 1959-64; contbr. articles to med. jours. Mem. vis. com. Grad. Sch. Edn., Harvard U., 1982-88; bd. dirs. Grantmakers in Health, 1985-89; bd. overseers, social scis. dept., Tufts U., 1990-94; bd. visitors U. Okla. Sch. Pub. Health, 1991-94. Capt. USAF, 1951-53. Recipient Martha M. Eliot award Am. Pub. Health Assn., 1976, Disting. Alumni award Cornell U. Med. Coll., 1987, 6 awards various pediatric socs., 1989; Markle scholar acad. medicine, 1962-67; fellow Ctr. for Advanced Study Behavioral Scis., Stanford, Calif., 1974-75. Mem. Assn. Med. Sch. Pediatric Dept. Chairmen (pres. 1969-70), Am. Assn. Poison Control Centers (pres. 1962-64), Am. Acad. Pediatrics (v.p., pres. 1983-85, Grulee award 1981, Dale Richmond award 1981, Aldrich award 1986, Job Smith award 1987, Abraham Jacobi award 1996), Am. Pediatric Soc. (Joseph St. Geme award 1989, John Howland award 1998), Ambulatory Pediatric Assn. (chmn. 1963-64, George Armstrong award 1969), Assn. Am. Med. Colls., Internat. Epidemiol. Assn., Soc. Pediatric Research (v.p. 1970-71), Inst. Medicine (council 1974-77, chmn. com. on prevention of mental illness 1992-93, chmn. steering com. nat. study quality assurance programs 1975-76, Gustave Lienhard award 1989), Primary Care Achievement award PEW Found. Health Professions Commn., 1994, N.Y. Acad. Medicine (trustee, sec. 1989-92), Brit. Paediatric Soc. (hon.), Am. Health Fedn. (trustee 1989-92), Alliance for Health Care for All (trustee 1991-94), Harvard Club (N.Y.C.), Phi Beta Kappa, Alpha Omega Alpha.

HAGGERTY, THOMAS FRANCIS, newspaper editor; b. Troy, N.Y., Dec. 28, 1938; s. Thomas Anthony and Dorothy Marie (MacCauley) H.; m. Joyce Elaine Schearer, Feb. 4, 1967 (div. 1981); 1 child, Lori Lee. Sports writer Troy Record, 1961-65, sports editor, 1965-73; copy editor Springfield (Mass.) Union and Sunday Republican, 1973-76, exec. city editor, 1976-77, mng. editor, 1977-91, mng. editor production, 1991—; prof. journalism Westfield State Coll., Mass., 1983-84, Western New Eng. Coll., 1985. Served with USAF, 1952-61. Mem. Assoc. Press Mng. Editors Assn. Roman Catholic. Home: 72 Barrett St Apt 20B Northampton MA 01060-1737 Office: Springfield Newspapers PO Box 2350 1860 Main St Springfield MA 01103-1000*

HAGGETT, ROSEMARY ROMANOWSKI, dean. BS summa cum laude in Biology, U. Bridgeport, 1974; PhD in Physiology, U. Va., 1979. Postdoctoral fellow Northwestern U., Evanston, Ill., 1979-82; asst. prof. biology Loyola U. Chgo., 1982-87; asst. rsch. scientist zoology U. Md., College Park, 1987-88; from program dir. to divsn. dir. animals and nutrition USDA, 1988-94, dep. assoc. adminstr., 1988-94; dean Coll. Agr., Forestry and Consumer Scis. W.Va. U., Morgantown. Mem. ESCOP, Adminstrv. Heads Sect. (sec. 1996-97, vice chair 1997-98, chair 1998-99, chair-elect bd. agrl. 1998-99), Assn. Women in Sci., Soc. Study of Reproduction (edn. com. 1992, awards com. 1993-94). Office: WVa U Coll Agr Forestry and Consumer Scis PO Box 6108 Morgantown WV 26506-6108

HAGGIS, ARTHUR GEORGE, JR., retired military officer, educator, publisher; b. Youngstown, Ohio, June 3, 1924; s. Arthur George Sr. and Mary Mildred (Campbell) H.; m. Lewanna Evalyn Strom, Apr. 7, 1944; children: Lynda Lee, Arthur George III, Richard Charles, Douglas Hood, Pamela Sue. *Lewanna and Arthur Haggis were members of the same church, entered Youngstown College together, and married during the turbulent years of World War II, Now in their 55th year of marriage, they are extremely proud of the accomplishments of their five children and spouses Thomas, Judy, Nancy, Diane, and Jeff; glorify in the expectations of their grandchildren Jill, Jennifer, Arthur IV, Jason, Robert, Matthew, Diane, Lynn, and Nathan; and marvel at the future of their great grandchildren Kathryn, Kelly, Jasmine, Kienan, Kayla, and all those to be born to the Haggis Clan. Truly, a marriage made in Heaven!.* BS in Edn., Wayne State U., 1957, MEd, 1959, EdD, 1961. Enlisted pvt. U.S. Army, 1943, advanced through enlisted grades to staff sgt., commd. 2d. lt., field artillery/Battle of the Bulge, 1945, advanced through ranks to Brig. Gen., 1964; bn. survey officer field artillery U.S. Army ETO, 1943-46; S-2 475th Field Artillery Battalion and asst. indsl. engr. U.S. Steel Corp., McDonald, Ohio, 1946-51; post dep. comdr., adj. 2d Armored Div. Trains, Bad Kreuznach, Fed. Republic Germany, 1951-54; spl. mil. asst. to Sec. of Army , Chief of Info. U.S. Army, Ft. Wayne, Mich., Detroit Arsenal, Mich. Mil. Dist.; with ordnance tank automotive command Washington and Detroit; mem. gen. staff U.S. Army, Washington, 1954-64; pres., CEO Haggis Assocs. Inc., Washington and Hollywood, D.C. and Fla., 1964-71, Atlantis Pvt. Schs., Inc., Hollywood, 1971—; chmn., CEO The Atlantis-Lewart Group, Inc., Hollywood, 1987—; pres., CEO Ednl. Cons., Washington and Hollywood, 1966—, Atlantis Pub. Co., Hollywood, 1978—, Atlantis Rsch. Insts., Inc., Hollywood, 1981—, Perfect Body Products, Inc., Hollywood, 1981—; apptd. gubernatorial mem. State of Fla. Bd. Correctional Edn., Correctional Edn. Sch. Authority, term ending 1994; aide-de-camp to Gen. of Army Omar N. Bradley, 1955; negotiator Dept. Def. Armed Forces res. Ann. Unit Tng. Clause, UAW-CIO/GM contract, 1956; comdr. Army Task Force Ground Zero, Operation Plumbbob, atmospheric nuclear exlposion experiment, Frenchman Flat, Nev., 1957; liaison Sec. of Army, 1st U.S. Satellite Explorer I, 1957-58; comdr. U.S. Joint Task Force Mackinac, Mackinac Bridge Dedication Ceremony Mich., 1958; originator Dept. Def. Nat. Com. for Employer Support of Guard and Res., 1955-58; developer Dept. Def. Armed Forces Week, 1955-61. Co-editor, Small Business Library, The Government Market, 1966, Selling to the U.S. Government and its Contractors, vol. I, 1966, Bids, Proposals, Contracts and Contract Administration, vol. II, 1966, Texts of Small Business Enterprise Institute, vol. III, 1966, Bids, Proposals and Contracts for Small Business Enterprise Course Handbook, vol. IV, 1966; author: Educational Evaluation Program: Predicting College Success, 1967; author: (with others) Edu-Care, the New School Concept, 1991, also supporting texts, Atlantis Beginning Language and Number Development Program, Books 1 and 2, 1981, Atlantis Basic Spelling Series, Books A-H, 1981-85, Atlantis Computer Series, Books I-VII, 1982-87, Atlantis Health Series, 1981-87. Sustaining mem. Freedoms Found. at Valley Forge, 1985—, Mus. of Art, 1986—, Opera Soc.; founder Performing Arts Ctr. Pacers, 1985; mem. Opera Guild, Inc., 1986—; pres. Wayne State U. Alumni Club Washington D.C., 1963-69; trustee Philharmonic Orchestra Fla., 1987—; mem. Rep. Presdl. Task Force, 1983—, Rep. Senatorial Inner Circle, Rep. Pres.' Club, 1984—, Mayor's Prayer Breakfast Com., Ft. Lauderdale, 1988—; mem. adv. coun. Broward Community Found., 1987—; sec. of def. appointee nat. com. for employer support of the guard and res. Dept. Def. Decorated Bronze Star, Purple Heart; recipient award City of St. Ignace, 1958, Nat. USO award 1959, citation City of Detroit, 1959, Exceptional Svc. Nat. award Assn. U.S. Army, 1990; decorated Nat. Soc. of SAR, 1985; U.S. Army doctoral scholar Wayne State U., 1960-61; grantee Detroit Edison Co., 1964-65, Litton Industries, 1965-66. Mem. Assn. U.S. Army (state pres., regional v.p. 1984-87, sustaining mem. Landpower Edn. Fund Inc. 1984, chmn. Fla. state exec. coun. 1985-87, bd. dirs. Fla. Gulf Stream chpt. 1984—, nat. adv. bd. dirs. 1990-96), Navy League (bd. dirs. Ft. Lauderdale coun. 1988—), USO (pres. greater Ft. Lauderdale Inc. coun. 1988—, Freedoms Found. at Valley Forge George Washington medal 1991), Nat. Assn. Atomic Vets., Mil. Order of Purple Heart (life), Ret. Officers Assn., Mil. Order of World Wars, Am. Legion, VFW, Disabled Am. Vets., Nat. Sojourners Inc., Nat. Order Battlefield Commns., Nat. Eagle Scout Assn., Vets. of Battle of the Bulge, Greater Ft. Lauderdale C. of C. (founding trustee 1989—), Air Force Assn. (citation 1961), Clan Campbell Soc. of Fla., Inc., Scots-Am. Soc. of Brevard, Army and Navy (Washington), Patrick AFB Officers, K.T., Masons. Republican. Lutheran. Avocations: woodworking, bridge, sailing, water sports. Office: Atlantis-Lewart Group Inc PO Box 254451 Patrick A F B FL 32925-0451

HAGGIS, LEWANNA STROM, educator, author, consultant; b. Youngstown, Ohio, Aug. 6, 1924; d. Charles Benjamin and Pearl (Simon) Strom; m. Arthur G. Haggis, Apr. 7, 1944; children: Lynda Lee, Arthur G. III, Richard Charles, Douglas Hood, Pamela Sue. BA, Youngstown Coll., 1946. Adminstr. top secret plans Office Dep. Chief Staff Mil. Ops. Dept. of the Army, The Pentagon, 1962-63; v.p. Haggis Assocs. Inc., Washington and Hollywood, Fla., 1964-71, Ednl. Cons. Inc., Washington and Hollywood, 1966—; v.p., prin. Atlantis Pvt. Schs., Inc., Hollywood, Fla., 1971—; bd. dirs., v.p. Atlantis Pub. Co., Hollywood, 1978—, Atlantis Rsch. Inst., Inc., Hollywood, 1981—; bd. dirs., vice chair. Atlantis-Lewart Group, Inc, Hollywood, 1988—; chmn. USO 1st Ann. Armed Forces Week Svc. Award, Ft. Lauderdale, Fla., 1990. Co-author: (books 1 and 2) Atlantis Beginning Language & Number Development Pro, 1981, (7 vols.) Atlantis Basic Spelling, 1982, (7 vols.) Atlantis Basic Arithmetic, 1982, EDU-CARE, The New School Concept, 1991. Founder, bd. dirs. USO Greater Ft. Lauderdale, Fla., 1988—; bd. dirs. Philharmonic Soc. Ft. Lauderdale, 1986—, Broward County chpt. Freedoms Found., Valley Forge, 1984—, Mayor's Prayer Breakfast Com., Ft. Lauderdale, 1988—; active The Opera Guild, Inc., Ft. Lauderdale, 1985—, Rep. Senatorial Inner Circle, Washington, 1985—; bd. dirs. Protestant Parish Chapel, Patrick AFB, 1994—. Recipient USO Founding Dirs. award, USO Greater Ft. Lauderdale, 1988, Y-100 and Mobile Message award, 1990, USO Disting. Svc. award, 1991, Army Wife Extraordinaire award, 1995. Mem. ASCD, Assn. of U.S. Army (corp. mem., chmn. Fla. Gulf Stream chpt. JROTC medal awards com. 1986-96, Cert. of Appreciation 1996), Ret. Officers Assn., Army Wives Group (chmn. 1995-96), Broward County Child Care and Kindergarten Assn., Officers Wives Club, North Arlington Newcomers Club (v.p. 1961-62). Republican. Lutheran. Home: 620 Verbenia Dr Ind Hbr Bch FL 32937-2533

HAGGLUND, CLARANCE EDWARD, lawyer, publishing company owner; b. Omaha, Feb. 17, 1927; s. Clarance Andrew and Esther May (Kelle) H.; m. Dorothy Souser, Mar. 27, 1953 (div. Aug. 1972); children: Laura, Bret, Katherine; m. Merle Patricia Hagglund, Oct. 28, 1972. BA, U. S.D., 1949; JD, William Mitchell Coll. Law, 1953. Bar: Minn. 1955, U.S. Ct. Appeals (8th cir.) 1974, U.S. Supreme Ct. 1963. Diplomate Am. Bd. Profl. Liability Attys. Ptnr. Hagglund & Johnson and predecessor firms, Mpls., 1973—; mem. Hagglund, Weimer and Speidel, PA; publ., pres. Common Law Publishing Inc., 1991—; pres. Internat. Control Sys., Inc., Mpls., 1979—, Hill River Corp., Mpls., 1976—; gen. counsel Minn. Assn. Profl. Ins. Agts., Inc., Mpls., 1965-86; CFO, Pro-Trac, software for profl. liability ins. industry. Contbr. articles to profl. jours. Served to lt. comdr. USNR, 1945-46, 50-69. Fellow Internat. Soc. Barristers; mem. Lawyers Pilots Bar Assn., U.S. Maritime Law Assn. (proctor), Acad. Cert. Trial Lawyers Minn. (dean 1983-85), Nat. Bd. Trial Advocacy (cert. in civil trial law, bd. dirs.), Douglas Amdahl Inns of Ct. (pres.), Ill. Athletic Club (Chgo.), Edina Country Club (Minn.), Calhoun Beach Club (Mpls.). Roman Catholic. Avocation: flying. Home: 3168 Dean Ct Minneapolis MN 55416-4386 Office: 5101 Olson Memorial Hwy Golden Valley MN 55422-5149

HAGGSTROM, JANE, mental health nursing educator, administrator; b. N.Y.C., June 11, 1947; d. Gustave August and Margaret (Cameron) H.; children: Daniel Haggstrom, Brian Haggstrom Tai. BSN, Duke U., 1969; MEd, Columbia U., 1974; PhD, U. Calif., Santa Barbara, 1994. RN, Calif. Dir. staff devel. Carrier Found., Belle Mead, N.J., 1975-78; assoc. dir. nursing Langley Porter Psychiat. Inst., San Francisco, 1978-82; exec. dir. Santa Barbara Homeless Coalition/Affordable Housing Assn., 1985-92; dir. staff devel. Pinecrest Hosp., Santa Barbara, 1982-87; dir. of nursing, mgr. Schick Shadel Hosp., Santa Barbara, 1989-93; pub. health nurse First Steps Perinatal Outreach Program, Isla Vista, Calif., 1989-92; mgr. inpatient psychiatry Alta Bates Med. Ctr., Berkeley, Calif., 1992—; mem. City County Com. on Homeless, Santa Barbara, 1985-90; mem. City County Task Force on the Homeless Mentally Ill, Santa Barbara, 1985-90; mem. Santa Barbara County Alcoholism Adv. Bd., 1986-89. Recipient Woman of Yr. award County Bd. Suprs., Calif. State Legislature, 1990, ACLU award, 1988; NIMH trainee, 1972-74. Democrat. Avocations: playing piano, hiking, camping, dancing. Office: Alta Bates Med Ctr Herrick Campus 20001 Dwight Way Berkeley CA 04704

HAGIWARA, NAOYUKI, English language and literature educator; b. Kyoto, Japan, Jan. 24, 1929; s. Chiyokichi and Tomiko (Hara) H.; m. Fusako Taguchi, Aug. 28, 1957; children: Motoyuki, Tomomichi. BA, Kyoto U., 1951. Rsch. assoc. of English Osaka Prefecture U., Sakai, Japan, 1951-58, lectr. of English, 1958-66, assoc. prof. English, 1966-73, prof. English, 1973-91, prof. cross-cultural comm. grad. sch., 1982-91, prof. emeritus, 1991—; grad. rschr. of English U. Warwick, Coventry, U.K., 1967-68; instr. simultaneous interpreting INTER Sch., Osaka, 1985-87; prof. English and cross-cultural comm. St. Andrew's U. and Grad. Sch., Izumi, Osaka, Japan, 1991-98; part-time lectr. comparative study of cultures Osaka Prefectural Coll. of Nursing, 1994-98; permanent judge Japan Univs. E.S.S. League, Tokyo, 1978-95; monitor Asahi Evening News. Co-author: Asia and Japan, 1990, The Utilization of Broadcasting English, 1986. Mem. Japan Inst. for Internat. Study, Japan Soc. of English Edn., Japan Pub. Univs. Soc. (spl. com. for the investigation of common primary test 1980-85), Japan Soc. of Stylistics, Japan Assn. of Coll. English Tchrs. (councilor 1981-98, reviewer 1988—), Japan English Forensics Assn. (permanent judge 1980-94), Am. Biog. Inst. Rsch. Assn. (dep. gov.), Internat. Biog. Ctr. (dep. dir. gen.), Order Internat. Fellowship U.K. Buddhism. Avocations: game of Go, calligraphy, table tennis. Home: 3-18-14 Minoo, Minoo 562-0001, Japan Office: St Andrew's Univ, 1-1 Manabino, Izumi 594-1198, Japan

HAGLER, JON LEWIS, investment executive; b. Harlingen, Tex., May 28, 1936; s. John Arthur and Helen (Starkey) H.; m. Jo Ann Winchester, Dec. 21, 1957; children: Elizabeth Ayn, Karin Jill. B.S., Tex. A&M, 1958; M.B.A., Harvard U., 1963. Investment analyst, portfolio mgr. Waddell & Reed, Inc., Kansas City, Mo., 1963-69; pres., chmn. Jennison Mgmt. Corp., N.Y.C., 1969-77; v.p., treas., chief investment officer Ford Found., N.Y.C., 1977-81; chmn. Hagler, Mastrovita & Hewitt, Inc., Boston, 1982-95; ptnr., chmn. gov. com., dir. Grantham, Mayo, Van Otterloo & Co., Boston, 1996—. Trustee Bennington Coll., 1976-80, Jon L. Hagler Found., 1985—, Tex. A&M Found., 1996—; bd. dirs. Assocs. of Harvard Bus. Sch., 1979-82; mem. investment adv. com. Africa-Am. Inst., N.Y.C., 1976—, trustee,

1991—; fin. com. Rockefeller Family Fund, N.Y.C., 1975-96; mem. investment adv. com. Tex. A&M U. Found., 1994-96; mem. pension fin. com. World Bank, 1978-87. Served with U.S. Army, 1958-61. Mem. N.Y. Soc. Security Analysts, Boston Soc. Security Analysts. Methodist. Club: Harvard of N.Y. Home: 2 Pleasant St Dover MA 02030-2049 Office: Grantham Mayo Van Otterloo & Co LLC 40 Rowes Wharf Boston MA 02110-3340

HAGLUND, BERNICE MARION, elementary school educator; b. Negaunee, Mich.; d. Paul and Bernice Cody; m. Charles Haglund; children: Christopher C., Mary. BA, No. Mich. U., 1971, MA, 1978. Tchr. Arnold Elem. Sch., Mich. Center Schs., Mich.; social sec., v.p., pres. Mich. Ctr. Jr. Child Study Group, 1979-83, com. mem. sci. com., dept. head to curriculum counsel, 1993—. V.p., treas., social sec. Commonwealth Wives, Jackson, 1971-82. Mich. State grantee U.S. Optical soc., 1993. Mem. AAUW (sec. social edn. area), ASCD, Bus. and Profl. Women (sec. 1969-71, coord. study group 1972—, sec., social, contact edn. chair, woemn's issues), Orton Soc. (workshop trainer), Mich. Dyslexia Inst., Mich. Sci. Tchrs. Assn., Nat. Sci. Tchrs., Acad. Orton Gillingham, Phi Delta Kappa. Roman Catholic. Home: 1840 Noon Rd Jackson MI 49201-9154

HAGLUND, THOMAS ROY, research biologist, consultant, educator; b. Beloit, Wis., Jan. 19, 1950; s. Roy Wilhelm and Marguerite Jean (Anderson) H.; m. Doris Anne Mendenhall, Oct. 22, 1988; 1 child, Victoria Tamsin. BS in Earth Sci., U. Wash., 1972; postgrad., U. Ill., Chgo., 1972-74; PhD in Biology, UCLA, 1981. Lectr., biology Calif. State Univ., L.A., 1981-83; sci. chair Windward Sch., L.A., 1983—; rsch. biologist UCLA, L.A., 1985—; adj. prof. biology Calif. State Poly. U., Pomona, 1991—; cons. U.S. Army C.E., L.A., 1979-80, Calif. Dept. Fish and Game, 1986—, Met. Water Dist., L.A., 1991, 93, 94, Dept. Pub. Works, Los Angeles County, 1991, 94—, U.S. Fish Wildlife Svc., 1992—; chair So. Calif. Native Fishes Working Group, 1996—. Contbr. chpt. to Historical Biogeography of North American Fish, 1991; contbr. articles to Jour. paleontology, Evolution Paleobiology, Biochem. Systematics Ecology, Copeia. Grantee NSF, 1978, Calif. Dept. Fish and Game, 1986, 87, 90, 91, 92, 93, 94. Mem. AAAS, Am. Soc. Ichthyology and Herpetology, Am. Fisheries Soc., Desert Fishes Coun. Achievements include research in systematics and population genetics of minnows, suckers and sticklebacks, conservation genetics of endangered North American fish. Office: UCLA Dept Biology Los Angeles CA 90024-1606 also: Windward Sch 11350 Palms Blvd Los Angeles CA 90066-2104

HAGMAN, HARLAN LAWRENCE, education educator; b. DeKalb, Ill., Sept. 8, 1911; s. Gus Carl and Emily Sophia (Peterson) H.; m. Mary Anna Cassels, May 23, 1943; children: William Gordon, Richard Harlan, Jean Cassels, Thomas Lawrence; foster children: James Evanson, Donald Jones. EdB, No. Ill. U., 1936; MA, Northwestern U., 1939, PhD, 1947. Formerly tchr. pub. schs., prin. and supt.; instr. Northwestern U., 1940-41; assoc. prof. Drake U., Des Moines, 1947-49; prof. edn. Drake U., 1949-50, dean coll. edn., 1950-57; prof. edn. Wayne State U., 1957-60, dean adminstrn., 1960-72; prof. higher edn., 1972—; Moderator fgn. policy radio broadcasts, nat. network. Author: A Handbook for the Schoolboard Member, 1941, The Administration of American Public Schools, 1951, (with Alfred Schwartz) Administration in Profile for School Executives, 1955, Administration of Elementary Schools, 1956, September Campus, 1977, Bright Michigan Morning: The Years of Governor Tom Mason, 1981, The Academic Life, 1983, A Seasonal Present and Other Stories, 1989, (with Howard Snyder) Second Balcony, 1990, Nathan Hale and John Andre: Reluctant Heroes of the American Revolution, 1991; editorial cons., McGraw-Hill Book Co., Internat. City Mgrs. Assn.; editor: We Hold These Truths: The Collected Sermons of Rt. Rev. Richard Emrich; contbr. to: Am. Peoples Ency.; also contbr. to ednl. jours.. Bd. dirs. Youth for Understanding, Internat. Edn. Exchange. Served as lt. comdr. USNR, World War II. Mem. Players Club, Circumnavigators Club. Home: 1017 Kensington Ave Grosse Pointe MI 48230-1402 Office: Wayne State U Coll of Education Detroit MI 48202

HAGMAN, LARRY, actor; b. Weatherford, Tex., Sept. 21, 1931; s. Benjamin and Mary (Martin) H.; m. Maj Axelsson, 1954; children: Heidi, Preston. Student, Bard Coll. Began career in off-Broadway shows; appeared in Broadway shows: God and Kate Murphy, 1959, The Nervous Set, 1959, The Warm Peninsula, 1959-60, The Beauty Part, 1962-63; numerous TV appearances from late 1950's to mid 1960's, including The Edge of Night; starred in: (TV series) I Dream of Jeannie, 1965-70, The Good Life, 1971-72, Here We Go Again, 1973, Dallas, 1978-91, Staying Afloat, 1993, Orleans, 1997; motion picture debut in Ensign Pulver, 1964; other films include Fail Safe, 1964, The Group, 1966, In Harm's Way, 1965, Beware! the Blob, 1972, Harry and Tonto, 1974, Mother, Jugs and Speed, 1976, The Eagle Has Landed, 1977, S.O.B., 1981, Nixon, 1995, Primary Colors, 1997; appeared in TV films including Dallas: The Early Years, 1986, J.R. Lives, 1996, Orleans, 1996, The Third Twin, 1997, Dallas: War of the Ewings, 1998; dir. USO shows for USAF in Europe. Office: c/o Richard Grant & Assocs 8484 Wilshire Blvd Ste 500 Beverly Hills CA 90211-3214*

HAGMANN, LILLIAN SUE, violin instructor; b. Fontana, Calif., Mar. 10, 1931; d. Riley Royston and Winifred Lillian (Humphry) Green; m. Armand P. Oueilhe, Dec. 17, 1950 (div. 1971); children: Ellen Lynne Oueilhe Keene, Karen Sue Oueilhe Stanton, A. Louis Oueilhe (dec. 1971), Gregoire Pierce Oueilhe; m. Rolf Hagmann, May 19, 1971. AA, Chaffey Coll., 1951; Travel Counselor, Internat. Travel Tng., Chgo., 1974; student, Suzuki Violin Tchr. Tng. Inst., Guelph, Can., 1992, Suzuki Violin Tchr. Tng. Inst., Forest Grove, Oreg., 1993, 97, Occidental Coll., Eagle Rock, Calif., 1994, Suzuki Violin Tchr. Tng. Inst., Stevens Point, Wis., 1995, Occidental Coll., Eagle Rock, Calif. Pricer MacNall Bldg. Materials, Santa Barbara, Calif., 1964-67; office mgr. Laguna Blanca Sch. Devel. Program, Santa Barbara, Calif., 1968; pub. rels. asst. to mgr. Goleta (Calif.) Savs. and Loan, 1969-71; travel counselor Around The World Travel, Palatine, Ill., 1974-77; travel mgr./dir. pub. rels. Newport Area Travel, Newport Beach, Calif., 1977-80; travel counselor Cresenta Valley Travel, La Crescenta, Calif., 1981; violin instr. Arise Acad. Arts, Pomona, Calif., 1989-94, U. Redlands (Calif.) Cmty. Sch. Music, 1995, Arts Encounter, Rowland Heights, Calif., 1996-97; del. 1st Stringed Instrument Edn. Del., China, 1997. Violinist Santa Barbara Symphony, 1962-70, Riverside (Calif.) City Coll. Symphony, 1990-97; life mem. Adams Sch. PTA, Santa Barbara, 1967—; bd. dirs. Calif. Congress PTA; organizer, pres. Assn. for Neurologically Handicapped Children, 1970-71; mem. choir Corona Cmty. Ch., 1995-97; organizer violin concerts for children/. Democrat. Avocations: gardening, artist. Home: 1143 Via Santiago Corona CA 91720-3950

HAGMEIER, CLARENCE HOWARD, retired anesthesiologist; b. Pitts., Dec. 23, 1914; s. Clarence Howard and Bertha May (Rogers) H.; m. Hilda Marie Bronder, Oct. 30, 1942; children: Clarence, Roberta, Susan, David, Michael. BS with honors, U. Pitts., 1943, MD, 1950. Diplomate Am. Bd. Anesthesiology; Oreg. State Bd. Med. Examiners. Intern Good Samaritan Hosp., Portland, Oreg., 1950-51; resident Oreg. Med. Sch. and Hosp., 1951-53; pvt. practice Portland, 1953-87; ret., 1987. Chmn. Multnomah County Rep. Com., 1980-82; pres. Portland Ronald McDonald House, 1991-93; mem. internat. adv. bd. Ronald McDonald House, 1993-95; mem. exec. com. Oreg. Presch. Immunization Consortium 1992—; sr. role model OASIS, 1993; Vols. of Am. Allstar, 1996. With USN, World War II. Fellow Am. Coll. Anesthesiologists, Internat. Coll. Surgeons; mem. Oreg. Med. Assn. (pres. 1976-77), Multnomah County Med. Soc. (pres. 1974), Rotary (pres. Portland club 1979-80, dist. gov. 1983-84, nat. coord. PolioPlus, 1986-88, mem. exec. com. Nat. PolioPlus Immunization Task Force 1992-94, Found. citation for meritorious svc. 1991, Svc. Above Self award 1993, Found. Disting. Svc. award 1995, del. to Coun. on Legis. 1995, 98), PolioPlus Partners Com., Theta Chi, Chi Rho Nu, Phi Rho Sigma. Republican. Avocation: gardening. Home: 4907 SW Canterbury Ln Portland OR 97219-3326

HAGN, GEORGE HUBERT, electrical engineer, researcher; b. Houston, Sept. 15, 1935; s. H. John and Lucile Emilie (Bohls) H.; m. Rose Marie Meier, Apr. 12, 1997; children: Cheryl Ann, David John. BSEE, Stanford U., 1959, MSEE, 1961. Registered elec. engr., Calif. Rsch. engr. Stanford Rsch. Inst. (name changed to SRI Internat. 1977), Menlo Park, Calif., 1959-69, sr. rsch. engr., 1969-73; asst. dir. SRI Washington Office, Arlington, Va., 1973-76, program mgr., 1976-80; program dir. SRI Telecomm. Sci. Ctr., Arlington, 1980-84; asst. dir. Telecom. Scis. Ctr. SRI Washington Office, Arlington, 1984-86, asst. dir. Info. Sci. and Tech. Ctr., 1986-88, asst. dir. Info. and Telecom. Scis. Ctr., 1988-91, sr. staff advisor Info. and Telecom. Scis. Ctr., 1991-93, sr. staff advisor Info. Telecom. and Automation Divsn., 1993-96, sr. staff advisor signals tech. program, 1996—; U.S. industry mem., electromagnetic propagation panel NATO Adv. Group for Aerospace R & D, 1989-91. Assoc. editor Radio Sci., 1975-78. Adult leader Boy Scouts Am., Annandale, Va.; bd. dirs. Annandale Christian Community for Action, 1990-93; active Annandale United Meth. Ch. Fellow IEEE (life, spectrum mgmt. and electromagnetic compatibility 1979, guest editor IEEE Transactions, EMC 1977, 81, spl. issues spectrum mgmt.), Washington Acad. Scis. (life, bd. mgrs. 1994-97, v.p. adminstrn. 1996-97); mem. AAAS, IEEE Antenna and Propagation Soc. (adminstrv. com. 1993-96, sec. wave propagation stds. com. 1989—, assoc. editor for stds. AP-S mag. 1991—), Am. Geophys. Union, N.Y. Acad. Sci., Internat. Union Radio Sci. (URSI chmn. U.S. com. 8 on radio noise 1974-75, chmn. internat. URSI com. E 1975-78, U.S. com. E on electromagnetic noise and interference 1975-78, chmn. internat. com. E on electromagnetic noise and interference 1978-81, vice chmn., treas. U.S. nat. com. 1978-91, mem. URSI liaison com. with Internat. Telecom. Union's Internat. Radio Consultative Com. and Internat. Telegraph and Telephony Consultative com. 1981-90, chmn. 1984-90). Home: 4208 Sleepy Hollow Rd Annandale VA 22003-2046 Office: SRI Internat 1611 N Kent St Ste 700 Arlington VA 22209-2102*

HAGOOD, LEWIS RUSSELL, lawyer; b. Persia, Tenn., July 13, 1930; s. Hobart Verlin and Stella Rose (Carter) H.; m. Mary Evelyn Morrisette, Mar. 15, 1952; children: Lewis Russell Jr., Mary Victoria, Paul Gregory. Student, Lincoln Meml. U., Harrogate, Tenn., 1947-49; BS, East Tenn. State U., 1952; JD, U. Tenn., 1963. Bar: Tenn. 1964, U.S. Dist. Ct. (ea. dist.) Tenn. 1964, U.S. Dist. Ct. (ea. dist.) Ky. 1975, U.S. Tax Ct. 1984, U.S. Ct. Appeals (6th cir.) 1968, U.S. Supreme Ct.; cert. fed. mediator for Ea. Dist. Tenn.; cert. mediator Tenn. Supreme Ct. Ptnr. McLellan, Wright, Hagood, Attys., Kingsport, Tenn., 1964-65; assoc. Arnett & Draper, Attys., Knoxville, Tenn., 1965-67; ptnr. Arnett, Draper & Hagood, Knoxville, 1967—; mem., sec. Tenn. Bd. Law Examiners, 1994—; spkr., lectr. in field. Editor-in-chief: Tennessee Law Review, 1963-64; contbr. articles to profl. jours. Bd. dirs. Knoxville Symphony Soc., 1977—; mem. East Tenn. chpt. March of Dimes, 1981-84; bd. dirs. Knoxville Teen Ctr., Inc., 1975-97. With U.S. Army, 1954-56. Fellow Tenn. Bar Found.; mem. ABA, Tenn. Bar Assn. (past chmn. labor law sect.), Knoxville Bar Assn. Republican. Presbyterian. Avocations: golf, fishing, antique autos. Office: Arnett Draper & Hagood Plz Towers Ste 2300 Knoxville TN 37929

HAGOOD, M. FELTON, surgeon; b. Marietta, Ga., Oct. 18, 1941; s. Murl Miller and Mary Evelyn (Jones) H.; m. Martha Addie James, June 20, 1965; children: Gregory Felton, Robert Miller, Richard James. MD, Emory U., 1966. Diplomate Am. Bd. Surgery. Am. Bd. Colon & Rectal Surgery. Intern U. Va. Hosp., Charlottesville, 1966-67, surg. resident, 1967-68; med. officer Charleston Naval Hosp. U.S. Navy, 1968-70; resident gen. surgery Med. U. S.C., 1970-73; fellow colon & rectal surgery Ochsner Found. Hosp., New Orleans, 1973-74; pvt. practice-colon & rectal surgery Kennestone Hosp., Marietta, 1974—. past pres. Am. Cancer Soc., 1978. Lt. cmdr. USNR, 1968-70. Mem. Cobb County Med. Soc. (pres. 1993-94), Kiwanis Club, Phi Beta Kappa, Alpha Omega Alpha. Methodist. Avocations: golf, boating. Home: 577 Keeler Woods Dr Marietta GA 30064 Office: Surg Assocs of Marietta 790 Church St NW Ste 570 Marietta GA 30060-8967

HAGOOD, SUSAN STEWART HAHN, clinical dietitian; b. Balt., May 31, 1953; d. Paul Gilbert and Phyllis Jeanette (Mann) Hahn; m. Thomas Richard Hagood, Jr., Nov. 25, 1978; 1 child, Margaret Foster. BS, Western Ky. U., 1975; MS, Ga. State U., 1992. Registered and lic. dietitian. Dietetic trainee U. Hosp., Jacksonville, Fla., 1975-76; clin. dietitian VA Med. Ctr., Lake City, Fla., 1976-80; in-service and staff devel. dietitian VA Med. Ctr., Lake City, 1980-85; clin. specialist Clayton Gen. Hosp., Riverdale, Ga., 1985-88; grad. teaching asst. Ga. State U., 1991; ambulatory care and rsch. dietitian VA Med. Ctr., Atlanta, 1992—. Pres. Lake City (Fla.) Hist. Preservation Bd., 1982-83; chmn. youth adv. com. Columbia County 4-H, Lake City, 1981-84; vol. instr. Tech. Assistance Health Resource Group, Lake City, 1982-84; co-chmn. Com. for Restoration Columbia County Hist. Mus., 1983-84; bd. dirs. Clayton County unit Am. Heart Assn., 1987-88; mem. Dekalb unit nutrition and cancer work group Am. Cancer Soc., 1993—; leader Avondale-Decatur svc. unit Girl Scouts U.S.A., 1993—. Mem. Am. Dietetic Assn., Atlanta Dist. Dietetic Assn., Atlanta English Speaking Union, DAR, Colonial Dames Am., Colonial Dames XVII Century, Phi Upsilon Omicron, Alpha Xi Delta. Republican. Presbyterian. Avocations: rug making, traveling, hiking, camping. Home: PO Box 982 Decatur GA 30031-0982 Office: VA Medical Ctr 1670 Clairmont Rd Decatur GA 30033-4004

HAGOOD, THOMAS RICHARD, JR., minister, publisher; b. Charlotte, N.C., Sept. 16, 1954; s. Thomas Richard and Donna Gwendolyn (Williams) H.; m. Susan Stewart Hahn, Nov. 25, 1978; 1 child, Margaret Foster. BA, Davidson Coll., 1976; MDiv, Columbia Theol. Sem., 1996. Ordained to Presbyn. Ch., 1997. Editor Columbia Publs., Inc., Decatur, Ga., 1976-88, publisher, 1988—; min. Barnesville (Ga.) Presbyn. Ch., 1997—; mem. small ch. com., com. preparation ministry Presbytery Greater Atlanta, 1998—, com. World Wide Mins. Scoutmaster Boy Scouts of Am., Lake City, Fla., 1982-85; pres. Columbian Countians, Lake City, 1982-85; mem. Govt. Study Com., Columbia County, Fla., 1984; elder Presbyn. Ch., Atlanta. Recipient Silver Beaver award North Fla. coun. Boy Scouts Am., 1986. Mem. English Speaking Union, Lake City Rotary (bd. dirs. 1982-85). Avocations: backpacking, camping, reading, woodworking. Home: PO Box 982 Decatur GA 30031-0982

HAGOORT, THOMAS HENRY, lawyer; b. Paterson, N.J., May 30, 1932; s. Nicholas Hugh and Rae (Sytsma) H.; m. Lois Ann Bennett, Sept. 6, 1954; children: Nancy Lynn Hagoort Treuhold, Susan Audrey Hagoort Bick. A.B. cum laude, Harvard U., 1954, LL.B. magna cum laude, 1957. Bar: N.Y. 1959. Assoc. firm Cleary, Gottlieb, Steen & Hamilton, N.Y.C., 1957-67, ptnr., 1968-90, of counsel, 1991—; gen. counsel Albany Internat. Corp., 1991—. Note editor, Harvard Law Rev., 1956-57. Pres. Mountainside Hosp., Montclair, N.J., 1983-85, chmn. bd. trustees, 1985-88; pres. Internat. Baccalaureate of N.Am., N.Y.C., 1980-91, Montclair Bd. Edn. 1966-70; mem., Coun. of Found. Internat. Baccalaureate Orgn., Geneva, 1982-96, pres. and chair exec. com., 1990-96. Mem. ABA, N.Y. State Bar Assn., Harvard Club of N.J. (pres. 1977-78), Montclair Golf Club, S.C. Yacht Club. Democrat. Home: PO Box 3229 Hilton Head Island SC 29928-0229

HAGOPIAN, JACOB, federal judge; b. Providence, July 3, 1927; s. Bedros and Varvar (Leylegian) H.; m. Mary L. Pomoranski, Aug. 14, 1953; children: Mark Jay, Dana Aquinas, Mary Lou, Jan Christian, Jon Gregory. AB, George Washington U., 1957; JD, Am. U., 1960; grad. in Internat. Law, Judge Advocate Gen.'s Sch., 1964; student, Indsl. Coll. Armed Forces, 1967. Bar: Va. 1961, R.I. 1964, U.S. Supreme Ct. 1964, U.S. Dist. Ct. R.I., U.S. Dist. Ct. (ea. dist.) Va., U.S. Ct. Appeals (D.C. cir.), U.S. Ct. Customs and Patent Appeals, U.S. Ct. Claims, U.S. Tax Ct. Enlisted U.S. Army, 1944, advanced through grades to 1st sgt. 11th Airborne Divsn., 2d lt. to 1st lt. 82d Airborne Divsn., 1948-50; capt. U.S. Army Security Agency, Washington, 1950-53, 56-60; with 501st Recon group U.S. Army Security Agency, Korea, 1953, Tokyo, 1954-56; advanced through grades to col. U.S. Army, 1953-68; appellate judge U.S. Ct. Mil. Rev. U.S. Army Ct. Criminal Appeals, Washington, 1968-70; ret. U.S. Army, 1970; appellate judge U.S. Army Judiciary, Washington, 1968-70; dir. law ctr. Roger Williams Coll., Providence, 1970-71; U.S. magistrate judge U.S. Dist. Ct., Providence, 1971—; legal adv. to intelligence cmty. Spl. Ops., Berlin, 1960-63; group supv. def. appellate divsn. USA Judiciary, Washington, 1964-66; dep. and chief criminal law divsn. OTJAG dept. of army The Pentagon, Washington, 1966-68; lectr. Fed. Jud. Ctr., Washington; adj. prof. Am. U., 1971—, Suffolk U. Law Sch.; vis. prof. U.S. Naval War Coll.; mem. faculty fellow AY, 1997—, hon. program, U. R.I. Contbr. articles to profl. jours. Decorated Legion of Merit (2) with first oak leaf cluster; recipient Army Commendation medal with oak leaf cluster. Mem. ABA (former cons. sect. criminal justice, vice chmn. com. on adequate def. and incentives in mil., former sec.-reporter com. mil. law, Houston Justice Assist award 1987), Fed. Bar Assn. (past pres. R.I. chpt., mem. nat. coun., mem. nat. chmn. com. criminal law, chmn. U.S. magistrate judge's com.), Am. Judges Assn., Inst. Jud. Adminstrn., U.S. Naval War Coll. Found., Nat. Def. U. Found. Office: US Dist Ct One Exchange Ter Providence RI 02903

HAGSTROM, JACK WALTER CARL KLING, retired pathology educator; b. Rockford, Ill., Dec. 2, 1933; s. Walter Carl Paul Hagstrom and Loretta Christine Kling Pearson. AB, Amherst Coll., 1955; MD, Cornell U., 1959. Instr. dept. pathology Cornell U. Med. Coll., N.Y.C., 1962-65, asst. prof., 1965-68; assoc. prof. Case We. Res. U., Cleve., 1968-70; assoc. prof. Columbia U., N.Y.C., 1970-75, prof. pathology, 1975-91, prof. emeritus, 1991—; attending pathologist U. Hosp., Cleve., 1968-70, Presbyn. Hosp., N.Y.C., 1975-91; dir. dept. pathology Harlem Hosp., N.Y.C., 1981-91; hon. curator modern poetry Amherst (Mass.) Coll. Libr., 1981—. Author: Thom Gunn: A Bibliography, 1979; contbr. articles to profl. jours. Mem. corporator Holden Arboretum, Mentor, Ohio. Fellow Am. Coll. Cardiology; mem. Garrick Club, Travellers' Club, Pratts Club, Grolier Club, Club Odd Vols., Jockey Club, Kiambu Club. Episcopalian. Home: PO Box 105 Seven Ponds Towd Rd New York NY 11976

HAGUE, PAUL CHRISTIAN, lawyer; b. Cleve., May 6, 1943; s. Joseph Anthony and Virginia Blanche (Galloway) H.; m. Marcia Beth Metz, Sept. 29, 1973; children: Suzanne Elizabeth, John Christian. BA, U. Dayton, 1965; JD, U. Pitts., 1968. Bar: Pa. 1969, Fla. 1983, U.S. Ct. Appeals (3rd cir.) 1970. Assoc. Meyer, Unkovic & Scott, Pitts., 1969-75; ptnr., 1975—. Bd. dirs. Pitts. Jaycees, 1969-72; trustee The Ellis Sch., Pitts. 1986-90. Mem. ABA, Allegheny County Bar Assn. (chmn. young lawyers sect. 1977, bd. govs. 1978, chair civil litigation sect. 1995), Pa. Bar Assn. (ho. of dels. 1995—) , Acad. Trial Lawyers Allegheny County, Pitts. Athletic Assn. (bd. dirs. 1986-89). Office: Meyer Unkovic & Scott 1300 Oliver Building Pittsburgh PA 15222-2300

HAGUE, WILLIAM EDWARD, editor, author; b. Duquesne, Pa., Feb. 2, 1919; s. William Edward and Edith (Osburn) H.; m. Margaret Cleland Anderson, July 22, 1950 (div.). A.B., Princeton U., 1940; postgrad., U. Pitts. Sch. Law, 1940-41. Assoc. editor Tide mag., 1947-49; promotion dir. Living for Young Homemakers mag., 1949-50, copy editor, 1951-54, mng. editor, 1954-61; editor Living's Guide to Home Planning mag., 1958-61; with Conde Nast Publs., N.Y.C.; sr. editor House & Garden, 1961; editor-in-chief House & Garden Guides, 1962-72; asst. account exec. Fitzgerald Advt. Agy., New Orleans, 1950-51. Author: How to Decorate With Color, 1964, What You Should Know About Furniture, 1965, Planning Your Vacation Home, 1968, Plan Your Baths for Beauty and Efficiency, 1969, Plan The Kitchen That Suits You, 1969, Making The Most of The One-Room Apartment, 1969, Your Vacation House, How To Plan It, 1972, Doubleday's Complete Basic Book of Home Decorating, 1976, Know Your America, California, 1978, Remodel, Don't Move, 1981, The New Complete Basic Book of Home Decorating, 1983; editor: Country Kitchens and Baths, 1987; contbg. editor: Reader's Digest's Household Hints, 1987. Recipient Dorothy Dawe award for disting. journalistic coverage in home furnishings field, 1969. Home: 49 E 73rd St Apt 5F New York NY 10021-3560

HAHIN, CHRISTOPHER, metallurgical engineer, corrosion engineer; b. Buffalo, Dec. 26, 1945; s. Leo Paul and Nancy (Morabito) H.; children: Bonnie L., Terence J., Jonathan R. *Son of Nancy Morabito Hahin and Leo Paul Hahin, marine engineer and commissioned officer, US Merchant Marine Academy; brother of Richard Hahin, professor of physiology at Northern Illinois University, Noreen Hahin-Evens, pharmacist, Linda Hahin, teacher, Mary Lou Hahin-Chuhaj, business manager, and Michael Hahin, artist and trainer of race horses.* BS, Mich. State U., 1968; MS, U. Ky., 1974. Cert. profl. engr., Ill., Calif. Missile facilities engr. USAF, Strategic Air Command, Minot AFB, N.D., 1968-72; rsch. metallurgist U.S. Army Corps of Engrs. Constrn. Engr. Rsch. Lab., Champaign, Ill., 1974-81; prin. engr. Container Corp. Am., Carol Stream, Ill., 1981-84; chief metallurgist Avondale Ind., Danly Machine Divsn., Chgo., 1984-86; engr. structural materials and bridge investigations Bur. Materials and Phys. Rsch., Ill. Dept. Transp., Springfield, 1987—; prin. assoc. Materials Protection Assn., Springfield, Ill., 1984—. Author: Book Science Baseball, 1983; contbr. Advanced Casting Technology Conf., Kalamazoo, 1986, ASM Metals Handbook vol. 13, 1987; patentee in field; contbr. over 120 articles to profl. jours. With USAF 1968-72. Fellow Ashland Oil U. Ky., 1971; decorated A.F.C.M. 1st Oak Leaf Cluster; recipient U.S. Army Spl. Act Svc., 1981. Mem. ASTM, Am. Soc. for Metals, Nat. Corrosion Engrs. Assn., Am. Welding Soc. Independent. Achievements include development of corrosion cost prediction models for utilities and structures using air, water, soil and air pollution data; determined lifting, earth moving and towing requirements for combat engineer vehicles using actual battle scenarios; introduced leaded free machining steels for use in mass production of improved carburized die set bushings for stamping industry; development of improved pin and link eyebar designs and materials for bridges; developed accurate and rapid method for determination of fatigue damage in bridges using stress frequency histograms and linear damage rule; developed as-welded notch toughness test for steel weldments using natural notches and other similar code authority qualification tests; proposed new mix design methodology for fibrous concrete which increase workability toughness and durability; development of a new corrosion fatigue equation for prediction of life of structural steels in various environments, new direct tension test which measures the plane-strain fracture toughness of portland cement concrete. Office: Ill Dept Transp 126 E Ash St Springfield IL 62704-4766

HAHLER, GARY EDWARDS, secondary school educator, coach; b. Nov. 11, 1955. BS in Edn., Greenville (Ill.) Coll., 1979; MS in Adminstrn., McNeese State U., 1995. Tchr., coach Andrew Jackson H.S., Chalmette, La., 1987-90, St Bernard (La.) H.S., 1991-92, Reeves (La.) H.S., 1992-93, Fairview H.S., Grant, La., 1993-95, De Ridder (La.) Jr. H.S., 1995-96, E. Beauregard H.S., Dry Creek, La., 1996—. E-mail: gehahler@century-inter.net. Home: PO Box 333 Grant LA 70644-0333

HAHM, DAVID EDGAR, classics educator; b. Milw., Sept. 30, 1938; s. Edgar David and Loraine Emily (Stebnitz) H.; m. Donna Lorraine Seifert, Aug. 8, 1964; children: Melanie Davida, Christopher David, Geoffrey Kenneth, Martha Maria. BA, Northwestern Coll., 1960; student, Wis. Luth. Sem., 1960-61; MA, U. Wis., 1962, PhD, 1966. Asst. prof. U. Mo., Columbia, 1966-69; asst. prof. Ohio State U., Columbus, 1969-72, assoc. prof., 1972-78, prof., 1978—; Vis. fellow Corpus Christi Coll., Cambridge, Eng., 1990-91. Author: The Origins of Stoic Cosmology, 1977; contbr. articles to jours., chpts. to books. Trustee Dublin Hist. Soc., 1974-79, pres., 1974-76; active Archtl. Rev. Bd., Dublin, Ohio, 1976-83, chmn., 1980-82; exec. bd. Worthingtonb Hist. Soc., 1981-89, 93—; trustee Old Dublin Assn., 1996—, treas., 1997—. Fellow Ctr. Hellenic Studies; mem. AAUP, Am. Philol. Assn., Am. Philos. Assn., Classical Assn., Mid. West and South, History of Sci. Soc., Soc. Ancient Greek Philosophy. Lutheran. E-mail: hahm.1@osu.edu. Office: Ohio State U Dept Greek and Latin 230 N Oval Mall Columbus OH 43210-1335

HAHN, BESSIE KING, library administrator, lecturer; b. Shanghai, People's Republic of China, May 14, 1939; came to U.S., 1959; d. Jen Fong and Wei (Lok) King; m. Roger Carl Hahn, 1962 (div. 1983); children: Angela Yee-mei, Michael King-yau, Belinda Shee-wei; m. David Ware Duhme, 1989. B.A., Mt. Marty Coll., Yankton, S.D., 1961; M.S.L.S., Syracuse U., 1972. Librarian Carrier Corp., Syracuse, N.Y., 1972; life sci. bibliographer Syracuse U. Libraries, 1973-75, head sci. and tech., 1975-78; asst. dir. reader services Johns Hopkins U. Library, Balt., 1978-81; dir. libraries Brandeis U., Waltham, Mass., 1981-96, asst. provost for librs., univ. libr., 1996—; cons. Shanghai Jiao Tong U. Library, Shanghai, 1983—, hon. prof., 1984. Editor Jour. Ednl. Media and Library Scis., 1983—; contbr. articles to profl. jours. Bd. govs. Abraham Lincoln Brigade Archives, 1989—; commr. New England Assoc. Schs. and Colls., Inc., 1991-97. Recipient Golden Cup award Johns Hopkins U. Class of 1980, 1980. Mem. ALA, Chinese-Am. Librarians Assn. (pres. 1982-83), Brandeis U. Nat. Women's Com. (hon. benefactor 1986, hon. life 1990—). E-mail: bhahn@brandeis.edu. Home: 148 Sudbury Rd Weston MA 02493-1351 Office: Brandeis U Libr 415 South St Waltham MA 02453-2728

HAHN, CATHY ANN CLIFFORD, sales executive; b. Celina, Ohio, June 6, 1947; d. William Eugene and Kathleen (McNally) Clifford; m. John Hahn (div.). BS, U. Dayton, 1969. Sales rep. J.T. Baker Instruments, Bridgeport, Conn., 1972-76, E.I. duPont de Nemours & Co., Dallas, 1976-81; new bus.

developer E.I. duPont de Nemours & Co., Wilmington, Del., 1981-83, sr. tng. designer, 1983-84, sales tng. mgr., 1984-85; ter. mgr., trainer E.I. duPont de Nemours & Co., Dallas, 1985-94; v.p. Planet Cadillac Clothing Co., Plano, Tex., 1994-95; owner Metaluna Ltd. Co., Dallas, Tex., 1996—. Vol. Am. Cancer Soc., Dallas, 1986—. Home and Office: 5217 Old Shepard Pl Plano TX 75093-5002

HAHN, DAVID BENNETT, hospital administrator, marketing professional; b. Louisville, Ohio, June 5, 1945; s. Bennett E. and Betty J. (McGaughey) H.; m. Elizabeth Burdine, Oct. 4, 1975; children: Stephen, Sarah, Scott. BS in Agrl. Econs., Ohio State U., 1967; MBA, U. Toledo, 1977. Social worker, supr. Franklin County Welfare, Columbus, Ohio, 1968-71; pers. asst. Franklin County Welfare, Columbus, 1971-73; pers. dir. Mansfield (Ohio) Gen. Hosp., 1973-76; adminstr. Kettering Hosp., Loudonville, Ohio, 1978-81; v.p. Marietta (Ohio) Hosp., 1981-92; CEO City Hosp., Bellaire, 1992-94, mktg. dir. med. integrated svcs., 1995-98; pres. Advanced Practice Systems, 1996—; v.p. Tech Risk Mat. Group, 1998—; coach St. Clairsville H.S. Soccer. Mem. East Muskingham Civic Assn. Bd., 1982-92; bd. dirs., recreation coord. Marietta Soccer League; v.p. Mid-Ohio Mktg. Assn., 1992; bd. dirs. Belmont County Salvation Army, 1992—. Fellow Am. Coll. Health Care Execs.; mem. Assn. MBA Execs., Am. Mktg. Assn. (local chpt. bd. dirs.), Ohio Hosp. Assn. Com., Ohio Hosp. Soc. for Planning and Mktg., Loudonville C. of C. (pres. bd. dirs. 1981), Bellaire C. of C. (bd. devel. com.), Wheeling Soccer Assn. (coach), St. Clairsville Area Soccer Assn. (bd. pres.), Pioneer Alumni Ohio State U. (bd. dirs., pres.), Rotary (bd. dirs. Loudonville club 1978-81), Lions (1st v.p.), Shriners, Masons. Mem. Calvary Presbyterian. Avocations: soccer, reading, gardening, running. Office: Tech Risk Mgmt Group Inc 401 N Michigan Ave Ste 2600 Chicago IL 60611-4246

HAHN, DOWON, pharmaceutical researcher, educator; b. Hoo-Chang, Korea, Nov. 20, 1931; came to U.S., 1955; s. Sung-Bum Hahn and Wan-Ok Cho; m. Myung Yun Kim, Aug. 31, 1963; children: Charles, Helen, Anna. BS in Agrl. Mechanics, Mich. State U., 1960, MS in Animal Breeding, 1963; PhD in Endocrinology, U. Mo., 1967. Assoc. scientist Ortho Pharm. Corp., Raritan, N.J., 1968-69, scientist, 1969-70, sr. scientist, 1970-72, group leader, 1973-74, sect. head, 1975-82, asst. dir., 1982-87, dir., 1987-92; Disting. rsch. fellow R.W. Johnson Pharm. Rsch. Inst., Raritan, N.J., 1993—; adj. prof. dept. animal sci. Rutgers U., New Brunswick, N.J., 1982—, dept. ob/gyn. Ea. Va. Med. Sch., Norfolk, 1987—;postdoctoral fellow Worcester Found., 1967-68. Recipient grant Danforth Found., 1958, fellowship Ford Found., 1967, Phillips B. Hoffman Rsch. Scientist award Johnson and Johnson, 1973, 85, Johnson medal Johnson and Johnson, 1990. Mem. Soc. for Study of Reproduction, Soc. for Gynecol. Investigation, The Endocrine Soc., Am. Soc. Reproductive Medicine, Am. Coll. Ob/gyn., Japan Soc. Ob/gyn. Home: 6 Shelton Rd Flemington NJ 08822-3356 Office: RW Johnson Pharm Rsch Inst US Hwy 202 Raritan NJ 08869

HAHN, ERWIN LOUIS, physicist, educator; b. Sharon, Pa., June 9, 1921; s. Israel and Mary Hahn; m. Marian Ethel Failing, Apr. 8, 1944 (dec. Sept. 1978); children: David L., Deborah A., Katherine L.; m. Natalie Woodford Hodgson, Apr. 12, 1980. B.S., Juniata Coll., 1943, D.Sc., 1966; M.S., U. Ill., 1947, Ph.D., 1949; D.Sc., Purdue U., 1975. Asst. Purdue U., 1943-44; research assoc. U. Ill., 1950; NRC fellow Stanford, 1950-51, instr., 1951-52; research physicist Watson IBM Lab., N.Y.C., 1952-55; assoc. Columbia U., 1952-55; faculty U. Calif., Berkeley, 1955—, prof. physics, 1961—, assoc. prof., then prof. Miller Inst. for Basic Rsch., 1958-59, 66-67, 85-86; Eastman vis. prof. Balliol Coll., Oxford, Eng., 1988-89; cons. Office Naval Rsch., Stanford, 1950-52, AEC, 1955—; spl. cons. USN, 1959; adv. panel mem. Nat. Bur. Stds., Radio Stds. div., 1961-64; mem. NAS/NRC com. on basic rsch.; advisor to U.S. Army Rsch. Office, 1967-69; faculty rsch. lectr. U. Calif., Berkeley, 1979. Author: (with T.P. Das) Nuclear Quadrupole Resonance Spectroscopy, 1958. Served with USNR, 1944-46. Fellow Guggenheim Found., 1961-62, 69-70, NSF, 1961-62; recipient prize Internat. Soc. Magnetic Resonance, 1971, Humboldt Found. award, 1977, 94, Alumni Achievement award Juniata Coll., 1986, citation U. Calif., Berkeley, 1991; co-winner prize in physics Wolf Found., 1984; named to Calif. Inventor Hall of Fame, 1984; vis. fellow Brasenose Coll., Oxford U., 1969-70, life hon. fellow, 1984—. Fellow AAAS, Internat. Soc. Electron Paramagnetic Resonance, Am. Phys. Soc. (past mem. exec. com. div. solid state physics, Oliver E. Buckley prize 1971); mem. NAS (co-recipient Comstock prize in electricity, magnetism and radiation 1993), Slovenian Acad. Scis. and Arts (fgn.), French Acad. Scis. (fgn. assoc.), Berkeley Fellows. Home: 69 Stevenson Ave Berkeley CA 94708-1732 Office: U Calif Dept Physics 367 Birge Berkeley CA 94720

HAHN, FRED, retired political science and history educator; b. Stankov, Czechoslovakia, May 28, 1906; came to U.S., 1939, naturalized, 1947; D.Law and Polit. Sci., U. Prague, 1929; M.A., Columbia U., 1951. s. Emil and Helen (Wilhelm) H.; m. Edith H. Friedman, Dec. 25, 1949; children: Susan Ann, Jeanette Emily. Atty. Prague, Czechoslovakia, 1929-39; self-employed N.Y.C., 1941-62; lectr. Fairleigh Dickinson U., Rutherford, Madison, N.J., 1962-64; assoc. prof. Trenton (N.J.) State Coll., 1964-69, prof., 1969-77, prof. emeritus, 1977—; guest prof. U. Frankfurt, Germany, 1968-69, 71, 73, 75; assoc. Inst. on East Central Europe, Columbia U., 1980-88, assoc. faculty seminar, 1987—. Author: Marxist and Utopian Socialists, 1965, History of Russia, 1968, Stürmer, 1978; co-author several books; contbr. articles to profl. jours. Fulbright grantee, 1968-69, 73. Mem. Am. Hist. Assn., Am. Assn. for Advancement Slavic Studies, Czechoslovakia Soc. Arts and Scis., Soc. for History Czechoslovak Jews (dir.), Internat. PEN. Fax: 212-865-9779. Home: 780 W End Ave New York NY 10025-5573

HAHN, FREDERIC LOUIS, lawyer; b. Chgo., Apr. 28, 1941; s. Max and Margery Ruth (Goodman) H.; m. Susan Firestone, Mar. 26, 1967; 1 child, Frederic Firestone. AB with highest distinction, Cornell U., 1962, MBA with highest distinction, 1963; JD magna cum laude, Harvard U., 1966. Bar: Ill. 1966; CPA, Ill. Assoc. Hopkins & Sutter, Chgo., 1966-72, ptnr., 1973-94; ptnr. Mayer, Brown & Platt, Chgo., 1994—. Bd. dirs. Lyric Opera of Chgo., 1988—. Recipient Gold medal (CPA exam) State of Ill., 1963. Mem. Phi Beta Kappa. Home: 1377 Scott Ave Winnetka IL 60093-1444 Office: Mayer Brown & Platt 190 S La Salle St Ste 3100 Chicago IL 60603-3441

HAHN, GEORGE LEROY, agricultural engineer, biometeorologist; b. Muncie, Kans., Nov. 12, 1934; s. Vernon Leslie and Marguerite Alberta (Breeden) H.; m. Clovice Elaine Christensen, Dec. 3, 1955; children—Valerie, Cecile, Steven, Melanie. B.S., U. Mo., Columbia, 1957, Ph.D., 1971; M.S., U. Calif., Davis, 1961. Agrl. engr., project leader and tech. advisor Agrl. Research Service, U.S. Dept. Agr., Columbia, Mo., 1957, Davis, Calif., 1958-61, Columbia, 1961-78, Clay Center, Nebr., 1978—. Contbr. articles to tech. jours. and books on impact of climatic and other environ. factors on livestock prodn., efficiency, and well-being, evaluation of methods of reducing impact and techniques for measuring dynamic responses and characterizing stress in meat animals. Recipient award Am. Soc. Agrl. Engrs.-Metal Bldgs. Mfrs. Assn., 1976. Fellow Am. Soc. Agrl. Engrs. (dir. prof. coun. 1991-93); mem. Am. Meteorol. Soc. (award for outstanding achievement in bioclimatology 1976), Internat. Soc. Biometeorology (treas. 1999—), Am. Soc. Animal Sci. Office: US Meat Animal Rsch Ctr PO Box 166 Clay Center NE 68933-0166

HAHN, GEORGE THOMAS, materials engineering educator, researcher; b. Vienna, Austria, July 28, 1930; came to U.S., 1938; s. Rudolph and Stella (Honig) H.; m. Charlotte Minovitz, June 10, 1956; children: Claudia Abbott, Elizabeth. BSME, NYU, 1952; MS in Metall. Engring., Columbia U., 1956; ScD in Metall. Engring., MIT, 1959. Rsch. engr. Westinghouse Rsch. Labs., Pitts., 1952; cons. Mfg. Labs., Cambridge, Mass., 1956-60; rsch. assoc. metal sci. sect. Battelle Meml. Inst., Columbus, Ohio, 1960-66, mgr. metal sci. sect., 1966-79; prof. materials sci. and engring. Vanderbilt U., Nashville, 1979-98, prof. materials sci. and engring. emeritus, 1998—, chmn. dept. materials sci. and engring/, 1988-93; co-dir. Ctr. Materials Tribology, Nashville, 1987-96; pres. Mechanics & Materials Techs. Inc., Nashville, 1988—. Co-editor: Fracture, 1959, Fast Fracture and Crack Arrest, 1977, Crack Arrest Methods, 1980; contbr. numerous articles to profl. jours. Capt. USAF, 1953-57. Fellow Am. Soc. Metals (Campbell Meml. Lectr. 1981), Metall. Soc., Am. Soc. Lubrication Engrs. Avocation: painting. Office: Vanderbilt U Dept Mech Engring Box 1592 Sta B Nashville TN 37235

HAHN, H. MICHAEL, advertising executive; b. Huron, Ohio, June 15, 1928; s. Herbert Henry and Florence (Hast) H.; m. Jacqueline Williams, Sept. 22, 1956; children: Bruce Williams, Timothy Ross. BA in English, Psychology, Western Res. U., 1951; hon. humanities degree, Tokyo U., 1953. Acct. exec. Howard Swink, Advt., Marion, Ohio, 1954-59; exec. v.p. Jaqua Advt., Grand Rapids, Mich., 1959-68, Norman Navan Advt., Grand Rapids, 1968-83; pres., owner Strategic Mktg., Grand Rapids, 1984—; speaker to schs., colls., Mich., 1959—; cons. Gen. Assembly, Presbyn. Ch. (USA), western Mich., 1980—. Sgt. maj. U.S. Army, 1951-54, Korea. Presbyterian. Office: Strategic Mktg Inc 3445 Lake Eastbrook Blvd SE Grand Rapids MI 49546-5943

HAHN, HELENE B., motion picture company executive; b. N.Y.C.. BA, Hofstra U.; JD, Loyola U., Calif., 1975. Bar: Calif. 1975. V.p. bus. affairs Paramount Pictures Corp., L.A., sr. v.p. bus. affairs, 1983-84; sr. v.p. bus. and legal Walt Disney Studios, Burbank, Calif., 1984-87, exec. v.p., 1987-94; with Dreamworks, 1994—. Recipient Frontrunner award in bus. Sara Lee Corp., 1991, Big Sisters Achievement award, 1992, Clairol Mentor award, 1993, Women in Bus. Magnificent Seven award, 1994. *

HAHN, JAMES KENNETH, lawyer; b. L.A., July 3, 1950; s. Kenneth and Ramona Hahn; m. Monica Ann Teson, May 19, 1984; children: Karina Natalie, Jackson Kenneth. BA in English magna cum laude, Pepperdine U., 1972, JD, 1975. Bar: Calif. 1975. Law clk. L.A. County Dist. Atty.'s Office; city pros. L.A. City Atty.'s Office, 1975-79; pvt. practice Marina del Rey, 1979-81; city contr. City of L.A., 1981-85, city atty., 1985—. Office: Office of the City Atty City of LA 1800 City Hall E 200 N Main St Los Angeles CA 90012-4110

HAHN, JAMES MAGLORIE, former librarian, farmer; b. Grey Eagle, Minn., June 2, 1936; s. Frank John and Mabel Leone H.; m. Ellen MacMonagle, Sept. 7, 1976; children by previous marriage: Michele Diane, Nichola Darcy, Jennifer Deirdre, Gillian Dana, Kristan Desiree. B.A., U. Minn., 1960, M.A., 1962, M.L.S., 1962. Dir. Libraries and Information Center, Minn. Dept. Corrections, 1961-63; chief librarian Royal Air Force, Lakenheath, Eng., 1963-68; asst. command librarian Hdqrs. U.S. Air Force Europe and Near East, Wiesbaden, Ger., 1968-69; staff librarian Hdqrs. 1st Air Force, Newburgh, N.Y., 1969; asst. chief for network devel. Library of Congress, Washington, 1970-75; chief library div. VA, Washington, 1975-79; dir. learning resources service VA, 1979-81, dir. continuing edn. resources services, 1981-89; treas. SABIL Inc., 1983-89; farmer Castleton, Va., 1988—; assoc. prof. library sci. Cath. U. Am., Washington, 1977-89; adviser on libraries and patient edn. Am. Hosp. Assn., 1977-89; bd. regents Nat. Library Medicine, 1980-89; farmer, 1987-94; sec./treas. Solitude Farms Property Owners Assn., 1994—. Home: 6437 Campground Ln Castleton VA 22716-1703

HAHN, JOAN CHRISTENSEN, retired drama educator, travel agent; b. Kemmerer, Wyo., May 9, 1933; d. Roy and Bernice (Pringle) Wainwright; m. Milton Angus Christensen, Dec. 29, 1952 (div. Oct. 1, 1971); children: Randall M., Carla J. Christensen Teasdale; m. Charles Henry Hahn, Nov. 15, 1972. BS, Brigham Young U., 1965. Profl. ballroom dancer, 1951-59; travel dir. E.T. World Travel, Salt Lake City, 1969—; tchr. drama Payson High Sch., Utah, 1965-71, Cottonwood High Sch., Salt Lake City, 1971-95; retired, 1995; dir. Performing European Tours, Salt Lake City, 1969-76; dir. Broadway theater tours, 1976—. Bd. dirs. Salem City Salem Days, Utah, 1965-75; regional dir. dance Latter-day Saints Ch., 1954-72. Named Best Dir. High Sch. Musicals, Green Sheet Newspapers, 1977, 82, 84, 90, Utah's Speech Educator of Yr., 1990, 91, named to Nat. Hall of Fame Ednl. Theatre Assn., 1991; recipient 1st place award Utah State Drama Tournament, 1974, 77, 78, 89, 90, 91, 94, 95, Tchr. of Yr. award Cottonwood High Sch., 1989-90, Limelight award, 1982, Exemplary Performance in teaching theater arts Granite Sch. Dist., Salt Lake City, 1982; named to Nat. Hall of Fame, Ednl. Theatre Assn., 1991, Cottonwood H.S. Hall of Fame, 1995; Joan C. Hahn Theatre named in her honor Cottonwood H.S., 1997; named Outstanding Educator, Utah Ho. Reps., 1995. Mem. Internat. Thespian Soc. (sponsor 1968—, internat. dir. 1982-84, trustee 1978-84), Utah Speech Arts Assn. (pres. 1976-78, 88-90), NEA, Utah Edn. Assn., Granite Edn. Assn., Profl. Travel Agts. Assn., Utah High Sch. Activities Assn. (drama rep. 1972-76), AAUW (pres. 1972-74). Republican. Mormon. Avocations: reading; travel; dancing. Home: PO Box 36 Salem UT 84653-0036

HAHN, LEWIS EDWIN, philosopher, retired educator; b. Swenson, Tex., Sept. 26, 1908; s. Edwin D. and Ione (Brewster) H.; m. Elizabeth Herring, June 30, 1932 (dec. 1991); children: Helen Elizabeth, Mary, Sharon; m. Mary Anne King, Sept. 1, 1992. BA, U. Tex., 1929, MA, 1929; PhD, U. Calif., 1939. Tchg. fellow U. Calif., 1931-34; from instr. philosophy to assoc. prof. U. Mo., Columbia, 1936-49; prof. philosophy Washington U., St. Louis, 1949-63, chmn. dept., 1949-63; from assoc. dean to dean Washington U. Grad. Sch. Arts and Scis., St. Louis, 1953-63; rsch. prof. philosophy So. Ill. U., Carbondale, 1963-77; prof. emeritus So. Ill. U., 1977—; vis. prof., editor So. Ill. U. Libr. of Living Philosophers, 1981—; disting. vis. prof. Baylor U., 1977-80; Mem. U.S. Nat. Commn. UNESCO, 1965-67; vis. lectr. Princeton U., 1947. Author: A Contextualistic Theory of Perception, 1942, (with others) Value: A Cooperative Inquiry, 1949, Enhancing Cultural Interflow Between East & West, 1998; co-author: Guide to the Works of John Dewey, 1970; editor: Library of Living Philosophers, 1981—; co-editor: The Philosophy of Gabriel Marcel, 1984, The Philosophy of W.V. Quine, 1986, expanded edit., 1998, The Philosophy of G.H. von Wright, 1989, Charles D. Tenney's Discovery of Discovery, 1991; editor: The Philosophy of Charles Hartshorne, 1991, The Philosophy of A.J. Ayer, 1992, The Philosophy of Paul Ricoeur, 1995, The Philosophy of Paul Weiss, 1995, The Philosophy of Hans-Georg Gadamer, 1997, The Philosophy of Roderick M. Chisholm, 1997, The Philosophy of P.F. Strawson, 1998. Recipient Disting. Svc. award So. Ill. U., 1993. Fellow AAAS; mem. Am. Philos. Assn. (exec. bd. 1950-54, 70-73, chmn. com. placement, available pers. 1951-54, sec.-treas. West divsn. 1949-51, sec.-treas. 1960-66, com. on internat. coop. 1967-80, history com. 1993), AAUP, Am. Soc. Aesthetics, S.W. Philos. Soc. (pres. 1955), Mo. Philos. Assn. (pres. 1949-50), So. Soc. for Philosophy and Psychology (pres. 1958-59), Ill. Philosophy Conf. (pres. 1969-71), Soc. Advancement Am. Philosophy (Herbert W. Schneider award 1998), Phi Beta Kappa. Home: 1951 N Reed Station Rd Carbondale IL 62901-7136 Office: So Ill U Dept Philosophy Carbondale IL 62901-4505

HAHN, LUCILLE DENISE, paper company executive, retired; b. Stony Point, N.Y., Oct. 8, 1940; d. Raymond and Catherine (Nobert) Hoyt. Lab. asst. Champion Internat. (formerly St. Regis Paper Co.), West Nyack, N.Y., 1972-74, technician, 1974-77, tech. asst., 1977-79, rsch. asst., 1979-82, technologist, 1982-84, sr. technologist, 1984-86, assoc. testing coord., 1986-89, testing engr., 1989-96, sr. quality engr., 1996—, ret., 1998; quality mgmt. rep. ISO 9000 Quality Sys., 1994-98. Author: Testing Guidebook, 1990, (videos) Testing the Strength Properties of Paper, 1991, Testing the Strength Properties of Board, 1991. Fellow TAPPI (sec. process and product quality divsn. 1987-88, vice chair 1989-90, chmn. 1991-92, bd. dirs. 1993-96); mem. NAFE.

HAHN, MARY DOWNING, author; b. Washington, Dec. 9, 1937; d. Kenneth Ernest and Anna Elisabeth (Sherwood) Downing; m. William Edward Hahn, Oct. 7, 1961 (div. 1977); children: Katherine Sherwood, Margaret Elizabeth; m. Norman Pearce Jacob, Apr. 24, 1982. BA in Fine Arts and English, U. Md., 1960, MA in English, 1969. Asst. libr. children's sect. Prince George's County (Md.) Meml. Libr. System, 1975-91; instr. English U. Md., College Park, 1970-74; free-lance illustrator PBS/WETA, Arlington, Va., 1973-75. Author: The Sara Summer, 1979, The Time of the Witch, 1982, Daphne's Book, 1983 (William Allen White Children's Choice award 1985-86), The Jellyfish Season, 1985, Wait Till Helen Comes: A Ghost Story, 1980 (11 Children's Choice awards), Tallahassee Higgins, 1987, Following the Mystery Man, 1988, December Stillness, 1988 (Book award Child Study Assn. 1989, Calif. Young Readers' medal 1990-91), The Doll in the Garden, 1989 (Md. Children's Book award 1990-91, 7 Children's Choice awards), The Dead Man in Indian Creek, 1990 (4 Children's Choice awards), The Spanish Kidnapping Disaster, 1991, Stepping on the Cracks, 1991 (Scott O'Dell Hist. Fiction award 1992, ALA notable 1991, Joan G. Sugarman award, Hedda Seisler Mason award, Children's Choice awards), The Wind Blows Backward, 1993 (ALA Best Books for Young Adults), Time for Andrew, 1994 (7 Children's Choice awards), Look for Me by Moonlight, 1995 (Yalsa Quick Picks for Reluctant Readers), The Gentleman Outlaw and Me-Eli, 1996, Following My Own Footsteps, 1996, As Ever, Gordy, 1998, Anna All Year Round, 1999. Recipient Scott O'Dell award for hist. fiction, 1992, author's award Md. Libr. Assn., 1997. Mem. Soc. Children's Book Writers, Washington Children's Book Guild. E-mail: mdh12937@aol.com.

HAHN, ROBERT SIMPSON, computer scientist, mechanical engineer; b. N.Y.C., Nov. 1, 1916; m. 1941; 3 children. ME, U. Cin., 1940, MSc, 1942, DSc in Applied Physics, 1944. Rsch. engr. Hearld Divsn. Cincinnati-Milacron, Worcester, Ohio, 1944-79; pres. Hahn Engring. Inc., Auburn, Mass., 1979—; cons., 1971-79. Recipient Lifetime Achievement award Am. Soc. Profl. Engrs. Mem. ASME (medal 1981), Nat. Acad. Engrs., Soc. Mfg. Engrs., Internat. Inst. Prodn. Engring. Rsch. Home: 218 E Hill Rd Oakham MA 01068-9623 Office: Hahn Engring Inc 160 Southbridge St Auburn MA 01501-2583*

HAHN, STANLEY ROBERT, JR., lawyer, financial executive; b. Louisville, Dec. 8, 1946; s. Stanley Robert and Dorothy Dodd (Moseley) H.; children from previous marriage: Laura, Valerie, Kathy; (div.); m. LaDonna Marie Dees, Nov. 9, 1996. BBA in Fin., Ga. State U., MBA; LLM in Litigation, Atlanta Law Sch., JD. Bar: Ga. 1983, U.S. Dist. Ct. (no. dist.) Ga. 1983, U.S. Ct. Appeals (11th cir.) 1983, U.S. Ct. Apppeals (4th cir.) 1985, U.S. Supreme Ct. 1986. Mgr. credit White-Westinghouse Corp., Atlanta, 1975-77; mgr. fin. Am. Can Co., Greenwich, Conn., 1977—; pvt. practice Atlanta, 1983—; bd. dirs. HDC Investments Inc., Atlanta, Interest Unltd. Inc., Atlanta. Mem. Assn. MBA Execs., Assn. Trial Lawyers Am., Nat. Assn. Credit Mgmt. Baptist. Avocations: golf, tennis, chess, billiards. Office: 5865 Jimmy Carter Blvd Ste 110 Norcross GA 30071-2921

HAHN, THOMAS JOONGHI, accountant; b. Seoul, Korea, Apr. 12, 1955; came to U.S., 1979; s. Sang Jin and Seong Soon (Hong) H.; m. Linda Young Kim, May 26, 1984; children: Gina K., Michael J., Catherine S. BS, U. Md., 1982. CPA, CFP. Jr. acct. VerKentenen, Anerbach & Olson, CPAs, Silver Springs, Md., 1982-83; sr. acct. Chough, Oh & Co., CPAs, Silver Springs, 1983-85; ptnr. Lee & Hahn, CPAs, Falls Church, Va., 1985-87; prin. Thomas J. Hahn, CPA, Falls Church, 1987—; bd. dirs. STG, Inc., Fairfax, Va. Host weekly radio talk show, 1996—. Recipient Svc. award Posung H. S. Alumni Assn. of Greater Washington Area, 1992. Mem. AICPA, Va. Soc. CPAs. Roman Catholic. Office: Thomas J Hahn CPA 7639 Leesburg Pike 1st Fl Falls Church VA 22043-2520

HAHN, WILLIAM ORR, psychologist, consultant; b. Pitts., Aug. 19, 1950; s. Edward Howard and Louise (Flowers) H.; m. April Diesel, Nov 5, 1977; children: William O. Jr., Amy Lee, Heather Ann. BS, Clarion U., 1972; MEd, Duquesne U., 1973; advanced degree, Ind. U. Pa., 1976; PhD, U. Pitts., 1984. Lic. psychologist, Pa.; cert. sch. psychologist, Pa.; nat. cert. sch. psychologist; bd. cert. and diplomate Acad. Experts in Traumatic Stress. Dir. Behavior Mgmt. Cons., New Kensington, Pa., 1982—; staff psychologist Forbes Regional Health Ctr., Monroeville, Pa., 1987—, chmn., 1988-90, sect. chair, 1997—; instr. Duquesne U. Grad. Sch., Pitts., 1990—. Author: Suicide and Children, 1986. Bd. dirs. Fellowship of Christian Athletes, Pa., 1990—. Mem. APA, Pa. Psychol. Assn., Nat. Assn. Sch. Psychologists, Assn. Sch. Psychologists Pa. (sec. 1985-86, pres. 1986-87). Roman Catholic. Office: Behavior Mgmt Cons 365 Freeport St New Kensington PA 15068-6076

HAHNE, C. E. (GENE HAHNE), computer services executive; b. Savannah, Ga., Sept. 21, 1940; s. Charles Eugene and Hortense (Kavanaugh) h.; m. Brenda Wike, Nov. 25, 1983; children: Gregory, Christopher, David, Stephanie. BS in Indsl. Mgmt., Ga. Inst. Tech., 1963. Sales mgr. Shell Oil Co., Cleve., 1969-72; head office rep. Shell Oil Co., Houston, 1973-75, mgr. tng., human resources and products, 1979-93; mgr. tng. and recruiting Shell Chem., Houston, 1976-78; CEO, chmn. bd. dirs. Intercom, The Woodlands, Tex., 1993-99; mng. ptnr. Strategic Directions, Humble, Tex., 1999—; mem. adv. coun. U. Houston, 1984-85, curriculum com., 1990-92; chair mktg. com. Houston C.C., 1987-90; speaker in field Europe, Can., S.Am., U.S. Author: Management Handbook, 1981, Training Handbook, 1986, Sales Training Handbook, 1991, Training and Development Handbook, 1995; contbr. articles to profl. jours. Mem. bus. and industry coun. Houston C.C., 1986—; mem. adv. coun. Tex. A&M U., College Station, 1985-88; chair fundraising com. Brookwood Cmty., Houston, 1986-88; bd. dirs. Interact, Houston, 1983, U. Tex., Austin, 1984-85, H.R. Comm. Recipient Speaker's award United Way, 1988, Pres. award Houston Community Coll., 1987, Tex. Vocat. Excellence award, 1990. Mem. ASTD (nat. bd. treas. 1981-86, Gordon M. Bliss award 1989, Torch award 1987, Lifetime Recognition award 1989, Disting. Contbn. to Cmty./Nation award 1984, James Ball award 1981), World Future Soc., Sales and Mktg. Execs. of Houston (bd. dirs. 1986-88), Soc. for Human Resource Mgmt. Republican. Home: 20210 Atascocita Lake Dr Humble TX 77346-1659

HAHNE HOFSTED, JANET LORRAINE, artist; b. Bklyn., Apr. 1, 1948; d. Lawrence Henry and Dorothy Lorraine Meyer; m. Ronald Charles Hahne, Nov. 22, 1976 (div. Oct. 1983); children: Jackson Noah, Carlena Amanda; m. Jolyon Gene Hofsted, Dec. 7, 1985. BS, SUNY, New Paltz, 1971. Dir., founder Maverick Art Ctr., Woodstock, N.Y., 1997—; lectr. in field. One-woman shows include Fletcher Gallery, 1997, Kingston (N.Y.) City Hall, 1986, Gracie Mansion Mus. Store, N.Y.C., 1986, Woodstock Artists Assn., 1986, 88, Hawthorn Gallery, 1988, Rage, Kingston, 1990; group shows include Helio Gallery, N.Y.C., 1986, Dome Gallery, N.Y.C., 1990, Fletcher Gallery, 1996, Sky's the Limit Gallery, Kingston, 1997, Maverick Art Ctr., Woodstock, 1997, Marcuse, Kingston, 1998. Mem. Woodstock Artists Assn. Home: 157 Maverick Rd Woodstock NY 12498 Office: Maverick Art Ctr 163 Maverick Rd Woodstock NY 12498

HAHNER, JUNE EDITH, history educator; b. N.Y.C., July 8, 1940; d. Fred and Edith (Konrad) H. BA, Earlham Coll., 1961; MA, Cornell U., 1963, PhD, 1966. Asst. prof. Tex. Tech U., Lubbock, 1966-68; prof. dept. history SUNY, Albany, 1968—; co-pres. Coord. Coun. on Women in History, 1998—. Author: Civilian-Military Relations in Brazil 1889-1898, 1969, Poverty and Politics: The Urban Poor in Brazil, 1986 (New Eng. Coun. Latin Am. Studies prize 1987), Emancipating the Female Sex: The Struggle for Women's Rights in Brazil, 1850-1940, 1990; editor: Women in Latin American History: Their Lives and Views, 1976, 80, Women Through Women's Eyes: Latin American Women in Nineteenth-Century Travel Accounts, 1998; mem. editl. bd. The Ams., 1974-92, Lat. Am. Rsch. Rev., 1994-96. Recipient rsch. and tchg. award Fulbright Commn., 1980; hon. fellow Woodrow Wilson Found., 1961-62, OAS, 1963, NEH, 1971, 82-83, Rockefeller Found., 1986-87. Mem. Am. Hist. Assn. (mem. com. women historians 1990-92), Northeastern Assn. Brazilianists (mem. exec. coun. 1993-95), New Eng. Con. Lat. Am. Studies (mem. exec. coun. 1977-79), Lat. Am. Studies Assn., Brazilian Studies Assn. Home: 534 Huron Rd Delmar NY 12054-2630 Office: SUNY Dept History 1400 Washington Ave Dept History Albany NY 12222-1000

HAHNER, LINDA R. R., artist, creative director; b. Healdsburg, Calif., Dec. 4, 1952; d. Ellison and Joan (Prenderville) Ruffner; m. Thomas G. Russell, Dec. 23, 1971 (div.); 1 child, Thomas Kristian Russell, 1 foster child, Eric J. Miklas; m. Wolfgang Andreas Hahner, Dec. 21, 1989. BA Fine Art/Creative Writing with honors, Principia Coll., Elsah, Ill., 1980; MFA, Washington U., St. Louis, 1986; student, Skowhegan Sch. Painting/Sculp., 1985, Acad. Fine Art, Helsinki, 1987. Painter, prof., artist London, Helsinki, Freiburg, 1986-95; pres., founder Out of the Blue Design LLC, San Francisco, 1995—. One-person shows include The Am. Ctr., Helsinki, 1986, Helsinki Art Hall, 1987, Millikin Gallery, Decatur, Ill., 1988, Hagelstam Gallery, Helsinki, 1990, Zimmerman Gallery, Breisach, Germany, 1994; exhibited in group shows Steinberg Gallery, St. Louis, 1986, B Z Wagman Gallery, St. Louis, 1988, Rislakki Collection, Helsinki, 1991; represented in permanent collections Boatman's Bank, 1st Nat. Bank of Columbia, Finland/U.S. Ednl. Exch. Commn., Trade-off OY, KOP Bank Finland, Veikko Savolainen, Arja and Kari Antilla. Fulbright fellow and travel grantee, 1986; Skowhegan award and grantee, 1985. Mem. Women in Multimedia, Multimedia Devel. Group., ACM & Siggraph. Office: Out of the Blue Design LLC 461 Second St Ste T552 San Francisco CA 94107-1641

HAIDOSTIAN, ALICE BERBERIAN, concert pianist, civic volunteer and fundraiser; b. Highland Park, Mich., Sept. 21, 1925; d. Harry M. and Siroun

Vartabedian Berberian; m. Berj H. Haidostian, Oct. 1, 1949; children: Cynthia Esther Haidostian Wilbanks, Christine Rebecca Haidostian Garry, Dicran Berj. MusB, U. Mich., 1946, MusM, 1949. Pvt. piano tchr., 1946-48; tchr. music Detroit Pub. Sch., 1953; dir. The Haidostians vocal trio, 1959-71; dir. Youth Choral Group Cultural Soc. Armenians from Istanbul, 1965-72; chmn. adv. coun. Armenian Studies Program, U. Mich., 1984—. Active 1st profl. prodn. Armenian nat. opera Anoush, Mich. Opera Theatre, 1981-82; dir. (vocal trio) The Haidostians, 1959-71, Youth Choral Group of Cultural Soc. Armenians from Istanbul, 1965-72. Active Centennial Celebration U. Mich. Sch. Music, Detroit, 1980; organist, choir dir. Armenian Congl. Ch. Detroit, 1946-48; mem. Westminster Ch. Detroit Chancel Choir, 1965-80, Armenian Gen. Benevolent Union Alex Manoogian Sch., 1981-91, Detroit chpt. core group com., 1992—, chmn. Marie Manoogian group, 1993—; mem. Detroit Symphony Orch., 1986-88, bd. dirs. Hall Vol. Coun., 1994-96; mem. Detroit Women's Symphony Orch., Mich. Opera, Mich. Opera Theatre, Oakway Symphony Orch., Save Orch. Hall, Women's Divsn. Project Hope, 1964—, pres. 1995-96; pres. Detroit Armenian Women's Club, 1964-65, 73-75. Recipient Spirit of Detroit award 1980, Heart of Gold award United Found. City Detroit, 1981, Nat. Svc. citation U. Mich. Alumnae Coun., 1980, Disting. Alumni Svc. award U. Mich., 1981, Magic Flute award Internat. Found. Mozarteum, Salzburg, Austria, 1989, Lifetime Achievement award Outstanding Woman Mich., 1998; named Armenian Mother of Yr., Internat. Inst. Detroit, 1981. Mem. Detroit Assn. Univ. Mich. Women (pres. 1969-71), Mich. Fedn. Music Clubs, Mich. State Med. Soc. Aux., Pro Mozart Soc. Greater Detroit (pres. 1982—), Pro Musica Detroit (sec. 1969-90, 1st v.p. 1990—), Tuesday Musicale Detroit (pres. 1970-72), Univ. Mich. Alumni Assn. (chmn. alumnae coun. 1977-79), Univ. Mich. Sch. Music Alumni Soc., Women's Assn. Detroit Symphony Orch. (pres. 1986-88), U. Mich. Alumni Assn. (bd. dirs.), U. Mich. Emeritus Club (pres. 1997-98). Avocation: playing piano by ear, travel. Home: 6838 Valley Spring Dr Bloomfield Hills MI 48301-2845

HAIES, EVELYN S(OLOMON), fundraiser, educator, writer; b. Bklyn., Oct. 26, 1944; d. Samuel and Marion (Dickstein) Solomon; m. Jay W. Haies, May 30, 1966; children: Elissa Rachel Grunwald, Deborah, Lila Shleifstein, Daniel, David. BA, Hunter Coll., 1964; MFA, Bklyn. Coll., 1989. Cert. jr. h.s. tchr. social studies, jr., sr. h.s. lang. arts & social studies. Tchr. N.Y.C., 1964—; finance profl. N.Y.C. Ins., 1986—; founder, pres. Rachel's Children Reclamation Found. Inc., N.Y.C., 1996—. Author: Four Years of Glory, 1964, (poetry) Frozen Shadows, 1989, Parallel Parashas, 1995; author lyrics We Are Rachel's Children, 1995, Hagolan & Od Josef Chai, 1996; contbr. articles to profl. jours. Bd. dirs. sisterhood Manhattan Beach Jewish Ctr., Bklyn., 1990—; nat. v.p. Women's Br., N.Y.C., 1994—, chair nat. conv., Washington, 1995. Recipient Women of Yr. award Prospect Park Yeshiva, Bklyn., 1975, Women United Redeption, Bklyn., 1996. Avocations: poetry readings, lecturing. Office: Rachels Children Reclamation Found PO Box 220 Valley Stream NY 11582-0220

HAIG, DAVID M., property and investment manager; b. New Rochelle, N.Y., May 20, 1951; s. Alexander Salusbury and Joan (Damon) H. Student, Marlboro Coll., 1974. Trustee Estate of S.M. Damon, Honolulu, 1982—; bd. dirs. BancWest Corp., First Hawaiian Bank, Honolulu. Bd. dirs. YMCA Met. Honolulu, 1985—; dir. Aloha United Way, 1990-94; trustee YMCA Retirement Fund, 1991—, Hawaii Pacific U., 1988-94; nat. bd. mem. YMCA of U.S.A., 1990-94, bd. dirs. internat. com., 1989-93; chmn. Hawaii Food Bank, 1990-94, dir., 1982-94. Mem. Young Pres.'s Orgn., Oahu Country Club, Waialae Country Club, Rotary, 200 Club, Pacific Club, Honolulu Club. Address: David M Haig Trustee 999 Bishop St #2800 Honolulu HI 96813-4423

HAIG, FRANK RAWLE, physics educator, clergyman; b. Phila., Sept. 11, 1928; s. Alexander M. and Regina A. (Murphy) H. A.B., Woodstock Coll., Md., 1952, S.T.L., 1960; Ph.L., Bellarmine Coll., Plattsburgh, N.Y., 1953; Ph.D., Catholic U., 1959; LHD honoris causa, SUNY, 1987. Ordained priest Roman Cath. Ch. 1960. Joined S.J., 1946; postdoctoral fellow U. Rochester, N.Y., 1962-63; asst. prof. Wheeling Coll., W.Va., 1963-66, pres., 1966-72; asst. and assoc. prof. Loyola Coll., Balt., 1972-81; pres. Le Moyne Coll., Syracuse, N.Y., 1981-87; prof. physics Loyola Coll., Balt., 1987—. Editor Jour. Md. Assn. Higher Edn., 1979-81; contbr. articles on nuclear physics, bibl. theology and internat. politics to profl. publs. Pres., Wheeling C. of C., 1969-71; pres. Syracuse Opera Co., 1983-85, chmn. bd., 1985-87; gen. campaign chmn. United Way Onondaga County, Syracuse, 1985-86. Recipient Mayor's Achievement award Mayor of Syracuse, 1983; Harry J. Carman award Middle States Council for Social Studies, 1985; NSF fellow, 1962-63. Mem. AAUP (v.p. Md. Conf. 1990-92, 95, pres., 1995-98), Am. Assn. Physics Tchrs. (pres. Chesapeake sect. 1976-77, 90-92), Am. Phys. Soc., Washington Acad. Scis. (pres. 1993-94), Sigma Xi. Republican. Roman Catholic. Office: Loyola Coll Dept Physics 4501 N Charles St Baltimore MD 21210-2601

HAIG, MONICA ELAINE NACHAJSKI, special education educator; b. Bay Shore, N.Y., Nov. 17, 1963; d. Walter Andrew and Elaine Gilda (Guerringue) Nachajski; m. Michael Haig, June 24, 1989; children: Kathleen Mary, Michael Christopher. BS in Edn., SUNY, Geneseo, 1985; MS in Edn. with high honors, L.I. U., 1989. Cert. permanent spl. and elem. edn. tchr., N.Y. Tchr. spl. edn. Convalescent Hosp. for Children, Rochester, N.Y., 1985, Patchogue-Medford Sch. Dist., Patchogue, N.Y., 1985—; edn. cons., mem. Suffolk County Exec.'s Conf. on Youth, Alcohol and hwy. Safety, Ronkonkoma, N.Y., 1990; participant seminars, workshops and confs. Mem. Coun. for Exceptional Children. Avocations: dance movement therapy, reading. Office: Tremont Elem Sch Oregon Ave Medford NY 11763

HAIG, ROBERT LEIGHTON, lawyer; b. Plainfield, N.J., July 30, 1947; s. Richard Randall and Edith (Remington) H. AB, Yale U., 1967; JD, Harvard U., 1970. Bar: N.Y. 1971, U.S. Dist. Ct. (so. and ea. dists.) N.Y., U.S. Ct. Appeals (2d cir.). Assoc. Kelley Drye & Warren, N.Y.C., 1970-79, ptnr., 1980—; mem. bd. advisers Law Dept. Mgmt. Adviser, 1995—. Co-author: Preparing for and Trying the Civil Lawsuit, 1987, 91, 94, 97, Federal Civil Practice, 1989, 93, 97, Federal Litigation Guide, 1992, 93, 94, Corporate Counsel's Guide, 1996, 97, Products Liability in New York, 1997; also contbr. chpts. to books; mem. bd. editors Fed. Litigation Guide Reporter, 1989—, In-House Law Practice Management, 1997—; editor-in-chief Comml. Litigation in N.Y. State Cts., 1995, Bus. and Comml. Litigation in Fed. Cts., 1998. Co-chair Comml. Cts. Task Force, 1995—; mem. legis. com. Com. for Modern Cts., N.Y.C., 1986—, bd. dirs., 1994—; mem. Am. Law Inst., 1998—; mem. N.Y. State Conf. Bar Leaders, exec. coun., 1988-90, dept. disciplinary com. appellate divsn., 1996—, hearing panel chair, 1999—; mem. N.Y. State Jud. Salary Commn., 1997—. Recipient award for excellence in continuing legal edn. Assn. Continuing Legal Edn. Adminstrs., 1991. Fellow Am. Bar Found., N.Y. Bar Found.; mem. ABA (del. 1991—, standing com. on jud. selection, tenure and compensation 1995-96, com. on bus. cts. 1996—, chair subcom. on rels. between inside and outside counsel 1997—), Assn. of Bar of City of N.Y. (mem. jud. com. 1985-88, chmn., 1989-92, mem. coun. on jud. adminstrn. 1989-92, chmn. 1996—), N.Y. County Lawyers Assn. (exec. com. 1986-95, v.p. 1986-92, pres. 1992-94, dir. 1985—, chmn. com. on supreme ct. 1984-86, chmn. fin. com. 1988-90, lectr. 1984—, pres. Found. 1992-94), N.Y. State Bar Assn. (chmn. com. on fed. cts. 1986-88, del. 1988—, chmn. comml. and fed. litig. sect. 1988-90, lectr. 1985—, exec. com. 1991-94, mem. steering com. on commerce and industry 1997—, chair com. on multi-disciplinary practice and the legal profn. 1998—, 1st Ann. award for Disting. Pub. Svc. comml. and fed. litig. sect. 1995). Office: Kelley Drye & Warren 101 Park Ave New York NY 10178-0002

HAIG, SUSAN, conductor. Conductor Windsor Symphnoy Orchestra, Windsor, ON. Office: Windsor Symphony Orch, 487 Ouellette Ave, Windsor, ON Canada N9A 4J2*

HAIGH, CHARLES, criminal justice educator; b. Paterson, N.J., Oct. 29, 1939; s. Wallace Glover and Myrtle (Lewis) H.; m. Patricia Brennan, Apr. 12, 1986; children: Michael C., Charles E. BS in Law Enforcement Adminstrn., U. New Haven, 1972, MPA, 1976; CAS in Ednl. Adminstrn./Supervision, Fairfield (Conn.) U., 1980; EdD in Ednl. Mgmt., U. Bridgeport, 1989. Dir. tng. Milford (Conn.) Police Dept., 1965-91; asst. prof., adj. prof. criminal justice program Ctrl. Conn. State U., New Britain, 1991—; adj. prof. criminal justice program U. New Haven, West Haven, Conn., 1979—. Adv. bd. criminal justice program Housatonic C.C., Bridgeport, 1985-92; deacon First United Ch. of Christ, Congl., Milford, 1993—, chmn., 1995. With USN, 1957-60. Ctrl. Conn. State U. grant, 1994. Mem. Acad. Criminal Justice Scis., Northeastern Assn. Criminal Justice Scis. (Outstanding Svc. to Assn. award 1994), Elks (chmn. Most Valuable Student scholarship program 1990—), Masons. Democrat. Avocations: golf, biking, swimming. Home: 25 Art St Milford CT 06460-4318

HAIGHT, CHARLES SHERMAN, JR., federal judge; b. N.Y.C., Sept. 23, 1930; s. Charles Sherman and Margaret (Edwards) H.; m. Mary Jane Peightal, June 30, 1953; children: Nina E., Susan P. B.A., Yale U., 1952, LL.B., 1955. Bar: N.Y. State 1955. Trial atty., admiralty and shipping dept. Dept. Justice, Washington, 1955-57; assoc. firm Haight, Gardner, Poor & Havens, N.Y.C., 1957-68; ptnr. Haight, Gardner, Poor & Havens, 1968-76; judge U.S. Dist. Ct. for So. Dist. N.Y., 1976—. Bd. dirs. Kennedy Child Study Ctr.; adv. trustee Am.-Scandinavian Found., chmn., 1970-76; bd. mgrs. Havens Fund. Mem. Maritime Law Assn., U.S., N.Y. State Bar Assn., Bar Assn. City N.Y., Fed. Bar Council. Episcopalian. Office: US Dist Ct US Courthouse 500 Pearl St New York NY 10007-1316

HAIGHT, DAVID B., church official. s. Hector C. and Clara Tuttle Haight; m. Ruby Olson, three children. Attended Utah State U; Former Mayor, Palo Alto, Calif.; Asst. to the twelve 1970-76, Apostle, Quorum of the Twelve, 1976—, Mormon Ch., Salt Lake City; Comdr. Navy, WW2. Office: LDS Church 50 E North Temple Salt Lake City UT 84150-0002 Office: Bonneville Internat Corp Broadcast House 55 E 3rd Ave Salt Lake City UT 84107-4722*

HAIGHT, JAMES THERON, lawyer, corporate executive; b. Racine, Wis., Dec. 10, 1924; s. Walter Lyman and Geraldine (Foley) H.; m. Patricia Aloe, Apr. 26, 1952; children: Alberta, Barbara, Catherine, Dorothy, Elaine. Student, U. Nebr., 1943-44, U. Bordeaux, France, 1947; diplome d'Etudes, U. Paris, 1948; B.A., U. Wis., 1950, LL.B., 1951. Bar: D.C. 1952, U.S. Supreme Ct. 1955, Calif. 1968. Atty. Covington & Burling, Washington, 1951-56, Goodyear Tire & Rubber Co., Goodyear Internat. Corp., Akron, Ohio, 1956-61; gen. counsel, sec. George J. Meyer Mfg. Co., Milw., 1961-66; sr. v.p., sec., chief corp. counsel Thrifty Corp., L.A., 1966-92, spl. counsel, 1992-96. Mem. adv. bd. Internat. and Comparative Law Ctr., Southwestern Legal Found., 1964-89; adv. bd. Edward Roybal Inst. Applied Gerontology, Calif. State U., L. Fellow Am. Bar Found. (life); mem. ABA (vice chmn. internat. law sect. 1965-67, chmn. 1974-75), Calif. Bar Assn., Los Angeles County Bar Assn., Pasadena Bar Assn., Am. Soc. Corp. Secs., Order of Coif. Home and Office: 1390 Ridge Way Pasadena CA 91106-4514

HAIGHT, SCOTT KERR, lawyer; b. Allentown, Pa., Oct. 5, 1961; s. Gordon Eugene and Barbara Lea (Kerr) H.; m. Virginia Valentine Fox, Aug. 27, 1983; children: Elizabeth Valentine, Andrew Steven. BA in History, Davidson Coll., 1983; JD, Emory U., 1986. Bar: Tenn. 1986, U.S. Dist. Ct. (we. dist.) Tenn. 1986, U.S. Ct. Appeals (5th cir.) 1987. Atty. Armstrong, Allen, Prewitt, Gentry, Johnston & Holmes, Memphis, 1986-87, Baker, Donelson, Bearman & Caldwell, P.C., Memphis, 1987-99, Garrison, Morris & Haight, PLLC, Memphis, 1999—; pres. bd. dirs. Lamplighter sch., Memphis, 1990-94, U.S. Legis. Com., I.N.T.A, N.Y.C., 1990-91, 92-96; mem. Legislative Analysis Comm., 1996—. Mng. editor Emory Jour. Internat. Dispute Resolution, 1985-86. Magistrar pres. Lamar Inn, Phi Delta Phi, 1985-86; precinct officer of election Shelby County Election Commn., Tenn., 1990-94; election inspector, 1994—, sr. warden, pres., vestry, bd. dirs. St. Georges Episcopal Ch., Germantown, Tenn., 1994-95, jr. warden, 1996—; bd. dirs. St. George's Day Sch., 1994-96, mem. governing commn., 1996-97. Mem. ABA (intellectual property sect., spl. com. security interests in intellectual property, bus. law sect., electronic practices subcom. of UCC com., internat. law sect.), Internat. Trademark Assn., Legis. Analysis Com. (chair security interests subcom. 1996-98, external affairs com., model state trademark bill subcom. 1999—), Internat. Bar Assn., Tenn. Bar Assn., Memphis Bar Assn., Fed. Bar Assn. Repulbian. Episcopalian. Office: Garrison Morris & Haight PLLC 5100 Poplar Ave Ste 2100 Memphis TN 38137

HAIGHT, WARREN GAZZAM, investor; b. Seattle, Sept. 7, 1929; s. Gilbert Pierce and Ruth (Gazzam) H.; m. Suzanne H., Sept. 1, 1951; children—Paula Lea, Ian Pierce; m. Ottina Mehau, June 25, 1985. A.B. in Econs, Stanford U., 1951. Asst. Treas. Hawaiian Pineapple Co., Honolulu, 1955-64; v.p., treas. Oceanic Properties, Inc., Honolulu, 1964-67; pres., dir. Oceanic Properties, Inc., 1967-85, chmn., 1983-85; pres. Hawaii, Castle & Cooke Inc., 1983-85, Warren G. Haight & Assocs., 1985—; chmn. Molokai Ranch, Ltd., 1996—; bd. dirs. Round Hill Enterprises, Inc., Las Positas Land Co., Inc., Baldwin Pacific Properties, Inc., Hawaii Project Mgmt., Inc., Transamerica Realty Advisors, Inc., Queen Emma Corp., Queens Devel. Corp., Dole Corp., Standard Fruit and Steamship Co., Inc., Bumble Bee Seafoods, Inc. Bd. dirs. Downtown Improvement Assn., Oahu Devel. Conf., Hawaii Island Econ. Devel. Bd., Econ. Devel. Corp. Honolulu, Intellect, Inc., Hawaii Resort Developers Conf., Homeless Solutions, Inc., Mutual Housing of Hawaii, Inc.; mem. Transit Coalition, Honolulu, Govs. Com. on Econ. Futures; pres., bd. dirs. Land Use Rsch. Found. of Hawaii, Pacific Found. for Cancer Rsch., Hawaii Nature Ctr.; mem. policy adv. bd. for elderly affairs State of Hawaii. Lt. USNR, 1951-55. Mem. Housing Coalition, Calif. Coastal Council. Clubs: Outrigger Canoe, Round Hill Country, Plaza, Pacific. Home: 319 Lala Pl Kailua HI 96734-3224 Office: 220 S King St Ste 1465 Honolulu HI 96813-4542

HAIGNERE, CLARA SUE, health education educator; b. Columbus, Ohio, Jan. 31, 1952; d. Eugene B. and Francis M. (Field) H.; m. Richard A. Bissell, June 17, 1973 (div. 1983); m. Robert S. Norman, July 19, 1986; 1 child, Samuel V. Norman-Haignere. BA, U. Calif., Davis, 1974; MA, U. Denver, 1980, PhD, 1983; MPH, Columbia U., 1985. Cert. health edn. specialist. Asst. prof. dept. health and nutrition Bklyn. Coll., 1985-86; exec. dir. teen advocacy Planned Parenthood Fedn., N.Y.C., 1986-88; exec. dir. AIDS and adolescence awareness project Columbia U., N.Y.C., 1988-90; asst. prof. cmty. health edn. Hunter Coll., N.Y.C., 1990-92; ednl. advisor AIDS/HIV tech. assistance project N.Y.C. Bd. Edn., 1992-93; asst. prof. dept. health studies Temple U., Phila., 1993—; mem., spkr. U.S. Out of El Salvador Com., Denver Cath. Archdiocese, 1980; cons., coord. Oscar Romero Holistic Health Care Ctr., 1986; HIV/AIDS educator Gay Men's Health Crisis, 1987; adj. prof. dept. health studies NYU, 1992-93; rsch. reviewer Nat. Inst. Child Health and Human Devel., Washington, 1992; rsch. cons. Project Reach Youth, Bklyn, 1991-92; collaborator, mem. Ctr. for Study of Family Policy, Hunter Coll., 1992; cons., advisor dept. nursing Coll. Allied Health Scis. Thomas Jefferson U., Phila., 1995; cons. N.Y.C. Bd. Edn., 1992; mem. various coms. Temple U., 1993—. Contbr. articles to profl. jours.; co-author: (video) AIDS NOT US, 1989, (curriculum) Adolescents Living Safely..., 1991. Mem. steering com. Youth Health Empowerment, Phila., 1995—; bd. dirs. AIDS and Adolescence Network of N.Y., N.Y.C., 1994-97; mem. N.J. HIV Prevention Planning Group, Sex Info. and Edn. Coun. of U.S. Recipient Nat. Rsch. award NIMH, 1983, postdoctoral fellow, 1983-85; grantee ARREST CDC, 1994, 95—, William Penn Found., 1996—. Mem. Am. Pub. Health Assn. (co-coord. investigative trip to El Salvador 1985), Am. Alliance for Health, Phys. Edn., Recreation and Dance, Pa. Pub. Health Assn., Internat. Union for Health Promotion and Edn., Soc. for Pub. Health Edn., Phila. Coll. Physicians and Surgeons (pub. health sector), Alpha Kappa Delta, Phi Kappa Phi, Phi Beta Kappa. Home: K18 Shirley Ln Lawrenceville NJ 08648-1420 Office: Dept Health Studies Temple U 301 E Vivacqua Hall Philadelphia PA 19122

HAIK, RICHARD T., SR., federal judge; b. 1950. BS, U. Southwestern La., 1971; JD, Loyola U., New Orleans, 1975. Assoc. Haik & Broussard, 1975-79; ptnr. Haik, Broussard & Haik, 1979-81, Haik, Haik & Minvielle, 1981-84; judge La. State Dist., New Iberia, 1984-91; dist. judge U.S. Dist. Ct. (we. dist.) La., 1991—. With USAR, 1978-81; USNG, 1971-78. Mem. ABA, La. Bar Assn., Iberia Parish Bar Assn., La. Dist. Judge's Assn. (exec. com. 1988-91), Nat. Coun. Juvenile and Family Ct. Judges (steering com. alcohol and substance abuse). Office: US Dist Ct Fed Bldg 705 Jefferson St Ste 213 Lafayette LA 70501-6936

HAILE, ALLEN CLEVELAND, educator and administrator; b. Forbes Rd., Pa., Aug. 26, 1930; s. Wesley Matthew and Mary Olivia (Hall) H.; m. Barbara Honey, Dec. 30, 1975; children: Mark, Brice, Scott, Marybeth, Jonathan, Courtney. AB, U. Nebr., Omaha, 1959; MS, U. So. Calif., 1966, MPA, 1971, PhD, 1971. Commd. 2d lt. USAF, 1953, advanced through grades to lt. col., retired, 1973; v.p. urban affairs Pepperdine U., L.A., 1969-73; sr. rschr. Dept. Info. Scis. Rand Corp., Santa Monica, Calif., 1972-73; regional rep. Pacific Basin U.S. Sec. Commerce, L.A., 1977-81; dept. mgr. human resources devel. Bechtel Civil, Inc., Jubail City, 1981-85, mgr. bus. devel. for bldgs. and infrastructure ops., 1985-87, mgr. mktg., 1987-89, mgr. infrastructure devel. Pacific Rim countries, 1991—; dean Coll. of Bus. Calif. Poly State U., San Luis Obispo, 1993-94, dir. cmty. and govt. rels., 1994—; adj. prof. Golden Gate Univ., 1992. V.p., bd. dirs. San Luis Obispo ARC, C. of C.; pres. Filipino Am C. of C., 1991; bd. dirs. United Way, San Luis Obispo, Econ. Forecast Project, San Luis Obispo, Larkin St. Youth Ctr., San Francisco Edn. Fund, Ct. Appointed Spl. Advocates for Children, Western Govtl. Rsch. Assn., pres. 1989; pres. San Francisco Social Svcs. Commn. 1989, San Francisco Planning and Urban Rsch. Assn., 1992. Decorated DFC and seven air medals. Mem. Am. Soc. Pub. Adminstrn. (bd. trustees found., chmn. constitution revision com. 1988, 89). Home: 1022 Islay St San Luis Obispo CA 93401-4026 Office: Calif Poly State U Office Corp Govt Rels San Luis Obispo CA 93407

HAILE, BENJAMIN CARROLL, JR., retired chemical and mechanical engineer; b. Shanghai, China, Apr. 6, 1918; came to U.S., 1925; s. Benjamin Carroll and Ruth Temple (Shreve) H.; m. Lola Pauline Lease, Dec. 28, 1957; children: Thomas Benjamin, Ronald Frederick. BS, U. Calif., Berkeley, 1941; cert., Harvard-MIT, 1945; postgrad., U. So. Calif., 1950-51. Registered profl. chem. and mech. engr., Calif. Chem. engr. Std. Oil of Calif. (Chevron), San Francisco, El Segundo, Calif., 1941-43, 46-48; sr. project chem. engr. C.F. Braun & Co., Alhambra, Calif., 1948-50, 54-56, 67-71, 72; contract chem. and mech. engr. Dow Chem., Stearns-Roger, Fluor et al, Tex., Colo., Ill., 1951-54, 56-57; sr. process engr. Aerojet-Gen. Corp., Sacramento and Covina, Calif., 1957-67; mech. engr. So. Calif. Edison Co., Rosemead, Calif., 1972-84; pvt. practice chem. engr. Fontana and Montclair, Calif., 1986, 88, 92; sr. mem. tech. staff Ralph M. Parsons Co., Pasadena, Calif., 1971, 88-91. 2d lt. USAAF, 1943-46. Mem. NSPE (life, Sacramento chpt. pres. 1960-62), Am. Inst. Chem. Engrs. (mem. emeritus), Toastmasters Internat. (chpt. v.p. 1979, Outstanding Toastmaster 1984), Psi Upsilon. Republican. Achievements include project, process and mech. engring. design of oil refineries, chem. plants, others, with estimated cumulative inflation adjusted value of one billion dollars during lifetime; project leader and process development of new fluid bed adsorption process for air separation; economic optimization studies of complete aerospace programs; static electricity protection study for Polaris propellant manufacturing facility; project leader and designer of one of the world's largest boring machines, 1952-53. Home: 159 N Country Club Rd Glendora CA 91741-3919

HAILE, GETATCHEW, archivist, educator; b. Shenkora, Shewa, Ethiopia, Apr. 19, 1931; came to U.S., 1976; s. Haile Woldeyes and Asseggedetch Wolde Yohannes; m. Misrak Emitu Amare, July 12, 1964; children: Rebecca, Sossina, Elizabeth, Dawit, Mariam-Sena, Yohannes. BD, Coptic Theol. Coll., Cairo, 1957; BA, Am. U. at Cairo, 1957; PhD, Tübingen (Fed. Republic Germany) U., 1962. Advisor Middle Eastern affairs Ethiopian Ministry Fgn. Affairs, Addis Ababa, 1962; prof. Ethiopian studies Addis Ababa U., 1962-73; mem. parliament State of Ethiopia, Addis Ababa, 1974-75; cataloguer Oriental manuscripts Hill Monastic Manuscript Libr. St. John's U., Collegeville, Minn., 1976-99, regents prof. medieval studies, 1988-99; Co-editor Acta Ethiopica, 1974-89; mem. internat. adv. bd. Jour. Ethiopian Studies, 1991—, Ethiopian Jour. of Edn., 1992—; contbg. editor Northeast African Studies; mem. adv. bd. Analecta Bellandiana, 1993—, Aethiopica, Zeitschrift für Äthiopistische Studien, 1996—; exec. editor Ethiopian Register, 1994—; author monographs and contbr. articles to scholarly jours. Mem. Cen. Com. of World Coun. of Chs., Geneva, 1968-74; mem. adv. bd. Ethiopian Orthodox Ch., Addis Ababa, 1973-74. MacArthur fellow, 1988. Corr. fellow Brit. Acad.; mem. Am. Oriental Soc. Home: 17903 County Road 9 Avon MN 56310-8624 Office: St John's U Hill Monastic Manuscpt Libr Collegeville MN 56321

HAILE, H. G., German language and literature educator; b. Brownwood, Tex., July 31, 1931; s. Frank and Neil (Goodson) H.; m. Mary Elizabeth Huff, Sept. 1, 1952; children: Jonathan, Christian, Constance Haile Hunsaker; m. Elizabeth Wade, Mar. 17, 1990. B.A., U. Ark., 1952, M.A., 1954; student, U. Cologne, Germany, 1955-56; Ph.D., U. Ill., 1957. Instr. U. Pa., 1956-57; asst. prof., then asso. prof. U. Houston, 1957-63; mem. faculty U. Ill., Urbana, 1963—; prof. German U. Ill., 1965—, head dept., 1964-73; asso. mem. U. Ill. (Center for Advanced Study), 1969—; vis. prof. U. Mich., U. Ga. Author: Das Faustbuch nach der Wolfenbuttler Handschrift, 1963, 95, The History of Doctor Johann Faustus, 1965, 1996, Artist in Chrysalis: A Biographical Study of Goethe in Italy, 1973, Invitation to Goethe's Faust, 1978, Luther: An Experiment in Biography, 1983; contbr. numerous articles to profl. and popular jours. Fulbright fellow, 1955; Fellow Am. Council Learned Socs., 1961-62. Office: U Ill 3072 Foreign Languages Urbana IL 61801 *A child of the Dust Bowl who became a foreign language teacher, I was skeptical about America. I have learned to accept skepticism as the American trait which protects us from correctness, collectivism and coercion.*

HAILE, LAWRENCE BARCLAY, lawyer; b. Atlanta, Feb. 19, 1938; children: Gretchen Vanderhoof, Eric McKenzie (dec.), Scott McAllister, m. Carole Chimko, Dec.1, 1998. BA in Econs, U. Tex., 1958, LLB, 1961. Bar: Tex. 1961, Calif. 1962. Law clk. to U.S. Judge Joseph M. Ingraham, Houston, 1961-62; pvt. practice law San Francisco, 1962-67, L.A., 1967—; instr. UCLA Civil Trial Clinics, 1974, 76; lectr. law Calif. Continuing Edn. of Bar, 1973-74, 80-89; mem. nat. panel arbitrators Am. Arbitration Assn., 1965—. Assoc. editor: Tex. Law Rev, 1960-61; Contbr. articles profl. publs. Mem. State Bar Calif., Tex., U.S. Supreme Ct. Bar Assn., Internat. Assn. Property Ins. Counsel (founding mem., pres. 1980), Vintage Auto Racing Assn. (bd. dirs.), Vintage Motorsports Coun. (pres.), Phi Delta Phi, Delta Sigma Rho. Office: 9925 Lancer Ct Beverly Hills CA 90210-1419 *Gold is like brass/Except less crass.*

HAILEY, ARTHUR, author; b. Luton, Eng., Apr. 5, 1920; arrived in Can., 1947, naturalized, 1952, (also Brit. citizen); s. George and Elsie (Wright) H.; m. Sheila Dunlop, July 28, 1951; children: Roger, John, Mark (by previous marriage), Jane, Steven, Diane. Student elementary schs., Eng. Author: Runway Zero-Eight, 1958 (with John Castle), The Final Diagnosis, 1959, In High Places, 1962, Hotel, 1965, Airport, 1968, Wheels, 1971, The Moneychangers, 1975, Overload, 1979, Strong Medicine, 1984, The Evening News, 1990, Detective, 1997; author novels pub. in 40 langs., 160 million copies in print; author 12 internat. TV plays including No Deadly Medicine (Emmy nomination 1957); (TV series) Hotel; collected plays Close-up on Writing for Television, 1960; motion pictures include Zero Hour, 1956, Time Lock, 1957, The Young Doctors, 1961, Hotel, 1966, Airport, 1970, The Moneychangers, 1976, Wheels, 1978, Strong Medicine, 1986; (poem) A Last Request; first editor RAF aircrew tng. mag, Airclues. Air Ministry staff officer, London, 1945-47; pilot, flight lt. RAF, 1939-47; commd. RCAF Res. flight lt., 1951. Recipient Air Efficiency award RAF; subject TV program This Is Your Life, Eng., 1991. Mem. Writers Guild Am. (life), Authors League Am., Alliance of Canadian Cinema, Television and Radio Artists (hon. life), Writers Guild Can. (life). Home: Lyford Cay, PO Box N-7776, Nassau The Bahamas Office: Nancy Stauffer Assocs PO Box 1203 Darien CT 06820-1203

HAILS, ROBERT EMMET, aerospace consultant, business executive, former air force officer; b. Miami, Fla., Jan. 20, 1923; s. Daniel Troy and Jean (Burke) H.; m. Ethel Fitzgerald Gayle, Mar. 2, 1957; children: Robert Emmet Jr., Merrily Hails Joiner, Florence T. Hails Patton, Laura Hails Smith. BS in Aero. Engring., Auburn U., 1947; MS in Indsl. Engring., Columbia U., 1950; postgrad., C&CS Air U., 1955; postgrad. AMP, Harvard U. Sch. Bus., 1965. Enlisted USAAF, 1942, commd. 2d lt., 1944, advanced through grades to lt. gen., 1974, combat pilot Pacific Theater, 1944-45; assigned to SAC, 1947-48; inspector gen. Hdqrs. USAF, 1950-53; program devel. officer Marcel Dassault Mystere IV Jet Aircraft, French Air Force Am. embassy, Paris, 1953-55; air staff project officer F-104/F-105 aircraft HQ USAF, 1956-60; comdr. procurement dist. USAF, San Francisco, 1960-62; mil. asst. for weapons systems acquisition Office Sec. AF, 1962-66; system program dir. Joint USAF/USN A-7D Aircraft Engring., Devel., Test & Prodn., AF Systems Cmmd., 1966-68; dep. chief staff maintenance engring. Air Force Logistics Command, 1968-71; comdr. Def. Pers. Support Ctr. Def. Log. Agy., Phila., 1971-72; comdr. Air Logistics Ctr. USAF, Warner Robins AFB, Ga., 1972-74; vice comdr. Tactical Air Command Langley AFB, Va., 1974-75; dep. chief staff systems and logistics Hdqrs. USAF, Washington, 1975-77; ret. USAF, Washington, 1977; mgmt. cons. Atlanta, 1978-80; sr. v.p. internat. ops. LTV Corp., Dallas, 1980-84; pres. Hails Assocs. Inc., Macon, Ga., 1984—; mem. sci. bd. Loral Corp., Macon, Ga., 1992-96. Regional exec. Boy Scouts Am.; mem. Auburn U. Alumni Engring. Coun.; bd. advisors Wesleyan Coll., 1985-90; mem. Found. Bd., Macon State Coll., 1998—. Decorated DSM with 2 oak leaf clusters, legion of Merit with 2 oak leaf clusters, Air medal with 2 oak leaf clusters; Order of Nat. Security (Korea); recipient Engring. Achievement award Auburn U., 1998. Mem. AIAA, Air Force Assn., Daedalians, Auburn U. SPADES, Army-Navy Country Club (Arlington, Va.), Idle Hour Golf and Country Club, Omicron Delta Kappa, Sigma Alpha Epsion. Roman Catholic. Office: PO Box 5290 Macon GA 31208-5290

HAILSTORK, ADOLPHUS CUNNINGHAM, composer; b. Rochester, N.Y., Apr. 17, 1941. B in Music, Howard U., Washington, 1963; studied with Nadia Boulanger, Am. Inst., Fountainebleau, France, 1963; MusB in Composition, MusM in Composition, Manhattan Sch. of Music, N.Y., 1965, 66; PhD, Mich. State U., East Lansing, 1971; studied with Jon Appleton and H. Howe, Dartmouth Coll., 1972. Grad. asst. Mich. State U., 1969-71; prof. Youngstown (Ohio) State U., 1971-77, Norfolk (Va.) State U., 1977—. Compositions include symphonic works and tone poems for orchestra; a piano concerto; numerous chamber works; duos for such combinations as horn and piano, clarinet and piano, tuba and piano, flute and piano, and others; a large number of songs, including songs for soprano, baritone, tenor, bass, mezzo-soprano, band transcriptions and many pieces for piano; compositions include: Phaedra tone poem, 1966, SA-1 for Jazz Ensemble, 1971, Bellevue, 1974, Concerto for Violin Horn and Orch., 1975, Celebration, 1975, American Landscape No. 1 for Concert Band, 1977, Epitaph: In Memoriam Martin Luther King, Jr., 1979, Norfolk Pride March for Concert Band, 1980, An American Port of Call, 1985, Done Made my Vow, 1985, I Will Lift Up Mine Eyes, 1989, Sonata da Chiesa, 1990, Trio, 1987, Trio Sonata, 1991. Recipient Ernest Bloch award for choral composition, 1971, Belwin-Mills/Max Winkler award for band composition, 1977, Virginia Band Dirs. award, 1987, numerous commissions; named Cultural Laureate of the State of Va., 1992. Office: Norfolk State Univ Dept of Music 2401 Corprew Ave Norfolk VA 23504-3993*

HAIMAN, FRANKLYN SAUL, author, communications educator; b. Cleve., June 23, 1921; s. Alfred Wilfred and Stella (Weiss) H.; m. Louise Goble, June 11, 1955; children—Mark David, Eric Saul. B.A., Case Western Res. U., 1942; M.A., Northwestern U., 1945, Ph.D., 1948. Mem. faculty Northwestern U., Evanston, Ill., 1948—; chmn. dept. communication studies Northwestern U., 1964-75, prof. communication studies, 1970-88, John Evans prof. communication studies, 1988-91, John Evans prof. emeritus, 1991—; adj. prof. U. of San Francisco, 1992—. Author: Group Leadership and Democratic Action, 1951, Freedom of Speech: Issues and Cases, 1965, Freedom of Speech, 1976, Speech and Law in a Free Society, 1981, "Speech Acts" and the First Amendment, 1993; co-author: The Dynamics of Discussion, 1960, 2d edit., 1980; editor: (book series) To Protect These Rights, 1976-77; contbr. articles to profl. jours. Pres. ACLU of Ill., 1964-75, nat. bd. dirs., 1965-96, nat. corp. sec., 1976-82, nat. v.p., 1987-96, vice chair nat. adv. coun., 1996—. With USAAF, 1942-45. Mem. ACLU, Nat. Comm. Assn., Am. Psychol. Assn., AAUP, Phi Beta Kappa. Home: 5283 Broadway Ter Apt 4-b Oakland CA 94618-1491

HAIMAN, IRWIN SANFORD, lawyer; b. Cleve., Mar. 19, 1916; s. Alfred W. and Stella H. (Weiss) H.; m. Jeanne D. Jaffee, Mar. 8, 1942; children: Karen H. Schenkel, Susan L. B.A., Western Res. U., 1937; LL.B., Cleve. Marshall Law Sch., 1941; J.D., Cleve. State U., 1969. Bar: Ohio 1941, U.S. Ct. Appeals (6th cir.) 1961, U.S. Supreme Ct. 1961. Asst. to pres. Tremco Mfg. Co., Cleve., 1936-42; house counsel William Edwards Co., Cleve., 1947-48; pvt. practice Cleve., 1948-68; ptnr. firm Garber, Simon, Haiman, Gutfeld, Friedman & Jacobs, 1968-80; ptnr. McCarthy, Lebit, Crystal & Haiman, 1981—; lectr. in speech Western Res. U., 1948-70; dir. Washington Fed. Savs. and Loan Assn.; asst. law dir., prosecutor City of Lyndhurst, Ohio, 1965-79, law dir., 1979-84. Trustee Montefiore Home, Cleve., 1974-88 (life trustee 1988—)—, East End Neighborhood House, 1962-68; councilman City of South Euclid, 1948-54, pres., 1952-54; pres. Young People's Congregation, Fairmount Temple, 1951-52; sec., trustee Surburban Temple, 1962-65, trustee, 1983—, pres., 1984-87; chmn. speakers div., bd. dirs. Cleve. chpt. ARC, 1959-62; chmn. speaker and film div. Cleve. United Appeal, 1961-62; chmn. speakers div. Jewish Welfare Fund Cleve., 1973-79. Served as 1st lt. AUS, 1943-47. Mem. Ohio, Cleve. bar assns., Assn. Trial Lawyers Am., Zeta Beta Tau. Clubs: Oakwood Country, Lake Forest Country (pres. 1971-72, 75-79). Home: 20201 N Park Blvd Cleveland OH 44118-5000

HAIMAN, ROBERT JAMES, newspaper editor, journalism educator, media consultant; b. Norwich, Conn., May 6, 1936; s. Albert and Letta (Cone) H.; m. Elizabeth Royce Greenlaw, Sept. 26, 1964 (div. Aug. 1996); 1 child, Robert Greenlaw. Student, U. Conn., 1953-55; BS, U. Fla., 1957. Reporter St. Petersburg (Fla.) Times, 1958-60, copy editor, 1962-63, nat. editor, 1964-66, mng. editor, 1966-76, exec. editor, 1976-83; pres., mng. dir. Poynter Inst. Media Studies, 1983-96, pres. emeritus, disting. editor in residence, 1997—; bd. dirs. Times Pub. Co., St. Petersburg; trustee Fla. InterAm. Scholarship Found.; mem. minority mgmt. task force Inst. Journalism Edn. Mem. pres. round table Eckerd Coll.; trustee Poynter Inst. Media Studies, St. Petersburg; mem. Pulitzer Prize jury, 1977, 90, 91, 96, 97; internat. adv. bd. Inst. Advancement Journalism, Johannesburg, South Africa; mem. nat. adv. bd. Inst. for Journalists and Pub. Policy Gordon Pub. Policy Ctr. Brandeis U. Mem. Pres.'s coun. U. Fla., U. South Fla.; chmn. campus adv. bd. U. South Fla., 1989-91; mem. journalism adv. bd. Knight Found., Inst. Current World Affairs, Hanover, N.H., Tampa Bay Com. Coun. on Fgn. Rels.; trustee Bayfront Ctr. Found.; elder Presbyn. Ch.; fellow Freedom Forum Media Studies Ctr., N.Y.C., 1998-99. With USMC, 1961. Named Disting. Alumnus, U. Fla., 1988. Mem. AP Mng. Editors Assn. (pres. 1982), Am. Soc. Newspaper Editors (dir. 1992-98), Internat. Press Inst. (Vienna), World Editors Forum (Paris), Interam. Press Assn., Racquet Club, St. Petersburg Yacht Club, Dragon Club, Quarterback Club, Golden Triangle Club, Soc. Profl. Journalists. Democrat. Home: Isla Key # 103 5155 Isla Key Blvd S Saint Petersburg FL 33715-2611 Office: 801 3rd St S Saint Petersburg FL 33701-4920

HAIMES, TODD, artistic director; m. Alison Haimes; children: Hilary, Andrew. Grad., Yale Sch. of Mgmt., U. Pa. Artistic dir. Roundabout Theatre Co., N.Y.C., 1990—. Office: Roundabout Theatre Co 1530 Broadway New York NY 10036-4002*

HAIMES, YACOV YOSSEPH, systems and civil engineering educator, consultant; b. Baghdad, Iraq, June 18, 1936; came to U.S., 1965, naturalized, 1972; s. Yosseph and Rose (Elani) H.; m. Sonia E. Jamison, June 16, 1968; children: Yosef, Michelle. BS, Hebrew U., Jerusalem, 1964; MS, U. Calif., 1967, PhD with distinction, 1970. Jr. petroleum engr. Ministry of Devel., Jerusalem, 1962-65; asst. prof. engring. Case-Western Reserve U., Cleve., 1970-71; assoc. prof. systems engring. Case-Western Reserve U., 1971-76, dir. grad. program water resources and systems engring., 1972-87, prof. systems engring. and civil engring., 1976-87, dir. Center for Large Scale Systems and Policy Analysis, 1980-84, chmn. systems engring. dept., 1983-86; Lawrence R. Quarles Prof. of Engring. and Applied Sci. U. Va., Charlottesville, 1987—; dir. Ctr. for Risk Mgmt. of Engring. Systems, U. Va., 1987—; pres. Environ. Systems Mgmt. Inc., Ohio, 1974—; mem. staff Office of Sci. and Tech. Policy, Exec. Office of President, 1977, Com. on Sci. and Tech., Ho. of Reps., 1978; cons. in field.; chmn. UNESCO Working Group on Water Resources Planning, 1980-87; mem. bd. on water sci. and tech. NRC, 1982-84; chmn. tech. adv. com. Internat. Ground Water Modeling Ctr. Holcomb Research Inst., 1985-88, mem. 1983-88; cons. Congl. Office of Tech. Assessment, 1977-89; cons. Sci. Adv. Bd. U.S. EPA, 1986-96, Oil and Gas Regulatory Commn. State of Ohio, 1986-87, chmn. regulatory com., 1986-87; active UNESCO Internat. Hydrological Program IV Panel on Water Resources, 1991—. Author: (with W.A. Hall and H.T. Freedman) Multiobjective Optimization in Water Resources Systems, 1975; Hierarchical Analyses of Water Resources Systems, 1977; (with V. Chankong) Multiobjective Decision Making: Theory and Methodology, 1983; (with J. Pet-Edwards, V. Chankong, H. Rosenkranz and F. Ennever) Risk Assessment and Decisionmaking Using Test Results: The Carcinogenicity Prediction and Battery Selection (CPBS) Approach, 1989; (with K. Tarvainen, T. Shima and J. Thadathil) Hierarchical Multiobjective Analysis of Large-Scale Systems, 1990; (with V. Chankong) Multiobjective Problems: Theory and Methods, 1996; Risk Modeling, Assessment, and Management, 1998; editor: Scientific, Technological and Institutional Aspects of Water Resource Policy, 1980; (with P. Laconte) Water Resources and Land Use Planning, 1982; Energy Auditing and Conservation, 1980; Risk/Benefit Analysis in Water Resources Planning and Management, 1981; Large Scale Systems, 1982; (with D. Allee) Multiobjective Analysis in Water Resources, 1984; (with V. Chankong) Decision Making with Multiple Objectives, 1985; (with J.H. Snyder) Groundwater Contamination, 1986; (with E.Z. Stakhiv) Risk-Based Decision Making in Water Resources, 1986; (with J. Kindler and E. Plate) The Process of Water Resources Planning: A Systems Approach, 1987; (with D. Baumann) Water Resources Planning and Management: The Role of the Social Sciences, 1988; (with E. Stakhiv) Risk Analysis and Management of Natural and Man-Made Hazards, 1989; (with J. Bear, F. Walters and G. Jousma) Modeling of Groundwater Contamination, 1989; (with E.Z. Stakhiv) Risk-Based Decision Making in Water Resources, 1990; (with E.Z. Stakhiv and D. Moser) Risk-Based Decision Making in Water Resources, 1992; (with E.Z. Stakhiv and D. Moser), Risk Based Decision Making in Water Resources) VI, 1994, (with E.Z. Stakhir and D. Moser), Risk Based Decision Making in Water Resources, VII, 1996; assoc. editor IEEE Trans. on Systems, Man and Cybernetics, 1979—, Automatica, 1981-92, Large Scale Systems: Theory and Applications, 1981-88, Jour. Control, Theory and Advanced Tech., 1985-92, Info. and Decision Techs., 1988-91, Reliability Engring. and Systems Safety, 1990—, Risk Analysis Internat. Jour., 1991—. Mem. UNESCO IHP IV Panel Water Resources, 1991-97. Case Centennial Scholar Case Inst. Tech., Case Western Res. U., 1980. Fellow IEEE, AAAS, ASCE (com. on water resources systems 1975-80, outstanding rsch. paper award 1990), AWRA, IWRA, SRA; Internat. Water Resources Assn., Am. Water Resources Assn. (pres. Ohio sect. 1974-75), IEEE Systems, Man and Cybernetics Soc. (v.p. for tech. activities 1990-91, v.p. for publs. 1992-93), Univs. Council on Water Resources (chmn. com. on environ. quality 1977-79, dir. 1979-85, v.p. 1983-84, pres. 1984-85, Pub. Svc. award 1991, Warren A. Hall medal 1997), Internat. Fedn. Automatic Control (chmn. working group on water resources 1973-87, vice-chmn. systems engring. com. 1987-90), Am. Automatic Control Council (vice-chmn. systems engring. com. 1976-79), Am. Geophys. Union (com. on water resources systems 1970-74, chmn. water resource environ. mgmt. com. 1980-82), Ops. Rsch. Soc. Am., Soc. for Risk Analysis (chmn. com. on confs. and workshops 1989-91), Multiple Criteria Decision Making Soc. (exec. com. 1984—), Sigma Xi (past pres. local chpt.), Tau Beta Pi. Home: 3160 Waverly Dr Charlottesville VA 22901-9576 Office: U Va Olsson Hall Rm 112 Dept Systems Engring Charlottesville VA 22903*

HAIMS, BRUCE DAVID, lawyer; b. N.Y.C., Nov. 25, 1940; s. Samuel Harold and Judith (Feller) H.; m. Judith Jackson; children: Carolyn, Daniel, Nolan. BS in Econs., U. Pa., 1962; LLB magna cum laude, Harvard U., 1965; LLM in Taxation, NYU, 1972. Bar: Conn. 1965, N.Y. 1967, U.S. Ct. Appeals (2d cir.) 1968, U.S. Tax Ct. 1972. Assoc. Debevoise & Plimpton, N.Y.C., 1967-72, ptnr., 1973—. Dir. Axe Houghton Found. Capt. U.S. Army, 1965-67. Mem. N.Y. State Bar Assn., Assn. of Bar of City of N.Y., Internat. Fiscal Assn. Home: 470 W End Ave Apt 14A New York NY 10024-4933 Office: Debevoise & Plimpton 875 3rd Ave Fl 23 New York NY 10022-6256

HAINES, CATHY JEAN, elementary education educator; b. Philipsburg, Pa., Nov. 21, 1949; d. George Clark and Mary Frances (Taylor) Moore; m. Don Haines; 1 chld, Franklin Cole Whitby. BS in Music Edn., U. Mary-Hardin Baylor, 1973; MA in Music Theory, U. Iowa, 1981, MA in Ednl. Adminstrn., 1990, postgrad., 1997. Cert. tchr., Tex., music tchr., secondary adminstr., Iowa. Tchg. asst. U. Iowa, Iowa City, 1976-77; tchr. Pulaski County Spl. Sch. Dist., Little Rock, 1979-83, Kennedy H.S., Pierce, Hiawatha and Nixon Elem. Schs., 1983-87; music tchr. Harding Mid. Sch., Cedar Rapids, 1983—; tchr. Interlochen (Mich.) Ctr. for Arts, 1993-96, Blue Lake Fine Arts Camp, 1999, Very Spl. Arts; mem. NCA evaulation team Anson Jr. H.S., Marshalltown, Iowa, 1990; mem. S.E. Iowa Symphony Orch., Iowa City Cmty. String Orch., Waterloo-Cedar Falls Symphony Orch., Ottumwa Symphony Orch., Oskaloosa Symphony Orch.; mem. summer chamber music workshops Raphael Trio, Adamant, Vt. Violinist Hancher Auditorium, Iowa City, Interlochen Ctr. for Arts; contbr. articles to profl. publs. Mem. NEA, ASCD, Nat. Sch. Orch. Assn. (nat. exec. bd. 1988-90, Disting. Svc. award), Iowans for Arts Edn. (state bd. dirs. 1988-90), Phi Delta Kappa (rec. sec. 1995-96). Office: Cedar Rapids Cmty Sch Dist Cedar Rapids IA 52246

HAINES, DENNIS G., military officer. BS in Bus. Adminstrn. and Mgmt., U. Wyo., 1968, MS in Bus. Adminstrn. and Mgmt., 1969; disting. grad., Squadron Officer Sch., 1972; grad., Air Command and Staff Coll., 1978. Commd. 2d lt. USAF, 1968, advanced through grades to maj. gen., 1997; maintenance control officer 19th Tactical Air Support Squadron, 314th Air Divsn., Osan Air Base, South Korea, 1972-73; chief, maintenance control divsn. comdr. 18th Equipment Maintenance Squadron, Kadena Air Base, Japan, 1980-83; dep. dir., dir. for maintenance engring. Hdqs. Pacific Air Forces, Hickam AFB, Hawaii, 1983-87; dep. comdr. for maintenance 37th Tactical Fighter Wing, Nellis AFB, Nev., 1988-90; chief fighter propulsion mgmt. divsn. San Antonio Air Logistics Ctr., Kelly AFB, Tex., 1990-91; dir. aircraft directorate Ogden Air Logistics Ctr., Hill AFB, Utah, 1991-93; dir. logistics Hdqs. Air Edn. and Tng. Command, Randolph AFB, Tex., 1993-95; dir. of supply Hdqs. USAF, Washington, 1995-96; dir. of logistics Hdqs. Air Force Materiel Command, Wright-Patterson AFB, Ohio, 1996-97, Hdqs. Air Combat Command, Langley AFB, Va., 1997—. Decorated Legion of Merit with oak leaf cluster, Meritorious Svc. medal with 4 oak leaf clusters. Office: HQ ACC/LG Ste 210 130 Douglas St Langley AFB VA 23665-2791

HAINES, JAMES B., JR., federal judge; b. 1948. BA, Wash. State U., 1970; JD, Willamette U., 1977. Bar: Wash., Maine. Law clk. to Hon. Eugene A. Wright, U.S. Ct. Appeals for 9th Circuit, 1977-78; assoc. Davis, Wright, Todd, Riese & Jones, Seattle; assoc. prof. law U. W.Va., Morgantown, 1980-83; assoc. Hewes, Culley & Beals, Portland, Maine, 1983-86; ptnr. Black, Lambert, Coffin & Haines, Portland, 1986-90; bankruptcy judge for Maine, U.S. Bankruptcy Ct., Bangor, 1990—. With USCG, 1970-74. Office: US Bankruptcy Ct Margaret Chase Smith Fed Bl POB 1327 202 Harlow St Ste 334 Bangor ME 04401-4901

HAINES, JOHN MEADE, poet, translator, writer; b. 1924. Homesteader in Alaska, 1947-69; poet-in-residence U. Alaska, Anchorage, 1972-73; vis. prof. English U. Wash., Seattle, 1974; vis. lectr. U. Mont., Missoula, 1974-75; Guggenheim fellowship, 1984-85; disting. vis. lectr. U. Calif., Santa Cruz, 1986; writer-in-residence Montalvo Ctr. for the Arts, 1987-88, Djerassi Found., 1988; vis. prof. Ohio U., Athens, 1989-90; vis. writer George Washington U., 1991-92; Elliston fellow in poetry U. Cin., 1992; chair in creative arts Austin Peay State U., Clarksville, Tenn., 1993—; vis. lectr. Ann. Summer Wordsworth Conf., Grasmere, Eng., 1996. Translator: El Amor Ascendia, 1967; author: Winter News: Poems, 1966, Suite for the Pied Piper, 1967, The Legend of Paper Plates, 1970, The Mirror, 1971, The Stone Harp, 1971, Twenty Poems, 1971, Leaves and Ashes: Poems, 1974, In Five Years Time, 1976; The Sun on Your Shoulder, 1976, Cicada, 1977, In a Dusty Light, 1977, Living Off the Country: Essays on Poetry and Place, 1981, Of Traps and Snares, 1981, Other Days, 1982, News from the Glacier: Selected Poems 1982, Forest Without Leaves, 1984, Stories We Listened To, 1986, The Stars, The Snow, The Fire, 1989, Meditation On a Skull Carved in Crystal, 1989, New Poems, 1980-88, 90, (poetry) Rain Country, 1990, The Owl in the Mask of the Dreamer, Collected Poems, 1993, A Guide to the Four-Chambered Heart, 1996, At the End of this Summer, 1948-54, 1997, (essay) Fables and Distances, New and Selected Essays, 1996. Recipient Acad. award in Lit. Am. Acad. of Arts and Letters, 1995; 63d fellow Acad. Am. Poets, 1997. Home: 509 Hollins Ave Helena MT 59601-2816

HAINES, KATHLEEN ANN, physician, educator; b. N.Y.C., July 28, 1949; d. George Raymond and Gertrude Ann (Driscoll) H.; m. Emil Claus Gotschlich, May 24, 1975; 1 child, Emily Claire. BA, CUNY, 1971; MD, Albert Einstein Coll. Medicine, 1975. Diplomate Am. Bd. Pediatrics, Am. Bd. Allergy and Immunology. Intern, resident N.Y. Hosp./Cornell U., N.Y.C., 1975-77, fellow in allergy/immunology, 1977-80; instr. in pediatrics NYU Sch. of Medicine, N.Y.C., 1980-84, asst. prof. pediatrics, 1984-91, asst. prof. medicine, 1989-91, assoc. prof. clin. pediatrics and medicine, 1991—; dir. pediat. rheumatology Hosp. for Joint Diseases/NYU Med. Ctr., 1994—; dir. clin. immunology lab. Hosp. for Joint Diseases, 1995—; mem. rsch. coun. N.Y. Heart Assn., 1988-90. Contbr. articles to profl. jours., chpts. to books in field. Grantee N.Y. Arthritis Found., 1990, 96, NIH, 1993-98. Fellow Am. Acad. Allergy and Immunology, Am. Acad. Pediatrics; mem. Am. Soc. Cell Biology, Am. Fedn. Clin. Rsch., Allergy, Asthma and Immunology Soc. of Greater N.Y. (sec. 1995-97, pres.-elect 1997-98, pres. 1998-99), Harvey Soc., Soc. Pediatric Rsch. Office: Hosp for Joint Diseases 303 2nd Ave New York NY 10003-2797

HAINES, KENNETH H., television broadcasting executive; b. Spokane, Sept. 5, 1942; s. Kenneth A. and Helen Elizabeth (Evans) H.; m. Stephanie Marie Phelps, Nov. 23, 1981; 1 child, Avery Jordan. *Father, Kenneth A. Haines, 50 years with United States Department of Agriculture, most recently Director of International Research, Washington, DC. Married 65 years to Helen Haines. Brother, Thomas R. Haines, 28 years employed by Washington State Department of Social and Health Services, currently as the Community Service Office Administrator, Seattle. Wife, Stephanie, BS Virginia Tech, MS Radford University. Faculty member in English, Central Piedmont College, Charlotte, received the college "teaching excellence" award, 1992. Daughter, Avery, student at Providence Day School Charlotte, selected as member of the National Junior Honor Society in 1999.* BA, Dakota Wesleyan U., 1964; MA, U. Wyo.; MS, Troy State U., 1970; EdD, Va. Tech., 1976. News dir. KORN TV, Mitchell, S.D., 1962-64; sta. mgr. KUWR Radio, Laramie, Wyo., 1965-67; gen. mgr. KLME Radio, Laramie, 1967-68; instr. flight ops. U.S. Army, Ft. Rucker, Ala., 1968-70; from dir. radio, tv, film to dir. pub. affairs, univ. rels. Va. Tech., Blacksburg, 1970-81; from dir. network ops. to exec. v.p., COO Raycom Sports, Charlotte, N.C., 1981—; bd. dirs. Charlotte Sports Commn., ACC Properties. *Kenneth Haines negotiates Raycom contracts for all network coverage and sports properties. He developed innovative projects such as "Glasnost Bowl", the "Blockbuster Bowl", the "Emmy Awards for Sports", LPGA golf tournaments, and live programming from Graceland. He authored studies of collegiate conferences initiating major restructuring of traditional college athletic alignments. In 1991, he negotiated a partnership with ABC-TV to produce all its college basketball games. A frequent speaker at sports marketing conferences, he travels extensively to college campuses and television studios, and frequently quoted by such publications as USA Today, The Wall Street Journal, Broadcasting and The Associated Press.* Bd. dirs. Sunshine Football Classic, 1989—, Charlotte Basketball Challenge, 1987—; tournament dir. LPGA Golf, 1997—. Named Reporter of Yr., UPI, 1967, Opperman Disting. Lectr., Dakota Wesleyan U., 1998; recipient golden award Coun. Support Higher Edn., 1978. Mem. Am. Assn. Agr. Writers, Am. Coll. Pub. Rels. Assn. (exceptional achievement award 1974), Va. Press Assn., Coun. for Advancement and Support of Edn. (pres. univ. faculty club 1980-82), Nat. Acad. TV Arts and Scis. (judge), Charlotte C. of C. (bd. dirs.), Phi Kappa Delta, Pi Delta Epsilon, Omicron Delta Kappa. Avocations: sports, photography, television, travel, reading. Home: 1909 Carmel Rd Charlotte NC 28226-5021 Office: Raycom Sports 2815 Coliseum Center Dr # 200 Charlotte NC 28217-2394

HAINES, LEE MARK, JR., religious denomination administrator; b. Marion, Ind., Dec. 9, 1927; s. Lee M. Sr. and Anna (Stevens); m. Maxine Louise Shockey, June 8, 1948; children: Mark Edward, Rhoda Lynn. B of Religion, Ind. Wesleyan U., 1950; MDiv, Christian Theol. Sem., Indpls., 1959; ThM, Christian Theol. Sem., 1973; D Ministry, Bethel Theol. Sem., St. Paul, 1981; DD (hon.), Ind. Wesleyan U., 1981; LittD (hon.), Houghton Coll., N.Y., 1981; DD (hon.), So. Wesleyan U., 1996. Ordained to ministry Wesleyan Ch., 1950. Pastor Peru (Ind.) Wesleyan Meth. Ch., 1948-51, Blue River Wesleyan Meth. Ch., Arlington, Ind., 1951-56, Jonesboro (Ind.) Wesleyan Meth. Ch., 1956-61; editor Adult Sunday Sch. Lessons Wesleyan Meth. Ch., Marion, Ind., 1961-63; pastor Eastlawn Wesleyan Ch., Indpls., 1963-70; assoc. prof. religion Ind. Wesleyan U., 1970-80; gen. sec. edn. and the ministry The Wesleyan Ch., Indpls., 1980-88, gen. supt., 1988—; historian The Wesleyan Ch., 1976-88; vice-chair Wesleyan World Fellowship, 1996—. Assoc. editor/writer: The Wesleyan Bible Commentary; co-author: An Outline History of the Wesleyan Church; co-editor: Conscience and Commitment: History of the Wesleyan Methodist Church, Days of Our Pilgrimage: History of the Pilgrim Holiness Church; contbg. author Reformers and Revivalists: The History of the Wesleyan Church. Mem. Evang. Theol. Soc., Wesleyan Theol. Soc. (editor 1978-81), Christian Holiness Partnership (treas. 1994-97). Office: Internat Ctr Wesleyan Ch PO Box 50434 Indianapolis IN 46250-0434 *God is the divine lover of each human person, and seeks through Jesus Christ to bring about a loving relationship with each one. Our highest task is to help bring that to pass.*

HAINES, LISA ANN, secondary education educator; b. Camden, N.J., Dec. 14, 1966; d. Sonia Joan (Kiriluk) F. BA, Rutgers U., Camden, 1990; postgrad., Rutgers U., 1993—. Cert. tchr. K-12, N.J. Tchr. Pennsauken (N.J.) Bd. of Edn., 1990—; mem. Pennsauken H.S. scholarship com., 1994-96, mem. prin.'s adv. com., 1996-97, Gold Card com., 1996-98, Century III Scholarship com., curriculum co-chair departmental in-svc. group, mem. faculty discipline com., prop mistress sch. show, faculty vol., co-editor The Looking Glass, co-adviser yearbook. Mem. Nat. Coun. Tchrs. of English, N.E. MLA, Kappa Delta Pi. Avocations: writing, poetry, travel, theater, rollerblading. Home: 31 N Maple Ave Apt 502 Marlton NJ 08053-1740

HAINES, MARTHA MAHAN, lawyer; b. Detroit, Feb. 4, 1952; d. Albert F. and Martha M. (Sager) Mahan; divorced; children: Ella Catherine, Emily Martha. Student, U. Utah, 1970-72; BA magna cum laude, Wayne State U., 1974; JD, U. Mich., 1977. Bar: Ill. 1978, U.S. Dist. Ct. (no. dist.) Ill. 1982. Assoc. Chapman and Cutler, Chgo., 1978-82, jr. ptnr., 1982-86; of counsel Altheimer & Gray, Chgo., 1986-90, ptnr., 1990-97; ptnr. Barnes & Thornburg, Chgo., 1997-99; atty. fellow Office Mcpl. Securities, SEC, Washington, 1999—. Bd. dirs. The Samaritan Inst. Mem. Nat. Assn. Bond Lawyers, Civic Fedn. Chgo., Mich. Shores Club. Democrat. Methodist. E-mail: hainesm@sec.gov. Office: Office Mpcl Securities SEC 450 5th St NW Washington DC 20549

HAINES, RANDA, film director; b. L.A., Feb. 20, 1945. Studied with Lee Strasberg; student, Am. Film Inst. Bd. advisors F.O.C.U.S. Inst. Film. Dir.: (TV spl.) Under the Sky, 1979, (PBS) The Jilting of Granny Weatherall,(TV movie) Something About Amelia, 1984, (Emmy award nomination for director of a limited series or spl.), (TV episodes) Hill St. Blues, 1982, (films) Children of a Lesser God, 1986, (DGA nomination best dir.), The Doctor, 1991, Wrestling Ernest Hemingway, 1993, Dance with Me, 1998; (prodr.) A Family Thing, 1996. Mem. Dirs. Guild Am. Office: Dirs Guild Am 7950 W Sunset Blvd Los Angeles CA 90046-3333 also: FOCUS-LA # 200 600 Corporate Pointe Ste 200 Culver City CA 90230-7658

HAINES, RICHARD FOSTER, psychologist; b. Seattle, May 19, 1937; s. Donald Hutchinson and Claudia May (Bennett) H.; m. Carol Taylor, June 17, 1961; children: Cynthia Lynn, Laura Anne. Student, U. Wash., 1955-57; BA, Pacific Luth. Coll., Tacoma, 1960; MA, Mich. State U., 1962, PhD, 1964. Predoctoral rsch. fellow NIH, 1964; Nat. Acad. Sci. postdoctoral resident rsch. assoc. Ames Rsch. Ctr./NASA, Moffett Field, Calif., 1964-67, rsch. scientist, 1967-86, chief of space human factors office, 1987-88, rsch. scientist Rsch. Inst. Advanced Computer Sci., 1988-90; assoc. prof. dept. psychology San Jose State U., 1988-89; computer scientist RECOM Techs., Inc., Moffett Field, Calif., 1993—; rsch. cons. to NASA Foothill Coll.; cons. Stanford U. Sch. medicine, 1966-67, TRW-Systems Group, 1969-70; mem. adv. com. on vision NRC; founding mem. advanced tech. applications com. Calif. Coun. AIAA and NASA, 1975-80; mem. adv. bd. Space Scis. Ctr.-Foothill Coll., 1976-78; bd. advisors Fund for UFO Rsch., Washington; chmn. bd. Novosibirsk Christian Pub.-Calif., 1993—. Author: UFO Phenomena and the Behavioral Scientist, 1979, Observing UFOs, 1980, Melbourne Episode: Case Study of a Missing Pilot, 1987, Advanced Aerial Devices Reported During the Korean War, 1990, Night Flying, 1992, Project Delta, 1994, Close Encounters of the Fifth Kind, 1999; mem. editl. bd. Jour. UFO Studies, Internat. UFO Reporter, Cuadernos de Ufologica; contbr. articles to profl. jours. Mem. Palo Alto (Calif.) Mayor's Com. on Youth Activities, 1967; chmn. adv. coun. Christian Cmty. Progress Corp., Menlo Park (Calif.); v.p., dir. Ctr. Counseling for Drug Abuse, Menlo Park; bd.

dirs., chmn. sci. adv. team Threshold Found.; founding co-dir. Joint Am.-Soviet Aerial Anomaly Fedn., 1991—. Named Alumnus of Yr., Pacific Luth. U., 1972. Fellow Aerospace Med. Assn. (assoc.); mem. Optical Soc. Am., Soc. for Sci. Exploration, Sigma Xi. Achievements include patents for device of advanced detection of glaucoma, optical projector of vision performance data for design engineers, visual simulator optical alignment device, grooming aid for use by astronauts in space. Home: 325 Langton Ave Los Altos CA 94022-1055 Office: RECOM Techs Inc Ames Rsch Ctr-NASA N269-4 Moffett Field CA 94035

HAINES, RONALD H., bishop; b. New Castle, Del., Aug. 14, 1934; m. Mary Ferrell; six children. BS in Engring., U. Del., 1956; student; M. Div., S.T.M., Gen. Theol. Sem. Ordained deacon Episcopal Ch., 1966, ordained priest, 1967. Bus. career; asst. St. Paul's Ch., Bronx, N.Y., 1967-68; rector St. Francis Ch., Rutherfordton, N.C., until 1981; bishop's dep. Diocese of Western N.C., 1981-86; suffragan bishop Diocese of Washington, 1986-90, bishop, 1990—. Address: Church House Mount St Alban Washington DC 20016

HAINES, STEPHEN JOHN, neurological surgeon; b. Burlington, Vt., Sept. 4, 1949; s. Gerald Leon and Frances Mary (Whitcomb) H.; m. Jennifer Lea Plombon; children: Christopher, Jeremy. AB, Dartmouth Coll., 1971; MD, U. Vt., 1975. Diplomate Am. Bd. Neurol. Surgery; diplomate Nat. Bd. Med. Examiners. Intern U. Minn., Mpls., 1975-76; neurol. surgery resident U. Pitts., 1976-81; asst. prof. neurosurgery U. Minn., Mpls., 1982-87, assoc. prof. neurosurgery and otolaryngology, 1987-93, prof. neurosurgery and otolaryngology and pediatrics, 1993-97, head. div. pediatric neurosurgery, 1985-97; prof. neurosurgery, otolaryngology and pediatrics, chmn. dept. neurosurgery Med. U. S.C., Charleston, 1997—. Contbr. articles to profl. jours. Fellow ACS; mem. AMA, Am. Assn. Neurol. Surgeons (Van Wagenen fellow 1981), Congress Neurol. Surgeons (pres. 1996), Soc. Clin. Trials, Neurosurg. Soc. Am., Am. Acad. Neurol. Surgery, Soc. Neurol. Surgeons. Office: Medical U SC Dept Neurol Surgery 171 Ashley Ave Charleston SC 29425-0001

HAINES, THOMAS DAVID, JR., lawyer; b. Dallas, Oct. 30, 1956; s. Thomas David Sr. and Carol V. (Mullins) H.; m. Nanette Cluck, Mar. 1, 1986; children: Bennett Ann, Maison Cluck. BS in Polit. Sci., Okla. State U., 1979; JD, U. Okla., 1982. Bar: Okla. 1982, N.Mex. 1983, U.S. Ct. Appeals (10th cir.) 1983, U.S. Dist. Ct. N.Mex. 1983. Assoc. Hinkle, Cox, Eaton, Coffield & Hensley, Roswell, N.Mex., 1982-87, ptnr., 1988—. Contbg. editor N.Mex. Tort and Worker's Compensation Reporter, 1987-90, Employment Law Deskbook for New Mexico Employers, 1997. Youth sponsor First United Meth. Ch., Roswell, 1986-88, chmn. stewardship com. 1990-91, chmn. adminstrv. coun., 1998—; coach Roswell Youth Soccer Assn., 1995—; trustee 1st United Meth. Ch., Roswell, 1996-98. Mem. State Bar Assn. N.Mex. (com. on continuing legal edn., young lawyers divsn. 1989—, mem. med.-legal rev. commn. 1988—), Chaves County Bar Assn., N.Mex. Def. Lawyer's Assn., N.Mex. Trial Lawyer's Assn., Kiwanis (Roswell club, Outstanding Club Sec. award 1993-95, pres. 1998-99, named one Outstanding Young Men in Am. 1990), Phi Delta Phi, Phi Kappa Phi. Republican. Avocations: golf, basketball, music, politics. Office: Hinkle Cox Eaton Coffield & Hensley 400 N Pennsylvania Ave Ste 700 Roswell NM 88201-4777

HAINES, THOMAS W. W., lawyer; b. Balt., Oct. 10, 1941; s. John Summer and Clara Elizabeth (Ward) H.; m. Vivienne Wilson, Jan. 3, 1981; children: Robert S., Elizabeth E., John M. BA, Cornell U., 1963; LLB, U. Md., 1967. Bar: Md. 1967, U.S. Dist. Ct. Md. 1968, U.S. Ct. Appeals (4th cir.) 1972, U.S. Tax Ct. 1973, U.S. Supreme Ct. 1975. Assoc. Semmes, Bowen & Semmes, Balt., 1968-75, ptnr., 1975-95; ptnr. Venable, Baetjer & Howard, LLP, Balt., 1995—. Fellow Am. Coll. Trust and Estate (counsel); mem. ABA, Md. Bar Assn., Bar Assn. Balt. City, Gibson Island Club, Maryland Club. Episcopalian. Office: Venable Baetjer & Howard 1800 Mercantile Bank Trust 2 Hopkins Plz Ste 2100 Baltimore MD 21201-2982

HAINES, WALTER WELLS, retired economics educator; b. Stamford, Conn., Dec. 1, 1918; s. Thomas Kelly Peterson and Carrie Hooker (Williams) H.; m. Hazel Ellen Maxwell, Jan. 1, 1945 (div.); children: Jennifer Jean, Deborah Lee, Pamela Ann, Christopher Alan, Liseli Ellen, Timothy Maxwell; m. Mary Lou Peck, Nov. 30, 1991. *Mother is daughter of Mosely Hooker Williams, congregational minister and editor for the American Sunday School Union. She is descended from Thomas Hooker, non-conformist minister, who arrived in America in 1663 and founded Hartford, Connecticut, in 1636. Father is a descendent of Richard and Margaret Haines, Quakers from Banbury Monthly Meeting in England, who came to Burlington, New Jersey, in 1682. He is the inventor of the Domart sewing box. Wife Mary Lou Peck, EdD, Columbia University, 1983, is associate professor of nursing, Russell Sage College, and was instrumental in establishing the Nurse Practitioner program in the Graduate School there.* BA, U. Pa., 1940, MA, 1941; MA, Harvard U., 1942, PhD (Lehman nat. fellow), 1943. Instr. econs. Kenyon Coll., 1946-47; mem. faculty NYU, 1947—, prof. econs., 1960-89, emeritus prof. of econs., 1989—, chmn. dept. Univ. Coll., 1956-68, dir. undergrad. studies, 1983-89; adminstr. Friends Hosp., Tiriki, Kenya, 1969-70; Fulbright prof. econs. U. Peshawar, Pakistan, 1962-63; Fulbright prof. environ. conservation Middle East Tech. U., Ankara, Turkey, 1973-74; lectr. Siena Coll., 1989-92. Author: Money, Prices and Policy, 1961, also articles. Lehman Nat. fellow Harvard U., 1941-43. Fellow Internat. Inst. for Social Econs.; mem. AAAS, World Future Soc., Internat. Assn. for Rsch. in Econ. Psychology, Fulbright Alumni Assn., Cultural Survival, Human Economy Ctr. (bd. dirs.), Am. Econ. Assn., Fellowship of Reconciliation, Fedn. Am. Scientists, Assn. for Social Econs., Soc. for Advancement of Socio-Econs., Internat. Soc. for Intercommunication New Ideas (Disting. fellow 1992, mem. consultative coun.), Internat. Soc. Ecol. Econs., Nat. Peace Inst. Found., Assn. World Edn., Global Edn. Associates, Amnesty Internat., World Federalists, Parliamentarians for Global Action, Economists Allied for Arms Reduction, Internat. Physicians for the Prevention of Nuclear War, Nature Conservancy, Nat. Wildlife Fedn., Wilderness Soc., Union of Concerned Scientists, Carter Ctr., Albert Einstein Inst., UN Assn. U.S., World Federalists, Habitat for Humanity, Natural Resources Def. Coun., Wilderness Soc., World Wildlife Fund, Phi Beta Kappa. Mem. Religious Soc. of Friends. Home: 196 Vosburgh Rd Averill Park NY 12018-5710 *The wellspring of my life is a belief that there is something of God in every person. From this universality of the divine spark emerge many principles of faith; the brotherhood of man, the importance of the golden rule, the primacy of love. These in turn call for social action to promote civil rights, nondiscrimination, peace, cooperation, democracy, world equality, the preservation of a quality environment, and conservation of resources for future generations. I have no illusion that this belief has brought me "success", but it has contributed much to the richness of life.*

HAINES, WILLIAM JOSEPH, pharmaceutical company executive; b. Crawfordsville, Ind., Sept. 26, 1919; s. Burt and Lala R. (Luster) H.; m. Wilma M. Hester, June 6, 1943; children: Paula Sue Haines Curtis-Burn, Eric J. AB summa cum laude, Wabash Coll., 1940, DSc (hon.), 1970; PhD, U. Ill., 1943; grad. exec. program in bus. adminstrn., Columbia Bus. Sch., 1965. Rsch. biochemist Upjohn Co., Kalamazoo, 1943-50, head dept. endocrinology rsch., 1950-54; tech. dir. Armour Labs., Kankakee, Ill., 1954-58; v.p. dir. rsch. Ortho Pharm. Corp., Raritan, N.J., 1958-65, exec. v.p., 1965-67; vice chmn. Johnson & Johnson Internat., 1967-69; dir., mem. exec. com. Johnson & Johnson, New Brunswick, N.J., 1969-79, v.p. corp. office sci. and tech., 1979-82; pres. Bucks-Tech Assocs., Inc. (cons. in mgmt., sci. and tech.), Doylestown, Pa., 1982—; chmn. sci. adv. com. Alliance Internat. Health Care Trust, 1983-87; former dir. Quidel Corp., La Jolla, Calif.; invited lectr. Laurentian Hormone Conf., 1952, Gordon Rsch. Conf., 1952. Contbr. numerous sci. articles to profl. jours., including pioneer paper on human requirement for essential amino acids, 1942. One of initial investigators to identify essential amino acids for human nutrition; patentee biosynthesis of adrenal cortex hormones, paper chromatography and automatic partition column chromatography of steroids. Trustee Wabash Coll., 1972-93, trustee emeritus, 1993—; trustee Hood Coll., 1975-87, vice chmn. bd., 1982-87, trustee emeritus, 1989—; Joslin Diabetes Found. Inc., Boston, 1974-79; elder Thompson Meml. Presbyn. Ch., New Hope, Pa. Recipient William E. Upjohn prize and medal, 1952, Alumni Merit award Nat. Assn. Wabash Men, 1973. Fellow AAAS, Am. Inst. Chemists; mem. Am. Chem. Soc. (med. cheistry div.), N.Y. Acad. Scis., Endocrine Soc., Am. Soc. Biol. Chemists, Soc. Chem. Industry (former chmn. Am. sect.), Pharm. Mfrs. Assn. (former chmn. R&D sec.), Assn. Rsch. Dirs., Indsl. Rsch. Inst., (dir. emeritus), N.J. Acad. Scis., Soc. Exptl. Biology and Medicine, Pacific Coast Fertility Soc., Am. Fertility Soc., Internat. Soc. Rsch. in Biology Reproduction (charter), Am. Inst. Mgmt. (exec. council), Am. Mgmt. Assn., Am. Found. Pharm. Edn. (Century Club), Ind. Covered Bridge Soc., Sons of Ind. (N.Y.C. chpt.), Chemists Club (N.Y.C.), Masons, Elks, Kiwanis (emeritus), Lake Naomi Club, Phi Beta Kappa, Phi Lambda Upsilon, Phi Kappa Phi, Sigma Xi, Alpha Chi Sigma. Republican. Home: 5 Bedford Dr Doylestown PA 18901-9463 Office: Johnson & Johnson 1 Johnson And Johnson Plz New Brunswick NJ 08933*

HAINING, JEANE, psychologist; b. Camden, N.J., May 2, 1952; d. Lester Edward and Adina (Rahn) H. BA in Psychology, Calif. State U., 1975; MA in Sch. Psychology, Pepperdine U., 1979; MS in Recreation Therapy, Calif. State U., 1982; PhD in Psychology, Calif. Sch. Profl. Psychology, 1985. Lic. clin. psychologist 1987, lic. ednl. psychologist 1982. Crisis counselor Calif. State U., Northridge, 1973-74; recreation therapist fieldwork Camarillo (Calif.) State Hosp.-Adolescent/Children's Units, 1974; Intern recreation therapist UCLA Neuropsychiatric Inst., L.A., 1975-76; substitute tchr./recreation therapist New Horizons Sch. for Mentally Retarded, Sepulveda, Calif., 1976-79; sch. psychologist Rialto (Calif.) Unified Sch. Dist., 1979-82; clin. psychologist field work San Joaquin County Dept. Mental Health, Stockton, Calif., 1982-83; intern clinical psychologist Fuller Theol. Sem. Psychology Ctr., Pasadena, Calif., 1984-85; clin. psychologist U.S. Dept. Justice, Terminal Island, Calif., 1985-86; cmty. mental health psychologist L.A. County Dept. Mental Health, 1987-89; clin. psychologist Calif. Dept. Corrections, Parole Outpatient Clinic, L.A., 1990—, Mary Magdeline Project, Commerce, Calif., 1992—; mem. psychiat.-psychol. panel adult and juvenile Superior Ct., L.A., 1992-98; mem. psychiat. panel U.S. Dist. Ct. (cen. dist.) Calif., L.A., 1989—; clin. psychologist O. Carl Simonton Cancer Ctr., Pacific Palisades, Calif., 1993—; evidence code experts panel Juvenile Dependency Ct., 1992—. Adv. bd. Camarillo (Calif.) State Hosp., 1994-97, vice-chmn. adv. bd., 1996-97; examiner Lic. Ednl. Psychologist Oral Examinations, Calif. Bd. Behavioral Sci. Examinations, Sacramento, 1985. Recipient award Outstanding Achievement Western Psychology Conf., Calif., 1974. Mem. APA, Forensic Mental Health Assn. (con. planning com. 1993). Democrat. Lutheran. Avocations: rock climbing, skiing, skating, tennis, piano.

HAINSWORTH, MELODY MAY, information professional, researcher; b. Vancouver, B.C., Can., May 13, 1946; m. Robert John Hainsworth, Jan. 6, 1968; children: Kaleeg William, Shane Alan. BA with honors, Simon Fraser U., Vancouver, 1968; MLS, Dalhousie U., Halifax, N.S., Can., 1976; PhD, Fla. State U., Tallahassee, 1992. Libr. Dept. Edn. of Tanzania, Mbeya, 1969-72, Dept. of Edn. of Zambia, Mwinilunga, 1972-74; law libr., deptl. libr. Dept. of Atty. Gen. of N.S., Halifax, 1975-77; regional libr. Provincial Ct. Librs. Dept. of Atty. Gen. of Alta., Calgary, 1977-80, So. Alta. Law Soc. libr., 1980-89; dir. librs. Keiser Coll., Tallahassee, 1992-93; v.p. info. resources and svcs. Internat. Coll., Naples, Fla., 1993—; adj. instr. Sch. Libr. and Info. Studies, Fla. State U., Tallahassee, 1990-91; speaker in field; rschr. in law and info. sci.; co-founder Naples Free-Net, World Class Acad.; active Women's Polit. Caucus; co-founder Naples Free-Net; rsch. in law and info. sci. World Class Acad. Author monographs; contbr. articles to profl. jours. Pres. Naples Free Net, 1993—; co-chair adv. com. com. on edn. and tech. Fla. State Bd. Ind. Colls. and Univs., 1993—; founding mem. Pub. Access to the Law of Fla., 1990—; mem. exec. bd. Calgary Legal Guidance, 1985-89, vice chmn., 1988-89, hon. life mem.; tech. grant com. Collier County Edn. Found., 1994-96, sec./webmaster World Class Collier; supt. search com., 1998; chair edn. com. East Naples Civic Assn., 1998. Student Leader Bursaries Simon Fraser U. scholar, 1966-68; H.W. Wilson scholar Dalhousie U., 1974; recipient Woman of Distinction award AAUW, 1999. Mem. Spl. Librs. Assn (pres. 1994-95), Assn. Online Profls., Fla. State, Ct. and County Librs. Assn., Tallahassee Law Librs. Assn., Fla. Libr. Assn., Assn. Libr. and Info. Sci. Edn., Alta. Legal Archives Soc. (hon. life), Collier County Bar Assn., Women's Polit. Caucus (webmaster 1999—), Tempo Internat. (webmaster 1999—), Naples Press Club. Avocations: squash, hiking, travel. Office: Internat Coll 2654 Tamiami Trl E Naples FL 34112-5707

HAIR, GILBERT MARTIN, foundation administrator; b. Manila, Philippines, Mar. 16, 1941; came to U.S., 1945; s. Jack and Jane McMahon Hair; m. Joanne Walsh, June 1966 (div.); m. Susan Christian, Apr. 5, 1969 (div. 1979); 1 child, Nicole. BA, Am. U., 1966; postgrad., San Fernando Valley Coll. Law, 1973-74. Cert. travel counsel, cert. Cruise Line Internat. Assn., Calif. Landscape Contractors Assn. With CIA, 1963-66; sales rep. Pan Am. World Airways, N.Y.C., 1966-71; dir. mktg. Continental Airlines, L.A., Micronesia, 1972-79; sr. v.p. mktg. Air North Am., Pasadena, Calif., 1979-83; instr., program dir. Jostens, Inc., L.A., Ventura, Calif., 1982-87; stockbroker, investment banker Thousand Oaks, Calif., 1987-93; pres., exec. dir. The Ctr. for Internee Rights Inc., Newbury Park, Calif., 1992—, Miami Beach, 1992—. Mem. Rep. Nat. com., Washington, 1964—; pres. Conejo Valley (Calif.) Rep. Action Com., 1992; mem. Beach Rep. Club, 1995—. With USMC, 1960-63. Mem. Westlake Tennis and Swim Club, Royal Bankok Sports Club (life). Roman Catholic. Avocations: golf, tennis, fishing, travel, politics, computers. E-mail: expows@bigfoot.com. Home: 6060 La George Dr Miami Beach FL 33140 Office: CFIR Inc 6060 La Gorce Dr Miami Beach FL 33140

HAIR, KITTIE ELLEN, secondary educator; b. Denver, June 12, 1948; d. William Edward and Jacqueline Jean (Holt) H. BA, Brigham Young U., 1971; MA in Social History, U. Nev., Las Vegas, 1987, cert. paralegal, 1995. cert. tchr., Nev. Health educator Peace Corps, Totota, Liberia, 1971-72; tchr. Clark County Sch. Dist., Las Vegas, Nev., 1972-77, 1979—; chair dept. social studies Clark County Sch. Dist., Las Vegas, 1993-95; missionary Ch. Jesus Christ Latter-Day Saints, Alta., Can., 1977-79. Recipient Outstanding Faculty award U. Nev./Southland Corp., Las Vegas, 1991; named Educator of Yr. Kiwanis Club, 1998-99. Mem. Phi Kappa Phi, Phi Alpha Theta, Delta Kappa Gamma (pres. Chi State, Iota chpt. 1996-98). Democrat. Avocations: collecting western and Native American art, gardening. Office: Advanced Technologies Acad 2501 Vegas Dr Las Vegas NV 89106-1643

HAIR, ROBERT EUGENE, editor, writer, historian; b. Winamac, Ind., Apr. 11, 1921; s. Charles Franklin and Lucy Agnes (Zellers) H.; m. Marian Martha Emerson, Dec. 11, 1949; children: Donald Edward, Martha Anne. AB, DePauw U., Greencastle, Ind., 1942; postgrad., U. Mich., Ann Arbor, 1943-44, 53-56. Newspaper writer and editor; editor Mich. Dept. Health, Lansing, 1956-60; asst. editor Encyclopedia Britannica, Chgo., 1960-64; exec. editor Battelle Rsch. Outlook, Columbus, 1964-69; editor Cordis Corp., Miami, 1969-80. Author: (books) Sturgis, Michigan: Its Story to 1930, 1992, Sturgis, Michigan: 1930-1945, 1996, Sturgis and Its Industrial Growth, 1998; contbr. articles to profl. jours. Pres. Civic Auditorium Bd., Sturgis, 1994, St. Joseph County Hist. Soc., Centreville, Mich., 1995; v.p. Sturgis Hist. Soc., Mich., 1996, Centennial Celebration Com., Sturgis, 1996. Recipient Award of Merit Hist. Soc. of Mich., 1996. Mem. Am. Med. Writers Assn., Soc. Profl. Journalists, Masonic Blue Lodge, Sturgis Exchg. Club (pres. 1951-52), Lambda Chi Alpha. Republican. Presbyterian. Avocations: preserving history, philately, music, photography, collecting antiques. Home: 428 Mortimer St Sturgis MI 49091-2228

HAIRALD, MARY PAYNE, vocational education educator, coordinator; b. Tupelo, Miss., Feb. 25, 1936; d. Will Burney and Ivey Lee (Berryhill) Payne; m. Leroy Utley Hairald, May 31, 1958; 1 child, Burney LeShawn. BS in Commerce, U. Miss., 1957, M in Bus. Edn., 1963; postgrad., Miss. Coll., 1964, Miss. State U., 1970, U. So. Miss., 1986-88, 90, U. Calif., Davis, summer 1997, Babson Coll., summer 1998. Bus. edn. tchr. John Rundle High Sch., Grenada, Miss., 1957-59; youth recreation leader City of Nettleton, Miss., summers 1960-61; tchr. social studies Nettleton Jr. High Sch., 1959-70; tchr.-coord. coop. vocat. edn. program Nettleton High Sch., 1970—; area mgr. World Book, Inc., Chgo., 1972-84; local coord. Am. Inst. for Fgn. Study, Greenwich, Conn., 1988—; instr. bus. Itawamba C.C., Tupelo, 1975-80; sponsor Cmty. Coord. for Program of Acad. Exch. (PAX), 1998—; advisor DECA, Nettleton, 1985—, state officers' advisor, 1995—; apptd. adv. coun. mem. Miss. Coop. Edn.-State Dept. Edn. Editor advisor State DECA Newsletter, 1987-92; contbr. articles on coop. edn. to newspapers. Co-organizer Nettleton Youth Recreation Booster Club; fundraiser Muscular Dystrophy Assn.; Sunday sch. tchr. coll. and career class Nettleton United Meth. Ch. Recipient 1st place Nat. Newsletter award Nat. DECA, 1988, 89, 90, 92, Excellence in Supervision award Am. Inst. for Fgn. Study, 1992; named Star Tchr., Miss. Econ. Coun., 1978, 95, Dist. II DECA Advisor of Yr., Miss. Assn. DECA, 1990, 93, Nat. DECA Hall of Fame charter mem., 1996; named tchr. of yr. Wal-Mart, 1997; recipient award for excellence Pub. Edn. Forum, 1997; award finalist Miss. Mfrs. Assn., 1997, 98; recipient Pub. Edn. Forum award, 1997. Mem. AAUW (charter), Am. Vocat. Assn. (Region IV Coop. Vocat. Edn. Tchr. of Yr. 1985, Region IV Mktg. Edn. Tchr. of Yr. 1988, Region IV New and Related Svcs. Tchr. of Yr. 1996, Region IV Outstanding Vocat. Tchr. of Yr. 1996, Nat. Tchr. of the Yr. 97), Coop. Work Experience Edn. Assn., Miss. Assn. Vocat. Educators (dist. sec.), Miss. Assn. Coop. Vocat. Edn. Tchrs. (v.p. 1980-83, pres. 1983-84, Miss. Tchr. of Yr. 1984, 87, 95), Miss. Assn. Mktg. Educators (Dist. II Tchr. of Yr. 1993, 94), Mktg. Edn. Assn., Nettleton Ladies Civitan Club (charter), Phi Delta Kappa (Phi Delta Kappa Kappan of Yr. 1998, found. rep.). Democrat. Methodist. Home: PO Box 166 Nettleton MS 38858-0166

HAIRE, JACK, magazine publisher; married; children: Billy, John. Grad., American U., D.C., 1974. With McGraw Hill, 1974-78; joined Time Inc., 1978; sales rep. Fortune mag., N.Y.C., 1978-80; mgr. New England sales office Fortune mag., Boston, 1980-82; mgr. Chgo. sales office Fortune mag., Chgo., 1982-84; dir. U.S. advt. sales Fortune mag., 1986-89, Time mag., 1989-91; v.p. advt. sales Entertainment Weekly mag., 1989-91; v.p. regional advt. sales Time Inc., Chgo., 1991-93; pub. Time mag., N.Y.C., 1993—. Office: Time Time & Life Bldg Rockefeller Ctr New York NY 10020-1393

HAIRSTON, HAROLD B., protective services official; m. Anne Hairston; children: Harold, Jr., Jennifer. Student, A&T Univ., N.C., Pa. State U., Abington. With Phila. Fire Dept., 1964—, lt. Ladder Co. # 6, 1971-78, chief battalion, dep. fire marshal, 1981-86, dep. chief, chief divsn. fire prevention, 1986-92, commr., 1992—; expert witness Mcpl. and Common Pleas Ct.; testifier Consumer Products Safety Commn., Washington. Bd. dirs. Delaware Valley Burn Found., Hero Scholarship Fund, Police Athletic League, ARC S.E. Pa. Mem. Nat. Fire Protection Assn., Urban Fire Forum, Bldg. Officals and Code Adminstrs., Internat. Assn. Black Profl. Firefighters, Internat. Assn. Fire Chiefs, Metro Fire Chiefs. Office: Fire Department Fire Administration Bldg 240 Spring Garden St Fl 2D Philadelphia PA 19123-2923

HAIRSTON, JAMES CHRISTOPHER, airline catering and distribution executive; b. Dallas, Nov. 23, 1960; s. James Loy and Beverly Gail (Van Duzen) H.; m. Cheryl Alice Wilson, Mar. 3, 1984; children: Mary Alice, Emily Elizabeth, James Christopher Jr., William Michael. Student, St. Edward's U., Austin, Tex., 1979; BS in Psychology, So. Meth. U., 1983; postgrad., U. Tex., Tyler, 1984-85. Sales rep. Hairston Produce Co., Dallas, 1980-83; pres. Bullet Distbg. Co., Dallas, 1981-82; sales mgr. Southland Corp./Dist. Ctr., Tyler, 1984-86; pres. Airline Distbn. Svcs., Inc., Dallas, 1986-93, Contra Pak, Inc., Dallas, 1993—; owner Milk Buds Co., 1994—; owner Hairston Produce Co., 1991-93; ptnr. HST Acquisition Group, 1996—. Contbr. numerous articles to trade jours. and newspapers. Mem. Rep. Nat. Com., 1984—; sponsor Dallas Can Acad., 1987—, Am. Heart Assn., 1987—; cand. Highland Park Ind. Sch. Dist. Sch. Bd., 1993, 97; Rep. precinct chmn., 1997—; Rep. election judge, 1997—. Mem. Tex. Restaurant Assn., Dallas Restaurant Assn., Dallas Jaycees, Masons, Shriners, Premier Club (Dallas). Roman Catholic. Avocation: golf, cycling, running, reading.

HAIRSTON, WALTER ALBERT, school system administrator; b. Winston-Salem, N.C., Sept. 14, 1928; s. Harvey and Ethel (Marshall) H.; m. Genell Rosella Bright, Mar. 10, 1951 (div. Sept. 12, 1972; m. Jeanette Olivia, Jan. 2, 1979; children: Jacqueline, Walter, Denice, Roslyn, Michael, Linda, Brenda. BS, Morgan State U., 1959; MEd, Loyola Coll., 1970; graduate, Command and Gen. Staff Coll., 1974, Nat. Def. U., 1979. Commd. U.S. Army, 1948, ret. Col., 1985; commandant 2071st U.S. Army Sch., 1979; mem. functional area assessment team Transp. Corps, U.S. Army, Fort Eustis, Va., 1984; chief evaluator and dir. Command Gen. Staff Coll., 1979-81; from tchr. to dean Balt. City Dept. Edn., 1960—. Col. U.S. Army, 1948-85. Mem. Masons, Kappa Alpha Psi, Kappa Delta Pi. Democrat. Presbyn. Avocations: golf, fishing, boating, woodwork. Home: 14300 Robcaste Rd Phoenix MD 21131-1426

HAISCH, BERNHARD MICHAEL, astronomer; b. Stuttgart-Bad Canstatt, Federal Republic of Germany, Aug. 23, 1949; s. Friedrich Wilhelm and Gertrud Paula (Dammbacher) H.; m. Pamela S. Eakins, July 29, 1977 (div. 1986); children: Katherine Stuart, Christopher Taylor; m. Marsha A. Sims, Aug. 23, 1986. Student, St. Meinrad (Ind.) Coll., 1967-68; BS in Astrophysics, Ind. U., 1971; PhD in Astronomy, U. Wis., 1975. Rsch. assoc. Joint Inst. Lab. Astrophysics, U. Colo., 1975-77, 78-79; vis. scientist space rsch. lab. U. Utrecht, The Netherlands, 1977-78; rsch. scientist Lockheed Rsch. Lab., Palo Alto, Calif., 1979-83, staff scientist, 1983—; dep. dir. Ctr. for EUV Astrophysics U. Calif., Berkeley, 1992-94; guest investigator Internat. Ultraviolet Explorer, Einstein Obs., Exosat, ROSAT Obs., EUVE Obs., Astro-D (ASCA), X-Ray Timing Explorer, 1980—; vis. fellow Max Planck Inst. Extraterr. Physik, Garching, Germany, 1991-94. Editor-in-chief Jour. Sci. Exploration, 1988—, Solar and Stellar Flares, 1989; sci. editor The Astrophys. Jour., 1993—; monograph The Many Faces of the Sun, 1999; mem. editl. bd. Solar Physics, 1992-95, Speculations in Sci. and Tech., 1995—; contbr. articles to profl. jours. Fellow Royal Astron. Soc., AIAA (assoc.); mem. Internat. Astron. Union, Am. Astron. Soc., European Astron. Soc., Commonwealth Club Calif., Sigma Xi, Phi Beta Kappa, Phi Kappa Phi. Avocations: Tae Kwon Do, international folk dance, downhill skiing, songwriting. Office: Lockheed Martin Solar and Astrophys Lab Div H1-12 Bldg 252 3251 Hanover St Palo Alto CA 94304-1121

HAISLETT, NICOLE, Olympic athlete. Gold medalist 200 Meter Freestyle, Barcelona, Spain, 1992. Address: care US Olympic Com 1750 E Boulder St Colorado Springs CO 80909-5724

HAIZLIP, HENRY HARDIN, JR., real estate consultant, former banker; b. Pine Bluff, Ark., Dec. 18, 1913; s. Henry Hardin and Rebecca (Porter) H.; m. Emily Williamson, Feb. 15, 1947; children: Henry Hardin III, Wilson, Jean Hunter, Selden. Student, Tulane U., 1932-33. With W.N. Ballou Cotton Co., Memphis, 1933-36; with First Nat. Bank Memphis, 1936-73, exec. v.p., 1968-70, chmn. exec. com., 1970-73; pres. First Memphis Realty Trust, 1970-73, chmn., 1973-76; pres. First Tenn. Corp., 1973-78; real estate cons. Haizlip/Lovitt, Memphis, 1979—; dir. Mid South Title Co., Union Service Industries Inc.; vice chmn. First Tenn. Nat. Corp., until 1979; ret.; instr. in mortgage financing La. State U., Ohio State U. Pres. Memphis Cotton Carnival Assn., 1966, bd. dirs., 1967—; vice chmn. Shelby United Good Neighbors, 1967-68; mem. Chickasaw coun. Boy Scouts Am.; pres. Future Memphis, Inc., 1974-77; bd. dirs. Memphis and Shelby County unit Am. Cancer Soc., 1967-68; trustee Comty. Found. Greater Memphis, chmn., 1978; mem. pres.'s coun. Tulane U., New Orleans, Rhodes Coll., Memphis; vice-chmn. The Trezevant Manor Episcopal Home. Capt. AUS, 1941-46. Mem. Am. Bankers Assn., Downtown Assn. Memphis (chmn. bd.), Kappa Alpha. Episcopalian. Clubs: Memphis Country; Menasha Hunting and Fishing (Turrell, Ark.); Memphis Hunt and Polo. Home: 965 Audubon Dr Memphis TN 38117-4601 Office: 6070 Quince Rd Memphis TN 38119-7254

HAJCAK, CATHERINE, geologist, consultant. BS in Geology with honors, Kent State U., 1990, BA in Math., 1995; MS in Geology, Miami U., Oxford, Ohio, 1992. Registered geologist, Ala., Mo., Wis.; notary pub., N.C. Mapper ctrl. regional geology br. U.S. Geol. Survey, Denver, 1989; rschr. Inst. for Sedimentary and Petroleum Geology, Geol. Survey Can., Calgary, Alta., 1990, 91; instr. Miami U., 1990-92; sr. geologist Environ. Strategies Corp., Reston, Va., 1992-98, Durham, N.C., 1998—. Contbr. articles to profl. jours., including Environ. Claims Jour., GSA Abstracts. Glenn W. Frank scholar Kent State U., 1988-89; thesis grantee U.S. Petroleum Assn., 1990-92, rsch. grantee Geol. Soc. Am., 1991. Mem. Nat. Ground Water Assn., Am. Assn. Petroleum Geologists, Groundwater Profls. N.C., Greater Raleigh C. of C., Cary C. of C., Sigma Gamma Epsilon. Avocations: travel, flying, fine wines, photography. E-mail: chajcak@earthlink.net. Office: Environ Strategies Corp 1000 Park Forty Plz Ste 300 Durham NC 27713

HAJEK, FRANCIS PAUL, lawyer; b. Hobart, Tasmania, Australia, Oct. 21, 1958; came to U.S., 1966; s. Frank Joseph and Kathleen Beatrice (Blake) H. BA, Yale U., 1980; JD, U. Richmond, 1984. Bar: Va. 1984, U.S. Dist.

Ct. (ea. dist.) Va. 1984, U.S. Ct. Appeals (4th cir.) 1986. Law clk. to presiding magistrate U.S. Dist Ct., Norfolk, Va., 1984-85; assoc. Seawell, Dalton, Hughes & Timms, Norfolk, 1985-87, Weinberg & Stein, Norfolk, 1987-89, Wilson, Hajek & Shapiro, P.C., Virginia Beach, Va., 1989—, l'Anson-Hoffman Am. Inn of Ct., 1991-97. Mem. ABA, ATLA, Am. Rail Labor Acad., Va. Bar Assn., Norfolk-Portsmouth Bar Assn. (chmn. exec. com. young lawyer's sect. 1990-91). Roman Catholic. Avocations: squash, tennis. Home: 2116 Windward Shore Dr Virginia Beach VA 23451-1726 Office: Wilson Hajek & Shapiro PO Box 5369 Virginia Beach VA 23471-0369

HAJEK, OTOMAR, mathematics educator; b. Beograd, Serbia, Jugoslavia, Dec. 22, 1930; came to U.S., 1966, naturalized, 1974; s. Frantisek Josef and Ruzena (Houdekova) H.; m. Olga Barbara Nemcova, Feb. 12, 1955, 1 son, Michael F.A. Diploma math., Caroline U., Prague, Czechoslovakia, 1953, Candidate Sci., 1963; RNDr, Caroline U., 1966. Asst. prof. Czech Inst. Tech., Prague, 1953-56; sr. asst. prof. Czech Inst. Tech., 1956-60; sci. officer Research Inst. Computing Machinery, Prague, 1960-65; sr. sci. officer Caroline U., Prague, 1965-66; assoc. prof. Case Western Res. U., Cleve., 1966-69, prof. math., 1969—, prof. systems engring., 1988-96; prof. emeritus, 1996—. Author: Dynamical Systems in the Plane, 1968, Pursuit Games, 1975, Control Systems in the Plane, 1991; co-author: Local Semi-Dynamical Systems, 1969; co-editor: Global Differentiable Dynamics, 1970. Recipient von Humboldt award, 1975; Deutsche Forschungsgemeinschaft fellow Bonn., 1979, 90, Fulbright fellow, 1990. Mem. Am. Math. Soc., Czechoslovak Soc. Arts and Scis., von Humboldt Assn., Fulbright Assn. Lutheran. Home: 11330 Savannah Dr Fredericksburg VA 22407-9109

HAJEK, ROBERT J., SR., lawyer, real estate broker, commodities broker, nursing home owner; b. Berwyn, Ill., May 17, 1943; s. James J., Sr., and Rita C. (Kalka) H.; m. Maris Ann Enright, June 19, 1965 (div. Oct. 1991); children: Maris Ann, Robert J., David, Mandie. BA, Loras Coll., 1965; JD, U. Ill., 1968. Bar: Ill. 1968, U.S. Tax Ct. 1970, U.S. dist. ct. (no. dist.) Ill. 1971, U.S. Ct. Appeals (7th cir.) 1972, U.S. Supreme Ct. 1972. Lic. real estate broker, Ill., Nat. Assn. Securities Dealers; registered U.S. Commodities Futures Trading Commn. ptnr. Hajek & Hajek, Berwyn, Ill., 1968-76; pres., bd. chmn. Hajek, Hajek, Koykar & Heying, Ltd., Westchester, Ill., 1976-85; pres., chief exec. officer Land of Lincoln Real Estate, Ltd., Glendale Heights, Ill., 1985-89, also bd. dirs.; ptnr., owner Camelot Manor Nursing Home, Streator, Ill., 1978—, Ottawa (Ill.) Care Ctr., 1981—, Glenwood House Nursing Home, Streator, Ill., 1988—, Sullivan House Nursing Home, Ottawa, Ill., 1991—, Law Centre Bldg., Westchester, 1976-91; exec. v.p., gen. counsel Ottawa Long Term Care, Inc.; owner Garfield Ridge Real Estate, Chgo., 1973-78, Centre Realty, Westchester, 1976-85; ptnr. Westbrook Commodities, Chgo., 1983; v.p., bd. mem., gen. counsel DeHart Gas and Oil Devel., Ltd., 1970-73; prin. Northeastern Okla. Oil and Gas Prodn. Venture, Tulsa, 1982—; exec. v.p., gen. counsel Garrett Plante Corp., 1978—; bd. dirs. Land of Lincoln Savs. and Loan, 1981-89, Home Title Services of Am., Inc., 1981-89, Land of Lincoln Ins. Agy., Inc., 1981-89, Medema Builders, Inc., 1983-88, Ptnrs. of Ill., Inc., 1984-89, The Ill. Co., 1984-88, Ill. Co. Properties, Inc., subs. of Ill. Co., 1984-87, Ottawa Long Term Care, Inc., 1982—, Garrett Plante Corp., 1978—, St. Mary's Living Square Chgo., 1985-92. Sr. boys' basketball coach Roselle Recreation Assn., Ill., 1981-83. Mem. ABA, Ill. Bar Assn., Nat. Assn. Realtors, Ill. Assn. Realtors, Northwest Suburban Bd. Realtors, Ill. Health Care Assn., Phi Alpha Delta. Republican. Episcopalian. Clubs: Amateur Radio, No. Ill. DX Assn.

HAJIM, EDMUND A., financial services executive; b. Los Angeles, July 26, 1936; s. Jack and Sophie H.; m. Barbara E. Melnick, Aug. 8, 1965; children: Geoffrey Blair, Jon Bradley, Corey Brooke. BS, U. Rochester, 1958; MBA, Harvard U., 1964. Research analyst Capital Research Co. subs. Capital Group, Inc., N.Y.C., 1964-66, office mgr., 1966-67; v.p., dir. Capital Mgmt. Service, 1967-69; pres. Greenwich Mgmt. Co., Conn., 1969; pres., dir. Growth Fund Am., 1969-70, Income Fund Am., 1970; sr. v.p. E.F. Hutton, Nat. Instl. Equity, N.Y.C., 1974-77; dir., mng. dir. Lehman Bros., N.Y.C., 1977, pres. securities divsn., 1977-79; chmn., CEO Lehman Mgmt. Co., N.Y.C., 1980-83, Furman, Selz L.L.C., N.Y.C., 1983-98; co-chmn. Ams., ING Barings, 1998—; CEO ING Furman Selz Asset Mgmt. Inc., N.Y.C., 1998—; ptnr., mng. dir. Lehman Bros. Kuhn Loeb & Kuhn Loeb Lehman Bros. Internat., N.Y.C., 1977-83, also bd. dirs.; chmn., bd. dirs. Lehman Corp., One William St. Fund, Lehman Cash Mgmt. Fund; chmn. Lehman Capital Fund, Greenwich, Conn., Bd. Trust Fund, Fund Source and FFB Funds Trust; bd. dirs. Xerox Fin. Svcs. Inc., Tosco Corp., NFO Rsch. Past chmn. bd. trustees Brunswick Sch., Greenwich; mem. pres. council U. Rochester, 1975—, now trustee. Served with USN, 1958-61. Mem. Inst. Chartered Fin. Analysts, Chief Execs. Orgn., N.Y. Soc. Security Analysts (past dir.), Bond Club, Harvard Club, Wall St. Club, Stanwich Country Club. Office: ING Furman Selz Asset Mgmt Inc 230 Park Ave New York NY 10169-0005

HAJJAR, DAVID PHILLIP, biochemist, educator. BA in Biochemistry, Am. Internat. Coll., 1974; MS, U. N.H., 1977, PhD, 1978. Rsch. fellow in biochemistry U. N.H., Durham, 1975-78; postdoct. fellow Med. Sch. Rockefeller U., 1978-80; rsch. asst. in pathology med. coll. Cornell U., Ithaca, N.Y., 1978-81; postdoct. fellow Med. Sch., 1980-81; asst. prof. biochemistry and pathology med. coll. Cornell U., Ithaca, N.Y., 1981-84, assoc. prof. med. coll., 1984-89, prof. biochemistry and pathology, 1989—; dir. Ctr. Vascular Biology; dean Cornell U. Grad. Sch. of Med. Scis., 1997—; sr. investigator N.Y. Heart Assn., 1981-84; mem. pathology A study sect. NIH, 1991-95; mem. review com. coun. on arteriosclerosis Am. Heart Assn., 1992—. Contbr. over 100 articles to profl. and sci. jours. Nat. Merit scholar, 1969; Predoctoral fellow N.H. chptr. Am. Heart Assn., 1976-78; PHS postdoctoral rsch. fellow NIH, 1978-81, New Investigator Rsch. award, 1981-84; recipient Tchr.-Scientist award Andrew Mellon Found., 1981-83, FASEB (AAP) Warner-Lambert/Parke Davis award, 1991, Cornell U. Med. Coll., Alumni award, 1997—. Fellow AAAS. Office: Cornell U Grad Sch Med Sci 445 E 69th St New York NY 10021-5603

HAKALA, JUDYTH ANN, data processing executive; b. Manistee, Mich., Sept. 19, 1955; d. John Emil and Reta Mae (Crain) H. BS, Taylor U., Upland, Ind., 1977. Cert. prodn. and inventory control. Tech. dir. Bowling & Rixom, Traverse City, Mich., 1981-82; programmer Systems for Profit, Inc., Grand Rapids, Mich., 1982-84, programmer, analyst, 1984-88, systems mgr., 1988-89; cons. Competitive Solutions, Inc., Grand Rapids, Mich., 1989-92, dir. of cons., 1992-96, design analyst, 1996-98, sys. arch., custom prodns. mgr., 1998—; ind. cons., 1981—. Mem. activist Right to Life Mich., Grand Rapids; bd. dirs. Reconciliation Met. Cmty. Ch., 1999—. Mem. Am. Prodn. and Inventory Control Soc., Finnish-Am. Soc. (membership com. 1988—, chmn. publicity com., 1989-92, sec. 1992—). Republican. Home: 3024 Woodbridge Dr SE Grand Rapids MI 49512-5639 Office: Competitive Solutions Inc 3855 Sparks Dr SE Grand Rapids MI 49546-6107

HAKALA, KAREN LOUISE, retired real estate adminstrator; b. Lansing, Mich., Dec. 8, 1941; d. Herod Maxon and Flora Belle (Barton) Mitchell; m. Paul Kenneth Hakala, June 24, 1959 (div. Nov. 1972); children: Chris, Craig. BS, No. Mich. U., Marquette, 1986. Real estate adminstr. The Cleve.-Cliffs Iron Co., Ishpeming, Mich., 1967-99; ret., 1999. Mem. devel. com. Planned Parenthood No. Mich., Marquette, 1996—; bd. dirs. Marquette Symphony Orch., 1998-99, treas. 1999—. Mem. AAUW (pub. policy rep. 1995-99, pres. 1999).

HAKE, THEODORE LOWELL, auction house owner, writer; b. York, Pa., Aug. 30, 1943; s. Theodore Russell and Ethel Amanda (Towson) H.; m. Jonell Ann Robinson, Aug. 25, 1973; 1 child, Theodore James. BA in Polit. Sci., U. Pitts., 1965; MA in Comm., U. Pa., 1969. Owner, operator Hake's Americana & Collectibles, York, 1967—. Author: Ency. of Polit. Buttons, 3 vols., 1974-77, Hake's Guide to Character Toy Premiums, 1996, 12 other reference books for collectors of Am. popular culture. Mem. Am. Polit. Items Collectors (bd. dirs. 1985-86, Hall of Fame 1985), Ephemera Soc. of Am., World's Fair Collectors Soc., Token and Medal Soc., Tin Container Collectors Assn., Nat. Fantasy Fan Club. Office: Hake's Americana & Collectibles PO Box 1444 York PA 17405-1444

HAKEEM, MUHAMMAD ABDUL, artist, educator; b. N.Y.C., Oct. 15, 1945; s. Cheveland and Ruby (Rountrea) Marshall; m. Sheron Fatima, Nov. 27, 1987. Student of sculpture and painting, Pratt Inst., Pietrasanta, Italy, 1972; BFA, Pratt Inst., 1974; MA, Tchr. Coll., 1976; MEd, Columbia U., 1980. Artist N.Y. Daily News, 1976-78; asst. technician Bklyn. Mus., 1980-81, instr. African Art, 1981; tchr. Holy Rosary Sch., Bklyn., 1982-89; arts and crafts specialist Fresh Air Fund Camp, Fishkill, N.Y., 1983 summer, Camp Merrimac, Contoo Cook, N.H., 1986-88 summer; art tchr. Middle Sch. 319, Bronx, N.Y., 1997-98; adj. prof. Naropa Inst., Boulder. One-man shows include Christ Hosp. Primary Care Ctr., Jersey City, N.J., 1997; exhibited in group shows at Bklyn. Mus., 1973, Lynn Kottler Galleries, 1974, Hansen Galleries, 1974, Galleries Internat., 1975, Cmty. Gallery, 1977, Waverly Gallery, Inc., 1977, Allan S. Park Gallery, 1978, Greenwich Bar and Restaurant, 1979, Macy Gallery, 1980, West Side Story, 1981, Lynn Kittler Galleries, 1981, World Trade Expo-Keane Mason Gallery, 1981, Tabor Gallery, 1982, Gallery II, St. George, Utah, 1984, Beaulahland, 1986, Morin-Miller Galleries, 1987, 89, Ednl. Alliance, 1988, Steamboat Springs (Colo.) Art Coun./Eleanor Bliss Ctr. for the Arts of the Depot (hon. mention), 1992, Boulder (Colo.) Art Ctr., 1993, Louisville (Colo.) Arts Ctr., 1993, Emmanuel Gallery-U. Colo., Denver, 1994, Cross Gallery, Boulder, 1995—, Cross Gallery, Denver, 1995, Bklyn. Children's Mus., 1996, The Christ Hosp. Primary Care Ctr., 1997; works represented at Kearon-Hempenstall Gallery, Jersey City; multimedia exhbn. at Colo. History Mus., 1996. Art tchr. Lower East Side Cmty Sch., N.Y.C., 1976-77, Urban League, Bklyn., 1969 summer; counselor Office of Cath. Edn., Bklyn., 1987-88; mem. customer panel Regional Transp. Divsn. Winner Cheekwood Nat. Contemporary Painting Competition, Cheekwood Mus. Art, Tenn., 1993. Mem. Kappa Delta Pi (Kappa chpt.). Home: 2133 S Eaton St Apt 31 Denver CO 80227-3665 Address: 2133 S Eaton St Apt 31 Denver CO 80227-3665

HAKEL, MILTON DANIEL, JR., psychology educator, consultant, publisher; b. Hutchinson, Minn., Aug. 1, 1941; s. Milton Daniel and Emily Ann (Kovar) H.; m. Lee Ellen Pervier, Sept. 1, 1962; children: Lane, Jennifer. BA, U. Minn., 1963, PhD, 1966. Diplomate in Indsl. and Organizational Psychology Am. Bd. Profl. Psychology. Prof. psychology Ohio State U., Columbus, 1968-85; prof. psychology U. Houston, 1985-91, chmn. dept., 1987-91; Ohio Bd. Regents eminent scholar, prof. Bowling Green State U., 1991—; pres. Organizational Research and Devel., 1977—; ptnr. Applied Research Group, 1984-87; trustee Am. Bd. Profl. Psychology, 1987-90; mem. com. on assessment and tchr. quality NRC, 1999—. Co-author (sr.): Making It Happen: Doing Research with Implementation in Mind, 1982; author: Beyond Multiple Choice: Evaluating Alternatives to Traditional Testing, 1998; editor Current Directions in Psychol. Sci., 1998—, Personnel Psychology, 1973-84, pub., 1984—; contbr. 36 articles to profl. jours. Chair Human Capital Initiative Coordinating Com., 1991-99. Recipient James McKeen Cattell award, 1965; Fulbright-Hays Sr. scholar, 1978; NSF grantee, 1966-73. Fellow Am. Psychol. Soc. (founding bd. dirs.); mem. Soc. for Indsl. and Orgnl. Psychology (pres. 1984, Disting. Svc. Contbrs. award 1995), Acad. Mgmt., Internat. Assn. Applied Psychology, Summit Conf. Presbyterian. Home: 1435 Cedar Ln Bowling Green OH 43402-1476 Office: Bowling Green State U Dept Psychology Bowling Green OH 43403

HAKEN, RUDOLF, music educator; b. Urbana, Ill., Dec. 23, 1965; s. Wolfang R.G. and Anna-Irmgard (von Bredow) H.; m. Leila Ann ramagopal, Nov. 11, 1989; children: Oliver, Sofia, Nicolas. BMusic, U. Ill., 1991; MMusic, Rice U., 1993. Music prof. W.Va. U., Morgantown, 1994-96, U. Ill., Urbana, 1996—; soloist, condr., composer Concert Halls in N.Am. and Europe, 1976—; competition judge Houston Symphony, 1998, Chgo. Viola Soc., Chgo., 1998, Midwest Young Artists, 1998. Composer 3 CDs of original works; composer Books of Complete Works, 1998. Avocation: marathon running. Office: U Ill Sch Music 1114 W Nevada St Urbana IL 61801-3859

HAKES, THOMAS BRION, manufacturing company executive, physician; b. Chgo., Dec. 27, 1944; s. L. Glenn and Vera M. (Brion) H.; m. Ellen D. Hallock, Apr. 6, 1990; children: Henrietta, John Bradford. BSEE, Rose-Hulman Inst. Tech., 1967; MD, Columbia U., 1973. Diplomate Am. Bd. Internal Medicine, Am. Bd. Oncology. Intern St. Luke's Hosp., N.Y.C., 1973-75; resident in medicine, fellow in oncology Meml. Hosp., N.Y.C., 1975-78; assoc. attending physician Meml. Sloan-Kettering Cancer Ctr., N.Y.C., 1978—; co-chmn. C/S Grp., Lebanon, N.J., 1994—. Office: C/S Group 3 Werner Way Lebanon NJ 08833-2223

HAKIM, BESIM SELIM, architecture and urban design educator, researcher; b. Paris, July 31, 1938; came to U.S., 1978; s. Selim D. and Meliha M. (Yamulki) H.; m. Fatina S. Hijab, Oct. 31, 1963 (div. July 1983); children: Omar, Lena, Sara; m. Mariam B. Bashayan, Dec. 31, 1984; 1 child, Malak. BArch, Liverpool (Eng.) U., 1962; MArch in Urban Design, Harvard U., 1971. Registered architect, Ariz. Asst. prof. Tech. U. of Nova Scotia, Halifax, Can., 1967-74, assoc. prof., 1974-80, adj. rsch. prof., 1980-83; adj. assoc. prof. U. N.Mex., Albuquerque, 1982-83; assoc. prof. King Fahd U. of Petroleum and Minerals, Dhahran, Saudi Arabia, 1984-85; assoc. prof. Coll. of Architecture and Planning King Faisal U., Dammam, Saudi Arabia, 1985-93; ind. scholar and cons., 1994—; vis. prof. McGill U., Montreal, 1974, Tech. Inst. Architecture and Urbanism, Tunis, Tunisia, 1975, King Saud U., Riyadh, Saudi Arabia, 1982, 87, 89, 92, MIT, 1977; vis. scholar MIT, 1981, Cornell U., 1995; cons. to Skidmore, Owings and Merrill, Architects/Engrs., Chgo., Keith Graham & Assocs., Architects, Halifax, Nova Scotia, others; architect, engr. King Khaled Internat. Airport, Riyadh, Saudi Arabia, 1983-84; lectr. numerous univs. and profl. confs. in U.S., Can., Eng., Japan, Greece, Turkey, Tunisia, Jordan, United Arab Emirates, Saudi Arabia, Morocco. Prin. works include urban design downtown Halifax, N.S., Coors Corridor Study, Albuquerque, Hist. Old Town, Albuquerque, 11 custom-built houses, 8-story office bldg., hosp. renovations/additions, apt. bldgs. and a religious facility, U.S., Can., Mid-East; author: Arabic-Islamic Cities: Building and Planning Principles, 1986, 2d edit., 1988, Japanese edit., 1990; contbr. articles to profl. jours. Recipient citation for rsch. Progressive Architecture, 1987, Edn. Honors award AIA, 1990. Mem. AIA, Am. Inst. Cert. Planners, Am. Planning Assn., Assn. Collegiate Schs. of Architecture, Middle East Studies Assn. N.Am., Halifax Bd. Trade (civic affairs com.). Home: 1832 Field Dr NE Albuquerque NM 87112-2834

HAKIM, FARES SAMIH, physician; b. Damascus, Syria, Nov. 5, 1963; came to U.S., 1989; s. Mohamed Samih and Raja (Abaza) H. BS, French Inst. Syria, Damascus, 1981; MD, Damascus U., 1987. Diplomate Am. Internal Medicine. Resident in internal medicine Cohchin Hosp., Paris, 1988-89; fellow surg. rsch. VA Hosp., Washington, 1990-92; rsch. assoc. Inst. Clin. Rsch., Washington, 1992-94; resident in internal medicine Med. Coll. Ga., Augusta, 1994-97, fellow in gastroenterology, hepatology, 1997—. Contbr. articles to profl. jours. Mem. AMA, ACP, Am. Gastroent. Assn., Am. Coll. Gastroent., Am. Assn. Gastrenterology Endoscopy, Am. Assn. Studies Liver Disease. Avocations: sports, travel, languages. Home: 1017 Stevens Creek Rd Augusta GA 30907-3205 Office: Med Coll Ga 1120 15th St BBR2541 Augusta GA 30912-0006

HAKIM, MICHEL, religious leader. Archéparque Ea. Rite Roman Cath. Ch. in Can., Montreal; archbishop of Saint-Sauveur for Greek-Melkite Caths. in Can., Montreal, 1980-98, archéparque emeritus, 1998—. Office: 12325 Pl de La Minerve, Montreal, PQ Canada H4J 1X3

HAKIMI, S. LOUIS, electrical and computer engineering educator; b. Meshed, Iran, Dec. 16, 1932; came to U.S., 1952, naturalized, 1967; s. A. Moshe and Miriam (Nabavian) H.; m. Mary Yomtob, Aug. 22, 1965; children: Alan, Carol, Diane. B.S. in Elec. Engring., U. Ill., Urbana, 1955, M.S. in Elec. Engring., 1957, Ph.D. in Elec. Engring., 1959. Asst. prof. elec. engring. U. Ill., 1959-61; assoc. prof. Northwestern U., Evanston, Ill., 1961-66; prof. Northwestern U., 1966-86, chmn. dept. elec. engring., 1972-77; prof. U. Calif., Davis, 1986—, chmn. elec. and computer engring., 1986-96. Assoc. editor Networks, 1975-90, adv. editor, 1990—; assoc. editor IEEE Transactions on Circuits and Systems, 1975-77; bd. adv. editors Transp. Sci., 1985—. Fellow IEEE; mem. Soc. Indsl. and Applied Math., Sigma Xi, Tau Beta Pi, Phi Kappa Phi. Home: 27017 E El Macero Dr El Macero CA 95618-1008 Office: U Calif Dept Elec & Computer Engring Davis CA 95616

HAKIMOGLU, AYHAN, electronics company executive; b. Erbaa, Turkey, Aug. 19, 1928; came to U.S., 1955; s. Mekki and Mediha H.; children by previous marriage: Zeynep B., Incigul R. O'Brien, Deborah A. Cueto, Leyla P.; m. Rachida Elmir, July 12, 1997. BSEE, Robert Coll., Istanbul, 1949; MSEE, U. Cin., 1950. Founder, pres., chmn. bd. Dynaplex Corp., Princeton, N.J., 1962-67; gen. mgr. Teledyne Telemetry Co., Los Angeles, 1966-67; founder, chmn. bd., pres. Aydin Corp., Horsham, Pa., 1967-96; cons. Aydin Corp., Plymouth Meeting, Pa.; investor. Served to lt. Turkish Army, 1951-52. Named Turkish Am. of Yr. Assembly Turkish Am. Assn., 1985; recipient Outstanding Pub. Svc. award, Assembly Turkish Am. Assns., 1988, 89, Disting. Alumni award U. Cin., 1991. Moslem.

HÄKKINEN, SIRPA MARJA ANNELI, oceanographer; b. Joutsa, Finland, Oct. 13, 1951; came to the U.S., 1981; d. Toivo Emil and Laura Saima Maria Häkkinen; m. George Leonard Johnson, July 31, 1989; 1 child, Lyuba. BS, U. Helsinki, Finland, 1974, MS in Physics, 1976, Licentiate in Philosophy in Nuc. Physics, 1978; PhD in Geophys. Fluid Dynamics, Fla. State U., 1984. Tchg. asst. dept. nuc. physics U. Helsinki, 1974-77; scientist Inst. Marine Rsch., Helsinki, 1977-80; internat. exch. visitor dept. oceanograph Fla. State U., Tallahassee, 1981, grad. rsch. asst. dept. oceanography, 1981-84, rsch. assoc. dept. oceanography, 1984-85; resident rsch. assoc. NASA Goddard Space Flight Ctr., Greenbelt, Md., 1985-87; oceanographer NASA Goddard Space Flight Ctr., Greenbelt, 1990—; scientist Univs. Space Rsch. Assn., Greenbelt, 1987-88; rsch. staff dept. geology Princeton (N.J.) U., 1988-90; proposal reviewer NASA, NSF, Nat. Oceanic and Atmospheric Adminstrn., Nat. Eviron. Rsch. Coun., Eng. Reviewer Jour. Phys. Oceanography, Geophys. Rsch. Letters, Jour. Geophys. Rsch., 1990—, Nature; contbr. articles to profl. jours. Pres. Finlandia Assn., Washington Chpt., 1992. Fellow NRC, Washington, 1985-87. Mem. Am. Geophys. Union, Finnish Geophys. Union, Finnish Math. and Phys. Soc., Oceanography Soc., Com. for Polar Oceanography. Avocation: gardening. Home: 7708 Lake Glen Dr Glenn Dale MD 20769-2027 Office: Goddard Space Flight Ctr Ocean and Ice Br Code 971 Greenbelt MD 20771

HAKUTANI, YOSHINOBU, English educator; b. Osaka, Japan, Mar. 27, 1935; s. Yoshiyuki and Shigeko H.; m. Michiko Watanabe, Feb. 1, 1967; children: Yoshiki, Naoki. BA, Hiroshima U., 1957; MA, U. Minn., 1959; PhD, Pa. State U., 1965. Instr. English S.D. State U., Brookings, 1959-61; asst. prof. English Calif. State U., Northridge, 1965-68; from asst. to assoc. prof. English Kent (Ohio) State U., 1968-79, prof. English, 1979—. Author: Young Dreiser, 1980, Richard Wright and Racial Discourse, 1996; editor various mag. articles; co-editor: The City in African-American Literature, 1995, Haiku: This Other World by Richard Wright, 1998; mem. editl. bd. Kent State U. Press, 1991-94, Dreiser Studies, 1993—; gen. editor Peter Lang Pub., Inc., 1994—. Faculty Rsch. grantee Kent State U., 1972-98. Mem. MLA, Am. Lit. Assn., Theodore Dreiser Soc. (pres. 1998—), Richard Wright Cir. (mem. adv. bd. 1991—). Avocations: sports fan, playing tennis, carpentry. E-mail: yhakutan@kent.edu. Office: Kent State U Dept English Kent OH 44242

HALABY, NAJEEB E., financier, lawyer; b. Dallas, Nov. 19, 1915; s. Najeeb Elias and Laura (Wilkins) H.; m. Doris Carlquist, Feb. 9, 1946 (div. 1977); children: Lisa (Queen Noor of Jordan), Christian, Alexa; m. Jane Allison Coates Frick, Oct. 1, 1980 (dec. 1996). A.B., Stanford U., 1937; student, U. Mich. Law Sch., 1937-38; LL.B., Yale, 1940; LL.D., Allegheny Coll., 1967, Loyola U., Los Angeles, 1968, Dowling Coll., 1985; &, Embry Riddle & Aero. U., 1993. Bar: Calif. 1940, D.C. 1948, N.Y. 1973. Pvt. practice L.A.; with O'Melveny & Myers, 1940-42; test pilot Lockheed Aircraft Corp., Burbank, Calif., 1942-43; fgn. affairs adviser to sec. def., 1948-53, dep. asst. sec. def., 1952-54; with L. S. Rockefeller and Bros., 1953-56; pres. Am. Tech. Corp.; sec.-treas., counsel Aerospace Corp.; faculty lectr. UCLA; dir. def. studies program; chmn. UCLA (1960 disarmament conf.); pvt. practice law Calif., 1959-61; adminstr. FAA, 1961-65; pres. Pan Am World Airways, 1968-72, chmn., chief exec. officer, 1969-72; pres. Halaby Internat. Corp., 1973—; chmn. Save The Children Found., 1992—, Dulles Access Rapid Transit, Inc., 1985—; with Nat. Ctr. for Atmospheric Rsch. Found., 1985—. Trustee Aspen Inst., chmn., Wolf Trap Found., (Va.), Jones Inst. Reproductive Biology, Flight Safety Found.; elected chmn. bd. visitors AOPA Flight Safety Found.; mem. adv. coun. Brookings Inst., Libr. of Congress, Smithsonian Instn., Nat. Gallery of Art, Stanford in Washington. Served as naval aviator USN World War II; asst. chief fighter sect. Naval Air Test Center Patuxent River, Md. Decorated Legion of Honor France; Order of Cedars Lebanon; medal of Independence Jordan; recipient Arthur Fleming award; Godfrey L. Cabot award; Monsanto Air Safety award; Glen Gilbert Air Traffic award, Nat. Air and Space Mus. trophy Smithsonian Instn., 1995. Fellow AIAA; mem. Soc. Exptl. Test Pilots, Corbey Ct., Coun. on Fgn. Rels. Clubs: Alibi, Metropolitan; Chevy Chase; Bohemian (San Francisco); Piping Rock (N.Y.C.), Explorers, Tower. Office: 175 Chain Bridge Rd Mc Lean VA 22101-1907*

HALABY, RAOUF JAMIL, English and art educator, consultant; b. Jerusalem, Nov. 22, 1945; came to U.S., 1965; s. Jamil Tanas and Katrina Helane (Halabi) H.: m. Rachel Dell Lollar, Dec. 26, 1970; children: Ramzy Truman, Ryan Nicola. BA, Ouachita Bapt. U., 1968, MS in Edn., 1970; EdD, East Tex. State U., 1973; postgrad., La. Tech. U., Rome, 1993. Asst. prof. English Ouachita Bapt. U., Arkadelphia, Ark., 1973-80, assoc. prof. English, 1980-85, prof. English and art, 1986—; cons. U. Minn., Mpls., 1982; vis. prof. U. Guadalahara, Mex., 1988; cons. linguistics, lit., and gifted and talented edn., 1980—. Contbr. columns and essays to newspapers, chpts. to books. Active Boy Scouts of Am., 1988—; chmn. bd. dirs. Group Living Inc., 1985-90; in charge of Univ. Art Gallery, Arkadelphia, 1992—; active in local elem. sch. art programs, Arkadelphia; elected mem. Ark. Humanities Bd. Gifted and Talented Summer Program grantee Ark. Dept. Edn., 1986-93. Baptist. Avocations: writing, beekeeping, sculpting, gardening, canoeing, fishing, reading. Office: Ouachita Bapt U PO Box 3785 Arkadelphia AR 71998-3785

HALABY, SAMIA ASAAD, artist, educator, computer artist; b. Jerusalem, Palestine, Dec. 12, 1936; s. Asaad Saba and Foutounie Assad (Atallah) H. BS in Design, U. Cin., 1959; MA in Painting, Mich. State U., 1960; MFA in Painting, Ind. U., 1963. Teaching asst. Ind. U., Bloomington, 1962-63; assoc. prof. Ind. U., 1969-72; instr. U. Hawaii, Honolulu, 1963-64; vis. lectr. U. Hawaii, summer 1966; asst. prof. Kansas City (Mo.) Art Inst., 1964-66, U. Mich., 1967-69; vis. lectr. art Yale U., 1972-73, assoc. prof., 1973-76, adj. assoc. prof., 1976-82; lectr. in field; vis. prof. U. Hawaii, Honolulu, 1985-86, U. South Fla., 1990; adj. instr. Cooper Union, 1989-92; artist-in-residence Tamarind Lithography Workshop, Albuquerque, 1972; presenter 4th Internat. Symposium on Electronic Art, Mpls., 1993, 7th symposium, Rotterdam, 1996. One-man shows include Gima Gallery, Honolulu, 1964, The Gallery, Bloomington, 1970, Phyllis Kind Gallery, Chgo., 1971, Yale Sch. Art Gallery, 1972, Spectrum Gallery, N.Y.C., 1973, Marilyn Pearl Gallery, N.Y.C., 1978, 22 Wooster Gallery, 1982, 83, Tossan-Tossan Gallery, N.Y.C., 1983, 88, Housatonic Mus., Bridgeport, 1983, Galaria de arte Palace, Granada, Spain, 1986, Gallery II U. Mich., Kalamazoo, 1989, 911 Gallery, Indpls., 1993, Darat Al-Funun, Amman, Jordan, 1995, Galerie Atassi, Damascus, Syria, 1997, Galerie Le Porte, Halab, Syria, 1997; group shows include Solomon R. Guggenheim Mus., N.Y.C., 1975, Susan Caldwell Gallery, N.Y.C., 1977, Iraqi Cultural Center, London, 1979, Kunsternes Hus, Oslo, Norway, 1981, U. Art Mus., N.Mex., 1985, Hudson Ctr. Gallery, N.Y.C., 1985, Tercera Bienal de la Habana, Cuba, 1989, Prix Ars Electronica, Linz, Austria, 1990, Art and Algorithm, Mpls. Coll. Art, 1991, Hilo Internat. Exhbn. of Works on Paper, U. Hawaii, 1990, Digitized and Manipulated, Sangre De Cristo Arts Ctr., Pueblo, Colo., 1991, opening exhbn. Darat Al Funun of Shoman Found., Amman, Jordan, 1993, Fourth Internat. Symposium Electronic Art, Mpls., 1993, Arab Women, Nat. Mus. Women in the Arts, Washington, 1994; performance art Bklyn. Mus., 1994, Poetry Project, N.Y.C., 1995, Lebanese Am. U., Beirut, 1995, HERE, N.Y.C., 1996; represented in permanent collections Solomon R. Guggenheim Mus., Inst. Du Monde Arab, Paris, Indpls. Mus. Art, Art Inst. Chgo., Nelson Rockhill Gallery Art, Kansas City, Ind. U. Mus., Mich. State U. Mus., Ft. Wayne (Ind.) Mus. Art, Detroit Inst. Art, Cleve. Mus. Art, Cin. Art Mus., Nat. Gallery Jordan, Amman, Yale U. Gallery, Tamarind Inst. Collection, Albuquerque, Alternative Mus., N.Y., Honolulu Acad. Arts, Ind. U. Mus., Bloomington, Mead Art Mus., Amherst, Conn., Palm Springs (Calif.) Desert Mus., Yale U. Gallery, New Haven, corp. collections, U.S. Steel, ATT Longlines, First Nat. Chgo, Kemper Ins. Chgo., S.E. Banking Corp. Fla., Witko Chem. Corp., Standard Oil Ohio, IBM, Arab Bank. Subj. of Prof. Publs.: Kansas City Coun. for Faculty Devel. traveling fellow, 1965; Creative Artists Pub. Svc. Program grantee, 1978-79. Studio: PO Box 965 New York NY 10013-0861

HALAMANDARIS, HARRY, aerospace executive; b. Sunnyside, Utah, Sept. 26, 1938; s. Gust and Olga (Konakis) H.; m. Sandra Susan Hansen, Aug. 4, 1961; children: Chris Harry, Gina Lee. AS, Carbon Coll., 1958; BS in Math., Utah State U., 1960, BSEE, 1961, MSEE, 1962. Instr. West Coast U., L.A., 1964-68; mem. tech. staff Hughes Aircraft, Culver City, Calif., 1962-65; sr. mem. tech. staff Litton Guidance & Controls, Woodland Hills, Calif., 1965-69; gen. mgr., exec. v.p. Satellite Positioning Corp., Encino, Calif., 1969-72; pres., asst. group exec. Teledyne Systems, Northridge, Calif., 1972-89; dir. corp. tech. Teledyne Industries, Inc., L.A., 1989-94; group exec. Kaiser Aerospace and Electronics, Van Nuys, Calif., 1994-95; corp. sr. v.p. Litton Industries, Inc., 1995—; mem. adv. coun. Coll. Ea. Utah; industry adv. bd. U. So. Calif., Calif. State U., L.A.; bd. dirs. Econ. Devel. Corp., 1992-94. Contbr. over 30 articles to profl. jours. Mem. bd. govs. Pacific Boys Lodge, Woodland Hills, Calif., 1986-88; aerospace chmn. United Way, L.A., 1988-89. NSF fellow, 1961-62. Mem. Am. Electronics Assn. (bd. dirs., exec. com. 1984-94, pres. Roundtable exec. com. 1989-92), Utah State Alumni, Masons, Sigma Xi (officer, v.p. 1960-61), Phi Kappa Phi, Tau Beta Pi. Democrat. Greek Orthodox. Avocations: racquetball, gardening, sports. Home: 21041 Nashville St Chatsworth CA 91311-1447 Office: Litton Industries Inc 21240 Burbank Blvd Woodland Hills CA 91367-6675

HALAS, CYNTHIA ANN, business information specialist; b. Norristown, Pa., July 24, 1961; d. George and Maria (Mitrik) H. Student, Temple U., 1979-80; AS in Bus. Adminstrn., Montgomery County Coll., Blue Bell, Pa., 1993; student, Springhouse Computer Sch., Exton, Pa., 1994-95. Columnist, corr. The Recorder, Conshohocken, Pa., 1980-81; claims supr. Liberty Mut. Ins. Co., Blue Bell, 1980-84; claims svc. rep. Met. Property & Liability Ins. Co., Wayne, Pa., 1984-87; model Frank James Assocs., Phila., 1986-87; auditor/tng. coord. Coresource, Inc., Wayne, 1987-94; sys. support analyst Del. Valley Fin. Svcs., Inc., Berwyn, Pa., 1994-95; sys. support coord. Aetna-U.S. Healthcare, Blue Bell, Pa., 1995—. Active Nat. Arbor Day Found. Mem. NAFE, U.S. Fencing Assn. Byzantine Catholic. Avocations: golf, fencing, horseback riding, needlepoint, travel. Office: Aetna-US Healthcare 930 Harvest Dr Blue Bell PA 19422-1959

HALAS, PAUL ANTHONY, JR., business appraisal and valuation specialist, consultant; b. Chgo., June 27, 1933; s. Paul Aloysius and Elonia Bernidene (Zelinski) H.; m. Shirley Donna Willis, Aug. 17, 1957 (dec.); children: Julie, Vickie, Jon, Carl, Jim. Student, Columbia Sch. Broadcasting, 1951-53, Northwestern U., 1957-59. Cert. mgmt. cons., N.Y. Rep. Solar Chgo. divsn. USI's, 1957-60; rep. J. W. Bolton, Inc., Lawrence, Mass., 1960-62; gen. sales mgr. Schimanek, Internat., Chgo., 1962-63; v.p. mktg. Products Engring. Co., Tinley Park, Ill., 1963-68; gen. sales mgr. Vacudyne Corp., Chicago Heights, Ill., 1968-70; mktg. mgr. Fastron Co., Franklin Park, Ill., 1970-72, Scandura, Inc., Charlotte, N.C., 1972-78; mgmt. cons. Halas & Assocs., Charlotte, 1978-85, valuation specialist, 1985—. Contbr. numerous articles on bus. valuation and appraisal. Recipient Printed award Grain Age Mag., 1976. Mem. BBB, ASME (coord. ANSI A90 com. 1974-77), Inst. Mgmt. Cons., Charlotte C. of C. Republican. Roman Catholic. Avocations: music, photography, vacation. Office: Halas & Assocs 425 Roselawn Pl Charlotte NC 28211-4162

HALASKA, THOMAS EDWARD, academic administrator, director, engineer; b. Childress, Tex., Aug. 4, 1945; s. Howard Edward and Ruth Marie (Reinders) H.; m. Marilyn Jean Walenta, June 7, 1969; 1 child, Jean Ellen. BSEE, Milw. Sch. Engring., 1969; MBA, Ga. State U., 1975; EdD, U. Ga., 1992. Plant engr. Tom's div. Gen. Mills, Inc., Columbus, Ga., 1969-74; dir. mfg. Stuckey Stores div. Pet, Inc., Eastman, Ga., 1974-82; dir. mgmt. info. systems Mid. Ga. Coll., Cochran, 1982-87, dir. instnl. rsch., 1987—; CIO Mid. Ga. Coll., 1992—. Mem. Soc. Coll. and Univ. Planning, Assn. for Instnl. Rsch., Univ. System Computer Network (regents adminstrv. com. info. tech.), Rotary (bd. dirs. Cochran chpt. 1986—). Republican. Roman Catholic. Avocation: pilot. Home: RR 6 Box 174 Eastman GA 31023-9029 Office: Mid Ga Coll 1100 2nd St SE Cochran GA 31014-1564

HALASZ, NICHOLAS ALEXIS, surgeon; b. Budapest, Hungary, Mar. 13, 1931; came to U.S., 1948; naturalized, 1954; s. Elek and Lilly (Boehm) H.; m. Margaret Diane Hinshaw, Dec. 5, 1964; children: Katherine Ann, Peter Nicholas. BS, Trinity Coll., 1950; MD, Yale U., 1954. Diplomate Am. Bd. Surgery, Am. Bd. Thoracic Surgery. Intern Yale-New Haven Med. Ctr., 1954-55, resident, 1956-62; asst. prof. UCLA, 1962-67; from assoc. prof. to prof. surgery U. Calif., San Diego, 1967-94, head div. anatomy, 1968-94; dir. transplantation svc. U. Calif.-San Diego Med. Ctr., 1974-94; prof. emeritus surgery U. Calif., San Diego, 1994—; chief surg. svc. VA Med. Ctr., San Diego, 1994—; dir. transplantation svc. U. Calif.-San Diego Med. Ctr., 1972-94; cons. U.S. Naval Hosps., San Diego and Camp Pendleton, Calif. Contbr. articles to profl. jours. Capt. M.C., U.S. Army, 1956-58. Grantee NIH, 1962-92, NSF, 1963-66, Am. Heart Assn., 1966-68; Markle Found. scholar in acad. medicine, 1966-71. Mem. ACS, AMA, Am. Surg. Assn., Soc. Univ. Surgeons, Transplantation Soc., Am. Soc. Transplantation Surgeons, Calif. Med. Assn., San Diego County Med. Soc., Phi Beta Kappa, Alpha Omega Alpha. Office: VA Med Ctr # 112 3350 La Jolla Village Dr San Diego CA 92161-0002

HALASZ, ROBERT JOSEPH, editor; b. Budapest, Hungary, June 11, 1937; s. Nicholas and Piroska (Szenes) H.; m. Miriam Sonia Jackson, Oct. 2, 1965 (div. 1968). BA, U. Chgo., 1959; MA, Roosevelt U., 1967. Editor Standard Edn. Corp., Chgo., 1960-79, Funk & Wagnalls Inc., N.Y.C., 1980-83. Author: The U.S. Marines, 1993. Mem. Editl. Freelancers Assn. Avocations: painting, skiing, tennis. Home: 276 Riverside Dr New York NY 10025-5204

HALASZ, STEPHEN JOSEPH, retired electro-optical systems engineer; b. Eger-Csehi, Hungary; s. Sandor and Ilona (Huszák) H.; children: Stepehn S., Christopher L. Jacqueline R. BS, Columbia U., 1955. Test engr. J.A. Maurer, Inc., N.Y.C., 1955-56; project engr. GE Co., Utica, N.Y., 1956-58; sr. physicist Avion divsn. ACF Industries, Paramus, N.J., 1958-65; head IR and Display Lab. Aerojet Gen., 1965-72; sr. specialist Xerox Electro-Optical, Pasadena, Calif., 1972-75, Ford Aeronutronic, Newport Beach, Calif., 1975-83; chief scientist Hughes Aircraft, El Segundo, Calif., 1983-92. Contbg. author: (handbook) IR Handbook, 1969. With U.S. Army, 1945. NRA. Republican. Roman Catholic. Achievements include numerous designs and research projects including optical guidance for satellite interception; IR moving target tracker; handheld thermal imager; scanned matrix for IR pattern recognition; high speed target acquisition with fused senors; others; patentee in field. Avocations: photography, antique guns. Home: 66887 San Carlos Rd Desert Hot Springs CA 92240-2622

HALBACH, EDWARD CHRISTIAN, JR., legal educator; b. Clinton, Iowa, Nov. 8, 1931; s. Edward Christian and Lewella (Sullivan) H.; m. Janet Elizabeth Bridges, July 25, 1953; children: Kristin Lynn, Edward Christian III, Kathleen Ann, Thomas Elliot, Elaine Diane. BA, U. Iowa, 1953, JD, 1958; LLM, Harvard U., 1959; LLD, U. Redlands, 1973. Assoc. prof. Sch. Law, U. Calif. at Berkeley, 1959-62, prof., 1963—, dean, 1966-75. Co-author: Materials on Decedents' Estates and Trusts, 1965, 73, 81, 87, 93, Materials on Future Interests, 1977, Death, Taxes and Family Property, 1977, California Will Drafting, 1965, 77, 92; author: Use of Trusts in Estate Planning, 1975, 81, 84, 86, 91, Fundamentals of Estate Planning, 1983, 86, 87, 89, 91, 93, 95, Summary of the Law of Trusts, 1990, 1998, Principles and Techniques of Estate Planning, 1995; reporter Uniform Probate Code, 1969, Restatement 3d Trusts Prudent Investor Rule, 1991; also articles. 1st lt. USAF, 1954-56. Mem. ABA (chmn. various coms. sect. individual rights and responsibilities and sect. real property probate adn trust law, dir. probate and trust divsn., sect. chmn.), Iowa Bar Assn., Am. Law Inst. (reporter Restatement 3d Trusts, advisor Restatement 2d, 3d Property), Am. Acad. Polit. and Social Scis., Am. Bar Found., Am. coll. Trust and Estate Counsel, Am. Coll. Tax Counsel, Internat. Acad. Estate and Trust Law (v.p., exec. com., pres.). Home: 679 San Luis Rd Berkeley CA 94707-1725 Office: U Calif Sch Law Boalt Hall Berkeley CA 94720

HALBERG, CHARLES JOHN AUGUST, JR., mathematics educator; b. Pasadena, Calif., Sept. 24, 1921; s. Charles John August and Anne Louise (Hansen) H.; m. Ariel Arfon Oliver, Nov. 1, 1941 (div. July 1969); children—Ariel (Mrs. William Walters), Charles Thomas, Niels Frederick; m. Barbro Linnea Samuelsson, Aug. 18, 1970 (dec. Jan. 1978); 1 stepchild, Ulf Erik Hjelm; m. Betty Reese Zimprich, July 27, 1985. B.A. summa cum laude, Pomona Coll., 1949; M.A. (William Lincoln Honnold fellow), UCLA, 1953, Ph.D., 1955. Instr. math. Pomona Coll., Claremont, Calif., 1949-50; assoc. math. UCLA, 1954-55; instr. math. U. Calif.-Riverside, 1955-56, asst. prof. math., 1956-61, assoc. prof. math., 1961-68, prof. math., 1968—, vice chancellor student affairs, 1964-65; dir. Scandinavian Study Center at Lund (Sweden) U., 1976-78; docent U. Goteborg, Sweden, 1969-70; bd. dirs. Fulbright Commn. for Ednl. Exchange between U.S. and Sweden, 1976-79. Author: Aftermath, 1996, (with John F. Devlin) Elementary Functions, 1967, (with Angus E. Taylor) Calculus with Analytic Geometry, 1969. Served with USAAF, 1945-46. NSF fellow U. Copenhagen, 1961-62. Mem. Math. Assn. Am. (chmn. So. Calif. sect. 1964-65, gov. 1968), Am. Math. Soc., Swedish Math. Soc., Sigma Xi, Phi Beta Kappa. Home: PO Box 2724 Carlsbad CA 92018-2724

HALBERSTAM, HEINI, mathematics educator; b. Most, Czechoslovakia, Sept. 11, 1926; came to Eng., 1939, naturalized, 1947; s. Michael and Judith (Honig) H.; m. Heather M. Peacock, Mar. 11, 1950 (dec. 1971); children: Naomi Deborah, Judith Marion, Lucy Rebecca, Michael Welsford; m. Doreen Bramley, Sept. 28, 1972. B.S. with honours, Univ. Coll., London U., 1946; M.S., London U., 1948, Ph.D., 1952. Lectr. math. U. Exeter, 1949-57; reader Royal Holloway Coll., London U., 1957-62; Erasmus Smith prof. Trinity Coll., Dublin, Ireland, 1962-64; prof. Nottingham U., England, 1964-80; prof. math. U. Ill., Urbana-Champaign, 1980-96, prof. emeritus, 1996—; vis. lectr. Brown U., 1955-56; vis. prof. U. Mich., 1966, U. Tel Aviv, 1973, U. Paris-South, 1972. Co-author: Sequences, 1966, 2d edit., 1983, Sieve Methods, 1975; co-editor math. papers of, W.R. Hamilton, H. Davenport; contbr. articles to profl. jours. Mem. London Math. Soc. (v.p. 1962-63, 74-77), Am. Math Soc.

HALBERSTAM, MALVINA, law educator, lawyer; b. Kempno, Poland, May 2, 1937; came to U.S., 1947; d. Marcus and Pearl (Halberstam) H.; m. Wolf Z. Guggenheim (separated 1981); children: Arye, Achiezer. BA cum laude, Bklyn. Coll., 1957; JD, Columbia U., 1961, MIA, 1964. Bar: N.Y. 1962, U.S. Dist. Ct. (so. dist.) N.Y. 1963, U.S. Ct. Appeals (2d cir.) 1965, U.S. Supreme Ct. 1966, Calif. 1968. Law clk. Judge Edmund L. Palmieri Fed. Dist. Ct. (so. dist.) N.Y., 1961-62; rsch. assoc. Columbia Project on Internat. Procedure, 1962-63; asst. dist. atty. N.Y. County, 1963-67; with Rifkind & Sterling, L.A., 1967-68; sr. atty. Nat. Legal Program on Health Problems of the Poor, L.A., 1969-70; prof. Sch. Law Loyola U., L.A., 1970-76; prof. Benjamin N. Cardozo Sch. Law Yeshiva U., N.Y.C., 1976—; vis. prof. Gould Law Ctr., U. Soc. Calif., L.A., 1972-73, U. Va. Sch. Law, 1975-76, U. Tex. Sch. Law, summer 1974, Hebrew U., Jerusalem, 1984-85; counselor on internat. law U.S. State Dept. Office of Legal Adviser, 1985-86; cons., 1986-92. Author: (with De Feis) Women's Legal Rights: International Agreements An Alternative to ERA?, 1987; articles and rev. editor Columbia Law Rev., 1960-61; reporter Am. Law Inst. Model Penal Code Commentaries, 1977-81; contbr. articles, commentary, book revs. to profl. publs. Mem. Bklyn. Coll. Alumni Adv. Bd. on Women's Career Devel. and Leadership Program.; mem. adv. com. to standing com. on law and nat. security, ABA; mem. study group on shape Arab-Israeli settlement, humanitarian, and demographic issues Coun. on Fgn. Rels. Kent scholar (2x); Stone scholar; recipient Jane Marks Murphy prize. Mem. Am. Law Inst., Am. Soc. Internat. Law, Assn. Bar City N.Y. (coun. on internat. affairs, com. on human rights), Internat. Law Assn. (exec. com., human rights com. Am. br.), Internat. Assn. Jewish Lawyers and Jurists (bd. govs., NGO rep. to UN), Columbia Law Sch. Alumni Assn., Phi Beta Kappa. Home: 160 Riverside Dr New York NY 10024-2106 Office: Yeshiva U Benjamin N Cardozo Sch Law 55 5th Ave Fl 10 New York NY 10003-4391

HALBERSTEIN, JOSEPH LEONARD, retired associate editor; b. Piqua, Ohio, Mar. 10, 1923; s. David and Mollie (Oberferst) H.; m. Lillian Friedman, Aug. 9, 1964; children: Richard Martin, Howard Louis. BA in Journalism, Ohio State U., 1944; postgrad., Pa. State U., 1976. Sportswriter Columbus (Ohio) Citizen, 1943-44; sports editor Lima (Ohio) News, 1944-49; circulation mgr. Town and Village, N.Y.C., 1950-52; sports editor, mng. editor Wilmington (Del.) Sunday Star, 1952-54; wire editor, sports editor Gainesville (Fla.) Sun, 1955-71; mng. editor, assoc. editor Bucks County Courier Times, Levittown, Pa., 1971-93, ret., 1993; lectr. various univs. Contbr. articles to profl. jours. Bd. dirs. ARC, Langhorne, Pa., 1971-80, Congregation Beth El, Levittown, 1978-85. Recipient 2d Pl. best column Nat. Newspaper Assn., 1961, 1st Pl. best column Keystone Press Assn., 1976, 2d Pl. best game story Basketball Writers Assn. Mem. Fla. Sportswriters Assn. (pres.), Pa. AP Mng. Editors Assn. (pres.), Soc. of Profl. Journalists (greater Phila. chpt. pres. 1981-82), Pa. Soc. of Newspaper Editors, Sigma Delta Chi. Avocations: walking, travel, computer study. Office: Bucks County Courier Times 8400 Route 13 Levittown PA 19057 *Newspapers bring information to people. Sometimes that information helps people make decisions that affect their lives or the lives of others. In journalism, one has to inform, to help, and, especially to care. Caring is what makes any endeavor a noble one.*

HALBERT, RONALD JOEL, preventive medicine physician, educator; b. Jacksboro, Tex., June 11, 1958; s. Arthur Joel and Ollie Matilda (Havens) H. BS in Biology magna cum laude, Abilene Christian U., 1979; MD, Baylor U., 1982; MPH in Epidemiology, U.C.L.A., 1990. Diplomate Am. Bd. Preventive Medicine. Pvt. practice Tex., 1985-95, Calif., 1985-95; assoc. dir. preventive medicine residency UCLA, 1992-97, lectr. Sch. Pub. Health, 1994-97; dir. clin. ops. quality initiatives divsn. Found. Health Sys., Inc., Woodland Hills, Calif., 1997-99; med. dir. Internat. Med. Corps., L.A., 1988, cons., 1992; epidemiologist Immunization Demonstration Project, L.A., 1991-93, Roybal Immunization Coalition, L.A., 1995; preventive medicine practitioner, Mission City Cmty. Network, Sepulveda, Calif., 1993; cons. U.S. Dept. Labor, Washington, 1993, Ctr. for the Study of Latino Health, L.A., 1995-96; adj. asst. prof. Sch. Pub. Health, UCLA, 1997—. Contbr. articles to profl. jours. Pres. Pan-Am. Inst. of Maritime Archaeology, San Francisco, 1993-95; dir. Internat. Med. and Ednl. Found., L.A., 1991-93, Westside Cmty. Outreach for Prevention & Edn., L.A., 1995—. Rsch. fellow Internat. Med. Corps., 1987, divsnl. fellow U.C.L.A. Sch. Pub. Health, 1988-89; recipient Humanitarian Med. award Com. for a Free Afghanistan, Washington, 1985. Fellow Am. Coll. Preventive Medicine, Adventurers' Club of L.A., Explorers Club; mem. APHA, Nat. Coun. for Internat. Health.

HALBFINGER, ANDREA SUE, journalist; b. Feb. 17, 1941. BA, Bennington Coll., 1962; MS in Journalism, Columbia U., 1963. News editor Valley Stream MAILeader, Mineola, N.Y., 1992-97, Lynbrook USA, Mineola, N.Y., 1997—; county reporter Nassau Cmty. Newspaper Group, Mineola, N.Y., 1997—. Home: 201 Mount Joy Ave Freeport NY 11520-1443

HALBOUTY, MICHEL THOMAS, geologist, petroleum engineer, petroleum operator; b. Beaumont, Tex., June 21, 1909; s. Tom Christian and Sodia (Manolley) H.; m. Billye Stevens, Dec. 27, 1981; 1 dau., Linda Fay. BS, Tex. A&M U., 1930, MS, 1931, Profl. Degree in Geol. Engring, 1956; D Eng. (hon.), Mont. Coll. Mineral Sci. and Tech., 1966; PhD in Geology (hon.), USSR Acad. Scis., 1990. Geologist, petroleum engr. Yount-Lee Oil Co., Beaumont, 1931-33; chief geologist, petroleum engr. Yount-Lee Oil Co., 1933-35; v.p., gen. mgr., chief geologist and petroleum engr. Glenn H. McCarthy, Inc., Houston, 1935-37; owner firm cons. geologists and petroleum engrs. Houston, 1937-81; chmn., chief exec. officer Michel T. Halbouty Energy Co., 1981—; discoverer numerous oil and gas fields La. and Tex.; adj. prof. Tex. Tech U.; vis. prof. Tex. A&M U.; hon. prof. geology Nanjing (China) U., 1993. Author several books. Contbr. numerous papers on geology and petroleum engring. to profl. jours. Served as lt. col. AUS, 1942-45. Recipient Tex. Mid-Continent Oil and Gas Assn. disting. service award for an ind., 1965; named engr. of yr. Tex. Soc. Profl. Engrs. and Engrs. Council, 1968; recipient Disting. Alumni award Tex. A&M U., 1968; Michel T. Halbouty Geoscis. Bldg. named for him, 1977; recipient DeGolyer Disting. Service medal Soc. Petroleum Engrs. of Am. Inst. Mining, Metall. and Petroleum Engrs., 1971; hon. mem. Spindletop sect., 1972; hon. mem. inst., 1973; Anthony F. Lucas Gold medal, 1975; Pecora award NASA, 1977; Horatio Alger award Am. Schs. and Colls. Assn., 1978, Spirit of Life award City of Hope, 1978, Breath of Life award Cystic-Fibrosis Found., 1981, merit medal Circum-Pacific Council for Energy and Mineral Resources, 1982, Hoover medal Am. Assn. Engring. Socs., 1982, disting. service award Paul Carrington chpt. SAR, 1983, Tex. Heritage award Angleton C. of C., Tex., 1983. Mem. AAAS, Am. Assn. Petroleum Geologists (hon., pres. 1966-67, Human Needs award 1975, Sidney Powers Meml. medal 1977), Am. Soc. Oceanography, Internat. Assn. Sedimentology, Inst. Petroleum, London, Am. Petroleum Inst., Am. Inst. Mining and Metall. Engrs., Soc. Econ. Paleontologists and Mineralogists, Soc. Econ. Geologists, Mineral. Soc. Am., Geol. Soc. Am., Soc. Exploration Geophysicists (hon.), Nat. Acad. Engring., Houston Geol. Soc. (hon.), N.Y. Acad. Sci., Tex. Acad. Sci. (Disting. Tex. Scientist of Yr. 1983), Am. Inst. Profl. Geologists, Am. Geol. Inst., Tex., Nat. socs. profl. engrs., Gulf Coast Assn. Geol. Socs. (hon.). Episcopalian. Clubs: Ramada, Houston, Petroleum, River Oaks Country (Houston); Dallas Petroleum; Eldorado Country, Vintage (Palm Desert, Calif.); New Orleans Petroleum; Cosmos (Washington); Broadmoor, Kissing Camels (Colorado Springs). Home: 2121 Kirby Dr Houston TX 77019-6035 Office: Halbouty Center 5100 Westheimer Rd Houston TX 77056-5596

HALBROOK, RITA ROBERTSHAW, artist, sculptor; b. Greenville, Miss., May 22, 1930; d. William Daniel and Artye Loree (Robinson) R.; m. David McCall Halbrook, Oct. 1, 1949; children: Ann L. Peden, D. M. Jr., Tina H. Donahoo, Andrew L. BFA, Delta State U., 1982. Bd. dirs. Miss. Art Colony, Utica, 1977-80, publicity dir., 1977-84. One-woman shows include Miss. ETV Studios, Jackson, 1985, Gulf South Gallery, McComb, Miss., 1987, State Capitol Rotunda, Jackson, State Dept. Agr. and Miss. Arts Commn., 1988, New Stage Theatre, Jackson, 1992, The Courthouse Racquet Club Galleries, Jackson, 1992; two-woman show Pegasus Gallery, Miss. State U., 1986; exhibited in group shows at Cottonlandia Mus., Greenwood, Miss., 1987, 93, Miss. Mus. Art, Jackson, 1989, 93, Gov.'s Mansion, Southeastern Crafts Conf., Jackson, 1991, Miss. Mus. Art, Jackson, Wiregrass Mus. Art, Dothan, Ala., 1993, Cork Gallery, Avery Fisher Hall, Lincoln Ctr. Pla., N.Y.C., 1994, others; commd. artist Delta Catfish Mus., Belzoni, Miss., 1993, St. Therese's Cath. Ch., Jackson, 1996, others; represented in collections Delta State U., Ernst and Whinney, Tatung, Inc. (Taiwan), Citizens Bank Yazoo City, former Pres. and Mrs. George Bush, The White House; subject in publs.: (books) Mississippi Artsts, 1977; Of Arts and Artists, 1980, Artists of the South, Vol. I, 1992, (newspaper) The Clarion Ledger-Jackson Daily News, 1985. Mem. county com. Miss. Republicans, 1963-69, inter-agy. coun. Partners in Health and Nutrition, 1989—, parish coun. All Saints Cath. Ch.; bd. dirs. Helping Hands Humphreys County, 1991—. Recipient Best in Show and Second award Miss. Art Colony, 1986, Best in Show, Nat. League Am. PEN Women, 1987, 95. Mem. Nat. League Am. Pen Women (pres. Delta, Miss. br. 1996—), Craftsmen's Guild Miss. (exhibiting, bd. dirs. 1993-96), Profl. Artists League Miss., Ofcl. Miss. Women's Club, Delta State U. Alumni Assn. (Disting. 1993). Democrat. Avocations: hiking, swimming, reading. Home: 501 Cohn St Belzoni MS 39038-3703 Studio: 501 Cohn St Rear Belzoni MS 39038-3703

HALDAR, FRANCES LOUISE, business educator, accountant, treasurer; b. Mineola, N.Y., July 2, 1948; d. Alfred Karl and Gudrun Maria (Lucks) Loschen; m. Kali S. Haldar, Feb. 29, 1972; children: Neil Alexander, Monica Joyce. AA, The Ohio Sate U., 1985, BSBA in Acctg. summa cum laude, 1989, MBA, 1991, PhD, 1999. Adminstrv. asst. Pam Am. World Airways Inc., N.Y.C., 1968-73; acct., treas. K.S. Haldar, MD, Inc., Mansfield, Ohio, 1978—; adj. prof. bus. to prof., then assoc. prof. acctg. N. Ctrl. Tech. Coll., Mansfield, 1991—, acad. advisor, 1991—, assoc. prof. bus., 1993-96, assoc. prof. acctg., 1996-99, prof. acctg., 1999—. Mem. ASCD, Nat. Bus. Edn. Assn., Am. Assn. C.C., Am. Acctg. Assn., Inst. Mgmt. Accts., Golden Key, Phi Kappa Phi, Beta Gamma Sigma. Avocations: reading, traveling. Office: N Ctrl Tech Coll PO Box 698 Mansfield OH 44901-0698

HALDEMAN, JOE WILLIAM, novelist; b. Oklahoma City, June 9, 1943; s. Jack Carroll and Lorena (Spivey) H.; m. Mary Gay Potter, Aug. 21, 1965. B.S. in Physics and Astronomy, U. Md., 1967; M.F.A. in English, U. Iowa, 1975. Assoc. prof. writing program MIT, 1983—. Author: War Year, 1972, The Forever War, 1975, Mindbridge, 1976, Planet of Judgement, 1977, All My Sins Remembered, 1977, Infinite Dreams, 1978, World Without End, 1979, Worlds, 1971, (with Jack C. Haldeman II) There Is No Darkness, 1983, Worlds Apart, 1993, Dealing in Futures, 1985, Tool of the Trade, 1987, Buying Time, 1989, The Hemingway Hoax, 1990, Worlds Enough and Time, 1993, 1968, 1995, None So Blind, 1996, Saul's Death and Other Poems, 1997, Forever Peace, 1997; editor: (with Martin H. Greenburg and Charles Waugh) Body Armor: 2000, 1986, Supertanks, 11987, Spacefighters, 1988; editor: Cosmic Laughter, 1974, Study War No More, 1977, Nebula Awards 17, 1983. Served with U.S. Army, 1967-69. Decorated Purple Heart; recipient Hugo award, 1976, 77, 91, 95, 98, Nebula award, 1975, 91, 93, Rhysling award, 1984, 91, World Fantasy award, 1993, John W. Campbell award, 1998. Mem. Sci. Fiction Writers Am. (treas. 1970-73, chmn. grievance com. 1977-79, pres. 1992-94), Authors Guild, Writers Guild, Poets and Writers, Inc., Nat. Space Inst.

HALDEMAN, SCOTT, neurology educator; b. June 23, 1943. DC, Palmer Coll. Chiropractic, 1964; BS, U. Pretoria, 1968, MS, 1970; PhD, U. B.C., 1973, MD, 1976. Clin. prof. dept. neurology U. Calif., Irvine, 1984—; adj. prof. rsch. dept. L.A. Chiropractic Coll., 1985—. Mem. N. Am. Spine Soc. (past pres. 1988-89), World Fedn. Chiropractic (chmn. rsch. coun. 1990—). E-mail: HaldemanMD@aol.com. Home: 1125 E 17th St Ste W127 Santa Ana CA 92701-2228

HALDEN, MARTHA ANN, pediatrics nurse, educator; b. Dallas, July 22, 1933; d. Ollie and Nona I. (Lavender) Gouger; m. William J. Halden, Oct. 23, 1954; children: William J., Sue Halden Albe, Daniel L., Mary Beth Sherman. Student, So. Meth. U., 1950-51; diploma, Meth. Hosp. of Dallas, 1954. RN. Pediatric nurse physician's office, Austin, Tex., Dallas. Mem. Tex. Nurses Assn.

HALE, ALLEAN LEMMON, writer, educator; b. Bethany, Nebr.; d. Clarence Eugene and Constance (Harlan) Lemmon; m. Mark Pendleton Hale, Dec. 31, 1936 (dec. Nov., 1977); children: Susanna, Mark Jr. AA, Columbia Coll., 1933; BA in English with Distinction, U. Mo., 1935; MA in Humanities, U. Iowa, 1962. Prodn. asst. in drama Chgo. Theol. Sem., 1941; alumni dir., editor Columbia (Mo.) Coll., 1951-56; instr. comm. U. Iowa, Iowa City, 1960-62; contract playwright Friendship Press, N.Y.C., 1960-75; instr. creative writing Adult Edn. Program, Urbana, Ill., 1965; editl. asst. Oscar Lewis Anthropologist, Urbana, 1966-69; instr. creative writing Parkland Coll., Champaign, Ill., 1979-80; editor Tenessee Williams Plays New Dirs. Publishers, N.Y.C., 1996-99; adj. prof. in theater U. Ill., Urbana, 1996—; editl. asst. to Lyle Leverich on Tom: The Unknown Tennessee Williams, 1986-87; mem. editl. bd. The Tennessee Williams Literary Jour., New Orleans, 1989—; lectr. Am. Playwrights Exhibit Humanities Rsch. Ctr., U. Tex., Austin, 1994; cons. to PBS Am. Masters Tennessee Williams: Orpheus of the American Stage, Internat. Cultural Programming, N.Y., 1995; photo cons. A&E Biography TV program Tennessee Williams, 1998. Author: (book)) Petticoat Pioneer, 1957, 2d. rev. edit., 1968; editor: (books) Tennessee Williams, The Notebook of Trigorin, 1997, Tennessee Williams, Not About Nightingales, 1998, Tennessee Williams, Stairs to the Roof, 1999; contbr. The Cambridge Companion to Tennessee Williams, 1997; playwright: The Hero (Samuel French Playwriting award 1933, Zeta Phi Eta Playwriting Contest 1st, 1933, Last Flight Over, Midwestern Intercollegiate Playwriting Contest 1st, 1935, The Red Bastard of Genesis, Mahan Story Contest, U. Mo. 1st, 1935, They Walk in Darkness, U. Mo. Dramatic Arts Contest, 1949; other plays include: Two in a Trap, 1966, The Second Coming of Mrs. C., 1971, The Battle at Liberty Courthouse, 1975; also 27 articles on Tennessee Williams published in literary jours., and presentations to univs., confs. literary festivals. Mem. Krannert Art Mus. Assocs., 1980—; Media chair Internat. Conf. on Women and Peace, U. Ill., 1989. Recipient 1st award best column in mag., Nat. Fedn. Presswomen, 1953, Distinguished Alumni award Columbia (Mo.) Coll., 1964. Mem. Champaign Social Sci. Club, U. Ill. Women's Club, Red Herring Fiction Workshop, Phi Beta Kappa. Democrat. Avocations: art, history, langs., aerobics. Home: 305 G H Baker Dr Urbana IL 61801-1160 Office: U Ill Dept Theatre 4-122 Krannert Ctr Pfm Arts 500 S Goodwin Ave Urbana IL 61801-3741

HALE, BRUCE DONALD, retired marketing professional; b. Oak Park, Ill., Dec. 21, 1933; s. Edward Garden and Mildred Lillian (Pelc) H.; m. Nancy Ann Novotny, July 2, 1955 (div. 1976); children: Jeffrey Bruce, Karen Jill Hale; m. Connie Luella Green Gunderson, Apr. 21, 1979. BA in Econs., Wesleyan U., Middletown, Conn., 1955. Trainee Caterpillar Tractor Co.,

Peoria, Ill., 1955-56, dealer tng. rep., 1956-59; dist. rep. Caterpillar Tractor Co., Albuquerque, 1959-62; asst. sales mgr. Rust Tractor Co., Albuquerque, 1962-65; gen. sales mgr. Rust Tractor Co., Albuqerque, 1965-71, v.p. sales, 1971-81, v.p. mktg., 1981-96; ret., 1996. Mem. Am. Mining Congress, Soc. Mining Engrs., Associated Contractors N.Mex., Associated Equipment Distbrs., Rocky Mountain Coal Mining Inst., N.Mex. Mining Assn., Albuquerque Country Club. Avocations: golf, fishing, music, classic cars. Home: 9508 Layton Pl NE Albuquerque NM 87111-1368

HALE, CHARLES DENNIS, education educator; b. L.A., Jan. 27, 1954; s. Roland Kieth Sr. and JoAnne (Steel) H.; m. Dilna Maria Victor, Sept. 10, 1977. BS, U. So. Miss., 1977; MA in Health Edn., U. Fla., 1982, EdS, 1986, EdD, 1989. Health edn. cons. Dist. Health Program Office, Gainesville, Fla., 1982-85; edn. specialist Alachua County Health Dept., Gainesville, 1985-87; project mgr. Family Resource Ctr., Gainesville, 1987; health educator U. Fla., Gainesville, 1988-89; assoc. prof., dept. chair St. Leo (Fla.) Coll., 1989-94; coord. acad. programs, assessment and evaluation U. Ga., 1994-96; assoc. prof., dir. grad. studies in edn. St. Leo (Fla.) Coll., 1996—. Contbr. articles to profl. publs. Recipient 6 grants. Mem. Am. Assn. for Higher Edn., Am. Ednl. Rsch. Assn., Assn. Continuing Higher Edn., Assn. for Instnl. Rsch., Assn. for Study of Higher Edn., Nat. Coun. Measurement in Edn. Roman Catholic. Avocations: writing, travel, learning. Office: Saint Leo Coll MC 2005 PO Box 6665 Saint Leo FL 33574-6665

HALE, CHARLES MARTIN, stockbroker; b. London, Jan. 19, 1936; s. Charles Sidney and Carmen Rosa (de Mora) H.; m. Kaaren Alexis Garfunkel, Feb. 11, 1967; children: Melissa Lauren, Amanda Suzanne. BS in Geology, Stanford U., 1957; MBA, Harvard U., 1963. Gen. ptnr. Hirsch & Co., N.Y.C., 1963-70; mng. dir. A.G. Becker & Co., London, 1970-83; gen. ptnr. Lehman Bros., Kuhn Loeb & Co., London, 1983-84; chmn. Donaldson Lufkin & Jenrette Internat., Ltd, London, 1984—; chmn. U.K. Assn. of NYSE mems. Served to lt. USN, 1958-61. Mem. The Pilgrim Soc., Harvard Club (N.Y.C.), City of London Club, Annabel's Club, Harry's Bar Club, Mark's Club, Hurlingham Club, Vanderbilt Club, Delta Kappa Epsilon. Republican. Episcopalian. Home: 33 Lyall Mews, London SW1X 8DJ, England Office: Donaldson Lufkin & Jenrette Internat, 99 Bishopgate, London EC2M 3XD, England

HALE, CHARLES RUSSELL, lawyer; b. Talpa, Tex., Oct. 17, 1916; s. Charles L. and Exa (Evans) H.; m. Clementine L. Moore, Jan. 5, 1946; children: Robert R., Norman B. AB, Stanford U., 1939; JD, Fordham U., 1950. Bar: N.Y. 1950, Calif. 1953. Supr., United Geophys. Co., Pasadena, Calif., 1940-46; mem. patent staff Bell Telephone Labs., N.Y.C., 1947-48, Sperry Gyroscope Co., Great Neck, N.Y., 1948-51; practiced in Pasadena, 1951-54; ptnr. Christie, Parker & Hale, Pasadena, 1954-87; retired, 1987. Mem. ABA, IEEE, Rancho Santa Fe (Calif.) Golf Club. Home: PO Box 616 Rancho Santa Fe CA 92067-0616 Office: Christie Parker & Hale 350 W Colorado Blvd Pasadena CA 91105-1855

HALE, CHRISTY, illustrator, designer, art educator; b. Southbridge, Mass., Jan. 21, 1955; d. Harold Charles and Eunice (Sherman) H.; m. Scott Julian Apostolou, Aug. 31, 1991; 1 child, Katherine Hale. BA, Lewis and Clark Coll., Portland, Oreg., 1977, MAT, 1980; BFA, Pratt Inst., 1986. Art asst. E.P. Dutton, N.Y.C., 1986-87; assoc. designer Aperture Books, N.Y.C., 1988-90; sr. designer G.P. Putnam's Sons & Philomel, N.Y.C., 1988-90; adj. prof. Pratt Inst., Bklyn., 1995—; interim art dir. Macmillan Children's Books, N.Y.C., 1990-91; art dir. Four Winds Press, N.Y.C., 1990-94, Lee & Low Books, N.Y.C., 1991—. Illustrator: Problems to Solve, 1993, Juan Bobo and the Pig, 1993, The Ancestor Tree, 1994, Paco and the Witch, 1995, Those Calculating Crows, 1996, Elizabeti's Doll, 1998. Democrat. Avocations: letterpress printing, travel.

HALE, CYNTHIA LYNETTE, religious organization administrator; b. Roanoke, Va., Oct. 27, 1952. BA, Hollins Coll., 1975; MDiv, Duke U., 1979; D in Ministry, United Theol. Sem., Dayton, Ohio, 1991. Ordained Disciples of Christ Ch., Va., 1977. Head resident Hollins (Va.) Coll., 1975-76; intern to minister St. Mark's United Meth. Ch., Charlotte, N.C., 1976; undergrad. counselor Office of Minority Affairs Duke U., Durham, N.C., 1976-77; intern to minister Staunton Meml. Ch., Pittsboro, N.C., 1977-78; coordinating counselor summer transitional program Duke U., Durham, N.C., 1978; chaplain Fed. Correctional Instn., Butner, N.C., 1978-83; chaplain, instr. staff tng. acad. Fed. Prison System, Glynco, Ga., 1983-85; pastor, developer Ray of Hope Christian Ch., Decatur, Ga., 1986—; 1st vice moderator Christian Ch. (Disciples of Christ), U.S. and Can., 1993—; bd. dirs. Coun. on Christian Unity, 1978-81; bd. trustees Disciples Nat. Convocation, 1980-86, pres. 1982-84, pres. ministers' fellowship, 1990—; task force on Renewal and Structural Reform, Disciples of Christ, 1980-87, adminstrv. com. 1982-87, gen. bd., 1982-88; bd. dirs. Disciples Divsn. Higher Edn., St. Louis, 1986-89; bd. trustees Lexington (Ky.) Theol. Sem., 1990—; bd. dirs. Disciples' Nat. Evangelic Assn., 1991—. Mem. governing bd. Nat. Coun. Chs., 1978-83, panel on bio-ethical concerns, 1980-82; mem. Project Impact-Dekalb. Recipient Liberation award Disciples Nat. Conv., 1984, Religion award DeKalb Br. NAACP, 1990, Religious award for dedicated svc. Ninety-Nine Breakfast Club, award Martin Luther King's Bd. of Preachers, 1993, Chosen award Atlanta Gospel Choice, 1998. Office: Ray of Hope Christian Ch 3936 Rainbow Dr Decatur GA 30034-2213

HALE, DANNY LYMAN, financial executive; b. Ft. Lauderdale, Fla., Mar. 23, 1944; s. Thomas Hatten and Marion June (Frizzell) H.; m. Reda Fay Kofahl, June 10, 1966; 1 child, Matthew Bryan. BA in Econs., Yale U., 1966. Cons. in fin. planning Gen. Electric Co., Fairfield, Conn., 1977-78; mgr. fin. stragety devel. Gen. Electric Co., Louisville, 1978-79, mgr. fin. ops., 1979-80; mgr. divsn. fin. ops. GE Credit Corp., Stamford, Conn., 1980-82, v.p., dept. gen. mgr., 1982-84; mng. dir., mgr. bus. devel. Kidder Peabody Group, N.Y.C., 1987-88; pres. chase Comml. Corp., Chase Manhattan Bank, Paramus, N.J., 1988-91; exec. v.p. U.S.F. & G. Corp., Balt., 1991, exec. v.p., CFO, 1993-98; exec. v.p., CFO Promus Hotel Corp., Memphis, 1999—. With U.S. Army, 1967-69. Republican. Congregationalist. Home: 2590 Johnson Rd Germantown TN 38139 Office: Promus Hotel Corp 755 Crossover Ln Memphis TN 38117-4900

HALE, DAVID CLOVIS, former state representative; b. Sacramento, Aug. 14, 1964; s. Clovis Ray and Judy Garland (Lee) H.; m. Shannon Lynn Ruyle, June 19, 1993. BA in Social Sci., Cedarville Coll., 1986; M in internat. bus., St. Louis U., 1995. Asst. mgr. Assocs. Fin. Corp., Fairborn, Ohio, 1986-87; br. fin. rep. Am. Family Fin. Svc., St. Louis, 1987-88; state rep. State of Mo., Jefferson City, 1989-94; mgr. external affairs AT&T Wireless Svcs., St. Louis, 1995—. Mem. Am. Legis. Exch. Coun. Health Care Task Force, 1989-93, Trade, Travel and Tourism Task Force, 1993-94, Missourians First Task Force, 1992-94; allocator United Way, 1990-93; active First Evang. Free Ch., St. Louis. Mem. World Affairs Coun. (bd. dirs.), St. Louis World Trade Club St. Louis. Home: 2065 Wealdwood Ct Kirkwood MO 63122-6735 Office: AT&T Wireless Svcs 400 S Woods Mill Rd Chesterfield MO 63017-3429

HALE, DAVID FREDRICK, health care company executive; b. Gadsden, Ala., Jan. 8, 1949; s. Millard and Mildred Earline (McElroy) H.; m. Linda Carol Sadorski, Mar. 14, 1975; children: Shane Michael, Tara Renee, Erin Nicole, David Garrett. BA, Jacksonville State U. Dir. product mgmt. Ortho Pharm. Corp. divsn. Johnson & Johnson, Raritan, N.J., 1978-80; v.p. mktg. BBL Microbiology Sys. divsn. Becton Dickinson & Co., Cockeysville, Md., 1980-81, v.p., gen. mgr., 1981-82; sr. v.p. mktg. and bus. devel. Hybritech, Inc., San Diego, 1982, pres., 1983-86, CEO, 1986-87; pres., CEO, bd. dirs. Gensia Sicor, Inc., San Diego, 1987-97, Women First HealthCare, Inc., 1998—; bd. dirs. Dura Pharms., LMA N.Am., Metabasis Therapeutics, Children's Hosp., Francis Parker Sch., U. Calif. San Diego Found., San Diego Econ. Devel. Corp., Biocom San Diego; founder CONNECT. Mem. Young Pres.'s Orgn. Republican. Episcopalian. Home: PO Box 8925 16596 Via Lago Azul Rancho Santa Fe CA 92067 Office: Women First HealthCare Inc 12220 El Camino Real Ste 400 San Diego CA 92130-2091

HALE, DEAN EDWARD, social services administrator; b. Balt., Aug. 4, 1950; s. James Russell and Marjorie Elinor (Hoerman) H.; m. Lucinda Hoyt Muniz, 1979; children: Christopher Deane, Lydia Alice JeeSoo. BA in Social Work, U. Pa., 1975; postgrad., U. London, 1974, U. Oreg., 1976, Portland State U., 1993, 95—. Dir. recreation Hoffman Homes for Children, Gettysburg, Pa., 1970; social worker Holt Adoption Program, Inc., Eugene, Oreg., 1975-78; supr. social svcs. Holt Internat. Children's Svcs., Eugene, 1978-84, Asia rep., 1984-90, program mgr., 1990-94, interim dir. internat. programs, 1994-95, dir. China, 1995-97, dir. social svcs. for India, 1997—; guest lectr. U. Oreg.; cons. internat. child welfare, 1982—; co-founder Family Opportunities Unltd. Inc., 1981—. Author: Adoption, A Family Affair, 1981, When Your Child Comes Home, 1986. Pres. Woodtique Heights Homeowners Assn., 1980-91, also bd. dirs.; pres. Our Saviour's Luth. Ch., 1981-85; bd. dirs. Greenpeace of Oreg., 1979-84; cons., campaign worker Defazio for Congress, 1988, 87-90; mem. Westside Neighborhood Quality Project, 1988. Named Outstanding New Jaycee, Gettysburg Jaycees, 1971. Mem. NASW (bd. dirs. 1978-80, sec. 1979-80), Nat. Assn. Christian Social Workers, Acad. Cert. Baccalaureate Social Workers. Fax: 541-683-4339. E-mail: halel@juno.com. Home: 931 Taylor St Eugene OR 97402-4451 Office: PO Box 2880 1195 City View St Eugene OR 97402-3325

HALE, JACK K., mathematics educator, research center administrator; b. Dudley, Ky., Oct. 3, 1928; s. James Marion and Cora Lee (Kelly) H.; m. Hazel Reynolds. BA in Math., Berea Coll., 1949; PhD in Math., Purdue U., 1953; DSc (hon.), Rijksuniveriteit-Gent, Belgium, 1983; doctor honoris causa, Stuttgart U., Federal Republic of Germany, 1988, Tech. U. Lisbon, 1991, Rostoch U., Federal Rep. Germany, 1999. Instr. Purdue U., West Lafayette, Ind., 1949-54; with Sandia Corp., Albuquerque, 1954-57, Remington-Rand Univac, St. Paul, 1957-58, Rsch. Inst. for Advanced Study, Balt., 1958-64; prof. div. applied math. Brown U., Providence, 1964-89, chmn., 1973-76; Regents' prof. Ga. Inst. Tech., Atlanta, 1988-98, dir. Ctr. for Dynamical Systems and Nonlinear Studies, 1989-98; regents prof. emeritus Ga. Inst. Tech., 1998—. Author: Oscillations in Nonlinear Systems, 1963, Functional Differential Equations, 1977, Ordinary Differential Equations, 1978, Methods of Bifurcate Theory, 1982, Introduction to Infinite Dimensional Dynamic Systems, 1984, Asymptomatic Behavior of Dissip. Systems, 1988, Dynamics and Bifurcation, 1992, Introduction to Fundamental Differential Equations, 1993; editor in chief Jour. Differential Equations, 1981—. Recipient Chauvenet prize Math. Assn. Am., 1965; Guggeheim fellow, 1979-80; disting. alumnus, Purdue, U., Berea Coll. Fellow Royal Soc. Edinburgh (hon.), Brazilian Acad. Sci. (corr.); mem. Polish Acad. Sci. (fgn.), Am. Math. Soc., Am. Acad. Mechanics, Brazilian Math. Soc. Home: 1480 Rainer Falls Dr NE Atlanta GA 30329-4104 Office: Dynamical Systems and Nonlinear Studies Ga Inst Tech Ctr Atlanta GA 30332

HALE, JAMES THOMAS, retail company executive, lawyer; b. Mpls., May 14, 1940; s. Thomas Taylor and Alice Louise (Mc Connon) H.; m. Sharon Sue Johnson, Aug. 27, 1960; children: David Scott, Eric James, Kristin Lynn. BA, Dartmouth Coll., 1962; LLB, U. Minn., 1965. Bar: Minn. Law clk. Chief Justice Earl Warren, U.S. Supreme Ct., 1965-66; asso. firm Faegre & Benson, Mpls., 1966-73; ptnr. Faegre & Benson, 1973-79; v.p., dir. corp. growth Gen. Mills, Inc., 1979-80, v.p. fin. and control consumer non-foods, 1981; sr. v.p., gen. counsel, corp. sec. Dayton-Hudson Corp., Mpls., 1981—; adj. prof. U. Minn., 1967-73; dir. N. Atlantic Life Ins. Co.; bd. dirs. Minn. Continuing Legal Edn. Mem. exec. com. Fund Legal Aid Soc., others. Mem. Hennepin County Bar Assn., Order of Coif, Phi Beta Kappa. Office: Dayton-Hudson Corp 777 Nicollet Mall Minneapolis MN 55402-2055*

HALE, JOSEPH RICE, church organization executive; b. Texarkana, Tex., Mar. 25, 1935; s. Alfred Clay and Bess (Akin) H.; m. Mary Richey, June 2, 1964; 1 son, Jeffrey Glen. BA, Asbury Coll., Wilmore, Ky., 1957; BD, So. Methodist U., 1960; DD, Asbury Theol. Sem., 1978; LHD (hon.), Fla. So. Coll., 1994. Ordained to ministry Meth. Ch., 1958. Pastor Meth. Ch., Sunset, Tex., 1958-60; evangelist, 1960-66; assoc. dir. dept. evangelism Bd. Evangelism, Meth. Ch., 1966-68, dir. ecumenical evangelism, 1968-74; dir. evangelization devel. Bd. Discipleship, United Meth. Ch., 1975-76; gen. sec. World Meth. Council, 1976—; exec. com. Key 73, 1970-73; sec. working group evangelism Nat. Council Chs., 1972; pres. Communications Found., Inc., 1974-75; world ambassador Internat. Prayer Fellowship, 1974; exec. com. Evangelization Forum, 1973-75; registrar World Meth. Evangelism Convocation, Jerusalem, 1974; mem. Conf. Secs. Christian World Communions, 1976—, chmn. Christian World Communions, 1983-86. Author: Design for Evangelism, 1970, Christ Matters!, 1971, God's Moment, 1972; contbr. articles to profl. jours.; producer: The Spirit is Moving, 1980 (video prodn.) Roots of Faith, 1979, To Live to God, 1984, Nairobi, 1986, Singapore, 1991, Rio de Janeiro,1996, Rio: Walking in the Spirit, 1996, One People In All the World, 1996; editor proc. 13th-17th World Meth. Confs. Recipient Key to City of Daytona Beach Fla., 1963-64, Asbury Coll. Alumni award, 1977, Disting. Svc. award for ecumenical rels. Christian Meth. Episcopal Ch., 1994, Philip award Nat. Assn. United Meth. Evangelists, 1998; named Ky. col., 1977; decorated Great Cross of Merit, Equestrian Order of the Holy Sepulchre in Jerusalem, 1992. Home: 34 Forest Park Dr Waynesville NC 28786-8231 Office: World Meth Coun PO Box 518 575 Lakeshore Dr Lake Junaluska NC 28745-9742

HALE, JUDSON DRAKE, SR., editor; b. Boston, Mar. 16, 1933; s. Roger Drake and Marian (Sagendorph) H.; m. Sara Huberlie, Sept. 6, 1958; children: Judson Drake, Daniel, Christopher. BA, Dartmouth Coll., 1958; D Journalism (hon.), New Eng. Coll., 1984; LittD (hon.), Franklin Pierce Coll., 1987; LHD (hon.), Keene State Coll., 1989. Asst. editor Yankee, Inc., Dublin, N.H., 1958-61, assoc. editor, 1961-63, mng. editor, 1963-69; editor-in-chief Yankee Mag., Old Farmers Almanac; v.p. Yankee Pub. Inc., Dublin, 1969—; editor, v.p. Old Farmers Almanac; dir. Solar Environ. Scis., Inc. Author: Inside New England, 1982, The Education of a Yankee, 1987; editor: That New England, 1968; editor The Best of Yankee mag., 1985, The Best of the Old Farmer's Almanac, 1991, The Old Farmer's Almanac Book of Everyday Advice. Trustee MacDowell Colony. Served with AUS, 1955-57. Mem. Cheshire County Dartmouth Alumni Club, Mass. Hist. Soc., Dublin Lake Club, Phi Kappa Psi. Democrat. Episcopalian. Home: Valley Rd Dublin NH 03444 Office: Yankee Pub Inc Main St Dublin NH 03444-0520

HALE, JUDY ANN, education educator; b. Tuscaloosa, Ala., Oct. 16, 1955; d. Rogene Bae and Berta Inez (Smelley) Hale. BA, David Lipscomb U., 1978; MEd, Ala. A&M U., 1989; PhD, Miss. State U., 1994. Art tchr. grades 7-8 Scottsboro (Ala.) Jr. High, 1978-81; headstart tchr. Bridgeport (Ala.) Elem. Sch., 1983-84, tchr. grade 1, 1984-87; migrant tchr. grades K-6 Stevenson (Ala.) Elem. Sch., 1987-89, kindergarten tchr., 1989-91; tchg. asst. Miss. State U., Starkville, 1991-94; asst. prof. Jacksonville (Ala.) State U., 1994—; owner, operator The Art Studio, Scottsboro, 1981-83; presenter in field. Mem. beautification coun. C. of C., Scottsboro, 1983; mem., v.p. Doctoral Student's Assn., Starkville, 1991-94. Faculty Rsch. grantee Jacksonville State U., 1994-96. Mem. AAUW (sec. 1987-89, pres. 1989-91), DAR, Am. Assn. for Edn. Young Children, Mid South Ednl. Rsch. Assn., Ala. Assn. for Young Children, Jacksonville Exch. Club, Beta Phi, Delta Kappa Gamma, Phi Delta Kappa (historian 1993-94). Avocations: traveling, home decorating, gardening, creative arts, racquetball.$D. Office: Jacksonville State Univ Ramona Wood Bldg 700 Pelham Rd N Jacksonville AL 36265-1623

HALE, KAYCEE, research marketing professional; b. Mount Hope, W.Va., July 18, 1947; d. Bernard McFadden and Virginia Lucille (Mosley) H. AA, Compton Coll., 1965; BS, Calif. State U., Dominguez Hills, 1981. Fashion model O'Bryant Talent Agy., L.A., 1967-77; faculty mem. L.A. Trade-Tech. Coll., 1969-71, Fashion Inst., L.A., 1969-77, 1975—; pres. The Fashion Co., L.A., 1970-75; co-host The Fashion Game TV Show, L.A., 1982-87; exec. dir. Fashion Inst. Design and Merchandising Resource & Rsch. Ctr., L.A., 1975—, Fashion Inst. Design and Merchandising Mus. and Libr., L.A., 1977-98; lectr. in field, internat., 1969—. Author: (brochure) What's Your I.Q. (Image Quotient)?; (tape) Image Builders; contbg. editor Library Management in Review; columnist The Public Image, 1990; contbr. Bowker Annual 1990-91, (newsletter) Northeast Library System, 1991. Adv. bd. Calif. State U., Long Beach, 1988-91. Mem. ALA, Spl. Librs. Assn. (pres. elect 1986—, pres. 1987-88, bd. dirs. So. Calif. chpt. 1985—), Spl. Librs. Adv. Coun. (pub. rels. com. 1987-89), SLA Libr. Mgmt. Div. (chmn.-elect 1987-88, chmn. 1988-89, pres.'s task force on image of libr./info. profl.), Textile Assn. L.A. (bd. dirs. 1985-87), Calif. Media and Libr. Educators Assn., Am. Mktg. Assn., Western Mus. Conf., Am. Mus. Assn., Costume Soc. Am. Office: Fashion Inst Design & Merchandising 919 S Grand Ave Los Angeles CA 90015-1421

HALE, KENNETH BYRON, retired law enforcement officer, eudcator; b. Caledonia, Mich., May 18, 1920; s. Herman and Lucille Florence (Rhead) H.; m. Erika Anna Justus, Mar. 10, 1943; children: Kenneth Byron, Thomas Gerard, Judith Eileen. BS in Police Adminstrn., Mich. State U., 1941. Agt. U.S. Secret Svc., Toledo, Ohio, Washington, 1941-42; spl. agt. U.S. Secret Svc., Chgo. and Washington, 1945-47, Detroit, 1949-55; spl. agt. in charge U.S. Secret Svc., Omaha and Indpls., 1955-71; adminstr., instr. Ind. Ctrl. Coll., Indpls., 1972-74; chief of police Police Dept., Indpls., 1974-75. Mem. Marion County Area Police Svcs., 1965-70; scoutmaster Boy Scouts Am., 1953-59; precinct insp. Marion County Election Bd., Indpls., 1977-98. Capt., Mil. Intelligence U.S. Army, 1942-45, 47-49 ETO. Mem. Internat. Assn. Chiefs of Police, Ind. Assn. Chiefs of Police, Police League Ind. (Officer of Yr. 1971), Assn. Former Agts. of U.S. Secret Svc. Republican. Lutheran. Avocations: bowling, fishing, genealogy.

HALE, LANCE MITCHELL, lawyer; b. Roanoke, Va., Oct. 14, 1956; s. Ralph M. and Ruby A. (Akers) H.; m. Terry Lynn Sprouse; children: Christina Nicole, Laura Michelle, Layna Maribeth, Logan Mitchell. BSBA, U. Va., 1979, MS in Acctg., 1981; JD, N.Y. Law Sch., 1984. Bar: Va. 1984, N.J. 1984; CPA, Va. Staff acct. Robert M. Mussleman, CPA, Atty. at Law, Charlottesville, Va., 1979-81; CPA Schapiro, Wisan & Krassner, P.C., N.Y.C., 1982-84; ptnr. King, Fulghum, Snead & Hale, P.C., Roanoke, 1984-89; pvt. practice Lance M. Hale Esquire, P. C., Roanoke, 1989—. Bd. dirs. estate planning coun. Ferrum Coll., Va., 1988. Mem. Am. Trial Lawyers Assn., Va. Trial Lawyers Assn., Va. Soc. CPAs, First Latvian/Am. Trade Conf., Phi Alpha Delta, Beta Alpha Psi. Avocations: hiking, camping, hunting. Home: 5 Breezewood Cir Vinton VA 24179-1801 Office: PO Box 1721 Roanoke VA 24008-1721

HALE, LEON, newspaper columnist. Columnist, features desk Houston Chronicle, 1983—; columnist Houston (Post) Chronicle, 1966—. Office: Houston Chronicle 801 Texas Ave Houston TX 77002-2996*

HALE, MARGARET SMITH, insurance company executive, educator; b. Browning, Mont., May 10, 1945; d. Stephen Howard and Evelyn Sarah (Beer) Smith; m. Lawrence L. Hale, Apr. 25, 1970 (div. Jan. 1984); children: Katherine Moore, Laura Ellen. BSBA, Boston U., 1967; AS in Risk Mgmt., Ins. Inst. Am., 1986. Underwriter Chubb & Son, Inc., N.Y.C., 1967-70; br. mgr., asst. v.p. Chubb & Son, Inc., Boston, 1970-80; asst. v.p., account exec. Marsh & McLennan Inc., Boston, 1980-84; sr. v.p. Frank B. Hall, Boston, 1984-87; resident v.p. Warwick Ins. Co., Needham, Mass., 1987-90; pres. Smith & Hale Assocs., Inc., South Orleans, Mass., 1990—; lectr. Risk and Ins. Mgrs. Soc., Boston, 1975-85; mem. fin. div. Babson Coll., Wellesley, Mass., 1987—. Bd. dirs. Lupus Erythematosus Assn., Boston, 1975-78, Parker Hill Med. Ctr., Boston, 1978-80; tchr. Congl. Ch. Sch., Needham, Mass., 1982—; chmn. ins. adv. com. Town of Needham, 1982—. Mem. Ins. Mgrs. Assn. (treas. Boston 1971-80), Ins. Library Assn. (dir. 1980-82). Home: 76 Lienau Dr Chatham MA 02633-2118 Office: Smith & Hale Assocs PO Box 136 South Orleans MA 02662

HALE, MARIE STONER, artistic director; b. Greenwood, Miss.. Student in Piano, U. Miss., Hattiesburg; studied with Richard Ellis, Christine du Boulay, Jo-Anna Kneeland, David Howard. Tchr. Ellis/du Boulay Sch., Chgo., Jo-Anna Kneeland Imperial Studios, Palm Beach County, Fla.; co-founder Ballet Arts Found., West Palm Beach, Fla., 1973-86; co-founder, artistic dir. Ballet Fla., West Palm Beach, 1986—. Office: Ballet Fla 500 Fern St West Palm Beach FL 33401-5726*

HALE, MARTIN DE MORA, investor; b. N.Y.C., Jan. 29, 1941; s. Charles S. and Carmen Rosa (de Mora) H.; m. Deborah Campbell, Sept. 27, 1969; children: Charles, Martin de Mora Jr. Grad., Yale U., 1962; student, Harvard U., 1967. Chmn., dir. Great Lakes Chem. Corp., West Lafayette, Ind., 1979—; pres., CEO Putnam Mgmt. Co., Boston, 1981-83; exec. v.p., dir. Hellman, Jordan, Boston, 1983—; bd. dirs. Octel Corp. Chmn. fin. com. Student Conservation Assn., Charlestown, N.H., 1991—; chmn. bd. govs. Sch. of the Mus. of Fine Arts, Boston, 1994—, trustee Mus. Fine Arts, 1994—. 1st lt. U.S. Army, 1965. Avocations: contemporary art, contemporary crafts. Office: Hellman Jordan Mgmt Co 75 State St Boston MA 02109-1817

HALE, MARY HELEN PARKER, university administrator; b. May 25, 1920; d. James Carroll and Mollie (Dear) Parker; m. George Erwin Hale, June 12, 1942; children: John Parker, James Milton, Nancy Anne. BA in English, La. Coll., 1940, BA in Music, 1940; MA in English, La. State U., 1942; PhD in Fine Arts (hon.), U. Alaska, 1965. Instr., dir. choral music Boston, 1944-45, Albany, N.Y., 1945, Washington, 1946-49, Anchorage, Alaska, 1949-50; dir. Anchorage Cmty. Chorus, 1951-59; founder, dir. Alaska Festival of Music, 1956-59; vice chmn. N.Am. Assembly of Arts Agys., 1968-70; coord. arts and cmty. affiliates office Anchorage C.C. and U. Alaska, Anchorage, 1970-86; dir. pub. svcs. Anchorage C.C., 1977-81, asst. to pres., 1979-81. Founder Alaska southcentral H.S. Music Festival, 1950; mem. Alaska Centennial Commn., 1963-65; charter mem. Alaska State Coun. on Arts, 1966, chmn., 1967-71; founder, mem., sec. Alaska Humanities Forum, 1974-79; mem. adv. bd. No. TV, Inc., 1979-98, endowment com. Anchorage Sr. Ctr., 1987-98; bd. dirs. Anchorage YMCA; vice-chmn. citizens adv. coun. Anchorage C.C., 1981, mem. adv. coun., 1981-86, founder Arts Fair and Women's Ctr. adv. com. Celebrating Alaska's Women, 1945-65, 86, 87; vice chmn. Claiotion C.C.s in Alaska, 1986-88. Recipient Mayor's Disting. Svc. award, Anchorage, 1965, 49'er award, Outstanding Vol. award U. Alaska, 1976, Outstanding Alumni award La. Coll., 1979, President's citation Anchorage C. of C., 1979, Disting. Svc. award Anchorage C.C., 1983, Denali award Alaska of Yr., 1991; named to Hall of Fame, Alaska Press Club, 1970, 72, Mary Hale Hall named in her honor Rehearsal Hall Alaska Performing Arts Ctr. Mem. LWV, AAUW, Anchorage Arts Coun. (charter mem.), U. Alaska Anchorage Alumni Assocs., Internat. Platform Assn., Nat. Assn. Women Deans, Adminstrs. and Counselors, Woman's Club, Soroptimists (pres. Anchorage chpt. 1956), Rep. Women's Club, Mu Phi Epsilon, Beta Sigma Phi (hon.). Home: 11601 Birch Rd Anchorage AK 99516-2326

HALE, NATHAN ROBERT, architect; b. Battle Creek, Mich., July 20, 1944; s. Nathan Shirley and Gertrude Anges (Barnes) H.; m. CarolAnn Purrington, May 28, 1966; children: Marilyce, Maile, Martha. BA, Syracuse U., 1967, BArch, 1971. Dir. Archs. Hawaii, Honolulu, 1971—. Served with AUS, 1968-70, Vietnam. Mem. AIA (bd. dirs. 1984, pres. 1992), Hawii C. of C. (exec. com. 1994—), Econ. Devel. Corp. Honolulu (chair 1993-96, bd. dirs. 1982—), Rotary Club (bd. dirs. 1986-88), Friends of Children's Advocacy Ctr. (pres. 1991, 93, bd. dirs., 1986—). Office: Architects Hawaii Ltd Pacific Tower 300 1001 Bishop St Honolulu HI 96813-3429

HALE, PAUL NOLEN, JR., engineering administrator, educator; b. Galveston, Tex., Dec. 5, 1941; s. Paul Nolen Hale and Margaret (Wentzel) Carroll; m. Frances Anne Andrews, Jan. 26, 1968; children: Tammy Lynn, Eric Timothy. BS in Indsl. Engring., Lamar Tech., Beaumont, Tex., 1965; MS in Indsl. Engring., U. Ark., 1966; PhD in Indsl. Engring., Tex. A&M U., 1970. Registered profl. engr., La., Tex. Asst. prof. indsl. engring. La. Poly. Inst., Ruston, 1966-67, Tex. A&M U., College Station, 1970-71; from asst. prof. to prof. indsl. engring. La. Tech. U., Ruston, 1971-84, head dept. indsl. engring., 1982-84, head dept. biomed. engring., 1984-85, 87-96, dir. rehab. engring. ctr., 1984-98, assoc. dean Coll. Engring. and Sci., 1999—; spl. tech. asst. Western Electric, Shreveport, La., 1966; safety cons. Continental Can Co., Hodge, La., 1972; v.p. C.H.& D. Tech. Cons., Ruston, 1967—; pres. Mgmt. Support Corp., Ruston, 1973—; keynote speaker Conf. of Assn. Driver Educators for Disabled, Ky., 1988; standards com. adaptive driving devices, Soc. Auto. Engrs., 1984—; adv. com. bioengring. div. NSF, 1989-92; program evaluator bioengring. Accreditation Bd. Engring. and Tech., 1990—. Author: (with others) Hazard Control Information Handbook, 1983, Ergonomics in Rehabilitation, 1988; editor: Rehabilitation Technical Services, 1989; co-editor: (proceedings) Technology for the Next Decade, 1989; mem. editorial bd. Assistive Tech., 1988—. Pres. Wesley Chapel Water System, Ruston, 1972-82; mem. Mayor's Com. for Disabled, Ruston, 1985-88; adminstrv. bd. Trinity Meth. Ch., Ruston, 1984-87; bd. dirs. Safety Coun. Greater Baton Rouge, 1984-87. Recipient Meritorious Svc. award Gov.'s Conf. for Handicapped, La., 1984. Fellow Am. Inst. Med. and Biol. Engring.; mem. Biomed. Engring. Soc. (bd. dirs. 1993-96, student affairs com. 1989-91, soc. affairs com. 1991-93), RESNA (bd. dirs. 1987-95), Coun.

of Chairs of Biomed. Engring. (chair 1992-93). Home: 3978 Highway 818 Ruston LA 71270-8304 Office: La Tech U PO Box 10348 Ruston LA 71272

HALE, RICHARD LEE, magazine editor; b. Formoso, Kans., Jan. 3, 1930; s. Glenn Becton and Ruby Tiarena (Johnson) H.; m. Nancy June Craig, Feb. 22, 1953; children—Steven Craig, Kristin Lee Hale Shurtz, Michael John, Sarah Johanna Hale Wilcher. BS in Journalism, U. Kans., 1952. Editor Bird City (Kans.) Times, 1955-58; editor, pub. St. Francis Herald, Kans., 1958-74; editor Golf Course Mgmt., Lawrence, Kans., 1974-76, PGA Mag., Palm Beach Gardens, Fla., 1976-80; dir. comm. GCSAA, Lawrence, 1980-82; editor Dental Econs., Penn Well Pub. Co., Tulsa, 1982-97, pub., 1989-97. Editor: (ann.) PGA Book of Golf, 1977-80; cons. editor Odontos Pub. Co., 1997—. Chmn. local com. Boy Scouts Am., St. Francis, 1970-74; trustee Trinity United Meth. Ch., Palm Beach Gardens, 1979-80, Am. Fund for Dental Health, 1989—. Spl. agt. CIC, U.S. Army, 1952-54. St. Francis Herald named Best Weekly Newspaper Kans. Press Assn., 1962. Mem. Am. Assn. Dental Editors, Am. Fund for Dental Health (trustee, advisor 1989-93), Kans. Press Assn. (bd. dirs. 1973-74), Golf Writers Assn. Am., Riverside Country Club (St. Francis; pres. 1971), Rotary (pres. local chpt. 1970). Democrat. Methodist. Avocation: golf, travel, nature walks. Home: 415 N Forest Ridge Blvd Broken Arrow OK 74014-2761

HALE, ROBERT FARGO, government official; b. Sacramento, Calif., Jan. 21, 1947; s. William David and Elizabeth (Wells) H.; m. Susan Kohn, June 23, 1973; children—Scott, Michael. B.S. with honors, Stanford U., 1968, M.S., 1969; M.B.A., George Washington U., 1976. Analyst, study dir. Ctr. for Naval Analysis, Washington, 1972-75; analyst Congl. Budget Office, Washington, 1975-78, dep. asst. dir., 1978-81, asst. dir. def. issues, 1981-94, asst. sec. fin. mgmt. USAF, 1994—. Served to lt. (j.g.) USNR, 1969-72. Mem. Phi Beta Kappa. Jewish. Home: 3357 Taleen Ct Annandale VA 22003-1161 Office: 1130 Air Force Pentagon Washington DC 20330-1130

HALE, ROGER LOUCKS, manufacturing company executive; b. Plainfield, N.J., Dec. 13, 1934; s. Lloyd and Elizabeth (Adams) H.; m. Sandra Johnston, June 10, 1961 (div.); children: Jocelyn, Leslie, Nina, Deirdre; m. Eleanor L. Hall, Nov. 24, 1989. BA, Brown U., 1956; MBA, Harvard U., 1961. With Tennant Co., Mpls., 1961—, pres., CEO, 1975-98, chmn., CEO, 1998-99, chmn., 1999, also bd. dirs.; bd. dirs. U.S. Bank Corp. Bd. dirs. Walker Art Ctr., 1970—, Ploughshares Fund, 1996—; chmn. Neighborhood Employment Network, 1980; bd. dirs., chmn. Pub. Radio Internat., 1990; chmn. Minn. Bus. Partnership, 1993-95. Named Exec. of Yr., Corp. Report mag., 1988, One of Minn.'s 5 Outstanding Corp. Dirs., Twin Cities Bus. Monthly, 1996; recipient Mpls. Spl. Recognition award for Svc. to City of Mpls., 1993. Office: Tennant 701 Lilac Dr N Minneapolis MN 55422-4687

HALE, STEPHEN MICHAEL, artist; b. St. Johnsbury, Vt., July 17, 1961; s. Richard Martin and Jeanne Rita (Cormier) H. Student, R.I. Sch. Design, 1979-82. Visual artist N.Y.C., 1982—. Represented by Bridgewater/Lustberg Gallery, N.Y.C., 1989—, Greathouse Gallery, N.Y.C., 1985-88, Damon Brandt Gallery, N.Y.C., 1983-84; freelance illustrator various mags., 1985-91; represented in permanent collections Ark. Arts Ctr., Little Rock, Mus. Art Carnegie Inst., Pitts. Fellow Nat. Endowment Arts, 1985, N.Y. Found. for Arts, 1988; grantee Pollock-Krasner Found., 1987. Democrat. Roman Catholic. Avocations: photography, film and video. Studio: 185 E 3rd St Apt 3G New York NY 10009-7411

HALE, WILLIAM BRYAN, JR., newspaper editor; b. Stephenville, Tex., Apr. 26, 1933; s. William Bryan and Gladys (Tittle) H.; divorced; children: Shandra Hale Reiss, Tamara Hale Cameron, Nicholas, Sabrina. Student, UCLA, 1953-54. Police beat/courts reporter Santa Monica (Calif.) Outlook, 1953-58; gen. reporter Ontario (Calif.) Daily Report, 1958-59; criminal court writer L.A. City News Service, 1959-60; gen. reporter L.A. Times, 1960-61; reporter Houston Chronicle, 1961-62; news editor Somerset (Pa.) American, 1962-63; night editor Elmira (N.Y.) Star-Gazette, 1963-64; copy editor, investigative reporter Milw. Jour., 1964-70; Tucson corr. Time mag./Time-Life Books, 1970-71; night city editor Tucson Citizen, 1970-71; nat. desk copy editor Los Angeles Times, 1971-90; sr. lectr. U. So. Calif., 1974-88; pres. Nat. Copy Editors Sch., Thousand Oaks, Calif., 1984-90; founder and dir. Australian Sub-Editors Sch., Sydney, Australia, 1989-94. Cpl. USMC, 1951-53. Avocations: horseback riding, hiking. Home: PO Box 35128 Tucson AZ 85740-5128

HALES, ALFRED WASHINGTON, mathematics educator, consultant; b. Pasadena, Calif., Nov. 30, 1938; s. Raleigh Stanton and Gwendolen (Washington) H.; m. Virginia Dart Greene, July 7, 1962; children—Andrew Stanton, Lisa Ruth, Katherine Washington. B.S., Calif. Inst. Tech., 1960, Ph.D., 1962. NSF postdoctoral fellow Cambridge U., Eng., 1962-63; Benjamin Peirce instr. Harvard U., 1963-66; faculty mem. UCLA, 1966-92, prof. math., 1973-92, prof. emeritus, 1992—; dir. Inst. Def. Analyses, Ctr. Comms. Rsch., La Jolla, Calif., 1992—; cons. Jet Propulsion Lab., La Canada, Calif., 1966-70, Inst. for Def. Analyses, Princeton, N.J. and LaJolla, Calif., 1964-65, 76, 79-92; vis. lectr. U. Wash., Seattle, 1970-71; vis. mem. U. Warwick Math. Inst., Coventry, Eng., 1977-78, Math. Sci. Rsch. Inst., Berkeley, 1986-87. Co-author: Shift Register Sequences, 1967, 82; contbr. articles to profl. jours. Bd. trustees Math. Sci. Rsch. Inst., Berkeley, 1995—. Mem. Am. Math. Soc., Math. Assn. Am., Soc. Indsl. and Applied Math. (Polya prize in combinatorics 1972), Sigma Xi. Clubs: Pasadena Badminton. Office: Ctr for Comm Rsch 4320 Westerra Ct San Diego CA 92121-1969

HALES, DANIEL B., lawyer; b. Oak Park, Ill., Sept. 29, 1941; s. Burton W. and Marion (Jones) H.; m. Deborah J. Dorr, June 4, 1966; children, Daniel R.J., Marion P., George B. BA in Econs., U. Mich., 1963; Juris Doctorate, Northwestern U., 1966. Bar: Ill.1966, U.S. Dist. Ct. (no. dist.) Ill. 1967, U.S. Ct. Appeals (7th cir.) 1968, U.S. Supreme Ct. 1977. Ptnr. Peterson, Ross, Schloerb & Seidel, Chgo.; gen. counsel The Philadelphia Soc., Chgo.; dir. Chgo. Crime Commn. Pres., dir. Americans for Effective Law Enforcement Inc., Chgo.; bd. dirs. Duncan YMCA, Chgo.; chmn. Ill. Lawyers for Reagan and Bush, 1980; gen. counsel New Trier Twp., Winnetka, Ill. Republican Orgn.; mem. bd. govs. United Rep. Fund of Ill. Mem. Chgo. Bar Assn. (trust law com. 1975—), Ill. State Bar Assn., The Law Club, N.E. Commonwealth Club, N.E. Federalist Soc. (advisor). Office: Peterson & Ross 200 E Randolph St Ste 7300 Chicago IL 60601-7012*

HALES, ROBERT D., church official; b. N.Y.C., Aug. 24, 1932; s. John Rulson and Vera Marie Holbrook Hales, m. Mary Elene Crandall; 2 children. Grad., U. Utah; MBA, Harvard U. Former exec. to 3 nat. cos.; from br. pres. to stake pres. counselor LDS Ch., from pres. Eng. London Mission to 1st counselor Sunday Sch. Gen. Presidency, until 1974, mem. Gen. Authority, from asst. to coun. of 12 apostles to 1st Quorum of Seventy, 1974-85, bishop, 1985-94, mem. coun. of 12 apostles, 1994—. Served USAF. *

HALEVI, MARCUS, photographer; b. Croton-on-Hudson, N.Y., Jan. 17, 1942; s. Henry and Zelma (Brenner) H. BArch, U. Mich., 1965. Arch. The Archs. Collaborative, Cambridge, Mass., 1969-72; freelance photographer Cambridge, 1972—. One person shows include Anchorage (Alaska) Fine Arts Mus., 1978, Peabody Mus., 1990, Carpenter Ctr. Arts Harvard U., 1995; exhibited in group shows Inst. Contemporary Art, Boston, 1977, NYU Art Gallery, 1980, Cambridge Multicultural Art Ctr., 1990, Soka Gakkai Mus., Hiroshima, Japan, 1990, Howard Yezerski Gallery, Boston, 1991, Nat. Press Club, Washington, 1992, Aidekman Art Gallery, Boston, 1998, De Cordova Mus, Lincoln, Mass., 1998; prin. works include refugees of Mekong River, land mine clearing in Cambodia, st. children of Bangkok, child prostitution, Agent Orange poisoning of Vietnam vets., Cambodian refugee camps, asylums of Romania, Russian prison sys., urban India, environ. vigilantes, rural post offices; photographer: (book) Alaska Crude: Visions of the Last Frontier, 1977; portfolio pub., 1998.. With USCG, 1967. Recipient Pulitzer Prize for gen. news, 1988, 1st prize Boston Photo-Arts, 1979, W. Eugene Smith Meml. award, 1989, 1st prize New Eng. Press Assn., 1991, 1st prize New Eng. AP awards, 1991, Picture of Yr. awards Nat. Press Photographers Assn. & U. Mo. Sch. Journalism including 2d prize for feature photograph, 1987, 3d prize for news picture story, 1990, 2d prize for spot news photography, 1990, judge's spl. recognition Canon photo-essayist, 1992; Nat. Endowment Arts photography grantee, 1992, Mass. Coun. for Arts and Humanities grantee, 1986, Mass. Cultural Coun. grantee, 1995. Home and Studio: 33 Cedar St Somerville MA 02143-2231

HALEY, CAIN CALMES, computer consultant; b. Greensville, S.C., Apr. 4, 1952; d. Julius French and Melville Cain (Calmes) H.; m. John Francis Blakeslee, Jr., Oct. 24, 1983. BA, U. S.C., 1974, MA, 1975. Sch. psychologist Allendale (S.C.) County Sch., 1976-77; sch. psychologist, tchr. Beaufort (S.C.) County Sch., 1977-80; editor South World Mag., Hilton Head, S.C., 1980-82; mgr. Acctg./Mgmt. Svcs., Hilton Head, S.C., 1982-83, Computer Gazebo, Hilton Head, 1983-84; owner, prin. Entre Computer Ctr., Hilton Head, 1984-92, Calcom Ventures, Hilton Head, 1987—; ptnr. Robbins & Haley, Atlanta, 1990-92; adv. to bd. dirs. Dunes Mktg. Group, Hilton Head, 1984-86. Mem. Hilton Head Planning Commn., 1987—; bd. dirs. Gov.'s Council Vocat. Edn., Hilton Head, 1987—. Mem. LWV (chmn. 1986-87), Profl. Women (pres. 1985-86), Hilton Head C. of C. (chmn. com. 1986-87), Nat. Assn. Female Execs., Zonta. Office: Calcom Ventures 52 New Orleans Rd Hilton Head Island SC 29928-4722

HALEY, DAVID ALAN, preferred provider organization executive; b. St. Louis, Aug. 29, 1943; s. John David and Helen Ermyl (Richardson) H.; m. Donna Lee Davis, Nov. 24, 1965; children: Trisha Lynn, Jason Alan, Eric Nathan. BA, So. Ill. U., Edwardsville, 1966; MPH magna cum laude, UCLA, 1971. Adminstrv. asst. Kaiser Found. Hosp., Panorama City, Calif., 1971; assoc. adminstr. Our Lady of Lourdes Hosp., Pasco, Wash., 1971-74, Garfield Hosp., Monterey Park, Calif., 1974-75; assoc. exec. dir. Gen. Hosp., Ft. Walton Beach, Fla., 1976-79; v.p. ops. Our Lady of the Lake Regional Med. Ctr., Baton Rouge, 1979-88; pres. Phoenix Connection, Baton Rouge, 1988-89; CEO Gibson Gen. Hosp., Princeton, Ind., 1989-93; pres., CEO Four States Physicians Assn., Joplin, Mo., 1993-94; exec. dir. MedQuest Health Resources, Inc., 1995-96; pres., ceo The Haley Group, 1996—; mem. Four Rivers Comprehensive Health Planning Agy., Richland, Wash., 1972-74; treas. S.E. Wash. State Hosp. Coun., Pasco, 1973, v.p. 1974; corp. mem. Mid La. Health Systems Agy., Baton Rouge, 1979-82; gubernatorial appointee La. Statewide Health Coord. Coun., Baton Rouge, 1984, Ind. Healthcare Facility Adminstrn. Bd., Indpls., 1991-93; sec.-treas. S.W. Ind. Hosp. Coun., Evansville, 1992-93. Served with USNR, 1967-69. USPHS fellow, 1969-71. Fellow Am. Coll. Healthcare Execs.; mem. Healthcare Fin. Mgmt. Assn., La. Hosp. Assn. (council on planning, 1984-87), Ind. Hosp. Assn. (mem. coun. pub. rels. 1992-93), Vis. Nurse Assn. Southwestern Ind. (bd. dirs. 1992-93), La. Assn. Bus. and Industry (health care council 1987). Republican. Lodge: Kiwanis. Home: 21408 Old North Church Rd Frankfort IL 60423-3019 Office: MedQuest Health Resources Inc 20060 Governors Dr Ste 102 Olympia Fields IL 60461-1029

HALEY, GEORGE, Romance languages educator; b. Lorain, Ohio, Oct. 19, 1929; s. George and Mary (Haley). AB, Oberlin Coll., 1948; MA, Brown U., 1951, PhD (Pres.'s fellow), 1956. Prof. U. Chgo., 1968—, chmn. dept. Romance langs., 1970-74. Author: Vicente Espinel and Marcos de Obregón, 1959, The Narrator in Don Quixote, 1965, Diario de un Estudiante de Salamanca, 1977, El Quijote de Cervantes, 1984; mem. editl. bd. Modern Philology, 1967—. Guggenheim fellow, 1962-63. Mem. MLA, Hispanic Soc. Am., Phi Beta Kappa. Home: 901 S Plymouth Ct Chicago IL 60605-2059 Office: 1050 E 59th St Chicago IL 60637-1559

HALEY, GEORGE BROCK, JR., lawyer; b. Atlanta, Feb. 9, 1926; s. George Brock and Naomi Esther (Alverson) H.; m. Marjorie Elizabeth Griffiths, June 24, 1950; children: Susan Haley Brumfield, Katherine Haley Herman, George Brock III, Victor Pearse. AB, Harvard U., 1948, LLB, 1951. Bar: Ga. 1951, D.C. 1976. Assoc. Kilpatrick & Cody (name changed to Kilpatrick Stockton), Atlanta, 1951-60, ptnr., 1960-93, of counsel, 1994—. Mem. Ga. Gov.'s Jud. Process Rev. Commn., Atlanta, 1988-89; trustee Frances Wood Wilson Found. Staff sgt. AUS, 1944-46, MTO. Mem. ABA, State Bar Ga., Atlanta Bar Assn., Atlanta Lawyers Club, Capital City Club. Methodist. Avocations: boating, hiking.

HALEY, GEORGE PATRICK, lawyer; b. Bad Axe, Mich., Sept. 23, 1948; s. Glen Kirk and Bernice (Cooper) H.; m. Theresa L. Thomas, Dec. 24, 1975. BS, U. Mich., 1970; MS, U. Calif., Berkeley, 1971; JD, Harvard U., 1974. Bar: Calif. 1974, U.S. Dist. Ct. (no. dist.) Calif. 1974, U.S. Dist. Ct. (ea. dist.) Calif. 1980. Assoc. Pillsbury Madison & Sutro, San Francisco, 1974-81, ptnr., 1982—; prof. U. Shanghai, Shanghai-San Francisco Sister City Program, 1986—. Author numerous articles uniform commercial code, project fin. Dir. Calif. Shakespeare Festival, Berkeley, 1986-93; dir. Nat. Writing Project, 1996—. Mem. ABA (chmn. com. 1976-93), State Bar Calif. (chmn. fin. instns. com. 1980, commercial code com. 1988). Republican. Methodist. Avocations: tai chi chuan, golf, cooking. Home: 1825 Marin Ave Berkeley CA 94707-2414

HALEY, JOHN CHARLES, financial executive; b. Akron, Ohio, July 24, 1929; s. Arthur and Katherine (Moore) H.; m. Rheba Hopkins, June 11, 1951; children: Alyson, Susan, John, Thomas. A.B., Miami U., Oxford, Ohio, 1950; M.S., Columbia Grad. Sch. Bus., 1951; LL.D. (hon.), Pace U., 1984. With Chase Manhattan Bank, N.Y.C., 1953—; asst. treas. Chase Manhattan Bank, 1959-62, asst. v.p., 1962-64, v.p., 1964-70; exec. v.p. Chase Manhattan Corp, 1975-84; dep. chmn. Kissinger Assocs., 1984-85; chmn., chief exec. officer Bus. Internat. Inc., N.Y.C., 1986-87; group pres. Orion Banking Group, London, 1970-73, dir. Armco Corp., chmn., bd. 1995-96. Trustee Siemens Found.; chmn. emeritus bd. trustees Pace U. Served with AUS, 1951-53. Mem. Union Club (N.Y.C.), New Canaan Country Club, Beta Theta Pi. Home and Office: 8 Deer Run Path Rutland VT 05701-9654

HALEY, JOHN DAVID, petroleum consulting company executive; b. Denver, Mar. 16, 1924; s. Peter Daniel and Margaret Dorothy (O'Haire) H.; m. Annie Loretta Breeden, June 20, 1951; children: Laura, Patricia, Brian, Sharon, Norine, Kathleen. Profl. engr., Colo. Sch. Mines, 1948. Registered profl. engr., Colo., Okla. Petroleum engr. Creole Petroleum, Venezuela, 1948-50; field engr. Texaco Inc., La., 1950-52; staff engr. Carter Oil (Exxon), Tulsa, 1954-56; petroleum cons. Earlougher Engring., Tulsa, 1956-61; v.p. prodn. Anschutz Corp., Denver, 1962-86; v.p. Circle A Drilling, Denver, 1967-78; dir. Circle A Mud, Denver, 1983-86; pres. Greylock Pipeline, Denver, 1983-86, Anschutz Pipeline, Denver, 1984-86, Haley Engring. Inc., 1987—. Mem. Pres.'s Coun., Colo. Sch. Mines, 1985—; bd. dirs. Alumni-Assn., 1992-97, pres., 1995; bd. dirs. CSM Found., 1996-98; Rep. committeeman, Littleton, Colo. Lt. comdr. USNR, 1943-46, 52-54. Recipient Outstanding Alumnus award Alumni Assn., 1997. Mem. Soc. Petroleum Engrs. (bd. dirs. Denver chpt. 1965), Soc. Petroleum Evaluation Engrs. (bd. dirs. 1992-95), Ind. Petroleum Assn. Mountain States, Am. Petroleum Inst. (citation for svc.), Internat. Assn. Drilling Contractors, Rocky Mountain Oil and Gas Assn. (bd. dirs. 1988-2000), Soc. Profl. Well Log Analysts, Petroleum Club (Denver chpt.). Roman Catholic. Home: 561 E Caley Dr Littleton CO 80121-2212

HALEY, JOHN HARVEY, lawyer; b. Hot Springs, Ark., May 29, 1931; s. Harvey H. and Anne (Tanner) H.; m. Cynthia Martin, Sept. 7, 1997. AB, Emory U., 1952; LLB, U. Ark., 1955. Bar: Ark. 1955, U.S. Dist. Ct. (we. dist.) Ark. 1955, U.S. Ct. Appeals (8th cir.) 1955, U.S. Supreme Ct. 1971. Clk. Ark. Supreme Ct., Little Rock, 1955-56; ptnr. Rose Law Firm, Little Rock, 1956-71, Haley, Young, Bogard & Gitchell, Little Rock, 1971-73, Laser, Sharp, Haley, Young & Boswell, Little Rock, 1973-82, Haley, Polk & Heister, Little Rock, 1982-86, Arnold, Grobmyer & Haley, Little Rock, 1986-96; owner Haley Law Firm, Little Rock, 1996—; bd. dirs. North Ark. Telephone Co., Flippin, Ark.; Munro and Co., Hot Springs, Ark., Binnacle Industries, Rose Creek Industries, Kappa Realty, Little Rock, Plaza Partnership, Talweg, LLC, Memphis; lectr. U. Ark. Law Sch., Little Rock, 1956-60, CLU instr., 1961-65; spl. counsel liquidation and rehab. Ark. Ins. Dept., 1967-71. Editor Ark. Law Rev., 1954-55. Chmn. Ark. State Bd. Correction, 1967-72, Ark. State Bd. Law Examiners, 1960-63, Election Rsch. Coun., Little Rock, 1961-64; dir. Wildwood Ctr. Performing Arts, Little Rock, 1994—, Florence Crittenden Home, Little Rock, 1994—; scoutmaster Second Presbyn. Ch. Troop, Little Rock, 1962-65. Methodist. Avocations: piloting, sailing, bicycling, underwater photography, skiing. Home: 3614 Doral Dr Little Rock AR 72212-2920 Office: Haley Law Firm PO Box 3730 Little Rock AR 72203-3730

HALEY, PRISCILLA JANE, artist, printmaker; b. Boston, June 22, 1926; d. Arthur Benjamin and Jessamy (Fountain) H.; m. Tadeusz Bilous, May 21, 1961. B.A., Oberlin Coll., Ohio, 1948; postgrad., Bklyn. Mus. Sch., 1955. Resident artist Yaddo Found., Saratoga Springs, N.Y., 1957. One-man show Village Art Ctr., N.Y.C., 1960; 3-man show Islip Art Mus., 1975; represented in permanent collection N.Y. Pub. Libr., Nat. Acad. Galleries, Bklyn. Mus., Libr. of Congress, Bowdoin Coll. Art Mus., Oberlin Coll., Addison Gallery art, Wesleyan U. Libr., Portland (Oreg.) Mus. Art, others; portfolio of prints and poems by Maine poets, The Island, 1961. Recipient Medal of Honor Audubon Artists, 1957, 1st prize Bablyon Arts Coun. Juried Exhbn., 1992; Louis Comfort Tiffany Found. grantee, 1959. Mem. Soc. Am. Graphic Artists. Home: 133 Livingston Ave Babylon NY 11702-1601

HALEY, RICHARD EDWARD, JR., computer scientist; b. Boston, Nov. 21, 1958; s. Richard Edward, Sr. and Margaret Anne (McLellan) H.; m. Lisa Ann Gillespie, Aug. 13, 1988. Grad. high sch., Plano, Tex. With U. Dallas, Irving, Tex., 1976-84, Dallas Co. Deaf Edn., Tex., 1982-87; dir. transp. Tex. Sch. Deaf, 1987-91; owner Writeswright Word Processing, Dallas, Tex., 1986-91; independent game devel., 1987-91; graphics programer Origin Sys., Austin, Tex., 1991-92; network programmer Data Interface, Austin, 1993-94; lan adminstrn. Infinity Group, Albuquerque, N.M., 1994-95; computer tech. Presbyn. Hosp., Albuquerque, 1995—; owner WWWritch, 1996—. Author (web page) Abraham Gutmann for Senate, 1996, Slugbaby, 1996; prodr., dir. Roundtable, 1995-96 (Cmty. Impact award 1995); prodr. ABQ Pub. Access TV, 1994—; crew mem. (TV show) Good Health, Good Life, 1995, Freedom Hour, 1996. Rep. Green Coun., N.M., 1994; vice chmn. Albuquerque Regional Greens, 1994; candidate for Ho. of Reps. from N.Mex. dist. 3, 1997; Green Party candidate for auditor State of N.Mex., 1998; founder Freedom Activist Coalition, 1998. Mem. Delta-9. Avocations: bikes, camping, sailing, hiking.

HALEY, ROGER KENDALL, librarian; b. Boston, Oct. 29, 1938; s. John F. and Rose (Walker) H.; m. Mary Hannon; 1 child, Michael J. A.B., Georgetown U., 1960; M.L.S., U. Md., 1976. Reference asst. U.S. Senate Library, Washington, 1964-71, asst. librarian, 1971-73, librarian, 1973-97. Mem. Spl. Librs. Assn. (John Cotton Dana award 1993), D.C. Libr. Assn., Am. Inst. Parliamentarians. Office: 1243 Independence Ave SE Washington DC 20003-1445

HALEY, ROSLYN TREZEVANT, educational program director; b. Washington, July 23, 1955; d. Morti Trezevant and Sara Roslyn Kebe; m. Darrell D. Haley, July 30, 1988; children: Jessica, Darrell Jr.; children from previous marriage: Donald Sumbry, Anthony Sumbry, Krystal Garth. BA in History, S.C. State U., 1976; MPA, Calif. State U., L.A., 1983; postgrad., UCLA. Faculty cert. U. Phoenix, 1996. Admissions evaluator UCLA, 1979-81, counselor Sch. Pub. Health, 1981-83, head counselor dept. theater, 1983-93; dir. student and counseling svcs. UCLA Sch. Theater, Film and TV, 1993—; adult edn. tchr. L.A. Unified Sch. Dist., 1984-93; lectr. U. Phoenix, Woodland Hills, Calif., 1996—; bd. mem. Palmdale (Calif.) H.S., Visual and Performing Arts Acad., 1999. Author of poetry. March organizer March for Jesus, L.A., 1994, Antelope Valley, 1995-99; adminstr. Command Ctr., Convoy of Hope, Palmdale, 1998; sch. site coun. Palmtree Elem. Sch., Palmdale, 1998-99; recruiter Boy Scouts Am. Western L.A. Coun. Bd., 1998-99. Recipient Outstanding Svc. award March for Jesus, L.A., 1994, Outstanding Svc. award First Missionary Bapt. Ch., Littlerock, Calif., 1997. Mem. Am. Assn. Ednl. Rsch. Republican. Avocations: reading, swimming, horseback riding, cycling. E-mail: rhaley@ucla.edu. and rhaley@emelnitz.ucla.edu. Fax: 310-825-3383. Home: 37518 Larchwood Dr Palmdale CA Office: UCLA Sch TFT 405 Hilgard Ave Los Angeles CA 90024

HALEY, ROY W., financial services executive; b. 1947. BS, MIT, 1969. With Arthur Andersen & Co., Houston, 1969-71, 73-88, Ruhmann Mfg. Co., Schulenburg, Tex., 1971-73; pres. Am. Gen. Fin. Inc. (formerly Credithrift Fin. Inc.), 1989-91; also exec. v.p. adminstrn. Am. Gen. Corp., Houston; chief exec. officer Am. Gen. Fin. Inc., Evansville, Ind., 1989-91; pres. Am. Gen. Corp., Houston, 1991-93; pres., CEO Wesco Distbn., Pitts., 1994—. Office: Wesco Distbn Inc Commerce Ct Ste 700 Four Sta Sq Pittsburgh PA 15219*

HALEY, THOMAS JOHN, retired pharmacologist; b. Crosby, Minn., Nov. 4, 1913; s. Thomas Edward and Ida May (Young) H.; m. Edna Baker, June 1, 1944 (div. Sept. 1963); m. Jeanne Wall, Sept. 24, 1964; children: Kathyleen, Barbara. BS, U. So. Calif., 1938, MS, 1942; PhD, U. Fla., 1945. Lic. pharmacist, Calif., Nev. Grad. asst. instr. U. Fla., Gainesville, 1942-45; med. dir. E.S. Miller Labs Inc., L.A., 1945-47; chief pharmacology toxicologist Lab. Nuclear Medicine UCLA, 1947-66; prof. pharmacology U. Hawaii Med. Sch., Honolulu, 1966-69; leader pharmacology & toxicology Rsch. Triangle Inst., Research Triangle Park, N.C., 1969-71; adj. prof. pharmacology & toxicology U. N.C. Med. Sch., Chapel Hill, 1969-71; pharmacologist Food & Drug Adminstrn. Nat. Ctr. Toxicology Rsch., Pine Bluff, Ark., 1971-82; adj. prof. pharmacology U. Ark. Med. Ctr., Little Rock, 1971-82. Author: Clinical Toxicology, 1948, 1972, Respiratory Nervous System Ion Radiology, 1962, 1964, Manual of Toxicology, 1987. Sci. com. air pollution L.A. County, 1948-66. Mem. Inst. Strahlenhemat & Biol. (internat. mem.), L.A. C. of C. (clean air com. 1954-56), Oceanside City Coun. (hazard waste com. 1986-91). Democrat. Roman Catholic. Avocation: stamp collecting. Home: 774 Rivertree Dr Oceanside CA 92054-7456

HALEY, VINCENT PETER, lawyer; b. Phila., Oct. 6, 1931; s. Vincent Paul and Madeline R. (McCrystal) H.; m. Mary Ann Harron, Apr. 14, 1956; children—Paul V., Kevin G., Maureen T., Patricia Ann M., Kathleen A., Brian M., Regina E., Christopher P., Megan A. B.S., Villanova, 1953, J.D. cum laude, 1959. Bar: Pa. 1960, Fla. 1979. Acct. Arthur Young & Co., CPAs, Phila., 1955-56; assoc. Schnader, Harrison, Segal & Lewis, Phila., 1959-67, ptnr., 1968—, mem. exec. com., 1985-88, 89-94; mem. bd. consultors Law Sch. Villanova U., 1985—; lectr. in field. Sec. Mercy Health Sys., Bala Cynwyd, Pa., 1969—; mem. Archdiocese of Phila. Bd. Edn., 1973-79, pres., 1977-79; mem., bd. dirs. Police Athletic League of Phila., 1994—. With USNR, 1953-55. Mem. Pa. Bar Assn. (chmn. corp., banking and bus. law sect. 1979-81), Phila. Bar Assn., Villanova U. Law Alumni Assn. (pres. 1962-63), Union League Club (Phila.), Huntingdon Valley Country Club, Roosevelt Racquet Club (Huntingdon Valley, Pa., bd. dirs. 1969-80, 91-94, treas. 1972-80), Order of Coif (chpt. v.p. 1962-63). Home: 305 Madison Rd Huntingdon Valley PA 19006-6713 Office: Schnader Harrison Segal et al 1600 Market St Ste 3600 Philadelphia PA 19103-7240

HALFACRE, ROBERT GORDON, landscape architect, horticulturist, educator; b. Newberry, S.C., June 22, 1941; s. Edwin Harvey and Lela (Ruff) H.; m. Carolyn F. Halfacre, Jan. 24, 1963 (div. Jan., 1980); children: Angela, Robert. BS, Clemson U., 1963, MS, 1965; PhD in Horticulture, Va. Poly. Inst., 1968; MLA, N.C. State U., 1973. Registered landscape architect, S.C. Asst. prof. N.C. State U., Raleigh, 1968-71, assoc. prof., 1971-74; assoc. prof. horticulture Clemson (S.C.) U., 1974-79, prof., 1979-90, Alumni disting. prof., 1990—, univ. ombudsman, 1998—; landscape architect Landscape Archtl. Svcs., Clemson, 1977—; mem. Planning Commn. City of Clemson, 1990-93; pres. faculty senate, Clemson U., 1989-90, bd. visitors, 1992-94, chmn. grievance bd., 1996-98, ombudsman, 1998—. Author: Carolina Landscape Plants, 1971, Keep 'em Growing, 1972, Fundamentals of Horticulture, 1975, Horticulture, 1979, Plant Science, 1987, Landscape Plants of the Southeast, 5th edit., 1989. Dir. Horticulture Gardens, Clemson U., 1974-77; pres. bd. dirs. Daniel H.S. P.T.A., Clemson, 1985-86; chmn. United Way Campaign, Clemson U., 1996-97. Recipient Silver Seal award Nat. Coun. State Garden Clubs, 1984, Helen S. Hull award, 1979, Sigma Xi Rsch. award, 1968, Outstanding Tchr. award N.C. State U., 1970, Outstanding Faculty award AAUP, 1997. award for Faculty Excellence, Clemson U. Bd. Trustees, 1997. Mem. Nat. Ombudsman Assn., Am. Soc. Landscape Architects, Am. Soc. for Hort. Sci. (L.M. Ware Outstanding Tchr. award So. region 1982, Julian C. Miller rsch. award 1968). Republican. Lutheran. Avocations: water skiing, writing, tennis, travel. Fax: 864-656-4373; e-mail: ombudsman@clemson.edu. Home: 136 Riverpoint Dr Clemson SC 29631-1049 Office: Clemson U 164 Poole Agrl Ctr Clemson SC 29634

HALFEN, DAVID, publishing executive; b. Newark, July 23, 1924; s. Abraham and Rachael (Sudit) H.; m. Geneviève Alberte Martin, Jan. 15, 1948; children: Daniel, William, Alexandre Anthony. BS with high honors, U. Wis., 1948; Diploma in French Civilization with high honors, U. Paris, 1949, PhD with highest honors, 1954. From asst. to chief cost acct. Atlas Constructors, Morocco, 1952-54; from asst. editor to editor-in-chief Hart Pub. Co., N.Y.C., 1954-56, 58-62; fgn. affairs editor Scholastic mag., N.Y.C.,

1956-58; from field editor to v.p., gen. mgr. Coll. divsn. Scott, Foresman and Co., Glenview, Ill., 1962-78, v.p., gen. mgr. Lifelong Learning divsn., 1978-87, ret., 1987; chmn. adv. com. USN Courses at Sea Program, 1987-92; sr. assoc. Middlesex Rsch. Ctr., Bethesda, Md., 1991-93; vol. exec. Internat. Exec. Svc. Corps, Zimbabwe, 1993, cons., 1994-96. Author: La Plume: Revue Symboliste 1889-1899, 1954. With AUS, 1943-46, PTO.

HALFORD, SHARON LEE, legal studies administrator, victimologist, educator; b. Clifton, Colo., July 22, 1946; d. Robert Lee and Florence V. (Kubly) Eighmy; m. Allen A. Dreher, Jan. 29, 1967 (div. Jan. 1979); children: Heidi Ann, Gretchen Christine, Kirsten Beth; m. Donald Gary Halford, May 23, 1986. BS in Edn., U. Colo., 1969; postgrad., U. Denver, 1981-83; M in Criminal Justice, U. Colo., 1987. Legal asst. 1st Jud. Dist. Atty., Golden, Colo., 1979-81, legal rschr., 1981-83; victim witness coord. 18th Jud. Dist. Atty., Englewood, Colo., 1983-92; mem. faculty Aurora (Colo.) C.C. Criminal Justice Dept., 1989-95, prof., chair pub. svc. dept., 1995—, dir. paralegal studies, 1995—, asst. v.p. instrn., 1999—, chair faculty senate, 1997-99, pres. faculty coun., 1997-99; mem. faculty Colo. Faculty Adv. Coun., 1993—; project coord. Lowry Family Ctr.; project coord. Svc. Learning, Colo. Campus Compact, 1997—; lectr. Law Enforcement Tng. Acad., 1994—. Contbg. author, editor: Colorado Crime Victims Rights Contitutional Amendment Outreach Manual and Implementation Manual, 1992-93; author: (book) Connecting Colleges, Communities and Careers, 1998. Mem. Domestic Violence Task Force, Douglas County, Colo., 1985-92, Arapahoe County, Colo., 1985-94; trainer Rape Assistance and Awareness Program, Denver, 1985-91, MADD, 1990-92, Colo. Victim Witness Coord. Coalition, 1991; mem. 18th Judicial Dist. Child Advocacy Ctr. Com., 1990—, Gov.'s Victims' Compensation and Assistance Coord. Com., 1991-95, Colo. Victim Asst. and Law Enforcement Bd., 1991-95, Criminal Justice Educators Task Force, 1992—, chair, 1995-98; mem. Colo. Corrections Consortium, 1992—, officer faculty senate, 1995-99; mem. Colo. Crime Victim Rights Constl. Amendment Com., 1990—; com. chair Colo. PACT Project, 1993-95; mem. Colo. C.C. Diversity Com., 1997—. Fellow Nat. Orgn. for Victim Assistance, Nat. Victim Ctr.; mem. AAUW, LWV, ACLU, Anti-Defamation League, Colo. Orgn. for Victim Assistance (pres. 1992-95), S.W. Criminal Justice Educators Assn., Acad. Criminal Justice Scis., Am. Assn. Paralegal Educators, Nat. Fedn. Paralegal Assns., Rocky Mountain Paralegal Assn., Nat. Criminal Justice Assn. Democrat. Methodist. Office: CC Aurora 16000 E Centretech Pky Aurora CO 80011-9057

HALFPENNY, JAMES CARSON, scientist, educator, author; b. Shreveport, La., Jan. 23, 1947; s. Donald Frazier and Dorothy (Carson) H. BS, U. Wyo., 1969, MS, 1970; PhD, U. Colo., 1980. Various positions with govt. conservation agys., parks and univ conservation programs, 1966—; coord. long-term ecol. rsch. program U. Colo., Boulder, 1980-91; rsch. assoc. Inst. Arctic and Alpine Rsch., U. Colo., 1980-87, 92, fellow, 1987-91, affiliate, 1991—; instr. Teton Sci. Sch., Kelly, Wyo., 1980—, affiliate, 1992—, Aspen (Colo.) Ctr. for Environ. Studies, 1984—, Yellowstone (Wyo.) Inst., 1984—, Rocky Mountain Nature Assn., 1987, 90, 92; pres. A Naturalist's World, Boulder, 1985—; staff trainer Colo. Div. Wildlife, 1979, 83, 91, sci. advisor 1982-85; staff trainer Yellowstone Nat. Park, 1985-86, 88, Grand Teton Nat. Park, 1990, Rocky Mountain Nat. Park, 1992; grant proposal rev. bd. NSF, 1984—, Nat. Geog. Sci., 1984—; trustee Thorne Ecol. Inst., Boulder, 1982-84; mem. Indian Peaks Wilderness Area Adv. Panel, Boulder, 1982-86, others; speaker mammal tracking, alpine and winter ecology, Republic of China's endangered wildlife. Author: A Field Guide to Mammal Tracking, 1986, Winter: An Ecological Handbook, 1989, (video) Living Among Ice Bears, (video) Tracking: Mastering the Basics, 1997, Scats and Tracks of the Rocky Mountains, 1998, Scats and Tracks of the Pacific Coast, 1999, (video) A Celebration of Bears, 1999; contbr. chpts. to Discovering Yellowstone Wolves: Wathcer's Guide; editor (booklets) Mountain Rsch. Sta.: its environment and rsch., 1982, Long Term Ecol. Rsch. in the U.S.: a network of rsch. sites, 1982, 83, 84; contbr. articles to profl. jours. and mags. on nat. history. Mem. sci. adv. panel EOP program U. Colo., 1982-84; mem. sci. coun. Greater Yellowstone Coalition; bd. advisors Teton Sci. Sch., Moran, 1985-89; bd. dirs. Nat. Outdoor Leadership Sch., Lander, Wyo., 1975-80, chmn., 1978-79. With USNR, 1969-71, Vietnam. Decorated Navy Achievement medal with combat "v", Vietnamese Gallantry Cross with palm (Republic Vietnam); recipient Book Plate award Denver Pub. Libr. Friends Found. Fellow The Explorer Club; mem. AAAS, Ecol. Soc. Am., Am. Inst. Biol. Scis., Am. Soc. Mammalogists, Internat. Soc. Cryptozoology, Southwestern Assn. Naturalists, N.W. Sci. Assn., Colo.-Wyo. Acad. Sci., Orgn. Biol. Field Stas., Sci. Coun. Greater Yellowstone Coalition, Sigma Xi. Achievements include classification of mammal tracks into gait patterns; interpretation of mammal trails; research on nutrient inputs from aeolian insects into the alpine tundra, on alpine disturbance from vole population irruption, and on long-term variability in subnivean environment. Avocations: nature photography, cross country skiing, hiking, country and folk dance. Office: A Naturalist's World PO Box 989 Gardiner MT 59030-0989

HALFVARSON, LUCILLE ROBERTSON, music educator; b. Petersburg, Ill., May 17, 1919; d. Harris Morton and Lucille (Fox) Robertson; m. Sten Gustaf Halfvarson, Aug. 8, 1946; children: Laura, Eric, Linnea, Mary. BA, Knox Coll., 1941; MusM, Am. Conservatory, 1969. Cert. tchr., Ill. Tchr. music and speech Freeman Elem. Sch., Aurora, Ill., 1941-44; choral dir. Galesburg (Ill.) Sr. H.S., 1944-46; dir. of music Our Savior Luth. Ch., Aurora, Ill., 1950-63; oratorio soloist, 1952-67; dir. of music Westminster Presbyn. Ch., Aurora, 1963-84; vocal instr. Merit Music Program, Chgo., 1982-93; ret., 1993; choir dir. 1st Meth. Ch., Galesburg, 1944-46; choral-vocal instr. Waubonsee C.C., Sugar Grove, Ill., 1967-79; organizer Jr. Coll. Music Festival, Waubonsee Coll., Sugar Grove, 1972-73; pvt. vocal instrn., Aurora, 1979—. Conductor Messiah Concert Waubonsee Coll., Paramount Arts Ctr., 1968—, 25th Concert, 1992. Co-chair Citizens Adv. Com. Paramount Arts. Ctr., Aurora, 1977-78; founder, pres. United Arts Bd. Fox Valley, 1977-82; chair Paramount Celebration Arts, 1985-86; residency dir. Met. Life Affiliate Artist, Aurora, 1982-83; bd. dirs. YWCA, 1984-91, chair corp. award com., 1994-95; dir. New Eng. Congl. Ch. Bell Choir, 1997—. Recipient Disting. Svc. award Cosmopolitan Club, Aurora, Ill., 1983; named Woman of Year YWCA, Aurora, 1976, Disting. Alumni Knox Coll., Galesburg, Ill., 1984. Mem. AAUW, DAR, PEO, Music Educators Nat. Conf., Am. Choral Dirs. Assn., Aurora C. of C. (Image Maker 1992), Phi Beta Kappa. Avocations: needlework, gardening, fishing, reading. Home: 1105 W Downer Pl Aurora IL 60506-4821

HALGREN, LEE A., academic administrator. V.p. acad. and student affairs State Coll. Colo., Denver, 1995—. Office: The State Coll Colo 1580 Lincoln St Ste 750 Denver CO 80203-1505

HALIO, JAY LEON, language professional, educator; b. N.Y.C., July 24, 1928; s. Samuel and Anna (Cohen) H.; children: Brian, Amy. BA, Syracuse U., 1950; MA, Yale U., 1951, PhD, 1956. Instr. English U. Calif., Davis, 1955-57, asst. prof., 1957-63, assoc. prof., 1963-68, prof., 1968; prof. U. Del., Newark, 1968—, assoc. provost for instrn., 1975-81, dir. Ctr. for Teaching Effectiveness, 1975-80, 86-87, dir. humanities semester, 1978-81; chmn. bd. editors U. Del. Press, 1985-97; mem. central exec. com. Folger Inst. Renaissance Studies, 1975-98; mem. adv. bd. Ctr. for Renaissance and Baroque Studies, U. Md., mem. editorial adv. bd. Coll. Literature, Jour. Theatre and Drama; Fulbright-Hays sr. lectr. U. Malaya, 1966-67, Buenos Aires, Argentina, 1974. Author: Angus Wilson, 1964, Understanding Shakespeare's Plays in Performance, 1988, Philip Roth Revisited, 1992, Shakespeare in Performance: A Midsummer Night's Dream, 1994, Romeo and Juliet: A Guide to the Play, 1998; editor: Approaches to Macbeth, 1966, Twentieth Century Interpretations of As You Like It, 1968, Volpone, 1968, Macbeth, 1972, King Lear, 1973; (with David Bevington) Shakespeare: Pattern of Excelling Nature, 1978, British Novelists Since 1960: Dictionary of Literary Biography, vol. 14, 1983, Romeo and Juliet: A Guide to the Play, 1998; (with Kenneth Muir, D.J. Palmer) Shakespeare, Man of the Theater, 1983; (with Barbara C. Millard) As You Like It: An Annotated Bibliography, 1985, Critical Essays on Angus Wilson, 1985, King Lear, 1992; (with Jerzy Limon) Shakespeare and His Contemporaries, 1992, The Merchant of Venice, 1993, The First Quarto of King Lear, 1994, Shakespeare's Romeo and Juliet: Texts, Contexts and Interpretation, 1995, Critical Essays on King Lear, 1996, (with Ben Siegel) Daughters of Valor: Contemporary Jewish American Women Writers, 1997, (with Hugh Richmond) Shakespearean Illuminations, 1998; contbr. essays and revs. to lit. jours. Mem. MLA, Am. Lit. Assn., Assn. Lit. Scholars and Critics, Internat. Shakespeare Assn., Shakespeare Assn. Am., Phi Beta Kappa. Club: Blue and Gold. Home: 8 Country Hill Dr Newark DE 19711-2526 Office: U Del Dept English Newark DE 19716

HALIW, ANDREW JEROME, III, lawyer, engineer; b. Ansbach, Fed. Republic of Germany, Aug. 8, 1946; came to U.S., 1950; s. Ilko and Sophie (Kindrat) H.; children: Larissa Andrea, Andrea Stephanie. BEE, Wayne State U., 1968, JD, 1972; postgrad. in Fin., U. Mich., 1993—. Bar: Mich. 1973, U.S. Dist. Ct. (ea. dist.) Mich. 1973, U.S. Supreme Ct. 1982, Mich. (6th cir.) 1986; lic. profl. engr., Mich., Fla.; registered patent & trademark atty. Divisional elec. engr. J & L div. LTV, Warren, Mich., 1968-72; ptr. bd. dirs. Sullivan & Leavitt P.C., Northville, Mich., 1972-79, ptnr., 1979-91, also bd. dirs.; ptnr. Haliw, Siciliano & Mychalowych, P.C., Farmington Hills, Mich., 1991—; bd. dirs. Am. Supplier Inst., Dearborn Mich.; chmn. Advanced Systems and Designs, Inc., Dearborn; vice chmn. ASI Internat.; commr. SMART, Oakland County. Atty. Ukrainian Cultural Ctr., Warren, 1984; del., dist. dir. Farmington Hills Reps., 1990—; chair Zoning Bd. Appeals, Farmington Hills. Mem. ABA, Detroit Bar Assn., Oakland County Bar Assn., Detroit Engring. Soc. (dist. bd. dirs.). Republican. Ukrainian Catholic. Home: 38250 Nine Mile Rd Northville MI 48167-9014 Office: Haliw Siciliano & Mychalowych PC 37000 Grand River Ave Ste 350 Farmington Hills MI 48335-2812

HALKETT, ALAN NEILSON, lawyer; b. Chungking, China, Oct. 5, 1931; came to U.S., 1940; s. James and Evelyn Alexandrina (Neilson) H.; m. Mary Lou Hickey, July 30, 1955; children—Kent, James, Kate. B.S., UCLA, 1953, LL.B., 1961. Bar: Calif. 1962. Mem. firm Latham & Watkins, L.A., 1961-95, mem. exec. com., 1968-72, chmn. litigation dept., 1980-86, chmn. succession com., 1986-87; state chmn. Am. Coll., Calif., 1992-94; designee CPR panel Disting. Neutrals, 1994—. Served to lt. USN, 1954-58. Fellow Am. Coll. Trial Lawyers; mem. Calif. Bar Assn., Chancery Club, UCLA Law Alumni Assn. (pres. 1968), Order of Coif. Republican. Clubs: Jonathan (Los Angeles); Palos Verdes Country (Palos Verdes Estates, Calif.). Avocations: golf; old cars. Office: Latham & Watkins 633 W 5th St Ste 4000 Los Angeles CA 90071-2005

HALKI, JOHN JOSEPH, retired military officer, physician; b. Fairchance, Pa., July 28, 1926; s. John Stephen and Ann Priscilla (Uhler) H.; m. Elizabeth Irvine Coogle, Apr. 30, 1960; children: Carla Ann, John J. II. BS in Pharmacy, W.Va. U., 1950, BS, 1954; MD, Med. Coll. Va., 1956; PhD in Pharmacology, U. Kans., 1973. Diplomate Am. Bd. Ob-Gyn. Pharmacist Fredlock's Pharmacy, Morgantown, Va., 1950-54; intern Ohio Valley Gen. Hosp., Wheeling, W.Va., 1956-57; resident in Ob-gyn Med. Coll. Va. Hosps., Richmond, 1957-60; commd. 1st lt. USAF, 1957, advanced through grades to brig. gen., 1979; chief ob-gyn service 5060th USAF Hosp., Ladd AFB, Alaska, 1960-62; chief pharmacy 5060th USAF Hosp., Ladd AFB, Ala., 1961-62; asst. chief ob-gyn service 7625th USAF Hosp. USAF Acad., Colorado Springs, Colo., 1963-65, chief ob-gyn service, 1965; chief surg. service 7625th USAF Hosp. USAF Acad., Colorado Springs, 1965; mem. dept. pharmacology Kans. U. Med. Ctr. Air Force Inst. Tech., Kansas City, 1965-68; asst. chmn. ob-gyn Wilford Hall USAF Med. Ctr., Lackland AFB, Tex., 1968-70, asst. dir. base med. services, 1969-70, chief flight medicine div. base med. services, 1969-70, chief med. processing div., 1969-70, asst. chief mil. pub. health base med. services, 1969-70, chmn. ob-gyn, 1970-73, program dir. residency tng. in ob-gyn, 1970-73, dir. hosp. services, 1973-75; comdr. USAF Med. Ctr., Wright-Patterson AFB, Ohio, 1975-79; dir. med. inspection Air Force Inspection and Safety Ctr., Norton AFB, Calif., 1979-81; ret. USAF, 1981; assoc. clin. prof. ob-gyn. Wright State U. Sch. Medicine, Dayton, Ohio, 1975-79, assoc. prof. ob-gyn., 1980-87, assoc. clin. prof. pharmacology, 1976-80, assoc. prof. pharmacology and toxicology, 1980-87, prof. ob-gyn., 1987-89, prof. pharmacology and toxicology, 1987-89, Nicholas J. Thompson prof. ob-gyn, 1985-89, prof. emeritus, 1989—, asst. dean air force affairs, 1976-79, chmn. ob-gyn., 1982-89, program dir. integrated ob-gyn residency program, 1982-89; dir. edn. ob-gyn Miami Valley Hosp., Dayton, 1984-89, emeritus med. staff, 1989—; cons. ob-gyn to surgeon gen. USAF, Washington, 1969-81, USAF Med. Ctr., Wright-Patterson AFB, 1982-89, United Services Dayton Area Inc., 1982-89; asst. clin. prof. ob-gyn U. Tex. Health Sci. Ctr., San Antonio, 1968-70, assoc. clin. prof. ob-gyn, 1970-75; med. dir. Frederick A. White Ctr. Ambulatory Care Wright State U., Dayton, 1981-82; mem. U.S. Pharmacopeial Com. on Revision, 1985-90, chmn. splty. adv. panel in ob-gyn, 1985-90. Active Boy Scouts Am., W.Va., Tex., Ohio, 1938-77; charter mem. Acad. Medicine Wright State U. Sch. Medicine, 1978-88. With USN, 1944-46; USAF, 1957-81. Decorated DSM, Legion of Merit (2), World War II Victory Medal, Nat. Def. medal, Am. Campaign medal, Asiatic-Pacific Campaign medal with 1 service star; recipient Air Force Outstanding Unit award with 2 oak leaf clusters, Merck award W.Va. U. Coll. Pharmacy, 1950, Teaching Recognition award Am. Acad. Family Physicians, 1982, Outstanding Alumnus award W.Va. U. Sch. Pharmacy, 1986; named hon. recruiter USAF Recruiting Svc., 1988. Fellow ACS (life), Am. Coll. Ob-Gyn. (life, sec.-treas. armed forces dist. 1971-74, vice chmn. 1984-87, Kermit Krantz Air Force award Armed Forces Dist. 1988); mem. AMA, VFW, Ohio State Med. Assn., Montgomery County Med. Assn., Air Force Soc. Clin. Surgeons (life, bd. govs. 1977-78), Assn. Profs. Gynecology and Obstetrics (life), Fed. Health Care Execs. Inst. Alumni Assn. (life), W.Va. U. Alumni Assn. (life), W.Va. U. Sch. Medicine Alumni Assn. (life.), W.Va. U. Sch. Pharmacy Alumni Assn., Alpha Omega Alpha, Rho Chi. Republican. Roman Catholic. Avocations: gardening, landscaping, music, sports spectator, photography. Office: Wright State U Sch Medicine Miami Valley Hosp Ob/gyn 128 E Apple St Ste 3800 Che Dayton OH 45409-2902

HALKIN, HUBERT, mathematics educator, research mathematician; b. Liege, Belgium, June 5, 1936; came to U.S., 1960; s. Leon E. and Denise (Daude) H.; m. Carolyn Mulliken, June 22, 1964 (div. 1971); children: Christopher, Sherrill-Anne; m. Katherine Hodges, Dec. 24, 1988. Ingenieur, Université de Liège, 1960; Ph.D., Stanford U., 1963. Mem. tech. staff Bell Telephone Labs., Whippany, N.J., 1963-65; assoc. prof. math. dept. U. Calif., San Diego, 1965-69; prof. U. Calif., 1969—; dept. chmn. U. Calif., San Diego, 1981-87. Editor Jour. Optimization Theory and Applications, 1968—, Revue Française d'Automatique de Recherche Operationnelle, 1973—. Guggenheim fellow, 1971-72. Club: Sierra. Office: U Calif San Diego Dept Math La Jolla CA 92093

HALL, ABRAM, publishing production manager; b. N.Y.C., Mar. 10, 1962; s. Abram Jr. and Daisy (Johnson) H. BFA, Pratt Inst., 1986. Prodn. mgr. Rockefeller Univ. Press, N.Y.C., 1987-88; prodn. coord. Sch. of Visual Arts Press, N.Y.C., 1988-89; prodn. mgr. Oxford Univ. Press, N.Y.C., 1989—; featured spkr. BookTech '99, Overseas Book Mfg.: Buying Tactics, 1999. Art dir., prodn. mgr.: (brochure) Infectivity, 1987 (Ga. Pacific award of excellence 1987); prodn. coord.: (book) Illustration Portfolio 9, 1988 (Rochester Club of Printing House Craftsmen 2d pl. award 1988); prodn. coord.: (book) Oscar's Orange Book, 1990 (N.Y. Book Show 2d pl. award 1990); prodn. mgr.: (book) Mr. Bug's Phonics Book, 1997 (N.Y. Book Show 1st pl. award 1997), Oxford Picture Dictionary, 1998 (N.Y. Book Show 3rd pl. award 1998). Deacon South Bushwick Reformed Ch., Bklyn., 1986-90; del. to Black coun. Reformed Ch. of Am., N.Y.C., 1987-90, del. to urban conf., Hoboken, N.J., 1997. Recipient Cert. of Recognition USIA, 1991. Mem. Graphic Arts Tech. Found., N.Y. Bookbinders' Guild. Democrat. Avocations: painting, drawing, writing, baseball, computers. Office: Oxford Univ Press 198 Madison Ave New York NY 10016-4308

HALL, ALAN CRAIG, library director; b. Marietta, Ohio, Mar. 9, 1954; s. Harry Edward and Flossie June (Heddleston) H.; m. Barbara Ann Metzger, May 23, 1981; 1 child, Shawn Alan. BS in Edn., W.Va. U., 1976; MLS, Case Western U., 1977. With circulation dept. Washington County Pub. Libr., Marietta, Ohio, 1970-75; with govt. documents dept. Freiberger Libr., Cleve., 1976-77; dir. Delphos (Ohio) Pub. Libr., 1977-83, Pub. Libr. of Steubenville and Jefferson County, 1983—; cons. Morgan County Libr., McConnelsville, Ohio, 1992-93, Barnesville (Ohio) Pub. Libr., 1991, Reed Meml. Libr., Ravenna, Ohio, 1997-98; chair Ohio Libr. Coun., Columbus, 1994, com. rev. bd. structure, 1999, co-chair Ohio statewide resource sharing com., 1998-99. Author: Marietta's Innkeeper, 1991, The Mary Thompson Collection, 1997; editor: The Papers of A.T. Nye, 1975, Abandoned Underground Coal Mines of Jefferson County, 1991, Richmond, Ohio Cemetery Book, 1995; compiler Historic Pages Series, 1975-76; editor: Steubenville (Ohio) Bicentennial History Book, 1996-97; contbr. articles to profl. publs. Chairperson Ohio Humanities Coun., Steubenville, 1991; pres. Ret. Sr. Vol. Program, Steubenville, 1989-90; ruling elder Starkdale Presbyn. Ch., 1985-88, 94-96, 98—, chmn. pastor nominating com., 1996-97. Mem. ALA, Jefferson County Hist. Soc., Steubenville Lions Club (pres. 1986-87), Ohio Libr. Assn. (pres. 1992-93, Libr. of Yr. 1989), Steubenville Rotary. Office: 407 S 4th St Steubenville OH 43952-2942

HALL, ALBERT L., lawyer, retired; b. Chgo., June 17, 1926; s. Albert L. and Orpah (Starratt) H.; m. Catherine Ann Comstock, Sept. 27, 1947; children: Terry Lee, David M., Margaret Ruth, Diane Marie. Grad., Lake Forest Acad., 1944; B.S., U. Ill., 1949, M.S., 1950; J.D., Northwestern U., 1955. Bar: Ill. 1955, U.S. Dist. Ct. (no. dist.) Ill. 1955. Tchr. Washington Park High Sch., Racine, Wis., 1950-52; ptnr. Hall, Roach, Johnston et al, Waukegan, Ill., 1958-91; of counsel Hall, Roach, Johnston et al, Ill., 1991-95, Bollman & Lesser, Lake Forest, Ill., 1996—; arbitrator Am. Arbitration Assn., 1975-90, 19th Jud. Cir. Ct. Ill., 1990-98. Bd. dirs. Lake County Children's Orthopedic Clinic, Inc., 1966—, pres., 1979-81. With USNR, 1944-46. Mem. Lake County Bar Assn., Waukegan-Lake County C. of C. (pres. 1968-69), Delta Tau Delta, Phi Alpha Delta. Club: City Club of Waukegan (pres. 1970). Home: 2048 Hickory St Waukegan IL 60087-5019

HALL, ANDREW CLIFFORD, lawyer; b. Warsaw, Poland, Sept. 16, 1944; s. Edmund and Maria (Hahn) H.; came to U.S., 1949, naturalized, 1954; children: Michael Ian, Adam Stuart, Hilary Meyers Azrael, Katie Meyers; m. Gail Meyers, 1993. BA, U. Fla., 1965, JD with high honors, 1968. Bar: Fla. 1968, U.S. Dist. Ct. (so. dist.) Fla. 1968, U.S. Dist. Ct. (no. dist.) Ga. 1971, U.S. Ct. Appeals (5th cir.) 1971, Ga. 1973, U.S. Supreme Ct. 1974, U.S. Ct. Appeals (D.C. cir.) 1974, U.S. Ct. Appeals (11th cir.) 1981. Law clk. to judge U.S. Dist. Ct.; assoc., Haas, Holland, Levison, Gilbert, Atlanta, 1970-72, Frates, Floyd, Pearson, Stewart, Miami, 1972-75; ptnr. Storace, Hall & Hauser, Miami, 1975-79, Hall & Hauser, 1979-82, Hall & O'Brien, P.A., Miami, 1982-95, Andrew Hall and Assoc., Pa., 1995-99; Hall, David and Joseph, P.A., 1999—; instr. bus. law U. Fla.; Trustee U. Fla., Coll. of Law Found. Bd. dirs. Greater Miami Jewish Fedn.; chmn., bd. trustees, bd. dirs Cen. Agy. Jewish Edn., Ash Ha Torah; mem. coun. of 100 Fla. Internat. U. Mem. ABA, Hebrew Immigrant Aid Assn. (nat. bd. mem.), Fla. State Bar, Am. Judicature Soc., U. Fla. Coll. Law Alumni (coun.), Acad. Fla. Trial Lawyers (diplomate), Assn. Trial Lawyers Am., Phi Kappa Phi, Phi Alpha Delta, Order of Coif. Democrat. Jewish. Home: 2000 S Bayshore Dr Miami FL 33133-3256 Office: Hall David and Joseph PA Att/Karen Fernandez 1428 Brickell Ave PH Miami FL 33131-3438

HALL, ANTHONY ELMITT, crop ecologist; b. Tickhill, Yorkshire, Eng., May 6, 1940; came to U.S., 1964; s. Elmitt and Mary Lisca (Schofield) H.; m. Bretta Reed, June 20, 1965; children: Kerry, Gina. Student, Harper Adams Agrl. Coll., Eng., 1958-60; student in agrl. engring., Essex Inst. Agrl. Engring., Eng., 1960-61; BS in Irrigation Sci., U. Calif., Davis, 1966, PhD in Plant Physiology, 1970. Farmer Dyon House, Austerfield, Eng., 1955-58; extension officer Ministry of Agr., Tanzania, 1961-63; research asst. U. Calif., Davis, 1964-70, asst. research scientist, 1971; research fellow Carnegie Inst., Stanford, Calif., 1970; prof. U. Calif., Riverside, 1971—, cons. on African agrl. devel., 1974—, chmn. dept botany and plant scis., 1994-97. Editor: Agriculture in Semi-Arid Environments, 1979, Stable Isotopes and Plant Carbon-Water Relations, 1993; mem. editl. adv. bd. (jour.) Field Crops Rsch., Vigna Crop Germplasm Com. USDA; contbr. articles to profl. jours. Fellow Am. Soc. Agronomy, Crop Sci. Soc. Am.; mem. Am. Soc. Plant Physiologists, Scandinavian Soc. Plant Physiology, Alpha Zeta, Gamma Sigma Delta, Phi Beta Kappa, Phi Kappa Phi. Achievements include design (with others) of a steady state porometer for measuring stomatal conductance; research on the physiology and breeding of heat and chilling tolerant, pest resistant and drought adapted cowpea cultivars. Office: U Calif Dept Botany and Plant Scis Riverside CA 92521

HALL, ANTHONY R., photographer; b. London, Mar. 18, 1950; s. Reynolds A. and Lilly Elizabeth Hall; m. Marie Quilon, Feb. 14, 1991; children: Coloma, Everest. AA English, Pierce Coll., 1969; BA in English, Calif. State U., 1971. Profl. photographer specialising in people, in comml. and fashion advt.; clients include: Warner Bros., A&M Records, L.A., UCLA, W.W. Norton Books, CableVision Industries, SpeakEasy Mag., Paris, Playboy Agy., Max Agy., Smash Agy., L.A., Brooks Coll. Fashion Design, Damen Industries, Dorothy Shreve Talent Agy., Palm Springs, many others; photography in pubs. including: L.A. Times, Image Mag., Valley Family, L.A. Family Mag., Dama Dinamica, Churokoron, Profl. Photographer, Black Pasion Vol. 2, ArtWeek, others; exhbns. include: Living Arts Gallery, 1983, Photography World Concerts for Humanity, 1984, L.A.V.A., 1985, Calif. State Regional Photographic, 1986, Calif. State U., Choco, 1989, Profl. Photographers Am. Western States, 1990, Internat., 1990, Chgo. Art Inst., 1990, Showcase 91, Beaverton Arts, Oreg., 1991, Soc. for Contemporary Photography, 1991, Orlando Gallery, sherman Oaks, 1991, Fla. Nationals, 1992, Mo. State U., Kirksville, 1992, FotoFest Internat., Houston, 1992, Orlando Gallery, 1993. Recipient 1st place award Calif. State U. Regional, 1986, Fla. Nationals, 1992, Cert. of Merit, Profl. Photographers of Am., 1990. Mem. Kodak Profl. Network of Photographers. Office: 12782 Sky Line Dr Desert Hot Springs CA 92240-4338

HALL, ARSENIO, actor, comedian; b. Cleveland, Feb. 12, 1955; s. Fred and Annie Hall. Student, Ohio U.; BA in speech, Kent State U. Began entertainment career as stand-up comic, Chgo.; TV appearances on Tonight Show with Johnny Carson, The Oprah Winfrey Show, Tonight Show with Jay Leno, The Rosie O'Donnell Show; host, exec. prodr. The Arsenio Hall Show, 1989-94; host The Late Show, 1987; co-host Thicke of the Night, 1983, MTV Awards, 1989-91; appeared in films Amazon Women on the Moon, 1987, Coming to America, 1988, Harlem Nights, 1989; prodr. The Party Machine, (film) Bopha, 1993; host: (home video) Time Out: The Truth about HIV, AIDS and You.

HALL, ARTHUR RAYMOND, JR., minister; b. Danville, Ill., Apr. 16, 1922; s. Arthur Raymond and Hetta Ada (Wheeler) H.; m. Lou Ann Benson, Mar. 16, 1946; children: Janet Marie Hall Graff, Laura Ann Hall Scott Abell, Nancy Marion Hall Berens. A.B., U. Ill., 1946, M.A., 1948; M.Div. cum laude, Union Theol. Sem., N.Y.C., 1951; D.D., Hanover Coll., 1961. Staff asst. McKinley Meml. Ch. and Found., Champaign, Ill., 1946-48; student asst. First Presbyn Ch., N.Y.C., 1948-50; ordained to ministry Presbyn. Ch., 1951; pastor First Presbyn. Ch., Monmouth, Ill., 1951-58, Cen. Presbyn. Ch., Louisville, 1958-67, Bradley Hills Presbyn. Ch., Bethesda, Md., 1967-89; pres. bd. Christian edn. United Presbyn. Ch., 1968-73; sec., bd. dirs. Louisville Presbyn. Sem., 1962-70; chmn. renewal and extension of ministry (United Presbyn. Gen. Assembly), 1965-68; mem. joint com. on Presbyn. Reunion, 1969-83; moderator Synod of Piedmont, 1974-75; trustee U.P. Ch., 1974-83; bd. dirs. U.P. Found., 1974-83; del. Uniting Assembly of World Alliance of Ref. Chs., Nairobi, Kenya, 1970; mem. com. on theol. edn. Presbyn. Ch., U.S.A., 1987, assoc. dir. 1988-90. Contbr. articles to periodicals. Pres. Citizens Met. Planning Coun., Louisville, 1962; chmn. Mayor's Adv. Com. for Community Devel., 1963-67; v.p. Louisville YMCA Downtown Bd., 1963; bd. dirs. Louisville Health and Welfare Coun., 1963-67, Greater Washington Coun. Chs., Johnson C. Smith Theol. Sem., Atlanta, 1973—, Interdenominational Theol. Ctr., Atlanta, 1974—; trustee Centre Coll. Ky., 1959-73, Union Theol. Sem., N.Y.C., 1975-84; trustee Travelers Aid Soc., Louisville, 1959-67, v.p., 1961-67. Lt. (j.g.) USNR, 1943-46. Mem. Am. Guild Organists, Washington Interchurch Club, Rotary, Beta Theta Pi, Phi Delta Phi. Democrat. Home: 580 Russell Ave Gaithersburg MD 20877-2868

HALL, ATLEE BURPEE, researcher; b. Talking Rock, Ga., Feb. 5, 1911; s. Thomas Sanford and Betulia Queen (Lambert) H.; m. Rhonwyn Fay Blevins, Apr. 9, 1933; children: Kilmer Lanier, Gloria Joyce, Rebecca Lou, Andrea Faith. Grad. high sch. Postmaster U.S. Postal Svc., Ider, Ala., 1935-56; elec. mechanic NASA, Huntsville, Ala., 1956-66; rschr. pvt. practice, Arab, Ala., 1966—. Author: Goodness and Mercy, 1989, Crossword Puzzle Dictionary, 1993, (booklets) Nature Study Calendar, 1972, Primitive Baptist Statistics, 1974. Avocations: amateur radio, weather log, religious history, primitive Bapt. min., amateur naturalist. Home: 1427 Fenton Rd Arab AL 35016-4629

HALL, BENNETT FREEMAN, minister; b. Macon, Ga., Nov. 30, 1914; s. Charles McDonald and Mary Elizabeth (Lyon) H.; m. Mae Elizabeth Wells, June 2, 1937; children: Mari, Laura, Louise, Ben. Student, Bryan U., 1934-

36; AB, Stetson U., 1938; ThM, So. Bapt. Theol. Sem., 1943; postgrad., Jewish Theol. Sem., 1968-71; ThM, Princeton Theol. Sem., 1975; DMin, Drew U., 1979. Ordained to ministry Bapt. Ch., 1936. Pastor Sale Creek, Tenn., 1935-36, Sorrento, Fla., 1936-38; pastor Union Gospel Mission, Louisville, Ky., 1938-39, Lucerne Park Ch., Orlando, Fla., 1939-41, Fayetteville and Williams, Ind., 1941-42, Falmouth (Ky.) Bapt. Ch., 1942-44, First Bapt. Ch., Titusville, Fla., 1944-49, Bay Haven Bapt. Ch., Sarasota, Fla., 1950-53, Southside Bapt. Ch., Bradenton, Fla., 1954-67, Somerset Hills Bapt. Ch., Bernardsville, N.J. (Now in Basking Ridge, N.J.), N.J., 1967-79, First Bapt. Ch., Lexington, Ky., 1982-85; trustee Bapt. Bible Inst., Fla., 1949-59; mem. state mission bd. Fla. Bapt. Conv., 1957-59; dean, tchr. extention dept. Stetson U., 1960-64; evangelist Jamaica Crusade, 1966; missions com. Met. N.Y. Bapt. Assn., 1968-72, chmn. constn. and credentials com., 1972-77; tchr., sem. extension Met. N.Y. Assn., 1976-78; adv. bd. Cumberland Coll., Williamsburg, Ky., 1982-91. Chmn. ARC, Titusville, 1944-46; mem. Mental Health Orgn., Bradenton, 1964-66. Home: 293 S Main St Winchester KY 40391-2471 *Two great statements, learned in college, have been the guiding principle of my life. The Socratic challenge: "Follow the truth wherever it leads." The other: "Learn to distinguish between the spiritual ointment and the spiritual neceptacle."*

HALL, BEVERLY ADELE, nursing educator; b. Houston, Aug. 19, 1935; d. Leslie Leo and Lois Mae (Pesnell) H. BS, Tex. Christian U., 1957; MA, NYU, 1961; PhD, U. Colo., 1974. RN, Tex., N.Y. With Ft. Worth (Tex.) Dept. Health, 1957-59; asst. prof. U. Mass., Amhurst, 1961-65; chief nurse N.Y.C. Med. Coll., 1965-67; asst. prof. U. Colo., Denver, 1967-70; assoc. prof. U. Washington, Seattle, 1974-80; prof., chmn. dept. U. Calif., San Francisco, 1980-84; Denton Cooley prof. nursing U. Tex., Austin, 1984—; mem. grad. faculty Sch. Biomed. Sci. U. Tex., Galveston; pres. med. svcs. Bd. Dir. Project Transitions; disting. prof. Coll. Nursing, Arts and Scis., Hyogo, Japan; mem. NIH Study Group; cons. HIV/AIDS Internat. Coun. fo Nurses. Author: Mental Health and the Elderly, 1985 (Book of Yr.); mem. editl. rev. bd. Advances in Nursing, Archives Psychiat. Nursing, Qualitative Health Rsch., Rsch. in Nursing and Health, Nursing Outlook, Jour. Profl. Nursing, Jour. of the Am. Psychiat. Nurses Assn.; contbr. articles to profl. jours., chpts. to books. Served to capt. U.S. Army, 1962-66. Recipient Tex. Excellence Teaching award U. Tex. Ex-Students Assn., 1994. Fellow Am. Acad. Nursing (governing bd., mem. fellowship selection com.), Am. Coll. Mental Health Adminstrn.; mem. ANA (divsn. gerontological practice), Coun. Nurse Rschrs., Am. Inst. Life Threatening Illness and Loss, So. Nursing Rsch. Soc. Home: 23 Jackson Ct San Antonio TX 78230-2569 Office: U Tex 1700 Red River St Austin TX 78701-1412

HALL, BEVERLY JOY, police officer; b. St. Paul, Minn., Dec. 31, 1957; d. Kenneth Ray and Harriet Kathleen (Fuller) H.; m. Charles Alan Neuman, Feb. 14, 1956. AAS in Law Enforcement, North Hennepin C.C., Brooklyn Park, Minn., 1977; BA in Law Enforcement Mgmt., Met. State U., St. Paul, 1999. Lic. peace officer, Minn. Community svc. officer Brooklyn Park Police Dept., 1977-79; police officer St. Paul Police Dept., 1979-86, police sgt., 1986-95, police lt., 1995—; hostage negotiator, St. Paul Police Dept., 1991-92, hostage negotiating team coord., 1992-96. Mem. Internat. Assn. Women Police (regional coord. 1988-94, bd. dirs.), Nat. Assn. Women Law Enforcement Execs., Minn. Assn. of Women Police (pres. 1982-86), Assn. Tng. Officers of Minn., Fed. Bur. of Investigations Nat. Acad. Assocs. Avocations: gardening, jogging, reading. Office: Saint Paul Police Dept 100 11th St E Ste 1 Saint Paul MN 55101-2296

HALL, BLAINE HILL, retired librarian; b. Wellsville, Utah, Dec. 12, 1932; s. James Owen and Agnes Effie (Hill) H.; m. Carol Stokes, 1959; children: Suzanne, Cheryl, Derek. BS, Brigham Young U., 1960, MA, 1965, MLS, 1971. Instr. English, Brigham Young U., Provo, Utah, 1963-72, humanities librarian, 1972-96; book reviewer Am. Reference Book Ann., 1984—. Author: Collection Assessment Manual, 1985, Saul Bellow Bibliography, 1987, Jerzy Kosinski Bibliography, 1991, Jewish American Fiction Writers Bibliography, 1991, Conversations with Grace Paley, 1997; editor: Utah Libraries, 1972-77 (periodical award ALA 1977); contbr. articles to profl. jours. Bd. dirs. Orem (Utah) Pub. Libr., 1977-84; mem. Orem Media Rev. Commn., 1984-86; chmn. Utah Adv. Commn. on Librs. With U.S. Army, 1953-54, Korea. Mem. ALA (coun. 1988-92), Utah Libr. Assn. (pres. 1980-81, Disting. Svc. award 1989), Mountain Plains Libr. Assn. (bd. dirs. 1978-83, editor newsletter 1978-83, pres. 1994-96, grantee 1979, 80, Disting. Svc. award 1991), Phi Kappa Phi. Mormon. Avocations: writing, photography, carpentry, family history, reading. Home: 230 E 1910 S Orem UT 84058-8161

HALL, BRAD BAILEY, orthopaedic surgeon, health care administrator; b. Lubbock, Tex., Nov. 16, 1951; s. John Robert and Anna Ruth (Marks) H.; m. Carol Lynn Martin, Dec. 20, 1975; children: Clint Berkeley, Kathryn Lynn. Student, Ariz. State U., 1970-72; MD, Tex. Tech U., 1977; MS in Healthcare Adminstrn., U. Colo., 1996. Diplomate Am. Bd. Orthopaedic Surgery. Resident in orthopaedic surgery Mayo Clinic, Rochester, Minn., 1977-82, cons. in orthopaedic surgery, 1982-83; spine fellow U. Toronto, Ont., Can., 1982; pvt. practice, San Antonio, 1983-97; sr. v.p. quality Bapt. Health Sys., San Antonio, 1997-98, v.p. med. mgmt., 1998—; med. dir. Bent Health Network, San Antonio, 1998—; clin. assoc. prof. U. Tex. Health Sci. Ctr., San Antonio, 1984—, med. dir. orthopaedic clinic, 1996-97; orthopaedic staff physician Audie L. Murphy Meml. VA Hosp., San Antonio, 1985—; chmn. dept. orthopaedics St. Luke's Luth. Hosp., San Antonio, 1986-88, dir. residency, 1987-94, chief of staff, bd. dirs., mem. fin. com., chmn. exec. staff com., 1992—; pres., bd. dirs. Musculoskeletal Assocs. So. Tex., P.A., 1994-97; presenter in field. Contbr. articles and abstracts to med. jours., chpts. to books. Grantee Orthopaedic Rsch. and Edn. Found., 1979; scholar Mayo Found., 1982. Mem. AMA (physicians recognition award 1984-87, 88-96), Orthopaedic Rsch. Soc., Am. Acad. Orthopaedic Surgeons, Mid-Am. Orthopaedic Assn., N.Am. Spine Soc., Clin. Orthopaedic Soc., Western Orthopaedic Assn., Tex. Spine Soc. (bd. dirs., pres. 1994-95), Tex. Med. Assn., Tex. Orthopaedic Assn., Bexar County Med. Soc., San Antonio Orthopaedic Assn. (pres.), Am. Coll. Physician Execs. Office: Bapt Health Sys 660 N Main Ave Ste 325 San Antonio TX 78205-1222

HALL, BRIAN KEITH, biology educator, author; b. Port Kembla, N.S.W., Australia, Oct. 28, 1941; s. Harry J. and Doris (Garrad) H.; m. June Denise Priestley, May 21, 1966; children: Derek Andrew, Imogen Elizabeth. BSc, U. New Eng., Australia, 1963, BSc with honors, 1965; PhD, U. New Eng., 1968, DSc, 1978. Teaching fellow U. New Eng., Armidale, 1965-68; asst. prof. biology Dalhousie U., Halifax, N.S., Can., 1968-72, assoc. prof., 1972-75, prof., 1975—, chmn. dept. biology, 1990-95, Killam rsch. prof., 1990-95; faculty sci., Killam prof. biology, 1996—; vis. prof. U. Guelph, 1975, U. Queensland, Australia, 1981, Southampton U., Eng., 1982; Rayne mem. vis. prof. U. Western Australia, 1993; mem. adv. com. on life scis. Natural Scis. and Engring. Rsch. Coun. Can., 1985; Turner-Newall lectr. U. Manchester, Eng., 1985; Frontiers in Biology lectr. Tex. A&M U., 1992; Von Hofsten lectr. Uppsala U., Sweden, 1993; Plenary lect. Internat. Congress of Vert. Morphol., 1994; Fry lectr. Can. Soc. Zoologists, 1994, Sarnat lectr. UCLA, 1994; Miller vis. res. prof. U. Calif., Berkeley, 1997; Landsdowne vis. prof. U. Victoria, 1998. Author: Developmental and Cellular Skeletal Biology, 1978, (with N. MacLean) Cell Commitment and Differentiation, 1987, The Neural Crest, 1988, Evolutionary Developmental Biology, 1992, 2d edit., 1998, The Neural Crest in Development and Evolution, 1999; editor: Cartilage, 3 vols., 1983, Bone, A Treatise, 9 vols., 1990-94; (with S. Newman) Cartilage: Molecular Aspects, 1991, (with J. Hanken) The Vertebrate Skull, 3 vols., 1993, Homology: The Hierarchical Basis of Comparative Biology, 1994, (with W.M. Wake) The Origin and Evolution of Larval Forms, 1999. Recipient Young Scientist of Yr. medal Atlantic Provinces Interuniv. com. in Scis., 1974, Fry medal Can. Soc. of Zoologists, 1994, Craniofacial Biology Rsch. award 1996; fellow Nuffield Found., 1982; Warwick James fellow London U., 1989; fellow Ctr. for Human Biology, U. Western Australia, 1993. Fellow Royal Soc. Can.; mem. AAAS, Coun. Biology of Can. (coun. 1979-81), Can. Nat. Com., Internat. Union Biol. Scis. Home: 2384 Armcrescent E, Halifax, NS Canada B3L 3C7

HALL, CARL LOREN, electrical distribution executive; b. Jenkins, Ky., Oct. 4, 1937; s. Carl Edwin and Josephine (Smith) H.; m. Barbara Kay Anderson, Aug. 21, 1956; children: Carl David, Michael, Elizabeth. BS, U. Cin., 1971. From warehouseman to sr. sales rep. Graybar Electric Co., Inc., Cin., 1959-74; br. mgr. Graybar Electric Co., Inc., Dayton, Ohio, 1975-76; dist. sales mgr. Graybar Electric Co., Inc., Cin., 1976-81; dist. mgr. Graybar Electric Co., Inc., Memphis, 1981-84, Houston, 1984-88; dist. mgr., dir. Graybar Electric Co., Inc., Chgo., 1988-94; exec. v.p. Graybar Electric Co., Inc., St. Louis, 1994-95, pres., CEO, 1995—. bd. dirs. Boatmen's Nat. Bank, St. Louis, St. Louis Repertory Theatre, Nat. Assn. Elec. Distbrs. With USAF, 1955-59. Mem. Medinah Country Club, Bellerive Country Club, St. Louis Club. Avocation: golf. Office: Graybar Electric Co Inc 34 N Meramec Ave Stop 1 Clayton MO 63105-3882*

HALL, CARL WILLIAM, agricultural and mechanical engineer; b. Tiffin, Ohio, Nov. 16, 1924; s. Lester and Irene (Routzahn) H.; m. Mildred Evelyn Wagner, Sept. 5, 1949; 1 dau., Claudia Elizabeth. B.S., B. in Agricultural Engring. summa cum laude, Ohio State U., 1948; M.M.E., U. Del., 1950; Ph.D., Mich. State U., 1952. Registered profl. engr., Mich., Ohio. Instr. U. Del., 1948-50, asst. prof., 1950-51; asst. prof. Mich. State U., 1951-53, assoc. prof., 1953-55, prof., 1955-70, chmn. dept. agrl. engring., 1964-70; dean, dir. research (Coll. Engring.); prof. mech. engring. Wash. State U., Pullman, 1970-82, pres. WSU Rsch. Found., 1973-82; dep. asst. dir. Directorate for Engring. NSF, 1982-90; ret., 1990; with ESCOE, Inc., Washington, 1979; dist. vis. prof. Ohio State U., 1991; rsch. con. U. P.R., 1957, 63; del. to USSR, 1958, 87; cons. U. Nacional de Colombia, 1960; cons. dairy engring., India, 1961, food engring., Taiwan, 1961, Mission to Ecuador, 1966, U. Nigeria, 1967, UNDP/SF Project 80 (higher edn. Latin Am.), 1964-70, world food and nutrition study Nat. Acad. Sci., 1976-77; mem. engring. edn. del. to People's Republic of China, 1978, Indonesia, 1978, 93, 94; co-chmn. NRC-India Nat. Sci. Acad. Workshop, New Delhi, 1979; with ACA, Inc. (cons. engring.), 1956-70, pres., 1962-70; chmn. Nat. Dairy Engring. Conf., 1953-66; mem. postgrad. edn. select com. USN, Monterey, Calif., 1975; rsch. fellow Jap. Soc. promotion Sci., 1991. Author: Drying Farm Crops, 1957, Agricultural Engineering Index 1907-60, 1961-70, 71-80, 81-90, (with others) Drying of Milk and Milk Products, 1966, 71, Agricultural Mechanization for Developing Countries, 1973; co-editor: Agricultural Engineers Handbook, 1960, Processing Equipment for Agricultural Products, 1963, 2d edit., 1979, Spanish edit., 1968, Milk Pasteurization, 1968, Ency. of Food Engineering, 1971, 86, Drying Cereal Grains, 1974, 2d edit., 1991, Dairy Technology and Engineering, 1976, Errors in Experimentation, 1977, Dictionary of Drying, 1979, Drying and Storage of Agricultural Products, 1980, Biomass as an Alternative Fuel, 1981, Dictionary of Energy, 1983, Food and Energy, 1984, Food and Natural Resources, 1988, Biomass Handbook, 1989, (with others) Drying and Storage of Grains, 1992, Literature of Agricultural Engineering, 1992, The Age of Synthesis, 1995; editor, emeritus: Drying Technology: Marcel Dekker, Inc.; contbr. yearbooks, encys., handbooks, over 400 articles to profl. jours. Served with AUS, 1943-46, ETO. Decorated Bronze Star and CIB; recipient Disting. Faculty award Mich. State U., 1963, Centennial Achievement award Ohio State U., 1970, Massey-Ferguson Edn. medal, 1976, Max Eyth medal, Germany, 1979, Medal du Merite, France, 1979, Silver medal, Paris, 1980, Cyrus Hall McCormick medal, 1984, Disting. Svc. award and medal NSF, 1988, Excellence in Drying award IDS, 1990, Food Engring. award and medal, 1993; named Engr. of Yr. D.C. Coun. of Engrs. and Architects, 1999. Fellow AAAS (life), ASME (life, v.p. rsch. 1993-95), ASAE (life, pres. 1974-75), Am. Inst. Med. and Biol. Engring., NAE, Accreditation Bd. Engring. and Tech.; mem. Am. Soc. Engring. Edn. (life), Am. Inst. Biol. Scis., Wash. Soc. Profl. Engrs. (nat. dir. 1975-79), Va. Soc. Profl. Engrs. (pres. No. Va. chpt. 1987-88), Internat. Commn. Agrl. Engrs. (v.p. 1965-74), Engrs. Coun. for Profl. Devel. (exec. com., bd. dirs., sec. 1973-74, chmn. engring. accreditation commn. 1979-80), 99th Inf. Divsn. Assn., VFW, Inst. Food Tech., Inst. Biol. Engring., Sigma Xi, Tau Beta Pi, Phi Kappa Phi, Gamma Sigma Delta, Phi Lambda Tau. Achievements include rsch. in energy, drying, food engring., properties of materials and biomass. Office: Engring Info Svcs 2454 N Rockingham St Arlington VA 22207-1033

HALL, CHARLES ADAMS, information systems specialist; b. Damoh, India, Aug. 6, 1949; s. Keith Burckle and Virginia (Bevan) H.; m. Nancy Louise Dahl, June 7, 1980; 1 child, Loren Jarrett. BA, Hiram (Ohio) Coll., 1972; AA, Ind. Vocat. Tech. Coll., 1983. Programmer Superior Supply, Inc., Marion, Ind., 1983-85, data processing mgr., 1985-89, dir. mgmt. info. systems, 1990-92; systems adminstr. Hi-Way Dispatch, Marion, 1992-94, B&M Investors, Marion, 1994-98; dir. mgmt. info. systems Wiljef Transp., 1998—; programmer Freel & Mason, Marion, 1985; programmer, chief programmer Bruce, Hall & Assocs., Marion, 1986-88. Developer computer game. Sec., treas. bd. dirs. Health Environ. for All Life, Marion, 1988—. With U.S. Army, 1973-76. Mem. Christian Ch. (Disciples of Christ). Office: PO Box 896 Marion IN 46952-0896

HALL, CHARLES ALLEN, aerospace and energy consultant; b. Wichita, Kans., Oct. 11, 1933; s. J. Raymond and Nila Mildred (Allen) H.; m. Berneida K. Dechant, Nov. 29, 1940; children: Melissa Sue Smith, Charles A. Rowden. BS in Engring. and Mgmt., U. Denver, 1968; MSCE, U. Colo., 1972, PhD, 1978. With Martin Marietta Corp., Denver, 1959-64, mgr. mech. engring., 1964-78, dir. mech. engring., 1978-82; v.p. engring. Martin Marietta Corp., Balt., 1982-84; dir. research, corp. Martin Marietta Corp., Bethesda, Md., 1984-86, v.p. engring., corp., 1986-88; v.p. tech. activities Energy Systems, Oak Ridge, Tenn., 1988-92, pres. splty. components, 1992-96; cons. in nuclear waste cleanup and aerospace fields, 1996—. Inventor O-Leak Fuel Tubing, 1980; concept for solar energy chem. furnace, 1977. Mem. Colo. State Air Quality Control Commn., Denver, 1978-82. Mem. Fla. Def. Conversion and Transition Commn., Bayou Club (Largo, Fla.), Black Diamond Ranch (Lecanto, Fla.). Avocation: golf. Home and Office: 7428 Watersilk Dr Pinellas Park FL 33782-4310

HALL, CHARLES FREDERICK, space scientist, government administrator; b. San Francisco, Apr. 7, 1920; s. Charles Rogers and Edna Mary (Gibson) H.; m. Constance Vivienne Andrews, Sept. 18, 1942; children—Steven R., Charles Frederick, Frank A. B.S., U. Calif., Berkeley, 1942. Aero. research scientist NACA (later NASA), Moffett Field, Calif., 1942-60; mem. staff space projects NACA (later NASA), 1960-63; mgr. Pioneer Project, NASA, 1963-80. Recipient Disting. Service medal NASA, 1974, Achievement award Am. Astronautical Soc., 1974, Spl. Achievement award Nat. Civil Service League, 1976, Astronautics Engr. award Nat. Space Club, 1979. Rsch., reports on performance of wings and inlets at transonic and supersonic speeds, on conical-cambered wings at transonic and supersonic speeds, 1942-60; pioneer project launched 4 solar orbiting, 2 Jupiter and 2 Venus spacecraft. Home: 817 Berry Ave Los Altos CA 94024-5416

HALL, CHARLES WASHINGTON, lawyer; b. Dallas, June 30, 1930; s. Albert Brown and Eleanor Pauline (Hopkins) H.; m. Mary Louise Watkins, Aug. 3, 1957; children: Katherine Louise, Allison Ash, Charles Washington III. BA, U. of South, 1951; JD, So. Meth. U., 1954, LLM in Taxation, 1959. Bar: Tex. 1954. Ptnr. Storey, Armstrong & Steger, Dallas, 1954-57; sr. ptnr. Fulbright & Jaworski, Houston, 1957—; mem. adv. com. on tax litigation Dept. Justice, 1979-80; dir. Friedman Ind., Inc., Tex. Med. Ctr., Inc. Houston; mem. Commr. Internal Revenue Adv. Group, 1990-91; mem. adv. coun. U.S. Claims Ct., 1988—. Pres., trustee Sarah Campbell Blaffer Found., Houston; dir. Goodwill Industry, Houston, 1977-84; trustee Inst. Religion, Houston, Killson Found., Houston, M.D. Anderson Found., Houston, Allbritton Found., Houston, Allbritton Art Inst., Houston, Southwestern Legal Found., Dallas, S.W. Rsch. Inst., San Antonio, Houston Child Guidance Ctr., 1984-86; gov. Houston Forum, 1992-95. Fellow Am. Bar Found.; mem. ABA (chmn. sect. taxation 1987-88, ho. dels. 1991-95, nat. conf. lawyers and CPAs chmn. from 1991), Houston Bar Assn., Dallas Bar Assn., State Bar Tex. (chmn. sect. taxation 1970-71), Internat. Bar Assn., Am. Coll. Tax Counsel (regent 1982-91), Am. Law Inst., River Oaks Country Club, Petroleum Club, Coronado (pres. 1982-83), Houston City Club, Met. Club (Washington), Order of St. Lazarus. Episcopalian. Office: Fulbright & Jaworski LLP 1301 Mckinney St Ste 5100 Houston TX 77010-3031

HALL, CHARLOTTE HAUCH, newspaper editor; b. Washington, Sept. 30, 1945; d. Charles Christian and Ruthadele Bertha (LaTourrette) H.; m. Robert Lindsay Hall, June 8, 1968; 1 child, Benjamin H. BA, Kalamazoo Co., 1966; MA, U. Chgo., 1967. Reporter, news editor The Ridgewood (N.J.) Newspapers, 1971-74; copy editor, news editor The Record, Hackensack, N.J., 1975-76; asst. mng. editor The Boston Herald Am., 1977-78; dep. met. editor The Washington Star, 1979-80; news editor, Nassau County editor, Washington news editor Newsday, Melville, N.Y., 1981-87, asst. mng. editor, 1988-94; mktg. dir. Newsday, Inc., Melville, 1994-96, mng. editor, 1997—. Trustee Kalamazoo Coll. Mem. Am. Soc. Newspaper Editors, Newspaper Assn. Am., Phi Beta Kappa. Office: Newsday Inc 235 Pinelawn Rd Melville NY 11747-4250

HALL, CHERYL, newspaper editor. Financial editor Dallas Morning News, Tex. Office: The Dallas Morning News Communciations Ctr 508 Young St Dallas TX 75202-4828*

HALL, CHRISTOPHER, political party official. Chmn. Maine Dem. Party, Augusta. Office: Maine Democratic Party PO Box 5258 Augusta ME 04332-5258

HALL, CHRISTOPHER GEORGE LONGDEN, management consultant; b. Coventry, Eng., June 7, 1956; came to U.S., 1980; s. Alfred Frederick and Margaret Anne (Robinson) H.; m. Avril Jacqueline Wardell, July 31, 1982. MA, Oxford U., 1977, DPhil, 1980; MS in Bus., Columbia U., 1983. Asst. to chmn. Gold Fields Am. Corp., N.Y.C., 1980-83; pres. Hall Mgmt. Assocs., San Francisco, 1983-87, Congden and Carpenter Co., Seekonk, Mass., 1987-88; mng. dir. Petralex Stainless Ltd., Malvern, Pa., 1985-86; v.p. planning Levinson Steel Co., Pitts., 1988-89; v.p. mktg. Thypin Steel Co., N.Y.C., 1989-95; ptnr. Stafford Bus. Advisors, Portland, ME, 1995—; internat. commercial arbitrator Am. Arbitration Assn., 1991—. Author: Britain, America and Arms Control, 1921-1937, 1987, Steel Phoenix, The Fall and Rise of the American Steel Industry, 1996, Ports and Railroads of the Atlantic Northeast, 1999. Councilman City of Oxford (Eng.), 1979-81; mem. Dem. Nat. Com., 1996-97; chmn. Maine Dem. Com., 1997-99; pres. Genesis Cmty. Loan Fund; bd. dirs. Maine Coun. Chs. Mem. United Oxford and Cambridge Univs. Club (London), Nat. Arts Club (N.Y.). Episcopalian. Avocations: travel, cricket, naval history. Office: 107 Exchange St Portland ME 04101-5001

HALL, CLARENCE ALBERT, JR., geologist, educator; b. L.A., Jan. 5, 1930; s. Clarence Albert and Margaret Olive (Fabrick) H.; children: Eric Robert, Kris Delorah. BS, Stanford U., 1952, MS, 1953, PhD, 1956. Instr. U. Oreg., Eugene, 1954-55; mem. faculty UCLA, 1956—, prof. geology, chmn. dept. geology, 1974-76, chmn. dept. geophysics and space physics, 1976, chmn. dept. earth and space scis., 1976-78, dean of phys. scis., 1983-94; dir. White Mountain Rsch. Sta. U. Calif. Systemwide, 1979-95. Contbr. articles to profl.jours.; editor Jour. Paleontology, 1971-71. Fulbright rsch. fellow in Italy, 1963-64, 70-71; recipient Dibblee medal, 1998. Fellow AAAS, Geol. Soc. Am., Paleontol. Soc. Office: UCLA Dept Earth And Scis Los Angeles CA 90095-1567

HALL, CONRAD ALDEN, history educator; b. Durham, N.C., June 3, 1971; s. William Charles Hall and Janet Ackermann Zucker. AB, Duke U., 1994, MAT, 1996. Tchr. history Canterbury Sch., Ft. Myers, fla., 1996-98, Cary (N.C.) Acad., 1998—. James Madison Meml. fellow. Mem. Duke U. Varsity Club. Avocation: running. Home: 129 Pinecrest Rd Durham NC 27705-5822

HALL, CONRAD L., cinematographer; b. Tahiti, 1926; s. James Norman H. Student, U. So. Calif. Early career in indsl. TV films, commls.; films include Incubus, 1961, The Wild Seed, 1965, Morituri, 1965, Harper, 1966, The Professionals, 1966, Cool Hand Luke, 1967, Divorce American Style, 1967, In Cold Blood, 1967, Hell in the Pacific, 1968, Butch Cassidy and the Sundance Kid, 1968, Tell Them Willie Boy Is Here, 1969, The Happy Ending, 1969, Fat City, 1972, Electra Glide in Blue, 1973, Smile, 1975, The Day of the Locust, 1975, Marathon Man, 1976, Black Widow, 1987, Tequila Sunrise, 1988, Class Action, 1989, Jennifer 8, 1992, Searching for Bobby Fisher, 1992 (Academy Award nominee, Best Cinematographer, 1993), Love Affair, 1994. Recipient Oscar award for Butch Cassidy and the Sundance Kid, 1969, Am. Soc. of Cinematographers award, 1989. *

HALL, CYNTHIA HOLCOMB, federal judge; b. Los Angeles, Feb. 19, 1929; d. Harold Romeyn and Mildred Gould (Kuck) Holcomb; m. John Harris Hall, June 6, 1970 (dec. Oct. 1980);. A.B., Stanford U., 1951, J.D., 1954; LL.M., NYU, 1960. Bar: Ariz. 1954, Calif. 1956. Law clk. to judge U.S. Ct. Appeals 9th Circuit, 1954-55; trial atty. tax div. Dept. Justice, 1960-64; atty.-adviser Office Tax Legis. Counsel, Treasury Dept., 1964-66; mem. firm Brawerman & Holcomb, Beverly Hills, Calif., 1966-72; judge U.S. Tax Ct., Washington, 1972-81, U.S. Dist. Ct. for central dist. Calif., Los Angeles, 1981-84; cir. judge U.S. Ct. Appeals (9th cir.), Pasadena, Calif., 1984—, sr. judge, 1997—. Served to lt. (j.g.) USNR, 1951-53. Office: US Ct Appeals 9th Cir 125 S Grand Ave Pasadena CA 91105-1621

HALL, DAVID, newspaper editor; b. Lebanon, Tenn., Mar. 7, 1943; s. Hal Turner Hall and Mildred (Durham) Hall Carson; m. Suzanne Lovell, Sept. 5, 1964; children: Carson, Matthew, Amanda. BS, U. Tenn., 1965, MA in Econs., 1966; postgrad., Northwestern U., 1995. Fin. news reporter, asst. fin. editor, Middle East corr., chief editorial writer, asst. mng. editor Chgo. Daily News, 1966-78; asst. mng. editor Chgo. Sun-Times, 1978; mng. editor St. Paul Pioneer Press, 1978-82; exec. editor St. Paul Pioneer Press and Dispatch, 1982-84; editor, v.p. The Denver Post, 1984-86, editor, sr. v.p., 1986-88; editor, v.p. The Record, Hackensack, N.J., 1988-92; editor The Plain Dealer, Cleve., 1992-99. Bd. dirs. Coun. on World Affairs. With U.S. Army, 1967-69, Vietnam. Recipient Disting. Alumni award Castle Heights Mil. Acad., Lebanon, 1984. Mem. Am. Soc. Newspaper Editors, Cleve. Com. on Fgn. Rels., Soc. Profl. Journalists, Scarabbean Soc., Cleve. City Club Found., Phi Gamma Delta. Presbyterian.

HALL, DAVID, sound archivist, writer; b. New Rochelle, N.Y., Dec. 16, 1916; s. Fairfax and Eleanor Rayburn (Remy) H.; married, June 8, 1940 (widowed Mar. 24, 1992); children: Marion Hall Hunt, Jonathan, Peter, Susannah. B.A., Yale U., 1939; postgrad., Columbia U., 1940-41. Advt. copy writer Columbia Records, Bridgeport, Conn., 1940-42; music program annotator NBC, N.Y.C., 1942-48; classics music dir. Mercury Record Corp., N.Y.C., 1948-56; music editor Stereo Rev., N.Y.C., 1957-62, contbg. editor, 1962-98; pres. Composers Rec., Inc., N.Y.C., 1963-67; curator Rodgers and Hammerstein Archives of Recorded Sound., N.Y. Pub. Library, N.Y.C., 1967-83, cons., 1983-85; dir. Music Ctr. Am.-Scandinavian Found., N.Y.C., 1950-57; Fulbright vis. scholar Copenhagen U., 1956-57; free-lance writer, lectr.; classical recordings cons., 1967—; mem. Commn. for the White House Record Libr., 1979. Author: The Record Book, 1940-48. Trustee Wilton Library Assn., Conn., 1975-79. Decorated knight Order of Lion, Finland. Mem. Nat. Acad. Rec. Arts and Scis. (trustee 1965-67), Nat. Music Council (dir. 1968-80), Assn. for Recorded Sound Collections (pres. 1980-82). Democrat. Home: PO Box 257 Castine ME 04421-0257

HALL, DAVID, law educator, dean; b. Savannah, May 26, 1950; s. Levi and Ethel H.; m. Marilyn Braithwaite-Hall; children: Sakile, Kiamsha, Rahsaan. BS in Polit. Sci., Kans. State U., 1972; MA in Human Rels., U. Okla., 1975, postgrad., 1975-78, JD, 1978; LLM, Harvard U., 1985, Doctor Juridical Scis., 1988. Bar: Ill., Mass., Okla. Profl. basketball player Spaidero Pallacanestro, Inc., Udine, Italy, 1972-74; grad. asst. human rels. dept. U. Okla., Norman, 1974-75; lawyer Chgo. regional office Fed. Trade Commn., 1978-80; assoc. prof. law Sch. Law U. Okla., Norman, 1983-85; asst. prof. law Sch. Law U. Miss., 1980-83; assoc. dean academic affairs Sch. Law Northeastern U., Boston, 1988-92, prof. law, 1985—, dean Sch. Law, 1993—; instr. ethnic studies dept. and law ctr. U. Okla., Norman, 1975-79; Robert D. Klien U. lectr. Northeastern U.; co-chair legal edn. forum Law Sch. Harvard U., Cambridge, Mass., 1984-85, co-coord. Nat. Symposium on the Constitution and Race, 1987; coord. law student outreach program Barron Assessment Ctr., Boston. Contbr. numerous articles to profl. jours. Mem. bd. Mass. Civil Liberties Union, 1987-88, Inst. Affirmative action, Boston, TransAfrica Forum Scholars Adv. Coun., Washington, commn. on equal justice Mass. Legal Assistance Corp., 1995—, Nat. Consumer Law Ctr., 1993—; pres. African Cultural Soc. St. Paul A.M.E. Ch., Cambridge, Mass.; bd. dirs. Gang Peace Inc., 1995—. named Professor of the Year NAACP, to Savannah Athletic Hall of Fame; honoree African Am. Ist. Oratory Competition; recipient Black Rose award Sigma Gamma Rho., Humanitarian award Nat. Conf. Cmty. and Justice. Fellow Am. Sociol. Assn.; mem. ABA (standing ocm. lawyers' pub. svc. responsibility 1995—), Assn. Law Sch. (diversity in legal edn. 1995-96), Boston Bar Assn., Mass. Bar Assn. (mem. bd. minorities in the profession 1995-96), Okla. Bar Assn. (Outstanding Sr. award), Nat. Conf. Black Lawyers (pres. Mass. chpt.

1986—), Black Faculty and Staff Orgn., Nat. Black Wholistic Soc. (pres. 1993, mem. bd. 1984—), Order of the Coif. Office: Northeastern U Sch Law Provost Office 400 Huntington Ave Boston MA 02115-5005

HALL, DAVID CHARLES, zoo director, veterinarian; b. St. Paul, Aug. 12, 1944; s. Wilhelm Frank and Estelle Elizabeth (Johnson) H.; m. Sandra Jean Prink, Oct. 2, 1945; children: Jason Wilhelm, Jeremy Marvin. BME, U. Minn., 1966, DVM, 1976. Sr. mktg. engr. Rosemount Engring. Co., Eden Prairie, Minn., 1966-75; ptnr. Oregon (Wis.) Vet. Med. Clinic, 1976-86; dir. Henry Vilas Zool. Pk., Madison, Wis., 1986—; advisor Food div. Wis. Dept. Agrl. Trade and Consumer Protection, Madison, 1985-86, Exam. sect. Wis. Dept. Regulation and Licensing, Madison, 1981-82. Recipient Caleb Dorr acad. award, U. Minn., 1972-76. Mem. AVMA, Am. Assn. Zoo Vets., Am. Assn. Zool. Pks. and Aquariums, Phi Kappa Phi, Phi Zeta. Lutheran. Lodge: Optimists (pres. 1980). Avocations: skiing, swimming, hiking, hunting, other outdoor sports. Home: 3162 Waucheeta Trl Madison WI 53711-5952 Office: Henry Vilas Park Zoo Office of the Dir 702 S Randall Ave Madison WI 53715-1665

HALL, DAVID EDWARD, lawyer; b. Syracuse, N.Y., June 28, 1940; s. Edward V. and Helen E. (Weisenburger) H.; m. Bonne Marie Paltz, July 31, 1965; children: David A., Katherine M. BS in Indsl. Rels. magna cum laude, Lemoyne Coll., 1962; LLB, Georgetown U., 1965. Bar: N.Y. 1965. Ptnr. Hodgson, Russ, Andrews, Woods & Goodyear, Buffalo, 1965, 1970—. Editor Georgetown Law Jour., 1964. Bd. dirs. Niagara Frontier Radio Reading Svc., Buffalo, 1989—, People Inc. found., 1998—. Capt. USAF, 1966-70. Decorated Meritorious Svc. medal. Mem. Indsl. Rels. Rsch. Assn. (bd. dirs. 1980—, exec. v.p. 1993-94, pres.-elect 1994, pres. 1995), Transit Valley Country Club. Roman Catholic. Avocations: tennis, golf. Office: Hodgson Russ Andrews et al 1800 One # M T Pla Buffalo NY 14203

HALL, DAVID RAMSAY, architect; b. Lansing, Mich., Oct. 24, 1945; s. Harold Wendell and Sarah Katherine (Schlademan) H.; m. Catherine Anne Weeks, Dec. 23, 1967; children: Sarah Catherine, Rebecca Jane. BArch, Wash. State U., 1968. Registered architect, Wash. Designer, draftsman Earl Flansburgh & Assocs., Cambridge, Mass., 1968-70, NBBJ, Seattle, 1970, Mel Streeter & Assoc., Seattle, 1971-72; designer, ptnr. Henry Klein Partnership, Architects, Mt. Vernon, Wash., 1972—. Author, designer, contbr. articles to profl. publs. Commr. Dike Dist. # 19, Skagit County, Wash., 1984-95; mem. adv. bd. Wash. State U., Pullman, 1990-96; bd. dirs. Self Help Housing, Mt. Vernon, 1980-84. Recipient Progressive Architecture Design award, 1972, Honor award Cedar Shake & Shingle, 1991, Am. Wood Coun., 1993, Sunset Mag. Western Home award. 1995. Mem. AIA (bd. dirs. N.W. chpt. 1985-88, Honor award Seattle chpt. 1991, N.W. chpt. 1991, 94, 96, 97, 98, Commendation award Seattle chpt. 1987). Avocations: watercolor painting, photography, hiking, gardening, fishing. Home: 5871 Farm To Market Rd Bow WA 98232-9213 Office: Henry Klein Partnership 314 Pine St Ste 205 Mount Vernon WA 98273-3852

HALL, DAVID WALTER, botanist; b. New Orleans, Sept. 6, 1940; s. Walter Knowlton and Lenna Anne (Guthrie) H.; m. Tiia Reet Karell, Nov. 25, 1981; children: Alexander, Elizabeth. BS, Ga. So. U., 1965, MS, 1967; PhD, U. Fla., 1978. Diplomate Am. Bd. Forensic Examiners; cert. expert in botany; registered profl. wetland scientist. Rsch. assoc. U. Fla., Gainesville, 1971-73, asst. in botany, 1973-81, dir. plant identification and info. svc., 1981-90; sr. scientist KBN Engring. and Applied Scis., Inc., Gainesville, 1990-96, Golder Assocs. Inc., Gainesville, 1996-97; pres. David W. Hall Cons., Inc., Gainesville, 1997—. Author: Illustrated Plants of Florida and the Coastal Plain, 1993; co-author spl. publs. Inst. Food and Agrl. Scis., U. Fla., 1987, 88, 89, 92, dept. civil engring. U. Fla., 1989; contbr. or co-contbr. chpts. to: Aquatic Pest Control Applicator Training Manual, 1991, Turf Weeds and Their Control, 1994, Forensic Taphonomy: The Post-Mortem Fate of Human Remains, 1997. Bd. dirs., v.p. Fla. Tennis Found., 1992—; tennis coach Ga. So. U., 1966-67; profl. racket stringer, 1963-90; pvt. instr. tennis, 1965-90; umpire various tennis tournaments, 1963-85; dir. profl. tennis tournaments, 1964-85; condr. tennis clinics for area high schs. and coll. programs, leagues, underprivileged children; organizer, mem. City of Gainesville Tennis Adv. Bd.; founder U. Fla. Gator Tennis Boosters, 1968; bd. dirs. tennis program 300 Club, Gainesville, 1975-76, organizer, tennis chmn.; organizer, dir. Fla. intercity adult tennis league; mem. dist. 4 Cmty. Devel. Com., 1994-95; commr. tennis Gainesville Sports Coun., 1989-90. Named one of Outstanding Young Men of Am., 1973; NDEA Title IV fellow U. Fla., 1967-70; Mercer Rsch. fellow Harvard U., 1968; recipient Disting. Svc. award Fla. Assn. County Agrl. Agts., 1990, Nat. Assn. County Agrl. Agts., 1990, Disting. Alumni award dept. biology Ga. So. U., 1991, Svc. award Fla. Dept. Environ. Regulation, 1988, Svc. Leadership award Augusta Coll., 1963; ranked in various coll. and other tennis tournaments, 1960-94. Fellow Am. Coll. Forensic Examiners, Am. Acad. Forensic Scis.; mem. AAAS, Am. Soc. Plant Taxonomists, Exotic Plant Pest Coun., Assn. Southea. Biologists, Soc. Wetland Scientists, Weed Sci. Soc. Am., So. Weed Sci. Soc., Fla. Acad. Scis., Fla. Native Plant Soc. (Green Palmetto Svc. award 1987), Nat. Assn. Environ. Profls., Fla. Assn. Environ. Profls., North Fla. Bot. Soc., Fla. Weed Sci. Soc. (pres. 1987-88, sec., treas. 1984-86, bd. dirs. 1984-90, Outstanding Weed Scientist 1999), Internat. Assn. for Identification (Fla. divsn.), Internat. Weed Sci. Soc., USTA (mem. exec. bd. 1991-93, mem. del.'s assembly 1991-93, mem. pres.'s com. 1989-91, active other coms.), Fla. Tennis Assn. (pres. 1989-91, 1st v.p. 1985-87, chmn. adult tennis coun. 1986-89, mem. exec. bd. 1982-95, USTA del. 1991-93, mem. Fla. Tennis Assn./USTA league appeals com. 1985-86, Man of Yr. 1984), Gainesville Area Tennis Orgn. (pres., bd. dirs. 1994—). Achievements include definition of discipline of forensic botany. Avocations: tennis, singing. Home and Office: 3666 NW 13th Pl Gainesville FL 32605-4823

HALL, DENNIS GENE, optics educator; b. Belleville, Ill., Mar. 7, 1948; s. Eugene and Mildred (Klein) H.; m. Rita Mae Winkelmann, June 12, 1970; children: Katherine, Christine, Gregory. BS in Physics, U. Ill., 1970; MS in Physics, So. Ill. U., 1972; PhD in Physics, U. Tenn., 1976. Asst. prof. physics So. Ill. U., Edwardsville, 1976-78; sr. engr. McDonnell Douglas Corp., St. Louis, 1978-80; asst. prof. Inst. Optics U. Rochester, N.Y., 1980-82, assoc. prof., 1982-87, prof., 1987—; William F. May prof. Inst. Optics U. Rochester, N.Y., 1995—, assoc. dir., 1992-93, dir., 1993—; grad. fellow Oak Ridge (Tenn.) Associated Univs., 1975. Contbr. articles to profl. publs., chpts. to books; patentee in field. Capt. USAFR, 1973-89. Fellow Optical Soc. Am. (bd. dirs. 1991-93), Am. Phys. Soc., Internat. Soc. Optical Engring.; mem. Am. Assn. Physics Tchrs. Avocation: tennis. Office: U Rochester Inst Optics Rochester NY 14627

HALL, DON ALAN, editor, writer; b. Indpls., Aug. 7, 1938; s. Oscar B. and Ruth Ann (Leak) H.; m. Roberta Louise Bash, Apr. 30, 1960; children: Alice Leigh, Nancy Elizabeth. B.A., Ind. U., 1960, M.A., 1968. News editor Rock Springs (Wyo.) Daily Rocket-Miner, 1960-63; mag. editor, picture editor Waukegan News-Sun, Ill., 1964-66; reporter, copy editor Salem Capital Jour., Oreg., 1966-70; free lance journalist Victoria, B.C., Can., 1970-74; copy editor, sci. writer, music reviewer Corvallis (Oreg.) Gazette-Times, 1974-78, copy desk chief, 1978-82, news editor, 1983-84, author weekly opinion column, 1985-87; author weekly nature column for Oreg. newspapers, 1976-85; instr. dept. journalism Oreg. State U., 1984-87. Author: On Top Of Oregon, 1975, Bird in the Bush, 1986; editor Mammoth Trumpet, Center for the Study of the First Americans, 1991—. Recipient Westinghouse-AAAS Sci. Writing award, 1977. Office: Oreg State Univ 355 Weniger Hall Corvallis OR 97331-8574

HALL, DONALD E., English educator; b. Aug. 16, 1960; s. Donald Eugene and Margie Davison Hall. BA, U. Ala., 1981; MA, U. Ill., 1984; PhD, U. Md., 1991. Vis. prof. English Nat. U. Rwanda, 1984-86; asst. prof. English Calif. State U., Northridge, 1991-95, assoc. prof., assoc. chair English, 1995-99, coord. humanities interdisciplinary program, 1995—, prof., 1999—; mem. adv. bd. Victorian Poetry, 1995—. Author: Fixing Patriarchy: Feminism and Mid-Victorian Male Novelists, 1996; editor: Muscular Christianity: Embodying the Victorian Age, 1994; co-editor: RePresenting Bisexualities: Subjects and Cultures of Fluid Desire, 1996; contbr. articles to profl. jours. Co-founder, bd. dirs. Inst. for Lesbian, Bisexual, Gay and Transgender Studies, Calif. State U., Northridge, 1995—. Calif. State U. grantee, 1991-95; fellow U. Ill., 1982-83, provost's fellow U. Md., 1986-88. Mem. MLA (nat. del. 1997—, mem. prose fiction exec. com. 1997—), Pacific Coast MLA, Victorian Interdisciplinary Studies Assn. of Western U.S., Phi Beta Kappa. E-mail: donald.hall@csun.edu. Office: Calif State U Northridge English Dept Northridge CA 91330-8248

HALL, DONALD JOYCE, greeting card company executive; b. Kansas City, Mo., July 9, 1928; s. Joyce Clyde and Elizabeth Ann (Dilday) H.; m. Adele Coryell, Nov. 28, 1953; children: Donald Joyce, Margaret Elizabeth, David Earl. A.B., Dartmouth, 1950; LL.D., William Jewell Coll., Denver U., 1977. With Hallmark Cards, Inc., Kansas City, Mo., 1953—, adminstrv. v.p., 1958-66, pres., chief exec. officer, 1966-83, chmn. bd., 1983—, chief exec. officer, 1983-86, also dir.; dir. United Telecommunications, Inc., Dayton-Hudson Corp., William E. Coutts Co., Ltd.; past dir. Fed. Res. Bank Kansas City, Mut. Benefit Life Ins. Co., Business Men's Assurance Co., Commerce Bank Kansas City, 1st Nat. Bank Lawrence. Pres. Civic Council Greater Kansas City; past chmn. bd. Kansas City Assn. Trusts and Founds.; Bd. dirs. Am. Royal Assn., Friends of Art, Eisenhower Found.; bd. dirs. Kansas City Minority Suppliers Devel. Council, Kans. City Minority Suppliers Devel. Council,Kansas City Symphony; past pres. Pembroke Country Day Sch., Civic Council of Greater Kansas City; trustee, past chmn. exec. com. Midwest Research Inst.; trustee Nelson-Atkins Museum of Art. Served to 1st lt. AUS, 1950-53. Recipient Eisenhower Medallion award, 1973; Parsons Sch. Design award, 1977; 3d Ann. Civic Service award Hebrew Acad. Kansas City, 1976; Chancellor's medal U. Mo., Kansas City, 1977; Disting. Service citation U. Kans., 1980. Mem. Kansas City C. of C. (named Mr. Kansas City 1972, dir.), AIA (hon.). Office: Hallmark Cards Inc PO Box 419580 2501 Mcgee St Kansas City MO 64141-6580

HALL, DONALD S., former planetarium administrator, pottery expert; b. Columbus, Ohio, June 3, 1940; s. William Kenneth and Irene Myra (Beltzhoover) H.; 1 child, Elizabeth Elaine. AB, Stetson U., 1962; MEd, U. N.C., 1965. Adminstrv. asst. Morehead Planetarium, Chapel Hill, N.C., 1962-64, asst. dir., 1965-67; edn. dir. Strasenbrugh Planetarium, Rochester, N.Y., 1968-69, dir., 1970-95; astronomy instr. U. N.C., 1966-67; U.S. astronaut instr. Morehead Planetarium, 1962-67. Contbr. numerous articles to profl. publs. Bd. dirs. Am. Theatre Organ Soc.; bd. dirs., program chmn. Rochester Theatre Organ Soc.; bd. dirs. Girl Scouts Genessee Valley; mem. adv. bd. dirs. Earth-Space-Sci. Edn. Ctr. Mem. Internat. Planetarium Soc. (pres. 1977-78), Internat. Planetary Dirs. Congress (v.p. 1987-93), Mid. Atlantic Planetary Soc., Gt. Lakes Planetary Soc., Am. Art Pottery Assn. (pres. 1999-2001). E-mail: dsh@multicom.org. Mailing: Box 10514 Rochester NY 14610-0514

HALL, DONALD VINCENT, social worker; b. Ft. Dodge, Iowa, June 13, 1955; s. John William and Helen Evelyn (Swanson) H.; m. Marla Jo Adamson, May 28, 1977; children: Lucas William, Jessica Lauren. BSW, U. Iowa, 1977; MSW, U. Kans., 1979. Cert. clin. social worker; lic. social worker, Iowa; diplomate bd. clin. social work; qualified clin. social worker. Social worker Heartland Edn. Agy., Johnston, Iowa, 1979-91, facilitator conflict resolution and concensus decision making, cons. long range planning, presenter workshops, 1989—; pvt. practice clin. social worker, psychotherapist children, individauls, couples, families, groups Counseling and Assessment Svcs., P.C., 1991—; participant Des Moines Family Therapy Tng. Inst., 1991—. Bd. dirs. Johnston (Iowa) Community Sch., 1984-90, pres. bd., 1987-90. Presbyterian (ordained elder). Home: 6845 NW Beaver Dr Johnston IA 50131-1245 Office: Counseling and Assessment Svcs PC 2404 Forest Dr Des Moines IA 50312-5400

HALL, DOUGLAS LEE, computer science educator; b. San Antonio, Feb. 5, 1947; s. Robert Arthur and Thelma (Stischer). AA in Foreign Lang., San Antonio Coll., 1967; BA in Spanish, U. Tex., 1969; MEd in Bilingual Edn., Pan Am. U., 1977; PhD, N. Tex. State U., 1987. Tchr. Edgewood Ind. Sch. Dist., San Antonio, 1969-73, Brownsville (Tex.) Ind. Sch. Dist., 1973-74, 76-78; precious metals specialist Nu-Metals, Inc., Dallas, 1974; tchr. DPC Am. Sch., Dubai, UAE, 1975-76; tng. dir. ABDick, San Antonio, 1978-79; bilingual tchr. Dallas Ind. Sch. Dist., 1979-82; computer cons. Taylor Mgmt. Systems, Dallas, 1982-83; lectr. in field N.Tex. State U., Denton, 1984-86; grad. advisor St. Mary's U., San Antonio, 1986—, chair dept. computer sci., 1990—, pres. faculty senate, 1992-93; dir. Deutscher Volkstanzverein, San Antonio, 1987—; asst. dir. San Antonio Folk Dance Fest, 1986—; advisor St. Mary's U. Chpt. Assn. for Computing Machinery, 1989—. Contbr. articles to profl. jours. Docent Inst. Texan Cultures, San Antonio, 1989—; pres. Crown Hill Pk. Homeowners, San Antonio, 1986-89; del. 1st U.S.-Japan Grassroots Summit, 1991. Named Tchr. of Yr., Brownsville Ind. Sch. Dist. 1974, 77, Outstanding Elem. Tchr. 1974, Disting. Grad. Faculty Mem., U. North Tex., 1991-92, Disting. Computer Sci. Alumnus, 1998. Mem. NEA, IEEE, ACM, Tex. State Tchrs. Assn., Am. Assn. Artificial Intelligence. Avocations: theology, genealogy, foreign languages. Home: 515 Marquis St San Antonio TX 78216-5217 Office: Saint Mary's U One Camino Santa Maria San Antonio TX 78228-8524

HALL, DOUGLAS SCOTT, astronomy educator; b. Lexington, Ky., May 30, 1940; s. William Scott and Catherine (Read) H.; m. Bonnie Schumacher, June 3, 1964 (div. 1978); children: Bruce Douglas, Brandon Scott; m. Mimi Kemp, Aug. 1, 1981. BA in Chemistry, Swarthmore Coll., 1962; MA in Astronomy, Ind. U., 1964, PhD in Astronomy, 1967. Rsch. assoc. Dyer Obs., Nashville, 1967; asst. prof. Vanderbilt U., Nashville, 1967-71, assoc. prof., 1971-80, prof., 1980—; dir. Dyer Obs., Nashville, 1986—; cons. Tenn. State U., Nashville, 1988—, adj. prof., 1991—. Co-author: Supernova 1987-A!, 1988, Photoelectric Photometry of Variable Stars, 1988; contbr. papers to profl. jours.; referee for various astron. jours. and rsch. found.; founder Internat. Amateur and Profl. Photoelectric Photometry Comms., 1980—, editor, 1984—; mem. edit. bd. Inf. Bull. Variable Stars, 1991—. Recipient U.S. Sr. Scientist award Alexander von Humbolt Found., Fed. Republic Germany, 1973-74; named Astronomer of Yr., Astron. League, 1984; rsch. grantee NSF, 1968-87, NASA, 1977-83, Rsch. Corp., 1979. Mem. Internat. Astron. Union, Am. Astron. Soc. (rsch. grantee 1988), Astron. Soc. of the Pacific (liaison), Internat. Amateur and Profl. Photoelectric Photometry (pres. 1980—), Am. Assn. Variable Star Observers (editorial bd. 1976—), Tenn. Acad. Sci. (editorial bd. 1972), Sigma Xi (pres. Vanderbilt chpt. 1987-89). Office: Arthur J. Dyer Observatory Vanderbilt Univ Nashville TN 37235

HALL, EDWARD PAYSON, JR., communication educator; b. St. Louis, Nov. 13, 1938; s. Edward Payson Sr. and Marjorie (LeMasters) H.; m. Jean Quintero. BA, U. Wash., 1972, PhD, 1980; MA, U. Hawaii, 1974. Asst. prof. comm. U. Del., Newark, 1980-84, U. Hawaii, Honolulu, 1984-86; asst. prof. comm. Radford (Va.) U., 1986-88, assoc. prof. comm., 1988-93, founding dir. comm. grad. program, 1986-90, coord. planning New Coll. Global Studies, 1989-93; assoc. prof. comm. Western N.Mex. U., Silver City, 1993-95, prof. comm., 1995—, coord. accreditation/self-study, 1995-97, founding dir. acad. support dept., 1997-98, coord. instnl. assessment, 1997—; manuscript reviewer Wadsworth Pub. Co., 1983, Progress in Communication Scis., Ablex Pub. Corp., 1984, 87; panel chair 5th Symposium on Lang. Studies, U. Del., Newark, 1983; presenter in field. Editor (procs.) Conference on Communication Research Needs, 1973; contbr. chpt. to book and articles to profl. jours. Pub. rels. cons. Pacific Luth. U., Tacoma, 1977; invited spkr. Nat. Assn. for Fgn. Student Affairs, Ashland, Oreg., 1979; ednl. cons. Filipino Am. Assn., Wilmington, Del., 1981-84; pub. rels. cons. Teamsters Local 174, Seattle, 1982; panel chair 5th Symposium on Lang. Studies, Del., 1983; hon. bd. mem. Global Soc., Radford, 1990-93; bd. mem. Global Lang. and Culture Inst., Silver City, 1993-98; mem. NAFTA Connection Coordinating Coun., 1994-95; merit badge counselor Boy Scouts Am., 1995—, others. Contbr. grantee U.S. Dept. Health, Edn. and Welfare, Seattle, 1972-74, Tacoma Sch. Dist., 1977, grad. study grantee East-West Ctr., Honolulu, 1972-74, Rsch.-travel grantee East-West Ctr., Honolulu, 1973, rsch. grantee Haas Found., 1977, Courseware devel. grantee Office Computer-Based Instrn., U. Del., 1983, grant-in-aide Coll. Arts and Sci., U. Del., 1984; planning grantee Commonwealth Va., Commn. on the U. of the 21st Century, Radford U., 1991. Mem. World Comm. Assn., Internat. Comm. Assn. (chair hospitality com. 1985-88, chair divsn. V 1990, 91, presenter, respondent), Internat. Assn. Intercultural Comm. Studies, Speech Comm. Assn. (mem. nominating com. internat. and intercultural divsn. 1990-91, chair internat. and intercultural divsn. 1991, 92, respondent), Assn. for Asian Studies, Philippine Studies Assn., Pacific and Asian Comm. Assn. Avocation: writing. Home: 20 Vista Grande Rd Silver City NM 88061 Office: Western NMex Univ PO Box 680 Silver City NM 88062

HALL, ELEANOR WILLIAMS, public relations executive; b. Boston; d. James Murray and Julia Eleanor (Williams) H. AB cum laude, Radcliffe Coll., 1945. Exec. sec. Am. Express Co., N.Y.C., 1950-62, adminstrv. asst. corp. mktg., 1963-65, mgr. corp. mktg., 1965-69, mgr. corp. pub. rels., 1969-71; mgr. mktg. svcs. Am. Express Internat. Banking Corp. (now Am. Express Bank Ltd.), N.Y.C., 1971-72, asst. treas. advt. and pub. rels., 1972-76, asst. v.p. advt. and pub. rels., 1976-82; pres. Eleanor Hall Assocs., Inc., 1982-90. Mem. Harvard-Radcliffe Club. Address: 342 102d Ave SE Ste 218 Bellevue WA 98004-6165

HALL, ELIZABETH MURCHIE, retired special education educator, consultant; b. Jan. 14, 1945. BA in Philosophy, Sarah Lawrence Coll., 1967; MEd in Spl. Edn., Ala. A&M U., 1977; PhD in Spl. Edn., Peabody/Vanderbilt U., 1981. Tchr. English Brevard County schs., Melbourne, Fla., 1972-75; tchr. spl. edn., program coord. Huntsville (Ala.) City Schs., 1977-80; prof. Athens (Ala.) State Coll., 1980-98; owner, cons. Skills for Success, Huntsville, 1999—. E-mail: skillsforsuccess@juno.com. Office: 7808 Bridgewell Run SE Huntsville AL 35802-3902

HALL, ELTON ARTHUR, philosophy educator; b. San Fernando, Calif., Sept. 18, 1940; s. Harwood Harry and Verna Florentina (Engelhardt) H.; m. Katherine May Lennard, Aug. 27, 1961; children: Helena Louise, Anita Virya. BA, Occidental Coll., 1963; MA, U. Calif., Santa Barbara, 1965, U. Calif., Santa Barbara, 1967. Asst. prof. philosophy Moorhead (Minn.) State U., 1967-69, Calif. State U., Fresno, 1969-75; head dep. social sci. Oxnard (Calif.) Coll., 1987-90, prof. philosophy, 1975-92, acting div. dir. arts, letters and sci., 1990-91, acting dean gen. edn., 1991-92; prof. philosophy Moorpark (Calif.) Coll., 1992—; pres. acad. senate, 1996-99; adj. prof. sociology Calif. Luth. U., 1994; tchr. trainer Calif. Assn. Schs. Cosmetoloty, Sacramento, 1988-91, Calif. Assn. Pvt. Postsecondary Schs., 1991-93. Contbr. articles to profl. jours. Chief negotiator local 1828 Am. Fedn. Tchrs., 1996—. Mem. Internat. Soc. Neoplatonic Studies, Muyiddin Ibn 'Arabi Soc. Avocations: religious studies, poetry, hiking. Office: Moorpark Coll 7075 Campus Rd Moorpark CA 93021-1605

HALL, FLOYD, retail executive; b. Duncan, Okla., Sept. 4, 1938; m. Janet Hall; children: Larry, Karen. Student, Bakersfield Jr. Coll., So. Meth. U., Harvard U., 1977. Nat. sales mgr. Montgomery Ward, Chgo., 1966-70; v.p., regional v.p. The Singer Co., Dallas, Tex., 1970-73; pres., CEO B. Dalton Book Seller, Mpls., 1973-81; chmn., CEO Target Stores, Mpls., 1981-84, Grand Union Co., Wayne, N.J., 1984-89; also bd. dirs. Grand Union Co.; chmn., CEO The Museum Co., East Rutherford, N.J., 1989-95, also bd. dirs.; chmn., pres., CEO Kmart Corp., Troy, Mich., 1995—, also bd. dirs.; bd. dirs. Lynx Techs., Kenwood Prodns. Trustee Bklyn. Mus.; bd. dirs. Give Kids The World, Jundt Growth Fund. Served with U.S. Army. Office: Kmart Corp 3100 W Big Beaver Rd Troy MI 48084-3163*

HALL, FREDERICK KEITH, chemist; b. Leeds, Eng., Jan. 3, 1930; naturalized, 1976; s. Frederick Stanley and Mary Elizabeth (Stocks) H.; m. Patricia Ellison, Aug. 25, 1956; children: Simon Keith, Stephanie Jane, Andrew Nicholas. BS with 1st class honors, U. Manchester, 1951; PhD, U. Leeds, 1954; grad. advanced mgmt. program, Harvard U., 1979. Rsch. chemist Courtaulds (Can.) Ltd., 1956-58, asst. tech. mgr., 1958-60, tech. mgr., 1960-63, plant mgr., 1963-66; dir. tech. svc. Internat. Paper Co., 1966-70, asst. dir. rsch. ctr., 1970-72, dir. primary process, 1972-75, corp. dir. rsch., 1975-77; dir. S & ED labs., 1977-79; chief scientist S & T labs., 1979-93, chief scientist, dir. rsch., 1994—; ret., 1995. With Brit. Army, 1953-55. Fellow TAPPI (pres. 1991-93), Royal Soc. Chemistry, Textile Inst., Am. Inst. Chemists; mem. Chem. Inst. Can., Can. Pulp and Paper Assn., Tuxedo Club. Office: Internat Paper Corp Rsch Ctr Long Meadow Rd Tuxedo Park NY 10987

HALL, GENE M., consumer protection agency administrator. Student, U. Del., 1964-68, Villanova Law Sch., 1968-71. Dep. atty. gen. State of Del., Wilmington, 1973-94; dir. Consumer Protection—Fraud Unit, Wilmington, 1994—. Mem. Nat. Dist. Attys. Assn., Del. Bar Assn. Office: Fraud/Consumer Protection Unit 820 N French St Wilmington DE 19801

HALL, GEORGIANNA LEE, special education educator; b. Greeley, Colo., Apr. 2, 1947; d. John Russell and Lois Louise (Urich) Martin; m. William James Bailey, 1970 (div. June 1972); m. Rex Henry Hall, Dec. 22, 1984; 1 stepchild, Jorri Colleen. AA, Fullerton (Calif.) Jr. Coll., 1967; BA, Calif. State U., Fullerton, 1969, elem. edn. credential, 1971, learning handicapped credential, 1976. Cert. resource specialist, lang. devel. specialist. Tutor Edn. Project for Disadvantaged Youth Savanna Sch. Dist., Stanton, Calif., 1965-69; math. tchr. Norwalk (Calif.)-LaMirada Sch. Dist., 1971-72; tchr. Cypress (Calif.) Sch. Dist., 1972-74, tchr. learning disability, 1974-80, tchr. learning handicapped, 1976, tchr. communicatively handicapped, 1981—, resource specialist, 1981—, dist. mentor tchr. for spl. edn., 1993—; dist. spl. edn. rep. for writing of Original Greater Anaheim Consortium Plan for Spl. Edn., 1980; dist. interview team for tchrs., prins., and aides, Cypress, 1985—, dist. staff devel. com., tchg. and assessment com., 1994-95; compliance program quality reviewer dist. leadership team rep. State Calif., Orange County, 1991—; Cypress dist. rep. for drug free schs. Cypress Sch. Dist.-U. Calif., Irvine, 1992—; King sch. rep. dist. drug alcohol tobacco edn.; mem. leadership team King Elem. Sch., Cypress, 1989—; lead tchr. for conflict mgr. tng., 1993—; coord. sch. intervention team, 1989—; coord. activities Svcs. for At-Risk Students, King Elem. Sch., 1990—, crisis intervention team, 1994—; dist. coord. CCR, 1994—; mem. Dist. Coord. Curriculum Com., 1994—; mem. dist. adv. com. Medi-Cal, 1994—; mem Dist. Testing and Assessment Com., 1994—; ACT tchr. rep. interview team for dir. instrn. and spl. edn., 1996, dist. interview team for instrnl. aides. Neighborhood rep. Muscular Dystrophy Assn., Huntington Beach, Calif., 1988—, Coun. for Paralyzed vets., Huntington Beach, 1989—; vol. reading tutor PLUS, Huntington Beach, 1992; publicity chmn. King Sch. PTA, 1992-93, 93-94; coord. resources needy families, King elem. sch. Recipient Hon. Svc. award PTA King Sch., Cypress, 1982; named Spl. Edn. Tchr. of Yr. Resource Specialists Calif., 1989. Mem. NEA, Calif. Tchrs. Assn., Assn. Cypress Tchrs. (sch. rep. 1974-76, 79-82, sec. 1976-77, 2d v.p. 1978-79, 1st v.p. 1979-80), Calif. Assn. Resource Specialists, Children with Attention Deficit Disorder, Learning Disability Assn., Calif. Assn. for Supervision and Curriculum Devel., Orange County Math. Assn., Coun. Exceptional Children, Coun. Learning Disabilities. Avocations: reading, travel, running, theatre. Office: King Elem Sch 8710 Moody St Cypress CA 90630-2220

HALL, GORDON R., retired state supreme court chief justice; b. Vernal, Utah, Dec. 14, 1926; s. Roscoe Jefferson and Clara Maud (Freestone) H.; m. Doris Gillespie, Sept. 6, 1947; children: Rick Jefferson, Craig Edwin. B.S., U. Utah, 1949, LL.B., 1951. Bar: Utah 1952. Solo practice Tooele, Utah, 1952-69; county atty. Tooele County, 1958-69; judge 3d Jud. Dist. Utah, 1969-77; assoc. justice Supreme Ct. Utah, 1977-81, chief justice, 1981-94; of counsel Snow, Christensen & Martineau, Salt Lake City, 1994-98; chmn. Utah Jud. Coun., 1983-94; pres. Conf. Chief Justices, 1988-89; chmn. Nat. Ctr. State Cts., 1988-89; pres. Utah Assn. Counties, 1965; mem. Pres.'s Adv. Com. OEO, 1965-66. Served with U.S. Maritime Svc., 1944-46. Mem. ABA, Utah Bar Assn. Office: 250 N Sandrun Rd Salt Lake City UT 84103-2239

HALL, GRACE ROSALIE, physicist, educator, literary scholar; b. Meriden, Conn., July 15, 1921; d. George John and Grace Cleora (Gleason) White; m. Eldon Conrad Hall, July 2, 1948; children: Brent Channing, Pamela Rosalie, Craig Gleason, Gordon Timothy. Spl. student, Pembroke Coll., 1940-41; BS in Chemistry, Ea. Nazarene Coll., 1946; MA in Physics, Boston U., 1946, postgrad., 1946-53; MA in English, Simmons Coll., 1975. Bookkeeper Cherry & Webb Co., Providence, 1939-42; sec. to registrar Eastern Nazarene Coll., Quincy, Mass., 1942-44, instr. physics, chemistry, 1945-46; teaching fellow physics Boston U., 1946-49; instr. physics lab. Northeastern U., Boston, 1956-57; instr. physics Simmons Coll., Boston, 1949; asst. prof. physics Eastern Nazarene Coll., Quincy, 1957-61, asst. prof. chemistry, 1969, asst. prof. phys. sci., 1974; instr. Shakespeare Barrington (R.I.) Coll., 1984; tchr. Westwood (Mass.) Sem., 1975; ch. sch. dir. 1st Parish, Westwood, 1977-81; chair sem. U. Louisville, 1988. Author: The Tempest as Mystery Play: Uncovering Religious Sources of Shakespear's Most Spiritual Work, 1999; contbr. (with others) Webs & Wardrobes, 1987; editor: Journey to the Moon: The History of the Apollo Guidance Computer, 1994; contbr. articles to profl. jours. Dir. South County Norfolk Assn. for Retarded Citizens, 1978-79, Westwood Interfaith Coun., 1985-89; judge H.S. Sci. Fairs, North

Quincy, Mass., 1960-64, 69-76, Regional Sci. Fairs, Bridgewater, Mass., 1960-62; chair City-Wide Bookfair, Quincy, 1962; pres. Ch. Women United, 1959. Faculty scholar Eastern Nazarene Coll., 1943-45; recipient Libr. Family of Yr. award City of Quincy, 1960; named to R.I. Honor Soc. Mem. MLA (session participant 1978, 84), Shakespeare Assn. Am. (seminar participant 1988-96), Christianity and Lit. Assn. (conf. participant 1984, 89-90, 95), MIT Women's League (editor activities guide and newsletter 1989—, adv. group 1998), New Eng. Hist. Geneal. Soc., Internat. Soc. Poets, Munro Soc., Clarendon Soc., Mythopoetic Soc., Phi Delta Lambda. Avocations: children's lit., recycling, grandparenting, snorkeling . E-mail: grwhall@aol.com.

HALL, HANSEL CRIMIEL, communications executive; b. Gary, Ind., Mar. 12, 1929; s. Alfred McKenzie and Grace Elizabeth (Crimiel) H. BS, Ind. U., 1953; LLB, Blackstone Sch. Law, 1982. Officer IRS, 1959-64; gasoline svc. sta. operator, then realtor Chgo., 1964-69; program specialist HUD, Chgo., 1969-73; dir. equal opportunity St. Paul, 1973-75; dir. fair housing Indpls., from 1975; human resource officer U.S. Fish and Wildlife Svc., Twin Cities, Minn. Cons. in civil rights; pres. bd. dirs. Riverview Towers Cooperative Assn., Inc., 1984-87; pres., CEO Crimiel Comms., Inc., 1988—; CFO, treas. Korean War Vets. Edn. Grant Corp., 1996—; del. U.S. Parliamentarian to Russia and Czechoslovakia, 1992; bd. dirs. Nat. Korean War Vets. Assn., 1992. With USAF, 1951-53, Korea. Recipient Amb. for Peace cert. Korean Vets. Assn., 1991, Korean Svc. medal Rep. of Korea, 1991. Mem. NAACP (Golden Heritage life mem.), Res. Officers Assn., Am. Inst. Parliamentarians, Nat. Assn. Parliamentarians, Minn. State Assn. Parliamentarians (pres. 1997-99), Toastmasters DTM, Ind. U. Alumni Assn., Omega Psi Phi.

HALL, HAROLD ROBERT, retired computer engineer; b. Bakersfield, Calif., Feb. 7, 1935; s. Edward Earl and Ethel Mae (Butner) H.; m. Tenniebee May Hall, Feb. 20, 1965. BS, U. Calif., Berkeley, 1956, MS, 1957, PhD, 1966. Chief engr. wave-filter div. Transonic, Inc., Bakersfield, 1957-60; chief design engr. Circuit Dyne Corp., Pasadena and Laguna Beach, Calif., 1960-61; sr. devel. engr. Robertshaw Controls Co., Anaheim, Calif., 1961-63; research engr. Naval Command, Control and Ocean Surveillance Ctr., rsch. and devel. divsn. Navy Research Lab., San Diego, 1966-95; bd. dirs. Circuit Dyne Corp., Pacific Coil Co. Treas. Pacific Beach Town Coun., San Diego, 1996-98, Friends of Ostomates Worldwide-U.S.A., Akron, Ohio, 1992—. Recipient Thomas Clair McFarland award U. Calif., Berkeley, 1956, NSF fellow, 1957. Mem. IEEE, Acoustical Soc. Am., Phi Beta Kappa. Home: 8585 Via Mallorca Unit 7 La Jolla CA 92037-2585

HALL, HENRY LYON, JR., lawyer; b. Boston, July 23, 1931; s. Henry Lyon and Edith Page (Blanchard) H.; m. Jean Elizabeth Haring, Sept. 13, 1958; children: Henry Lyon, George B. A.B., U. Mass., 1953; J.D., George Washington U., 1962. Bar: Va. 1963, Mass. 1963. Assoc. Ropes & Gray, Boston, 1963-73, ptnr., 1973-97, of counsel, 1998—; lectr., panelist seminars. Mem. Mass. Gov.'s Comm. Sch. Dist. Orgn., 1971-73; mem. sch. com. Minuteman Reg. Vocat. Sch. Dist., 1971-83, chmn. 1971-75; mem. permanent audit com. town of Belmont, Mass., 1979—, chmn. 1982-92; chmn. by law rev. com. 1979-83, bylaw rev. com., 1983-91; town moderator, Belmont, 1991—; corporator, trustee Belmont Savs. Bank. Served in U.S. Army, 1953-56. Mem. ABA, Mass. Bar Assn., Mass. Moderators Assn. (bd. dirs. 1995—, 1st v.p. 1997-98, pres. 1998-99), Nat. Assn. Bond Lawyers, Va. State Bar, Boston Bar Assn., Mass. Taxpayers Found., Govt. Fin. Officers Assn., Mass. Charitable Soc., Mass. Mcpl. Assn., Order of Coif, Phi Delta Phi. Home: 22 Randolph St Belmont MA 02478-3540 Office: One International Place Boston MA 02110-2624

HALL, HOMER L., journalism educator; b. Reeds, Mo., June 11, 1939; s. Columbus Terry and MArgie (Fain) H.; m. Lea Ann (Watson), Sept. 4, 1960; children: Lynlea, Ashley. BS in Edn., U. Mo., 1960; MS in Edn., U. Kans., 1965; postgrad. various insts. Tchr. North Kirkwood (Mo.) Jr. High, 1963-68, 70-73, Shawnee Mission, Kans., 1968-69; reporter Sedalia (Mo.) Democrat, 1969; tchr. Sedalia High Sch., 1969-70, Kirkwood High Sch., 1973-99; dir. journalism workshops Ball State U., Muncie, Ind., 1983-85, 87; tchr. summer journalism workshops, Mo., Ill., Tex., Ind., Calif., Wash., R.I., Iowa, Hawaii, Ariz., Kans., Oreg. Author: (textbooks) Junior High Journalism, 1969, rev. edit., 1993, 1998, Senior High Journalism, 1985, rev. edit., 1993, 1998, Yearbook Guidebook, 1981, rev. 4 times, Observe, React, Think, Write, 1998; contbr. numerous articles to journalism publs. Tchr. Sunday sch. Kirkwood Baptist Ch., 1982—, deacon, 1985—. Served to 1st lt. U.S. Army, 1961-63. Named Mo. Journalism Tchr. of Yr., Mo. Interscholastic Press Assn., 1973, Mo. Tchr. of Yr., Mo. Dept. of Edn., 1979, Merit medal Journalism Edn. Assn., 1979, Nat. Journalism Tchr. of Yr., Dow Jones Newspaper Fund, 1982; recipient Gold Key award Columbia Scholastic Press Assn., 1982, Pioneer award Nat. Scholastic Press Assn., 1982, Horace Mann award Mo. Nat. Edn. Assn., 1983, Scholastic Journalism award Ball State U., 1993, Nat. Yearbook Adviser of Yr. award, 1996; named to Scholastic Journalism Hall of Fame, Okla. U., 1992, Mo. Interscholastic Press Assn. Hall of Fame, 1997. Mem. Mo. Journalism Edn. Assn. (past pres.), Kirkwood Community Tchrs. Assn. (past pres.), Sponsors of Sch. Publs. Greater St. Louis (sec., past pres.), Nat. Journalism Edn. Assn. (sec., cert. commn. chair, v.p., pres., Carl Towley award, nat. yearbook adviser of yr. 1996), Phi Delta Kappa. Avocations: tennis, reading, writing, bridge, square dancing. Home: 104 W Harbor Ct Hendersonville TN 37075 Office: Kirkwood High Sch 801 W Essex Ave Saint Louis MO 63122-3646

HALL, HOWARD TRACY, chemist; b. Ogden, Utah, Oct. 20, 1919; s. Howard and Florence (Tracy) H.; m. Ida Rose Langford, Sept. 24, 1941; children—Sherlene, Howard Tracy Jr., David Richard, Elizabeth, Virginia, Charlotte, Nancy. A.S., Weber Coll., 1939; B.S., U. Utah, 1942, M.S., 1943, Ph.D., 1948; D.Sc. (hon.), Brigham Young U., 1971; HHD (hon.), Weber State U., 1987. Registered patent agt. Chemist U.S. Bur. Mines, Salt Lake City, 1942-44, 46; research asso. Gen. Electric Research Lab., Schenectady, 1948-55; dir. research, prof. chemistry Brigham Young U., 1955-67, disting. prof. chemistry, 1967-80, disting. prof. emeritus, 1980—. Contbr. articles to profl. jours. Served as ensign USNR, 1944-46. Co-recipient Research medal Am. Soc. Tool Mfg. Engrs., 1962; Modern Pioneers Creative Industry award NAM, 1965; Engring. Materials Achievement award Am. Soc. Metals, 1973; Man of Yr. award Abrasive Engring. Soc., 1980; Alfred P. Sloan Found. research fellow, 1959-63. Fellow Am. Inst. Chemists (Chem. Pioneer award 1970), AAAS; mem. Am. Chem. Soc. (Creative Invention award 1972), Am. Phys. Soc. (co-winner Internat. Prize for New Materials 1977), Sigma Xi, Phi Kappa Phi. Patentee in field; pioneer in synthesizing of diamond. Home: 1711 Lambert Ln Provo UT 84604-1858 Office: Brigham Young Univ Dept Chemistry Provo UT 84602

HALL, J. MICHAEL, federal agency administrator, oceanographer. Program dir. climate & global change program Nat. Oceanic & Atmospheric Adminstrn., Silver Spring, Md. Recipient Spl. award Am. Meteorol. Assn., 1999. Office: Nat Oceanic & Atmospheric Adminstrn Global Programs 1100 Wayne Ave Ste 1210 Silver Spring MD 20910-5603*

HALL, J. TILLMAN, physical education educator, administrator, writer; b. Big Sandy, Tenn., Jan. 16, 1916; s. Travis M. and Sophia (Kirk) H.; m. Louise Babb, June 16, 1940; children: Nancy Sweeny, Jody Esser. BA, Pepperdine U., L.A., 1940; MA, U. So. Calif., 1947, EdD, 1951. Head dept. phys. edn. Pepperdine U., L.A., 1946-50; head dept. phys. edn. U. So.Calif., L.A., 1950-87, dir. Emeriti Ctr., Emeriti Coll., 1988-96. Author 10 books on phys. edn., recreation and dance; editor books on golf and tennis. Mem. Area Agy. on Aging. With USN, 1941-45. Recipient R. Tait McKenzie Disting. Prof. award AAHPERD, 1978, Disting. Retiree award, 1997. Mem. Internat. Sr. Citizen Assn.

HALL, JAMES EVAN, federal agency administrator, lawyer; m. Anne Stewart Impink; 2 daughters. Degree, U. Tenn. Counsel U.S. Senate Subcom. on Intergovtl. Rels.; staff U.S. Senator Al Gore, Sr.; pvt. practice Chattanooga; cabinet staff Tenn. Gov. Ned McWherter; dir. Tenn. State Planning Office; chief of staff U.S. Senator Harlan Mathews; mem. Nat. Transp. Safety Bd., Washington, 1993—, vice-chmn., 1994, chmn., 1994—. With U.S. Army, Vietnam. Decorated Bronze Star. Office: Nat Transp Safety Bd Office of the Chmn 490 L'Enfant Plz SW Washington DC 20594-0003*

HALL, JAMES FREDERICK, retired college president; b. Detroit, Dec. 30, 1921; s. Cortez Rogers and Bertha Wilhelmina H.; m. Betty Louise Stark, Sept. 17, 1949; children—Kristine Martha, Jay Charles. Student, U. Mich., 1939-41; B.A., Wayne State U., 1947, M.A., 1948; Ed.D., Tchrs. Coll., Columbia U., 1954. Instr. Highland Park Jr. Coll., 1948-49; adminstrv. asst., instr. N.Y.C. Community Coll., 1950-51; dir. student personnel services, dept. head Orange County Community Coll., Middletown, N.Y., 1952-55; dean collegiate tech. div., exec. asst. to pres. Ferris State U., 1955-57; founding pres. Dutchess Community Coll., 1957-72; pres. Cape Cod Community Coll., 1972-87; trustee, Mass. rep., Gov.'s appointment New Eng. Bd. Higher Edn., 1975-87; chmn. Pres.'s Council of Regional Community Colls. in Mass., 1976-78; mem. Mass. Postsecondary Edn. Commn., 1978-85; trustee Middle States Assn. Schs. and Colls., 1966-72; mem. mgmt. team Labor Negotiations for Regional Bd. Community Colls., 1978; bd. incorporators Bass River Savs. Bank, 1979-85. Bd. dirs. Cape Code Conservatory, West Barnstable, Mass., 1973-87, Cape Code YMCA, 1991—; trustee Cape Cod Hosp., Hyannis, Mass., 1978-87; mem. Mass. Health Facilities Appeal Bd., 1988-91; mem. Gov. Oversight Com., Town of Yarmouth, Mass., 1992—; mem. Town of Yarmouth Appeals Bd., 1992-93; apptd. Town of Yarmouth Rep. to Steam Ship Authority, 1997-98; bd. trustees Hist. Soc. Old Yarmouth, 1994—. Lt. (j.g.) USNR, 1942-46. Mem. New Eng. Assn. Schs. and Colls. (accreditation teams 1975-77), Southeastern Assn. Cooperation in Higher Edn. in Mass. (dir. 1972-79, pres. 1976, treas. 1978), Mass. Adminstrs. in Community Colls. (pres. 1974-75), Associated Colls of Mid-Hudson Area (chmn. bd. trustees 1963-64, 72, trustee 1963-72), Internat. Edn. Consortium (chmn. Coll. Consortium Internat. Studies, bd. dirs. 1985-87), South Yarmouth Lawn and Tennis Club (bd. dirs. 1991-93). Home: 29 Liverpool Dr Yarmouth Port MA 02675-1526

HALL, JAMES H(ERRICK), JR., philosophy educator, author; b. Houston, Oct. 20, 1933; s. James Herrick and Loula Ben (Vining) H.; m. Bonlyn Goodwin, 1957 (div. 1977); children: Christopher Vining, Jonathan Goodwin; m. Myfanwy Seaver Monroe, 1977; 1 child, Charles Trevor. AB, Johns Hopkins U., 1955; BD, Southeastern Sem., Wake Forest, N.C., 1958, ThM, 1960; PhD, U. N.C., Chapel Hill, 1964. Instr. philosophy U. N.C., Chapel Hill, 1960-62; asst. prof. Furman U., Greenville, S.C., 1963-65; assoc. prof. U. Richmond, Va., 1965-74, chmn. dept. philosophy, 1965-89, 94-96, prof., 1974—, The Thomas chair, 1982—. Author: Knowledge Belief and Transcendence, 1975, Logic Problems, 1991; (with others) Biblical and Secular Ethics, 1988. Mem. vestry St. Paul's Episc. Ch., Richmond, 1988-91; profl. ch. musician, Chapel Hill, Raleigh, Balt., Washington, Richmond. Coun. for Philosophic Studies fellow, Grand Rapids, 1973, U. Warwick fellow, Coventry, U.K., 1989-90, Kenan fellow U. N.C., 1960-61; rsch. grantee Duke Found., Durham, 1964, Mednick Trust, 1973-74. Mem. AAUP (chpt. pres. 1991-92), Am. Philos. Assn., Soc. for Philosophy of Religion, So. Soc. for Philosophy and Psychology, Omicron Delta Kappa. Democrat. Episcopalian. Avocations: choral music, camping, computers, travel. Home: 209 Wood Rd Richmond VA 23229-7538 Office: U Richmond Dept Philosophy North Ct University Of Richmond VA 23173

HALL, JAMES RAYFORD, III, adult education educator; b. Chgo., Sept. 4, 1946; s. James Rayford and Hortense Elizabeth (Jones) H. BA, Langston U., 1968; MA, Ball State U., 1970. History tchr. Chgo. Bd. Edn., 1968-86; history instr. Joliet (Ill.) Jr. Coll., 1970-71, Kennedy-King Coll., Chgo., 1987-91; instr. Gary (Ind.) Community Schs., 1987—, at-risk specialist, 1988-89; history instr. Calumet Coll., Whiting, Ind., 1989-91; polit. sci. and sociology instr. Ivy Tech State Coll., Gary, Ind., 1996—. Precinct Capt. 17th Ward Democratic Party, Chgo., 1978-81. Fellow Polit. Socialization of Disadvantage Youth, Ball State U. Office of Edn., 1969. Mem. Nat. Tchrs. Assn., Am.Fedn. Tchrs., Am. Polit. Sci. Assn., Am. Black Polit. Scientist Assn., TransAfrica. Democrat. Baptist. Avocations: photography, writing. Home: 584 Roosevelt St Gary IN 46404-1310 Office: Interplanetary Music BMI 584 Roosevelt St Gary IN 46404-1310

HALL, JAMES ROBERT, secondary education educator; b. Salem, Ill., Dec. 24, 1947; s. James Wesley and Patricia Joyce (Ellis) H. BS, U. Ill., 1970. Cert. secondary tchr., Ill. Tchr. Murphysboro (Ill.) H.S., 1970—. Author, compiler (tng. manual) Key Club Faculty Advisors, 1975. Sunday sch tchr. United Meth. Ch., Murphysboro, 1973-76, youth dir., 1973-76, mem. coun. on ministries, 1984—, trustee, 1984—; founder, dir. Christian Lay Coun. Youth Coffeehouse, 1973-75; mem. Murphysboro Recreation Bd., 1974-76, pres. 1975-76; cmty. amb. So. Ill. U. Area Svcs., 1975—; bd. dirs. Murphysboro Heart Fund, 1973-76, co-chmn. 1975-76; chmn. Murphysboro Muscular Dystrophy Assn., 1971-74; counsellor Little Grassy Youth Ch. Camp, 1973; mem. steering com. Murphysboro Apple Festival, 1975—, exec. com., 1983—; bd. dirs. Murphysboro United Way, 1978-83, Murphysboro Sr. Citizens Coun., 1980-83, Resource Reclamation Inc., 1979-85; vice chmn. Murphysboro Swimming Pool Project Commn., 1983-84, chmn. 1984-88; active Murphysboro Tourism Commn., 1995—; chmn. Murphysboro Mainstreet Promotions Commn., 1998—. Named on of Oytstanding Young men of Am. 1975, 84; recipient Citizenship award Sta. WTAO Radio, 1983, 84, Ann. Cmty. Svc. award Modern Woodmen Am., 1982, Citizen of Yr. award Murphysboro C. of C., 1984, Disting. Educator award Phi Delta Kappa, 1991. Mem. NEA, Ill. Edn. Assn., Murphysboro Edn. Assn., Key Club (advisor 1972—, adminstr. Ill.-Eastern Iowa dist. 1985-96, Key Club Internats. 1996, James R. Hall Achievement award 1999), Kiwanis (pres. 1977-78, lt. gov. dist. divsn. 1984-85, chmn. spl. club svcs. Ill.-Eastern Iowa dist. 1984-85, Mid. Sch. Builders Club advisor 1993—, cert. trainer 1993—, gov.-elect 1995-96, gov. 1996-97, Target 2000, long range planning com. for Key Club, Dr. Luis V. Amador medallion 1995, G. Harold Martin fellow 1996, George F. Hixson fellow Diamond 2 Levil i 1996-98). Avocations: collecting books and plates, bowling, tennis. Home: 28 Candy Ln Murphysboro IL 62966-2953 Office: Murphysboro H S 16 Blackwood Dr Murphysboro IL 62966-2937

HALL, J(AMES) R(OBERT), English educator; b. Rochester, N.Y., Mar. 17, 1946; s. James Robert and Helen Grace (Schauseil) H.; m. Joan Marie Wylie, Aug. 17, 1974; children: Jennifer Joy Wylie Hall, Justin James Wylie Hall. BA, St. John Fisher Coll., 1968; MA, U. Notre Dame, 1970, PhD, 1973. Vis. lectr. U. Ill., Urbana, 1973-74; instr. English St. Mary-of-Woods (Ind.) Coll., 1975; asst. prof. U. Miss., University, 1978-84, assoc. prof., 1984-90, prof., 1990—; scholarship reveiwer Old English Newsletter Western Mich. U., 1976—; referee scholarly manuscripts; cons. Nat. Endowment Humanities, Washington, 1990—. Contbr. essays to profl. jours. Adviser Old Miss Coll. Reps., University, 1995—. Am. Coun. Learned Socs. rsch. fellow, 1981-82, Harvard U. tchg.-rsch. fellow, 1983-84, NEH, 1993-94. Mem. Medieval Acad. Am., Internat. Soc. Anglo-Saxonists, South Atlantic Modern Lang. Assn., Am. Friends Bodleian Libr. Roman Catholic. Home: 1705 Johnson Ave Oxford MS 38655-4725 Office: U Miss Dept English University MS 38677

HALL, JAMES STANLEY, jazz guitarist, composer; b. Buffalo, Dec. 4, 1930; s. Harold S. and Louella (Cowles) H.; m. Jane Susan Yuckman, Sept. 9, 1965; 1 dau., Debra Jean. Mus.B., Cleve. Inst. Music, 1955; PhD in Music (hon.), Berklee Sch. Music, Boston, 1995. Author: Exploring Jazz Guitar; joined chico Hamilton, 1955; mem. Jimmy Giuffre Trio, 1957, tour U.S. and Europe with Jazz at Philharmonic, 1958, 59, Europe and S.A. with Ella Fitzgerald, 1959, 60; featured by Sonny Rollins, 1961-62; formed quartet with Art Farmer, 1962-64; leader own trio and quartet, 1962—; performed at White House, 1969; albums include Jazz Guitar, 1957, Undercurrent, All Across the City, Dedications & Inspirations, Diaglogues, Textures, 1997. By Arrangement, 1998, Jim Hall and Pat Metheny, 1999; motion picture appearance in Jazz on a Summer's Day, 1958; appearance on Ralph Gleason's TV Show, 1962-63, BBC, 1964, Jim Hall Invitational Concert, 1990, Tonite show, 1992; tour Europe, 1967, 69, 79-82, 86-87, 89—, Japan, 1970, 76, 79, 87, 90—; (documentary film) A Life in Progress. Recipient award Downbeat Critics Poll, 1963-65, 74, 76-80, 82-88, 89-90, 91-93, award Downbeat Readers' Poll, 1965-66, award Playboy Mag. All-Star Poll for Guitar, 1968-71; named Best Performer Jazz Mag., 1965-66, Best Composer-Arranger, Jazz Critics Circle N.Y., 1997; winner Jazz Times poll as Best Guitar, 1991, Jazzpar prize, Denmark, 1998, Disting. Alumni award Cleve. Inst. Music. Mem. BMI.

HALL, JANET C., lawyer; b. Lowell, Mass., Sept. 15, 1948. AB magna cum laude, Mt. Holyoke Coll., 1970; JD, NYU, 1973. Bar: Mass. 1973, U.S. Dist. Ct. Mass. 1974, D.C. 1976, U.S. Ct. Appeals (4th cir.) 1979, Conn. 1980, U.S. Dist. Ct. Conn. 1980, U.S. Ct. Appeals (2d cir.) 1987. Trial atty. antitrust divsn. U.S. Dept. Justice, 1975-79; ptnr. Robinson & Cole, Hartford, Conn. Rsch. editor: Annual Survey of American Law, 1972-73. Mem. ABA (litigation and antitrust law sects.), Conn. Bar Assn. (mem. exec. com. fed practice sect., antitrust sect. 1982—, ho. delegates 1990—). Office: Robinson & Cole 1 Comml Plz 280 Trumbull St Ste 26 Hartford CT 06103-3599

HALL, JANET FORESMAN, retired English language, science educator; b. Warsaw, Ind., Mar. 23, 1936; d. Eugene Harold and Mildred Florence (Johnson) Foresman; m. James David Hall, Aug. 17, 1958; children: Joel James Hall, Jeremy James Hall. BA, DePauw U., 1958; MS, Ind. U., South Bend, 1985. English tchr. Warsaw (Ind.) Cmty. Schs., 1958-59; genetics rsch. asst. Ind. U., Bloomington, 1959-61; newspaper corr. Montgomery County Sentinel, Rockville, Md., 1965-67; biochemistry rsch. asst. Notre Dame U., Ind., 1978-79; English, sci. instr. Ivy Tech. State Coll., South Bend, Ind., 1989-97; ret., 1997; advisor Phi Theta Kappa Ivy Tech. State Coll., 1995-97, writing across curriculum, 1990-92. Den leader Boy Scouts Am., South Bend, Ind., 1970-71, asst. den leader, 1978-79; jr. great books leader, South Bend, 1969, 72-73; docent Snite Mus., Notre Dame, Ind., 1978-82; mem. Scholarship Found. of St. Joseph County, 1982—, pres., 1987-88; sustaining mem. Children's Dispensary, pres., 1985-86. Recipient Horizon award Phi Theta Kappa, Indpls., 1997. Mem. Nat. Assn. Humanities Educators (conf. presenter), Hoosier Art Patrons, Pi Beta Phi (pres. 1972-73). Methodist. Avocations: gardening, traveling, reading, water color painting. Home: 21266 Sail Bay Dr Cassopolis MI 49031-9300

HALL, JAY, social psychologist; b. Houston, Oct. 18, 1932; s. Ernest James and Jamie (Clark) H.; m. Missy Hall; children: Kelly, Allison, Jeffrey. BA in Psychology, U. Tex., 1959, MA in Psychology, 1961, PhD in Psychology, 1963. Lectr. dept. psychology U. Tex., Austin, 1961-63, dir. S.W. Ctr. for Law and Behavioral Scis., 1964-66, assoc. prof. Grad. Sch. Bus., 1966-69; assoc. dir. Nat. Parole Insts., Austin, 1963-64; founder, chmn. bd. Teleometrics Internat., The Woodlands, Tex., 1969-93; CEO, chmn. Leadership Systems Internat., The Woodlands, Tex., 1996—. Author: Ponderables: Essays on Managerial Choice-Past and Future, 1982, The Competence Connection: A Blueprint for Excellence, 1988, Models for Management: The Structure of Competence, 1988, The Executive Trap, 1992, Why Some Leaders are Better than Others, 1995; contbr. numerous articles and psychol. tests to profl. publs.; inventor Halford Grip sports/grip prosthesis. Trustee The Woodlands Med. Ctr., 1980-91, Community Life Found., 1985-88, The John Cooper Sch., The Woodlands, 1986-91; dir. Interfaith, The Woodlands, 1980-88. 1st lt. U.S. Army, 1955-58. Mem. Am. Psychol. Assn., AAAS, N.Y. Acad. Sci., Sigma Xi. Episcopalian. Avocation: golf.

HALL, JEAN QUINTERO, communication educator; b. Manila, July 28, 1946; came to U.S., 1963; d. Evan Drake Moody and Victoria (Quintero) Bombon; m. Edward Payson Hall. BA in Comm., U. Wash., 1978; MPA, U. Del., 1984. Faculty Kapiolani C.C., Honolulu, 1984-85; cmty. developer Cath. Social Svcs., Honolulu, 1985; adminstr. City & County of Honolulu, 1985-86; faculty New River C.C., Dublin, Va., 1986-90; adminstr. Radford (Va.) U., 1987-89, faculty, 1989-92; pres. Global Soc., Radford, 1989-92; ind. cons. Silver City, N.Mex., 1992-94; faculty Western N.Mex. U., Silver City, 1994—; spkr. in field; columnist Filipino-Am. J., Phoenix, 1999—. Author: Desiderate Melodies, 1990, Rizal - Our Beloved Beacon, 1996. Grantee Commonwealth Va., 1991. Mem. Pacific & Asian Comm. Assn., Asian Studies/Philippine Studies Group, Filipino Am. Educators Assn., Filipino Cultural Heritage Soc., Filipino Am. Assn. N.Mex., Sigma Iota Epsilon. Avocation: writing. Home: 20 Vista Grande Silver City NM 88061-6613

HALL, JEROME WILLIAM, research engineering educator; b. Brunswick, Ga., Dec. 1, 1943; s. William L. and Frances K. (Wickie) H.; m. Loretta E. Hood, Aug. 28, 1965; children: Jennifer, Bridget, Bernadette. BS in Physics, Harvey Mudd Coll., 1965; MS in Engring., U. Wash., 1968, PhDCE, 1969. Registered profl. engr., D.C., N.Mex., Va. Asst. prof. civil engring. U. Md., College Park, 1970-73, assoc. prof., 1973-77; assoc. prof. U. N.Mex., Albuquerque, 1977-80, prof., 1980—, dir. bur. engring. research, 1981-88, asst. dean engring., 1985-88, chmn. dept. of civil engring., 1990-97; cons. in field, 1971—. Contbr. articles to profl. jours. Recipient Teetor award Soc. Automotive Engrs., 1975; Pub. Partnership award Alliance For Transportation Rsch., 1997. Fellow Inst. Transp. Engrs. (pres. N.Mex. sect. 1984-86, sec.-treas. western dist. 1987-88, v.p. 1988-89, pres. 1989-90, internat. bd. dirs. 1993-95); mem. Transp. Rsch. Bd. (chmn. com. 1986-92, chmn. group coun. 1992-95, panel chmn. 1990—), Am. Soc. Engring. Edn., Am. Rd. and Transp. Builders Assn. Republican. Roman Catholic. Office: U of New Mexico Civil Engring Dept Albuquerque NM 87131-1351

HALL, JOAN M., lawyer; b. Inman, Nebr., Apr. 13, 1939; d. Warren J. and Delia E. (Allyn) McClurg; m. George J. Cotsirilos, Dec. 4, 1988; children: Colin Michael, Justin Allyn. BA, Nebr. Wesleyan U., 1961; JD, Yale U., 1965. Bar: Ill. 1965, U.S. Dist. Ct. (no. dist.) Ill. 1965, U.S. Ct. Appeals (7th cir.) 1965. Assoc. Jenner & Block, Chgo., 1965-71, sr. ptnr., 1971—; chmn. character and fitness Ill. Supreme Ct., 1988-89; mem. dist. admissions com. U.S. Dist. Ct. (no. dist.) Ill. Mem. exec. com. Yale Law Sch. Assn., 1976-86, treas., 1982-85; bd. dirs. Yale Law Sch. FUnd, 1978—, chmn., 1984-86; bd. dirs. Chgo. Lawyer's Com. Civil Rights Under the Law, 1978—, chmn., 1983-84; bd. dirs. Legal Assistance Found. Chgo., 1979-82; trustee Rush-Presbyn. St. Luke's Hosp., 1984—; mem. Gannon-Proctor Commn., 1982-84; trustee, bd. govs. Nebr. Wesleyan U., 1983—; bd. dirs. Goodman Theatre, Ill. Sports Facility Authority, 1986-96; mem. vis. com. Northwestern U. Sch. Law, 1987-92; mem. adv. coun. De Paul U. Sch. Law, 1987-94; bd. govs. Chgo. Lighthouse for the Blind. Fellow Am. Coll. Trial Lawyers; mem. ABA (chmn. litig. sect. 1982-83, fed. judiciary com. 1985-91, resource devel. coun. 1984-85, Ho. of Dels. 1991-93), Comml. Club (sec. 1995—), Econ. Club (Chgo., dir.). Office: Jenner & Block 1 E Ibm Plz Fl 4000 Chicago IL 60611-7603

HALL, JOHN EMMETT, orthopedic surgeon, educator; b. Wadena, Sask., Can., Apr. 23, 1925; came to U.S., 1971; s. Emmett Matthew and Isobel Mary (Parker) H.; m. Frances Norma Walsh, May 31, 1952; children: Maureen, Susan, Bruce, Peter, Martha, Thomas, David. BA, U. Sask., 1948; MD, CM, McGill U., Montreal, 1952. Diplomate Am. Bd. Orthop. Surgery. Orthop. surgeon Hosp. Sick Children, Toronto, 1958-71; chief orthop. surgeon Hosp. Sick Children, 1966-71; asst. prof. medicine U. Toronto, 1966-71; prof. orthop. surgery Harvard U. Med. Sch., 1971—; clin. chief orthop. Children's Hosp. Med. Ctr., Boston, 1971-81, sr. assoc. in orthop. surgery, 1981-86; orthop. surgeon-in-chief Boston Children's Hosp., 1986-94, sr. assoc. in orthop. surgery, 1995—. Contbr. articles med. jours. Served with RCAF, 1942-46. Fellow ACS, Royal Coll. Surgeons Can.; mem. AMA, Can. Med. Assn., Am. Orthop. Assn., Can. Orthop. Assn., Acad. Orthop. Surgeons, Scoliosis Rsch. Soc. (pres. 1968-70), Pediat. Orthop. Assn. (pres. 1978-80), Harvard Club. Roman Catholic. Home: 36 Codman Rd Brookline MA 02445-7555 Office: Children's Hosp in Boston 300 Longwood Ave Boston MA 02115-5724*

HALL, JOHN FRY, psychologist, educator; b. Phila., Apr. 24, 1919; s. Harry R. and Alta (Herner) H.; m. Jean Midlam, May 14, 1943; 1 son, John. B.S., Ohio U., 1946; M.A., Ohio State U., 1947, Ph.D., 1949. Mem. faculty Pa. State U., University Park, 1949—; prof. psychology Pa. State U., 1958—; prof. emeritus, 1985—; Program dir. psychobiology NSF, Washington, 1966-67; vis. prof. U. Va., 1952, U. Wis., 1954, U. Calif. at Berkeley, 1962, U. Hawaii, 1968, Fla. State U., 1975-76. Author: Psychology of Motivation, 1961, Psychology of Learning, 1966, Readings in the Psychology of Learning, 1967, Verbal Learning and Retention, 1971, Classical Conditioning and Instrumental Learning, 1976, An Invitation to Learning and Memory, 1982, Learning and Memory, 1989; contbr. articles to profl. jours. Mem. Am. Psychol. Assn., Psychonomics Soc., A.A.A.S. Home: 334 Caloosa Palms Ct Sun City Center FL 33573-6938

HALL, JOHN HOPKINS, retired lawyer; b. Dallas, May 10, 1925; s. Albert Brown and Eleanor Pauline (Hopkins) H.; m. Marion Martin, Nov. 23, 1957; children: Ellen Martin, John Hopkins II. Student, U. Tex., 1942, U. of South, Sewanee, Tenn., 1942-43; LL.B., So. Meth. U., 1949. Bar: Tex. bar 1949. Ptnr. Strasburger & Price, Dallas, 1957-93, ret., 1993. Served with U.S. Army, 1943-45. Fellow Tex. Bar Found., Am. Bar Found., Internat. Acad. Trial Lawyers, Am. Coll. Trial Lawyers; mem. Tex. Bar Assn.,

Tex. Assn. Def. Counsel, Internat. Assn. Def. Counsel, Fin and Feather Club. Episcopalian.

HALL, JOHN LEWIS, physicist, researcher; b. Denver, Aug. 21, 1934; s. John Ernest and Elizabeth Rae (Long) H.; m. Marilyn Charlene Robinson, Mar. 1, 1958; children: Thomas Charles, Carolyn Gay, Jonathan Lawrence. BS in Physics, Carnegie Mellon U., 1956, MS in Physics, 1958, PhD in Physics, 1961; PhD (hon.), U. Paris XIII, 1989. Postdoctoral rsch. assoc. Nat. Bur. Standards, Washington, 1961-62; physicist Nat. Bur. Standards, Boulder, Colo., 1962-75, sr. scientist, 1975—; cons. Los Alamos (N.Mex.) Sci. Labs., 1963-65; lectr. U. Colo., Boulder, 1977—; cons. numerous firms in laser industry, 1974—. Contbr. numerous tech. papers to profl. jours.; patentee in laser tech.; editor: Laser Spectroscopy 3, 1977. Recipient IR-100 award IR Mag., 1975, 77, Gold medal Nat. Bur. Stds., 1974, Stratton award, 1971, E.U. Condon award, 1979, Gold medal Dept. Commerce, 1969, Presdl. Meritorious Exec. award, 1980, Meritorious Alumnus award Carnegie Mellon U., 1985. Fellow Optical Soc. Am. (bd. dirs. 1980-82, Charles H. Townes award 1984, Frederic Ives medal 1991), Am. Phys. Soc. (Davisson-Germer award 1988, Arthur L. Schawlow prize 1993); mem. NAS, Comite Consultatif pour la Definition du Metre. Office: JILA-Nat Bur of Standards 325 Broadway St Boulder CO 80303-3337

HALL, JOHN RAYMOND, JR., fire protection executive; b. Washington, Feb. 25, 1948; s. John Raymond and Elizabeth Florence (Lord) H.; m. Jean Baird Horky, Dec. 2, 1972. BA cum laude, Brown U., 1967; PhD, U. Pa., 1972. Rsch. analyst Resource Mgmt. Corp., Bethesda, Md., 1972-73; sr. rsch. assoc. Urban Inst., Washington, 1973-79; ops. rsch. analyst U.S. Fire Adminstrn., within Fed. Emergency Mgmt. Agy., Washington, 1979-82, Ctr. for Fire Rsch., within Nat. Bur. of Stds, Gaithersburg, Md., 1982-84; asst. v.p. fire analysis and rsch. Nat. Fire Protection Assn., Quincy, Mass., 1984—; exec. sec. rsch. sect. Nat. Fire Protection Assn., 1990—; chair OR/MS Bd., Balt., 1994; past pres. Inst. for Ops. Rsch. and the Mgmt. Scis., Balt. and Providence, 1995, mem. fin. com. 1997-98; v.p. for mem. activities Inst. of Mgmt. Scis., Providence, 1983-86, sec. 1979-83, mem. at-large of coun., 1977-79, chmn. orgn. and bylaws com., 1979-94, pres. Washington chpt. 1978-79, v.p. for membership coll. on pub. programs and processes, 1982-85; trustee Washington Ops. Rsch./Mgmt. Sci. Coun., 1980-81, 83-84. Author: (with others) Procedures for Improving the Measurement of Local Fire Protection Effectiveness, 1976, How Effective Are Your Community Services?, 1977, 92, The SFPE Handbook of Fire Protection Engineering, 1988, 95, Fire Protection Handbook, 1986, 97; editor TIMS Chpts. Newsletter, 1976-79; columnist Mgmt. Sci. Update, 1980-81; columnist/editor Applications Rev., 1976-88; contbr. articles to profl. jours. Chmn. Fire Protection Commn., Norwood, Mass., 1986—. Recipient (4) Cert. of Outstanding Performance Fed. Emergency Mgmt. Agy., 1981-83, Cert. of Spl. Achievement, 1982, Cert. of Recognition Nat. Bur. of Stds., 1983-84, Leadership Giving award United Way of Neponset Valley, 1991. Mem. AAAS, ASTM (E5 exec. com. 1996—, 4th vice chair 1998—), Internat. Assn. for Fire Safety Sci. (exec. com. 1994—, programme com. 1991—, newsletter editor 1994—), Ops. Rsch. Soc. Am. (tech. sects. com. 1972-76), Soc. for Risk Analysis, Am. Mgmt. Assn., Inst. Mgmt. Scis., Combustion Inst., Phi Beta Kappa, Sigma Xi. Democrat. Achievements include rsch. on the modeling and conceptual framework innovations in fire risk analysis in the USA. Home: 10 Alden Dr Norwood MA 02062-5326 Office: Nat Fire Protection Assn PO Box 9101 1 Batterymarch Park Quincy MA 02269-9101

HALL, JOHN THOMAS, lawyer; b. Phila., May 14, 1938; s. John Thomas and Florence Sara (Robinson) H.; m. Carolyn Park Currie, May 26, 1968; children: Daniel Currie, Kathleen Currie. AB, Dickinson Coll., 1960; MA, U. Md., 1963; JD, U. N.C., 1972. Bar: N.C. 1972. Chmn. dept. speech Mercersburg (Pa.) Acad., 1960-63, U. Balt., 1963-69; research asst. N.C. Ct. Appeals, Raleigh, 1972-73, dir. pre-hearing research staff, 1974-75, asst. clk., marshall, librarian, 1980-81; counsel Dorothea Dix Hosp., Raleigh, 1974; asst. dist. atty. State of N.C., Raleigh, 1975-80, 81-83; pvt. practice Raleigh, 1973-74, 83—; mem. faculty King's Bus. Coll., Raleigh, 1973-75, N.C. Bar Assn., 1987—; undercover inmate Cen. Prison Duke Ctr. on Law and Poverty, Durham, N.C., 1970. Mem. Raleigh Little Theatre, Theatre in the Park, Raleigh; charter mem. Wake County Dem. Men's Club, 1977—. Named Best Actor, Raleigh Little Theatre, 1975, 77, 80, 82, 85, 86, 93, 98. Mem. ABA, N.C. Bar Assn., Wake County Bar Assn. (bd. dirs. 1986-89, vice chmn. exec. com. 1986-87), 10th Jud. Dist. Bar Assn. (bd. dirs. 1986-89, chmn. grievance com. 1987-90), Wake County Acad. Criminal Trial Lawyers (v.p. 1986-87), Scottish Clan Gunn Soc., Neuse River Valley Model R.R. (Raleigh). Roman Catholic. Avocations: model railroading, walking, reading. Office: PO Box 1207 Raleigh NC 27602-1207

HALL, JOHN WESLEY, JR., lawyer; b. Watertown, N.Y., Jan. 28, 1948; s. John Wesley and Mary Louise (Hodge) H.; m. Alison Hall; children: Justin William, Mark Daniel, Juliana Sanchez. BA, Hendrix Coll., 1970; JD, U. Ark., 1973. Bar: Ark. 1973, U.S. Dist. Ct. (ea. and we. dists.) Ark. 1973, U.S. Ct. Appeals (8th cir.) 1973, D.C. 1975, U.S. Ct. Appeals (5th cir.) 1976, U.S. Supreme Ct. 1976, Tenn. 1988, U.S. Ct. Appeals (fed. cir.) 1988, U.S. Ct. Appeals (6th cir.) 1991, Nev. 1993, U.S. Ct. Appeals (9th cir.) 1995, N.Y. 1996. Dep. pros. atty., Office Pros. Atty., Little Rock, 1973-79; head career criminal divsn. Little Rock, 1978-79; law clk. Ark. Supreme Ct., Little Rock, 1974; pvt. practice, Ark. Supreme Ct., 1974—; instr. trial advocacy Ark. Pros. Attys. Assn., 1977-79; adj. prof. Sch. Law, Grad. Sch. Criminal Justice, U. Ark., Little Rock, 1985, 88, 91; speaker to lawyer and police groups. Author: Search and Seizure, 1982, 3d edit., 1993, Professional Responsibility of the Criminal Lawyer, 1987, 2d edit., 1996, Trial Handbook for Arkansas Lawyers, 1986, 3d edit., 1998; editor, author: Arkansas Prosecutor's Trial Manual, 1976-77, Arkansas Extradition Manual, 1978; editor: (with B. Scheck and P. Neufield) DNA: Understanding, Controlling, and Depleting the New Evidence of the 90's, 1990; contbr. articles to law jours. Mem. NACDL (life, bd. dirs. 1989-95, 97-000), Am. Bd. Criminal Lawyers, Assn. Responsible Lawyers, Ark. Bar Assn. (ho. of dels. 1976-79), Ark. Assn. Criminal Def. Lawyers (pres. 1987-89). Episcopalian. Home: 300 Rice St Little Rock AR 72205-6141 Office: 523 W 3d St Little Rock AR 72201-2309

HALL, JULIE JANE, community health nurse, administrator; b. Berkeley, Calif., Jan. 14, 1951; d. Dale and Patricia Hall; m. Norman Charles Weinstein, Mar. 22, 1986. ADN, Boise State U., 1980, BS, 1983; MPH in Health Svcs. Adminstrn., U. Minn., 1997. Cert. community health nurse. Staff nurse St. Luke's Regional Med. Ctr., Boise, Idaho, 1980-84; hospice nurse Mountain States Tumor Insts., Boise, 1983-84; staff devel. coord. Hillcrest Care Ctr., Boise, 1986-87; asst. mgr. St. Alphonus Home Health, Boise, 1987-90, adminstr., 1990-99. Mem. APHA, Idaho Hosp. Assn. Home Care Soc. (pres. 1993-94, 97-99), Leadership Boise (v.p. 1994-95), Idaho Nurses Assn., Sigma Theta Tau.

HALL, KATHRYN WALT, ambassador; m. Craig Hall; 2 children, 4 stepchildren. AB in Econs., U. Calif., Berkeley, JD. Asst. city atty. Berkeley, Calif.; with Safeway Stores; pres. Kathryn Hall Vineyards, Inc., Walt Mgmt., Inc.; mng. dir., ptnr. Hall Fin. Group, Inc.; amb. to Austria Vienna, 1997—; mem. hunger adv. com. U.S. Ho. of Reps. Co-founder North Tex. Food Bank; mem. Nat. Adv. Coun. for Violence Against Women; trustee Woodrow Wilson Internat. Ctr. for Scholars; former bd. dirs., v.p. Tex. Mental Health Assn. Mem. Dallas Area C. of C., Comml. Real Estate Women, Tex. Retailers Assn. Office: Am Embassy Vienna Austria Dept State Washington DC 20521-9900*

HALL, KEITH R., federal official; b. Rockville Centre, N.Y., June 30, 1947; m. Linda Judith Merker, 1969; children: Jennifer, Jason. BA in History and Polit. Sci., Alfred U., 1969; MPA, Clark U., 1979. Commd. 2 lt. U.S. Army, 1970, advanced through grades to capt.; chief intelligence collection mgmt., comdr. human source collection U.S. Army, Augsburg, W. Ger., 1970-74; commd. tactical signals intelligence co. U.S. Army, Pyongtaek, Rep. Korea, 1974-75; supr. divsn. signals intelligence ops. tng. Army Intelligence Sch. U.S. Army, Ft. Devens, Mass., 1976-79; resigned U.S. Army, 1979; budget examiner Office Mgmt. and Budget, Washington, 1979-83; dep. staff dir., budget dir. Senate Select Com. Intelligence, Washington, 1983-91; dep. asst. sec. defense intelligence Office of Sec. of Defense, Washington, 1991-95; exec. dir. for intelligence cmty. affairs Office of Dir. Ctrl. Intelligence/CIA, Washington, 1995-96; dep. dir., acting dir. Nat. Reconnaissance Office, Washington, 1996-97, asst. sec. of Air Force (space), dir., 1997—; Presdl. mgmt. intern U.S. Office Personnel Mgmt., Washington, 1979-81. Mem. Security Affairs Support Assn., Nat. Milit. Intelligence Assn. (bd. dirs. 1988-97). Lutheran. Avocations: reading, baseball, hiking, bicycling, postal history.

HALL, KENDRA JEAN, neuroscience nurse, researcher, educator; b. L.A., June 26, 1945; d. Kenneth Eugene and Loretta Gene (Hurlburt) H.; children: Madelyn Elizabeth Behrman, Rose Lorraine Behrman. BA in Psychology, U. Calif., Davis, 1970; AS with highest honors, Sacramento City Coll., 1980; BSN, Calif. State U., Sacramento, 1982, postgrad. Clin. nurse, neurosurg. ICU U. Calif. Davis Med. Ctr., Sacramento, 1981-86; asst. dir. nurses Sutter Healthcare Systems, Sacramento, 1987; instr. med.-surg. nursing Sacramento City Coll., 1988; rsch. and pain care nurse, dept. anesthesia U. Calif. Davis Med. Ctr., Sacramento, 1988-91; neurology nurse clinician, rsch. nurse VA No Calif Health Care System, Sacramento, 1991-98; rsch. assoc. Consol. Sci., Inc. for Crossroads Program, Stockton, Calif., 1998—; lectr. neurology Sacramento Cmty. Critical Care Course. Mem. AAUW (Stockton br.), ANA, Calif. Nurses Assn., Am. Assn. Neurosci. Nurses, No. Calif. Nursing Rsch. Network, Ctrl. Valley Birding Consortium, Assistance League, Sierra Club, Audubon, Sigma Theta Tau, Phi Kappa Phi.

HALL, KENNETH RICHARD, chemical engineering educator, consultant; b. Tulsa, Okla., Nov. 5, 1939; s. Snipes Webster and Selina Rose (Scarpin) H.; m. Janet Beulah Blood, June, 1964 (div. 1975); children: Tara Marie, Deirdre Rene; m. Frieda Maria Karner, Mar. 12, 1976; children: Kent Max, Keith Anton, Krysta Maria. BS ChemE, U. Tulsa, 1962; MS, U. Calif., Berkeley, 1964; PhD, U. Okla., 1967. Registered engr., Tex. Asst. prof. U. Va., Charlottesville, 1967-70, 71-74; asst. to pres. ChemShare Corp., Norman, Okla., 1970; sr. research engr. AMOCO, Tulsa, 1970-71; vis. prof. U. Louvain, Belgium, 1971-72; assoc. prof. Tex. A&M U., College Station, 1974-78, prof., 1978—, dir. thermodynamics research ctr., 1979-85, 97—, asst. dir. Tex. engring. experiment sta., 1985-88, assoc. dean engring., 1987-94, assoc. dir., 1988, dep. dir., 1988-94, assoc. dep. chancellor for engring., 1990-94, interim head chem. engring., 1994; dir. CTS divsn. NSF, Va., 1994-96; cons. OPC Engring., Houston, 1980-85, Quantum Tech., Houston, 1981-85; cons. Precision Measurement Inc., Duncanville, Tex., 1981-90, also bd. dirs. Lorax Corp., 1991—. U.S. editor Flow Measurement and Instrumentation; contbr. over 175 articles to profl. jours. Recipient numerous grants for research. Mem. ASTM (chmn. D-3 1985-91, 94—), Am. Chem. Soc., Am. Soc. Engring. Edn., Am. Inst. Chem. Engrs. (chmn. ctrl. Va. chpt. 1969, chmn. cyyogenics 1977-79, exec. position II South Tex. sect. 1991-92, bd. dirs. fuels and petrochems. divsn. 1992-94). Avocations: sports, reading. Home: 1401 Millcreek Ct College Station TX 77845-8352 Office: Tex A&M U Dept Chem Engring College Station TX 77843

HALL, LARRY D., energy company executive, lawyer; b. Hastings, Nebr., Nov. 8, 1942; s. Willis E. and Stella W. (Eckoff) H.; m. Jeffe D. Bryant, July 5, 1985; children: Scott, Jeff, Mike, Bryan. BA in Bus., U. Nebr., Kearney; JD, U. Nebr. Bar: Nebr., Colo. Ptnr. Wright, Simmons, Hancock & Hall, Scottsbluff, Nebr., 1967-71; atty., asst. treas. KN Energy Inc., Hastings, 1971-73, dir. regulatory affairs, 1973-76; v.p. law divsn. KN Energy Inc., Lakewood, Colo., 1976-82, sr. v.p., 1982-85, exec. v.p., 1985-88, pres., COO, 1988-94, pres., CEO, 1994—, also bd. dirs., 1988-94, chmn., CEO, pres., 1996—; bd. dirs. Colo. Assn. Commerce and Industry, Gas Rsch. Inst., Colo. Alliance for Bus., MLA, Intrasar, Inc.; chmn. Natural Gas Coun., 1998. Dir. Boy Scouts Am., Colo. Mem. ABA, Colo. Assn. Commerce and Industry (bd. dirs.), Interstate Natural Gas Assn. Am. (chmn. 1997), Midwest Gas Assn., CAB (bd. dirs.), Fed. Energy Bar Assn., Nebr. Bar Assn., Colo. Bar Assn., Pres. Assn., Midwest Gas Assn. (chmn.), Hiwan Country Club, Desert Mountain, Elks, Club 30. Presbyterian. Avocations: skiing, golf, photography. Home: 1892 Sugarbush Dr Evergreen CO 80439-9415 Office: KN Energy Inc PO Box 15265 Lakewood CO 80215

HALL, LAWRIE PLATT, consumer products executive, public community corporate philanthropy executive; b. Balt., Mar. 26, 1942; d. William Henry and Virginia (Stein) Pitcher. AB in Fine Arts, Goucher Coll., Balt., 1960; Cert. Middle Mgmt., Simmons Grad. Sch., Boston, 1977. Advt/ writer, prodn. asst. Hutzlers Dept. Stores, Balt., 1964-66; pub. rels. asst. Balt. Mus. Art, 1966-68; pub. info. officer U. Balt., 1969-70; pub. rels. dir. Balt. Assn. for Retarded Citizens, 1971; advt. supr., pub. rels. asst. Sierra Pacific Power Co., Reno, Nev., 1972-74; dir. local govt. rels. to dir. we. state and local rels. Atlantic Richfield Co., L.A., 1974-79; group exec. govt. affairs Greater Cin. C. of C., 1980-86; owner Pitcher Platt & Assocs., 1981-90; exec. dir. Crime Commn., Orlando, Fla., 1982-83; staff dir. Office of Mayor, City of Orlando, 1983-88; pub. rels. and cmty. affairs dir. Tupperware Home Parties U.S., Orlando, 1988-90; dir. external affairs Tupperware Worldwide, Orlando, 1990-96, Tupperware Corp., Orlando, 1996—. Bd. dirs. Sta. WMFE, pub. broadcasting, Orlando, 1987-90, Metro Orlando Urban League, 1984-89, Cen. Fla. Women's Resource Ctr., 1984-87, vice-chmn., 1986, 87; memb. bd. Heart of Fla. United Way, campaign chmn. Osceola County, 1992; bd. dirs. Cultural Alliance Cen. Fla., 1988-90, chmn., 1990; bd. dirs. Boys and Girls Clubs Ctr.. Fla., 1994—, chmn. mktg. com., 1997, 98; chmn. Arts Svcs. Coun., Inc., 1990-91, Chamber Found., 1994-96; alumni Leadership Orlando Class of 1982, Orange Blossom Trail Devel. Bd. Orlando and Orange County, 1990-93, Leadership Fla. Class of 1987-88; mem. mktg. adv. com. Boys and Girls Clubs Am., 1994—; bd. dirs. Valencia C.C. Found., 1995-97. Mem. Pub. Rels. Soc. Am., Fla. Exec. Women, Fla. Women's Alliance (bd. dirs. 1994-98, 99—), Greater Orlando C. of C. (bd. dirs. 1990-91, 97-98, 99—), Fla. C. of C. (bd. dirs. 1990-92), Kissimmee-Osceola C. of C. (bd. dirs. 1988-96, 99—), Community Vision Inc. (bd. dirs. 1998—), Citrus Club. Democrat. Avocations: reading, canoeing, writing, needlepoint, ballot issues campaigns. Office: Tupperware Corp PO Box 2353 Orlando FL 32802-2353

HALL, LEE BOAZ, publishing company consultant, author; b. Little Rock, Oct. 8, 1928; s. Graham Roots and Louise (Boaz) H.; m. Mary Louise Reed, Nov. 29, 1951 (div.); children: Gwendolyn, Ann Valerie, Graham; m. Sarah Moore, Dec. 15, 1978. B.A., Yale U., 1950. Reporter Ark. Gazette, Little Rock, 1950-51; officer Dept. Def., Washington, 1951-52, W.Ger., 1952-53; reporter Washington Post, 1953-55; with Life mag., 1955-70; bur. chief Life mag., Latin Am., 1958-59, Paris, 1963-66; editor Life en Espanol, 1966-69; editor internat. edits. Life, N.Y.C., 1970; pres. Tomorrow Pub. Co., N.Y.C., 1970-72; sr. v.p. internat. pub. Playboy Enterprises, Inc., Chgo., 1972-86; pres. Int Pub., Inc., 1986—, Donlee, Inc., Little Rock, 1986—. Author: International Magazine and Book Licensing, 1983. Served with U.S. Army, 1950-51. Mem. Federation Internationale de la Presse Periodique (liaison), Racquet Club, Montecito Country Club. Home and Office: 1180 Camino Dr PO Box 763 Summerland CA 93067-0763 *Two words "fair play" define the principles and standards of conduct I try to adhere to in my life. Professionally, negotiating as I do with people of many cultures, fairness is of the essence. Too many Americans, isolated by oceans, guided by strict interpretation of the Puritan ethic and misled by the trappings of their power, lord their tastes, their customs and their wealth over those they perceive as less fortunate.*

HALL, LYDIA JANE, geriatrics nurse; b. Ravenwood, Mo., Mar. 4, 1939; d. George G. and Lydia G. (Lambert) Griffin; m. Clifford Ray Hall, Sept. 18, 1987; children: Ray Ballin, Ronald Ballin, Janet Goad, Julia Newton. Assoc. Nursing, Butler County Community Coll., Eldorado, Kans., 1983; student, Arkansas City Community Coll., 1984, Kans. Newman Coll., Wichita, 1985. Staff nurse Arkansas City Meml. Hosp., 1983-85, St. Joseph Med. Ctr., Wichita, Kans., 1985-86, Heritage House, Winfield, Kans., 1986; evening and night charge nurse Health Concepts IV-Cedar Vale (Kans.) Regional Hosp., 1986-87, 88-89; staff nurse St. Luke's Hosp., Wellington, Kans., 1988, Augusta (Kans.) Med. Complex, Inc., 1989; night charge nurse Cumbernauld Village, Winfield, Kans., 1990; DON Grouse Valley Manor, Dexter, Kans., 1991-97; charge nurse Med. Lodge East, Arkansas City, Kans., 1997-98, Presbyn. Manor, Arkansas City, 1998—. Mem. sch. bd. Unified Sch. Dist. 462, Burden, Kans., 1975-79; mem., chmn. Cowley County Spl. Edn. Bd., 1975-79. Home: 1021 E 2nd Ave Winfield KS 67156-2302

HALL, MARCIA JOY, non-profit organization administrator; b. Long Beach, Calif., June 24, 1947; d. Royal Waltz and Norine (Parker) Stanton; m. Stephen Christopher Hall, March 29, 1969; children: Geoffrey Michael, Christopher Stanton. AA, Foothill Coll., 1967; student, U. Oreg., 1967-68; BA, U. Washington, Seattle, 1969. Instr. aide Glen Yermo Sch., Mission Viejo, Calif., 1979-80; market rsch. interviewer Rsch. Data, Framingham, Mass., 1982-83; adult edn. instr. Community Sch. Use Program, Milford, Mass., 1982-83; career info. ctr. coord. Milford High Sch., 1983-86; corp. rels. dir. Sch. Vols. for Milford, Inc., 1985-86; N.E. area coord. YWCA of Annapolis and Anne Arundel County, Severna Park, Md, 1987-89; exec. dir. West Anne Arundel County C. of C., Odenton, Md., 1989—, also exec. dir. Found., Inc.; v.p. Corridor Transp. Corp. Pres. PTO, Mission Viejo, 1979-80, Milford, 1981-84; consumer assistance vol., Calif. Pub. Interest Rsch. Group, 1977-78; chmn. grant com. 21st Century Edn. Found., Ann Arundel Pub. Schs., Leadership Anne Arundel. Mem. Am. Bus. Women's Assn., Md. Assn. C. of C. Execs. (v.p.), Toastmasters (treas. 1988—, pres. 1989—). Avocations: piano, music composition, bridge, reading. Home: 507 Devonshire Ln Severna Park MD 21146-1017

HALL, MARILEE ALICE, elementary education educator; b. Kingwood, W.Va., Sept. 6, 1947; d. George Forest Sr. and Jessie Alice (Hill) Sypolt; m. David Leroy Hall, June 19, 1971. BS in Edn., W.Va. U., 1974, MS in Journalism, 1983. Cert. profl. tchr., W.Va. Tchr. Monongalia County Schs., Morgantown, W.Va., 1975-77, Preston County Schs., Kingwood, W.Va., 1978—; grant writer Valley Eme. Sch., Arthurdale, W.Va., 1994—. Author: School Public Relations Handbook, 1983. Pres., chair, mem. Arthurdale Heritage Inc., 1985—; co-chair, mem. Valley Dist. Fair, Reedsville, W.Va., 1987—; founder, editor, pub. Restoring Yesterday for Tomorrow, 1985—. Recipient Vol.-of-Month award Arthurdale Heritage Inc., 1996, 97. Mem. NEA, W.Va. Edn. Assn., Preston County Edn. Assn., VFW Ladies Assn., Preston County & W.Va. Reading Couns. (chair young writers 1990-93), Kappa Tau Alpha. Democrat. Avocation: freelance writing, public relations. Home: PO Box 211 Arthurdale WV 26520-0211 Office: Arthurdale Heritage Inc PO Box 850 Arthurdale WV 26520-0850

HALL, MARILYN MARGARET, occupational health nurse; b. Bay City, Mich., Mar. 1, 1941; d. Oscar and Esther (Kolb) Pfannes; m. Harold D. Hall, June 5, 1965; children: Veronica Hall Henley, Gregory H. Diploma in nursing, Saginaw (Mich.) Gen. Hosp., 1962. RN, Ala., S.C.; cert. occupational health nurse-specialist; cert. in pulmonary function testing, audiometrics; cert. breach analipis testing, breath alcohol testing. Occupational health nurse GM, Athens, Ala., MEMC Materials Inc., Spartanburg, S.C., Hoechsl Diafoil, Greer, S.C., 1997-98, Mitsubishi Polyester Film, L.L.C.; mem. Spartanburg Regional Med. Occupl. Health Bd. Mem. Patnership for Nursing, S.C., 1990-92. Mem. Am. Assn. Occupational Health Nurses, S.C. Assn. Occupational Health Nurses, Saginaw Gen. Hosp. Sch. Nursing Alumni Assn. Home: 312 Tearose Ln Simpsonville SC 29681-5847

HALL, MARION TRUFANT, botany educator, arboretum director; b. Gorman, Tex., Sept. 6, 1920; s. Frank Marion and Nora Gertrude (Wharton) H.; m. Virginia Riddle, Nov. 9, 1944; children: Susan, Alan Lee, John Lane. BS, U. Okla., 1943, MS, 1947; PhD, Washington U., St. Louis, 1951; DSc (hon.), North Central Coll., Ill., 1977. Ranger Nat. Park Service, Dept. Interior, 1942; instr. botany U. Okla., 1946-47; curator Bebb Herbarium, 1949; field botanist, instr. Tex. Nature Camp, Nat. Audubon Soc., Kerrville, Tex., 1948; grad. asst. zoology, teaching fellow Washington U., 1948-50; spl. lectr. genetics and evolution Henry Shaw Sch. Botany, 1952; botanist Cranbrook Inst. Sci., Bloomfield Hills, Mich., 1950-56; acting dir. Cranbrook Inst. Sci., 1955-56; prof., head dept. botany Butler U., 1956-62; vis. prof. botany U. Okla., 1962; dir. Stovall Mus. Sci. and History, 1962-66; dir. Morton Arboretum, Lisle, Ill., 1966-90, dir. emeritus, 1990—; prof. botany, acting dir. U. Mich. Bot. Gardens, 1963-64; prof. horticulture U. Ill., Urbana; adj. prof. biology No. Ill. U.; cons. Mich. Dept. Conservation, Handbook Biol. Materials for Museums, also cons. on conservation issues, open space preservation & mgmt., vegetational analysis, land use rating. Contbr. numerous research articles to profl. jours. Bd. dirs. Joyce Found., Chgo. Henrietta Heerman scholar Washington U., 1951; recipient award for professionalism Am. Assn. Bot. Gardens and Arboreta Inc., citation for svcs. to U.S. govt. Inst. Mus. Svcs., Alumni Achievement award U. Okla., 1953, Liberty Hyde Bailey medal for outstanding achievement in Am. horticulture Am. Hort. Soc., 1990, Hutchinson medal for outstanding svc. to horticulture, 1990; NSF grantee. Fellow Ind. Acad. Sci., Cranbrook Inst. Sci.; mem. Ecol. Soc. Am., Asa Gray Meml. Assn., Mich. Natural Areas Coun., Okla. Acad. Sci., Mich. Bot. Club (past pres. Detroit), Phi Beta Kappa, Sigma Xi, Phi Sigma. Home and Office: 2016 Northwood Dr Maryville TN 37803-6365

HALL, MARY ANN, English language educator; b. Pitts., Aug. 4, 1946; d. George G. and Helen K. (Summers) H. BA in Lit., U. Pitts., 1977, MFA in Writing, 1981, PhD in Lit., 1990. Tchr. asst., fellow U. Pitts., 1979-85, part-time instr., 1986-88; instr. U. Pitts., Titusville, Pa., 1988-93; asst. prof. U. Pitts., Titusville, 1993-98, assoc. prof., 1998—. Contbr. articles to profl. jours. Mem. Nat. Coun. Tchrs. of English (sec. Assembly for Tchg. of English Grammar 1992-94), Assn. Bus. Comm. Office: U Pitts at Titusville Brown St Titusville PA 16354

HALL, MARY TAUSSIG, volunteer; b. St. Louis, Feb. 21, 1911; d. Frederick Joseph and Florence (Gottschalk) Taussig; m. Louis Benoist Tompkins, June 17, 1941 (dec. Oct. 1950); children: Frederick Kingsbury Tompkins, Mary Waterman Tompkins (Mrs. Neil Houghton); m. Thomas Steele Hall, Oct. 21, 1952 (dec. 1990). BA, Bryn Mawr Coll., 1933; MSW, Washington U., St. Louis, 1938; LHD (hon.), Lindenwood Coll., 1979. Cert. social worker. Caseworker New England Home for Little Wanderers, Boston, 1938-39. Editor: Stones for Bread, 1940. Pres., Mo. Assn. Social Welfare, 1942-44, bd. dirs., 1942-48; bd. dirs., chair industry com. Urban League Greater St. Louis, 1943-52; bd. dirs. Family and Children's Svcs., St. Louis, 1944-57; apptd. by gov. state commr. Children's Code Commn., 1945, Bd. Children's Guardians, 1946-55; apptd. by mayor bd. dirs. City Hosp. # 2 during racial integration; founding bd. dirs. Washington U. Med. Ctr. Child Guidance Clinic, St. Louis, 1948-52; chmn. bd. Divsn. Children's Svcs., St. Louis, 1955-66; nat. com. policy Child Welfare League Am., 1955-57; nat. coun. Internat. Social Svc., 1968-88; mem. world coun. YWCA, N.Y.C., 1963—; pres. St. Louis chpt. bd. UN Assn., 1977-80, nat. steering com. coun. chpt. pres., 1979-82, nat. bd. govs. UN Assn. USA, 1980-90; mem. nat. coun. UN Assn. USA, 1991—. Rcipient alumni award Washington U., 1956, Woman of Achievement award for Social Concern, City of St. Louis, 1979, Arnold Goodman Nat. Leadership award UN Assn. U.S.A., 1994. Mem. Cosmopolitan Club (N.Y.C.). Avocations: garden, travel. Home: 4969 Pershing Pl Saint Louis MO 63108-1220

HALL, MICHAEL L., business educator; b. Beaumont, Tex., Nov. 24, 1949; s. William Lindsay and Mary Elizabeth Hall; m. Linda Gail Townley, Dec. 29, 1989; children: Lindsay Shannon, Leigha Katherine, Logan Richard. BA with honors, Lamar U., 1972; MA, U. Okla., 1977, PhD, 1977. Asst. prof. Bowling Green (Ohio) State U., 1977-78, Russell Sage Coll., Troy, N.Y., 1978-87; assoc. prof. Russell Sage Coll., Albany, N.Y., 1987-98; dir. policy rsch. Profman Corp., Glens Falls, N.Y., 1998—. Contbr. articles to profl. jours. Vol. WMHT Pub. TV, Albany, 1981-84, Ctr. for the Disabled, Albany, 1989; bd. mem. New Covenant Presbyn. Ch., Albany, 1991-93. REcipient Arch. of Democracy award USIA, Bulgaria, 1993-94. Mem. ASPA (program chair Capital dist. 1980-81), Nat. Assn. Schs. Pub. Adminstrn. (sect. chair 1992-93). Democrat. Avocations: health and fitness, American films, University Oklahoma athletics. E-mail: mhalletalbany.net. Home: 54 Eliot Ave Albany NY 12203 Office: Profman Corp 37 Evertts Ave Glen Falls NY 12312

HALL, MICHAEL LEE, federal government agency grants administrator; b. San Antonio, Jan. 2, 1946; s. John Edward and Lorraine Louise (Horn) Hall; m. Joy Lynn Schmidt, Aug. 28, 1966. BA, U. Tex., 1968, MA, 1972; MA, Johns Hopkins U., 1974, PhD, 1977. Asst. prof. Centenary Coll. La., Shreveport, 1976-80; assoc. prof. Centenary Coll. La., 1980-87, chmn. dept. English, 1980-83; program officer Nat. Endowment for the Humanities, Washington, 1987-88, asst. dir. for seminars div. fellowships and seminars, 1988-95, sr. program officer collaborative rsch., 1996—; humanities adminstr. NEH, Washington, 1985-87; program adminstr. LC/Ameritech Nat. Digital Libr. Competition Libr. of Congress, Washington, 1998-99; instr. (part-time) Georgetown U., Washington, 1989, U. Md., 1992, 94—; dir. summer seminar for secondary sch. tchrs. NEH, Centenary Coll. La., Shreveport, 1984. Co-editor: LIT: Literature and Interpretive Techniques, 1986; poetry editor Poet Lit. Mag., Oklahoma City, 1985-96; contbr. articles and revs. on Brit. lit. to profl. jours. Nat. Endowment for the Humanities fellow in residence U. Chgo, 1978-79. Mem. MLA, Nat. Coun. Tchrs. English, John Donne Soc. Democrat. Presbyterian. Avocations: traveling, swimming, photography, writing. Office: NEH 1100 Pennsylvania Ave NW Washington DC 20004-2501

HALL, MIKE BURT (MARSHALL B.), artist, educator; b. Ashland, Wis., June 18, 1932; s. Burt Carolus Hall and Ruby Alvina Bekken. Studied with Percy Mannser. Tchr. art Oreg. Soc. Artists, 1962; pvt. tchr. One man shows include Oreg. Soc. Artists, Portland, 1962, Maryhill (Wash.) Mus. Fine Arts, 1964, 66, Abbot Hall Gallery William Temple House, 1993; group shows include Soc. Western Artists De Young Mus., San Francisco, 1965, 67, 68, Charles and Emma Frye Mus. Art, Seattle, 1968, 69, Am. Artists Profl. League, 1982, 83, 84, 85, 86, Soc. Western Artists Rosicrucian Mus., San Jose, Calif., 1976, Morseburg Gallery, L.A., 1965, Qraz Gallery, Seattle, 1967, Husberg Fine Arts Gallery, Sedona, Ariz., 1970, First Ave Galleries, Scottsdale, Ariz., 1971, McAdoo Gallery, Santa Fe, N. Mex., 1971; permanent collections include Maryhill Mus. Fine Arts, West Coast Picture Frame Co., Concordia U., Mt. Hood C.C., The Halton Co., numerous pvt. collections Wash., Oreg., Calif., Ariz., Nev., N. Mex., Conn., others. Recipient Edmund Ayling award and degree of honor Soc. Western Artists, 1968, medal of honor Am. Artists Profl. League, 1984; Best of Show award Lake Oswego (Oreg.) Festival of Art, 1984. Avocation: collecting art. Home and Studio: 2715 NE Saratoga St Portland OR 97211-5961

HALL, MILES LEWIS, JR., lawyer; b. Fort Lauderdale, Fla., Aug. 14, 1924; s. Miles Lewis and Mary Frances (Dawson) H.; m. Muriel M. Fisher, Nov. 4, 1950; children: Miles Lewis III, Don Thomas. A.B., Princeton U., 1947; J.D., Harvard U., 1950. Bar: Fla. 1951, U.S. Supreme Ct., 1972, U.S. Ct. Appeals (11th cir.), U.S. Dist. Ct. (so. dist.) Fla. Since practiced in Miami; ptnr. Hall & Hedrick, Miami, 1953—; dir. Gen. Portland, Inc., 1974-81. Author: Election of Remedies, Vol. VIII, Fla. Law and Practice, 1958. Pres. Orange Bowl Com., 1964-65, dir., 1950—, sec., treas. 1984-86; vice-chmn., dir. Dade County (Fla.) ARC, 1961-62, chmn., 1963-64, dir., 1967-73; nat. fund cons. ARC, 1963, 66-68, trustee, 1985—; pres. Ransom Sch. Parents Assn., 1966; chmn. South Fla. Gov.'s Scholarship Ball, 1966; mem. exec. bd. South Fla. council Boy Scouts Am., 1966-67; citizens bd. U. Miami, 1961-66; mem. Fla. Council of 100, 1961-97, vice chmn., 1961-62; mem. Coral Gables (Fla.) Biltmore Devel. Com., 1972-73; mem. bd. visitors Coll. Law, Fla. State U., 1974-77; bd. dirs. Coral Gables War Meml. Youth Ctr., 1967—, pres., 1969-72; bd. dirs. Salvation Army, Miami, 1968-83, Fla. Citizens Against Crime 1984-89; bd. dirs. Bok Tower Gardens Found. Inc., 1987—, sec., 1991—; trustee St. Thomas U., 1990-96, vice chmn., 1993-96; trustee Fla. Supreme Ct. Hist. Soc., 1988—, v.p., 1991-92, pres., 1993-95. 2d lt. USAAF, 1943-45. Fellow Am. Bar Found., Fla. Bar Found.; mem. ABA (Fla. c-chmn. membership com. sect. corp. banking and bus. law 1968-72), Dade County Bar Assn. (dir. 1964-65, pres. 1967-68), Fla. Bar Assn., Am. Judicature Soc., Miami-Dade County C. of C. (v.p. 1962-64, dir. 1966-68), Harvard Law Sch. Assn. Fla. (dir. 1964-66), Cottage Club, Harvard Club, The Miami Club (v.p., dir. 1989-91, pres. 1990-91), Princeton Club So. Fla. (past pres.), Alpha Tau Omega. Methodist. Home: 8134 SE Hall Dr Arcadia FL 34266 Office: Hall & Hedrick 25 SE 2nd Ave Ste 1105 Miami FL 33131-1605

HALL, MILTON L., bishop. Bishop 1st Jurisdiction of Ind., Ch. of God in Christ, Kokomo, 1988—. Office: 1st Jurisdiction of Ind Ch of God in Christ 1417 N Delphos St Kokomo IN 46901-2566*

HALL, MILTON REESE, retired oil company executive; b. Vicksburg, Miss., July 5, 1932; s. Alvin Howard and Adelle Vera (McKay) H.; m. Margaret Louise Bailey, Feb. 17, 1957; children: Mark Russell, Stacy Elaine. BS in Acctg., Miss. So. U., 1953; MBA in Acctg., U. Miss., 1956; postgrad., La. State U., 1958-62. CPA, Miss. Trainee, div. contr. Kaiser Aluminum & Chem. Co., various locations, 1956-66; analyst Tex. Instruments, Inc., Dallas, 1966-67; contr., v.p. Koch Industries, Inc., Wichita, Kans., 1967-92; retired, 1993. With U.S. Army, 1953-55. Republican. Baptist. Avocations: music, snow skiing.

HALL, MONTY, television producer, actor; b. Winnipeg, Man., Can., Aug. 25, 1921; came to U.S., 1955; s. Maurice Harvey and Rose (Rusen) Halparin; m. Marilyn Doreen Plottel, Sept. 28, 1947; children: Joanna, Richard David, Sharon Fay. BS, U. Man., 1945, LLD (hon.), 1987; D Human Scis. (hon.), Hanneman U., 1988; PhD (hon.), Haifa U., 1989. TV personality, emcee N.Y.C. and Hollywood, Calif., 1955—; Lectr. broadcasting and fund raising various charities. Actor, U. Man., Canadian Army shows; emcee: NBC-Radio, Monitor on NBC-TV, Keep Talking, Byline: Monty Hall, Video Village on CBS-TV, ABC-TV; host Let's Make a Deal, 1964-86, Split Second, 1986-87; Author: Emcee: Monty Hall, 1974; producer (TV show) Your First Impression; guest appearances numerous TV series: starring role (stage prodn.) High Button Shoes, 1978. Bd. dirs. numerous charitable orgns.; bd. govs. Cedars-Sinai Med. Ctr.; active numerous orgns. on behalf of Israel; hon. mayor, Hollywood, 1973-79. Decorated officer Order of Can.; recipient star on Hollywood's Walk of Fame, 1973, on Palm Springs Walk of Fame, 1996; Internat. Humanitarian award Variety Clubs, 1983, over 500 other awards, including Monty Hall floor at U. Calif./L.A. Hosp., Johns Hopkins U., Balt., Mt. Sinai Hosp., Toronto, Hahneman Hosp., Phila. Mem. AFTRA, Screen Actors Guild, Variety Clubs (internat. pres. 1975-77, internat. chmn. 1981—). Club: Hillcrest Country. Avocations: golf, tennis. *The longer I live, the more I am obsessed with man's inhumanity directed against his fellow man. Is there a basic flaw in man's makeup which prevents the good from overtaking and defeating the evil? I have spent my adult life dedicated to helping children around the world, the diseased, handicapped and the underprivileged. The rewards tangible and intangible have shaped my life, have given me an inner peace with myself, and yet a frustration at what could be and is not. The same holds for nation against nation. What could be—and is not. Is this the order of things past and things to come? I pray with all my heart that the teachings of peace shall prevail.*

HALL, NANCY CHRISTENSEN, publishing company executive, author, editor; b. N.Y.C., Nov. 14, 1946; d. Henry Norman and Elvira (Dugan) Christensen; m. John R. Hall Jr., June 12, 1968; children: Jonathan Scott, Kirsten Marie. B.A., Manhattanville Coll., 1968; postgrad., Old Dominion U., 1970-71. Sr. assoc. editor Cahners Pub. Co., N.Y.C., 1972-74; freelance editor N.Y.C., 1974-78; sr. editor Grosset and Dunlap, N.Y.C., 1978-81; exec. editor, asst. v.p. Macmillan Pub. Co., N.Y.C., 1981-84; assoc. pub., v.p. Simon & Schuster Pub. Co., N.Y.C., 1984-85; founder, prin. Nancy Hall, Inc., juvenile book devel co., N.Y.C., 1986—; founder, ptnr. Hall Assocs., Inc., 1996—. Author: Monsters: Creatures of Mystery, 1980, Macmillan Fairy Tale Alphabet Book 1983; editor: Platt and Munk Treasury of Stories for Children, 1981, Favorite Tales from Hans Christian Andersen, 1988; prodr. series: Macmillan Jumbo Seasonal Patterns, Macmillan Manipulatives, Sesame Street Early Learning Games, Mickey's Young Readers Libr., Disney's Small World Libr., My First Hello Readers, and others. Office: Nancy Hall Inc 23 E 22nd St New York NY 10010-5304

HALL, NECHIE TESITOR, advertising and public relations executive; b. May 10, 1946; d. Carl and Elsie Marie (Lenzini) Tesitor; m. James William hall, Nov. 25, 1967; 1 child, Meredith Elyse. BFA, U. Colo., 1967; postgrad., U. Colo., Colorado Springs, 1971. Asst. mktg. dir. Woodmoor Corp., Monument, Colo., 1968-69, dir. pub. rels., 1969-70; pres., ptnr. Praco, Ltd., Colorado Springs, 1970—; cons. in field. Bd. dirs. fund raising chmn. Alcoholic Recovery Ctr., Colorado Springs, 1974-77, El Pomar Renewal Ctr., Colorado Springs, 1977-80; bd. dirs. Pauline Meml. Sch., Colorado Springs, 1980-82, Rocky Mountain Rehab. Ctr., Colo. Amateur Sports Corp., treas., 1990-91; bd. dirs. St. Francis Hosp., Endowment Found., Goodwill Industries; asst. overall chmn. Nat. Sports Festival I & II U.S. Olympic Com., Colorado Springs, 1978-79; CASA chmn. bd., chmn. pub. rels. Nat. Sports Festival V, 1983; bd. dirs. Colorado Springs Fine Arts Ctr.; co-chmn. task force Olympic Hall of Fame; mem. bus. adv. coun. U. Colo., Colorado Springs; vice chmn. bd. dirs. Econ. Devel. Corp. Colorado Springs; trustee Pioneer's Mus.; mem. El Paso County Med. Soc. Found. Recipient Silver medal Am. Advt., 1987; named bus. Citizen of Yr. Colorado Springs C. of C., 1988. Mem. Pub. Rels. Soc. Am. (v.p. Pikes Peak chpt. 1978-80), Pikes Peak Ad Fedn. (Silver medalist 1987), Exec. Women Internat., Colorado Springs Press Club, Internat. Assn. Bus. Communicators, Country Club of Colo., Broadmoor Golf Club, C. of C. (bd. dirs.), Kappa Alpha Theta. Republican. Roman Catholic. Home: 100 Gardner Pl Colorado Springs CO 80906-3314 Office: Praco Ltd PO Box 387 Colorado Springs CO 80901-0387

HALL, OGDEN HENDERSON, retired allied health educator; b. Clayton, La., Nov. 8, 1922; s. William A. and Gladys (Denham) H.; m. Barbara Beale, Jan. 9, 1948; children: Michelle, Ogden Jr., Jennifer. B.S., La. State U., 1948, M.B.A., 1961, Ph.D., 1963. Office mgr. William Wolf Bakery, Baton Rouge, 1947-50; owner-mgr. Hall-Denham Hardware, Denham Springs, La., 1948-62; asso. prof. bus. Va. Poly. Inst., 1963-68; prof. dept. mgmt. and marketing U. New Orleans, 1968-83; clin. prof. allied health La. State U. Med. Ctr., 1984—; now ret.; cons. in field. Pres. Denham Springs C. of C., 1958; bd. dirs. Credit Bur. Baton Rouge, 1959. Served with AUS, 1943-44; Served with USAAF, 1944-46. Mem. Acad. Mgmt., Ea. Acad. Mgmt. (pres. 1968), So. Mgmt. Assn. (pres. 1978), Decision Sci. Inst., Inst. Gen. Semantics. Home: 130 White Stork Dr Slidell LA 70461-3206

HALL, PAMELA BRIGHT, school health nurse; b. Pasquotank County, N.C., Nov. 23, 1955; d. Erna Dare and Virginia Lee (Edwards) Bright; m. Randy Byrd Hall, Apr. 6, 1975; children: Alton Paul, Randy Byrd. AS, Coll. of the Albemarle, Elizabeth City, N.C., 1987; BSN, E. Carolina U., 1994. Cert. CPR instr., AHA; cert. sch. health nurse, Nat. Bd. Sch. Nurses. Pub. health nurse Albemarle Home Care, Elizabeth City, 1988-89; staff nurse ICU Albemarle Hosp., Elizabeth City, 1987-95; sch. health nurse Elizabeth City-Pasquotank Sch. Sys., 1994—; mem. Pasquotank County Rescue Squad, 1985-88. Recipient Captains award Pasquotank County Rescue Squad, 1986. Home: 1191 Consolidated Rd Elizabeth City NC 27909-7897

HALL, PAMELA S., environmental consulting firm executive; b. Hartford, Conn., Sept. 4, 1944; d. LeRoy Warren and Frances May (Murray) Sheely; m. Stuart R. Hall, July 21, 1967. BA in Zoology, U. Conn., 1966; MS in Zoology, U. N.H., 1969, BS summa cum laude, 1982; student spl. grad. studies program, Tufts U., 1986-90. Curatorial asst. U. Conn., Storrs, 1966; rsch. asst. Field Mus. Natural History, Chgo., 1966-67; tchg. asst. U. N.H., Durham, 1967-70; program mgr. Normandeau Assocs. Inc., Portsmouth, N.H., 1971-79, marine lab. dir., 1979-81; programs and ops. mgr. Normandeau Assocs. Inc., Bedford, N.H., 1981-83; v.p. Normandeau Assocs. Inc., Bedford, 1983-85, sr. v.p., 1986-87, pres., 1987—. Mem. Conservation Commn., Portsmouth, 1977-90, Wells, Estuarine Rsch. Res. Rev.Commn., 1986-88, Great Bay (N.H.) Estuarine Rsch. Res. Tech. Working Group, 1987-89; trustee Trust for N.H. Lands, 1990-93; trustee N.H. chpt. Nature Conservancy, 1991—, chair 1995—, chair emeritus, 1999—, incorporator N.H. Charitable Fund, 1991-99; bd. advisors Vivamos Mejor, USA, 1990—; bd. dirs. Environ. Bus. Coun. New England, 1995—, treas. 1997—; bd. emeritus Ecosystems Inst., 1997—; commr. N.H. Land and Cmty Heritage Commn., commr. N.H. Land and Heritage Commn., 1998—. Graham Found. fellow, 1966; NDEA fellow, 1970-71. Mem. ASTM, The Nature Conservancy, Soc. of the Protection of N.H. Forests, The Audubon Soc., Nat. Assn. Environ. Profls., Sigma Xi. Home: 4 Pleasant Point Dr Portsmouth NH 03801-5275 Office: Normandeau Assocs Inc 25 Nashua Rd Bedford NH 03110-5500

HALL, PAUL J., lawyer; b. San Diego, Jan. 13, 1951. AB with highest honors, U. Calif., Santa Cruz, 1972; postgrad, Yale U.; JD, U. Calif., Berkeley, 1975. Bar: Calif. 1975. Mem. Manatt, Phelps & Phillips, L.A., 1975-94, Stein & Lubin LLP, San Francisco, 1995-98, Lillick & Charles LLP, San Francisco, 1998—; bd. regents U. Calif., 1992-93, regent designate, 1991-92. Trustee U. Calif. Santa Cruz Found., 1986—. Mem. Calif. State Bar, Boalt Hall Alumni Assn. (bd. dirs. 1983-90, treas. 1985-86, sec. 1986-87, v.p. 1987-89, pres.-elect 1989-90, pres. 1990-91), U. Calif. Santa Cruz Alumni Assn. (bd. dirs. 1983-90, pres. 1986-90). Address: Lillick & Charles 2 Embarcadero Ctr Ste 2700 San Francisco CA 94111-3996*

HALL, PENELOPE COKER, magazine editor; b. Charlotte, N.C., Mar. 19, 1932; d. James Lide and Elizabeth (Boatwright) Coker; m. William Parmenter Wilson, Sept. 6, 1964 (div. 1971); 1 child, Eliza Wilson Ingle; m. Mortimer Waddhams Hall, Dec. 8, 1972; stepchildren: Dorothy, Margaret, Mary Howland, Matthew. Student, Sarah Lawrence Coll., Bronxville, N.Y., 1954. Sr. editor, biographer Cleveland Amory's Celebrity Register, N.Y.C.; prodr., commentator Wrap-Up with Mike Wallace, N.Y.C.; co-prodr., interviewer for series of hr. long spls. NBC-TV, N.Y.C.; co-host 10 Around Town Channel 10 TV, Phila.; co-host The New Yorkers Channel 5 TV, N.Y.C., 1968-70; reporter, Sunday anchor 10 O'Clock News, Channel 5, N.Y.C., 1970-73; host cable cooking show Cooking Cable, Millbrook, N.Y., 1975—; editor-in-chief Dutchess Mag., N.Y.C., 1992-98, editor-at-large, columnist, 1998—. Contbr. numerous articles to profl. jours.; author: Fancy and the Cement Patch, 1966, The Wish Bottle, 1967, Riding High, 1990. Bd. trustees Spoleto Festival, Charleston, S.C., 1997—, Coker Coll., Hartsville, S.C.; bd. dirs. Bardaven theatre, Poughkeepsie, 1985-92; nat. bd. for women in medicine Med. Coll. Pa., Phila., 1995—; fund raiser Dem. Nominess for Dutchess County. Mem. Author League, Sandanona Beagles, Millbrook Hounds, Century Club, Millbrook Golf and Tennis Club (bd. dirs. 1989-93), Cosmopolitan Club (seminar com. 1990—). Democrat. Episcopalian. Avocations: painting, horseback riding, boating. Home: PO Box 516 Millbrook NY 12545-0516

HALL, PETER FRANCIS, physiologist; b. Sydney, Australia, Dec. 12, 1924; s. William and Ruby Alice (Price) H.; m. Helen Ruth Godfrey, Nov. 10, 1968; children: Philip Charles, Warwick David. M.B.B.S., U. Sydney, 1947, M.D., 1956; Ph.D., U. Utah, 1962. Sr. med. officer Royal Prince Alfred Hosp., Sydney, 1947-50; registrar Guys Hosp., 1954-59; hon. med. officer Sydney Hosp., 1954-59; NIH fellow U. Utah, 1959-62; asst. prof. dept. physiology U. Pitts., 1962-64; prof. biochemistry Melbourne U., 1964-71; prof., chmn. dept. physiology U. Calif.-Irvine, 1971-78; prin. scientist Worcester Found. Exptl. Biology, Shrewsbury, Mass., 1978-86; chmn. endocrinology U. New South Wales and Prince Henry/Prince of Wales Hosps., Sydney, 1986—. Author: Gynaecomastia, 1959, Function of the Endocrine Glands, 1959; Contbr. articles to med. jours. Recipient Merck prize for chemistry, 1959. Fellow Royal Australian Coll. Physicians, Royal Coll. Physicians (London); mem. Am. Physiol. Soc., Am. Soc. Cell Biology, Am. Soc. Biol. Chemistry, Endocrine Soc. Mem. Ch. of Eng. Home: 81 Ocean St, Woollahra NSW 2025, Australia Office: Prince of Wales Hosp, Dept Endocrinology High Street, Randwick NSW 2031, Australia

HALL, SIR PETER GEOFFREY, urban and regional planning educator; b. London, Mar. 19, 1932; came to U.S., 1980; s. Arthru Vickers and Bertha (Keefe) H.; m. Carla Maria Wartenberg, Sept. 7, 1962 (div. 1967); m. Magda Mroz, Feb. 13, 1967. BA in Geography, Cambridge (Eng.) U., 1953, PhD, 1959; DDS (hon.), Birmingham (Eng.) U., 1991; PhD (hon.), Lund (Sweden) U., 1992; DLitt (hon.), Sheffield, 1995, Newcastle, 1995; DEng (hon.), Tech. U. Nova Scotia, Can., 1996; ArtsD (hon.), Oxford Brookes U., 1997. Lectr. Birkbeck Coll., U. London, 1957-65; reader London Sch. Econs., 1966-67; prof. U. Reading, Eng., 1968-89, chmn., 1971-77, dean faculty urban and regional studies, 1975-78, bd. mgmt., 1983-86, prof. emeritus, 1989—; prof. dept. city and regional planning U. Calif., Berkeley, 1980-92, assoc. dir. Inst. Urban and Regional Devel., 1988-88, dir., 1989-92, prof. emeritus, 1993—; chmn. of planning The Bartlett, Univ. Coll., London, 1992—, dir. sch. pub. policy, 1996-97; spl. advisor Dept. of Environ., London, 1991-94; mem. Urban Task Force, 1998-99. Author: The World Cities, 1966, 3d edit., 1984, Europe 2000, 1977 (Bentinck prize 1979), Great Planning Disasters, 1980, The Inner City in Context, 1981, Silicon Landscapes, 1985, Can Rail Save the City?, 1985, High-Tech America, 1986, Western Sunrise, 1987, Cities of Tomorrow, 1988, London 2001, 1989, Cities and Civilization, 1998; co-author: The Rise of the Gunbelt, 1991, Technopoles of the World, 1994, Sociable Cities, 1998, Cities in Civilization, 1998. Advisor Social Dem. party, 1983-85; active S.E. Econ. Planning Coun., 1966-79, Social Sci. Rsch. Coun., 1974-79. Fellow Brit. Acad., Royal Geog. Soc. (Gill Meml. prize 1968, Founder's medal 1991), St. Catharine's Coll. (hon.); mem. Royal Town Planning Inst. (hon.), Am. Planning Assn., Athenaeum Club, Royal Acad. Avocations: reading, travelling. Home: 12 Queen's Rd, London W5 2SA, England Office: The Bartlett Sch Arch & Planning, Wates House 22 Gordon St, London WC1H 0QB, England

HALL, PETER MICHAEL, physics educator, electronics researcher; b. Belmont, N.Y., July 31, 1934; s. Harris Tremaine and Dorothy Lou (Harris) H.; m. Betty Jane Bressell, Dec. 21, 1956; children: Michael, Ann, Sarah, Philip. BA, Hobart Coll., 1954; MS, Iowa State U., 1956, PhD, 1959. Registered profl. engr., N.C. Mem. tech. staff AT&T Bell Labs., Murray Hill, N.J., 1959-64; fellow AT&T Bell Labs., Allentown, Pa., 1964-90; Disting. prof. physics Johnson C. Smith U., Charlotte, N.C., 1990—. Co-author: Thin Film Technology, 1968; contbr. articles to profl. jours., chpt. to book; patentee on fabrication of circuit packages. Recipient award for best paper Electronic Components Conf., 1984. Fellow IEEE (components, hybrids and mfg. tech. group, best paper award 1988); mem. ASME (editor 1989-95), Am. Phys. Soc., Am. Assn. Physics Tchrs., Phi Beta Kappa, Sigma Xi. Democrat. Episcopalian. Avocation: sailing. Home: 10308 Katelyn Dr Charlotte NC 28269-1401 Office: Johnson C Smith U 100 Beatties Ford Rd Charlotte NC 28216-5398

HALL, PHYLLIS CHARLENE, therapist, counselor; b. L.A., Mar. 18, 1957; d. Clellan James Jr. and Yvonne Rayedith (Ralls) H. BA, Whittier Coll., 1979; MS in Phys. Edn., Calif. State U., Fullerton, 1985, MS in Counseling, 1988; PhD in Psychology, U.S. Internat. U., 1996. Cert. critical incident debriefing. Coach varsity girls basketball, softball Calif. High Sch., Whittier, 1979-80; counselor Rio Hondo Coll., Whittier, 1980-88; coach asst. girls varsity basketball Long Beach (Calif.) Wilson High Sch., 1985-88; therapist intern Turning Point Counseling, Garden Grove, Calif., 1988-89; counselor Long Beach City Coll., 1988—, girls acad. advisor, 1989-94, asst. coach girls basketball, 1993-94; psychologist asst./intern Family Svcs. Long Beach, 1994-98; bd. dirs. Long Beach City Coll.; mem. adv. bd. U. Calif. C.C., 1997—; exec. bd. Long Beach City Coll., 1997—. Author: Liberators from Planet Liberx, 1985. Mem. cmty. adv. coun. U. Calif., 1996-98; co-sponsor African Am. in Unity Long Beach City Coll., 1990-92; com. mem. 1st Annual African Am. Achievement Conf., San Diego, 1994. Recipient PhD Student Achievement award USIU Dept. MFT, 1996. Mem. Calif. Tchrs. Assn., Long Beach City Coll. Counselors Assn., Women in Arts (founding mem.). Avocations: reading African culture and history, basketball, racquetball, writing. Office: Long Beach City Coll 1305 E Pch Long Beach CA 90806

HALL, PIKE, JR., lawyer; b. Shreveport, La., May 27, 1931; s. Pike and Hazel (Tucker) H.; m. Anne Oden Hall, Dec. 24, 1951; children: Brevard Hall Knight, Pike III. BA, La. State U., 1951, JD, 1953. Bar: La. 1953. Asst. city atty. City of Shreveport, 1954-58; elected mem. Caddo Prish Sch. Bd., Shreveport, 1964-70; judge 2d Cir. Ct. Appeal, Shreveport, 1971-85, chief judge, 1985-90; assoc. justice Supreme Ct. La., 1990-94; counsel Blanchard, Walker, O'Quin & Roberts, Shreveport, 1994—; past chmn. La. Conf. of Ct. Appeal Judges; past bd. govs., vice chmn. La. Jud. Coll.; chmn. La. Jud. Bugetary Control Bd., 1992-94. Mem. adminstrv. bd. First United Meth. Ch., Shreveport. Mem. ABA, La. State Bar Assn. (past bd. govs., past Ho. of Dels.), Shreveport Bar Assn., Order of Coif. Democrat. Avocations: golf, fishing, hunting. Home: 1018 Delaware St Shreveport LA 71106-1402

HALL, RALPH C., retired architect, mechanical engineer; b. Lowell, Ohio, June 9, 1925; s. Joseph R. and Florence E. (Misel) H.; m. Elizabeth Ruth Lenox, June 28, 1947; children: Nancy Elaine Hall Bell, Stephen Mark. BME, Ohio State U., 1948; MDiv, Grace Theol. Sem., Winona Lake, Ind., 1951; ThD, Christian Bible Coll./Sem., Independence, Mo., 1996. Registered architect, Ohio, 20 other states; registered profl. engr., Ind., Fla., Va. Architect, CEO Brethren Archtl. Svc., Winona Lake, Ind., 1960-74; architect, profl. engr. Ralph C. Hall, P.E., R.A., Winona Lake, 1974-84, Bradenton, Fla., 1984-96; ret., 1996. Chmn. bd. dirs. Brethren Retirement Homes, Winona Lake, 1976-84; chmn. plan commn. Town of Winona Lake, 1976-79. Republican. Grace Brethren Ch. Avocations: photography, travel. Home: 5708 34th Ct W Bradenton FL 34210-3549

HALL, RALPH CARR, lawyer, real estate consultant; b. Chgo., Mar. 28, 1928; s. Rupert Irving and Pauline Martha (Prime) H.; m. Barbara Fordyce, Jan. 21, 1950; children: Brett C., Brian C., Judson P., Trudy A. LLB, Tulsa U., 1952. Bar: Okla. 1952, Tex. 1974. V.P. Hall Investment Co., Tulsa, 1948-58; pres. Realty Constrn. Co., Tulsa, 1958-61; real estate investment rep. Am. Oil Co., Birmingham, Ala., 1961-63; div. real estate mgr. Kroger Co., Nashville and Charlotte, N.C., 1963-66; v.p., real estate counsel H.E.B. Properties, Corpus Christi, Tex., 1966-85; pvt. practice, Corpus Chirsti, 1985-97; real estate cons., 1985—; mediator Nueces County Dispute Resolution Ctr., 1994-97. Pres., bd. dirs. Goodwill Ind. South Tex., Corpus Christi, 1969-88; planning commr. City of Corpus Christi, 1990-95. Mem. Tex. Bar Assn., Nueces County Bar Assn., Corpus Christi Pistol and Rifle Club (pres. bd. dirs. 1980). Republican. Episcopalian.

HALL, RALPH MOODY, congressman; b. Rockwall, Tex., May 3, 1923; s. Hugh O. and Maude Hall; m. Mary Ellen Murphy, Nov. 14, 1944; children: Hampton, Brett, Blakeley. Student, U. Tex., Tex. Christian U., So. Meth. U.; LLB, So. Meth. U. Bar: Tex. County judge Rockwall County, Tex., 1950-62; mem. Tex. Senate, 1962-72; past pres., chief exec. officer Tex. Aluminum Corp.; past gen. counsel Tex. Extrusion Co., Inc.; past organizer, chmn. bd. Lakeside Nat. Bank of Rockwall; chmn. bd. Bank of Crowley; past chmn. bd. dirs. Lakeside News, Inc.; chmn. bd. Linrock Inc.; pres. Crowley Holding Co.; mem. 97th-106th Congresses from 4th Tex. dist., Washington, D.C., 1980—; mem. commerce com., mem. sci. com., ranking minority mem. energy and power subcom. Served with USNR, 1942-45. Mem. Am. Legion, VFW. Methodist. Lodge: Rotary (past pres.). Office: US Ho of Reps 2221 Rayburn House of C Bldg Washington DC 20515*

HALL, RAYMOND, sociology educator; b. Marshall, Tex., Feb. 2, 1938. BA, Wiley Coll., 1962; MA, Stephen F. Austin State U., 1968; cert. in Ea. African Studies, Syracuse U., 1971, PhD, 1972; MA (hon.), Dartmouth Coll., 1993. Asst. prof. history and sociology Bishop Coll., Dallas, 1968-69, asst. prof. polit. sci. dept., 1971-72; asst. prof. sociology Dartmouth U., 1972-78, assoc. prof. sociology, 1978-86, prof. sociology, 1986, dir. dept. sociology, 1990, Orvil E. Dryfoos prof. of pub. affairs, 1994; prin. Emekuku Cmty. Tech. Secondary Sch., Owerri, Nigeria, 1964-66; chmn. polit. sci. dept. Bishop Coll., Dallas, 1971-72; dir. Dartmouth MIT Urban Studies Program, 1975-77; chmn. Dartmouth-Talladega Title III Exch. com., 1973-78; dir. Dartmouth-Boston Urban Studies Program, 1978-80; chmn. urban studies program Dartmouth, 1981-84, acting chmn. dept. sociology, 1984, chmn. dept. sociology, 1985-91, 94-97; faculty adv. bd. The Beacon of Dartmouth, 1990—; cons. P.E.A.C.E., Inc., Syracuse 1969, Dallas Ind. Sch. Dist., 1968, 80, U.S. Dept. of Edn., 1992, field reader, sch. partnership program, 1988, field reader titles III & IX U.S. Dept. Edn., 1982—; field reader and tech. advisor title I and title III programs Dept. of Health, Edn. and Welfare, Dept. Human Svcs., 1975-81; cons. to curriculum com. Dallas Ind. Schs. Dist., 1969; spl. cons. NIH, Harvard Sch. of Pub. Health, 1993. Editl. bd. Gnosis, 1987—; contbr. numerous articles to profl. jours. Bd. trustees Wiley Coll., 1989-91, chair acad. programs com.; bd. dirs. The Forum for U.S.-Soviet Dialogue, 1983-86, A Better Chance, Hanover, N.H., 1973-75, Martin Luther King Recreation Ctr., Dallas, 1968-69, Dallas Opportunities Indsl. Coops., 1968-69. Served U.S. Army, 1962-64. Vis. scholar Social Sci. Rsch. Coun., 1975; Salzburg Seminar Presdl. fellow, 1994, 95; Jr. faculty fellowship Dartmouth Coll., 1977, IBM Faculty fellowship, 1971-73, Richard King Mellon fellowship, The Maxwell Sch., Syracuse U., 1969-70; grantee Spencer Found., Hewlett Found., 1989, Dickey Endowment, 1988-89, Rockefeller Interdisciplinary, 1987-88, Sr. Faculty, Dartmouth Coll., 1981-82, Ford Found. Faculty, 1969-70. Mem. ACLU, Am. Sociol. Assn., Ea. Sociol. Assn., African Heritage Studies Assn., Soc. for the Study of Social Problems, Phi Beta Sigma. Home: 8 Pinewood Village West Lebanon NH 03784-3123 Office: Dept of Sociology Dartmouth Coll 106 Silsby Hall Hanover NH 03755

HALL, REBEKAH A., journalist, editor; b. Kansas City, Mo., June 13, 1973; d. Nelson E. Hall and Maria Teresa Gomez. BS in Journalism, U. Kans., 1997. Intern Am. Bus. Women's Assn., Kansas City, 1995-96, 96, Atlanta Mag., 1997; editor Our Kids Mag., Atlanta, 1997—. Mem. Soc. Profl. Journalists, Atlanta Press Club. Avocations: reading, walking. E-mail: ourkids@family.com. Home: Ste D389 2221 Peachtree St Atlanta GA 30309

HALL, RICHARD CLYDE, JR., religious educational administrator; b. Florence, Ala., Apr. 13, 1931; s. Richard Clyde Sr. and Annie Hazel (Darrah) H.; m. Mildred Marie Denham, May 19, 1957; children: Richard Denham, Darralyn Marie, Kevin Clyde, Edward Earnest. AA, U. Fla., 1950, BA, 1953; MRE, Southwestern Bapt. Theol. Sem., 1958, DRE, 1966, EdD, 1975, MA, 1984. Ordained to gospel ministry So. Bapt. Conv., 1955. Youth dir. 1st Bapt. Ch., Miami, Fla., 1953; ednl. sec., youth dir. Ave. J Bapt. Ch., Ft. Worth, 1953-54; dir. Bapt. Student Union Fla. Bapt. Conv.,

Jacksonville, 1954-57; min. edn. Eastover Bapt. Ch., Ft. Worth, 1957-61; minister edn. 1st Bapt. Ch., Elizabethton, Tenn., 1961-63, Gambrell Street Bapt. Ch., Ft. Worth, 1963-65; assoc. ch. tng. dept. Bapt. Gen. Conv. Tex., Dallas, 1965-72, sec. ch. tng. dept., 1972-73; mgmt. cons. Pro., Inc., San Diego, 1973-74; cons. adult work ch. tng. dept. Bapt. Sunday Sch. Bd., Nashville, 1974-75, cons. gen. adminstrn. ch. tng. dept., 1975-76, mgr. youth sect. discipleship tng. dept., 1976—; teaching fellow religious psychology and drama Southwestern Bapt. Theol. Sem., Ft. Worth, 1960-61; del. Bapt. World Alliance, Tokyo, 1970; instr. youth edn. Sem. Extension, 1981—; discipleship workshop leader, family group leader Bapt. Youth World Conf., Buenas Aires, 1984; conf. leader, coord. numerous youth confs. Queensland, Australia, New South Wales, Australia, Auckland, New Zealand, Gaza City, Gaza, 1997-98, Victoria, Australia, Windhoek, Namibia, Gaza City, Gaza; conf. leader Caribbean Bapt. Fellowship, Montego Bay, Jamaica, 1986; sem. leader Bapt. Youth World Conf., Glasgow, Scotland, 1988, chaplain, Harare, Zimbabwe, 1993; del. Lausanne II-World Congress on Evangelism, Manila, Philippines, 1989; teaching fellow religious psychology and drama Southwestern Bapt. Theol. Sem., Ft. Worth, 1960-61; guest lectr. Southwestern Bapt. Theol. Sem., New Orleans Bapt. Theol. Sem., So. Bapt. Theol. Sem., Midwestern Bapt. Theol. Sem., Southeastern Bapt. Theol. Sem. and Golden Gate Bapt. Theol. Sem., 1985—; adj. prof. New Orleans Bapt. Theol. Sem., Golden Gate Bapt. Theol. Sem. and Midwestern Bapt. Theol. Sem., 1985—; instr. Okla. Bapt. U., 1991—. Author: Source, 1967-70, Church Training, 1970—; (cassette and workbook) The Work of the Associational Age Group Leader, 1980; (filmstrip) DiscipleLife: Training Youth in Discipleship, 1981, DiscipleLife, 1984; compiler: Youth Leadership Training Pak, 1982, DiscipleHelps: A Daily Quiet Time Guide and Journal, 1985; (with Joe Ford) DiscipleYouth I Kit, 1982, DiscipleYouth I Notebook, 1982, DiscipleYouth II Kit, 1985, DiscipleYouth II Notebook, 1985, DiscipleYouth Library, 1992, (with Dean Finley) The Notebook: A Disciple Youth Experience, 1996; (with Wesley Black) DiscipleNow Manual; (with Valerie Hardy) Mission Trip Administrative Manual. Trauma Center Plus, Handbook for Youth Discipleship, Basic Church Stuff: A Guide for Assimulating New Youth Church Members, Compiler. Recipient Career of Excellence award LifeWay Christian Resources, 1998. Mem. ASTD, Internat. Religious Edn. Assn., So. Bapt. Religious Edn. Assn. (sec.-treas. 1982-83), Ea. Bapt. Religious Edn. Assn. (sec.-treas. 1975-79, pres. 1980), Southwestern Bapt. Religious Edn. Assn., Adult Edn. Assn. Office: LifeWar Christian Resources 2720 Windemere Dr Nashville TN 37214

HALL, RICHARD MURRAY, JR., finance executive, consultant; b. St. Joseph, Mo., Jan. 1, 1947; s. Richard Murray and Alice Elaine (Huff) H.; m. Joyce Ann Stearns, Mar. 28, 1971 (div. Nov. 1983). BBA in Econs., Wichita State U., 1969, MS in Fin., 1972; Grad. Degree in Banking, So. Meth. U., 1975. Asst. v.p. Fourth Nat. Bank & Trust, Wichita, Kans., 1969-75; v.p. Citizens Frost Bank, San Antonio, 1975-77, United Bank Denver, 1977-84; pres. Am. Nat. Bank/United Bank-City Ctr., Aurora, Colo., 1984-86; sr. v.p. Corp. Fin. Asocs., Denver, 1987-89; dir. Colo. Nat. Leasing, Inc., Denver, 1989-95, pres., 1989-95, chmn. bd. dirs., 1993-95; v.p. and gen. mgr. comml. banking divsn. Colo. Nat. Bank, Denver, 1992-94; pres., chmn. bd. dirs. Colo. Bus. Leasing, Inc., Denver, 1995—; bd. dirs. Health Agys. of Colo., chmn., 1998—. Dir. Am. Heart Assn. Colo., 1980—, pres., 1987-88; mem. Leadership Denver Assn., 1981, dir., 1990-95, pres. 1994-95; chmn. ArtReach, Inc., Denver, 1988, 89; bd. dirs. Colo. Spl. Olympics, 1994—, vice chmn., 1997, 99; bd. dirs. Health Agys. of Colo., 1997—, chmn., 1998—. Mem. Denver Athletic Club, Meridian Golf Club. Republican. Avocations: golf, skiing, writing. Office: Colo Bus Leasing Inc 999 18th St Ste 2400 Denver CO 80202-2424

HALL, RICKEY LEE, academic administrator; b. Waterloo, Iowa, Dec. 31, 1968; s. Mattie Mae Walker. BA in Am. Studies, U. Iowa, 1992, MA in Higher Edn., 1995. Tchg. asst. Office Campus Programs U. Iowa, Iowa City, 1994-95; resident advisor Project ACHIEVE Belin/Blank Ctr., U. Iowa, Iowa City, 1994, 95, 96, coord. Project ACHIEVE, 1997; customer svc. specialist Toyota Motor Ins. Svc., Cedar Rapids, Iowa, 1992-94; dir. diversity programs Wartburg Coll., Waverly, Iowa, 1995-98; dir. minority student program U. Minn., Morris, 1998—; mem. conf. planning com., profl. devel. com. Iowa Student Pers. Assn. Amb. Club advisor Roosevelt Elem. Sch., Waterloo, 1997-98. Mem. Am. Coll. Pers. Assn., Nat. Assn. Student Pers. Adminstrs., Mid-Am. Assn. Ednl. Opportunity Program Pers., Phi Beta Sigma. Democrat. Baptist. E-mail: hallrl@mrs.umn.edu. Fax: 320-589-6090. Office: Univ Minn Morris 600 E 4th St Morris MN

HALL, ROBERT, art educator, artist; b. Pitts., Dec. 21, 1931; s. Fred Lee and Margaret Finklea H.; m. Gudrun Guttzeit; 1 child, Renda Leigh. BA, Fla. State U., 1960; MEd, U. Fla., 1970. Chair visual arts Flagler Coll., St. Augustine, Fla., 1970—; vis. prof., dir. Fed. Project, Jacksonville, Fla., 1967; resource tchr. Duval County, Jacksonville, 1959-68; cons. in field. Sec. Presidio commn. City of St. Augustine, 1981-89; mem. Planning and Zoning com. City of St. Augustine, 1978-79. With USN, 1950-55. Mem. Historic Fla. Militia. Democrat. Avocations: motor sports, military history. Home: 42 Spanish St St Augustine FL 32084

HALL, ROBERT ALAN, financial company executive; b. Montgomery, Ala., Oct. 30, 1958; s. Mack Luverne and Miriam (Johnston) H. BS in Commerce and Bus. Adminstrn., U. Ala., 1981. CPA, Ala., cert. internal auditor. Sr. acct. Jackson and Thornton, CPAs, Montgomery, 1981-83; sr. auditor Vulcan Materials Co., Birmingham, Ala., 1983-86, supr. internal audit, 1986-87; mgr., fin. and adminstrn. Saudi Arabian Vulcan Ltd., Jubail, Saudi Arabia, 1987-90; spl. assignments analyst Vulcan Materials Co., 1990-91; contr., treas., asst. sec. Bill Harbert Internat. Constrn. Inc., Birmingham, Ala., 1991-95, v.p., CFO, 1995—; presdl. appointee White House Conf. on Small Bus., 1995; mem. Pres.'s Bus. Adv. Coun., Washington, 1995—; mem. profl. adv. bd. Sch. Accountancy/U. Ala., 1991—. Charter mem. Rep. Presdl. Task Force, Washington, 1984-86; presdl. appointee White House Conf. Small Bus., 1995. Recipient presdl. achievement award Pres. Ronald Reagan, 1983, Cert. of Appreciation, Gov. of Ala., 1988; named hon. citizen City of L.A., 1984, hon. asst. atty. gen. State of Ala., 1984, hon. gov. of Tex., 1995, hon. lt. gov. of Ala., 1998; named one of Outstanding Young Men of Am., 1986. Mem. AICPA, Ala. Soc. CPAs, Am. Businessmen's Assn. Saudi Arabia (bd. dirs. 1988-90), U. Ala. Sr. Execs. Club., Coll. Commerce, Hon. Order Ky. Cols. Baptist. Home: 416 Old Brook Cir Birmingham AL 35242-2658 Mailing Address: PO Box 531390 Birmingham AL 35253-1390

HALL, ROBERT DALE, mathematician, educator, physicist; b. West Palm Beach, Fla., Mar. 31, 1960; s. Robert Dale Sr. and Eula Katherine (Daniels) H.; m. Joanna Joy Binder, Nov. 23, 1984; children: Charity Ann, Jared Michael. BS in Secondary Edn., Pensacola (Fla.) Christian Coll., 1982. Writer, pub. A Beka Book, Pensacola, 1982-87; chmn. math., physics Grace Christian Sch., Brandon, Fla., 1987—; coach FACCS Brainbowl, 1989—, Mathcourts, 1990—, Brandon, Fla. Mem. Nat. Coun. Tchrs. Math. Republican. Avocations: sports. E-mail: djcjhall@hotmail.com. Office: Grace Christian Sch PO Box 843 Brandon FL 33509

HALL, ROBERT EMMETT, JR., investment banker, realtor; b. Sioux City, Iowa, Apr. 28, 1936; s. Robert Emmett and Alvina (Faden) H.; m. Marna Thiel, 1969. BA, U. S.D., 1958, MA, 1959; MBA, U. Santa Clara, 1976; grad. Am. Inst. Banking, Realtors Inst. Grad. asst. U. S.D., Vermillion, 1958-59; mgr. ins. dept., asst. mgr. installment loan dept. Northwestern Nat. Bank of Sioux Falls, S.D., 1959-61, asst. cashier, 1961-65; asst. mgr. Crocker Nat. Bank, San Francisco, 1965-67, loan officer, 1967-69, asst. v.p., asst. mgr. San Mateo br., 1969-72; v.p., Western regional mgr. Internat. Investments & Realty, Inc., Washington, 1972—; owner Hall Enterprises Co., 1976—; pres. Almaden Oaks Realtors, Inc., 1976—; instr. West Valley Coll., Saratoga, Calif., 1972-82, Grad. Sch. Bus., U. Santa Clara (Calif.), 1981-82, Evergreen Valley Coll., San Jose, Calif. Treas., Minnehaha Leukemia Soc., 1963, Lake County Heart Fund Assn., 1962, Minnehaha Young Republican Club, 1963. Mem. Am. Inst. Banking, Calif. Assn. Realtors (vice chmn.), Beta Theta Pi. Republican. Clubs: Elks, Rotary (past pres.), K.C., Almaden Country. Home: 6951 Castlerock Dr San Jose CA 95120-4705 Office: Hall Enterprises 6501 Crown Blvd Ste 106 San Jose CA 95120-2903

HALL, ROBERT ERNEST, economics educator; b. Palo Alto, Calif., Aug. 13, 1943; s. Victor Ernest and Frances Marie (Gould) H.; m. Susan E. Woodward; children: Jonathan, Andrew, Christopher, Anne. BA, U. Calif.-Berkeley, 1964; PhD, MIT, 1967. Asst. prof., acting assoc. prof. U. Calif., Berkeley, 1967-70; from assoc. prof. to prof. MIT, Cambridge, 1970-78; prof., sr. fellow Stanford U. (Calif.), 1978—, Robert and Carole McNeil joint prof. and sr. fellow, 1998; dir. econ. fluctuation program Nat. Bur. Econ. Research, Cambridge, 1978—; adv. com. Exec. Office of Pres., Washington, 1981-82. Author: Macroeconomics, 1985, 5th rev. edit., 1997, Booms and Recessions in a Noisy Economy, 1990, The Rational Consumer: Theory and Evidence, 1990, Flat Tax, 1995, Economics, 1997, rev. edit.; editor: Inflation, 1983. Woodrow Wilson fellow, 1964; Ford Found. faculty rsch. fellow, 1969. Fellow Econometric Soc., Am. Acad. Arts and Scis.; mem. Am. Econs. Assn., Am. Statis Assn. Democrat. Office: Stanford U Hoover Instn Stanford CA 94305*

HALL, ROBERT J., newspaper executive; b. Phila.. BS in accounting, Drexel U. CPA in 1968. With Inquirer & Daily News, Phila., Pa., 1973-85; exec. v.p. & gen. mgr. Detroit Free Press, 1985, pub., chmn.; pub., chmn. Phila. Inquirer and Daily News, 1990—. Bd. of Trustees at Drexel U., vice chmn. of the Greater Phila. First Corp., chmn. of the Phila. Comm. for the 1994 World Cup Bid and chmn. of the Fairmount Pk. Historic Houses Project. mem. of the Bd. of the Police Athletic League, Greater Phila. C. of C., Phila. Convention and Visitors Bur., Phila. Sports Congress, Met. Sunday Newspapers and Newspapers First Corp. Office: The Phila Inquirer PO Box 8263 400 N Broad St Philadelphia PA 19101-4099*

HALL, ROBERT JOSEPH, physician, medical educator; b. Buffalo, June 4, 1926; s. Joseph M. and Florence C. (Kirst) H.; m. Dorothy Nowak, Aug. 28, 1948; children: Thomas R., Kathleen A. Hall Noble, Mary J. Hall Stuart, Michael F., Steven E. Student, Canisius Coll., Buffalo, 1943-45; MD, U. Buffalo, 1948. Diplomate Am. Bd. Internal Medicine, Sub Bd. Cardiovascular Disease (mem. cardiovascular disease sect. 1969-75). Intern Mercy Hosp., Buffalo, 1948-49; commd. 1st lt. M.C. U.S. Army, 1948, advanced through grades to col., 1966; resident in internal medicine Walter Reed Gen. Hosp., Washington, 1949-52; resident in cardiovascular diseases Walter Reed Gen. Hosp., 1956-57; asst. cardiovascular research Walter Reed Army Inst. Research, 1957-58; service in Korea and Japan, 1952-55; chief cardiology service Brooke Gen. Hosp., Ft. Sam Houston, Tex., 1961-66, Walter Reed Gen. Hosp., 1966-69; ret., 1969; clin. assoc. prof. medicine Georgetown U. Med. Sch., 1967-69; clin. prof. medicine Baylor U. Coll. Medicine, Houston, 1969—, U. Tex. Med. Sch., Houston, 1977—; med. dir. Tex. Heart Inst., Houston, 1969-93; chmn. exec. com. profl. staff Tex. Heart Inst., 1969-93; dir. div. cardiology St. Luke's Episcopal Hosp., Houston, 1969-95; assoc. chief med. service St. Luke's Episcopal Hosp., 1970-83; dir. edn., cardiology Tex. Heart Inst. Tex. Heart Inst. and St. Luke's Episcopal Hosp., 1992—; cons. Tex. Children's, VA, Brooke Gen. hosps., M.D. Anderson Hosp. and Tumor Inst.; mem. cardiovascular study sect. NIH, 1958-61; mem. phys. evaluation team Gemini project NASA, 1958-61; mem. nat. adv. heart counseil Dept. Def., 1966-69; adv. council Mended Hearts, 1970-78. Contbr. numerous articles med. jours. Mem. President's Adv. Panel Heart Disease. Decorated Legion of Merit; recipient Disting. Alumnus award Canisius Coll., 1995. Fellow A.C.P., Am. Coll. Cardiology (gov. 1968-71-74, chmn. bd. govs. and trustee 1973-74); mem. Am. Heart Assn. (fellow council clin. cardiology; pres. Houston chpt. 1974-75, advisor corp. cabinet 1980-86), Assn. Mil. Surgeons U.S., Assn. Advancement Med. Instrumentation, Pan Am. Med. Assn. (chmn. sect. cardiovascular diseases 1978-81), Assn. Univ. Cardiologists, Tex. Med. Assn., Tex. Cardiology Club, Harris County Med. Soc., Houston Cardiology Soc. (chmn. 1976-77), Houston Soc. Internal Medicine, Alpha Omega Alpha, 1948—. Home: 5504 Sturbridge Dr Houston TX 77056-1623 Office: 6624 Fannin St Ste 2480 Houston TX 77030-2309

HALL, ROBERT PAUL, social services administrator; b. Salisbury, Md., July 5, 1952; s. R. Paul and Elizabeth (Satterfield) H.; m. Conee Nelson, May 28, 1994. BA, U. Md., 1974; MDiv, Wesley Theol. Sem., 1977. Dir. planning Community Action of Greater Wilmington, Wilmington, Del., 1980-82; dir. devel. ARC, Wilmington, 1983-84; exec. dir. Delawareans United to Prevent Child Abuse, Wilmington, Del., 1984-96, Del. Assn. Home and Cmty. Care, Montchanin, 1997-98, Del. Ecumenical Coun. Children & Families, Wilmington, 1997—. Contbr. articles to profl. jours. Winner Commr's. award, 1991. Mem. NASW, Am. Counseling Assn., Am. Mental Health Counselors Assn. (task force on childhood and adolescence). Home: PO Box 260 Montchanin DE 19710-0260

HALL, ROBERT WILLIAM, philosophy and religion educator; b. Arlington, Mass., Apr. 6, 1928; s. Samuel Harry and Agness (Babikian) H.; m. Mary Alice Starritt, Oct. 25, 1958; children—Christopher Allen, Jonathan Brooks, Pamela Leigh, Timothy Randall, Jennifer Lane, Nicholas Ramsay. A.B., Harvard, 1949, M.A., 1951, Ph.D., 1953. Vis. asst. prof. philosophy Vanderbilt U., 1955-57; asst. prof. philosophy and religion U. Vt., Burlington, 1957-63; assoc. prof. U. Vt., 1963-67, prof., 1967—, Marsh prof. intellectual and moral philosophy, 1985, chmn. dept., 1963-72. Author: Plato and the Individual, 1963, Studies in Religious Philosophy, 1969, Plato, 1981; editor: APEIRON, 1966-87. Served with CIC AUS, 1953-55. Shedd fellow in religion in higher edn., 1968-69. Mem. Am. Philos. Assn., Soc. Ancient Greek Philosophy (sec.-treas. 1963-72), Am. Soc. Aesthetics, Phi Beta Kappa. Home: 165 N Prospect St Burlington VT 05401-1607 Office: 70 S Williams St Burlington VT 05401-3404

HALL, ROGER LEE, musicologist, educator, composer; b. Glen Ridge, N.J., Nov. 13, 1942. Cert., Trinity Coll., London, 1967; BA, Rutgers U., 1970; MA, SUNY, 1972. Music cons. Nat. Geographic Soc., Washington, 1972; lectr. various colls., mus., 1974—; researcher, writer various jours., mags., 1975—; instr. Stonehill Coll., North Easton, Mass., 1979-82, Brookline (Mass.) Adult and Community Edn. Program, 1983-96; composer ASCAP, N.Y.C., 1985—; cable TV producer Pinetree Prodns., Stoughton, Mass., 1987—; cons. Paul Revere House, Boston, 1981, The Shaker Seminar, Pittsfield, Mass., 1984-87. *An American music specialist with over 25 years of experience. Music consultant for recordings, seminars and workshops. Coordinator for two festivals dealing with early American music. Music historian for the oldest choral society in America and chairman of its Bicentennial Committee. Teacher and lecturer on classical and popular music topics. Local music history project for use in public schools and by residents. Founder of Pine Tree Productions, an audio and video music service. Award-winning compositions. Arrangements and editions of Shaker folk music included on several recordings. Producer of cable television and radio programs, including a series on American songs.* Editor (music collection) The Happy Journey, 1982, Love Is Little, 1992, Joy of Angels, 1995; composer: Piano Variations, 1984, Peace - A Patriotic Ode, 1989, A Little Theatre Music, 1990, Three Shaker Poems, 1996; feature writer The World of Shaker, Holland, Mich., 1985-96; prodr., host Continental Cablevision, Stoughton, Mass., 1986; author: (pamphlet) Singing Stoughton, 1985, (booklets) Story of Simple Gifts, 1987, Music in Stoughton, 1989, The Stoughton Songster, 1991, A Guide to Film Music, 1997, A Guide to Shaker Music, 1997, New England Songster, 1997, A guide to George Gershwin, 1998, Remembering Radio, 1998.; radio tributes Sta. WBET-AM, 1985-93, Sta. WGBH-FM, 1981-95. Chmn. bd. Stoughton Arts Coun., 1980-84; mem. Town Hall Centennial Com., Stoughton, 1981. Served with U.S. Army, 1960-63. SUNY assistantship, 1971-72; Title IV fellow Case Western Res. U., 1972-74; Mass. Arts Lottery grantee, 1985-90. Mem. Old Stoughton Mus. Soc. (v.p. 1978-86), The Sonneck Soc. Lutheran. Club: Shaker Study Group (pres. 1987-89). Avocations: collecting autographs, poetry, photography. E-mail: musbuff@aol.com. Home and Office: 235 Prospect St Stoughton MA 02072-4163

HALL, SHELLEY STEVENSON, special education educator; b. Bridgeport, Conn., May 8, 1949; d. Norman and Fay Leah (Taubman) Stevenson; m. Thomas Lewis Hall, Sept. 5, 1971; children: Karla Luisa, John William. BS, U. Bridgeport, 1971; MA, Fairfield U., 1976, cert. of advanced studies, 1980; postgrad., Sacred Heart U., Bridgeport, 1976, So. Conn. State U., 1978. Cert. spl. edn., English and social studies tchr., Conn.; initial educator's cert. in adminstrn. and supervision. Tchr. spl. edn. Norwalk (Conn.) Bd. Edn., 1975-80, Weston (Conn.) Bd. Edn., 1980—; ednl. tutor Dr. Jerome Schiller, Fairfield, Conn., 1985—; adj. prof. Fairfield U., 1988—; tchr. assessor Best Assessor Program State of Conn., 1989—, cooperating tchr./mentor, 1990—, trainer of mentors and cooperating tchrs., 1991; editor Blue ribbon application for nat. recognition of Weston H.S., 1996. Sec. Hadassah Med. Orgn., Trumbull, Conn., 1985—. Recipient Outstanding Svc. to Weston Cmty. award Weston Bd. Edn., 1988, Hadassah Leadership award, 1990; honoree Hadassah Hand of Healing, 1990; named Hadassah Woman of Yr., 1998, Hadassah Vol. of Yr., 1997. Mem. Coun. for Exceptional Children (pres. chpt. 1977-78), Orgn. for Rehab. and Tng., Hadassah Med. Orgn., Phi Delta Kappa (sec. 1991-93). Jewish. Avocations: reading, travel, baking, entertaining. Home: 35 Coach House Rd Stratford CT 06497-1037

HALL, STANTON HARRIS, dental educator, orthodontist; b. Boise, Idaho, Apr. 8, 1940; s. Perce and Orpha (Harris) H; m. Sharon Viola Price, June 30, 1962; children: Jennifer Ann, Camille Elaine, Matthew Ridd. MS, DDS, Northwestern U., 1967; PhD, U. Wash., 1974. Cert. orthodontist, 1977; diplomate Am. Bd. Orthodontics, 1991. Research assoc. Nat. Inst. Health, Bethesda, Md., 1974-77; assoc. prof. dept. orthodontics U. Wash., Seattle, 1979—. Contbr. articles and poetry to profl. publs. Mem., counselor stake presidency Ch. Jesus Christ Latter-Day Saints, 1984-93, bishop, 1979-84, 93—; councilman Aurora Dist. Boy Scouts Am., Seattle, 1984-87. Capt. USAF, 1967-69, comdr. USPHS, 1974-77. Fellow USPHS, 1964-67; recipient C.V. Mosby award for scholarship, Northwestern U. Dental Sch., 1967. Mem. ADA, AAAS, Wash. Assn. Dental Specialities (sec.-treas. 1988-89, pres. 1989-91), Wash. State Soc. Orthodontists (bd. dirs., publ. chmn. 1982-87, sec.-treas. 1987-88, v.p. 1988-89, pres. 1989-90), Pacific Coast Soc. Orthodontists (Wash. state dir., bd. dirs. 1994-97), Am. Assn. Orthodontists, Omicron Kappa Upsilon. Home: 4549 Thackeray Pl NE Seattle WA 98105-4841 Office: U Wash Dept Orthodontics Seattle WA 98195 also: 12817 120th Ave NE Kirkland WA 98034-3001

HALL, STEPHEN CHARLES, lawyer; b. Carmel, Calif., Sept. 14, 1948; s. Melvin Wiley and Dorothy Louise (Hoyt) H.; m. Kristi Lee Roberts, Feb. 23, 1983; children: Spencer Stephen Rodrigo, Rachel Genevieve Cristina, Trevor Charles. AB, Dickinson Coll., 1971; JD, Vt. Law Sch., 1977. Bar: Pa. 1978, Va. 1979, U.S. Dist. Ct. (ea. dist.) Va. 1982, U.S. Dist. Ct. (we. dist.) Va. 1990, U.S. Ct. Appeals (4th cir.) 1982. Title atty. Chgo. Title Inst. Co., Richmond, 1978-79; assoc. Edward E. Willey Jr., P.C., Richmond, 1979-82; ptnr. Willey & Hall, P.C., Richmond, 1983-88; assoc. Hazel & Thomas, P.C., Richmond, 1988-90, ptnr., 1990-94; ptnr. Keith & Hall, Richmond, 1994—. Contbr. articles to profl. jours. Past chmn. bd. trustees St. Michael's Episcopal Sch. Mem. Richmond Bar Assn. (past chmn. publs. com.), Chesterfield Bar Assn. (chmn. mem. com. 1990-), Bon Air Bus. and Profl. Assn. (past pres.). Episcopalian. Avocations: golf, photography. Office: Keith & Hall 2727 Mcrae Rd Richmond VA 23235-3055

HALL, STEVE HARRIS, educator; b. Bellsburg, Tenn., Apr. 10, 1949; s. Herman Albert and Francis Lewis H.; children: Joshua Lewis, Rachel Payne. BS in Edn., Memphis State U., 1971; MSc, Tenn. State U., 1980. Cert. tchr., Tenn. Tchr. Metro Nashville Schs., 1971-73, Cheatham County Schs., Ashland City, Tenn., 1974—. Sch. Safety com. Tenn. State Bd. Edn., Nashville, 1994, Sch. Safety coord. Cheatham County Schs., Ashland City, 1998. Named Secondary Tchr. of Yr. Cheatham County, 1988-89, Systemwide Secondary Tchr. of Yr., 1992-93. Mem. Nat. Ednl. Assn., Tenn. Tchrs. Assn. (distinguished classroom tchr. award 1989), Masonic Lodge. Avocations: ballroom dancing, fly fishing, reading, geneology. Home: 1021 Hardesty Rd Ashland City TN 37015-5004 Office: Cheatham County Central High School Number One Cub Circle Ashland City TN 37015

HALL, SUSAN LAUREL, artist, educator, writer; b. Point Reyes Sta., Calif., Mar. 19, 1943; d. Earl Morris and Avis Mary (Brown) H. BFA, Calif. Coll. Arts & Crafts, Oakland, 1965; MA, U. Calif., Berkeley, 1967. Mem. faculty Sch. Visual Arts, N.Y.C., 1981-92. Artist: one person shows San Francisco Mus. of Art, 1967, Quay Gallery, San Francisco, 1969, Phyllis Kind Gallery, Chgo., 1971, 98 Greene St. Loft, N.Y.C., Whitney Mus. Modern Art, N.Y.C., 1972, Nancy Hoffman Gallery N.Y.C., 1973, 75, Henderson Mus. U. Col., Boulder, 1973, U. R.I. Gallery, Kingston, 1976, Harcus Krakow Rosen Sonnabend Gallery, Boston, 1976, Hal Bromm and Getler-Pall Galleries, N.Y.C., 1978, Helene Shlien Gallery, Boston, 1978, Hamilton Gallery N.Y.C., 1978, 79, 81, 83, Ovsey Gallery, L.A., 1981, 82, 84, 87, 89, 91, Paule Anglim Gallery, San Francisco, 1975-83, Ted Greenwald Gallery, N.Y.C., 1986, Trabia Macafee Gallery N.Y.C., 1988, 89, Wyckoff Gallery, Aspen, Colo., 1990-92, Milagros Contemporary Art, San Antonio, 1995, Brendan Walter Gallery, L.A., 1995, U. Tex. San Antonio, 1996, Jan Holloway Gallery, San Francisco, 1997, San Francisco Mus. Art Rental Gallery, 1998, Gail Harvey Gallery, L.A., 1999, Bergamot Sta., L.A., 1999, Frank Lloyd Wright Civic Ctr., San Rafael, 1999, Frank Lloyd Wright Civic Ctr., San Rafael, 1999, Jernigan Wicker Gallery, San Francisco, 1999; group shows include Whitney Mus. of Am. Art, San Francisco Mus., Oakland Mus., Balt. Mus., Inst. Contemporary Art, Phila., Hudson River Mus., Bklyn. Mus., Nat. Mus. Women in the Arts, Mus. Fine Arts, Boston, Aldrich Mus. Contemporary Art, G.W. Einstein Gallery, Blum Helman Downtown, Leo Castelli Gallery Uptown, Graham Modern, N.Y.C., Kunstmus. Luzern, Switzerland, Landesmus., Bonn, Germany; represented in pub. collections at Whitney Mus. Am. Art, San Francisco Mus., Bklyn. Mus., Carnegie Inst., St. Louis Mus., Nat. Mus. Women in the Arts and others. Nat. Endowment Arts fellow, 1979-87, Adolph Gottleib Found. fellow, 1995; grantee: Pollack Krasner Found., N.Y. State Coun. on Arts; recipient Marin Arts Coun. Bd. Dirs. award, 1999.

HALL, TERESA JOANNE KEYS, manufacturing engineer, professor; b. Chanute, Kans., 1954; d. William Milton and Mary Joanne (Greve) Keys; m. Douglas Wayne Hall, Jan 31, 1986; 1 child, Benjamin Alan. BA in Industry, U. Northern Iowa, 1988, MA in Tech., 1991; PhD in Indsl. Edn. and Tech., Iowa State U., 1997. Cert. mfg. engr. Dept. mgr. Cooks Inc., Waterloo, Iowa, 1974-76; grounds maintenance City of Waterloo, 1976-77; trades mechanic Deere & Co., Waterloo, 1977-79, foundry maintenance planner, 1979-82, metals analyst, 1982-84, sr. maintenance planner, 1984-87; pvt. practice Waterloo, 1988-91; instr. U. Northern Iowa, Cedar Falls, 1992-96, asst. prof., 1997—; expert witness mfg. fabrication & safety issues. Contbr. articles to profl. jours. Grantee NSF, 1996, 98, Tchr. Edn. Alliance, 1997. Mem. AAUW, Soc. Mfg. Engrs. (faculty advisor 1993—), Am. Mensa Ltd., Nat. Assn. Indsl. Technologists, Epsilon Pi Tau. Avocations: gardening, expert witness: safety & engineering design litigation. Office: U Northern Iowa Dept Indsl Tech Cedar Falls IA 50614

HALL, THOR, religion educator; b. Larvik, Norway, Mar. 15, 1927; came to U.S., 1957, naturalized, 1973; s. Jens Martin and Margit Elvira (Petersen) H.; m. Gerd Hellstrom, July 15, 1950 (dec.); 1 child, Jan Tore; m. Nancy Varnell, Mar. 12, 1999. Diploma in theology, Scandinavian Methodist Sem., 1950; postgrad., Selly Oak Colls., Birmingham, Eng., 1950-51; M.R.E., Duke U., 1959, Ph.D., 1962. Ordained deacon Methodist Ch., 1952, elder, 1954. Minister Kongsvinger-Odal Meth. Ch., Norway, 1951-53; exec. sec. youth dept. Meth. Ch., Norway, 1953-57; minister Ansonville (N.C.) Meth. Ch., 1958-59; asst. minister 1st Presbyn. Ch., Durham, N.C., 1960-62; asst. prof. preaching and theology Duke U., 1962-68, assoc. prof., 1968-72; disting. prof. religious studies U. Tenn., Chattanooga, 1972-94, LeRoy A. Martin disting. prof. religious studies, 1987-94, prof. emeritus, 1994—; vis. prof. Oslo U., 1977, Liberia, 1980, U. Copenhagen, 1984, 96; mem. Gen. Bd. Evangelism, Meth. Ch., 1968-72; mem. Oxford Inst. Meth. Theol. Studies, 1982-92; cons. Ecumenical Prayer Seminars, 1967-80, Army, Navy, Air Force Chaplaiins Corps, 1967-68, 71-72; James Sprunt lectr. Union Theol. Sem., Richmond, Va., 1970; Voigt lectr. So. Ill. conf. United Meth. Ch., 1979; Goodsonlectr. Va. conf., 1983; mem. Tenn. Com. for Humanities, 1978-82, chmn. subcom. on devel., mem. exec. com., 1979-82; Stahley lectr. Ferrum Coll., Va., 1987. Author: A Theology of Christian Devotion, 1969, A Framework for Faith, 1970, The Future Shape of Preaching, 1971, Whatever Happened to the Gospel, 1973, (with others) Advent-Christmas (Proclamation B), 1975, Anders Nygren, 1978, Systematic Theology Today, Part I, 1978, The Evolution of Christology, 1982, Pentecost (Proclamation 4B), 1990; editor: Var Ungdom, 1953-57, The Unfinished Pyramid (Charles P. Bowles), 1967, A Directory of Systematic Theologians in North America, 1977; translator: A Political Dogmatic (Jens Glebe-Möller) 1987, Jesus and Theology (Glebe-Möller), 1989, Forgiveness (Carl-Reinhold Bråkenhielm), 1993; contbr. articles to profl. jours. World Council Chs. scholar, 1950-51; Crusade scholar, 1957-59; Gurney Harris Kearns fellow, 1959-60; Angier Duke Meml. fellow, 1960-61; James B. Duke fellow, 1961-62; Am. Assn. Theol. Schs. faculty fellow, 1968-69; Fulbright-Hays travel grantee, 1984. Mem. AAUP, Soc. Sci. Study Religion, Am. Acad. Religion (v.p. Southeastern region 1984-85, pres. 1985-86), SE Commn. for the Study Religion (exec. dir. 1987-91), Soc. Philosophy of Religion. Home: 1102 Montvale Cir Signal Mountain TN 37377-2511 *The greatest factor contributing to personal growth and professional development is the full utilization of opportunities available at the present and the fulfillment of one's responsibilities, whatever they are.*

HALL, TIMOTHY COUZENS, biology educator, consultant; b. Darlington, Durham, Eng., Aug. 29, 1937; came to U.S., 1965; s. Gilbert Leslie and Dorothea Olive (Lindemann) H.; m. Sandra Severn, Aug. 20, 1960; children: Alexandra Vikki Anna, Liza Bryony, Peter Marcus Jeremy. BSc with honors, U. Nottingham, Eng., 1962, PhD in Plant Physiology, 1965. Louis W. and Maud Hill postdoctoral fellow dept. hort. sci. U. Minn., St. Paul, 1965-66; asst. prof. horticulture U. Wis., Madison, 1966-70, assoc. prof., 1970-75, prof., 1975-82, adj. prof. biophysics and genetics, 1982-84; dir. Agrigenetics Advanced Rsch. Div., Madison, 1980-84, Agrigenetics Rsch. Corp., Boulder, Colo., 1981-84; Disting. prof., head dept. biology Tex. A&M U., College Station, 1984-92, dir. Inst. Devel. and Molecular Biology, 1992—; sr. biotech. cons. Rhône-Poulenc Agrochimie, Lyon, France, 1985—; chair, organizer Gordon Conf. on Plant Molecular Biology, 1987; cons. plant biotech. Novartis, 1997-98; co-chair, co-organizer Juan March Workshop on Chromation and DNA Modification, 1998. Editor: (with J.W. Davies) Nucleic Acids in Plants, 2 vols., 1979, (with L. van Vloten-Doting and G.S.P. Groot) Molecular Form and Function of the Plant Genome, 1985; mem. editl. bd. Oxford Surveys Plant Molecular and Cell Biology, 1983-80, Transgenic Rsch., 1991-95, Plant Jour., 1991—, Jour. Virology, 1996—; contbr. numerous articles to profl. jours., book chpts.; patentee in field. Pilot Royal Air Force, 1956-58. Grantee NIH, NSF, USDA, NATO, Rhône-Poulenc Agrochimie, Internat. Paper Co., Tex. Advanced Tech. Program, Rockefeller Found. Fellow Indian Virol. Soc.; mem. AAAS, RNA Soc., Am. Soc. for Biochemistry and Molecular Biology, Am. Soc. for Microbiology, Am. Soc. Plant Physiologists (organizer Juan March workshop on chromatin and DNA modividation Madrid, 1998), Am. Soc. for Virology, Am. Phytopathol. Soc., Soc. Gen. Microbiology, Fedn. Am. Socs. Exptl. Biology, Biochem. Soc., Internat. Soc. for Molecular-Plant Microbe Interactions, Internat. Soc. Plant Molecular Biology, Soc. for In Vitro Biology, RNA Soc., Squash Club Tex. A&M U., Sigma Xi. Avocations: squash, racquetball, bridge, travel. E-mail: tim@idmb.tamu.edu. Office: Tex A&M U Inst Devel-Molecular Biol College Station TX 77843-3155

HALL, TONY P., congressman; b. Dayton, Ohio, Jan. 16, 1942; m. Janet Dick, 1973; 1 child, Jyl. Student, Ohio State U.; AB, Denison U., 1964; LLD (hon.), Asbury Coll., Eastern Coll. Vol. Peace Corps, Thailand, 1966-67; mem. Ohio Ho. of Reps., 1969-72, Ohio Senate, 1973-78, 96th-106th Congresses from 3d Ohio dist., Washington, D.C., 1979—. Founder, mem. steering com. Congl. Friends of Human Rights Monitors; mem. bd. mgrs. Air Force Mus. Found.; trustee Holiday Aid; mem. adv. com. Emergency Resource Bank; chmn. Dem. Caucus Task Force on Hunger. Recipient Disting. Svc. Against Hunger award Bread for the World, 1984, 87, Tree of Life award Jewish Nat. Fund, 1986, Golden Apple award Nat. Assn. Nutrition and Aging Svcs. Programs, 1986, Freedom award Asian Pacific Am. C. of C., 1986, Presdl. End Hunger award, 1988, Silver Anniversary award NCAA, 1989, Silver World Food Day medal Food and Agriculture Orgn. of UN, Ptnrs. award Oxfam Am., 1992; nominated for Nobel Peace prize, 1998. Mem. Nat. Assn. Women, Infants & Children (Leadership award 1991). Democrat. Office: 1432 Longworth Bldg Ofc Washington DC 20515-3503*

HALL, WILBUR DALLAS, JR., medical educator; b. Calhoun, Ga., June 22, 1938; m. Marguerite Holt, July 4, 1992; children: Ashley, Brent, Marianne, Tommy. MD, Emory U., 1963. Diplomate Am. Bd. Internal Medicine and Nephrology. Chief med. resident Grady Meml. Hosp., 1966; prof. medicine, dir. div. hypertension Emory U., Atlanta, 1976-97, prof. emeritus, 1997—, program dir. Gen. Clin. Rsch. Ctr., 1988-97. Author 3 books; contbr. 75 chpts. to books, over 100 articles to profl. jours. Master ACP; mem. Ga. Heart Assn. (pres. 1984-85). Home: 1100 Parker Pl NE Atlanta GA 30324-5402

HALL, WILEY A., columnist, journalist; b. Washington, Feb. 11, 1953; s. Wiley A. Jr. and Mildred C. (Whitehead) H.; m. Allyson Holley, Sept. 3, 1977 (div. 1991); children: Wiley A. IV, James A. Student, Macalester Coll., 1971-75, U. Ghana, 1974. Reporter Balt. Evening Sun, 1975-85; columnist Baltimore Sun, 1985-95, Baltimore African-American, 1996—; dir. comm. Morgan State U., Balt., 1995—. Author: Urban Rhythms, Urban Blues, 1996; contbr. to anthology Thinking Black, 1996. Bd. dirs. Associated Black Charities, Balt., 1996—, Balt. Symphony Orch., 1987—; mem. adv. com. Ctr. Stage, Balt., 1993; bd. dirs. Arena Players, Inc., Balt., 1995. Recipient Unity award in media Lincoln U., 1984, Benjamin Fine award Nat. Assn. Secondary Sch. Prins., 1991; and numerous others. Mem. Nat. Assn. Black Journalists (Frederick Douglass award 1984), Soc. Profl. Journalists, The Trotter Group (founding mem.), Balt. Urban League. Home: 6140 Little Foxes Run Columbia MD 21045-5643*

HALL, WILLIAM DARLINGTON, lawyer; b. Elkins, W.Va., Jan. 12, 1914; s. Nathan I. and Grace (Darlington) H.; m. Louise Brown, Aug. 3, 1949; children—Carolyn L., Dorothy K., Beverly G. B.E.E., W.Va. U., 1934, M.E.E., 1935, E.E., 1940; J.D., George Washington U., 1946. Bar: D.C. 1945. Engr. Gen. Electric Co., Lynn, Mass., 1936-39; radio engr., patent adviser Signal Corps U.S. Army, Washington, 1939-47; chief patent sect., 1946-47; practiced in Washington Washington, 1947—; partner firm Hall, Myers and Rose, 1974-89; of counsel Shlesinger & Myers, Bethesda, Md., 1989, Myers, Rose & Liniak, Bethesda, Md., 1990-92, Myers, Liniak and Berenato, Bethesda, Md., 1992-98; arbitrator Am. Arbitration Assn., 1970—; mem. Army-Navy Patent Adv. Bd., 1946-47. Home: 10850 Stanmore Dr Rockville MD 20854-1522 Office: Hall Priddy & Myers 10220 River Rd Potomac MD 20854-4916

HALL, WILLIAM EDWARD, JR., insurance agency executive; b. Roanoke, Va., Oct. 15, 1951; s. William Edward and Virginia (Moomaw) H., m. Emily Ayers Rierson, May 27, 1972; children: Amanda Marie, John William. BA in Econs., U. N.C., Chapel Hill, 1973, MBA (Bus. Found. fellow), 1977; MS in Fin. Svcs., Am. Coll., 1989. CPA, CLU, ChFC. Coll. agt. Northwestern Mut. Life, Chapel Hill, 1972-73, 75-77, spl. agt., Greensboro, N.C., 1973-75, 78—; staff acct. Price Waterhouse & Co., Charlotte, N.C., 1977-78; ptnr. Sprinkle & Assocs., life ins. agy., Greensboro, 1978-87; sr. v.p., ptnr. Todd Orgn. of the Carolinas, 1987—. Bd. dirs. cen. N.C. chpt. Nat. Multiple Sclerosis Soc.; active Leadership Greensboro Alumni Assn. Mem. AICPA, Nat. Assn. Accts., Estate Planning Council, Am. Soc. CLUs, Greensboro CLU & ChFC Chpt. (bd. dirs. 1980-83, sec., treas. 1988-89, pres. 1990-91), Assn. Advanced Life Underwriters, Todd Nat. (legis. chmn. 1991—), Greensboro Country Club, Kiwanis, Phi Beta Kappa, Beta Gamma Sigma, Beta Theta Pi. Republican. Presbyterian. Home: 1912 Lafayette Ave Greensboro NC 27408-7204 Office: Todd Orgn of The Carolinas Ste 300 620 Green Valley Rd Greensboro NC 27408-7725

HALL, WILLIAM JOEL, civil engineer, educator; b. Berkeley, Calif., Apr. 13, 1926; s. Eugene Raymond and Mary (Harkey) H.; m. Elaine Frances Thalman, Dec. 18, 1948; children: Martha Jane, James Frederick, Carolyn Marie. Student, U. Calif., Berkeley, 1943-44, Kings Point, 1944-45; BSCE, U. Kans., 1948; MS, U. Ill., Urbana, 1951, PhD, 1954. Teaching asst. U. Kans., 1947-48; engr. Sohio Pipe Line Co., 1948-49; mem. faculty U. Ill., Urbana, 1949-93; prof. civil engring. U. Ill., 1959-93, head dept. civil engring., 1984-91; prof. emeritus, 1993—; cons. structural dynamics, seismic, materials to govt. orgns. and industry. Author books, articles, chpts. in books, revs. Recipient A. Epstein Meml. award U. Ill., 1958, Halliburton Engring. Edn. Leadership award, 1980, Disting. Engring. Svc. award U. Kans., 1985; Univ. scholar, U. Ill., 1986-89. Fellow AAAS; mem. NAE, ASME, ASTM, ASCE (hon., pres. Ctrl. Ill. sect. 1967-68, chmn. structural divsn. exec. com. 1973—, chmn. tech. coun. on lifeline earthquake engring. exec. com. 1982—, Kans. sect. award 1948, Walter L. Huber award 1963, Howard award 1984, Newmark medal 1984, C. Martin Duke award 1990, Norman medal 1992), Am. Concrete Inst., Am. Welding Soc. (Adams Meml. membership award 1967), Earthquake Engring. Rsch. Inst. (Housner medal 1998), Seismol. Soc. Am., Structural Engrs. Assn. Ill. (John Parmer award 1990), Sigma Xi, Tau Beta Pi (Daniel C. Drucker eminent faculty award 1993), Sigma Tau, Chi Epsilon (nat. honor mem. 1998), Phi Kappa Phi. Home: 3105 Valley Brook Dr Champaign IL 61822-6111 Office: U Ill Civil Engring Lab 2106 Newmark 205 N Mathews Ave Urbana IL 61801-2350

HALL, WILLIAM KEARNEY, retired dermatologist; b. Springfield, Mo., Oct. 9, 1918; s. Edward Bennington and Mary Katharine (Kearney) H. BS, Yale U., 1939; MD, Harvard U., 1942. Commd. ensign USN, 1942, advanced through grades to capt., 1956, ret., 1962; intern U.S. Naval Hosp., Chelsea, Mass., 1942-43; resident U.S. Naval Hosp., Phila., 1953-56; pvt. practice St. Charles, Mo., 1962-83. Avocation: genealogy. Home: 33 Westmoreland Pl Saint Louis MO 63108-1227

HALL, WILLIAM SMITH, JR., land surveyor; b. Milford, Conn., Nov. 10, 1941; s. William Smith and Elizabeth (Brodeur) H.; m. Joy Collette Herrick, Sep. 13, 1969; children: William Smith 3d, Amber-Dawn. Student, U. Conn., 1959-60; AS in Civil Engring., Hartford State Tech. Coll., 1972. Lic. land surveyor, Conn.; cert. sr. civil engring. technician, notary public. Rodman-transitman Mcpl. Engring. Dept., Milford, 1960-67; road insp., survey party chief Mcpl. Engring. Dept., Trumbull, Conn., 1967-70; transitman, party chief Leonard Surveyors, Norwalk, Conn., 1970; transitman Donald Disbrow, P.E. & RLS, Hamden, Conn., 1970-72; lic. land surveyor Kasper Assocs., PE & LS, Bridgeport, Conn., 1972-77; owner, mgr., lic. land surveyor Hall Surveyors, Plymouth, Conn., 1973—; mem. adv. com. civil dept. Capitol Commty. Tech. Coll., Hartford, Conn., 1984—, surveying instr., 1991—; Am. Congress Surveying and Mapping com. mem. film on land surveying A Matter of Degrees, 1983-86. Capt. Woodmont Vol. Fire Co. 5, Milford, 1969; chmn. bd. trustees Terryville Congl. Ch., Plymouth, 1986; mem. Plymouth Zoning Bd. Appeals, 1980—, vice chmn., 1985—, acting chmn., 1988. Mem. Conn. Assn. Land Surveyors (sec. 1979-82, pres. 1982-84, county bd. dirs. 1984—, code revision com. 1991-93, com. chmn. "Statute of Limitations" legis., Appreciation awards 1984), Surveyor's Proprietor's Coun. (sec.-treas. 1989, v.p. 1990, pres. 1991). Democrat. Avocations: bowling, sailing, swimming, boating, camping. Office: 350 Lake Plymouth Blvd Plymouth CT 06782-2703

HALL, ZACH WINTER, academic administrator; b. Atlanta, Sept. 15, 1937; s. Dixon Winter and Marjorie Elizabeth (Owens) H.; m. Anne Browning, June 1958 (div. Aug. 1960); m. Marion Nestle, Dec. 1973 (div. June 1985); m. Julie Ann Giacobassi, Nov. 9, 1987. BA, Yale U., 1958; PhD, Harvard U., 1966. Asst. prof., then assoc. prof. Harvard Med. Sch., Boston, 1968-76; prof. U. Calif., San Francisco, 1976-94; dir. Nat. Inst. Neurol. Disorders and Stroke, Bethesda, Md., 1994-97; assoc. dean for rsch. U. Calif., San Francisco, 1997-98, vice chancellor rsch., 1998—; mem. Med. Adv. Bd., Chevy Chase, Md., 1995-99, Howard Hughes Med. Inst.; Alexander Forbes lectr. Grass Found., 1994; David Nachmanson lectr. Weigmann Inst., Rehovath, Israel, 1996. Author, editor: Molecular Neurobiology, 1992; editor jour. Neuron, 1988-94. Fellow AAAS; mem. Am. Acad. Arts and Scis., Inst. Medicine. Office: U Calif San Francisco Sch Medicine Parnassus Ave San Francisco CA 94143

HALLA, BRIAN, electronics company executive; b. Springfield, Ill., 1946. BSEE, U. Nebr., 1969. Applications engr. Control Data Corp., 1969-74; dir. mktg. Intel Corp., 1974-78; exec. v.p. LSI Logic, 1988-96; chmn. bd., pres., CEO Nat. Semiconductor Corp., Santa Clara, Calif., 1996—. Mem. Semi-Conductor Indsl. Assn. (bd. dirs.). Office: National Semiconductor Corp 2900 Semiconductor Dr Santa Clara CA 95051-0695

HALLADAY, LAURIE ANN, public relations consultant, former franchise executive; b. Monroe, Mich., Aug. 18, 1945; d. Alvin John and Florence (Lowrey) Kohler; m. Edward L. Howell, Aug. 27, 1966; m. 2d Fredric R. Halladay, May 24, 1980. BJ, U. Mo., 1967. Reporter, staff writer Copley Newspapers, L.A., 1967-69; account exec. Furman Assocs., L.A., 1969-71, v.p., 1971-74; account supr. Bob Thomas & Assocs., L.A., 1974-76, v.p., 1976-78; v.p., sr. ptnr. Fleishman-Hillard, Inc., St. Louis, 1980-84; owner, operator McDonald's, Portland, Oreg., 1984-87, McDonald's McStop of Mid.-Mo., Kingdom City, 1988-92; chmn. press ops. for Budweiser/G.I. Joe's Portland 200 Indy Car Race, 1984-87; mem. advt., promotions com. Hollywood Boosters, 1986. Bd. dirs. Waterman Place Assn., St. Louis, 1983; mem. pub. rels. com. Winston Churchill Meml., Fulton, 1988-92. Recipient Merit award Calif. Press Women, 1969, Lulu award Los Angeles Women's Ad Club, 1976, McDonald's Outstanding Store award, 1985, 86, 89, 90, 91. Mem. PRSA (Prism award 1977), Soc. Am. travel Writers (assoc. 1981-84), Women in Comm. (dir. St. Louis 1980-82), Nat. Tour Assn., Mo. Travel Coun., Mission Valley Country Club, Delta Delta Delta (alumna adviser 1989, 90,, v.p. Delta Xi House Corp. 1991, collegiate dist. officer 1991, 94, regional program chmn. 1994, program resource team pub. rels. specialist 1995-96, nat. chmn. pub. rels. 1996). Home: 242 Hidden Bay Dr #301 Osprey FL 34229

HALLAGIN, JANET ELAINE, consultant, writer, editor; b. Great Bend, Kans., May 2, 1948; d. John Wesley and Eva Rhae (Skinner) Maclean Simpson; m. Garry L. Hallagin, June 6, 1968; children: William John, Lee Andrew. AA in Math., Neosho County C.C., Chanute, Kans., 1984, AA in Drafting, 1977; PhB, U. Kans., 1986; postgrad., The Inst. Children's Lit., West Redding, Conn., 1992. Nurse's aid, sec., 1968-69, ins. investigator, 1969-70, spl. edn. tchr.'s aide, 1971-72, sewing machine operator, 1973-74, swim instr., lifeguard, 1973-74; structural steel draftsman Chanute (Kans.) Mfg. Co., Inc., 1977-81; draftsman, prog. mgr. GEO Churchill, Chanute, 1981-83; free lance writer Buffalo, Kans., 1986-91, West Des Moines, 1991—; mem. judiciary bd., adv. bd. scholarship hall sys. U. Kans., Lawrence, 1984-85, project cons. Steamboat Resorts, M.C. Gilbertson, Steamboat Springs, Colo., 1988-96; editor, project cons. Beaver Creek (Colo.) promotional project John Simpson Enterprises, 1996. Author: (childrens adventure) The Way of Courage, 1993, Escape In The Night, 1994, (essays) Living Philosophy, 1996; prin. works include 3 dimensional clay scultures created under Creature Fair. Co-founder Chanute Cmty. Theater, Inc., 1976-84; founding pres. local chpt. Chronic Fatigue Syndrome Info. and Self-Help, Chanute, 1986; mem. Grace Episcopal Ch., dir. edn. 1975-80, youth coord., 1976-78. Recipient outstanding merit award Hooper-Holmes, Kans. City, Mo., 1970, outstanding merit spl. edn. award Douglasville (Ga.) Sch. Dist., 1971-72, cert. of achievement award The Pumping Inst., Tex., Kans., 1981; chancellor's outstanding achievement scholar U. Kans., 1984-85, 85-86. Mem. Elks (ladies aux. 1975-84, sec.-treas. 1976, v.p. 1977, pres. 1978), Phi Beta Kappa, Phi Theta Kappa. Republican. Avocation: three dimensional and relief wood carving. Home: 1221 63rd St West Des Moines IA 50266-5854

HALLAM, ARLITA WARRICK, quality of life administrator; b. Peoria, Ill., June 28, 1944; d. Jesse Edward and Hazel Winifred (McClister) Warrick; m. Julian Morgan Austin, June 28, 1964 (div. 1975); m. Donald Owen Hallam, Sept. 15, 1978. BS, Ill. State U., Normal, 1965; MS, U. Ill., 1968; PhD, U. Tex., Arlington, 1992. Dir. Normal Pub. Libr., 1965-67, Fondulac Dist. Libr., East Peoria, Ill., 1967-74; instr. Ill. Ctrl. Coll., East Peoria, 1970-74; regional coord. Ill. Bicentennial Commn., Springfield, 1974-76; exec. dir. Ft. Crevecoeur, Creve Coeur, Ill., 1976-77; dir. sales and mktg. Group V Devel. Co., East Peoria, 1977-78; prin. libr. Abilene (Tex.) Pub. Libr., 1978-82; dir. North Richland Hills (Tex.) Pub. Libr., 1982-92, Clearwater (Fla.) Pub. Libr. Sys., 1992-98; quality of life adminstr. City of Clearwater, 1998—. Author articles. Grad. Leadership N.E., Ft. Worth, 1990, Exec. Fellows Program, Tampa, 1993, Leadership Pinellas, Clearwater, 1994. Named among Top Ten Women of Yr., Am. Bus. Women's Assn., Denver, 1974. Mem. ALA, Pub. Libr. Assn., Fla. Libr. Assn., Fla. Assn. Christian Librs. (pres. 1997-99), Rotary. Nazarene. Avocations: reading, travel, history, museums. Home: 80 Rogers St 6D Clearwater FL 33756-5275 Office: City of Clearwater 100 N Osceola Ave Clearwater FL 33755-4029

HALLAM, BEVERLY (BEVERLY LINNEY), artist; b. Lynn, Mass., Nov. 22, 1923; d. Edwin Francis and Alice (Linney) Hallam Murphy. BS in Edn, Mass. Coll. Art, 1945; postgrad., Cranbrook Acad. Art, Mich., 1948; MFA, Syracuse U., 1953. Chmn. dept. art Lasell Jr. Coll., Auburndale, Mass., 1945-49; assoc. prof. Mass. Coll. Art, 1949-62; bd. dirs. Barn Gallery Associates, Inc., Ogunquit, Maine. One-person shows include Joe and Emily Lowe Art Center, Syracuse U., 1953, DeCordova Mus., Lincoln, Mass., 1954, Shore Galleries, Boston, 1959, 62, 68, 73, 74, Witte Meml. Mus., San Antonio, 1968, U. Maine, 1969, Lamont Gallery, Exeter, N.H., 1969, Addison Gallery, Andover, Mass., 1971, Fitchburg Art Mus., 1972, Fairweather Hardin Gallery, Chgo., 1972, Hobe Sound (Fla.) Galleries, 1973, Inst. Contemporary Art, Boston, 1977, PS Galleries, Maine, 1981, Payson-Weisberg Gallery, N.Y.C., 1984, Farnsworth Mus., Rockland, Maine, 1984, 98, Midtown Galleries, N.Y.C., 1988, Francesca Anderson Gallery, Boston, 1988, Hobe Sound Galleries North, Portland, Maine, 1988, Evansville (Ind.) Mus. Arts and Sci., 1990, Sheldon Swope Mus., Terre Haute, Ind., 1990, Art Mus. S.E. Tex., Beaumont, 1990, Bergen Mus. Art and Sci., Paramus, N.J., 1990, Polk Mus. Art, Lakeland, Fla., 1991, Ogunquit Art Assn., 1999; two-person show, Inst. Contemporary Art, Boston, 1956, numerous group shows including Barn Gallery, 1954-94, Busch-Reisinger Mus., Harvard U., 1956, 59, 60, Portland Mus., 1959, 84, 92, 93, 97, Mus. Fine Arts, Boston, 1960, Inst. Contemporary Art, Boston, 1960, 63, 68, 77, Pace Gallery, Boston, 1962, DeCordova Mus., 1963, 64, 68, 69, 70, 71, 75, Ward-Nasse Gallery, N.Y.C., 1971-72, Ogunquit (Maine) Mus. Am. Art, 1964, 70, 71, 78, 80, 84, 89, 91-93, 95, R.I. Arts Festival, 1966, Smithsonian Instn., Washington, 1966, Am. Water Color Soc. Traveling Exhibition, 1967, Watercolor U.S.A., Springfield, Mo., 1968, Maine State Mus., 1976, Maine Coast Artists, 1974, 75, 77, 83, 89, 92, 93, Joan Whitney Payson Gallery of Art, Maine, 1980, Farnsworth Art Mus., 1982, 87, 92, 95, 96, Bowdoin Coll. Mus. Art, 1984, 92, Midtown Payson Galleries, N.Y.C., 1985, 87, 90, 92, Expo '92, Seville, Spain, Barbara Scott Gallery, Bay Harbor Island, Fla., 1993, Fitchburg (Mass.) Art Mus., 1994, Monmouth (N.J.) Mus., 1995, Evansville Mus. Arts and Sci., 1996; represented in permanent collections Rose Art Mus. Brandeis U., Fogg Art Mus., Cambridge, Mass.; Corcoran Gallery Am. Art, Washington, Witte Meml. Mus., San Antonio, DeCordova Mus., Lincoln, Addison Gallery, Andover, Bowdoin Coll. Mus. Art, Fitchburg Art Mus., Ogunquit Mus. Am. Art, Portland Mus., Colby Coll., U. Maine, Currier Gallery Art, Manchester N.H., Farnsworth Library and Art Mus., Rockland, Maine, U. N.H. Art Galleries, Durham, Everson Mus., Syracuse, First Nat. Bank, Boston, Ernst and Ernst, Chgo., Carnegie Corp., N.Y., Nat. Mus. Women in the Arts, Washington, Gouws Capital Mgmt., Inc., Portland, Maine, Marion Koogler Art Mus., San Antonio, Tex., others, also, pvt. collections, U.S. Can., Paris, Switzerland; Publ. Beverly Hallam, Paintings, Drawings and Monotypes, 1956-71, 1971; subject of book and video Beverly Hallam: The Flower Paintings, 1990, An Odyssey in Art, 1998. Recipient Pearl Safir award Silvermine Guild Artists, New Canaan, Conn., 1955, Painting prize Boston Arts Festival, 1957, Blanche E. Colman Found. award, 1960, Hatfield awards Boston Soc. Watercolor Painters, 1960, 64, 1st prize Edwin Webster award, 1962, Am. Artist Achievement award, 1993. Mem. Ogunquit Art Assn. (past pres.), Archives of Am. Art, Artists Equity. Avocations: gardening, photography. Home: 30 Surf Point Rd York ME 03909-5053

HALLAM, ROBERT G., wholesale distribution executive; b. Dallas, 1941. Diploma, U. Tex., 1964, JD, 1966. Chmn., CEO Ben E. Keith Co., Ft. Worth. Office: Ben E Keith Co PO Box 36629 Dallas TX 75235-1629*

HALLANAN, ELIZABETH V., federal judge; b. Charleston, W.Va., Jan. 10, 1925; d. Walter Simms and Imogene (Burns) H. U. Charleston, 1946; JD, W.Va. U., 1951; postgrad. U. Mich., 1964. Atty. Crichton & Hallanan, Charleston, 1952-59; mem. W.Va. State Bd. Edn., Charleston, 1955-57, Ho. of Dels., W.Va. Legis., Charleston, 1957-58; asst. commr. pub. instns. Charleston, 1958-59; mem., chmn. W.Va. Pub. Service Commn., Charleston, 1969-75; atty. Lopinsky, Bland, Hallanan, Dodson, Deutsch & Hallanan, Charleston, 1975-84; sr. judge U.S. Dist. Ct. for So. Dist. W.Va., Charleston, 1983—. Recipient Hannah G. Solomon award Nat. Coun. Jewish Women, 1997, Justitia Officium awrd W.Va. U. Coll. Law, 1997; named Woman of Achievement, YWCA, 1997, West Virginian of Yr., Charleston Gazette, 1997. Mem. W.Va. Bar Assn. Office: US Dist Ct PO Box 2546 Charleston WV 25329-2546

HALLARD, WAYNE BRUCE, economist; b. Plainfield, N.J., Dec. 28, 1951; s. Donald Jay and Patricia (Adelmann) H.; m. Grace Elizabeth Farrell, Apr. 29, 1972 (div. 1979); 1 child, Travis; m. Deborah Jane Russo, Aug. 16, 1987. Student, Brown U., 1970-71; AA in Bus., Union Coll., 1977; BS in Econs., Fairleigh Dickinson U., 1980, MBA in Econs., 1984; postgrad., N.Y.U., 1984-87. Store mgr. Wine Art of N.J., Watchung, 1972; mgr. Bell Atlantic, Newark, 1972—; cons. N.J. Coun. of Savs. Instns., West Orange, 1987-95, F.A. Russo Assocs., Scotch Plains, N.J., 1989—. Trustee, treas. Lehmen Found., Newark, 1979-84; bd. dirs., treas. Vol. Ctr. of Greater Essex County, 1990-97; mem. Mental Health Assn., East Orange, 1979-80, Newark Mus., 1987—; trustee, past sec., treas. Newark Jaycees Internat. Senators Scholarship Found., 1986—; umpire Scotch Plains-Fanwood Youth Baseball Assn., 1982—; trustee, past pres. Brotherhood Temple Sharey Tefilo Israel, South Orange, N.J., 1980—; mem. ACLU. With USAFR, 1971-80. Recipient Cert. of Appreciation Cts. and Corrections Assn. N.J. 1982; named One of Outstanding Young Men of Am., 1981, 83, 85, 86, 88. Mem. ACLU, Am. Econ. Assn., Greater Newark C. of C. (bd. dirs. 1980-82), Telephone Pioneers Am., Internat. Platform Assn., Fairleigh Dickinson Univ. Alumni Assn. (bd. govs. 1997—), Am. Sealyham Terrier Club (past bd. dirs.), Garden State All Terrier Club (past treas.), Mastiff Club Am., Aircraft Owners and Pilots Assn., Stewards Club Am., ARZA, Jewish Chatauqua Soc., Delta Mu Delta. Republican. Jewish. Avocations: gourmet cooking, reading, show dogs, pvt. pilot. Home: 518 Jerusalem Rd Scotch Plains NJ 07076-2011 Office: Bell Atlantic 540 Broad St Newark NJ 07102-3112

HALLAS, EVELYN MARGARET, physical therapist; b. Ambridge, Pa., May 25, 1922; d. George and Suzanne (Metro) H. BS in Phys. Therapy, Boston U., 1950. Lic. phys. therapist. Mech. engr. Pitts. Forgings Co., Coraopolis, Pa., 1942-43; phys. therapist Dept. Vets. Affairs, 1950-92; rsch. therapist N.Mex. Maternal Child Health, Albuquerque, 1966; ednl. activities coord. Tex. Inst. Rsch./Rehab., Houston, 1972; chief phys. therapy VA Outpatient Clinic, Las Vegas, Nev., 1990-97; semi-ret. phys. therapist Las Vegas, 1997—; cons. Nat. Found. Infantile Paralysis, N.Y.C., 1950-54, Govt. of Guam, Agana, 1965; lectr. Kantonsspital, Zurich, Switzerland, 1963; physical therapist cons. Mem. Am. Phys. Therapy Assn. (life, VA sect. initiator 1970's, regional rep., liaison geriatric sect., phys. therapy historian for Dept. Vets. Affairs, Prime Timers and Nev. chpt., Nev. state geriatric liaison, co-chmn. ho. of dels. extension of Prime Timers), Altrusa (past pres.), Prime Timers (sec.), Toastmasters Internat. Republican. Roman Catholic. Avocations: photography, hiking, swimming, travel. Home: 7601 W Charleston Blvd Apt 15 Las Vegas NV 89117-1418

HALLAUER, ARNEL ROY, geneticist; b. Netawaka, Kans., May 4, 1932; s. Roy Virgil and Mabel Fern (Bohnenkemper) H.; m. Janet Yvonne Goodmanson, Aug. 29, 1964; children: Elizabeth, Paul. B.S., Kans. State U., 1954; M.S., Iowa State U., 1958, Ph.D., 1960. Rsch. agronomist UDSA, Ames, Iowa, 1958-60; geneticist UDSA, Raleigh, N.C., 1961-62; rsch. geneticist UDSA, Ames, 1963-89; prof. Iowa State U., 1990—, C.F. Curtiss Disting. prof. agr., 1991—. Author: (with J.B. Miranda) Quantitative Genetics in Maize Breeding, 1981, 2d edit., 1988; editor: Specialty Corns, 1994. 1st lt. U.S. Army, 1954-56. Recipient Applied Rsch. and Ext. award 1981, Henry A. Wallace award for disting.svc. to agr., 1992, Disting. Alumni Achievement citation, 1996, Iowa State U., Genetics and Plant Breeding award Nat. Coun. Plant Breeding, 1984, Gov.'s Sci. medal State of Iowa, 1990, Burlington No. Career Rsch. Achievement award Iowa State Found., 1991, Centennial medal Phi Kappa Phi, 1997; USDA grantee, 1982, 85, 87, 90; named to USDA/Agrl. Rsch. Sci. Hall of Fame, 1992. Fellow Am. Soc. Agronomy (Agronomic Achievement award for crops 1989, Agronomy Rsch. award 1992), Crop Sci. Soc. (Dekalb Pfizer Crop Sci. award 1981), Iowa Acad. Sci. (disting. fellow 1985); mem. NAS, Nat. Agri-Mktg. Assn. (nat. award for excellence in rsch. 1993), Am. Genetic Assn., Am. Statis. Assn., Kans. State U. Alumni Assn. (alumni fellow 1997), Iowa State Alumni Assn. (faculty citation 1987, Disting. Achievement Citation 1995), Gamma Sigma Delta (Disting. Svc. to Agr. award 1990, Rsch. Award of Merit 1999). Republican. Lutheran. Home: 516 Luther Dr Ames IA 50010-4735 Office: Iowa State U 1505 Dept Agronomy Ames IA 50010

HALL-BARRON, DEBORAH, lawyer; b. Oakland, Calif., Oct. 7, 1949; d. John Standish Hall and Mary (Swinson) H.; m. Eric Levin Meadow, Feb. 1973 (div. June 1982); 1 child, Jesse Standish Meadow Hall; m. Richie Barron, 1997. Paralegal cert., Sonoma State U., Rohnert Park, Calif., 1984; JD, John F. Kennedy U., Walnut Creek, Calif., 1990. Bar: Calif. 1991. Paralegal Law Offices Marc Libarle/Quentin Kopp, Cotati, Calif., 1983-84, MacGregor & Buckley, Larkspur, Calif., 1984-86, Law Offices Melvin Belli, San Francisco, 1987-88, Steinhart & Falconer, San Francisco, 1988; mgr. Computerized Litigation Assocs., San Francisco, 1996; law clk. Morton & Lacy, San Francisco, 1989-91, assoc., 1991-96; atty. Law Offices of Charlotte Venner, San Francisco, 1996-97, Plastiras & Terrizzi, San Francisco, San Rafael, Calif., 1998, Bishop, Barry, Howe, Haney & Ryder, San Francisco,

Calif., 1998—. Atty. Vol. Legal Svcs., San Francisco, 1991-96; judge San Francisco Youth Ct., 1995-97; com. chmn. Point Richmond (Calif.) coun., 1994-96. Recipient Whiley Manuel Pro Bono award State Bar Calif., 1993. Mem. Nat. Assn. Ins. Women, Def. Rsch. Inst., Bar Assn. San Francisco (del. 4th world conf. on women 1995, chair product liability com.), Internat. Com. Lawyers for Tibet (litigation com. 1991-97, co-chair women's com.), Ins. Claims Assn. (chmn. membership com. 1994-96), Hon. Order of Blue Goose Internat., Queen's Bench (chmn. employment com. 1994-97, bd. dirs. 1996—), BASF intellectual property/entertainment law). Democrat. Avocations: sailing, playing guitar and saxaphone, home brewing, mountain biking, human rights advocate.

HALLBAUER, ROSALIE CARLOTTA, business educator; b. Chgo., Dec. 8, 1939; d. Ernest Ludwig and Kathryn Marquerite (Ramm) H. BS, Rollins Coll., 1961; MBA, U. Chgo., 1963; PhD, U. Fla., 1973. CPA, Ill.; cert. mgmt. acct., cost analyst, profl. estimator, cert. cash mgr. Assoc. prof. acctg. Fla. Internat. U., Miami, 1972—. Office: Fla Internat Univ University Park Campus Miami FL 33199

HALLBERG, BENGT O., systems strategy director, fiber optic specialist; b. Stockholm, Dec. 31, 1943; s. Olle E.S. and Anne-Marie K. H.; m. Lena M. Tengelin, June 13, 1975; children: Niklas O., Mattias A., Andreas E. MS in Physics, Royal Inst. Tech., Stockholm, 1978. Constrnl. engr. AB Svenska Bostäder, Stockholm, 1965-76; scientist Inst. of Optical Rsch., Stockholm, 1976-81; pres. Scan Fiber Opto AB, Stockholm, 1988-92, BOH Optical AB, Stockholm, 1981-95; dir. Fiber Network Application Lab, Ericsson, Stockholm, 1995-97; dir. sys. strategy Residential Access, Ericsson Inc., N.Y.C., 1998—. Inventor airborne multispectral radiometer, fiber optic communication system based on WDM; patentee frequency and output regulation in laser diodes. Mem. Optical Soc. Am., Internat. Soc. Optical Engring., European Optical Soc., Swedish Optical Soc. Office: Ericsson Inc 100 Park Ave New York NY 10017-5516

HALLBERG, BUDD JAYE, management consulting firm executive; b. Ottumwa, Iowa, Oct. 2, 1942; s. Melvin Kenneth and Janet Berina (Dowden) H.; m. Diana May Pierce, Dec. 30, 1962; children: Cynthia Ann Hallberg-Walker, Amy Christine. BA, Parsons Coll., 1965; MA, Goddard Coll., 1980; BS, SUNY, 1981; diploma, Command & Gen. Staff Coll., 1981; cert., Wharton Sch., 1984, Yale U., 1996. Account exec. Francis I. duPont & Co., Moline, Ill., 1966-69; sales mgr. Francis I. duPont & Co., N.Y.C., 1969-70; br. mgr. Francis I. duPont & Co., Toledo, 1970-71; v.p. Dominick & Dominick, Inc., N.Y.C., 1971-72, Hornblower & Weeks, Inc., N.Y.C., 1972-74; mem. N.Y. Mercantile Exchange, N.Y.C., 1974-76; dir. U.S. Commodity Future Trading Commn., Washington, 1976-83; v.p. Heinold Commodities, Inc., N.Y.C., 1983-85; pres. SCAN Mgmt. Inc., Gettysburg, Pa., 1985—. Contbr. articles to profl. jours. Fund raiser Rep. party Old Greenwich, Conn., 1974, Gettysburg, Pa., 1995, St. Saviours Episc. Ch., Old Greenwich, 1975, Prince of Peace Episc. Ch., Gettysburg, 1985—. Lt. col. USAR. Mem. Futures Industry Assn., Nat. Futures Assn. (assoc.), Army & Navy Club Wash., Met. Club, Down Town Assn. (N.Y.C.), Rotary, Masons (32 deg.), Scottish Rite, The William Soc., Sons of Union Vets of Civil War. Avocations: fishing, hunting, tennis, jogging, golf. Home: 320 Spangler School Rd Gettysburg PA 17325-8639 Office: SCAN Mgmt Inc PO Box 4835 Gettysburg PA 17325-4835

HALLE, MORRIS, linguist, educator; b. Liepaja, Latvia, July 23, 1923; s. Irving and Lisa (Kahan) H.; m. Rosamond Thaxter Strong, July 2, 1955; children—David S., John G., M. Timothy. Student, CCNY, 1941-43; MA, U. Chgo., 1948, DHL (hon.), 1992; postgrad., Columbia, 1948-49; PhD, Harvard U., 1955; DSc (hon.), Brandeis U., 1989. Mem. faculty Mass. Inst. Tech., Cambridge, 1951-96; prof. modern langs. and linguistics Mass. Inst. Tech., 1961-76, Ferrari P. Ward prof. modern langs. and linguistics, 1976-81, Inst. Prof., 1981-96; prof. emeritus Mass. Inst. Tech., Cambridge, 1996—; James R. Killian, Jr. Faculty Achievement Award lectr., 1978-79. Author: (with R. Jakobson and C.G.M. Fant) Preliminaries to Speech Analysis, 1952, The Sound Pattern of Russian, 1959, (with N. Chomsky) The Sound Pattern of English, 1968, (with S.J. Keyser) English Stress: Its Form, Its Growth, and Its Use in Verse, 1971, (with G.N. Clements) Problem Book in Phonology, 1983, (with J. R. Vergnaud) An Essay on Stress, 1987, On Stress and Accent in Indo-European, 1997. Served with AUS, 1943-46. Recipient Union des Assurances de Paris Sci. prize, 1991; Guggenheim fellow, 1960-61; Am. Acad. Arts and Scis. fellow, 1963—. Mem. NAS, Linguistic Soc. Am. (v.p. 1973, pres. 1974). Home: 10 Arlington St Cambridge MA 02140-2713 Office: MIT 77 Massachusetts Ave Cambridge MA 02139-4307

HALLECK, CHARLES WHITE, lawyer, former judge; b. Rensselaer, Ind., July 6, 1929; s. Charles Abraham and Blanche (White) H.; m. Carolyn L. Wood, Dec. 23, 1950 (div. Oct. 1969); children: Holly Louise, Charles White, Todd Alexander, Heather Leigh, Heidi Lynne, William Hemsley, Hope Leslie; m. Jeanne Wahl, May 16, 1970. A.B., Williams Coll., 1951; J.D., George Washington U., 1957; LL.D. (hon.), St. Joseph's Coll., 1971; AA in Photography, Foothill Coll., Los Altos Hills, Calif., 1996. Asst. U.S. atty. for D.C., 1957-59; assoc. Hogan and Hartson, Washington, 1959-65; judge Superior Ct. D.C., 1965-77; mem. firm Lamb, Halleck & Keats, Washington, 1977-80; sole practice, 1980-86, photojournalist, 1986—. Served with USNR, 1951-55; to lt. Res. (ret.). Mem. Beta Theta Pi, Phi Delta Phi.

HALLECK, LOIS RENEE, critical care and emergency room nurse; b. Vineland, N.J., Aug. 24, 1961; d. Nicholas Sr. and Stella Carmella (Ciapanna) Calvelli. Diploma, Presbyn.-U. Pa. Sch. Nursing, Phila., 1982; BSN, Jefferson U., 1990. RN, N.J., Pa. Staff nurse Underwood Meml. Hosp., Woodbury, N.J., 1982-87, Thomas Jefferson U. Hosp., Phila., 1987-92; flight nurse USAF, McGuire AFB, N.J., 1991—. Mem. ACLS (advanced burn life support, trauma nurse care cert., emergency nurse pediat. course cert.), Emergency Nurses Assn. (CEN), N.J. Nurses Assn., Pa. Nurses Assn., Res. Officers Assn., Nat. Flight Nurse Assn., Sigma Theta Tau.

HALLENBECK, HARRY C., architect. Dir. State of Calif., Sacramento, 1997; dir. planning and design svc. Vanir Constrn. Mgmt., Inc., Sacramento, 1997—. Recipient Edward C. Kemper award Archtl. Inst. Am., 1994. Office: Vanir Constrn Mgmt Inc State & Consumer Svc Agy 980 9th St Ste 900 Sacramento CA 95814-2719 also: 7485 Rush River Dr # 333 Sacramento CA 95831-5259

HALLENBECK, KENNETH LUSTER, numismatist; b. Ann Arbor, Mich., Oct. 20, 1931; s. Kenneth Luster and Ethel (Apfel) H.; m. June Eugenia Miekka, July 2, 1955; children: Kevin L., Thomas G., Scott A., Sheryl A. AB in Geography, U. Mich., 1955. Planning analyst Lincoln Nat. Life Ins. Co., Ft. Wayne, Ind., 1957-70, sr. planning analyst, 1970-72, asst. mgr. policy issue, 1972-77; bd. govs. Am. Numismatic Assn., Colorado Springs, Colo., 1971-87, mus. curator, 1977-82, v.p., 1987-89, pres., 1989-91; pres., owner Ken Hallenbeck Coin Gallery, Inc., Colorado Springs, 1983—; apptd. by Pres. Nixon to U.S. Assay Commn. 1974; testified before Congl. subcom. on coinage and consumer affairs for commemorative coinage, mem. design selection com. for Olympic coin designs, 1992. Contbr. numerous articles to mags. Mem. Rep. Cen. Com., Ft. Wayne, 1972-77, Better Bus. Bur., Colorado Springs; alternate del. to Rep. County and 5th Congl. Dist. Caucuses. With U.S. Army, 1955-57. Fellow Life Mgmt. Inst.; mem. Colorado Springs C. of C., Tokens and Medals Soc. (past pres.), Masons, also numerous local, regional and nat. coin clubs. Republican. Congregationalist. Avocations: numismatics, western history. Office: Ken Hallenbeck Coin Gallery Inc 711 N Nevada Ave Colorado Springs CO 80903-1007

HALLENBERG, ROBERT LEWIS, lawyer; b. Louisville, Oct. 21, 1948; s. Daniel Ward and Anna Mae (Lewis) H.; m. Susan Annette Shaffer, Nov. 29, 1980; children: Shea F., Jonathan E.R., Robert Lewis Jr. BA, U. Ky., 1970, JD, 1973; LLM in Taxation, U. Miami (Fla.), 1974. Bar: Ky. 1973, U.S. Dist. Ct. (we. dist.) Ky. 1975, U.S. Tax Ct. 1986. Ptnr. firm Woodward, Hobson & Fulton, Louisville, 1974—; adj. prof. U. Louisville Sch. Law, 1974-80. Bd. dirs. Louisville Theatrical Assocs., 1980-90, v.p., sec., 1985-90; bd. dirs. Goodwill Industries Ky., 1987-93, sec. 1988-91; pres. Louisville Estate Planning Coun., 1979-80; Bd. dirs. Louisville Estate Planning Forum, 1986-93, sec., 1992-93; mem. Estate Planning Coun. of Louisville, bd. dirs. 1989-95, pres. 1993-94. Fellow Am. Coll. Trust and Estate Counsel; mem. ABA (subchpt. com. 1974-77, real property, probate and trust com. 1985—), Ky. Bar Assn. (sec. tax com. 1984-85). Republican. Episcopalian. Clubs: Pendennis, Owl Creek Country (bd. dirs. 1988-91, pres. 1989-90, treas. 1990-91). Office: Woodward Hobson & Fulton 2500 Nat City Tower Louisville KY 40202

HALLER, ANN CORDWELL, secondary school educator; b. Denver, July 2, 1944; d. Robert William and Dorothy Warne (Dahlberg) Cordwell; m. Frederick Ray Haller, Sept. 18, 1965; children: Michael Frederick, Lori Ann. BA in Pre-Med. Scis., Univ. Montana, 1966; MA in Anatomy, Univ. N.D., 1969; PhD in Anatomy, La. State Univ., 1975. Instr. dept. anatomy, sch. medicine Univ. N.D., Grand Forks, 1969-71; instr. dept. biol. scis. Univ. New Orleans, 1975-76; tchr. Kellogg (Idaho) Joint Sch. Dist. #391, 1978—; head class adv. Kellogg H.S., 1980—; mem. faculty adv. com. Nat. Honor Soc., Kellogg. Bd. dirs. Nat. Sci. Scholars Program, Idaho, other scholarship bds., West Shoshone Hosp., Kellogg, 1977-79; mem. Idaho health Sys. Agy., Boise, 1976-79. Recipient Centennial Tchr. Idaho award NIH, 1986. Mem. DAR, Lamaze Internat. (Lamaze childbirth instr. 1978—), Nat. Sci. Tchrs. Assn., Philanthropic Ednl. Orgn., Sigma Xi, Delta Kappa Gamma. Lutheran. Avocations: gardening, reading, classical music, dog training, travel. Home: 804 Country Club Ln PO Box 923 Pinehurst ID 83850-0923 Office: Kellogg Joint Sch Dist 391 Jacobs Gulch Rd Kellogg ID 83837

HALLER, ARCHIBALD ORBEN, sociologist, educator; b. San Diego, Jan. 15, 1926; s. Archie O. and Eleanor (Brizzee) H.; m. Hazel Laura Zimmerman, Feb. 15, 1947 (dec. 1985); children: Elizabeth Ann, Stephanie Lynn Bylin, William John; m. Maria Camila Omegna Rocha, Apr. 12, 1986 (div. 1987); m. Maria Cristina Del Peloso, Sept. 16, 1989; stepchildren: Graziella, Camila. BA magna cum laude, Hamline U., 1950; MA, U. Minn., 1951; PhD, U. Wis., 1954. Assoc. prof., then prof. sociology Mich. State U., East Lansing, 1956-65; postdoctoral rschr. U. Wis., Madison, 1954-56, vis. prof., summer 1964, prof. sociology and rural sociology, 1965-94, emeritus prof., 1994—; affiliated faculty Indsl. Rels. Rsch. Inst., U. Wis., Madison, 1975-94; faculty in Latin Am. and Iberian studies U. Wis., Madison, 1965-94; affiliated faculty Inst. Environ. Studies, U. Wis., Madison, 1990-94; Fulbright prof. sociology Rural U. of Brazil, 1962, U. Sao Paulo, 1974, 87-90, Fulbright travel grantee Univs. Sao Paulo, Brasilia, Pernambuco, Paraiba, and Ceara, Brazil, 1979; vis. prof. Brigham Young U., Provo, Utah, 1973, Fed. U. Minas Gerais, Brazil, 1998; disting. vis. prof. rural sociology Ohio State U., 1982-83; vis. fellow Australian Nat. U., 1981; cons. Fed. U., Pernambuco, 1994, UNESCO, 1989; cons. on Amazonian rsch. Govt. of Brazil, 1991-94, 97; cons. for nat. social change to Pres. of Brazil, 1994-96, others; organizer symposia on Brazil; faculty of agrarian scis. of Pará, 1997, 98, Ind. U., Bangladesh, 1998. Author: The Occupational Aspiration Scale: Theory, Structure and Correlates, 1963, 71, The Socioeconomic Macroregions of Brazil--1970, 1983; co-editor (with R.M. Hauser et al) Social Structure and Behavior: Essays in Honor of William Hamilton Sewell, 1982; editor spl. issues Luso-Brazilian Rev.; author rsch. monographs and tech. articles; contbr. articles to profl. jours.; contbr. to theories of societal status allocation, to the demographic structure of societal inequality, to identifying of the socioeconomic development regions of Brazil, and to the measurement of internat. devel. Mem. Mich. Com. on Mental Health Policies, 1961-62, Nat. Exec. Res., 1959-66; mem. sociology fellowship panel Coun. on Internat. Exch. Scholars, 1977-81, chmn., 1981. Decorated Grand Officer Order of Merit of Labor, Govt. of Brazil, 1981; univ. fellow U. Wis., 1954. Fellow AAAS, Am. Sociol. Assn.; mem. Internat. Rural Sociol. Assn., Internat. Sociol. Assn., L.Am. Rural Sociol. Assn., Midwest Sociol. Assn., Sociol. Rsch. Assn., L.Am. Studies Assn., N.Y. Acad. Scis., Rural Sociol. Soc. (pres. 1970-71, rep. AAAS 1973-86, Disting. Rural Sociologist 1990), Univ. Club, Sigma Xi, Gamma Sigma Delta, Phi Beta Kappa. Home: 529 Edward St Madison WI 53711-1207 Office: U Wis 311 Agriculture Hall Madison WI 53706

HALLER, CALVIN JOHN, banker; b. Buffalo, July 9, 1925; s. John Martin and and Emelia (George) H.; m. Yvette Ann Hogrewe, June 12, 1948; children: Cary John, Darlene Ann Haller Kalfahs. B.S. in Bus. Adminstrn. with distinction, U. Buffalo, 1949. With Buffalo Savs. Bank (now Goldome), from 1949, now ret. pres. Western N.Y. Bd. dirs. Niagara Luth. Nursing Homes, Cerebral Palsy Assn., Buffalo, Children's Found., Erie County, Buffalo Fedn. of Nieghborhood Ctrs.; bd. trustees Niagara Luth. Homes Found., Inc.; trustee, past pres. Met. YMCA Buffalo and Erie County; chmn. bd. trustees YMCA Greater Buffalo; trustee emeritus, past chmn. bd. Keuka Coll. Lt. (j.g.) USNR, 1943-46. Mem. N.Y. Soc. Security Analysts, Newcomen Soc. N.Am., Nat. Assn. Bus. Economists, U. Buffalo Alumni Assn., Beta Gamma Sigma. Lutheran. Clubs: Mason. Clubs (Buffalo), Country (Buffalo), Bond (Buffalo), Buffalo (Buffalo), Equality (Buffalo). Home: 235 Westfall Dr Tonawanda NY 14150-7136

HALLER, CHARLES EDWARD, engineering consultant; b. Fairfield, Conn., Sept. 5, 1924; s. William Charles and Gertrude Ida Mae (Belinski) H.; m. Eleanor Margret Hoffman, Oct. 11, 1950; children: Carolyn, Debra Lynn, Mark, Charles. Student, Yale U., 1943-44; BEE, Rensselaer Poly. Inst., 1947. Project engr. Western Union Telco., N.Y.C., 1948-56; assoc. lab. dir. ITT Labs., Nutley, N.J., 1956-62; v.p., dir. ops. ITT Worldcom, N.Y.C., 1962-67; pres. ITT Def. Communications, Nutley, N.J., 1967-74; mng. dir. I.O. ITT Telecom N.Am., Nutley, N.J., 1974-83; group gen. mgr., pres. ITT Asia Pacific, N.Y.C., 1983-87; cons. Internat. Enterprises, Kinnelon, N.J., 1987—; Author: Communications Switching Systems, 1964. With USN, 1943-46. Fellow IEEE (life). Republican. Avocations: politics, bowling, golf, reading, travel. Home and Office: 134 Summit Ter Kinnelon NJ 07405-2420

HALLER, EUGENE ERNEST, materials scientist, educator; b. Basel, Switzerland, Jan. 5, 1943; s. Eugen and Maria Anne Haller; m. Marianne Elisabeth Schlittler, May 26, 1973; children: Nicole Marianne, Isabelle Cathrine. Diploma in Physics, U. Basel, 1967, PhD in Physics, 1970. Postdoctoral asst. Lawrence Berkeley (Calif.) Lab., 1971-73, staff scientist, then sr. staff scientist, 1973-80, faculty sr. scientist, 1980—; assoc. prof. U. Calif., Berkeley, 1980-82, prof. materials sci., 1982—; co-chmn. Materials Rsch. Soc. Symposia, Boston, 1982, 89, Internat. Conf. on Shallow Levels in Semiconductors, Berkeley, 1984, 94; chair 20th Internat. Conf. on Defects in Semicondrs., 1999; mem. rev. com. instrument div. Brookhaven Nat. Lab., Upton, N.Y., 1987-93; mem. Japanese tech. panel on sensors NSF-Nat. Acad. Sci., Washington, 1988; vis. prof. Imperial Coll. Sci., Tech. and Medicine, London, 1991. Editorial adv. bd. Jour. Phys. and Chem. Solids, 1993—, Material Sci. Founds., 1998—; contbr. to numerous profl. publs. U.S. Sr. scientist award Alexander von Humboldt Soc., Germany, 1986, Max-Planck Rsch. award, 1994; rsch. fellow Miller Inst. Basic Rsch., Berkeley, 1990. Fellow Am. Phys. Soc. (James C. McGroddy prize in new materials 1999); mem. AAAS, Materials Rsch. Soc., Swiss Phys. Soc., Sigma Xi. Achievements include patents in surface passivation of semiconductors, synthesis of crystalline carbon nitride potentially a superhard material, and far infrared germanium laser. Office: U Calif Berkeley 553 Evans Hall Berkeley CA 94720

HALLER, IRMA TOGNOLA, secondary education educator; b. Bainbridge, N.Y., Aug. 25, 1937; d. Tullio and Margaretha (Fuchs) Tognola; m. Hans R. Haller, July 11, 1964. BA, SUNY, Albany, 1959; MEd in Teaching of Social Studies, Boston U., 1962. Tchr. social studies Chenango Valley Jr.-Sr. High Sch., Binghamton, N.Y., 1959-64; tchr. social studies and English Sidney (N.Y.) High Sch., 1964—, chair dept. social studies, 1986—; mem. tchr. edn. adv. bd. SUNY, Oneonta, 1983-97, chair, 1985-88, 93-94; active local sch. improvement coms. Mem. steering com. Sidney Ctrl. Schs. Bus. Edn. Cmty. Partnership, 1992—. N.Y. State Electric and Gas Corp. grantee, 1985; Catskill Regional Tchr. Ctr. grantee, 1985, 87, 89. Mem. Nat. Coun. Social Studies, N.Y. State Social Studies Coun., N.Y. State United Tchrs., Catskill Area Social Studies Coun. (newsletter editor 1989-90), Sidney Tchrs. Assn., Phi Delta Kappa. Avocations: reading, walking. Office: Sidney H S 95 W Main St Sidney NY 13838-1601

HALLER, KAREN SUE, writer; b. St. Louis, Apr. 25, 1935; d. Frank Michael and Frieda Catherine (Hartmann) Kratoville; m. Albert John Haller; children: Christopher Karl, Debra Lynn. BS in Edn., U. Mo., 1956. Tchr. elem. sch. Ladue (Mo.) Sch. Dist., 1956-60; hearing testing tech. Spl. Sch. Dist. St. Louis County, 1975, 76. Author, photographer: Walking with Wildflowers, 1994; contbg. photographer: Wildflowers of Arkansas, 1984, Sensitive Plants of St. Francis National Forests, 1984, Wildflowers of North America, 1987. Asst. leader, leader brownie troop Girl Scouts Am., 1969, 70, jr. girl scouts troop, 1970, 71; advisor Co-ed explorer post Boy Scouts Am., 1976-80; bus tour guide, chmn. St. Louis Vis. Ctr., 1966-70; mem. mortar bd. U. Mo., Columbia, 1955; vol. interpreter Sophie M. Sachs Butterfly House, 1998-99; Earthwatch vol. Bees and Orchids of Brazil project, 1998. Mem. Nat. Audubon Soc. (program chmn. 1987-90, awards chmn. 1990, Dorr scholar 1989), Mo. Native Plant Soc. (pres. 1991-93, Erna R. Eisendrath Edn. award 1994), Webster Groves Nature Study Soc. (pres. 1978-80, conservation chmn. 1983-86), Sierra Club, Naiads (v.p., pres., treas., sec.). Avocations: hiking, canoeing, camping, sewing, travel. Home and Office: 618 Spring Meadows Dr Ballwin MO 63011-3451

HALLER, KATHLEEN, nursing educator, family nurse practitioner; b. Eagle Bend, Minn., May 6, 1936; d. William John and Violet (Roach) Juola; m. Christian A. Haller, Dec. 27, 1958; children: Anne Marie Haller Wildfong, Barbara Jane Haller Moser, Joyce Ellen Haller Weise. Diploma in Nursing, Rockford (Ill.) Meml. Hosp., 1957; BSN, No. Ill. U., 1975; MSN, Mich. State U., 1994. Obstet. instr. Rockford Meml. Hosp., 1958-59, nurse labor and delivery, 1957-58, 59-61, nursing educator, 1973-74; sch. nurse Rockford Bd. Edn., 1974; psychiat. staff nurse Singer Zone Ctr., Rockford, 1975-76; staff devel. dir. Butterworth Hosp., Grand Rapids, Mich., 1976-83; mem. faculty Grand Valley State U., Allendale, Mich., 1991—; mem. staff devel. coordinating com. Butterworth Hosp., 1983. Mem. adminstrv. bd. 1st United Meth. Ch., Grand Rapids, 1988; active Hist. Commn., Wyoming, Mich., 1994. Mem. ANA, Mich. Nurses Assn. (mem. human rights com. 1989), Am. Congress on Nursing and Health Care Econs., Sigma Theta Tau. Democrat. Avocations: needlework, reading. Office: Grand Valley State U Lake Michigan Dr Allendale MI 49401

HALLER, WILLIAM PAUL, analytical chemist, robotics specialist; b. Orange, N.J., Nov. 23, 1957; s. William Charles and Patricia Marie (Scavone) H.; children: Robert William, Alicia Ann. BS in Biochemistry, Fairleigh Dickinson U., 1980. Rsch. chemist Internat. Paint Co., Union, N.J., 1980-83; analytical quality assurance chemist Ortho-McNeil Pharm. Corp., Raritan, N.J., 1983—; quality assurance robotics specialist Ortho Pharm. Corp., Raritan, N.J., 1985—; steering com. Johnson & Johnson Intercompany Robotics Interest Group, Raritan, 1985-87, Johnson & Johnson Tech. Forum Group, 1995—. Co-author: Advances in Laboratory Automation-Robotics, 1986, 90. Recipient Johnson & Johnson Achievement award, 1991, Pioneer in Lab. Robotics award, 1995. Mem. AAAS, Am. Chem. Soc., Lab. Robotics Interest Group (exec. com.). Democrat. Achievements include development of protocols and criteria for the validation of robotic systems in the analytical lab., automate analytical methods to robotic systems, customized apparatus to help in automating analytical methods to robotic systems, development of standardized platforms and criteria for robotic systems to be used within the J&J family of companies worldwide allowing for easier and more efficient transfer of technology between operating cos. and maintaining a high level of compliance with regulatory agencies. Office: Ortho-McNeil Pharm Corp PO Box 300 Rt 202 Raritan NJ 08869-0602

HALLETT, CAROL BOYD, air transportation executive; b. Oakland, Calif., Oct. 16, 1937; married. Student, U. Oreg., San Francisco State Coll. Assemblywoman Calif. State Assembly, Sacramento, 1976-82, minority floor leader, 1979-82; cons., dir. Found. for Individual and Econ. Freedom, Sacramento, 1982-86; dir. of parks and recreation Calif., 1982-83; western regional dir. Citizens For Am., Sacramento, 1983-84; asst. to U.S. Sec. Interior, 1984-85; nat. field dir. Citizens For Am., Washington, 1985-86; amb. Am. embassy, Nassau, Bahamas, 1986-89; U.S. commr. of customs U.S. Customs Svc., Washington, 1989-93; sr. govt. rels. advisor Collier, Shannon, Rill & Scott, Washington, 1993-95; pres., CEO Air Transport Assn. Am., Washington, 1995; head U.S. Presdl. del. for celebration St. Kitts and Nevis, 1983; mem. ofcl. U.S. Presdl. del. to observe Guatemalan presdl. election, 1985; cons. trade Clark Co., Paso Robles, Calif., 1993-95. Recipient Order of Merit King Juan Carlos I of Spain, 1994; named Woman of Yr., Bahamian Rev. mag., 1988; Paul Harris fellow Rotary, Nassau, 1989. Office: Air Transport Assn Am Ste 1100 1301 Pennsylvania Ave NW Washington DC 20004-1707

HALLETT, CHARLES ARTHUR, JR., English and humanities educator; b. New Haven, July 19, 1935; s. Charles Arthur and Bridie D. (McIntyre) H.; m. Elaine Stewartson, Nov. 7, 1958. BA, New Sch. for Social Rsch., 1961; MA, Columbia U., 1963; DFA, Yale U., 1967. Mem. faculty Fordham U., Bronx, N.Y., 1967—, assoc. prof. English, 1971-81, prof., 1981—; asst. project dir. NEH Shakespeare Summerfest, N.Y.C., 1981; vis. prof. U. Warwick, Eng., 1978, Loyola U., New Orleans, 1994. Author: Middleton's Cynics, 1975, The Revenger's Madness, 1981, Analyzing Shakespeare's Action, 1991; (play) Aaron Burr, also articles; contbr. to Ency. Americana. Fellow Lawrence Langner Theatre Guild Found., 1965-66; Am. Coun. Learned Socs. grantee, 1981. Home: 116 E 91st St Apt 5 New York NY 10128-1667 Office: English Dept Fordham U Bronx NY 10458

HALLETT, E. BRUCE, III, publishing executive; b. Rochester, N.Y., Sept. 22, 1949; s. E. Bruce and Constance (Carpenter) H.; m. Deborah Ann Donahue, May 8, 1982; children: Cleary Carpenter, E. Bruce IV, Katherine Thrall, Thomas Henry Walker, Emma Brewster. BA, Princeton U., 1967-71; MBA, Columbia U., 1979-80. Writer, editor N.Y. Daily News, N.Y.C., 1971-79; financial analyst Time Inc., N.Y.C., 1980-81, group dir. devel., 1986, asst. bus. mgr. Sports Illustrated, 1981-82, bus. mgr. Sports Illustrated, 1982-84, asst. to pub. Sports Illustrated, 1985-86, internat. gen. mgr. TIME Mag., 1987-88, mng. dir. Time Inc. mags. Australia, 1988-95, pres. TIME Mag., 1995—. Mem. Elanora Country Club (Narabeen, NSW, Australia), Baltusrol Golf Club. Office: Time Mag 1271 Avenue Of The Americas New York NY 10020-1300

HALLETT, MARK, physician, neurologist, health research institute administrator; b. Phila., Oct. 22, 1943; s. Joseph Woodrow and Estelle (Barg) H.; m. Judith E. Peller, June 26, 1966; children: Nicholas L., Victoria C. B.A. magna cum laude, Harvard U., 1965, M.D. cum laude, 1969. Diplomate Am. Bd. Psychiatry and Neurology. Resident in neurology Mass. Gen. Hosp., Boston, 1972-75; Moseley fellow Harvard U., London, 1975-76; lectr., assoc. prof. neurology Harvard U., Boston, 1976-84; head clin. neurophysiology lab. Brigham and Women's Hosp., Boston, 1976-84; clin. dir. Nat. Inst. Neurol. Disorders and Stroke, NIH, Bethesda, Md., 1984—. Author: (with others) Entrapment Neuropathies, 1990, 3rd edit., 1998; editor: (with J. Jankovic) Therapy with Botulinum Toxin, 1994; contbr. numerous articles to profl. jours. Bd. dirs. Easter Seals Rsch. Found., Chgo., 1985-87; mem. med. adv. bd. Nat. Parkinson Found., Miami, 1985—, Dystonia Med. Rsch. Found., Chgo., 1989-93, Benign Essential Blepharospasm Rsch. Found., Beaumont, 1990—, Myoclonus Rsch. Found., Fort Lee, N.J., 1989—. Mem. Am. Assn. Electrodiagnostic Medicine (pres. 1991-92), Am. Acad. Neurology, Am. Neurol. Assn., Am. Clin. Neurophysiology Soc., Soc. for Neurosci., Movement Disorder Soc. (pres. 1999—), Phi Beta Kappa, Alpha Omega Alpha. Democrat. Jewish. Home: 5147 Westbard Ave Bethesda MD 20816-1413 Office: NINDS NIH Bldg 10 Rm 5N226 10 Center Dr MSC 1428 Bethesda MD 20892-1428

HALLETT, WILLIAM JARED, nuclear engineer; b. Rock Springs, Wyo., Apr. 12, 1923; s. William Jared and Florence Myrtle (Miller) H.; m. Marjorie Louise Taylor, Dec. 25, 1942; children—Katherine O. Hallett Rembert, Carolyn R. Hallett Kortangen, Helen L. Hallett Warren, David William. B.S. in Chem. Engring., U. Colo., 1944; postgrad., UCLA, 1957-58, 62-70, No. Ill. U., 1973. Registered profl. nuclear engr., Calif. Engr. Tenn. Eastman Corp., Oak Ridge, 1944-47; sect. head Fairchild E & A Corp., Oak Ridge, 1947-50; project mgr. AI Div. Rockwell Internat., Canoga Park, Calif., 1950-66; div. dir., mgr. Argonne Nat. Lab., Ill., 1968-86; ret., 1986. Contbg. author: Nuclear Reactor Engineering, 1963; Nuclear Power and Its Environmental Effects, 1980. Bd. dirs. Simi Valley Unified Sch. Dist., Calif., 1965-68. Republican. Methodist. Avocations: photography, art collecting, travel.

HALLEY, DIANE ESTHER, artist; b. Jasper, Ind., May 14, 1939; d. John and Esther Margaret (Kruse) Darden; m. Norman B. Halley, May 21, 1966; 1 child, William Tull Halley. BS in Elem. Edn., Ind. State U., 1961. Tchr. 4th grade New Albany, Ind., 1961, Seymour, Ind., 1962-64, Westminster, Colo., 1964-68; portrait artist Arvada, Colo., 1979—. Paintings (included in books) Colorado, 1990, Best of Watercolor Painting Textures, 1997. Pres. Clear Creek Valley Med. Aux., Lakewood, Colo., 1973-74, 91-92. Recipient Founders award Colo. Watercolor Soc., 1992, Grumbacher award Pikes Peak Watercolor Soc., 1995, Pres.'s award Colo. Watercolor Soc., 1994. Mem. Nat. Assn. Women Artists (Cecil Schapiro Meml. award 1998), Nat. Watercolor Soc. (Del Mar Coll. award 1982), Catherine Lorillard Wolf Art Club (Adriana Zahn award 1985, Cynthia Goodgal award 1986), Rocky Mountain Nat. Watermedia Soc., Kans. Watercolor Soc. (Am. artist cash award 1999). Avocations: Bible study, snow skiing, playing bridge, gardening. Home: 6631 Osceola Ct Arvada CO 80003-6426

HALLEY, JAMES WOODS, physics educator; b. Chgo., Nov. 16, 1938; m. Merile Hobbs; 2 children. BS, MIT, 1961; PhD, U. Calif., Berkeley, 1965. Tchg. asst. U. Calif., Berkeley, 1961-63, NSF predoctoral fellow, 1963-65; NSF postdoctoral fellow Faculte des Scis., Orsay, France, 1965-66; asst. prof. U. Calif., Berkeley, 1966-68; assoc. prof. U. Minn., Mpls., 1968-77, prof. physics, 1977—, fellow Supercomputer Inst., 1989—, grad. faculty materials sci., 1989—; vis. prof. Oxford U., 1973, Harwell AERE, 1973, U. Oreg., 1975, Yale U., 1976, Brookhaven U., 1976, 79, Harvard U., 1979, Mich. State U., 1980, Argonne, 1981—, Inst. for Theoretical Physics, Santa Barbara, 1983, 97, 98, chemistry dept. U. Calif., Santa Barbara, 1984, U. Calif., Berkeley, 1993; IBM Almaden Rsch. Ctr., 1987, Australian Nat. U., 1988; cons. 3M, 1985-89, UNESCO, 1986, GM Corp., 1989-90, Ednl. Testing Svc., 1989; mem. GRE bd. examiners Ednl. Testing Svc., 1991-96. Author: Physics of Human Motion, 1981; editor 5 books; contbr. over 150 articles to profl. jours. Recipient George Taylor Tchg. award, 1979, McMillan professorship, 1979; Bush fellow, 1983-84; grantee NSF, 1972-79, 95—, Rsch. Corp., 1970-72, Corrosion Ctr., 1980-92, Ednl. Devel. Program, 1973, 79, 3M, 1982, IBM Advanced Edn. Project, 1985, Dept. Edn., 1986, US-Australia travel grantee NSF, 1987, rsch. grantee IBM, 1988-90, grantee Electric Power Rsch. Inst., 1988-90, Dept. Energy, 1990—, Sumitomo Metal Industries, 1992-93, NASA, 1992-95. Fellow Am. Phys. Soc.; mem. AAAS, Materials Rsch. Soc. Achievements include research in theory of disorder in condensed matter, statistics and dynamics of polymers, physics of the fluid-solid interface, high temperature superconductivity, condensate fraction in bose superfluids. Office: Univ Minn Sch Physics and Astronomy Minneapolis MN 55455

HALLEY, JANET CARNAHAN, secondary education educator; b. Tulsa, Okla., Nov. 19, 1930; d. Chester Carroll and Auretta Ida (Stephens) Carnahan; 1 child, Carol Anne Goodhue. Student, Coll. of Emporia, Kans., 1948-50; BS, Iona Coll., 1981, MS in Edn., 1986. Tchr. K-8 Lyon County Rural Sch., Olpe, Kans., 1950-51; home and substitute tchr. Union Free Sch. Dist., Lyndenhurst, N.Y., 1953-56; tchr., adminstr. Far Hills (N.J.) Country Day Sch., 1956-77; adminstr. K-8 Convent of the Sacred Heart, Greenwich, Conn., 1977-79; tchr. mid. sch. Convent of the Sacred Heart, Greenwich, 1979—; mem. network faculty devel. com. Network of Sacred Heart Schs., Newton, Mass., 1992-94, mem. inst. planning com., 1990-91, 92-93, mem. editl. bd., 1996—. Life deacon, ch. coun. pres. United Ch. of Christ, 1999—. Mem. Nat. Coun. Tchrs. of English, Phi Delta Kappa. Avocations: reading, classical music, creative writing, walking, computers. Office: Convent of Sacred Heart 1177 King St Greenwich CT 06831-2998

HALLEY, PETER, painter, educator; b. N.Y.C., Sept. 24, 1953. BA, Yale U.; MFA, U. New Orleans. instr. painting and sculpture Sch. Visual Arts, N.Y.C., 1989—. Exhibited works at Whitney Mus., N.Y., 1987, Guggenheim Mus., N.Y., 1988, Mus. Fine Arts, Boston, 1988, Carnegie Mus. Art, Pitts., 1988, Ft. Worth Mus. Tex., 1989, Ringling Mus. Art, Sarasota, Fla., 1989, Bklyn. Mus., N.Y., 1989, Touring Europ Retrospective, Switzerland, France, Spain and Amsterdam, 1991-92; commd. artist Chase Manhattan Bank, N.Y., 1989. Office: Peter Halley Studios 526 W 26th St Rm 920 New York NY 10001-5541*

HALLEY, SAMUEL HAMPTON, III, architect; b. Lexington, Ky., Feb. 8, 1941; s. Samuel Hampton and Mary Ford (Offutt) H.; m. Suzanne Shelby Fish, Aug. 4, 1962; children: Samuel Hampton IV, Benjamin Helm, Elizabeth Simpson. BArch, U. Ky., 1966. Registered architect Ky., Fla., Ohio, Ill., Ind., N.C., W.Va. Intern architect Chrisman Miller & Wallace, Lexington, Ky., 1964-70; architect McLoney & Tune, Lexington, 1970-71; ptnr. Hill-Halley Architects, Danville, Ky., 1971-74; architect Scruggs & Hammond, Lexington, 1974-75; pres. Omni Architects, Lexington, 1975—; mem. adv. com. dept. landscape arch. U. Ky., Lexington, 1992—, chair, 1987-92; mem. adv. com. Lexington C.C., 1982-88;. Author: (computer software) Project Mgmt. 1, 1981, Project Mgmt. 2, 1982. Mem. Lexington Fayette Urban County Govt. City Coun., Lexington, 1993; bd. dirs. Emerson Ctr., Lexington, 1986—; pres. Gardenside Neighborhood Assn., Lexington, 1981—. Recipient Disting. Svc. award U. Ky., 1982, Am. Soc. Landscape Architects, 1986. Mem. AIA (East Ky. chpt. pres. 1976, Student Medal award 1966), Ky. Soc. Architects (pres. 1981, C. Julian Oberwarth Svc. award 1992, Disting. Svc. award 1986), C. of C. (CEO Roundtable 1990-94). Avocation: boating. Office: Omni Architects 212 N Upper St Ste 200 Lexington KY 40507-1001

HALLGREN, RICHARD EDWIN, meteorologist; b. Kersey, Pa., Mar. 15, 1932; s. Edwin Leonard and Edith Marie H.; m. Maxine Hope Anderson, Apr. 17, 1954; children: Scott, Douglas, Lynette. BS, Pa. State U., 1953, PhD, 1960; DSc (hon.), SUNY, 1989. Systems engr. IBM Corp., 1960-64; sci. adv. to asst. sec. of commerce, 1964-66; dir. world weather systems ESSA, Rockville, Md., 1966-69; asst. adminstrn. ESSA, 1969-70; asst. adminstr. NOAA, Rockville, 1970-71; asso. adminstr. environ. monitoring and prediction NOAA, 1971-73, asst. adminstr. for ocean and atmospheric scis., 1977-79; dep. dir. Nat. Weather Service, Silver Spring, Md., 1973-77; dir. Nat. Weather Service, 1979-88; exec. dir. Am. Meteorol. Soc., 1988—; permanent U.S. rep. World Meteorol. Orgn., 1980-88. Contbr. articles to sci. jours. Served with USAF, 1954-56. Recipient Arthur S. Flemming award U.S. C. of C., 1968, Gold medal Dept. Commerce, 1969, Internat. Meteorol. Orgn. prize World Meteorol. Orgn., 1990; named Meritorious Sr. Exec., 1980, Disting. Sr. Exec., 1986; alumni fellow Pa. State U., 1987. Fellow AAAS, Am. Meteorol. Soc. (pres., C.F. Brooks award); mem. Oceanographic Soc., Am. Geogphys. Union, Sigma Xi. Lutheran. Home: 11428 Cedar Ridge Dr Potomac MD 20854-3761 Office: Am Meteorol Svc 1200 New York Ave NW Ste 410 Washington DC 20005-6115

HALLIDAY, ALAN WOOD, neurologist; b. West Point, N.Y., Dec. 16, 1953; s. Willis Wood Jr. and Ruth Marcella (Bartlow) H.; m. Ann Elizabeth O'Connor, Dec. 18, 1982; children: Stephen, Connor. BS, Ind. U. of Pa., 1976; MD, Pa. State U., 1980. Diplomate Am. Bd. Psychiatry and Neurology. Staff neurologist Brooke Army Med. Ctr., San Antonio, 1984-85, asst. chief dept. neurology, 1985-87, chief dept. neurology, 1987—; prof. neurology U. Tex. Health Sci. Ctr., San Antonio, 1996—, USUHS, Bethesda, Md., 1994—. Col. U.S. Army, 1980—. Fellow Am. Acad. Neurology, Uniformed Svcs. Orgn. Neurologists (sec.-treasx. 1994—). Episcopalian. E-mail:colualanuhalliday@smtplink.bamc.amedd.army.mil. HOme: 18227 Open Forest San Antonio TX 78259 Office: Brooke Army Med Ctr 3851 Roger Brooke Dr Fort Sam Houston TX 78234

HALLIDAY, IAN, astronomer; b. Lloydminster, Sask., Can., Nov. 10, 1928; s. Clarence Peter and Edith Victoria (Phillips) H.; m. Norma Lillian Mobley, July 7, 1951; children—John Douglas, Janet Elizabeth. B.A., U. Toronto, 1949, M.A., 1950, Ph.D., 1954. Sr. sci. officer Dominion Obs., Dept. Energy, Mines and Resources, Ottawa, 1952-70; sr. research officer Herzberg Inst. Astrophysics, Nat. Research Council Can., Ottawa, 1970-90, guest worker, 1990-96. Author research papers in field; editor: Jour. Royal Astron. Soc. Can, 1970-75; co-editor: Solid Particles in the Solar System, 1980. Recipient Queen's Silver Jubilee medal, 1977, Polish Medal of Merit, 1976. Fellow Royal Soc. Can.; mem. Internat. Astron. Union (pres. commn. 22 1976-79), Royal Astron. Soc. Can. (pres. 1980-82, hon. pres. 1989-93), Can. Astron. Soc., Am. Astron. Soc., Meteoritical Soc., Planetary Soc., Internat. Halley Watch (chmn. steering group 1985-90). Home: 825 Killeen Ave, Ottawa, ON Canada K2A 2X8

HALLIDAY, JOHN MEECH, investment company executive; b. St. Louis, Oct. 16, 1936; s. William Norman and Vivian Viola (Meech) H.; m. Martha Layne Griggs, June 30, 1962; children: Richard M., Elizabeth Halliday Traut. BS, U.S. Naval Acad., 1958; MBA, Harvard U., 1964. Dir. budgeting and planning Automatic Tape Control, Bloomington, Ill., 1964-66; dir. planning Ralston-Purina, St. Louis, 1966-67, v.p. subsidiary, 1967-68, dir. internat. banking, 1967-68; v.p. Servicetime Corp., St. Louis, 1968-70; assoc. R.W. Halliday Assocs., Boise, Idaho, 1970-87; v.p. Sawtooth Comm. Corp., Boise, 1970-73, Comdr. Corp., 1979-81; pres., CEO, bd. dirs. ML, Ltd., San Francisco, 1979—, H.W.L. Inc., San Francisco, 1985-93; pres. Halliday Labs., Inc., 1980-91; exec. v.p., bd. dirs. Franchise Fin. Corp. Am., Phoenix, 1980-85; bd. dirs., v.p. Harvard Bus. Sch. Assn. No. Calif., 1980-87; pres., CEO, bd. dirs. Cycletorl Diversified Industries, Inc., 1992—; guest lectr. U. Calif. Berkeley, 1991—, Calif. Bus.-Higher Edn. Forum, 1995-98. Pres. Big Bros. San Francisco, 1978-81; trustee, pres. U. Calif.-Santa Cruz Found., 1988—; mem. ad hoc com. on corrections Calif. State Senate, 1995-96; fellow bd. visitors and fellows viticulture and enology U. Calif., Davis, 1999. Mem. Restaurant Assn. (v.p. 1969-70), Olympic Club (San Francisco), Scott Valley Tennis Club (Mill Valley, Calif.). Republican. Episcopalian. Home: 351 Corte Madera Ave Mill Valley CA 94941-1013 Office: 55 New Montgomer St San Francisco CA 94105-3402

HALLIDAY, JOSEPH WILLIAM, lawyer; b. N.Y.C., Aug. 9, 1938; s. Joseph John and Marie (Marro) H.; m. Vivian Ross Talbird, July 10, 1960; children: Katherine Ann Langan, Mary Allison Shaw. AB, Fordham U., 1960, LLB, 1963. Bar: N.Y. 1964, D.C. 1965. Assoc. White & Case, N.Y.C., 1965-72, ptnr., 1972-85; ptnr. Skadden Arps Slate Meagher & Flom, LLP, N.Y.C., 1985—; lectr. Ctr. for Internat. Banking Studies, U. Va., Banking Law Inst., Inst. Internat. Rsch., Law and Bus., Euromoney, Practicing Law Inst. Editor-in-chief Fordham Law Rev., 1962-63. Served to 1st lt. U.S. Army, 1963-65. Mem. ABA, N.Y. State Bar Assn., Assn. Bar City N.Y., N.Y. County Lawyers Assn., Larchmont Yacht Club (commodore 1985-86). Republican. Roman Catholic. Avocations: yachting, skiing, golf. Office: Skadden Arps Slate Meagher & Flom LLP 919 3rd Ave New York NY 10022-3902

HALLIDAY, WILLIAM ROSS, retired physician, speleologist, writer; b. Atlanta, May 9, 1926; s. William Ross and Jane (Wakefield) H.; m. Eleanore Hartvedt, July 2, 1951 (dec. 1983); children: Marcia Lynn, Patricia Anne, William Ross III; m. Louise Baird Kinnard, May 7, 1988. BA, Swarthmore Coll., 1946; MD, George Washington U., 1948. Diplomate Am. Bd. Vocat. Experts. Intern Huntington Meml. Hosp., Pasadena, Calif., 1948-49; resident King County Hosp., Seattle, Denver Children's Hosp., L.D.S. Hosp., Salt Lake City, 1950-57; pvt. practice Seattle, 1957-65; with Wash. State Dept. Labor and Industries, Olympia, 1965-76; med. dir. Wash. State Div. Vocat. Rehab., 1976-82; staff physican N.W. Occupational Health Ctr., Seattle, 1983-84; med. dir. N.W. Vocat. Rehab. Group, Seattle, 1984, Comprehensive Med. Rehab. Ctr., Brentwood, Tenn., 1984-87; dep. coroner, King County, Wash., 1964-66; internat. mining speleol. com. on volcanic caves, 1992-98; chmn. Hawaii Speleol. Survey, 1989-97; dir. Western Speleol. Survey, 1957-83, dir. rsch., 1983-96. Author: Adventure Is Underground, 1959, Depths of the Earth, 1966, 76, American Caves and Caving, 1974, 82; co-author: (with Robert Nymeyer) Carlsbad Cavern: The Early Years, 1991; editor Jour. Spelean History, 1968-73; contbr. articles to profl. jours. Mem. Gov.'s North Cascades Study Com., 1967-76; mem. North Cascades Conservation Coun., v.p., 1962-63; pres. Internat. Speleological Found., 1981-87, Internat. Union Speleol. Com. on Volcanic Caves, 1992-98; asst. dir. Internat. Glaciospeleological Survey, 1972-76; chmn. Hawaii Speleol. Survey, 1989-97; bd. dirs. We. Speleol. Survey, 1957-83, dir. rsch., 1983-96. Served to lt. comdr. USNR, 1949-50, 55-57. Recipient medal Geol. Soc. China; named Alumnus of Yr., George Sch., 1992. Fellow Am. Coll. Chest Physicians, Nat. Speleological Soc. (hon. mem. 1965, bd. govs. 1950-94), Explorers Club; mem. AMA, Nat. Trust (Scotland), Mountaineers Club (past trustee), Seattle Tennis Club.

HALLIGAN, JAMES EDMUND, university administrator, chemical engineer; b. Moorland, Iowa, June 23, 1936; s. Raymond Anthony and Margaret Ann (Crawford) H.; m. Ann Elizabeth Sorenson, June 29, 1957; children: Michael, Patrick, Christopher. M.S. in Chem. Engring, Iowa State U., 1962, M.S., 1965, Ph.D., 1968. Registered profl. engr., Okla. Process engr. Humble Oil Co., 1962-64; mem. faculty Tex. Tech U., 1968-77; dean engring. U. Mo., Rolla, 1977-79; dean engring. U. Ark., Fayetteville, 1979-82, vice chancellor for acad. affairs, 1982-83, interim chancellor, 1983-84; pres. N.Mex. State U., Las Cruces, 1984-94, Okla. State U., Stillwater, 1994—; v.p. engring. Kandahar Cons. Ltd.; mem. Gov. Tex. Energy Adv. Council, 1972-74; prof. achievement citation engr. Iowa State U. Coll. Engring., 1984. Served with USAF, 1954-58. Recipient Disting. Teaching award Tex. Tech U., 1972, Disting. Research award, 1975, 76; Disting. Teaching award U. Mo., Rolla, 1978, Disting. Achievement citation Iowa State U. Alumni Assn., 1996. Mem. AIChE, NSPE, Am. Chem. Soc., Am. Soc. Engring. Edn., Rotary, Tau Beta Pi, Phi Kappa Phi, Pi Mu Epsilon. Roman Catholic. Office: Okla State U 107 Whitehurst Stillwater OK 74078-1010

HALLIGAN, KEVIN LEO, lawyer; b. South Orange, N.J., Feb. 1, 1964; s. Kevin Richard and Catherine Ann (Sullivan) H. BA, John Carroll U., 1986; JD, Creighton U., 1989. Bar: Ill. 1989, U.S. Ct. Appeals (7th cir.) 1992, Iowa 1995, U.S. Dist. Ct. (cent. dist.) Ill. 1995, U.S. Dist. Ct. (so. dist.) Iowa 1996. Prosecutor Sangamon County States Attys. Office, Springfield, Ill., 1990-91; assoc. Delano Law Offices, P.C., Springfield, 1991-95, Brooke & O'Brien, P.L.C., Davenport, Iowa, 1995—; corp. dir. H&H Food Sales, Davenport, 1995—. Mem. Dillon Inn of Ct., Kiwanis. Roman Catholic. Avocations: tennis, basketball, fishing, golf. Home: 2546 Middle Rd Davenport IA 52803-3640 Office: Brooke & O'Brien PLC 2322 E Kimberly Rd Davenport IA 52807-7205

HALLIN, DANIEL CLARK, communications educator; b. Palo Alto, Calif., June 11, 1953. BA in Polit. Sci. with honors, U. Calif., Berkeley, 1973, MA in Polit. Sci., 1974, PhD in Polit. Sci., 1980. Rsch. asst. U. Calif., Berkeley, 1974-76, tchg. asst., 1974-75, 78; fellow Freedom Forum Media Studies Ctr., Columbia U., N.Y.C., 1991-92; prof. dept. comm., adj. prof. polit. sci. U. Calif., San Diego, 1992—, chairperson, 1994-97; assoc. Ctr. for War, Peace and News Media; presenter, keynot spkr. various ednl. symposia and confs., most recently at Mid. Tenn. State U., 1993, U. Calif., Berkeley, 1993, U. Pa., 1994, U. Stirling, Scotland, 1994, U. Autonoma de Baja California, Tijuana, Mex., 1994, XIX Ann. Congress of L.Am. Studies Assn., Guadalajara, 1997, U. Brasilia, 1996, Seoul Nat. U., 1997, Westminster U., London, 1998, Nat. U., Athens, Greece, 1998. Author: The "Uncensored War": The Media and Vietnam, 1989, The Presidency, The Press and the People, 1992, We Keep America on Top of the World: Television Journalism and the Public Sphere, 1994; contbr. chpt. to: Critical Theory and Public Life, 1985, Political Communication: Approaches, Studies, Assessments, 1987, Reading the News, 1986, Watching Television, 1986, Is the Cold War Over? Images of the USA and the USSR in Soviet and American Media, 1991, Comparatively Speaking, 1992, Viewing War: How the Media Handled the Persian Gulf, 1994; co-contbr. chpt. to: Taken by Storm: The Media, Public Opinion and U.S. Foreign Policy in the Gulf War, 1994, Mass Media and Society, 1996; mem. editl. bd. Polit. Comm.; acting editor-in-chief Comm. Rev.; contbr. articles and revs. to profl. publs. Pres. Binat. Assn. Schs. of Comm. of the Californias. Recipient 1st prize media studies project essay contest Woodrow Wilson Internat. Ctr. for Scholars, 1990. Mem. Am. Polit. Sci. Assn., L.Am. Studies Assn., Internat. Comm. Assn., Union for Dem. Comm. Home: 3315 31st St San Diego CA 92104-4619 Office: Univ Calif San Diego Dept Comm 0503 La Jolla CA 92093

HALLINAN, JOHN CORNELIUS, mechanical engineering consultant; b. Phila., Feb. 12, 1919; s. John Joseph and Ellen Bridget (Sullivan) H.; m. Eleanor Ruth Denny, July 7, 1945; children: Ann, Mary, Kathleen, Claire (dec.), Joan, John, Patricia, Mark, Michael, Joseph, William, Theresa. BSME, Villanova U., 1940. Design and lab. engr. Am. Bosch, Springfield, Mass., 1946-47; lab. mgr. Baldwin Lima Hamilton, Eddystone, Pa., 1947-54; rsch. engr. Caterpillar Inc., Peoria, Ill., 1954-62, lab. mgr., 1962-72, engring. mgr., 1972-85; engring. cons., Washington, Ill., 1985—. Contbr. articles to profl. jours. Trustee St. Patrick Parish, Washington, 1962-93, lector, 1978—. With USN, 1943-46. Named Engr. of Yr., Peoria Engring. Coun., 1975, Recipient Internal Combustion Engine award Am. Soc. of Mechanical Engineers, 1995. Mem. ASME (chmn. ctrl. Ill. sect. 1962-63, other sectional and regional offices, chmn. Soichiro Honda medal com., divsn. for disting. tech. svc. to diesel engine industry 1992, Internal Combustion Engine award 1995), Soc. Automotive Engrs., Submarine Vets. WWII. Achievements include direction and management of the design and development of large engines, turbocharging of engines, conversion of diesel to spark ignited engines. Home and Office: 700 Crestview Dr Washington IL 61571-1605

HALLINAN, JOSEPH THOMAS, journalist, correspondent; b. Barberton, Ohio, Sept. 3, 1960; s. Neil Patrick and Judith Ann (Tonovitz) H. BS magna cum laude, Boston U., 1984. Reporter The Indpls. Star, 1984-91; nat. corr. Newhouse News Svc., Washington, 1991-99; reporter Chgo. Tribune, 1999—. Recipient Pulitzer prize for investigative reporting, 1991; named Disting. Alumni, Boston U., 1992; Nieman fellow Harvard U., 1997-98. Roman Catholic. Avocations: scuba diving, fishing, travel. Office: Newhouse News Svc 435 N Michigan Ave Chicago IL 60611

HALLINGBY, PAUL, JR., investment banker; b. L.A., Sept. 27, 1919; s. Paul and Ethel Marie (Sutor) H.; m. Allison Lazo, Oct. 9, 1943 (dec. 1965); children: Leigh, Paul Lazo, Allison H. Dodge; m. Jo Ann Davis, Nov. 17, 1994. BA, Stanford U., 1941; postgrad, Harvard U., 1941-42. Salesman First Boston Corp., N.Y.C., 1946-48; v.p. E.F. Hutton & Co., N.Y.C., 1948-52, Middle South Utilities Inc., N.Y.C., 1952-58; chmn., chief exec. officer White, Weld & Co. (merger Merrill Lynch, Pierce, Fenner & Smith Inc.), N.Y.C., 1958-78; vice chmn. Merrill Lynch, Pierce, Fenner & Smith, N.Y.C., 1978-80; mng. dir. emeritus Bear, Stearns & Co., N.Y.C., 1980—. Mem. adv. bd. Skin Cancer Found., N.Y.C. Lt. comdr. USNR, 1942-46. Marconi fellow, N.Y.C. Mem. River Club, Meadow Club, Shinnecock Hills Club, Bathing Corp. Club, Lyford Cay Club, Meadow Brook Club. Republican. Presbyterian. Home: 1 Sutton Pl S New York NY 10022-2471 Office: 245 Park Ave New York NY 10167-0002

HALLION, RICHARD PAUL, aerospace historian, museum consultant; b. Washington, May 17, 1948; s. Richard Paul and Marie Elizabeth (Flynn). BA with high honors in History, U. Md., 1970, PhD, 1975. Curator sci. and tech., curator space sci. and exploration Nat. Air and Space Mus., Smithsonian Instn., 1974-80; prof. history, instr. aerospace engring., U. Md., College Park, 1980-81, assoc. prof. gen. adminstrn., Univ. Coll., 1980-81; historian Air Force Flight Test Ctr., Edwards AFB, Calif., 1982-86; dir. spl. staff office Aeronautical Systems Div., Wright-Patterson AFB, Ohio, 1986-87; vis. prof. mil. history U.S. Army War Coll., Carlisle Barracks, Pa., 1987-88, exec. staff advanced projects office Air Force Systems Command, Andrews AFB, Md., 1988-90; sr. analyst, sec. Air Force Staff Group, 1990-91; Lindbergh vis. prof. Smithsonian Instn., 1991, chief air force history, 1992—; founder Paralog Assocs.; cons. mus. Author: Supersonic Flight, 1972, Legacy of Flight: The Guggenheim Contribution to American Aviation, 1977, The Wright Brothers: Heirs of Prometheus, 1978, (with Tom D. Crouch) Apollo: Ten Years since Tranquility Base, 1979, Test Pilots: The Frontiersmen of Flight, 1981, Designers and Test Pilots, 1982, Rise of the Fighter, 1984, Naval Air War in Korea, 1986, The Hypersonic Revolution, 1988; Strike From the Sky, 1988, Storm Over Iraq, 1992, Air Power Confronts an Unstable World, 1997, The Literature of Aeronautics, Astronautics and Air Power; contbr. articles to profl. jours. Recipient Dr. Robert H. Goddard Hist. Essay award Nat. Space Club, 1980; Daniel and Florence Guggenheim fellow, 1974-75. Mem. AIAA (History Manuscript award 1976, Young Engr./Scientist award Nat. Capitol sect. 1979), Aviation/Space Writers Assn. (Writing citation 1977-78, Space Lit. award 1979), Internat. Footprinters Assn., Air Force Hist. Found. (mem. editorial adv. bd.), Air Force Assn. (life), U. Md. Alumni Assn. (life), Precision Strike Assoc., Internatl. Order of Characters. Office: AF/HO 200 McChord St Box 94 Bolling AFB DC 20332-1111

HALLION, THOMAS FRANCIS, umpire; b. Saugerties, N.Y., Sept. 5, 1956; m. Elizabeth Carnright, Sept. 11, 1983; children: Corey, Kyle, Jacob. Student, U. Buffalo. Umpire N.Y.-Pa. League, Carolina League, Ea. League, Am. Assn., Nat. League, N.Y.C., 1985—. Avocations: golf, tennis, antiques. Office: Nat League 350 Park Ave New York NY 10022 Office: Umpires Union 1735 Market St Philadelphia PA 19103

HALLISSEY, MICHAEL, strategic consultant; b. Southampton, England, Mar. 6, 1943; s. John Francis and Mary (Kendall) H. Grad., Magdalen Coll., Oxford U., Eng., 1964. Chartered acct., Eng. With Price Waterhouse, 1964-98; asst. mgr. Price Waterhouse, Melbourne, Australia, 1968, Milan, Italy, 1969; ptnr. Price Waterhouse, London, 1974-98, head practice devel., 1979-81; head strategic planning, 1981-82, head corp. fin. services, 1983-88; dir. strategy Price Waterhouse Europe, 1988-98; vis. fellow Imperial Coll. Sci. and Tech., London, 1998—. Contbr. articles to profl. publs. Fellow Royal Soc. of Arts; mem. Inst. Chartered Accts. Eng. and Wales. Mem. Conservative Party. Mem. Ch. of Eng. Avocations: politics, sailing, music, opera. Home: 66 Waterside Point, Anhalt Rd, London SW11 4PD, England Office: Imperial Coll Sci & Tech, 53 Prince's Gate, London SW7 2PG, England

HALLMAN, GARY L., photographer, educator; b. St. Paul, Aug. 7, 1940; s. Jack J. and Helen A. Hallman; 1 child, Peter J. BA, U. Minn., 1966, MFA, 1971. Mem. faculty dept. studio arts U. Minn., Mpls., 1970—; assoc. prof. photography U. Minn., 1976—; vis. adj. prof. R.I. Sch. Design, 1977-78; vis. exchange prof. U. N.Mex., 1984-85; vis. assoc. prof. The Colo. Coll., Colorado Springs, Colo., 1990; mem. visual arts adv. bd. Minn. State Arts Council, 1973-76; bd. dirs. Minn. Artists Exhbn. Program, 1989-91. Exhbns. include, Internat. Mus. Photography, George Eastman House, 1974, Light Gallery, N.Y.C., 1975, Balt. Mus., 1975, Mus. Modern Art, N.Y.C., 1978, Mpls. Inst. of Arts, Minn., 1996, B. Gray Gallery East Carolina Univ., Greenville, N.C., 1997, Nat. Mus. of Am., Washington, 1984. Frederick R. Weisman Art Mus., Mpls., 1998, The State Russian Mus., St. Petersburg, 1998; represented in permanent collections, Mus. Modern Art, N.Y.C., Internat. Mus. Photography, Rochester, N.Y., Nat. Gallery Can., Fogg Art Mus., Harvard U., Princeton U. Art Mus., Nat. Mus. Am. Art, Smithsonian Instn., Washington. Served with USN, 1958-61. Nat. Endowment Arts fellow, 1975-76; Bush Found. fellow, 1976-77; McKnight Found. fellow, 1982, 90, Artist Assistance fellowship grant, 1996. Mem. Soc. Photog. Edn., Coll. Art Assn. Am. Office: U Minn Dept Studio Arts Minneapolis MN 55455

HALLMAN, H(ENRY) THEODORE, JR., artist, textile designer; b. Bucks County, Pa., Dec. 23, 1933; s. H. Theodore and Mildred Eleanor (Brumbaugh) H. Cert., Fontainebleau Sch. Fine Arts, France, 1955; BFA, BS in Edn, Temple U., 1956; MFA in Painting, Cranbrook Acad. Art, 1957, MFA in Textiles, 1958; studied at, Bundestextilschule, Austria, 1962; PhD in Edn, U. Calif., Berkeley, 1974. workshop tchr. in design, textiles, handweaving, color, U.S., Eng., Can.; lectr. in design, textile structures; chmn. Haystack Sch., Deer Isle, Maine, 1958-60, Penland (N.C.) Sch., summers 1963-70, 96, U. Calif., Berkeley, 1973-74, Calif. State U., San Francisco, 1970, Bklyn. Mus. Sch., 1973; lectr. teaching workshops Inst. Am. Indian Art, Sante Fe, No. N.Mex. C.C., El Rito, N.Mex., Nancy Block Studio, Sante Fe; head dept. textile design Moore Coll. Art, 1963-69; head of textiles, Ont. Coll. Art, Toronto, 1975-99, initiating summer programs in Florence, Italy, Como, Italy, Kyoto, Japan, Paris; bd. dirs. S.W. Craft Center, San Antonio; adv. bd. Pacific Basin Sch. Textile Arts, Berkeley, Calif.; bd. advisers Toronto (Ont., Can.) Mus. Textiles. One-man shows include Phila. Art Alliance, 1960, Loch Haven Art Center, Orlando, Fla., 1970, Woodmere Art Gallery, Phila., 1971, Royal Ont. Mus., Toronto, 1978, Renwick of Smithsonian, Washington, 1980, Centre des Arts Visuels, Montreal, Mendel Art Gallery, Saskatchewan, Moore Coll. Art, Phila., McMillan Meml. Gallery, Lincoln, Nebr., S.W. Craft Center, San Antonio, Tex., Fashion Inst. Tech., N.Y.C., 1983, Bklyn. Mus. Art, 1984, Tokyo Gallery Space '21, 1985, Kyoto Am. Ctr., 1985, Hamilton Art Gallery, 1985, Columbus Cultural Art Ctr., 1995, 97, Cambridge Gallery, Ont., 1994, Allentown Art Mus., 1998; two-man show Chgo. Art Inst., 1969, Disciples of Reenchantment, 1997, Art Expo at Javitz Ctr., N.Y.C., 1990, Allentown Art Mus., 1998; four-person show at Columbus Cultural Art Ctr.; group shows include Talkative Textiles, San Francisco and Sante Fe, 1992-93, opening show Barbara Okun Gallery, Santa Fe, 1992, Envision Gallery, Taos, N.Mex., 1993, Helen Drutt Gallery, Phila., 1994, Internationales Kunsthandwerk, Stuttgart, Germany, The Art Fabric: Mainstream, Miniature Weavings, London, Am. Fedn. Arts travelling exhbn., 1981-82, Milw. Art Mus., 1986, 5 Decades of Am. Fiber Art, Am. Craft Mus., N.Y.C., 1995, Ont. Craft Gallery, also numerous U.S. Govt. Agy. travelling shows; represented in permanent collections, Met. Mus. Art, N.Y.C., Victoria and Albert Mus., London, Royal Ont. Mus., Toronto, Bklyn., Mus. Art, Cooper Hewitt Mus., N.Y.C., Smithsonian Inst., Washington, Phila. Mus. Art, Oakland (Calif.) Mus. Art, Cin. Art Mus., Utah Mus. Fine Arts, Mus. Contemporary Crafts, N.Y.C., Addison Gallery Am. Art, Andover, Mass., Mus. Decorative Arts, Chateau Dufresene, Montreal Que., Textile Mus., Toronto; exhbn. N.Y. Art Expo '90; invited show Helen Drutt Gallery, Phila.; work represented in numerous art, design and craft jours. and books. Adv. bd. Pacific Basin Sch., Berkeley, Calif. L.C. Tiffany grantee, 1962; Oscar D'Italia 85, Calvatore, Italy; elected Coll. of Fellows by Am. Craft Council, N.Y.C. Mem. Internat. Soc. Arts and Letters (hon. life), World Craft Council (invited lectr. conf., Mexico 1976), Ont. Craft Council (dir.). Address: PO Box 250 Lederach PA 19450-0250 Address: PO Box 281 Lederach PA 19450-0281

HALLMAN, PATRICIA ANN, music educator; b. Lincolnton, N.C., May 24, 1948; d. Glen Rodney and Tessie Juanita (Crowder) Fox; m. Larry Reeves Hallman, Aug. 24, 1969; 1 child, Jeremy Reeves. BA in Music Edn. and Sacred Music, Gardner Webb U., Boiling Springs, N.C., 1982; Orff-Schulwerk Level I Cert., Radford (Va.) U., 1984; Orff-Schulwerk Level II Cert., Hofstra U., 1985; Orff-Schulwerk Level III Cert., Memphis State U., 1987. Cert. music educator, N.C. Minister of music Oak Grove Bapt. Ch., Lincolnton, N.C., 1975-77, Reepsville Bapt. Ch., Lincolnton, N.C., 1980-83; minister youth and activities New Hope Bapt. Ch., Earle, N.C., 1983-84; minister of music Mountain View Bapt. Ch., Lincolnton, 1984-86, Boger City Bapt. Ch., Lincolnton, 1990-92; tchr. music Lincoln County Schs., Lincolnton, 1984—; minister of music Lawings Chapel Bapt. Ch., Lincolnton, 1994, Calvary Bapt. Ch., Lincolnton, 1996-98; tchr. pvt. piano and voice lessons, 1986—; conducted crusades in field, 1993, 94, 95, 96, 98. Bd. dirs. Local Chpt. N.C. State Symphony, Lincolnton, 1987-92. Mem. N.C. Assn. Educators, Am. Orff-Schulwerk Assn. (bd. dirs. 1993, composer From Us To You 1993), South-fork Bapt. Assn. (children's choir coord. 1984—). Baptist. Avocations: swimming, traveling, singing, performing, cooking. Home: 2536 Pickwick Pl Lincolnton NC 28092-7749 Office: Iron Station Elem Sch 4207 W Highway 27 Lincolnton NC 28092-0713

HALLMARK, DONALD PARKER, museum director, lecturer; b. McPherson, Kans., Feb. 16, 1945; s. Daniel Clell and Esther Ione (Hart) H.; m. Linda Lorraine Lego, June 10, 1967; m. Monica Lynn, Amy Kristen. BFA, U. Ill., 1967; MA, U. Iowa, 1970; PhD, St. Louis U., 1980. From asst. prof. to prof. Greenville (Ill.) Coll., 1970-81, chmn. art dept., 1976-81; dir. Richard W. Bock Sculpture Collection, Greenville, 1975-81, Frank Lloyd Wright's Dana-Thomas House Hist. Site, Springfield, Ill., 1981—; founding bd. mem. Frank Lloyd Wright Bldg Conservancy, Chgo., 1988-96; adj. prof. Sangamon State U., Springfield, 1986-90; lectr. in field. Author: (booklet) The Dana-Thomas House: Its History, Acquisition and Preservation, 1992, (catalogue) Paul Ashbrook, 1990 (illustrated book) The Natural Pattern of Structure, 1995; TV interview appearance Bob Vila's Guide to Historic Homes, The Dana-Thomas House, 1996; editor newsletter Guidelines for the Conservation of Frank Lloyd Wright Decorative Arts, 1996. Cons., sponsor Ill. Govt. Intern Program, Springfield, 1985—; libr. cons., vol. Michael Victor II Libr. Springfield Art Assn., 1988-93. Faculty grantee Shell Found., 1975; Grad. fellow St. Louis U., 1976. Mem. Am. Assn. Mus. Presbyterian. Avocations: slide library collecting, antique collecting, travel, ground and garden maintenance. Home: 605 W Sheridan St Petersburg IL 62675-1359 Office: Ill Hist Preservation Agy 301 E Lawrence Ave Springfield IL 62703-2232

HALLO, WILLIAM WOLFGANG, Assyriologist; b. Kassel, Germany, Mar. 9, 1928; came to U.S., 1940, naturalized, 1946; s. Rudolf and Gertrude (Rubensohn) H.; m. Edith Sylvia Pinto, June 22, 1952 (dec. Oct. 1994); children: Ralph Ethan, Jacqueline Louise; m. Nanette Stahl, Oct. 18, 1998. BA magna cum laude, Harvard U., 1950; candidatus Litterarum Semiticarum, U. Leiden, Netherlands, 1951; MA, U. Chgo., 1953, PhD, 1955; MA (hon.), Yale U., 1965; DHL (hon.), Hebrew Union Coll.-Jewish Inst. Religion, 1986. Research asst. Oriental Inst., U. Chgo., 1954-56; from instr. to asst. prof. Bible and Semitic langs. Hebrew Union Coll.-Jewish Inst. Religion, Cin., 1956-62; mem. faculty Yale U., 1962—; prof. Assyriology, 1965-75, William M. Laffan prof. Assyriology and Babylonian lit., 1976—; curator Babylonian collection, 1963—; master Morse Coll., 1982-87; chmn. dept. Near Eastern langs. and civilizations, 1975-82, 85-89; chmn. Univ. (now adv.) com. on Judaic Studies, 1979-84, acting chmn., 1998; vis. prof. Mid. Eastern civilization Columbia U., 1970-71, 80, Jewish Theol. Sem. 1981, 82-83; Franz Rosenzweig guest prof. U. Kassel, Germany, 1991. Author: Early Mesopotamian Royal Titles, 1957, (with J.J.A. van Dijk) The Exaltation of Inanna, 1968; (with W.K. Simpson) The Ancient Near East: A History, 1971, 2d edit., 1998; Sumerian Archival Texts, 1973; (with Briggs Buchanan) Early Near Eastern Seals in the Yale Babylonian Collection, 1981, The Book of the People, 1991, Origins: The Ancient Near Eastern Background of Some Modern Western Institutions, 1996; co-author: The Torah: A Modern Commentary, 1981, Heritage: Civilization and the Jews, 2 vols., 1984; editor: Essays in Memory of E.A. Speiser, 1968, (with Carl D. Evans and John B. White) Scripture in Context: Essays on the Comparative Method, 1980, (with James C. Moyer and Leo G. Perdue) Scripture in Context II: More Essays on the Comparative Method, 1983, (with Bruce W. Jones and Gerald L. Mattingly) The Bible in Light of Cuneiform Literature: Scripture in Context III, 1990 (with K. Lawson Younger Jr. and Bernard F. Batto) The Biblical Canon in Comparative Perspective: Scripture in Context IV, 1991, (with K. Lawson Younger Jr.) The Context of Scripture, vol. I: Canonical Compostitions from the Biblical World, 1997; translator: The Star of Redemption, 1971. Contbr. numerous articles, revs. on Assyriology and Bibl. archeology; mem. editl. com. Yale Near Eastern Researches, 1967—; editor, 1970—; mem. editl. bd. Moment Mag., Bible Rev., Archaology Odyssey. Mem. commn. Jewish edn. Union Am. Hebrew Congregations, 1967-71; co-founder, dir., mem. exec. com. Assn. Jewish Studies, 1970-71, v.p., 1972-74. Guggenheim fellow, 1965-66, Fulbright scholar, 1950-51, fellow Inst. Advanced Studies, Hebrew U., Jerusalem, 1978-79, Nat. Humanities Inst., 1987-88; honored by an anniversary volume: The Tablet and the Scroll: Near Eastern Studies in Honor of William W. Hallo, 1993. Mem. Am. Oriental Soc. (assoc. editor, 1965-71, chmn. Ancient Near East sect. 1971-78, v.p. 1987-88, pres. 1988-89), World Union Jewish Studies, Harvard Club (So. Conn.), Yale Club (N.Y.C.), Phi Beta Kappa. Home: 245 Blake Rd Hamden CT 06517-3324 Office: Babylonian Collection Yale Univ New Haven CT 06520-8240

HALLOCK, C. WILES, JR., athletic official; b. Denver, Feb. 17, 1918; s. Claude Wiles and Mary (Bassler) H.; m. Marjorie Louise Eldred, Mar. 23, 1944; children: Lucinda Eldred Hallock Rinne, Michael Eldred. A.B., U. Denver, 1939. Sports info. dir. U. Wyo., 1949-60, track coach, 1952-56; sports info. dir. U. Calif., Berkeley, 1960-63; dir. pub. relations Nat. Collegiate Athletic Assn., 1963-68; dir. Nat. Collegiate Sports Services, 1967-68; commr. Western Athletic Conf., 1968-71; exec. dir. Pacific-8 Conf. (now Pacific-10 conf.), San Francisco and Walnut Creek, Calif., 1971-83; historian Pacific 10 Conf., 1983. Mem. Laramie (Wyo.) City Council, 1958-60. Served to lt. comdr. USNR, World War II. Decorated Air medal; mem. Nat. Football Found. and Hall of Fame Honors Ct. Mem. Nat. Collegiate Athletic Assn., Nat. Assn. Collegiate Dirs. Athletics (Corbett award 1983), Collegiate Commrs. Assn., Coll. Sports Info. Dirs. Am. (Arch Ward award 1963), Football Writers Assn. Am. (past dir.), U.S. Basketball Writers Assn., Lambda Chi Alpha. Presbyn. Home: 235 Western Hills Dr Pleasant Hill CA 94523-3167 Office: 800 S Broadway Walnut Creek CA 94596-5218*

HALLOCK, JAMES ANTHONY, pediatrician, school dean; b. Paterson, N.J., Oct. 28, 1942; s. Anthony E. and Alice S. (Dahab) H.; m. Jeanne LaRossa, June 27, 1965; children: James A. Jr., Jeffrey D., Julie E. AB, Seton Hall U., 1963; MD, Georgetown U., 1967. Diplomate Am. Bd. Pediatrics. Resident in pediatrics Children's Hosp. of Phila., 1967-69; chief resident in pediatrics Hosp. of U. Pa., 1969-70; asst. prof. pediatrics U. South Fla., Tampa, 1972-75, assoc. prof., 1975-80, prof., 1980-88, assoc. dean, 1978-83, dep. dean, 1983-85; exec. dean U. South Fla., Tampa and St. Petersburg, 1985-88; prof. pediatrics, dean East Carolina U. Sch. Medicine, Greenville, N.C., 1988—; vice chancellor for health scis., 1990. Contbr. articles to profl. jours. Maj. USAF, 1970-72. Fellow Am. Acad. Pediatrics; mem. N.C. Med. Soc., N.C. Biomed. Rsch. (bd. dirs. 1989), Pitt County Med. Soc., Pitt/Greenville C. of C. (bd. dirs. 1989), Rotary (St. Petersburg and Greenville chpts.). Office: East Carolina U Office Vice Chancellor & Dean Sch Medicine Greenville NC 27858-4354

HALLOCK, ROBERT BRUCE, physics educator; b. Washington, Dec. 9, 1943; s. Robert Frederick and Dorothy (Mengel) H.; m. Norma Evelyn Hayward, Jun 19, 1965; children: Robert William, Kevin Frederick. BS, U. Mass., 1965; MS, Stanford U., 1967, PhD, 1969, postdoctoral, 1969-70. Asst. prof. U. Mass., Amherst, 1970-74, assoc. prof., 1974-79, prof., 1979—; dir. lab. low temp. physics, 1978—, head dept. physics and astronomy, 1985-93; vis. assoc. prof. Brown U., Providence, 1975, Cornell U., Ithaca, N.Y., 1977-78; co-chair Gordon Rsch. Conf. on Quantum Fluids and Solids, 1982; adj. prof. dept. polymer sci. and engring. U. Mass., 1985—; mem. five colls. Radio Astronomy Policy Bd., 1985-87; mem. Rsch. Corp. Grants Adv. Bd., 1989-96; mem. fundamental physics discipline working group NASA, 1997—; chair Quantum Fluids & Solids Internat. Conf., 1998. Author, editor: Superfluid Helium, 1983; contbr. articles to profl. jours. Leader Cub Scout Am., Hadley, Mass., 1975-80. Woodrow Wilson Found. fellow, 1965, Air Force Office of Sci. Rsch.-NRC fellow, 1969, A.P. Sloan Found. rsch. fellow, 1972-76, U. Mass. fellow, 1974, 93, J.S. Guggenheim Meml. fellow, 1992-93. Fellow Am. Phys. Soc. (exec. coun. New Eng. sect. 1986-89); mem. Phi Beta Kappa, Sigma Xi. Avocation: photography. Office: U Mass Dept Physics & Astronomy Amherst MA 01003

HALLORAN, BRIAN PAUL, lawyer; b. Covington, Ky., Sept. 22, 1969; s. Kenneth Anthony and Ann Carole (Rymarquis) H. BA in History, Ea. Ky. U., 1990; JD, Salmon P. Chase Coll. Law, 1994. Bar: Ky. 1994, U.S. Dist. Ct. (ea. dist.) Ky. 1996. Pvt. practice, Newport, Ky., 1994—; cons. Globoleochem Cons., Covington, 1994—; counsel Rogue Predator Pictures, LLC, & Rogue Ptnrrrs., LP., L.A. Mem. Campell County Rep. Com., Alexandria, Ky., 1996—. Mem. Ky. Bar Assn., Ky. Assn. Trial Attys., No. Ky. Bar Assn., Kenton County Jaycees. Roman Catholic. Avocations: music, golf, soccer, softball, computers. Office: 300 E 3d St Newport KY 41071-1841

HALLORAN, JAMES VINCENT, III, technical writer; b. Greenwich, Conn., May 12, 1942; s. James Vincent and Rita Lucy (Keator) H.; m. Barbara Sharon Case, Sept. 7, 1974. BME, Cath. U. Am., 1964; MBA, U. Chgo., 1973. Mktg. rep. Rockwell Internat., El Segundo, Calif., 1973-76, bus. area mgr., 1976-80, bus. analysis mgr., 1980-84; asst. dir. market analysis H. Silver & Assocs. Inc., Torrance, Calif., 1984-87, dir. mktg., 1987-90; program mgr. Tech. Tng. Corp., Torrance, 1990-91; prin. Bus. Info. & Analysis, Redondo Beach, Calif., 1991-94; mgr. spl. projects Wyle Labs., El Segundo, Calif., 1994—. Commr. Redondo Beach Housing Adv. and Appeals Bd., 1985-89; mem. citizens adv. bd. South Bay Union High Sch. Dist., Redondo Beach, 1983; dir. Project Tomahawk, Curtiss-Wright Hist. Assn., 1995—, newsletter editor, 1995-98, spl. events chmn., 1998—. Capt. USAF, 1964-68. Libertarian. Avocations: cycling, photography, traveling abroad. Home: 612 S Gertruda Ave Redondo Beach CA 90277-4245 Office: Wyle Labs 128 Maryland St El Segundo CA 90245-4115

HALLORAN, KATHLEEN L., financial executive, accountant; b. Sandwich, Ill., July 19, 1952; d. Oscar L. and Gertrude L. Huber; divorced. BA in Acctg., Lewis U., 1974; MBA, No. Ill. U., 1979. CPA, Ill. With No. Ill. Gas subs. NICOR, Inc., Naperville, 1974-84, asst. sec., 1983-84, asst. contr., 1984; sec., treas. NICOR Inc., Naperville, 1984-87; sec., contr. NICOR, Inc., Naperville, 1987-89, v.p., sec., contr., 1989-92; v.p. info svcs. and gen. acctg. No. Ill. Gas, Aurora, 1992-94, v.p. info. svcs. and rates, 1994-95, v.p. info. svcs., rates and human resources, 1995-96, sr. v.p. adminstrn., 1996—. Bd. dirs. Voices for Ill. Children, Wynscape Nursing & Rehab. Ctr., Castle BancGroup, Inc. Mem. Am. Gas Assn., Chgo. Econs. Club. Office: Nicor Gas Co PO Box 190 Aurora IL 60507-0190

HALLORAN, LEO AUGUSTINE, retired financial executive; b. Schenectady, N.Y., Apr. 2, 1931; s. Leo Augustine Halloran and Helen (O'Hare) Pagel; m. Marilyn Elizabeth Gobeli, Dec. 29, 1956; children: Patricia Garvey, Michael, Kevin. AB in Econs., Union Coll., Schenectady, N.Y., 1953. With fin. mgmt. program Gen. Electric Co., Schenectady, 1956-60, mem. corp. audit staff, 1961-64, mgr. fin., 1965-70; mgr. fin. Consumer Products Group, Fairfield, Conn., 1971-75; sr. v.p., chief fin. officer Gen. Electric Capital Corp., Stamford, Conn., 1976-89. Sgt. U.S. Army, 1953-55. Avocations: basketball, reading, traveling. Address: 524 E 72nd St New York NY 10021-9801

HALLORAN, MICHAEL JAMES, lawyer; b. Berkeley, Calif., May 20, 1941; s. James Joseph and Fern (Ogden) H.; m. Virginia Smedberg, Sept. 6, 1964; children: Pamela, Peter, Shelley. BS, U. Calif., Berkeley, 1962, LLB, 1965. Bar: Calif. 1966, D.C. 1979, Wyo. 1996. Assoc. Keatinge & Sterling, L.A., 1965-67; assoc. Pillsbury, Madison & Sutro, San Francisco, 1967-72, ptnr., 1973-90, 97—; mng. ptnr. Pillsbury, Madison & Sutro, Washington, 1979-82; exec. v.p., gen. counsel BankAm. Corp. and Bank of Am., San Francisco, 1990-96; mem. legal adv. com. N.Y. Stock Exch., 1993-96; bd. overseers Inst. Civil Justice, 1994-98; chair sect. corp. securities banking and emerging cos. Pillsbury Madison & Sutro, 1997—. Editor: Venture Capital and Public Offering Negotiation, 1982—. Mem. corp. governance, shareholder rights and securities transactions com. Calif. Senate Commn., 1986-98; bd. dirs. Am. Conservatory Theater. Mem. ABA (chmn. state regulation of securities com. 1981-84, mem. coun. of sect. of bus. law 1986-90, chmn. banking law com. 1992-96, mem. corp. laws com. 1997—), Bar Assn. San Francisco (bd. dirs. 1993-96), Orinda Country Club. Avocations: skiing, golf, fishing, hiking. Office: Pillsbury Madison & Sutro LLP 235 Montgomery St Fl 16 San Francisco CA 94104-3074 also: 2550 Hanover St Palo Alto CA 94304-1115

HALLORAN, MICHAEL JOHN, lawyer; b. St. Louis, June 4, 1951; s. Edward Anthony Halloran and Helen M. (Kickham) Phillips; m. Gwen V. Carroll, July 25, 1983 (div. Oct. 1984). BS in Commerce, St. Louis U., 1972, JD, 1975. Bar: Ill. 1975, U.S. Dist. Ct. (no. dist.) Ill. 1975, U.S. Ct. Appeals (7th cir.) 1975. Assoc. Seyfarth, Shaw, Fairweather & Geraldson, Chgo., 1975-76, 77-78, Washington, 1976-77; atty. Beinhauer & Rouhana, N.Y.C., 1978-79; assoc. William B. Hanley & Assocs., Chgo., 1979-81; assoc. Bell, Boyd & Lloyd, Chgo., 1981-83, ptnr., 1983-86; pvt. practice, Chgo., 1987—. Home: 1017 W Washington St Apt 6F Chicago IL 60607-2112 Office: 53 W Jackson Blvd Ste 319 Chicago IL 60604-3608

HALLORAN, RICHARD COLBY, writer, former research executive, former news correspondent; b. Washington, Mar. 2, 1930; s. Paul James and Catherine (Lenihan) H.; m. Carol Prins, June 21, 1958; children: Christopher Paul, Laura Colby, Catherine Anne; m. Fumiko Mori, Nov. 11, 1978. AB with distinction, Dartmouth Coll., 1951; MA, U. Mich., 1957. Staff writer, then asst. fgn. editor Business Week mag., 1957-61; Tokyo bur. chief McGraw-Hill World News, 1962-64; Asia specialist Washington Post, 1965-66; bur. chief Washington Post, Tokyo, 1966-68; Washington corr. Washington Post, 1968-69; Washington corr. N.Y. Times, 1969-72, Tokyo bur. chief, 1972-76, investigative reporter Washington Bur., 1976-78, energy corr., 1978-79, def. corr., 1979-84, mil. corr., 1984-89; dir. comm. and journalism East-West Ctr., Honolulu, 1990-94; ind. writer Honolulu, 1994—; adj. fellow Pacific Forum-Ctr. Strategic and Internat. Studies, Ctr. War, Peace , and News Media, Cambridge, Mass.; vis. lectr. U. Hawaii, 1995-96; bd. dirs. Hawaiian Electric Industries Power Corp. Author: Japan: Images and Realities, 1969, Conflict and Compromise: The Dynamics of American Foreign Policy, 1973, To Arm a Nation: Rebuilding America's Endangered Defenses, 1986, Serving America: Prospects for the Volunteer Force, 1988. Mem. Honolulu Com. Fgn. Rels., Pacific and Asian Affairs Coun., bd. govs. Japanese Cultural Ctr. of Hawaii. 1st lt. U.S. Army, 1952-55. Recipient citation for interpretation fgn. affairs Overseas Press Club, 1969, George Polk award for nat. reporting L.I. U., 1982, Gerald R. Ford prize for disting. reporting on nat. def. Gerald R. Ford Found., 1988, Outstanding Civilian Svc. medal U.S. Army, 1989, Japan's Order Sacred Treasure, Gold Rays with Rosette, 1998; Ford Found. fellow Columbia U., 1964-65. Woodrow Wilson nat. fellow Furman U., Luther Coll., S.C. Iowa, Union Coll., N.Y., U. Redlands, Calif., Linfield Coll., Oreg., Goucher Coll., Md., Ohio Wesleyan U., McMurry U., Tex., Trinity Coll., Vt., St. Mary's Coll., Calif., Wabash Coll. Ind. Mem. 100th Infantry Bn. Vet. Assn. (hon.), Fgn. Corrs. Club Japan. Roman Catholic. Home: 1065 Kao'opulu Pl Honolulu HI 96825-1364

HALLOWELL, JOHN H, minister; b. L.I., Oct. 30, 1953; s. John Wentworth and Ann Marie (Burkhard) H.; m. Kathryn Margaret Allen, Dec. 30, 1978; children: David, Marke, Matthew. BA in Classical Langs.,

Calif. State U., Long Beach, 1979. Ordained min. Calvary Chapel, Capistrano Beach, Calif., 1985—, pastoral rschr., 1985—. Mem. Am. Acad. Religion. Soc. Bibl. Lit. Home: 27251 Rosario Mission Viejo CA 92692-3512 Office: Calvary Chapel 25975 Domingo Ave Capo Beach CA 92624-1115

HALLOWELL SCHEMMER, SHANNON, nurse anesthetist; b. Orlando, Fla., Jan. 6, 1965; d. Albert Valentine and Ginger (Stanley) H. BSN, Clemson U., 1986; MSN, U. N.C., Charlotte, 1994. RN, N.C., S.C.; cert. critical care nurse; ACLS instr. Staff nurse III Greenville (S.C.) Meml. Hosp., 1986-89; asst. nurse mgr. PACU Carolinas Med. Ctr., Charlotte, 1989-91, staff nurse emergency dept., 1993, nurse anaesthetist, 1994—; cons. Nellcor, Inc., Pleasanton, Calif., 1991-92. Mem. AACN, Am. Assn. Nurse Anesthetists, Golden Key Honor Soc., Sigma Theta Tau, Phi Kappa Phi. Republican. Avocations: water & snow skiing, cycling, running, hiking. Home: 2914 Sharon Rd Charlotte NC 28211-2130

HALLSTED, NANCY RUTH EVERETT, pianist, music educator; b. Reno, Nev., Dec. 28, 1938; d. Marion Kenneth and Ruth Elizabeth (Zollinger) Everett; m. Byron Leon Hallsted, June 10, 1962; children: Sheila Ann Hallsted-Baumert, John Edmond. BA, LaSierra U., Riverside, Calif., 1960; MA, U. So. Calif., L.A., 1965. Permanent tchg. cert. MTNA. Ind. pvt. tchr. piano Bethesda, Md., 1971—; faculty piano, profl. studies The Levine Sch. of Music, Washington, 1988—; presenter, performer internat. piano workshops; adjudicator for concerti, solo and piano ensemble competitions. Performed chamber music Gaithersburg Libr. Series, The Fairfax Symphony Musicales, Hamilton House, The Chevy Chase Club, others; contbr. numerous articles to profl. jours. Arts adminstr., pres. Friday Morning Music Club, Washington; bd. dirs. Washington Performing Arts Soc.; adv. planning bd. in music Strathmore Hall Arts Ctr., Rockville, Md. Recipient Bank of Am. Award in Fine Arts, 1956, Santa Fe award, 1956; U. So. Calif. scholar, 1960. Mem. Montgomery County Music Tchrs. Assn. (past pres.), Md. State Music Tchrs. Assn. Home: 9212 Villa Dr Bethesda MD 20817-3310

HALLSTRAND, SARAH LAYMON, denomination executive; b. Nashville, Oct. 25, 1944; d. Charles Martin and Lillian Christina (Stenberg) Laymon; m. John Peter Hallstrand, July 6, 1974; 1 child, Lillian Johanna. BA cum laude, Fla. So. Coll., 1966; ThM, Boston U., 1971; D of Ministry, McCormick Theol. Sem., 1985; grad., Coll. for Fin. Planning, Denver, 1990. Ordained Am. Baptist Ch., 1976; certified retirement counselor. Dir. Christian edn. Trinity United Meth. Ch., Bradenton, Fla., 1968-70, Univ. United Meth. Ch., Syracuse, N.Y., 1971-73; assoc. min. First Bapt. Ch., Syracuse, 1973-78; pastor Oneida (N.Y.) Bapt. Ch., 1978-80; midwest rep. Mins. and Missionaries Benefit Bd., Am. Bapt. Chs., Oak Park, Ill., 1981—; leader retirement planning seminars Am. Bapt. Assembly, Green Lake, Wis., 1985—; mem. rep. Midwest Ministerial Leadership Commn., Valley Forge, Pa., 1985—; adj. prof., pastoral care McCormick Theol. Sem., Chgo., 1986—; adj. prof. retirement planning The Divinity Sch., Rochester, N.Y., 1994; vis. scholar Am. Bapt. Bd. Ednl. Ministries, Valley Forge, 1986-87; bd. dirs. Midwest Career Devel. Svc., Chgo., 1987—, chair, 1993-96; bd. dirs. The Gathering Place Retreat Ctr., Gosport, Ind., 1988-95; mem. program com. and women in ministry rep. Roger Williams Fellowship, 1988-95; mem. nat. continuing edn. team Am. Bapt. Chs., Valley Forge, Pa., 1991-98; conf. leader for women's spiritual renewal weekends; speaker in field. Contbg. author: Songs of Miriam: A Women's Book of Devotions, 1994; contbr. articles to profl. jours. Mem. Am. Bapt. Chs. Mins. Coun., Inst. Cert. Fin. Planners (cert.), Internat. Soc. Retirement Planners, Alpha Gamma Delta. Democrat. Office: Mins and Missionaries Benefit Bd PO Box 549 Oak Park IL 60303-0549 *The church has not been called to be successful as measured by the world's standards. It has always been and will always be that the true goal of the church is faithfulness as measured by the liberating and transforming gospel of Jesus Christ.*

HALLSTROM, LASSE, director; b. Stockholm, 1946. Dir. feature films, including A Lover and His Lass, 1975, Abba: The Movie, 1977, Father to Be, 1979, The Rooster, 1981, Happy We, 1983, My Life as a Dog, 1985, Children of Bullerby Village, 1987, Once Around, 1991, What's Eating Gilbert Grape, 1993, Something To Talk About, 1995, The Cider House Rules, 1999. Office: ICM 8942 Wilshire Blvd Beverly Hills CA 90211-1934 also: Wayne Mejia de Blois Mejia & Co 9171 Wilshire Blvd Ste 541 Beverly Hills CA 90210-5515

HALLSTROM, ROBERT CHRIS, government actuary; b. Sacramento, June 8, 1953; s. Clifford Clarence and Billee June (Plunkett) H.; m. Pamela Jane Pracht, Apr. 25, 1987; 1 child, Kelsey Kathlene. BA in Math. with honors, Calif. State U., Sacramento, 1974, MS in Math., 1976. Cert. math. tchr. c.c., Calif. Asst. actuary Transam. Ins. Co., L.A., 1976-80; actuary Cal-Farm Ins. Co., Sacramento, 1980-84; instr. math. Sacramento City Coll., 1985, Sierra Coll., Rocklin, Calif., 1985; sr. casualty actuary Calif. Dept. Ins., San Francisco, 1985—. Fellow Casualty Actuarial Soc.; mem. Internat. Actuarial Assn. Avocations: mathematics, collecting books and phonograph records, reading. Office: Calif Dept Ins 45 Fremont St Fl 24 San Francisco CA 94105-2204

HALLWAS, JOHN EDWARD, English language educator; b. Waukegan, Ill., May 24, 1945; s. Emil Ferdinand and Ruth Edna (Wells) H.; m. Garnette Verna Stockstad, Jan. 3, 1966; children: John Darrin, Evan Bradley. BS in Edn., Western Ill. U., Macomb, 1967, MA, 1968; PhD, U. Fla., 1972. Grad. asst. Western Ill. U., Macomb, 1967-68, prof. English dept., 1970—. Author: Western Illinois Heritage, 1983, Illinois Literature: The 19th Century, 1986, Macomb: A Pictorial History, 1990, Spoon River Anthology: An Annotated Edition, 1992, The Bootlegger: A Story of Small-Town America, 1998, others; editor Western Ill. Regional Studies, 1978-92; co-editor: Tales From Two Rivers book series, 1981—, Prairie State Books, 1987—; newspaper columnist Macomb Jour., 1981-84, Jacksonville (Ill.) Jour. Courier, 1984-85, 87-88. NDEA fellow U. Fla., Gainesville, 1968-70; recipient Faculty Svc. award Nat. U. Continuing Edn. Assn., 1981, Alumni Achievement award Western Ill. U., Macomb, 1983, MidAm. award, Soc. for Study of Midwestern Lit., 1994; named faculty lectr. Western Ill. U., Macomb, 1983, Disting. prof., 1992. Mem. Soc. for Study Midwestern Lit., Ill. State Hist. Soc. (adv. bd. 1990—), McDonough County Hist. Soc. (pres. 1981-83), Phi Beta Kappa, Phi Kappa Phi. Avocations: nature study, fitness walking, skiing. Home: 8 Hickory Bow Macomb IL 61455-1018 Office: Western Ill U Libr Macomb IL 61455

HALM, JAMES MAURICE, retired chemist, poet; b. Chgo., Oct. 11, 1930; s. James Albert and Sadie (Olejnick) H.; m. Carol Ann Wenzelburger, June 3, 1934; children: Cynthia, Jennifer, Rebecca, Elizabeth. BS in Chemistry, U. Ill., 1953; MS in Chemistry, St. Louis U., 1955; PhD in Chemistry, Va. Tech., 1972. Prof. chemistry Morton Coll., Cicero, Ill., 1957-67; rsch. asst. Va. Tech., Blacksburg, 1968-72; rsch. chemist Adressograph-Multigraph, Warrensville Heights, Ohio, 1972-74; rsch. assoc., project leader A.B. Dick Co., Chgo., 1974-81; sr. scientist St. Regis Paper Co., West Nyack, N.Y., 1981-85; prof. chemistry Norwich U., Northfield, Vt., 1986-90; scientist Internat. Paper, Tuxedo, N.Y., 1990-93, Erie, Pa., 1993-96; adj. prof. chemistry William Rainey Harper Coll., Palatine, Ill., 1975-80; chemistry cons., Hendersonville, N.C., 1996—. Patentee in field; contbr. articles to sci. jours.; contbg. poet to numerous mags. and jours. With U.S. Army, 1954-56. Avocations: photography, classical music, gardening. Home: 3 Ridgestone Dr Hendersonville NC 28792-9488

HALM, NANCYE STUDD, private school administrator; b. Jamestown, N.Y., Mar. 26, 1932; d. Thomas Howerton and Margaret Hazel (LeRoy) Neathery; m. David Philip Mack, Aug. 25, 1951 (div. 1972); children: Margaret, Jennifer, Geoffrey, Peter; m. Loris L. Studd, July 6, 1974; m. James Richard Halm, Aug. 30, 1991. BS in Edn., SUNY, Fredonia, 1954, postgrad.; postgrad., St. Bonaventure U. Tchr. Morning Sun (Iowa) Consolidated Schs., 1956-57, Panama (N.Y.) Cen. Schs., 1958-65, Jamestown (N.Y.) Pub. Schs., 1967-69, Olean (N.Y.) Pub. Schs. 1969-72, Jamestown Pub. Schs., 1972-73; pers. mgr. F.W. Woolworth Co., Lakewood, N.Y., 1972-79; dir. Nat. Conf. Christians & Jews, Jamestown, 1979-86; counselor N.Y. State Div. for Youth, Jamestown, 1979-89; exec. rep. Am. Bapt. Found., Valley Forge, Pa., 1989-94; adminstr. New Castle Christian Acad., 1996—. Nat. bd. dirs. Am. Bapt. Chs. U.S.A., Valley Forge, Pa. 1988-89; v.p. Chautauqua County Am. Bapt. Women, 1981-90; pres. Falconer Bapt. women, 1986-90; love gifft chmn. Pitts. Bapt. Assn., 1990-91; trustee and chair of Endowment Fund Chautauqua Baptist Union at Chautauqua Inst., 1982—. Recipient Cert. of Merit Cassadaga Job Corp, 1984. Mem. Rebekah. Republican. Avocations: quilting, reading, crafts. Home: 1702 W Washington St New Castle PA 16101-1360

HALMER, JUDITH R., writing and literature educator; b. Buffalo, Nov. 4, 1951; d. Hermann and Rose (Rosenthal) Weinheimer; m. Bruce J. Chalmer, Aug. 8, 1971; children: Micah, Seth, Eli. BA, Goddard Coll., 1975; MFA, Norwich U., 1991. Asst. prof. writing and lit. Norwich U., Montpelier, Vt., 1992—. Author: Out of History's Junk Jar, 1995. Recipient 1st prize New Eng. Writers Assn., 1991.

HALMI, ROBERT, film producer; b. Budapest, Hungary, Jan. 22, 1924; s. Bela and Sarah (Deri) H.; m. Esther Szirmay, Sept. 9, 1980; children: Kevin Gorman, Kim Gorman, Robert, Bill. Grad., U. Budapest, 1946. Mag. photographer, 1946-52; photographer Life mag., 1952-62; documentary producer, 1962-75; chmn. Hallmark Entertainment, N.Y.C., 1993—. Producer over 200 TV movies, miniseries and theatrical features including Grand Larceny, 1987, Mayflower Madam, 1987, Call of the Wild, 1993, The Yearling, 1994, Getting Out, 1994, The Sunshine Boys, 1995, Kidnapped, 1995, Bye Bye Birdie, 1995, Gulliver's Travells, 1996, Captain Courageous, 1996, 20,000 Leagues Under the Sea, 1997, Moby Dick, 1998, Merlin, 1998, Crime & Punishment, 1998, Rear Window, 1998, Land of Oz, 1999, Don Quixote, 1999, Cleopatra, 1999, Arabian Nights, 1999, Alice in Wonderland, 1999, Noah's Ark, 1999, Mr. & Mrs. Bridge, Gypsy, The Incident, Lily in Love, Barnum, Pack of Lies, ; author: Into Your Hands Are They Delivered, Animals of Africa, Animals of North America, Sports Cars of the World, How To Photograph Women, Zoos of the World,. Recipient 15 Emmy awards, Peabody award, Christopher award, Genesis award, CINE Golden Eagle award, numerous Houston Film Festival awards. Address: Hallmark Entertainment 21st Fl 1325 Avenue of the Americas New York NY 10019-6026*

HALMOS, PAUL RICHARD, mathematician, educator; b. Budapest, Hungary, Mar. 3, 1916; came to U.S., 1929; s. Alexander Charles and Paula (Rosenberg) H.; m. Dorothy Moyer, Jan. 1, 1934 (div. Mar. 1945); m. Virginia Templeton Pritchett, Apr. 7, 1945. BS, U. Ill., 1934, MS, 1935, PhD, 1938; DSc (hon.), U. St. Andrews, Scotland, 1984; D Math. (hon.), U. Waterloo, Can., 1990. Instr. U. Ill., Urbana, 1938-39, assoc., 1942-43; fellow, asst. Inst. for Advanced Study, Princeton, N.J., 1939-42; asst. prof. Syracuse (N.Y.) U., 1943-46; from asst. prof. to prof. U. Chgo., 1946-61; prof. U. Mich., Ann Arbor, 1961-68; prof., chmn. dept. U. Hawaii, Honolulu, 1968-69; prof., then Disting. prof. Ind. U., Bloomington, 1969-85; prof. Santa Clara (Calif.) U., 1985-96, prof. emeritus, 1996—. Author: Finite Dimensional Vector Spaces, 1942, Measure Theory, 1950, A Hilbert Space Problem Book, 1967, I Want to Be a Mathematician, 1985, others. Mem. Math. Assn. Am. (Haimo award for Dist. Coll. & Univ. Teaching of Mat., 1994), Am. Math. Soc., others. Avocations: photography, walking. Home: 110 Wood Rd Apt I-203 Los Gatos CA 95030-6720 Office: Santa Clara U Dept Math Santa Clara CA 95053

HALMOS, PETER, entrepreneur; b. Budapest, Hungary, July 4, 1943; came to U.S., 1951; s. George Anthony and Clara (Sacher) H.; m. Vicki Carol Knight, Dec. 31, 1978; children: Nicholas, Gregory. BS, MBA, U. Fla., 1969; postgrad., Harvard U., 1976. Chmn. bd. Safecard Svcs., Inc., Ft. Lauderdale, Fla., 1969-90, exec. mgmt. cons., 1990-92; v.p. High Plains Capital Corp., Cheyenne, Wyo., 1978-92, chmn., 1992—; chmn., CEO Credit Ln. Corp., 1990—, Passport Ins. Co., Inc., Bismark, N.D., 1990—, Your Life Pub. Corp., 1997—, PAH Corp., 1996—, Peter Halmos & Sons, Inc., 1997—, Intelligence Svcs. Corp., 1998—; chmn. Trucks, Podell, Stoll, Blank, Horowitz & Halmos Jam Music Corp., 1998—. Trustee Palm Beach (Fla.) Day Sch., 1988-91; trustee, chmn. Peter Halmos Family Found., Inc., 1984—; bd. dirs. Pinecrest Sch., Ft. Lauderdale, 1985-92; trustee Preservation Found., Palm Beach, 1988—, Palm Beach Community Chest United Way, 1988-92, Am. Cancer Soc., Palm Beach, 1988—. Independent. Episcopalian. Home: 315 Clarke Ave Palm Beach FL 33480-6126

HALOPOFF, WILLIAM EVON, industrial designer, consultant; b. Los Angeles, May 31, 1934; s. William John Halopoff and Dorothy E. (Foote) Lawrence; m. Nancy J. Ragsdale, July 12, 1960; children: Guy William and Carolee Nichole. BS, Art Ctr. Coll. Design, 1968. Internat. indsl. design cons. FMC Corp. Cen. Engring. Lab., Santa Clara, Calif., 1969-81; mgr. indsl. design Tandem Computers, Cupertino, Calif., 1981-93; design cons. Halopoff Assocs., San Jose, Calif., 1984—. Patentee in field. Served with U.S. Army, 1957-59. Mem. Indsl. Designers Soc. Am., Soc. Automotive Engrs. (chmn. subcom. 29 1979-85). Avocation: fine art. Home and Office: 17544 Holiday Dr Morgan Hill CA 95037-6303

HALPENNY, DIANA DORIS, lawyer; b. San Francisco, Jan. 18, 1951; d. William Frederick and Doris E. Halpenny. BA, Calif. State Coll., 1973; JD Order of Coif, Univ. Pacific, 1980. Bar: Calif. 1980. Bookkeeper, sales clk. Farmers Empire Drugs, Santa Rosa, Calif., 1971-73; activity dir. Beverly Manor Convalescent Hosp., Anaheim, Calif., 1973-74; instructional aide LA County Supt. Schs., Downey, Calif., 1974-76, sub. tchr., 1976-77; assoc. Littler, Mendelson, Fastiff & Tichy, San Jose, Calif., 1980-82, Walters & Shelburne, Sacramento, 1982-84, Kronick Moskovitz Tiedemann & Girard, Sacramento, 1984-85; legal advisor Pub. Employment Rels. Bd., 1985-87; gen. counsel San Juan Unified Sch. Dist., 1987—. Founding mem. In-house Sch. Attys No. Calif.; past pres. no. sect. Sch. Law Study Sect. County Counsels Assn., 1991-92; legal adv. com. Calif. Sch. Bd. Assn. Edn. Legal Alliance; exec. bd. Calif. Edn. Mandated Cost Network, 1987—, chair 1998—. Mem. Calif. Coun. Sch. Attys. (v.p. programs 1993, pres. elect 1994, pres. 1995, exec. bd. dirs. 1993—). Office: San Juan Unified Sch Dist 3738 Walnut Ave Carmichael CA 95608-3099

HALPER, EMANUEL B(ARRY), real estate lawyer, developer, consultant, author; b. Bronx, N.Y., June 24, 1933; s. Nathan N. and Molly (Rabinowitz) H.; m. Ilona Rubinstein, Mar. 5, 1961; children: Eve Brook, Dan Reed. AB, CCNY, 1954; JD, Columbia U., 1957. Bar: N.Y. 1958, Minn. 1982; real estate broker, N.Y. House counsel Howard Stores Corp., Bklyn., 1960; ptnr. Zissu, Berman, Halper & Gumbinger, N.Y.C., 1965-87, of counsel, 1987—; ptnr. Can. Pacific Realty Co., N.Y.C., 1970—; v.p. devel. Chase Enterprises, Hartford, Conn., 1987-89; pres. Am. Devel. and Cons. Corp., Greenvale, N.Y., 1989—, Texam. Horizon Ventures, 1989-93; adj. prof. real estate NYU, 1973-83; spl. prof. law Hofstra U., 1998—. Author: Wonderful World of Real Estate, 1975 (republished as Conversations in Real Estate, 1990), Shopping Center and Store Leases, 1979, Ground Leases and Land Acquisition Contracts, 1988; columnist N.Y. Law Jour., 1982—; contbg. editor Real Estate Review, N.Y.C., 1973—; chmn. editorial policy com. Internat. Property Investment Jour., Hempstead, N.Y., 1982-87. With USAR, 1957-63. Recipient Disting. Teaching award NYU, 1978, Dean's award Hofstra U. Law Sch., 1987. Mem. ABA (chmn. comml. leasing com. 1986-93, chmn. comml. and indsl. leasing group 1993-94, mem. supervisory coun. of real property, probate and trust law sect. 1994—, mem. standing com. on CLE, 1994-96, mem. standing com. pubs. 1997-98, Gavel award 1977), World Assn. Lawyers (chmn. internat. real estate com. 1982-90), Internat. Inst. for Real Estate Studies (chmn. bd. 1980-87), Am. Coll. Real Estate Lawyers. Jewish. Avocations: writing, painting, gardening, yoga, running. Office: PO Box 261 Greenvale NY 11548-0261

HALPER, JUNE ANN, human resource development consultant; b. N.Y.C., Dec. 13, 1949; d. Harold Herbert and Sophy (Cohen) H. BS in Edn. magna cum laude, Syracuse U., 1970; MA in Guidance and Counseling, Columbia U., 1971, MEd, 1973. Asst. mgmt. devel. and tng. Philip Morris, USA, N.Y.C., 1971-75; mgr. orgnl. devel. and tng. RCA Missile and Surface Radar, Moorestown, N.J., 1975-80; prin. cons. Ebasco Svcs., Inc., N.Y.C., 1980-86; prin. The Halper Group, Ltd., N.Y.C., 1986—; sr. cons. Guttman Devel. Strategies, Inc., 1995—; adj. instr. Am. Mgmt. Assn. Mem. N.Y. Human Resource Planners, Am. Soc. for Tng. and Devel.

HALPER, THOMAS, political science educator; b. Bklyn., Dec. 1, 1942; s. Albert and Pauline (Friedman) H.; m. Marilyn S. Snyder, Jan. 14, 1979; 1 dau., Pauline. A.B., St. Lawrence U., 1963; M.A., Vanderbilt U., 1967, Ph.D., 1970. Instr. Tulane U., 1967-68; asst. prof. polit. sci. Coe Coll., 1968-74; asst. prof. polit. sci. Baruch Coll., 1974-76, prof., chmn. dept., 1976—. Author: Foreign Policy Crises, 1971, Power, Politics and American Democracy, 1981, The Misfortunes of Others, 1989; contbr. articles to profl. jours. Mem. Am. Polit. Sci. Assn. Home: 75 Livingston St Brooklyn NY 11201-5054 Office: Baruch Coll Dept Polit Sci 17 Lexington Ave Dept Polit New York NY 10010-5518

HALPERIN, BERTRAND ISRAEL, physics educator; b. Bklyn., Dec. 6, 1941; s. Morris and Eva (Teplitsky) H.; m. Helena Stacy French, Sept. 23, 1962; children: Jeffery Arnold, Julia Stacy. A.B., Harvard U., 1961; A.M., U. Calif., 1963, Ph.D., 1965; vis. grad. student, Princeton U., 1964-65. NSF postdoctoral fellow U. Paris, 1965-66; mem. tech. staff Bell Labs., Murray Hill, N.J., 1966-76; lectr. Harvard U., 1969-70, prof. physics, 1976—, chmn. dept. physics, 1988-91, Hollis prof. maths. and natural philosophy, 1992—; cons. Lucent Technologies, Schlumberger-Doll Rsch. Labs. Assoc. editor: Revs. Modern Physics, 1973-80. Fellow Am. Phys. Soc. (Oliver Buckley prize 1982), Am. Acad. Arts and Scis.; mem. NAS, Am. Philos. Soc. Rsch. in solid state theory, statis. physics. Office: Harvard U Dept Physics Cambridge MA 02138

HALPERIN, JEROME ARTHUR, pharmaceutical executive; b. Paterson, N.J., Feb. 21, 1937; s. Harry Nathan and Frieda (Niestat) H.; m. Barbara Anne Hott, Sept. 1, 1963; children: Alicia Jennifer Odom, Rachel Elizabeth Carr. BS, Rutgers U., 1958; MPH, Johns Hopkins U., 1962; MS, MIT, 1974; DSc (hon.), Mercer U., 1993, Mass. Coll. Pharm., 1995, Phila. Coll. Pharmacy and Sci., 1996. Commd. officer USPHS, 1958, advanced through grades to asst. surgeon gen. (rear adm.), 1983; staff pharmacist USPHS Hosps., Dept. HEW, Albuquerque and N.Y.C., 1958-61; radiol. health specialist Calif. Health Dept., Berkeley, 1962-65; agreement states coord. Bur. Radiol. Health, Rockville, Md., 1965-66; dir. indsl. radiation and air hygiene Kans. Dept. Health, Topeka, 1966-68; regional rep. Bur. Radiol. Health, Chgo., 1968-71; dir. Northeastern Radiol. Health Lab., FDA, HEW, Winchester, Mass., 1971-73; dep. assoc. dir. new drug evaluation Bur. Drugs, FDA, HEW, Rockville, Md., 1974-77, dep. dir., 1977-82; acting dir. Office of Drugs Nat. Ctr. for Drugs and Biologics FDA, Rockville, 1982-83; v.p. tech. CIBA Consumer Pharms., Edison, N.J., 1983-89; exec. dir. U.S. Pharmacopeial Conv., Inc., Rockville, Md., 1989-95, exec. v.p., CEO, 1995—; chmn. Conf. on Pharmacy 21st Century Va., 1984; cons. WHO, 1979—; trustee Am. Inst. History of Pharmacy, Food & Drug Law Inst., Am. Found. for Pharm. Edn. Contbr. articles to profl. jours. Mem. Bd. Health, Hoffman Estates, Ill., 1971; bd. dirs. Perspective Woods Citizen Assn., Olney, Md., 1977-80. Named Alumnus of Yr., Rutgers U. Coll. of Pharmacy, 1981; recipient Outstanding Svc. award Federally Employed Women's Assn., 1983. Fellow AAAS, APHA, Am. Assn. of Pharm. Scientists; mem. Drug Info. Assn., Am. Pharm. Assn., Internat. Pharm. Fedn. (mem. bd. pharm. scis.). Jewish. Office: US Pharmacopeia 12601 Twinbrook Pkwy Rockville MD 20852-1790

HALPERIN, JOHN STEPHEN, mathematics educator; b. Kingston, Ont., Can., Feb. 1, 1942; s. Israel and Mary Esther (Sawdey) H.; m. Janet R.P. Thorgrimsson, Apr. 14, 1979; children: Nicole, Adam. BSc, U. Toronto, 1965, MSc, 1966; PhD, Cornell U., 1970. Asst. prof. math. U. Toronto, Ont., Can., 1970-74, assoc. prof. math., 1975-79, prof. math., 1979—, chmn. dept., 1991-98, sr. advisor to v.p. rsch. and internat. rels., 1998—; vis. prof. U. de Lille, France, 1976-77, 82, 89, U. Nice, France, 1982, 86, Stockholm U., 1985, U. Louvain-la-Neuve, Belgium, 1979, 88, 90; program leader MITACS, network ctrs. of excellence, 1998—; Jeffery-Williams lectr., 1998. Author: Connections, Curvature and Cohomology, 1972, 2d vol., 1974, 3d vol., 1976. Contbr. articles to profl. jours. Nat. Scis. and Engring. Research Council grantee, 1971—; NATO grantee, 1985—. Fellow Royal Soc. Can.; mem. Can. Math. Soc., Am. Math. Soc. Home: 75 Wembley Rd, Toronto, ON Canada M6C 2G3 Office: Univ Toronto, Dept Math, Toronto, ON Canada M5S 1A1

HALPERIN, JOHN WILLIAM, English literature educator; b. Chgo., Sept. 15, 1941; s. S. William and Elaine P. H. AB, Bowdoin Coll., 1963; MA, U. N.H., 1966, Johns Hopkins U., 1968; PhD, Johns Hopkins U., 1969. Asst. prof. English SUNY, Stony Brook, 1969-72; dir. summer session SUNY, 1969-72, asst. to acad. v.p., 1971-72; assoc. prof. English U. So. Calif., 1972-77, prof., 1977-83, dir. grad. studies in English, 1973-75; Centennial prof. English Vanderbilt U., Nashville, 1983—; fellow Wolfson Coll., Oxford U., 1976; vis. prof. U. Sheffield, Eng., 1979-80. Author: The Language of Meditation, 1973, Egoism and Self-Discovery in the Victorian Novel, 1974, (with Janet Kunert) Plots and Characters in the Fiction of Jane Austen, The Brontes and George Eliot, 1976, Trollope and Politics, 1977, Gissing: A Life in Books, 1982, C.P. Snow: An Oral Biography, 1983, The Life of Jane Austen, 1984, reprint, 1996, Jane Austen's Lovers and Other Essays, 1988, Novelists in Their Youth, 1990, Eminent Georgians, 1995, reprinted, 1998; editor: Henry James, The Golden Bowl, 1972, The Theory of the Novel, 1974, Jane Austen: Bicentenary Essays, 1975, George Gissing, Denzil Quarrier, 1979, Anthony Trollope, Lord Palmerston, 1981, Anthony Trollope, Sir Harry Hotspur of Humblethwaite, 1981, Trollope Centenary Essays, 1982, Anthony Trollope, Dr. Wortle's School, 1984, George Meredith, The Ordeal of Richard Feverel, 1984, George Gissing, The Emancipated, 1985, George Gissing, Will Warburton, 1985, Anthony Trollope, The Belton Estate, 1986, Anthony Trollope, The American Senator, 1986, George Gissing, In The Year of Jubilee, 1987, Proust, 1988, Gissing, New Grub Street, 1992, Anthony Trollope, The Vicar of Bullhampton, 1997; contbr. articles and essays to profl. jours. With U.S. Army, 1963-69. NDEA fellow, 1966-69, Rockefeller Found. fellow, 1976, Am. Philos. Soc. fellow, 1978, Guggenheim fellow, 1978-79, 85-86, Am. Coun. Learned Socs. fellow, 1981. Fellow Royal Soc. Lit.; mem. MLA, PEN. Office: Vanderbilt U Dept English Nashville TN 37235

HALPERIN, KRISTINE BRIGGS, insurance sales and marketing professional; b. Pocatello, Idaho, July 25, 1947; d. Fergus and Shirley (Tanner) Briggs; m. Michael Lauren Halperin, Aug. 5, 1995; children: Anthony Ted Rojas, Nancy Kristine Rojas. Student, Idaho State U., 1965-66. Tech. coord. Farmers Ins. Group, Pocatello, 1971-81; svc. rep. All Seasons Ins. Agy., Ventura, Calif., 1982; sr. comml. underwriting asst. Royal Ins. Co., Ventura, 1982-85; sr. comml. lines underwriter Andreini & Co., Ventura, 1985-88; large comml. account unit coord. Frank B. Hall, Inc., Oxnard, Calif., 1988-93; mgr. comml. lines dept. Fox Ins. Agy. Inc., Camarillo, Calif., 1993—. Editor (bulletin) News Waves, 1985-87, 98—; artist various works specializing in charcoal portraits. Mem. NAFE, Ins. Women Ventura County (treas. 1987-88, v.p. 1988-90, 96-97, pres. 1990-91, 97-98, corr. sec. 1991-92, bd. dirs. 1986, Woman of Yr. 1989-90), Nat. Assn. Ins. Women. Republican. Baptist. Avocations: belly dancing, gardening, reading, hiking, carpentry. Home: 2197 Brookhill Dr Camarillo CA 93010-2107 Office: Fox Ins Agy Inc 2301 Daily Dr Ste 200 Camarillo CA 93010-6680

HALPERIN, MORTON H., political scientist; b. Bklyn., June 13, 1938; s. Harry and Lillian (Neubert) H.; m. Ina Elaine Weinstein, June 19, 1960 (div. Dec. 1979); children: David, Mark, Gary; m. Carol Pitchersky, Sept. 29, 1991. A.B., Columbia U., 1958; M.A., Yale U., 1959, Ph.D., 1961. Research assoc. Harvard U., 1960-66, asst. prof., 1963-66; dep. asst. sec. U.S. Dept. Def., Washington, 1966-69; sr. staff mem. Nat. Security Council, Washington, 1969; sr. fellow Brookings Instn., Washington, 1969-73; research project dir. Twentieth Century Fund, Washington, 1974-75; dir. Ctr. Nat. Security Studies, Washington, 1975-92; dir. Washington office ACLU, 1985-92; sr. assoc. Carnegie Endowment for Internat. Peace, 1992-94; Barer Prof. Internat. Rels. The George Washington U., Washington, 1992-94; spl. asst. to pres., sr. dir. for democracy Nat. Security Coun., Washington, 1994-96; sr. fellow Cou. Fgn. Rels., Washington, 1996-98; sr. v.p. Twentieth Century Fund/Century Found., Washington, 1997-98; dir. policy planning staff Dept. of State, 1998—. Author: Limited War in the Nuclear Age, 1963, Contemporary Military Strategy, 1967, Bureaucratic Politics and Foreign Policy, 1974, Top Secret, 1977, Nuclear Fallacy, 1987, Self-Determination in a New World Order, 1992. Recipient Meritorious Civilian Service award U.S. Dept. Def., 1969; recipient Hugh M. Hefner 1st Amendment Playboy Found., 1981, W. Lucius Cross medal Yale Grad. Sch. Alumni Assn., 1983, John Jay award Columbia Coll., 1986; MacArthur Found. fellow, 1981-85. Mem. ACLU, Coun. Fgn. Rels., Fedn. Am. Scientists Internat., Inst. Strategic Studies. Democrat. Jewish. Home: 2101 Connecticut Ave NW Washington DC 20008-1728

HALPERIN, RICHARD E., lawyer, holding company executive; b. N.Y.C., Dec. 7, 1954; s. Alvin M. and Anne (Beecher) H.; m. Lucy Landesman, Oct. 5, 1980. BS cum laude, Boston U., 1976; JD, New Eng. Sch. of Law, 1979. Bar: N.Y. 1980. Adminstrv. asst. to atty. gen. N.Y. State Exec. Bur., 1979-84; pres. R.O.P. Aviation, Teterboro, N.J., 1984-99; exec. v.p., spl. counsel to the chmn. Revlon Group Inc., N.Y.C., 1985-99, MacAndrews & Forbes Group, Inc., N.Y.C., 1984-99; founder, CEO Vebcity Group LLC, N.Y.C., 1999—; pres. Revlon Found., 1985—, MacAndrews & Forbes Found., N.Y.C., 1984—. Office: Vebcity Group LLC 38 E 63nd St New York NY 10021

HALPERIN, RICHARD GEORGE, information technology executive; b. Chgo., Apr. 5, 1948; s. Robert Charles and Phyllis Dorothy (Jewel) H.; m. Carolyn A'Della Bacino, Oct. 5, 1974; children: Nicole, Heidi, Erik. BSBA, Northwestern U., 1970. Mktg. mgr. IBM, Des Plaines, Ill., 1970-79; nat. sales mgr. Kast Metals, Shreveport, La., 1979-83; area dir. Wang Labs., Rolling Meadows, Ill., 1983-85; v.p. sales and svcs. System Software Assoc., Chgo., 1985-89; sr. v.p. Software Group XL Datacomp, Hinsdale, Ill., 1989-91; pres. Ex, Inc., Chgo., 1991-92; pres., CEO JBA Internat., Inc., Birmingham, Eng., 1992—, also bd. dirs.; bd. dirs. JBA Internat., Birmingham, Genesis, Glenview, Ill., Advanced Graphical Applications, Schaumburg, Am. Indian Svcs., Phoenix, Alliance, Anderson Cons., Chgo.; partnership CADDO Petroleum, Shreveport, La., 1981-86, BLM, Shreveport, 1981—. Named Top Dist. Mgr., Wang, Chgo., and Rome, 1984. Mem. Internat. Soc. Philos. Enquiry, Data Processing Mgrs. Assn., Info. Tech. Assn. Am., Northwestern Club of Chgo., Delta Upsilon, N Club Mens. Address: 641 Golf Rd Crystal Lake IL 60014-5650

HALPERIN, ROBERT MILTON, retired electrical machinery company executive; b. Chgo., June 1, 1928; s. Herman and Edna Pearl (Rosenberg) H.; m. Ruth Levison, June 19, 1955; children: Mark, Margaret, Philip. Ph.B., U. Chgo., 1949; B.Mech. Engring., Cornell U., 1949; M.B.A., Harvard U., 1952. Engr. Electro-Motive div. Gen. Motors Corp., La Grange, Ill., 1949-50; trust rep. Bank of Am., San Francisco, 1954-56; adminstr. Dumont Corp., San Rafael, Calif., 1956-57; vice chmn., bd. dirs. Raychem Corp., Menlo Park, Calif., 1957-94; bd. dirs. Avid Tech. Inc., Wildlife Comms., Inc. Bd. trustees U. Chgo.; bd. dirs. Harvard Bus. Sch. Pub. Co., Stanford Health Svcs. Lt. USAF, 1952-63. Mem. Harvard Club of N.Y.C. Office: Ste 100 755 Page Mill Rd Bldg A Palo Alto CA 94304-1018

HALPERIN, SAMUEL, education and training policy analyst; b. Chgo., May 10, 1930; married; 2 children. Student (scholar), Ill. Inst. Tech., 1948-49; A.B., A.M. (scholar 1950-52), Washington U., St. Louis, 1952, Ph.D. in Polit. Sci. (fellow 1954-56), 1956; postgrad. (fellow), Columbia U., 1953-54. Asst. prof. polit. sci. Wayne State U., 1956-60; Am. Polit. Sci. Assn. congl. fellow Com. on Edn. and Labor, U.S. Ho. of Reps., 1960-61; legis. asst. to Hon. Cleveland M. Bailey and Adam C. Powell, 1960-61; cons. to subcom. on edn. and Senator Wayne Morse, Com. on Labor and Public Welfare, U.S. Senate, 1961, subcom. on reorgn., research and internat. orgns., 1970-73; specialist, dir. legis. services br. U.S. Office Edn., Washington, 1961-64; asst. U.S. commr. edn. for legis. and dir. office legis. and congl. relations, 1964-66; dep. asst. sec. for legis. HEW, Washington, 1966-69; dir. Ednl. Staff Seminar, Washington, 1969-73; dir. Inst. for Ednl. Leadership, George Washington U., 1973-81, pres., 1981, sr. fellow, 1981-86; fellow Jerusalem Ctr. Pub. Affairs, 1981-84; coordinator Relief Activities in South Lebanon, Am. Jewish Joint Distbn. Com., 1982; dir. Am. Youth Policy Forum, Washington, 1993-99; professorial lectr. Am. U., 1962-63; adj. prof. Tchrs. Coll. Columbia U., 1966-68; lectr. in edn. policy Duke U. Inst. Policy Scis. and Public Affairs, 1974-75; Alfred N. Whitehead fellow for advanced study in edn. Harvard U., 1969; mem. vis. com. Harvard Grad. Sch. Edn., 1973-79; mem. Urban Edn. Task Force, Nat. Urban Coalition; mem. profl. rev. panels; cons. speaker, guest lectr. in field; mem. nat. adv. bd. U.S. Peace Corps, Exec. High Sch. Internships Am., Nat. Sch. Vol. Program, HEW Steering Com. on Life-Long Learning, Nat. Student Ednl. Fund, Am. Council Edn.'s Nat. Identification Program for Advancement Women in Higher Edn. Adminstrn., United Student Aid Funds; mem. Sec. of Navy's Adv. Bd. on Edn. and Tng.; mem. adv. panel on human resources research Rand Corp. Author: The Political World of American Zionism, 1961, 2d edit., 1985, A University in the Web of Politics, 1960, Essays on Federal Education Policy, 1975, A Guide for the Powerless, 1981, Any Home a Campus: Open University of Israel, 1984, The forgotten Half Revisited, 1998; co-editor, contbg. author: Perspectives on Federal Educational Policy, 1976, Federalism at the Crossroads, Improving Educational Policymaking, 1976; contbr. numerous articles, revs. to profl. publs.; cons. Change mag.; mem. nat. adv. bd. Crossreference, Jour. Multi-Cultural Edn. Mem. nat. adv. bd. Am. Jewish Com.; founder, sec. D.C. Youth Svc. Corps.; mem. Nat. Adv. Coun. on Sch.-to-Work, D.C. Commn. on Nat. Svc.; mem. exec. bd. Coalition for Nat. And Cmty. Svc.; bd. dirs. Learning Matters: The Merrow Report on PBS, Ctr. for Youth as Resources, Assocs. for Renewal in Edn. Maj. ROTC, 1948-52. Recipient Superior Svc. award HEW, 1964, 67, Disting. Svc. award, 1968; award of merit Nat. Assn. Pub. Sch. Adult Edn.; Disting. Svc. awards Nat. Assn. State Bds. Edn., 1977, Nat. Assn. of Svc. and Conservation Corps., 1990, 97, Jobs for the Future, 1994, Pres.'s medal George Washington U., 1994, Harry S. Truman award Am. Assn. C.C., 1995, Lewis Hine Award, 1999; AFL-CIO rsch. grantee, 1959-60, Wayne State U. faculty rsch. grantee, 1958-59; Rockefeller Found. fellow, Bellagio, 1981, 92. Mem. D.C. Pvt. Industry Coun., Phi Beta Kappa, Pi Sigma Alpha (pres.). E-mail: shalperin@aypf.org. Home: 3041 Normanstone Ter NW Washington DC 20008-2731 Office: Am Youth Policy Forum 1836 Jefferson Pl NW Washington DC 20036-2505

HALPERIN, STUART, entertainment company executive; b. Bklyn., June 20, 1963. Newswriter CNN; various mktg. positions New Line Cinema, 20th Century Fox Internat., Universal Pictures; co-founder, exec. v.p. Hollywood Online, Santa Monica, Calif. Office: Hollywood Online 1620 26th St Ste 370 South Santa Monica CA 90404-4040

HALPERN, ABRAHAM LEON, psychiatrist; b. Warsaw, Poland, Feb. 2, 1925; came to U.S., 1957, naturalized, 1962; s. Rubin M. and Helen (Perelman) H.; m. Marilyn Lois Benjamin; children: Howard, Lon, Marnen, Heather Halpern Schneid, Mark, Emily Halpern Lewis. John. M.D., U. Toronto, Ont., Can., 1952. Diplomate Am. Psychiatry and Neurology with cert. in forensic psychiatry, Am. Bd. Forensic Psychiatry; cert. mental hosp. adminstr. Intern Toronto Western Hosp., 1952-53; resident Warren (Pa.) State Hosp., 1957-60, Ea. Pa. Psychiat. Inst., Phila., 1959; assoc. research scientist Mental Health Research Unit, Syracuse, N.Y., 1961-62; commr. mental health Onondaga County, 1962-67; practice medicine specializing in psychiatry Mamaroneck, N.Y., 1967—; dir. psychiatry United Hosp. Med. Ctr., Port Chester, 1967-91; attending psychiatrist Beth Israel Hosp., N.Y.C., 1968-73, Westchester County Med. Ctr., 1971—; cons. forensic psychiatry High Point Hosp., Port Chester, 1969-93; cons. St. Vincent's Hosp., Harrison, N.Y., 1973-93; clin. assoc. prof. psychiatry N.Y. Med. Coll., Valhalla, N.Y., 1973-80, clin. prof. psychiatry, 1980-94; prof. emeritus of psychiatry N.Y. Med. Coll., Valhalla, 1994—; cons. Rye (N.Y.) Hosp. Ctr., 1994—; attending psychiatrist Kirby Forensic Psychiat. Ctr., Ward's Island, N.Y., 1994-95; attending psychiatrist dept. alcohol/substance abuse treatment Yonkers (N.Y.) Gen. Hosp., 1995-96; clin. dir. mental health svcs. Dept. Correctional Program, Westchester County, N.Y., 1996; clin. asst. prof. SUNY, Syracuse, 1964-67; asst. clin. prof. Mt. Sinai Sch. Medicine, 1970-74; clin. assoc. prof. N.Y. Med. Coll., 1973-80, clin. prof. psychiatry, 1980-94, prof. emeritus, 1994—; clin. prof. forensic psychiatry, N.Y. Sch. Psychiatry, 1979-82; mem. med. adv. com. Vis. Nurse Assn., Syracuse, 1962-67; mem. N.Y. State Mental Hygiene Med. Rev. Bd., 1982-86; bd. govs. High Point Hosp., 1989-92. Assoc. editor Bull. Am. Acad. Psychiatry and the Law, 1982-88; mem. editorial bd. Psychiat. Jour. of U. Ottawa, 1979-91; mem. exec. editorial com. Psychiat. Quar., 1982-90, assoc. editor, 1990—. Chmn. Syracuse chpt. Com. to Abolish Capital Punishment, 1962-65; mem. profl. adv. com. N.Y. State Assn. for Mental Health, 1964-67; mem. N.Y. State Law Revision Adv. Com. on the Insanity Def., 1979-80; mem. Westchester County Community Mental Health Bd., 1976-78, chmn., 1977-78; mem. Westchester County Hosp. Bd., 1992—; bd. visitors Harlem Valley Psychiat. Center, 1978-82; mem. N.Y. State Correction Med. Rev. Bd., 1980-87, N.Y. State Mental Hygiene Med. Rev. Bd., 1982-85; bd. dirs. Westchester Council on Alcoholism, 1980-85. Served to surgeon lt. comdr. Royal Can. Navy, 1942-45, 53-57. Recipient Citizenship award N.Y. State Bar Assn., 1966, Liberty Bell award Onondaga County Bar Assn., 1966. Fellow ACP, Am. Acad. Forensic Scis., Am. Coll. Psychiatrists, Am. Psychiat. Assn. (com. psychiatry and law 1973-75, com. on abuse and misuse psychiatry and psychiatrists 1993—), Am. Assn. Psychoanalytic Physicians (dir. 1978-84), Am. Pub. Health Assn., Academia, Medicinae and Psychiatriae Found.

(charter); mem. AMA, N.Y. State Med. Soc. (com. on mental health, com. bioethical issues, com. on child abuse and domestic violence), Internat. Assn. Forensic Psychotherapy, Pan Am. Med. Assn. (mem. council sect. on psychiatry 1983-85), Westchester County Med. Soc., Westchester Psychiat. Soc. (pres. 1973-74), Soc. Med. Jurisprudence (trustee 1980-85, 99—), Internat. Acad. Law and Mental Health (pres. 1983-87), Am. Acad. Psychoanalysis (sci. assoc. 1987), Am. Acad. Psychiatry and Law (councilor 1978-81, pres. elect 1981-82, pres. 1982-83, Golden Apple award 1987), Accreditation Coun. on Fellowships in Forensic Psychiatry (pres. 1990-93), Internat. Coun. on Prison Med. Svcs. (v.p. 1991—). Home and Office: 720 The Pky Mamaroneck NY 10543-4227

HALPERN, ALVIN MICHAEL, physicist, educator; b. N.Y.C., July 17, 1938; s. Bernard and Gilda (Reiss) H.; m. Mariarosa Roffi, Dec. 2, 1966; children: Kenneth, Marc. AB, Columbia U., 1959, MA, 1961, PhD, 1965. Instr. Pratt Inst., N.Y.C., 1964-65; instr. physics Bklyn. Coll., 1965-66, asst. prof., 1966-69, assoc. prof., 1970-74, prof., 1975—, chmn. dept., 1980-90; exec. dir. Applied Scis. Inst., 1990-93; univ. dir. rsch. devel., v.p. rsch. found. CUNY, 1993-97, univ. dean rsch., acting pres. rsch. found., 1997—. Contbr. articles to profl. jours. Recipient awards CUNY, 1976, 78, 80, 81, 84; Pfister fellow Columbia U., 1961-64, NSF predoctoral fellow Columbia U., 1959-61; NSF grantee, 1970, 72, 73, 78-80, 79-80, 80-82. Mem. AAAS, AAUP, Am. Phys. Soc., Am. Assn. Physics Tchrs., N.Y. Acad. Scis. Office: Rsch Found CUNY 30 W Broadway New York NY 10007-2192

HALPERN, BARRY DAVID, lawyer; b. Champaign, Ill., Feb. 25, 1949; s. I.L. and Trula M. H.; m. Cynthia Ann Zedler, Aug. 4, 1972; children: Amanda M., Trevor H. BA, U. Kans., 1971, JD, 1973. Bar: Kans. 1973, Fla. 1975, Ariz. 1978, Colo. 1991, U.S. Dist. Ct. Kans. 1973, U.S. Dist. Ct. Ariz. 1978, U.S. Supreme Ct. 1976. Ptnr. Snell & Wilmer, Phoenix, 1978—. Bd. dirs. Crisis Nursery, Phoenix, 1987, Friends of Foster Children, Phoenix, 1987, Phoenix Symphony; bd. dirs. Combined Orgn. Met. Phoenix Arts and Scis., pres., 1996-97. Mem. ABA, State Bar Ariz., State Bar, Fla., State Bar Kans., State Bar Colo., Maricopa County Bar Assn. (chmn. med.-legal com. 1995-96). Office: Snell & Wilmer 1 Arizona Ctr Phoenix AZ 85004-0001

HALPERN, BRUCE PETER, academic administrator, researcher, educator; b. Newark, Aug. 18, 1933; s. Leo and Thelma (Rubin) H.; m. Pauline Touber Anklowitz, June 9, 1956; children: Michael Touber, Stacey Rachael. A.B., Rutgers U., 1955; M.Sc., Brown U., 1957, Ph.D., 1959. Asst. prof. physiology SUNY Health Sci. Ctr., Syracuse, N.Y., 1961-66; assoc. prof. psychology, neurobiology and behavior Cornell U., Ithaca, N.Y., 1966-73, prof., 1973-95, chmn. dept. psychology, 1974-90, 91-96, Susan Linn Sage prof. psychology, 1995—, prof. neurobiology and behavior, 1974—; mem. Adv. Panel Sensory Physiology and Perception NSF, 1976-79; mem. adv. com. Nat. Inst. Neurol. and Communicative Disorders and Stroke, NIH, 1978-79, 85-87, Internat. Commn. on Olfaction and Taste, Union of Physiol. Scis., 1986-94; Fogarty sr. internat. fellow, vis. prof. oral physiology Osaka U., 1982-83; chmn. Gordon Conf. on Chem. Senses: Taste and Smell, 1987-90; PHS-NIMH postdoctoral fellow physiology, rsch. assoc., lect. psychology Cornell U., Ithaca, N.Y., 1959-61; vis. scientist Monell Chem. Senses Ctr., 1996-97. Exec. editor Chem. Senses, 1984-88; contbr. articles to profl. jours. NIMH grantee, 1958-62; NIH grantee, 1963-72; NSF grantee, 1972-90. Mem. Am. Physiol. Soc., Assn. Chemoreception Scis. (pres. 1982-83). Office: Cornell U Dept Psychology Dept Psychology Behavior Uris Hall Ithaca NY 14853-7601 *For those with power: As one's ability to influence or control the actions of others increases, one must become increasingly unwilling to use that ability. For scholars: Any generally accepted scientific idea is an ideal area for creative research, since the idea is almost certainly incorrect.*

HALPERN, DANIEL, poet, editor, educator; b. Syracuse, N.Y., Sept. 11, 1945; s. Irving Daniel Halpern and Rosemary (Glueck) Nelson; m. Jeanne Catherine Carter, Dec. 31, 1982. BA, Calif. State U., Northridge, 1969; MFA, Columbia U., 1972. Pub., editor in chief Ecco Press-Antaeus, N.Y.C., 1970—; adj. prof. writing Columbia U., N.Y.C., 1975—, chmn. grad. writing divsn., 1980-84; dir. Nat. Poetry Series, N.Y.C., 1978—. Author: Traveling on Credit, 1972 (Gt. Lakes Colls. Nat. Book award 1973), Street Fire, 1975, Life Among Others, 1978, Seasonal Rights, 1982, The Good Food: Soups, Stews, and Pastas, 1985, Tango, 1987, Halpern's Guide to the Essentials Restaurants of Italy, 1990, Foreign Neon, 1991, Antaeus Theme Issues, 1994, Selected Poems, 1994, Something Shining, 1999; editor: Borges on Writing, 1973, The American Poetry Anthology, 1975, The Art of the Tale: An International Anthology of Short Stories, 1986, Writers on Artists, 1986, On Nature, 1987, Journals, Notebooks, and Diaries, 1988, Versions of Dante's Inferno: Translations by 20 Contemporary Poets, 1993, Not for Bread Alone: Writers on Food, Wine and the Art of Eating, 1993; transls.: Orchard Lamps, Poems by Ivan Drach, 1973, The Poems of Mririda n'Ait Attik, 1975. Fellow NEA, 1973-74, 86, N.Y. State Coun. on Arts, 1978, Robert Frost fellow, 1974; recipient Jessie Rehder Poetry award, 1971, YMHA Discovery award, Pen Publisher citation, 1993. Office: Ecco Press Ltd 100 W Broad St Hopewell NJ 08525-1926

HALPERN, ERIC FRANKLIN, university publishing director; b. Portsmouth, N.H., Feb. 28, 1952; s. Stephen and Irene Sally (Needle) H.; m. Frances Jane Weatherburn; children: Helen Augusta, Ian Henry. BA, U. Calif., Santa Cruz, 1974, Oxford U., 1977; MA, Stanford U., 1980. Asst. editor Acquisitions Cornell Univ. Press., Ithaca, N.Y., 1981-84; editor Humanities Johns Hopkins Univ. Press., Balt., 1984-90, editor-in-chief, 1990-96; dir. Univ. Pa. Press, Phila., 1996—. Mem. Modern Lang. Assn., Classical Assn. Atlantic States. Office: Univ Pa Press 4200 Pine St Philadelphia PA 19104-4011

HALPERN, JACK, chemist, educator; b. Poland, Jan. 19, 1925; came to U.S., 1962, naturalized; s. Philip and Anna (Sass) H.; m. Helen Peritz, June 30, 1949; children: Janice Henry, Nina Phyllis. BS, McGill U., 1946, PhD, 1949; DSc (hon.), U. B.C., 1986, McGill U., 1997. Postdoctorate overseas fellow NRC, U. Manchester, Eng., 1949-50; instr. chemistry U. B.C., 1950, prof., 1961-62; Nuffield Found. traveling fellow Cambridge (Eng.) U., 1959-60; prof. chemistry U. Chgo., 1962-71, Louis Block prof. chemistry, 1971-83, Louis Block Disting. Service prof., 1983—; vis. prof. U. Minn., 1962, Harvard, 1966-67, Calif. Inst. Tech., 1968-69, Princeton U., 1970-71, Max. Planck Institut, Mulheim, Fed. Republic Germany, 1983—, U. Copenhagen, 1978; Sherman Fairchild Disting. scholar Calif. Inst. Tech., 1979; guest scholar Kyoto U., 1981; Firth vis. prof. U. Sheffield, 1982, Phi Beta Kappa vis. scholar, 1990; R.B. Woodward vis. prof. Harvard U., 1991; numerous guest lectureships; cons. editor Macmillan Co., 1963-65, Oxford U. Press; cons. Am. Oil Co., Monsanto Co., Argonne Nat. Lab., IBM, Air Products Co., Enimont, Rohm and Haas; mem. adv. panel on chemistry NSF, 1967-70; mem. adv. bd. Am. Chem. Soc. Petroleum Research Fund, 1972-74; mem. medicinal chemistry sect. NIH, 1975-78, chmn., 1976-78; mem. chemistry adv. council Princeton U., 1982—; mem. univ. adv. com. Ency. Brit., 1985—; mem. chemistry vis. com. Calif. Inst. Tech., 1991—; chmn. German-Am. Acad. Coun., 1993-96, chmn. bd. trustees, 1996—. Assoc. editor: Inorganica Chimica Acta, Jour. Am. Chem. Soc.; co-editor: Collected Accounts of Transition Metal Chemistry, vol. 1, 1973, vol. 2, 1977, Procs. NAS, Oxford Univ. Press, Internat. Series Monographs on Chemistry; mem. editl. bd. Jour. Organometallic Chemistry, Accounts Chem. Rsch., Catalysis Revs., Jour. Catalysis, Jour. Molecular Catalysis, Jour. Coord. Chemistry, Gazzetta Chimica Italiana, Organometallics, Catalysis Letters, Kinetics and Catalysis Letters; contbr. articles to Ency. Britannica, rsch. jours. Trustee Gordon Rsch. Confs., 1968-70; bd. govs. David and Arthur Smart Mus., U. Chgo., 1988—; bd. dirs. Ct. Theatre, 1989—. Recipient Young Author's prize Electrochem. Soc., 1953, award in catalysis Noble Metals Chem. Soc., London, 1976, Humboldt award, 1977, Richard Kokes award Johns Hopkins U., 1978, Willard Gibbs medal, 1986, Bailar medal U. Ill., 1986, Wilhelm von Hoffman medal German Chem. Soc., 1988, Chem. Pioneer's award Am. Inst. Chemists, 1991, Paracelsus prize Swiss Chem. Soc., 1992, Basolo Medal, Northwestern U., 1993, Robert A. Welch award, 1994, Henry J. Albert award Internat. Precious Metals Inst., 1995, award in Organometallic Chem. Am. Chem. Soc., 1995, Order of Merit Federal Republic of Germany, 1996. Fellow AAAS, Royal Soc. London, Am. Acad. Arts and Scis., Chem. Inst. Can., Royal Soc. Chemistry London (hon.), N.Y. Acad. Scis., Japan Soc. for Promotion Sci.; mem. NAS (fgn. assoc. 1984-85, mem. coun. 1990—, chmn. chemistry sect. 1991-93, v.p. 1993—), Am. Chem. Soc. (editl. bd. Advances in Chemistry series 1963-65, 78-81, chmn. inorganic chemistry 1985, award in inorganic chemistry 1968, award for disting. svc. in advancement of inorganic chemistry 1985, award in organometallic chemistry 1995), Max Planck Soc. (sci. mem. 1983—), Art Inst. Chgo., Renaissance Soc. (bd. dirs. 1985—), New Swiss Chem. Soc. (Paracelsus prize 1992), Sigma Xi. Home: 5630 S Dorchester Ave Chicago IL 60637-1722 Office: U Chgo Dept Chemistry Chicago IL 60637

HALPERN, JAMES BLADEN, lawyer; b. Buffalo, Apr. 20, 1936; s. Philip and Goldene P. (Friedman) H.; m. Jessie Malkoff, July 6, 1958 (div.); 1 child, Jennifer; m. Niesa N. Brateman, Aug. 26, 1979; 1 child, Sheri. B.A., Harvard U., 1958, J.D., 1961. Bar: N.Y. 1961, D.C. 1970. Atty. corp. fin. div. SEC, Washington, 1961-64; chief counsel-instns., instl. investor study, 1969-70; assoc. firm Proskauer Rose Goetz & Mendelsohn, N.Y.C., 1964-69; assoc. Arent Fox Kintner Plotkin & Kahn, PLLC, Washington, 1971-73, mem., 1974—. Mem. ABA, D.C. Bar Assn., Assn. Bar City N.Y., Am. Law Inst. Democrat. Jewish. Office: Arent Fox Kintner Et Al 1050 Connecticut Ave NW Washington DC 20036-5339

HALPERN, JAMES S., federal judge; b. N.Y.C., Oct. 16, 1945; s. William and Marion (Kohn) H.; m. Nancy A. Nord, Mar. 8, 1984; children: W. Dyer, Hilary A. BS cum laude, U. Pa., 1967, JD, 1972; LLM in Taxation, NYU, 1975. Bar: N.Y. 1973, D.C. 1983. Assoc. Mudge, Rose, Guthrie & Alexander, N.Y.C.; asst. prof. law sch. Washington and Lee U., Va., 1972-74, St. John's U., N.Y., 1976-78; vis. prof. law sch. NYU, 1978-79; assoc. Roberts & Holland, N.Y.C., 1979-80; prin. tech. advisor IRS, Dept. Treas., 1980-83; ptnr. Baker & Hostetler, Washington, 1983-90; judge U.S. Tax Ct., Washington, 1990—. Col. USAR. Mem. ABA (tax sect.). Office: US Tax Ct 400 2nd St NW Washington DC 20217*

HALPERN, JEFFREY, advertising company executive; b. Bronx, N.Y., Nov. 11, 1959; s. Marvin and Ethel Dora Halpern. BS in Journalism, W.Va. U., 1981. Group dir. Sutton Pub. Rels., N.Y.C., 1991-92; v.p. Medicus Pub. Rels., N.Y.C., 1992-94; copy/account supr. Medicus Advt., N.Y.C., 1994-95; copy supr. Cline Davis Mann, N.Y.C., 1995-96; v.p., group copy supr. healthcare advt. Harrison Star, N.Y.C., 1996-97, v.p., group copy supr., 1997—. Recipient N.Y. Pyramid awards, 1994, 95, CIpRA award, 1995, DuPont Employee Recognition award, 1994. Home: 60 W Broad St Mount Vernon NY 10552 Office: Harrison Star 16 W 22d St New York NY 10010

HALPERN, JOEL MARTIN, anthropologist, photographer; b. N.Y.C., Apr. 8, 1929; s. Carl M. and Nettie M. (Cantor) H.; m. Barbara D. Kerewsky, Oct. 26, 1952; children: Kay L., Susannah L. Cargill, Carla A. BA, U. Mich., 1950; PhD, Columbia U., 1956. Rsch. assoc., human rels. area files Am. U., Washington, 1956; field svc. officer FSR/ICA/Dept. State, Laos, 1956-58; asst. prof. dep. anthropology UCLA, 1958-63; assoc. prof. dept. anthropology Brandeis U., Waltham, Mass., 1963-67; assoc. Russ Rsch. Ctr./Harvard U., Cambridge, Mass., 1965-67; assoc. prof. anthropology U. Mass., Amherst, 1967-69, prof., 1969-92, prof. emeritus, 1992—; vis. prof. U. Freiburg, Germany, 1970-71; sr. rsch. assoc. Inst. Southeastern European Studies U. Graz (Austria), 1993—, vis. prof., 1994; resident fellow MIT-Harvard Joint Ctr. Urban Studies, Cambridge, 1969-70; cons. RAND Corp., 1959-61. Author: A Serbian Village, 1958, 2d edit., 1967, The Changing Village Community, 1967, Government and Politics in Laos, 1964; author, editor: The Far East comes Near, 1989; featured in catalogues. Chair Meking com. Asia Soc./U.S. AID, 1968-70; legal cons. immigration cases, 1984—; cons. U.S. AID/Bosnia, 1996, U.S. Congress, 1998-99. NSF grantee, various yrs.; NEH rsch. grantee, 1974-77, NIMH-NICHHD, 1974-77; IREX rsch. adv., 1993-94. Fellow Am. Anthrop. Assn.; mem. Am. Assn. for Advancement of Slavic Studies, Assn. for Asian Studies, Current Anthropology, Am. Assn. S.E. European Studies. Office: U Mass Dept Anthropology Amherst MA 01003

HALPERN, JOSEPH ALAN, physician; b. Bklyn., Feb. 28, 1952; s. Lester A. and Adele Janet (Tax) H.; m. Cynthia Gould, Sept. 1, 1979; 1 child, Elyza. AB, Bard Coll., Annandale on Hudson, N.Y., 1974; MD, N.Y. Med. Coll., Valhalla, 1978. Diplomate ABEM, ABIM. Resident family practice SUNY, Buffalo, 1978-79; resident in medicine Norwalk (Conn.) Hosp., 1979-81, chief resident medicine, 1981-82; emergency physician Kent and Queen Anne Hosp., Chestertown, Md., 1982-83, North Arundel Hosp., Glen Burnie, Md., 1983-85; attending emergency physician John Hopkins Hosp., Balt., 1986-87; emergency physician Anne Arundel Med. Ctr., Annapolis, Md., 1987—; attending physician Bayview Med. Ctr., Balt., 1992-94. Fellow Am. Coll. Emergency Physicians; mem. ACP, Med. Chi. Md. Avocations: sailing, bicycling. Home: 2 Waters Rd Severna Park MD 21146-4642 Office: Anne Arundel Med Ctr Franklin at Cathedral St Annapolis MD 21401

HALPERN, MANFRED, political science educator; b. Mittweida, Germany, Feb. 1, 1924; came to U.S., 1937; naturalized, 1944; s. Jacob and Edith (Aron) H.; m. Betsy Steele, Nov. 5, 1948; children: Jeffrey Kim, Tamara Steele, Katrina Ann, David Nicholas; m. Cynthia L. Perwin, Nov. 16, 1978; 1 child, Joshua Christopher. BA, UCLA, 1947; MA, Sch. Advanced Internat. Studies, Washington, 1948; PhD, Johns Hopkins U., 1960. Rsch. analyst div. rsch. for Europe Dept. of State, Washington, 1948, rsch. analyst, 1950-53, spl. asst. to chief div. rsch. for Near East, S. Asia and Africa, 1953-58; prof. politics Princeton U., 1958-94; prof. politics emeritus, 1994—; mem. faculty Johns Hopkins, 1956, George Washington U., 1951-53; lectr. Nat. War Coll. Fgn. Svc. Inst., Strategic Intelligence Sch.; cons. Rand Corp., 1958-66, Dept. State, 1963-67. Author: The Politics of Social Change in the Middle East and North Africa, 1963, The Dialectics of Transformation in Politics, Personality and History, 1973. Chmn. chpt. Student for Dem. Action, Washington, 1947-50; mem. nat. bd. Ams. for Dem. Action, 1949-50. With inf., AUS, 1944-45. Fellow Middle East Studies Assn. N.Am. (program chmn.), Middle East Inst., African Studies Assn. (program chmn.), Adlai Stevenson Inst. Internat. Affairs; mem. Am. Polit. Sci. Assn., Am. Soc. Social Psychiatry (coun.), Phi Beta Kappa. Home: 27 Maclean Cir Princeton NJ 08540-5620 Office: Princeton U Dept Politics Princeton NJ 08540

HALPERN, MARCIA LYNN, neurologist. MD, U. Pa., 1980. Diplomate Am. Bd. Psychiatry and Neurology. Intern UCLA, Los Angeles, 1980-81; resident Dept. Neurology Hosp. U. Penn., Phila., 1981-84; staff Fox Chase Neurologic Assocs., Phila., 1984—. Office: Fox Chase Neurologic Assocs 7602 Central Ave Philadelphia PA 19111

HALPERN, MERRIL MARK, investment banker; b. Bayonne, N.J., May 4, 1934; s. Samuel and Belle (Schwartz) H.; BS, Rutgers U., 1956; MBA, Harvard, 1962; m. Phyllis Goldstein, June 14, 1960 (div.); children: Belle Linda, Jennifer, Samuel, Isaac; m. Dolores M.Eckersley, Aug. 28, 1991. With Ernst & Ernst, N.Y.C., 1956-60, sr. acct., 1958-60; with McDonnell & Co., Inc., 1962-68, v.p., 1967-68; ptnr., dir. corp. fin. H. Hentz & Co., N.Y.C., 1969-70; prin. Merril M. Halpern & Co., N.Y.C., 1970-73; pres. Charterhouse Group Internat., Inc., N.Y.C., 1973-84, chmn. bd., 1984—; dir. Microwave Power Devices, Inc., 1995—, United Road Svcs. Inc., 1998—. Served with AUS, 1957-58. Office: Charterhouse Group Internat Inc 535 Madison Ave New York NY 10022-4212

HALPERN, NATHAN LOREN, communications company executive; b. Sioux City, Iowa, Oct. 22, 1914; s. Aaron and Lena (Robin) H.; m. Edith Kessel, Oct. 7, 1938; 1 son, Michael. B.A., U. So. Calif., 1936; LL.B. cum laude, Harvard, 1939. Bar: Calif., D.C. 1939. Asst. to chmn. SEC, Washington, 1939-41; exec. asst. to dir. WPB, Washington, 1941-42, USIS, France, 1945; asst. to pres. CBS, N.Y.C., 1945-49; pres. TNT Communications, Inc., N.Y.C., 1949—; Former pres. Internat. Center Photography; pres. East Hampton Beach Preservation Soc.; trustee N.Y. Central Park Conservancy. Benefactor, mem. corp. Met. Mus. of Art. Served with USNR, 1942-44. Mem. Soc. Motion Picture and TV Engrs., Phi Beta Kappa. Clubs: Harvard, Players. Home: 993 5th Ave New York NY 10028-0105 Office: 575 Madison Ave New York NY 10022-2511

HALPERN, PAUL G., history educator; b. N.Y.C., Jan. 27, 1937; s. Harry and Teresa (Ritter) H. BA with honors, U. Va., 1958; MA, Harvard U., 1961, PhD, 1966. Instr. Fla. State U., Tallahassee, 1965-66; asst. prof. Fla. State U., 1966-70, assoc. prof., 1970-74; prof. dept. history, 1974—; vis. prof. strategy dept. Naval War Coll., Newport, R.I., 1986-87. Author: The Mediterranean Naval Situation, 1908-14, 1971, The Naval War in the Mediterranean, 1914-18 1987, A Naval History of World War I, 1994, Anton Haus: Österreich-Ungarns Grossadmiral, 1998; editor: The Keyes Papers, 3 vols., 1972-81, The Royal Navy in the Mediterranean, 1915-1918, 1987. Mem. Naval Aviation Mus. Found., Pensacola, Fla., Naval War Coll. Found., Newport, R.I. 1st lt. U.S. Army, 1958-60. Fellow Woodrow Wilson Nat. Fellowship Found., 1958. Fellow Royal Hist. Soc.; mem. Am. Hist. Assn., The Navy Records Soc. (coun. 1968-72, 82-86), Naval Rev., U.S. Naval Inst., Royal United Svcs. Inst. Def. Studies, Friends of Imperial War Mus., Friends of Nat. Maritime Mus., Phi Beta Kappa, Phi Eta Sigma. Avocations: model ship collecting, book collecting, model soldier collection. Home: 3103 Brandemere Dr Tallahassee FL 32312-2423 Office: Fla State U Dept History Bellamy Bldg Tallahassee FL 32306

HALPERN, PHILIP MORGAN, lawyer; b. Derby, Conn., Apr. 17, 1956; s. Edwin Vincent and Carol Veronica (Gallagher) H.; m. Carolyn G. McElwreath, Mar. 11, 1989. BS magna cum laude, Fordham U., 1977; JD, Pace U., 1980. Bar: N.Y. 1981, U.S. Dist. Ct. (so. and ea. dists.) N.Y. 1981, U.S. Ct. Appeals (2d cir.) 1982, U.S. Tax Ct. 1984, U.S. Supreme Ct. 1985, U.S. Dist. Ct. Conn. 1989, Conn. 1989, U.S. Ct. Appeals (3d cir.) 1991. Law clk. to sr. judge U.S. Dist. Ct. (so. dist.) N.Y., N.Y.C., 1980-82; assoc. litigation dept. Kimmelman, Sexter & Sobel, N.Y.C., 1982-83; ptnr. Pirro, Collier, Cohen, & Halpern LLP, N.Y.C., 1983—; mng. ptnr. Pirro, Collier, Cohen, & Halpern LLP, White Plains, N.Y., 1996—; arbitrator Civil Ct. City N.Y. and Am. Arbitration Assn., 1987-96; adv. coun. Bd. of Judges, So. Dist. of N.Y., 1995—; mediator U.S. Dist. (so. dist.) N.Y., 1998—, mem. adv. com. on civil practice, 1999—. Author: Age Discrimination in Employment Act: Employers Can Enforce Releases Too!, 1992, Fair Value Proceedings: Fixing Fair Value in New York, 1996. Chmn. Young Reps., Tuckahoe, N.Y., 1975-77; chmn. taxi commn. Village of Mamaroneck, N.Y., 1986-87, mem. planning bd., 1987-89. Mem. ABA, N.Y. State Bar Assn. (com. on lawyer competency, com. on fed. judiciary), Assn. of Bar of City of N.Y., Assn. Trial Lawyers Am., N.Y. Trial Lawyers Assn., N.Y. County Lawyers Assn., Fed. Bar Coun., Profl. Golfers Assn. (adv. coun. metro. sect. 1992—), Westchester Country Club. Roman Catholic. Office: Pirro Collier Cohen & Halpern One N Lexington Ave White Plains NY 10601 also: 99 Park Ave New York NY 10016-1601

HALPERN, RALPH LAWRENCE, lawyer; b. Buffalo, May 12, 1929; s. Julius and Mary C. (Kaminker) H.; m. Harriet Chasin, June 29, 1958; children: Eric B., Steven R., Julie B. LL.B. cum laude, U. Buffalo, 1953. Bar: N.Y. 1953. Teaching assoc. Northwestern U. Law Sch., 1953-54; assoc. firm Jaeckle, Fleischmann, Kelly, Swart & Augspurger, Buffalo, 1957-58; asso. firm Raichle, Banning, Weiss & Halpern (and predecessors), 1958-59, ptnr., 1959-86; ptnr. Jaeckle, Fleischmann & Mugel, Buffalo, 1986—. Pres. Buffalo Coun. World Affairs, 1972-74, Temple Beth Zion, Buffalo, 1981-83; chmn. Buffalo chpt. Am. Jewish Com., 1975-77; bd. govs. United Jewish Fedn., Buffalo, 1972-78, 91-97, v.p., 1992-95. Served to capt. JAGC U.S. Army, 1954-57. Mem. ABA (ho. dels. 1989-95, 97-99), N.Y. State Bar Assn. (chmn. com. profl. ethics 1971-76, chmn. com. jud. election monitoring 1983-86, chmn. spl. com. to consider adoption of ABA model rules of profl. conduct 1983-85, sec. internat. law and practice sect. 1992-93, vice chmn. 1993-95), Erie County Bar Assn., Am. Judicature Soc., Am. Law Inst. Home: 88 Middlesex Rd Buffalo NY 14216-3618 Office: Jaeckle Fleischmann & Mugel 800 Fleet Bank Bldg Buffalo NY 14202-2292

HALPERN, RICHARD I., lawyer; b. Pitts., June 10, 1949. BA with distinction, Stanford U., 1971; MBA, U. Pa., 1973; JD, NYU, 1976. Bar: Pa. 1976. Ptnr. Eckert, Seamans Cherin & Mellott, Pitts. Mem. ABA. Office: Eckert Seamans Cherin & Mellott 600 Grant St Ste 42 Pittsburgh PA 15219-2703*

HALPERN, STEVEN JAY, editor, newspaper columnist, freelance writer; b. New Rochelle, N.Y., May 20, 1959; s. Barry and Carol (Gussow) H. BA, Brandeis U., 1981. Editor, pub., pres. Dick Davis Pub., Ft. Lauderdale, Fla., 1982—; freelance fin. writer nationwide, 1985—, guest speaker radio, TV and seminars, 1986—; nationally syndicated fin. columnist Knight-Ridder Newspapers, Miami, Fla., 1988—; pres. Internet Global Comm., 1998—; speaker various investment clubs, seminars, etc., U.S. Contbr. articles to profl. jours. Fundraiser Outreach Broward, Ft. Lauderdale, 1986—; bd. dirs. The Solomon Project, Ft. Lauderdale, 1988—; pres. Ctr. One, Ft. Lauderdale, 1991—. Recipient Up-and-Comer award South Fla. Mag., 1992. Democrat. Jewish. Avocations: tennis, skiing, adventure travel. Office: Dick Davis Pub 899 W Cypress Creek Rd Fort Lauderdale FL 33309-2072

HALPERSON, MICHAEL ALLEN, publishing company executive; b. Boston, Sept. 11, 1946; s. Bertram David and Rose (Doolan) H. AB, Union Coll., 1968; MA in Teaching, U. Mass., 1970. Asst. to group v.p. Plymouth Rubber Co., Inc., Canton, Mass., 1972-73; corp. dir. pers. and indsl. rels. Plymouth Rubber Co., Inc., Canton, 1973-79, mgr. mktg., cons. products, 1979-81, dir. sales and mktg., 1981-85, v.p., 1985-92; v.p., gen. mgr. Plymouth Office Products a Hon Industries Co., Pawtucket, R.I., 1992-93; exec. v.p., COO Kryptonite Corp., Canton, Mass., 1994-95; exec. v.p. Dome Pub. Co. Inc., Warwick, R.I., 1995—, Data Binding, Inc., Warwick, R.I., 1995—; v.p. Parkway Realty, Inc., Warwick, R.I., 1995—, Dome Industries, Inc., Warwick, R.I., 1995—; bd. dirs., v.p. Cape Cod Sea Camps, Inc., Capt. Del Assocs., Inc., Brewster, Mass.; bd. dirs. Kryptonite Corp., Canton, Mass., bd. dirs., treas. Camp Wono, Inc., Brewster, Mass. Bd. dirs. Canton Assn. Industries, Inc., 1977-92, Neponset Valley Nursing Assn., Inc., 1979-97, Southwood Cmty. Hosp., Norfolk, Mass., 1983-92, Neponset Valley Hospice, 1993-97, Norfolk-Bristol Homemakers Svc., Inc.; bd. dirs. Neponset Valley Health Sys., Inc., Norwood, Mass., 1985-92, chmn., 1990-92; bd. dirs. Norwood Hosp., Inc., 1983-92, chmn., 1988-90; bd. overseers Boston Ballet, 1992-93, Boston Symphony Orch., 1995—; trustee Boston Ballet Ctr. for Dance Edn., 1993-96, Boston Ballet, 1996—. With USAF, 1970-72. Mem. Bus. Products Industry Assn., (bd. dirs. 1996—), Office Products Mfrs. Assn. (bd. dirs. 1985—, pres. 1989, chmn. 1990); St. Botolph Club, Boston, Williams Club, N.Y.C. Avocations: reading, swimming. Home: 78 Cannon Forge Dr Foxborough MA 02035-5217 Office: Dome Pub Co Inc PO Box 1220 Ten New England Way Warwick RI 02887-1220

HALPERT, DOUGLAS JOSHUA, immigration lawyer; b. Bklyn., Nov. 9, 1962; s. Eugene and Miriam (Feigenbaum) H.; m. Yee-Wen Chen, July 22, 1989. BA in English Lit., U. Chgo., 1984; JD, Fordham Law Sch., 1988. Bar: N.Y. 1989, Ohio 1994. Immigration atty. Cohen, Swados, Wright, Hanifin, Bradford & Brett, Buffalo, 1988-94, Frost & Jacobs, Cin., 1994—. Recipient Vol. Lawyer of Yr. award Cin. Bar Assn., 1998. Mem. Am. Immigration Lawyers Assn., Cin. Bar Assn., Alumni Schs. Com. of U. Chgo. Avocations: lit., writing, movies, sports. Office: Frost & Jacobs 2500 PNC Ctr 201 E 5th St Ste 2500 Cincinnati OH 45202-4182

HALPERT, LEONARD WALTER, retired editor; b. Bklyn., July 7, 1924; s. Daniel and Kate (Hollander) H.; m. Shirley Small, May 25, 1952; 1 child, Melinda. B.A., Bklyn. Coll., N.Y., 1947; M.S. in Journalism, Northwestern U., Evanston, Ill., 1948. Editorial writer Washington Times-Herald, Washington, D.C., 1950-51; reporter Buffalo Evening News, 1948-50, editorial writer, 1951-80, editorial page editor, 1980-89; ret., 1989. Served with AUS, 1943-45. Mem. Am. Soc. Newspaper Editors, Nat. Conf. Editorial Writers, Soc. Profl. Journalists. Home: 12 Neumann Pky Buffalo NY 14223-1429

HALPERT, RICHARD LEE, lawyer; b. Kalamazoo, Mich., Nov. 1, 1947; s. Samuel K. and Rosalie (Zuravel) H.; m. Mary K. Sydlaske, June 24, 1973; children: David, Michael. BA, Kalamazoo Coll., 1969; JD cum laude, Ind. U., 1972. Bar: Mich. 1973, U.S. Dist. Ct. (we. dist.) Mich. 1980, U.S. Supreme Ct. 1985. Trial atty. Van Buren County Pros. Attys. Office, Paw Paw, Mich., 1972-74, Kreis, Enderle, Halpert, Borsos & Ford, Kalamazoo, 1974-82, Halpert & Koning, Kalamazoo, 1982-87, Howard & Howard, Kalamazoo, 1987-95, Halpert, Weston, Wuori & Sawusch, P.C., Kalamazoo, 1996—; lectr. in field. Co-author over 30 manuals for Inst. Continuing Legal Edn.; note editor Ind. Law Jour., 1971-72. Bd. dirs. YMCA, Kalamazoo, 1989-94, bd. trustees, 1998—; Kalamazoo County Rep. Exec. Com., 1975, Kalamazoo County Humane Soc.; trustee Ctrl. Mich. U., Mt. Pleasant, 1981-83. Mem. ATLA, Mich. Trial Lawyers Assn., Am. Burn Assn. (spl. mem. 1984—, rehab. com. 1997—), Internat. Soc. for Burn Injuries (spl. mem.), State Bar Mich. (negligence sect., com. on profl. and jud. ethics 1980-82), Kalamazoo Bar Assn. (chmn. com. on profl. responsibility 1981-83), Phoenix Soc. for Burn Injuries (bd. trustees and exec. com.), Am. Arbitration Assn. Avocations: bicycling, nature photography, hiking. Office: Halpert Weston

Wuori and Sawusch PC Ste 1050 136 E Michigan Ave Kalamazoo MI 49007-3947

HALPERT, STUART D., real estate company executive. BS, Brown U.; JD, George Washington U. Counsel house banking com. U.S. Congress; pvt. practice; co-founder, chmn. First Washington Mgmt., Inc., 1983—; chmn. bd. dirs. First Washington Realty Trust, Inc., Bethesda, Md., '; outside mem. bd. dirs. ElderTrust. Mem. Internat. Coun. Shopping Ctrs. Fax: 301-907-4911. Office: 4350 East-West Hwy Ste 400 Bethesda MD 20814

HALPIN, ANNA MARIE, architect; b. Murphysboro, Ill., July 24, 1923; d. John William and Anna Christina (Weilmuenster) H. B.S. in Architecture, U. Ill., 1948. Designer, project architect various firms,, San Francisco, Rome, N.Y.C., 1948-67; editorial dir. Sweet's div. McGraw-Hill, Inc., N.Y.C., 1967-88; ret. Sweet's div. McGraw-Hill, Inc.; freelance cons., 1988-98; rep. to Constrn. Industries Coordination Com., Am. Nat. Metric Council, 1974-80. Mem. AIA (treas., dir. N.Y. chpt. 1974-78, coll. fellows 1976, nat. dir. 1977-79, nat. v.p. 1980, dir. Found. 1980, Richard Upjohn fellow 1991), Women's Equity Action League (pres. N.Y. state orgn. 1976-77), Constrn. Specifications Inst., Alliance Women in Architecture. Home: 519 E 86th St New York NY 10028-7541

HALPIN, DANIEL WILLIAM, civil engineering educator, consultant; b. Covington, Ky., Sept. 29, 1938; s. Jordan W. and Gladys E. (Moore) H.; m. Maria Kirchner, Feb. 8, 1963; 1 son, Rainer. B.S., U.S. Mil. Acad., 1961; M.S.C.E., U. Ill., 1969, Ph.D., 1973. Research analyst Constrn. Engring. Research Lab., Champaign, Ill., 1970-72; faculty U. Ill., Urbana, 1972-73; mem. faculty Ga. Inst. Tech., Atlanta, 1973-85, prof., 1981-85; A.J. Clark prof., dir. Constrn. Engring. and Mgmt. U. Md., 1985-87; dir. div. Constrn. Engring. and Mgmt. Purdue U., 1987—; cons. constrn. mgmt.; vis. assoc. prof. U. Sydney, Australia, 1981; vis. prof. Swiss Fed. Inst. Tech., 1985, U. Karlsruhe, Germany, 1998; vis. scholar Tech. U., Munich, 1979; vis. lectr. Ctr. Cybernetics in Constrn., Bucharest, Romania, 1973; cons. office tech. assessment U.S. Congress, 1986-87; mem. JTEC Team to evaluate constrn. tech., Japan, 1990. Author: Design of Construction and Process Operations, 1976, Construction Management, 1980, Planung und Kontrolle von Bauproduktionsprozessen, 1979, Constructo - A Heuristic Game for Construction Management, 1973, Financial and Cost Control Concepts for Construction Management, 1985, Planning and Analysis of Construction Operations, 1992, Construction Management, 2d edit., 1997. Served with C.E., U.S. Army, 1961-67. Decorated Bronze Star; recipient Walter L. Huber prize ASCE, 1979, Peurifoy Constrn. Rsch. award, 1992; grantee NSF, Dept. Energy. Mem. ASCE (past sect. pres. 1981-82, chmn. constrn. rsch. coun. 1985-86, Peurifoy Constrn. Rsch. award 1992), Am. Soc. Engring. Edn., Sigma Xi. Methodist.

HALPIN, JAMES, retail computer stores executive. V.p., sr. merchandising mgr. Zayre Copr., 1984-88; pres. BJ's Wholesale Club, 1988-90; exec. v.p. Waban, Inc., 1990-92; pres. HomeBase, 1991-92; pres., CEO, bd. dirs. CompUSA, Dallas, 1993—; bd. dirs. Interphase Corp., Invincible Techs. Corp., Remington Products, Toy Biz, Inc. Mem. gov. bd. Jr. Achievement, Dallas; fundraiser Cardinal Cushing Sch., Hanover, Mass. Office: CompUSA Inc 14951 Dallas Pkwy Dallas TX 75240-7570*

HALPIN, PETER G., investment company executive; b. Chgo., Nov. 23, 1949; s. Francis W. and Jeanne C. H.; m. Jennifer Jelley, De.c 8, 1984; children: Patrick, Kelley. BA in Polit. Sci., Ill. Benedictine Coll., 1971; MS, Loyola U., 1975. Sr. planning analyst dept. pub. works Chgo of Chgo., 1971-76; adminstrv. asst. Ill. State Senate Pres. Thomas Hynes, Springfield, 1976-78; dir. Office of Cook County Assessor, Chgo., 1985-89; pres. Peter Halpin & Assocs., Chgo., 1989-93; dir. comm. & external affairs U.S. Dept. Transp., Fed. Transit Adminstrn., Washington, 1993-95; dir. congrl. affairs dept. transp. Office of the Sec., Washington, 1995-97; mng. dir. congrl. & intergovt. affairs Overseas Pvt. Investment Corp., Washington, 1997—. Deputy campaign mgr. Thomas Hynes for Mayor, Chgo., 1986; mem. Ill. Commn. Handgun Control. Mem. Ill. State Soc., Landmarks Preservation Coun., Am. Rivers. Democrat. Office: Overseas Pvt Investment co 1200 New York Ave NW Washington DC 20527

HALPIN, TIMOTHY PATRICK, former air force officer; b. Worcester, Mass., Mar. 13, 1960; s. Daniel Joseph Halpin and Angelina (Ferranti) Wilkes; m. Rachel Esther Hanneman, Aug. 3, 1991; children: Alyssa Kristin, Patrick Stephan, Joseph Marvin, Nathan Erick. BBA in Mgmt., U. Mass., 1982; MBA, Embry-Riddle Aero. U., 1994; JD, Regent U., 1998. Bar: Va. 1998. Commd. 2d lt. USAF, 1982, advanced through grades to capt., 1986; instr. electronic warfare USAF, various locations, 1984-89, 93d Bomb Wing, Castle AFB, Calif., 1989-95; resigned, 1995; atty. Lambert & Lambert, Virginia Beach, Va., 1997—. Decorated DFC, Air medal (3). Mem. VFW. Republican. Avocations: cross country and downhill skiing, ice hockey, politics, theology. Home: 3704 Kings Point Arch Virginia Beach VA 23452-3204 Office: Lambert & Lambert 335 S Witchduck Rd Virginia Beach VA 23462-3645

HALPRIN, ANNA SCHUMAN (MRS. LAWRENCE HALPRIN), dancer; b. Wilmette, Ill., July 13, 1920; d. Isadore and Ida (Schiff) Schuman; m. Lawrence Halprin, Sept. 19, 1940; children: Daria, Rana. Student, Bennington Summer Sch. Dance, 1938-39; BS in Dance, U. Wis., 1943, PhD (hon.), 1994; PhD in Human Services (hon.), Sierra U., 1987. presenter opening invocation STate of the World Forum by spl. invitation from Mikhail S. Gorbachev. Founder, choreographer, dir., performer, Dancers' Workshop of San Francisco, N.Y.C., 1973; appeared in: films The Bed; master tchr. films, Esalen Inst., U. Calif. at Berkeley, UCLA, U. Ill., Reed Coll., Harvard Sch. Design, Environmental Sch. Design, U. Calif., San Francisco State Coll., U. Mich.; coord., dir. Profl. Tng. Program, 1978—; choreographed: Jerusalem, 1973; films Golden Positions, others; mem. Regional Bay Area Arts Coun., San Francisco Arts Resource Devel. Com., Gestalt Inst., San Francisco; founder, dir., Marin Dance Coop.; dir. Tampala Inst.; workshop performances A Workshop for the People of San Francisco, 1975-76, Dances with the People of San Francisco, 1976-77, Am. Dance Festival, 1976, Search for Living Myths and Rituals through Dance and the Environment, 1982, Return to the Mountain, 2 day performance, 1983, Run to the Mountain, 1984, Circle the Mountain, 1985, Circle the Earth, A Peace Dance, 1986, Circle the Earth, A Dance in the Spirit of Peace, 1987, The Planetary Dance, 1987, 95, Circle the Earth, 1988, Circle the Earth: Dancing with Life on the Line, 1989, Circle the Earth in the Spirit of Freedom, Zurich, Switzerland, 1989, Circle the Earth for the Greening of the Earth, Phila., 1989, Circle the Earch, Italy, Germany and Japan, 1991, Carry Me Home, Every Beat Is A Prayer; founder: Impulse mag; author: Exit to Enter, 1973, Collected Writings, 1973, A School Comes Home, 1973, Collected Writings II, Movement Ritual I, 1980, Circle the Earth Manual, 1987, Collected Writings III, 1989, Moving Toward Life: Five Decades of Transformational Dance, 1995, Dance as a Healing Art, A Manual for Teachers of People with Cancer, 1997, (videotapes) Dance for Your Life, A Ritual of Life/Death, Circle the Earth, (documentary) Circle The Earth: Dancing with Life on the Line, (performance) Circle the Earth, 1989, (theatre piece) Carry Me Home, 1990; founder, dir. Positive Motion, Moving Towards Life; an hour performance Anna & Lawrence Halprin - Inner Spaces KGED Pub. TV, 1991, Dances in Nature videos, 1995. Bd. dirs. East West Holistic Healing Inst.; mem. Gov.'s Coun. on Phys. Fitness and Wellness. Recipient award Am. Dance Guild, 1980, Guggenheim award, 1970-71, Woman of Wisdom award Bay Area Profl. Women's Network, Tchr. of Yr. award Calif. Tchrs. Assn., 1988, Lifetime Achievement award in visual and performing arts San Francisco Bay Guardian newspaper, 1990, Women of Achievement, Vision and Excellence award, 1992, Balasaraswati/Joy Ann Dewey Bieneke chair for disting. tchg. Am. Dance Festival, 1996, Lifetime Achievement in Modern Dance award Am. Dance Festival, 1997; named to Isadora Duncan Hall of Fame, Bay Area Dance Coalition, 1986; Nat. Endowment Arts Choreographers grantee, 1976, NEA choreography grantee, 1977, San Francisco Found. grantee, 1981, Calif. Arts. Coun. grantee, 1990—; inductee Marin Women's Hall of Fame, 1998. Fellow Am. Expressive Therapy Assn.; mem. Assn. Am. Dance, Conscientious Artists Am., San Francisco C. of C. Home and Office: 15 Ravine Way Kentfield CA 94904-2713 *Today I am deeply involved in making a contribution as an artist to world peace. I'm interested in the development of public workshops and dance rituals to create harmony and understanding in social and healing interactions in communities. I am taking dances on a planetary scale.*

HALSBAND, FRANCES, architect; b. N.Y.C., Oct. 30, 1943; d. Samuel and Ruth H.; m. Robert Michael Kliment, May 1, 1971; 1 child, Alexander H. BA, Swarthmore Coll., 1965; MArch, Columbia U., 1968. Registered architect, N.Y., N.J., Mass., Conn., Ohio, Va., N.H.; cert. Nat. Coun. Archtl. Reg. Bds. Arch. Mitchell/Giurgola Archs., N.Y.C., 1968-72; ptnr. R.M. Kliment & Frances Halsband Archs., N.Y.C., 1972—; vis. critic archtl. design Columbia U., 1975-78, 87, N.C. State U., 1978, Rice U., 1979, U. Va., 1980, Harvard U., 1981, U. Pa., 1981, U. Calif., Berkeley, 1997; dean Sch. Architecture, Pratt Inst., 1991-94; Freidman prof. U. Calif., Berkeley, 1997; mem. N.Y.C. Landmarks Preservation Commn., 1984-87; lectr. U. So. Calif., U. Va., Temple U., Washington U., Tulane U., Harvard U., U. Oreg., U. Washington. Projects include: computer Sci. Bldg., Columbia U. (AIA Nat. Honor award 1987), Gilmer Hall addition U. Va., Town Hall, Salisbury Conn., Computer Sci. Bldg., Princeton U. (AIA Nat. Honor award 1994), Case Western Res. Adelbert Hall restoration (AIA Nat. Honor award 1994), Alvin Ailey Am. Dance Theater Found., N.Y.C., hdqs. Marsh & McLennan Co., Ind. Bank Hdqs., Bklyn. Coll. Master Plan, Entrance Pavillion L.I. Rail Rd. Penn Sta., U.S. Courthouse, Bklyn., Yale Div. Sch., Dartmouth Roth Ctr. for Jewish Life; works exhibited in Cooper-Hewitt Mus., Bklyn. Mus., Nat. Acad. Design, Deutsches Architekturmuseum, Frankfourt; author: Annotated Bibliography of Technical Resources for Small Museums, 1983. Trustee Nat. Inst. Archtl. Edn., 1988-93; mem. GSA GPO Courthouse Bklyn., Roth Ctr. for Jewish Life Dartmouth; master plan Lamont Doherty Earth Obs., Palisades, N.Y.; mem. archtl. rev. panel Fed. Res. Sys., 1993—. Fellow AIA (exec. bd. N.Y.C. chpt. 1979, pres. N.Y.C. chpt. 1991-92), Century Assn.; mem. Archtl. League N.Y. (exec. bd. 1975—, v.p. arch. 1981-85, pres. 1985-89), Assn. Collegiate Schs. Architecture (N.E. regional dir. 1993-95). Office: RM Kliment & Frances Halsband 255 W 26th St New York NY 10001-8001

HALSELL, GEORGE KAY, music educator; b. Bryan, Tex., 1956; s. Kay and Jo Inez (Wootten) H.; m. Melanie Lynn Marsh, 1984. MusB, Johns Hopkins Univ., 1979; MusM, U. Tex., 1980, DMA, 1989. Instr. music West Va. Univ., Morgantown, 1983-84; adj. instr. music Essex C.C., Balt., 1985-90, Frederick (Md.) C.C., 1985-90; asst. prof. music Adams State Coll., Alamosa, Colo., 1990-91; adj. instr. music Pikes Peak C.C., Colorado Springs, 1992-94, U. So. Colo., Pueblo, 1992-94; asst. prof. Music Coll. So. Idaho, Twin Falls, 1994—; freelance musician; lectr. Pueblo Symphony Orch., 1992-94. Office: Coll So Idaho 315 Falls Ave Twin Falls ID 83301-3367

HALSETH, JAMES A., academic administrator; b. Pine City, Minn., Aug. 19, 1940; s. Allwyn Yvone and Ester Clarice (Raymond) H.; m. Mary Rossi, June 10, 1965. BA, Concordia Coll., 1962; MA, Ea. N.Mex. U., 1963; PhD, Tex. Tech U., 1973. Chair dept. social sci. Pacific Luth. U., Tacoma, Wash., 1975-81; v.p. acad. affairs, dean Tex. Luth. Coll., Seguin, 1981-86, CEO, 1983; v.p., dean Calif. Luth. U., Thousand Oaks, Calif., 1986-90, univ. provost, 1990-94; v.p., dean Olivet (Mich.) Coll., 1994—; cons. Bennington (Vt.) Coll., 1995-96. Chair Family & Children Ctr., Tacoma, Wash., 1978-79; mem. adv. bd. Seguin Retired Sr. Vol., 1981-85; bd. dirs. Luth. Inst. Theol., Seguin, 1982-86, Luth. Inst. Religious Studies, 1983-85; mem. Small Bus. Inst., Ventura County, Calif., 1983-86; supr. Partnership Quality Learning, Olivet, 1994-98, cons., 1996-98. Grantee Office Internat. Edn. & Fgn. Lang. Dept. Edn., 1978, 84, Trio Programs, 1987-92, Mich. Office Ednl. Equity, 1995-98, W. K. Kellogg Found., 1996. Office: Olivet Coll Mott 206 Olivet MI 49076

HALSETH, MICHAEL JAMES, medical center administrator; b. Bagley, Minn., Nov. 3, 1944; s. Alden Edmore and Christine (Knutson) H.; m. Jill Gwendolyn Utter, Feb. 18, 1967; children: Keith Henry, Holly Lynn, Katherine Jean. BS, Cailf. State U., 1967; MS, U. N.D., 1971. Indsl. engr., dir. pers. St. Agnes Hosp., Fresno, Calif., 1971-75; resident mgr. systems engring. McDonnell Douglas Automation, San Francisco, 1975-76; dir. mgmt. engring. Providence Meml. Hosp., El Paso, Tex., 1976-77; assoc. dir. All Sts. Episcopal Hosp., Ft. Worth, 1977-82; adminstr., chief oper. officer U. Va. Med. Ctr., Charlottesville, 1982-89, interim exec. dir., 1989-90, exec. dir., 1990—. Cpt. USAF, 1967-71. Mem. Am. Coll. Healthcare Execs., Va. Hosp. Assn., Univ. Hosp. Consortium (bd. dirs. 1985-95). Avocations: hobbies, golf. Office: U Va Med Ctr # 148 Jefferson Park Ave Charlottesville VA 22902-0148*

HALSEY, ASHLEY, III, newspaper editor; b. Phila., Aug. 4, 1952; s. Ashley Jr. and Margaret (Woods) H.; m. Laura Jean Ketchum, Apr. 14, 1984; 1 child, Graham Ketchum Halsey. BA, Temple U., 1974. Reporter Germantown Courier, Phila., 1972, sports editor, 1973, mng. editor, 1975-77; reporter Phila. Bull., 1977-79; reporter Phila. Inquirer, 1980-81, nat. corr., 1982-85, asst. nat. editor, 1985-86, dep. nat. editor, 1986-88, dep. fgn. editor, 1989-91, nat. editor, 1991-96, travel editor, 1996-97; asst. city editor Washington Post, 1997-98, deputy Md. editor, 1999—. Avocations: sailing, running. Office: The Washington Post 1150 15th St NW Washington DC 20071-0002

HALSEY, DOUGLAS MARTIN, lawyer; b. Warwick, R.I., Apr. 24, 1953; s. Donald Post Jr. and Marita H.; m. Amy Klinow, Sept. 5, 1976; children: Mark, Meredith. BA, Columbia U., 1976; JD cum laude, U. Miami, 1979. Bar: Fla. 1979, U.S. Ct. Appeals (11th cir.), U.S. Dist. Ct. (so. dist.) Fla. Assoc. Paul & Thomson, Miami, Fla., 1979-83; ptnr. Thomson, Bohrer, Werth & Razook, Miami, 1985-88, Douglas M. Halsey, P.A., Miami, 1989-97, Halsey & Burns, P.A., Miami, 1997—. Rsch. editor U. Miami Law Review, 1978-79. Mem. United Way of Miami-Dade County, 1995—; chair-elect Children's Home Soc. Fla., 1998-99; bd. dirs. Ctr. for Fla.'s Children, Tallahassee, 1995-99. Mem. Fla. Bar (chmn. environ. and land use law sect. 1993-94, President's Pro Bono Svc. award 1991), Alexis de Tocqueville Soc. Office: First Union Fin Ctr 200 S Biscayne Blvd Ste 4980 Miami FL 33131-5309

HALSEY, GARY, illustrator; b. Dayton, Ohio, Sept. 26, 1951; s. Donald and Elizabeth Halsey. Postgrad., Art Students League of N.Y., 1978-79; BFA, Wright State U., 1977; MFA, U. Cin., 1982. painter/designer theatre, tv, corp., hotel and residential clients, U.S., Eng., 1977—; illustrator book jackets and interiors; muralist, painting conservation. Sgt. USAF, 1970-74. Avocations: vol. work, benefitting charitable causes.

HALSEY, JAMES ALBERT, international entertainment impressario, theatrical producer, talent manager; b. Independence, Kans., Oct. 7, 1930; s. Harry Edward and Carrie Lee (Messick) H.; m. Minisa Crumbo; children: Sherman Brooks, Gina, Cris, Woody. Student, Independence Community Coll., 1948-50, U. Kans.; doctorate of Fine Arts honoris causa, Baker Univ., 1992. Pres. Thunderbird Artists, Inc., Independence, from 1950, Jim Halsey Co., Inc., Tulsa, from 1952, Norwood Advt. Agy., James Halsey Property Mgmt. Co., Tulsa Proud Country Entertainment, Stas. KTOW/KGOW, J.H. Radio Mgmt., Cyclone Records, Tulsa Records, J.H. Lighting and Sound Co., Singin' T Prodns.; v.p. Gen. Artists Corp., Beverly Hills, Calif., 1966; chmn., chief exec. officer Century City Artists Corp., Tulsa, Nashville; personal mgr. various entertainment personalities; pres. Internat. Fedn. Festival Orgns.; internat. jurist Golden Orpheus Festival, Bulgaria, 1981-82, 84, 88, 94; ptnr. Billboard Song Contest; cons. William Morris Agy., 1990-95; producer shows for auditoriums, fairs, rodeos, TV, internat. music fests also others in U.S. and internationally including Tulsa Internat. Music Festival, 1977-80, Neewollah Internat. Music Festival, 1981-83; gen. ptnr. Parker Ranch, Tulsa; bd. dirs. Merc. Bank and Trust, Tulsa, Citizens Nat. Bank, Independence, Farmers & Mchts. Bank, Mound City, Kans., Nashville Symphony; chmn. mus. bus. dept. Okla. City U., 1994—; lectr., speaker colls., univs., 1992—. Trustee Philbrook Art Ctr., Tulsa; bd. dirs. Thomas Gilcrease Mus. Assn., Tulsa Philharm. Assn., Roy Clark Celebrity Golf Classic, UNICEF, Nashville Symphony, Nat. Music Coun. Served with U.S. Army, 1954-56. Recipient Disting. Service award U.S. Jr. C. of C., 1959, Ambassador of Country Music award SESAC Corp., 1978, citation Cashbox Mag., 1980, citation Golden Orpheus Festival, 1982, Hubert Long award Wembley Festival, Eng., 1982, commendation Los Angeles Mayor Tom Bradley, Gov.'s medal Kans. Commn., 1986, Frederic Chopin medal Polish Artist Bur., 1987; named Disting. Kansan Topeka Capital Jour. Mem. Country Music Assn. (bd. dirs. 1963-64, 70-71, v.p. 1979-80, Founding Pres.'s award 1985), Acad. Country Music (bd. dirs. 1969-70, 73-74, v.p. 1975-76, 78-79, 79-80, 88-89, Jim Reeves Meml. award 1977), Internat. Fedn. Festival Orgns. (Am. pres., Oscar Midem award 1982). Home: Spirit Horse Ranch Rte 3 Box 708 Mounds OK 74047-9022

HALSEY, JOYCE LESLIE, secondary education educator; b. Sedalia, Mo., Oct. 29, 1959; d. Kenneth H. and Bessie G. (Woodward) Leslie; m. Randall Halsey, Dec. 29, 1990. BEd, Ctrl. Mo. State U., Warrensburg, 1982, MEd, 1987. Tchr., coach Lee's Summit (Mo.) R-7 Schs., 1982-97; internat. baccalaureate coord., tchr., golf coach Lee's Summit North H.S., 1997—; cons. Modern Red Schoolhouse, Indpls., 1995-96; mem. adv. bd. MSHSAA Girls Golf., Mo. Arts in Edn., Jefferson City. Recipient Excellence in Tchg. and Expect the Best awards Lee's Summit C. of C. and R-7 Sch. Dist., 1992, Silver Shoe award Lee's Summit North Faculty, 1996; Coun. for Basic Edn. fellow, 1995; Nat. Endowment for Humanities grantee, 1989, 92, 95. Mem. Nat. Coun. Tchrs. English, Mo. Assn. Tchrs. English, Mule Train Athletic Booster club. Office: Lee's Summit North HS 901 NE Douglas St Lees Summit MO 64086-4505

HALSEY, MARTHA TALIAFERRO, Spanish language educator; b. Richmond, Va., May 5, 1932; d. James Dillard and Martha (Taliaferro) H. AB, Goucher Coll., 1954; MA, U. Iowa, 1956; PhD, Ohio State U., 1964. Asst. prof. Spanish, Pa. State U., University Park, 1964-70, assoc. prof., 1970-79, prof., 1979-85, prof. emerita, 1995—; vis. Olive B. O'Connor prof. lit. Colgate U., Hamilton, N.Y., 1983. Author: Antonio Buero Vallejo, 1973, Dictatorship to Democracy: the Recent Plays of Buero Vallejo (La Fundación to Mósica cercana), 1994; editor: Madrugada, 1969, Hoy es fiesta, 1978, Los incocentes de la Moncloa, 1980, El enganao, Caballos desbocaos, 1981, (with Phyllis Zatlin) The Contemporary Spanish Theater: A Collection of Critical Essays, 1988, Entre actas: Diálogos sobre teatro espanol entre siglos, 1999, Estreno, 1992-98; gen. editor Estreno Contemporary Spaish Plays, 1992-98, Estreno: Studies in Contemporary Spanish Theater, 1998—; mem. editl bd. Modern Internat. Drama, 1968-75, Ky. Romance Quar., 1970-76, Annals Contemporary Spanish Lit., 1991—, Tesserae: Jour. Iberian and Latin Studies, 1997—; contbr. articles to profl. jours. Grantee Am. Philos. Soc., 1970, 78, Inst. for Arts and Humanistic Studies, 1977,Program Cultural Cooperation bewteen Spanish Ministry Culture and U.S. univs., 1992, 94-95. Fellow Hispanic Soc. Am. (hon. assoc.); mem. MLA, N.E. MLA, Assn. Assn. Tchrs. Spanish and Portuguese, Fellowship of Reconciliation, War Resisters League, Phi Beta Kappa, Phi Sigma Iota, Sigma Delta Pi. Democrat. Episcopalian. Home: 151 W Prospect Ave State College PA 16801-5248 Office: Pa State U Dept Spanish University Park PA 16802

HALSO, ROBERT, real estate company executive. Pres. Pulte Homes of Michigan. Office: Pulte Home Corp 33 Bloomfield Hills Pkwy Bloomfield Hills MI 48304*

HALSTEAD, SCOTT BARKER, medical research administrator; b. Lucknow, India, Jan. 23, 1930; came to U.S., 1932; s. Gordon Brinkerhoff and Helen (Honsinger) H.; m. Edna Gertrude Fishburn, May 28, 1955; children: Rodd, Layne, Geoffrey. BA, Yale U., 1951; MD, Columbia U., 1955; MD (hon.), Mahidol U., Bangkok, 1990. Commd. 2d lt. U.S. Army, 1957, advanced through grade to lt. col., 1967, retired, 1968; prof., chmn. U. Hawaii Sch. Medicine, Dept. Tropical Medicine, Honolulu, 1968-83; prof. U. Hawaii Sch. Public Health, Honolulu, 1968-83; dep. and acting dir. health scis. divsn. Rockefeller Found., N.Y.C., 1983-95; dir. infectious disease rsch. USN, Bethesda, Md., 1995-97; chief scientist Office Naval Rsch., 1997-99, cons., 1999—; advisor AIDS vaccine NIH, Bethesda, Md., 1988—, advisor infectious diseases, Ctrs. Disease Control, Atlanta, 1989-96, Langmuir lectr., 1981, Smadel lectr., 1997; mem. Armed Forces Epidemiology Bd., Washington, 1987-93, Naval Rsch. Adv. Comm., 1995-98; advisor Program for Vaccine Devel., WHO, 1989-94; co-founder Children's Vaccine Initiative, 1990; pres.-elect Am. Bur. Med. Advancement in China, 1998—. Fogarty Sr. fellow, NIH, 1975. Mem. Am. Soc. Tropical Medicine and Hygiene (pres. 1990-91), Internat. Fedn. Tropical Medicine (pres. 1992-96). Home and Office: 5824 Edson Ln North Bethesda MD 20852-2933

HALSTED, DAVID CRANE, diplomat; b. Plainfield, N.J., Sept. 7, 1941; s. Osborne and Katharine (Patterson) C.; m. Michele Vautrain, Mar. 8, 1996; children: Edward, Sarah, David Jr., Charles. BA, Dartmouth Coll., 1963; MA, George Washington U., 1968. Dep. chief of mission U.S. Embassy, Kampala, Uganda, 1979-81; dep. dir. Vietnam, Laos, Cambodia desk State Dept., 1982-84; polit./econ. counselor U.S. Embassy, Rangoon, Burma, 1984-86; dep. dir. West African Affairs State Dept., Washington, 1986-89, dir. African Regional Affairs, 1989-91; U.S. Consul Gen. U.S. Consulate Gen., Capetown, South Africa, 1991-93; U.S. ambassador to Chad, 1996—. Lt. (j.g.) USNR, 1963-67. Office: Am Embassy N'Djamena Dept Of State Washington DC 20521-2410*

HALSTRÖM, FREDERIC NORMAN, lawyer; b. Boston, Feb. 26, 1944; s. Reginald F. and Margaret M. (Graham) H.; divorced, 1989; children: Ingrid Alexandra, Reginald Frederic II. Student, Northeastern U., 1961-63, USAF Acad., 1963-65; AB, Georgetown U., 1967; JD, Boston Coll., 1970. Bar: Mass. 1970, U.S. Dist. Ct. Mass., 1971, U.S. Dist. Ct. R.I. 1981, U.S. Tax Ct., 1981, U.S. Ct. Appeals (1st cir.) 1971, U.S. Ct. Appeals (11th cir.) 1991. Assoc. Schneider and Reilly, P.C., Boston, 1970-73; ptnr. Parker, Coolter, Daley and White, Boston, 1973-78; prin. Halström Law Office, Boston, 1978—; spl. prosecutor Dist. Atty., Norfolk County, 1969-70; spl. asst. city solicitor City of Quincy, 1980. Editor Mass. Law Quar., 1972; contbr. articles to profl. jours. Fellow Boston Coll. Law Sch., v.p. 1988-91, pres. 1991—, benefactor Frederic N. Halström Nat. Moot Ct. Team. Mem. ABA (chmn. products liability com. gen. practice sect. 1980-85, award of achievement young lawyers divsn. 1978, vice chmn. taxation on ins. cos. sect. 1986-88), Assn. Trial Lawyers Am. (gov. 1981-84, 87—), state del. 1976-78, 86-87, chair various coms.), Mass. Acad. Trial Attys. (co-chmn. tort law sect. 1980—, bd. of govs. 1976—, sec. 1987-88, pres.-elect 1995-96, pres. 1996-97), Mass. Bar Assn. (pres. young lawyers divsn. 1977-78, bd. dels. 1978-80), Middlesex County Bar Assn., Trial Lawyers Pub. Justice (sustaining founder, v.p. 1989—), Thomas F. Lambert Jr. Endowed Chair Trust), Algonquin Club, Univ. Club (Boston). Fax: 617-426-4791. E-mail: FHalstrom@aol.com. Home: 483 River Rd Carlisle MA 01741-1873 Office: 132 Boylston St Boston MA 02116-4616

HALT, JAMES GEORGE, advertising executive, graphic designer; b. Buffalo, Feb. 16, 1937; s. Clemens George Halt and Marion Helen Smith; m. July 6, 1963; children: Shannon, Kevin, Sean, Christopher. BFA, U. Buffalo, 1961. Artist, designer Thomas Lowes Assocs., Buffalo, 1961-63, art dir., 1963-69, creative dir., 1969-77; pres., owner James Halt Graphic Design, Buffalo, 1977—; cons. Hammermill Paper Co., Erie, Pa. and Memphis, 1978—. Co-author, designer: Graphic Design USA, 1986, 89-90; designer: Trademarks USA, 1968, The Book of American Trademarks, vol. I, 1972, vol. II, 1973, Novum Gebruchsgraphik, 1980. Mem. Albright Knox Art Gallery, 1987—, Buffalo Mus. Sci., 1988—, Buffalo/Erie County Hist. Soc., 1993—, Zool. Soc. Buffalo, 1988—. Recipient Freedom Found. medal, Freedom Found. at Valley Forge, 1966, Creativity Certificate of Distinction, Art Direction Magazine Book/Show, N.Y.C., 1971, 73-79, 82-83. Mem. Art Dirs. Communicators of Buffalo (recipient over 75 awards 1961—). Democrat. Roman Catholic. Avocations: golf, woodworking, gardening. Home: 351 Springville Ave Amherst NY 14226-2857 Office: James Halt Graphic Design 166 Niagara Falls Blvd Buffalo NY 14223-3025

HALTAM, MICHAEL PATRICK, medical device manufacturing executive; b. Buffalo, N.Y., July 19, 1965; s. Harold George and Joan Irene H.; m. Patricia Marie Johel, July 14, 1989; children: Sean Michael, Erin Ann. BS in Bus. Adminstrn., SUNY, Buffalo, 1988. Ops. mgr. Del. North Cos. Inc., 1990-93; account mgr. Frontier Bus. Systems Inc., 1993-96; terr. mgr. U.S. Surg. Corp., 1996-97; regional specialist, implantable device divsn. Accon Internat. Inc., 1997—. Republican. Roman Cath. Avocations: skeet shooting, hockey, reading. E-mail: mhaltam@aol.com. Home: 28 Skylark Ct East Amherst NY 14051

HALTER, H(ENRY) JAMES, JR. (DIAMOND JIM HALTER), retail executive; b. Fernandina, Fla., Feb. 28, 1947; s. Henry James and Grace (Bealey) H.; m. Wanda O'Quinn, Mar. 15, 1970; children: Jennifer, John, Elizabeth, Amelia. BS in Mgmt., Valdosta State Coll., 1970. Sales mgr. Southwestern Co., Nashville, 1969; collection mgr. Fla. Title & Mortgage Co., Jacksonville, 1970-72; appraiser Richard Hamilton & Assocs., Jacksonville Beach, 1972-74; exec. v.p. Developers Investors Svc. Corp., Jacksonville, 1975-78; pres. A-Coin and Stamp Gallery, Inc., Jacksonville, 1978-81; ptnr. Jacksonville Precious Metals, 1981, Sidetrack Video Arcade Chain, Ga., 1982-84; pres. Diamond House Corp., Valdosta, Ga., 1985—, J-Mart Jewelry Outlets, Inc., Tifton, Ga., 1988-91; chmn. bd. J-Mart Jewelry Outlets, Inc., 1990-91; pres. K&H Ltd., Valdosta, 1992-94; exec. dir. Soc. for Legalization of Drugs, Valdosta, 1994-97; bus. cons., 1996—. Author: May I Help You, 1988, LIZ, Inc., 1998. Bd. dirs. Park Ave. United Meth. Ch., Valdosta, 1986-88, Alapaha coun. Boy Scouts Am., 1982—; mem. Alumni Bd. Valdosta State U.; youth spkr. Atlanta Com. for the Olympic Games, selected local hero torch bearer Olympic Games, Atlanta, 1996; co-author Olympic Awareness Award for 1996 Olympic Games, 1994-95; mem. Ga. Small Bus. Task Force. Recipient Addy award, 1980, 83, God and Svc. nat. award Meth. Ch. and BSA, Cmty. Hero Torch Bearer, Coca Cola Olympic Torch Relay, 1996; named Adm. in Ga. Navy, 1983, Outstanding Ga. Citizen, 1990. Mem. Nat. Speakers Assn., Toastmasters, Sertoma, Vigil Honor, Order of the Arrow, Rotary, Sigma Iota (pres. charter), Alpha Phi Omega. Avocations: motivational speaking, antique paper money, wiregrass Ga. history, civic speaker on Ga. history. Home and Office: 208 Breckenridge Dr Valdosta GA 31605-6402

HALTER, JEFFREY BRIAN, internal medicine educator, geriatrician; b. Mpls., Aug. 25, 1945; s. Cyril Joel and Marcella (Medoff) H.; m. Ellen Laura Kuper, June 25, 1972; children: Alexander, Loren, Ethan, Amy. BA magna cum laude, U. Minn., 1966, BS, MD, 1969. Diplomate Am. Bd. Internal Medicine (test com. on geriatrics 1986-88), Am. Bd. Endocrinology and Metabolism. Intern, then resident in internal medicine Harbor Gen. Hosp., Torrance, Calif., 1969-71; resident U. Wash. Sch. Medicine, Seattle, 1973-74, fellow div. metabolism, endocrinology and gerontology, 1975-77, acting instr., asst. prof., then assoc. prof. dept. medicine, 1974-84; staff physician VA Med. Ctr., Seattle, 1974-75, assoc. dir. Geriatric Rsch., Edn. and Clin. Ctr., 1978-84; prof. internal medicine, chief div. geriatric medicine U. Mich. Med. Sch., Ann Arbor, 1984—, rsch. scientist, med. dir. Inst. Gerontology, 1984—, dir. Geriatrics Ctr., 1988—; chief geriatric sect. Ann Arbor VA Med. Ctr., 1984-92, dir. Geriatric Rsch., Edn. and Clin. Ctr., 1988-99; participant, presenter numerous congresses, symposia, confs., workshops in field; vis. prof. numerous univs., including Karolinska Inst., Stockholm, 1983, U. Copenhagen, 1983, Johns Hopkins U., 1985, 91, U. So. Calif., 1985, Harvard Med. Sch., 1987, 89, UCLA, 1991, U. Chgo., 1991, U. Melbourne, 1991, U. Adelaide, 1991, McGill U., 1991, U. Md., 1994; cons. Nat. Inst. on Aging; numerous others. Mem. editl. bd. Jour. Clin. Endocrinology and Metabolism, 1984-88, Am. Jour. Physiology: Endocrinology and Metabolism, 1985-91, Diabetes, 1986-88, Yr. Book Endocrinology, 1986-91, Jour. Gerontology: Med. Scis., 1988-92; mem. editl. bd. Jour. Am. Geriatrics Soc., 1990-93, assoc. editor, 1993-97; guest editor Supplement on Diabetes in Elderly, Diabetes Care, 1990; contbr. over 300 articles and abstracts to med. jours., chpts. to books. With USPHS, 1971-73. AMA Goldberger fellow U. Geneva Inst. Clin. Biochemistry, 1969; grantee VA, 1978—, Nat. Inst. on Aging, 1985—, Nat. Inst. Diabetes, Digestive and Kidney Diseases, John A. Hartford Found., 1988-94, Am. Fedn. for Aging Rsch., 1994-95, Univers Found., 1991—. Fellow AAAS; mem. Am. Diabetes Assn. (chmn. com. on rsch. rev. 1989-90), Endocrine Soc., Am. Fedn. Clin. Rsch., Western Soc. Clin. Investigation, Am. Soc. Clin. Investigation, Gerontol. Soc. Am. (rsch., edn.-practice com. 1984-87, chmn. rsch. com. clin. medicine sect. 1986-87, chmn. clin. medicine sect., v.p. 1992-93), Am. Geriatrics Soc. (bd. dirs. 1990—, pub. policy com. 1993-97, chmn. long range planning com. 1995-97, pres. elect 1997-98, pres. 1998-99), Ctrl. Soc. Clin. Rsch. (chmn. endocrinology coun. 1993-94, chmn. geriatrics coun. 1995-96), Am. Physiol. Soc., Phi Beta Kappa, Alpha Omega Alpha. Avocations: running, swimming, skiing. Office: U Mich Geriatrics Ctr CCGCB Room 1111 1500 E Medical Center Dr Ann Arbor MI 48109-0926

HALTER, JON CHARLES, magazine editor, writer; b. Hamilton, Ohio, Nov. 24, 1941; s. Sam Lesher and Helen Louise (Olds) H.; m. Corina Garcia, Feb. 14, 1968; children: Jon Julian, Helen Margaret. BA, Syracuse U., 1964, MA, 1966. Vol. U.S. Peace Corps, Venezuela, 1966-68; asst. editor Nat. Petroleum News mag. McGraw-Hill Inc., N.Y.C., 1968-72; editor, writer Boys' Life mag. Boy Scouts Am., North Brunswick, N.J., 1972-79; editor, writer Boys' Life mag. Boy Scouts Am., Irving, Tex., 1979-90, exec. editor Scouting Mag., 1990-94; editor Scouting Mag., Exploring Mag., Irving, 1994—. Author: Bill Bradley: One to Remember, 1974, Reggie Jackson: All-Star in Right, 1975, Top Secret Projects of World War II, 1978, Their Backs to the Wall: Famous Last Stands, 1980. Mem. Soc. Profl. Journalists, Authors Guild. Democrat. Presbyterian. Avocations: reading, model building, tennis, running. Home: 505 E Huitt Ln Euless TX 76040-5532 Office: Boy Scouts Am Scouting Mag PO Box 152079 1325 W Walnut Hill Ln Irving TX 75038-3008

HALTERMAN, MARTHA LEE, social services administrator, counselor; b. Poole, Ky., Feb. 4, 1940; d. Byron Lee and Mary Helen (Reinhardt) Melton; m. John David Halterman Jr., Apr. 26, 1968; 1 child, Rebecca Marie. B in Psychology and Sociology, Henderson (Ky.) C.C., 1975, Brescia Coll., 1977; M in Psychology, U. Evansville, Ind., 1980; cert. in mgmt., U. So. Ind., 1990. Lic. clin. social worker, social worker, marriage and family therapist, intervention tng. I and II, Am. Mgmt. Assn., dir. Rainbow for All Children. Office cashier J. J. Newberry Co., Henderson, 1958-63; regional trainer, office cashier C.I.T. Fin. Corp., Henderson, 1965-74; intern Redbanks Nursing Home, Henderson, 1975; dir. counseling and family svcs. Cath. Charities Bur., 1978—; supr. family & children svcs. Cath. Charities Bur. Family Life Diocese of Evansville, 1985-94; counseling and family svcs. dir., 1994—; coord. family life Cath. Charities Bur. Family Life Diocese of Evansville, 1987-94, coord. total svcs., 1993-94. Diocesan rep. Ind. Pro-Life Task Force, Indpls., 1987-94; sec. Domestic Violence Task Force, Evansville, 1980-88; bd. dirs. v.p. Birthright, Evansville, 1983-94; mem. Green River Regional Mental Health and Mental Retardation Bd., Owensboro, Ky., 1990-94. Mem. Evansville Psychol. Assn., Am. Assn. Marriage and Family Therapy (clin.). Roman Catholic. Avocations: reading, walking, swimming, gardening, sewing. Home: 117 N Bobolink Run Henderson KY 42420-4701 Office: Cath Charities 123 NW 4th St Rm 603 Evansville IN 47708-1790

HALTIWANGER, ROBERT SIDNEY, JR., book publishing executive; b. Winston-Salem, N.C., Mar. 15, 1923; s. Robert Sidney and Janie Love (Couch) H.; m. Marguarite C. LaBelle, Aug. 23, 1994. AB, Harvard U., 1947. Coll. field rep. Prentice-Hall Inc., Atlanta, 1947-56, Southeast regional mgr., 1956-65; dir. Two Year div. Prentice-Hall Inc., Englewood Cliffs, N.J., 1965-71; v.p. sales Prentice-Hall Inc. Englewood Cliffs, N.J., 1971-80, exec. v.p. coll. div., 1980-85; pres. sales and mktg. coll. div. Prentice-Hall Inc, 1985—; cons. Simon & Shuster, 1988-89. Served to 1st lt. USAF, 1943-46, PTO. Recipient Chmn. award Gulf and Western, 1985, Frank Enenbach award Prentice-Hall Coll. Div., 1987. Mem. Am. Assn. Pubs. (liason com. 1975-82), Harvard Club (N.Y.C. chpt.), Knickerbocker Club. Democrat. Presbyterian. Home: 1 Horizon Rd Fort Lee NJ 07024-6502 Office: Prentice Hall Inc Englewood Cliffs NJ 07632

HALTOM, CRISTEN EDDY, psychologist; b. Albion, N.Y., Oct. 22, 1948; d. Arthur Benedict and Susan (Cooper) Eddy; m. Maurice Haltom Jr., Apr. 5, 1980; children: Jhakeem, Ajemo, Rebecca. BA, Albion Coll., 1970; MS, Cornell U., 1974, PhD, 1978. Lic. psychologist, N.Y. Instr. Eisenhower Coll., Seneca Falls, N.Y., 1976, Elmira (N.Y.) Coll., 1976-77, Cornell U., Ithaca, N.Y., 1977-78; clin. psychology intern Benjamin Rush Ctr. Mental Health and Mental Retardation, Phila., 1978-79; assoc. psychologist Elmira Psychiat. Ctr., 1979-84; pvt. practice Ithaca, 1984—. Co-editor: Women and Problem Drinking, 1980; contbr. articles to profl. jours. Panelist Cable Channel 7 TV, Ithaca, 1988, arts & scis. career ctr. Cornell U., 1994, 97; foster care parent tng. Tompkins Co. Dept. Social Svcs., 1997, 98, 99. Mem. APA, Ctrl. N.Y. Psychol. Assn., N.Y. State Psychol. Assn., World Fedn. Mental Health, Christian Assn. Psychologists. Avocations: drawing, tennis, dance, windsurfing. Office: 215 N Geneva St Ithaca NY 14850-4135

HALTOM, ELBERT BERTRAM, JR., retired federal judge; b. Florence, Ala., Dec. 26, 1922; s. Elbert Bertram and Elva Mae (Simpson) H.; m. Constance Boyd Morris, Aug. 19, 1949; 1 dau., Emily Haltom Olsen. Student, Florence State U., 1940-42; JD, U. Ala., 1948. Bar: Ala. 1948. Practiced in Florence, 1948-80; mem. firm Bradshaw, Barnett & Haltom, 1948-58, Haltom & Patterson, 1959-80; judge U.S. Dist. Ct. (no. dist.) Ala., Huntsville & Birmingham, 1980-91; sr. judge U.S. Dist. Ct. (no. dist.) Ala., Florence, 1992-98; bar commr. 11th Jud. Cir. Ala., 1976-80. Mem. Ala. Ho. of Reps., 1954-58; mem. Ala. Senate, 1958-62; candidate lt. gov. Ala., 1962; mem. Ala. Democratic Exec. Com., 1966-80. Served with USAAF, 1944-45. Decorated Air medal with four oak leaf clusters. Fellow Internat. Soc. Barristers, Am. Coll. Trial Lawyers; mem. ABA, Ala. Bar Assn., Am. Legion, VFW, Florence Rotary Club, Phi Gamma Delta, Phi Delta Phi. Methodist.

HALTZEL, MICHAEL HARRIS, federal agency administrator; b. N.Y.C., Mar. 28, 1941; s. Henry and Lillian (Feinberg) H.; m. Helen Scull Hitchman, June 12, 1966; children: Rebecca A. Haltzel-Haas, Andrew. BA, Yale U., 1963; MA, Harvard U., 1966, PhD, 1971. Asst. prof. history Hamilton Coll., Clinton, N.Y., 1971-75; dep. dir. Aspen Inst. Berlin, 1975-78; assoc. Russell Reynolds Assocs., Inc., N.Y.C., 1980-82; v.p. acad. affairs Longwood Coll., Farmville, Va., 1982-84; sr. v.p. Internat. Mgmt. and Devel. Inst., Washington, 1984-85; dir. West European studies Woodrow Wilson Internat. Ctr. Scholars, Washington, 1985-92; chief European divsn. Libr. Congress, Washington, 1992-94; dir. dem. staff, subcom. European Affairs U.S. Senate Foreign Rels. Com., Washington, 1994—; mem. adv. com. Council Foreign Rels., Washington, 1997—, chmn. study group nationalities and ethnic conflict in Europe, 1992-93; election monitor Orgn. Security and Cooperation Europe, Bosnia and Herzegovina, 1996; mem. U.S. del. Conf. Security Coop. Europe Human Dimension, Copenhagen, 1990, Wehrkunde Security Conf., Munich, 1993; mem. review panel U.S. Info. Agency, Washington, 1992; mem. adv. com. Inst. World Affairs, 1990—; advisor Congl. Study Group Germany, 1989—. Author: Der Abbau der deutschen staendischen Selbstverwaltung in den Ostseeprovinzen Russlands, 1855-1905, 1977; co-editor: Between the Blocs: Problems and Prospects for Europe's Neutral and Nonaligned States, 1989, Northern Ireland and the Politics of Reconciliation, 1993; contbr. articles to newspapers and jours. Foreign Area fellow Am. Coun. Learned Socs., 1968-71; fellow Fulbright, 1963-64, Woodrow Wilson Nat., 1964-65, NDEA, 1965-66. Mem. Yale '63 Class Coun. Democrat. Jewish. Avocations: hiking, tennis, canoeing, travel. Home: 2105 Wakefield St Alexandria VA 22308-2750 Office: Com Foreign Rels US Senate Washington DC 20510-6225

HALUSHYNSKY, GEORGE DOBROSLAV, systems engineer; b. Lviv, Ukraine, Jan. 10, 1935; came to U.S., 1949; s. Bohdan and Irene (Mryc) H.; m. Mary Stephany Onuferko, Aug. 6, 1960; children: Helene Irene, Martha Christine. BSEE with honors, Case Western Reserve U., 1956; MEA, George Washington U., 1970. Engr. RCA, Camden, N.J., 1958-63, Bunker-Ramo Corp., Silver Spring, Md., 1963-66; sr. engr. Page Comms., Washington, 1966-68, Vitro Corp., Silver Spring, 1968-76; asst. prof. lectr. George Washington U., Washington, 1976-77; sr. prof. staff Johns Hopkins U. Applied Physics Lab., Laurel, Md., 1977-95; sr. engr. Unisys Corp., Reston, Va., 1995-97; prin. applications analyst Litton PRC, Alexandria, Va., 1997—. Author tech. publs. Recipient commendation awards USN, 1990-91. Mem. Armed Forces Comm. and Electronics Assn., Nat. Def. Indsl. Assn., Eta Kappa Nu, Tau Beta Pi.

HALVER, JOHN EMIL, nutritional biochemist; b. Woodinville, Wash., Apr. 21, 1922; s. John Emil and Helen Henrietta (Hansen) H.; m. Jane Loren, July 21, 1944; children: John Emil, Nancylee Halver Hadley, Janet Ann Halver Fix, Peter Loren, Deborah Kay Halver Hanson. BS, Wash. State U., 1944, MS in Organic Chemistry, 1948; PhD in Med. Biochemistry, U. Wash., 1953. Plant chemist Assoc. Frozen Foods, Kent, Wash., 1946-47; asst. chemist Purdue U., 1948-49; instr. U. Wash., Seattle, 1949-50; affiliate prof. U. Wash., 1960-75; prof. U. Wash. Sch. Fisheries, 1978-92; prof. emeritus U. Wash., 1992—; condr. research on vitamin and amino acid requirements for fish; identified aflatoxin B1 as specific carcinogen for rainbow trout hematoma, identified vitamin C2 for fish; dir. Western Fish Nutrition Lab., U.S. Fish and Wildlife Service, Dept. Interior, Cook, Wash., 1950-75, sr. scientist, nutrition, Seattle, 1975-78; cons. FAO, UNDP, Internat. Union Nutrition Scientists, Nat. Fish Research Inst., Hungary, World Bank, Euroconsult, UNDP, IDRC; affiliate prof. U. Oreg. Med. Sch., 1965-69; vis. prof. Marine Sci. Inst., U. Tex., Port Arkansas; pres. Fisheries Devel. Technology, Inc., 1980-90, Halver Corp., 1978—. Capt. U.S. Army, World War II; col. USAR. Decorated Purple Heart, Bronze Star with oak leaf cluster, Meritorious Service Conduct medal. Fellow Am. Inst. Fishery Research Biologists, Am. Inst. Nutrition; mem. Soc. Exptl. Biol. Medicine, Nat. Acad. Sci., Am. Sci. Affiliation, Am. Chem. Soc., Am. Fishery Soc., World Aquaculture Soc., Phi Lambda Upsilon, Pi Mu Epsilon, Alpha Chi Sigma. Methodist (lay leader 1965-70). Club: Rotary. Home: 16502 41st Ave NE Seattle WA 98155-5610 Office: U Wash Box 355100 Sch Fisheries Seattle WA 98195

HALVERSON, GEORGE CLARENCE, business administration educator; b. Greece, N.Y., Apr. 22, 1914; s. Nils and Bertha (Flodquist) H.; m. Thelma Lee Cunningham, Sept. 9, 1949; children: Kristine, John. A.B. in Govt. and Econs, Antioch Coll., Yellow Springs, Ohio, 1938; M.A. in Internat. Adminstrn, Columbia U., 1944; Ph.D. in Labor Econs, London Sch. Econs., 1952. Field examiner NLRB, 1938-41, 48-49; head bus. adminstrn. extension U. Calif., Berkeley, 1952-57; asst. dean Sch. Bus. U. Calif., 1955-56; coordinator mgmt. devel. Ampex Corp., Redwood City, Calif., 1957-61; v.p. Hergenrather Assos., San Francisco, 1961-62; mem. faculty San Jose State U., Calif., 1962-85, prof. Sch. Bus., 1965-85; prof. emeritus San Jose State U., 1985—, dean Sch. Bus., 1974-81, chmn. manpower adminstrn. dept., 1963-68, asst. to pres., 1970-74. Co-author: Causes of Industrial Peace: Lockheed Aircraft Corp. and the Machinists, 1955; Contbr. articles to profl. jours. Hon. bd. dirs. Better Bus. Bur., San Jose, 1975-81 ; bd. dirs. Industry Edn. Council Calif., 1977-81 , Center Creative Arts and Scis., 1978-81 , Applied Human Develop. Inc., 1980-89, Community Assn. for Retarded, 1982-84. Served with USCGR, 1942-46. Fulbright fellow, 1949-51. Mem. Acad. Mgmt. Democrat. Unitarian. Home: 149 N Gordon Way Los Altos CA 94022-3043

HALVERSON, STEVEN THOMAS, lawyer, construction executive; b. Enid, Okla., Aug. 29, 1954; s. Robert James Halverson and Ramona Mae (Ludke) Selenski; m. Diane Mary Schueller, Aug. 21, 1976; children: John Thomas, Anne Kirsten. BA cum laude, St. John's U., 1976; JD, Am. U., 1979. Bar: Va. 1979. Asst. project dir. ABA, Washington, 1977-79; with Briggs & Morgan, St Paul., 1980-83; sr. v.p. M.A. Mortenson Cos., Denver, 1984—; bd. dirs. Ctr. for New West, Rocky Mountain World Trade Ctr., Regis U., Ctrl. City Opera, Lowell Whiteman Sch., Design Build Inst. Am. Co-author: Federal Grant Law, 1982, The Future of Construction, 1997; contbr. articles to profl. jours. Republican. Roman Catholic. Home: 1821 Via Arriba Palos Verdes Peninsula CA 90274 Office: 800 Wilshire Blvd # 1650 Los Angeles CA 90017

HALVERSTADT, DONALD BRUCE, urologist, educator; b. Cleve., July 6, 1934; s. Lauren Oscar and Lillian Frances (Jones) H.; m. Margaret Ann Marcy, Aug. 4, 1956; children: Donna, Jeffrey, Amy. B.A. magna cum laude, Princeton U., 1956; M.D. cum laude, Harvard U., 1960. Diplomate Am. Bd. Urology. Intern, then resident in surgery Mass. Gen. Hosp., Boston, 1960-62, resident in urology, 1964-67; pvt. practice medicine specializing in urology Oklahoma City, 1967—; chief pediatric urology svc. Okla. Children's Meml. Hosp., Oklahoma City, 1967—, chief staff, 1974-79; clin. prof. urology and pediatrics U. Okla. Med. Sch., 1970—, vice chair dept. urology, 1982—; interim provost U. Okla. for Health Scis., Oklahoma City, 1979-80; spl. asst. to pres. for hosp. affairs Oklahoma U., 1980-84; CEO State of Okla. Teaching Hosps., 1980-83, also bd. dirs.: CEO State Regents for Higher Edn., 1988-93; mem. U. Okla. Bd. Regents, 1993-99, chmn. 1999; founder, vice chmn., dir. Lincoln Nat. Bank, Oklahoma City; vice chair bd. govs. Okla. Med. Ctr. Hosp. Sys., 1998—. Contbr. articles to med. jours. Vice chair bd. govs. Univ. Health Ptnrs.; pres., chmn. bd. Okla. Ind. Phys. Svcs. Corp., 1986-96; trustee Columbia Presbyn. Hosp., 1990—, chmn., 1995-96; bd. govs. Okla. Med. Ctr. Hosps., 1998—, vice chair, 1998. Fellow ACS; mem. AMA (physicians recognition award 1969, 72, 79, 82, 85, 91, 94, 96, 99), Am. Urol. Assn., Am. Acad. Pediat., Soc. Pediat. Urology, Am. Soc. Nephrology, Soc. Univ. Urologists, So. Med. Assn., Okla. Med. Assn., Oklahoma County Med. Soc., Okla. State Regents for Higher Edn., Am. Coll. Physician Execs., Assn. Governing Bds. Colls. and Univs. (bd. dirs., sec. 1996-97, treas. 1997-98). Presbyterian. Home: 2932 Lamp Post Ln Oklahoma City OK 73120-6105 Office: 711 Stanton L Young Blvd Oklahoma City OK 73104-5023

HALVERSTADT, ROBERT DALE, mechanical engineer, metals manufacturing company; b. Warren, Ohio, Jan. 25, 1920; s. Roscoe B. and Dorothy (Grubbs) H.; m. Maryella Green, Dec. 31, 1941; children: Marta Jean Halverstadt Carmen, Linda Anne Halverstadt Orelup, Sally Jo Halverstadt Ham. BS in Mech. Engring., Case Inst. Tech., 1951. Registered profl. engr., N.Y., Ohio. Journeyman machinist Republic Steel Corp., Cleve., 1939-51; design engr. GE, Evendale, Ohio, 1951-53; supr. Metalworking Lab., 1953-58; corp. cons. N.Y.C., 1958-59; mgr. Thomson Engring. Lab., Lynn, Mass., 1959-63; gen. mgr. engring. Continental Can Co., N.Y.C., 1963-64; group v.p. Booz, Allen & Hamilton Inc., N.Y.C., 1964-73; CEO Foster D. Snell Inc. subs., N.Y.C., 1964-73; pres. Design and Devel., Inc. subs., N.Y.C., 1966-70; v.p. tech. Singer Co., N.Y.C., 1973-74; pres. Spl. Metals Corp. subs. Allegheny Ludlum Industries, Inc., New Hartford, N.Y., 1974-82, Materials Tech. Group, New Hartford, 1981-83; mng. dir. Allegheny Ludlum Industries Ltd., New Hartford; sr. staff v.p. Allegheny Internat., New Hartford, 1983-85; pres. AIMe Assocs., New Canaan, Conn., 1985—; co-chmn. Titanium Metals Corp. Am., 1980-83; dir. Oneida Nat. Bank, 1979-83, Carus Corp., Centrex Labs., 1975-80; mem. adv. bd. Flexmedics, Inc., 1982-92; chmn. bd. Spl. Metals Corp., 1987—. Mem. editl. bd. Internat. Jour. Turbo and Jet Engine Tech.; patentee in field. Pres. Industry, Labor and Edn. Coun. Mohawk Valley, Inc., 1975-80. Lt. (j.g.) USCGR, 1942-45. Recipient Jubilee of Victory medal Govt. France, 1996. Fellow Am. Soc. Metals (trustee, treas. 1988-91); mem. ASME, Woodway Country Club, Univ. Club (N.Y.C.), Sigma Xi, Tau Beta Pi, Theta Tau. Mem. United Ch. of Christ. Home: 333 Oenoke Rdg New Canaan CT 06840-4114 Office: Spl Metal Corp PO Box 1649 New Canaan CT 06840-1649

HALVORSEN, MORRIE EDWARD, trade association administrator; b. Ft. Pierce, Fla., May 23, 1931; s. Ray George and Marion Emily H.; m. Patsy Ann Buck, Jan. 11, 1958; 1 dau., Georgia Ann. Student, Denison U., 1949-51; BS in Econs., U. Wis., 1953. V.p. mktg. Milw. Elec. Tool Corp., 1957-72, ITT Phillips, 1973-77; now exec dir. Splty. Tools & Fasteners Distbrs. Assn., Elm Grove, Wis. With U.S. Army, 1953-55. Office: Splty Tools & Fasteners Distbrs Assn PO Box 44 Elm Grove WI 53122-0044

HALVORSON, ALFRED RUBIN, retired mayor, consultant, education educator; b. Milan, Minn., Jan. 22, 1921; s. Chris and Alice (Kleven) H.; m. Dorothy F. Boxrud, Apr. 23, 1944; children: Gary A., Joan D. Halvorson Felice. BS, U. Minn., 1944, PhD, 1949. County extension agt. Agr. Extension Svc. of Minn., St. Paul, 1945; soil fertility researcher Oreg. State U., Klamath Falls, 1949-54; extension agronomist Purdue U., Lafayette, Ind., 1954-57; extension soil scientist Wash. State U., Pullman, 1957-86, prof. emeritus, 1986—; cons. ACF & Shirley Fetilizer Ltd., Brisbane, Australia, 1964, Saudi Arabia Farming Ops., Riyadh, 1984, U.S. AID, Sanaa, North Yemen, 1987. City councilman, City of Pullman, 1987-91, mayor, 1991-95. With M.C. U.S. Army, 1945. Mem. Kiwanis (chair com. Pullman chpt.). Republican. Lutheran. Avocations: hiking, backpacking, gardening, reading, classics. Home and Office: 325 SE Nebraska St Pullman WA 99163-2239

HALVORSON, ARDELL DAVID, soil scientist; b. Rugby, N.D., May 31, 1945; s. Albert F. and Karen Halvorson; m. Linda Halvorson; children: Renae, Rhonda. BS, N.D. State U., 1967; MS, Colo. State U., 1969, PhD, 1971. Soil scientist Agr. Rsch. Svc., USDA, Sidney, Mont., 1971-83; soil scientist Agr. Rsch. Svc., USDA, Akron, Colo., 1983-88, rsch. leader, 1988-94; lab. dir. USDA-Agr. Rsch. Svc., Mandan, N.D., 1994-97; soil scientist USDA-Agr. Rsch. Svc., Ft. Collins, Colo., 1997—. Contbr. more than 160 articles to profl. publs. Fellow Am. Soc. Agronomy (assoc. editor 1983-87), Soil Sci. Soc. Am. (chmn. divsn. S-8 1989), Soil and Water Conservation Soc. (chpt. pres. 1991); mem. Crop Sci. Soc. Am. Office: USDA-ARS PO Box E Fort Collins CO 80522-0470

HALVORSON, NEWMAN THORBUS, JR., lawyer; b. Detroit, Dec. 17, 1936; s. Newman Thorbus and Virginia Westbrook (Markle) H.; m. Sally Clark Stone, May 3, 1969; children: Christina English, Charles Burgess Westbrook. AB, Princeton U., 1958; LLB, Harvard U., 1961. Bar: Ohio 1962, D.C. 1963, U.S. Supreme Ct. 1965. Assoc. Covington & Burling, Washington, 1962-70, ptnr., 1970-83, 85—; asst. U.S. atty. Office of U.S. Atty., Washington, 1983-85; assoc. ind. counsel (spl. prosecutor under Ethics in Govt. Act), 1987-90. Editor, Harvard Law Rev., 1960-61; author: Intermediate Sanctions Regs: Many Questions Remain, Tax Notes, 1998. Sr. warden, Jr. warden, vestryman Christ Ch. Georgetown, Washington, 1983-86, 89-92, chmn. fin. com., 1992-96; bd. dirs. Lupus Found. D.C., 1974-85; mem., bd. dirs. Eugene and Agnes E. Meyer Found., Washington, 1976-91, chmn., 1989-90; bd. mgrs. Hist. Soc. Washington, 1995—; bd. dirs. Coun. for Ct. Excellence, Washington, 1995—; trustee Potomac Sch., McLean, Va., 1980-86, chmn., 1981-83; mem. com. of 100 on Federal City, 1970—, trustee, treas., 1975-79; bd. trustees, mem. exec. com. Greater Washington Rsch. Ctr., 1997—; v.p., trustee Cleveland Park Hist. Soc., 1997—. With USMCR, 1961-67. Mem. ABA, D.C. Bar. Republican. Episcopalian. Clubs: Met. (Washington), Chevy Chase (Md.). Home: 3500 Lowell St NW Washington DC 20016-5025 Office: Covington & Burling 1201 Pennsylvania Ave NW PO Box 7566 Washington DC 20044-7566

HALWIG, J. MICHAEL, allergist; b. Denver, Apr. 15, 1954; s. John Philip and Hilda (Fuggis) H.; m. Nancy Diane Graupman, June 14, 1975; children: Courtney Elizabeth, J. Christopher. BA, Johns Hopkins U., 1975; MD, Northwestern U., Chgo., 1980. Diplomate Am. Bd. Allergy and Immunology, Am. Bd. Internal Medicine. Intern in internal medicine Northwestern U. Meml. Hosps., Chgo., 1980-81, resident in internal medicine, 1981-83; allergy fellowship Northwestern U. Med. Sch., Chgo., 1983-85; practice medicine specializing in allergy, asthma, immunology Atlanta, 1985—; instr. Northwestern U. Med. Sch., Chgo., 1984-85, admissions amb., 1989—; clin. asst. prof. Emory U. Sch. Medicine, 1989—. bd. dirs. Am. Lung Assn. Ga., 1996—. Fellow Am. Coll. Allergy, Asthma and Immunology (allergy practice and practice guidelines com. 1992—), Am. Acad. Allergy, Asthma and Immunology (Managed Care Key Contact Network 1996—); mem. AMA, Asthma and Allergy Found. of Am. (nat. chpt. bd. dirs., chpt. rels. and devel. com. 1997—, mktg. and fundraising com. 1997—, Ga. chpt. founding mem., bd. dirs., med. dir. 1995—, chmn. med. adv. com. 1995—), Joint Coun. on Allergy and Immunology, Med. Assn. Ga. (rep. Coun. on Legislation 1989-95), Allergy, Asthma and Immunology Soc. Ga. (pres. 1993-95, v.p. 1991-93, program chmn. 1991-93, co-chmn. third party payors com. 1992—, rep. bengin medicare carrier adv. com. 1993—, Gengia medicare carrier adv. com.), So. Med. Assn., Cobb County Med. Assn., Cobb Area Pediat. Soc., Wellstar Health Care Sys. (pediat. asthma task force 1996—, asthma/COPD task force 1998—), Ga. Partnership for Caring. Presbyterian. Avocations: running, listening to jazz, golf. Office: 1700 Hospital South Dr Ste 404 Austell GA 30106-8116

HALWIG, NANCY DIANE, banker; b. Rochester, N.Y., Sept. 17, 1954; d. Norman Charles and Elizabeth Marie (Callemyn) Graupman; m. John Michael Halwig, June 14, 1975; children: Courtney Elizabeth, John Christopher. BA in Elem. Edn. with honors, Goucher Coll., 1975; M. Mgmt. in Fin., Northwestern U., 1979. Br. adminstrv. mgmt. trainee Md. Nat. Bank, Balt., 1975-76; comml. banking officer Am. Nat. Bank Chgo., 1976-80; v.p. relationship mgr. Citicorp USA-Chgo., 1980-85; v.p., team leader Citicorp N.Am., Atlanta, 1985-89, v.p. region credit officer, 1986-90; v.p., regional mgr. Kredietbank-Atlanta, 1990-95; regional v.p. Bank of Am., FSB, Atlanta, 1995-96, sr. v.p., 1996-98; regional mktg. mgr., sr. v.p. Congress Fin. Corp., Atlanta, 1999—; mem. contbns. com. Citicorp, Chgo., Atlanta, 1984-90; sec., bd. dirs. S.W. Cobb Allergy and Asthma, P.C., 1989-97. Mem. fin. com. Big Bros./Big Sisters, Atlanta, 1987-91; mem. leadership forum Scottish Rite Hosp., Atlanta, 1988-92; contbns. contact Scitrek Mus., Atlanta, 1988-90, mem. pres.'s coun., 1990-91; mem. steering com. N.W. Ga. Girl Scouts Friendship Circle, 1993-94, mem. Friendship Circle, 1993—, Juliette Low assoc., 1998—; troop treas. Girl Scouts U.S., 1994-96; sustainer Atlanta Women's Fund, 1995-99; co-chair Atlanta Women in Fin., 1999. Named one of Atlanta Women to Watch, Atlanta Bus. Chronicle, 1988. Mem. Fin. Women Internat. (Paragon Cir., futures com. 1996-97, nominating com. 1997-98), Nat. Assn. Bank Women (found. trustee 1984-85, treas. found. 1985-86, bd. dirs. and chmn. fin. com. 1987-88, chmn. task force on child care financing alternatives, restructuring task force 1988-89, nat. conf. program chmn. 1991-92), Aux. Am. Coll. Allergy, Asthma & Immunology, Women's Fin. Exch. (founding bd. dirs.), Atlanta C. of C. (bd. advisors), Atlanta Venture Forum, Assn. Corp. Growth, Turnaround Mgmt.

Assn., Comml. Fin. Assn., Northwestern Univ. Club of Atlanta, Phi Beta Kappa. Republican. Avocations: running, Stair Master, swimming, jogging. Home: 4400 Woodland Brook Dr NW Atlanta GA 30339-5365 Office: Congress Fin Corp 200 Galleria Pky Ste 1500 Atlanta GA 30339

HALYARD, RAYMOND JAMES, aerospace engineer, mathematics educator; b. Evansville, Ind., Oct. 23, 1939; s. Ragon James and Leona (Barfield) H.; m. Peggy Earle Travis, July 29, 1965; children: Debra Jo, Michael Travis, David James. BS in Aero. Engring., Purdue U., 1962; MCE, U. Houston, 1972. Registered profl. engr., Tex. Propulsion analysis engr. Rocketdyne Co., Canoga Park, Calif., 1963-65; propulsion analysis engr. McDonnell Douglas Corp., Houston, 1965-73, booster sys. flight contr., 1978-86; environ. engr. Lummus Co., Houston, 1973-75; avionics test engr. Rockwell Internat. Corp., Houston, 1975-78; engring. supr. shuttle booster sys. Rockwell Space Ops. Co., Houston, 1986-94; analysis engr. space sta. power sys. United Space Alliance, Houston, 1994—; instr. math. San Jacinto Coll., Pasadena, Tex., 1991—. Author: The Quest for Water Planets, 1996; contbr. articles to sci. jours. Vol. youth mentor Crossroads Svc. Orgn., Houston, 1997—. Recipient Astronaut Silver Snoopy award NASA/Johnson Space Ctr., Houston, 1978, 88, cert. of appreciation for manned flight awareness from adminstr. NASA, 1988. Mem. Nat. Space Soc. Avocation: space futurist. Home: 15723 Fathom Ln Houston TX 77062-4435 Office: United Space Alliance 600 Gemini St Houston TX 77058-2783

HAM, INYONG, industrial engineering educator; b. Hwangzu, Korea, Dec. 22, 1925; came to U.S., 1954, naturalized, 1975; s. Dukjung and Kwangdo (Kim) H.; m. Hyunduk Kim, Nov. 14, 1949; children: Taewoo, Taewuk. B.Engring., Seoul Nat. U., Korea, 1948; M.Sc., U. Nebr., 1956; Ph.D., U. Wis., 1958, hon. doctorate, Nanjing Aero. Inst., People's Republic China, 1988. Prof. indsl. engring. Pa. State U., University Park, 1958-95, FANUC prof., 1989-92, Disting. prof., 1991-95, emeritus prof., 1995; dir. Mfg. Rsch. Ctr., 1990-92; dir. industry and asst. min. of industry Republic of Korea, Seoul, 1960-62; cons. Asian Productivity Orgn., Tokyo, UN Indsl. Devel. Orgn., World Bank, others; Fulbright prof. USSR, 1981; cons. prof. Xian Jiaotong U., Beijing Inst. Tech., Harvin Tech. U., People's Republic of China, 1993; hon. prof. Jilin Tech. U. and Yenbin U., People's Republic of China, 1993; chair, vis. prof. U. Tokyo, 1989, Russel Severance Springer vis. prof. U. Calif., Berkeley, 1991; endowed chair vis. prof. Seoul Nat. U., Korea, 1994-95. Author: Design of Cutting Tools, 1968; Group Technology, 1985. Recipient CAM-I award Computer Aided Mfg. Internat., 1978, Disting. Svc. citation, U. Wis., 1985. Fellow ASME, Inst. Indsl. Engring. (mfg. systems div. award 1981), Soc. Mfg. Engrs. (Internat. Edn. award 1985, Albert M. Sargent Progress award 1990); mem. N.Am. Mfg. Rsch. Inst. (pres. 1985-86), Internat. Inst. Prodn. Engring. Rsch. (pres. 1994-95), Korea Scientist and Engrs. in Am. (pres. 1973-74). Home: 980 Mccormick Ave State College PA 16801-6529 Office: Pa State U Dept Indsl Engring University Park PA 16802

HAM, KAREN, music educator; b. Bklyn., Apr. 13, 1952; d. Irving and Eva (Walker) H. AA, Staten Island Coll., 1974; BA, CUNY, 1978; MA, NYU, 1983; student in piano, French Conservatory Music, N.Y.C., 1990—. Tchr. Assn. Black Social Workers, Bklyn., 1978-85, Bklyn. Music Sch., 1985-87; tchr., condr. Holy Innocents Sch., Bklyn., 1985—. Roman Catholic. Avocations: research of American songwriters, American musical films. Home: 235 W 102nd St # D New York NY 10025-8400 Office: Holy Innocents Sch 249 E 17th St Brooklyn NY 11226-4601

HAM, LEE EDWARD, civil engineer; b. San Francisco, Dec. 19, 1919; s. Lloyd Burley and Helen Mary (Atkinson) H.; 6, 1942; children by previous marriage: Elizabeth, Peter, Charles, Barbara; m. Elizabeth Chapman, Aug. 29, 1986. B.C.E., U. Calif., Berkeley, 1942. Civil engr. Wilsey & Broughton, S., San Francisco, 1946-52; v.p. Wilsey & Ham, Foster City, Calif., 1952-57, pres., 1957-84, chmn. bd. dirs., 1985-88, pres., chmn. bd., 1988—, founder, 1998; past bd. dirs. Calif. Health Systems, Mills Peninsula Corp. Author: The Corporate New Town, 1971. Vice pres. Western region Boy Scouts Am. Served with U.S. Army, 1941-46. Decorated Bronze Star; recipient Eminent Engr. award Tau Beta Pi, 1988. Fellow ASCE, Am. Cons. Engrs. Council; mem. Lambda Alpha. Designer new town of Foster City, 1960. Home: 225 Roblar Ave Hillsborough CA 94010-7026 Office: 383A Vintage Park Dr Foster City CA 94404-1147

HAMADA, DUANE TAKUMI, architect; b. Honolulu, Aug. 12, 1954; s. Robert Kensaku and Jean Hakue (Masutani) H.; m. Martha S.P. Lee, Dec. 22, 1991; children: Erin, Robyn, David. BFA in Environ. Design, U. Hawaii, 1977, BArch, 1979. Registered architect, Hawaii, Guam, Florida, Puerto Rico, Saipan. Intern Edward Sullam, FAIA & Assocs., Honolulu, 1979-80; assoc. Design Ptnrs., Inc., Honolulu, 1980-86; prin. AM Ptnrs., Inc., Honolulu, 1986-98; dir. Design Ptnrs. Inc., Honolulu, 1998—. Chmn. 31st Ann. Cherry Blossom Festival Fashion Show, Honolulu, 1982, 32d Ann. Cherry Blossom Festival Cooking Show, 1983, mem. steering com., 1982, 83. Recipient Gold Key award for Excellence in Interior Design Am. Hotel and Motel Assn., 1990, Renaissance '90 Merit award Nat. Assn. Home Builder's Remodeler Coun., Merit award Honolulu mag., 1990, Cert. of Appreciation PACDIV USN, 1992, Gold Nugget award of Merit, 1997. Mem. AIA (jury student awards 1997, 98, jury profl. awards 1999), Constrn. Specifications Inst., Nat. Coun. Archtl. Registration Bds., Colegio de Arcquitectos de P.R., Japanese C. of C. Hawaii, Japan-Am. Soc., Hawaiian Astron. Soc. Avocations: astronomy, music. Office: Design Ptnrs Inc 1580 Makaloa St Ste 1100 Honolulu HI 96814

HAMADA, OMAR LOUIS, physician; b. Tallahassee, June 10, 1966; s. Louis Bahjat and Ann Hanan (Souki) Hamada; m. Tara Lee Newton, Sept. 30, 1995. BS, Union U., 1986; MA, Columbia Bibl. Seminary, S.C., 1988; MD, U. Tenn., 1993. Diplomate Am. Bd. Family Practice, Nat. Bd. Med. Examiners, Am. Bd. Sports Medicine. Intern Bapt. Meml. Hosp., Memphis, 1992-93, resident in family practice, 1993-95, staff, 1995—; staff LeBohneur Children's Hosp., Memphis, 1995—, U. Tenn. Bowld. Rsch. Hosp., Memphis, 1995—, St. Francis Hosp., Memphis, 1995—; courtesy staff Meth. Hosp., Memphis, 1995—; dir. predoctoral affairs, clerkship dir. U. Tenn., Memphis, 1995—, asst. prof., 1997—; staff Regional Med. Ctr., Memphis, 1995—, Bapt. Meml. Hosp., Memphis, 1995—; vis. prof./lectr. in field; peer reviewer Lebanese Med. Jour. Contbr. articles to profl. jours. Exec. dir. Hamada Evangelistic Outreach, Jackson, Tenn., 1988—; exec. bd. dirs. Youth For Christ, Memphis, 1995—. Flight Surgeon and Hyperbaric Med. Officer U.S. Spl. Forces. Recipient Golden Apple Excellence in Tchg. award 1997, 98, Mead Johnson award for Grad. Med. Edn., 1994; named Top 40 under 40 Memphis Bus. Jour., 1998. Fellow Am. Acad. Family Physicians; mem. AMA, Am. Acad. Family Practitioners, Tenn. Med. Assn., Tenn. Acad. Family Physicians, Am. Lebanese Med. Assn., Undersea and Hyperbaric Med. Soc., Spl. Ops. Med. Assn., Assn. Mil. Surgeons U.S., Aerospace Med. Assn., U.S. Army Assn. Flight Surgeons, Mensa. Office: Healthplex Family Medicine 1121 Union Ave Memphis TN 38104-3306

HAMADA, ROBERT S(EIJI), economist, educator; b. San Francisco, Aug. 17, 1937; s. Horace T. and Maki G. H.; m. Anne Marcus, June 16, 1962; children: Matthew, Janet. BE, Yale U., 1959; SM, MIT, 1961, PhD, 1969. Economist Sun Oil Co., Phila., 1961-63; instr. U. Chgo., 1966-68, asst. prof. fin., 1968-71, assoc. prof., 1971-77, prof., 1977-89, Edward Eagle Brown prof., 1989-93, Edward Eagle Brown Disting. Svc. prof., 1993—, dir. Ctr. for Rsch. in Security Prices, 1980-85, dir. Ctr. Internat. Bus. Edn. and Rsch., 1992-93; dep. dean for faculty Grad. Sch. Bus. U. Chgo., 1985-90, dean, 1993—; vis. prof. univs. including London Grad. Sch. Bus. Studies, 1973, 79-80, UCLA, 1971, U. Wash., Seattle, 1971-72, U. B.C., Vancouver, Can., 1976; bd. dirs. A.M. Castle & Co., No. Trust Corp.; pub. dir. Chgo. Bd. Trade; cons. numerous fin. instns., banks, mfg., mgmt. cons., acctg. and law firms. Past assoc. editor: Jour. Fin., Jour. Fin. and Quantitative Analysis, Jour. Applied Corp. Fin.; cons. editor: Scott, Foresman & Co. fin. series; contbr. numerous articles to profl. jours. Bd. dirs. numerous neighborhood non-profit orgns., including Hyde Park Neighborhood Club, Chgo., Harper Ct. Found., Chgo., Hyde Park Co-op., U. Chgo. Lab Schs., Window to the World Comms., Inc. (WTTW-TV). Recipient First Outstanding Tchr. award Grad. Sch. Bus., U. Chgo., 1970, McKinsey Teaching prize, 1981; named to 8 Outstanding Bus. Sch. Profs., Fortune Mag., 1982; Sloan Found. fellow, 1959-61, Ford Found. fellow, 1963-65, Standard Oil Found. fellow, 1965-66; MIT scholar, 1959-61, Yale scholar, 1955-59. Mem. Am. Fin. Assn. (bd. dirs. 1982-85), Econometric Soc., Nat. Bur. Econ. Rsch. (bd. dirs., mem. investment and exec. coms.), Am. Econ. Assn. (investment com.), Inst. Mgmt. Scis. (investment com.), Tau Beta Pi. Office: U Chgo Grad Sch Bus 1101 E 58th St Chicago IL 60637-1511

HAMALAINEN, PEKKA KALEVI, historian, educator; b. Finland, Dec. 28, 1938; s. Olavi Simeon and Aili Aliisa (Laiho) H.; m. Patricia Beth Dunlap; 1965; children: Kim Ilkka, Leija-Lee Louise Aili, Timothy Pekka Olavi, Kai Kalevi Edward. A.B., Ind. U., 1961, Ph.D., 1966. Acting asst. prof. history U. Calif., Santa Barbara, 1965-66; asst. prof. history U. Calif., 1966-70; assoc. prof. history U. Wis., Madison, 1970-76; prof. U. Wis., 1976—, chmn. Western European area studies program, 1977—; nat. screening com. Scandinavian area Inst. Internat. Edn., Fulbright Hays Program; cons. Dept. State., Washington, 1991—; chair grad. edn. coun. U. Wis., 1996—, Vilas assoc. Author: Kielitaistelu Suomessa 1917-1939, 1968, Nationalitetskampen och sprakstriden i Finland 1917-1939, 1969, In Time of Storm: Revolution, Civil War and the Ethnolinguistic Issue in Finland, 1978, Luokka ja Kieli Vallankumouksen Suomessa, 1978, Uniting Germany: Actions and Reactions, 1994; contbr. articles to profl. publs. and jours. Served to lt. Finnish Navy, 1957-58. Faculty research grantee U. Calif., 1966-69; faculty summer fellow, 1969; Ford Found. grantee, 1967; faculty research grantee U. Wis., Madison, 1970—; Am. Philos. Soc. research grantee, 1973; Am. Council Learned Socs. fellow, 1976; research grantee, 1978. Mem. AAUP, Am. Hist. Assn., German Studies Assn., Soc. Advancement Scandinavian Study (adv. com. exec. coun.), Fin. Hist. Assn. (corr. emem.), Coun. European Studies, Paasikivi Seura, Ind. U. Alumni Assn. Office: U Wis 3211 Humanities 455 N Park St Madison WI 53706-1405

HAMAN, RAYMOND WILLIAM, lawyer; b. St. Maries, Idaho, Jan. 22, 1927; s. William and Eva Kate (Colliver) H.; m. Phyllis Maxine Garrett, June 24, 1948; children: Lorinda Ann, Bradley Lawrence (dec.). Student, Whitman Coll., 1947-49; JD, Washington and Lee U., 1952. Bar: Wash., 1952, U.S. Dist. Ct. (we. dist.) Wash. 1952, U.S. Ct. Appeals (9th cir.), U.S. Supreme Ct. Assoc. Evans, McLaren, Lane, Powell & Beeks, Seattle, 1952-59, ptnr., 1959-66; ptnr. Lane Powell Moss & Miller, Seattle, 1966-89; ptnr. Lane Powell Spears Lubersky, Seattle, 1989-91, of counsel, 1991—; legal counsel Gov. Daniel J. Evans, Olympia, Wash., 1965, 67; mem. statute Law Com., 1966-95, chmn. 1988-95. Trustee, past pres. Lighthouse for the Blind, Inc., Seattle, 1964—; bd. dirs. Mercer Island (Wash.) Sch. Dist., 1967-72, Island County (Wash.) United Way, 1993—, pres., 1997-98. With USMC, 1945-46, PTO. Mem. ABA, Wash. Bar Assn., King County Bar Assn., Order of the Coif. Republican. Episcopalian. Home: PO Box 926 Langley WA 98260-0926 Office: Lane Powell Spears Lubersky 1420 5th Ave Ste 4100 Seattle WA 98101-2338

HAMANN, JANET MARIAN, educational psychology educator; b. San Francisco, Feb. 29, 1940; d. Lawrence Henry and Esther Abigail (Long) H.; m. Wayne R. Sutton, July 30, 1960 (div. July 1969); children: Karin, Jessica, Paul, Roger. BA, UCLA, 1960, MA, 1976, PhD, 1989. Cert. secondary sch. tchr., Calif. Tchr., counselor L.A. City Schs., 1961-74; sr. rsch. asst. UCLA Sch. Edn., 1978-86; lectr., evaluator Mt. St. Mary's Coll., L.A., 1982-92; lectr. Loyola Marymount U., L.A., 1989-90, Calif. Poly. U., Pomona, 1991-92; rschr. UCLA Sociobehavioral Group, 1989-93; instrnl. specialist Moorpark (Calif.) Coll., 1993-96; asst. prof. tchr. edn. Calif. State U., Bakersfield, 1996—. Contbr. articles to profl. jours. Recipient UCLA Dissertation award, 1988; Pi Lambda theta scholar, 1987; UCLA Sociobehavioral Group Postdoctoral fellow, 1989. Mem. World Federalist Assn., Internat. Found. for Integral Psychology, Am. Ednl. Rsch. Assn., Sierra Club. Democrat. Avocations: reading, music, sketching, hiking, dancing. Home: 6700 Nottingham Ln Apt 45 Bakersfield CA 93309-8038 Office: California State Univ-Bakersfield Dept Tchr Edn 9001 Stockdale Hwy Bakersfield CA 93311-1022

HAMARNEH, SAMI KHALAF, historian of pharmacy, medicine and science, author; b. Madaba, Jordan, Feb. 2, 1925; came to U.S., 1952, naturalized, 1957; s. Khalaf and Nura A. (Zumut) H.; m. Nazha T. Ajaj, July 4, 1948; 1 son, Faris. BSc in Pharmacy, Syrian U., Damascus, 1948; MSc in Pharm. Chemistry, N.D. State U., Fargo, 1956; PhD in History of Pharmacy and Medicine, U. Wis., 1959; DLitt (hon.), Hamdard U., Karachi, Pakistan, 1998. Curator charge divsn. med. scis. Mus. History and Tech., U.S. Nat. Mus., Smithsonian Instn., Washington, 1959-72; historian dept. sci. and tech. Nat. Mus. Am. History U.S. Nat. Mus., Smithsonian Instn., 1972-77; curator emeritus Mus. History and Tech., U.S. Nat. Mus., Smithsonian Instn., 1977—; prof. history Islamic med. scis. King Fahd Med. Rsch. Ctr./Abdulaziz U., Jeddah, Saudi Arabia, 1982-83; med. historian faculty medicine Allied Sci. Sch. Pub. Health/Yarmouk U., Irbid, Jordan, 1984-86; prof. U. Jordan, Amman, 1987-90; prof. Islamic medicine Internat. Inst. Islamic Thought and Civilization, Kuala Lumpur, Malaysia, 1993-99; vis. assoc. prof. George Washington U., 1963-64; vis. prof. history of sci. U. Pa., Phila., 1969; vis. prof. U. Aleppo, Syria, 1977-79; spl. research med. scis., profl. ethics and edn. in medieval Islam. Author: Bibliography of Medicine and Pharmacy in Medieval Islam, 1964, Index of Arabic Manuscripts on Medicine and Pharmacy at the National Library of Cairo, 1967, Index of Manuscripts on Medicine and Pharmacy in the Zahiriyah Library, 1969, Temples of the Muses and a History of Pharmacy Museums, 1972, Origins of Pharmacy and Therapy in the Near East, 1973, The Physician, Therapist and Surgeon Ibn al-Quff, 1974, Catalogue of Arabic Manuscripts on Medicine and Pharmacy at Brit. Library, 1975, Directory of Historians of Arabic-Islamic Science, 1980, Pharmacy Museums USA, 1981, Health Scis. in Early Islam, Collected Papers, 2 vols., 1983-85, Background of History of Arabic Medicine and Allied Sciences, 1986, Promises, Heritage and Peace, 1986, Introduction on Al-Biruni's Book on Precious Stones, 1988, Ibn al-Quff al-Karaki's Book on the Preservation of Health, 1989, Ibn al-Quff al-Karaki's on Surgery, 1994, Directory of Historians of Islamic Medicine and the Allied Sciences, 1995, Arabic-Islamic Medicine and Pharmacy During the Golden Age, 1997; editor: Jour. History Arabic Sci., 1976-80; mem. adv. bd. Hamdard Medicus, 1980—; contbr. articles to profl. jours. Recipient Star of Jordan medal, 1965; E. Kremers award for distinguished pharmaco-hist. writings, 1966, Citation of Merit, U. Wis., 1997. Mem. Inst. History Arabic Sci. (founding mem. 1976), Am. Inst. History Pharmacy (pres. 1979-81), Arab Soc. for History Pharmacy (Cairo) (founding mem. 1976), Arab Acad. of Damascus (corr. mem.), Royal Acad. for Islamic Civilization Inst. (corr. mem. 1983—). Home: 4631 Massachusetts Ave NW Washington DC 20016-2361 Office: Smithsonian Instn Nmah Rm 5003 Washington DC 20560

HAMARSTROM, PATRICIA ANN, director, animation/multimedia specialist; b. Kans. City, Mo., Aug. 13, 1952; d. Harold Melchor and Nettie Ann (Wussow) H.; m. John D. Williams, Mar. 10, 1972 (div. 1980): 1 child, Jeffrey D. MFA, U. Mo., Kansas City, Mo., 1981; PhD, U. Tex., Richardson, Tex, 1988. Exec. prodr. video and prodn. mgr. Multi-Image Resources, Inc., Dallas, 1982-85; pres., CEO Hamar Prodns., Inc., Dallas, 1985-97; dir. sch. design & media arts Ill. Inst. Art, Chgo., 1997—; mem. sr. faculty in computer animation/multimedia Art Inst. Dallas, 1985-97; guest lectr./dramaturg Dallas Theatre Ctr., 1985-91; lectr. U. Tex., Richardson, 1985-88; dir. Playwrighting Program New Arts Theatre, Dallas, 1983-85; founder, pres. Chgo. S.I.G.G.R.A.P.H. Dir. plays, including: The King and I, 1985, Othello, Shakespeare in the Pk., 1988, Long Day's Journey Into Night, Nat. Theatre Yugoslavia, 1988-92; prodr., translator, adapter play: A Tomb for Boris Davidovich, 1986; prodr., dir., screenwriter films: Long Day's Journey Into Night, 1988, Tom, Dick and Harry, 1990, A Tomb for Boris Davidovich, 1991, Dance of the Tigers, 1992, Texas Women, 1992; organizer, artistic dir. Women's Performance and Art Festival, 1991-94. Del. Dem. Nat. Conv., Kansas City, Mo., 1976, Dem. State Conv., Houston, 1992; bd. dirs. Addison Ctr. Theatre, 1984-88; mem. Adv. Bd. Humanities Forum, Dallas Theatre Ctr., 1986-87; chairperson tech. com. Art Inst. Dallas; U.S. cultural rep. to Yugoslavia USIA, 1988. Mem. SIGGRAPH, ACM, AAUW, Internat. TV Assn., Am. Ctr. for Design, Women in Film, Assn. of Theatre In Higher Edn., Am. Film Inst., Women in Animation, Assn. of Multimedia Communicators. Avocations: yoga, computer, music, movies, singing. Office: Ill Inst Art 350 N Orleans St Chicago IL 60654-1502

HAMBEL, HENRY PETER, clinical hypnotherapist, forensic security consultant, educator; b. Bklyn., Apr. 11, 1951; s. Henry Thomas and Doris Ada (Mawhinney) H.; m. Carole Ann. AAS in Criminal Justice, Suffolk County Community Coll., 1977; BS in Criminal Justice, Pacific Western U., 1988, PhD in Criminal Justice and Forensic Psychology, 1992; postgrad., Newport U. Sch. Law, 1992; DSc, Clayton Col. Nat. Health, Ala., 1993. Cert., registered hypnotherapist Nat. Guild Hypnotists; cert. security guard instr., N.Y., Fla.; diplomate Am. Bd. Law Enforcement Experts, Am. Bd. Psychol.-Specialties in Hypnosis, Am. Col. Forensic Examiners, Am. Bd. Forensic Examiners, Am. Psychotherapy Assn. Park police Suffolk County Park's Dept., Sayville, N.Y., 1973; deputy sheriff Suffolk County Sheriff's Dept., Riverhead, N.Y., 1973-80; police officer, undercover narcotics detective Suffolk County Police Dept., Yaphank, N.Y., 1980-88; pres., owner Pvt. Security Officer Agy., Eastport, N.Y., 1982-88; expert witness, forensic security cons., pvt. practice Eastport, N.Y., 1988—, Port St. Lucie, Fla., 1988—; clin. hypnotherapist, adminstr. Hambel Inst.; adj. prof. Clayton Col. Natural Health, Birmingham, Ala.; active Nassau-Suffolk Tobacco Control Task Force. Author: Last Call: The Party's Over: The Reality of Alcohol and Other Drug Use, 1990. Apptd. supr., mem. Olympic Games Security Team, Atlanta, 1996. Mem. Am. Soc. Indsl. Security (cert. protection profl.), Soc. Police Black Belts, Internat. Police Assn. (life), Nat. Assn. Chiefs of Police (nat. v.p. forensic and tech.), Nat. Sheriffs Assn., Fraternal Order of Police, Ret. Detectives Assn. Suffolk County, Ret. Police Assn. N.Y., Ret. and Disabled Police of Am. (membership coord.). Avocations: animal rights advocacy, vegetarianism, anti-alcohol, drugs and tobacco, pistol shooting. Fax: 561-878-1679. E-mail: Henry.Hambel@GTE.NET. Office: 907 SW Lake Charles Cir Port St Lucie FL 34986-3421

HAMBERG, MARCELLE ROBERT, retired urologist; b. Anderson, S.C., July 4, 1931; s. Robert Clark and Pauline Elizabeth H.; m. Cheryl Ann Jones, Dec. 14, 1961; children: Marcelle R. Hamberg Jr., Gabrielle C. Hamberg Buchanan. BS, Hampton U., 1953; MD, Meharry Med. Coll., 1957. Diplomate Am. Bd. Urology. Rotationg intern Hubbard Hosp., Nashville, 1957-58, resident in surgery, 1958-59, resident in urology, 1959-62; Newman van Horne spl., fellow in cancer urology Mem. Sloan-Kettering Cancer Ctr., N.Y.C., 1962-63; ret., 1997; tchg. staff U. Louisville, 1968-69; sr. attending VA Hosp., Louisville, 1968-69; chief urology, assoc. prof. Meharry Med. Coll., Nashville, 1974-82. 1st lt. U.S. Army Res., 1958-68. Mem. Am. Urol. Assn., Anthrop. Assn. (Southea. sect.). Democrat. Avocations: woodworking, reading, lawn gardening. Home: 4474 Clarksville Pike Nashville TN 37218-1526

HAMBIDGE, DOUGLAS WALTER, archbishop; b. London, Mar. 6, 1927; emigrated to Can., 1956; s. Douglas and Florence (Driscoll) H.; m. Denise Colvill Lown, June 9, 1956; children: Caryl Denise, Stephen Douglas, Graham Andrew. ALCd, London U., 1953, BD, 1958, DD, 1969. Ordained deacon Church of England, 1953, priest, 1954, consecrated bishop, 1969; asst. curate St. Mark's Ch., Dalston, London, 1953-55; priest-in-charge St. Mark's Ch., 1955-56; incumbent All Saints Ch., Cassiar, B.C., Can., 1956-58; rector St. James Parish, Smithers, B.C., 1958-64, North Peace Parish, Ft. St. John, B.C., 1964-69; canon St. Andrew's Cathedral, 1965; lord bishop of Caledonia, 1969-80, New Westminster, B.C., 1980-81; lord archbishop of New Westminster and metropolitan of B.C., 1981-93; prin. St. Mark's Theol. Coll., Dar es Salaam, Tanzania, 1993-95; asst. bishop Diocese of Dar es Salaam, Dar es Salaam, 1993-95; mem. Anglican Consultative Coun., 1985-93; chancellor Vancouver Sch. Theology, 1999. E-mail: hambidge@nanaimo.ark.com.

HAMBLEN, LAPSLEY WALKER, JR., judge; b. Chattanooga, Tenn., Dec. 25, 1926; s. Lapsley Walker Sr. and Libby (Shipley) H.; m. Claudia Royster Terrell, Mar. 20, 1971; children by previous marriage: Lapsley Walker III, Allen M., William Shipley. BA, U. Va., 1949, LLB, 1953. Bar: W.Va. 1954, Ohio 1955, Va. 1957. Trial atty. IRS, Atlanta, 1955; atty. advisor U.S. Tax Ct., 1956; ptnr. Caskie Frost Hobbs & Hamblen and predecessor firms, Lynchburg, Va., 1957-82; dep. asst. atty. gen. tax div. U.S. Dept. Justice, 1982; judge U.S. Tax Ct., Washington, 1982-92, chief judge, 1992-94, 94-96, sr. judge, 1996—; mem. adv. bd. Va. tax rev. U. Va. Law Sch., Charlottesville, 1990—; former trustee So. Fed. Tax Inst.; former co-dir. ann. conf. on fed. taxation U. Va. Served with USN, 1945-46. Fellow Am. Coll. Tax Counsel, Am. Coll. Trust and Estate Counsel, Raven Soc., Order of Coif, Omicron Delta Kappa, Phi Alpha Delta. Presbyterian. Office: US Tax Ct 400 2nd St NW Washington DC 20217

HAMBLETON, GEORGE BLOW ELLIOTT, management consultant; b. Balt., Dec. 20, 1929; s. John Adams Hambleton and Margaret (Elliott) Carey; m. Janet Findlay MacLaren, Mar. 17, 1962 (dec. 1991); children: Anne Carey, Charles MacLaren, James Elliott; m. Diana Lea Walker, June 29, 1998. AB, Princeton U., 1952; program for mgmt. devel., Harvard U., 1964. Various positions with Latin American div. Pan Am, 1955-62; asst. div. service mgr. Pan Am, Miami, Fla., 1963-64; dir. USSR Pan Am, Moscow, 1966-70; dir. internat. affairs Pan Am, Washington, 1971-76; dir. comml. sales Pan Am, N.Y.C., 1977-80; v.p. mktg. N.Y. Airways, N.Y.C., 1976-77; exec. dir., vice chmn. Project Orbis, Inc., N.Y.C., 1980-83; pres. Andrews MacLaren, Inc., N.Y.C., 1983-86; dep. asst. sec., dep. dir. gen. U.S. and fgn. comml. svc. Dept. Commerce, Washington, 1986-88; sr. v.p. Mgmt. Internat. Inc., Westport, Conn., 1988—; bd. dirs. Flight Found., Inc., Washington, Andrews MacLaren Ltd., Northants, Eng. Dir. Fgn. Policy Discussion Group, Washington, 1975-96; mem. N.J. Conservation Found.; mem. adv. com. East-West Trade, U.S. Dept. Commerce, 1973-79; mem. dist. export coun. U.S. Dept. Commerce, Conn., 1989-93; bd. dirs. River Blindness Found., Houston, 1990-95, Coll. of the Atlantic, Bar Harbor, Maine, 1996—. 1st lt. U.S. Army, 1952-55, Korea. Mem. Upper Raritan Watershed Assn., Brook Club (N.Y.), Met. Club (Washington), Naval and Mil. Club (London), Md. Club (Balt.), Princeton Club (N.Y.), Essex Hunt Club (Far Hills, N.J.), Union Club (N.Y.), Harvard Bus. Sch. Club (Washington, v.p. 1973-76), Wings Club (N.Y.), Soc. Colonial Wars (N.Y.). Republican. Episcopalian. Avocations: flying, fishing, skiing, running, hunting. Home: PO Box 943 Far Hills NJ 07931 Office: Mgmt Internat Inc Ste 11G 130 E 67th St New York NY 10021

HAMBLIN, KENNETH LORENZO, radio talk show host, columnist; b. Bklyn., Oct. 22, 1940; m. Sue Ann Hoover, Oct. 22, 1972; children: Kenneth Lawrence, Linda. Grad., George W. Wingate H.S., 1957. Radio host Sta. KOA, 1982-86, Sta. KNUS, 1986-87, 92-94, Sta. KUVO, 1987-89, Sta. KBXG, 1989-90; columnist Denver Post, 1990—; with N.Y. Times Syndicate, 1994—; host syndicated radio talk show Entertainment Radio Networks, 1994—; panelist TV show Feisty After Fifty; guest host CNBC-TV weekend talk series. Staff photographer Detroit Free Press; free-lance photographer; prodr., cinematographer numerous documentaries; host, prodr. Sta. WTVS, Detroit Pub. TV.; prodr. ski films, mgr. cable TV sta., Dillon, Colo. Voted Denver's Best Talk Host by Westword Newspaper; recipient numerous Colo. broadcaster awards, Sigma Delta Chi Broadcaster awards. Avocations: pilot (lic.), scuba diving (cert.), fly fishing, parachutist. Office: Denver Post 1560 Broadway Denver CO 80202-5177*

HAMBRECHT, PATRICIA G., auction house administrator; b. New Orleans; m. George A. Hambrecht; children: Amanda, Elliot. B in History summa cum laude, Yale Coll., 1975; JD, Harvard U., 1978. bd. dirs. Internat. Found. for Art Rsch., Vol. Lawyers for the Arts. Assoc. Hughes Hubbard and Reed; gen. counsel Christie's, 1988-95, mng. dir., 1995-97; pres. Christie's North and South Am., 1997—. Avocations: collecting 19th and 20th century drawings, theater, ballet, opera. Office: Christie's 502 Park Ave New York NY 10022-1108*

HAMBRECHT, WILLIAM R., retired venture capitalist; b. 1935; married; 5 children. Student, Princeton U. Broker Francis I. DuPont & Co., San Francisco; mng. ptnr. Hambrecht & Quist, San Francisco, 1968-97, past pres., CEO, chmn. bd. dirs., ret., 1997; founder, CEO W.R. Hambrecht & Co., San Francisco, 1997—; bd. dirs. People Express, Inc., Internet Travel Network, Adobe Sys. Inc., Calyx and Corolla, LXR Biotech. Inc. Bd. dirs. pub. radio and TV sta. KQED Inc., San Francisco. *

HAMBRICK, ERNESTINE, retired colon and rectal surgeon; b. Griffin, Ga., Mar. 31, 1941; d. Jack Daniel and Nannie (Harper) Hambrick Rubens. BS, U. Md., 1963; MD, U. Ill., 1967. Diplomate Am. Bd. Colon and Rectal Surgery, Am. Bd. Surgery. Intern in surgery Cook County Hosp., Chgo., 1967-68, resident in gen. surgery, 1968-72, fellow colon and rectal surgery, 1972-73, attending surgeon, 1973-74, part-time attending surgeon, 1974-80; pvt. practice colon and rectal surgery Chgo., 1974-97; pres. med. staff Michael Reese Hosp., Chgo., 1990-92, chief surgery, 1993-95;

founder STOP Colon/Rectal Cancer Found., 1997—; mem. Nat. Colorectal Cancer Prevention Round Table, 1997—. *After twenty three and a half years as a colon and rectal surgeon, Ernestine Hambrick stepped out of clinical practice on January 1st, 1998 to create a national education initiative directed towards the eradication of colon and rectal cancer. To that end, she founded the STOP Colon/Rectal Cancer Foundation in November, 1997. This foundation promotes public awareness, screening and early detection of colorectal cancer, and preventive life-style changes. In December, 1997, she was named to the National Colorectal Cancer Roundtable - a federally funded group charged with developing a national prevention strategy.* Contbr. articles to profl. jours. Trustee Rsch. and Edn. Found., Michael Reese Med. Staff, Chgo., 1994-98, treas., 1994-98. Mem. ACS, Am. Soc. Colon and Rectal Surgeons (v.p. 1992-93, trustee Rsch. Found. 1992-98), Am. Coll. Gastroenterology. Avocations: travel, photography, scuba diving, flying, writing. Office: 30 N Michigan Ave Ste 1118 Chicago IL 60602-3503

HAMBRICK, GEORGE WALTER, JR., dermatologist, educator; b. Charlottesville, Va., Dec. 4, 1922; s. George W. and Sallie Anna (McCallum) H. BS, Concord Coll., 1944; MD, U. Va., 1946. Intern Hosp. U. Iowa, 1946-47; asst. resident dermatology U. Va. Hosp., 1947-48; resident Columbia-Presbyn. Hosp., N.Y.C., 1950-51; fellow dermatology Duke Hosp., Durham, N.C., 1951-52; assoc. dermatology Duke Hosp., 1953; instr. Columbia, 1953-55, assoc., 1955-57, asst. prof., 1957-62; assoc. prof. U. Pa., 1962-66; assoc. prof. Johns Hopkins U., 1966-69, prof., 1969-76, dir. dermatology Johns Hopkins Med. Inst., 1967-76; prof. U. Cin., 1976-81, dir. dermatology, 1976-81; prof. Cornell U. Coll. Medicine, 1981-96; chief dermatology N.Y. Hosp., 1981-96; prof emeritus, 1996—. Served as capt., M.C. AUS, 1948-50. Fellow ACP; mem. AMA (del. 1981-90), Soc. Investigative Dermatology (pres. 1971-72, hon. mem.), Dermatology Found. (trustee, pres. 1974), Assn. Profs. Dermatology, Am. Dermatol. Assn., Am. Acad. Dermatology (dir. 1978), Am. Skin Assn. (pres. 1988-93), Alpha Omega Alpha. Home: 3071 Stony Point Rd Charlottesville VA 21911 Office: Philips Ambulatory Care Ctr Dept Dermatology 10 Union Sq E New York NY 10002

HAMBURG, BEATRIX ANN, medical educator, researcher; b. Jacksonville, Fla., Oct. 19, 1923; d. Francis Minor and Beatrix McCleary; married, May 25, 1951; children: Eric N., Margaret A. A.B., Vassar Coll., 1944; M.D., Yale U., 1948; DHL (hon.), Northwestern U., 1994. Diplomate: Nat. Bd. Med. Examiners. Intern Grace-New Haven Hosp., 1948-49; resident Yale Psychiat. Inst., New Haven, 1949-50; resident in pediatrics Children's Hosp., Cin., 1950-51; resident in psychiatry Inst. Juvenile Research, 1951-53; research assoc. Stanford U. Med. Sch. (Calif.), 1961-71, assoc. prof. psychiatry, 1976-80; assoc. prof. Harvard Med. Sch., Boston, 1980-83; exec. dir. Div. Health Policy Research, 1981-83; prof. psychiatry and pediatrics Mt. Sinai Med. Sch., N.Y.C., 1983—, dir. div. child and adolescent psychiatry, 1988-92; pres. William T Grant Found, NYC, 1992—; assoc. dir. Lab. of Stress and Conflict, Stanford U. Med. Sch., 1974-76; sr. research psychiatrist NIMH, Bethesda, Md., 1978-80; dir. studies Pres.'s Commn. Mental Health, 1977-78; mem. vis. com. Sch. Pub. Health, Harvard U., 1977-80, commn. on behavior and soc., Nat. Acad. Scis., 1983—. Author: Behavioral and Psychosocial Issues in Diabetes, 1980, School Age Pregnancy and Parenthood, 1986; contbr. numerous sci. articles to profl. jours. Trustee W.T. Grant Found., 1978—; bd. dirs. New World Found., 1978-83, Bush Found., Revson Found., Greenwall Found., 1986—; mem. Pub. Health Coun. State of N.Y., 1978-80. Vis. scholar Ctr. Advanced Study Behavioral Scis., 1967-68; recipient Outstanding Achievement award Alcohol, Drug Abuse and Mental Health Adminstrn., 1980. Fellow Am. Acad. Child Psychiatry; mem. AAAS (bd. dirs. 1987-91), NIMH (nat. adv. mental health coun.), Inst. of Medicine of NAS, Soc. Profs. Child Psychiatry (program com. 1972-74), Am. Acad. Child Psychiatry (adolescent com. 1977-81), Soc. Adolescent Medicine, APHA (adolescent com. 1978-80), Soc. Study of Social Biology, Acad. Rsch. in Behavioral Medicine (exec. coun. 1980), N.Y. Acad. Medicine (bd. trustees 1992), Century Club, Phi Beta Kappa. Office: William T Grant Found 570 Lexington Ave New York NY 10022-6837

HAMBURG, CHARLES BRUCE, lawyer; b. Bklyn., June 30, 1939; s. Albert Hamburg and Goldie (Blume) H.; m. Stephanie Barbara Steingesser, June 23, 1962; children: Jeanne M., Louise E. B.Chem. Engring., Poly. Inst. Bklyn., 1960; JD, George Washington U., 1964. Bar: N.Y. 1964. Patent examiner U.S. Patent Office, 1960-63; patent atty. Celanese Corp. Am., N.Y.C., 1963-65; patent atty. Burns, Lobato & Zelnick, N.Y.C., 1965-67; patent atty. Nolte & Nolte, N.Y.C., 1967-75; prin. C. Bruce Hamburg, N.Y.C., 1976-79; ptnr. Jordan & Hamburg, L.L.P., N.Y.C., 1979—. Recipient Superior Service award (2) U.S. Patent Office, 1963, 63. Mem. ABA, Am. Intellectual Property Law Assn., N.Y. Patent Trademark Copyright Law Assn., Internat. Assn. Protection Intellectual Property, Queens Bar Assn., Bklyn. Bar Assn., Licensing Execs. Soc., Internat. Fedn. Intellectual Property Attys. Club: Masons. Author: Patent Fraud and Inequitable Conduct, 1972, 78; Patent Law Handbook, 1983-84, 84-85, 85-86, Doctrine of Equivalents in U.S., 1995 (Japanese), 2d edit., 1998 (Korean); monthly columnist Patent and Trademark Rev., 1976-85; U.S. corr. Patents and Licensing, Japan, 1986—. Office: 122 E 42nd St New York NY 10168-0002

HAMBURG, DAVID A., psychiatrist, foundation executive; b. Evansville, Ind., 1925. M.D., Ind. U., 1947, D.Sc. (hon.), 1976; D.Sc. (hon.), Rush U., 1977, Mt. Sinai Sch. Medicine, 1980, U. Rochester, 1981, U. Ill., Chgo., 1984, Albert Einstein Sch. Medicine, 1985, U. Pitts., U. So. Calif., Hahnemann U., 1986; LHD (hon.), Ramapo Coll., 1991, Duke U., 1993. Diplomate Am. Bd. Psychiatry and Neurology. Intern Michael Reese Hosp., Chgo., 1947-48, resident in psychiatry, 1949-50; resident in psychiatry Yale U.-New Haven Hosp., 1948-49; staff psychiatrist Brooke Army Hosp., San Antonio, 1950-52; practice medicine specializing in psychiatry, 1950-75; research psychiatrist Walter Reed Army Inst. Research, Washington, 1952-53; assoc. dir. Psychosomatic and Psychiat. Inst., Michael Reese Hosp., Chgo., 1954-56; fellow Center for Advanced Study in Behavioral Scis., Palo Alto, Calif., 1957-58, 67-68; chief Adult Psychiat. Br. NIMH, Bethesda, Md., 1958-61; prof., chmn. dept. psychiatry Stanford U. Med. Sch., 1961-72, Reed-Hodgson prof. human biology, 1972-76; Sherman Fairchild Disting. scholar Calif. Inst. Tech., Pasadena, 1974-75; pres. Inst. Medicine Nat. Acad. Scis., Washington, 1975-80; dir. div. health policy research and edn., John D. MacArthur prof. health policy and mgmt. Harvard U., Cambridge, Mass., 1980-82; pres. Carnegie Corp., N.Y.C., 1983-97, pres. emeritus, 1997—; adv. com. med. rsch. WHO, 1975-86; mem. exec. panel adv. com. Chief of Naval Ops, 1984-92; chmn. sci. adv. bd. NIMH, 1986-87; sec. Energy Adv. Bd., 1990-94; mem. Ctr. for Naval Analysis, 1990-93. Bd. dirs. Rockefeller U., 1979—, Mt. Sinai Med. Ctr., N.Y.C., 1984—; trustee Stanford U., 1988-94, Internat. Devel. Rsch. Ctr., Ottawa, Ont., Can., 1990-94, Am. Mus. Natural History, N.Y.C., 1990—, Pres.'s Coun. on Advisors on Sci. and Tech., 1994—; dep. chmn. Fed. Res. Bank N.Y., Def. Policy Bd., U.S. Dept. Def., 1994-95. Recipient numerous awards including: Pres.'s medal Michael Reese Med. Ctr., 1974; A.C.P. award, 1977; MIT Bicentennial medal, 1977, Presdl. Medal of Freedom, 1996. Mem. Am. Psychiat. Assn. (Vestermark award 1977, Disting. Svc. award 1991, Pres.'s medal Bank St. Coll. 1994, Charter medallion Radcliffe Coll. 1994), Nat. Acad. Scis. (com. on internat. security and arms control 1981-86, Pub. Welfare medal 1998), AAAS (pres. 1984-85, chmn. bd. 1985-86), Assn. Rsch. Nervous and Mental Disease (pres. 1967-68), Am. Philos. Soc., Am. Acad. Arts and Scis., Phi Beta Kappa, Alpha Omega Alpha. Address: Carnegie Corp NY 437 Madison Ave New York NY 10022-7001

HAMBURG, JOSEPH, physician, educator; b. Phila., Sept. 9, 1922; s. Thomas and Gertrude (Shulitzky) H.; m. Minerva Glickman, July 10, 1949 (dec. June 6, 1983); children: Jay, Marianne, Bonnie; m. Estelle Guttman, Aug. 25, 1985. Student, Temple U., 1938-42; MD, Hahnemann Med. Coll., 1951, ScD, 1979; LHD (hon.), Thomas Jefferson U., 1993. Diplomate: Am. Bd. Family Practice. Intern Stamford (Conn.) Hosp., 1951-52; pvt. practice medicine Stamford, 1952-63; asst. prof. Coll. Medicine U. Ky., Lexington, 1963-66; dean Coll. Allied Health Professions, 1966-84, prof. medicine, community medicine and allied health edn., 1971-91, dean and prof. emeritus, 1992—; cons. in field; pres. Ky. Peer Rev. Orgn., 1980; chmn. Nat. Coun. for Edn. Health Profls. in Health Promotion, 1986-97. Gen. editor: Review of Allied Health Education, Vols. 1-5, 1972-85. Served with U.S. Army, 1942-46. Mem. Am. Soc. Allied Health Professions (pres. 1972), AMA, Inst. Medicine, Ky. Med. Assn., Am. Acad. Family Practice, Ky. Acad. Family Practice. Home: 3212 S Ocean Blvd Apt 608 Highland Bch FL 33487-2587 Office: U Ky Coll Allied Health Professions Lexington KY 40536

HAMBURG, MARGARET ANN (PEGGY HAMBURG), city commissioner; b. Chgo., July 12, 1955; d. David Alan and Beatrix Ann (Mc Cleary) H.; m. Peter Fitzhugh Brown, May 23, 1992; children: Rachel Ann Hamburg Brown, Evan David Addison Brown. BA magna cum laude, Harvard/Radcliffe Coll., 1978; MD, Harvard, 1983. Diplomate Am. Bd. Internal Medicine, Nat. Bd. Med. Examiners. Intern, resident in internal medicine The N.Y. Hosp., Cornell Med. Coll., N.Y.C., 1983-86; spl. asst. to the dir., office of disease prevention and health promotion, office of the asst. sec. for health U.S. Dept. Health and Human Svcs., Washington, 1986-88; spl. asst. to the dir. Nat. Inst. Allergy and Infectious Diseases, NIH, Bethesda, Md., 1988-89, asst. dir., 1989-90; deputy commr. Family Health Svcs., N.Y.C. Dept. Health, N.Y.C., 1990-91; commr. of health N.Y.C. Dept. Health, N.Y.C., 1991-97; planning and evaluation asst. sec. HHS, Washington, 1997—; guest investigator The Rockefeller U., N.Y.C., 1985-86; clin. instr. dept. medicine Georgetown U. Sch. Medicine, Washington, 1986-90; asst. prof. clin. pub. health Columbia U. Sch. Pub. Health, N.Y.C., 1991—; adj. asst. prof. medicine Cornell U. Med. Coll., N.Y.C., 1991—; scholar Pub. Health Leadership Inst. Ctr. for Disease Control U. Calif., 1992; bd. dirs. N.Y.C. Health Systems Agy., Med. and Health Rsch. Assn., Health Hosps. Corp, Nat. Coun. on Women's Health, Primary Care Devel. Corp.; steering com. women and aids NIH, 1991; bd. govs. Greater N.Y. Hosp. Assn., 1991—; mem. bd. sci. advisors. Nat. Pub. Radio, 1992—; com. mem. on substance abuse mental health issues in aids rsch., 1993—; advisory bd. mem. Medunsa Trust, Inc., Med. U. So. Africa, 1993—; mem. defense sci. bd. task force on Gulf War Syndrome U.S. Dept. Defense, 1993—; bd. mem. sci. counselors Nat. Ctr. Infectious Diseases, U.S. Ctrs. for Disease, 1994—. Editorial bd. mem. Jour. N.Y. Acad. Sci., 1992—, The Bull. of N.Y. Acad. Medicine, 1992—, Current Reviews in Pub. Health, 1993—; contbr. to numerous profl. jours. Vol. attending physician The Washington Free Clinic, Washington, 1988-90. Recipient commendation Pub. Health Svc., 1988, 90, Spl. Recognition award Pub. Health Svc., 1990, cert. of Honor The Women's Club of N.Y., 1993, N.Y. Rotary Club award, 1993, Robert F. Wagner Pub. Svc. award NYU, 1993. Fellow AAAS (med. scis. section com. 1989—); mem. ACP, APHA, Am. Med. Women's Assn., Coun. on Fgn. Rels., Health Care Exec. Forum, N.Y. Acad. Medicine, Pub. Health Assn. N.Y.C., Inst. Medicine, Soc. Social Biology, Women in Health Mgmt. Office: Dept HHS Planning and Evaluation 200 Independence Ave SW Washington DC 20201-0004*

HAMBURG, MARIAN VIRGINIA, health science educator; b. St. Louis, Oct. 20, 1918; d. Oliver John and Hazel (Klein) Miller; m. Morris Hamburg, Dec. 27, 1955; children: Jean, Jacalyn. Student, U. Wis., 1936-37; B.Sc., U. Mo., 1940; M.A., N.Y. U., 1945; Ed.D., Columbia U., 1955. Cert. health edn. specialist. Dir. health edn. YWCA, Chgo., 1946-48; health edn. coordinator Stephen F. Austin State U., Nacogdoches, Tex., 1948-49; sch. health cons. Nassau County Tb and Public Health Assn., Garden City, N.Y., 1949-51; asst. dir. pub. edn. Nat. Found., N.Y.C., 1951-54; sch. health cons. Am. Heart Assn., N.Y.C., 1954-64; mem. faculty NYU, 1964-87, assoc. prof. edn., 1966-69, prof., 1969-87, prof. emeritus, 1987—, dir. health edn., 1967-73, chmn. dept. health edn., 1974-86; dir. Alcohol Studies Project, 1975-79; dir. Nat. Inst. Sex Edn. in Elem. Sch.,k 1968-72; mem. White House Conf. on Food, Nutrition and Health, 1969; mem. com. sch. health and health careers Am. Heart Assn., 1964-66; mem. task force sch. health edn. study Nat. Health Coun., 1965=68; del. Nat. Interagy. Coun. on Smoking and Health, 1967; dir. Sex. Info. and Edn. Coun. U.S., 1980-90; chmn. adv. com. Nat. Ctr. Health Edn., 1982-86; mem. Coun. Edn. Pub. Health, 1983-89; bd. dirs. Nat. Commn. for Health Edn. Credentialing, 1991—. Author: (with Morris Hamburg) Health and Social Problems in Schools: Case Studies for School Personnel, 1968; mem. editorial bd. Jour. Sch. Health, 1980-86. Bd. dirs. South Nassau Communities Hosp., 1992-93; mem. com. community programs Nat. coun. YMCA, 1968. Recipient award Mortar Bd., 1940, Women's Centennial Honor award U. Mo., 1968, Disting. Service award N.Y. State Assn. Health, Phys. Edn., Recreation, 1970, U. Mo. Alumni award, 1978, Disting. Service award Assn. for Advancement Health Edn., 1981, Scholar award, 1984, Honor award Am. Alliance for Health, Phys. Edn., R & D, 1988. Mem. APHA (governing coun. 1979-84, Disting. Career award), Am. Sch. Health Assn. (Disting. Svc. award 1969), Assn. for Advancement Health Edn. (bd. dirs. 1986-89), Soc. Pub. Health Edn. (honor award 1987), Am. Coll. Health Assn. (assoc. editor Jour. 1979-82, v.p. 1983-85), Internat. Union Health Edn. (pres. N.Am. region 1979-82, v.p.), Am. Assn. World Health (bd. dirs.), Pi Lambda Theta (award 1940), Eta Sigma Gamma (nat. honor award 1990). Home: 16916 Hierba Dr Apt 258 San Diego CA 92128-2691

HAMBURGER, MARY ANN, medical management consultant; b. Newark, Aug. 25, 1939; d. Herman and Sylvia (Strauss) Marcus; div. June 1966; children: Bruce David, Marc Laurence. AA, U. Bridgeport (Conn.), 1960. Office mgr. Millburn, N.J., 1970-84; propr., mgr. Mary Ann Hamburger, Assocs., med. mgmt. cons. co., Maplewood, N.J., 1984-; tchr. adult edn. South Orange Maplewood Bd. Edn., 1975-83; cons. Wellcare of N.Y.; profl. physician recruiter, N.Y., N.J.; broker med. practices. Mem. NAFE. Democrat. Jewish. Avocations: reading, music, needlepoint, theatre, sports. Home and Office: 74 Hudson Ave Maplewood NJ 07040-1403

HAMBURGER, PHILIP (PAUL), writer; b. Wheeling, W. Va., July 2, 1914; s. Harry and Janet (Kraft) H.; m. Edith Iglauer, Dec. 24, 1942 (div. 1966); children: Jay Philip, Richard Shaw; m. Anna Walling Matson, Oct. 27, 1968. B.A., Johns Hopkins U., 1935; M.S., Grad. Sch. Journalism, Columbia, 1938. Mem. staff New Yorker mag., 1939—, writer Profiles, Talk of the Town, Reporter-at-Large articles, Notes for a Gazetteer, Letters from Fgn. Places, Casuals, music critic, 1948-49, TV critic, 1949-55; on leave from New Yorker as writer, Office of Facts and Figures and O.W.I., 1941-43; Frank R. Kent Meml. lectr., Johns Hopkins U., 1986; past mem. adv. bd. George Foster Peabody Radio and Television Awards; bd. dirs. Authors League Fund.; Condr. non-fiction workshop Ind. U. Writers' Conf., 1969, 75. Author (for govt.): Divide and Conquer, The Unconquered People, Tale of a City; Author: The Oblong Blur and Other Odysseys, 1949, J.P. Marquand, Esquire, 1952, Mayor Watching and Other Pleasures, 1958, Our Man Stanley, 1963, An American Notebook, 1965, Curious World: A New Yorker At Large, 1987, Friends Talking in the Night, 1999. Recipient 50th Anniversary Honors medal Grad. Sch. Journalism, Columbia U., 1963, N.Y. Pub. Libr. Lit. Lion award, 1986, George Polk career award, 1994, Columbia Journalism Alumni award, 1997. Mem. Authors League Am., Authors Guild (quondam council), P.E.N., Nat. Press Club (Washington), Century Assn. (N.Y.C.). Home: 151 E 80th St New York NY 10021-0442 also: PO Box 1453 Wellfleet MA 02667-1453 Office: care The New Yorker 20 W 43rd St New York NY 10036-7400

HAMBURGER, ROBERT N., pediatrics educator, consultant; b. N.Y.C., Jan. 26, 1923; s. Samuel B. and Harriet (Newfield) H.; m. Sonia Gross, Nov. 9, 1943; children: Hilary, Debre (dec.), Lisa. BA, U. N.C., 1947; MD, Yale U., 1951. Diplomate Am. Bd. Pediatrics, Am. Bd. Allergy and Immunology. Instr., asst. clin. prof. sch. medicine Yale U., New Haven, 1951-60; assoc. prof. biology U. Calif. San Diego, La Jolla, 1960-64, assoc. prof. pediatrics, 1964-67, prof., 1970-90, prof. emeritus, 1990—, asst. dean sch. medicine, 1964-70, lab. dir., 1970—, head fellows tng. program allergy and immunology divsn., 1970-90; pres. RNA and Co., Inc., 1997—; cons. various cos., Calif., Sweden, Switzerland, 1986—; bd. dirs. La Jolla Diagnostics, Inc. Author 1 book; contbr. articles to profl. jours.; patentee allergy peptides, allergen detector. Vol. physician, educator Children of the Californias, Calif. and Baja California, Mex., 1993—. 1st lt. Air Corps, U.S. Army, 1943-45. Grantee NIH and USPHS, 1960-64, 64-84; Fulbright fellow, 1980, Disting. fellow Am. Coll. Allergy, Asthma, Immunology, 1986. Mem. U. Calif. San Diego Emeriti Assn. (pres. 1992-94). Avocations: flying, skiing, writing. Office: U Calif San Diego Allergy Immunology Lab La Jolla CA 92093-0950

HAMBURGER, RONALD OWEN, structural engineering executive; b. N.Y.C., May 22, 1952; s. Stanley Cellar and Claire (Oppenheimer) H.; m. Deborah Ann Osborne, Aug. 26, 1979; children: Kathryn Marie, Robert Steven. BS in Civil Engring., Poly. Inst. N.Y., 1974, MS in Civil Engring., 1974; MBA in Project Mgmt., Golden Gate U., 1986. Registered profl. civil engr. Calif., La., Utah, Guam; registered profl. structural engr. Calif., Guam. Engr. Bechtel Assocs. Profl. Corp., N.Y.C., 1974-76; supervising engr. Bechtel Corp., San Francisco, 1976-86; sr. v.p. EQE Internat., Inc., San Francisco, 1986—; project dir. SAC Joint Venture, Sacramento, 1994—; chair tech. subcom. 2 Bldg. Seismic Safety Coun., 1995—. Contbr. articles to profl. publs. Commr. Pacifica (Calif.) Transp. and Safety Commn., 1982-85; commr. bikeway com. San Mateo (Calif.) Regional Planning Commn., 1985. Mem. Structural Engrs. Assn. Calif. (dir. 1995—), Structural Engrs. Assn. No. Calif. (chair seismology com. 1993-94, pres. 1995-96), Earth Engrng. Rsch. Inst. (dir. 1997—, chair existing bldgs. forum 1995—, v.p. 1999). Republican. Jewish. Avocations: private pilot, equestrian, martial arts. Office: EQE Internat Inc 44 Montgomery St Fl 32 San Francisco CA 94104-4602

HAMBURGER, VIKTOR, retired biology educator; b. Landeshut, Silesia, Germany, July 9, 1900; came to U.S., 1932, naturalized, 1940; s. Max and Elsbeth (Gradenwitz) H.; children—Doris Sloan, Carola Marte. Ph.D., U. Freiburg, Germany, 1925; D.S. (hon.), Washington U., St. Louis, 1976; Ph.D. (hon.), Uppsala U., Sweden, 1984; DS (hon.), Rockefeller U., 1996. Prof. zoology Washington U., 1941-68, E. Mallinckrodt disting prof. emeritus, 1968—. Editor: (with Willier and Weiss) Analysis of Development, 1955, The Heritage of Experimental Embryology (Hans Spemann and the Organizer), 1988, Viktor Hamburger, Neuroembryology, The Selected Papers, 1990. Recipient F.O. Schmitt medal in neurosci., 1976, R.G. Harrison prize Internat. Soc. Devel. Biology, 1981, Louise Gross Horwitz prize, 1983, Fidia Georgetown Neurosci. award, 1987, National medal Science, 1989, Karl Spencer Lashley award, Amer. Philosophical Soc., 1990. Mem. AAAS (chmn. sect. F), Soc. Devel. Biology, Internat. Soc. Devel. Biology, Soc. Neuroscis. (Ralph Gerard prize 1985). Home: 740 Trinity Ave Saint Louis MO 63130-3142 Office: Washington U Dept Biology Saint Louis MO 63130

HAMBY, BARBARA JEAN, writer, poet; b. Chico, Calif., Apr. 20, 1929; d. Frank Llewellyn Fairfield and Grace Ellen Mann; separated; children: Gail D. Wilson Anderson, Kurt E. Deutscher. Student, U. Wash., 1947-48, Clark Coll., 1990—. Author: My Muse Has Many Moods, 1995, Trilogy: Love Lines, Life Lines, Laugh Lines, 1998. Named Golden Poet, World of Poetry, 1987, 91, Silver Poet, 1989, People to People Amb. to South Africa, Women Writers, 1998. Mem. NOW, Older Women's League, Oreg. State Poetry Assn. (2nd prize 1995), Wash. State Poets (3rd prize 1995), Southwest Wash. Writers, Columbia Poets (1st prize 1990). Democrat. Unitarian. Avocations: swimming, walking, traveling. Office: Drummer Pub PO Box 65596 Vancouver WA 98665

HAMBY, ROBERT KEVIN, lawyer; b. Ft. Worth, Aug. 1, 1959; s. Thorton Estill and Ara Lina (Parker) H.; m. Terri Kondik, Jan. 1, 1985; 1 child, Austin Kindred. BA, U. Tex., 1981; JD, Cath. U. of Am., 1993. Pub. affairs specialist Dallas, 1982-87, Tex. Water Commn., Austin, 1987-91; legal clk. U.S. Dept. Justice, Washington, 1991-93; atty. Fulbright & Jaworski L.L.P., Dallas, 1994-98; assoc. gen. counsel, sr. v.p. Tex. Credit Union League, 1998—; law clk. Office of V.P., Washington, 1992, Superior Ct., Washington, 1993; mem. citizens adv. bd. Richardson Ind. Sch. Dist. Former bd. trustees Dallas Mental Health and Mental Retardation Ctr., co-creator Hispanic task force; assoc. mem. Greater Dallas Crime Commn.; mem. youth crime commn., liaison to Washington H.S. crime commn., 1995-96; former chair, mem. Addison Planning and Zoning Commn.; former pres. Valley of Bent Tree Homeowners Assn.; coord. Dallas City Bond Campaign, 1982; mem. Greater Dallas Rep. Forum, Rep. Assembly; mem. citizens rev. bd. Richardson Ind. Sch. Dist. Mem. Dallas Bar Assn. (chair media. rels. com., chair legislation/new laws, tellers com., publns. com., chair judges in cmty. com.), Phi Delta Phi. Republican. Office: Ste 1000 4455 LBJ Freeway Farmers Branch TX 75244

HAMED, MARTHA ELLEN, government administrator; b. Washington, Jan. 14, 1950; d. Rockford Norris and Dorothy Hope (Lough) H. AA, George Washington U., 1985, BA in Psychology and Sociology, 1989; MS in Adminstrn., Ctrl. Mich. U., 1999. Command fed. women's program mgr. U.S. Atlantic Fleet, Norfolk, Va., 1978-79; fed. women's program mgr. Naval Ordnance Sta., Indian Head, Md., 1979-80; pers. mgr., Equal Employment Opportunity course dir. Naval Civilian Pers. Command, Arlington, Va., 1980-83; dep. Equal Employment Opportunity officer, site mgr. Ship R&D Ctr., Bethesda, Md., 1983-85, Naval Surface Weapons Ctr., Silver Spring, Md., 1985; command fed. women's program mgr. Naval Sea Sys. Command, Washington, 1985-87, mgr. command tng. programs, 19987-88, asst. dir. awards and performance appraisal programs, 1988-89; asst. mgmt. analysis Office of Insp. Gen., 1989-92; project mgr. Office of Under Sec. of Def., 1992—; chief interagy. Bus. Process Re-engring. divsn. Def. Human Resource Activity Office Under Sec. Def., 1998—. Commr. Anne Arundel County Women's Commn., 1990-92. Recipient V.P. Hammer award for bus. processing re-engring., 1995, VA Vets. Benefits Adminstrn. Commendation award, 1996; named to Outstanding Young Women Am., U.S. Jaycees, 1983. Mem. AAUW, Federally Employed Women. Democrat. Avocations: natural history, cats, salt-water fishing. Office: Office of Undersec Def 4015 Wilson Blvd Arlington VA 22203-1954

HAMEKA, HENDRIK FREDERIK, chemist, educator; b. Rotterdam, Holland, May 25, 1931; came to U.S., 1960, naturalized, 1963; s. Dirk C. and Johanna (Mannebeck) H.; m. Charlotte C. Procacci, Aug. 2, 1972. Drs., U. Leiden, The Netherlands, 1953, D.Sc., 1956; M.A. (hon.), U. Pa., 1971. Rsch. assoc. U. Rome, Italy, 1956-57; fellow Carnegie Inst. Tech., 1957-58; rsch. physicist N. V. Philips Lamps, Eindhoven, The Netherlands, 1958-60; asst. prof. chemistry Johns Hopkins, 1960-62; assoc. prof. chemistry U. Pa., 1962-67, prof. chemistry, 1967—; disting. vis. rsch. prof. USAF Acad., 1986-87. Author: Advanced Quantum Chemistry, 1965, Introductory Quantum Theory, 1967, Physical Chemistry, 1977; Contbr. numerous articles to sci. jours. Recipient Alexander von Humboldt prize, 1981; Alfred P. Sloan Research fellow, 1963-67. Achievements include research on theory of molecular structure and optical and magnetic properties of molecules; calculations of spin-orbit and spin-spin coupling; theory of resonance optical rotation, spectral predictions. Home: 1503 Argyle Rd Berwyn PA 19312-1905 Office: U Pa Dept Chemistry Philadelphia PA 19104

HAMEL, DANA BERTRAND, academic administrator; b. Rumford, Maine, Aug. 9, 1923; s. Donat H. and Louise (Kenison) H.; m. Shirley Elmeree Smith Knavel, Dec. 19, 1945; children—Dana Randolph, Michelle, April. AB, Ashland (Ohio) Coll., 1951; MA, Ohio State U., 1952; EdD, U Cin., 1962; AA in Humanities (hon.), Southside Va. C.C. Watchmaker Thomas J. Apryle & Sons, Johnstown, Pa., 1946; owner Hamels, Jewelers, Conemaugh, Pa., 1946-48; mem. mgmt. dept. Gen. Motors Inst., Flint, Mich., 1955-57; dean adminstrv. affairs Ohio Coll. Applied Sci. and Ohio Mechanics Inst., Cin., 1957-63, acting pres., 1961-62; exec. v.p., dean of faculties Ohio Coll. Applied Sci. and Ohio Mechanics Inst., 1962-63; dir. Roanoke Tech. Inst., 1963-64, Va. Dept. Tech. Edn., Richmond, 1964-66; chancellor Va. Community Coll. System, Richmond, 1966-79; cons. Va. Community Coll. System, 1979-80; cons. to pres., dir. spl. acad. programs Va. State U., Petersburg, 1980-961980—; exec. dir. Va. Ctr. Pub./Pvt. Initiatives; pres. Hamel & Assocs., Richmond, 1996—; coord. for offices of Va. Sec. of Edn. and Dept. of Edn. for WorkForce 2000, V-Quest Programs, 1992-96; co-chair Metro Richmond 2000; acting dir. Adminstrv. Affairs, CEBAF. Gov.'s liaison SURA/Continuous Electron Beam Accelerator Facility, 1983—; trustee, v.p. 1983-99, Southeastern Univs. Rsch. Assn., Inc., 1981—; mem. Va. Adv. Coun. Vocat. Edn.; bd. dris. Richmond Eye and Ear Hosp. Authority, 1989—, Ctr. of Excellence, Inc., Richmond Community High Sch., 1981—; chmn. bd. Va. Edn. Rsch. 1981-85, Network for Supercomputers, 1986—; sr. cons. 1986-93, So. Growth Policies Bd. Tech. Coun., 1987-95; Va. coord. Vamanuf Networking, 1990—; exec. dir. Mfg. Networking and Indsl. Modernization Project, 1992—; interim exec. dir. Va. Alliance Mfg. Competitiveness, 1993—; interim dir. Sch. to Work Program, 1994-95. Wth USAAF, 1942-45. Mem. So. Assn. Schs. and Colls. (former pres.), Am. Assn. Jr. Colls.. (commn. on legis.), Nat. Coun. State Dirs. (former chmn.), Am. Soc. Engring. Edn., Am. Psychology and Guidance Assn., Nat. Assn. for Gifted Children, Am. Coll. Pers. Assn., Cin. Guidance and Pers. Assn., Va. League Nursing (pres. 1987), Forum Club, Masons, Kiwanians, Phi Delta Kappa, Psi Chi, Iota Lambda Sigma. Home and Office: Hamel & Assocs 300 Coalport Rd Richmond VA 23229-7019

HAMEL, LOUIS H., JR., lawyer; b. Haverhill, Mass., June 30, 1934; s. Louis H. and Dorothy A. (Berry) H.; m. Geraldine T. Griffin, Dec. 28, 1959 (div. 1977); children: Juliana, Louis III, Lucy, Paul, Mark J. BA, St. Paul's Coll., 1956; MA, Fordham U., 1959; JD, Harvard U., 1969. Bar: Mass. 1969, U.S. Dist. Ct. Mass. Instr. Manhattanville Coll., Purchase, N.Y., 1959-60; pres. Hamel Realty, Haverhill, Mass., 1961-69; assoc. Hale and Dorr, Boston, 1969-72, jr. ptnr., 1972-76, sr. ptnr., 1976-97, of counsel, 1998—. Contbr. articles to profl. jours. Bd. trustees Boston Chamber Music Soc., 1987—, pres., 1996—. Office: Hale and Dorr 60 State St Ste 25 Boston MA 02109-1816 also: 955 Main St Ste 202 Winchester MA 01890-4302

HAMEL, LOUIS REGINALD, systems analysis consultant; b. Lowell, Mass., July 23, 1945; s. Wilfred John and Angelina Lucienne (Paradis) H.; m. Roi Anne Roberts, Mar. 24, 1967 (dec.); 1 child, Felicia Antoinette; m. Anne Louise Staup, July 2, 1972; children: Shawna Michelle, Louis Reginald III. AA, Kellogg C.C., 1978. Retail mgr. Marshall Dept. Stores, Beverly, Mass., 1972-73; tech. svc. rep. Monarch Marking Systems, Framington, Mass., 1973-74; employment specialist Dept. Labor, Battle Creek, Mich., 1977-78; v.p. corp. Keith Polygraph Cons. and Investigative Svc., Inc., Battle Creek, 1978-79; indsl. engr., engine components divsn. Eaton Corp., Battle Creek, 1979-82; tooling and process engr. Kelley Tech. Svcs., Battle Creek, 1983-84, Clark Equipment Inc., 1983-84; tooling and mfg. engr., mfg. mgr. Trans Guard Industries Inc., Angola, Ind., 1983-85; facilitator employee involvement, safety dir. Wohlert Corp., Lansing, Mich., 1985—; workers compensation adminstr., tng. dir. Wohlert Corp., Lansing, 1985—, system analysis cons., 1975—; systems analysis consultant; b. Lowell, Mass., July 23, 1945; s. Wilfred John and Angelina Lucienne (Paradis) H.; AA, Kellogg Community Coll., 1978; m. Roi Anne Roberts, Mar. 24, 1967 (dec.); 1 child, Felicia Antoinette; m. Anne Louise Staup, July 2, 1972; children: Shawna Michelle, Louis Reginald III. Retail mgr. Marshalls Dept. Stores, Beverly, Mass., 1972-73; tech. service rep. Monarch Marking Systems, Framingham, Mass., 1973-74; employment specialist Dept. Labor, Battle Creek, Mich., 1977-78; v.p. corp. Keith Polygraph Cons. and Investigative Service, Inc., Battle Creek, Mich., 1978-79; indsl. engr., engine components div. Eaton Corp., Battle Creek, Mich., 1979-82; tooling and process engr. Kelley Tech. Services, Battle Creek, Mich., Clark Equipment Inc., 1983-84; tooling and mfg. engr., mfg. mgr. Trans Guard Industries Inc., Angola, Ind., 1983-85; facilitator employee involvement, safety dir., workers compensation adminstr., tng. dir. Wohlert Corp., Lansing, Mich., 1985—; systems analysis cons., 1975—. Mem. Calhoun County Com. on Employment of Handicapped, Battle Creek, Mich., 1977-78; mem. Capital Area Labor Mgmt. Com., 1986-91. With USN, 1963-71, Vietnam. Recipient Services to Handicapped award Internat. Assn. Personnel in Employment Security, Mich. chpt., 1978. Mem. VFW, Nat. Geog. Soc., Mich. Assn. Concerned Vets. (dir.), Nat. Assn. Concerned Vets. Democrat. Roman Catholic. E-mail: Lhand@mvcc.com. Mem. Calhoun County Com. on Employment of Handicapped, Battle Creek, Mich., 1977-78; mem. Capital Area Labor Mgmt. Com., 1986-91. With USN, 1963-71, Vietnam. Recipient Svcs. to Handicapped award Internat. Assn. Pers. in Employment Security, Mich. chpt. 1978. Mem. VFW, Nat. Geog. Soc., Mich. Assn. Concerned Vets. (dir.), Nat. Assn. Concerned Vets. Democrat. Roman Catholic. E-mail: lhand@mvcc.com. Home and Office: 12240 S M 66 Hwy Bellevue MI 49021-9639 *Personal philosophy: A warm handshake, with a smile, will give more people a lift than all the elevators in the world.*

HAMEL, MANETTE C., artist, writer; b. Amersfoort, The Netherlands, Aug. 4, 1913; d. Hendrik Cramer and Maria Christina Hey Ligers; m. Diederik A. van Hamel, Feb. 6, 1940; children: Alfred, Jan Willem, Martine. *Diederik Van Hamel was a career diplomat. His last post was general consul for the Netherlands in New York City. When he retired, he fulfilled his dream to make violins and violas. He died on August 30, 1997.* Student, Conservatory Music, Holland; studied art with Rolph Scarlett. profl. pianist and violinist. One-woman shows include Stedelijk Mus., Amsterdam, 1968, Rosenthal Studio Haus, N.Y.C., 1968; exhibited in group show at Cooper Hewitt Mus., N.Y.C., 1978; prin. works include wearable sculpture Jewelry Mus., Phorzheim, Germany, 1973; represented in permanent collections including Metropolitan Mus. Art, Stedelyk Mus.; author numerous short stories. Recipient 1st prize CNE Toronto, 1965, 1st prize Craftsmen N.Y., 1970. Avocations: chamber music. E-mail: mvamam@I.B.M.net. Home: 6 Lower Byrdcliffe Rd Woodstock NY 12497

HAMEL, MICHAEL A., military officer. BS in Aero. Engring., USAF Acad., 1972; MBA, Calif. State U., Dominguez Hills, 1974; grad., Squadron Officer Sch., 1975, Air Command and Staff Coll., 1980. Commd. 2d lt. USAF, 1972, advanced through grades to brigadier gen.; staff devel. planner Space and Missile Sys. Orgn., L.A. AFB, 1972-75; missile analyst fgn. tech. divsn. Lowry AFB, Colo., 1975-77; mission dir. Aerospace Data Facility, Buckley Air N.G. Base, Colo., 1977-79; air staff tng. officer R&D Hdqs. USAf, Washington, 1979-80; project mgr., manned spaceflight engr. Office of Sec. of Air Force for Spl. Projects, L.A. AFB, 1980-86; program element monitor, exec. officer Hdqs. USAF, Washington, 1986-90; chief plans divsn. Hdqs. Air Force Space Command, Peterson AFB, Colo., 1991-94; comdr. 750th Space Group, Onizuka Air Sta., Calif., 1994-95; vice comdr. 21st Space Wing, Peterson AFB, 1995-96; mil. adviser to v.p. The White House, Washington, 1996-98; vice comdr. Space and Missile Sys. Ctr., L.A. AFB, 1998—. Decorated Def. Superior Svc. medal, Legion of Merit, Meritorious Svc. medal with 3 oak leaf clusters. Office: SMCICV Ste 6037 2430 E El Segundo Blvd El Segundo CA 90245

HAMEL, RODOLPHE, lawyer, pharmaceutical company executive; b. Lewiston, Maine, June 3, 1929; s. Rodolphe and Alvina Melanie (Bilodeau) H.; m. Marilyn Vivian Johnsen, June 10, 1957; children: Matthew Edward, Anne Melanie. BA, Yale U., 1950; LLB, Harvard U., 1953. Bar: Maine 1953, D.C. 1953, N.Y. 1957. Assoc. firm Shearman & Sterling, N.Y.C., 1956-66; v.p., corp. sec., gen. counsel Macmillan Inc., N.Y.C., 1972-73; internat. counsel Bristol-Myers Squibb Co. (formerly Bristol-Myers Co.), N.Y.C., 1966-72, 73, v.p., counsel internat. div., 1974-81, assoc. gen. counsel, 1978-89, v.p., 1983-92, gen. counsel, 1989-94, sr. v.p., 1992-94; cons., 1995—. 1st lt. AUS, 1953-56. Mem. ABA, N.Y. State Bar Assn., Assn. of Bar of City of N.Y., Yale Club. Office: Bristol-Myers Squibb Co 345 Park Ave New York NY 10022-6000

HAMEL, WILLIAM JOHN, church administrator, minister; b. Marquette, Mich., July 30, 1947; s. John Peter and Jayne B. (Berklund) H.; m. Karen Margaret Holleen, Aug. 10, 1968; children: Krista Joy, Kari Elise. BS, Wheaton Coll., 1969; MDiv, Trinity Evang. Div. Sch., Deerfield, Ill., 1972; DD, Trinity Internat. U., 1998; DCM, Trinity Western U., 1998. Ordained minister Evang. Free Ch. Am., 1978. Pastor West Bloomington (Minn.) Evang. Free Ch., 1972-86; dist. supt. Midwest Dist. Evang. Free Ch. Am., Kearney, Nebr., 1986-90; exec. v.p. Evang. Free Ch. Am., Mpls., 1990-97, pres., 1997—. Office: Evang Free Ch Am 901 E 78th St Minneapolis MN 55420-1334

HAMELIN, JEAN-GUY, bishop; b. St.-Severin, Que., Can., Oct. 8, 1925; s. Bernard and Gertrude (Bordeleau) H. B.A., Sem. Trois-Rivieres, Que., Can., 1945; Lic. Theology, Angelicum, Rome, 1953; Lic. Social Scis., Gregoriana, Rome, 1955. Ordained priest Roman Catholic Ch., 1949; consecrated bishop, 1974. Tchr. secondary sch. Trois-Rivieres, Que., Can., 1949-52; mem. faculty Sem. Trois-Rivieres, Que., Can., 1955-58; chaplain to various social orgns. Shawinigan, Que., Can., 1958-64; dir. social action dept. Bishop's Conf., Ottawa, Ont., Can., 1964-68; gen. sec. Bishop's Conf., Montreal, Que., Can., 1968-74; bishop Diocese of Rouyn-Noranda, Que., Can., 1974—; v.p. Can. Conf. Cath. Bishops, 1983-85; 91-93, pres., 1993-95; ecclesiastical advisor Cooperation Internat. for Devel. and Solidarity, Brussels, 1988-94. Mem. exec. com. Assembly of Druibic Bishops, 1998—. Address: Chancery Office, 515 Cuddihy, Rouyn, PQ Canada J9X 4C5

HAMELIN, MARCEL, historian, educator; b. Saint-Narcisse, Que., Can., Sept. 18, 1937; m. Judy Purcell, Aug. 18, 1962; children—Danielle, Christine, Marc. Doctorat es Lettres, Universite Laval, Can. Faculty U. Ottawa, Ont., Can., prof. history, 1966—, chmn. dept. history, 1968-70, vice dean sch. grad. studies, 1972-74, dean faculty of arts, 1974-90, rector, vice chancellor, 1990—. Author: History of the Province of Quebec. Mem. Canadian Hist. Assn., Assn. Canadienne-francaise pour l'avancement des Scis. (pres. 1976-77), Royal Soc. Can. Fax: (613) 562-5103. Office: 550 Cumberland, Ottawa, ON Canada K1N 6N5

HAMER, FORREST MICHAEL, psychologist; b. Goldsboro, N.C., Aug. 31, 1956; s. Forrest Theophilus and Bertha Elizabeth (Barnes) H. BA, Yale U., 1978; PhD, U. Calif., 1987. Lic. psychologist, Calif. Psychologist pvt. practice, Oakland, Calif., 1991—; lectr. U. Calif., Berkeley, 1988—. Author of poems (Beatrice Hawley award 1995). Home: 5275 Miles Ave Oakland CA 94618 Office: 5305 College Ave Oakland CA 94618

HAMER, WALTER JAY, chemical consultant, science writer; b. Altoona, Pa., Nov. 5, 1907; s. Jesse James and Naomi Gertrude (Roland) H.; m. Alma Robinson, Mar. 19, 1941; 1 child, Margaret. BS, Juniata Coll., Huntingdon, Pa., 1929, DSc (hon.), 1966; PhD, Yale U., 1932. Asst. instr. Juniata Coll., 1926-29; fellow Yale U., New Haven, 1932-34; rsch. assoc. MIT, Cambridge, 1934-35; rsch. chemist Nat. Bur. Standards, Washington, 1935-50, chief electrochemistry, 1950-70, dir. Electrolyte Ctr., 1968-72; chem. cons. Washington, 1972—; adj. prof. Georgetown U., Cath. U., govt. agys. commerce and agr., 1940-50; rsch. chemist Manhattan Project, Washington, 1943-45; adj. examiner Civil Svc. Commn., 1948-50; cons. U.S. Dept. Def., 1951-53; mem. electrochem. soc. Internat. Union Pure and Applied Chemistry, 1958-68; vis. panel mem. Electrochemistry Lab., U. Pa., Phila., 1962-63; lectr. in field. Contbr. articles to profl. jours.; editor: Electrochemical Constants, 1953, The Structure of Electrolytic Solutions, 1959. Recipient cert. of merit Manhattan Project, 1945, OSRD, 1945; Superior Accomplishment award U.S. Dept. Commerce, 1954, 62, 65, Disting. Svc. gold medal, 1966; 1st prize for paper IEEE, 1955. Mem. The Electrochem. Soc., Inc. (hon., v.p. 1960-63, pres. 1963-64, Robert T. Foley award Nat. Capital sect. 1991), Yale Chemists Assn. (pres. 1958-61), Cosmos Club. Republican. Episcopalian. Achievements include discovery of the electromotive series of the elements in Molten Systems, of the primary pH Standard for Aqueous Systems from 0 to 60 degrees Celsius, of the ionization constant of water from 0 to 60 degrees Celsius; research in determining the Faraday Constant, method to set standards for electrolytic conductance, maintenance of U.S. national standard of voltage. Home and Office: 407 Russell Ave Apt 305 Gaithersburg MD 20877-2830

HAMERLY, MICHAEL T., librarian, historian; b. Seattle, Sept. 23, 1940; s. James Charles Riley and Harriet Elinor (Jackson) H.; m. Carmen Victoria Flores Rosero, Jan. 19, 1963; 1 child, Michael Charles. BA, U. Wash., 1963, MA, 1965, M in Librarianship, 1979; PhD, U. Fla., 1970. From instr. to asst. prof. U. No. Colo., Greeley, 1970-74; dir. Archivo Arzobispal, Ecuador, 1975-78; rschr. Dept. Historia Maritima, Armada del Ecuador, 1975-77; vis. sr. lectr. dept. Spanish and Latin Am. studies Hebrew U., Jerusalem, 1981; cataloguer Pre-Columbian studies Dumbarton Oaks Rsch. Library and Collections, 1983-84; bibliographer, cataloguer Latin Am. Bibliographic Found., Redlands, Calif., 1985-88; catalog librarian, assoc. prof. Pacific collection Micronesian Area Rsch. Ctr., U. Guam, Mangilao, 1988-91; collection devel. lib., assoc. prof. to prof. Robert F. Kennedy Meml. Lib. U. Guam, 1991-98, chmn. press coun., 1990-97, prof., curriculum resources ctr. coord., 1997; catalogue libr. John Carter Brown Libr., Providence, 1998—. Contbr. articles to profl. jours.; Andean area editor The Americas; a quar. rev. of Inter-Am. Cultural history, 1974-88; assoc. editor Revista del Archivo Historico del Guayas, 1975—; contbg. editor Handbook of Latin Am. Studies, 1971—; mem. editl. bd. Plantation Soc. Ams., 1979—. NDEA, Title VI, Doherty and Fulbright-Hays grantee, fellow; Am. Coun. Learned Socs. and Social Sci. Rsch. Coun. grantee. Mem. Latin-Am. Studies Assn., Conf. on Latin-Am. History, Centro de Investigaciones Historicas de Guayaquil, Acad. Arquidiocesana de Historia Eclesiastica, Asian-Pacific Am. Librs. Assn., Assn. Historiadores Ecuatorianos, Acad. Nat. Historia, Fulbright Assn., Guam Libr. Assn., Pacific Islands Assn. Librs. and Archives, Beta Phi Mu. Fax: 401-863-3477. E-mail: michaelúhamerly@brown.edu. Home: 9416 1st Ave NE Ste 113 Seattle WA 98115-2749 Office: John Carter Brown Libr PO Box 1894 Providence RI 02912-1894

HAMERMESH, DANIEL SELIM, economics educator; b. Cambridge, Mass., Oct. 20, 1943; s. Morton and Madeline (Goldberg) H.; m. Frances Witty, Dec. 18, 1966; children: David J., Matthew A. AB, U. Chgo., 1965; PhD, Yale U., 1969. Asst. prof. Princeton (N.J.) U., 1969-73; assoc. prof. Mich. State U., East Lansing, 1973-76, prof., 1976-93, chmn. dept., 1984-88; Edward Everett Hale centennial prof. econs. U. Tex., Austin, 1993—; rsch. dir. ASPER-U.S. Dept. Labor, Washington, 1974-75; vis. prof. Harvard U., Cambridge, Mass., 1981, Latrobe U., Melbourne, Australia, 1987, Gadjah Mada U., Indonesia, 1990, Australian Nat. U., 1991, Rijksuniversiteit Limburg, The Netherlands, 1992, New Econ. Sch., Moscow, 1993, Hebrew U., Jerusalem, 1995, Erasmus U., The Netherlands, 1997; mem. econ. adv. panel NSF, 1995-97; rsch. assoc. Nat. Bur. Econ. Rsch., 1979—. Mem. bd. editors Am. Econ. Rev., 1990-94; co-editor Econ. Letters, 1994-98, Labour Econs., 1996—. Pres. Congregation Kehillat Israel, Lansing, 1988-90. Recipient Best Article award Western Econ. Assn., 1987, Parents' Assn. Centennial Teaching fellow U. Tex., 1995-96; NSF rsch. grantee, 1980-82, 84-86, 86-91, 95—. Fellow Econometric Soc.; mem. Am. Econ. Assn., Midwest Econ. Assn. (pres. 1988-89), Soc. Labor Economists (2nd v.p. 1999). Jewish. Avocations: running, classical music. Office: U Tex Dept Econs Austin TX 78712

HAMERMESH, MORTON, physicist, educator; b. N.Y.C., Dec. 27, 1915; s. Isador J. and Rose (Kornhauser) H.; m. Madeline Goldberg, 1941; children—Daniel S., Deborah R., Lawrence A. B.S., Coll. City N.Y., 1936; Ph.D., N.Y.U., 1940. Instr. physics Coll. City N.Y., 1941, Stanford, 1941-43; research asso. Radio Research Lab., Harvard, 1943-46; asst. prof. physics N.Y.U., 1946-47, asso. prof., 1947-48; sr. physicist Argonne Nat. Lab., 1948-50, asso. dir. physics div., 1950-59, dir. physics div., 1959-63, assoc. lab. dir. basic research, 1963-65; prof. U. Minn., Mpls., 1965-69, 70-86, prof. emeritus, 1986—; head Sch. Physics and Astronomy, 1965-69, 70-73; prof. physics, chmn. dept. physics State U. N.Y., Stony Brook, 1969-70. Translator: Classical Theory of Fields (by Landau and Lifshitz), 1951; numerous papers in field. Fellow Am. Phys. Soc.; mem. Research Soc. Am. Office: Univ Minn Physics Dept Minneapolis MN 55455

HAMEROW, THEODORE STEPHEN, history educator; b. Warsaw, Poland, Aug. 24, 1920; came to U.S., 1930, naturalized, 1929; s. Haim Schneyer and Bella (Rubinlicht) H.; m. Margarete Lotter, Aug. 16, 1954 (div. Dec. 27, 1996); children: Judith Margarete, Helena Francisca; m. Diane Franzen, Oct. 4, 1997. B.A., CUNY, 1942; M.A., Columbia U., 1947; Ph.D., Yale U., 1951. Instr. Wellesley Coll., 1950-51, U. Md., 1951-52; instr., asst. prof., then asso. prof. U. Ill. 1952-58; mem. faculty U. Wis., 1958-91, prof. history, 1961-91, G. P. Gooch prof. history, 1978-91, chmn. dept. history, 1973-76; cons. editor Dorsey Press, 1961-71; mem. coun. Internat. Exch. Scholars, 1983-85, Nat. Coun. on Humanities, 1992-99. Author: Restoration, Revolution, Reaction, 1958, Otto von Bismarck: A Historical Assessment, 1962, The Social Foundations of German Unification 1858-1871, 2 vols, 1969-72, The Birth of a New Europe: State and Society in the Nineteenth Century, 1983, Reflections on History and Historians, 1987, From the Finland Station: The Graying of Revolution in the Twentieth Century, 1990, On the Road to the Wolf's Lair: German Resistance to Hitler, 1997; co-author: History of the World, 1960, A History of the Western World, 1969; editor: Otto von Bismarck, Reflections and Reminiscences, 1962, The Age of Bismarck, 1973; editorial bd.: Jour. Modern History, 1967-70, Central European History, 1968-72, Revs. in European History, 1974-78. Served with inf. AUS, 1943-46. Mem. Am. Hist. Assn., Conf. Group Central European History (sec.-treas. 1960-62, chmn. 1976), Wis. Assn. of Scholars (pres. 1989-91). Home: 885 Terry Pl Madison WI 53711-1956

HAMERS, ROBERT J., chemistry educator, researcher. Prof. chemistry U. Wis., Madison, Evan P. Helfaer chair, 1996—. Recipient Peter Mark Meml. award Am. Vacuum Soc., 1994; NSF fellow, 1992-97. Fellow Am. Vacuum Soc. Fax: 608-262-0453. Office: U Wisconsin Dept Chemistry 1101 University Ave Madison WI 53706-1322

HAMES, CARL MARTIN, educational administrator, art dealer, consultant; b. Birmingham, Ala., July 12, 1938; s. William Geda and Mary Anna (Martin) H. BA, Birmingham So. Coll., 1958; MA, Samford U., 1971, MS, 1980. Cert. tchr. in English, History and Spanish; cert. sch. adminstr. Tchr. Birmingham Pub. Schs., 1958-64; tchr. Birmingham U. Sch., 1964-69, asst. headmaster, 1969-75; coll. counselor The Altamont Sch., Birmingham, 1975-91, dean of students, 1975-89, asst. headmaster, 1989-91, headmaster, 1991—; dir. Town Hall Gallery, Birmingham, 1965—; chmn. Birmingham Nat. Coll. Fair, 1995, 96, 97. Writer poetry. Ethnic heritage chmn. Birmingham Hist. Soc., 1989—; active Birmingham Mus. Art, 1958-92; com. ann meeting Am. Hort. Soc., 1991; chmn. visual arts com. Arts Council Birmingham So. Coll., 1995—, founder, chmn. "Writing Today" Writers' Conf., 1980; featured spkr. Ind. Presbyn. Ch./Ind. Arts Festival, 1998. Recipient Silver Bowl awards in drama, visual arts Birmingham Festival of Arts, Disting. Alumnus award Birmingham-So. Coll., 1993, 1st Pl. Hackney prize for poetry State of Ala., 1996; named Barton Hill Head Instr. in the Humanities the Altamont Sch., 1986, named a Gem of Birmingham Black & White newspaper, 1996;. Mem. Nat. Coun. Tchrs. English, Ala. Assn. Ind. Schs. (bd. dirs. 1991—, chmn. biennial conf. 1994, v.p. 1997-99, pres. 1999—), Nat. Assn. Coll. Admissions Counselors (chmn. Nat. Coll. Fair Sept. 1995, 96, 97), So. Assn. Coll. Admissions Counselors (chmn. Coll. Fair 1994), Birmingham Bot. Soc., Birmingham Art Assn. (editor), Nat. Soc. of Arts and Letters (co-hmn. lit. competition 1998), Birmingham Mus. Art (editor), The Club, Phi Delta Kappa. Democrat. Roman Catholic. Avocations: collecting art, travel, gardening. Home: 3963 Montclair Rd Birmingham AL 35213-2414 Office: The Altamont Sch PO Box 131429 Birmingham AL 35213-6429

HAMES, WILLIAM LESTER, lawyer; b. Pasco, Wash., June 21, 1947; s. Arlie Franklin and Nina Lee (Ryals) H.; m. Pamella Kay Rust, June 3, 1967; children: Robert Alan, Michael Jonathan. *Mr. Hames' father was a blue collar worker. Mr. Hames' mother was a housewife who enrolled her three children in music lessons and enforced three hour per day practice sessions for all three. She instilled a work ethic and discipline which has resulted in Mr. Hames' successful legal career. Brother, Frank, is a partner in a successful music production company in Dallas, Texas. Sister, Gina, is a History Professor at Pacific Lutheran University in Tacoma, Washington. Thanks Mom!.* BS in Psychology, U. Wash., 1974; JD, Willamette U., 1981. Bar: Wash. 1981, U.S. Dist. Ct. (ea. dist.) Wash. 1982, U.S. Ct. Appeals (9th cir.) 1985, U.S. Dist. Ct. (we. dist.) Wash. 1985. Counselor Wash. Juvenile Ct., Walla Walla, Wash., 1974-76; reactor operator control rm. United Nuclear Inc., Richland, Wash., 1976-77; assoc. Sonderman, Egan & Hames, Kennewick, Wash., 1981-84, Timmons & Hames, Kennewick, 1984-86, Sonderman, Timmons & Hames, Kennewick, 1987-88; ptnr. Hames, Anderson & Whitlow, Kennewick, 1988—. *In addition to a thriving personal injury firm, Mr. Hames is the immediate past-President of the Bankruptcy Bar Association for the Eastern District of Washington. He is co-Chairman of the Association's annual seminar and retreat which attracts national caliber speakers. He has been chosen twice as the presenter at the Annual Western and Eastern Washington Bankruptcy Judges Conference.* Mem. Am. Trial Lawyers Assn., Wash. State Bar Assn., Wash. State Trial Lawyers Assn., Benton-Franklin County Bar Assn., Bankruptcy Bar Assn. (bd. dirs.), Fed. Bar Assn. (bd. dirs.). Democrat. Methodist. Home: 410 W 21st St Kennewick WA 99337 Office: Hames Anderson & Whitlow PO Box 5498 Kennewick WA 99336-0498

HAMID, MICHAEL, electrical engineering educator, consultant; b. Danaba, Tulkarm, Jordan, June 7, 1934; arrived in Can., 1958; m. Khetam Dahlah; Sept. 1, 1973; children: Rumsey, Sammy, Nady, Reema. BEE, McGill U., 1960, MEE, 1962; PhDEE, U. Toronto, 1966. Registered profl. engr., Ont., Man. Asst., assoc., full prof. U. Man., Winnipeg, Can., 1965; dean scholar's affairs Universite Internacional, Ann Arbor, Mich., 1972-75; chmn. grad. studies elec. engring dept. U. Man., Can., 1983-88; prof. elec. engring. U. South Ala., Mobile; mem. Can. Del. to Internat. Union of Radio Sci., 1965; pres., bd. dirs., treas. Internat. Microwave Power inst., 1969-73; adj. prof. Agrl. Engring., U. Man., 1970-77; vis. prof. U. Ctrl. Fla., Orlando, 1987-89; W.W. Clyde chair dept. elec. engring. U. Utah, 1987; mem. Man. Rsch. Coun., Prov. of Man., 1971-75; gen. chmn. Microwave Power Symposium, Monterey, Calif., 1971; vis. prof. Defence Rsch. Establishment, Dept. Nat. Defence Can., Ottawa, 1972; cons. Defence Rsch. Bd. Can., 1971-73; chmn. Internat. Conf. Biol. Effects of Microwaves and Ultrasound, U. Man., 1969; session organizer and chmn., invited speaker, Internat. Union Radio Sci. Gen. Assembly, Commn. VI., Warsaw, Poland, 1972; invited speaker Microwave State-of-the-Art Internat., IEEE Microwave Theory and Techniques Symposium, Chgo., 1972; ; mem. Man. Rsch. Counc. and chmn. of Elec. and Electronics Products Rsch. Com., 1971-75, Nat. Rsch. Coun. Can. Assoc. Com. on Bird Hazards to Aircraft, 1972-77, Policy Com. and Grants Selection com., Transp. Inst., U. Man., 1972-78; session organizer, invited speaker, Internat. URSI-IEEE-Antennas and Propagation Symposium, U. Colo., 1973; chmn. IEEE edn. activities bd., 1972; invited speaker Brazilian Soc. for Advancement Sci., 25th meeting, Sao Paulo, 1973; invited speaker, mem. Internat. Organizing Com., Colloquium on Microwave Communication, Hungarian Acad. Sci., 1970—; invited speaker NATO Adv. Group for Aerospace R&D E.M. Wave Propagation Panel, The Netherlands, 1974; adj. prof. Naval Postgrad. Sch., Monterey Calif., 1979-81; invited speaker Internat. Conf. on Communications Cirs. and Systems, India, 1981; invited speaker and mem. tech. program com., Internat. Symposium on Microwaves and Communication, Kharagpur, India, 1981; chmn. libr. and fin. coms., U. Man. Transport Inst., 1982-84; mem. Radar Subcom. of Radarsat, Can. Adv. Com. on Remote Sensing, Ottawa, 1983-88; mem. Grad. Studies Awards Com, U. Man., 1984-88; session chmn. URSI/IEEE-Antennas and Propagation Soc. Internat. Symposium, U. B.C., Vancouver, 1985; me. Antenna Tech. and Applied Electromagnetics Conf. Program Com., U. Man., 1986—; expert witness Andrew Antennas vs. Gabriel Electronics, patent infringement litigation, Portland, Maine, 1984-86; expert witness radio interference litigation WKRG, Inc. vs. State of Ala., 1990-91; invited speaker, 78th meeting of N.D. Acad. Sci., U. N.D., Grand Forks, 1986; vis. prof. U. Cen. Fla., dept. elect. engring., 1987—; gen. chmn. Symposium on Electromagnetic Detection of Latent Objects, 1989; me. Internat. Adv. and Tech. Program Com., Internat. Symposium on Recent Advances in Microwave Tech., Beijing, 1989, Reno, 1991, New Delhi, 1993. Author or co-author 292 tech. articles, 7 monographs and book chpts., 178 conf. papers, 26 rsch. reports, 25 patents; assoc. editor Jour. Microwave Power, 1969-77; mem. editorial bd. Microwave Jour., Jour. Microwave Power, IEEE Transactions on Microwave Theory and Techniques, 1969—. Fellow IEE, IEEE (award for contbns. to electromagnetic scattering and diffraction, devel. dielectric-loaded waveguides, resonators and antennas), Internat. Microwave Power Inst., Electromagnetics Acad. (invited mem.), Am. Assn. of Engring Soc., Phi Eta Sigma, Tau Beta Pi. Office: U South Ala Dept Elec Engring Mobile AL 36688

HAMIDZADEH, HAMID REZA, mechanical engineer, educator, consultant; b. Tehran, Iran, July 22, 1952; came to U.S., 1982; s. Khodadad and Nosrat (Fassieh) H. m. Azar Mofid, July 2, 1987; children: Cyrus, Archer. BSc, Arya Meher U. of Tehran, 1974; MSc, Imperial Coll. U. London, 1975, PhD, 1978. Postdoctoral rsch. asst. Imperial Coll., London, 1978-82; lectr., assoc. mem. grad. sch. U. Md., College Park, 1982-83; asst. prof. U. So. Colo., Pueblo, 1983-86; assoc. prof. S.D. State U., Brookings, 1986-90, prof., 1990—, prin. investigator mech. engring., 1994-96; sr. design cons. Cummins Engine Co., Columbus, Ind., 1995; organizer numerous tech. confs.; rev. manuscripts of tech. books for pubs. Contbr. more than 55 articles to profl. jours. including Jour. Shock and Vibration, ASME, among others. Recipient numerous grants. Mem. ASME (sr. del NSSC com. 1988-93, regional chair bd. minority and women 1989-92, profl. devel. com. 1993-96, Faculty Advisor of Yr. 1991). Avocations: swimming, poetry. Home: 6015 S Mustang Ave Sioux Falls SD 57108-3800 Office: SD State U Dept Mech Engring 214 Crothers Engring Hall Brookings SD 57007

HAMILL, DOROTHY STUART, professional ice skater; b. Chgo., 1957; d. Chalmers C. and Carolyn C. (Clough) H.; m. Dean Paul Martin, 1982, (div. 1984); m. Kenneth Forsythe, 1987; 1 child, Alexandra. Student, Colo. Acad., Greenwich High Sch. Co-owner, pres. The Ice Capades, 1993-95; with Winter Tour World Figure Skating Champions, 1997. Profl. skater: Ice Capades, 1977—; former tour co. Dorothy Hamill on Ice, 1985—; author: Dorothy Hamill On or Off the Ice. Mem. Pres.'s Council Phys. Fitness. Olympic Gold medalist, 1976; world figure skating champion, 1976; U.S. figure skating champion; Emmy award Romeo and Juliet on Ice, 1984. *

HAMILL, JOHN P., bank executive; b. N.Y.C., 1940; married. A.B., Holy Cross Coll., 1961; Master's Degree in Taxation, NYU Sch. Law, 1964. Bar: N.Y., Ohio. Dep. gen. counsel legal dept. Chem. Bank N.Y.; pres., chief exec. officer Galbreath Mortgage Co.; pres., chief exec. officer trust affiliate, pres. mortgage banking affiliate Banc One Corp., Columbus, Ohio, prior to 1980; exec. v.p., gen. counsel Shawmut Corp., Boston, 1980-81, pres., 1981—; pres. Shawmut; dir. Shawmut Bank N.A., 1981—; vice chmn., dir. Shawmut Nat. Corp., Boston, 1988—; pres. Fleet Bank of Mass., Boston,

1992, pres., bd. dirs., 1993—. Office: Fleet Bank-MA One Federal St 37th Fl Boston MA 02110*

HAMILL, MARK RICHARD, actor; b. Oakland, Calif., Sept. 25, 1951; m. Marilou York, 1978; children: Nathan, Griffin, Chelsea. Student, L.A. City Coll., 1969-70. Performed at Renaissance Faire, Agoura, Calif., 3 seasons; appearances include (TV series) Texas Wheelers, 1974, Bruno the Kid, 1996, Batman: Gotham Knights, 1997; (TV movies) Eric, Sarah T.: Portrait of a Teen-age Alcoholic, 1975, Delancey Street: The Crisis Within, 1975, Mallory, Circumstantial Evidence, 1976, The City, 1977, 1983, Earth Angel, 1991, (other TV roles) Bill Cosby Show, 1990, General Hospital, 1972-73, Partridge Family, 1971, Owen Marshll Counselor at Law, 1972, Night Gallery, 1972, The FBI, 1972, Room 222, 1973, The Magician, 1973, Manhunter, 1974, Cannon, 1974, Bronk, 1975, Lucas Tanner, 1975, Streets of San Francisco, 1975, Petrocelli, 1975, Med. Ctr., 1976, Marcus Welby, M.D., 1976, One Day at a Time, 1976, (pilot) Eight Is Enough, 1977, The Muppet Show, 1980, Amazing Stories, 1986, Alfred Hitchcock Presents, 1987, Hooperman, 1989, The Flash, 1991, Burke's Law, 1994, SeaQuest, 1994, Outer Limits, 1996, (motion pictures) Star Wars, 1977, Corvette Summer, 1978, The Big Red One, 1980, The Empire Strikes Back, 1980, Night the Lights Went Out in Georgia, 1981, Return of the Jedi, 1983, Britannia Hospital, 1983, Slipstream, 1988, Black Magic Woman, 1991, Picture Perfect, 1991, Sleepwalkers, 1992, The Guyver, 1992, Time Runner, 1993, Midnight Ride, 1993, John Carpenter Presents: Body Bags, 1993, Batman: Mask of the Phatasm, 1993, Village of the Damned, 1995, Silk Degrees, 1996, The Raffle, 1995, Wing Commander Academy, 1996, Glen 13, 1997, Star Wars, 1997, Laserhawk, 1997, Watchers Reborn, 1998, Hamilton, 1998, Scooby Doo on Zombie Island, 1998, Walking Across Egypt, 1999, Sinbad: Beyond the Veil of the Mists, 1999, Wing Commander (voice), 1999; (theatre) Broadway debut in Elephant Man, 1981, also Amadeus, 1982, Harrigan 'n Hart, 1985, The Nerd, 1987, (off Broadway) Harrigan 'n Hart, 1984, Room Service, 1986; other voice work in radio. Address: The Hamill Exch care Nacolle Parsons PO Box 526177 Salt Lake City UT 84152-6177*

HAMILL, (WILLIAM) PETE, newspaper columnist, author, editor; b. Bklyn., June 24, 1935; s. William and Anne (Devlin) H.; m. Ramona Negron, Feb. 3, 1962 (div. 1970); children—Adriene, Deirdre; m. Fukiko Aoki, May 23, 1987. Student, Pratt Inst., 1952, Mexico City (Mexico) Coll., 1956-57. Comml. artist, 1957-60; reporter N.Y. Post, later columnist, 1960-74; columnist N.Y. Daily News, 1975-79, 82-84; contbg. editor Saturday Evening Post, 1963-64; contbr. Village Voice, New York Mag., N.Y.C., 1974—; editor Mexico City News, 1986-87; columnist Esquire, 1989-91, N.Y. Post, 1988-93, N.Y. Newsday, 1994—; editor-in-chief N.Y. Daily News, 1997. Author: (novels) A Killing for Christ, 1968, The Gift, 1973, Flesh and Blood, 1977, Loving Women, 1990, Snow in August, 1997, (nonfiction) Irrational Ravings, 1972, A Drinking Life: A Memoir, 1994, Tools as Art, 1995, Piecework, 1996, News is a Verb, 1998, Why Sinatra Matters, 1998, Diego Rivera, 1999, (short stories) The Invisible City: A New York Sketchbook, 1980, Tokyo Sketches, 1993, (screenplays) Doc, 1971, Badge, 373, 1973, Liberty, 1986, Neon Empire, 1987; contbr. articles to numerous mags. Trustee Mus. City N.Y.; coun. mem. Writers Guild Am. Past. Served with USN, 1952-54. Recipient Meyer Berger award Columbia Sch. Journalism, 1962, award Newspaper Reporters Assn., 1962, 25 Yr. Achievement award Soc. of Silurians, 1989, Peter Kihss award, Silurians, 1992. Mem. PEN, Nat. Assn. Hispanic Journalists, Silurians. Democrat.

HAMILL, PETER VANVECHTEN, physician, epidemiologist, consultant; b. Balt., Apr. 16, 1926; s. Northmore Wilbur and Priscilla VanVechten H.; m. Margot Joan Henry, June 12, 1952; children: Jan Elizabeth, Peter VanVechten Jr., Hannah Elizabeth, Northmore Wilbur II. BA, U. Mich., 1947, MD, 1953; MPH, Johns Hopkins U., 1962. Diplomate Am. Coll. Epidemiology, Am. Coll. Preventive Medicine, Am. Coll. Occupl. and Environ. Medicine. Commd. ensign USN, 1944, various assignments, 1944-53; commd. med. officer in charge Alaska Native Hosp. USPHS, 1955-57; chief epidemiologic investigations air pollution program USPHS, Washington, 1958-62, staff dir., med. adviser, surgeon gen. com. on smoking and health, 1962-64, chief med. advisor U.S. Nat. Health Survey, 1964-78; ship explorer med. officer USCG, Aleutian Islands, 1957-58; pres. Hamill Assocs., Inc., Annapolis, Md., 1978—; vis. prof. epidemiology U. Mass., Amherst, 1978-79; sr. med. advisor Olin Corp., Stamford, Conn., 1978-87; prof. epidemiology and preventive medicine U. Md., Balt., 1979-81; sr. med. cons. Occidental Chem. Corp., Dallas, 1986—; expert advisor TelTech, Mpls., 1989—. Pres. Key Sch. Bd. Trustees, Annapolis, 1968-70. Fellow Am. Coll. Occupl. and Environ. Medicine, Am. Coll. Epidemiology, Am. Coll. Preventive Medicine, Soc. Cin., Army and Navy Club, Explorer's Club. Republican. Episcopal. Avocations: sailing, collecting fine wines and books. Home: 1001 Whitehall Cove Annapolis MD 21401

HAMILTON, ALBERT CHARLES, English language educator; b. Winnipeg, Man., Can., July 20, 1921; s. Clifford Goddard and Mary (Briggs) H.; m. Mary E. McFarlane, July 2, 1950; children: Ian, Malcolm, Peter, Ross. B.A. with honors, U. Man., 1945; M.A., U. Toronto, 1948; Ph.D., U. Cambridge, Eng., 1953. Supr. English Cambridge (Eng.) U., 1950-52; prof. English U. Wash., 1952-68, Queen's U., Kingston, Ont., Can., 1968—; Cappon prof. emeritus English Queen's U., 1981—; vis. fellow St. John's Coll., Cambridge, 1974-75; vis. prof. U. Toronto, 1961-62, Harvard U., 1969, Kumamoto U., 1988. Author: Structure of Allegory in Spenser's Faerie Queene, 1961, The Early Shakespeare, 1967, Sir Philip Sidney: A Study of his Life and Works, 1977, Northrop Frye: Anatomy of His Criticism, 1990; editor: Selected Poetry of Spenser, 1966, Spenser's Faerie Queene, 1977; gen. editor: The Spenser Ency., 1990. Huntington Library fellow, 1959-60, Humanities Rsch. Centre (Australia), 1987. Fellow Royal Soc. Can.; mem. MLA, Renaissance Soc. Am., Assn. Can. U. Tchrs. of English, Spenser Soc. Am., Internat. Assn. U. Profs. Office: Queen's U, Dept English, Kingston, ON Canada K7L 3N6

HAMILTON, ALLAN CORNING, retired oil company executive; b. Chgo., June 9, 1921; s. Daniel Sprague and Mildred (Corning) H.; m. Edith Johnson, June 3, 1950 (div. 1995); children: Kimball C., Scott W., Dean C., Gail W.; m. Geraldine C. Berndt, Jan. 27, 1996. BS in Econs., Haverford Coll., 1943; LLD (hon.), Union Coll., Schenectady, N.Y., 1979. With Standard Oil Co., N.J., 1946-51, Esso Export Corp., 1951-56; treas. Internat. Petroleum co. Ltd., Coral Gables, Fla., 1956-61, Esso Internat. Inc., 1961-66; with Exxon Corp. (formerly Standard Oil Co., N.J.), N.Y.C., 1966-83, treas., v.p., prin. fin. officer, 1970-83. Lt. USNR, 1943-46. Clubs: Dalton Ranch Golf (Durango, Colo.), Explorers, Metropolitan (N.Y.C.).

HAMILTON, ALLEN PHILIP, financial advisor; b. Albany, Calif., Oct. 17, 1937; s. Allen Philip Sr. and Barbara Louise (Martin) H.; m. Mary Williams, July 18, 1981 (div. Mar. 1987). BA in Bus. Mgmt., St. Mary's U., San Jose, Calif., 1961; AA, Contra Costa State Coll., 1957; Bus. Assoc. degree, NW Mo. State U., 1969; postgrad., San Jose State U., 1959-61. Cert. fin. planner. Fin. advisor Consol. Investment Svcs., Kansas City, Mo., 1968-70; pres., CEO, Balanced Mgmt. Assn., Mission, Kans., 1969-72, Advanced Svc. Assn., Overland Park, Kans., 1971-78; divisional mgr. Waddell & Reed, Inc., Kansas City, 1978-81; sr. v.p., regional dir. WZW Fin. Svcs., Kansas City, 1981-86; exec.v.p. Skaife & Co., Orinda, Calif., 1986-88; v.p., mktg. dir. Consol. Securities Corp., Walnut Creek, Calif., 1988; sr. dir. and cert. trainer Club Am., Inc., L.A., 1990—; CFP, prin. Hamilton Fin. Adv., Am. Investment Svcs., Pleasant Hill, Calif., 1989—; silver mktg. distbr., corp. trainer, Can. mktg. distbr. and trainer Nikken, Inc. Internat., numerous fgn. countries, 1991—; sales mgr., ind. distributor, sales trainer Alpine Industries, 1992—; prin. advisor Environ. Solutions Internat.; exec. dir., C.E.O. Environ. Air Quality and Health Found. (Environ. Solutions Internat.), 1998—; sales, mktg. dir. Exthel Wireless Communications Inc., 1998-99; trainer, presdl. dir. Builders Referral Inc., Orange County, Calif., 1998—; exec. v.p., v.p. mktg. Performance Mktg. Group, Orange County, 1999—; sr. dir. Club Am. OTC Pink Shts., L.A., 1990-92; presdl. dir. FundAmerica, Irvine, Calif., 1988—; guest speaker in field. Author: (with others) The Financial Planner A New Profession, 1986. Asst. dist. commr. Boy Scouts Am., Kansas City, Kans., 1970-79; corp. dir. United Campaign, Overland Park, Kans., 1965-73; active TV show Kidney Found., Kansas City, Mo., 1969-70; sr. arbitrator San Francisco Bay Area Better Bus. Bur., 1986—. Lt. U.S. Army, 1963-65. Recipient Citation Nat. Campaign Re-election 1992, 1992m Senatorial Commn. Rep. Senatorial Inner Circle, 1991. Mem. Inst. Cert. Fin. Planners, Internat. Assn. for Fin. Planning (v.p., bd. dirs. 1982-87, practitioner div.), Registry of Fin. Planning Practitioners, Mt. Diablo Distbrs. Assn. Republican. Avocations: cars, outdoors, tennis, travel, boating. Home: 8 Robin Ridge Aliso Viejo CA 92656

HAMILTON, BARRY ALAN, aerospace engineer, software engrineer; b. Sterling, Colo., Oct. 5, 1967; s. Harold Oren and Gail Emaline (Marconi) H. BS in Aerospace Engring., U. Colo., 1991. Sr. assoc. engr. Lockheed Missiles and Space Co., Sunnyvale, Calif., 1991-94; mem. profl. staff Advanced Systems Engring., Denver, 1994-98; pres. Priority Data Systems, Denver, 1998—. Mem. AIAA (chair nat. career enhancement com. 1994-98, young mems. dir. San Francisco sect. 1993-94, 3rd Pl. award 1994, Citation 1998). Republican. Avocations: mountain biking, snow boarding, sports. Fax: 303-977-4994. E-mail: barry.a.hamilton@lmco.com. Home: 124 E Colorado Ave Ste B Denver CO 80210 Office: Priority Data Systems 124 E Colorado Ave #B Denver CO 80210

HAMILTON, BEVERLY EDITH, former nurse educator; b. Daytona Beach, Fla., June 3, 1912; d. Harry and Edith (Wolf) Horn; m. Joseph William Hamilton, Mar. 4, 1939; children: Joseph, Homer, Judith. BSN, Fla. State U., 1937. RN. Instr., trainer ARC, Dover, Ohio, 1945-90. Methodist. Home: 508 Evergreen Dr Dover OH 44622-1302

HAMILTON, BEVERLY LANNQUIST, investment management professional; b. Roxbury, Mass., Oct. 19, 1946; d. Arthur and Nancy Lannquist. BA cum laude, U. Mich., 1968; postgrad., NYU, 1969-70. Prin. Auerbach, Pollak & Richardson, N.Y.C., 1972-75; v.p. Morgan Stanley & Co., N.Y.C., 1975-80, United Techs., Hartford, Conn., 1980-87; dep. comptr. City of N.Y., 1987-91; pres. ARCO Investment Mgmt Co, L.A., 1991—; also v.p. Atlantic Richfield Co., L.A.; bd. dirs. Conn. Natural Gas Co., Mass. Mut. Investment Mgmt., Emerging Markets Growth Fund, United Asset Mgmt. Trustee Hartford Coll. for Women, 1981-87, Stanford Univ. Mgmt. Co., 1991—; bd. dirs. Inst. for Living, 1983-87. Mem. NCCJ (bd. dirs. 1987-91). Office: ARCO Investment Mgmt Co 515 S Flower St Los Angeles CA 90071-2201

HAMILTON, BOBBY, professional race car driver; b. Nashville, May 29, 1957; m. Debbie Hamilton; 1 child, Bobby Jr. former Nashville Speedway track champion; NASCAR Winston Cup Series debut 1991, winner Dura-Lube 500, Phoenix, 1996; 1997 season includes winner Rockingham; 1998 season includes winner Martinsville, 2 top-5s, 8 top-10s, top 15 in points. Recipient NASCAR Winston Cup Series Rookie of Yr. award, 1991. Office: c/o Morgan-McClure Motorsports 26502 Newbanks Rd Abingdon VA 24211*

HAMILTON, CARL HULET, retired academic administrator; b. Morris, Okla., Sept. 30, 1934; s. Alva H. and Olah E. (Pryor) H.; m. Gloria Joyce Gore, Sept. 3, 1954; children: Ray, Carla Jo, Deanna Jean. ThB, Southwestern Coll., 1956; BA, Oklahoma City U., 1957; MA, U. Tulsa, 1962; PhD, U. Ark., 1968. English tchr. Southwestern Coll., Oklahoma City, 1957-60; editor Oral Roberts Evangelistic Assn., Tulsa, 1960-62; English tchr., editor Oral Roberts U., Tulsa, 1966-68; acad. dean, 1968-75; provost Oral Roberts U., Tulsa, 1975-84; adminstr. World Evangelism, San Diego, 1984-86; chief of staff Feed the Children, Oklahoma City, 1986-88; provost, chief acad. officer Oral Roberts U., 1989-98. Min. of adminstrn. First United Meth. Ch., 1999—. Mem. Rotary. Republican. Methodist. Avocations: fishing, water sports, motorcycling. Home: PO Box 488 Disney OK 74340-0488

HAMILTON, CARLOS ROBERT, JR., internist, endocrinologist; b. Houston, June 12, 1939; s. Carlos Robert and Berta (Denman) H.; m. Carolyn Burton, Aug. 12, 1961; children: Carlos R. III, Patricia Frances. BA, U. Tex., 1961; MS, MD with honors, Baylor Coll. Medicine, 1966. Diplomate Am. Bd. Internal Medicine, Am. Bd. Endocrinology and Metabolic Diseases; lic. physician, Tex. Intern in internal medicine The Johns Hopkins Hosp., Balt., 1966-67, asst. resident in internal medicine, 1967-69, chief resident in medicine, 1970-71; clin. and rsch. fellow Harvard Med. Sch./Mass. Gen. Hosp., Boston, 1969-70; asst. prof. medicine Johns Hopkins U. and Hosp., Balt., 1971-72; staff endocrinologist Wilford Hall USAF Med. Ctr., San Antonio, 1972-74; clin. assoc. prof. medicine Baylor Coll. Medicine, Houston, 1974—; cons. endocrinology and internal medicine Med. Clinic of Houston, L.L.P., 1974—; med. advisor employee benefit com. Southwestern Bell Tel. Co., 1975-93; attending physician in endocrinology Ben Taub Gen. Hosp./Baylor Coll. Medicine, 1980—; attending physician, mem. active staff The Meth. Hosp., Houston, 1974—. Contbr. articles to profl. jours. Dist. and coun. chair, area pres., regional bd. dirs., v.p. Boy Scouts Am., Houston, Atlanta, Irving, Tex., 1980—; bd. regents Tex. Woman's U., 1999—. Recipient Dist. award of merit, Silver Beaver award, Silver Antelope award, Disting. Eagle Scout award, Silver Buffalo award Boy Scouts Am., 1982-95. Fellow ACP (bd. dirs. Tex. chpt., Mead-Johnson Residency scholar 1970, bd. dirs. Tex. Acad. Internal Medicine and ACP-ASIM health and pub. policy com.), Am. Coll. Clin. Endocrinology; mem. SAR (bd. dirs. Paul Carrington chpt. 1992—, pres. 1993), Am. Soc. Internal Medicine (bd. dirs. polit. action com. 1995-98, Key Congl. Contact of Yr. 1996), Am. Assn. Clin. Endocrinologists (bd. dirs. 1995—, chair legis. and regulatory com. 1998—), Tex. Med. Assn. (exec. com. polit. action com. 1989—, chair 1995, 96), Harris County Med. Soc. (bd. dirs. 1992—, pres.-elect 1998, pres. 1999), Kiwanis (bd. dirs. Houston chpt. 1986-95, pres. 1995), Alpha Omega Alpha, Sigma Xi. E-Mail: chamilton@mchllp.com. Home: 3713 Chevy Chase Houston TX 77019 Office: Med Clinic of Houston LLP 1707 Sunset Blvd Houston TX 77005

HAMILTON, CAROL JEAN, English educator, writer, storyteller; b. Enid, Okla., Aug. 23, 1935; d. Clarence DeWitt and Ruby Raye (Settles) Barber; m. Joseph Jefferson Hamilton, Aug. 25, 1956 (div. May 1994); children: Debra Susan Hamilton Havenar, Christopher David, Stephen Anthony. BS, Phillips U., 1957; MA, U. Ctrl. Okla., 1978. Tchr. North Haven (Conn.) Schs., 1956-59, Indpls. Pub. Schs., 1970-71, Tinker Elem., Mid-Del. Schs., Tinker AFB, Okla., 1971-82, Acad. Ctr. for Enrichment, Midwest City, Okla., 1982-93; Spanish tutor, tchr. Mid-Del Schs., Midwest City, 1985-88; instr. English and Spanish, Rose State Coll., Midwest City, 1988-98; prof. creative studies divsn. U. Ctrl. Okla., Edmond, 1996—; artist-in-residence Contemporary Arts Found., Oklahoma City, 1971-79; former instr. U. Okla., Norman; instr. Okla. Quartz Mountain Arts Inst., 1993—; instr., spkr. Okla. Writing Project, 1993—; chmn. tchr. rights Mid-Del Schs., 1980-83. Author: (children's novels) The Dawn Seekers, 1987 (S.W. Book award 1988), Mystery of Black Mesa, 1995 (Cherubim award 1995), (poetry) Once the Dust, 1992 (Okla. Book award 1992, Pegasus award), Daring the Wind, 1987, Legends of Poland, 1992. Recipient Byline lit. award Byline mag., 1987-92; named Poet Laureate of Okla., 1995. Mem. Soc. Children's Book Writers, Acad. Am. Poetry, Am. Astron. League, Poetry Soc. Okla. (past pres., other offices), Mid-Okla. Writers, Individual Artists Okla. (sec. bd. dirs. 1978-85), Creative Writers Inst., Sierra Club. Democrat. Mem. Christian Ch. (Disciples of Christ). Avocations: interpreting, storytelling. Home: 9608 Sonata Ct Midwest City OK 73130-6416 Office: U Ctrl Okla 100 N University Dr Edmond OK 73034-5207

HAMILTON, CHARLES HOWARD, metallurgy educator; b. Pueblo, Colo., Mar. 17, 1935; s. George Edwin and Eva Eleanor (Watson) H.; m. Joy Edith Richmond, Sept. 7, 1968; children: Curtis Gene, Krista Kathleen, Brady Glenn. BS, Colo. Sch. Mines, 1959; MS, U. So. Calif., 1965; PhD, Case Western Res. U., 1968. Research engr. Space div. Rockwell Internat., Downey, Calif., 1959-65; mem. tech. staff Los Angeles div. Rockwell Internat., 1968-75; tech. staff, phys. metallurgy Sci. Ctr., Thousand Oaks, Calif., 1975-77, group mgr. metals processing, 1977-79, prin. scientist, 1979-81, dir. materials synthesis and processing dept., 1982-84; assoc. prof. metallurgy Wash. State U., Pullman, 1984-87, prof., 1987—; chmn. Rockwell Corp. tech. panel, materials research and engring; co-organizer 1st Internat. Symposium Superplastic Forming, 1982, Internat. Conf. on Superplasticity and Superplastic Forming, 1988. Sr. editor Jour. Materials Shaping Tech.; dep. editor Scripta Metallurgica et Materialia, 1989—; contbr. tech. articles to profl. publs.; patentee advanced metalworking and tech. Named Rockwell Engr. of Yr., 1979; recipient IR 100 award Indsl. Research mag., 1976, 80. Fellow Am. Soc. Metals; mem. AIME (shaping and forming com.), Sigma Xi. Home: 410 SE Crestview St Pullman WA 99163-2213

HAMILTON, CHERYL LOUISE, elementary education educator; b. Indpls., Oct. 13, 1951; d. Roy and Ellen Elizabeth (Grinstead) H. BS, Ind. U., Indpls., 1973; MS in Edn., Butler U., Indpls., 1985. Cert. elem. tchr., Ind. Tchr.'s aide Indpls. Public Schs., 1969, tchr., 1974—; student intern Nat. Education Assn., Indpls., 1972; campus coord. Ind. State Teachrs Assn., Indpls., 1972-73; resident camp dir. Hoosier Capital Girl Scouts Coun., Indpls., 1977-78; cons. Outdoor Edn. Curriculum, 1986, Nat. Gardening Assn., 1993; environ. edn. workshop leader, 1986, 95, 97; mem. Indpls. Pub. Schs. Energy Cadre, 1980—. Instr. Am. Red Cross, Indpls., 1987--; mem. Girl Scouts U.S., 1959--, (recipient Thanks Badge, 1989), leader Hoosier Capital Girl Scouts, 1975--, master trainer 1989--; past dir. PTO. Recipient Above and Beyond Call of Duty award Indpls. Edn. Found., 1990, 92, Conservation Tchr. of Yr. award Marion County Soil and Water Dist., 1991; Hoosier scholar State of Ind., 1971; fellow Eli Lilly Found., 1984. Mem. Ind. State Tchrs. Assn., Indpls. Edn. Assn., Nat. Wildlife Fedn., Nat. Gardening Assn. (grow lab. cons. 1993), Delta Kappa Gamma. Avocations: camping, singing. Home: 3507 Luewan Dr Indianapolis IN 46235-2217

HAMILTON, CLYDE HENRY, federal judge; b. Edgefield, S.C., Feb. 8, 1934; s. Clyde H. and Edwina (Odom) H.; children: John C., James W. BS, Wofford Coll., 1956; JD with honors, George Washington U., 1961. Bar: S.C. 1961. Assoc. J.R. Folk, Edgefield, 1961-63; assoc., gen. ptnr. Butler, Means, Evins & Browne, Spartanburg, S.C., 1963-81; judge U.S. Dist. Ct. S.C., Columbia, 1981-91, U.S. Ct. Appeals (4th cir.), Richmond, Va., 1991—; reference asst. U.S. Senate Library, Washington, 1958-61; gen. counsel Synalloy Corp., Spartanburg, 1969-80. Mem. editorial staff Cumulative Index of Congl. Com. Hearings, 1935-58; bd. editors George Washington Law Rev., 1959-60. Pres., Spartanburg County Arts Council, 1971-73; pres. Spartanburg Day Sch., 1972-74, sustaining trustee, 1975-81; past mem. steering com. undergrad. merit fellowship program and estate planning council Converse Coll., Spartanburg; trustee Spartanburg Methodist Coll., 1979-84; mem. S.C. Supreme Ct. Bd. Commrs. on Grievances and Discipline, 1980-81; del. Spartanburg County, 4th Congl. Dist. and S.C. Republican Convs., 1976, 80; mem., past chmn. fin. com. and adminstrv. bd. Trinity United Meth. Ch., Spartanburg, trustee, 1980-83. Served to capt. USAR, 1956-62. Recipient Alumni Disting. Svc. award Wofford Coll., 1991. Mem. S.C. Bar Assn., Piedmont Club (bd. govs. 1979-81). Office: US Ct Appeals 4th Cir 1901 Main St Columbia SC 29201-2443

HAMILTON, DAGMAR STRANDBERG, lawyer, educator; b. Phila., Jan. 10, 1932; d. Eric Wilhelm and Anna Elizabeth (Sjöström) Strandberg; A.B., Swarthmore Coll., 1953; J.D., U. Chgo. Law Sch., 1956; J.D., Am. U., 1961; m. Robert W. Hamilton, June 26, 1953; children: Eric Clark, Robert Andrew Hale, Meredith Hope. Admitted to Tex. bar, 1972; atty., civil rights div. U.S. Dept. Justice, Washington, 1965-66; asst. instr. govt. U. Tex.-Austin, 1966-71; lectr. Law Sch. U. Ariz., Tucson, 1971-72; editor, researcher Assoc. Justice William O. Douglas, U.S. Supreme Ct., 1962-73, 75-76; editor, rschr. Douglas autobiography Random House Co., 1972-73; staff counsel Judiciary Com., U.S. Ho. of Reps., 1973-74; asst. prof. L.B. Johnson Sch. Pub. Affairs, U. Tex., Austin, 1974-77, assoc. prof., 1977-83, prof., 1983—, assoc. dean, 1983-87; interdisciplinary prof. U. Tex. Law Sch., 1983—; vis. prof. Washington U. Law Sch., St. Louis, 1982, U. Maine, Portland, 1992; vis. fellow Univ. London, QMW sch. law, 1987-88, Univ. Oxford Inst European & Comparative Law, 1998. Mem. Tex. Bar Assn., Am. Law Inst., Assn. Pub. Policy Analysis and Mgmt., Swarthmore Coll. Alumni Coun. (rep.), Kappa Beta Phi (hon.), Phi Kappa Phi (hon.). Democrat. Quaker. Contbr. to various publs. Home: 403 Allegro Ln Austin TX 78746-4301 Office: U Tex LBJ Sch Pub Affairs Austin TX 78713

HAMILTON, DANIEL STEPHEN, clergyman; b. Cedarhurst, N.Y., Jan. 7, 1932; s. Richard Samuel and Catherine Mary (Liston) H. B.A., Cathedral Coll., 1954; S.T.B., Cath. U. Am., 1958; Ph.D., Greenwich U., 1991. Ordained priest Roman Catholic Ch., 1958; asst. pastor St. Anne's Ch., Garden City, N.Y., 1958-61; campus chaplain Adelphi U., Garden City, 1959-61; prof. St. Pius X Preparatory Sem., Uniondale, N.Y., 1961-68; campus chaplain Hofstra U., Hempstead, N.Y., 1961-66; columnist L.I. Catholic, Hempstead, 1962-85; editor L.I. Catholic, 1975-85; dir. Bur. Public Info., Diocese Rockville Centre, 1968-85; chmn. Ecumenical Commn., 1968-88; resident priest St. William the Abbot Parish, Seaford, N.Y., 1971-85; pastor Our Lady of Perpetual Help Parish, Lindenhurst, N.Y., 1985—. Named hon. papal prelate, 1980. Mem. Cath. Theol. Soc. Am., Fellowship Cath. Scholars. Home and Office: 210 S Wellwood Ave Lindenhurst NY 11757-4927

HAMILTON, DARDEN COLE, flight test engineer; b. Pitts., Nov. 28, 1956; s. Isaac Herman Hamilton and Grace Osborne (Fish) Thorp; m. Linda Susanne Moser, Aug. 7, 1976; children: Christopher Moser Hamilton, Elijah Cole Hamilton. BS in Aeronautics, St. Louis U., Cahokia, Ill., 1977; postgrad., Ariz. State U. Lic. pilot, airframe and power mechanic. Engr. McDonnell Douglas Aircraft Co., St. Louis, Mo., 1977-80; group leader, engring. Cessna Aircraft Co., Wichita, Kans., 1980-83, sr. flight test engr., 1983-85; sr. flight test engr. Allied-Signal Aerospace Co., Phoenix, 1986-92, flight test engr. specialist, 1992-98, prin. engr., 1998—. Editor Family Proponent Newsletter, 1994-98. Mem. Ariz. Gov.'s Constnl. Commemoration Com., 1997-99; bd. dirs. Ariz. House and Senate Chaplaincy, 1997-98, chmn. bd. advisors, 1998—; Desert Sky precinct committeeman Glendale Rep. Com.; vol. coord. legis. dist. 16 campaign John Shadegg for Congress, 1994-96; elected dist. 16 for Ariz. Senate, 1999—; mem. adult edn. dept. Rivers Cmty. Ch.; del. Ariz. dist. 16 Ariz. Rep. Conv., 1995—; resolutions com. Ariz. Rep. Com., Ariz. govs. mil. base retention task force, 1999—; chmn. Ariz. Senate domestic violence task force, 1999—. Mem. NRA (life, cert. instr.), Soc. Flight Test Engrs., Am. Helicopter Soc., Am. Legis. Exch. Coun., Ariz. State Rifle and Pistol Assn. (life). Avocations: horses, target shooting, camping. Home: 5533 W Christy Dr Glendale AZ 85304-3889 Office: Allied-Signal Aerospace Co Allied Signal Engines Inc 111 S 34th St Phoenix AZ 85034-2802

HAMILTON, DAVID EUGENE, minister, educator; b. Pyeng Yang, Korea, Jan. 21, 1929; m. Marilyn Long Hamilton; children: Beth Jean Hamilton Stanton, Rebecca Sue Hamilton Vierling, Sarah Ruth Hamilton Goeglein, Jill Linette Hamilton Martin. AB in Theology, Gordon Coll., 1950; BD, Gordon Div. Sch., 1953; ThM, Columbia Theol. Seminary, Decatur, Ga., 1960, Fuller Theol. Seminary, 1983. Ordained to ministry Presbyn. Ch. of U.S., 1954. Asst. to pastor McIlwain Presbyn. Ch., Pensacola, Fla., 1954-55; founding pastor Fairfield Presbyn. Ch., Pensacola, 1956-60; pastor El Presbiterio del Pacifico ch., Teloloapan, Mexico, 1961-66, Northside Presbyn. Ch., Burlington, N.C., 1972-76; moderator Pacific Presbytery of the PCA; dir. Bible Inst., Telolapan; missionary Mexico; dean of students, dir. field edn. Westminster Theol. Seminary, Escondido, Calif., 1984-87; min. to srs. Ind. Presbyn. Ch., Memphis, 1987-96; dir. evangelistic mins. Grace Evangelical Ch., Germantown, Tenn., 1997—; involved numerous ch. and missionary endeavors, including coord. ch. planting team in Quito, Ecuador, 1977-81, dir. Cosecha dept., Radio Sta. HCJB, establisher Family Counseling ministry, leader weekly Bible studies; organizer Gideon camp to distribute Bibles in Acapulco; interim pastor Covenant Presbyn. Ch., Bakersfield, Calif., 1982, others. Avocations: reading, classical music, ministry to people with needs, all sports.

HAMILTON, DAVID F., judge; b. 1957. BA magna cum laude, Haverford Coll., 1979; JD, Yale U., 1983. Law clk. to Hon. Richard D. Cudahy U.S. Ct. Appeals (7th cir.), 1983-84; atty. Barnes & Thornburg, Indpls., 1984-88, 91-94; judge U.S. Dist. Ct. (so. dist.) Ind., Indpls., 1994—; counsel to Gov. of Ind., 1989-91; chair Ind. State Ethics Commn., 1991-94. V.p. for litigation, bd. dirs. Ind. Civil Liberties Union, 1987-88. Fulbright scholar, 1979-80; recipient Sagamore of the Wabash, Gov. Evan Bayh, 1991. Office: US Dist Ct So Dist Ind 46 E Ohio St Rm 330 Indianapolis IN 46204-1921*

HAMILTON, DAVID JOHN, business systems/technology manager; b. Bryn Mawr, Pa., Apr. 28, 1956; s. John A. and Eleanor N. H; m. Janet Ellen Gardner, Aug. 3, 1986; children: Sara Ashley, Sean Christopher. BME, U. Del., 1978; MBA, Widener U., Chester, Pa., 1981. Registered profl. engr., Del.; cert. in prodn. and inventory mgmt., cert. computer systems integrator. Prodn. engr. Stuart Pharms., Wilmington, Del., 1978-79, planning asst., 1979; planner, scheduler Stuart Pharms., Newark, 1979-80, supr. inventory and materials control, 1980-83, plant systems coord., 1983-84; prodn. systems adminstr. ICI Pharms., Wilmington, 1984-85; materials mgr. ICI Pharms., Pasadena, Calif., 1985-88; mgr. bus. planning ICI Films, Wilmington, 1988-93; mgr. bus. reengineering ZENECA Inc., Wilmington, 1993-

95; mgr. supply chain reengring. ICI Explosives, Inc., Dallas, 1995-96; bus. sys./tech. mgr. ICI Acrylics, Inc., Memphis, 1996—; instr. Widener U., Chester, 1983-85, 88-95; MRP II project leader Stuart Pharms., Wilmington, 1983-85. Author: Cycle Counting: An Approach to Inventory Record Accuracy, 1981; contbr. articles to profl. jours. Mem. Rep. Nat. Com., 1977-81; v.p. Woodside Pines, Arcadia, Calif., 1985-88. Mem. Am. Prodn. and Inventory Control Soc. (v.p. bd. dirs. 1984-85, 89—, instr., 1988, 89), Nat. Soc. Profl. Engrs., Inst. Indsl. Engrs., Am. Soc. Quality Control, Am. Assn. Artificial Intelligence, Del. Assn. Profl. Engrs., Coun. Logistics Mgmt. Republican. Lutheran. Home: 9879 Frank Rd Germantown TN 38139-8000 Office: ICI Acrylics Inc The Lucite Ctr 7275 Goodlett Farms Pkwy Cordova TN 38018-4909

HAMILTON, DAVID LEE, retired environmental company executive; b. Pitts., Mar. 26, 1937; s. James Arthur and Margaret (Kennett) H.; m. Molly Anne Wolford, June 27, 1959; children: David Scott, Bryan Lee, Timothy Drew. BSChemE, Bucknell U., 1957; MBA, U. Pitts., 1965. Various positions Exxon Co., USA, 1957-79; exec. asst. to pres. Exxon Corp., N.Y.C., 1979-80, dep. mgr. dept. petroleum products, 1983-85; v.p. supply and transp. Exxon Internat. Co., N.Y.C., 1980-82, sr. v.p., 1982-83; v.p. Esso Europe, London, 1985-86; v.p. mktg. Exxon Co., Internat., Florham Park, N.J., 1986-88; exec. v.p. OHM Corp., Findlay, Ohio, 1989-92. Bd. dirs. The Std. Steamship P&I Club, Bermuda, 1982-85, Concord Resource Group, Lawrenceville, N.J., 1989-91; trustee Bucknell U., Lewisburg, Pa., 1984—; pres. Dallas Tennis Assn., 1994-97; treas. U.S. Tennis Assn., 1997-99, pres., 1999—, chair mktg. coun., 1999—. Mem. TBarM Racquet Club (Dallas), Sigma Chi (Significant Sig award 1985), Beta Gamma Sigma, Omicron Delta Kappa. Avocations: tennis, golf, travel, reading. Home: 12115 Elysian Ct Dallas TX 75230-2221

HAMILTON, DAVID MIKE, publishing company executive; b. Little Rock, 1951; s. Ralph Franklin and Mickey Garnette H.; m. Carol Nancy McKenna, Oct. 25, 1975; children: Elisabeth Michelle, Caroline Ellen. BA, Pitzer Coll., 1973; MLS, UCLA, 1976. Cert. tchr. library sci., Calif. Editor Sullivan Assocs., Palo Alto, Calif., 1973-75; curator Henry E. Huntington Library, San Marino, Calif., 1976-80; mgr. prodn., mktg. William Kaufmann Pubs., Los Altos, Calif., 1980-84; pres. The Live Oak Press, Palo Alto, 1984—; cons. editor, gen. ptnr. Sensitive Expressions Pub. Co., Palo Alto, 1985—; consulting dir. AAAI Press, 1994—; mng. editor and pub. AI Mag. Author: To the Yukon with Jack London, 1980, The Tools of My Trade, 1986, Making A Digital Book, 1994; contbg. editor and webmaster AAAI world-wide web site, 1995—; contbg. author Small Press jour., 1986, Making a Digital Book, 1995, (books) Book Club of California Quarterly, 1985, Research Guide to Biography and Criticism, 1986. Sec. vestry Trinity Parish, Menlo Park, 1986, bd. dirs., 1985-87; trustee Jack London Ednl. Found., San Francisco; bd. dirs. ISYS Forum, Palo Alto, 1987-96; pres. site coun., mem. supt.'s adv. com. Palo Alto Unified Sch. Dist.; mem. Wellesley Coll. Parent's Coun., 1997—. Mem. ALA, Coun. on Scholarly, Med. and Ednl. Publs., Am. Assn. Artificial Intelligence (bd. dirs. 1984—, dir. publs.), Bookbuilders West (book show com. 1983), Author's Guild, Soc. Tech. Communication (judge 1984), Assn. Computing Machinery (chmn. pub. com. 1984), Soc. Scholarly Pubs. (program com. 1999), Sierra Club (life), Book Club Calif. Democrat. Episcopalian. Avocations: backpacking, camping, hiking, book collecting. Home: 2620 Emerson St Palo Alto CA 94306-2310 Office: The Live Oak Press PO Box 60036 Palo Alto CA 94306-0036

HAMILTON, DAVID WENDELL, medical services executive; b. Gregory, S.D., Feb. 20, 1953; s. Wendell Ralph and Doris Marie (Jacobsen) H.; m. Priscilla Ann Boyer, Mar. 12, 1983. BS in Math., U. Nebr., 1979, MBA, 1984. Mgr. spl. devel. Profl. Bus. Sys. Author: Programming Windows NT-Unleashed, 1996. Democrat. Lutheran. Avocations: reading, flying, hunting, fishing. Home: 5950 Bartholomew Cir Lincoln NE 68512-1804 Office: 3140 O St Lincoln NE 68510-1533

HAMILTON, DONALD BENGTSSON, author; b. Uppsala, Sweden, Mar. 24, 1916; s. Bengt L.K. and Elise (Neovius) H.; m. Kathleen Stick, 1941 (dec. Oct. 28, 1989); children: Hugo, Elise, Gordon, Victoria. B.S., U. Chgo., 1938. Writer and photographer, 1946—. Creator Matt Helm series; author books including Death of a Citizen, 1960, The Wrecking Crew, 1960, The Removers, 1961, The Silencers, 1962, Murderer's Row, 1962, The Ambushers, 1963, The Ravagers, 1963, The Shadowers, 1964, The Devastators, 1965, The Betrayers, 1966, The Menacers, 1968, The Interlopers, 1969, The Intriguers, 1972, The Intimidators, 1974, The Terminators, 1975, The Terrorizers, 1977, The Retaliators, 1976, The Poisoners, 1971, Cruises with Kathleen, 1980, The Mona Intercept, 1980, The Revengers, 1982, The Annihilators, 1983, The Infiltrators, 1984, The Detonators, 1985, The Vanishers, 1986, The Demolishers, 1987, The Frighteners, 1989, The Threateners, 1992, The Damagers, 1993; contbr. articles on hunting, yachting, and photography to mags. Mem. Mystery Writers Am., Western Writers Am., Outdoor Writers Assn. Am. Home and Office: c/o Lezon 19 Putnam Rd Ipswich MA 01938-2123

HAMILTON, DONALD DOW WEBB, publisher, freelance writer; b. Akron, Ohio, Feb. 6, 1940; s. Charles Bartow Webb and Grace Virginia (Crummet) H. Diploma, U.S. Army Sch. of Info., Ft. Slocum, N.Y., 1963, U.S. Army Psywar Sch., Ft. Bragg, N.C., 1963. Asst. fashion editor N.Y. Times, N.Y.C., 1961; asst. prodn. mgr. Coll. Books, N.Y.C., 1961; pub. rels. mgr. Akron (Ohio) Goodwill Industry, 1971-73; pres. Akron Manuscript Club, Akron, 1980-82; freelance writer, 1959—; editor news report Two Edged Sword, 1986—; editor news svc. Rock Update, 1988—; editor news jour. Editor's Jour., 1990—. Key contbr. Messenger, 1995—. Mem. Presdl. Task Force, Washington, 1988—; judge adjutent VFW-Cuyahoga Falls, Ohio, 1990. With U.S. Army, 1962-65. Recipient Cert. of merit Broadcasting & Visual Activities, 1965, Congl. Order of Liberty, Washington, 1993. Mem. VFW. Avocations: speaking, music, walking. Home: 327 Portage Trl Cuyahoga Falls OH 44221-3233

HAMILTON, DONALD GORDON, religious association administrator; b. Toronto, Ont., Can., June 21, 1934; m. Joan Mackenzie Sept. 1, 1956 (dec. Oct. 1995); children: John, Mark, Sharon, Philip; m. Shirley Ohlman, June 8, 1997. Grad. with honours, Jarvis Collegiate Inst., Toronto, 1953; diploma, London Bible Inst., 1956; BTh, London Theol. Sem., 1957; MMin, Internat. Sch. Theology, 1981; DMin, Trinity Evang. Seminary, 1996; DDiv, Briercrest Biblical Sem., 1996. Ordained to ministry Gospel Ch., 1957. Pastor Westmount Park Ch., Weston, Ont., 1957-66, Ch. Redeemer, Niagara Falls, Ont., 1966-71; sr. pastor Peoples Ch. Montreal, Que., 1971-78, Pky. Bible Ch., Scarborough, Ont., 1978-87, Grace Ch., Newmarket, Ont., 1987-90; pres., chief adminstrv. officer Associated Gospel Chs., Burlington, Ont., 1990—; summer pastor United Bapt. Ch., Clark's Harbour, N.S., 1955; pastoral charge United Maritime Bapt. Conv., Pubnico and Argyle, N.S., 1955; nat. bd. dirs. Child Evangelism Fellowship, Can.; bd. reference Ptnrs. Internat. Christian Nats. Evangelism Commn., Can.; mem. faculty evening sch. Ont. Bible Coll., Toronto. Sec. Aide-Olympique, Montreal, 1976. Mem. l'Assn. Pour l'Évangélisation des Enfants de Québec (chmn. provincial com.), Greater Toronto Sunday Sch. Assn. (co-founder, dir.), Assoc. Gospel Chs. (chmn. com. Christian edn., chmn. com. edn. and ministry, chmn. com. French work in Can.), Slavic Gospel Assn. (adv. coun.). Office: Assoc Gospel Chs. Wikwemikong Fellowship, Box 193, Manitowaning, ON Canada P0P 1N0*

HAMILTON, DOROTHY JEAN, acute care nurse practitioner in cardiology; b. Gaffney, S.C., Oct. 17, 1954; d. J.C. and Martha Jean (Long) Phillips; m. Moses Marshall, May 20, 1989 (div.); children: Doricia, Maurice Jr., Angelina, Michelle, Melissa. ADN, Cuyagoga C.C., Cleve., 1979; BSN, Cleve. State U., 1988; MSN, Case Western Res. U., 1996. RN, Ohio; CCRN; cert. acute care nurse practitioner; cert. ACLS provider and instr. Staff nurse Cleve. Clinic Found., 1979-86, asst. nurse mgr., 1986-93, clin. instr. cardiac, 1993-96; acute care nurse practitioner in cardiology Univ. Hosps. of Cleve., 1998—. Mentor John Haye H.S., Cleve., 1993-98. Mem. AACN, ANA, Soc. Critical Care Medicine. Avocations: dancing, reading. Home: 3975 Colony Rd Cleveland OH 44118-2305 Office: Univ Hosps of Cleve 11100 Euclid Ave Cleveland OH 44106-1736

HAMILTON, EDWARD TEDJASUKMANA, automotive executive, small business owner; b. Indonesia, Jan. 7, 1943; came to U.S., 1950.; s. Alexander and Maryam H.; m. Silvia Elizabeth Büettner, July 1, 1982; children: Adam, Krystle. Student, Cornell U., 1960-65; MBA, Mich. State U., 1967—. Mgr. Chrysler Corp. (now Daimler Chrysler AG), Auburn Hills, Mich., 1967—. Co-author (dictionary) English-Indonesian Lang.; co-inventor (with others) Mini Van, 1980. 41st House Dist. Candidate, Troy, Mich., 1994; nominee Oakland County Exec., 1996; candidate for Gov. Mich., 1997, 98; pres. Troy Rep. Club; outreach chmn. Rep. 12th Congl. Dist.; mem. fin. com. Oakland County Rep. Com. Mem. LWV, Soc. Automotive Engrs., Engring. Soc. Detroit, Ind. Women's Forum, Detroit C. of C., Detroit Inst. Arts, Heritage Found., Ducks Unltd., Chrysler Mgmt. Club. Home: 1745 McManus Dr Troy MI 48084

HAMILTON, FRANK STRAWN, jazz musician, folksinger, composer and arranger, educator; b. N.Y.C., Aug. 3, 1934; s. Frank Strawn and Gladys (Bley) Hamilton; m. Sheila Lofton, Nov. 7, 1957 (div. Nov. 1971); children: Cameron Auguste, Evan Baird, Liam Christopher, Heather Alexa; m. Deeanne Lee Walter, May 5, 1972 (div. Oct. 1980); m. Mary Doyle, Jan. 15, 1983. Student, Los Angeles City Coll., 1952-53, Chgo. Mus. Coll., 1959-62, L.A. Valley Coll., 1963-64. Organizer, head teaching staff, v.p., co-founder Old Town Sch. Folk Music, Chgo., 1957-62; ho. musician Gate of Horn, Chgo., 1959-61; mem. The Weavers, 1962-63; founder The Hot Club of Atlanta, 1995. Appeared Asheville (N.C.) Folk Festival, 1953, Newport Folk Festival, 1959; motion picture appearance in Subterraneans, 1958; performed with trio Meridian for spl. children's programs Young Audiences in Atlanta Pub. Sch. System, 1987-99, with wife Mary; rec. artist Folkways, Vanguard records; devel. method annotation folk guitar and 5 string banjo; film score: A Time Out of War, 1952; TV score: Survival; folk singer with wife Mary, The Hamiltons. Mem. Irish Arts Atlanta. Mem. ACLU, UN Assn., Dramatist Guild, Chgo. Hist. Soc. (hon.). Home: 852 Cinderella Ct Decatur GA 30033-5812

HAMILTON, HAROLD PHILIP, fund raising executive; b. High Point, N.C., Apr. 26, 1924; s. Alfred McKinley and Dora Elizabeth (Surratt) H.; m. Agnes Marie Kametz, Sept. 4, 1944; children: Dawn Elizabeth, Deborah Anne, Harold Philip, Elaine Denise. Student, Lehigh U., 1943-44; B.A. cum laude, High Point Coll., 1947, L.H.D., 1965; B.D. (Myers Park scholar), Duke, 1950, Ph.D., 1954. Asst. prof. philosophy and religion N.C. State Coll., 1953-55; dean of faculty, asso. prof. Christian thought Ky. Wesleyan Coll., 1955-58, dean of coll., prof., 1958-59, dean of coll., acting pres., 1959-60, pres., prof. Christian thought, 1960-70; pres. Central Meth. Coll., 1970-76; asst. state treas. Commonwealth of Ky., 1976-80; adminstr. Timken Mercy Med. Center, 1980-83; pres. Deaconess Hosp. Found., 1983-85; v.p. planned giving Ohio Presbyn. Retirement Svcs. Found., 1985-95; pres. Oxford Inst. Meth. Theol. Studies, 1958, Ctrl. Ohio Planned Giving Coun. Served with AUS, World War II. Mem. Am. Renaissance Soc., Central States Faculty Conf. (exec. com.), Am. Soc. Ch. History, Inst. Higher Edn., Fayette C. of C., NEA, Nat. Assn. for Hosp. Devel., Newcomen Soc. N.Am., Phi Delta Theta, Phi Alpha Theta, Phi Beta Patron, Omicron Delta Kappa. Methodist (lay leader, ofcl. bd., tchr., elder). Lodges: Rotary (v.p.), Round Table. Home: 1459 Firwood Dr Columbus OH 43229-3434 Office: Ohio Presbyn Retirement Svcs Found 1001 Kingsmill Pkwy Columbus OH 43229-1129

HAMILTON, HARRY LEMUEL, JR., academic administrator; b. Charleston, S.C., May 26, 1938; s. Harry Lemuel and Velma Fern (Bell) H.; m. LaVerne McDaniel, June 26, 1965 (div. 1978); children: David M., Lisa L.; m. Mary MacIntyre, May 10, 1997. BA in Physics, Beloit Coll., 1960; MS in Meteorology, U. Wis., 1962, PhD in Meteorology, 1965. Asst. prof. atmospheric sci. SUNY, Albany, 1965-71, assoc. prof., 1971-90, dir. ednl. opportunity program, 1968-71, chairperson atmospheric sci., 1976-83; dean undergrad. studies, assoc. v.p. academic affairs SUNY, 1983-88; rsch. scientist GE, Schenectady, N.Y., 1973-75; sr. v.p., provost Chapman U., Orange, Calif., 1990—. Trustee Beloit (Wis.) Coll., 1972—; bd. dirs. Albany Med. Ctr., 1988-90, Mohawk Hudson Cmty. Found., 1988-90; pres. Empire State Inst. for Performing Arts, Albany, 1986-90; bd. dirs. world affairs coun. Orange County, 1995—; treas. Arts Orange County, 1995—; bd. dirs. Discovery Sci. Ctr., 1998—. Mem. Am. Meteorol. Soc., Am. Assn. for Higher Edn., Sigma Xi. Office: Chapman U 333 N Glassell St Orange CA 92866-1099

HAMILTON, HOWARD LAVERNE, zoology educator; b. Lone Tree, Iowa, July 20, 1916; s. Harry Stephen and Gertrude Ruth (Shibley) H.; m. Alison Phillips, Dec. 22, 1945 (dec. 1972); children: Christina Helen, Phillips Howard, Martha Jayne; m. Elizabeth Burnley Bentley, June 18, 1975; children: Elizabeth Marshall, Catherine Randolph. B.A. with highest distinction, State U. Iowa, 1937, M.S., 1938; postgrad., U. Rochester, 1938-40; Ph.D., Johns Hopkins U., 1941. Asst. prof. to prof. zoology Iowa State U., 1946-62, acting head, 1960-61, chmn. dept. zoology and entomology, 1961-62; prof. biology U. Va., 1962-82, prof. emeritus, 1982—. Author: Lillie's Development of the Chick, 1952; cons. editor, McGraw-Hill Ency. Sci. and Tech., 1962-78; mng. editor: The Am. Zoologist, 1965-70; Author: (with Viktor Hamburger) Citation Classic: A Series of Normal Stages in the Development of the Chick, 1951. Served to capt. Med. Adminstrv. Corp., AUS, 1941-45, to col. USAR, 1945-69. Mem. Am. Soc. Zoologists, Am. Soc. Naturalists, Soc. Developmental Biology, Internat. Inst. Devel. Biology, Am. Inst. Biol. Sci., Nat. Soc. Ams. of Royal Descent (pres. gen. 1974-80, hon. life pres. gen. 1980—), SAR (nat. exec. com., pres. Va. Soc. 1979-80, registrar gen. 1980-82, pres. gen. 1982-83, Minuteman award and Gold Good Citizenship medal), Order of Three Crusades 1096-1192 (historian gen. 1976-83, 1st v.p. gen. 1983—), Assn. Preservation Va. Antiquities, Va. Hist. Soc. Club: Farmington Country. Home: Jumping Branch Farm 1906 Garth Rd Charlottesville VA 22901-5411 Office: U Va Dept Biology Gilmer Hall Charlottesville VA 22901

HAMILTON, J. LEONARD, college basketball coach; b. Gastonia, N.C., Aug. 4, 1948; m. Claudette Hale; children: Lenny, Allison. Student, Gaston (N.C.) C.C.; BS in Phys. Edn., U. Tenn., Martin, 1971; MA in Phys. and Health Edn., Austin Peay State U., 1973. Asst. coach Austin Peay State U., 1972-74; asst. coach U. Ky., 1974-80, assoc. head coach, 1980-86; head coach Okla. State U. Cowboys, 1986-90, reached Big 8 Tournament, advanced to 2d round of Nat. Invitiation Tournament, 1988-89, 89-90; head coach U. Miami Hurricanes, Fla., 1990—; played NCAA Tournament, 1998, ranked 12th in NCAA, 1998-99. Charter mem. Hall of Fame, U. Tenn., Martin, 1983; named. Big EAST COnf. Coach of Yr., 1995, UPI Nat. Coach of Yr., 1995. Office: c/o Intercoll Athletics U Miami PO Box 248167 Coral Gables FL 33124-0820*

HAMILTON, JACQUELINE, art consultant; b. Tulsa, Mar. 28, 1942; d. James Merton and Nina Faye (Andrews) H.; m. Richard Sanford Piper, Jan. 2, 1968 (div. June 1976). BA, Tex. Christian U., 1965; grad., Stockholm U., 1967; postgrad., Harvard U., 1972-73, Tufts U., 1971, Rice U., 1982-83, Houston C.C., 1986-87. Art cons. for corps., pvt. collectors and mus., Houston, 1979—; expert witness in lawsuits regarding art. Contbr. articles to profl. publs. Active Cultural Arts Council of Houston. Mem. Assn. Corp. Art Curators, Nat. Assn. Corp. Art Mgmt., Rice Design Alliance, Tex. Arts Alliance, The Houstonian Club, The Forum Club, L'Alliance Francaise, Swedish Club, Norwegian-Am. C. of C., Swedish-Am. C. of C., French-Am. C. of C. Presbyterian. Office: PO Box 1483 Houston TX 77251-1483

HAMILTON, JAMES WILLIAM, lawyer; b. Omaha, Sept. 6, 1932; s. James William and Mary (Morgans) H.; m. Carol Lorraine Kircher, July 10, 1954; children: Theodore, Evelyn, Bonnie. BA, Stanford U., 1954, LLB, 1959. Bar: Calif. 1960, D.C. 1983. Assoc. Paul, Hastings, Janofsky & Walker, L.A., 1959-65; ptnr. Paul, Hastings, Janofsky & Walker, L.A., 1965-93, sr. counsel, 1993—; ptnr. Paul, Hastings, Janofsky & Walker, Costa Mesa, Calif., 1974-82, 85-93; ptnr. Paul, Hastings, Janofsky & Walker, Washington, 1982-85, of counsel, 1993—; bd. dirs. Nat. Bank So. Calif., Newport Beach. Bd. dirs. Art Inst. So. Calif., Laguna Beach, Opportunity Internat., Chgo.; bd. visitors Stanford U. Law Sch., 1978-81, 96—. 1st lt. USAF, 1954-56. Mem. ABA, Los Angeles County Bar Assn. (chmn. corp. sect. 1973-74, editor bull. 1970-71), Orange County Bar Assn., Big Canyon Country Club (Newport Beach), Ironwood Country Club (Palm Desert, Calif.), Phi Gamma Delta. Republican. Presbyterian. Avocations: golf, skiing, swimming. Home: 895 Cliff Dr Laguna Beach CA 92651-1410 Office: Paul Hastings Janofsky & Walker 695 Town Center Dr Fl 17 Costa Mesa CA 92626-1924*

HAMILTON, JAQUELINE BUCKNER, artist, landscaper; b. Nov. 22, 1936. AA, Stephens Coll., 1954-56; student, Marshall U., 1956-58, Prince Georges U., 1984-86. Juried artist Torpedo Factory Art Ctr., Alexandria, Va., 1989-93; pvt. practice Clinton, Md., 1993—. Exhibited in group shows at Gallery West, 1989, 90, Prince George's Cmty. Coll., 1991, Md. nat. Capital Park and Planning Show, 1991, Newberry Farms Art Gallery, 1991-92, Doctor's Hosp. Art Show, 1992, 96, Bread and Chocolate, 1993-94, 1994-96. Recipient Nyborg award Mid-Atlantic Regional, 1990, Dick Blick award 1991, Silver Medal award 1996. Home: 9409 Michael Dr Clinton MD 20735-3244

HAMILTON, JEAN CONSTANCE, judge; b. St. Louis, Nov. 12, 1945; d. Aubrey Bertrand and Rosemary (Crocker) H. A.B., Wellesley Coll., 1968; J.D., Washington U., St. Louis, 1971; LL.M., Yale U., 1982. Bar: Mo. 1971. Atty. Dept. of Justice, Washington, 1971-73, asst. U.S. atty., St. Louis, 1973-78; atty. Southwestern Bell Telephone Co., St. Louis, 1978-81; judge 22d Jud. Circuit, State of Mo., St. Louis, 1982-88; judge Mo. Ct. Appeals (ea. dist.), 1988-90; U.S. dist. judge U.S. Dist. Ct. (ea. dist.) Mo., 1990—, chief judge, 1995—. Mem. ABA, Bar Assn. Met. St. Louis, Women Lawyers Assn. Met. St. Louis, Nat. Assn. Women Judges, Am. Law Inst. Episcopalian. Office: US Court and Custom House 1114 Market St Fl 1 Saint Louis MO 63101-2043

HAMILTON, JERALD, musician; b. Wichita, Kans., Mar. 19, 1927; s. Robert James and Lillie May (Rishel) H.; m. Phyllis Jean Searle, Sept. 8, 1954; children: Barbara Helen, Elizabeth Sarah, Catharine Sandra. MusB, U. Kans., Lawrence, 1948, MusM, 1950; postgrad., Royal Sch. Ch. Music, Croydon, Eng., summer 1955, Union Theol. Sem. Sch. Sacred Music, N.Y.C., summer 1960; studies with, Laurel Everette Anderson, Andre Marchal, Catharine Crozier, Gustav Leonhardt. From instr. to asst. prof. organ and theory Washburn U., Topeka, 1949-59; dir. Washburn Singers and Choir, 1955-59; asst. prof. organ, dir. univ. singers and chorus Ohio U., Athens, 1959-60; asst. prof. organ and ch. music U. Tex., Austin, 1960-63; lectr. ch. music Episcopal Theol. Sem. S.W., Austin, 1961-63; mem. faculty U. Ill., Urbana-Champaign, 1963-88, prof. music, 1967-88, prof. emeritus, 1988—; organist, choirmaster chs. in Kans. and Tex., 1942-63; organist, choirmaster Episcopal Ch. St. John the Divine, Champaign, 1963-88; organist, choirmaster St. John's Cathedral, Albuquerque, 1988-93, organist-choirmaster emeritus, 1994—; mem., chmn. commn. ch. music Episc. Diocese Kans., 1951-59; mem. bishop's commn. ch. music Episc. Diocese of Springfield, 1978-80, 82-88; concert organist, 1955-96. Author (with Marilou Kratzenstein) Four Centuries of Organ Music, Detroit Studies in Music Bibliography No. 51, 1984. Fulbright scholar, 1954-55. Mem. Assn. Anglican Musicians, Omicron Delta Kappa, Pi Kappa Lambda, Phi Mu Alpha. Episcopalian. Home: PO Box 3836 Edgewood NM 87015-3836

HAMILTON, JIMMY RAY, secondary education educator; b. McDowell, Ky., Mar. 4, 1949; s. Victor and Lola (Tackett) H.; children: Victor William, Madelin Mae Reinersmann; m. Christa Karin Weinkotz, Apr. 7, 1974; children: Margaret Ann Long, Nathaniel Ray. Student, Def. Info. Sch., 1969, 70, 72; BA in English and Secondary Edn., Ariz. State U., 1987; postgrad., U. Phoenix, 1994-95, Grand Canyon Coll., 1994-95. Cert. English and secondary edn. tchr., ESL and bilingual edn. Tchr. adult based edn. Marcos DeNiza H.S., Tempe, Ariz., 1987-89; tchr. English IV Red Mesa (Ariz.) H.S., 1989-90; tchr. English and drama, drama coach Many Farms (Ariz.) H.S., 1991-96; head coach boys' varsity basketball, 1996-98; head coach girls' volleyball Ariz. Interscholastic Assn., Phoenix, 1993—. Contbg. editor: Writing For the Workplace, 1998; pub., editor: Come On, Act Navajo, 1998. Mem. Pres. Nixon Inaugural Com., Washington, 1973. Recipient Dir.'s award for best play Native Am. Drama Festival, Tuba City, 1991-92, 92-93, Dir.'s award Four Corners Classic Drama and Fine Arts Festival, 1994, 95. Avocations: guitar, writing, fishing, hunting. Home: PO Box 65 Many Farms AZ 86538-3065

HAMILTON, JOE, executive. BA in Math., Fordham U.; MBA in Fin., U. Calif., Berkeley. Numerous positions including sr. v.p. capital markets divsn. Crocker Nat. Bank; chief adminstrv. officer, CFO Grubb & Ellis Co.; exec. dir. Brobeck, Phleger & Harrison Law Firm; C.O.O. and pres. Cunningham Comm., Inc., Palo Alto, Calif.; bd. dirs. Cunningham Comm., Inc. Office: 1510 Page Mill Rd Palo Alto CA 94304-1125*

HAMILTON, JOHN J., JR., airport executive; b. Elizabethtown, N.Y., July 1, 1940; married; 2 children. BA, St. Michael's Coll., 1961. With USN; dir. ops. Burlington (Vt.) Internat. Airport, dir. aviation. With Vt. Air NG. Office: Burlington Internat Airport 1200 Airport Dr Ste 1 South Burlington VT 05403*

HAMILTON, JOHN KENNEDY, state treasurer. Treas. State of Ky., Frankfort. Office: State Treas Office Capitol Annex Rm 183 Frankfort KY 40601*

HAMILTON, JOHN MAXWELL, university dean, writer; b. Evanston, Ill., Mar. 28, 1947; s. Maxwell Millings and Elizabeth Curran (Carlson) H.; m. Regina Frances Nalewajek, Aug. 19, 1975; 1 child, Maxwell Janek. BA in Journalism, Marquette U., Milw., 1969; postgrad., U. N.H., 1971-73; MS in Journalism, Boston U., 1974; PhD in Am. Civilization, George Washington U., 1983. Reporter Milw. Jour., 1967-69; free-lance journalist Washington, 1973-75; fgn. corres. L.Am., 1976-78; spl. asst., asst. adminstr. Agy. for Internat. Devel., Washington, 1978-81; staff assoc. House Fgn. Affairs Subcom. Internat. Econ. Policy/Trade, Washington, 1981-82; chief U.S. fgn. policy corres. Internat. Reporting Info. Sys., Washington, 1982-83; dir. Main St. Am. and the Third World, Washington, 1985-87; sr. counselor World Bank, Washington, 1983-85, 87-92; dean and prof. Manship Sch. Mass. Comm. La. State U., Baton Rouge, 1992—, Hopkins Braezele prof., 1998; commentator MarketPlace Pub. Radio Internat., 1991—; bd. dirs., treas. Internat. Ctr. for Journalists; guest lectr. U.S. Info. Svc., Brazil, 1993. Author: Main Street America and the Third World, 1986, 2d edit., 1989, Edgar Snow: A Biography, 1988 (Critic's Choice, L.A. Times, Frank Luther Mott-Kappa Tau Alpha Rsch. award 1988), Entangling Alliances: How the Third World Shapes Our Lives, 1990; co-author: (with George Krimsky) Hold the Press: The Inside Story on Newspapers, 1996; author chpts. in books; contbr. numerous articles to profl. jours. including Atlanta Constn., Balt. Sun, Bull. of Atomic Scientists, Boston Globe, Chicago Tribune, Christian Sci. Monitor, Columbia Journalism Rev., Jour. Commerce, New York Times, The Nation, others. Capt. USMC, 1969-73. Grantee Ford Found., Carnegie Inst., U.S. AID, numerous others, 1985-94. Mem. Assn. of Schs. of Journalism and Mass Comm. (chair task force on alliances 1992-94), Soc. Profl. Journalists. Democrat. Home: 567 L S U Ave Baton Rouge LA 70808-4643 Office: La State Univ Manship Sch Mass Comm Baton Rouge LA 70803

HAMILTON, JOHN MCFARLAND, plastic surgeon, bank director; b. Lebanon, Tenn., July 5, 1925; s. Courtnay Cowper and Sarah Louise (Williamson) H.; m. Imogene Nicholson, Dec. 19, 1951; children: Susan Richards Hamilton Churuti, John McFarland Jr., Courtnay C., Scott Deering. BS, Tulane U., 1946; MD, La. State U., 1949. Diplomate Am. Bd. Plastic Surgery. Inter, resident in gen. surgery George Washington U. Hosp., Washington, 1949-51; resident in gen. and plastic surgery Baylor Med. Sch., Houston, 1953-56, instr. plastic surgery, 1956-57; pvt. practice, St. Petersburg, Fla., 1957—; dir. cleft palate team All Children's Hosp., St. Petersburg, 1957-77; chief staff Children's Hosp., St. Petersburg, 1962-63, Bayfront Med. Ctr., St. Petersburg, 1982-83; lectr. med. jurisprudence Stetson U. Law Coll., St. Petersburg, 1974-80; bd. dirs. Premier Cmty. Bank, Largo, Fla.; vice chmn. Bayfront Life Svcs., St. Petersburg, 1985-86, Fla. Med. Polit. Action Com., Tallahassee, 1982-83. Assoc. editor Fla. Med. Jour., 1969-79; contbr. articles to med. jours., including Plastic and Reconstructive Surgery, Fla. Med. Jour., So. Med. Jour., Aesthetic Surgery Jour., Tech. Forum. Founder, treas. Pinellas County Polit. Action Com., St. Petersburg, 1963—; bd. dirs. Fla. Orch., Tampa, 1998—. Lt. USN, 1943-46; capt. USAF, 1950-53, Korea. Recipient A.J. Gorday award Bayfront Med. Ctr., 1986, Fund Raiser of Yr. award for Fla. West Coast Nat. Soc. Fund Raising Execs., 1987, Golden Baton award Fla. Orch., 1998. Fellow ACS; mem. AMA, Southeastern Soc. Plastic and Reconstructive Surgeons (editor

Bull. 1964-68, pres. 1976), Fla. Med. Assn. (del. 1970-78), Fla. Soc. Plastic Surgeons (founding, pres. 1967-68), Pinellas County Med. Soc. (pres. 1975-76, achievement award 1978, svc. award 1988). Republican. Methodist. Avocations: photography, clarinet, poetry. Home: 430 Brightwaters Blvd NE Saint Petersburg FL 33704-3712 Office: 424 Beach Dr NE Saint Petersburg FL 33701-3020

HAMILTON, JOHN THOMAS, JR., lawyer; b. Delhi, N.Y., Apr. 17, 1951; s. John Thomas and Theresa Anastasia (L'Ecuyer) H.; m. Julia Ann Whitlow, Sept. 3, 1977; children: John Thomas III, Sara Baer. BS, Hamilton Coll., 1973; JD cum laude, Union U., Albany, N.Y., 1976. Bar: N.Y. 1977, U.S. Dist. Ct. (no., so., ea. and we. dists.) N.Y., U.S. Ct. Appeals (2d cir.). Law clerk Lynn & Lynn, PC, Albany, 1974-75; law clk. Solomon & Solomon, P.C., Albany, 1975-77; assoc. Solomon & Solomon, P.C., 1977, George S. Evans, N.Y.C., 1977-78, Frank E. Maher, Bklyn., 1978-80; pvt. practice, Delhi, 1980—; atty., counsel Sen. Chas. D. Cook, Albany, 1981-98; counsel N.Y.C. Watershed Negotiations, 1990-97; counsel local govt. com. N.Y. Senate, 1983-92, agrl. com., 1981-82, asst. counsel to majority leader, 1999—. Mem. Assn. Retarded Children (life); v.p. Del. County Hist. Assoc., 1985-87, pres. 1988-96; chmn., treas. Cook for Senate, 1978-98; exec. bd. dirs. Otschodela coun. Boy Scouts Am., 1992—. Mem. ATLA, N.Y. State Bar Assn., N.Y. County Lawyers Assn., N.Y. State Trial Lawyers Assn., Del. County Bar Assn. Republican. Home and Office: 145 Main St Delhi NY 13753-1282

HAMILTON, JUDITH HALL, computer company executive; b. Washington, June 15, 1944; d. George Woods and Jane Fromm (Brogger) Hall; m. Stephen T. McClellan, Oct. 29, 1988. BA, Ind. U., 1966; postgrad., Boston U., 1966-68; postgrad. Exec. Sch. Mgmt., UCLA, 1980-81. Programmer System Devel. Corp., Santa Monica, Calif., 1968-69, dir. programming, 1975-80; systems analyst Daylin, Inc., Beverly Hills, Calif., 1969-71; systems mgr. Audio Magnetics, Gardena, Calif., 1971-73; pres. Databasics, Inc., Santa Monica, 1973-75; v.p. Computer Scis. Corp., El Segundo, Calif., 1980-87; ptnr. Ernst & Young, L.A., 1987-89, N.Y.C., 1989-91; sr. v.p., gen. mgr. Locus Computing Corp., L.A., 1991-92; pres., CEO Dataquest, Inc., a Dun & Bradstreet Corp., San Jose, Calif., 1992-95, First Floor Software, Mountain View, Calif., 1996-98, Classrm. Connect, El Segundo, Calif., 1999—; bd. dirs. R.R. Donnelley, Software.com, Sentry Group, Silicon Valley Joint Venture. Bd. dirs. Wildlife Conservation Soc. No. Calif., 1994—, Cmty. Breast Health Project 1994—. Mem. Assn. Data Processing Svc. Orgns. (bd. dirs., chmn.), Info. Tech. Assn. Am., Commonwealth Club Silicon Valley (bd. dirs. 1997—), Kappa Alpha Theta. Office: First Floor Software 444 Castro St Ste 200 Mountain View CA 94041-2051

HAMILTON, KATHLEEN ALLEN, secondary education educator; b. Corpus christi, Tex., Sept. 2, 1952; d. William Francis and Lyla Lemont (Thomas) Allen; m. Paul Martin Hamilton, June 8, 1974; children: Jason, John. BBA, U. Houston, 1974, MEd, 1980. Rsch. statis. aide U. Tex. Health Sci. Ctr., Houston, 1974-75; svc. rep. Southwestern Bell Telephone, Houston, 1975-77; sec. Tex. Commerce Bank, Houston, 1979-80; tchr. Aransas Pass (Tex.) Ind. Sch. Dist., 1983—. Treas. First United Meth. Ch., Aransas Pass, 1997—, mem. nominating com., mem. fin. com. Avocation: fishing. Office: Aransas Pass Ind Sch 450 S Avenue A Aransas Pass TX 78336-4602

HAMILTON, KATHRYN BORYS, marketing communications consultant; b. Lodi, N.J., Aug. 22, 1950; d. Daniel Francis and Julia Rose (Boreijsza) Borys; m. Thomas Michael Hamilton, May 24, 1984. BA in English, William Paterson Coll., 1972. Acct. exec. Peter Martin Assoc., N.Y.C., 1974-77; editor Banner Books, N.Y.C., 1977-79; ea. editor Bldgs. Mag., N.Y.C., 1979-85; v.p. Rubenstein Assoc., N.Y.C., 1985-87; dir. mktg. comm. Skidmore, Owings & Merrill, N.Y.C., 1987-93; prin. Hamilton Ink, Katonah, N.Y., 1993—. Editor: The 1st Children's Encyclopedia, 1977; creative dir. (direct mktg. piece) Open Stores Faster, 1997 (Silver medal Ad Club Westchester), (comm. package) Cerami & Assoc., 1996 (Silver medal Bus. Mktg. Assn.). Bd. dirs. Chappaqua (N.Y.) Drama Group, 1994-95. Mem. Assn. Women in Comm. (bd. dirs. local chpt. 1998—, Silver Commendation p.r. campaign 1998). Office: Hamilton Ink 101 Allison Rd Katonah NY 10536-3429

HAMILTON, KIMBERLY DARLENE, diversified service company executive; b. Seminole, Okla., Jan. 16, 1960; d. Lynn Vernon Eidson and Louetta Darlene (Allen) Vannoy. Student, Richland Coll., 1985, Brookhaven Coll., 1985-87. Mgr. graphic info. svcs. Grace Energy Corp., Dallas, 1977-92; bus. mgr. Bob's Best Termite & Pest Lic. Pest Control Tech., Tex., 1992-97. Mem. Assn. Records Mgrs. Adminstrn., Assn. Info. Image Mgmt. (bd. dirs., editor newsletter The Spittin' Image), In-Plant Printing Mgmt. Assn., Postal Customer Coun., NAFE. Republican. Home: 2117 Wimpole Ct E Roanoke TX 76262-6879

HAMILTON, LEE HERBERT, educational organization administrator, former congressman; b. Daytona Beach, Fla., Apr. 20, 1931; m. Nancy Ann Nelson, Aug. 21, 1954; children: Tracy Lynn, Deborah Lee, Douglas Nelson. AB, DePauw U., 1952, hon. degree; scholar, Goethe U., Germany, 1952-53; JD, Ind. U., 1956; hon. degree, Hanover Coll., Detroit Coll. Law, Ball State U., U. S. Ind., Wabash Coll., Union Coll., Ind. U., Am. Univ., Marian Coll., Suffolk U. Mem. 89th-105th Congresses from 9th Dist. Ind., Washington, 1965-99; ranking minority mem. House com. internat. rels.; former chmn. select. com. to investigate covert arms transactions with Iran U.S. Congress, mem. joint econ. com., former chmn. fgn. affairs com., former co chair Joint com. Orgn. Congress, former chmn. Ho. intelligence com., former chmn. Ho. com. investigate Oct. surprise; dir. Woodrow Wilson Ctr. Internat. Scholars Smithsonian Instn., Washington, 1999—. Democrat. Office: Woodrow Wilson Ctr Internat Scholars One Woodrow Wilson Plz 1300 Pennsylvania Ave NW Washington DC 20523*

HAMILTON, LEONARD DERWENT, physician, molecular biologist; b. Manchester, Eng., May 7, 1921; came to U.S., 1949, naturalized, 1964; s. Jacob and Sara (Sandelson) H.; m. Ann Twynam Blake, July 20, 1945; children: Jane Derwent, Stephen David, Robin Michael. BA, Balliol Coll., Oxford U., Eng., 1943, BM, 1945, MA, 1946, DM, 1951; MA, Trinity Coll., Cambridge U., Eng., 1948, PhD, 1952. Diplomate Am. Bd. Pathology. USPHS rsch. fellow U. Utah, 1949-50; staff Sloan-Kettering Inst., N.Y.C., 1950-79, head isotope studies sect., 1957-64, assoc. scientist, 1965-79; staff Meml. Hosp., N.Y.C., 1950-65; faculty Sloan-Kettering div. Grad. Sch. Med. Scis. Cornell U., 1956-64; sr. scientist, head divsn. microbiology Med. Research Ctr. Brookhaven Nat. Lab., Upton, N.Y., 1964-76; head biomed. and environ. assessment divsn. Office. Environ. Policy Analysis, 1973-94; attending physician Hosp. Med. Research Ctr., 1964-85; dir. WHO Collaborating Ctr. for Assessment of Health and Environ. Effects of Energy Systems, 1983-97, WHO focal point on health and environ. effects of energy systems and mem. expert adv. panel on environ. hazards, 1983—; prof. medicine Health Sci. Ctr., SUNY, Stony Brook, 1968—; adj. prof. biometry and epidemiology Med. U. S.C., Charleston, 1996—; cons. HEW, Ctr. Disease Control, Nat. Inst. Occupational Safety and Health, epidemiology study of Portsmouth Naval Shipyard, 1978-88; vis. fellow St. Catherine's Coll., Oxford U., 1972-73; internat. panel experts on fossil fuel UN Environment Programme, 1978, panel on nuclear energy, 1978-79, panel on renewable sources and comparative assessment of different sources, 1980; com. mem. Nat. Acad. Sci.-NRC, Washington, 1975-80; mem. N.Y.C. Mayor's Tech. Adv. Com. on Radiation, 1963-77, N.Y.C. Commr. of Health Tech. Adv. Com. on Radiation, 1978—; energy panel WHO Commn. on Health & Environment, 1990-91; mem. Interant. Expert Group 3, Comparative Environ. and Health Effects of Different Energy Systems for Electricity Generation, 1990-91; sr. expert Symposium on Electricity and the Environ., Helsinki, Finland, 1991. Editor: Gerrard Winstanley, Selections from His Works, 1944; Physical Factors and Modification of Radiation Injury, 1964; The Health and Environmental Effects of Electricity Generation-a Preliminary Report, 1974. Recipient Fed. Lab. Consortium award, 1990; Am. Cancer Soc. scholar, 1953-58; Commonwealth Fund grantee, 1955-62. Mem. AMA, Am. Assn. Cancer Rsch., Am. Soc. Clin. Investigation, Am. Soc. for Investigative Pathology, Soc. for Risk Analysis, Harvey Soc., Internat. Soc. Environ. Epidemiology, Cosmos Club (Washington). Home: Childs Ln Old Field Setauket NY 11733 Office: Brookhaven Nat Lab Environ Policy Analysis Upton NY 11973

HAMILTON, LINDA HELEN, clinical psychologist; b. N.Y.C., Dec. 2, 1952; d. Peter and Helen (Casey) Homek; m. Terrence White, Aug. 10, 1974 (div. 1983); m. William Garnett Hamilton, Dec. 29, 1984. BA summa cum laude, Fordham U., 1984; MA, Adelphi U., 1986, PhD, 1989. Lic. psychologist, N.Y. Dancer N.Y.C. Ballet, 1969-88; clin. psychologist Fair Oaks Hosp., Summit, N.J., 1989-90, Miller Inst. for Performing Artists, N.Y.C., 1989-95; pvt. practice N.Y.C., 1991—; rsch. assoc. Miller Inst. Performing Artists, N.Y.C., 1987-95; chair dance com. MedArt U.S.A., N.Y.C., 1990-92; cons. psychologist Sch. Am. Ballet, N.Y.C., 1991—, Alvin Ailey Am. Dance Ctr., N.Y.C., 1996—; advice columnist Dance Mag., 1992—, sr. editor, 1997—; assoc. prof. Fordham U., 1998—; co-leader Performing Arts Medicine Delegation to Russia and Ea. Europe, 1992. Contbr. articles to profl. jours. and popular mags.; author: The Person Behind the Mask: A Guide to Performing Arts Psychology, Advice for Dancers; featured in a documentary by European Media Support. Mem. exec. com. BFA Dance Program, Fordham U., 1997—. Miller Inst. Performing Artists grantee, 1987. Mem. APA (Daniel E. Berlyne award 1993), Internat. Assn. Dance Medicine and Sci., Performing Arts Medicine Assn., Dance Profls. Assocs. (bd. dirs. 1997—). Avocations: travel, reading, opera, ballet. Office: 2000 Broadway New York NY 10023-5028

HAMILTON, LORRAINE REBEKAH, adult education consultant; b. York, Pa., Jan. 17, 1960; d. Robert Stephen Sheely and Emma Estella (Taylor) Ford; m. Ronald Dana Hamilton, Apr. 14, 1990. Diploma in Drafting and Design Tech., Cumberland-Perry Tech. Sch., Mechanicsburg, Pa., 1978; BS in Psychology, U. Houston, 1992, MA in Gen. Behavioral Scis., 1994. Drafter aluminum products Capitol Products, Camp Hill, Pa., 1978-81; drafter oil field equipment Continental Emsco, Houston, 1981-82; coll. prof. Coll. of the Mainland, Texas City, Tex., 1983-87; contract drafter/piping Astech Svcs., Houston, 1985-86; computer specialist Amoco Oil Co., Texas City, 1986-92; ind. cons. Sage Learning Method, 1994—; owner Synergy Sys., 1994-95, E-Three, 1996—; founder EntertaiNET Networking Party, 1996—. Convenor Women's Studies Student Assn., Houston, 1994; treas., forum rep. NOW, Houston, 1992; vol. Landmark Edn. Corp., Houston, 1992-94. Mem. Omicron Delta Kappa. Home: PO Box 22653 Houston TX 77227-2653

HAMILTON, LYMAN CRITCHFIELD, JR., telecommunications industry executive; b. L.A., Aug. 29, 1926; s. Lyman Critchfield and Edna Lorraine (Gluck) H.; m. Mary W. Shepard, June 25, 1949 (div. 1984); children: William, Richard, Douglas, David; m. Beverly C. Lannquist, Nov. 17, 1984. Student, U. Redlands, 1944-45; BA, Principia Coll., 1947; MPA, Harvard U., 1949; LLD (hon.), Waynesburg Coll., 1979. Budget examiner U.S. Bur. of Budget, Washington, 1950-56; asst. adminstr. U.S. Civil Adminstrn. of Ryukyu Islands, Okinawa, Japan, 1956-60; investment officer World Bank & IFC, Washington, 1960-62; with Internat. Telephone & Telegraph Corp., N.Y.C., 1962-79, treas., 1967-76, v.p., 1968-73, sr. v.p., 1973-74, exec. v.p., 1974-77, pres., 1977-79, chief oper. officer, 1977, chief exec., 1978-79; chmn., pres. Tamco Enterprises, Inc., N.Y.C., 1980-89; chmn., pres., chief exec. officer Imperial Corp. of Am., 1989-90; pres., chief exec. officer Alpine Polyvision, Inc., 1991-93, chmn., 1993; bd. dirs. Scan Optics, Inc., Manchester, Conn., Polyvision Inc., N.Y.C., Ibnet, N.Y.C.; chmn. Video Net, Inc., Dallas. Lt. (j.g.) USNR, 1944-46. Mem. L.A. Country Club, Farmington Woods Country Club, Univ. Club. Republican.

HAMILTON, MALCOLM COWAN, librarian, editor, indexer, personnel professional; b. Bath, Maine, Jan. 29, 1938; s. Newell Cowan and Laura Emma (Munro) H. BA, U. Maine, 1961; MS, Simmons Coll., Boston, 1968. Cert. libr., tchr.; sr. profl. human resources cert. Tchr. English Chelmsford High Sch., Mass., 1961-67; librarian Harvard Grad. Sch. Edn., Cambridge, Mass., 1967-80; librarian John F. Kennedy Sch. Govt. Harvard, Cambridge, Mass., 1980-96, also univ. pers. libr., 1987—; project mgr. project adapt Harvard U., Cambridge, 1996-98, sr. cons. office of human resources, 1998—. Author: Travel Index, 1988; editor, indexer: Education Literature, 1907-1932, 11 vols., 1979; compiler: Directory of Educational Statistics: A Guide to Sources, 1974; assoc. editor Jour. Policy Analysis and Mgmt., 1981-87. Mem. ALA, Assn. Coll. and Rsch. Librs., Spl. Librs. Assn. (chmn. ednl. div. 1975-76, chmn. social scis. div. 1985-86, pres. Boston chpt. 1987-88), Soc. for Human Resources Mgmt. Democrat. Anglican. Avocation: travel. Home: 24 Elmore St Arlington MA 02476-5928 Office: Harvard U Office of Human Resources Holyoke Ctr 1350 Massachussetts Ave Cambridge MA 02138

HAMILTON, MARK ALAN, electrical engineer; b. Amarillo, Tex., Aug. 19, 1960; s. Larry Don and June Rae (Jones) H. BSEE, Kans. State U., 1984. Electronics engr. U.S. Army Comm.-Electronics Command, Ft. Monmouth, N.J., 1984-90, Ft. Leavenworth, Kans., 1990-97; computer specialist Def. Info. Sys. Agy.-Ctrl. Comm. Office, Ft. Leavenworth, Kans., 1997-98; computer specialist customer svc. ctr. Combined Arms Command-Ft. Leavenworth Directorate Info. Mgmt, Ft. Leavenworth, 1998—. Mem. Tau Beta Pi, Eta Kappa Nu. Roman Catholic. Avocations: reading, chess. Home: 1434 Columbia Ave Leavenworth KS 66048-3140

HAMILTON, MICHAEL A., medical educator; b. Nice, France, Sept. 26, 1935; children: Sebastian, Sunita. MusB, U. Rochester, 1955, MD, 1964; postgrad., Cath. U., 1957-59; MPH in Epidemiology, U. N.C., 1971. Pediatric intern U. Calif., San Francisco, 1964-65; U.S. Peace Corps vol. U. Nangrahar, Jalalabad, Afghanistan, 1965-67; med. resident U. Ky., Lexington, 1967-69; preventive medicine resident U. N.C., Chapel Hill, 1969-71; internist, adj. in medicine Lincoln Cmty. Health Ctr., Durham, 1971-75; dir. physician's asst. program Duke U., Durham, 1974-85; dir. diet and fitness ctr. Duke U. Med. Ctr., Durham, 1985—; cons. Nat. Bd. Med. Examiners, 1975, mem. recertifying examination com., mem. std. setting com., mem. test devel. com., chmn. patient mgmt. program test com. for physician asst. certifying exam.; cons. to Govt. of Guyana, 1983. Co0author: Reduction of Atherogenic Risk Factors on Short-Term Weight Reduction, 1987, Duke University Medical Center Book of Diet and Fitness, 1990; co-editor: Medicine and Pediatrics, 1988. Home: 1011 Dacian Ave Durham NC 27701-1709 Office: 804 W Trinity Ave Durham NC 27701-1826*

HAMILTON, NANCY BETH, business executive; b. Lakewood, Ohio, July 22, 1948; d. Edward Douglas and Gloria Jean (Blessing) Familo; m. Thomas Woolman Hamilton, June 10, 1970; children: Susan Elizabeth, Catherine Anne. BA, Denison U., 1970. Cert. secondary edn. tchr., Fla. Tchr. Orange County (Fla.) Bd. Edn., 1970-71; registrar Jones Coll., Orlando, Fla., 1971-72; mgr. service dept. Am. Lawyers Co., Cleve., 1972-79, mgr. data processing dept., 1980-95, corp. sec.-treas., 1995—. Mem. editl. bd. Comml. Law Jour., 1991—. Trustee, treas. Westshore Montessori Assn., Rocky River, Ohio, 1984-88; bd. dirs. Holly Ln. PTA, Westlake, Ohio, 1988-94, treas., 1992-94; bd. dirs. Parkside PTA, Westlake, 1991-97, treas., 1994-96; treas. Westlake Coun. PTAs, 1999—, Westlake H.S. PTA, 1995-98, pres., 1998—. Mem. Comml. Law League Am. (chmn. com. 1989-94, membership chmn. 1994-96, com. chair 1997—), Comml. Law League of Am. (Midwestern dist. rec. sec. 1997—), Westwood Country Club, Alpha Phi (pres. Cleve. Westshore chpt. alumnae 1986-88). Republican. Methodist. Avocations: skiing, travel. Office: Am Lawyers Co 853 Westpoint Pky Ste 710 Cleveland OH 44145-1532

HAMILTON, NANCY RICHEY, critical care nurse, educator; b. Alexandria, La., Oct. 8, 1950; d. Allen M. and Beryl M. (Price) Richey; m. James G. Hamilton, July 15; 1 child, April Michele. BS, Northwestern State U., Natchitoches, La., 1972; postgrad., U. Md., 1973-74; ADN, Hinds Jr. Coll., Raymond, Miss., 1983; BSN, Northwestern State U., 1994. RN Tenn., N.C., La.; cert. ACLS instr., TNCC, intensive and coronary care. Charge nurse Jefferson Meml. Hosp., Jefferson City, Tenn., St. Mary's Med. Ctr., Knoxville, Tenn.; asst. head nurse Duke U. Med. Ctr., Durham, N.C.; tchr. biology high sch., 1972-75; asst. head nurse, emergency rm. St. Frances Cabrini Hosp., Alexandria, 1990-92, critical care instr., 1990-92; insvc. dir./supr. health care divsn. La. State U. Med. Ctr.-Huey P. Long Med. Ctr., Pineville, La., 1992-94, area mgr. critical care, critical care dir./educator, 1994—; guest lectr. nursing Northwestern State U., La. Coll. Mem. AACN, Tenn. Nurses Assn., N.C. Nurses Assn.

HAMILTON, PATRICIA ROSE, artist's agent; b. Phila., Oct. 21, 1948; d. William Alexis and Lillian Marie (Sloan) Hamilton. BA, Temple U., 1971; MA, Rutgers U., 1971. Sec. to curator Whitney Mus., N.Y.C., 1971-73; sr. editor Art in Am., 1973; curator exhbns. Crispo Gallery, 1974-75; dir. Hamilton Gallery, 1976-84; artist's agt., 1984—. Democrat. Avocations: tennis, swimming, cooking. Home and Office: 6753 Milner Rd Los Angeles CA 90068-3207

HAMILTON, PETER BANNERMAN, business executive, lawyer; b. Phila., Oct. 22, 1946; s. William George Jr. and Elizabeth Jane (McCullough) H.; m. Elizabeth Anne Arthur, May 8, 1982; children—Peter Bannerman, Jr., Brian Arthur. A.B., Princeton U., 1968; J.D., Yale U., 1971. Bar: D.C. 1972, Pa. 1972, Ind. 1985. Mem. staff Office Asst. Sec. Def. for Systems Analysis and Office Gen. Counsel, Dept. Def., Washington, 1971-74; mem. firm Williams & Connolly, Washington, 1974-77; gen. counsel Dept. Air Force, Washington, 1977-78; dep. gen. counsel HEW, Washington, 1979; exec. asst. to sec. HEW, 1979; spl. asst. to Sec. and Dep. Sec. Def., Washington, 1979-80; ptnr. Califano, Ross & Heineman, Washington, 1980-82; v.p., gen. counsel, sec. Cummins Engine Co., Inc., 1983-86, v.p. law and treasury, 1987-88, v.p., CFO, 1988-95; sr. v.p., CFO, Brunswick Corp., Lake Forest, Ill., 1996-98; exec. v.p., CFO, chmn. Indoor Recreation Group, 1998—; bd. dirs. Kemper Nat. Ins. Cos., Scotsman Industries, Inc. Articles editor: Yale Law Jour, 1970-71. Served to lt. USN, 1971-74. Home: 970 E Deerpath Lake Forest IL 60045-2212 Office: Brunswick Corp 1 N Field Ct Lake Forest IL 60045-4811

HAMILTON, PHILLIP DOUGLAS, lawyer; b. Pasadena, Calif., Oct. 16, 1954; s. Ivan and Annette O. (Brown) H.; m. Gerry Messner, Sept. 17, 1976 (div. Feb. 1984); m. Janet L. Hester, Apr. 22, 1984; children: Melissa, John, Mark Charles. BA, U. Pa., 1976; JD, Pepperdine U., 1979. Bar: Calif. 1979, U.S. Dist. Ct. (cen. dist.) Calif. 1980. Assoc., Offices of James J. DiCesare, Santa Ana, Calif., 1979-84; sole practice, Newport Beach, Calif., 1984—. Bd. dirs. Juvenile Diabetes Found., Orange County, 1988, pres., 1989, 90, 91. Recipient Am. Jurisprudence award, 1980. Mem. Assn. Trial Lawyers Am., Orange County Trial Lawyers Assn., Calif. Trial Lawyers Assn., Calif. Trial Lawyers Polit. Action Com., Orange County Bar Assn. Presbyterian. Office: 535 Anton Blvd Ste 1150 Costa Mesa CA 92626-1969

HAMILTON, PHYLLIS, principal. Prin. Arnold Jr. High Sch., Houston, 1986—. Recipient Blue Ribbon award U.S. Dept. Edn., 1990-91. Office: Arnold Jr High Sch 11111 Telge Rd Cypress TX 77429-3390*

HAMILTON, RANDY HASKELL, city manager; b. N.Y.C., Dec. 27, 1921; s. Harry and Adelaide Beatrice (Haskell) H.; m. Ruth Manning (div. May 1961); children: Sarah Beth, Leander Munhall III; m. Louanne McKernan, Apr. 29, 1962; children: Jill Katherine, Jennifer Sabrina. BA, U. N.C., 1943, MA in Pub. Adminstrn., 1947, MA in City and Regional Planning, 1949; PhD, U. Zurich, Switzerland, 1963. City mgr. City of Carolina Beach, N.C., 1949-52; dir., assoc. dir. Nat. League Cities, Washington, 1952-56; city mgr., mcpl. adv. Royal Govt. Thailand, Bangkok, 1956-64; dir. comparative urban studies project UN/IPA, N.Y.C., 1964-65; spl. project dir. League Calif. Cities, Berkeley, Calif., 1965-73; dean Grad. Sch. Pub. Adminstrn., Golden Gate U., San Francisco, 1973-90; vis. scholar Inst. Govtl. Studies, U. Calif., Berkeley, 1990—. Mem. editl. bd. Pub. Adminstrn. Rev., 1970-75, Internat. Jour. Pub. Adminstrn., 1977—, State and Local Govt. Rev., 1980-86; editor Western Govtl. Rsch. Jour., 1990-92. Chmn. Gov.'s Adv. Coord. Coun. Pub. Personnel, Sacramento, 1973; chmn. adv. com. Calif. State Welfare Grant, Sacramento, 1972, State Calif., Sacramento, 1975; chmn. Highland Hosp. Found., Oakland, Calif., 1991-93. Capt. USAF, 1943-46. Decorated comdr. Royal Order of Crown (Thailand); named Man of Yr., N.C. Lion's Club, 1950; recipient spl. citation U.S. CSC, 1975. Fellow Nat. Acad. Pub. Adminstrn.; mem. Internat. City Mgmt. Assn. (Stephen B. Sweeney award 1980), Am. Soc. for Pub. Adminstrn. (nat. pres. 1976). Republican. Presbyterian. Office: U Calif Inst Govtl Studies 109 Moses Hall Berkeley CA 94720-2370

HAMILTON, RHODA LILLIAN ROSEN, guidance counselor, language educator, consultant; b. Chgo., May 8, 1915; d. Reinhold August and Olga (Peterson) Rosen; m. Douglas Edward Hamilton, Jan. 23, 1936 (div. Feb. 1952); remarried, Aug. 1995 (dec. 1997); children: Perry Douglas, John Richard. Grad., Moser Coll., Chgo., 1932-33; BS in Edn., U. Wis., 1953, postgrad., 1976; MAT, Rollins Coll., 1967; postgrad., Ohio State U., 1959-60; postgrad. in clin. psychology, Mich. State U., 1971, 76, 79,, Mich. State U., 80; postgrad., Yale U., 1972, Loma Linda U., 1972; postgrad. in computer mgmt. sys., U. Okla., 1976; postgrad. in edn., U. Calif., Berkeley, 1980. Exec. sect. to pres. Ansul Chem. Co., Marinette, Wis., 1934-36; pers. counselor Burneice Larson's Med. Bur., Chgo., 1954-56; adminstrv. asst. to Ernst C. Schmidt Lake Geneva, Wis., 1956-58; assoc. prof. fin. aid Ohio State U., 1958-60; tchr. English to spkrs. of other langs. Istanbul, Turkey, 1960-65; counselor Groveland (Fla.) H.S., 1965-68; guidance counselor and psychol. cons. early childhood edn. Dept. Def. Overseas Dependents Sch., Okinawa, 1968-85; instr./lectr. early childhood Lake Jr. Coll., Leesburg, Fla., 1986-88; pres. Hamilton Assocs., Groveland, Fla., 1986—; vis. lectr. Okla. State U., 1980; co-owner plumbing, heating bus., Marinette, 1943-49; journalist Rockford (Ill.) Morning Star, 1956-58, Istanbul AP, 1960; lectr. Lake Sumter C.C., 1989—, Lake Sumter Jr. Coll., 1989. Author poetry on Middle East, 1959-64; Career Awareness, 1978; Listen Up, 1997-98. Vol. instr. U.S. citizenship classes, Okinawa, 1971-72; judge Gold Scholarships Okinawa Christian Schs., 1983, 84. Mem. Am. Fedn. Govt. Employees, Fla. Retired Educators, Order Ea. Star (organist), Shuri Chpt. #One Okinawa Japan (life mem. Trillium No. 208 Wis., dual mem.), Marinette Woman's Club (Wis., pres. 1949-51), Groveland Woman's Club (Fla.), Phi Delta Gamma. Episcopalian. Home: 2408 Ellsworth Way Apt 1A Frederick MD 21702-3124

HAMILTON, RHONDA LYNN, librarian; b. Marion, Ind., June 20, 1955; d. Rex L. and Ruth L. Kline; m. Mark L. Hamilton, Oct. 26, 1974; children, LesliMarie, Ashley Erin. Student, Ind. U.-Purdue U., Fort Wayne; cert. libr. sci., U. Wis., 1999. Dir. Markle (Ind.) Pub. Libr., 1992—. Home: 2820 W 300 N Bluffton IN 46714 Office: Markle Pub Libr 155 Sparks St Markle IN 46770

HAMILTON, ROBERT APPLEBY, JR., insurance company executive; b. Boston, Feb. 20, 1940; s. Robert A. and Alice Margaret (Dowdall) H.; m. Ellen Kuhlen, Aug. 13, 1966; children: Jennifer, Robert Appleby III, Elizabeth. Student, Miami U. (Ohio), 1958-62. CLU; chartered fin. cons. With Travelers Ins. Co., various locations, 1962-65, New Eng. Mut. Life Ins. Co., various locations, 1965-90; regional pension rep. New Eng. Mut. Life Ins. Co., Boston, 1968-71; regional mgr. New Eng. Mut. Life Ins. Co., Chgo., 1972-83; sr. pension cons. New Eng. Mut. Life Ins. Co., 1983-90; mktg. and fin. cons. Snowbeck Enterprises, Inc., Geneva, Ill., 1990-97, ret., 1997. Producer Sta. WCTV; mem. Rep. Town Com., Wenham, Mass., 1970-72, Milton Twp., Ill., 1973-75; mem. Wenham Water Commn., 1970-72. Mem. Midwest Pension Conf. (chmn. 1989-90), Am. Soc. Pension Actuaries (assoc.), Am. Soc. CLUs, Am. Assn. Fin. Planners, Project Sharing Coun. Am., Chgo. Coun. Fgn. Rels., Alpha Epsilon Rho. Republican. Home: 110 Hamilton Ct Wheaton IL 60187

HAMILTON, ROBERT MORRISON, geophysicist; b. Houston, June 20, 1936; s. Robert Gilbert and Marieta Josephine (Heisser) H. Geophys. Engr., Colo. Sch. Mines, 1958; MA, U. Calif., Berkeley, 1963, PhD, 1965. Rsch. seismologist N.Z. Dept. Sci. and Indsl. Rsch., Wellington, 1965-68; geophysicist U.S. Geol. Survey, Menlo Park, Calif., 1968-72; dep. for earthquake geophysics then chief Office Earthquake Studies U.S. Geol. Survey, Reston, Va., 1972-78, rsch. geophysicist Office Earthquake Studies, 1978-82, chief geologist geologic div., 1982-87, rsch. geophysicist, 1987-90; acting dir., secretariat Internat. Decade for Natural Disaster Reduction UN, Geneva, 1990-92; geophysicist, chmn. subcom. on natural disaster reduction/Nat. Sci. and Tech. Coun. U.S. Geol. Survey, Reston, 1992-97, acting chief office earthquakes, volcanoes, and engring., 1994-96; mem. sci. and tech. com. Internat. Decade for Natural Disaster Reduction/UN, 1996—; exec. dir. commn. on geoscis., environment and resources NRC/NAS, 1997—. Served with AUS, 1959. Nat. scholar, 1954-58; Socony-Mobil Oil Co. scholar, 1958; Pan Am. Petroleum Found. scholar, 1963-64; recipient Cecil Green medal for outstanding geophysics grad., 1958, Dept. Interior Meritorious Service award, 1978, Disting. Service award, 1986, U.S. Govt. Merit Rank award, 1986; Alumni Disting. Achievement medal Colo. Sch. Mines, 1984. Fellow AAAS, Geol. Soc. Am.; mem. Am. Geophys. Union (pres. elect seismology sect. 1986-88, pres. 1988-90), Seismological Soc. Am. (pres., bd.

dirs.). Office: NAS Comn on Geoscis Environment Res 2101 Constitution Ave NW Washington DC 20418-0007*

HAMILTON, RONALD RAY, minister; b. Evansville, Ind., May 6, 1932; s. Floyd Ray Hamilton and Ruby Dixon (Chism) Hahn; m. Norma Jean Robertson, Mar. 25, 1956; children: Ronnetta Jean, Andrea, Robert Rae. BA, U. Evansville, 1955; BD, Garrett Theol. Sem., 1958, MDiv, 1972; PhD, Oxford Grad. Sch., Eng., Dayton, Tenn., 1989. Ordained elder United Meth. Ch. Minister Scobey (Mont.) Meth. Ch., 1958-61, St. Andrew Meth. Ch., Littleton, Colo., 1961-67; sr. minister First Meth. Ch., Grand Junction, Colo., 1967-75, Christ United Meth. Ch., Salt Lake City, 1975-80, Littleton United Meth., 1980-86, U. Park United Meth., Denver, 1986-91, First United Meth. Ch., Sun City, Ariz., 1992-98; chaplain Sun Health Corp., Sun City, 1998—. Author: The Way to Success, 1972, The Greatest Prayer, 1983, A Chosen People, 1986; editor jour., 1978. Recipient Spl. award Mental Health Assn., Mesa County, Colo., 1974, Goodwill Rehab. Inc., 1975. Mem. Lions Club, Rotary Club, Civitan (chaplain 1964-67). Republican. Avocations: acting, directing, travel, chess. Home: 4509 E Frye Rd Phoenix AZ 85044-7601

HAMILTON, RUSSELL GEORGE, JR., academic dean, Spanish and Portuguese language educator; b. New Haven, Aug. 31, 1934; s. Russell George Sr. and Lucinda (Brown) H.; m. Cherie Yvonne Van Nockay, July 3, 1956; children: Cherie Andrea Hamilton Newton, Russell Malcolm, Melissa Elena, David Dean. BA, U. Conn., 1956; MA, U. Wis., Madison, 1957; PhD, Yale U., 1965. Instr. Portuguese Yale U., New Haven, 1962-64; asst. prof. Spanish and Portuguese U. Minn., Mpls., 1964-67, assoc. prof. Spanish and Portuguese, 1967-71, prof. Spanish and Portuguese, 1971-84, assoc. dean Coll. of Liberal Arts, 1982-84; dean grad. studies and rsch. Vanderbilt U., Nashville, 1984-98, dean Grad. Sch., 1998—; vis. prof. winter lit. U. Calif., San Diego, 1976; vis. prof. Spanish and Portuguese U. Va., Charlottesville, 1981-82; cons. N.Y. State Bd. Edn., NYU, 1976, Voice of Am. (Portuguese in Africa), Washington, 1986—, U. Mass. (Spanish and Portuguese), Amherst, Mass., 1987, La. Bd. of Higher Edn., Baton Rouge, 1987, 91. Author: Voices From An Empire: A History of Afro-Portuguese Literature, 1975, Literatura Africana, Literatura Necessaria, vol. 1, 1981, vol. 2, 1983. Recipient Wilbur L. Cross medal Yale Grad. Sch. Alumni Assn., 1991; Fulbright grantee, 1960-62, 70-71, Gulbenkian grantee, 1971, Social Sci. Rsch. Coun. grantee, 1978-79. Mem. Grad. Record Exam. Bd. (exec. com., chmn. minority com. 1986-90), Assn. Grad. Schs. (chair minority com. 1986-90), Teaching of English as a Fgn. Lang. Coun., Coun. Grad. Sch. (chmn. bd. 1990). Club: Wednesday Night (Nashville). Office: Vanderbilt U Grad Sch 411 Kirkland Hall Nashville TN 37240*

HAMILTON, RUTH HELLMANN, design company owner; b. Millboro, S.D., Oct. 15; d. Walter Otto and Laura Ethel (King) Hellmann; m. Gordon Eugene Hamilton, June 11, 1950; children: Kristin Goodnight, Bret Hamilton, Lori O'Toole, Lynnelle Anderson. AB, Nebr. Wesleyan U., Lincoln, 1948; MEd and Humanities, So. Meth. U., 1952. Owner, chief exec. officer Sonoran Desert Designs, Tucson, 1976-98; lectr. Ariz. Desert Mus., Tucson, 1985-86, Tohono Chul Mus., Tucson, 1986-95, Prescott Coll., Tucson, 1987, Tucson Bot. Gardens, 1985-98, Elderhostel, 1991-92; tchr. design student classes. Exhibited displays for Old Pueblo Mus. at Foothills Mall, 1987-90; demonstrations of desert designs Ariz. State Conv. Garden Clubs N.Mex., 1987, 89; one-woman shows at Tucson Garden Club, 1988, 90; original designs published by Nat. Coun. Garden Clubs Calendars, 1984, 87, 89, 95, 98, 99. Mem. pub. svcs. bd. KVOA-TV, 1969-74. Named hon. sr. St. Andrew's Presbyn. Ch. Mem. Los Cerros Garden Club (pres. 1984-85, 94-95). Avocation: flower arrangement and spacial design. Home: 7720 N Sendero De Juana Tucson AZ 85718-7517

HAMILTON, SCOTT SCOVELL, professional figure skater, former Olympic athlete; b. Toledo, Aug. 28, 1958; adopted s. Ernest Scovell and Dorothy (McIntosh) H. Grad. high sch., Bowling Green, Ohio, 1976; student, Metro State Coll., 1979. nat. spokesman Discover Card youth programs, 1995—. Amateur competitive career includes Nat. Figure Skating Championships: jr. men's 1st pl., 1976, sr. men's 9th pl., 1977, 3d pl., 1978, 4th pl., 1979, 3d pl., 1980, 1st pl., 1981, 82, 83, 84, Mid-Western Figure Skating Championships: sr. men's 3d pl., 1977, 78, 79, Norton Skate Championships (now Skate Am.): men's divsn. 1st pl., 1979, 80, 81, 82, South Atlantic Figure Skating Championships: sr. men's divsn. 1st pl., 1980, Eastern Figure Skating Championships: sr. men's 1st pl., 1980, 81, 82, 83, 84, World Figure Skating Championships: men's divsn. 5th pl., 1980, 1st pl. 81, 82, 83, 84, Nat. Sports Festival Championships: 1st pl. men's divsn., 1981; Winter Olympics: men's divsn. 5th pl., Lake Placid, N.Y., 1980, 1st pl., Sarajevo, Yugoslavia, 1984, Nippon Hoso Kykai Figure Skating Championships, men's divsn. 1st pl., 1982, Golden Spin of Zagreb Championships, men's divsn. 1st pl., 1983; Profl. competitive career includes Nutrasweet/NBC-TV World Profl. Figure Skating Championships mens. divsn., 1st pl., 1984, 86, 2d pl., 85, 87, 88, 89, 91; World Challenge Champions/ABC-TV men's divsn., 2d pl., 1985, 1st pl., 1986; U.S. Open men's divsn. 1st pl., 1990, 2d pl., 1991, Diet Coke Profl. Skaters Championship men's divsn. 1st pl., 1992, Hershey's Kisses Pro-Am. Figure Skating Championships 2d Place Men's divsn. 1993, Sun Valley Men's Outdoor Championship 2d pl., 1994, The Gold Championship men's divsn. 1st pl., 1994, Can. Profl. Skating Championship men's divsn. 1st pl., 1994, Fox's Rock and Roll Skating Championship men's divsn. 1st pl., 1994; profl. performances include Nat. Arena Tour Ice Capades, 1984-85, 85-86, star Scott Hamilton's Am. Tour, 1986-87, 1990-91, co-star Concert On Ice, Harrah's Hotel, Lake Tahoe, Nev., 1987, spl. guest star Festival On Ice, Nat. Theatre Tour, 1987, star Discover Card Stars On Ice Nat. Arena Tour, 1987-88, 88-89, star Festival On Ice, Harrah's Hotel, 1988, guest star ABC-TV spl. Ice Capades With Kirk Cameron, 1988, A Very Special Christmas, ABC-TV, 1988, An Olympic, Calgary Christmas, ABC-TV, 1988, star and mus. comedy and acting debut Broadway On Ice, Harrah's Hotel and Nat. Theatre Tour, 1989; CBS-TV Sports Figure Skating Commentator 1984-91 various skating competitions and CBS-TV coverage Winter Olympics, Albertville, France, 1992, Lillehammer, Norway, 1994; star, dir., producer Scott Hamilton's Celebration On Ice, Sea World of Calif., 1988, Scott Hamilton's Time Traveler: An Odyssey On Ice, Sea World of Calif., 1989; host, guest star TV spl. A Salute To Dorothy Hamill, 1988; star, co-producer Discover Card Stars On Ice, Nat. Arena Tour, 1989-91; guest star CBS-TV spl. Disney's Christmas on Ice, 1990; co-producer, star Discover Card Stars on Ice Nat. Arena Tour, 1991-92; co-host, star HBO TV spl. Vail Skating Festival, 1992; co-prodr., star Discover Card Stars on Ice Nat. Arena Tour, 1992-93, 93-94, 94-95, Canadian Nat. Tour, 1995; guest TV spl. A Disney Christmas on Ice, 1992, CBS-TV spl. Disney on Ice, 1992, HBO-TV spl. Vail Skating Festival, 1993, Skates of Gold I, Boston, 1993, Skates of Gold II, Cin., 1994, CBS-TV Disney Fantasy on Ice, 1993, CBS-TV spl. Nancy Kerrigan & Friends, 1994, CBS-TV spl. Disney's Greatest Hits, 1994, CBS-TV spl. Dreams on Ice, 1995; creator original concepts in arena figure skating. Cons. Friends of Scott Hamilton Found. named in his honor to fundraise and benefit youth oriented causes throughout U.S., 1988, Scott Hamilton's Friends and Legends 1st Annual Celebrity Charity Golf Tournament, Ford's Colony, Williamsburg, Va., 1991; participant fund-raising Athletes for Reagan, March of Dimes, Am. Cancer Soc., Spl. Olympics, Starlight Found., United Way Adoption Home Socs., Make A Wish Found, Big Bros., 1984—, Athletes For Bush, Adult and Ped. AIDS Rsch., Edn. and Funding, 1988—, Homeless, 1989—, Great Am. Workout for Pres.'s Coun. Phys. Fitness & Sports, 1990, 92; nat. spokesman Discover Card youth programs, 1995—. Winner Olympic Gold medal, Sarajevo, 1984; U.S. Olympic Com. awards and honors include carrier Am. Flag in opening ceremonies Lake Placid, 1980, Figure Skating Athlete of Yr., 1981, 82, 83, 84, Athlete of Yr., 1981, Olympic Spirit award, 1987; recipient Olympia award Southland Corp., 1984, Achievement award March of Dimes, 1984, Colo. Athlete of Yr. award Denver Athletic Club, 1984, Most Courageous Athlete award Phila. Sportswriters Assn., 1985, Profl. Skater of Yr. award Am. Skating World mag., 1986, Jacques Favart award Internat. Skating Union, 1988, The Crown Royal Achievement award from House of Seagrams and Jimmy Heuga Ctr., 1991, Clairol's Personal Best award, 1991, Spirit of Giving award U.S. Figure Skating Assn., 1993, 9th Ann. Great Sports Legends award Nick Buonoconti Fund The Miami Project, 1994, Ritter F. Shumway award U.S. Figure Skating Assn., 1994; inducted U.S. Olympic Hall of Fame, 1990, World Figure Skating Hall of Fame, 1990; honoree nat. com. for adoption, 1992. Hon. mem. Phila. Skating Club, Humane Soc. Republican. Avocation: golf. Office: 4242 Van Nuys Blvd Sherman Oaks CA 91403-3710 Address: CBS Sports/CBS Inc 7800 Beverly Blvd Los Angeles CA 90036-2112

HAMILTON, SHIRLEY ANN, nursing administrator; b. Charleston, W.Va., Dec. 21, 1936; d. Leslie and Mae Elizabeth (Westfall) Wolfe; m. Jennings W. Hamilton, Mar. 1, 1958; children: Anthony Scott, Yvonne Alane. Diploma in nursing, Charleston (W.Va.) Gen. Hosp., 1957; BSN, Elizabethtown Coll., 1976. RN, W.Va., Pa. Head nurse Charleston Gen. hosp., 1960-65; staff nurse York (Pa.) Hosp., 1966-67, supr., 1969-90, DON, 1990-94, adminstrv. coord., 1994—; supr. York Meml. Hosp., 1967-69. Pres. Manchester (Pa.) Twp. Lioness, 1990-92. Home: 2315 Mayfield St York PA 17402-1205 Office: York Hosp 1001 S George St York PA 17403-3645*

HAMILTON, SUSAN OWENS, transportation company executive, lawyer; b. Birmingham, Ala., Aug. 7, 1951; d. William Lewis and Vonnette (Wilson) Owens; m. M. Raymond Hamilton, June 8, 1974. BA, Auburn U., 1973; JD, Samford U., 1977. Bar: Ala., Fla. Claim agt. Seaboard System R.R. and predecessor cos., Birmingham, Ala., 1977-78; atty. Seaboard System R.R. and predecessor cos., Louisville, 1978-80, claims atty., 1980-81; asst. gen. atty. Seaboard System R.R. and predecessor cos., Jacksonville, Fla., 1981-83, asst. gen. solicitor, 1983-84, gen. mgr. freight claim services, 1984-85; asst. v.p. casualty prevention Chessie System R.R.'s, Balt. and Jacksonville, 1985-86; asst. v.p. freight damage prevention and claims CSX Transp., Jacksonville, 1986-87, asst. v.p. adminstrv. svcs., 1987-90, sr. asst. v.p. adminstrv. svcs., 1990-95; v.p., gen. counsel CTI, a Unit of CSX, 1995—; gen. mgr. Crew Mgmt. Ctr., CSX Transp., Jacksonville, Fla., 1997—. Vice chair fund distbn. com., United Way of N.E. Fla., 1991-93, chmn., 1993-94, mem. exec. com., 1992-97, chmn. bd. dirs., 1996-97; mem. Gator Bowl Com., 1993—, Gator Bowl officer, 1995—, exec. com., 1998—. Mem. ABA, Jacksonville Bar Assn., Bus. and Profl. Women (pres. Jacksonville chpt. 1984-85), Fla. Bus. and Profl. Women (Outstanding Young Career Woman 1982), Uptown Civitan (bd. dirs. Jacksonville club 1982-84, v.p., pres. elect. 1993, pres. 1993-94). Methodist. Avocations: music, reading, sports. Home: 8224 Sabal Oak Lane Jacksonville FL 32256-7373 Office: J501 500 Water St Jacksonville FL 32202

HAMILTON, THOMAS ALLEN, independent insurance agent; b. Oklahoma City, July 7, 1947; s. Vernon Carlton and Hazel (Margie) H.; children: Travis Matthew, Heather Lynne. BBA Mktg. and Mgmt., Okla. U., 1969. Registered securities rep. Dept. mgr. J.C. Penney, Oklahoma City, 1969-71; spl. agt. CNA Ins., Oklahoma City, 1971-74; group cons. Mass. Mut. Ins. Co., Oklahoma City, 1974-79, qualified plan cons.; bus./estate ins. cons. Mass Mut. Ins. Co., Oklahoma City, 1979-93; ins. investment cons. Sun Fin. Group, Oklahoma City, 1993-95; ind. ins. agt. specializing in life/health, 1996—; registered rep. LifeMark Securities, Oklahoma City, 1995—; owner Advantage Golf Southwest, Oklahoma City. Past chmn. troop 177 Boy Scouts Am., Oklahoma City, 1987-88. Mem. Nat. Assn. Life Underwriters, Am. Bus. Clubs, Oklahoma City Art Mus., Integris Med. Ctr. Okla. Found., Oklahoma City Ski Club. Republican. Protestant. Home and Office: 6500 Dulane Cir Oklahoma City OK 73132-2005

HAMILTON, THOMAS MICHAEL, marketing executive; b. Bronxville, N.Y., Jan. 8, 1947; s. Harold Thomas and Mary Theresa (Byrne) H.; m. Kathryn Borys, May 24, 1984. BS, SUNY, Buffalo. Sales mgr. Herk, Inc., N.Y.C., 1971-73; account exec. William Esty Co., Inc., N.Y.C., 1973-77, account supr., 1977-80, v.p., assoc. dir. sales promotion, 1980-83, sr. v.p., dir. sales promotion, 1983-88; pres. Hamilton Promotions, Inc., Katonah, N.Y., 1988-89; v.p. mktg. Harrington, Righter & Parsons Inc., N.Y.C., 1989-84; prin. The Hamilton Way, Katonah, N.Y., 1994—. Fundraiser United Way of Greater N.Y., 1976-84; council mem. HIP Consumer Council, N.Y.C., 1985; mem. North East Katonah (N.Y.) Community League, 1987—. Served to 1st lt. USAF, 1968-71. Mem. Mktg. Communications Execs. Internat. (bd. dirs. 1983-86), Promotion Mktg. Assn. Am. (bd. dirs. 1986-93, exec. com. 1987-93, vice-chmn. 1989-90, chmn.-elect 1990-91, chmn. bd. 1991-92, chmn. emeritus 1993-94). Avocations: golf, travel.

HAMILTON, THOMAS STEWART, physician, hospital administrator; b. Detroit, June 19, 1911; s. J.T. Stewart and Lucy (Safford) H.; m. Amy Washburn, June 30, 1937; children: Ann Washburn Hamilton Brainerd, Barbara Hamilton Almy, Jeanne. Grad., Philips Exeter Acad., 1930; A.B., Williams Coll., 1934, D.Sc. (hon.), 1969; postgrad., Harvard, 1934-36; M.B., Wayne U., 1938, M.D., 1939; D.Sc. (hon.), Trinity Coll., 1962, U. Hartford, 1975. Intern, asst. resident Harper Hosp., Detroit, 1938-40; gen. practice medicine Truro, Cape Cod, Mass., 1940-41; asst. dir. Mass. Gen. Hosp., Boston, 1941-42, 45-46; dir. Newton-Wellesley Hosp., Newton Lower Falls, Mass., 1946-54; exec. dir. Hartford (Conn.) Hosp., 1954-76, pres., 1969-76, pres. emeritus, 1976—; prof. U. Conn. Sch. Medicine, 1978-86, prof. emeritus, 1986—; dir. Phoenix Mut. L.I.C., 1962-82. Contbr. articles to profl. jours. Trustee Soc. for Savs., 1961-70, McLean Fund, 1968-89; commr. Joint Commn. Accreditation Hosps., 1960-66; mem. cancer control com. USPHS, 1964-70, mem. liaison com. on med. edn., 1969-75; regent U. Hartford, 1962-68. Served to lt. col. M.C. AUS, 1942-45. Recipient Disting. Alumnus award Wayne State U. Sch. Medicine, 1970, Disting. Pub. Service award Conn. Bar Assn., 1975, Gold Medal award New Eng. Hosp. Assembly, 1975; inducted into Modern Health Care Hall of Fame, 1999. Fellow Am. Coll. Hosp. Adminstrs. (regent New Eng. 1953-57, Gold Medal award 1971); mem. AMA (mem. internship rev. com. 1958-68), Mass. Med. Assn., Conn. Med. Assn., Hartford County Med. Assn., Assn. Am. Med. Colls. (sec.-treas. 1968-70), Council Teaching Hosps. (chmn. 1970), Am. Hosp. Assn. (pres., chmn. bd. trustees 1962-63, Disting. Service award 1969), Conn. Hosp. Assn. (pres. 1966, Disting. Service award 1970), Mass. Hosp. Assn. (pres. 1951), Soc. Med. Adminstrs. (pres. 1968-70), Med. Adminstrs. Conf., Marine Hist. Soc. Club: Masons Island Yacht. Home: 80 Loeffler Rd Apt G315 Bloomfield CT 06002-2290 Office: Hartford Hosp 80 Seymour St Hartford CT 06115-2701

HAMILTON, THOMAS WOOLMAN, publishing company executive; b. Somerville, N.J., Aug. 25, 1948; s. John Wesley and Evelyne (Woolman) H.; m. Nancy Beth Familo, June 10, 1970; children: Susan Elizabeth, Catherine Anne. BA, Denison U., 1970; MBA, Rollins Coll., 1972. V.p. Continental Bank, Cleve., 1972-76; exec. v.p., gen. mgr. Am. Lawyers Co., Cleve. and N.Y.C., 1976—. Contbr. articles to profl. jours. Active Rep. Nat. Com.; bd. dirs. Morris Weissman Found., 1979—. Capt. USAF, 1972. Mem. Comml. Law League Am. (bd. dirs. 1983-86, bd. dirs. fund for pub. edn. 1986-89), Am. Comml. Collectors Assn., Assn. Lawlist Pubs. (pres. 1982-83, 89-90, 98-99), Greater Cleve. Growth Assn., Westwood Country Club, Cleve. Yachting Club, Midday Club, Debt. Buyers Assn. Avocations: skiing, golf. Office: Am Lawyers Co 853 Westpoint Pky Cleveland OH 44145-1532

HAMILTON, VIRGINIA (MRS. ARNOLD ADOFF), author; b. Yellow Springs, Ohio, Mar. 12, 1936; d. Kenneth James and Etta Belle (Perry) H.; m. Arnold Adoff, Mar. 19, 1960; children: Leigh Hamilton, Jaime Levi. Student, Antioch Coll., 1952-55, Ohio State U., 1957-58, New Sch. for Social Research; LLD (hon.), Wright State U., Ohio. May Hill Arbuthnot honor lectr., 1992. Author: Zeely, 1967 (Nancy Block Meml. award Downtown Community Sch. Awards Com.), The House of Dies Drear, 1968 (Edgar Allan Poe award for best juvenile mystery 1969), The Time-Ago Tales of Jadhu, 1969, The Planet of Junior Brown, 1971 (John Newbery Honor Book award 1971), W. E. B. DuBois: A Biography, 1972, Time-Ago Lost: More Tales of Jahdu, 1973, M. C. Higgins, the Great, 1974 (Lewis Carroll Shelf award 1974, Boston Globe/Horn Book award 1974, John Newbery medal 1975, Nat. Book award 1975), Paul Robeson: The Life and Times of a Free Black Man, 1974, Arilla Sun Down, 1976, Illusion and Reality, 1976, Justice and Her Brothers, 1978, Jahdu, 1980, Dustland, 1980, The Gathering, 1981, Sweet Whispers, Brother Rush, 1982 (John Newbery Honor Book award 1983, Coretta Scott King award 1983, Boston Globe/Horn Book award 1983, Am. Book award nomination 1983), The Magical Adventures of Pretty Pearl, 1983, Willie Bea and the Time the Martians Landed, 1983, A Little Love, 1984 (Horn Book Fanfare award 1985), Junius Over Far, 1985, The People Could Fly: American Black Folktales, 1985 (Coretta Scott King award 1986, N.Y. Times Best Illustrated Children's Book award 1986), The Mystery of Drear House, 1987, A White Romance, 1987, In the Beginning: Creation Stories from Around the World, 1988 (John Newbery Honor Book award 1989), Anthony Burns: The Defeat and Triumph of a Fugitive Slave, 1988 (Boston Globe/Horn Book award 1988, Coretta Scott King award 1989), The Bells of Christmas, 1989, The Dark Way: Stories from the Spirit World, 1990, Cousins, 1990, The All Jahdu Storybook, 1991, Many Thousands Gone, 1992, Plain City, 1993, Jaguarundi, 1994, Her Story: African American Folktales. 1995; editor The Writings of W. E. B. DuBois, 1975. Recipient Ohioana Lit. award, 1969, 84, Ohioana Lit. award for body of work, 1981, Regina medal Cath. Libr. Assn., 1990, Hans Christian Andersen medal awarded for body of work 1992, Laura Ingalls Wilder medal ALA, 1995, John D. and Catherine T. MacArthur Genius award fellow, 1995. Address: care Arnold Adoff Agy PO Box 293 Yellow Springs OH 45387-0293*

HAMILTON, VIRGINIA VAN DER VEER, historian, educator; b. Kansas City, Mo., Sept. 7, 1921; d. McClellan and Dorothy (Rainold) Van der Veer; A.B., Birmingham (Ala.)-So. Coll., 1941, M.A. (Ford Found. Fund for Adult Edn. fellow), 1961; Ph.D., U. Ala., Tuscaloosa, 1968; LittD, U. Ala., 1992; m. Lowell S. Hamilton, Aug. 4, 1946; children—Carol, David. Staff writer AP, Washington, 1942-46, Birmingham News, 1948-50; asst. prof. history U. Montevallo (Ala.), 1951-55; asst. prof., asst. to pres. for pub. relations Birmingham-So. Coll., 1955-65; lectr. in history U. Ala., Birmingham, 1965-68, asst. prof., 1968-71, asso. prof., 1971-75, prof., 1975-87, prof. emerita, 1987—. U. Ala. at Tuscaloosa faculty research grantee, 1969; U. Ala. at Birmingham faculty research grantee, 1973-74, 74-75. Mem. So., Am. hist. assns., Orgn. Am. Historians, Soc. Am. Historians, Am. Assn. State, local History, Ala. Assn. Historians, Ala. Hist. Soc., Oral History Assn. Author; Hugo Black: The Alabama Years, 1972, Alabama: A History, 1977, The Story of Alabama, 1980, Your Alabama, 1980, Seeing Historic Alabama, 1982, rev. edit., 1996, Lister Hill: Statesman from the South, 1987, Looking For Clark Gable and Other 20th Century Pursuits, 1996; editor: Hugo Black and the Bill of Rights, 1978. Home: 3246 Overbrook Rd Birmingham AL 35213-3928

HAMILTON, W. W., church administrator. Gen. sec. The Church of God in Christ, Memphis. Office: Church of God in Christ Office of the Gen Sec 1620 Broadway Ave Seaside CA 93955*

HAMILTON, WILLIAM BERRY, JR., shipping company executive; b. Birmingham, Ala., Apr. 4, 1929; s. William Berry and Nettie (Whatley) H.; m. Jean Lucile Patteson, Feb. 1, 1951; children: Jean Lucile, Ann Elizabeth, William Berry III. B.A., Vanderbilt U., 1951. Accountant Hiwassee Constructors, Chattanooga, 1952; cert. pub. acct. O.E. Johnson & Assocs., Chattanooga, 1952-54; controller, gen. mgr. Spl. Products Co., Inc., Chattanooga, 1954-59; v.p., controller Ryder Truck Lines, Inc., Jacksonville, Fla., 1959-65; v.p. finance Chgo. Rawhide Mfg. Co., 1965-67; v.p., controller-treas. Sea-Land Service Inc., Elizabeth, N.J., 1967-69; exec. v.p. adminstrn., dir. Sea-Land Service Inc., 1969-75; v.p., treas., asst. sec. McLean Industries, Inc., Elizabeth, 1968-74; pres. Monterey Transp. Co., Inc. (subs. R.J. Reynolds Industries, Inc.), Winston-Salem, N.C., 1975-77; pres., dir. Security-First Corp., Jacksonville, Fla., 1977-82; chmn. bd., pres. St. John's Marine Fin. Co. Inc., 1979—; chmn., chief exec. officer Port of Monmouth Devel. Corp., 1983-87; dir., mem. exec. com. J.J. Henry Co., Inc., N.Y.C., 1981-85; chmn. bd. Henry Laurel Co. Inc., 1983-87; dir. Henry Properties Ltd., L.I. Devel. Co. Ltd.; instr. acctg. U. Chattanooga, 1953-54. Served with USAF, 1951-52. Recipient Guest Lectr. award U. Fla., 1965. Mem. Am. Bur. Shipping, Soc. Naval Architects and Marine Engrs., Am. Inst. C.P.A.s, Financial Execs. Inst., Am. Trucking Assn. (nat. bd. dirs., chmn. methods and procedures nat. accounting 1959—), Nat. Def. Transp. Assn., Nat. Assn. Accountants (named most valuable mem. Jacksonville 1959-60, chpt. v.p., bd. dirs. 1960-63), Tenn. Soc. C.P.A.s, Am. Accounting Assn., Nat. Officer Mgmt. Assn., Am. Mgmt. Assn., U.S. Power Squadron, USCG Aux., Propeller Club of U.S., Navy League, Phi Delta Theta, Pi Delta Epsilon. Episcopalian (vestryman). Clubs: Fla. Yacht, River (Jacksonville); Ponte Vedra, Sawgrass (Ponte Vedra Beach, Fla.); Sea Bright (N.J.) Beach; N.Y. Yacht, World Trade Center, Vanderbilt Alumni, Whitehall (N.Y.C.); Twin-City (Winston-Salem); Cat Cay (Bahamas). Lodge: Kiwanis. Home: 695B Ponte Vedra Blvd #103 Ponte Vedra Beach FL 32082-2783

HAMILTON, WILLIAM EUGENE, JR., electrical engineer; b. Washington, Sept. 14, 1942; s. William Eugene and Esther Arlene (Richards) H.; m. Linda Julia Schoch, Apr. 28, 1973; children: Brett, Derek. BSEE, Iowa State U., 1964; MSEE, Purdue U., 1966, PhD, 1970. Sys. engr. Comptek Rsch., Inc., Buffalo, 1972-75, Sierra Rsch. Corp., Buffalo, 1975-78; sect. head software devel. to tech. cons. Moog Inc., Hydra-Point divsn., Cheektowaga, N.Y., 1978-82; staff engr. Aircraft Controls divsn. Moog Inc., East Aurora, N.Y., 1982-83; sr. rsch. engr. GM R&D Ctr., Warren, Mich., 1983-87, staff rsch. engr., 1987—. Contbr. articles to profl. jours. Clk. of session Faith Evang. Presbyn. Ch., Orion, Mich., 1993-97, elder, 1988—. Capt. U.S. Army, 1970-72. Decorated Bronze Star medal. Mem. Am. Sci. Affiliation. Avocations: study of faith/science issues, theology, church history.

HAMILTON, WILLIAM HOWARD, laboratory executive; b. Greenville, Pa., Apr. 2, 1918; s. Simeon Milo and Mary (Baer) H.; m. Ellinor Kistler, Feb. 9, 1944; children: William H. Jr., Nancy Hamilton Lopez. B.S. in Math. and Physics, Washington and Jefferson Coll., 1940; M.S. in Math. and Physics, U. Pitts., 1948. With Westinghouse Electric Corp., 1940-80; gen. mgr. Bettis Atomic Power Lab., West Mifflin, Pa., 1970-79; cons., 1979—; chmn. Tech. Adv. Group TMI-2 Cleanup; chmn. tech. oversight com. Ft. St. Vrains; chmn. sr. ind. rev. panel Molten Salt Reactor Experiment, Oak Ridge; chmn. High Level Weste Rev. Com., Savannah River. Pres. Edgewood Council, Pitts., 1965-77. Served to lt. comdr. U.S. Navy, 1942-45. Recipient Westinghouse Order of Merit, 1958. Fellow IEEE. Republican. Presbyterian. Clubs: Duquesne (Pitts.); Rolling Rock (Ligonier, Pa.). Patentee continous wave acoustic guidance system, 1965.

HAMILTON, WILLIAM MILTON, manufacturing executive; b. Phila., Feb. 5, 1925; s. Louis Valentine and Elsie Marie (Walter) H.; m. Edith Marie Busey, June 9, 1947; children: Barbara Marie, William Milton Jr., Patricia Ann. B.S. in Indsl. Mgmt., Ga. Inst. Tech., 1947. Asst. br. mgr. Swift & Co., Atlanta, 1947-48; treas. R.K. Price Co., Fayetteville, Ga., 1954-55; br. mgr. N.Y. Wire Cloth Co., Atlanta, 1955-56; from ops. mgr. to pres. Premier Indsl. Corp., Cleve., 1956-91, dir., cons., 1991-96, spl. asst. to chmn., 1998—, also bd. dirs.; CEO product mfg. group Premier Farnell, Cleve., 1996-98, spl. asst. to CEO, 1998—, pres., CEO, 1998—. Served to lt. USN, 1943-46, 48-54. Mem. Elyria Country Club (Ohio), Jonathan Landing Golf Club (Fla.). Methodist. Home: 2222 Pebblebrook Cleveland OH 44145-4378 Office: Premier Farnell 4500 Euclid Ave Cleveland OH 44103-3736

HAMILTON-KEMP, THOMAS ROGERS, organic chemist, educator; b. Lebanon, Ky., May 13, 1942; s. Thomas Rogers and Catherine Rose (Hamilton) K.; m. Lois Ann Groce, Sept. 13, 1980. AA, St. Catharine Coll., 1962; BA, U. Ky., 1964, PhD in Chemistry, 1970. Mem. faculty U. Ky., Lexington, 1970—, asst. prof. natural products chemistry, 1970-75, assoc. prof., 1975-85, prof., 1985—. Rschr. on isolation, identification and biol. effects of natural compounds including antimicrobials; contbr. articles to profl. jours. Mem. AAAS, SAR, Am. Chem. Soc., Am. Soc. Hort. Sci., Sigma Xi, Gamma Sigma Delta, The Filson Club. Democrat. Catholic. Home: 2025 Williamsburg Rd Lexington KY 40504-3015 Office: U Ky Agrl Sci Ctr N # N 308 Lexington KY 40546

HAMISTER, DONALD BRUCE, retired electronics company executive; b. Cleve., Nov. 29, 1920; s. Victor Carl and Bess Irene (Sutherl) H.; m. Margaret Irene Singiser, Dec. 22, 1946; children: Don Bruce, Tracy. A.B. cum laude, Kenyon Coll., 1947, LLD (hon.), 1989; postgrad., Stanford U., 1948-49, U. Chgo., 1957; LLD (hon.), Kenyon Coll., 1989. Application engr. S.E. Joslyn Co., Cin., 1947-48; regional sales mgr. Joslyn Mfg. and Supply Co., St. Louis, 1950-52; mktg. mgr. Joslyn Mfg. and Supply Co., Chgo., 1953-55, asst. to pres., 1956-57, mgr. aircraft arrester dept., 1958-62, gen. mgr. electronic systems div., 1962-71; v.p., gen. mgr., dir. Joslyn Mfg. and Supply Co., Goleta, Calif., 1973-78, group v.p. indsl. products, 1974-78, pres., chief exec. officer, 1978-85, chmn., 1979-94, ret. chmn., 1994; chmn. Joslyn Mfg. and Supply Co. named changed to Joslyn Corp., 1986; also bd. dirs. Joslyn Corp., 1973—; pres. Joslyn Stainless; chmn. emeritus Joslyn Corp., Goleta, 1995—; pres., dir. Joslyn Stamping Co.; pres., chmn., dir. Joslyn Def. Systems, Inc., 1981—; dir. Brewer Tichener Corp.; chief exec. officer Joslyn Corp., Chgo., 1991-94, ret., 1994. Served to lt. USNR, 1942-46. Mem. IEEE, Airline Avionics Inst. (pres., chmn. 1972-74). Club: Univ. (Chgo.). Office: Joslyn Corp Chicago IL 60606

HAMIT, FRANCIS GRANGER, freelance writer; b. N.Y.C., Oct. 6, 1944; s. Harold Francis and Ethel Cordelia (Granger) H.; m. Doris Elaine Pratt Kaesser, May 31, 1974 (div. Mar. 1978). B of Gen. Studies, U. Iowa, 1972, MFA in English, 1976. Freelance writer Iowa City, Chgo., L.A., 1975—; area capt. RRS Security, Ill., 1977; sales rep. Wells Fargo Co. Inc., Chgo., 1979-80; assoc. editor Video Action Mag., Chgo., 1982; factory rep. Hoover Co., L.A., 1987-88; v.p. sales and mktg. EPIC Pvt. Security, West Covina, Calif., 1989-90. Author: Virtual Reality and the Exploration of Cyberspace, 1993; author, dir.: (play) Marlowe: An Elizabethan Tragedy, 1988; contbg. editor: Security Technology and Design Mag., 1993—, Advanced Imaging Mag., 1994—; contbr. 15th edit. Ency. Britannica, 1981-82. With U.S. Army, 1967-71, Vietnam, Germany. Mem. Am. Soc. Indsl. Security, Nat. Mil. Intelligence Assn., L.A. Sci. Fantasy Soc., Assn. Former Intelligence Officers. Democrat. Buddhist.

HAMLETT, JAMES GORDON, electronics engineer, management consultant, educator; b. Utica, N.Y.. BSEE, Syracuse U., 1947-49; BSBA, SUNY, Syracuse, 1985; MBA, City U., Seattle, 1991. Cert. profl. cons.; chartered cons.; cert. vocat. edn. tchr., N.Y.; 1st class radiotel. lic. with ship radar endorsement, FCC. Engr.-writer Warner, N.Y., Inc., Syracuse, 1952-54; vocation edn. tchr. evenings adult edn. Syracuse Cen. Tech. H.S., 1956-62; project leader GE, Syracuse, 1966-90; mgmt. cons. Syracuse, 1990—; adj. faculty City U., Seattle; pres., mgmt. cons. IntraGlobal Mgmt., Inc., Syracuse, N.Y., 1994—; lectr. City Univ. Trencin, Slovakia, 1995; steering com. Empire State Coll. SUNY, 1995—; spkr. in field. Author: Your Television Set, 1953, Engineering-Related Abbreviations, 1980-84 (VIP award 1980). Prin. Onondaga (N.Y.) Flood Control Com., 1962; tennis coach U.S. Jaycees, North Syracuse, N.Y., 1968; mem. steering com., sec., mem. exec. com. L.C. Smith Coll. Engring. and Computer Sci., Syracuse U., 1991, founding officer Alumni Assn., 1994—; keynote spkr. VA Regional Hosp., 1995. With U.S. Army, 1942-45, ETO. Recipient Cert. of Appreciation for Outstanding Dedication L.C. Smith Coll. Engring and Computer Sci. Syracuse U., 1993, Testimonial-Belgium Remembers (Battle of the Bulge), Ctr. Rsch. and Info. of Battle of Ardennes, Liége, Belgium, 1996, Citation for disting. svc. during Battle of Bulge, N.Y. State Senate Dist., 1996, N.Y. State Conspicuous Svc. medal, 1997; Bus. and Mgmt. Lectureship Ctrl. European grant, Slovakia, 1994-95. Fellow Soc. for Tech. Commn. (internat. stem mgr., mgmt. theory and practice 1980, exec. com.); mem. IEEE (life sr., exec. com. Cert. 1981, editor Syracuse Scanner 1959-69), VFW, N.Y. Acad. Scis. (cert. 1985), Am. Mgmt. Assn. Internat., Profl. Cons. Assn. Ctrl. N.Y., Am. Cons. League, Internat. Platform Assn., Syracuse GE Engrs. Assn., Greater Syracuse C. of C., Syracuse U. Alumni Assn., Am. Soc. Tng. and Devel., Empire State Coll. Alumni Assn. (pres. Syracuse area alumni/student assn.), City U. Alumni (life), Vets. Battle of the Bulge (life, historian, treas.), Order of the Engr. Avocations: tournament tennis (Wimbledon, Eng. 1969), reading management practice, music. Home: 330 Everingham Rd Syracuse NY 13205-3258*

HAMLETT, ROBERT BARKSDALE, systems engineer; b. Richmond, Va., Nov. 3, 1949; s. Thomas Coleman and Kathleen Pendleton (Snow) H.; m. Linda Lane Moody, June 24, 1972 (div. Dec. 1982); 1 child, Sarah Barksdale; m. Karen Ann Carwile, Jan. 19, 1985; children: John Coleman, Robert Barksdale Jr. BS in Physics cum laude, Hampden-Sydney Coll., 1972. Programmer United Va. Bank, Richmond, 1972-74, systems programmer, 1975-78, systems programming officer, 1979-82, mgr. tech. support, 1983-84; account systems engr. IBM Corp., Richmond, 1984-87, adv. systems engr., 1987-93; advisory svcs. specialist IBM Corp., Richmond, Va., 1993-96; sr. I/T specialist IBM Corp., Richmond, 1997—. Clk. Grace Bapt. Ch., Richmond, 1986-88, treas. 1997. Home: 5223 Willane Rd Glen Allen VA 23059 Office: IBM Corp 9201 Arboretum Pkwy Richmond VA 23236-3469

HAMLIN, DON AUER, financial executive; b. Klamath Falls, Oreg., Oct. 6, 1934; s. Don Fessler and Margaret May (Auer) H.; m. Karen Ruth Wagner; children by previous marriage: Michael, Kathryn, Stephen, Mary, Mark, John, Matthew. BBA, Loyola U. of South, New Orleans, 1955; grad. USAF Command and Staff Coll., 1967; MS in Bus. Adminstrn., George Washington U., 1968. Commnd. 2d lt. U.S. Army, 1955, advanced through grades to lt. col., 1975; served with inf., ordnance, M.P., various locations, 1955-64; inf. comdr. and staff officer, Alaska, Hawaii, Vietnam, 1964-68; cost analyst and dep. agy. comdr. Pentagon Gen. Staff, Washington, 1968-72; inf. adviser, Vietnam, 1972; comptroller Ft. Sam Houston, Tex., 1972-75; ret., 1975; comptroller Severance & Assos., San Antonio, 1975-81; sec.-treas., dir. Severance Reference Lab., Inc., San Antonio, Tex., 1981-82; co-founder, pres. Engring. Cybernetics, Inc., San Antonio, 1982-85; dir. fin. Whittaker Health Services, Austin, Tex., 1985-86; v.p. fin. Metlife Healthcare Network, 1986-88; Harris Meth. Health Plan, Ft. Worth, 1989-91; sr. v.p./CEO, Harris Meth. Health Plan, pres. Harris Meth. Health Ins. Co., 1991-94; CEO Heritage Southwest Med. Group, Irving, Tex., 1994-96; healthcare mgmt. cons., 1996—; treas. San Vicente Artists, Silver City NM, 1996—, mem. bd. trustees Gila Regional Med. Ctr., Grant County NM, 1998—, bd. dirs. Mimbres Region Arts Coun., Silver City, NM, 1997—, bd. dirs. Copper Crest Country Club, 1999—, pvt. investor, 1983—; dir. Data Terminal Corp., San Antonio, 1981; pres. Balance Point Youth Ranch, San Antonio, 1980-81. Pres., St. Pius X Bd. Edn., San Antonio, 1979. Decorated Legion of Merit with oak leaf cluster, Bronze Star with oak leaf cluster, Air medal with oak leaf cluster, Purple Heart with oak leaf cluster. Mem. San Antonio Med. Mgrs. Assn. (pres. 1982-84), Med. Group Mgrs. Assn., San Antonio Mus. Assn., Mexican-Am. Cultural Center, San Antonio C. of C. Home and Office: PO Box 5162 Silver City NM 88062-5162

HAMLIN, EDMUND MARTIN, JR., engineering manager; b. Utica, N.Y., June 9, 1949; s. Edmund Martin and Catherine Mary (Humphreys) H.; m. Nancy Ann Christensen, June 26, 1971; children: Benjamin John (dec.), Eleanor Mary, Edmund Alexander. BSEE, Clarkson U., 1971; MBA, UCLA, 1993. Lic. airframe and powerplant mechanic, 1994. Engr. NASA Flight Rsch. Ctr., Edwards, Calif., 1971-75; sr. engr. NASA Flight Rsch. Ctr., Edwards, 1976-79; project engr. Sundstrand Energy Systems Div., Belvidere, Ill., 1975-76; sr. engr. Teleco Oilfield Svcs., Meriden, Conn., 1979-80, mgr. electronic systems, 1980-83, the sr. staff engr., 1984; sr. engr. NASA Ames-Dryden, Edwards, Calif., 1984-85; asst. chief flight sys. NASA Ames-Dryden, Edwards, 1985-90, chief flight instrumentation, 1990-94, asst. dir. rsch., 1994-98, asst. dir. safety & flight assurance, 1998—. Inventor: position measurement system, 1976, method for determining and correcting magnetic interference in boreholes, 1988, method for computing borehole azimuth while rotating, 1989. Pres. bd. trustees Tehachapi (Calif.) Unified Sch. Dist., 1989-94. Mem. AIAA, Instrument Soc. Am., Aircraft Owners and Pilots Assn., Exptl. Aircraft Assn., Ea. European Adoption Coalition (dir.). Avocations: flying, aircraft restoration, fly fishing, camping, carpentry. Office: NASA Ames-Dryden Flight Rsch Facility PO Box 273 Edwards CA 93523

HAMLIN, EDWIN CLIBURN, sales consultant; b. Eden, N.C., Nov. 17, 1961; s. James Henry and Odessa (Strong) H.; m. DeWanna Thomas, Feb. 16, 1986; children: Erran, Catherine. B Bus. Adminstrn. and Acctg., Catawba Coll., 1984. Corp. mgmt. assoc. dept. corp. tng. Wachovia Corp., Winston-Salem, N.C., 1984-85, loan adminstrn. rep. dept. gen. loan adminstrn., 1985-86; sr. analyst dept. asset-based finances Wachovia Bank, Winston-Salem, 1986-87, asst. v.p., corp. lending officer, 1987-90, mgr. corp. tng. and devel., 1990-91; account exec. Supermarket Info. Systems Inc., Winston-Salem, 1991-95, sales cons., 1995-97, regional sales exec., 1997-99, nat. bus. devel. mgr., 1999—; instr. Living Well Fitness Ctr., 1988-89, Power House Gym Aerobics and Fitness, 1996—. Chmn. bd. trustees Cleveland Avenue Christian Ch. Disciples of Christ, 1991, deacon, 1992—, chmn. ofcl. bd., 1992—; vol., team leader United Way, March of Dimes, Piedmont Team Walk, 1984-93; v.p. Griffin Elem. Sch. PTA, 1992-94, Jefferson Davis Diggs, 1995—, Winston-Salem Leadership, 1988-99. Avocations: aerobics, running, cycling, reading, modeling. Home: 1791 Greencedar Ln Winston Salem NC 27127-7355 Office: Supermarket Info Systems Inc 4045 University Pkwy Winston Salem NC 27106-3325

HAMLIN, HARRY ROBINSON, actor; b. Pasadena, Calif., Oct. 30, 1951; s. Chauncey Jerome and Bernice (Robinson) H.; 1 son by previous marriage, Dimitri Alexander; m. Lisa Rinna, Mar. 29, 1997. B.A., Yale U.; postgrad., Am. Conservatory Theatre, San Francisco. Performances include: (films) Movie Movie, 1979, Clash of The Titans, 1981, King of the Mountain, 1981, Making Love, 1982, Blue Skies Again, 1983, Maxie, 1985, Dinner At Eight, 1990, The Celluloid Closet, 1995, Badge of Betrayal, 1996; (TV mini-series) Studs Lonigan, Master of the Game, 1984, Space, 1985, Favorite Son, 1988, Night Sins, 1997; (TV films) Laguna Heat, 1987, Deceptions, 1990, Deadly Intentions...Again?, 1991, Deliver Them From Evil: The Taking of Alta View, 1991, Save Me, 1992, Under Investigation, 1993, Poisoned by Love: The Kern County Murders, 1993, In the Best of Families: Marriage, Pride and Madness, 1994, Tom Clancy's Op Center, 1995, Her Deadly Rival, 1995; (TV series) L.A. Law, 1986-91; (Broadway debut) Awake and Sing!, 1984, Movie Stars, 1999. ITT Fulbright grantee, 1977. Office: care Larry Taub Gersh Agency Inc 232 N Canon Dr Beverly Hills CA 90210-5302*

HAMLIN, JAMES TURNER, III, university dean, physician; b. Danville, Va., Feb. 6, 1929; s. James T. and Nell (Davis) H.; m. Mary Caperton, June 9, 1955; children: Helen Austin, Mary Davis, James Turner. A.B., Va. Mil. Inst., 1951; M.D., U. Va., 1955. Intern Peter Bent Brigham Hosp., Boston, 1955; also resident; instr. medicine N.Y. Med. Coll., 1959-60; guest investigator Rockefeller Inst., N.Y.C., 1960-62; asst. prof. medicine Med. Coll. Ga., Augusta, 1962-64; asso. prof. Med. Coll. Ga., 1964-66; asso. prof. medicine U. Va., Charlottesville, 1966-73; dir. clin. research center U. Va., 1966-71, asst. dean, 1970-71, acting dean sch. medicine, 1971-72, asso. dean, 1972-73; vice dean sch. medicine Tulane U., New Orleans, 1973-75; dean Tulane U., 1975-88, dean emeritus, 1989—, prof. medicine, 1973-88, prof. emeritus, 1989—. Contbr. articles to med. jours. Mem. Am. Fedn. for Clin. Research, So. Soc. for Clin. Investigation, AAAS, AMA, Med. Soc. Va., Albemarle County, La. State, Orleans Parish med. socs., Sigma Xi, Alpha Omega Alpha. Republican. Presbyterian. Home: 199 Fairmont Cir Danville VA 24541-5210 Office: 1430 Tulane Ave New Orleans LA 70112-2699

HAMLIN, KATHRYN F., geriatrics nurse, administrator; b. New Haven, Mar. 17, 1951; d. Joseph P. and Marjorie E. (Chagnon) Fitzgerald; m. Chester G. Hamlin, Feb. 14, 1980; children: Kandi, Timothy, David, Keith, Jessica. Diploma, St. Francis Sch. Nursing, Hartford, Conn., 1972; BS cum laude, Post Coll., Waterbury, Conn., 1988; MS in Healthcare Mgmt., Hartford Grad. Ctr., 1990. Cert. in nursing adminstrn. Staff nurse, med.-surg. VA Hosp., West Haven, Conn.; nursing supr. Hebrew Home and Hosp., Hartford, Conn.; asst. dir. nursing Hebrew Home and Hosp., West Hartford, Conn., v.p. for nursing. Mem. Conn. Nurse Assn., Conn. Orgn. Nurse Execs. Home: 96 Talcott Rd Glastonbury CT 06033-2919

HAMLIN, KENNETH ELDRED, JR., retired pharmaceutical company executive; b. Balt., Mar. 27, 1917; s. Kenneth Eldred and Julia (Gallup) H.; m. Janet Hoy, June 18, 1941; children: Kathleen Ann, Kenneth Thomas. B.S., U. Md., 1938, Ph.D., 1941. Research assoc. U. Ill., Urbana, 1941-42; instr. U. Md., 1942-43; research chemist, asst. head organic research, head organic research, asst. dir. chem. research Abbott Labs., North Chicago, Ill., 1943-61; dir. research Abbott Labs., 1961-66; v.p. research and devel. Cutter Labs., Inc., Berkeley, Calif., 1966-73; v.p. research and quality assurance Cutter Labs., Inc., 1973-74, sr. v.p. sci. ops., 1974-81, vice chmn. bd. dirs., 1980-81, dir., 1968-81; vol. tchr. gen. sci., computer sci. Author: (with Jenkins, Hartung, Hamlin and Data) The Chemistry of Organic Medicinal Products, 1957. Mem. Am. Pharm. Assn., Am. Chem. Soc., AAAS, Sigma Xi, Rho Chi, Alpha Chi Sigma. Republican. Home: 3270 Terra Granada Dr # 1A Walnut Creek CA 94595-3526

HAMLIN, ROBERT HENRY, public health educator, management consultant; b. Cambridge, Mass., Apr. 2, 1923; s. Howard E. and Margaret E. (Henry) H.; m. Beate Kraschewski, Dec. 16, 1960; 1 son, Andrew Werner. A.B. summa cum laude, Ohio State U., 1944; B.S.M., Northwestern Med. Sch., 1945, B.M., 1946, M.D. with honors, 1947; M.P.H. magna cum laude, Harvard, 1952, JD, 1953. Diplomate: Am. Bd. Preventive Medicine. Intern Johns Hopkins Hosp., Balt., 1946-47; cons. Mass. commn. reporting, preparing and promulgating legislation on pub. and mental health and pub. welfare, 1950-53; 1st asst. to commnr. pub. health Mass., 1952-53; asst. prof. legal medicine Harvard Law Sch., 1952-57; lectr. pub. health law and adminstrn. Harvard Sch. Pub. Health, 1952-57, asso. prof. pub. health adminstrn., 1959-62, Roger Irving Lee prof. pub. health, 1962-65, chmn. dept. pub. health practice, 1963-65; v.p. Booz, Allen and Hamilton (mgmt. cons.), 1965-67; ind. mgmt. cons., 1968; chmn. bd. MACRO Systems, Inc. (mgmt. cons.), Washington, 1969-80; clin. prof. dept. comprehensive medicine Coll. Medicine, U. South Fla., 1980-83; acting dir., prof. pub. health program Coll. Pub. Health, U. South Fla., 1983; pres. United Health Techs., Inc. (mgmt. cons.), 1981—; adj. prof. health adminstrn. Columbia U. Sch. Public Health and Adminstrv. Medicine, 1972-80; cons. Rockefeller Found., 1959-61; staff dir. spel. commn. Harvard health services, 1953-54; mem. U.S. Commn. for UNESCO, 1958-60; dir. pub. health, Brookline, Mass., 1953-57; cons. Hoover Commn. II, 1954-55; asst. to sec. health, edn. and welfare, 1957-59; vis. lectr. pub. health adminstrn. and law Harvard, 1957-59. Contbr. articles profl. publs. U.S. del. 10th session gen. conf. UNESCO, Paris, 1958, pub. health adminstrn. cons. to pvt. orgns., state and local govts. Served as apprentice seaman USN, 1943-46; lt. (j.g.) M.C. USNR, 1947-49. Fellow Am. Pub. Health Assn.; mem. Am. Pub. Welfare Assn., Am. Acad. Health Adminstrn. (dir. 1976-81), Mass. Med. Soc., Phi Beta Kappa, Phi Eta Sigma, Alpha Epsilon Delta, Alpha Omega Alpha, Delta Omega. Office: United Health Techs 13300 Indian Rocks Rd-1904 Largo FL 33774-2010

HAMLIN, TOM, radio and television sportcaster, realtor; b. West Middletown, Ohio, Aug. 20, 1930; s. Harlin and Martha (Selby) H.: m. Phyllis Ann Hazelwood, June 20, 1953; children: Margo Ann, Thomas Charles. BA in Journalism, Ohio Wesleyan U., 1951. Sports dir. Sta. WLOK-AM-TV, Lima, Ohio, 1953-54, Sta. WMAN, Mansfield, Ohio, 1954-56, Stas. WAPI-AM and WABT-TV, Birmingham, Ala., 1956-60, Sta. WHIO-AM-TV, Dayton, Ohio, 1960-77, Sta. WKEF-TV, Dayton, 1979-85; freelance TV and radio announcer Voice of Ohio State football network, 1973-75, Tampa Bay Bucs network, 1976-77; freelance TV and radio sports announcer, 1971—, Ctrl. State U. Football, Ohio, 1987-96, N.A.I.A. Championship Games, 1990-92.; game analyst NCAA Basketball Final Four finals Sports Network Inc., 1963; Rose Bowl play-by-play announcer NBC Radio, 1974, 75. Bd. dirs. Greater Dayton Humane Soc., 1968-95, v.p., 1984-86. With USMC, 1945-46. Named Ala. Sportscaster of Yr. Nat. Sportswriters-Sportscasters Assn., 1959, Citizen of Yr., Dayton Jaycees, 1968; 6 nominations Ohio Sportscaster of the Yr. Mem. Ohio Sportscasters Assn. (pres. 1966-67), Dayton Area Bd. Realtors, Agonis Club (pres. 1991-92). Presbyterian. Home: 401 Canterbury Dr Dayton OH 45429-1441 Office: Big Hill Realty Corp 5580 Far Hills Ave Dayton OH 45429-2285

HAMLISCH, MARVIN, composer, conductor, pianist, entertainer; b. N.Y.C., June 2, 1944; s. Max and Lilly (Schachter) H.; m. Terre Blair, 1989. B.A., Queen's Coll., 1967; student, Juilliard Sch. Music, 1951-64. Principal pops conductor Pittsburgh Symphony, Pittsburgh, 1994—, Balt. Symphony Orch., 1996—. Rehearsal pianist Broadway shows, including Funny Girl, Fade Out--Fade In, also TV series Bell Telephone Hour, early 1960's; first composition for film The Swimmer, starring Burt Lancaster, 1968; other film scores include Take the Money and Run, 1969, Bananas, 1971, Save The Tiger, 1973, Kotch, 1971, The Way We Were (Best Original Song and Best Original Dramatic Score, Acad. Motion Picture Arts Scis. 1974), The Sting, (Best Adaptation award Acad. Motion Picture Arts Scis. 1974), Same Time Next Year, 1979, Ice Castles, 1979, Chapter Two, 1979, Starting Over, 1979, Ordinary People, 1980, Sophie's Choice, 1982, Frankie and Johnny, 1991, Switched at Birth, 1991; composer songs for films Three Men and a Baby; popular songs include Sunshine, Lollipops and Rainbows, 1960, Nobody Does It Better, 1977; Broadway musicals: A Chorus Line, 1975 (Pulitzer and Tony awards), They're Playing Our Song, 1979, The Goodbye Girl, 1993; theme song for Good Morning, America, 1975; composer symphonic work in one movement "Anatomy of Peace", 1991, (performed by Dallas Symphony Orch., London Symphony Orch., Symphony for U.N. at Carnegie Hall; composer music for global anthem "One Song"; lyrics by Alan and Marilyn Bergman (internat. debut at Barcelona Olympics, 1992); author: The Way I Was, 1992. recipient Outstanding Music Direction & Music and Lyrics Emmy awards for Barbra Streisand: The Concert, 1994.

HAMM, CHARLES JOHN, banker; b. Bklyn., May 11, 1937; s. Frank Coleman and Lisbeth (Higgins) H.; m. Irene Frail, Aug. 14, 1960; children: Charles William, Liza Higgins. BA, Harvard U., 1959; MBA, NYU, 1967. Vice pres., mgmt. supr. Wells Rich Greene Inc., N.Y.C., 1967-74; sr. v.p., mgmt. rep. Foote Cone & Belding Inc., N.Y.C., 1974-75; pres., chief operating officer F. William Free Inc., N.Y.C., 1975-77; exec. v.p. McCann-Erickson Inc., Atlanta, 1977-79; vice chmn. U.S.A. McCann-Erickson Inc., 1979-83; exec. v.p. McCann-Erickson World Wide, 1983-85, also dir.; pres. Independence Savs. Bank, Bklyn., 1985—, chief exec. officer, 1986—, chmn., 1996—; trustee Ind. Savs. Bank, N.Y.C., 1974—; dir. Cmty. Preservation Corp., 1994—, N.Y. State Banking Bd., 1994—; bd. dirs., com. on econ. devel., com. on edn. N.Y.C. Partnership; bd. dirs., chmn. com. pub. affairs Savs. Banks Assn. N.Y. State, 1988-94; bd. dirs. N.Y. region Fed. Home Loan Bank, mem. exec. com., 1992-97, chmn. mktg. com., 1994-97; mem. exec. com., bd. dirs. Cmty. Banks Assn. N.Y. State, mem. long-range planning com., 1995-96; bd. dirs. N.Y. Investment Fund, 1997—. Apptd. com. Bklyn. Waterfront Devel., 1995-96; mem. alumni coun. Phillips Exeter (N.H.) Acad., 1980-96, mem. fund raising adv. com., 1989-94; bd. dirs. Bklyn. Bur. Cmty. Svcs., 1985—, chmn., 1989-98; bd. dirs. Bklyn. Hist. Soc., 1986-89, Bklyn. Botanic Garden, 1987—, mem. exec. com., 1994—; bd. dirs. MSB fund Inc., 1987-90, Mason's Island Property Owners Assn., 1991-95, Pratt Inst. Bklyn., 1991—, chair fin. com., 1996-98; bd. dirs. Bklyn. Hosp. Ctr., Prospect Park Alliance, Bklyn., 1997—; chmn. devel. com. Pratt Inst., 1993-96; dir. The Friend Group, Cin., 1993—. 1st lt. C.E. U.S. Army, 1959-61. Recipient Robert E. Healey award Interpub. Group of Cos., 1979. Mem. Nat. Coun. Savs. Instns. (bd. dirs. 1991-92), Bklyn. C. of C. (bd. dirs. 1985-95, vice chmn. 1989-95, exec. com. 1989-95), Cmty. Banks Assn. N.Y. State (chmn. group IV/V, mem. exec. com. 1989-93), Univ. Club, Heights Casino Club (N.Y.C.), Bronxville Field Club (N.Y.), Mason's Island Yacht Club (Conn.), Hillsboro (Pompano Beach, Fla.). Office: Independence Savs Bank 195 Montague St Brooklyn NY 11201-3631

HAMM, DAVID BERNARD, lawyer; b. Bklyn., Oct. 6, 1948; s. Isidore I. and Sarah (Lamm) H.; m. Margaret Weiss, June 20, 1971; children: Jennifer A. Maltz, Michael S. BA cum laude, CUNY, Bklyn., 1971; JD magna cum laude, N.Y. Law Sch., 1977. Bar: N.Y. 1978, U.S. Dist. Ct. (no. dist.) N.Y. 1978, U.S. Dist. Ct. (so. and ea. dists.) N.Y. 1979, U.S. Supreme Ct. 1981, U.S. Ct. Appeals (2d cir.) 1982, (3d cir.) 1988. Law clk. to presiding judges N.Y. State Ct. Appeals, Albany, 1977-79; assoc. Herzfeld & Rubin P.C., N.Y.C., 1979-85, mem., 1986—. Mem. Commn. Legis. and Civic Action Agudath Israel of Am., N.Y.C., 1979—. Recipient Community Service award Agudath Israel of Am., 1986. Mem. ABA, N.Y. State Bar Assn. (com. civil practice law and rules), N.Y. County Lawyers Assn. (torts law sect., appellate advocacy com.), Jewish Lawyers Guild, N.Y. Law Sch. Alumni Assn. (Prof. Vincent LoLordo award 1977). Democrat. Home: 2015 E 22nd St Brooklyn NY 11229-3615 Office: Herzfeld & Rubin PC 40 Wall St Fl 54 New York NY 10005-2349

HAMM, GEORGE ARDEIL, retired secondary education educator, hypnotherapist, consultant; b. San Diego, Aug. 13, 1934; s. Charles Ardeil and Vada Lillian (Sharrah) H.; m. Marilyn Kay Nichols, July 1, 1972; children—Robert Barry, Charles Ardeil II, Patricia Ann. B.S. in Music, No. Ariz. U., 1958, M.A. in Music Edn., 1961; M.A. in Ednl. Adminstrn., Calif. Lutheran Coll., 1978, M.S. in Guidance and Counseling, 1981, PhD, U. Mass., 1998. Cert. secondary sch. tchr., adminstr. pupil pers. svcs., Calif., clin. hyprotherapist. Tchr. music Needles (Calif.) H.S., 1958-61; music sociology, psychology tchr, counselor Hueneme H.S., Oxnard, Calif., 1961-93; ret. dean instrn. U. Martial Arts and Scis.; founder Nat. Judo Inst., Colorado Springs, Colo., Coll. Sport Sci., Nat. Judo Inst.; cons. applied sport hypnotherapy; creator tchg. program. Served with USMC, 1953-55; Korea. Mem. Am. Fedn. Tchrs., Am. Coun. Hypnotist Examiners, U.S. Judo Assn. Inc. (7th degree black belt of Judo, 8th degrees black belt of Ju Ji Tsu, master level coach of Judo, 1980, cert. sr. rank examiner), Phi Delta Kappa, Kappa Delta Pi. Republican. Mormon. Contbr. numerous articles to nat. and internat. Judo jours. Pioneer ednl. hypnosis. Home: 2560 Ruby Dr Oxnard CA 93030-8607

HAMM, MARIEL MARGARET, soccer player; b. Selma, Ala., Mar. 17, 1972; m. Christian Corry. BS in Polit. Sci., U. N.C., 1994. Forward U.S. Women's Nat. Soccer Team, Chgo., 1987—. Named U.S. Soccer Female Athlete of Yr., 1994-95, MVP of U.S. Women's Cup, 1995; recipient Gold medal Atlanta Olympics, 1996; World Cup 1999. Office: US Soccer Fedn US Soccer House 1801 S Prairie Ave Chicago IL 60616-1357*

HAMM, RICHARD L., church administrator; b. Crawfordsville, Ind., Dec. 21, 1947; m. Melinda Ann Fishbaugh; children: David Lee, Laura Ann. Student, St. Petersburg Jr. Coll., 1966-67; BA in Religion, Butler U., 1970; D of Ministry, Christian Theol. Sem., 1974. Pastor Abington (Ind.) Christian Ch., 1968, Little Eagle Creek Christian Ch., Westfield, Ind., 1970; assoc. pastor Ctrl. Christian ch., Kansas City, Kans., 1974; founding pastor North Oak Christian ch., Kansas City, Mo., 1975-82; sr. pastor 1st Christian Ch., Ft. Wayne, Ind., 1982-90; regional min. Christian Ch. (Disciples of Christ) Tenn., 1990-93; gen. min., pres. Christian Ch. (Disciples of Christ) U.S. and Can., 1993—; bd. dirs. mid-Am. region Christian Ch. (Disciples of Christ), 1977-81, bd. dirs. Kans. region, 1980-81, bd. dirs. Ind. region, 1983-90, chair area new ch. com. Ind. region, 1984-87, 89, mem. commn. ministry Ind. region, 1985-87, 89, mem. gen. bd., 1986-90, bd. dirs. divsn. overseas ministries, 1991—, commn. on ministry, 1991—, mem. task force mission funding, 1992; moderator Christian Ch. Greater Kansas City, 1980-81; advisor/participant World Coun. Chs. Ctrl. Com., Geneva, 1992; convener Chs. Covenant Communion workshops, Tenn., 1992; v.p. Nat. Coun. Chs., 1996; mem. ctrl. com. World Coun. Chs., 1998—. Author: From Mainline to Front Line, 1997. Mem. Mayor's Task Force Domestic Violence, 1990. Recipient Recognition award North Kansas City Edn. Assn., 1979, Recognition award Ft. Wayne, Ind., Edn. Assn. and Ft. Wayne Community Schs., 1984, Ind. Region's Model Ministry award, 1990; named Ecumenist of Yr. of Tenn., 1993. Mem. Tenn. Assn. Chs. (pres.-elect 1992), Clergy United Action (pres. 1984-86), Associated Chs. Ft. Wayne and Allen County (bd. dirs., officer 1982-90), Rotary. Office: Christian Church (Disciples of Christ) PO Box 1986 Indianapolis IN 46206-1986

HAMM, (CHARLES) STAN(LEY), telecommunications company executive; b. Winston-Salem, N.C.; m. Sara Hamm; 2 children. Grad., Wake Forest U. From sales rep. to regional mgr. IBM, 18 years; v.p., gen. mgr. Eczel Corp., Raleigh, N.C.; pres., CEO, Am. Cellular Comm. Corp.; pres. BellSouth Cellular Corp., Atlanta; group pres. mobile sys. BellSouth, Atlanta, 1993—. Office: BellSouth Corp 1100 Peach St NE Atlanta GA 30309*

HAMM, VERNON LOUIS, JR., management and financial consultant; b. East St. Louis, Ill., Mar. 14, 1951; s. Vernon Louis and Colleen Ann Hamm; B.S., Murray (Ky.) State U., 1973; M.B.A., St. Louis U., 1975; postgrad. Stanford U., 1975. Jr. exec. corp. accounts Brown Group, Inc., St. Louis, 1973-75; group supr. APC Skills Co., Palm Beach, Fla., 1975-77; account mgr. Inst. Mgmt. Resources, Los Angeles, 1977-78; dir. mgmt. devel. Naus & Newlyn, Inc., Paoli, Pa., 1978-82; pres. Mgmt. Alternatives Ltd., 1982—; mgmt., fin. and energy cons., 1975—; bd. dirs. Ryan's Family Steakhouses, Inc., Psychosystems Mgmt. Corp., N.Y.C., MAL Ventures, Detroit. Mem. Am. Soc. for Tng. and Devel., Am. Prodn. and Inventory Control Soc., Murray State U. Alumni Assn. Contbr. articles to profl. publs.

HAMM, WILLIAM JOSEPH, retired physics educator; b. Belleville, Ill., July 26, 1910; s. William Hamm and Catherine Tiehess. BS, U. Dayton, 1930; MS, Cath. U. Am., 1935; PhD, Washington U., St. Louis, 1942. Joined Soc. Mary, Roman Cath. Ch., 1927. Asst. prof. St. Mary's U., San Antonio, 1935-37, prof. physics, 1942-44, 46-78, 79-87, Minnie Stevens Piper Found. prof., 1958, prof. emeritus, 1987—; asst. prof. Maryhurst Normal Sch., Kirkwood, Mo., 1937-40; prin. St. Michael's Cen. Cath. High Sch., Chgo., 1944-46; researcher NRC, Brooks AFB, Tex., 1978-79; chmn. San Antonio chpt. Inst. Radio Engrs., 1951-53, chmn. conf., 1953; extramural assoc. NIH, Bethesda, Md., 1977—; participant Balt. Longitudinal Study Aging, NIH, 1977—; bd. dirs. Tex. State Surplus Porperty Agy., Austin, 1971; rsch. asso.c NRC, Washington, 1978. Named Piper prof. Minnie Stevens Piper Found., 1958. Fellow IEEE; mem. Am. Inst. Physics, Am. Phys. Soc., Am. Amateur Radio Relay League, Am. Amateur Satellite Inc., Internat. Mission Radio Assn., Quarter Century Wireless Assn., Soc. of Mary (St. Louis province). Avocations: amateur radio, jogging. Home: Marianist Residence 1 Camino Santa Maria St San Antonio TX 78228-5433 Office: St Marys U Dept Physics 1 Camino Santa Maria St San Antonio TX 78228-8500

HAMMACK, JULIA DIXON, music educator; b. Sturgis, Ky., Oct. 11, 1913; d. Augustus Rees and Ethel Lysle (McKeaig) H. B Music Edn., Murray State U., 1937; M Music Edn., Am. Conservatory Music, 1943. Cert. tchr. (life). Vocal and instrumental dir. grades 1-12 Dixon (Ky.) Schs., 1937-41; vocal supr.-dir. grades 1-12 Clarksville (Tenn.) Schs., 1941-45; piano tchr., choir dir. Union U., Jackson, Tenn., 1945-47; piano tchr. Tift Coll. Women, Forsyth, Ga., 1947-51; program dir., talent coord. U.S. Army, Stuttgart, Germany, 1952-54; asst. prof. of music Wis. State U., Whitewater, 1955-59; pvt. piano tchr., 1937-93; ch. choir dir. Salem Luth. Ch., Indpls., 1983-90, 1st Bapt. Ch., Forsyth, 1947-51. Fin. supporter AAUW, 1997—, Am. Pianist Assn., 1992—, Indpls. Symphony Orch., 1980-98. Mem. Matinee Musicale (profl. assoc.), Christ Ch. Episcopal Cathedral (St. Teresa's guild, altar guild 1990-98), Sigma Alpha Iota (Indpls. alumnae chpt., life, corr. sec., editor 1986-90, Rose of Honor 1990, also other honors 1997). Episcopalian. Avocations: writing, travel, concerts, reading, letter writing. Home: 2625 N Meridian St Apt 408 Indianapolis IN 46208-7704

HAMMAD, ALAM E., international business consultant, educator; b. Cairo, Egypt, Sept. 24, 1943; s. Mohammad Attia H.; m. Dyannoelle Elizabeth, Jan. 19, 1978; 1 child, Adam. BA in Commerce, Cairo Poly. Inst., 1965; MS in Mktg., La. State U., 1971; D of Bus. Adminstrn., George Washington U., 1977. Advisor Min. State & Gov. of Dhofar, Salalah, Oman, 1977-79; advisor Min. Petroleum andMinerals, Muscat, Oman, 1979; advisor to min., head planning Min. Agr. and Fisheries, Muscat, Oman, 1979-83; pres., founder Pyramex Fin. Internat., Va., 1983-84; chmn. MicroAge Computers Corp., Va., 1984-86; prof., lectr. George Washington U., Washington, 1984-88; pres., found Pizza Club, Inc., Va., 1987-97; contractor, builder, internat. cons., 1984—; sr. assoc. Ctr. Strategic & Inernat. Studies, 1997—; mem. found. com. Sultan Qaboos U., 1981-86; pres. Info. Security Found., 1991-93; vis. prof. George Washington U., 1988-90; chmn. found. com. Oman Nat. Fisheries Co., 1980-81, Oman Bank Agr., 1981-82; bd. dirs. Oman Sun Farms Co., 1979, Oman Devel. Bank, 1979-83; pres. Am. Global Pub., 1992—; pub. policy expert The Heritage Found., 1996—; writer Okaz Saudi Newspaper, 1996—, Gulf News, 1992-93. Author: Development of Agriculture and Fisheries in Oman, 1981, Agriculture, Animal Wealth, Water Resources and Fisheries of Oman, 1987, Islamic Banking: Theory and Practice, 1989; Encyclopedia of Computer Terms, English-Arabic, 1994; Dictionary of Computer Terms, English-Arabic, 1994; contbr. articles to profl. jours. Chmn. pub. affairs, exec. vice chmn., 1st vice chmn. Alexandria Rep. City Com.; pres. Nat. Arab-Am. Rep. coun.; mem. George Washington Dist. Com., Boy Scouts Am.; bd. visitors, trustee George Mason U., 1994-98, vice rector, 1996-98; commr. Alexandria Indsl. Devel. Authority, 1996-98; mem. Nat. Policy Coun., Nat. Alumni Found., Heritage Found., No. Va. Rep. Bus. Forum, Com. for a Safe Va., Campaign for Honest Change, Empower Am., Rep. Nat. Com., Bachelor 95 & Master Commr. Sci. 97 U. Scouting. Decorated Order of Sultan Qaboos. Mem. Assn. Governing Bds. Univs. and Colls., Acad. Internat. Bus., Friendship Vets. Fire Engine Assn., Beta Gamma Sigma. Home: 819 S Fairfax St Alexandria VA 22314-4311

HAMMAKER, PAUL M., retail executive, business educator, author; b. Dayton, Ohio, Jan. 25, 1903; s. Wilbur Emory and Willamine (Weihrauch) H.; m. Patricia Curry, Sept. 5, 1929 (dec. 1955); children—Robert, John, David; m. Adrienne V. S. Stokes, June 15, 1956 (dec. 1970); m. Susan Ford, Nov. 24, 1989. B.C.S., U. Ill., 1925; LL.D., MacMurray Coll., 1957. With Marshall Field & Co., 1943-57, divisional v.p., 1948; gen. mdse. mgr., sr. v.p., asst. gen. mgr. Chgo. and suburban stores, until 1957; exec. v.p., gen. mgr. Montgomery Ward, 1957-59, mem. bd. dir., 1958-61, pres., 1959-61; dir. The Fair Store, Montgomery Ward Real Estate Corp., Montgomery Ward Credit Corp., Standard T Chem. Co., Inc.; Prof. bus adminstrn. Grad. Sch. Bus. Adminstrn., U. Va., 1962-73; sr. fellow Center for Study Applied Ethics, 1973—; founder, partner Old Dominion Assos. (Mgmt. Cons.), 1964-89. Author: (with Louis T. Rader) Plain Talk About Managing. Mem. Alpha Tau Omega, Beta Gamma Sigma. Clubs: Farmington Country (Charlottesville, Va.), Greencroft (Charlottesville, Va.), Commercial (Chgo.). Home: 317 E Beverley St Staunton VA 24401-4328

HAMMAM, M. SHAWKY, electrical engineer, educator; b. Aug. 5, 1919. BSc, U. London, Eng., 1943, PhD, 1946. Registered profl. engr., N.Y. Sr. lectr. Alexandria U., Egypt, 1948-55; assoc. prof. Ein Shamus U., Egypt, 1955-63; vis assoc. prof. U. Kans., 1963-64; prof. Clarkson U., Potsdam, N.Y., 1964—; Niagara Mowhawk Power prof. Clarkson U., 1965. Fellow IEEE; mem. Inst. Elec. Engrs. (U.K.), Inst. Physics.

HAMMAR, DAVID BRUCE, clergyman; b. Ridgewood, N.J., Jan. 17, 1947; s. Russell Alfred and Mildred Phyllis (Peters) H.; m. Linda Kaye Bergy, Aug. 18, 1968; children: Steven, Mark, Catherine, Sarah. AB, U. Redlands, 1968; MDiv, Colgate Rochester Div. Sch., 1971. Ordained to ministry Am. Bapt. Chs., USA, 1971. Min. Christian edn. North Scituate (R.I.) Bapt. Ch., 1971-77; assoc. pastor United Ch. Los Alamos, N.Mex., 1977-85; pastor Bethel Bapt. Ch., Casper, Wyo., 1985-95, 1st Bapt. Ch., Ft. Dodge, Iowa, 1995—; mem. min's. coun. Am. Bapt. Ch. USA, 1971—; mem. policy bd.Am. Bapt. Chs. Rocky Mountains, Denver, 1986-88; mem. chaplaincy bd. Wyo. Med. Ctr., Casper, 1993-95; chair ministry com. area 5 Mid-Am. Baptist Ch., 1999—. Composer, arranger religious music. Soccer coach Los Alamos Youth Soccer, 1980-84, Casper Youth Soccer, 1986-88, 91, Ft. Dodge Youth Soccer, 1995, 97; percussionist Los Alamos Sinfonietta, 1977-85, Ft. Dodge Area Symphony, 1995—; vice chmn. bd. Samaritan Counseling Ctr., Casper, 1990-94. Mem. Ft. Dodge Ministerial Assn., Ft. Dodge Interfaith Forum. Avocations: music, tennis, photography, camping, reading. Office: 1st Bapt Ch 28 N 10th St Fort Dodge IA 50501-3913

HAMMAR, LESTER EVERETT, health care manufacturing company executive; b. Tillamook, Oreg., Dec. 15, 1927; s. Leo E. and Harriet L. (Parsons) H.; m. Margrit Steigl, May 9, 1964; children: Lawrence, Thomas, Stephanie. B.S., Oreg. State U., 1950; M.B.A., Washington U., 1964. With Montsanto Co., 1952-69; controller Monsanto-Europe, 1966-69; v.p., controller Smith Kline & French Labs., Phila., 1969-72, Abbott Labs., North Chgo., Ill., 1972-88; ret.; bd. dirs. Mulitflex, Inc.; bd. trustees Asia House Investments; project mgr. Exec. Svc. Corp. Chgo. Mem. audit com. City of Lake Forest; ruling elder, clk. of session 1st Presbyn. Ch. of Lake Forest; bd. dirs. Haven, Clara Abbott Fund. 1st lt. F.A., AUS, 1951-52. Mem. Fin Execs. Inst., Am. Mgmt. Assn. (former chmn. fin. coun., bd. mem.), 100 of Lake Country Club. Home and Office: 911 Gloucester Xing Lake Forest IL 60045-4901

HAMMARGREN, LONNIE, former lieutenant governor; b. Dec. 25, 1937; married. BA, U. Minn., 1958, MA in Psychol., 1960, BS, 1964, MD, 1964, MS in Neurosurgery, 1974. Diplomate Am. Bd. Neurological Surgery; med. license Nev., Minn. Flight surgeon for the astronauts NASA Manned Space Craft Ctr.; former lt. gov., pres. of the senate State of Nev., 1995-98; med. pvt. practice Las Vegas, 1998—; assoc. clin. prof. neurosurgery U. Nev. Sch. Medicine, Reno; clin. assoc. prof. surgery U. Calif., San Diego, 1982; chair Commn. Econ. Devel., Commn. Tourism; bd. dirs. Nev. Dept. Transp. Bd. regents U. and C.C. Sys. Nev., 1988-94; adv. bd. mem. Gov.'s com. for Employment of Handicapped; mem. State Bd. Edn., 1984-88; bd. mem. March of Dimes, Aid to Adoption of Spl. Kids. Mem. Spinal Cord Injury Program of Nev. (pres.), Cancer Soc., Aerospace Med. Assn., U Med. Ctr. Rehabilitation Unit (dir.), U. Med. Ctr. (chmn. neurosurgery dept.), Help Them Walk Again Found. (Nat. Dir.), Spina Bifida and Hydrocephalus Soc. (med. dir.), Internat. Ctr. for Rehabilitation Engring. (med. dir.), Pacific World Med. Found. (treas.), Paramed. and Emergency Care Bd. (adv.). Office: 3196 Maryland Pkwy Ste 106 Las Vegas NV 89109

HAMME, DAVID CODRINGTON, architect; b. York, Pa., Oct. 8, 1931. BA magna cum laude, Gettysburg Coll., 1952; BArch, U. Pa., 1960, MArch, 1962. Archtl. designer J. Alfred Hamme and Assocs., York, Pa., 1961-62; planner U. Pa. Planning Office, Phila., 1962; sr. designer Phila. City Planning Commn., 1962-66; project dir. Wallace, McHarg, Roberts & Todd, Phila., 1966-68, sr. assoc., 1968-79; sr. assoc. Wallace Roberts & Todd, Phila., 1980-81, ptnr., 1981-90, mng. ptnr., 1990—; assoc. prof. dept. architecture Drexel U., Phila., 1965-73, adj. prof., 1973—, asst. dir. dept. architecture, 1985-86; lectr. dept. landscape architecture U. Pa., Phila., 1975-78, 1981-88. Theophilus Parson Chandler scholar; recipient Design award HUD, 1968, Honor award Am. Soc. Landscape Designers, 1973, Honor award for mgmt. approaches HUD, 1974, Arthur Spayd Brooke Gold medal for design, Charles Merrick Gay prize, Paul Philippe Cret medal for design, Warren Powers Laird medal for design. Mem. AIA (numerous medals and awards). Office: Wallace Roberts Todd 260 S Broad St Fl 8 Philadelphia PA 19102-5075*

HAMMEL, HAROLD THEODORE, physiology and biophysics educator, researcher; b. Huntington, Ind., May 8, 1921; s. Audry Harold and Ferne Jane (Wiles) H.; m. Dorothy King, Dec. 29, 1948; children: Nannette, Heidi. BS in Physics, Purdue U., 1943; MS in Physics, Cornell U., 1950, PhD in Zoology, 1953; DSc (hon.), Huntington Coll., 1999. Jr. physicist Los Alamos (N.Mex.) Lab., 1944-46, staff physicist, 1948-49; from instr. to asst. prof. U. Pa., Phila., 1953-61; assoc. prof., fellow John B. Pierce Lab. Yale U., New Haven, 1961-68; prof. Scripps Instn. of Oceanography U. Calif., San Diego, 1968-88, emeritus prof., 1988—; adj. prof. physiology and biophysics Ind. U., Bloomington, 1989—; fgn. sci. mem. Max Planck Inst. for Physiol. & Clin. Rsch., 1978—; U.S. sr. scientist Alexander von Humboldt Found., 1981. Author: (with Scholander) Osmosis and Tensile Solvent, 1976; contbr. over 200 articles to profl. jours. Fellow AAAS; mem. Am. Phys. Soc., Am. Physiol. Soc. (Fifth August Krogh Disting. lectureship 1998, Honor award Environtl. and Exersize sect. 1996), Am. Soc. mammology, Norwegian Acad. Sci. & Letters. Democrat. Achievements include first measurement of phloem sap pressure in higher plants, and of xylem sap pressure in higher plants; explanation of freezing without cavitation in evergreen plants; extension and application of kinetic theory to Hulett's theory of solvent tension; research in theory of adjustable set point and gain for regulation of body temperature in vertebrates, in temperature regulation, in osmoregulation, and in osmosis and fluid transport in plants. Home: 1605 Ridgeway Dr Ellettsville IN 47429-9474 Office: Ind U Med Scis Program Bloomington IN 47405

HAMMEL, JOHN WINGATE, lawyer; b. Indpls., Dec. 25, 1943; s. Walter Francis and Mary Vivian (Patterson) H.; m. Linda Ann Yarling, Dec. 22, 1972; children: William Wingate II, Kathryn Christine, Rebecca Ann. BS, Butler U., 1967; postgrad., So. Ill. U., 1967-68; JD, Ind. U., 1975. Bar: Ind. 1975, U.S. Dist. Ct. (so. dist.) Ind. 1975, U.S. Ct. Mil. Appeals 1978, U.S. Ct. Appeals (7th crct.) 1982. Assoc. Yarling, Winter, Tunnell & Robinson, Indpls., 1975-86; ptnr. Yarling & Robinson, Indpls., 1986—. Lt. col. Ind. Army N.G. Mem. ABA, Ind. Bar Assn., Indpls. Bar Assn., 7th Cir. Bar Assn. Republican. Home: 5242 Rucker Cir Indianapolis IN 46250-2329 Office: Yarling & Robinson Ste 1535 Market Sq Ctr 151 N Delaware St Indianapolis IN 46204-2526

HAMMELL, GRANDIN GAUNT, real estate consultant; b. Rumson, N.J., Aug. 10, 1945; s. Grandin Kenneth and Catherine Elizabeth (Conklin) H.; m. Darlene Faye Settje, Nov. 21, 1972; children: Grandin Jeffrey, Heidi Grechen. B of Bus. Sci., Calif. State U., Los Angeles, 1979; grad., Realtor Inst., 1994. V.p. Security Pacific Bank, N.A., Los Angeles, 1973-87; exec. v.p. The Wellington Group, Rolling Hills Estate, Calif., 1987-89; bus. cons. Cambridge Bus. Forms, Burbank, Calif., 1991-93; real estate cons. Fowler Real Estate Better Homes & Gardens, Boulder, Colo., 1993—; speaker seminars on estate planning, so. Calif., 1983-90. Exec. producer radio program The World of Money. Mem. planned giving com. of So. Calif. chpt. Arthritis Found., 1987-93; v.p. Burbank Ednl. Found., 1984-93; chmn. fund raising com. L.A. County Natural History Mus.; trustee Realtor Cmty. Action Com., Inc., 1996—. Mem. Glendale Estate Planning Commn., Burbank C. of C. (ednl. com. 1989-93, devel. com.). Avocations: pub. speaking, retirement groups. Office: Fowler Real Estate Better Homes & Gardens 2970 Wilderness Pl Ste 200 Boulder CO 80301-5412

HAMMER, ALFRED EMIL, artist, educator; b. New Haven, Jan. 11, 1925, s. Forrester L. and Eugenie (Bauer-Enquist) H.; m. Marian Valle, Aug. 14, 1948; children: Alfred Emil, Paul Forrester, Eric Valdemar, Eugenie Bauer; m. Jeanne Baker, Dec. 18, 1966; children: Stephen Drake, Rosamond Swan. BFA, R.I. Sch. Design, 1950; BFA, Yale U., 1951, MFA, 1952. Instr. to assoc. prof. painting and drawing R.I. Sch. Design, Providence, 1952-69, chmn. grad. studies, 1958-60, dean students, 1960-61; dean Cleve. Inst. Art, 1969-74; dir., prof. Sch. Art, U. Man., Winnipeg, Can., 1974-82; dir. Pacific N.W. Coll. Art, Portland, Oreg., 1982-83; prof. Hartford Art Sch., U. Hartford, Conn., 1983-88, dean, 1983-86; freelance artist, 1988—. Exhibited group shows R.I. Ann. (recipient 1st prize award 1952), Providence Art Club Ann. (recipient 1st prize award 1953, 54, 55, 57), Newport Ann. (recipient 1st prize 1959), Boston Arts Festival, 1958, Shippee Gallery, N.Y.C., 1985, Joseloff Gallery U. Hartford, 1992; one-man shows include: U. Man., 1980, Thomas Gallery, 1980, Melnyschenko Gallery, Winnipeg, 1981, Movie House Studio Gallery, Millerton, N.Y., 1992; represented in collections Agnes Gund, Jr. C. of C., Nat. Mus. Israel, R.I. Sch. Design Mus., Portland Art Mus., Conn. Bank and Trust Co., Northeast Savs., Hartford, Corp. Hdqrs. Otis Elevator Corp., Farmington, Conn., Bank of New Eng., Boston, Shawmut Bank, Hartford, Aetna Ins., Hartford, Govt. of Man., Can., Gov.'s Coll. of Conn. Artists, Prize Winning Oil Paintings, 1960. Mem. Conn. Watercolor Soc., Lyme Art Assn. Home: 165 Tunxis Ave Bloomfield CT 06002-1737

HAMMER, DAVID LINDLEY, lawyer, author; b. Newton, Iowa, June 6, 1929; s. Neal paul and Agnes Marilyn (Reece) H.; m. Audrey Lowe, June 20, 1953; children: Julie, Lisa, David. BA, Grinnell Coll., 1951; JD, U. Iowa, 1956. Bar: Iowa 1956, U.S. Dist. Ct. (no. dist.) Iowa 1959, U.S. Dist. Ct. (so. dist.) Iowa 1969, U.S. Ct. Appeals (8th cir.) 1996, U.S. Supreme Ct. 1977. Ptnr. Hammer Simon & Jensen, Galena, Ill. and, Iowa; mem. grievance commn. Iowa Supreme Ct., 1973-85; mem. adv. rules com., 1986-92. Author: Poems from the Ledge, 1980, The Game is Afoot, 1983, For the Sake of the Game, 1986, The 22nd Man, 1989, To Play the Game, 1986, The Quest, 1993, My Dear Watson, 1994, The Before Breakfast Pipe, 1995, A Dangerous Game, 1997, The Vital Essence, 1999. Bd. dirs. Linwood Cemetery Assn., 1973—, pres., 1983-84; bd. dirs., past pres. Finley Hosp., hon. dir.; bd. dirs. Finley Found., 1988-95; past campaign chmn., past pres. United Way; past bd. dirs. Carnegie Stout Pub. Libr. With U.S. Army, 1951-53. Fellow Am. Coll. Trial Lawyers; mem. ABA, Young Lawyers Iowa (past pres.), Iowa Def. Counsel Assn. (pres. 1991-92, del. to Def. Rsch. Inst. 1992-93), Assn. Def. Trial Attys. (exec. coun. 1983-86, past chmn. Iowa chpt.), Iowa State Bar Assn. (past chmn. continuing legal edn. com.), Iowa Acad. Trial Lawyers, Dubuque County Bar Assn. (past pres.), Baker St. Irregulars. Republican. Congregationalist. Office: 700 Locust St Ste 190 Dubuque IA 52001-6824

HAMMER, DEBORAH MARIE, librarian, paralegal; b. Bronx, N.Y., Nov. 16, 1947; d. Ben and Helen (Lorenz) Halprin; m. Mark Stewart Hammer, May 30, 1976; 1 child, Joshua Robert. BA, CCNY, 1968; MLS, Rutgers U., 1969. Cert. libr. N.Y. Gen. asst. info., tel. ref. div. Queens Borough Pub. Libr., 1969-71, gen. asst. popular libr., 1972-80; asst. div. head history, travel & biography Queens Borough Pub. Libr., Jamaica, N.Y., 1972-81; div. head history, travel & biography Queens Borough Pub. Libr., 1981-92, div. mgr. social scis., 1992-98; libr. cons. Halimer Ent., New Hyde Park, 1998—; fee conciliation coord. Nassau County Bar Assn., 1999—. Democrat. Avocations: reading, cooking, handcrafts, camping, cross-country skiing. Home and Office: 1647 Park Ave New Hyde Park NY 11040-4324

HAMMER, DONALD PRICE, librarian; b. Pottsville, Pa., Dec. 16, 1921; s. Edward Price and Gertrude Mae (Schaeffer) H.; m. Louise Eleanore Kohler, May 26, 1947; 1 child, Donald Edward. *Donald Hammer's wife, Louise, was a professional librarian through fifty-one years of married life. Starting in school libraries, she served as a reference librarian at the University of Illinois and at Purdue University. She was a research librarian for the Wabash Valley Education Center, West Lafayette, Indiana, and an Assistant Professor of Education at Purdue University training school media librarians. In retirement she held seminars for training lay people to develop and administer church libraries.* B.S., Kutztown (Pa.) State Coll., 1948; M.L.S., George Peabody Coll., 1955; postgrad., U. Pitts., Moody Bible Inst. Asst. librarian Gettysburg (Pa.) Coll. Library, 1948-50; gifts and exchange librarian, then law librarian Pa. State Library, Harrisburg, 1950-55; bookstack librarian U. Ill., Urbana, 1955-58; head serials unit, then head systems devel. Purdue U. Library, 1959-71; assoc. dir. U. Mass. Library, 1972-73; exec. dir. Library and Info. Tech. Assn.-Library Adminstrn. and Mgmt. Assn., Chgo., 1973-79, Library and Info. Tech. Assn., 1973-86; mem. coms. Am. Nat. Standards Inst.; cons. in field. *Mr. Hammer is involved with the development, promotion, and use of automation technology in libraries, from its earliest days of punched cards to the use of satellites and net-working today. He organized national and regional conferences for many years, and sponsored by the American Library and Information Technology Association these provided a forum for discussion, an environment for learning, and a program for action on the design, development, and implementation of automated and technological systems in the library information science field.* Author: The Information Age—Its Development, Its Impact, 1976; also articles, chpts. in books. Chmn. Wheeling (Ill.) Sr. Citizen Commn., 1987-89, chmn. 1996-98, Wheeling (Ill.) Ad Hoc Human Rights Com., 1993-95; counselor Ill. Dept. of Ins., Sr. Health Ins. Program, 1993-98; chmn. Wheeling 2000 and Beyond Project Cmty. Svcs. Com., 1995-98, leader current events class, 1989-98, super sr., 1994, commr., 1998. With USAF, 1942-44. Grantee Library Services and Constrn. Act, 1968-71. Mem. ALA (pres.-elect Info. Sci. and Automation Div. 1972-73), Am. Soc. Info. Sci. (chmn.-elect Ind. chpt. 1971-72), Beta Phi Mu. Baptist. Home: 203 Stafford Dr Wheeling IL 60090-3159

HAMMER, EMANUEL FREDERICK, clinical psychologist, psychoanalyst; b. N.Y.C., Aug. 15, 1926; s. Isadore and Rebecca (Lieberman) H.; m. Lila Maralyn King, June 4, 1950; children: Diane Robin, Cary Marc. Student, Bklyn. Coll., 1944-45, 46-47; BA magna cum laude, Syracuse U., 1948; PhD, NYU, 1951. Diplomate in clin. psychology Am. Bd. Profl. Psychology; cert. psychologist N.Y. Dir. intern tng. Lynchburg (Va.) State Colony, 1951-52; sr. research scientist N.Y. State Psychiat. Inst., 1952-55; dir. dept. psychology, Psychiat. Clinic N.Y.C. Criminal Cts., 1955-72; dir. Am. Projective Drawing Inst., N.Y.C., 1956—; chief psychologist Lincoln Inst. for Psychotherapy, N.Y.C., 1960-68; lectr. Bklyn. Coll., 1958-63, New Sch. for Social Research, 1972; adj. asso. prof. N.Y. U. Grad. Sch. Arts and Scis., 1966-76; psychiat. cons., therapist United Presbyn. Ch., 1966-80; prof. grad. art therapy dept. Pratt Inst., 1978-88; clin. prof. Postdoctoral Inst. Advanced Psychol. Studies, Adelphi U., 1980—. Author: The Clinical Application of Projective Drawings, 1958, Creativity, 1961, Use of Interpretation in Treatment, 1968, Antiachievement: Perspectives on School Drop-Outs, 1970, Creativity, Talent and Personality, 1984, Reaching the Affect: Style in the Psychodynamic Therapies, 1990, Advances in Projective Drawing Interpretation, 1997, also 75 profl. papers. Served with USAF, 1945-46, PTO. Fellow APA, Am. Anthrop. Assn. (liaison fellow); mem. Nat. Psychol. Assn. for Psychoanalysis (dir. admissions, sr. mem. and faculty), Soc. Personality Assessment (sec.), N.Y. Soc. Clin. Psychologists (pres. 1964-65). Home and Office: 381 W End Ave New York NY 10024-6104

HAMMER, HAROLD HARLAN, oil company financial executive; b. Chgo., May 23, 1920; s. B. James and Frances (Halbren) H.; m. Hannah Richmond, Mar. 1, 1956; children: John, Elizabeth. B.S., Northwestern U., 1941; M.B.A., N.Y. U., 1950, J.D., 1955. Bar: N.Y. State 1955. Accountant U.S. Steel Corp., 1941-42; asst. sec.-treas. Duraloy Co., Scottdale, Pa., 1945-48; financial analyst, asst. controller Port of N.Y. Authority, 1948-50; investment counsel N.Y.C., 1950—, since practiced in; v.p. finance, dir. Control Data Corp., Mpls., 1966-72; chmn. finance com., dir. Gen. Refractories Co., 1963-66; with Gulf Oil Corp., Pitts., 1972—; sr. v.p. Gulf Oil Corp., 1972-73, exec. v.p., 1973-81, chief adminstrv. officer, 1981-85; chmn. MMC Group Inc., 1986—; bd. dirs., chmn. J.C. Horne & Co., Standard-Thomson Corp. Author: Financing the Port of New York Authority, 1957, also articles in field. Bd. dirs. W. Penn Hosp. Served as lt. USNR, World War II. Mem. ABA, Fed., N.Y. Bar Assns., Phi Alpha Delta. Methodist. Clubs: Fox Meadow Tennis (gov. 1966); Duquesne (Pitts.), Fox Chapel Golf (Pitts.); Rolling Rock (Ligonier, Pa.). Office: MMC Group Inc 1 Oliver Plz Pittsburgh PA 15222-2600

HAMMER, JACOB MYER, physicist, consultant; b. N.Y.C., Sept. 14, 1927; s. Joseph Israel Hammer and Miriam Silverman; m. Rose Kizner (div. 1975); children: Daniel, Jonathan, Miriam; m. Katrina Schuyler, July 10, 1982; 1 stepson, David Reisberg. BS in Engring. Physics, NYU, 1950, PhD in Physics, 1956; MS in Physics, U. Ill., 1951. Mem. tech. staff Bell Telephone Labs., Murray Hill, N.J., 1956-59, RCA Labs., Princeton, N.J., 1959-68; mem. tech. staff David Sarnoff Rsch. Ctr., Princeton, 1970-87, cons., 1987—; sr. visitor Cavendish Lab., Cambridge U., 1968-69. Coauthor: Integrated Optics, 1975, Fiber & Integrated Optics, 1979; co-editor: Surface Emitting Semiconductor Lasers and Arrays, 1993; contbr. numerous articles to profl. jours.; patentee in field. With AUS, 1946-47. Fellow IEEE (life, assoc. editor Jour. Quantum Electronics, 1987-90); mem. Am. Phs. Soc., Optical Soc. Am. Office: 42 City Gate Ln Annapolis MD 21401-2736

HAMMER, JOHN HENRY, II, hospital administrator; b. Bartlesville, Okla., Dec. 27, 1943; s. John Henry and Lucy (Macias) H.; BBA, St. Joseph's Coll., 1966; student U. Md. (Europe), 1968-69; MBA, U. Ill., 1984; m. Maria Lynn Adams; children: John Henry, Erica, Chassity Russell, Colby Russell, Megan. Project mgr. Econ. & Manpower Corp., N.Y.C., 1971-73; asst. dir. human resources St. Catherine Hosp., East Chicago, Ind., 1974-80, pres. Employees Credit Union, 1974-80; dir. pers. Lakeview Med. Ctr., Danville, Ill., 1980-84, v.p., 1984-88, v.p. United Samaritans Med. Ctr., Danville, Ill., 1988-95; adminstrv. dir. U. Ill., Illini Union, 1997—; bd. dirs. East Cen. Ill. Health Systems Agy., East Cen. Ill. Health Planning Orgn., Vermilion Area Cmty. Health Ctr. Chmn. De La Garza Career Ctr. Program Com., 1974-80, bd. dirs. Jr. Achievement of Danville, 1990-95, vice chmn., 1991, chmn. 1993-95. Capt. USAF, 1967-71, to lt. col. USAFR, 1974-93. Mem. Ind. Soc. Hosp. Personnel Adminstrn. (chmn. 1976-77, dir. 1977-79, pres. 1979-80), Am. Coll. Healthcare Execs., Rotary (bd. dirs. 1990-92, pres. 1991) Roman Catholic. Office: 218 W Ellsworth St Westville IL 61883-1232

HAMMER, KATHERINE GONET, software company executive; b. Shreveport, La., Jan. 5, 1946; d. Joseph Peter and Bernice Evelyn (Post) Gonet; m. Gael Warren Hammer, May 25, 1965 (div.); children: Katherine Elizabeth, Evelyn Alice; m. Ronald R. Scott, Feb. 14, 1982 (div.). BA in English, U. Iowa, 1967, MA in Linguistics, 1969; PhD in English Linguistics, 1973. Asst. prof. Coe Coll., Cedar Rapids, Iowa, 1973-75; asst. prof. in linguistics Wash. State U., Pullman, 1975-80; vis. scholar Ctr. for Cognitive Sci. U. Tex., Austin, 1980-81; software devel. mgr. Tex. Instruments, Austin, 1981-84; mem. tech. staff Microelectronics and Computer Tech. Corp., Austin, 1984-90; pres., chief exec. officer Evolutionary Techs. Internat., Inc., Austin, 1991—. Avocation: sculpting. Office: Evolutionary Techs Internat 816 Congress Ave Ste 1300 Austin TX 78701

HAMMER, LINDA See LINDROTH, LINDA

HAMMER, MARION PRICE, association executive; b. Columbia, S.C., Apr. 26, 1939; 3 children. Exec. dir. Unified Sportsmen of Fla., Fairfax, Va., 1978—; pres. NRA, Fairfax, Va.; bd. dirs. NRA, Tallahassee, Fla. Registered lobbyist for pro-gun issues. Recipient Harlon B. Carter Legis. Achievement award, 1992, SCOPE ann. 2d Amendment award, 1987, Roy Rogers Man of Yr. award, Outstanding Cmty. Svc. award Nat. Safety Coun., 1993, Nat. Edn. award Am. Legion, Sybil Ludington award. Mem. NRA (life, cert. firearm instr., chmn. legal policy com., chmn. task force on hunter safety legislation, vice chmn. women's policies com., mem. nominating com., pub. affairs com., ethics com., membership coms.). Office: NRA PO Box 7530 Tallahassee FL 32314*

HAMMER, ROBERT EUGENE, psychologist; b. Faribault, Minn., Aug. 7, 1931; s. Rolf Walter and Verona (Bakken) H.; m. M. Kitti Nations, Apr. 30, 1967 (div. Jan. 1988); children: Gregory Clay, Cynthia Beth; m. Bonnie Jo French, Nov. 12, 1988. BS in Counseling Psychology, U. Houston, 1959, MA, 1963; PhD in Spl. Edn. Adminstrn., U. Iowa, 1970. Lic. psychologist, Iowa; cert. health svc. provider in psychology. Tchr. educable mentally retarded Houston Ind. Sch. Dist., 1961-63; testing supr. U. Houston Counseling Ctr., 1963-65; child psychologist Mental Health Inst., Independence, Iowa, 1965-67, dir. adolescent treatment unit, 1969-74, dir. psychol. svcs., 1969-97, dir. adolescent treatment unit, 1989—; rsch. dir. Iowa Div. State Mental Health Resources; pvt. practice counseling and cons. psychologist, 1974—. Bd. dirs. Iowa Nursing Found.; vol. fireman; mem. men's gospel quartet United Parish Ch. Served with USAF, 1950-53. Mem. Am. Psychol. Assn., Nat. Assn. Rural Mental Health, Am. Soc. Quality Control, State Mental Health Dirs. Assn., Iowa Psychol. Assn., Houston TKE Alumni Assn., SPEBSQSA, U.S. Chess Fedn., Evaluation Network, Am. Legion, Lions, Masons. Contbr. articles to profl. jours. Home: PO Box 0257 120 2nd St S Coggon IA 52218-0257

HAMMER, TERENCE MICHAEL, physician; b. Chgo., May 7, 1946; s. Albert S. and Minnetta Elizabeth (Nichols) H.; 1 child, Kathryn Gyo Hammer. BS, U. Ill., 1968; MD, Stanford U., 1973. Diplomate Am. Bd. Family Practice. Intern L.A. County-U. So. Calif. Med. Ctr., 1973-74; med. dir. Long Beach (Calif.) Health Dept. Drug Program, 1974-75; resident in family medicine Contra Costa Med. Svcs., Martinez, Calif., 1975-77; pvt. practice in family medicine Redondo Beach (Calif.) Med. Group, 1977-81, Family Practice Assocs., Torrance, Calif., 1981-96, Med. Inst. Little Co. of Mary Hosp., Torrance, 1996—; lectr. in field. Bd. trustees Peninsula Edn. Found., Palos Verdes, Calif., 1991—; bd. examiners Malcolm Baldridge Nat. Quality Awards, 1999. Mem. Am. Coll. Physician Execs., Premier Health Med. Group (pres. 1991—), South Bay Ind. Physicians Med. Group (pres. emeritus), Soc. Chief Med. Officers, Phi Beta Kappa. Lutheran. Avocations: white water rafting, skiing, modern art collecting, swimming, writing. Office: Med Inst Little Co Mary Hosp 20911 Earl St Ste 400 Torrance CA 90503-4355

HAMMER, WADE BURKE, retired oral and maxillofacial surgeon, educator; b. Lakeland, Fla., Apr. 21, 1932; s. Orval Seown and Lilly Pearl (Wade) H.; m. Betty Dean Webb, June 22, 1956; children: Robert Burke Hammer, Joanna Wade Hammer Dykes. A.A., U. Fla., 1956; D.D.S., Emory U., 1960. Diplomate Am. Bd. Oral and Maxillofacial Surgery. Pvt. practice dentistry Orange Park, Fla., 1960-61; resident in oral and maxillofacial surgery U. Pa. Grad. Sch. Medicine, Phila., 1961-62, Grady Meml. Hosp., Atlanta and Emory U., 1962-65; practice dentistry specializing in oral and maxillofacial surgery Atlanta, 1965-68; mem. staff Med. Coll. of Ga. Hosp., Augusta; asst. prof. oral and maxillofacial surgery Med. Coll. Ga., Augusta, 1968-71, assoc. prof., 1971-75, prof., 1975-93, prof. emeritus oral and maxillofacial surgery, 1993; staff VA Hosp. Complex, Augusta, 1969-99; cons. Ft. Gordon Army Med. Ctr., 1970-93, Univ. Hosp., Augusta, 1968-93. Contbr. articles to profl. jours. Chmn. exec. com. Gen. Faculty Orgn. Med. Coll. Ga., 1988. With USN, 1950-54, col. USAR, 1976-92, ret. Decorated Legion of Merit, Meritorious Svc. medal, Army Commendation medal (5), Knight Hospitalar Order St. John of Jerusalem, Knight Sovereign Mil. Order of the Temple of Jerusalem. Fellow Am. Assn. Oral and Maxillofacial Surgeons (life), Am. Coll. Dentists, Am. Soc. Dental Anesthesiology; mem. ADA (life), Internat. Assn. Dental Rsch., Ga. Dental Assn., Ea. Dist. Dental Assn., Am. Assn. Dental Schs., Augusta Dental Soc., Ga. Soc. Oral and Maxillofacial Surgeons, Southeastern Soc. Oral and Maxillofacial Surgeons (pres. 1984-85), Res. Officers Assn. (Nat. Dental Surgeon 1990-92, Dept. of Ga. Pres. 1998-99), Interallied Confedn. of Res. Officers (US. del. 1992—), Assn. Mil. Surgeons, USCG Aux., Exptl. Aircraft Assn., Am. Legion, VFW, U.S. Army Order Mil. Merit, U.S. Sailing Assn., Boat-U.S., The Ret. Officers Assn., Sigma Xi, Omicron Kappa Upsilon (pres. Supreme chpt. 1980-81). Methodist.

HAMMER, WILLIAM ROY, paleontologist, educator; b. Detroit, Nov. 15, 1949. BS, Wayne State U., 1971, MS, 1973, PhD, 1979. Asst. prof. geology Wayne State U., Detroit, 1980-81; asst. prof. geology Augustana Coll., Rock Island, Ill., 1981-87, assoc. prof., 1987-94, prof., chair dept. geology, dir. Fryxell Geology Mus., 1988—, Fritiof Fryxell endowed chair, 1998—; rsch. assoc. Field Mus. Natural History, Chgo., 1993—; prin. investigator grants for Antarctic Rsch. NSF, Washington, 1981—; Am. Assn. Petroleum Geologists Disting. lectr., 1996-97. Contbr. articles to profl. jours.; contbg. author to 12 books and 3 field guidebooks. Mem. AAAS (mem.-at-large com. on geology and geography 1998—), Soc. Vertebrate Paleontology (chair Skinner prize com. 1998—), Paleontological Soc. (chair N/C sect. 1989-90), Soc. Econ. Paleontologists and Mineralogists (v.p. Great Lakes sect. 1985-86). Achievements include discovery of many new fossil reptiles and amphibians from Antarctica, including the first Jurassic dinosaurs from that continent. Office: Augustana Coll Dept Geology Rock Island IL 61201

HAMMERLE, FREDRIC JOSEPH, metal processing executive; b. Newark, Jan. 2, 1944; s. Fredric Frank and Catherine G. (Wankmuller) H.; m. Nancy Elizabeth Looby, June 16, 1979; children: Oliver, Dora. BA, Rutgers U., 1966, MBA, 1967. Prodn. mgr. Engelhard Corp., Plainville, Mass., 1967-72, group v.p., 1978-86; v.p. mfg. Franklin Mint Corp., Franklin Center, Pa., 1972-78; exec. v.p., chief operating officer Stern Metals, Inc., Attleboro, Mass., 1986—; bd. dirs., treas. Internat. Precious Metals Inst. Referee Amateur Hockey Assn. U.S., 1980—; bd. dirs., sec. Sturdy Meml. Hosp., 1989—. Sgt. USMCR, 1966-72. Mem. Mfg. Jewelers Silversmiths of Am. (bd. dirs. 1983—, pres.), Gold Filled Assn. (bd. dirs. 1980—, sec., pres.), Boston Jewelers Club (bd. dirs. 1995—), 24 Karat Club N.Y., Jewelry Info. Ctr., Silver Users Assn. (bd. dirs. 1985—, pres.), Bass Anglers Sportsman Soc. (Montgomery, Ala.). Roman Catholic. Avocations: ice hockey, restoring autos, fishing. Office: Stern Metals Inc 110 Mossberg Dr Attleboro MA 02703-4632

HAMMERLINDL, DONALD JAMES, petroleum consultant; b. Milden, Sask., Can., July 31, 1944; came to U.S., 1968; s. Joseph Harold and Winnifred Jane (Adams) H. BS in Engring., U. Wyo., 1970. Ops. engr. ARCO Oil and Gas, Corpus Christi, Tex., 1970-73; reservoir engr. ARCO Oil and Gas, Dallas, 1973-80; chief engr. Triton Energy, Dallas, 1980-81; pres. Toltec Royalty, Dallas, 1981-82; v.p. DeGolyer and MacNaughton, Dallas, 1983—. Contbr. articles to profl. jours. Mem. Soc. Petroleum Engrs. (disting.), The Petroleum Soc., Assn. Profl. Engrs., Geologists and Geophysicists of Alta., Tex. State Bd. Registration of Profl. Engrs., Calgary Petroleum Club, The Hickory Creek Hunt. Avocation: horses. Home: 1721 Spring Lake Dr Arlington TX 76012 Office: DeGolyer and MacNaughton 400 One Energy Sq Dallas TX 75206

HAMMERMAN, MARC RANDALL, nephrologist, educator; b. St. Louis, Sept. 29, 1947; s. Elmer and Lillian (Gaylor) H.; m. Nancy Tutt, Aug. 9, 1974; children: Seth, Megan. AB, Washington U., St. Louis, 1969, MD, 1972. Intern Barnes Hosp., St. Louis, 1972-73, resident, 1973-74; resident Mass. Gen. Hosp., Boston, 1976-77; instr. Washington U., St. Louis, 1977-78, asst. prof., 1979-84, assoc. prof., 1984-89, prof., 1989—, dir. renal div. Sch. Medicine, 1991—; mem. study sect. NIH, 1990-95; investigator Am. Heart Assn., 1984. Contbr. over 100 sci. articles, revs. to profl. pubs., chpts. to books. Lt. comdr. USPHS, 1974-76. NIH grantee, 1980—. Mem. Am. Fedn. for Clin. Rsch., Am. Soc. Clin. Investigation, Assn. Am. Physicians. Office: Washington U Sch Medicine Renal Div Box 8126 660 S Euclid Ave Saint Louis MO 63110-1010

HAMMERMAN, STEPHEN LAWRENCE, lawyer, financial services company executive; b. Bklyn., Apr. 18, 1938; s. David S. and Hannah (Chaimowitz) H.; m. Eleanor Draizen; children—Ira, Charles, Michael, Caryn. B.S. in Econs., U. Pa., 1959; LL.B., NYU, 1962. Bar: N.Y. 1962. Assoc. Dewey and Ballantine, N.Y.C., 1962-64; asst. U.S. Atty. U.S. Attys. Office, N.Y.C., 1964-68; assoc. Paul and Weiss, N.Y.C., 1968-69; sr. v.p., gen. counsel White, Weld & Co., N.Y.C., 1969-78; mng. dir., gen. counsel Merrill Lynch-White Weld Capital Markets, N.Y.C., 1978-79; N.Y. regional adminstr. SEC, N.Y.C., 1979-81; asst. to pres., v.p., gen. counsel Merrill Lynch, Pierce, Fenner & Smith Inc., N.Y.C., 1981-84; sr. v.p., gen. counsel Merrill Lynch & Co. Inc., N.Y.C., 1984-85, exec. v.p., officer, gen. counsel, 1985-92, vice chmn., gen. counsel, 1992—; dir. Merrill Lynch & Co., N.Y.C., 1985—. Author: Securities Law Techniques, 1985. Mem. N.Y. Stock Exchange (legal adv. com.), Securities Industry Assn. (fed. regulation com), N.Y.C. Bar Assn. (investment com. chmn.). Home: 1495 Bay Blvd Atlantic Beach NY 11509-1648 Office: Merrill Lynch & Co Inc World Fin Ctr 250 Vesey St Fl 4 New York NY 10080-0002*

HAMMERSCHMIDT, JOHN PAUL, retired congressman, lumber company executive; b. Harrison, AR, May 4, 1922; s. Arthur Paul and Junie (Taylor) H.; m. Virginia Sharp; 1 child, John Arthur. Student, The Citadel, U. Ark., Okla. State U. Chmn. bd. Hammerschmidt Lumber Co., Harrison, 1946-84; mem. 90th-102d Congresses from 3d Ark. Dist., 1967-93; mem. Pub. Works and Transp. Com., 1967-93, ranking mem., 1987-93; mem. V.A. Com., 1967-93, ranking mem., 1973-86; bd. dirs. 1st Fed. Bank of Ark.; bd. dirs. Dillard's Dept. Store, Southwestern Energy Co., Am. Freightways; bd. trustees U. of the Ozarks; mem. adv. bd. Winrock Internat.; chmn. N.W. Ark. Coun.; state chmn. Ark. Citizen of Yr. Com.; mem. Presdl. Commn. on Aviation Security and Terrorism; mem. Claude and Mildred Pepper Found., 1989-90 (PVA Speedy award), bd. Met. Washington Airports Authority. Chmn. Ark. Republican Com., 1964-66; mem. Rep. Nat. Finance Com., 1960-64, nat. Rep. committeeman from, Ark., 1976-80; mem. Harrison City Coun., 1948, 60, 62. Served as pilot USAAF, World War II, CBI. Decorated Air medal with 4 oak leaf clusters, D.F.C. with 3 oak leaf clusters, 3 Battle Stars, The China War Meml. medal, Meritorious Svc. award VFW Congl. award, Silver Helmet award, Nat. Order Trenchrats Legis. Svc. award, Award for Life Svc. to Vets.; named. Ark. Citizen of Yr., 1991, Ark. Aerospace Found. Hall of Fame, 1991. Mem. Ark. Lumber Dealers Assn. (past pres.), Midwest Lumbermens Assn. (past pres.), Harrison C. of C. (named Man of Yr. 1965), Am. Legion. Presbyn. (ordained elder, deacon). Lodges: Masons (33 degree-Grand Cross), Shriners, Jesters, Elks, Rotary (past pres. Harrison).

HAMMERSCHMIDT, MARILYN KAY, health services administrator; b. Belpre, Kans., Mar. 28, 1944; d. Lawrence Ferdinand and Frances Elizabeth (Schmitt) Koett; m. Harold Francis Hammerschmidt, Dec. 1, 1973; children: Kevin Frances, Brian James. BSN, St. Mary of the Plains Coll., 1969. RN, Colo., Kans. Staff nurse Great Bend (Kans.) Med. Ctr., 1967-68; relief charge nurse St. Anthony's Hosp., Dodge City, Kans., 1968-69; county health nurse Pawnee County Health Dept., Larned, Kans., 1969-71; pub. health nurse Wichita (Kans.) Sedge County Health Dept., 1971-72; relief charge nurse orthopaedics Wesley Med. Ctr., Wichita, 1972-73; home health nurse St. Frances Home Health, Grand Island, Nebr., 1976-77; evening charge nurse orthopaedics-pediats. Ft. Hamilton Hughes Hosp., Hamilton, Ohio, 1984-88; nursing supr. home health Am. Nursing Care, Cin., 1988-92; dir. health svcs. Lakewood (Colo.) Meridian Retirement Comty., 1992—; mem. nursing adv. bd. Red Rocks C.C., Denver, 1994, 95. Author: (tape) Care of Death and Dying, 1991. Democrat. Roman Catholic. Avocations: crafts, sewing, Tai Chi Chih, water aerobics. Home: 8970 W Portland Ave Littleton CO 80128-8011

HAMMES, GORDON G., chemistry educator; b. Fond du Lac, Wis., Aug. 10, 1934; s. Jacob and Betty (Sadoff) H.; m. Judith Ellen Frank, June 14, 1959; children: Laura Anne, Stephen R., Sharon Lyn. A.B., Princeton, 1956; Ph.D., U. Wis., 1959. NSF postdoctoral fellow Max Planck Inst. fur physikalische Chemie, Göttingen, Germany, 1959-60; from instr. to assoc. prof. Mass. Inst. Tech., Cambridge, 1960-65; prof. Cornell U., Ithaca, N.Y., 1965-88; chmn. dept. chemistry Cornell U., 1970-75, Horace White prof. chemistry and biochemistry, 1975-88, dir. biotech. program, 1983-88; prof. U. Calif., Santa Barbara, 1988-91, vice chancellor, 1988-91; prof. Duke U., Durham, N.C., 1991—; vice chancellor Duke U. Med. Ctr., Durham, N.C., 1991-98; univ. disting. svc. prof. biochemistry Duke U., Durham, N.C., 1996—; mem. physiol. chemistry sect., phys. biochemistry study sect., Tng. grant com. NIH; bd. counselors Nat. Cancer Inst., 1976-80; mem. adv. coun. chemistry dept., Princeton, 1970-75, Poly. Inst. N.Y., 1977-78, Boston U., 1977-92; mem. NRC, U.S. nat. com. for biochemistry, 1989-95. Author: Principles of Chemical Kinetics, Enzyme Catalysis and Regulation, (with I. Amdur) Chemical Kinetics: Principles and Selected Topics; editor: Biochemistry, 1992—; also articles. NSF sr. postdoctoral fellow, 1968-69; NIH Fogarty scholar, 1975-76. Mem. NAS, Am. Acad. Arts and Scis., Am. Chem. Soc. (award biol. chemistry 1967, editorial bd. jours., exec. com. div. phys. chemistry 1976-79, exec. com. div. biol. chemistry 1977-88, com. profl. tng. 1985-92, task force on biotech. 1989-90), Am. Soc. Biochemistry and Molecular Biology (coun., editorial bd. jour. pres.), Phi Beta Kappa, Sigma Xi, Phi Lambda Upsilon. Home: 11 Staley Pl Durham NC 27705-2421

HAMMESFAHR, ROBERT WINTER, lawyer; b. Pittsfield, Mass., May 17, 1954; s. Frederick W. and Patricia Lue (Winter) H.; m. Susan J. Gardner (dec.); 1 child, Scott Gardner. BA, Colgate U., 1975; JD, Northwestern U., Chgo., 1978. Bar: Ill. 1978, U.S. Dist. Ct. (no. dist.) Ill. 1978, N.Y. 1991, U.S. Supreme Ct. 1989. Ptnr. Blatt, Hammesfahr & Eaton, Chgo., 1994-97, mng. ptnr., 1997—. Author: (with others) Punitive Damages: A Guide to the Insurability of Punitive Damages in the United States and Its Territories, 1988, Punitive Damages: A State-By-State Guide to Law and Practice, 1991, (pocket parts 1993, 96, Japanese edit., 1995), The Law of Reinsurance Claims, 1994, Supplement 1997; chmn. editl. bd. Andrews Internat. Reins. Dispute Reporter; contbr. articles to profl. jours. Mem. ABA, Chgo. Bar Assn. Avocations: tennis, skiing. Office: Blatt Hammesfahr & Eaton 333 W Wacker Dr Ste 1900 Chicago IL 60606-1226

HAMMILL, DICK, advertising and marketing executive. Sr. v.p. mktg. and comm. The Home Depot, Inc., Atlanta. Office: The Home Depot Inc 2455 Paces Ferry Rd SE Atlanta GA 30339-4024*

HAMMILLER, RUTH ELLEN, school psychologist; b. Burlington, Wis., May 6, 1952; d. Cyril Charles and Marion Frances (Rhodes) H. BS in Elem. Edn., U. Wis., Whitewater, Wis., 1974, MS in Edn. in Sch. Psychology, 1982, Sch. Psychologist Letter of Recognition, 1983; PhD in Ednl. Adminstrn., U. Wis., Madison, Wis., 1994. Cert. education, sch. psychologist, ednl. adminstr., Ind. Tour guide Nestle Co., Burlington, Wis., 1970-74; tchr. Brodhead (Wis.) Pub. Schs., 1974-82; vocat. guidance counselor U. Wis., Whitewater, 1982-83, grad. asst., 1982-83; tchr. Brodhead (Wis.) Pub. Schs., 1983-84; testing coord. Lake Mills (Wis.) Pub. Schs., 1989-91; program asst. U. Wis.-Edn. Adminstrns., Madison, 1992-93; sch. psychologist Lake Mills (Wis.) Pub. Schs., 1984-99; dir. pupil svcs. Palmyra (Wis.)-Eagle Area Sch. Dist., 1999—; psychol. cons. Divsn. on Ch. and Ministry-S.W. Assn. United Ch. of Christ, Madison, 1995—. Contbr. articles to profl. jours. Youth ministries mem., chair First Congl. Ch., Fort Atkinson, 1984-90, vice-moderator, 1992-93, 150th anniversary chairperson, 1991-92, long range planning chairperson, 1990-91, diaconat mem., 1994-99, vice-moderator, 1999—. Recipient Arvil S. Barr fellowship U. Wis., 1993-94, Netzer-Eye scholarship, 1992-93, UCEA Grad. Student Seminar award U. Coun. Ednl. Adminstrs., 1993,. Mem. NEA, Am. Ednl. Rsch. Assn. (rsch. evaluator 1993—) (Nat. Grad. Student Rsch. Seminar award 1993), Nat. Assn. Sch. Psychologists, Wis. Assn. Sch. Psychologist, Wis. Edn. Assn., Phi Kappa Phi, Kappa Delta Phi, Psi Chi C Honor Soc. Avocations: music, golf, travel, writing, reading. Home: 1125 Seminole Dr Fort Atkinson WI 53538-1083 Office: Palmyra Eagle Area Sch Dist PO Box 901 Palmyra WI 53156

HAMMON, NORMAN HAROLD, fundraising counsel and development consultant; b. McAlester, Okla., Dec. 26, 1952; s. Duane E. and Mary Maxine (Donley) H.; m. Sheryl L. Martin, 1994. AA in Sociology, Tulsa Jr. Coll., 1974; BSW, U. Okla., 1977, MSW, 1978; ed. grantwriting tng. program, Funding Ctr., Oklahoma City, 1984; peer adv. program cons. tng., Mid Am. Arts Aliance, Kansas City, Mo., 1993. Presentance investigator Mcpl. Ct., Tulsa, 1971-72; exec. dir. Open Line Crisis Ctr., Tulsa, 1970-74; asst. dir. Number Nyne Crisis Ctr., U. Okla., Norman, 1975-76; bus. mgr., co-founder Street Players Theatre, Norman, Okla., 1980-85, devel. dir., 1985-88; cons. fund raising, devel. and planning Hammon & Assocs., Norman, 1985—; cons. profl. orgns., including Jazz in June Ann. Festival, 1988, Okla. Shakespeare in the Park, 1990—, Sta. KGOU Pub. Radio, I. Okla., 1990, others; condr. workshops and seminars various non-profit orgns., 1994—; advisor funding devel., proposal writer various non-profit orgns., 1978—; prodr., bus. mgr. 2X4 Prodns., Norman. Contbr. articles to area newspaper, profl. pubs.; author: (book) Fund Raising . . . for the rest of us, 1998. Human rights commr. City of Norman, 1978-81, mem. arts roundtable for design of arts grants program, 1980; mem. City Coun., Norman, 1981-83; co-designer ind. artists/emerging orgns. grant program Norman Arts and Humanities Coun., 1981, chair Roundtable, 1986; project assistance panelist/evaluator Okla. Arts Coun., 1986-89, mem., 1991—; trainer/cons. client svcs. delivery team Ctr. Non-Profit Mgmt. Recipient Mayor's Proclamation in Appreciation for Svc., City of Norman, 1988. Mem. Okla. Cmty. Theatre Assn. (bd. dirs. 1989, mem. cons.-in-residence program, condr. seminars 1987, 89, Officer of Yr. 1989). Democrat. Mem. Christian Ch. (Disciples of Christ). Avocations: camping, hiking, cycling, geography, reading. Office: Hammon & Assocs PO Box 2356 Norman OK 73070-2356

HAMMOND, BENJAMIN FRANKLIN, microbiologist, educator; b. Austin, Tex., Feb. 28, 1934; s. Virgil Thomas and Helen Marguerite (Smith) H. B.A., U. Kans., 1954; D.D.S., Meharry Med. Coll., 1958; Ph.D., U. Pa., 1962. Mem. faculty U. Pa. Sch. Dental Medicine, Phila., 1958—, prof. microbiology, 1970—, chmn. dept., 1972-85; Pres.'s lectr. U. Pa., 1981, assoc. dean acad. affairs, 1984, dir. periodontal microbiology lab., 1985—; prof. of medicine, dir. oral microbiology testing svc. lab. Med. Coll. Pa., 1991—; mem. oral biology and medicine study sect. NIH, 1972-75, 95-99; mem. Nat. Adv. Dental Rsch. Coun., 1975—; Ralph Metcalf disting. vis. prof. Marquette U., 1986; disting. lectr. U. Paul Sabatier, Toulouse, France, 1991. Recipient USPHS Research Career Devel. award, 1965, Lindback award U. Pa., 1969; Silver medal City of Paris, 1978; NIH grantee, 1981—. Mem. Am. Soc. Microbiology, Internat. Assn. Dental Rsch. (E.H. Hatton award 1959), Am. Assn. Dental Rsch.(pres. 1978-79), Coll. Physicians of Phila., Phila. Mus. Art (trustee), The Phila. Club. Home: 560 N 23rd St Philadelphia PA 19130-3132

HAMMOND, BILL, publishing executive; b. Boston, Nov. 5, 1947. BA, Groton U., 1970; MA, Babson Coll., 1984. Sales rep. Little Brown & Co., Boston, 1974-76, asst. sales mgr., 1976-78, nat. sales mgr., 1978-81; mng. dir. Concord (Mass.) Pub., 1985-94; pub. Hazelden Pub. & Edn., Center City, Minn., 1995—. Office: Hazelden Pub & Edn Box 176 15251 Pleasant Valaay Rd Center City MN 55012-0176*

HAMMOND, BLAINE RANDOL, priest; b. Lincoln, Nebr., Oct. 30, 1946; s. Blaine Gibson and Mary Eloise (Carlson) H.; m. Elizabeth Dianne Forbes, Sept. 18, 1965; children: Dawn Marie, Sheila Dianne, Justin David. BA in English, U. Wash., Seattle, 1979; MDiv, Iliff Sch. Theology, 1982; cert. Anglican studies, Ch. Divinity Sch. of Pacific, 1988. Ordained deacon Episcopal Ch., 1988; priest, 1989. Vicar St. Irenaeus Episcopal Mission, Lyons, Colo., 1988-89; interim rector Christ Episcopal Ch., Castle Rock, Colo., 1989, curate, 1989-91; chmn., founder peace and justice com. Diocese of Colo., 1989-91; mem. world peace and global affairs com. Colo. Coun. Chs., Denver, 1988-90. Co-founder Colo. Coalition on Religion and the Environment, 1989. Home: 4000 Clayton Rd Concord CA 94521-2617 *We have such a strong tendency to see religion as a scientific inquiry. But to me, it can only be understood as poetry—the poetry of relationship.*

HAMMOND, CHARLES AINLEY, clergyman; b. Asheville, N.C., Aug. 7, 1933; s. George Bradley and Eleanor Maria (Gantz) H.; m. Barbro Stigsdotter Laurell, July 16, 1960; children: Stig Bradley, Inga Allison. B.A., Occidental Coll., Los Angeles, 1955; B.D., Princeton Theol. Sem., 1958; D.D., Missouri Valley Coll., 1981, Wabash Coll., 1982. Ordained to ministry United Presbyn. Ch., 1958; pastor chs. in Pa. and Calif., 1958-75; exec. presbyter Presbytery Wabash Valley, West Lafayette, Ind., 1975-87, Presbytery Phila., 1987-98; int. pastor 192d gen. assembly United Presbyn. Ch., New Providence, N.J., 1998—; moderator 192d gen. assembly United Presbyn. Ch., 1980-81; chmn. Gen. Assembly Mission Coun., 1982-83. Author: Newtonian Polity in an Age of Relativity, 1977, Seven Deadly Sins of Dissent, 1979. Sec. Hallam (Pa.) Borough Planning Commn., 1962-64, Westchester Cmty. Plans, L.A., 1966-68, Pasadena (Calif.) Planning Commn., 1971-75; chmn. pvt. land use com., 1972-73, chmn. pub. land use com., 1973-74; mem. Presbyn. Ch. (U.S.A.), 1983-91; bd. dirs. Met. Coun. Chs. of Phila., 1990-95; trustee Beaver Coll., 1991—; gen. assembly Permanent Jud. Com., 1995—; mem. bd. corporators Pres. Min. Found. Recipient Disting. Alumnus award Princeton Theol. Sem., 1981. Mem. Assn. Presbyn. Ch. Educators, Friends of Old Pine (trustee). Republican. Club: Union League (Phila.), Athaneum (Phila.). Office: 2200 Locust St Philadelphia PA 19103-5511

HAMMOND, CHARLES BESSELLIEU, obstetrician, gynecologist, educator; b. Ft. Leavenworth, Kans., July 24, 1936; s. Claude G. and Alice (Sims) H.; m. Peggy A. Hammond, jUne 21, 1958; children: Sharon L., Charles B. BS, The Citadel, 1957, Duke U., 1961. Diplomate Am. Bd. Ob-Gyn. Intern in surgery Duke U., 1961-62, resident in ob-gyn, 1962-63, 66-69, fellow in reproductive endocrinology, 1963-64, asst. prof. dept. ob-gyn, 1969-73, assoc. prof., 1973-78, prof., 1978-81, E.C. Hamblen prof., 1981—, chmn., 1980—. Contbr. in field. Served with USPHS, 1964-66. Fellow (hon.) Royal Coll. Ob-gyn (ad eundeum), 1998; mem. Am. Fertility Soc. (pres. 1985), Am. Coll. Ob.-Gyn. (chmn. dist. IV 1997-2000), Am. Assn. Ob-Gyn. Found. (pres. 1996—), Assn. Profs. Obstetrics and Gynecology, Am. Gynecol. and Obstet. Soc. (pres. 1993-94), Soc. Gynecol. Investigation, N.C. Med. Soc., N.C. Soc. Obstetricians and Gynecologists (pres. 1985), Am. Gynecol. Club (pres. 1994). Presbyterian. Home: 2827 Mcdowell Rd Durham NC 27705-5604 Office: Duke U Med Ctr PO Box 3244 Durham NC 27715-3244

HAMMOND, C(LARKE) RANDOLPH, healthcare executive; b. Anniston, Ala., July 3, 1945; s. Clarke MacAlpin and Edna Odell (Webb) H.; m. Carolyn Jane Milam, Oct. 26, 1974; children: Chadwick, Kyle, Amanda. BS in BA, U. So. Miss., 1968; M.Health Adminstrn., U. Ala., Birmingham, 1978. CPA, Ark. Asst. adminstr., controller Helena (Ark.) Hosp., 1971-74; asst. adminstr. S. Highlands Hosp., Birmingham, 1974-77; adminstr. Brookwood Health Svcs., Rocky Mt., N.C., 1977-79; v.p. ops. Brookwood Health Svcs., Birmingham, 1979-81; pres., CEO Medlab, Birmingham, 1981-88; asst. v.p. Hoffman-LaRoche, Birmingham, 1988-90; sr. v.p., Roche Biomed. Lab., Birmingham, 1988-90; v.p. Jemison Investment Co., Birmingham, 1990-92; CEO, pres. Textile Resource & Mktg., Dalton, Ga., 1990-92; COO, sr. v.p. ops. Diagnostic Health Corp., Birmingham, 1992-94; sr. v.p. ops. Healthsouth Corp., 1994-95; pres., CEO Monitor MEDX, Inc., Birmingham, 1996-97; CEO Mens Focus Health Ctrs., Inc., Birmingham, 1997-98; COO Mens Focus Health Ctrs., Inc., 1998—; bd. dirs. Med Occ, Birmingham, Ala., Kustom Threads, Birmingham, Puckett Labs., Hattiesburg, Miss. Pres. Diabetes Trust Fund, Birmingham, 1989, bd. dirs., 1984-89; chmn. deacons Valleydale Bapt. Ch., Birmingham, 1983, strategic planning com., 1983; chmn. bd. Liberty Recreation Ctr., Inc., Pensacola, 1989—. With USN, 1968-70. Mem. Am. Assn. Health Care Execs., Health Fin. Mgmt. Assn., U. Ala. Health Adminstrs. Alumni Soc. (pres. 1989), U. Ala. Alumni Assn. (bd. dirs. 1988-90), The Club, Shoal Creek Golf Club, N. River Yacht Club, Inverness Country Club, Greystone Country Club. Republican. Baptist. Avocations: flying, scuba diving. Home: 1011 Greymoor Rd Birmingham AL 35242-7210 Office: Mens Focus Health Ctr Inc 100 Corporate Rdg N Ste 104 Birmingham AL 35242-5415

HAMMOND, DAVID ALAN, stage director, educator; b. N.Y.C., June 3, 1948; s. Jack and Elizabeth Alida (Furno) H. B.A. magna cum laude, Harvard U., 1970; M.F.A., Carnegie-Mellon U., 1972. Mem. faculty Juilliard Theatre Center, N.Y.C., 1972-74; asst. conservatory dir. Am. Conservatory Theatre, San Francisco, 1974-81; assoc. stage dir. Am. Conservatory Theatre, 1974-78; dir. Summer Tng. Congress, 1976-80, resident stage dir., 1979-81; adj. assoc. prof. acting and directing Yale Sch. Drama, New Haven, 1981-85; adj. prof. dept. dramatic art U. N.C., Chapel Hill, 1985-88, prof., 1988—; artistic dir. PlayMakers Repertory Co., Chapel Hill, 1985-92, assoc. producing dir., 1992-99; guest artist Pacific Conservatory Performing Arts, 1976, U. Wash., 1977, SUNY, Purchase, 1979; guest dir. Aspen Music Festival, Colo., 1974-75, San Francisco Opera, 1978, Carmel (Calif.) Bach Festival, 1979-80, Sherwood Shakespeare Festival, Oxnard, Calif., 1981, Valley Shakespeare Festival, Saratoga, Calif., 1984, 86, 88, Shakespeare Festival of Dallas, 1990, Teatro Alianza, Montevideo, 1992, 94, 97, Teatro El Galpon, Montevideo, 1995, Opera Co. N.C., 1998, 99; resident dir. Yale Repertory Theatre, New Haven, 1981-85; dir. Roundabout Theatre, N.Y.C., 1983; Arts Am. cultural specialist U.S. Info. Svc., 1992, 94. Recipient Drama-Logue Critics award, L.A., 1980, 81, Florencio award, Montevideo, Uruguay, 1992. Mem. Soc. Stage Dirs. and Choreographers, Actors' Equity, Am. Guild Mus. Artists, Nat. Theater Conf. Office: PlayMakers Repertory Co 203 N Graham St # 3235cb Chapel Hill NC 27516-2208

HAMMOND, DONALD LEROY, computer company executive; b. Kansas City, Mo., Aug. 7, 1927; s. Clark E. and Laila G. (Morris) H.; m. Kathryn Shinkmay, Aug. 21, 1949; children—Debora Ruth, Katherine Eileen, Carol Linda, Nancy Louise, Paul David. B.S. in Physics, Colo. State U., 1950, M.S., 1952, D.Sc. (hon.), 1974; D.Sc. (hon.), Bristol U., 1987. Chief crystal rsch. U.S. Army Electronics, Ft. Monmouth, N.J., 1952-56; dir. rsch. Sci. Electronic Products, Loveland, Colo., 1956-59; mgr. precision crystals time and frequency Hewlett-Packard Labs., Palo Alto, Calif., 1959-64, mgr. phys. rsch. and devel., 1964-66, dir. phys. elec. lab., 1966-79, dir. physics rsch. ctr., 1979-84, dir. Europe rsch. ctr., 1984-86, acting dir., 1986-87, dep. dir. corporate devel., 1987-88; mem. CB Sawyer Frequency Control Symposium, 1970; bd. dirs. several corps. Mem. bd. edn. Palo Unified Sch. Dist., 1971-81, also pres. Served as ensign USN, 1945-52. Fellow IEEE; mem. NAE, Am. Inst. Physics. Home: 12660 Corte Madera Ln Los Altos CA 94022-2614

HAMMOND, EDWARD H., university president; b. McAllen, Tex., May 4, 1944; s. Will J. and Bergit A. (Lund) H.; m. Vivian hammeke, Aug. 26, 1967; children: Kelly Edvidge, Lance Edward, Julie Marie. BS in Speech, Kans.

State Tchrs. Coll., 1966, MS, 1967; PhD, U. MO., 1971. Asst. dir. of field svcs. Kans. State Tchrs. Coll., Emporia, 1966-67; dir. student affairs Purdue U. North Cen. campus, Westville, Ind., 1967-68; counselor housing office U. Mo., Columbia, 1969-70; asst. dean of students So. Ill. U., Carbondale, 1970, asst. to pres. for student rels., 1970-73; v.p. student affairs Seton Hall U., S. Orange, N.J., 1973-76, U. Louisville, 1976-87; pres. Fort Hays State U., Hays, Kans., 1987—; chair bd. trustees Boost Alcohol Consciousness Concerning the Health of U. Students of the U.S. Inc., 1987-93; trustee The Lincoln Found., 1979-87; mem. Inter-Assn. Task Force on Coll. Alcohol Abuse and Misuse, 1984—; vis. faculty mem. Ind. U., Bloomington, 1972-83; cons. in field. Contbr. articles to profl. jours. NDEA fellow U. Mo., 1968-70; named to Mid-Am. Edn. Hall of Fame, 1997. Mem. Am. Coun. on Edn., Am. Assn. State Colls. and Univs., Am. Assn. Univ. Adminstrs., Nat. Assn. Student Pers. Adminstrs. (nat. pres. 1983, John Jones award 1986), Kans. C. of C. and Industry (bd. dirs. 1990—), Pi Kappa Delta, Sigma Phi Epsilon. Avocations: golf, racquetball, water sports, tennis. Office: Fort Hays State U 600 Park St Bldg 1 Hays KS 67601-4099

HAMMOND, FRANK JEFFERSON, III, lawyer; b. Moss Point, Miss., Sept. 18, 1953; s. Frank Jefferson Jr. and Jane (Laird) H.; m. Gale Ray, May 30, 1975; children—Katharine Blakeney, Benjamin Laird. B.B.A., U. Miss., 1974, J.D., 1976; LL.M., U. Fla., 1978. Bar: Miss. 1977, U.S. Dist. Ct. (no. dist.) Miss. 1977, U.S. Dist. Ct. (so. dist.) Miss. 1977, U.S. Ct. Appeals (5th cir.) 1977, U.S. Tax Ct. 1978, U.S. Ct. Appeals (11th cir.) 1980, U.S. Supreme Ct. 1989. Mem. Corlew, Krebs & Hammond, P.A., Pascagoula, Miss., 1978-84; mem. Watkins & Eager, PLLC, Jackson, Miss., 1984—; adj. prof. U. Ala. Sch. Law, Mobile, 1983; adj. faculty U. So. Miss., Gautier, 1983-84; bd. dirs. Merchants and Marine Bank, Pascagoula, Miss. Trustee Dantzler Meml. Meth. Ch., Moss Point, Miss., 1981-84. U. Fla. Grad. Council fellow, 1977; Richard B. Stephens scholar, 1978. Mem. ABA, Miss. State Bar (chmn. sect. estates and trusts 1988-89), Phi Kappa Phi, Beta Alpha Psi, Beta Gamma Sigma, Omicron Delta Kappa. Home: PO Box 650 Jackson MS 39205-0650 Office: Watkins & Eager PLLC 400 E Capitol St Ste 300 Jackson MS 39201-2610

HAMMOND, GEORGE SIMMS, chemist, consultant; b. Auburn, Maine, May 22, 1921; s. Oswald Kenric and Marjorie (Thomas) H.; m. Marian Reese, June 8, 1945 (div. 1977); children: Kenric, Janet, Steven, Barbara, Jeremy; m. Eva L. Menger, May 22, 1977; stepchildren—Kirsten Menger-Anderson, Lenore Menger-Anderson. BS, Bates Coll., 1963; MS, PhD, Harvard U., 1947; DSc (hon.), Wittenberg U., 1972, Bates Coll., 1973; Dr. honoris causa, U. Ghent, 1973, Georgetown U., 1985, Bowling Green State U., 1990, Weizman Inst. Sci., 1993. Postdoctoral fellow UCLA, 1947-48; mem. faculty Iowa State Coll., 1948-58, prof. chemistry, 1956-58; vis. assoc. prof. U. Ill., summer 1953; prof. organic chemistry Calif. Inst. Tech., Pasadena, 1958-72; div. chemistry and chem. engring. Calif. Inst. Tech., 1968-72; Arthur Amos Noyes prof. chemistry; vice chancellor natural scis. U. Calif.-Santa Cruz, 1972-74, prof. chemistry, 1972-78; exec. dir. for biosci., metals and ceramics Allied Corp., Morristown, N.J., 1978-88; cons., 1988—; mem. chem. adv. panel NSF, 1962-65; fgn. sec. Nat. Acad. Scis., 1974-78. Author: (with J. S. Fritz) Quantitative Organic Analysis, 1956, (with D.J. Cram) Organic Chemistry, 1958, (with J. Osteryoung, T. Crawford and H. Gray) Models in Chemical Science, 1971; co-editor: Advances in Photochemistry, 1961; mem. editorial bd. Jour. Am. Chem. Soc, 1967—. Recipient James Flack Norris award in phys. organic chemistry, 1968, National Medal of Science, 1994. Mem. NAS (foreign soc.), Am. Chem. Soc. (award in petroleum chemistry 1960, Priestly medal 1976, Nat. medal of sci. 1994, Seaborg medal 1994), Am. Acad. Arts and Scis., Materials Rsch. Soc., Inter-Am. Photochem. Soc., European Photochem. Soc., Phi Beta Kappa, Sigma Xi. Home: 930 SW 197th Ave Beaverton OR 97006-2471

HAMMOND, GLENN BARRY, SR., lawyer, electrical engineer; b. Roanoke, Va., Sept. 3, 1947; s. Howard Reichard and Billie (Cromer) H.; m. Vickie McComb, Dec. 29, 1973 (div.); 1 child, Glenn Barry II. BA, Va. Mil. Inst., 1969; MBA, So. Ill. U., 1974; JD, U. Richmond, 1978; BS elec. engring., Nova Coll., 1995. Bar: Va. 1979, U.S. Dist. Ct. (we. dist.) Va. 1979, U.S. Ct. Appeals (4th cir.) 1981, U.S. Ct. Mil. Appeals 1989, Air Force Ct. Mil. Rev. 1989, U.S. Supreme Ct., 1992. Assoc. Wilson, Hawthorne & Vogel, Roanoke, 1978-79; pvt. practice Roanoke, 1979-80, 86—; atty., advisor to chief adminstrv. law judge Social Security Adminstrn., HHS, Roanoke, 1980-86; ptnr. Wooten & Hart P.C., 1995-98; pres. R.F. Cons., Inc., Roanoke, Va., 1998—; pres. LCH Broadcasting Group, Inc. Roanoke, also bd. dirs. Editor: Psychiatry in Military Law, 1988. Sr. vice comdr. Mil. Order World Wars, Roanoke, 1981. Col. JAGC, USAF, 1969-75, Res. 1975—. Mem. Air Command Assn. (life), DAV (life), VFW (life), AFA (life), Nat. Mil. Intelligence Assn. (life), Armed Forces Comms. Electronics Assn., Nat. Orgn. Social Security Claimants Reps., Masons. Office: 1612 Tinker Mountain Rd Troutville VA 24175

HAMMOND, HERBERT J., lawyer; b. Santa Fe, May 19, 1951. BS magna cum laude, U. N.Mex., 1973; JD, NYU, 1976. Bar: Tex. 1977, U.S. Patent and Trademark Office 1977, U.S. Dist. Ct. (no., so., we. and ea. dists.) Tex. 1977, U.S. Dist. Ct. Nebr. 1985, U.S. Dist. Ct. Wis. (ea. dist.) 1987, U.S. Ct. Appeals (5th and 11th cirs.) Tex. 1981, U.S. Ct. Appeals (fed. cir.) Tex. 1982, U.S. Tax Ct. 1983, U.S. Claims Ct. 1987. Shareholder Thompson & Knight, Dallas. Contbr. to law jours. Mem. State Bar Tex. (vice chmn. com. on computerization of the profession 1989-92, chair computer sect. 1994-95, newsletter editor computer sect.), Am. Intellectual Property Law Assn., Dallas Bar Assn. (chair intellectual property sect. 1998), Phi Beta Kappa, Phi Kappa Phi, Kappa Mu Epsilon. Office: Thompson & Knight 1700 Pacific Ave Ste 3300 Dallas TX 75201-4693

HAMMOND, HOWARD DAVID, retired botanist and editor; b. Phila., Feb. 10, 1924; s. Clarence Elwood Jr. and Myrtle Iva (Sprowles) H.; m. Sarah Lichtenberg, Apr. 30, 1955; 1 child, Julia Ethel. BS, Rutgers U., 1945, MS, 1947; PhD, U. Pa., 1952. Asst. prof. U. Del., Newark, 1957-58, Howard U., Washington, 1958-68; from asst. prof. to assoc. prof. SUNY, Brockport, 1968-83; assoc. editor N.Y. Bot. Garden, Bronx, 1984-92. Co-editor: Floristic Inventory Tropical Countries, 1989, Southwestern Rare and Endangered Plants: Proceedings of the Second Conference/USDA Forest Service, 1996. Vol. Deaver Herbarium, No. Ariz. U., 1993—; mem. pub. art adv. com. City of Flagstaff, 1996—; adj. curator botany Mus. No. Ariz., 1998—. Mem. Am. Inst. Biol. Scis., Bot. Soc. Am., Torrey Bot. Soc.(editor 1976-82, 87-92, pres. 1992), Sigma Xi. Home: 4025 Lake Mary Rd Apt 33 Flagstaff AZ 86001-8608

HAMMOND, ISAAC WILLIAM, physician, epidemiologist; b. Cape Coast, Ghana, Mar. 17, 1951; s. Charles Williams and Beatrice Hammond; m. Marilyn Barker, June 11, 1977 (div. May 1981); 1 child, Allotey; m. Hoora Rahimi, Aug. 31, 1982; children: Mohammed, Mustafa, Reza, Mahjub, Sarah. BS, Calif. State U., 1976; MPH, Ind. State U., 1979; PhD, U. Okla., 1982; MD, U. Fla., 1989. Fellow U. Okla. Health Sci. Ctr., Oklahoma City, 1979-82; NIH fellow Cornell U. Med. Ctr., N.Y.C., N.Y., 1982-84; intern, resident Emory U. Med. sch., Atlanta, 1989-92; resident Tulane U. Med. Sch., New Orleans, 1992-93; staff physician, dir. hypertension clin. VA Med. Ctr., New Orleans, 1993-96; adj. assoc. prof. Tulane U. Sch. Pub. Health & Tropical Medicine, 1994-98; pres., dir. clin. rsch., dir. outcomes rsch. and disease state mgmt. Am. Rsch. Assocs., 1996—; reviewer FDA, 1996-98, Eli Lilly & Co., 1998—; assoc. prof. Ind. U., 1999—, U. North Tex., 1997—. Grantee NIH, Astra-Merck, Am. Heart Assn., WHO, Nat. Heart, Lung & Blood Inst. Mem. AMA, Am. Coll. Physicians, Am. Fedn. Clin. Rsch., Am. Soc. Hypertension, Am. Soc. Internal Medicine, Internat. Soc. Hypertension in Blacks, Nat. Med. Assn., N.Y. Acad. Sci., Royal Soc. Health, Soc. Epidemiol. Rsch., Soc. Gen. Internal Medicine, So. Med. Assn. Office: Am Rsch Assocs PO Box 3572 Carmel IN 46033

HAMMOND, J. D., university dean, insurance executive; b. Maitland, Mo., Nov. 14, 1933; s. William Byron and Lillian Irene (Goodpasture) H.; m. Marian Jane Idle, Aug. 20, 1960; children: Nancy Lee, Michael James. AB, N.W. Mo. State U., 1955; PhD, U. Pa., 1961. Asst. prof. econs. Ohio State U., Columbus, 1959-64, assoc. prof. bus. adminstrn., 1964-69, prof. ins., 1969-82, William Elliot prof. ins., 1982-86, William Elliot endowed chairholder, 1986—; dean Smeal Coll. Bus. Adminstrn. Pa. State U., University Park, 1989—; pres. Risk Theory Seminar, 1973-74; bd. dirs. Atlantic Mut. Ins. Co., Penn State Rsch. Found.; disinterested trustee Scudder, Steven & Clark, 1985—, Scudder Vairable Life Fund, 1985—, Scudder Pathway Fund, 1997—, Scudder Instl. Fund, 1997—; chmn. workforce diversity task force Am. Assembly Collegiate Schs. of Bus., 1993. Chair campaign Pa. chpt. United Way. Office: Smeal Coll Bus Admnistrn Pa State U 801 Business Admin Bldg University Park PA 16802-3008

HAMMOND, JEROME JERALD, government program administrator, agricultural economist; b. Davenport, Wash., Mar. 16, 1942; s. Gerald Hammond and Mary Avis (Felton) Koch; m. Melissa Martin, Aug. 27, 1991. AA, Skagit Valley Coll., 1963; BA in Econs., Ctrl. Wash. U., 1968; PhD in Agrl. Econs., Wash. State U., 1974. Cert. total quality mgmt. facilitator ODI, 1990-91. Economist Econ. Rsch. Svc. U.S. Dept. Agr., Washington, 1974-77; leader Asia programs Office Internat. Cooperation and Devel., 1977-80; dir. divsn. internat. conservation Soil Conservation Svc., 1980-94; dir. resource econs. and social scis. divsn. USDA Natural Resources Conservation Svc., 1995-97, dir. internat. program divsn., 1997—; tech. mem. Sci. and Tech. Exch. Negotiating Team, Sofia, Bulgaria, Bucharest, Romania, Budapest, Hungary, 1985; agy. rep. U.S. Agrl. Attache Conf., Manila, 1980, mem. sci. and tech. exch. agrl. working group meetings, Paris and Bonn, Germany, 1983, Bucharest, Romania, 1987; U.S. del. UN-FAO Conf., Arusha, Tanzania, 1978, New Delhi, 1980; profl. assoc. East-West Ctr., Honolulu, 1985; cert. candidate Sr. Exec. SVc., U.S. Office Pers. Mgmt., 1988. Contbr. numerous articles and reports to profl. jours.; spkr. in field; mem. Intermountain Econ. Rev., assoc. editor, 1969-70. Agy. coord. Combined Fed. Campaign, Washington, 1979; divsn. rep. ARC, Washington, 1980-81; dep. chmn. EEOC Soil Conservation Svc., Washington, 1985; legis. fellow Office U.S. Senator Thad Cochran, 1989. Staff sgt. USAF, 1963-67. Recipient Cert. of Merit, USDA, 1975, 82, 89, 97, Combined Fed. Campaign-Honor award Sec. of Agr., 1979, Meritorious Svc. award Soil Conservation Svc., 1984, Agy. coord. savs. bond campaign, 1992, award patriotism U.S. Savs. Bond program Sec. of Treasury, 1985, 92, Internat. Honor award USDA Office Internat. Coop. and Devel., 1986, CFC Spl. Svc. award Sec. of Energy, 1989, Cert. Recognition Sec. Vet. Affairs, 1990. Fellow Am. Agrl. Econs. Assn., Soil and Water Conservation Soc. (sec. Washington chpt. 1988, pres.-elect 1990, pres. 1991, chmn. internat. activities com. 198-92, Commendation award 1989, Outstanding Svc. award 1991); mem. World Assn. Soil and Water Conservation (regional v.p. for N.Am. 1988-94, 97—), Chinese Soil and Water Conservation Soc., Resource Policy Consortium (sec.-treas. 1996-97, vice chair 1997-98, chair 1998-99), USDA Economists Group (pres. 1997, 98), Am. Legion. Presbyterian. Avocations: running, hiking, gardening, hunting, fishing. Home: 8413 Ft Hunt Rd Alexandria VA 22308-1839 Office: USDA Natural Resources Conservation Svc PO Box 2890 Washington DC 20013-2890

HAMMOND, JUDITH ANNE, family nurse practitioner; b. Newburgh, N.Y., Jan. 2, 1945; d. Barney and Violet (Cervoni) Carfarone; children: Michael, Teresa. Diploma, St. Francis Hosp. Sch. Nursing, Poughkeepsie, N.Y., 1966; BSN cum laude, Mt. St. Mary Coll., Newburgh, 1982; MS in Family Primary Care, Pace U., 1990. RN, cert. nurse practitioner in family health, sch. nurse-tchr. Staff nurse St. Luke's Hosp., Newburgh, 1966-69; pvt. duty nursing, 1974-75; sch. health nurse Mt. St. Mary Coll., Newburgh, 1976-79; occupational health nurse IBM Corp., Poughkeepsie, 1984-85, 87-88; nurse practitioner, sch. nurse-tchr. Newburgh Enlarged City Sch. Dist., 1989—; adj. instr. Dutchess Community Coll., Poughkeepsie, 1988-89, coord. nursing/health-related program, 1989. Mem. ANA, N.Y. State Nurses Assn., Nat. Assn. Sch. Nurses, N.Y. State Coalition of Nurse Practitioners, Am. Acad. Nurse Practitioners, Sigma Theta Tau Internat. (Mu Epsilon chpt., Zeta Omega chpt.).

HAMMOND, JUDY MCLAIN, business services executive; b. Downey, Calif., June 24, 1956; d. Ernest Richard and Bernice Elaine (Thompson) McLain; m. Dennis Francis Hammond, Aug. 15, 1981. BS in Mgmt., Pepperdine U., 1982; MBA, U. So. Calif., 1986. Br. mgr. Kelly Svcs., Encino, Calif., 1978-81; mktg. mgr. Payco Am. Corp., Encino, 1981-83, GC Svcs. Corp., Santa Ana, Calif., 1983-86; pres. Resource Mgmt. Svcs. Inc., Norwalk, Calif., 1986—; founder, pres. The Debt Marketplace, Inc., Norwalk, 1994—; founder, pres. The Debt Marketplace, Inc., 1994—; cons., expert in collection and recovery. Author: Collect More From Collection Agencies. Mem. Toastmasters. Avocations: scuba diving, underwater photography. Office: 10440 Pioneer Blvd Ste 2 Santa Fe Springs CA 90670-8235

HAMMOND, KAREN SMITH, marketing professional, paralegal; b. Baton Rouge, Dec. 20, 1954; d. James Wilbur Smith and Carolyn (May) Carper; m. Ralph Edwin Hammond, Dec. 17, 1985. Student, La. State U., 1973-75, Colo. Women's Coll., 1976; BJ, U. Colo., 1978; cert. paralegal, U. Tex., 1981. Newspaper reporter Lakewood (Colo.) Sentinel, 1978; paralegal Office U.S. Atty. No. Dist. Tex.; sales rep. Arlington Citizen Jour. newspaper, 1979-80; legal asst. Oscar H. Mauzy Atty.-at-Law, Dallas, 1981; editor Ennis (Tex.) Press, 1981-82; sales rep. VEU Subscription TV, Dallas, 1983-84; comml. account rep. U.S. Telecom, Dallas, 1984; with The Movie Channel/Showtime, 1985; mktg. rep. Allnet Comm., Dallas, 1985-87, ChemLawn Svcs. Inc., Plano, Tex., 1992, Accuroof, 1994, Diversified Info. Svcs., Plano, 1994, Elite Roofing, Plano, 1994—; advt. sales rep. Legal Asst. Today Mag., 1987; sales rep. Telecable Inc., Richardson, Tex., 1988-91; account exec. Brewer Comm., Carrollton, Tex., 1988-89, Plano (Tex.) Cellular, 1989-90; telemktg. sales Toyota of Dallas, 1995—; salesperson Linkcell, 1996-98; with Sears Home Improvement, 1998—; salesperson Publishing Concepts, Dallas; triex agt. Pkwy. Pontiac, Dallas, 1983-86; free lance writer Dallas Metro mag., 1991—. Bus. writer Mid-Cities Daily News, 1981. Campaign mgr. Mark Bielamowicz for Mayor, Cedar Hill, Tex., 1979; active campaigns Martin Frost for U.S. Congress, Dallas, 1978, Jimmy Carter for Pres., Ft. Worth, 1980, Ann Richards for Gov., Tex., 1990; vol. Clinton/Gore Reelection Campaign, 1996, Collin County Dem. Party, vol. George McGovern for Pres. campaign, 1972. Mem. NAFE, NOW, Women in Comms. (fin. com. 1979), Dallas Assn. Legal Assts., Soc. Profl. Journalist, Dallas C. of C., Nat. Org. for Women. Democrat. Home: PO Box 14139 Arlington TX 76094-1139 Address: 439 Bowen Rd # 30 Arlington TX 76012

HAMMOND, KATHLEEN ANN, nutrition support dietitian and nurse; b. Lowell, Mass., Jan. 18, 1960; d. Louis D. and Vera M. (Scalph) Pesce; m. Maxwell Hammond, May 25, 1991; children: Matthew Scott, Mark Lee. Diploma, Piedmont Hosp. Sch. Nursing, 1981; BS, U. Ga., 1985, MS, 1987; BSN, 1994. RN, Ga.; cert. nutrition support nurse., nutrition support dietitian. Staff nurse med.-surg. and ICU Clayton Gen. Hosp., Riverdale, Ga., 1981-85; staff nurse Piedmont Hosp., Atlanta, 1987-90; nutrition support nurse DeKalb Med. Ctr., Decatur, Ga., 1988-92; dir. clin. edn. Home Nutritional Svcs., Marietta, 1992-94; cons. in field Lilburn, Ga., 1994—; continuing edn. coord. Nations Healthcare, 1995—; clin. instr. nutrition support U. Ga., Athens, 1987—; lectr. nursing Shallowford Ctr., Dunwoody, Ga., 1992-96; course dir. nutrition physician asst. program Emory U. Contbg. author: (booklet) Groshong, Kickman and Port Catheters, 1991, Transitional Feedings in Nursing Core Curriculum, Am. Soc. Parenteral and Enteral Nutrition, 1995, Guidelines for Nutrition Care, 1996, Contemporary Nutrition Support Practices, 1998, Quick Reference to Clinical Dietetics, 1997, Physical Assessment in Nursing Clinics, 1997, Physical Assessment in A.S.P.E.N. Nutrition Support Practice Manual, 1998; contbr. article to Internat. Jour. Nutrition. Mem. Am. Soc. Parenteral and Enteral Nutrition, Ga. Area Soc. Parenteral and Enter Nutrition (pres. 1992-93, bd. dirs. 1994—), Sigma Xi. Home: 4063 Deerbrook Way SW Lilburn GA 30047-3220

HAMMOND, KEN, newspaper magazine editor. Editor Texas Magazine, Houston Chronicle, Tex. Office: Houston Chronicle Pub Co 801 Texas Ave Houston TX 77002-2996

HAMMOND, LAUREN ROCHELLE, senate consultant; b. L.A., Nov. 27, 1955; d. David Frederick and Percy Winona (McIntyre) H. BA in Govt., Calif. State U., Sacramento, 1977; AA in Gen. Edn., Sacramento City Coll., 1977; postgrad., U. of Pacific, 1978-81. Fellow State Atty. Gen., Sacramento, 1980-81; asst. spl. svcs. Calif. Senate, Sacramento, 1981-85, prodn. asst. newsletter program, 1985-88, adminstrv. asst. rules com., 1988-93, cons. rules com., 1993—; cons. Sacramento County Bd. Edn., 1992; advisor various Dem. candidates L.A., Sacramento, 1991-96; mem. Assembly Dist. 9 Com. Mem. County Health Coun., Sacramento, 1994; treas. African Am. caucus Calif. Dem. Party, 1994-96; vice chair, commr. County Project Planning Com., Sacramento, 1995-97; del. Dem. Nat. Conv., Chgo., 1996; elected mem. Sacramento City Coun., Dist. 5, 1997, re-elected, 1998. Recipient Cmty. Svc. award Women's Civic Improvement Club, Sacramento, 1992. Mem. NAACP, Africa's Daughters Rising PAC (founding officer, sec. 1993-95), Calif. State U. Sacramento Alumni Assn. (Svc. award 1993). Roman Catholic. Avocations: softball, golf, recreational boating, computers. Office: Senate Rules Com Calif Legislature 1020 N St Ste 255 Sacramento CA 95814-5624 also: City Hall Rm 205 Sacramento CA 95814-2672

HAMMOND, LOU RENA CHARLOTTE, public relations executive; b. Muenster, Tex.; d. Louis Martin and Regina L. (Schoech) Wolf; m. Christopher Weymouth Hammond, Sept. 6, 1964; 1 child, Stephen. BA, U. Houston, 1962. Rep. pub. rels. Pan Am. Airways, N.Y.C., 1968-76, mgr. pub. rels., 1977-79, dir. pub. rels., 1980-81, dir. pub. affairs, 1981; pres., ptnr. Taylor and Hammond, N.Y.C., 1981-84; prin., pres. Lou Hammond and Assocs., N.Y.C., 1984—; mem. adv. bd. Ctr. for Tourism and Travel at NYU. Editor: (calendar) Avenue mag., 1976-79. Mem. Women's Bd. of Madison Sq. Boys and Girls Club, N.Y.C. Recipient Matrix award in pub. rels., 1992, Winthrop W. Grice award Hotel Sales and Mktg. Assoc. Internat., 1992, Inside PR Mag.'s All-Star award, 1992. Mem. Soc. Am. Travel Writers, Fashion Group, Assn. Better N.Y., Les DAmes de Escoffier, Women's Forum, Women Execs. in Pub. Rels., Doubles Club. Roman Catholic. Avocations: bridge, tennis, 18th Century antiques. E-mail: louh@lhammond.com. Office: Lou Hammond & Assocs Inc 39 E 51st St New York NY 10022-5916

HAMMOND, MARGARET, lawyer; b. Winterville, N.C., June 2, 1949; d. Hoyt and Mary Hammond. BS, N.C. A&T State U., 1971; MA, Atlanta U., 1983; JD, Loyola U., New Orleans, 1984. Bar: La. 1984, U.S. Dist. Ct. (ea. dist.) La. 1987. Instr. polit. sci. N.C. A&T State U., Greensboro, 1973-76, So. U., New Orleans, 1979-82; edn. cons. Edn. Services and Programs Inc., New Orleans, 1982-84, Loyola U., New Orleans, 1982-84; asst. dist. atty. Parish of Orleans, New Orleans, 1984-86; staff atty. Orleans Indigent Defender Program, New Orleans, 1986-92; pvt. practice New Orleans, 1986—. Ford Found. fellow, 1971-73, Earl Warren Found. fellow, 1981-84. Mem. La. Bar Assn., New Orleans Bar Assn., Sorority Inc., Alpha Kappa Alpha. Democrat. Avocations: travel, music. Office: 200 Commercial Sq Slidell LA 70460

HAMMOND, MICHAEL PETER, music educator, dean; b. Kenosha, Wis., June 13, 1932; s. Laurence Cyril and Beatrice Jean (Slater) H.; m. Anne Lilley, June 11, 1966; children: Benjamin, Thomas. BA in Classics and Philosophy with honors, Lawrence U., 1954, LHD (hon.), 1975; postgrad., Delhi (India) U., 1954-55; BA with honors, Oxford (Eng.) U., 1959, MA, 1961; postgrad., U. Wis., 1963. Research fellow neuroanatomy U. Wis., 1959, instr. physiology, 1963; NIH postdoctoral research fellow med. sch. Marquette U., Milw., 1962-63; instr. music theory, ensemble condr., asst. to dir. Music for Youth, Milw., 1964-65; dir. composition studies, instr. orchestration, dir. Wis. Conservatory Music, Milw., 1966-68; assoc. prof. music SUNY, Purchase, 1968-70, prof., 1970-86, dean music, 1968-77, acting dean of dance, 1976-77, coll. pres., 1977-80, mem. Chancellor's Council Pres.'s, 1977-86; Elma Schneider prof. music, dean music Rice U., Houston, 1986—; rector Prague Mozart Acad., 1991—; condr. Ars Musica Chamber Orch., 1969-71, Milw. Civic Orch., 1966-68; asst. condr. Am. Symphony Orch., 1969-71; condr., music dir. Bergen (N.J.) Philharm., 1972-74; condr. Dessoff Choir, N.Y.C., 1973-84, Canticum Vocal Ensemble, Houston, 1988—; composer in residence Milw. Repertory Theater, 1963-68; rector Prague Mozart Acad., 1991—. Compositions include: Canticum Novum - Chamber Cantata for four soloists, chorus and five instruments, 1969, Three Pieces for two oboes, 1969, Sonatina for piano, 1968, Merchant of Venice - music for the play, 1966, Under Milkwood - songs and settings for the play, 1966, Puntila - keyboard music and songs for the play, 1966, Amphytrion 38 - harp music for the play, 1965, Homage and Variations on the Name Bach - for lg. orch., 1970, And Death Shall Have No Dominion for tenor, chorus and piano, 1979, Performing verse translation of Berlioz L'Enfance du Christ, 1990. Rotary Found. Internat. fellow, 1954-55, HEW fellow, India, 1976; Rhodes scholar, 1959. Mem. Am. Symphony Orch. League. Office: Rice U Shepherd Sch Music Office of the Dean PO Box 1892t # S532 Houston TX 77251*

HAMMOND, NORMAN DAVID CURLE, archaeology educator, researcher; b. Brighton, Eng., July 10, 1944. BA, U. Cambridge, Eng., 1966, Diploma in Classical Archaeology, 1967, MA, 1970, PhD, 1972, ScD, 1987, DSc (hon.), 1999. Rsch. faculty Cambridge U., Eng., 1967-75; faculty Bradford U., Eng., 1975-77; vis. prof. Rutgers U., 1977-78, faculty, 1978-88, assoc. prof., 1978-84, prof., 1984-88; member staff Peabody Mus., Harvard U., 1988—; prof. archaeology Boston U., 1988—; vis. prof. U. Calif., Berkeley, 1977, Jilin U., China, 1981, Calif. Acad. Sci., 1984-85, U. Paris, 1987, Acad. Scis., USSR, 1991, U. Bonn, 1994; vis. faculty U. Cambridge, 1981-82, 91, 96-97, U. Oxford, 1989; archaeology corr. The Times, London (Press award, Brit. Archaeol. Awards 1994, 98), 1967—; field work in North Africa, Afghanistan, Greece, Guatemala, Belize, Ecuador; disting. lectr. Montana State U., 1996, Bushnell lectr. Cambridge U., 1997, Stone lectr. Arch. Inst. of Am., 1998. Author: (with F.R. Allchin) The Archaeology of Afghanistan, 1977, (with G.R. Willey) Maya Archaeology and Ethnohistory, 1979, Ancient Maya Civilization, 1982, 5th edit., 1994, various foreign edits., Cuello: An Early Maya Community in Belize, 1991; numerous monographs on excavations in No. Belize, 1973, 75, 76, Lubaantun, 1975, Nohmul, 1985; gen. editor: Procs., 44th Internat. Congress of Americanists, 1982-84. Dumbarton Oaks fellow, 1988; Rockefeller Found. scholar, 1997. Fellow Royal Asiatic Soc., Soc. Antiquaries London, British Acad. Office: Boston Univ Dept Archaeology 675 Commonwealth Ave Boston MA 02215-1406

HAMMOND, PAUL YOUNG, political scientist, educator; b. Salt Lake City, Feb. 24, 1929; s. James Thaddeus and Hortense Clair (Young) H.; m. Merylyn Felt Simmons, Aug. 29, 1950; children: Paul Brett, Wendy Simmons, Robyn Simmons, Spencer Blair, Clifford Simmons. B.A., U. Utah, 1949; M.A., Harvard U., 1951, Ph.D., 1953; postgrad. Fulbright scholar, London Sch. Econs., 1952-53. Instr. govt. Harvard U., Cambridge, Mass., 1953-55; lectr. Columbia U., N.Y.C., 1956-57; asst. prof. polit. sci. Yale U., New Haven, 1957-62; research asso. Washington Center Fgn. Policy Research, Johns Hopkins U., 1962-64; mem. research staff Rand Corp., Santa Monica, Calif., 1964-76; head social sci. dept. Rand Corp., 1973-76; vis. research polit. scientist U. Calif., Berkeley, 1971-72; Edward R. Weidlein prof. environ. and pub. policy studies U. Pitts., 1976-83, disting. service prof. pub. and internat. affairs, 1983—; dir. Ridgway Ctr. of Internat. Security Studies, 1988-91, Energy and Environ. Center, 1979-81; Fulbright rsch. prof. Inst. of S.E. Asian Studies, Singapore, 1993-94; lectr. U. Tex., U. So. Calif., U. Calif., Santa Barbara and Los Angeles; cons. in field. Author: Organizing for Defense: The Adminstration of the American Military Establishment, 1961, The Cold War Years: American Foreign Policy Since 1945, 1969, Cold War and Detente: The American Foreign Policy Process Since 1945, 1975, NATO Strategic Planning: Preparations That Do No Harm, 1988, Fulfilling the Promise of the Goldwater-Nichols Act: Operational Planning and Command, 1989, NATO: The Infrastructure of Reassurance, 1989, What Future For the U.S. Military Presence in Europe, 1990, LBJ and the Presidential Management of Foreign Relations, 1992, Towards a Workable European Architecture: Political-Military Problems in the New Europe, 1994, Doing Without America?, 1996, On Taking Peacekeeping Seriously, 1997, Culture Versus Civilization: A Critique of Huntington, 1997; co-author: The American Civil-Military Decisions, 1963, Information System Applications for a High Level Staff, 1972, Social Choice and Soviet Strategic Decision Making, 1977, Regional Energy Policy Alternatives, 1977, Administration of Security Assistance: Systems and Process, 1978, Individual Energy Conservation Behaviors, 1980, The Reluctant Supplier, 1983, Alternative Organizational Structures for NATO, 1992; co-editor: Political Dynamics in the Middle East, 1971. Forrestal fellow in naval history, 1955, Stimson Fund fellow Yale U., 1959, Rockefeller fellow in internat. studies, 1963-64, Fulbright fellow Singapore, 1993; Fulbright scholar London Sch. Econs., 1952-53. Mem. Am. Polit. Sci. Assn., Internat. Studies Assn., Internat Inst. Strategic Studies. Mem. LDS Ch. Office: Grad Sch Pub & Internat Affairs Forbes Quadrangle University of Pittsburgh Pittsburgh PA 15260

HAMMOND, R. PHILIP, chemical engineer; b. Creston, Iowa, May 28, 1916; s. Robert Hugh and Helen Hammond; m. Amy L. Farmer, Feb. 28, 1941 (div. 1969); children: Allen L., David M., Jean Phyllis, Stanley W.; m.

Vivienne Fox, 1972. BSChemE, U. So. Calif., 1938; Ph.D. in Phys. and Inorganic Chemistry (Naval Research fellow), U. Chgo., 1947. Registered profl. engr., Ill., Calif. Chief chemist Lindsay Chem. Co., West Chicago, Ill., 1938-46; group leader Los Alamos Sci. Lab., 1947-62, assoc. div. leader reactor devel. div., 1960-62; dir. nuclear desalination program Oak Ridge Nat. Lab., 1962-73; adj. prof. U. Calif. at Los Angeles, 1972—; head energy group R & D Assos. Corp., Santa Monica, Calif., 1973-83; desalination cons., 1987—; leader advanced sea water evaporator design Met. Water Dist. of So. Calif., L.A., 1989—. Author articles on nuclear power reactors, nuclear wastes, reactor safety econs., energy centers, metallurgy of plutonium and refractory metals, rare earths, radiation chemistry, remote control engring.; contbr. to fusion energy concept using underground containment, to Ency. Brit. Mem. U.S. delegation Conf. on Peaceful Uses Atomic Energy, Geneva, Switzerland, 1955, 65, 71, IAEA Panel on Desalination, Vienna, Austria, 1964, 65, 66, 71; mem. U.S. team to USSR on desalination, 1964. Mem. Am. Nuclear Soc. (charter), Am. Chem. Soc., Am. Inst. Chem. Engrs., Sigma Xi, Phi Kappa Phi, Phi Lambda Upsilon. Achievements include patents for improved safety for high speed rail transport, for devices for preventing collisions at sea and for storing nuclear waste; orgination of advanced concepts in sea water evaporator construction, and efficient coupling to nuclear energy sources; design (with others) of advanced reactor containment system capable of withstanding melt-down accidents with zero leakage, and of automotive engine using liquid air and liquid natural gas as fuel. Home and Office: PO Box 3971 Laguna Hills CA 92654-3971 *With our achievements in desalination, efficient agriculture, and nuclear power, it is now clear that the food producing ability of the earth is not limited by technology. But our political and social institutions have not kept up. We are beset by poor leadership, indecision, tremendous waste and ignorance of the money value of time. Here is the challenge for youth.*

HAMMOND, RALPH CHARLES, real estate executive; b. Valley Head, Ala., Feb. 1, 1916; s. William Bleve and Alice Corina Jane (Holleman) H.; student Snead Jr. Coll., 1938-39, Berea Coll., 1940-41; AB, U. Ala., 1945; DLitt, Livingston U., 1992; m. Myra Leak, June 20, 1954; children—James, Ben. Press sec. to gov. Ala., Montgomery, 1946-50, exec. sec., 1955-59; gen. rep. ARC, Greensboro, N.C., 1950-54; mayor of Arab (Ala.), 1963-69; pres. City Ctr., Inc., Arab, 1959—. Commr. from Ala., U.S. Study Commn. S.E. River Basins, 1958-64; bd. dirs. Ala. Tb Assn., 1956-83, pres., 1972-74; hon. Christmas Seal chmn., Ala. Served with AUS, 1941-45. Commd. Poet Laureate of Ala., 1991-95; Paul Harris fellow Rotary Internat., 1992. Mem. Ky. Hist. Soc., Phillip Hamman Family Assn. Am. (pres. 1972-78), Ala. Poetry Soc. (pres. 1981-84, Ala. Poet of Yr. 1985), Ala. Writers' Conclave (pres. 1987-89), Nat. Fedn. State Poetry Socs. (treas. 1985-86, 2d v.p. 1990-92, 1st v.p. 1993-94, pres. 1994-96). Democrat. Methodist. Lodge: Masons. Author: My GI Aching Back, 1945; Ante Bellum Mansions of Alabama, 1951; Philip Hamman, Man of Valor, 1976; Song of Appalachia, 1982; How High the Stars, 1982; Upon the Wings of the Wind, 1982; One Golden Apple a Day, 1983; Collected Poems, 1983; Wisdom Is, 1984; Edging Through the Grass (Book of Yr. Ala. Poetry Soc.), 1985; editor: Alabama Poets: A Contemporary Anthology, 1989, A Blossoming of Sonnets, 1990, Upper Alabama-Poems Out of Light (George Washington Honor medal Freedoms Found. Valley Forge 1993, Book of Yr. award Ala. Poetry Soc. 1993), Crossing Many Rivers-Poems Along the Way, 1995 (Book of Yr. award Ala. Poetry Soc. 1995), Vincent Van Gogh--A Narrative Journey, 1997; contbr. short stories and feature articles to jours., mags.; poems pub. in 40 jours. Home: 1280 Guntersville Rd Arab AL 35016-1618 Office: PO Box 486 Arab AL 35016-0486

HAMMOND, ROBERT LEE, retired feed company executive; b. Farmington, Minn., Oct. 23, 1926; s. Lee L. and Mae Francis (Kingston) H.; m. Helene Germaine Haven, May 8, 1948; children—Robert Lee, Jr., Jane Kay Kipling. Student, U. Dubuque, 1944-45; student, Northwestern U., 1945-46. Co-owner Hammond Oil Co., Estherville, Iowa, 1952-60; asst. sales mgr. Golden Sun Feeds Inc., Estherville, Iowa, 1960-62; plant mgr. Golden Sun Feeds Inc., Des Moines, 1962-64; exec. v.p. sales mgr. Golden Sun Feeds Inc., Estherville, 1964-71, pres., 1971-88; bd. dirs. Golden Sun Feeds Inc., chmn. bd. 1988-91; chmn. bd. Am. Feed Industry Ins., 1987-91. Pres. Indsl. Devel. Commn., Estherville, 1966-67. Served with USN, 1944-46. Am. Feed Industry Assn. (dir., com. chmn. 1971-74, nat. chmn. 1986-87), Iowa Grain and Feed Assn. (dir., treas. 1969-72), Estherville C. of C. (dir. 1958-60). Republican. Episcopalian. Lodges: Elks, Masons, Rotary. Avocations: hunting; golf; fishing; travel.

HAMMOND, ROY JOSEPH, reinsurance company executive; b. St. Louis, Jan. 9, 1929; s. Edward Herman and Alvera Ann (Herzog) H.; m. Donna LaSalle Perkins, Apr. 12, 1951; children—Douglas Edward, Donald Erwin, Laura Ann Hammond Budniakiewicz. BS, Northwestern U., 1954; JD, DePaul U., Chgo., 1959. Bar: Ill. bar 1959. With Am. Mut. Reins. Co., Chgo., 1963-91; v.p., then sr. v.p., gen. counsel and sec. Am. Mut. Reins. Co., 1967-76, pres., chief exec. officer, bd. dirs., 1976-91; pres., chief exec. officer Whitehall Consts., Ltd., Camden, N.C., 1991—; pres. Wheeling (Ill.) Mcpl. Park Dist., 1963-65; past mem. Reins. Assn. Am., bd. dirs., 1976-86. Served with AUS, 1946-48. Mem. ABA, Ill. State Bar Assn., Internat. Assn. Def. Counsel, Fedn. Ins. and Corp. Counsel, Chgo. Casualty Adjusters Assn. (pres. 1972-73), Chgo. Yacht Club. Republican. Presbyterian. Home and Office: Whitehall Shores 201 Azalea Dr Camden NC 27921-6991

HAMMOND, TEENA GAY, editor; b. Louisville, Dec. 3, 1967; d. Jimmie Howard and Rosetta (Gay) H. Student, U. Louisville, 1985-87, Ariz. State U., 1989-93. Bus. reporter Bus. Jour., Phoenix, 1993-95; dir. mktg. and pub. rels. Murro Cons., Phoenix, 1995-96; bus. reporter Bus. Press, Ontario, Calif., 1996-97; West Coast retail editor Women's Wear Daily, Fairchild Publs., L.A., 1997—; West Coast fashion and features editor W mag., Fairchild Publs., L.A., 1997—. Recipient 1st place award for gen. reporting Ariz. Press Club, 1994, 1st place awward for sustained coverage series, 1994, 3rd place award for gen. reporting, 1994; 2d place award for journalistic achievement Ariz. Newspaper Assn., 1994. Avocations: skydiving, scuba, hiking. Office: 7th Fl 11100 Santa Monica Blvd Los Angeles CA 90025

HAMMOND, VERNON FRANCIS, school administrator; b. Grand Rapids, Mich., Sept. 27, 1931; s. Rodney Clyve and Wylida Helen (Bonner) H.; m. Anne Louise Seeley, Dec. 10, 1954; children; Michelle, Milissa, Milanie, Michael. BA, Bob Jones U., 1959, MA, 1960; postgrad., Butler U., 1968-69, Pepperdine U., 1969-72; MEd, Lynchburg Coll., 1975. Cert. ednl. adminstrn. Tchr., coach, vice prin. Cen. Bapt. Schs., Anaheim, Calif., 1963-68; tchr. Indpls. Christian Acad., 1968-69; tchr., coach Faith Bapt. Schs., Canoga Park, Calif., 1969-72; prin. Lynchburg (Va.) Christian Acad., 1972-75, Bethany Christian Sch., Troy, Mich., 1975-84, Heart to Heart Christian Acad., Phoenix, 1984-88; administr. Temple Christian Schs., Lakeland, Fla., 1989-97; girls head basketball coach Temple Christian Sch., 1990-97; instr. Ind. Bapt. Coll., Indpls., 1968-69, Lynchburg Bapt. Coll., 1973-75; sec.-treas. Mich. Assn. Christian Schs., Troy, 1982-83; bd. dirs. Western Fellowship Christian Schs., Phoenix, 1985-88; conv. spkr. Christian Edn. Assn., S.E., Pensacola, Fla.; founder, pres. Vand A Enterprises, 1994—. Del. Mich. Rep. Conv., 1980, 82; precinct del. Mich. Rep. Party, Troy, 1980-84; precinct leader Ariz. Rep. Party, Phoenix, 1986-89; bd. dirs. Bethany Villa, Troy, 1975-84. With USN, 1951-55. Coach of Fla. Christian Girls Conf. State Championship Basketball Team, 1993-94. Mem. adv. bd. Sketch Erickson Nat. Ministries, Lakeland, Fla., 1995—. Avocations: reading, gardening, woodworking, coaching.

HAMMOND, WELDON WOOLF, JR., hydrogeologist; b. San Antonio, May 17, 1937; s. Weldon Woolf and Thelma Evangeline (Vandever) H.; m. Linda Lou Cowden, Aug. 3, 1963; children: Weldon Woolf III, Rory Cowden. BA, U. Tex., 1960, MA, 1969, PhD, 1984. Geologist, dist. mgr. Tex. Water Devel. Bd., Austin, San Antonio, 1964-71; ecologist Alamo Area Coun. Govt., San Antonio, 1971-77; from lectr. to assoc. prof. U. Tex. San Antonio, 1977-90, dir. divsn. earth and phys. scis., 1993—, dir. ctr. water rsch., 1986—, McNutt Disting. prof. geology, 1999—; cons. San Antonio, 1979—; McNutt Disting. prof. geology, U. Tex. San Antonio, 1999—. Capt. USN, 1960-63, 90-91. Mem. Assn. Engring. Geologists, Geol. Soc. Am., Assn. Ground Water Scientists and Engrs., Internat. Assn. Hydrogeologists. Home: 4 Lazy Ln San Antonio TX 78209-2833 Office: Univ Tex San Antonio 6900 N Loop 1604 W San Antonio TX 78249-0663

HAMMOND-ALLEN, JEANETTE CAROL, operating room nurse; b. Bristow, Okla., Oct. 10, 1956; d. Willie Henry and Vivian Marcaine (Williams) H.; m. Horace Mike Allen. BS in Biology, Langston U., 1977; BSN, U. Okla., Oklahoma City, 1980; MS in Health Svcs. Adminstrn., Ctrl. Mich. U., 1989. CNOR. Commd. 2d lt. U.S. Army, 1980, advanced through grades to lt. col., 1997; staff nurse med.-surg. Letterman Army Med. Ctr., San Francisco, 1980-82, 121 Evacuation Hosp., Seoul, Korea, 1982-83; staff nurse oper. rm. Ireland Army Community Hosp., Ft. Knox, Ky., 1983-84, asst. chief oper. rm./ctrl. material svcs., 1985-86; head nurse oper. rm./ctrl. material svcs. 42d Field Hosp., Ft. Knox, 1984-86; staff nurse oper. rm. Tripler Army Med. Ctr., Honolulu, 1986-88, asst. chief ctrl. material svcs., 1988-89, chief ctrl. material svcs., 1989-90; head nurse oper. rm./ctrl. material svcs. McDonald Army Community Hosp., Ft. Eustis, Va., 1990-94; sr. clin. nurse oper. rm. Walter Reed Army Med. Ctr., Washington, 1994-97, chief ctrl. materiel svcs., 1997—; mem. 91 Delta operating rm. technician task selection bd. U.S. Army, Ft. Sam Houston, Tex., 1993, Tri-Svc. Standardization Bd., Ft. Detrick, Md., 1998—. Decorated Army Commendation medal, Achievement award, Meritorious Svc. medal. Baptist. Avocations: reading, gardening, cross stitching, crafts, computers. Office: Walter Reed Army Med Ctr Georgia Ave Washington DC 20307-5001

HAMMOND-BLESSING, DIANN A., elementary education educator; b. Cedar Rapids, Iowa, May 24, 1943; d. Russell Irving and Ola Arline (Leonard) Hammond; m. Dale Fredrick Blessing, June 10, 1979. BA in Edn., U. Wyo., 1966, MEd, 1973. Cert. elem. tchr., Colo. Tchr. German and social studies Deaver-Frannie Schs., Deaver, Wyo., 1966-68, Alliance (Nebr.) City Schs., 1968-70; tchr. elem. Jefferson County Schs., Arvada, Colo., 1971—; del. Colo. Del. Assembly, 1974-79; sec. Argonauts Investment Group, 1986-87, v.p., 1989, pres., 1990, treas.-elect, 1993, treas., 1994. Coauthor curriculum units Our Changing Langauge, 1978. mem. Record Keeping Task Force, Jefferson County, Colo., 1974-75, 84; del. Dem. County and State Convention, Colo., 1976, 80; mem. polit. action com. Jefferson County Schs., 1979-80; precint chair Dem. Com., Colo., 1984. Mem. NEA, AAUW (editor newspaper 1985-87), PTA, Internat. Reading Assn. (Colo. coun., Colo. Edn. Assn., Colo. Reading Assn., Jefferson County Edn. Assn. (mem. com., rep. 1973-82, 94-95, 96-97, 97-98, bd. dirs. 1974-79), Jefferson County Internat. Reading Assn., Instrnl. Profl. Devel. Avocations: special event and interior decorating, assembly and design of clothing, elegant crafts. Home: 6626 S Yukon Way Littleton CO 80123-3070 Office: Warder Elem Sch 7840 Carr Dr Arvada CO 80005-4420

HAMMOND-KOMINSKY, CYNTHIA CECELIA, optometrist; b. Dearborn, Mich., Sept. 1, 1957; d. Andrew and Angeline (Laorno) Kominsky; m. Theodore Glen Hammond, Sept. 21, 1985. Student Oakland U., Rochester, Mich., 1976-77; OD magna cum laude, Ferris Coll. Optometry, 1981. Lic. optometrist, Mich.; cert. diagnostic and therapeutic pharm. agt. Intern, Optometric Inst. and Clinic of Detroit, 1980, Ferris State Coll., Big Rapids, Mich., 1980, Jackson Prison (Mich.), 1981; assoc. in pvt. practice, Warren, Mich., 1981-82; optometrist Pearle Vision Ctr., Sterling Heights, Mich., 1982-87, K-Mart Optical Ctr., Sterling Heights, 1982-87, Royal Optical, Sterling Heights, 1988—; provided eye care to nursing homes, Mt. Clemens, Mich. Head vol. caregivers and organ donation programs St. Therese of Lisieux Ch., Shelby Twp., Mich. Inventer binocular low vision aid device. Avocations: music, sports, clogging, gardening, antique crystal. Home: 47626 Cheryl Ct Shelby Township MI 48315-4708 Office: Royal Optical Lakeside Mall 14300 Lakeside Cir Sterling Heights MI 48313-1326

HAMMONDS, TIMOTHY MERRILL, scientific association executive, economist; b. Cortland, N.Y., June 5, 1944; s. Robert Merrill and Helen Marie (Conrad) H.; m. Karen Stein, June 17, 1966; 1 child, Lynn Vanessa. MBA, Cornell U., 1967, PhD, 1970. Assoc. prof. agrl. econs. Oreg. State U., Corvallis, 1970-75; sr. v.p. Food Mktg. Inst., Washington, 1975-93, pres., CEO, 1993—; mem. bd. on agr. NAS, 1988-91; bd. dirs. Nat. Minority Supplier Devel. Coun., Acad. Food Mktg., St. Joseph's U., 1996—, Sloan Found. Ctr. for Retail Food Industry, U. Minn., 1995—; mem. adv. bd. Cornell U. Sch. Agrl. Econs., 1994—. Editor Agribus. Jour., 1985-93; mem. editl. bd. Am. Jour. Agrl. Econs., 1978-80; contbr. articles to profl. jours. Recipient Rainbow/PUSH Coalition Ptnrs. award, 1998; Mem. Am. Agrl. Econs. Assn., Phi Kappa Phi. Republican. Methodist. Office: Food Mktg Inst 800 Connecticut Ave NW Washington DC 20006-2709

HAMMONS, BRIAN KENT, lawyer, business executive; b. Wurzburg, Federal Republic Germany, Mar. 6, 1958; came to U.S. 1958; s. R. Dwain and Donna G. (Carender) H.; m. Kimberly M. Pflumm, July 26, 1980; children: April Michelle, David Dwain, Adam Carender. BS summa cum laude, S.W. Mo. State U., Springfield, 1980; JD cum laude, So. Meth. U., Dallas, 1985. Bar: Mo. 1985. Exec., treas., v.p. Hammons Products Co., Stockton, Mo., 1980-86; exec. v.p., sec. Hammons Products Co., 1987-96, pres., COO, 1997—; assoc. Stinson, Mag & Fizzell, Kansas City, Mo., 1986-87. Mem. Stockton Airport Bd., 1987-89, Stockton City Coun., 1989-91; cub scout leader Boy Scouts Am.; Sunday sch. tchr.; soccer coach. Mem. Mo. Bar Assn., Masons (sec. 1980-81), Lions (pres. 1990-91), Leadership Mo., Young Presidents Orgn., Phi Delta Phi. Republican. Methodist. Avocations: running, flying, tennis, golf, hunting, politics. Office: Hammons Products Co 105 Hammons Dr PO Box H Stockton MO 65785

HAMMONS, ERNST WILLIAM, public relations executive; b. Louisville, Sept. 8, 1937; s. William M. and Mary R. (Ernst) H.; m. Margaret McCloskey, Nov. 16, 1963 (div. 1984); children: James, Melanie, Michael, David. AB in Journalism, U. Ky., 1959. Asst. bus. editor Cin. Enquirer, 1962-65; asst. account exec. to v.p./client service mgr. Burson-Marsteller, Chgo., 1965-77, v.p./dir. editorial services, 1977-80, v.p./asst. to pres., 1977-83; sr. v.p. human resources Burson-Marsteller, N.Y.C., 1983-87, sr. v.p./dir. of tng. and devel. worldwide, 1987—. 1st lt. USAF, 1959-62. Recipient Golden Trumpet award Publicity Club, Chgo., 1970, 72, 74, 77; Cert. of Excellence Communications Collaborative, Chgo., 1976. Mem. Pub. Relations Soc. Am. (Silver Anvil award 1973, chmn. Chgo. Counselors Acad. 1979-81), Soc. Profl. Journalists, Am. Soc. Tng. and Devel. Democrat. Office: Burson-Marsteller 230 Park Ave S New York NY 10003-1513

HAMMONS, JAMES HUTCHINSON, chemistry educator, researcher; b. Chgo., Aug. 8, 1934; s. Harry Edgar and Rhoda Anita (Zimmermann) H.; m. Elisabeth Grant Netherwood, Aug. 18, 1956; children: Laura N., James B. B.A., Amherst Coll., 1956; M.A., Johns Hopkins U., 1958, Ph.D., 1962. Faculty Swarthmore Coll., Pa., 1964—, instr., 1964-66, asst. prof, 1966-70, assoc. prof., 1970-76, prof., 1976-97; prof. emeritus Swarthmore Coll., 1997—; chmn. dept. chemistry Swarthmore Coll., Pa., 1976-81, chmn. div. natural scis. and engring., 1986-87. Contbr. chpts. to publs. in field. Recipient NSF Coll. Faculty Rsch. Opportunity award U. Washington, 1989. Home: 17 Furness Ln Wallingford PA 19086-6057 Office: Swarthmore Coll Dept Chemistry 500 College Ave Ste 2 Swarthmore PA 19081-1390

HAMMONS, JOHN Q., hotel executive. Chmn., CEO John Q. Hammons Hotels, Inc. and Cos., Springfield, Mo. Office: John Q Hammons Hotels Inc & Cos #900 300 John Q Hammons Pkwy Springfield MO 65806

HAMNER, CHARLES, company executive. Pres. N.C. Bio-Tech. Ctr., Research Triangle Park, N.C. Office: PO Box 13547 Research Triangle Park NC 27709*

HAMNER, EUGENIE LAMBERT, English educator; b. Darlington, Ala., May 24, 1936; d. Robert Eugene Jr. and Helen (Burford) Lambert; m. Gustavus O. Hamner, 1966 (div. 1988); children: Helen Gaussen, Nicholas Feagin. BA in English & history, Huntingdon Coll., 1958; MA in English, U. N.C., 1959, PhD in English, 1965. Instr. English Winthrop Coll., Rock Hill, S.C., 1959-60; instr. U. N.C., Chapel Hill, 1963-64; asst. prof. Huntingdon Coll., Montgomery, Ala., 1964-65, U. Ga., Athens, 1965-66; from asst. prof. to prof. U. So. Ala., Mobile, 1969-96. Co-editor: Ways of Knowing: Essays on Marge Piercy, 1991, (children's book) A Kitten for Julie and Christopher, 1997. Bd. dirs. Mobile Mus. Art, 1984-88; mem. Mobile Hist. Devel. Commn., 1987-92; elem. sch. vol. Rolling Readers USA. Alpha Beta scholar, 1958, Sigma Sigma Sigma scholar, 1958. Mem. Assn. Coll. English Tchrs. Ala., South Atlantic Modern Lang. Assn., Habitat for Humanity (family sel. com. 1995—), Mobile Opera Guild, Nat. Soc. Colonial Dames of Am., Omicron Delta Kappa. Democrat. Episcopalian. Avocations: reading, gardening, travel, children. Home: 3764 Mordecai Ln Mobile AL 36608-2007

HAMNER, LANCE DALTON, prosecutor; b. Fukuoka, Japan, Sept. 18, 1955; parents Am. citizens; s. Louie D. and Mary Louise (Sloan) H.; m. Karla Jean Cleverly, Sept. 22, 1980; children: Lance Dalton Jr., Nicholas James, Louie Alexander, Samuel Sean, Victoria Jean. BS summa cum laude, Weber State Coll., 1984; JD magna cum laude, Ind. U., 1987. Bar: Ind., U.S. Dist. Ct. (no., so. dist.) Ind. 1988. Atty. Barnes & Thornburg, Indpls., 1988-89; dep. prosecuting atty. Marion County Prosecutor's Office, Indpls., 1989-90; pros. atty. Johnson County, Franklin, Ind., 1990—; legal corrs. WGGR radio news, Indpls., 1995; adj. prof. law Sch. Law Ind. U., Indpls., 1995-96, Bloomington, 1996—; frequent spkr. on legal topics including search and seizure and interrogation law; legal corr. WGGR Radio, 1995; lectr. Ind. Continuing Legal Edn. Forum, Indpls., 1992; frequent spkr. on legal topics, including search and seizure and interrogation law; faculty mem. Newly-Elected Pros. Sch., Ind. Pros. Attys. Coun. 1999. Editor Ind. Law Jour., 1987; contbr. articles to profl. jours. Asst. scoutmaster Boy Scouts Am., Franklin, Ind., 1995—. Mem. Nat. Dist. Attys. Assn., Ind. Prosecuting Atty.'s Coun., Nat. Eagle Scout Assn., Order of the Coif. Republican. Mormon. Avocations: family, fitness, writing. Office: Prosecutor's Office Courthouse Annex N 18 W Jefferson St Franklin IN 46131-2353

HAMNER, REGINALD TURNER, lawyer; b. Tuscaloosa, Ala., June 4, 1939; s. Raiford Samuel and Ellie Wells (Turner) H.; m. Anne Eleen Young, Nov. 8, 1969; children: Patrick Turner, William Christian. BS, U. Ala., 1961, JD, 1965. Bar: Ala. 1965, U.S. Dist. Ct. (mid. dist.) Ala. 1966, U.S. Ct. Appeals (5th cir.) 1966, U.S. Ct. Mil. Appeals 1968, U.S. Supreme Ct. 1968, U.S. Ct. Appeals (11th and 5th cirs.) 1981. Law clk. Supreme Ct. Ala., 1965; dir. legal-legis. affairs The Med. Assn., State of Ala., 1968-69; sec., exec. dir. Ala. State Bar, Montgomery, 1969-94, U.S. Dist. Ct. (mid. dist.) Ala., 1995—; coord. ct. project, U.S. Dist. Ct. (mid. dist.) Ala., 1995—. Bd. dirs. SE br., YMCA, Montgomery, 1978-81; former legal counsel govtl. adv. panels investigating Ala. Prison System; vice chmn. State Child Welfare Com.; dir. Attys. Ins. Mut. of Ala., Inc.; sec., treas. Ala. Law Found., 1987-93; chmn. Ala. Rhodes Scholarship Com., 1989-94. With USAF, 1965-68, col. USAFR, ret. Fellow Am. Bar Found. (life state chmn. 1994-95); mem. ABA (numerous coms., mem. ho. of dels. 1972-76, 85-89, 93, 96—), Am. Judicature Soc., Nat. Assn. Bar Execs. (pres. 1978-79), Am. Soc. Assn. Execs. (commr. certification com. 1991-94), Ala. Coun. Assn. Execs. (pres. 1984), Ala. Law Inst. (council), Jud. Conf. U.S. Ct. Appeals (11th cir. 1981-95), Ala. Nat. Alumni Assn. (pres. 1989-90), Montgomery Country Club, Omicron Delta Kappa, Alpha Epsilon Delta, Phi Alpha Delta, Delta Tau Delta. Episcopalian. Home: 9853 Wynchase Cir Montgomery AL 36117-5185 Office: US Dist Ct 15 Lee St Montgomery AL 36104-4056*

HAMNER, W. EASLEY, architect; b. Altavista, Va., Sept. 22, 1937; s. Robert Wilbourne and Isabelle (Easley) H.; m. Suzanne Leath, June 18, 1961; children: Janine, Michael. Diploma, Ecole de Beaux Arts, Fontainebleau, France, 1959; BArch, N.C. State U., 1960; MArch, Harvard U., 1967. Registered arch. Mass. Assoc. Thompson B. Burk, New Orleans, 1961-66; prin. The Stubbins Assocs., Cambridge, Mass., 1967—; Architect Citicorp Ctr., 1970-77; bd. dirs. Hyman/Stubbins, Inc. Prin. works include Riverpark, Norwalk, Conn. (award), The MITRE Corp. (award), O'Neill Fed. Bldg., Boston, Bristol-Myers Rsch. Labs, Wallingford, Conn. (award), Suffolk County Jail, Boston (2 awards), Suffolk County House of Corrections, Boston (award), Anhui Internat. Trade Ctr., Hefei, China, Sands Hotel/Casino, Las Vegas, Shezhen City (China) Plz. Pres. Cambridge Cmty. Svcs., 1982—, Ellery Sq. Owners Assn., 1983-85; chmn. bd. trustees Pro Arte Chamber Orch., 1993—; bd. dirs. Cambridge Cmty. Found., 1993—; elected mem. Harvard Grad. Sch. Design Alumni Coun., chmn. com. of five, 1983-84. Lt. U.S. Army Intelligence, 1960. Fellow AIA; mem. Am. Planning Assn., Boston Soc. Arch., Urban Land Inst. (vice-chmn. urban devel. mixed use coun.), Harvard U. Alumni Assn. (dir. 1984-88), Cambridge Club (pres. 1988-89), Boston Harbor Yacht Club. Democrat. Office: The Stubbins Assocs Inc 1033 Massachusetts Ave Cambridge MA 02138-5319

HAMOLSKY, MILTON WILLIAM, physician; b. Lynn, Mass., May 25, 1921; s. Israel and Sophie (Cremer) H.; m. Sandra Oelbaum, Feb. 18, 1979; children—Deborah Lynne, John Stephen, David James. A.B., Harvard U., 1943, M.D., 1946; Ad Eundum, Brown U., 1964. Diplomate Am. Bd. Internal Medicine. Intern Beth Israel Hosp., Boston, 1946-47; resident Beth Israel Hosp., 1947-48, 50-51, asst. physician, dir. endocrine clinic, 1957-63; instr. Harvard U. Med. Sch., 1951-55, asst. prof. medicine, 1955-63; prof. med. sci. Brown U., 1963-87, prof. emeritus, 1987—; physician-in-chief R.I. Hosp., Providence, 1963-87, W&I Hosp., Providence, 1981-87; vis. asst. prof. biochemistry Brandeis U., 1958-59; vis. Commonwealth fellow Coll. de France, 1960-62; chief adminstrv. officer R.I. Bd. Med. Licensure and Discipline, 1987—; exec. com. Diet Counseling Svc. Obstet. Health Care Com.; pres. Zlinkoff Found. Med. Edn. and Rsch., 1989-95; pres. Dolen Found., 1989—; chmn. adv. com. Comty. Health Ctrs., 1990—; cons. to hosps. Author: Thyroid Testing, 1968; contbr. numerous articles on endocrinology to profl. publs. Trustee Planned Parenthood, Providence, R.I. Child Guidance Clinic, Camp Jori, Providence, R.I. Hosp., 1986—. Served as capt. M.C., U.S. Army, 1948-50. Recipient Henry A. Christian award Harvard U. Med. Sch., 1946, Mallinckrodt award as founder nuclear medicine, 1977, W.W. Keen disting. svc. award Brown U.; named to R.I. Heritage Hall of Fame, 1996. Mem. A.C.P. (master gov. R.I. chpt.), AMA, Am. Thyroid Assn., Endocrine Soc., Am. Physiol. Soc., Soc. Clin. Investigation, Am. Fedn. Clin. Research, R.I. Diabetes Soc. (pres.), R.I. Heart Assn. (pres.). Home: 150 Arlington Ave Providence RI 02906-2330 Office: RI Dept Health 3 Capitol Hl Ste 1 Providence RI 02908-5097*

HAMON, RICHARD GRADY, lawyer; b. Corpus Christi, Tex., Dec. 30, 1937; s. Richard Paul and Dorothy Ileen (Norris) H.; m. Mary Lynn Farmer, Mar. 2, 1963; children; Leigh Ann, Clark Everett. AA, Del Mar Jr. Coll., 1957; BBA, Baylor U., 1959, JD, 1962. Ptnr. Blanchette, Hamon, Tabor & Coke, Dallas, 1962-76; stockholder, v.p. Winstead, Sechrest & Minick, Dallas, 1976-94, of counsel, 1994—. Mem. ABA, State Bar Tex. So. Baptist. Office: Winstead Sechrest & Minick 5400 Renaissance Tower Dallas TX 75270

HAMOND, KAREN MARIE KOCH, secondary education educator; b. Arlington, Mass., Dec. 12, 1954; d. James Walter and Dorothy Mary (Buchanan) Koch; m. Norman Roy Hamond, Oct. 9, 1976; children: Jeremy Michael, Jason Matthew, Jillian Marie, Jennifer Margaret. BA, Salem (Mass.) State Coll., 1976; MS, Lowell (Mass.) U., 1983; Cert. Advanced Studies, Harvard U., 1992. Cert. secondary maths. tchr., Mass. Tchr. St. Mary's High Sch., Lawrence, Mass., 1976-77, Peabody (Mass.) Vets. Meml. High Sch., 1977-78; tchr. Triton Regional High Sch., Byfield, Mass., 1978—, math. team advisor, 1980-91; prof. math. Western New Eng. Coll., Springfield, Mass., 1992—; tchr. summer sch. Gov. Dummer Acad., Byfield, Mass., 1993—. Mem ASCD, Nat. Coun. Tchrs. of Maths., Math. Assn. Am., NEA, Mass. Tchrs. Assn.. Am. Math. Soc. Avocations: camping, skiing, travel. Home: 14 Riverview Dr Newbury MA 01951

HAMOR, KATHY VIRGINIA, consultant; b. Port Jervis, N.Y., Aug. 2, 1957; d. John Barry and Grace Marion (Carpenter) H. BA, Elmira Coll., 1979; MPA, U. S.C., 1983. Paralegal Bergson, Borkland, Margolis & Adler, Washington, 1979-81; presdl. mgmt. intern U.S. Customs Svc., Washington, 1983-85, project mgr., 1986-88, pub. affairs officer, 1989-90, chief press ops. br., 1991-92; cons., lobbyist Mehl & Pickens Assocs., Inc., Washington, 1992-94; pres. Capital Concepts, Washington, 1994—; exec. dir. The Savings Coalition of America, 1994—. Home: 2844 Little Falls Pl Falls Church VA 22042-1730

HAMORY, BRUCE HILL, health facility administrator; b. Lancaster, Pa., Sept. 14, 1947; s. Eugene M. and Dorothy E. Hamory; m. Ann M. Ziebol, Jan. 8, 1972; children: Matthew, Joan. BS in Microbiology, U. Tenn., 1967; MD, Baylor, 1971. Diplomate Am. Bd. Internal Medicine, Am. Bd. Infectious Diseases. Intern Vanderbilt U. Hosp., Nashville, 1971-72, resident, 1972-74; fellow in virology and epidemiology U. Va. Hosp., 1974-76; asst. prof., assoc. prof. medicine U. Mo.-Columbia Sch. Medicine, 1978-87; assoc. prof. medicine Pa. State U. Coll. Medicine, Hershey, 1987-93, prof., 1993—, asst. dean. clin. affairs, 1993-94, assoc. dean clin. affairs, 1994-96, COO

Hershey Med. Ctr., exec. dir. univ. hosps., 1996-97; exec. v.p. and chief med. officer Pa. State Geisinger Health Sys., 1997—. Lt. comdr., M.C. USNR, 1976-78. Fellow ACP, Infectious Disease Soc. Am. Office: Pa State Geisinger Health Sys 2601 Market Pl Harrisburg PA 17110-9363

HAMOVITCH, WILLIAM, economist, educator, university official; b. Montreal, Que., Can., Sept. 1, 1922; came to U.S., 1946, naturalized, 1953; s. Abraham and Tillie (Weisenfeld) H.; m. Mitzi Berger, May 30, 1946 (dec. Dec. 31, 1992); children: Alan, Susan. B.Com., McGill U., 1943; M.P.A. (Adminstrn. fellow), Harvard, 1945, M.A., 1946, Ph.D., 1949. Lectr., asst. prof. U. Buffalo, 1946-53; asst. prof., assoc. prof., prof. Queens Coll. City U. N.Y., Queens, 1953-86; chmn. dept. econs. Queens Coll. City U. N.Y., 1965-76, provost, acad. v.p., 1976-84, acting pres., 1985; v.p. acad. affairs William Paterson Coll. N.J., Wayne, 1986-92, ret., 1992; research scientist N.Y.C. Temp. Commn. on City Finances, 1965; Chmn. Commn. on Off-Track Betting in Nassau County, 1970. Author: Conflict and Stability in Labor Relations: A Case Study, 1952; Editor: The Federal Deficit: Fiscal Imprudence or Policy Weapon?, 1965, Monetary Policy: The Argument From Keynes' Treatise to Friedman, 1966, Employment and Occupation Projections for Nassau-Suffolk to 1985, 1968. Fellow Royal Econ. Soc.; mem. Am. Econ. Assn. Home: 77 Westminster Rd Great Neck NY 11020-1272

HAMOY, CAROL, artist; b. N.Y.C., May 22, 1934; d. Morris David and Selma (Essex) Cohen. Student, Newark (N.J.) Sch. Fine Art, 1952-54, Art Students League, N.Y.C., various yrs. Lectr., spkr. in field. Solo shows include USMA/West Point, N.Y., 1978, Katonah (N.Y.) Gallery, 1983, Lower Manhattan Cultural Coun., N.Y.C., 1986, May Mus./Lawrence, N.Y. Ceres, N.Y.C., 1992, MTA-Arts for Transit, N.Y.C., 1993, Robert Kahn Gallery, Houston, 1993, Temple Judea Mus., Elkins Park, Pa., 1993, Univ. Art Ctr., Shreveport, La., 1994, Ceres, N.Y.C., 1995, 98, 99, Goldman Art Gallery, Rockville, Md., 1996, Nat. Mus. Am. Jewish History, Phila., 1996, Broadway Windows, N.Y.C., 1997, Ellis Island Immigration Mus., N.Y.C., 1997, Mizel Mus., Denver, 1997, Breman Heritage Mus., Atlanta, 1998, Eldridge St. Project, N.Y.C., 1998, Inter-Am. Gallery, Miami, Fla., 1998, Skirball Mus., Cincinnati, 1999, Franklin Marshall Coll., Lancaster Pa., 1999, Margolis Gallery, Houston, 1999, Lower East Side Tenement Mus., N.Y., 1999; group shows include Pelham (N.Y.) Art Ctr., 1988, U. Ky., Lexington, 1989, HUC, N.Y.C., 1989, Kentuck Mus., Northport, Ala., 1989, Clough Hansen Gallery, Memphis, 1989, JRC Gallery, Evanston, Ill., 1992, Soho 20, N.Y.C., 1993, Charach-Epstein Mus., West Bloomfield, Mich., 1994, 97, Nat. Jewish Mus., Washington, 1995, Fine Arts Rosen Mus., Boca Raton, Fla., 1995, Right Brain Gallery, Atlanta, 1999; permanent collections include Nat. Mus. Women in the Arts, Nat. Jewish Mus., Washington, others. Grantee Va. Ctr. for Creative Arts, Sweet Briar, Va., 1980, Artists' Space, N.Y.C., 1981, Hillwood Art Mus., N.Y. State Coun. for Creative Arts, 1992, MTA-Arts for Transit, N.Y.C., 1993, Lucius N. Littauer Found. Bessemere Trust Co. NA, 1997. Studio: 340 E 66th St New York NY 10021-6821

HAMPEL, ROBERT EDWARD, advertising executive; b. Cin., Apr. 29, 1941; s. John Edward and Ruth Elizabeth (Pister) H.; m. Nanci Jean Nau, Aug. 24, 1963; 1 child, Jeffrey Braam. BBA, U. Cin., 1964; MBA, U. Evansville, 1980. Asst. account mgr. Procter and Gamble, Balt., 1965; corp. forecaster Procter and Gamble, Cin., 1966-68; asst. contr. Keller-Crescent Co., Evansville, Ind., 1968-71; dir. mgmt. info. svcs. Keller-Crescent div. Am. Standards, Evansville, 1971-76, exec. v.p. fin., 1976-85, sr. exec. v.p., 1985-86; sr. exec. v.p., sec., treas., CFO Keller-Crescent Co., Inc., Evansville, 1987—, bd. dirs.; bd. dirs. Hahn, Inc. Pres. Jr. Achievement of S.W. Ind., Evansville, 1976-77, Evansville Philharm., 1981-82; pres. United Way of S.W. Ind., 1988-89; bd. dirs. Evansville Mus. Arts and Scis., 1988-95, treas., 1987-88; treas. Evansville Regional Econ. Devel. Corp., 1994—. Mem. Nat. Assn. Accts. (pres. Evansville chpt. 1980-81, nat. bd. dirs. 1984-85, nat. com. 1985-87). Home: 10727 Coach Light Dr Evansville IN 47711-8674 Office: Keller-Crescent Co Inc 1100 E Louisiana St PO Box 3 Evansville IN 47701-0003

HAMPL, MARY NOTERMANN, program manager; b. Mpls., Feb. 3, 1945; d. Joseph and Fern Irene (Ladwig) Little; m. Richard L. Notermann, Aug. 2, 1968 (div. July 1981); children: Jennifer Anne, Jason Richard; m. Werner Heinz Hampl, July 6, 1985; stepchildren: Matthew H., Carrie Elizabeth. BA, U. Minn., 1974; cert. spl. studies, Harvard U. Ext., 1989. Caseworker Outreach Ctr. Retarded Citizens, Mpls., 1974-75; exec. dir. South Side Svc. Retarded Citizens, Mpls., 1975-79; material control adminstr. Honeywell, Inc., Mpls., 1979-81; sr. buyer, planner NBI, Inc., Boulder, Colo., 1981-85; materials mgr. Zymacom, Inc., Westford, Mass., 1985-88; materials purchasing Roll Sys., Inc., Burlington, Mass., 1989-91; purchasing mgr. Medisense, Inc., Bedford, Mass., 1991-97; program mgr. Sun Microsystems, Burlington, Mass., 1998—; sec. Reubin Lindh Day Care Ctr., Mpls., 1977-79. Mem. LWV, Am. Assn. Purchasing Mgmt., Am. Prodn. and Inventory Control Soc. (cert.), Mensa. Avocations: reading, swimming, skiing, travel. Home: 17 Arborwood Dr Burlington MA 01803-3816 Office: Sun Microsystems One Network Dr Burlington MA 01803

HAMPSHIRE, JOHN CARR, III, artist, educator; b. Chgo., Nov. 30, 1971; s. John Carr and Linda (Tedesco) H. BS, Skidmore Coll., Saratoga Springs, N.Y., 1994; MFA in Painting, SUNY, Albany, 1997. With Mangino's Restaurant, Saratoga Springs, 1990-93, cook, 1993—; tchg. asst. Skidmore Coll., Saratoga Springs, 1993-94, SUNY, Albany, 1995-97; adj. prof. art SAGE JCA, Albany, 1997—; lectr. Berkshire C.C., Pittsfield, Mass., 1997; lectr. in field. One man shows include Berkshire C.C., 1977, UnCommon Grounds, 1997, SCAC Gallery, 1998, SUNY Cobleskill, 1999. Tchr. in enrichment program Saratoga-Warren County BOCES, Malta Ave. Elem. sch., 1997. Recipient Kebco Graphics award, 1990; N.Y. State Bd. Regents scholar, 1990. Mem. Periclean Honor Soc. Roman Catholic. Home: 236 4th St Troy NY 12180

HAMPSON, THOMAS MEREDITH, lawyer; b. Ann Arbor, Mich., Feb. 18, 1929; s. Harold Snover and Louise Susan (Goetchius) H.; m. Margaret H. Clark, Nov. 24, 1951 (div. Dec. 1969); children: Melissa Clark Hampson, Douglas Meredith; m. Zena Collier, Dec. 30, 1969. BA, Cornell U., 1951, LLB with distinction, 1955. Bar: N.Y. 1955, U.S. Dist. Ct. (we. dist.) N.Y. 1955, U.S. Supreme Ct. 1964. Assoc. Harris, Beach, Wilcox, Rubin & Levey, Rochester, N.Y., 1955-62; ptnr. Harris, Beach & Wilcox, Rochester, N.Y., 1962—; vis. instr. Cornell Law Sch., Ithaca, N.Y., 1969-75. Radio broadcaster The Jazz Scene, 1960-80, Jazz Notes, 1979-81, Mostly Jazz, 1985—; newspaper columnist, 1985-88. Chmn. Monroe County Fair Campaign Practices Com., Rochester, 1977-91; trustee Rochester Pub. Libr., 1976-98; dir. Cornell Lab. Ornithology, Ithaca, N.Y., 1984-90, Hawk Mountain Sanctuary Assn., 1990-98, Rundel Libr. Found., 1995—; bd. dirs. N.Y. State Civil Liberties Union, N.Y.C., 1963-69; commr. Rochester Civil Svc. Commn., 1997—. 1st lt. USAF, 1951-53. Recipient Civil Liberties award N.Y. Civil Liberties Union, Genesee Valley chpt., 1987. Mem. ABA, N.Y. State Bar Assn., Monroe County Bar Assn., City Club (pres. 1965-66), Philosophers' Club (pres. 1985-88). Democrat. Unitarian. Avocations: birding, jazz. Home: 83 Berkeley St Rochester NY 14607-2207 Office: Harris Beach & Wilcox 130 Main St E Rochester NY 14604-1687

HAMPTON, BENJAMIN BERTRAM, brokerage house executive; b. N.Y.C., Aug. 3, 1925; s. max and Pauline (Weinberger) H.; m. Elizabeth Golub-Cohen, Oct. 16, 1975; 1 child by previous marriage, Roger Neil; stepchildren: Laurence, James, Lisa. B Aero. Engring., NYU, 1947; cert. in mech. engring., Pa. State Coll., 1945; MBA, Harvard U., 1949. Sales mgr. Carew Products, Inc., N.Y.C., 1949-51; project mgr. Emerson Radio & TV Corp., 1951-52; div. mgr. Paragon Oil Co., Mineola, N.Y., 1952-55; mgmt. cons. E.N. Kagan & co., N.Y.C., 1955-60; exec. asst. to pres. mktg. sect. Fed. Pacific Electric co., Newark, 1960-62; asst. to pres. Seagrave Corp., N.Y.C., 1962-63; v.p. Swingline Inc., Long Island City, N.Y., 1963-68, exec. v.p., 1968-71, bd. dirs., 1970-71; exec. v.p., bd. dirs. Poloron Products Inc., New Rochelle, N.Y., 1971-73, pres., chief exec. officer, 1973-74; exec. v.p., bd. dirs. West Chem. Products, Inc., Long Island City, 1975-78; prin. Hampton Assocs., 1979-82; v.p. Merrill Lynch Pierce Fenner & Smith; Great Neck, N.Y., 1982—. Co-chmn. N.Y. State fin. com. J.F. Kennedy presdl. campaign, 1960. With AUS, 1944-46. Mem. Harvard Club, Pi Lambda Phi. Home: 339 E Shore Rd Great Neck NY 11023-1707 Office: Merrill Lynch 200 Middle Neck Rd Ste 1E Great Neck NY 11021-1134

HAMPTON, CHARLES EDWIN, lawyer, mathematician, computer programmer; b. Oct. 22, 1948; s. Roy Mizell and Hazel Lucretia (Cooper) H.; m. Cynthia Torrance, Sept. 14, 1968; children: Charles Edwin Jr., Adam Ethan. Student, Baylor U., 1967, Rice U., 1967-68; BA with highest honors, U. Tex., 1971, JD with high honors, 1977; MA, U. Calif., Berkeley, 1972, Candidate in Philosophy in Math., 1975. Bar: Tex. 1977, U.S. dist. Ct. (we. dist.) Tex. 1979, U.S. Dist. Ct. (no. dist.) Tex. 1980, U.S. Ct. Appeals (5th cir.) 1986. Rsch. asst. U. Calif., 1974-75; briefing atty. to justice Tex. Supreme Ct., 1977-78; assoc. Law Offices Don L. Baker, P.C., Austin, 1981-96; legal counsel Office Ct. Adminstrn., Tex. Jud. Coun., Austin, 1981; staff atty. Supreme Ct. Tex., Austin, 1981-96; assoc. Rinehart & Nugent, 1984-87; mem. vis. com. dept. math. U. Tex. at Austin, 1987-95. NSF fellow, 1971-74; Moody Found. scholar. Mem. ABA, State Bar Tex., Travis County Bar Assn., Chancellors, Order of Coif, Lions, Phi Kappa Phi, Phi Delta Phi. Office: Gammage Hampton Marcin & Ray PO Box 164191 611 W 15th St Ste 200 Austin TX 78701-1513

HAMPTON, EDWARD JOHN, engineering company executive; b. Pitts., July 28, 1952; s. Edward Aloysius and Helen (Litz) H.; BSME, U. Dayton, 1973; PhD, Westinghouse Program, 1982; m. Rebecca Ann Franklin, Jan. 5, 1974; 1 child, Edward Steven. With Westinghouse Energy Systems, Pa., 1973-82, mgr. product integrity and design assurance, 1981-82; sr. v.p. bus. devel. SMC O'Donnell, Inc., Pitts., 1982-92, also bd. dirs.; pres., chmn. bd., CEO Engring. Applied Scis., Inc., Export, Pa., 1992—; sr. v.p. Atomic Energy Authority, United Kingdom, 1991; engring. cons. in structural integrity, fracture mechanics, fatigue and finite element computer analyses at Sci. mgt. Corp. Recipient Engineering Excellence award Westinghouse, 1981; Tech. Excellence award O'Donnell & Assocs., 1983. Mem. ASME, Nat. Soc. Profl. Engrs., Soc. Mech. Engrs., Gamma Beta. Contbr. 47 articles on engring., plant life extension and mechanics to profl. jours.; co-inventor 17 patents. Achievements include institutionalize several programs for design assurance in both foreign and domestic reactors and fossil boilers; work with nuc. reactors using Pu weapons grade material; fissile materials; dry cask storage units for filtration and validation. Office: Engring Applied Scis Inc 4 Triangle Ln Ste 120 Export PA 15632-9326

HAMPTON, JOHN JAMES, university dean, consulting company executive; b. Jersey City, June 24, 1942; s. John Charles Reilly and Anna Marie (Antonaccio) Hampton; m. Doreen Tango, Oct. 14, 1989. AB in History, Stetson U., 1964; MBA, George Washington U., 1969, D Bus. Adminstrn., 1971. Assoc. prof. Towson (Md.) State Coll., 1969-75; v.p. Marine Transport Lines, N.Y.C., 1975-77; prof. fin. Seton Hall U., South Orange, N.J., 1977-83, dean Sch. Bus., 1983-87; provost Coll. Ins., N.Y.C., 1987-91; pres. Princeton Cons. Group, Litchfield, Conn., 1991—; dean Sch. Bus., Ctrl. Conn. State U., New Britain, 1995—. Author: Financial Precision Making, 1975, 4th edit., 1986; gen. editor: AMA Management Handbook, 1993. Capt. U.S. Army, 1964-68. Office: Ctrl Conn State U Sch Bus New Britain CT 06050

HAMPTON, JOHN LEWIS, retired newspaper editor; b. Verda, Ky., Jan. 13, 1935; s. John Lewis and Ruby Lillian (Slagle) H.; m. Lillian Valls; children from previous marriage: Rachel Hampton Midence, Jessica Hampton Fazio, Jonathan Hugh. A.B. in Journalism (Outstanding Journalism Grad. award 1959), U. Ky., 1959; M.A. in Communications and Journalism (grad. fellow 1960), Stanford U., 1960. Staff writer AP, Lexington, Ky., 1960-61; bur. chief Louisville (Ky.) Courier-Jour., 1961-67; staff writer Nat. Observer, Washington, 1967-71; sr. editor, then asst. mng. editor Nat. Observer, 1971-77; mem. editorial bd. Miami (Fla.) Herald, 1977, editor, 1978-99. Served with AUS, 1953-56. Named to Hall Disting. Alumni U. Ky.; recipient Pulitzer prize in editorial writing, 1983. Mem. Am. Soc. Newspaper Editors, Inter Am. Press Assn. (bd. dirs. 1987-99), Fla. Soc. Newspaper Editors. Office: Miami Herald 1 Herald Plz Miami FL 33132-1693

HAMPTON, LEROY, retired chemical company executive; b. Ingalls, Ark., Apr. 20, 1927; s. Ed Levi and Kitty Annie (Larry) H.; m. Anne Neris Herndon, July 11, 1954; children: Mary Louise, Gloria, Stanley Lamar, Cedric Leroy, Candice La Neris. B.S., U. Colo., 1950; M.S., Denver U., 1960. Registered pharmacist, Colo., Mich. Registered pharmacist Rocky Mountain Drug Co., Denver, 1950-53; scientist-chemist Dow Chem. Co., Golden, Colo., 1953-58; profl. scientist-chemist in charge Dow Chem. Co., 1958-61, devel. chemist, 1961-63, devel. leader, 1963-67; recruiting supr. Dow Chem. Co., Midland, Mich., 1967-68; recruiting mgr. N.E. Region, 1968-70, mgr. minority employee relations, 1970-75; dir. Dow Chem. Employees Credit Union, 1975-95, pres., 1979, 85, v.p., 1991, pres., chmn., 1992; mgr. issue analysis Dow Chem. Co., 1976-80, rsch. assoc., 1981-86; owner, operator hardware store, Denver, 1965-67. Bd. dirs. Midland Kiwanis Club Found., 1973-74, 90-95, v.p., 1992, pres., 1994-95; bd. dirs. Midland chpt. ARC, 1974-76; mem. Midland Bd. Edn., 1978-82, sec., 1979-80, v.p., 1981-82; dir. affirmative action Saginaw Valley State U., Univ. Ctr., Mich., 1987-90; bd. dirs. Midland Assn. Retarded Citizens, 1982-88, v.p., 1985-86, treas., 1986-87; deacon Meml. Presbyn. Ch., Midland, Mich., 1985-87, 95-97. With USNR, 1945-46. Mem. Am. Chem. Soc., Am. Pharm. Assn., Mich. Pharmacists Assn., Alpha Phi Alpha. Democrat. Presbyterian (deacon 1985-87, 95-97). Club: Kiwanis (pres. Midland club 1976-77). Home: 2206 Burlington Dr Midland MI 48642-3895

HAMPTON, MARK GARRISON, architect; b. Tampa, Fla., July 17, 1923; s. Ham Stonewall and Laura (Bingenheimer) H. B.S., B.Arch., Ga. Inst. Tech., 1949. Owner Mark Hampton, Architect, Tampa, 1952-65, Miami, Fla., 1974—; partner Herbert H. Johnson Assocs., Miami, 1966-73. Prin. works include Chemistry and Life Sci. bldgs, U. So. Fla., Tampa, 1961, First Fed. Office Bldg, Sarasota, 1973. Bd. dirs. Lannan Found., Palm Beach, Fla., 1972-88; pres. Tampa Art Inst., 1958, 64. Served with inf. AUS, 1943-46. Decorated Bronze Star, Purple Heart; recipient award Homes for Better Living competition, 1957, 62; Nat. Design award Horizon Home program, 1963. Fellow AIA (juror Nat. Honor awards 1963, 64, medal of honor for design Fla. Central chpt. 1974, award of honor for design 1987, test of time award 1987). Episcopalian. Office: Mark Hampton Architect FAIA 3900 Loquat Ave Miami FL 33133-5622

HAMPTON, PHILIP MCCUNE, banker; b. Whittier, Calif., Oct. 6, 1932; s. Philip and Margaret McCune (Andrew) H.; m. Elaina Frutiger, July 8, 1972; children: Mark Lawrence, John Andrew. BA, Miami U., Oxford, Ohio, 1954. With Bankers Trust Co., N.Y.C., 1954-89, sr. v.p., 1976-79, exec. v.p., 1979-86, vice chmn., 1986-89; chmn. Metzler Corp., N.Y.C., 1989-96; pres., CEO Metzler N.Am. Corp., Seattle, 1996-98; exec. v.p. fin. Avesta Sheffield, East, Balt., 1998—; dir. Tyco Labs., Inc., HemaSure, Inc.; former ptnr. N.Y. Partnership. Trustee Village of Croton-on-Hudson, N.Y., 1971-72. Mem. Empire State C. of C. (past bd. dirs.), N.Y. State Bankers Assn. (past bd. dirs.). Home: 1838 Hurricane Harbor Ln Naples FL 34102-5130*

HAMPTON, PHILLIP JEWEL, artist, educator; b. Kansas City, Mo., Apr. 23, 1922; s. Cordell Bernard Daniels and Goldie Kelley Powell; m. Dorothy Louise Smith, Sept. 28, 1946 (dec. Oct. 1986); children: Harry James, Robert Keith. Student, Drake U., 1947-48; BFA, Kansas City U., 1951; MFA, Kansas City Art Inst., 1952. Dir. art program Savannah (Ga.) State Coll., 1952-69; prof. art So. Ill. U., Edwardsville, 1969-92, emeritus prof. fine arts, 1992—; artist, spl. projects Hampton Studio, Edwardsville, 1992—; dir. day camp City of Kansas City Recreation, 1952; art cons. U.S. GSA, East St. Louis, Ill., 1995-98; curator 2 spl. exhbns. St. Louis Artists Guild, 1998—. Author: (catalogs) 3d World Drawings, 1979, Schemata of Ethnic Minority Artists, 1980; artist book/promotional materials Symphony Kids, KFUO-99FM, 1996; represnet in permanent collection at St. Louis Art Mus. Mem. adv. bd. West Broad YMCA, Savannah, 1966-69; bd. dirs. United Fund, Edwardsville, 1971-74; mem. Citizens Adv. Coun. Dist. 7, Edwardsville, 1973-75. Recipient Gov.'s award for best-in-show Ill. State Fair Profl. Art Exhbn., 1990, others. mem. St. Louis Art Mus., Art St. Louis, St. Louis Artist's Guild. Presbyterian. Avocations: reading, writing, chess, market studies. Home: 832 Holyoake Rd Edwardsville IL 62025-2315

HAMPTON, PHILLIP MICHAEL, consulting engineering company executive; b. Asheville, N.C., Sept. 5, 1932; s. Boyd Walker and Helen Reba (Smith) H.; m. Wilma Christine Gross, July 7, 1951; children: Philip Michael, Deborah Lynn, Gregg Ashley. A.B. in Geology, Berea Coll., 1954. Draftsman-designer Johnson & Anderson, Inc., Pontiac, Mich., 1955-57; designer, also project mgr. Johnson & Anderson, Inc., 1957-59, dir. bus. devel., 1962-76, v.p., 1966-74, exec. v.p., 1974-76; v.p. Spalding G. DeDecker & Assos., Inc., Madison Heights, Mich., 1976-84; founder, pres. Hampton Engring. Assocs., Inc., 1985—; pres. HMA Consultants Inc., 1977—, Geo Internat., Inc., 1978—; v.p. JAVLEN Internat., 1971-73, Micuda-Hampton Assocs., Inc., 1985-86; co-founder, owner My World Shops and Hampton Galleries, Ltd., 1976-90; co-owner Hampton-Tyedten Galleries Ltd., 1979-81; mem. public adv. panel GSA, 1977-78; chmn. task force of com. fed. procurement of architect/engr. svcs. ABA, 1977-79. Editor: Total Scope, 1963-71. Pres. Waterford Bd. Edn., 1969-71; mem. state resolution com. Democratic Conv., 1972; exec. com. Oakland County Dem. Com., 1973-74; precinct del., 1972-76, 80—; trustee Environ. Research Assocs., sec.-treas., 1969-71, pres., 1971-73; chmn. Waterford Cable Communications Commn., 1981-88; mem. Cultural Council Pontiac, 1987-90; bd. dirs. Oakland C. of C., 1972-74; chmn. utilities com. Oakland Bus. Roundtable, 1993—; vice chmn. Pontiac Urban League, 1996—. Named to Honorable Order Ky. Colonels. Fellow Am. Cons. Engrs. Coun. (internat. engring. com. 1971-76, vice chmn. pub. rels. com. 1970-72, chmn. publs. com. 1972-74, chmn. ABA model procurement code com. 1977-79, nat. dir. 1986-89, mem. com. fellows 1988—, Pres. award 1990); ASCE, AAAS, mem. Nat. Water Well Assn. (chmn. tech. div. 1969-71), Cons. Engrs. Coun. Mich. (awards com. 1970-74), Am. Arbitration Assn. (comml. panel 1977—), Pontiac C. of C. (co-founder 1989). Presbyterian. Clubs: Pontiac Exchange, Pontiac-Detroit Lions Quarterback Club. Home and Office: 2440 Ostrum St Waterford MI 48328-1829 Office: 35 W Huron St Ste 801 Pontiac MI 48342-2128 *My first employment, at age 13, was as a janitor. The superintendent of facilities taught me to pay attention to detail. He advised, "clean under the stairwells and the entrance will take care of itself." I understood his meaning and adopted the philosophy as my own in many areas of my life and career.*

HAMPTON, RAYMOND, painter; b. Orangeburg, S.C., Mar. 19, 1956; s. James K.C. and Annie Mae (Broderick) H. BFA, High Mus./Atlanta Coll. Art, 1979; MFA, U. Wis., 1981; student, North Light Art Sch., Cin., 1989, Internat. Corr. Sch. Art, 1995-96. Prodn. lab. technician asst.-film District Photo Inc., Beltsville, Md., 1979-80; freelance sign painter Orangeburg area, 1980—; prodn. stock clk. Woody's Prodn., Orangeburg, 1987-90; prodn. mgr. D&F Prodns., Orangeburg, 1990-94; visual artist self employed, 1981—; freelance designer African-Am. flag competition Ethnics United, The Carnegie Mus. of Art, Pitts., 1997. Exhibited works at Three Rivers Arts Festival, Pitts., 1997, Greyfox Gallery, Bozeman, Mont., 1995, I.P. Stanback Mus. and Planetarium, Orangeburg, 1993, Westside Jewish Cmty. Ctr., L.A., 1995, 96, Snowgrass Inst. Art Gallery, Cashmere, Wash., 1995, Art Addiction Internat. Gallery, Stockholm, 1997, Mus. Internat. Contemporary Art, Florianopolis, Brazil, 1998, Southeastern Wildlife Exposition, Charleston, S.C., 1998, others. Advanced Opportunity fellow U. Wis., 1980-81; recipient several awards for art. Mem. Boston Mus. Fine Arts, Smithsonian Instn. Baptist. Avocations: collecting contemporary junk mail, photographs, museum shop posters. Home: 249 Fair St NE Orangeburg SC 29115-5023

HAMPTON, REX HERBERT, former mining executive, director; b. Chgo., Aug. 3, 1918; s. John William and Alice Grace (Melling) H.; m. Ruth Lorraine Gibbons, Sept. 30, 1940 (dec. May 1994); children: Hope, Rex Herbert, Robin Virgil, Maryalice. B.S. in Forest Mgmt, Utah State U., 1942; M.A. in Internat. Affairs, George Washington U., 1963; Grad., U.S. Air Force War Coll., 1973. Real estate broker, Colo. Commd. 2d lt. U.S. Army, 1942, advanced through grades to brig. gen., 1968; ret., 1972; mgr. Bennett Shellenberger Realty, Colorado Springs, Colo., 1975-80; chmn. bd., pres., CEO Golden Cycle Gold Corp., Colorado Springs, 1980-93, ret., 1993; dir. Golden Cycle Gold Corp.; cons. ATE Enterprises Liquidating Trust, Cin. Decorated D.S.M., Legion of Merit with cluster, Bronze Star, others. Mem. DAV, VFW, Ret. Officers Assn. (past pres. chpt.), El Paso Club, Peterson Field Officers Club, Broadmoor Golf Club (Colorado Springs), IOOB. Republican. Mormon. Clubs: Peterson Field Officers, Broadmoor Golf (Colorado Springs).

HAMPTON, RICHARD CLINTON, JR., clergy member, therapist; b. Kittanning, Pa., June 9, 1942; s. Richard Clinton Sr. and Virginia Leona (Kriner) H.; m. Nancy Louise McDivitt, Apr. 2, 1965; children: Lisa Louise, Caleb Richard. BS in Edn., Indiana U. Pa., 1965; BTh in Bible, Manahath Sch. Theology, 1971; MDiv, Berean Christian Coll. & Sem., 1972, ThD of Ministries, 1974; DD (hon.), Am. Bible Inst., 1973. Ordained to ministry Am. Bapt. Ch. U.S.A, 1970; cert. addictions counselor Pa. Chem. Abuse Certification Bd., internat. drug and abuse counselor Internat. Certification and Reciprocity Consortium/Alcohol and Other Drug Abuse, Inc.; lic. clin. pastoral counselor Nat. Christian Counselors Assn. Tchr. Elkland (Pa.) H.S., 1965-66, Averill Park (N.Y.) Mid. Sch., 1966-68; claims examiner Allstate Ins. Co., Latham, N.Y., 1968-69; pastor First Bapt. Ch., Johnsonburg, Pa., 1969-72, Scottdale, Pa., 1972-78; pastor St. Clair Ave. Bapt. Ch., Hamilton, Ohio, 1978-80; ea. dist. dir. Pa. Coun. Alcohol Problems, Harrisburg, 1980-88; pastor Berean Bapt. Ch., Reading, Pa., 1988-94; therapist, cons. Caron Found., Wernersville, Pa., 1994—. Republican. Home: 813 Lorane Rd Reading PA 19606-3722 Office: Caron Counseling Svcs 845 N Park Rd Wyomissing PA 19610-1340

HAMPTON, SHELLEY LYNN, hearing impaired educator; b. Muskegon, Mich., Nov. 27, 1951; d. Donald Henry and Ruth Marie (Heinanen) Tamblyn; m. John Pershing Hampton Jr., Aug. 10, 1985; 1 child, Sarah Elizabeth. BA, Mich. State U., 1973, MA, 1978. Cert. tchr., Wash., Mich., N.Y. Tchr. presch. thru 3d grade N.Y. State Sch. for Deaf, Rome, 1973-78; cons. Ingham Intermediate Sch. Dist., Lansing, Mich., 1978-81; hearing impaired coord. Shoreline Sch. Dist., Seattle, 1981—; N.W. rep. Bur. of Edn. Handicapped, N.Y.C., 1978; N.Y. del. Humanities in Edn., 1977; adv. bd. State Libr. for the Blind, Lansing, 1980-81; adj. prof. Mich. State U., 1979-81, Seattle Pacific U., 1984-86; participant World Cong. Edn. and Tech., Vancouver, B.C., 1986; computer resource technician Spl. Programs, 1988-92, collegial team leader, 1992-95; rep. Site-Based Mgmt. Coun., Seattle, 1992-95. Writer: Social/Emotional Aspects of Deafness, 1983-84. Del. N.Y. State Assn. for Edn. of Deaf, N.Y.C., 1974-78; N.Y. del. Humanities in Edn., 1977; mem. bd. Plymouth Congl. Ch., Seattle, 1983-87. Recipient Gov.'s Plaque of Commendable Svc., State of Mich., 1981; grantee State of Wash., 1979, 82, Very Spl. Arts Festival, 1979-81; recipient Outstanding Svc. award Mich. Sch. for the Blind, 1980. Mem. NEA, Wash. State Edn. Assn., Shoreline Edn. Assn., Alexander Graham Bell Assn., Regional Hearing Impaired Coop. for Edn., Internat. Orgn. Educators of the Hearing Impaired, Auditory-Verbal Internat., U.S. Pub. Sch. Caucus, Conf. Ednl. Adminstrs. Serving the Deaf. Home: 14723 62nd Dr SE Everett WA 98208-9383 Office: Shoreline Hearing Program 16516 10th Ave NE Seattle WA 98155-5904

HAMPTON, VERNE CHURCHILL, II, lawyer; b. Pontiac, Mich., Jan. 5, 1934; s. Verne Churchill and Mildred (Peck) H.; m. Stephanie Hall, Oct. 5, 1973; children: J. Howard, Timothy H., Julia C. Thibodeau. BA, Mich. State U., 1955; LLB, U. Va., 1958. Bar: Mich. 1958. Since practiced in Detroit; ptnr. firm Dickinson Wright, 1967—; bd. dirs., sec. Carhartt, Inc., KPSI Radio Corp. Mem. Mich. Rep. Fin. Com.; bd. dirs. Detroit Bus./Edn. Alliance; corp. mem. Boys' Clubs Met. Detroit. Mem. ABA, State Bar Mich. (chmn. bus. law sect. 1980-84), Detroit Athletic Club, Country Club Detroit, Yondotega Club, Sigma Alpha Epsilon, Phi Alpha Delta. Republican. Episcopalian. Home: 510 Oxford Rd Grosse Pointe MI 48236-1842 Office: Dickinson & Wright 500 Woodward Ave Ste 4000 Detroit MI 48226-3416

HAMRE, GARY LESLIE WILLIAM, entrepreneur; b. Mpls., July 28, 1939; s. Hiram O. and Mayme R. (Sorensen) H.; m. Margaret Ann Renshaw, July 14, 1958 (div. 1981); children: Jeffrey A.C., Cheryl L., Dayna L.; m. Karen Sue Link, Nov. 30, 1984. BA, U. Minn., 1966; postgrad., Ohio State U., 1978. Lic. real estate sales cons. Area mgr. Union Oil Co. Calif., Mpls., 1963-71, Columbus, Ohio, 1971-78; pres. G.L.W.H. Ent., Inc., Ohio, 1978—; owner 76 Halfway House Truck Stop, 1978-90; sales cons. comml. real estate, 1990—. Dep. sheriff Franklin County Sheriff's Office, Columbus, 1977—, cpl., 1999—; sustaining mem. Rep. Nat. Com., Washington, 1981—; bd. dirs., com. chmn. Am. Diabetes Assn., 1988-91. Mem. NRA (life), Fraternal Order of Police, Nat. Restaurant Assn., Ohio Restaurant Assn., Ctrl. Ohio Restaurant Assn. (bd. dirs. 1984-92, pres. 1990, chmn. bd. 1991), Nat. Assn. Truckstop Operators (assignment com. 1986-90), Sales and Mktg. Execs. Internat., Nat. Fedn. Ind. Businessmen, U.S. C. of C., Columbus C.

of C., Sales Execs. Club, Lions (pres. Powell, Ohio 1986-87, Lion of Yr. 1985-86, zone chmn. 1987-88, Melvin Jones fellow 1991, dist. 13F gov. 1990-91, chmn. state constn. and by-laws 1993-96), Masons, Shriners (provost), Moose. Lutheran. Avocations: golf, boating, snowmobiling, hunting, fishing. Home: 22 Barrhill Dr Delaware OH 43015-7608

HAMREN, NANCY VAN BRASCH, bookkeeper; b. L.A., Feb. 2, 1947; d. Milton Carl and Winifred (Taylor) Van Brasch; m. Jerome Arthur Hamren, Feb. 14, 1981; children: Emily Allison, Meredith Ann. Student, Pasadena City Coll., 1964-65, San Francisco State Coll., 1966-67, U. Oreg., 1975-79. Bookkeeper/office mgr. Springfield Creamery, Eugene, Oreg., 1969—, also bd. dirs.; originator Nancy's Yogurt, Nancy's Cultured Dairy Products. Active mem. Oreg. Shakespearean Festival, Ashland, 1986, Oreg. Nat. Abortion Rights Action League, Planned Parenthood, Sta. KLCC-PBS Radio; bd. dirs. BRING Recycling. Mem. Oreg. Dairy Assn., Audubon Soc., N.Am. Truffling Soc., The Wilderness Soc., Oreg. Pub. Broadcasting, Buhl (Idaho) Arts Coun., Conservation Internat, Provender Alliance (bd. dirs.). Democrat. Unitarian. Avocations: gourmet cooking, gardening, walking, wine tasting. Home: 1315 Ravenswood Dr Eugene OR 97401-1912 Office: Springfield Creamery 29440 Airport Rd Eugene OR 97402-9524

HAMRICK, BILL ALLEN, principal, retired; b. Brownwood, Tex., Sept. 23, 1925; s. William Rufus and Gladys Myril (Elms) H.; m. Mary Edith Loyd Hamrick, May 27, 1949; children: Billy Don, Jerry Neal. BA, Howard Payne Coll., Brownwood, Tex., 1950; MEd, U. Houston, 1963. School administration. Prin. and coach Bangs I.S.D., Bangs, Tex., 1950-51; coach and A.D. Round Rock I.S.D., Round Rock, Tex., 1951-52, Angleton I.S.D., Angleton, Tex., 1952-59, Rosenberg I.S.D., Rosenberg, Tex., 1959-63, Athens I.S.D., Athens, Tex., 1963-67, Carroll High Corpus Christi I.S.D., Corpus Christi, Tex., 1967-76; asst. prin. Martin Jr. High, Corpus Christi, Tex., 1976-78, King High Sch., Corpus Christi, Tex., 1978-80; prin. Wynn Seale Jr. High, Corpus Christi, Tex., 1980-85, W.B. Ray High Sch., Corpus Christi, Tex., 1985-95; retired, 1995; pres. Corpus Christi Coaches Assn., Corpus Christi Prin. Assn., Corpus Christi, Tex.; bd. dirs. Tex. High Sch. Coaches Assn., Austin, Tex.; prin. Flour Bluff H.S.; founder, dir. Richard Milburn Acad., Corpus Christi. Sec. bd. trustees Corpus Christi Ind. Sch. Dist. Fellowship I.D.E.A. Kitering Found., Columbus, Mo., Tex. A&M Found., College Station. Mem. Tex. Assn. of Secondary Prin., Corpus Christi Prin. Assn., Parent and Tchrs. Assn. Democrat. Methodist. Avocations: oil painting, golf. Fax: 512-225-4945. Home: 54 Townhouse Ln Corpus Christi TX 78412-4269 Office: Richard Milburn Acad 5155 Flynn Pky Corpus Christi TX 78411-2530

HAMRICK, LEON COLUMBUS, surgeon, medical director; b. Ludville, Ga., Nov. 11, 1925; s. Harlie Monroe and Hattie Mae (Ballew) H.; m. Frances Marion Brannan, June 7, 1949; children: Martha, Leon Jr., Mary Nell, Catherine, Margaret Susan. BS, Emory U., 1949, MD, 1952; LLD (hon.), Birmingham So. Coll., 1993. Diplomate Am. Bd. Surgery. Intern Columbus (Ga.) City Hosp., 1952-53; resident surgery Lloyd Noland Hosp., Fairfield, Ala., 1953-57; assoc. in surgery Lloyd Noland Hosp., Fairfield, 1957-72, med. dir., 1972-98; chm. bd. dirs. Lloyd Noland Found., Fairfield, 1972—; mem. city adv. bd. AM South Bank, Birmingham, 1974-94; founding dir. Mutual Assurance Soc. Ala., Birmingham, 1977—; clin. prof. surgery U. Ala. Sch. Medicine, Birmingham, 1983—; trustee Miles Coll., Fairfield, Ala., 1990—; bd. dirs. Health Maintenance Group Ala., Birmingham, 1977-97. Mem. State Com. Pub. Health, Montgomery, Ala., 1972-81, chmn., 1975-81; mem. Ala. Bd. Med. Examiners, Montgomery, 1972-81, chmn., 1975-81; mem. State Bd. Censors, Med. Assn. State of Ala., Montgomery, 1972-81, chmn., 1975-81; mem. Ala. Med. Licensure Commn., Montgomery, 1981—, chmn., 1981-92; mem. Cert. of Need Rev. Bd., Montgomery, 1984-87; del. Gen. and Jurisdictional Confs. United Meth. Ch., 1984-96; dir. World Meth. Coun., 1985-96, Gen. Coun. on Ministries United Meth. Ch., 1988-96; mem. Jurisdictional Episcopy Com. United Meth. Ch., 1988-96; chmn. Episcopacy com. North Ala. Conf. United Meth. Ch., 1992-96. With USN, 1943-46, ETO, PTO. Recipient Disting. Svc. award Ala. Hosp. Assn., Montgomery, 1986. Fellow ACS; mem. AMA, Med. Assn. State Ala. (Disting. Svc. award 1986), Jefferson County Med. Soc. Avocations: gardening, fishing. Home: 3656 Rockhill Rd Birmingham AL 35223-1520 Office: Lloyd Noland Hosp 701 Lloyd Noland Pkwy Fairfield AL 35064-2699

HAMRICK, LESLIE WILFORD, JR., metallurgy supervisor; b. Charleston, W.Va., Dec. 26, 1946; s. Leslie Wilford and Olive Marie (Means) H.; m. Margaret C. Hamrick, Sept. 20, 1970 (div. Jan. 1976); m. Mary Lee Smathers, Aug. 6, 1978; 1 child, Hannah Chance. BA, U. Charleston, 1969. Shift coord. FMC, South Charleston, W.Va., 1973-79; maint. supr. Foote Mineral Co., Graham, W.Va., 1979-86; maint. foreman Century (W.Va.) Aluminum, 1986-92; metallurgy supr. Ravenswood (W.Va.) Aluminum, 1992—. Author: Hating Hugh, 1991 (2d place award 1991), Wozzek's Price, 1990 (2d place award 1992); (short story) Reconciliation, 1992 (3d place award 1993), Roots and Wings - The Family Record of Benjamin Hamrick, 1997. Trustee Point Mountain/Hamrick Reunion, 1995, chmn., 1998. With USN, 1969-73. Republican. Avocation: geneaology. Home: RR 2 Box 157aaa Ravenswood WV 26164-9794

HAMRICK, LINDA L., educator; b. Fort Wayne, Ind., Feb. 14, 1954. BS in Edn., Ball State U., 1977; MS in Edn., Ind. U., 1980; EdD in Ednl. Leadership, Ball State U., 1991. Cert. tchr., sch. adminstr., supt., Ind. Tchr. Fort Wayne (Ind.) Cmty. Schs., 1978—; adminstrv. intern Ft. Wayne (Ind.) Cmty. Schs., 1997—; educator-YIC Whitley County Probation, Columbia City, Ind., 1997—; assoc. faculty Ind. U., 1987, 88; sch. supt. internship N.W. Allen County Schs., Fort Wayne, 1990-91. Site dir. youth basketball Ft. Wayne YMCA, 1982-86; site supr. Ft. Wayne Park Dept., 1980-85. Mem. AAPHERD, Ind. Middle Level Educators Assn., Internat. Reading Assn., Am. Endurance Ride Conf., Internat. Arabian Horse Assn., Upper Midwest Endurance Ride Conf. Avocations: horse riding endurance, snowmobiling, downhill skiing, boating, water skiing. Office: South Side HS 3601 S Calhoun Fort Wayne IN 46807

HAMRICK, MIKE ALAN, athletic director; b. Charleston, W.Va., Aug. 24, 1957; m. Soletta Prino, Aug. 1, 1981; children: Brett and Justin (twins), Mollie Ann. BA in Edn., Marshall U., 1980; MS in Sports Adminstrn., Ohio U., 1981. Asst. football coach Ohio U., Athens, 1980; dir. athletic promotions U. Nev., Las Vegas, 1981-82; asst. to dir. athletics U. Kans., 1982-84; asst. athletic dir. Ill. State U., 1984-90; dir. athletics U. Ark., Little Rock, 1990-95, East Carolina State U., Greenville, N.C., 1995—. Office: Easr Carolina U Ficklen Dr Greenville NC 27858-4353

HAMROCK, MARGARET MARY, retired educator, writer; b. Campbell, Ohio, Apr. 2, 1910; d. Louis Francis and Mary (Augustin) H. BS in Edn., Kent State U., 1946. Tchr. Campbell (Ohio) Bd. Edn., 1927-75; ret., 1975. Author: Tell Me I'm Somebody, 1994; composer of songs; over 100 letters to editor pub. in Cleve. Plain Dealer, Youngstown Vindicator, nat. mags. Mem. Ohio Ret. Tchrs. Assn. (life), Kent State U. Alumni Assn. Avocations: reading, writing.

HAMROFF, MICHAEL SCOTT, archives executive; b. Queens, N.Y., Mar. 12, 1963; s. Sheldon and Zelda (Lurie) H.; m. Iris Eden, Mar. 29, 1987; children: Samantha, Brooke, Brandon. BA cum laude, Hofstra U., 1985. Exec. Comprehensive Archives, Richmond Hill, N.Y., 1985—. Mem. Assn. Record Mgrs., Profl. Records and Info. Svc. Mgrs. Avocation: golf. Office: Comprehensive Archives Inc 87-46 123d St Richmond Hill NY 11418

HAN, CHIEN-PAI, statistics educator; b. Hunan, China, Dec. 17, 1936; came to U.S., 1960; s. Chung-Shih and Pei-Wen Han; M. Maria Han, Aug. 28, 1965; children: Richard, Julie. BA, Nat. Taiwan U., Taipei, 1958; MA, U. Minn., 1962; PhD, Harvard U., 1967. Asst. prof. stats. Iowa State U., Ames, 1967-69, assoc. prof., 1970-75, prof., 1975-82; prof. math. U. Tex.-Arlington, 1982—; statis. cons. Mus. N.Mex., Santa Fe, 1965; vis. asst. prof. Harvard U., Cambridge, Mass., 1970. Author: (with T.A. Bancroft) Statistical Theory and Inference in Research, 1981; mem. editl. bd. Comms. in Stats. Theory and Methods, 1975-92, Jour. Statis. Rsch., 1994; assoc. editor Comms. in Stats., 1993—. Fellow Am. Statis. Assn. (pres. Iowa chpt. 1971-72); mem. Internat. Statis Inst. (elected), Inst. Math. Stats., Internat. Assn. Survey Statisticians, Internat. Chinese Statis. Assn. (bd. dirs. 1987-92), Sigma Xi, Mu Sigma Rho. Office: U Tex Dept Math PO Box 19408 Arlington TX 76019

HAN, CHINGPING JIM, industrial engineer, educator; b. Shanghai, People's Republic China, Aug. 24, 1957; came to U.S., 1983; s. Bao-San Zhang and Xiao-xian Han; m. Man-xia Maria Zhang, Feb. 22, 1982; children: George, Elaine. PRC, BSME, Dalian Inst. Tech., Dalian, 1982; MS in Indsl. Engring., Pa. State U., 1985, PhD, 1988. Asst. prof. mfg. systems engring. Fla. Atlantic U., Boca Raton, 1988-93, assoc. prof. and assoc. dir. mfg. systems engring., 1993—. Contbr. articles to profl. jours., procs. Avocations: classical music, travel. E-mail: han@fau.edu. Home: 19571 Black Olive Ln Boca Raton FL 33498-4827 Office: Fla Atlantic Univ 777 Glades Rd Boca Raton FL 33431-6498

HAN, D(ONGYEON) PETER, urologist; b. Seoul, Republic of Korea, Mar. 16, 1959; came to U.S., 1985; m. Ruth Han, Mar. 30, 1985; children: Pierce, Tatiana. BS, Yale U., 1982; MD, U. Chgo., 1986. Diplomate Am. Bd. Urology. Resident in urology Portsmouth (Va.) Naval Hosp., 1995; staff urologist Camp Lejeune (N.C.) Naval Hosp., 1995-97, head urology dept., 1997; mng. physician in urology Tidewater Physicians, Newport News, Va., 1997—; lab. dir. Tidewater Physicians Multispecialty Group, Newport News, 1998—. Contbr. articles to profl. jours. Comdr. USNR, 1984—. Mem. Am. Urol. Assn. (mid-Atlantic sect. 1995—), Soc. Govt. Svc. Urologists, Va. Urol. Soc. Presbyterian. Office: Tidewater Physicians Group # 109 813 Diligence Dr Newport News VA 23606

HAN, ITTAH, lawyer, political economist, high technology and financial strategist, computer engineer; b. Java, Indonesia, Jan. 29, 1939; came to the U.S., 1956, naturalized, 1972; s. Hongtjioe and Tsuiying (Chow) H. BS in Mech. Engring. and Elec. Engring., Walla Walla Coll., 1960; MS in Elec. Engring., U. Colo., 1961; BA in French, U. Colo., Boulder, 1965; MA in Math., U. Calif., Berkeley, 1962; MSE in Computer Info. & Control Engring., U. Mich., 1970; MS in Computer Sci., U. Wis., Madison, 1971; MBA in Mgmt., U. Miami, Fla., 1973; BA in Econs., U. Nev., 1977; MBA in Tax, Golden Gate U., 1978, MBA in Real Estate, MBA in Fin., 1979; MBA in Banking, 1980, MPA in Adminstrv. Orgn. and Mgmt., 1984; ME in Comp. Engrg., U. Idaho, 1991; JD, Whittier Coll., 1991; PhD in Ethics and Tech., The Union Inst., 1994; MS in Comp. Based Learning, Nova Southeastern U., 1994; MA in Edn. and Human Development, George Wash. U., 1995; MS in Instrl. and Performance Tech., Boise State U., 1995; MA in Humanities, Calif. State U., Dominguez Hills, CA, 1995; MA in Human Resources Devel., Webster Univ., 1997; MS in Space Studies, U of North Dakota, Grandforks, 1998; MA in Liberal Studies, Lang. and Comm., Regis U., Denver, 1998; MA in Labor and Policy Studies, State U. of NY, Empire State Coll., Saratoga Spgs., 1999. CFP. Salesman Watkins Products, Walla Walla, Wash., 1956-60; instr. Sch. Engring. U. Colo., Denver, 1964-66; sys. engr. IBM Corp., Oakland, Calif., 1967-69, Scidata, Inc., Miami, Fla., 1971-72; chief of data processing Golden Gate Bridge, Hwy. and Transp. Dist., San Francisco, 1973-74; mgr. info. sys. tech. and advanced sys. devel. Summa Corp., Las Vegas, Nev., 1975-78; mgr. sys. devel. Fred Harvey, Inc., Brisbane, Calif., 1978-80; chmn. corp. sys. steering com., mgr. sys. planning Amfac Hotel & Resorts, Inc., 1978-80; tax strategy planner, innovative turnaround fin. strategy planner, chief exec. Ittahhan Corp., 1980-95; instr. U. Nev. Sch. Elec. Engring., Reno, 1981; exec. v.p. Developers Unltd. Group, Las Vegas, 1982-84, John H. Midby and Assocs., Las Vegas, 1982-84, 86-95; sec., treas., dir. River Resorts, Inc., Las Vegas, 1983-84; sec., treas. Goldriver Ltd., Las Vegas, 1983-84; v.p. Fidelity Fin. Co., Las Vegas, 1984-85; pres. Weststar Gen. Ptnr. Co., 1984-85, Developers Group Svc. Co., 1984-86, Orion Land Devel. Co., Las Vegas, 1987-89, Very High Tech. Computer Engring., Inc., Las Vegas, 1988-95; CEO, pres. Very High Tech. Polit. Economy Turnaround Mgmt. Strategist, Inc., 1986-95, Artificial Intelligence Computer Engring. and Expert Sys. Engring., Inc. (named changed to Turnaround Strategist and Artificial Intelligence Engring., Inc.), 1986—; sys. designer, cons. in field. Mem. Internat. Bd. Stds. and Practices for CFP, Inc., Calif. Bar Assn., Am. Contract Bridge League. Republican. Home and Office: 2501 Fulano Way Las Vegas NV 89102-2034

HAN, JIAHUAI, medical researcher. BS in Biochemistry, Beijing U., 1982, MS in Protein Biochemistry, 1988; PhD in Molecular Biology, U. Brussels, 1990. Rsch. fellow Dept. Internal Medicine and Howard Hughes Med. Inst., U. Tex. Southwestern Med. Ctr., Dallas, 1987-92; rsch. assoc. Dept. Immunology, The Scripps Rsch. Inst., La Jolla, Calif., 1992-93, sr. rsch. assoc., 1993-96, asst. mem., 1996—. Contbr. articles to profl. jours. Recipient Established Investigator award Am. Heart Assn., 1995. Office: Scripps Rsch Inst 10550 N Torrey Pines Rd La Jolla CA 92037-1000*

HAN, KENNETH, dean; b. Seoul, Korea, July 3, 1938; came to U.S., 1965; s. Chyi-Kyung and Taeksoon (Shim) H.; m. Helen Hyi-won Rho, Sept. 1, 1967; children: Iris, Vincent, Allison. BS, Seoul Nat. U., 1961, MS, 1963; MS, U. Ill., 1967; PhD, U. Calif., Berkeley, 1971. Lectr. Monash U., Melbourne, Australia, 1971-74, sr. lectr., 1974-81; assoc. prof. S.D. Sch. Mines, Rapid City, 1981-84, prof., 1984-87, dept. head metallurgy, 1987-94, dean, 1994—. Author: Mineral Processing and Extractive Metallurgy, 1981, Recovery and Sampling of Precious Metals, 1989; editor-in-chief Gordon & Breach, 1986—; patentee in field. Recipient Arthur F. Taggett award, 1995, Milton Wadsworth award, 1995, Ernest L. Buckley award, 1994. Mem. AIME (disting. mem., chmn. 1996-97), NAE, Soc. Mining, Metallurgy and Exploration. Republican. Home: SD Sch Mines 5499 Blue Stem Ct Rapid City SD 57702-8205 Office: SD Sch Mines 501 E Saint Joseph St Rapid City SD 57701-3995

HAN, MAO-TANG, surgeon, researcher; b. Jinan, Shandong, China, Aug. 28, 1934; came to U.S., 1989; s. Houngwen Han and Shie Sun; m. Hui-Fong Wang, Aug. 28, 1960; children: Han Qiang, Han Shan. Student, Chee-Loo U., 1951-52; MD, Tongj Medical Sch., Wuhan, China, 1952-57. Resident gen. surgery Simo (Province of Yunan) Dist. Hosp., 1957-60, Tonjee Teaching Hosp. Medical U. Tonjee, Wuhan, Province of Hubei, 1960-61; resident in pediatric surgery Tianjin Children's Hosp., Tianjin, 1963-64, chief resident in pediatric surgery, 1964-65, attending surgeon, 1965-79; postgrad. fellow Shanghai Chest Hosp., 1975-76; vis. physician, fellow dept. surgery The Mayo Clinic, Rochester, Minn., 1979-82; chief surgeon dept. surgery Tianjin Children's Hosp., Tianjin, 1984-89; assoc. editor Chinese Jour. Pediat. Surgery; organizer 1st and 2d Internat. Symposia on Pediat. Surgery of China, 1984, 88. Contbr. chpts. to books; contbr. articles to profl. jours. Mem. Assn. of Chinese Pediatric Surgery, Chinese Medical Assn., Am. Coll. Chest Physicians, Asian Assn. Pediatric Surgeons, Pacific Assn. Pediatric Surgeons. Achievements include pioneering of clinical surgery in neonatal esophageal atresia, hypoglycemic hyperinsulinemia, and pediatric hepatic cancer surgery. Home: 4009 NE 70th St Seattle WA 98115-6021

HAN, MOO-YOUNG, physicist; b. Seoul, Korea, Nov. 30, 1934; came to U.S., 1954; s. Sunghoon and Kiejer (Kim) H.; m. Changki Hong, Aug. 29, 1959; children: Grace, Chris, Tony. BS, Carroll Coll., Waukesha, Wis., 1957; PhD, U. Rochester, 1964. Research assoc. Syracuse U., 1964-65; asst. prof. U. Pitts., 1965-67; asst. prof. physics Duke U., Durham, N.C., 1967-71; assoc. prof. Duke U., 1971-77, prof., 1977—; vis. prof. Kyoto U., 1974, Korea Advanced Inst. of Sci., 1982. Author: The Secret Life of Quanta, 1990, The Probable Universe, 1992, Quarks and Gluons, 1999; editor Korean Am. Sci. and Tech. News, 1995—. Recipient Outstanding Prof. award Duke U., 1971, Disting. Tchg. award Duke U., 1972, Disting. Fgn. Scholar award Kyoto U., 1974, Global award Mich. State U., 1998. Mem. Soc. Korean-Am. Scholars, Golden Key (hon.). Home: 615 Duluth St Durham NC 27705-1824 Office: Duke U Dept Physics Durham NC 27708

HAN, NONG, artist, sculptor, painter; b. Seoul, Korea, Oct. 10, 1930; came to U.S., 1952, naturalized, 1958; Commr. Asian Art Commn. Asian Art Mus. San Francisco, The Avery Brundage Collection, City and County of San Francisco, 1981-84. One-man exhbns. paintings and/or sculpture include Ft. Lauderdale (Fla.) Mus. Arts, Santa Barbara (Calif.) Mus. Art, Crocker Art Mus., Sacramento, Calif., 1965, Ga. Mus. Art, Athens, 1967, El Paso (Tex.) Mus. Art, 1967, Nat. Mus. History, Taiwan, 1971, Nihonbashi Gallery, Tokyo, Japan, 1971, Shinsegye Gallery, Seoul, Korea, 1975, Nat. Mus. Modern Art, Seoul, 1975, San Francisco Zool. Garden, 1975, Tongin Art Gallery, Seoul, 1978, Consulate Gen. Republic of Korea, L.A., 1982, Choon Chu Gallery, Seoul, 1982, Mee Gallery, Seoul, 1984, 86, Leema Art Mus., Seoul, 1985, Tong-A Dept. Store, Taegu, Korea, 1986, Tongso Gallery, Masan, Korea, 1986, Han Kwang Art Mus., Pusan, Korea, 1986, Union de Arte, Barcelona, Spain, 1987, Acad. de Belles Arts, Sabadell, Spain, 1987, Nong Hyup Art Mus., Ft. Lee, N.J., 1995, The Info. Ctr. Korean Embassy, Washington, 1997; Gallery Art Exchange, N.Y.C., 1998; numerous group exhibits Mus. and Art Ctr., Douglaston, N.Y., 1961, Nat. Collection Fine Arts, Smithsonian Instn., Washington, 1961, Mus. Fine Arts, Springfield, Mass., 1961, Conn. Acad. Fine Arts, Hartford, Conn., 1962, Charles and Emma Frye Art Mus., Seattle, 1962, The Denver Art Mus., 1965, Jersey City Mus., 1967, U. Santa Clara (Calif.) Mus., 1967, U. Calif., Berkeley, 1968, Maison de la Culture du Havre, Le Havre, France, 1970, Oakland (Calif.) Art Mus., 1971, Gallerie des Champs Elysees, Paris, 1971, Nat. Sculpture Soc., Lever House, N.Y.C., 1971, Taipei Provincial Mus., Republic of China, 1971, San Francisco Mus. Modern Art, 1972, Galerie Hexagramme, Paris, 1975, Galeria de Arte Misrachi, Mexico City, 1979, The Mun Ye Art Ctr., Seoul, 1986, Salon de Artistes Francais, Paris, France, 1971, Salon d'Automne, Paris, 1969-71, Salon Grands et Jeunes d'Aujourd'hui, Paris, 1971-77, The Jane Voorhees Zimmerli Art Mus. Rutgers, New Brunswick, N.J., 1997, Chgo. Cultural Ctr., 1997, Mus. Contemporary Art, Washington D.C., 1997, Taipei Gallery Taiwanese Cultural Ctr., N.Y.C., 1998, Fisher Gallery U. So. Calif., L.A., 1998, Japanese Am. Nat. Mus., L.A., 1998, Bedford Gallery, Dean Lesker Regl. Ctr. for the Arts, Walnut Creek, 1998, The Kaohsing Museum of Fine Art, 1998, Taipei Museum of Fine Arts, 1998, Marugame Genichiro Inokuma Mus. of Contemporary Art, Japan, 1999, Fukuoka Asian Art Mus., Fukuoka City, 1999, Akita Senshu Mus. Art, Akita City, 1999; represented in numerous permanent collections including, Santa Barbara Mus. Art, Anchorage (Alaska) Hist. and Fine Art Mus., Museo de Arte, Lima, Peru, Govt. Peru, Nat. Mus. History, Govt. of Republic of China, Oakland (Calif.) Art Mus., Ga. Mus. Art, Athens, Korean Embassy, Lima, Peru, Nat. Mus. of Modern Art, Nat. Mus. Korea, Govt. of Republic of Korea, Seoul, Nat. Gallery of Modern Art, New Delhi, India, Asian Art Mus. San Francisco, Govt. of People's Republic China, Beijing and Shanghai, Palacio de la Zarzuela, Madrid, Palacio de la Moncloa, Madrid, The Korean Embassy, Madrid, Mus. Art de Sabadell, Spain, Mus. Nat. des Beaux-Arts, Monte Carlo, Monaco, The Philatelic Mus. Palais des Nations, Geneva, others; author: Nong Questions, 1982. Chmn. San Francisco-Seoul Sister City Com., City and County San Francisco, 1981-84. Served with U.S. Army, 1956-59; Served with USAF, 1959-60. Recipient numerous awards including citations from Republic of Korea, Cert. Disting. Achievement State of Calif., 1982, Proclamation City and County of San Francisco, 1982; Nong Stamp issued in his honor UNISEF, 1996. Home: 7360 Locust Run Dr Marshall VA 20115-2103 *Beauty and ugliness, good and bad, right and wrong. Which test should I choose to measure these? Then, how long can I rely on the test I choose?.*

HAN, SYUNG D., international trade consultant, financier; b. Seoul City, Republic of Korea, Mar. 3, 1943; U.S. citizen; s. Young and Kum J. Han. PhD (hon.), Oddessa (USSR) U., 1991; PhD, KW U., 1993; postgrad., Harvard U., 1994, 96, George Washington U., 1994, Columbia U., 1997. Pres. Sunnyland Ent., Inc., Westminster, Calif., 1972-74; CEO, chmn. Global Economies Analysis, Inc., Falls Church, Va., 1974—; pres. S.D. Sunnyland Ent., Inc., Falls Church, 1974—, Sunnyland Holding Inc., Falls Church, 1994—. Recipient medal of peace Peace Found., USSR, 1991, medal of freedom Rep. Party, Washington, 1993. Mem. Nat. Def. Preparation Assn., Acad. Polit. Sci., Washington Internat. Trade Assn., Commonwealth of Va. (public notary). Roman Catholic. Office: SD Sunnyland Ent Inc 6231 Leesburg Pike Falls Church VA 22044-2102

HAN, TIMOTHY WAYNE, drug abuse professional, public health educator; b. Seoul, Korea, Aug. 31, 1953; came to U.S., 1977; s. Ki Cho and Man (Soo) H.; m. Kimmy Jin Sook, Apr. 14, 1991. BS, Mercy Coll., 1982; BA, CUNY, 1986, MEd, MS, 1987. Health resource coord. N.Y.C. Dept. Health, 1987-91, AIDS tng. specialist, pub. health adviser Bur. AIDS, 1989—, substance abuse prevention specialist, 1991—; lectr., educator Asian-Am. communication Columbia U., N.Y.C., 1993—; cons. N.Y.C. Bd. Edn., Bronx, 1991—, child crisis intervention team, 1987—. Teen columnist: N.Y. Korea Times, 1989—; weekly radio talk show host: (Korean Christian Broadcasting Network) The Parade of Youth, 1993—; contbr. articles to profl. jours. Counselor YWCA, 1989, teen dir., 1986-90; youth leader Greater N.Y. Conf., 1992, youth dir., 1984—. Mem. APHA, AMA. Avocations: camping, music, playing piano and guitar, travel, climbing. Home: 3530 Henry Hudson Pky E Bronx NY 10463-1306

HAN, YOUNG JO, agricultural engineer, educator; b. Seoul, Korea, Oct. 7, 1956; came to U.S., 1981; s. Chung Sup Han and Daehee Kim Han; m. Inyee Yoo, Dec. 22, 1984; 1 child, Christopher J. BS, Seoul Nat. U., 1979, MS, 1981; PhD, U. Ill., 1986. Registered profl. engr., S.C. Civh. asst. U. Ill., Urbana, 1982-85, vis. asst. prof., 1986; asst. prof. agrl. engring. Clemson (S.C.) U., 1986-92, assoc. prof. agrl. and biol. engring., 1992-96, prof. agrl. and biol. engring., 1996—. Contbr. articles to profl. jours. Adviser Clemson Table Tennis Assn., 1989-94, Tae Kwon Do Club, 1996—. Wright fellow in agr. U. Ill., 1981-82, Hunter fellow in agr., 1982-83. Mem. Am. Soc. Agrl. Engrs. (Blue Ribbon award 1986, Outstanding Paper award 1993), Soc. Mfg. Engrs. and Machine Vision Assn., Sigma Xi, Phi Kappa Phi, Tau Beta Pi, Alpha Epsilon, Gamma Sigma Delta. Avocations: table tennis, tennis, golf. Home: 202 Sedgefield Dr Clemson SC 29631-1796 Office: Clemson U 229 Mcadams Hall Clemson SC 29634-0357

HANAFUSA, HIDESABURO, virologist; b. Nishinomiya, Japan, Dec. 1, 1929; came to U.S., 1961; s. Kamehachi and Tomi H.; m. Teruko Inoue, May 11, 1958; 1 dau., Kei. B.S., Osaka (Japan) U., 1953, Ph.D., 1960. Research assoc. Research Inst. for Microbial Diseases, Osaka U., 1958-61; postdoctoral fellow virus lab. U. Calif., Berkeley, 1961-64; vis. scientist College de France, Paris, 1964-66; assoc. mem., chief dept. viral oncology Public Health Research Inst. of City N.Y. Inc., 1966-68, mem., 1968-73; prof. Rockefeller U., 1973—, Leon Hess prof., 1986—. Mem. editorial bd. Jour. Virology, 1975—, Molecular Cell Biology, 1984—; contbr. articles to profl. jours. Recipient Howar Taylor Ricketts award, 1981, Albert Lasker Basic Med. Rsch. award, 1982, Asahi Press prize, 1984, Nat. Acad. Sci. award, 1985, Clowes Meml. award, 1986, Culture Merit award, Japan, 1991, Alfred Sloan prize Gen. Motors, 1993, Order of Culture, Japan, 1995; Nat Cancer Inst. grantee, 1966—. Mem. Am. Soc. Microbiology, Am. Soc. Virology, AAAS, N.Y. Acad. Sci., Am. Soc. Biol. Chemistry, Am. Assn. Cancer Rsch. Achievements include research on retroviruses and oncogenes. Home: 500 E 63rd St New York NY 10021-7946 Office: Rockefeller U 1230 York Ave New York NY 10021-6399

HANAHAN, DONALD JAMES, biochemist, educator; b. Springfield, Ill., May 13, 1919; s. James Francis and Clara (Schiller) H.; m. Lillian Marie Larsen, June 21, 1947; children—Douglas A., Laura J., Timothy J., Colleen J., Carolyn M. B.S., U. Ill., 1941, Ph.D., 1944. Research asso. Manhattan Project, 1944-45; postdoctoral fellow U. Calif., Berkeley, 1945-47; faculty U. Wash., Seattle, 1948-67; prof. biochemistry U. Wash., 1958-67; prof., head dept. biochemistry U. Ariz., Tucson, 1967-76; prof. biochemistry U. Tex. Health Sci. Center, San Antonio, 1976—; chmn. dept. U. Tex. Health Sci. Center, 1976-84; prof. emeritus U. Tex. Health Sci. Center, San Antonio, 1994-98. Author: Lipid Chemistry, 1960, A Guide to Phospholipid Chemistry, 1997; contbr. articles to profl. jours. Guggenheim Found. fellow, 1955; NIH spl. fellow, 1965-66; Macy faculty scholar, 1974. Mem. Am. Chem. Soc., Am. Soc. Biol. Chemists. Home: 2892 Pine St San Francisco CA 94115 Office: U Tex Health Sci Ctr Dept Biochemistry San Antonio TX 78284

HANAHAN, JAMES LAKE, insurance executive; b. Burlington, Iowa, Aug. 27, 1932; s. Thomas J. and Clarice P. (Lorey) H.; m. Marilyn R. Lowe, Dec. 27, 1952; children: Bridget Sue Bahlke, Erin Rose Savage. BS, Drake U., 1955; postgrad., George Williams Coll., 1956. Phys dir. Monmouth (Ill.) YMCA, 1955-56; cmty. rels. staff Caterpillar Tractor Co., Peoria, Ill., 1956-57; rep. Conn. Gen. Life Ins. Co., Des Moines, 1957-59, asst. mgr., 1959-63; mgr. group ins. ops. Conn. Gen. Life Ins. Co., Tampa, Fla., 1963-80; pres., chief exec. officer WHP, First In Employee Benefits Inc., 1980-91, J&H Cons. Group Inc., 1980-91; v.p. AON Cons., 1991—; instr. C.P.C.U. courses; seminar leader C.L.U. workshop; cons. ins. seminar Fla. State U.; guest instr. U. South Fla., Hillsborough County Schs. Great Am. Teach-In. Bd. dirs. West Coast Employee Benefit Coun., Tampa Sports Found., Jr. Achievement, Tampa Bay Acad.; chmn. joint bd. trustees Town and Country Hosp. and Meml. Hosp. Tampa; past pres. Pinellas Emergency Mental Health Svcs.; mem. Hillsborough County Health Coun. Recipient double D award Drake U., PEMHS Cmty. Svc. award. Mem. Sales Mktg. Execs.

Tampa (past pres., Exec. of Yr. 1982), Nat. Risk Mgmt. Soc., Greater Tampa C. of C., Mineral Soc. Tampa, Tampa Sports and Recreation Coun. (bd. dirs.), Self Ins. Assn. Am., Pinellas Econ. Devel. Coun. (chmn.), Health Ins. Inst. Am., Profl. Benefit Adminstrs. Assn., Com. of 100, Nat. D Club (Drake U.; dir.), Timber Greens Country Club, Pres.'s Assn., Phi Sigma. Democrat. Roman Catholic. Home: 6659 Garden Palm Ct New Port Richey FL 34655-5117

HANAN, LAURA MOLEN, artist; b. Ft. Monmouth, N.J., Jan. 30, 1954; d. Richard Eugene Molen and Agnes Arlene (Stahlhacke) Rose; m. John Morris Hanan, Apr. 26, 1985; 1 child, Whitney Anne. BS, U. Calif. Berkeley, 1978; BA in Journalism, Humboldt State U., 1980; AOS in Visual Comm., Northwest Coll. Art, 1992. Reporter, city editor Contra Costa Sun, Moraga, Calif., 1980-81; sports reporter, photographer The Canby (Oreg.) Herald, 1981-82; sr. technical writer MDS Qantel Bus. Computers, Hayward, Calif., 1982-84; bus. mgr., owner, designer Hanan Constrn. and Design Co., Inc., Alameda, Calif., 1986-90; dir. admissions Northwest Coll. Art, Poulsbo, Wash., 1992-93; fine artist, graphic artist Laura Hanan Art, Gig Harbor, Seattle, Wash., 1993—; creative dir. Pacific Pipeline, Kent, Wash., 1992-93; co-owner The Watermark Gallery, Village Art Gallery, Freighthouse Gallery, Gig Harbor, Tacoma, 1993-96; art dir., cons. Exec. Office Svcs., Gig Harbor, Beaverton, Oreg., 1996-97. Exhibited in group shows Emerald City Fine Art Gallery, Seattle, 1996-97, Nicholas Joseph Fine Art, N.Y.C., 1997-98, Hastings-Ray Gallery, Southern Pines, N.C., 1997—, Peninsula Br. Libr., Gig Harbor, 1994, 95, 96, Tacoma Art Mus., 1999; represented in permanent collection Pierce County Libr., also pvt. collections. Recipient First Place prize Peninsula Art League, 1995, 2d place, 1996, 3d place, 1997, Peoples Choice award Peninsula Art League, 1997; nominated for 1999 Tacoma Art Mus. juried fundraiser "The Night Tacoma Danced". Avocations: swimming, fishing, sewing, computers, walking.

HANAN, PATRICK DEWES, foreign language professional, educator; b. New Zealand, Jan. 4, 1927; s. Frederick Arthur and Ida Helen (Dewes) H.; m. Anneliese Drube, July 1951; 1 son, Rupert Guy. B.A., Auckland U., 1948, M.A., 1949; B.A., U. London, 1953, Ph.D., 1960. Lectr. Sch. Oriental and African Studies, 1954-63; assoc. prof., then prof. Stanford U., 1963-68; prof. Chinese lit. Harvard U., Cambridge, Mass., 1968-89, Victor S. Thomas prof. Chinese lit., 1989-98, Victor S. Thomas rsch. prof. Chinese lit., 1998—; dir. Harvard-Yenching Inst., 1987-95. Author: The Chinese Short Story, 1973, The Chinese Vernacular Story, 1981, The Invention of Li Yu, 1988; transl.: The Carnal Prayer Mat, 1990, Silent Operas, 1990, A Tower for the Summer Heat, 1995, The Sea of Regret, 1995, The Money Demon, 1999. Fellow Am. Council Learned Socs., Guggenheim Found.; Mem. Am. Acad. Arts and Scis. Office: 2 Divinity Ave Cambridge MA 02138-2020

HANANIA, NICOLA ALEXANDER, physician; b. Jerusalem, Aug. 10, 1960; came to U.S., 1988; s. Alexander Nicola and Leila Doris (Mouchabeck) H.; m. Khoulood Farid Fakhoury, Jan. 8, 1988; children: Alexander Nicola, Hannah Laila. MB, BS, U. Jordan, 1984. Diplomate Am. Bd. Internal Medicine, Am. Bd. Pulmonary Medicine, Am. Bd. Critical Care Medicine. Rotating intern U. Jordan, Amman, 1984-85, resident in internal medicine, 1985-88; resident in internal medicine U. Toronto, 1988-91, fellow in pulmonary medicine, 1991-94; fellow in critical care medicine Coll. Medicine Baylor U., Houston, 1994, asst. prof. medicine, 1995—; presneter Am. Coll. Chest Physicians, Chgo., 1992, Ont. Thoracic Soc., 1993, Asthma Control and Treatment Conf., Collingwood, Ont., 1993, Am. Thoracic Soc., San Francisco, 1993, Boston, 1994, Royal Coll. Physicians and Surgeons Can., Vancouver, 1993, Nat. Conf. on Asthma and Edn., Toronto, 1993, Toronto Hosp., 1994. Contbr. articles to profl. jours. Recipient scholarship U. Toronto, 1992, Rsch. award Toronto Hosp., 1993, 94; grantee Glaxo Can., Inc., 1994. Fellow Royal Coll. Physicians (Can.); mem. ACP, Am. Thoracic Soc., Am. Coll. Chest Physicians (Dupont Pharms. award 1993), Coll. Physicians and Surgeons Ont., Ont. Thoracic Soc., Soc. Critical Care Medicine, Jordanian Assn. Internal Medicine, Jordan Med. Assn. Greek Orthodox. Avocations: stamp collecting, swimming, reading. Office: Baylor U Coll Medicine One Baylor Plz Houston TX 77030

HANARD, PATRICIA ANN, family nurse practitioner; b. Searcy, Ark., Dec. 19, 1943; d. Claudis E. and H. Frances (Stringfellow) Byrum; m. Marcel Roger-Andre Hanard II, Apr. 19, 1964; children: Marcel III, Samantha, Brendan, Dominic. AAS, Ill. Cen. Coll., 1971; BS with honors, Coll. St. Francis, Joliet, Ill., 1985; MLS, Bradley U.; MSN in Pub. Health Nursing, U. Ill., 1996. RN, Ill.; cert. family nurse practitioner; cert. in reproductive endocrinology and infertility; registered med. lab. technician. Nurse emergency rm. Proctor Hosp., Peoria, Ill., 1972-78; head nurse, mgr. office Midwest Med. Svcs., Peoria, 1978-87; head nurse ob/gyn Coll. Medicine U. Ill., Peoria; clin. nurse specialist, office mgr. Fertility and Reproductive Medicine Ctr. of Ctrl. Ill., 1987-97; family nurse practitioner Midwest Urol. Assn., 1997—. Capt. USAR. Mem. AWHONN, Am. Fertility Soc., Am. Med. Technologists, Ill. State Assn. Med. Technologists, ANA, Ill. Nurses Assn., Soc. Urologic Nurses Assn., Alpha Chi Omega, Phi Theta Kappa, Phi Kappa Phi, Sigma Theta Tau. Home: 1023 W Hiawatha Ct Dunlap IL 61525-9543

HANAU, KENNETH JOHN, III, venture capitalist; b. Ridgewood, N.J., Apr. 30, 1965; s. Kenneth John Jr. and Carol Lee (Rossner) H.; m. Ann Ranson Smith, June 4, 1994; 1 child, Lindsay Lee. BA magna cum laude, Amherst Coll, 1988; MBA, Harvard U., 1993. CPA, Vt. Assoc. Coopers & Lybrand, Boston, 1989-90; asst. to pres. K&H Corrugated Case Corp., Walden, N.Y., 1990-91; assoc. Morgan Stanley & Co., Inc., N.Y.C., 1993-94; prin. Weiss, Peck & Greer, Private Equity Ptnrs., LLC, N.Y.C., 1994—; Bd. dirs. K&H Corrugated Case Corp., Walden, N.Y., Shelter Distbn., Inc., Indpls., Richelieu Foods, Inc., Northbrook, Ill., Color Assocs., Inc., St. Louis, Lionheart Newspaper Inc., Fort Worth, Tex., Regent Comm., Inc., Covington, Ky. Mem. Siwanoy Country Club, Harvard Club N.Y.C., Madison Beach Club, Hay Harbor Club. Avocations: reading, music, golf. Home: 21 Gladwin Pl Bronxville NY 10708-2712 Office: Weiss Peck Greer LLC One New York Plaza New York NY 10004

HANAUER, JOE FRANKLIN, real estate executive; b. Stuttgart, Fed. Republic Germany, July 8, 1937; came to U.S., 1938; s. Otto and Betty (Zurndorfer) H.; m. Jane Boyle, Oct. 20, 1972; children: Jill, Wendy, Jason, Elizabeth. BS, Roosevelt U., 1963. Pres. Thorsen Realty, Oak Brook, Ill., 1974-80; sr. v.p. Coldwell Banker, Newport Beach, Calif., 1980-83, pres., 1984, chmn. bd., CEO, 1984-88; prin. Combined Investments LP, Laguna Beach, Calif., 1989—; chmn. bd. dirs. Grubb & Ellis Co., San Francisco, 1993-97; bd. dirs. MAF Bancorp, Chgo., Grubb & Ellie Co., Chgo.; chmn. policy adv. bd. Joint Ctr. for Housing Studies Harvard U., 1995-96. Bd. dirs. Chgo. Chamber Orch., 1976—; trustee Roosevelt U. Mem. Nat. Assn. Realtors (exec. com.). Home: 105 S La Senda Dr Laguna Beach CA 92651-6731 Office: Combined Investments LP 361 Forest Ave Ste 200 Laguna Beach CA 92651-2146

HANAWALT, PHILIP COURTLAND, biology educator, researcher; b. Akron, Ohio, Aug. 25, 1931; s. Joseph Donald and Lenore (Smith) H.; m. Joanna Thomas, Nov. 2, 1957 (div. Oct. 1977); children: David, Steven; m. Graciela Spivak, Sept. 10, 1978; children: Alex, Lisa. Student, Deep Springs Coll., 1949-50; BA, Oberlin Coll., 1954; MS, Yale U., 1955, PhD, 1959; ScD (hon.), Oberlin Coll., 1997. Postdoctoral fellow U. Copenhagen, Denmark, 1958-60, Calif. Inst. Tech., Pasadena, 1960-61; rsch. biophysicist, lectr. Stanford U., Calif., 1961-65, assoc. prof., 1965-70, prof., 1970—; Howard H. and Jessie T. Watkins univ. prof. Stanford U., 1997—; chmn. dept. biol. scis. Stanford U., Calif., 1982-89; mem. physiol. chemistry study sect. NIH, Bethesda, Md., 1966-70, mem. chem. pathology study sect., 1981-84; mem. sci. adv. com. Am. Cancer Soc., N.Y.C., 1972-76, Coun. for Extramural Grants, 1998—; chmn. 2d ad hoc senate com. on professoriate Stanford U., 1988-90; mem. NSF fellowship rev. panel, 1985; mem. carcinogen identification com. Calif. EPA, 1995-98; mem. toxicology adv. com. Burroughs-Welcome Fund, 1995—, chmn., 1997—; mem. sci. adv. bd. Fogarty Internat. Ctr., NIH, 1995-99; chmn. Gordon Conf. on Mutagenesis, 1996; chmn. Gordon Conf. on Mammalian DNA Repair, 1999; mem. bd. on radiation effects rschr. NAS Commn. on Life Scis., 1996-98; trustee Oberlin Coll., 1998—. Author: Molecular Photobiology, 1969; author, editor: DNA Repair: Techniques, 1981, 83, 88, Molecular Basis of Life, 1968, Molecules to Living Cells, 1980; mng. editor DNA Repair Jour., 1982-93; assoc. editor Jour. Cancer Rsch., Molecular Carcinogenesis, Environ. Health Perspectives, Biotechniques; bd. rev. editors Sci.; contbr. more than 370 articles to profl. jours. Recipient Outstanding Investigator award Nat. Cancer Inst., 1987—, Excellence in Tchg. award No. Calif. Phi Beta Kappa, 1991, Environ. Mutagen Soc. Ann. Rsch. award, 1992, Peter and Helen Bing award for Disting. Tchg., 1992, Am. Soc. for Photobiology Rsch. award, 1996, Internat. Mutation Rsch. award, 1997; Hans Falk lectr. Nat. Inst. Environ. Health Scis., 1990, Severo Ochoa Meml. Hons. lectr. NYU, 1996, IBM-Princess Takamatsu lectr. Japan, 1999; Fogarty sr. rsch. fellow, 1993. Fellow AAAS, Am. Acad. Microbiology; mem. NAS, Am. Assn. Cancer Rsch. (bd. dirs. 1994-97), Genetics Soc., Biophys. Soc. (exec. bd. 1969-71), Am. Soc. Biochemistry and Molecular Biology, Environ. Mutagen Soc. (pres. 1993-94), Radiation Rsch. Soc. Achievements include co-discovery of DNA excision-repair and transcription-coupled DNA repair. Home: 317 Shasta Dr Palo Alto CA 94306-4542 Office: Stanford U Herrin Biology Labs Stanford CA 94305-5020

HANBACK, HAZEL MARIE SMALLWOOD, management consultant; b. Washington, Sept. 19, 1918; d. Archibald Carlisle and Mary Louise (Mayhugh) Smallwood; m. William B. Hanback, Sept. 26, 1942; 1 child, Christopher Brecht. AB, George Washington U., 1940; MPA, Am. U., 1968. Archivist, U.S. Office Housing Expediter, 1948-50; mgmt. engr. U.S. Archives, 1950-51; spl. asst.-indsl. specialist Sec. Def., 1951-53; dir. documentation div. Naval Facilities Engring., Alexandria, Va., 1953-81; mgmt. cons., 1981—. Author: Military Color Book, 1960—, Status of Women in a Cybernetically Oriented Soc., 1968—, (newsletter) Worms Eye View, 1982—, The Military Industrial Complex, 1982—. Pres., West End Citizens Assn., Washington, 1956-58; trustee George Washington U., 1979—. Nominee Rockefeller Pub. Service award, 1969, Fed. Woman's award, 1969; recipient cert. of merit Dep. Def., 1965. Mem. Mortar Bd., Phi Delta Gamma, Sigma Kappa. Democrat. Episcopalian. Clubs: George Washington U. (chmn. bd. 1971-75), Columbian Women (pres. George Washington U. Club 1967-69), Order Ea. Star. Home: 2152 F St NW Washington DC 20037-2712

HANBURY, GEORGE LAFAYETTE, II, academic administrator; b. Norfolk, Va., Sept. 20, 1943; s. Emmette Cecil and Ada Christine (Nelligar) H.; m. Jana Hanbury; 1 stepchild, Jia; children from previous marriage: George Lafayette III, Melissa Lee. BS in Pub. Adminstrn, Va. Poly. Inst., 1965; MPA, Old Dominion U., 1977; postgrad., Sr. Exec. Inst. Govt., U. Va., 1985. Asst. to city mgr. Norfolk, 1967-70; asst. city mgr. Virginia Beach, Va., 1970-74; city mgr. Virginia Beach, 1974-82, Portsmouth, Va., 1982-90, Ft. Lauderdale, Fla., 1990-98; exec. v.p. Nova Southeastern U., Ft. Lauderdale, 1998—. Mem. Internat. City Mgmt. Assn., Am. Soc. Pub. Adminstrs., Pi Alpha Alpha. Home: The Four Seasons 333 Sunset Dr Apt 807 Fort Lauderdale FL 33301-2655 Office: Nova Southeastern Univ 3301 College Ave Fort Lauderdale FL 33314-7796

HANCE, JAMES HENRY, JR., bank executive; b. St. Joseph, Mo., Sept. 16, 1944; s. James Henry Sr. and Kathryn (Lichty) H.; m. Beverly Vaughan Smith, May 20, 1960; children: Samantha, Lindsay, Meredith, Blair. BA in Econs., Westminster Coll., Fulton, Mo., 1966; MBA in Fin., Washington U., St. Louis, 1968. CPA. Ptnr. Price Waterhouse, Phila. and Charlotte, N.C., 1968-85; chmn. bd. Consolidated Coin Caterers Corp., Charlotte, 1985-86; exec. v.p., chief acctg. officer NCNB Corp., Charlotte, 1987-88; CFO, co-vice-chmn. Nationsbank Corp. (now Bank of Am.), Charlotte, N.C., 1988—; bd. dirs. Nationsbank of Tenn., D.C., Md., Charlotte, N.C. Bd. dirs. Microelectronics Ctr. N.C., Research Triangle Park, 1988; trustee Presbyn. Hosp. and Presbyn. Hosp. Health Svcs. Corp., Charlotte, 1989, Charlotte Country Day Sch., 1990; mem. acctg. and fin. commn. Bank Adminstrn. Inst., Rolling Meadows, Ill., 1989. Fellow Soc. Internat. Bus. Fellows. Republican. Presbyterian. Office: Bank of Am 100 N Tryon St Fl 58 Charlotte NC 28202-4000*

HANCE, WILEY FRANCIS, executive producer; b. Arlington, Mo., Oct. 30, 1923; s. Francis Marion and Hattie Blanche (Loughridge) H. BA, Washington U., 1950; MA, Cornell U., 1951. Dir. pub. affairs ABC Radio/TV, N.Y.C., 1951-71; dir. pilot project Time-Life Films, N.Y.C., 1972-74; pres., prodr. Times Four Prodns., Inc., N.Y.C., 1974-83; exec. prodr. Western N.Y. Pub. TV, Buffalo, 1977-83; prodr. HanSan Prodns., Inc., N.Y.C., 1988—; prodr. N.Y. Area Emmy Awards, N.Y.C., 1988—. Prodr. TV series Mark Russell Comedy Spls., 1975—, TV spls. El Greco, 1971, The Changing Image, 1972, We Are Not Alone, 1988, Lost in the Stars, 1989; prodr., creator TV series The Music Room, 1982-83, Directions, 1961-71, Meet the Professor, 1961-64, Dean Pike/Bishop Pike, 1955-60. With U.S. Army, 1942-45. Recipient Grand award Internat. Film and TV Festival, 1971, Gold Medal, 1972, Chris award Columbus Film Festival, 1971, 4 nat. Emmy nominations. Mem. NATAS (trustee, pres. N.Y. chpt. 1993-95, gov. 1955), Assn. of Ind. TV Prodrs., Am. Film and Video Assn., Am. Film Inst., Sigma Alpha Iota. Avocation: painting. Home: 405 E 54th St Apt 2A New York NY 10022-5176 Office: HanSan Prodns Inc 405 E 54th St Apt 2A New York NY 10022-5176

HANCHETT-SERBIN, KAREN LYNN, community college administrator; b. Tokyo, Japan, June 29, 1966; came to U.S., 1968; d. James Edward and Jeanne Marie Hanchett; m. David Nathan Serbin, Oct. 27, 1993; children: Isabelle Marie, Hilary Lynn. BA, Westminster Coll., 1988; MEd, Ariz. State U., 1993. Asst. dir. Lorrain (Ohio) County C.C., 1989-90; orientation intern. instr. SUNY, Binghamton, summer 1990, mgr. pottery studio, 1991-92; resident dir. Manhattanville Coll., Purchase, N.Y., 1990-91; IVEP coord., cons. Gateway C.C., Phoenix, 1992-93, adminstrn. counselor, 1993; camp dir. Moscow, Russia, 1994; cons. student affairs Carnegie Mellon U., Pitts., 1998—; tng. cons. Am. Bus. Tng., Moscow, Russia, 1994-95, Ctr. for Bus. Skills Devel., 1995-96. Mktg. advisor Nat. Coun. on Comty. and Justice, Pitts. Avocations: swimming, pottery, interior design. E-mail: kserbin@aol.com. Home: 7016 Blackhawk St Pittsburgh PA 15218

HANCHEY, JAMES CLINTON, lawyer; b. DeQuincy, La., Jan. 10, 1936; s. Clinton W. and Alice Pearl (Harrell) H.; m. Nancy Lee Ligon, Sept. 4, 1993. BA, La. State U., 1958, JD, 1960. Law clk. U.S. Dist. Ct. Appeals (3d cir.), Lake Charles, La., 1960-61; spl. asst. atty. gen. State of La., Baton Rouge, 1960; ptnr. Jones, Tête, Nolen, Hanchey, Fonti & Balfoue, 1961—. Past bd. dirs. YMBC, Lake Charles, La.; past pres. Arts Coun. S.W. La., past v.p. Lake Charles Symphony, bd. dirs. Art Assocs. Lake Charles. Avocations: reading, travel. Office: PO Box 910 Lake Charles LA 70602-0910

HANCOCK, CHARLES CAVANAUGH, JR., scientific association administrator; b. Riverside, Calif., Oct. 19, 1935; s. Charles Cavanaugh and Mary Elizabeth (Riordan) H.; children: Christopher Alan, Stephen Edward. B.S. in Chem. Engring, Stanford U., 1958; M.S. in Indsl. Engring, Tex. Tech U., 1967. Commd. 2d lt. U.S. Air Force, 1958, advanced through grades to lt. col., 1974; worldwide locations in research and devel. and logistics, to, 1979, ret., 1979; exec. officer Am. Soc. Biochem. and Molecular Biology, Bethesda, Md., 1979—; also mgr. Jour. Biol. Chemistry.; gen. sec. 17th Congress of Biochemistry and Molecular Biology; bd. dirs. Chem. Heritage Found., 1993-94. Decorated Meritorious Service medal with 3 oak leaf clusters. Mem. AAAS, Inst. Indsl. Engrs. (sr.), Coun. Engring. and Sci. Soc. Execs., Conv. Liaison Coun. (chmn. 1991-92), Profl. Conv. Mgmt. Assn., Coun. Biology Editors, Soc. Scholarly Pub., Sigma Xi, Alpha Pi Mu, Univ. Club San Diego. Club: Univ. Club. Office: Am Soc Biochem & Molecular Biology 9650 Rockville Pike Bethesda MD 20814-3998

HANCOCK, DON RAY, researcher; b. Muncie, Ind., Apr. 9, 1948; s. Charles David and Jane Lamoine (Krey) H. BA, DePauw U., 1970. Cmty. worker Fla. Meth. Spanish Ministry, Miami, 1970-73; seminar designer United Meth. Seminars, Washington, 1973-75; info. coord. S.W. Rsch. and Info. Ctr., Albuquerque, 1975—; cons. State Planning Coun. on Radiactive Waste Mgmt., Washington, 1980-81; task force mem. Gov.'s Socioecon. Com., Santa Fe, 1983; pub. adv. bd. WIPP Socioecon. Study, Albuquerque, 1979-81. Contbr. articles to profl. jours. Bd. chmn. Roadrunner Food Bank, Albuquerque, 1981-92, N.Mex. Coalition Agaist Hunger, 1978-85; bd. dirs. Albuquerque Housing and Neighborhood Econ. Devel. Com., 1994—, United Meth. Bd. of Ch. and Soc., Washington, 1976-80. Mem. Univ. Heights Assn. (bd. dirs. 1977-82, 85, 88-89, 90-99). Democrat. Office: SW Rsch and Info Ctr PO Box 4524 Albuquerque NM 87196-4524

HANCOCK, GERRE EDWARD, musician; b. Lubbock, Tex., Feb. 21, 1934; s. Ervin Edward and Flake (Steger) H.; m. Judith Duffield Eckerman, July 22, 1961; children: Deborah, Lisa. MusB, U. Tex., 1955; diploma, U. Sorbonne, Paris, 1956; M in Sacred Music, Union Theol. Sem., N.Y.C., 1961; MusD, Nashotah House Episcopal Sem., 1986, U. South, 1999. Asst. organist St. Bartholomew's Ch., N.Y.C., 1960-62; organist, choirmaster Christ Ch. Cathedral, Cin., 1962-71; mem. artist faculty Coll.-Conservatory Music, U. Cin., 1964-71; organist, master choristers St. Thomas Ch., N.Y.C., 1971—; faculty Juilliard Sch., N.Y.C., 1971—, Inst. Sacred Music, Yale U., New Haven, 1974—, Eastman Sch. Music, U. Rochester, N.Y., 1996—; concert organist McFarlane Mgmt., Cleve., 1964—; condr. choral festivals, U.S. and Europe, 1964—; clinician organ and choral workshops, Australia and Republic of South Africa, 1964—. Author: Organ Improvisations, 1976, Improvising: How to Master the Art, 1994; composer: (cantata) Plum Line and City, 1967, (choral works) Missa Resurrectionis, 1979; performer concerts throughout U.S. Europe, South Africa, Australia, Japan. Served with U.S. Army, 1956-58. Fellow Royal Sch. Ch. Music, Am. Guild Organists (past mem. coun.), Royal Coll. Organists (hon.); mem. Assn. Anglican Musicians (past pres.), Phi Mu Alpha Sinfonia (past pres.), Pi Kappa Lambda. Republican. Episcopalian. Club: St. Wilfrid (N.Y.C.) (pres. 1973-74). Avocation: tennis. Office: St Thomas Ch 1 W 53rd St New York NY 10019-5496

HANCOCK, HERBERT JEFFREY (HERBIE HANCOCK), composer, pianist, publisher; b. Chgo., Apr. 12, 1940; s. Wayman Edward and Winnie (Griffin) H.; m. Gudrun Meixner, Aug. 31, 1968. Student, Grinnell (Iowa) Coll., 1956-60, Roosevelt U., Chgo., 1960, Manhattan Sch. Music, 1962, New Sch. Social Research, 1967. owner-pub. Hancock Music Co., 1962—; founder Hancock and Joe Prodns., 1989—; pres. Harlem Jazz Music Center, Inc. Performed with Chgo. Symphony Orch., 1952, Coleman Hawkins, Chgo., 1960, Donald Byrd, 1960-63, Miles Davis Quintet, 1963-68; recorded with Chick Corea; scored films Blow Up, 1966, The Spook Who Sat By the Door, 1973, Death Wish, 1974, A Soldier's Story, 1984, Jo Jo Dancer, Your Life is Calling, 1986, Action Jackson, 1988, Colors, 1988, Harlem Nights, 1989, Livin' Large, 1991; scored and appeared in film 'Round Midnight, 1986 (Academy award best original score 1986); albums include Takin' Off, 1963, Succotash, 1964, Speak Like a Child, 1968, Fat Albert Rotunda, 1969, Mwandishi, 1971, Crossings, 1972, Sextant, 1972, Headhunters, 1973, Thrust, 1974, The Best of Herbie Hancock, 1974, Man-Child, 1975, The Quintet, 1977, V.S.O.P., 1977, Sunlight, 1978, An Evening with Herbie Hancock and Chick Corea in Concert, 1979, Feets Don't Fail Me Now, 1979, Monster, 1980, Greatest Hits, 1980, Lite Me Up, 1982, Future Shock, 1983, (with Foday Musa Suso) Village Life, 1985, (with Dexter Gordon) The Other Side of 'Round Midnight, 1987, Perfect Machine, 1988, Jamming, 1992, Cantaloupe Island, 1994, Tribute to Miles, 1994, Dis Is Da Drum, 1995, The New Standard, 1996, 1+, 1997, Gershwin's World, 1998 (Grammy). Recipient citation of achievement Broadcast Music, Inc., 1963; Jay award Jazz mag., 1964; critics poll for talent deserving wider recognition Down Beat mag., 1967; 1st place piano category, 1968, 69, 70; composer award, 1971; All-Star Band New Artist award Record World, 1968; named top jazz artist Black Music mag., 1974; recipient Grammy award for best rhythm and blues instrumental performance, 1983, 84, for best jazz instrumental composition (co-composer), 1987, best jazz instrumental performance, 1995. Mem. Nat. Acad. Rec. Arts and Scis., Jazz Musicians Assn., Nat. Acad. TV Arts and Scis., Broadcast Music. Club: Pioneer (Grinnell Col.). Address: Hancock Music 1250 N Doheny Dr Los Angeles CA 90069-1723*

HANCOCK, IAN FRANCIS (O YANKO LE REDŽOSKO), linguistics educator; b. London, Aug. 29, 1942; came to U.S., 1972; s. John Redzo and Kathleen Elsa (Palmer) H.; married; children: Julian Marko, Adrian Lee Imre, Meilinne Khim, Colin Malik. Diploma in Oriental and African Studies, U. London, 1969, Ph.D., 1971. Reporter, photographer Daily Free Press, B.C., 1959-60; various positions Europe, 1961-74; display advt. staff Sears Roebuck Co., B.C., 1964-65; compiler literary index Vancouver Pub. Library, 1971-72; prof. linguistics U. Tex., Austin, 1972—; mem. Jewish Studies Adv. Bd. U. Tex., 1986—; mem. Adv. Coun. on Jewish Affairs, Haifa, 1983; U.S. rep. UNICEF; spl. advisor U.S. Holocaust Meml. Coun., 1985-87; pres. UN Praesidium Head for Internat. Romani Union, 1990—, Internat. Roma Fedn., Inc., 1993—; bd. dirs., mem. Romani adv. coun. Project on Ethnic Rels., 1993—; mem. U.S. State Dept. Diplomatic Team, Joint Coun. Europe/Orgn. for Security and Coop. in Europe meeting on Roma, Warsaw, 1994; White House apptd. U.S. Holocause Meml. Coun., 1997. Author: (with David De Camp) Pidgins and Creoles: Current Trends and Prospects, 1974, (with John Reinecke and others) Bibliography of Pidgin and Creole Languages, 1975, Problems in the Creation of Standard Dialect of Romanes, 1975, The Pariah Syndrome, 1987, (with Loreto Todd) Internat. English Usage, 1986, A Handbook of Romani, 1995; editor: Romani Sociolinguistics, 1979, Readings in Creole Studies, 1979, (with John Reinecke and others) Jour. of Creole Studies, 1972; mem. editl. bd. Jour. of Gypsy Lore Soc., 1975, Roma, 1973, Jour. of Krio Lit. Soc., 1970; contbr. (with John Reinecke and others) articles to profl. jours. Bd. dirs. Gullah Connection Com., 1990—; mem. Phila. Ctr. on the Holocaust. Recipient Rafto Internat. Human Rights prize, Norway, 1997; named Gamaliel chair in Peace & Justice, 1998. Office: U Tex Dept English Parlin Hall Austin TX 78712 also: Internat Union (USA) Manchaca TX 78652-0822*

HANCOCK, JOAN HERRIN, retired executive search company executive; b. Indpls., Apr. 16, 1930; d. Roy Silvey and Glenna Olive (Metsker) Herrin; widowed; children: Glenna Jill Hancock Smith, Jeri Lee Hancock Moore, John Norman. BA, Butler U., 1953. Cert. profl. cons. Career counselor Career Cons. Inc., Indpls., 1974-82; counselor, corp. officer Unique Alternatives Inc., Indpls., 1982-84, Alternatives Plus Inc., Indpls., 1984-92; pres. Herrin & Assocs., 1992-99; ret. 1999. Precinct Committeeperson Dem. Com., Indpls, 1960-67, 86-95, 98—; pres. Sch. # 59 PTA, 1964, CWF, 1957-59, bd. dirs., 1957—, chair centennial com., 1996; past group leader Camp Fire Girls; past mem. of chmn.'s club Marion County Dem. Cen. Com.; 50th reunion com. Broad Ripple H.S., 1998—; active Buller U. 1953 Reunion Com., Allisonville Christian Ch. Mem. Blueridge Garden Club (program chmn., 1998—, v.p., 1998—). Home and Office: 6040 Knyghton Rd Indianapolis IN 46220-4956

HANCOCK, JOHN ALVA, legislative staff member; b. Columbia, S.C., Mar. 7, 1955; s. Jack Grant and Barbara Ann (Schwartz) H.; m. Maura Ann Carroll, Apr. 7, 1979; children: Jonathan Grant, Kyle Francis. BS, U.S. Naval Acad., 1978; MA, U. So. Calif., 1991; PhD, George Mason U., 1999. Commd. ens. USN, 1978, advanced through grades to comdr.; main propulsion asst. USS Tautog, Pearl Harbor, Hawaii, 1980-84; navigator, ops. officer USS Gnelard P. Lipscomb, Norfolk, Va., 1984-86; radiol. controls. officer USS Hunley, Norfolk and Holy Loch, Scotland, 1987-88; submarine ops. officer Naval Forces Europe, London, 1988-91; exec. officer USS Von Steuben, Charleston, S.C., 1991-93; assoc. chair dept. weapons and sys. engring. U.S. Naval Acad., Annapolis, Md., 1993-98; ret. USN, 1998; dep. chief of staff Senator Kay Bailey Hutchison, Washington, 1999—. Mem. Assn. Public Polich Analysis and Mgmt., Acad. Polit. Sci. Republican. Presbyterian. Office: Office of Senator Kay Bailey Hutchison 284 Russell Senate Office Washington DC 20510

HANCOCK, JOHN COULTER, telecommunications company executive; b. Martinsville, Ind., Oct. 21, 1929; s. Floyd A. and Catherine (Coulter) H.; m. Betty Jane Holden, Feb. 6, 1949; children: Debbie, Dwight, Marilyn, Virginia. BSEE, Purdue U., 1951, MEE, 1955, PhD, 1957. Engr. Naval Avionics Facility, Indpls., 1951-57; asst. prof. elec. engring. Purdue U., West Lafayette, Ind., 1957-60, assoc. prof. elec. engring., 1960-63, prof. elec. engring., 1963-65, head Sch. Elec. Engring., 1965-72, dean Schs. Engring., 1972-84; exec. v.p., chief tech. officer Sprint, Inc., Kansas City, Mo., 1984-86; exec. v.p. corp. devel. and tech. United Telecommunications, Inc., Kansas City, Mo., 1986-88, cons., 1988—; mem. Nat. Sci. Bd., 1986—; bd. dirs. Hillenbrand Industries, Batesville, Ind. Author: An Introduction to the Principles of Communications Theory, 1961. Fellow IEEE, AAAS, Am. Soc. Engring. Edn. (pres. 1983-84, Lamme award 1980); mem. Nat. Acad. Engring., Sigma Xi, Eta Kappa Nu, Tau Beta Pi.

HANCOCK, JOHN WALKER, III, banker; b. Long Beach, Calif., Mar. 8, 1937; s. John Walker and Bernice H.; m. Elizabeth Hoien, June 20, 1959; children: Suzanne, Donna, Randy, David. BA in Econs, Stanford U., 1958, MBA, 1960. With Security Pacific Nat. Bank, L.A., 1960-92, v.p., 1968-77, sr. v.p., 1977-84, exec. v.p., 1984-92; pres. Bancap Investment Group, Long Beach, Calif., 1992—; bd. dirs. Harbor Bank; chmn. Meml. Med. Ctr.; commr. Port of Long Beach. Bd. dirs. Long Beach Symphony, Meml. Hosp., Long Beach City Coll. Found. Mem. Stanford U. Alumni Assn., Calif. Club (L.A.), Va. Country Club, Balboa Bay Club, Pacific Club. Republican. Home: 258 Roycroft Ave Long Beach CA 90803-1717 Office: Bancap Investment Group 6265 E 2nd St Long Beach CA 90803-4613*

HANCOCK, M(ARION) DONALD, political science educator; b. McAllen, Tex., Aug. 20, 1939; s. Robert Nicklas and Florence Olive (Norquest) H.; children: Erik Lorans, Kendra Lee. BA, U. Tex., 1961; postgrad., U. Bonn, Germany, 1959-60; MA, Columbia U., 1962, PhD, 1966; postgrad., U. Stockholm, 1963-64. Instr. Columbia U., spring 1965; asst. prof. polit. sci. U. Tex., Austin, 1965-69; assoc. prof. U. Tex., 1969-75, prof., 1975—, dir. Center for European Studies, 1970-79, assoc. dean, Coll. Social and Behavioral Scis., 1976-79; prof. Vanderbilt U., Nashville, 1979—, dir. Title VI Nat. Resource Ctr. on Western Europe, 1992-95; dir. Center for European Studies, 1981—; co-chmn. Coun. for European Studies, 1981-85; vis. prof. Columbia U., 1967, U. Bielefeld, 1973, U. Mannheim, 1977, U. Regensburg, 1986-87; Washington del. representing Commn. of the European Cmty. (Team Europe); lectr. in field. Author: Sweden: The Politics of Postindustrial Change, 1972, West Germany: Politics of Democratic Corporatism, 1989; co-author: (with John Logue and Bernt Schiller) Managing Modern Capitalism, 1991, (with Helga Welsh) German Unification: Process and Outcomes, 1994; editor, co-author: Politics in Western Europe, 2d edit., 1998, (with Gideon Sjoberg) Politics in the Post-Welfare State: Responses to the New Individualism, 1972; co-editor: 10th ann. spl. issue Comparative Politics, 1978. Woodrow Wilson fellow, 1961-62; Dept. State Internat. Affairs fellow, summer 1962; Council Fgn. Relations internat. affairs fellow, 1972-73. Mem. Am. Polit. Sci. Assn., So. Polit. Sci. Assn., Coun. European Studies Soc. Advancement Scandinavian Studies, European Cmty. Studies Assn. (exec. com.), Conf. Group on German Politics (pres. 1990-92). Democrat. Episcopalian. Office: Vanderbilt U Dept Polit Sci Nashville TN 37235

HANCOCK, NANNETTE BEATRICE FINLEY, mental health educator, consultant; b. Birmingham, Ala., Aug. 24, 1937; d. James L. and Minnie (Mason) Finley; m. Frank J. Hancock Jr., Dec. 27, 1958 (div. May 1976); children: Andria Denise, Frank J. III, Cheryl René. BSN, Dillard U., 1958; MPH in Pub. Health, U. Calif., Berkeley, 1970; PhD in Psychology, Western Colo. U., 1977; MA in Clin. Psychology, John F. Kennedy U., 1991. Lic. marriage, family and child therapist. 2d lt. staff nurse U.S. Army Nurse's Corp, Denver, 1958-59; staff nurse, head nurse St. Francis Hosp., Evanston, Ill., 1960-64, Richmond (Calif.) Hosp., 1964-65; sch. nurse Richmond Unified Sch. Dist., 1965-69; prof. Contra Costa Coll., San Pablo, Calif., 1970—; pvt. practice mental health cons. Richmond, 1977—; founder, owner Nannette's Beauty and Figure Salon, 1982-86; head mental health component Bay Area Black Consortium for Quality Health Care AIDS Minority Health Initiative, Oakland, Calif., 1994—. Mem. Social Heritage Group, 1964—, human rels. com., 1966-70, Easter Hill Meth. Ch., 1964—. Col. Army Nurse's Corp. USAR, 1978—. Mem. Calif. Assn. Marriage and Family Therapy, Calif. Nurse's Assn., Bay Area Assn. Black Psychologists, Res. Officer's Assn. Avocations: water skiing, opera, symphony, theatre, reading. Home: 4801 Reece Ct Richmond CA 94804-3444 Office: 1440 Broadway Ste 209 Oakland CA 94612-2022

HANCOCK, S. LEE, lawyer; b. Knoxville, Tenn., Aug. 11, 1955; s. Melton Donald and Alma Helen (McDaniel) H.; m. Kathleen Ann Koll, July 26, 1986. BS summa cum laude, Southwest Mo. State U., 1975; JD cum laude, So. Meth. U., 1979. Bar: Mo. 1979, U.S. Dist. Ct. (we. dist.) Mo. 1979, U.S. Tax Ct. 1982, U.S. Ct. Claims Calif. 1983, Calif. 1988, U.S. Supreme Ct., 1992; CPA, Mo. Assoc. Blackwell, Sanders, Matheny, Weary & Lombardi, Kansas City, Mo., 1979-83, ptnr., 1984-88; ptnr. Allen, Matkins, Leck, Gamble & Mallory, Newport Beach, Calif., 1988-98, of counsel, 1999—; CEO G02 Systems, Inc., Newport Beach, Calif., 1998—; pres., CEO Go2 Systems, Inc. Bd. dirs. U. Calif./Orange County Venture Forum, 1988-95, Orange County Cmty. Found., 1991—, sec. 1994-95, pres. 1995-97. Mem. ABA, Young Execs. Am. (bd. dirs. Orange County chpt. 1992-96, pres. 1994-95), Calif. Bar Assn., Mo. Bar Assn., Orange County Bar Assn., Lawyers Assn. Kansas City (pres. young lawyers sect. 1986-87, bd. dirs. 1986-87), Order of coif, Mensa. Republican. Avocations: flying, sailing, skiing, photography. Home: 4 Hampshire Ct Newport Beach CA 92660-4933 Office: G02 Systems, Inc. 18400 Von Karman Fl 4 Newport Beach CA 92715

HANCOCK, STEWART F., JR., state judge; b. Syracuse, N.Y., Feb. 2, 1923; s. Stewart F. and Marion (MCLennan) H. BS, U.S. Naval Acad., 1945; LLB, Cornell U., 1950; LLD (hon.), Syracuse U., 1993, Le Moyne Coll., 1999. Corp. counsel, chief legal officer City of Syracuse, 1961-63; justice 5th judicial dist. N.Y. Supreme Ct., 1971-77, assoc. justice appellate divsn. 4th judicial dept., 1977-86; assoc. judge N.Y. Ct. Appeals, Albany, 1986-93; disting. vis. prof. law, jurist in residence Syracuse U., 1994—; counsel Hancock & Estabrook, Syracuse, 1994—; mem. N.Y. State Com. on Profession and the Cts., 1994—. Rep. chmn. Onondaga County, 1964-66; Rep. candidate for Congress, 1966; former mem. Onondaga County Met. Water Bd.; mem. Syracuse Bd. Edn., ARC, Dunbar Ctr., Pebble Hill Sch., Crouse-Irving Meml. Hosp., Syracuse Symphony; mem. First Presbyn. Ch., Cazenovia. Line officer USN, 1945-47, lt. (s.g.) USNR, 1950-51. Fellow Am. Bar Found., New York State Bar Found.; mem. ABA, N.Y. State Bar Assn., Onondaga County Bar Assn. Office: Hancock & Estabrook 1500 Mony Tower 1 PO Box 4976 # 1 Syracuse NY 13221-4976

HANCOCK, WILLIAM JOHN, career officer; b. Davenport, Iowa, Oct. 23, 1942; s. Tom and Jane (McGinn) H.; m. Gayle Redmond, May 29, 1969; 1 child, Jeffrey Alan. BS, U.S. Naval Acad., 1965; student, Guided Missle Sch., 1965, AMPHIP Sch., 1966, Destroyer Sch., 1968, PCO Pipeline, 1980-81; MS, USN Postgrad. Sch., Monterey, Calif., 1972. Commd. ensign USN, 1965, advanced through grades to vice adm., 1996; 1st lt. USS Tattnall, 1965-66; officer in charge Coastal Div. 14, 1966-67; weapons/chief engr. USS Brooke (DEG 1), 1968-70; analyst OPNAV, 1972-74; exec. officer USS PFFoster (DD 964), 1975-77; exec. asst. Sec. Navy (OPA), 1977-79, adminstrv. aide, 1979-80; comdg. officer USS Towers (DDG 9), 1981-83; tng. officer, asst. ops. officer 7th Fleet Staff, 1983-85; br. head OPNAV, 1985-86, exec. asst., 1986-87; comdg. officer USS Worden (CG-18), 1987-89; br. chief, dep. dir. for combat support ops. JCS, 1989-90; dir. for ops. Div. Office Budget and Reports, 1990-91; comdr. Cruiser-Destroyer Group One, 1991-93; dir. Cinc Liaison Divsn., Budget & Reports, 1993-96, dep. chief naval ops.-logistics, 1996—. Recipient Vice Adm. Stockdale award for inspirational leadership, 1983. Avocation: skiing. Office: Dep Chief Naval Ops (Logistics) 2000 Navy Pentagon Washington DC 20350-2000

HANCOCK, WILLIAM MARVIN, computer security and network engrng. executive; b. Portsmouth, Va., Feb. 10, 1957; s. William H. and Marjorie E. (Davis) H. BA in Computer Sci., Thomas A. Edison Sr. Coll., 1992; MS in Computer Sci., Greenwich U., 1993, PhD in Computer Sci., 1994. Cert. info. systems security profl., network expert. Programmer Tex. Instruments, Dallas, 1972-74; cons. Digital Equipment Corp., Dallas, 1979-82; div. analyst Standard Oil of Ohio, Dallas, 1982-84; v.p. engrng. New Leaf Techs., Arlington, Tex., 1984-90, Network 1 Inc., Arlington, 1990-94; exec. v.p. and chief tech. officer Network 1, Boston, 1990—; U.S. network expert Am. Nat. Stds. Inst., N.Y.C., 1985-87; stds. editor Internat. Orgn. for Stds., Geneva, 1986-88. Author: Designing and Implementing Ethernet Networks, 1988, Network Concepts and Architectures, 1989, Issues and Problems in Computer Networks, 1990, Advanced Ethernet/802.3 Management and Performance, 1992, Computer Consulting is a Very Funny Business, 1993, Designing and Implementing ATM Networks, 1994, Applied Networking, 1996, Advanced Network Architecture, 1996, Everything You Wanted to Know About Networks But Were Afraid to Ask, 1998, Windows-NT Network Security, 1998, Networking Explained, 1999; editor-in-chief Computers and Security Mag.; columnist Network Security Mag. With USN, 1974-79. Recipient Arnold Fletcher award, 1992. Mem. IEEE, NSOR, ANSI, Digital Equipment Computer Users Soc. (Tech. Excellence award 1992), Assn. for Computing Machinery, Computer Security Inst. Achievements include design of over 4300 computer networks. Six-time world aikido champion. Office: Network -1 Security Solutions Inc 1601 Trapelo Rd Waltham MA 02451

HANCOX, DAVID ROBERT, audit administrator, educator; b. Albany, N.Y., Aug. 1, 1951; s. Robert F. and Elaine C. (Morgart) H.; m. Judith A. Gaylord, Jan. 17, 1975; children: Robert, Bradford, Ryan D. AS, Hudson Valley Community Coll., 1973; BBA, Siena Coll., 1975. Cert. internal auditor; cert. govt. fin. mgr. State auditor N.Y. State Comptr., Albany, 1974—; lectr. Albany Bus. Coll., 1982-83, Schenectady (N.Y.) Community Coll., 1988, Siena Coll., Loudonville, N.Y., 1991—, Sage Coll., Albany, 1992-97; dir. state audits N.Y. State Comptr., 1989—. Co-author: State and Local Government, Program Control and Audit: Handbook for Managers and Auditors, 1997. Chair adminstrn. com., v.p. parish coun. St. James Ch., 1994-98, pres. parish coun., 1998-99; cluster leader Albany Diocese, 1995-96. Mem. Assn. Govt. Accts. (pres. N.Y. Capital chpt. 1986-87, bd. dirs. 1987-89, Arlington, Va. regional v.p. 1990—, Gold award 1991), Inst. Internal Auditors (Albany chpt. bd. govs. 1988-90, 93-96, pres. 1996-97). Roman Catholic. Avocations: reading, computers, exercising. Home: 21 Magnolia Ter Albany NY 12209-1714 Office: N Y State Comptr AE Smith Bldg Albany NY 12236

HANCOX, STEVEN J., auditor, state official; b. Dec. 26, 1957. BBA, Siena Coll., 1979. Audit supr. mgmt. audit group N.Y. State Comptr.'s Office, Albany, 1986-95; mgr. strategic planning N.Y. State Comptr.'s Office, Albany, 1995-97, asst. to dep. comptr., 1997—. E-mail: sjhancox@osc.state.ny.us. Home: 50 S Main Ave Albany NY 12208-2508 Office: NY State Comptr's Office AE Smith Office Bldg 6th Fl Albany NY 12236-0001

HAND, CADET HAMMOND, JR., marine biologist, educator; b. Patchogue, N.Y., Apr. 23, 1920; s. Cadet Hammond and Myra (Wells) H.; m. Winifred Werdelin, June 6, 1942; children—Cadet Hammond III, Gary Alan. B.S., U. Conn., 1946; M.A., U. Calif. at Berkeley, 1948, Ph.D., 1951. Instr. Mills Coll., 1948-50, asst. prof., 1950-51; research biologist Scripps Inst. Oceanography, 1951-53; mem. faculty U. Calif. at Berkeley, 1953—, prof. zoology, 1963-85, prof. emeritus, 1985—; dir. Bodega Marine Lab., 1961-85; Cons. NIH, 1964-66, NSF, 1964-69; mem. atomic safety and licensing bd. panel Nuclear Regulatory Commn., 1971-92, adminstrv. judge atomic safety and licensing bd. panel, 1980-92; NSF sr. postdoctoral fellow, 1959-60; Guggenheim fellow, 1967-68. Contbr. articles to profl. jours. Fellow Calif., Wash. acads. scis.; mem. No. Calif. Malacozool. Soc. (pres. 1963-87), Soc. Systematic Zoology, Ecol. Soc. Am., Ray Soc. (Gt. Britain), Am. Soc. Zoologists (chmn. div. invertebrate zoology 1977-78), Am. Soc. Limnology and Oceanography. Home: 305 McChristian Ave Bodega Bay CA 94923 Office: Bodega Marine Lab Bodega Bay CA 94923

HAND, DALE L., pharmacist; b. Boise, Idaho, Oct. 21, 1947; s. Robert Ray and Evelyn Mabel (McKenzie) H.; m. Gloria J. Lassen, Dec. 19, 1970; children: Travis D., Jason D. Student, Walla Walla Coll., 1965-66; B Pharmacy, Idaho State U., 1970; MS in Health Svcs. Adminstrn., Coll. St. Francis, Joliet, Ill., 1985. Intern Clinic Pharmacy, Pocatello, Idaho, 1968-70; pharmacognosy lab. tchng. asst. Idaho State U., 1969-70; hosp. pharmacy internship St. Luke's Hosp., Boise, 1970-71, clin. staff pharmacist, 1971-77; various to dir. pharmacy svcs. Porter Meml. Hosp., Denver, 1981-92, adminstrv. dir. dept. pharm. care, 1992—; pharmacy extern preceptor U. Colo., 1981—; cons. pharmacist McNamara Hosp. and Nursing Home, Fairplay, Colo., 1981-83; cons. Edn. Design, Inc., 1993—; lectr. in field.; chmn. various hosp. coms. Contbr. articles to profl. jours. Bd. dirs. Arapahoe Sertoma, 1991-98. Mem. Am. Soc. Health Sys. Pharmacists, Colo. Soc. Health Sys. Pharmacists. Seventh-Day Adventist. Avocations: golf, softball, snow-skiing, landscape design, music. Home: 7269 W Chestnut Dr Littleton CO 80128-5699 Office: Porter Adventist Hosp 2525 S Downing St Denver CO 80210-5817

HAND, JANET L., medical, surgical and critical care nurse, educator; b. Joplin, Mo., Aug. 13, 1948; d. George Henry and Alice Loue (Leonard) Ritter; m. Robert Wayne Hand, June 15, 1968; chldren: Jeffrey Scott, Misty Michele. BS in Biology, West Tex. State U., Canyon, 1970, BSN, 1983. Cert. to enucleate eyes from donors, 1984; cert. secondary level tchr., Tex., 1971. Office nurse for internist Amarillo, Tex., 1984-86; infection control nurse, edn. coord. Palo Duro Hosp., Canyon, 1986-87, charge nurse, med.-surg. floor, 1987-92; charge 5B-DSU unit High Plains Bapt. Hosp., Amarillo, 1987-89, staff nurse and quality assurance for DSU unit, 1992—; office nurse, 1st surg. asst. gynecologist's office, Amarillo, 1989-90; auditor charts Northwest Hosp., 1990-93; part-time weekend staff nurse gynecology floor N.W. Tex. Hosp., Amarillo, 1992-94. Mem. Assn. Operating Room Nurses, Am. Acad. Ophthalmic Nurses, Tex. Assn. Post Anesthesia Nurses.

HAND, JOHN OLIVER, museum curator; b. N.Y.C., Aug. 17, 1941; s. John Osborn and LaBelle (Bridges) H. B.A., Denison U., Granville, Ohio, 1963; M.A., U. Chgo., 1967; M.F.A. (Samuel Kress Found. fellow 1969-72), Princeton U., 1971, Ph.D. (Belgian Am. Found. fellow 1972-73), 1978. With edn. dept. Nat. Gallery Art, Washington, 1965-69; curator No. Renaissance painting Nat. Gallery Art, 1973—; preceptor Princeton U., 1971. Author papers in field. Office: Nat Gallery Art Washington DC 20565

HAND, PETER JAMES, neurobiologist, educator; b. Oak Park, Ill., Jan. 5, 1937; s. James Harold and Edna Mae (Watson) H.; m. Mary Minnis, Sept. 16, 1958; children—Katherine Patricia, Carol Jane, Margaret Anne, Robin Lynn, Stephen Douglas, Peter James; m. Carol Louise Corson, Oct. 23, 1976; m. Christine L. Arnold, Sept. 19, 1986. VMD, U. Pa., 1961, PhD, 1964. Faculty U. Pa., Phila., 1964—, prof. anatomy, 1979—, head dept. anatomy, 1980-87, 91-97; mem. NIH rev. com. Regional Primate Ctrs., 1985-89; mem. nominating com. Lifu Acad. award in Chinese Medicine. Contbr. articles to profl. jours. Pres. USO Council, Cape May, N.J., 1972-73, nat. del.; trustee Mid-Atlantic Ctr. for Arts, Cape May, 1973-74; bd. dirs. Cape May Taxpayers Assn., 1972-74, Univ. City Hist. Soc., Phila., 1978-80. NIH grantee, 1970-82, 86-92, 95—. Mem. Am. Assn. Anatomists, Am. Assn. Vet. Anatomists, Soc. Neurosci. (pres. Phila. chpt. 1984-85), Internat. Brain Rsch. Orgn., World Assn. Vet. Anatomists, Internat. Assn. for Study of Pain, Am. Coll. Acupuncture (pres. 1997-98), Internat. Coll. Acupuncture and Electro-Therapeutics, Sigma Xi, Alpha Psi (trustee 1965-87). Republican. Home: 5290 SE Joshua Tree Ter Hobe Sound FL 33455-7891 Office: Sch Vet Medicine U Pa Philadelphia PA 19104

HAND, ROGER, physician, educator; b. Bklyn., Sept. 25, 1938; s. Morton and Angela (Belvedere) H.; children: Christopher, Jessica. BS, NYU, 1959, MD, 1962. Intern, then resident in internal medicine NYU Med. Ctr., 1962-68; postdoctoral fellow, asst. prof. Rockefeller U., N.Y.C., 1968-73; clin. asst. prof. medicine Cornell U. Med. Coll., N.Y.C., 1970-73; asst. prof., then assoc. prof. medicine McGill U., Montreal, Que., Can., 1973-80; prof. medicine, dir. McGill Cancer Ctr., 1980-84; sr. physician Royal Victoria Hosp., Montreal, 1980-84; chmn. internal medicine Ill. Masonic Ctr., Chgo., 1984-88; prof. medicine U. Ill., Chgo., 1984—, chief sect. gen. internal medicine, 1988-95, prof. health policy and adminstrn. Sch. Pub. Health, 1995—; prin. clin. coord. Ill. Found. Quality Health Care, Chgo., 1996—. Contbr. articles to profl. jours. Brig. gen. USAR, 1963-71, 85—. Decorated Air medal, Meritorious Svc. medal, Army Commendation medal; med. rsch. grantee. Fellow ACP, Royal Coll. Physicians and Surgeons, Am. Coll. Med. Quality; mem. Am. Soc. Clin. Investigation, Am. Soc. Biol. Chemists, Am. Assn. Cancer Research, Am. Soc. Clin. Oncology, Infectious Disease Soc., Can. Soc. Clin. Investigation, Cen. Soc. Clin. Rsch., Am. Cancer Soc.(bd. dirs. Ill. div.), Am. Health Quality Assn. Office: IFQHC Ste 104 South 2625 Butterfield Rd Oak Brook IL 60523-1234

HAND, VIRGINIA SAXTON, home health nurse; b. Phila., July 21, 1956; d. John Grant and Grace Marie (Palermo) Saxton; m. Arthur L. Hand III, June 2, 1979; children: Arthur IV, Katherine, Ryan, Sean. RN, St. Agnes Med. Ctr. Sch., Nursing, Phila., 1977. RN, Pa. Staff nurse St. Agnes Med. Ctr., Phila., 1977-78, head nurse, 1979-81; staff nurse Frankford Hosp., Phila., 1985-93; home health nurse Phila., 1993—. Vol. meals to shut-ins St. Matthew Outreach, Phila., 1989—; group facilitator St. Matthew's Mothers of PreTeens, Phila., 1994—; mem. Precana team St. Matthew's Ch., 1990—; mem. St. Matthew Sacremental Prep Team, 1994—; parish nurse, 1999—. Roman Catholic. Home: 3212 Cottman Ave Philadelphia PA 19149-1511

HAND, WILLIAM BREVARD, federal judge; b. Mobile, Ala., Jan. 18, 1924; s. Charles C. and Irma W. H.; m. Allison Denby, June 17, 1948; children: Jane Connor Hand Dukes, Virginia Alan Hand Hollis, Allison Hand Peebles. BS in Commerce and Bus. Adminstrn., U. Ala., 1947, JD, 1949; LLD (hon.), U. Mobile, 1990. Bar: Ala. 1949. Assoc. Hand, Arendall, Bedsole, Greaves & Johnston, Mobile, 1949-71; chief judge, then sr. judge U.S. Dist. Ct. (so. dist.) Ala., Mobile, 1971—. Chmn. Mobile County Rep. Exec. Com., 1968-71. Served with U.S. Army, 1943-46. Decorated Bronze Star medal. Mem. Am., Fed., Ala., Mobile bar assns. Methodist. Office: US Dist Ct US Courthouse 113 Saint Joseph St # 7 Mobile AL 36602-3606*

HANDA, EUGENIE QUAN, graphic designer; b. Oakland, Calif., Oct. 18, 1957; d. Eugene Ernest and Ruby (Louie) Quan; m. Mark Richard Handa, Feb. 14, 1981; children: Sharice Quan, Chaz Quan. BFA in Graphic Design with distinction, Calif. Coll. Arts and Crafts, 1979. Graphic artist Bemis Corp., Union City, Calif., 1979-80; graphic designer Hubbert, Ltd. Advtsg., Santa Clara, Calif., 1980-81, Darien, Russell & Hill Advtsg., San Jose, Calif., 1981-82, KNTV, Inc.-Channel 11, San Jose, 1982-83; owner, graphic designer Quanda Design, San Jose and Danville, Calif., 1983—; vol. graphic designer, cons. Sycamore Valley Elem. Sch., Danville, Calif., 1994—. Work includes design for No. Calif. Hyatt Hotels, 1983-88, Lifescan Quality Awards Program, 1984-87, Hewlett-Packard Collateral, 1987—, Jadtec Computer Group Collateral, 1987-95, Am. Med. Writer's Assn. Booklets, 1993-94, others. Art dir. fundraiser East Valley Ednl. Found., San Jose, Calif., 1986; adv. sch. bond Sycamore Valley PTA, Danville, Calif., 1995-98; legis. rep. San Ramon Valley Unified Sch. Dist., Sacramento, 1997—; mem. standing com. PTA, newsletter and directory chmn., 1995-97; troop team mem., designer, coord. sibling care San Francisco Bay Coun. Girl Scouts USA, 1996-97. Recipient Sam Seagull award Advtsg. Club Monterey Peninsula, 1982, Outstanding Vol. award San Francisco Bay Girl Scout Coun., 1997. Mem. Calif. Coll. Arts and Crafts Alumni, PTA. Avocations: volunteering for children's education, providing senior citizen care. Office: Quanda Design 118 Lasata Ct Danville CA 94526-4401

HANDBERG, IRENE DEAK, educational organization executive; b. Jamaica, N.Y.; d. Paul and Irene (Dyroff) Deak; children: Roger B. III, Ryan Paul. BS, Fla. State U.; MEd, U. N.C., 1970. Cert. tchr. in reading and math., N.C. Lead tchr., reading specialist Chapel Hill (N.C.) City Schs., 1966-69; dir. learning lab. Seminole Community Coll., Sanford, Fla., 1974-78; basic skills cons. EDL/McGraw-Hill Book Co., Orlando, Fla., 1978-82; regional dir. EDL/Arista Pub., Orlando, 1982-84; mktg. mgr., product mgr. Arista/Regents/EDL-Hachette, N.Y.C., 1984-85; v.p. mktg. and sales Raintree Pubs., Milw., 1985, gen. mgr., pub., 1985-87; dir. spl. projects Simon & Schuster, Englewood Cliffs, N.J., 1987-88; v.p. corp. devel. Simon & Schuster, N.Y.C., 1988-90, sr. v.p., 1990-91; chmn. Irene Handberg Internat., N.Y.C., 1991—; pres. The Learning Connection, Frostproof, Fla., 1991—. Co-author: EDL/McGraw-Hill Teacher's Guide. Elected precinct woman com. Dem. County Com., Fla.; capt. Nat. Cancer So., Fla., chmn. Sch. Adv. Com., Fla. NSF fellow U. N.C., 1969; recipient Svc. award Jr. Achievement. Mem. Chief Exec. Officers Group (coun. small bus. execs.), Sales and Mktg. Execs., Profl. Dimensions, Chief Exec. Officers Club. Lutheran. Avocations: spectator sports, art, music, skiing. Office: The Learning Connection 300 E 93rd St Apt 29C New York NY 10128-6109

HANDEL, BERNARD, accountant, actuarial and insurance consultant, lawyer; b. N.Y.C., Sept. 25, 1926; s. Louis and Sarah (Brody) H.; m. Shirley M. Krom. BBA, CUNY; JD, Pace U. With Eisner & Lubin, CPAs, N.Y.C., 1946-52; v.p. Davis Assocs., N.Y.C., 1952-56; pres. Handel Group divsn. H.D.L. Assocs., Inc., Poughkeepsie, N.Y., 1956—, Hudson Valley Planning, Poughkeepsie, 1961—; sr. cons. Milliman & Robertson, Inc., 1992-94. Bd. dirs. First Ameritas Life Ins. Co.; bd. dirs. Hudson Valley Health Sys. Agy., pres., 1982-84, Dutchess County Health Planning Coun., 1976-96, Dutchess County chpt. ARC, Am. Health Planning Assocs., 1982-85, Bardavon Opera House, 1985-92; treas. Dutchess County Assn. Sr. Citizens, 1976; past insp. N.Y. State Athletic Commn.; mem. N.Y. State Hosp. Rev. and Planning Coun., 1978-92; trustee Vassar Bros. Hosp., 1986—, vice-chmn., 1991-92, chmn., 1993-95; trustee, sec. Mid-Hudson Health, 1993—. Served with U.S. Army, 1945-46. Mem. Internat. Found. Employee Benefit Plans (chmn. cons. actuaries com., chmn. health care svc. com. 1980-83, 88-90, chmn. health care data base com., 1986-87, dir. 1981-83, 85-87, 90-91, 94-96, 99—), IS-CEBS (fellow, gov. coun. 1982-84), chmn. Human Resources Dutchess County Econ. Zone, 1996—, N.Y. State Soc. CPAs, ABA, N.Y. State Bar Assn., Rotary, Poughkeepsie Tennis Club. Author books and articles in field; editorial bd. Benefits Quarterly, Pension Mgmt., Corporate Health Care Report, Health and Welfare Benefits Alert. Office: 53 Academy St Poughkeepsie NY 12601-4113

HANDEL, DAVID JONATHAN, health care administrator; b. N.Y.C., Jan. 2, 1946; s. Milton M. and Ruth (Stamer) H.; m. Julia Elizabeth Noll, June 26, 1971; children: Daniel, Jennifer. BS, Cornell U., 1966; MBA, U. Chgo., 1968. Assoc. planning coordinator for health scis. Northwestern U., Chgo., 1970-73, adminstr. Northwestern U. Med. Clinics and Med. Assocs., 1973-76; dir. planning and implementation Mid-Ohio Health Planning Fedn., Columbus, Ohio, 1976-79; assoc. hosp. adminstr. Vanderbilt U. Hosps., Nashville, 1979-82, assoc. dir. ops., 1982-85; dir. Ind. U. Hosps., Indpls., 1985-96; exec. v.p. ops., COO Clarian Health Ptnrs., Inc., Indpls., 1997—; v.p. United Hosp. Svcs., Indpls., 1986-88, pres., 1989-90, Bedford Reg. Med. Ctr., 1997—, La Porte Regional Health Sys., Inc., 1998—. Contbr. articles to profl. jours. Sr. asst. health svcs. officer USPHS, 1968-70. Fellow Am. Coll. Health Care Execs.; mem. Ind. Hosp. Assn. (bd. dirs. 1994-97). Office: Clarian Health 550 University Blvd Indianapolis IN 46202-5149

HANDEL, MORTON EMANUEL, management consultation executive; b. N.Y.C., Apr. 12, 1935; s. Benjamin and Mollie (Heller) H.; m. Irma Ruby, Aug. 5, 1956; children: Mark, Gary, Karen. BA, U. Pa., 1956; postgrad., NYU, 1957-59. V.p. Dale Plastic Playing Card Corp., N.Y.C., 1955-57; gen. mgr. Handel Nets & Fabrics Corp., N.Y.C., 1957-62; pres. A.M. Industries, Inc., Farmingdale, N.Y., 1962-68, Allan Marine, Inc., Deer Park, N.Y., 1969-71; chmn. bd. Marlow Yacht Corp., Deer Park, 1969-71; v.p. fin., sec.-treas. Aurora Products Corp. (subs. Nabisco Inc.), 1971-73, sr. v.p., chief fin. officer, 1973-74; v.p. Rowe Industries Inc., 1971-74; v.p., dir. Aurora Nederland N.V., 1971-74, Aurora Plastics Can. Ltd., 1971-74; v.p. fin., chief fin. officer Coleco Industries Inc., 1974-78, sr. v.p., chief fin. officer, 1978-82, exec. v.p. fin. and adminstrn., 1982-83, exec. v.p. corp. com., 1983-85, exec. v.p. corp. devel., 1985-88, chmn., dir., chief exec. officer, 1988-90; pres., dir. S&H Cons., Ltd, Bloomfield, Conn., 1990—; bd. dirs. Concurrent Computer Corp., Ft. Lauderdale, Fla., CompUSA, Dallas, Ithaca Industries, Inc., Wilkes Boro, N.C.; pres., dir. Ranger Industries, Inc., Bloomfield, Conn., 1997—; chmn. bd. dirs. Marvel Enterprises, Inc., N.Y.C.; trustee Aurora Products Profit Sharing Trust, 1971-74, Coleco Industries Inc. Pension Plan, 1975-90. Pres. Rochdale Village Civic Assn., 1964-65; pres. bd. dirs. Hartford Symphony Orch., 1976—; bd. dirs. Jewish Children's Svc. Corp., 1976-78; corporator St. Francis Hosp., 1982—; bd. dirs. One Thousand Corp., 1983—, Greater Hartford Arts Coun., Inc., 1987-89, Hebrew Home for the Aged, 1989—; vice chmn. bd. regents U. Hartford, 1992—; trustee, vice chmn. Hartt Sch. Music, 1991—; bd. dirs. Jewish Fedn. of Greater Hartford, 1996—, Hartford Dispensary Inc., 1996—. Mem. Am. Mgmt. Assn., Fin. Execs. Inst., Alpha Epsilon Pi. Home: 41 Ranger Ln West Hartford CT 06117-3040 Office: S&H Cons Ltd One Regency Dr Bloomfield CT 06002-2404

HANDEL, RICHARD CRAIG, lawyer; b. Hamilton, Ohio, Aug. 11, 1945; s. Alexander F. and Marguerite (Wilks) H.; m. Katharine Jean Carter, Jan. 10, 1970. AB, U. Mich., 1967; MA, Mich. State U., 1968; JD summa cum laude, Ohio State U., 1974; LLM in Taxation, NYU, 1978. Bar: Ohio 1974, S.C. 1983, U.S. Dist. Ct. (so. dist.) Ohio 1975, U.S. Dist. Ct. S.C. 1979, U.S. Tax Ct. 1977, U.S. Ct. Appeals (4th cir.) 1979, U.S. Supreme Ct. 1979; cert. tax specialist. Assoc. Smith & Schnacke, Dayton, Ohio, 1974-77; asst. prof. U. S.C. Sch. Law, Columbia, 1978-83; ptnr. Nexsen, Pruet, Jacobs & Pollard, Columbia, 1983-87, Moore & Van Allen, Columbia, 1987-88, Nexsen Pruet Jacobs & Pollard, Columbia, 1988-89; chief tax policy and appeals S.C. Tax Commn., Columbia, 1989-95; chief coun. Policy S.C. Dept. of Revenue, Columbia, 1995—; adj. prof. U. S.C. Sch. Law, 1990—. Contbr. articles to legal jours. bd. dirs. Friends of Richland County Pub. Libr. Served with U.S. Army, 1969-70, Vietnam. Gerald L. Wallace scholar, 1977-78; recipient Outstanding Law Prof. award, 1980-81. Mem. ABA (com. state and local taxes, chmn. membership com. 1997—, vice-chmn. com. tax procedures

1993-94, com. stds. tax practice), S.C. Bar Assn., Order of Coif. Office: SC Dept Revenue PO Box 125 301 Gervais St Columbia SC 29201-3041

HANDEL, WILLIAM KEATING, advertising and sales executive; b. N.Y.C., Mar. 23, 1935; s. Irving Nathaniel and Marguerite Mary (Keating) H.; m. Margaret Inez Sitton; children: William Keating II, David Roger. BA in Journalism, U. S.C., 1959, MA in English Lit., 1960. Account supr. Ketchum, MacLeod & Grove, Pitts., 1960-67; mgr. advt. and pub. rels. ITT Gen. Controls, Glendale, Calif., 1967-80; mgr. corp. comm. Fairchild Camera and Instrument Corp., 1980-84; dist. mgr. Cahners Pub. Co., 1984-90; western regional sales mgr. Quality Publ. Co., 1990—; pub. rels. counsel Calif. Pvt. Edn. Schs., 1978-87; chmn. exhibits Mini/Micro Computer Conf. Bd. dirs. West Valley Athletic League, L.A. chpt. USMC Scholarship Found.; pub. rels. cons. Ensenada, Mexico Tourist Commn., 1978; chmn., master of ceremonies USMC Birthday Ball, L.A., 1979-82. With USMC, 1950-53. Decorated Silver Star, Bronze Star, Purple Heart (4), Navy Commendation medal with combat V; recipient Pub. Svc. award L.A. Heart Assn., 1971-73. Mem. Bus. and Profl. Advt. Assn. (cert. bus. communicator, past pres.), 1st Marine Divsn. Assn., Navy League (bd. dirs.), AdLinx Golf Club of So. Calif., Torrey Pines Golf Club, Griffith Pk. Golf Club, Nueva España Boat Club, Bajamar Country Club, Ensenada Country Club, Baja Country Club, Ensenada Fish and Game Club (Baja, Mex.), U. S.C. Alumni Club (founder/pres. L.A. chpt.), Sigma Chi (chpt. adv.). Republican. Roman Catholic. Home: 2428 Badajoz Pl Rancho La Costa CA 92009-8006

HANDELMAN, ALICE SAMUELS, public relations professional, writer, former social worker; b. Bklyn., Mar. 17, 1943; d. Ned Harlan and Margaret (Isaacs) Samuels; m. Howard Talbot Handelman, Aug. 29, 1965; children: Karen Handelman Hirshman, Patricia Handelman Bloom, Marjorie Lynn Handelman. BJ, U. Mo., 1965. Intern reporter Miami (Fla.) News, summer 1964; staff feature writer St. Louis Blues, 1968-77; freelance writer St. Louis, 1967—; cmty. rels. assoc. Jewish Ctr. for Aged of Greater St. Louis, Chesterfield, Mo., 1981-85; dir. cmty. rels. Jewish Ctr. for Aged of Greater St. Louis, Chesterfield, 1985—; bd. dirs. Mideast Area Agy. on Aging, 1997—; pub. rels. cons. Jewish Family and Children's Svc., St. Louis, 1983, 89; guest lectr. Maryville U., 1997. Author, photographer: LaSalle Street--A History of the St. Louis Wholesale Flower market, 1987; freelance writer, contbr. to St. louis Globe-Dem., St. Louis Post-Dispatch, N.Y. Times, St. Louis Jewish Light, St. Louis Blues Goal Mag., Hockey News, Hockey World, Ladue News, Sporting News, Nat. Hockey League, Hockey Pictorial, Suburban Jour. Newspapers; writer copy for Knight's Catalogue, 1983. Instr. hockey for women Meramec C.C., St. Louis, 1976-77; adv. com. vis. prof. program JCA Assocs., 1981-83, Gerontol. Inst., St. Louis, 1981-83; pub. rels. chmn. Nat. Coun. Jewish Women, 1981-83, publicity chmn. fashion sale, 1985; pres. Weber Sch. PTA, Creve Coeur, Mo., 1982; mem. Women's Am. ORT, 1965—; life mem. Jewish Hosp. Aux., 1965—, Jewish Ctr. for Aged Aux., 1986—, Nat. Coun. Jewish Women; pres. Young Women's Coun. on Edn. of Jewish Fedn. St. Louis, 1969; mem. ctrl. advancement team Pkwy. Ctrl. H.S., 1985-89; photographer Tour de Cure bicycle ride to benefit Am. Diabetes Assn., 1992, 93; bd. dirs. Mideast Area Agy. on Aging, 1997—; sec., bd. dirs. Gateway Elder Svcs., 1998—. Recipient William Randolph Hearst award Hearst Found., Columbia, Mo., 1965, United Way Graphic Design award, 1986, United Way Photography award, 1987, 89, 2d place award Guide to Jewish Life in St. Louis photo contest, 1989, 2d place award Jewish Hosp. St. Louis Generations of Women photo contest, 1989, Star Communicator comm. program award Unied Way Greater St. Louis, 1990, Bronze Photography award, 1995, 15 Yr. Svc. award Jewish Ctr. for Aged, 1997, Fred Goldstein Communal Svc. award Jewish Fedn. St. Louis, 1998; Besse Marks Meml. scholar, 1964-65. Mem. Nat. Fedn. Press Women (1st place award comm. contest, 3d place photo feature 1989, 3d place award advt. photography 1993, hon. mention advt. photo, 2d place mktg. new svc. award, 2d place mag. advt., 1996, 3d place direct mail mktg. fundraising lit., 2d place direct mail advt.-fund raising Ann. NFPW Comm. Contest 1996, 3d place Color mag. advt. 1996), Jewish Ctr. for Aged Aux., Fellows of Jewish Hosp., Mo. Press Women (1st place corp. newsletter category state feature writing comm. contest 1988, 93, 1st place advt. photography, 2d place feature article, 3 1st place awards 1994, 1st place not for profit newsletter 1994, 5 1st place comm. awards 1995, 1st place newsletter award Mo. Assn. of Homes for the Aging 1994, planning com. Fair St. Louis Srs. Day 1995-98, planning com. Srs. Day VP Fair 1994), Mo. Assn. Homes for the Aging (publicity com., Outstanding 1st Place Newsletter award), Nat. Fedn. Press Women (1st place feature photo 1994, 4 1st place awards Mo. affiliate 1999), Mo. Press Women (pub. chmn. 1994), Women in Comm. (Ruth Philpott Collins award 1984, Best in the Midwest 2d place feature writing 1992). Jewish. Home: 12 Terry Hill Ln Saint Louis MO 63131-2422 Office: Jewish Ctr for Aged of Greater St Louis 13190 S Outer 40 Chesterfield MO 63017-5998

HANDELMAN, HOWARD, political scientist, educator; b. N.Y.C., Apr. 29, 1943; s. Victor and Ruth (Goodman) H.; m. Nancy Rae Forster, Sept. 22, 1967; 1 child, Michael Jesse. Student, London Sch. Econs., 1963-64; BA, U. Pa., 1965; MA in polit. sci., U. Wis., 1967; PhD in polit. sci., U.Wis., 1971. Instr. Ctr. for Latin Am., U. Milw., 1970-71, asst. prof., 1971-76, assoc. prof., 1976-81, prof., 1981—; faculty assoc. Am. Universities Field Staff, Hanover, N.H., 1978-80. Author: Struggle in the Andes, 1974, Military Rule and the Road to Democracy in South America, 1981, The Politics of Rural Change in Asia and Latin America, 1981; co-author, editor: Paying the Costs of Austerity in South America, 1989; co-author: Politics in a Changing World, 1993, 2d edit., 1998, The Challenge of Third World Development, 1996, Mexican Politics, 1997. Mem. Latin Am. Studies Assn. Jewish. Avocations: jogging, music, raquetball. Office: U Wis-Milw Polit Sci Dept PO Box 413 Milwaukee WI 53201-0413*

HANDELSMAN, LAWRENCE MARC, lawyer; b. N.Y.C., Jan. 17, 1945; s. David and Ruth (Litner) H.; m. Sara Pruzan, June 10, 1967; children: Sharon, Carolyn. BBA, CCNY, 1965; JD, NYU, 1968. Bar: N.Y. 1968, U.S. Ct. Mil. Appeals 1969, U.S. Dist. Ct. (so. and ea. dists.) N.Y. 1973, U.S. Ct. Appeals (2d cir.) 1973, Fla. 1978. Assoc. Stroock & Stroock & Lavan, N.Y.C., 1973-78, ptnr., 1979—. Served to capt. JAGC, U.S. Army, 1969-73. Mem. ABA (bus. bankruptcy com. 1969—), Assn. of Bar of City of N.Y. (bankruptcy com. 1974-77, 1985—). Home: 22 Scarsdale Farm Rd Scarsdale NY 10583-1919 Office: Stroock & Stroock & Lavan 180 Maiden Ln New York NY 10038-4925

HANDELSMAN, WALT, cartoonist. Cartoonist Picayuna New Orleans Times-Picayune, 1989—. Recipient Pulitzer prize for edtl. cartooning, 1997. Office: New Orleans Times Picayune 3800 Howard Ave New Orleans LA 70125-1429*

HANDELSMAN, YEHUDA, endocrinologist, internal medicine physician; b. Tel Aviv, Israel, Aug. 22, 1947; came to U.S., 1969; s. Jacob and Zahava (Lewin) H.; m. Nava Dina Pedazur, Feb. 22, 1986; children: Tomer Lee, Roy Gil. AA with honors, San Joaquin Delta Coll., Stockton, Calif., 1973; BA summa cum laude, U. of the Pacific, Stockton, Calif., 1975; MD, Tel Aviv U., 1984; postdoctoral fellow, U. So. Calif., 1988-89. Diplomate Am. Bd. Internal Medicine. Intern Beekman Downtown Hosp., N.Y.C., 1985-86; resident in internal medicine Beekman Downtown Hosp., 1986-88; clin. fellow in diabetes and endocrinology L.A. County-U. So. Calif. Med. Ctr., L.A., 1988-89; attending physician Midway Hosp., L.A., 1990-93, Granada Hills (Calif.) Cmty. Hosp., 1991—, Encino-Tarzana (Calif.) Med. Ctr., 1991—; cons., bd. dirs. Dynamic Home Care, L.A., Las Vegas, 1991-97; cons. Yad B'yad-Human Saving Fund, L.A., 1991-97; clin. instr. medicine U. So. Calif. Med. Sch., 1988-90; dir. endocrine quar. conf. encino-Tarzana Med. Ctr., dir. monthly diabetes edn. seminars, 1995-98; mem. diabetes edn. faculty Bristol Myers Squibb, 1997, 98; mem. spkrs. bur. Parke-Davis, 1997, 98. Med. columnist Israel Shelanu, 1992-94, L.A. News, 1989-91. Bd. dirs. Diabetes Care Ctr. Encino-Tarzana Hosp., 1994-98; dir. Israeli Spl. Olympic Games, 1968-82. Mem. AMA (Physician Recognition award 1988, 95), ACP, Am. Assn. Clin. Endocrinologists, Calif. Med. Assn. (Physician Recognition award 1995), N.Am. Menopause Soc., Nat. Osteoporosis Found., Am. Diabetes Assn., Am. Israeli Med. Soc., L.A. County Med. Assn., Calif. Med. House Staff Assn., Am. Med. Student Assn., Phi Kappa Phi, Theta Alpha Phi, Alpha Gamma Sigma, Delta Sy Omega. Avocations: talk show host, theater, basketball, politics, music. Office: 18370 Burbank Blvd Ste 704 Tarzana CA 91356-2820

HANDFORD, MARTIN JOHN, illustrator, author; b. London, Sept. 27, 1956; s. Ruth Winter. BA, Maidstone Art Coll., 1980. Author, illustrator: Where's Waldo?, 1987, Find Waldo Now, 1988, The Great Waldo Search, 1989, Where's Waldo? The Ultimate Fun Book, 1990, Where's Waldo? The Magnificent Poster Book, 1991, Fun With Waldo, 1992, More Fun With Waldo, 1992, Where's Waldo? In Hollywood, 1993, Where's Waldo? The Dazzling Deep-Sea Divers Sticker Book, 1994, Where's Waldo? The Wildly Wonderful Activity Book, 1995, Where's Waldo? The Simply Sensational Activity Book, 1995. Office: care Candlewick Press 2067 Massachusetts Ave Cambridge MA 02140-1340

HANDLER, ALAN B., state supreme court justice; b. Newark, July 20, 1931; m. Rose Marie H.; 5 children. AB, Princeton U., 1953; LLB, Harvard U., 1956. Bar: N.J. 1956. Dep. atty. gen., 1961-64, 1st asst. atty. gen., 1964-68; justice Superior Ct., 1968-73; spl. counsel to gov., 1976-77; assoc. justice N.J. Supreme Ct., Trenton, 1977—. Mem. Harvard Law Sch. Assn. of N.J. (past pres.), Phi Beta Kappa. Office: NJ Supreme Ct Richard J Hughes Justice Complex CN023 Trenton NJ 08625-0979*

HANDLER, ARTHUR M., lawyer; b. N.Y.C., Feb. 16, 1937. BS, Queens Coll., 1957; LLB, Columbia U., 1960. Bar: N.Y. 1960, U.S. Dist. Ct. (ea. dist.) N.Y. 1960, U.S. Dist. Ct. (so. dist.) N.Y. 1963, U.S. Tax Ct. 1971, U.S. Ct. Appeals (2d cir.) 1971, U.S. Supreme Ct. 1965. Staff counsel SEC, Washington, 1960-61; law clk. U.S. Dist. Ct. for So. Dist.N.Y., N.Y.C., 1961-62; asst. U.S. atty. So. Dist. N.Y., N.Y.C., 1962-65; assoc. Proskauer, Rose, Goetz & Mendelsohn, N.Y.C., 1965-67; assoc. Golenbock and Barell, N.Y.C., 1967-70, ptnr., 1970-89; ptnr. Whitman & Ransom, N.Y.C., 1990-93, Burns Handler & Burns, N.Y.C., 1993—; arbitrator Am. Stock Exchange, N.Y.C., 1986—. Vol. atty. Pres.'s Com. for Civil Rights under Law, Jackson, Miss., 1966. Mem. ABA, N.Y. State Bar Assn., Bar Assn. of City of N.Y., Fed. Bar Council, Am. Arbitration Assn. (arbitrator 1969—). Clubs: University (N.Y.C.); Lords Valley Country (Hawley, Pa.) (bd. govs. 1977-80). Avocations: golf, skiing, theatre, travel. Office: Burns Handler & Burns 220 E 42nd St Rm 3000 New York NY 10017-5806

HANDLER, EVELYN, science administrator; b. Budapest, Hungary, May 5, 1933; U.S. citizen; m. 1965; two children. BA, Hunter Coll., 1954; MSc, NYU, 1962, PhD in Biology, 1963; LHD (hon.), Rivier Coll., 1982, U. Pitts., 1987, Hunter Coll., 1988. Rsch. assoc. Sloan-Kettering Inst., 1958-60, Merck Inst. Therapeutic Rsch., 1958-60; lectr. Hunter Coll., 1962-64, from asst. to prof. biol. sci., 1965-80, dean sci. and math., 1977-80; pres. U. N.H., 1980-83, Brandeis U., 1983-91; exec. dir. Calif. Acad. Scis., San Francisco, 1994-98; ret.; vis. scientist Karolinska Inst., 1971-72; evaluator Com. Higher Edn., Middle States Assn., 1972—; vice chmn. univ. faculty senate CUNY, 1974-76; generalist, mem. Am. Coun. Pharm. Edn., 1978-83; bd. dirs. New Eng. Life Ins. Co., Student Loan Corp. Trustee Bay Area Biosci. Ctr., 1995—, Mills Coll., 1995—. Sr. fellow Carnegie Found. Advanced Tchg., 1990-92; scholar in residence Harvard U., 1991-92, assoc. in edn. 1992-93; rsch. grantee NIH, 1964-69, 73-76, NSF, 1965-67, 70-72, CUNY, 1972-74. Fellow AAAS, N.Y. Acad. Sci.; mem. Internat. Soc. Hematology, Harvey Soc. Office: Calif Acad Scis Golden Gate Park San Francisco CA 94118

HANDLER, HAROLD ROBERT, lawyer; b. Jersey City, Aug. 24, 1935; s. Morris Sidney and Fan (Krieger) H.; m. Lynne Tishman; children: Maren, Jeremy, Jolyon. BS, Lehigh U., 1957; LLM, Columbia U., 1961. Bar: N.Y. 1961, U.S. Tax Ct. 1963, U.S. Ct. Appeals (2d cir.) 1980. Atty., advisor U.S. Tax Ct., Washington, 1961-63; assoc. Simpson Thacher & Bartlett, N.Y.C., 1963-69, ptnr., 1970-97, of counsel, 1998—; adj. assoc. prof. law NYU, 1978-80. Chmn. fin. com., citizens adv. com. Met. Transp. Authority, N.Y.C., 1975-79; trustee Citizens Budget Commn.; chmn. Bd. Jewish Cmty. Ctr. on Upper West Side, N.Y.C. Fellow Am. Coll. Tax Counsel; mem. ABA, N.Y. State Bar Assn. (chmn. subcom. tax sect. 1979-83, mem. exec. com. tax sect. 1990—, officer 1996-2000, chair 1999-20000), Assn. of Bar of City of N.Y. (chmn. tax com. 1983-86, mem. tax coun. 1990-98), Am. Law Inst., Inst. Fed. Taxation (panelist), Inst. Securities Regulation (panelist corp. taxation, personal income taxation).

HANDLER, JEROME SIDNEY, anthropology educator; b. N.Y.C., Sept. 3, 1933; s. Sam and Sara (Wieder) H.; children—Joshua Martin, Lisa Frances. BA, UCLA, 1956, MA, 1959; PhD, Brandeis U., 1965. From asst. prof. to prof. anthropology So. Ill. U., Carbondale, 1964-93, prof. Black Am. studies, 1993-95, prof. emeritus, 1995—; Olive B. O'Connor vis. prof. Am. instns. Colgate U., Hamilton, N.Y., 1971-72; hon. rsch. asst. Univ. Coll., London, 1966-67; staff archaeologist New World Archaeol. Found., Chiapas, Mex., 1957; cons. AID, fall, 1964, Peace Corps, summer 1969; cons. Libr. of Congress, 1998, 99, panelist NEH, 1977-79, 82; mem. adv. com. African Burial Ground, N.Y.C., GSA, 1991-93. Author: A Guide to Source Materials for the Study of Barbados History, 1627-1834, 1971, The Unappropriated People: Freedmen in the Slave Society of Barbados, 1974, Supplement to A Guide to Source Materials for the Study of Barbados History, 1991; co-author: Plantation Slavery in Barbados: An Archaeological and Historical Investigation, 1978, Searching for a Slave Cemetery in Barbados: A Bioarcheological and Ethnohistorical Investigation, 1989. Vis. Rsch. fellow U. W.I., Jamaica, 1969-70, Barbados, 1983; research assoc. Research Inst. for Study of Man, N.Y.C., 1978-79; vis. scholar Center for Afro-Am. Studies, UCLA, 1980, Dept. Afro-Am. Studies, Harvard U., summer 1992; Rsch. grantee NSF, 1966-67, 71-73, Wenner-Gren Found. Anthrop. Rsch., 1971-72, 87, Rsch. Inst. Study Man, 1962, 70, NIH, 1965, Am. Philos. Soc., 1968, Nat. Geographic Soc., 1987, Nat. Endowment for Humanities Inst. for Coll. Tchrs., 1997-98; Nat. Endowment for Humanities fellow, 1969-70, 75-76, 79; Travel grant Am. Coun. Learned Socs., 1977, grantee Social Sci. Rsch. Coun. and Am. Coun. Learned Socs. Joint Com. on Latin Am. Studies, 1983; Nat. Humanities Ctr. fellow, 1982-83, John Carter Brown Library fellow, 1985, 88, DuBois Inst. Afro-Am. Rsch. fellow Harvard, 1989-90, Va. Found. Humanities fellow, 1995-99. Fellow Am. Anthrop. Assn. (rep. to Am. Coun. Learned Socs. 1985-90); mem. Caribbean Studies Assn. (past mem. exec. council). Home: 146-10 Ivy Dr Charlottesvle VA 22903 Office: Va Found Humanities 145 Ednam Dr Charlottesville VA 22903-4629

HANDLER, LAUREN E., lawyer; b. Jersey City, Mar. 13, 1953. BA cum laude, Tufts U., 1975; JD with honors, George Washington U., 1978. Bar: N.J. 1978, U.S. Dist. Ct. N.J. 1978, N.Y. 1984, U.S. Dist. Ct. (ea. and so. dists.) N.Y. 1986. Mem. Porzio, Bromberg & Newman PC, Morristown, N.J.; arbitrator U.S. Dist. Ct. N.J., 1985—. Mem. ABA (sects. on torts and ins. practice, litigation, employment), Am. Bd. Trial Attorneys, Am. Coll. Trial Lawyers, N.J. State Bar Assn. (cert. trial attys. sect., mem. exec. com. civil trial bar sect. 1986-91, sec. 1989-91, vice chair 1992, employment law sect.), Trial Attys. N.J., Morris County Bar Assn. (chair med.-legal cooperation com. 1988-96, treas. 1996, 2nd v.p. 1997, 1st v.p. 1998), Def. Rsch. Inst., Internat. Assn. Def. Counsel. Office: Porzio Bromberg & Newman PC 163 Madison Ave Ste 6 Morristown NJ 07962*

HANDLERY, PAUL ROBERT, hotel executive; b. St. Helena, Calif., Apr. 8, 1920; s. Harry and Rose Helen (Braun) H.; m. Ardyce Arlene Lundquist, June 1, 1945; children: Barbara Kim (Mrs. David R. Metcalf), Michael Kent, Nancy Liane, Jon Steven, Lane Ardyce. A.A., U. Calif. at Berkeley, 1940; B.S. with honors, Sch. Hotel Adminstrn., Cornell U., 1943; LLD (hon.), Golden Gate U., 1991. Cert. hotel adminstr. V.p. Handlery Hotels Inc., San Francisco, 1946-63, pres., 1963-86, chmn. bd., chief exec. officer, 1986—; past pres., bd. dirs. San Francisco Conv. and Visitors Bur.; bd. dirs. Civic Bank of Commerce, Oakland. Past chmn., mem. adv. bd. Salvation Army; past pres., trustee No. Calif. chpt. Leukemia Soc. Am.; hon. regent John F. Kennedy U., Orinda, Calif.; mem. adv. bd. Hotel and Restaurant Sch., Calif. Poly. U., Pomona, City Coll. San Francisco (past chmn. bd.), U. San Francisco, Golden Gate U., San Francisco (hospitality mgmt. bd.); pres. Hotel and Restaurant Found.; past pres., trustee, hon. chmn. for life Am. Hotel Found. Capt. AUS. Named to Men of Distinction Innkeeping mag., 1963, Hall of Fame Hospitality mag., 1966, Man of Year Pacific Hotel-Motel News, 1970, Man of Year Nat. Jewish Hosp., Denver, 1973, Hall of Fame, Calif. Restaurant Assn. Ednl. Found., 1996; recipient U. San Francisco pres.'s medallion, 1993, Peter Goldman award of Excellence Hotel Coun. of San Francisco, 1993, Hon. Col. award Salvation Army, 1996. Mem. Am. Hotel and Motel Assn. (dir., pres. 1974, chmn. bd. 1975, past trustee amb. Ednl. Inst., IHA bd. dirs. AHMA liaison com. with Internat. Hotel Assn., chmn., cert. hotel adminstr. emeritus Ednl. Inst. 1995), Calif. Hotel and Motel Assn. (past pres., dir. emeritus, Hall of Fame award 1991), Union Sq. Assn., San Francisco (bd. dirs., past pres.), East Bay Hotel Assn. (past pres.), Hotel Employers Assn. San Francisco (past pres.), Cornell Soc. Hotelmen, Cornell U. Coun. Commonwealth Club, Bermuda Dunes Country Club, Moraga Country Club. Office: 180 Geary St Suite 700 San Francisco CA 94108*

HANDLEY, GERALD MATTHEW, lawyer; b. Phila., Dec. 7, 1942; s. John F. and Helen E. (Gerdelman) H.; m. Sandra I. Martin, June 13, 1970; children: Christopher, Elizabeth. BBA, La Salle Coll., Phila., 1965; JD, U. Mo., Kansas City, 1972. Bar: Mo. 1972, U.S. Dist. Ct. (we. dist.) Mo. 1972, U.S.Supreme Ct., 1976, U.S. Ct. Appeals (8th and 10th cirs.) 1980, U.S Dist. Ct. Kans. 1998. Asst. pub. defender Office Pub. Defender, Kansas City, Mo., 1972-73; 1st asst. pub. defender Office Pub. Defender, Kansas City, 1973-75, interim pub. defender, 1975-76; ptnr. Speck & Handley, Kansas City, 1980-90; pvt. practice Law Offices of G. Handley, 1991, ptnr., 1991—; lectr. Rockhurst Coll., Kansas City, 1976-78; instr. U. Mo. Sch. Law. Contbr. chpts. to law books. Pres., Home Owners Assn., Kansas City, 1980. Served with U.S. Army, 1966-67, Vietnam. Fellow Am. Bd. Criminal Lawyers; mem. ABA, NACDL, Mo. Bar Assn., (Lon Hocker Trial Lawyer award 1977), Mo. Assn. Criminal Def. Lawyers (pres. 1980, hon. bd. dirs.), U.S. Supreme Ct. Bar Assn., Kansas City Met. Bar Assn. Roman Catholic. Avocations: golf, gardening. Home: 22 W 54th St Kansas City MO 64112-2816 Office: 1101 Walnut St Ste 1400 Kansas City MO 64106

HANDLEY, LEON HUNTER, lawyer; b. Lakeland, Fla., Sept. 9, 1927; s. Driskle Hubert and Mamie (Denmark) H.; m. Mary Virginia Wolfe, May 2, 1953; children: Leon Hunter, Mary Ellen, Laura Catherine, Leann Virginia; BSBA with honors, U. Fla., 1949, JD, 1951. Bar: Fla. 1951, U.S. Dist. Ct. (so. dist.) Fla. 1952, U.S. Dist. Ct. (mid. dist.) Fla. 1962, U.S. Supreme Ct. 1956, U.S. Ct. of Appeals (5th cir.) 1960, U.S. Ct. Appeals (11th cir.) 1981; pres. Gurney & Handley, Orlando, Fla., 1951—; bd. dirs. Beneficial Savs. Bank, chmn.; bd. dirs. Orlando/Tampa, Cracker Groves Inc., Orlando, 1964—; v.p., bd. dirs. So. Indsl. Savs. Bank, Orlando, Mine & Mill Supply Co., Lakeland, 1966—, Claude H. Wolfe, Inc., Orlando, 1969—; gen. counsel, life dir., past pres. Cen. Fla. Fair; chmn. bd. trustees Sta. WMFE-TV. Pres. Chesley Magruder Charitable Trust; elder Presbyn. Ch. Warrant officer U.S. Maritime Svc., 1945-46, ETO; sgt. U.S. Army, 1946-48, Korea; capt. USAFR, 1949-59. Fellow Am. Coll. Trial Lawyers; mem. ABA, Am. Bd. Trial Advocates (Fla. Trial Lawyer of Yr. 1996, advocate), Orange County Bar Assn. (past pres.), Fla. Bar Assn. (past pres. sta. jr. bar sect., bd. govs. 1959-60), Fedn. Ins. and Corp. Counsel, Internat. Assn. Def. Counsel, Assn. Def. Trial Attys., Trial Attys. Am., Am. Judicature Soc. (listed Best Lawyers in Am.), Pres.'s Coun. (founder U. Fla. chpt.), Citrus Club, Orlando Country Club, Univ. Club, Masons (grand orator Fla. 1982, 86) K.T., Shriners, Scottish Rite (33d degree, insp. gen. hon. 1979), Rotary (pres. Orlando chpt. 1984, Paul Harris fellow), Travelers' Century Club, Fla. Blue Key (pres. 1951), Phi Delta Phi, Alpha Tau Omega (prs. U. of Fla. chpt. 1951), Phi Kappa Phi, Alpha Kappa Psi, Beta Gamma Sigma (U. Fla. Hall of Fame). Republican. Avocations: jogging, handball. Home: 1621 Spring Lake Dr Orlando FL 32804-7111 Office: Gurney & Handley 225 E Robinson St Ste 450 Orlando FL 32801-1905

HANDLEY, MARGIE LEE, business executive; b. Bakersfield, Calif., Sept. 29, 1939; d. Robert E. and Jayne A. (Knoblock) Harrah; children: Steven Daniel Lovell, David Robert Lovell, Ronald Eugene Lovell; m. Leon C. Handley, Sr., Oct. 28, 1975. Grad. H.S., Willits, Calif. Lic. gen. engrng. contractor. Owner, operator Shasta Pallet Co., Montague, 1966-70, Lovell's Tack 'n Togs, Yreka, Calif., 1970-73; v.p. Microphor, Inc., Willits, 1974-81; pres. Harrah Industries, Inc., Willits, 1981—; gen. ptnr. Madrone Profl. Group, Willits, 1982—; pres. Hot Rocks, Inc., Willits, 1983-89; co-ptnr. Running Wild Ostriches, 1994—; bd. dirs. Nat. Bank of the Redwoods, NBR Mortgage Co., Howard Found., Willits Electronics Assembly, Inc.; active State of Calif. Employment Tng. Panel, 1993-95, coord. State Calif. Timber Transition, 1994-95; apptd. mem. State of Calif. Econ. Strategy Panel, 1995—. Sec. Willits Cmty. Scholarships, Inc., 1962; trustee Montague Meth. Ch., 1966-73; sec. Montague PTA, 1969; clk. bd. trustees Montague Sch. Dist., 1970-73; del. Calif. State Conf. Small Bus., 1984; alt. del. Rep. Nat. Conv., Kansas City, Detroit, 1976, 80; 3d dist. chmn. Mendocino County Rep. Ctrl. Com., 1978-84; mem. Calif. State Rep. Ctrl. Com., 19985, 86, 87; Rep. nominee for State Senate Calif. 2nd Senate Dist., 1990, 93; mem. Rep. Congl. Leadership Coun., 1980-82; Mendocino County chmn. Reagan/Bush, 1980, 84; Mendocino County co-chmn. Deukmejian for Gov., 1982; mem. Region IX Small Bus. Adminstrn. Adv. Coun., 1982-93; mem. Gov.'s Adv. Coun., 1983-90; Rep. nominee State Assembly 1st Assembly Dist.; del., asst. sgt. of arms Rep. Nat. Conv., Dallas, 1984, del., New Orleans, 1988, San Diego, 1996; vice chmn. Mendocino County Rep. Ctrl. Com., 1985; active Calif. Transp. Commn., 1986-90; state dir. Nroth Bay Dist. Hwy. Grading and Heavy Engring. divsn., 1986; dir. Lit. Vols. Am. Named Mendocino 12th Dist. Fair Woman of the Yr. 1987. Mem. No. Coast Builders Exch., Soroptimist Internat., Rotary Club, Willits C. of C. (hon.). Home: PO Box 1329 Willits CA 95490-1329 Office: Harrah Industries Inc 42 Madrone St Willits CA 95490-4206

HANDLEY, WILLIAM ROSS, English educator; b. Salt Lake City, Jan. 6, 1963; s. George Kenneth and Kate Browning H. BA, MA, Stanford U., 1986; MPhil, DPhil, Oxford U., 1988; PhD, UCLA, 1997. Asst. prof. English Harvard U., Cambridge, Mass., 1995-99, U. So. Calif., L.A., 1999—. Contbr. articles to profl. jours. Rhodes scholar Rhodes Trust, 1986-89; Chancellor's fellow UCLA, 1989-90, 94-95; Keck Rsch. fellow Huntington Libr., 1998. Mem. MLA, Am. Studies Assn., We. Lit. Assn., Phi Beta Kappa. Democrat. Mem. LDS Ch. Avocation: piano. Office: U So Calif Dept English 420 Taper Hall Univ Park Los Angeles CA 90089

HANDS, TERENCE DAVID (TERRY HANDS), theater and opera director; b. Jan. 9, 1941; s. Joseph Ronald and Luise Berthe (Kohler) H.; m. Josephine Barstow, 1964 (div. 1967); m. Luarila Mikaël, 1974 (div. 1980; life ptnr. Julia Lintott; 2 children. BA in Eng. Lang. and Lit. with honors, Birmingham (Eng.) U., 1962, DLitt (hon.), 1988; diploma with honors, RADA, 1964; DLitt (hon.), Middlesex U., 1997. Founder, artistic dir. Liverpool (Eng.) Everyman Theatre, 1964-66; artistic dir. RSC Theatreground, 1966-67; from assoc. dir. to dir. emeritus Royal Shakespeare Co., England, 1967-91, dir. emeritus, 1991—; cons. Comedie Francaise, 1975-80, Theatre Clwyd, 1996-97, dir. 1997; contbr. to Theatre 72, Playback pubs.; translator of plays. Dir.: (plays) Hamlet, 1994, Merry Wives of Windsor, 1995, The Pretenders, 1996, The Royal Hunt of The Sun, 1996, The Importance of Being Ernest, 1997, A Christmas Carol, 1997, Equus, 1997, The Journey of Mary Kelly, 1998, The Seagull, 1998, The Norman Conquests, 1998, others. Recipient Chevalier des Arts et des Lettres, 1975, Pragnell Shakespeare award 1991. Fellow Shakespeare Inst. (hon.). Office: Clwyd Theatr Cymru, Mold Flintshire, North Wales CH7 1YA, England

HANDSCHUMACHER, ROBERT EDMUND, biochemistry educator; b. Abington, Pa., Oct. 16, 1927; m. Joan A. Goddard; children: Kurt, Mark. BSChemE, Drexel Inst., 1949; MS in Biochemistry, U. Wis., 1951, PhD in Biochemistry, 1953. Postdoctoral fellow Lister Inst., 1953-54; postdoctoral fellow pharm. Yale U. Sch. Medicine, New Haven, 1955-56, asst. prof. pharm., 1956-60, assoc. prof. pharm., 1960-64, dir. div. biol. scis., 1969-72, chmn. dept. pharm., 1974-77, prof. pharm., 1964-95, prof. emeritus, 1996—; chmn. Eleanor Roosevelt Internat. Fellowship Com., 1966-73, Am. Cancer Soc. Coun. Rsch. Grants, 1977-78, sci. rev. com. Ludwig Cancer Unit, Brussels, 1980-84, health and med. care com. Commn. Acad. Sci., 1984—; sec., treas. Am. Assn. Cancer Rsch., Phila., 1982-88; rsch. prof. Am. Cancer Soc., 1977-95; Philips Meml. lectr. Meml. Sloan-Kettering, N.Y.C., 1985; chmn. exp. therap. adv. bd. B-W Fund, 1990-93; coun. mem. Nat. Inst. Environ. Health Scis., 1987-91. Author 250 articles, book chpts., etc. Sci. dir. Anna Fuller Fund, Yale U. Sch. Medicine, 1973-88; chmn. Samuel Roberts Noble Found. Adv. Bd., Okla., 1982-90; mem. bd. govs. Yale U. Press, New Haven, 1989-93. Fellow AAAS; mem. Conn. Acad. Sci. & Engring. (charter). Democrat. Lutheran. Achievements include development of new cancer treatments involving Asparaginase, 5-Fluorouracil; initial purification of the Lymphokine IL-1; discovery of receptor for the transplantation drug Cyclosporin. Home: 97 Great Harbor Rd Guilford CT 06437-3036 Office: Yale U Sch Medicine 333 Cedar St New Haven CT 06510-3289

HANDY, CAROLYN, newspaper editor; b. Bennington, Vt., Dec. 20, 1950; d. Herbert Lewis and Barbara (Lindsay) H.; 1 child, Hannibal Lloyd. AA, Greenfield (Mass.) C.C., 1972; B in English, Sch. Lifelong Learning, Lee, N.H., 1991; M in English, U. N.H., 1995. Staff reporter Tri-Town Transcript, Dover, N.H., 1989-93; editor Tri-Town Transcript, Dover, 1993—; staff reporter Shipyard News, Portsmouth, N.H., 1992-93; editor Shipyard News, Portsmouth, 1993-95; reporter Granite State Vacationer, Dover, 1992-94; editor U. N.H., Durham, 1993—. Mem. Toastmasters Internat. (chpt. v.p. pub. rels. 1996—, Competent Toastmasters recognition 1997), Mensa. Office: Tri-Town Transcript 270 Central Ave Dover NH 03820-4131

HANDY, CHARLES BROOKS, accountant, educator; b. Coffey, Mo., Apr. 26, 1924; s. Herbert Franklyn and Laura Ada Margaret (Mueller) H.; m. Donna Jean Peters, June 29, 1958 (dec.); children: William Mark, Karen Lynne; m. Mary C. O'Brien McGrane, Nov. 5, 1994. B.A., Westminster Coll., Fulton, Mo., 1947; M.A., U. Iowa, 1956; Ph.D., Iowa State U., 1970. C.P.A., Iowa. Staff acct. McGladrey, Hansen, Dunn & Co. (now McGladrey & Pullen), Davenport, Iowa, 1955-58; instr. acctg. Iowa State U., Ames, 1958-60; asst. prof. Iowa State U., 1960-70, assoc. prof., 1970-75, prof., 1975-92, chmn. supervisory com. bus. adminstrv. scis., 1975-78, acctg. coordinator, 1977-78, chmn. dept. indsl. adminstrn., 1978-80, dir. Sch. Bus. Adminstrn., 1980-84, dean Coll. Bus. Adminstrn., 1984-89, ret. dean emeritus, 1992. Served to lt. (j.g.) USNR, 1943-46. Mem. AICPA's, Iowa Soc. CPA's, Beta Alpha Psi, Omicron Delta Epsilon. Republican. Presbyterian. Home: 57 High Point Cir Unit 205 Naples FL 34103-4246

HANDY, EDWARD OTIS, JR., financial services executive; b. Akron, Ohio, Jan. 9, 1929; s. Edward Otis and Alice (Saalfield) H.; m. Susan Eastabrooks, May 12, 1951; children: Susan Littlefield, John E., Edward O. III, Seth H. AB, Harvard U., 1951, LLB, 1956. Bar: R.I. 1956, U.S. Dist. Ct. R.I. 1956. Assoc. Edwards & Angell, Providence, 1956-59; staff atty. Textron Inc., Providence, 1960-74, asst. gen. counsel, 1974-76, v.p. employee benefits, 1976-87, v.p., sec., 1987-91; ret., 1991. Bd. dirs. ERISA Industries Com., 1982-91, vice chmn., 1990-91; pres., bd. dirs. Providence Athenaeum, 1972-78; trustee various orgns. Capt. USMC, 1951-53, Korea. Mem. Providence Art Club, Hyannisport Club. Republican. Unitarian.

HANDY, LYMAN LEE, petroleum engineer, chemist, educator; b. Payette, Idaho, Aug. 4, 1919; s. Clarence Lee and Lillie (Hall) H.; m. Lenore E. Ross, Aug. 28, 1948; children—Mark Ross, Gail Eileen. Student, Western Wash. Coll., 1938-40; B.S., U. Wash., 1942, Ph.D., 1951. With Chevron Oil Field Rsch. Co., 1951-66; mem. faculty U. So. Calif., 1966-89, prof. chem. and petroleum engring., chmn. petroleum engring., 1966-86, chmn. chem. engring., 1969-76, Omar B. Milligan prof. petroleum engring., 1976-89, prof. emeritus, 1989—; cons. in field. Mem. editorial bd., Trans. Am. Inst. Mining Engrs., 1960, 68, 69; contbr. articles to profl. jours. Served to lt. USNR, 1942-46. Fulbright fellow, 1989. Mem. Am. Chem. Soc. (chmn. Orange County sect. 1969), Soc. Petroleum Engrs. (dir. Los Angeles basin sect. 1971-75, chmn. 1974, nat. dir.-at-large 1978-81), Am. Inst. Chem. Engrs., Phi Beta Kappa, Sigma Xi, Phi Lambda Upsilon, Tau Beta Pi, Phi Kappa Phi. Home: 1401 Dana Pl Fullerton CA 92831-1110 Office: U So Calif University Park Los Angeles CA 90089

HANDY, RICHARD LINCOLN, civil engineer, educator; b. Chariton, Iowa, Feb. 12, 1929; s. Walter Newton and Florence Elizabeth (Shoemaker) H.; married, Apr. 18, 1964 (div. 1980); 1 child, Beth Susan.; m. Kathryn Etona Claussen, Feb. 13, 1982. BS in Geology, Iowa State U., 1951, MS, 1953, PhD in Soil Engring. and Geology, 1956. Asst. prof. civil engring. Iowa State U., Ames, 1956-59; assoc. prof. Iowa State U., 1959-63, prof., 1963-87, disting. prof., 1987-91, disting. prof. emeritus, 1991—; prof.-in-charge Spangler Geotech. Lab., 1963-91; cons. in soil engring., soil and rock testing, landslide stabilization; v.p. research W.N. Handy Co., 1958-91, chmn. bd., 1986-90; pres. Handy Geotech. Instruments, Inc., 1980-93, chmn. bd. dirs., 1993—; mem., chmn. bd. dirs. Geopier Found. Co., L.C., 1993-95. Author: The Day the House Fell, 1995; co-author: (with M.G. Spangler) Soil Engineering 3rd edit., 1972, 4th edit. 1983; contbr. articles to profl. jours. Recipient faculty citation Iowa State U., 1976; named Anson Marston Disting. Prof. Engring., Iowa State U., 1987. Fellow AAAS, Geol. Soc. Am., Iowa Acad. Sci.; mem. ASCE (Thomas A. Middlebrooks award 1986), Soil Sci. Soc. Am., Internat. Soc. Soil Mech. and Found. Engrs. Achievements include patents in soils field. Home and Office: 1502 270th St Madrid IA 50156-7522

HANDY, ROBERT MAXWELL, patent lawyer; b. Buffalo, Apr. 1, 1931; s. John Abner and Yvonne Fernande (Blaise) H.; m. Berniece Emily Reist, July 2, 1955; children: Mary, Robert, David. B.S., Trinity Coll., 1953; M.S., Northwestern U., 1958, Ph.D., 1962; J.D., Ariz. State U., 1984. New product devel. research mgr. Westinghouse Electric Co., Pitts., 1961-69; product mgr. Semiconductor div. Motorola, Inc., Phoenix, 1969-72, corp. dir. research, 1972-75; exec. dir. Ariz. Solar Energy Research Commn., 1975-76; dir. bus. and tech. planning Integrated Circuits div. Motorola, Inc., Mesa, Ariz., 1976-80; sr. patent counsel Motorola, Inc., Phoenix, 1980-88; group patent counsel Motorola, Inc., 1988-94; intellectual property counsel Ea. Europe, Mid. East, and Africa Motorola GmbH, Weisbaden, Germany, 1995-98; pvt. practice Gilbert, Ariz., 1999—; instr. Carnegie Mellon U., 1967. Served to lt. (j.g.) USNR, 1954-57. Royall A. Cabell fellow, 1959-60. Mem. ABA, IEEE, Am. Phys. Soc., Phi Beta Kappa. Office: 1700 E Lakeside Dr #17 Gilbert AZ 85234-4978

HANDY, ROBERT TRUMAN, association administrator; b. Portland, Oreg., May 1, 1941; s. Royal Sheppard and Eloise (Yeager) H.; m. Linda Rose Andreas, Aug. 26, 1967 (div. 1976); 1 child, Heather Andreas Handy Zimmerman; m. Janet Lee Ward, Jan. 14, 1979; stepchildren: Christopher W. Ward, Elizabeth Leigh Ward Schmidt. BS in History, Polit. Sci., Portland State U., 1969, MA in Am. Diplomatic History, 1971. Dir. community svcs. Coll. of the Mainland, Texas City, Tex., 1972-74, dir. internat. programs, 1975-76; founder and exec. dir. Gulf Coast World Affairs Coun., 1976-84; exec. dir. Houston World Trade Assn., 1984-88; pres. Devel. Resources Internat., Houston, 1988—; exec. dir. Brazoria County Hist. Mus., Angleton, Tex., 1992—; adj. faculty Alvin (Tex.) C.C., 1994-98. Pub., editor Jour. Fgn. Affairs; internat. editor In Between Mag.; book reviewer Houston Chronicle. Bd. dirs. Galveston County Community Action Coun., Galveston, Tex., 1973, La Marque (Tex.) Aid and Guidance Coun., 1979; mem. La Marque Econ. Devel. Coun., 1980; del. European Community Visitors Program, Belgium, Fed. Republic Germany, France, Eng., 1981; chmn. Galveston County Coun. of Chambers, 1988; appointee European Community "Team 1992", 1989. With USN, 1959-62. Mem. Brazosport C. of C. (chmn. internat. com. 1992-93), Am. Assn. Museums, Am. Assn. State & Local Hist., Angelton C. of C. Democrat. Avocations: racquetball, jogging. Home: 2910 Frostwood Cir Dickinson TX 77539-4207 Office: 100 E Cedar Courthouse Sq Angleton TX 77515

HANDY, ROLLO LEROY, philosopher, research executive; b. Kenyon, Minn., Feb. 20, 1927; s. John R. and Alice (Kispert) H.; m. Toni Scheiner, Sept. 17, 1950 (dec. July 1997); children: Jonathan, Ellen, Benjamin. BA, Carleton Coll., Northfield, Minn., 1950; MA, Sarah Lawrence Coll., 1951; postgrad., U. Minn., 1951-52; Ph.D., U. Buffalo, 1954. Mem. faculty U. S.D., 1954-60, prof. philosophy, head dept., 1959-60; assoc. prof. Union Coll., Schenectady, N.Y., 1960-61; mem. faculty SUNY, Buffalo, 1961-76, prof. philosophy, 1964-76, chmn. dept., 1961-67, chmn. divsn. philosophy and social scis., 1965-67, provost faculty ednl. studies, 1967-76; pres. Behavioral Rsch. Coun., Great Barrington, Mass., 1976-84; pres. Am. Inst. Econ. Rsch., Great Barrington, Mass., 1977-91, pres. emeritus, 1991—. Author: Methodology of the Behavioral Sciences, 1964, Value Theory and the Behavioral Sciences, 1969, The Measurement of Values, 1970, (with Paul Kurtz) A Current Appraisal of the Behavioral Sciences, 1964; (with E.C. Harwood) rev. edit., 1973, (with E.C. Harwood) Useful Procedures of Inquiry, 1973; co-editor: Philosophical Perspectives on Punishment, 1968, The Behavioral Sciences, 1968, The Idea of God, 1968. With USNR, 1945-46. Mem. AAUP (chpt. pres. 1964-65), Am. Anthrop. Assn., Am. Philos. Assn. Home: 750 Weaver Dairy Rd Apt 159 Chapel Hill NC 27514-1440

HANDZEL, STEVEN JEFFREY, accountant; b. Phila., Nov. 9, 1954; s. Joseph Leo and Dori Lou (Kistler) H.; m. Beth Ann Barrick, Apr. 20, 1985; children: Samantha Nicole, Patrick Ryan, Daniel Joseph. BBA, Coll. of William and Mary, 1976; MBA, West Chester U., 1991. CPA, Pa. Staff auditor Peat, Marwick, Mitchell & Co., Phila., 1976-79, supr. sr., 1979-80; mgr. fin. reporting U.S. Cold Storage, Inc., Phila., 1980-83, treas. fed. credit union, 1982-83; audit mgr. Barbacane, Thornton & Co., Wilmington, Del., 1983-86; audit supr. Chester County, West Chester, Pa., 1986-88, acctg. mgr., 1988-92; pvt. practice Steven J. Handzel, CPA, West Chester, Pa., 1993—; CFO Gorelick & Assocs., 1997—; bd. dirs., treas. J.L. Handzel Marine Engring. Svcs., Inc., Pa. Rep. committeeman Chester County, 1977-94; mem. coun. West Chester Borough, 1980-88, v.p. couns., 1980-81; mem. sch. bd. West Chester Area Sch. Dist., 1989-93, 95—, pres. 1997-98; treas. West Chester Recreation Commn., 1987-88, Chester County Assn. Boroughs, 1983, sec., 1984, v.p., 1985, pres., 1986-87; mem. Chester County Intermediate Unit Sch. Bd., 1991-93, 95—, v.p., 1997-98, pres. 1999—; pres. West Chester Jaycees, 1990-91, dist. dir. Pa. Jaycees, 1991-92, regional dir., 1992-93, state v.p., 1993-94, state treas., 1994, Eyreman award, 1990, Statesman award, 1991. Mem. AICPA, Pa. Inst. CPAs (local gov. auditing and acctg. com., non-profit orgns. com. 1994-96), Del. Soc. CPAs, Govt. Fin. Officers Assn. (spl. rev. com. 1990—), Lions. Methodist. Avocations: skiing, sailing, gardening. Home: 302 N High St West Chester PA 19380-2614 Office: PO Box 3492 West Chester PA 19381-3492

HANDZLIK, JAN LAWRENCE, lawyer; b. N.Y.C., Sept. 21, 1945; s. Felix Munso and Anna Jean Handzlik; children: Grant, Craig, Anna. BA, U. So. Calif., 1967; JD, UCLA, 1970. Bar: Calif. 1971, U.S. Dist. Ct. (cen. dist.) Calif. 1971, U.S. Ct. Appeals (9th cir.) 1971, U.S. Supreme Ct. 1975, U.S. Tax Ct. 1979, U.S. Dist. Ct. (no. dist.) Calif. 1979, U.S. Dist. Ct. (ea. dist.) Calif. 1981, U.S. Dist. Ct. (so. dist.) Calif. 1982, U.S. Ct. Appeals (2d cir.) 1984, U.S. Ct. Internat. Trade 1984. Law clk. to Hon. Francis C. Whelan, U.S. Dist. Ct. (cen. dist.) Calif., L.A., 1970-71; asst. U.S. atty. fraud and spl. prosecutions unit criminal div. U.S. Dept. Justice, L.A., 1971-76; assoc. Greenberg & Glusker, L.A., 1976-78; ptnr., prin. Stilz, Boyd, Levine & Handzlik, P.C., L.A., 1978-84; prin. Jan Lawrence Handzlik, P.C., L.A., 1984-91; ptnr. Kirkland & Ellis, L.A., 1991—; del. U.S. Ct. Appeals for 9th cir. Jud. Conf., L.A., 1983-85; counsel to ind. Christopher Commn. Study of the L.A. Police Dept., 1991; dep. gen. counsel to Hon. William H. Webster, spl. advisor to L.A. Police Commn. for Investigation of Response to Urban Disorders, 1992; mem. adv. com. for Office of L.A. County Dist. Atty., 1994-96. Mem. editl. adv. bd. DOJ Alert, 1994-95. Bd. dirs. Friends of Child Advs., L.A., 1987-91, Inner City Law Ctr., L.A., 1993—; mem. bd. judges Nat. and Calif. Moot Ct. Competition Teams, UCLA Moot Ct. honors program. Mem. ABA (sect. criminal justice nat. com. on white collar crime 1991—, vice-chair 1998—, co-chair securities fraud subcom. 1994-98, west coast white collar crime com., exec. com. 1993—, vice-chair 1994-96, chair 1996-98, mem. sect. litigation, criminal litigation com. 1989—), Fed. Bar Assn., State Bar Calif. (sects. on criminal law and litigation), L.A. County Bar Assn. (mem. exec. com. criminal justice sect. 1997—, coms. on fed. cts. 1988—, chair criminal practice subcom. 1989-90, fed. appts. evaluation 1989-93, white collar crime com. 1991-97, exec. com. 1991-97). Office: Kirkland & Ellis 300 S Grand Ave Ste 3000 Los Angeles CA 90071-3140

HANE, MIKISO, history educator; b. Hollister, Calif., Jan. 16, 1922; s. Ichitaro and Hifuyo (Taoka) H.; m. Rose Michiko Kanemoto, Sept. 19, 1948; children: Laurie Shizue, Jennifer Kazuko. BA, Yale U., 1952, MA, 1953, PhD, 1957. Asst. prof. history U. Toledo, Ohio, 1959-61; asst. prof. history Knox Coll., Galesburg, Ill., 1961-66, assoc. prof. history, 1966-72, prof. history, 1972-92, prof. emeritus, 1993—. Author: Japan, A Historical Survey, 1972, Peasants, Rebels and Outcasts, 1982, Emperor Hirohito and His Chief Aide, 1982; editor, translator: Reflections on the Way to the Gallows, 1988, Eastern Phoenix: Japan Since 1945, 1996. Fulbright grantee, 1957-58, Japan Found. grantee, 1973, NEH grantee, 1979-80. Mem. Assn. for Asian Studies (bd. dirs. 1985-88), Am. Hist. Assn. (teaching div. 1980-83), Midwest Conf. on Asian Affairs (pres. 1988), Nat. Coun. on Humanities. Buddhist. Home: 2285 N Broad St Galesburg IL 61401-1454 Office: Knox Coll History Dept South St Galesburg IL 61401

HANEKE, DIANNE MYERS, education educator; b. San Francisco, Feb. 23, 1941; d. Wayne and Dorothy (Johnson) Myers; m. John Paul Haneke, Apr. 10, 1965; children: Mark, Debra, Julie. BA in Social Sci., Edn., So. Calif. Coll., 1964; MS in Edn., SUNY, Albany, 1971, cert. advanced studies, 1990, postgrad., 1990—, PhD in Reading, 1998. Cert. elem., social studies and reading tchr., N.Y. Reading specialist Greenville (N.Y.) Elem. Sch., 1971-72, 84-85, Durham (N.Y.) Elem. Sch., 1972-74, Cairo (N.Y.) Durham Schs., 1979-82, 86-89; counselor Capital Area Christian Counseling, Delmar, N.Y., 1980-81; instr. psychology Columbia Greene C.C., Hudson, N.Y., 1982-83; reading specialist Hunter (N.Y.)-Tannersville Schs., 1985-86; instr. edn. and reading Mt. St. Mary Coll., Newburgh, N.Y., 1990-92; adj. prof. reading edn. Concordia U., Austin, Tex., 1993—. Author: A Woman After God's Own Heart, 1982, A View From the Inside: An Action Plan for Gender Equity in New York State Educational Administration, 1990. Instr. water safety ARC, 1978-91; host parents Youth for Understanding, 1984-85, 88-89; leader, resource person Girl Scouts Am., 1978-90. Myers-Haneke Edn. scholar So. Calif. Coll., 1971—; recipient Alumnus of Yr. award So. Calif. Coll., 1979, Disting. Contbr. award So. Calif. Coll. Alumni Assn., 1988, Disting. Svc. award So. Calif. Coll. Edn. Dept., 1988, So. Calif. Coll. Alumni Assn., 1994. Mem. ASCD, Am. Ednl. Rsch. Assn., Assn. Tchr. Educators, Capital Area Reading Coun., Christian Educators' Assn. Internat., Coll. Reading Assn., Nat. Reading Conf., Internat. Coun. Tchrs. English, Tex. State Reading Assn., Delta Kappa Gamma, Phi Delta Kappa. Republican. Avocations: swimming, tennis, vocal and instrumental music, travel, Special Olympics. Office: Concordia Univ Edn Divsn 3400 Interstate 35 N Austin TX 78705-2799

HANEKE, G. DONALD, federal judge; b. 1945. AB, St. Peters Coll., 1967; JD, NYU, 1970. Bar: N.J. 1970. Law clk. to Hon. Harold Kolovsky, N.J. Superior Ct., 1970-71; asst. U.S. atty. for dist. N.J., U.S. Dept. Justice, 1971-74, 78-82; assoc. Drazin and Warshaw, Newark, 1974-78; magistrate judge for N.J., U.S. Magistrate Ct., Newark, 1982—. Office: King Fed Bldg-US Courthouse 50 Walnut St Rm 2066 Newark NJ 07102-3506

HANES, DONALD KEITH, cooperative executive; b. Oregon, Ill., Apr. 4, 1933; s. Harold Samuel and Ruth Lucille (Burke) H.; m. Patricia Elsberg, July 30, 1960; children: Deborah Ann, Dawn Michele, Katherine Elizabeth. BS in Journalism and Comm., U. Ill., 1955. Publs. advt. mgr. Watt Pub. Co., Mt. Morris, Ill., 1957-61; agrl. promotion specialist Portland Cement Assn., Chgo., 1961-65; asst. dir. advt. and pub. rels. Am. Breeders Svc., DeForest, Wis., 1965-68; dir. info. and edn. Farm Electrification Coun., Oakbrook, Ill., 1968-71; from dir. to v.p. pub. rels. Nat. Coun. Farmer Coops., Washington, 1971-82, v.p. comm., 1982-90, v.p., mem. instnl. rels., 1990-96; ret., 1996; bd. dirs. Coop. Devel. Found., Washington, 1986-94, United Coop. Svcs., Washington, 1980-81, 89, vice chmn. bd., 1981-83, 84-85, 90—, del.-at-large, 1983-84, 88, chmn. bd., 1985-87, United Coop Appeal, 1995; chmn. Md. Coop. Law Coalition, 1983-88. Producer (film) From This Land, 1979 (Cine Golden Eagle award 1979, Gold Camera U.S. Indsl. Film Festival 1980), (video) Cooperative Benefits, 1992; co-producer: (video) The Cooperative Spirit, 1994. Served to capt. USAR, 1955-65. Recipient Coop Communications award, 1984, Coop Career award Nat. Planning com. for Coop Month, 1996. Mem. Coop Communicators Assn. (hon. mem., pres. 1975-76, H.E. Klinefelter award 1979), Agrl. Rels. Coun. (sr. mem., Founders award 1977, pres. 1982-83), Advt. Coun. Coops. (pres. 1982-84, Leadership award 1984), Nat. Agrimktg. Assn. (co-founder Chesapeake chpt. 1982, bd. dirs. 1982-84). Republican. Methodist. Club: Nat. Press (Washington). Lodge: Masons. Avocations: Am. hist., fishing, swimming, horseback riding, travel. Home: 1100 Cedrus Way Rockville MD 20854-5534

HANES, JOHN GRIER, lawyer, state legislator; b. Cheyenne, Wyo., 1936; s. Harold H. and Mary Elizabeth (Grier) H.; m. Liv Paul; children: Greg, Clint. BS in Bus. Adminstrn., U. Wyo., 1958, JD, 1960. Bar: Wyo. 1960, U.S. Ct. Appeals (10th cir.) 1960, U.S. Ct. Mil. Appeals, 1960, U.S. Supreme Ct. 1964. Dep. sec. of state State of Wyo., 1963-65; prin. Burke Woodard & Bishop, Cheyenne, 1965-90, of counsel, 1990—; atty. Wyo. Senate, 1967-71; mcpl. judge City of Cheyenne, 1970-73; mem. Burke, Woodard & O'Donnell, Cheyenne, Wyo., until 1990; of counsel Burke & Woodard, P.C. and predecessor firms, Cheyenne, Wyo., 1990—; mem. Wyo. Ho. of Reps., 1993-99, Wyo. Senate, 1999—. Vol. Cheyenne Frontier Days; mem. Heels; Rep. precinct committeeman, 1976-94. With U.S. Army JAGC. Mem. C. of C., Rotary (pres. 1982-83, dist. gov. 1990-91), Sigma Nu. Avocations: outdoor sports, travelling. Home: 848 Creighton St Cheyenne WY 82009-3231 Office: 600 Boyd Bldg 1720 Carey Ave Cheyenne WY 82001-4429

HANES, JOHN WARD, sculptor, civil engineer consultant; b. San Francisco, June 5, 1936; s. Ward Herbert and Ruth Florence (Jacks) H.; m. Virginia Rae Meadows, Nov. 27, 1957 (div. Feb. 1966); children: Derek S., Kim R., Mark A.; m. Meda Lee Walter, June 29, 1968; 1 child, Ward W. BS in Engring., U. Calif., Davis, 1979. Registered civil engr., Calif. From engr. technician to civil engr. Soil Conservation Svc., USDA, Berkeley, Calif., 1960-79; civil engr. Soil Conservation Svc., USDA, Davis, 1979-83, hydraulic engr., 1983-90; sculptor, consulting civil engr. Boonville, Calif., 1990—. Pres. Santa Rosa (Calif.) Ski Club, 1971. Mem. Gualala Arts Ctr., Mendocino Arts Ctr., Nat. Sculpture Soc. Avocations: private pilot, multi media art, hunting, camping, fishing. Home: Box 510 29000 Mountain View Rd Boonville CA 95415

HANES, RALPH PHILIP, JR., former textiles executive, arts patron, cattle farmer; b. Winston-Salem, N.C., Feb. 25, 1926; s. Ralph Philip and Dewitt (Chatham) H.; m. Joan Audrey Humpstone, Jan. 14, 1950 (dec. Jan. 1983); m. Mary Charlotte Metz, Dec. 23, 1984. Grad., Woodberry Forest Sch., 1944; student, U. N.C., 1944-46; B.A., Yale U., 1949; L.H.D. (hon.), St. Andrews Coll., Laurinburg, N.C., 1981; DFA (hon.), N.C. Sch. of Arts, 1987; HHD (hon.), Wake Forest U., 1990. With Hanes Cos. Inc. (formerly Hanes Dye and Finishing Co.), Winston-Salem, N.C., 1950-93; pres. Hanes Dye and Finishing Co., 1965-68, chmn. bd., 1968-88, chmn. emeritus, 1988-93; chmn. bd. Ampersand, Inc., 1976-85; mem. coun. of sr. fellows Salzburg Seminars in Am. Studies. Cons. editor Performing Arts Rev., 1981-85, Jour. Arts Mgmt. and Law, 1981-86; editorial adv. bd. Art Economist, 1982-86. Bd. dirs. (apptd. by Pres. J.F. Kennedy) Nat. Cultural Ctr. for Performing Arts, 1962-65; mem. (apptd. by Pres. L.B. Johnson) Nat. Council Arts, 1965-70, mem. adv. music panel, 1970-72; bd. dirs. Am. Symphony Orch. League, 1958-61, Moravian Music Found., 1963-65; founder, mem. bd. visitors N.C. Sch. Arts, 1985—; trustee Salem Coll., 1961-64; bd. dirs. Jargon Soc. Inc., 1968—, pres., 1968-75; founder N.C. State Arts Coun., chmn. 1964-66; founder Ams. for the Arts (formerly Am. Coun. Arts), bd. dirs., 1960-69, pres., 1964-66, vice chmn., 1967-69; bd. visitors Barter Theatre, State Theatre of Va., 1967-75; mem. nat. adv. com. Brevard Sch. Music, 1969-74; trustee, exec. com, N.C. Sch. Arts, 1966-78; mem. nat. adv. com. Am. Crafts Coun., 1970-72, Appalachian Trail Conf., 1973-76; assoc. fellow Jonathan Edward Coll., Yale U., 1971-74; chmn. Yale U. Council Com. on Music, 1970-73; bd. dirs. Nat. Audubon Soc., 1972-78, John W. and Anna H. Hanes Found., 1974—, So. Appalachian Highlands Conservancy, 1974-78, Old Salem, Inc., 1974-77, Isaak Walton League Am., 1974-78, Nature Conservancy, 1975-79, (apptd. by Pres. Gerald Ford) Kennedy Center for the Performing Arts, 1975-80; mem. internat. council Mus. Modern Art, 1978-93; bd. dirs. Salzburg Seminar of Am. Studies, 1978-82, Spoleto Festival, 1979-86, 87-93; arts cons. govts. of, Austria, 1978, P.R., 1978; bd. dirs. Nat. Council Friends of Kennedy Ctr., 1975-80, Nat. Mus. Am. Art, Renwick Gallery, 1976-89, Alliance for Arts Edn., 1976-79; mem. exec. com. Nat. Coun. for Arts and Edn., 1976-79; mem. adv. coun. on arts Fed. Res. Bank of Richmond (Va.), 1977-78; bd. dirs. Am. Land Trust, 1976-93, Bus. Com. for Arts, 1980-86, Arena Stage, Washington, 1990-93; mem. Gov.'s Coun. Bus., Arts and Humanities, 1977-85; mem. fine arts com. Fed. Res. Bank of Washington, 1979-81; mem. adv. bd. Pauline Koner Dance Consort, 1977-80; bd. dirs. Arts Internat., 1981-85, Arts Resources Corp., 1981-83; adv. com. Am. Farmland Trust, 1983-97; mem. internat. coun. N.Y.C. Ballet, 1984-86; chmn. Am. Art Forum, 1986-87, bd. dirs. 1986-90; bd. dirs. Arena Stage, 1990-92; com. mem. State of N.C. Award, 1993, Yr. of Mountains Commn., N.C., 1995-96; corporate mem. Woods Hole Oceanog. Inst., 1994-98; mem. founding com. Agri-Rsch. Extension Network of N.Am., 1995-97; mem. coun. advisors Blue Ridge Pky., 1998—; mem. amb.'s steering com. Nat. Coun. Arts, 1999—; chmn. cabinet Spl. Olympics World Games, 1999. Named Young Man of Yr. Winston-Salem Jaycees, 1958, Young Man of Yr. N.C. Jaycees, 1958, Hon. Comdr., USS N.C., 1998; recipient Chmn.'s award NEA, 1966, Gov.'s award for preservation of natural area, 1969, pub. svc. award State of N.C., 1976, Morrison award for the Arts, 1977, Swan award, Tenn., 1970, N.C. Soc. of N.Y.C. award, 1979, Cmty. Svc. award Winston-Salem Urban League, 1979, Conservation award Isaac Walton League Am., 1982, award for disting. svc. to arts Nat. Gov.'s Assn., 1982, N.C. Gov.'s award in fine arts, 1982, awards Winston-Salem chpt. NAACP, 1983, Nat. Medal of Arts Amb. for the Arts presented by Pres. George Bush, 1991, award Piedmont Opera Theatre, 1992; tribute Nat. Arts Club, N.Y.C., 1995, Southeastern Ctr. for Contemporary Arts Leadership award, 1998. Mem. Am. League Anglers, Potomac Appalachian Mountain Club, S.E. Coun. on Founds., Trout Unltd., World Bus. Coun., Appalachian Consortium, East African Wildlife Soc., Isaac Walton League, Nat. Wildlife Fedn., N.Am. Mycological Assn., Pa. Acad. Fine Arts, Ut Prosim Soc., Royal Soc. Arts, Wilderness Soc., Walpole Soc., Appalachian Trail Conf., Century Assn. (N.Y.C.), Yale Club (N.Y.C.), Lotos Club (N.Y.C.), Met. Club (Washington), Peale for Visual Arts (Phila.), Piedmont Club, Twin City Club, Cane River Club, Bohemian Club, Currituck Club, Roaring Gap. Home: PO Box 1704 Winston Salem NC 27102-1704 Office: Hanes Cos Inc PO Box 202 Winston Salem NC 27102-0202

HANESIAN, DERAN, chemical engineer, chemistry and environmental science educator, consultant; b. Niagara Falls, N.Y., Sept. 26, 1927; s. Vahan and Anna (Kabasakallian) H.; m. Eva Hanesian. BChE, Cornell U., 1952, PhD, 1961. Registered profl. engr., N.Y., N.J. Prodn. engr. E.I. duPont de Nemours, Niagara Falls, 1952-57; research engr. E.I. duPont de Nemours, Deepwater, N.J., 1960-63; prof. dept. chem. engring., chemistry and environ. sci. N.J. Inst. Tech., 1963—, chmn. dept. chem. engring., chemistry and environ. sci., 1975-88; research engr. E.I. duPont, 1964-66, Exxon, Florham Park, N.J., 1967-70; tchr. Celanese, 1977, 80, Algerian Petroleum Inst., 1978; vis. prof. U. Edinburgh, 1981, Yerevan Poly. Inst., Armenia, USSR, 1983; acting dep. dir., vis. prof. Ctr. for Plastics Recycling Rsch., Rutgers U., Piscataway, N.J., 1989-93. Served with U.S. Army, 1945-46. Recipient Robert Van Houten award N.J. Inst. Tech., 1977, Outstanding Profl. Devel. by Tenured Faculty Mem. award, 1994, Excellence in Tchg. (lower divsn. undergrad.) award, N.J. Inst. Tech., 1998; grantee NSF, 1967, 72, 91, German Acad. Exch. Svc., 1982, Fulbright grantee Yerevan Poly. Inst., 1982. Fellow AIChE and emeritus mem; AAUP, Am. Chem. Soc., Am. Soc. Engring. Edn. life mem. and fellow, Mid-Atlantic AT&T Found. (award 1986, Centennial cert. award 1993, John Fluke award for excellence in lab. instrn. 1994, Mid. Atlantic Disting. Tchg. award 1997, Mid. Atlantic Outstanding Campus Rep. award 1999, The Professor Dicran H. Kabakjian Science Award), Armenian Students Assoc. of Amer., Inc., 1998; Order of the Engr., Fulbright Assn., Sigma Xi, Omega Chi Epsilon, Alpha Chi Sigma, Tau Beta Pi, Omicron Delta Kappa. Armenian Apostolic. Home: 51 Shepard Pl Nutley NJ 07110-2730 Office: NJ Inst Tech 323 Dr ML King Blvd Newark NJ 07102

HANEY, HARRY L., JR., forestry specialist, educator; b. Baileyton, Ala., Sept. 28, 1937; m. Jacqueline Taylor; 1 child, J. Lee. BS, Auburn U., 1959; M in Forestry, Yale U., 1969, MPhil, 1972, MS, 1973, PhD, 1975. Procurement and logging supervisor Melvin & Quitman Lumber Co., Ala., Miss., 1959, 62-65; forest mgr. St. Regis Paper Co., Fla., 1965-67; forestry econs. Weyerhauser Co., Washington, 1970; Garland Gray prof. forestry Va. Tech. U., Blacksburg, 1975—; cons. in field. Co-author: Essentials of Forestry Investment Analysis, 1984, Estate Planning for Forest Landowners: What Will Become of Your Timberland?, 1993, Forest Owner's Guide to the Federal Income Tax, 1995. Fellow Soc. Am. Foresters (chair Appalachian Soc. 1985); mem. Va. Forestry Assn (bd. dirs. 1985-91, 92-95). Office: Va Tech Coll Forestry & Wildlife Resources 324 Cheatham Hall Blacksburg VA 24061-0324*

HANEY, JAMES KEVIN, lawyer; b. New Brunswick, N.J., Apr. 11, 1966; s. James Alexander and Caroline Martha (Smolinski) H.; m. Elaine M. (Larsen), June 25, 1995. BA, U. Pa., 1988; JD with honors, St. John's U., 1991; MBA, Seton Hall U., 1998. Bar: N.J. 1991, U.S. Dist. Ct. N.J. 1991, N.Y. 1992, U.S. Ct. Appeals (3d and fed. cirs.) 1998, U.S. Supreme Ct. 1998. Twp. engring. inspector East Brunswick (N.J.) Twp., 1986-89; law clk. to Hon. June Strelecki N.J. Superior Ct., Monmouth County, 1991-92; assoc. Magee, Pagano & Isherwood, Wall, N.J., 1992-93, Zucker, Facher & Zucker, West Orange, N.J., 1993-99, Gilberg & Kiernan, Parsippany, N.J., 1999—. Mem. ABA, Assn. Def. Trial Attys., Def. Rsch. Inst., N.J. Def. Assn., N.J. State Bar Assn., N.Y. State Bar Assn., Ctrl. N.J. Alumni Club U. Pa., St.

John's Alumni Assn., Phi Delta Phi. Address: Gilberg & Keieknan 140 Littleton Rd Ste 201 Parsippany NJ 07054

HANEY, KEVIN SCOTT, admnitrator; b. Monongahela, Pa., Nov. 27, 1958; s. Robert George and Rita Ethel H.; m. Dawn Colleen Williams, May 23, 1980; chilre: Donovan, Shannoin, Devin. Cert., Washington (Pa.) Inst. Tech., 1983. Engring. lab. tech. Honeywell, Albuquerque, 1983-87; prin. Bernalille (N.Mex.) Acad., 1987-89, Christina Life Acad., Rio Rancho, N.Mex., 1989—; youth dir. Celebration Bapt. Ch., Rio Rancho, N.Mex., 1999—. Republican. Home: 3305 19th St SW Ri Rancho NM 87124 Office: Christian Life Acad 3910-A 19th Ave SE Rio Rancho NM 87124

HANEY, ROBERT LOCKE, retired insurance company executive; b. Morgantown, W.Va., June 14, 1928; s. John Ward and Katherine Eugenia (Locke) H. BA, U. Calif., Berkeley, 1949. Sr. engr. Pacific Telephone Co., San Francisco, 1952-58; mgmt. analyst Lockheed Missiles & Space Co., Sunnyvale, Calif., 1958-64; sr. cons. John Diebold, N.Y.C., 1964-65; sr. indsl. economist Mgmt. & Econs. Research, Inc., Palo Alto, Calif., 1965-67; prin. economist Midwest Research Inst., Kansas City, Mo., 1967-69; dir. mktg. coordination Transam. Corp., San Francisco, 1969-73; staff exec. Transam. Ins. Corp., L.A., 1974-82; 2d v.p. Transam. Life Cos., L.A., 1982-93; ret., 1993; cons. in field. Co-author: Creating the Human Environment, 1970. Lt. (j.g.) USN, 1949-52. Mem. Scabbard & Blade. Republican. Episcopalian. Avocations: photography, gardening, cycling. Home: 2743 Tiburon Ave Carlsbad CA 92008-7908

HANF, JAMES ALPHONSO, poet, government official; b. Chehalis, Wash., Feb. 3, 1923; s. William G. and Willa DeForest (Davis) H.; m. Ruth G. Eyler, Aug. 16, 1947; 1 child, Maureen Ruth. Grad. Centralia Jr. Coll., 1943, DLitt (hon.) World U. Ariz., 1980 Naval architect technician P.F. Spaulding, naval architects, Seattle, 1955-56, Puget Sound Bridge & Dredge Co. (Wash.), 1953-55, Puget Sound Naval Shipyard, 1951-53, 56-93; cons. Anderson & Assocs., ship bldg.; cons. The Rsch. Bd. Advs., Am. Biographical Inst., Inc.; guest lectr. on poetry and geneal. rsch. methods to various lit. socs., 1969—; contbr. hundreds of poems to lit. jours., anthologies and popular mags.; poetry editor Coffee Break, 1977-82. Recipient Poet Laureate Recognition award Internat. Biog. Centre of Cambridge, Eng., grand prize World Poetry Soc. Conv., 1985, 86, , 90, Golden Poet award World of Poetry in Calif., 1985-90, Silver Poet award Calif. sponsored nat. contest, 1989, numerous other awards. Judge poetry contest, Australia and India, 1985; named Man of Yr. Abaas, 1989—; named Internat. Eminent Poet Internat. Poet Acad. of Madras, India, 1987. Mem Internat. Poetry Soc. (Poet Laureate Wash. State award 1981), World of Poetry Soc. (Golden Poet award 1985-88, Poet Laureate award 1979), Kitsap County Writers Club (pres. 1977-78), Internat. Fedn. Tech. Engrs., Nat. Hist. Locomotive Soc., Kitsap County Hist. Soc., Puget Sound Geneal. Soc., Western World Haiku Soc., Olympic Geneal. Soc. (pres. 1974-75), N.Y. Poetry Forum, World Poets Resource Ctr., Literarische Union, Académie Européenne des Scis., Des Arts Et Des Letters (corr.), Internat. Soc. Poets Md. (hon. charter), Internat. Platform Assn., Calif. Fedn. Chaparral Poets, World Sadhak Soc. (hon.), Nat. Libr. Poetry (hon. mem.). Baptist. Home: PO Box 374 Bremerton WA 98337-0075

HANFORD, AGNES RUTLEDGE, financial adviser; b. Far Rockaway, N.Y., Aug. 26, 1927; d. Warren Day and Agnes Beatrice (Kane) H. Grad., Convent of Sacred Heart Prep. Sch., N.Y.C.; BA in English, French, Newton Coll., 1950. Asst. clk. rules com U.S. Ho. of Reps., Washington, 1953-56; account exec. W.E. Hutton & Co., N.Y.C., 1956-74; fin. cons. Thomson McKinnon Securities, N.Y.C., 1974-80, Tampa, Fla., 1980-89; fin. adviser Prudential Securities, Inc., Tampa, 1989-94. Mem. Hillsborough County Rep. Exec. Com., Tampa, 1980-93, Women's Econ. Coun., N.Y., 1979-80, Tampa Mus. Art, 1980—, Tampa Bay History Ctr., 1995—; mem. Friends of Plant Park, 1995—, bd. dirs., 1997—; mem. adv. coun. U. South Fla. Contemporary Art Mus., 1996—. Mem. Women's Nat. Rep. Club (mem. bd. govs. 1970-75, v.p. 1975-76), Tampa Yacht and Country Club, Lawrence Beach Club. Roman Catholic. Home: 4141 Bayshore Blvd Tampa FL 33611

HANFORD, GEORGE HYDE, retired educational administrator; b. Cambridge, Mass., July 29, 1920; s. Alfred Chester and Ruth Hyde H.; m. Elaine Halstead, Sept. 15, 1942; children: Anne Catherine, Mary Lee Hanford Wile. B.A., Harvard U., 1941, M.B.A., 1943; L.L.D. (hon.), W.Va. Wesleyan Coll.; EdD (hon.), Thomas Edison State Coll. Asst. dean Harvard Grad. Sch. Bus. Adminstrn., 1946-48; treas., bus. mgr., tchr., coach N. Shore Country Day Sch., Winnetka, Ill., 1948-55; treas., then v.p., exec. v.p. Coll. Entrance Exam. Bd., N.Y.C., 1955-79; pres. Coll. Entrance Exam. Bd., 1979-86, pres. emeritus, 1987—. Author: Life with the SAT, 1991, A Tale of Three Cities in One, 1996, For the Entertainment of Strangers, 1997. Former trustee Nat. Scholarship Svc. and Fund Negro Students, Dwight Sch., Ednl. Testing Svc., Am. Coun. on Edn., Ea. Ednl. Consortium, United Bd. Coll. Devel., Thomas A. Edison State Coll., N.J. Inst. Collegiate Tchg. and Learning, Nat. Coun. for Excellence in Critical Thinking. With USNR, 1943-46. Recipient disting. or spl. svc. awards Am. Sch. Counselors Assn., Nat. Assn. Coll. Admissions Counselors, Nat. Assn. Secondary Sch. Prins., Nat. Assn. Student Fin. Aid Adminstrs., Johnson C. Smith Univ.; inducted into Harvard Varsity Club Hall of Fame. Mem. Exec. Svc. Corps of New Eng., Hawaiian Mission Children's Soc., Cambridge Hist. Soc. (pres. 1995-97), Canterbury Soc. (symposiarch 1993—), Belmont Hill Club, Cambridge Boat Club, Tenafly Tennis Club. Episcopalian.

HANFORD, GRAIL STEVENSON, writer; b. Far Rockaway, N.Y., Apr. 10, 1932; d. Warren Day and Agnes Beatrice (Kane) Hanford. BA, Smith Coll., 1954. Reporter Tustin (Calif.) News, 1955; newspaper editorial asst. The Register, Santa Ana, Calif., 1955; assoc. editor Am. Mercury Mag., N.Y.C., 1956-59; freelance writer N.Y.C., 1959-60; editor Royal Ins. Cos., N.Y.C., 1960-62; book editor/copy editor Am. Legion Mag., N.Y.C., 1962-75; sr. editor Am. Legion Mag., Washington and Indpls., 1976-82; asst. editor Am. Legion Mag., Indpls., 1982-83; sr. writer Writers For Bus., Indpls., 1983-88, Tampa, Fla., 1988—. Contbr. articles to profl. jours. Bd. dirs. Cathedral Sch. of St. Mary, Garden City, N.Y., 1967-71, pres. Alumna Assn., 1967-69; bd. dirs. Hort. Soc. Indpls. Mus. of Art, 1981-86; pres. Smith Coll. Club Indpls., 1982-84. Mem. Fla. Motion Picture and TV Assn., Nat. Book Critics Cir., Indpls. Press Club (bd. dirs. 1980), Am. News Women's Club, West Fla. Smith Coll. Club (v.p. 1992-94. pres. 1996-99), Ivy League Club of Tampa Bay (bd. dirs. 1989-96, sec. 1990, v.p. 1991). Republican. Roman Catholic. Office: Writers For Bus 4141 Bayshore Blvd Tampa FL 33611-1800

HANFT, RUTH S. SAMUELS (MRS. HERBERT HANFT), health care consultant, educator, economist; b. N.Y.C., July 12, 1929; d. Max Joseph and Ethel (Schechter) Samuels; m. Herbert Hanft, June 17, 1951; children: Marjorie Jane, Jonathan Mark. BS, Cornell U., 1949; MA, Hunter Coll., 1963; PhD, George Washington U., 1989; ScD (hon.), U. Osteo. Med & Health Scis., 1993. Cons. Urban Med. Econs. Project, Hunter Coll., N.Y.C. and D.C. Dept. Health, 1962-63; health economist Office of Rsch. and Stats., Social Security Adminstrn., Washington, 1964-66; chief grants mgmt. health div. Office Econ. Opportunity, Washington, 1966-68; sr. health analyst Office of Asst. Sec. Planning and Evaluation HEW, Washington, 1968-71, spl. asst., asst. sec. health, 1971-72; dep. asst. sec. for health policy, rsch. and stats. Office of Asst. Sec. for Health HEW, 1977-79, dep. asst. sec. for health rsch., stats. and tech., 1979-81; health care cons., 1981-88; cons., rsch. prof. dept. health svcs. mgmt. and policy George Washington U., Washington, 1988-91, prof., 1991-95; cons., 1995—; vis. prof. Dartmouth Med. Sch., 1976—; sr. rsch. assoc. Inst. Medicine-NAS, Washington, 1972-76. Contbr. articles to profl. jours. Mem. Med. Assistance Svc. Bd. Commonwealth Va., 1984-89, Meharry Med. Coll. Bd. Trustees, 1989-94. Fellow Hastings Ctr., Assn. Health Svcs. Rsch., Inst. Medicine; mem. Nat. Acad. Sci., Cosmos Club. Jewish. Home: 3340 Brookside Dr Charlottesville VA 22901-9566

HANIFEN, RICHARD CHARLES, bishop; b. Denver, June 15, 1931; s. Edward Anselm and Dorothy Elizabeth (Ranous) H. B.S., Regis Coll., 1953; S.T.B., Cath. U., 1959, M.A., 1966; J.C.L., Pontifical Lateran U., Italy, 1968. Ordained priest Roman Catholic Ch., 1959; asst. pastor Cathedral Parish, Denver, 1959-66; sec. to archbishop Archdiocese Denver, 1968-69, chancellor, 1969-76; aux. bishop of Denver, 1974-83; 1st bishop of Colorado Springs, Colo., 1984—. Office: Bishop of Colo Springs 29 W Kiowa St Colorado Springs CO 80903-1403

HANIGAN, LAWRENCE, retired railway executive; b. Notre-Dame-de, Stanbridge, Can., Apr. 3, 1925; s. John Henry and Alice (Lareau) H.; m. Anita Martin, July 20, 1946; children: Carmen, Doris, Guy, Patricia, Michael. Sales mgr. Boisse Lumber Co., Montreal, 1950-52; regional mgr. Cooper-Widman Ltd., Montreal, 1952-70; mem. City of Montreal Exec. Com., 1970-78; chmn. Montreal Urban Community Exec. Com., 1972-78; chmn., gen. mgr. Montreal Urban Community Transit Commn., 1974-85; chmn. VIA Rail Canada Inc., 1985-93. Home: 358 du Baron St, Saint Sauveur, PQ Canada J0R 1R4

HANIKA, STEPHEN D., advertising executive. Sr. ptnr., group acctg. dir. Euro RSCG Tatham (formerly Tatham Euro RSCG), Chgo. Office: Euro RSCG Tatham 980 N Michigan Ave Ste 500 Chicago IL 60611-4519*

HANIN, ISRAEL, pharmacologist, educator; b. Shanghai, China, Mar. 29, 1937; s. Arie and Rebecca (Lubarsky) H.; m. Leda Toni, June 12, 1960; children: Adam, Dahlia. BS, UCLA, 1962, MS, 1965, PhD in Pharmacology, 1968. Vis. scientist dept. toxicology Karolinska Inst., Stockholm, 1968; staff pharmacologist Lab. Preclin. Pharmacology, NIMH, Washington, 1969-73; from asst. prof. to assoc. prof. psychiatry and pharmacology U. Pitts. Sch. Medicine, 1973-81, prof., 1981-86; prof., chmn. Dept. Pharmacology and Exptl. Therapeutics, dir. Inst. Neurosci. and Aging, dir. MD/PhD program Loyola U. Chgo. Stritch Sch. Medicine, Maywood, Ill., 1986—; mem. rsch. grant rev. com. NIMH, 1979-82, Nat. Inst. Aging, 1987-92, NIH Res., 1991-95; mem. pharmacology test com. Nat. Bd. Med. Examiners, 1987-90; mem. sci. adv. bd. Interneuron Pharms., Inc., Lexington, Mass., 1991—; cons. UCB Pharm., Brussels, 1981-98; mem. Alzheimer's Disease Rsch. Fund Panel Ill. Dept. Pub. Health, 1995—; mem. AMVETS Rsch. Initiative Com. Hines VA Hosp., 1996—. Editor 14 books; contbr. articles to profl. jours. Served to 2d lt. Armored Corps, Israeli Army, 1955-58. NIMH, NIH, Nat. Inst. Aging grantee, 1965—. Mem. Neurosci. Soc. (pres. Pitts. chpt. 1982-83, pres. Chgo. chpt., 1990-91), Am. Chem. Soc., Am. Soc. Pharmacology and Exptl. Therapeutics (co-founder Great Lakes chpt. 1987, pres. 1990-92), Am. Soc. Neurochemistry, Am. Coll. Neuropsychopharmacology. Address: Loyola U Chgo Stritch Sch Medicine Dept Pharm Rm 3621 Bldg 102 Maywood IL 60153

HANISEE, MARK STEVEN, employee benefits professional; b. Logansport, Ind., Dec. 23, 1958; s. William Bernard and Nancy (Thomas) H.; m. Patricia Jean Lauria, Jan. 7, 1989. BS, Fla. So. Coll., 1981. Account exec. Canon, Tampa, Fla., 1981-83; group sales exec. John Alden Life Co., Tampa, 1983-85; group account exec. State Mut. Cos., Tampa, 1985-89; sr. account exec., v.p. sales Bankers Risk Mgmt. Svcs., Inc., St. Petersburg, Fla., 1989-93; ptnr. Pension Investors Corp., Inc., 1993-94; pres. Tampa Bay Group Ins. Assn., 1993; sales exec. Sedgwick Noble Lowndes, 1994-96; candidate for State Rep., 1996-98; mktg. dir. Admin. Svc. Inc., 1998-99; benefits dir. Team Staff, 1999—. Mem. Leadership Hillsborough, 1996, Tiger Bay Club, 1996. Mem. Internat. Assn. Fin. Planning (bd. dirs. 1989-92), Employee Benefit Coun., Health Underwriters, Nat. Polit. Action Com. Chair, 1997—, Life Underwriters, Tampa C. of C. (health care task force com.), West Tampa bus. Alliance (bd. dirs.), Krewe Sant'Yago (com. chmn. 1990-91, sec., bd. dirs. 1992-93, grand marshall night parade 1994, large exec. bd.), Lincoln Club (sec. 1995), Merry Makers Club, Tampa Club, Rough Riders, Masons. Republican. Roman Catholic. Avocations: sailing, boating, fishing, tennis. Home: 6374 2nd Ave S Saint Petersburg FL 33707-1406 Office: Pension Investors Corp 3820 Northdale Blvd Ste 102B Tampa FL 33624-1834

HANISKO, JOHN-CYRIL PATRICK, electronics engineer, physicist; b. Detroit, Mar. 17, 1937; s. John Joseph and Pauline Victoria (Vrabel) H. BEE, U. Detroit, 1963, MSEE, 1965; MA, Wayne State U., 1972, PhD in Physics, 1988. Engr. Burroughs, Detroit, 1962-65; rsch. engr. Boeing, Seattle, 1965-67; sr. engr. Eastman Kodak, Rochester, N.Y., 1967-68; staff engr. Kent-Moore Corp., Warren, Mich., 1971-73; rsch. engr. Udylite, Warren, 1973-75; cons. Southfield, Mich., 1975-76; project engr. Bendix, Troy, Mich., 1976-80; staff engr. TRW, Farmington Hills, Mich., 1980-94; sr. engr. Eaton Corp., Southfield, Mich., 1994—. Contbr. articles to profl. jours. Mem. Cath. League for Civil and Religious Rights, N.Y., Nat. Tax Limitation Com., Washington, Nat. Right to Life Com., Washington. Named Design of Yr. EDN Mag., 1977. Mem. IEEE (sr.). Roman Catholic. Achievements include 10 patents for Electrical Control Apparatus for Internal Combustion Engines, for Sequential Injection Timing Apparatus, for Voltage Controlled Oscillator Having Ratiometric and Temperature Compensation, for Automotive Anti-theft Device, for brake-sensor signal processing, for resistive brake lining wear and temperature sensing system, for method and apparatus for trimming gain of an accelerometer, for method and apparatus for detecting operational failure of a digital accelerometer, for single-wire brake sensing system. Home: 21888 Murray Crescent Dr Southfield MI 48076-1619 Office: Eaton Corp 26201 Northwestern Hwy Southfield MI 48076-3926

HANKE, BYRON REIDT, residential land planning and community associations consultant; b. Mount Pleasant, Pa., Oct. 28, 1911; s. Emil and Augusta T. (Graf) H.; m. Anne Damon Fisher, Oct. 12, 1938; children: Carol Elizabeth Hanke Teich, Emily Anne Hanke VanZee. B.A., Colgate U., 1933; M.Landscape Architecture, Harvard U., 1937, Charles Eliot fellow, 1938, M.Urban Planning, 1940. Land planning cons. FHA, 1940-45, dir. land planning, 1945-72; dir. homes assn. study Urban Land Inst., Washington, 1962-64; pres. Byron R. Hanke Assocs.; cons. residential land planning and community assns. Byron R. Hanke Assocs., Washington, 1972-96; land planning cons. U.S. Govt. in Dominican Republic, 1967, Japan, 1970; cons. founding Community Assns. Inst., 1973-74. Author: Planned-Unit Development with a Homes Association, 1963, The Homes Association Handbook, 1964, Urban Densities in the U.S. and Japan, 1971, Design Review ... Architectural Control, 1978, Information System for Community Association Practitioners, 1983, Now You Are on the Board, 1992; co-author reports, handbooks. Recipient Merit award Nat. Assn. Home Builders, 1969. Fellow Am. Soc. Landscape Architects; mem. Am. Inst. Cert. Planners, Community Assns. Inst. (trustee, Disting. Svc. award 1978), Urban Land Inst. (life coun.), Phi Beta Kappa, Lambda Alpha (awards innovations and publs. 1972). Office: Byron R Hanke Assocs 3545 Alder Rd Scientist's Cliffs Port Republic MD 20676-2625

HANKENSON, E(DWARD) CRAIG, JR., performing arts executive; b. Mankato, Minn., Apr. 12, 1935; s. Edward Craig and Ethel Irene (Favre) H.; m. Francis Joyce Hall, Mar. 23, 1957 (div. 1978); 1 child, Meridith Joyce.; m. Catherine Ann Donaldson, 1981; 1 child, Jennifer Leigh. MusB, Eastman Sch. Music, 1957, MusM, 1959. Head voice and opera dept. Auburn U., Ala., 1959-62; bus. mgr. Chautauqua Opera Assn., N.Y., 1958-61; stage mgr. Chautauqua Opera Assn., 1957-59, stage dir., 1962; mgmt. intern San Francisco Opera Co., 1962-65; assoc. dir. Brevard Mus. Center, N.C., 1965-68; gen. mgr. Saratoga Performing Arts Ctr., N.Y., 1968-75; dir. Saratoga Performing Arts Ctr., 1975-78; exec. dir. Wolf Trap Found. Performing Arts, Vienna, Va., 1978-81; pres. Producers, Inc., 1980; dir., chmn. dept. arts mgmt. and events U. South Fla., Tampa, 1983-86; pres. KiddyCart Inc., 1987—, Producers, Inc., 1981—; chmn. bd. PICASTAR, 1985—; dir. Rochester Community Opera, N.Y., 1957-59; mem. Title III adv. council N.Y. Dept. Edn., 1969-75, N.Y. Gov.'s Commn. on Arts in Edn., 1978; cons. N.Y. Council on Arts; council bd. Rensselaer Poly. Inst.; cons. theater constrn. and mgmt. Concord Pavillion, Calif., Robin Hood Dell, Phila. Producer: (TV spls.) Snow White, PBS, 1973, Al Hirt and Pete Fountain Together, PBS, 1979, Great Jazz Pianists, PBS, 1979-81, Brigadoon, Majestic Theatre, N.Y.C., 1980-81, Lionel Hampton's Return to the Paradise, PBS, 1988, Thames Live Cinema, Radio City Music Hall, 1988; nat. tour of Show Boat, 1980, Kiss Me Kate and Taming of the Shrew, Washington Internat. Jazz Festival, 1980, nat. tour Pete Fountain, Jerry Mulligan and Al Hirt, 1982, 83, Tom Paxton, Dab O' Dixie, 1987, translator: Haydn's Lo Speziale, 1958, Smetana's Bartered Bride, 1964; creator Ticket Reservation Systems, 1968, prodr. of Glenn Miller, Artie Shaw, Woodie Herman, Helen O'Connell, Warren Covington, Don Cornell, Pied Pipers BigBand Nat. Tour Show, 1993. Bd. dirs. Capitol Area Resident Opera Co., 1969-71; mem. alumni adv. bd. Eastman Sch. Music, 1974-78; mem. com. performing arts Leukemia Soc. Am., Inc.,; mem. spl. adv. com. on spl. projects and presenting orgns. Nat. Endowment for the Arts, 1979-80; elder, mem. ruling session Temple Ter. Presbyn. Ch., 1990—, chmn. rsch. and planning, 1992—; bd. dirs., sec. Ter. Landings Assn. Recipient citation Central Theaters, Moscow, 1973. Mem. Internat. Assn. Concert and Festival Mgrs. (dir.), Performing Arts Assn. N.Y. (pres. 1972-78), Orgn. Summer Festival Mgrs. (moderator 1971-79 , dir), N.Y. Fedn. Music Clubs (dir.), Saratoga Springs C. of C. (dir. 1969-72, chmn. promotion com. 1970-72), Council of Pres.'s, Albany League Arts, Saratoga Springs PTA (pres. 1972-73), Temple Terrace C. of C. (spl. events com.), Rotary. Creator startup cons. for Ticketron ticket system. Office: Producers Inc 11806 N 56th St Ste B Tampa FL 33617-1652*

HANKERSON, CHARLIE EDWARD, JR., music educator; b. Ft. Lauderdale, Fla., Oct. 16, 1934; s. Charlie Edward Sr. and Pearl Lee (Patterson) H.; m. Orcenia Rookard, Oct. 14, 1962 (div. Feb. 1985); children: Anita Lynn, Leslie Arnetta, Charles III; m. Gwendolyn Araminta Betancourt, Apr. 6, 1985. BS in Instrumental Music, Fla. A&M U., 1956; MusM in Edn., Cath. U. Am., 1971. Commd. 2d lt. U.S. Army, 1956; advanced through grades to col. USAR, 1987; counselor Dist. Tng. Sch., Laurel, Md., 1961-62; music tchr. Loudoun County Schs., Leesburg, Va., 1962-67, D.C. Pub. Schs., Washington, 1968-94. Bd. dirs. South Potomac Citizens Assn., Ft. Washington, Md., 1990-91. Recipient Army Commendation medal Dept. Army, 1975, Army Achievement medal, Sec. of Army, 1983, Cert. of Appreciation, Chief USAR, 1987, Meritorious Svc. medal Dept. Army, 1987. Mem. Omega Psi Phi. Avocations: fishing, sports. Home: 9715 Traverse Way Fort Washington MD 20744-5745

HANKET, MARK JOHN, lawyer; b. Jan. 28, 1943; s. Lassie W. and Florence J. (Kubat) H.; m. Carole A. Dalpiaz, Sept. 14, 1968; children: Gregory, Jennifer, Sarah. AB magna cum laude, John Carroll U., 1965; JD cum laude, Ohio State U., 1968; MBA, Zavier U., 1977. Bar: Ohio 1968, Mich. 1993. Atty. Chemed Corp., Cin., 1973-77, asst. sec., 1977-82, sec., 1982-84; v.p., sec. Chemed Corp., 1984-86; v.p., gen counsel DuBois Chems. Divsn., 1986-87; v.p., sec. gen. counsel DuBois Chems., Inc., 1987-91; sec. gen. counsel Diversey Corp., 1991-94, v.p., sec. gen. counsel, 1994-96; v.p. law and people excellence, sec. Americlean Sys., Inc., 1996-99; asst. gen. counsel Diversey Lever, Inc., 1999—. Capt. U.S. Army, 1968-73. Decorated Meritorious Svc. medal, Army Commendation medal with oak leaf cluster. Mem. ABA, Mich. Bar Assn., Oakland County Bar Assn., Am. Corp. Coun. Assn., Ohio Bar Assn. Office: AmeriClean Sys 26935 Northwestern Hwy Ste 400 Southfield MI 48034-8449

HANKIN, CHARLES EDWARD, sculptor; b. Phila., Apr. 10, 1948; s. William Henry and Martha Willits (Parry) H.; m. Mary Margavitch (dec. Dec. 1984). BFA, Phila. Coll. Art, 1975; MFA, N.Y. Acad. Art, 1992. dir. Tri-State chpt. Artists Equity, Phila., 1997. One-man shows Ursinus Coll., Collegeville, Pa., 1981; exhibited in group show including Phila. Coll. Art, 1969-74, Plymouth Friends Sch., Plymouth Meeting, Pa., 1978, William Jeanes Libr., Lafayette Hill, Pa., 1978, Upstairs Gallery, Reading, Pa., 1980, Allerbescht Gallery, Harleysville, Pa., 1981, Allentown (Pa.) Art Mus., 1982, Woodmere Art Mus., Phila., 1983, 97, More Gallery, Phila., 1984, Haverford (Pa.) Gallery, 1989, Upper Merion Cultural Cr., King of Prussia, Pa., 1990, N.Y. Acad. Art, N.Y.C., 1992, Windlestrae Ctr. for Arts, Montgomeryville, Pa., 1995, Gloucester County Coll., N.J., 1994, Art Inst., Phila., 1997; mural executed North Wales (Pa.) Elem. Sch., 1997; also pvt. commns.; important sculptures include female figure Woodmere Art Mus., 1997. Avocations: tennis, skiing. E-mail: art4beauty@aol.com.

HANKIN, JOSEPH NATHAN, college president; b. N.Y.C., Apr. 6, 1940; s. Harry and Beatrice H.; m. Carole G. Hankin, Aug. 20, 1960; children—Marc, Laura, Brian. BA in Social Scis. (N.Y. State Regents scholar), CCNY, 1961; M.A. in History, Columbia U., 1962, Ed.D. in Adminstrn. Higher Edn. (Kellogg fellow), 1967; postgrad. seminar, Harvard U. Grad. Sch. Bus., 1979; Litt.D. (hon.), Mercy Coll., 1979. N.Y. State Regents coll. teaching fellow, 1961-63; fellow dept. history CCNY, 1962-63, lectr., 1963-65; lectr. history Bklyn. Coll. CUNY, summer 1963, lectr. history Queens Coll., summer 1964; course asst. dept. higher and adult edn. Tchrs. Coll., Columbia U., spring 1965, occasional lectr., 1965—, adj. prof. higher and adult edn., 1976—; dir. evening div. and summer session Harford Jr. Coll., Bel Air, Md., 1965-66, dean continuing edn. and summer session, 1966-67, pres., 1967-71; pres. Westchester C.C., Valhalla, N.Y., 1971—; bd. dirs. Mut. Funds Trust, 1988—; mem. task force on study higher edn. in D.C., 1966-67; spkr., panelist and cons. in field; condr. workshops and seminars. Contbr. articles and revs. to profl. publs. and newspapers. Mem. adv. com. Columbia U. Tchrs. Coll. C.C. Ctr., 1970—; bd. dirs., mem. exec. com. Westchester C.C. Found., 1971—; mem. Tri-State Coll. Consortium (now Eastern Ednl. Consortium), 1975—, pres., 1977-89, fin. com., 1982-87; mem. adv. com. SUNY Ednl. Opportunity Ctr., 1975—; mem. Coun. for Arts in Westchester, N.Y., 1971—, mem. coll. adv. com., 1971, mem. arts action plan for Westchester com., 1974-75, mem. Friends of Arts, 1976—, mem. benefit com., 1983-86, trustee, 1983-85; mem. Westchester Rockland Newspapers Lend-A-Hand Adv. Bd., 1974—; mem. Friends Harrison Pub. Libr., 1980—, Friends Neuberger Mus., 1979—; bd. advisors Hudson River Mus., 1985—; mem. adv. bd. Westchester County Hist. Soc., 1981-84; trustee Westchester Econ. Understanding Found., 1979, Harford Family Found., 1984—. Recipient Disting. Service award Bel Air (Md.) Jaycees, 1968, Brotherhood award Westchester region NCCJ, 1975, Arabic Soc. plaque, 1977, Plaque Pres. Ea. Ednl. Consortium, 1978, Championship of Youth award Youth Services div. B'nai B'rith, 1978, Community Svc. award Soc. Italian-Am. Orgns., 1986, plaque Alpha Beta Gamma and Drucker Mgmt. Soc., 1983, plaque Italian Club, 1984, plaque French Club, 1977, Honor award AIA, 1983, Cert. Vol. Services United Way Westchester, 1986, Cert. Appreciation Westchester 2000, 1988. Mem. Am. Assn. Jr. Colls. (v.p. 1971-74, bd. dirs. 1971-74, pres.'s acad. 1976—, various coms., Cert. Recognition 1981), Am. Assn. Higher Edn. (charter, life), Assn. Pres.'s Public C.C.s (legis. com. 1974-76, 86—, exec. com., mem.-at-large 1987-88), Faculty Student Assn. Westchester C.C. (dir. 1971—), Coll. Consortium for Internat. Studies (exec. com. 1974-88, sec.-treas. 1984-88, mem. ad hoc com. on bylaws 1983), Middle States Assn. Colls. and Schs. (ad hoc com. centennial celebration 1985—, pres. 1999) N.Y. State Assn. Jr. Colls., Young Presidents Orgn. (pres.'s forum 1979-90, founding dir. 1979-80, 84-85, day chairperson 1977-89), CEO Orgn., World Pres. Orgn., Westchester County C. of C. (bd. dirs. 1981-85, chmn. 1988, reaccreditation task force com. on staff 1982-83, chmn. nomination com. 1983-85), Phi Delta Kappa, Alpha Beta Gamma (hon.), Phi Theta Kappa. Home: 4 Merion Dr Purchase NY 10577-1302 Office: Westchester Community Coll 75 Grasslands Rd Valhalla NY 10595-1636 *In order to succeed, to do the best we can at whatever level on whatever path we choose, we do not need brilliance, nor money, nor luck, nor successful parents, nor benign climate, nor even perfect health. We do need belief and hope, imagination and inventiveness, foresight, preparation, and also motivation and perseverance, as well as hard work.*

HANKIN, MITCHELL ROBERT, lawyer; b. Phila., May 16, 1949; s. Samuel and Harriet (Cohen) H. BA, Trinity Coll., Hartford, Conn., 1971; JD, Columbia U., 1974. Bar: Pa. 1974, U.S. Dist. Ct. (ea. dist.) Pa. 1975, U.S. Ct. Appeals (3d cir.) 1975. Assoc. Blank, Romeklaus, Comisky, Phila., 1974-75; asst. U.S. atty. U.S. Atty.'s Office, Phila., 1975-76; ptnr. Hankin Enterprises, Willow Grove, Pa., 1976—; bd. dirs. Bank of Old York, Bank of King of Prussia (Pa.), Royal Bank of Pa. Mem. ABA, Pa. Bar Assn., Montgomery County Bar Assn., Phila. Bar Assn., Phi Beta Kappa. Home: 1115 Barberry Rd Bryn Mawr PA 19010-1907

HANKINS, KATHERINE ELIZABETH, obstetrician-gynecologist; b. Springfield, Ohio, Nov. 25, 1952; d. Raymond Richard and Helen Louise Stasiak; m. Jordan Henry Hankins, Aug. 17, 1974; children: Nancy Virginia, Richard Jordan. BA, U. Miss., University, 1975; MD, U. Miss., Jackson, 1979. Intern in ob-gyn La. State U. Med. Ctr., Shreveport, 1979-80; resident Wake Forest U. Bowman Gray Sch. Medicine, Winston-Salem, N.C., 1981-83; health officer Chattanooga and Hamilton County Health Dept., 1984-87; rsch. assoc. in ob-gyn Creighton U. Med. Ctr., Omaha, 1988-89, resident in family practice, 1989—; ob-gyn cons. Tenn. Dept. Health and Environ., Nashville, 1984-87; mem. adv. bd. Regional Tng. Ctr. for Family Planning, Emory U. Sch. Medicine, 1986-87; guest lectr. Teen Pregnancy, TV series, 1987; moderator Sexually Transmitted Disease, PBS, 1987. Mem. newsletter staff Fertility News, 1984-85. Sunday sch. tchr. St. Timothy's Episcopal Ch., Winston-Salem, 1983; cons. Girl Scouts U.S.A., Omaha, 1990. Recipient Disting. Leadership award March of Dimes, 1987, cert. of merit Tenn. Dept.

Health and Environ., 1987, Outstanding Resident award Creighton U. Med. Ctr., 1990. Fellow Am. Coll. Ob-Gyn. (jr., chmn. Tenn. sect. 1984-85, program dir. ann. meeting 1985), Am. Soc. for Colposcopy and Cervical Pathology; mem. AMA, Am. Fertility Soc. (exec. com. women's coun. 1983-86, co-chmn. com. 1982-84, chmn. 1984-89, Society Devel. fellow 1986-87), Assn. Women Surgeons. Avocations: family activiies, church youth, Bible study, exercise, weightlifting. Office: Creighton U Med Ctr 601 N 30th St Omaha NE 68131-2137

HANKINSON, TIM, soccer coach; b. Feb. 18, 1955. BS in Athletic Adminstrn., U. S.C., 1977. Lic. coach U.S. Soccer Fedn. Head coach Oglethorpe U., Atlanta, 1978-80, Ala. A&M, 1980-81, De Paul U., 1982, Datagraphic Soccer Club, 1984, Syracuse U., 1985-90, UMF Tindastol, Iceland 2nd Divsn., 1991; head coach, gen. mgr., owner Charleston Battery, USISL, 1992-94; gen. mgr. Raleigh Flyers, USISL, 1995; dir. player devel. Major League Soccer, 1996-98; head coach Tampa Bay Mutiny, 1998—; former coach U.S. Pro-40 Select team; former chmn. mktg. com. USISL. Named Big East Conf. Coach of Yr., 1986, Nat. Coach of Yr., USISL, 1994. Led Ala. A&M to NCAA Final Four, 1980, 81, Datagraphic Soccer Club to U.S. Amateur Cup semifinals, 1984, Syracuse U. to Big East Conf. Tournament Championship, 1985. Office: care Tampa Bay Mutiny 4042 N Himes Ave Tampa FL 33607*

HANKS, ALAN R., chemistry educator; b. Balt., Nov. 30, 1939; s. Raymond Hanks and Lillian (Simon) Miller; m. Beverly Jean Hinson, Jan. 17, 1961; children: Craig, Denise, Leta. BS in Physics, West Tex. State U., 1962; MS in Biophys. Chemistry, N. Mex. Highlands U., 1964; PhD in Biophysics, Pa. State U., 1967. Nuclear med. sci. officer Armed Forces Inst. Pathology, Washington, 1967-69; from asst. to prof. biochemistry, biophysics Tex. A&M U., Coll. Sta., Tex., 1969-82; state chemist, seed commnr., prof. Purdue U., West Lafayette, Ind., 1982—; corr. mem., liaison Collaborative Internat. Pesticide Analytical Coun., 1988; mem. Food and Agrl. Orgn. UN expert group on pesticides, 1991—. Contbr. articles to profl. jours. Fellow Assn. Ofcl. Analytical Chemists (chmn. methods bd. 1986-89, bd. dirs. 1990-96, sec.-treas. 1992-93, pres.-elect 1993-94, pres. 1994-95, immediate past pres. 1995-96, chmn. liaison com. 1997—); mem. Assn. Am. Feed Control Ofcls. (chmn. minerals com. 1985-96, pres.-elect 1998-99, pres. 1999—, lab. methods and svc. com. 1988-93, bd. dirs. 1996—), Assn. Am. Plant Food Control Ofcls. (chmn. Magruder check sample com. 1988-90, bd. dirs. 1989-94, chmn. environ. affairs com. 1990—, pres.-elect 1991-92, pres. 1992-93, past pres. 1993-94). Avocations: fishing, gardening, sports, travel. Home: PO Box 2627 West Lafayette IN 47996-2627 Office: Purdue U 1154 Biochemistry West Lafayette IN 47907-1154

HANKS, EUGENE RALPH, land developer, cattle rancher, forester, retired naval officer; b. Corning, Calif., Dec. 11, 1918; s. Eugene and Lorena B. Hanks; m. Frances Elliot Herrick, Mar. 4, 1945; children: Herrick, Russell, Stephen, Nina. Student, Calif. Poly. Coll., 1939-41, U. So. Calif., 1949-50, Am. U., 1958-59; grad., Command and Staff Coll., Norfolk, Va., 1960. With Naval Aviation Flight Tng.,V-5 Program USN, 1941-42, commd. ensign, 1942, advanced through ranks to capt., 1963; carrier fighter pilot, Am. Ace, six victories, 1942-45; test pilot Naval Air Test Ctr., 1946-48; mem. Navy Flight Exhbn. Team Blue Angels, 1950; commdg. officer fighter squadrons including Navy's 1st squadron of F4 Phantoms, Mach II Missile Fighters, Miramar, Calif., 1952-61; 1st ops. officer U.S.S. Constellation, 1961-62; dir. ops. Naval Missile Test Ctr., 1963-66; test dir. Joint Task Force Two, Albuquerque, 1966-69; ret., 1969; owner, developer Christmas Tree Canyon, Cebolla Springs and Mountain River subdivs., Mora, N.Mex., 1969-98. Decorated Navy Cross, DFC with star (2), Air medal (7), Legion of merit; named Citizen of Yr., Citizen's Com. for Right to Bear Arms, 1987, 93, to Dun and Bradstreet's Million Dollar Club. Mem. Ret. Officers Assn., Am. Fighter Aces Assn., Combat Pilots Assn., Assn. Naval Aviation, Am. Forestry Assn., NRA, Blue Angels Assn., Naval Aviation Museum Found., Am. Aviation Mus. Gt. Britain, Legion of Valor. Republican. Home and Office: Christmas Tree Canyon PO Box 239 Mora NM 87732-0239

HANKS, GERALD E., oncologist; b. Ellensburg, Wash., Sept. 21, 1934; m. Barbara L. Fowble. BS cum laude, Wash. State Coll., 1955; MD cum laude, Washington U., St. Louis, 1959. Diplomate Am. Bd. Radiology. Intern in medicine Yale Univ. Svc./Grace-New Haven (Conn.) Hosp., 1959-60; fellow Divsn. Radiotherapy Stanford (Calif.) U., 1960-63, chief resident, Divsn. Radiotherapy, 1962-63; various faculty positions to prof. with tenure U. Pa. Sch. Medicine, Phila., 1985-92; chmn. dept. radiation oncology Fox Chase Cancer Ctr., 1985—; prof., chmn. dept. radiation oncology Med. Coll. of Pa., 1992—; various adminstrv. positions to vice-chmn. dept. radiation U. Pa., Phila., 1985-92, acting chmn. dept. radiation therapy, 1985-86, chmn. dept. radiation therapy, 1985—; cons. scientific adv. bd. dept. radiation oncology, U. Ariz., 1987; peer rev. cons. NIH; lectr. in field. Editorial bd.: Internat. Jour. of Radiation Oncology Biology Physics, Clin. Oncology: A Jour. of the Royal Coll. of Radiologists, Jour. of Surg. Oncology; contbr. numerous articles to profl. jours. and publs.; chpts. to books. With Med. Corp., USN Rev., 1959-63; active duty USN, 1963-65. Recipient C.V. Mosby Book award for scholastic excellence, 1959; recipient numerous grants in field including Radiation Therapy Oncology Group, 1981-86, 85-89, 89-92, 92-95, Patterns of Care Studies, 1980-85, 88-92, 92-93, 94-97, others. Fellow Am. Coll. Radiology (numerous offices and bds., gold medal 1996); mem. Am. Cancer Soc., Am. Soc. Clin. Oncology, AMA, Am. Radium Soc. (pres.-elect 1985, pres. 1986), Am. Soc. Therapeutic Radiology and Oncology (Gold medal 1994), Internat. Commn. on Radiation Units and Measurements, Internat. Congress of Radiation Oncology, InterSoc. Coun. for Radiation Oncology (pres. 1988-91), Joint Commn. on Accreditation of Health Care Orgns., Radiation Therapy Oncology Group, Nat. Coun. on Radiation Protection and Measurements Patterns of Care Study (prin. investigator 1988—), Calif. Radiation Therapy Assn. (pres. 1975-76), Calif. Radiologic Soc. (exec. com. 1976-83), No. Calif. Radiation Therapy Assn. (pres. 1974-75), others. Avocations: viticulture, gardening. Office: Fox Chase Cancer Ctr 7701 Burholme Ave Philadelphia PA 19111-2412*

HANKS, JAMES JUDGE, JR., lawyer; b. Washington, Jan. 31, 1943; s. James Judge and Dorothy (Teeple) H. AB, Princeton U., 1964; LLB, U. Md., 1967; LLM, Harvard U., 1969. Bar: Md. 1967. Law clk. to judge U.S. Ct. Appeals (D.C. cir.), 1967-68; assoc. Weinberg and Green Law Firm, Balt., 1969-74; ptnr. Weinberg and Green, Balt., 1975-93, Ballard Spahr Andrews & Ingersoll, Baltimore, Md., 1993—; vis. prof. of law Cornell Law Sch., 1993, adj. prof. law 1994—, adj. prof. mgmt., 1999; adj. prof. law Northwestern Law Sch., 1997; lectr. various profl. orgns. and law schs. Author: Maryland Corporation Law; co-author: Legal Capital, 3d edit.; contbr. articles to profl. jours. Fellow Am. Bar Found.; mem. ABA, Am. Law Inst., Md. State Bar Assn. (chmn. bus. law sect. 1982-83), Md. Club. Democrat. Episcopalian. Home: 1159 Riverside Ave Baltimore MD 21230-4119 Office: Ballard Spahr Andrews & Ingersoll 300 E Lombard St Baltimore MD 21202-3219

HANKS, MERTON EDWARD, professional football player; b. Dallas, Tex., Mar. 12, 1968. BA, liberal arts, U. Iowa, 1990. With San Francisco 49ers, 1991—. Named to Sporting News NFL All-Pro Team, 1994-95, Pro Bowl, 1994-96. Dr. Z's All-Pro team, 1994; played in Super Bowl XXVIV, 1994. Office: San Francisco 49ers 4949 Centennial Blvd Santa Clara CA 95054-1229*

HANKS, TOM, actor; b. Concord, Calif., July 9, 1956; m. Samantha Lewes, 1978 (div. 1985); 2 children; m. Rita Wilson, Apr. 1988; children: Chester, Truman Theodore. Student, Calif. State U., Sacramento. Motion picture appearances include He Knows You're Alone, 1980, Splash, 1984, Bachelor Party, 1984, Volunteers, 1985, The Man with One Red Shoe, 1985, The Money Pit, 1986, Nothing in Common, 1986, Every Time We Say Goodbye, 1986, Dragnet, 1987, Big, 1988, Punchline, 1988, Turner and Hooch, 1989, The 'Burbs, 1989, Joe Versus the Volcano, 1990, Bonfire of the Vanities, 1990, Radio Flyer, 1992, A League of Their Own, 1992, Sleepless in Seattle, 1993, Philadelphia, 1993 (Golden Globe for Best Actor - Drama 1994, Academy Award for Best Actor 1994), Forrest Gump, 1994 (Academy Award for Best Actor 1995), Apollo 13, 1995, Celluloid Closet, 1995, Toy Story (voice), 1995, Saving Private Ryan, 1998 (nominated Acad. awards), You've Got Mail, 1998, Toy Story 2 (voice), 1999, The Green Mile, 1999; actor, dir., writer That Thing You Do!, 1996; TV movie appearances include Mazes and Monsters, 1982, I Am Your Child, 1997, (TV series) Bosom Buddies, 1980-82, (TV mini-series) From the Earth to the Moon, 1998; guest star (TV shows) Saturday Night Live, 1985, The Tonight Show, Late Night with David Letterman, Tales from the Crypt (None But the Lonely Heart, also dir.), Fallen Angels (I'll Be Waiting), also dir., 1993. Recipient Louella O. Parsons Awd., Hollywood Women's Press Club, 1994; named Man of the Yr., Harvard's Hasty Pudding Theater Club, 1995. Mem. Actors' Equity Assn., Screen Actors Guild, AFTRA. Office: CAA 9830 Wilshire Blvd Beverly Hills CA 90212-1804*

HANKS-DECRESCENZO, JAME MELISSE, insurance company executive; b. Midland, Tex., June 19, 1955; d. James Edward and Hari Jean (Jackson) Hanks; m. Michael Harry DeCrescenzo; children: Alexandra, Andrew. BA, U. Md., Spain, 1975; BSN, Tex. Women's U., 1980; MA magna cum laude, U. Tex., 1984. RN. Dir. spl. accounts Dey Labs., Dallas, 1978-80; salesman SMI, Dallas, 1980-83; ind. oil and gas investor Dallas, 1983-88; with Am. Gen. Ins. Co., 1988; dir. devel. Travelers Ins. Co., Richardson, Tex., 1990-94; dir. provider devel. Found. Health, A Tex. Health Plan, Dallas, 1994-97; v.p. managed care Patient-Physician Network, Plano, Tex., 1997—. Republican. Unitarian.

HANLE, PAUL ARTHUR, museum administrator; b. Newark, N.J., Oct. 27, 1947; s. John Edward and Claire (Kane) H.; m. Joan duBois Burroughs, Oct. 1979. A.B. in Physics, Princeton U., 1969; M.S. in Physics, Yale U., 1972, M.Phil., 1972, Ph.D. in History of Sci, 1975. Research fellow Smithsonian Instn., Washington, 1973-74; assoc. curator Nat. Air and Space Mus., Smithsonian Instn., 1974-78, curator of sci. and tech., 1978-80, acting chmn. space sci. and exploration dept., 1980-81, chmn. dept., 1981-84, assoc. dir. for research, 1984-86; assoc. dir. acad. affairs, 1987; exec. dir. Md. Sci. Ctr., Balt., 1987-96; pres. Acad. Natural Scis., Phila., 1996—; mem. Inst. Advanced Study, Princeton, 1983-84. Author: (with Paul Forman) Einstein. A Centenary Exhibition, 1979, Bringing Aerodynamics to America, 1982; editor: High Technology on Earth, 1979; (with Von Del Chamberlain) Space Science Comes of Age, 1981; contbr. The Space Telescope, by Robert W. Smith, 1989, 2nd edit., 1994. NSF intern, 1971; NSF traineeship, 1971-72; recipient Research award Smithsonian Instn., 1978; Robert H. Goddard Hist. Essay award, 1979. Mem. Assn. Sci. & Tech. Ctrs., Am. Assn. Mus., Soc. for History Tech., AAAS, Sigma Xi. Office: Acad Natural Scis 1900 Benjamin Franklin Pkwy Philadelphia PA 19103-1195

HANLE, ROBERT V., museum administrator; b. Pitts., Mar. 30, 1940. BA, Elizabethtown Coll., 1962; MA, U. Pa., 1968, PhD, 1973. Ordained to ministry Congl. Ch. Min. Congl. Ch.; tchr. high sch. Milton Hershey Sch., Hershey, Pa.; assoc. prof., dean faculty Elizabethtown Coll., 1964-76; investment mgr.; prof., v.p. acad. affairs Met. State U., St. Paul, Minn., 1976-86; assoc. dean, dir. external rels. Inst. Tech., U. Minn., Mpls., 1984-89, v.p., dir. devel. U. Minn. Found., 1989-97; exec. dir. for devel., overseer Office Membership-Devel., Smithsonian Instn., Washington, 1997—. Fax: 202-633-8978. Office: Smithsonian Instn Office Exec Dir for Devel 1000 Jefferson Dr SW Rm 105 Washington DC 20560-0027*

HANLEY, EDWARD J., federal agency administrator. Sr. dep. contr. adminstrn., CFO Dept. of Treasury, Washington, 1998—. Office: Dept of Treasury 250 E St SW Washington DC 20219

HANLEY, EDWARD JOHN, federal government executive; b. Endicott, N.Y., Dec. 14, 1941; s. Loftus Lawrence and Grace Cecilia (Martiny) H; m. Katherine Anne Keith, Aug. 6, 1966; children: Cecilia Anne, Patrick Keith. BA, Colgate U., 1963. Presdl. mgmt. intern U.S. PO Dept., Washington, 1965-68; assoc. cons. Fry Cons. Inc., Washington, 1968-70; v.p., ptnr. Lewin & Assocs. Inc., Washington, 1970-76; mng. ptr. Hanco Ltd. Partnership, Mt. Lake Pk., Md., 1976-78; dep. asst. adminstr. U.S. EPA, Washington, 1979-80, dir. facilities and info. svcs., 1981-82, dir. info. resources mgmt., 1983—; chairperson Interagy. Commn. on Info. Resources Mgmt., Washington, 1987-88, exec. bd. mem., 1986—. With U.S. Army, 1963. Recipient Meritorious Exec. award, Pres. of U.S., 1988. Mem. Assn. of Pub. Policy and Mgmt. Avocations: reading, hunting, fishing, skiing. Office: Environ Protection Agy Info Resources Mgmt 401 M St SW Washington DC 20024-2610

HANLEY, FRANK, labor union official; b. N.Y.C., July 5, 1930; s. Simon P. and Sally Hanley; m. Patricia Healy, 1959; 6 children. Student, U. Notre Dame, 1954-58, trade union program, Harvard U., 1959. Mem. Internat. Union Oper. Engrs., Washington, 1948—, asst. to gen. pres., 1959-74, v.p., 1974-79, sec.-treas., 1979-89, gen. pres., 1990—. Mem. VFW, Notre Dame Club. Office: Internat Union Operating Engrs 1125 17th St NW Washington DC 20036-4707

HANLEY, FRED WILLIAM, librarian, educator; b. Booneville, Miss., May 13, 1939; s. John Martin and Ethel May (Robertson) H.; m. Bethany Nell Holt, June 21, 1971; children: Seth Patrick, Cassandra May. BS, Lambuth Coll., Jackson, Tenn., 1961; MDiv, Meth. Theol. Sch., Delaware, Ohio, 1964; MA in History, Ariz. State U., 1966, MA in Counseling, 1968. Cert. secondary tchr., Ariz. Assoc. pastor Prospect Street Meth. Ch., Marion, Ohio, 1961-64; tchr. history Phoenix Union High Sch. Dist., 1965-74, curriculum coord., 1974-78, chmn. English dept., 1978-89, chmn. libr. dept., 1989—, chmn. tech. com., 1991—. Editor Ariz. Health Svcs. jour., 1965. Bd. dirs. Wesley Found., Tempe, Ariz., 1964-69; vol. Am. Cancer Soc., Phoenix, 1985-91; chmn. Phoenix Symphony Guild Symphonette Orch., 1993—; mem. exec. com. Phoenix Symphony Guild Orchestral Tng. Program, 1994—; libr. Phoenix Symphony Guild, 1998—. Recipient Tchr. of Yr. award West High Sch., Phoenix, 1969, Disting. Alumnae award Lambuth Coll., 1979. Mem. ALA, NEA, Ariz. Edn. Assn., Ariz. Libr. Assn., N. Cen. Assn. of Sec. Schs. Accreditation Team for Ariz., Nat. Coun. Tchrs. English., Phi Alpha Theta. Democrat. Avocations: marathon running, golf, hiking. Home: 10411 W Flower St Avondale AZ 85323-4403 Office: Alhambra High Sch 3839 W Camelback Rd Phoenix AZ 85019-2598

HANLEY, HOWARD JAMES MASON, research scientist; b. Hove, Sussex, Aug. 19, 1937; arrived in U.S., 1962; s. Charles Edward Mason and Evelyn Agnes (Palmer) H.; m. Janet Mary Kettlewell, July 29, 1964; 1 child, Elizabeth Mary. BSc, London U., 1959, PhD, 1963. Rsch. assoc. Dept. Chemistry, Pa. State U., State College, 1963-65; phys. chemist Nat. Bur. of Stds., Boulder, 1965-83; fellow Nat. Inst. of Stds. and Tech., Boulder, 1983—; adj. prof. Dept. Chem. Engring., U. Colo., 1974—, vis. prof. 1969; vis. rsch. fellow, 1973-74, 78-79, 87, 88, 92; vis. scientist Inst. Laue-Langevin, Grenoble, France, 1984, 85; fellow Wissenschaftskolleg zu Berlin, Berlin Inst. Advanced Studies, 1989-90; rsch. adv. com. Nat. Bur. Stds., 1980-83; Australian Nuclear Sci. and Tech. Orgn. vis. prof. Rsch. Sch. Chemistry, Australian Nat. U., 1998—. Author/editor: Transport Phenomena in Fluids, 1969, Turner in Dorset, 1992; cons. editor Marcel Dekker Inc., N.Y., 1968—; editor NIST Jour. of Rsch., 1975-88; adv. editor Internat. Jour. of Thermophysics, 1981—; contbr. articles to profl. jours. Recipient Silver medal U.S. Dept. of Commerce, 1982, Gold medal, 1985; recipient Humboldt Rsch. prize, 1992. Fellow Royal Chem. Soc.; mem. ASME (com. thermophys. properties 1980-94, chmn. 1980-85), Internat. Union Pure and Applied Chemistry (transport properties com. 1976-88, com. on quantum fluids), MaryLeBone Cricket Club. Avocations: landscape art, English literature, social history, music, cricket. Office: Nat Inst Stds and Tech 325 Broadway Boulder CO 80303-3337

HANLEY, KEVIN LANCE, maintenance manager; b. Oil City, Pa., Nov. 25, 1961; s. Harold Edward and Helen Louise (Banta) H.; m. Patricia Yolanda DeLeon, Sept. 29, 1984; children: Jennifer Jessica, Kevin Lance Jr. Grad. high sch., Titusville, Pa.; diploma, McDonald's Regional Hdqs., L.A., 1986. Maintenance supr. Paschen Mgmt. Corp. McDonald's, Camarillo, Calif., 1980-86, asst. mgr., 1986-88, 95, maintenance cons., 1988-89; mgr. phys. plant Westmont Coll., Santa Barbara, Calif., 1988—; apartment mgr. Bartlein & Co., Ventura, Calif., 1990-97; 3rd class petty officer USNR, Port Hueneme, Calif., 1994—; gen. cons. "R" Cleaning Maintenance, Santa Paula, Calif., 1989-91; owner Custodial-Plus Svcs., Ventura, Calif., 1996—. Sec.-treas. Ch. of God of Prophecy, Carpinteria, Calif., 1987-95, 98—, co-pastor, 1988-95. With USNR, 1994—. Recipient Navy and Marine Corp Achievement Medal, 1998. Republican. Avocations: backpacking, bowling, camping. Office: Westmont Coll 955 La Paz Rd Santa Barbara CA 93108-1023

HANLEY, THOMAS PATRICK, obstetrician, gynecologist; b. St. Louis, Apr. 16, 1951; s. Thomas P. and Virginia Barbara (Lydon) H.; m. Patricia Ann McHargue, Dec. 27, 1975; children: Colleen, Thomas III, Timothy, Matthew. BA, St. Louis U., 1973, MD, 1977. Diplomate Am. Bd. Ob-gyn. Intern St. Louis U., 1977-78, resident, 1978-81; practice medicine specializing in ob-gyn St. Louis, 1981—; pres. med. staff St. Mary's Health Ctr., 1993; mem. staff Mo. Bapt. Hosp., Deaconess Hosp.; assoc. clin. prof. St. Louis U. Med. Sch., 1983—; mem. exec. com. St. Louis Med. Group, 1995—. Mem. AMA (Physicians Recognition award 1981—), Am. Coll. Ob-Gyn. (Physicians Excellence award 1986, 89, 92, 95), Gynecol. Laser Soc., St. Louis Gynecol. Soc. (pres. 1989-90), St. Louis Met. Med. Soc., West Borough Country Club. Republican. Roman Catholic. Avocation: golf. Office: 1035 Bellevue Ave Ste 208 Saint Louis MO 63117-1846

HANLEY, THOMAS RICHARD, engineering educator; b. Logan, W.Va., July 26, 1945; s. Thomas Jesse and Dorothy Louise (Hay) H.; m. Norma Kathryn Decker, Dec. 27, 1979; children: Thomas Jeffrey, Alan Michael, Andrew Richard, Caitlin Marisa. BSChemE, Va. Poly. Inst., 1967; MSChemE, Va. Poly. Inst. and State U., 1971, PhDChemE, 1972; MBA in Mgmt., Wright State U., 1975. Registered profl. engr., La., Ky. Devel. engr. AF Materials Lab., Wright Patterson AFB, Ohio, 1972-75; asst. prof. Tulane U., New Orleans, 1975-79; assoc. prof. Rose-Hulman Inst. Tech., 1979-83; prof., dept. head La. Tech. U., Ruston, 1983-85; prof., chmn. dept. Fla. State U., Fla. A&M U., Tallahassee, 1985-91; dean Speed Sci. Sch. U. Louisville, 1991—; cons. TASA, Blue Bell, Pa.; divsn. advisor NSF, Washington, 1987-93; presenter at numerous nat. and internat. profl. confs. Contbr. articles to profl. jours. Capt. USAF, 1972-75. Recipient award Soc. Am. Mil. Engrs., 1966, 67, Acad. award Am. Legion, 1967, Ralph R. Teetor Ednl. award SAE, 1989, Outstanding Engr. in Edn. award Ky. Soc. Profl. Engrs., 1994; grantee NSF, GE, Colgate-Palmolive, United Catalysts, IKA Works, Swan Biomass, Toro, Olin, Stone and Webster. Fellow AIChE (profl. devel. recognition cert. 1980, student chpt. advisor award 1979); mem. Am. Soc. Engring. Edn., Nat. Assn. Basketball Coaches, Sigma Xi, Phi Kappa Phi, Tau Beta Pi, Phi Lambda Upsilon, Omega Chi Epsilon. Office: U Louisville Speed Sci School Louisville KY 40292

HANLEY, WILLIAM H., association executive; b. S.I., N.Y., July 12, 1942; s. John J. and Norma M. (Freeman) H.; m. Irene A. Petrou, June 28, 1969; children: Matthew D., Elizabeth A. BA, Manhattan Coll., 1964; MA, Marquette U., 1966. Instr. Manhattan Coll., Riverdale, N.Y., 1966-68; assoc. prof. Rockland Community Coll., Suffern, N.Y., 1968-79; exec. adminstr. Soc. Cosmetic Chemists, N.Y.C., 1979-88; exec. v.p. Illuminating Engrng. Soc. N.Am., N.Y.C., 1988—. Mem. Am. Soc. Assn. Execs. (cert.), N.Y. Soc. Assn. Execs. (bd. dirs. 1990—), Coun. Engring. and Sci. Soc. Execs. Roman Catholic. Office: Illuminating Engring Soc NAm 120 Wall St Apt 17 New York NY 10005-4001*

HANLINE, MANNING HAROLD, internist; s. Manning Harold and Anne (Sekerka) H.; m. Margaret, June 18, 1977; children: Trinity, Andrew, John. AA, Pensacola (Fla.) Jr. Coll., 1971; BS in Biology cum laude, Tulane U., 1973, MD, 1977. Diplomate Am. Bd. Internal Medicine, Am. Bd. Emergency Medicine. Intern, resident in internal medicine Univ. Hosp., Jacksonville, Fla., 1977-80; fellow in critical care medicine Md. Inst. Emergency Med. Svcs. Sys., Balt., 1981-82; pvt. practice internal medicine, 1984—; med. dir. Pensacola Cluster Facility, 1987—, Escambia County Jail, Pensacola, 1994—; apptd. Fla. Bd. Medicine, 1989-93; chief dept. medicine Bapt. Hosp., Pensacola, 1995—. Lt. col. USARMC, 1991—. Fellow Am. Coll. Physicians, Am. Coll. Emergency Physicians; mem. AMA, Fla. Med. Assn., Fla. Coll. Emergency Physicians, Soc. Critical Care Medicine, Escambia County Med. Soc. Home: 2740 Sunrunner Ln Gulf Breeze FL 32561-5509 Office: 1717 N E St Pensacola FL 32501-6339*

HANLON, CYRIL ROLLINS, physician, educator; b. Balt., Feb. 8, 1915; s. Bernard and Harriet (Rollins) H.; m. Margaret M. Hammond, May 28, 1949; children: Philip, Paul, Richard, Christine, Thomas, Mary, Martha, Sarah. A.B., Loyola Coll., Balt., 1934; M.D., Johns Hopkins U., 1938; D.Sc. (hon.), Georgetown U., 1976, U. Ill., 1986, St. Louis U., 1986. Diplomate Am. Bd. Surgery (chmn. 1966-67). Intern John Hopkins Hosp., 1938-39, W.S. Halsted fellow in surgery, 1939-40, instr. surgery, 1946-48, asst. prof., 1948-50, assoc. prof., 1950; asst. resident, resident in surgery Cin. Gen. Hosp., 1940-41, 43-44; exchange fellow surgery U. Calif., 1941-42; prof. surgery, chmn. dept. St. Louis U., 1950-69; prof. surgery Northwestern U. Med. Sch., 1969-85, prof. emeritus, 1985—; Chmn. surgery study sect. NIH, 1965-66; pres. Council Med. Specialty Socs., 1974-75; chmn. Coordinating Council on Med. Edn., 1976-77. Contbr. articles to profl. jours. Served to lt. (j.g.) M.C. USNR, 1944-46, CBI. Recipient Fleur-de-lis award St. Louis U., 1968; Statesmen in Medicine award Airlie Found., 1974. Founder group Am. Bd. Thoracic Surgery (1949); fellow ACS (gov., regent 1967-69, exec. dir. 1969-86, pres. elect 1986-87, pres. 1987-88), Royal Australasian Coll. Surgeons (hon.), Royal Coll. Surgeons of Eng. (hon.), Royal Coll. Surgeons in Ireland (hon.), Royal Coll. Surgeons of Can. (hon.), Am. Assn. Surgery of Trauma (hon.), Am. Urol. Assn. (hon.), Am. Hosp. Assn. (hon.); mem. Am. Heart Assn. (surgery research study com. 1966-68), Internat. Cardiovascular Soc. (pres. N.Am. chpt. 1963-64), Soc. Vascular Surgery (pres. 1968), AMA, Am. Surg. Assn. (sec. 1968-69, pres. 1981-82), Western Surg. Assn., So. Surg. Assn., Soc. Thoracic Surgeons, Central Surg. Assn., Am. Assn. Thoracic Surgery (treas. 1962-68), Soc. U. Surgeons (pres. 1958), Soc. Clin. Surgery (pres. 1968-70), St. Louis Surg. Soc., Johns Hopkins Med. and Surg. Assn. (v.p. 1975-77), Johns Hopkins Soc. Scholars, Cosmos Club, Alpha Omega Alpha. Roman Catholic. Address: 633 N Saint Clair St Chicago IL 60611-3211

HANLON, JAMES ALLISON, confectionery company executive; b. Oak Park, Ill., Nov. 27, 1937; s. James Graves and Frances (Allison) H.; m. June Weiland, May 30, 1959; children: Perian, Loretta, Jill, James. BA, U. Notre Dame, 1959; postgrad., U. London, 1979, U. Pa., 1980. Mgr. accounts Needham Harper Steers Advt., Chgo., 1959-67; mgr. mktg. L.S. Heath & Co., Inc., Robinson, Ill., 1967-70; v.p. mktg. Peter Paul Cadbury, Naugatuck, Conn., 1970-79, pres., chief exec. officer, 1983-86; pres. Cadbury Can., Toronto, Ont., 1979-83, also bd. dirs.; pres., chief exec. officer Leaf N.Am., Bannockburn, Ill., 1988-95; chmn., CEO, pres. Harmony Foods, Santa Cruz, Calif., 1996—. Nat. trustee Boy's Clubs of Am. With USMCR, 1956-59. Named Mktg. Warrior of Yr., AMR, Inc., 1979, Most Motivated Exec., 1992; recipient Kettle award Confectionary Industry, 1992. Mem. New Haven Country Club. Roman Catholic. Home: 61 Morningside Dr Milford CT 06460-7713 *Life unfolds itself at it's own pace...Any grand plans should be tempered by the unaticipated events.*

HANLON, R(OBERT) TIMOTHY, lawyer; b. St. Louis, Feb. 23, 1937; s. Robert Francis and G. Lucille (Johnson) H.; m. Marilyn Teresa Yans, Aug. 24, 1963; children: Margaret Ann, Elizabeth, R. Timothy Jr., Mary Alyssa. AB, St. Louis U., 1958; JD, Harvard U., 1961. Ptnr. Shaw, Pittman, Potts & Trowbridge, Washington, 1964—; cons. Pres.'s Adv. Coun. on Exec. Orgn., Washington, 1970. Capt. USAF, 1958-64. Roman Catholic. Home: 3609 Thornapple St Bethesda MD 20815-4113 Office: Shaw Pittman Potts & Trowbridge 2300 N St NW Fl 5 Washington DC 20037-1172

HANMAN, TED E., music educator, choral conductor; b. St. Louis, July 28, 1961; s. Gary Edwin and Shirley Anne (Warren) H.; m. Elizabeth Janet Campbell, Aug. 11, 1984; children: Peter Edwin, Michael Campbell, Lydia Elizabeth May. MusBE, Ctrl. Meth. Coll., 1983; post grad. cert. in Edn., Southlands Coll., Wibledon, England, 1988; MA in Music Edn., Inst. Edn., London U., 1991. Cert. vocal and instrumental edn. Instrumental music tchr. Croydon Music Tchg. Agy., London, 1988-91, North Platte Schs., Dearborn, Mo., 1992-95, Atchison Pub. Schs., Kans., 1995—; guest lectr. London U., 1991. Vol. Voluntary Svc. Overseas, London, 1985-87; conductor Croydon Young Musicians, London, 1988-91, Atchison Cmty. Band, 1997; guest clinician Pasao Music Acad., Kansas City, Mo., 1997; adjudicator Kans. Music Educators Dist. 1, Baldwin, Kans., 1997. Choral fellow Ctrl. Meth. Coll., 1981-83, presdl. scholar, 1982-83. Mem. Kans. Music Educators Conf., Kans. Bandmasters Assn. Methodist. Avocations: composition, chess, reading, tennis. E-mail: thanman@msn.com.

HANMER, STEPHEN READ, JR., retired government executive; b. Denver, Aug. 15, 1933; s. Stephen Read and Mary Virginia (Marchant) H.; m. Lois Eileen Boteler, June 25, 1955; children: Susan Eileen Hanmer Alexander, Stephen Read III, Sara Lynn. B.S. in Phys., Va. Mil. Inst., Lexington, 1955; MS in Aerospace Engring., MSME, U. So. Calif., 1964. Commd. 2d lt. U.S. Army, 1956, major, 1965, lt. col., 1968; commanding officer 6th bn., 32d Artillery U.S. Army, Republic of Vietnam, 1968; col. U.S. Army, 1975, retired, 1977; assoc. prof. dept. mechanics U.S. Mil. Acad., 1964-67; def. plans div. staff mem. U.S. Mission to NATO, Brussels, 1978-81; dir. theater nuclear force policy Office of Sec., Dept. Def., Washington, 1981-84; prin. dep. asst. sec. Internat. Security Policy Dept. Def., Washington, 1984-85; amb., dep. head U.S. del. Strategic Arms Reduction Talks, 1985-87, amb., chief U.S. del., 1988-89; dep. dir. ACDA, 1989-93; asst. to pres. Kaman Scis. Corp., Alexandria, Va., 1993-98; ret., 1998. Decorated Legion of Merit, Bronze Star; recipient Meritorious Civilian Svc. medal U.S. Dept. Def., 1981, Sec. of Def. medal, 1987, Sr. Exec. Svc. Disting. Exec. award, 1988, Sec. State Superior Honor award, 1993, Disting. Honor award ACDA, 1993. Mem. St. Andrews Soc. Washington (sec. 1995, 96, v.p. 1997), Sertoma Club (bd. dirs. 1977), Internat. Inst. for Strategic Studies, Am. Def. Preparedness Assn. Republican. Episcopalian.

HANNA, CAREY MCCONNELL, securities and investments executive; b. Huntsville, Ala., Mar. 5, 1941; s. Elzaphan McConnell and Evelyn Adella (White) H.; m. Anna Estelle Giaffis, Aug. 5, 1961; children: James, Catherine, Christopher, David. BS, U. S.C., 1965, MEd, 1979. CLU, ChFC, registered fin. cons. Asst. v.p. First State Nat. Bank, Jackson, S.C., 1964-66; agt. The Prudential, Aiken, S.C., 1966-69; tchr., coach, dept. head Aiken County Schs., 1969-79; state editor, metro editor The Augusta (Ga.) Chronicle, 1970-78; pres. Hanna Fin. Advisors, Aiken, 1978—; registered rep. Multi-Fin. Securities Corp., Denver, Colo., 1991—; moderator Life Underwriter Tng. Coun., Aiken, 1990-96. Coach Aiken H.S. acad. team, 1991—; pres. Aiken Jaycees, 1971; pres. Schofield Mid. Sch. PTO, Aiken, 1982, 83; trustee Mead Hall Parish Day Sch., Aiken, 1991-92; vestry St. Thaddeus Episcopal Ch., Aiken, 1991-92. Recipient Ga. AP Pub. Svc. award, 1975; named Outstanding State Chmn. S.C. Jaycees, 1967. Fellow Life Underwriter Tng. Coun.; mem. Nat. Assn. Life Underwriters (Nat. Quality award, Nat. Sales Achievement award), Internat. Assn. Registered Fin. Planners (founding), Million Dollar Roundtable, Aiken Assn. Life Underwriters (pres. 1986), Aiken County Estate Planning Coun., Nat. Eagle Scout Assn. Avocations: sports, reading, family activities, ch. activities. Home: 1212 Williams Dr Aiken SC 29803-5364 *We are called to a life of stewardship. In all things and in all ways, we are given opportunities to serve. However, we may think we have been called to serve those who can benefit us the most, but true service comes from helping those who need it most and from whom there is no monetary award. A simple thank you can be the most powerful gift of all.*

HANNA, COLIN ARTHUR, county official, management and computer consultant; b. Abington, Pa., Dec. 3, 1946; s. Arthur and Jean Victoria (McClure) H.; AB, U. Pa., 1968; m. Anne Price Hemphill, Dec. 28, 1967; children: Jean Price, Colin Alexander. With CBS, Inc., 1969-76; account exec. CBS Radio Spot Sales, N.Y.C., 1969-70; mgr. creative services CBS-Viacom Group, N.Y.C., 1970-71; account exec. CBS Radio Spot Sales, N.Y.C., 1971-72, sales mgr., Phila., 1974-76; account exec. WCAU Radio, Phila., 1972-74; dir. sales devel. WCAU-TV, Phila., 1976; pres. Hanna & Wile Advt., Wayne, Pa., 1976-77, Tri-State Trade Exchange, Inc., West Chester, Pa., 1978-80, Hanna Enterprises Ltd., 1980—; prin. Whittlesey and Assocs., West Chester, 1980-85; pres. The Cheshire Group, West Chester, 1985-91, The Bank Execs. Network, Inc., 1988-90, PC Helper, 1991-95, Vestryman Ch. of Good Samaritan, Paoli, Pa.; mem. bd. overseers Sch. Arts and Scis. U. Pa.; elected mem. Chester County Rep. Com., 1992—; county commr. Chester County, 1992—, chmn. bd. commrs., 1998; bd. mem. Delaware Valley Regional Planning Commn., 1996—, chmn., 1996-97, 98—. With USNR, 1968-69. Mem. Shakespere Soc. Phila., Newcomen Soc. N.Am., Coll. Alumni Soc. U. Pa. (pres.), Gen. Alumni Soc. U. Pa. (v.p.), Alumni Assn. U. Pa. (pres.), County Commrs. Assn. Pa., Mensa. Republican. Episcopalian. Clubs: Racquet (Phila.); Radley Run Country (West Chester); Tred Avon Yacht (Oxford, Md.). Home and Office: 603 Fairway Rd West Chester PA 19382-2013

HANNA, FRANK JOSEPH, credit company executive; b. Douglas, Ga., Apr. 20, 1939; s. Frank Joseph and Josephine (Nahoom) H. m. Vail Deadwyler, Sept. 15, 1960; children: Frank, Lisa, David. BBA, U. Ga., 1961. Credit mgr. Sears, Roebuck & Co., Atlanta, 1961-63, Gen. Motors Corp., Atlanta, 1963-65; gen. mgr. Rollins Acceptance Corp., Atlanta, 1965-81; with Credit Claims & Collections, 1981-90, First Fin. Mgmt. Corp., 1990-93, Worldwide Capital, Inc., Atlanta, 1993—; real estate developer, 1968. Office: Two Ravinia Dr Ste 1750 Atlanta GA 30346

HANNA, GEORGE VERNER, III, lawyer; b. Shelby, N.C., Mar. 2, 1943; s. George and Mildred Mae (McSwain) H.; m. Linda Faye Tyndall, May 4, 1982 (div.); children: George Verner IV, Mark W., Elizabeth P.; m. Deborah Henson Hannon, Apr. 14, 1984. AB, U. N.C., 1965, JD, 1968. Bar: N.C. 1968, U.S. Dist. Ct. (we. dist.) N.C. 1969, U.S. Dist. Ct. (ea. dist.) N.C. 1972, U.S. Dist. Ct. (mid. dist.) 1974, U.S. Ct. Appeals (4th cir.) 1976, U.S. Supreme Ct. 1976. Law clk. N.C. Supreme Ct., Raleigh, 1968-69; assoc. Moore & Van Allen, PLLC, Charlotte, N.C., 1969-73, ptnr., 1974—; arbitrator Am. Arbitration Assn. Com. chmn. Mecklenburg Coun. Boy Scouts Am.; former mem. bd. mgrs. Harris YMCA, Charlotte; bd. mgrs. McCrorey YMCA, Charlotte; past pres., bd. dirs. So. Piedmont Legal Svcs., Charlotte; past pres. bd. dirs. Children's Law Ctr., Charlotte. Fellow Am. Bar Found; mem. ABA, N.C. Bar Assn. (bd. govs., mem. exec. com.), Mecklenburg County Bar Found. (pres. bd. dirs.), Mecklenburg County Bar Assn., Quail Hollow Club, Charlotte Tower Club. Methodist. Home: 244 Hempstead Pl Charlotte NC 28207-1922 Office: Moore & Van Allen PLLC NationsBank Corp Ctr 100 N Tryon St Fl 47 Charlotte NC 28202-4003

HANNA, HARRY MITCHELL, lawyer; b. Portland, Oreg., Jan. 13, 1936; s. Joseph John and Amelia Cecelia (Rask) H.; m. Patricia Ann Shelly, Feb. 4, 1967; 1 child, Harry M. Jr. BS, U. Oreg., 1958; JD, Lewis and Clark Coll., 1966. Bar: Oreg. 1966, U.S. Tax Ct. 1967, U.S. Dist. Ct. Oreg. 1970, U.S. Supreme Ct. 1971, U.S. Ct. Appeals (9th cir.) 1973, U.S. Ct. Claims 1973. Airport mgr. Port of Portland, 1964-66; mng. ptnr. Hanna & Purcella, Portland, 1966-80, Niehaus, Hanna, Murphy, Green, Holloway & Connolly, Portland, 1980-88; shareholder, v.p. Hanna, Kerns & Strader, P.C., Portland, 1988—; judge pro-tempore U.S. Dist. Ct. Oreg., 1973-78; adj. prof. N.W. Sch. Law, Lewis and Clark Coll., Portland, 1976-77. Trustee Emanuel Med. Ctr. Found., 1989—; pres. Ctrl. Cath. H.S. Bd., 1992-95; vice chair Life Flight Devel. Bd., 1994-97, chair, 1997—. Mem. ABA, Fed. Bar Assn., Oreg. State Bar Assn., Multnomah Bar Assn., Rotary (pres. East Portland club 1989-90). Avocations: tennis, hunting, fishing, coaching youth athletics. Office: Hanna Kerns & Strader PC 1300 SW 6th Ave Ste 300 Portland OR 97201-3461

HANNA, JAMES CURTIS, state official; b. Takoma Park, Md., July 14, 1935; s. Frederick G. Hanna and Seona E. (Shenk) Young; m. Carol Patche, 1956 (div. 1973); children: Laurie Jane, Daniel Frederick; m. Janet M. Reese, 1985. AA, U. Fla., 1956; BA, U. Miami, 1964. Registered architect, Fla., Md. Draftsman Philpott, Ross & Saarinen, Ft. Lauderdale, Fla., 1964-74; constrn. mgr. Enterprise Developers, Ft. Lauderdale, 1974-75; engring. mgr. Bailey & Assoc., Ft. Lauderdale, 1975-77; staff arch. Md. Dept. Housing and Comty. Devel., Annapolis, 1977-84, adminstr. arch. and constrn., 1984-90; dir. codes adminstrn. Md. Dept. Housing and Comty. Devel., Crownsville, 1990—; Dept. of Housing and Comty. Devel. rep. Md. Emergency Mgmt. Agy.; Dept. Housing and Comty. Devel. subject matter expert Ams. with Disabilities Act., Gov.'s Emergency Mgmt. Adv. Coun. mem.; mem. steering com., co-chair ea. region Coun. of State Adminstrv. Agys. Bd. dirs. Sylvan Shores Svcs. Corp., Riva, Md., 1987-93, sec.-treas., 1993; mem. Nat. Trust for Hist. Preservation, 1986-91; appted. Gov.'s Mgmt. Adv. Coun., 1996, 99. Mem. Nat. Conf. State Bldg. Codes and Stds. (del., bd. dirs., pres., so. regional dir.), Coun. of State Adminstrv. Agys. (steering com., co-chair ea. region), Nat. Inst. Bldg. Scis., N.Am. Fireman's Assn., Md. Bldg. Ofcls. Assn. (bd. dirs., sec. 1997, 98, 91-99). Avocations: water sports, antiques, computers. Office: State of Md Dept Housing Comty Devel 100 Community Pl Crownsville MD 21032-2022

HANNA, LEE ANN, critical care nurse; b. Little Rock, June 16, 1961; d. David Lee and Betty Lou (Pope) Redmond; m. Anthony Warren Hanna, June 18, 1986; children: Thomas Dale, Katherine Elizabeth. AS in Nursing, Belmont Coll., 1980; BSN, Union U., 1983; MSN, Vanderbilt U., 1993. RN, Tenn. Critical care nurse Select Splty. Hosp., Nashville, 1980-95; mgr. continuous quality improvement edn. Am. Transitional Hosp., Nashville, 1995—; instr.: ACLS, BCLS and PALS; lectr. in field. Mem. AACCN (cert.), Nat. Assn. Healthcare Quality (cert.).

HANNA, MARTIN SHAD, lawyer; b. Bowling Green, Ohio, Aug. 4, 1940; s. Martin Lester and Julia Loyal (Moor) H.; m. Ann I. Amos; children: Jennifer Lynn, Jonathan Moor, Katharine Anne. Student, Bowling Green State U.; B.S., Purdue U., 1962; J.D., Am. U., 1965. Bar: Ohio 1965, D.C. 1967, U.S. Supreme Ct. 1969. Ptnr. Hanna, Middleton & Roebke, 1965-70; ptnr. Hanna & Hanna, Bowling Green, 1971—; spl. counsel for atty. gen. Ohio, 1969-71, 82-85, Ohio Bd. Regents, 1974; instr. Bowling Green State U., 1970, Ohio Div. Vocat. Edn., 1970—, Ohio Peace Officer Tng. Council, 1968; legal adviser NW Ohio Vol. Firemen's Assn., 1970—. Contbr. articles to profl. publs. Elder, lay minister Presbyn. Ch.; state chmn. Ohio League Young Republican Clubs, 1972-73; nat. vice chmn. Young Rep. Nat. Fedn., 1973-75, counselor to chmn., 1975-77; cive chmn. Wood County Rep. Exec. Com., Ohio, 1972-80, precinct committeeman, 1968-80; trustee Bowling Green State U., 1976-86; mem. Ohio State Fire Commn., 1979-87; mem. Ohio Rural Fire coun., 1993—. Recipient George Washington honor medal award Freedoms Found. at Valley Forge, 1969, award of merit Ohio Legal Ctr. Inst., 1973, Robert A. Taft Disting. Service award, 1974, James A. Rhodes Leadership award, 1975; named one of 10 Outstanding Young Men, Ohio Jaycees, 1968. Mem. ABA, D.C. Bar Assn., Ohio Bar Assn., Northwest Ohio Bar Assn., Wood County Bar Assn., Toledo Bar Assn., Am. Trauma Soc. (trauma and law com.), Phi Delta Phi, Pi Kappa Delta, Omicron Delta Kappa. Home: PO Box 1137 Bowling Green OH 43402-1137 Office: 700 N Main St Bowling Green OH 43402-1815

HANNA, MICHAEL GEORGE, JR., immunologist, institute administrator; b. Cleve., July 7, 1936; s. Michael George and Camella (Karem) H.; m. Barbara Ann Pearson, Sept. 6, 1958; children: Michael George, Christina Louise, Suzanne Kathleen. B.S. in Biology, Baldwin-Wallace Coll., 1958; M.S. in Biology, Notre Dame U., 1960; Ph.D., U. Tenn., 1964. Research biologist biology div. Oak Ridge Nat. Lab., 1964-68, dir. immunology of carcinogenesis group, 1968-75; dir. cancer biology, head host tumor interaction sect. cancer biology program Nat. Cancer Inst. Frederick (Md.) Cancer Research Facility, 1975-79; dir. Nat. Cancer Inst. Frederick (Md.) Cancer Research Facility, 1979-82; dir. Litton Inst. Applied Biotech., Rockville, Md., 1982-85; sr. v.p., COO Biotech. Rsch. Inst., Rockville, Md., 1985-94; pres., CEO PerImmune, Inc., Rockville, Md., 1994-98; chmn., chief sci. officer Intracel, 1998—; cons. NASA Lunar Receiving Lab., 1968-70; chmn. tech. adv. com. on biotech. U.S. Dept. Commerce, 1985-90; mem. working group on biotech. U.S. Dept. Def., 1984-90; mem. bd. overseers Ctr. for Advanced Rsch. in Biotech., 1984-88. Gen. editor: Contemporary Topics in Immunobiology, 1971—, Vaccine Rsch., 1991—; mem. editorial bd. Immunopharmacology, 1978—, Cancer Rsch., 1978-92, Jour. Biol. Response Modifiers, 1982—, Cancer Metastasis, 1984—. Recipient Charles Thornton award Litton Industries, 1984. Mem. Soc. Exptl. Pathology, Am. Assn. Cancer Rsch., Am. Assn. Immunologists, Internat. Soc. Immunopharmacology (coun. 1991—). Achievements include 300 publications, patents (with others) for Tumor Specific Monoclonal Antibodies, Tumor Associated Monoclonal Antibodies Derived from Human B-Cell Line, Active Specific Immunotherapy of Carcinomas. Office: 1330 Piccard Dr Rockville MD 20850-4330

HANNA, MICHAEL K., state legislator; b. Lock Haven, Pa., Aug. 25, 1953; m. Susan K. Hanna. BA, Lock Haven U., 1977; JD, U. Pitts., 1980. State rep. dist. 76 Pa. Ho. of Reps., Clinton City, 1990—; former pvt. practice as atty. E-mail: http://www.pahouse.net/hanna/index.htm. or http://ww.kenet.org/Government/StateGovernment/hanna.htm. Office: 29 Bellefonte Ave Lock Haven PA 17745-1207*

HANNA, NESSIM, marketing educator; b. Assiut, Egypt, Apr. 30, 1938; came to U.S., 1961, naturalized, 1973; s. Yanni and Lulu Shehata (Oweda) H.; m. Dana Lascu, Aug. 28, 1987 (div. 1988); m. Margaret Ann Curzan, 1996. BS in Commerce, Cairo U., 1958; MS in Mktg., U. Ill., 1964, PhD in Mktg, 1969. Asst. prof., chmn. dept. mktg. W.Va. Inst. Tech., Montgomery, 1968-69; asso. prof. bus. adminstrn. Middle Tenn. State U., Murfreesboro, 1969-70; prof. mktg. No. Ill. U., De Kalb, 1970—; mktg. cons. Arab Research and Admintrn. Center, 1975-77, Investments Cons. Internat., 1974-77; vis. prof. mktg. U. Petroleum and Minirals, Dharan, Saudi Arabia, 1980-81, Norwegian Sch. Mgmt., Oslo, 1988; chmn. dept. mktg., dir. research inst. King Saud U., Kassim, Saudi Arabia, 1983-84; vis. scholar Hong Kong Bapt. U., fall 1991. Author: Marketing Opportunities in Egypt: A Business Guide, 1977, Principles of Marketing, 1985, Pricing Policies and Procedures, 1995, Winning Strategies, 1991, Consumer Behavior: An Applied Approach, 1999; contbr. articles to profl. jours. Named Outstanding Citizen Citizenship Council Met. Chgo., 1974. Mem. Southwestern Social Sci. Assn., Am. Mktg. Assn., Midwest Bus. Adminstrn. Assn., Assn. Egyptian-Am. Scholars (treas.), Acad. Mktg. Sci., Am. Inst. Decision Scis., Phi Beta Lambda, Beta Gamma Sigma, Phi Kappa Phi, Alpha Mu Alpha. Republican. Christian Orthodox. Avocation: overseas travel. Home: 580 Normal Rd Dekalb IL 60115 Office: No Ill U Dept Mktg De Kalb IL 60115

HANNA, NOREEN ANELDA, retired adult education administrator, consultant; b. Napa, Calif., Nov. 28, 1939; d. Thomas James and Eileen Anelda (Jordan) H.; m. Leon O'bine Gotcher, Aug. 14, 1971 (div. Nov. 1980); children: John Allen, Tamara Kay. BA, San Francisco State U., 1963; postgrad., Sonoma State U., 1974-81, Ctr. for Leadership Devel., 1982-83; MA, U. San Francisco, 1989. Cert. gen. elem., specialist in reading, gen. adminstrv. svcs. Classroom tchr. Ullom Elem. Sch., Las Vegas, Nev., 1963; classroom tchr. J. L. Shearer Elem. Sch., Napa, 1963-78, reading resource tchr., 1978-80; asst. prin. Napa Valley Adult Sch., Napa, 1980-81, acting prin., 1981-82; prin. El Centro Elem. Sch., Napa, 1982-83; adminstr. J.T.P.A./Gain Programs, Napa, 1983-90; prin. Napa Valley Adult Sch., Napa, 1983-99, retired, 1999; commn. mem. Calif. Post Secondary Edn., 1987-89; cons. Calif. Dept. Edn., Sacramento, 1988—, Staff Devel. Inst., Sacramento, 1999—; adv. bd. dir. Ctr. for Adult Edn., San Francisco (Calif.) State U., 1988-95; adv. bd. mem. Immigration Reform & Control Act, Sacramento, 1989-92; presenter and cons. in field. Exec. bd. dirs. Leadership Napa Valley, 1985-93; sec. Leadership Napa Valley Found., 1988—. State Edn. scholar Calif. PTA, 1976, Grad. Edn. scholar Delta Kappa Gamma, Napa, 1977; recipient Cmty. Leadership award Napa Valley Unified Sch. Dist., 1988, Assn. Calif. Adminstrs. Adult Edn. Adminstr. of yr. award, 1992, George C. Mann Discing. Svc. award Calif. Coun. for Adult Edn., 1994. Mem. ASCD, Am. Assn. for Adult and Continuing Edn., Assn. Calif. Sch. Adminstrs. (chair to state adult edn. com. 1988-89, 93—, state rep. assembly del. 1989-92, state adult edn. com. chairperson 1989-92, others), Calif. Coun. for Adult Edn. (North Coast chpt. bd. dirs. 1988-99), Napa C. of C. (bd. dirs. 1985-88, edn./bus. com. 1985-99, others), Correctional Educators Assn., Soroptimist Internat. of Napa, Napa Valley Historical Soc. (pres. 1999-01), Phi Delta Kappa, Delta Kappa Gamma. Republican. Roman Catholic. Avocations: needlepoint, reading, sailing, swimming, hot air ballooning.

HANNA, RONALD EVERETTE, art educator, consultant; b. Miami, Fla., Dec. 17, 1953; s. Frederick Bruce and Bettye (Mathis) H.; children: Tina Maria, Vanessa Annette. BS in Edn., Fla. A & M U., 1974. Cert. tchr. Therapist Perdue Extended Art Facility, Miami, 1989-90; instr. English for speaker of other langs. Lindsey Hopkins Adult Edn. Ctr., Miami, 1989-91; art educator Dade County Pub. Sch. System, Miami, 1975—; pvt. art tutor, Miami, 1979—; free lance art cons., Miami, 1985—; art show judge various contests, 1980-94. Cmty. coord. City of Hialeah (Fla.) Arts Bd., 1982-84; mentor 500 Male Role Models, Miami, 1993—. Named Region III Tchr. of Yr., 1993-94, Mainstream Tchr. of Yr.; recipient awards AAA Safety Coun., Dade County Youth Fair, The Links Inc., City of Miami Beach Fine Arts, Metro Dade County award, Fedn. Women's Club. Mem. NEA (Recognition award 1978), Nat. Alliance Black Sch. Educators, Dade County Art Edn. Assn., Am. Mensa (Recognition award 1982—), Elks (Recognition award 1975, 82, 93), Mason (Recognition award 1993), Order Eastern Star, Alpha Omega (Recognition award 1993). Democrat. Episcopalian. Avocations: computer networking, reading, health, art. Home: 3676 SW 27th St Miami FL 33133-2712 Office: Van E Blanton Elem Sch 10327 NW 11th Ave Miami FL 33150-1094

HANNA, SUZANNE LOUISE, nurse; b. Mankato, Minn., Aug. 31, 1953; d. Frank Edward and Phyllis Ruth (Moeller) Wilkins; m. Thomas Ray Hanna, Sept. 15, 1973; children: Elizabeth Amy, Joseph Ryan, Thomas Wilkins. Diploma in nursing with highest honors, Iowa Western C.C., Council Bluffs, 1991. RN, Iowa; cert. provider ACLS, Am. Heart Assn. Exec. sec. First Nat. Bank, Mpls., 1971-72, Nat. Bank of Am., Salina, Kans., 1972; receptionist The Evening Sentinel, Shenandoah, Iowa, 1972-73; ins. sec. Wilson Ins. Agy., Shenandoah, 1973-79; med./surg. staff nurse Shenandoah Meml. Hosp., 1980-81; office nurse Dr. Floyd A. Jones, Shenandoah, 1983-95; clin. nurse Great Plains Physician Group, Omaha, Nebr., 1995-98; emergency rm. nurse Shenandoah Meml. Hosp., 1992-95; clin. nurse Nebr. Health Sys., 1998—; bd. dirs. Ag-Pro Corp., Shenandoah; co-chairperson family life com., 1989-90. Alt. Rep. Page County Convs., 1988, 92; active ladies guild St. Mary Ch., Shenandoah, 1986—, mem. parish coun. bd., pres. parish coun., 1989-92, instr. religious edn., 1988-90, mem. choir, 1991—, organist, song leader, 1992—, liturgy planning com., 1996—; bd. dirs. Shenandoah Music Assn., 1996—; mem. local Am. Legion Aux., 1994—; Park Bd. Commr., 1998—. Mem. Beta Sigma Phi (pres. 1979-80). Roman Catholic. Avocations: volleyball, aerobics, swimming. Home: 1302 Johnson Dr Shenandoah IA 51601-2606 Office: 1 Jack Foster Ave Shenandoah IA 51601-2606

HANNA, TERRY ROSS, lawyer, small business owner; b. Wadsworth, Ohio, May 17, 1947; s. Harry Ross and Geraldine (Frensley) H.; m. Max Anna Hindes, Jan. 20, 1968; children: Travis, Taylor, Molly. BBA, U. Okla., 1968, JD, 1972; LLM, NYU, 1973; MA in Bibl Studies, Dallas Theol. Sem., 1988. Bar: Okla. 1972, U.S. Tax Ct. 1974, U.S. Ct. Appeals (10th cir.) 1979, U.S. Supreme Ct. 1989; CPA, Okla. Mem. McAfee & Taft, Oklahoma City, 1972-80; pres. P 356 Inc., Oklahoma City, 1980—; of counsel Crowe & Dunlevy, Oklahoma City, 1987—; pres. H.J. Freede, Inc., Oklahoma City, 1998—; owner Mo Jo Video, 1995—; spl. lectr. Oklahoma City U. Sch. Law, 1974-75. Editor Okla. U. Law Rev., 1970-72. Mem. internat. com. Boy Scouts Am., 1988—; dir. U.S. Found. for Internat. Scouting, Irving, 1989—. Baden-Powell fellow World Scout Found., 1988—; recipient Silver Beaver award Boy Scouts Am., 1988. Mem. Okla. Bar Assn. (pres. taxation sect. 1978-79), Sports Lawyers Assn., Order of Arrow (lodge advisor 1989—), Kappa Sigma (chpt. advisor 1974-75), Phi Delta Phi (magister 1972). Republican. Mem. Christian Ch. Avocations: coach, patch collector, fishing, softball, computers. Home: 2600 W Coffee Creek Rd Edmond OK 73003-3326 Office: Crowe & Dunlevy 1800 Mid America Towers Oklahoma City OK 73102

HANNA, VAIL DEADWYLER, critical care nurse; b. Atlanta, Jan. 28, 1942; d. George B. and Dorothy (Heffernan) Deadwyler; children: Frank, Lisa, David. ADN, Kennesaw (Ga.) Jr. Coll., 1976; BSN, Ga. State U., Atlanta, 1983; MA, Ga. Sch. Profl. Psychology, 1996. RN, Ga.; lic. assoc. profl. counselor, Ga. Staff nurse ICU, recovery room Cobb Gen. Hosp., Austell, Ga., 1976-84; staff nurse ICU, recovery room St. Joseph's Hosp., Atlanta, 1984-87, clin. mgr. coronary care unit, 1987-89; post anesthesia care unit staff nurse St. Joseph's Hosp., 1991-92; staff nurse adolescent unit CPC Parkwood Behavioral Health Care, 1994-95; staff nurse Charter Peachford Hosp., 1995-98; psychometrist, 1995-97; psychotherapist Three Rivers Behavioral Health Svcs., 1997-98; nurse and counselor Day One Life Mgmt., 1998—. Chmn. quality assurance coun. St. Joseph's Hosp., 1988-89, chmn. nursing staff, 1988-89. Cert. of Commendation, Kennesaw Jr. Coll., 1976, Evangeline Lane Founder's award, 1983. Mem. ANA, AACN, APA, ACA, Lic. Profl. Counselors Assn., Ga. Nurses Assn., Am. Heart Assn., Golden Key, Northside Women's Club, Phi Kappa Phi, Mu Rho Sigma. Home: 4621 Sharon Valley Ct Dunwoody GA 30338-5953

HANNA, WILLIAM BROOKS, book publisher; b. Montreal, Feb. 22, 1936; s. George Spencer and Phyllis Edith (Brooks) H.; children: Catherine Frances, Philip Spencer; m. Frances Ann Gerhardt, Nov. 20, 1982. Grad., Upper Can. Coll., 1954; B.A. in Modern History, U. Toronto, 1958. Successively coll. sales mgr., sch. sales mgr., editor-in-chief Collier-Macmillan-Can., Ltd., 19S8-65; pres. Pergamon of Can., Ltd.; also dep. chmn. bd. Pergamon of Can., Ltd., Toronto, 1967-68; exec. v.p., dir. Pergamon Press, Inc., 1966-68; v.p., dir. Burns & MacEachern, Ltd., Toronto, 1968-70; pres., dir. GLC Pubs., Toronto, 1970-75; pres., chief exec. officer, dir. Holt Rinehart & Winston of Can., Ltd., Toronto, 1975-78; pub. joint UNICEF/Red Cross Com. for 1979 Internat. Yr. of Child, 1978-79; v.p. Gen. Pub. Co. Ltd., Toronto, 1979-94, Stoddart Pub. Co. Ltd., Toronto, 1984—. Chmn. convocation Trinity Coll., U. Toronto, 1994-96, trustee 1996—; chmn. export coun. Can. Book Publ. Coun., 1993-95. Mem. Overseas Press Club Am., Assn. Can. Pubs. (rep. to 25th Congress of Internat. Assn. Can. Pubs. (dir. CANCOPY 1997-98), chmn. copyright com., Arbor award U. Toronto 1998), Faculty Club U. Toronto. Home: 51 Acacia Rd, Toronto, ON Canada M4S 2K6 Office: 30 Lesmill Rd, North York, ON Canada M3B 2T6

HANNA, WILLIAM DENBY, motion picture and television producer, cartoonist; b. Melrose, N.M., July 14, 1910; s. William John and Avice Joyce (Denby) H.; m. Violet B. Wogatzke, Aug. 7, 1936; children: David William, Bonnie Jean. Animator, scriptwriter, lyricist, composer Harman-Ising Animation Studios, Hollywood, 1933-37; animation dir., prodr., story editor MGM, Hollywood, 1937-57, head animation dept., 1955-57; co-founder (with Joseph Barbera) Hanna-Barbera Prodns., Hollywood, 1957—. Dir. with Barbera of short animated films including Puss Gets the Boot, 1940 (Academy award nomination best animated short subject 1940), The Nightmare Before Christmas, 1940 (Academy award best animated short subject 1941), Yankee Doodle Mouse, 1943 (Academy award best animated short subject 1943), Mouse Trouble, 1944 (Academy award best animated short subject 1944), Quiet, Please!, 1945 (Academy award best animated short subject 1945), The Cat Concerto, 1946 (Academy award best animated short subject 1946), Dr. Jekyll and Mr. Mouse, 1947 (Academy award nomination best animated short subject 1947), The Little Orphan, 1948 (Academy award best animated short subject 1948), Hatch Up Your Troubles, 1949 (Academy award nomination best animated short subject 1949), Jerry's Cousin, 1950 (Academy award nomination best animated short subject 1950), The Two Mouseketeers, 1951 (Academy award best animated short subject 1951), Johann Mouse, 1952 (Academy award best animated short subject 1952), Touche, Pussy Cat, 1954 (Academy award nomination best animated short subject 1954), Good Will to Men, 1955 (Academy award nomination best animated short subject 1954), One Droopy Knight, 1957 (Academy award nomination best animated short subject 1957; animated programming series with Barbera include The Ruff & Reddy Show, 1957-60, The Huckleberry Hound Show, 1958-62 (Emmy award 1960), Yogi Bear, 1958-62, The Quick Draw McGraw Show, 1959-62, The Flintstones, 1960-66 (Golden Globe award 1965), Top Cat, 1961-62, Lippt the Lion, 1962, Touche Turtle, 1962, Wally Gator, 1962, The Jetsons, 1962-67, 69-76, 79-81, 82-83, 85, The Adeventures of Jonny Quest, 1964-65, 67-72, 79, 80-81, The Magilla Gorilla Show, 1964-67, The Peter Potamus Show, 1964-67, Tom and Jerry, 1965-72, 75-78, 80-82, The Atom Ant/Secret Squirrel Show, 1965-68, Sinbad, Jr., the Sailor, 1966, The Abbott and Costello Cartoon Show, 1966, Laurel and Hardy, 1966-67, Space Kiddettes, 1966-67, Space Ghost, 1966-68, Frankenstein, Jr. and the Impossibles, 1966-68, Sampson and Goliath, 1967-68, Birdman and the Galaxy Trio, 1967-68, The Herculoids, 1967-69, Moby Dick and the Mighty Mightor, 1967-69, Shazzan!, 1967-69, The Fantastic Four, 1967-70, The Wacky Races, 1968-70, The Adventures of Gulliver, 1969-70, The Perils of Penelope Pitstop, 1969-71, The Cattanooga Cats, 1969-71, Dastardly and Mutley in Their Flying Machines, 1969-71, Scooby-Doo, Where Are You?, 1969-74, Where's Huddles?, 1970-71, The Harlem Globetrotters, 1970-73, Josie and the Pussycats, 1970-76, Pebbles and Bamm Bamm, 1971-72, Help! It's the Hair Bear Bunch, 1971-72, The Funky Phantom, 1971-72, Wait Til Your Father Gets Home, 1972, Sealab 2020, 1972-73, The Roman Holidays, 1972-73, The Amazing Chan and the Chan Clan, 1972-74, The Flintstones Comedy Hour, 1972-74, Josie and the Pussycats in Outer Space, 1972-74, Speed Buggy, 1971-74, Butch Cassidy and the Sundance Kids, 1973-74, Peter Puck, 1973-74, Inch High, Private Eye, 1973-74, Yogi's Gang, 1973-75, Jeannie, 1973-75, Goober and the Ghost Chasers, 1973-75, The Addams Family, 1973-75, Super Friends, 1973-83, Wheelie and the Chopper Bunch, 1974-75, The Partridge Family: 2200 A.D., 1974-75, Hong Kong Phooey, 1974-76, These Are the Days, 1974-76, Devlin, 1974-76, Valley of the Dinosaurs, 1974-76, The Scooby-Doo/Dynomutt Hour, 1976-77, Mumbly, 1976-77, Jabberjaw, 1976-78, The Skatebirds, 1977-78, The Tom and Jerry/Great Grape Ape Show, 1977-78, Scooby's All-Star Laff-a-Lympics, 1977-78, Fred Flintstone and Friends, 1977-78, Captain Caveman and the Teen Angels, 1980, The Scooby-Doo and Scrappy-Doo

Show, 1980-82, The Drak Pack, 1980-82, Fonz and the Happy Days Gang, 1980-82, The Richie Rich Show, 1980-82, The Kwicky Koala Show, 1981-82, Trollkins, 1981-82, Laverne and Shirley in the Army, 1981-82, The Smurfs, 1981-90 (Emmy award 1982, 83, Bronze award Internat. Film & TV Festival N.Y. 1987, Humanitas award for best animated program 1987), Laverne and Shirley with the Fonz, 1982-83, Scooby, Scrappy, and Yabba Doo, 1982-83, The Smurf's Springtime Spl., 1982 (Bronze award Internat. Film & TV Festival of N.Y. 1982, Golden Reel award 1982), The Smurf's Games, 1984 (Bronze award N.Y. Internat. Film Festival 1984), Snorks, 1984-86, The Greatest Adventure: Stories from the Bible, Episodes 1-6, 1985 (Gold Angel award for excellence in media 1986, 88, Disting. Svc. award Nat. Religious Broadcasters 1987, Excellence award Film Adv. Bd. 1987, 88, Golden Eagle award Nat. Religious Broadcasters 1988), The Funtastic World Hanna-Barbera, 1986-87, 87-88, Pound Puppies, 1986-87, The Flintstones Kids, 1986-87 (Best Animation Series Youth in Film award 1987, Pioneer award Broadcast Music Inc 1987, Humanitas award for best animated program 1988), The Flintstones Kids-Just Say No Spl., 1989 (Commendation plaque Pasadena Jr. C. of C. 1989), The Little Troll Prince, 1986 (Silver Angel award for excellence in media 1988, Golden Halo award for outstanding prodn. and unique values 1988, Bronze Halo award for quality of writing So. Calif. Motion Picture Coun. 1988), Wildfire, 1986-87, Foofur, 1986-87, Popeye and Son, 1987-88, Galtar and the Golden Lance, 1987 (Golden Reel award for sound editing 1988), The Jetsons Oldies, 1987-88 (Best Animation Series award Youth in Film 1987), The Completely Mental Misadventures of Ed Grimley, 1988-89 (Outstanding Creativity Mobius awards 1988), The Dreamer of Oz, 1990 (Christopher award 1991, Cine Golden Eagle award 1991, Merit cert. Chgo. Internat. Film Festival, 1991), The Last Halloween, 1991 (Emmy award 1992); animated spls. include Alice in Wonderland, 1966, Jack and the Beanstalk, 1967 (Emmy award 1967), The Last of the Curlews, 1972 (Emmy award 1973), My Smurfy Valentine, 1982, Smurfily-Ever-After, 1985, The Flintstones' 25th Anniversary Celebration, 1986, The Jetsons Meet the Flintstones, 1987, Hanna-Barbera's 50th: A Yabba Dabba Doo Celebration, 1989, I Yabba Dabba Doo!, 1993 (Bronze award Worldfest Houston Internat. Film & Video awards 1993), The Adams Family, 1992, (Bronze award Worldfest Houston Internat. Film & Video 1993, Silver award Children's Entertainment Internat. Acad. Comm. Arts & Scis. 1993, Emmy award for graphics and title design 1994), The Pirates of Dark Water, 1992 (Bronze award Internat. Acad. Comm. Arts & Scis. 1993), The New Adventures of Captain Planet, 1993 (Environ. Media award Environ. Media Assn. 1994, Bronze plaque Columbus Internat. Film & Video Festival 1994), The Halloween Tree, 1993 (Emmy award for writing in an animated program 1994), Hard Luck Duck, 1992, Dexter's Laboratory, 1995 (ASIFA Annie award 1995), Daisy-Head Mayzie, 1995 (Cable Ace award 1995, Silver medal N.Y. Festival 1995; live action spls. include The Runaways, 1974 (Emmy award 1974); live action TV movies include Hardcase, 1972, Shootout in a One-Dog Town, 1974, The Gathering, 1977 (Christopher award 1978, Emmy award 1978), The Gathering Part II, 1979, Stone Fox, 1987; animated feature include films Hey There, It's Yogi Bear, 1964, A Man Called Flintstone, 1966, Charlotte's Web, 1973 (Annie award 1977), Heidi's Song, 1982, Once Upon a Forest, 1993; live action feature films C.H.O.M.P.S., 1979, The Flintstones, 1994; autobiography A Cast of Friends, 1996. Recipient Gov.'s award Acad. TV Arts and Scis., 1988; named to Acad. TV Arts and Scis. Hall of Fame, 1994. Office: Hanna-Barbera Inc 15303 Ventura Blvd Ste 1409 Sherman Oaks CA 91403-5810*

HANNA, WILLIAM JOHNSON, electrical engineering educator; b. Longmont, Colo., Feb. 7, 1922; s. William Grant and Anna Christina (Johnson) H.; m. Katherine Fagan, Apr. 25, 1944 (dec. 1993); children: Daniel August, Paul William; m. Helen Yeager McCarty, Sept. 19, 1996. BSEE, U. Colo., 1943, MS, 1948, D in Elec. Engring., 1951. Registered profl. engr., Colo., Kans. Mem. faculty U. Colo., 1946-91, prof. elec. engring., 1962-91, prof. emeritus, 1991—; cons. in field; mem. Colo. Bd. Engring. Examiners, 1973-85; with Ponderosa Assocs., Lafayette, Colo. Author articles, reports. Served to 1st lt. AUS, 1943-46. Recipient Faculty Recognition award Students Assn. U. Colo., 1956, 61, Alfred J. Ryan award, 1978, Archimedes award Calif. Soc. Profl. Engrs., 1978, Outstanding Engring. Alumnus award U. Colo., 1983, Faculty Service award, 1983; named Colo. Engr. of Yr. Profl. Engrs. Colo., 1968; named to Hon. Order of Ky. Cols. Mem. IEEE, Am. Soc. Engring. Edn., Nat. Soc. Profl. Engrs. (pres. Colo. 1967-68), Nat. Coun. Engring. Examiners (pres. 1977-78, Disting. Svc. award with spl. commendation 1990), AIEE (chmn. Denver 1961-62). Republican. Presbyterian. Club: Masons. Home and Office: 27 Silver Spruce Nederland Star Rt Boulder CO 80302-9604 *Honors and awards I have received are but a reflection of the character of my friends and associates. To them and my family go the accolades.*

HANNAFORD, PETER DOR, public relations executive, writer; b. Glendale, Calif., Sept. 21, 1932; s. Donald R. and Elinor (Nielsen) H.; m. Irene Dorothy Harville, Aug. 14, 1954; children: Richard Harville, Donald R. II. AB, U. Calif., 1954. Acct. exec. Helen A. Kennedy Advt., 1956; v.p. Kennedy-Hannaford, Inc., San Francisco and Oakland, Calif., 1957-62; pres. Kennedy-Hannaford, Inc., 1962-67, Pettler & Hannaford, Inc., Oakland, 1967-69; v.p. Wilton, Coombs & Colnett, Inc., 1969-72; pres. Hannaford & Assocs., Oakland, 1973; asst. to Gov. of Calif.; dir. pub. affairs Govs.' Office, 1974; chmn. bd. Hannaford Co., Inc. (formerly Deaver & Hannaford, Inc.), 1975-95; mng. dir. The Franklin Firm, Washington, 1996-98; pub. Ferndale (Calif.) Enterprise, 1996-98; pres. Hannaford Enterprises Inc., 1998—; nat. pres. Mut. Advt. Agy. Network, 1968-69; vice chmn. Calif. Gov.'s Consumer Fraud Task Force, 1972-73; bd. dirs. Gridcore Sys. Internat. Corp., Eberle Comms. Group Inc. Author: The Reagans: A Political Portrait, 1983, Talking Back to the Media, 1986 (Japanese edit. 1990); co-author: Remembering Reagan, 1994, Recollections of Reagan, 1997, My Heart Goes Home: A Hudson Valley Memoir, 1997, The Quotable Ronald Reagan, 1998. Mem. Alameda County Rep. Ctrl. Com., Rep. State Cttl. Com. Calif., 1968-74, The Commonwealth Fund's Commn. on Elderly People Living Alone, 1986-91; Rep. nominee for U.S. Congress, 1972; governing bd. Tahoe Regional Planning Agy., 1973-74; trustee White House Preservation Fund, 1981-89, pub. rels. adv. com. USIA, 1981-92; bd. dirs. Am. Spectator Ednl. Found., 1984—, Washington Internat. Horse Show, 1986-91; mem. adv. com. Mt. Vernon, 1991-96; mem. bd. of session Georgetown Presbyn. Ch., Washington, 1999—. 1st lt. Signal Corps, U.S. Army, 1954-56. Mem. Univ. Club (N.Y.C.), Cosmos Club, Potomac Polo Club, Theta Xi. Presbyterian. Office: Hannaford Enterprises Inc Ste 800 W 1299 Pennsylvania Ave NW Washington DC 20004-2424

HANNAH, BARBARA ANN, nurse, educator; b. Pawnee, Okla., Sept. 25, 1943; d. Harold Ray and Betty Jean (Newport) Norris; m. Charles Bush Hannah, Mar. 25, 1971; children: Charles Douglas, Harry William. AS, Rogers State Coll., Claremore, Okla., 1974; BS in nursing, Tulsa U., 1976; MS, Okla U., 1985; EdD, Okla. State U., 1998. RN, Okla.; cert. BLS, ACLS, PALS. Nurse St. Francis Hosp., Tulsa, 1968-77, edn. specialist, 1986-90, clin. mgr. post-anesthesia care unit, 1991-96, critical care edn. coord., 1996—; dir. clin. prodn. CSI Prodns. for Medcom Inc., Tulsa, 1977-86; asst. adminstr. nursing Cleveland (Okla.) Area Hosp., 1990-91; cons. St. Anthony Hosp., Oklahoma City, 1985; mem. affiliate faculty, chmn. emergency cardiac care com. Am. Heart Assn., 1986, mem. nat. faculty, 1990—, chmn. bd. Okla. affiliate, 1996-98; bd. dirs. Citizen CPR, 1986-91, chmn. comprehensive monitoring com., 1990-91. Producer audio-visual programs for nursing edn., 1977-86. Mem. Food & Refreshment Com. Channel 8 fund raising drive, Tulsa, 1985, 86. Recipient spl. awards and honors All Heart Vol., 1988, Lifetime Achievement award Am. Heart Assn.; named Woman of Yr., 1998. Mem. NAFE, Acute Care Nurses Assn. (seminar dir., treas. Greater Tulsa area chpt.), Okla. Nurses Assn. (dist. 2 com. on profl. practice), Am. Heart Assn. (v.p. program com. 1990—, chmn. faculty BLS task force Woman of Yr., Okla. affiliate 1993, 97, chmn. Okla. affiliate 1994, 95-96, Lifetime Achievement award 1998), Am. Soc. Post Anesthesia Nurses (1st pl. poster award Nat. Ann. Conf. 1993, alt. del. from Okla. 1994), Okla. Soc. Post Anesthesia Nurses (pres. Tulsa chpt. 1993), Am. Soc. Peri Anesthesia Nurses (Okla. del. to bd. 1996—), Sigma Theta Tau. Avocations: biking, hiking, quilting, travel. Home: PO Box 112 Skiatook OK 74070-0112 Office: St Francis Hosp 6161 S Yale Ave Tulsa OK 74136-1992

HANNAH, GREGG S., business educator. AB, Dartmouth Coll., 1965; MBA, Northwestern U., 1972. V.p., mgr., employee benefits investment divsn. Norwest Bank, Mpls., 1981-85; pres., dir. Marquette Capital Mgmt. Corp., Mpls., 1985-87; sec., treas. Hannah & Assocs., Inc., Pomfret, Conn., 1987—; assoc. prof. bus. mgmt. Nichols Coll., Dudley, Mass., 1988—; trustee, chmn. fin. adminstrn. and devel. com. Conn. State U. Sys., Hartford, 1992—.

HANNAH, JOHN HENRY, JR., judge; b. 1939; 1 child, John III. BS, Sam Houston State U., 1966; postgrad., South Tex. Sch. Law, 1970. Mem. Tex. Ho. of Reps., 1967-73; pvt. practice Lufkin, Tex., 1971-73; dist. atty. Angelina County, Tex., 1973-77; atty. Hannah & Welch, Lufkin, 1977-81; U.S. atty. Ea. Dist. Tex., 1977-81; prin. John Hannah Law Office, 1981-91; sec. of state State of Tex., Austin, 1991-94; dist. judge U.S. Dist. Ct. (ea. dist.), Tyler, 1994—; legal counsel Common Cause, Austin, 1975. Served USN, 1961. Grad. Tchg. fellow Sam Houston U., 1965-66. Mem. Am. Bd. Trial Advocates, State Bar Tex., Tex. Dist. and County Attys. Assn., Tex. Trial Lawyers Assn., Tex. Criminal Def. Lawyers Assn., Phi Gamma Mu. Office: US Dist Ct Ea Dist Tex 104 N Third St Lufkin TX 75901*

HANNAH, JOHN ROBERT, SR., accountant; b. Monroe, La., Aug. 11, 1939; s. Robert Ruskin Hannah and Berta (Gilliland) Nelson; m. Elizabeth Girdner, Dec. 26, 1965; children: Allison, John Robert Jr. BS, La. State U., 1960. CPA, Tex. Acct. Arthur Young & Co., Houston, 1960-70, Peters & Smith, Midland, Tex., 1970-71; ptnr. Hannah & Trott, Midland, 1971-72; contr. Western States Producing Co., San Antonio, 1972-73; v.p. fin. Sommers Drug Stores Co., San Antonio, 1973-77; pvt. practice acctg. San Antonio, 1987—; ptnr. Peters, Anders & Hannah, San Antonio, 1978-86; seminar speaker Bexar County Med. Soc., San Antonio, 1981. Fin. chmn. YMCA, San Antonio, 1975-82, chmn., 1982-83; adminstr. Bible Study Fellowship, San Antonio, 1977-83; bd. dirs. Morningside Ministries, 1991, Christian Ministry Assistance, 1992, treas.; chmn. bd. trustees Alamo Heights United Meth. Ch., 1998. Lt. USN, 1961-65. Mem. Am. Inst. CPA's, Tex. Soc. CPa's, Fin. Execs. Internat., Execs. Internat. Club (San Antonio, pres. 1975-76). Methodist. Home: 102 Castleoaks Dr San Antonio TX 78213-2303 Office: 800 Navarro St Ste 210 San Antonio TX 78205-1725

HANNAH, WAYNE ROBERTSON, JR., lawyer; b. Freeport, Ill., Aug. 18, 1931; s. Wayne Robertson and Edith (Biene) H.; m. Patricia Anne Matthews, June 1, 1957; children—Tamara Lee, Wendy, Wayne Robertson III. B.A., Ill. Coll., 1953; J.D., NYU, 1957. Bar: Ill. 1957, U.S. Dist. Ct. (no. dist.) Ill., U.S. Supreme Ct. Ptnr. Sonnenschein, Nath & Rosenthal, Chgo., 1965—; dir. Checker Motors Corp., N.Y.C. and Kalamazoo, 1982-86; lectr. Ill. Inst. Continuing Edn. Sec. 7th cir. Root-Tilden Scholarship Program NYU, 1967-94; chmn. Root-Tilden-Kern scholarship com., 1981-86, trustee law ctr., 1985—; pres. bd. Firman Cmty. Svcs, Chgo., 1972-75; trustee, pres., chmn. bd. Chgo. City Ballet, 1982-86. 2d lt. USMC, 1951-54. Root-Tilden scholar NYU, 1954-57; Fulbright scholar, 1953-54. Mem. ABA (real estate com.), Chgo. Bar Assn. (chmn. condominium subcom. real estate com. 1977-78, sec., dir. condominium assn. 1991—), Ill. Bar Assn. (real estate com.), Econ. Club (Chgo.), Skokie Country Club (Glencoe, Ill.). Presbyterian. Avocations: tennis; golf. Office: Sonnenschein Nath and Rosenthal 233 S Wacker Dr Ste 8000 Chicago IL 60606-6342

HANNAHS, DOROTHY GENE, library director; m. James R. Hannahs, June 25, 1966; children: Timothy, Todd, Amy. BS in Edn., Miami U., 1966. Substitute tchr. Licking County Pub. Schs., Ohio, 1986-94; dir. Alexandria (Ohio) Pub. Libr., 1994—. Treas. Concord Willing Workers Club, Johnstown, 1989—. Mem. Ohio Libr. Coun. Office: Alexandria Pub Libr PO Box 67 10 Maple Dr Alexandria OH 43001-0067

HANNAN, BRADLEY, educational publishing consultant and executive; b. Rochester, N.Y., Apr. 24, 1935; d. Jack Seymour MacArthur and Alice E. (Knapp) Staley; m. William J. Hannan, Jr., June 15, 1957 (div. 1977); children: Megan, Timothy, Patrick, Moira. BA, Ariz. State U., 1957. Tchr. various sch. dists. Ariz., 1957-62; English language cons. Evanston (Ill.) Twp. High Sch., 1963-65; editor, then sr. editor Harper & Row Pubs., Evanston, 1965-75; sr. reading text editor Scott, Foresman & Co., Glenview, Ill., 1975-78, sr. editor lang. arts, 1982-87; dir. reading McDougal Littell & Co., Evanston, 1978-81; project dir. spelling Ednl. Challenges, Alexandria, Va., 1981-82; dir. curriculum and product mgmt. for reading and lang. arts texts Open Court Pub. Co., Chgo. and Peru, Ill., 1987-88; cons., project dir. lang. arts texts Harcourt Brace, Orlando, Fla., 1988-89; sr. mng. editor reading, lang. arts, social studies Sci. Rsch. Assocs., Chgo., 1989; cons. ednl. pub. Chgo., 1989-90; dir. reading, lang. arts, social studies Proof Positive/Farrowlyne Assocs., Chgo., 1990-98; editor ALA, Chgo., 1998; editl. cons., 1998—; speaker Internat. Reading Assn., New Orleans, 1981, Chgo. Women in Publishing, 1981, Childrens' Reading Roundtable, Chgo., 1985; developer reading textbook series. Mem. Internat. Reading Assn., Chgo. Book Clinic, Chgo. Women in Pub. Avocations: language acquisition and development, reading competence, book production, phonics. Home: 800 Judson Ave Apt 301 Evanston IL 60202-2451

HANNAN, PHILIP MATTHEW, bishop; b. Washington, D.C., May 20, 1913; s. Patrick Francis and Lillian Louise (Keefe) H. Student, St. Charles Coll., 1931-33; A.B., Cath. U., 1935, M.A., 1936, J.C.D., 1949; student, N.Am. Coll., 1936-40; S.T.B., S.T.L., Gregorian U., Rome, 1940. Ordained priest Roman Catholic Ch., 1939; clerical appt. St. Thomas Aquinas Ch., Balt., 1940-42; vice chancellor Cath. Diocese Washington, 1948-51, chancellor, 1951-62, vicar gen., 1960-65; adminstr. St. Patrick's Ch., Washington, 1951-56; pastor St. Patrick's Ch., 1956-65; aux. bishop Archdiocese Washington; also editor-in-chief Catholic Standard of D.C., 1956-65; archbishop New Orleans, 1965-89; organizer housing program for elderly Christopher Homes, Inc.; Chmn. ad hoc com. Nat. Conf. Cath. Bishops Office Priestly Life and Ministry, 1971-74; chmn. bd. trustees Cath. U. Am., Washington, 1973-76, 78-82; nat. chaplain Cath. Daus. Am., 1974-78; mem. communications com. U.S. Cath. Conf. Bishops, 1979-82; pres. Claravision, 1999—. Mem. goals com. Met. Area Com. New Orleans; mem. White House Conf. on Children and Youth, 1970; mem. exec. bd. New Orleans council Boy Scouts Am., 1970-78; mem. bd., past chmn. interfaith com. United Fund New Orleans. Served as chaplain USAAF, 1942-46. Recipient George Washington medal Freedoms Found., Headliner of Yr. award Press Club New Orleans, Loving Cup for Community Service Times-Picayune newspaper; Hannan Hall Cath. U. Am. named in his honor, 1987. Home: 1451 Moss St New Orleans LA 70119*

HANNAWALT, WILLIS DALE, retired lawyer; b. Delaware, Ohio, Apr. 28, 1928; s. Othello Erwin and Dorothy (Sherbourne) H.; m. Vivian Nina Chaya, Sept. 8, 1950; children: Nina Jo, James Frederick, Rachel Beth. A.B., U. Chgo., 1950, J.D., 1954. Bar: Calif. 1955, U.S. Dist. Ct. (no. dist.) Calif. 1955, (ea. dist) Calif. 1980, U.S. Ct. Appeals (9th ctrl) 1955, U.S. Supreme Ct. 1970. Teaching fellow Stanford U., Palo Alto, Calif., 1954-55; assoc. Pillsbury, Madison & Sutro, San Francisco, 1955-65, ptnr., 1965-98; ret., 1998; mem. faculty Golden Gate Law Sch., San Francisco, 1958-68; cons. Hudson Inst., Tarrytown, N.Y., 1964. Chmn. State Bar Jour. Com., 1964. Served with USCG, 1946-47, 51-53. Mem. FBA, NRA (life), Calif. State Bar, Bar Assn. San Francisco, San Francisco Lawyer's Club, Am. Legion, Calif. Rifle and Pistol Assn. (life), World Trade Club. Office: Pillsbury Madison & Sutro 235 Montgomery St # 540 San Francisco CA 94104-2902

HANNAY, WILLIAM MOUAT, III, lawyer; b. Kansas City, Mo., Dec. 3, 1944; s. William Mouat and Gladys (Capron) H.; m. Donna Jean Harkins, Sept. 30, 1978; children: Capron Grace, Blaike Ann, William Mouat IV. BA, Yale U., 1966; JD, Georgetown U., 1973. Bar: Mo. 1973, D.C. 1974, N.Y. 1975, Ill. 1980. Law clk. to Judge Myron Bright, U.S. Ct. Appeals, 8th Circuit, St. Louis 1973-74, to Justice Tom Clark, U.S. Supreme Ct., Washington, 1974-75; assoc. Weil Gotshal & Manges, N.Y.C., 1975-77; asst. dist. atty. New York County Dist. Atty.'s Office, N.Y.C., 1977-79; ptnr. Schiff Hardin & Waite, Chgo., 1979—; adj. prof. IIT/Chgo.-Kent Law Sch., 1983—. Author: International Trade: Avoiding Criminal Risks, 1991, Designing an Effective Antitrust Compliance Program, 1996, Tying Arrangements, 1997; contbr. articles to profl. jours. Chmn. bd. dirs. Gilbert and Sullivan Soc. of Chgo., 1984-87. Served with U.S. Army, 1967-68, Vietnam. Mem. ABA (chair sect. internat. law & practice 1998-99), Chgo. Bar Assn. (chmn. antitrust com. 1986-87). Democrat. Episcopalian. Clubs: Yale (pres. 1987-89), Chgo. Yacht, Union League (Chgo.). Home: 591 Plum Tree Rd Barrington Hills IL 60010-2329 Office: Schiff Hardin & Waite 7200 Sears Tower Chicago IL 60606

HANNEKEN, DAVID WILLIAM, advertising executive; b. Milw., Feb. 2, 1962; s. Clemens B. and Mary E. (Miller) H.; m. Mary Alice Kreiter, July 27, 1985; children: Sarah, Kevin, Kyle. BA in Mktg., BA in Journalism, Marquette U., 1986. Copywriter Curro/Eichenbaum Advt., Milw., 1986-89; sr. copywriter Ogilvy & Mather, Hawaii, Honolulu, 1989-91, Cramer-Krasselt, Milw., 1991-93; v.p., creative dir. Hoffman York & Compton, Milw., 1993-97; creative dir., ptnr. Kohnke Hanneken, Milw., 1997—. *

HANNEMAN, ELAINE ESTHER, salesperson; b. Waupaca, Wis., Aug. 28, 1928; d. Martin Fred Strey and Laura Rucks; m. Alfred Adam Hanneman, Feb. 14, 1948; children: Karen, Dale, Sally, Sandra. High sch. grad., 1946. Acct. AAL Life Ins. Co., Appleton, Wis., 1946-48; salesperson Cinderella Cosmetics, 1948-60; sales Artex Paint, Milw., 1960-74, Car Ins. and Memberships (AAA), Appleton, Wis., 1974-78, Am. Family Life, Columbus, Ga., 1979—. Mem. Gold Century Club, Pres. Club, Am. Family Life. Lutheran. Avocations: travel, reading, swimming, crafts. Home: PO Box 244 Weyauwega WI 54983-0244 also: 1842 Edgewater Dr Amherst WI 54407 also: 8742 Edge Water Dr Amherst Junction WI 54407

HANNEMAN, RODNEY ELTON, metallurgical engineer; b. Spokane, Wash., Mar. 14, 1936; s. Christie Luther and Viva Helen (Sugrue) H.; married; 3 children. BS in Phys. Metallurgy, Wash. State U., 1959; MS in Metallurgy, MIT, 1961, PhD, 1964; grad., GE Mgmt. Devel. Inst., 1979. With GE Co., Schenectady, 1963-81; mgr. materials characterization lab. GE Co., 1977-80, mgr. materials programs, 1980-81; v.p. research, devel. and energy resources Reynolds Metals Co., Richmond, Va., 1981-85; v.p. quality assurance and tech. op. Reynolds Metals Co., 1985-98; pres. Mgmt. and Tech. Consultants, Richmond, Va., 1998—; dir. Face Internat. Corp., 1998—; mem. vis. com. dept. materials sci. and engring. MIT, 1975-80, mem. adv. bd. Materials Processing Ctr., 1980-97; mem. adv. bd. U. Va., 1982-87, chmn. indsl. adv. bd. grad. engring. program, 1983-86; chmn. rsch. coordinating coun. Gas Rsch. Inst., 1985-87, adv. coun., 1988—; bd. dirs. Materials Properties Coun., 1982-90; mem. ind. adv. bd. ASME, 1987-97; mem. adv. com. Va. Ctr. for Innovative Tech., 1999—. Mem. found. bd. Sci. Mus. Va., 1989—; v.p. Civic Assn., 1990-92. Recipient Alumni Achievement award Wash. State U., 1978; Joint Engring. Council award, 1984. Mem. AIME, MAPI, SAE, Am. Soc. Metals (Geisler award 1971, Engring. Materials Achievement award 1973), Am. Chem. Soc. (Chem. Innovator award 1970, Edison medallion 1979), Indsl. Rsch. Inst., Aluminum Assn. (chmn. tech. com. 1989-97), Sigma Xi. Achievements include patents in field.

HANNETT, FREDERICK JAMES, healthcare consulting company executive; b. Seattle, Sept. 12, 1950; m. JoAnne Thompson, May 10, 1980; children: Tom, Emily. Pres., COO The Jefferson Group, Washington, 1987-96; mng. prin. The Capitol Alliance, Washington, 1997—. Mem. Va. Bd. Health; bd. advisors Dem. Leadership Coun., Washington. Avocations: tennis, skiing, golf. Office: The Capitol Alliance 1350 I St NW Ste 870 Washington DC 20005-3386*

HANNEWALD, NORMAN EUGENE, secondary school educator; b. Stockbridge, Mich., Aug. 4, 1945; s. Martin Carl and Helen Pauline (Archenbronn) H.; m. Penny Lynn Boyer, Jan. 28, 1967; children: Marcia, Gregory, Mark. BS, Ea. Mich. U., 1967, MS, 1972. Sci. tchr. mid. sch. Northville (Mich.) Pub. Schs., mem. after sch. gifted sci. program. Mem. Nat. Sci. Tchrs. Assn., Mich. Sci. Tchrs. Assn.

HANNIBAL, EDWARD LEO, copywriter; b. Manchester, Mass., Aug. 24, 1936; s. Joseph Leary and Loretta Louise (McCarthy) H.; m. Margaret Adele Twomey, June 14, 1958; children: Mary Ellen, Edward J., Eleanor, John, Julia. BA, Boston Coll., 1958. Copywriter Kenyon & Eckhardt, N.Y.C., 1962-63, Norman, Craig & Kummel, N.Y.C., 1963-64; v.p. asoc, creative dir. Benton & Bowles, Inc., N.Y.C., 1965-68; exec. v.p., creative dir. Wayne Jervis Assocs., N.Y.C., 1968-1970; v.p., creative supr. Grey Advt., 1975-79; exec. v.p., co-creative dir. Hannibal Figliola Advt., N.Y.C., 1980-83; sr. v.p., group creative dir. Grey Advt., N.Y.C., 1985—. Author: Chocolate Days, Popsicle Weeks, 1970, Dancing Man, 1973, Liberty Square Station, 1977, (with Robert Boris) Blood Feud, 1979, A Trace of Red, 1982. Mem. PEN. Democrat. Roman Catholic. Avocations: reading, running. Office: Grey Advt 777 3rd Ave New York NY 10017-1401

HANNING, GARY WILLIAM, utility executive, water company executive, consultant; b. Sherman, Tex., Aug. 30, 1942; s. William Homer and Mary Maxine (Harshbarger) H.; m. Robin Dale Smith, June 8, 1974; children: TJ, Lorissa Diane. BS, Rollins Coll., 1974; MBA, Stetson U., 1976. Mgr., co-owner Hanning Water Systems, Denison, Tex., 1963-66; engring. technician Gen. Dynamics, Ft. Worth, 1966-67; engr. supr. Bendix Field, Pasadena, Calif., 1967-70; engr. Philco-Ford Corp., Cape Kennedy, Fla., 1970-73, Jet Propulsion Lab., Pasadena, Calif., 1973-74; sect. mgr. Planning Rsch. Corp., Kennedy Space Ctr., 1974-77; pres. S.S.S. Water Systems, Inc., Denison, 1978-83, Texoma Svcs. Corp., Pottsboro, Tex., 1980-99, Tanglewood Water Co., 1994-99; exec. Tecon Water Cos. Inc., 1999—; bd. dirs. Ind. Water and Sewer Co. Tex. Inc., Austin, Boy Scouts Am., Circle Ten, Dallas; entrepreneur Bells Discount Supply, Tex., 1983-87. Contbr. articles to profl. jours. Mem. City Coun., Pottsboro, Tex., 1992—. With USN, 1960-63. Mem. Tanglewood Golf Assn. (sec.-treas. 1992), Am. Legion, C. of C. Mem. Ch. of Christ. Avocations: inventing, camping, reading, golfing, boating, hunting. Office: Tecon Water Cos Inc 1437 W Georgetown Rd Pottsboro TX 75076

HANNON, BRUCE MICHAEL, engineer, educator; b. Champaign, Ill., Aug. 14, 1934; s. Walter Leo and Kathleen Rose (Phalen) H.; m. Patricia Claire Coffey, Aug. 11, 1956; children: Claire, Laura, Brian. BSCE, U. Ill., 1956, MS in Engring. Mechanics, 1966, PhD in Engring. Mechanics, 1970. Engr. with chem. industry, 1957-66; instr. U. Ill., Urbana, 1966-71, assoc. prof. energy rsch., 1974-83, prof. regional sci., 1983—, Jubilee prof. liberal arts and scis., 1991—; vis. prof. Nat. Ctr. for Supercomputing Applications; cons. NSF, NAS, NAE, chem. industry, various fed. energy agys; patentee in field. Contbr. articles to profl. jours. 1st lt. C.E. AUS, 1956-57. Named Engring. Tchr. of Yr., U. Ill., 1970, Man of Yr., Sierra Club, 1971; recipient 1st prize Mitchell Award Club of Rome, 1975. Home: 1208 W Union St Champaign IL 61821-3229 Office: U Ill 220 Daven Hall Urbana IL 61801

HANNON, JOHN ROBERT, investment company executive; b. Atlanta, Aug. 9, 1945; s. George Franklin and Elizabeth (Broadfield) H.; m. Jackie Lyn Wagner, Apr. 28, 1984; children: Kimberly Mishkind, Melissa Watlington. BA, Duke U., 1967. CFA, CLU, CPCU. Group sales rep. The Prudential Ins. Co. of Am., Charlotte, N.C., 1967-69, group ins. mgr., 1969-72; assoc. dir. group ins. The Prudential Ins. Co. of Am., Newark, 1972-74; regional group mgr. The Prudential Ins. Co. of Am., Jacksonville, Fla., 1974-79, dir. group mktg., 1979-81; v.p. group credit mktg. The Prudential Ins. Co. of Am., Newark, 1981-83; v.p. group ins. mktg. The Prudential Ins. Co. of Am., Roseland, N.J., 1983-85, v.p. group credit ins. ops., 1985-87, v.p. corp. group mktg. communications, 1987-88; sr. v.p. Prudential Capital Corp., Newark, 1988-91, Prudential Investment Corp., Newark, 1991; pres. Prudential Affiliated Investors, Newark, 1991-92, chmn., chief exec. officer, 1992-94; sr. mng. dir. Prudential Asset Mgmt. Group, Newark, 1994-95, Prudential Pvt. & Internat. Investors, Newark, 1995; sr. v.p. Enhanced Investment Technologies, Inc. (INTECH), Palm Beach Gardens, Fla., 1995-98; pres., CEO Hannon Consulting Group, Inc., 1999—; mem. vis. faculty Bus. Sch. U. North Fla., Jacksonville, 1979-80. Elder Presbyn. Ch., 1977—, deacon, 1987—; vol. campaign U.S. Senate Challenger, State of Fla., 1980; mem. nat. Eagle Scout Assn. With USN, 1963-67. Mem. Fin. Analysts Fedn., Assn. Investment Mgmt. and Rsch., N.Y. Soc. Security Analysts, Mensa, Rudder Club (commodore 1979-80), PGA Nat. Golf and Sports Club. Home and Office: PGA Nat 86 Dunbar Rd E Palm Bch Gdns FL 33418-6815

HANNON, KEMP, state senator; s. James Michael and Evelyn (Kemp) H.; m. Bronwyn Hannon. AB, Boston Coll., 1967; JD, Fordham U., 1970. Dep. county atty. Nassau County, N.Y., 1971-74; assemblyman State of N.Y., 1977-89, minority leader pro tem, 1983-89, sen., 1989—; chair health com., 1995—; of counsel Farrel Fritz PC Law Firm, Albany, 1986—; gen. counsel Nassau Regional OTB Corp., N.Y., 1974-76. Mem. N.Y. State Bar Assn., Nassau County Bar Assn., Delta Sigma Pi. Office: 609 Legis Office Bldg Albany NY 12247*

HANNON, PATRICIA ANN, library director; b. Passaic, N.J., Jan. 1, 1947; d. L. Robert and Frances Laurent Hannon. BA in Math., Caldwell Coll., 1968; MLS, L.I. U., 1972. Libr. Hackensack (N.J.) Pub. Libr., 1968-75; dir. Wood-Ridge (N.J.) Pub. Libr., 1975-81, Wanaque (N.J.) Pub. Libr., 1983-84, Oakland (N.J.) Pub. Libr., 1984-88, Emerson (N.J.) Pub. Libr., 1988—. Pres. St. Joseph's Parish Coun., E. Rutherford, N.J., 1979, Regency Pk. Condominium Assn., Ramsey, N.J., 1990-91. Named Outstanding Young Women of Am., 1977. Mem. N.J. Libr. Assn. (mem. exec. bd. 1974-76, conf. chair 1978-80, chair bldg. symposium 1994-97), Emerson C. of C. (sec. 1992-94, 97—), Bergen County Libr. Coop. Sys. (pres. 1988, 97), Highlands Regional Libr. Coop. (v.p. 1998-99, pres. 1999—), Beta Phi Mu. Avocations: guitar, needlepoint, houses. E-mail: Hannon@bccls.org. Office: Emerson Pub Libr 20 Palisade Ave Emerson NJ 07630

HANNON, RICHARD W., director budget bureau. BA, Syracuse U.; MA, St. Johns Fisher, Rochester, N.Y. Dir. budget bureau City Hall, Rochester, N.Y., 1994—. Bd. dirs. YMCA, Rochester. Mem. N.Y. State Finance Officers Assn. Office: City Hall Budget Bureau 30 Church St Rm 200A Rochester NY 14614-1291*

HANNON, TIMOTHY PATRICK, lawyer, educator; b. Culver City, Calif., Nov. 29, 1948; s. Justin Aloysius and Ann Elizabeth (Ford) H.; m. Patricia Ann Hanson, May 1, 1976; children: Sean Patrick, James Patrick. Student, U. Vienna, 1968-69, Naval War Coll., 1988; BA, U. Santa Clara, 1970, JD cum laude, 1974. Bar: Calif. 1974, U.S. Dist. Ct. (no. dist.) Calif. 1974, U.S. Dist. Ct. (so. and dists.) Calif. 1978, U.S. Ct. Appeals (9th cir.) 1978, Ct. Appeals Armed Forces 1979, D.C. 1981, U.S. Tax Ct. 1983, U.S. Ct. Claims 1983; cert. trial and def. lawyer Univorm Code Mil. Justice. Assoc. N. Perry Moerdyke, Jr., Palo Alto, Calif., 1975-81; ptnr. Myerdyke & Hannon, Palo Alto, 1982-84, Attwood, Hurst, Knox & Anderson, 1984-86; pvt. practice Campbell, Calif., 1986-97; U.S. Adminstrv. law judge Social Security Adminstrn., 1997—; instr. San Jose State U., 1985-89; instr. De Anza Jr. Coll., Cupertino, Calif., 1987—, instr. extension courses U. Calif., Santa Cruz, 1982-83; lectr. Lincoln Law Sch., San Jose, Calif., 1988—; arbitrator Santa Clara County Superior Ct., Santa Clara County Mcpl. Ct.; sr. mil. mem. expanded Internat. Mil. Edn. Tng., Uganda; judge pro temp Santa Clara County Mcpl. Ct. Chmn., Menlo Park Housing Commn., 1979-81; mem. allocations com. vol. United Way Clara County, 1987-90; mem. San Jose Vets. Meml. Com., 1993-99, treas., 1996-99. Admiral, pilot Tex. Navy, 1998. With Calif. Army NG, 1970-76, capt., USNR, 1979—. Mem. Santa Clara County Bar Assn. (exec. com.), Santa Clara U. Nat. Alumni, U. Santa Clara Law Alumni Assn. (bd. dirs. 1980-81, sec. 1981-83, v.p. 1983-85, pres. 1985-87), Kiwanis. Roman Catholic. Avocation: flying. Home: 806 Buckwood Ct San Jose CA 95120-3306 Office: 280 S 1st St # 300 San Jose CA 95113-3002

HANNON, VIOLET MARIE, surgical nurse; b. Wayne, Mich., Sept. 11, 1943; d. John R. and Ethel L. (Goudy) Hines; children: Judith, Susan. Diploma, Grace Hosp. Sch. Nursing, Detroit, 1964; BS summa cum laude, U. Detroit, 1985; postgrad., Cen. Mich. U., 1990—. Cert. ACLS, CNOR. Staff nurse Grace Hosp., 1964-67, Sinai Hosp., Detroit, 1971-75, Oakwood Hosp., Dearborn, Mich., 1967-71, 1975-86; ophthalca svcs. nurse Henry Ford Hosp., 1987-93, HCIA, Inc., 1993-98, Eisenhower Hosp., 1999—. Mem. Assn. Operating Room Nurses, ASORN. Home: 13476 Little Bend Trail Palm Desert CA 92260

HANNULA, TARMO, photographer. BA in Aesthetic Studies and Music, U. Calif., Santa Cruz, 1982. Freelance photographer, 1982-97; staff photographer Register-Pajaronian, Watsonville, Calif., 1997—. Mem. Nat. Press Photography Assn. Office: Register-Pajaronian 1000 Main St Watsonville CA 95076

HANNUM, GERALD LUTHER (LOU HANNUM), retired tire manufacturing company official; b. Syracuse, N.Y., May 31, 1915; s. Ralph Charles and Coral (Snyder) H.; m. Carolyn Russell Osgood, Nov. 29, 1941; children: Nancy, Susan, Jean. AB, Syracuse U., 1937; MA, Kent State U., 1971. Supr. forecasting and inventory control B.F. Goodrich, Arkon, Ohio, 1961-67; econ. planning specialist, staff for v.p. planning B.F. Goodrich Co., 1967-75, econ. planner, 1946-75; ret., 1975. Councilman City of Medford, Oreg., 1977-82, 89-92, mayor, 1983-86, water commr., 1997—; bd. dirs. United Way, Medford, 1986—; pres. Crater Lake coun. Boy Scouts Am., 1987-90. Lt. USNR, 1943-52, PTO. Recipient Silver Beaver award Boy Scouts Am., 1987. Mem. League Oreg. Cities (pres. 1983, Richards award 1989), Rotary. Avocations: hiking, photography. Home: 2900 Seckel St Medford OR 97504-8150

HANOVER, R(AYMOND) SCOTT, tennis management professional; b. Des Moines, June 10, 1964; s. Norman E. and Jo Ann (Taylor) H.; m. Marla J. Boicourt, Apr. 23, 1988. BA, Grand View Coll., 1986. Staff writer, news asst. Des Moines Register, 1985-90; sch. dir. Missouri Valley sect. U.S. Tennis Assn., Kansas City, Mo., 1990-96; mgr. Plaza Tennis Ctr., Kansas City, Mo., 1996—. Editor U.S. Profl. Tennis Assn. Missouri Valley divsn. newsletter, 1992-95. Dir. Heart of Am. Dist. Tennis., 1996—, sec., 1999—; co-founder, bd. dirs. Kansas City Met. Tennis Assn. Recipient Svc. award Nebr. AHPERD, 1991, Missouri Valley Tennis Assn. and Heart of Am. Tennis Assn. Facility of Yr. award, 1997. Mem. U.S. Tennis Assn. (life, referee 1997—, liaison to Club Mgrs. Assn. 1998—, Mo. Valley nominating com. 1998, Outstanding Pub. Facility award 1998, Heart of Am. Orgn. of Yr. award 1998), Missouri Valley Tennis Assn. (chmn. pub. rels. com. 1989-90, chmn. cmty. devel. com. 1996-98), U.S. Profl. Tennis Registry, Grand View Alumni Coun. (pres. 1988-90). Office: Kansas City Parks/Recreation 4747 JC Nichols Pkwy Kansas City MO 64112-1627

HANOWELL, ERNEST GODDIN, physician; b. Newport News, Va., Jan. 31, 1920; a. George Frederick and Ruby Augustine (Goddin) H.; m. Para Jean Hall, June 10, 1945; children: Ernest D., Deborah J. Hanowell Orick, Leland H., Dee P. Hanowell Martinmaas, Robert G. Diplomate Am. Bd. Internal Medicine. Intern USPHS Hosp., Norfolk, Va., 1948-49; resident in internal medicine USPHS Hosp., Seattle, 1952-55; fellow in cardiology New Eng. Ctr. Hosp., Boston, 1961-62; chief medicine USPHS Hosp., Ft. Worth, 1955-57; dept. chief medicine USPHS Hosp., Boston, 1957-59; chief medicine USPHS Hosp., Memphis, 1964-65, Monterey County Gen. Hosp., 1969-70; ret. med. dir., col. USPHS; mem. internal medicine and cardiology staff Kaiser Permanente Med. Group, Sacramento, 1971-87; writer, Auburn, Calif., 1987—; clin. asst. Tufts Med. Sch., 1960-61; cons. chest disease Phila. Gen. Hosp., 1960-61; asst. prof. U. Md. Med. Sch., 1961-64; instr. U. Tenn. Med. Sch., 1964-65; asst. clin. prof. Sch. Medicine, U. Calif., Davis, 1973-81; mem. attending staff Cardiac Clinic Stanford U. Med. Sch. 1967-69; mem. sr. adv. bd. Area 4 Agy. on Aging. Mem. sch. bd. Salinas, Calif., 1968-69; bd. dirs. Am. Heart Assn., Tb and Health Assn.; advisor sr. adv. com. 7 counties area 4, Placer County, Calif. Served with AUS, 1943-46. Fellow ACP, Am. Coll. Chest Diseases; mem. Crocker Art Mus. Assn., Rotary, Phi Chi. Home and Office: 1158 Racquet Club Dr Auburn CA 95603-3042

HANRAHAN, BARBARA, university press executive; b. Boston, July 7, 1947. BA summa cum laude, Wheaton Coll., Mass., 1969; MA, U. Chgo., 1970. Humanities editor U. Chgo. Press, 1974-82; sr. acquisitions editor U. Wis. Press, Madison, 1985-92; editor-in-chief U. N.C. Press, Chapel Hill, 1992-96; dir. Ohio State U. Press, Columbus, 1996—. Office: Ohio State U Press 1070 Carmack Rd Columbus OH 43210-1002*

HANRAHAN, LAWRENCE MARTIN, healthcare consultant; b. Cin., Mar. 9, 1961; adopted s. Robert Donald and Mary Francis (Doran) H.; biol. s. Barry Wright and Kathryn Regina Kinkaid. AB in Chemistry, Miami U., 1983; MD, U. Cin. Coll. Medicine, 1988; MBA, U. Tex. Grad. Sch. Bus., Austin, 1992. Founder, owner Landscaping group, Cin., 1975-85; chief ultrasound tech., instr., rsch. assoc. The Good Samaritan Hosp. Peripheral Vascular Lab., Cin., 1983-84; instr., technologist The Christ Hosp. Clin. Vascular Lab., Cin., 1986; tech. cons., instr. Biosound, Inc., Indpls., 1983-89; surg. rsch. fellow divsn. surgery Boston U. Sch. Medicine; peripheral vascular technologist, instr. Seton Med. Ctr., Austin, 1991; summer assoc. health care ops. Deloitte & Touche, Houston, 1991, cons. health care ops., 1991-92, sr. cons., 1992-94, mgr. health care ops., 1994—; sr. assoc. healthcare provider cons. William M. Mercer, Inc., Houston, 1995-97; founder Hanrahan Williams LLC, Houston, 1997—; founder, chmn., pres. CORE Med. Techs., Inc., Houston, 1992—; treas. Miami Med. Edn. and Devel., Miami U., 1975-79; com. mem. Disting. Lecture Series, U. Tex. Sch. Bus., Austin; founding pres. Tex. Bus. Hall of Fame Found. Scholarship Alumni Assn., 1992-93; bd. dirs., exec. com., 1992-93. Contbr. 10 articles to profl. jours.; co-inventor 2 U.S. patents. Finalist ACS resident competition, 1990, San Diego State U. Entrepreneurship competition; winner New Eng. Surg. Soc. resident competition, 1990; Tex. Bus. Hall of Fame Found. scholar, 1991, Abell-Hanger Endowed presdl. scholar, 1991. Mem. AMA, Soc. for Vascular Tech., Tex. Med. Assn., Mass. Med. Soc., Harris County Med. Soc., Med. Student Surgical Soc., Beta Theta Pi Frat. Avocation: jazz music.

HANRAHAN, MICHAEL G., lawyer, business consultant; b. Mount Vernon, N.Y., June 1, 1949; s. G. Michael and Florence M. (Quinn) H.; m. Barbara L. Fluhr, June 11, 1977; children: Thomas M., Elizabeth L. BA, Saint Bonaventure U., 1971; JD, Fordham U., 1974. Bar: N.Y., 1975; U.S. Dist. Ct. (ea. dist.) N.Y. 1975, U.S. Ct. Appeals (2nd cir.) 1975, Supreme Ct. 1997. Ptnr. Hanrahan & Hanrahan, Pelham, N.Y., 1975—, Hanrahan & Curley, Chappaqua, N.Y., 1995—; bd. dirs. John Langenbacher Co., Inc., Bronx, N.Y., U.S. Veneer Co., Inc., 1985—; counsel Entrepreneurial Ctr., Inc., Purchase, N.Y., 1995—. Pres., dir. Pelham (N.Y.) Family Svc., Inc., 1976-80. Mem. Rotary Internat. (pres., dir. 1976—, Paul Harris fellow 1988). Office: Hanrahan & Hanrahan 438 5th Ave Pelham NY 10803-1257

HANRAHAN, ROBERT JOSEPH, chemist, educator; b. Chgo., Jan. 7, 1932; s. James Richard and Lucille Florence (Granger) H.; m. Mary Ellen Hogan, Oct. 28, 1957; children: Ann Marie, Sheila Frances, Robert Joseph, Margaret Evyleen. B.S., Loyola U., Chgo., 1953; Ph.D., U. Wis., Madison, 1957. Research chemist Pure Oil Co., Crystal Lake, Ill., 1953; teaching asst., research asst. Monsanto research fellow U. Wis., Madison, 1953-57; NSF postdoctoral fellow Leeds (Eng.) U., 1957-58; asst. prof. phys. chemistry U. Fla., 1958-64, assoc. prof., 1964-71, prof., 1971—, chmn. phys. chemistry div., 1977-86; vis. sci. Hahn-Meitner Inst. Nuclear Research, Berlin, 1976; cons. in field. Patentee in field; contbr. articles to profl. jours. AEC rsch. grantee, 1963-74; ERDA grantee, 1975-77; Dept. Energy grantee, 1977-88; Dreyfus Found. grantee, 1983. Mem. Am. Chem. Soc., Am. Phys. Soc., Radiation Research Soc., AAAS, Am. Soc. Mass Spectrometry, Inter-Am. Photochem. Soc. Democrat. Roman Catholic. Rsch. on chem. effects of nuclear radiation and on solar energy systems. Home: 3730 NW 16th Pl Gainesville FL 32605-4848 Office: U Fla Dept Chemistry Gainesville FL 32611

HANRATH, LINDA CAROL, librarian, archivist; b. Chgo., Aug. 22, 1949; d. John Stanley and Victoria (Fraint) Grzesiakowski; m. Richard Alan Hanrath, Nov. 1, 1980; 1 child, Emily. BA in History, Rosary Coll., 1971, MA in Library Sci., 1974. Tchr. social studies Notre Dame High Sch., Chgo., 1971-75; outreach libr. Indian Trails Pub. Libr., Wheeling, Ill., 1975-76, Arlington Heights (Ill.) Meml. Libr., 1976-78; corp. libr. William Wrigley Jr. Co., Chgo., 1978—. Mem. Spl. Librs. Assn. (chmn. libr. jobline com. 1981-83, 86-87, food agrl. and nutrition divsn. 1988-89, sec. Ill. chpt. 1984-86, pres.-elect 1993-94, pres. Ill. chpt. 1994-95, conf. bd. info. svcs. adv. coun. 1990—, winner outstanding achievement award 1997), Assn. Records Mgrs. and Adminstrs., Soc. Am. Archivists, Midwest Archives Conf., Beta Phi Mu. Avocations: needlework, skiing, reading, gourmet cooking. Home: 715 E Devon Ave Roselle IL 60172-1461 Office: William Wrigley Jr Co 410 N Michigan Ave Chicago IL 60611-4213

HANRATTY, THOMAS JOSEPH, chemical engineer, educator; b. Phila., Nov. 9, 1926; s. John Joseph and Elizabeth Marie (O'Connor) H.; m. Joan L. Hertel, Aug. 25, 1956; children: John, Vincent, Maria, Michael, Peter. BS Chem. Engring., Villanova U., 1947; hon. doctorate, 1979; M.S., Ohio State U., 1950; Ph.D., Princeton U., 1953. Engr. Fischer & Porter, 1947-48; research engr. Battelle Meml. Inst., 1948-50; engr. Rohm & Haas, Phila., summer 1951; research engr. Shell Devel. Co., Emeryville, Calif., 1954; faculty U. Ill., Urbana, 1953—, assoc. prof., 1958-63, prof. chem. engring., 1963—, James W. Westwater prof. chem. engring., 1989-97; cons. in field; vis. assoc. prof. Brown U., 1962-63. Contbr. articles to profl. jours. NSF sr. postdoctoral fellow, 1962; recipient Curtis W. McGraw award Am. Soc. Engring. Edn., 1963, Sr. Research award, 1979; Disting. Engring. Alumnus award Ohio State U., 1984; Shell Disting. prof., 1981-86; 1st winner Internat. prize for rsch. in multiphase flow, 1998; Sr. Univ. Scholar, U. Ill., 1987, Lamme award Ohio State Univ., 1997. Fellow Am. Phys. Soc.; mem. NAE, Am. Acad. Arts and Scis., AIChE (Colburn award 1957, Walker award 1964, Profl. Progress award 1967, Ernest Thiele award Chgo. sect. 1986), Serra Internat. Club. Roman Catholic. Home: 1019 W Charles St Champaign IL 61821-4525 Office: U Ill 205 Roger Adams Lab 600 S Mathews Ave Urbana IL 61801-3602

HANS, MARY CLARE, aquatics director, red cross trainer; b. Buffalo, N.Y., Aug. 2, 1936; d. Aloysius William and Gertrude Elizabeth Huber; m. Edward Donald Hans, Oct. 1, 1955; children: Edward W., Robert D., Marie E., Kenneth J., James A. Sec., bookkeeper Brennan's Mens Wear, Buffalo, N.Y., 1974-77; pvt. investor Hammer Security, Buffalo, N.Y., 1977-79; prin., owner Claiborn Liquors, Buffalo, N.Y., 1979-93; aquatic dir. Jewish Cmty. Ctr., Buffalo, N.Y., 1993—. Vol., instr. Am. Red Cross, Buffalo, 1969—. Recipient Team Competition award Nat. Championship Synchronized Swimming, Portland, Oreg., 1998. Mem. Aquatic Exercise Assn. Democrat. Roman Cath. Avocations: masters speed and synchronized swimmer. Home: 322 Dearborn St Buffalo NY 14207-2719

HANSBURY, STEPHAN CHARLES, lawyer; b. Mt. Holly, N.J., Nov. 3, 1946; s. Charles Clark and Kathryn Irene (Meyer) H.; m. Sharon Buckley; children: Elizabeth Kathryn, Jillian Judith, Stephanie Clark. BA, Allegheny Coll., 1968; MBA, Fairleigh Dickinson U., 1973; JD, Seton Hall U., 1977; cert. civil trial atty., Supreme Ct. N.J., 1989. Bar: N.J. 1977, U.S. Dist. Ct. (no. dist.) N.J. 1977, U.S. Supreme Ct. 1982. Dir. spl. programs Bloomfield (N.J.) Coll., 1968-71; dir. fin. aid Monmouth Coll., West Long Branch, N.J., 1971-72; asst. adminstr. Morris View, Morris Plains, N.J., 1972-78; assoc. Hansbury, Martin & Knapp, Morris Plains, 1978-87, pres., 1987-92; ptnr. Kummer Knox, Naughton & Hansbury, Parsippany, N.J., 1992—, pres., 1996—; mem., gen. counsel Cheshire Home, Florham Park, N.J., 1978—, Ciba-Geigy Corp., Summit, N.J., 1980-92. Legis. aide Assemblyman Arthur Albohn, Morristown, N.J., 1980-83; mem. Morris County Bd. of Social Svcs., 1989-96, chmn. 1992-94. Mem. ABA, N.J. Bar Assn., Morris County Bar Assn. (trustee 1987-90), Rotary (bd. dirs. Morris Plains 1981-83, v.p. 1996-97, pres.-elect 1997-98, pres. 1998—), Morristown Club. Republican. Episcopalian. Avocations: tennis, golf, reading. Office: Kummer Knox Naughton & Hansbury 299 Cherry Hill Rd Parsippany NJ 07054-1111

HANSCHEN, PETER WALTER, lawyer; b. San Francisco, July 7, 1945; s. Walter A. and Dorothy E. (Watkins) H.; m. Brenda C. Hanschen, Feb. 7, 1987. BA, San Francisco State U., 1967; JD, U. Calif.-Berkeley, 1971. Bar: Calif. 1972, U.S. Supreme Ct. 1985, U.S. Ct. Appeals D.C. Cir. 1975. Assoc. Lawler, Felix & Hall, L.A., 1971-73; atty. Pacific Gas Transmission Co., San Francisco, 1973-76, Pacific Gas & Elec. Co., San Francisco, 1976-79; gen. counsel Pacific Gas Transmission, San Francisco, 1979-83; asst. gen. counsel Pacific Gas & Elec. Co., San Francisco, 1983-88; ptnr. Graham & James, San Francisco, 1988-99, Morrison & Foerster, San Francisco, 1999—. Mem. ABA, Internat. Bar Assn., Fed. Energy Bar Assn., Counsel of Calif. Pub. Utilities. Avocations: golf, gardening, sports. Office: Morrison & Foerster LLP 425 Market St San Francisco CA 94105-2482

HANSEL, PAUL GEORGE, physicist, consultant; b. Grand Island, Nebr., June 22, 1917; s. Arthur Hiram and Wilma D. (Amick) H.; m. Helen Stephens; children: Stephen, James, Gregory. BS in Engring. Physics, U. Kans., 1946. Engr. Signal Corps Labs., Ft. Monmouth, N.J., 1941-47; chief radio engr. Servo Corp. Am., Hicksville, N.Y., 1947-61; v.p. rsch. and engring. Electronic Communications, Inc., St. Petersburg, Fla., 1961-79; cons. Advanced Tech. Cons.'s, St. Petersburg, 1979—. Contbr. articles, reports to sci. and tech. jours.; patentee radio direction finding, navigation. Mem. adv. coun. U. Fla. Coll. Engring., Gainesville, 1965-89; pres. adv. coun. U. Fla., 1976-86. Recipient Apollo award NASA, 1972, citation for inventions War Dept. (now Dept. Def.), 1946. Fellow IEEE (Pioneer award 1970); mem. AAAS, N.Y. Acad. Scis., Fla. Acad. Scis. Avocations: writing, lecturing, flying. Home: 1374 Monterey Blvd NE Saint Petersburg FL 33704-2316

HANSEL, STEPHEN ARTHUR, holding company executive; b. Long Branch, N.J., Aug. 13, 1947; s. Paul George and Helen (Stephens) H.; children: Alexander, Nicholas, Derek, Andrew, Paula. B.A., Wesleyan U., 1969; M.B.A., Darden Sch. Bus. Adminstrn., 1971; cert. Advanced Mgmt. Program, Harvard Bus. Sch. Pres., CEO Hibernia Corp., Hibernia Nat. Bank, New Orleans. Founder, pres. Found. for Pulmonary Hypertension, Inc.; trustee Wesleyan U., New Orleans Mus. of Art; mem. greater New Orleans bus. coun. Republican. Office: Hibernia Corp PO Box 61540 313 Carondelet St New Orleans LA 70130-3109

HANSEL, WILLIAM, biology educator; b. Vale Summit, Md., Sept. 16, 1918; s. John W. and Helen M. (Sperlein) H.; m. Milbrey Downey, Aug. 16, 1942; children: Barbara, Kay. MS, Cornell U., 1947, PhD, 1949. Asst. prof. Cornell U., Ithaca, N.Y., 1949-52, assoc. prof., 1952-61, prof., 1961-90, Liberty Hyde Bailey prof., 1983-90, chmn. physiology dept., 1978-83; Gordon D. Cain prof. La. State U., Baton Rouge, 1990—; scientific adv. Merck, Sharp and Dohme, Rahway, 1980-85, Smith, Kline, Beecham, Westchester, Pa., 1986-91. Author: Genetic Engineering of Animals, 1990, Nutrition and Reproduction, 1998; contbr. over 300 articles to profl. jours. Maj. U.S. Army, 1941-46, ETO. Fellow AAAS; mem. Soc. Study Reprodn. (pres. 1976), Am. Physiol. Soc., Endocrine Soc., Soc. Exptl. Biology and Medicine (treas. 1975), Gamma Sigma Delta, Sigma Xi, Phi Kappa Phi. Achievements include isolation and identification of causative agent of bovine x-disease; developed a successful technique for estrous cycle regulation in cattle, pioneered in development of assays for hormones in blood of animals; discovered control mechanisms for corpus luteum function in cattle; demonstrated the relationships between nutrition and reproduction in cattle. Office: Pennington Biomed Rsch Ctr B-1047 Baton Rouge LA 70808

HANSELL, DEAN, lawyer; b. Bridgeport, Conn., Mar. 24, 1952. BA, Denison U., 1974; JD, Northwestern U., 1977. Bar: Ill. 1977, U.S. Dist. Ct. (no. dist.) Ill. 1977, U.S. Ct. Appeals (7th cir.) 1978, U.S. Ct. Appeals (D.C. cir.) 1978, U.S. Ct. Appeals (9th cir.) 1979, Calif. 1980, U.S. Dist. Ct. (cen. dist.) Calif. 1981, U.S. Dist. Ct. (so. dist.) Calif. 1989, U.S. Supreme Ct. 1998. Asst. atty. gen. for environ. control State of Ill., Chgo., 1977-80; atty. FTC, L.A., 1980-83; assoc. Lillick, McHose & Charles, L.A., 1983-84, Donovan Leisure Newton & Irvine, L.A., 1984-86; ptnr. LeBoeuf, Lamb, Greene & MacRae, L.A., 1986—; adj. assoc. prof. Southwestern U. Sch. Law, L.A., 1982-86; mem. Ill. Solar Resources Adv. Panel, 1978-80; judge pro tem L.A. County Mcpl. Ct., 1987-97, L.A. County Superior Ct., 1989—; mem. adv. bd. Fayette Haywood Legal Svcs., Tenn., 1979-83, Nat. Inst. for Citizen Edn. in Law, 1989-94. Bd. dirs. Jewish Fedn. Coun. Met. L.A. Region, 1984-87, Project LEAP, Legal Elections in All Precincts, Chgo., 1976-80, Martin Luther King, Jr. Ctr. Nonviolence, L.A., 1991-95, L.A. Pub. Libr. Found., 1997—; commr. L.A. Bd. Police Commrs., 1997—. Mem. editl. bd. L.A. Lawyer Mag., 1995—, Internat. Reins. Dispute Reporter, 1996—; contbr. articles to profl. jours. Mem. L.A. County Bar Assn. (mem. exec. com. antitrust sect. 1982-92, chair 1989-90), Calif. Bar Assn., L.A. Complex Litigation Inn Ct., Phi Beta Kappa, Omicron Delta Kappa. Office: LeBoeuf Lamb Greene & MacRae 725 S Figueroa St Ste 3600 Los Angeles CA 90017-5436

HANSELL, EDGAR FRANK, lawyer; b. Leon, Iowa, Oct. 12, 1937; s. Edgar Noble and Celestia Delphine (Skinner) H.; m. Phyllis Wray Silvey, June 24, 1961; children—John Joseph, Jordan Burke. AA, Graceland Coll., 1957; BBA, U. Iowa, 1959, JD, 1961. Bar: Iowa 1961. Assoc. Nyemaster, Goode, McLaughlin, Voigts, West, Hansell & O'Brien, P.C., Des Moines, 1964-68, ptnr., shareholder, 1968—; bd. dirs. The Vernon Co., Des Moines Devel. Corp., Des Moines Internat. Airport; adj. prof. law Drake U., Des Moines, 1990-98. Mem. editorial adv. bd. Jour. Corp. Law, 1985—. Bd. dirs. Des Moines Child Guidance Ctr., 1972-78, 81-87, pres., 1977-78; trustee Iowa Law Sch. Found., 1975-90, pres., 1983-87; bd. dirs. Iowa Natural Heritage Found., 1988-93, Iowa Sports Found., 1986-97; bd. dirs. Iowa State Bar Found., 1991—, prs., 1996—. With USAF, 1961-64. Mem. ABA, Iowa Bar Assn. (pres. young lawyers sect. 1971-72, bd. govs. 1971-72, 85-87, mem. grievance commn. 1973-78, Merit award young lawyers sect. 1977, chmn. corp. and bus. law com. 1979-85, pres. 1989-90), Polk County Bar Assn., Des Moines Club (pres. 1979-80). Home: 139-37th Des Moines IA 50312-4303 Office: Nyemaster Goode Voigts West Hansell & O'Brien PC 700 Walnut St Ste 1600 Des Moines IA 50309-3800

HANSELL, JOHN ROYER, retired physician; b. Phila., June 30, 1931; s. Henry Lewis and Elizabeth (Campbell) H. AB, U. Pa., 1953; MD, Jefferson Med. Coll., 1957. Diplomate Am. Bd. Pathology, Am. Bd. Nuclear Medicine (chmn. 1988-89). Intern Germantown Hosp., Phila., 1957-58, resident, pathologist, 1956-61; resident, pathologist Bryn Mawr (Pa.) Hosp., 1961-62; pathology fellow New Eng. Deaconess Hosp., Boston, 1962-63; resident Mayo Clinic, Rochester, Minn., 1966-67; chief nuclear medicine VA Med Ctr., Phila., 1967-93. Contbr. chpts. to books and articles to profl. jours. Comdr. USPHS, 1963-66. Fellow Soc. Nuclear Medicine, Coll. Am. Pathologists. Republican. Episcopalian. Avocations: antiques, gardening.

HANSELL, RICHARD STANLEY, obstetrician, gynecologist, educator; b. Indpls., Nov. 18, 1950; s. Robert Mathey and Jewell (Martin) H.; m. Cathy C., Oct. 7, 1995; children: Elizabeth, Victoria. BA, DePauw U., 1972; MD, Ind. U., 1976. Cert. Am. Bd. Obstetrics and Gynecology. Practice medicine specializing in ob-gyn Cedarwood Med. Ctr., St. Joseph, Mich., 1980-86; asst. prof. ob-gyn. Ind. U., Indpls., 1986-93, assoc. prof. ob-gyn, 1993—; instr. Western Mich. U., Kalamazoo, 1980-86; med. bd. Planned Parenthood, Benton Harbor, Mich., 1980-86; med. dir. Planned Parenthood of Ctrl. Ind., 1991-95; examiner Am. Bd. Ob-gyn., 1994—. Mem. AMA, Am. Coll. Ob-Gyn, Assn. of Profs. of Gynecology and Obstetrics, Ind. State Med. Soc., Ctrl. Assn. Ob/gyn., Indpls. Med. Soc. Presbyterian. Lodge: Kiwanis. Avocations: golf, fishing. Office: Ind U Med Sch Dept Ob-Gyn 1001 W 10th St Indianapolis IN 46202-2859

HANSELMAN, RICHARD WILSON, entrepreneur; b. Cin., Oct. 8, 1927; s. Wendell Forest and Helen E. (Beiderwelle) H.; m. Beverly Baker White, Oct. 16, 1954; children: Charles Fielding, II, Jane White. BA in Econs, Dartmouth Coll., 1949. V.p. merchandising RCA Sales Corp., Indpls., 1964-66, v.p. product planning, 1966-69, v.p. product mgmt., 1969-70; pres. luggage div. Samsonite Corp., Denver, 1970-73, pres. luggage group, 1973-74, exec. v.p. ops., 1974-75, pres., 1975-77; sr. v.p. Beatrice Foods Co., Chgo., 1976-77, exec. v.p., 1977-80; pres., chief operating officer, dir. Genesco Inc., Nashville, 1980-86, chief exec. officer, 1981-86, pvt. investor, corp. dir., 1986—; bd. dirs. Becton Dickinson and Co., Arvin Industries, Bradford Funds, Inc., Found. Health Systems Inc., Wollin Products Inc. (chmn.). Trustee Com. for Econ. Devel. Served with U.S. Army, 1950-52. Mem. Belle Meade Country Club, Union League, Chgo. Club, Golf Club of Tenn., Phi Kappa Psi. Office: 3017 Poston Ave Nashville TN 37203-1313

HANSELMANN, FREDRICK CHARLES, lawyer; b. Phila., Sept. 1, 1955; s. Helmuth Fredrick and Maria Elizabeth (Dougherty) H.; m. Mary Nina Johnson, May 7, 1983; children: Elizabeth Ryan, Peter Cornelius, Kevin Andrew, Charlotte Mary. BA magna cum laude, La Salle Coll., 1977; JD, U. Notre Dame, 1980. Bar: Pa. 1980, U.S. Dist. Ct. (ea. dist.) Pa. 1981, U.S. Dist. Ct. (mid. dist.) Pa. 1987, U.S. Ct. Appeals (3d cir.) 1981. Assoc. German, Gallagher & Murtagh, P.C., Phila., 1981-85, Wilson, Elser, Moskowitz, Edelman & Dicker, Phila., 1985-90; ptnr. Mylotte David & Fitzpatrick, Phila., 1990—. Mem. ABA, Pa. Bar Assn., Phila. Bar Assn., Def. Rsch. Inst., Profl. Liability Underwriting Soc., Lawyers Club Phila., Notre Dame Club Phila., Avalon Yacht Club, Glen Lake (Mich.) Assn. Republican. Roman Catholic. Home: 118 Azalea Way Flourtown PA 19031-2008 Office: Mylotte David & Fitzpatrick 1635 Market St Fl 9 Philadelphia PA 19103-2217

HANSEN, ALAN EDWARD, mental health nurse; b. Hettinger, N.D., Jan. 12, 1953; s. Eugene and Evelyn (Tkachenko) H.; m. Rayleen Weisz, June 8, 1975; children: Derek, Brooke. BS in Nursing, Union Coll., Lincoln, Nebr., 1974; MHS, Whitworth Coll., Spokane, Wash., 1983. RN, Wash., Nebr. Psychiatric staff nurse State of Iowa Penal System, Oakdale, 1979-80, Sacred Heart Med. Ctr., Spokane, Wash., 1980-83; instr. Meth. Coll. Nursing, Omaha, Nebr., 1983-86; staff nurse Meth. Hosp., Omaha, 1986-90; chem. dependency nurse St. Francis Drug and Alcohol Treatment Ctr., Grand Island, Nebr., 1990-92, St. Francis Med. Ctr. Emergency Rm., Grand Island, Nebr., 1992—.

HANSEN, ANDREW MARIUS, retired library association executive; b. Storm Lake, Iowa, Mar. 25, 1929; s. Andrew Marius and Margaret Mary (Van Wagenen) H.; m. Rina M. Smith, Feb. 24, 1967; 1 child, Neil S. B.A., U. Omaha, 1951; postgrad., U. Md., 1955; M.A., U. Minn., 1962; postgrad, U. Iowa, 1968-71. Librarian Bismarck (N.D.) Public Library, 1957-63, Sioux City (Iowa) Public Library, 1963-67; instr. Sch. of Library Sci., U. Iowa, Iowa City, 1967-71; exec. sec. ALA, Chgo., 1971-80; exec. dir. reference and adult services div. ALA, 1980-94; vis. asst. prof. Ind. State U., Terre Haute, 1966. Pres. Friends of Wilmette Pub. Library, 1984-85. Served with USAF, 1951-55. Mem. ALA (Mudge-Bowker award 1993), N.D. Libr. Assn. (pres. 1958-59, sec.-treas. 1962-63), Iowa Libr. Assn. (pres. 1967-68), Coalition Adult Edn. Orgns. (bd. dirs. 1972-93), Ch. and Synagogue Libr. Assn. (treas. Northeastern Ill. chpt. 1985-91), Chgo. Libr. Club (sec. 1983-84), Rotary. Presbyterian. Home: 314 Skokie Blvd Wilmette IL 60091-3002

HANSEN, ARTHUR GENE, former academic administrator, consultant; b. Sturgeon Bay, Wis., Feb. 28, 1925; s. Henry A. and Ruth (Anderson) H. BSEE, Purdue U., 1946, MS in Math., 1948, DEng (hon.), 1971; PhD in Math., Case Inst. Tech., 1958; DSc (hon.), Ind. U., 1982. Research scientist NASA, 1948-49, 50-58; tchr. U. Md., 1949-50; sect. head Cornell Aero. Lab., Buffalo, 1958-59; mem. faculty mech. engring. U. Mich., 1959-66; dean Ga. Inst. Tech., 1966-69, pres., 1969-71; pres. Purdue U., 1971-82; chancellor Tex. A&M U. System, 1982-86; dir. rsch. Hudson Inst., 1987-88; prof. mech. engring. Tuskegee Inst., 1965; sr. rsch. engr. Douglas Aircraft Co., 1964; cons. to industry, 1961-70; chmn. bd. Corp. for Edn. Tech., 1992-94; chmn. Atlanta Civic Design Commn., 1968-79, Ga. Sci. and Tech. Commn., 1968-71, Ga. Ocean Sci. Ctr. of Atlantic Commn., Atlanta, 1968-71; mem. adv. coun. Skidaway Oceanographic Inst. for Univ. System Ga., 1968-71; pres. Ind. Conf. Higher Edn., 1975; chmn. com. on minorities in engring. NRC, 1974-76; bd. dirs. Nat. Action Coun. for Minorities in Engring., Inc., 1984-86; mem. energy rsch. adv. bd. Dept. Energy; chmn. adv. coun. Electric Power Rsch. Inst., 1973-79; chmn. bd. Ind. State Symphony Soc., 1989-91. Author: Similarity Analyses of Boundary Value Problems in Engineering, 1964, Fluid Mechanics, 1967. Chmn. bd. visitors Air U., 1974-77; bd. visitors Air Force Inst. Tech., 1987-89; trustee Nat. Fund Minority Engring. Students, 1980-81; mem. acad. adv. bd. U.S. Naval Acad., 1975-79; past chmn. Tex. Com. Employer Support of Guard and Res.; past chmn. Tex. Sci. and Tech. Coun.; chmn. Ind. Commn. for Higher Edn., 1994—; bd. dirs. CUNY Rsch. Found., 1994-97. With USMCR, 1943-46. Recipient Leather medal Sigma Delta Chi, Disting. Svc. medal Dept. Def., 1985; named Ind. Engr. of Yr., 1979, Purdue Disting. Alumnus, 1979. Fellow AAAS; mem. NAE, Gas Rsch. Inst. (chmn. adv. coun. 1976-79), Sigma Xi, Eta Kappa Nu, Pi Tau Sigma, Tau Beta Pi, Phi Kappa Phi, Omicron Delta Kappa, Phi Eta Sigma, Kappa Kappa Psi. Home: 815 Sugarbush Rdg Zionsville IN 46077-1911

HANSEN, ARTHUR MAGNE, engineering and manufacturing executive; b. N.Y.C., Apr. 19, 1946; s. Magne S. and Astrid M. Hansen; m. Ann E. Heisinger, Apr. 3, 1971; 3 children. BSME, N.J. Inst. Tech., 1968. With Foster Wheeler Corp., Livingston, N.J., 1968-82, 84-89, field service engr., 1968-71, distbn. mgr. Pitts. br., 1971-73, dept. mgr., Livingston, 1976-79, dir. svcs. and design, 1979-80, exec. v.p., 1984-89; pres., chief ops. officer Foster Wheeler Ltd., St. Catherine, Ont., Can., 1981-82, also bd. dirs.; pres., chief exec. officer Foster Wheeler Energy Corp., Clinton, N.J., 1990-95, also bd. dirs., chmn., v.p., chief engr.; v.p., chief engr. Wheeler Energy Internat., 1995—; bd. dirs. Generadones de Vapor FW, Spain. Mem. ASME (assoc.). Office: Foster Wheeler Energy Internat Perryville Corporate Park Clinton NJ 08809-4000*

HANSEN, BARBARA CALEEN, physiology educator, scientist; b. Boston, Nov. 24, 1941; d. Reynold L. and Dorothy (Richardson) Caleen; m. Kenneth Dale Hansen, Oct. 8, 1976; 1 son, David Scott. B.S., UCLA, 1964, M.S., 1965; Ph.D., U. Wash., 1971. Asst. prof. then assoc. prof. U. Wash., Seattle, 1971-76; prof., assoc. dean U. Mich., Ann Arbor, 1977-82; assoc. v.p. acad. affairs and research, dean grad. sch. So. Ill. U., Carbondale, 1982-85; v.p. for grad. studies and research U. Md., Balt. and Baltimore County, 1985-90; prof. physiology, dir. obesity and diabetes rsch. ctr. U. Md., 1990—; mem. adv. com. to dir. NIH, Washington, 1979-83; mem. joint health policy com. Assn. Am. Univs., Nat. Assn. State Univs. and Land-Grant Colls., Am. Coun. on Edn., Washington, 1982-86; mem. nutrition study sect. NIH, 1979-83; mem. program com. Inst. Medicine-NAS, Washington, 1982-84; mem. Armed Forces Epidemiology Bd., 1991-95, Bd. Sci. Counselors, Nat. Toxicology Bd., NIEHS, NIH, 1992-94; mem. search com. Office of Rsch. Integrity, NIH, 1992-93. Author: The Commonsense Guide to Weight Loss for People with Diabetes, 1998; editor: Controversies in Obesity, 1983; chpts. on physiology; contbr. articles to profl. jours. Mem. adv. com. Am. Bur. Med. Advancement China, N.Y.C., 1982-85, Robert Wood Johnson Found., Princeton, N.J., 1982-91; mem. adv. bd. African-Am. Inst. 1987-91. U. Pa. Inst. Neurosci. fellow, 1966-68; Arthur Patch McKinley scholar of Phi Beta Kappa, 1964. Mem. Am. Physiol. Soc., Inst. Medicine of NAS, Am. Soc. for Nutritional Scis., Am. Soc. for Clin. Nutrition (v.p., pres.-elect 1994-95, pres. 1995-96), Internat. Assn. for Study of Obesity (pres. 1986-90), N.Am. Assn. for Study of Obesity (pres. 1984-85, 86—), Nat. Assn. State Univs. and Land Grant Colls. (chaiperson coun. on rsch. policy and grad. edn. 1986-87), Phi Beta Kappa. Republican. Presbyterian. Achievements include discovery of periodic (10-14 min.) cycling pattern of pancreas insulin secretion; identification of the pattern of progressive defects in insulin secretion and insulin action preceding overt clinical type 2 diabetes mellitus; showed prevention of obesity prevents most type 2 diabetes. Office: U Md-Balt Sch Medicine Obesity-Diabetes Rsch Ctr 10 S Pine St MSTF 600 Baltimore MD 21201-1116*

HANSEN, BERNARD J., alderman; b. Nov. 26, 1944; m. Annette; children: Paul, David. Student, Wrights Jr. Coll. Dep. sheriff; ward supt. dept. streets and sanitation City of Chgo., alderman ward 44, 1983—; chmn. Econ. and Capital Devel. Com.; mem. Budget and Govt. Ops. Com., Rules and Ethics Com., Fin. Com., Human Rels. Com., Spl. Events and Cultural Affairs Com., Zoning Com. Office: 1057 W Belmont Ave Chicago IL 60657-3327*

HANSEN, BEVERLY ANNE, environmental policy educator; b. Johnson City, N.Y., Jan. 12, 1955; d. Robert Charles and Doris Therese Frankis; m. Emerson Wade Hansen, June 19, 1982; children: Katie, Alyssa, Erin. BS in Biology, Niagara U., 1977; MS in Environ. Sci., SUNY, Syracuse, 1984; MBA, Syracuse U., 1984; postgrad., SUNY, Syracuse, 1994-97. Cert. tchr., N.Y. Microbiologist Syracuse Rsch. Corp., 1979-82, Packaging Cons. Internat., Inc., Syracuse, 1984-86, 92-94, 1997-98; rschr. Randolph G. Pack Environ. Inst., Syracuse, 1996, 98, 99; part-time prof. SUNY, Oswego, 1994—; part-time instr. SUNY Coll. Environ. Scis. and Forestry, Syracuse, 1998. Co-editor jour. Adirondacks and Beyond, 1998. Mem. ASPA, Am. Polit. Sci. Assn., Democrat. Roman Catholic. E-mail: ewh3@juno.com. Home: 3306 Tuccamore Cir Baldwinsville NY 13027

HANSEN, C. LEROY, judge. BS, U. Iowa, 1956; JD, U. N.Mex., 1961. Judge U.S. Dist. Ct. N.Mex., 1992—. Office: US Courthouse Ste 660 333 Lomas Blvd NW Albuquerque NM 87102

HANSEN, CARL R., management consultant, b. Chgo., May 2, 1926; s. Carl M. and Anna C. (Roge) H.; m. Christia Marie Loeser, Dec. 31, 1952; 1 child, Lothar. MBA, U. Chgo., 1954. Dir. market rsch. Kitchens of Sara Lee, Deerfield, Ill., Earle Ludgin & Co., Chgo.; svc. v.p. Market Rsch. Corp. Am., 1956-67; pres. Chgo. Assoc. Inc., 1967—. Chmn. Ill. adv. coun. SBA, 1973-74; mem. exec. com. Ill. Gov.'s Adv. Coun., 1969-72; resident officer U.S. High Commn. Germany, 1949-52; vice chmn. Rep. Cen. Com. Cook County; chmn. Cook County Young Reps., 1957-58, 12th Congl. Dist. Rep. Orgn., 1971-74, 78-82, Suburban Rep. Orgn., 1974-78, 82-86; del. Rep. Nat. Conv., 1968, 84, 92; chmn. Legis. Dist. Ill., 1964—; del. Rep. State Conv., 1962-96; Elk Grove Twp. Rep. committeeman, 1962—; pres. John Ericsson Rep. League Ill., 1975-76; Rep. presdl. elector Ill., 1972; chmn. Viking Ship Restoration Com., mem. Cook County Bd. Commrs., 1970, 74—, chmn. legis. com., adminstrn. com.; mem. bd. dirs. Nat. Assn. Counties; mem. Am. Scandinavian Found. 1st lt. AUS, 1944-48, maj. Res. Mem. Am. Mktg. Assn., Am. Statis. Assn., Nat. Assn. Counties (dir.), Res. Officers Assn., Chgo. Hist. Soc., Planning Forum, Am. Legion, VFW, Dania Soc., Sons of Norway, Swedish Am. Hist. Soc., Lions, Masons, Shriners. Home: 110 S Edward St Mount Prospect IL 60056-3414 Office: 118 N Clark St Chicago IL 60602-1304

HANSEN, CHARLES, lawyer; b. Jersey City, May 23, 1926; s. Charles Henry and Katherine (Bensch) H.; m. Carolyn P. Smith, Sept. 26, 1953; children: Mark, Melissa. B.S., U. Mich., 1946; J.D., Mich. Law Sch., 1950. Bar: N.Y. 1951, Wis. 1961, Mo. 1980. Engr. Westinghouse Electric Co., 1946; assoc. Mudge, Stern, Williams & Tucker, 1950-53; chief labor counsel, div. counsel Sylvania Electric Products, 1953-61; sec., gen. counsel Trane Co., La Crosse, Wis., 1961-69, exec. v.p., 1968-73; pres. Cutler-Hammer World Trade, Inc., 1973-77; v.p. Cutler-Hammer, Inc., 1973-77, exec. v.p., 1977-79; sr. v.p. law Emerson Electric Co., 1979-84, sr. v.p., sec., gen. counsel, 1984-89; ptnr. Bryan Cave, 1989-95, of counsel, 1995—; adj. prof. Sch. Law St. Louis U., 1987—. Served to lt. (j.g.) USNR, 1943-46. Mem. ABA, Wis., Mo. bar assns., Am. Law Inst., Order of Coif, Tau Beta Pi. Home: 8 Wydown Ter Saint Louis MO 63105-2217 Office: 211 N Broadway 1 Metropolitan Sq Ste 3000 Saint Louis MO 63102-2750

HANSEN, CHARLES MORTON, genealogy editor, retired military officer; b. Huntington Park, Calif., Sept. 27, 1933; s. Andrew Hansen and Lena S. Andrew. BA in History, UCLA, 1955; MA in History, San Francisco State U., 1985. Commd. 2d lt. U.S. Army, 1955, advanced through grades to col., 1977; platoon leader U.S. Army, Korea, 1957-59; sr. adv. U.S. Army, Viet Nam, 1965-66; ret. U.S. Army, 1982; contbg. editor The Am. Genealogist, 1988—; editor The Genealogist, 1996—. Contbr. articles to profl. jours. Decorated Legion of Merit, Bronze star, Combat Infantry Badge, Cross of Gallantry Republic of Vietnam; recipient Coddington award for Merit New England Hist. Geneaol. Soc., 1995. Fellow Am. Soc. of Genealogists; mem. Soc. of Genealogists (London), Heraldry Soc. (London), Soc. Heraldica Scandinavia (Denmark), Ninth Infantry Regiment Assn., Harbor Point Racquet Club. Methodist. Avocation: tennis. Home: 25 Rodeo Ave 22 Sausalito CA 94965-1783

HANSEN, CHERRY A. FISHER, special education educator; b. Jackson, Minn., Nov. 9, 1951; d. Marlo Argene and Mary Ellen (Walsh) Fisher; m. Paul Herbert Hansen, June 26, 1977; children: Angela, Rachel. BA, U. No. Iowa, 1974; MS, Drake U., 1994. Cert. tchr., Iowa, cons. endorsement behavior disorders. Tchr. of emotionally disturbed Pottawattamie County Agy., Council Bluffs, Iowa, 1974-76; behavior disorders tchr. Council Bluffs (Iowa) Cmty. Schs., 1974-78, 87-91; adult edn. tchr. Iowa Western C.C., Council Bluffs, 1984-86; behavior disorders tchr. Area Edn. Agy. # 13, Council Bluffs, 1991—, state para conv. com., summer 1997, compliance writing com., fall 1997, lead tchr., 1994—. Mem. altar guild, com. head, Bible sch. St. John's Luth. Ch., Honey Creek, Iowa; treas. LWML Evening Group, 1997; del., rep. Camp Okoboji; mem. bd. dirs. Human Care. Avocations: antiquing, sewing, stained glass, crafts, cooking. Home: 30063 Coldwater Ave Honey Creek IA 51542-4187

HANSEN, CHRISTIAN ANDREAS, JR., plastics and chemical company executive; b. New Braunsfels, Tex., Sept. 12, 1926; s. Christian Andreas and Velma Arbeda (Ivy) H.; m. Emily Dann; B.S., Rice U., 1948; Exec. With Exxon, 21 years, last position gen. mgr., Linden, N.J.; dir. mfg. chem. div. G.A.F. Corp., N.Y.C., 1969-71; chmn. bd., chief exec. officer, pres., founder Hanlin Group, Inc., Linden Chlorine Products, Inc., 1971-93; LCP/Nat. Plastics, Inc., 1977-93; retired, 1993.; chmn. Chem. Industry Council N.J., Trenton, 1977-82; mem. N.J. Gov.'s Commn. on Hazardous Waste Disposal. Founder, chmn., CEO, pres. Pathways, Inc., 1994—; Hansen Plastics, Inc., 1994—; real estate agent Weichert Realtors, N.J.; pres. Union County (N.J.) United Fund, 1967-69; councilman City of Baytown (Tex.), 1961-63; leader Boy Scouts, Sea Scouts. Served to lt. USNR, 1943-46. Named Man of the Year, Union County United Fund, 1970. Mem. Am. Inst. Chem. Engrs., Chlorine Inst. (past pres., past bd. dirs.), Eastern Union County C. of C. (v.p. 1968-69). Pub.: God's Bible and Jesus' Papers, 1994; patentee in field. Home and Office: 1 Scenic Dr Highlands NJ 07732-1329

HANSEN, CHRISTOPHER AGNEW, lawyer; b. Yakima, Wash., Dec. 10, 1934; s. Raymond Walter and Christine F.M. (Agnew) H.: m. Sandra Ridgely Pindell, Aug. 4, 1959; Anne Ridgely, Christopher Agnew Jr., Eric Bruce. BS, Cornell U., 1957; JD, U. Md., 1963. Bar: Md. 1963, U.S. Supreme Ct. 1973, U.S. Ct. Appeals (4th cir.) D.C. 1978. Law clk. Cir. Ct. for Balt. County, Towson, Md., 1960-63; assoc. Piper & Marbury, Balt., 1963-74; pvt. practice Towson, 1974-83, 95—; of counsel Casey, Scott, Canfield & Heggestad PC, Washington, 1982-93, Heggestad & Weiss, PC, Washington, 1993—; ptnr. Constable, Alexander & Skeen, Towson, 1984-86, Parks, Hansen & Ditch, Towson, 1986-94. With U.S. Army, 1957-60. Mem. ABA, D.C. Bar, Md. State Bar Assn., Bar Assn. Balt. County, Balt. City Bar Assn., Md. Assn. Def. Trial Counsel, Phi Alpha Delta. Episcopalian. Office: 7313 York Rd Ste 200 Towson MD 21204-7617

HANSEN, CLAIRE V., financial executive; b. Thornton, Iowa, June 3, 1925; s. Charles F. and Grace B. (Miller) H.; m. Renee C. Hansen, Aug. 17, 1946; children: Charles James, Christopher David, Peter Chrissis. BSc, U. Notre Dame, 1947; MBA, Harvard U., 1948. Chartered fin. analyst. With Salk, Ward & Salk, Inc.; v.p. Salk Inst. Agency, 1954-59; with Duff, Anderson & Clark, Chgo., 1959-67; v.p., dir. Duff, Anderson & Clark, 1967-71; dir. Duff and Phelps, Inc., 1972-88; exec. v.p. Duff & Phelps, 1973-75, pres., chief exec. officer, 1975-84, chmn., chief exec. officer, 1984-87; chmn., bd. dirs. Duff & Phelps Utilities Income, Inc., Chgo., 1987—. Bd. dirs. Chgo. Lung Assn., 1962-80, pres. 1973-75; bd. dirs. Am. Lung Assn., 1971-83, Ctr. Religion and Psychotherapy in Chgo., 1979-83; trustee Glenwood Sch. for Boys, 1974-95, chmn., 1983-87; bd. dirs. Auditorium Theatre Coun., 1983-88, treas., 1987-88; bd. dirs. Schwab Rehab. Hosp., 1978-82, pres., 1980-82; bd. dirs. Pelican Bay Found. Inc., 1993-99, treas., 1993-96, pres., 1996-97. Mem. Inst. Chartered Fin. Analysts, Mid-Am. Club, Univ. Club, Chgo. Club, Olympia Fields Country Club, Club Pelican Bay, Hole-in-the-Wall Golf Club. Republican. Episcopalian. Home: 5601 Turtle Bay Dr Apt 2001 Naples FL 34108-2703 Office: 55 W Monroe St Ste 3600 Chicago IL 60603-5011

HANSEN, CURTIS LEROY, federal judge; b. 1933. BS, U. Iowa, 1956; JD, U. N.Mex., 1961. Bar: N.Mex. Law clk. to Hon. Irwin S. Moise N.Mex. Supreme Ct., 1961-62; ptnr. Snead & Hansen, Albuquerque, 1962-64, Richard C. Civerolo, Albuquerque, 1964-71, Civerolo, Hansen & Wolf, P.A., 1971-92; dist. judge U.S. Dist. Ct., N.Mex., 1992—. Mem. State Bar N.Mex., Albuquerque Bar Assn., Am. Coll. Trial Lawyers, Am. Bd. Trial Advocates, Albuquerque Country Club. Office: US Courthouse Chambers 660 333 Lomas Blvd NW Albuquerque NM 87102

HANSEN, DAVID RASMUSSEN, federal judge; b. 1938. BA, N.W. Mo. State U., 1960; JD, George Washington U., 1963. Asst. clk. to minority House Appropriations Com. Ho. of Reps., 1960-61; adminstrv. aide 7th Dist. Iowa, 1962-63; pvt. practice law Jones, Cambridge & Carl, Atlantic, Iowa, 1963-64; capt., judge advocate General's Corps U.S. Army, 1964-68; pvt. practice law Barker, Hansen & McNeal, Iowa Falls, Iowa, 1968-76; ptnr. Win-Gin Farms, Iowa Falls, 1971—; judge Police Ct., Iowa, 1969-73, 2d Jud. Dist. Iowa Dist. Ct., 1976-86, U.S. Dist. Ct. (no. dist.) Iowa, Cedar Rapids, 1986-91, U.S. Ct. Appeals (8th cir.), Cedar Rapids, 1991—. Office: US Courthouse 101 1st St SE Cedar Rapids IA 52401*

HANSEN, DONALD CURTIS, retired manufacturing executive; b. Marinette, Wis., Mar. 13, 1929; s. Curtis Albert and Dagmar Anne (Johnson) H.; m. Joan Mary Crant, Nov. 9, 1973. BBA, Carroll Coll., 1952. Purchasing agt. Prescott/Sterling Co., Menominee, Mich., 1954-62; mfrs. rep. Don C. Hansen Assocs., Phoenix, 1962-63; sales mgr. Karolton Envelope Co., San Francisco, 1964-72; owner, pres. San Francisco Envelope Co., 1972-79; owner Curtis Swann Cards, San Francisco, 1977-79; pres., owner Don C. Hansen, Inc. (doing bus. as The Envelope Co.), Oakland, Calif., 1979-95; ret., 1995. Mgr., organizer Twin City Civic Chorus, Menominee, 1959; bd. dirs. Menominee C. of C., 1958. Served with U.S. Army, 1952-54. Mem. Envelope Printing Specialists Assn. (bd. dirs. 1983—, pres. 1983-84), Envelope Mfrs. Assn. Am., San Francisco Lithograph and Craftsmans Club, Printing Industries of No. Calif. (bd. dirs. 1980-94), San Francisco Tennis Club (bd. govs. 1989-92), Terravita Country Club (Scottsdale, Ariz.; bd. dirs. 1997-98), Masons, Shriners, Desert Foothills Bridge Club (mgr. 1998—). Republican. Avocations: tennis, skiing, bridge, golf, dominoes.

HANSEN, DONALD MARTY, journalist, accountant; b. Elmhurst, Ill., July 6, 1935; s. Donald Joseph Hansen and Vivian Leona (Bourgart) Guthrie; m. Rose Ann Baumeister, Aug. 12, 1961 (div.); children: Teresa Lynn, Donna Louise, David Lawrence, Daniel Leonard. Assoc. in Acctg., Racine Tech., 1971. Drill press operator J.I. Case Co., Racine, Wis., 1964-70; acct. Scott Petersen Meat Co., Chgo., 1974-95, Crosby Freezer, Inc., Chgo., 1995—; editor, pub. Don Hansen's Nat. Weekly Football and Basketball Gazettes, Brookfield, Ill., 1987—; columnist USA Today Online, 1998—; stringer Football News, Miami, 1981—, The Sporting News, St. Louis, 1987—, USA Today, Arlington, Va., 1987—; mem. Melberger award selection com. Downtown Wilkes-Barre Touchtown Club, 1993—; mem. com. for NCAA Divsn. III Player of the Yr., John Gagliardi award, 1993—. Contbr. articles to profl. jours. Originator, promoter, operator annual summer wrestling tournament Oak Park-River Forest (Ill.) H.S., 1978-80; mem. selection com. Farm All-Am. Football Team, 1999—; mem. selection com. NCAA Divsn. II Hall of Fame Football, 1999—. With USN, 1952-54. Recipient Leadership trophy Chase Park (Chgo.), 1947, Celebrity Cert. of Appreciation ARC, 1992, Statistician of the Yr. Oak Park-River Forest H.S., 1981. Mem. CO-SIDA Coll. Sports Info. Dirs. Am. Republican. Mem. Assembly of God Ch. e-mail: fbgazette@thc.to; website: www.thc.to/fbgazette. Home: 8802 45th Pl Apt 11 Brookfield IL 60513-2563 Office: Don Hansen's Nat Weekly Football Gazette PO Box 514 Brookfield IL 60513-0514

HANSEN, DONALD W., insurance and financial services executive; b. Chgo., June 9, 1924; s. Chris M. and Violet Louise (Anderson) H.; m. Nancy SanRoman, Dec. 21, 1944; children: Donald W. II, Scott D., Debra Anne. B.S. in Bus. and Econs, Ill. Inst. Tech., 1948; postgrad., U. Chgo. Grad. Sch. Bus., 1957. Fin. rep., mgr. bank relations Comml. Credit Co., Chgo., 1948-57; pres. Sears Roebuck Acceptance Co., Wilmington, Del., 1957-63; v.p. fin. services Allstate Ins. Co., 1963-75, v.p. money center and banking adminstrn., 1971-76; pres. Allstate Fin. Corp., 1964-74; chmn. bd. Allstate Savs. & Loan Assn., 1963-66; pres., chief exec. officer Allstate Enterprises Mortgage Corp., Anaheim, Calif., 1972-74, First Farwest Corp., Portland, Oreg., 1976-78, Midwestern United Life Ins. Co., Ft. Wayne, Ind., 1978-83, United Equitable Corp., Lincolnwood, Ill., 1983-86; pvt. practice fin. services cons. Scottsdale, Ariz., 1986—. Active Young Pres. Orgn., 1959-73. Served to 1st lt. AUS, 1943-46. Mem. Scottsdale Young Country Club, Internat. Portland City Club, Baja Beach and Tennis Club (Punta Bonda, Baja, Mex.). Republican. Presbyterian. Home: 11040 N 77th St Scottsdale AZ 85260-5564

HANSEN, DONNA LAUREE, court reporting educator; b. Concordia, Kans., Dec. 25, 1939; d. Peter August and Lynda Bernice (Carlson) H. BA, Bethany Coll., 1961; MS, Kans. State U., 1986. Cert. tchr., Kans., notary pub., Kans. Tchr. Munden (Kans.) High Sch., 1961-64; instr. typing Brown Mackie Coll., Salina, Kans., 1964-74, instr. ct. reporting, 1974-77, chair ct. reporting, 1977-88, 96-98, cons., instr., 1989—, chair med. office dept., 1998—; instr. shorthand workshop Pittsburg (Kans.) State U., 1978, Emporia (Kans.) State U., 1978; adminstr. social work spl. project City of Camden, N.J., summers 1962, 63. Compiler (books) Court Reporting Procedures, 1981, Court Reporting Theory Review Books 1, 2, 3, 1983, Court Reporting Advanced Theory Review, Vols. I, II, III, 1984. Bd. dirs. YWCA, Salina, 1991-93, membership chair, 1992-93; mem. alumni bd. Bethany Coll., Lindsborg, Kans., 1979-81. Mem. AAUW (pres 1995-97, numerous offices, Outstanding Mem. 1980), Kans. Bus. Tchrs. Assn., Nat. Bus. Tchrs. Assn., Kans. Shorthand Reporters Assn., Nat. Shorthand Reporters, Delta Kappa Gamma (numerous offices). Republican. Lutheran. Avocations: reading, swimming, cooking, sewing. Office: Brown Mackie Coll 126 S Santa Fe Ave Salina KS 67401-2810

HANSEN, ELAINE T., academic administrator. AB with greatest distinction cum laude, Mt. Holyoke Coll., 1969; MA, U. Minn., 1972; PhD, U. Wash., 1975. Asst. editor Mid. English dictionary U. Mich., 1975-77, assoc. rsch. editor, 1978-80; from asst. prof. to assoc. prof. dept. English Haverford (Pa.) Coll., 1980-90, dept. chair, 1989-92, prof. dept. English, 1991—, provost, 1995—; lectr. in field. Author: The Solomon Complex: Reading Wisdom in Old English Poetry, 1988, Chaucer and the Fictions of Gender, 1992, Mother Without Child: Contemporary Fiction and the Crisis of Motherhood, 1997; mem. editl. bd. Coll. Lit.; reader manuscripts for jours. and univ. presses; contbr. articles to profl. jours., also revs. and papers. NEH Summer stipendee, 1981; Mellon grantee for faculty devel. in humanities, 1983-84, Whitehead grantee for faculty in the humanities, 1987-88; Am. Coun. Learned Socs. fellow, 1993-94. Mem. MLA (mem. Chaucer divsn. exec. com. 1995—, divsn. rep. to del. assembly 1996—, com. on acad. freedom and profl. rights and responsibilities 1997—), Am. Coun. Learned Socs. (prescreener Cen. Fellowship Program), Medieval Acad., New Chaucer Soc., Nat. Women's Studies Assn., Soc. for Feminist Medieval Scholarship (pres. 1993-95). Office: Haverford Coll 370 Lancaster Ave Haverford PA 19041

HANSEN, ELIZABETH JEAN, appraiser, author; b. Redwood City, Calif., Sept. 14, 1930; d. Conrad and Macil (Gibbsen) H. Postgrad., U. So. Calif., L.A. Antique entrepreneur, appraiser, estate liquidator, 1961—; founder, owner Hansen's Assn. Appraisers and Liquidators, Watsonville, Calif., 1972-89. Contbg. writer antique pubs. including The West Coast Peddler, Antique Today, Tri-State Weekly, Arts and Antiques mag., Antiques and Collecting Hobbies mag., Antique Dealer, Art and Antique Adventure, Antique Gazette's eastern pub., others; author: Furniture Manuals Vol. I-V, Appraisal Manuals Vol. I and II, Oriental Art Manual Vol. I-IV, Book of Marks, Porcelain/Pottery, 15 State of the Art manuals of bus. and antiques, Porcelain Manual Vol. I, Silver Manual Vol. I and II, Art and Pattern Glass Manual Vol. I, Jewelry Manuals Vol. I-IV, Textile Manual Vol. I and II, Cut Glass Working Manual, Business Manuals Vol. I-V, Code of Ethics and Standards for Appraisers. Recipient Cert. of Merit for Disting. Svc., Cambridge, Eng., 1988. Office: 49 Blanca Ln Spc 305 Watsonville CA 95076-2155

HANSEN, ENID EILEEN, secondary education educator; b. Daykin, Nebr., Aug. 5, 1943; d. Albert Carl and Irene Marie (Houser) M.; m. Gary Allen Hansen, Mar. 28, 1964;children: Rachelle, Galen, Bryan. BA, U. Nebr., Kearney, 1964, MA, 1992. Cert. secondary sch. tchr. English, comm., drama, Nebr. Tchr. English, Chester-Hubbel H.S., Chester, Nebr., 1964-65; tchr. lang. arts and vocal music Ruskin (Nebr.) H.S., 1965-66; tchr. English and speech Sandy Creek H.S., Fairfield, Nebr., 1987—. Recipient Christa McAuliffe recognition Lincoln Jour. Star, 1996, Tchr. Achievement award for excellence in classroom tchg. Peter Kiewit Assn., 1998. Mem. Music Tchrs. Assn., Nebr. Music Tchrs. Assn., Nat. Piano Guild, Nat Coun. Tchrs. English, Nebr. English and Lang. Arts Coun., Nebr. Comm. and Theatre Assn., Delta Kappa Gamma.

HANSEN, ERIC LLOYD, accountant; b. Hastings, Nebr., Jan. 1, 1949; s. William Lloyd and Dorothy Barbara (Uerling) H.; m. Lana Jean Perry; children: Kelly, Timothy. BBA, U. Kans., 1971, JD, 1974. CPA, Mo. Tax staff Touche, Ross & Co., Kansas City, Mo., 1974-78, supr., 1978-80, mgr., 1980-84, ptnr., 1984—. Pres. Trinity Luth. Found., Shawnee Mission, Kans., 1986—. Mem. Am. Inst. CPA's, Mo. Soc. CPA's, Kansas City Bar Assn. Avocation: golf. Home: 7514 Caenen Lake Dr Shawnee Mission KS 66216-3082 Office: Touche Ross & Co 1010 Grand Suite 400 Kansas City MO 64106

HANSEN, FLORENCE MARIE CONGIOLOSI (MRS. JAMES S. HANSEN), social worker; b. Middletown, N.Y., Jan. 7, 1934; d. Joseph James and Florence (Harrigan) Congiolosi; m. James S. Hansen, June 16, 1959 (dec. Nov. 1989); 1 child, Florence M. BA, Coll. New Rochelle, 1955; MSW, Fla. State U., 1960; PhD, Union Inst., 1992. Caseworker, Orange County Dept. Pub. Welfare, N.Y., 1955-57, Cath. Welfare Bur., Miami, Fla., 1957-58; supr. Cath. Family Service, Spokane, Wash., 1960, Cuban Children's Program, Spokane, 1962-66; founder, dir. social service dept. Sacred Heart Med. Ctr., 1968-85, dir. Kidney Ctr., 1967-91. Asst. in program devel. St. Margaret's Hall, Spokane, 1961-62; trustee Family Counseling Svc. Spokane County, 1981—, also bd. dirs.; mem. budget allocation panel United Way, 1964-76, mem. planning com., 1968-77, mem. admissions com., 1969-70, chmn. projects com. 1972-73; mem. kidney disease adv. com. Wash.-Alaska Regional Med. Program, 1970-73. Mem. Spokane Quality of Life Commn., 1974-75; vol. Primary Health Care Nangoma Health Ctr., 1992—; cons. CARE Internat., Zambia, 1993-95. Recipient Ursula Laurus citation Coll. New Rochelle, 1990, Angela Merici medal, 1995. Mem. Nat. Assn. Social Workers (Wash. chpt. pres. 1972-74, Wash. State Social Worker of Yr. 1991, Nat. Social Worker of Yr. 1991), Acad. Cert. Social Workers (charter). Roman Catholic. Home: 5609 W Northwest Blvd Spokane WA 99205-2039 Office: Nangoma Health Ctr, Box 830022, Mumbwa Zambia

HANSEN, GRANT LEWIS, retired aerospace and information systems executive; b. Bancroft, Idaho, Nov. 5, 1921; s. Paul Ezra and Leona Sarah (Lewis) H.; m. Iris Rose Heyden, Apr. 21, 1945; children: Alan Lee, Brian Craig, Carol Margaret, David James, Ellen Diane. B.S. in Elec. Engring., Ill. Inst. Tech., 1948; postgrad. engring. and mgmt., UCLA, Calif. Inst. Tech.; D.Sc., Nat. U., 1978. With Douglas Aircraft Co., 1948-60; v.p., program dir. for Centaur (Convair div.), 1960-65; v.p. launch vehicle programs Convair div. Gen. Dynamics Corp., 1965-69, v.p., gen. mgr., 1973-78; asst. sec. air force for research and devel., 1969-73; v.p. Gen. Dynamics Corp., San Diego, 1974-78; exec. v.p. System Devel. Corp., Santa Monica, Calif., 1978-86; also pres. SDC Systems Group, 1978-84; U.S. del. NATO (Adv. Group for Aerospace Research and Devel.), 1969-73; U.S. mem. sci. com. for nat. reps. SHAPE Tech. Center, The Hague, Netherlands, 1969-73; mem. research and tech. adv. council NASA, 1971-73; mem. sci. adv. bd. Dept. Air Force, 1976-86. Served with USNR, World War II. Decorated Purple Heart; recipient Pub. Service award NASA, 1966, Disting. Pub. Service award NASA, 1975, Alumni Recognition award Ill. Inst. Tech., 1967, USAF Exceptional Civilian Service medal, 1973, 83; inducted Ill. Inst. Tech. Hall of Fame, 1984. Fellow AIAA (nat. pres. 1975), Am. Astronautical Soc., AAAS, Internat. Acad. Astronautics; mem. IEEE (sr.), German Soc. Air and Space Travel (corr.), Nat. Acad. Engring., NRC, Eta Kappa Nu, Tau Beta Pi. Home: 10737 Fuerte Dr La Mesa CA 91941-5740 *I've given my whole self to each challenge I've accepted, believing that what's best for my future is an honest day's effort today. I have great faith in my God and my country.*

HANSEN, H. JACK, management consultant; b. Chgo., Mar. 28, 1922; s. Herbert Christian John and Laura Eliabeth (Osterman) H.; m. Joan Dorothy Norum, Nov. 28, 1980; children: Marilyn Joan, Gail Jean, Mark John, Jacquelyn Lee. BSME, Ill. Inst. Tech., 1944. Cert. mgmt. cons. Mech. and indsl. engr. Harper Wyman Co., Chgo., 1944-51; chief indsl. engr. Shakeproof divsn. Ill. Tool Works, Des Plaines, 1951-53; cons., prin. A.T. Kearney & Co., Chgo. and N.Y.C., 1953-71; pres. H.J. Hansen Co., Elburn, Ill., 1971—; acting. mfg. enring. mgr. European operation Hobart Corp., 1974-78; owner, mgmt. cons. Hansen Mgmt. Search Co., Mt. Prospect, Ill., 1980-93. Pioneerd use of Should Cost studies for U.S. Dept. Def., conceptualized and developed procedure for gain sharing productivity improvement; active turnaround cons., 1992—. Mem. Planning Commn., Village of Elburn, 1995-97, trustee, 1997—, chmn. Pers. Commn., mem. Fin. Commn., mem. Pub. Works Commn.; pres. Good Shepherd Luth. Ch., Des Palines, Ill., 1988-90, Men's Club, 1987-90; active mem. mcpl. legis. com. DuKane Valley Coun. With AUS, 1945-46. Mem. Inst. Mgmt. Cons. (founding), Methods-Time Measurement Assn. (bd. dirs. 1964-70, pres. 1967-68), Am. Arbirtion Assn., Soc. Advancement Mgmt. (past bd. dirs.), coun. for Internat. Progress in Mgmt. (past bd. dirs.), Found. Internat. Progress in Mgmt. (past bd. dirs.), Elburn C. of C. Office: H J Hansen Co 317 Prairie Valley St Elburn IL 60119-8977

HANSEN, H. REESE, dean, educator; b. Logan, Utah, Apr. 8, 1942; s. Howard F. and Loila Gayle (Reese) H.; m. Kathryn Traveller, June 8, 1962; children: Brian T., Mark T., Dale T., Curtis T. BS, Utah State U., 1964; JD, U. Utah, 1972. Bar: Utah, 1974. Atty. Strong, Poelman & Fox, Salt Lake City, 1972-74; from asst. prof. to assoc. prof. Brigham Young U., Provo, Utah, 1974-79, prof., 1979—, from asst. dean to assoc. dean, 1974-89, dean, 1989—; commr. ex officio Utah State Bar, Salt Lake City, 1989—; commr. Nat. Conf. Commrs. on Uniform State Laws, 1988-95. Co-author: Idaho Probate System, 1977, Utah Probate System, 1977, Cases and Text on Laws of Trusts, 6th edit., 1991; editor: Manual for Justices of Peace--Utah, 1978; contbr. articles to profl. jours. Mem. LDS Ch. Office: Brigham Young U 348A Jrcb Provo UT 84602-1029

HANSEN, HAL T., investment company executive. Pres. Cargill Investor Svcs., Chgo., ret. 1998; founder Viking Investors Svcs., Lake Forest, Ill., 1998—; exec. cons. CP Risk Mgmt. (subs. Chgo. Ptnrs.), 1998—. Nat. Futures Assn. (former chmn.). *

HANSEN, HAROLD B., JR., principal; b. Sewickley, Pa., July 3, 1955; s. Harold B. and Mary Clara (VanderVort) H.; m. Patty Jo Gabhart, Sept. 19, 1976; children: Jeremiah James, Joshua Andrew, Esther Beth, Christopher Seth. BA in Elem. Edn., Purdue U., 1980; MA in Sch. Adminstrn., Western N.Mex. U., 1987. Cert. secondary lang. arts and spl. edn. tchr., TESL tchr., instrnl. leader, sch. adminstr., elem. tchr., coach, N.Mex. Resource rm. tchr. Flossmoor/Homewood (Ill.) Pub. Schs., 1981, Newcomb (N.Mex.) H.S., 1981-82; tchr. self-contained spl. edn. Chester (Mont.) Pub. Schs., 1982-84; adminstr., prin., tchr. Bennett (Colo.) Bapt. Ch. Sch., 1984; propr., tutor Hemispheric Learning Tutorial Svcs., 1982—; tchr. resource room, coach cross county, wrestling, track and field Gallup-McKinley County Pub. Schs., Tohatchi/Navajo Reserv., N.Mex., 1985-90; elem. tchr. phys. edn. and health, at-risk tchr. Tohatchi Elem. Sch. Gallup-McKinley County Pub. Schs., Tohatchi, 1990-98, 5th grade track & field head coach, 1991-98, 5th grade boys' and girls' basketball asst. coach, 1995-98; prin. Smith Lake Elem. Sch., Gallup-McKinley County Pub. Schs., 1998—; mem. various sch. coms. Gallup-McKinley County Pub. Schs., 1990-98; seminar leader on hemispherecity; dep. registration officer McKinley County, N.Mex., 1986—. Past pres. Village of Hope, substance abuse tng. ctr.; co-founder, past bd. dirs. Christian Home Educators Assn.; dir. Approved Workmen Are Not Ashamed; coord. Jump Rope for Heart, Am. Heart Assn.; mem. Coun. for Curricular Excellence, McKinley County; TESOL rep. for Western N.Mex. U.'s Gallup Grad. Ctr.'s Adv. Coun., 1997—. Named to Outstanding Young Men of Am., 1987. Mem. ASCD, N.Mex. Assn. Health, Phys. Edn., Recreation and Dance, Christian HomeEducators Assn., Aesthetic Realism Found. E-mail: HaniibaazH@aol.com. Fax: 505-786-5542. Home: PO Box 100 Smith Lake NM 87365-0100

HANSEN, HAROLD JOHN (HARRY), artist, educator; b. Chgo., June 18, 1942; s. Harold Melbourne and Florence Marion (O'Connell) H.; m. Martha Dianne Lyon, May 8, 1965; children: Daniel Charles, Susan Elizabeth. BFA, U. Ill., 1964; MFA, U. Mich., 1966. Instr. Kendall Sch. Design, Grand Rapids, Mich., 1966-69; asst. prof. art Ferris State Coll., Big Rapids, Mich., 1969-70; asst. prof. art U. S.C., Columbia, 1970-75, assoc. prof. art, 1975-86, prof. art, 1986—; guest curator S.C. State Mus., Columbia, 1997. Exhibited watercolors and other works at some 60 solo and maj. exhbns. Recipient some 35 awards for art work; grantee S.C. Humanities Coun., 1994-95, S.C. Arts Commn. and NEA, 1975. Mem. S.C. Watercolor Soc. (bd. dirs. 1989—). Office: U SC Dept Art Columbia SC 29208

HANSEN, HUGH JUSTIN, agricultural engineer; b. Thief River Falls, Minn., Mar. 30, 1923; s. Oscar Edward and Othelia C. (Olen) H.; m. JoAnne Skeim, Aug. 28, 1949; children: Susan Marie, Christopher Hugh, Mark Alexander. B.S. in Agrl. Engring, N.D. State U., 1951; M.S., Cornell U., 1952. Asst. prof. agrl. engring. Purdue U., 1952-55; with Reuben H. Donnelley Corp., N.Y.C., 1955-71; pub. Reuben H. Donnelley Corp., 1962-71; group pub. Dun-Donnelly Pub. Corp., N.Y.C., 1971-74; mgr. Western Regional Agrl. Engring. Service, Oreg. State U., Corvallis, 1974-78; extension energy engr. Western Regional Agrl. Engring. Service, Oreg. State U., 1978-90; acting head Agrl. Engring. Dept., June-Nov. 1986; prof. emeritus Oreg. State U., Corvallis, 1990—. Served with USMCR, 1942-46. Fellow Am. Soc. Agrl. Engrs. (bd. dirs. 1964-66, pres. 1971-72); Mem. Am. Soc. Engring. Edn., Am. Agrl. Editors Assn. Home: 3018 NW Lisa Pl Corvallis OR 97330-3216 Office: Oreg State U Bioresources Engring Dept Corvallis OR 97331 *Helping farmers do a good job of producing high quality food and fiber with a minimum of labor and a fair return on their investment with a reasonable profit has been and continues to be my lifetime professional objective.*

HANSEN, JAMES ALLEN, state agency administrator; b. West Point, Nebr., Jan. 10, 1939; s. Walter J. and Dorothy (Kay) H.; m. Janice A. Wenke, June 27, 1964 (div. 1975); m. Rebecca A. Bayer, Nov. 28, 1975. BA, Wayne State Coll., 1965. Pres. Farmers State Bank, Lexington, Nebr., 1972-80, No. Bank, Omaha, 1980-86, 1st Nat. Bank, Fremont, Nebr., 1986-87; regional v.p. Am. First Co., Omaha, 1987-90; mng. agt. FDIC/RTC, Burnsville, Minn., 1990; dir. Nebr. Dept. Banking & Fin., Lincoln, 1991-98; chmn., CEO Centennial Bank, Omaha, 1999—; chmn., bd. dirs. Conf. of State Bank Suprs., Washington, 1992-97. Mem. group study exch. team to Australia, Rotary Internat., 1970. 1st lt. U.S. Army N.G., 1960-66. Home: 1233 S 116th Ave Omaha NE 68144-1717 Office: Centennial Bank 9003 S 145th St Omaha NE 68134

HANSEN, JAMES E., physicist, meteorologist, federal agency administrator; b. Mar. 29, 1941. BA in Physics and Math. with highest distinction, U. Iowa, 1963, MS in Astronomy, 1965; postgrad., U. Kyoto and Tokyo U., 1965-66; PhD in Physics, U. Iowa, 1967. NAS-NRC resident rsch. assoc. Goddard Inst. for Space Studies, N.Y.C., 1967-69; NSF postdoctoral fellow Leiden Observatory, Netherlands, 1969; rsch. assoc. Columbia U., 1969-72; mem. staff, space scientist, mgr. planetary and climate programs Goddard Inst. for Space Studies, 1972-81, head, 1981—; adj. assoc. prof. dept. geol. scis. Columbia U., 1978-85, adj. prof., 1985—; co-prin. investigator AEROPOL Project, 1971-74; co-investigator Voyager Photopolarimeter Experiment, 1972-85; prin. investigator Pioneer Venus Orbiter Cloud-Photopolarimeter Experiment, 1974-78, co-investigator, 1978—; prin. investigator Galileo Photopolarimeter Radiometer Experiment, 1977—, Earth Observing System Interdisciplinary Investigation, 1989—. Author: (with others) Radiation in the Atmosphere, 1978, Carbon Dioxide Review, 1982. Am. Geophys. Union fellow, 1992; recipient Goddard Spl. Achievement award, 1977, Group Achievement award NASA, 1982, 93, Exceptional Svc. medal NASA, 1984, Presdl. Rank award NASA, 1990. Achievements include research in radiative transfer in planetary atmospheres, interpretation of remote sounding of planetary atmospheres, development of simplified climate models and 3-D global climate models, climate mechanisms such as the role of clouds in climate, current climate trends from observational data and projections of man's impact on climate. Office: Goddard Inst Space Studies 2880 Broadway New York NY 10025-7886*

HANSEN, JAMES JOHN, accountant; b. Madison, Wis., Sept. 13, 1971; s. John Charles and Judith Ann (Gust) H. Assoc. degree, Madison (Wis.) Area Tech. Coll, 1991; BS summa cum laude, Edgewood Coll., 1997. Acct. Callahan & Co., Stoughton, Wis., 1991-96; staff acct. Meicher & Assoc., LLP, Madison, Wis., 1996—. Mem. AICPA, Wis. Inst. of CPAs. Avocations: computers. Home: 1406 Frisch Rd Madison WI 53711-3242 Office: Meicher & Assoc LLP 406 Science Dr Ste 310 Madison WI 53711-1068

HANSEN, JAMES LEE, sculptor; b. Tacoma, Wash., June 13, 1925; s. Hildreth Justine and Mary Elizabeth Hansen; m. Annabelle Hair, Aug. 31, 1946 (dec. Sept. 1993); children: Valinda Jean, Yauna Marie; m. Jane Lucas, May 13, 1994. Grad., Portland Art Mus. Sch. Faculty Oreg. State U., Corvallis, 1957-58, U. Calif., Berkeley, 1958, Portland State U., 1964-90. One-man shows include Fountain Gallery, Portland, Oreg., 1966, 69, 77-81, U. Oreg. Art Mus., Eugene, 1970, Seligman (Seders Gallery), Seattle, 1970, Portland Art Mus., 1971, Cheney Cowles Meml. Mus., Spokane, Wash., 1972, Polly Freidlander Gallery, Seattle, 1973, 75-76, Smithsonian Instn., Washington, 1974, Hodges/Banks Gallery (now Linda Hodges Gallery), Seattle, 1983, Abanté Gallery, Portland, 1986, 88, 92, Maryhill Mus. of Art, Goldendale, Wash., 1997-98, Bryan Ohno Gallery, Seattle, 1997; exhibited in group shows at N.W. Ann. Painters and Sculptors, Seattle, 1952-73, Oreg. Ann. Painters and Sculptors, Portland Art Mus., 1952-75, Whitney Mus. Am. Art, N.Y.C., 1953, Santa Barbara (Calif.) Mus. Art, 1959-60, Denver Art Mus., 1960, San Francisco Art Mus., 1960, Smithsonian Instn., Washington, 1974, Wash. State U., Pullman, 1975, Benton County Hist. Mus., 1998; represented in permanent collections Graphic Arts Center, State Capitol, Olympia, Wash., U. Oreg., Eugene, Salem (Oreg.) Civic Center, Clark Coll., Vancouver, Wash., Portland Art Mus., Transit Mall, Portland, Seattle Art Mus., Gresham Town Fair (Oreg.), Oreg. Health Scis. U., Portland, Vancouver Sculpture Park, others; represented by Abanté Gallery, Portland, Hansen Studio, Vancouver, Peter Bartlow Gallery, Chgo., Bryan Ohno Gallery, Seattle. Address: 28219 NE 63rd Ave Battle Ground WA 98604-7107

HANSEN, JAMES VEAR, congressman; b. Salt Lake City, Aug. 14, 1932; s. J. Vear and Sena H.; m. Ann Burgoyne, 1958; children: Susan, Joseph James, David Burgoyne, Paul William, Jennifer. BS, U. Utah, 1960. Mem. Utah Ho. of Reps., 1973-80; spkr. of the house U.S. Ho. of Reps., 1979-80; mem. 97th-106th Congresses from 1st Utah dist., Washington, 1981—; pres. James V. Hansen Ins. Agy., Woodland Springs Devel. Co. Office: Ho of Reps 2466 Rayburn Bldg Washington DC 20515-4401*

HANSEN, JEAN MARIE, math and computer educator; b. Detroit, Mar. 8, 1937; d. Harvey Francis and Ida Marie (Hay) Chapman; m. Donald Edward Hansen, Aug. 29, 1968; children: Jennifer Lynn, John Francis. BA, U. Mich., 1959, MA, 1960. Cert. Secondary Sch. Tchr. Tchr. Detroit Pub. Schs., 1959-60, Newark (Calif.) Sch. Dist., 1960-65, Dept. Def., Zweibruken, Germany, 1965-67, Livonia (Mich.) Pub. Schs., 1967-69; instr. Ford Livonia Transmission Plant, 1990—; trustee/pres. Northville (Mich.) Bd. Edn., 1981—. Author: California People and Their Government, 1965, Voices of Government, 1969-70. Named Disting. Bd. Mem., Mich. Assn. Sch. Bds., 1991, Citizen of Yr., Northville C. of C., 1991. Mem. AAUW (v.p. Northville bd. 1982-86, pres. 1987-89, Mich. chpt. Agt. of Change award, edn. area 1985), LWV, Kiwanis, Northville Women's Club. Republican. Avocations: weaving, basket weaving, skiing, golf, travel. Home: 229 Linden St Northville MI 48167-1426

HANSEN, JOHN HERBERT, university administrator, accountant; b. Milw., Mar. 20, 1945; s. John Herbert and Elsie F. (Patri) H.; m. Christina Ann Laniey, Sept. 5, 1970. BBA, U. Wis., 1969; M in Acctg., U. Ill., 1973. CPA, Wis. Dir. treas. svcs. Marquette U., Milw., 1973—. With USAF, 1970-73. Mem. Am. Inst. CPA's, Milw. Bond Club. Republican. Club: Merrill Hills Country. Avocations: golf, gardening. Office: Marquette U PO Box 1881 Milwaukee WI 53201-1881

HANSEN, JOHN PAUL, metallurgical engineer; b. Bain, Minn., Feb. 11, 1928; s. Charles George and Henrietta Eva (Taylor) H.; m. Doris Alma Dropps, Sept. 9, 1950; children: Steven Michael, Bradley Paul, Kurt Lewis. B.S., U. Minn., 1954, M.S., 1955, Ph.D., 1958. Registered profl. engr., Ala. Metall. engr. U.S. Bur. Mines, Mpls., 1958-63; chief Tuscaloosa Metallurgy Rsch. Lab. U.S. Bur. Mines, Tuscaloosa, 1967-70; prof. metall. engring. U. Ala., University, 1963-87, head chem. and metall. engring. dept., 1970-73; prof. emeritus metall. engring. U. Ala., Tuscaloosa, 1988—; lectr. U. Ala.; cons. Army Missile Command, Ala. Geol. Survey. Served with AUS, 1946-49, 50-52. Mem. AIME, Sigma Xi, Tau Beta Pi, Alpha Sigma Mu, Omega Chi Epsilon. Lutheran. Club: University Faculty (pres. 1973). Research reduction of iron ores and prereduced iron ore pellets. Home: 1245 E Highpoint St Springfield MO 65804-7605

HANSEN, KAREN THORNLEY, accountant; b. Chgo., June 1, 1945. BA, Marycrest Coll., Davenport, Iowa, 1967. CPA, N.Y.; cert. med. technician. Med. staff tech. Mercy Hosp., Davenport, Iowa, 1967-68, St. Joseph Hosp., Chgo., 1968, Spl. Hematology, Wilford Hall, USAF Hosp., Lackland AFB, Tex., 1973-78; staff acct. Lewittes & Co., Poughkeepsie, N.Y., 1980-81; sr. acct. Urbach, Kahn & Werlin, Poughkeepsie, 1981-82; ptnr. Hansen & Dunn, CPA's, Poughkeepsie, 1982-94, Hansen & Arnold, Poughkeepsie, 1995—. Bd. dirs., sec. United Way Dutchess County, Poughkeepsie, 1988—; bd. dirs. YMCA Dutchess County, Girl Scouts U.S.A., 1983-87, Mid-Hudson Civic Ctr., Inc., 1993-95; mem. Jr. League Poughkeepsie, 1979—; bd. dirs. Civic Properties, Inc., 1992—; mem. membership com. and econ. devel. com. Poughkeepsie Partnership, Inc.; trustee St. Martin de Porres Ch. Mem. AICPA, N.Y. State Soc. CPAs, Greater Poughkeepsie Area C. of C. (bd. dirs. 1986—, 1st vice chair 1996, chair, 1997, sec. exec. com. 1991, Amrita Club (bd. dirs. 1982-92, pres. 1990), Poughkeepsie Tennis Club. Republican. Roman Catholic. Office: Hansen & Arnold 309 Main Mall Poughkeepsie NY 12601-3116

HANSEN, KENNETH D., lawyer, ophthalmologist; b. Seattle, Mar. 26, 1947; s. George R. and Elaine D. (Jacobsen) H.; m. Barbara Caleen, Oct. 8, 1976; 1 son, David Scott. BS in Psychology, U. Wash., 1969, JD, 1972, MD with honors, 1976. Bar: Wash. 1972, Mich. 1977, Ill. 1984, D.C. 1986, U.S. Supreme Ct. 1981. Diplomate Am. Bd. Ophthalmology. Legal counsel Assn. Wash. Bus., Olympia, 1972-73; asst. atty. gen. State of Wash., Seattle, 1973-74; v.p., gen. counsel Northwest Med. Rsch. Found. Seattle, 1976-86; pres. Internat. Health Found., 1986—; intern medicine U. Mich. Hosp., Ann Arbor, 1977, resident in ophthalmology, 1978-80; sr. med. staff Henry Ford Hosp., Detroit, 1981-82; dir. ophthalmology Carbondale Clinic, Ill., 1983-86, chmn. dept. surgery, gen. counsel, 1984-86; clin. asst. prof. ophthalmology and med. humanities So. Ill. U., Carbondale 1983-86; clin. asst. prof. ophthalmology U. Md., Balt., 1986—; med.-legal adv. com. U. Mich. Hosp. System; cons. Nat. Def. Med. Coll., China; charter coun. mem. practicing physicians adv. coun. to Sec. of U.S. Dept. Health and Human Svcs., 1992-97; internat. med.-legal lectr. Assoc. editor Trauma, 1995—. Recipient U. Wash. Med. Thesis Award, Gold Medal Egyptian Med. Syndicate, 1986; William Wallice Wilshire Meml. scholar; Anna C. Dunlap Meml. scholar; Grad. Research fellow, 1975—; recipient Red Rose award Soc. Rsch. Adminstrs., 1989. Fellow Am. Coll. Legal Medicine (jud. council, model statutes com., Pres's. award 1989), Internat. Coll. Surgeons; mem. ABA, AMA, Wash. State Bar Assn. Mich. Bar Assn., Ill. Med. Soc. (med.-legal council), Ill. Bar Assn., Mich. Med. Schs. Council Deans (med.-legal adv. com.), Mich. Ophthalmology Soc. (research award 1981), Am. Acad. Ophthalmology, D.C. Bar Assn., Phi Delta Pi, Phi Eta Sigma, Pi Sigma Epsilon. Baptist. Assoc. editor Wash. Law Rev., 1971-72; contbr. articles to legal and med. profl. jours., publs. Home: 6501 Bright Mountain Rd Mc Lean VA 22101-1701 Office: 4601 Fairfax Dr Ste 100 Arlington VA 22203-1524

HANSEN, KENT, public relations professional, consultant; b. Alliance, Ohio, Dec. 1, 1947; s. Robert Kent and Sue (Shiflet) H.; m. Grace Goffredo, Oct. 30, 1971; children: Emily, Melissa, Gabriel, Megan, P.J., Katie. BA in History/Theater Arts, U. of State of N.Y., 1988; MS in Human Resource Mgmt., Chapman U., 1991. Commd. ensign USN, 1967, advanced through grades to chief petty officer; pub. affairs officer Naval Air Res. Unit, Whidbey Island, Wash., 1977-81; pub. affairs office mgr. USS Coral Sea, Alameda, Calif., 1981-83; chief of bur. Pacific Stars and Stripes, Tokyo, 1983-86; dep. pub. affairs officer Comdr. U.S. Naval Forces Japan, Yokosuka, Japan, 1986-89; exec. prodr. (Japan) Navy Broadcasting Svc., Yokosuka, 1989-92; exec. prodr. (west coast) Navy Broadcasting Svc., San Diego, 1992-93; comty. rels. dir. Utah Dept. Transp., Salt Lake City, 1994—; ret., 1993; cons. joint task force aesthetic design Am. Assn. State Hwy and Transp. Ofcls., Washington, 1996, mem. subcom. pub. affairs, 1994—. Author: (play) Something's Rotten at the Sawmill, 1995; illustrator: (periodical) U.S. C. of C. in Tokyo Jour., 1986, (fgn. lang. texts) Conversational Spanish for Professionals, 1977. Artistic dir. Terrace Plaza Playhouse, Ogden, Utah, 1995. Mem. Pub. Rels. Soc. Am. (Golden Spike award of excellence 1995). Mormon. Avocations: community theater, Boy Scout activities. Office: Utah Dept Transp 4501 S 2700 W Salt Lake City UT 84119-5977

HANSEN, KENT FORREST, nuclear engineering educator; b. Chgo., Aug. 10, 1931; s. Kay Frost and Mary (Cummins) H.; m. Katherine Elizabeth Kavanagh, June 13, 1959 (dec. Dec. 1975); children: Thomas Kay, Katherine Mary; m. Deborah Lea Hill, June 26, 1977, (div. Aug. 1991); 1 child, Gordon Benedict; m. Léonie Andrews Work, June 11, 1992. S.B., Mass. Inst. Tech., 1953, Sc.D., 1959. Sr. engr. Sylvania Electric Products, Waltham, Mass., 1957-58; asst. prof. nuclear engring. MIT, Cambridge, Mass., 1960-64, assoc. prof., 1964-68, prof., 1968—, assoc. dean engring., 1979-81, assoc. dir. energy lab., 1984-90; bd. dirs. EG&G, Inc., Stone & Webster, Inc.; cons. to industry. Co-author: Numerical Methods of Reactor Analysis, 1964, Advances in Nuclear Science and Technology, Vol. 8, 1975. Ford postdoctoral fellow, 1960-61. Fellow Am. Nuclear Soc. (dir., Arthur Holly Compton award 1978); mem. Am. Nuclear Soc., Nat. Acad. Engring., Sigma Xi, Sigma Chi. Home: 23 Phillips Pond Rd Natick MA 01760-5643 Office: MIT Energy Lab Massachusetts Ave Cambridge MA 02139-4325

HANSEN, LELAND JOE, communications executive; b. Spokane, Wash., Mar. 26, 1944; s. Herman Johnny and Emma Irene (Borth) H.; m. Jonni Krajeski, Apr. 15, 1979. Creative dir., dir., producer Mel Blanc and Assocs., Beverly Hills, Calif., 1971-73; creative dir., writer, producer, dir. nat. TV and radio commls. and entertainment programs ABC Watermark, Universal City, Calif., 1973-80; pres., chief exec. officer, writer, producer, dir. film and TV GDE Prodns. Inc., Sherman Oaks, Calif., 1980-87; sr. writer, dir. video svcs. Rockwell Internat., Canoga Park, Calif., 1987-95; ind. film, video and multimedia audio prodr. specializing in mktg. videos for corps., 1995—; voice-over artist nat. TV and radio. Dir. American Top Forty, 1973-77, The Elvis Presley Story, Soundtrack of the Sixties; creator, producer, dir. Alien Worlds, 1973-80. Founding mem. Am. Forces Radio, Saigon, Socialist Republic of Vietnam, 1963-64. Served with U.S. Army, 1962-65, Vietnam. Recipient Belding award The Advt. Club Los Angeles, 1977. Mem. AFTRA. Avocations: pilot, architectural design, model builder.

HANSEN, MARION JOYCE, nursing administrator; b. Wadena, Minn., Oct. 20, 1951; d. Charles R. and Dorothy M. (Hennen) Hillig; m. Keith Hansen, June 2, 1979; children: Adam, Angela, John James, Jason. Diploma, St. Luke's Hosp. Sch. Nursing, Duluth, Minn., 1972; BS, Moorhead State U., 1991. Lic. nursing home adminstr. Staff RN ICCU Tri-County Hosp., Wadena, 1972-74, house supr. ICCU, staff RN, edn. dir., ICCU coor., 1974-89, asst. adminstr.; dir. of nursing Elders' Home, Inc., New York Mills, Minn., 1989-96; contr. risk mgr. Elders' Home, 1996-97; adminstr. Heritage Manor Assisted Living, 1997-98, Elders' Home, 1997-98; DON Heritage Living Ctr., Park Rapids, Minn., 1999—; claims coord. workers compensation; grant writer HUD sect. 202 Minn. Dept. of Transp. Mem. Am. Cancer Soc. (comms. chair, past pres.), Minn. Health and Housing Alliance, Am. Assn. Homes and Svcs. for the Aging, Retirement Housing Profls. Program. Home: 28287 Cord 23 Sebeka MN 56477 Office: Heritage Living Ctr 619 W 6th St Park Rapids MN 56470

HANSEN, MATILDA, state legislator; b. Paullina, Iowa, Sept. 4, 1929; d. Arthur J. and Sada G. (Thompson) Henderson; m. Robert B. Michener, 1950 (div. 1963); children: Eric J., Douglas E.; m. Hugh G. Hansen (dec.). BA, U. Colo., 1963; MA, U. Wyo., 1970. Tchr. history Englewood (Colo.) Sr. High Sch., 1963-65; dir. Albany County Adult Learning Ctr., Laramie, Wyo., 1966-78, Laramie Plains Civic Ctr., 1979-83; treas. Wyo. Territorial Prison Corp., Laramie, 1988-93, also bd. dirs.; bd. dirs. Wyo. Territorial Park. Author: (textbooks) To Help Adults Learn, 1975, Let's Play Together, 1978. Legislator Wyo. Ho. of Reps., Cheyenne, 1975-95, minority whip, 1987-88, asst. minority leader, 1991-92, 93-94; mem. mgmt. coun. Wyo. State Legislature, Cheyenne, 1983-84; chair Com. for Dem. Legislature, Cheyenne, 1990-94, Wyo. State Dems., 1995-99. GE fellow in econs. for high sch. tchrs., 1963; named Pub. Citizen of Yr., Wyo. Assn. Social Workers, 1980-81. Mem. LWV Wyo. (v.p. 1966-68), LWV Laramie (bd. dirs. 1966-72, Nat. Conf. State Legislators (vice chair human resources 1983, nat. exec. com. 1990-94), Laramie Area C. of C., Laramie Women's Club, Faculty Women's Club. Mem. Soc. of Friends. Avocations: gardening, quilting, mountaineering. Home: 1306 E Kearney St Laramie WY 82070-4142 Office: 1306 E Kearney St Laramie WY 82070-4199

HANSEN, MICHELE SIMONE, secondary education educator; b. Nashua, N.H., Feb. 19, 1947; d. Real Louis and Eleanore Marie (Desbiens) Bujold; widowed; 1 child, Karl Alexander. BA cum laude, Rivier Coll., 1968, MA cum laude, 1988. Cert. tchr., N.H. Reporter Nashua Telegraph, 1968-69, editor, 1969-70; editor USAF Community Newspaper, Izmir, Turkey, 1972-74, USAF Wives Mag., Ramstein, Fed. Republic Germany, 1975-78; tchr. journalism and English Nashua Sr. High Sch., 1980—. Chair publicity Adopt-A-Sch. Com., Nashua, 1985-95; mem., treas. St. Joseph's Choir, 1982-97; bd. dirs. Yankee Pen, 1992—. Named N.H. Journalism Tchr. of Yr., Union Leader, 1992, Young Career Woman of Yr., Nashua Bus./Profl. Women's Club, 1968. Mem. Nat. Coun. Tchrs. English, N.H. Coun. Tchrs. English, Journalism Edn. assn. (N.H. state dir. 1998—), Ret. Officers Assn., DAV Aux., USCG Acad. Parents Assn., Rivier Coll. Alumni Assn. (bd. dirs. 1980-84). Democrat. Roman Catholic. Avocations: travel, singing. Office: Nashua Sr High Sch 36 Riverside Dr Nashua NH 03062-1254

HANSEN, NANETTE ELIZABETH, anchorwoman, correspondent; b. Orange, N.J., Mar. 26, 1963; d. James Kent and Maureen Ellen (Dowdell) H. BA in Comm., Boston Coll., 1985. Anchor, reporter Sta. WAVI Radio,

Portsmouth, N.H., 1986-87, Sta. WMUR-TV, Manchester, N.H., 1987-94; corr. CBS News, N.Y.C., 1994-95, anchor, 1995—. Vol., telethon host Easter Seal Soc., Manchester, 1990-94; telethon host Children's Miracle Network, Manchester, 1992-93. Mem. Boston Coll. Club of N.H. (Alumni of Yr. 1994). Avocations: showing Cavalier King Charles Spaniels, skiing, golf. Office: CBS News 524 W 57th St New York NY 10019-2924

HANSEN, NILES MAURICE, economics educator; b. Louisville, Jan. 2, 1937; s. Kristian and Alma (Jensen) H.; m. Josephine Drescher, Aug. 22, 1959; children: Karen, Eric, Laura; m. Koren Sherrill, Feb. 9, 1979; 1 child, Stephen. B.A., Centre Coll. Ky., 1958; M.A., Ind. U., 1959, Ph.D., 1963. Asst. and assoc. prof. U. Tex., 1963-67; prof. econs., assoc. dir. Ctr. for Devel. Change U. Ky., 1967-69; prof. econs., dir. Ctr. for Econ. Devel. U. Tex., Austin, 1969-75; head urban and regional systems, acting chmn. human settlements and svcs., rsch. scholar Internat. Inst. for Applied Systems Analysis, Laxenburg, Austria, 1975-77; vis. fellow Can. Inst. for Rsch. on Regional Devel., Moncton, New Brunswick, 1987; vis. scholar Regional U. d'Aix-Marseille, Aix-en-Provence, France, 1988; Leroy G. Denman Jr. regents prof. econs. U. Tex. Author: French Regional Planning, 1968, France in the Modern World, 1969, Rural Poverty and the Urban Crisis, 1970, Intermediate-Size Cities as Growth Centers, 1971, Growth Centers and Regional Development, 1972, Location Preferences, Migration and Regional Growth, 1973, The Future of Nonmetropolitan America, 1973, Public Policy and Regional Development, 1974, The Challenge of Urban Growth, 1975, Improving Access to Economic Opportunity, 1976, The Border Economy, 1981; co-author: Regional Policy in a Changing World, 1990; editor: Human Settlement Systems: International Perspectives on Structure Change and Public Policy, 1977, The Border Economy: Regional Development in the Southwest, 1981, Regional Policy and Regional Integration, 1996; contbr. articles to profl. jours. NSF fellow U. Paris, 1965-66, Fulbright 40th Ann. Disting. fellow, Turkey, 1987. Mem. Am. Econ. Assn., So. Regional Sci. Assn. (pres. 1979, elected fellow 1993), Western Regional Sci. Assn. (pres. 1982), French Speaking Regional Economists, N.Am. Regional Sci. Assn. (pres. 1992). Home: 807 Rock Creek Dr Austin TX 78746-4529 Office: U Tex Dept Econs Austin TX 78712

HANSEN, OLE, physicist; b. Frederiksberg, Denmark, May 14, 1934; came to U.S., 1981; s. Victor and Bodil (Olsén) H.; m. Ruth Gaarn Bastiansen, Apr. 26, 1958; children: Lars, Sven, Bjorn, Maj Britt. Mag. scient, U. Copenhagen, 1958, Dr. Phil., 1967. Lectr. U. Copenhagen, 1960-68, 72-74, prof., 1974-82; prof. U. Pa., Phila., 1969-70; staff mem. Los Alamos (N.Mex.) Nat. Lab., 1969-72, 74-75; sr. scientist Brookhaven Nat. Lab., Upton, N.Y., 1981-92; dir. Niels Bohr Inst. Astronomy, Physics and Geophysics, Copenhagen, 1992-99; mem. nat. sci. coun. Ministry of Edn. and Rsch., Denmark, 1979-81; mem. adv. panel Los Alamos Nat. Lab., 1982-87; mem. nuclear sci. adv. com. Dept. Energy, Washington, 1984-88; mem. bd. Danish Nat. Rsch. Found., 1991-99, Danish Space Rsch. Inst., 1995-98; bd. dirs. Norditat. Author: (with others) Two-neutron Transfer Reactions and the Pairing Model, 1973; contbr. articles to profl. jours. Recipient Ole Romer award, 1968, Humboldt award, 1988. Mem. Danish Sci. Edn. Coun. Achievements include discovery of pairing vibration in nuclei (with O. Nathan), systematically measured quantum mechanical effects in heavy ion transfer reactions, and strangenes enhancement in ultra relativistic nucleus-nucleus collisions (E-802 collaboration). Office: Niels Bohr Inst, Blegdamsvej 17, DK 2100 Copenhagen Denmark

HANSEN, OLE VIGGO, chemical engineer; b. Detroit, May 6, 1934; s. Oluf Viggo and Carrie Alma (Wary) H.; m. Shirley Elizabeth Ford, Dec. 29, 1966; 1 child, Victoria Louisa. BSChemE, Wayne State U., 1956; equivalent of BS in Meteorology, Tex. A & M Univ., 1958. Registered profl. engr., Mich. Engr. tech. svcs. 3M Co., Detroit, 1956-57; chem. engr. Fisher Body div. Gen. Motors, Detroit, 1960-64; mgr. mktg. Monsanto Co., St. Louis and Australia, 1964-76; dir. tech. mktg. Beltran Assocs., Inc., N.Y.C., 1976-78; leader mist eliminator profit ctr. Koch - Glitsch, Inc., Wichita, Kans., 1978—; bd. dirs. Divmesh of Canada, Ltd., Calgary, Alta., 1984-85. Contbr. articles to profl. jours.; patentee in field. Served to capt. USAF, 1956-60. Mem. Am. Inst. Chem. Engrs. (session chmn. nat. meeting 1980), Am. Meteorol. Soc., Soc. Automotive Engrs. Australasia. Avocations: 19th century history, classical music, travel. Home: 7800 Killarney Pl Wichita KS 67206-1633 Office: Koch-Glitsch Inc 4111 E 37th St N Wichita KS 67220-3203

HANSEN, ORVAL, lawyer, former congressman, think tank executive; b. Firth, Idaho, Aug. 3, 1926; s. Farrel L. and Lily (Wahlquist) H.; m. June Duncan, Dec. 31, 1955; children: Margaret, Elizabeth, James, Katherine, John, Mary, Sarah. BA, U. Idaho, 1950, LLD (hon.), 1988; JD, George Washington U., 1954, LLM, 1973, PhD, 1986. Bar: Idaho 1954, D.C. 1954. Practice law Idaho Falls, 1956-68; staff asst. to Senator Henry Dworshak, 1950-54; mem. Idaho Ho. of Reps., 1956-62, 64-66, house majority leader, 1961-62; mem. Idaho Senate, 1966-68, 91st-93d congresses from 2d Idaho Dist.; former mem. Cook, Purcell, Hansen & Henderson, Washington; of counsel Hopkins, Roden, Crockett, Hansen & Hoopes, PLLC, Washington. Trustee John F. Kennedy Ctr. for Performing Arts, 1976-86; pres. Columbia Inst. for Polit. Rsch. With USNR, 1944-46; lt. col. USAFR, ret. Rotary Found. fellow U. London (Eng.) Sch. Econs., 1954-55. Mem. D.C. Bar Assn., Am. Legion, V.F.W., Phi Beta Kappa, Sigma Chi, Phi Alpha Delta. Republican. Mormon. Home: 5555 Little Falls Rd Arlington VA 22207-1525 Office: Columbia Institute 1215 17th St NW Washington DC 20036-3008

HANSEN, PAUL WALDEN, conservation organization executive; b. Bridgeport, Conn., Feb. 22, 1952; s. Carl Bernard and Phyllis Marie (Adler) H.; m. Kay Ann Stratman, May 27, 1989. BA in Biology, Antioc Coll., 1975, MA in Natural Resources Adminstrn., 1979. Coord. acid rain project Izaak Walton League Am., Gaithersburg, Md., 1982-84; office opener Izaak Walton League Am., Mpls., 1984-89, dir. office, 1989-94; assoc. exec. dir. Izaak Walton League Am., Gaithersburg, 1994-95, exec. dir., 1995—; cons. on acid rain and other bilateral environ. issues Can. Dept. Environ. and Dept. External Affairs, 1981-90; testifier before U.S. Ho. of Reps. and Can. Parlaiment coms., also numerous state legis. and regulatory procs.; com. mem. 7th Forest Conf., Nat. Shooting Range Symposium, also others. Named Am. Friend of Can. by speaker Can. Ho. of Commons, 1987. Mem. Outdoor Writers Assn. Am. (coms.), Internat. Assn. Fish and Wildlife Agys. (coms.). Office: Izaak Walton League Am 707 Conservation Ln Gaithersburg MD 20878-2982*

HANSEN, PER BRINCH, computer scientist; b. Copenhagen, Nov. 13, 1938; came to U.S., 1970, naturalized, 1992; s. Jorgen Brinch and Elsebeth (Ring) H.; m. Milena Marija Hrastar, Mar. 27, 1965; children: Mette, Thomas. MS, Tech. U. Denmark, Copenhagen, 1963, Dr. Tech., 1978. Systems programmer Regnecentralen, Copenhagen, 1963-70, mgr. software devel., 1967-70; rsch. assoc. Carnegie-Mellon U., Pitts., 1970-72; assoc. prof. Calif. Inst. Tech., Pasadena, 1972-76; chmn. dept. computer sci. U. So. Calif., L.A., 1976-77, prof., 1976-84, Henry Salvatori prof., 1982-84; prof. U. Copenhagen, 1984-87; disting. prof. Syracuse (N.Y.) U., 1987—; cons. Burroughs, Honeywell, IBM, JPL, Mostek, TRW, others. Author: Operating System Principles, 1973, The Architecture of Concurrent Programs, 1977, Programming a Personal Computer, 1982, On Pascal Compilers, 1985, Studies in Computational Science, 1995, The Search for Simplicity, 1996, Programming for Everyone, 1999; mem. editl. bd. Acta Informatica, Concurrency, Software, Lecture Notes in Computer Sci.; contbr. articles to profl. jours.; inventor of programming langs. Concurrent Pascal, Edison, Joyce, SuperPascal. Recipient Chancellor's medal Syracuse U., 1989; grantee NSF, Army Rsch. Office, Office Naval Rsch., Rome Air Devel. Ctr. Fellow IEEE; mem. Assn. for Computing Machinery. Avocations: history, photography, jazz. Home: 5070 Pine Valley Dr Fayetteville NY 13066-9723 Office: Syracuse U 2-175 CST Syracuse NY 13244

HANSEN, PETER, international organization executive. Under sec.-gen. Commr.-Gen. of UNRWA, N.Y.C. Office: Commr-Gen UNRWA UN Room DC2-1755 New York NY 10017 also: Vienna Internat Ctr, PO Box 700, A-1400 Vienna Austria also: PO Box 140157, Amman 11814, Jordan*

HANSEN, RANDALL GLENN, school psychologist, consultant; b. Fayetteville, N.C., Dec. 9, 1946; s. Glenn Sidney and Ramona Mary (Blocker) H.; m. Wanda Kay Moller (div. Dec. 1990); 1 child, Nicholas Glenn. BS in Secondary Edn., Black Hills State U., Spearfish, S.D., 1971; BA in Social Work, Chadron (Nebr.) State Coll., 1978; MEd in Counseling-Guidance-Pers. Svcs., S.D. State U., 1982; cert. sch. psychology licensing program, Moorhead (Minn.) State U., 1986; PhD in Clin. Sch. Psychology, Walden U., Mpls., 1991. Clin./sch. psychology nat. cert. counselor; cert. cognitive-behavioral therapist; lic. profl. counselor, marriage family therapist, ednl. psychologist, S.D.; nat. cert. sch. psychologist; diplomate Am. Psychotherapy Assn. Tchr., counselor Sky Ranch for Boys, Camp Crook, S.D., 1971-72; social worker I, S.D. Dept. Social Svcs., Rapid City, 1972-73; multi-county svc. area supr. S.D. Dept. Social Svcs., Mitchell and Sioux Falls, 1979-85; asst. mgr. Pioneer Market, North Platte, Nebr., 1973-74; county dir. Frontier County Div. Pub. Welfare, Curtis, Nebr., 1974-75; quality control reviewer Nebr. Dept. Pub. Welfare, Scottsbluff, 1975-77, asst. income maintenance rep., 1977-79; sch. psychologist Tracy (Minn.), Milroy, Balaton and Walnut Grove Schs., 1985-88, Palo Verde Unified Sch. Dist., Blythe, Calif., 1988—; pvt. practice Blythe Family Counseling Ctr., 1995—; sch. psychol. cons. Desert Ctr. Unified Sch. Dist., Eagle Mountain, Calif., 1988-94; pub. spkr. on learning disabilities and how mind processes info., 1986—. Author: (psychol. test) Children's Attention-Deficit Hyperactivity Inventory, 1991. Bd. dirs. Food Svcs. Ctr., Sioux Falls, 1980-85, Educators Interested in Spl. Edn., Marshall, Minn., 1985-88; counselor Crisis Line, Sioux Falls, 1981-85; softball coach Project Awareness, Sioux Falls, 1984. Named Vol. of Month, Crisis Line, 1984. Mem. ACA, APA, NASP, Nat. Assn. Cognitive Behavioral Therapists, Riverside Assn. Sch. Psychologists, Menninger Found. Democrat. Avocations: golf, motorcycle riding, spending time with son. Home: 8401 E Hobson Way Spc 34 Blythe CA 92225-2100 Office: Counseling Ctr 689 N Lovekin Blvd Blythe CA 92225-1136 also: 110 N Spring St Blythe CA 92225

HANSEN, RICHARD ARTHUR, insurance company executive, psychologist; b. Jersey City, Apr. 28, 1941; s. Arthur Henry and Borghild Marie (Johnson) H.; m. Julie Rae Horns, Sept. 6, 1965; 1 child, Jane Marie. BA, Columbia U., 1962, MA, 1966, PhD, 1969. Lic. psychologist, N.Y. Assoc. prof. CCNY, 1969-76; sr. rsch. assoc. Psychol. Corp., N.Y.C., 1976-78; sr. v.p. N.Y. Life, N.Y.C., 1978—; trustee Mackay Shields Mainstay Series Mut. Fund, 1989-93. Bd. dirs. Sunbridge Coll., 1993-98. Lt. (j.g.) USNR, 1962-64. Republican. Presbyterian. Office: NY Life Ins Co 51 Madison Ave New York NY 10010-1603

HANSEN, RICHARD BUDDIE, English educator, chef; b. Redfield, S.D., May 15, 1946; s. Rueben Buddie and Beryl Lucille Hansen; children: Wendy, Holly. BS in English, Bus. Edn., No. State U., Aberdeen, S.D., 1969; grad. strategic planning, Bill Cook Sch., 1994; grad., Apollo Reservation Tng., 1995. Cert. tchr., S.D., Minn. English tchr. Wilmot (S.D.) Sch. Dist., 1969-95, computer instr., 1992-95; chef Shady Beach Supper Club, Corona, S.D., 1985-93; cook Silver's Bar and Grill, Corona, S.D., 1994-95; bus. edn. tchr. Lisbon (N.D.) Sch. Dist., 1995-96; chef Holiday Inn, Alexandria, Minn., 1996—, Isabelle's Dining and Cocktails, Alexandria, Minn., 1996—; English tchr. Brandon (Minn.) Sch. Dist., 1996—; exec. chef Best Western, Fergus Falls, Minn., 1999—; facilitator coop. learning devel. prog. Wilmot Sch. Dist., 1992, oral interpretation coach, drama coach, Wolfton sch. newspaper adviser; developer tech. prep. curriculum Wilmot Sch. Dist., 1993-95; strategic planner Wilmot Sch. Dist., 1994-95; modernization site dir. Wilmot Sch. Dist., 1994-95; driver's edn. instr. Wilmot Sch. Dist., Summer 1994; travel svc. assoc. Rosenbluth Internat., Fargo., N.D., 1995. Author ABC grant for curriculum integration for Wilmot Sch. Dist., 1992; presenter in field. Mem. Wilmot City Coun.; trustee, session mem., clk. session ch. bd. First Presbyn. Ch. Mem. NEA, Nat. Coun. Tchrs. English, S.D. Edn. Assn., N.D. Edn. Assn., Minn. Edn. Assn., Wilmot Edn. Assn. (sec. treas. 1969-97, pres. 1970-90), Lisbon Edn. Assn., Brandon Edn. Assn. Home: PO Box 231 Brandon MN 56315-0231 Office: Brandon Sch Dist Third & Stowe Brandon MN 56315

HANSEN, ROBERT CLINTON, electrical engineering consultant; b. St. Louis, Aug. 3, 1926; m. 1952; 2 children. BS, U. Mo., 1949, D of Eng. (hon.), 1975; MS, U. Ill., 1950, PhD, 1955. Rsch. assoc. antenna lab. U. Ill., 1950-55; sr. staff engr. microwave lab. Hughes Aircraft Co., 1955-59; sr. staff engr. telecomm. lab. Space Technol. Labs., 1959-60; dir. test mission analysis office Aerospace Corp., Calif., 1960-67; head electronics divsn. KMS Technol. Ctr., 1967-71; pres., cons. R.C. Hansen, Inc., Tarzana, Calif., 1971—; mem. commn. B, Internat. Sci. Radio Union. Editor: Microwave Scanning Antennas, 1964-65, Significant Phased Array Papers, 1973, Geometric Theory of Diffraction, 1981, Moment Methods in Antennas and Scattering, 1990; author: Phased Array Antennas, 1998. Recipient Disting. Alumnus award U. Ill. Elect. Engring. Dept., 1981, Disting. Alumnus Svc. medal, 1986. Fellow IEEE (pres. antennas and propagation soc. 1964, 80), Aerospace & Electronic Sys. Soc. (Barry Carlton award 1991, AP Disting. Achievement award 1994), Inst. Elec. Engrs. (London); mem. NAE, Am. Phys. Soc. Office: RC Hansen Inc PO Box 570215 Tarzana CA 91357-0215

HANSEN, ROBERT GUNNARD, philatelist, entrepreneur; b. Chgo., Aug. 16, 1939; s. Earl F. and Mildred E. (Hargrave) H.; A.A., Lincoln Coll., 1960; B.A., Culver Stockton Coll., 1962; M.B.A., U. So. Calif., 1966; postgrad. UCLA Extension, 1962-67; m. Bertha Golds, Aug. 10, 1960; children—Karin Lee, Lisa Marie. With Litton Industries, 1962-63, Sterer Engring., 1963-69; mktg. and contracts ofcl. Santa Barbara Research Ctr., 1969-73; pres., chief exec. officer, R.G. Hansen & Assocs., Santa Barbara, 1974— ; pres., owner The Silver Penny and Santa Barbara Stamp & Coin, 1969—; owner, CEO, pres. Univ. Travel Bureau, 1990-95; guest lectr. Santa Barbara City Coll. Mem. Am. Vacuum Soc., Am. Philatelic Soc. (life), Am. Numismatic Assn., Hawaii Numismatic Assn., Sci. and Engring. Coun. Santa Barbara (pres. 1989), Token and Medal Soc., Masons, York Rite. Scottish Rite, Shriners, Royal Order of Scotland, Channel City, Royal Arch Masons, trustee Santa Barbara Historical Soc., Rotary Internat. (Paul Harris fellow 1990, 96). Research and publs. on cryogenics, electro-optics, infrared radiation; patentee in field. Republican. Presbyterian. Office: 631 Chapala St Santa Barbara CA 93101-3311

HANSEN, ROBERT WILLIAM, artist, educator; b. Osceola, Nebr., Jan. 1, 1924; s. William Otto and Gladys Marie (Miller) H.; m. Margaret Helen Kuhlman, Mar. 21, 1948; children: Eric Pat, Fritz Gerald. AB, U. Nebr., 1948, BFA, 1948; Maestro de Bellas Artes, Escuela U. de Bellas Artes, San Miguel de Allende, Mex., 1949; postgrad., U. de Michoacan, Morelia, Mex., 1952-53. Asst. prof. art Bradley U., 1949-55, U. Hawaii, 1955-56; asst. prof. Occidental Coll., 1955-60, assoc. prof., 1960-67, prof., 1967-87, prof. emeritus, 1987—. One-man shows include Ferus Gallery, L.A., 1957, Comara Gallery, L.A., 1964, 66, 68, 70, 72, 75, Castellane Gallery, N.Y.C., 1964, L.A. Mcpl. Gallery, 1973, Brand Gallery, 1976, Mich. State U. Gallery, 1980, Oranges/Sardines Gallery, L.A., 1981-82, Occidental Coll., 1987; group shows include, Mus. Modern Art, N.Y.C., 1961, Carnegie Internat., Pitts., 1961, 64, The New Vein Show, Europe and S. Am., 1969-71; represented in permanent collections, Mus. Modern Art, N.Y.C., Whitney Mus., N.Y.C., Fine Arts Gallery of San Diego; translator: Curvilinear Perspective, 1988. Founder (1989), pres. Carpinteria Creek Com. With U.S. Army, 1943-46. Guggenheim fellow, India, S.E. Asia, 1961-62; Fulbright sr. rsch. grantee, India, 1961-62; Tamarind lithographic fellow, 1964-65. Mem. ACLU, Phi Beta Kappa. Home: 1498 Santa Ynez Ave Carpinteria CA 93013-1312

HANSEN, ROBYN L., lawyer; b. Terre Haute, Ind., Dec. 2, 1949; d. Robert Louis and Shirley (Nagel) Wieman; m. Gary Hansen, Aug. 21, 1971 (div. 1985); children: Nathan Ross Hansen, Brian Michael Hansen; m. John Marley Clarey, Jan. 1, 1986. BA, Gustavus Adolphus, 1971; JD cum laude, William Mitchell Coll. Law, 1977. Bar: Minn. 1977, U.S. Dist. Ct. Minn. 1977. Atty. Briggs and Morgan P.A., St. Paul, 1977-93, Leonard, Street and Deinard, Mpls., 1993—. Trustee Actors Theatre St. Paul, 1980-88, Minn. Mus. Am. Art, 1994-97; bd. dirs. St. Paul Downtown Coun., 1985-93, Met. State U. Found., 1993—, St. Paul Area Conv. and Vis. Bur., 1995—, chair, 1999—; bd. dirs. Capital City Partnership, 1997—; exec. dir. Minn. Inst. Pub. Fin., 1987-93, bd. dirs., 1993-95, pres., 1995. Mem. ABA, Minn. Bar Assn., Ramsey County Bar Assn., Nat. Assn. Bond Lawyers, St. Paul Area C. of C. (bd. dirs., exec. com. 1997—). Office: Leonard Street and Deinard 2270 World Trade Ctr Saint Paul MN 55101

HANSEN, RUTH LUCILLE HOFER, business owner, consultant; b. Wellman, Iowa, Feb. 8, 1916; d. Harve Hiram and Frances Ada (Fitzsimmons) Hofer; m. Donald Edward Hansen, June 26, 1937 (dec. Feb. 1996); children: James Edward, Sandra Kaye. Student, Upper Iowa U., 1958, U. Northern Iowa, 1959. Co-founder, v.p. H & H Distbg. Co., West Union, Iowa, 1946-59; cons. H & H Distbg. Co.; v.p., gen. ptnr., sec., treas. Don E. Hansen Family Partnership Ltd. Pres. United Presbyn. Women of Bethel Presbyn. Ch., West Union, Iowa, 1967—, mem. comty. planning and devel. commn.; pres. Lakes & Prairies Presbyterial, Cedar Rapids, Iowa, 1972-75; elder Bethel Presbyn. Ch., West Union, 1960-63; v.p., program chmn., camp dir., leader Camp Wyo. Ch. Camp; dist. Wapsipinicon coun. Girl Scouts, 1972-75; tchr. Vacation Bible Sch., Ch. Sch. for Adults, 1970; rep. John Knox Presbytery. Mem. Bus. and Profl. Women (pres.). Avocations: community plays, sewing, dancing, golfing, bridge. Home: 704 N Vine St West Union IA 52175-1018 Home (winter): 10549 W Bayside Rd Sun City AZ 85351-2729

HANSEN, STEPHEN CHRISTIAN, banker; b. N.Y.C., July 3, 1940; s. Norbert C. and Harriet C. H.; m. Ethel Olmsted, June 12, 1971; 1 son, Lee Christian. A.B., Princeton U., 1962; LL.B., U. Va., 1966; postgrad., Brown U. Grad. Sch. Banking. Bar: N.Y. 1966. Assoc. Alexander & Green, N.Y.C., 1966-68; mem. N.Y. State Legislature, 1968-70; spl. asst. to under-sec. HUD, Washington, 1970-73; spl. asst. to chmn. FDIC, Washington, 1973-76; sr. v.p. Dollar Bank, Pitts., 1976-78, pres., 1978—, pres., CEO, 1982—; chmn. Regional Indusl. Devel. Corp. Mem. PennSouthwest, Carnegie Inst., Carnegie Sci. Ctr.; former mem. Cleve. Dist. Pitts. Fed. Res. Bd. Mem. N.Y. State Bar Assn. Office: Dollar Bank PO Box 987 Pittsburgh PA 15230-0987

HANSEN, STEVEN ALAN, construction executive; b. Key West, Fla., July 5, 1949; s. Baron Lewis Hansen and June Marie (Ferree) Correll; m. Sally Jo Cooper, Nov. 13, 1976; children: Blake, Carter, Reid. BA in Govt. and Religion, Ind. U., 1972. V.p. Hansen-Haberman Constrn., Aspen, Colo., 1978-82; pres. Hansen Constrn. Inc., Aspen, 1982—. Avocations: oil painting, sketching. Office: Hansen Constrn Inc PO Box 10493 Aspen CO 81612-7329

HANSEN, STEVEN MICHAEL, fiber scientist, researcher; b. St. Paul, June 15, 1953; s. John P. and Doris A. (Dropps) H.; m. Sharon A. Walker, Dec. 20, 1977; 1 child, Kathryn D. BS in Chem. Engring., U. Ala., Tuscaloosa, 1975, MS in Chem. Engring., 1977, PhD, 1981. Assoc. chem. engr. Texaco Product Rsch. Lab., Bellaire, Tex., 1977-78; instr. U. Ala., Tuscaloosa, 1978-81; rsch. engr. DuPont Pioneering Rsch. Lab., Wilmington, Del., 1981-83; rsch. engr. DuPont Dacron Rsch. Lab., Kinston, N.C., 1983-85, rsch. assoc., 1985-96; asst. prof. Ga. Texh. Sch. Textiles, Atlanta, 1985-87; sr. rsch. assoc. DuPont Dacron, Wilmington, N.C., 1996—; mem. external adv. bd. Sch. Textiles, Ga. Inst. Tech., 1996—. Contbr. articles to profl. jours.; patentee in field. Vol. St. James Episcopal Ch., Wilmington. Mem. Fiber Soc. (indsl. lectr. 1995-97), Sigma Xi. Avocations: fishing, bridge. Home: 7008 Eschol Ct Wilmington NC 28409-2687 Office: Dacron Tech PO Box 2042 Wilmington NC 28402-2042

HANSEN, THOMAS NANASTAD, pediatrician, health facility administrator; b. Neenah, Wis., Oct. 11, 1947; m. Cheryl Bailey, June 9, 1979; children: Elaine Christ, William Thomas. BS in Physics summa cum laude, Tex. Christian U., 1970; MD, Baylor Coll. Medicine, 1973. Diplomate Am. Bd. Pediatrics. Intern in pediatrics Baylor Coll. Medicine, Houston, 1973-74, resident in pediatrics, 1974-76, postdoctoral fellow in neonatal perinatal medicine, 1976-78; postdoctoral fellow in pediatric pulmonary disease U. Calif., San Francisco, 1978-81; asst. prof. pediatrics Baylor Coll. Medicine, 1978-84, assoc. prof. pediatrics, 1984-89; prof. pediatrics and cell biology Tex. Children's Hosp. Found., Houston, 1989-95; head sect. on neonatology Baylor Coll. of Medicine, 1987-95, vice-chmn. rsch. dept. pediatrics, 1994-95, dir. child health rsch. ctr., 1994-95, co-dir. ctr. for tng. in molecular medicine, 1994-95; chmn. pediat., CEO Children's Hosp., Columbus, Ohio, 1995—; mem. exam com. Am. Bd. Pediatrics, 1982—, sub-bd. neonatal-perinatal medicine, 1992—, chmn. credentials com., 1993—, chmn.-elect sub-bd. neonaatal perinatal medicine, 1994. Contbr. numerous articles to profl. jours. Trustee Tex. Women's Hosp., 1988-91. Mem. Western Soc. for Pediatric Rsch., So. Soc. for Pediaatric Rsch., Soc. for Pediatric Rsch. (sec.-treas. 1986-91, chmn. student rsch. com. 1990—, trustee internat. chpt. 1992—), Am. Physiol. Soc., Am. Pediatric Soc., Am. Fedn. for Clin. Rsch., Am. Thoracic Soc., Am. Acad. of Pediatrics, N.Y. Acad. of Scis., Am. Soc. for Cell Biology, Assn. of Med. Sch. Pediatric Dept. Chmn., Sigma Xi. Home: 4328 Vaux Link New Albany OH 43054-9681 Office: Med Dir's Office Childrens Hosp 700 Childrens Dr Columbus OH 43205-2664*

HANSEN, TOM, lawyer. Ptnr. Hansen Jacobson & Teller, Beverly Hills, Calif. Office: Hansen Jacobson & Teller 450 N Roxbury Dr #8 Beverly Hills CA 90210-4222*

HANSEN, W. LEE, economics educator, author; b. Racine, Wis., Nov. 8, 1928; s. William R. and Gertrude M. (Spillum) H.; m. Sally Ann Porch, Dec. 26, 1955; children—Ellen J., Martha L. BA, U. Wis.-Madison, 1950, MA, 1955; PhD, Johns Hopkins U., 1958. Asst. prof. econs. UCLA, from 1958, assoc. prof., to 1965; assoc. prof. econs. U. Wis.-Madison, from 1965, prof., prof. emeritus, 1996—; sr. staff economist Pres.'s Coun. Econ. Advisers, Washington, 1964-65; trustee Nat. Coun. on Econ. Edn., N.Y.C., 1976; sec. NCEE, 1996—. Author: Benefits, Costs, and Finance of Public Higher Education, 1969, Education, Income, and Human Capital, 1970, The Labor Market for Scientists and Engineers, 1973, Perspectives on Economic Education, 1977, A Framework for Teaching Basic Economic Concepts, 1984, The End of Mandatory Retirement, 1989, Unemployment Insurance: The Second Half-Century, 1990, Academic Freedom on Trial: 100 Years of Sifting and Winnowing at the University of Wisconsin, 1998; contbr. articles to profl. jours. Served as sgt. U.S. Army, 1951-53. Recipient Amoco Disting. Tchg. award U. Wis., 1982, Hilldale award, 1988, Disting. Svc. award Nat. Coun. on Econs. Edn., 1991, Marvin Bower award, 1994, Tchr. Acad. U. Wis., 1994, Outstanding Postsecondary Educator award nat. Fedn. Ind. Bus. Found., 1992, Leavey award for excellence in pvt. enterprise edn. Freedoms Found., 1996; Guggenheim fellow, 1969-70; Fulbright sr. scholar, Australia, 1988. Mem. AAUP (chair com. on the econ. status of the profession 1979-86, mem. nat. coun. 1980-82, retirement com. 1985—), Am. Econ. Assn. (chmn. com. on econ. edn. 1983-88, exec. sec. commn. grad. edn. econs. 1988-91), Indsl. Rels. Rsch. Assn., Midwest Econs. Assn. (pres. 1987), Phi Beta Kappa. Unitarian. Office: U Wis Dept Econs 1180 Observatory Dr Madison WI 53706-1320

HANSEN, WAYNE W., lawyer; b. Clintonville, Wis., June 7, 1942; s. William W. and Berniece M. (Kuehn) H.; m. Carolyn M. Lemke, Dec. 21, 1969; children: Drew D., Janna J. BBA, U. Wis., 1965, JD, 1967. Bar: Wis. 1967, U.S. Dist. Ct. (we. dist.) Wis. 1971, U.S. Ct. Appeals (7th cir.) 1972, U.S. Dist. Ct. (ea. dist.) Wis. 1975, Wash. 1979, U.S. Dist. Ct. (we. dist.) Wash. 1979, U.S. Ct. Appeals (9th cir.) 1982, U.S. Dist. Ct. (ea. dist.) Wash. 1986. Atty. NLRB, Mpls., 1967-70, Schmitt Nolan Hansen & Hartley, Merrill, Wis., 1970-79; ptnr. Lane Powell Spears Lubersky, Seattle, 1979-98; mng. ptnr. Jackson Lewis Schnitzler & Krupman, Seattle, 1998—. Contbg. author: Developing Labor Law, 1971, Doing Business in Washington State—Guide for Foreign Business, 1989. Office: Jackson Lewis Schnitzler & Krupman 1420 5th Ave Ste 2000 Seattle WA 98101-4087*

HANSEN, WENDELL JAY, clergyman, gospel broadcaster; b. Waukegan, Ill., May 28, 1910; s. Christian Hans and Anna Sophia (Termansen) H.; m. Bertelle Kathryn Budman, Mar. 9, 1933 (dec. Jan. 6, 1956); 1 child, Sylvia Marie; m. Eunice Evaline Irvine, Nov. 2, 1957; 1 child, Dean. Grad., Cleve. Bible Coll., 1932; A.B., William Penn Coll., 1938; postgrad., Gletch Berg Skule, Switzerland, 1939; MA, U. Iowa, 1940, PhD, 1947. Ordained to ministry Recorded Friends, 1936, Evang. Reformed Ch., 1944. Pastor chs., Grinnell, Iowa, Mpls., Iowa City, 1934-47; evangelist with talking and performing birds, 1946—; past mgr. gospel radio stas. Two Rivers, Wis., Menomonie, Wis., Peru, Ind., Wabash, Ind., East St., Louis, Ill., Indpls., 1952—; pres., chmn. of bd. WESL Inc., East St. Louis, 1962—; cons. radio and TV, 1970—, appointed adv. com. to Indpls. Prosecutor, 1986; Appeared on Fuji Network, Tokyo and Channel X, London. *The Lorine L. Reynolds Foundation is translating a new purified version of the Bible from the Hebrew and the Greek. The Gospel, and other books of the Old and New Testaments have already been completed. When unhappy people decide to trust in God, they become valuable. They find happiness in serving. Through* *speaking, entertaining, writing, radio and TV, without begging for money, I have tried to help people receive this happiness.* Contbr. articles to popular mags. Dir. St. Paul Inter-racial Work Camp, 1939; chmn. Minn. Joint Refuge Com., 1940-41; trustee Lorine L. Reynolds Found., 1995—. Recipient honor citation Internat. Assn. Broadcasters, 1980; Boss of Yr. award Hamilton County Broadcasters, 1979, award Boys Town, 1983, award Women of Faith, St. Louis, 1984. Mem. Internat. Platform Assn., Internat. Assn. Christian Magicians, Ind. Bird Fanciers, East St. Louis C. of C. (bd. dirs. 1981-86), Pi Kappa Delta. Club: Ind. Pigeon (best exotic bird award 1969, 75, 80). Lodge: Kiwanis (East St. Louis bd. dirs. 1980-84). Republican. Quaker.

HANSEN-FLASCHEN, JOHN HYMAN, medical educator, researcher; b. Hamilton, Ohio, June 25, 1950; s. Steward Samuel and Joyce (Davies) Flaschen; m. Susan Lauretta Hansen, Aug. 22, 1951; children: Lynn, Lauren. AB, Brown U., 1972; MD, NYU, 1976. Diplomate in internal medicine, pulmonary medicine, critical care medicine Am. Bd. Internal Medicine. Resident in medicine U. Pa., Phila., 1976-79, chief resident in medicine, 1980-81, pulmonary fellow, 1979-80, 81-82, attending physician, 1982—, dir. edn. and tng. programs in pulmonary and critical care, 1983-90, asst. prof. medicine, 1982-87, assoc. prof., 1988-98, prof., 1999—, dir. pulmonary, allergy and critical care divsn., 1996—, chief, 1998—, dir. Pa. Lung Ctr., 1996—. Mem. editl. bd. Clin. Pulmonary Medicine, Respiratory Medicine, Up to Date in Pulmonary and Critical Care Medicine; contbr. articles to profl. jours. Mem. steering com. Nat. Emphysema Treatment Trial, 1997—. Recipient Spl. Investigator award Am. Heart Assn., 1982-84, Lindback Tchg. award U. Pa., 1999; Measey Found. fellow, 1982-83. Fellow ACP, Am. Coll. Chest Physicians, Coll. Physicians Phila.; mem. Am. Thoracic Soc. (chmn. postgrad. edn. com. 1995—, clin. problems long range planning com. 1997-99), Soc. for Critical Care Medicine, Soc. for Bioethics Consultation, Laennec Soc. Phila. (pres. 1990-91), Drinker Soc. for Critical Care in Phila. (founder, 1st pres. 1988-90), Sigma Xi, Alpha Omega Alpha. Democrat. Home: 365 Penn Rd Wynnewood PA 19096-1401 Office: Hosp of U Pa 873 Mahoney Bldg 3400 Spruce St Philadelphia PA 19104-4204

HANSEN-RACHOR, SHARON ANN, conductor, choral music educator; b. Omaha, Nebr., Aug. 22, 1954; d. Joseph Anthony Busch and Helen Marie Prokop Krustev; m. David John Rachor, May 27, 1991; 1 stepchild, Stephanie Rachor. BM, U. Nebr., Omaha, 1975; MM, U. Nebr., Lincoln, 1978; postgrad., U. Ill., 1981-82; DMA, U. Mo., Kansas City, 1986. Pub. sch. music tchr. Millard and Springfield (Nebr.) schs., 1975-83; grad. teaching asst. U. Ill., 1981-82, U. Mo., Kansas City, 1983-86; assoc. prof. choral music and conducting U. No. Iowa, Cedar Falls, 1986-94; assoc. prof. choral music and conducting, dir. choral activities U. Wis., Milw., 1994—, chair dept. music, 1996-98; vis. prof. orchestral studies U. Regensburg, Germany, 1993; guest condr. Moldavian Philharm. Choir, 1997, Bucharest Radio Choir, 1998, Craiova Philharm. Choir, 1998 ; cons. in field. Author: Helmuth Rilling: Conductor-Teacher, 1997; contbr. articles to profl. jours.; mem. editl. bd. Choral Jour. U. No. Iowa grantee, Amsterdam, 1991, Stuttgart, Germany, 1993-94; Kemper fellow U. Mo., Kansas City, 1986; U. Wis. Milw. grantee, Romania, 1997, 98. Mem. Am. Choral Dirs. Assn., Internat. Fedn. Choral Music, Gachinger Kantorei Stuttgart, Phi Kappa Lambda, Mu Phi Epsilon, Pi Kappa Pi, Alpha Lambda Delta. Avocations: reading, gardening, gourmet cooking, travel, outdoor activities. Home: 2512 E Linnwood Ave Milwaukee WI 53211-3342 Office: U Wis Milw Dept Music PO Box 413 Milwaukee WI 53201-0413

HANSER, FREDERICK O., professional sports team executive; b. St. Louis, Apr. 13, 1942; s. S. Albert Hanser and Olive D. Mullen; m. Katharine Thomson; children: Tim, Kara. BA in Econs., Yale U., 1963; JD, Wash. U., 1966. Lawyer Fordyoe & Mayne, 1966-78; ptnr. Armstrong & Teasdale, LLP, St. Louis, 1978-96; pres., dir. Gateway Group Inc., 1996—; chmn. St. Louis Cardinals, 1996—; mem. exec. com., bd. dirs. Miss. Valley Bancshares Inc. Mem. exec. bd. Greater St. Louis area coun. Boy Scouts Am.; bd. dirs. St. Louis Children's Hosp., mem. devel. bd.; bd. dirs. St. Louis Country Day Sch., Easter Seal Soc. Office: St Louis Cardinals 250 Stadium Plz Saint Louis MO 63102

HANSER, RUSSELL P., lawyer; b. N.Y.C., Apr. 2, 1972; s. Barry Elliot and Terry Claire Hanser; m. Kimberly Hope Nelson, Aug. 24, 1997. BA in Polit. Sci., Amherst Coll., 1994; JD, Harvard U., 1997. Bar: Mass. Litigation atty. Ropes & Gray, Boston, 1996, 97-99; law clk. judge Norman Stahl U.S. Ct. Appeals, Concord, N.H., 1999—. Editor: Harvard Law Rev., 1995-96, primary editor, 1996-97. Olin fellow in law and econs. Harvard Law Sch., Cambridge, Mass., 1996-97. Mem. ABA, Mass. Bar Assn. E-mail: hanser@hotmail.com.

HANSFORD, LARRY CLARENCE, computer consultant company executive; b. La Porte, Ind., Oct. 15, 1945; s. Curtis Edgar and Eva Maree (Owens) H.; m. Mabel Darlene Miller, June 27, 1970; 1 child, Patrick Robert. BEE, Ga. Inst. Tech., 1975. Asst. purchasing agent Dobbs House, Inc., Atlanta, 1963-65; enlisted USAF, 1965; commd. 2nd lt., 1975, advanced through grades to capt., 1986; computer sys. analyst Mil. Airlift Command Scott AFB, Ill., 1976-80; Air Force comms. command, 1980-82; comms. liaison officer Wright-Patterson AFB, Ohio, 1982-86; pres., chmn. bd. Milk-N-Honey Acres, Inc., Baldwin, Ill., 1978-79; owner, 1980-82; pres., chmn. bd. Creative Computer Cons., Inc., 1982-86; owner, 1987-91; mgr. telecomms. Martin Marietta, 1987-93; program mgr. Sci. Applications Internat. Corp., Dayton, Ohio, 1993-94; pres., chmn. bd. dirs. Creative Data Solutions, Inc., New Carlisle, Ohio, 1994—. Supt. edn. Skyland United Meth. Ch., Atlanta, 1973-75; sec. enlistment 1st United Med. Ch., Sparta, Ill., 1978-82, chmn. bd., New Carlisle, Ohio, 1985-87, 90-91; trustee Ginghamburg United Meth. Ch., Tipp City, Ohio, 1992-96. Mem. IEEE, Assn. Sys. Mgmt. Republican. Home: PO Box 503 New Carlisle OH 45344-0503

HANSHAW, JAMES BARRY, physician, educator; b. Scarsdale, N.Y., Dec. 23, 1928; s. George Lee and Kathryn Frances (Reilly) H.; m. Marian Christine Kernan, Aug. 14, 1954; children: Thomas, Lee, Elizabeth, John, Margaret. AB, Syracuse U., 1950; MD, SUNY, Syracuse, 1953, DSc (hon.), 1991. Intern Cin. Gen. Hosp., 1953-54; resident pediatrics U. Rochester Med. Center, 1956-58; Nat. Found. postdoctoral fellow virology Harvard U. Sch. Pub. Health, 1958-60; academic medicine, specializing in pediatrics Rochester, N.Y., 1960-75; instr. to prof. pediatrics and microbiology U. Rochester Sch. Medicine, 1960-75; prof., chmn. dept. pediatrics U. Mass., Worcester, 1975-85; interim vice chancellor, acad. dean U. Mass., 1985-86, provost, dean, 1986-89, dean emeritus, prof. pediatrics, 1989—, interim chmn. dept. pediatrics, 1997-98; chmn. dept. pediatrics Meml. Health Care, 1993-98; lectr. pediatrics Harvard U. Med. Sch., 1975—; vis. prof. Inst. Child Health, London U. and Hosp. for Sick Children, London, 1971-72; cons. USPHS, Am. Acad. Pediatrics, Mass. Dept. Pub. Health. Author: (with J.A. Dudgeon) Viral Infections Fetus and Newborn, 1978, 2d edit. (with Dudgeon and W.C. Marshall), 1985. Served with USAF, 1953-56. Buswell fellow U. Rochester, 1960-62; NIH grantee, 1962-75. Mem. AMA, Am. Pediatric Soc., Soc. Pediatric Research, Am. Acad. Pediatrics, Infectious Diseases Soc. Am., New Eng. Pediatric Soc., Sigma Xi, Alpha Omega Alpha. Home: 18 Baypath Dr Boylston MA 01505-1427 Office: 119 Belmont St Worcester MA 01605-2903

HANSLEY, LEE, art gallery owner, curator; b. Roanoke Rapids, N.C., Jan. 11, 1948; s. Lonnie L. and Kathleen (Crumpler) H. Student, U. N.C., 1966-70. City editor The Daily Herald, Roanoke Rapids, 1970-73; editor The Northampton News, Jackson, N.C., 1973-75, Roanoke-Chowan News-Herald, Ahoskie, N.C., 1976, Halifax (N.C.) County This Week, 1976-78, The Suburbanite Newspaper, Winston-Salem, N.C., 1978-80; exhbns. curator Southeastern Ctr. Contemporary Art, Winston-Salem, 1980-86; pub. rels. dir. WUNC Radio, Chapel Hill., N.C., 1986-91; ind. cons. Durham (N.C.) Arts Coun., 1992; proprietor Lee Hansley Gallery, Raleigh, N.C., 1993—; cons. art exhibits Duke U. Law Sch., Durham, 1995—. Curator: Edith London: A Retrospective, 1992; editor: (exhbn. catalogs) Award in Visual Arts, 1981, 83, 86. Mem. Raleigh Arts Commn., 1989-95, chmn., 1991-93; mem. Durham Art Guild, 1991-97; bd. dirs. City Gallery, Raleigh, 1989-93; pub. rels. bd. Nat. Pub. Radio, Washington, 1989-91; mem. City of Raleigh Pub. Art Com., 1989—. Recipient Gen. Excellence award N.C. Press Assn., Chapel Hill, 1978, Investigative Reporting award, 1978. Mem. N.C. Mus. Art., Mus. Modern Art, Smithsonian Instn., Weatherspoon Gallery, Ackland Art Mus. Democrat. Avocations: gardening, non-fiction, art collecting. Home: 804 N King Charles Rd Raleigh NC 27610-1628 Office: Lee Hansley Gallery 16 W Martin St Ste 201 Raleigh NC 27601-2931

HANSMAN, ROBERT G., art educator, artist. BFA, U. Kans., 1970. Asst. prof. Washington U., St. Louis; instr. dept. parks and recreation Project Artspark, 1993, Arts Connection/City Faces, 1994—; instr. juvenile detention program Children's Art Cir., 1995. One-man shows include St. Louis C.C. at Forest Park, 1988, MJF Arts Studio Gallery, 1990, University City Pub. Lib., 1992, 95, Bonsack Gallery, 1995; represented in permanent collection St. Louis C.C. at Forest Park. Mem. pub. housing revitalization focus group Darst-Webbe, 1995. Recipient First Pl. award/Best of Show, St. Louis Artists Guild, 1988, 92, Componere Gallery, 1990, Not Just An Art Dirs. Club, 1990, The Gallery Connection, 1991, Art St. Louis Gallery, 1991, World of Difference award City Faces, 1996, Mo. Arts award Mo. Arts Coun., 1997; named Reader's Poll Best Local Artist, The Riverfront Times, 1995; Bi-State Arts in Transit Project grantee, 1995, 96, 97. E-mail: hansman@arch.wustl.edu. Office: Washington U Sch Arch Campus Box 1079 One Brookings Dr St. Louis MO 63130

HANSMANN, HENRY BAETHKE, law educator; b. Highland Park, Ill., Oct. 5, 1945; s. Elwood Hansmann and Louise Frances (Baethke) Moore; m. Marina Santilli, 1992; 1 child, Lisa Santilli. BA, Brown U., 1967; JD, Yale U., 1974, PhD, 1978. Asst. prof. law U. Pa. Law Sch., Phila., 1975-81, assoc. prof. law, econs. and pub. policy, 1981-83; prof. law Yale U., New Haven, 1983-88, Harris prof., 1988—. Author: The Ownership of Enterprise, 1996. John Simon Guggenheim Found. fellow, 1985-86. Mem. Am. Econ. Assn., Am. Law and Econ. Assn. Home: 340 Livingston St New Haven CT 06511-1336 Office: Yale U Law Sch PO Box 208215 New Haven CT 06520-8215

HANSMANN, RALPH EMIL, investment executive; b. Utica, N.Y., May 25, 1918; s. Emil C. and Friedericka (Fuchs) H.; m. Doris Macdonald, Oct. 16, 1943; children: Robert E., Jane C. AB, Hamilton Coll., 1940, LLD, 1992; MBA, Harvard, 1942. Investment assoc. Harold F. Linder, William T. Golden, N.Y.C., 1945-48, 53—; staff Gen. Am. Investors Co., Inc., 1949-52; bd. advisors First Eagle Fund Am. Emeritus trustee Inst. Advanced Study, Princeton, N.J.; life trustee Hamilton Coll., Clinton, N.Y.; trustee, treas. N.Y. Pub. Libr. Served as lt. USNR, 1942-45. Mem. Downtown Assn. (N.Y.C.), Ridgewood (N.J.) Country Club, Phi Beta Kappa. Home: 385 Manchester Rd Ridgewood NJ 07450-1212 Office: 40 Wall St New York NY 10005-2301

HANSMEIER, BARBARA JO, elementary education educator; b. Jacksonville, Ill., Aug. 1, 1954; d. Samuel Farrell and Harriett Josephine (Moss) H. BA, Ill. Coll., 1976; MS in Elem. Edn., So. Ill. U., Edwardsville, 1993. Cert. tchr., Ill. Tchr. 4th and 5th grades Jacksonville Sch. Dist. 117, 1977-78, tchr. 3d grade, 1978-81; head counselor summer enrichment program for the gifted MacMurray Coll., Jacksonville, 1981-85; tchr. 1st grade Jacksonville Sch. Dist. 117, 1981—; tchr. 1st, 2d and 3d grades MacMurray Coll., Prairie Scholars, Jacksonville, 1988—, chaperone, tour leader, summers, 1986-87, 90. Mem. Jacksonville Art Assn., 1990—, trustee, 1996—; mem. exec. bd. Women's Crisis Ctr., Jacksonville, 1990-95; lifetime mem. aux. Passavant Area Hosp.; mem. Grace United Meth. Ch. Mem. NEA, ASCD, DAR, Ill. Edn. Assn., Jacksonville Edn. Assn., Phi Delta Kappa (sec. 1991-93), Delta Kappa Gamma (chmn. fin. com. 1988-96). Methodist. Avocations: music, walking, nature, crafts, antiques. Home: 3 Baldwin Rd Jacksonville IL 62650-2721 Office: Franklin Elem Sch 352 Franklin St Jacksonville IL 62650-2924

HANSON, A. STUART, health facility administrator, physician; b. Mpls., Mar. 10, 1937; s. Arthur Emanuel and Frances Elenor (Larson) H.; m. Gail Joan Taylor, June 16, 1963; children: Marta Eileen, Peter Arthur. BA, Dartmouth Coll., 1959; MD, U. Minn., 1963. Diplomate Am. Bd. Internal Medicine, Am. Bd. Pulmonary Disease. Cons. Park Nicollet Clinic, Mpls., 1971—, med. dir., 1975-82, v.p. legis. and cmty. affairs, 1982-86; dir. med. edn. Park Nicollet Med. Found., Mpls., 1982-86; pres., CEO Inst. Rsch. & Edn. Healthsys. Minn., Mpls., 1986—; bd. dirs. Minn. Health Data Inst., 1993—. Pres., bd. chair Minn. Smoke Free Coalition, 1989-88, 96-98; chmn. bd. Smoke Free Generation Minn., 1984-90. Recipient Cmty. Leaderhip award Am. Lung Assn. Henepin County, 1987, Harvey H. Rogers Meml. award Minn. Pub. Health Assn., 1988, award for excellence in health promotion Minn. Health Commr., 1989. Fellow ACP, AMA (del., chmn.), Am. Coll. Chest Physicians; mem. Minn. Med. Assn. (pres. 1992-93, Stop the Violence award 1994, Disting. Svc. award 1998), Minn. Healthcare Coalition on Violence, Hennepin County Med. Soc. (pres. 1990-91, Charles Bolles Bolles-Rogers award). Universalist. Avocations: birding, gardening, physical fitness, reading, traveling. Office: Inst Rsch & Edn 3800 Park Nicollet Blvd Minneapolis MN 55416-2527

HANSON, AL, financial newsletter editor and publisher; b. Mpls., May 15, 1930; s. Albert and Lillie (Hanse) H.; m. Janette Ladonna Vansickle, June 27, 1952; children: Sharon, Susan, Shirley, Sandra. BA, Augsburg Coll., 1952. Product mgr. Uniroyal, Indpls., 1960-70; mem., seat owner Mpls. Grain Exch., 1970-76, Intermountain Stock Exch., Salt Lake City, 1971-77; editor Al Hanson Newsletter, Ottertail, Minn., 1982—; pres. Internat. Cons., Buenos Aires, 1989—. Author: Personal Witnessing in Jail, 1989; contbr. several hundred articles to profl. jours. Founder Lutheran Prison Ministry, 1980. Lt. U.S. Army, 1950-60. Home: 312 College Dr Concordia MO 64020 Office: Internat Cons PO Box 9 Ottertail MN 56571-0009 Address: PO Box 168 Concordia MO 64020

HANSON, ANN M., women's health care nurse practitioner; b. Norwich, Conn., June 17, 1965; d. John H. Curran and Dolores C. (Bell) Hudyma; m. James W. Hanson, Jan. 2, 1987; children: Elizabeth Ann, Andrew James. BSN, U. Conn., 1987, MS, 1998. RNC, APRN Conn.; cert. clin. nurse III, cert. in high risk obstetrics and fetal assessment, in neonatal resuscitation, instr. for neonatal resuscitation provider program. Instr. fetal heart monitoring principles and practice program Assn. Women's Health, Obstetrics and Neonatal Nurses; staff nurse pediatrics unit Mt. Sinai Hosp., Hartford, Conn., 1987-888; staff nurse pediatrics unit Lawrence Meml. Hosp., New London, Conn., 1988-98, clin. nurse III labor and delivery room, 1998—; clin. rsch. coord., nurse practitioner Thameside Ob-Gyn Ctr., Groton, Conn. Active Boy Scouts Am.; tchr. religion edn. Sacred Heart Ch., Groton. Mem. Am. Acad. Nurse Practitioners, Assn. Women's Health, Obstetric and Neonatal Nurses, Sigma Theta Tau Internat., Honor Soc. Nursing.

HANSON, ANNE MARIE LALONDE, speech and theatre educator; b. Avon, Ohio, Jan. 18, 1955; d. Robert James and Marjory Verl (Eckstein) LaL.; m. Bruce Arden Hanson, June 4, 1985; 1 child, Eric Loren. BA, Baldwin-Wallace Coll., 1977; MA, Ariz. State U., 1983; postgrad., U. Kans., 1989-91. Tech. dir. Phoenix Ctr. Performing Arts, 1978-79; grad. teaching asst. Schiller Coll., Strasbourg, France, 1977, Ariz. State U., Tempe, 1978-79; asst. prof. theatre and English Benedictine Coll., Atchison, Kans., 1979-84; instr. theatre and speech Northeastern State U., Tahlequah, Okla., 1984-89; grad. teaching asst. U. Kans., Lawrence, 1989-91; instr. speech Haskell Indian Nations U., Lawrence, 1991—. Tech. dir., costume and scene designer Benedictine Coll. Theatre, 1979-84; costume/scenic designer River City Players Summer Theatre, 1985-90. Summer fellow Grad. Coll. U. Kans., Lawrence, 1990. Mem. AAUW, Speech Comm. Assn., U.S. Inst. Theatre Tech. Avocations: antique garment collecting and restoration, needlework, sewing. Home: 1436 S Olive St Ottawa KS 66067-3447 Office: Haskell Indian Nations U 155 Indian Ave Lawrence KS 66046-4817

HANSON, ARNOLD PHILIP, retired lawyer; b. Berlin, N.H., July 11, 1924; s. Arnold H. and Evelyn (Renaud) H.; m. Della Ann Lavernoich, June 26, 1948; children: Arnold Philip, Caryl Hanson Brensinger, Julie E. Hanson Mook. BA, U. N.H., 1948; JD, Boston, 1951. Bar: N.H. 1951. Pvt. practice Berlin, N.H., 1951-60; ptnr. Bergeron & Hanson, Berlin, 1960-80, Bergeron & Hanson, P.A., Berlin, 1980-87, Bergeron, Hanson & Bornstein, P.A., Berlin, 1988-91; county atty. Coos County, N.H., 1952-56; mem. ct. accreditation com. State of N.H., 1970-77, Regional Criminal Justice Planning Coun., 1978-88; ptnr. North Country TV Cable Co., Groveton, N.H., 1962-89; chmn. bd., chmn. exec. com. Berlin City Bank, 1975-87. Chmn. city Republican Conv., Berlin, 1952-54; bd. dirs. Rep. State Com., 1958-60; del. Rep. Nat Com., 1964; trustee A.V. Hosp., 1976-85, mem. coms., 1976-86; area chmn. fundraising campaigns including ARC, U. N.H. Centennial Fund, Crippled Children, N.H. Children's Aid Soc., Boy Scouts Am., Boston U. Law Sch. Centennial Fund, St. Paul's Sch. Advanced Studies Program, A.V. Hosp. Bldg. Fund maj. gifts program, Frank Kenison Fund Boston U. Law Sch.; mem. U. N.H. 50th Reunion Fund Raising Class of 1948, 1996-98. Served with USN, 1943-46. Recipient Silver Shingle award Boston U. Sch. Law, 1977, Alumni Meritorius award U. N.H., 1986. Fellow Am. Bar Found.; mem. N.H. Bar Assn. (pres. 1974-75, bd. govs. 1973-76), Coos County Bar Assn. (pres. various yrs.), Tri-Legal County Svcs., N.H. Alumni Assn. (bd. dirs. 1974-77), Boston U. Alumni Assn., Am. Legion (post judge adv. 1952-64), VFW (post judge adv. 1952-93), Sky Meadow Country Club (Nashua, N.H.), Vines Country Club (Ft. Myers, Fla.), Kiwanis (pres. 1966). Lutheran. Home: 55 Hawthorne Village Rd Nashua NH 03062-2271 also: 13190 Oakmont Drive #8 Fort Myers FL 33907-8020

HANSON, BARBARA JEAN, education educator; b. Pawtucket, R.I., June 4, 1940; d. Joseph Leo and Gladys May (Knowles) Wahl; m. Donald Roland Hanson, June 16, 1962 (div. 1996); children: Erika, Jake. B in Edn., R.I. Coll., 1962; MEd, Bridgewater State Coll., 1993. Tchr. Attleboro (Mass.) Sch. Sys., 1962-65, 68—, Pattonville (Mo.) Sch., 1965-67; lectr. in field. Tchr. leader P.A.L.M.S. Mass. Tchr. fellow. Mem. NEA, Attleboro Tchrs. Assn., Eastern Star, Alpha Delta Kappa. Avocations: nature, arts, singing, crafts. Home: Unit 13 41 Deerfield Rd Unit 13 South Attleboro MA 02703

HANSON, BRUCE EUGENE, lawyer; b. Lincoln, Nebr., Aug. 25, 1942; s. Lester E. and Gladys (Diessner) H.; m. Peggy Pardun, Dec. 25, 1972 (dec. Nov. 1989). BA, U. Minn., 1965, JD, 1966. Bar: Minn. 1966, U.S. Dist. Ct. Minn. 1966, U.S. Tax Ct. 1973, U.S. Ct. Appeals (8th cir.) 1973, U.S. Ct. Appeals (fed. cir.) 1983, U.S. Supreme Ct. 1970. Shareholder Doherty, Rumble & Butler, P.A., St. Paul, 1966—; lawyer; b. Lincoln, Nebr., Aug. 25, 1942; s. Lester E. and Gladys (Diessner) H.; m. Peggy Pardun, Dec. 25, 1972 (dec. Nov. 1989). BA, U. Minn., 1965, JD, 1966. Bar: Minn. 1966, U.S. Dist. Ct. Minn. 1966, U.S. Tax Ct. 1973, U.S. Ct. Appeals (8th cir.) 1973, U.S. Ct. Appeals (fed. cir.) 1983, U.S. Supreme Ct. 1970. Shareholder, Doherty, Rumble & Butler, P.A., St. Paul, 1966—. Dir., sec. Am. Saddlebred Horse Assn.; bd. trustees, chair United Hosp., 1996-98. Mem. ATLA, Ramsey County Bar Assn., Minn. State Bar Assn., Am. Health Lawyers Assn., Minn. Soc. Hosp. Attys., North Oaks Golf Club, Order of Coif, Phi Delta Phi. Dir., sec. Am. Saddlebred Horse Assn.; bd. trustees, chair United Hosp., 1996-98. Mem. ATLA, Ramsey County Bar Assn., Minn. State Bar Assn., Am. Health Lawyers Assn., Minn. Soc. Hosp. Attys., N. Oaks Golf Club, Order of Coif, Phi Delta Phi. Home: 23 Evergreen Rd Saint Paul MN 55127-2077 Office: Doherty Rumble & Butler 2800 Minn World Trade Ctr Saint Paul MN 55101

HANSON, BYRON WINSLADE, music educator; b. Mpls., Feb. 27, 1942; s. Byron Willard and Louisemay (Leim) H.; m. Ann Louise Herkelmann, Aug. 28, 1982; children: Meredith, Lindsay. BMus, Eastman Sch. Music, 1963, MusM, 1965. Tchr. Interlochen (Mich.) Arts Acad., 1965-93; dir. music Interlochen Ctr. for Arts, 1993—; orch. cond. Interlochen Arts Acad., 1971-93; musician Peninsula Music Festival, Fish Creek, Wis., 1968-93; bd. dirs. Youth Orch. Divsn. Am. Symphony Orch. League, Washington. Trustee Pathfinder Sch., Traverse City, Mich., 1990-96, bd. pres. 1994-95. Avocations: reading, history, theatre. Home: PO Box 122 Interlochen MI 49643-0122 Office: Interlochen Ctr for Arts PO Box 199 Interlochen MI 49643-0199

HANSON, CAPPY LOVE, writer, musician, singer, composer; b. Berkeley, Calif., May 12, 1946; d. David Nathaniel and Jeanne Ardath (Warner) Taylor. Contbr. poems to Writer's Digest, Transworld Snowboarding, ByLine, The Los Alamos Monitor, The Santa Fe New Mexican, New Frontiers, Blue Mesa Rev., Poetpourri, three anthologies. Placed 1st Writer's Digest Annual Poetry Competition, 1993, 2nd New Mexican, 1993, 3rd Poetry Soc. Tenn., 1995; recipient Hougthon award New England Poetry Club, 1994. Avocations: bird-watching, snowboarding. Home: 131 Peak Pl Trlr 121 Santa Fe NM 87501-8998

HANSON, CARL MALMROSE, financial company executive; b. Boston, Aug. 25, 1941. BA, U. Mass., 1963; MBA, Dartmouth Coll., 1969. CPA, Mass. Acct. Coopers Lybrand, Boston, 1969-73; chief fin. officer South Shore Bank, Quincy, Mass., 1973-76; v.p. Multibank Fin. Corp., Quincy, Mass., 1976-79; pres. Multibank Leasing Corp., Quincy, Mass., 1979-80; contr. State St. Boston Corp., 1980-84; chief fin. officer Chase Bank Fla., St. Petersburg, 1984-87; contr. Bank New England, Boston, 1987-89; chief fin. officer Amoskeag Bank Shares, Manchester, N.H., 1989-92; exec. v.p. Kirchman Corp., Orlando, Fla., 1992-94, Globex Techknowledge Corp., Heathrow, Fla., 1994-95; pvt. practice fin. cons., 1995—. Lt. USN, 1964-68. Mem. Fin. Execs. Inst. (treas. 1989-91).

HANSON, CHARLES R(ICHARD), manufacturing company executive; b. Appleton, Wis., Mar. 24, 1948; s. Floyd P. and Edna (Vincent) H.; m. Deborah L. Dembowski, June 23, 1973. Student, U. Wis., Madison, 1975, 76—. Auto. mechanic Dave's Cert. Svc., Appleton, 1968-72; svc. mgr. Lien Chem., Milw., 1972-73; tech. coordinator Laminations Corp., Neenah, Wis., 1973-75; gen. foreman Laminations Corp., 1975-79, prodn. supt., 1979-80, prodn. mgr., 1980—; prodn. cons. Laminations West, Ontario, Calif., 1976-99; dir. mfg. Laminations Corp., Neenah, Wis., Allentown, Pa., Wilsonville, Oreg., 1990—. Factory fundraiser United Way, Neenah, Wis., 1981, 88, 91. Mem. ASME (sr. mem.), Internat. Maint. Inst. Avocations: computers, electronics, automobile customizing, auto racing, amateur radio. Home: N254 Pinecrest Blvd Appleton WI 54915-9461 Office: Laminations Corporation 2254 Harrison St # 469 Neenah WI 54956-5901

HANSON, CURTIS, director, writer; b. Mar. 24, 1945. Dir., screenwriter (film) Sweet Kill, 1972, The Bedroom Window, 1988; dir., co-producer (film) The Little Dragons, 1977; dir. (film) The Arousers, 1970, Losin' It, 1983, Bad Influence, 1990, The Hand That Rocks the Cradle, 1992, The River Wild, 1994, L.A. Confidential, 1997, Wonder Boys, 1999; screenwriter: The Dunwich Horror, 1970, The Silent Partner, 1978, White Dog, 1982, Never Cry Wolf, 1983. Office: United Talent Agy 9560 Wilshire Blvd Fl 5 Beverly Hills CA 90212-2400*

HANSON, DALE S., banker; b. Milw., Nov. 11, 1938; s. Yngve Holger and Evelyn (Johnson) H.; m. Joan Benton, July 15, 1961; children—Thomas S., Tim B. B.A. in Econs., Carlton Coll., 1960; postgrad. Exec. Program, Credit and Fin. Mgmt. Stanford U., 1966-67. Asst. cashier First Bank, St. Paul, 1964-66, asst. v.p., 1966-68, v.p., 1968-82, sr. v.p., 1982-83, exec. v.p., 1983-84, pres., 1984-88; pres., mng. ptnr. FBS Mcht. Banking Group, 1987-90; mng. ptnr. Matrix Leasing Internat., 1989-90; exec. v.p. 1st Bank System, Mpls., 1984-91; v.p., treas., chief fin. officer C.H. Robinson Co., Mpls., 1991—, also bd. dirs.; bd. dirs. W.A. Lang Co., Edwards Mfg. Co. Mem. Corp. Health One, Inc.; bd. dirs. St. Paul Chamber Orch., Twin City Pub. TV, St. Paul Riverfront Devel. Corp., 1985-91. 1st lt. USNG, 1961-67. Mem. Robert Morris Assocs. (pres. 1982-83), Fin. Execs. Inst. (bd. dirs. Twin Cities chpt.), Somerset Golf Club, Mpls. Club, Minn. Club (St. Paul). Republican. Presbyterian. Avocations: Skiing; sailing; golfing; photography. Office: care C H Robinson Co 8100 Mitchell Rd Ste 200 Eden Prairie MN 55344-2178*

HANSON, DAVID GORDON, otolaryngologist, surgeon; b. Seattle, Nov. 16, 1943; m. Terri Dangerfield, Jan. 22, 1976. BS, Wheaton Coll., 1966; MD, U. Wash., 1970; MS, U. Minn., 1976. Intern Hennepin County Gen. Hosp., Mpls., 1971-72; resident in surgery and otolaryngology U. Minn., Mpls., 1972-76; sr. surgeon NIH, Nat. Inst. Neurol. and Communicative Disorders and Stroke, USPHS, Bethesda, Md., 1975-78; asst. prof. surgery UCLA Sch. Medicine, 1978-83, assoc. prof., vice chief divsn. head and neck surgery, 1983-89; prof., chmn. dept. otolaryngology Northwestern U. Med. Sch., Chgo., 1989—; chmn. otolaryngology Northwestern Meml. Hosp., Chgo., 1989—; chief sect. head and neck surgery VA Med. Ctr., West Los Angeles, 1983-89. Contbr. articles to profl. jours. Served to comdr. USPHS, 1975-78. NIH grantee, 1983—. Fellow ACS, Triological Soc., Am. Laryngological Assn, Am. Broncho-Esophagol. Assn., Am. Soc. Head and Neck Surgery, Am. Acad. Otolaryngology (Award of Honor, 1985); mem. AMA. Avocations: skiing, sailing.

HANSON, DAVID JAMES, lawyer; b. Neenah, Wis., July 20, 1943; s. Vernon James and Dorothy O. Hanson; m. Diana G. Severson, Aug. 25, 1965 (div. Sept. 1982); children: Matthew Vernon, Maja Kirsten, Brian Edward; m. Linda Hughes Bochert, May 23, 1983; children: Scott Charles, Sarah Katherine. BS, U. Wis., 1965, JD, 1968. Bar: Wis. 1968, U.S. Dist. Ct. (we. dist.) Wis. 1968, U.S. Dist. Ct. (ea. dist.) Wis. 1969, U.S. Ct. Appeals (7th cir.) 1970, U.S. Supreme Ct. 1976. Asst. atty. gen. State of Wis. Dept. of Justice, Madison, 1968-71, dep. atty. gen., 1976-81; asst. chancellor, chief legal counsel U. Wis., Madison, 1971-76; ptnr. Michael, Best & Friedrich, Madison, 1981—; part-time lectr. Law Sch., U. Wis., Madison, 1972-75; bd. dirs., chair govt. law sect. State Bar Wis., Madison, 1979-88. Author monograph: The Lowered Age of Majority: It's Impact on Higher Education, 1975; contbr. articles to profl. publs. Wis. Epilepsy Assn., Madiso n, 1986—; bd. dirs. Sand County Found., Madison, 1988—, Wis. Ctr. for Academically Talented Youth, Madison, 1991-94, bd. trustees Edgewood Coll., Madison, 1987—. Mem. Madison Club, Amer. Bar Assn. Democrat. Unitarian. Avocations: canoeing, skiing, tennis, biking, hunting. Office: Michael Best & Friedrich PO Box 1806 Madison WI 53701-1806

HANSON, DENNIS MICHAEL, medical imaging executive; b. Cleve., Aug. 20, 1943; s. John Joseph and Victoria (Tucholski) H. BBA, Cleve. State U., 1971; MPH, U. Pitts., 1974. Asst. adminstr. Huron Rd. Hosp., Cleve., 1974-76; adminstr. asst. Mt. Sinai Med. Ctr., Cleve., 1976-80; dir. radiology U. Louisville, Ky., 1980-84, assoc. prof., 1982-86; sr. cons. Honeywell, Mpls., 1986-87; mgr. radiology U. N.C., Chapel Hill, 1987-90; mgr. diagnostic imaging Kaiser Hosp., Honolulu, 1990-97; coord. diagnostic imaging Bapt. Regional Med. Ctr., Corbin, Ky., 1999—. Councilman City of Meadowbrook Farm, Ky., 1982-86. With USAF, 1961-65. Named Ky. Colonel, 1984. Fellow Am. Coll. Healthcare Execs.; mem. Am. Hosp. Assn., Am. Hosp. Radiology Adminstrs.

HANSON, DIANE CHARSKE, management consultant; b. Cleve., May 15, 1946; d. Howard Carl and Emma Katherine (Lange) Charske; m. William James Hanson, June 30, 1973. BS, Cornell U., 1968; MS, U. Pa., 1989. Home service rep. Rochester Gas and Electric, N.Y., 1968-70; home economist U. Conn., Storrs, 1970-72; job analyst personnel dept. State of Conn., Hartford, 1972-73; sales rep. Ayerst Labs., Waterbury, Conn., 1973-80, sales trainer, 1979-80; dist. sales mgr. Phila., 1980-87; pres. Creative Resource Devel., W. Chester, Pa., 1986—; developer, pres. Womens Referral Network, West Chester, 1987-89. Vice-pres., bd. dirs., aux. pres. Chester County Soc. for Prevention Cruelty to Animals, 1986-97, pres. bd. dirs., 1992-94, mem. exec. com., 1994-95. Mem. ASTD (v.p. comm. Del. chpt. 1991-92, pres. Del. chpt. 1999—), Internat. Soc. for Performance Improvement (v.p. programs Great Valley chpt. 1993-94, pres.-elect 1995, pres. 1996), Pa. State Tech. Devel. Ctr. (bd. dirs. 1991-92), Assn. Quality and Participation, Phila. Soc. for Human Resources, Phila. Human Resources Planning Group, Phila. Orgn. Devel. Network, Chester County Human Resources Assn. (program chair 1991-92), Greater Valley Forge Human Resources Assn. (bd. dirs. 1993-94). Avocations: skiing, tennis, gardening, sailing, exercise. E-mail: hanson@worldaxes.com. Home and Office: 824 W Strasburg Rd West Chester PA 19382-1927

HANSON, EDWARD ALVIN, technical writer; b. Pomona, Calif., Sept. 28, 1950; s. Donald Raymond Hanson and Joan Lillian (Beisner) Stout; m. Maureen McDonald, Apr. 28, 1980 (div. Jan. 1995); 1 child, Terra Lowansa. AS in Geology, Chaffey C.C., 1970; AS in Computer Sci., Victor Valley Coll., 1987. Chemist Occidental Rsch. Corp., LaVerne, Calif., 1975-78, Scott Specialty Gases, San Bernardino, Calif., 1985-91, Geneva Pharms., Broomfield, Colo., 1993-98, TTS, Inc., Aurora, Colo., 1998—; freelance writer Bear Tracks Comm., 1998—. Contbr. poems to profl. publs. (Pres. award 1998, Diamond award 1998). Mem. Internat. Soc. Poets., Soc. Tech. Comms. Home: 7630 Leyden Ln Commerce City CO 80022-1320

HANSON, EILEEN, principal; b. Camden, N.J., Mar. 3, 1948; d. Thomas Edward and Rita Theresa (Madison) Bannan; m. Kenneth Wesley Hanson, Mar. 22, 1975; 1 child, Michelle Eileen. BA, San Diego State U., 1970; teaching cert., Calif. State U., Dominguez Hills, 1974, cert. adminstr., 1976. Cert. tchr., adminstr., Calif.; cert. mediator, Calif. Prin. St. Anthony Sch., El Segundo, Calif., 1976-80; dir. St. Charles Catechetical Program, San Diego, 1980-87; prin. Holy Family Sch., San Diego, 1987-92, St. Pius X Sch., Chula Vista, Calif., 1992—; grant project coord. for Cath. Schs. San Diego, 1992-94. Mem. ASCD, Nat. Cath. Educators Assn., Greater Math. Assn., San Diego Child Care and Devel. Com., San Diego Alcohol and Tobacco Edn. Assn., Western Cath. Ednl. Assn., Western Assn. Schs. and Colls. Home: 942 Grove Ave Imperial Beach CA 91932-3347 Office: 37 E Emerson St Chula Vista CA 91911-3507

HANSON, ERIK BRIAN, professional baseball player; b. Kinnelon, N.J., May 18, 1965. Student, Wake Forest U. With Seattle Mariners, 1988-93, Cin. Reds, 1994; pitcher Boston Red Sox, 1995-97, Toronto Blue Jays, Can., 1997—. Selected to A.L All-Star Team, 1995.

HANSON, FLOYD BLISS, applied mathematician, computational scientist, mathematical biologist; b. Bklyn., Mar. 9, 1939; s. Charles Keld and Violet Ellen (Bliss) H.; m. Ethel Louisa Hutchins, July 27, 1962; 1 child, Lisa Kirsten. BS, Antioch Coll., 1962; MS, Brown U., 1964, PhD, 1968. Space technician Convair Astronautics, San Diego, 1961; applied mathematician Arthur D. Little, Inc., Cambridge, Mass., 1961; physicist Wright-Patterson AFB, Dayton, Ohio, 1962; assoc. research scientist Courant Inst., N.Y.C., 1967-68; asst. prof. U. Ill., Chgo., 1969-75, assoc. prof., 1975-83, prof., 1983—, assoc. dir. Lab. for Advanced Computing, 1990—; faculty rsch. participant Argonne (Ill.) Nat. Lab., 1985-87, faculty rsch. leave, 1987-88, rsch. assoc., 1988—; vis. prof., divsn. applied math. Brown U., 1994; mem. vis. faculty Sch. Civil and Environ. Engring., Cornell U., 1995. Assoc. editor-in-chief Applied and Computational Control Signals and Circuits, 1996—; author: (with others) Control and Dynamical Systems: Advances in Theory and Applications, 1996; contbr. articles in field to profl. jours. NSF rsch. grantee, 1970-83, 88—, NSF equipment grantee, 1973; Nat. Ctr. for Supercomputer Applications Computer grantee, 1986—; supercomputer grantee Los Alamos Nat. Lab., 1990-97, Cornell Theory Ctr., 1993-96, Pitts. Supercomputer Ctr., 1993-98, San Diego grantee Super Computer Ctr., 1998—. Mem. Soc. Indsl. and Applied Math., Computer Soc. of IEEE, Control Soc. of IEEE, Resource Modeling Assn. Home: 5435 S East View Park Chicago IL 60615-5915 Office: U Ill Dept Math Stats and Computer Sci M/C 249 851 S Morgan St Rm 322 Chicago IL 60607-7042

HANSON, GEORGE, music director, conductor; m. Dawn Hanson. Degree, Ind. U. Resident conductor Atlanta Symphony; asst. to Leonard Bernstein Vienna Stae Opera; asst. Giuseppe Patane La Scala, Covent Garden, Munich Opera Houses; mus. dir. Anchorage Symphony; asst. conductor N.Y. Philharmonic; conductor Tucson Symphony Orchestra; appeared with sixty orchestras and operas in sixteen countries. Named Winner of the Leopold Stokowski Competition at Carnegie Hall, N.Y.C., Hungarian Internat. Coducting Competition, Budapest, Young Musician of 1990 Musical Am. Address: Tucson Symphony Orchestra-TSO 2175 N 6th Ave Tucson AZ 85705-5606

HANSON, GERALD EUGENE, oral and maxillofacial surgeon; b. Lincoln, Nebr., July 18, 1947; s. Gerald Stephen and Ferne Althea (Russell) H. DDS, MPH, Loma Linda U., 1973; oral & maxillofacial surgery cert., U. Minn., 1976. Diplomate Am. Bd. Forensic Dentistry. Pvt. practice Palm Desert, Calif., 1976-78, Las Vegas, Nev., 1978—; mem. com. edn. & rsch. Eisenhower Med. Ctr., Rancho Mirage, Calif., 1977, dir. continuing dental edn. program, 1977-78; chief divsn. oral & maxillofacial surgery Sunrise Hosp., 1984-94, Columbia Mountain View Hosp., 1995—. Rep. environ. reference com. joint policy coun. APHA, Washington, 1977; bd. dirs. Clark County chpt. Am. Cancer Soc., 1979-83; chmn. oral cancer screening clinics Jaycees State Fair & Annual Health Fair, Las Vegas, 1981; adv. bd. Clark County C.C., Las Vegal, 1979; mem. Nev. State Bd. Health, 1990-95; bd. dirs. Am. Assn. Oral and Maxillofacial Surgery Found., 1995—. Fellow Pierre Fauchard Acad., Internat. Coll. Dentists, Western Soc. Oral & Maxillofacial Surgeons (bd. dirs. 1981-83, 91-97, pres. 1995-96), Am. Assn. Oral & Maxillofacial Surgeons (trustee Dist. VI 1984-88, Nev. del. 1979-83, sec.-treas. 1988-91), Am. Coll. Dentistry; mem. ADA (chmn. sci. session 1982, mem. coun. hosp. affairs 1985-89, AAOMS rep. interprofl. rels. com. 1987), Nev. Dental Assn. (co-chmn. group care & hosp. svcs. com. 1979-84, Clark County del. Ho. Dels. 1980-84, pres. 1987), Am. Coll. Oral & Maxillofacial Surgeons, Nev. Soc. of Oral and Maxillofacial Surgeons (pres. 1983-85), Am. Assn. Oral and Maxillofacial Surgery Found. (bd. dirs. 1995—), Las Vegas Execs. Assn., Clark County Aviation Assn., Clark County Dental Soc. (pres. 1982-83). Avocations: flying, antique airplane collecting, music, diving, skiing. Office: 2585 S Jones Blvd Ste 1A Las Vegas NV 89146-5604

HANSON, GERALD WARNER, retired county official; b. Alexandria, Minn., Dec. 25, 1938; s. Lewis Lincoln and Dorothy Hazel (Warner) H.; m. Sandra June Wheeler, July 9, 1960; 1 child, Cynthia R. AA, San Bernardino Valley (Calif.) Coll., 1959; BA, U. Redlands (Calif.), 1979; MA, U. Redlands, 1981; EdD, Pepperdine U., 1995. Cert. advanced metrication specialist. Dep. sealer San Bernardino (Calif.) County, 1964-80, div. chief, 1980-85, dir. weights and measures, 1985-94; CATV cons. City of Redlands, 1996—, City of Yucaipa, 1998—; substitute tchr. Redlands Unified Sch. Dist., 1996—. Chmn. Redlands Rent Rev. Bd., 1985-99; bd. dirs. House Neighborly Svc., Redlands, 1972-73, Boys Club, Redlands, 1985-86; mem. Redlands Planning commn., 1990-98. With USN. Fellow U.S. Metric Assn. (treas. 1986-88, 92—); mem. NRA (life), Nat. Conf. on Weights and Measures (life, asst. treas. 1986-94), Western Weights and Measures Assn. (life, pres. 1987-88), Calif. Assn. Weights and Measures Ofcls. (life, 1st v.p. 1987), Calif. Rifle and Pistol Assn. (life), Masons, Shriners, Kiwanis (treas. Redlands club 1983-95), Over the Hill Gang (San Bernardino, newsletter editor 1998—). Avocations: golf, digital photography, mechanics, microcomputers. Home: 225 E Palm Ave Redlands CA 92373-6131

HANSON, GILBERT NIKOLAI, geochemistry educator; b. Mpls., Apr. 30, 1936; s. John Jacob and Evelyn Bernice (Huikko) H.; m. Janet Rae Hillman, Sept. 15, 1963; children: Lynn Carol, Kevin Andrew, Darlene Annette. BA, U. Minn., 1958, MS, 1962, PhD, 1964. Rsch. assoc. Minn. Geol. Survey, Mpls., 1964-65, Swiss Fed. Inst. Tech., Zurich, Switzerland, 1965-66; asst. prof. geochemistry SUNY, Stony Brook, 1966-70, assoc. prof. geochemistry, 1970-75, prof. geochemistry, 1975—, chmn. dept. earth and space scis., 1983-93. Contbr. numerous articles to profl. jours. Grantee NSF, NASA, Dept. Energy, Am. Chem. Soc. Mem. AAAS, Geol. Soc. Am., Am. Geophys. Union, Geochemical Soc., Geol. Soc. India. Democrat. Unitarian. Avocations: bicycling, skiing, inline skating, reading. Home: 7 Pilgrim Dr Prt Jefferson NY 11777-1409 Office: SUNY at Stony Brook Dept Geosciences Stony Brook NY 11794-2100

HANSON, HAROLD PALMER, physicist, government official, editor, academic administrator; b. Virginia, Minn., Dec. 27, 1921; s. Martin Bernhard and Elvida Elaine (Paulsen) H.; m. Mary Jean Stevenson, June 22, 1944; children: Steven Bernard, Barbara Jean. BS, Superior (Wis.) State Coll., 1942; MS, U. Wis., 1944, PhD, 1948. Mem. faculty U. Fla., 1948-54, dean grad. sch., 1969-71, v.p. acad. affairs, 1971-74, exec. v.p., 1974-78, exec. v.p. emeritus, 1990—; mem. faculty U. Tex., Austin, 1954-69, prof. physics, 1961-69, chmn. dept., 1962-69; provost Boston U., 1978-79; exec. dir. Com. on Sci. and Tech., U.S. Ho. of Reps., Washington, 1979-82, 84-90; provost Wayne State U., Detroit, 1982-84; summer rsch. physicist Lincoln Labs., MIT, 1953, Gen. Atomic Co., San Diego, 1964; summer vis. lectr. U. Wis., 1957; Fulbright rsch. scholar, Norway, 1960-61. Editor DELOS, 1991—. Bd. dirs. N. Central Fla. Health Planning Coun.; mem. steering com. Fla. Ednl. Computer Network. With USNR, 1944-46. Decorated St. Olav's medal Norway, Order of North Star 1st class Sweden; U. Fla. presdl. scholar, 1976. Fellow Am. Phys. Soc.; mem. Sigma Xi, Sigma Pi Sigma, Omicron Delta Kappa. Clubs: Town and Gown (Austin); Rotary. Office: U Fla 118 440 2346 NPB Gainesville FL 32611-2085

HANSON, HEIDI ELIZABETH, lawyer; b. Portsmouth, Ohio, Nov. 13, 1954. BS, U. Ill., 1975, JD, 1978. Bar: Ill. 1978, U.S. Dist. Ct. (no. dist.) Ill., U.S. Ct. Appeals (7th cir.). Atty. water, air and land pollution divs. Ill. EPA, Springfield, Ill., 1978-85; atty. water pollution div. Ill. EPA, Maywood, Ill., 1985-86; assoc. Ross & Hardies, Chgo., 1987-89, ptnr., 1990-94; founder H.E. Hanson Law Offices, Western Springs, Ill., 1994—. Mem. Chgo. Bar Assn., Air and Waste Mgmt. Assn., Indsl. Water, Waste and Sewer Group. Avocation: gardening. Office: 4721 Franklin Ave Ste 1500 Western Springs IL 60558-1720

HANSON, JANICE CRAWFORD, artist, financial analyst; b. Norwalk, Conn., Oct. 8, 1952; d. Arthur James and Jean Alice (MacKinnon) Crawford; m. Jeffrey Becker Hanson, May 29, 1976; children: Forrest James, Shane Crawford. BA, Wellesley Coll., 1974; MBA, U. Denver, 1979. CFA. Sec. to assoc. dean Yale Sch. of Music, New Haven, Conn., 1975-76; adminstrv. asst. to dir. of internships Inst. Policy Scis. Duke U., Durham, N.C., 1976-78; fiscal analyst Denver Water Bd., 1979-84; fin. analyst Englewood, Colo., 1984; part-time fin. analyst Jeffrey B. Hanson M.D., P.C., Granger, Ind., 1989-92; part-time watercolorist Englewood, Colo., 1989—. Exhibited in group shows at Watercolor West XXVII Exhbn., Riverside, Calif., 1995, Western Colo. Watercolor Soc. Nat. Juried Exhbn., Grand Junction, 1994, 95, 96, Rocky Mountain Nat. Watermedia Exhbn., Golden, Colo., 1996, 98, Pikes Peak Watercolor Soc. Nat. Exhbn., Colorado Springs, Colo., 1997, 98, Am. Women Artists Nat. Juried Competition, Taos, N.M., 1999. Vol. Denver Dumb Friends League, 1986-88, Cherry Creek Schs., Englewood, Colo., 1992—. Recipient Best of Show award Nat. Greeley Art Mart, 1994, Platinum award, Nat. Greeley Art Mart, 1995, Dean Witter award for originality Colo. Watercolor Soc. State Juried Exhbn., Denver, Colo., 1996. Mem. Assn. for Investment Mgmt. and Rsch., Watercolor West (juried assoc.), Colo. Watercolor Soc. (signature), Western Colo. Watercolor Soc. (signature), Denver Soc. Security Analysts. Avocations: running, fiber arts, needlework, photography.

HANSON, JASON DAVID, lawyer; b. L.A., Feb. 14, 1969; s. William Dean and Merrilyn Ethyl (Coleman) H. BS, Cornell U., 1991; JD, Duke U., 1994. Bar: Md. 1994, D.C. 1995. Assoc. Arnold & Porter, Washington, 1994-97; trial atty. anti trust divsn. U.S. Dept. Justice, Washington, 1997-99; global litigation counsel GE Med. Systems, Milwaukee, Wis., 1999—. Staff editor: Duke Law Jour., 1993-94. Mem. ABA. Office: GE 3000 Grandview W-400 Waukesha WI 53188

HANSON, JEAN ELIZABETH, lawyer; b. Alexandria, Minn., June 28, 1949; d. Carroll Melvin and Alice Clarissa (Frykman) H.; m. H. Barndt Hauptfuhrer, May 15, 1982; children: Catherine Jean, Benjamin Colman (twins). BA, Luther Coll., 1971; JD, U. Minn., 1976. Bar: N.Y. 1977, U.S. Dist. Ct. (so. dist.) 1977. Probation officer Hennepin County, Mpls., 1972-73; law clk. Minn. State Pub. Defender, Mpls., 1975-76; assoc. Fried, Frank, Harris, Shriver & Jacobson, N.Y.C., 1976-83, ptnr., 1983-93, 94—; gen. counsel U.S. Treasury, Washington, 1993-94; Mem. bd. regents Luther Coll.; mem. bd. visitors Law Sch. U. Minn. Recipient Disting. Svc. award Luther Coll., 1991, Outstanding Achievement award U. Minn., 1999. Mem. ABA, N.Y. State Bar Assn., Assn. of Bar of City of N.Y. (securities regulation com. 1991-98, mem. task force women in the profession 1995-98), U. Minn. Law Alumni Assn. Democrat. Lutheran. Office: Fried Frank Harris Shriver & Jacobson One New York Plaza New York NY 10004

HANSON, JIM HENRY, veterinarian; b. Sioux Falls, S.D., Mar. 8, 1967; s. Henry Albert and Alice Mae (Shove) H.; m. Marie Elnora Cummings. BS in biology, BS in chemistry, Southwest State U., Marshall, Minn., 1989; DVM, U. Minn., 1993. Veterinarian Dakota Large Animal Clinic, Harrisburg, S.D., 1993-96; pvt. practice Adrian, Minn., 1996—. Mem. AVMA, Am. Assn. Equine Practitioners. Home: 29371 Durfee Ave Adrian MN 56110-9747 Office: Hanson Veterinary Svcs 29371 Durfee Ave Adrian MN 56110-9747

HANSON, JO, artist; b. Carbondale, Ill.; d. Thomas A. and Carrie M. H. MA in Art, San Francisco State U.; MA in Edn, U. Ill. Instr. sculpture U. Calif., Berkeley, Calif. Coll. Arts and Crafts, Oakland; participant art panels Women's Caucus for Art and Coll. Art Assn., 1979, 81, 89, 91, 93, 99, Exploratorium Symposium, "Rising Above Our Garbage", San Francisco, 1994; co-curator Living in Balance, San Francisco Internat. Airport and Richmond Art Ctr., 1993, 94, Dear Mother Earth, Marin County Civic Ctr., 1998. Author: Artists' Taxes, The Hands-on Guide, 1987; one-woman shows of sculpture and installations include, Corcoran Gallery Art, Washington, 1974, Pa. Acad. Fine Arts, Phila., 1976, Utah Mus. Fine Arts, Salt Lake City, 1977, San Francisco Mus. Modern Art, 1976, 80, Internat. Sculpture Conf., San Francisco, 1982, Internat. Conf. Health Cities, San Francisco, 1993, Dublin (Calif.) Civic Ctr., 1994; exhibited in numerous group shows including San Francisco Mus. Modern Art, 1978, Otis Art Inst., 1978, Museau de Arte Contemporanea da U. de São Paulo, Brazil, 1980, Pratt Manhattan Center, N.Y.C., 1981, Auckland City Art Gallery, N.Z., 1985, Municipal Art Soc., N.Y. 1990, Regional Ctr. for the Arts, Walnut Creek, Calif., 1993-95, Ariz. State U., 1995; represented in permanent collections including Bank of Am., San Francisco, Herbert F. Johnson Mus. Cornell U., Fresno (Calif.) Art Mus., Mills Coll., Oakland, Calif., Oakland Mus. of Art, San Francisco Arts Commn., San Francisco Mus. Modern Art, numerous pvt. collections; co-prodr. Women Environmental Artists Directory, 1999. Mem. San Francisco Arts Commn., 1982-89; mem. adv. bd. artist-in-residence Exploratorium, San Francisco, 1983-91; advisor artist-in-residence program San. Fill Co., San Francisco. Recipient citation San Francisco Bd. Suprs., 1980, San Francisco mayor, 1989; named Disting. Woman Artist of Yr., Fresno (Calif.) Art Mus., 1998; Nat. Endowment for Arts fellow, 1977, grantee, 1980. Mem. Coll. Art Assn., Women's Caucus for Art (Regional Lifetime Achievement award 1992, Nat. Lifetime Achievement award 1997), Pacific Rim Sculptors Group. Subject of articles in numerous newspapers, mags. and books.

HANSON, JOHN, federal agency administrator; b. Tuscaloosa, Ala., May 16, 1950; m. Julie Clifford. BA, Ga. State U. Staff mem. Gov. George Busbee, Ga., 1977-79; dep. dir. state svcs. Nat. Govs. Assn., 1979-83; dir. vet. affairs and rehab. divsn. Am. Legion; spl. asst. to asst. sec. for pub. and intergovtl. affairs Dept. Vets. Affairs, Washington, 1994, dep. asst. sec. intergovtl. affairs, 1995, acting asst. sec. for pub. and intergovtl. affairs, 1998—. With USAF, 1971-74, Vietnam. Office: Dept Vets Affairs 810 Vermont Ave NW Washington DC 20420

HANSON, JOHN C., investment company executive. Ltd. ptnr. Brown Bros. Harriman & Co., N.Y.C. Office: Brown Bros Harriman & Co 59 Wall St New York NY 10005-2808

HANSON, JOHN J., lawyer; b. Aurora, Nebr., Oct. 22, 1922; s. Peter E. and Hazel Marion (Lounsbury) H.; m. Elizabeth Anne Moss, July 1, 1973; children from their previous marriages—Mark, Eric, Gregory. A.B., U. Denver, 1948; LL.B. cum laude, Harvard U., 1951. Bar: N.Y. bar 1952, Calif. bar 1955. Asso. firm Dewey, Ballantine, Bushby, Palmer & Wood, N.Y.C., 1951-54; ptnr. firm Gibson, Dunn & Crutcher, L.A, 1954—; mem. exec. com. Gibson, Dunn & Crutcher, 1978-87, adv. ptnr., 1991—. Contbr. articles to profl. jours. Trustee Palos Verdes (Calif.) Sch. Dist., 1969-73. Served with U.S. Navy, 1942-45. Fellow Am. Coll. Trial Lawyers; mem. Am. Bar Assn., Los Angeles County Bar Assn. (chmn. antitrust sect. 1979-80), Bel Air Country Club. Home: 953 Linda Flora Dr Los Angeles CA 90049-1630 Office: Gibson Dunn & Crutcher 333 S Grand Ave Ste 4400 Los Angeles CA 90071-3197

HANSON, JOHN M., civil engineering and construction educator; b. Brookings, S.D., Nov. 16, 1932; m. Mary Josephson, Jan. 16, 1960 (dec. 1999). B.S.C.E., S.D. State U., 1949; M.S. in Structural Engring., Iowa State U., 1957; Ph.D. in Civil Engring., Lehigh U., 1964. Profl. engr. Ill., N.C., Colo., Oreg., Mich. Structural engr. J.T. Banner & Assoc., Laramie, Wyo., 1957-58, Phillips, Carter, Osborn, Denver, 1958-60; research inst. prof. Lehigh U., Bethlehem, Pa., 1960-65; engr., asst. mgr. structural devel. Portland Cement Assn., Skokie, Ill., 1965-72; rsch. dir., v.p., pres. Wiss, Janney, Elstner, Northbrook, Ill., 1972-92; disting. prof. civil engring. and constrn. N.C. State U., Raleigh, 1993—. Contbr. articles to profl. jours. Served to lt. USAF, 1953-55, Korea. Recipient Disting. Engr. award S.D. State U., 1979; Profl. Achievement citation Iowa State U., 1980. Fellow ASCE (State of Art award 1974, Reese award 1976, 88, T.Y. Lin award 1979, Boase award 1995, forensic engring. award 1999), Am. Concrete Inst. (hon., bd. dirs. 1981-84, 88-94, v.p. 1988-89, pres. 1990, Bloem award 1976, Henry Crown award Ill. chpt. 1993), Prestressed Concrete Inst. (bd. dirs. 1977-80, 93-95, Korn award 1978); mem. NAE, Internat. Assn. Bridge and Structural Engring. (hon., pres. 1993-97), Internat. Concrete Repair Inst., Transp. Rsch. Bd. Lutheran. Office: NC State U Dept Civil Engring Campus Box 7908 Raleigh NC 27695-7908

HANSON, KAREN, philosopher, educator; b. Lincoln, Nebr., Apr. 11, 1947; d. Lester Eugene and Gladys (Diessner) H.; m. Dennis Michael Senchuk, Aug. 22, 1970; children: Tia Elizabeth, Chloe Miranda. BA summa cum laude, U. Minn., 1970; MA, Harvard U., 1980, PhD, 1980. Lectr. to assoc. prof. Ind. U., Bloomington, 1976-91, prof. philosophy, 1991—, adj. prof. Am. studies, women's studies, and comparative lit., 1991—, chair philosophy, 1997—; mem. governing bd. Ind. U. Inst. for Advanced Study, Bloomington, 1992-95; mem. editorial bd. Peirce Edition Project, Indpls., 1982-89, 90—. Author: The Self Imagined, 1986; co-editor: Romantic Revolutions, 1990; assoc. editor Jour. Social Philosophy, 1982-86; edtl. bd. Philosophy of Music Edn. Rev., 1992—; edtl. cons. Am. Philos. Quar., 1995—; contbr. articles to profl. books and jours. Del. Am. Coun. Learned Socs., 1993-98 (exec. com., 1994-98); officer John Dewey Found., 1989—. Office of Women's Affairs disting. scholar, 1995. Mem. Am. Philos. Assn. (exec. officer 1986-91, program com. 1984-91, nominating com. 1993-94, 95-96, com. priorities and problems 1998—), Am. Soc. for Aesthetics (program com. 1989-90, 98-99, 99-00, trustee 1997—), Soc. for Women in Philosophy, Phi Beta Kappa (exec. com. Gamma of Ind. chpt. 1993-97, officer 1995-97, pres. 1996-97). Home: 1606 S Woodruff Ln Bloomington IN 47401-4448 Office: Ind U Dept of Philosophy Sycamore 026 Bloomington IN 47405

HANSON, KENT BRYAN, lawyer; b. Litchfield, Minn., Sept. 17, 1954; s. Calvin Bryan and Muriel (Wessman) H.; m. Barbara Jane Ehlenbaus, Aug. 24, 1974; children: Lindsay Michal, Taylor Jordan, Chase Philip. AA with high honors, Trinity Western Coll., 1974; BA, U. B.C., Vancouver, 1976; JD magna cum laude, U. Minn., 1979. Bar: Minn. 1979, U.S. Dist. Ct. Minn. 1980, U.S. Ct. Appeals (8th cir.) 1980, U.S. Dist. Ct. (we. dist.) Wis. 1983, Wis. 1985, U.S. Ct. Appeals (9th cir.) 1989, U.S. Dist. Ct. Ariz. 1992, Ohio 1993, Calif. 1994. Assoc. Grossman, Karlins, Siegel & Brill, Mpls., 1979-81, Gray, Plant, Mooty, Mooty & Bennett, Mpls., 1981-85; ptnr. Bowman & Brooke, Mpls., 1986-95; CEO Hanson, Marek, Bolkcom & Greene, Ltd., Mpls., 1996—. Bd. dirs. Inner City Boys Club, Ctrl. Free Ch., Mpls., 1979-81; 12th ward del. Mpls. Dem. Farmer Labor Com. Conv., 1982; mem. exec. bd. Ctrl. Free Ch., Mpls., 1986; chair exec. bd. Ctrl. Community Ch., 1993-96. Mem. ABA, State Bar Assn. Wis., Minn. Def. Lawyers Assn., Minn. State Bar Assn., Hennepin County Bar Assn., Calif. State Bar Assn., State Bar of Ohio, Def. Rsch. Inst. Avocations: classical music, golf, tennis, computers, theology. Office: Hanson Marek Bolkcom & Greene Ltd 2200 Rand Tower 527 Marquette Ave Minneapolis MN 55402-1302

HANSON, KERMIT OSMOND, business administration educator, university dean emeritus; b. Troy Twp., Iowa, May 14, 1916; s. Gerhard Severin and Sunniva Fosmark (Borge) H.; m. Jane Elizabeth Haugen, Aug. 17, 1940; children: James Stephen, Katherine Jane, Paul Richard, Daniel Gerhard. A.B. cum laude, Luther Coll., Decorah, Iowa, 1938; M.S., Iowa State U., 1940, Ph.D., 1950; D.Sc. (hon.), Luther Coll., 1981. Ops. analyst Fed. Land Bank, Omaha, 1941-43; chief statis. service sect. VA br. office, Seattle, 1946-47; mem. faculty Sch. Bus. Adminstrn., U. Wash., Seattle, 1948-81; prof. acctg., finance and statistics Sch. Bus. Adminstrn., U. Wash., 1954-81, chmn. dept. accounting, finance and statistics, 1955-60, assoc. dean, 1959-64; dean Sch. Bus. Adminstrn., U. Wash. (Grad. Sch. Bus. Adminstrn.), 1964-81, dean emeritus, 1981—; John F. Mee Disting. prof. Sch. Bus. Adminstrn. Pacific Luth. U., 1985-86; instr., ednl. dir. Pacific Coast Banking Sch., 1948-81, also mem. bd. dirs.; exec. dir Pacific Rim Bankers Program, 1977-89, vice chmn. bd. dirs., 1979-98, chmn. emeritus, 1998—; bd. dirs. Pacific Horizon Funds, Inc., 1982-98, Wash. Fed. Savs. & Loan Assn., 1966—, Seafirst Retirement trust, 1993-97, Safeco Corp., 1976-81; cons. GAO, 1970-78; chmn. Wash. Gov.'s Adv. Coun. on Productivity, 1974-75; mem. bd. adv. Naval Postgrad. Sch., Monterey, Calif., 1976-84. Author: Managerial Statistics, 1955, 2d edit. (with G. Brabb), 1961, (with M. Tomich) (monograph) Pacific Rim Bankers Program—A Brief History—The First Ten Years 1977-1986, 1987, The Pacific Coast Banking School—The First 50 Years, 1988. Mem. adv. com. Chief Seattle coun. Boy Scouts Am., 1958—, pres., 1967-69; bd. trustees Horizon House, 1990-96, pres., 1994-96; mem. adv. bd. U. Miami (Fla.) Sch. Bus., 1983-88, Pacific Luth. U. Sch. Bus., Tacoma, 1987-90, Seattle Pacific U. Sch. Bus., 1985-90; bd. dirs. Journey for Perspective Found., 1964-76. Lt. USNR, 1943-46. Recipient

Silver Beaver award Seattle council Boy Scouts Am., 1963, Disting. Service award U. Wash., 1981, Pioneer Meml. award Luther Coll., 1997. Mem. Am. Assn.. Collegiate Schs. Bus. (pres. 1971-72), Am. Accounting Assn., Am. Finance Assn., Financial Execs. Inst., Beta Gamma Sigma, Beta Alpha Psi, Alpha Kappa Psi. Lutheran. Home: 17760 14th Ave NW Shoreline WA 98177-3207

HANSON, LARRY KEITH, plastics company executive; b. Hawkins, Wis., Aug. 14, 1932; s. Harold and Clara Pauline (Lund) H.; m. Patricia Rosalie Sammarco, Aug. 6, 1955; children: Lawrence Keith, John Steven, James Paul. BS, U.S. Mcht. Marine Acad., 1955. Engr. Curtis-Wright Corp., Woodridge, N.J., 1955-58; sales engr. Gits Bros. Mfg. Co., Chgo., 1958-66, Aeroquip Corp., Burbank, Calif., 1966-70; exec. v.p. Furon Co., Laguna Niguel, Calif., 1970-97; mng. dir. Furon SA/NV subs. Furon Co., Kontich, Belgium, 1983-90; exec. v.p. Furon Co., Laguna Niguel, Calif., 1990-97; retired, 1997; cons. (part-time) Furon Co., Laguna Niguel, 1997—. Patentee in field. Mem. ASME, Soc. Automotive Engrs. Avocations: fly fishing, drawing, inventions. Office: Furon Co. 4412 Corporate Center Dr Los Alamitos CA 90720-2400*

HANSON, LOWELL KNUTE, seminar developer and leader, information systems consultant; b. Langford, S.D., Sept. 28, 1935; s. Hans Jacob and Katherine Sofie (Hoines) H.; m. Mary Lou Heeney, Oct. 24, 1964; children: Victoria Lynn Hanson Wheeler, Thomas Lowell, Ronald Richard. BSEE, S.D. Sch. Mines and Tech., 1961. Cert. Cisco trainer. Field engr. supr. Control Data, Sunnyvale, Calif., 1961-62; mgr. systems test Control Data, Mpls., 1962-69; mgr. product mgmt. Control Data, France, 1969-71; mgr. test and integration Control Data, Mpls., 1971-74; communications cons. Control Data, Republic of South Africa, 1974-76; prin. applications engr. Control Data, Mpls., 1976-85; prin. systems engr. Martin Marrietta, Washington, 1986; pres. Viking Svcs., Centreville, Va., 1986—; LAN seminar dir. The Am. Inst., N.Y., 1987, 89; dir. and cons. Bus. Comm. Rev., Hinsdale, Ill., 1990-93, Am. Rsch. Group, 1993—. Author, presenter Trouble Shooting LANs seminar, 1988, Hands on LAN, 1990, Maintaining and Trouble Shooting Novell LANs, 1990. Pres. Homeowner Assn., Maple Grove, Minn., 1983-84. Fellow IEEE; mem. Toastmasters (pres. Maple Grove chpt. 1981-82, Capital area gov. 1986, Toastmaster of Yr. Maple Grove chpt. 1983, past pres. worldwide 84, Club of Yr. 84 Toastmasters). Republican. Avocations: reading, personal development, hiking, plays, movies. Office: Viking Svcs 6418 Overcoat Ln Centreville VA 20121-2314

HANSON, MARK TOD, engineering mechanics educator; b. Montevideo, Minn., Nov. 14, 1960; s. Curtis Dewayne and Maxie Lou (Todt) H. BS in Civil Engring., N.D. State U., 1983; MS in Structural Engring., U. Wash., 1985; PhD in Applied Mechanics, Northwestern U., 1989. Asst. prof. engring. mechanics U. Ky., Lexington, 1989-95, assoc. prof. engring. mechanics, 1994—; vis. prof. dept. mech. engring. Kyushu U., Fukuoka, Japan, 1990; spkr. in field univs., confs.; organizer, chair conf. sessions. Assoc. editor Stress Intensity Factors Handbook; reviewer jours. in field; contbr. articles to profl. jours., book chpts.; pub. conf. proceedings. Mem. ASME (Henry Hess award 1993), ASCE (elasticity com. 1991—), Tau Beta Pi, Phi Kappa Phi. Avocations: skiing, fishing, cycling, hunting. Office: Univ of Kentucky Dept of Engring Mechanics 467 Anderson Hall Lexington KY 40506-0046

HANSON, MARTIN PHILIP, mechanical engineer, farmer; b. Watseka, Ill., Feb. 4, 1937; s. Philip Andrew and Mary Jane (Martin) H.; m. Virginia Ann Garfield, Jan. 2, 1960; children: Martin Philip Jr., Adam Gunnar. BS, U.S. Naval Acad., 1959. Registered profl. engr., Mich., Ill., La., Maine, N.H., Tex. Commd. ensign USN, 1959, advanced through grades to lt. comdr., 1968; reactor mech. asst. USS Enterprise (CVAN-65), Alameda, Calif., 1968-69; resigned, 1969; project engr. Consumers Power Co., Jackson, Mich., 1969-74; project engring. mgr. United Engrs. and Constructors Inc., Phila., 1974-77, Seabrook, N.H., 1977-82, Glen Rose, Tex., 1982-83, Washington, 1983-87; project control specialist Systematic Mgmt. Svcs., Argonne, Ill., 1987-92; project engr. Mac Tech. Svcs. Co., Argonne, 1992-95; sr. project mgmt. specialist Aguirre Engrs., Inc., Argonne, 1995-97; v.p. RERC Environ., Inc., Chgo., 1997—; sec. repository coordination group Dept. Energy, Washington, 1983-86, sec. repository change control, 1984-86. Capt. USNR, 1969-92, comdr. res. regts. Mem. ASME (past chmn. New England sect.), Am. Nuc. Soc., Chgo. Computer Soc., Naval Res. Assn., Organ Transplant Support (past dir.-at-large), Transplant Recipients Internat., Nat. Soc. SAR. Achievements include organizing new programs for continuous fiber ceramic composites and other technologies. Avocations: automobiles, tax preparation, classical music. Home: 1009 Troutlilly Ln Darien IL 60561-8819 Office: RERC Environ Inc 2 N Lasalle St Ste 730 Chicago IL 60602-3703

HANSON, MARY LOUISE, retired social services administrator; b. Walsenburg, Colo., Nov. 8, 1928; d. Norman Francis and Ellen Matilda (Peterson) Kastner; m. Peter R. Hanson, Sept. 1, 1951 (dec. Dec. 1991); children: Sherod Day, Janell Marie, Kari Annette. BA, U. Wyo., 1951, MA, 1958. Bookkeeper Rawlins Nat. (Wyo.) Bank, 1948-49; scholarship sec. U. Wyo., Laramie, 1962-64; dist. counselor Vocational Rehab., Laramie, 1964-71; exec. dir. Laramie Sr. Ctr., 1973-92; ptnr. First St. Gallery, Laramie, 1996—; pres. Laramie Sr. Housing, Inc., 1982-92, Laramie Housing, Inc., 1988-96. Developer 1st counseling and tng. programs for vocat. rehab. Albany and Platte Counties, Wyo., 1964-71; dir. renovation hist. bldgs., Laramie, 1973-92. Fed. and Wyo. State grantee, 1964-71, Divsn. Aging., 1973-92. Mem. Albany County Hist. Soc., Laramie Plains Mus., Colo. Reservation Assn., U. Wyo. Alumni Assn. Avocations: cycling, cooking, crocheting, writing, skiing. Home: PO Box 2001 Laramie WY 82073-2001 Office: First St Gallery 121 S 1st St Laramie WY 82070-3026

HANSON, MURRAY LYNN, minister; b. Albert Lea, Minn., May 26, 1948; s. Palmer J. and Betty (Lyle) H.; m. Mary Ann Eastwold, Dec. 26, 1970; children: Andrew, Rebecca. BA, Mankato State U., 1970; MDiv, Dubuque Theol. Sem., 1973, D Ministry, 1980. Ordained to ministry Presbyn. Ch. (U.S.A.), 1973. Intern Sunnyside Presbyn. Ch., South Bend, Ind., 1972; supply pastor Hazelton (Iowa) Presbyn. Ch., 1973; assoc. pastor Lakeside Presbyn. Ch., Storm Lake, Iowa, 1973-77; pastor 3d Presbyn. Ch., Rockford, Ill., 1977—; supr. field edn. McCormick/Dubuque Sems., Chgo., Dubuque, 1979—; commr. Gen. Assembly, Presbyn. Ch. (U.S.A.), No. Ill., 1989. Author: An Examination of the Influence of the Roman Catholic Religious Affiliation of Alfred Smith and John Kennedy in the Presidential Elections of 1928 and 1960, 1970, 71, A Self-Assessment Manual for Local Congregations, 1980, Self-Assessment Study of Third Presbyterian Church, 1980. Bd. dirs. Protestant Community Svcs., Rockford, 1985-87, Regional "For Kids' Sake), No. Ill./So. Wis., 1990-95; tour organizer, host to Eng., Scotland, Jordan, Israel, Egypt, Denmark, Norway, Sweden, 1985—. Recipient U. Dubuque Theol. Sem. Alumni award, 1992. Office: 3d Presbyn Ch 1221 Custer Ave Rockford IL 61103-4667

HANSON, NOEL RODGER, management consultant; b. L.A., Jan. 19, 1942; s. Albert and Madelyne Gladys (Pobanz) H.; B.S. in Indsl. Mgmt., U. So. Calif., 1963, M.B.A. in Fin., 1966; m. Carol Lynn Travis, June 17, 1967 (div.); 1 son, Eric Rodger. Asst. dir. alumni fund, then dir. ann. funds U. So. Calif., 1964-66; asst. to Walt Disney for Cal-Arts, Retlaw Enterprises, Glendale, Calif., 1966-68, asst. dir. joint devel. Claremont U. Center, 1968-69; v.p. adminstrn. Robert Johnston Co., Los Angeles, 1969-70; partner Hale, Hanson & Co., Pasadena, Calif., 1970-82, Hanson, Olson & Co., 1982—; pres. Pasadena Services, Inc., 1977—; dir. Pasadena Fin. Cons., Inc., Wilihire Funding, Inc., 1988—. Mem. Pasadena City Traffic Adv. Commn., 1997—; trustee Oakhurst Sch., Pasadena, 1973-75; bd. advisers Girls Club Pasadena, 1977—; mem. U. So. Calif. Assos., 1979—, U. So. Calif. Commerce Assos., 1965—. Republican. Presbyterian. Club: Jonathan (Los Angeles). Home: 1051 La Loma Rd Pasadena CA 91105-2208 Office: Hanson & Co 21 W Dayton St Pasadena CA 91105-2001

HANSON, NORMAN, lawyer; b. Roy, Mont., Feb. 12, 1916; s. Peder and Ida S. (Olson) H.; m. Constance Brown, Sept. 5, 1946; children: David, Margaret, Sara. BA with honors, U. Mont., 1937, JD with honors, 1940. Bar: Mont. 1940, U.S. Dist. Ct. Mont. 1940, U.S. Supreme Ct. 1960. Assoc. Brown and Davis, Billings, Mont., 1940; spl. agent FBI, Washington, 1941-42; assoc., ptnr. Brown, Davis and Hanson, Billings, 1946-51; ptnr. Coleman, Jameson and Lamey, Billings, 1952-57; ptnr. Crowley, Haughey, Hanson, Toole and Dietrich, Billings, 1958-88, of counsel, 1989—; spl asst. to Atty. Gen. of U.S., 1954-55; trustee Rocky Mountain Mineral Law Found., Denver, 1969—, pres. 1982-83; lectr. bus. law Montana State U., Billings, 1989. Co-founder, editor: Mont. Law Rev., 1939-40; contbr. articles to profl. jours. Bd. dirs. Mont. Heart Assn., 1956-62, Sch. Dist. 2; numerous cmty. orgns.; com. mem. Gov.'s Com. Edn. Maj. USAF, 1943-46, War Crimes Br., USFET, 1946. Mem. State Bar Mont., Yellowstone County Bar Assn. (pres. 1955-56). Republican. Congregational. Clubs: Rotary (Billings) (pres. 1965-66), Billings Petroleum. Lodge: Masons. Avocations: service with charitable orgns., bridge, golf. Home: 2026 Pryor Ln Billings MT 59102-1656 Office: Crowley Haughey Hanson Toole & Dietrich PO Box 2529 Billings MT 59103-2529

HANSON, PATTI LYNN, human resources administrator; b. Kennewick, Wash., Apr. 21, 1953; d. Lyle Harry and Ellene Lavonne (McGrath) Morgan; m. Dale R. Hanson, Jan. 18, 1995. AS, El Paso C.C., Colorado Springs, Colo., 1972; BS, Regis Coll., 1982; M in Human Resources Devel., Webster U., 1994. Sec. Adams County Sch. Dist., Thornton, Colo., 1972-73; sec. Montgomery Ward & Co., Denver, 1973-77, computer operator, 1977-79, sec., 1979-83, pers. supr., 1983-84; pers. mgr. Montgomery Ward & Co., Shawnee Mission, Kans., 1984-86; govt. funds coord. Montgomery Ward & Co., Kansas City, Mo., 1986; div. tng. mgr. Montgomery Ward & Co., Kansas City, 1986-88; regional human resource mgr. KFC Nat. Mgmt. Co., Irving, Tex., 1988-90; human resources dir. Businessland, Inc./JWP, Lenexa, Kans., 1990-91; v.p. human resources tech. acquisition svcs. divsn. Entex Info. Svcs., Overland Park, Kans., 1992—. Active Big Sisters Am., Denver, 1984. Mem. Human Resource Mgmt. Assn. Republican. Avocations: golf, piano, jogging, tennis. Home: 11978 Connell Dr Shawnee Mission KS 66213-2514 Office: Entex 8717 W 110th St Overland Park KS 66210-2101

HANSON, PAUL ANTHONY, publisher; b. Sheboygan, Wis., July 13, 1958; s. Roger Dean and Mary Helen (Bradley) Hanson-Tritch. BA in Humanistic Studies/Sociology, U. Wis., Green Bay, 1979, 83; postgrad., U. Wis., Stevens Point, 1985-87, U Minn., Duluth, 1993-97. Page Brown County Libr., Green Bay, 1978-79; with Sun Valley retirement Home, Green Bay, 1982-84; sr. bookseller Waldenbooks, Methuen, Mass., 1988-89; sales clk. Filene's Basement, Methuen, 1988-89; with Paper Box & Specialty, Sheboygan, Wis., 1990-95; server Annie's American Cafe, Sheboygan, 1995—; Editor/pub.: (chapbooks) Duluth's Split Rock, 1994, Geography Lessons Lessens Geography, 1995, The Independent Dependent Kind, 1996, Anybody Here is Here for History, 1997. Mem. Rebecca Nurse Homestead, Peabody Essex Inst. Mem. Sheboygan County Writers Club. Home: 1527 N 36th St Sheboygan WI 53081-1810

HANSON, PHILLIP JOHN, united way executive; b. Omaha, Feb. 22, 1960; s. Harold D. and Margaret D. (Langenfeld) H.; m. Nancy Marie Pierson, Apr. 23, 1983; children: Mark, John, Katherine. BA, Rockhurst Coll., 1982; MPA, U. Mo., Kansas City, 1988. Mgmt. trainee United Way of Am., Alexandria, Va., 1982-83; various positions Heart of Am. United Way, Kansas City, Mo., 1983-95; exec. v.p. resource devel. Heart of Am. United Way, Kansas City, 1996—. Bd. dirs. Habitat for Humanity, Kansas City, Mo., 1986-92, Seton Ctr., Kansas City, 1994—; pres. Kansas City Tomorrow Alumni Bd., 1997. Mem. Nat. Soc. Fund Raising Execs. (cert. fund raising exec., treas. mid Am. chpt. 1996-97), Rockhurst Coll. Alumni Bd. (pres. 1993-94). Roman Catholic. Office: Heart Am United Way 1080 Washington St Kansas City MO 64105-2216

HANSON, RICHARD A., state commissioner; m. Sharon Kinney. B in Engring., Kans. State U.; MBA, Washington U.; postgrad., U. Mo. Engr. pvt. industry; dep. commr. Office of Adminstrn.; asst. state treas.; commr., chief adminstrv. officer Mo. Commr. Adminstrn., 1993—; interim Sec. of State, 1994; bd. mem. State Employees Retirement Sys., Consol. Health Care Plan, Deferred Compensation Commn., Voluntary Life Ins. Commn., Pub. Entity Risk Mgmt. Bd., Commn. on Intergovernmental Rels., Minority Bus. Adv. Commn., Bd. Fund Commrs., Show Me State Games, others. Named State Exec. of Yr., Fed. Exec. Inst. Alumni Assn., Pub. Adminstr. of Yr., Mo. Inst. Pub. Adminstrs., Statesman of Month, Jefferson City Post-Tribune. Mem. Jefferson City Leadership Forum, Jefferson City Area C. of C. (bd. mem.). Office: Adminstrn Office PO Box 809 Jefferson City MO 65102-0809

HANSON, RICHARD EDWIN, civil engineer; b. Sioux City, Iowa, July 22, 1931; s. Gustav Edwin and Delia Thelma (Horton) H.; m. Joann Gager Terhune, Nov. 6, 1954 (div. Jan. 1971); children: Richard Edwin Jr., John William, Tamara Terhune; m. Lillie Gwenette Capitanio, Feb. 21, 1987. BSCE, Iowa State U., 1953; postgrad., U.S. Army Gen. Staff Coll. Registered profl. engr., Iowa. Engr.-in-tng. U.S. Army Corps Engrs., Washington, 1957-58; sr. co. engr. Dickinson Constrn. Co., Chgo., 1959-62; asst. chief constrn. mgmt. Goddard Space Flight Ctr., NASA, Greenbelt, Md., 1963-69; chief project mgmt. U.S. Postal Svc., Washington, 1969-70; chief Air Force project mgmt. U.S. Army Corps Engrs., Washington, 1971-77; chief of constrn. U.S. Army Corps Engrs., Balt., 1977-81; chief of constrn. South Atlantic div. U.S. Army Corps Engrs., Atlanta, 1982-85; chief of constrn. U.S. Army Corps Engrs., Washington, 1986-91; dir. constrn. ops. Pacific Ocean div. U.S. Army Corps Engrs., Honolulu, 1991-96; cons. in engring. and constrn. mgmt., 1996—. Editor: Corps Engrs. Constrn. Newsletter, 1988-91. Pres. Walbrooke Manor Citizens Assn., Lanham, Md., 1963-64. 1st lt. C.E., U.S. Army, 1953-57. Mem. ASCE, NSPE, Army Engr. Assn., Soc. Am. Mil. Engrs. (bd. dirs. Washington chpt. 1988-91), Beta Theta Pi. Republican. Avocations: flying, golf, skiing, fishing, sailing. Home: 44-125 Kahinani Way Kaneohe HI 96744-2569

HANSON, RICHARD WINFIELD, biochemist, educator; b. Oxford, N.Y., Nov. 10, 1935; s. John Vincent and Agatha Helen H.; m. Gloria M. Lucchesi, June 10, 1961; children: Paul, Benjamin, Daria. BS, Northeastern U., 1959; MS, Brown U., 1961, PhD, 1963. Asst. prof to prof. biochemistry Temple U. Sch. Medicine, Phila., 1965-78; prof., chmn. dept. biochemistry Case Western U. Sch. Medicine, Cleve., 1978—, Leonard and Jean Sheggs prof. biochemistry, 1993—; cons. USPHS, FDA. Assoc. editor Jour. Biol. Chemistry; contbr. articles to profl. jours. Served to capt. Med. Service Corps, U.S. Army, 1963-65. Recipient Mead-Johnson award, 1971, Kaiser Permenante award, 1982, Maurice Saltzman award, 1991, Osborne Mendel award, 1995, William C. Rose award, 1999. Mem. AAAS, Inst. Medicine NAS, Am. Soc. Biochemistry and Molecular Biology (rpes. 1999), Am. Soc. for Gene Therapy. Office: Case Western Res U Dept of Biochemistry 2119 Abington Rd Cleveland OH 44106-4935

HANSON, ROBERT DELOLLE, lawyer; b. Harrisburg, Pa., Dec. 13, 1916; s. Henry W. A. and Elizabeth (Painter) H.; BA, Gettysburg Coll., 1939; LLB, Dickinson Law Sch., 1942; m. Barbara Esmer, Apr. 22, 1949. Bar: Pa. 1942; practiced in Harrisburg, 1946-98; solicitor, Dauphin County, 1958-76, Dauphin County Redevel. Authority, 1959-98. Pres. Family and Children's Service of Harrisburg, 1956-57; mem. Harrisburg Sch. Bd., 1952-57, Dauphin County Housing Authority, 1960; gen. chmn. Tri-County United Fund, 1969, pres., 1971-72; trustee Gettysburg Coll., 1974—, sec., 1980, vice chmn., 1983-86; pres. Keystone area council Boy Scouts Am., 1980-82 (Silver Beaver award 1980, Eagle award 1990). Maj. inf. AUS, 1942-46; ETO. Recipient Alexis de Tocqueville award United Way Am., 1991 Others award Salvation Army, 1992; decorated Bronze Star, Purple Heart. Mem. Am., Pa. (sec., treas. taxation sect. 1948-59), Dauphin County (dir. 1958-59) bar assns., Gettysburg Coll. Alumni Assn. (treas. 1958-59, v.p. 1968-71, pres. 1971-72), Phi Beta Kappa. Lutheran (pres. council of congregation 1953-55, 57-59). Clubs: Masons (33 deg., past master, pres. bd. trustees 1982-85), Execs. (pres. 1953), Tuesday, Harrisburg Rotary (pres. 1979). Home: 2500 N 2nd St Harrisburg PA 17110-1106 Office: 111 Locust St Harrisburg PA 17101-1426

HANSON, ROBERT DUANE, civil engineering educator; b. Albert Lea., Minn., July 27, 1935; s. James Edwin and Gertie (Kvale) H.; m. Kaye Lynn Nielsen, June 7, 1959; children: Craig Robert, Eric Neil. Student, St. Olaf Coll., Northfield, Minn., 1953-54; BSE, U. Minn., 1957, MS in Civil Engring., 1958; PhD, Calif. Inst. Tech., Pasadena, 1965. Registered profl. engr., Mich., N.D. Design engr. Pitts.-Des Moines Stel, Des Moines, 1958-59; asst. prof. U. N.D., Grand Forks, 1959-61; research engr. Calif. Inst. Tech., 1965; asst. prof. U. Calif.-Davis, 1965-66; from asst. prof. to prof. civil engring. U. Mich., Ann Arbor, 1966—; chmn. dept. civil engring. U. Mich., 1976-84; sr. earthquake engr. Fed. Emergency Mgmt. Agy., Ariz., 1994—; vis. prof., dir. Earthquake Engring. Rsch. Ctr., U. Calif., Berkeley, 1991; dir. BCS divsn. NSF, Washington, 1989-90; cons. NSF, 1979-88, 92-94; cons. Bechtel Corp., Ann Arbor, 1976-87, Sensei Engrs., Ann Arbor, 1977-90, Bldg. Seismic Safety Coun., 1988-94, Fed. Emergency Mgmt. Agy., 1992-94. Contbr. articles to profl. jours. Recipient Reese Research award ASCE, 1980; recipient Disting. Service award U. Mich., 1969; teaching award Chi Epsilon, 1985, Attwood Engr. Excellence award, 1986. Mem. NAE, ASCE (com. chmn. 1975-94), Earthquake Engring. Rsch. Inst. (v.p. 1977-79, bd. dirs. 1976-79, 88-92, pres.-elect 1988, pres. 1989-91, past pres. 1991-92). Lutheran. Home: 2256 N Middlecoff Dr Mesa AZ 85215-2634 Office: U Mich Dept Civil and Environ Engring Ann Arbor MI 48109-2125 also: Fed Emergency Mgmt Agy 2256 N Middlecoff Dr Mesa AZ 85215-2634

HANSON, RONALD WILLIAM, lawyer; b. LaCrosse, Wis., Aug. 3, 1950; s. Orlin Eugene and Irene Agnes H.; m. Sandra Kay Cook, Aug. 21, 1971; children: Alec Evan, Corinn Michele. BA summa cum laude, St. Olaf Coll., 1972; JD cum laude, U. Chgo., 1975. Bar: Ill. 1975, U.S. Dist. Ct. (no. dist.) Ill. 1975, U.S. Ct. Appeals (7th cir.) 1978, U.S. Ct. Appeals (10th cir.) 1989. Assoc. Sidley & Austin, Chgo., 1975-83, ptnr., 1983-88, Latham & Watkins, Chgo., 1988—; ofcl. advisor to Nat. Conf. of Commrs. on Uniform State Laws; lectr. Ill. Inst. Continuing Legal Edn., Springfield, 1979—, Am. Bankruptcy Inst., Washington, 1984—, Banking Law Inst., 1985, Practicing Law Inst., 1985—, Am. Law Inst., 1987. Contbr. articles to profl. jours. Mem. ABA, Ill. Bar Assn., Order of Coif, Met. Club, Phi Beta Kappa. Republican. Lutheran. Home: 664 W 58th St Hinsdale IL 60521-5104 Office: Latham & Watkins Sears Tower Ste 5800 Chicago IL 60606-6306*

HANSON, THOR, retired health agency executive and naval officer; b. Amarillo, Tex., May 7, 1928; s. Carl Joseph Emanuel and Lillian (Nelson) H.; m. Charlotte Ann Edens, Oct. 6, 1956; children: Inge Rew, Erica Karen, Ivor Carl, Lars Jon, Ursula Edens. B.S., U.S. Naval Acad., 1950; M.A., Oxford U., Eng., 1954. Commd. ensign U.S. Navy, 1950, advanced through grades to vice adm., 1979; service in Korea and Vietnam; naval aide, exec. asst. to sec. Navy, 1970-72; comdg. officer Naval Sta. Pearl Harbor, 1973-74; chief U.S. Naval Mission to Brazil, 1974-76; comdr. Cruiser-Destroyer Group 8; also comdr. Attack Carrier Striking Group 2, U.S. 6th Fleet, 1976-77; mil. asst. to sec. def., 1977-79; dir. joint staff Office Joint Chiefs Staff, 1979-82, ret., 1982; mil. analyst Cable News Network, 1982; pres., CEO Nat. Multiple Sclerosis Soc., 1982-92, pres. emeritus, 1992—; chmn. Nat. Health Coun., 1991-93; hon. bd. dirs. Rsch.! Am.; bd. dirs. AUSA Life Ins. Co. Bd. dirs. East End Seaport and Marine Found.; pres. Southold Citizens for Safe Roads. Decorated Def. D.S.M. with oak leaf cluster, Legion of Merit, Bronze Star with combat V, Meritorious Service medal, Joint Service Commendation medal; Vietnam Navy Distinguished Service medal; Brazilian Naval Order of Merit; Rhodes scholar, 1951-54. Mem. Am. Assn. Rhodes Scholars, Coun. on Fgn. Rels., U.S. Naval Inst., U.S. Naval Acad. Alumni Assn., Am. Fedn. Musicians (hon. life), Century Assn., N.Y. Yacht Club, Orient Yacht Club, Leander Rowing Club (England), Ends of the Earth Club, Digressionsits Club. Episcopalian. Home: Interwellen PO Box 112 900 Birdseye Ln Orient NY 11957-0112

HANSON, VICTOR HENRY, II, newspaper publisher; b. Augusta, Ga., Aug. 17, 1930; s. Clarence Bloodworth, Jr. and Elizabeth (Fletcher) H.; m. Elizabeth Stallworth, Dec. 29, 1953; children: Clarence Bloodworth III, Victor Henry III, Elizabeth Mickel, Mary Fletcher, Robert Stallworth. Grad., Choate Sch., 1949; student, U. Va., 1949-51; B.A., U. Ala., 1954. With Birmingham (Ala.) News & Post Herald, 1946-54, 57—, gen. mgr., 1963-83; with advt. and prodn. dept. WAPI-TV, Birmingham, 1954-55; v.p. Birmingham News Co., 1960-79, pres., 1979—, pub., 1983—. Trustee So. Rsch. Inst., Birmingham, Birmingham Mus. of Art; mem. exec. com. Met. Arts Council; mem. bd. dirs. Pub. Affairs Rsch. Coun. of Ala.; trustee Endowment Development Com. of United Way of Central Ala.; Presbyn. Ch. elder. Served to capt. USAF, 1955-57. Mem. SAR, Birmingham C. of C., Soc. of Cinn., N.C. Soc. of Cinn., Birmingham Country Club, Summit Club, Mountain Brook Club, Kappa Alpha. Home: 3910 Hunters Ln Birmingham AL 35243-5920 Office: Birmingham News 2200 4th Ave N Birmingham AL 35203-3840

HANSON, WENDY KAREN, chemical engineer; b. Mpls., May 29, 1954; d. Curtis Harley Hanson and Patricia Lou (Vogler) Schweiger. BS, U. Minn., 1976; BA, U. Colo., Denver, 1984; postgrad., U. Calif., La Jolla, 1984-87. Chem. technician Shasta Beverages, Mpls., 1977-78, Conwed, Roseville, Minn., 1978-80; geologist Century Geophys. Corp., Grand Junction, Colo., 1980, Tooke Engring., Grand Junction, 1980-82; sr. scientist Sci. Ventures, San Diego, 1987-96; engr. Parker-Hannifin Corp., San Diego, 1996-97. Patentee magnesium separation from Dolomitic phosphate by sulfuric acid leaching. Judge San Diego (Calif.) Sci. and Engring. Fair, 1987-96; leader, publs. editor San Diego (Calif.) Wilderness Assn., 1989-97. Mem. Am. Chem. Soc. Avocations: backpacking, gardening, spitoon collecting.

HANSON, WILLIAM LEWIS, lawyer; b. Shanghai, China, Oct. 1, 1924; came to U.S., 1927; s. Victor and Lucia Mae (Parks) H.; m. Elen Stella Hanson, June 26, 1949; children: Raiha Ballard, Victoria Berman, Emily Hanson-McMullen. AB cum laude, high hons., U. Redlands, Calif., 1946; JD, Harvard U., 1950. Bar: Wash., Fed. Tax Ct., 1976, U.S. Supreme Ct., 1983, U.S. Ct. Appeals (9th cir.), 1969. Coll. and peace edn. sec. Am. Friends Svc., Seattle, 1954-59; pvt. practice law Seattle, 1959-70, 73—; tchr. law/history Lakeside Sch., Seattle, 1970-73; arbitrator Arbitration Panel of Superior Ct. of King County. Co-author: A New China Policy, 1965, Uncommon Controversy: Indian Fishing Rights in the Northwest, 1970; author: (booklet) Peace in China, 1958. Bd. dirs., vol. atty. Am. Friends Svc., 1959-69, ACLU, 1965-78; bd. dirs., commentator Jack Straw Found., Seattle, 1972—; bd. dirs. Jack Straw Found., 1985-91, pres. 1991-92; trustee Friends Ednl. Trust, 1992—; bd. dirs. Inst. for Global Security Studies, Seattle, 1991-98; vol., past pres. World Peace Through Law Sect. of Wash. Bar Assn., 1970-91, 96—; planner, chmn. Bar Assn. Conf. on World Law, 1985-96, leader trip to China/Tibet, 1993. Recipient Cmty. Svc. for Peace Ann. award Unitarian Ch., Seattle, 1968. Democrat. Soc. of Friends. Avocations: photography, Chinese art, biking (built titanium bike Seattle Bike Show, 1997). Home and Office: 4819 NE 103rd St Seattle WA 98125-8141

HANTHORN, DENNIS WAYNE, performing arts association administrator; b. Lima, Ohio, Dec. 21, 1951; s. Floyd Wilber and June J. (Rummel) H.; m. Rebecca R. Hackler, Aug. 2, 1975; children: Rachel R., Micah A, Hanna. BS in Music Edn., Southwest Mo. State, Springfield, 1975; MusM in French Horn, U. Wis., 1977. Instr. U. Ala., 1978-79; gen. mgr. Cin. Chamber Orch., 1980-82; founder, dir. Queen City Brass, 1979-83; mng. dir. Dayton (Ohio) Opera, 1982-89; gen. dir. Florentine Opera Co., Milw., 1989—. Home: N75w5434 Georgetown Dr Cedarburg WI 53012-1557 Office: Florentine Opera Co 735 N Water St Ste 1315 Milwaukee WI 53202-4106*

HANTMAN, BARRY G., software engineer; b. Boston, May 22, 1962; s. Leonard M. and Barbara R.; m. Susan Chapman, June 2, 1985; 1 child, Noam Seth. BA, Brandeis U., 1984; postgrad., Fitchburg State Coll., 1984-86. Cons. Wicat Sys., Waltham, Mass., 1982-84; mgr. operational software Raytheon Co., Bedford, Mass., 1984—; Open Software Found. primary rep. Raytheon Co., Tewksbury, 1991-93, CAD Framework Initiative primary rep., 1993-94, program mgr. Dept. Def. Microwave/Millimeter Advanced Computational Environ. Program, 1992-97, Dept. Def. Mfg. Automation and Design Engring. Program, 1996. Lodge chief Order of Arrow, Stoneham, Mass., 1979-81; chmn. Town of Danville (N.H.) Planning Bd.; chmn. Cable TV Com., Rockingham County (N.H.) Planning Commn. Mem. IEEE Computer Soc., U.S. Holocaust Meml. Coun., African Wildlife Found., World Wildlife Fund, Wildlife Conservation Soc., Assn. Computing Machinery, Mentor Graphics User Group (pres. 1988-90, v.p. 1987-88, mem. steering com. 1985-87, 90-92). Jewish. Avocations: foreign travel, video editing. Home: 52 Justin Dr Danville NH 03819-5109 Office: Raytheon Co S3SG10 180 Hartwell Rd Bedford MA 01730

HANTON, E(MILE) MICHAEL, public and personnel relations consultant; b. Gary, Ind.; s. Zachary and Maria (Suciu) H. AB, Ind. U., 1951, MA, 1955; grad., USAF Air War Coll., 1968. Various prodn. positions U.S. Steel Corp., Gary, 1940-41, 50; prodn. contr. Douglas Aircraft Corp., Santa Monica, Calif., 1946-47; classified advt. mgr Weaver Pub. Co., Santa Monica,

1947-48; reporter Muncie (Ind.) Evening Press, 1952, Gary Post-Tribune, 1952-53; head cashier Office Lake County Treas., Gary, 1955-60; pub. and pers. rels. cons. Gary, 1960—, Plattsburgh, N.Y., 1968—; asst. prof. State U. Coll. Arts & Scis., Plattsburgh, 1966-67; cons. community rels. and fund raising. Author: The New Nurse, 1973. With USAAF, 1941-45, USAF active res. 1945-69, ret. Decorated Air medal, Purple Heart. Mem. Am. Med. Writers Assn., Assn. Edn. in Journalism and Mass Communications, Health Scis. Comm. Assn., Am. Acad. Advt., Nat. League Nursing, Gary C. of C., Plattsburgh C. of C., Air Force Assn., Res. Officers Assn., Nat. Arts Club, Steel Club, Caterpillar Club, Flying Boot Club. Office: PO Box 803 Plattsburgh NY 12901-0803

HANUS, JEROME GEORGE, archbishop; b. May 26, 1940. Attended, Conception Sem., Mo., St. Anselm U., Rome, Italy, Princeton Theol. Sem., Princeton U. Ordained priest Roman Cath. Ch., 1966. Abbot Conception Abbey, 1977-87; pres. Swiss Am. Benedictine Congregation, 1984-87; bishop Diocese of St. Cloud, Minn., 1987-94; coadjuctor archbishop Dubuque, Iowa, 1994-95, archbishop, 1995—. Office: PO Box 479 Dubuque IA 52004-0479*

HANUSA, GEORGE LEONARD, minister; b. Alma Center, Wis., Sept. 30, 1932; s. Edward and Clara (Terasa) H.; m. Janet Louise Westphal, Aug. 4, 1956; children: Ellen Louise, Julie Marie. BA, Wartburg Coll., 1954; BD, Wartburg Theol. Sem., Dubuque, Iowa, 1958, MST, 1967. Pastor Zion Luth. Ch., Alta Vista, and St. John's Luth. Ch., Boyd, Iowa, 1958-61, Salem Luth. Ch., Andrew, Iowa, 1961-65, Bethel Luth. Ch., Parkersburg, Iowa, 1966-68, St. Paul's Luth. Ch., Waverly, Iowa, 1968-76; asst. to bishop Iowa Dist. Luth. Ch., Des Moines, 1976-86; dir., v.p. comm. and devel. Luth. Social Svc. Iowa, Des Moines, 1987-94, dir. pub. rels. and ch. rels., 1994-97, ret., 1997. Author: Hope for All Generations, 1996. Democrat. Avocations: writing, photography, gardening, traveling. Home: 7204 Reite Ave Des Moines IA 50311-1304

HANUSHEK, ERIC ALAN, economics educator; b. Lakewood, Ohio, May 22, 1943; s. Vernon F. and Ruth (Hostetler) H.; m. Nancy L. Keleher, June 11, 1965 (div.); children: Eric Alan, Megan E. B.S., U.S. Air Force Acad., 1965; Ph.D. in Econs., MIT, 1968. Sr. staff economist Coun. Econ. Advisers, Washington, 1971-72; assoc. prof. USAF Acad., Colo., 1972-73; sr. economist Cost of Living Coun., Washington, 1973-74; assoc. prof. econs. Yale U., New Haven, 1975-78; dir. pub. policy analysis U. Rochester, N.Y., 1978-83, prof. econs. and polit. sci., 1978—, chmn. dept. econs., 1982-87, 88-90, dir. W. Allen Wallis Inst. Polit. Economy, 1992—; rsch. assoc. Nat. Bur. Econ. Rsch., 1996—; dep. dir. Congl. Budget Office, Washington, 1984-85; mem. com. nat. stats. Nat. Rsch. Coun., 1992-98; cons. World Bank 1984—, U.S. Com. on Civil Rights, 1986-89. Author: Education and Race, 1972, (with J. Jackson) Statistical Methods for Social Scientists 1977, (with C. Citro) Improving Information for Social Policy Decisions, 1991, (with R. Harbison) Education Performance of the Poor, 1992, Making Schools Work, 1994, (with J. Banks) Modern Political Economy, 1995, (with N. Maritato) Assessing Knowledge of Retirement Behavior, 1996, (with Dale W. Jorgenson) Improving America's Schools, 1996, (with Constance F. Citro) Assessing Policies for Retirement Income, 1997. Served to capt. USAF, 1965-74. Mem. Internat. Acad. Edn., Assn. Pub. Policy Analysis and Mgmt. (v.p. 1986-87, pres. 1988-89), Am. Econ. Assn., Econometric Soc., Am. Statis. Assn. Office: U Rochester Dept Econs Rochester NY 14627

HANVIK, JAN MICHAEL, arts promoter, writer; b. Mpls., Nov. 9, 1950; s. William Joseph and Geneva Margaret (Dicks) H. BFA in Dance, CUNY, 1982; MA in L.Am. and Caribbean Studies, NYU, 1985. Exec. dir. Pan Am. Musical Art Rsch. Inc. (PAMAR), N.Y.C., 1987—; cons. Ford Found., N.Y.C., 1995-96, NEA, 1995-97, Compton Found., 1997, N.Y. State Coun. Arts, 1982—, Nat. Inst. Fine Arts, Mexico City, 1995-96. Contbr. articles to Dictionary of 20th Century Cultures, 1996, International Encyclopedia of Dance, 1996, also to mags. Bd. dirs. World Dance Alliance Ams. Ctr., N.Y.C., 1997—. Recipient Fulbright award USIA, El Salvador, 1990-91, Fundacion Banco De Boston, Uruguay, 1999, Am. Cultural Specialist award, Bolivia, 1988. Mem. Ams. Soc., Assn. Performing Arts Presenters. Soc. of Friends. Avocations: gardening, travel, kayaking. E-mail: pamarj@aol.com. Office: PAMAR Inc 198 Broadway Rm 807 New York NY 10038-2515

HANWAY, DONALD GRANT, retired agronomist, educator; b. Broadwater, Nebr., Aug. 6, 1918; s. Frank Pierce and Emma Terrissa (Twist) H.; m. Blanche Elizabeth Larson, Sept. 26, 1942 (dec. Aug. 1996); children: Donald Grant, Wayne Edward, Janice Kay; m. Susanne Ruth Pennington, Apr. 10, 1999. B.S., U. Nebr., 1942, M.S., 1948; Ph.D., Iowa State Coll., 1954. Tchr. rural schs., Morrill County, Nebr., 1936-40; mem. faculty dept. agronomy U. Nebr., Lincoln, 1947-84, chmn. faculty dept. agronomy, 1955-76, prof. emeritus, 1984—; also extension agronomist, chief of party univ. mission to Ataturk U. U. Nebr., Erzurum, Turkey, 1965-67; agronomic cons., Nigeria, Columbia, Morocco, Tunisia; mem. Plant Variety Protection Adv. Bd., 1987-90. Contbr. articles to profl. jours. Mem. Nebr. Commn. on Status of Women, 1986-89. With USAAF, 1942-46. Honoree Nebr. Hall of Agrl. Achievement, 1988. Fellow AAAS, Am. Soc. Agronomy, Crop Sci. Soc.; mem. Soil Sci. Soc. Am., Soil and Water Conservation Soc., Am. Inst. Biol. Scis., Phi Beta Kappa, Sigma Xi, Alpha Zeta, Gamma Sigma Delta. Episcopalian. Home: 5610 Pioneers Blvd Apt 197 Lincoln NE 68506-5192

HANWAY, DONALD GRANT, Episcopal priest; b. Lincoln, Nebr., Dec. 9, 1943; s. Donald Grant Sr. and Blanche Elizabeth (Larson) H.; m. Nadine Young Kingman, May 28, 1966; children: Laura, Stephen, Julie. BA, U. Nebr., 1965, MA, 1967; MDiv, Va. Theol. Seminary, 1971, D of Ministry, 1997. Vicar St. Elizabeth's Ch., Holdrege, Nebr., 1971-75; curate St. Luke's Episcopal Ch., Kalamazoo, 1975-77; rector Christ Ch. Episcopal, Beatrice, Nebr., 1977-81; vicar, chaplain St. Mark's on the Campus, Lincoln, Nebr., 1981—; charter mem., then pres. leadership devel. task force Interchurch Ministries Nebr., Lincoln, 1981-93; charter mem. instnl. rev. bd. U. Nebr., Lincoln, 1993-95. Editor: The Nebraska Churchman, 1972-74. 1st lt. U.S. Army, 1966-68, Vietnam. Recipient Bronze Star U.S. Army, 1968. Mem. Assn. Campus Religious Workers (pres. 1996-98), Lincoln Torch Club, Lincoln Elks Lodge, Phi Beta Kappa. Avocations: movies, golf. Home: 3016 Browning St Lincoln NE 68516-4606 Office: St Mark's on the Campus 1309 R St Lincoln NE 68508-1219

HANZAK, GARY A. JOHN, credit and leasing executive; b. Cleve., June 21, 1957; s. Richard and Amelia Maria (Sarna) H.; m. Veronica Lee Myers, Sept. 28, 1980 (div. Feb. 1987); m. Frances Watson Peay Herring, Aug. 11, 1990; 1 child, Heather Deniese. AAS summa cum laude., J. Sargeant Reynolds Coll., 1991. Dept. mgr. Progressive Cos., Cleve., 1979-85; pres. Com Pro, Richmond, Va., 1984-85; state contract adminstr. Copy Systems Inc., Richmond, 1985-86; recovery mgr. Freedlander Mortgage, Richmond, 1986-88; dir. adminstrn. Ikon Office Solutions, Richmond, 1988—; mem. Alco Capital Resource Task Force, 1993. Author (fiction) Blackhawk, 1998, (corp. newsletter) Leasing Leader. Vol. Virginia Aveni Election Campaign, Cleve., 1974, YMCA Camp for the Deaf, Cleve., 1976. Recipient achievement award Dun & Bradstreet, 1990, Ace award, 1993. Mem. Pres. Club. Roman Catholic. Avocations: woodworking, photography, writing. Office: PO Box 6819 Richmond VA 23230-0819

HANZLIK, RAYBURN DEMARA, lawyer; b. L.A., June 7, 1938; s. Rayburn Otto and Ethel Winifred (Membery) H.; m. Carolyn Marie Williams; children: Kristina, Rayburn N., Alexander, Geoffrey. BS, Principia Coll., 1960; MA, Woodrow Wilson Sch. Fgn. Affairs, U. Va., 1968; JD, U. Va., 1974. Bar: Va. 1975, D.C. 1977. Staff asst. to Pres. U.S., Washington, 1971-73; assoc. dir. White House Domestic Council, 1975-77; of counsel Danzansky Dickey Tydings Quint & Gordon, Washington, 1977-78, Akin Gump Strauss Hauer & Feld, Washington, 1978-79; pvt. practice L.A., 1979-81; adminstr. Econ. Regulatory Adminstrn., Dept. Energy, Washington, 1981-85; ptnr. Heidrick and Struggles, Inc., 1985-91, McKenna & Hanzlik, Irvine, Calif., 1991-92; chmn. Lanxide Sports Internat., Inc., San Diego, 1992-95, Stealth Propulsion Internat., Ltd., San Diego, Calif. and Melbourne, Australia, 1994-97; exec. v.p. Commodore Corp., N.Y.C. and McLean, Va., 1997-98; mng. dir. Brewer-Hanzlik Nuclear Ptnrs., LLC, 1998—. Contbg. author: Global Politics and Nuclear Energy, 1971, Soviet Foreign Relations and World Communism, 1965. Alt. del. Republican Nat. Conv., 1980; dir. Calif. Rep. Victory Fund, 1980; candidate U.S. Senate, 1980. Served to lt. USN, 1963-68, Vietnam. Mem. ABA, Va. Bar Assn., D.C. Bar Assn. Republican. Christian Scientist.

HAPGOOD, ROBERT DERRY, English educator; b. Lompoc, Calif., Dec. 11, 1928; s. Arthur Richard and Elsie Rachel (Brown) H.; m. Marilyn Janelle Oliver, July 16, 1950; children—Miranda Kristin, Susanna Elizabeth. B.A. with highest honors, U. Calif., Berkeley, 1950, M.A., 1951, Ph.D., 1955. Instr. English Ind. U., 1955-57; vis. prof. Am. lit. and civilization Dijon (France) U., 1957-58; instr. U. Calif., Berkeley, 1958-59; asst. prof. U. Calif., Riverside, 1959-65; mem. faculty U. N.H., Durham, 1965—; prof. English U. N.H., 1969-95; prof. emeritus English, 1996—; chmn. dept. U. N.H., 1972-75, dir. London program, 1986-89; dir. U. N.H./Cambridge U. summer program, 1982-85; exchange prof. Osaka (Japan) U., 1977-79; vis. prof. Shoin Women's U., Japan, 1992; dir. Shakespeare Workshop, Bowdoin Coll., summers 1972-75. Author: Shakespeare the Theatre-poet, 1988; editor: Hamlet - Shekespeare in Production, 1999; mem. editorial bd. Univ. Press New Eng., 1975-77. Served with AUS, 1953-55. Recipient essay prize English Inst., 1968, Lindberg award for Outstanding Scholar-Tchr., 1990; fellow Inst. Renaissance Studies, Ashland, Oreg., 1961; Mellon postdoctoral fellow, 1964-65; fellow Southeastern Inst. Medieval and Renaissance Studies, Chapel Hill, N.C., 1969; Am. Coun. Learned Socs. fellow, 1979-80, Folger Inst. fellow, 1987, NEH summer fellow, 1994. Mem. MLA, Shakespeare Assn. Am., Internat. Shakespeare Assn. Home: Cove Rd PO Box 451 Cape Neddick ME 03902-0451 Office: U NH English Dept Hamilton Smith Hall Durham NH 03824

HAPKA, CATHERINE M., internet executive. BS, U. Minn.; MBA, U. Chgo. Gen. mgr. Gen. Electric, 198-487; pres. Data Svcs., 1989-91; pres., COO Interprise, U.S. West Comms., 1991-94, exec. v.p., 1994-96; pres., CEO, founder Rhythms NetConnections, Englewood, Colo., 1996—.

HAPNER, MARY LOU, securities trader and dealer; b. Fort Wayne, Ind., Nov. 9, 1937; d. Paul Kenneth Brooks and Eileen (Summers) H. BS with honors, Ariz. State U., 1966, MS, 1967. Stockbroker Young, Smith & Peacock, Phoenix, Ariz., 1971-76, v.p., 1976-89; v.p. Peacock, Hislop, Staley & Given, Phoenix, 1989-90, 1st v.p., 1990—. Author: Career Courage, 1984; author numerous poems. Chmn. March of Dimes, Sun City, Ariz., 1983; trustee St. Lukes, Phoenix, 1978; mem. fin. com. YWCA, Phoenix, 1975; chair budget com. Ch. of Beatitudes, Phoenix, mem. exec. coun., 1991; bd. dirs. Ariz. Children's Found., 1998. Recipient Spirit of Philanthropy award, 1997. Mem. Charter 100 (chair membership 1979-81, pres. 1980, pres. 1982, v.p. 1981, treas., membership chair 1995). Republican. Lutheran. Avocations: golf, singing with concert choirs, writing poetry.

HAPP, HARVEY HEINZ, electrical engineer, educator; b. Berlin, June 27, 1928; came to U.S., 1947, naturalized, 1953; s. Harry and Hertha (Friedmann) H.; m. Ruth Hollander, Nov. 17, 1951; children: Deborah Ann, Sandra Eva. B.S. in Elec. Engring, Ill. Inst. Tech., 1954; M.E.E., Rensselaer Poly. Inst., Troy, N.Y., 1958; D.Sc., U. Belgrade, Yugoslavia, 1962. Registered profl. engr., N.Y. With Gen. Electric Co., 1954-88; sr. application engr. Gen. Electric Co., Schenectady, 1968-72; mgr. analytical engring. services Gen. Electric Co., 1972-77, mgr. advanced system tech., 1977-82, mgr. system analysis, 1982-87, cons., 1987-88, also mem. faculty power system engring. course; with N.Y. State Dept. Pub. Service, 1988—; lectr. colls. Author: Diakoptics and Networks (translated into Russian and Romanian), 1971, Piecewise Methods and Applications to Power Systems (translated into Chinese), 1980; editor: Gabriel Kron and Systems Theory, 1973; mem. editorial bd. Procs. IEEE, 1979-84; contbr. numerous articles and book revs. to profl. jours., chpts. to tech. books. Fellow IEEE (life; Prize Paper award Region 5 1962, power sys. engring. com. 1977, Region 1 award 1980); mem. Tensor Soc. Gt. Britain (v.p. 1972-82), Conf. Internat. des Grands Reseaux Electrique a Haute Tension, Internat. Power Sys. Computations Conf. (co-founder 1962), Gen. Electric Co. Engrs. and Scientists Assn. (chmn. policy com. 1968-70), Ill. Inst. Tech. Alumni Assn., Sigma Xi, Tau Beta Pi, Eta Kappa Nu. Home: 2211 Webster Dr Niskayuna NY 12309-3930 Office: NY State Dept Pub Svc 3 Empire State Plz Albany NY 12223-1000

HAPPEL, JOHN, chemical engineer, researcher; b. Bklyn., Apr. 1, 1908; s. John and Emilie (Weinkauf) H.; m. Dorothy Merriam, 1951; children: Jill, George, Ruth. BS, MIT, 1929, MS, 1930; DChemE, Poly. Inst. Bklyn., 1948. Registered profl. engr., N.Y. With Socony Vacuum Oil Co., 1930-48; prof. chem. engring., chmn. dept. chem. engring. NYU, N.Y.C., 1949-73, prof. emeritus, 1973—; adj. prof. Columbia U., N.Y.C., 1973—, spl. rsch. assoc., 1976—; emeritus mem. bd. mgrs. Mohonk Consultations, Inc.; mem. petroleum industry war coun., 1942-45; mem. tech. com. in charge constrn. and operation of world's largest butadiene plant for synthetic rubber, 1942-47; cons. petroleum chems. various cos. Author: Chemical Process Economics, 1958, 2d edit. (with Donald Jordan), 1974, (with Howard Brenner) Low Reynolds Number Hydrodynamics, 1965, 2d edit., 1973, paperback edit., 1983; translator: (with M.F. Delleo Jr., G. Dembinski, A.H. Weiss) Catalysis by Non-Metals (from Russian by O.V. Krylov), 1970, (with Miguel Hnatow and Laimonis Bajars) Base Metal Oxide Catalysts, 1977, Isotopic Assessment of Heterogeneous Catalysts, 1986; mem. editorial adv. bd. Ency. Chem. Processing and Design, Oxidation Communications; contbr. articles to profl. jours., chpts. to tech. books; patentee in field. Recipient Certificate of Distinction Poly. Inst. Bklyn.; Tyler award N.Y. sect. Am. Inst. Chem. Engrs.; Vols. 82, 83 Chem. Engring. Communications honored 80th birthday. Fellow N.Y. Acad. Scis. (v.p. 1977), Am. Inst. Chem. Engrs. (Founders award 1987); mem. Am. Chem. Soc. (Honor Scroll), Nat. Acad. Engring., Chemists Club, Sigma Xi, Alpha Chi Sigma, Phi Lambda Upsilon, Tau Beta Pi. Episcopalian. Home: 69 Tompkins Ave Hastings Hdsn NY 10706-3944 Office: Columbia U New York NY 10027

HAPPER, WILLIAM, JR., physicist, educator; b. Vellore, India, July 27, 1939; came to U.S., 1941, naturalized, 1961; s. William and Gladys (Morgan) H.; m. Barbara Jean Baker, June 10, 1967; children: James William, Gladys Anne. BS, U. N.C., 1960; PhD, Princeton U., 1964. Rsch. assoc. Radiation Lab., Columbia U., N.Y.C., 1964; asst. prof. physics Radiation Lab., Columbia U., 1967-70, assoc. prof., 1970-74, prof., 1974-80; dir. Radiation Lab., Columbia U. (Radiation Lab.), 1976-79; prof. Princeton (N.J.) U., 1980-91, 93—; dir. office energy rsch. U.S. Dept. Energy, Washington, D.C., 1991-93; dir. Magnetic Imaging Technologies, Inc.; chmn. Jason/Mitre, 1987-90; trustee Mitre Corp.; cons. in field. Alfred P. Sloan fellow, 1967; recipient Alexander von Humboldt award Germany, 1976. Fellow Am. Phys. Soc. (Herbert Broida prize 1997), Am. Acad. Arts and Scis., Nat. Acad. Scis., Am. Philos. Soc. Home: 559 Riverside Dr Princeton NJ 08540-4007 Office: Princeton U Dept Physics Princeton NJ 08544

HAQ, BILAL UL, national science foundation program director, researcher; b. Gorakhpur, India, Oct. 8, 1943; came to U.S., 1968; s. Fazli and Sorraya (Rabbani) H.; m. Nazli Azam, June 11, 1975. MSc, U. Panjab, Pakistan, 1963; PhD, U. Stockholm, 1967, DSc, 1972. UNESCO scholar U. Vienna, Austria, 1964-65; Swedish Internat. Devel. Authority rsch. scholar U. Stockholm, 1965-68; rsch. scientist Woods Hole (Mass.) Oceanographic Inst., 1968-82, Exxon Prodn. Rsch. Co., Houston, 1982-88; program dir. divsn. marine geology and geophysics NSF, Washington, 1988—; rsch. assoc. Smithsonian Inst., Washington, 1988-92; vis. prof. U. Copenhagen, Geol. Survey of Denmark, 1991; keynote spkr. Bur. Mineral Resources, Canberra, Australia, 1988, Internat. Geol. Congress, Washington, 1989, Kyoto, Japan, 1992, Linnean Soc. Conf. on the Indus River and Its Civilization, London, 1994, Intergovt. Oceanographic Commn. Conf. on Integrated Coastal Zone Mgmt., Karachi, Pakistan, 1994, Internat. Sedimentol. Congress, Alicante, Spain, 1998; vis. com. for Brit Geol. Survey, U.K. Nat. Environ. Rsch. Coun., Swindon, 1990-91; mem. panel U.S., Japan Coop. Program Natural Resources, Tokyo, 1991-92; on assignment White House Office Mgmt. and Budget, 1992, World Bank environ. dept., 1993; hon. prof. Tongji U., Shanghai, China, 1997—. Author, editor: Introduction to Marine Micropaleontology, 1978, 98, Marine Geology and Oceanography of Arabian Sea, 1984, Ocean Drilling on Exmouth Plateau, 1990, Calcareous Nannoplankton, 1984, Nannofossil Biostratigraphy, 1984, Sequence Stratigraphy and Facies Association, 1993, Sequence Stratigraphy and Depositional Response to Eustatic, Tectonic and Climatic Forcing, 1995, Sea Level Rise and Coastal Subsidence: Causes, Consequences and Strategies, 1995, Coastal Zone Management Imperative for Developing Maritime Nations, 1997; prodr. video film Sequence Stratigraphy and the Danian Succession, 1993. Recipient 1998 Francis P. Shepard medal Soc. for Sedimentary Geology. Fellow Geol. Soc. Am., Geol. Soc. London; mem. Am. Assn. Petroleum Geologists (disting. lectr. 1989), Am. Geophys. Union. Achievements include research in global sea level and environmental change. Office: NSF 4201 Wilson Blvd Arlington VA 22230-0001

HAQUE, AKHLAQUE UL, educator, researcher; b. Oct. 20, 1963. MA in Econs., Cleve. State U., 1990, PhD, 1994. Project mgr., asst. prof. U. Ala., Birmingham, 1995—; adj. faculty Cleve. State U., 1994-95. E-mail: ahaque@uab.edu.

HAQUE, MOHAMMED SHAHIDUL, electrical engineer; b. Dhaka, Bangladesh, May 12, 1965; came to U.S., 1991; s. Shamsul and Hafiza (Akter) H.; m. Aynun Naher, June 14, 1994; children: Afsara, Sakib. BSEE, Bangladesh U. Engring. & Tech., Dhaka, 1989; MSEE, U. Ark., 1992, PhD, 1997. Tchg. asst., dept. elec. engr. Bangladesh U. Engring. and Tech., 1990; rsch. asst., dept. elec. engr. U. Ark., Fayetteville, 1991-92; sr. rsch. asst. U. Ark., 1993-97, rsch. asst. prof., 1997; process devel. engr. Novellus Systems Inc., San Jose, 1997—; lectr. in field. Contbr. articles to Jour. Applied Physics, Solar Energy Materials and solar Cells, Jour. Elec. Materials, others. Mem. IEEE, Electrochemical Soc. Islamic. Achievements include research in microelectronic materials for solar cell applications and multichip module packaging technology; invention of a low temperature silicon solar cell fabrication process; contribution to understanding and quality improvement of chemical vapor deposited silicon dioxide and diamond dielectric films. Avocations: music, philately, photography. Home: 2200 Monroe St Apt 1001 Santa Clara CA 95050 Office: Novellus Sys Inc 3970 N 1st St San Jose CA 95134

HARA, GEORGE, software company executive; b. Osaka, Japan, Oct. 10, 1952; s. Nobutaro and Mitsuko (Kuroda) H.; m. Junko Hara, Oct. 8, 1988. LLB, Keio U., Tokyo, 1975; MS in Engring., Stanford U., 1981, MABA in Bus. Fin. officer UN Capital Devel. Fund, N.Y.C., 1980-81; founder, pres. Gekee Fiberoptics Inc., Palo Alto, Calif., 1981-83; pres. Data Control Ltd., Osaka, 1984-85; v.p. Pacific Catalyst Group, L.A., 1984—; gen. ptnr. Japan Incubation Capital, Tokyo, 1985-88; pres., chief exec. officer Data Control Ltd., Osaka, Tokyo and Palo Alto, 1985—; founder, mng. ptnr. DEFTA, Palo Alto and San Francisco, 1986—; founder, advisor Control Tech. Ltd., Osaka, 1986—; bd. dirs. Wollongong Group Inc., Palo Alto, IDA Bldg. (USA) Corp., San Francisco, Plantec Inc., Tokyo, Borland Internat.; chief exec. advisor Hankyo Corp., Osaka., 1989—. Advisor coll. bus. U. San Francisco, 1987—, advisor to pres., 1988—; advisor to gov. Prefecture of Osaka, 1986-88; active task force for econ. devel. Osaka Kansai Keizaidoyukai, 1981; bd. dirs. Metadigm Found., Calif. Mem. Archaeol. Inst. Am., Japan-Cen. Am. Soc. (pres. 1976-78), Shotosha Found. (chmn. 1977—), Japan Software Rsch. Found. (bd. dirs. 1988—), Networking Japan (pres. 1985), Alliance Japan (pres. 1986, chmn. 1989), Alliance 90 (chmn. 1990), Smithsonian Inst., Calif. Acad. Sci., Stanford Assn. Japan, U.S.-Japan High Tech. Trade and Strategic Alliance Com. (pres. 1989—) Cen. Am. Mita Assn., Kansai Stanford Assn. (mus. soc. officer), Nat. Venture Capital Assn. Office: DEFTA Ptnrs 111 Pine St Ste 1410 San Francisco CA 94111-5616 also: One Embarcadero Ctr San Francisco CA 94111*

HARA, TADAO, educational administrator; b. Shimonoseki, Japan, Oct. 21, 1926; s. Ikuhisa and Chitose Hara; m. Suzuko Hara, May 12; children: Nobumichi, Izumi. BA, Tamagawa U., Machida, Japan, 1952; MA in Bibl. Theology, N.W. Coll., 1958; MA in Ednl. Psychology, Calif. State U., Long Beach, 1965; LittD (hon.), N.W. Coll., 1990. Ordained to ministry Assembly of God Ch. Fgn. student counselor Calif. State U., Long Beach, 1965-68; prof. edn. Tamagawa U., 1969-79, dean students, 1973-77, dir. internat. edn., 1976-79; founder, prin. Internat. Bilingual Sch., Palos Verdes Estates, Calif. Mem. adv. bd. Calif. State U. Long Beach Coll. Edn., 1985-88. Recipient Disting. Alumnus award Coll. Edn., Calif. State U., Long Beach, 1994. Mem. ASCD, Nat. Assn. Internat. Educators, Delta Upsilon Chi. Home: 3992 Toland Cir Los Alamitos CA 90720-2261 Office: 300 Paseo Del Mar # B Palos Verdes Estates CA 90274

HARAD, GEORGE JAY, manufacturing company executive; b. Newark, Apr. 24, 1944; m. Beverly Marcia Harad, June 12, 1966; children: Alyssa Dawn, Matthew Corde. BA, Franklin and Marshall Coll., 1965; MBA with high distinction, Harvard Bus. Sch., 1971. Staff cons. Boston Cons. Group, 1970-71; asst. to sr. v.p. housing Boise Cascade Corp., 1971; asst. to v.p. Boise Cascade Corp., Palo Alto, Calif., 1971; fin. mgr. Boise Cascade Realty Group, Palo Alto, Calif., 1972-76; mgr. corp. devel. Boise Cascade Corp., Boise, ID, 1976-80; dir. retirement funds, risk mgmt. Boise Cascade Corp., 1980-82, v.p., contr., 1982-84, sr. v.p., chief fin. officer, 1984-89, exec. v.p., chief fin. officer, 1989-90, exec. v.p. paper, 1990-91; pres., COO Boise Cascade Corp., Boise, ID, 1991-94, pres., CEO, 1994-95; chmn., bd. dirs. Boise Cascade Corp., 1995; chmn., dir. Boise Cascade Office Products Corp.; CEO, chmn. Boise Cascade Corp., Boise, ID, 1995—; bd. dirs. Allendale Ins. Co.; bd. govs. Nat. Coun. of Paper Industry for Air and Stream Improvement Inc. Founder, pres. Boise Coun. for Gifted and Talented Students, 1977-79; bd. dirs. Boise Philharm. Assn., 1983-84; dir. bd. trustees Coll. Idaho, 1986-91. Grad. Prize fellow Harvard Grad. Sch. Arts and Scis., 1965-69, Frederick Roe fellow Harvard U. Sch. Bus., 1971; George F. Baker scholar, 1970-71. Mem. NAM (bd. dirs.), Am. Forest and Paper Assn. (bd. dirs., mem. exec. com. 1984-94), Century Club (Boston), Arid Club, Crane Creek Country Club. Office: Boise Cascade Corp PO Box 50 Boise ID 83728-0001

HARAGAN, DONALD ROBERT, university administrator, geosciences educator; b. Houston, Apr. 15, 1936; s. Donald William and Mary (Thompson) H.; m. Willie Mae O'Berry, July 2, 1966; children—Shannon Lea, Shelley Jo. B.S., U. Tex., 1959, Ph.D., 1969; M.S., Tex. A & M U., 1960. Registered profl. engr., Tex. Research asst. Tex. A & M U., College Station, 1959-60; research scientist U. Tex., Austin, 1960-66, instr., 1966-69; asst. prof. Tex. Tech. U., Lubbock, 1969-72; assoc. prof. Tex. Tech U., Lubbock, 1972-78, prof. geosci., 1978—, dept. chmn., 1972-77, 80-83, interim dean, 1985, interim v.p., 1985-86, v.p. for acad. affairs and research, 1986-88, exec. v.p., provost, 1988—; interim pres. Tex. Tech. U., Lubbock, 1996, pres., 1996—. Contbr. articles in field to profl. jours. Mem. Am. Soc. Civil Engrs., AAAS, Am. Meteorol. Soc., Am. Water Resources Assn., Tex. Acad. Sci. Home: 6914 Nashville Dr Lubbock TX 79413-6002 Office: Tex Tech U Office of Provost Lubbock TX 79409

HARA-ISA, NANCY JEANNE, graphic designer, county official; b. San Francisco, May 14, 1961; d. Toshiro and Masaye Hara; m. Stanley Takeo Isa, June 15, 1985. Student, UCLA, 1979-82; BA in Art and Design, Calif. State U., L.A., 1985. Salesperson May Co., L.A., 1981; svc. rep. Hallmark Cards Co., L.A., 1981-83; prodn. artist Calif. State U., L.A., 1983, Audio-Stats Internat. Inc., L.A., 1983; prodn. asst. Auto-Graphics Inc., Pomona, Calif., 1984-85, lead supr., 1985-86; art dir., contbg. staff writer CFW Enterprises, Burbank, Calif., 1987-88; graphic designer, prodn. mgr. Bonny Jularbal Graphics, Las Vegas, Nev., 1988-90; graphic designer Weddle Caldwell Advt., Las Vegas, 1990-92; owner Nancy Hara-Isa Designs, 1992—; graphic artist Regional Transp. Commn. of Clark County, Las Vegas, 1993-98; mgmt. analyst Clark County Dept. Aviation, Las Vegas, 1998—; freelance designer Caesars Palace. Writer Action Pursuit Games mag. Parade asst., mem. carnival staff Nisei Week., L.A., 1980-84; asst. mem. Summit Orgn., L.A., 1987—; mem. selection com. United Way; alumni grad. Clark County Leadership Forum, 1996. Mem. NAFE, Women in Profl. Graphic Svcs. (acting 1st v.p. 1990, 2d v.p. 1991), Women in Comms., Green Valley Rep. Women's Club, Am. Soc. Public Adminstrs., (coun. mem. 1998-99). Presbyterian. Avocations: photography, swimming, horseback riding, shooting. Home: 367 Cavos Way Henderson NV 89014-3555

HARALAMPU, GEORGE STELIOS, electric power engineer, former engineering executive electric utility company; b. Lynchburg, Va., Mar. 20, 1925; s. Stelios P. and Thelxiope (Hagipalaiologous) H.; m. Helen Avtges, June 14, 1953; children: Evelyn, Stephen. BSEE, Tufts U., 1952; MSEE, Northeastern U., 1960. Registered profl. engr., Mass. Successively jr. engr., asst. engr., engr., protection engr. New Eng. Electric System, Boston, 1952-69; protection and planning engr. New Eng. Electric System, Westborough, Mass., 1969-73, asst. chief engr., 1973-75, dir. elec. engring., 1975-84, dir. engring., 1984-91, v.p. engring., 1988-91, ret., 1991; mem. steering com. Edison Electric Inst., Washington, 1968-73; chmn. system protection T.F., N.E. Power Coordinating Coun., N.Y.C., 1978-83; mem. system design task force New Eng. Power Pool, Springfield, Mass., 1969-70, chmn. transient voltage analysis, 1971-77. Contbr. articles to profl. jours. Sgt. U.S. Army, 1943-46, ETO. Fellow IEEE (chmn. surge protective devices com. 1979-80, com. award 1988); mem. IEEE Power Engrng. Soc. (Laurence Cleveland award 1987), Power Engrng. Soc. Boston (sr., chmn. 1967-68), Masons. Republican. Greek Orthodox. Avocations: furniture making, gardening, traveling, symphony. Home: 60 Long Ave Belmont MA 02478-2963

HARALICK, ROBERT MARTIN, electrical engineering educator; b. N.Y.C., Sept. 30, 1943; s. David and Yetta (Stier) H.; m. Joy Gold, Aug. 20, 1967 (div. July 1977); 1 child, Tammy-Beth; m. Linda G. Shapiro, Feb. 12, 1978 (div. Aug. 1992); 1 child, Michael Aaron; m. Ihsin T. Phillips, Dec. 1993. BA, U. Kans., 1964, BS, 1966, MS, 1967, PhD, 1969. Asst. prof. elec. engring. U. Kans., Lawrence, 1969-71, assoc. prof., 1971-75, prof., 1975-78; prof. Va. Poly. Inst. and State U., 1979-84; v.p. rsch. Machine Vision Internat., Ann Arbor, Mich., 1984-86; Boeing Clairmont Egtvedt prof. elec. engring., adj. prof. computer sci. U. Wash., Seattle, 1986—; pres. Mnemonics Inc., 1979—; co-dir. NATO Advanced Study Inst. Image Processing, 1978; co-chmn. NATO Advanced Study Inst. on Image Processing, 1980, Robust Computer Vision Workshop, 1990, 92, 94; vice chmn. 5th Internat. Conf. on Pattern Recognition, Miami, 1980; dir. NATO Advanced Study Inst. on Pictorial Data Analysis, 1982; adj. prof. Ctr. Bioengring. U. Wash., Seattle, 1988—; program chmn. 10th annual ICPR Conf. on Pattern Recognition Systems and Applications, 1990; program co-chmn. Internat. Conf. on Document Analysis and Recognition, 1991, vice chmn., 1997; co-chmn. Evaluation and Validation of Computer Vision Algorithm, 1998. Author: (with T. Creese) Differential Equations for Engineers, 1977; Pictorial Data Analysis, 1983, (with L. Shapiro) Computer and Robost Vision, Vol I and II, 1992, The Inner Meaning of Hebrew Letters, 1995, (with M. Glazerson) The Torah Codes and Israel Today, 1996; editor: (with J. C. Simon) Issues in Digital Image Processing, 1980, Digital Image Processing, 1981; assoc. editor Computer Vision, Graphics and Image Processing, 1975-93, Pattern Recognition, 1977-93, Communication of the ACM, Image Processing, 1982-92, IEEE Transactions on Systems, Man and Cybernetics, 1979-88, IEEE Transactions on Image Processing, 1992-96, Jour. of Electronic Imaging, 1994—; mem. editorial bd. IEEE Transactions on Pattern Analysis and Machine Intelligence, 1981-84, IEEE Expert, 1986-90, Machine Vision and Applications, 1987—, Real Time Imaging, 1994—, mem. editl. com. IEEE Transactions on Pattern Analysis and Machine Intelligence, 1979-84, mem. adv. bd. IEEE Transactions on Pattern Analysis and Machine Intelligence, 1984-93, Image and Vision Computing, 1984-93; mem. adv. program com. Structural & Syntactic Pattern Recognition, 1990; contbr. over 500 articles to profl. jours.; digital computer art exhibitions include William Rockhill Nelson Gallery, Kansas City, Mo., 1971, Nat. History Mus., U. Kans., 1971, Dulin Gallery Art, 1971 (2 purchase awards), Nat. Invitational Print Show, U. R.I., 1972, Fla. State U., 1972, San Diego State Coll., 1972. Recipient Dow Chem. Young Outstanding Faculty award Am. Soc. Engring. Educators, 1975, Outstanding Young Elec. Engrs. Honorable Mention award Eta Kappa Nu, 1975, Best Paper award 5th Ann. Symposium on Automatic Imagery Pattern Recognition, 1975, Best Paper award Pattern Recognition Soc., 1989; NSF faculty fellow, 1977-79. Fellow IEEE, IAPR; mem. IEEE Computer Soc. (chmn. pattern analysis and machine intelligence tech. com. 1975-82, acoustics, signal and speech processing, sys., man and cybernetics, pattern recognition tech. subcom. 1975-81, data structures and pattern recognition subcom. 1975-81, biomed. pattern recognition subcom. 1975-81, internat. assn. for pattern recognition gov. bd. 1986—, program com. pattern and image processing conf. 1978, 4th internat. joint conf. on pattern recognition 1978, conf. B-pattern recognition methods and sys. program com. 11th internat. conf. on pattern recognition 1992, structural and syntactic pattern recognition 1992, 2d internat. conf. on document analysis and recognition 1993, chairperson various workshops and confs., Cert. Appreciation award 1978, 84), Pattern Recognition Soc., Internat. Assn. for Pattern Recognition (pres. 1996-98), Am. Assn. Artificial Intelligence, Assn. Computing Machinery. Avocation: hammered dulcimer. Home: 8651 Inverness Dr NE Seattle WA 98115-3987 Office: U of Wash Dept of Elec Engring EE/CSE Bldg Rm 253 Seattle WA 98195

HARALSON, LINDA JANE, communications executive; b. St. Louis, Mar. 24, 1959; d. James Benjamin and Betty Jane (Myers) N.; married. BA summa cum laude, William Woods Coll., 1981; MA, Webster U., 1982. Radio intern Stas.-KFAL/KKCA, Fulton, Mo., 1981; paralegal Herzog, Kral, Burroughs & Specter, St. Louis, 1981-82; staffing coord. then mktg. coord. Spectrum Emergency Care, St. Louis, 1982-85, mktg. mgr., 1985-87; dir. mktg. and recruitment Carondelet Rehab. Ctrs. Am., Culver City, Calif., 1987—; mktg. dir. outpatient and corp. svcs. Calif. Med. Ctr., L.A., 1987-88; mktg. dir. Valley Meml. Hosp., Livermore, Calif., 1988-89; account exec. Laurel Comm., Medford, Oreg., 1989-91; cmty. rels. dir. Rogue Valley Med. Ctr., Medford, 1991-95; cmty. pub. rels. dir. Rogue Valley Manor, Medford, 1995-97; pvt. practice in comms. and mktg., 1997—. Party chmn. Heart Assn., St. Louis, 1982—; bd. dirs. Am. Lung Assn. Oreg. Recipient Flair award Advt. Fedn. St. Louis, 1984, Hosps. award Hagen Mktg. Rsch. and Hosps. mag., 1984; Presdl. Acad. scholar William Woods Coll., Fulton, 1977-81. Mem. AAUW, Britt Music Festivals, Alpha Phi Alumnae Assn. (pres. chpt. 1985-87). Republican. Avocations: running, travel, sports, French, needlepoint. Home and Office: 4546 NE East Devils Lake Rd Otis OR 97368-9614

HARARI, HANANIAH, artist; b. Rochester, N.Y., Aug. 29, 1912; s. Israel Ely and Sarah (Berger) H.; m. Freda Emanuel, May 10, 1936 (dec. 1977); 1 son, Michael John; m. Shirley Lewis, Sept. 1, 1979. Student, Coll. Fine Arts, Syracuse (N.Y.) U., 1930-32; apprentice, Fernand Leger, André Lhote, Marcel Gromaire, Paris, 1932-34; student, Fontainebleau Ecole de Fresque, Paris, 1933. Tchr. painting Am. Artists Sch., N.Y.C., 1938-40, New Sch. Social Rsch., 1974, Sch. Visual Arts, 1974-90, Art Students League, 1984—; tchr. illustration Workshop Sch. Art, 1950-52. One-man shows Mercury Gallery, 1939, Pinacotheca, 1941, 43, Laurel Gallery, 1948, 51, new Sch. Social Rsch., 1974, Nardin Galleries, 1979, 86, Martin Diamond Fine Arts, Inc., 1981, Susan Teller Gallery, 1995; retrospectives Neuberger Mus. of Art, N.Y.C., 1997, Montclair Art Mus., N.J., 1997, Gallery Dai Ichi Arts, 1997Mem. Art Gallery, Rochester, N.Y., 1998; exhbns. include Mus. Modern Art, 1938, 42-43, Whitney Mus., 1942, 43, 44, 46, 47, 81, 90, Met. Mus., 1943, Met. Mus., 1986, 96, Toledo Mus., 1947, San Francisco Palace Legion of Honor, 1947, Art Dirs. Ann., 1947-48, 50, 52, Albright Art Gallery, Buffalo, Cleve. Mus. Art, Art Gallery of Toronto, Art Mus. N.Mex., Albuquerque, 1977, Portsmouth Gallery (Va.), 1982, Lowe Art Mus., Miami, Fla., 1983, Ashville (N.C.) Art Mus., 1997, Ga. Mus. Art, Athens, 1998, Laguna (Calif.) Art Mus., 1998, others; represented in permanent collections Met. Mus., Phila. Mus. Art, Whitney Mus., Albright Art Gallery, U. Ariz., Tucson, N.Y. Pub. Libr., Yale U. Art Gallery, Nat. Mus. Am. Art, Smithsonian Inst., Phoenix Art Mus., Amon Carter Mus., Brit. Mus., Worcester Art Mus., Wichita Art Mus., Del. Art Mus., Cleve. Mus. Art, Bklyn. Mus., Mus. City of N.Y., Nat. Acad. of Design, Montclair Mus., Meml. Art Gallery, Rochester, N.Y., Libr. of Congress, Affiliated Portraits, Inc., Nardin Galleries, Michael Rosenfeld Gallery, Susan Teller Gallery. Served with AUS, 1943-45. Recipient Hallgarten prize N.A.D., 1942, Emy Herzfeld award 4th Ann. Audubon Artists Exhbn., 1945, Binney & Smith award Audubon Artists, 1987, Art Students League award Audubon Artists, 1991, 92, Emily Lowe award Audubon Artists, 1993; grantee Richard Florsheim Found., 1996, Westchester Arts Coun., 1996. *In appreciation of the gift of life, I aspire to leave some lively and harmonious tracks.*

HARARY, KEITH, research scientist, author, science journalist; b. N.Y.C., Feb. 9, 1953; s. Victor and Lillian (Mazur) H.; m. Darlene Moore, Oct. 22, 1985. BA in Psychology, Duke U., 1975; PhD, Union Inst., 1986. Crisis counselor Durham (N.C.) Mental Health Ctr., 1972-76; rsch. assoc. Psychical Rsch. Found., Durham, 1972-76; rsch. assoc. dept. psychiatry Maimonides Med. Ctr., Bklyn., 1976-79; dir. counseling Human Freedom Ctr., Berkeley, Calif., 1979; rsch. cons. SRI Internat., Menlo Park, Calif., 1980-82; design cons. Atari Corp., Sunnyvale, Calif., 1983-85; pres., rsch. dir. Inst. for Advanced Psychology, San Francisco, 1986—; freelance sci. journalist, 1988-98; editor-at-large Omni Mag., 1996-98; sr. v.p., rsch. dir. Capital Access/Resource Group Internat., 1996—; invited lectr. Duke U., 1995; lectr. in field; adj. prof. Antioch U., San Francisco, 1985, 86; guest lectr. Lyceum Sch. for Gifted Children, 1985-89; vis. rschr. USSR Acad. Scis., 1983; rsch. cons. Am. Soc. for Psychical Rsch., 1971-72, Found. for Rsch. on Nature of Man, 1972, sci. applications Internat. Corp., 1991-93; psychol. cons., nat. media spokesperson Budget Rent A Car Corp., 1997-99; psychol. cons., media spokesperson Sears Corp., 1997; psychol. cons. Microsoft Corp., 1998-99. Co-author: The Mind Race, 1984, 85, 30-Day Altered States of Consciousness Series, 1989-91, rev. edits., 1999, Who Do You Think You Are? Explore Your Many-Sided Self With the Berkeley Personality Profile, 1994, CD-ROM edit., 1996; featured monthly columnist in The Omni Mind Brain Lab in Omni Mag., 1995-98; contbr. over 100 articles to profl. jours., other publs. Mem. APA, Am. Psychol. Soc., Assn. for Media Psychology, Am. Soc. for Psychical Rsch. (bd. dirs. 1994—). Achievements include first to develop reflective approach to personality profiling; development of advanced human perception research, including original training methodologies in altered states induction, and extended perception; development of original scientific terminology adapted and used in specialized theoretical areas in advanced perceptual research, including extended perception, extended human abilities, mental noise, paranormal hysteria, stress apparitions, others; development of original clinical approaches to crisis intervention. Home and Office: PO Box 910 Tiburon CA 94920-2517

HARATUNIAN, MICHAEL, engineering company executive; b. 1933. Various positions STV Group, Inc., Douglasville, Pa., 1972—, pres., COO, 1988—, chmn. bd. dirs., CEO, 1991-99, chmn. bd., 1999—. Office: 225 Park Ave S New York NY 10003-1604

HARAVON COLLINS, LESLEA, women's studies educator; b. Mt. Kisco, N.Y., Feb. 13, 1967; d. Aristide and Alda (Saporta) H. BA, Swarthmore Coll., 1989; MA, U. Iowa, 1993, PhD, 1996. Tchg. asst. U. Iowa, Iowa City, 1991-96, adj. asst. prof. women's studies, 1996—. Mem. N.Am. Soc. Sociology of Sport, Profl. Instrs. Alliance, Lesbian, Gay, Bisexual Faculty & Staff Assn., Coun. on the Stutus of Women. Avocations: yoga instructor. Home: 24 Woodcrest Ln NE Iowa City IA 52240-9502

HARAYDA, JANICE, newspaper book editor, author; b. New Brunswick, N.J., July 31, 1949; d. John and Marel (Boyer) H. BA cum laude, U. N.H., 1970. Editl. asst. Mademoiselle mag., N.Y.C., 1970; asst. to travel editor Saturday Rev., N.Y.C., 1971; sr. editor, contbg. editor Glamour mag., N.Y.C., 1971-78; editl. dir. Boston mag., 1978-81; freelance writer Boston, 1981-87; book editor Plain Dealer, Cleve., 1987-98; editor-in-chief N.J. Life mag., Lambertville, 1998, Princeton (N.J.) Alumni Weekly, 1999—; lectr. Radcliffe Pub., Cambridge, Mass., 1979, 80, Cath Conf., among others; instr. writing Marymount Coll., N.Y.C., 1977; instr. journalism Boston U. Sch. Pub. Comm., 1979; freelance writer. Author: The Joy of Being Single, 1986; contbg. author: Rooms with No View, 1974, Titters, 1979, Women: A Book for Men, 1979, The Accidental Bride, 1999. Adminstrv. bd. Park Ave. United Meth. Ch., N.Y.C., 1975-78, active civic, corp. and religious groups, 1988—. Recipient award for Excellence in Journalism Cleve. Press. Club, 1994; named guest editor Mademoiselle mag., 1970. Mem. Am. Soc. Journalists and Authors, Nat. Book Critics Cir. (bd. dirs. 1997—, v.p. awards 1998—), Royal Scottish Country Dance Soc., Clan Donald USA. Avocations: opera, theater, ballet, travel, dancing with Scottish country dance troupes. Office: Princeton Alumni Weekly 194 Nassau St Princeton NJ 08542

HARB, MAC, Canadian government official. BS, U. Ottawa, Ont., Can., MSEE. Alderman City of Ottawa, 1985-88, dep. mayor, 1987-88; mem. of parliment Ho. of Commons, Ottawa, 1988—, sec. to min. for internat. trade, 1993-95. Former vice-chmn. Ottawa Non-Profit Housing Corp, Ottawa Econ. Affairs Com.; bd. mgmt. Preston St. bus. improvement bd. Mem. Assn. Profl. Engrs. on Ont. Avocations: cooking, gardening, travel. Office: Ho of Commons, Ctr Block Rm 552D, Ottawa, ON Canada K1A 0A6

HARBATER, DAVID, mathematician; b. N.Y.C., Dec. 19, 1952; s. Maurice and Marilyn (Haber) H. AB summa cum laude, Harvard U., 1974; MS in Math., Brandeis U., 1975; PhD in Math., MIT, 1978; MA (hon.), U. Pa., 1984. Asst. prof. U. Pa., Phila., 1978-83, assoc. prof., 1983-91, prof., 1991-96, E. Otis Kendall prof. math., 1996—. Contbr. articles to profl. jours. Fellow NSF, 1975-78, 82-83, Sloan Found., 1984-87, Lindback award for disting. tchg. U. Pa., 1995. Mem. Am. Math. Soc. (postdoctoral fellow 1978-79, Frank Nelson Cole Prize in Algebra, 1995), Phi Beta Kappa, Sigma Xi. Democrat. Jewish. Home: 2400 Chestnut St Philadelphia PA 19103-4316 Office: U Pa Dept Math 209 S 33rd St Dept Math Philadelphia PA 19104-6317

HARBAUGH, DANIEL PAUL, lawyer; b. Wendell, Idaho, May 18, 1948; s. Myron and Manuelita (Garcia) H. BA, Gonzaga U., 1970, JD, 1974. Bar: Washington 1974, U.S. Dist. Ct. (ea. dist.) Wash. 1977, U.S. Ct. Appeals (9th cir.) 1978. Asst. atty. gen. State of Wash., Spokane, 1974-77; ptnr. Richter, Wimberley & Ericson, Spokane, 1977-83, Harbaugh & Bloom, P.S., Spokane, 1983—; bd. dirs. Spokane Legal Svcs., 1982-86; bd. govs. LAWPAC, Seattle, 1980-92. Bd. dirs. Spokane Ballet, 1983-88; chpt. dir. Les Amis du Vin, Spokane, 1985-88; mem. Spokane County Civil Svc. Commn., 1991—, chmn., 1999—, Gonzaga U. Pres'. Coun., 1991—. Mem. ATLA, Wash. State Bar Assn. (spl. dist. counsel 1982-95, mem. com. rules for profl. conduct 1989-92, mem. legis. com. 1995-96), Spokane County Bar Assn. (chair med.-legal com. 1991), Wash. State Trial Lawyers Assn. (v.p. 1988-89, co-chair worker's compensation sect. 1992, 93, spl. select. com. on workers' corp. 1990—, forum 1994—, vice-chmn. 1994-97, mem. legis. com. 1995—), Nat. Orgn. Social Security Claimants Reps., Internat. Wine and Food Soc. (pres. local chpt. 1989-91, cellar master 1994-96), Spokane Club, Spokane Country Club (adminstrv. com. 1995-98, chmn. 1991-98, trustee 1996—, sec.-treas. 1997-98, pres. 1998—), Alpha Sigma Nu, Phi Alpha Delta. Roman Catholic. Office: Harbaugh & Bloom PS PO Box 1461 Spokane WA 99210-1461

HARBAUGH, JAMES JOSEPH, professional football player; b. Toledo, Ohio, Dec. 23, 1963. Degree in comm., U. Mich., 1987. Quarterback Chgo. Bears, 1987-93, Indpls. Colts, 1994-98, Balt. Ravens, 1998-99, San Diego Chargers, 1999—. Selected to Pro Bowl, 1995. Office: San Diego Chargers Qualcomm Stadium San Diego CA 92160*

HARBAUGH, JOHN WARVELLE, applied earth sciences educator; b. Madison, Wis., Aug. 6, 1926; s. Marion Dwight and Marjorie (Warvelle) H.; m. Josephine Taylor, Nov. 24, 1951 (dec. Dec. 25, 1985); children: Robert, Dwight, Richard. BS, U. Kans., 1948, MS, 1950; PhD, U. Wis., 1955. Prodn. geologist Carter Oil Co., Tulsa, 1951-53; prof. geol. sci. Stanford U., 1955—. Author: (with G. Bonham Carter) Computer Simulation in Geology, 1970, (with D.M. Tezlaff) Simulating Clastic Sedimentation, 1989, (with P. Martinez) Simulating Nearshore Environments, 1993, (with R. Slingerland and K. Furlong) Simulating Clastic Sedimentary Basins, 1994, (with J.C. Davis and J. Wendebourg) Computing Risk for Oil Prospects: Principles and Programs, 1995, (with J. Wendebourg) Simulating Oil Entrapment in Clastic Sequences, 1997. Recipient Haworth Disting. Alumni award U. Kans., 1968, Krumbein medal Internat. Assn. Math. Geologists, 1986. Fellow Geol. Soc. Am.; mem. Am. Assn. Petroleum Geologists (Levorsen award 1970, Disting. Svc. award 1987, Disting. Edn. award Pacific sect. 1999). Republican. Home: 683 Salvatierra St Stanford CA 94305-8539 Office: Stanford U Dept Geol Scis 229 Geology Bldg Stanford CA 94305-2115

HARBAUGH, LOIS JENSEN, secondary education educator; b. Elmhurst, Ill., Sept. 16, 1942; d. G. E. and Dorothy G. (Madsen) Jensen; m. Lou L. W. Harbaugh Jr., Aug. 8, 1964; children: Michelle, Bill. BA, Wheaton Coll., 1964; MAT in Sci. Edn., U. Tex., Dallas, 1978. Cert. composite secondary sci. tchr., Tex. Tchr. Troy Mills (Iowa) Sch., 1965-66, Richardson (Tex.) Jr. High Sch., 1969-71; tchr., chair sci. First Bapt. Acad., Dallas, 1975-81, Lake Highlands Jr. High Sch., Richardson, 1981-98, Woodrow Wilson H.S., Dallas, 1998—; mem. Tex. State Textbook Com., Tex. Edn. Agy., 1990, 94, 97. Bd. dirs. Crisis Pregnancy Ctr., Dallas, 1983-88; bd. dirs. and educators Found. for Thought and Ethics, Richardson, 1988—. Christa McAuliffe fellow Dept. Edn., 1988; grantee Recognizing Innovation for Student Edn. (RISE) Found., 1989; recipient Nat. Radio Astronomy Observatory (NRAO) Inst. award NSF, 1988, Newmast award NASA, 1989, Tchr. Cons. award Tex. Instruments, 1991. Mem. Nat. Sci. Tchrs. Assn., Nat. Sci. Suprs. Assn. (sec. 1988-92), Sci. Tchrs. Assn. Tex., Richardson Assn. Tex. Profl. Educators (pres. 1994-96), Assn. Tex. Profl. Edn. (region X sec. 1996-98), Tex. Earth Sci. Tchrs. Assn., Mensa. Achievements include amateur radio. Office: Woodrow Wilson HS 100 S Glasgow Dallas TX 75214

HARBAUGH, TERESA GABRIEL, publisher, artist; b. San Bernardino, Calif., Feb. 5, 1948; d. Louis Paul and Doris (Peters) Gabriel; m. Paul Harrison Harbaugh, Sept. 1, 1973; children: Phaedra Gabriel, Jerad Harrison. BFA, U. Santa Clara, 1969; secondary tchg. cert., U. San Diego, 1970. Owner, pres. Azusa, Englewood, Colo., 1981—. Avocations: collecting beads, button, antique purses, postcards, photographs, yoga, swimming, ceramics/pottery. Office: Azusa Pub Inc 3575 S Fox St Englewood CO 80110

HARBECK, WILLIAM JAMES, real estate executive, lawyer, international consultant; b. Glenview, Ill., Dec. 16, 1921; s. Christian Frederick and Anna (Gaeth) H.; m. Jean Marie Allsopp, Jan. 20, 1945; children: John, Stephen, Timothy, Mark, Christopher. B.A., Wabash (Ind.) Coll., 1947; J.D., Northwestern U., 1950. Bar: Ill. 1950. Land acquisition atty. Chgo. Land Clearance Commn., 1950-51; regional real estate dir. Montgomery Ward & Co., Chgo., 1951-68; asst. to pres., dir. corp. facilities Montgomery Ward & Co., 1968-70, v.p., dir. facilities devel., 1970-81; v.p. Montgomery Ward Devel. Corp., 1972-81; pres., chief exec. officer Montgomery Ward Properties Corp., 1974-81; pres. William J. Harbeck Assocs., 1981—; bd. dirs. Randhurst Corp., 1972-81, mem. exec. com., 1975-79. Mem. editorial bd. profl. jours.; contbr. articles to profl. jours. Bd. dirs. Chgo. Lawson YMCA, 1973-89, chmn. devel. com., 1979-89, mem. exec. com., 1985-89; bd. dirs. Greater North Michigan Ave Assn., Chgo., 1979-81; chmn. constrn. com. Chgo. United, 1979-81; co-chmn. Chgo. Bus. Opportunities Fair, 1980-81; mem. real estate com. Chgo. Met. YMCA, 1982-89, chmn. Bldg. Task Force, 1985-90; mem. pres.'s coun. Concordia U., River Forest, Ill., 1969-87, mem. bd. regents, 1987-96, mem. strategic planning com., 1989-91; bd. trustee Concordia U. Found., 1996-97; mem. planning com. Inst. for Philanthropic Mgmt., 1985-89; youth Bible and Bethel instr. Redeemer Luth. Ch., Highland Pk., Ill., 1965-89, congregation pres., 1968-70, 85-87, chmn. ch. growth com., 1982-89; mem. Eternal Shepherd Luth. Ch., Salem, S.C., 1990—, bd. elders, 1991-96, chmn., 1993-96; trustee Luth. Ch. Mo. Synod Found., 1975-76, 81-90, bd. mems., 1992-98, mem. Synodical mission study commn., 1974-75, mem. dist. rsch. and planning com., 1981-90, mem. task force on synodical constn. by-laws and structure, 1975-79; bd. mems. Luth. Ch. ext. fund, 1989-92; mem. rsch. and planning com. No. Ill. Dist. Luth. Ch. Mo. Synod, 1984-89; nat. mem. Luth. Ch. Ext. Fund. Bd., 1992-96; sponsor Luth. Chs. for Career Devel., 1979-88; corp. chmn. U.S. Bond drive, Chgo., 1976; chief crusader Chgo. Crusade Mercy, 1976-78; divsn. chmn. Chgo. Cerebral Palsy campaign, 1977-78. Lt. (j.g.) USNR, 1942-46. Mem. Ill. Bar Assn., Internat. Coun. Shopping Ctrs. (bd. dirs. 1972-78, exec. com. 1975-78, govt. affairs com. 1977-89, awards com. 1980-83, urban com. 1980-83, lectr. 1969-89), Luth. Layman's League, Alpha Sigma Kappa, Phi Alpha Delta. Home and Office: 23 Eastern Point Keowee Harbours Salem SC 29676

HARBERGER, ARNOLD CARL, economist, educator; b. Newark, July 27, 1924; s. Ferdinand C. and Martha (Bucher) H.; m. Ana Beatriz Valjalo, Mar. 15, 1958; children: Paul Vincent, Carl David. Student, Johns Hopkins U., 1941-43; MA, U. Chgo., 1947, PhD, 1950; Doctor honoris causa, U. Tucuman, 1979, Cath. U. Chile, 1988, Tech. U. Cen. Am., 1989. Asst. prof. polit. economy Johns Hopkins U., 1949-53; asso. prof. econs. U. Chgo., 1953-59, prof., 1959—, chmn. dept., 1964-71, 75-80, Gustavus F. and Ann M. Swift disting. svc. prof., 1977-91, prof. emeritus, 1991—, dir. Ctr. Latin Am. Econ. Studies, 1965-92; vis. prof. MIT (Ctr. Internat. Studies), New Delhi, 1961-62, Econ. Devel. Inst., IBRD, 1965, Harvard U., 1971-72, Princeton U., 1973-74, UCLA, 1983, 84, U. Paris, 1986; prof. econs. UCLA, 1984—; cons. IMF, 1950, 89, U.S. Pres.'s Materials Policy Commn., 1951-52, U.S. Treasury Dept., 1961-75, Com. Econ. devel., 1961-78, Planning Commn., India, 1961-62, 73, Pan Am. Union, 1962-76, Dept. State, 1962-76, Cen. Bank, Chile, 1965-70, Dominican Republic, 1989, Nicaragua, 1990, China, 1995, Ecuador, 1996, Planning Dept., Panama, 1963-77, Colombia, 1969-71, Nicaragua, 1990; cons. Ford Found., 1967-77, Planning Commn., El Salvador, 1973-75, Budget and Planning Office, Uruguay, 1974-75, Can. Dept. Regional Econ. Expansion, 1975-77, Econ. Min. Argentina, 1994—, Fin. Ministry, Bolivia, 1976, Mex., 1976—; cons. Can. Dept. Employment and Migration, 1980-82, Indonesian Ministry Fin., 1981-82, 86, Can. Dept. Fin., 1982-88, Can. Dept. Industry, Sci. and Tech., 1991—, Chinese Ministry Fin., 1983; ministry fin., Malawi, 1988, Venezuela, 1989, Colombia, 1991, 94, Dominican Republic, 1996, 97; mem. internat. adv. coun. Inst. Internat. Studies, Stanford U., 1991—; v.p., chmn. adv. coun. Inst. for Policy Reform. *In 1999 he completed 50 years of graduate teaching in economics. His students have made notable contributions both in the academic world and in public policy formation. Over half a dozen have been rectors or presidents of universities, and literally scores have been economics deans or department heads. In economic policymaking, over a dozen have been heads of their countries central banks, and over two dozen have been cabinet ministers (secretaries). In Latin America, and especially in Chile, Argentina and Mexico, his former students have been important leaders in the liberalization and modernization of economic policy.* Author: Project Evaluation, 1972, Taxation and Welfare, 1974; Editor: Demand for Durable Goods, 1960, The Taxation of Income from Capital, 1968, Key Problems of Economic Policy In Latin America, 1970, World Economic Growth, 1985; contbr. sci. papers to profl. jours. and govt. publs. With AUS, 1943-46. Guggenheim fellow; Fulbright scholar; faculty rsch. fellow Social Sci. Rsch. Coun.; Ford Found. faculty rsch. fellow, 1968-69. Fellow Econometric Soc., Am. Acad. Arts and Scis.; mem. Am. Econ. Assn. (mem. exec. com. 1970-72, v.p. 1992, pres.-elect 1996, pres. 1997), Western Econ. Assn. (v.p. 1987-88, pres. 1989-90), Royal Econ. Soc., Nat. Tax Assn., NAS, Phi Beta Kappa. Home: 136 Buckskin Rd Bell Canyon CA 91307-1125 Office: UCLA PO Box 951477 405 Hilgard Ave Los Angeles CA 90095-9000

HARBERT, BILL LEBOLD, construction corporation executive; b. Indianola, Miss., July 21, 1923; s. John Murdock and Mae (Schooling) H.; m. Mary Joyce Patrick, June 28, 1952; children—Anne Harbert Moulton, Elizabeth Harbert Cornay, Billy L., Jr. B.S., Auburn U., 1948; Advanced Mgmt. Program, Harvard U., 1966. Lic. profl. engr. and land surveyor, Ala. Exec. v.p. Harbert Constrn. Corp., Birmingham, Ala., 1948-79; pres. Harbert Constrn. Corp., Birmingham, 1979-81; pres., chief oper. officer Harbert Internat., Inc., Birmingham, 1981-90, vice chmn., 1990-91, pres., chmn. bd., 1991-98; pres., chmn. bd. dirs. Bill Harbert Internat. Constrn., Inc., 1992—, chmn., CEO, 1998—. Trustee, co-chmn. Laborers Nat. Pension Fund, Dallas, 1968—; bd. dirs. U. Ala. Health Service Found., Birmingham, 1983-95, Met. Devel. Bd. of Birmingham, 1980-83, AMI Brookwood Med. Ctr., 1990—. Served to sgt. U.S. Army, 1943-46. Mem. Birmingham Area C. of C. Methodist. Clubs: Vestavia Country (pres. 1971), Riverchase Country (pres. 1980). Home: 205 Vestavia Cir Birmingham AL 35216-1351

HARBERT, GUY MORLEY, JR., retired obstetrician, gynecologist; b. Fredericksburg, Va., Dec. 19, 1929; s. Guy Morley and Hannah (Turman) H.; m. Peggy Ann Simpson, Sept. 8, 1951; children—Lucille Hannah, Guy Morley, III, Michael Simpson. B.A., U. Va., 1952, M.D., 1956. Diplomate: Am. Bd. Ob-Gyn (maternal-fetal medicine). Intern Barnes Hosp., St. Louis, 1956-57; resident in ob-gyn U. Va. Hosp., 1959-63; med. faculty U. Va. Med. Sch., 1963—, prof. ob-gyn, 1976-95, prof. emeritus, 1995; mem. human embryology and devel. study sect. NIH, 1975-79. Author articles in profl. jours., chpts. in books. Served as officer M.C. USAF, 1957-59. Mem. Soc. Gynecol. Investigation (exec. council 1973-76), Perinatal Research Soc. (exec. council 1977-79), So. Perinatal Assn. (exec. council 1974-77), Am. Gynecol. Soc., Am. Assn. Obstetricians and Gynecologists, N.Y. Acad. Scis., Am. Coll. Obstetricians and Gynecologists, Assn. Profs. Ob-Gyn, S. Atlantic Assn. Obstetricians and Gynecologists, Sigma Xi. Presbyterian. Office: U Va Hosps Jefferson Park Ave Charlottesville VA 22908

HARBIN, CALVIN EDWARD, retired educator; b. Puxico, Mo., Mar. 26, 1916; s. Samuel Wesley and Ada Maria (Shelton) H.; m. Dorothy Comoh, June 26, 1947; chilren: Maria, Ruth, Charles. BS, S.E. Mo. State U., 1949; MA, Peabody-Vanderbilt U., 1949; EdD, U. Mo., 1952; LLD (hon.), Rio Grande Coll., 1976. Prof., dean Ft. Hays State U., Hays, Kans., 1952-81; cons. faculty mem. U.S. Army Command and Gen. Staff Coll., Ft. Leavenworth, Kans., 1968-72; counselor Hansen Found., Logan, Kans., 1981—. Author: Teaching Power, 1967; co-author (with Dane and Polly Bales): Kate Hansen, Beloved Teacher, America's Cultural Ambassador to Japan, 1999; contbr. articles to profl. jours.; composer hymns. Col. U.S. Army, 1941-76, ETO. Mem. SAR. Republican. Presbyterian. Avocations: gardening, writing, senior citizen's organizations. Home: 303 W 19th St Hays KS 67601-3116

HARBIN, MERLINE JOHNSON, social service agency administrator; b. Pensacola, Fla., Mar. 10, 1938; d. Harry Frederick and Nettie Merline (Sutherland) Johnson; m. Paul Burrell Jenkins, Aug. 19, 1961 (div. Nov. 1967); 1 child, Davalyn Jenkins; m. Nelson Sherman Harbin, Feb. 9, 1973; children: Michael Johnson, Janice Rachael Harbin Owen. BS in Edn., Fla. State U., 1960. Cert. Girl Scout Exec. Dir. Tchr. girls' phys. edn. Mowat Jr. H.S., Lynn Haven, Fla., 1960-62; sales clk. Velma's Ladies Shop, Panama City, Fla., 1962-63, buyer, asst. mgr., 1963-69; tchr. English and girls' phys.edn. Auburndale (Fla.) Jr. H.S., 1969-70; receptionist, ins. clk. pvt. dental office, Jacksonville, 1971-73; field dir. Gateway Girl Scout Coun., Jacksonville, Fla., 1979-81, asst. exec. dir., 1981-89, asst. exec. dir. properties and fin., 1989-94, asst. exec. dir. properties and risk mgmt., 1994-96; exec. dir. Apalachee Bend Girl Scout Coun., Tallahassee, Fla., 1996—; vice-chair Youth Enrichment League, Jacksonville, 1983-85; membership chair Fla. sect. Assn. of Girl Scout Exec. Staff, Fla., 1986-88. Editor: (monthly newsletter) Trail Sign, 1979-89. Mem. Big Bend chpt. Stand for Children, Tallahassee, Fla., 1997—. Recipient Archtl. Design Excellence award Girl Scouts of USA, 1993. Mem. Jacksonville C. of C. (mem. Mandarin coun. 1991-96), Fla. State U. Alumni Assn., Tallahassee C. of C., Rotary Club Tallahassee, Kappa Delta Pi, Phi Delta Pi, Alpha Xi Delta Alumni Assn. Republican. Mem. Church of Christ. Avocations: sailing, sewing. Fax: (850) 386-2093. E-mail: nharbin@talweb.com. Office: Apalachee Bend Girl Scout Coun 250 Pinewood Dr Tallahassee FL 32303-4838

HARBIN, MICHAEL ALLEN, religion educator, writer; b. Vincennes, Ind., May 24, 1947; s. Hugh Allen and Norma June (Palmer) H.; m. Esther Marie Rinas, May 31, 1971; children: Athena Colleen, Heidi Elizabeth, Douglas Allen. BS, U.S. Naval Acad., 1969; ThM, Dallas Theol. Sem., 1980, ThD, 1988; MA, Calif. State U., Carson, 1993. Instr. Dallas Bible Coll., 1984-86; freelance writer Garland, Tex., 1986-93; assoc. prof. Taylor U., Upland, Ind., 1993—; mem. elder bd. South Garland Bible Ch., Garland, Tex., 1981-93, chmn. elder bd., 1982-86; mem. elder bd. Upland Evangel. Mennonite Ch., 1995—. Author: To Serve Other Gods, 1994; contbr. articles to profl. jours. Del. 16th Senatorial Dist. Rep. Conv., Dallas, 1990, 92; alt. del. State Rep. Conv., Ft. Worth, 1990. Capt. USNR, ret. Fellow Inst. of Bibl. Rsch.; mem. Soc. Bibl. Lit., Bibl. Archaeol. Soc., Bible Sci. Assn. (cons. spkr.), Evang. Theol. Soc., Am. Legion, Near Ea. Archaeol. Soc. Home: 629 W South St Upland IN 46989-9016 *I owe whatever success I have achieved to the fact that I have always tried to take God and his Word seriously and apply the implications to my life.*

HARBISON, JAMES PRESCOTT, research physicist; b. Phila., Apr. 5, 1951; s. Robert James III and Elizabeth (Thompson) H.; m. Susan Foster, June 17, 1973; children: Thomas Foster, Daniel Robert, Elizabeth Thompson Harbison. AB in Physics, Harvard Coll., 1973, SM in Applied Physics, 1974, PhD in Applied Physics/Materials Sci., 1977. IBM postdoctoral fellow Harvard U., Cambridge, Mass., 1977-78; mem. tech. staff Bell Labs., Murray Hill, N.J., 1978-84, Bellcore, Red Bank, N.J., 1984-95; rsch. scientist Bellcore, Morristown, N.J., 1996-97; sr. scientist Bellcore, Morristown, 1997-99, Telcordia Techs., Morristown, 1999—. Contbr. articles to profl. jours.; patentee in field. Mem. Am. Phys. Soc., Am. Vacuum soc., Minerals, Metals and Materials Soc., Materials Rsch. Soc. Unitarian. Home: 53 Tyson Dr Fair Haven NJ 07704-3036 Office: Telcordia Techs MCC 1C-341B 445 South St Morristown NJ 07960-6438*

HARBISON, JAMES WESLEY, JR., lawyer; b. Mooresville, N.C., Aug. 30, 1934; s. James Wesley and Ola Mae (Bonney) H.; m. Margaret Geddes Morgan, Apr. 15, 1961; children: Anne, James. AB, Duke U., 1956; LLB, Yale U., 1959. Bar: N.C. 1959, N.Y. 1960, U.S. Dist. Ct. (so. and ea. dists.) N.Y. 1961, U.S. Ct. Appeals (2d cir.) 1962, U.S. Supreme Ct. 1968, U.S. Ct. Appeals (7th cir.) 1970, U.S. Ct. Appeals (5th cir.) 1975. Assoc. Simpson, Thacher & Bartlett, N.Y.C., 1960-73; ptnr. Wickes, Riddell, Bloomer, Jacobi & McGuire, N.Y.C., 1973-78, Morgan, Lewis & Bockius LLP, N.Y.C., 1979—. Served to capt. USAF, 1959-60, N.Y. A.N.G., 1960-68. Mem. ABA, N.C. Bar Assn., N.Y. State Bar Assn., Assn. of Bar of City of N.Y., Fed. Bar Council, Am. Judicature Soc. Democrat. Methodist. Clubs: Met., Yale (N.Y.C.). Home: 30 E End Ave New York NY 10028-7053 Office: Morgan Lewis & Bockius LLP 101 Park Ave New York NY 10178*

HARBOR, KINGSLEY OKORO, communications and journalism educator, researcher; b. Aro, Abia, Nigeria, Apr. 5, 1951; came to U.S., 1977; s. Robert and Victoria Imuche (Okoro) H.; m. Victoria Nwamuru Oti, Dec. 27, 1987; children: Emmanuel, Janet, Chibuzo. Diploma in Telecomm. Engring., P & T Tech. Sch., Oshodi, Lagos, Nigeria, 1976; BS in Tech., U. Houston, 1983; MEd in Mass Comm., So. Univ. A&M, 1985; PhD in Journalism, So. Ill. U., 1993. Postal officer Fed. Ministry Comm., Umuahia, Nigeria, 1972-73; internat. rels. officer Fed. Ministry Comm., Lagos, Nigeria, 1976-77; asst. tech. officer in tng. P & T Tech. Sch., Oshodi, Lagos, Nigeria, 1973-76; adminstrv. asst. So. Ill. U., Carbondale, 1988-89, tchg. asst., 1989-92; instr. mass comm. Shaw U., Raleigh, N.C., 1992-93; asst. prof. journalism Miss. Valley State U., Itta Bena, 1993-98, coord. of comm., 1993-94, acting chmn. dept. mass. comms., 1994-95, founding chmn. dept. mass. comms., 1995—, assoc. prof. journalism, 1998—; budget dir. Miss. Valley State U. Activity I Fed. Grant, Itta Bena, 1993—; founder, editor-in-chief MassComm Newsletter Miss. Valley State U., 1996—; fiscal officer Delta Devil's Gazette Newspaper, Itta Bena, 1996—. Fin. contbr. United Way, Itta Bena, Greenwood, Miss., 1995, Miss. Valley State U. Alumni Orgn., Itta Bena, 1996; mem. St. Francis of Assissi Sch. PTA, Greenwood, Miss., 1995. Named most valuable staff, Richmond (Tex.) State Sch., 1983, Instr. of Year, Shaw U. students, Raleigh, N.C., 1992; recipient journalism award Sch. Journalism, So. Ill. U., Carbondale, 1991; dissertation rsch. fellow So. Ill. U., 1992. Mem. Assn. for Edn. in Journalism and Mass Comm. (internat. comm. divsn., mass. comm. divsn., law divsn., minorities and comm. div.), Nat. Comm. Assn., Assn. Schs. Journalism and Mass Comm., Greenwood-LeFlore C. of C. Avocations: soccer, swimming, table tennis, singing, reading. Home: PO Box 8401 Greenwood MS 38935-8401 Office: Miss Valley State Univ 14000 Highway 82 W Itta Bena MS 38941-1400

HARBORDT, CHARLES MICHAEL, forest products executive; b. Houston, Apr. 8, 1942; s. Charles and Mary Lydia (Shumard) H.; m. Jackie Ward, June 23, 1960; children: Michelle, Katherine, Julie. BS, Stephen F. Austin U., Nacogdoches, Tex., 1963; MS, So. Meth. U., 1965; PhD, Tex. A&M U., 1970. Cert. environ. profl., Nat. Assn. Environ. Profls., Nat. Registry Environ. Profls.; registered environ. profl., environ. assessor. Assoc. chemist Texaco, Inc., Bellaire, Tex., 1965-67, sr. chemist, 1970-71; environ. dir. Temple Industries, Diboll, Tex., 1971-75; environ. dir. Temple-Eastex Inc., Diboll, 1975-80, energy, environ. and individual hygiene dir., 1980-90; v.p. Temple-Inland Forest Products Corp., Diboll, 1990—, Temple-Inland, Diboll, 1996—; mem. oper. com. Nat. Coun. Air and Stream Improvement, 1994—, chmn. chem. health effects and mgmt., 1994-97. Apptd. Tex. Regional Water Devel. Bd., 1998; v.p. United Fund, Lufkin, Tex., 1976; mem. adminstrn. bd. Lufkin Meth. Ch., chmn. bd. trustees, 1989-91, trustee, 1996—; chmn. career edn. com. Lufkin H.S., 1980-86; trustee Stephen F. Austin U. Found., 1996—; bd. dirs. Stephen F. Austin U. Real Estate Found., 1997—, Bus. Coun. for Sustainable Devel., Gulf of Mexico, 1993—. Robert A. Welch Found. fellow, 1963-65, Stephen F. Austin U. Disting. alumnus, 1994. Fellow Am. Inst. Chemists; mem. Am. Hardboard Assn. (chmn. environ. com. 1982-85, chmn. environ. com. 1983-85), TAPPI, Air Pollution Control Assn., Water Pollution Control Fedn., Diboll Jaycees, Angelina County (Tex.) C. of C. (bus. com. 1979, mem. edn. coun. 1984), Phi Kappa Phi, Phi Lambda Upsilon. Avocations: hunting, photography, reading, travel. Office: Temple Inland Inc PO Drawer N Diboll TX 75941

HARBOTTLE, GARMAN, chemist; b. Dayton, Ohio, Sept. 25, 1923; s. William Edwin and Susan (Garman) H.; m. Naomi Perkiss, June 10, 1949; 1 child, Laura. BS, Calif. Inst. Tech., 1944; PhD, Columbia U., 1949. Chemist Brookhaven Nat. Lab., Upton, N.Y., 1949—; dir. Internat. Atomic Energy Agy., Vienna, Austria, 1965-67; rsch. collaborator Met. Museum of Art, 1990—; adj. prof. SUNY, Stony Brook, 1985-93; guest prof. U. Sci. Tech. China, Hefei, 1997. Assoc. editor Archaeometry Jour., 1981-96, Jour. Radioanalytical Chemistry, 1982—. Trustee Vanderbilt Mus., Centerport, N.Y., 1979-87, Inc. Village of Old Field, N.Y., 1980-86. Atomic Energy Commn. postdoctoral fellow, 1951-52, Guggenheim fellow, 1957-58; recipient George von Hevesy medal, 1983, Glenn T. Seaborg medal Am. Nuclear Soc., 1995, Roald Fryxell medal Soc. for Am. Archaeology, 1994. Mem. Soc. for Archaeol. Scis. (pres. 1987). E-mail: garman@bnl.gov. Office: Brookhaven Nat Lab Upton NY 11973

HARBOUR, PATRICIA ANN MONROE, poet; b. Winchester, Ind.; d. Cecil James and Opal (Crouse) Monroe; m. James Claude Harbour, July 29, 1972; children: Eric Arif Monroe Khan, Reneé Ann Monroe Harbour. A in Bus., Ball State U., 1956. Typist Lincoln Life Ins. Co., Ft. Wayne, Ind., 1957; office sec. Lincoln Life Ins. Co., Dallas, 1957; legal exec. sec. Russell E. Wise Law Firm, Union City, Ind., 1958-63; sales assoc., sr. sales assoc. Palais Royal (SRI Retailers, Inc.), Katy, Tex., 1993, sr. sales assoc., cosmetician, cons., 1994; instr. tap dancing, swimming. Contbr. poems World of Poetry (honorable award 1991), Sparrowgrass Poetry Forum, Inc., 1992, The Poetry Center Anthology, Arcadia Poetry Anthology (honorable award 1992), On the Threshold of a Dream. Vol. III (Outstanding Poets of 1994: Nat. Libr. of Poetry, Editor's Choice Outstanding Achievement award 1994, 97). Elected into Internat. Poetry Hall of Fame, 1997, 98. Mem. Internat. Soc. Poets (Poet of Merit award, 1992, 93, Editor's Choice award Best Poems of 1997, 1997), Sigma Sigma Sigma. Avocations: dog walking, interior decorating, designing and painting wall graphics, line dancing. Home: 310 Buckeye Dr Katy TX 77450-1633

HARBOUR, ROBERT RANDALL, state agency administrator; b. Oklahoma City, Dec. 13, 1949; s. Robert Roy and Anna Belle (Boatner) H.; m. Patti Rae Levine, Apr. 4, 1981; children: Ann Joelle, Robert Daniel. BA in Pub. Adminstrn., U. Ctrl. Okla., 1975. Clk. Okla. Dept. Human Svcs., Oklahoma City, 1974-76; interviewer Okla. Employment Security Commn., Oklahoma City, 1976-80, sr. interviewer, 1980-89, local office mgr. I, 1989-93, trainer, mgr. I, 1993—, tng. program writer, presenter, 1993—; job search workshop presenter, employment svc. programs presenter Okla. Employment Security Commn., Oklahoma City, 1987-93; facilitator job fair Gov.'s Coun. Small Bus., Oklahoma City, 1990, Mayor's Employer Adv. Coun., Oklahoma City, 1992, Oklahoma City C.C., 1991. Contbr: (workbook) Job Search Workshop Workbook, 1989; writer: (tng. programs) State-Mandated Manager Training Program, 1993, Non-Supervisory Employee Training Program, 1993, New Employee Training Program, 1993. Recipient Spl. Merit award Mil. Order Purple Heart, Oklahoma City, 1991, Career Day Program Appreciation award Pvt. Industry Coun., Oklahoma City, 1991, Honorable Mention award ASTD Tng. Manual, 1994. Mem. ASTD (Honorable Mention for tng. manual ctrl. Okla. chpt. 1994, Honorable Mention award for program design ctrl. Okla. chpt. 1995), Internat. Assn. Pers. in Employment Svc., Nat. Forensic League, Internat. Platform Assn. Democrat. Avocations: public speaking, writing, reading, bowling, tennis. Home: 1740 Carlisle Rd Oklahoma City OK 73120-1117 Office: Okla Employment Security Commn 2401 N Lincoln Blvd Rm 200 Oklahoma City OK 73105-4495

HARBUCK, EDWIN CHARLES, insurance agent; b. Shreveport, La., Mar. 5, 1934; s. Charles Adam and Elsie (Owens) H.; m. Delores Threlkeld, June 10, 1955; children: Jonathan S., Edwin Seth, Christopher L., Charles Adam II. BS, Centenary Coll., 1956. CLU. Vice pres., gen. mgr. Harbuck Sporting Goods, Inc., Shreveport, 1958-63; agt. Prudential Ins. Co. of Am., Shreveport, 1963—. Chmn. bd. trustees First Bapt. Ch. Sch., Shreveport, 1978, 98-99; mem. La. State Civil Svc. Commn., 1981-93; chmn. Centenary Coll. Gt. Tchrs. Scholar Campaign, Shreveport, 1992-93; campaign chmn. United Way N.W. La., Shreveport, 1989, pres., 1993; trustee Centenary Coll. La., 1990, vice chmn. bd. trustees, 1999; v.p. La. Civil Svc. League, 1994—. Recipient Monte M. Lemann Pub. Svc. award La. Civil Svc. League, New Orleans, 1985, Clyde E. Fant Meml. award for Cmty. Svc., 1994; named Shreveport Outstanding Young Man, Jaycees, 1962, Outstanding Young Men in Am., U.S. Jaycees, Washington, 1970. Mem. Chartered Life Underwriters (pres. Shreveport chpt. 1976), Tax Inst. Arklatex, Estate Planning Coun., Shreveport Assn. Life Underwriters, Million Dollar Roundtable (life), Shreveport Club, Pierremont Oaks Tennis Club. Baptist. Avocations: tennis, hunting, fishing, scuba diving. Home: 4364 Richmond Ave Shreveport LA 71106-1418 Office: Harbuck & Ridley LLC 400 Travis St Ste 808 Shreveport LA 71101-3111

HARCOURT, MICHAEL FRANKLIN, retired premier of Province of British Columbia, lawyer, educator; b. Edmonton, Alta., Can., Jan. 6, 1943; s. Frank Norman and Stella Louise (Good) H.; m. Mai-Gret Wibecke Salo, June 26, 1971; 1 son, Justen Michael. BA, U. B.C., 1965, LLB, 1968. Bar: B.C. 1969. Founder dir. Vancouver Cmty. Legal Assistance Soc., 1969-71; ptnr. firm Lew, Fraser & Harcourt, 1971-79; pres. Housing and Econ. Devel. Cons. Firm, Vancouver, from 1977; alderman City of Vancouver, 1972-80, mayor, 1980-86; mem. Legis. Assembly, 1986-96; leader New Dem. Party of B.C., 1987-96; premier Province of B.C., 1991-96, ret., 1996; former leader of opposition, leader of govt.; sr. assoc. Sustainable Devel. Inst., Vancouver, B.C., 1996—; asst. dir. Justice Devel. Commn., Vancouver; dir. Housing Corp. B.C.; adj. prof. faculty grad. studies U. B.C., 1996—; bd. dirs. Vancouver Internat. Airport, Vancouver Port Authority. Bd. dirs. Asia-Pacific Found. Mem. Law Soc. B.C., Nat. Rountable Environ. and Economy (chmn. fgn. rels. com.), Jericho Tennis Club. New Democrat. Mem. United Ch. Can. Avocations: tennis, golf, skiing, jogging, basketball. Office: HU B5-2202 Main Mall, Vancouver, BC Canada V6T1Z4

HARCOURT, ROBERT NEFF, educational administrator, journalist, genealogist; b. East Orange, N.J., Oct. 19, 1932; s. Stanton Hinde and Mary Elizabeth (Neff) H. *Son of Stanton Hinde Harcourt, U.S. Naval Academy 1925, Harcourt shares a great grandfather with publisher Alfred Harcourt, one of founders of Harcourt, Brace & Co. thru direct lineal descent from John Howland and John Tilley, both signers of the November 11, 1620 "Mayflower Compact". He shares ancestors with American Presidents Franklin Roosevelt, Gerald Ford, Richard Nixon, and George Bush. He is descended from John Hobby, one of the founders of Greenwich, CT., who served for several terms in Connecticut's general assembly. On mother's side (Neff family), he is descended from Swiss hero Adam N f who, in 1531, saved the Banner of Zurich at the Battle at Kappel Am Albis. The N f sword is today on display at Zurich's Swiss National Museum. Harcourt is the grandson of John Peter Neff, former Vice-President of American Arch & Co. of NYC, whose patented locomotive was displayed at the 1939 New York World's Fair. His mother, Mary E. Neff Harcourt served for forty-five years as a Westfield, N.J. Red Cross volunteer.* BA, Gettysburg Coll., 1958; MA, Columbia U., 1961. Cert guidance, secondary edn., career and vocational guidance, N.Mex. Social case worker N.J. State Bd. Child Welfare, Newark and Morristown, 1958-61; asst. registrar Hofstra U., 1961-62; asst. to evening dean of students CCNY, 1961-62; housing staff U. Denver, 1962-64; fin. aid and placement dir. Inst. Am. Indian Arts (IAIA), Santa Fe, 1965-95, contract cons., 1999; appointed by corp. pres. to adv. bd. Genre Ltd. Art Pubs., L.A., 1986—; nat. color ad participant The Bradford Exchange, Chgo., 1986—; Truman scholar coordinator. *In 1955-56, Mr. Harcourt was the personnel and public relations specialist with the U.S. Army's first Atomic Cannon Unit in Neckarsulm, Germany. He presented his research paper, "Cyclic Regeneration" to the International Conference on General Semantics in Denver, Colorado, in August, 1968, S.I. Hayakawa Honorary Chairman. Using photographic works, he participated in the spring 1973 Institute of American Indian Arts Faculty Exhibit at the Kennedy Center, Washington D.C. Mr. Harcourt took selected graduate courses at the University of Denver (Post Master's Fellowship), Northern Arizona University, San Francisco State University, University of Hawaii, Rutgers University and Worcester College of Oxford University in England.* Donor Am. Indian Lib. collection Gettysburg (Pa.) Coll., active Santa Fe Civic Chorus, 1977-78, art judge, 3d and 4th ann. Aspen Fundraiser Nat. Mus. Am. Indian, 1993, 94, vol. Inst. for Preservation Original Langs. Am. (IPOLA). With U.S.Army, 1954-56. Ger. Named Hon. Okie, Gov. Dewey F. Bartlett (decorated Nat. Def. medal), 1970, postmasters fellow U. Denver, 1962-64, col. a.d.c. to N.Mex. Gov. David F. Cargo, 1970, IAIA Truman scholar; recipient disting. Alumni award Gettysburg Coll. Alumni Assn., 1995. Mem. Am. Contract Bridge League (exec. bd., v.p., Santa Fe unit, life master, ACBL dist. 17 rep.), SAR, Santa Fe Coun. Internat. Rels., Am. Assn. Counseling and Devel., New England Historic Genealogical Soc., Assn. Specialists in Group Work (charter), Adult Student Personnel Assn. (charter), Southwestern Assn. Indian Affairs, Neff Family Hist. Soc., St. Andrew Scottish Soc. of N.Mex., Gen. Soc. Mayflower Descendents, Pilgrim John Howland Soc., Upson Family Assn., Order of the Founders and Patriots of Am., Mil. Order of the Loyal Legion of the U.S., Military Order of Fgn. Wars of U.S., Phi Delta Kappa (past mem. exec. bd. local chpt.), Alpha Tau Omega, Alpha Phi Omega, Safari Club Internat. Home: 2980 Viaje Pavo Real Santa Fe NM 87505-5344

HARCROW, E. EARL, lawyer; b. Carrizozo, N.Mex., Mar. 4, 1954; s. James Earl and Nettie (McInnes) H.; m. Julie A., Apr. 16, 1987; children: Ashley Nicole, James Earl. BS, Tex. Tech. U., 1976, JD, 1979. Bar: Tex. 1979, U.S. Dist. Ct. (no. dist.) Tex., U.S. Ct. Appeals (5th cir.) 1979. Asst. dist. atty. Lubbock (Tex.) Dist. Atty. Office, 1979-80, Tarrant Dist. Atty. Office, Ft. Worth, 1980-83; ptnr. Shannon, Gracey, Ratliff & Miller, Ft. Worth, 1983-99; mng. ptnr. Shannon, Gracey, Ratliff & Miller, 1995-96, ptnr. in charge of tech., 1996-99; ptnr. Haynes & Boone, Ft. Worth, 1999—; gen. counsel Dallas Ft. Worth Med. Ctr., 1990—; pres. Tex. Healthcare Resources, 1993—. Dir. Planned Parenthood N. Tex., 1987-92; fellow Tex. Bar Found., 1991—; pres. JAMM Group Inc., 1996—.

HARD, BRIAN, truck leasing company executive. CEO Penske Truck Leasing Co., Reading, Pa. Office: Penske Truck Leasing Co RR 10 Reading PA 19603-9810*

HARDAWAY, ANFERNEE DEON (PENNY HARDAWAY), professional basketball player; b. Memphis, July 18, 1972. Grad., Memphis State U. Guard, forward Orlando Magic, 1993—. Appeared in film Blue Chips, 1994. Named to Newcomer of Yr. in the BMC, 1992-93, NBA All-Rookie First Team, 1993, Eastern Conf. All-Star Team, 1994-95, 95-96, All NBA First Team, 1995, Dream Team III, 1996; Nat. H.S. Player of Yr. award Paracle Mag., 1990-91; 1st team All Am. Memphis State U., 1992-93; honored by retiring of Jersey at Memphis State U., 1994. Mem. Eastern Conf. Champions Orlando Magic, 1994-95. Office: Orlando Magic 2 Magic Pl 8701 Maitland Summit Blvd Orlando FL 32810*

HARDAWAY, ERNEST, II, oral and maxillofacial surgeon, public health official. BS, Howard U., 1957, DDS, 1966, cert. in oral and maxillofacial surgery, 1972; MPH, Johns Hopkins U., 1973. Intern, then chief resident oral and maxillofacial surgery Howard U. Med. Ctr., Washington, 1969-72; asst. prof., mem. attending staff Howard U. Coll. Medicine and Med. Ctr., Washington, 1974—; with Bur. Quality Assurance, HHS, Washington, 1974-77; various adminstrv. positions Bur. Med. Services and Health Services Adminstrn., USPHS, 1977-80; dep. commr., then commr. pub. health City of Washington, 1982-84; acting v.p. fin. and adminstrv. affairs Mile Sq. Health Ctr., Inc., 1984; asst. to regional health adminstr. Fed. Employee Occupational Health Program, 1985; exec. v.p. Fed. Employee Occupational Health Program, Chgo., 1986—; mem. profl. staff Com. on Ways and Means, U.S. Ho. of Reps., 1972; spl. asst. to dir. Office Policy Planning and Evaluation, HEW, 1973; presenter at numerous profl. meetings. Contbr. articles to dental jours. Mem. D.C. Emergency Med. Care Adv. Com., D.C. Long-Term Planning Group, 1983, D.C. Health Coordinating Council, D.C. Commn. on Homelessness, 1984; mem. adv. bd. Rosemont Health Ctr., 1984; sec. D.C. Commn. on Licensure to Practice Healing Art, 1983; bd. dirs. United Black Fund, 1984, Potomac Valley Myastenia Gravis Found., 1984. Global Community Health fellow HEW, 1971, Louise C. Ball fellow, 1969; recipient Meritorious Service award USPHS, 1982, J.B. Johnson Nursing Ctr. award, 1983, Outstanding Service placque D.C. Village Choir, 1984, Disting. Service cert. Concerned Citizens for Alcohol Abuse, 1984, Whitman-Walker award for AIDS effort, 1984, Exceptional Accomplishment award Regional Health Adminstr., 1987. Fellow Am. Assn. Oral and Maxillofacial Surgeons (ho. of dels. 1977-80), Internat. Coll. Dentistry, Royal Soc. Health, Acad. Dentistry Internat., Am. Coll. Dentistry; mem. ADA (cons. council hosp. dental care 1976-77), D.C. Soc. Oral and Maxillofacial Surgeons (sec.-treas. 1979-81), Nat. Dental Assn. (Dentist of Yr. 1983, 1st ann. Disting. Service award 1984), Omicron Kappa Upsilon, Chi Delta Mu, Sigma Pi Phi. Home: 88 W Schiller St Apt 1204 Chicago IL 60610-2037

HARDAWAY, ROBERT MORRIS, III, physician, educator, retired army officer; b. Camp John Hay, Philippines, Jan. 9, 1916; s. Robert Morris and Olive (Gray) H.; m. Lee H. Harkey, June 12, 1939; children—Robert Morris IV, Elizabeth J., Thomas G. II, Christopher L. A.B., U. Denver, 1936; postgrad., U. Colo. Med. Sch., 1935-37; M.D., Washington U., St. Louis, 1939. Diplomate Am. Bd. Surgery. Commd. 1st lt., M.C. U.S. Army, 1939, advanced through grades to brig. gen., 1970; ward officer, surg. service Fitzsimons Gen. Hosp., Denver, 1940-41, N. Sector Gen. Hosp., Hawaii, 1941-43; tchr. Med. Field Service Sch., Carlysle Barracks, Pa., 1943-45; surg. trainee Nichols Gen. Hosp., Louisville, 1945-46; resident surgery Madigan Gen. Hosp., Tacoma, 1946-47, Fitzsimons Gen. Hosp., 1949-50; chief surg. service 34th Gen. Hosp., Korea, 1947-49, Sta. Hosp., Ft. Belvoir, Va., 1950-54, 97th Gen. Hosp., Frankfurt, Germany, 1954-58, Martin Army Hosp., Ft. Benning, Ga., 1958-60; dir. div. surgery Walter Reed Army Inst. Research, Washington, 1960-67; comdg. officer 97th Gen. Hosp., Frankfurt, Germany, 1967-70; comdg. gen. William Beaumont Army Med. Ctr., El Paso, 1970-75; prof. surgery Tex. Tech U. Sch. Medicine, El Paso, 1976—; staff R.E. Thomason Gen. Hosp., El Paso, 1975—. Author: Syndromes of Disseminated Intravascular Coagulation, 1966, Clinical Management of Shock, Surgical and Medical, 1968, Capillary Perfusion in Health and Disease, 1981, Shock—the Reversible Stage of Dying, 1988, Treatment of Wounded in Vietnam, 1988, Blood Problems in Critical Care, 1989; contbr. articles on intravascular coagulation and hemorrhagic shock to jours. and books. Decorated Army Commendation medal with oak leaf cluster, Legion of Merit with oak leaf cluster, D.S.M.; recipient 2d prize for exhibit A.M.A., 1964; Silver award exhibit Am. Soc. Clin. Pathologists-Coll. Am. Pathologists, 1964; certificate of outstanding achievement U.S. Army Sci. Conf., 1964. Fellow ACS, Am. Coll. Angiology, Am. Assn. for Surgery Trauma, Microcirculation Assn.; mem. Assn. Mil. Surgeons U.S., AMA, Alpha Omega Alpha. Episcopalian. Office: Tex Tech U Sch Medicine 4800 Alberta Ave El Paso TX 79905-2709 *Nothing we know, (or think we know) is the ultimate truth.*

HARDAWAY, ROGER DALE, historian, educator; b. Manchester, Tenn., Aug. 1, 1949; s. Hubert and Kitty Ruth (Shelton) H. BS, Mid. Tenn. State U., 1971; BS in Edn., U. Memphis, 1976, JD, 1977; MA, N.Mex. State U., 1979, Ea. N.Mex. U., 1985; MA in Tchg., U. Wyo., 1985; ArtsD, U. N.D., 1994. Asst. to pres. Ea. N.Mex. U., Portales, 1980-82, instr. history, polit. sci., 1982-83; sole practice law Portales, 1983-85; instr. history & polit. sci. Ea. N.Mex. U., Clovis, 1985-90; from asst. to assoc. prof. Northwestern Okla. State U., Alva, 1990—, chair history dept., 1998—. Author: A Narrative Bibliography of the African American Frontier, 1995; co-editor: African Americans on the Western Frontier, 1998. Mem. N.Mex. Commn. on Indian Affairs, 1981-85. Served in U.S. Army, 1971. Mem. Nat. Assn. African Am. Studies, Assn. Study of Afro-Am. Life and History, Assn. Caribbean Studies, Wyo. State Hist. Soc., Okla. Hist. Soc., Western History Assn. Democrat. Methodist. Avocations: watching TV, reading, movies, spectator sports. Home: 1800 Oklahoma Blvd Apt 200 Alva OK 73717-1747

HARDAWAY, TIMOTHY DUANE, basketball player; b. Chgo., Sept. 1, 1966. Grad., U. Tex. at El Paso, 1989. With Golden State Warriors, 1989-95, Miami Heat, 1995—. Named to NBA All-Rookie team, 1990, All-Star team, 1991, 92, 93. Office: Miami Heat SunTrust Int'l Ctr One SE 3rd Ave Ste 2300 Miami FL 33131*

HARDBERGER, PHILLIP DUANE, judge, lawyer, journalist; b. Morton, Tex., July 27, 1934; s. Homer Reeves and Bess (Scott) H.; m. Linda Morgan, May 1968; children: Amy, Kimberlea Jones. B.A., Baylor U., 1955; M.S., Columbia U., 1960; LL.B., Georgetown U., 1965. Reporter Waco (Tex.) News Tribune, 1952-54; press rep. Tex. Baptist Conv., 1958-59; assoc. editor Mil. Pub. Inst., N.Y.C., 1961; exec. sec. Peace Corps, 1962-66; spl. asst. to dir. OEO, 1967-68; trial lawyer, 1968-94; chief justice Fourth Ct. of Appeals, State of Tex., San Antonio, 1994—. Author: Texas Courtroom Evidence, Texas Workers' Compensation Trial Manual; contbr. articles to profl. jours. Served to capt. USAF, 1955-58. Home: 319 W Hollywood Ave San Antonio TX 78212-2211 Office: Fourth Ct of Appeals 300 Dolorosa Ste 3200 San Antonio TX 78205

HARDEE, LEWIS JEFFERSON, JR., educator; b. Wilmington, N.C., Jan. 17, 1937; s. Lewis Jefferson and Dorothy (Dosher) H. BA, U. N.C., 1959, MA, 1971. Instr. Am. Acad. Dramatic Arts, N.Y.C., 1970-84; asst. prof. Wagner Coll., S.I., N.Y., 1984-89, assoc. prof., 1989-95, prof., 1995—; head dept., producer Wagner Coll. Theatre, S.I., N.Y., 1994—; music dir., composer in residence Penny Bridge Players, Bklyn., 1981-84, music dir. Wagner

Coll. Theatre, S.I., 1984-94. Author: A Brief History of the Lambs, 1997; composer Revolution!; composer, author, lyricist The Prince and the Pauper, 1978, revised, 1992, Treasure Island, 1979, Christopher Columbus, 1981, 92, Christopher Columbus His Story, 1991, Hansel and Gretel, 1981, Nothing to Hide, 1983, Robin Hood, Build Me A Bridge, 1983, Goldilocks, 1983, Sweet Land of Liberty, 1986, The Little Prince, 1987, Three Southern Families, A History, 1994; editor, The Lambi Script, 1997; co-author: Nothing to Hide, 1983; editor: The Lambs, 1997. Bd. dirs. The Lambs, N.Y.C., 1987—, historian, 1996—, corr. sec., 1998—; bd. dirs. Inter-Cities Performing Arts, Inc., Union City, N.J., 1988-89, Brunswick Performing Arts Ctr., Inc., Southport, N.C., 1989-94. With U.S. Army, 1960-62. Grantee Meet the Composer, Inc., 1982, N.C. Coun. for Arts, 1976; recipient Award of Merit Eleanor Gay Lee Gallery Found., 1983; Parade Grand Marshall, N.C. Fourth of July Festival, 1998. Mem. ASCAP, Dramatists Guild, Assoc. Artists Southport (hon. life), Omicron Delta Kappa. Avocation: history. Home: 320 E 57th St New York NY 10022-2948 Office: Wagner Coll Grymes Hill Staten Island NY 10301

HARDEE, LUELLEN CARROLL HOOKS, school psychologist; b. Dublin, N.C., May 19, 1948; d. Charlie Lee Thomas and Mary Lou (Lewis) Carroll; m. Richard Eugene Hooks Jr., Dec. 20, 1969 (div. Jan. 1986); m. Jasper Ronald Hardee, Apr. 29, 1995. BS in Speech Pathology and Audiology, East Carolina U., 1969; MEd in Counseling, U. N.C., Charlotte, 1978; PhD in Sch. Psychology, N.C. State U., 1989. Speech pathologist, audiologist Robeson County Schs., Lumberton, N.C., 1970-71, Rowan County Schs., Salisbury, N.C., 1971, Stanly County Schs., Albemarle, N.C., 1971-78; counselor exceptional children, psychologist Montgomery County Schs., Troy, N.C., 1978-81; psychol. asst. Lions Clinic for the Blind N.C. State U., Raleigh, 1981; coord. psychol. svcs. Brunswick County Schs., Southport, N.C., 1981-83; psychology instr. Carteret Community Coll., Morehead City, N.C., 1984; part-time sch. psychologist Carteret County Schs., Beaufort, N.C., 1985-87, sch. psychologist, 1989—; speech pathologist Stanly County Headstart, Albemarle, summers 1971-73, dir., 1973-76, coord. handicapped children programs, summer 1977. Solicitor Cancer Fund Drive, Albemarle, 1977-78; mem. com. N.C. Azalea Festival, Wilmington, 1981—; hostess Hospice-Festival of Trees, Beaufort, 1989; bd. dirs. Carteret County Domestic Violence Program, 1992-96, chair fashion show, 1993-95, chair edn. com., 1994-96; mem. Carteret Residents for Excellence in Edn., 1990-95, Carteret County Child Rev. and Child Protection Teams, 1990-97, chair, 1992-93, Carteret County Literacy Council, 1996—, Carteret County Human Rights Advisory Committee, 1998—. Mem. NCSPA (treas. 1990-92). Avocations: interior design, water sports, travel. Home: 104 Rattan Ln Morehead City NC 28557-9677 Office: Carteret County Bd Edn PO Box 600 Beaufort NC 28516-0600

HARDEGREE, GLORIA JEAN FORE, health services administrator; b. Atlanta, July 18, 1940; d. Lee Harrison and Corine Joan (Atkinson) Fore; m. Guy H. Hardegree Jr., Jan. 23, 1960; children: Pamela Jean Reas, Sherrie Etta Drew. Diploma in nursing, Crawford W. Long Hosp., 1971; BS, Coll. St. Francis, 1982; M in Counseling, Liberty U. RN, Ga.; cert. occupational health nurse; cert. case mgr. Occupational health nurse Dobbs House Inc., Dallas, 1974-75, AT&T, Atlanta, 1974; occupational health nurse Ga. Power Co., Atlanta, 1976—, coord. Wellness Program. Recipient Schering award, 1987, Nurse of Yr. award, Med. Products S.E., 1991, Mayor's work award, 1995. Mem. Ga. Assn. Occupational Health Nurses (recording sec., Nurse Yr. award, 1987), Atlanta Assn. Occupational Health Nurses. Office: Southern Co Bin 10013 241 Ralph McGill Blvd NE Atlanta GA 30308-3328

HARDEN, BLAINE CHARLES, journalist; b. Moses Lake, Wash., Apr. 4, 1952; s. Arno E. and Betty (Thoe) H. BA in Polit. Sci. and Philosophy, Gonzaga U., 1974; MA in Journalism, Syracuse U., 1976. Reporter Trenton (N.J.) Times, 1976-78; reporter The Washington Post, 1979-83, Africa corr., 1985-89, Ea. Europe corr., 1989-93, investigative staff, 1994-95, nat. polit. reporter, 1995-96, N.Y. bur. chief, 1997-98; reporter N.Y. Times, N.Y.C., 1999—. Author: Africa: Dispatches from a Fragile Continent, 1990, A River Lost: The Life and Death of the Columbia, 1996. Recipient Livingston award, 1986, non-deadline writing writing award Am. Soc. Newspapers Editors, Washington, 1988, Ernie Pyle award for human interest, 1993; Alicia Patterson rsch. fellow, 1993. Office: NY Times 229 W 43d St New York NY 10036*

HARDEN, CLINTON DEWEY, JR., restaurant owner, state official; b. Belen, N.Mex., Apr. 12, 1947; s. Clinton Dewey and Doretha E. (Miller) H.; m. Kathrine H. Harden, Aug. 5, 1968; children: Danielle, Dionne, Dustin. BS in Bus. Mgmt., U. Utah, 1970; MBA, Ea. N.Mex. U., 1994. Account exec. Continental Ins., Salt Lake City, 1970-78; owner restaurant Twin Cronnie Enterprises, Clovis, N.Mex., 1978—; cabinet sec. Dept. Labor, Albuquerque, 1995—; chmn. Cabinet Coun. on State Pers., Santa Fe, 1995—. Mem. Sch.-to-Work Adv. Bd., Santa Fe, 1995—, Pardon and Parole Com., Santa Fe, 1995—, Human Resource Investment Coun., Santa Fe, 1995—, Gov.'s Com. for the Concerns of the Handicapped, 1998; pres. Clovis chpt. Amateur Athletic Union; mem., coach Clovis Girls Athletic Assn.; mem. Mayor's Coun. on Juvenile Crime, Clovis; mem. Children Youth and Families Interag. Coord. Group, 1995—; bd. dirs. Interstate Conf. of Employment Security Agencies, 1995—; rep. Nat. Gov.'s Assn. Human Resources Coun., 1995—; lead sec. Workforce Devel. Reform, 1996—. Mem. Clovis C. of C. (v.p.). Republican. Methodist. Office: Labor Dept PO Box 1928 Albuquerque NM 87103-1928

HARDEN, DOYLE BENJAMIN, import-export company executive; b. Banks, Ala., Oct. 15, 1935; s. J.C. and Gladis C. (Romine) H.; m. Elvira Harden; children: Janet Denice, Misty Lyn, Dusty Lyn, Wesley Doyle. Student pub. schs. Salesman, Gordon Foods, Atlanta, 1955-64; pres. Kwik Shop Markets, Columbus, Ga., 1964-73, Exportaciones Chico, S.A., Juarez, Mex., 1973-76, Chico Arts, El Paso, Tex., 1976—, Transp. Interoceanica, S.A., Honduras, C.Am., 1975-80. Office: 1045 Humble Pl El Paso TX 79915-1008

HARDEN, GAIL BROOKS, elementary school educator; b. Fulton County, Ga., Feb. 7, 1950; d. Dorsey D. and Gippie C. Brooks; m. Jack H. Harden, July 14, 1978; children: Kevin G. Jackson, Jeremy J., Erin B. BS, Brenau Coll., Gainesville, Ga., 1974; MEd, U. Ga., 1978; EdS, West Ga. Coll., 1991. Cert. reading specialist, Ga. Tchr. Barrow County Schs., Winder, Ga., 1974-78; with Sand Hill Sch., Carrollton, Ga., 1980—, coord. elem. testing, 1988-89; dir. Sand Hill after-sch. program Carroll County Schs., Carrollton, Ga., 1989-90; coord. elem. testing Sand Hill Sch., tech. coord., 1992—. Named Tchr. of Yr., Sand Hill Sch., 1986. Mem. Internat. Reading Assn., Christian Educators Assn. Internat. Office: Sand Hill Sch 45 Sandhill School Rd Carrollton GA 30116-9736

HARDEN, HARVEY, director civil service department, Spokane; b. Blackwell, Okla., July 6, 1940. BBA, Walla Walla Coll., 1963; MBA in Bus. Edn., Ea. Washington U., 1969. Bus. instr. Rainer (Wash.) Sch. Dist., 1966-67; mem. testing staff Spokane Civil Svc. Dept., 1968-70, mem. classification staff, 1970-77, director, 1977—. Mem. Internat. Pers. Mgmt. Assn. Office: City of Spokane Civil Svc Dept 808 W Spokane Falls Blvd Spokane WA 99201-3333

HARDEN, JON BIXBY, publishing executive; b. Fitzgerald, Ga., Mar. 7, 1944; s. William Harmon and Mary Bixby (Brewster) H.; m. Lynne Ann Lumsden, May 3, 1986; children: Gregory Ross, Heather Lynne. AAS, Rochester Inst. Tech., 1965; BS, Univ. Rochester, 1967; MBA, U Pa., 1969. Research analyst Doubleday & Co., Inc., N.Y.C., 1969-72, mgr. corp. research, 1972-74, pub. group mgr., 1974-77; dir. bus. devel. McGraw-Hill Book Co., N.Y.C., 1977-80, dir. planning and devel. Internat. div., 1980-84; v.p. corp. devel. and strategic planning Simon & Schuster, Inc., N.Y.C., 1984-85; pres. Dodd, Mead & Co., Inc., N.Y.C., 1985-88; gen. mgr. Romaine Pierson Pubs., Inc., Port Washington, 1988-89; pres. JBH Communications, Inc., 1989—; editor, pub. The Hartford News, Conn., 1989—; pub. Hartford Tonite!, 1996—. bd. dirs. SCAN Vol. Parents Aids Assn., Inc., 1980-89, v.p., 1985-89; bd. mgrs. West Side YMCA, 1985-89, vice-chmn., 1987-89. Mem. The Hartford Club, The Hartford Golf Club. Home: 16 Oak Ridge Ln West Hartford CT 06107-3505 Office: JBH Comms Inc 191 Franklin Ave Hartford CT 06114-1386

HARDEN, MARVIN, artist, educator; b. Austin, Tex.; s. Theodore R. and Ethel (Sneed) H. BA in Fine Arts, UCLA, 1959, MA in Creative Painting, 1963. Tchr. art Calif. State U., Northridge, 1968-97, prof. emeritus, 1997—; Tchr. art Santa Monica (Calif.) City Coll., 1968; mem. art faculty UCLA Extension, 1964-68; prof. emeritus Calif. State U., 1997; mem: visual arts fellowship, painting panel NEA, 1985. One-man shows include Ceeje Galleries, L.A., 1964, 66, 67, L.A. City Coll., 1968, Occidental Coll., L.A., 1969, Whitney Mus. Am. Art, N.Y.C., 1971, Eugenia Butler Gallery, L.A., 1971, Rath Mus., Geneva, Switzerland, 1971, Irving Blum Gallery, L.A., 1972, Los Angeles Harbor Coll., 1972, David Stuart Galleries, L.A., 1975, Coll. Creative Studies, U. Calif., Santa Barbara, 1976, James Corcoran Gallery, L.A., 1978, Newport Harbor Art Mus., 1979, L.A. Mcpl. Art Gallery, 1982, Conejo Valley Art Mus., 1983, Simard Gallery, L.A., 1985, The Armory Ctr. for the Arts, Pasadena, Calif., 1994, Ventura (Calif.) Coll. Art Gallery, 1997; group shows include U.S. State Dept. Touring Exhbn., USSR, 1966, Oakland (Calif.) Mus. Art, 1966, UCLA, 1966, Mpls. Inst. Art, 1968, San Francisco Mus. Art, 1969, Phila. Civic Ctr. Mus., 1969, Mus. Art, R.I. Sch. Design, 1969, N.S. State Mus., 1969, Everson Mus. Art, Syracuse, 1969, La Jolla (Calif.) Mus., 1969, 70, High Mus. Art, Atlanta, 1969, Flint (Mich.) Inst. Arts, 1969, Ft. Worth Art Center Mus., 1969, Contemporary Arts Assn., Houston, 1970, U. N.Mex., 1974, U. So. Calif., 1975, Bklyn. Mus., 1976, Los Angeles County Mus. Art, 1977, 96, Newport Harbor Art Mus., 1977, Frederick S. Wight Gallery, UCLA, 1978, Cirrus Editions, Ltd., L.A., 1979, Franklin Furnace, N.Y.C., 1980, Art Ctr. Coll. Design, L.A., 1981, Alternative Mus., N.Y.C., 1981, Laguna Beach Mus. (Calif.), 1982, L.A. Inst. Contemporary Art, 1982, Mus. Contemporary Art, Chgo., 1983, Mint Mus., Charlotte, N.C., 1983, DeCordova and Dana Mus. and Park, Lincoln, Mass., 1983, Equitable Gallery, N.Y.C., 1984, L.A. Municipal Art Gallery, 1984, 1985, Cirrus, L.A., 1986, 1990, Heal the Bay, Surfboard Art Invitational, 1990, Pasadena Armory Ctr. for the Arts, 1992, Claremont Coll. West Gallery, L.A., 1992, Grolier Club, N.Y.C., 1993, Calif. State U., San Luis Obispo, 1994, Cheney Cowles Mus., Spokane, Wash., 1995, Louis Stern Fine Art, L.A., 1995, 98, Porter Troup Gallery, San Diego, 1995, Armory Ctr. for the Arts, Pasadena, 1996, 97, Tel Aviv Mus. Art, 1998, Palos Verdes Art Ctr., 1999; represented in permanent collections include Whitney Mus. Am. Art, N.Y.C., Mus. Modern Art, N.Y.C., N.Y. Pub. Libr. Spence Collection, Getty Ctr. for Arts and Humanities, L.A. County Mus. Art, Atlantic Richfield Co. Corp. Art Coll., Grunwald Ctr. Graphic Arts UCLA, City of Los Angeles, Metromedia, Inc., L.A., San Diego Jewish Community Center, Berkeley (Calif.) U. Mus., Home Savs. & Loan Assn., L.A., also pvt. collections. Bd. dirs. Images & Issues, 1980-86; mem. artists adv. bd. L.A. Mcpl. Art Gallery Assn., 1983-86. Recipient UCLA Art Council award, 1963, Disting. Prof. award Calif. State U. Northridge, 1984, Exceptional Merit Service award Calif. State U. Northridge, 1984; Nat. Endowment Arts fellow, 1972; awards in Visual Arts, 1983; Guggenheim fellow, 1983. Mem. L.A. Inst. Contemporary Art (co-founder 1972). Home: PO Box 1793 Cambria CA 93428-1793

HARDEN, OLETA ELIZABETH, English educator, university administrator; b. Jamestown, Ky., Nov. 22, 1935; d. Stanley Virgil and Myrtie Alice (Stearns) McWhorter; m. Dennis Clarence Harden, July 23, 1966. BA, Western Ky. U., 1956; MA in English, U. Ark., 1958, PhD, 1965. Teaching asst. U. Ark., Fayetteville, 1956-57, 58-59, 61-63; instr. S.W. Mo. State Coll., Springfield, 1957-58, Murray (Ky.) U., 1959-61; asst. prof. English Northeastern State Coll., Tahlequah, Okla., 1963-65; asst. prof. Wichita (Kans.) State U., 1965-66; asst. prof. English Wright State U., Dayton, Ohio, 1966-68, assoc. prof., 1968-72, prof., 1972-93, asst. chmn. English dept., 1967-70, asst. dean, 1971-73, assoc. dean, 1973-74, exec. dir. gen. univ. services, 1974-76, pres. of faculty, 1984-85; prof. emerita Wright State U., Dayton, 1993—; pres. Wright State Retirees Assn., 1995-96. Author: Maria Edgeworth's Art of Prose Fiction, 1971, Maria Edgeworth, 1984. Wright State U. rsch. and devel. grantee, 1969, 78, Ford Found. grantee, 1971, Wright State U. sabbatical grantee Oxford U., Eng., 1978-79, 86-87; recipient Presdl. award for Outstanding Svc. Wright State U., 1986, Alumni Teaching Excellence award, 1993. Mem. MLA, Coll. English Assn., AAUP, Women's Caucus for Modern Langs., Am. Conf. for Irish Studies (conf. presenter 1989, 91, 95). Home: 2618 Big Woods Trl Fairborn OH 45324-1704 Office: Wright State U Dept English 7751 Colonel Glenn Hwy Dayton OH 45431-1674

HARDEN, PATRICIA KEEGAN, financial aid officer; b. Rye, N.Y., May 18, 1937; d. Vincent L. and Eleanor Cassidy Keegan; m. David O. Harden, Apr. 15, 1978. BS, Simmons Coll., 1958. Dir. fin. aid Simmons Coll., Boston, 1970-78; asst. mgr. Capt.'s Quars. Inn, Saba, Netherlands Antilles, 1977-81; dir. fin. aid Endicott Coll., Beverly, Mass., 1981-84, Emmanuel Coll., Boston, 1984-96; fin. aid coord. Urban Coll. Boston, 1997—; cons. Mass. Higher Edn. Info. Group, Newton, 1998—. Vol. asst. Beacon Hill Civic Assn., Boston, 1992-94. Mem. Mass. Assn. Student Fin. Aid (pres. 1992-95). Office: Urban Coll Boston 178 Tremont St Boston MA 02111-1006

HARDEN, PATRICK ALAN, journalist; b. Twickenham, Eng., Aug. 13, 1936; s. Ernest William and Annie Ceridwen (Jones) H.; m. Connie Marie Graham, Nov. 2, 1963; children: Marc Graham, Ceri Marie. Cert. in journalism, Ealing (Eng.) Tech. Coll., 1957. With UPI, 1960-78; regional exec. UPI, London, 1968-69; European picture mgr. UPI, London and Brussels, 1969-72; regional exec. UPI, Detroit, 1973-75; gen. mgr. UPI Can. Ltd., Montreal, 1976-78, UP Can., Toronto, 1979-82; dir., sec. UP Can., 1979-82; treas. UPI Can. Ltd.; gen. mgr. Edmonton (Alta.) Sun, 1982-84, pub., 1984-92; v.p. Toronto Sun Pub. Corp., 1989-94; v.p., bur. chief Washington, 1992-94; Washington columnist Toronto Sun Pub. Corp., 1994-97; freelance writer, 1997-98; Washington bur. chief LRP Pubs., Alexandria, Va., 1998—. Mem. senate U. Alta, 1991-92. Recipient Merit award City of Edmonton, 1992.

HARDER, CHERIE S., public information officer. BA in Govt. magna cum laude, Harvard U., 1991; post-grad. diploma in English lit., U. Queensland, St. Lucia, Australia, 1994. Asst. editor Let's Go: Italy 1991 Travel Guide, 1990; legis. asst. Office of Rep. Joe Skeen, 1992-93; dep. policy dir. Empower Am., 1993-94, 95-97; domestic policy dir. Office of Senator Sam Brownback, 1997—; speech writer. Contbr. articles to profl. jours. Office: 303 Hart Senate Office Bldg Washington DC 20510-1604

HARDER, EDWIN L., electrical engineer; b. Buffalo, N.Y., 1905. EE, Cornell Univ., 1926; MS, Univ. Pitts., 1930, PhD, 1946. Sr. cons. Westinghouse Elec. Co., 1970—. Recipient Lamme award Am. Inst. Elec. Engrs., Disting. Svc. award Am. Fedn. Info Processing Socs., Centennial award Am. Inst. Elec. Engrs., George Westinghouse Lifetime Innovation award, 1990. Mem. Nat. Acad. Engrs., Am. Inst. Elec. Engrs., Am. Math. Soc. Home: 1204 Milton St Pittsburgh PA 15218-1233

HARDER, JOHN E., electrical engineer; b. Wilkinsburg, Pa., Dec. 8, 1930; s. Edwin L. and Esther (Kunkle) H.; m. Marilyn Reed, Aug. 9, 1958; children—Anita R., Susan R., Jean R. BS, Carnegie Mellon U., 1952; postgrad., U. Pitts., 1953-58; MBA, Ind. U., 1961, MS, 1971. Registered profl. engr., Ind. Engr., Westinghouse Electric Corp., Pitts. and Bloomington, Ind., 1952-69; adv. engr. Westinghouse Electric Corp., Bloomington, Ind., 1969-89, ABB Power T&D Co., Bloomington, 1990-94; pvt. practice applications cons., 1995—. Contbr. articles to tech. jours. Served as pvt. U.S. Army, 1955-56. Fellow IEEE (various coms. 1973—); mem. ASME (various coms. 1963—), Internat. Conf. Large High Voltage Electric Systems. Republican. Lutheran. E-mail: 73704.337@compuserve.com. Address: 97 N Hartstrait Rd Bloomington IN 47404-9700

HARDER, KELSIE BROWN, retired language professional, educator; b. Pope, Tenn., Aug. 23, 1922; s. Prince William and Belle (MaGee) H.; m. Louise Maron, Oct. 9, 1960; children: Kelsie Terry, Gerald William, Dennis Prince, Frank Maron, Thomas Brown, Ann Leslie, Marcia Louise. B.A. magna cum laude, Vanderbilt U., 1950, M.A., 1951; Ph.D., U. Fla., 1954. Asst. prof. English Youngstown U., 1954-58, assoc. prof., 1958-60, prof., 1960-64; Fulbright lectr. India, 1962-63; prof. English SUNY, Potsdam, 1964-89, chmn. English and drama depts., 1964-78, chmn. faculty, 1985-89, chmn. governance com. SUNY faculty senate, 1988-91, Disting. Teaching prof., 1989-94, Disting. Prof. English Emeritus, 1994—; chair Symposium on Contemporary American Fiction, 1995; Fulbright vis. prof. U. Lodz, Poland, 1971-72; cons. Office Edn., Washington, summers 1966, 67, Random House Dictionary of the English Lang., Dictionary of American Reg. English; mem. Com. on Place Name Survey of U.S., SUNY Awards Com., 1976-81; dir. Place Name Survey of U.S., 1988-91. Guest appearances: Cable News Network, stas. WXYZ, WEWS.; Editor: Names, 1966-68, 81-87 , Illustrated Dictionary of Place Names: Canada and the United States, 1976, 2d edit., 1985, Favorite Baby Names, 1985, Names and Their Varieties: A Collection of Essays in Onomastics, 1986; mem. adv. bd.: American Speech, 1960-61, 80-81, Unusual and Most Popular Baby Names, 1988; co-editor: A Dictionary of Am. Proverbs, 1992; co-author: Claims to Name, 1993; contbr. articles to profl. jours. Served with AUS, 1944-46. Recipient SUNY Best award, 1989. Mem. Publ. MLA, Am. Name Soc. (past exec. sec.-treas., v.p., pres.), MLA, Ohio Folklore Soc. (past pres.), Tenn. Folklore Soc., Miss. Folklore Soc., N.Y. Folklore Soc. (exec. com.), Internat. Ctr. of Onomastics (Belgium), Am. Dialect Soc. (proverbs chmn., mem. usage com.), St. Lawrence County Hist. Assn. (past pres., trustee), Milton Soc. (life), Spenser Soc. (life), Phi Beta Kappa, Sigma Phi Epsilon (dist. gov. 1965-66), Eta Sigma Phi, Sigma Delta Pi, Phi Kappa Phi (chpt. pres. 1993), Phi Kappa Sigma (counselor). Home: 5 Lawrence Ave Potsdam NY 13676-1815 Office: SUNY English Dept Potsdam NY 13676

HARDER, LEWIS BRADLEY, ore bodies development company executive; b. N.Y.C., July 23, 1918; s. Lewis Francis and Gertrude Burbank (Harris) H.; m. Dorothy Dyer Butler, Sept. 7, 1941; children: Deirdre Butler, Diana. B.A., Harvard U., 1941. Analyst Morgan Stanley & Co., N.Y.C., 1941; customers man Harris Upham & Co., 1945-51, partner, 1951-54; pres. South Am. Gold & Platinum, 1954-63, dir., 1952-63; pres., dir. Colamer Co; chmn. bd. dirs., CEO, Internat. Mining Corp.; bd. dirs. Pitts. and W.Va. Ry. Co. Served to lt. USNR, 1942-45. Decorated D.F.C. Roman Catholic. Clubs: Bedford Golf and Tennis. Home: 120 Mt Holly Rd Katonah NY 10536-3540 Office: 220 E 42nd St Ste 505 New York NY 10017-5806

HARDER, ROBERT CLARENCE, state official; b. Horton, Kans., June 4, 1929; s. Clarence L. and Olympia E. (Kubik) H.; m. Dorothy Lou Welty, July 31, 1953; children: Anne, James David. AB, Baker U., Baldwin, Kans., 1951; MTh, So. Meth. U., 1954; ThD in Social Ethics, Boston U., 1958; LHD (hon.), Baker U., 1983, Ottawa U., 1991. Ordained to ministry Meth. Ch., 1959; pastor East Topeka Meth. Ch., 1958-64; mem. Kans. Ho. of Reps., 1961-67; rsch. assoc. Menninger Found., Topeka, 1964-65; instr. Washburn U., Topeka, 1964, 68, 69; dir. Topeka Office of Econ. Opportunity, 1965-67; tech. asst. coordinator Office of Gov. of Kans., 1967-68; dir. community resources devel. League of Kans. Municipalities, 1968-69; dir. Kans. Dept. Social Welfare, Topeka, 1969-73; sec. Kans. Dept. Social Welfare, 1973-87; projects adminstr. Topeka State Hosp., 1987-89; adj. prof. pub. adminstrn. Kans. U., 1987-95, instr. Sch. Social Welfare, 1971-87; cons. Menninger Topeka, 1991-92; sec. Kans. Dept. Health and Environment, 1992-95. Contbr. articles to profl. jours. Recipient Disting. Svc. award East Topeka Civic Assn., 1963, Romana Hood award, 1965, Cert. of Recognition, State of Kans., 1979, 87, Spl. Commendation award Kans. Senate, 1987, Spl. Commendation, Kans. Ho. of Reps., 1987; named Outstanding Pub. Ofcl. of the Yr., 1987. Mem. Am. Soc. Public Adminstrs. (Public Adminstr. of Yr. Kans. chpt. 1980), Am. Public Welfare Assn., Kans. Health Care Commn., Kans. Conf. Social Welfare (Outstanding Person of Yr. 1987). Democrat.

HARDER, ROLF PETER, graphic designer, painter; b. Hamburg, Germany, July 10, 1929; came to Can., 1955; s. Henry and Henriette (Loeffler) H.; m. Maria-Inger Rumberg, May 3, 1958; children—Christopher, Vivian. Student, State Art Sch. (Acad. Fine Arts), Hamburg, 1948-52. Designer Rolf Ruehle Werbung, Hamburg, 1952-55; designer Schneider Cardon Ltd, Montreal, Que, Can, 1955-56; art dir. George Ferguson Assocs., Montreal, 1956-57; visualizer Lintas GmbH, Hamburg, 1957-59; designer, owner Rolf Harder Design, Montreal, 1959-65; co-founder, designer Design Collaborative, Montreal, 1965-77; pres., designer Rolf Harder & Assocs., Montreal, 1977—; mem. internat. adv. bd. Typos Mag., London, 1979—; co-organizer exhibition The Visual Image of the Munich Games, Mus. Fine Arts, Montreal, 1972. Co-publisher: Pitseolak: Pictures Out Of My Life, 1972, Arts of the Eskimo: Prints, 1974; works published and exhibited in U.S., Can., Europe, Japan, Korea, S. Am., USSR; represented in permanent collections at Nat. Archives of Can., Ottawa, Die Neue Sammlung, Munich, Design Austria, Vienna, U. of Reading, Eng., Library of Congress, Musée de la Publicité, Palais du Louvre, Paris, Washington, AGI Archives, Essen, Germany, SUNY, Fredonia, U. Que. Poster Collection, Montreal. Coach Beaconsfield Soccer Assn., Montreal, 1966-69. Recipient over 100 nat. and internat. design awards. Fellow Soc. Graphic Designers of Can.; mem. Royal Canadian Acad. Arts, Alliance Graphique Internationale (pres. Can. group 1975-97), Am. Inst. Graphic Arts, Internat. Ctr. for Typographic Arts. Clubs: Clearpoint Tennis, West-Island Tennis (Montreal). Avocations: tennis, music. Home: 43 Lakeshore Rd, Beaconsfield, PQ Canada H9W 4H6

HARDER, V. PETER, government official; b. Winnipeg, Man., Can., 1952. BA in Polit. Sci. with honors, U. Waterloo; MA, Queen's U. Fgn. svc. officer Dept. External Affairs, Canada, 1977; chief of staff Canada; with Canadian Nat., Montreal; exec. dir. Immigration and Refugee Bd., Canada, 1988-91, assoc. dep. min., 1991-93, dep. solicitor gen., 1993, dep. min., 1993-95; sec. Treas. Bd., Comptroller Gen. Can., 1995—. Office: Sec of Treasury Bd &, Comptroller Gen of Can, Ottawa, ON Canada K1A OR5

HARDER, VIRGIL EUGENE, business administration educator; b. Ness City, Kans., July 19, 1923; s. Walter J. and Fern B. (Pausch) H.; m. Dona Maurine Dobson, Feb. 4, 1951; children—Christine Elaine, Donald Walter. B.S., U. Iowa, 1950, M.A., 1950; Ph.D., U. Ill., 1958. Instr. bus. adminstrn. U. Ill., Urbana, 1950-55; asst. prof. U. Wash., Seattle, 1955-59, assoc. prof., 1959-67, prof., 1967-86, prof. emeritus, 1986—, asso. dean sch. bus. adminstrn., 1966-74; dir. Inst. Fin. Edn. Sch. for Exec. Devel., Seattle, 1974-83. Served with AUS, 1943-45. Fellow Am. Bus. Communications Assn. (pres. 1965). Club: Trail Blazers. Office: U Wash Sch Bus Adminstrn Seattle WA 98195

HARDER, WENDY WETZEL, communications executive; b. Oceanside, Calif., Feb. 14, 1951; d. Burt Louis and Marjorie Jean (Evans) W.; m. Peter N. Harder, Dec. 1, 1984; 1 child, Jonathan Russell. AA, Palomar Coll., 1971; BA in Communications, U. So. Calif., 1973; MBA, Pepperdine U., 1988. Pub. rels. dir. Orange County Community Devel. Coun., Santa Ana, Calif., 1975-76; assoc. producer Sta. KOCE-TV, Huntington Beach, Calif., 1976-77, reporter, 1977-79, anchor, assoc. producer, 1979-82; sr. adminstr. communications Mission Viejo (Calif.) Co., 1983-84, mgr. corp. affairs, 1984-85, dir. corp. affairs, 1985-91, v.p. corp. affairs, 1991-93, v.p. mktg. and corp. comm., 1993-97; dir. cmty. rels. Soka Univ. Am., 1998—. 1st v.p. Aliso Viejo (Calif.) Cmty. Found., 1988-93, pres., 1993-97, Saddleback Coll. Found., Mission Viejo, 1989-94; co-chmn. The Ctr. on Tour-Schs. Com., Orange County, Calif., 1989-92; v.p. Found. for Vocat. Visions, 1996—, Found. for Vocat. Visions, 1996—; bd. dirs. Dunaj Internat. Dance Ensemble, Orange County, 1985—. Recipient Golden Mike award Radio & TV News Assn., 1981; co-recipient Best Spl. Event award, Pub. Rels. Soc. Am., 1986, Golden Mike award Radio & TV News Assn., 1979. Mem. Pub. Rels. Soc. Am., Orange County Press Club (Best Feature Release award 1983). Republican. Lutheran. Avocations: folk dancing, reading. Office: Soka Univ Am 85 Argonaut Aliso Viejo CA 92656-4132

HARDESTY, DAVID CARTER, JR., university president; b. Philadelphia, Miss., Sept. 20, 1945; m. Susan B. Hardesty, 1968; children: Ashley, D(avid) Carter III. AB, W.Va. U., 1967; MA, Oxford (Eng.) U., 1969; JD, Harvard U., 1973. Bar: W.Va. 1973. Tax commr., sec. Econ. Devel. Authority, State of W.Va., Charleston, 1977-80, chmn. Mcpl. Bond Comm., 1977-80; assoc. Bowles Rice McDavid Graff & Love, Charleston, 1973-77, ptnr., 1981-95; pres. W.Va. U., Morgantown, 1995—; chmn. W.Va. Tax Study Commn., 1982-84; mem. W.Va. Asian Trade Missions, 1978-79, 95; chmn. W.Va. Roundtable, Inc., 1994—; frequent speaker at CLE and bus. group meetings. Chancellor United Meth. Ch., W.Va., 1986-95; trustee Univ. Sys., 1989-95, 1st chmn., 1989-91; trustee W.Va. Wesleyan Coll., 1986-94; mem. W.Va. Rhodes Scholar Selection Com., 1980—, sec., 1991—; bd. advisors W.Va. U., 1980-89, chmn. bd. advisors, 1987-89; bd. dirs. United Meth. Charities W.Va., 1978-94; bd. dirs. Greater Kanawha Valley Found., 1980-89, chmn., 1988-90. Rhodes scholar, 1969. Mem. ABA, W.Va. Bar Assn., 4th Cir. Jud. Conf. Office: WVa U Office of Pres PO Box 6001 Morgantown WV 26506-6001

HARDESTY, HIRAM HAINES, ophthalmologist, educator; b. Paulding, Ohio, Jan. 16, 1914; s. Eugene and Ida (Underwood) H.; m. Mary Lee Bill, June 12, 1940; children—Susan Hardesty Corcoran, Thomas Haines, John Lee. A.B., Miami U., Oxford, Ohio, 1936; M.D., Western Res. U., 1940; postgrad., U. Pa., 1945-46. Diplomate: Am. Bd. Ophthalmology. Resident ophthalmology Univ. Hosps., Cleve., 1946-48, mem. tchg. staff, 1948—, assoc. clin. prof., 1960-96, ret., 1996, emeritus staff, 1996—. Contbr. articles to profl. jours. Active local United Appeal.; Bd. dirs. Cleve. Soc. for Blind; bd. dirs., past pres. Allen Meml. Library. Served with USAAF, 1941-45. Fellow Am. Acad. Ophthalmology and Otolaryngology; mem. Cleve. Ophthalmology Club (past pres.), Am. Assn. Pediatric Ophthalmology (bd. dirs.), Ohio Soc. Prevention Blindness (bd. dirs.), Am. Orthoptic Council, Assn. Research Strabismus (bd. dirs.). Home: 7337 Girdle Rd West Farmington OH 44491-9792

HARDESTY, ROBERT LYNCH, surgeon, educator; b. New Brighton, Pa., Sept. 12, 1940; s. Robert and Cora Belva (Cable) H.; m. Catherine Ann Steward, Oct. 3, 1965; children: Lara Ann, Derek John, Kieran Steward. Student, U. Pitts., 1958-59, MD, 1966; BS, Allegheny Coll., 1962. Diplomate Am. Bd. Surgery, Am. Bd. Thoracic Surgery. Resident in surgery U. Pitts., 1966-71, resident in cardiothoracic surgery, 1971-72, asst. prof. surgery, 1974-80, assoc. prof., 1980-86, prof., 1986—. Author: Extracorporeal Membrane Oxygenation (ECMO) for Neonatal Pulmonary Insufficiency, 1974, Cardiac Transplantation, 1981, Cardiac and Pulmonary Transplantation, 1982. Maj. USAF, 1972-74. Recipient Man of Yr. award Pitts. Acad. Medicine, 1986, Man of Yr. award in sci. vectors Alpha Omega Alpha, 1987. Fellow Am. Soc. for Artificial Internal Organs; mem. Am. Surg. Assn., Am. Assn. Thoracic Surgery, Soc. Univ. Surgeons, Transplantation Soc., Phi Eta Sigma. Republican. Roman Catholic. Avocation: woodworking. Home: 1050 Fox Chapel Rd Pittsburgh PA 15238-2014 Office: U Pitts Med Ctr Dept Surgery C-700 Presbyn U Hosp Pittsburgh PA 15213

HARDESTY, STEPHEN DON, secondary education educator; b. Oak Park, Ill., Feb. 23, 1945; s. Donald A. and Corinne M. (Wilson) H.; m. Linda C. Shafer, Aug. 2, 1968; 1 child, Heather Anne. BA in Geology, U. South Fla., 1967; postgrad., U. Mo., 1968; MS in Bus., Rollins Coll., 1977. Cert. tchr., Fla. Tchr. earth sci. and math. Maitland (Fla.) Jr. H.S., 1968-69; tchr. earth, life and physical scis., geography Conway Jr. H.S., Orlando, 1969-87, chmn. sci. dept., 1981-87; adj. instr. earth sci., astronomy, meteorology Valencia C.C., 1977—; tchr. earth and environ. sci., astronomy, dual enrollment geology Dr. Phillips Sr. H.S., Orlando, 1987—; tchr. for tchr. inservice insts. in earth scis. Orange County Schs./Valencia C.C., 1982-88; instr. summer inst. in oceanography/hist. geology Valencia C.C.; mem. earth/space scis. middle/jr. sect. State Ednl. Frameworks Com., 1985; chmn. earth/space scis. State Ednl. Materials Coun., 1986-88; mem. earth/space scis. sr. high and middle/jr. sects. State Course Performance Standards Com., 1986-87; mem. earth/space sci. sect. State Tchr. Cert. Writing Team, U. South Fla., 1987-89, State Tchr. Cert. Specialization Validation Team, 1987-88, mem. State Minimum Performance Statdards in Sci. Writing and Review Coms., 1987-88; mem. State Tchr. Cert.-Passing Score Com. Earth Sci., U. Ctrl. Fla., 1989; mem. student performace test writing team Fla. State U., 1989-90; owner, tartan weaving instr. Caithness Shuttle Crafts. Past pres. Greenview Homeowners Assn., Orlando. Mem. Nat. Assn. Geology Tchrs. (Fla. Earth Sci. Tchr. of Yr. 1992), Nat. Earth Sci. Tchrs. Assn., Soc. Econ. Paleontologists and Mineralogists, Fla. Assn. Sci. Tchrs., Fla. Earth Scis. Tchrs. Assn., St. Andrews Soc. Ctrl. Fla. (past pres.), Scottish-Am. Soc. Ctrl. Fla. (past chmn. bd.), Clan Gunn Soc. North Am. (past pres.). Republican. Office: Dr Phillips HS 6500 Turkey Lake Rd Orlando FL 32819-4743*

HARDGROVE, JAMES ALAN, lawyer; b. Chgo., Feb. 20, 1945; s. Albert John and Ruth (Noonen) H.; m. Kathleen M. Peterson, June 15, 1968; children: Jennifer Anne, Amy Kristine, Michael Sheridan. BA, U. Notre Dame, 1967; cert. English law, U. Coll. Law, 1969; JD, U. Notre Dame, 1970. Bar: Ill. 1970, U.S. Ct. Appeals (7th cir.) 1970, U.S. Dist. Ct. (no. dist.) Ill. 1970, U.S. Dist. Ct. (cen. dist.) Ill. 1978, U.S. Supreme Ct. 1980. Law clk. to presiding justice U.S. Ct. Appeals (7th cir.), Chgo., 1970-71; assoc. Sidley & Austin, Chgo., 1971-76, ptnr., 1977—. Mem. ABA, Ill. Bar Assn., Chgo. Bar Assn., Legal Club. Home: 948 Ridge Ave Evanston IL 60202-1720 Office: Sidley & Austin 1 First Natl Plz Chicago IL 60603-2003

HARDIE, ANTHONY D., legislative staff member, social welfare administrator; b. Chippewa Falls, Wis., Feb. 15, 1968; s. David L. and Lois R. (West) H. Student, Def. Language Inst., 1988; BS with honors, U. Wis., 1998. Mem. vets. adv. com. U.S. Senator Russell Feingold, 1998—, U.S. Senator Herb Kohl, 1998—; constituent liaison and spl. projects coord. U.S. Rep. Tammy Baldwin, 1999—. Program dir. VIP of Dane County, Inc., Madison, Wis., 1997-99, youth mentor, 1995—. With U.S. Army, 1986-93. Decorated Bronze Star; Wingspread fellow U. Wis., 1995. Life mem. DAV (officer of the day 1997-98); mem. Nat. Gulf War Resource Ctr. (nat. sec. 1997—, bd. dirs. 1997—), Gulf War Vets. Wis. (pres. 1996—), Nat. Coalition Student Vets. (vice-chair 1997-98), U.S. Student Assn. (bd. dirs. 1997-98), Vets. Foreign Wars, Am. Legion, U. Wis.-Madison Pre-Law Soc. (sr. exec. v.p. 1995-98), Pi Sigma Alpha, Phi Eta Sigma, Golden Key Nat. Honorary Soc. Office: 33 University Sq Ste 252 Madison WI 53715-1042

HARDIE, JAMES CARL, college administrator; b. Pitts., June 10, 1922; s. Stanley Frank and Helen Katherine (Wassel) H.; m. Emma Kathryn Cepko, Jan. 28, 1956; children: James Matthew, Lynn Anne. BA, U. Pitts., 1943, ML, 1948. Counselor U. Pitts., 1946; dir. housing, head men's dormitories Carnegie Inst. Tech., Pitts., 1946-47; dir. athletic publicity U. Pitts., 1947-48; dir. campaign Ketchum, Inc., Pitts., 1948-57; dir. devel., v.p. Case Inst. Tech., Cleve., 1957-67; v.p. Case We. Res. U., Cleve., 1967-69; cons. to more than 60 non-profit instns. Cleve., 1969—. Chmn. bd. dirs. Jennings Found. Yardstick Project, 1968-81; founder Corp. 1% Program for Higher Edn., 1961-69; trustee George S. Dively Found., 1985-97. Lt. U.S. Army, 1943-45. Recipient Disting. Svc. award Ohio Coun. Fund-Raising Execs., 1988, Citation Coun. Fin. Aid to Edn., 1979; named Outstanding Profl. Nat. Soc. Fund-Raising Profls., 1991. Mem. Union Club Cleve., Grand Harbor Country Club, Grenelefe Country Club, Omicron Delta Kappa, Delta Sigma Rho. Republican. Avocations: golf, reading, gardening, piano, writing. Home and Office: 245 Springdale Ln Moreland Hills OH 44022 also: 1508 Ocean Dr Apt 103 Vero Beach FL 32963-5346

HARDIE, JAMES HILLER, lawyer; b. Pitts., Dec. 1, 1929; s. James H. and Elizabeth Gillespie (Alcorn) H.; m. Frances P. Curtis, Dec. 5, 1953; children: J. Hiller, Janet Hardie Harvey, Andrew G., Michael C., Rachel Hardie Share. A.B., Princeton U., 1951; LL.B., Harvard U., 1954. Bar: Pa. 1955. Assoc. Reed Smith Shaw & McClay, Pitts., 1954-62, ptnr., 1962—. Mem. ABA, Am. Law Inst., Pa. Bar Assn. Office: Reed Smith Shaw & McClay PO Box 2009 Pittsburgh PA 15230-2009

HARDIE, ROBERT C., newspaper publishing executive; b. Glendale, Calif., Mar. 15, 1921; s. Robert Victor and Helen Gardener (Clyde) H.; m. Mary Jane Hoiles, July 15, 1945; children: Douglas, Melissa, David, Steven. BA, U. Calif., Berkeley, 1943. Pub. Freedom Newspapers, Marysville, Calif., 1946—; chmn. bd. dirs. Freedom Comms. Inc., Irvine, Calif., 1981—. Lt. (j.g.) USN, 1943-45. Mem. Rotary, Elks. Avocation: tennis. Office: Freedom Comms Inc PO Box 19549 Irvine CA 92623-9549 also: Freedom Newspapers 30 S Prospect St PO Box 1779 Colorado Springs CO 80901-1779*

HARDIMAN, DAVID ALEXANDER, music educator; b. Indpls., June 15, 1939; s. Nathan C. and Sadie F. (Lyles) H.; m. Juanita Harris (div. June 1971); 1 child, David Anthony. B of Music Edn., Ind. U., 1959; MusM, Butler U., 1971. Student tchr. Ondpls. Pub. Schs., 1959, substitute tchr., 1959-61, tchr. elem. sch., 1961-63, tchr. instrumental music, 1963-71; tchr. instrumental music Berkeley (Calif.) Unified Sch. Dist., 1971-74; instr. Contra Costa C.C., Richmond, Calif., 1974-75, Alameda (Calif.) Coll., 1974-76, City Coll. San Francisco, 1974—. Mem. Nat. Assn. Negro Musicians, Am. Fedn. Musicians, Oakland Jazz Bomplex (bd. dirs.), Bay Area Jazz Soc. (pres. 1984-86), Jazz Action Movement, Phi Mu Alpha. Home: 38 Bradford St San Francisco CA 94110 Office: City Coll San Francisco Box A-50 50 Phelan Ave San Francisco CA 94112

HARDIMAN, JOSEPH RAYMOND, securities industry executive; b. Salisbury, Md., May 27, 1937; s. Leonard Roy and Virginia Mildred (Darden) H.; m. Katherine McCampbell, Mar. 23, 1963; children: Katherine Hughes, Elizabeth Gore. BA, U. Md., 1959, LLB, 1962. Bar: Md. 1962. Law clk. to Hon. Hall Hammond Md. Ct. of Appeals, 1962-63; assoc. Miles & Stockbridge, Balt., 1963-68; exec. v.p., sec., dir. Robert Garrett & Sons, Inc., Balt., 1968-75; gen. ptnr. Alex. Brown & Sons, 1975-87, mng. dir., COO, 1984-87; pres., CEO, dir. Nat. Assn. Securities Dealers, Inc., 1987-97, Nasdaq Stock Market, Inc., 1987-97; bd. dirs. Intellectual Devel. Sys., Inc., Flag Investors Funds, ISI Funds, Nevis Fund, Wit Capital Group, Inc. Bd. dirs. Arthritis Found., Md., 1975-79, pres., 1976-78; bd. dirs. Balt. Urban Coalition, 1975-78, U. Md. Med. Sys., 1980-86, Fund for Ednl. Excellence, 1984-91, Ctr. for the Study of the Presidency, 1992-97, U. Md. Found., 1992—; mem. steering com. Baltimore County Charter Rev. Commn., 1977-78; trustee St. Paul's Sch. for Girls, 1978-86, Securities Industry Found. Econ. Edn., 1988-96; mem. adv. bd. U. Calif. Securities Regulation Inst., 1988-97; bd. visitors U. Md. Sch. Law, 1990—; mem. Am. Bus. Conf., Con. on Competitiveness, 1994-97. Mem. Md. Club, Elkridge Club (Balt.), Met. Club (D.C.), Links Club (N.Y.C.), Gulfstream Club (Fla.), Order of Coif, Phi Delta Theta, Omicron Delta Kappa. Home: 8 Bowen Mill Rd Baltimore MD 21212-1053

HARDIMAN, THERESE ANNE, lawyer; b. Chestnut Hill, Pa., Mar. 2, 1956; d. Edward Joseph and Grace Joan (Shaw) Hardiman; m. David J.P. Malecki, Feb. 3, 1990; 1 child, Christine Mary; BA in History, BA in Psychology, Mt. St. Mary's Coll., 1978; JD, Thomas M. Cooley Law Sch., 1983. Bar: Pa. 1983, U.S. Dist. Ct. (ea. dist.) Pa. 1983, U.S. Ct. Appeals (3d cir.) 1984, U.S. Dist. Ct. (mid. dist.) Pa. 1989. Staff rsch. asst. Internat. Brotherhood of Teamsters, Washington, 1978-79; law clk. Richard R. Rashid, Atty. at Law, Lansing, Mich., 1981-82; law clk. Pearlstine, Salkin, Hardiman & Robinson, Landsdale, Pa., 1981; staff asst. Employment Rels. Bd., Mich. Dept. Civil Svc., Lansing, 1982; mem. Pearlstine, Salkin, Hardiman & Robinson, Landsdale, 1983-86; v.p. Edward J. Hardiman & Assocs. P.C., 1986-94; sole practitioner, 1995—. Editor-in-chief Pridwin, 1978, layout editor, 1977. Recipient Golden Key award, Delta Theta Phi, 1981; Outstanding Student award Student Bar Assn., Thomas M. Cooley Law Sch., 1982. Mem. ABA, Assn. Trial Lawyers Am., Pa. Assn. Trial Lawyers, Pa. Bar Assn., Monroe County Bar Assn., Montgomery County Bar Assn., Delta Theta Phi. Republican. Roman Catholic. Office: PO Box 66 Pocono Pines PA 18350-0066

HARDIN, ADLAI STEVENSON, JR., judge; b. Norwalk, Conn., Sept. 20, 1937; s. Adlai S. and Carol (Moore) H. BA, Princeton U., 1959; LLB, Columbia U., 1962. Bar: N.Y. 1963, U.S. Dist. Ct. (so. and ea. dists.) N.Y. 1965, U.S. Supreme Ct. 1967, U.S. Ct. Appeals (2d cir.) 1965, U.S. Ct. Appeals (5th cir.) 1974, U.S. Ct. Appeals (3d cir.) 1977, U.S. Ct. Appeals (9th cir.) 1982, U.S. Ct. Appeals (4th and D.C. cirs.) 1985, U.S. Ct. Appeals (7th cir.) 1988. Assoc. Milbank, Tweed, Hadley & McCloy, N.Y.C., 1963, ptnr., 1971; judge U.S. Bankruptcy Ct., 1995—. Trustee Spence Sch., 1981-87; former elder, trustee Madison Ave. Presbyn. Ch. With USAR, 1962-68. Mem. ABA (past chmn. N.Y. State membership com., antitrust sect., litigation sect.), Fed. Bar Coun. (trustee 1983-92, v.p. 1986-88, chmn. bd. dirs. 1990-92), Fed. Bar Found. (pres. 1992-94), N.Y. State Bar Assn. (mem. com. on profl. ethics, mem. jud. election monitoring com., mem. internat. litigation com.), Assn. of Bar of City of N.Y. (sec. 1979-82, chmn. com. on profl. and jud. ethics 1970-73, mem. spl. com. on lawyers role in securities transactions, mem. spl. com. to cooperate with ABA in revision of Canons of Ethics, mem. nominating com., mem. com. on membership, mem. com. on profl. discipline), Nat. Conf. Bankruptcy Judges, Am. Bankruptcy Inst. Office: US Courthouse 300 Quarropas St White Plains NY 10601-4140

HARDIN, CHRISTOPHER DEMAREST, medical educator; b. Syracuse, N.Y., July 31, 1961. BS, Cornell U., 1983; MS in Physiology and Biophysics, U. Rochester, 1986; PhD, U. Cin., 1989. Sr. fellow Dept. Radiology U. Wash., 1989-91, rsch. asst. prof., 1991—; asst. prof. physiology U. Mo., Columbia, 1993—; tutor, mentor in field; spkr. in field. Contbr. articles to profl. jours. Albert J. Ryan fellow, 1986-89, tng. grant fellow U. Cin., 1985-86, univ. grad. fellow U. Rochester, 1983-85; Jeffrey D. Doane Meml. award, 1987, Nat. Rsch. Svc. award, 1989-92. Mem. AAAS, Internat. Soc. Heart Rsch. (N.Am. sect), Am. Heart Assn. Sci. Coun. (basic sci.), Am. Physiol. Soc., Harold Lamport award Outstanding Young Invesitgator 1995), Biophysical Soc. Home: 1210 Sunset Dr Columbia MO 65203-2348 Office: Univ of Missouri Dept of Physiology MA415 Med Scis Bldg Columbia MO 65212

HARDIN, CLIFFORD MORRIS, retired university chancellor, cabinet member; b. Knightstown, Ind., Oct. 9, 1915; s. James Alvin and Mabel (Macy) H.; m. Martha Love Wood, June 28, 1939; children: Susan Carol (Mrs. L.W. Wood), Clifford Wood, Cynthia (Mrs. Robert Milligan), Nancy Ann (Mrs. Douglas L. Rogers), James. BS, Purdue U., 1937, MS, 1939, PhD, 1941, DSc (hon.), 1952; Farm Found. scholar, U. Chgo., 1939-40; LLD, Creighton U., 1956, Ill. State U., 1973; Dr. honoris causa, Nat. U. Colombia, 1968; DSc, Mich. State U., 1969, N.D. State U., 1969, U. Nebr., 1978, Okla. Christian Coll., 1979. Instr. U. Wis., 1941-42, asst. prof. agrl. econs., 1942-44; assoc. prof. agrl. econs. Mich. State Coll., 1944-46, prof., chmn. agrl. econs. dept., 1946-48, dir. expt. sta., 1949-53, dean agr., 1953-54; chancellor U. Nebr., 1954-69; sec. U.S. Dept. Agr., Washington, 1969-71; vice chmn. bd., dir. Ralston Purina Co., St. Louis, 1971-80; dir. Center for Study of Am. Bus., Washington U., St. Louis, 1981-83, scholar-in-residence, 1983-85; cons., dir. Stifel, Nicolaus & Co., St. Louis, 1980-87; bd. dirs. Gallup, Inc., Lincoln, Nebr.; bd. dirs. Omaha br. Fed. Res. Bank of Kansas City, 1961-67, chmn., 1962-67. Editor: Overcoming World Hunger, 1969. Trustee Rockefeller Found., 1961-69, 72-81, Winrock, Internat., Morrilton, Ark., 1984-94, Am. Assembly, 1975—, U. Nebr. Found., 1975—; mem. Pres.'s Com. to Stregthen Security Free World, 1963. Mem. Assn. State Univs. and Land-Grant Colls. (pres. 1960, chmn. exec. com. 1961).

HARDIN, ELIZABETH ANN, academic administrator; b. Charlotte, N.C., Nov. 21, 1959; d. William Gregg and Ann (Astin) H. BBA magna cum laude, U. Ga., 1981; MBA, Harvard U., 1985. Spl. project coord. NCNB Corp., Charlotte, 1981-82, investment officer, 1982-83; cons. Booz, Allen & Hamilton, Atlanta, 1985-86; asst. placement dir. Harvard U. Bus. Sch., Boston, 1986-87, dir. MBA program adminstrn., 1987-89, acting placement dir., 1988-89; mgr. employment Sara Lee Hosiery, Winston-Salem, N.C., 1990-92, mfg. mgr., 1992-93; dir. product devel. Sara Lee Hosiery, Winston-Salem, 1993-94; mng. cons. Info. Sci. Assocs., Charlotte, N.C., 1994-95; assoc. vice chancellor for bus. planning U. N.C., Charlotte, 1995—; cons., developer adminstrv. policy guide Chelsea (Mass.) Pub. Schs., 1989-90. Mem. adv. bd. Harvard Non-Profit Fellowship, 1986—; chmn. Harvard Non-Profit Mgmt. Fellowship, 1989-96; active AIDS Action Com. Mass., Holy Comforter, Charlotte; mem. total quality edn. task force N.C. Bus. Com. on Edn., 1992-93; troop leader Girl Scouts U.S.A.; mem. Leadership Charlotte, 1996—; mem. grant panel Arts and Scis. Coun., 1998, 99. Fellow State Farm Co. Found., 1980, Delta Gamma Found., 1983. Mem. Assn. for Corp. Growth (bd. advisors 1996—), Harvard Bus. Sch. Assn., Phi Kappa Phi, Delta Gamma (pres. alumnae Charlotte 1982-83). Republican. Avocations: reading, writing, public policy, photography. Office: U of NC at Charlotte Charlotte NC 28223

HARDIN, EUGENE BROOKS, JR., retired banker; b. Wilmington, N.C., Oct. 18, 1930; s. Eugene Brooks Hardin and Roberta Gilmour (Sterling) Demme; m. Olivia Lynch, Aug. 16, 1958; children: John Haywood II, Olivia Cary. B.S., U. N.C., 1952. With Wachovia Bank & Trust Co., Wilmington, 1956—, asst. v.p., 1957-60, v.p., 1962-68, sr. v.p., 1969-72; sr. v.p., regional exec. Wachovia Bank & Trust Co., Raleigh, 1972-79, regional v.p., 1979-95; cashier Burlington, N.C., 1961-62; ret., 1995; bd. dirs. Wachovia Bank, Raleigh, N.C. Pres., bd. dirs. Babies Hosp., Wilmington, 1968-72; pres. United Fund, 1970; treas., trustee Episcopalian Diocese East Carolina, 1965-72; chmn. Raleigh Civic Center Authority, 1978-81; chmn. Raleigh-Durham Airport Authority, 1981-82; chmn. bd. trustees St. Mary's Coll., 1979-85; bd. dirs. Children's Home Soc. N.C. Served with USNR, 1948-49; to 1st lt. USAF, 1952-56. Mem. Robert Morris Assos. Clubs: Civitan (pres. Wilmington 1971-72); Carolina Yacht (Wrightsville Beach); Carolina Country (Raleigh); Cape Fear Country (Wilmington); Land Fall (Wilmington). Home: 404 Drummond Dr Raleigh NC 27609-7006

HARDIN, FRANKIE CREAMER, elementary education educator; b. Asheville, N.C., Oct. 2, 1940; d. Frank Calvin and Lillie Anne (Wilson) Creamer; m. Jack Thomas Hardin Sr., Aug. 12, 1993; 1 stepchild, Jack Thomas. AA, Anderson Coll., 1960; BA, Furman U., 1962; MA, Ind. U., 1970. Tchr. L.P. Hollis Jr. High Sch., Greenville, S.C., 1963-66, Seneca (S.C.) Northside Elem. Sch., 1966-67, Scipio (Ind.) Elem. Sch., 1967-69, Crothersville (Ind.) Elem. Sch., 1969-70, OWenton (Ky.) Elem. Sch., 1970-71, Phyllis Wheatley Elem. Sch., Louisville, 1970, Glen Arden (N.C.) Elem. Sch., 1971, Eminence (Ind.) Elem. Sch., 1972-77, Indpls. Pub. Schs., 1978-79; cons. Cmty. Sch. Corp. So. Hancock, New Palestine, Ind., 1979-84; tchr. Greenville County (S.C.) Sch. Dist., 1984-96, 98; presenter reg., state and nat. workshops on standardized testing and state mandated tests, vocabulary growth, and At-Risk students, Vocabulary and Improving Standardized Test Scores. Recipient Tchr. of the Yr. award S.W. Area PTA, 1994; Baker's grantee, 1992-95. Mem. Internat. Reading Assn., Coun. Exceptional Children, Assn. Supervision and Curriculum Devel., Nat. Coun. Tchrs. Math., Am. Vets. Assn., Retired Tchrs. Assn., Am. Legion Aux., Order of the Eastern Star. Republican. Baptist. Avocations: travel, reading, writing, sports. Home: 9 Glenwaye Dr Greenville SC 29615-3311 Office: Bakers Chapel Elem Sch 555 S Old Piedmont Hwy Greenville SC 29611-6109

HARDIN, GEORGE CECIL, JR., petroleum consultant; b. Oakwood, Tex., Oct. 6, 1920; s. George Cecil and Pearl (Moore) H.; m. Virginia Howard, Nov. 21, 1942; children—George Howard, Susan. B.S. in Geology and Petroleum Engring, Tex. A&M U., 1941; Ph.D. in Geology (Van Hise fellow 1941), U. Wis., 1942. Registered engr., Tex., Okla. Mining engr. Victory Fluorspar Mine, Cave In Rock, Ill., 1942; geologist U.S. Geol. Survey, 1942-45, party chief, 1944-45; geologist Carter Gragg Oil Co., Palestine, Tex., 1945-46; geologist, petroleum engr. M.T. Halbouty Cons. Firm, Houston, 1946-51; exploration and prodn. mgr. M.T. Halbouty Oil and Gas Interests, Houston, 1951-59; gen. mgr. M.T. Halbouty Oil and Gas Interests, 1959-61; exec. v.p., dir. Halbouty Alaska Oil Co., 1957-61; partner Hardin and Hardin (cons. geologists), Houston, 1961-65; mgr. oil and gas expln. Kerr-McGee Oil Ind., Inc., 1964-65; v.p. N.Am. Oil & Gas Exploration, 1965-67, v.p. oil, gas and minerals exploration, 1967-68, group v.p. exploration, 1968; v.p. Kerr-McGee, Argentina, 1967-68, Kerr-McGee Can., Ltd., 1967-68, Kerr-McGee Australia, Ltd., 1967-68; pres. Royal Resources Corp., 1968-70, Ada Oil Exploration Corp., 1970-71, Ashland Exploration Co., 1971-80; sr. v.p. Ashland Oil Inc., 1971-80; dir. Ashland Oil Can Ltd., 1976-79, Allied Bank of Tex., Houston, 1956-78; mem. exec. com. Allied Bank of Tex., 1956-62, chmn. auditing com., 1962-65; vice-chmn., dir. Integrated Energy, Inc., 1981-83. Author articles in field. Fellow Geol. Soc. Am.; mem. Houston Geol. Soc. (pres. 1961-62), Gulf Coast Assn. Geol. Socs. (pres. 1959), Am. Assn. Petroleum Geologist (sec.-treas. 1964-66), Am. Inst. Profl. Geologists. Clubs: Petroleum (bd. dirs. 1956-58), Grandfather Country (Linville, N.C.). Home: 205 Ridge Creek Dr Morrisville NC 27560-7802

HARDIN, HAL D., lawyer, former United States attorney, former judge; b. Davidson County, Tenn., June 29, 1941. BA, Middle Tenn. State U., 1966; JD, Vanderbilt U., 1968; postgrad., State Jud. Coll., Reno, 1976. Bar: Tenn. 1969, D.C. 1983, Tex. 1990, U.S. Ct. Claims, 1983, U.S. Tax Ct., 1983, U.S. Ct. Mil. Appeals, 1983, U.S. Supreme Ct., 1973. Fingerprint technician FBI, 1961; dir. St. Louis Job Corps Ctr., 1968; asst. dist. atty. Nashville, 1969-71; pvt. practice, 1971-75; presiding judge Nashville Trial Cts., 1976-77; judge Spl. Ct. of Appeals, 1977; U.S. atty. Middle Dist. Tenn., 1977-81; practice law Nashville, 1981—; instr. govt. Aquinas Coll., Tenn. State Coll., 1975-76; adj. instr. fed. sentencing, criminal practice and procedure Nashville Sch. Law, 1994-99. Bd. dirs. Leadership Nashville, 1983, Capital Case Resource Ctr., 1988-95, Nat. Assn. Former U.S. Attys., 1993-96; vol. Peace Corps, Colombia, S.Am., 1963-65. Named one of Best Lawyers in Am., 1993-98. Fellow Tenn. Bar Found.; mem. Nashville Bar Assn. (bd. dirs. 1983-85, v.p. 1985), Tenn. Bar Assn. (gen. counsel 1982-90), D.C. Bar, Tex. Bar Assn., Tenn. Criminal Def. Attys., Am. Bd. Trial Advs. (sec. Tenn. chpt. 1987, nat. bd. dirs. 1988-89, pres. Tenn. chpt. 1990), Inns of Ct. (master). Office: 218 3d Ave N Nashville TN 37201

HARDIN, JAMES, retail food company executive; b. 1936. BBA, East Tex. State U., 1961. Pres. Brookshire Grocery Co. Inc., Tyler, Tex., CEO, 1999. Office: Brookshire Grocery Co PO Box 75710 1600 SW Loop 323 Tyler TX 75701*

HARDIN, JAMES NEAL, German and comparative literature educator, publisher; b. Nashville, Tenn., Feb. 17, 1939; s. James N. and Ina M. (Anderson) H.; m. Anne Farr. AB, Washington and Lee U., 1960; postgrad., U. Berlin, 1960-61; PhD, U. N.C., 1967. Prof. German lit. U. S.C., Columbia, 1969—; pres. Hardin Pub. Inc. Author: Johann Beer, 1983, Johann Beer Bibliographie, 1984, Christian Gryphius Bibliographie, 1985, J.C. Ettner Bibliographie, 1988; editor: Der Verliebte Oesterreicher, 1977, Dictionary of Lit. Biography, Vols. 59, 66, 69, 81, 85, 90, 94, 97, 118, 124, 129, 133, 138, 148, 194 and 168, Goethe's Wilhelm Meister's Travels, 1991; founder, co-editor: Studies in German Language, Literature and Linguistics, Works of Christian Gryphius, 2 vols., 1985; contbr. articles to profl. jours. and mags. Capt. U.S. Army, 1967-69. Decorated Army Commendation medal; recipient Alexander von Humbolt award, 1974-75, Russell award for scholarship, 1979; Fulbright scholar, 1960-61. Mem. MLA, Am. Assn. Tchrs. of German, South Atlantic MLA, Am. Soc. German Lit. 16th and 17th Centuries, Internat. Verein fuer Germanistik. Home: 228 Mallet Hill Rd Columbia SC 29223-3205 Office: Camden House PO Box 2025 Columbia SC 29202-2025

HARDIN, JAMES W., botanist, herbarium curator, educator; b. Mar. 31, 1929. BS, Fla. So. Coll., 1950; MS, U. Tenn., 1951; PhD, U. Mich., 1957. Instr. U. Mich., 1956-57; from asst. prof. to prof. N.C. State U., Raleigh, 1957-68, prof., 1968-96, emeritus prof., 1996—, curator herbarium, 1957-96; vis. prof. Mountain Lake Biological Sta. U.Va., summers 1962, 64, 83, U. Okla. Biological Sta., summers 1967, 70; mem. exec. com. Flora Southeastern U.S., 1966-97; endangered species com. N.C. Dept. Natural & Econ. Resources, 1973-74, natural areas adv. com., 1973-79; mem. plant conservation sci. com. N.C. Dept. Agriculture, 1980-97, chmn. 1987-97; mem. endangered species com. N.C. Wildlife Resources Commn., 1976-78, N.C. State Mus. Natural Hist., 1975-78; pres. Highlands Biological Station, Inc., 1963-69, trustee, 1958-69, sec., 1960-63; invited symposium speaker. Author: Human Poisoning, 1974, Textbook of Dendrology, 1996; editor ASB Bull., 1980-86; mem. editorial com. Am. Jour. Botany, 1964-66; mem. editorial bd. Brittonia, 1964-67, Brimleyana, 1975-97; reviewer jours. in field. Trustee Highlands Biol. Found., 1976-99. Mem. Am. Soc. Plant Taxonomists (pub. policy com. 1976-78, editorial bd. 1964-67, editor-in-chief Systematic Botany 1985-91, pres. elect 1991-92, pres. 1992-93, past pres. 1993-94, Cooley award 1958), Southern Appalachian Botanical Club (v.p. 1959-60, pres. 1964-65, Bartholomew award 1994), Botanical Soc. Am. (editorial com. 1964-66, chair southeastern sect. 1968-69), Assn. Southeastern Biologists (Meritorious Teaching award 1991, chmn. local arrangements 1966, 77, v.p. 1968-69, pres. 1970-80, editor 1980-86), Internat. Assn. Plant Taxonomy, Soc. Economic Botany (chmn. local arrangements 1979), Torrey Botanical Club, Coun. Biology Editors (reference style com. 1986-89), Gamma Sigma Delta (sec.-treas. N.C. chpt. 1972-73), Phi Kappa Phi, Sigma Xi (exec. com. N.C. chpt. 1962-63, sec. 1965-66, treas. 1966-67, v.p. 1967-68, program chmn. 1968-69, pres. 1969-70). Office: N C State Univ Dept Botany Raleigh NC 27695-7612

HARDIN, LOWELL STEWART, retired economics educator; b. nr. Knightstown, Ind., Nov. 16, 1917; s. J. Fred and Mildred (Stewart) H.; m. Mary J. Cooley, Sept. 21, 1940; children: Thomas Stewart, Joyce Ann, Peter Lowell. BS, Purdue U., 1939, DAgr (hon), 1990; PhD, Cornell U., 1943. Grad. asst., instr. Cornell U., 1939-43; instr., asst. and assoc. prof., prof. Purdue U., 1943-65, adj. prof. agrl. econs., 1965-66, prof., 1981-84, emeritus prof., asst. dir. internat. programs, 1984—, acting head dept. agrl. econs., 1954-57, head dept., 1957-65; also dir. Purdue Work Simplification Lab.; program adviser agr. Ford Found., 1965-66, program officer agr., 1966-81; former trustee Internat. Food Policy Rsch. Inst., Washington, Internat. Ctr. for Agrl. Rsch. in Dry Areas, Aleppo, Syria, Internat. Svc. for Nat. Agrl. Rsch., The Hague, The Netherlands, Winrock Internat. Inst. for Agrl. Devel., Morrilton, Ark. Author: (with L.M. Vaughan) Farm Work Simplification, 1949. Fellow AAAS, Am. Agrl. Econ. Assn. (pres. 1963-64); mem. Internat. Assn. Agrl. Economists, Sigma Xi, Alpha Gamma Rho, Phi Kappa Phi, Alpha Zeta, Sigma Delta Chi. Federated Church. Home: 2628 Calvin Ct Lafayette IN 47906-1402

HARDIN, PAUL, III, law educator; b. Charlotte, N.C., June 11, 1931; s. Paul and Dorothy (Reel) H.; m. Barbara Russell, June 8, 1954; children: Paul Russell, Sandra Mikush, Dorothy Holmes. AB, Duke U., 1952, JD, 1954; LHD (hon.), Clemson U., 1970; LLD (hon.), Coker Coll., 1972; LittD (hon.), Nebr. Wesleyan U., 1978; LLD (hon.), Adrian Coll., 1987, Monmouth Coll., 1988; HHD (hon.), Wofford Coll., 1989; LLD (hon.), Rider Coll., 1990; LHD (hon.), Duke U., 1994. Bar: Ala. 1954. Practiced in Birmingham, 1954, 56-58; asst. prof. Duke Law Sch., 1958-61, assoc. prof., 1961-63, prof., 1963-68, univ. trustee, 1969-74, 1995—; pres. Wofford Coll., Spartanburg, S.C., 1968-72, So. Methodist U., Dallas, 1972-74, Drew U., Madison, N.J., 1975-88; chancellor U. N.C., Chapel Hill, 1988-95, chancellor emeritus, prof. law, 1995—; vis. prof. U. Tex., summer 1960, U. Pa., 1962-63, U. Va., 1974; dir. Smith Barney mut. funds, Italy Fund, Inc. Author: (with Sullivan, others) The Administration of Criminal Justice, 1966, (with Sullivan) Evidence, Cases and Materials, 1968; contbr. articles to profl. jours. law revs. Chmn. Human Relations Com., Durham, N.C., 1961-62; mem. gen. conf. United Meth. Ch., 1968, 76, 80, 84; pres. Nat. Assn. Schs. and Colls. of United Meth. Ch., 1984; chmn. Nat. Commn. on United Meth. Higher Edn., 1975-77. Served with CIC, AUS, 1954-56. Mem. Carnegie Found. for Advancement Teaching (bd. dirs. 1990-98), Order of Coif, Phi Beta Kappa.

HARDIN, SARA JANE, consumer products company executive; b. Kansas City, Mo.; d. Ira Lucas Hardin and Gertrude Mary Griffith. BA, Yale Coll., 1974; JD, George Washington U., 1978. Asst. dir. adv. com. on housing and urban growth ABA, Washington, 1974-75; atty. advisor U.S. Dept. HUD, Washington, 1979-80; exec. dir. Nat. Rural Housing Coalition, Washington, 1980-82; cons. Washington, 1982-85, 86-90; govt. rels. specialist Atty. Gen. Counsel's Office Nat. Corp. Housing Partnerships, Washington, 1985-86; sr. program specialist AARP, Washington, 1990—; mem. adv. com. Stds. Energy Efficiency Appliances; bd. dirs. Nat. Low-Income Energy Consortium. Bd. dirs. Cleve. Park Hist. Soc., Washington, 1988-90. Avocation: reading. E-mail: jhardin@aarp.org. Home: 3726 Connecticut Ave NW Washington DC 20008 Office: AARP Consumer Issues 601 E St NW Washington DC 20049

HARDIN, SHERRIE ANN ASFOURY, commercial photographer; b. Saratoga Springs, N.Y., May 28, 1950; d. Edward Asfoury and Olivia Dorethea (Rehm) Melrose; m. Lin Hardin, Feb. 13, 1972. Student, Polk Community Coll., Winter Haven, Fla., 1968-69, 77, La Harbor Coll., Wilmington, Calif., 1984-85, El Camino Coll., Hawthorne, Calif., 1985-87. Dep. Polk County Sheriff's Office, Bartow, Fla., 1975-78; freelance comml. artist Winter Haven, Fla., Sacramento, Calif., 1978-84; photographer Nissan Motor Corp. in USA, Gardena, Calif., 1985-86; gen. mgr. Awards-Rex Group, Hawthorne, 1986-88; photog. coord. Meisel, Atlanta, 1988-89; owner, mgr. Sherrie Hardin, Photographer, 1985—; ptnr. LS Advtg. & Graphics, 1998—; mentor Cartersville Md. Sch., 1996-98. Photog. work includes stock, indsl., environ. and nature photography, restorations of old damaged photographs and fine art photography. Chairperson 7th Dist. Ann. Congl. H.S. Art Comp., 1998—; grad. Jedco-Polk Leadearship XI. Mem. Etowah Creative Art Coun. (bd. dirs.), Rockmart Art Coun., Environ. Def. Fund, Nat. Trust for Hist. Preservation, High Mus. of Art, Cartersville-Bartow County C. of C., Polk County C. of C., Northwest Ga. Travel Assn. Avocations: golf, fishing, sculpting, painting, gardening. Office: 844 Terry White Rd Aragon GA 30104-2032

HARDIN, TERRENCE ARMSTRONG, radio broadcasting manager; b. Cin., Sept. 10, 1961; s. Oliver Wendell and Carol Lockwood H.; m. Dayna Lynn Glasson, Oct. 8, 1994. BFA in Radio, TV Comms., So. Meth. U., 1985. Cert. radio mktg. cons. Nat. sales mgr. Sta. WBAP and Sta. KSCS-FM, Dallas, 1986-88; gen. sales mgr. Sta. WMJI-FM, Cleve., 1988-90, Stas. KCBQ-AM-FM and Sta. KIHI-FM, Denver and San Diego, 1990-92, Sta. WPNT-FM, Chgo., 1992-95; v.p., gen. mgr. Stas. KYOT-FM, KZON-FM, KOY and KISO, Phoenix, 1995—; guest speaker Ariz. State U., Tempe, 1995; advisor Glaser Capital, Cin., 1990—. Mem. awards com. Medallion of Merit Scholarship Found., Ariz. State U., Tempe, 1995-96; fund raiser Children's Cancer Ctr., Phoenix, 1995-96; exec. coun. Boys and Girls Club of Met. Phoenix. Mem. Am. Diabetes Assn. Avocations: travel, golf, mountain biking. Office: The Phoenix Radio Stas 840 N Central Ave Phoenix AZ 85004-2003*

HARDIN, THOMAS JEFFERSON, II, investment counsel; b. Richmond, Va., Jan. 19, 1945; s. Nathaniel Arnold and Margaret Fatio (L'Engle) H.; m. Catherine Merrifield Hoar, Feb. 24, 1968 (div. Sept. 1991); children: Maria L'E., T. Jefferson III. Student, Ga. State U., 1965; BS in Commerce, Washington and Lee U., 1967; MBA in Fin., Emory U., 1971. Security analyst J.C. Bradford & Co., Nashville, 1971-72; v.p., sr. security analyst N.C. Nat. Bank, Charlotte, 1972-79; v.p., dir. Forsyth Twine & Cordage Co., Charlotte, 1979-82; v.p., sr. security analyst Interstate Securities Corp., Charlotte, 1982-84; v.p., dir. rsch. Portfolio Capital Mgmt. Inc., Charlotte, 1984-85; pres. ATIM, Inc. (formerly A.T. Investment Mgmt., Inc.), Charlotte, 1985—; bus. mgr. M-B LLC, 1993—; co-mgr. Russelville Mgmt. LLC, 1996—; participant Fin. Analysts' Fedn. Rockford Sem., Ill., 1973, Ctr. Rsch. SEcurities Pricing U. Chgo., 1975-76, AIMR sem. Chgo., 1992; exec. dir. Alliance for Clean Energy, Washington, 1985-89. V.p., dir. Barclay Downs Homeowners Assn., Charlotte, 1977-78, Foxcroft Homeowners Assn., Charlotte, 1982-86; mem. chpt. svcs. com., support group leader, peer counselor Multiple Sclerosis Soc., Charlotte, 1987-94. 1st lt. U.S. Army, 1967-69. Named Master Forest Mgr., N.C. Agrl. Extension Svc., 1987. Fellow Assn. Investment Mgmt. Rsch.; mem. Am. Forestry Assn. (life), N.C. Soc. Fin. Analysts, Mecklenburg Forestry Assn. (chmn. 1988-91), Bald Head Island Club, Piedmont Driving Club, Washington and Lee Alumni Assn., Emory Grad. Bus. Assn. Avocations: hunting, swimming. Home: 1976 Ferncliff Rd Charlotte NC 28211-2704 Office: ATIM Inc PO Box 15333 Charlotte NC 28211-0601

HARDIN, WILLIAM BEAMON, JR., electrical engineer; b. Lumberton, N.C., Jan. 28, 1953; s. William Beamon and Virginia Ruth (Conner) H.; m. Mary Wanda Livingston, Jan. 22, 1971; children: William David, Christopher Wayne, David Wayne. BEE, Thomas A. Edison State Coll., 1990. Cert. plant engr., worldwide energy mgr., lighting efficiency profl.; lic. elec. contractor, N.C. Elec. engr. Barnhill Electric Engr. Co., Fayetteville, N.C., 1973-76; indsl. contractor Red Springs, N.C., 1976-78; plant engr. Waverly Mills, Laurinburg, N.C., 1978-81; chief elec. engr. Sharon-Harris Nuclear Power Plant, Raleigh, N.C., 1981-82; group engr. J.P. Stevens & Co., Inc., Great Falls, S.C., 1982-86; mgr. plant engrng. and energy mgr. Springs Industries, Laurel Hill, N.C., 1986—; advisor indsl. adv. com. Alternative Energy Corp., Raleigh, N.C., 1988—, state edn. adv. com., 1990—, Indsl. Energy Textile Focus Group N.C., Raleigh, 1991, indsl. maintenance and elec. installation adv. com. Richmond Community Coll. Engrng. Dept., Rockingham, N.C., 1990—. Chmn. Laurinburg (N.C.) C. of C. Edn. Com., 1991—. Named Vol. of Yr. Laurel Hill Sch., 1992. Mem. Cogeneration Inst. Environ. Engrs. and Mgrs., Am. Inst. Plant Engrs., Environ. Engrs. and Mgrs., Environ. Engrs. and Mgrs. Inst. Assn. Energy Engrs. (Regional Energy Engr. of Yr. 1992, Regional Energy Mgr. of Yr. 1990, Energy Engr. of Yr. 1989, 90), Elec. Industry Evaluation Panel, Scotch Meadows Country Club. Republican. Baptist. Achievements include development of Energy Patrol program involving students in efficient school energy usage by monitoring lights, leaks and thermostat settings. Home: 1373 Meadowlakes Rd Rock Hill SC 29732-9098

HARDIN, WILLIAM DOWNER, retired lawyer; b. Newark, Sept. 27, 1926; s. Charles R. and Emma (Downer) H.; m. Rosemarie Koellhoffer, Jan. 19, 1952 (dec. Mar. 1996); children: William Downer, David Gerth, Peter Roe. A.B., Princeton, 1948; LL.B., Columbia, 1951. Bar: N.J. 1951. Law clk. N.J. Superior Ct., 1951-52; since practiced in Newark and Morristown; mem. firm Pitney, Hardin, Kipp & Szuch, Morristown, 1957-96; mem. N.J. Bd. Bar Examiners, 1964-68, chmn., 1968; mem. local draft bd. SSS, 1953-74, chmn., 1970-74; mem. Family Svc. Bur., Newark, 1953-75, pres., 1960-66; mem. Family Svc. Morris County, 1976-85, 87-98, pres., 1979-82, 95-97, v.p., 1992-95; mem. membership com. Family Svc. Assn. Am., 1965-78, dir., 1971-79, 89-95; mem. Nat. Budget and Consultation Com., 1966-71, Coun. on Accreditation Svcs. for Families and Children, 1978-80. Trustee Newark Acad., 1952-85, pres., 1969-72, chmn., 1976-78; mem. Legal Svcs. of N.J., 1983—, chmn., 1990-96; mem. Legal Aid Soc. of Morris County, N.J., 1984-93, pres., 1989-90. With USNR, 1944-46. Mem. ABA, Fed. Bar Assn., N.J. Bar Assn., Essex County Bar Assn., Morris County Bar Assn., Morristown Club, Nassau Club, Coral Beach and Tennis Club, Short Hills Club. Episcopalian. Home: 15 Gapview Rd Short Hills NJ 07078-2077 Office: 200 Campus Dr Florham Park NJ 07932-1007

HARDING, BARRY, school system administrator, educational consultant; b. Lumberton, N.C., 1952; s. Stephen and Berlie Mae (Brewington) H.; m. Cheryl Ann Blanks, Nov. 19, 1978; children: Laura Beth, Stephen Barry. BS in Elem. Edn., Pembroke (N.C.) State U., 1975, MA in Ednl. Adminstrn., 1978; EdS, East Carolina U., Greenville, N.C., 1983; EdD, S.C. State Coll., Orangeburg, S.C., 1990. Tchr. grades 4-6 Allenton Sch., Lumberton, bldg. prin., 1978-79; prin. Pembroke Middle Sch., 1979-83, Green Grove Elem. Sch., Fairmont, N.C., 1983-89, Peterson Elem. Sch., Red Springs, N.C., 1989-93; asst. supt. adminstrn. Pub. Sch. Robeson County, 1993—, supt., 1999—; mem. N.C. Sch. Improvement Panel, 1995-96; local and state cons. to schs. and civic orgns.; speaker in field; presenter Internat. Reading Assn., 1995. Author: The Saddletree Church of God Organizational Handbook-"Who We Are", 1st edit., 1992, 2nd edit., 1995. People to People del. to China, 1988; selected as mem. The Z. Smith Reynolds Found. Inc. N.C.; mem. laymens bd. dirs. N.C. Ch. of God, 1994—; bd. dirs. East Coast Bible Coll. Recipient Disting. Educator award Charles F. Kettering Found., 1983, award for sch. improvement project N.C. Inst. Govt., 1986, Prin. of Yr. Pub. Schs. of Robeson County Wachovia, 1992, others. Mem. Nat. Assn. Elem. Sch. Adminstrs., N.C. Assn. Sch. Adminstrs., Tarheel Prins. Assn., Robeson County Prins. Assn. (pres. 1986), Phi Delta Kappa, Kappa Delta Pi. Avocations: reading, golfing, fishing. Home: 107 Camellia Ln Lumberton NC 28360-8101

HARDING, ENOCH, JR., clothing executive; b. Greenville, S.C., Apr. 7, 1931; s. Enoch and Nell (Evans) H.; m. Sarah Tomlinson, Dec. 26, 1953 (div. 1978); children: Enoch III, Earle T., David H., Elizabeth W.; m. Virginia Black, Sept., 1978. BS, Presbyn. Coll., Clinton, S.C., 1953. Div. mgr. Stone Mfg. Co., Columbia, S.C., 1955-62, Oxford Industries, Columbia, 1962-71; div. pres. Kellwood Co., N.Y.C., 1971-77, 83-95, corp. exec. v.p. opers., 1995—; pres. Vanity Fair Mills, Reading, Pa., 1977-83. Vice chmn. Midlands Tech. Coll., Columbia, 1961-71. 1st lt. U.S. Army, 1953-55. Mem. Union League Club N.Y.C. Avocation: sailing. Home: 36 Harleston Pl Charleston SC 29401-1268

HARDING, FANN, health scientist, administrator; b. Henderson, Ky., Jan. 29, 1930; d. James Hilary and Lucy (Caldwell) H. Student, Western Coll., Oxford Ohio, 1947-48; A.B. in Biology, Coker Coll., Hartsville, S.C., 1951; M.S. in Anatomy, Med. U. S.C., Charleston, 1954, Ph.D., 1958. Research and teaching asst. dept. anatomy Med. U. S.C., 1951-53, teaching fellow, 1953-55, research fellow, 1955-58; analyst pub. health research program, research and tng. grants br. Nat. Heart Inst., Bethesda, Md., 1958-61; scientist adminstr. research and tng. grants br. Nat. Heart Inst., 1961-64, chmn. nat. adv. heart council statements com., 1961-64, sr. health scientist adminstr. research grants br. (sect. chief), 1964-69, sr. health scientist adminstr. thrombosis and hemorrhagic diseases br. (acting chief), extramural program, also arteriosclerosis program, 1969-72; mem. Nat. Heart Inst. (Fellowship Bd.), 1966-68; sr. health scientist adminstr. thrombosis and hemorrhagic diseases program (acting chief), div. blood diseases and resources Nat. Heart and Lung Inst. (name changed to Nat. Heart, Lung and Blood Inst. 1976), Bethesda, 1972-74; asst. to dir. div. blood diseases and resources Nat. Heart, Lung and Blood Inst., 1974—, program dir. extramural research tng. and career devel. in blood diseases and transfusion medicine, exec. sec. blood diseases and resources adv. com., 1974-95; asst. coordinator U.S.-USSR Health Exchange Program, 1974-95; ret., 1996, sculptor, 1996—; mem. Women's Action Program Adv. Coun., HEW, 1971-72; cons. James H. Mitchell Found., Washington, 1962-67, Washington VA Hosp., 1968-70; environ. cons. Henderson (Ky.) Citizens Com., 1974-76; bd. dirs. Lupus Found. Am., 1985-88; initiated and implemented concept of transfusion medicine, 1982—. Editorial bd.: Lupus News, 1988—. Organizer NIH Orgn. for Women, 1970; bd. dirs. Assn. Women in Sci. Edn. Found., 1973-77; bd. visitors Coker Coll., 1974-78; bd. dirs., sec., treas. Nat. Children's Choir, Washington, 1981-91. Recipient Ruth Patrick award, 1951, NIH sustained performance award, 1973, Nat. award Fedn. Orgns. for Profl. Women, 1977, Disting. Svc. award Transfusion Medicine Acad. Award Program, Am. Assn. Blood Banks, 1990, Disting. Alumni award Coker Coll., 1992, award of Merit for Transfusion Medicine, NIH, 1993, Founder's award for Pioneering Contbns. to Advance Women in the Professions, Fedn. Orgns. for Profl. Women, 1995. Fellow Sigma Delta Epsilon; mem. AAAS (panel on women in sci. 1973-77), Nat. Women's Polit. Caucus (charter), Assn. Women in Sci. (founding mem. 1971, exec. bd. 1973-75), Fedn. Orgn. Profl. Women (founding pres., exec. bd. 1972—), Nat. Womans Party (bd. dirs. 1981—, corr. sec. 1989-91, rec. sec. 1991-96), Microcirculatory Soc. (charter), Reticuloendothelial Soc. (charter), Am. Assn. Blood Banks, Internat. Soc. Thrombosis & Haemostasis, Internat. Soc. Blood Transfusion, Internat. Soc. Lymphology. E-mail: fharding@erols.com. Fax: (202) 265-3267. Home: 2119 S Street NW Washington DC 20008-4011

HARDING, JAMES RAYMOND, II, special education educator; b. Chgo., Sept. 30, 1966; s. James Raymond and Sara Victoria Harding. BS, Wright State U., 1991; MEd, U. West Fla., 1993; EdS, Fla. State U., 1996, EdD in Higher Edn., 1999. Cert. tchr., Fla. Cons. in disability related issues ADA, Fla., 1991—; tchr. Escambia County Schs., Pensacola, Fla., 1993-94; substitute tchr. Leon County Schs., Fla., 1993—; intern, edn. unit Gov.'s Budget Office, Fla., 1995; intern, appropriations com. Fla. Ho. of Reps., Tallahassee, 1996. Mem. steering com., Forging Tallahassee, 1998-99, Rep. Nat. Congress; youth state coord., Jeb for Gov., Tallahassee, 1998. Recipient Svc. award Flas. Student Assn. 1996-98, Disting. Mem. award Rep. Party Fla., 1999. Mem. Nat. Assn. on Alcohol, Drugs, and Disabilities (bd. dirs.), Fla. Bd. of Regents (Svc. award, 1998), Fla. Paralyzed Vets. Assn. Roman Catholic. Home: FSU U-Box 65788 Tallahassee FL 32313

HARDING, JAMES WARREN, finance company executive; b. Montoursville, Pa., Nov. 9, 1918; s. James John and Alda (Edkin) H.; m. Emily Sue Landes, Mar. 22, 1941 (dec. Mar., 1992); 1 child, Connie Sue Harding; m. Mary Briand, Jan. 15, 1994. B.A., Lycoming Coll., 1938, LL.D. (hon.); M.A., U. Chgo., 1940. With Kemper Cos., Chgo., 1940-84; accountant Kemper Cos., 1940-50, comptroller, 1960-68, exec. v.p., 1969; chmn. bd. Bank of Chgo., from 1969; pres. Kemper Corp., 1969-84, ret.; pres. Am. Underwriting Corp., Central Mortgage Co.; pres. Nat. Agts. Service Co., 1969—, also bd. dirs.; bd. dirs. Kemper Fin. Svcs. Contbr. articles to ins. and trade mags. Finance chmn. Crusade of Mercy, Chgo., 1964-65; trustee James S. Kemper Found., Mundelein Coll.; adv. bd. U. Chgo., Brigham Young U. Served with USNR, 1943-44. Recipient Hardy award Ins. Inst., 1946. Mem Fin. Execs. Inst., Phi Kappa Sigma. Republican. Methodist. Clubs: Chgo. University, Indian Wells Country Club. Home: 1230 Thornbury Ln Libertyville IL 60048-2361

HARDING, JESSICA ROSE, public affairs specialist, journalist; b. Provincetown, Mass., Jan. 10, 1942; d. Joseph Anthony and Jessica Henrietta (Grace) Lema; m. Jan. 7, 1960 (dec. Sept. 1990); children: Victoria Lee Harding Johnston, H. William, David Charles. BS in Journalism, U. Md., 1996. Legal asst., paralegal Dept. Energy, Washington, 1977-82; aide to asst. dir. Automated Sys. Office, Libr. of Congress, Washington, 1982-84; spl. asst. for internat. security Office of Sec. Def., Washington, 1984-85; pub. affairs officer Army Chief Chaplains, Washington, 1985-88; pub. affairs specialist Navy Drug and Alcohol Program, Washington, 1988-98; pres., CEO The Write Angle, Crofton, Md.; weekly columnist From a Woman's Point of View, Enterprise and Inner Harbor News, Balt.; freelance writer; founder The Write Angle, Inc., Crofton, Md.; producer videotape prodns. for drug and alcohol program edn. and tng. br. USN, 1992-98. Mem. chorus Annapolis (Md.) chpt. Sweet Adelines, 1975-85; group facilitator Single Again, Crofton, Md., 1988-92. Roman Catholic. Office: The Write Angle PO Box 3673 Crofton MD 21114-3673

HARDING, JOHN HIBBARD, insurance company executive; b. Plainfield, N.J., Jan. 12, 1936; s. Ernest Reginald and Emily (Hibbard) H.; m. Joan Edith Tarro, Nov. 29, 1973; children—David, Philip, Robert, Brooke, Ashley. B.A., Princeton U., 1958. Asst. actuary Nat. Life Ins. Co., Montpelier, Vt., 1965-67; assoc. actuary Nat. Life Ins. Co., Montpelier, 1967-69, actuary R&D, 1969-72, v.p., actuary, 1972-80, sr. v.p., chief actuary, 1980-83, exec. v.p., 1983-85, vice chmn. bd., dir., 1985-87, pres., COO, 1987-96; v.p., chief actuary Blue Cross-Blue Shield of Vt., 1997—; chmn., CEO Adminstrv. Svcs., Inc.; dir. Equity Svcs., Inc., Nat. Life Investment Mgmt. Co., Sentinel Advisors, Inc., 1987-96. Fellow Soc. Actuaries (bd. govs. 1993-95); mem. Am. Acad. Actuaries (bd. dirs. 1982-85, v.p. 1988-90, pres.-elect 1991-92, pres. 1992-93, immediate past pres. 1993-94). Home: PO Box 180 East Calais VT 05650-0180

HARDING, JOHN T., journalist; b. Morristown, N.J., Jan. 6, 1937; s. Thomas and Mary Rose (McHarg) H.; m. Sandra Kelley, Apr. 20, 1968; children: Lisa, Thomas Alexander. BA cum laude, Montclair State U., 1987, MA, 1996. Bus. writer and editor The Star-Ledger, Newark, N.J., 1970—. Author and editor newsletter Editor's Revenge, 1975-85. Trustee Milton Sch., Millburn, N.J., 1989—. With U.S. Army, 1959-62. Recipient Excellence in Real Estate Journalism award N.J. Assn. Realtors, 1994, Media Excellence award for disting. journalism N.J. Builders Assn., 1996. Mem. Nat. Assn. Real Estate Editors (pres. 1993, Best Newspaper Report award 1989), Soc. Profl. Journalists, Soc. Am. Bus. Editors and Writers, Phi Kappa Phi. Avocations: music, celtic history.

HARDING, JOHN WALTER, art critic; b. L.A., Aug. 16, 1947; s. Walter Ellis and Elizabeth Alice (Link) H.; m. Georgina R. Markovich, May 2, 1974; 1 child, Jessica Elizabeth. AA, Long Beach City Coll., 1967; BA, UCLA, Westwood, 1973. Theater and film critic Patuxent Pub. Co., Columbia, Md., 1982-88; arts editor Patuxent Pub. Co., Columbia, 1988—. Home: 10053 Carillon Dr Ellicott City MD 21042-6207

HARDING, LINDA OTTO, gerontological nurse; b. Calicoon, N.Y., Apr. 30, 1944; d. Max Hermann and Leona (Kleb) Otto; m. Bruce Nelson Harding, June 4, 1966; children: Jonathan, Linette. Diploma, Robert Packer Hosp. Sch. of Nursing, Sayre, Pa., 1965; student, Phillips U., Enid, Okla., 1967-68. RN, N.Y., Pa.; cert. personal care home administr.; cert. gerontol. nurse; cert. diabetes educator. Psychiat. nurse Meth. Hosp., Indpls., 1969-71; Tb control nurse Madison County Dept. Health, Anderson, Ind., 1971-73; charge nurse Milford (Pa.) Valley Convalescent Home, 1974-83; office nurse Tri State Med. Assocs., Matamoras, Pa., 1983-91; dir. resident health svcs. Twin Cedars Assisted Living Ctr., Shohola, Pa., 1990—. Founder Tri State Alzheimer's Support Group; dir. Share-Care Diabetes Support Group; welcome sec. Bethany Christian Fellowship. Named Vol. of Yr., Mercy Cmty. Hosp., 1997. Mem. ANA, Pa. State Nurses Assn. (newsletter editor, past treas., v.p.), Am. Assn. Diabetes Educators, N.E. Pa. Assn. Diabetes Educators. Home: 360 Little Walker Rd Shohola PA 18458-9737

HARDING, MAJOR BEST, state supreme court chief justice; b. Charlotte, N.C., Oct. 13, 1935; m. Jane Lewis, Dec., 1958; children: Major B. Jr., David L., Alice Harding Sanderson. BS, Wake Forest U., 1957; LLM, U. Va., 1995; LLD (hon.), Stetson U., 1991, Fla. Coastal Sch. Law, 1999; LLM in Jud. Process, U. Va., 1995. Bar: N.C. 1959, Fla. 1960. Staff judge adv. hdqrs. Ft. Gordon, Ga., 1960-62; asst. county solicitor Criminal Ct. of Record, Duval County, Fla., 1962-63; pvt. practice law, 1964-68; judge Juvenile Ct., Duval County, 1968-70; judge 4th Jud. Cir. of Fla., 1970-74, chief judge, 1974-77; justice Supreme Ct. of Fla., Tallahassee, 1991—, chief justice, 1998—; supervisory judge Family Mediation Unit, 1984-90; mem. Matrimonial Law Commn. and Gender Bias Study Commn.; chair Fla. Ct. Edn. Coun., past mem. Jud. Conf.; 1st dean New Judges Coll., 1975, faculty mem. in probate and juvenile areas, until 1979; dean Fla. Jud. Coll., 1984-92, mem. bench-bar commn.; chmn. Supreme Ct. com. on law-related edn., 1997—. Bd. dirs. Legal Aid Assn., Family Consultation Svc., Daniel Meml. Home; past pres. Rotary Club of Riverside, Jacksonville, Fla., Rotary Club of Tallahassee; chmn. U.S. Constn. Bicentennial Commn., Jacksonville; past mem., deacon, elder St. John's Presbyn. Ch.; commr. Gen. Assembly Presbyn. Ch. U.S., 1971; mem. Christ Presbyn. Ch., Tallahassee, clk. of session, elder. Recipient Award for Outstanding Contbn. to Field of Matrimonial Law Am. Acad. Matrimonial Lawyers, 1986, Harry Lee Anstead Professionalism award Dade County Trial Lawyers Assn., 1998. Mem. ABA, The Fla. Bar, N.C. State Bar Assn., Chester Bedell Inn of Ct. (past pres.), Scabbard and Blade, Tallahassee Am. Inn of Ct., Tallahassee Bar Assn., Sigma Chi (Significant Sig award 1997), Phi Delta Phi. Office: Supreme Ct of Fla 500 S Duval St Tallahassee FL 32399-6556

HARDING, MARGARET TYREE, minister; b. Lynchburg, Va., May 28, 1951; d. Aubrey Nathaniel and Audrey (Riley) Tyree; m. William R. Harding, Sep. 11, 1993. BA, Averett Coll., 1978; MDiv, Southeastern Bapt. Theol. Sem., Wake Forest, N.C., 1981. Ordained to ministry So. Bapt. Conv., 1982. Min. youth Moffett Meml. Bapt. Ch., Danville, Va., 1976-78, West Main Bapt. Ch., Danville, 1979-81; min. edn. and youth North Run Bapt. Ch., Richmond, Va., 1981-84; min. edn., youth and adminstrn. Grandin Ct. Bapt. Ch., Roanoke, Va., 1984—. Contbr. articles to profl. jours. Devotional officer Jr. Women's Club, Madison Heights, Va., 1971-75; alumni rep. Averett Coll., Danville, 1984—, mem. mins. adv. com., 1991; usher Mill Mountain Theater, Roanoke, Va., 1990—. Mem. Religious Edn. Assn. U.S. and Can. (bd. dirs. 1991), Va. Bapt. Gen. Assn. (gen. bd. 1989—), Va. Bapt. Religious Assn. (pres. 1989), So. Bapt. Religious Edn. Assn. (asst. sec. 1994-95), Roanoke Area Religious Edn. Assn. (pres. 1991). Home: 3613 Martinell Ave Roanoke VA 24018-4033 Office: Grandin Ct Bapt Ch 2660 Brambleton Ave SW Roanoke VA 24015-4306 *Make the most of every movement of your life. It is given to you by God to be enjoyed and lived to the fullest.*

HARDING, MARIE, ecological executive, artist; b. Glen Cove, N.Y., Nov. 13, 1941; d. Charles Lewis and Marie (Parish) H.; m. John P. Allen, Jan. 29, 1965 (div. Oct., 1991); 1 child, Eden A. Harding. BA, Sarah Lawrence Coll., 1964; postgrad., Arts Students League, N.Y.C., 1965. Founder Synergia Ranch for Wellness, Innovation, Retreats and Confs., Santa Fe, 1969; founding mem., actress Theater of All Possibilities, Santa Fe, 1971-86; founding mem., dir. Inst. Ecotechnics, Santa Fe, also London, 1974—; bd. dirs. Synopco Corp., N. Mex., 1974-81; bd. dirs., founding mem. Savannah Systems Pty., Ltd., Kimberly region, Australia, 1976—, Outback Sta. Pty. Ltd., Kimberly region, Australia, 1976-94; chair, dir. EcoWorld, Inc., Santa Fe, 1982-94; dir., founding mem., CFO Space Biospheres Ventures, Biosphere 2, Ariz., 1984-94; chair, CEO Oceans Expdns., Inc., 1986-92; pres. ecol. and biosphere R&D/implementation project Global Ecotechnics Corp., Santa Fe, 1994—; pres. Decisions Team, Inc. Ecol. Project Mgmt., Santa Fe, Ariz., 1994—, Syneco LLC, retreats and confs.; particpant in constrn. and fin. Capt. R. Heraclitus rsch. vessel, Oakland, Calif., 1974; bd. dirs. Hotel Vajra, Kathamdu, Nepal, 1976-94, Caravan of Dreams Performing Arts Ctr., Ft. Worth, 1983-94, Synergetic Press, London and Ariz., 1984—. Artist: paintings shown in exhibitions San Francisco, London, Ft. Worth, Santa Fe, Biosphere 2, Ariz., 1979-93, Biosphere 2 Paintings Exhbn., London, 1996; project dir., artist mural project History of Jazz, Dance, Theater, Ft. Worth, 1982-83; producer, dir. (films) Bryon Gysin Loves ya, Project Charlie, The Search, Synergia History, Planet Earth Conf. Vol. Swallows, Madras, India, 1964, Project Concern, Vietnam, Hong Kong, 1964-65; artist, founder, trustee October Gallery Trust, internat. artists forum, London, 1979; mem. Planetary Coral Reef Found., Inc., 1993—. Mem. Friends of Tibet, N.Mex. Black Belt Club, Tae Kwon Doe Inst. N.Mex. Avocations: ecological project implementation, endangered lifestyles/cultures, painting, landscape gardening, retreat faciliatation. Home and Office: Synergia Ranch 26 Synergia Rd Santa Fe NM 87505-0900

HARDING, RAY MURRAY, JR., judge; b. Logan, Utah, Nov. 23, 1953; s. Ray M. Sr. and Martha (Rasmussen) H.; m. Jeri Lynn; children: Michelle, Nicole, Justin, Skyler. BS, Brigham Young U., 1975; JD, J. Reuben Clark Law Sch., 1978. Bar: Utah 1978. Ptnr. Harding & Harding, American Fork and Pleasant Grove, Utah, 1978-85; owner Harding & Assoc., American Fork and Pleasant Grove, 1986-95; judge 4th Jud. Dist. Ct. Utah County, State of Utah, 1995—; atty. Lindon City and Pleasant Grove City, Utah, 1983-95, Alpine City, 1985-94, American Fork, Utah, 1985-95. Bd. trustees Utah Valley State Coll., 1986-95, chmn., 1991-93. Named Businessman of Yr., Future Bus. Leaders of Am., 1983. Mem. ABA, ATLA, Utah State Bar Assn., Utah Trial Lawyers Assn., Utah County Bar Assn., Pleasant Grove C. of C. (pres. 1983), Kiwanis (local bd. dirs. 1982-83). Avocations: skiing, scuba diving, hiking, hunting, travel. Home: 11165 Yarrow Cir Highland UT 84003-9598 Office: 4th Judicial Dist Ct 125 N 100 W Provo UT 84601-2849

HARDING, WAYNE EDWARD, III, software company executive, accountant; b. Topeka, Sept. 29, 1954; s. Wayne Edward and Nancy M. (Gean) H.; BS with honors in Bus. Adminstrn., U. Denver, 1976, MBA, 1983; m. Janet Mary O'Shaughnessy, Sept. 5, 1979 (div. Mar. 1985); m. Karen Ruttan, Oct. 10, 1987. Partner, HKG Assocs., Denver, 1976-77; staff auditor Peat, Marwick, Mitchell & Co., Denver, 1976-78; auditor Marshall Hornstein, P.C., Wheat Ridge, Colo., 1978-79; sr. auditor Touche Ross & Co., Denver, 1979-80; controller Mortgage Plus Inc., 1980-81; sec.-treas. Sunlight Systems Energy Corp., 1980-81; ptnr. Harding, Newman, Sobule & Thrush, Ltd., Denver, 1981-82; pvt. practice specializing in microcomputer applications and litigation support, 1982-89; acct., v.p. Great Plains Software, Fargo, N.D., also dir. CPA ptnr. rels.; founder Discount Computer Rentals, Inc., 1985; dir. Harding Transp., Harding Tech. Leasing, Crown Parking Products; lectr. to various profl. groups on computer tech. Class agt., mem. alumni council Phillips Exeter Acad., Exeter, N.H., 1973-83, class agt., 1993—; bd. dirs., treas. Legal Center for Handicapped Citizens, Denver, 1979-80; vol. Denver Bridge, 1984-85. Mem. AICPA (instr., mem. tech. rsch. com. 1994—), Colo. Soc. CPAs (chmn. CPE com. 1987-89, instr., mem. bd. dirs. 1994-97, v.p. 1996-97), Beta Alpha Psi, Pi Gamma Mu, Beta Gamma Sigma. Libertarian. Mem. editorial bd. Practical Acct. Mag.; contbr. articles in field of microcomputers to profl. jours. including Jour. of Accountancy. Home and Office: 5206 S Hanover Way Englewood CO 80111-6240

HARDING, WAYNE MICHAEL, sociologist, researcher; b. Boston, Jan. 10, 1947; s. Lawrence Robert and Genevieve Ruth (Ewell) H.; m. Kathleen Mary Fraser, Sept. 27, 1971; 1 child, Alexander Fraser. AB in Sociology magna cum laude, Brandeis U., 1970; EdM, Harvard U., 1971; PhD, Brandeis U., 1992. Evaluation cons. to exemplary program in occupational edn. Cardinal Cushing Ctr. for the Spanish Speaking, Boston, 1970-71; asst. dir. edn. The Sanctuary, Inc., Cambridge, Mass., 1971-73; rsch. asst. analytical studies and planning group Mass. Inst. Tech., Cambridge, 1974; rsch. assoc. The North Charles Mental Health Rsch. and Tng. Found., Cambridge, 1974—; dir. projects, officer, co-founder Social and Behavioral Rsch., Inc., Cambridge, 1980-85, Social Sci. Rsch. and Evaluation, Inc., Lincoln, Mass., 1984—; lectr. on psychiatry Harvard Med. Sch., Cambridge, 1984—; ptnr., co-founder Social Sci. Rsch. Enterprises, Lincoln, 1987—; sr. rsch. scientist Gemini Industries, Inc., Burlington, Mass., 1989-81, Rainbow Tech., Inc., Olney, Md., 1994—. Bd. dirs., treas. Rogers Pierce Children's Ctr., Arlington, Mass., 1980-84; mem. Burlington bd. Appeals. Avocations: gardening, skiing. Home: 16 Chadwick Rd Burlington MA 01803-3604 Office: Social Sci Rsch Evaluation 121 Middlesex Tpke Burlington MA 01803-4990

HARDIS, STEPHEN ROGER, manufacturing company executive; b. N.Y.C., July 13, 1935; s. Abraham I. and Ethel (Krinsky) H; m. Sondra Joyce Rolbin, Sept. 15, 1957; children: Julia Faye, Andrew Martin, Joanna Halley. B.A. with distinction, Cornell U., 1956; M.P.A. in Econs., Woodrow Wilson Sch. of Pub. and Internat. Affairs Princeton U., 1960. Asst. to controller Gen. Dynamics, 1960-61; fin. analyst Pfaudler Permutit Inc., 1961-64; staff asst. to controller, 1964; mgr. corp. long-range planning Ritter Pfaudler Corp., 1965-68, dir. corporate planning, 1968; treas. Sybron Corp., Rochester, N.Y., 1969—; v.p. fin. Sybron Corp., 1970-77, exec. v.p. fin. and planning, 1977-79; vice chmn., chief fin. and adminstrv. officer Eaton Corp., Cleve., 1979—, vice chmn., CEO, 1995, chmn., CEO, 1996—; bd. dirs. Key Corp., Progressive Corp., Nordson Corp., Lexmark Corp., Marsh & McLennan. Past mem. Gov.'s Task Force on High Tech. Industry; past mem. bd. dirs. Rochester Area Hosp. Corp., Rochester Area Ednl. TV Sta., Genesee Hosp.; trustee Cleve. Clinic, Inc., Playhouse Square Found., Musical Arts Assn. (Cleve. Orchestra); mem. Leadership Cleve.; mem. Cleve. Tomorrow; trustee Greater Cleve. Growth Assn. With USNR, 1956-58. Mem. Phi Beta Kappa. Office: Eaton Corp 1111 Superior Ave E Cleveland OH 44114-2584

HARDISON, DIANE SORRELL PARKER, special education educator; d. W.J. and Hazel G. Sorrell; 1 child, MeAnn. BS in Elem. Edn., Atlantic Christian Coll., 1968; M in Mental Retardation, East Carolina U., 1972, EdS in Supervision, 1984. Cert. in learning disabilities, supr. Tchr. 3rd grade Wilson (N.C.) County Schs., 1968-70, tchr. mentally handicapped, 1970-71, 73-75, dir. programs for exceptional children, 1975-96; regional coord. spl. edn. East Carolina U., 1997—; developer program for severely handicapped students, 1973; co-founder Wilson County Parent/Staff Liaison Com. Exceptional Children, 1979; lectr. in field. Vol. Spl. Olympics, Wilson. Named Tchr. of Yr., N.C. Assn. Retarded Citizens, 1974; recipient Outstanding Spl. Edn. Adminstr. award N.C. Coun. Adminstrs Spl. Edn., 1995.

HARDISON, DONALD LEIGH, architect; b. Fillmore, Calif., Mar. 23, 1916; s. Leigh Winter and Myrtle Glenn (Thorpe) H.; m. Betty Jane Decker, June 14, 1942; children—Stephen Decker, Janet Leigh Hardison Brown. A.B., U. Calif.-Berkeley, 1938. Lic. architect, Calif. Prin. Hardison & Assocs., Richmond, Calif., 1948-56; ptnr. Hardison & Komatsu, Richmond, 1956-64; pres. Hardison & Komatsu, San Francisco, 1965-78; chmn. bd. Hardison Komatsu Ivelich & Tucker, San Francisco, 1978-87. Prin. works include Sonoma State Coll. Residence Hall, 1972 (AIA award 1977), Chevron Cafeteria-Tech. Ctr., Richmond, 1981, McAllister Tower, San Francisco, 1982, (co-architect) U. Calif.-Berkeley Student Ctr. Complex, 1970 (AIA award 1970). Mem. Richmond Planning Commn., 1952-55; mem. Calif. Commn. on Housing and Community Devel., 1969-74; bd. dirs. Art Ctr., Richmond, 1965-70, Richmond Mus. of History, 1990—. Fellow AIA (bd. dirs. 1978-80, chancellor Coll. Fellows 1985, pres. East Bay chpt. 1954, pres. Calif. council 1965, Calif. council Disting. Service citation 1984). Republican. Presbyterian. Club: Commonwealth (San Francisco). Lodge: Rotary (pres. Richmond, Calif. 1986-87). Office: Hardison Komatsu Ivelich & Tucker 400 2nd St San Francisco CA 94107-1488

HARDISTER, DARRELL EDWARD, insurance executive; b. Davidson County, N.C., Sept. 17, 1934; s. George Herbert and Myrtle Rosa (Parrish) H.; m. Miriam Smith; children: Debra Sue, Pamela Louise, Myrtle Darlene. Grad., Am. Coll. CLU, ChFC, LUTCF. Asst. mgr. Correct Craft Boat Co., Titusville, Fla., 1952-57; sales rep. Napa/Stradley's Motor Supply, Titusville, 1957-59; sales rep., mgr. Peninsular Life Ins. Co., Brevard County, Fla., 1959-64; previous owner, mgr. D.E. Hardister, CLU & Assocs. Ins. Agency, Titusville, 1964-96; speaker at convs. in field. Contbr. articles to profl. publs. and company publs. Pres. North Brevard County Devel. Com., 1979, 80; mem. Gov.'s Adv. Coun., Fla.; pres. Titusville High Choir Parents Assn., 1979-83; past advisor Fla. Theater Restoration Com., Titusville; past chmn. bd. dirs. North Brevard YMCA; past mem. Brevard County Zoning Bd. Recipient Key to City of Titusville. Mem. Nat. Assn. Life Underwriters, North Brevard Assn. Life Underwriters (pres. 1969-70, bd. dirs.), Rotary (pres. local chpt. 1976-77, Paul Harris Fellow), Lions (pres., sec. local chpt. 1961, 64). Republican. Avocations: photography, boating, fishing, drag racing. Home: 3305 Royal Palm Ct Titusville FL 32780-5648 Office: 3305 Royal Palm Ct Titusville FL 32780-5648

HARDISTY, WILLIAM LEE, English language educator; b. Creston, Iowa, Feb. 14, 1946; s. Ernest Dale and Velda Marie (Schaffer) H.; m. Bernadine Maxine Reimers, July 30, 1967; children: Lance William, Chad Eugene. AA, Creston (Iowa) C.C., 1965; BS, N.W. Mo. State U., Maryville, 1967, MA, 1972; postgrad., U. No. Iowa, Cedar Falls, 1988. Cert. tchr., Iowa, Mo. Instr. Iowa Western Coll., Council Bluffs, 1987—; chmn. lang. arts A-H-S-T H.S., Avoca, Iowa, 1967—; drama dir. A-S-T High Sch., Avoca, Iowa, 1967-92; presenter Iowa Tchrs. English, Des Moines, 1991-95, Iowa Conservation Edn. Coun., Ames, 1995, Iowa State Edn. Assn., 1982-95. Dist. chmn. Mid-Am. coun. Boy Scouts Am., 1984-98, coun. com., 1998; chmn. Rep. Party Knox Twp., Avoca, 1988-98; pres. Iowa Assn. County Conservation Bds., Des Moines, 1990; pres. Pott count R.E.A.P. Bd. Council Bluffs, 1992; elder Presbyn. Ch., 1969—; mem. Sheriff's Dept. Citizens Adv. Bd., 1994—. Mem. NRA (life), NEA (life), Nat. Coun. Tchrs. English (life), Pheasants Forever (bd. dirs. 1990-91), Iowa State Edn. Assn., Southwest Unitserv Unit (exec. bd. 1994—), Phi Delta Kappa. Avocations: writing, hunting, hiking, canoeing, travel. Home: 317 E Jaycee St Avoca IA 51521-5104 Office: A-H-S-T High Sch 768 S Maple Avoca IA 51521

HARDMAN, CORLISTA HELENA, school system administrator; b. Charleston, W.Va., Feb. 5, 1948; d. Curtis Thomas and Maelena Hardman; 1 child, Bruce. BS in Edn., W.Va. State Coll., 1969; MEd, Baldwin-Wallace Coll., 1977. CErt. tchr., Ohio. Tchr. Cleve. City Schs., 1969—; supr. Cleve. State U., 1981—; adj. prof. John Carroll U., 1996. Fin. sec. Everlasting Bapt. Ch., Cleve., 1978—; leader Lake Erie coun. Girl Scouts U.S., 1989—. Martha Holden Jennings scholar, 1985; named Tchr. in Excellence Nat. Coun. Negro Women, 1992; recipient Presdl. award elem. sci., 1997. Mem. Ohio Coun. Tchrs. English and Lang. Arts, Cleve. Tchrs. Union, Cleve. Regional Coun. Sci. Tchrs. (co-pres. 1998), Ctr. City Profl. Devel. (chair 1986—), Alpha Kappa Alpha (Excellence in Sci. and Math. Tchg. 1997). Avocations: reading, aerobics. Office: Orchard Elem Sch 4200 Bailey Ave Cleveland OH 44113-3821

HARDMAN, DANIEL CLARKE, accountant; b. Gadsden, Ala., Aug. 10, 1954; s. Edgar Paul and Juanette Lorena (Hall) H.; m. Elwanda Denise Holland, June 6, 1976; children: Benjamin M., Adam L. BS with honors, Jacksonville State U., 1976. CPA, Ala. Acctg. mgr. Ernst & Whinney, Birmingham, Ala., 1976-81; prin. Hardman, Guess, Frost & Cummings, P.C., Birmingham, 1981—; bd. dirs. Exec. Techs., Inc., Birmingham. Dist. commr. Boy Scouts Am., Birmingham, 1982-84; bd. dirs. Highlands Day Sch.; chmn. tax com. Bus. Coun. Ala., 1986-97. Mem. Am. Inst. CPA's, Ala. Soc. CPA's, Nat. Assn. Accts. (bd. dirs. Ala. 1981), Birmingham C. of C. (pres.' com. 1981). Republican. Methodist. Club: Exchange (bd. dirs. Birmingham 1986). Avocations: hunting, canoeing. Home: 5200 Meadow Brook Rd Birmingham AL 35242-3312 Office: Hardman Guess et al 2120 16th Ave S Ste 300 Birmingham AL 35205-5046

HARDMAN, DELLA BROWN TAYLOR, art educator, retired; b. Charleston, W.Va., May 20, 1922; d. Anderson Hunt and Captolia Monette (Casey) Brown; m. Francis Coolidge Taylor, Mar. 30, 1945 (dec. Apr. 1978); children: Andrea, Francis Jr., Faith; m. Leon Herman Hardman, June 1987 (dec. Mar. 1995). BS in Edn., W.Va. State Coll., 1943; MA, Boston U., 1945; PhD, Kent State U., 1994. Prof. art W.Va. State Coll., Institute, 1956-86; art lectr. part time Nathan Mayhew Seminars, Vineyard Haven, Mass., 1991—, also bd. dirs. Columnist Vineyard Gazette, 1998—. Trustee Oak Bluffs (Mass.) Libr., 1997. Inducted into Nat. Black Coll. Hall of Fame, 1998. Mem. Vis. Nurses Assn. (corporator 1996—). Democrat. Baptist. Home: PO Box 2035 27 DeBettencourt Pl Oak Bluffs MA 02557

HARDMAN, HAROLD FRANCIS, pharmacology educator; b. East Orange, N.J., Aug. 2, 1927; s. Harold Maine and Agnes Lillian (McGovern) H.; m. Jean Ely Dettmer, June 27, 1950; children—David, Timothy, John, Susan. B.Sc. (Am. Found. Pharm. Edn. scholar), Rutgers U., 1949; M.Sc. (Am. Found. Pharm. Edn. fellow), U. Ill. at Chgo., 1951; Ph.D. (Am. Found. Pharm. Edn. fellow), U. Mich., 1954, M.D., 1958. Asst. prof. pharmacology U. Mich., 1958-60; assoc. prof. pharmacology Marquette U., Milw., 1960-62; prof. pharmacology, chmn. dept. Med. Coll. of Wis. at Milw., 1962—, chmn. dept., 1962-88, assoc. dean basic scis., 1968-70; prof. emeritus, 1992—, chmn. retirees, 1993-95; Bd. dirs. Med. Coll. Wis., 1980-82; trustee Biosis, 1988-91. Served to sgt. AUS, 1946-47. John and Mary Markle scholar acad. medicine, 1958-62; recipient Outstanding Alumni award U. Mich., 1989, Disting. Svc. award Med. Coll. Wis., 1985, Med. Alumni recognition award, 1995, Pharmacology Grad. Student Recognition award, 1995; Citation Esteem, Dean and Bd. Dirs. Med. Coll. Wis., 1988. Mem. Am. Soc. Pharmacology and Exptl. Therapeutics (chmn. program com. 1973-76, councillor 1976-79, pres.-elect 1981-82, pres. 1982-83), Fedn. Am. Socs. Exptl. Biology (pres. 1983-84), Assn. Med. Sch. Pharmacology Chairmen (sec. 1970-72, pres. 1978-80), Milw. Acad. Medicine (pres. 1974-75). Achievements include rsch. in cardiovascular pharmacology with continuous support from NIH for 32 yrs. Studied the effect of drug and receptor ionization upon pharmacological activity with emphasis upon beta adrenergic receptor agonists and antagonists. Also conducted studies on the behavioral and cardiovascular actions of marijuana and derivatives. Home: 1120 Indianwood Dr Brookfield WI 53005-5705

HARDMAN, JOEL GRIFFETH, pharmacologist; b. Colbert, Ga., Nov. 7, 1933; s. Joel Carlton and Ruby Lee (Griffeth) H.; m. Georgette Johnson, July 16, 1955; children: Pamela Hope, Frances Leigh, Mary George, Joel Carlton. B.S. in Pharmacy, U. Ga., 1954, M.S. in Pharmacy, 1959; Ph.D. in Pharmacology, Emory U., 1964. Instr. pharmacy U. Ga., Athens, 1957-60; predoctoral fellow dept. pharmacology Emory U., Atlanta, 1960-64; instr. physiology Vanderbilt U., Nashville, 1964-67; asst. prof. Vanderbilt U., 1967-70, assoc. prof., 1970-72, prof. physiology, 1972-75, prof., chmn. dept. pharmacology, 1975-90, assoc. vice chancellor for health affairs, 1991-97, prof. pharmacology emeritus, 1998; Francqui fgn. vis. prof. Free U. Brussels, 1974; mem. pharmacology study sect. NIH, 1975-79, chmn., 1977-79; mem. research com. Tenn. Heart Assn., 1976-79; mem. adv. Bd. Advances in Cyclic Nucleotide Research. Mem. editl. bd. Jour. Biol. Chemistry, 1975-80, Jour. Cyclic Nucleotide Rsch., 1974-94, Circulation Rsch., 1980-86; contbr. sci. papers in field to profl. publs.; editor: Molecular Pharmacology, 1983-85; co-editor-in-chief The Pharmacological Basis of Therapeutics, 9th edit., 1996. Recipient H.B. Van Dyke award Columbia U., 1981. Mem. AAAS, Am. Soc. Pharmacology and Exptl. Therapeutics (pres. 1993-94), Am. Heart Assn. (rsch. com. 1979-84), Alpha Omega Alpha.

HARDMON, LADY, professional athlete; b. Sept. 12, 1970. Guard Utah Starzz, 1997-99, Sacramento Monarchs, 1999—. Named to All-SEC team, 1990, 92, SEC All-Tournament team, 1990, 92, Hon. Mention Kodak All-Am.; winner bronze medal World Univ. Games in Buffalo, 1993, gold medal, 1992; played in 1989 Jr. World Championship. Avocations: working out, speaking to young people at church. Office: Sacramento Monarchs Utah Starzz One Sports Pky Sacramento CA 95834*

HARDOUIN, BERNARD MICHAEL, III, fitness specialist; b. Dayton, Ohio, Feb. 10, 1972; s. Bernard Michael Jr. and Clara (Betancourt) H.; m. Susan Carole Eason, July 26, 1997. BS, U. So. Miss., 1994; MA, U. N.C., 1996. Fitness trainer U. So. Miss., Hattiesburg, 1990-94; phys. educator U. N.C., Chapel Hill, 1994-96; corp. fitness specialist Imperial Athletic Club, Durham, N.C., 1996; youth fitness dir. McLeod Regional Med. Ctr., Florence, S.C., 1996—. Author: Safari Slim and the Search for the Fat-Loss Secret, 1997. Home: 738 Arlington Cir Florence SC 29501-4667 Office: McLeod Health & Fitness Ctr 1945 W Palmetto St Florence SC 29501-3919

HARDRICK, MARIA DARSHELL, government official, tax examiner; b. Milw., Feb. 5, 1966; d. Dorotha G. Hardrick. BS, Wilberforce U., 1988. CPA, Ohio. Internat. tax examiner IRS, Cin., 1988—. Vol. Project Friendship. Mem. Nat. Assn. Black Accts., Black Profl. Assn. Baptist. Avocations: aerobics, tennis, reading, theatre. Home: 11963 Crossings Dr Cincinnati OH 45246 Office: IRS 550 Main St Cincinnati OH 45202

HARDS, RICHARD CHARLES, artist; b. Logan, UT, Aug. 18, 1961. BFA, Utah State U., 1985; MFA, U. Wis., Madison, 1989. Artist Carl Hammer Gallery, Chgo., 1993—, Lisa Sette Gallery, Scottsdale, Ariz., 1996—, Catharine Clark Gallery, San Francisco, 1998—. Home: 1951 S Canalport Ave Chicago IL 60616-1044

HARDWAY, JAMES EDWARD, vocational and rehabilitative specialist; b. Pueblo, Colo., Nov. 26, 1944; s. William Jeremiah and Margaret Ann (Rinker) H.; m. Mary Frances Walker, Sept. 9, 1967; children: Tina Marie, Catherine Ann, William James. BA, U. So. Colo., 1969; MS, U. Wis.-Stout, Menomonie, 1971; postgrad., U. Toledo, 1972—. Cert. vocat. evaluator, work adjustment specialist. Counselor Pueblo (Colo.) Diversified Industries, 1969-70; vocat. evaluator Penta County Vocat. Schs., Perrysburg, Ohio, 1971-82; dept. mgr. Magic City Enterprises, Cheyenne, Wyo., 1982-88; case mgr. Profl. Rehab. Mgmt., Cheyenne, 1989-91, regional mgr., 1992-94; pvt. practice vocational expert Cheyenne, 1994—; speaker State of Ohio Spl. Needs Conf., Ohio, 1972-80; cons. Wyo. State Tng. Sch., Lander, 1977. Pres. bd. dirs. Laramie County Community Action, Cheyenne; bd. dirs. Handicapped Employment Agy., Cheyenne, Wyo. Alzheimer's Assn. With U.S. Army, 1962-65. Fellow Am. Bd. Vocat. Experts; mem. Kiwanis (bd. dirs.). Home: 12309 White Eagle Rd Cheyenne WY 82009-8640

HARDWAY, WENDELL GARY, former college president; b. Bolair, W.Va., Mar. 5, 1927; s. Ressie Bruce and Elsie Clennen (Miller) H.; m. Hannah Lou Garrett, July 12, 1950. B.S., W.Va. U., 1949, M.S., 1953; Ph.D., Ohio State U., 1959. Tchr. Troy (W.Va.) High Sch., 1949-54; asst. prof. sci. Glenville (W.Va.) State Coll., 1954-57, assoc. prof. edn., 1959-61, prof., chmn. div. edn., dir. student teaching, 1961-66; pres. Bluefield (W.Va.) State Coll., 1966-73; pres. Fairmont (W.Va.) State Coll., 1973-88, ret., 1988; bd. dirs. One Valley Bank, Morgantown. Pres. United Way, Fairmont, 1976; mem. Glenville City Council, 1958-64; pres. W.Va. Intercollegiate Athletic Conf., 1977-78. Served with AUS, 1945-46. Named Man of Yr., Bluefield Jaycees, 1969, Disting. Pioneer, Glenville State Coll., 1985, Outstanding Alumnus, W.Va. U. Coll. Agr., 1987. Hardway Libr. at Bluefield State Coll. and Hardway Hall (adminstrn. bldg.) at Fairmont State Coll. named in his honor. Mem. Marion County C. of C. (prime min.), Ambassadors Club, Phi Delta Theta, Gamma Sigma Delta, Phi Delta Kappa, Kappa Delta Pi. Methodist. Home: 4 Bel Manor Dr Fairmont WV 26554-1206

HARDWICK, DAVID FRANCIS, pathologist; b. Vancouver, B.C., Can., Jan. 24, 1934; s. Walter H. W. and Iris L. (Hyndman) H.; m. Margaret M. Lang, Aug. 22, 1956; children: Margaret F., Heather I., David J. M.D., U. B.C., 1957. Intern Montreal (Que., Can.) Gen. Hosp., 1957-58; resident Vancouver Gen. Hosp., 1958-59, Children's Hosp., Los Angeles, 1959-62; research assoc. U. So. Calif., 1961-62; clin. instr. U. B.C., Vancouver, 1963-65; asst. prof. pathology U. B.C., 1965-69, assoc. prof., 1969-74, prof., 1974—, head dept. pathology, 1976-90, assoc. dean rsch. and planning, 1990-96; dir. labs. Children's Hosp., Vancouver, 1969-92, Vancouver Gen. Hosp., 1976-90; chmn. M.A.C., Children's Hosp., 1970-87; dir. interinstitutional planning U. B.C. Medicine, 1996—; mem. U. B.C. Senate, 1966-71. Author: Acid Base Balance and Blood Gas Studies, 1968, Intermediary Metabolism of Liver, 1971, Directing the Clinical Laboratory, 1990; contbr. numerous articles to profl. publs. Recipient Queen's Centennial medal Govt. Can., 1978, U. B.C. Faculty Citation Teaching award, 1987, Wallace Wilson Leadership award, 1990, William Boyd Lectureship award Canadian Assn. Path, 1994, Sydney Israels Founders award B.C. Rsch. Inst. Children and Family, 1997, Univ. medal for Outstanding Svc., U. B.C., 1997; Sydney Farber lectr., Soc. Ped. Path., 1998. Fellow Royal Coll. Physicians (Can.), Coll. Am. Pathologists; mem. Internat. Acad. Pathology (pres. 1996), Can. Med. Assn., B.C. Assn. Lab. Medicine, B.C. Med. Assn., N.Y. Acad. Sci., Soc. Pediat. Pathology, Internat. Acad. Pathology (Disting. Svc. award 1994), U.S. Acad. Pathology, Can. Assn. Pathology, Alpha Omega Alpha. Home: 727 W 23rd Ave, Vancouver, BC Canada V5Z 2A7 Office: U BC, Dept Pathology, 2211 Wesbrook Mall, Vancouver, BC Canada V6T 1W5

HARDWICK, ELIZABETH, author; b. Lexington, Ky., July 27, 1916; d. Eugene Allen and Mary (Ramsey) H.; m. Robert Lowell, July 28, 1949 (div. Oct. 1972); 1 child, Harriet. AB, U. Ky., 1938, MA, 1939; postgrad., Columbia U., 1939-41. Adj. assoc. prof. Barnard Coll. Author: (novels) The Ghostly Lover, 1945, The Simple Truth, 1955, Sleepless Nights, 1979, (essays) A View of My Own, 1962, Seduction and Betrayal, 1974, Bartleby in Manhattan, 1983, Sight Readings, 1998; editor: The Selected Letters of William James, 1960; adv. editor: N.Y. Rev. Books. Recipient George Jean Nathan award for dramatic criticism, 1966, gold medal for criticism Am. Acad. Arts and Letters, 1993; Guggenheim fellow, 1947. Mem. Am. Acad. and Inst. Arts and Letters, Acad. Arts and Scis. Home: 15 W 67th St New York NY 10023-6226

HARDWICK, JAMES CARLTON, JR., business and financial planner; b. Atlanta, Sept. 11, 1943; s. James Carlton and Agnes (Kelley) H.; B.A. in Econs., Davidson Coll., 1965; M.B.A. in Fin., Harvard U., 1970; m. Mary Gettys Robinson, Sept. 25, 1965; children—James Carlton, Benjamin Robinson. Cert. real estate broker; registered investment advisor; mgmt. acct. With R.J. Reynolds Industries, Inc., 1970-88, sr. fin. analyst, 1970-73, sr. systems analyst, 1973-75, mgr. corp. acctg. analysis, 1975-78, asst. treas. Aminoil, Houston, 1978-79, budget mgr., Winston-Salem, N.C., 1979-88; pres. Bent Tree Group, Inc., Winston-Salem, 1990—; procurement officer Wachovia Bank, 1989-90. Served with U.S. Army, 1966-68. Cert. in mgmt. acctg. Mem. Winston-Salem C. of C., Inst. Mgmt. Coun. for Entrepreneurial Devel., Fin. Entrepreneurial Network, Mensa. Democrat. Methodist. Clubs: Forsyth Country. Home: One Sheffield Pl Winston-Salem NC 27104 Office: 380 Knollwood St Ste 635 Winston Salem NC 27103-1870

HARDY, ASHTON RICHARD, lawyer; b. Gulfport, Miss., Aug. 31, 1935; s. Ashton Maurice and Alice (Baumbach) H.; m. Katherine Ketelsen, Sept. 4, 1959; children: Karin H. Wood, Katherine H. Foster. BBA, Tulane U., 1958, JD, 1962. Bar: La. 1962, FCC, 1976. Ptnr. Jones, Walker, Waechter, Poitevent, Carrere & Denegre, New Orleans, 1962-74, 76-82; gen. counsel FCC, Washington, 1974-76; ptnr. Fawer, Brian, Hardy, Zatzkis, New Orleans, 1982-86, Hardy & Popham, 1986-88, Walker, Bordelon, Hamlin, Theriot & Hardy, New Orleans, 1988-92, Hardy & Carey, New Orleans, 1992—; gen. counsel La. Assn. Broadcasters, 1976-86, Greater New Orleans Assn. Broadcasters, 1976—, La. Assn. Advt. Agys., 1982-86; lectr. in field; advance rep. to Pres. U.S., 1971-74. Bd. dirs. New Orleans Mission, 1989—, Met. Crime Commn. New Orleans, 1993—, vice-chmn., 1997—, United Christian Charities, 1993—. Lt. USN, 1958-60. Mem. La. Bar Assn. (del. ho. of dels. 1987-92), FCC Bar Assn., Nat. Religious Broadcasters (bd. dirs. S.W. chpt. 1994—), Christian Legal Soc., Metairie Country Club (pres. 1986), Comm Club. Home: 306 Cedar Dr Metairie LA 70005-3902 Office: Hardy & Carey Ste 300 110 Veterans Memorial Blvd Metairie LA 70005-3024

HARDY, BRIDGET MCCOLL, screenwriter; b. Laramie, Wyo., Oct. 2, 1959; d. Eugene Nicholas and Deborah Wells Hardy. BA cum laude with honors, Smith Coll., 1984; MA, Jackson Sch. Internat. Studies, 1993; cert. in lit. fiction, U. Wash. Ext., 1995. Founder, pres. Am. Beyond Lang. Edn., Tokyo, Seattle, 1986-91; freelance screenwriter Seattle, 1995—; Japan-Am. cross-cultural cons. Am. Beyond Lang. Edn., Tokyo, Seattle, 1984-92, design asst. lang. immersion camp, Seattle, 1990; various positions Microsoft, Redmond, Wash., 1995-96.; Vol. and hospitality chair Japan-Am. Soc., 1990—; orientation tchr. Youth for Understanding, Seattle, 1991; vol. and interpreter Internat. Children's Festival, Seattle, 1991, 92, 95; vol. Greenworks, Seattle, 1994—; youth team leader Youth Vol. Corps, Redmond, 1994. Recipient Metro Bus Poetry award Seattle Metro, 1996; Earthwatch scholar, 1982. Avocations: scuba diving, Aikido, travel, gardening, adventure seeking.

HARDY, CHARLES LEACH, federal judge; b. L.A., Jan. 24, 1919; s. Charles Little and Dorothy (Leach) H.; m. Jean McRae, Jan. 26, 1947; children: Charles M., Caroline, Catherine, John L. Julianne, Eileen, Sterling A., Steven W., Janette. BS, U. Ariz., 1947, LLB, 1950. Bar: Ariz. 1949. Pvt. practice Phoenix, 1949-66; dep. county atty. Maricopa County, Ariz., 1952-55; asst. atty. gen. State of Ariz., 1956-59; judge Ariz. Superior Ct., 1966-80; U.S. dist. judge Ariz. Dist., Phoenix, 1980—; now sr. judge. Pres. Young Democratic Clubs Ariz., 1956-57, nat. committeeman, 1957-58; chmn. Maricopa County Dem. Cen. Com., 1958-59; mem. Ariz. Bd. Crippled Children's Services, 1965. Served with F.A. AUS, 1941-45. Decorated Bronze Star. Mem. ABA, Am. Judicature Soc., State Bar Ariz., Maricopa County Bar Assn. Mem. LDS Ch. Office: US Dist Ct US Courthouse & Fed Bldg Rm 7025 3017 US Courthouse3 Phoenix AZ 85025-0005*

HARDY, CLARENCE EARL, JR., human resources executive; b. Edenton, N.C., July 2, 1944; m. Mae A. Brewer; children: Clarence, Melva. BA in Polit. Sci. and Econs., N.C. Ctrl. U., 1967; MPA in Pub. Adminstrn., Syracuse U., 1969; diploma in sr. mgrs. in govt. program, Harvard U., 1990. Pers. mgmt. analyst Atomic Energy Commn., 1971-73; pers. officer, mgmt. analyst Atomic Energy Commn. Energy Rsch. and Devel. Adminstrn., 1973-75, sr. mgmt. analyst, program evaluation officer, 1975-76, chief hqrs. pers. ops. br., 1976-77; pers. officer Fed. Energy Regulatory Commn., 1978; chief pers. mgmt. svcs. Dept. Energy Hqrs., 1977-78, dep. dir. hqrs. pers. ops. divsn., 1978-79; chief pers. divsn. Nat. Bur. Standards, 1979; dir. pers. mgmt. EPA, 1979-88, dep. dir. Office of Human Resources Mgmt., 1988-97; dir. Office Cooperative Environ. Mgmt., 1997—; prof. George Mason U., 1998—. N.C. Ctrl U. Polit. Sci. scholar, 1966, 67; Maxwell fellow, 1968, 69, Congl. fellow Brookings Instn., 1996. Mem. Internat. Pers. Mgmt. Assn., Internat. Platform Assn., Am. Soc. Pub. Adminstrn., Am. Mgmt. Assn., Am. Judicature Soc., Acad. Polit. and Social Sci., Am. Polit. Sci. Assn., World Future Soc., Acad. Mgmt., Nat. Assn. Environ. Profls.

HARDY, DEBORAH WELLES, history educator; b. Milw., Nov. 2, 1927; d. Frank M. and Doris (Berger) Hursley; widowed; children: Scott, Jonathan, Bridget. Student, Swarthmore Coll., 1945-47; BA, Stanford U., 1949; MA, U. Calif., 1950; PhD, U. Wash., 1968. TV writer, 1964-72; mem. faculty U. Wyo., Laramie, 1967-93, prof. history, 1978-93, head dept., 1980-85, prof.

emeritus, 1993—; free-lance TV writer, 1964-74; mem. Wyo. Council Humanities, 1972-76. Author: Petr. Tkachev: The Critic as Jacobin, 1977, Wyoming University: The First Hundred Years, 1986, Land and Freedom: The Origins of Russian Terrorism, 1987; also articles. Grantee Social Sci. Research Council, summer 1971, Am. Philos. Soc., 1976; Internat. Research and Exchanges Bd. scholar, 1987. Mem. Am. Hist. Assn., Am. Assn. Advancement of Slavic Studies, Western Social Sci. Assn., Western Slavic Assn., Phi Beta Kappa. Home: 2450 E Park Ave Laramie WY 82070-4858 Office: U Wyo History Dept Laramie WY 82071

HARDY, DORCAS RUTH, business and government relations executive; b. Newark, N.J., July 18, 1946; d. C. Colburn and Ruth (Hart) H.; m. Samuel V. Spagnolo. B.A., Conn. Coll., 1964-68; M.B.A., Pepperdine U., 1976. Legis. rsch. asst. U.S. Senator Clifford P. Case, Washington, 1970; spl. asst. White House Conf. Children and Youth, Washington, 1970-71; exec. dir. Health Svcs. Industry Commn., Cost of Living Coun., Washington, 1971-73; asst. sec. Calif. Dept. Health, Sacramento, 1973-74; assoc. dir. U. So. Calif. Ctr. Health Svcs. Rsch., 1974-81; asst. sec. human devel. svcs. HHS, Washington, 1981-86; commr. Social Security Washington, DC, 1986-89; pres. Dorcas R. Hardy & Assocs., Spotsylvania, Va., 1989—; chmn. bd. dirs., and CEO Work Recovery, Inc., Tucson, 1996-98; bd. dirs. First Coast Svc. Options, Inc., Options Clearing Corp., Wright Investors Svc. Managed Funds. Author: Social Insecurity: The Crisis in America's Social Security System and How to Plan Now for Your Own Financial Survival, 1992. Mem. Girl Scouts USA; bd. dirs. Com. on Developing Am. Capitalism; former chmn. Pres.'s Task Force on Legal Equity for Women. Office: Washington Metro Office 11407 Stonewall Jackson Dr Spotsylvania VA 22553-4608

HARDY, GORDON ALFRED, music educator, music school president; b. Hudson, Ind., Aug. 18, 1918; s. Carl Alfred and Gayle (Pike) H.; m. Lillian Studebaker, May 19, 1945; children—John Studebaker, Christopher Bartlett, Susan, Jeffrey Pike. B.A., B.Mus., U. Mich., 1941, M.Mus., 1946; B.S., Juilliard Sch. Music, 1952. Teaching fellow Juilliard Sch. Music, 1952-53, teaching asst., 1953-54, mem. faculty lit. and materials of music dept., 1954—, asso. dean, 1963-69, dean students, 1970-76; dean Aspen (Colo.) Music Sch., 1963-66, exec. v.p., 1966-75, pres., 1976-89, pres. emeritus, 1990—. Author: (with Arnold Fish) Music Literature-A Workbook for Analysis, vol. I, Homophony, 1963, vol. II, Polyphony, 1966. Bd. dirs. Juilliard Repertory Project, 1968, Juilliard Inst. Spl. Studies, 1969. Served to lt. USNR, 1942-45. Mem. Theta Chi. Home: 149 E 73rd St New York NY 10021-3592

HARDY, HARVEY LOUCHARD, lawyer; b. Dallas, Dec. 2, 1914; s. Nat L. and Winifred H. (Fouraker) H.; m. Edna Vivian Bedell, Feb. 14, 1948; children: Victoria Elizabeth Hardy Pursch, Alice Anne Hardy Gannon. Bar: Tex. 1936, U.S. Dist. Ct. (so. and we. dists.) Tex. 1946, U.S. Ct. Appeals (5th cir.) 1946, U.S. Supreme Ct. 1949. First asst. dist. atty. Bexar County, San Antonio, 1947-50, acting dist. atty., 1950-51; city atty., San Antonio, 1952-53, Castle Hills, Tex., 1959-96, Leon Valley, Tex., 1967-96, Roma, Tex., 1973-96, Helotes, Tex., 1984-96, Fair Oaks Ranch, Tex. 1986-96; legal advisor bd. trustees Firemen and Policemen's Pension Fund of San Antonio, 1956-96; of counsel Hardy Jacobson Gazda & Jacobson, San Antonio, 1996—; legal advisor Grey Forest Utilities, 1986-96. Author: A Lifetime at the Bar: A Lawyer's Memoir. Served to 1st lt. inf. U.S. Army, 1941-45. Decorated Bronze Star with cluster. Fellow Tex. Bar Found.; mem. Nat. Inst. Mcpl. Legal Officers, Tex. Bar Assn., San Antonio Bar Found., Tex. Assn. City Attys., San Antonio Bar Assn. Methodist. Home: 215 Atwater Dr San Antonio TX 78213-3321

HARDY, HUGH, architect; b. Spain, July 26, 1932; s. Gelston Hardy and Barbara Hardy LaVenture; m. Tiziana Spadea, Jan. 29, 1966; children: Sebastian, Penelope. B.Arch., Princeton U., 1954, M.F.A. in Architecture, 1956. Archtl. asst. to Jo Mielziner, N.Y.C., 1958-62; founder Hugh Hardy & Assocs., N.Y.C., 1962-67; ptnr. Hardy Holzman Pfeiffer Assocs., N.Y.C. and L.A., 1967—; Davenport vis. prof. archtl. design Yale U., 1976; Saarinen vis. prof. Yale U., 1987; past chmn. Design Arts Adv. Panel Nat. Endowment for the Arts; apptd. to Nat. Council on the Arts by Pres. of U.S., 1992; cons., lectr. in field. Designer: Orchestra Hall, Mpls., 1974, Cooper-Hewitt Mus., N.Y.C., 1976, St. Louis Art Mus., 1977, The Joyce Theater, N.Y.C., 1982, Rizzoli Bookstore, N.Y.C., New Victory Theater, 1995, Bryant Park Restaurant, 1995, Windows in the World, 1996, New Amsterdam Theater, 1997. Bd. dirs. Isamu Noguchi Found., Mcpl. Art Soc. N.Y., N.Y.C., 1976—, v.p., 1981—, lifetime dir., 1992—; bd. mem. N.Y.C. Hist. House Trust, 1989—. Recipient D'Amato prize Princeton U., 1954, Brunner prize in architecture Nat. Inst. Arts and Letters, 1974, Benjamin West Clinedinst medal Artists' Fellowship Inc., 1988. Fellow AIA (N.Y. chpt. medal of honor 1978, Archtl. Firm award 1981, several honor awards); mem. Archtl. League N.Y. (v.p. for architecture 1977-81, bd. dirs. 1987—), Nat. Acad. Design (assoc.), Am. Acad. Arts and Letters, Century Assn. Office: Hardy Holzman Pfeiffer Assocs 902 Broadway Fl 19 New York NY 10010-6082*

HARDY, JAMES CHESTER, speech pathologist, educator; b. Salina, Kans., Apr. 14, 1930; s. James Chester and Mary Ellen (Baker) H.; m. Dolores Nadine McFarland, May 23, 1953 (div. Dec. 1988); children: Allan James, Charles Thomas, Matthew Hurt. BS, N.E. Mo. State U., 1951; MA, U. Iowa, 1957, PhD, 1962. Speech correctionist Pub. Schs., Poplar Bluff, Mo., 1954-55; grad. asst. dept. speech pathology & audiology U. Iowa, Iowa City, 1955-56, grad. asst. U. Hosp. Sch., 1956, speech therapist, 1956-57, supr. speech and hearing dept. U. Hosp. Sch., 1967, asst. prof. dept. speech pathology and audiology, 1961-64, assoc. prof., 1964-69, assoc. prof. dept. pediatrics, 1966-69, prof. dept. speech pathology and audiology, 1969-97, prof. dept. pediatrics, 1969-97, dir. speech and hearing clinic, 1972-79, dir. profl. svcs. div. devel. disabilities, dept. pediatrics, 1979-97, dir. Iowa program for assistive tech., 1990-97, ret., 1997; cons. Iowa Newborn Hearing Evaluation Referral Project, 1998, Iowa Sch., 1999—. Author: Cerebral Palsy: Remediation of Communication Problems, 1983; contbr. articles to profl. jours., chpts. to textbooks. Bd. dirs. Optimist Club of Iowa City, 1966-67, pres., 1966-67; scout master Boy Scouts Am., Iowa City, 1973-78, chmn., troop com., 1977-78. With U.S. Army, 1952-54. Fellow Am. Acad. for Cerebral Palsy and Devel. Medicine, Am. Speech-Language-Hearing Assn.; mem. Iowa Speech and Hearing Assn. (pres. 1963, Louis DiCarlo award 1987).

HARDY, JANE ELIZABETH, communications educator; b. Fenelon Falls, Ont., Can., Mar. 27, 1930; came to U.S., 1956, naturalized, 1976; d. Charles Edward and Augusta Miriam (Lang) Little; m. Ernest E. Hardy, Sept. 3, 1955; children: Edward Harold, Robert Ernest. BS with distinction, Cornell U., 1953. Garden editor and writer Can. Homes Mag., Maclean-Hunter Pub. Co., Ltd., Toronto, Ont., 1954-55, 56-62; contbg. editor Can. Homes, Southam Pub. Co., Toronto, Ont., 1962-66; instr. Cornell U., 1966-73, sr. lectr. in comm., 1979-96; mem. Cornell U. Provost's Adv. Com. on Status of Women, 1977-81; lectr., condr. workshops on writing. Author: Writing for Practical Purposes, 1996; editor pro-tem Cornell Plantations Quar., 1981-82; author numerous publs. including brochures, slide set scripts, contbr. numerous articles in mags. Chmn. bd. dirs. Matrix Found., 1998—. Mem. Women in Comms. Inc. (faculty advisor 1977-95, liaison 1986-94, chair, adv.mem. 1988-90), Assn. for Women in Comms. (nat. bd. dirs. 1997—), Royal Hort. Soc., Ithaca Garden Club, Ithaca Women's Club, Pi Alpha Xi, Phi Kappa Phi, Alpha Omicron Pi. Home: 215 Enfield Falls Rd Ithaca NY 14850-8797

HARDY, JOHN CHRISTOPHER, physicist, educator; b. Montreal, Que., Can., July 10, 1941; s. Noel Woodburn and Ethel May (Collins) H.; m. Lynn Helen Frederick, June 3, 1964 (div.); children: Ericka, Kirsten, Bruce, Alana; m. June Dennie, July 5, 1997. BSc, McGill U., Montreal, 1961, MSc, 1963, PhD (D.W. Ambridge prize 1965), 1965. NRC Can. postdoctoral fellow Oxford (Eng.) Nuc. Physics Lab., 1965-67; Miller rsch. fellow Lawrence Radiation Lab., Berkeley, Calif., 1967-69, staff physicist, 1969-70; assoc. rsch. officer Atomic Energy Can. Ltd., Chalk River, Ont., 1970-74, sr. rsch. officer, 1975-83, head nuc. physics br., 1983-86, asst. v.p., 1986-89, dir. TASCC divsn., 1989-97; prof. physics Tex. A&M U., College Station, 1997—; sci. assoc. CERN, Geneva, 1976-77. Contbr. articles to profl. jours. and books; editor North Renfrew Times, 1972-97; mem. editl. bd. Nuc. Physics News Internat., 1995-97, Phys. Rev. C. Jour., 1980-82, 95-97. Chmn. bd. dirs. Deep River Sci. Acad., 1986-97, trustee 1997—; mem. adv. bd. TRIUMF, 1992-98; mem. program adv. coms. Oak Ridge Nat. Lab., UNISOR, 1979-85, Lawrence Berkeley Lab., Super HILAC, 1983-86, Oak Ridge Nat. Lab., HHIRL, 1991-92, Nat. Superconducting Cyclotron Lab., 1990-93, Lawrence Berkeley Lab., Cyclotron, 1994-99, Oak Ridge Nat. Lab., HRIBF, 1999—. Fellow Royal Soc. Can. (Rutherford medal in physics 1981, v.p. Acad. III 1992-95, chmn. fundraising com. 1994-97), Am. Phys. Soc.; mem. Can. Assn. Physicists (Herzberg medal 1976). Office: Cyclotron Inst Tex A&M U College Station TX 77843

HARDY, JOHN EDWARD, English language educator, author; b. Baton Rouge, Apr. 3, 1922; s. Roger Barlow and Mary (McCoy) H.; m. Marie Elam, Dec. 30, 1942 (div.); children: Margot (Mrs. Timm Ferguson), Leonore (Mrs. David Dvorkin), Catherine (Mrs. Didier Pouligny), Laura, Anne (Mrs. George Biswell), Eve (Mrs. Daryl Joiner); m. Willene Schaefer, June 25, 1969. B.A., La. State U., 1944; M.A., State U. Iowa, 1946; Ph.D., Johns Hopkins U., 1956. Mem. English faculties U. Detroit, 1945-46, Yale U., 1946-48, U. Okla., 1948-52, Johns Hopkins U., 1952-54; mem. faculty U. Notre Dame, 1954-66, prof. English, 1964-66, mem. acad. council, 1963-66, grad. council, 1963-66; prof. English, chmn. dept. U. South Ala., 1966-69; prof. English U. Colo., Boulder, 1969-70; prof. English, chmn. dept. U. Mo., St. Louis, 1970-72; dir. grad. studies in English U. Ill.-Chgo., 1972-75, prof. English, 1972-92; prof. emeritus, 1992—; head dept. English U. Ill.-Chgo., 1984-89, mem. grad. coll. exec. com., 1974-76, 81-82. Author: (with Cleanth Brooks) Poems of Mr. John Milton, 1951, The Curious Frame, 1962, Man in the Modern Novel, 1964, Katherine Anne Porter, 1973, Certain Poems, 1958, The Fiction of Walker Percy, 1987; Editor: The Modern Talent, 1964, (with Seymour L. Gross) Images of the Negro in American Literature, 1966. Fulbright prof. Am. lit. U. Munich, Germany, 1959-61; Ford Faculty Study fellow, 1952-53; Rockefeller fellow poetry, 1954; fellow Inst. for Humanities U. Ill. Chgo., 1989-90. Mem. MLA, Phi Beta Kappa. Home: 6033 Riverbend Lakes Dr Baton Rouge LA 70820-5050

HARDY, JOSEPH A., SR., wholesale distribution executive; b. 1923. Retail jeweler Hardy & Hayes Corp., Pitts., 1946-56; founder Eighty Four Cash & Carry Inc., 1956-89; pres., CEO Eighty Four Associates Inc., Eighty Four, Pa., 1989—, chmn., 1993—. With U.S. Army, 1942-46. Office: 84 Lumber Co Rt 519 Eighty Four PA 15330*

HARDY, LEE PATRICK, humanities educator; b. Ventura, Calif., May 27, 1950; s. Jess Earle and Anne Leeds Hardy; m. Judith Claire Knoops, June 6, 1976; children: Katrina, Andrew, Ian, Grace. BA, Trinity Christian Coll., Palos Heights, Ill., 1976; MA, Duquesne U., 1979, PhD, 1987; MA, U. Pitts., 1981. Instr. Calvin Coll., Grand Rapids, Mich., 1981-85, from asst. prof. to assoc. prof., 1985-89, prof. philosophy, 1989—; sr. fellow Lilly Fellows Program, Valparaiso, Ind., 1992-93. Author: Fabric of This World, 1990; editor: Phenomenology of Natural Science, 1992; translator: Husserl's Transcendental Phenomenology, 1993, The Idea of Phenomenology, 1999. Mem. Am. Philos. Assn., Soc. Christian Philosophers. Office: Calvin Coll Dept Philosophy 3201 Burton St SE Grand Rapids MI 49546-4388

HARDY, LINDA LEA STERLOCK, media specialist; b. Balt., Aug. 15, 1947; d. George Allen and Dorothy Lea (Briggs) Sterlock; m. John Edward Hardy III, Apr. 25, 1970; 1 child, Roger Wayne. BA in History, N.C. Wesleyan Coll., 1969; MEd in History, East Carolina U., 1972, MLS, 1990. Cert. tchr., N.C. History tchr. Halifax (N.C.) County Schs., 1972-83, learning lab tchr., 1983-91, computer lab tchr., 1990-95; media specialist Nash-Rocky Mount (N.C.) Schs., 1995—; part-time history instr. Nash C.C., 1993. Mem. AAUW (pres. Rocky Mount br. 1993-95, sec. 1997-99, Named Gift award 1987), Bus. and Profl. Women (pres. Rocky Mount chpt. 1986-87, 90-91, treas. 1992-97, sec.-treas. dist X 1989-90, state election chmn. 1989-90, 93-95, state credentials chmn. 1997-98, sec.-treas. dist. 6 1997-98, Girl Friday award 1981, 98, Woman of Yr. award 1986, 97, state found. fin. chair 1996-97), Nat. Assn. Educators, N.C. Assn. Educators, Nash/Rocky Mount Assn. Educators (faculty rep. 1995—), Phi Delta Kappa, Pi Gamma Mu. Republican. Methodist. Avocations: reading, travel, needlepoint, computers. Office: Red Oak Middle School 3170 Red Oak Battleboro Rd Battleboro NC 27809

HARDY, LOIS LYNN, educational training company executive; b. Seattle, Aug. 20, 1928; d. Stanley Milton and Helen Berniece (Conner) Croonquist; m. John Weston Hardy, July 29, 1951 (div. 1974); children: Sarah Lynn, Laura Lynn; m. Joseph Freeman Smith, Jr., Apr. 18, 1981. BA, Stanford U., 1950, MA, 1952; postgrad., U. Calif., Berkeley, 1957-78, U. San Francisco, 1978-81. Cert. life secondary tchr., life counselor, adminstr., Calif.; lic. career and ednl. counselor, Calif. Tchr., counselor Eastside Union High Sch. Dist., San Jose, Calif., 1951-55; dir. Lois Lynn Hardy Music Studio, Danville, Calif., 1955-69; high sch. tchr. San Ramon Unified Sch. Dist., Danville, 1969-71, counselor, 1971-83; dir. Growth Dynamics Inst., Alamo, Calif., 1976—; instr. Fresno (Calif.) Pacific Coll., 1976-79, Dominican Coll., San Rafael, Calif., 1979—; cons., trainer Personal Dynamics Inst., Mpls., 1976—, Performax Internat., Mpls., 1979—, San Jose Unified Sch. Dist., 1986-86, Novato (Calif.) Unified Sch. Dist., 1985-86, IBM, San Francisco, 1984, corp. and ednl. cons., 1951—. Author: How To Study in High School, 1952, 3d edit., 1973; (with B. Santa) How To Use the Library, 1954; How To Learn Faster and Succeed: A How to Study Workbook For Grades 1-14, 1982, rev., 1985; author various seminars; contbr. numerous articles to profl. jours. Choir dir., organist Community Presbyn. Ch., Danville, 1966-68, elder, 1974-75; speaker to numerous orgns., 1955—. Named Musician of Yr., Contra Costa County, 1978, Counselor of Yr., No. Calif. Personnel and Guidance Assn., 1980; Olive S. Lathrop scholar, 1948, AAUW scholar, 1950; recipient Colonial Dames prize in Am. History, 1950. Mem. Am. Assn. Counseling and Devel., Calif. Assn. Counseling and Devel., Calif. Tchrs. Assn., Calif. Career Guidance Assn., Nat. Speakers Assn., Am. Guild Organists, Stanford U. Alumni Assn., Calif. Assn. for the Gifted, Delta Zeta. Democrat. Presbyterian. Avocations: writing, music, art, building houses. Office: Growth Dynamics Inst PO Box 1053 Alamo CA 94507-7053

HARDY, MICHAEL C., performing arts administrator; b. Durham, N.C., July 14, 1945; s. William Marion Hardy and Eloise Frances (Carrington) Schipke; children: Miranda, Christopher. AB, Duke U., 1966; MA, U. N.C., 1968; PhD, U. Mich., 1971. Gen. mgr. drama dept. East Carolina U., 1971-73; prodr. Krannert Ctr. Performing Arts at U. Ill., 1973-79, dir., 1979-83; pres., CEO Snug Harbor Cultural Ctr., Inc., N.Y.C., 1983-88; ind. cons., 1988-91; exec. dir. Internat. Soc. for the Performing Arts, Grand Rapids, Mich., 1991-98; pres. Ky. Ctr. for the Arts, Louisville, 1998—; cons. dir. Coll. Fine Arts Performing Arts Complex U. Tex., Austin, 1978-79. Stage dir., prodr. for theatre and opera productions including The Real Inspector Hound, La Boheme, Three Penny Opera, Carmen, Dames at Sea, Ten Little Indians, Hay Fever, Kiss Me Kate, Much Ado About Nothing, Dark of the Moon, La Ronde; contbr. articles to profl. jours. Bd. dirs. St. Vincent's Hosp., S.I., N.Y., 1985-88; with N.Y. Cultural Inst. Group, 1984-88; CIG chair Mayor Ed Koch's Commn. Cultural Affairs, N.Y.C., 1987-88. Recipient Carolina Playmaker's Mask award U. N.C., 1968, Commendation for Achievement award N.Y. State Legis., 1988, Dept. Parks and Recreation citation N.Y.C., 1988. Mem. Am. Soc. Assn. Execs. Office: Ky Ctr for the Arts 501 W Main St Ste 1 Louisville KY 40202-2989*

HARDY, MICHAEL LYNN, lawyer; b. St. Louis, Aug. 28, 1947; s. William Frost and Ruth (Shea) H.; m. Martha Bond, Sept. 2, 1972; children: Brian M., Kevin S. AB, John Carroll U., 1969; JD, U. Mich., 1972. Bar: Ohio 1972. Assoc. Guren, Merritt, et al, Cleve., 1972-77, ptnr., 1977-84; ptnr. Thompson, Hine & Flory, LLP, Cleve., 1984—. Editor-in-chief Ohio Environ. Monthly, 1989-94, Ohio Environ. Law, 1992; bd. advisors Harvard Environ. Law Rev., 1976-78, The Environ. Counselor, 1988—. Capt. U.S. Army, 1969-74. Mem. ABA (nat. resources sect.), Ohio State Bar Assn. (sec. environ. law com. 1983-84, vice-chmn. 1984-86, chmn. 1987-91), Def. Rsch. Inst. (chmn. industrywide litig. com. 1989-91), Canterbury Golf Club. Home: 30649 Summit Ln Cleveland OH 44124-5836 Office: Thompson Hine & Flory LLP 3900 Key Ctr 127 Public Sq Cleveland OH 44114-1216*

HARDY, RALPH W. F., biochemist, biotechnology executive; b. Lindsay, Ont., Can., July 27, 1934; s. Wilbur and Elsie H.; m. Jacqueline M. Thayer, Dec. 26, 1954; children: Steven, Chris, Barbara, Ralph (dec.), Jon. BSA, U. Toronto, 1956; MS, U. Wis.-Madison, 1958, PhD, 1959; DSc (hon.), U. Guelph, 1997. Asst. prof. U. Guelph, Ont., Can., 1960-63; research biochemist DuPont deNemours & Co., Wilmington, Del., 1963-67, research supr., 1967-74, assoc. dir., 1974-79, dir. life scis., 1979-84; pres. Bio Technica Internat., Inc., Peoria, Ill., 1984-86; pres., CEO Boyce Thompson Inst., Inc., Ithaca, N.Y., 1986-95; dep. chmn. Bio Technica Internat., Inc., 1986-90, cons., bd. dirs., 1990-99; pres. Nat. Agrl. Biotech. Coun., Ithaca, N.Y., 1996—; mem. exec. com. bd. agr. NRC, 1982-88, mem. commn. life scis., 1984-90, bd. biology, 1984-90, com. on biotech, 1988-95, chmn. com. 1993-94, bd. sci. technol. internat. devel., 1990-93, chmn. com. on biol. control, 1992-95, chmn. com. on biol. nitrogen fixation, 1992-94, chmn. com. on natural products, 1996-97; mem. com. genetic experimentation Internat. Coun. Sci. Union, 1981-95; chmn., founder Nat. Agrl. Biotech. coun., 1988-93; mem. sci. adv. com. U.S. Dept. Energy, 1991-95; mem. alt. agr. rsch. comml. bd. USDA, 1992-96, mem. and corp. sec. alt. agrl. rsch. comml. corp., 1996—; mem. Can. reallocations com. NSERC, 1997-98; mem. Can. Found. for Innovation, 1998—. Author: Nitrogen Fixation, 1975, A Treatise on Dinitrogen Fixation, 3 vols., 1977-79; contbr. over 150 articles to sci. jours. Mem. biotech. exec. bd. Cornell U., 1986-95, adv. coun. Vet. Coll., 1989-96; mem. gov. bd. Cornell Ctr. for Environment, 1991-95. Recipient Gov. Gen.'s Silver medal, 1956, Sterling Henricks award 1986; WARF fellow, 1956-58; DuPont fellow, 1958-59. Mem. Indsl. Biotech. Assn. (bd. dirs. 1986-89), Agr. Rsch. Inst. (bd. govs. 1988-91), Am. Chem. Soc. (exec. com. biol. chemistry divsn. 1978-81, Del. award 1969), Am. Soc. Biol. Chemists and Molecular Biologists, Am. Soc. Plant Physiology (exec. com., treas. 1974-77), Am. Soc. Agronomy, Am. Soc. Microbiology. Episcopalian.

HARDY, RICHARD EARL, rehabilitation counseling educator, clinical psychologist; b. Victoria, Va., Oct. 11, 1938; s. Clifford E. and Louise (Hamilton) H.; 1 son, Jason Elliott. BS, Va. Poly. Inst. and State U., 1960, MS, 1962, EdD, 1966. Lic. clin. psychologist Va.; cert. cons. trainer Am. Soc. Clin. Hypnosis. Rehab. counselor State of Va., Richmond, 1961-63; rehab. advisor HHS, Washington, 1964-66; chief psychologist S.C. Dept. Rehab., Columbia, 1966-68; prof. chmn. dept. rehab. counseling Med. Coll. Va., Richmond, 1968-96; chmn., prof. emeritus Med. Coll. Va., 1996—; former bd. mem. S.C. State Bd. Psychology; internat. cons. to numerous countries including Turkey, Iraq, Peru, Uruguay, South Africa, Brazil, Thailand. Author, editor: International Rehabilitation: Approaches and Programs, Hemingway: A Psychological Portrait, 1988, Gestalt Psychotherapy, 1991, Hispaniola Episode: A Mental Health Allegory, 1992, (with J.G. Cull) The Brass Chalice: Drug Prevention Stories and Information for Children and Youth, 1994, Rehabilitation Counseling in the Rehabilitation Process, 1999, numerous others. Recipient Nat. award Nat. Rehab. Assn., 1976; recipient Nat. award Am. Assn. Workers for Blind, 1976, Outstanding Grad. award Med. Coll. Va./Va. Commonwealth U., Dept. Rehab. Counseling, 1997, Richard E. Hardy endowed scholarship Med. Coll. Va., 1998. Fellow APA, Assn. Allied & Preventive Psychology; mem. Am. Assn. Vol. Action Scholars, Phi Kappa Phi. Office: Va Commonwealth U 921 W Franklin St Richmond VA 23284-9007

HARDY, THOMAS AUSTIN, sculptor; b. Redmond, Oreg., Nov. 30, 1921; s. Orlando Buell and Marie Jane (Austin) H. BS, U. Oreg., 1942, MFA, 1952. Lectr. U. Calif., Berkeley, 1956-58; assoc. prof. sculpture Tulane Univ., New Orleans, 1958-59; artist-in-residence Reed Coll., Portland, Oreg., 1959-61; prof. sculpture Univ. Wyo., Laramie, 1975-76. One man shows include De Young Mus., San Francisco, 1957, Oakland (Calif.) Art Mus., 1958, Pensacola (Fla.) Art Center, 1958, Columbia U., 1959, Seattle Art Mus., 1954, Stanford U. Gallery, 1955, group shows include, Met. Mus., N.Y.C., 1952, Am. Mus. Natural History, 1958, Pa. Acad., Phila., 1958, Mus. Modern Art, N.Y.C., 1959; represented in permanent collections Whitney Mus. Am. Art, N.Y.C., Seattle Art Mus., Portland (Oreg.) Art Mus., Lloyd Center, Portland, Hilton Hotel, Portland, Chandler Meml. Pavilion, Los Angeles, Fed. Bldg., Juneau, Alaska, Western Forestry Center, Portland, Civic Center, Salem, U. Calif., Berkeley, Clackamas Town Center, Portland, Seattle Center, High Desert Mus., Bend, Oreg., Santa Barbara (Calif.) Art Mus., Willamette U., Salem, Oreg., Oreg. Hist. Soc., Portland, Tuality Hosp., Hillsboro, Oreg., Umpqua Community Coll., Oreg., Franklin Delano Roosevelt Meml., Washington, D.C. Bd. govs. Pacific Northwest Coll. Art. Recipient Disting. service award U. Oreg., 1966, Gov.'s award Oreg. Art Commn., 1986, Webfoot award U. Oreg. Alumni Assn., 1986. Mem. Portland Art Assn., Audubon Soc., Am. Mus. Natural History, Kappa Sigma. Democrat. Avocation: dealer in fine books. Home: #203 1530 SW Harrison St Apt 203 Portland OR 97201-2585 Office: Kraushaar Galleries 724 5th Ave New York NY 10019-4106*

HARDY, THOMAS CRESSON, insurance company executive; b. Hoisington, Kans., 1942; s. C.C. and Delia Hardy; children—Jay C., Glenn W. B.A., U. Kans., 1963; M.B.A., Wharton Sch., U. Pa., 1965. CLU, CPCU, FLMI. With Exxon Corp., N.Y.C., 1965-69; treas. Keene Corp., N.Y.C., 1969-73; exec. v.p. fin. Fidelity Union Life Ins. Co., Dallas, 1973-79; (co. acquired by Allianz of Am. 1979); v.p. Allianz of Am.; pres. Allianz Investment Corp., Dallas, 1979-82; pres., chief exec. officer Gt. Am. Res. Ins. Co., 1983-88; exec. v.p., COO Provident Life & Accident Ins. Co., Chattanooga, 1988-94; pres., CEO, bd. dirs. Loewen Life Ins. Group, 1997—, Mayflower Nat. Life Ins. Co.; chmn. bd. dirs. Security Instnl. Co.; pres., CEO, bd. dirs. Nat. Capitol Life. Bd. dirs., pres. Chattanooga Symphony & Opera Assn., 1989-97; bd. dirs. exec. com. Chattanooga Allied Arts, 1992-97; mem. U. Kans. Bus. Sch. Adv. Bd.; bd. visitors Berry Coll., 1992-99. Mem. Fin. Execs. Inst. (chpt. pres., nat. bd. dirs.). Home: 920 State St New Orleans LA 70118-5909

HARDY, TOM CHARLES, JR., medical equipment company; b. Galveston, Tex., Apr. 19, 1945; s. Tom Charles Sr. and Joyce (Pounds) H.; m. Penelope Berry; children: Kris, Michael. BA, Austin Coll., 1967; MBA in Fin., U. Tex., 1970. CPA, Tenn., Tex.; cert. mgmt. acctg. Acct., analyst Shell Oil Co., Houston, 1970-73; fin. analyst Gen. Portland Inc., Dallas, 1973-74; cost acctg. mgr. Gen. Portland Inc., Tampa, Fla., 1974-75; div. acctg. mgr. Gen. Portland Inc., Chattanooga, 1975-77; div. contr. Gen. Portland Inc., Wichita, Kans., 1978-82; mgr. corp. planning Gen. Portland Inc., Dallas, 1982-83, treas., 1983-85; corp. sec. Lafarge Corp., Dallas, 1985-88; v.p., treas., chief fin. officer United Medicorp, Inc., Dallas, 1989-91; v.p., CFO, treas., sec. Healthtronix Med. Equipment, Inc., Dallas, 1991—. Mem. Fin. Execs. Inst., Tex. Soc. CPAs. Avocations: tennis, folk guitar. Office: Healthtronix Med Equipment Inc 811 E Plano Pkwy Ste 111 Plano TX 75074-6747

HARDY, WALTER NEWBOLD, physics educator, researcher; b. Vancouver, B.C., Mar. 25, 1940; s. Walter Thomas and Julia Marguerite (Mulroy) H.; m. Sheila Lorraine Hughes, July 10, 1959; children: Kevin James, Steven Wayne. BSc in Math and Physics with honors, U. B.C., 1961; PhD in Physics, Univ. B.C., 1965. Postdoctoral fellow Centre d'Etudes Nucleaires de Saclay, France, 1964-66; mem. tech. staff N.Am. Rockwell, Thousand Oaks, Calif., 1966-71; assoc. prof. physics U. B.C., 1971-76, prof., 1976—; vis. scientist Ecole Normale Superieure, Paris, 1980-81, 85, 95. Contbr. articles to sci. jours.; patentee precision microwave instrumentation. Recipient Stacie prize NRC of Can., 1978, Gold medal B.C. Sci. Coun., 1989; Rutherford Meml. scholar, 1964; Alfred P. Sloan fellow, 1972-74; Can. Coun. Rsch. fellow, 1984-86. Mem. Can. Assn. Physicists (Herzberg medal 1978, gold medal for achievement in physics, 1993, Brookhouse medal 1999), Am. Phys. Soc. Office: UBC, Dept Physics, Vancouver, BC Canada V6T 1Z1

HARDY, WAYNE RUSSELL, insurance and investment broker; b. Denver, Sept. 5, 1931; s. Russell Hinton and Victoria Katherine (Anderson) H.; m. Carolyn Lucille Carvell, Aug. 1, 1958 (July 1977); children: James Russell Hardy, Jann Miller Hardy. *Son James R. Hardy (Jim) graduated from Phillips University in Enid, Oklahoma in 1984 with a BA in Mass Communications. He works for Bob Hope as a producer and editor and is a writer. He and wife Selene live in Burbank, California. They have 3 children: Eric, Jin Jin, and Tommy. Daughter Jann Hardy graduated from the University of Colorado in 1987 with a Bachelors in Fine Arts and a BA in Psychology. She is an artist living in Denver and works for a major company there. She is an avid hockey player and fan.* BSCE, U. Colo., 1954; MS in Fin. Svcs., Am. Coll., 1989. CLU; chartered fin. cons. Western dist. mgr. Fenestra, Inc., San Francisco, 1956-63; ins. and investment broker John Hancock Fin. Svcs., Denver, 1963—, Wayne R. Hardy Assocs., Denver, 1963—; speaker convs. and sales seminars, 1977, 81, 84, 85, 89; v.p. CLU assn. John Hancock, 1979-80, chmn. agt.'s adv. com., 1983-84; active State of Colo. Ins. Adv. Bd., 1991-93. Chmn. Colo. Coun. Camera Clubs, Denver,

1962; bd. dirs. Porter Charitable Found., Denver, 1983-85; deacon, class pres. South Broadway Christian Ch., 1961-65; mem. Denver Art Mus., Denver Botanic Gardens, Rocky Mountain Estate Planning Coun., Mensa, Alliance Francaise. Capt. U.S. Army, 1954-56, Korea, USAR, 1956-80. Mem. Am. Soc. CLU and ChFC (pres. Rocky Mountain chpt. 1990-91), Nat. Assn. Life Underwriters (pres. Denver chpt. 1983-84, Nat. Quality award 1968—, expert witness ins. litigation, Disting. Life Underwriters award 1970-83), Nat. Football Found. (bd. dirs. Denver chpt. 1992—), Million Dollar Round Table (life), U. Colo. Alumni (bd. dirs. 1990-92), U. Colo. Alumni C Club (bd. dirs. 1972-74), Univ. Club, Greenwood Athletic Club, Village Tennis Club, Rocky Mountain Optimist Club (pres. 1984-85). Republican. Avocations: tennis, photography, foreign languages, art, travel. Home and Office: 6178 E Hinsdale Ct Englewood CO 80112-1534

HARDY, WILLIAM MCDONALD, JR., clergyman, physician assistant; b. Madisonville, Tex., Feb. 7, 1957; s. William McDonald and Frankie Beatrice (Bell) H.; m. Kathryn Joyce Phillips, Jan. 19, 1980; children: Karen R., Karla J., Kimberly A., Klarissa D., William M. III. Student, Tex. A&M U., 1975-77; BS, Howard U., 1980; MSPA (psychiatry), U. NebraskaColl. Med., 1998. Lic. Okla. Bd. Med. Examiners, cert. Correctional Health Profl. (CCHP), 1998. Physician asst. John A. Kenney M.D., Washington, 1980-82; D.C. Dept. of Correction, Lorton, Va., 1982, Fed. Prison Hosp., El Reno, Okla., 1982-89, Okla. Army Nat. Guard, Midwest City, Okla., 1983-89, VA Medical Ctr., Oklahoma City, 1989-95; instr. CPR Emergency Care, ARC, Edgewater, Md., 1982; admissions officer VA Hosp., patient referral coord., clinical instr., 1989-95, pres.-elect of Assn. of Psychiatric Phys. Assts., 1998, Univ. Tex. Med. Branch Managed Care Clin. Systems Coord., 1996—. Author: Protocol for Psychiatric Physician Assistants, 1997; Contbr. articles to Am. Jour. Psychiatry. Vol. ARC; vice chmn. Citizens' Participation Com., 1989; bd. dirs. Lincoln Terrace Neighborhood Assn., Okla City, 1991; emergency medical svc. Huntsville Police dept., 1975, EMT Madisonville County Hosp., 1976-77, Capt., Tex. Army Natl. Guard, 1996—. Recipient Cert. of Appreciation AMC, 1987, Cert. of Commendation Okla. Army Nat. Guard, 1983, Cert. of Svc. U.S. Army, 1983, Letter of Commendation D.C. Dept. Corrections, 1982; named Outstanding Young Men of Am. U.S. Jaycees, 1983. Mem. Amer. Acad. of Phys. Assts. House of Delegates, 1998—, Tex. Acad. of Phys. Assts., 1997—. Avocation: writing. Home: 12686 Sunset Dr Tyler TX 75704

HARDY, WILLIAM ROBINSON, lawyer; b. Cin., June 14, 1934; s. William B. and Chastine M. (Sprague) H.; m. Barbro Anita Medin, Oct. 11, 1964; children: Anita Christina, William Robinson Jr. AB magna cum laude, Princeton U., 1956; JD, Harvard U., 1963. Bar: Ohio 1963, U.S. Supreme Ct. 1975. Life underwriter New Eng. Mut. Life Ins. Co., 1956-63; assoc. Graydon, Head & Ritchey, Cin., 1963-68, ptnr., 1968-98; mem. panel comml. arbitrators Am. Arbitration Assn., 1972—, mem. panel large complex case program, 1993—, panel of mediators, 1993—, comml. arbitrator tng. faculty, 1998—; reporter joint com. for revision of rules of U.S. Dist. Ct. for So. Dist. Ohio, 1975, 80, 83, mem., 1990—. Bd. dirs. Cin. Union Bethel, 1968-82, pres., 1977-82, emeritus, 1982—; bd. dirs. Ohio Valley Goodwill Industries Rehab. Ctr., Cin., 1970—, pres., 1981-92; mem. Cin. Bd. Bldg. Appeals, 1976—, vice chmn., 1983, chmn., 1983—; pres. Hamilton County (Ohio) Alcohol and Drug Addiction Svcs. Bd., 1990-92; trustee Substance Abuse Mgmt. and Devel. Inc., 1998—. Capt. USAR, 1956-68; maj. gen. Ohio Mil. Res., insp. gen., 1988-89, TJAG, 1989-93, dep. comdr., 1993-96, comdr., 1996—. Recipient award of merit Ohio Legal Ctr. Inst., 1975, 76. Mem. ABA, AAAS, Ohio Bar Assn., Cin. Bar Assn., Ohio Acad. Trial Lawyers, 6th Cir. Jud. Conf. (life), Ohio Soc. Colonial Wars (gov. 1979), Phi Beta Kappa. Mem. Ch. of Redeemer. Club: Princeton (N.Y.C.). Office: 432 Walnut St Ste 206 Cincinnati OH 45202-3909

HARDY-BRAZ, STEVEN THOMAS, psychologist; b. Rockville, Conn., Dec. 22, 1966; s. Milton Bradford and Ellen Blake Hardy; m. Liza Hardy Braz, Aug. 12, 1995. Cert. mgmt. substance abuse treatment, South Ctrl. C.C., New Haven, 1990; BA in Clin. Counseling Psychology, U. New Haven, 1990, BS in Criminal Justice, 1990; MA in Devel. Psychology, Gallaudet U., 1991, specialist in psychology, 1995, cert. instr. instrumental enrichment, 1996; cert. dynamic assessment, Touro Coll., 1996. Sch. psychologist Ea. N.C. Sch. for the Deaf, Wilson, 1996—; ednl. specialist Ctr. for Devel. and Learning U. N.C., Chapel Hill, 1998—; asst. to dir. re-entry Elan One Corp., 1986; logistics coord. Family Life Program/Learning Vacation, 1990-91; instr. psychology dept. Gallaudet U., 1991-92, staff mem. personal discovery program, 1992—, rsch. instr. Rsch. Inst./Mental Health, 1993-94; asst. boys basketball coach Scranton State Sch. for the Deaf, 1994-95; sign lang. interpreter, 1994—; contract sch. psychologist, 1995—; psychol. assoc. Dr. William Kachman, Md., 1995—; adv. bd. mem. N.C. State Mental Health Svcs. for the Deaf, Raleigh, 1997—; presenter in field. Mem. editl. bd. The Ednl. Forum, 1995—; contbr. chpt. to book. Mem. APA, Nat. Assn. Sch. Psychologists (nat. cert. sch. psychologist), Wilson Assn. Sch. Deaf, Mensa. Avocations: Aikido, rock climbing. E-mail: Steven-Hardy-Braz@ncmail.net. Office: Ea NC Sch for the Deaf Hwy 301 North Wilson NC 27894-2768

HARDY DE JESUS, GEORGETTE MARILYN, university administrator; b. Phila., Dec. 17, 1948; d. Joseph Neil and Ellanora Delores Mae Townsend-Hardy; m. Juan De Jesus, July 15, 1989; 1 child, Arden Juan. BA cum laude, Howard U., 1973, MEd, 1974. Cert. NCC, PADI, profl. counselor. Ednl. program administr. Univ. D.C., Washington; guidance facilitator Howard U., Washington; field reader U.S. Dept. of Edn., Washington; dir. pre-coll. programs Upward Bound Program and Math. Sci. Initiative, U. Md., College Park; active Md. Exec. Coun. for Ednl. Opportunity. Mem. ACA, Am. Coll. Counseling Assn., Am. Psychological Assn., Am. Mental Health Counselors Assn., Mid-Ea. Assn. Ednl. Opportunity (program pers.), Kappa delta Pi, Delta Sigma Theta.

HARDYMON, DAVID WAYNE, lawyer; b. Columbus, Ohio, Aug. 22, 1949; s. Philip Barbour and Margaret Evelyn (Bowers) H.; m. Monica Ella Sleep, Mar. 13, 1982; children: Philip Garnet, Teresa Jeanette. BA in History, Bowling Green State U., 1971; JD, Capital U., Columbus, Ohio, 1976. ssss Ohio 1976, U.S. Dist. Ct. (so. dist.) Ohio 1976; U.S. Supreme Ct. 1980, U.S. Ct. Appeals (6th cir.) 1982. Asst. prosecuting atty. Franklin County Prosecuter's Office, Columbus, Ohio, 1976-81; assoc. Vorys, Sater, Seymour & Pease, Columbus, 1981-86, ptnr., 1987—. Mem. Chmn's. Club Franklin Country Rep. Orgn., 1983. Fellow Columbus Bar Found.; mem. Ohio State Bar Assn., Columbus Bar Assn. Avocation: sailing. Office: Vorys Sater Seymour & Pease PO Box 1008 52 E Gay St Columbus OH 43215-3161

HARDYMON, JAMES FRANKLIN, retired diversified products company executive; b. Maysville, Ky., Nov. 11, 1934; s. Kenneth Thomas and Pauline (Strode) H.; m. Rebecca Gay Garred, June 25, 1960; children: Jennifer, Frank. BSCE, U. Ky., 1956, MSCE, 1958. V.p. planning and devel. Browning divsn. Browning div. Emerson Electric Co., Maysville, 1970-73, exec. v.p., 1973-76; pres. spl. products divsn. Emerson Electric Co., St. Louis, Ky., 1976-79; v.p. corp. group and pres. Skil divsn. Emerson Electric Co., Chgo., 1979-83; exec. v.p. Emerson Electric Co., St. Louis, 1989-91, vice chmn., 1986-88, COO, 1986-89, pres., 1988-89; COO Textron, Inc., Providence, 1989-90, CEO, 1991-98, chmn., also dir. With U.S. Army, 1958-59, 61-62. Recipient Corp. Devel. award ASME, 1976. Republican. Mem. Christian Ch. (Disciples of Christ). Office: care Textron Inc 40 Westminster St Providence RI 02903*

HARE, DAVID, playwright; b. St. Leonards, Sussex, Eng., June 5, 1947; s. Clifford Theodore and Agnes (Gilmour) H.; m. Margaret Matheson, Aug. 1970 (div. 1980); children: Joe, Lewis, Darcy; m. Nicole Farhi, 1992. MA, Cambridge U., 1968. Founder Portable Theatre, 1968, Joint Stock Theatre Group, 1974, Greenpoint Films, 1983; assoc. dir. Royal Nat. Theatre, London, 1984-88, 89-97. Author: (plays) Slag, 1970 (Evening Standard Drama award 1970), The Great Exhibition, 1972, (with Howard Brenton) Brassneck, 1973, Knuckle, 1974 (John Llewlyn Rhys award 1975), Teeth 'n' Smiles, 1975, (with others) Deeds, 1978, Plenty, 1978 (N.Y. Drama Critics Circle Best Fgn. Play award 1983, Best Play Tony award nominee 1983), A Map of the World, 1982 (Dramalogue award), (with Brenton) Pravda, 1985 (Evening Standard Drama award 1985, Plays and Players best play award 1985, City Limits best play award 1985), The Bay at Nice, 1986, Wrecked Eggs, 1986, The Knife, 1987, The Secret Rapture, 1988 (Plays and Players Best Play award 1988, Drama mag. Best Play award 1988, Drama Desk Best Play award nominee 1990), Racing Demon, 1990, 93, 95 (Olivier Best Play award 1990, Time Out Theatre award 1990, Plays and Players best play award 1990, London Critics Circle Best Play award 1990, Tony award nominee 1996), Murmuring Judges, 1991, 92, 93, The Absence of War, 1993, Skylight, 1995, 96, 97 (Olivier Best Play award), Amy's View, 1996, 97, 98, 99, The Judas Kiss, 1997, 98, Via Dolorosa, 98, 99; (adaptations) Fanshen (William Hinton), 1975, Rules of the Game (Luigi Pirandello), 1971, 92, The Life of Galileo (Bertolt Brecht), 1994, Mother Courage and Her Children (Brecht), 1995, Ivanov (Anton Chekhov), 1997, The Blue Room (Schnitzler), 1998; plays performed U.S.-Broadway, Pub. Theatre, N.Y.C., Goodman Theatre, Chgo., Arena Theatre, Washington, Lincoln Ctr., and other places; (TV films) Man Above Men, 1973, Licking Hitler (Brit. Acad. Film and TV Arts Best Play award 1978), Dreams of Leaving, 1980, Saigon: Year of the Cat, 1983, Heading Home, 1990, The Absence of War, 1995; (screenplays) Plenty, 1985, Wetherby, 1985 (Golden Bear award best film Berlin Film Festival 1985), Paris By Night, 1988, Strapless, 1989, Damage, 1992, The Secret Rapture, 1993, Feasting with Panthers, 1995; (essays) Writing Lefthanded, 1991, Asking Around, 1993; dir: (theatre) Inside Out, 1968, Christie in Love, 1969, Purity, 1969, Fruit, 1970, Blow Job, 1971, England's Ireland, 1972, Brassneck, 1973, The Pleasure Principle, 1973, The Provoked Wife, 1973, The Party, 1974, Teeth 'n' Smiles, 1975, Weapons of Happiness, 1976, Devil's Island, 1977, Plenty, 1978, Total Eclipse, 1981, A Map of the World, 1983, Pravda, 1985-86, King Lear, 1986, The Bay at Nice and Wrecked Eggs, 1986-87, The Knife, 1987, The Secret Rapture, 1989, The Designated Mourner, 1996; (films) Wetherby, 1985, Paris by Night, 1989, Strapless, 1989, (TV) Licking Hitler, 1978, Dreams of Leaving, 1980, Heading Home, 1992, The Designated Mourner, 1996, Heartbreak House, 1997; (opera libretto) The Knife, 1988; author: (books) Writing Left-handed, 1991, Asking Around, 1993, Acting Up, 1999. Fellow Royal Soc. Lit.; mem. Officiers de l'ordre des Artes et Lettres, Dramatists Club. Office: c/o Casarotto Ramsay, 60 Wardour St, London W1, England

HARE, ELEANOR O'MEARA, computer science educator; b. Charlottesville, Va., Apr. 6, 1936; d. Edward King and Eleanor Worthington (Selden) O'Meara; m. John Leonard Ging, Feb. 4, 1961 (div. 1972); 1 child, Catherine Eleanor Ging Huddle; m. William Ray Hare, Jr., May 24, 1973. BA, Hollins Coll., 1958; MS, Clemson U., 1973, PhD, 1989. Rsch. asst. cancer rsch. U. Va. Hosp., Charlottesville, 1957-58; rsch. specialist rsch. labs. engring. sci. U. Va., Charlottesville, 1959-64; tchr. Pendleton (S.C.) High Sch., 1964-65; vis. instr. dept. math. sci. Clemson (S.C.) U., 1974-79, instr. dept. computer sci., 1979-83, lectr. dept. computer sci., 1983-90, asst. prof. dept. computer sci., 1990-98, assoc. prof. dept. computer sci., 1998—. Contbr. articles to profl. jours. Bd. dirs. LWV of the Clemson Area, 1988-96; chmn. nursing home study LWV of S.C., 1988-92; oboe and English horn player Anderson (S.C.) Symphony, 1980—. Fellow Inst. Combinatorics and its Applications; mem. AAUP, Assn. for Computing Machinery. Office: Clemson U Dept Computer Sci Clemson SC 29634-1906

HARE, FREDERICK KENNETH, geography and environmental educator, university official; b. Wylye, Eng., Feb. 5, 1919; s. Frederick Eli and Irene (Smith) H.; m. Suzanne Alice Bates, Aug. 23, 1941 (div. 1952); 1 son, Christopher John; m. Helen Neilson Morrill, Dec. 26, 1953; children: Elissa Beatrice, Robin Gilbert. B.S. 1st class honors, U. London, 1939; Ph.D., U. Montreal, 1950; LL.D., Queens U., 1964, U. Western Ont., 1968, Trent U., 1979, Meml. U., 1985; D.Sc., McGill U., 1969, Adelaide U., 1974, York U., 1978; DLitt, Thorneloe Coll. Laurentian U., 1983; grad. (hon. cert.), Nat. Def. Coll.; D.Sc., Windsor U., 1988, Guelsh U., 1995. Asst. prof. geography McGill U., 1945-49, prof., chmn. dept. geography, 1950-62, prof. geography and meteorology, dean faculty arts and scis., 1962-64; dir. Arctic Meteorology Research Group, McGill Sub-Arctic Research Lab., 1954-62; prof. geography King's Coll., U. London, 1964-66; master of Birkbeck Coll., U. London, 1966-68; pres. U. B.C., Vancouver, Can., 1968-69; prof. geography and physics U. Toronto, Ont., Can., 1969-84; chmn. adv. bd. Inst. Internat. Programs U. Toronto, Ont., 1990-94; Univ. prof. U. Toronto, 1976-84, univ. prof. emeritus, 1984—; dir. Inst. Environ. Studies, 1974-79; provost Trinity Coll., 1979-86; gov. Trinity Coll. Sch., 1979-86; chancellor Trent U., Peterborough, Ont., 1988-95; dir.-gen. rsch. coordination Can. Dept. of Environment, 1972-73, sci. adviser, 1972-74; mem. NRC, Can., 1962-64; mem. Natural Environment Research Coun., U.K., 1965-68; bd. dirs. Resources for the Future, 1968-80; mem. spl. programme panel on ecoscis. NATO, 1972-75, chmn., 1974-75; mem. Can. Environ. Adv. Council, 1973-78; mem. corp. Woods Hole Oceanographic Inst., 1976-79; chmn. Canadian Climate Program Planning Bd., 1979-90; chmn. Royal Soc. Can. Commn. on Lead in the Environment, 1984-86, tech. adv. com. on R & D Atomic Energy of Can. Rsch. Ltd., 1991-95; mem. Resources for the Future, 1990—; chmn. Tech. Adv. Panel on Nuclear Safety, Ont. Hydro, 1990-94, active, 1994-99; commr. Ont. Nuclear Safety Rev., 1986-88; chmn. Internat. Programs Adv. Bd., U. Toronto, 1990-93. Author: The Restless Atmosphere, 1953, On University Freedom, 1967, (with M.K. Thomas) Climate Canada, 1974, 2d edit., 1979; author, editor: (with R.A. Bryson) Climates of North America; Contbr. (with R.A. Bryson) articles to sci. publs. Served as meteorologist Brit. Air Ministry, 1941-45; flight lt., meteorol. br. R.A.F.V.R., 1943-45, Gt. Britain. Fellow King's Coll., 1967, Trinity Coll. 1991—; Recipient Patterson medal, 1973, Massey medal, 1974; Patron's medal Royal Geog. Soc., 1977; decorated Officer Order Can., 1978, promoted to Companion, 1987; recipient U. Toronto Alumni Faculty award, 1982, Internat. Meteorol. Orgn. Prize, 1989. Fellow AAAS, Royal Soc. Can. (Centenary medal 1982, Dawson medal 1988, Climate Inst. award 1991), Royal Meteorol. Soc. (past pres.), Royal Geog. Soc., Am. Geog. Soc. (hon. fellow), Arctic Inst. N.Am. (past chmn.), Am. Meteorol. Soc. (emeritus).

HARE, JERRY WAYNE, communications executive; b. Claremore, Okla., Nov. 16, 1937; s. Curb and Metheta Evelyn (Doss) H.; m. Mary Jo Sellers, Nov. 15, 1956; children: Pamela S., Anthony W., Rhonda S. Calhoun, LaDonna E. Girdner. Indstl. elec. technician, Okla. State U., 1960. Founder, owner Sooner TV, Tahlequah, Okla., 1963—; founder, owner Crystal Creek Ranch, Tahlequah, 1968—, Bird-Link Sys., Tahlequah, 1984—, Crystal Creek Dairy, Tahlequah, 1990—. Mem. Profl. Svc. Assn. Inc., Nat. Fedn. Ind. Businessman, Nat. Write Your Congressman, Tahlequah Area C. of C., U.S. C. of C., Masons (32nd degree award 1968), Okla. Cattlemen Assn. Democrat. Avocations: fishing, hunting, family activities. Office: Sooner TV Bird Link Sys 405 E Downing St Tahlequah OK 74464-3015

HARE, JOHN, radio station executive. With ABC Radio, Houston, Washington, 1969-80, Detroit, 1980; group pres. ABC Group Radio, 1997-99; v.p., gen. mgr. Sta. KTKS-FM, Dallas/Ft. Worth, 1984-86; pres., gen. mgr. Sta. WBAP, Arlington, Tex., 1986-96, Sta. KSCS-FM, Dallas/Ft. Worth, 1996-97; pres. ABC Radio, Dallas, 1999—. Office: ABC Radio 13725 Montfort Dr Dallas TX 75240*

HARE, LEROY, JR., pharmaceutical company executive; b. Topeka, Nov. 1, 1955; s. LeRoy and Carol Darlene (Johnson) H.; m. Margaret Ann Burke, Dec. 30, 1982; children: Susan Audrey and Sarah Jean (twins). Student, Kans. State U., 1974-76; BBA, Washburn U., 1978. Book buyer Palmer News, Inc., Topeka, 1978-81; store mgr. Town Crier Book Store, Topeka, 1980-81; field sales rep. USV Labs., Topeka, 1981-84; field sales rep. Glaxo Inc, Topeka, 1985-90, field sales trainer, 1988-90, regional sales trainer, 1989-90, mem. profl. devel. program, 1989, managed care area account mgr., 1990-94; dist. sales mgr., 1994-95; co-founder Info Tec, LLC, DAPS, 1995-96; account mgr. Networks Plus, 1996—, dist. sales mgr., 1996; acct. mgr. ENTEX Info. Svcs., Inc., Lenexa, Kans., 1996-97; account mgr. Info. Mgmt. Network Comm., 1997; account mgr. NetStandard, Inc., 1997-98, sales mgr., 1998; V.p. Gateway Fin. Svc., 1998—. Author sales tng. manual. Mem. adv. panel Marian Clinic, Topeka, 1989-94, Black Health Care Coalition, 1994-95. Avocations: golf, landscaping, snow skiing.

HARE, PETER HEWITT, philosophy educator; b. N.Y.C., Mar. 12, 1935; s. Michael Meredith and Jane Perry (Jopling) H.; m. Daphne Joan Kean, May 30, 1959 (dec. Aug. 1995); children: Clare Kean, Gwendolyn Meigs. BA, Yale U., 1957; MA, Columbia U., 1962, PhD, 1965. Lectr. philosophy SUNY, Buffalo, 1962-65, from asst. prof. to prof., 1965-97, disting. svc. prof., 1997—, asst. chmn. dept., 1965-68, chmn. dept. 1971-75, 85-94, assoc. dean divsn. undergrad. edn., 1980-82; vis. prof. Moscow State U., 1989; bd. advisors, Peirce Edition Project, Ind. U./Purdue U., 1998—. Author: A Woman's Quest for Science, 1985; (with others) Evil and the Concept of God, 1968, Causing, Perceiving and Believing, 1975; editor: Doing Philosophy Historically, 1988, (with others) History, Religion and Spiritual Democracy, 1980, Naturalism and Rationality, 1986, series Frontiers of Philosophy, Prometheus Books, 1986—; mem. editl. bd. Am. Philos. Quar., 1978-87, Jour. Speculative Philosophy, 1987—. Chmn. joint awards coun. SUNY, 1982-83. NEH fellow 1968, recipient Conf. award, 1987, 90. Mem. Am. Philos. Assn. (nominating com. Eastern divsn. 1990-92, program com. Eastern divsn. 1993-95, chmn. program com. 1994-95, nat. bd. officers 1996-99, chmn. com. career opportunities 1996-99, Ombudsman 1996-99), Peirce Soc. (editor Transactions 1974—, pres. 1975-76), N.Y. State Philos. Assn. (pres. 1975-77), Soc. Advancement Am. Philosophy (exec. com. 1977-80, pres. 1988-90, Herbert W. Schneider award 1996), Elizabethan Club. Avocations: sailing, photography. Home: 219 Depew Ave Buffalo NY 14214-1621 Office: SUNY Dept Philosophy Baldy Hall Buffalo NY 14260

HARE, ROBERT YATES, music history educator; b. McGrann, Pa., June 14, 1921; s. Robert Deemar and Beulah (Yates) H.; m. Constance King Rutherford, Mar. 31, 1948; children: Stephen, Beverly, Madeleine. Mus.B., U. Detroit, 1948; M.A., Wayne State U., 1950; Ph.D., U. Iowa, 1959. Instr. Marietta (Ohio) Coll., 1949-51, Del Mar Coll., Corpus Christi, Tex., 1951-55; prof., chmn. grad. studies San Jose (Calif.) State U., 1956-65; prof., dean Eastern Ill. U. Music, 1965-74; prof. music history and lit. Ohio State U., Columbus, 1974-86, prof. emeritus, 1986—; dir. Sch. Music Ohio State U., 1974-78, dir. audio-rec. engring., 1979-82, arts adminstr. research and faculty devel., 1982-86; cons. in field; Mem. council music edn. in higher edn. Ill. Music Educators Assn., 1969-74. Condr. coll. symphony band, 1956-63, San Jose Youth Symphony, 1957-59, univ. symphony, 1968-74, Ea. Ill. U. Symphony, 1968-74; French horn recitals, Carnegie Music Hall, Pitts., 1940, 42; French hornist, Pitts. Symphony Orch., 1941-43, 44-45, Buffalo Philharmonic, 1943-44, Cin. Summer Opera Co., 1945, Indpls. Symphony Orch., 1945-46, San Antonio Symphony Orch., 1947-49; orchestrator, San Antonio Symphony Orch., 1947-49; recs. include Pitts. Symphony Orch., Indpls. Symphony Orch. (as French hornist), San Jose State U. Symphonic Band (as condr.); contbr. articles to profl. jours. Mem. com. grad. and profl. edn. in arts and humanities Ill. Bd. Higher Edn., 1969-70; mem. performing arts commn. Ill. Sesquicentennial, 1967; mem. exec. bd. Greater Columbus Arts Council, 1974-76, Ohio Alliance for Arts in Edn., 1974-76; trustee Columbus Symphony Orch., 1975-79. Profl. Promise scholar Carnegie-Mellon U., 1939. Mem. Music Educators Nat. Conf. (publs. planning com. 1970-76), Am. Musicol. Soc., Coll. Music Soc., Phi Mu Alpha, Sinfonia (hon.), Pi Kappa Lambda (hon.), Delta Omicron (hon.). Lodges: Masons; Shriners. Home: 2494 Farleigh Rd Columbus OH 43221-2618 Office: Ohio State U Coll Arts 305 Mershon Auditorium Columbus OH 43210

HARELL, GEORGE S., radiologist; b. Vienna, Austria, Apr. 27, 1937; came to U.S., 1940; s. Isidore and Zinaida (Hilferding) Silbermann; m. Carol Deane Wright, Mar. 21, 1970, children: Mark, Ben. AB, Oberlin Coll., 1959; MD, Columbia U., 1963. Resident in radiology Med. Sch., Stanford (Calif.) U., 1967-71, asst. prof., 1971-78, assoc. prof., 1978-82; radiologist dept. radiology East Jefferson Gen. Hosp., Metairie, La., 1982-84, chmn. dept. radiology, 1984-94; clin. prof. radiology Tulane U., New Orleans, 1987—; project officer NIH, Washington, 1965-67. Contbr. chpt. to: The Oesophagus, 1986, 92, 97. Lt. comdr. USPHS, 1963-65. James C. Picker Found. grantee, 1972-74, NIH grantee, 1977-80, 82-85, Am. Heart Assn. grantee, 1981-83. Mem. Soc. Computed Body Tomography/Magnetic Resonances, Soc. Gastrointestinal Radiologists, Am. Coll. Radiology, Phi Beta Kappa. Office: 4009 Rivage Ct Metairie LA 70002-1345

HARENBERG, PAUL E., state legislator; b. N.Y.C.; m. Sylvia Ann Mervin; children: Paul, Peter, David, Jennifer. BA in Liberal Arts, Columbia Coll., N.Y.C.; MA in Pub. Law & Govt., Columbia U.; PhD in Edn., NYU; D of Civil Law (hon.), Dowling Coll. Mem. N.Y. State Assembly, Albany, 1975—, chmn. commn. on aging, 1981-96, chmn. steering com., 1997-99; past tchr. social studies, Russian lang. Bauport-Blue Point H.S., Bayport, N.Y.; past assoc. prof. govt. N.Y. inst. Tech., Central Islip; assoc. prof. SUNY, Stony Brook, Sch. Social Welfare. Author: (textbook) American Government; also study reports. Fulbright-Hays Exch. teaching fellow Loughborough Coll., Eng.; named Man of Yr. Geriatric Com. of L.I., Sayville H.S. Key Club, John XXIII Humanitarian of Yr. Sisters of St. Dominic, Legislator of Yr. L.I. Coun. Sr. Citizens; numerous others. Democrat. Avocations: sailing, reading, opera, music. Office: NY State Assembly Albany NY 12248

HARENZA, BRIAN JAMES, international banker; b. Chambersburg, Pa., Feb. 16, 1974; s. James Anthony Harenza and Christine Marilyn Hill. BA, Dickinson Coll., 1996. Internat. banker DG Bank, N.Y.C., 1996—. Winfield scholar Dickinson Coll., 1996.

HARF, PATRICIA JEAN KOLE, syndicated columnist, educational consultant, lecturer, clinical psychologist, family therapist; b. Berea, Ohio, Oct. 14, 1937; d. Paul Frederic and Mena (Labordes) Kole; m. Fredric Henry Harf, June 21, 1969. BS in Edn. with honors, Baldwin-Wallace Coll., Berea, Ohio, 1959; MS in Edn., U. Akron, 1966; Dr. in Edn., Ariz. State U., 1972; PhD, London Inst. Applied Rsch., 1995; HHD, World Acad., 1994; PhD, London Inst. Applied Rsch., 1995. Rsch. Ednl. Rsch. Coun. Am., 1967-69; tchr. Berea City Schs., Cleve. and Parma, Ohio, 1969-73; asst. prof. Cleve. State U., 1975—; corr., columnist, freelance writer, syndicated columnist Chronicle-Telegram, Elyria, Ohio, 1986-89; owner Harf's Comms. Inc., Berea, Ohio, 1993—; ednl. cons. State of Ohio; syndicated columnist Universal Press, Cleve. Plain Dealer; diagnostician of reading difficulties; trustee Coalition for Children's Media; cons. learning disabilities; guest lectr.; TV guest appearances; court appointed spl. cons. for juveniles, 1996-97; mem. Reading Enrichment for Adult Devel.; mem. Coun. of Higher Learning. Author teaching materials and tchr. and children's texts; contbr. articles to profl. jours. ; also advisor to book pubs. and magazines. Pres. Berea Hist. Soc., World Found. Successful Women; mem. Cleve. Orch. Women's Com., Nat. Mus. Women in Arts, Coun. Exceptional Children, Ohio Town Forum, Ohio Arts Festival, com. 500 Project READ; advisor Cleve. Radio and TV Coun.; tutor Project Learn, Cleve.; mem. Berea Rep. Precinct Com.; founder Preventive Parenting; dep. senator Internat. Parliament Safety & Peace Italy; mem. Children's TV Workshop, 1995-96; trustee Meth. Childrens Found. and Home, 1996-97. Named Intellectual Woman of Yr., 1991-92, Emminent fellow in Universe of Mankind, 1994, Ohio Ednl. Woman of Yr., Ohio Educator of Yr. and Outstanding Educator, Outstanding Citizen Berea C. of C., Outstanding Berea High Grad. awd., 1997; Ohio Edn. Woman of Yr., 1991, Most Admired woman of Yr., 1993, Lifetime Fellow and Hon. Prof. Australian Inst. for Coordinated Rsch., 1995; recipient Women's Inner Cir. of Achievement award, 1992, Woman of Yr. commemorative medal Order of Internat. Fellowship, 1994, Excellence in Journalism award 1990-93, World Lifetime Achievement award, 1996; named baroness Royal Order Bohemian Crown, 1994. Mem. NEA, NOW, AAUW, LWV, Am. Writers Assn., Am. Women in Radio and TV, Inc., Soc. Profl. Journalists (Excellence in Journalism award 1990, Ohio Live, Woman Source directory 1998-00), Women in Journalism, Assn. Tchrs. of Learning Disabilities, Am. Assn. Women in Bus., Berea C. of C. (Outstanding Citizen 1965), Bus. Profl. Women Assn., Australian Inst. Coordinated Rsch. (fellow, hon. prof.), Berea Hist. Soc., Berea Bus. and Profl. Women, Women in Comm. Inc., Internat. Women's Media, Internat. Reading Assn. (cons. and writer for reading tchrs.), Nat. Edn. Assn., Ohio Edn. Assn. (Woman of Yr. in Comms. 1991), Internat. Platform Assn., World Found. of Successful Women, Nat. Assn. Women (Internat. Leaders in Achievement award 1996), Profl. Educators Assn., Learning Disability Assn., Nat. Assn. Psychologists, Ohio Assn. Psychologists, Nat. Assn. Women in the Arts, Western Res. Rep. Women's Assn., S.W. Women Rep. Assn., Kiwanis (sec., v.p.), Berea Rep. Club (Mayoral Volunteerism award 1987), Press Club of Cleve. (award 1996), Cleve. Women's City Club, Berentown Forum. Republican. Methodist. Avocations: reading, golf, flower arranging, politics, crafts. Home: 323 Westbridge Dr Berea OH 44017-1562

HARFF, CHARLES HENRY, lawyer, retired diversified industrial company executive; b. Wesel, Germany, Sept. 27, 1929; s. Philip and Stephanie (Dreyfuss) H.; m. Marion Haines MacAfee, July 19, 1958; children—Pamela Haines, John Blair, Todd Philip. B.A., Colgate U., 1951; LL.B., Harvard U., 1954; postgrad., U. Bonn, Fed. Republic Germany, 1955. Bar: N.Y. 1955. Assoc. Chadbourne & Parke, N.Y.C., 1955-64, ptnr., 1964-84; sr. v.p., gen. counsel, sec. Rockwell Internat. Corp., Pitts., 1984-94, sr. v.p., spl. counsel, 1994-96, ret., 1996; cons., 1996—; bd. dirs. Meritor Automotive Inc.

Trustee Christian Johnson Endeavor Found., N.Y.C., 1984—; bd. dirs. Atlantic Legal Found., 1989-98, Fulbright Assn., 1995—. Fulbright scholar U. Bonn, Germany, 1955. Mem. ABA, N.Y. State Bar Assn., The Assn. Gen. Counsel, Econ. Club N.Y., Harvard Club, Duquesne Club, Allegheny Country Club, Laurel Valley Golf Club, Farm Neck Golf Club (Martha's Vineyard, Mass.). Home: Blackburn Rd Sewickley PA 15143-8386 Office: Rockwell Internat Corp 625 Liberty Ave Pittsburgh PA 15222-3110

HARFORD, JAMES JOSEPH, aerospace historian; b. Jersey City, Aug. 19, 1924; s. Thomas William and Jane Hume (Henderson) H.; m. Mildred Rita Waters, Apr. 19, 1952; children: Susan Gately, James Joseph, Peter Benedict (dec.), Jennifer, Christopher. BSME, Yale U., 1945. Sales engr. Worthington Corp., 1946-49; assoc. editor Modern Industry, 1950-52; free-lance writer Europe, 1952-53; exec. sec. Am. Rocket Soc., 1953-63; exec. dir. Am. Inst. Aeros. and Astronautics, 1963-88, exec. dir. emeritus, 1988—; v.p. Internat. Astronautical Fedn., 1988-90. Author: Korolev (How One Man Masterminded the Soviet Drive to Beat America to the Moon), 1997, (with others) China Space Report, 1979. Mem. 1945W class coun Yale U.; trustee Friends of Princeton Pub. Libr., 1996—; bd. mem. Princeton Adult Edn. Sch., 1996—. Ensign USNR, 1945-46. Recipient NASA Pub. Svc. award, 1985, Air Force Exceptional Svc. award, 1987, Nat. Space Club Robert Goddard Hist. Essay prize, 1995, Internat. Astron. Fedn. award, 1997; Verville fellow Nat. Air and Space Mus. Fellow AIAA (Disting. SAvc. award 1988, Internat. Coop. Aerospace award 1995), AAAS, Brit. Interplanetary Soc., Royal Aero. Soc. (assoc.); mem. Internat. Acad. Astronautics. Home and Office: 601 Lake Dr Princeton NJ 08540-5634

HARGADON, BERNARD JOSEPH, JR., retired consumer goods company executive; b. Ardmore, Pa., Dec. 27, 1927; s. Bernard Joseph and Anna Mendenhall (Lancaster) H.; m. Jill Dinwiddie, Dec. 15, 1990; children from previous marriage: Geoffrey, Robert, Louise, Lawrence (dec.), David. BS, Drexel U., 1952, MBA, 1959. Auditor Gen. Motors Corp., 1955-57; prof. acctg. Drexel U., 1957-59; with AID, Colombia, 1960-63, McKesson, San Francisco, 1964—; pres. McKesson Internat., 1980-95, ret., 1995; adj. prof. internat. bus. Golden Gate U. Author: in Spanish Principles of Accounting, 1964, Principles of Cost Accounting, 1971. Trustee Golden Gate U.; bd. dirs. World Affairs Coun. No. Calif. With USN, 1945-48. Mem. World Trade Club, Orinda Country Club, City Club San Francisco. Roman Catholic.

HARGAN, CHARLES JAMES, lithographer, village official; b. Clarion, Iowa, June 24, 1941; s. Vernon Garney and Olive Lucile (Tourtelotte) H.; m. Carol Ann Moze, Nov. 25, 1961 (div. June 1981); children: Robert, James, Susan; m. Inga Lynn Johnson, Oct. 6, 1984; 1 child, David. Lithographer W.A. Krueger Co. (now World Color), Brookfield, Wis., 1962—. Pres. Village of Germantown, wis., 1993—, trustee, 1986-93. With U.S. Army, 1958-62. Mem. Am. Legion. Republican. Lutheran. Avocations: bowling, fishing, writing, travel, history. Office: Village of Germantown PO Box 337 Germantown WI 53022-0337

HARGENS, CHARLES WILLIAM, III, electrical engineer, consultant; b. Phila., Oct. 21, 1918; s. Charles William Jr. and Marjorie (Garman) H.; m. Mary K. Johnson, June 14, 1941; children: William Garman, Mary Van Deusen, Roger Snow. SB, MIT, 1941. Registered profl. engr., Pa. Design engr. Lockheed Aircraft, Burbank, Calif., 1941-42; group engr. Gilfillan Bros., L.A., 1942-43; vis. staff mem. MIT Radiation Labs., Cambridge, 1942-44; group engr. RCA, Camden, N.J., 1945-47; sr. engr., tech. dir., inst. fellow Franklin Inst. Labs., Phila., 1947-88; assoc. prof. Temple U., Phila., 1976-77, Drexel U., Phila., 1978-87; noise control cons. air mgmt. div. City of Phila., 1978—; rsch. assoc. Wills Eye Hosp., 1970; cons., prof. acoustics; invited lectr. U. Wis., 1962, 63, 64. Co-author: Studies in Medicine, Physics and Voice, 1968, (chpts.) Bioengineering and the Skin, 1981, Handbook of Noninvasive Methods and the Skin, 1994; contbr. articles to Jour. Ophthalmic Surgery, Jour. Acoustical Soc. Am., Investigative Dermatology, Indsl. Rsch., Electronics Jour. Instrument Soc. Am., Jour. Franklin Inst., IEEE Transactions. Mem. adv. com. Spring Garden Coll., Phila., 1972-76; rsch. assoc. Bd. of City Trusts, 1970. Recipient Diploma, War Manpower Commn., 1944, Citation Mayor City of Phila., 1974. Fellow IEEE (Phila. Sect. Appreciation award 1972); mem. ASTM (Citation 1982), Franklin Inst. (com. sci. and arts 1981), MIT Alumni Assn. (life, Bronze Beaver award 1976), Numerical Control Soc. (founder), Sigma Xi. Episcopalian. Achievements include 12 patents for radio, electronics, computation, instrumentation optics and measurement; development of specialized instruments for dermatologists, brain tissue and other researchers. Home and Office: 1006 Preston Rd Glenside PA 19038-7333 *Never retire completely from your profession, unless health forces it upon you. It is foolish to give up all the experience, knowledge, and associations acquired over a productive lifetime.*

HARGESHEIMER, ELBERT, III, lawyer; b. Cleve., Jan. 4, 1944; s. Elbert and Agnes Mary (Heckman) H.; children: Heather Leigh, Elbert IV, Jon-Erik, Piper Elizabeth, Kevin R. Cross, Mark R. Dziob. AB, Cornell U., 1966; JD, SUNY, Buffalo, 1969. Bar: N.Y. 1970, U.S. Dist. Ct. (we. dist.) N.Y. 1971. Assoc. Miller, Bouvier, O'Connor & Cegielski, Buffalo, 1970-73, ptnr., 1973-74; ptnr. Godinho & Hargesheimer, Hamburg, N.Y., 1974-84; pvt. practice law Hamburg, 1984—; chief counsel Joint Legis. Commn. to Revise Bus. and Corp. Law, N.Y. State Assembly and Senate, 1974-75; prosecutor Village of Blasdell (N.Y.), 1978-80, 83-87, village atty. 1980-82; fund chmn. South Towns Hosp. Found., Inc., 1973-76, fin. chmn., bd. dirs., 1976-77, v.p., 1978-82; chmn. Hamburg Town Rep. Com., 1978-88; coord. Erie County Pretrial Svcs. Program, 1987-88; counsel Erie County Rep. Com., 1980-92; mem. Erie County Bd. Ethics, 1979-89, chmn. 1983.; charter mem., counsel S.W. Hamburg Taxpayers Assn. Named Mr. Rep., Town of Hamburg Rep. Club, 1982, Rep. of Yr., Hamburg Twon Rep. Com., 1988. Mem. N.Y. State Bar Assn., Western N.Y. Trial Lawyer's Assn., Theta Chi. Methodist. Home and Office: 22 Buffalo St Hamburg NY 14075-5002

HARGISS, JAMES LEONARD, ophthalmologist; b. Manhattan, Kans., June 15, 1921; s. Meade Thomas and Julia Baldwin (Wayland) H.; m. Helen Natalie Berglund, July 19, 1947; children: Phillip M., Craig T., D. Reid. BS, U. Wash., 1942; MD, St. Louis U., 1945; MSc in Medicine, U. Pa., 1952. Diplomate Nat. Bd. Med. Examiners, Am. Bd. Ophthalmology. Intern U.S. Naval Hosp., PSNS Bremerton, Washington, 1945-46; resident physician G.F. Geisinger Meml. Hosp. and Foss Clinic, Danville, Pa., 1949-51; practice medicine specializing in ophthalmic surgery Seattle, 1951-58; ophthalmic surgeon Eye Clinic of Seattle, 1958-94, pres., 1962-91, CEO, 1985-91; ophthalmic cons. Eye Assocs. N.W., Seattle, 1994—; asst. clin. prof. Sch. Medicine, U. Wash., 1995—. Contbr. chapter to book, 1987, articles to Ophthalmology, 1964-80. Dist. chmn. King County Rep. Cen. Com., 1962-70. Served as physician/surgeon with USNR, 1945-48. Recipient Citation of Merit Washington State Med. Assn., 1959; Wendell F. Hughes fellow, 1960. Fellow AMA (Cert. of award 1960), Am. Coll. Surgeons (fellows leadership soc.), Leadership Soc., Am. Acad. Ophthalmology (Honor award 1975), Am. Soc. Ophthalmic Plastic and Reconstructive Surgery (charter) (Lester T. Jones award 1979), De Bourg Soc. of St. Louis U., Pacific Coast Oto-Ophthalmology Soc. (v.p.), Lions (Lake City pres. 1960-61), Gullwing Group Internat., Alpha Omega Alpha. Avocations: golf, skiing, art, classic cars. Office: Eye Assocs NW 1101 Madison St Ste 600 Seattle WA 98104

HARGRAVE, JAMES LEE, editor, consultant; b. Granite City, Ill., Sept. 19, 1951; s. Donald Jean and Doris Jean Hargrave; m. Sharon Kay Chapman, Sept. 9, 1972; 1 child, Jane Elizabeth. BS, So. Ill. U., 1976; MA, So. Bapt. Theol. Sem., Louisville, 1985. Ordained min. to Bapt. Ch., 1986. Art supr. Madison (Ill.) Pub. Sch. Sys., 1976-78; advt. mgr. Dicor Photographic Co., Belleville, Ill., 1978-82; children's ministry St. Matthews Bapt. Ch., Louisville, 1982-85; children's mus. First Bapt. Ch. Ferguson, St. Louis, 1985-89; state Sun. sch. assoc. Ala. Bapt. Conv., Montgomery, 1989-93; editor, cons. Lifeway Christian Resources, Nashville, 1993—. Author: Children's Sunday School for a New Century, 1999; co-author: Towards 2000: Leading Chidlren in Sunday School, 1995, Crayons, Computers, and Kids, 1996. Mem. adv. bd. Nat. Presch. Children's Conv., Nashville, 1996—; mem. steering com. Nat. Leadership Summit, Nashville, 1995-97. Mem. ASCD, Soc. Am. Magicians, Internat. Brotherhood Magicians, So. Bapt. Religious Edn. Assn. Avocations: magic, music, art, cooking, drama. E-mail: jhargra@lifway.com. Office: Lifeway Christian Resources MSN 178 127 Ninth Ave N Nashville TN 37234

HARGRAVE, ROBERT WARREN, hair styling salon chain executive; b. Meridian, Miss., Sept. 15, 1944; s. George Herbert and Clara (Gibson) H.; m. Janeice Stodghill, Dec. 23, 1967; 1 child, Jennifer Lyn. Student, Tyler Jr. Coll., 1963-65; BS, Baylor U., 1967; postgrad., East Tex. State U., 1968. Lic. nursing home adminstr., Tex. Nursing home adminstr. ARA-Nat. Living Ctrs., Waco, Tex., 1969-71; dir. personnel and spl. programs ARA-Nat. Living Ctrs., Houston, 1971-75; exec. v.p. ARA-Geriatrics, Colo., Tex. 1975-79; founder, owner 16 hair styling salons San Antonio Enterprises, Inc., 1979—; tchr. nursing home adminstrn., McLennan Community Coll., Waco, 1970, mem. steering com. to establish nursing home license program, 1970; mem. Nat. Bd. Salon Franchises, Cutco Insustries, Inc., N.Y.C., 1985-87, pres. Direct Licensees' Assn., 1991-92; adv. com. Tex. Cosmetology Commn., 1994—. Mem. adv. bd. cosmetology dept. South San High Sch., 1987—, adv. coun. for career and tech. edn. N. East Ind. Sch. Dist., 1994—. Mem. Am. Salon Assn., Tex. Salon Assn., San Antonio Salon Assn., Tex. Nursing Home Assn. (chpt. pres. 1970), Colo. Health Care Assn. (del. for nat. fire safety 1978), Am. Health Care Assn., Nat. Parks and Recreation Assn., Nat. Therapeutic Recreational Soc., Gideons Internat. Avocations: boating, fishing. Office: San Antonio Enterprises Inc 4221 Centergate St San Antonio TX 78217-4802

HARGRAVE, SARAH QUESENBERRY, consulting company executive; b. Mt. Airy, N.C., Dec. 11, 1944; d. Teddie W. and Lois Knight (Slusher) Quesenberry. Student, Radford Coll., 1963-64, Va. Poly. Inst. and State U., 1964-67. Mgmt. trainee Thalhimer Bros. Dept. Store, Richmond, Va., 1967-68; Cen. Va. fashion and publicity dir. Sears Roebuck & Co., Richmond, 1968-73; nat. decorating sch. coord. Sears Roebuck & Co., Chgo., 1973-74, nat. dir. bus. and profl. women's programs, 1974-76; v.p., treas., program dir. Sears-Roebuck Found., Chgo., 1976-87, program mgr. corp. contbns. and memberships, 1981-84, dir. corp. mktg. and pub. affairs, 1984-87; v.p. personal fin. svcs. and mktg. Northern Trust Co., Chgo., 1987-89; pres. Hargrave Consulting, 1989—; spkr., seminar leader in field. Bd. dirs. Am. Assembly Collegiate Schs. Bus., 1979-82, mem. vis. com., 1979-82, mem. fin. and audit com., 1980-82, mem. task force on doctoral supply and demand, 1980-82; mem. Com. for Equal Opportunity for Women, 1976-81; chmn., 1978-79, 80-81; mem. bus. adv. coun. Walter E. Heller Coll. Bus. Adminstrn., Roosevelt U., 1979-89; co-dir. Ill. Internat. Women's Yr. Ctr., 1975. Named Outstanding Young Women of Yr. Ill., 1976; named Women of Achievement State Street Bus. and Profl. Woman's Club, 1978. Mem. Eddystone Condominium Assn. (v.p. 1978-86), Profl. Women's Network. Home and Office: 34 Fairlawn Ave Daly City CA 94015-3425*

HARGRAVES, MARTHA ANN, health services administrator, educator; b. Mexia, Tex., July 24, 1946; d. Willie Henry and Luerean (Edmond) Houston; m. Archie Lee Hargraves, June 10, 1965 (div. 1975); 1 child, Sharon Denise. BSBA, Jarvis Christian Coll., 1967; M in Pub. Health, U. Tex., 1975, PhD in Mgmt./Policy Scis., 1992. Chief interagy. coordination Dept. of Health and Human Svcs., Washington, 1975-77, spl. asst. Office of Sec., 1977-79; dep. asst. sec. licensing and regulation Dept. of Health and Human Svcs., State of La., 1979-81; program mgmt. officer Ctrs. for Disease Control USPHS, Atlanta, 1981-88; faculty assoc., rsch. assoc. U. Tex. Sch. of Pub. Health Ctr. for Health Policy, Houston, 1988-92, postdoctoral fellow Office of the Pres., 1992-93; asst. prof., dir. health policy and health svcs. rsch. U. Tex. Sch. of Pub. Health Ctr. for Health Policy, Galveston, 1993—; com. mem. osteoporosis adv. com. Tex. Dept. of Health, Austin, Tex., 1996-98; com. mem. mayor's com. for the advancement of families and children, Galveston, 1988—; mem. panel of experts U.S. Dept. Health and Human Svcs., USPHS, 1998—. Contbr. articles to profl. jours. Bd. dirs. YMCA, Galveston, 1994-96, San Jacinto Girl Scouts, Houston, 1990-93. Recipient Disting. Alumni Citation of Yr. Nat. Assn. for Equal Opportunity in Higher Edn., 1997. Mem. Soc. for the Study of Social Problems (com. of budget and fin. 1999—, chair minority grad. scholarship com. 1998), Chauncey Leake History of Medicine Soc., Consortium of Doctors, Ltd., Phi Kappa Phi. Avocations: cooking, walking, travel. Fax: 409-747-4991. E-mail: mhargrav@utmb.edu. Office: U Tex Med Br at Galveston 301 Clinical Scis Bldg 301 University Blvd Galveston TX 77555

HARGRAVES, RUDOLPH, state supreme court justice; b. Shawnee, Okla., Feb. 15, 1925; s. John Hubert and Daisy (Holmes) H.; m. Madeline Hargrave, May 29, 1949; children: Cindy Lu, John Robert, Jana Sue. LLB, U. Okla., 1949. Bar: Okla. 1949. Pvt. practice Wewoka, Okla., 1949; asst. county atty. Seminole County, 1951-55; judge Seminole County Ct., 1964-67, Seminole County Superior Ct., 1967-69; dist. judge Okla. Dist. Ct., Dist. 22, 1969-79; assoc. justice Okla. Supreme Ct., Oklahoma City, 1979, former vice chief justice, former chief justice, justice, 1979—. Mem. Seminole County Bar Assn., Okla. Bar Assn., ABA. Democrat. Methodist. Lodges: Lions; Masons. Office: Okla Supreme Ct State Capitol Bldg Room 202 Oklahoma City OK 73105*

HARGREAVES, DAVID WILLIAM, communications company executive; b. Akron, Ohio, May 4, 1943; s. William B. and Helen Grace (Slusser) H.; m. Sandra Jean Tessier, Sept. 4, 1965; children: Kristen Elizabeth, Cinda Anne, Gregory David. BSEE, U. Maine, Orono, 1965; MBA, U. Rochester, 1967. Sales engr. Mobile Communications div. Gen. Electric, Lynchburg, Va., 1970-74, mgr. systems projects, 1974-75, mgr. systems bids/proposals, 1975-78; mgr. internat. mktg. Gen. Electric Powerline Carrier Bus., Lynchburg, 1978-80; gen. mgr. Gen. Electric Microwave Link Operation, Owensboro, Ky., 1980-84; mng. dir. Alpha Telecom div. Alpha Industries, Methuen, Mass., 1984-86; pres. Dynatech Tactical Comms. Inc. (formerly Controlonics Corp.), Nashua, N.H., 1986-97; pres., CEO DTC Comms. Inc., Nashua, 1997—; condr. seminars in field. Contbr. articles to profl. jours. Chmn. bd. Gen. Electric United Way Pacesetter campaign, Lynchburg, 1978; advisor Jr. Achievement project bus., Owensboro, 1982, 83. Served to capt. U.S. Army, 1968-70, Vietnam. Decorated Bronze Star, D.S.C., 1970. Mem. Am. Mktg. Pres.'s Assn., Massibesic Yacht Club, Eta Kappa Nu, Tau Beta Pi. Republican. Avocations: sailing, skiing, amateur radio. Home: 191 Buttrick Rd Hampstead NH 03841-2183 Office: DTC Comms Inc 75 Northeastern Blvd Nashua NH 03062-3128

HARGREAVES, GEORGE HENRY, civil and agricultural engineer, researcher; b. Chico, Calif., Apr. 2, 1916; s. Carey and Luella May (Raymond) H.; m. Elizabeth Ann Gardner, Aug. 9, 1941 (dec. Dec. 1948); 1 child, Margaret Ann Hargreaves Stolpmann; m. Sara Etna Romero, Jan. 6, 1951; children: Mark Romero, Sonia Maria Hargreaves Hart, George Leo. B.S. in Soils, U. Calif.-Berkeley, 1939; B.S.C.E., U. Wyo., 1943. Civil engr. U.S. Bur. Reclamation, Sacramento, 1946-48; reclamation engr. U.S. Army C.E., Greece, 1948-49; engr. AID, Greece, Peru, Haiti, Philippines, Brazil and Colombia, 1950-68; chief civil engr. engrng. branch Natural Resources Divsn. Inter-Am. Geudetic Survey, Ft. Clayton, C.Z., 1968-70; research engr. in irrigation Utah State U., Logan, 1970-86, dir. research Internat. Irrigation Ctr., 1980-86, research prof. emeritus, 1986—. Author: World Water for Agriculture, 1977; co-author: Irrigation Fundamentals, 1998. Contbr. numerous articles to profl. jours. Served to lt. (j.g.) USNr, 1943-46; PTO. Fellow ASCE (chmn. surface water com. 1974-75); mem. Am. Soc. Agrl. Engrs. (chmn. Rocky Mountain sect. 1974), Internat. Commn. Irrigation and Drainage (chmn. U.S. com. on crops and water use 1992-96). Recipient Royce J. Tipton award 1987. Home: 1660 E 1220 N Logan UT 84341-3040 Office: Utah State U Internat Irrigation Ctr Dept Biol/Irrigation Engring Logan UT 84322-4150

HARGROVE, DON, state senator; b. Bozeman, Mont., Mar. 16, 1933; s. Ora Augustus and Helen Victoria (Drizle) H.; m. Eloise Marilyn Fellbaum, Aug. 20, 1955; children: Mark, Dan, David. BS, Mont. State U., 1956; MS, U. So. Calif., L.A., 1966. Commd. 2d lt. USAF, 1956, advanced through grades to col., 1976, comdr. 41st Mil. Airlift Squadron, comdr. 63d Mil. Airlift Group, def. attache to Bolivia; senator Mont. State Senate, Helena, 1995—; aviation advisor Colombian Nat. Narcotics Police, 1986-91. Republican. Home: 37 Big Chief Trl Bozeman MT 59718-9419 Office: Montana State Senate State Capitol Dist 16 Helena MT 59620

HARGROVE, ERWIN C., political scientist, educator; b. St. Joseph, Mo.; s. Erwin C. and Gladys Lenore (France) H.; m. Julia Mosher, Sept. 21, 1991. BA, Yale U., 1953, PhD, 1963. Faculty Brown U., Providence, R.I., 1960-76, Vanderbilt U., Nashville, 1976—; vis. scholar Inst. Ednl. Policy Studies, Grad. Sch. Edn. Harvard U., 1980. Author: Presidential Leadership, Personality and Political Style, 1966, Professional Roles in Society and Government: The English Case, The Power of the Modern Presidency, 1974, The Missing Link: The Study of the Implementation of Social Policy, 1975, Jimmy Carter as President, Leadership and the Politics of the Public Good, 1988 (Richard E. Neustadt award), Prisoners of Myth: Leadership of the Tennessee Valley Authority, 1933-1990, 1994, The President as Leader: Attending to the Better Angels of Our Nature, 1998; (with Michael Nelson) Presidents, Politics and Policy, 1984; co-editor, author: TVA, Fifty Years of Grass-roots Bureacracy, 1983; co-editor: The President and the Council of Economic Advisors: Interviews with CEA Chairmen, 1984, Leadership and Innovation: A Biographical Perspective on Entrepreneurs in Government, 1987, 2nd edit. 1990, Impossible Jobs in Public Management, 1990. Assoc. Chubb fellow, Yale U., 1959-60, Social Sci. Rsch. Coun. Faculty fellow, Yale U., 1967-68, Howard Found. fellow, 1967-68, Summer fellow NEH, 1989.

HARGROVE, ERWIN CHARLES, JR., political science educator; b. St. Joseph, Mo., Oct. 11, 1930; s. Erwin Charles and Gladys Lenore (France) H.; m. Lynne Douglas, Apr. 10, 1961 (div. Jan., 1991); children: John, Amy, Sarah; m. Julia Mosher, Sept. 21, 1991. BA, Yale U., 1953, PhD, 1963. From asst. prof. to prof. polit. sci. Brown U., Providence, R.I., 1960-71; prof., dept. chair polit. sci. Brown U., Providence, 1971-73; sr. fellow Urban Inst., Washington, 1973-75; prof. polit. sci., dir. Inst. for Pub. Policy Studies Vanderbilt U., Nashville, Tenn., 1976-85; chmn. dept. polit. sci. Vanderbilt U., Nashville, 1992-96. Author: Presidential Leadership, Personality and Political Style, 1966, Professional Roles in Society and Government: The English Case, 1972, The Power of the Modern Presidency, 1974, The Missing Link: The Study of Implementation of Social Policy, 1975, Jimmy Carter as President, Leadership and the Politics of the Public Good, 1988 (Richard E. Neustadt award 1988), Prisoners of Myth: Leadership o f the Tennessee Valley Authority, 1933-1990, 1994, The President as Leader: Appending to the Better Angels of Our Nature, 1998; co-author: (with Michael Nelson) Presidents, Politics and Policy, 1984; co-editor: (with Paul Conkin) TVA, Fifty Years of Grass Roots Bureaucracy, 1983, (with Samuel Morley) The President and the Council of Economic Advisers: Interviews with CEA Chairmen, 1984, (with Jameson Doig), Leadership and Innovation: A Bigraphical Perspective on Entrepreneurs in Government, 1987, (with John Glidewell) Impossible Jobs in Public Management, 1990. With U.S. Army, 1954-56. Democrat. Episcopalian. Home: 662 Timber Ln Nashville TN 37215-1120 Office: Vanderbilt Univ Polit Sci Dept Nashville TN 37235

HARGROVE, JAMES WARD, financial consultant; b. Shreveport, La., Oct. 31, 1922; s. Reginald H. and Hallie (Ward) H.; m. Marion Elizabeth Smith, Aug. 25, 1942; children: James W., Florence, Thomas M., William H. Grad., Sewanee Mil. Acad., 1939; B.A., Rice U., 1943. Sec., treas. Caddo Abstract Co., 1946-47; with Tex. Eastern Transmission Corp., 1947-69, sr. v.p., 1967-69; asst. postmaster gen. finance and adminstrn. U.S. Postal Service, Washington, 1969-71; sr. asst. postmaster gen. support U.S. Postal Service, 1971-72; fin. cons. Houston, 1972-76; U.S. ambassador Australia, 1976-77; chmn. Vaughan, Nelson & Hargrove, Inc. (investment counselors), 1977—83; gov.-adviser Rice U.; chmn. Entrix Inc., 1989—. Mem. Phi Beta Kappa. Home: 60 Tiel Way Houston TX 77019-1510

HARGROVE, JERRY EDWARD, JR., minister; b. Camden, Ark., Dec. 11, 1949; s. Jerry Edward and Fannie Lee (Blake) H.; B.A., U. Ark., 1972; postgrad. Cath. U. Am., 1972-76; M.S., Loyola Coll., 1982; PhD, Loyola Coll., 1997. Cert. nat. counselor; cert. clin. mental health conselor. Tchr., elem. secondary schs. and colls., 1955-76; ordained priest Roman Catholic Ch., 1976; assoc. pastor Nativity Ch., 1976-79; asst. pastor St. Peters Ch., Washington, 1979-83 ; assoc. pastor Holy Name Ch., Washington, 1983-86, pastor, 1986-93; dir., chaplain Howard U. Newman Ctr., 1994—; chaplain Seaton High Sch., 1984; tchr./counselor St. Cecilia High Sch., Washington, 1974-78; chaplain D.C. N.G., 1978. Mem. NAACP (life), Am. Counseling Assn., Mil. Chaplains Assn., Phi Mu Alpha, Alpha Phi Alpha (life). Clubs: K.C., Knights of St. John. Home and Office: 206 New York Ave NW Washington DC 20001-1232

HARGROVE, JOHN JAMES, bankruptcy judge; b. Bay Shore, N.Y., May 4, 1942; s. John A. and Cecelia L. Hargrove; m. Jane A Nagle, Oct. 21, 1967; children: David, Kristin, Kelly, Kathryn. BAin Polit. Sci., U. Notre Dame, 1964, JD, 1967. Bar: N.Y. 1968, Calif. 1971. Atty. Gant & Asaro, San Diego, 1972-76; ptnr. Weeks, Willis, Hoffman & Hargrove, San Diego, 1976-79, Strauss, Kissane, Davis & Hargrove, San Diego, 1979-83, Britton & Hargrove, San Diego, 1983-84; prin. John J. Hargrove & Assocs., San Diego, 1984-85; judge U.S. Bankruptcy Ct., San Diego, 1985—; adj. prof. Calif. Western Sch. Law, 1986. Coach University City Bobby Sox Softball Team; lector Our Mother of Confidence Roman Cath. Ch.; trustee U. Notre Dame, 1987-89. Lt. col. USMCR, 1968-90. Mem. U. Notre Dame Alumni Assn. (bd. dirs. 1985-89, pres. 1988-89). Republican. Avocations: basketball, softball, running. Office: US Bankruptcy Ct So Dist Calif 325 W F St San Diego CA 92101-6989*

HARGROVE, JOHN RUSSELL, lawyer; b. Chgo., Jan. 20, 1947; s. John Francis and Dolly (Arzich) H.; m. Mary Cheryl Fuller, Feb. 12, 1972; children: John Ashby, James Fuller. BS, Butler U., 1969; JD magna cum laude, Ind. U., 1972. Bar: Ind. 1972, Fla. 1974, U.S. Tax Ct. 1975, U.S. Supreme Ct. 1976. Law clk. to Hon Roy L. Stephenson U.S. Ct. Appeals Ind., 1971-72, U.S. Ct. Appeals (8th cir.), 1972-74; mng. dir. and shareholder Heinrich, Gordon, Hargrove, Weihe & James, P.A., Ft. Lauderdale, Fla., 1985-91. Lead articles and book rev. editor Ind. Law Rev., 1971-72. Bd. visitors Ind. U. Sch. Law, 1995—; bd. dirs. EV Ready Broward, 1996-98; nat. co-chair Franciscan Games, 1996. Schofield scholar. Recipient Faculty award Ind. U. Sch. of Law, 1972. Fellow Fla. Acad. Probate and Trust Litigation; mem. ABA, Fed. Bar Assn. (Broward County Fla. chpt., exec. com. 1979-80, v.p. 1980-81, pres. 1981-82), Fla. Bar Assn., Ind. Bar Assn. (mem. bd. vis. Sch. of Law 1995—). Roman Catholic. Office: 500 E Broward Blvd Ste 1000 Fort Lauderdale FL 33394-3000*

HARGROVE, MICHAEL B., transportation executive; b. Georgetown, Ky., Apr. 15, 1941; s. B. Walton and Zellaca Mae (Isbell) H.; m. F. Marion Hanson, June 25, 1966. BS in Chemistry, U. Ky., 1963, MS in Econs., 1966, PhD in Econs., 1971. Chemist Ky. Hwy. Dept., Frankfort, 1963-64; rsch. asst. Ky. Hwy. Labs., Lexington, 1964-65; teaching asst. U. Ky., Lexington, 1965-66, rsch. assoc., 1966-68; lectr. U. Md., College Park, 1968-71, asst. prof., 1971-77; prin. Tempus Assocs., University Park, Md., 1974-79; mgr., engrng. economist Assn. Am. R.R.s, Washington, 1979-84, dir., engrng. economist, 1984—. Contbr. articles to profl. jours. U. Md. rsch. fellow, 1977. Mem. Am. Econs. Assn., Am. Statis. Assn., Am. R.R. Engrng. Assn., Transp. Rsch. Forum, Decision Sci. Inst. Democrat. Methodist. Avocations: sailing, golf. Home: 61 St Andrews Rd Severna Park MD 21146-1433 Office: Assn Am RRs 50 F St NW Washington DC 20001-1530

HARGROVE, MIKE (DUDLEY MICHAEL HARGROVE), professional baseball team manager; b. Perryton, Tex., Oct. 26, 1949; m. Sharon Ruprecht, Dec. 12, 1970; children: Kimberly Denise, Melissa Kathryn, Pamela Christine, Andrew Michael, Cynthia Michelle. BS in Phys. Edn. and Social Scis., Northwestern Okla. State U. Baseball player Tex. Rangers, 1974-78, San Diego Padres, 1979; baseball player Cleve. Indians, 1979-85, coach minor league team, 1986, mgr. minor league team, 1987-89, coach, 1990-91, mgr., 1991—. Named Am. League Rookie of Yr. Baseball Writers' Assn. Am., 1974, Am. League Rookie Player of Yr. Sporting News, 1974; named to All-Star team, 1975, Am. League Mgr. of Yr. Sporting News, 1995. Mgr. Am. League championship team, 1995. Office: Cleveland Indians 2401 Ontario St Cleveland OH 44115-4003*

HARI, KENNETH STEPHEN, painter, sculptor, writer; b. Perth Amboy, N.J., Mar. 31, 1947; s. Stephen John and Jeannette Anna (Matuszewsky) H. Diploma, Newark Sch. Fine and Indsl. Arts, 1966; BFA, Md. Inst. Art, 1968, Yale U., 1970; postgrad., NYU, 1988. cons. various cos. One man exhbns. include ctrl. Ala., 1996, Beijing, 1996; group exhbns. include Md. State Mus., 1967, Union Coll., Schenectady, 1969, Monmouth (N.J.) Coll., 1970, Newark Mus., 1971, Trenton State Coll., 1972, one-man exhbns. include C.C. Price Gallery, N.Y.C., H.S. Graphics, Ltd., Keasbey, N.J.; represented in permanent collections of over 390 mus. throughout world, including Vatican, Lincoln Center Gallery for Performing Arts, N.Y.C., Va. Poly. Inst., Blacksburg, N.J. State Mus., Trenton, Grand Ole Opry House, Nashville, Xiaoyi Liu collection, Mus. Kenneth Hari, Beijing, China, established 1991, other pub. and pvt. collections; Important works include portraits of, W.H. Auden, N.Y.C., 1969, M. Moore, N.Y.C., 1969, Pablo Casals, Marlboro, Vt., 1970, Andres Segovia, N.Y.C., 1972, James Michener, Piperville, Pa., 1973, Marcel Marceau, N.Y.C., 1973, Donald Delue, N.Y.C., 1973, Dr. Allan Callow, Boston, 1973, Kurt Vonnegut, Jr., 1973, Buckminster Fuller, 1973, Lord Hailsham, London, 1978, Dr. Linus Pauling for Pauling Inst., Menlo Park, Calif., 1979, Paul Robeson for Paul Robeson Center, Rutgers U., Newark, 1979 (Hay award recipients.); Zhao Peng Fei, Beijing, Philip Johnson, N.Y.C., Paul Roache, Spain, Chen Chi, N.Y.C., Liu Zongyu, Beijing, Zhongguo Shengj, Living Treasure of China, 1999, Hiroko Seta, Tokyo, Japan, 1999, Rosemary Clooney, Beverly Hills, Calif., 1999; Paul Robeson exibited Johnson & Johnson , New Brunswick Travel Exhibition, The Angel of Revelation Mural, N.J., 1990; Original lithographs pub. Prophet, 1971, Lovers of Our Time, 1971, Vermont, 1972, Folk Singer, Marcel Marceau, 1973, Abraham, 1973, Ernest Hemingway, 1978, Homage to Virginia, 1980, Tropical Ladies, 1981, The Pearl, 1999. Bd. dirs. N.J. Art Festival, 1973—. Office: Eastman & John Watson Art Galleries Care John Eastman PO Box 243 Keasbey NJ 08832-0243 *Art is the soul of man, and without it he is lost.*

HARIJAN, RAM, computer scientist, technology transfer researcher; b. Keecheri, Kerala, India, June 3, 1938; s. Narayanan and Devaki (Amma) Nambiar; m. Lakshmi VP, Aug. 19, 1977; 1 child, Pooja Devi. BA with honors, Madras U., India; MA with award, Southampton U., Eng.; PhD, Reading U., Eng. Lectr. Kerala (India) U.; mining officer Singareni Collieries, India; sch. tchr. Barnstaple Grammar Sch., Eng.; lectr. Bosworth Coll., Eng.; tutor cons. Open U., Eng.; researcher Centre for Studies in Tech. Transfer, Eng.; involved in formulating computerisation policies of Indian Govt., 1985-89; vis. prof. U. Madras, 1982, Calicut U., 1985. Contbr. The Phenomenon of Late-Development Syndrome and Ways of Combating the Syndrome in Late-Developing Countries, The Phenomenon of Late-Development Syndrome in Late-Developing Societies, Combating the Syndrome Through Technology Transfer, Targeted Inputting of Computers to Combat India's Late-Development Syndrome. Chmn. North Devon Dist. Labour Party, 1972-77, North Devon Assn. Racial Equality, 1978-80; vol. social worker Helping the Disabled and Disadvantaged. Avocations: bridge, chess. Home: 30 Norfolk Rd, Leicester LE9 9HR, England

HARINCK, JOHN GORDON, sales executive, hydraulics engineer; b. Detroit, Sept. 6, 1939; s. Peter Gordon and Mary Alice (Hooper) H.; m. Dorothy Elizabeth Wallace, Nov. 17, 1959 (div. Feb. 1984); children: Jeffery John, Elizabeth Mary, Pamela Ann, Timothy Alan, Shannon Elizabeth; m. Sally Ann Sperry, Feb. 9, 1985. BSME, Lawrence Inst. Tech., Southfield, Mich., 1965. Cert. fluid power specialist. Applications engr. Vickers, Inc., Troy, Mich., 1960-67; sales engr., sales supr., product mgr., gen. sales mgr. Eaton Corp., Marshall, Mich., 1967-74; Midwest regional mgr. Pall Corp., Glen Cove, N.Y., 1974-78; account mgr., branch mgr. Fauver Co., Inc., Madison Heights, Mich., 1978-84; nat. accounts mgr., regional mgr., Double A Products Co. Vickers, Inc., Troy, Mich., 1984-97; fluid power specialist DTS Fluid Power, Grandville, Mich., 1997-99; owner, operator Housemaster Home Inspection Svc., Tucson, 1999—. Mem. Jaycees, Marshall, 1967-72. Mem. Engr. Soc. of Detroit, Nat. Fluidpower Assn., Fluid Power Soc., Soc. Automotive Engrs., Moose. Republican. Episcopalian. Avocations: skiing, golf, woodworking, fishing. Home and Office: 8330 N La Oesta Ave Tucson AZ 85704-3412

HARING, ELLEN STONE (MRS. E. S. HARING), philosophy educator; b. L.A., 1921; d. Earl E. and Eleanor (Pritchard) Stone; m. Philip S. Haring, Dec. 1942 (div. June 1951). BA, Bryn Mawr Coll., 1942; MA, Radcliffe Coll., 1943, PhD (AAUW fellow), 1959. Adminstrv. worker ARC, Boston, 1943; mem. faculty Wheaton Coll., Norton, Mass., 1944-45; mem. faculty Wellesley Coll., 1945-72, assoc. prof., 1958-64, prof. philosophy, 1964-72; prof. philosophy U. Fla., Gainesville, 1972-93, prof. emerita, 1993—; chmn. dept. U. Fla., 1972-80. Mem. Am. Philos. Assn., Metaphys. Soc. Am. Office: U Fla Griffin-Floyd 330 Gainesville FL 32611-8545

HARING, EUGENE MILLER, lawyer; b. Washington, May 16, 1927; s. Horace E. and Edith (Miller) H.; m. Janet K. Marshall, Apr. 10, 1971. A.B. summa cum laude, Princeton U., 1949, A.M. (Woodrow Wilson fellow), 1951; LL.B., Harvard U., 1955. Bar: N.J. 1955, N.Y. 1983, U.S. Dist. Ct. N.J. 1955, U.S. Dist. Ct. (so. and ea. dists.) N.Y. 1992, U.S. Ct. Appeals (3d cir.) 1962, U.S. Supreme Ct. 1969. Asst. in instrn. Princeton U., 1950-52; assoc. McCarter & English, Newark, 1955-61, ptnr., 1961-97, chmn. exec. com., 1982-97, of counsel, 1997—; cert. mediator U.S. Dist. Ct., 1994—; mediator CPR Inst. for Dispute Resolution, N.J. Panel, 1994—; mem. roster of mediators Judiciary of State of N.J.; mem. civil justice reform act adv. com. U.S. Dist. Ct. N.J., 1997—. Contbr. articles to profl. jours. Chmn. Princeton Twp. Zoning Bd. Adjustment, 1979-80, mem. bd., 1975-79; vestryman Trinity Episc. Ch., Princeton, 1975-79, 97—, warden, 1980-84; mem. com. on constn. and canons Episc. Diocese of N.J., 1980-87, chancellor, 1983-94; trustee Gen. Theol. Sem., N.Y., 1987-90; mem. vis. com. Rutgers U. Law Sch., 1994—; trustee N.J. Jersey Shore Found., 1988-92. Served with USNR, 1945-46. Fellow Am. Bar Found., Lawyers Adv. Com. (U.S. Ct. Appeals 3d cir. 1990-93, U.S. Dist. Ct. N.J. 1997—); mem. ABA, N.J. Bar Assn. (ins. com. 1972-74, chmn. 1981-83), N.J. State Bar Found. (trustee 1986-87, v.p. 1987-88, chmn. 1988-90), Essex County Bar Assn., Mercer County Bar Assn., Am. Law Inst. (life), Am. Judicature Soc., Internat. Assn. Def. Counsel, Harvard Law Sch. Assn. N.J. (pres. 1971-72, nat. v.p. 1972-73), Hist. Soc. U.S. Dist. Ct. for Dist. N.J. (trustee 1987-90, 97—), Hist. Soc. 3d Cir. Ct. Appeals (bd., dirs. 1993—), Nassau Club, Princeton, Springdale Golf Club, Princeton, Monmouth Hunt Club, Phi Beta Kappa. Republican. Avocation: horseback riding, golf. Home: 75 Rosedale Ln Princeton NJ 08540-2417 Office: McCarter & English Gateway 4 100 Mulberry St Newark NJ 07102-4004

HARING, HOWARD JACK, newsletter editor; b. Boyertown, Pa., Aug. 7, 1924; s. Howard and Beulah (Rose) H.; m. Rosalind Kenyon Hoyle, Dec. 10, 1949; children: Christopher, Jeffrey, Douglas, Andrea, Eric. AB, Muhlenberg Coll., 1948; MJ, Columbia U., 1949. Reporter Providence Jour.-Bull., 1949; editor Boyertown (Pa.) Times, 1950; reporter Allentown (Pa.) Morning Call, 1951-53; sports columnist, TV mag. editor Washington Star, 1954-58; assoc. editor Saturday Evening Post, Phila., 1958-62; copy chief Ladies Home Jour., N.Y.C., 1963-69; exec. editor Boy's Life mag., North Brunswick, N.J., 1970-71; editor Exploring mag., 1972-74; sr. editor Guideposts mag., N.Y.C., 1975-81, mng. editor, 1982-88, contbg. editor, 1989-95; editor newsletter South County (R.I.) Ctr. for Arts, 1991—, Richmond (R.I.) Sr. Citizens, 1995—; instr. editing newspapers and periodicals Am. U., Washington, 1955-58; mem. Am. Soc. Mag. Editors, 1972-90. Editor numerous books for Curtis Pub. Co., Scribner's and Reader's Digest Books; revised and edited: Pete Martin's Jerry Giesler, 1959. Vice-chmn. Indsl. Commn. West Windsor Twp., N.J., 1970-72, chmn., 1973-74. With AUS, 1942-46. Decorated Purple Heart. Home and Office: 87 Beaver River Rd West Kingston RI 02892-1135

HARING, KATHRYN ANN, special education educator, research scientist; b. Syracuse, N.Y., Oct. 1, 1955; d. Norris G. and Dorothy M. (Borgens) H.; m. David L. Lovett, Nov. 11, 1950; children: Momaur, Bastick, Kokopellie. BS, U. Western Wash., 1977; PhD, U. N.Mex., 1987. Tchr., coach Federal Way (Wash.) Schs., 1979-82; clin. supr. U. N.Mex., Albuquerque, 1983-84; tchr. Albuquerque Pub. Schs., 1985-86; asst. prof. Utah State U., Logan, 1986-90; coord. rsch. scientist San Francisco State U., 1987-90; prin. investigator, assoc. prof. spl. edn. U. Okla., Norman, 1990—; adv., expert N.Mex. Protection and Advocacy, Albuquerque, 1983-86; witness for people with disabilities and their families ACLU, San Francisco, 1987-90, Okla. Indigent Def. Fund, 1996—. Author, editor: Integrated Lifecycle Services for People with Disabilities, 1992. Faculty advisor Students for Exceptional Children, Norman, Okla., 1990-97, Habitat for Humanity, Norman, 1996—; mem. exec. bd., treas. Assn. for People with Severe Disabilities, 1994-96. Mem. Am. Assn. Learning Disabilities (pres. 1984-86), Coun. Exceptional Children (divsn. rsch. treas 1986-88, divsn. early childhood editl. bd. 1992—), Grad. Student Assn. U. N.Mex. (pres. 1983-86). Democrat. Unitarian. Avocations: running, hiking, vegetarian cooking, dance, gardening. Home: 4612 Crystal Lake Rd Norman OK 73072-9739 Office: Univ Okla 820 Van Vleet Oval # 321 Norman OK 73019-2040

HARING, OLGA MUNK, retired medical educator, physician; b. Oradea, Bihor, Romania, Aug. 25, 1917; came to U.S., 1949; d. Moris and Ilona (Lindenbaum) Munk; m. Tibor J. Haring, Feb. 20, 1938 (div. Jan. 1961); 1 dau., Claire. BA, Jewish Girls Gymnasium, Budapest, Hungary, 1932; MD, U. Vienna, 1938, Leon U., Nicaragua, 1939; postgrad., Sorbonne U., Paris, 1947-49. Diplomate Am. Bd. Internal Medicine. Med. dir. pub. health dept. Health Ctr. 1, Managua, Nicaragua, 1940-46; chief of service cardiology ward Gen. Hosp., Managua, 1946-47; fgn. asst. cardiology Laribosiere Hosp., Paris, 1947-49; intern St. Francis Sanitorium for Cardiac Children, Roslyn, N.Y., 1950; research assoc. div. cardiology Chgo. Med. Sch., 1950-57, clin. assoc. in medicine, 1953-57; assoc. of chief of service Univ.-La Rabida Sanitarium, 1952-57; Hektoen Inst. fellow in pediatric cardiology Cook County Children's Hosp., 1951; rotating intern Mt. Sinai Hosp., Chgo., 1952, chief cardiac pediatric clinic, 1952-57; resident in medicine Chgo. Wesley Meml. Hosp., 1960-61, Cook County Hosp., Chgo., 1961-62; rsch. assoc. in teratology Congenital Heart Disease Research and Tng. Ctr.-Hektoen Inst. Med. Research, Chgo., 1962-66; assoc. attending physician div. medicine Cook County Hosp.-Northwestern U. Med. Sch., Chgo., 1964—; mem. univ. faculty dept. medicine Northwestern U. Med. Sch., Chgo., 1965—, prof., 1974-87, prof. dept. cmty. health and preventive medicine, 1974-87, prof. emeritus, 1987—, dir. med. sch. cardio-pulmonary-renal clinics, 1965-75, dir. cardiac clinics, 1975-87, prof. Grad. Sch., 1972-87; attending staff physician Northwestern Meml. Hosp., Chgo., 1966-87, sr. attending staff, 1987—; attending physician VA Lakeside Hosp., Chgo., 1975-87. Contbr. numerous articles, abstracts to profl. jours. Fellow in social pediatrics UN Children's Emergency Fund-U., Paris, 1948; grantee NIH, 1956-61, 67-73, Chgo. Heart Assn., 1962-66, Health Resources Adminstrn., 1972-76, Nat. Heart and Lung Inst., 1974-79, 77-82. Fellow ACP, Am. Coll. Cardiology, Am. Heart Assn. (council on circulation), Inst. Medicine in Chgo., Sigma Xi; mem. Am. Fedn. Clin. Research, AAAS, Assn. Computing Machinery, Assn. Health Records, AAUP, Am. Med. Women's Assn., Am. Geriatrics Assn., Am. Gerontology Soc. Democrat. Jewish. Home: 1201 Judson Ave Evanston IL 60202-1316

HARING, ROBERT WESTING, newspaper editor; b. Salem, Mo., Nov. 13, 1932; s. Arthur S. and Martha I. (Westing) H.; m. Jo M. Houser, June 1, 1957 (dec. Nov. 1991); children: Robert A., Joel B., Jon G.; m. Carolyn Scudder, May 20, 1995. AA, Kansas City (Mo.) Jr. Coll., 1951; BJ, BA in History, U. Mo., 1954. Reporter So. Illinoisan, Carbondale, Ill., 1954-55, city editor, 1957-59; writer AP, Little Rock, 1959-61; corr. AP, Tulsa, 1961-64; asst. bur. chief AP, Columbus, Ohio, 1964-67; bur. chief AP, Newark, 1967-71; exec. AP, N.Y.C., 1971-75; Sunday editor Tulsa World, 1975-81, exec. editor, 1981-95; ret., 1998. Chmn. Goodwill Industries, Tulsa, 1990-94; bd. dirs. River Parks Authority, Tulsa, 1985-93; pres. Tulsa Zoofriends, 1994-96; chmn. Tulsa Mentoring Coun., Tulsa Lit. Coalition, 1996-98; initiated price earnings ratio in newspaper stock tables, 1973. With U.S. Army, 1955-57. Avocations: running, tennis, bicycling. Home: 1620 S Detroit Ave Tulsa OK 74120-6214

HARINGTON, CHARLES RICHARD, vertebrate paleontologist; b. Calgary, Alta., Can., May 22, 1933; s. Charles Frederic and Florence Katherine (Shillington) H.; m. Gail Doreen Rice, Sept. 15, 1994. BA, U. Alta., 1954, BSc, 1957, PhD, 1977; MSc, McGill U., 1961. Wildlife biologist Can. Wildlife Svc., Ottawa, Ont., 1960-65; vertebrate paleontologist Can. Mus. Nature, Ottawa, 1965—; coord. climatic change in Can. program Nat. Mus. Natural Scis., Ottawa, 1978—; chmn. Can. Com. on Climatic Fluctuations and Man, Ottawa, 1985-90. Author: Quaternary Vertebrate Faunas of Canada and Alaska, 1978; editor: Climatic Change in Canada, 5 vols., 1980-85, Canada's Missing Dimension: Science and History in the Canadian Arctic Islands, 1990, The Year Without a Summer?: World Climate in 1816, 1992; contbr. articles to profl. jours., popular publs. and revs. Recipient Can. Assn. Geographers prize, 1957, meritorious svc. award Yukon Govt. for contbns. to paleontology in Yukon Terr., 1998. Fellow Royal Geog. Soc. (Eng.), Royal Can. Geog. Soc. (Massey medal 1987), Arctic Inst. N.Am. Avocations: travel, camping, reading, canoeing, bicycling. Office: Paleobiology, Can Mus of Nature, Ottawa, ON Canada K1P 6P4

HARIRI, GISUE, architect, educator; b. Abadan, Iran, May 16, 1956; came to U.S., 1974; d. Karim Hariri and Behjat (Isphahani) Saboonchi. BArch, Cornell U., 1980. Apprentice Jennings and Stout, San Francisco, 1980-82; Paolo Soleri, Arcosanti, Ariz., 1982-83; apprentice Paul Segal Assocs. Architects, N.Y.C., 1983-85; ptnr. Hariri & Hariri, N.Y.C., 1986—; lighting and furniture designer, 1993—; participant in Urban Housing Festival, The Hague, The Netherlands, 1991; lectr. in field. Work exhibited in Storefront for Art and Architecture, N.Y.C., 1988, Parson Sch. Design, N.Y.C., 1988, Princeton (N.J.) U., 1988, Archtl. League N.Y., 1990, Kent (Ohio) State U., 1991, Richard Anderson Gallery, N.Y.C., 1993, Cornell U., Ithaca, N.Y., 1993, Contemporary Arts Ctr., Cin., 1993, others, also in various profl. publs.; Monograph: Hariri & Hariri Work in Progress, 1996, Kliczkowski Casas Internat., 1997. Recipient Young Architects Forum award Archtl. League N.Y., 1990. Mem. Internat. Interior Design Assn. Media Stars, 1998. Office: Hariri & Hariri 18 E 12th St New York NY 10003-4458

HARITOS, GEORGE KONSTANTINOS, engineer, educator, military officer; b. Athens, Nov. 29, 1947; came to the U.S., 1964; naturalized, 1970; s. Konstantinos G. and Maria K. (Yiakoumakis) H.; m. Mary Jeannette Martell, June 20, 1971; children: Konstantinos, Marika. BS in Engring., U. Ill., Chgo., 1969, MS in Mechanics and Materials, 1970; PhD in Structural Mechanics, Northwestern U., 1978. Commd. 2d lt. USAF, 1971, advanced through grades to col., 1993; aero. structures engr. aero. systems divsn. USAF, Dayton, Ohio, 1971-75; prof. engring. mechanics USAF Acad., Colorado Springs, 1978-82; prof. aeronautics and astronautics Air Force Inst. Tech., Dayton, 1982-85; program mgr. mechanics of materials Air Force Office Scientific Rsch., Washington, 1986-89, dir. aerospace scis., 1989-90, assoc. dir., 1990-91, dep. dir. and comdr., 1993-95; chief flight vehicles divsn. Hdqrs. Air Force Systems Command, Washington, 1991-92; chief air vehicles br. Hdqrs. Air Force Materiel Command, Dayton, 1992-93; assoc. dean Grad. Sch. Engring. Air Force Inst. Tech., Dayton, Ohio, 1995-98, vice comdt., 1998-99, comdt., 1999—; mem. Def. Com. on Rsch., Washington, 1993-95, OSR Rsch. Coun., Washington, 1993-95. Editor: Damage Mechanics in Composites, 1987, Smart Structures and Materials, 1991; assoc. editor: Internat. Jour. Damage Mechanics, 1990—; contbr. articles to profl. jours. Walter P. Murphy fellow Northwestern U., 1975; decorated meritorious svc. medal with five oak leaf clusters, Air Force commendation medal with one oak leaf cluster. Fellow AIAA (assoc.); mem. Am. Acad. Mechanics, Am. Soc. for Engring. Edn., ASME (materials and structures com. 1986—). Achievements include research in fracture mechanics; fatigue at elevated temperature; engineering mechanics and materials; initiated international research thrusts in mesomechanics for connecting the behavior of materials to their microstructural makeup, and in biomimetics for synthesizing multifunctional materials that imitate biological materials. Office: Air Force Inst Tech Grad Sch Engring 2950 P St Bldg 125 Wright Pat OH 45433-7765

HARJO, JEANNE, pediatrics nurse; b. Cin., Oct. 6, 1953; d. Nancy (Schwierjohann) Hines; m. James Harjo, Aug. 18, 1972; children: James, Christina. Diploma, Good Samaritan Hosp., Cin., 1974. Staff nurse Children's Hosp., Cin., 1978-98, discharge planning coord., 1998—. Author: Neonatal Surgery A Nursing Perspective, 1988; contbg. author: Comprehensive Neonatal Nursing A Physiological Perspective, 1993, 2d edit., 1998. Mem. Nat. Assn. Neonatal Nurses, Am. Pediatric Surg. Nurses Assn. Home: 4657 N Edgewood Ave Cincinnati OH 45232-1758

HARK, WILLIAM HENRY, medical executive, retired military officer; b. Charleston, W.Va., Nov. 1, 1932; s. Zundel and Esther Sylvia (Henry) H.; m. Claudette Berkeley Watson, Apr. 14, 1961; 1 child, William Tucker. AB, W.Va. U., 1954, BS, 1955; MD, Med. Coll. Va., 1957; MPH, Harvard U., 1963. Diplomate Am. Bd. Preventive Medicine. Intern Walter Reed Gen. Hosp., Washington, 1957-58; resident in aerospace medicine U.S. Army, 1962-65, advanced through grades to col., physician, aviation med. cons., 1957-76, ret., 1976; mgr. med. specialites divsn. FAA, Washington, 1980-92, dep. fed. air surgeon, 1992—; adv. group for aerospace R&D, NATO, Brussels, 1969-71; mem. joint com. on aviation pathology Dept. of Def., Washington, 1969-71. Decorated Legion of Merit, Air medal, Bronze Star, Vietnam Campaign medal U.S. Army, 1968. Fellow Am. Coll. Preventive Medicine, Aerospace Med. Assn.; mem. Assn. Mil. Surgeons U.S., So. Med. Assn. Avocations: photography, computers. Home: 4317 Southwood Dr Alexandria VA 22309-2822 Office: FAA 800 Independence Ave SW Washington DC 20591-0001

HARKARVY, BENJAMIN, artistic director. Artistic dir. Royal Winnipeg (Can.) Ballet, 1957-58; artistic dir., founder The Netherlands Dance Theatre, 1959-69; artistic dir. Harkness Ballet, N.Y.C., 1969-70, Dutch Nat. Ballet, The Netherlands, 1970-71, Pa. Ballet, Phila., 1972-82; freelance choreographer various ballet cos., 1982-91; artistic dir. dance divsn. Juilliard Sch., N.Y.C., 1992—; dir. ballet project Jacob's Pillow, 1983-89. Choreographer ballets Time Passed Summer, Recital for Cello and 8 Dancers, Cinque Madrigali, Frames. Office: Juilliard Sch 60 Lincoln Center Plz New York NY 10023-6588

HARKEN, ALDEN HOOD, surgeon, thoracic surgeon; b. Boston, 1941. MD, Case Western Reserve U., 1967. Diplomate Am. Bd. Surgeons, Am. Bd. Thoracic Surgeons. Intern Peter Bent Brigham Hosp., Boston, 1967-68, resident surgery, 1968-70, resident thoracic surgery, 1971-73; fellow cardio-vascular surgery Boston Children's Hosp., 1970-71; surgeon U. Colo. Hosp., Denver; prof., chmn. surgery dept. U. Colo. Sch. Medicine, Denver; part time pvt. practice surgery Denver. Mem. Am. Assn. Thoracic Surgeons, Soc. Univ. Surgeons. Office: U Colo Med Sch Dept Surg 4200 E 9th Ave Denver CO 80220-3706

HARKER, JOSEPH EDWARD, construction, industrial and steel company executive; b. Provo, Utah, Jan. 20, 1936; s. Joseph Alton and Virginia (Packard) H.; student U. Utah, 1954-58; m. Betty Steen, Aug. 20, 1952; children: Joseph Steven, Debra Lynn, Todd Edward. Jr. civil engr. Morrison Knudson Co., Boise, Idaho, 1950-53; welder Utah Sprocket Co., Salt Lake City, 1953-58; engr. draftsman U.S. Steel, Geneva, Utah, 1958-62, field engr., 1962-64, field engr., San Francisco, 1964-66, constrn. engr., Chgo., 1966-72, supt. constrn., 1972-74, mgr. constrn. Eastern dist., Pitts., 1974-78, gen. mgr. constrn., mgmt., 1978-81, v.p. Am. Bridge div., 1981-84; v.p. Edward Gray Corp., 1984-85; pres. Eichleay Corp., Pitts., 1985-86; pres., CEO Harker Assocs., McMurray, Pa., 1986-90, CEO, 1990-93; sr. v.p. Am. Bridge Co., Pitts., 1994—; co-owner Greystone Environ. Techs. Group, Birmingham, Ala., chmn. Active Boy Scouts Am., 1954—. Served with USAR, 1955-60. Mem. Soc. Mining Engrs. of AIME, Am. Inst. Steel Engrs., Engrs. Soc. Western Pa., Valley Brook Country Club (McMurray), Oakmont Country Club. Republican. Mem. LDS Ch. Home: 109 Druid Dr Canonsburg PA 15317-3607

HARKES, JOHN, professional soccer player; b. Kearny, N.J., Mar. 8, 1967; m. Cindy; children: Ian, Lauren. Student, U. Va. With U.S. Nat. Team, 1987—, capt.; midfielder, capt. D.C. United Team; midfielder West Ham United English Premier League, 1995-96, Derby County Football Club. Named Player of Yr., Mo. Athletic Club, 1987, Player of Yr., Atlantic Coast Conf., 1987, Most Valuable Player, U.S. Cup, 1990, First Am. to play in F.A. Cup Final, 1993, First Am. to score goal in Coca-Cola League Cup Final, 1993, C0-Most Valuable Player, Copa Am., 1995. Achievements include captaining D.C. United to first-ever MLS Championship, 1996, scoring English League's Goal of Yr., 1990. Office: DC United 13832 Redskin Dr Herndon VA 20171-3208*

HARKEY, JOHN NORMAN, judge; b. Russellville, Ark., Feb. 25, 1933; s. Olga John and Margaret (Fleming) H.; m. Willa Moreau Charlton, May 24, 1959; children—John Adam, Sarah Leigh. AS, Marion (Ala.) Inst., 1952; LLB, U. Ark., 1959, BS, BSL, 1959, JD, 1969. Bar: Ark. 1959. Since practiced in Batesville; pros. atty. 3d Jud. Dist. Ark., 1961-65; ins. commr. Ark., 1967-68; chmn. Ark. Commerce Commn., 1968-69; spl. justice Ark. Supreme Ct., 1988; judge juvenile divsn. Ark. 16th Dist., 1989-90; sr. ptnr. Harkey, Walmsley and related firms, Batesville, 1970-92; chancery and probate judge 16th Jud. Dist., Ark., 1993-98, cir., chancery judge, 1999—. 1st lt. USMCR, Korea. Mem. Ark. Bar Assn., Am. Bar Register, U.S. Marine Corps League. Home: 490 Harkey Rd Batesville AR 72501-9294 Office: PO Box 2656 Batesville AR 72503-2656

HARKEY, ROBERT SHELTON, lawyer; b. Charlotte, N.C., Dec. 22, 1940; s. Charles Nathan and Josephine Lenora (McKenzie) H.; m. Barbara Carole Payne, Apr. 2, 1983; 1 child, Elizabeth McKenzie. BA, Emory U., 1963, LLB, 1965. Bar: Ga. 1964, U.S. Dist. Ct. (no. dist.) Ga. 1964, U.S. Ct. Appeals (1st, 5th, 7th, 9th and 11th cirs.) 1964-86, U.S. Supreme Ct. Assoc. Swift, Currie, McGhee & Hiers, Atlanta, 1965-68; atty. Delta Air Lines, Atlanta, 1968-74, gen. atty., 1974-79, asst. v.p. law, 1979-85, assoc. gen. counsel, v.p., 1985-88; gen counsel, v.p., 1988-90; gen. counsel, sr. v.p. Delta Air Lines, Atlanta, 1990-94, gen. counsel, sr. v.p., sec., 1994—; mem. coun. Emory U. Law Sch., 1997—. Unit chmn. United Way, Atlanta, 1985; trustee Woodruff Arts Ctr., 1995—; bd. visitors Emory U., 1996—. Mem. ABA (com. gen. counsels), Air Transport Assn. (chmn. law coun. 1996-98), State Bar Ga. (chmn. corp. counsel sect. 1992-93), Atlanta Bar Assn., Corp. Counsel Assn. Greater Atlanta (bd. dirs. 1990), Commerce Club. Presbyterian. Avocations: tennis, reading. Office: Delta Air Lines Hartsfield Atlanta Internat Airport Atlanta GA 30320

HARKIN, MICHAEL EUGENE, anthropologist, educator, writer; b. Muncie, Ind., Aug. 16, 1958; s. Roy Eugene and Sandra Arlene (Satterthwaite) H.; m. Alison Margaret Quaggin; children: Caroline Margaret, James Michael, William Evan. BA with honors, U. N.C., 1980; AM, U. Chgo., 1984, PhD, 1988. Vis. asst. prof. U. Wyo., Laramie, 1989-90, asst. prof., 1993-96, assoc. prof. anthropology, 1996—; vis. asst. prof. Mont. State U., Bozeman, 1990-91; asst. prof. Emory U., Atlanta, 1991-93. Author: The Heiltsuks, 1997; assoc. editor Ethnohistory, 1997—; contbr. articles to profl. jours. Nat. Endowment for the Humanities fellow, 1999—. Fellow Am. Anthrop. Assn.; mem. Am. Soc. for Ethnohistory, Am. Ethnol. Soc., Am. Soc. for Psychol. Anthropology. Democrat. Episcopalian. Avocation: cross-country skiing. Office: University of Wyoming Dept Anthropology PO Box 3431 Laramie WY 82071-3431

HARKIN, THOMAS RICHARD, senator; b. Cumming, Iowa, Nov. 19, 1939; s. Patrick and Frances H.; m. Ruth Raduenz, 1968; children: Amy, Jenny. BS, Iowa State U., 1962; JD, Cath. U. Am., 1972. Mem. staff Ho. of Reps. Select Com. U.S. Involvement in S.E. Asia, 1970; mem. 94th-98th Congresses from 5th Iowa Dist., mem. sci. and tech. com., mem. agr., nutrition and forestry coms.; U.S. Senator from Iowa, 1984—; mem. Dem. Steering Com., com. labor and human resources; ranking minority mem. Appropriations Subcom. on Labor, Health and Human Svcs and Edn.; ranking minority mem. Subcom. on Disability Policy; ranking minority mem. Agr., Nutrition, and Forestry subcom. on Rsch., Nutrition, and Gen. Legis.; mem. Small Bus. Com.; prin. author Ams. with Disabilities Act. Co-author: (with C.E. Thomas) Five Minutes to Midnight: Why the Nuclear Threat is Growing Faster than Ever, 1990. Dem. candidate for Presidency of U.S., 1992. Served with USN, 1962-67. Named Outstanding Young Alumnus Iowa State U. Alumni Assn., 1974. Democrat. Office: US Senate 731 Hart Senate Bldg Washington DC 20510-1502*

HARKINS, EDWIN L., music educator, performer; b. Decatur, Ill., Nov. 20, 1940; s. Hoyle Edward and Lucile (McBride) H.; m. Bonnie Lu Turpin, June 17, 1962. BM in Trumpet, Ill. Wesleyan U., 1963; MusM in Trumpet, Yale U., 1965; postgrad., U. Chgo., 1965-66; PhD in Composition, U. Iowa, 1968. Instr. New. England Conservatory of Music, Boston, 1968-70, Neighborhood Sch. Music, New Haven, Conn., 1970-72; instr. U. Calif., San Diego, 1972-76, asst. prof., 1976-78, assoc. prof., 1980-84, prof., 1984—. Trumpeter with SONOR, La Jolla, Calif., 1976—; mem. N.H. Symphony, 1963-65, 20th Century music ensembles U. Chgo., 1965-66, U. Iowa, 1966-68, U. Calif., San Diego, 1972-76, appears on 4 records; guest soloist Hartford Symphony, 1963, Arch Ensemble, 1981, CONTINUUM, 1985; as vocalist mem. Extended Vocal Techniques Ensemble, 1975-85, appears on 3 records; as composer, performer co-founder (with Philip Larson) of (THE); composer Vis-à-Vis, 1986; author: (book) Maynard Ferguson: A Jazz Discography, 1976; contbr. articles to profl. jours.; designed and built programmable rhythm sequencer (with Rob Gross), 1975; designed computer program LASAR, 1978. Grantee Calif. Arts Council, 1984, 85, Nat. Endowment Arts, 1986, 87; Calif. Arts Council fellow, 1976, U. Calif. fellow, 1973-76. Mem. Soc. Music Theory, Internat. Trumpet Guild. Democrat. Avocations: golf, baseball statistics. Office: U Calif 9500 Gilman Dr La Jolla CA 92093-0326*

HARKINS, HERBERT PERRIN, otolaryngologist, educator; b. Scranton, Pa., Aug. 13, 1912; s. Percy Stoner and Myra (Perrin) H.; BS, Lafayette Coll., 1934; MD, Hahnemann Med. Coll., 1937; MSc, U. Pa., 1942; m. Anna Catherine Shepler, July 16, 1938; children: Herbert P., Sally Anne, Nancy Shepler. Lectr. otolaryngology Hahnemann Med. Coll., 1939-44, asso. prof., 1944-51, prof. head dept. otolaryngology, 1951; asst. prof. otolaryngology Grad. Sch. Medicine, U. Pa., 1951—; sr. staff otolaryngology Lankenau Hosp. Bd. Studies in Higher Edn. Trustee, Lafayette Coll. Served as comdr. U.S. Navy, 1945-48; Res. Diplomate Am. Bd. Otolaryngology. Fellow ACS; Am. Otorhinol. Soc. Plastic Surgery; mem. Am. Soc. Ophthalmic and Otolaryngologic Allergy (pres.), Am., Pa. acads. ophthalmology and otolaryngology, Coll. Physicians Phila., Phila. Laryngol. Soc., Phila County Med. Soc., AMA, Am. Laryngol., Rhinol. and Otol. Soc. Clubs: Union League, Phila. Country, Bachelors Barge. Contbr. numerous articles on ear, nose and throat to med. jours. Home: 701 Woodleave Rd Bryn Mawr PA 19010-1708

HARKINS, JOHN GRAHAM, JR., lawyer; b. Phila., May 9, 1931; s. John Graham and Elizabeth Taylor (Bowers) H.; m. Beatrice Gibson McIlvain, June 30, 1955; children: John Graham III, Alida McIlvain. B.A. with honors, U. Pa., 1953, LL.B. summa cum laude, 1958. Bar: Pa. 1959, U.S. Supreme Ct. 1971. Assoc. firm Pepper, Hamilton & Scheetz, Phila., 1958-63; partner Pepper, Hamilton & Scheetz, 1963-92, co-chmn., 1982-86, chmn., 1986-92; ptnr. Harkins Cunningham, Phila., 1992—; instr. U. Pa., 1956-58, lectr. Law Sch., former bd. overseers-law, 1981-95; mem. adv. com. Inst. Law and Econs., 1981—, com. chmn., 1981-91. Editor-in-chief: U. Pa. Law Rev, 1957-58. Supr. Easttown Twp., Pa., 1972-77; past bd. dirs. Chester County Hosp.; past trustee Curtis Inst. Music; trustee U. Pa., 1987-97, trustee emeritus, 1998—; trustee U. Pa. Health Sys., 1988—, vice chmn., 1991—; mem. bd. overseers U. Pa. Med. Sch., 1990—, chmn., 1991—. With U.S. Army, 1953-55. Fellow Salzburg Seminar in Am. Studies, 1961. Mem. Am. Coll. Trial Lawyers, Am. Law Inst., Am. Bar Assn., Pa. Bar Assn., Phila. Bar Assn., Jud. Conf. U.S. Ct. of Appeals for 3d Circuit, Order of Coif, Phi Beta Kappa. Clubs: Merion Cricket, Radnor Hunt. Home: Lowbrook PO Box 813 Devon PA 19333-0813 Office: Harkins Cunningham 2800 One Commerce Sq 2005 Market St Philadelphia PA 19103-7042

HARKINS, KENNETH R., federal judge; b. Cadiz, Ohio, Sept. 1, 1921; m. Helen Mae Dozer, Dec. 26, 1942; children—M. Elaine, Richard A. BA in Econs., Ohio State U., 1943, LLB, 1948, JD, 1967. Bar: Ohio 1949. Atty. U.S. Housing and Home Fin. Agy., 1949-51; trial atty. antitrust div. U.S. Dept. Justice, Washington, 1951-55; co-counsel Antitrust subcom. Judiciary Com. Ho. of Reps., Washington, 1955-60; gen. counsel Stromberg Carlson div. and electronics div. Gen. Dynamics Corp., 1960-64; chief counsel Antitrust subcom. Judiciary Com. Ho. Reps., Washington, 1964-71; commr. U.S. Ct. Claims, Washington, 1971-82, judge, 1982—; now sr. judge. Served to 1st lt. U.S. Army, 1943-46. Office: US Ct of Federal Claims 717 Madison Pl NW Washington DC 20005-1011

HARKINS, RICHARD WESLEY, marine engineer, naval architect; b. Duluth, Minn., Oct. 11, 1946; s. Wesley Ray and Vivian G. (LaBrosse) H.; m. Deborah Ann deGonzaque, Aug. 17, 1974; children: Ryan Wesley, Blair Ashley, Danielle Ashley. BS, U.S. Mcht. Marine Acad., Kings Point, N.Y., 1971; MSE in Naval Architecture and Marine Engring., U. Mich., 1976. Registered profl. engr., Ohio. 3d asst. engr. Hanna Steamship Corp., Cleve., 1971; 1st asst. engr. Poling Transp. Corp., N.Y.C., 1971-72; engr. Ingalls Shipbuilding Co., Pascagoula, Miss., 1972-74; fleet supt. Interlake Steamship Co., Cleve., 1976-94; v.p. ops. Lake Carriers' Assn., Cleve., 1994—. Author: (tech. paper) Investigation of Fuel Injection Cavitation, 1985 (Best Paper of 1985 Soc. Naval Architects and Marine Engrs.). Mem. Soc. Naval Architects and Marine Engrs. (ship machinery com. 1985, chmn. diesel panel 1985—, chmn. papers com. 1985-87, local sect. rep. 1985-87). Roman Catholic. Avocations: cross-country skiing, running, antique autos, golf. Home: 2771 Hampton Rd Cleveland OH 44116-2548 Office: 614 W Superior Ave Ste 915 Cleveland OH 44113-1306

HARKNESS, DONALD RICHARD, retired hematologist, educator; b. Mitchell, S.D., Aug. 23, 1932; s. Kenneth McKenzie and Marguerite (Sherwood) H.; m. Mary Hideko Nishi, Aug. 22, 1954; children: Laurel Jean, Kenneth Bruce, Susan Marie, Jane Elizabeth. B.A. with highest honors in Zoology, U. Calif.-Berkeley, 1954; M.D. magna cum laude, Washington U., St. Louis, 1958. Med. intern Barnes Hosp.-Washington U., 1958-59, med. resident, 1959-60; research assoc. U.S. Pub. Health Service, NIH, 1960-64; asst. prof. med. faculty U. Miami, Fla., 1964-68, assoc. prof., 1968-73, prof., 1973-80; Love prof. medicine U. Wis., Madison, 1980-97, chmn. dept., 1980-93, asst. dean for continuing med. edn. Med. Sch., 1996-99; emeritus prof., 1997—; dir. Radiation Effects Rsch. Found., Hiroshima, 1993-95; mem. adv. com. on sickle cell disease NIH, Bethesda, Md., 1974-75; dir. Miami Comprehensive Sickle Cell Ctr., 1973-78; program specialist in hematology VA Central Office, Washington, 1974-77; chmn. bd. Univ. Health Care, Inc., 1983-91. Researcher in hematology; contbr. writing to profl. publs. John and Mary Markle Found. scholar in acad. medicine, 1966-71. Fellow ACP; mem. Am. Soc. Hematology (councilor 1978-81), Am. Soc. Clin. Investigation, Assn. Am. Physicians, Ctrl. Soc. for Clin. Rsch. (councilor 1986-88), Midwest Blood Club (councilor 1981-85), Nat. Blood Club (sec.-treas. 1976-77), So. Blood Club (pres. 1979-80), Alpha Omega Alpha. Republican. Presbyterian. Address: 110 Standish Ct Madison WI 53705-5131

HARKNESS, JOHN CHEESMAN, architect; b. N.Y.C., Nov. 30, 1916; s. Albert and Sara Arden (Cheesman) H.; m. Sarah Pillsbury, June 14, 1941 (separated); children: Sara Harkness Super, Joan Harkness Hantz, Nell, Timothy, Alice, Frederick, John Pillsbury. BFA cum laude, Harvard U., 1938, BArch, MArch, 1941. Registered architect Fla., Maine, Mass., Minn., R.I., Va. Architect Saarinen and Swanson, Birmingham, Mich., Harrison, Fouilhoux and Abramovitz, N.Y.C., Skidmore, Owings and Merrill, N.Y.C., prior to 1945; prin. The Architects Collaborative, Cambridge, Mass., 1945-95, pres., 1966-67, 77-84, also bd. dirs., chmn. bd. prins., 1984-86; mem. design faculty Harvard Grad. Sch. Design, 1946-50, mem. vis. com.; mem. vis. com. R.I. Sch. Design; mem. capitol area planning bd., Minn. State; archtl. advisor Boston Redevel. Authority for Park Pla., Mass. Design Competition. Author: Encyclopedia of Architecture, 1989; prin.-in-charge projects Martin County Libr., Fla., Creative Arts Ctr., master plan, Squires addition Student Activities Ctr., Biology Bldg., all at Va. Poly. Inst. and State U., Blacksburg, Univ. Ctrs., Coll. William and Mary, Va., Sci. Bldg. Middlebury (Vt.) Coll., Hillside Office Bldg., Waltham, Mass., CBS Office Bldg., Mt. Pleasant, N.Y., master plan and 6 med. bldgs. Children's Hosp. Med. Ctr., Boston (Harleston Parker medal Boston Soc. Architects, Honor award AIA), hdqrs. CIGNA, Bloomfield, Conn. (award N.Eng. Regional Coun. AIA, award excellence Am. Inst. Steel Constrn. 1985), Hoffman Lab. Exptl. Geology (Boston Arts Festival award 1964), athletic facilities, addition Mus. Comparative Zoology, med. sch. Lab. Reprodn. and Reproductive Biology, all at Harvard U., master plan indsl. complex, Jubail, Saudi Arabia, master plan and office bldg. Summit at Westchester, Mt. Pleasant, Cen. Nat. Mus., Riyadh, Saudia Arabia, hdqrs. Shawmut Bank Boston, Amoskeag Bank, Manchester, N.H., Montego Bay (Jamaica) Hosp., Ainsworth Gymnasium Smith Coll., Northampton, Mass. (honor award N.Eng. Regional Coun. AIA), U. Tunis Libr. and Sch. Law, Econs., and Bus. Adminstrn., Tunisia, James L. Hanley Edn. Ctr., Providence (award), New Trier Twp. High Sch., Winnetka, Ill, Blue Hills Regional Vocat. Sch., Canton, Mass., Wayland (Mass.) High Sch. Ambulance driver Am. Field Svc., 1943-44. Pvt. U.S. Army, 1945, ETO, NATOUSA, bronze cross of merit with swords from Polish Rep. for action at the Battle of Casino, Italy. Recipient various competition and archtl. design awards including 6 awards Am. Assn. Sch. Adminstrs., 1960-67, William Ware award, Boston Soc. Architects honor award, 1993; named Harvard Athletic Hall of Fame, NCAA Wrestling champion, 1938, lifetime svc. to wrestling award Nat. Wresting Hall of Fame, 1999. Fellow AIA (archtl. juror various design programs, 2d award alt. to Appleton Travelling fellowship); mem. NAD, Boston Soc. Architects (past pres., 1st prize 1940), Mass. State Assn. Architects (past pres.), Archtl. League N.Y., Harvard Grad. Sch. Design Alumni Assn. (past pres.), Harvard U. Alumni Assn. (former dir. 1988). Home: 223 Oakland Ave Arlington MA 02476-7253 Office: Fletcher Harkness Cohen Moneyhun Inc 560 Harrison Ave Boston MA 02118-2436

HARKNESS, PETER ANTHONY, editor, publisher; b. Washington, July 31, 1943; s. Richard Long and Gladys (Suiter) H.; m. Patricia French, Apr. 10, 1971; children: Wyeth Long, Rollin Charles. Student, U. N.C., 1961-63, 64-65; BA in Journalism, Am. U., 1966. Mng. editor Congl. Quar., Washington, 1980-84, exec. editor, 1984-87; editor, pub. Governing Mag., Washington, 1988—. Author: China and U.S. Far East Policy, 1945-1966, 1967. Bd. dirs. Ptnrs. for Livable Communities, Washington, 1993—. With Army N.G., 1969-75. Recipient Raymond Clapper award for investigative reporting White House Corr. Assn., 1974. Fellow Nat. Acad. Pub. Adminstrn. Avocations: biking, skiing, sailing. *

HARKNESS, R. KENNETH, restaurant chain executive; b. Warren, Ohio, Aug. 22, 1949; s. Roy K. and Yvonne D. (Howitt) H.; m. Marianne Loprete, Sept. 28, 1974 (div. Apr. 1999); 1 child, Austin Blaine. BS in Bus., Rutgers U., 1972, MBA in Acctg., 1973. Pres., chief exec. officer N.Y. Sub Inc., Dallas, 1974-81, 85—, Fox Hunt Realty, Inc., Far Hills, N.J., 1981-85, Kenco Restaurants, Inc., Dallas, 1987—. Mem. University Park Master Plan Com. Mem. Nat. Restaurant Assn., Tex. Restaurant Assn., Rep. Inner Circle. Episcopalian. Office: NY Sub Inc 3411 Asbury St Dallas TX 75205-1844

HARKRADER, MILTON KEENE, JR., corporate executive; b. Cranford, N.J., Apr. 8, 1939; s. Milton Keene and Elizabeth Dyer (Evans) H.; m. Nina B. Salo, June 25, 1960; children: Nina Elizabeth, Milton Keene III, Eric Scott. AB, Hamilton Coll., 1958; MBA, U. Pa., 1960. Account exec. Dancer Fitzgerald Sample, Inc., N.Y.C., 1960-63; product mgr. Colgate Palmolive Co., N.Y.C., 1963-65; account exec. Foote Cone & Belding, Inc., N.Y.C., 1965-66; v.p., account supr. Young & Rubicam, Inc., N.Y.C., 1966-73; exec. v.p. Isidore Lefkowitz Elgort, Inc., N.Y.C., 1973-79; group v.p. DDB Needham Worldwide, N.Y.C., 1979-91; v.p. comm. and devel. Hamilton Coll., Clinton, N.Y., 1991-94; exec. v.p. Nordico Mktg. Devel. Inc., N.Y.C., 1994—; dir. Good Friends Film Prodns., Inc. Mem. DKE Club, Univ. Club, Weston Field Club. Home: 81 Field Point Dr Fairfield CT 06430-6329

HARL, NEIL EUGENE, economist, lawyer, educator; b. Appanoose County, Iowa, Oct. 9, 1933; s. Herbert Peter and Bertha Catherine (Bonner) H.; m. Darlene Ramona Harris, Sept. 7, 1952; children: James Brent, Rodney Scott. BS, Iowa State U., 1955, PhD, 1965; JD, U. Iowa, 1961. Bar: Iowa 1961. Field editor Wallace's Farmer, 1957-58; research assoc. U.S. Dept. Agr., Iowa City and Ames, Iowa, 1958-64; assoc. prof. econs. Iowa State U., Ames, 1964-67; prof. Iowa State U., 1967—, Charles F. Curtiss Disting. prof., 1976—, dir. Ctr. Internat. Agrl. Fin., 1990—; mem. adv. group to commr. IRS, 1979-80; mem. adv. com. Heckerling Inst. on Estate Planning, Miami, Fla., 1983-96; mem. adv. com. Office Tech. Assessment, U.S. Congress, 1988-95, vice chair, 1992-93, chair, 1993-94; mem. exec. bd. U.S. West Comms., Iowa, 1989-90; lectr. in field. Author: Farm Estate and Business Planning, 1973, 14th edit., 1999, Legal and Tax Guide for Agricultural Lenders, 1984, supplement, 1987, Agricultural Law, 15 vols., 1980-81, Agricultural Law Manual, 1985, The Farm Debt Crisis of the 1980s, 1990; co-author: Farmland, 1982, Principles of Agricultural Law, 1997, The Family Owned Business Exclusion, 1998, Taxation of Cooperatives, 1999; author, actor films and videotape programs; contbr. articles to profl. jours. Trustee Iowa State U. Agrl. Found., 1969-90. 1st lt. AUS, 1955-57. Recipient Outstanding Tchr. award Iowa State U., 1973, Disting Svc. to Agr. award Am. Soc. Farm Mgrs. and Rural Appraisers, 1977, Iowa sect. 1996, Faculty Svc. award Nat. Univ. Ext. Assn., 1980, Disting. Svc. award Am. Agrl. Editors Assn., 1984, Disting. Achievement citation Iowa State U., 1985, Disting. Svc. to State Govt. award Nat. Gov.'s Assn., 1986, Disting. Svc. award Iowa State U., 1986, Farm Leader of Yr. award Des Moines Register, 1986, Henry A. Wallace award, 1987, Superior Svc. award USDA, 1987, Disting. Svc. to Iowa Agr. award Iowa Farm Bur., 1992, Faculty Excellence award, Iowa Bd. Regents, 1993, Charles A. Black award Coun. Agrl. Sci. Tech., 1997, Excellence in Internat. Agr. award Iowa State U., 1999. Fellow Am. Coll. Trusts and Estates Counsel, Am. Agrl. Econs. Assn. (exec. bd. 1979-85, pres. 1983-84, bd. dirs. Am. Agrl. Econs. Found. 1992-94, pres. 1993-94, Outstanding Ext. Program award 1970, Excellence in Communicating Rsch. Results award 1975, Disting. Undergrad. Tchr. award 1976), ABA Rsch. Found., Iowa State Bar Found.; mem. ABA, Iowa Bar Assn. (Pres. award 1991), Am. Agrl. Law Assn. (pres. 1980-81, Disting. Svc. award 1984). Home: 2821 Duff Ave Ames IA 50010-4709 Office: Iowa State U Dept Econs Ames IA 50011

HARLAN, HEATHER GORDON, reporter; b. Balt., June 13, 1972; d. Charles Walton and Mary Dell Gordon Harlan. BS, Boston U., 1994. Reporter Ind. Newspapers, Inc., Dover, Del., 1994-96; bur. chief The Press of Atlantic City, 1996—. Vol. St. Francis Ctr., Long Beach Twp., N.J., 1998—, Interfaith Health and Support Svcs. So. Ocean County, N.J., 1998—. Recipient First Amendment award N.J. Press Assn., 1998, Feature Writing award North Jersey Press Club, 1999. Mem. U.S. Tennis Assn., Soc. Profl. Journalists, Investigative Reporters and Editors, Press Club Atlantic City (sec. 1997-98, v.p. 1998-99). Presbyterian. Avocations: tennis, rollerblading, traveling. E-mail: hgharlan@aol.com. Office: Press Atlantic City 185 N Main St Manahawkin NJ 08050

HARLAN, JACK RODNEY, geneticist, emeritus educator; b. Washington, June 7, 1917; s. Harry Vaughn and Augusta (Griffing) H.; m. Jean Yocum, Aug. 4, 1939; children: Sue (Mrs. Robert Hughes), Harry, Sherry (Mrs. Mark Wilson), Richard Edwin. B.S. in Botany with distinction, George Washington U., 1938; Ph.D. in Genetics, U. Calif. at Berkeley, 1942. Research asst. Tela R.R. Co., Honduras, 1942; geneticist Dept. Agr., Woodward, Okla., 1942-51, Stillwater, Okla., 1951-61; prof. agronomy Okla. State U., Stillwater, 1951-66; prof. genetics U. Ill. at Urbana, 1966-84, prof. emeritus, 1984—; botanist Dept. of Agr. (plant exploration and introduction), Turkey, Syria and Iraq, 1948, Dept. of Agr., Iran, Afghanistan, Pakistan, India and Ethiopia, 1960; sr. staff mem. Iranian prehistoric project Oriental Inst. U. Chgo., 1960, sr. staff mem. Turkish prehistoric project, 1964; mem. Dead Sea Archaeol. Project, 1977, 79, 83; plant exploration, Africa, Asia, Latin Am.; cons. FAO, 1970-71, internat. bd. Plant Genetic Resources, 1974-79, Nabta Playa Archaeol. Project, Egypt, 1994. Contbr. to profl. jours. Fellow AAAS, Am. Soc. Agronomy, Am. Acad. Arts and Sci.; mem. Nat. Acad. Scis., Crop Sci. Soc. Am. (pres. 1966), Am. Inst. Biol. Scientists, Bot. Soc. Am., Am. Soc. Agronomy, Soc. for Econ. Botany, Phi Beta Kappa, Sigma Xi, Phi Kappa Phi. Presbyn. (elder).

HARLAN, JOHN MARSHALL, construction company executive; b. Detroit; s. Campbell Allen and Ivabell Lucile (Campbell) H.; m. Elizabeth Henninger, Feb. 18, 1956; children: Patricia G. Harlan Schumacher, Diana L. Harlan Stein, Sandra S. Harlan McAndrews. BSEE, U. Mich., 1956. Electrician Harlan Electric Co., Detroit, 1956-60, estimator, then contract mgr. and v.p., 1960-63; pres., bd. dirs. Harlan Electric Co., Southfield, Mich., 1963-72, pres., chmn., 1972-94; dir. MYR Group Inc., 1995—; pres., bd. dirs. Federated Elec. Contractors, 1968-73; chmn., bd. dirs. Contractors Mut. Assn., Washington, 1973-81; bd. dirs. Nat. Constrn. Employers Coun., Washington, 1978-82; fellow, bd. dirs. Engring. Soc. Detroit, 1982-88. Pres., bd. dirs. Sci. and Engring. Fair Met. Detroit, 1964-95; trustee Lawrence Tech. U., Southfield, 1981-98. Fellow Acad. Elec. Contracting; mem. Nat. Elec. Contractors Assn. (bd. dirs., pres. Southeastern Mich. chpt. 1968-95), Constrn. Assn. Mich. (chmn. bd. dirs. 1990-98), Tau Beta Pi, Eta Kappa Nu. Home: 7769 Clearwater Dr Williamsburg MI 49690-9579

HARLAN, JOHN W., physician; b. Feb. 5, 1946. MD, U. Kans., 1974. Diplomate Am. Bd. Surgery, Am. Bd. Plastic Surgery; bd. certified Am. Acad. Wound Care. Gen. surgeon Polson, Mont., 1978-80, Helena, Mont., 1980-91; chief resident assoc., fellow plastic/reconstructive surgery Mayo Clinic/Mayo Grad. Sch. Medicine, Rochester, Minn., 1992-93; plastic surgeon Spokane (Wash.) Plastic Surgeons, 1993-95, Aesthetic Plastic Surgery Ctr., Missoula, Mont., 1995—. Maj. U.S. Army, 1981-88. Fellow ACS; mem. Am. Soc. Plastic and Reconstructive Surgeons, Alpha Omega Alpha. Office: 900 N Orange St Ste 306 Missoula MT 59802-2951

HARLAN, KATHLEEN TROY (KAY HARLAN), business consultant, professional speaker and seminar leader; b. Bremerton, Wash., June 9, 1934; d. Floyd K. and Rosemary (Parkhurst) Troy; m. John L. Harlan, Feb. 16, 1952 (div. 1975); children: Pamela Kay, Kenneth Lynwood, Lianna Sue; m. Stuart Friedman, Nov. 10, 1991. Chair Kitsap-North Mason United Way, 1968-70; owner, operator Safeguard N.W. Systems, Tacoma, 1969-79; devel., mgr. Poulsbo (Wash.) Profl. Bldg., 1969-75; pres. Greenapple Graphics, Inc., Tacoma, 1976-79; owner, mgr. Iskrem Hus Restaurant, Poulsbo, 1972-75; pres. Bus. Seminars, Tacoma, 1977-82; owner, mgr. Safeguard Computer Ctr., Tacoma, 1982-91; owner Total Systems Ctr., Tacoma, 1983-88; mem. Orgnl. Renewal, Inc., Tacoma, 1983-88; assoc. mem. Effectiveness Resource Group, Inc., Tacoma, 1979-80; pres. New Image Confs., Tacoma, 1979-82; spkr. on mgmt. and survival in small bus.; CEO Manage Ability, Inc., profl. mgmt. firm, 1991-97; exec. dir. Another Door to Learning, 1996-97; dir. ops. CEO Read Inc., , 1997-98, pres., 1998—. Contbg. author: Here is Genius!, 1980; author small bus. manuals. Mem. Wash. State br. Boundary Rev. for Kitsap County, 1970-76, Selective Svc. Bd. 19, 1969-76; co-chair Wash. State Small Bus. Improvement Coun., 1986; del. White House Conf. on Small Bus., 1986; chair Wash. State Conf. on Small Bus., 1987; founder, mem. exec. bd. Am. Leadership Forum, 1988-94; dir. Bus. Leadership Week, Wash. State, 1990-96; chair Pro-Tech Pierce County, 1992-94; chair Allenmore Hosp., 1993-96; founding mem. Multicare Health Found., 1995-98. Recipient Nellie Cashman award; named Woman Entrepreneur of Yr. for Wash. State, 1986, 87. Mem. Tacoma-Pierce County C. of C. (lifetime exec. bd. 1985—, chair spl. task force on small bus. for Pierce County 1986-89, treas. 1987-88, chair-elect 1988-90, chair 1990-91).

HARLAN, LOUIS RUDOLPH, history educator, writer; b. West Point, Miss., July 13, 1922; s. Allen Dorset and Isabel (Knaffl) H.; m. Sadie Morton, Sept. 6, 1947; children—Louis Knaffl, Benjamin Wailes. BA, Emory U., 1943; MA, Vanderbilt U., 1948; PhD, Johns Hopkins U., 1955. From asst. to assoc. prof. East Tex. State Coll., 1950-59; from assoc. prof. to prof. U. Cin., 1959-66; prof. history U. Md., College Park, 1966-84, Disting. prof. history, 1984-92, prof. emeritus, 1992—; mem. Nat. Hist. Publs. and Records Commn., 1984-88. Author: Separate and Unequal, 1958, Booker T. Washington, Vol. 1, 1972 (Bancroft award 1973), Booker T. Washington, Vol. 2, 1983 (Beveridge award, Bancroft award, Pulitzer Prize 1984), All at Sea: Coming of Age in World War II, 1996; editor: Booker T. Washington Papers, 14 vol. series, 1972-89. Bd. dirs. ACLU, Cin., 1963-66, Montgomery County, Md., 1967-72. Lt. (j.g.) USN, 1943-46; ETO, PTO. Fellow Am. Coun. of Learned Socs., 1962, Guggenheim Found., 1975, Inst. Advanced Study in Behavioral Scis., 1980, award for disting. svc. in documentary preservation and publ. Nat. Hist. Publs. and Records Commn., 1991. Fellow Soc. Am. Historians; mem. Am. Hist. Assn. (pres. 1989), So. Hist. Assn. (exec. bd. 1983-85, pres. 1989-90), Assn. for Documentary Editing (Julian P. Boyd award 1989), Assn. Study Afro-Am. Life and History (exec. bd. 1968-75), Orgn. Am. Historians (pres. 1989-90), Phi Beta Kappa, Phi Kappa Phi. Democrat. Avocations: tennis; swimming. Home: Carol Woods Retirement Cmty 750 Weaver Dairy Rd # 160 Chapel Hill NC 27514-1502

HARLAN, NEIL EUGENE, retired healthcare company executive; b. Cherry Valley, Ark., June 2, 1921; s. William and Mary Nina (Ellis) H.; m. Martha Almlov, Sept. 27, 1952; children: Lindsey Beth, Neil Eugene, Sarah Ellis. Student, U. Edinburgh, Scotland, 1946; BS, U. Ark., 1947, LLD, 1969; MBA, Harvard U., 1950, DBA, 1956. Mem. faculty Grad. Sch. Bus. Adminstrn. Harvard U., 1951-62, asst. prof., 1954-58, assoc. prof., 1958-61, prof., 1962; asst. sec. Air Force Washington, 1962-64; exec. v.p. Anderson, Clayton & Co., 1964-67; dir. McKinsey & Co., Inc., 1967-74; dir. McKesson Corp., San Francisco, 1974-93, chmn., CEO, 1984-86, 89-90. Author: Management Control in Air Frame Subcontracting, 1956, (with R.H. Hassler) Cases in Controllership, 1958, Cases in Accounting Policy, 1961, Managerial Economics, 1962. Chmn. San Francisco Ballet, 1982-85; trustee exec. com. World Affairs Coun. No. Calif., 1983—; vice-chmn., dir. Nat. Park Found., 1986-92; bd. govs. San Francisco Symphony, 1985-88; mem. Calif. Com. on Campaign Fin., Calif. Bus. Roundtable, 1984-87; vis. com. Harvard Bus. Sch., 1984-87. Served with AUS, 1943-46. Mem. Webhannet Golf Club, Edgecomb Tennis Club (Kennebunk Beach, Maine), Bohemian Club, Pacific Union Club (San Francisco), Links Club (N.Y.C.). Home: 1170 Sacramento St # 13D San Francisco CA 94108-1943 Office: McKesson Corp 1 Post St Ste 3275 San Francisco CA 94104-5292

HARLAN, NORMAN RALPH, construction executive; b. Dayton, Ohio, Dec. 21, 1914; s. Joseph and Anna (Kaplan) H.; Indsl. Engring. degree U. Cin., 1937; m. Thelma Katz, Sept. 4, 1955; children: Leslie, Todd. Chmn. Am. Constrn. Corp., Dayton, 1949—, Harlan, Inc., realtors; ptnr. Norman Estates. Mem. Dayton Real Estate Bd., Ohio Real Estate Assn., Nat. Assn. Real Estate Bds., C. of C., Pi Lambda Phi. Home: 303 Glenridge Rd Kettering OH 45429-1631 Office: Am Constrn Corp 2451 S Dixie Dr Dayton OH 45409-1861

HARLAN, RAYMOND CARTER, communication executive, computer application developer; b. Shreveport, La., Nov. 13, 1943; s. Ross E. and Margaret (Burns) H.; m. Nancy K. Munson, 1966 (div. 1978); children: Kathleen Marie, Patrick Raymond; m. Sarah J. Kinzel, 1979 (div. 1982); m. Linda Frances Gerdes, Mar. 30, 1985; stepchildren: Kimberly Jo Gillis, Kellie Leigh Raffa, Ryan William Gerdes. BA in Speech and Drama cum laude, Southwestern U., 1966; MA in English, U. Tex., 1968; MA in Speech & Theatre Arts, Bradley U., 1976. Commd. 2d lt. USAF, 1968, advanced through grades to maj., 1980, ret., 1988; pres. ComSkills Tng., Aurora, Colo., 1988—; asst. prof. Bradley U., Peoria, Ill., 1972-76; instr., asst. prof., course dir. Air Force Acad., Colorado Springs, 1976-81; asst. prof. Air Force Inst. Tech., Dayton, Ohio, 1987-88; internat. trainer Inst. for Internat. Rsch., London, 1990-92; presenter in field. Author: The Confident Speaker, 1993; co-author: Telemarketing That Works, 1991, Interactive Telemarketing, 1995; contbr. articles and revs. to profl. jours. Decorated Air Force Commendation medal with three oak leaf clusters, Air Force Meritorious Svc. medal with one oak leaf cluster; recipient George Washington Honor Medal Freedom Found., 1983, Leo A. Codd award Am. Def. Preparedness Assn., 1st Prize ann. poetry contest Ariz. State Poetry Soc., 1979. Mem. ASTD, Ret. Officers Assn., Soc. for Tech. Comm. Lutheran. Avocations: skiing, cycling, gardening. Office: ComSkills 17544 E Wesley Pl Aurora CO 80013-4174

HARLAN, ROBERT DALE, information studies educator, academic administrator; b. Hastings, Nebr., Aug. 4, 1929; s. Hugh Allan and Madge Keister (Newmyer) H. BA, Hastings Coll., 1950; MA in Library Sci., U. Mich., 1956, MA, 1958, PhD, 1960. Head book order sect. Library U. Mich., Ann Arbor, 1956-58, lectr., 1960; asst. prof. Sch. Library Sci. U. So. Calif., Los Angeles, 1960-63; asst. prof. library and info. studies U. Calif., Berkeley, 1963-70, assoc. prof., 1970-76, prof., 1976-94, prof. emeritus, 1994—; assoc. dean Sch. Library and Info. Studies, 1971-74, 77-82; acting dean Sch. Library and Info. Studies U. Calif., Berkeley, 1985-86; vis. assoc. prof. Sch. Libr. Sci. UCLA, summer 1973; cons. NEH, Washington; proprietor Park Hills Press. Author: John Henry Nash, 1970, Bibliography of the Grabhorn and Grabhorn-Hoyem Presses, 1977, George L. Harding, 1978, The Colonial Printer: Two Views, 1978, Chapter Nine, 1982, William Doxey's Publishing Venture: At the Sign of the Lark, 1983, The Two Hundredth Book, 1993; chmn. edit. bd. catalogues and bibliographies series U. Calif. Press, 1982—; contbr. numerous articles and revs. to profl. jours. Rackham pre-doctoral fellow, U. Mich., 1958-60, summer faculty fellow U. Calif., Berkeley, 1964; grantee Assn. Coll. and Research Libraries, 1960, 63. Mem. Bibliog. Soc. Am., Bibliog. Soc. U. Va., Am. Soc. 18th Century Studies, Will Cather Pioneer Meml. Soc., Fine Press Book Assn., Book of Calif. Club (bd. dirs. 1982-88, sec. bd. 1987-88). Office: Univ of Calif Sch Info Mgmt Berkeley CA 94720

HARLAN, ROBERT ERNEST, professional football team executive; b. Des Moines, Sept. 9, 1936; m. Madeline Harlan; children: Kevin, Bryan, Michael. BJ, Marquette U., 1958. Former gen. reporter UPI, Milw.; sports info. dir. Marquette U., Milw., 1959; dir. community rels. St. Louis Cardinals baseball team, 1966-68, dir. pub. rels., 1968-71; asst. gen. mgr. Green Bay (Wis.) Packers, 1971-75, corp. gen. mgr., 1975-81, corp. asst. to pres., 1981-88, exec. v.p. adminstrn., 1988-89, pres., chief exec. officer, 1989—; bd. dirs. Firstar Bank, Green Bay. Mem. exec. bd. Packer 65 Roses Sports Club. Served with U.S. Army. Mem. bd. of trustees, St. Norbert Coll., Wis. Avocation: golf. Office: Green Bay Packers 1265 Lombardi Ave Green Bay WI 54304-3997 also: Green Bay Packers Lambeau Field PO Box 10628 Green Bay WI 54307-0628*

HARLAN, ROSS EDGAR, retired utility company executive, writer, lecturer, consultant; b. Poteau, Okla., July 11, 1919; s. Edgar Leslie and Leola (Carter) H.; m. Margaret Burns, May 31, 1942; children: Raymond Carter, Rosemary, Marvin Allen, Scott Lee. Student, Southeastern Okla. State U.,

1937-38, Eastern Okla. State Coll., 1938-39; B.S.B.A., Okla. State U., 1941; postgrad., Harvard U., 1942. Mem. faculty, coach Poteau High Sch., 1945-46, Poteau Jr. Coll., 1945-46; with Okla. Gas & Electric Co., Oklahoma City, 1946-85, mgr. rates and contracts dept., 1954-64, v.p., 1964-78, sr. v.p. div. mgmt., 1978-80, sr. v.p. adminstrn. and public affairs, 1980-85, ret.; ind. cons., writer Oklahoma City, 1985—; cons. spl. books div. Reader's Digest, 1985—; mem. bd. govs. Ea. Okla. State Coll. Devel. Found. Author: Strikes, 1946, Frontier Oklahoma-The Twin Territories, 1994. Pres. Okla. Council on Econ. Edn., 1977-79; bd. govs. Nat. Wrestling Hall of Fame, 1977-85; pres. adv. bd. Okla. State U. Coll. Bus. Assos.; mem. adv. bd. Okla. State U. Tech. Inst.; bd. govs. Okla. State U. Found. Served with Army N.G., 1937-38; to lt. col. USAAF, 1941-46. Named to Okla. State U. Coll. Bus. Hall of Fame, 1980, Eastern Okla. State Coll. Hall of Fame, 1992; recipient George Washington Honor medal Freedoms Found. Am., 1970, Disting. Alumnus award Okla. State U., 1979; named Boss of Yr., Nat. Secs. Assn., 1977; charter mem. Poteau (Okla.) Athletic Hall of Fame. Mem. Oklahoma City C. of C., Toastmasters Internat. (comm. and leadership award 1985), Am. Legion, VFW, Mil. Order of World Wars, Disabled Am. Vets., Beta Gamma Sigma. Methodist. Home and Office: 2639 N Eagle Ln Oklahoma City OK 73127-1166

HARLAN, WILLIAM ROBERT, JR., physician, educator, researcher; b. Richmond, Va., Nov. 1, 1930; s. William Robert and Helen J. (Weaver) H.; m. Linda Carol Mavencamp, Aug. 23, 1980; children: Elizabeth, William, Christopher, Nicole. B.A., U. Va., 1951; M.D. magna cum laude, Med. Coll. Va., 1955. Diplomate: Am. Bd. Internal Medicine, Am. Bd. Family Practice. Intern U. Wis., Madison, 1955-56; resident in medicine Duke U. Hosp., Durham, N.C., 1958-62; dir. Clin. Research Center, Med. Coll. Va., 1963-70; asso. dean U. Ala. Med. Sch., 1970-72; prof. medicine and community health scis. Duke U., 1972-74; prof. medicine and postgrad. medicine U. Mich., Ann Arbor, 1974-88; asst. dean Med. Sch. U. Mich.; dir. div. epidemiology and clin. applications Nat. Heart, Lung and Blood Inst., 1988-91; assoc. dir. for disease prevention Nat. Insts. of Health, Bethesda, 1991—; cons. World Bank; mem. sci. adv. bd. U.S. Air Force; mem. Armed Forces Epidemiology Bd., NIH study sects. and adv. councils. Contbr. articles to med. jours. Served with M.C. USN, 1956-58. Fellow ACP; mem. Am. Heart Assn., N.Y. Acad. Sci., Sigma Xi, Alpha Omega Alpha. Episcopalian. Home: 3503 Windsor Pl Chevy Chase MD 20815-4001 also: 155 N Sea Pines Dr Hilton Head Island MD 29928

HARLAND, WILLIAM ROBERT, SR., painter; b. Cambridge, Mass., July 7, 1943; s. Samuel William Harland and Theresa May (Butt) Besco; m. Ellen Regina Leavis, Apr. 4, 1970; children: William, Amy, Andrew. Cert., Vesper George Sch. of Art, Boston, 1970. Field artist USN; art dir. SMP Industries Trade Publs., 1972-76; visual artist, tchr. Littleton, Mass.; studio artist, numerous comms.; tchr. in field. Designer book plates and cover designs; prodr. (tv series) A Way of Art; course originator Drawing for the Strait Line Impaired. With USN, 1962-66. Mem. Am. Watercolor Soc. (assoc.), New Eng. Watercolor Soc. (assoc.), Concord Art Assn. (Disting. Artist Mem. 1980), Leominster Art Assn. (painting master 1990), Kirkwood Gallery New Eng. Artists. Avocation: fishing, music. Home: 50 Jennifer St Littleton MA 01460-1709 Office: Bill Harland Studio PO Box 553 Littleton MA 01460-0553

HARLEM, SUSAN LYNN, librarian; b. L.A., Oct. 1, 1950; d. Frank Joseph and Esther Frances (Bomell) H.; m. Anthony Stephen Hacsi, Aug. 31, 1990. BA, UCLA, 1972, MLS, 1976. Libr. U. Md., College Park, 1976-79, U.S. Dept. Edn., Washington, 1979-82, GSA, Washington, 1982-87, NLRB, Washington, 1988—; tutor Washington Lit. Coun., 1992—. Co-author: Washington on Foot, 1984. Office: NLRB Libr 1099 14th St NW Washington DC 20570

HARLEMAN, ANN, English educator, writer. BA in English, Douglass Coll., 1967; PhD in Linguistics, Princeton U., 1972; MFA in Creative Writing, Brown U., 1988. Asst. prof. dept. English, Rutgers U., New Brunswick, N.J., 1973-74; asst. prof. dept. English, U. Wash., Seattle, 1974-79, assoc. prof., 1979-84; vis. assoc. prof., rsch. affiliate writing program MIT, Cambridge, 1984-86; vis. scholar program in Am. civilization Brown U., Providence, 1986—; Cole disting. prof. Wheaton (Mass.) Coll., 1992-93; prof. English, RISD, Providence, 1994—; Fulbright-Hays lectr., 1980-81. Author: Graphic Representation of Models in Linguistic Theory, 1976, (with Bruce A. Rosenberg) Ian Fleming: A Critical Biograhy, 1989, Happiness, 1994, Bitter Lake, 1996; translator: Mute Phone Calls, 1992; contbr. over 50 articles to scholarly publs., transls. and revs., poems and short stories to lit. mags. Recipient Raymond Carver prize, 1986, Nelson Algren runner-up award Chgo. Tribune, 1987, 3d prize Judith Siegal Pearson award, 1988, Chris O'Malley fiction prize Madison Rev., 1990, Judith Siegal Pearson award, 1991, syndicated fiction award PEN, 1991, Iowa short fiction award, 1993; Guggenheim fellow, 1976-77, fellow Huntington Libr., 1979-80, MacDowell Colony, 1988, Am. Coun. Learned Socs., 1992, Wurlitzer Found., 1992; sr. scholar Am. Coun. Learned Socs./IREX, 1976-77; grantee NEH, 1988, Rockefeller Found., 1989, Bogliasco Found., 1998; fellow R.I. Coun. Arts, 1989, 97. Mem. PEN Am. Ctr. Home: 55 Summit Ave Providence RI 02906-2709 Office: Brown U Program In Am Civilization Providence RI 02912

HARLEMAN, DONALD ROBERT FERGUSSON, environmental engineering educator; b. Palmerton, Pa., Dec. 5, 1922; s. Robert Roy and Nora (Curry) H.; m. Martha Havens, Oct. 21, 1950; children: Kathleen T., Robert I.H., Anne C. BSCE, Pa. State U., 1943; MS, MIT, 1947, DSc, 1950. Design engr. Curtiss-Wright Corp., Columbus, Ohio, 1944-45; from research asst. to research assoc. Hydrodynamics Lab. MIT, Cambridge, Mass., 1945-50, asst. prof. hydraulics, 1950-56, assoc. prof., 1956-62, prof. civil engring., 1963-75, Ford prof. engring., 1975-91, Ford prof. engring. emeritus, 1991—, head water resources and environ. engring. div., 1972-83, dir. R.M. Parsons Lab., 1973-83; vis. prof. Calif. Inst. Tech., 1962-63; del. U.S.-Japan Joint Sci. Seminar on Coastal Engring., 1964, 74;; sr. visitor applied math. and theoretical physics Cambridge (Eng.), 1968-69; vis. scientist Internat. Inst. Applied Systems Analysis, Vienna, 1977-78; mem. Water Pollution Control Fedn.; mem. U.S. nat. com. Internat. Assn. Water Pollution Research. Mem. bd. editors Jour. Hydraulic Research. Guggenheim fellow, 1968-69; named Outstanding Alumnus Coll. Engring., Pa. State U., 1979. Mem. ASCE (Research prize 1960, Karl Hilgard Hydraulic prize 1971, 73, J.C. Stevens award, 1973, W.W. Horner award 1983, hon. 1989), Boston Soc. Civil Engrs. (Desmond Fitzgerald medal 1967, hon. mem. 1987), Am. Geophys. Union, Internat. Assn. for Hydraulic Research, Am. Soc. Limnology and Oceanography, Nat. Acad. Engring. Home: 100 Memorial Dr Cambridge MA 02142-1314 Office: MIT Dept Civil Engring Cambridge MA 02139

HARLEY, HALVOR LARSON, banker, lawyer; b. Atlantic City, N.J., Oct. 7, 1948; s. Robison Dooling and Loyde Hazel (Gauchnauer) H. BSc, U. S.C., 1971, MA, 1973; JD, Widener U., 1981. Bar: Pa. 1982, D.C. 1989, U.S. Ct. Appeals (3d cir.) 1987, U.S. Dist. Ct. (ea. dist.) Pa. 1987, U.S. Supreme Ct., 1988, U.S. Ct. Appeals D.C., 1989. Staff psychologist Columbia Area Mental Health Ctr., S.C., 1971-73; dir. Motivational Rsch. Cons., Columbia, 1973-79; psychologist Family Ct. Del., Wilmington, 1979; pvt. practice law Phila., 1982; v.p. investment banking Union Bank, L.A., 1982-88; v.p., mgr. Tokai Bank, Newport Beach, Calif., 1988-94; v.p., mgr. Mellon Pvt. Asset Mgmt., Newport Beach, 1994-97, first v.p., 1994—; regional sales mgr. So. Calif. Pvt. Asset Mgmt., 1994—. Author: Help for Herpes, 1982; contbr. articles to profl. jours. Fundraiser Orange County Performing Art Ctr., 1983-84; trustee, exec. com. Orange County Mus. Arts; vol. Hosp. Ship HOPE, Sri Lanka, 1968-69; bd. dirs., v.p. exec. com. alzheimers Assn. Orange County; bd. dirs. Lido Sands Homeowners Assn., Newport Beach, 1984-85, So. Calif. Entrepreneurship Acad., 1995—; bd. dirs. United Cerebral Palsy of Orange County, chmn. Bastile Day com. Mem. ATLA, Calif. Bankers Assn., Am. Judicature Soc., Indsl. League Orange County (membership com. 1983-84), Am. Bankers Assn., World Trade Ctr. Assocs. Orange County (directing com. 1983-85), Orange County Performing Arts Fraternity (trustee), Psi Chi (chpt. pres. 1971-73). Home: 5015 Lido Sands Dr Newport Beach CA 92663-2403 Office: Mellon Bank 4695 Macarthur Ct Ste 240 Newport Beach CA 92660-8851

HARLEY, NAOMI HALLDEN, radiation specialist, environmental medicine educator; b. N.Y.C., Aug. 4, 1932; d. Carl Edward and Ida Wilson (Palmer) Hallden; m. John Henry Harley, Sept. 11, 1964. BS, Cooper Union U., N.Y.C., 1959; MS, NYU, 1967, PhD, 1971, Advanced Profl. Cert., 1983. Phys. scientist U.S. AEC, N.Y.C., 1951-65; rsch. prof. environ. medicine NYU, 1965—; coun. mem., sci. com. chmn. Nat. Coun. on Radiation Protection and Measurement, Washington, 1982—. Contbr. articles to profl. jours. Adviser to UN Sci. Com. on Effects of Atomic Radiation (UNSCEAR), 1989—. USPHS fellow, 1988. Fellow AAAS, Health Physics Soc. Democrat. Office: NYU Sch of Medicine Dept Environ Medicine 550 1st Ave New York NY 10016-6481

HARLEY, ROBISON DOOLING, physician, educator; b. Pleasantville, N.J., Feb. 27, 1911; s. Halvor L. and Alice (Robison) H.; children—Robison Dooling, Ardee R., Heather L., Halvor L. II, William W. B.Sc., Rutgers U., 1932; M.D., U. Pa., 1936; Ph.D., U. Minn., 1949. Diplomate Am. Bd. Ophthalmology. Intern Phila. Gen. Hosp., 1936-38; fellowship Mayo Clinic, Rochester, Minn., 1938-41; jr. staff cons. Mayo Clinic, 1941-42; pvt. practice as ophthalmologist and ophthalmic surgeon Atlantic City and Phila., 1947-67; attending surgeon, dir. ophthalmology St. Christopher's Hosp. for Children, Phila., 1958-70; chief surgeon Atlantic City Hosp., 1950-67; cons. Shore Meml. Hosp., Somers Point, 1958-67; attending surgeon Temple U. Hosp., Phila., 1947-87; also Wills Eye Hosp. and Research Inst.; cons. Betty Bacharach Home for Children; cons. surgeon Wills Eye Hosp.; attending surgeon, dir. dept. pediatrics and motility; formerly prof., chmn. ophthalmology, prof. pediatrics Temple U. Health Sci. Ctr., Phila.; now prof. emeritus; dir. Overseas Eye Programs: Project Hope, Care-Medico, Internat. Eye Surgeons, Project Orbis; adj. prof. Thomas Jefferson U.; A.L. Morgan lectr., Toronto, 1972, Antonio Navas lectr., P.R., 1979, Frank Costenbader lectr., Washington., 1979. Author 152 med. publs. indluding book chpts. and 4 textbooks; contbg. author: Textbook of Pediatrics, 1975, 77, 79, 98; contbr. chpt. Pediatric Ophthalmological Surgery; editor: Pediatric Ophthalmology, 1975, Pediatric Opthalmology textbook, 2 vols., 1983, 3d edit., 1992; contbr. articles to profl. jours., chpts. to books; mem. editorial bd.: Jour. Pediatric Ophthalmology and Strabismus. Mem. exec. bd. Atlantic area coun. Boy Scouts Am., 1949—; mem. Fight for Signt Inc., N.Y.C., Retinitis Pigmentosa Found. Served to lt. col. AUS, 1942-47. Decorated Legion of Merit from Panama (Vasco Nunez de Balboa). Fellow A.C.S. (gov. 1959-62), Am. Acad. Ophthalmology (assoc. sec. continuing edn.); mem. Assn. Research Ophthalmology, Pan-Am. Congress Ophthalmology, Am. Ophthal. Soc., Del. Assn. Blind. (pres.), Phi Beta Kappa, Sigma Xi. Clubs: Explorers N.Y.C., Brigantine (N.J.) Yacht (commodore); Union League (Phila.); Corinthian Yacht (Cape May, N.J.). Home: The Devon Apt 704 2401 Pennsylvania Ave Wilmington DE 19806-2135

HARLEY, ROBISON DOOLING, JR., lawyer, educator; b. Ancon, Panama, July 6, 1946; s. Robison Dooling and Loyde Hazel (Goehenauer) H.; m. Suzanne Purviance Bendel, Aug. 9, 1975; children: Arianne Erin, Lauren Loyde. BA, Brown U., 1968; JD, Temple U., 1971; LLM, U. San Diego, 1985. Bar: Pa. 1971, U.S. Ct. Mil. Appeals 1972, Calif. 1976, U.S. Dist. Ct. (cen. and so. dists) Calif. 1976, N.J. 1977, U.S. Dist. Ct. N.J. 1977, U.S. Supreme Ct. 1980, D.C. 1981, U.S. Ct. Appeals (9th cir.) 1982, U.S. Dist. Ct. (ea. dist.) Pa. 1987, U.S. Ct. Appeals (3rd cir.) 1986. Cert. criminal law specialist Calif. Bd. Legal Specialization, 1981, recertified 1986, 91, 96; cert. criminal trial adv. Nat. Bd. Trial Advocacy, 1982, recertified, 1987, 92, 97. Asst. agy. dir. Safeco Title Ins. Co., L.A., 1975-77; ptnr. Cohen, Stokke & Davis, Santa Ana, Calif., 1977-85; prin. Harley Law Offices, Santa Ana, Calif., 1985—; adj. prof. Orange County Coll. Trial Advocacy, adj. prof., paralegal program U. Calif., trial adv. programs U.S. Army, USN, USAF, USMC; judge pro-tem Orange County Cts. Author: Orange County Trial Lawyers Drunk Driving Syllabus; contbr. articles to profl. jours. and reports. Bd. dirs. Orange County Legal Aid Soc. Served to lt. col. JAGC, USMCR, 1975-94; trial counsel, def. counsel, mil. judge, asst. staff judge adv. USMC, 1971-75, regional def. counsel Western Region, 1986-90, instr., program coord. Army, Navy, Air Force, Marines, Coast Guard Trial Adv. Programs worldwide. Recipient Commendation medal U.S. Navy, Nat. Defense Svc. medal, Reserve medal, 23 Certs. of Commendation and/or Congratulations. Mem. ABA, ATLA, Orange County Bar Assn. (judiciary com., criminal law sect., adminstrn. of justice com.), Orange County Trial Lawyers Assn., Calif. Trial Lawyers Assn., Calif. Attys. for Criminal Justice, Calif. Pub. Defenders Assn., Nat. Assn. for Criminal Def. Attys., Assn. Specialized Criminal Def. Advs., Orange County Criminal Lawyers Assn. (found. com.), Res. Officers Assn., Marine Corps Reserve Officers Assn., Marine Corps Assn. Republican. Avocations: sports, physical fitness, reading. Home: 31211 Paseo Miraloma San Juan Capistrano CA 92675-5505 Office: Harley Law Offices 825 N Ross St Santa Ana CA 92701-3419

HARLEY, RUTH, artist, educator; b. Phila.; children: Peter Wells Bressler, Tori Angela. Student, Pa. State U., 1941; BFA, Phila. Coll. Art, 1945; postgrad., U. N.H., 1971, Hampshire Coll., 1970. Former instr. Phila. Mus. Art, 1946-59; former art supt. Ventnor (N.J.) City Bd. Edn., 1959-61; art tchr. The Print Club, Phila., Allens Lane Art Ctr., Phila., Suburban Ctr. Arts, Lower Merion, Pa., Radner (Pa.) Twp. Adult Ctr., 1949-59, Atlantic City Adult Ctr., 1959-60. *The great use of life is to spend it for that which outlasts it. Be still, be quiet, and watch how magically life unfolds. The 1990's decade brought a new period of work which is now based on a spectrum from white (pure light) to violet. Her canvases depict the energetic transformation of the spiritual journey or visions of ecstasy was the name of the first showing of these paintings. They express the artists most intense emotions, pain, love, sorrow and mostly joy. Natural and psychic unleashed energy create abstract images that fleetingly imply water, weather and movements of angels.* One-woman shows include Dubin-Lush Galleries, Phila., 1956, Contemporary Art Assn., Phila., 1957, Vernon Art Exhbns., Germantown, Pa., 1958, Detroit Inst. Arts, 1958, Phila. Mus. Art, 1957, 59, Moore Inst., Phila., 1962-68, Greenhill Galleries, Phila., 1974, Phila. Civic Ctr., 1978, Natal Rio Grande du Norte, Brazil, 1979, Galerie Novel Esprit, Tampa, Fla., 1992-95, Mind's Eye Gallery, St. Petersburg, Fla., 1993, Ga. Tech. Art Ctr., 1998, Robert Ferst Ctr. for the Arts Ga. Inst. Tech., 1998-99; exhibited in various group shows, including Group 55, Phila., 1955, Print Club, Phila., 1955, Nat. Tours 1956-59, Pa. Acad. Fine Arts, 1957, Vernon Art Exhbns., 1958, Detroit Inst. Arts, 1958, Phila. Mus. Art, 1959, Moore Inst., 1962, Phila. Civic Ctr. Mus., 1975, Galerie Nouvel Esprit Assemblage Russe, 1992, Kenneth Raymond Gallery, Boca Raton, 1992-93, Mind's Eye Gallery, 1993, Polk Mus. Art, Lakeland, Fla., 1993, Don Roll Gallery, Sarasota, Fla., 1994-95, Las Vegas (Nev.) Internat. Art Expo, 1994, Heim Am. Gallery, Fisher Island, Fla., 1996, McLean Gallery, Malibu, Calif., 1997, 98, 99, Robert Ferst Ctr. Arts, Ga. Tech. U., 1998,99, Christina Gallery, Atlanta, 1999; represented in permanent collections at U. Villanova (Pa.) Mus., Temple U. Law Sch., Pa., Woodmere Mus., Phila.; included in Art in America Ann. Guide, 1993-99; 1973 photo sculpture commd. through Phila. Re-Devel. Authority. Contbr. art prize to Ventnor N.J. Sch. Sys. Address: PO Box 433 Melrose FL 32666-0433

HARLIN, MARILYN MILER, marine botany educator, researcher, consultant; b. Oakland, Calif., May 30, 1934; d. George T. and Gertrude (Turula) Miler; m. John E. Harlin II, Oct. 25, 1955 (dec. Feb. 1966); children: John E. III, Andrea M. Harlin Cilento. AB, Stanford U., 1955, MA, 1956; PhD, U. Wash., 1971. Instr. Am. Coll. Switzerland and Leysin, 1964-66; asst. prof. Pacific Marine Sta., Dillon Beach, Calif., 1969; asst. prof. marine biology U. R.I., Kingston, 1971-75, assoc. prof., 1975-83, prof., 1983—, chair botany dept., chair dept. biol. scis.; guest scientist Atlantic Regional Lab., Halifax, N.S., Can., 1973-78; hon. vis.prof. LaTrobe U., Bundoora, Victoria, Australia, 1984; resource person R.I. Coastal Resource Mgmt. Coun., 1980—, R.I. Dept. Environ. Mgmt., 1980; cons. Applied Sci. Assocs., Narragansett, R.I., 1988—, Western Australia Water Authority, Perth, 1994; rsch. assoc. U. Calif., Santa Cruz, 1993. Co-editor: Marine Ecology, 1976, Freshwater and Marine Plants of Rhode Island, 1988. Bd. dirs. Westminster Unitarian Ch., East Greenwich, R.I., 1987; bd. govs. Women's Ctr., Kingston, 1989-90. Grantee NOAA, 1975-81, Dept. Environ. Mgmt./EPA, 1989-91, U.S. Fish and Wildlife, 1995. Mem. Internat. Phycological Soc., Phycological Soc. Am. (editor newsletter 1982-84, editorial bd. 1988-90), N.E. Algal Soc. (exec. com.), Sigma Xi (pres., sec. 1979-82). Avocations: yoga, hiking, cross-country skiing, reading, writing. Office: U RI Biol Scis Ranger Hall Kingston RI 02881

HARLIN, RENNY (RENNY LAURI MAURITZ HARJOLA), film director; b. Helsinki, Finland, 1959; m. Geena Davis, 1993. dir: (feature films) Born American, 1986, Prison 1988, A Nightmare on Elm Street 4: The Dream Master, 1988, Die Hard 2, 1990, The Adventures of Ford Fairlane, 1990, Cliffhanger, 1993; (T.V.) Freddy's Nightmares, 1990; dir & prodr.: (feature films) Rambling Rose, 1991; Cutthroat Island, 1995, Speechless, 1994, Long Kiss Goodnight, 1996, Deep Blue Sea, 1999. Office: care International Creative Mgmt Jim Wiatt-agent 8942 Wilshire Blvd Beverly Hills CA 90211-1934*

HARLLEE, MARY BETH, social worker, educator; b. Statesville, N.C., Apr. 20, 1946; d. Zimmie Edward and Anna Beth (Morrison) Tharpe; m. Thomas Cannon Harllee, Nov. 12, 1972. AA, Mitchell Jr. Coll., 1966; BA, Catawba Coll., 1968; MEd, U. N.C., Charlotte, 1977; MSW, U. S.C., Columbia, 1990. Lic. social worker, N.C., S.C. Child welfare specialist City of Danville, Va., 1968-72; personnel cons. Golden Door, Charlotte, 1972-74; reading specialist, program coord. Learning Found., Charlotte, 1974-76; human svcs. asst. City of Charlotte, 1977-87; svc. rep. Kelly Svcs., Charlotte, 1987-88; social worker S.C. State Hosp., Columbia, 1989-90, Harris Psychiat. Hosp., Anderson, S.C., 1990—; dir. Project Cope, Hartsville, S.C., 1995—; adj. prof. Coke Coll., Hartsville, S.C., 1995—. Chair social com. N.C. Literacy Bd., Charlotte, 1984-88; mem. gov.'s Adv. Bd. Alzheimer's Assn. Named Social Worker of Yr. Dept. Health and Environ. Control, Florence, S.C., 1992, 95. Mem. Nat. Assn. Clin. Social Workers. Democrat. Avocations: dance, cooking, writing poetry, reading. Office: Harris Psychiat Hosp PO Box 2907 Anderson SC 29622-2907

HARLOW, CHARLES VENDALE, JR., finance educator, consultant; b. Long Beach, Calif., May 18, 1931; s. Charles Vendale and Lucille (Morris) H.; m. Luann Jones, July 6, 1956; children: Jeffrey, Pamela, John. BA, Stanford U., 1953; MBA, U. So. Calif., 1960, DBA, 1968. Ptnr. Harlow & Harlow Investments, Long Beach, 1955-68; pres. Cambistics, Inc., Long Beach, 1968-88; asst. prof. Calif. State U., Long Beach, 1968-71, assoc. prof., 1971-75, prof. fin., 1975-94; prof. fin. Pepperdine U., 1995—; mng. dir. Cambistics Securities Corp., Long Beach, 1990—*. Co-author: The Commodity Futures Trading Guide, 1969 (100 Best Books in Bus. award), The Futures Game, 1974, How to Shoot From the Hip Without Getting Shot in the Foot: Making Smart Strategic Choices Every Day, 1990. 1st lt. USMC, 1953-55. NSF grantee, 1968. Republican. Avocations: running, golf, amateur radio, writing.

HARLOW, EDWARD E., JR., oncologist. BS in Microbiology, U. Okla., 1974, MS, 1978; PhD, U. London, 1982. Rsch. microbiologist McDonnell Douglas Aerospace, St. Louis, 1974-75; fellow of the Lady Tata Meml. Trust Imperial Cancer Rsch. Fund Labs., London, 1978-81, vis. fellow, 1982; prof. genetics, dir. rsch. Mass. Gen. Hosp. Cancer Ctr., Charlestown; mem. selection jury Lasker Prize; mem. awards assembly GM Cancer Rsch. Found.; mem. new investigator rsch. adv. com. Med. Found.; mem. external adv. bd. UCLA Jonsson Comprehensive Cancer Ctr., Washington U. Cancer Ctr.; mem. sci. adv. bd. Children's Hosp., Boston, Found. for Advanced Cancer Studies; Eppley vis. prof. U. Nebr. Med. Ctr., 1991; Ralph R. Braund vis. prof. Forum on Cancer Rsch., 1993; Richard C. Parker meml. lectr. Columbis U., 1993; Charles L. Spurr prof. oncology Wake Forest U., 1994; William Sokolow vis. lectr. U. Calif., San Francisco, 1995; Eudoxia Dutkevich meml. lectr. U. Toronto, Can., 1996; Charles B. Smith vis. rsch. prof. Meml. Sloan-Kettering Cancer Ctr., 1996; Howard Hughes lectr. MIT, 1996. Author: (with D. Lane) Antibodies: A Laboratory Manual, 1988, Using Antibodies: A Laboratory Manual, 1998; editor: (with F. Alt and E. Ziff) Current Communications in Molecular Biology, Nuclear Oncogenes, 1987, (with J. Brugge, T. Curran and F. McCormick) Origins of Human Cancer, 1992; contbr. articles to profl. jours. Trustee Cold Spring Harbor Lab. Recipient Alfred P. Sloan, Jr. medal GM Cancer Rsch. Found., 1995. Office: Mass Gen Hosp Cancer Ctr Lab Molecular Oncology Bldg 149 13th St Mailcode 1497330 Charlestown MA 02129*

HARLOW, JOAN BEVERLEY, writer; b. Malden, Mass., July 25, 1932; d. Albert Ernest and Marguerite Wells (Small) Hiatt; m. Richard Lee Harlow, Aug. 17, 1951; children: Deborah, Lisa, Kristan, Scott, Jennifer. Cert., Stenotype Inst., Boston, 1950. lectr. in field. Author: (children's books) Poems Are for Everything, 1973, Shadow Bear, 1981, The Mysterious Dr. Chen, 1996. Mem. Soc. Children's Book Writers & Illustrators.

HARMAN, ANGELA DIANE, construction company executive; b. Ozark, Ark., June 5, 1972; d. Juanita Kenney. BA in History and Polit. Sci., Ark. tech. U., 1994. Transp. mgr. Am. Quality Mfg., Conway, Ark., 1994-96; asst. project mgr. Nabholz Constrn., Conway, 1996-97; project adminstr. C.A. Walker Constrn., Houston, 1997—. Editor/writer Dover Times, 1990; pub. Shadows mag., 1990. Mem. Justice for All, Houston, 1998; pres. Cardinal Key, Russellville, 1993-94. Recipient Award for Acad. Excellence, Ark. Tech. U., 1991, 92, 93, acad. scholar, 1990. Avocations: writing, painting, reading, collecting antique books. Home: 1819 Augusta Dr Apt 432 Houston TX 77057-3142 Office: C A Walker Constrn 1543 Silber Rd Houston TX 77055-5331

HARMAN, CHARLES MORGAN, mechanical engineer; b. Cannonsburg, Pa., July 25, 1929; s. Charles Nash and Mildred (Barker) H.; m. Althea Ann Ashton, June 12, 1956 (div.); children—Ruth Ann, Charles Morgan, Samuel Stuart. B.S., U. Md., 1954; M.S., U. N.D., 1957; Ph.D., U. Wis., 1961. Registered profl. engr., Wis., N.C. Asst. prof. mech. engring. Duke U., Durham, N.C., 1961-70, prof. mech. engring., 1970—, assoc. dean Grad. Sch., 1970-80, dir. grad. studies, 1986—; pres. Synergy Research Corp., 1983-84; engring. cons. Douglas Aircraft Co., 1961-64, Army Research Office, Durham, 1964—. Contbr. articles to profl. jours.; editor: Jour. Advanced Transp, 1976—. Served with USN, 1949-51. Ford Found. fellow, 1960-61; recipient Profl. Achievement citation Douglas Aircraft Co., 1964. Mem. ASME, ASHRAE, Advanced Transit Assn. Home: 1701 Tisdale St Durham NC 27705-5631 Office: Duke U Dept Mech Engring Durham NC 27708-0301

HARMAN, GEORGE GIBSON, physicist, consultant; b. Norfolk, Va., Dec. 7, 1924; s. George Gibson and Annie Wall (Baldwin) H.; m. Ann Worischek, Jan. 31, 1953 (div. 1985); children: Joyce Catherine, Arthur Lawrence, Stewart Thomas; m. Donna K. Williamson, 1986. B.S. in Physics, Va. Poly. Inst., 1949; M.S. in Physics, U. Md., 1959. With Nat. Inst. Stds. and Tech. (formerly Nat. Bur. Stds.), Washington, 1950—, sr. rsch. scientist, 1976-93; fellow Nat. Inst. Stds. and Tech. (formerly Nat. Bur. Stds.), Washington, Eng., 1993—; rsch. fellow Reading (Eng.) U., 1962-63. Author 2 books; contbr. articles to profl. jours.; patentee (4). Served with U.S. Army, 1943-46. Recipient Silver medal U.S. Dept. Commerce, 1973, Gold medal, 1979, Achievement award Internat. Electronics Packaging Soc., 1988. Fellow IEEE (Centennial medal 1984, chmn. fellows and awards com., Outstanding Contbns. award 1992, 93, 15-Yr. Outstanding Contbns. to ECT Conf. 1993, Harry Diamond Meml. award, 1996), Internat. Microelectronics Packaging Soc. (chpt. pres. 1980-82, tech. achievement award 1981, Lewis F. Miller award 1984, regional dir. 1985-87, chmn. found. grants com., Disting. Svc. award 1986, 87, Daniel C. Hughes award 1989, chmn. nat. tech. program com. 1990-92, nat. pres. 1995, DVS European Electronic Packaging award 1998); mem. ASTM, Am. Phys. Soc., Sigma Xi, Sigma Pi Sigma. Club: Cosmos (Washington). Home: 4719 Dorset Ave Bethesda MD 20815-5445 Office: Nat Inst Standards and Tech Div # 812 Gaithersburg MD 20899

HARMAN, GILBERT HELMS, philosophy educator; b. East Orange, N.J., May 26, 1938; s. William Henry and Marguerite Variel (Page) H.; m. Lucy Newman, Aug. 14, 1970; children: Elizabeth, Olivia. BA, Swarthmore Coll., 1960; PhD, Harvard U., 1964. With dept. philosophy Princeton (N.J.) U., 1963—, prof., 1971—, chair cognitive studies program, 1992-97. Author: Thought, 1973, The Nature of Morality, 1977, Change in View, 1986, Skepticism and the Definition of Knowledge, 1990, (with Judith Jarvis Thomson) Moral Relativism and Moral Objectivity, 1996, Reasoning, Meaning, and Mind, 1999; editor: On Noam Chomsky, 1974, (with Donald Davidson) Semantics of Natural Language, 1971, The Logic of Grammar, 1975, Conceptions of the Human Mind, 1993. Mem. Am. Philos. Assn., Philosophy of Sci. Assn., Soc. for Philosophy and Psychology. Home: 106 Broadmead St Princeton NJ 08540-7216 Office: Princeton Univ Dept Philosophy Princeton NJ 08544-1006

HARMAN, HENRY M., JR., accountant, educator; b. Schenectady, N.Y., May 28, 1924; s. Henry Martyn Harman and Adelaide Phillips; m. Jane Robertson, Dec. 2, 1944; children: Linda, Owen, David, Carol. BS, Lehigh

U., 1956; MBA, U. Bridgeport, 1972. CPA, Pa., Conn.; cert. inventory mgmt. practitioner, ICMA. Controller CT Hard Rubber, New Haven, 1951-63; internal auditor Gen. Dynamics, Ft. Worth, 1952-53; acct. Touche Ross CPA, Phila., 1952-54; controller Tech. Measurement, North Haven, Conn., 1964-68; v.p. fin. Cott Corp., New Haven, 1968-72; dir. Cott Corp., New Haven, Conn., 1970-72; controller Henry Richards Co., Hamden, 1972-76; asst. prof. Ctrl. Conn. State U., New Britain, 1976-85; treas. JK Harman INc., Hamden, 1984—; assoc. prof. Meth. Coll., Fayetteville, N.C., 1985-87; cons. Montgomery Assocs., Woodbridge, Conn. Author: Book of Reports, 1984. Treas. Seven Lakes Landowners Assn., West End, N.C., 1992-94. Mem. Nat. Assn. Accts. (chpt. pres., dir. 1978-88, cert. inventory mgmt. practitioner). Avocations: golfing, bridge, computers. Home: 2152 7 Lks S West End NC 27376-9613

HARMAN, JANE, congresswoman, lawyer; b. N.Y.C., June 28, 1945; d. A. N. and Lucille (Geier) Lakes; m. Sidney Harman, Aug. 30, 1980; children: Brian Lakes, Hilary Lakes, Daniel Geier, Justine Leigh. BA, Smith Coll., 1966; JD, Harvard U., 1969. Bar: D.C. 1969, U.S. Ct. Appeals (D.C. cir.) 1972, U.S. Supreme Ct. 1975. Spl. asst. Commn. of Chs. on Internat. Affairs, Geneva, Switzerland, 1969-70; assoc. Surrey & Morse, Washington, 1970-72; chief legis. asst. Senator John V. Tunney, Washington, 1972-73; chief counsel, staff dir. Subcom. on Rep. Citizen Interests, Com. on Judiciary, Washington, 1973-75; adj. prof. Georgetown Law Ctr., Washington, 1974-75; chief counsel, staff dir. Subcom. on Constl. Rights, Com. on Judiciary, Washington, 1975-77; dep. sec. to cabinet The White House, Washington, 1977-78; spl. counsel Dept. Def., Washington, 1979; ptnr. Manatt, Phelps, Rothenberg & Tunney, Washington, 1979-82, Surrey & Morse, Washington, 1982-86; of counsel Jones, Day, Reavis & Pogue, Washington, 1987-92; mem. 103rd-105th Congresses from 36th Calif. dist., 1992—, mem. nat. security com., intelligence com.; mem. vis. coms. Harvard Law Sch., 1976-82, Kennedy Sch. Govt., 1990-96. Counsel Dem. Platform Com., Washington, 1984; vice-chmn. Ctr. for Nat. Policy, Washington, 1981-90; chmn. Dem. Nat. Com. Nat. Lawyers' Coun., Washington, 1986-90. Mem. Phi Beta Kappa. Democrat. Office: US House Reps 325 Cannon Bldg Ofc Bldg Washington DC 20515-0003 also: 1217 El Prado Ave Torrance CA 90501-2708*

HARMAN, JO ANN SNYDER, secondary school educator; b. Lahmansville, W.Va., Aug. 30, 1940; d. Lloyd Neil and Eva Lucretia (Parker) Snyder; m. Robert L. Harman, June 17, 1962; children: Kenton Snyder, Brenton Robert. BA summa cum laude, Fairmont (W.Va.) State Coll., 1962; MA, W.Va. U., 1986. Cert. in gifted edn., French, English. Sec. tchr. Fairfax (Va.) County Bd. Edn., 1962-64; adult edn. instr. Shepherd Coll., Petersburg, W.Va., 1986—; sec. tchr. Grant County Bd. Edn., Petersburg, W.Va., 1964—; pres. Petersburg H.S. Faculty Senate; coord., instr. summer program gifted and talented students Collegiate Acad. of Learning; presenter insvc. sessions and profl. programs on writing, creativity, and gifted edn.; dir., sponsor student trips; mentor new tchrs.; invited participant Pearl S. Buck Centennial Celebration, China; selected pilot program for French book for Am. Schs. Libraire Hachette, France; mem. North Ctrl. Evaluation Team; participant confs. in field; tchr., mentor, supr.; supervising tchr. for student tchrs. from France. Contbr. articles to profl. jours. Sponsor Nat. Honor Soc. and French Club; mem. and clk. of session Petersburg Presbyn. Ch.; originator tribute for Pearl S. Buck Centennial, 1991. Recipient Presdl. citation from W.Va. Gov.'s Honors Acad., Tchr. Achievement award Ashland Oil, 1992; named Grant County Tchr. of Yr., 1992, 96, W.Va. Tchr. of Yr., 1996, W.Va. English Tchr. of Yr., 1998; 9 mini-grants for edn. Mem. NEA, ASCD, W.Va. Edn. Assn., Grant County Edn. Assn., Nat. Coun. Tchrs. English, W.Va. Assn. for Gifted, Internat. Platform Assn., Nat. Assn. Student Activity Advisors, World of Poetry, Order Eastern Star (past grand officer and grand rep.), Delta Kappa Gamma (chpt. pres.), Kappa Delta Pi, Pi Lambda Theta. E-mail: jharman@hardynet.com. Home: HC 84 Box 26 Lahmansville WV 26731-9701

HARMAN, JOHN ROYDEN, lawyer; b. Elkhart, Ind., June 30, 1921; s. James Lewis and Bessie Bell (Mountjoy) H.; m. Elizabeth Rae Crosier, Dec. 12, 1943 (dec. May 1995); 1 child, James Richard. B.S., U. Ill., 1943; J.D., Ind. U., 1949. Bar: Ind. 1949. Assoc. Proctor & Proctor, Elkhart, 1949-51; pvt. practice, Elkhart, 1952-60; ptnr. Cawley & Harman, 1960-65, Thornburg, McGill, Deahl, Harman, Carey & Murray, 1965-82, Barnes & Thornburg, Elkhart, 1982-89; ret., 1989; atty. City of Elkhart, 1952-60. State del. Ind. Republican Com., 1962-70; pres., bd. dirs. Crippled Childrens Soc.; bd. dirs. United Community Services Elkhart County. 1st lt., F.A., AUS, 1943-46, PTO. Fellow Ind. Bar Found; mem. ABA, Ind. Bar Assn. , Elkhart County Bar Assn. (pres. 1977), Elkhart City Bar Assn. (pres. 1970), Elkhart C. of C. (pres. 1977, bd. dirs. 1972-75), Elcona Country Club (bd. dirs.), Phi Kappa Psi, Alpha Kappa Psi, Phi Delta Phi. Republican. Presbyterian. Avocation: golf. Office: NBD Bank Bldg 121 W Franklin St Ste 200 Elkhart IN 46516-3200 *Be honest and forthright—think positively—continually try to enhance the cause of mankind.*

HARMAN, MARK, English educator; b. Mar. 6, 1951. BA, U. Coll., 1972, MA, 1974; MA, Yale U., 1976, MPhil in German, 1977, PhD in German, 1980. Instr. Dartmouth Coll., 1979-80, asst. prof. in German, 1980-84; asst. prof. in German Franklin & Marshall Coll., 1985-90; vis. assoc. prof. of English Elizabethtown Coll., 1998—; vis. assoc. prof. of English Elizabeth Coll., 1998—. Recipient Henry Hutchinson Stewart prize in modern langs. Nat. U. of Ireland, 1970; scholarships U. Coll., 1969-71, The Thomas MacDonah 1916 Commemoration scholarship, 1969-72, German Acad. Exch. scholarship, 1972-73, scholarship German Acad. Exch., 1977-78, rsch. grant Yale Coun. on West European Studies, 1977; Pro Helvetia grant for rsch. and translation, 1986, grant for translation Austrian Ministry for Edn. and Art, 1994; Wilmarth Lewis fellowship, 1975-77. E-mail: mhar103@aol.com. Home: 809 Martha Ave Lancaster PA 17601

HARMAN, NANCY JUNE, elementary education educator, principal; b. WaKeeney, Kans., June 23, 1954; d. Don Raymond and Ida Berdena (Hildebrand) Legere; m. Roger Dean Harman, May 24, 1975; children: Michael James, Jennifer Legere. BS in Elem. Edn., Ft. Hays State U., 1975, MS in Edn. Adminstrn., 1993. Cert. early childhood, elem. tchr., elem. adminstr., Kans. Tchr. Catherine Elem. Sch., Hays, Kans., 1975-76, Dodge Elem. Sch., Wichita, Kans., 1977-80, Franklin Elem. Sch., Wichita, 1981-82, Felten Mid. Sch., Hays, 1987-90; prin. O'Loughlin Elem. Sch., Hays, 1990-98, 1998—; mem. nat. leadership team Operation Primary Phys. Sci., 1996—. Mem. com. Sternberg Discovery Rm., Hays, 1993-94; mem. Hays Book Guild, 1987—; past mem. bd. dirs. Hays Arts Coun. Recipient Presdl. award for excellence in math. and sci. tchg., 1997. Mem. ASCD, PEO, Nat. Coun. Tchrs. English, Kans. Reading Assn., Kans. Assn. Tchrs. English (state bd. dirs. 1993-96), Kans. Comm. Arts (stds. writers com.), Kans. Assn. Tchrs. Math., Phi Delta Kappa (pres. 1997—), Alpha Delta Kappa (pres. 1988-93). Presbyterian. Avocations: running, reading, collecting antiques. Home: 2306 Plum St Hays KS 67601-3035 Office: O Loughlin Elem Sch 1401 Hall St Hays KS 67601-3753

HARMAN, ROBERT JOHN, religious organization administrator; b. Elmhurst, Ill., Oct. 10, 1937; s. Clifford Martin and Anna Elizabeth (Johnson) H.; m. Marcia Bornemeier, Aug. 1, 1959; children: Scott, Michael. BA, North Cen. Coll., 1959; BD, Garett Evang. Theol. Sem., 1962; postgrad., Union Theol. Sem., 1973-74, 69-72; MPA, NYU, 1975. Ordained to ministry Evang. United Brethren Ch., 1962; (merged with United Meth. Ch. 1968). Sr. pastor Community United Meth. Ch., Naperville, Ill., 1968-73; planner, nat. div. Gen. Bd. Global Ministries, N.Y.C., 1975-84; dist. supt. No. Ill. Conf. Meth. Chs., Chgo., 1984-85; dir. planning United Meth. Ch. Gen. Bd. of Global Ministries, N.Y.C., 1985-89, dep. gen. sec., world div., 1989—; unit dir. Nat. Coun. Chs., N.Y.C., 1978-83, 89-96; del. World Coun. Chs., Geneva, 1991, mem. unit II commn. on chs. in mission; health, edn. and witness, 1992—; mem. exec. com. World Meth. Coun., 1991. Mem. editorial bd., pres. Christianity and Crisis Jour., 1982-84; contbr. articles to profl. jours. Dep. gen. sec. Cmty. and Institutional Ministries, Evangelization of Ch. Growth. Recipient numerous fellowships. Office: Gen Bd Global Ministries United Meth Ch 475 Riverside Dr New York NY 10115-0122

HARMAN, WALLACE PATRICK, lawyer; b. El Paso, Tex., Jan. 22, 1949; s. Wallace Irvin and Dorothy Louise (Pearson) H.; m. Gina Marie Ries, Dec. 31, 1988; children: Loren Patrick, Claire Marie. BA, Stanford U., 1972; JD, U. Calif., 1977. Bar: Calif. 1977, U.S. Ct. Appeals (9th cir.) 1977, N.Mex. 1978, U.S. Dist. Ct. N.Mex. 1978, U.S. Ct. Appeals (10th cir.) 1978. Zone adminstrn. mgr. Am. Motors Corp., Burlingame, Calif., 1972-74; atty., shareholder Sutin, Thayer & Browne, APC, Albuquerque, N.Mex., 1977-87, group leader comml. group, 1985-87; atty., shareholder, mng. ptnr., leader bus. group The Payne Law Firm, P.C., Albuquerque, 1987-91; atty., ptnr. Hisey & Wainwright, P.A., Albuquerque, 1991-92; atty., pres., chief exec. officer The Harman Law Firm, P.C., Albuquerque, 1992—; mem. N.Mex. Supreme Ct. Med.-Legal Panel, Albuquerque, 1978-80, 91—; mem. N.Mex. Supreme Ct. Lawyers Assistance Com., Albuquerque, 1991—; area rep. The Taft Sch., Watertown, Conn., 1992—; mem. mentorship program Hatings Coll. Law. Co-author: Recent Developments in Commerical Law, University of New Mexico Law Review, 1989. Bd. advisors Lovelace Med. Ctr., Albuquerque, 1980-89; mem. state bd. trustees The Nature Conservancy, N.Mex., 1984-88; adv. bd. Assistance League Albuquerque, 1982-89, Jr. League Albuquerque, 1984-87, Make-a-Wish Found. of N.Mex., Inc., 1996-97. Recipient AV Rating award Martindale-Hubbell, 1990. Mem. ABA, Albuquerque Bar Assn. Democrat. Avocations: photography, sports, computers, landscaping, writing. E-mail: harman@sandia.net.

HARMAN, WILLARD NELSON, malacologist, educator; b. Geneva, N.Y., Apr. 20, 1937; s. Samuel Willard and Mary Nelson (Covert) H.; m. Susan Beth Mead, June 12, 1968 (div. 1980); children—Rebecca Mary, Willard Wade; m. Barbara Ann Stong, June 8, 1981; children—Jessica Mary, Samuel Willard. Student, Hobart Coll., 1954-55; B.S., Coll. Environ. Sci. and Forestry, SUNY, 1965; Ph.D., Cornell U., 1968; postgrad., Marine Biol. Lab., Woods Hole, Mass., 1968. Asst. prof. SUNY, Oneonta, 1968-69, assoc. prof., 1969-76, prof. biology, 1976—, chmn. dept. biology, 1981-89, dir. Biol. Field Sta., 1989—; resource advisor N.Y. State Dept. Environ. Conservation, Albany, 1980—. Contbr. articles to profl. jours. Rep. Otsego County Republican Com., N.Y., 1973-76; chmn. planning bd., Springfield, N.Y., 1984-96 . Served with USN, 1956-61. Recipient Chancellor's award SUNY, 1974-75, Quality award EPA, 1989, Excellence award SUNY, 1990. Mem. Soc. Limnology and Oceanography, N.Am. Benthological Soc., Soc. for Exptl. and Descriptive Malacology, Am. Malocological Union, Otsego County Conservation Assn. (bd. dirs. 1970—, pres. 1974-78, 80-81, chmn. lake com. 1981—). Episcopalian. Avocations: sailing; fishing; scuba diving; skiing. Home: RR 2 Box 829 Cooperstown NY 13326-9327 Office: Biol Field Sta RR 2 Box 1066 Cooperstown NY 13326-9330

HARMAN, WILLIAM BOYS, JR., lawyer; b. Newport News, Va., June 5, 1930; s. William Boys and Helen (Conner) H.; children: Susan Carol, Thomas Scott, Ann Carrington. AB, Coll. William and Mary, 1951, JD, 1956; LLM, Georgetown U., 1960. Bar: Va. 1956, D.C. 1961. Tax atty. Gen. Motors Corp., Detroit, 1956-58; atty. Office Chief Counsel, IRS, Washington, 1958-59, Office of Tax Legis. Counsel, U.S. Treasury Dept., Washington, 1959-61; atty. firm Cummings & Sellers, Washington, 1961-62; asso. gen. counsel Am. Life Conv., Washington, 1962-67; gen. counsel Am. Life Conv., 1968-72; v.p. law Am. Life Ins. Assn., 1973-75; exec. v.p. Am. Council Life Ins., 1976-78; partner firm Sutherland, Asbill & Brennan, Washington, 1978-85, Davis & Harman, Washington, 1985—. Served with USCGR, 1952-54. Mem. ABA, Va. State Bar, D.C. Bar Assn., Assn. Life Ins. Counsel, Am. Law Inst., SAR, William and Mary Law Sch. Assn., Order of Coif, Washington Golf and Country Club, Metropolitan Club, Phi Beta Kappa, Phi Alpha Delta, Sigma Alpha Epsilon. Home: 3839 N Tazewell St Arlington VA 22207-4568 Office: Davis & Harman Ste 1200 1455 Pennsylvania Ave NW Washington DC 20004-1008

HARMEL, MEREL HILBER, anesthesiologist, educator; b. Cleve., May 19, 1917; s. Louis and Hermine (Greenbaum) H.; m. Armide Chilcoat, July 2, 1944 (dec. 1988); children: Nancy Armide, Ruth Courtney, Priscilla Gover, Mary Louise; m. Ernestine Friedl Levy, Dec. 27, 1990.. BA, Johns Hopkins U., 1938, MD, 1943. Diplomate Am. Bd. Anesthesiology. Fellow in anesthesiology NRC; anesthesiologist-in-chief Albany Med. Ctr., 1948-52; anesthesiologist-in-chief Kings County Med. Ctr., Bklyn., 1952-68, pres. med. bd., 1958-62, chmn. exec. com., 1964-65; cons. L.I. Jewish, St. Albans Naval, Maimonides, St. John's Episcopal, VA hosps., N.C. Eye and Ear Hosp., Durham; assoc. prof. anesthesiology (surgery) Albany Med. Coll., 1948-52; prof., chmn. dept. anesthesiology SUNY Downstate Med. Ctr., 1952-68, Pritzker Sch. Medicine, U. Chgo., 1968-71; prof. anesthesiology Duke Med. Ctr., Durham, N.C., 1971—, chmn. dept. anesthesiology ctr., 1971-83; prof. anesthesiology Duke Med. Center, 1983-87, prof. Emeritus, 1987—; vis. prof. dept. anesthesiology Sch. Medicine, Johns Hopkins U., 1985—. Contbr. articles to profl. jours. Commonwealth fellow Oxford U., 1961-62, hon. mem. Sr. Common Rm., Pembroke Coll., 1961; Merel Harmel vis. lectureship established Duke U. Med. Ctr., 1983. Fellow Am. Coll. Anesthesiology (bd. govs.), Royal Coll. Anaesthesia Faculty; mem. AMA, Am. Soc. Anesthesiologists (Living History Series), Assn. Univ. Anesthetists, Duke U. Med. Ctr. Founders Soc., Johns Hopkins U. Soc. Scholars, Japan Soc. Anesthesiologists (hon.), Assn. Anesthesiologists Français (hon.), Oxford Soc. Carolinas (hon. sec. 1990—). Office: Duke U Med Ctr Dept Anesthesiology PO Box 3094 Durham NC 27715-3094

HARMELIN, STEPHEN JOSEPH, lawyer; b. Phila., May 7, 1939; s. Louis M. and Ethel (Katz) H.; m. Julia Tose, June 18, 1995; children: Alison Kate, Melina Alexis. BA cum laude, U. Pa., 1960; LLB, Harvard U., 1963. Bar: Pa. 1964, U.S. Supreme Ct. 1968. Atty. broadcast bur. FCC, Washington, 1964; aide White House, Washington, 1964-65; assoc. Dilworth, Paxson, Kalish & Dilks (name now Dilworth, Paxson), Phila., 1965-70; ptnr. Dilworth, Paxson, Kalish & Dilks, Phila., 1970-86; co-chmn. corp. dept. Dilworth, Paxson, Kalish & Dilks (name now Dilworth, Paxson, Kalish & Kauffman), Phila., 1986-91, mng. ptnr., 1991—; bd. dirs., chmn. CONFAB, Inc., King of Prussia, Pa., 1996-97; chmn. Publicker Industries, Greenwich, Conn., 1980-84; lectr. Phila. Coll. Art, 1970-72. Spl. asst. dist. atty. City of Phila., 1970; commr. Pa. Conv. Ctr. Authority, Phila., 1989, 91; gen. counsel Pa. Legis. Reapportionment Commn., 1982-98; chmn. Thomas Skelton Harrison Found., sec. Nat. Constitution Ctr., Phila., 1982, Found. of the Phila. Heart Inst., 1988; bd. dirs. Phila. div. Am. Cancer Soc., 1986, crusade chmn., 1987-88. With USCGR, 1963-69. Mem. ABA, Phila. Bar Assn., Union League Club. Republican. Jewish. Office: Dilworth Paxson LLP 1735 Market St Philadelphia PA 19103-7501

HARMELINK, HERMAN, III, clergyman, author, educator, ecumenist; b. Sheldon, Pa., Dec. 26, 1933; s. Herman II, and Thyrza (Eringa) H.; m. Barbara Mary Conibear, Aug. 11, 1959; children: Herman IV Alan, Lindsay Alexandra (Mrs. Richard L. LeMay, Jr.). BA cum laude, Central Coll., 1954; MA, Columbia U., 1955; postgrad., U. London, 1955; M.Div., New Brunswick Theol. Sem., 1958; World Coun. Chs. scholar, U. Heidelberg, 1959; S.T.M. magna cum laude, Union Theol. Sem., N.Y.C., 1964, M.Phil., 1978. Ordained to ministry Reformed Ch. Am., 1959; min. Community Ch., Glen Rock, N.J., 1959-64, Woodcliff Community Ch., Woodcliff-on-Hudson, N.J., 1964-71, Ref. Ch., Poughkeepsie, N.Y., 1971—; mem. adj. faculty in philosophy SUNY, 1983—, Marist Coll., 1990—; vice chmn. Faith and Order Commn., Nat. Coun. Chs., 1976-79, mem. Commn. on Regional and Local Ecumenism, 1981-84; pres. Synod of N.J., 1969; chmn. interch. rels. Ref. Ch. Am., 1964-71; chmn. Ecumenical Rels. Commn. Internat. Coun. of Cmty. Chs., 1994—; del. 18th Plenary Consultation on Ch. Union, St. Louis, 1999; pres. Dutchess Interfaith Coun., 1977-78, mem. development retirement community com., 1989—, bd. dirs., 1998—; del. gen. coun. World Alliance Ref. Chs., Frankfurt, 1964, Nairobi, 1970; advisor 4th Gen. Assembly World Coun. Chs., Uppsala, Sweden, 1968; U.S. del. 50th Anniversary Faith and Order Commn., Lausanne, Switzerland, 1977; del. Nat. Coun. Chs. Gen. Assembly, 1999—. Author: Ecumenism and the Reformed Church, 1968; The Reformed Church in New Jersey, 1969; Another Look at Frelinghuysen and His Awakening, 1969; contbg. author to Piety and Patriotism, 1976, Vision from the Hill, 1984, The Livingston Legacy, 1987. Trustee Peter A. Lindsay Trust Imperial Coll. U. London; trustee St. Francis Hosp., 1979—, mem. exec. com. of bd., 1981—, joint conf. com., 1986—, chmn. planning com., 1987—; bd. dirs. Dutchess County Hist. Soc., 1974-78, also life mem.; bd. dirs. Dutchess County Arts Coun., 1976-80, Bardavon 1869 Opera House, 1978-79; mem. allocation and planning divs. United Way of Dutchess County; mem. Dutchess County Execs. Com. on Med. Ethics, 1991—; sec. bd. dirs. Rehab. Programs, Inc., 1977-79; bd. dirs. Collingwood Repertory Theatre, 1978-80; Mid-Hudson Meml. Soc., 1981-84; pres. Poughkeepsie Generating Community, 1974—; bd. dir. Literacy Vol. of Dutchess County, 1985—, pres. 1987-89; bd. dirs. Literacy Vols. Am., N.Y., 1989—, chmn., pers. comm., 1989—, mem. program com., 1990—, pres.-elect, 1992-93, pres. 1993—, bd. dirs. nat. bd. Lit. Vols. Am., 1993—; Poughkeepsie Rural Cemetery, 1986—, chmn. fin. com., 1989—; pres. Ranfurly Library Svc. of N.Y. Inc., 1982—, Town of Poughkeepsie Dem. Com., Dutchess County Dem. Com.; participant U.S.-S. African Leader Exchange Program, 1971; adv. bd. Wartburg Luth. Svcs., 1993—; bd. mem. Anderson Ednl. Found., 1993—; chmn. Anderson Sch. Wine Showcase, 1995—. Lt. USNR, 1957-61. Fulbright travel grantee to Germany, 1958-59. Mem. N.Am. Acad. Ecumenists, Am. Soc. Ch. History, Presbyn. Hist. Soc., Poughkeepsie C. of C., Dutchess Interfaith Coun., Dutchess County Clergy Club, Poughkeepsie Rotary (pres. 1977-79, sec. 1979—, sec. Dist. 721, 1980-81, gov. 1982-83, chmn. World Community Svc. 1986—, Rotary Internat. Coun. on Legis., Monte Carlo, 1983, Rotary Internat. pres.'s rep. to dist. confs. 1984, 88, Paul Harris fellow, sect. leader internat. conv., Portland, 1990), Lumanites (sec.-treas.), 251, Poughkeepsie Social Reading Club (past pres.), Circumnavigators Club (N.Y.C.), The Club, Travelers Century Club (life mem.), Fjord Club, Mil Order Fgn. Wars of U.S. (life vet. companion, mem. coun. N.Y. commandery), Fulbright Assn. (life), St. George's Soc. N.Y. (life), Chevalier du Tastevin (France). Office: 70 Hooker Ave Poughkeepsie NY 12601-4612 *In the words of John Bunyan, "He who would valiant be 'gainst all disaster, let him in constancy follow the Master. There's no discouragement shall make him once relent his first avowed intent to be a pilgrim."*

HARMER, DON STUTLER, physics and nuclear engineering educator; m. Carolyn Wood, 1952 (div. 1964); children: Diana H. Brown, Katherina H. Lucey, Nancy H. Wiggers; m. Lee DeLoache, Dec. 22, 1965; children: David Stutler, Muffin Louise Blakeney, Jonathan Aubrey. Student, USN Electronics Schs., Great Lakes, Ill. and Washington, 1946-47; BS in Chemistry cum laude, George Washington U., 1952; PhD in Nuclear Chemistry, UCLA, 1956; postgrad., N.C. State U., 1960. Postdoctoral fellow Brookhaven Nat. Labs., Upton, N.Y., 1956-59; prof. physics and nuclear engring. Ga. Inst. Tech., Atlanta, 1959—; cons. on solar neutrino experimental physics rsch. Brookhaven Nat. Labs., 1959-67; cons. computer systems design Digital Equipment Corp., Maynard, Mass., 1967-76; cons. hardware and software design, systems tng. CompuCom Inc., Atlanta, 1986-89; performed experimental rsch. on blood coagulation and in vitro tagging Ferst Rsch. Ctr., Atlanta, 1960-67; designed and implemented numerous on-line computer data acquistion and control systems. Contbg. author (textbook) Introduction to Computer Technology and Interfacing, 1970; contbr. more than 80 articles on physics and computer systems to profl. jours.; patentee in field. With USN, 1946-48, USNR, 1948-53. Recipient Outstanding Mentor award, 1992; named Faculty Mem. of Yr., 1992-93. Fellow Am. Inst. Chemists, Am. Inst. Physics, Am. Nuclear Soc., Southeastern MGT Register (past pres.), Peachtree MG Registry, MG Car Club, Sigma Nu. Episcopalian. Home: 3926 Harts Mill Ln NE Atlanta GA 30319-1854

HARMEYER, GEORGE H., military career officer; b. Havre de Grace, Md., Oct. 1, 1943; m. Phyllis Harmeyer; 1 child, Will. Grad., Western Md. Coll., 1965; MA in Geography, U. Wash.; grad., Army War Coll. Commd. officer U.S. Army, 1965, advanced through grades to maj. gen.; cavalry platoon leader, troop exec. officer, troop comdr. U.S. Army, Fulda, Germany; asst. squadron S3, troop comdr., squadron motor officer U.S. Army, Vietnam, 1968-69; troop comdr., squadron S3 2d Squadron, 2d Armored Cavalry U.S. Army, Bamburg, Germany; S3, 4th Phoenix Brigade, Divsn. C3, ops. officer, dep. G3 U.S. Army, Ft. Hood, Tex.; manpower survey staff officer SHAPE U.S. Army, Mons, Belgium, 1981; comdr. 1st Bn., 70th Armor, 4th Brigade, 4th Inf. Divsn. U.S. Army, Wiesbaden, Germany, 1982; chief tng. support divsn. hdqrs. Dept. of Army, ODCSOPS U.S. Army; chief of staff, 2d Armored Divsn., comdr. 1st Ironhorse U.S. Army, Ft. Hood, Tex., 1988; comdr. ops. group Nat. Tng. Ctr. U.S. Army, Ft. Irwin, Calif.; asst. divsn. comdr. (maneuver), 3d Inf. Divsn., comdr. U.S. Army, Schweinfurt, Germany; V Corps chief of staff U.S. Army, Heidelberg, Germany; comdr. 7th Army Tng. Command U.S. Army, Grafenwoehr, Germany, 1995—; tchr. U.S. Mil. Acad. Decorated Legion of Merit, Bronze Star with V device and second award, Meritorious Svc. medal, Def. Meritorious Svc. medal, Air medal, Army Commendation medal with V device, Army Achievement medal. Office: US Army Armor Ctr Fort Knox KY 40121

HARMON, ANGIE, actress; b. Dallas, Aug. 10, 1972. Actress starring in TV series: Baywatch Nights, 1995, C-16: FBI, 1997, Law & Order, 1998—; appeared in Lawn Dogs, 1997; TV guest appearances include Renegade, 1995. Office: Wolf Films Inc c/o Universal TV 100 Universal City Plz #69 Universal City CA 91608-1085*

HARMON, BUD GENE, animal sciences educator, consultant; b. Camden, Ind., July 2, 1931; s. Orvie M. and Margaret (Cooke) H.; m. Mary Lynne Jones, June 7, 1953; children: Brad Lee, Beth Ann, Jana Renee. BS, Purdue U., 1958; PhD, Mich. State U., 1962. Rsch. tchr. U. Ill., Urbana, 1962-75; rsch. dir. Ralston Purina, St. Louis, 1975-86; head dept. animal sci. Purdue U., West Lafayette, 1986—, now prof.; mem. sci. adv. bd. Farmland Industries, 1992—. With USN, 1951-55. Mem. Am. Soc. Animal Sci. (pres. 1994). Office: Purdue U Dept Animal Scis West Lafayette IN 47907*

HARMON, CLARENCE, mayor; m. Janet Kelley; 4 children. BS, Northeast Mo. State U.; MA in Criminal Justice Administrn. and Pub. Administrn., Webster U.; past postgrad., Harvard U. Past sec. to bd. commrs. City of St. Louis; with St. Louis Police Dept., 1969-1995, chief, 1991-95; dir. bus. devel., dir. dept. mkt. rsch. and analysis United Van Lines, Inc., 1995-97; mayor City of St. Louis, 1997—. Bd. dirs. United Way, St. Louis, St. Louis Symphony, Mo. Bot. Garden, Fair St. Louis; trustee Webster U., St. Louis Sci. Ctr. Fanforth Found. fellow; recipient Reach Out award St. Vincent Home, 1992, Dr. Martin Luther King, Jr. Life and Legacy award, 1992; named Mo. Police Chief of Year Mo. Police Chiefs' Assn., 1995. Mem. Am. Assn. Indsl. Mgmt. (bd. dirs.). Fax: 314-622-4061. Office: Office of Mayor 200 City Hall 1200 Market St Saint Louis MO 63103-2826*

HARMON, DANIEL PATRICK, classics educator; b. Chgo., May 3, 1938; s. Bernard Leonard and Dorothy Mildred (Lesser) H. AB, Loyola U., Chgo., 1962; MA, Northwestern U., 1965, PhD, 1968; postdoctoral, Am. Sch. Classical Studies in Athens, 1975. Acting asst. prof. U. Wash., Seattle, 1967-68, asst. prof. classics, 1968-75, assoc. prof., 1975-76, assoc. prof. classics and comparative lit., 1976-84, prof. classics, 1984—, chmn. classics, 1976-91; dir. U. Wash. Rome Ctr., 1992—. Contbr. articles and revs. to profl. jours. Mem. Am. Philol. Assn., Archaeol. Inst. Am., Société des Études Latines, County Louth (Ireland) Archaeol. and Hist. Soc., Classical Assn. Pacific Northwest (pres. 1974-75). Avocations: painting, photography, music. Home: 3149 NE 83rd St Seattle WA 98115-4751 Office: U Wash Dept Classics PO Box 353110 Seattle WA 98195-3110

HARMON, DAVID, finance company executive; b. 1938. MBA, Mich. State U., 1965. With Electronic Memories and Magnetics, Hawthorne, Calif., 1965-78; CEO El Camino Resources Ltd., Woodland Hills, Calif., 1978—; with El Camino Resources Internat., Woodland Hills, 1986—. Office: 21051 Warner Center Ln Woodland Hills CA 91367-6512*

HARMON, DAVID ANDREW, historian, researcher; b. Kingsport, Tenn., July 1, 1961; s. Allen LeRoy and Betty Ann (Bailey) H. BA, U. Tenn., 1983; MA, Emory U., 1987, PhD, 1993. Grad. student intern Martin Luther King Ctr. for Nonviolent Change, Atlanta, 1986-87; tchg. asst. Emory U., Atlanta, 1987, grad. asst., 1990; rsch. asst. Ctr. for Contemporary Film Media, Atlanta, 1988; sr. rschr. Ala. Pub. TV, Montgomery, 1994—. Author: Beneath the Image of the Civil Rights Movement and Race Relations, 1996; contbg. author: Ency. of African-Am. Civil Rights, 1992; rschr.: (documentary) Dawn's Early Light: Ralph McGill and the Segregated South, 1988; contbr. book revs. So. Historian, 1987. Mem. Am. Hist. Assn., Orgn. Am. Historians, So. Hist. Assn., Ala. Hist. Assn. Democrat. Methodist. Home: 5715 Calmar Dr Apt 2 Montgomery AL 36116-1829 Office: Ala Pub TV 1255 Madison Ave Montgomery AL 36107-1221

HARMON, DAVID EUGENE, optometrist, geneticist; b. Greeneville, Tenn., July 27, 1951; s. Carl Eugene and Kathryn Elizabeth (Colyer) H. BS, U. Tenn., 1973, MS, 1975; PhD, U. Ga., 1978; OD, New Eng. Coll. Optometry, 1989. Fellow U. Ga., Athens, 1978, U. Fla., Gainesville, 1979; vis. asst. prof. So. Ill. U., Carbondale, 1980-82; asst. prof. Clemson (S.C.) U., 1982-85, assoc. prof., 1985; internist VA Hosp., Boston, 1988, Children's

Hosp., Boston, 1988-89, Dimock Community Health Ctr., Boston, 1989; eye specialist Morristown, Tenn., 1989—; geneticist Morristown, 1989—; genetic cons. Nigerian Govt., 1980—. Contbr. articles to profl. jours. Mem. Sunday sch. Trinity United Meth. Ch., Greeneville, 1954—; sch. rep. New Eng. Coll. Optometry, 1987; coach nat. winning dairy cattle judging team, 1980, 81. Recipient Breeder All-Am. Dairy Animal award Am. Guernsey Cattle Club, 1973. Mem. Am. Optometric Assn., Am. Dairy Assn., Am. Soc. Animal Sci., Tenn. Optometric Assn., So. Coun. Optometrists, Am. Holstein Assn., Morristown C. of C., New Eng. Coll. Optometry Alumni Assn. (life), Lions Club Morristown, Sigma Xi, Alpha Zeta. Avocations: camping, hiking, table tennis. Home and Office: 131 N Henry St Morristown TN 37814-4626

HARMON, DEBRA MAE, journalist; b. Bagley, Minn., Apr. 4, 1968; d. Alvin Eugene and Betty Ann (Dahl) H. BS, Bemidji (Minn.) State U., 1989. Editor Warroad (Minn.) Pioneer, 1990-91, Page One Publ, Warroad, 1991-92; asst. editor Farmers Pub., Bagley, 1992-98; freelance editor Bagley Pub. Sch., 1992—; freelance writer Bagley Elem. Kids Place, 1998—, tech. coord., 1999—; spl. publ. editor Farmers Independent, Bagley, 1994-98. Treas. Berean Bapt. Ch., Bagley, 1989-98. Mem. Soc. Profl. Journalists, Bagley Jaycees. Avocations: photography, writing, skiing, biking.

HARMON, (LOREN) FOSTER, art consultant; b. Judsonia, Ark., Nov. 5, 1912; s. Alfred Roscoe and Mae (Foster) H.; m. Martha Rowles Foster, July 25, 1943. Student, Ind. U., 1930-32, Ohio U., 1932-33; BA, U. Iowa, 1935, MFA, 1936; DFA (hon.) Ohio U., 1992. Dir. Univ. and Exptl. Theatre, Ind. U., Bloomington, 1936-42; pub. relations mgr. Sta. WKBN Broadcasting Corp., Youngstown, Ohio, 1943-48; owner, developer, dir. Pine Shores Park, Sarasota, Fla., 1950-54 v.p., dir. Players, Sarasota, 1955-57; pub. relations dir. Ringling Mus. Art, 1958-59; dir. Oehlschlaeger Galleries, Sarasota, 1961-70; v.p. Vandium Tool Co., Athens, Ohio, 1954-64; founder, owner, dir. Harmon Gallery, Naples, Fla., 1964-79; owner, dir. Foster Harmon Galleries Am. Art, Sarasota, 1979-93; bd. trustees, advisor Ohio U. Mus. Am. Art, Fla. Artists Group Mus. and Gallery, 1974-87; founder Foster and Martha Harmon Am. Art Study Ctr. and Archives Ohio U., 1995. Active Ringling Mus. Coun., 1957—; trustee Ringling Sch. Art, Sarasota, 1981—; bd. dirs. Asolo State Theater 1982-89, Sarasota Opera Assn., 1983—, Van Wezel Performing Arts Hall Found., 1987—, Players, 1989—. Recipient cert. of merit Ohio U., 1970. Mem. Am. Ednl. Theatre Assn. (founder), Am. Fedn. Arts, Sarasota Art Assn. (pres. 1959-60), Fla. League Arts, Smithsonian Inst., Archives Am. Art, Sarasota Arts Council, St. Armands Assn. (pres. 1957-58), Internat. Platform Assn. Methodist. Clubs: Sarasota Yacht, Univ. (Sarasota). Home: 1255 N Gulfstream Ave Apt 1102 Sarasota FL 34236-8932

HARMON, GEORGE MARION, college president; b. Memphis, Aug. 12, 1934; s. George Marion and Madie P. (Foster) H.; m. Bessie W. Porter, Dec. 27, 1958; children: Nancy R., Mary K., Elizabeth T., George Marion III. BA, Rhodes Coll., 1956; MBA, Emory U., 1957; DBA, Harvard U., 1963. Market research analyst Continental Oil Co., Houston, 1957; research assoc. Harvard U., 1960-63; asst. prof. Coll. Bus. Adminstrn., dir. Salzberg Meml. Transp. Program Syracuse U., N.Y., 1963-66; sr. assoc. systems econs. div. Planning Research Corp., Washington, 1966-67; prof., chmn. dept econs. and bus. adminstrn., dir. continuing edn. program in econs. and bus. adminstrn. Southwestern U. (name changed to Rhodes Coll.), Memphis, 1967-74; prof., dean div. bus. and mgmt. W.Va. Coll. Grad. Studies, Charleston, 1974-75; prof., dean Sch. Bus. and Mgmt. Saginaw Valley State Coll., University Center, Mich., 1975-78; pres. Millsaps Coll., Jackson, Miss., 1978—; mem. faculty fin. Sch. Banking of the South, La. State U., 1968-72; dir. Audio Visual Systems, Inc., Tenn., 1970-72; v.p., treas. Allen Industries, Inc., Tenn., 1970-72; co-founder, v.p. Computer Survey Systems, Inc., Tenn., 1972-73; bd. dirs., chmn. exec. compensation com. MacCarty Farms, Inc., Magee, Miss., 1982-95; bd. dirs. Entex, Inc., Houston, 1981-99; mem. So. Regional Edn. Bd., Atlanta, 1994—; bd. dirs. Union Planters Bank, 1994-98. Contbr. articles on bus. adminstrn. to profl. jours. Bd. dirs. Fayetteville-Manlius Cen. Sch. Dist., N.Y., 1961-63, John Houston Wear Found., Jackson; trustee, chmn. pers. and labor rels. com. Saginaw Osteo. Hosp., 1977-78; bd. dirs. Jackson Symphony Orch. Assn., 1981-85, Miss. Opera Assn., 1981-86; chmn. So. Colls. and Univs. Union, 1983-88, Miss. Found. Ind. Colls., 1982; univ. senate United Meth. Ch., 1990—; comm. and sec. Jackson Internat. Airport Authority, 1991-97; chmn., bd. dirs. Jackson Med. Edn. Dist., 1998—. Mem. NCAA (coun. 1986-92), Jackson C. of C. (bd. dirs. 1981-84; chmn. bd. dirs. Jackson Med. Dist. 1998—), Soc. Internat. Bus. Fellows, Jackson Country Club, Univ. Club, Petroleum Club, Harvard Club (N.Y.C.), Rotary, Phi Beta Kappa, Beta Sigma Gamma, Omicron Delta Kappa. Methodist. Home: 104 Adderbury Ct Ridgeland MS 39157-8709 Office: Millsaps Coll 1701 N State St Jackson MS 39210-0002

HARMON, HARRY WILLIAM, architect, former university administrator; b. San Francisco, Feb. 8, 1918; s. Harry A. and Isabel (Quagelli) A.; m. Lois Anna Holtin, July 28, 1953; children: Bruce Gregory, Mark Brian, Patricia Andree. B.Arch., U. So. Calif., 1941. Draftsman Kaufmann, Lippincott & Eggers (architects), Los Angeles, 1945-48; project architect UCLA, 1948-50, sr. architect, 1952-62; chief coll. facilities planning Calif. State Colls., Inglewood, Calif., 1962-67; asst. vice chancellor Calif. State Colls., Los Angeles, 1967-69; vice chancellor phys. planning, devel. Calif. State Colls., 1969-75, exec. vice chancellor, 1975-83, exec. vice chancellor emeritus, 1983—; spl. cons. FAO; mem. Nat. Panel Arbitrators. Chmn. bd. visitors USAF Installation Devel. for USAF Directorate of Engring. Svcs., 1989—. Lt. USNR, 1942-45; lt. comdr. 1950-51; capt. Res. ret. Fellow AIA (nat. dir. 1977-80, sec. 1981-85, Disting. Svc. award Calif. coun. 1985, Edward C. Kemper award 1986, chair nat. jud. coun. 1986-88, mem. coun. 1986-93), Assn. Univ. Architects; mem. Coun. Ednl. Facility Planners Internat., Soc. Coll. and U. Planners, Am. Arbitration Assn., U. So. Calif. Alumni Assn., Blue Key, Alpha Rho Chi. Home: 1410 La Plaza Dr San Marcos CA 92069-4712

HARMON, JAMES ALLEN, federal agency administrator; b. N.Y.C., Oct. 12, 1935; s. Bert and Belle (Kirschner) H.; m. Jane Elizabeth Theaman, Aug. 11, 1957; children—Deborah Lynn, Douglas Lee, Jennifer Ann. B.A., Brown U., 1957; M.B.A., Wharton Grad. Sch., U. Pa., 1959. With N.Y. Hanseatic Corp., N.Y.C., 1959-74, sr. v.p., 1969-74; gen. ptnr. Wertheim & Co., Inc., N.Y.C., 1975-97, vice chmn., 1980-86; chmn. and CEO Schroder Wertheim & Co., Inc., N.Y.C., 1986-96; sr. chmn. Schroder Wertheim & Co., Inc., N.Y.C., London, 1996-97; pres., chmn. Export-Import Bank U.S., 1997—. Trustee emeritus Barnard Coll., Brown U.

HARMON, JANE, theatrical producer. With Jane Harmon Assocs., N.Y.C.; bd. dirs. Young Playwrights Inc. Prodr. Buried Child, A Life in the Theatre, The Robber Bridegroom, Driving Miss Daisy, The Last Night of Ballyhoo, also nat. and internat. tours and prodns.; co-prodr. Asinamali!, Beloved Friend. Office: Jane Harmon Assocs One Lincoln Plaza Ste 28-0 New York NY 10023*

HARMON, KAY MADELON, occupational therapist; b. Galveston, Tex., Feb. 5, 1949; d. Roger Q. and Alma Faye (Hall) H.; m. Stanley Davis Mitchell, June 24, 1967 (div. Nov. 1968). BA in Sociology, East Tex. Bapt. U., Marshall, 1980; advanced cert. in Occupational Therapy, Tex. Woman's U., Denton/Dallas, 1989. Lic. occupational therapist, Tex., Ark. Staff occupational therapist N.E. Ark. Rehab. Hosp., Jonesboro, 1989-91; dir. clin. svcs. Marshall (Tex.) Phys. Therapy, 1991-93; staff occupational therapist Pro Care Rehab., Mountain Home, Ark., 1993-96, Premier Rehab., Texarkana, Ark., 1993-96, CMS Therapies Rehab., Longview, Tex., 1993-96; regional occupational therapy supr. Sundance Rehab., Northeast, Tex., 1996; outpatient occupational therapist and home health Marshall (Tex.) Regional Med. Ctr., 1996-99; cons. Rehab. Choice in local nursing homes, Marshall, 1997-99; encor in nursing homes Mena, Mt. Ida, Hot Springs, Ark., 1999—. Mem. Am. Occupational Therapy Assn., Tex. Occupational Therapy Assn., Am. Soc. Hand Therapists (assoc. Tex. chpt.), Am. Orchid Soc., Shreveport Orchid Soc., Phi Theta Epsilon. Baptist. Avocation: growing orchids. Home: PO Box 1399 Mount Ida AR 71957

HARMON, KAY YVONNE, elementary education educator; b. Albert Lea, Minn., Dec. 12, 1942; d. Melvin Harold and Bertha Loretta (Sorensen) Vogelsang; m. Perry Dean Harmon, Aug. 14, 1971; children: Kristine Kay, Phillip Dean. BA, Luther Coll., 1963; BS, U. Minn., 1966. Tchr. elem. Grand Meadow (Minn.) Pub. Sch., 1963-65; tchr. secondary art edn. Little Falls (Minn.) Pub. Sch., 1966-68; secondary art tchr. Robinsdale Pub. Sch., New Hope, Minn., 1968-73; arts and crafts leader Crystal (Minn.) Park and Recreation, summer 1969; dir. chpt. I, art secondary tchr. Ulen (Minn.)-Hitterdal Pub. Sch., 1982—; instr. Community Edn., Ulen, 1986-88, Hawley, Minn., 1987-88, 91. Adult leader Eglon Hawks 4-H Club, 1984-93; mem. Hawley Art Show Com., 1987—; mem. Hawley Friends of Fine Arts, 1989—, sec.-treas., 1991-96. Mem. ASCD, NEA, Nat. Art Educators Assn., Minn. Edn. Assn., Art Educators Minn., Minn. Alliance for Arts, Ulen-Hitterdal Edn. Assn. (pres. 1990, treas. 1996—, membership chair 1997—), Alpha Delta Kappa (chpt. chaplain 1996-98, chpt. rec. sec. 1994-96). Methodist. Avocations: reading, drawing, bowling, golf, painting. Home: RR 1 Box 109 Hawley MN 56549-9753 Office: Ulen-Hitterdal Pub Sch PO Box 389 Ulen MN 56585-0389

HARMON, MARIAN SANDERS, writer, sculptor; b. Detroit, Jan. 16, 1916; d. Joseph and Anne (Stern) Sanders; m. Edward Stein, Jan. 15, 1950 (dec. 1960); m. Leonard Byron Harmon, 1963. BA, U. Mich., 1937. Dir. radio and TV Simons Michelson, Detroit, 1948-60; editor Table Talk Bridge Newspaper, 1954-62; writer ABC-TV, N.Y.C., 1960-65; organizer, pres. Visual Arts Forum, 1981-93. Author: (poems) The Hourglass, 1982, East of Morning, 1998, Widows' Walk, 1999; editor AAUW, East Hampton, 1984-87, various newspapers, 1945-65; first editor Northwest Detroiter, 1947; freelance writer for newspapers and mags.; computer art in invitational art shows, 1995, 96, 97. Recipient Best Sculpture in Show award Guild Hall East Hampton, 1989. Home: PO Box 1547 East Hampton NY 11937-0795

HARMON, MARY CAROL, writer; b. Phila.; Apr. 19, 1949; d. Alfred L. and Grace W. (Williams) Creager; m. Jeffrey A. Thomas, June 22, 1985; 1 child, Devin J. BA, NYU, 1982. Tng. asst. Price Waterhouse & Co., N.Y.C., 1969-72; writer Marsteller, Inc., N.Y.C., 1973-81; freelance writer N.Y.C., 1979—. Contbr. articles to consumer and bus. publs. Mem. Am. Soc. Journalists and Authors. Avocation: kayaking. Home: 291 Baltic St Brooklyn NY 11201-6404

HARMON, MELINDA FURCHE, federal judge; b. Port Arthur, Tex., Nov. 1, 1946; d. Frank Cantrell and Wilma (Parish) Furche; m. Frank G. Harmon III, Oct. 16, 1976; children: Mary Elizabeth, Phelps, Francis. AB, Harvard U., 1969; JD, U. Tex., 1972. Bar: Tex. 1973, U.S. Dist. Ct. (so. dist.) Tex. 1974, U.S. Dist. Ct. (no. dist.) Tex. 1975, U.S. Dist. Ct. (ea. dist.) Tex. 1978, U.S. Ct. Appeals (5th and 11th cirs.) 1981, U.S. Supreme Ct. 1982, U.S. Ct. Claims 1987. Law clk. to presiding judge U.S. Dist. Ct. (so. dist.) Tex., Houston, 1973-75; atty. Exxon Co., Houston, 1975-88; judge 280th Jud. Dist. Ct. Tex. State Trial Ct., ctrl. jurisdiction, 1988-89; judge U.S. Dist. Ct. (so. dist.) Tex., Houston, 1989—. Mem. Tex. Bar Assn., Am. Inns of Ct., Houston Bar Assn., Harvard Radcliffe Club. Roman Catholic. Office: US Dist Ct US Courthouse 515 Rusk Ave Ste 9114 Houston TX 77002-2605*

HARMON, PATRICK, newspaperman; b. St. Louis, Sept. 2, 1916; s. Jack and Laura (Duchesne) H.; m. Anne M. Worland, Aug. 31, 1940; children—Michael, Timothy, Kathleen, Daniel, John, Sheila, Peggy, Brigid, Kevin, Teresa, Christopher. A.B., U. Ill., 1939. Sports editor News-Gazette, Champaign, Ill., 1942-47, Gazette, Cedar Rapids, Iowa, 1947-51, Post, Cin., 1951-85; ret., 1985; sports commentator Sta. WCPO-TV, 1953-56, Sta. WKRC, 1958, Sta. WLW-TV, 1958-68; curator, historian Coll. Football Hall of Fame, Kings Island, Ohio, 1986-95; historian, 1995—. Contbg. sports editor: World Book, 1959—. Recipient Fred Hutchinson Meml. award for community service, 1969; named Internat. Churchmen's Sports Writer of Year, 1973. Mem. Sigma Chi. Home and Office: 19 Walnut Ave Cincinnati OH 45215-4335

HARMON, RICHARD WINGATE, management consultant; b. Exeter, N.H., July 16, 1958; s. William Wingate and Elaine (Waters) H.; m. Kathleen Hayward Harmon, Aug. 8, 1987; children: David Wingate, Sarah Elizabeth. BS in Adminstrn., U. N.H., 1981; MBA in Adminstrn., N.H. Coll., 1986. Lic. comml. pilot and flight instr. Founder, owner Harmon Aviation, Exeter, N.H., 1988—; owner, pres. Harmon Realty Investments, Exeter, 1985—; founder, owner Exeter Storage Depot, Inc., 1989—; owner, pres. Harmon-Waters, Exeter, 1982—; founder, owner Williamsburg Ridge Devel. Co. Inc., Exeter, 1996—; venture capital cons., constrn. mgmt. cons., bus. turnaround cons., bus. start-up cons. Mem. Aircraft Owners and Pilots Assn., Exptl. Aircraft Assn., Seaplane Pilots Assn., Exeter Area C. of C., N.H. Coll. Alumni Assn., U. N.H. Alumni Assn., Sigma Alpha Epsilon. Avocations: music, golf, skiing, travel, aviation. Office: Harmon-Waters 95 High St Exeter NH 03833-2927

HARMON, ROBERT GERALD, health company administrator, educator; b. Barnsdall, Okla., Mar. 20, 1944; s. Thomas Frederick and Eleandor Virginia (Colley) H.; m. Carol Louise Kalnitsky, Aug. 22, 1971; children: Rex, Susan. BA, Washington U., St. Louis, 1966, MD, 1970; MPH, Johns Hopkins U., 1977. Diplomate Am. Bd. Preventive Medicine. Intern, then resident U. Colo. Med. Ctr., Denver, 1970-73; asst. prof. health svcs. and internal medicine U. Wash., Seattle, 1977-80; chmn. dept. community medicine Maricopa Med. Ctr., Phoenix, 1980-85; dep. dir. Maricopa County Divsn. Pub. Health, Phoenix, 1980-82, dir., 1983-85; dir. Dept. Health State of Mo., Jefferson City, 1986-90; clin. prof. U. Mo. Sch. Medicine, Columbia, 1986-90; adminstr. Health Resources Svcs. Adminstrn. USPHS/HHS, Rockville, Md., 1990-93; sr. v.p. MetraHealth Ctr. for Corp. Health Inc., Oakton, Va., 1994-95; nat. med. dir. Optum divsn. United Health Group, McLean, Va., 1996—; adj. assoc. prof. sch. medicine U. Ariz., Tucson, 1981-85; cons. community medicine Project Health Opportunity for People Everywhere, Jamaica, 1973, 76; Pan Am. Health Orgn., Carribean, 1979, U.S. AID, Africa, 1978, 79. Contbr. articles to profl. jours. With USPHS, 1974-75. Fellow Am. Coll. Preventive Medicine (bd. regents 1983-88, 96—); mem. Nat. Assn. County Health Ofcls. (pres. 1983-85), Am. Pub. Health Assn. (gov. councilor 1984-88), Assn. State and Territorial Health Ofcls. (exec. com. 1987-90), Ariz. County Health Ofcls. (pres. 1984-85), Omicron Delta Kappa. Avocation: sports. Office: Optum Divsn United Health Group 8201 Greensboro Dr Ste 500 Mc Lean VA 22102-3824

HARMON, ROBERT WAYNE, electrical engineering executive; b. Winchester, Ind., Oct. 22, 1929; s. Wayne and Theresa (Bishop) H.; m. Mary Louise Cobb; children: Wayne Charles, Keith Robert, Arthur Dean, Frederic Bruce. BSEE with highest distinction, Purdue U, 1951, MSEE, 1955. Engr. Aro, Inc., Tullahoma, Tenn., 1951-54; devel. engr. Ohio Brass Co., Barberton, Ohio, 1955-63, dir. new product devel., 1963-68; chief engr. A.B. Chance Co., Centralia, Mo., 1968-95; cons. and legal tech. expert witness in field. Holder 30 patents in insulation, elect. apparatus. Fellow IEEE (life); mem. ASTM, Nat. Elec. Mfgrs. Assn. Avocations: geology, archaelogy, whitewater canoeing. Home and Office: 19001 N Jay Jay Centralia MO 65240-3510

HARMON, STEPHEN ALBERT, history educator; b. St. Louis, June 15, 1945; s. James Weldon and Alice Caroline (Jameton) H.; m. Fredrika Drosten, June 12, 1968 (div. Sept. 1979); 1 child, Cyrus Leben; m. Binnette Traore, Dec. 24, 1985; 1 child, James Ahmad. BA, San Francisco State U., 1979; MA, UCLA, 1981, PhD, 1988. Asst. prof. Ark. State U., Jonesboro, 1989-94; lectr. Pittsburg (Kans.) State U., 1994—; vis. prof. SUNY, Oswego, 1988-89. Soccer coach YMCA, Pittsburg, 1995—. Fulbright-Hayes grantee, 1983-84, 90-91. Mem. African Studies Assn., Kans. History Tchrs. Assn. Avocation: fly fishing. E-mail: sharmon@pittstate.edu. Office: Pittsburg State U Dept History 1700 S Broadway Pittsburg KS 66762

HARMON, TIM JAMES, construction executive; b. Evanston, Ill.; s. James Richard Harmon and Muriel Joan (Schneider) Mortell; m. Debra Moore, 1975 (div. 1977); m. Maribeth Bailey, Dec. 20, 1980; 1 child, Avraham. G-rad. high sch., Indpls. Pres. Emmanuel Hot Line Inc., Indpls., 1969-71; pres., owner Ginkomyer Bros. Inc., Indpls., 1972-75; mgr. Tech. 300 Near Eastside Multi-Svc. Ctr., Indpls., 1975-76; owner, ptnr. Earth Garden Cafe Inc., Indpls., 1977-81; owner Tim J. Harmon Builder, Indpls., 1979-86, Cottage Home Antiques, Indpls., 1986—; pres., owner Restoration Svcs., Indpls., 1986-92; owner Tim & Billy's Salvage Store, Indpls., 1992—; pres. Cottage Home Neighborhood Assn., 1984-85, 89-90, bd. dirs., 1984-86, 89-91. Mem. Near Eastside Cmty. Orgn., VISTA adv. com., 1988-90; bd. dirs. Mayor's Drug Abuse Task Force, 1972-73, Rehab Resource, 1989-90; precinct chair Dem. Com., 1988-91; bd. dirs. Amazing Space, 1993-95. Democrat. Mem. Christian Ch. Office: Tim & Billy's Salvage Store 970 Ft Wayne Ave Indianapolis IN 46202-3334 also: Tim & Billy's Really Small Corp 970 Fort Wayne Ave Indianapolis IN 46202-3334

HARMON, W. DAVID, academic administrator; b. Akron, Ohio, Feb. 21, 1943; s. W.D. Sr. and Joy Marie (Johnson) H.; m. Patricia Ann Stewart, Nov. 12, 1963; children: David Christopher, Mark Aric. BS, SUNY, Buffalo, 1964; MS, Hofstra U., 1970; PhD, St. John's U., Jamaica, N.Y., 1980. Tchr. East Meadow (N.Y.) Sch. Dist., East Meadow, 1964-70; dir. counseling ctr. St. John's U., Jamaica, N.Y., 1970—; instr. SUNY, Old Westbury, 1984—; cons. Rudolph Clark Assocs., Westbury, 1985—, N.Y.C. Police Dept., 1986, Am. Assn. Retired Persons, Queens, N.Y. 1987; adj. assoc. prof. psychology, St. John's U., Jamaica, N.Y. Chmn. Nassau County Human Rights Commn., Mineola, N.Y., 1986—; adj. leader Ethical Humanist Soc. L.I., 1989—; bd. dirs. St. Mary's Children and Family Svcs., Syosset, N.Y. Mem. Am. Coll. Personnel Assn., Assn. Non-White Concerns in Counseling, Com. on Multi-Cultural Affairs, Am. Psychol. Assn., Nat. Assn. Neuro-Linguistic Programmers. Republican. Club: 100 Black Men of Nassau/Suffolk, Inc. (Westbury) (2d v.p.). Avocations: pistol shooting, fishing, computers. Home: 199 W Seaman Ave Freeport NY 11520-1540 Office: St John's U Counseling Ctr 8000 Utopia Pkwy Jamaica NY 11432-1343

HARMON BROWN, VALARIE JEAN, hospital laboratory director, information systems executive; b. Peoria, Ill., June 21, 1948; d. Donald Joseph and Frances Elizabeth (Classen) Harmon; m. James Roger Brown, Aug. 21, 1982 (dec. May 1994). BSMT, Northwestern U., Chgo., 1970. Med. tech. Evanston (Ill.) Hosp., 1970-71, chief tech., 1971-75; med. tech. II M.D. Anderson Hosp., Houston, 1975-76; dir. lab. Physicians Ref. Lab., Houston, 1978-81, Med. Ctr. Hosp., Conroe, Tex., 1981-91, Palo Pinto Gen. Hosp., Mineral Wells, Tex., 1993-94; sales mgr. Long Beach (Calif.) Meml. Med. Ctr., 1995-96; quality assurance/regulatory affairs mgr. Consol. Med. Labs., Lake Bluff, Ill., 1996-97; admissions dir. Bio-Diagnostics Labs., Torrance, Calif., 1997—; lab. cons. Texaco Chem. Wellness Program, Conroe, 1989; health career sponsor Willis Ind. Sch. Dist., Tex., 1989, 90; mem. adv. bd. Med. Lab. Technician program Weatherford Coll., 1994. Coord. blood drive Gulf Coast Region Blood Ctr., 1986-91; sponsor colon cancer screening Montgomery County Health Fair, 1986; sponsor Camp Sunshine/Lions Club, 1988; sponsor cholesterol screening Med. Ctr. Hosp. Health Fair, 1989. Mem. NAFE, Am. Soc. Clin. Pathologists, Am. Soc. Med. Technologists, Clin. Lab. Mgmt. Assn. Republican. Roman Catholic. Avocations: embroidery, reading, antiques. Home: 23850 Nicole Way Yorba Linda CA 92887-5626 Office: 20221 Hamilton Ave Ste 200 Torrance CA 90502-1313

HARMOND, RICHARD PETER, historian, educator; b. N.Y.C., Mar. 19, 1929; s. William and Violet (Makein) H. BA, Fordham U., 1951; MA, Columbia U., 1954, PhD, 1966. Assoc. prof. St. John's U., N.Y.C., 1957—. Co-author: Long Island as America, 1977; co-editor: Technology in the 20th Century, 1983, Biographical Dictionary of American and Canadian Naturalists and Environmentalists, 1997; editor: (newsletter) L.I. Archives Conf., 1982—; assoc. editor: L.I. Hist. jour., 1988—; contbr. articles to profl. jours. With U.S. Army, 1951-53. Mem. Orgn. Am. Historians, Soc. History of Tech., Theodore Roosevelt Assn. (trustee 1994—), Phi Alpha Theta (paper prize com. 1994-97). Office: St John's U Hist Dept Jamaica NY 11439

HARMONY, MARLIN DALE, chemistry educator; b. Lincoln, Nebr., Mar. 2, 1936; s. Philip and Helen Irene (Michal) H. A.A., Kansas City (Mo.) Jr. Coll., 1956; B.S. in Chem. Engring., U. Kans., 1958; Ph.D. in Chemistry, U. Calif.-Berkeley, 1961. Asst. prof. U. Kans., Lawrence, 1962-67, assoc. prof., 1967-71, prof., 1971-98; chmn. U. Kans., 1980-88, prof. emeritus, 1998—; panel mem. NRC-Nat. Bur. Standards., 1969-78; mem. review panel NSF, 1977, 92. Author: Introduction to Molecular Energies and Spectra, 1972; contbg. editor: Physics Vade Mecum, 1981; mem. editorial bd. Structural Chemistry; contbr. articles to profl. jours.; patentee in field. Postdoctoral fellow NSF Harvard U., 1961-62. Fellow AAAS; mem. Am. Chem. Soc., Am. Phys. Soc., Sigma Xi, Alpha Chi Sigma, Phi Lambda Upsilon, Tau Beta Pi. Democrat. Home: 1033 Avalon Rd Lawrence KS 66044-2505 Office: U Kans Dept Chemistry Lawrence KS 66045

HARMS, DAVID JACOB, agricultural consultant; b. Springfield, Ill., Jan. 10, 1943; s. Jacob Dietrich and Onita Ruth (Schnapp) H.; children: Jacob, Johanna, Anika. BS in Agr., U. Ill., 1967. Cert. profl. crop cons. Field rep. Monsanto Corp., St. Louis and Manhattan, Kans., 1967-70; product mgr. Masonite Corp., Chgo., 1970-73; biochem. rep. P.P.G. Industries, Chgo., 1973-76; pres. Crop Pro-Tech, Inc., Naperville, Ill., 1976—; v.p., evaluation of rsch. for United Soybean Bd./Global Harvest Enterprises, Inc., 1993; pres. Profl. Crop Cons. Ill., 1984-86, treas., 1993—. Contbg. author tng. manual for privatization of agriculture in Egypt. Named to Cons. Hall of Fame, Ag. Cons. and Fieldman Mag., 1984; recipient Green Chemistry award, 1996. Mem. Am. Soc. Agronomy (cert. profl. agronomist, cert. profl. crop specialist), Nat. Alliance Ind. Crop Cons. (founding mem. 1978, pres. 1988, chair steering com., Communicator of Yr. award 1992, Cons. of Yr. cen. region 1993, mem. editl. bd. AgriFin mag. 1992-93, chair crops bd. 1992—), ARCPACS (chmn. adv. coun. 1997-98, Svc. to Agr. award 1999, pres. Cert. Adv. Coun.). Achievements include patents in field; research in herbicide by hybrid sensitivity, herbicide/hybrid/insecticide sensitivity. Office: Crop Pro-Tech Inc 2019 S Main St Bloomington IL 61704-7303

HARMS, DEBORAH GAYLE, psychologist; b. Ft. Worth; d. Raymond O. Smith and Billie (Allen) Greenwade; m. Joel Randall Harms; children: J. Christopher, Ryan R., Catherine R. BA with honors with high distinction, Wayne State U., 1977; MA in Clin. Psychology, U. Detroit, 1979, PhD in Clin. Psychology, 1984. Lic. psychologist. Trainee in psychology Henry Ford Hosp., Troy, Mich., 1978-79; intern in psychology Detroit Psychiat. Inst., 1979-82; staff psychologist Eastwood Clinic, Harper Woods, Mich., 1983-86; pvt. practice Harms and Harms, PC, Birmingham, Mich., 1985—; staff psychologist Dominican Consultation Ctr., Detroit, 1986-89; sr. psychologist Oakland County Probate Ct., Pontiac, Mich., 1990. Teaching fellow U. Detroit, 1978-79. Mem. APA, Nat. Register Health Care Providers in Psychology, Mich. Psychol. Assn., Mich. Women Psychologists, Mensa, Phi Beta Kappa. Avocations: reading, tennis, bridge, ballet, English riding. Home: 21783 Corsaut Ln Beverly Hills MI 48025-2607 Office: Harms and Harms PC 199 W Brown St Birmingham MI 48009-6022

HARMS, ELIZABETH LOUISE, artist; b. Milw., May 26, 1924; d. Frederick George and Veva (Sanderson) H.; m. Douglas Derwood Craft, Sept. 8, 1951. Diploma, Sch. Art Inst. Chgo., 1950, BFA, 1963, MFA, 1964. One-man shows: 55 Mercer St., N.Y.C., 1980, Fischbach Gallery, N.Y.C., 1975, Carnegie Inst. Mus. Art, 1969, Condeso/Lawler, 1982, 84, 85, 86, 90, 93, Gallery Jupiter, Little Silver, N.J., 1987, Jersey City Mus., 1988; group shows include Moravian Coll., Bethlehem, Pa., 1978, Jersey City Mus., 1980, 86, North of New Brunswick, South of N.Y., Rutgers-Newark, 1981, Coll. of New Rochelle, 1982, T. Bell Invitational, Condeso/Lawler, 1985, Montclair (N.J.) Art Mus., 1984, 86, Robeson Mus., Rutgers, Newark, 1988, Invitational Acad. & Inst. for Arts & Scis., N.Y.C., 1992, Skidmore Coll., Saratoga Springs, N.Y., 1993, So. Allegheny Mus. Art, Loretto, Pa., 1994. Recipient Armstrong prize Art Inst. Chgo., 1962; Tiffany Found. grantee, 1977. Home: PO Box 245 Jeffersonville NY 12748-0245

HARMS, ROBERT THOMAS, linguist, educator; b. Peoria, Ill., Apr. 12, 1932; s. Wilbert Erwin and Mildred Matilda (Thomas) H.; m. Sirpa Helina Aaltonen, July 1, 1956; children: Kirsti Maria, Ritva Helena, Eerik Thomas, Timo Kalevi. A.B., U. Chgo., 1952, A.M. in Slavic Langs, 1956, Ph.D. in Linguistics, 1960; postgrad. (Fulbright scholar), U. Helsinki, Finland, 1954-56; U.S.-Soviet exchange, Leningrad State U., 1962-63. Instr. U. Tex., Austin, 1958-61; asst. prof. linguistics U. Tex., 1961-64, asso. prof., 1965-67, prof., 1967—, chmn. dept. linguistics, 1973-77; Vis. asst. prof. Columbia U., 1960, vis. asso. prof., 1965; vis. asso. prof. Ohio State U., 1964; U.S.-Hungary exchange prof. U. Szeged (Hungarian Acad. Scis.), Budapest, 1967-68. Author: Estonian Grammar, 1962, Finnish Structural Sketch, 1964, Introduction to Phonological Theory, 1968; Editor: (with Emmon Bach) Universals in Linguistic Theory, 1968. Fulbright research grantee Finland, 1968; Nat. Acad. Scis. exchange prof. Acad. Scis. USSR and Estonian Acad. Scis. Mem. Linguistic Soc. Am., Finno-Ugrian Soc., Phi Beta Kappa. Lutheran. Home: 2609 Deerfoot Trl Austin TX 78704-2715 Office: U Tex Dept Linguistics Austin TX 78712

HARMS, STEVEN ALAN, lawyer; b. Detroit, Feb. 15, 1949; s. Herbert Rudolph and Elsa Jane (McClelland) H.; m. Nancy Gayle Banta, June 26, 1971; children: Jennifer Elizabeth, Heather Lynn, Robin Ann. BA, Hope Coll., 1970; JD, Detroit Coll. Law, 1975. Bar: Mich. 1975, U.S. Dist. Ct. (so. dist.) Mich. 1975, U.S. Ct. Appeals (6th cir.) 1982; bd. cert. creditors rights specialist. Ptnr. Muller, Muller, Richmond, Harms, Myers & Sgroi, P.C., Birmingham, Mich.; sec. gen. practice session State Bar Mich., 1982-83; mediator Oakland County Cir. Ct., 1990—; lectr. in field; adj. prof. Bus. Law Walsh Coll., Troy, Mich., 1990—. Author: Successful Collection of a Judgement, 1981; Rights of Commercial Creditors, 1982, Post Judgement Collection, 1988, Handling the Collection Case in Michigan, 1989, revised edit., 1998; co-author: Atty Fee Agreements, 1995; contbg. editor Michigan Business Formbook, 1997, revised edit., 1998, Michigan Civil Procedure, 1997; editor: General Practitioner, State Bar Mich., 1978-82. Bd. dirs. fin. com. YMCA, North Oakland County, Mich., 1987—, chmn. bd., 1990-91. Republican. Club: Pearson Yacht Owners Assn. (commodore 1988-90), Hunter Sailing Assn. (vice commodore 1985-86, commodore 1987-88). Office: Muller Muller Richmond Harms Myers & Sgroi PC 33233 Woodward Ave Birmingham MI 48009-0903

HARMSEN, TYRUS GEORGE, librarian; b. Pomona, Calif., July 24, 1924; s. Fred H. and Hazel (Weigle) H.; m. Lois Spaulding, Apr. 15, 1955; children—Mark Spaulding, Caroline Lora. A.B., Stanford, 1947, M.A., 1950; A.B. in L.S, U. Mich., 1948. Cataloguer dept. manuscripts Henry E. Huntington Library, San Marino, Calif., 1948-49, 50-59; coll. librarian Occidental Coll., Los Angeles, 1959-86, dir. book arts program, prof. bibliography, 1986-91; vis. lectr. Sch. Library Sci., U. So. Calif., 1958, 68. Author: The Plantin Press of Saul and Lillian Marks, 1960, Joseph Arnold Foster, Printer, 1998. Served with AUS, 1943-46. Council on Library Resources fellow, 1969. Presbyterian. Clubs: Zamorano, Rounce and Coffin (Los Angeles) (treas. 1956-91). Home: 1300 Medford Rd Pasadena CA 91107-1603

HARMSTON, ROBERT ALBERT, secondary education educator; b. Ayer, Mass., Jan. 13, 1942; s. Robert Nelson Harmston and Cecile Lillian (Lessard) Ross; m. Susan Jeannette Mosher, Oct. 29, 1966; children: Wendy Colleen, Robert Glenn. AA, San Bernardino Valley Coll., 1966; MusB, Calif. State U., Fullerton, 1969, BA in Anthropology, 1975, MA in Music Edn., 1981. Life tchg. credential grades K-14. Tchr. Pomona (Calif.) Unified Schs., 1970-72, Orange (Calif.) Unified Schs., 1972—; percussionist Orange County Symphony, 1968-70, profl. drummer, 1968—; percussionist Fullerton Cmty. Band, 1978—; tchr. Fullerton (Calif.) C.C., 1986. Cubmaster, asst. scoutmaster, commr. Boy Scouts Am., Fullerton, 1988— (Dist. Merit award 1998, Coun. Silver Beaver 1999). With U.S. Army, 1961-64. Mem. NEA (life), Am. Numismatic Assn., Calif. Tchrs. Assn., So. Calif. Sch. Band and Orch. Assn. (honor band mgr., cert. 1994), Orange Unified Educators Assn. (rep.), Amateur Radio Relay League (life), Phi Mu Alpha (life). Roman Catholic. Avocations: teaching U.S. history, chess, anthropology, coin and stamp collecting, ham radio operator.

HARNACK, DON STEGER, lawyer; b. Milw., June 19, 1928; s. Benjamin John and Katherine (Steger) H.; m. Rose Marie Ball, Oct. 17, 1959; children: Christopher Wallen, Gretchen Marie, Pamela Ann. BS, U. Wis., 1950; LLB, Harvard U., 1953. Bar: Wis. 1953, U.S. Dist. Ct. (ea. dist.) Wis. 1955, U.S. Tax Ct. 1957, Ill. 1959, U.S. Dist. Ct. (no. dist.) Ill. 1962, U.S. Ct. Appeals (6th and 7th cirs.) 1963, U.S. Ct. Claims 1966, U.S. Ct. Appeals (8th cir.) 1971, U.S. Supreme Ct. 1972. Assoc. Quarles, Spence & Quarles, Milw., 1955-57; trial atty. regional counsel IRS, Chgo., 1957-61; assoc. Dixon, Todhunter, Knouf & Holmes, Chgo., 1961-65; ptnr. McDermott, Will & Emery, Chgo., 1965-96, of counsel, 1997-98. Contbr. articles to profl. jours. Active Winnetka (Ill.) Zoning Bd., 1971-75; park bd. atty. Winnetka Park Dist., 1978-83; pres. N.E. Ill. coun. Boy Scouts Am., 1982-83; life trustee ULC Boys and Girls Club, Chgo.; trustee Village of Winnetka, 1984-88. Lt. USNR. Recipient Silver Beaver award Boy Scouts Am., 1984, named distinguished Eagle Scout, 1996. Mem. ABA, Ill. Bar Assn., Wis. Bar Assn., Union League Club (bd. dirs., officer, v.p. 1981-87, pres. 1987-88). Republican. Avocations: fishing, golf, reading, flying.

HARNER, MICHAEL JAMES, anthropologist, educator, author; b. Washington, Apr. 27, 1929; s. Charles Emory and Virginia (Paxton) H.; m. June Knight Kocher, 1951; children: Teresa J., James E.; m. Sandra Ferial Dickey, 1966. A.B., U. Calif., Berkeley, 1953, Ph.D., 1963. Asst. prof. Ariz. State U., Tempe, 1958-61; from sr. mus. anthropologist to assoc. rsch. anthropologist and asst. dir. Hearst Mus. Anthropology U. Calif., Berkeley, 1961-66; from vis. assoc. prof. to assoc. prof. Columbia U., N.Y.C., 1966-70; from assoc. prof. to prof. grad. faculty New Sch. Social Research, N.Y.C., 1970-87, chmn. dept. anthropology, 1973-77; internat. tchr. shamanism, 1977—; founder, dir. Ctr. for Shamanic Studies, Norwalk, Conn., 1979-87; pres., bd. dirs. Found. for Shamanic Studies, Mill Valley, Calif., 1985—; researcher Harvard U. Upper Gila expdn., 1948, Upper Amazon basin, 1956-57, 64, 69, 73, Am. Mus. of Natural History expdn. 1960-61, Western N.Am., 1951-53, 59, 65, 76, 78, Lapland, 1983, 84, Can. Arctic, 1987; vis. assoc. prof. U. Calif., Berkeley, 1971-72, vis. prof., 1975; vis. assoc. prof. Yale U., New Haven, 1970. Author: The Jivaro: People of the Sacred Waterfalls, 1972, 2d edit., 1984, Music of the Jivaro of Ecuador, 1972, Cannibal, 1979, The Way of the Shaman, 1980, 3d edit., 1990; editor: Hallucinogens and Shamanism, 1973; cons. editor: Revision Mag. Social Sci. Rsch. Coun., Doherty Found., Am. Mus. Nat. History fellow. Fellow AAAS, Am. Anthrop. Assn., Royal Anthrop. Inst. G.B. and Ireland, N.Y. Acad. Scis. (co-chmn. anthropology sect. 1980-81); mem. Am. Ethnol. Soc., Soc. Am. Archaeology, Soc. Ethnohistory, Assn. Transpersonal Psychology, Internat. Transpersonal Assn. (bd. dirs. 1982-85, 89-91), Assn. for the Anthropology of Consciousness, Xat Medicine Men's Soc., Inst. Andean Studies, Explorers Club (fellow). Office: Found for Shamanic Studies PO Box 1939 Mill Valley CA 94942-1939

HARNESS, DAVID KEITH, pastor; b. Beech Grove, Ind., Nov. 25, 1946; s. George Lewis and Evelyn Pauline (Reeves) H.; m. Peggy Ann Kyle, Feb. 14, 1993; children: Jonathan D., Ronald K., Rebecca L. Harness Lewis, Timothy Mayfield, Kimberly Mayfield. B in Theology, Apostolic Bible Inst., 1983. Pastor United Pentecostal Ch., Council Bluffs, Iowa, 1973-76, Internat. Ministerial Assn., Indpls., 1984-96; Global Network of Christian Ministries, 1997—; CEO Nat. Christian Outreach; pastor Compassion Ctr. Fellowship; bd. dirs. Christian Super Hwy. Network, Indpls.; asst. chaplain Marion County Jail, Indpls., 1997. Author: The Gospel According to a Grandpa, 1996. Pres. New Life Ch., Inc., Indpls., 1984-94; active Multiple Sclerosis Soc. Avocation: radio announcing. Home: 4331 Little Leaf Ct Indianapolis IN 46203-6226

HARNESS, WILLIAM EDWARD, tenor; b. Pendleton, Oreg., Nov. 26, 1940; s. Edward Cleo and Edna Margaret (Senn) H.; m. Anna Marie Ward, Jan. 11, 1964; children—Janine Kay, Heidi Maurine, William Edward, Shaana Marie, Shane Michael. Student pub. schs., Spokane, Wash. Gen. carpenter Rainway Mfg. Co., Spokane, 1958-61; with Wash. Water Power Co., Spokane, 1961-62; tech. service rep. Nat. Cash Register Co., Seattle, 1962-73. Concert and opera tenor various opera cos. and symphonies, 1973—; released 10 sacred recs., U.S. and Can.; profl. debut, San Francisco Opera Co., 1973, debut with N.Y.C. Opera, 1976, Met. Opera, N.Y.C., 1977, Hamberg (West Germany) Opera, 1978, maj. symphony debuts include Vancouver (B.C., Can.), Seattle, Los Angeles Philharm., San Francisco, Minn., Milw. Symphonies, sacred concert artist, 1978—; roles include: Edmondo in Manon Lescaut, Tonio in Daughter of the Regiment, Alfredo in La Traviata, Rodolfo in La Boheme, Count Almaviva in The Barber of Seville, Tamino in The Magic Flute, Faust in Faust, Cauaradossi in Tosca, Prince Calof in Turandot, Riccardo in Un Ballo in Maschera; sacred concert artist, U.S. and Can., South Africa, Latvia, Romania, Croatia. Recipient V.I.P. award Nat. Cash Register Co., 1970; Florence Bruce award San Francisco Opera, 1972; Enrico Caruso award, 1973; Cecilia Schultz award Seattle Opera, 1972; Distinguished Citizen award State of Wash., 1974; Nat. Opera Inst. fellow, 1973-74; Martha Baird Rockefeller grantee, 1974-76. Address: PO Box 328 Washougal WA 98671 Office: PO Box Ee Torrance CA 90508-0408

HARNESS, WILLIAM WALTER, lawyer; b. Ottumwa, Iowa, Apr. 14, 1945; s. Walter W. and Mary E. (Bukowski) H.; m. Carolyn Margaret Barnes, Jan 4, 1969; children: Matthew William, Michael Andrew. BA, U. Iowa, 1967; JD, Cleve. State U., 1974. Bar: Ohio 1975, U.S. Dist. Ct. (no. dist.) Ohio 1975, D.C. 1976, U.S. Dist. Ct. D.C. 1976, U.S. Ct. Appeals (D.C. cir.) 1976, U.S. Ct. Appeals (5th cir.) 1981, U.S. Dist. Ct. (we. dist.) N.C. 1979, U.S. Ct. Appeals (1st cir.) 1980, U.S. Ct. Appeals (4th cir.) 1981, U.S. Ct. Appeals (11th cir.) 1981. Mem. labor rels. staff Monogram Industries, Cleve., 1970-75; asst. counsel Nat. Treasury Employees Union, Washington, 1975-77, nat. counsel, Atlanta, 1977—; lectr. Emory U., Atlanta, 1978—; participant various seminars Ga. State U. Pres. Spring Mill-Kingsborough Ct. Corp., Atlanta. Served to 1st lt. U.S. Army, 1967-70. Mem. ABA (com. on fed. labor-mgmt. 1981-84), D.C. Bar Assn. (bd. dirs.), Soc. Fed. Labor Relations Profls., Indsl. Relations Research Assn. Home: 1285 Mile Post Dr Atlanta GA 30338-4756 Office: Nat Treasury Employees Union 2801 Buford Hwy NE Ste 430 Atlanta GA 30329-2137

HARNETT, JOSEPH DURHAM, oil company executive; b. Paterson, N.J., Aug. 23, 1917; s. James Harold and EMily (Steele) H.; m. Wilhelmina Nordstrom, June 21, 1941 (dec. July 1958); children: Gordon D., Linda C., Ralph H., David S.; m. Nancy Beam. B.S., Purdue U., 1939. With Consol. Edison Co., N.Y.C., 1939, Worthington Pump & Machinery Corp., 1940; with Standard Oil Co., Cleve., 1941-80, v.p., 1957-68, sr. v.p., 1968-70, exec. v.p., 1970-77, pres., 1977-80, now bd. dirs. Mem. Am. Petroleum Inst. (bd. dirs.), Country Club Cleve., Pepper Pike Club, Everglades Club, Lost Tree Club. Presbyterian. Home: 11090 Turtle Beach Rd # 204 No Palm Beach FL 33408-3423 Office: Moore and Ellrich 4400 P G A Blvd Ste 400 Palm Beach Gardens FL 33410

HARNETT, LILA, retired publisher; b. Bklyn., Oct. 4, 1926; d. Milton Samuel and Claire S. (Merahn) Mogan; m. Joel William Harnett. BA, CUNY, 1946; postgrad., New Sch. for Social Rsch., 1950. Pers. exec. Walter Lowen Agy., N.Y.C., 1947-52; pub. Bus. Atomics Report, N.Y.C., 1953-63; weekly columnist N.Y. State Newspapers, 1964-74; fine arts editor Cue Mag., N.Y., 1975-80; founder, contbg. editor Phoenix Home & Garden mag., 1980—, assoc. pub., 1988—, editor, 1996-99; pub. Scottsdale (Ariz.) Scene mag., 1992-98. Trustee Phoenix Art Mus., 1999—. Home: 4523 E Clearwater Pkwy Paradise Vly AZ 85253-2815 Office: Phoenix Home & Garden 4041 N Central Ave Phoenix AZ 85012-3330

HARNEY, KENNETH ROBERT, editor, columnist; b. Jersey City, Mar. 25, 1944; s. Carroll John and Agnes Theresa (Flanagan) H.; m. Lynne Andrea Leon, Aug. 26, 1967; children: Alexandra Erin, Brendan Leon, Timothy Andrew. AB cum laude, Princeton U., 1966; postgrad. (grad. fellow), U. Pa., 1966-67. Program analyst U.S. Office Econ. Opportunity, 1970-72; exec. editor, ptnr. The Housing & Devel. Reporter, Washington, 1972-82; syndicated columnist Washington Post, 1974—; exec. dir. Inst. Profl. & Exec. Devel., Inc., Washington, 1977-82; pres. Harney Corp., Bethesda, Md., 1980—; exec. dir. Nat. Real Estate Devel. Ctr., 1983—; pres. Rehab. Investor Corp., 1983—; mng. dir. Fin. Svcs. Inst., 1997—; mem. Fed. Res. Bd. Consumer Adv. Coun., 1995-98. Author: Beating Inflation with Real Estate, 1979, Guide to Federal Housing Programs, 1982, Exchange Your Real Estate: Why Pay Taxes, 1991. Councilman, vice-chmn. Village of Chevy Chase, Sect. 3, Chevy Chase, Md., 1987-94; bd. dirs. Nat. Housing Conf., 1988—; mem. consumer adv. coun. Federal Res., 1995-98. Recipient First prize Nat. Journalism Achievement Competition Nat. Assn. Realtors, 1979, Golden Hammer award Nat. Assn. Home Builders, 1980. Mem. Nat. Assn. Real Estate Editors, Nat. Press Club. Home: 3801 Bradley Ln Bethesda MD 20815-4254 Office: Rehab Investor Corp 6900 Wisconsin Ave Ste 602 Bethesda MD 20815-6100

HARNEY, PATRICIA RAE, nuclear analyst; b. Oklahoma City, Sept. 8, 1960; d. Donald R. Thompson and Donaleen L. (Turner) Robinson; m. Timothy D. Harney, Dec. 2, 1997; 1 child, Adrian. AAS in Ct. Reporting, Mile Hi Coll. Ct. Reporting, 1985; student, Front Range C.C., Westminster, Colo., 1993—. Cert. in hazardous materials; cert. Dept. Transp. Pvt. practice ct. reporter Denver, 1985-91; facility adminstr. Allen Bradley Co., Englewood, Colo., 1990-91; nuc. analyst Rocky Flats Environ. Tech. Site, Golden, Colo., 1991-95; tech. writer/analyst Y-12 Nuc. Plant, Oak Ridge, Tenn., 1995-96; nuc. safety sys. engr. Rocky Flats Environ. Tech. Site, Golden, 1996—; com. mem. Pro Bono Com., Denver, 1989-91. Mem. Non-Profit Orgn. for Abused Children, Denver, 1984-86. Recipient Productivity Improvement award for centralized waste storage facility EG&G Rocky Flats, 1994. Mem. Am. Nuc. Soc., Phi Theta Kappa. Avocations: reading, skiing, scuba diving, biking. Home: 8722 W Ute Dr Littleton CO 80128-6964

HARNEY, THOMAS C., lawyer; b. Dec. 21, 1942. BS, U. N.C., 1965; JD, U. So. Calif., 1972. Bar: Ga. 1972, U.S. Dist. Ct. N.D., Ga. 1972, U.S. Ct. Appeals (11th cir.). Atty., ptnr. Kilpatrick Stockton, Atlanta, 1972—. Trustee Galloway Sch., Atlanta. Lt. USN, 1965-68, Vietnam. Recipient Bronze Star medal with combat V, 1968. Office: Kilpatrick Stockton 1100 Peachtree St NE Ste 2800 Atlanta GA 30309-4501*

HARNICK, SHELDON MAYER, lyricist; b. Chgo., Apr. 30, 1924; s. Harry M. and Esther (Kanter) H.; m. Mary Boatner, Aug. 29, 1950 (annulled May 1957); m. Elaine May, Mar. 25, 1962 (div. May 1963); m. Margery Gray, Oct. 8, 1965; children: Beth, Matthew. MusB, Northwestern U., 1949. Writer light verse, songs; contbr. songs ann. musical Waa-Mu Show, Northwestern U., 1946-50; writer songs Broadway, off-Broadway shows Two's Company, 1953, New Faces of 1952, John Murray Anderson's Almanac, 1954, The Shoestring Revue 1955, The Littlest Revue 1956, Shoestring '57, 1957; (with composer Jerry Bock) Body Beautiful, 1958, Fiorello, 1959 (Pulitzer Prize, Tony award, N.Y. Drama Critics Circle award), Tenderloin, 1960, She Loves Me, 1963 (Grammy award), Fiddler on the Roof, 1964 (Tony award), Apple Tree, 1966, The Rothschilds, 1970, (with composer David Baker) Smiling the Boy Fell Dead, 1961, (with composer Richard Rodgers) Rex, 1976, (with composer Jack Beeson) Capt. Jinks of the Horse Marines, 1975, Dr. Heidegger's Fountain of Youth, 1978, (with composer Michel Legrand) A Christmas Carol, 1981 (with composer Joe Raposo) A Wonderful Life, 1986, Cyrano, 1994, co-author English lyrics, Ghetto, Mark Taper Forum, L.A., 1986-87; TV The Way They Were, 1963 (Grammy nom.); translator The Umbrellas of Cherbourg, 1979; composer 1-act mini-opera Frustration; translator, adaptor The Merry Widow, San Diego Civic Ctr., 1977, Carmen, Houston Opera, 1981, L'oca del Cairo, Lyric Opera of Kansas City, 1982, Songs of the Auvergne, N.Y.C., 1982; translator Bach Cantatas The Contest Between Phoebus and Pan, 1988, The Appeasement of Aeolus, 1990; librettist Love in Two Countries, 1991; album: A Evening with Sheldon Harnick, 1992. Served with Signal Corps, AUS, 1943-46. Recipient Marc Blitzstein Memorial award for musical theatre, Am. Acad. of Arts & Letters, 1993. Mem. Broadcast Music Inc., Songwriters Guild Am., Dramatists Guild. Jewish. Office: Deutsch & Blasband C/O Alvin Deutsch 800 3rd Ave New York NY 10022-7604*

HAROLD, FRAN POWELL, historic site director; b. Greensboro, N.C., June 16, 1951. BSA, U. Ga., 1973; MSA, U. N.C., Greensboro, 1978. Tchr. art Shamrock (Ga.) Edn. Sys., 1974-75; curator Danville Mus. Fine Arts and History, Danbury, Conn., 1975-77; head E. O. Smith Art Sch. U. Conn., Hartford, 1977-79; exec. dir. Juliette Gordon Low Birthplace, Savannah, Ga., 1982—. Mem. Rotary Clubs. Office: Juliette Gordon Low Birthplace 142 Bull St Savannah GA 31401-3723*

HARON, DAVID LAWRENCE, lawyer; b. Detroit, Sept. 24, 1944; s. Percy Hyman and Bess (Holland) H.; m. Pamela Kay Colburn, May 25, 1969; children: Eric, Andrea. BA, U. Mich., 1966, JD, 1969. Bar: Mich. 1969, U.S. Dist. Ct. (ea. dist.) Mich., 1969, U.S. Supreme Ct. 1974, U.S. Ct. of Appeals (6th cir.) 1996. Law clk. to chief judge Mich. Ct. Appeals, Detroit, 1969-70; assoc. Barris, Sott, Denn & Driker, Detroit, 1970-74; sr. ptnr. Josephson, Tennen, Haron and Bennett, Southfield, Mich., 1974-90; prin., shareholder, sr. v.p. Frank, Stefani, Haron and Hall, Troy, Mich., 1990—; arbitrator Mich. Prudential Securities, Inc. Expedited Arbitrations, 1994-96; cons. Universe Computer Software, 1985; pres., bd. dirs. S&H Licensing Corp., Southfield; panelist Ct. TV Law Ctr. Bar Assn. Mem. editorial bd. Prospectus Jour. Law Reform, 1969, (newsletter) Atty.'s Mktg. Report, 1986-88; contbr. articles to profl. jours. Commr. Farmington Hills Planning Commn., 1996—; vol. handicap parking enforcement officer Farmington Hills Police Dept., 1990-93; bd. dirs. Forest Elem. Sch. PTO, 1983, 87-88; v.p. North Farmington Baseball for Youth, 1984; mem. Sta. WTVS Auction, Detroit, 1985-88; trustee Caring Athletes Team for Children's and Henry Ford Hosps., 1996—, Temple Israel, West Bloomfield, Mich., 1987-93, tchr. Sunday Sch., 1986-88, chmn. Ritual com., 1988-93, advisor youth group, 1987-90; chmn. Farmington Hills Com. to Increase Voter Participation, 1987-89; bd. dirs. Met. Detroit chpt. Zionist Orgn. Am., 1987-90; pres. North Farmington H.S. Parent Club, 1989-95; mem. bd. advisors Farmington Hills Corps.-Salvation Army, 1997—; mem. site selection com. South Oakland County Habitat for Humanity; chair Cardozo Law Soc. of the Jewish Fedn. Met. Detroit, 1999—. Recipient Outstanding Alumnus award Mumford H.S., Detroit, 1985, Cert. recognition City of Farmington Hills, 1986. Fellow The Roscoe Pound Found.; mem. ABA (mem. com. on comml. leasing 1987—, real property, probate and trust law sect., mem. bus. law sect. com. on fed. regulation of securities, mem. subcom. on alternative dispute resolution, SEC enforcement matters), ASTM (mem. com. on environ. assessment 1992—), ATLA, Nat. Health Lawyers Assn., Mich. Trial Lawyers Assn., Am. Soc. Writers on Legal Subjects, Internat. Assn. Jewish Lawyers and Jurists, Million Dollar Advocates Forum, State Bar Mich. (mem. pro bono com. real property sect. 1996-98, professionalism com. 1994-98, chmn. unauthorized practice of law com. 1990-92, chmn. Ct. Appeals com. 1977-78), Nat. Assn. Securities Dealers (mediator 1996—, arbitrator 1997—), Am. Arbitration Assn. (arbitrator, mediator, spkr.), Comml. Law League Am., Detroit Bar Assn., Detroit Cordozo Law Soc. (chmn. 1999—), Oakland County Bar Assn. (participant Mich. law-related edn. project 1988-89, real estate com. 1990—, environ. law com. 1992-95, lawyer dispute conciliator, spkr. 1993, chmn. professionalism com. 1995-97, Cir. Ct. facilitator, master Inn of Ct. 1997—), Oakland Bar Adams Pratt Found. (trustee), Jewish Fedn. Met. Detroit, U. Mich. Alumni Assn., U. Mich. Victor's Club, Zionist Orgn. (bd. dirs. Detroit 1987-90), Tau Epsilon Rho, Tau Delta Phi. Jewish. Fax: 248-952-0890. E-mail: dharon@fsh-law.com. Home: 34685 Old Timber Rd Farmington MI 48331-1436 Office: Frank Stefani & Haron 5435 Corporate Dr Ste 225 Troy MI 48098-2624

HAROS, JOANN, critical care nurse; b. N.Y.C., Aug. 26, 1940; d. Charles and Genevieve (Toback) Manicaro; m. William Haros, Aug. 29, 1964; children: William, Nicholas. RN, Sacred Heart Hosp., Allentown, Pa., 1961. RN, Pa., Fla.; cert. perioperative nurse. Staff nurse Sacred Heart Hosp., Allentown, 1961-67, 76-84; office nurse/surg. asst. Wescosville (Pa.) Ob-Gyn. Assocs., 1984-86; specialty coord. gynecology, mem. Laser Team, chair-elect profl. nurse coun. The Allentown Hosp.-Lehigh Valley Hosp. Ctr., 1986-91; oper. rm. supr. Muhlenberg Hosp. Ctr., Bethlehem, Pa., 1992-95; patient care mgr. Intracoastal Health Systems, Inc., Good Samaritan Med. Ctr., West Palm Beach, Fla., 1996-98; staff nurse Good Samaritan Med. Ctr., West Palm Beach, Fla., 1998—; past chmn. unit based quality assurance com., past mem. divisional quality assurance com., presenter hosp. wide program "Achieving Excellence in Patient Care Through Quality Assurance"; co-chmn. Peer Rev. Coun. Mem. ANA, Assn. Oper. Rm. Nurses (past chmn. legis. com., splty. mgmt. assembly, splty. ambulatory surgery assembly), Pa. Coun. Oper. Rm. Nurses (past pres.), Mideastern Pa. Assn. Oper. Rm. Nurses (past pres.), Pa. Nurses Assn., Fla. Coun. Oper. Rm. Nurses (industry adv. com.), Sacred Heart Hosp. Alumnae Assn. Nurses, Ea. Area Regional Nurse Mgrs. Home: 2320 SW 22nd Ave Apt 204 Delray Beach FL 33445-7711

HARP, JOHN ANDERSON, lawyer; b. Helena, Ark., Nov. 30, 1950; s. Bert Seth and Mary Eleanor (Jolley) H.; m. Jane Van Cleave, Apr. 26, 1980; children: Anderson, Elizabeth, William, Hamilton. BA, Am. U., Washington, 1973; JD, Mercer U., Macon, Ga., 1980. Bar: Ga., Ala. Ptnr. Taylor, Harp & Callier, Columbus, Ga., 1985—. Co-author: Litigating Head Trauma Cases, 1991; bd. editors Neurolaw Letter, 1991—, IATROGENICS, 1992-93, Topics in Spinal Cord Injury Rehab., 1994—; contbr. articles to profl. jours. Reservist USMCR with Office of Asst. Sec. of Def., The Pentagon, 1996—. Col., USMCR, 1995—. Mem. ABA, ATLA, Ga. Bar Assn., Ala. Bar Assn., Nat. Spinal Cord Assn. (bd. dirs. 1987-95), Marine Corps Res. Officers Assn. (bd. dirs. 1995-98, nat. pres. 1997-98, vice-chmn. bd. dirs. 1998-99, Non Sibi Sed Patriae award), Mercer U. Law Sch. Alumni Assn. (nat. v.p. 1997-98, nat. pres.-elect 1998-99, nat. pres. 1999—). Avocations: running, skiing. Office: Taylor Harp & Callier 233 12th St Ste 900 Columbus GA 31901-2449

HARP, SOLOMON, III, former airport executive; s. Solomon Harp and Minnie (Allen) Mason; m. Carolyn White, July 25, 1954; children: Sharon, Cassandra, Joyce, Lisa. BA in Biology, Lincoln U., 1952; MS in Systems Mgmt., U. So. Calif., 1979. Commd. USAF, advanced through grades to colonel, comdr. 80th Tactical Fighter Squadron, 1971-72; comdr. U.S. Joint Task Force U.S. Readiness Command, 1973-74; deputy comdr. of ops., 8th tactical fighter wing USAF, 1975-76; sr. air force rep. U.S. Army Armor Ctr., 1976-80; dept. comdr. of plans 20th Norad region, Norad command, 1980-81; assoc. dir. facilities Montgomery Coll., Rockville, Md., 1982-83; pres. Harp Construction Co., Columbia, Md., 1983-85; mgr., airport ops. ctr. Balt./Washington Internat. Airport, 1985-90, dir. ops., 1990-97. Avocations: sports, music. *

HARP, TONI N., state legislator; b. San Francisco. BA, Roosevelt U.; MEd, Yale U. Mem. New Haven Bd. Aldermen, 1988-92, Commn. Affirmative Action, 1990-92; Conn. state senator, 1993—, chair pub. health com., 1997; project coord. health svcs. Democrat. Address: PO Box 9493 New Haven CT 06534-0493 Office: Conn State Senate State Capitol Hartford CT 06106*

HARPEL, GERALD ROBERT, obstetrician-gynecologist; b. Boston, Mar. 25, 1946; s. Aaron and Dorothy (Goldring) H.; m. Cassie M. Lemaster, Nov. 4, 1989; children: Crystal L. Lemaster, Aaron B. (dec.), Michael A. BA, Boston U., 1967; MPH, Yale U., 1969; MD, Boston U., 1973. Diplomate Am. Bd. Ob-Gyn. Intern R.I. Hosp.-Brown U., 1973-74; resident in ob-gyn. Good Samaritan Hosp., Phoenix, 1974-77; chief of staff Harrison Meml. Hosp., Cynthiana, Ky., 1994—; pvt. practice Just for Women-Ob-Gyn, Cynthiana; clin. prof. emeritus ob-gyn. U. So. Calif., 1995; cons. Harrison Meml. Hosp., Cynthiana, 1996—; vis. prof. Harrison County Dept. Edn., Cynthiana, 1995—. Fellow ACS, Am. Coll. Ob-Gyn., Internat. Coll. Surgery, L.A. Ob-Gyn. Soc.; mem. APHA, sn. Gynecol. Laproscopists, Am. Fertility Soc., Ky. Med. Assn., Ky. Pub. Health Assn., Calif. Med.Assn., Los Angeles County Med. Assn., Inquisitors Club. Office: Just for Women-Ob-Gyn PO Box 68 Cynthiana KY 41031-0068

HARPENDING, HENRY COSAD, anthropologist, educator; b. Penn Yan, N.Y., Jan. 13, 1944; married, 1966; 1 child. AB, Hamilton Coll., 1964; MA, Harvard U., 1965, PhD in Anthropology, 1972. Asst. prof. anthropology Yale U., 1971-72; from asst. prof. to prof. anthropology U. N.Mex., 1972-96; prof. anthropology Pa. State U., 1996-97, U. Utah, 1997—. Mem. Nat. Acad. Sci., Am. Assn. Phys. Anthropology, Am. Assn. Anthrop. Genetics, Human Behavior Evolution Soc. Office: U. Utah Dept. Anthropology, Stuart Salt Lake City UT 84112*

HARPER, ALFRED JOHN, II, lawyer; b. El Paso, Tex., Aug. 11, 1942; s. Mosely Lloyd and Marion M. (McClintock) H.; m. Cynthia Newkam; children—A. John, Leslie J. BA, North Tex. State U., 1964; LLB cum laude, So. Meth. U., 1967. Bar: Tex. 1967, U.S. Dist. Ct. (so. dist.) Tex. 1967, U.S. Dist. Ct. (no. dist.) Tex. 1975, U.S. Dist. Ct. (we. dist.) Tex. 1976, U.S. Dist. Ct. (ea. dist.) Tex. 1995, U.S. Ct. Appeals (5th cir.) 1968, (9th cir.) 1976, (11th cir.) 1982, (10th cir.) 1984, (6th cir.) 1990, (1st cir.) 1991, (2d cir.) 1995, U.S. Supreme Ct. 1971. Assoc. Fulbright & Jaworski, L.L.P., Houston, 1967-74, ptnr., 1974—; cert. labor and employment law specialist State Bar Tex. bd. legal specialization. Editor Jour. Air Law and Commerce, 1966-67; contbr. articles to profl. jours. With USMCR, 1960-66. Fellow Coll. Labor and Employment Lawyers; mem. ABA (former coun., labor and employment law sect., past mgmt. co-chmn. com. on devel. law under Nat. Labor Rels. Act, mgmt. co-chmn. meetings and insts. com., labor law sect.), Tex. Bar Assn., Order of Coif, Houston Country Club. Republican. Methodist. Office: Fulbright & Jaworski 1301 Mckinney St Houston TX 77010-3031

HARPER, CHARLES LITTLE, JR., foundation administrator, planetary scientist; b. Evanston, Ill., Dec. 29, 1958; s. Charles Little and Alice Patterson (Fall) H.; m. Susan Gilbert Billington, June 24, 1984; children: Rebecca Anne, Charles L. III, Katherine Comfort, Sarah Newkirk. BS in Civil and Geol. Engring. cum laude, Princeton U., 1980; DPhil, Oxford (Eng.) U., 1988, Dipl.Theol., 1988; cert. ion adminstrn. and mgmt., Harvard U., 1997. NRC rsch. fellow Johnson Space Ctr. NASA, Houston, 1988-91;

rsch. assoc. dept. earth and planetary scis. Harvard U., Cambridge, Mass., 1991-96, assoc. Coll. Obs., 1995—; exec. dir., sr. v.p. John Templeton Found., Radnor, Pa., 1996—; crisis counselor Youth for Christ, Oreg., 1980-81. Former mem. Mt. Hood Mountain Rescue Team. Squire-Marriot scholar, 1988. Fellow Am. Astron. Soc.; mem. Am. Geophys. Union, Geochem. Soc. Avocations: mountain climbing, scuba diving, sailing, winter camping, ice climbing. Office: John Templeton Found 2 Radnor Corp Ctr Ste 320 100 Matsonford Rd Radnor PA 19087

HARPER, CHARLES MICHEL, food company executive; b. Lansing, Mich., Sept. 26, 1927; s. Charles Frost and Alma (Michel) H.; m. Joan Frances Bruggema, June 24, 1950; children: Kathleen Harper Wenngatz, Carolyn Harper Haney, Charles Michel, Elizabeth Harper Murphy. BS in Mech. Engring, Purdue U., 1949; MBA, U. Chgo., 1950; LHD (hon.), U. Nebr., 1986; hon. degree, Coll. St. Mary, 1986; DEng (hon.), Purdue U., 1989; LHD (hon.), Kearney State U., 1990, U. Nebr., 1986; JD (hon.), Law Coll. of St. Mary, 1986; LHD (hon.), Bellevue Coll., 1993. Supr. methods engring. Oldsmobile div. Gen. Motors Corp., Detroit, 1950-54; indsl. engr. Pillsbury Co., Mpls., 1954-55, dir. indsl. engring., 1955-60, dir. engring., 1961-66, v.p. rsch., devel. and new products, 1965-70, group v.p.-poultry, food svc. and venture bus., 1970-74; exec. v.p., COO, dir. ConAgra Inc., Omaha, 1974-76, pres., CEO, 1976-81, chmn. bd., CEO, dir., 1981-93; chmn. bd., CEO RJR Nabisco Holdings Corp., N.Y.C., 1993-95, chmn. bd., 1995-96; bd. dirs. Valmont Industries, Inc., Peter Kiewit Sons', Inc., ConAgra, Inc.; mem. exec. com. Nat. Commn. on Agrl., Trade and Export Policy, 1984-86. Mem. coun. Village of Excelsior (Minn.), 1965-70, mayor, 1974; trustee Bishop Clarkson Meml. Hosp.; hon. chmn. Urban League Nebr. Membership Campaign, 1987; pres. Mid-Am. Coun. Boy Scouts Am., 1983-84. Served with AUS, 1946-48. Named Alumnus of Yr. U. Chgo. Grad. Sch. of Bus., 1991. Mem. U.S. C. of C. (bd. dirs., chmn. food and agrl. com.), Omaha C. of C. (chmn. 1979), Ak-Sar-Ben (gov.), U. Nebr. Lincoln Coll. Bus. Adminstrn. Alumni Assn. (hon. life), Beta Theta Pi. Office: One Ctrl Park Plz North Tower Ste 1500 Omaha NE 68102*

HARPER, CHRISTINE JOHNSON, psychiatric clinical nurse, administrator; b. Tyler, Tex., June 26, 1952; d. Reinhold P. and Alice G. (Levingston) Johnson; m. James H. Harper, Sept. 4, 1982; 1 child, Timothy Wright. BSN, U. Tex., 1974; MS, U. Tex., Tyler, 1981; MSN, Tex. Woman's U., 1992. RN, Tex.; cert. clin. nurse specialist in psychiat. mental health. Instr. Tyler Jr. Coll., 1976-87; sr. lectr. U. Tex., Tyler, 1987-91, adj. nursing faculty, 1994—; clin. specialist Rusk (Tex.) State Hosp., 1992-94, dir. nursing svcs., 1994—; mem. nurse practice orgn. exec. com. Tex. Dept. Mental Health/Mental Retardation, 1995-97; bd. dirs. nurse examiners State of Tex. Adv. Com. on Edn. Mem. Tex. Nurses Assn. (bd. dirs. dist. 19, ho. of dels., past pres., Exemplary Leadership in Tex. Nursing award 1988), Tex. Bd. Nurse Examiners (adv. com. edn. 1996—), Tex. Mental Health Mental Retardation Nurse Practice Orgn. (exec. com. 1995-97), Am. Psychiat. Nurses Assn. (Tex. rep. 1995), Sigma Theta Tau (chmn. nominations Iota Nu chpt.).

HARPER, CONRAD KENNETH, lawyer, former government official; b. Detroit, Dec. 2, 1940; s. Archibald Leonard and Georgia Florence (Hall) H.; m. Marsha Louise Wilson, July 17, 1965; children: Warren Wilson, Adam Woodburn. BA, Howard U., 1962; LLB, Harvard U., 1965; LLD (hon.), CUNY, 1990, Vt. Law Sch., 1994. Bar: N.Y. 1966. Law clk. NAACP Legal Def. and Ednl. Fund, N.Y.C., 1965-66, staff lawyer, 1966-70; assoc. Simpson Thacher & Bartlett, N.Y.C., 1971-74, ptnr., 1974-93, 96—; legal adviser U.S. Dept. of State, Washington, 1993-96; lectr. law Rutgers U., 1969-70; vis. lectr. law Yale U., 1977-81; cons. HEW, 1977; chmn. admissions and grievances com. U.S. Ct. Appeals, 2d cir., 1987-93; co-chmn. Lawyers' Com. for Civil Rights Under Law, 1987-89; mem. Permanent Ct. of Arbitration, The Hague, 1993-96, 98—, Adminstrv. Conf. U.S., 1993-95; bd. dirs. N.Y. Life Ins. Co., Pub. Svc. Enterprise Group, Pub. Svc. Electric & Gas. Trustee Inst. Internat. Edn., 1992-93, N.Y. Pub. Libr., chmn. exec. com., 1990-93, vice chmn. bd. trustees, 1991-93; trustee William Nelson Cromwell Found., 1990—, Met. Mus. of Art, 1996—; bd. mgrs. Lewis Walpole Libr., 1989-93; bd. visitors Fordham Law Sch., 1990-93, CUNY, 1989-93; vestryman Ch. of St. Barnabas, Irvington, N.Y., 1982-85; bd. dirs. Phi Beta Kappa Assocs., 1992-93; chancellor The Episc. Diocese of N.Y., 1987-92; mem. bd. legal advisors Martindale-Hubbell, 1990-93. Fellow Am. Bar Found., N.Y. Bar Found., Am. Coll. Trial Lawyers, Am. Acad. Arts and Scis.; mem. ABA (bd. editors jour. 1980-86), Internat. Bar Assn., Nat. Bar Assn., N.Y. State Bar Assn., Assn. of Bar of City of N.Y. (chmn. exec. com. 1979-80, pres. 1990-92), Am. Law Inst. (mem. coun. 1985—, 2nd v.p. 1998—), Am. Assn. for Internat. Commn. Jurists (bd. dirs. 1988-93), Am. Soc. Internat. Law (mem. exec. coun. 1997—, mem. exec. com. 1998—), Met. Black Bar Assn., Internat. Law Assn., N.Y. Law Inst. (mem. exec. com. 1997—), Am. Arbitration Assn. (bd. dirs. 1990-93, 97—, mem. exec. com. 1998—), Acad. Polit. Sci. (bd. dirs. 1998—), Coun. Fgn. Rels., Acad. Am. Poets (bd. dirs. 1990-93), Grolier Club (coun. mem. 1993, 97—), Century Assn., Harvard Club (mem. bd. mgrs. 1993), Yale Club, Phi Beta Kappa. Democrat. Episcopalian. Office: 425 Lexington Ave New York NY 10017-3954

HARPER, DAVID VIRGIL, water system operator; b. Mar. 2, 1955. AA, Jacksonville Jr. Coll., 1974; BS in Bus. Adminstrn., Libery U., 1987. Nuclear regulatory specialist Ark. Power & Light, Little Rock, 1979-81, Fla. Power Corp., St. Petersburg, 1981-90, United Energy Svcs., Aiken, S.C., 1990-92; water sys. operator West Saline Water, New Edinburg, Ark., 1992—. E-mail: theharpers4@juno.com. Home: 164 Bradley 8N Warren AR 71671

HARPER, DEREK, professional basketball player; b. Oct. 13, 1961; m. Sheila; children: Darius, Danielle, Dana, Daria. Guard Dallas Mavericks, 1983-94, 96-97, 1998—, N.Y. Knicks, 1994-96, Orlando Magic, 97-98. Namd to All-Defensive 2nd Team NBA, 1987, 90. Office: Los Angeles Lakers 3900 W Manchester Blvd Inglewood CA 90306*

HARPER, DIXON LADD, broadcast director; b. Ames, Iowa, Nov. 29, 1922; s. Harlan Howard and Mary Joan (Parsons) H.; student Mich. State U., 1943; B.S., Iowa State U., 1948; m. Shirley Thevenin, Mar. 22, 1947; children—Susan Shirley, Tod Dixon. Vice pres. broadcast Aubrey, Finlay, Marley & Hodgson, Chgo., 1956-63; account supr. Foote, Cone & Belding, Inc., Chgo., 1963-70; v.p. Lennen & Newall, Inc., Chgo., 1970-72; mgmt. supr. Clinton E. Frank, Inc., Chgo., 1972-75; pub. Specialized Agrl. Publs., Raleigh, N.C., 1975-82; dir. agrl. prodns. Capitol Broadcasting Co., 1982—; cons. Nat. Project in Agrl. Communications. With USAAF, 1943-44. Recipient Disting. Svc. award Nat. Pork Producers Coun., 1990. Mem. N.C. Assn. Farm Writers and Broadcasters, Nat. Agrl. Mktg. Assn., Nat. Agrimktg. Conf. (chmn.), Nat. Assn. Farm Broadcasters (pres. 1988, Meritorious Svc. award 1959), Wake County Agribus. Council (pres.), Soc. Profl. Journalists, Car/Va Speaker's Bur. (chmn.). Democrat. Methodist. Office: PO Box 12800 Raleigh NC 27605-2800

HARPER, DONALD VICTOR, transportation and logistics educator; b. Chgo., Mar. 27, 1927; s. Victor Rudolph and Mildred Victoria (Safbom) H.; children: Christine Ann, Diane Elizabeth, David Victor. Student, Wright Jr. Coll., 1945, 46-47; B.S. in Journalism, U. Ill., Urbana, 1950, Ph.D. in Econs., 1957. Instr. Coll. Commerce and Bus. adminstrn. U. Ill., Urbana, 1953-56; lectr. Carlson Sch. Mgmt. U. Minn., Mpls., 1956, asst. prof. Carlson Sch. Mgmt., 1956-59, assoc. prof., 1959-65, prof. transp. and logistics, 1965—, chmn. dept. mgmt. and transp., 1967-70, dir. MBA and PhD programs, 1970-79, dir. PhD program, 1979-80, chmn. dept. mktg. and logistics mgmt., 1991-96; cons. to bus. and govt. agys. Author: Economic Regulation of the Motor Trucking Industry by the States, 1959, Price Policy and Procedure, 1966, Transportation in America: Users, Carriers, Government, 2d edit. 1982; contbr. articles to profl. jours. Served with USNR, 1945-46. Mem. Am. Econ. Assn. (Disting. Mem. award transp. and pub. utilities group 1988), Am. Mktg. Assn., Transp. Research Forum, Am. Soc. Transp. and Logistics, Council of Logistics Mgmt., Transp. Club Mpls. and St. Paul, Assn. Transp. Law, Logistics and Policy. Home: 2451 Sheldon St Saint Paul MN 55113-3138 Office: U Minn Carlson Sch Mgmt 321 19th Ave S Minneapolis MN 55455-0438

HARPER, DOREEN C., nursing educator. Student, Albertus Magnus Coll., 1966-68; BSN, Cornell U., 1971; MSN, Catholic U., 1974; PhD in Human Devel., U. Md., 1980. Cert. adult nurse practitioner ANA. Home care nurse Child Devel. Ctr. R.I. Hosp., Providence, 1971; pub. health nurse Fairfax County Health Dept., Fairfax, Va., 1971-72; charge nurse adolescent mental health unit The Bancroft Inst., Falls Church, Va., 1973; college health nurse Trinity Coll., Washington, 1973-84; asst. prof. nursing dept. nursing George Mason U., Fairfax, Va., 1974-77, assoc. prof. nursing dept. nursing, 1980-82, 1987—; project dir. adult and gerontological nurse practitioner trg. grant George Mason U., Fairfax, 1988-91, adult nurse practitioner student health svcs., 1990—, coord. nurse practitioner program Coll. Nursing and Health Scis., 1991—; adult nurse practioner Kaiser/Georgetown Cmty. Health Plan, Springfield, 1979-81; chair RN to BSN program, asst. prof.Sch. Nursing U. Md., Catonsville, 1982-86; adult nurse practitioner OB-GYN Assocs., Alexandria, Va., 1987-1990; dir. nurse practitioner program Sch. Medicine and Health Scis. George Washington U., Washington, 1994—; cons. in field; principal investigator Nat. Ctr. Nursing Rsch. NIH, 1989-92; presenter in field; mem. nursing task force Va. Area Health Edn. Ctrs., 1993—. Editor: Nursing Connections, 1987-89; editl. review bd. Advances in Nursing Sci., 1989-93; contbr. numerous chpts., articles to profl. jours. and books. Predoctoral rsch. fellow Nursing Rsch. Svcs. Adminstrn.U. Md., 1977-80; recipient: Nat. Inst. Mental Health traineeship award Dept. Health, Edn. and Welfare Catholic U. Am., 1972-74. Fellow Am. Acad. Nursing (nat. peer review com. 1980-88); mem. Va. Nurses Assn. (dist. VIII Outstanding Nurse of the Year award 1975, del. 1976, 81 conv., mem. joint med./nursing practice com. 1976-78, dist. 8 chmn. nominating com. 1981-82), Sigma Theta Tau (Kappa chpt. nominating com. 1978-79, Epsilon Zeta chpt. 1987—, nominating com. 1989-91). Home: 6121 River Dr Lorton VA 22079-4123 Office: George Mason U Nursing Graduate Program 4400 University Dr MSN 3C4 Fairfax VA 22030-4444*

HARPER, EMERY WALTER, lawyer; b. Hackensack, N.J., Feb. 25, 1936; s. Walter Van Saun and Dorothy Charlotte (Schmidt) H.; m. Judith Van Nest Hover, Sept. 9, 1961 (div. 1991); 1 child, Caroline Curry. BA cum laude, Amherst Coll., 1958; LLB, Yale U., 1961. Bar: N.Y. 1962. Assoc. Lord Day & Lord, Barrett Smith, N.Y.C., 1961-69, ptnr., 1970-93; ptnr. Schnader, Harrison, Segal & Lewis, N.Y.C., 1993-96, chmn. internat. maritime group, 1993-95; pres. Harper Cons., Inc., N.Y.C., 1997—; of counsel Inman Deming LLP, 1998—; bd. dirs. The Shipping Network, Inc.; bd. dirs., founding mem. The Admiralty/Fin. Forum, Inc.; lectr. on maritime law Dalian, PRC, 1984; advisor U.S. del. to joint working group on liens and mortgages Internat. Maritime Orgn., 1st, 2d, 5th and 6th sessions UN Conf. on Trade and Devel., 1986-89; lectr. on admiralty and maritime financing; lectr. on ship fin. topics, Mex., Panama, Chile, Thailand, 1993-95; course dir. practice and techniques Financing Marine Assets and Ops., N.Y., 1995; organizer, pres. Am. Corps. in Coastwise Trade; participant U.S. Delegation to IMO/UNCTAD Joint Diplomatic Conf. on Maritime Liens and Mortgages, Geneva, 1993; cons. Inman Deming Internat., LLC, Washington, 1998—; del. to diplomatic conf. arrest of ships Internat. C. of C., 1999. Co-author: Essays on Maritime Liens and Mortgages and on Arrest of Ships, 1985; contbr. articles to profl. publs. Bd. trustees The Gateway Sch., N.Y., 1975-83; deacon Brick Presbyn. Ch., 1970-76, elder, 1976-82, trustee, corp. sec., 1982-88; mem. legal adv. com. Liberian Shipowners Coun., 1988—; chmn. Subcom. on Liberian Maritime Law Revision, 1993—. With USAFR, 1961-67. Mem. ABA, Assn. of Bar of City of N.Y. (chmn. admiralty com. 1977-80), Maritime Law Assn. (founding chmn. com. on Marine financing 1978-87), Com. Maritime Internat. (internat. subcom. on maritime liens and mortgages), N.Y. Amherst Alumni Assn. (pres. 1975-77), Pilgrims Soc., Union Club, Down Town Club. Fax: 202-347-6013. Office: Hamilton Sq Ste 600 600 Fourteenth St NW Washington DC 20005-2004 also: 18 East 50th St 7th Fl New York NY 10022

HARPER, GEORGE MILLS, English language educator; b. Linn Creek, Mo., Nov. 5, 1914; s. Charles Avery and Grace (Shipman) H.; m. Mary Jane Hughes, June 15, 1944; children: Margaret Mills, Ann Christian. A.B., Culver-Stockton Coll., 1940; M.A., U. Fla., 1947; Ph.D., U. N.C., 1951; D.Litt. (hon.), Trinity Coll., Dublin, 1980. From instr. to prof. English, U. N.C., 1950-66, asso. dean arts and scis., 1955-60, chmn. English dept., 1962-66, chmn. faculty, 1961-64, chmn. humanities, 1962-65; prof., chmn. English dept. U. Fla., 1966-69; dean arts and scis., Univ. prof. Va. Poly. Inst., 1969-70; chmn. English dept. Fla. State U., Tallahassee, 1970-73; prof. Fla. State U., 1970-90, Disting. prof., 1978-90; ret. Fla. State U., 1990; cons. U.S. Office Edn., 1967, 68, 69; lectr. Yeats Internat. Summer Sch., Ireland, 1964, 65, 68, 72, 74, 75, Internat. Congress Comparative Lit., Fribourg, Switzerland, 1964. Author: Neoplatonism of William Blake, 1961, Yeats's Quest for Eden, 1966, Yeats's Golden Dawn, 1974, Yeats's Theory of Theatre, 1975, W. B. Yeats and W. T. Horton, 1980; editor: (with Kathleen Raine) Thomas Taylor the Platonist, 1969 (with others), Yeats and the Occult, 1975, (with others) Letters to W.B. Yeats, 1977, (with W. K. Hood) A Critical Edition of Yeats's A Vision (1925), 1978, The Making of Yeats's "A Vision," 1987; gen. editor Yeats's "Vision" Papers, 1992; contbr. articles to profl. jours. Pres. Chapel Hill (N.C.) C. of C., 1965; bd. govs. Chapel Hill Pub. Library, 1959-65. Served to lt. comdr. USNR, 1942-46; comdr. Res. Mem. MLA (chmn. Celtic group 1967, 75), South Atlantic MLA (v.p. 1985, pres. 1986-87), Coll. English Assn. (pres. 1975-76). Democrat. Methodist. Home: 407 Plantation Rd Tallahassee FL 32303-4205

HARPER, GERARD EDWARD, lawyer; b. N.Y.C., Feb. 2, 1953; s. Eugene Walter and Muriel (Drumgoole) H.; m. Devereux Chatillon, Oct. 8, 1983; children: Amanda, Julia. BA, Rutgers U., 1975; JD, NYU, 1978. Bar: N.Y. 1980, U.S. Supreme Ct. 1986, D.C. 1989, U.S. Ct. Appeals (9th cir.) 1988), U.S. Ct. Appeals (2d cir.) 1991, U.S. Dist. Ct. (so. and ea. dists.) 1980, N.Y. 1985, U.S. Dist. Ct. (no. dist.) Calif., U.S. Dist. Ct. (D.C. cir.). Law clk. to Justice George MacKinnon U.S. Cir. Ct., Washington, 1978-79; assoc. Paul, Weiss, Rifkind, Wharton & Garrison, N.Y.C., 1979-86, ptnr., 1986—. Editor-in-chief NYU Law Rev., 1977-78. Gen. counsel, chmn. law com., mem. exec. com. N.Y. Dem. State Com., N.Y.C., 1987—. Mem. ABA, N.Y. State Bar Assn., N.Y. County Lawyers' Assn., Assn. of Bar of City of N.Y., Order of Coif. Roman Catholic. Office: Paul Weiss Rifkind Wharton & Garrison Ste 3700 1285 Avenue Of The Americas Fl 21 New York NY 10019-6065

HARPER, GLORIA JANET, artist, educator; children: Dan Conyers, Jan Girvan. Student, Famous Artists Sch., 1967-69, 69-71; BA in Comml. Art, Portland C.c., 1981; postgrad., Valley View Art Sch., 1982-89, Carrizzo Art Sch., 1983-89, Holdens Portrait Sch., 1989; studied with Daniel Greene, 1989, postgrad. in paralegal studies. Cert. art educator. Artist, art instr. Art By Gloria, 1980—; owner Art By Gloria Art Sch. and Gallery, Pendleton, Oreg., 1991—; lectr., workshop presenter in field, 1980—. Paintings and prints included in various mags. Mem. NAFE, Nat. Assn. Fine Artists, Water Color Soc. Am., Nat. Mus. Women in Arts, So. Career Inst. Profl. Legal Assts. (area rep.), Northwest Pastel Soc., Profl. Legal Assts., Pendleton C. of C. Avocations: photography and art of nature, hiking, gardening, learning. Home: PO Box 1734 Pendleton OR 97801-0570 Office: Art By Gloria 404 SE Dorion Ave Ste 204 Pendleton OR 97801-2531

HARPER, HARLAN, JR., lawyer; b. San Antonio, Sept. 15, 1928; s. Harlan and Julia Viola (Kelley) H.; m. Linda A. Steere, July 16, 1960; children: Anne Elizabeth, David Harlan. BA, So. Methodist U., Dallas, 1953, JD, 1957. Bar: Tex. 1957, U.S Dist. Ct. (no., ea. and we. dists.) Tex. 1957. Assoc. McNees & McNees, 1957, John Harrison, 1958-61; sr. ptnr. Fanning, Harper, Martinson, P.C. and predecessors, Dallas, 1961-97; semi-ret., 1997—. Served with USAF, 1953-55. Mem. Tex. Bar Assn., Pi Kappa Alpha. Baptist.

HARPER, HENRY H., military officer, retired; b. Ft. Benning, Ga., Aug. 24, 1934; s. H.M. and Frances Louise (Hearn) Harper; m. Helen Harpe, Apr. 2, 1960; children: Cynthia Jane, Linda Leigh. BS, U. Md., 1964; MA, George Washington U., 1965; Disting. grad., Indsl. Coll. Armed Forces, 1973. Commd. officer U.S. Army, 1954, advanced through grades to maj. gen., 1980; dep. comdg. gen. Armaments Command U.S. Army, Rock Island, Ill., 1977-79; dir. logistics U.S. European Command U.S. Army, Stuttgart, Fed. Republic Germany, 1979-82; comdg. gen. Depot System Command U.S. Army, Chambersburg, Pa., 1982-86; retired U.S. Army, 1986; corp. sr. v.p. Synovus Fin. Corp., Columbus, Ga., 1986-95; ret., 1995. Chmn. bd. dirs. Easter Seals West Ga., Inc.; chmn., bd. dirs. Goodwill Industries, Springer Opera House; bd. dirs. Universal Bank. Mem. Assn. U.S. Army (bd. govs., dir. Chambers Fort chpt. 1982-85), Columbus C. of C. (bd. dirs.). Episcopalian. Avocations: golf; jogging.

HARPER, JAMES EUGENE, plant physiologist; b. Syracuse, Kans., Jan. 19, 1940; s. Vernon C. and Margaret Harper; m. LaVerna J. Kesinger, July 24, 1964; children: Pamela S., Craig V. BS, Kans. State U., 1962, MS, 1966, PhD, 1968. Plant physiologist USDA, Urbana, Ill., 1968-81, 82-91, rsch. leader, location coord., 1991—, acting nat. program leader, 1993; vis. sci. Commonwealth Scis. and Indsl. Rsch. Orgn., Canberra, Australia, 1981-82. Editor: Physiological Limitations on Crop Growth, 1984; assoc. editor Crop Sci., 1980-83, tech. editor, 1983-85; assoc. editor Plant Physiology, 1987-92; contbr. more than 100 articles to profl. jours. in field. Bd. dirs. Sch. Dist. # 208, Homer, Ill., 1987-88. 1st lt. USANG, 1964-68. Fellow Am. Soc. Agronomy (bd. dirs. 1990-93), Crop Sci. Soc. Am. (bd. dirs. 1990-93); mem. Am. Soybean Assn. (tour recipient 1985), Am. Soc. Plant Physiologists, Lions (sec., pres. 1985-88). Avocations: automobile restoration, woodworking. Home: 1173 County Road 2400 E Saint Joseph IL 61873-9726 Office: USDA/ARS 1201 W Gregory Dr Urbana IL 61801-3838

HARPER, JAMES HOWARD, psychologist, hospital official; b. Jacksonville, Tex., Sept. 15, 1949; s. Howard and Ila Geneva (Cotton) H.; m. Christine Louise Johnson, Sept. 4, 1982; children: Timothy Wright, James Adam. BSc, Stephen F. Austin State U., Nacogdoches, Tex., 1971, MEd, 1976; postgrad., Tex. A&M U., Commerce, 1988-95. Lic. psychol. assoc., Tex. Social worker Rusk (Tex.) State Hosp., 1971-76, psychologist, 1976-85; psychologist University Park Hosp, Tyler, Tex., 1985-88, MHMR Regional Ctr., Tyler, 1988-90, Trinity Counseling Svc., Jacksonville, Tex., 1980-83, Tex. Dept. Criminal Justice, Rusk, 1990-91; psychologist, program adminstr. Rusk State Hosp., 1991—; pres. bd. dirs. Trinity Counseling, Jacksonville, 1980-83; bd. dirs. Tex. Assn. Alcohol and Drug Abuse Counselling, 1980-85. Author poetry and articles. Foreman, Smith County Grand Jury, Tyler, 1986; mayor pro tem, councilman City of Gallatin, Tex., 1980-82; elder Trinity Luth. Ch., Tyler, 1984-86; bd. dirs. Cherokee Civic Theatre, Rusk, 1993-95. Lutheran. Avocations: acting, photography, historical preservation, golf, poetry. Office: Rusk State Hosp PO Box 318 Rusk TX 75785-0318

HARPER, JAMES ROBERT, graphic designer; b. Chgo., Oct. 15, 1954. BFA, No. Ill. U., 1976; MA, Gov.'s State U., 1979; AAS, Tompkins Cortland C.C., Dryden, N.Y., 1985; postgrad., Cornell U., 1987-89. Instr. metalsmithing NCU Craft Studio Cornell U., Ithaca, N.Y., 1979-81; art dir. Shepard Advt., Inc., Ithaca, 1981-82; computer cons. Advt. Assocs., Inc., Ithaca, 1984-86; computer analyst, cons. Cornell U., Ithaca, 1989-95; pres. Jim Harper Designs, Ithaca, 1980—. Sec. IthacaNet, Inc., 1996-98.

HARPER, JAMES WELDON, III, finance consultant; b. Frederick, Md., Mar. 3, 1937; s. James Weldon Jr. and Mildred Mary (Conaway) H. Student, Duke U. Coll. rep. Time, Inc., 1955-59; jr. exec. trainee Merrill Lynch Pierce Fenner and Smith, N.Y.C., 1959-60; v.p. fin. planning Haight and Co., Inc., Washington, 1961-72; pres. fin. cons. Weldon Enterprises Ltd., Washington, 1973-95; founder, chmn., CEO Enviro Tek Corp., Waterford, Va., 1994—; former pres. U.S. Energy Conservation Service, Inc.; cons. Aries Corp.; nat. coord. Nat. Planned Giving Assocs., Inc., 1983-92; bd. dirs. 6 cos., 1962-91; involved in 115 corps., 98 partnerships; conservator Nat. Real Estate Trust for Health Care, Inc., 1987-92. Author 3 manuals. With U.S. Army, 1959. Methodist. Office: Enviro Tek Corp PO Box 366 Waterford VA 20197-0366

HARPER, JANET SUTHERLIN LANE, educational administrator, writer; b. La Grange, Ga., Apr. 2, 1940; d. Clarence Wilner and Imogene (Thompson); m. William Sterling Lane, June 28, 1964, (div. Jan. 1981); children: David Alan, Jennifer Ruth; m. John F. Harper, June 9, 1990. BA in English and Applied Music, LaGrange Coll., 1961; postgrad., Auburn U., 1963; MA in Journalism, U. Ga., Athens, 1979. Music and drama critic The Brunswick News, Brunswick, Ga., 1979—; info. asst. Glynn County Schs., Brunswick, 1979-82; adj. prof. Brunswick Coll., Ga., 1981-87; dir. pub. info. and publs. Glynn County Schs., Brunswick, 1982—. Contbg. editor Ga. Jour., 1981-84; editor, writer GAEL Conf. Jours., 1987-89. Organist St. Simons United Meth. Ch., 1981—; mem. Jekyll Island Music Theater Bd., 1994—, pres., 1994-97; mem. Golden Isles Arts and Humanities Bd., 1997—, pres., 1985-86, exec. bd., 1981-87, 96—, sec., 1998—; mem. adv. bd. Glynn County Ptnrs. in Edn., 1991—; mem. bd. Am. Cancer Soc., 1998—. Recipient award of excellence in sch. and cmty. rels. Ga. Bd. Edn., 1984, 92, Edn. Leadership award, Ga., 1989, disting. svc. award Ga. Sch. Pub. Rels. Assn., 1991. Mem. Nat. Sch. Pub. Rels. Assn. (Golden Achievement award 1985, 2 awards 1988, 90, 3 awards 1991, 92, 94), Ga. Sch. Pub. Rels. Assn. (pres. 1985-86), Ga. Assn. Ednl. Leaders (media rels. 1983—), Brunswick Press-Advt. Club (award of excellence in pub. rels. 1992), Brunswick Golden Isles C. of C., Mozart Soc., Phi Delta Kappa, Phi Kappa Phi, Sigma Delta Chi. Office: Glynn County Schs 1313 Egmont St Brunswick GA 31520-7244

HARPER, JOHN FRANK, cardiologist; b. Akron, Ohio, July 21, 1946; s. Frank E. and Jean E. (Sigmond) H.; m. Laurie Spencer, Dec. 20, 1969; children: David, Jonathan, Andrew, Anne. BA, So. Meth. U., 1968; MD, U. Tex. Dallas, 1972. Diplomate Am. Bd. Med. Examiners, Am. Bd. Internal Medicine, Cardiovascular Diseases. Intern Parkland Meml. Hosp., Dallas, 1972-73; resident, cardiology fellow VA Hosp., Dallas, 1973-75, 77-79; cardiologist Presby. Hosp. Dallas, 1979-92, chief cardiology sect., 1992—; sr. ptnr. North Tex. Heart Ctr., Dallas, 1991—; med. dir. Finley Ewing Cardiovascular Rehab. Ctr., Dallas, 1985-95. Maj. USAF, 1975-77. Fellow Am. Coll. Cardiology, Am. Heart Assn. (clin. coun. cardiology); mem. Tex. Med. Assn., Tex. Club Internists, Dallas County Med. Assn. Republican. Avocations: golf, running. Home: 4305 Lorraine Ave Dallas TX 75205-3707

HARPER, JUDSON MORSE, university administrator, consultant, educator; b. Lincoln, Nebr., Aug. 25, 1936; s. Floyd Sprague and Eda Elizabeth (Kelley) H.; m. Patricia Ann Kennedy, June 15, 1958; children: Jayson K., Stuart H., Neal K. B.S., Iowa State U., 1958, M.S., 1960, Ph.D., 1963. Registered profl. engr., Minn. Instr. Iowa State U., Ames, 1958-63; dept. head Gen. Mills, Inc., Mpls., 1964-69, venture mgr., 1969-70; prof., dept. head agrl. and chem. engring. Colo. State U., Ft. Collins, 1970-82, v.p. rsch. and info. tech., 1982—; Lady Davis scholar Technion, Haifa, Israel, 1978-79; interim pres. Colo. State U., Ft. Collins, 1989-90, cons. USAID, Washington, 1972-74, various comml. firms., 1975—. Author: Extrusion of Foods, 1982, Extrusion Cooking, 1989; editor newsletter Food, Pharm. & Bioengring. News, 1979-83, LEC Newsletter, 1976-89; contbr. articles to profl. publs.; patentee. Mem. sch. bd. St. Louis Park, Minn., 1968-70. Recipient Disting. Svc. award Colo. State U., 1977, Fulbright-Hayes scholar, 1978, Svc. award Centro de Investigaviones y Asistencia Technologica de Estado de Chihuahua, Chihuahua, Mex., 1980, Food Engring. award Dairy and Food Industry Supply Assn. and Am. Soc. Agrl. Engrs., 1983, Cert. of Merit, USDA Office Internat. Coop. and Devel., 1983, Cert. of Merit, Consejo Nacional de Ciencia y Technologie en Mexico, Mexico City, 1984, Profl. Achievement Citation Iowa State U., 1986, Cert. Appreciation Chinese Inst. of Food Tech., 1987, Charles Lory Pub. Svc. award, 1993, Hammer award The Nat. Performance Rev., 1994. Fellow Inst. Food Technologists (Internat. award 1990), AAAS; mem. Am. Inst. Chem. Engring. (dir. 1981-84), Am. Soc. Agrl. Engrs. (com. chmn. 1973-78, hon. engr. Rocky Mountain region), Am. Chem. Soc., Am. Soc. Engring. Edn. (com. chmn. 1976-77). Mem. Ind. United Methodist Ch. E-mail: jharper@research.colostate.edu. Home: 1818 Westview Rd Fort Collins CO 80524-1891 Office: Colo State U Office VP Rsch & Info Tech Fort Collins CO 80523-2001

HARPER, KENNETH CHARLES, clergyman; b. Detroit, Aug. 31, 1946; s. Charles Burdett and Marion Anna (Pankau) H.; m. Charlene Elizabeth Gates, Apr. 14, 1996; children: Charles William, David Peter, Andrew Scott. BS in Edn., Ill. State U., 1969; MDiv, Trinity Evang. Div. Sch., Deerfield, Ill., 1973; ThM, Princeton (N.J.) Theol. Sem., 1976; D of Ministry, San Francisco Theol. Sem., San Anselmo, Calif., 1986; postgrad., Pepperdine U., 1989-93. Ordained to ministry Presbyn. Ch., 1974. Edn. advisor Amwell Valley Commn., Reaville, N.J., 1973-74; asst. pastor 1st Presbyn. Ch., Mt. Holly, N.J., 1974-77; pastor 1st Presbyn. Ch., Herrin, Ill., 1977-82; sr. pastor 1st Presbyn. Ch., Westminster, Calif., 1982-94; pastor Chula Vista (Calif.) Presbyn. Ch., 1994-97, Ctrl. Presbyn. Ch., Miami, 1997—. Contbr. book revs. and articles to religious jours. Mem. Evang. Theol. Soc., Presbyns. for Renewal, Assn. Psychol. Type. Democrat. Office: Central Presbyn Ch 12455 SW 104th St Miami FL 33186*

HARPER, KENNETH FRANKLIN, retired state legislator, real estate broker; b. Covington, Ky., Jan. 15, 1931; s. Kenneth Wellington and Elizabeth Mary (Brickler) H.; m. Eileen Ann Kathman, May 16, 1953; children: Gregory, Scott, Glenn, Bryan, Lesley. Ed., U. Ky. Mem. Ky. Ho. of Reps., 1964-68; asst. commr. Ky. Dept. Child Welfare, 1969-70; commr. Ky. Dept. Pub. Info., 1970; sec. of state Commonwealth of Ky., 1971; broker, owner, pres. Harper Realty, 1986—; sr. cons. Shandwick USA Pub. Rels., Cin. and No. Ky.; mem. from 63d dist. Ky. Ho. of Reps., 1963-68, 82-94, vice chmn. tourism and energy com.; mem. adv. bd. Firstar Bank, N.A., Ctrl. Ky. Mem. exec. com. Kenton County Rep. Party, No. Ky.; chmn. No. Ky. Univ. Found.; past mem. Rep. State Ctrl. com.; commr. No. Ky. Conv. and Visitors Bur., chmn., 1991-92; mem. Southbank Ptnrs.; past state co-chmn. Am. Legis. Exch. Coun.; mem. No. Ky. Assn. for the Retarded; mem. Exec. Task Force on Hist. Preservation; mem. Greater Cin. Tall Stacks Commn., Greater Cin. film Commn.; bd. dirs. Anthem Blue Cross & Blue Shield, Midwest, No. Ky. U. Small Bus. Incubator. Recipient numerous Jaycee awards, Boss of Yr. award Nat. Secs. Assn., 1971, Walter L. Pieschel award No. Ky. C. of C., 1980, KMI Alumni Spirit of Excellence award, 1993, numerous others; Paul Harris fellow Rotary Internat., 1989; named to Outstanding Young Men of Am., 1964. Mem. Nat. Assn. Realtors, Ky. Assn. Realtors, No. Ky. Assn. Realtors, Nat. Rep. Legislators Assn. (past pres.). Roman Catholic. Home and Office: Harper Group LLC PO Box 17717 2700 Main Chase Ln Crestview Hills KY 41017

HARPER, LAWRENCE VERNON, human development educator; b. Oakland, Calif., July 7, 1935; s. Lawrence Averell and Anna Virginia (McCune) H.; m. Katherine Andrew Rayburn, Aug. 16, 1964; children: Michael James, Lisa Michele. BA in Sociology, U. Calif., Berkeley, 1957, PhD in Psychology, 1966. Staff fellow NIMH, Bethesda, Md., 1966-69; from asst. prof. to prof. human development U. Calif., Davis, 1969—, chmn. dept., 1990-98. Author: The Nurture of Human Behavior, 1989; co-author: Child Effects on Adults, 1977. Lt. (j.g.) USNR, 1957-59. Mem. AAAS, Animal Behavior Soc., Soc. for Rsch. in Child Devel., Internat. Soc. for Developmental Psychobiology. Avocations: hunting, restoring vintage automobiles. Office: U Calif Human & Commun Devel Davis CA 95616*

HARPER, LINDA RUTH, disabilities educator, consultant; b. Wilson, N.C., Dec. 16, 1943; d. John Hoover and Mary Edna (Finch) Lamm; m. Thomas Oliver Harper, Sr., Aug. 12, 1962; children: Thomas O., John Walter, Stephen Timothy. BS in home econs., Bob Jones Univ., 1967; MEd, Univ. S.C., 1976. Tchr. S.C. Pub. Schs., Camden, Greenville,, S.C., 1968-77; tchr., prin. Ga. Christian Sch., Union Point, 1979-86; asst. prin. N.C. Christian Sch., Goldsboro, N.C., 1986-87; tchr. AG & SP cons. program specialist N.C. Pub. Schs., Goldsboro, N.C., 1987—; del., presenter Am. Assn. Mental Retardation, Rep. of China, 1996; edn. con. O'Berry Ctr., Goldsboro, N.C., 1990—. Author: Meal Preparation Teaching Individuals with DD to Cook, 1998, Frozen Foods, 1961. Co-founder Bethel Christian Sch., 1979; state historian 4-H Club, 1961, co-presenter4-H Demonstration Cooperative Program, 1959; sunday sch. tchr., pianist, 1963—, women's club pres., 1996-97, mission trips at various chs., 1992-97. Recipient Leadership Achievement award Nash County 4-H Club, 1961, Nat. Honor Club award, 1961, Nat. Key Club, 1962. pres. of local chap. of NCAE (North Carolina Assn. of Educators, Inc.), 1998-99, Mem. NEA, Am. Assn. Mental Retardation (southeast region chair 1997-99, exec. bd. 1997—), Coun. for Exceptional Children, State Employees Assn., Edn. Leadership Prog., East CArolina Univ., 1999. Baptist. Avocations: sewing, piano, singing, flower arranging, food preparation. Office: O'Berry Ctr 400 Old Smithfield Rd Goldsboro NC 27530-8464

HARPER, MICHAEL JOHN KENNEDY, obstetrics and gynecology educator; b. London, Feb. 25, 1935; came to U.S., 1964; s. John Kennedy and Helen Malvina (Koeller) H.; m. Marian Wedd, July 23, 1960 (div. Feb. 1982); children: Charlotte G.K. Prather, Tristram J.K., Felicity W.K.; m. Ann Carlene Vandeventer, Feb. 16, 1985; 1 child, Helen H.K. BA in Agr., U. Cambridge, Eng., 1957, MA, 1961, PhD in Reproductive Physiology, 1962, ScD, 1979; post-grad. diploma, U. Reading, Eng., 1958; MBA, U. Tex., San Antonio, 1984. Tech. officer pharm. div. Imperial Chem. Industries Ltd., Cheshire, Eng., 1960-64, 65-66; vis. scientist Worcester Found. for Exptl. Biology, Shrewsbury, Mass., 1964-65; staff scientist Worcester Found. for Exptl. Biology, Shrewsbury, 1966-68, sr. scientist, 1968-72; med. officer Human Reproduction Sect. WHO, Geneva, 1972-75; assoc. prof. U. Tex. Health Sci. Ctr., San Antonio, 1975-81, prof. ob-gyn. and physiology, 1981-93; prof. ob-gyn. and cell biology Baylor Coll. Medicine, Houston, 1993-95; prof. ob-gyn Eastern Va. Med. Sch., Arlington, 1995—, dir. Consortium for Indsl. Collaboration in Contraceptive Rsch./ CONRAD Program, 1995—; lectr. Clark U., 1971; cons. NIH, Bethesda, Md., 1970—, WHO, Geneva, 1974-87, USAID, Arlington, Va., 1988—, Andrew W. Mellon Found., N.Y.C., 1991—; mem. com. reporting on Contraceptive Rsch. and Devel.: Looking to the Future, 1996, also others. Author: Birth Control Technologies, 1983, paperback edit., 1985; contbr. numerous articles to profl. jours.; inventor alkene/alkanol derivatives (Tamoxifen), 1963, alkene devivatives, 1985. Recipient Woodman prize, U. of Cambridge, 1956, Agr. Food Products prize, U. Reading, Eng., 1958, Rsch. Career Devel. award, NIH, Bethesda, Md., 1968-72. Fellow Inst. of Biology (Eng.); mem. Soc. for Endocrinology (Eng.), Soc. for Study of Fertility (Eng.), Endocrine Soc., Am. Assn. of Anatomists, Soc. for Study of Reproduction, Soc. for Gynecologic Investigation, Am. Physiol. Soc. Avocations: classical music, reading, hunting, automobiles, genealogy. Office: Conrad Program E Va Medical Sch 1611 N Kent St Ste 806 Arlington VA 22209-2111 *Honesty, integrity and the fortitude to withstand disappointment are key ingredients for a career in life science. Progress in biological research is slow and often imperceptible. By encouraging one's juniors to grow professionally, one's own growth is enhanced.*

HARPER, PATRICIA M., state legislator; b. Cresco, Dec. 4, 1932; d. Patrick Mullaney and Martha Gossman; 1 child, Susan. BA, U. No. Iowa, MA. Tchr. secondary math. and sci., 1955-86; mem. Iowa Ho. of Reps., 1987-90, 92-96, Iowa Senate, 1997—. Bd. dirs. Black Hawk/Grundy Mental Health Ctr., Grin and Grow Day Care Ctrs. Mem. AAUW, LWV, Waterloo Edn. Assn., Alliance for Mentally Ill. Democrat. Home: 3336 Santa Maria Dr Waterloo IA 50702-5334 Office: Iowa Senate State Capitol Des Moines IA 50319

HARPER, RICHARD HENRY, film producer, director; b. San Jose, Calif., Sept. 15, 1950; s. Walter Henry and Priscilla Alden (Browne) H.; m. Ann Marie Morgan, June 19, 1976; children: Christine Ann, Paul Richard, James Richard. Show designer Walt Disney Imagineering, Glendale, Calif., 1971-76; motion picture producer, dir. Harper Films, Inc., La Canada, Calif., 1976—. Producer, dir. (films) Impressions de France, Disney World, Fla., 1982, Magic Carpet Round the World, Disneyland, Tokyo, 1983, American Journeys, Disneyland, Calif., 1985, Collecting America, Nat. Gallery Art, Washington, 1988, Hillwood Mus., Washington, 1989, Journey Into the 4th Dimension for Sanrio World, Journey Into Nature for Sanrio World, Japan, 1990, Masters of Illusion, Nat. Gallery of Art, Washington, 1992. Recipient more than 150 awards world-wide for outstanding motion picture prodn. including Silver trophy Cannes Internat. Film Festival, 2 Gold awards Internat. Festival of the Ams., 1981, 82, 14 Golden Eagle C.I.N.E. awards, 1977-92, Emmy award Nat. Acad. TV Arts and Scis., 1993. Mem. Acad. of Motion Picture Arts and Scis.

HARPER, ROB MARCH, artist, educator; b. Chico, Calif., Oct. 5, 1942; s. Robert Wreathal and Lorene Marie (March) H.; m. Georgia Lee Schiller, May 31, 1971. BFA, San Francisco Art Inst., 1971; MFA, Washington U., St. Louis, 1974. Artist/illustrator Oakland, Calif., 1974-88; tchr. adult edn. Alameda County Pub. Schs., Oakland, Hayward, 1988—; tchr./artist Oakland Parks and Recreation dept., 1988—. One person show at Lucien Labaudt Art Gallery, San Francisco, 1974; exhibited in shows including Nelson Gallery Art, Kansas City, Mo., 1974, St. Louis Art Mus., 1974, Butler Inst. Am. Art, Youngstown, Ohio, 1975, Cooperstown (N.Y.) Art Assn., 1975, 77, E.B. Crocker Art Gallery, Sacramento, Calif., 1976, Civic Arts Gallery, Walnut Creek, Calif., 1976, Marrietta (Ohio) Coll., 1976, Chautauqua (N.Y.) Art Assn., 1977, Miniature Painters, Sculptors and Gravers Soc. Washington, Arts Club of Washington, 1977, 79, Nat. Soc. Painters in Casein and Acrylic, Inc., The Am. Acad. and Inst. Arts and Letters, N.Y.C., 1979, Lynn House Gallery, Antioch, Calif., 1994, Chico (Calif.) Art Ctr., 1994, Sarratt Gallery, Vanderbilt U., Nashville, 1996, Maude Kerns Art Ctr., Eugene, Oreg., 1996, Spartanburg (S.C.) County Mus. Art, 1996, Rosewood Arts Centre Gallery, Kettering, Ohio, 1999, San Francisco Mus. of Modern Art Rental Gallery-Group Show, 1999; represented in permanent collection O.K. Harris Gallery, N.Y.C., also pvt. collections. Recipient Hallmark award-purchase, 1973-74, Butler Inst. Am. Art purchase prize, 1975. Home: 3099 California St Oakland CA 94602-3907

HARPER, ROBERT, actor; b. N.Y.C., May 19, 1951. BA in English with high distinction, Rutgers Coll., 1974. Mem. repertory co. Arena Stage, Washington, 1974-76; actor, 1974—; guest artist Rutgers U., New Brunswick, N.J., 1977, 84. Actor Long Wharf Theater, New Haven, Conn., 1978, 84, Theater for New City, N.Y.C., 1981, (Broadway) Once in a Lifetime, 1978, The Inspector General, 1978, (featured actor Broadway) The American Clock, 1980, (TV films) J. Edgar Hoover, The Wrong Man, Not Quite Human, Payoff, Running Mates, The Story of Bill W, Paper Angels, Ruby Ridge, (guest actor TV series) Newhart, Roseanne, Murphy Brown, Wiseguy, L.A. Law, NYPD Blue, Law and Order, (featured actor TV series) Frank's Place, 1987-88, (films) Creepshow, 1982, Once Upon a Time in America, 1984, Amazing Grace and Chuck, 1987, Twins, 1989, Final Analysis, 1992, Deconstructing Harry, 1997, Molly, 1999. Advisor charity events The Laugh Factory, Hollywood, 1981—. Recipient Regents fellowship U. Calif., 1974, Kennedy Ctr. award Am. Coll. Theater Festival, 1974. Mem. MLA (spkr. conv. 1996), ACLU (sponsor Garden Event 1994), Acad. Motion Picture Arts and Scis., Acad. TV Arts and Scis., Am. Soc. Aesthetics, Screen Actor's Guild, Actor's Equity Assn. Office: 8721 Santa Monica Blvd Ste 151 West Hollywood CA 90069-4507

HARPER, ROBERT ALLAN, consulting psychologist, retired; b. Dayton, Ohio, Apr. 25, 1915; s. Earl Paull and Mary (Belden) H.; m. Flora Mie Bridges; children: Robert Belden, John Paull. Student, U. Dayton, 1934-36; B.A., Ohio State U., 1938, M.A., 1939, Ph.D., 1942. Instr. Kent State U., 1942-43; analyst War Manpower Commn., 1943; assoc. prof. Wagner Coll., 1943-45; psychiat. social worker U.S. Army, 1945-46; asst. prof. Ohio State U., 1946-50, dir. marriage counseling clinic, 1949-50; chmn. family life dept., dir. marriage counseling service Merrill-Palmer Inst., Detroit, 1950-53; pvt. practice psychotheraphy Washington, 1953-92. Author: (with John F. Cuber) Problems of American Society, 1948, Marriage, 1949, Psychoanalysis and Psychotherapy: 36 Systems, 1959, (with Albert Ellis) Creative Marriage, 1961, A Guide to Rational Living, 1961, 75, 98, (with Walter R. Stokes) 45 Levels to Sexual Understanding and Enjoyment, 1971, The New Psychotherapies, 1975; Cons. editor: Jour. Sex Edn. and Therapy, Psychotherapy, Jour. Rational-Emotive Therapy, Jour. Contemporary Psychotherapy, Internat. Jour. Family Therapy. Fellow Am. Psychol. Assn. (pres. div. psychotherapy 1978-79, pres. div. cons. psychology 1980-81, pres. div. humanistic psychology 1983-84, exec. bd. div. ind. practice, coun. reps. 1978-84, 90-96), Am. Assn. Marriage Counselors (sec. 1954-58, pres. 1960-62), Nat. Coun. Family Rels. (dir. 1951-55), Am. Acad. Psychotherapists (pres. 1961-63), Am. Group Psychotheraphy Assn., Eastern Psychol. Assn., D.C. Psychol. Assn. (dir. 1982-85); mem. Am. Soc. Psychologists in Pvt. Practice (exec. com.), Soc. Sci. Study Sex, Interam. Soc. Psychologists, Am. Soc. Group Psychotherapy and Psychodrama, Internat. Council Psychologists (exec. bd. 1971-74), N.Y. Acad. Scis., Internat. Soc. Gen. Semantics, Inst. Rational Living (bd.), ACLU, Washington Soc. Clin. Psychologists (exec. com.), Nat. Acads. Practice (treas. 1982-88), Phi Beta Kappa. Club: Cosmos. Home: 4903 Potomac Ave NW Washington DC 20007-1541

HARPER, S. BIRNIE, business brokerage company owner; b. Ft. Smith, Ark., June 8, 1944; s. S. Birnie and Margaret (Marshall) H.; m. Fern Dodson, 1969; children—Eliza, Sam, Dodson, Sara. BS in Commerce, Washington and Lee U., 1966; MBA, Harvard U., 1968. With Mid-Am. Industries Inc., Ft. Smith, 1968-88, v.p. fin., 1975-79, exec. v.p., 1979-82, CFO, 1982-95, exec. v.p., COO, 1985-86, pres., 1986-88, also bd. dirs.; pres. Wortz Co., Poteau, Okla., 1989-90, pres., CEO, 1990-95, also bd. dirs.; pres., owner Sunbelt Bus. Brokers, Ft. Smith, 1995—. Pres., bd. dirs. Ft. Smith Boys Club, 1982—; trustee Sparks Regional Med. Ctr., 1978-84, 94—; bd. dirs. Old Ft. Mus., 1982-85, 86-90, pres., 1983, 89; sr. warden St. John's Episcopal Ch., 1982-83; bd. dirs. United Way Ft. Smith, 1976-78. Home: 2502 Greenridge Dr Fort Smith AR 72903-5104 Office: Sunbelt Bus Brokers 423 Rogers Ave Fort Smith AR 72901-1911

HARPER, SANDRA STECHER, university administrator; b. Dallas, Sept. 21, 1952; d. Lee Roy and Carmen (Crespo) Stecher; m. Dave Harper, July 6, 1974; children: Justin, Jonathan. BS in Edn., Tex. Tech. U., 1974; MS, U. N. Tex., 1979, PhD, 1985. Speech/reading tchr. Nazareth (Tex.) High Sch., 1974-75; speech/English tchr. Collinsville (Tex.) High Sch., 1975-77, Pottsboro (Tex.) High Sch., 1977-79; instr. comm. Austin Coll., Sherman, Tex., 1980-82; rsch. asst. U. N. Tex., Denton, 1982-84; vis. instr. comm. Austin Coll., Sherman, 1985; from asst. prof. to assoc. prof. comms. McMurry Coll., Abilene, Tex., 1985-95; dean Coll. Arts and Scis. McMurry U., Abilene, Tex., 1990-95; v.p. for acad. affairs Oklahoma City U., 1995-98; asst. dir. NEH univ. core curriculum project McMurry U., Abilene, Tex.; provost, v.p. for acad. affairs Tex. A&M, Corpus Christi, 1998—, prof. comms., 1998—; CIES mentor for Russian adminstr. from Moscow State U., Ulyanovsk, 1995-96; mem. adv. bd. Coll. Am. Indian Devel., 1995-98; critic judge Univ. Interscholastic League, Austin, 1980-93; mem. adv. bd. Univ. Rsch. Consortium, Abilene, 1990-95. Contbr. articles to profl. jours.; author: To Serve the Present Age, 1990; co-author U.S. Dept. Edn. Title III Grant. Planner TEAM Abilene, 1991; del. Tex. Commn. for Libr. and Info. Svcs., Austin, 1991; chair Abilene Children Today: Life and Cmty. Skills Task Force, 1994-95; del. Oklahoma City Ednl. TV Consortium, 1997-98; bd. dirs. South Tex. Pub. Broadcasting, 1998—, Leadership Corpus Christi. Named Outstanding Faculty Mem., McMurry U., 1988, Outstanding Adminstrv., 1993; Media Rsch. scholar, Ctr. for Population Options, 1989. Mem. Nat. Communication Assn., Am. Assn. of Higher Edn. Democrat. Roman Catholic. Office: Tex A&M Corpus Christi 6300 Ocean Dr Corpus Christi TX 78412-5503

HARPER, SHIRLEY FAY, nutritionist, educator, consultant, lecturer; b. Auburn, Ky., Apr. 23, 1943; d. Charles Henry and Annabelle (Gregory) Belcher; m. Robert Vance Harper, May 19, 1973; children: Glenda, Debra, Teresa, Suzanna, Cynthia. BS, Western Ky. U., 1966, MS, 1982. Cert. nutritionist and lic. dietitian, Ky. Dir. dietetics Logan County Hosp., Russellville, Ky., 1965-80; cons. Western State Hosp., Hopkinsville, Ky., 1983-84, instnl. dietetic adminstr., 1984-88; dietitian Rivendell Children's Psychiat. Hosp., Bowling Green, Ky., 1988-90; instr. nutrition Western Ky. U., Bowling Green, 1990-92; cons. Auburn (Ky.) Nursing Ctr., 1976-95, Belle Meade Home, Greenville, Ky., 1980—, Brookfield Manor, Hopkinsville, Ky., 1983—, Sparks Nursing Ctr., Central City, Ky., 1983—, Muhlenberg Cmty. Hosp., Greenville, 1989—, Russellville (Ky.) Health Care Manor, 1978-83, 92—, Westlake Cumberland Hosp., Columbia, Ky., 1993—, Franklin-Simpson Meml. Hosp., Franklin, Ky., 1993—; nutrition instr. Madisonville (Ky.) Cmty. Coll., 1995-98. Mem. regional bd. dirs. ARC of Ky., Frankfort, 1990-96; vice chair ARC of Logan County, 1992-93, chmn., 1993-96, 97—; bd. dirs. Logan County ARC United Way, 1993—; co-chair adv. coun. devel. disabilities Lifeskills, 1992-93, adv. coun. Lifeskills Residential Living Group Home, 1993—, human rights adv. coun., 1994—; chair Let's Build our Future Campaign; nutrition del. Citizen Am. Program to USSR, 1990; adv. chair for vocat. edn., Russellville; mem. adv. coun. for home econs. and family living, We. Ky. U., 1990-93; bd. dirs. ARC of Logan County for United Way, 1993—; del. 24th Internat. Congress on Arts and Comm., Oxford (Eng.) U., 1997. Recipient Outstanding Svc. award Am. Dietetic Assn. Found., 1993, Outstanding Svc. award Barren River Mental Health-Mental Retardation Bd., 1987, Svc. Appreciation award Logan-Russellville Assn. for Retarded Citizens, 1987, Internat. Woman of Yr. award for contribution to Nutrition and Humanity, Internat. Biographical Assn., 1993-94, World Lifetime Achievement award Am. Biographical Inst., 1995; inaugurated Lifetime Dep. Gov., Am. Biographical Rsch. Bd., 1995, Pres.'s award ARC of Logan County, 1996, award of excellence Oxford, Eng. Internat. Congress on Arts and Comm., Internat. Sash of Acad., Am. Biograph. Inst., 1997. Mem. Am. Dietetic Assn., Nat. Nutrition Network, Ky. Dietetic Assn. (pres. Western dist. 1976-77, Outstanding Dietitian award 1984), Bowling Green-Warren County Nutrition Coun., Nat. Ctr. for Nutrition and Dietetics (charter), Ky. Nutrition Coun., Logan County Home Economist Club (sec. 1994-95, v.p. 1995-96, pres. 1996-97), Internat. Biog. Assn., Internat. Platform Assn., Gerontol. Nutritionist, Oncology Nutrition, Diabetes Care and Edn., Dietitians in Nutrition Support, Dietitians in Gen. Clin. Practice, Cons. Dietitians in Health Care, Dietetic Educators of Practice Nutrition, Edn. of Health Profls., Nutrition Rsch. and Nutrition Edn. for Pub. Practice Groups, Phi Upsilon Omicron (pres. Beta Delta alumni chpt. 1994-96, Outstanding Alumni award 1997). Avocations: music, drawing and art, poetry, reading, cake decorating. Home and Office: 443 Hopkinsville Rd Russellville KY 42276-1286

HARPER, VERNE JAY, petroleum landman; b. Longview, Tex., Oct. 8, 1952; s. John D. and Vesta P. (Bray) H.; m. Marilyn C. Harper; children: Shanda, Jeremy, Weston, Skyler. Student, Kilgore (Tex.) Coll., 1984—. Draftsman King Tool, Longview, 1978-79; petroleum landman Longview, 1979—. Contbr. (anthology) An Angry White Male, 1995. Avocations: auto racing, baseball, football. Office: PO Box 9624 Longview TX 75608-9624

HARPER, W(ALTER) JOSEPH, financial consultant; b. Columbus, Ohio, Apr. 6, 1947; s. J. Joseph and Patricia A. (Whetzle) H.; m. J. Lynn Rutherford, Aug. 1, 1970; children: Tracy, Kelly, Brett. BS in Edn., Ohio State U., 1970. Cert. fin. planner; registered investment advisor, Ohio. Tchr., coach Lake Wales (Fla.) Schs., 1970-71, Westerville (Ohio) Pub. Schs., 1971-74; securities salesman, fin. planner Investors Diversified Svcs., Columbus, 1974-83; fin. planner, investment mgr. Harper Assocs., Columbus, 1983—. Mem. golf team Ohio State U., 1966-69. Mem. Nat. Assn. Personal Fin. Advisors, Internat. Assn. Fin. Planning, Inst. Cert. Fin. Planners (bd. dirs., pres. Ctrl. Ohio Soc.), Rotary, Scioto Country Club, Worthington Hills Country Club. Republican. Avocations: sports, children's activities, duck hunting. *

HARPER, WILLIAM LLOYD, federal judge; b. 1931. AB, Emory U., 1954, JD, 1956. Atty. Dorsey & Dorsey, Atlanta, 1959-61; asst. atty. gen. State of Ga., 1961-71; exec. counsel Gov. of Ga., 1971-77; U.S. atty. No. Dist. Ga., 1977-81; atty. Hurt, Richardson, Garner, Todd & Cadenhead, 1981-84; magistrate judge U.S. Dist. Ct. (no. dist.) Ga., Atlanta, 1984—. 1st lt. USAF, 1956-58, maj. gen. USAFR ret. Office: 1629 US Courthouse 75 Spring St SW Atlanta GA 30303-3309

HARPER, WILLIAM WAYNE, broadcast executive; b. Peoria, Ill., 1943. BA, Sanamon State U., 1985; MSA, Ctrl. Mich. U., 1991. Dir. Sta. WAND-TV, Decatur, Ill., 1962-70; account exec. Sta. WTWD-TV, Terre Haute, Ill., 1970-74, Sta. WFIE-TV, Evansville, Ind., 1974-77, Sta. WAND-TV, Decatur, 1977-80; gen. sales mgr. Sta. WRSP-TV, Springfield, Ill., 1980-83; v.p., gen. mgr. Sta. WVFT-TV, Roanoke, Va., 1983-84, Sta. WSMH-TV, Flint, Mich., 1984-90, Sta. WBRE-TV, Wilkes-Barre, Pa., 1990-94; gen. mgr. Sta. WBBJ-TV, Jackson, Tenn., 1994-95, Sta. WRSP/WCCU-TV, Springfield, 1997—. Office: Sta WRSP/WCCO-TV 3003 Old Rochester Rd Springfield IL 62703-5664

HARPHAM, VIRGINIA RUTH, violinist; b. Huntington, Ind., Dec. 10, 1917; d. Pyrl John and Nellie Grace (Whitaker) Harpham; m. Dale Lamar Harpham, Dec. 25, 1938; children: Evelyn, George. AB, Morehead State U., 1939. Violinist, Nat. Symphony Orch., Washington, 1956-90, prin. of second violin sect., 1964-90; mem. Lywen String Quartet, 1960-69. Nat. Symphony String Quartet, 1973-82. Episcopalian. Home: 5354 43d St NW Washington DC 20015-2008

HARPOOTLIAN, RICHARD ARA, lawyer, political party official; b. Bklyn., Jan. 23, 1949; s. Harold C. and Joan (Williams) H.; m. Pamela McCreery, Jan. 1, 1972. BS, Clemson U., 1971; JD, U. S.C., 1974. Bar: S.C. 1974. Asst. solicitor Solicitor's Office (5th cir.), Columbia, S.C., 1975-77, dep. solicitor, 1977-83; ptnr. Swerling & Harpootlian, Columbia, 1983-90; solicitor Solicator's Office (5th cir.), Cola, S.C., 1991-95; pvt. practice, 1995—. Chmn. S.C. Dem. Party, 1998—. Methodist. Home: 1721 Enoree Ave Columbia SC 29205-2907 Office: 1720 Main St Suite 304 Columbia SC 29201*

HARPRING, LINDA JEAN, critical care and psychiatric nurse; b. Louisville, Ky., Mar. 28, 1956; d. James Phillip and Ellabelle Jean (Crowder) Anderson; children: Bradley, Vanessa, Frances, Joseph. BSN, U. Louisville, 1989, postgrad., 1995—. RN, Ky. Staff nurse Audubon Regional Med. Ctr., Louisville, 1989-90; nurse clinician Visiting Nurses Assn. Louisville, 1990-95; staff nurse Southwest Hosp., Louisville, 1990-98; rsch. coord. electrophysiology-cardiology U. Louisville, 1993-94; staff nurse Ctr. for Behavioral Health Bapt. East Hosp., 1996—. Mem. alumni bd. govs. U. Louisville Sch. Nursing, 1988-97. Mem. Sigma Theta Tau. Avocations: watercolor painting, charcoal & pencil sketching, poetry, flute. Home: 2234 Arthur Ford Ct #3 Louisville KY 40217

HARPSTER, JAMES ERVING, lawyer; b. Milw., Dec. 24, 1923; s. Philo E. and Pauline (Daanen) H. PhB, Marquette U., 1950, LLB, 1952. Bar: Wis. 1952, Tenn. 1953; dir. info. svcs. Nat. Cotton Council Am., Memphis, 1952-55; dir. public rels. Christian Bros. Coll., 1956; mgr. govt. affairs dept. Memphis C. of C., 1956-62; exec. v.p. Rep. Assn. Memphis and Shelby County, 1962-64; individual practice law, Memphis, 1965; ptnr. Rickey, Shankman, Blanchard, Agee & Harpster, and predecessor firm, Memphis, 1966-80, Harpster & Baird, 1980-83; pvt. practice, Memphis, 1984—. Mem. Shelby County Tax Assessor's Adv. Com., 1960-61; editor, asst. counsel Memphis and Shelby County Charter Com., 1962; mem. Shelby County Election Commn., 1968-70; mem. Tenn. State Bd. Elections, 1970-72, sec., 1972; mem. Tenn. State Election Commn., 1973-83, chmn., 1974, sec., 1975-83; a founder Lions Inst. for Visually Handicapped Children, 1954, chmn. E. H. Crump Meml. Football Game for Blind, 1956; pres. Siena Student Aid Found., 1960; bd. dirs. Memphis Public Affairs Forum; mem. Civic Rsch. Com., Inc., Citizens Assn. Memphis and Shelby County; Republican candidate Tenn. Gen. Assembly, 1964; v.p. Nat. Council Rep. Workshops, 1967-69; pres. Rep. Workshop Shelby County, 1967, 71, 77, 78, Rep. Assn. Memphis and Shelby County, 1966-67; chmn. St. Michael the Defender chpt. Catholics United for the Faith, 1973, 75, 89-92. With USAAF, 1942-46. Mem. Tenn. Bar Assn., Wis. Bar Assn., Navy League U.S., Cardinal Mindszenty Found., Am. Legion, Latin Liturgy Assn. Roman Catholic. Home: 3032 E Glengarry Rd Memphis TN 38128-2984 Office: 100 N Main St Ste 3217 Memphis TN 38103-0539

HARPSTER, ROBERT EUGENE, engineering geologist; b. Olney, Ill., Sept. 25, 1930; s. Christian Edward and Margaret (Tatum) H.; m. Carol Ann Dewald, Nov. 25, 1977; step-children: Larry Britt, Charla Britt. BS, Beloit Coll., 1952; MA, U. Tex., 1957. Registered geologist Calif.; cert. engring. geologist Calif., cert. quality assurance lead auditor. Petroleum geologist Geo Svc. Co., Abilene, Tex., 1952; engring. soil instr. Corp Engrs., Ft. Belvoir, Va., 1952-54; project geologist Bechtel Corp., Vernon, Calif., 1956-57; sr. project engr. geologist dept. water resources State Calif., Sacramento, 1957-73; sr. project engr. geologist Woodward-Clyde Cons., San Francisco, 1973-80, mgr. and implementator for internat. engring. projects, v.p. quality assurance/applied sci., 1980-88; quality assurance, organizer and implementor Woodward-Cyde Coms., Las Vegas, Nev., 1988-93; sr. quality assurance specialist, design rev. MACTEC, CER/SAIC, Las Vegas, Nev., 1993—; mem. tech. rev. bds. U.S. Gov. and pvt. industries, San Francisco, 1972--; instr. Antelope Community Coll., Lancaster, Calif., 1969-72; del. People to People, USSR, 1991. Author: Selected Clays used for Dam/Fills Construction, 1979, Methods of Investigating Faults, 1979. coach swimming Antelope Valley YMCA, Lancaster, 1969-72. Sgt. U.S. Army, 1952-54. Fellow Geological Soc. Am., Assn. Engring. Geologist (mem. chmn., v.p. 1961-63, vice chmn. 1959-62), Am. Soc. Civil Engrs., Am. Soc. for Quality Control, Earthquake Engr. Rsch. Inst., Interanl Clay Mineral Soc. Achievements include field methods for investigating faulting, and development of x-ray diffraction studies for relative age dating of paleosoils. Home: 5735 Buena Vista Ave Oakland CA 94618-2120

HARR, LAWRENCE FRANCIS, lawyer; b. Broken Bow, Nebr., Sept. 1, 1938; s. Joseph and Dorothy (Gleason) H.; m. Susan Smithberger; children: Sharyl, Steve, Brian, Burke, BSBA, Creighton U., 1960, JD, 1962. Bar: Nebr. 1962, Ill. 1971. Dept. atty. Nebr. Ins. Dept., Lincoln, 1963-69; gen. counsel, chief adminstrv. officer Consumer Credit Ins. Assn., Chgo., 1969-75; exec. v.p., exec. counsel Mut. of Omaha Ins. Cos., 1975—; chmn. Nebr. Guarantee Assn.; chmn. Nat. Orgn. of Life & Health Ins. Guaranty Assn.; bd. dirs. Omaha Indemnity Co., Mutual of Omaha Investors Svcs., Inc., Omaha Property and Casualty. Mem. exec. com., former chmn. Nebr. Ins. Fedn.,

Lincoln. Capt. U.S. Army 1962-1963. Mem. ABA, Nebr. Bar Assn., Omaha Bar Assn., Omaha C. of C. (past chmn. ins. execs. com.). Roman Catholic. Home: 9834 Harney Pkwy N Omaha NE 68114-4945 Office: Mut of Omaha Ins Co Mutual of Omaha Plz Omaha NE 68175

HARR, ROBERT FRANCIS, physicist; b. Washington, Nov. 23, 1962; s. Robert J. and N. Grace H. BS in Physics, Carnegie-Mellon U., 1984; MS in Physics, U. Calif., Berkeley, 1987, PhD in Physics, 1990. Assoc. rsch. physicist Yale U., New Haven, Conn., 1990-94, rsch. physicst, 1994-95; asst. prof. Wayne State U., Detroit, 1995-96, asst. prof. physics, 1996—. Contbr. articles to profl. jours. Wayne State U. Rsch. grantee, 1997; Tex. Nat. Rsch. Lab. Commn. fellow, 1993-94. Mem. IEEE, Am. Phys. Soc. Office: Wayne State U Dept Physics 666 W Hancock St Detroit MI 48201

HARRAWOOD, PAUL, civil engineering educator; b. Akin, Ill., Aug. 28, 1928; s. Raymond E. and Verdie Alma (Galbraith) H.; m. June Anne Harris, Nov. 28, 1953; 1 child, Laura Anne. B.S., U. Mo.-Rolla, 1951, M.S., 1956; Ph.D. (NSF fellow), N.C. State U., 1967. Instr. civil engring. U. Mo., Rolla, 1954-56; asst. prof. Duke U., Durham, N.C., 1956-67, asst. dean engring., 1961-62; assoc. prof. Vanderbilt U., Nashville, 1967-70, dir. engring. sci. div., 1967-71, prof., 1970—, assoc. dean engring., 1967-79, acting dean engring., 1970-71, dean engring., 1979-86; prof. emeritus civil engring, dean emeritus Sch. of Engring., Vanderbilt U., Nashville, 1997—; test engr. McDonnell Aircraft Corp., 1957; constrn. mgmt. engr. U.S. Army C.E., 1958. Served with USNR, 1951-54. Named Engr. of Year Tenn. Soc. Profl. Engrs., 1986. Mem. ASCE, Soc. Am. Mil. Engrs., Am. Soc. Engring. Edn., Am. Assn. Higher Edn., AAAS, Sigma Xi, Tau Beta Pi, Chi Epsilon. Home: 5314 Camelot Ct Brentwood TN 37027-4114 Office: Vanderbilt U PO Box 1607 Nashville TN 37202-1607

HARRE, ALAN FREDERICK, university president; b. Nashville, Ill., June 12, 1940; s. Adolph Henry and Hilda (Vogt) H.; m. Diane Carole Mack, Aug. 9, 1964; children: Andrea Lyn, Jennifer Leigh, Eric Stephen. BA, Concordia Sr. Coll., 1962; MDiv, Concordia Sem., St. Louis, 1966; MA, Presbyn. Sch. Christian Edn., Richmond, Va., 1967; PhD, Wayne State U., 1976. Ordained to ministry Luth. Ch. Asst. pastor St. James Luth. Ch. of Grosse Pointe, Grosse Pointe Farms, Mich., 1967-73; asst. prof. theology Concordia Tchrs. Coll., Seward, Nebr., 1973-78, asst. to pres., 1981, assoc. prof. theology, 1978-84, dean student affairs, 1982-84, acting pres., 1984; pres. Concordia Coll., St. Paul, 1984-88, Valparaiso (Ind.) U., 1988—. Author: Close the Back Door, 1984. Bd. dirs. Munster Med. Rsch. Found., Northwest Ind. Forum, Ind. Campus Compact, Independent Colls. Ind. Found., Luth. Ednl. Conf. Am., The Luther Inst. Mem. Am. Assn. Higher Edn., Ind. Conf. of Higher Edn., Ind. Soc. Chgo. Union League Club of Chgo. Home: 3900 Hemlock St Valparaiso IN 46383-1814 Office: Valparaiso U Office of the President Valparaiso IN 46383-9978

HARRELD, JAMES BRUCE, computer company executive; b. Gallipolis, Ohio, Dec. 12, 1950; s. James Baldwin and Ann Elizabeth (Lascu) H.; m. Mary E. Gillilan; children: Sara Elisabeth, Kelly Lynn, James Christopher, Matthew Parker. B.S., Purdue U., 1972; M.B.A., Harvard U., 1975. Asst. to exec. sec. Sigma Chi, Evanston, Ill., 1972-73; asst. to pres. Epsilon Data Mgmt., Boston, 1973-74; v.p., dir. Boston Cons. Group, Boston, Munich, Chgo., 1975-82; v.p. Dart & Kraft, Northbrook, Ill., 1982-84; sr. v.p. Kraft, Inc., Glenview, Ill., 1984-88, sr. v.p., chief info. officer, 1988-89; sr. v.p., chief info. officer Kraft Gen. Foods, Glenview, 1989-92, sr. v.p. mktg. svcs. and info. systems, 1992-93; pres. and dir. Boston Chicken, Inc., Golden, Colo., 1993-95; sr. v.p., chief strategist Internat. Bus. Machines, Armonk, 1995—; adj. prof. mgmt. Kellogg Grad. Sch. Bus., Northwestern U., 1993—. Co-author: Survival Manual, 1973. Recipient Balfour Province award Sigma Chi, 1972, Significant Sig award, 1989; recipient Purdue U. Disting. Engring. Alumnus award, 1991. Mem. Harvard Club (Boston), Denver Country Club, Hot Springs Club, Tau Beta Pi, Alpha Pi Mu. Republican. Presbyterian. Avocations: reading; golf. Office: IBM PO Box 4086 Old Orchard Rd Armonk NY 10504

HARRELL, (BENJAMIN) CARLTON, columnist, retired editor; b. Mamie, N.C., Oct. 1, 1929; s. Taylor Smith Jr. and Nellie Augusta (Gallop) H.; m. Audrey (Jeanine) Tarkenton, Apr. 26, 1952; children: Melissa Ann, Sheila Lynn. Student, U. N.C., 1947-49. Reporter Daily Advance, Elizabeth City, N.C., 1950-52, 53-56, Goldsboro (N.C.) News-Argus, 1956-57; reporter Durham (N.C.) Sun, 1957-64, state editor, 1964-65, asst. city editor, 1965-69, city editor, 1969-72, mng. editor, 1972-90; assoc. editor Herald-Sun, Durham, 1991-96, editor emeritus, columnist, 1996—. 2d lt. U.S. Army, 1952-53. Mem. Am. Soc. Newspaper Editors, Hist. Preservation Soc. Durham. Office: Herald Sun 410 Argonne Dr Durham NC 27704-1428

HARRELL, EDWARD HARDING, newspaper executive; b. Richmond, Va., Dec. 1, 1939; s. Emmett Livingston Harrell and Martha Mason (Harding) Harrell Owen; m. Diane Greer Dickerson, July 18, 1965 (dec.); children: Sara Wesley, Katherine Harding. BA, U. Va., 1962. Advt. salesman Richmond Newspapers, 1963-68, asst. advt. dir., 1975-82; gen. mgr. Westover Pub., Richmond, 1968-71; mktg. dir. Media Gen. Fin., Richmond, 1971-74; asst. gen. mgr. Pitts. Press, 1982-86; pres. Harrell Assocs., 1986-89, Tribune Rev., 1989—. Bd. dirs. Conv. and Vis. Bur., Pitts., 1985-87, Pitts. Dance Coun., 1985—; pres., bd. dirs. Sweetwater Arts Ctr., Sewickley, Pa., 1985-94, Va. Mus. Natural Hist., 1987-94, City Theatre, 1994-99, Pitts. Downtown Partnership, 1994, Pitts. Cultural Trust Bd., 1994—, Phipps Conservatory, 1997—, Housing Opportunities Made Equal Bd., 1997—, Press Club Western Pa., 1995—. Capt. U.S. Army, 1962-66. Mem. Newspaper Assn. Am., Duquesne Club (Pitts.), Edgeworth Club (Sewickley). Democrat. Episcopalian. Avocations: sailing, reading. Office: 665 Rodi Rd Pittsburgh PA 15235-4566

HARRELL, GARY PAUL, lawyer; b. Texas City, Tex., July 8, 1952; s. James Eugene Jr. and Mary Alice Harrell; m. Leigh Evans, May 27, 1978. BS, U. Tex., 1977, MA, 1979; cert. mgmt. healthcare facilities, UCLA, 1984; JD cum laude, Lewis & Clark Coll., 1991. Bar: Oreg. 1991, U.S. Dist. Ct. (fed. dist.) Oreg. 1991; diplomate Am. Coll. Healthcare Execs. Staff/charge nurse Healthcare Facilties, Austin, Tex., 1972-78; gen. mgr. Nursing Support Svcs., Austin, 1978-80; dir. edn. Downey (Calif.) Cmty. Hosp., 1980-84; v.p. patient care Grande Ronde Hosp., La Grande, Oreg., 1984-88; assoc. Lane Powell Spears Lubersky, Portland, Oreg., 1990-94; ptnr. Harrell & Nester, LLP, Portland, 1994—; adj. prof., asst. prof. Calif. State U., Long Beach, 1980-84; pres. Oreg. State Bd. Nursing, Portland, 1987-90. Contbr. chpts. to books. With USNR, 1970-74. Recipient Am. Jurisprudence award, 1989. Fellow Healthcare Fin. Mgmt. Assn. (v.p. Oreg. chpt.); mem. Oreg. Assn. Nurse Attys. (treas., past pres.), Am. Coll. Health Care Adminstrs. (past pres. Oreg. chpt.), Am. Health Lawyers Assn., Oreg. Health Care Assn. (chair assoc. com.). Avocations: flying, sailing, motorcycling. E-mail: gharrell@health-law.net. Office: Harrell & Nester LLP 1515 SW 5th Ave Ste 510 Portland OR 97201-5450

HARRELL, HENRY HOWZE, tobacco company executive; b. Richmond, Va., Sept. 18, 1939; s. Theron Rice and Susan Howze (Haskell) H.; m. Jean Covington Camp, Feb. 7, 1970; children—Susan Hampton, Shelby Madison. A.B., Washington and Lee U. V.p. Universal Leaf Tobacco Co., Inc., Richmond, 1974-81, sr. v.p., 1981-82, exec. v.p., 1982-86, pres., 1986-88, pres., chief exec. officer, 1988-91; chmn., chief exec. officer Universal Corp. (formerly Universal Leaf Tobacco Co., Inc.), 1991—; dir. Universal Corp.; bd. dirs. Jefferson Bankshares Inc., Charlottesville, Va.; mem. bd. visitors James Madison U., Harrisonburg, Va. Mem. Forum Club, Commonwealth Club, Phi Beta Kappa, Omicron Delta Kappa. Republican. Episcopalian. Clubs: Country of Va., Deep Run Hunt (bd. dirs. 1981-83). Avocations: fishing; gardening. *

HARRELL, INA PERRY, maternal/women's and medical/surgical nurse; b. Gates County, N.C., Dec. 26, 1930; d. Willie Lee and Willa Maris (Tinkham) Perry; m. Reuben Brooks Harrell, Dec. 19, 1954; children: Brooks Lee, David Austin. Diploma in nursing, Norfolk Gen. Hosp., 1952; diploma in obstetrics, Providence Lying-In Hosp., 1953. RN, N.C., Va.; cert. obstet. labor and delivery nurse, in CPR, admissions assessment nurse. Staff nurse obstetrics unit, labor and delivery room Norfolk (Va.) Gen. Hosp., Asheville, N.C., 1953-54; head nurse labor and delivery room and obstetrics unit Meml. Mission Hosp., Asheville, 1956-67; office nurse Dr. Bruce J. Franz, Asheville, N.C., 1967-77; staff nurse St. Joseph's Hosp., Asheville, 1977-95, ret., 1995. Mem. Nat. Bapt. Nurses Fellowship, N.C. Nurses Assn., Norfolk Gen. Hosp. Alumni Assn.

HARRELL, JAMES EARL, SR., radiologist, educator; b. El Dorado, Ark., Dec. 25, 1931; s. Wilson M. and Edna Irene (Slater) H.; m. Betty Jacqueline (Rogers) Martin, Aug. 23, 1951 (div. 1977); children: James Earl, David Alan; m. Joan Marie Cordes, Oct. 20, 1977. B.A., Ouachita Baptist Coll., 1953, postgrad., 1956-57; M.D., U. Ark., 1962. Am. Bd. Radiology. Commd. 2d lt. U.S. Army, 1953, advanced through grades to lt. col., 1970; radiologist Walter Reed Gen. Hosp., 1963-71, Washington Hosp. Ctr., 1971-72; radiologist Methodist Hosp., Houston, 1972—, chief of radiology, 1976—; prof., chmn. dept. radiology Baylor Coll. Medicine, Houston, 1976—; physician-in-charge dept. radiology Harris County Hosp. Dist., Houston, 1976—; pres. Houston Radiology Associated, 1976—; chief of radiology Jasper (Tex.) Meml. Hosp., 1981-94, Lafayette (La.) Gen. Hosp., 1983-88; resigned U.S. Army, 1971. Served to maj. gen. USAR; dep. surgeon gen. for mobzn. and res. affairs USAR, 1983-86. Fellow Am. Coll. Radiology; mem. AMA, Harris County Med. Soc., Tex. Med. Assn. Republican. Office: Baylor Coll Medicine Dept Radiology 1 Baylor Plz Houston TX 77030-3411 also: Meth Hosp 6565 Fannin St # M2214 Houston TX 77030-2704*

HARRELL, LIMMIE LEE, JR., lawyer; b. Jackson, Tenn., Aug. 15, 1941; s. Limmie Lee Sr. and Mary Benthal (Nowell) H.; m. Betsy D. Harrell; children: Limmie Lee III, Mary Kimberley. BS, Memphis State U., 1963, JD, 1966. Bar: Tenn. 1966, U.S. Dist. Ct. (we. dist.) Tenn. 1968, U.S. Supreme Ct. Ptnr. Harrell & Harrell, Attys., Trenton, Tenn., 1966—; chmn. bd. dirs. Bank of Commerce, Trenton. Pres. Gibson County Young Dems., Trenton, Tenn., 1968. Named one of Outstanding Young Men in Am. Mem. ABA, Tenn. Bar Assn., Gibson County Bar Assn., Assn. Trial Lawyers Am., Tenn. Trial Lawyers Assn., Memphis State Alumni Assn. (pres. 1984-85). Baptist. Club: Pinecrest Country Club (Trenton, Tenn.) (pres. (3) terms). Lodges: Elks (exalted ruler 1971-72), Moose. Avocations: golf, fishing, hunting, water skiing. Home: 300 Rosemont Dr Trenton TN 38382-3116 Office: Harrell & Harrell Attys Court Sq Trenton TN 38382-1862

HARRELL, LYNN MORRIS, cellist; b. N.Y.C., Jan. 30, 1944; s. Mack and Marjorie (Fulton) H.; m. Linda Blandford, Sept. 7, 1976. Student, Juilliard Sch. Music, Curtis Inst. Music; D (hon.), Cleve. Inst. Music, 1994. Piatigorsky prof. cello U. So. Calif., L.A., 1987-93; prof. internat. cello studies Royal Acad. Music, London, 1988-93, prin., 1993-95; artistic dir. L.A. Philharm. Inst., 1988-91. Prin. cellist, Cleve. Orch., 1963-71; debut Carnegie Hall, N.Y.C., 1963 ; soloist with maj. orchs. U.S. and Europe; rec. artist London/Decca Records, EMI/Angel, RCA, CBS, Deutsche Grammaphon; soloist meml. concert for Holocaust victims Vatican, 1994. Recipient 1st Piatigorsky award, Grammy award, 1981, 87, 88; co-recipient 1st Avery Fisher award, 1975. Office: care IMG 420 W 45th St New York NY 10036-3503

HARRELL, MICHAEL V., hospitality company executive. BS, U. Evansville. Ptnr. Lufkin Properties, 1970; with Servico, Inc., exec. v.p., COO; founder Vista Host, chmn. bd., CEO; pres. adv. coun. Hampton Inn. Mem. Internat. Assn. of Holiday Inns (bd. dirs. 1981-88, pres. 1985-86, past pres. coun.). Office: Vista Host Inc 10370 Richmond #150 Houston TX 77042

HARRELL, MICHELLE, special education educator; b. Smithfield, N.C., Aug. 8, 1965; d. Harold Lee Stanley and Rosa Lee (Wood) Watson; m. Michael Dean Harrell, Dec. 5, 1986. AA, Wayne C.C., 1993; MS in Spl. Edn., East Carolina U., 1996, postgrad. Cert. in spl. edn. Tchr.'s asst. East Carolina U., Greenville, 1993-95; tutor after-sch. program various schs. Greenville and Goldsboro, N.C., 1994-96; spl. edn. educator primary level Edgewood Comty. Devel. Sch. Wayne County Pub. Schs., Goldsboro, 1996—; mem. sounding bd. com. Wayne County Pub. Schs., Goldsboro, 1996—; mem. curriculum com. Edgewood Comty. Devel. Sch., Goldsboro, 1997-2000. Cert. coach Spl. Olympics, Goldsboro and Greenville, 1994-97. Mem. CEC. Avocations: enhancing computer skills, reading children's literature, horseback riding, beaches and mountains of North Carolina. E-mail: shellsped@pindigital.net. Home: 3589 Pikeville Princeton Rd Princeton NC 27569

HARRELL, ROY G., JR., lawyer; b. Norfolk, Va., Sept. 14, 1944; s. Roy G. and Winifred B. H. BS with honors, The Citadel; LLB cum laude, Washington & Lee. Bar: Fla.; cert. in real property. Assoc. Jennings, Watts, Clarke & Hamilton, Jacksonville, Fla., 1971-75; assoc. Greene, Mann, Rowe, Stanton, Mastry & Burton, St. Petersburg, Fla., 1975-76, ptnr., 1976-83; founding ptnr. Baynard, Harrell, Ostow & Ulrich (formerly Baynard, Harrell, Mascara & Ostow), St. Petersburg, 1983-94; of counsel Carlton, Fields, Ward, Emmanuel, Smith & Cutler, P.A., St. Petersburg, 1994-98; ptnr. Holland & Knight LLP, St. Petersburg, 1998—; coun. Am. Lawyer's Auxiliary, 1992-93. Notes editor Washington & Lee Law Review. Past chmn. governing bd. S.W. Fla. Water Mgmt. Dist., 1985-98; past co-chair Pinellas Anclote River Basin Bd.; former mem. policy com. Tampa Bay Nat. Estuary Program; former mem. Tampa Bay Water Coordinating Coun.; pres. United Way, Pinella County, 1986; grad. leadership St. Petersburg, 1976, Leadership Tampa Bay; past chmn. campus adv. bd. U. South Fla. Bayboro Campus; former bd. dirs. Bayfront Ctr. Found.; mem. Citizens Vision 2000; former bd. dirs. 1000 Friends of Fla.; immediate past chmn. bd. dirs. St. Anthony's Devel. Found.; former mem. bd. dirs. ARC, Tampa. Capt. U.S. Army, 1969-71. Recipient Leadership award Leadership St. Pete, 1986, Leadership award Nat. Assn. Leadership Orgn., 1986, PACE award Pinellas Emergency Mental Health Svcs. 1986, Human Svcs. award, 1987. Mem. ABA (mem. various coms.), Am. Coll. Mortgage Attys., Va. Bar Assn., Fla. Bar, St. Petersburg Bar Assn., Greater St. Petersburg C. of C. (Mem. of Yr. award 1981, pres. 1986-87), Leadership St. Pete Alumni Assn. (former chair bd. dirs.), Dragon Club, St. Petersburg Yacht Club, Suncoasters, Suncoast Tiger Bay Club, Anthonians (former pres.), Phi Sigma Alpha, Phi Alpha Delta. Office: Holland & Knight LLP 200 Central Ave Ste 1600 Saint Petersburg FL 33701

HARRELL, ROY HARRISON, JR., minister; b. San Angelo, Tex., July 13, 1928; s. Roy Harrison and Melinda (Garza) H.; m. Iris Ann Keeton, Dec. 15, 1951 (div. Aug. 1982); children: Amy Sue Dopson, Patrick Roy, Paula Ann Hahn; m. Iva Helen Odeen Dunton, Apr. 21, 1990. BA, Hardin Simmons U., 1949; MDiv, SW Bapt. Theol. Sem., 1956. Ordained to ministry So. Bapt. Conv., Aug. 1946. Campus min. Draughns Bus. Coll., Ft. Worth, 1952-53; youth min. Polytechnic Bapt. Ch., Ft. Worth, 1953-56; campus min. Tex. Wesleyan Coll., Ft. Worth, 1953-56; instr., asst. prof. Religion, campus min. Baylor U., Med. Ctr., Dallas, 1956-62; campus min. Baylor U., Waco, Tex., 1962-68; asst. pastor U. Bapt. Ch., Abilene, Tex., 1969, Pk. Cities Bapt. Ch., Dallas, 1970-82; pastor Ross Ave. Bapt. Ch., Dallas, 1983-95, pastor emeritus, 1995—; pres. East Dallas Coop. Parish, 1991-92. Contbr. articles to profl. jours. Bd. dirs. United Way Met. Dallas, 1992—, mem. faith com., 1994—, co-chair, 1994-95, exec. com. 1996-97, mem. nominating com., 1998-99; mem. exec. com. East Dallas Coop. Parish Coun., 1985-95, pres., 1993-94; mem. Youth Crime Commn. of Greater Dallas Crime Commn., Dallas Pub. Schs. Religious Cmty. Task Force; mem. chapel com. Thanks-Giving Sq., 1991—, chair, 1995-98, cons., 1997—; chair Dallas Observance of Nat Day of Prayer Breakfast, 1996; hon. supporter Dallas Observance Isreal Independence Day, 1998; founding bd. mem. Dallas-Our Kids, 1998—; mem. adv. bd. East Dallas Cmty. Org., cons. Thanksgiving Square for special projects. Mem. Dallas Pastors Assn. (sec.-treas. 1990-91, v.p. 1991-92, pres. 1992-94), Rotary Club Dallas (chair literacy com.), chair Rotary Internat. Dist. 5810 Ethics in Bus. and Govt. Com. (bd. dirs. 1999-01), Dallas Mus. of Art. Home: 3521 Villanova St Dallas TX 75225-5008 *The church is the only institution dedicated to changing the lives of people at their very heart. A minister therefore has the gravest of responsibility.*

HARRELL, SAMUEL MACY, agribusiness executive; b. Indpls., Jan. 4, 1931; s. Samuel Runnels and Mary (Evans) H.; m. Sally Bowers, Sept. 2, 1958 (div.); children: Samuel D., Holly Evans, Kevin Bowers, Karen Susan, Donald Runnels, Kenneth Macy. B.S. in Econs., Wharton Sch., U. Pa., 1953. Pres., chmn. bd., chief exec. officer, chmn., exec. com. Early & Daniel Industries, Cin., 1971—; chmn. bd., chmn. exec. com. Early & Daniel Co., Cin., 1971—; chmn. bd., chief exec. officer, chmn. exec. com. Tidewater Grain Co., Phila., 1971—; dir. Harriman Inst. Columbia U.; bd. dirs. Wainwright Bank & Trust Co., Wainright Abstract Co., Nat. Grain Trade Council, U.S. Feed Grains Council; mem. Chgo. bd. Trade. *Mr. Harrell was CEO for 20 years of a $650 million multi-national corporation, which was listed in Fortune Magazine's Top 100 Service Organizations. We are business appraisers. We value closely held businesses of all sizes, from small proprietorships such as medical practices to large multinational corporations. In the course of our work, we value specific intangible business assets such as patients, trademarks, copyrights, employment agreements and goodwill. In addition, we value minority equity interests, debt securities, preferred stock and stock options. Purposes for business appraisals include estate taxation, gift taxation, buy-sell agreements, divorce distributions and securities litigation.* Contbg. author: The Status of Agribusiness in Russia and the CIS. Dir. Harriman Inst., Columbia U. With AUS, 1953-55. Mem. Nat. Assn. Cert. Valuation Analysts, Inst. Bus. Appraisers, Am. Soc. Farm Mgrs. & Rural Appraisers, Am. Soc. Agrl. Cons., Internat. Bus. Brokers Assn., Young Pres.'s Orgn., U. Pa. Alumni Assn. (past pres.), Terminal Elevator Grain Mchts. Assn. (dir.), Millers Nat. Fedn. (dir.), Assn. Operative Millers, Am. Soc. Bakery Engrs., Am. Fin. Assn., Council on Fgn. Relations, Fin. Exec. Inst., N.Am. Grain Export Assn. (dir.), Mpls. Grain Exchange, St. Louis Mchts. Grain Exchange, Buffalo Corn Exchange, Delta Tau Delta (Past prs. Ind. alumni). Presbyterian. Clubs: Columbia, Indpls. Athletic, Woodstock, Traders Point Hunt, Dramatic, Players, Lambs (Indpls.); Racquet (Phila.); University (Washington and N.Y.C.). Lodges: Masons, Rotary. Home: 9495 Whitegate Ln Cincinnati OH 45243-1647 Office: EDI Internat Inc PO Box 43400 Cincinnati OH 45243-0400

HARRELL, WANDA FAYE, retail executive; b. Littlefield, Tex., June 3, 1942; d. Woodrow Wilson and B. Florence (Adams) Frazier; m. William Robert Harrell, Dec. 10, 1959; children: Wesley Roger, Debra Lanette. Bookeeper Harrell Bldg. Supply, Inc., Levelland, Tex., 1963-81; v.p. Harrell Bldg. Supply, Inc., Anton, Tex., 1981—, also sec., mem. bd. dirs.; bookkeeper Harrell Bldg. Supply Inc., Levelland, Tex. Author: Under the Rainbow: The Harrells, 1986, Pot's of Gold, Harrell's Cookin 1990; editor, author (ch. bulletin) The Anton Herald, 1973; writer: The Anton Tale Spinner, 1994. Sec., treas., life and charter mem. Anton Mus. Assn., 1986—. Named Citizen of Yr. Anton, Tex., 1996. Mem. S.W. Hardware Assn., Hardware Wholesalers Assn., Tex. Genealogy Assn., Ark. Genealogy Assn., Genealogy Helper of Iowa, Anton Jr. Home Demonstration (pres. 1974-76), Garden Club (Anton), Hockley County Home Demonstration Levelland (chmn. 1976), Littlefield Ex-Students Assn., Cotter and Co., Inc. Democrat. Mem. Ch. of Christ. Home: 410 Hickory St Levelland TX 79336-5710

HARRELSON, CLYDE LEE, secondary school educator; b. Baton Rouge, Nov. 20, 1946; s. Hezzie Clyde and Marguerite Lucille (Tucker) H. BA, Southeastern La. U., 1968; MA, La. State U., 1974, EdS, 1980, postgrad.; postgrad., So. U. Cert. social studies and English tchr., prin., supr., La. Tchr. English, East Baton Rouge Parish Sch. Bd., 1970—; tchr. English, McKinley Mid. Magnet Sch., Baton Rouge, 1982—, now dean of students; mem. Mid. Sch. Lang. Arts Curriculum Com. Mem. Arts Coun. Greater Baton Rouge, Found. for Hist. La., La. Preservation Alliance, Nat. Trust for Hist. Preservation, Colonial Williamsburg Found., NCCJ, Cmty. Assn. for Welfare Sch. Children, La. Dem. Com., Nat. Dem. Com. Mem. NEA, ASCD, Nat. Coun. Tchrs. English, La. Coun. Tchrs. English, East Baton Rouge Coun. Tchrs. English, East Baton Rouge Parish Dem. Exec. Com., La. Assn. Educators, East Baton Rouge Parish Assn. Educators, Kiwanis, Phi Delta Kappa. Episcopalian. Home: 3710 Prescott Rd Baton Rouge LA 70805-5055

HARRELSON, WALTER JOSEPH, minister, religion educator emeritus; b. Winnabow, N.C., Nov. 28, 1919; s. Isham Danvis and Mabel (Rich) H.; m. Idella Aydlett, Sept. 20, 1942; children: Marianne McIver, David Aydlett, Robert Joseph. Student, Mars Hill (N.C.) Coll., 1940-41, Litt.D. (hon.), 1977; A.B., U. N.C., 1947, Litt.D. (hon.), 1994; B.D., Union Theol. Sem., 1949, Th.D., 1953; postgrad., U. Basel, Switzerland, 1950-51, Harvard, 1951-53; D.D. (hon.), U. of South, 1974, Christian Theol. Sem., 1992. Instr. philosophy U. N.C., 1947; ordained to ministry Baptist Ch., 1949; tutor asst. Union Theol. Sem., 1949-50; prof. Old Testament Andover Newton Theol. Sch., 1951-55; dean, assoc. prof. Old Testament U. Chgo. Div. Sch., 1955-60; prof. Old Testament Div. Sch., Vanderbilt U., Nashville, 1960-75; chmn. grad. dept. religion Div. Sch., Vanderbilt U., 1962-67, dean, 1967-75, Disting. prof. Hebrew Bible, 1975-90, prof. emeritus, 1990—, dir. Lilly Ministry Project, 1990-94; interim dean Disciples Div. House, 1993-94; prof. Wake Forest U., 1994-96, adj. univ. prof. Divinity Sch., 1996—; dir. Ecumenical Inst. Advanced Theol. Studies, Jerusalem, 1977-78, 78-79; vice-chmn. transl. com. Rev. Standard Version of the Bible; vis. prof. Brite Div. Sch. Tex. Christian U., 1992, Boston Coll., 1991, 93; mem. ch. rels. com. U.S. Holocause Meml. Mus. Author: Jeremiah, Prophet to the Nations, 1959, Interpreting the Old Testament, 1964, From Fertility Cult to Worship, 1969, 80, The Ten Commandments and Human Rights, 1980, rev. edit., 1997, (with Rabbi R.M. Falk) Jews and Christians: A Troubled Family, 1990, (with Bruce M. Metzger and Robert C. Dentan) The Making of the New Revised Standard Version of the Bible, 1991, (with Rabbi R.M. Falk) Jews and Christians: In Pursuit of Social Justice, 1996; co-author, editor: Teaching the Biblical Languages, 1967; editor, contbr.: Israel's Prophetic Heritage, 1962; editl. chmn. Religious Studies Rev., 1974-80; assoc. editor Mercer Dictionary of the Bible, 1990; assoc. editor Mercer Commentary on the Bible, 1995. Dir. project to film Ethiopian Manuscripts, NEH, 1972-84; bd. dirs. Dead Sea Scrolls Found., 1991—, Planned Parenthood Assn., Nashville; active ch. rels. com. U.S. Holocaust Meml. Coun. Traveling fellow Union Theol. Sem., 1949; Am. Coun. Learned Socs. fellow, 1950-51, 70; exch. fellow U. Basel, 1950-51; Fulbright rsch. scholar, Rome, 1962-63; Harvie Branscomb Disting. prof. Vanderbilt U., 1977-78, Alexander Heard Disting. Svc. prof., 1985-86; NEH fellow, Rome, 1983-84; recipient Thomas Jefferson prize, 1987-88, Alumni/ae award Vanderbilt U., 1989, Festschrift, Justice and the Holy, 1989. Mem. NAS (mem. coun. Inst. Medicine), Soc. for Values in Higher Edn. (pres. 1972-74), Soc. Bibl. Lit. (pres. 1972), Am. Acad. Religion, Cath. Bibl. Assn., Phi Beta Kappa. Home and Office: 708 E Moore St Southport NC 28461-4029

HARRIE, DANIEL ANDREW, newspaper reporter; b. Salt Lake City, May 1, 1955; s. Delmar P. and Lenore (Gregerson) H.; m. Billie D. Hunsaker, June 28, 1980; children: Sam, Andrew, Ryan. BA in Comm., U. Utah, 1985. Staff writer UPI, Salt Lake City, 1985-90; staff writer/polit. The Salt Lake Tribune, 1990—. Recipient William H. Cowles III Meml. award AP, 1996, First place Gen. Reporting, 1998. Mem. Soc. Profl. Journalists (state chpt. pres. 1995, state bd. dirs. 1986—, 1st place winner in investigative reporting 1996, 1st place in deadline reporting 1996, 1st place in polit./non-deadline reporting 1997, 2d place incomprehensive reporting 1998). Office: The Salt Lake Tribune 143 S Main St Ste 400 Salt Lake City UT 84111-1945

HARRIES, KARSTEN, philosophy educator, researcher; b. Jena, Thuringia, Germany, Jan. 25, 1937; came to U.S., 1951; s. Wolfgang and Ilse (Grossmann) H.; m. Elizabeth Wanning, July 4, 1959; children: Lisa, Peter, Martin; 2d m., Elizabeth L. Langhorne, Mar. 14, 1991. BA, Yale U., 1958, PhD, 1962. Instr. Yale U., New Haven, 1961-63, asst. prof. philosophy, 1965-66, assoc. prof., 1966-70, prof., 1970—, Mellon prof., 1986-91; asst. prof. U. Tex., Austin, 1963-65; lectr. U. Bonn, Fed. Republic Germany, winters 1965-66, 68-69. Author: The Meaning of Modern Art, 1967, The Bavarian Rococo Church, 1983, The Broken Frame, 1989, The Ethical Function of Architecture, 1996 (Winner of 8th Ann. AIA Internat. Architecture Book award for criticism); editor: (with Christoph Jamme) Martin Heidegger: Kunst, Politik, Technik, 1992, Martin Heidegger: Politics, Art, and Technology, 1994; contbr. numerous articles and revs. to profl. jours. Recipient Disting. Teaching Effectiveness award U. Tex., 1964; Morse fellow Yale U., 1965-66, Guggenheim fellow, N.Y.C., 1971-72. Mem. Am. Philos. Assn., Am. Soc. for Aesthetics, Soc. for Eighteenth Century Studies, Cusanus Soc. Home: 16 Morris St Hamden CT 06517-3423 Office: Yale U Dept Philosophy New Haven CT 06520

HARRIETT, REBECCA, park director. BS in Park Mgmt., N.C. State U., 1981. With Nat. Park Svcs., 1981—; supt. Booker T. Washington Monument, Hardy, Va., 1995—. Mem. Rotary Internat., Assn. Nat. Park Rangers. Office: 12130 Booker T Washington Hwy Hardy VA 24101-3968*

HARRIFF, SUZANNA ELIZABETH BAHNER, advertising consultant; b. Vicksburg, Miss., Dec. 30, 1953; d. David S. and F. Suzanna (McElwee)

Bahner; m. James R. Harriff, Sept. 10, 1977; 1 child, Michael James. B.A. summa cum laude, SUNY-Fredonia, 1976; postgrad. Cornell U. Law Sch., 1981; MDiv with distinction Colgate Rochester Divinity Sch., 1995. Ordained to ministry Am. Bapt. Chs. USA, 1995. Media asst. Comstock Advt., Syracuse, N.Y., and Buffalo, 1976-77; media buyer/planner G. Andre Delporte, Syracuse, 1979-81; media dir. Roberts Advt., Syracuse, 1982; dir. media services Signet Advt., Syracuse, 1982-84; owner, pres. MediaMarCon, Syracuse, 1984—. Music dir., pianist Manlius United Methodist Ch., N.Y., 1983-92, youth dir., 1983-85; dir. music First Bapt. Ch., Manlius, 1993-96; assoc. pastor Andrews Meml. UMC, 1996—; tchr. Am. Bapt. Chs. N.Y. state lay studies program, Bethel Bible Sem., Syracuse; interim dir. mktg. and comm. Onondaga C.C., 1998—; co-chair St. Nicholas Ecumenical Festival, 1992-98; co-chair Am. Bapt. Ch. Nat. Biennial Conf., 1995; Pheresis donor ARC, 1987—; vol. Sta. WCNY-TV pub. TV auction drive, chair media div., 1986-97, gen. chair, 1994; accompanist musicals and chorus Manlius-Pebble Hill Sch., 1991-96; resource devel. chair Winterfest, Syracuse, 1992; lead female vocalist Aspen Dreams, 1996—. Recipient 500 Hour Svc. pin WCNY, 1996. Mem. NAFE, Syracuse Advt. Club (dir. 1985-88, program chair 1986-88, pres. 1988-89), Irish-Am. Cultural Inst. Syracuse, Phi Beta Kappa. Democrat. Avocations: music; theatre. Home: 8180 Bluffview Dr Manlius NY 13104-9740

HARRIGAN, ANTHONY HART, author; b. N.Y.C., Oct. 27, 1925; s. Anthony Hart and Elizabeth Elliott (Hutson) H.; m. Elizabeth McP. Ravenel, Aug. 16, 1950; children: Anthony Hart, Elizabeth Chardon, Elliott McP., Mary Ravenel. Student, Bard Coll., Kenyon Coll., Gambier, Ohio, U. Va. Reporter Virginian-Pilot, Norfolk, 1953-55; reporter Charleston (S.C.) News & Courier, assoc. editor, 1957-70; exec. v.p. U.S. Indsl. Coun., Nashville, 1970-78; pres. U.S. Indsl. Coun., 1978-90; pres. U.S. Bus. and Indsl. Coun. Ednl. Found., 1978-90; editl. advisor The Howard Ctr., 1999—; trustee, rsch. fellow Nat. Humanities Inst.; lectr. Harvard U., Nat. War Coll., Vanderbilt U., U. Colo.; past mem. rsch. com. S.C. Commn. Higher Edn. Author: Ten Poets Anthology, 1947, The Editor and the Republic, 1952, Red Star Over Africa, 1964, The New Republic, 1965, Defense Against Total Attack, 1966, A Guide to the War in Vietnam, 1965, American Perspectives, 1974, American Perspectives II, 1977; co-author: The Indian Ocean and the Threat to the West, 1976, The Southern Oceans and the Security of the Free World, 1978, Putting America First, 1987, American Economic Preeminence, 1989; co-author or editor other works, 1978; editl. adv. bd. Modern Age, 1955—; author newspaper column, 1970-90, also numerous articles in nat. jours. Bd. dirs. Howard Ctr., Rockford, Ill., 1999—. Served with USMCR, World War II. Recipient Mil. Rev. award U.S. Army Command and Gen. Staff Coll., 1965; grantee Relm Found., 1966, Wilbur Found., 1992, 95, Earhart Found., 1993. Mem. Soc. Colonial Wars in S.C., Nat. Press Club, Carolina Yacht Club. Anglican.

HARRIGAN, EDMUND PATRICK, physician, researcher; b. Springfield, Mass., Jan. 31, 1953; s. Edmund Lawrence and Kathleen Marie (Griffin) H.; m. Julie Marie Burghardt, Apr. 22, 1950; children: Eamon Patrick, David Russell, Jeffrey Conor, Paul William. BA in Chemistry magna cum laude, St. Anselm Coll., Manchester, N.H., 1974; postgrad., UCLA, 1975; MD, U. Mass., 1979. Diplomate Am. Bd. Psychiatry and Neurology. Intern in internal medicine Berkshire Med. Ctr., Pittsfield, Mass., 1979-80; resident in neurology Boston U., 1980-83, teaching fellow in neurology, 1980-83; pres. Coastal Neurology Svcs., Inc., Somersworth, N.H., 1985-90; dir. CIBA Geigy Pharm., Summit, N.J., 1990-92; with Pfizer Ctrl. Rsch., Groton, Conn., 1992—. Contbr. articles to profl. jours., chpt. to book. Mem. AMA, Am. Acad. Neurology, Am. Soc. Exptl. Neuro-Therapeutics (mem. exec. com.). Office: Pfizer Ctrl Rsch Eastern Point Rd Groton CT 06340

HARRIGAN, JOHN THOMAS, JR., physician, obstetrician-gynecologist; b. Perth Amboy, N.J., Apr. 20, 1929; s. John T. and Mary E. (Czapp) H.; m. Marlene Lulka, Apr. 14, 1961 (div.); children: John, Alisa, Edmund; m. Karen Tiejen, Aug. 23, 1992. Student, U. Va., 1946-49; M.D., George Washington U., 1953. Diplomate Am. Bd. Ob-Gyn. Intern Doctors Hosp., Washington, 1953-54; resident in ob-gyn Luth. Hosp., Balt., 1954-55, Providence Hosp., Washington, 1957-58, Free Hosp. for Women, Boston, 1958-59; practice medicine specializing in ob-gyn, sub specialist in maternal-fetal medicine Jersey City, 1960-65, Colonia, N.J., 1962-70, Madison Twp., N.J., 1965-70; asst. attending in ob-gyn Margaret Hague Hosp., Jersey City, 1960-65; attending physician in ob-gyn Rahway Hosp., N.J., 1962-70, South Amboy Hosp., N.J., 1965-73; sec. to med. staff South Amboy Hosp., 1970; attending in ob-gyn Martland Hosp. Unit, Newark, 1970-74; dir. dept. ob-gyn Monmouth Med. Ctr., Long Branch, N.J., 1974-76; dir. regional perinatal edn. program Monmouth Med. Ctr., 1975-78; dir. Monmouth Perinatal Ctr., Long Branch, 1975-78; sr. attending in ob-gyn St. Peter's Med. Ctr., 1978—; assoc. prof. ob-gyn Hahnemann Med. Coll., Phila., 1975-78; prof. dir. div. maternal-fetal medicine Rutgers Med. Sch., Piscataway, N.J., 1978—; prof. ob-gyn., dir. div. maternal-fetal medicine Rutgers Med. Sch., 1978-86, U. Medicine and Dentistry N.J., Robert Wood Med. Sch., 1986—; cons. in maternal-fetal medicine to physicians, Eastern N.J.; mem. maternal and infant care services com. N.J. Dept. Health, 1975—; dir. statewide premature delivery prevention project; med.-legal expert cons.; tech. adv. panel Healthstart program, N.J. Health Dept. Contbr. articles to med. jours.; reviewer med. jours. Mem. task force on biomed. causes and pub. rels. Gov.'s Coun. on Prevention Mental Retardation, N.J., task force on genetics and fetal defects, 1984—; mem. pub. affairs com. MOD Birth Defects Found.; pres. Perinatal Assn. N.J., 1991-93; mem. N.J. Commn. of Health and Parental and Child Health adv. Com., 1993—, vice chmn., 1995—. Capt. M.C. U.S. Army, 1955-57. Fellow ACOG (vice chmn. N.J. sect. 1979-82, chmn. N.J. sect. 1982—, nat. adv. coun. 1982—, legis. rep., treas. dist. III 1986); mem. AMA, Med. Soc. N.J. (maternal infant care com. 1988—), Am. Inst. Ultrasound in Medicine (legis. com. 1994), Am. Fertility Soc., N.J. Perinatal Assn. (v.p. 1980-90, pres. 1990), N.J. Perinatal Tech. adv. Com. Baker channing Soc., N.J. Ob-gyn. Soc. (coun.), N.J. Maternal Fetal Medicine Soc. (pres. 1994-95). Democrat. Roman Catholic. Home: 301 Sussex Ave Spring Lake NJ 07762-1231 Office: Jersey Shore Med Ctr Perinatal Inst 1943 State Route 33 Neptune NJ 07753-4843

HARRIGAN, KELLY A., human resources professional; b. Flushing, N.Y., Jan. 16, 1973. BA, SUNY, Stony Brook, 1995. Human resources rep. Ind. Fin., Westchester, N.Y., 1995-97; benefits adminstr. Swissre Am., N.Y.C., 1998; acting human resources mgr. Clarion Mktg. and Comms. Inc., Greenwich, Conn., 1999—. Mem. Soc. of Human Resources Mgmt. Office: Clarion Mktg and Comms Inc Greenwich Office Parks Greenwich CT 06831

HARRIGAN, RICHARD GEORGE, salesperson; b. Joliet, Ill., Feb. 12, 1952; s. William Francis and Margaret (Ruettiger) H.; m. Patricia Rae Bowman, Aug. 12, 1989; children: Michelle Freeman, Kimberly Freeman; children from a previous marriage: Jennifer Harrigan, Michelle Harrigan, Richard Harrigan, Sarah Harrigan, Samantha Harrigan. AS in Heating and Refrigeration, Joliet Jr. Coll., 1980. Salesman G.W. Berkheimer, Gary, Ind., 1978-92; owner, operator East-West Ent., Hobart, Ind., 1992—. Mem. IBR, NHAW. Roman Catholic. Avocation: travel. Home: PO Box C Hobart IN 46342-0016 Office: East-West Ent PO Box C Hobart IN 46342-0016

HARRIGAN, ROSANNE CAROL, nursing educator; b. Miami, Feb. 24, 1945; d. John H. and Rose (Hnatow) Harrigan; children: Dennis, Michael, John. BS, St. Xavier Coll., 1965; MS in Nursing, Ind. U., 1974, EdD in Nursing and Edn., 1979. Staff nurse, recovery rm. Mercy Hosp., Chgo., 1965, evening charge nurse, 1965-66; head nurse Chgo. State Hosp., 1966-67; nurse practitioner Health and Hosp. Corp. Marion County, Indpls., 1975-80; assoc. prof. Ind. U. Sch. Nursing, Indpls., 1978-82; nurse practitioner devel. follow-up program Riley Hosp. for Children, Indpls., 1980-85; chief nursing sect. Riley Hosp. Child Devel. Ctr., Indpls., 1982-85; prof. Ind. U. Sch. Nursing, Indpls., 1982-85; chmn., prof. maternal child health Loyola U. Niehoff Sch. Nursing, Chgo., 1985-92; dean U. Hawaii, Honolulu, 1992—; lecturer Ind. U. Sch. Nursing, 1974-75, chmn. dept. pediatrics, family and women's health, 1980-85; adj. prof. of pediatrics Ind. U. Sch. Med., 1982-85; editorial bd. Jour. Maternal Child Health Nursing, 1984-86, Jour. Perinatal Neonatal, 1985—, Jour. Perinatology, 1989—, Loyola U. Press, 1988—; adv. bd. Symposia Medicus, 1982-84, Proctor and Gamble Rsch. Adv. Com. Blue Ribbon Panel; scientific review panel NIH, 1985; cons. in field. Contbr. articles to profl. jours. bd. dirs. March of Dimes Cen. Ind. Chpt., 1974-76, med. adv., 1979-85; med. and rsch. adv. March of Dimes Nat. Found., 1985—, chmn. Task Force on Rsch. Named Nat. Nurse of Yr. March of Dimes, 1983; faculty research grantee Ind. U., 1978, Pediatric Pulmonary Nursing Tng. grant Am. Lung Assn., 1982-85, Attitudes, Interests and Competence of Ob-Gyn Nurses Rsch. grant Nurses Assn. Am. Coll. Ob-Gyn., 1986, Attitudes, Interests and Priorities of Neonatal Nurses Rsch. grant Nat. Assn. Neonatal Nurses, 1987, Biomedical Rsch. Support grant, 1988; Doctoral fellow Am. Lung Assn. Ind. Tng. Program, 1981-86. Mem. AAAS, ANA (Maternal Child Nurse of Yr. 1983), Assn. Women's Health, Obstetrical and Neonatal Nursing (chmn. com. on rsch. 1983-86), Am. Nurses Found., Nat. Assn. Neonatal Nurses, Nat. Perinatal Assn. (bd. dirs. 1978-85, rsch. com. 1986), Midwest Nursing Rsch. Soc. (theory devel. sect.), Ill. Nurses Assn. (commn. rsch. chmn. 1990-91), Ind. Nurses Assn., Hawaii Nurses Assn., Ind. Perinatal Assn. (pres. 1981-83), N.Y. Acad. Sci., Ind U. Alumni Assn. (Disting. Alumni 1985), Sigma Xi, Pi Lambda Theta, Sigma Theta Tau (chpt. pres. 1988-90).

HARRIMAN, GERALD EUGENE, retired business administrator, economics educator; b. Dell Rapids, S.D., May 30, 1924; s. Roy L. and Margaret (Schrantz) H.; m. Eileen Bernadine Bensman, June 10, 1950; children—G. Peter, Mary K., Margaret C., Elizabeth A. B.S., U. Notre Dame, 1947; A.M., U. S.D., 1949; Ph.D., U. Cin., 1957. Expediter Minn. Mining & Mfg. Co., 1947-48; from instr. to asst. dean, chmn. dept. bus. adminstrn. and finance Xavier U., 1949-66; prof. bus. adminstrn., chmn. div. bus. and econs. Ind. U. at South Bend, 1966-75, prof. bus. adminstrn. and econs., 1975-89, prof. emeritus, 1989—, dean faculties, 1975-87, acting chancellor, 1979, vice chancellor acad. affairs, 1987-89; ret., 1989; vis. prof. fin. U. S.D., 1962; chmn. acad. deans Ind. Conf. Higher Edn., 1981-82; cons. in field. Mem. citizens adv. coun. long range fin. planning Coun. of City of Cin., 1963; mem. Community Edn. Roundtable, 1984—; mem. Scholarship Found. of St. Joseph County, Inc., 1992. Served with USNR, 1942-45. Mem. Am. Econs. Assn., Am. Finance Assn., Beta Gamma Sigma. Home: 16600 Gerald St Granger IN 46530-9579 Office: 1700 Mishawaka Ave South Bend IN 46615-1408

HARRIMAN, JOHN HOWLAND, lawyer; b. Buffalo, Apr. 14, 1920; s. Lewis Gildersleeve and Grace (Bastine) H.; m. Barbara Ann Brunmark, June 12, 1943; children—Walter Brunmark, Constance Bastine, John Howland. A.B. summa cum laude, Dartmouth, 1942; J.D., Stanford U., 1949. Bar: Calif. 1949. Assoc. firm Lawler, Felix & Hall, Los Angeles, 1949-55; asst. v.p., then v.p. Security Pacific Nat. Bank, Los Angeles, 1955-72; sr. v.p. Security Pacific Nat. Bank, 1972-85; of counsel Argue Freston Pearson Harbison & Myers, 1985-86; sec. Security Pacific Corp., 1971-85; dir. Master Metal Works. Mem. L.A. adv. coun. Episcopal Ch. Found., 1977-79; mem. Republican Assocs., 1951—, trustee, 1962-72; mem. Calif. Rep. Central Com., 1956-69, 81—, exec. com., 1960-62, 81-84; mem. L.A. County Rep. Central Com., 1958-70, exec. com., 1960-62, vice chmn., 1962; chmn. Calif. 15th Congl. Dist. Rep. Central Com., 1960-62, Calif. 30th Congl. Dist. Rep. Central Com., 1962; treas. United Rep. Fin. Com. L.A. County, 1969-70; chmn. L.A. County Reagan-Bush campaign, 1980, co-chmn., 1984; exec. dir. Calif. Rep. Party, 1985-86. With USAAF, 1943-46. Mem. Am. Bar Assn., Am. Soc. Corp. Secs. (pres. Los Angeles region 1970-71), State Bar Calif., Phi Beta Kappa, Theta Delta Chi, Phi Alpha Delta. Clubs: California (Los Angeles); Lincoln, Breakfast Panel (pres. 1970-71).

HARRIMAN, MALCOLM BRUCE, investment advisor; b. Sandusky, Ohio, Feb. 25, 1950; s. Robert Byron and Catherine (Nicholson) H.; m. Carla J. Holgren, Sept. 19, 1971 (div. Mar. 1980); m. Suzan Gwen Alexander, June 27, 1980 (div. Dec. 1985); 1 child, Sasha Bryn; m. Alysa Ellen Gelband, Apr. 19, 1986; children: Sarah Ashley, Catherine Nicole. BA, Antioch Coll., 1976; MA, U. Md., 1980. Lic. ins. agt., Fla.; registered rep. Nat. Assn. Securities Dealers, N.Y. Stock Exch., Chgo. Bd. Options Exch., Am. Stock Exch., Phila. Stock Exch. Child care worker Ft. Wayne (Ind.) Children's Home, 1971-72; adolescent program supr. Taylor Manor Hosp., Ellicott City, Md., 1972-76; program coord. child and adolescent svcs. Horizon Hosp, Clearwater, Fla., 1981-82, mktg. specialist, 1983-86; v.p., prin. ptnr. Am. Residential Ctrs., Tampa, Fla., 1986-89; pres., prin. ptnr. Continuum Psychiat. (formerly Am. Residential Ctrs.), 1989-95; exec. dir., COO Tampa Bay Acad., Riverview, Fla., 1988-94; chmn. bd., 1994-96; pres., chief exec. officer HealthExpert Systems, Inc. (formerly HealthWare, Inc.), 1989-97; chief clin. officer Echo Mgmt. Group, Tampa, 1997; fin. advisor Raymond James & Assocs., Inc., Tampa, Fla., 1997—; bd. dirs. Sr. Care Group, Inc.; assoc. dept. psychiatry U. South Fla. Med. Sch., Tampa, 1980-81; mem. severely emotionally disturbed network project adv. coun. Pinellas County, Fla., 1985-86. Mem. corp. adv. bd. Behavioral Healthcare Tomorrow, 1994-97. Gubernatorial appointee Project Freeway Task Force, HRS Dist. V, Fla., 1985-86; mem. adv. bd. Behavioral Informatics Tomorrow, Inst. Behavioral Healthcare, San Francisco, 1993-98; mem. adv. com. Cognitive Rehab. Inst. Tampa, Fla., 1993-94; bd. dirs. Friends of Rsch. in Psychiatry Coll. Medicine, U. South Fla., 1998—; mem. adv. coun. Personal Enrichment through Mental Health Svcs. (PEMHS), 1998—. Mem. Am. Assn. Individual Investors, Nat. Assn. Psychiat. Treatment Ctr. for Children (bd. dirs. 1989-95), Assn. for Ambulatory Behaviorial Healthcare (outcome task force 1993-94, cons. bd. dirs. 1994-98), Suncoast C. of C. (edn. com., del. youth svcs. adv. coun. 1982-86), Brandon C. of C. Republican. Presbyterian. E-mail: mharriman@33t.rjf.com. Fax: 813-221-5576. Office: Raymond James & Assoc 100 S Ashley Dr Tampa FL 33602-5360

HARRIMAN, PHILIP DARLING, geneticist, science foundation executive; b. San Rafael, Calif., Nov. 24, 1937; s. Theodore Darling and Luciel Harriet (Muller) H.; m. Jenny Elizabeth Flack, June 12, 1959; 1 child, Marc Stuart. BS in Physics, Calif. Inst. Tech., 1959; PhD in Biophysics, U. Calif., Berkeley, 1964. Postdoctoral fellow U. Cologne (Germany), 1964-65, Pasteur Inst., Paris, 1965-66, Cold Spring Harbor (N.Y.) Lab., 1966-68; asst. prof. biochemistry Duke U. Med. Ctr., Durham, N.C., 1968-75; assoc. prof. biology U. Mo., Kansas City, 1975-77; program dir. genetic biology NSF, Washington, 1977—; sr. scientist office asst. dir. biology, behavioral scis., 1981-82; vis. prof. Johns Hopkins U. Med. Sch., Balt., 1987-88. Contbr. articles to profl. jours. Legis. asst. Congressman Dave McCurdy of Okla., 1980-81. 1st lt. USAFR, 1962—. Congl. fellow U.S. Office Personnel Mgmt., 1980-81. Fellow AAAS; mem. Genetics Soc. Am., Am. Soc. Microbiology. Unitarian. Achievements include research in genetics, genetic engineering, and molecular biology.

HARRIMAN, RICHARD LEE, performing arts administrator, educator; b. Independence, Mo., Sept. 10, 1932; s. Walter S. and M. Eloise (Faulkner) H.; AB, William Jewell Coll., 1953, LittD (hon.), 1983. MA, Stanford U., 1959. Instr., asst. prof. English U. Dubuque, Iowa, 1960-62; asst. prof. English, William Jewell Coll., Liberty, Mo., 1962, acting head English dept., 1965-69, dir. fine arts program, 1965—, asso. prof., 1966—. Treas. Kansas City Arts Council, 1980, sec., 1981; sec. Kansas City Am. Arts Festival, 1988-89. Served with, AUS, 1953-55. Woodrow Wilson fellow, 1957. Mem. MLA, AAUP, Internatl. Soc. of Performing Arts, Shakespeare Assn. Am., Assn. Performing Arts Presenters (nat. exec. bd. 1975-78), Lambda Chi Alpha, Sigma Tau Delta, Alpha Psi Omega. Methodist. Home: 1043 E Highway H Apt 3 Liberty MO 64068-4303

HARRIMAN, STEPHEN A., state public health commissioner; m. Priscilla Harriman. BA in Govt., Syracuse U.; MA, U. Conn. Exec. asst. to commr. of health State of Conn., Hartford, 1975-76; exec. dir. Conn. Med. Examining Bd., Hartford, 1976-78; dir. med. quality assurance divsn. Conn. Dept. Health, Hartford, 1978-82; chief bur. health systems regulation Conn. Dept. Pub. Health, Hartford, 1982-95; commr. Conn. Dept. Pub. Health, 1995—. Office: Conn Dept Pub Health Office of Commr PO Box 340308 Hartford CT 06134-0308

HARRINGER, OLAF CARL, architect, museum consultant; b. Hamburg, Germany, Apr. 29, 1919; came to U.S., 1927; s. Henry Theodore and Anke (Berger) H.; m. Helen Ehrat Hedges, Dec. 20, 1975; children—Carla, Brita, Eric. Student, Evanston Acad. Fine Arts, The New Bauhaus, 1937-38, Ill. Inst. Tech., 1942-45. Designer Raymond Loewy Assos., Chgo., 1946-49, H. Allan Majestic Assos., Chgo., 1949-51, Dickens, Inc., Chgo., 1951-52, Olaf Harringer and Assos. (architects/designers), Chgo., 1952-62; account exec. several exhibit firms Chgo., 1962-68; dir. exhibits Mus. Sci. and Industry, Chgo., 1957-60, 68-80; prin. Olaf Harringer Assos., Chgo., 1981-95. Mem. AIA (emeritus). Home: 3650 N 36th Ave # Villa5 Hollywood FL 33021-2543

HARRINGTON, ANNE, science historian; b. N.Y.C., June 15, 1960; d. Gerard Jr. and Sue Leia (Sayer) H.; m. Godehard Oepen, Sept. 10, 1989 (div. 1997). BA summa cum laude, Harvard U., 1982; PhD, Oxford U., 1985. Rsch. fellow Wellcome Inst., London, 1985-86; Humboldt rsch. fellow Freiburg (Germany) U., 1986-88; asst. prof. Harvard U., Cambridge, Mass., 1988-91, Morris Kahn assoc. prof., 1991-95, prof., 1995—; cons. Network on Mind-Body Interactions, MacArthur Found., Chgo, 1992-99; fellow Mind-Brain-Behavior Initiative, Harvard U., Cambridge, 1993—, governing bd., 1994—, assoc. dir., 1996-97, co-dir., 1997—. Author: Medicine, Mind and the Double Brain, 1987, Reenchanted Science, 1996; editor: So Human A Brain, 1992, The Placebo Effect: An Interdisciplinary Exploration, 1997. Recipient Capt. Jonathan Fay prize Radcliffe Coll., 1982, Bowdoin prize Harvard U., 1982, Marshall Trust scholarship, 1982-85, Wellcome Trust Postdoctoral Rsch. fellowship at Oxford and London, 1985-86, Alexander von Humboldt Postdoctoral Rsch. fellowship Freiburg U., 1986-88; grantee Nat. Libr. Medicine, 1991, NSF, 1991, Spencer Found., 1993. Mem. AAAS, History of Sci. Soc. Avocations: skiing, scuba diving, literature, travel. Office: Harvard U Dept History of Sci Sci Ctr 235 Cambridge MA 02138

HARRINGTON, ANNE WILSON, medical librarian; b. Phila., June 18, 1926; d. Edgar Myers and Jean Gould (DeHaven) Wilson; m. James Paul Harrington, June 11, 1948; children: Barbara Gould Harrington Murphy, Ian Edgar, Eric Bradley. BA, U. Pa., Phila., 1948; MS in Libr. Sci., Villanova U., 1977. Clk. Princeton U., 1948-51; CEO, ptnr. Teesdale Co., West Chester, Pa., 1954—; libr. asst. Franklin Inst., Phila., 1974-76; med. staff libr. The Chester County Hosp., West Chester, 1977—; mem., treas., chmn. sub-com. Consortium Health Info., Chester, 1977—. Trustee, sec., com. chmn. Wilmington (Del.) Friends Sch., 1963-72, 89; treas. com. on edn. Phila. Yearly Meeting Soc. Friends, 1980-91; mem., rep. Friends Coun. on Edn., Phila., 1991-96; overseer Quaker Info. Ctr., Phila., 1992-96; bd. mem., subcom. chmn. cmty. bd. Kendal Corp. CCRC, Kennett Square, Pa., 1973-97. Mem. Med. Libr. Assn., Acad. Health Info. Profls. (sr.), Phila. Area Med. Library Assn., Lake Paupac Club (chmn. environ. com., bd. dirs. 1990-96), Friends Med. Soc. Democrat. Avocations: music, reading, walking, sailing, tennis. Home: 1117 Talleyrand Rd West Chester PA 19382-7416 Office: Chester County Hosp West Chester PA 19380

HARRINGTON, ANTHONY ROSS, radio announcer, educator; b. Sanford, N.C., Feb. 18, 1958; s. Refus Roy and Pauline (Kelly) H. Diploma, Cen. Carolina Tech. Coll., 1977; BS summa cum laude, Campbell U., 1985, MEd, 1988, EdS, 1993; postgrad., N.C. State U., 1995—. Cert. tchr., N.C., lic. FCC radiotelephone operator. News announcer Sandhills Community Broadcasters, Southern Pines, N.C., 1977-78; announcer, engr. Harnett Broadcast, Inc., Lillington, N.C., 1978-88; bus driver Harnett County Schs., Lillington, 1974-76, instr. social studies, 1985—; mgr. radio sta., instr. radio-TV, mem. transfer adv. bd. Cen. Carolina Community Coll., 1988—. Mem. Cen. Carolina C.C. Tri-County English Alliance, 1989—; support N.C. Dems., Raleigh, 1986—. Pres.'s scholar Campbell U., 1983-85, Coates-Rodgers History scholar Campbell U., 1983-85. Mem. ASCD, NEA, Nat. Assn. Secondary Sch. Prins., North Carolina Assn. Educators, North Carolina Assn. Broadcasters, Nat. Coun. Social Studies, Century Club (N.C.), Campbell U. Century Club, Masons (chaplain 1983, jr. steward 1984, sr. steward 1990, sec. 1991-97), Ctrl. Carolina C.C. Century Club, Profl. Educators of N.C., Masons, N.C. Shriners. Presbyterian. Avocations: photography, singing popular and religious music. Home: 4224 Mt Pisgah Church Rd Broadway NC 27505-9629 Office: Harnett County Schs N Main St Lillington NC 27546 also: Ctrl Carolina CC 1105 Kelly Dr Sanford NC 27330-9059 also: Sta WUAW-FM Triton H S 215 Maynard Lake Rd Erwin NC 28339-8507

HARRINGTON, ANTHONY STEPHEN, lawyer; b. Taylorsville, N.C., Mar. 9, 1941; s. Atwell Lee and Louise (Chapman) H.; m. Hope Reynolds, Sept. 25, 1971; children: Adam Reynolds, Michael Addison. AB, U. N.C., 1963; LLB, Duke U., 1966. Bar: N.C. 1966, D.C. 1968, U.S. Supreme Ct. 1970. Asst. dean Duke Law Sch., Durham, N.C., 1966-68; assoc. Hogan & Hartson, Washington, 1968-73, ptnr., 1974—; bd. dirs. Ovation, Inc., Ctr. for Democracy, SouthernNet Inc., Southeastern Metal Products, Werres Corp., Rosemount Ctr.; co-chair Nat. Alliance to End Homelessness; vice-chmn. Pres. Fgn. Intelligence Adv. Bd., 1993—; mem. Commn. on Roles and Capabilities of Intelligence Cmty., 1995; chmn. Intelligence Oversight Bd., 1994—. Gen. Counsel Clinton/Gore Presdl. Campaign, 1992, Dem. Nat. Com., Washington, 1981-85. Episcopal. Clubs: Met., City (Washington). Avocations: politics, reading, gardening, tennis. Home: Ratcliffe Manor 7768 Ratcliffe Manor Rd Easton MD 21601-7432 also: 701 Pennsylvania Ave NW Washington DC 20004-2608 Office: Hogan & Hartson 555 13th St NW Ste 800E Washington DC 20004-1161

HARRINGTON, BENJAMIN FRANKLIN, III, retired business consultant; b. Princess Anne, Md., Dec. 8, 1922; s. Benjamin Franklin and Etta Maurice (Dashiell) H.; m. Jean Cameron Gilliam, July 21, 1962; children: Benjamin Franklin, Charles MacAlester. AA, Salisbury State Coll., 1951; JD, LaSalle U., 1955. Examiner Fed. Res. Bank, Richmond, Va., 1951-61; exec. v.p. Truckers Bank, Salisbury, Md., 1961-69; pres. Peoples Bank, Elkton, Md., 1969-91, bd. dirs., 1973-92; cons. Atlantic Fed. Savs. Bank, Elkton; lectr. in field.; bd. dirs., Delmar council Boy Scouts Am., 1973—; bd. dirs., treas. Cecil County Assn. for Retarded, 1972-88; bd. dirs. YMCA of Cecil County, 1975-88; bd. dirs., past pres. United Way of Cecil County; bd. dirs., treas. Cecil County Library, 1982-92; bd. dirs., past pres. Cecil County Hist. Soc.; bd. dirs. Cecil County Community Coll. Found. Named Citizen of Yr., C. of C., Elkton, 1984. Mem. Ind. Bankers Assn. (dir. 1973-80, 87-90), Md. Bankers Assn., Lions (pres. 1971-72, 94-95, 99—). Democrat. Methodist. Home: 402 Elkton Blvd Elkton MD 21921-5420

HARRINGTON, BETTY BYRD, entrepreneur; b. Longview, Tex., July 11, 1936; d. William Henry Byrd and Minnie Lee Tidwell; 1 child, Randy Lee Harrington. AA, Cedar Valley DCCCD, Dallas, 1988. Actress, model, entertainer Kathy King Entertainment Agy., DeSoto, Tex., 1956—; owner Gateway to Success/Career Devel. & Placement, DeSoto, Tex., 1981—, Resume Writing and Career Counseling Svc., DeSoto, 1987—. Author: The Dallas Dazzler, Job Search and Interview Techniques, (poetry) She Has Been Faithful, 1996, Pity the Children, 1996. Mem. AFTRA, AGVA, DeSoto C. of C., Greater Dallas C. of C. Republican. Baptist. Home and Office: 1338 E Parkerville Rd De Soto TX 75115-6421

HARRINGTON, BEVERLY, museum director. BS, Carnegie Mellon U., 1959; BAE, U. Wis., Oshkosh, 1967, MST, 1971; MSA, U. Wis., Milw., 1977. With art dept. U. Wis., Oshkosh, 1977-87; curator collections and exhibitions at arboretum Paine Art Ctr., Oshkosh, 1983-90; dir. Hearthstone Mus., Appleton, Wis., 1991—. Office: Hearthstone Hist House Mus 625 W Prospect Ave Appleton WI 54911-6042

HARRINGTON, BRUCE MICHAEL, lawyer, investor; b. Houston, Mar. 12, 1933; s. George Haymond Harrington and Doris (Gladden) Maginnis; m. Anne Griffith Lawhon, Feb. 15, 1958; children: Julia Griffith, Martha Gladden, Susan McIver. B.A., U. Tex., 1960, J.D. with honors, 1961. Bar: Tex. 1961, U.S. Dist. Ct. (so. dist.) Tex. 1962, U.S. Ct. Appeals (5th cir.) 1962, U.S. Supreme Ct. 1973. Assoc. Andrews & Kurth and predecessor firm, Houston, 1961-73, ptnr., 1973-84; dir. Offenhauser Co., Houston, Allied Metals, Inc., Houston. Trustee St. John's Sch., Houston, 1981-92, chmn. bd., CEO, 1986-92; chmn. bd. Covenant House, Tex., 1991-95; trustee St. Luke's Episcopal Hosp., Tex. Med. Ctr., Houston, 1983-86; bd. dirs. YMCA Bd. Mgmt., Am. Cancer Soc., 1992-94, Ctr. for Hearing and Speech, 1993, chmn. bd., 1995-98; vice chmn. Gateway Found., 1993-95; mem. adv. com. Assn. Governing Bds. of Colls. and Univs. Mem. ABA, Nat. Assn. Ind. Schs. (chmn. trustee com.), Ind. Schs. Assn. S.W. (chmn. trustee com., bd. exec. com.), Tex. Bar Assn., Houston Bar Assn., The Mil. and Hosp. Order of St. Lazarus, The Venerable Order of St. John (U.K.), The Order of Saints Maurice and Lazarus (Savoy), Houston Country Club, Petroleum Club, Houston Club, Phi Delta Phi, Order of Coif. Republican. Episcopalian. Home: 3608 Overbrook Ln Houston TX 77027-4128

HARRINGTON, CAROL A., lawyer; b. Geneva, Ill., Feb. 13, 1953; d. Eugene P. and M. Ruth (Bowersox) Kloubec; m. Warren J. Harrington, Aug. 19, 1972; children: Jennifer Ruth, Carrie Anne. BS summa cum laude, U. Ill., 1974, JD magna cum laude, 1977. Bar: Ill. 1977, U.S. Dist. Ct. (no. dist.) Ill. 1977, U.S. Tax Ct. 1979. Assoc. Winston & Strawn, Chgo., 1977-

84, ptnr., 1984-88; ptnr. McDermott, Will & Emery, 1988—; speaker in field. Co-author: The New Generation Skipping Tax, 1986, Generation Skipping Tax BNA Management, 1996, Generation-Skipping Transfer Tax, Warren, Gorham & Lamont, 1995; contbr. articles to profl. jours., Trustee and Estate mag. Fellow Am. Coll. Trusts and Estate Coun. (bd. regents 1999—); mem. ABA (chmn. B-1 generation skipping transfer com. 1987-92, coun. real property, probate and trust law sect. 1992-98), Ill. State Bar Assn., Chgo. Bar Assn. (trust law com. divsn. 1), Chgo. Estate Planning Coun. Office: McDermott Will & Emery 227 W Monroe St Ste 3100 Chicago IL 60606-5096

HARRINGTON, CHARLENE ANN, sociology and health policy educator; b. Concordia, Kans., Sept. 28, 1941; d. Lyman K. and Maxine (Boucher) Harrington; m. Ben Yerger, Aug. 28, 1976. BSN, U. Kans., Kansas City, 1963; MA in Cmty. Health, U. Wash., 1968; PhD in Sociology and Higher Edn., U. Calif., Berkeley, 1975. Staff nurse Good Samaritan Hosp., Portland, Oreg., 1963-64; sch. nurse U.S. Army Dependent Schs., Heilbronn, Germany, 1964-65; pub. health nurse Seattle King County and Group Health, Seattle, 1966-68; asst. prof., nursing program U. Kans., Kansas City, 1968-70; dep. dir., spl. asst. Calif. State Dept. Health, Sacramento, 1975-78; dir. Golden Empire Health Planning Agy., Sacramento, 1978-80; sr. rschr. Inst. for Health and Aging, U. Calif., San Francisco, 1980-83, asst. prof. Sch. Nursing, 1983-85, assoc. prof. dept. social and behavioral scis. Sch. Nursing, 1985-89, prof., vice chair dept. social and behavioral scis., 1989-93; chair dept. social and behavioral scis. U. Calif., San Francisco, 1994-96, prof. social and behavioral scis., 1997—; assoc. dir. Inst. for Health and Aging, U. Calif., San Francisco, 1981-94; cons. Nat. Coalition for Nursing Home Reform, Washington, 1987—; com. on regulation nursing homes Inst. Medicine, 1984-86, com. on nursing staff, 1994-96. Author: Long Term Care, 1985, Health Policy and Nursing, 2d edit., 1996; contbr. chpts. to books, articles to profl. jours. Fellow Am. Acad. Nursing (chair commn. on health policy 1991-93); mem. ANA, APHA, Nursing Econs. (bd. dirs. 1985-93), Inst. Medicine (com. nurse staffing 1995-96, roundtable of quality 1997-98, com. on quality in long-term care 1997—), Am. Sociol. Assn. (sect. coun. mem. 1992-94), Elected Inst. of Medicine (com. on longterm care quality 1998—, round table on quality 1997-98), Sigma Theta Tau. Democrat. Avocation: gardening. Office: U Calif Sch Nursing 3333 California St San Francisco CA 94143-0612

HARRINGTON, DONALD JAMES, university president; b. Bklyn., Oct. 2, 1945; s. John Joseph and Ruth Mary (Cummings) H. BA, Mary Immaculate Sem., Northampton, Pa., 1969, MDiv, 1972, ThM, 1973; LLD (hon.), St. John's U., 1985; postgrad., U. Toronto, 1980-82; PhD (hon.), Fu Jen U., Taipei, Taiwan, 1994; DHum (hon.), Am. U. Rome, 1994, Dowling Coll., 1996. Ordained priest Roman Catholic Ch., 1973. Instr. Niagara U., Niagara University, N.Y., 1973-80, dir. student activities, 1974-77, dean student activities, 1977-80, exec. v.p., 1981-84, pres., 1984-89; pres. St. John's U., Jamaica, N.Y., 1989—; bd. dirs. The Bear Stearns Cos., Inc., 1993—, Commn. Ind. Colls. and Univs., Albany, N.Y., 1987-89; mem. bd. Cath. edn. Diocese of Buffalo, 1987-89. Trustee Niagara U., 1984—, St. John's U., 1986—, DePaul U., 1988-91, Sem. Immaculate Conception, 1990-97, Res. Group, 1988—, Sisters Hosp., Buffalo, 1988-89; chair adv. com. Love Canal Land Use, 1988-89; bd. dirs., mem. exec. com. Commn. Ind. Colls. and Univs., 1991—; chair Big East Athletic Conf., 1994-97; mem. sanctity of life com. Diocese of Bklyn., 1990-97; chair Western N.Y. Consortium for Higher Edn., 1989-89, mem. exec. com., 1985-89; mem. adv. bd. New Yorkers Caring for N.Y.-N.Y. Med. Coll., 1998—; mem. Commr.'s Coun. on Higher Edn., 1998—. Mem. Assn. Cath. Colls. and Univs. (bd. dirs. 1997—). Office: St John's U Office of Pres Jamaica NY 11439

HARRINGTON, EDWARD F., federal judge; b. 1933. AB, Holy Cross Coll., Worcester, Mass., 1955; JD, Boston Coll., 1960. Law clk. to Hon. Paul C. Reardon Mass. Superior Ct., 1960-61; spl. trial atty. criminal div. U.S. Dept. Justice, 1961-65, atty.-in-charge Strike Force Against Organized Crime, 1970-73; asst. U.S. atty. Mass., 1965-69; assoc. Offices of Paul T. Smith, Boston, 1961, Offices of Melvin Louison, Taunton, Mass., 1969; mem. firm Peloquin, McKeon & Reilly, Boston, 1973-75, Gargan, Harrington & Markham, Boston, 1975-77; U.S. atty. Mass., 1977-81; mem. firm Sheridan, Garrahan & Lander, Framingham, Mass., 1981-88; dist. judge Mass., 1988—. Contbr. articles to profl. jours. Chmn. Alcoholic Beverages Control Commn., 1975-77; candidate Dem. Party for Atty. Gen., Mass., 1974; nominee Rep. Party for Atty. Gen., Mass., 1986; campaign chmn. Shriver for Pres. Campaign Com., 1976; advisor Nat. Commn. on Violence, 1968-69; cons. Nat. Commn. on Rev. of Nat. Policy Toward Gambling, 1974-76. Lt. (j.g.) USN, 1955-57; with USNR, 1957-72. Recipient Letter of Commendation FBI Dir. Edgar Hoover, 1968. Office: US Court District US Courthouse 1 Courthouse Way Boston MA 02210*

HARRINGTON, GARY BURNES, retired controller; b. Parkville, Mo., Nov. 8, 1934; s. George Burnes and Ethel Mae (Burge) H.; m. Doris Ann Scott, Oct. 28, 1953; children: Gary Burnes Jr., Sherri Ann, Michael Scott, John Patrick, Heather May. Student, Oklahoma City U., 1962-67. Acctg. supr. CIT Fin. Svcs., Oklahoma City, 1952-76; sr. auditor CIT Fin. Corp., N.Y.C., 1976-83; sr. supervising auditor CIT Fin. Corp., Livingston, N.J., 1983-86; audit officer Mfrs. Hanover Corp., N.Y.C. and Atlanta, 1986-88, The CIT Group/Sales Fin., Livingston and Oklahoma City, 1988-89; asst. contr. The CIT Group/Sales Financing, Livingston and Oklahoma City, 1989-95; ret. The CIT Group/Sales Financing, 1995. Various positions from Webelo leader to dist. commr. Boy Scouts Am., Oklahoma City and Norman, Okla., 1967—. Sgt. USAF, 1947-48, USAFR. Mem. Inst. Internal Auditors (1st v.p. 1979-80, pres. 1980-81, bd. chmn. 1981-82, Dist. Svc. award 1982), Am. Legion. Democrat. Baptist. Avocations: woodworking, Fishing, Camping, Hunting. Home: 2308 Edgewood St Moore OK 73160-4234

HARRINGTON, JAMES TIMOTHY, lawyer; b. Chgo., Sept. 4, 1942; s. John Paul and Margaret Rita (Cunneen) H.; m. Roseanne Strupeck, Sept. 4, 1965; children: James Timothy, Roseanne, Maris Zajdela. BA, U. Notre Dame, 1964, JD, 1967. Bar: Ill. 1967, Ind. 1968, U.S. Dist. Ct. (no. dist.) Ill. 1967, U.S. Dist. Ct. (no. and so. dists.) Ind. 1968, U.S. Ct. Appeals (7th cir.) 1969, U.S. Ct. Appeals (4th cir.) 1977, U.S. Ct. Appeals (8th cir.) 1979, U.S. Ct. Appeals (3d cir.) 1981, U.S. Supreme Ct. 1979, U.S. Ct. Appeals (D.C. cir.) 1993. Law clk. U.S. Dist. Ct. (no. dist.) Ind., 1967-69; assoc. Rooks, Pitts & Poust, Chgo., 1969-75, ptnr., 1976-87; ptnr. Ross & Hardies, Chgo., 1987—; lectr. environ. law, fed. procedures, adminstrv. law, 1960—. Vice chmn. Mid Am. Legal Found.; bd. dirs. Ill. Safety Coun. Fellow Am. Bar Found.; mem. Ill. Bar Assn., Ind. Bar Assn., Chgo. Bar Assn. (environ. law com., real estate com.), Indsl. Water Waste and Sewer Group (past chmn.), Air and Waste Mgmt. Assn., Assn. Environ. Law Inst., Ill. Assn. Environ. Profls., Law Club Chgo., Legal Club Chgo., Exec. Club Chgo., Union League Club Chgo. Roman Catholic. Home: 746 Foxdale Ave Winnetka IL 60093-1908 Office: Ross & Hardies 150 N Michigan Ave Ste 2500 Chicago IL 60601-7567

HARRINGTON, JEAN PATRICE, college president; b. Denver; d. James Michael and Katherine Ann (Holl) H. BA, Coll. Mt. St. Joseph, 1953; MA, Creighton U., 1958; PhD, U. Colo., 1967; LHD (hon.), Xavier U., 1983, Ohio Dominican Coll., 1988; LLD (hon.), St. Thomas Inst., Cin., 1985, Coll. Mt. St. Joseph, 1988, Hebrew Union Coll., 1990; D. Tech. Studies (hon.), Cin. Tech., 1988; LLD (hon.), No. Ky. U., 1996, U. Dayton, 1999. Joined Sisters of Charity of Cin., 1940; prin. St. Rose of Lima, Denver, 1953-56; tchr. Cathedral H.S., Denver, 1956-58, prin., 1958-68; dir. instl. rsch. Coll. Mt. St. Joseph, Cin., 1968-69, pres., 1977-87; exec. dir. Cin. Youth Collaborative, 1988-90; interim pres. Cin. State Coll., 1997. Bd. dirs. Penrose Hosp., Colorado Springs, 1976-86, St. Mary Corwin Hosp., Pueblo, Colo., 1972-80, Cin. Bicentennial Commn., 1982-89, Samaritan Health Resources, Inc., 1983-96, St. Rita Sch. for Deaf, 1983-86, United Appeal Cabinet, 1983, Cin. Cmty. Chest, 1988-95, Dan Beard coun. Boy Scouts Am., 1988-91; trustee Good Samaritan Hosp. and Health Ctr., Dayton, Ohio, 1978-80, 89-97, bd. dirs., 1989-96; trustee Miami U., 1989-97, chmn. 1994-97; bd. dirs. Coll. of Mt. St. Joseph, 1995—. Recipient Disting. Svc. citation NCCJ, 1987, Women Helping Women award Sorpotimist Internat., 1990, Statesman award Cin. Assn. Execs., 1988, St. Francis award Friars Club, 1994, Daniel Ransahoff Initiative award, 1994, Lincoln award No. Ky. U., 1994, Gt. Living Cincinnatian award C. of C., 1996, Svc. to Edn. award Ohiana Libr. Assn., 1998, Children's Advocate award Beech Acres; named Career Woman of Achievement YWCA, 1981, Disting. Bus. and Profl. Woman of Yr., 1982; inductee Hall of Excellence of Ohio Fedn. of Ind. Colls., 1990. Mem. Nat. Assn. Ind. Colls. and Univs., Assn. Cath. Colls. and Univs. (bd. dirs.), Ohio Found. Ind. Colls., Greater Cin. Consortium Colls. and Univs. (vice chmn. 1980-82), Coun. Ind. Colls. (bd. dirs. 1981-85), Cin. C. of C. (bd. dirs. 1978-84, trustee 1981-85, sec. 1979-85). Roman Catholic.

HARRINGTON, JEREMY THOMAS, clergyman, publisher; b. Lafayette, Ind., Oct. 7, 1932; s. William and Ellen (Cain) H. B.A., Duns Scotus Coll., 1955; postgrad., U. Detroit, 1955, Marquette U., 1961; M.A., Xavier U., Cin., 1965; M.S. in Journalism, Northwestern U., 1967. Joined Order Friars Minor, 1950; ordained priest Roman Catholic Ch., 1959; tchr. Roger Bacon High Sch., Cin., 1960-64; assoc. editor St. Anthony Messenger, Cin., 1964-66; editor St. Anthony Messenger, 1966-81, pub., 1975-81, pub., CEO, 1991—; mem. bd. Franciscan Province Cin., 1969-72, 75-81, chief exec. bd., 1981-90. Author: Your Wedding: Planning Your Own Ceremony, 1974; Editor: Conscience in Today's World, 1970, Jesus: Superstar or Savior?, 1972. Mem. Catholic Press Assn. (pres. 1975-77, dir.), Kappa Tau Alpha. Home: 2014 Springdale Rd Cincinnati OH 45231-1802 Office: St Anthony Messenger 1615 Republic St Cincinnati OH 45210-1298 *My success has been made by others. As a priest, as well as an editor and publisher, my challenge is to discover, recognize, encourage and make available to others the talents of authors and artists. To me, that's a parable of life. The more we can discover, appreciate and foster the good qualities and strengths of others, the more "successful" we are. Success in life is realizing how many gifts are made available to us by God and our fellow human beings.*

HARRINGTON, JOHN LEO, baseball company executive; b. Boston, July 12, 1936; s. John Joseph and Catherine (Quinn) H.; m. Maureen Helen Fitzgibbon, Oct. 3, 1959; children: Debra, Brian, Sean. BS in Bus. Adminstrn., Boston Coll., 1957, MBA, 1966. CPA, Mass. Asst. prof. Boston Coll., 1965-69; treas. Boston Red Sox, 1970-78; sr. v.p. Kaler, Carney Ins. Group, Boston, 1979-80; v.p. JRY Corp., 1981-86, pres., 1987—; gen. ptnr. of Boston Red Sox, 1981—, now CEO; exec. dir., trustee Yawkey Found., Dedham, Mass., 1981—; cons. NASA, Cambridge, 1966-69; bd. dirs. Computer Systems of Am., Boston, 1969-75, Fleet Bank NA, Health and Retirement Properties Trust, 1990-95, N.E. Sports Network, Inc., Hospitality Properties Trust, 1995—. Trustee Dana Farber Cancer Ctr.,-Jimmy Fund, Boston, 1970—, U.S. Little League Baseball Found.; treas. Town of Westwood, Mass., 1979-83; pres., bd. dirs. Boston Coll. Alumni, 1973-77, bd. dir. Nat. Baseball Hall of Fame, 1992—; trustee John F. Kennedy Libr. Found., 1997—. Served to lt. USNR, 1958-65. Recipient Presdl. award Boston Coll., 1976. Mem. AICPAs, Mass. Soc. CPAs, Beta Gamma Sigma. Avocations: sailing, skiing, tennis. Home: 34 Bridle Path Westwood MA 02090-2942 Office: Boston Red Sox 4 Yawkey Way Boston MA 02215-3496*

HARRINGTON, JOHN MICHAEL, JR., lawyer; b. Boston, July 5, 1921; s. John Michael and Marie Bernadine (Ratchford) H.; m. Ellen Patricia White, May 12, 1951; children—John Michael III, Marc W., Francis X. B., Ellen M., Matthew J., Patrick W. A.B., Harvard U., 1943, LL.B., 1949. Bar: Mass. 1949, U.S. Dist. Ct. (Mass.) 1950, U.S. Ct. Appeals (1st cir.) 1956, U.S. Supreme Ct. 1968. Law clk. Supreme Jud. Ct. Mass., Boston, 1949-50; assoc. Ropes & Gray, Boston, 1950-55, 57-61, ptnr., 1961-93, counsel, 1994—; asst. U.S. atty. Dist. of Mass., Boston, 1955-57; trustee Winchester Sav. Bank, Mass., 1966-91; mem. Mass. Jud. Conduct Commn., Boston, 1978-81. Trustee Roxbury Latin Sch., Boston, 1962-67, St. Sebastian's County Day Sch., Needham, Mass., 1973-86; mem. fin. com. Town of Winchester, 1959-62. Served to capt. field arty. U.S. Army, 1943-46, ETO. Fellow Am. Coll. Trial Lawyers, Am. Bar Found.; mem. ABA (standing com. on fed. judiciary 1st cir. 1978-84), Boston Bar Assn. Democrat. Roman Catholic. Clubs: Union (v.p. 1982-86, pres. 1986-88), Curtis, Harvard (Boston). Home: 19 Cabot St Winchester MA 01890-3501 Office: Ropes & Gray One International Pl Boston MA 02110-2624

HARRINGTON, JOHN TIMOTHY, lawyer; b. Madison, Wis., May 26, 1921; s. Cornelius Louis and Emily (Chisholm) H.; m. Deborah Reynolds, May 23, 1948; children—Elizabeth Chisholm, Samuel Parker, Hannah Quincy, Jane McRae. B.S., Harvard U., 1942, LL.B., 1948. Bar: Wis. 1949. Assoc. Quarles & Brady and predecessor firms, Milw., 1948-58; ptnr. Quarles & Brady and predecessor firms, 1958-91; ret., 1991—. Served to lt. comdr. USNR, 1942-46, PTO. Mem. ABA, Wis. Bar Assn., Milw. Bar Assn., Milw. Club. Republican. Home: 924 E Juneau Ave Milwaukee WI 53202-2748 Office: Quarles & Brady 411 E Wisconsin Ave Ste 2550 Milwaukee WI 53202-4497

HARRINGTON, JOHN VINCENT, retired communications company executive, engineer, educator; b. N.Y.C., May 9, 1919; s. John Joseph and Dorothy (Neisel) H.; m. Frances Cullinane, Jan. 23, 1943; children: John F., Nancy Harrington Higgins, Jeffrey, Richard, Brian. B.E.E., Cooper Union, 1940; M.E.E., Poly. Inst. Bklyn., 1948; Sc.D., Mass. Inst. Tech., 1957. Research engr. U.S. Air Force Cambridge Research Lab., Mass., 1946-51; leader data transmission group Lincoln Lab., M.I.T., Cambridge, 1951-56; asso. div. head aircraft control and warning Lincoln Lab., M.I.T., 1956-58, head radio physics div., 1958-63; prof. aeros., astronautics and elec. engring., 1st dir. Center Space Research, M.I.T., 1963-73; v.p. research and engring. Communications Satellite Corp., Washington, 1973-79; sr. v.p. research and devel., dir. COMSAT Labs., Clarksburg, Md., 1979-84; dir. Epsco, Inc., 1964-72, Shawmut County Bank, Cambridge, 1964-73, COMSAT Gen. Telesystems, Inc., Washington, 1973-81, Environ. Research and Tech., Inc., Concord, Mass., 1981-82; mem. Space Applications Bd., NRC, 1975-81. Contbr. articles to profl. jours. Lt. USNR, 1942-46. Recipient Exceptional Civilian Service medal U.S. Air Force, 1952, Exceptional Profl. Achievement citation Cooper Union, 1965, Gano Dunn award Cooper Union, 1983. Fellow IEEE, AAAS, AIAA; mem. St. Andrews South Golf CLub (Fla.), Isles Yacht Club (Fla.). Home: 1048 San Mateo Dr Punta Gorda FL 33950-6364

HARRINGTON, JOSEPH FRANCIS, educational company executive, history educator; b. Boston, Oct. 24, 1938; s. Joseph Francis and Mary Virginia (Lynch) H.; m. Brenda Marie Crowley, Sept. 3, 1966; children: Megan Marie, Christopher Joseph John. BS, Boston Coll., 1960; MA, Georgetown U., 1963, PhD, 1971. Instr. Framingham (Mass.) State Coll., 1966-68, asst. prof., 1968-70, assoc. prof., 1970-72, prof., 1972—, bd. chmn. dept. history, 1972-82; pres. Learning, Inc., Stoughton, 1979—, also bd. dirs.; treas. The East European Rsch. Ctr., 1989—. Author: Masters of War, Makers of Peace, 1985, Powers, Pawns and Parleys, 1978, Tweaking the Nose of the Russians: American-Romanian Relations, 1940-90; editorial bd. dirs. New England Jour. of History, 1991—, mng. editor, 1995—; editor: The Creative Child and Adult Quarterly, 1991-94; contbr. articles to profl. jours. Mem. Stoughton, Mass. Sch. Com., 1971-77, 82-87, 91-94. With U.S. Army, 1962-65. Tchg. fellow Georgetown U., Washington, 1960-62, 65-66, hon. fellow Kennedy Presdl. Libr., 1986-93. Mem. Mass. Assn. for Advancement of Individual Potential (bd. dirs., pres. 1987-89, 90-92, v.p. for R&D 1989), Nat. Assn. Creative Children and Adults (bd. dirs. 1985-92, editor The Creative Child and Adult Quar. 1991-93), New Eng. Slavic Assn. (v.p. 1990-91, treas. 1991-98), Soc. for Romanian Studies (pres. 1994-97, bd. dirs. 1997—), Kennedy Libr. Acad. Adv. Coun. Roman Catholic. Avocations: reading, racquetball. Home: 119 Holmes Ave Stoughton MA 02072-1926 Office: Framingham State Coll State St Framingham MA 01701

HARRINGTON, JOSEPH JOHN, environmental engineering educator; b. N.Y.C., Jan. 17, 1937; s. Joseph John and Eileen Patricia (Cannon) H.; m. Maryalice Lawlor, Aug. 25, 1962; children: Karen, Beth. BCE, Manhattan Coll., 1958; AM, Harvard U., 1959, PhD, 1963. Registered profl. engr., N.Y., Mass., N.H.; diplomate Am. Acad. Environ. Engrs. Cons. engr. Thomas Crimmins Contracting Co., Malcolm Pirnie Engrs., N.Y.C., 1957-59; mem. faculty Harvard U., Cambridge, Mass., 1963—, prof. environ. engring., 1964—, Gordon McKay prof., 1974—, acting dir. Ctr. for Population Studies, 1980-81, acting chmn. dept. population scis., 1980-81, dir. phys. scis. and engring. program, 1982-86, chmn. dept. environ. sci. and physiology, 1982-86, acting dir. occupational health program, 1988-89; v.p., dir. Process Rsch. Inc., Cambridge, 1967-76; cons. Environ. Rsch. and Tech. Inc., Concord, Mass., 1976-78, Metasystems Inc., Cambridge, 1968-80, USPHS, NIH, other fed. agys., 1959—; mem. com. on coastal flooding from hurricanes NAS, 1981-83. Mem. water supply com. Town of Hingham, Mass., 1973-82; mem. long-range solid waste disposal recycling com., 1975-82, City of Cambridge, Mass., tech. advisor water bd., 1992-94, pres., 1995—. Indo-Am. fellow U. Delhi, India, 1977. Fellow APHA, AAAS, Water Environment Fedn., Air and Waste Mgmt. Assn., Chi Epsilon. Home: 18 Highland Ave Cambridge MA 02139-1016 Office: Harvard U Dept Environ Health 665 Huntington Ave Boston MA 02115-6021

HARRINGTON, JUDITH REGINA, English language educator; b. Torrance, Calif., Oct. 1, 1944; d. Dale Lawrence and Ruth Marian (Luttner) H.; m. Robert Landon Wickham; children: Angela, Steven. BA in English, U. Dallas, 1966; MA in English, U. Denver, 1970, postgrad. in gifted edn., 1976-79; postgrad. in English Lit., U. Colo., 1984-89. English tchr. Air Acad. H.S., Colorado Springs, Colo., 1971-81; tchr. English, dept. chair, gifted program coord. Rampart H.S., Colorado Springs, 1981-93; Fulbright Exch. tchr. Turkey, 1993-94; AP English lang., gifted edn. tchr. Rampart H.S., 1995-98, chair dept. English, coord. gifted and talend program, 1998-99, internat. baccalaureate planning coord., 1997-98; planning cadre, tchr. Pine Creek H.S., 1998—; part-time instr. Expository Writing Program U. Colo., Boulder, 1984-85; part-time instr. English Pikes Peak C.C., Colorado Springs, 1985—. Author: (poetry) White Feathers, 1990, Ninth Direction, 1989, (short stories) The Flame and the Log, 1966, A Move Toward the Lost, 1968, (novels) Ghost Giver, 1991, Marriage Museum, 1994; contbg. author Prentice Hall's Masterpieces in World Literature, 1991, Multi-Media Schools, 1998, 99. Asst. coord. City-wide Gifted Edn. Program, U. Colo., Colorado Springs, 1981. Recipient Excellence in Edn. award Colo. Com. for Women's History, 1990; named Tchr. of the Yr., Rampart High Sch., 1991. Home: PO Box 99 Palmer Lake CO 80133-0099

HARRINGTON, KEVIN PAUL, lawyer; b. Paterson, N.J., Jan. 1, 1951; s. James John and theresa Elizabeth (Giblin) H. BA, Niagara U., 1973; JD, N. E. Sch. Law, Boston, 1978. Bar: N.J. 1978, U.S. Dist. Ct. N.J. 1978, U.S. Supreme Ct. 1983. Judicial clerkship to hon. Thomas R. Rumana Paterson, N.J., 1978-79; asst. prosecutor Passaic County Prosecutor's Office, Paterson, N.J., 1979-80; assoc. DeYoe & Guiney, Paterson, N.J., 1980-87; ptnr. Catania & Harrington, N. Haledon, N.J., 1987—. Pres., bd. trustees Clinic for Mental Health Svc., Paterson, N.J., 1990—. Recipient Civil Trial Atty. cert., Supreme Ct. N.J., 1986—. Mem. ATLA (bd. govs.), N.J. Def. Assn., N.J. Bar Assn., Passaic County Bar Assn. (trustee), Def. Rsch. Inst. Avocations: sports, golf, scuba diving. Office: Catania & Harrington 909 Belmont Ave Ste 3 North Haledon NJ 07508-2500

HARRINGTON, LAMAR, curator, museum director; b. Guthrie Center, Iowa, Nov. 2, 1917; d. Arthur Sylvester and Anna Mary (Landkamer) Hannes; m. Stanley John Harrington, 1938 (div. 1972); 1 dau., Linda Harrington Chace. Student, Cornish Sch. Fine Arts, Seattle, 1945-50; BA in History of Art, U. Wash., 1979. Staff Henry Art Gallery, U. Wash., Seattle, 1957-75; assoc. dir. Henry Art Gallery, U. Wash., 1969-75; curator, rsch. assoc. Archives Northwest Art, U. Wash. Libr., 1975-77; dir., chief curator Bellevue Art Mus., Wash., 1985-90; cons. in arts, 1977—; mem. panel visual arts divsn. NEA, 1976-78; juror fellowships Western States Arts Fedn., 1989; pres. Western Assn. Art Mus., 1973-75; trustee Pacific N.W. Arts Ctr., 1971-74; exec. com. Living Treasures video series N.W. Designer-Craftsmen, 1996—, Pacific N.W. Arts Coun. of Seattle Art Mus., 1976, mem. steering com. photography coun., 1977-78; v.p. Pottery Northwest, 1977-78; participant 1st Symposium on Scholarship and Lang., Nat. Endowments for Humanities and Arts, 1981; mem. adv. com. N.W. Oral History Project, Archives Am. Art, 1981; mem. Pilchuck adv. coun., 1992-95; trustee, chmn. archives Pilchuck Glass Sch., 1981-87, Internat. Coun., 1987-92; trustee Seattle bd. Santa Fe Chamber Music Festival, 1981-87, adv. bd. Santa Fe, 1985-89; trustee Puget Sound Chamber Music Soc., 1987-88; lectr. in field, organizer exhbns., leader seminars, mem. art juries, appearances on KCTS TV, 1963-73. Author: Ceramics in the Pacific Northwest: A History, 1979, Washington Craft Forms: an Historical Perspective, 1981; founder: Archives of N.W. Art, U. Wash., 1969, Index of Art in Pacific N.W., U. Wash. Press, 1970; curator Third Wyoming Biennial Exhbn., 1988-89, James W. Washington Jr.: The Spirit in the Stone Bellevue Art Mus., 1989; resident curator, mgr. Frank Lloyd Wright: In the Realm of Ideas Bellevue Art Mus., 1989; curator: Between Night and Morning: The Work of Guy Anderson, 1990, Eternal Laughter: A Sixty-Yr. Retrospective of George Tsutakawa Bellevue Art Mus., 1990; contbr. author, curator The History of Twentieth Century Am. Craft, Am. Craft Mus., 1996. Recipient Friends of Crafts award Seattle, 1972, Woman of Achievement award Women in Communications, 1974, Gov. Writer's award, 1980, Arts Svc. award King County Arts Commn., 1987, Gov. Wash. Art award, 1988, Bellevue Art Commn. Arts award, 1989, Community Svc. award Am. Inst. Interior Designers, 1990, Pyramid award Corp. Coun. for Arts, 1990; establishment of LaMar Harrington endowment Bellevue Art Mus., 1991. Fellow Am. Crafts Coun. (hon.); mem. AIA (hon.), Pacific N.W. Arts and Crafts Assn. (pres. 1957-59), Allied Arts Seattle (trustee 1962-81), Japan-Am. Soc. Wash. (trustee 1986-88), U. Washington Retirement Assn. (exec. com. 1992-94, curator art collection Univ. House at Wallingford 1995—). Home: Apt 319 4400 Stone Way N Seattle WA 98103

HARRINGTON, MARION RAY, ophthalmologist; b. Dallas, Sept. 20, 1924; s. Silas Fredrick and Mary Katherine (Ray) H.; m. Nan Puckhober, Oct. 1, 1942; 1 child, Nan Katherine Kern. Student, U. Tex., 1942, M.D., 1947. Diplomate: Am. Bd. Ophthalmology. Intern St. Paul Hosp., Dallas, 1941-48; chief ophthalmology Portsmouth (Va.) Naval Hosp., 1950-52; practice medicine specializing in ophthalmology Dallas, 1952—; mem. faculty U. Tex., Southwestern Med. Sch., Dallas, 1952—; clin. prof. U. Tex., Southwestern Med. Sch., 1975—. Served with USN, 1947-48, 50-52. Fellow ACS, Internat. Coll. Surgeons; mem. AMA, Tex. Med. Assn., Dallas County Med. Soc., So. Med. Soc., Am. Acad. Ophthalmology, Am. Assn. Ophthalmology, Tex. Acad. Ophthalmology and Otolaryngology, Tex. Ophthalmologic Assn., Dallas Acad. Ophthalmologists, Royal Soc. Medicine, Internat. Lens Implant Soc., Contact Lens Soc. Episcopalian. Home: 3620 Overbrook Dr Dallas TX 75205-4327

HARRINGTON, MARY EVELINA PAULSON (POLLY HARRINGTON), religious journalist, writer, educator; b. Chgo.; d. Henry Thomas and Evelina (Belden) Paulson; m. Gordon Keith Harrington, Sept. 7, 1957; children: Jonathan Henry, Charles Scranton. BA, Oberlin Coll., 1946; postgrad., Northwestern U., Evanston, Ill., Chgo., 1946-49, Weber State U., Ogden, Utah, 1970s, 80s; MA, U. Chgo.-Chgo. Theol. Sem., 1956. Publicist Nat. Coun. Chs., N.Y.C., 1950-51; mem. press staff 2d assembly World Coun. Chs., Evanston, Chgo., 1954; mgr. Midwest Office Communication, United Ch. of Christ, Chgo., 1955-59; staff writer United Ch. Herald, N.Y.C., St. Louis, 1959-61; affiliate missionary to Asia, United Ch. Bd. for World Ministries, N.Y.C., 1978-79; freelance writer and lectr., 1961—; corr. Religious News Svc., 1962—; prin. lectr. Women & Family Life in Asia series to numerous librs., Utah, 1981, 81-82; pub. rels. coord. Utah Energy Conservation/Energy Mgmt. Program, 1984-85; tchr. writing Ogden Cmty. Schs., 1985-89; adj. instr. writing for publs. Weber State U., 1986—; instr. Acad. Lifelong Learning, Ogden, 1992—, Eccles Cmty. Art Ctr., Ogden, 1993—; dir. comm. Shared Ministry, Salt Lake City, 1983—; chmn. comm. Intermountain Conf., Rocky Mountain Conf., Utah Assn. United Ch. of Christ, 1970-78, 82—, Ind. Coun. Chs., 1960-63; chmn. comm. Ch. Women United Utah, 1974-78, Ogden rep., 1980—, hostess Northern Utah, 1998. Editor: Sunshine and Moonscapes: An Anthology of Essays, Poems, Short Stories, 1994, (booklet) Family Counseling Service: Thirty Years of Service to Northern Utah, 1996; contbr. numerous articles and essays to religious and other publs. Pres. T.O. Smith Sch. PTA, 1976-78, Ogden City Coun. PTA, 1983-85; assoc. dir. Region II, Utah PTA, Salt Lake City, 1981-83, mem. State Edn. Commn., 1982-87; chmn. state internat. hospitality and aid Utah Fedn. Women's Clubs, 1982-86; v.p. Ogden dist., 1990-92, pres. Ogden dist., 1992-96, state resolutions com., 1996—; trustee Family Counseling Svc. No. Utah, Ogden, 1983-95, emeritus trustee, 1995—; Utah rep. to nat. bd. Challenger Films, Inc., 1986—; state pres. Rocky Mountain Conf. Women in Mission, United Ch. of Christ, 1974-77, sec., 1981-84, vice moderator Utah Assn., 1992-94. Recipient Ecumenical Svc. citation Ind. Coun. Chs., 1962, Outstanding Local Pres. award Utah PTA, 1978, Outstanding Latchkey Child Project award, 1985, Cmty. Svc. award City of Ogden, 1980, 81, 82, Celebration of Gifts of Lay Woman Nat. award United Ch. of Christ, 1987, Excellence in the Arts in Art Edn. award Ogden City Arts Commn., 1993, Spirit of Am. Woman in Arts and Humanities award Your Cmty. Connection, Ogden, 1994; Utah Endowment for Humanities grantee, 1981, 81-82. Mem. Nat. League Am. Penwomen (chmn. Utah conv. 1973, 11 awards for articles and essays 1987-95, 1st pl. news award 1992, 1st pl. short stories 1997, 3d pl. articles 1997), AAUW (state edn. rep. 1982-86), League of Utah Writers (Publ. Quill award 1998). Democrat. Avocation: building miniature world of peace each Christmas by family in the home. Home and Office: 722 Boughton St Ogden UT 84403-1152

HARRINGTON, MICHAEL BALLOU, health economist, systems engineer; b. Denver, Sept. 26, 1940; s. Theodore Charles Ballou and DeEtte June (Krastetter) H.; m. Mary Lynn Kijanka, Nov. 17, 1978; 1 child, Meredith Ballou. MS, U. Calif., Irvine, 1969, PhD (NDEA fellow), 1972. With Fgn. Service, Dept. State, 1972-74, Arthur Young & Co., 1975-78; sr. health economist/systems engr. GEOMET Technologies, Inc., Gaithersburg, Md., 1978-80; group leader The Mitre Corp., 1980-87, lead scientist, 1987-96, prin. info. tech. economist, 1997—; adj. prof. Grad. Inst. Bus. and Pub. Affairs, Washington, George Mason U., Fairfax, Va. With USMC, 1958-61. Mem. numerous profl. socs. Club: Potomac Valley Srs. Track. Avocation: writing. Contbr. articles to profl. jours.

HARRINGTON, NANCY D., college president. Pres. Salem (Mass.) State Coll., 1990—. Office: Salem State Coll Office Pres 352 Lafayette St Salem MA 01970-5348*

HARRINGTON, NANCY LYNN, tax accountant; b. Maple Heights, Ohio, Oct. 20, 1971; d. Robert J. Suchan and Donna L. (Josephites) Mansfield; m. Brian P. Harrington, May 21, 1994; 1 child, Meghan Elise. BS, Case Western Res. U., 1994. CPA, Ohio. Retail clk. K-mart, Solon, Ohio, 1988-92; acctg. asst. A.M. McGregor Home, East Cleveland, Ohio, 1993-94; tax sr. Arthur Andersen LLP, Cleve., 1994-98; tax supr. Am. Greetings Corp., Cleve., 1998—. Vol. tutor Project Step-Up, Cleve., 1993-94; vol. tchr. elem. edn. Jr. Achievement, Cleve., 1997—. Mem. AICPA, Ohio Soc. CPA's, Case Western Res. U. Alumni Orgn. (program com. 1996—). Democrat. Roman Catholic. Home: 4468 W 146th St Cleveland OH 44135-2836 Office: Am Greetings Corp 1 American Rd Cleveland OH 44144

HARRINGTON, NANCY REGINA O'CONNOR, volunteer; b. Chgo., Oct. 28, 1928; d. John Roland and Ethel Catherine (Constable) O'Connor; m. James Edward Harrington, Sept. 8, 1951; children: Mary Beth Grayson, Janet Gaines, Gail, Nancy Chartier. BA in art edn., Rosary Coll., River Forest, 1946-50. Cert. art tchr., Ill. Artist Chgo. Park Dist., 1949; art tchr. Chgo. elem. schs., 1951-52; color coord. homes Palos Park (Ill.) Builder, 1957-58; vol. Art Inst. of Chgo., 1980-86. Exhibited in Loyola Ramble, 1970s, Wilmette, 1960s, Palos Park, Ill., Evergreen Park, Ill., Chgo., Osprey, Fla., 1990s, Glenview, Ill., 1980s, 1990s. Bd. mem. Acad. Our Lady H.S. Alumni Bd., 1960's; pres. Mothers Club, v.p. Parents Club Regina Dominican H.S., Wilmette, Ill., 1972-73; vol. Judge Robert Downing Dem. Party, Glenview, Ill., 1974; 1st forelady of criminal ct. Cook County Ct. Sys., Chgo., 1980s; assoc. mem. Art Inst. Chgo., 1990—; vol. Resurrection House Daycare Ctr. for Homeless, Sarasota, Fla., 1993-98, Juvenile Diabetes Found., 1998—; colleague Ringling Mus. Art, Sarasota, 1994—; gen. chair Beaux Arts Festival, The Oaks C.C., 1996; mem. women's bd. Rosary Coll., 1990-98; hostess Hist. Spanish Pointe Fla. Luncheon, 1998, 99; mem. women's bd. dirs. Dominican U., 1997—. Recipient medallion Regina Dominican H.S. Mothers Club, 1972-73, Kemeny Lion medallion Art Inst. Chgo., 1980s, Resurrection House medallion, 1999; Honored vol. Sarasota Arts Coun., 1992. Mem. AAUW, Natl. Heritage Soc., North Shore Country Club (gen. chairperson 9-hole golf, gen. chairperson art festival, 1996), Oaks Country Club (mem. garden club, 1991—, ad hoc archtl. rev. bd., 1991-92, women's bd., 1993, Dominican Univ. Women's Bd., 1997—, vo;. Juvenille Diabetes Found., Sarasota, Fla. 1998, 99, Hostess of Mrs. Potter Palmer Luncheon Historic Spanish Pointe, Osprey, Fla., Ringling Sch. of Art and Design Libr., Chairing Art Seminar of 25th Internat. Congress on Arts and Comm., New Orleans, 1998; gen. chairperson art festival, 1995—, gen. chairperson Oaks Celebrates Arts, 1994, chairperson Art Club, 1993-94; founder Art Appreciation Club, 1993, Artist of Month Column (author) 1994—); founding mem. Nat. Women's Art Museum. Roman Catholic. Avocations: travel, reading, aquacize, opera, duplicate bridge. Home: 210 Saint James Park Osprey FL 34229-9065

HARRINGTON, PETER TYRUS, emergency management company executive, public relations consultant, author, photographer; b. N.Y.C., Aug. 28, 1951; s. Don and Gerry S. (Spolane) H. BA, Union Coll., 1973, MA in Am. Labor, 1975. Spl. investigator U.S. Dept. of Commerce, 1970; staff dir. N.Y. State Assembly, N.Y.C., 1971-73; editorial staff mem., writer, photographer Nat. Geographic Mag., Washington, 1974-76; ptnr. Don Harrington Assocs., Wilton, Conn., 1977—; pres. Harrington Comm., Wilton, 1980—; pub. affairs officer Fed. Emergency-Mgmt. Agy., Washington, 1983—, Fed. Catastrophic "Red" Team, 1996—, exec. officer Hurricane Andrew recovery, 1992-94; chief-of-staff to chmn. County Bd. Commrs., Dade County, Fla., 1994-95; cons. IBM, Armonk, N.Y., 1984-85; contbr. GE Capitol Corp.; contbg. editor Taxfax Mktg. Mag., 1985—; spl. cons. So. Conn. Newspaper Syndicate (Greenwich Time, Stamford Advocate); cons. Expeditions Inc., New Canaan, Conn., 1987-88; contbg. corr. Los Angeles Times, Washington Post Syndicate. Author: The Last Cathedral, 1979 (Book of Yr. award 1979), Never Too Old, 1981; author and photographer, The Sailing Chef, 1978, Maine, 1989; contbr. Murdock, Travel Marketing, Intrepid, Discovery, People, Yankee, Video and TV Guide mags., Smithsonian, Arizona Republic, Chicago Tribune, N.Y. Times, Wall Street Journal, Miami Herald, Boston Herald; contbr. and photographer of many articles with expertise in Amazon and Polar Region. Scoutmaster troop, Boy Scouts Am., Albany, N.Y., 1971-73; exec. dir. ACLU, Albany, 1972-73; mem. bd. Annapolis Youth Ctr., Md., 1978; past pres. Wilton Summer Playshop, 1972—; mem. adv. bd. ARC, Conn. Recipient Pub. Service Citation, Fed. Govt., 1985, Metro-Dade (Fla.), 1993; Fellow Author's Guild, Nat. Press Found., Soros Found.; mem. Washington Writers Assn., Nat. Press Club, Legis. Councils Assn., Am. Soc. Mag. Photographers. Office: Don Harrington Assocs 271 Wilson Ave Satellite Bch FL 32937-2933

HARRINGTON, RICHARD J., newspaper publishing executive; b. 1938. Pres., CEO Thomson Newspapers, Inc., Des Plaines, Ill., 1993—; now pres., CEO The Thomson Corp., Stamford, Conn.; bd. dirs. Associated Press, Newspaper Assn. of America. Office: Thomson Corp The Metro Center One Station Pl 6th Fl Stamford CT 06902*

HARRINGTON, ROBERT DUDLEY, JR., printing company executive; b. Worcester, Mass., Dec. 19, 1932; s. Robert Dudley and Anne Victoria Harrington; m. Melissa Banks Hubner, Mar. 25, 1978 (div.). AB, Brown U., 1955; MBA, Columbia U., 1957. With Morgan Guaranty Trust Co., N.Y.C., 1957-59; v.p. Faulkner, Dawkins & Sullivan, N.Y.C., 1959-69; pres. Printers Express Co., Inc., Greenwich, Conn., 1976—. Trustee, mem. Woods Hole Oceanographic Instn. Corp., pres. Assocs. Mem. N.Y. Yacht Club, Edgartown Yacht Club, Round Hill Club, Edgartown Reading Rm., Holland Lodge, Athelstan Lodge, The Pilgrims, Edgartown Yacht Club (commodore). Office: Printers Express Co Inc 333 Greenwich Ave Greenwich CT 06830-6505

HARRINGTON, ROGER FULLER, electrical engineering educator, consultant; b. Buffalo, Dec. 24, 1925; s. Henry Bassett and Emilie (Fuller) H.; m. Juanita L. Crawford, Aug. 7, 1954; m. Sandra, Judith, Alan, Laura. BS, Syracuse U., 1948, MS, 1950; PhD, Ohio State U., 1952. Instr. Syracuse U., N.Y., 1948-50, asst. prof., 1952-56, assoc. prof., 1956-60, prof., 1960-94, dir. Electromagnetics Ctr., 1982-94; vis. prof. U. Ill., Urbana, 1959-60, U. Calif., Berkeley, 1964, E. China Normal U., 1983, Ecole Poly. Fédéral de Lausanne, Switzerland, 1991; guest prof. Tech. U. Denmark, Lyngby, 1969; cons. in field. Author: Introduction to EM Engineering, 1956, Time-Harmonic EM Fields, 1961, Field Computation by Moment Methods, 1968. Served with USN, 1944-46. Research fellow Ohio State U., Columbus, 1950-52; Fulbright lectr., Denmark, eng., 1969; named Disting. Alumni Ohio State U., 1970; recipient Chancellor's Citation Syracuse U., 1984, URSI van der Pol Gold medal, 1996, jubilee medal Nicola Tesla Found., 1998. Mem. IEEE (Centennial medal 1984, Disting. Achievement award 1989), AAUP, Sigma Xi, Sigma Nu. Home: 5424 N Strada De Rubino Tucson AZ 85750-6061 Office: U Ariz Dept ECE Tucson AZ 85721

HARRINGTON, ROY EDWARDS, agricultural engineer, author; b. Atlanta, Mo., Oct. 23, 1925; s. Quincy K. and Sally Ethel (Edwards) H.; m. Dorose Oleta Zink, Sept. 6, 1953; children: Ellen Joyce Thompson, Janet Lisa Fish, Linda Carol Timmons. BS in Agrl. Engring., U. Mo., 1950. Registered profl. engr., Ill. Product devel. mgr. Deere & Co., Moline, Ill., 1950-66, mgr. product planning, 1971-86, ret., 1986; agrl. engr. Ford Found., New Delhi, 1966-71; cons. farm mechanization Winrock Internat., Ill., 1992, , New Delhi, 1987, Vols. in Tech. Asst., Peshawar, Pakistan, 1989, World Bank, Hungary, 1986; spkr. in field. Author: A Tractor Goes Farming, 1995, Grandpa's John Deere tractors, 1996, How John Deere Tractors & Implements Work, 1997; co-author: John Deere Tractors and Equipment, 1991; author: (booklet) Agricultural Mechanization in India, 1973; holder 21 tractor and farm implement patents, 1953-68; contbr. articles to profl. jours. Pres. Quad Cities World Affairs Coun., Moline, 1981-82; farm equipment mgr. Great Collections of Quad Cities, Moline, 1993; vol. exec. Internat. Exec. Svcs. Corps., Ludhiana, India, 1997. Served to sgt. inf. U.S. Army, 1944-46. Fellow Am. Soc. Agrl. Engrs. (v.p. 1987-90), Indian Soc. Agrl. Engrs.; mem. Soc. Automotive Engrs. Baptist. Avocations: photography, bulldozer operation. Home: 3500 27th Avenue Ct Moline IL 61265-5366

HARRINGTON, THOMAS BARRETT, judge; b. Alexandria, La., Feb. 15, 1936; s. Robert Lee and Clara (Barrett) H.; m. Elizabeth Wheeler; children: Thomas Barrett Jr., Mary Kathryn Harrington Peltier. BS, La. State U., 1958; JD, Tulane U., 1962; grad., Nat. Coll. Criminal Def. Lawyers, 1978. Asst. dist. atty. 15th Jud. Dist., 1970-72; city judge Crowley, 1983—; judge pro tempore 15th Jud. Dist. Ct., Acadia, Lafayette and Vermilion Parish, 1983. Mem. ABA, La. State Bar Assn., Fed. Bar Assn., Assn. Trial Lawyers Am., La. Trial Lawyers Assn., Nat. Assn. Criminal Def. Lawyers. Office: PO Box 225 Crowley LA 70527-0225

HARRINGTON, WALTER HOWARD, JR., judge; b. San Francisco, Aug. 14, 1926; s. Walter Howard and Doris Ellen (Daniels) H.; BS, Stanford, 1947; JD, Hastings Coll., U. Calif., 1952; m. Barbara Bryant, June 1952 (div. 1973); children: Stacey Doreen, Sara Duval; m. 2d, Hertha Bahrs, Sept. 1974. Admitted to Calif. bar, 1953; dep. legislative counsel State of Calif., Sacramento, 1953-54, 55; mem. firm Walner & Harrington, Sacramento, 1954; dep. dist. atty. San Mateo County, Redwood City, Calif., 1955-62; pvt. practice in Redwood City, 1962-84; judge San Mateo County Mcpl. Ct., 1984-90, Superior Ct., 1990-96. Chmn., San Mateo County Criminal Justice Council, 1971-76, San Mateo County Adult Correctional Facilities Com., 1969-71; pro tem referee San Mateo County Juvenile Ct., 1967-72. Ensign USNR, 1944-46. Mem. San Mateo County Bar Assn. (pres. 1969, editor publs. 1964-74), State Bar Calif. (editorial bd. 1968-81, vice chmn. 1969, 74-75, chmn., editor 1975-76), San Mateo County Legal Aid Soc. (pres. 1971-72), Order of Coif, Delta Theta Phi. Republican. Episcopalian. Office: Hall of Justice 400 County Ctr Redwood City CA 94063-1636

HARRINGTON-AUSTIN, ELEANOR JOYCE, educator; b. Florence, S.C., Nov. 12, 1951; d. James Willie and Miriam Hart H.; m. William James Austin, Aug. 19, 1978 (div. April 1982); 1 child, Larry S. Howard III. AB, Duke U., 1973; MA, Tulane U., 1977, PhD, 1995. Tchr. english Hillside High Sch., Durham, S.C., 1973-76, Isidore Newman Sch., New Orleans, 1980-82, Chapel Hill (N.C.) High Sch., 1982-85; program dir. Durham (N.C.) Tech. Cmty. Coll., 1985-90; vis. asst. prof. N.C. Ctrl. U., Durham, 1990—; vis. lectr. N.C. State U., Raleigh, 1998—. Author: Shelley's Post Colonialisty, 1999, (with others) Asia Loves Prometheus, 1999. Dem. precinct sec. Flat River Precinct, Peirson County, N.C., 1992-95; county sec. Peirson County (N.C.) Dem. Party, 1995-99. Grantee Nat. Endowment for the Humanities, 1992-93; fellow Tulane U., New Orleans, 1976-77. Mem. MLA, Keats-Shelley Assn., Triangle South Asia Consortium. Roman Cath. Avocations: poetry writing, collectibles, gardening, sewing. Office: Dept English NC Central Univ Fayetteville Street Durham NC 27707

HARRIS, AARON, management consultant; b. Birmingham, Ala., Oct. 27, 1930; s. Moses and Fannie (Williams) H.; m. Edna Mabel Turner, May 13, 1954; children: Kevin Brian, Edwin Maurice. B.A., Talladega Coll., 1952; M.S., Columbia U., 1959; postgrad., Princeton U., 1961. Trainee Bklyn. Pub. Library, 1956-59; asst. librarian Burroughs Wellcome Co., Tuckahoe, N.Y., 1959-64; assoc. librarian IBM Corp., East Fishkill, N.Y., 1964-66; library mgr. IBM Research Lab., San Jose, Calif., 1966-73; personnel exec. IBM Corp., San Jose, 1973-77; data processing mgr. IBM, 1977-80, mgr. tng. and devel., 1980-84, mgr. human resources info. systems, 1985-88; program mgr. mgmt. devel. Rolm Systems, Santa Clara, Calif., 1988-91; cons.; pres. Amistad Assocs. Gen. chmn. Citizens Com. on Schs., San Jose, 1969-71; mem. San Jose CSC, 1974-78; foreman pro tem Santa Clara County Grand Jury, 1979-80; candidate San Jose Sch. Bd., 1969, 73; past bd. dirs. Santa Clara chpt. ARC, Mus. Art, San Jose; bd. dirs. ACLU of Ala., Opera San Jose, 1986-92, Santa Clara County Urban League, 1984-87; San Jose Planning Commr., 1989-92; bd. dirs. Am. Civil Liberties Union Ala., 1996—. With AUS, 1952-55. Recipient Citizen of Year award Omega Psi Phi, 1970. Mem. Talladega Coll. Alumni Assn. (pres. Birmingham chpt. 1995—). Mem. AME Zion Ch. Home and Office: 341 Turnberry Rd Birmingham AL 35244-3291 *Those who have presented obstacles for failure have been overwhelmed by my confidence. Those who longed for my success have been supportive with encouragement and opportunity. The principles embodied in the golden rule are my constant aim.*

HARRIS, ALICE CARMICHAEL, linguist, educator; b. Columbus, Ga., Nov. 23, 1947; d. Joseph Clarence and Georgia (Walker) H.; m. James Vaughan Staros, Aug. 7, 1976; children: Joseph Vaughan, Alice Carmichael. BA, Randolph-Macon Woman's Coll., 1969; MA, U. Essex (Eng.), 1972; PhD, Harvard U., 1976. Tchg. fellow linguistics Harvard U., Cambridge, Mass., 1972-74, 75-76; lectr. linguistics Harvard U., Cambridge, 1976-77, rsch. fellow linguistics, 1977-79; rsch. asst. prof. linguistics Vanderbilt U., Nashville, 1979-84, assoc. prof. linguistics, 1985-91, assoc. prof. anthropology, 1986-92, prof. linguistics, 1991—, prof. anthropology, 1992—, chair dept. Germanic, Slavic langs., 1993—; chair faculty coun. Coll. Arts and Scis., 1995-96; vice chair grad. faculty coun., 1993-94, sec. faculty senate, 1993-94; assoc. rsch. U. Tbilisi, USSR, 1974-75; tutor linguistics Dunster House, Harvard U., Cambridge, 1975-77; cons. to Simon and Schuster; Erskine vis. prof. U. of Canterbury, Christchurch, New Zealand, 1999. Author: Georgian Syntax, 1981, Diachronic Syntax, 1985, The Indigenous Languages of the Caucasus, 1991; co-author: Historical Syntax in Cross-Linguistic Perspective, 1995 (Leonard Bloomfield book award 1998); mem. editl. bd. Natural Language and Linguistic Theory, 1987-90, assoc. ed. Language, 1988-89; mem. editl. bd. Diachronica, 1994—; mem. adv. com. Publs. MLA, 1995-97; contbr. articles to profl. jours. Sinclair Kennedy fellow Harvard U., 1974-75, NSF Nat. Needs Postdoctoral fellow, 1978-79; grantee Internat. Rsch. and Exch. Bd., 1973, 74-75, 77, 81, 89, 92, Linguistic Soc. Am., 1981, NSF 1980-83, 81-83, 83-85, 85-89, 97-99, NEH, 1990-91, Deutscher Adademischer Austausch Dienst, 1994; scholar Harvard U. 1972-73, Georgetown U., 1973; recipient Mellon Found. Regional Faculty Devel. award 1981, ACLS travel award, 1988, venture fund Vanderbilt U., 1987, 92, 94. Mem. Internat. Soc. Hist. Linguistics (mem. exec. com. 1995—), Linguistic Soc. Am. (cons., com. status women in linguistics, nominating com.), Southeastern Conf. Linguistics, Soc. for Study of Caucasia (exec. coun. 1990—), Societas Caucasologica Europaea (v.p. 1990-92, exec. com. 1992-94, 94—), Modern Lang. Assn., Phi Beta Kappa (Earl Sutherland prize for rsch. Vanderbilt U. 1998). Office: Vanderbilt U Program in Linguistics PO Box 37 Nashville TN 37202-0037

HARRIS, ANN BIRGITTA SUTHERLAND, art historian; b. Cambridge, Eng., Nov. 4, 1937; came to U.S., 1965, naturalized, 1996; d. Gordon B.B.M. and Gunborg Elizabeth (Wahlström) Sutherland; m. William Vernon Harris, July 13, 1965; 1 son, Neil William Orlando Sutherland. B.A. with 1st class honours, Courtauld Inst., U. London, 1961, Ph.D., 1965. Asst. lectr. U. Leeds, 1964-65; asst. prof. art history Columbia U., N.Y.C., 1965-71, Hunter Coll., N.Y.C., 1971-73; assoc. prof. SUNY, Albany, 1973-77; chmn. for acad. affairs Met. Mus. Art, N.Y.C., 1977-80; part-time faculty Juilliard Sch., N.Y.C., 1978-84; prof. U. Pitts., 1984—; founder, 1st pres. Women's Caucus for Art, 1973-76; disting. vis. prof. U. Tex.-Arlington, fall 1982; Mellon prof. history of art U. Pitts., spring 1984; vis. prof. history of art So. Meth. U., Dallas, fall 1993. Author: Andrea Sacchi, 1977, Selected Drawings of Gian Lorenzo Bernini, 1977; co-author: Die Zeichnungen von Andrea Sacchi and Carlo Maratta, 1967, Women Artists: 1550-1950, exhbn. catalogue, 1977, Landscape Painting in Rome, 1575-1675, exhbn. catalogue, 1985. Fellow Guggenheim Found., 1971, Ford Found., 1975-76, NEH, 1981-82, rsch. fellow Getty Mus. Art, 1988. Mem. Coll. Art Assn., Women's Caucus for Art. Office: U Pittsburgh Dept History of Art Pittsburgh PA 15260

HARRIS, ANNIE RENE, elementary school teacher; b. Eden, Miss., Aug. 20, 1946; d. Tommie L. and Rosetta (Tolbert) H. BS in Edn., Jackson (Miss.) State Coll., 1968, MS, 1972, EdS, 1974; EdD, Ind. U., 1983. Cert. elem. tchr., Miss. Elem. tchr. Jackson Pub. Schs.; asst. prof. edn. Ky. State U., Frankfort, Western Ky. U., Bowling Green; elem. tchr. Atlanta Pub. Schs.; guest lectr. home econs. dept. Indiana U., Bloomington, 1982-83; elem. tchr. Atlant Pub. Schs. Former leadership team chairperson E.L. Connally Sch., Atlantic Pub. Schs. Olympics Com., chair Red Cross and March of Dimes for E.L. Connally Elem. Sch.; rep. Am. Heart Fund; mem. PTA. Recipient Outstanding Elem. Tchr. Am. award, 1975, Finer Womanhood award Nat. Coun. Negro Women, 1980, Disting. Svc. citation United Negro Coll. Fund, 1979-80, Ky. Amb. Goodwill award, 1986, Atlanta Asssn. Educators cert., 1996-97, Achievement cert. Atlanta Fedn. Tchrs., 1996-97, Spl. Congrl. Recognition for Edn. cert. Rep. John Lewis, 1997, Spl. Recognition in Edn. cert. Phi Delta Kappa Soroity, 1997, John Herkiotz award for outstanding contbns. of tchg. democracy for work in mock election NASSP, 1997, Cert. of Appreciation Am. Red Cross Mem. Enrollment Campaign, 1997-98; named Tchr. of Yr., Connally Elem. Sch., 1996-97, Coca-Cola, 1996-97. Mem. NEA, Coun. for Exceptional Children.

HARRIS, ARTHUR HORNE, biology educator; b. Middleborough, Mass., May 18, 1931; s. Frank Arthur and Winifred Stevens (Deane) H.; div.; children: Tina Melissa, Rebecca Ann, Megan Aneen. BA, U. N.Mex., 1958, MS, 1959, PhD, 1965; postgrad., U. Ariz., 1959-60. Asst. prof. Ft. Hays Kans. State Coll., 1962-65; from asst. prof. to prof. U. Tex.-El Paso, 1965—; curator vertebrate paleobiology, 1967—, co-dir. resource collections lab. environ. biology, 1980-93, curator higher vertebrates, 1983—, dir. lab environ. biology, 1993—; biology educator; b. Middleborough, Mass., May 18, 1931; s. Frank Arthur and Winifred Stevens (Deane) H.; div.; children—Tina Melissa, Rebecca Ann, Megan Aneen. B.A., U. N.Mex., 1958, M.S., 1959, Ph.D., 1965; postgrad. U. Ariz., 1959-60. Asst. prof. Ft. Hays Kans. State Coll., 1962-65; from asst. prof. to prof. U. Tex.-El Paso, 1965—, curator vertebrate paleobiology, 1967—, co-dir. resource collections lab. environ. biology, 1980-93, , curator higher vertebrates, 1983—, dir. lab environ. biology, 1993—. Co-author: The Mammals of New Mexico, 1975, The Faunal Remains from Arroyo Hondo Pueblo, 1984; author: Late Pleistocene Vertebrate Paleocology of the West, 1985. Served with U.S. Army, 1951-53. NSF grantee, 1967-70; Nat. Geog. Soc. grantee, 1971-73, 84-86; recipient Faculty Research award U. Tex.-El Paso, 1976. Mem. Am. Soc. Mammalogists, Soc. Vertebrate Paleontology, Southwestern Assn. Naturalists (editor 1978-82), Soc. Systematic Biology, Am. Quaternary Assn. Democrat. Co-author: The Mammals of New Mexico, 1975, The Faunal Remains from Arroyo Hondo Pueblo, 1984; author: Late Pleistocene Vertebrate Paleocology of the West, 1985. Served with U.S. Army, 1951-53. NSF grantee, 1967-70; Nat. Geog. Soc. grantee, 1971-73, 84-86; recipient Faculty Research award U. Tex.-El Paso, 1976. Mem. Am. Soc. Mammalogists, Soc. Vertebrate Paleontology, Southwestern Assn. Naturalists (editor 1978-82), Soc. Systematic Biology, Am. Quaternary Assn. Democrat. Home: 665 Stedham Cir El Paso TX 79927-4202 Office: University of Texas Laboratory for Environmental BIO Centennial Mus and Dept Of Biology El Paso TX 79968

HARRIS, BARBARA C(LEMENTINE), bishop; b. Phila., 1930. Grad., Charles Morris Price Sch. Advt. and Journalism, Phila.; student, Villanova U., Urban Theology Unit, Sheffield, Eng.; D in Sacred Theology (hon.), Hobart and William Smith Colls., 1981; DD (hon.), Gen. Theol. Sem., 1989, Episc. Div. Sch., 1989, Amherst Coll., 1989. Ordained to ministry Episcopal Ch. as deacon, 1979, as priest, 1980. Pres. Joseph V. Baker Assocs., Phila., 1958-68; sr. staff cons., mem. community rels. dept. Sun Oil Co.; priest-in-charge St. Augustine of Hippo, Norristown, Pa.; interim rector Ch. of the Advocate, Phila.; exec. dir. Episc. Ch. Pub. Co., 1984-88; suffragan bishop Episcopal Diocese of Mass., Boston, 1989—; trustee Episc. Div. Sch. Address: Episc Diocese of Mass 138 Tremont St Boston MA 02111-1319

HARRIS, BAYARD EASTER, lawyer; b. Washington, July 22, 1944; s. Edward Bledsoe and Grace (Childrey) H.; m. Rebecca Bond Jeffress, June 10, 1967; children: Nicholas Bayard, Nathan Bedford (dec. 1989), Ellen Coley. AB in History, U. N.C., 1966; JD cum laude, U. S.C., 1973. Bar: Va. 1974, U.S. Dist. Ct. (we. dist.) Va. 1974, U.S. Ct. Appeals (4th cir.) 1974, U.S. Supreme Ct. 1982. Assoc. Woods, Rogers, Muse, Walker & Thornton, Roanoke, Va., 1973-79, ptnr., 1979-85; ptnr. Woods, Rogers & Hazlegrove, Roanoke, 1985-90; pres. Ctr. for Employment Law, Roanoke, 1991-98; of counsel Woods, Rogers and Hazlegrove, PLC, 1998—; mem. Transp. Safety Bd., 1992-96. Comments and rsch. editor U. S.C. Law Rev., 1972-73. Chpt. chmn. ARC, Roanoke Valley, 1985-87, chmn. ea. ops. hdqrs., 1988-91. Lt. USNR, 1966-70. Recipient Clara Barton award ARC Roanoke Valley chpt., 1986. Mem. ABA (labor and employment sect. 1974—), Va. Bar Assn. (labor and employment com. and sect. 1974—), Rotary. Republican. Episcopalian. Avocations: golf, gardening. Office: Woods Rogers & Hazlegrove 10 S Jefferson St Ste 1400 Roanoke VA 24011-1314

HARRIS, BEN M., education educator; b. Chgo., Feb. 8, 1923; s. Eva Mae (Barber) Sands; m. Mary Lee Christian, Sept. 28, 1948; children: Kim Christian, Tamara Lee. AA, Glendale Coll., 1943; BA, UCLA, 1948, MEd, 1951; EdD, U. Calif., Berkeley, 1958. Cert. elem. tchr., secondary tchr., prin., sch. adminstr., Calif. Chemist Desert Chem. Co., Twenty Nine Palms, Calif., 1943-44; tchr. Burbank (Calif.) Jr. High Sch., 1948-51; curriculum coordinator Inyo County Schs., Independence, Calif., 1951-54; tchr. Lafayette (Calif.) Elem. Sch., 1954-55; dir. curriculum Lafayette Sch. Dist., 1955-56, dir. pers., 1956-57; acad. asst. dept. edn. U. Calif., Berkeley, 1957-58; asst., then assoc. prof. U. Tex., Austin, 1958-68, prof. edn. adminstrn., 1968-87, M.K. Hage Centennial prof. edn., 1987, prof. emeritus, 1988—; cons. Ministry Edn., Venezuela, 1973, Bahrain, 1985, Effective Border Schs. R&D Initiative, 1995-96; vis. prof. U. Wash., Seattle, 1976, U. Tex., San Antonio, 1989, U. Tex. Pan Am., Edinburg, 1992; planning cons. Ministry of Edn., Egypt, 1987, Venezuela, 1973, 75, Malaysia, 1989, 91; UNESCO advisor U. Cordoba, Spain, 1971, U. Petroleum and Minerals, Dharan, 1979; advisor Lagoven, S.A. Venezuela Petroleum, 1991-92, Am. 2000 New Generation Schs. Project, Austin, 1991-92; vis. lectr. Taiwan Tchrs. Coll., Taichung/Kaochsfungand, 1994. Author: Supervisory Behavior in Education, 1963, 3d edit., 1985, Developmental Teacher Evaluation, 1986, Inservice Education for Staff Development, 1980, 2d edit., 1989; (with others) Inservice Education: A Guide to Better Practice, 1969, Personnel Administration in Education, 1980, 3d edit., 1992, Invention—Developmental Teacher Evaluation Kit, 1982, co-developer Diagnostic Executive Competency Assessment System, 1988. Served with USNR, 1944-46. Fulbright scholar U. Teheran, Iran, 1962-63, Bahrain, 1985. Mem. ASCD (nat. bd. dirs. 1973-75, 80-82), Am. Edn. Rsch. Assn., Coun. Profs. of Instrnl. Supervision (pres. 1976-77), Sam Bass Theatre Assn., Trad. Jaszz Club, Fulbright Alumni Assn., Phi Delta Kappa. Avocations: country and western dancing, singing, gardening. Office: U Tex Austin Dept Ednl Adminstrn George Sanchez Bldg # 310 Austin TX 78712

HARRIS, BENJAMIN HARTE, JR., lawyer; b. Mobile, Ala., Sept. 12, 1937; s. Ben H. and Mary Cade (Aldridge) H.; m. Martha Elliott Lambeth, Aug. 26, 1961; children: Benjamin Harte, Wayt. AB, Davidson Coll., 1959; JD, U. Ala., 1962. Bar: Ala. 1962, U.S. Dist. Ct. (so. dist.) Ala. 1964, U.S. Ct. Appeals (5th cir.) 1981, U.S. Supreme Ct. 1971, U.S. Ct. Appeals (11th cir.) 1981. Assoc. Johnstone, Adams, Bailey, Gordon & Harris (formerly Johnstone, Adams, May, Howard & Hill, L.L.C.), Mobile, Ala., 1964-70, mem., 1971—; chmn. Atty's Ins. Mut. Ala., bd. dirs. Past chmn. bd. dirs. Boys' Club, 1989-95; past chmn., past trustee UMS Prep Sch.; v.p., bd. dirs. Gordon Smith Ctr.; mem. standards com. United Way. Life fellow Am. Bar Found.; fellow Ala. Law Found.; mem. ABA (past ho. of dels., past bd. govs.), Ala. Law Found. (past pres., trustee), Mobile County Bar Assn. (exec. com. 1980-87), Ala. State Bar (bd. commrs. 1978-87, mem. exec. com., trustee bar found., past chmn. disciplinary commn., past pres.), Ala. Law Inst., Ala. Law Sch. Found. (past pres., trustee), Ala. Def. Lawyers Assn., Am. Judicature Soc., Am. Arbitration Assn., Ala. Jud. Commn., 11th Cir Ct. Appeals Hist. Soc. (trustee, v.p.), Nat. Conf. Bar Pres. (past exec. coun.), Brock Inn of Ct. (pres. 1996-98), Mobile Rotary Club (Paul Harris fellow), Athelstan Club. Episcopalian. Office: PO Box 1988 Mobile AL 36633-1988

HARRIS, BENJAMIN LOUIS, chemical engineer, consultant; b. Savannah, Ga., Aug. 1, 1917; s. Raymond Branson and Edith (Kontner) H.; m. Janet Diekmann, Oct. 4, 1942; children: Benjamin S., Stefanie Harris Hunt, Deborah Harris Kommalan, Penelope Harris Clifton, Rebecca Harris Gutin. BE, Johns Hopkins U., 1938, PhD, 1941; diploma, Indsl. Coll. Armed Forces, Washington, 1965. Registered profl. engr., Md. Asst. prof. Johns Hopkins U., Balt., 1946-53; with R & D Command U.S. Army, Edgewood Arsenal, Md., 1952-66; dep. asst. dir. def. R & D U.S. Office Sec. Def., Alexandria, Va., 1966-70; tech. dir. U.S. Army Chem. Rsch., Devel. and Engrng. Ctr., Aberdeen, Md., 1970-81; pres. Engrng. Rsch. Co. of Glenarm, Md., 1981-83; cons. in field, 1981—; pres. Profl. Engrs. Bd., Md., 1987-88, v.p., 1988-98. Editor St. George Philatelic Soc. Newsletter, 1988-96; patentee in field, contbr. articles to profl. jours. Mem. Gov.'s Exec. Adv. Coun., Md., 1988-95; mem. exec. bd. Balt. Area coun. Boy Scouts Am., 1964—; mem. adv. com. USCG, NRC, Washington, 1967-77; mem. com. ethics and professionalism Nat. Coun. Examiners Engrng. and Surveying. Maj. U.S. Army, 1941-46, Res., 1938-41, 46-77, ret. col., 1977. Recipient Silver Beaver award Boy Scouts Am., 1952, Silver Antelope award, 1987, Disting. Eagle award, 1976, Lamb award Luth. Ch., 1964, St. George award Cath. Ch., 1983; named Ky. Col. Fellow AAAS, AIChE; mem. SAR (past pres. Col. Nicholas Ruxton Moore chpt.), Am. Chem. Soc., Order Founders and Patriots Am. (gov. gen. 1996-98), Sons and Daus. of Pilgrims (gov. Md. br. 1996-98), Soc. Boonesborough, Nat. Congress Patriotic Orgns., Descendants of Ancient Planters, Sons of Confederate Vets., Soc. of Colonial Wars State of Md., Order of the Crown of Charlemgne USA, Order Honorable Arty. Co., St. George Soc. Balt., St. Andrews Soc. Balt., Ancient and Honorable Mech. Co. of Balt., Nat. Gavel Soc., Mil. Order World Wars (past comdr. Balt.-Devereaux chpt.), Ret. Officers Assn., Res. Officers Assn., Chem. Corps Regtl. Assn., Soc. of War of 1812 in State of Md. Democrat. Lutheran. Avocations: genealogy, philately, crafts, gardening. Home and Office: 11323 Glen Arm Rd Glen Arm MD 21057-9434

HARRIS, BILL DEAN, card services manager; b. Seminole, Okla., Sept. 24, 1954; s. Fay D. and Wanda J. (Pope) H.; m. Cheryl L. Kassin, May 31, 1980; 1 child, Cory. Diploma in banking adminstrn., Okla. Sch. Banking and Bus., 1973; student, Okla. League Savs. Instns., 1978. V.p. Homestead Savs., Woodward, Okla., 1973-84, First Fed. Savs., Hutchinson, Kans., 1984-90; asst. v.p. Cimarron Fed. Savs., Muskogee, Okla., 1990-91; card svcs. mgr. Data Ctr., Inc., Hutchinson, Kans., 1991—; cons. Landmark Fed. Bank, Dodge City, Kans., 1996. Mem. The Adv. Group, Akron, Ohio, 1993—. Named one of Outstanding Young Men in Am., 1982. Mem. Masons (sec., treas. Woodward lodge 189 1976-80). Republican. Mem. Christian Ch. (Disciples of Christ). Avocations: reading, swimming, walking. Home: 3310 Nutmeg Ln Hutchinson KS 67502-2928 Office: Data Ctr Inc 220 E Sherman St Hutchinson KS 67501-7189

HARRIS, BOB L(EE), retired educational administrator; b. Chesapeake, Ohio, Mar. 7, 1938; s. Hiram Hurston and Emma Louise (Bevans) H.; m. Beverly Sue Fuller, June 17, 1959; children: Robert Todd, Amy Beth Harris Bane. Cert. cadet, Rio Grande Coll., 1957, BS in Elem. Edn., 1965; M of Ednl. Adminstrn., Marshall U., 1975, cert. postmasters supt., 1981. Tchr. Chesapeake East Elem. Sch., 1957-58, 60-71, occupational work adjustment coord., 1971-74; tchr. Chesapeake West Elem. Sch., 1958-60, asst. prin., 1974-75, prin., 1975-97; ret., 1997. Mem., asst. PTA, Chesapeake, 1975—. Mem. Ohio Ret. Tchrs. Assn. (life), Ohio Assn. Track and C.C. Coaches (dist. rep. 1964-75, 81-88, ofcl., interpreter local rules 1964-90, Hall of Fame inductee 1982), Athletic Congress (ofcl. 1980-92, U.S.A. Track and Field ofcl. 1992—). Republican. Mem. Ch. of Christ. Home: 98 Township Road 1364 Chesapeake OH 45619-7096

HARRIS, BRENDA LEE, college administrator; b. Marlbough, Mass., Apr. 22, 1966; d. James Joseph and Jean Patricia (Gabrielsen) Burke. BBA in Fin. and Ins., Radford U., 1988; MSEd in Higher Edn. Adminstrn., Old Dominion U., 1996. Fin. aid dir. Va. Inst. Tech., Virginia Beach, 1988-89, Computer Dynamics Inst., Virginia Beach, 1989-92; placement dir. Tidewater Tech. Inst., Virginia Beach, 1992-93; enrollment svcs. specialist Tidewater C.C., Chesapeake, Va., 1993—. Mem. Va. C.C. Assn. (support staff showcase person 1997), Tidewater C.C. Classified Assn. (pres. 1997-98), Va. Assn. Fin. Aid Adminstrs. (co-chair membership 1997-98, award 1997). Roman Catholic. Avocations: cross-stitch, reading. Home: Lakes of Greenbrier 1128 Merchants Ct #2B Chesapeake VA 23320 Office: Tidewater CC 1428 Cedar Rd Chesapeake VA 23322-7108

HARRIS, BRENT RICHARD, investment company executive; b. Portland, Oreg., Aug. 6, 1959; s. Richard Thomas and Joan Kathleen (Robison) H.; m. Elizabeth Edwards, Sept. 20, 1986. BA in Econs. cum laude, Claremont McKenna Coll., 1981; MBA, Harvard U., 1985. CFA; chartered investment counselor. Sr. rsch. assoc. Claremont (Calif.) Econs. Inst., 1981-83; account mgr. Pacific Investment Mgmt. Co., Newport Beach, Calif., 1985-87, v.p., 1987-90, sr. v.p., 1990-91, mng. dir., 1991—; chmn. PIMCO Funds, 1992—; bd. dirs. Harris Holdings, Portland. Mem. L.A. Soc. Fin. Analysts. Republican. Avocations: golf, hiking. Office: PIMCO 840 Newport Center Dr Newport Beach CA 92660-6310

HARRIS, BRIAN CRAIG, lawyer; b. Newark, Sept. 8, 1941; s. Louis W. and Lillian (Frankel) H.; m. Ellen M. Davis, Aug. 20, 1978; children: Andrea, Keith. BS, boston U., 1963; JD, Rutgers U., 1966. Bar: N.J. 1968, D.C. 1968, U.S. Ct. Appeals (3d cir.) 1968, N.Y. 1984, U.S. Ct. Appeals (2d cir.) 1985. Asst. corp. counsel Newark, 1968-70; assoc. Braff, Litvak & Ertag, East Orange, N.J., 1970-72; ptnr. Braff, Litvak, Ertag, Wortmann & Harris, East Orange, 1972-85, Braff, Ertag, wortmann, Harris & Sukoneck, Livingston, N.J., 1985-91, Braff, Harris & Sukoneck, 1991—; adj. lectr. law and medicine Seton Hall U., South Orange, N.J., 1982-83, trial preparation Rutgers U. Law Sch., 1983, strategy of def. United Tech. Corp., Chgo., 1986. Sustaining mem. Product Liability Adv. Coun., Inc.; contbg. mem. Nat. Ileitis found., N.Y.C., 1983—. Named Master of Inns. of Ct., Arthur J. Vanderbilt Sect., 1988. Mem. ABA (employment law sect., tort and ins. sect.), Internat. Assn. Def. Counsel, Profl. Liability Underwriters Soc., N.Y. State Bar Assn., N.Y. Trial Lawyers Assn., Essex County Trial Lawyers Assn., Middlesex County Trial Lawyers Assn., Def. Rsch. Inst. (mem. com. employment law, mem. com. profl. liability, trustee Hamonie Group), N.J. Trial Lawyers Assn., N.J. Def. Assn., East Hampton Indoor Outdoor Tennis Club, Orange Lawn Tennis Club. Jewish. Avocations: running, basketball, theater, tennis, study of military strategy of land forces in World War II. Home: Llewellyn Pk West Orange NJ 07052-5402 Office: Braff Harris & Sukoneck 570 W Mt Pleasant Ave Livingston NJ 07039-1619 also: 305 Broadway Fl 7 New York NY 10007-1109

HARRIS, BURTON H., surgeon; b. N.Y.C., Jan. 30, 1941; s. Mark and Nettie (Bilsky) H.; m. Kathleen Mary Donnelly; children: David, Robert, Eileen, Mark. BA, Hobart Coll., 1961; MD, SUNY, N.Y.C., 1965. Intern, resident, and chief resident in surgery SUNY, 1965-71; chief resident in pediatric surgery Children's Hosp., Columbus, Ohio, 1971-73; prin. Drs. Wilkinson, Webb & Harris P.A., Jacksonville, Fla., 1973-81; dir. Kiwanis Pediat. Trauma Inst. New Eng. Med. Ctr., Boston, 1981-95, chief div. pediatric surgery, 1985-95; surgeon-in-chief Georgetown Children's Med. Ctr., Washington, 1995-98; dir. pediat. surgery Meml. Hosp., Colorado Springs, 1998—; Orvar Swenson prof. pediatric surgery Tufts U. Sch. Medicine, Boston, 1981-95; prof. surgery & pediat. Sch. Medicine Georgetown U., 1995-98. Editor: Progress in Pediatric Trauma, 1985, 87, 89, 92; assoc. editor Jour. Pediat. Surgery; contbr. articles to profl. jours. Med. advisor Profl. Golf Assn. Tour, Ponte Vedra, Fla., 1977-95. Brig. gen. (OM) USAR, 1966-93; ret. Decorated Legion of Merit, D.S.M.; NIH fellow, 1961-64, Am. Cancer Soc. clin. fellow, 1971-73. Fellow ACS (chpt. pres. 1980-81, state com. chmn. 1989-95), Am. Coll. Emergency Physicians, Am. Cancer Soc., Am. Pediatric Surg. Assn., Am. Acad. Pediatrics, Soc. Pediatric Trauma (pres. 1989-91), Ea. Assn. for Surgery Trauma (pres. 1989-90), Am. Trauma Soc. (dir. 1986-92), Internat. Soc. Aeromed. Svcs. (pres. 1988-90), New Eng. Pediatric Surg. Soc. (pres. 1988-95), Wellesley (Mass.) Country Club, Broadmoor Golf Club (Colorado Springs). Republican. Avocations: golf, baroque music.

HARRIS, CARLEINA HAMPTON, muncipal or county official, educator. BSN, Winston-Salem State U., 1963; postgrad., U. Md., 1969; MA in Health Sci. Adminstrn., Jersey City State Coll., 1974; postgrad., Montclair State Coll., 1978. Cert. nursing adminstr. Clin. instr. Hunter/Bellevue Sch. Nursing, N.Y.C., 1972-74; adj. prof. St. Joseph Coll., Bklyn., 1975-80; asst. dir. nursing dept. surgery Harlem Hosp. Ctr., N.Y.C., 1981-85; from dir. nursing to mng. dir. cmty. health edn. United Hosps. Med. Ctr., Newark, 1985-94; mgr. divsn. social svcs. City of Newark, 1994—; dir. sch. practical nursing City of Newark, 1977-81; instr., supr. Harlem Hosp. Sch. Nursing, N.Y.C., 1970-77. Cmty. adv. bd. Essex County Coll. Equal Opportunity Fund; Essex County Adv. Bd. on Status of Women. Recipient Black Achiever of Bus. and Edn. award. Mem. ANA, NAFE, Nat. League Nursing, Nat. Assn. Negro Bus. and Profl. Women's Club (N.J. unit), Black Nurses Assn., N.J. State Nurses Assn., N.J. Soc. Healthcare Edn. and Tng., Winston-Salem State U. Alumni Assn., Alpha Kappa Alpha. Fax: 973 733-4499. Office: City of Newark Divsn Social Svcs 94 William St Newark NJ 07102-1316*

HARRIS, CAROLE RUTH, educational consultant, researcher; b. N.Y.C., Nov. 29, 1933; d. Erwin and Fay (Fisher) Marks; m. Donald Schulkind, Jan. 23, 1955 (div. Oct. 1980); children: Laura Margaret, Heidi Elyse; m. John Nathaniel Harris, May 19, 1983. BA in English, Hunter Coll. CUNY, 1955; MA in English, Adelphi U., 1966; EdD in Curriculum/Tchg./Edn. Gifted, Columbia U., 1987; postgrad. various specialized edn. studies and English literature, SUNY, Stony Brook and Albany; postgrad. various specialized edn. studies, Empire State Coll., U. So. Calif. Los Angeles, U. Hawaii. Tchr. English N.Y.C. Pub. Schs., 1955-57; instr. dept. English Adelphi U., Garden City, N.Y., 1966-68; teaching asst. SUNY, Stonybrook, 1968-70, supr. elem. undergrad. student teaching, 1970-72; master tchr., cons. creative writing and humanities BOCES Inst. Gifted and Talented Youth, 1972-76; instr. gifted edn. U. Hawaii, Honolulu and Marshall Islands, 1977-81; prin. investigator Research Corp. of the Univ. of Hawaii, Marshall Islands, 1977-81; dir. Creatively Gifted Devel. Cons., Inc., Honolulu, 1981-83; researcher dept. spl. edn. Tchrs. Coll., Columbia U., N.Y.C., 1984-88; assoc. in edn., dept. of human devel. Harvard Grad. Sch. of Edn., Harvard U., Cambridge, Mass., 1989—; mem. faculty Sch. of Edn. grad. div. U. Mass., Lowell, 1990-99, also rsch. assoc.; adj. prof. edn. Northeastern U., Boston, 1999—; cons. gifted edn. Scraggy Hill Sch., Port Jefferson, L.I., 1972, Shoreham-Wading River Pub. Schs., L.I., 1975, N.Y. State Dept. Edn., 1976; undergrad. English instr. Nassau Community Coll., 1973; instr. gifted edn. Three-Village Schs., Setauket, N.Y., 1974; dir. Leadership Tng. Ctr., Marshall Islands, 1977-81; dir. pre-Kindergarden-Grade 8 program, Ebeye, Marshall Islands, 1984-85; fed. evaluator Magnet Schs. Lowell; speaker numerous profl. and non-profl. groups., schs., univs. world wide; mem. Nat. Task Force on the Culturally Different Gifted. Contbr. articles to profl. jours.; author: (poetry) Mountain Image at Gruyere, 1976, other poems in lit. mags. and jours.; author: (with others) Worldwide Perspectives on Disadvantaged Gifted, 1993, (with Mervin Lynch) Creativity for Children: Fostering Its Developing Through Theory and Practice, 1999, (chpt.) Kaleidoscope, 1995, others; editor Proc. N.Y. NOW Conf. on Feminist Edn., 1973. Grantee Research Corp. U. Hawaii, 1977-81. Fellow Nat. Acad. Ednl. Rsch. (governing bd. 1997—); mem. Council Exceptional Children (TAG div.), Nat. Assn. Gifted Children (chair subcom. Asian/Pacific populations, nat. task force on diversity, other coms., John C. Gowen award), Nat. Assn. Asian and Pacific Am. Edn., World Council Gifted and Talented Children (mem. gifted child internat. network), Am. Ednl. Rsch. Assn., Ea. Ednl. Rsch. Assn. (chmn. gifted), Assn. Advancement Ednl. Rsch. (dir. symposiums), Comparative and Internat. Edn. Soc., Kappa Delta Pi, Sigma Tau Delta. Jewish. Avocations: painting, directing community theater, crewel, Hawaiian quilting. Office: GATES Rsch and Evaluation 600 Main St Winchester MA 01890-4304

HARRIS, CASPA, JR., lawyer, educator, association administrator; b. Washington, May 20, 1928. BS in Acctg., Am. U., 1958, JD, 1967. Bar: D.C., Va., Supreme Ct.; CPA, Va. Staff pub. rels. NIH, Bethesda, Md., 1955-58; sr. auditor KPMG Peat Marwick, Washington, 1958-62; chief internal auditor Howard U., Washington, 962-65, comptroller, 1965-71, v.p. bus. and fiscal affairs, treas., 1971-87; pres. Nat. Assn. Coll. and Univ. Bus. Officers, Washington, 1987-95; lawyer, cons. pvt. practice, Waterford, Va., 1995—; prof. sch. of law Howard U., Washington, 1968-87, Kaufman-Cades CPA Rev. Sch., 1978-87, U. Ky., 1976—, U. Calif. Santa Barbara, 1984—; chmn., bd. dirs. Coll. Constrn. Loan Assn., Coll. Constrn. Loan Ins. Co.; bd. dirs. Nat. Harmony Meml. Park, The Common Fund; adv. coun. Met. Life Pension dept., Systems & Computer Tech. Corp.; treas. bd. State of Va., 1982-86, mem. Civil Rights Appellate Rev. Divsn. U.S. Dept. Edn., 1988-90; adv. bd. on colls. and univs. IRS, 1984-95; Presdl. adv. bd. on Historically Black Colls. and Univs., 1990-93; cons. Cassidy & Assocs., Washington, Nat. Heart Inst. Past chmn. of bd. Nat. Assn. Coll. & Univ. Bus. Officers Assns., also other offices; past pres. Ea. Assn. Coll. and Univ. Bus. Officers; bd. dirs. Salvation Army Met. Washington, 1970-76; mem. USO Fin. Com., 1970-71, Health Welfare Coun. and United Givers Fund D.C., 1970-72, nat. scholarship com. Lone Star Industries, Inc., 1983-90; treas. and dir. Nat. Capital Area Health Care Coalition, 1983-84; bd. dirs., vice chmn. D.C. chpt. ARC, 1981-86; chmn. fin. com., dir., The College Bd., 1983-88,. Recipient Am. Univ. Disting. Alumni award 1968, Ea. Assn. Coll. & Univ. Bus. Officers, KPMG Peat Marwick award 1995, Nat. Assn. Coll. Stores, Earl Kintner award, 1995. Mem. AICPA (minority recruitment com. 1969-72), Va. Soc. CPAs, Va. State Bar Assn., Bar Assn. D.C., Reston Lions Club (pres. 1978-79). Home: 39109 John Wolford Rd Waterford VA 20197-1616*

HARRIS, CHARLES EDGAR, retired wholesale distribution company executive; b. Englewood, Tenn., Nov. 6, 1915; s. Charles Leonard and Minnie Beatrice (Borin) H.; m. Dorothy Sarah Wilson, Aug. 20, 1938; children: Charles Edgar, William John. Pres., chmn., CEO H.T. Hackney Co., Knoxville, Tenn., 1972-83; ret.; former chmn. bd., chief exec. officer, dir. various corps. in Tenn., Ky., N.C., and Ga.; former bd. dirs. Park Nat. Bank, 1st Am. Nat. Bank Knoxville; dir. U.S. Indsl. Coun. Former bd. dirs. Downtown Knoxville Assn., Greater Knoxville Smoky Mountain coun. Bou Scouts Am., Met. YMCA, Knoxville, United Way Knoxville; mem. budget com. 1982 World's Fair, Knoxville; deacon, trustee Ctrl. Bapt. Ch., Knox County Assn. Bapt.; mem. exec. bd. Tenn. Bapt. Conv., Nashville; assoc. chmn. Layman's Nat. Bible Week, Washington; trustee Carson Newman Coll., Jefferson City, Tenn.; dir. Tenn. Taxpayers Assn.; dir. Religious Heritage of Am., St. Louis; bd. dirs. Tenn. Bapt. Children's Homes. Recipient Outstanding Community Leadership award Religious Heritage Am., Red Triangle award and Silver Triangle award YMCA. Mem. Greater Knoxville C. of C. (bd. dirs., Outstanding Corp. Citizenship award), Nat. Assn. Wholesalers-Distbrs., LeConte Club (charter), Knoxville Execs. Club (bd. dirs.), Rotary (officer, bd. dirs.). Home: 7914 Gleason Rd Apt 1071 Knoxville TN 37919-5477

HARRIS, CHARLES ELMER, lawyer; b. Williamsburg, Iowa, Nov. 26, 1922; s. Charles Elmer and Loretto (Judge) H.; m. Marjorie Clark, Jul. 9, 1949 (div. June. 1969); m. Linda Rae Slaymaker, Nov. 25, 1992; children: Martha Ann, Julie Ann, Charles Elmer III. Student, St. Ambrose Coll., 1940-42; B.S.C., U. Iowa, 1946, J.D., 1949. Bar: Iowa 1949. Mem. firm Brody, Parker, Roberts, Thoma & Harris, Des Moines, 1949-66, Herrick, Langdon, Belin Harris, Langdon & Helmick, Des Moines, 1966-78, Belin Harris Helmick, P.C., Des Moines, 1978-91, Belin, Harris, Lamson, McCormick, P.C., Des Moines, 1991-96; pvt. practice, Des Moines, 1997-99; ret., 1999; lectr. tax schs., meetings, 1951, 55, 67, 69, 77-84, 90, 91. Comments editor: Iowa Law Rev., 1948-49. Bd. dirs. NCCJ, 1964-67, Iowa Bar Found., 1977-92, Iowa Law Sch. Found., 1977-90, United Way Found., 1981-89. Lt. (j.g.) USNR, 1943-46. Fellow Am. Coll. Trust and Estate Counsel; mem. ABA, Iowa Bar Assn. (bd. govs. 1973-80, Merit award 1980), Polk County Bar Assn. (pres. 1972-73), Polk County Jr. Bar Assn. (pres. 1952-53), Order of Coif, Sigma Chi, Delta Theta Phi. Roman Catholic. Home: 5141 Robertson Dr Des Moines IA 50312-2170

HARRIS, CHARLES UPCHURCH, seminary president, clergyman; b. Raleigh, N.C., May 2, 1914; s. Charles Upchurch and Saidee (Robbins) H.; m. Janet Jeffrey Carlile, June 17, 1940; children: John C., Diana Jeffrey (Mrs. Melvin). BA, Wake Forest Coll., 1935, DHL (hon.), 1979; BD, Va. Theol. Sem., 1938, DD (hon.), 1958; postgrad., Union Theol. Sem., 1939-40; DCL (hon.), Seabury-Western Sem., 1972. Ordained deacon P.E. Ch., 1938, priest, 1939; rector All Saints Ch., Roanoke Rapids, N.C., 1938-39; asst. rector St. Bartholomew's Ch., N.Y.C., 1939-40; rector Trinity Ch., Roslyn, L.I., 1940-46, Highland Park, Ill., 1946-57; pres., dean Seabury-Western Theol. Sem., Evanston, Ill., 1957-72; pres., dean emeritus Seabury-Western Theol. Sem., 1972—; dean Lake Shore Deanery; vicar St. John's Ch., Harbor Springs, Mich., 1969-85, vicar emeritus, 1985—; founder St. Gregory's Ch., Deerfield, Ill.; hon. canon St. James Cathedral, Chgo., 1975-82; pres. Episc. Theol. Sch., Claremont, Calif., 1977-82; trustee Sch. of Theology, Claremont, 1979-82; chmn. exam. chaplains 5th and 6th provinces Episcopal Ch.; cons. nat. dept. Christian edn.; pres. Chgo. Inst. Advanced Theol. Studies, 1968-70; sec. Drafting Com. on Holy Eucharist, 1970-79; pres. Chgo. Inter-Sem. Faculties Union, 1971-72; vice chmn. N. Am. com. St. George's Coll., Jerusalem, 1981-83, pres, 1985-91; pres. Cyprus-Am. Archaeol. Inst., 1985-91, chmn., 1991, 98—; mem. exec. com. Nat. Cathedral, Washington, 1978-84, 95; v.p. Chgo. Inst. Advanced Theol. Studies, 1967-72; mem. Anglican Theol. Rev. Bd., 1959—, editor, 1971-72, pres., 1968-85, v.p., 1985—, pres. emeritus, 1991; mem. Am. Schs. Oriental Rsch., 1959—, trustee, 1969-72, 76-78, treas., 1984-87, chmn., CEO, 1992-94; hon. chmn. Inst. Christianity & Antiquities, Calif., 1996—; hon. pres. Cyprus Am. Archaeol. Rsch. Inst., 1997-98, chmn., 1998—. Author: (with A. LeCroy) Harris-Lecroy Report, 1975; contbr.: Sermons on Death and Dying, 1975; asst. editor Anglican Theol. Rev., 1958-71, editor, 1971-72. Trustee Little Traverse Conservancy, 1986; mem. bd. visitors Wake Forest U., 1979-94, Div. Sch. U. Chgo.; mem. bd. coun. Am. Rsch. Ctrs. Overseas, 1989-94, treas., 1991-95; mem. adv. com. Inst. for Antiquity and Christianity, 1987-94; mem. Com. of 40, Va. Theol. Sem., 1988-92. Mem. Am. Theol. Soc., Am. Acad. Religion, Soc. Bibl. Lit., Soc. Colonial Warriors, SAR, Conf. of Anglican Theologians. Clubs: University, Wequetonsing Golf (Harbor Springs); Little Sturgeon Trout; Desert Forest (Carefree, Ariz.). Home: Flint Hill Farm 3114 Longview Ln Delaplane VA 20144-2200

HARRIS, CHARLES WESLEY, political science educator; b. Auburn, Ala., Sept. 12, 1929; s. John Wesley and Leila (Magby) H.; m. Edna Verdell Jefferson, Sept. 1954 (div.); children: Neeka, Angela. BA cum laude, Morehouse Coll., 1949; MA, U. Pa., 1950; PhD, U. Wis., 1959. Assoc. prof. polit. sci. Grambling (La.) Coll., 1959-61; prof., chmn. divsn. social scis. Coppin State Coll., Balt., 1961-68, prof., dir. grad. studies, 1969-70; prof., acting chmn. dept. polit. sci. Howard U., Washington, 1970-71; chief govt. divsn. Congl. Rsch. Svc., Lib. of Congress, Washington, 1971-74; prof., chmn. dept. polit. sci. Howard U., 1971-74, prof., dir. grad. program in pub. affairs, 1977-88, assoc. dean Coll. Arts and Sci., 1988-92, grad. prof. polit. sci., 1992—; vis. fellow Xerox Corp., Rochester, N.Y., 1968; vis. scholar Brookings Instn., 1987; cons. D.C. Agenda Project and Fed. City Coun., 1996-97, D.C. Fin. Responsibility and Mgmt. Assistance Authority, Washington, 1997—; Woodrow Wilson Ctr. fellow, 1992-93. Author: Regional Councils of Government and the Central City, 1970, Resolving the Legislative Veto Issue, 1979, Perspectives of Political Power in D.C., 1981, Congress and the Governance of the Nation's Capital, 1995, Foreign Capital City Governance, 1997; contbr. articles to profl. jours. With U.S. Army, 1946-47. Recipient James Fund fellowship U. Wis., 1956, Advanced Studies grant Ford Found., 1968-69. Mem. ASPA, Am. Polit. Sci. Assn. (rsch. com. 1993-96, Outstanding Scholar award 1983), Nat. Conf. Black Polit. Scientists (coun. 1978-81), Alpha Phi Alpha. Baptist. Avocations: tennis, gardening. Office: Howard Univ Dept Polit Sci 2400 6th St NW Washington DC 20059-0002

HARRIS, CHAUNCY DENNISON, geographer, educator; b. Logan, Utah, Jan. 31, 1914; s. Franklin Stewart and Estella (Spilsbury) H.; m. Edith Young, Sept. 5, 1940; 1 child, Margaret (Mrs. Philip A. Straus, Jr.). AB, Brigham Young U., 1933; BA, Oxford U., 1936, MA, 1943, DLitt, 1973; postgrad., London Sch. Econs., 1936-37; PhD, U. Chgo., 1940; DEcon (honoris causa), Catholic U., Chile, 1956; LLD (honoris causa), Ind. U., 1979; DSc (honoris causa), Bonn U., 1991, U. Wis., Milw., 1991. Instr. in geography Ind. U., 1939-41; asst. prof. geography U. Nebr., 1941-43; asst. prof. geography U. Chgo., 1943-46, assoc. prof., 1946-47, prof., 1947-84, prof. emeritus, 1984—, dean social scis., 1955-60, chmn. non western area programs and internat. studies, 1960-66, dir. ctr. for internat. studies, 1966-84, chmn. dept. geography, 1967-69, Samuel N. Harper Disting. Svc. prof., 1969-84, spl. asst. to pres., 1973-75, v.p. acad. resources, 1975-78; del. Internat. Geog. Congress, Lisbon, 1949, Washington, 1952, Rio de Janeiro, 1956, Stockholm, 1960, London, 1964, New Delhi, 1968, Montreal, 1972, Moscow, 1976, Tokyo, 1980, Paris, 1984, Sydney, Australia, 1988, Washington, 1992, The Hague, 1996; v.p. Internat. Geog. Union, 1956-64, sec.-treas., 1968-76; mem. adv. com. for internat. orgns. and programs Nat. Acad. Scis., 1969-73, mem. bd. internat. orgns. and programs, 1973-76; U.S. del. 17th Gen. Conf. UNESCO, Paris, 1972; exec. com. div. behavioral scis. NRC, 1967-70; hon. cons. geography Libr. of Congress, 1974-80, mem. coun. of scholars, 1980-83, Conseil de la Bibliographie Géographique Internationale, 1986-94. Author: Cities of the Soviet Union, 1970; editor: Economic Geography of the U.S.S.R, 1949, International List of Geographical Serials, 1960, 71, 80, Annotated World List of Selected Current Geographical Serials, 1960, 64, 71, 80, Soviet Geography: Accomplishments and Tasks, 1962, Guide to Geographical Bibliographies and Reference Works in Russian or on the Soviet Union, 1975, Bibliography of Geography, Part I, Introduction to General Aids, 1976, Part 2, Regional, vol. 1, U.S., 1984, A Geographical Bibliography for American Libraries, 1985, Directory of Soviet Geographers 1946-87, 1988; contbr. Sources of Information in the Social Sciences, 1973, 86, Encyclopedia Britannica, 1989, Columbia Gazetteer of the World, 1998; contbg. editor: The Geog. Rev., 1960-73, Soviet Geography, 1987-91, Post-Soviet Geography and Economics, 1992—; hon. editor Urban Geography, 1984—; contbr. articles to profl. jours. Life mem. vis. com. U. Chgo. Libr. Recipient Alexander Csoma de Körösi Meml. medal Hungarian Geog. Soc., 1971, Lauréat d'Honneur Internat. Geog. Union, 1976; Alexander von Humboldt Gold Medal Gesellschaft für Erdkunde zu Berlin, 1978; spl. award Utah Geog. Soc., 1985; Rhodes scholar, 1934-37. Fellow Japan Soc. Promotion of Sci.; mem. Assn. Am. Geographers (sec. 1946-48, v.p. 1956, pres. 1957, Honors award 1976), Am. Geog. Soc. (coun. 1962-74, v.p. 1969-74; Cullum Geog. medal 1985), Am. Assn. Advancement Slavic Studies (pres. 1962, award for disting. contbns. 1978), Am. Acad. Arts and Scis., Social Sci. Rsch. Coun. (bd. dir. 1959-70, vice-chmn. 1963-65, exec. com. 1967-70), Internat. Coun. Sci. Unions (exec. com. 1969-76), Internat. Rsch. and Exchs. Bd. (exec. com. 1968-71), Nat. Coun. Soviet and East European Rsch. (bd. dir. 1977-83), Nat. Coun. for Geog. Edn. (Master Tchr. award 1986); hon. mem. Royal Geog. Soc. (Victoria medal 1987), Geog. Socs. Berlin, Frankfurt, Rome, Florence, Paris, Warsaw, Belgrade, Japan, Chgo. (Disting. Svc. award 1965, bd. dir. 1954-69, 82-90), Polish Acad. Scis. (fgn. mem.). Home: Apt 906 5550 S South Shore Dr Chicago IL 60637-5033 Office: U Chgo Com on Geog Studies 5828 S University Ave Chicago IL 60637-1583

HARRIS, CHRISTIE LUCY, author; b. Newark, Nov. 21, 1907; d. Edward and Matilda (Christie) Irwin; m. Thomas A. Harris, Feb. 13, 1932; children: Michael, Moira, Sheilagh, Brian, Gerald. Tchrs. cert., Provincial Normal Sch., Vancouver, B.C., Can., 1925. Tchr. B.C., 1925-32; free-lance scriptwriter Canadian Broadcasting Corp. radio, 1936-63; women's editor B.C. News Weekly, Abbotsford, 1951-57. Author: Raven's Cry, 1966, 92, Mouse Woman books (3), 1976, 77, 79, The Trouble With Princesses, 1980, Something Weird Is Going On, 1994, others. Decorated Order of Can., 1981; recipient Can. Book of Yr. medal for Children's book, 1967, 77; Can. Council Children's Lit. prize, 1981; recipient Lifetime Achievement award BC Gas, 1998. Mem. Writers' Union Can. (life). Address: c/o Sheilagh Simpson, 2323 Badger Rd, North Vancouver, BC Canada V7G 1S9 *Storytelling is a constant adventure.*

HARRIS, CHRISTOPHER, publisher, designer, editor; b. Plainfield, N.J., June 7, 1933; s. Maynard Lawrence and Edith Johnson (Bushnell) H.; m. Linda Martin Robinson, Oct. 8, 1955 (dec. 1967); children—Katherine Hamilton, Stephen Christopher, Andrea Lawrence; m. Sarah Pickett Hargrove Sullivan, Aug. 18, 1977. B.A., Yale U., 1955. Book mfg. coordinator Rand McNally & Co., Hammond, Ind., and N.Y.C., 1955-60; mng. editor Studio Books div. Viking Press, N.Y.C., 1960-70; editor, pres. Chatham Press, Riverside and Old Greenwich, Conn., 1970-76; dir. design and prodn. Yale U. Press, New Haven, 1977-88; dir. Summer Hill Books, 1978—; editor Proctor Libr. Newsletter, Weathersfield, Vt., 1996; auditor Town of Weathersfield, 1996-97. Democrat. Home and Office: 304 Beaver Pond Rd Perkinsville VT 05151-9558

HARRIS, CHRISTOPHER KIRK, lawyer; b. Albuquerque, July 6, 1951; s. Paul and Marguerite (Kirk) H. BA, Yale Coll., 1973; MSc, London Sch. Econs., 1974; JD, Boston Coll., 1977. Bar: Mass. 1977, D.C. 1980, U.S. Supreme Ct. 1981, Mont. 1986. Atty. GAO, Washington, 1977-78; chief counsel U.S. Senate Judiciary Subcom., 1979; atty. land and natural resources div. U.S. Dept. Justice, Washington, 1979-83; counsel Ho. of Reps. Energy and Commerce Com., Washington, 1983-84; ptnr. McCutchen Doyle

Brown & Enersen, 1991-94; ptnr. Harris, Tarlow & Stonecipher, Bozeman, Mont., 1994—. gen. counsel Nat. Oil Recyclers Assn., 1985—. Author: Hazardous Waste: Confronting the Challenge, 1987, Report That Spill!, 1990, Environmental Crimes, 1992, Hazardous Chemicals and the Right to Know, 1993, Used Oil: Management Practices and Potential Liability, 1988, (with others) Environmental Litigation, 1999. Recipient cert. of merit energy and minerals div. GAO, 1978; spl. achievement award U.S. Atty. Gen., 1981. Office: Harris Tarlow & Stonecipher 1439 W Babcock St Bozeman MT 59715-4101

HARRIS, CHRISTY FRANKLIN, lawyer; b. Greensboro, N.C., Dec. 8, 1945; s. Luther Franklin and Rebecca Ann (Bluster) H.; children: Stacey Lynn, Aubrey Leigh. AA, Oxford Coll., Emory U.; BA, U. Fla., 1967, JD with honors, 1970. Bar: Fla. 1970, U.S. Dist. Ct. (mid. dist.) Fla. 1970, U.S. Ct. Mil. Appeals 1971, U.S. Ct. Appeals (11th cir.) 1984. Assoc. Holland & Knight, Lakeland, Fla., 1970, 1973-74; pres. Canan & Harris P.A., Lakeland, 1974-76; pres., sr. atty. Harris, Midyette & Clements P.A., Lakeland, 1976-89, Harris & Midyette, P.A., Lakeland, 1989-91, Harris, Midyette, Geary, Darby & Morrell, P.A., Lakeland, Fla., 1991-98, Harris, Midyette & Darby, P.A., Lakeland, Fla., 1998—; mem. 10th cir. Grievance Com., Lakeland, 1976-79, 83-86, chmn. 1979, vice chmn., 1986; mem. Unauthorized Practice of Law Com., 1983-86; bd. dirs. Internat. Speedway Corp., 1986—. Bd. dirs. Program to Aid Drug Abusers, Lakeland, 1975-76, Campfire, 1979-85. Served to capt. USMCR, 1968-73, mil. judge. Named to Hon. Order of Ky. Cols., 1974. Mem. Fla. Bar, Lakeland Bar Assn., Attys. Title Ins. Fund, Order of Coif, Phi Beta Kappa, Phi Kappa Phi. Republican. Avocations: motor sports, sport fishing. Home: 1335 Longoak Dr N Lakeland FL 33811-2146 Office: Harris Midyette & Darby PA 2012 S Florida Ave PO Box 2451 Lakeland FL 33806-2451

HARRIS, CLAYTON, police chief; b. Cleve., Feb. 1, 1955; s. Lawrence and Christine P. (Hawkins) H.; m. Kimberly Joy Hawkins, Oct. 7, 1992; children: Joshua, Keturah, Valerie. AA in Law Enforcement, Cuyahoga C.C., Cleve., 1977; BS in Criminal Justice, Ohio U., 1979. Patrol officer Cuyahoga Met. Housing Police Dept., 1979-80; firefighter City of East Cleveland, 1980; comdr. East Cleveland Police Dept., 1980-94, Cleve. Police Dept., 1994-95; chief of police Cuyahoga C.C., 1995—; mem. adv. bd. Atty. Gen. Law Enforcement Conf., 1994—, Cuyahoga Regional Info. System. Author: Urban Police Mountain Bike Training Techniques, 1994-97, CCC Bike Safety Rodeo, 1996-97; dir./founder: (gospel quartet) Divine Creation Ministries, 1987. Pres. Cleve. chpt. NOBLE, 1989—; chmn. tng. com. Mayor's Minority Recruitment Com., 1997; mem. Mayor's Black on Black Crime com., 1997. Recipient Appreciation awards Cops and Kids, Inc., 1995-97, Ohio Law Enforcement Games, 1997. Mem. FOP, IACP (Internatl. Assn. of Chief's Police), IACLEA (Internatl. Assn. of Campus Law Enforcement Admin.) others. Avocations: golf, basketball, jogging, writing, music. Office: Cuyahoga Cmty Coll 2900 Community College Ave Cleveland OH 44115-3123

HARRIS, COLIN CYRIL, mineral engineer, educator; b. Leeds, Eng., 1928; came to U.S., 1960; m. Sylvia Glonstein, Apr. 16, 1964 (dec. Oct. 1979). B.Sc. in Math. and Physics (Brit. Govt. scholar), London U., 1952; Ph.D. in Mineral Engring. and Coal Preparation, Leeds (Eng.) U., 1959. Chartered engr., Gt. Britain. Rsch. asst. Leeds U., 1952-57; lectr. in coal preparation and mineral processing, 1957-60, 61-63; vis. asst. prof. mineral engring. Columbia U., 1960-61, assoc. prof. mineral engring., 1963-70, prof., 1970-99; adv. on faculty appointments, research and grad. programs to U.S. and fgn. univs.; external examiner fgn. univs.; adv. on research proposals to govt. funding agys.; adv., cons. to mining, research and mfg. cos.; mem. organizing coms. for several internat. confs. on mineral processing. Contbr. numerous articles on theory of mineral processing ops. to profl. publs.; editor: Symposium on Coal Preparation, 1957; assoc. editor: Internat. Jour. Mineral Processing, 1973-86 ; mem. editorial bd. Mineral Processing and Extractive Metallurgy Rev.— An Internat. Jour., Minerals and Metall. Processing; adv. to internat. jours. Served as sgt. Brit. Armed Forces, 1946-49. Nat. Coal Bd. Rsch. grantee, 1957-60, 62-63, Clean Coal Rsch. grantee U.S. Dept. Energy, U.S. Bur. Mines, Comm. Ctr., others. Mem. AIME (past chmn. publs. com., mem. awards. com., student affairs com.), AIME Soc. for Mining, Metallurgy and Exploration (A.M. Gaudin award and lectr. 1990), Operational Rsch. Soc. (London), Assn. Univs. Tchrs. (Gt. Brit.), Instn. Mining and Metallurgy (London), Leeds U. Record Club (libr. 1954-59). Office: Columbia U Sch Mines 907 Engring Ctr New York NY 10027

HARRIS, COURTENEY FRANCHELLE, program manager; b. Nuremberg, Germany, Aug. 5, 1972; came to U.S., 1973; p. Orville Dwain and Melba Joyce Harris. BA in English, Xavier U., 1994; MPA, Tex. So. U., 1999. Student intern Vinson & Elkins LLP, Houston, 1993; legis. aide Tex. State Ho. of Reps., Austin, 1994-95; clk. Legis. Black Caucus, Austin, 1994-95; membership svcs. exec. San Jacinto Girl Scouts Coun., Houston, 1995-97, program mgr., 1997—; mem. Assn. Girl Scout Exec. Staff, Houston, 1995—; protege Nat. Forum for Black Pub. Adminstrs., Houston, 1998—. Election bd. chairperson Student Govt. Assn., Xavier U., New Orleans, 1993-94; breast cancer health info. extender Baylor U., Houston, 1994; asst. coord. Juneteenth USA, Houston, 1995; life mem. Girl Scouts USA, 1995—. Scholar Nat. Collegiate Women, New Orleans, 1992. Mem. Order Ea. Star, Delta Sigma Theta (Pan Hellenic coun. rep. 1996—). Democrat. Roman Catholic. Avocations: reading, writing, racquetball. E-mail: charris@sjgs.org. and charris1@pdq.net. Fax: 713-292-0330. Office: San Jacinto Girl Scout Coun 3110 Southwest Freeway Houston TX 77098

HARRIS, CURTIS C., physician. MD, U. Kans. Intern and resident in internal medicine and oncology; chief Lab. Human Carcinogenesis Nat. Cancer Inst., NIH, Bethesda, Md., also head molecular genetics and carcinogenesis sect.; Deichmann lectr. VII Internat. Congress of Toxicology, 1995. Editor 10 books; exec. editor Carcinogenesis; contbr. over 450 articles and revs. to profl. jours. Alton Ochsner Relating Smoking and Health award, 1993, Walter Hubert Award, Lectr. British Assoc. Cancer Res., 1995. Mem. Internat. Soc. Gastroentergol. Carcinogenesis (Charles Heidelberger award 1999), Chem. Industry Inst. Toxicology (mem. sci. adv. panel, chmn. 1989-94, Founder's award 1995), Am. Assn. Cancer Rsch. Office: NIH Nat Cancer Inst Lab Carcinogenesis Rm 2C01 37 Convent Dr Bldg 37 Bethesda MD 20892-4255

HARRIS, CYRIL MANTON, physicist, engineering and architecture educator, consulting acoustical engineer; b. Detroit; s. Bernard O. and Ida (Moss) H.; m. Ann Schakne; children: Nicholas Bennett, Katherine Anne. B.A., UCLA, 1938, M.A., 1940; Ph.D., MIT, 1945; Sc.D. (hon.), N.J. Inst. Tech., 1981, Northwestern U., 1989. Rsch. asst. Carnegie Instn. Washington, 1941; mem. staff Bell Telephone Labs., 1945-51; cons. Office Naval Research, London, Eng., 1951; Fulbright lectr. Tech. U., Delft, Holland, 1951-52; Charles Batchelor prof. elec. engring., prof. architecture and past chmn. div. archtl. tech. Columbia U.; now prof. emeritus; vis. Fulbright prof. U. Tokyo, 1960; acoustical cons. Met. Opera House, N.Y.C., John F. Kennedy Ctr. Performing Arts, Washington, Krannert Ctr. Performing Arts, U. Ill., Powell Symphony Hall, St. Louis, Nat. Acad. Scis. Auditorium, Washington, Minn. Orch. Hall, Mpls., Nat. Ctr. Performing Arts, Bombay, Avery Fisher Hall, N.Y. State Theater reconstructions, Lincoln Ctr., N.Y.C., Symphony Hall, Salt Lake City, Benaroya Hall, Seattle; past dir. Inst. Theatre Tech.; mem. noise control group, mem. com. on undersea warfare NRC, 1955-57, mem. bldg. adv. bd., 1977-79; mem. coun. hearing and bioacoustics Armed Forces-NRC, 1953-55; mem. adv. panel 213 to Nat. Bur. Standards, 1966-69, chmn., 1969-71. Author: (with V.O. Knudsen) Acoustical Designing in Architecture, 1950, rev., 1980, Handbook of Noise Control, 1957, 2d edit., 1979, 3d edit retitled Handbook of Acoustical Measurements and Noise Control, 1991; Shock and Vibration Handbook, 4th edit., 1996, Dictionary of Architecture and Construction, 1975, 2d edition 1993; Historic Architecture Sourcebook, 1977, Illustrated Dictionary of Historic Architecture, 1983; Handbook of Utilities and Services for Buildings, 1990, Noise Control in Buildings, 1993, American Architecture: An Illustrated Encyclopedia, 1998; contbr. articles to profl. jours.; editorial adv. bd.: Physics Today, 1955-66. Bd. dirs. Armstrong Meml. Research Found., 1976—; hon. trustee St. Louis Symphony Soc., 1977—; mem. nat. adv. bd. Utah Symphony Orch., 1976-85. Recipient Franklin medal, 1977; Emile Berliner award, 1977; Hon. award U.S. ITT, 1977; Wallace Clement Sabine medal, 1979; AIA medal, 1980; Gold Medal Audio Engring. Soc., 1984; award of honor for sci. and tech. City of N.Y., 1985; Alumni award UCLA, 1989, Pupin medal Columbia U., 1998. Fellow IEEE, Acoustical Soc. Am. (pres. 1964-65, assoc. editor jour. 1959-70, Gold medal), Audio Engring. Soc. (hon.); mem. NAS, NAE, Am. Inst. Physics (governing bd. 1965-66), N.Y. Acad. Scis. (pres. 1991-93, chmn. bd. 1992-94), Am. Philos. Soc., Century Assn., Sigma Xi, Tau Beta Pi. Office: Columbia U Mudd Bldg New York NY 10027

HARRIS, D. GEORGE, entrepreneur; b. 1933; married. B.S.Ch.E., U. Mo., 1954. Internat. sales mgr. Calgon Corp., 1966-69; mng. dir. Chemviron SA, Brussels, 1969-75; pres., chief exec. officer Rhone-Poulenc Inc., 1975-81; v.p., pres. chem. div. SCM Corp., N.Y.C., 1981-85; corp. pres., chief operating officer SCM Corp., 1985-87; dir., sr. investment advisor Robert Fleming & Co., PLC, N.Y.C. and London, 1987-88; chmn., CEO N.Am. Salt Co., 1988-93; chmn. Great Salt Lake Minerals & Chems. Corp., Salt Lake City, 1989-93, N.Am. Chem. Corp., 1991-93, Salt Union Ltd., U.K., 1992—, Matthes & Weber, Germany, 1993—, Harris Chem. Group, Inc., 1993—, Harris Specialty Chems., Inc., 1994—, Novacarb, France, 1996—; founder, chmn. D. George Harris and Assocs., 1987—, U.S. Silica, 1996—, Penrice Sode Products, Pty. Ltd., 1996—; mem. Pres.'s Adv. Com. Trade Policy and Negotiations., 1990—; trustee Tax Free Fund Utah, 1992—; non-exec. chmn. McWhorter Techs., Inc., 1996, bd. dirs., 1996—. Served to 1st lt. U.S. Army, 1954-56. Recipient Winthrop-Sears award, 1990. Office: D George Harris & Assocs 399 Park Ave Fl 32 New York NY 10022-4614*

HARRIS, DALE RAY, lawyer; b. Crab Orchard, Ill., May 11, 1937; s. Ray B. and Aurelia M. (Davis) H.; m. Toni K. Shapkoff, June 26, 1960; children: Kristen Dee, Julie Diane. BA in Math., U. Colo., 1959; LLB, Harvard U., 1962. Bar: Colo. 1962, U.S. Dist. Ct. Colo. 1962, U.S. Ct. Appeals (10th cir.) 1962, U.S. Supreme Ct. 1981. Assoc. Davis, Graham & Stubbs, Denver, 1962-67, ptnr., 1967—, chmn. mgmt. com., 1982-85; spkr., instr. various antitrust and comml. litig. seminars; bd. dirs. Lend-A-Lawyer, Inc., 1989-94. Mem. campaign cabinet Mile High United Way, 1986-87, chmn., atty. adv. com., 1988, sec., legal counsel, trustee, mem. exec. com., 1989-94, chmn. bd. trustees, 1996, 97; trustee The Spaceship Earth Fund, 1986-89; trustee Legal Aid Found. Colo., 1989-95; mem. devel. coun. U. Colo. Arts and Scis. dept., 1985-93; area chmn. law sch. fund Harvard U., 1978-81; bd. dirs. Colo. Jud. Inst., 1994—, vice chair, 1998—; bd. dirs. Colo. Lawyers Trust Account Found., 1996—; steering com. Youth-At-Work, 1994, School-To-Work, 1995. With USAR, 1962-68. Receipient Williams award, Rocky Mountain Arthritis Found., 1999. Fellow Am. Bar Found. (Colo. state chmn. 1998—); mem. ABA (antitrust and litigation sects.), Colo. Bar Found., Colo. Bar Assn. (chmn. antitrust com. 1980-84, coun. corp. banking and bus. law sect. 1978-83, bd. govs. 1991-95, exec. com. 1993-94, chmn. family violence task force 1996—, pres.-elect 1999), Denver Bar Assn. (chmn. centennial com. 1990-91, pres.-elect 1992-93, pres. 1993-94, bd. trustees 1992-95, Merit award 1997), Colo. Assn. Corp. Counsel (pres. 1973-74), Denver Law Club (pres. 1976-77, Lifetime Achievement award 1997), The Two Percent Club (exec. com. 1994—), Citizens Against Amendment 12 Com. (exec. com. 1994), Phi Beta Kappa, Univ. Club, Rotary (Denver). Home: 2032 Bellaire St Denver CO 80207-3722 Office: Davis Graham & Stubbs 370 17th St PO Box 185 Denver CO 80201-0185

HARRIS, DARRYL WAYNE, publishing executive; b. Emmett, Idaho, July 29, 1941; s. Reed Ingval and Evelyn Faye (Wengreen) H.; m. Christine Sorenson, Sept. 10, 1965; children: Charles Reed, Michael Wayne, Jason Darryl, Stephanie, Ryan Joseph. B.A., Brigham Young U., 1966. Staff writer Deseret News, Salt Lake City, 1965, Post-Register, Idaho Falls, 1966-67; tech. editor Idaho Nuclear Corp., Idaho Falls, 1967-68; account exec. David W. Evans & Assos. Advt., Salt Lake City, 1968-71; pres. Harris Pub., Inc., Idaho Falls, 1971—; pub. Potato Grower of Idaho mag., 1972—, Snowmobile West mag., 1974—, Sugar Producer mag., 1974—, Blue Ribbon mag., 1987-90; Modstock mag., 1992—; pub. SnowAction mag., 1987—, Western Guide to Snowmobiling, 1988—, Houseboat Mag., 1990—, Pontoon and Deck Boat Mag., 1995—. Campaign mgr. George Hansen for Congress Com., 1974, 76; campaign chmn. Mel Richardson for Congress Com., 1986; 1st counselor to pres. Korean Mission, Ch. Jesus Christ of Latter-day Saints, Seoul, Korea, 1963, area public communications dir., Eastern Idaho, 1976-86; pres. Korea Seoul Mission, 1997—; High Priest, LDS Ch., 1987-91, high coun. Idaho Falls Ammon Stake, 1987-91, Ammon 8th Ward Bishopric, 1991-96; founder Blue Ribbon Coalition, 1987; v.p. Teton Peaks Council Boy Scouts Am., 1987-92; publicity chmn. Upper Snake River Scout Encampment, 1988; founder , pres. Our Land Soc., 1989-92. Mem. Agr. Editors Assn., Internat. Snowmobile Industry Assn. (Best Overall Reporting journalism award 1979, 80), Western Publs. Assn., World Champion Cutter and Chariot Racing Assn. (historian 1966-80), Nat. Snowmobile Found. (founder 1988), Kappa Tau Alpha. Lodge: Idaho Falls Kiwanis (pres. 1978, Disting. Club Pres. award 1978). Office: Harris Pub Inc 520 Park Ave Idaho Falls ID 83402-3516

HARRIS, DAVID ALAN, not-for-profit organization executive; b. Santa Monica, Calif., Sept. 23, 1949; s. Eric Albert and Nelly (Chender) H.; m. Giulia Boukhobza, Jan. 14, 1979; children: Daniel, Michael, Joshua. BA, U. Pa., 1971; MS, London Sch. Econs., 1972, postgrad., 1975-77; postgrad., Oxford (Eng.) U., 1977-78. Dir. govt. and internat. affairs Am. Jewish Com., N.Y.C., 1987-90, exec. dir., 1990—; nat. coord. Freedom Sunday for Soviet Jewry rally, Washington, 1987; pub. mem. U.S. Del. to Conf. on Security and Coop. in Europe. Author: The Jokes of Oppression, 1988, Entering a New Culture, 5th edit., 1989, The Jewish World, 1989; contbr. over 100 articles to mags. and newspapers. Cited by Lifestyles mag. and Jewish monthly as Jewish leader. Office: Am Jewish Com 165 E 56th St New York NY 10022-2709

HARRIS, DAVID FORD, management consultant, retired government official; b. Hillsboro, Mo., Feb. 14, 1931; s. Walter Dunklin and Nelle (Landrigan) H.; m. Erna Beckmann, Mar. 5, 1964; children: Christopher Beckmann, Stefanie Ford. BS, U.S. Mil. Acad., West Point, 1954; MBA, Stanford U., 1961. Budget officer Post Office Dept., Washington, 1964-68; spl. asst. postmaster gen. Post Office Dept., 1968-70; chief adminstrv. officer, sec. Postal Rate Commn., Washington, 1970-83; sec. to bd. govs. U.S. Postal Svc., Washington, 1983-95; ret., 1995; mgmt. cons. representing N.Am. for CB Group, Santiago, Chile, 1996—. Capt. U.S. Army, 1954-64. Mem. West Point Alumni Assn., Stanford Alumni Assn., Alexandria Sportsman's Club. Roman Catholic. Home and Office: 3643 Trinity Dr Alexandria VA 22304-1840

HARRIS, DAVID HENRY, retired life insurance company executive; b. N.Y.C., May 7, 1924; s. Julian A. and May L. (Wilenski) H.; 1 child, Jean Harris Haig; m. Cassandra Sturman, Feb. 20, 1987. Student, Sherborne (Eng.) Sch., 1937-40. With Prudential Ins. Co. Am., 1940-43; with Equitable Life Assurance Soc. U.S., N.Y.C., 1946-86, exec. v.p., 1973-77, exec. v.p., chief adminstrv. officer, 1977-80, exec. v.p., chief staff, 1981-86, bd. dirs., 1977-86; pres. Equitable Found., 1986-88; chmn. bd. Equimatics, Inc., 1971-73, Informatics, Inc., 1974-75; vice chmn. Equitable Variable Life Ins. Co., 1975-76, chmn., 1976-77. Bd. dirs. Can. Life of Am. Series Fund; trustee Chappaqua Libr., 1991-94. With AUS, 1943-46. Fellow Soc. Actuaries; mem. Lotos Club (N.Y.). Home: 130 E 67th St New York NY 10021-6136

HARRIS, DAVID JOEL, financial planner; b. Miller, S.D., Sept. 22, 1950; s. Joel Chips and Amy Ruth (Rietz) H.; m. Susan Claire Hagius, June 30, 1979 (div. 1997); children: John, Jennifer. BA, Earlham Coll., Richmond, Ind., 1972; MS, Purdue U., 1975; PhD, U. Hawaii, 1983. Vis. rsch. asst. Internat. Ctr. Tropical Agr., Cali, Colombia, 1975-76; sr. rsch. fellow Internat. Ctr. Tropical Agr., 1984-87; rsch. assoc. U. Hawaii, Honolulu, 1976-83; sr. rsch. fellow Internat. Ctr. Tropical Agr., 1984-87; mgr. Calif.-Nev. United Meth. Found., San Francisco, 1988-92; exec. v.p. Calif.-Nev. United Meth. Found., Sacramento, 1992-97; charitable trust planner Legacy Solutions, Santa Rosa, Calif., 1997—; treas. Nat. Assn. United Meth. Found., 1992-94. Contbr. articles to profl. jours. Pres. Mothers Against Drunk Driving, Sonoma County, Calif., 1989-91. Grad. fellow Purdue U., 1972, fellow NSF, 1973, 75-77. Mem. Nat. Com. on Planned Giving, Commonwealth Club Calif., Phi Beta Kappa. Methodist. Avocations: travel, computers, dogs, environment. Home: 355 Gemma Cir Santa Rosa CA 95404-2733 Office: David Harris Co Legacy Sols 1275 4th St Ste 388 Santa Rosa CA 95404-4049

HARRIS, DAVID THOMAS, immunology educator; b. Jonesboro, Ark., May 9, 1956; s. Marm Melton and Lucille Luretha (Buck) H.; m. Francoise Jacqueline Besencon, June 24, 1989; children: Alexandre M., Stefanie L., Leticia M. BS in Biology, Math. and Psychology, Wake Forest U., 1978, MS, 1980, PhD in Microbiology and Immunology, 1982. Fellow Ludwig Inst. Cancer Rsch., Lausanne, Switzerland, 1982-85; rsch. asst. prof. U. N.C., Chapel Hill, 1985-89; assoc. prof. U. Ariz., Tucson, 1989-96, prof., 1996—; cons. Teltech, Inc. Mpls., 1990—, Advanced Biosci. Resources, 1994-95; bd. sci. advisors Cryo-Cell Internat., 1992-95; bd. dirs. Ageria, Inc., Tuscon; dir. Cord Blood Stem Cell Bank, 1992—; mem. Ariz. Cancer Ctr., Steele Meml. Children's Rsch. Ctr., Ariz. Arthritis Ctr. Program, sci. adv. bd. Cord Blood Registry, Inc., chief sci. div. Cord Blood Registry, Inc. Coauthor chpts. to sci. books, articles to profls. jours.; reviewer sci. jours.; coholder 5 scientific patents. Grantee local and fed. rsch. grants, 1988—. Mem. AAAS, Am. Assn. Immunologists, Reticuleondothelial Soc., Internat. Soc. Hematotherapy and Graft Engring., Internat. Soc. Devel. and Comparative Immunology, Scandanavian Soc. Immunology, Sigma Xi,. Democrat. Mem. Ch. of Christ. Avocations: tennis, hiking, jogging, skiing, travel. Office: U Ariz Dept Microbiology Bldg 90 Tucson AZ 85721

HARRIS, DEL WILLIAM, professional basketball coach; b. Plainfield, Ind., June 18, 1937. BA, Milligan Coll., Tenn., 1959; MA, Ind. U., 1965. Ordained minister, Christian Ch., 1958. High sch. coach, 1959-64; head basketball coach Earlham Coll., Richmond, Ind., 1965-74; asst. coach Utah Stars, Am. Basketball Assn., 1974-75, U. Utah, 1975-76; asst. coach Houston Rockets, NBA, 1976-79, basketball coach, 1979-83; scout Milw. Bucks, Nat. Basketball Assn., 1983-86, asst. coach, 1986-87, head coach, 1987-91; v.p. ops. Milw. Bucks, from 1987; head coach Los Angeles Lakers, 1994—; asst. coach Team USA World Games, 1998; speaker on motivation Intercontinental Tng. Systems Inc., 1982-84. Author: Multiple Defenses, 1971, Zone Offense, 1975, Winning Defense, 1995; juvenile novel Playing the Game, 1982; appeared in (movie) Space Jam, 1996, (TV) Diagnosis Murder, 1996, In the House, 1997 (TV), Over The Top, 1997 (TV). Bd. dirs. Wis. Leukemia Soc., 1989, Milw. Athletes Against Childhood Cancer Fund; hon. chairperson Easter Seals Milw. High Sch. Classic, Vince Lombardi Golf Classic, Leukemia 6 Hours for Life Telethon; spokesperson St. Francis Children's Ctr., Milw., Spl. Olympics. Recipient Disting. Houstonian award, 1981, Coach of Yr. award NBA, 1995; Eli Lilly fellow, 1965. Office: Los Angeles Lakers PO Box 10 3900 W Manchester Blvd Inglewood CA 90306

HARRIS, DELMARIE JONES, elementary education educator; b. New Orleans, Mar. 16, 1947; d. Ralph and Ruth Lena (Ackerson) Jones; m. Hosey W. Williams (div. 1974); children: Hosey Willie, Sabrena Michelle; m. Ronald Andrew Harris, Mar. 7, 1978; 1 child, Rene Andrea. Student, Southern U., New Orleans, 1967-70; BA, Southern U., 1971. Tchr. St. Mary of Angels, New Orleans, La., 1971-73, J.F. Gauthier Elem. Sch., Poydras, La., 1973—; grade chmn. J.F. Gauthier steering com. bull. 741, 1987, language arts textbook adoption rep., 1992-93; recorder St. Bernard Parish Discipline Dress Code Adoption Com., 1988-90, math. rep., 1990, primary tchr.; mem. com. to rewrite curriculum for math. State of La., 1996. Mem. NEA, Nat. Coun. Tchrs. Math., Internat. Reading Assn., La. Assn. Educators, St. Bernard Assn. Educators. Democrat. Roman Catholic. Avocations: interior decorating, dancing.

HARRIS, DIANE CAROL, merger and acquisition consulting firm executive; b. Rockville Centre, N.Y., Dec. 25, 1942; d. Daniel Christopher and Laura Louise (Schmitt) Quigley; m. Wayne Manley Harris, Sept. 30, 1978. BA, Cath. U. Am., 1964; MS, Rensselaer Poly. Inst., 1967. With Bausch & Lomb, Rochester, N.Y., 1967-96, dir. applications lab., 1972-74, dir. tech. mktg. analytical systems div., 1974-76, bus. line mgr., 1976-77, v.p. planning and bus. programs, 1977-78, v.p. planning and bus. devel. Soflens div., 1978-80, corp. dir. planning, 1980-81, v.p. corp. devel., 1981-96; v.p. RID-N.Y. State, 1980-83; pres. Hypotenuse Enterprises, Inc., 1994—; mem. adv. bd. Merger Mgmt. Report, 1986-92; internat. bd. dirs. Assn. Corp. Growth, v.p. corp. mem. affairs, 1993-94, v.p. internat. expansion, 1994-95, pres. elect, 1996-97, pres. 1997-98; bd. dirs. Delta Labs., Inc., Flowserve Corp. (formerly Duriron Co.), 1993—. Contbr. articles to profl. jours. Pres. Rochester Against Intoxicated Driving, 1979-83, chmn. polit. action com., 1983, 86; bd. dirs., chmn. long-range planning com. Rochester area Nat. Council on Alcoholism, 1980-84; bd. dirs. Rochester Rehab. Ctr., 1982-84, Friends of Bristol Valley Playhouse Found., 1983-87; mem. Stop DWI Adv. panel to Monroe County Legislature, 1982-87, N.Y. State Coalition for Safety Belt Use, 1984-85; mem. key exec. group Rensselaer Poly. Inst., 1993-96; mem. Com. 200, 1993—; mem. ACG spkrs. bur., 1993—; mem. catalyst adv. com., 1995. Recipient Disting. Citizen's award Monroe County, 1979, Tribute to Women in Industry and Service award YWCA, 1983, Pres.'s 21st Century Leadership award-Women's Hall of Fame, 1995; NSF grantee, 1963; selected as one of 50 Women to Watch in Corp. Am., Bus. Week mag., 1987, 92, one of 100 Women To Watch, Duns Bus. Rev., 1988; Assn. For Corp. Growth Meritorious Svc. award, 1995. Mem. Am. Mgmt. Assn., Fin. Execs. Inst., Assn. Corp. Growth, C. of C. (pub. safety com. Rochester Area chpt., task force on hwy. safety and legis. 1981-86, high tech. Rochester adv. panel 1989-91), Nat. Assn. Women Bus. Owners, Internat. Alliance and Rochester Women's Network, Phi Beta Kappa, Sigma Xi, Delta Epsilon Sigma. Home: 60 Mendon Center Rd Honeoye Falls NY 14472-9363 Office: Hypotenuse Enterprises Inc 1545 East Ave Rochester NY 14610-1614

HARRIS, DON VICTOR, JR., lawyer; b. Nottingham Twp., Ind., Jan. 16, 1921; s. Don Victor and Nellie Florence (Dukes) H.; m. Joan Elliott Haffler, Aug. 15, 1959; children: Leigh Elliott (Mrs. John A. Hay), Meghan St. Clair. A.B., DePauw U., 1943; J.D., Harvard U., 1945. Bar: D.C. 1947. Law clk. to judge U.S. Ct. Appeals 2d Circuit, 1945-46; assoc. firm Covington & Burling, Washington, 1946-57; ptnr. Covington & Burling, 1957—; lectr. in law George Washington U., 1963-64; lectr. tax insts.; mem. IRS Commr.'s Adv. Group, 1976. Contbr. articles to law jours.; Case editor: Harvard Law Rev. Bd. dirs. Oak Hill Cemetery Co.; bd. dirs. Found. for Preservation Historic Georgetown. Fellow Am. Coll. Tax Counsel, Am. Bar Found. (life); mem. Am. Law Inst. (life), ABA (chmn. sect. taxation 1976-77), D.C. Bar Assn., Fed. Bar Assn., Phi Beta Kappa, Beta Theta Pi, Am. Camellia Soc. (judge), Met Club, Chevy Chase Club, John's Island Club (Fla.). Episcopalian. Home: 2803 P St NW Washington DC 20007-3067 also: John's Island 777 Sea Oak Dr No 715 Vero Beach FL 32963-3541 Office: 1201 Pennsylvania Ave NW PO Box 7566 Washington DC 20044-7566

HARRIS, DONALD, composer; b. St. Paul, Apr. 7, 1931; s. Barney William and Hattie (Paper) H.; m. Marilyn Hackett, 1983; children: Daniel, Jeremy. Mus.B., U. Mich., 1952, Mus.M., 1954. Music cons. Am. Cultural Center, USIS, Paris, 1965-67; asst. to pres. for acad. affairs New Eng. Conservatory Music, Boston, 1967-71; v.p. New Eng. Conservatory Music, 1971-74, exec. v.p., 1974-77, mem. teaching faculty depts. composition and music lit., 1967-77; composer-in-residence, prof. music, chmn. composition and theory Hartt Sch. of Music, U. Hartford, Conn., 1977-80; dean Hartt Sch. of Music, U. Hartford, 1981-88; dean Coll. of the Arts The Ohio State U., 1988-97, prof. composition, 1997—; vis. prof. music George Washington U., 1998; pres. Internat. Coun. Fine Arts Deans, 1994-96. Composer: Piano Sonata, 1956, Fantasy for Violin and Piano, 1957, Symphony in Two Movements, 1961, String Quartet, 1965, Ludus for 10 Instruments, 1966, Ludus II for 5 Instruments, 1973, Charmes for Voice and Orchestra, 1977, On Variations, 1976, For the Night to Wear (Hortense Flexner), mezzo-soprano and 7 instruments, 1978, Balladen for solo piano, 1979, Of Hartford in a Purple Light (Wallace Stevens) for soprano and piano, 1979, Prelude to a Concert in Connecticut, 1981, Les Mains (Marguerite Yourcenar) for mezzo-soprano and piano, 1983, Meditations for Solo Organ, 1984, Three Fanfares for Four Horns, 1984, Canzona & Carol for Double Brass Quintet and Timpani, 1986, Pierrot Lieder (soprano & 5 instruments), 1988, Mermaid Variations (chamber orch.), 1993; recs., CRI, Delos, Golden Crest Records; co-editor: The Correspondence Between Arnold Schoenberg and Alban Berg, 1986. Recipient commns. from Serge Koussevitzky Music Found., 1977, Elizabeth Sprague Coolidge Found., 1977, Goethe Inst., 1978, Conn. Commn. Arts, 1979, French Nat. Radio, 1972, Festival Contemporary Am. Music at Tanglewood, 1965, Boston Musica Viva, 1973, Cleve. Orch., 1975, Arnold Schoenberg Inst., 1988, Cleve. Chamber Orchestra, 1991; recipient Louisville Orch. award, 1954, Prince Rainier of Monaco Composition prize, 1960, award Am. Acad. and Inst. Arts and Letters, 1991; grantee-in-aid Rockefeller Found., 1969; grantee-in-aid Chapelbrook Found., 1970; fellowship grantee Nat. Endowment for Arts, 1974; Fulbright scholar, 1956;

Guggenheim fellow, 1965. Mem. ASCAP (Deems Taylor award 1989, others 1973—). Address: 5257 Courtney Pl Columbus OH 43235-3474

HARRIS, DONALD J., economics educator. BA, London U., 1960; PhD, U. Calif., Berkeley, 1965. Asst. prof. econs. U. Ill., Urbana, 1965-67; assoc. prof. U. Wis., Madison, 1968-72; prof. Stanford (Calif.) U., 1972—; econ. cons. UN, N.Y.C., 1966-67, Inter-Am. Devel. Bank, Washington, 1993-94; vis. fellow Cambridge (Eng.) U., 1966, 68, 77, 82, assoc. fellow Trinity Coll., 1982; disting. vis. prof. Yale U., New Haven, 1977-78; Fulbright scholar, Brazil, 1990-91, Mex., 1992. Author: Capital Accumulation and Income Distribution, 1978, Japanese ed., 1982, Spanish edit., 1984, Jamaica's Export Economy, 1997; mem. bd. editors Jour. Econ. Lit., 1979-84; contbr. articles to profl. jours. Ford Found. fellow, 1984-85. Mem. Am. Econ. Assn., Nat. Econ. Assn. Avocations: music, theater. Office: Stanford U Dept Econs Stanford CA 94305

HARRIS, DONALD RAY, lawyer; b. Lake Preston, S.D., Apr. 21, 1938; s. Raymond H. and Nona (Trousdale) H.; children: Beverly, Scott, Bradley, Lindi; m. Sharon K. Brown, Sept. 4, 1982. BA, State U. Iowa, 1959; JD, U. Iowa, 1961. Bar: Ill. 1963, U.S. Dist. Ct. (no. dist.) Ill. 1963, U.S. Ct. Appeals (3d, 4th, 6th, 7th, 9th and fed. cirs.) 1966-95, U.S. Dist. Ct. (we. dist.) Tex. 1989, U.S. Supreme Ct. 1977. Assoc. firm Jenner & Block, Chgo., 1963-70, ptnr., 1970—. Lt. inf. U.S. Army, 1961-63. Mem. ABA, Ill. Bar Assn., Chgo. Bar Assn., Bar Assn. 7th Cir., Chgo. Council Lawyers, Am. Coll. Trial Lawyers, Chgo. Legal Club, Chgo. Law Club. Office: Jenner & Block One IBM Plz Chicago IL 60611-3586

HARRIS, DONALD WAYNE, research scientist; b. Ft. Scott, Kans., Sept. 23, 1942; s. Carl Raymond Harris and Kathryn Francis (Peare) Hayes; m. Louisa Dudley Beisser, Aug. 1, 1998; children: Daniel Duane (dec. 1994), Sheila, Lynette, Crystal Ann. BS, U. Mo., 1966, PhD, 1974. From scientist to mgr. carbohydrate polymer rsch. Clinton (Iowa) Corn Processing Co., 1974-84; sr. rsch. scientist AE Staley Mfg. Co., Decatur, Ill., 1984-92; rsch. fellow AE Staley Mfg. Co., Lafayette, Ind., 1992—. Patentee in field; contbr. articles to profl. jours. With U.S. Army, 1968-70. Mem. Am. Chem. Soc., Am. Assn. Cereal Chemists, Phi Lambda Upsilon. Avocations: walking, hiking, hunting, fishing. Home: 5208 Cameron Ln Lafayette IN 47905-7581

HARRIS, DORIS ANN, nurse; b. Sayre, Pa., Mar. 5, 1947; d. Allan N. and Ruth E. (Stafford) H. Student, RPH Sch. Nursing, Sayre, 1968; BSPA, St. Joseph's Coll., Windham, Maine. RN, Conn. Staff nurse Conn. Hospice, Inc., Branford, 1980-88; spl. procedures nurse Yale Gynecology-Oncology Clinic, New Haven, 1988-90; nurse oncology unit Middlesex Hosp., Middletown, Conn., 1990-94; staff nurse The Madison (Conn.) House, 1994-98, Middlesex Hosp. Home Care, Clinton, Conn., 1998—. Mem. Nat. League for Nursing, Oncology Nursing Soc. (Conn. chpt.), Ind. Assn. Hospice Caregivers (co-founder, co-dir. 1987—). Home: 131 Liberty St Clinton CT 06413-1739

HARRIS, DOUGLAS CLAY, newspaper executive; b. Owensboro, Ky., Oct. 9, 1939; s. Marvin Dudley and Elizabeth (Adelman) H. BS, Murray State U., 1961; MS, Ind. U., 1964, EdD, 1968; grad. advanced mgmt. program, Harvard U., 1987. Counselor, asst. to dean of students Ind. U., Bloomington, 1965-68; mgmt. appraisal specialist United Air Lines, Elk Grove Village, Ill., 1968-69; dir. manpower div. Computer Age Industries, Washington, 1969; area personnel dir. Peat Marwick Mitchell & Co., N.Y.C., 1969-72; v.p. personnel Knight-Ridder, Inc., Miami, Fla., 1972-85, v.p., sec., 1986—. Served to capt. U.S. Army, 1961-62. Mem. APA, Inst. CFP's, Internat. Assn. Fin. Planners, Fla. Psychol. Assn., Southeastern Psychol. Assn. Democrat. Home: 30730 Watson Blvd Big Pine Key FL 33043-5009 Office: 1 Herald Plz Miami FL 33132-1609

HARRIS, E. LYNN, writer; b. Little Rock, 1955. Degree in journalism, U. Ark., 1977. Salesman IBM, 1977-88; writer, 1988—. Author: Invisible Life, 1991 (Best 10 Novels of 1991 Essence mag.), Just As I Am, 1994, And This Too Shall Pass, 1996. Office: care Double Day 1540 Broadway New York NY 10036-4039

HARRIS, ECON NIGEL, rheumatologist, internist; b. Georgetown, Guyana, S.Am.; came to U.S., 1987; s. T. Wilson and Cicely H.; m. Yvette Williams, 1981; children: Zaman Rashid, Tamia Alisha, Sandhya Caroline. BS, Howard U., 1968; MPhil, Yale U., 1970; MD, U. Pa., 1976; PhD in Medicine, U. West Indies, Kingston, Jamaica, 1982. Diplomate Am. Bd. Internal Medicine, Am. Bd. Rheumatology. Intern U. of the West Indies, Kingston, Jamaica, 1977; resident U. of the West Indies, Kingston, 1978-81; lectr. U. West Indies, Kingston, 1981-83; rheumatology fellow Hammersmith Hosp., London, 1983-85; dir. Lupus rsch. lab. St. Thomas Hosp., London, 1985-87; asst. prof. U. Louisville, Ky., 1987-91, assoc. prof., 1991-96; dean, v.p. acad. affairs Morehouse Sch. of Medicine, Atlanta, prof. dept. medicine; chief div. rheumatology U. Louisville; med. adv. bd. Lupus Found. Am. Editor: Phospholipid Binding Antibodies, 1991; contbr. articles to profl. jours. Recipient Internat. League Against Rheumatism prize Ciba-Geigy, 1993. Fellow Am. Coll. Rheumatology (chmn. antiphospholipid study group 1993—); mem. Phi Beta Kappa, Alpha Omega Alpha. Office: Morehouse Sch of Medicine 720 Westview Dr SW Atlanta GA 30310-1458*

HARRIS, ED JEROME, retired judge; b. May 19, 1920; m. June Brickson, Mar. 25, 1945; children: Edward J., Ann Harris Chaffin. Grad., Southwestern U., Georgetown, Tex., 1941; LLB, JD, U. Wis., 1948; MA, So. Meth. U., 1949. Cert. mediator. Sr. ptnr. Harris, Martin, Carmona, Cruse, Micks & Dunten, 1956-77; mem. Tex. Ho. of Reps., Austin, 1962-77; state dist. judge, 1977-93, ret., 1993. Del. Dem. Nat. Conv., N.Y.C., 1976; councilman, Galveston City, 1961-63; mem. adminstrv. bd. Moody Meml. First United Meth. Ch.; admiral Tex. Navy. Recipient 1st Ann. Independence award North Galveston County Dems., 1991. Mem. Am. Judges Assn., Coll. State Bar Tex., Wis. Bar Assn., Tex. Bar Assn., Galveston County Bar Assn., Montgomery County Bar Assn., Houston Area Ret. Officers Assn., Navy League, Ret. Officers Assn., VFW, U. Wis. Alumni Assn., Judiciary Tex. Coll. Advanced Jud. Studies, Galveston Coffee Club, Galveston Rifle and Pistol Club, Kiwanis, Eagles, Knights of Momus. Avocation: bicycling in Houston-Austin annual multiple sclerosis bike tour.

HARRIS, ED(WARD ALLEN), actor; b. Englewood, N.J., Nov. 28, 1950; s. Bob L. and Margaret Harris; m. Amy Madigan. Student, Columbia U., 1969-71, U. Okla., Norman, 1972-73; BFA, Calif. Inst. of Arts, Valencia, 1975. Appeared in plays A Streetcar Named Desire, Sweet Bird of Youth, Julius Caesar, Hamlet, Camelot, Are You Lookin?, Time of Your Life, Learned Ladies, Kingdom of Earth, Grapes of Wrath, Present Laughter, Balaam, Killers' Head, Fool for Love (Obie award 1983), Prairie Avenue (L.A. Drama Critics Circle award 1981), Scar, 1985 (San Francisco Critics award), Precious Sons, 1986 (Theater World award), Simpatico, 1994, 95, Taking Sides, 1996; appeared in films including Come, 1978, Borderline, 1978, Knightriders, 1980, Creepshow, 1981, The Right Stuff, 1982, Swing Shift, 1982, Under Fire, 1982, A Flash of Green, 1983, Places in the Heart, 1983, Alamo Bay, 1984, Sweet Dreams, 1985, Code Name: Emerald, 1985, Walker, 1987, To Kill a Priest, 1988, Jacknife, 1989, The Abyss, 1989, State of Grace, 1990, Paris Trout, 1991, Glengarry Glen Ross, 1992, Needful Things, 1993, The Firm, 1993, China Moon, 1994, Milk Money, 1994, Apollo 13, 1995 (Acad. award nominee for best supporting actor 1996, SAG award 1996), Just Cause, 1995, Eye for an Eye, 1995, Nixon, 1995, The Rock, 1996, Riders of the Purple Sage, 1996; TV movies include The Amazing Howard Hughes, 1977, The Seekers, 1979, The Aliens Are Coming, 1980, The Last Innocent Man, 1987, Running Mates, 1992, The Stand, 1994 (unbilled cameo), Absolute Power, 1997, Stepmom, 1998, The Truman Show, 1998 (nominated for Best Supporting Actor), The Third Miracles, 1999. Trustee Calif. Inst. of Arts, Valencia, 1985—. Mem. Screen Actors Guild, Equity. Address: 22031 Carbon Mesa Rd Malibu CA 90265-5008*

HARRIS, EDWARD D., JR., physician; b. Phila., July 7, 1937; children: Ned, Tom, Chandler. A.B., Dartmouth Coll., 1958, grad. with honors, 1960; M.D. cum laude, Harvard U., 1962. Diplomate Am. Bd. Internal Medicine and Rheumatology (chmn. subsplty. bd. in rheumatology 1986-88). Intern Mass. Gen. Hosp., Boston, 1962-63, asst. resident, 1963-64, sr. resident, 1966-67, clin. research fellow arthritis unit, 1967-69; asst. prof. Harvard Med. Sch., Boston, 1970; from asst. prof. to prof. Dartmouth Med. Sch., Hanover, N.H., 1970-83, Eugene W. Leonard prof., 1979-83, chief connective tissue disease sect., 1970-83; mem. staff Mary Hitchcock Meml. Hosp., 1970-83; chief med. service Middlesex Gen. U. Hosp., New Brunswick, N.J., 1983—; asst. prof. Harvard U. Med. Sch., Boston, 1970; prof., chmn. medicine U. Medicine and Dentistry N.J.-Rutgers U. Med. Sch., New Brunswick, 1983-88; Arthur L. Bloomfield prof. medicine Stanford U. Sch. Medicine, 1988-95, chmn. dept. medicine, 1988-95, George DeForest Barnett prof. medicine, pres. med. staff, 1988—; chief med. svc. Stanford U. Hosp., 1988-95; dir. Ctr. for Musculoskeletal Diseases, Stanford, 1996—; pres. med. staff, Stanford U. Hosp., 1997-99; med. dir. Internat. Med. Svc., 1997—. Editor The Pharos, 1997—. Fellow ACP; mem. Am. Rheumatism Assn. (numerous coms. 1967—, pres. 1985-86), Alpha Omega Alpha (exec. sec. 1997—). Office: Stanford U 1000 Welch Rd Ste 203 Palo Alto CA 94304-1808

HARRIS, EDWARD FREDERICK, orthodontics educator; b. San Jose, Calif., Oct. 2, 1947; s. Roy Hayward and Bonnie (Keeble) H.; m. Karen J. Morse, May 29, 1970 (div. July 1983); children: Jeremy T., Emily J. BA, San Jose State U., 1969; MA, Ariz. State U., 1972, PhD, 1977. Asst. prof. orthodontics U. Conn., Farmington, 1978-80; prof. orthodontics Coll. Dentistry U. Tenn. Ctr. for Health Scis., Memphis, 1980—. Contbr. articles to profl. jours. NIH fellow, 1973-80. Mem. Am. Assn. Phys. Anthropologists, Internat. Assn. Dental Rsch., Sigma Xi. Republican. Methodist. Office: 875 Union Ave # 301S Memphis TN 38163-3513

HARRIS, EDWIN B., educator, administrator; b. Syracuse, N.Y., Mar. 26, 1949; s. E. Burdett and Helen T. Harris; m. Barbara M. Mryglot, Sept. 1, 1973; children: Brendan P., Sean T., Colin M. BA, LeMoyne Coll., 1971; MA, Ohio State U., 1974; PhD, Syracuse U., 1984. Assoc. dir. fin. aid U. Notre Dame, South Bend, Ind., 1984-88; dir. admissions LeMoyne Coll., Syracuse, N.Y., 1988-95, St. Louis U., 1995—. Author: A Profession in Transition: Trends in Financial Aid Administrator Characteristics and Attitudes 1977-87, 1987; contbr. articles to profl. jours. Chair Conf. Jesuit Enrollment Mgrs.; trustee DeSmet Jesuit H.S., Creve Coeur, Mo., 1998—, Baxter Oaks, Chesterfield, Mo., 1998—. Mem. Nat. Cath. Coll. Admission Assn. (Midwest II regional coord.), Nat. Assn. Coll. Admission Counselors, Am. Assn. Higher Edn. Democrat. Roman Catholic. Avocations: running, reading, biking, rollerblading. E-mail: harrisb@slu.edu. Office: St Louis U 221 N Grand Blvd Saint Louis MO 63103

HARRIS, ELAINE K., medical consultant; b. N.Y.C., Mar. 17, 1924; d. Julius and Bertha (Wecker) Kirschbuam; m. Herbert Harris, Aug. 1, 1948; children: Gail, Linda, Geoffrey. AB Bus. Economics cum laude, Hunter Coll.; AM Bus. Edn., Columbia U. Lic. tchr. bus., N.Y. Founder, pres. Sjogren's Syndrome Found., 1983-91, exec. dir., 1991-94; cons. in field; v.p. exec. bd. Nat. Alliance for Oral Health; developer Sjogren's Syndrome Ednl. Symposia for lay and profls., nat. and internat. support group network. Editor: Moisture Seekers Newsletter, 1984-94, Sjogren's Syndrome Handbook: An Authoritative Guide for Patients, 1989; editor: The New Sjogren's Syndrome Handbook, 1998; contbg. author: Sjogren's Syndrome: Clinical and Immunologic Aspects, 1987, Self-Help, Concepts and Applications, 1992; contbr. articles to profl. jours. Founded Nassau-Suffolk Chpt. Hunter Coll. Alumni Assn., 1949; treas. Youth Employment Svc., Great Neck (N.Y.) Pub. Schs., former chair of Broader Horizons Com., PTO, Great Neck Pub. Sch., others; active Jewish communal field. Recipient Women's Living Legacy, Women's Internat. Ctr., 1994, Third Internat. Conf. on Sjogren's Syndrome, Greece, 1991; elected to Hunter Coll. Hall of Fame, 1989. Mem. Pi Lambda Theta. Avocations: gardening, baking, photography, grandparenting.

HARRIS, E(LEANOR) LYNN(E), religious studies and literature educator; b. Villa Park, Ill., July 7; d. Robert Carl and Karin Elizabeth (Peterson) Karlström. BA, U. Chgo., MA; MDiv, No. Bapt. Theol. Sem., 1975; D of Ministry, Chgo. Theol. Sem., 1980; PhD, NYU, 1980. Ordained min. United Ch. of Christ, 1987. Prof. U. Ill. Chgo., 1970—; interim min. Union Congl. Ch., Moline, Ill., 1997; min. Glen Ellyn (Ill.) Congl. Ch., 1987-89; adj. faculty religious studies Loyola U., Chgo.; adj. faculty English Ind. U. Northwest, DePaul U., Ill. Benedictine U.; sec. Bd. Christian Witness in Soc., 1984-88; presenter in fields. Author: The Mystic Spirituality of A.W. Tozer, A Twentieth Century American Protestant, 1992; contbr. poems and articles to profl. jours. Recipient Lucia Queen of Light award City of Chgo., 1970. Mem. MLA, Am. Acad. Religion, Soc. Sci. Study Religion, Am.-Scandinavian Found., Mensa. Avocations: art, music, travel, folk dancing, camping. Home: PO Box 412 Wheaton IL 60189-0412

HARRIS, ELLIOTT STANLEY, toxicologist; b. Bklyn., June 27, 1922; s. Edward Bernard and Bertha (Ruden) H.; m. Almeda Butler, Mar. 15, 1945; children: Jennifer Jo, Catherine Ann. B.A., U. Colo., 1948; M.S., U. So. Calif., 1950, Ph.D., 1954. Rosenstiehl postdoctoral fellow Roswell Park Meml. Inst., Buffalo, 1954-55; dir. clin. chemistry lab. Roswell Park Meml. Inst., 1955-56; research biochemist Wyeth Labs., Radnor, Pa., 1956-62; sr. research scientist Space Scis. Lab., Gen. Electric Co., Valley Forge, Pa., 1962-63; toxicologist, chief health services br. NASA, 1963-73; dir. div. biomed. and behavioral scis. Nat. Inst. Occupational Safety and Health, Cin., 1973-81; dep. inst. dir. Nat. Inst. Occupational Safety and Health, 1981-86; cons. occupational safety and health, 1986—; adj. assoc. prof. U. Cin., 1974—, Emory U. Sch. Medicine, 1985—; vis. prof. U. Ariz., 1980-81. Author numerous papers in field. Served with USAAF, 1943-45. Decorated D.F.C., Air medal with 3 oak leaf clusters. Fellow AAAS, Soc. Kettering Fellows; mem. Am. Assn. Clin. Chemists, Am. Pub. Health Assn., Am. Indsl. Hygiene Soc., Soc. Toxicology, Am. Conf. Govt. Indsl. Hygienists (hon. life), Soc. Ecotoxicology, Amateur Radio Relay League, Sigma Xi, Phi Lambda Upsilon, Alpha Epsilon Delta.

HARRIS, ELMER BESELER, electric utility executive; b. Chilton County, Ala., Apr. 8, 1939; s. Alton Clauton and Lera (Mitchell) H.; m. Glenda Steele, Sept. 15, 1962; children: Lera Lorraine, Thomas Alton. B.S. in Elec. Engring., Auburn U., 1962, M.S., 1968, M.B.A., 1970; student, U.S. Air Force Flight Sch., Tex., 1964, Air Command and Staff Coll., Maxwell AFB, Montgomery, Ala., 1970. With Ala. Power Co., Birmingham, Ala., 1958—, asst. v.p., 1975, asst. v.p., asst. treas., 1975-76, v.p. corp. fin. and planning, 1976, sr. v.p., 1978, exec. v.p., chief fin. officer, 1979, dir., 1980-85; exec. v.p., dir. Ga. Power Co., Atlanta, 1985-86; sr. exec. v.p., dir. Ga. Power Co., 1986-89; pres., chief exec. officer Ala. Power Co., Birmingham, 1989—; bd. dirs. So. Electric Gen. Co., Birmingham, Ala. Property Co., So. Electric Generating Co., AmSouth Bank, N.A. Bd. dirs. Ala. Coun. Econ. Edn., Birmingham Area coun. Boy Scouts of Am., Pub. Affairs Rsch. Coun. Ala., United Way; trustee Samford U., So. Rsch. Inst.; mem. adv. bd. St. Vincent Hosp. Mem. Edison Electric Inst., Southeastern Electric Exch., Soc. Am. Mil. Engrs., Summit Club, Montgomery Club, Rotary. Office: Ala Power Co PO Box 2641 600 18th St N Birmingham AL 35291-0001*

HARRIS, EMILY LOUISE, special education educator; b. New London, Conn., Nov. 16, 1932; d. Frank Sr. and Tanzatter (McCleese) Brown; m. John Everett Harris Sr., Sept. 10, 1955; children: John Everett Jr., Jocelyn E. (dec.). *Emily Harris's grandparents were William and Emma McCleese and William and Louise Brown.* BS, U. Conn., 1955; MEd, Northeastern U., 1969. Cert. tchr. elem. spl. subject sci., Mass., spl. subject reading, secondary prin., elem. prin. Tchr. New Haven Sch. Dept., 1957-59, Boston Sch. Dept., 1966-68, Natick (Mass.) Sch. Dept., 1969-72; cert. nurse's asst. The Hebrew Rehab. Ctr., Roslindale, Mass., 1973-75; spl. edn. educator Boston Sch. Dept., 1975-76, 78—, support tchr., 1976-78; site coord. Tchr. Corps., 1977-81; leader, co-leader Harvard U. Student Tchrs. at Dorchester H.S. Sem., 1995—; tchr. adviser Future Educators Am. Dorchester H.S. *Emily Harris is a member of the School of Base Management at Dorchester High School. She was College Faculty Wife at the Brown University Sepia Club and served as Vice-President from 1956-57. She was a member of the Yale Dames from 1958-59. She also served as M.I.T. Matron from 1968-69 and a Boston University Faculty Wife from 1969-87. Her biographical sketches appear in Who's Who in America in 1998, Who's Who of American Women in 1997, and The World's Who's Who of Women in 1997. She was a member of The National Association of Female Executives and the Baptist Church in Boston, Massachusetts from 1975 to the present.* Editor, compiler: Cooking With the Stars, 1989; contbr. article to profl. jours. Mem.-del. Mass. Fedn. Tchrs., Boston, 1993-96; elected rep. AFL-CIO (Boston Tchrs. Union), 1986-96; registrar of voters Dorchester (Mass.) H.S., 1986—; adv. bd. New England Assn. Schs. and Colls., 1980-93; 1st v.p., bd. dirs. League of Women for Comty. Svcs., Boston, 1976-80, Cynthia Sickle-Cell Anemia Fund, Boston, 1976-80. Recipient Tchg. award Urban League Guild Mass., 1993. Mem. AAUW, Zeta Phi Beta (Zeta of Yr. 1994), Alpha Delta Kappa, Kappa Delta Pi, Order Ea. Star (past worthy matron Prince Hall chpt. 1983-84), Delta Omicron Zeta, Phi Delta Kappa. Baptist. Avocations: reading, sewing. Home: 36 Dietz Rd Hyde Park MA 02136-1134

HARRIS, ERIC R., policy analyst, county official; b. Rochester, N.Y., Jan. 20, 1965; s. Roger Edwin and Helen Amanda (Kenyon) H. BA in Polit. Sci. cum laude, Boston U., 1987; MPA, U. Albany, 1993. Rsch. asst. Pub. Employees Fedn., Albany, N.Y., 1993; pub. mgmt. intern N.Y. State Dept. Social Svcs., Albany, 1994-95; policy analyst Office of County Exec., Albany, N.Y., 1995-96; dir. personnel svcs. Albany County, N.Y., 1996-98; resource and rev. specialist N.Y. State Office Mental Retardation and Devel. Disabilities, Albany, N.Y., 1998—. Lt. (j.g.) USN, 1987-90; lt. USNR, 1992—. Decorated Nat. Def. medal, others. Mem. Golden Key, Pi Alpha Alpha. Democrat. Office: Div Rev Support NYS OmRDD 44 Holland Ave Fl 5 Albany NY 12208-3411

HARRIS, EVA, molecular biology educator; b. N.Y.C., Aug. 6, 1965. BA, Harvard U., 1987; PhD in Molecular and Cell Biology, U. Calif., Berkeley, 1993. Dir. applied molecular biology/appropriate technol. transfer program U. Calif., San Francisco, 1993—, asst. adj. prof., 1997-98; asst. prof. Sch. Pub. Health U. Calif., Berkeley, 1998—. John D. and Catherine T. MacArthur Found. fellow, 1997. Mem. AAAS, Am. Soc. Microbiology. Office: U Calif Sch of Pub Health 239 Warren Hall Berkeley CA 94720*

HARRIS, F. CHANDLER, retired university administrator; b. Neligh, Nebr., Nov. 5, 1914; s. James Carlton and Helen Ayres (Boyd) H.; m. Barbara Ann Hull, Aug. 10, 1946; children: Victoria Williams, Randolph Boyd. AB, UCLA, 1936. Assoc. editor Telegraph Delivery Spirit, L.A., 1937-39; writer, pub. svc. network radio programs Univ. Explorer, Sci. Editor, U. Calif., 1939-61; pub. info. mgr. UCLA, 1961-75, dir., 1975-82, dir. emeritus, 1982—. Mem. pub. rels. com., western region United Way, 1972-75; bd. dirs. Am. Youth Symphony, L.A., 1978-98, v.p., 1983-98; bd. dirs. Hathaway Home for Children, 1982-88. Recipient 1st prize NBC Radio Inst., 1944; Harvey Hebert medal Delta Sigma Phi, 1947, Mr. Delta Sig award, 1972; Adam award Assistance League Mannequins, 1980, Univ. Service award UCLA Alumni Assn., 1986; bd. dirs. Western L.A. Regional C. of C., 1976-80. Mem. U. Calif. Retirees Assn. L.A. (pres. 1985-87), Sigma Delta Chi, Delta Sigma Phi (nat. pres. 1959-63), UCLA Faculty Club (sec. bd. govs. 1968-72). Editor Interfraternity Rsch. Adv. Coun. Bull., 1949-50, Carnation, 1969-80, Royce Hall, 1985. Home: 7774 Skyhill Dr Los Angeles CA 90068-1232

HARRIS, FRAN, sportscaster, former basketball player; b. Mar. 12, 1965; 1 child, Brittany. B of Journalism, U. Tex., 1986, M of Journalism. Guard Cesena, Italy, 1987-88, 89, WMBA - Houston Comets, 1997; WNBA basketball analyst Lifetime TV, 1999—; sports analyst ESPN and Fox Sports, 1999—. Author: About My Sisters Business: The Black Woman's Road Map to Successful Entrepreneurship, 1996, In the Black: An African-American Parent's Guide to Raising Financially Responsible Children, 1998. Named to U.S. Team Goodwill Games, 1986, All Am., 1985, Southwest Conf. Player of Yr., 1984, 85, 86, NCAA All Tourament Team. Office: care of Jill Smoller ICM 8942 Wilshire Blvd Beverly Hills CA 90211*

HARRIS, FRED, orthotist, prosthetist; b. Bklyn., Sept. 29, 1941; s. Fred and Eva H.; m. Sheila, Sept. 1966; children: Freddie, Jeffrey, Ted. AAS, N.Y.C. C.C., 1974; BS, CUNY, 1980. Orthotist, prosthetist VA Med. Ctr., N.Y.C., 1963—. With U.S. Army, 1960-62. Mem. AAAS, NAACP, Am. Congress Rehab. Medicine, Am. Acad. Orthotics & Prosthetics, N.Y. Acad. Scis., N.Y. Orthotic & Prosthetic Assn., N.Y. State Am. Acad. Orthotist & Prosthetists, Lower Limb Orthotics Soc., Cad/Cam Soc., Upper Limb Soc., Internat. Soc., N.Y. State Rifle Pistol Assn., Prescription Footwear Assn., Prosthetics & Orthotics, Sierra Club, Libr. of Congress Assn. Baptist. Avocations: reading, music, softball, basketball, bowling. Home: 633 Hegeman Ave Brooklyn NY 11207-7103

HARRIS, FRED R., political science educator, former senator; b. Walters, Okla., Nov. 13, 1930; s. Fred Byron and Alene (Person) H.; m. LaDonna Crawford, Apr. 8, 1949 (div. 1981); children: Kathryn, Byron, Laura.; m. Margaret S. Elliston, Sept. 5, 1982. B.A. in Polit. Sci, U. Okla., 1952, J.D. with distinction, 1954. Bar: Okla. bar 1954. Founder, sr. partner firm Harris, Newcombe, Redman & Doolin, Lawton, Okla., 1954-64; mem. Okla Senate, 1956-64, U.S. Senate from Okla., 1964-73; prof. polit. sci. U. N.Mex., Albuquerque, 1976—. Author: Alarms and Hopes, 1969, Now Is The Time, 1971, The State of the Cities: Report of the Commission on Cities in the 70's, 1972, Social Science and National Policy: The New Populism, 1973, Potomac Fever, 1977, America's Democracy, 1980, 3d edit., 1985, Readings on the Body Politic, 1987, Deadlock or Decision, 1993, In Defense of Congress, 1994; co-author: America's Legislative Processes, 1983, Understanding American Government, 1988, Quiet Riots, 1988, America's Government, 1990, Locked in the Poorhouse, 1998. Mem. Nat. Adv. Commn. Civil Disorders, 1967-68; Chmn. Democratic Nat. Com., 1969-70. Mem. Order of Coif, Phi Beta Kappa. Office: U New Mexico Dept Polit Sci Albuquerque NM 87131

HARRIS, FREDERICK GEORGE, publishing company executive; b. Niles, Ohio, Apr. 12, 1922; s. William H. and Nell H. (Zempkey) H.; m. Marjorie E. Bork, Sept. 10, 1950; children—Frederick, David, Joyce. B.S. in Bus. Adminstrn, Ohio State U., 1948. Staff accountant Lybrand, Ross Bros. & Montgomery, 1948-56; with Dow Jones & Co., Inc., 1956-87, comptroller-asst. sec., 1970-76, mem. mgmt. com., 1972—, v.p., comptroller, 1976-77, v.p. fin., 1977-84, sr. v.p., chief fin. officer, 1984-87; v.p., treas. Dow Jones-Bunker Ramo News Retrieval Service, Inc., 1971-78. Trustee Trenton Lutheran Housing Corp., 1969-81, treas., 1974-80; Chmn. local troop Boy Scouts Am., 1965-67. Served with USAAF, 1942-45. Mem. Fin. Execs. Inst. (chmn. orgn. planning com. N.Y. chpt. 1963-64), Nat. Assn. Accountants (asso. dir. N.Y. chpt. 1959-61), Inst. Newspaper Controllers and Finance Officers (dir. 1964-72, chmn. steering com. 1968-69, pres. 1970-71, Walter F. Carley award 1970, 73, 77), Hopewell Valley Golf Club, Delta Sigma Pi. Lutheran (v [illegible] ch. 1967-68, council 1965-71). Home: 113 Lewis Brook Rd Pennington NJ 08534-1909

HARRIS, FREDERICK JOHN, foreign language and literature educator; b. N.Y.C., July 29, 1943; s. Frederick and Anna (Guttmann) H. BA, Fordham U., 1965; MA, Columbia U., 1966, PhD, 1969. Asst. prof. Fordham U., N.Y.C., 1970-79, assoc. prof., 1979-84, prof. French and comparative lit., 1984—, chmn. div. humanities, 1979-85, chmn. dept. modern langs. and lits. (bi-campus); bd. dirs. Fordham U. Press, N.Y.C.; mem. adv. com. Krieg und Literatur/War and Literature. Author: André Gide-Romain Rolland: Two Men Divided, 1973, Encounters with Darkness: French and German Writers on World War II, 1983; contbr. articles to profl. jours. Mem. MLA, Am. Assn. Tchrs. French, Internat. Comparative Lit. Assn., Am. Comparative Lit. Assn., Assn. des Amis d'André Gide, Société des Professeurs Français et Francophones d'Amérique (bd. dirs. 1995-98), Stewart Hall (v.p. 1989-90, bd. dirs.). Roman Catholic. Office: Rose Hill Campus Lincoln Center Campus Fordham U New York NY 10023

HARRIS, FREDERICK PHILIP, retired philosophy educator; b. Portland, Oreg., Aug. 28, 1911; s. Philip Henry and Nellie Louise (Humpage) H.; m. Hester Almira Larson, July 15, 1943; children: Judith, Jacquelyn, Jennifer, Elizabeth, Marcia, Frederick (dec.). AB, Willamette U., 1935; MA, Columbia U., 1937, PhD, 1944; cert. in Japanese, U. Mich., 1944. Tutor Horace Mann Sch. for Boys, N.Y.C., 1935-41; instr. English Rutgers U., New Brunswick, N.J., 1941-42; psychologist Bur. Psychol. Svcs., U. Mich., Ann Arbor, 1946; assoc. prof. philosophy Case Western Res. U., Cleve., 1946-55, chmn. dept., 1948-57; headmaster Am. Sch. in Japan, Tokyo, 1957-66; prof. Oreg. State U., Corvallis, 1967-80, chmn. dept. philosophy, 1967-76; Fulbright vis. prof. faculty edn. Kyoto (Japan) U., 1955-57; prof. Rockefeller Found. Am. Studies Seminar, Doshisha U. Japan, 1956; vis. prof. U. Oreg., Eugene, summer 1950, U. Hawaii, Honolulu, summer 1966, Lewis & Clark Coll., Portland, 1966-67; dir. Oreg. Study Ctr. Waseda U., Tokyo, 1977-80; vis. prof. Grad. Sch. Commerce Waseda U., 1980, Open Coll., 1982-

92; pres. Tokyo Internat. Co., 1986-92; advisor Japan Intercultural Comm. Soc., Tokyo, 1980-82. Author: The Neo-Idealist Political Theory, 1944; editor: The Teaching of Philosophy, 1950; editor Perspectives, Japan Intercultural Comm. Soc., 1981-82. Trustee Internat. Sch., Nagoya, Japan, 1963-66, Sendai Am. Sch., Japan, 1963-65; del. 1st Am.-Japan Student Conf., Aoyama Gakuin, Tokyo, 1934. Staff sgt. U.S. Army, 1942-45. Fulbright grantee Kyoto U., 1955, 56; Frederick Philip Harris Libr. named in his honor Am. Sch. in Japan, Tokyo, 1966. Mem. Am. Philos. Assn., Asiatic Soc. Japan (counselor 1986-89), Japan English Forensics Assn., Dem. Nat. Com., Nature Conservancy, Wilderness Soc. Methodist. Avocations: swimming, hiking, mountain climbing, pottery, travel. Home: 3050 SW Ridgewood Ave Portland OR 97225-3363

HARRIS, GERALD WAYNE, retired radio advertising sales executive; b. Durham, N.C., Oct. 21, 1933; s. Erskine Owen Harris and Lora (Poole) Bryant; m. Shirley Eileen Cheek, July 10, 1954 (div. 1979); children: Ann, John, Guy, Sammy. Spl. corr. News-Leader, Richmond, Va., 1960-69; ops. mgr., news dir. WINA AM-FM, Charlottesville, Va., 1962-67; news reporter WSVA-TV, Harrisonburg, Va., 1967-69; gen. mgr. WTHO AM-FM, Thomson, Ga., 1969-71; news reporter WSPA AM-FM-TV, Spartanburg, S.C., 1971-77; advt. rep. WKDY Radio, Spartanburg, S.C., 1977-88, WNNC-WIRC-WXRC, Newton, Hickory, N.C., 1988-99; ret., 1999. Republican. Baptist. Home: 19 N Davis Ave Newton NC 28658-2328

HARRIS, GLENDA STANGE, medical transcriptionist, writer; b. Jacksonville, Fla., Jan. 11, 1954; d. Robert Lee and Wynelle (Jowers) S.; m. David Michael Harris Sr., Aug. 11, 1973; children: David Michael Jr., Mason Andrew. AA, Fla. Jr. Coll., Jacksonville, 1980. Asst. adminstr. Primary Health Care Ctr., Orange Park, Fla., 1980-83; med. transcriptionist Ctr. for Plastic and Reconstructive Surgery, Orlando, Fla., 1984-90, Sentinel Health Ptnrs., Fayetteville, 1991—. Author: (newspaper column) Grand Slam News, 1991-94. Republican. Methodist. Avocations: reading, travel, tennis, writing, gardening. Home: 135 Mark Ln Fayetteville GA 30214-7202 Office: Fayette Med Clinic 101 Yorktown Dr Fayetteville GA 30214-1568

HARRIS, GREGORY SCOTT, management services executive; b. Denver, June 5, 1955; s. Herbert E. and Marcia Jean (Raabe) H. B.S. in Journalism with honors, U. Colo., 1977; M.B.A., Loyola U., Chgo., 1981. Dir. public relations IMPACT Internat., Inc., Chgo., 1977-78; dir. edn. Nat. Home Furnishings Assn. (NHFA), Chgo., 1978-79, v.p. industry affairs, 1981-87, exec. v.p., chief operating officer, 1987-88; exec. dir. Interior Design Soc., Chgo., 1979-82; sec. NHFA Service Corp., 1986-87, v.p., 1986-87, pres., 1987-91, also bd. dirs.; pres. Open Hand: Chgo. Found., 1988-91; chief of staff Chgo. City Coun., 1992—; mem. Devel. Adv. Coun. City of Chgo., 1990-92; bd. dirs. Nonprofit Fin. Ctr.; mem. advocacy and pub. policy com. AFC. Trustee Design Found., Chgo., 1980-88; chmn. bd. dirs. AIDS Walk Found., 1990-91; bd. dirs. AIDS Legal Coun., 1992-94, Heartland Alliance for Human Needs and Human Rights; fin. dir. Simpson for Congress Com., 1991-92. Recipient Leadership in Marketing award Newspaper Pubs. Assn., 1983, Outstanding Young Chicagoan award Chgo. Jaycees, 1992, Outstanding Svc. to Immigrant and Refugee Cmty. award, 1996, Uptown C. of C. Ann. award, 1996, Voice of People Cmty. award, 1994, Equality award Human Rigts Campaign, 1997, W. Clement Stone award, 1998; named to City of Chgo. Hall of Fame, 1996. Office: Chgo City Coun City Hall 121 N La Salle St Chicago IL 60602-1202

HARRIS, GRETCHEN ELIZABETH, treasury analyst, consultant; b. Buffalo, Jan. 11, 1973; d. Orville Paul and Patricia Louise (Therre) H. BA cum laude, U. Rochester, 1995; postgrad., Simon Sch. Bus./U. Rochester. Asst. to COO Harter, Secrest & Emery, Rochester, N.Y., 1994-97; contract cons. Xerox, Rochester, N.Y., 1997; treasury analyst EDS, Rochester, 1998—; cons. Xerox, 1998—. Soup kitchen vol. Blessed Sacrement Ch., Rochester, 1997—; nursing home vol. Apple Gate Manor, Medina, N.Y., 1996—. Recipient Regents scholarship N.Y. State, 1991, Mildred Burton summer study grant U. Rochester, summer 1992, Alumni scholarship U. Rochester, 1991-95. Mem. Hartford Soc., U. Rochester Career Source (vol.). Episcopalian. Avocations: equestrian events, music, antiques, reading, architecture.

HARRIS, GUY HENDRICKSON, chemical research engineer; b. San Bernardino, Calif., Oct. 2, 1914; s. Edwin James and Nellie Mae (Hendrickson) H.; m. Elsie Mary Dietsch, Mar. 15, 1940; children: Alice, Robert, Mary, Sara. AA, San Bernardino Valley Coll., 1934; BS, U. Calif., Berkeley, 1937; AM, Stanford U., 1939, PhD, 1941. Analytical chemist Shell Devel. Co., Emeryville, Calif., 1937-38; organic chemist William S. Merrell Co., Cin., 1941-45; rsch. chemist Fiber Bd., Emeryville, 1945-46; from organic chemist to assoc. scientist The Dow Chem. Co., Pittsburg, Calif., 1946-62; assoc. scientist The Dow Chem. Co., Walnut Creek, Calif., 1964-82; sr. lectr. U. Ghana, Legon Accra, 1962-64; chmn. dept. chemistry John F. Kennedy U., Orinda, Calif., 1964-69; pvt. practice cons. Concord, Calif., 1982-88; rsch. engr. U. Calif., Berkeley, 1988—. Contbr. K & O Encyclopedia Chem. Tech., 1959, 70, 84, 97, Reagents in Mineral Tech., 1990. Fellow AAAS, Royal Soc. Chemistry; mem. AIME, Soc. Mining Engrs. (disting. mem.), Bus. Men's Fellowship USA, The Commonwealth Club, Sigma Xi. Roman Catholic. Achievements include 51 patents in field of mineral processing reagents in particular Z200 (R) agricultural chemicals and process for manufacture. Home: 1673 Georgia Dr Concord CA 94519-1921 Office: Univ California 386 Evans Hall # 1760 Berkeley CA 94720

HARRIS, HARRY H., television director; b. Kansas City, Mo., Sept. 8, 1922; s. Harry Howard Sr. and Jennie Harris; m. Patricia A. Pulici, Aug. 18, 1939; children: Susanne and Joanne. Student, UCLA, 1940-41. film editor Desilu Prodns., 1949-57. Prodr., dir. (TV movie): Eight is Enough Reunion, 1987; dir (TV movies): Alice in Wonderland, 1984, The Waltons Thanksgiving Special, 1993, The Runaways, 1974, Swiss Family Robinson,1976, Rivkin Bounty Hunter, 1980, The Young Pioneers, 1978; dir. (TV pilots): House Detective, 1985, Private Life of T.K. Dearing, 1975, Carousel Horse, 1986 (Emmy nomination), Kowalski Loves Ya, 1986, Tom Swift, 1982, Apple's Way, 1975, The Home Front, 1980, Scamps, 1969; dir (TV episodes): In the Heat of the Night, 1988-93, Remington Steele, 1984-88, Magnum P.I., 1985-88, Cagney & Lacey, 1983, Bodies of Evidence, 1992, Spenser for Hire, Jake and the Fatman, 1991, MacGyver, 1989-90, Father Dowling Mysteries, 1990, Scarecrow and Mrs. King, 1984, Hawaii 5-0, 1976, Blue Knight, 1985, Hunter, 1976, Oldest Rookie, 1987, Naked City, 1972, Mission Impossible, 1972, Perry Mason, 1972, Shell Game, 1976, Shaft, 1975, The D.A., Adam-12, 1974, T.H.E. Cat, 1965, Fame, 1982 (Emmy award 1982), The Waltons, 1972-82 (Emmy award nominee 1973, Humanitas award 1976), Eight is Enough, 1977-80, Our House, 1986, Boone, Apple's Way, 1975, Sisters, 1992-96 (Genesis award 1992, Golden Reel award 1995), Tom Swift, 1982, Falcon Crest, 1982-87, Dallas, 1981, 85, Hotel, 1983; Kung-Fu, 1975, A Fine Romance, 1989, Nurse, 1981, Mississippi, 1983, Supercarrier, 1988, Love American Style, 1968, Doc Elliot, 1975, Gibbsville, 1976, Spencer's Pilots, 1976, The Islanders, 1959, McCall of the Wild, 1989, Hearts are Wild, 1982, Dante's Inferno, 1968, Stick With Me Kid, 1994, The Cape, 1996, 7th Heaven, 1988-89, Beverly Hills 90210, 1988-89, Eight Is Enough Reunion, 1987, University Hospital, 1994-95, Savannah, 1995, Dr. Quinn Medicine Woman, 1994, Gunsmoke, 1961-66, Guns of Paradise, 1991, Wanted Dead or Alive, 1958-60, Rawhide, 1963-64, Jesse James, 1963, Wells Fargo, High Chapparral, 1967-70, Bonanza, 1968, Daniel Boone, 1964-68, Pistols N' Petticoats, 1967, Hondo, 1968, Stagecoach West, 1959, MacKenzies of Paradise Cove, 1978, Swiss Family Robinson, 1976, Man from Atlantis, 1977, Voyage to the Bottom of the Sea, 1968-72, Land of the Giants, 1968-70, Lost in Space, 1965-68, Time Tunnel, 1966, Road West, 1969, The Texan, 1958-59, Death Valley Days, 1968, Man Called Shenandoah, 1965, The Virginian, 1970, Men of Shiloh, 1970, Branded, 1964-66, Young Pioneers, 1978. 2nd Lt. USAF, 1944. Mem. Dirs. Guild Am., Motion Picture Film Editors (life). Avocation: amateur radio.

HARRIS, HENRY WILLIAM, physician; b. Catawba, N.C., Jan. 6, 1919; s. Henry William and Katie (Coulter) H.; m. Margaret Ann Roberts, Nov. 29, 1950; children: Henry William, John R., James P. B.A., U.N.C., 1940; M.D. cum laude, Harvard U., 1943. Diplomate: in pulmonary disease Am. Bd. Internal Medicine. Intern Harvard Med. Service, Boston City Hosp., 1944-45, asst. resident medicine, 1945-46; resident fellow Thorndike Meml. Lab., 1944, 46; resident chest service Bellevue Hosp., N.Y.C., 1947; staff physician Gunderson Clinic, LaCrosse, Wis., 1948-53; asst. prof. medicine U. Utah Coll. Medicine, 1955-59, asso. prof., 1959-60; chief pulmonary disease service VA Hosp., Salt Lake City, 1955-60; prof. chmn. dept. medicine Woman's Med. Coll. of Pa., 1960-67; chmn. dept. medicine Catholic Med. Center Bklyn. and Queens, 1967-70; asso. prof. clin. medicine N.Y.U. Sch. Medicine, 1969-70, prof., 1970—; acting dir. chest svc. Bellevue Hosp., N.Y.C., 1983-89, attending: with Tisch-Univ. Hosp., N.Y.C., Gouveneur Hosp., N.Y.C.; cons. VA Hosp., N.Y.C.; med. coord. Bur. Tuberculosis, Dept. of Health, N.Y.C. Mem. editorial bd.: Annals of Internal Medicine, 1976-80; Contbr. articles to profl. pubs. Bd. dirs. Am. Lung Assn., 1961-79, v.p., 1972-73; bd. dirs. N.Y. Lung Assn., 1974-95, v.p., 1983—, pres. 1987-90; bd. dirs. Am. Bur. Med. Advancement in China., 1978—, v.p., 1983-87, pres. 1987-92, chmn. H. Wm. Harris vis. prof. com., 1986-96. Served to capt., M.C. AUS, 1953-55. Fellow ACP; mem. Am. Thoracic Soc. (pres. 1962-63). Home: 111 7th St Apt 306 Garden City NY 11530-5716 Office: Chest Service Bellevue Hosp 1st Ave New York NY 10016

HARRIS, HENRY WOOD, cable television executive; b. Raleigh, N.C., June 11, 1938; s. Henry W. and Charlotte Louise (Allen) H.; m. Mary Margaret Durham, June 10, 1960; children—Stephen Gregory, Charlotte Durham. B.S. in Bus. Adminstrn, U. N.C., 1960, M.B.A., 1964. Loan officer Trust Co. Bank, Atlanta, 1964-66; operating v.p. Cox Cable Communications Co., Atlanta, 1966-69; pres. Cox Cable Communications Co., 1969-79; exec. v.p. Cox Broadcasting Corp., Atlanta, 1977-79; pres. Metrovision, Inc., Atlanta, 1979-95; divsn. pres. Time Warner Cable, Atlanta, 1995—. Mem. lay adv. bd. Marist Sch.; deacon Peachtree Presbyterian Ch. Served with USMCR, 1960-63. Mem. Phi Beta Kappa, Phi Eta Sigma. Club: Capital City. Home: 641 Wesley Rd NW Atlanta GA 30327-1240 Office: Ste 1530 115 Perimeter Center Pl NE Atlanta GA 30346-1238*

HARRIS, HOLTON EDWIN, plastics machinery manufacturing executive; b. N.Y.C., Aug. 24, 1923; s. David William and Mildred (Stoutborough) H.; m. Jeanne Deming, Feb. 22, 1963; children: Walter Deming, Dorothy Stoutenborough. BSEE, MIT, 1947, MSEE, 1948. Engr. GE, Syracuse, N.Y., 1948-49; sect. sales mgr. GE, Schenectady, N.Y., 1949-52; asst. to pres. R.W. Cramer Co., Centerbrook, Conn., 1952-53; sales mgr. Ea. Air Devices, Dover, N.H., 1953-54; mgr. comml. products Reeves Instrument Corp., Carle Place, N.Y., 1954-58; pres. Harrel, Inc., Norwalk, Conn., 1958—; lectr. in field. Contbg. author: Modern Plastics Ency., Blow Molding Handbook; patentee in field; contbr. articles to profl. jours. Dep. moderator Representative Town Meeting, Westport, Conn., chmn. fin. com.; chmn. Rep. Town. Com., Westport; mem. Charter Revision Comm., Westport. With U.S. Army Signal Corp., 1943-46, South Pacific. Mem. IEEE (life), Soc. Plastics Engrs. (sr.), Instrument Soc. Am. (sr.). Avocations: amateur radio. Home: 5 Newtown Tpke Westport CT 06880-1802 Office: Harrel Inc 16 Fitch St Norwalk CT 06855-1392

HARRIS, HOWARD HUNTER, oil company executive; b. Cushing, Okla., Dec. 7, 1924; s. Oscar Hunter and Gertie Lee (Stark) H.; m. Gwendolyne J. Moyers, Dec. 31, 1945; children: Howard Sidney, Rodney Craig. B.S. in Bus. Adminstrn., U. Okla., 1949, J.D., 1949; postgrad. in advt. mgmt., Stanford U., 1971. Atty. Emery & Harris, Cushing and Stillwater, Okla., 1949-50; staff atty. Sun Oil Co., Tulsa, 1950-54; div. atty. Marathon Oil Co., Tulsa, 1954-63; staff atty Marathon Internat. Oil Co., Findlay, Ohio, 1963-65; mgr. legal affairs Deutsche Marathon Petroleum Gmbh., Frankfurt and Munich, 1965-70; mktg. atty. and assoc. gen. counsel Marathon Oil Co., Findlay, Ohio, 1970-74, v.p. corp. external affairs, 1974-86; ret. Marathon Oil Co. Pres. Gainey Ranch Cmty. Assn., 1995-98. Served with AUS, 1943-45. Decorated Bronze Star. Mem. Am. Petroleum Inst., ABA, Ohio Bar Assn., Okla. Bar Assn., Order of Coif, Beta Gamma Sigma. Republican. Episcopalian. Lodges: Masons.

HARRIS, HOWARD JEFFREY, marketing and printing company executive; b. Denver, June 9, 1949; s. Gerald Victor and Leona Lee (Tepper) H.; m. Michele Whealen, Feb. 6, 1975; children: Kimberly, Valerie. BFA with honors, Kansas City Art Inst., 1973; M of Indsl. Design with honors, Pratt Inst., 1975; postgrad. Graphic Arts Rsch. Ctr., Rochester Inst. Tech., 1977; cert. mktg. exec., U. Utah, 1987. Indsl. designer Kivett & Myers, Architects, 1970-71; indsl. designer United Rsch. Corp., Denver, 1971-72; indsl. designer, asst. to v.p., pres. JFN Assos., N.Y.C., 1972-73; dir. facility planning Abt & Assos., Cambridge, Mass., 1973-74; v.p. design, prodn., and rsch. Eagle Direct, Denver, 1974—; pres. Eagle Direct, Denver. Vol., chmn. dirs. Stepping Stones (multi-religious orgn.). Recipient SBA Small Bus. Person of the Year award for Ste of Colo., 1997. Mem. Indsl. Designers Soc. Am., Graphic Arts Tech. Found., Design Methods Group, Cable TV Adminstrn. Mktg. Assn., Mail Advt. Assn., Am. Advt. Fedn., Nat. Assn. Printers and Lithographers (bd. dirs., chmn. mktg. com.). Democrat. Jewish. Office: 5105 E 41st Ave Denver CO 80216-4420

HARRIS, IRA STEPHEN, secondary education educator, administrator; b. Bklyn., July 13, 1945; s. Simon and Vera (Vichness) H.; m. Arlene Cramer, Dec. 25, 1971; children: Elliot, David, Sara. BS, Fairleigh Dickinson U., 1968; MS, L.I. U., 1970, Profl. Diploma magna cum laude, 1978. Sci. educator 158Q Marie Curie H.S., Bayside, N.Y., 1968-76; tchr. math., sci. and social studies, media specialist Campbell Jr. H.S. 218Q, Flushing, N.Y., 1976-79, Beard Jr. H.S. 189Q, Flushing, 1979-86; tech. specialist Carson Intermediate Sch. 237Q, Flushing, 1986—, asst. prin., 1995—. Commodore Newbridge Boat Club, Bellmore, N.Y.; v.p., edn. chmn. Bellmore Jewish Ctr.; pres. East Bay Civic Assn., Bellmore. Mem. N.Y. Acad. Scis. (judge sci. fair N.Y.C. 1985—). Republican. Home: 2729 Claudia Ct Bellmore NY 11710-4740

HARRIS, IRVING, lawyer; b. Cin., May 23, 1927; s. Albert and Sadye H.; m. Selma Schottenstein, June 18, 1950; children: Jeffrey Philip, Jonathan Lindley (dec.), Lisa Ann Hollister. Undergrad. degree, U. Cin., 1948, LLB, 1951. Ptnr. Cors, Hair & Hartsock, 1954-81, Hartsock, Harris & Schneider, Cin., 1981-82, Porter, Wright, Morris & Arthur, Cin., 1982-89; ptnr. firm Harris, Harris, Field Schacter & Bardach Ltd., Cin., 1989—; mem. Ohio Trade Mission to Orient, 1973, to Eng. and Germany, 1974; spl. counsel to Atty. Gen. Ohio, 1963-71; del. 6th Cir. Jud. Conf., 1991—; lectr. Advising, Oper. and Rebuilding the Financially Distressed Co., 1991; bd. dirs. Bank One, Cin., HRC Ltd. Partnership (Hyatt Regency (Cin.) Cin. Mem. Ohio Devel. Financing Commn., 1974-84, vice chmn., 1978-79; spl. counsel Ohio Atty. Gen.'s Office for the Police and Firemen's Disability and Pension Fund, 1994-97; trustee Skidmore Coll., 1976-90, trustee emeritus, 1991—; trustee emeritus Big Bros.; trustee Cin. Symphony Orch., 1989-96; mem. Hamilton County Steering Com., Dem. Party, 1980-91; bd. overseers U. Cin. Law Sch. With USN, 1945-46. Mem. ABA (Sherman Act com., sect. on antitrust and bus. law 1969—, subcoms. on derivative actions, bankruptcy, litigation of bus. and corp. litigation 1992—), Ohio Bar Assn., Cin. Bar Assn., Am. Judicature Soc., Am. Arbitration Assn. (arbitrator), Potter Stewart Inn of Ct. (master of the bench), Queen City Club, Univ. Club, Camargo Hunt Club, Cin. Tennis Club, Snowmass Country Club. Home: 18 Grandin Ln Cincinnati OH 45208-3365 Office: Harris Harris Field Schacter & Bardach Carew Tower Fl 41 Cincinnati OH 45202

HARRIS, IRVING BROOKS, cosmetics executive; b. St. Paul, Aug. 4, 1910; s. William and Mildred (Brooks) H.; m. Joan White; children: Roxanne, Virginia, William. AB, Yale U., 1931, hon. degree, 1990; hon. degree, Loyola U., 1976, Kenyon Coll., 1986, Columbia Coll., 1987, Lesley Coll., 1988, Bank Street Coll. Edn., 1988, De Pauw U., 1989; hon. deg., U. Ill., 1992, Roosevelt U., 1996; hon. degree, Gov.'s State U., 1997. Exec. in finance business, 1931-42, aircraft part bus., 1944-46; exec. Toni Home Permanent Co., after 1946; (sold stockholdings in Toni Co. to Gillette Safety Razor Co.), 1948; dir. Gillette Safety Razor Co., 1948-60; exec. v.p. Toni Co., 1946-52; chmn. bd. Sci. Research Assos., 1953-58; pres. Michael Reese Hosp. and Med. Center, Chgo., 1958-61, Harris Group, Inc., 1959-76; chmn. exec. com. Pittway Corp.; pres. William Harris Investors, 1987—. Trustee U. Chgo., Nat. Ctr. Clin. Infant Programs, Chgo. Ednl. TV Assn.; chmn. emeritus Family Focus; chmn. Harris Found.; pres. emeritus Erikson Inst.; pres., co-founder The Ounce of Prevention Fund, 1982—, chmn. emeritus, 1997—; trustee Am. Jewish Com.; chmn. adv. bd. Ill. Dept. Children and Family Svcs. Tng. Inst., Ill. Competitive Access and Reimbursement Equity Program; vice chmn. Gov.'s Task Force on Future of Mental Health in Ill.; spl. counselor to select com. on children Ill. Gen. Assembly; served with Bd. Econ. Warfare OPA, 1942-44. Recipient Chgo. UNICEF World of Children award, 1985, hon. membership award Chgo. Pediatric Soc., 1986, Am. Orthopsychiat. Assn. award, 1986, Salesman of Yr. award Harvard Club Chgo., 1989, Disting. Svc. to State Govt. award Nat. Gov.'s Assn., 1990, Amicus Certus award Luth. Soc. Svcs. of Ill., 1990, Cmty. Partnership award United Neighborhood Orgn., Chgo., 1990, As They Grow award Parents, 1991, Citizen fellow Inst. Medicine Chgo., 1990, Service to Young Children award Chgo. Met. Assn. for Edn. of Young Children, 1995; Clifford Beers lectr. Yale U., 1987. Fellow Am. Acad. Pediatrics (hon.), Am. Acad. Arts and Scis.; mem. NAS (pres.'s circle 1989), Am. Orthopsychiatric Assn. (award 1986, Marian F. Langer award 1995), Chgo. Pediatric Soc. (hon.). Clubs: Standard, Midday, Saddle and Cycle, Comml. (Chgo.). Home: 209 E Lake Shore Dr Chicago IL 60611-1307 Office: Pittway Corp 2 N La Salle St Ste 400 Chicago IL 60602-3703

HARRIS, J(ACOB) GEORGE, health care company executive; b. Kings Mountain, N.C., Sept. 5, 1938; s. James A. and Carolyn (Hord) H.; m. Sondra Gilbert, Mar. 29, 1959; children: Cynthia, Susan, David. BA in Math., Duke U., 1960. With Am. Hosp. Supply Corp., 1960-84; region mgr. Am. Hosp. Supply Corp., South San Francisco, 1964-67; pres. Am. Hosp. Supply Corp., Port Credit, Ont., Can., 1967-70; v.p. ops. Am. Hosp. Supply Corp., Evanston, Ill., 1970-71; pres. dietary products div. Am. Hosp. Supply Corp., McGaw Park, Ill., 1971-74; corp. v.p. Am. Hosp. Supply Corp., Evanston, 1974-78; exec. v.p. Am. Hosp. Supply Corp., 1978-84; chmn., chief exec. officer Health Group Inc., Nashville, 1984-85; founder, pres., CEO Pinnacle Care Corp. (merged Mariner Health Group), 1985-94; pres., COO Mariner Health Group, 1994; ret., 1994; formerly bd. dirs. Mariner Health Group; bd. dirs. Union Spl. Corp., Chgo., Monoclonal Antibodies, Inc., Mountain View, Calif., Electro Neucleonics Inc., Health Group, Electro-Biology Inc., Dialogic Comm. Corp. Bd. dirs. Highland Park (Ill.) Hosp., 1981-84; trustee McCormick Sem., Chgo. Mem. Scientific Apparatus Mfrs. Assn., Richland Country Club. Home: 1204 Beddington Park Nashville TN 37215-5810

HARRIS, JAMES ARTHUR, SR., school system administrator, economist, consultant; b. Portsmouth, Va., June 20, 1928; s. Ambrose Edward and Annie Eula Pitts (Lawson) H.; m. Ursula Harris, June 7, 1954; children: James A. Jr., Edmond F. AB, Va. State Univ., 1956; MA, NYU, 1959; PhD, Pacific Western U., 1983. Adj. assoc. prof. in econs. St. John's U., Jamaica, N.Y.; advisor to sr. v.p. econ. devel., dir. minority and women bus. lendinq N.Y. State Urban Devel. Corp., N.Y.C.; sr. faculty, adj. assoc. prof. mgmt. NYU, N.Y.C.; pres. Acquitech Systems, Inc., Bklyn., 1988-93; supt. Buffalo Pub. Schs., 1996—; cons. in field; leader cons. team evaluation mission Bur. Africa programs UN Devel. Program, N.Y.C.; mem. roster cons. and tech. assistance experts UN Devel. Program, UN Indsl. Devel. Orgn., African Devel. Bank, West African Devel. Bank, World Bank, UN Ctr. for Human Settlements, UN Econ. Commn. for Africa, UN Econ. and Social Commn. for Africa, UN Econ. and Social Commn. for Asia and Pacific, Asian Devel. Bank, UN Econ. and Social Commn. for Western Asia, Internat. Fund. for Agrl. Devel., UN Conf. Trade and Devel./GATT, Internat. Trade Ctr., Geneva. Contbr. articles to profl. pubs. Recipient award for teaching excellence and outstanding talent as tchr. NYU Sch. Continuing Edn., 1986, Great Tchr. award in recognition of superb accomplishment NYU Alumni Coun., 1994. Mem. Am. Econ. Assn., Nat. Econ. Assn., N.Y. Acad. Scis., Internat. Studies Assn., Internat. Polit. Sci. Assn., Assn. for Study Afro-Am. Life History, Am. Arbitration Assn. (internat. arbitration panel). Home: 195 Adams St Brooklyn NY 11201-1851*

HARRIS, JAMES HAROLD, III, lawyer, educator; b. Texarkana, Tex., Apr. 26, 1943; s. James Harold Jr. and Mildred (Freeman) H. BA, Dartmouth Coll., 1964; JD, Vanderbilt U., 1967. Bar: Tenn. 1967, U.S. Dist. Ct. (mid. dist.) Tenn. 1972, U.S. Ct. Appeals (6th cir.) 1972. Asst. dean Vanderbilt U. Sch. Law, Nashville, 1971; atty. Met. Govt. Nashville, Nashville, 1972-75; ptnr. Harris & Leach, Nashville, 1975-87, Harris & Baydoun, Nashville, 1987-90; counsel Wyatt, Tarrant, Combs, Gilbert & Milom, Nashville, 1990-93, Gordon, Martin, Jones & Harris, Nashville, 1994—. Capt. USNR, 1967—. Mem. ABA, Tenn. Bar Assn., Nashville Bar Assn., Nashville Entertainment Assn. (legal counsel). Home: 103 Burlington Ct Nashville TN 37215-1843 Office: Gordon Martin Jones Et Al 49 Music Sq W Ste 600 Nashville TN 37203-3231

HARRIS, JAMES THOMAS, III, college administrator, educator; b. Findlay, Ohio, July 31, 1958; s. James Thomas II and Carolyn Sue (Cairns) H.; m. Mary Catherine Kurdila, June 27, 1981; children: Zachary James, Braden Gerald. BE in Secondary Edn., U. Toledo, 1980; MEd in Ednl. Adminstrn., Edinboro U., 1983; EdD in Higher Edn. Adminstrn., Pa. State U., 1988; postgrad. Inst. Ednl. Mgmt., Harvard U., 1993. Secondary tchr., dept. chair Highland H.S., Sparta, Ohio, 1980-81, Ctrl. Cath. H.S., Toledo, Ohio, 1981-82; grad. asst., acad. advisor Edinboro (Pa.) State U., 1982-83; fin. aid adminstr. Pa. State U., University Park, 1983-86, assoc. dir. Corp. and Found. Rels. dept., 1986-88; v.p. Coll. Mt. St. Joseph, Cin., 1988-91, Wright State U., Dayton, Ohio, 1991-94; pres. Defiance (Ohio) Coll., 1994—; faculty mem. 10 Case Confs., 1986—; spkr., workshop presenter in field. Contbr. articles to profl. jours. Bd. dirs. West Hamilton (Ohio) Econs. Coun., 1988-91, Vol. Action Ctr., State College, Pa., 1987-88, Dayton 2003 Fund, Leadership Defiance, Defiance Area Soc. for Handicapped, Leadership Dayton, vice chair, 1992—; vol. ARC, Cin., 1988-91; vol. advisor St. Joseph Ch. and Elem. Sch., 1988-91; grad. Leadership Dayton, 1992; coach Nat. Collegiate Boxing Assn., Brunei, 1985, USSR, 1988. Recipient fellowship Am. Assn. Higher Edn. Resource and Index Ctr., 1987. Mem. NAACP, Am. Assn. Higher Edn., Rotary, Young President's Orgn., Legatus, Alpha Kappa Delta, Pi Lambda Theta. Roman Catholic. Avocations: reading, blues music, jogging. Office: Defiance Coll 701 N Clinton St Defiance OH 43512-1610*

HARRIS, JAN CAPLAN, health care administrator; b. Ithaca, N.Y., Jan. 15, 1944; d. Frank and Shirley Ellen (Rickard) Caplan; m. Sonny G. Harris, Mar. 23, 1990; children: Josh, Greg, Irene, Mike, Ginger, Morgan, J.B. BSN, Cornell U., 1966; MA in Liberal Studies, Dartmouth Coll., 1974; MS in Healthcare Adminstrn., U. Colo., 1989. Diplomate Am. Coll. Healthcare Execs. Coord. fed. programs, dir. instrn., tech. ctr. Northwest Arctic Sch. Dist., Kotzebue, Alaska, 1976-82; dir. planning and devel., interim pres., ops. exec. Maniilaq Assn., Kotzebue, 1985-93; adminstr., v.p. health svcs. Maniilaq Health Ctr., Kotzebue, 1993-97; propr. Harris Cons., Anchorage, 1997—; sr. health care quality improvement coord. PRO-West, Anchorage, 1998—; cons. Walrus Works, Anchorage, 1982-85, Harris Consulting, 1997—. Recipient Svc. award PHS/Indian Health Svc. Mem. Am. Soc. Quality, Healthcare Forum. Home: 3168 Cassius Ct Anchorage AK 99508-3334 Office: 721 Sesame St Ste 1A Anchorage AK 99503-6632

HARRIS, JANA, writer, educator; b. San Francisco, Sept. 21, 1950; m. Mark A. Botwell, Aug. 19, 1977. BS in Math., U. Oregon, 1969; MA in Creative Writing, San Francisco State U., 1972. Cons. math. Lawrence Hall Sci. U. Calif., Berkeley, 1972-75; instr. creative writing Modesto (Calif.) Jr. Coll., 1975-78, N.Y.U., 1980; dir. writers in performance Manhattan Theatre Club, N.Y.C., 1980-86; instr. creative writing U. Wash., Seattle, 1986—; writer in residence Popular Lit. Project NEH, New Brunswick, N.J., 1981-82; vis. writer in residence Pacific Luth. U., Tacoma, Wash., 1988, U. Wash., Seattle, 1988, 1990-92, Pollock vis. writer in residence, 1995-96; farmer High and Dry Farm, Sultan, Wash., (Sport Horse farm), 1986—. Author: (novels) Alaska, 1980 (Alt. Book of the Month), The Pearl of Ruby City, 1998; (poetry books) The Clackamas, 1979 (Elliston Book award finalist), Manhattan as a Second Language, 1982 (Pulitzer prize nominee), The Sourlands, 1989, Oh How Can I Keep on Singing? Voices of Pioneer Women, 1993 (Wash. Gov.'s writer's award 1994, Pulitzer prize nominee, PEN W. Ctr. award finalist), The Dust of Everyday Life, An Epic Poem of the Pacific Northwest, 1997; also short fiction, poems essays in numerous pubs. including The Nation, Ms, The Feminist Rev. of Books, U.S. Congressional Record; (plays) The Poetry of Jana Harris Adapted for the Stage and Screen: Fair Sex, by Lynn Middleton, 1984, Festival of the Bards, 1978; co-founder, assoc. editor Poetry Flash, San Francisco, 1972-78, assoc. editor Libera, 1972-3; founder and editor-in-chief Switched-on-Gutenberg, 1995. Named Calif. State fellow San Francisco State U., 1970-71, Poetry fellow N.J. State Coun. on the Arts, 1981-82, Washington State Arts Commn., 1993; winner Triton Coll. All Nations Poetry Contest, 1976; hon. mention Acad. Am. Poets Coll. Prize, 1970; grantee Berkeley Civic Arts Commn., 1974. Mem. PEN, Nat. Book Critics Cir., Associated Writing Programs, Poetry Soc.

Am., Poets and Writers Inc. Avocation: horse raising. E-mail: jnh@U.washington.edu.

HARRIS, JAY ROBERT, radiation oncologist; b. Weehawken, N.J., June 29, 1944. MD, Stanford U. Sch. Medicine, 1970. Resident in radiation therapy Joint Ctr. Radiation Therapy, Boston, 1973-77; fellow Harvard Med. Sch., Boston, 1976-77, prof. radiation oncology; chief radiation oncology Brigham & Women's Hosp., Dana Farber Cancer Inst., Boston. Mem. ASTRO, ASCO. Office: Dana-Farber Cancer Inst Brigham & Women's Hosp 44 Binney St Boston MA 02115-6013

HARRIS, JAY TERRENCE, newspaper editor; b. Washington, Dec. 3, 1948; s. Richard James and Margaret Estelle (Burr) H.; m. Eliza Melinda Dowell, June 14, 1969 (div.); 1 child, Taifa Akida; m. Anna Christine Harris, Oct. 25, 1980; children: Jamarah Kai, Shala Marie. BA, Lincoln U., 1970, LHD (hon.), 1988. Reporter Wilmington (Del.) News-Jour., 1970-73, spl. project editor, 1974-75; instr. journalism and urban affairs Medill Sch. Journalism, Northwestern U., Evanston, Ill., 1973-75, asst. prof., 1975-82, asst. dean, 1977-82; nat. corr. Gannett News Service, Washington, 1982-84, columnist Gannet newspapers and USA Today, 1984-85; exec. editor Phila. Daily News, 1985—; v.p. Phila. Newspapers, Inc., 1987—; chmn., pub. San Jose Mercury News, 1995—; asst. dir. Frank E. Gannett Urban Journalism Ctr., Northwestern U., 1977-82; founder, exec. dir. Consortium for Advancement of Minorities in Journalism Edn., Evanston, 1978-81; dir. Dow Jones Newspaper Fund, Princeton, N.J., 1980—; bd. visitors John S. Knight Profl. Journalism Fellowships, Palo Alto, Calif., 1982—; head Minorities and Communication Div. Assn. for Edn. in Journalism, 1982-83. Author: (annual census) Minority Employment in Daily Newspapers, 1978-82; co-author series articles on drug trafficking in Wilmington, 1972 (Pub. Service awards AP Mng. Editors Assn. 1972, Greater Phila. chpt. Sigma Delta Chi 1973). Past mem. bd. advisors Sch. Journalism U. Mo. Frank E. Gannett Urban Journalism fellow, 1973-74; recipient Pub. Service award Greater Phila. chpt. Sigma Delta Chi, 1973; Pub. Service award AP Mng. Editors Assn., 1972; Spl. Citation Nat. Urban Coalition, 1979; Par Excellence Disting. Service in Journalism award Operation PUSH, 1984; Drum Maj. for Justice award Southern Christian Leadership Conf., 1985. Mem. Am. Soc. Newspaper Editors (chmn. readership and rsch. com.), Women in Communication, Nat. Assn. Black Journalists, Omega Psi Phi. Office: San Jose Mercury News 750 Ridder Park Dr San Jose CA 95190

HARRIS, JEAN LOUISE, physician; b. Richmond, Va., Nov. 24, 1931; d. Vernon Joseph and Jean Louise (Pace) H.; m. Leslie John Ellis Jr., Sept. 24, 1955; children: Karen Denise, Pamela Diane, Cynthia Suzanne. BS, Va. Union U., 1951; MD, Med. Coll. Va., 1955; ScD (hon.), U. Richmond, 1981. Intern Med. Coll. Va., Richmond, 1955-56, resident internal medicine, 1956-58; fellow Strong Meml. Hosp.-U. Rochester (N.Y.) Sch. Medicine, 1958-60; rsch. assoc. Walter Reed Army Inst. Rsch., Washington, 1960-63; pvt. practice medicine specializing in internal medicine allergy Washington, 1964-71; instr. medicine Howard U. Coll. Medicine, Washington, 1960-68, asst. prof. dept. community health practice, 1969-72; prof. family practice Med. Coll. Va., Va. Commonwealth U., 1973-78; also dir. Center Community Health, 1973-78; sec. Human Resources Commonwealth of Va., 1978-82; v.p. state mktg. programs Control Data Corp., 1982-84, v.p. state govt. affairs, 1984-86, v.p. bus. devel., 1986-88; pres., chief exec. officer Ramsey Found., 1988-92; sr. assoc. dir., dir. med. affairs U. Minn. Hosp. and Clinic, Mpls., 1992-96; lectr. dept. med. care and hosps. Johns Hopkins, Balt., 1971-73; asst. clin. prof. dept. community medicine Charles R. Drew Postgrad. Med. Sch., L.A., 1970-73; adj. asst. prof. dept. preventive and social medicine UCLA, 1970-72; chief bur. resources devel. D.C. Dept. Health, 1967-69; exec. dir. Nat. Med. Assn. Found., Washington, 1969-72; Cons. div. health manpower intelligence HEW, 1969; mem. recombinant DNA adv. com. HEW USPHS-NIH, 1979-82; vice chmn. Nat. Commn. on Alcoholism and Alcohol Related Diseases, 1980-81; mem. Pres.'s Pvt. Sctor Initiatives Task Force, 1981-82, Def. Adv. Com. on Women in the Service, 1985-88, Eden Prairie City Coun., 1987-94, mayor, 1995—. Trustee U. Richmond, 1982-90; bd. dirs. Neighborhood Health Care Network, Women's Health Leadership Trust, Allina Found., Am. Composers Forum, Women's Econ. Roundtable. Recipient award East End Civic Assn. Richmond, Va., 1955, 1st Ann. Serwa award Va. Commonwealth chpt. Nat. Coalition of 100 Black Women, 1989, Leadership award S.W. Suburban Twin Cities chpt. NAACP, 1989; named one of Top 100 Black Bus. and Profl. Women, Dollars and Sense mag., 1985. Mem. Nat. Med. Assn., Inst. Medicine of NAS, Am. Coll. Physician Execs., NAACP, Women's Econ. Roundtable, Rotary, Sigma Xi, Beta Kappa Chi, Alpha Kappa Mu, Delta Sigma Theta. Home: 10860 Forestview Cir Eden Prairie MN 55347-2022 Office: 8080 Mitchell Rd Eden Prairie MN 55344-2230 *Life is an exciting continuum of choices. None of us is so fortunate as to always select the "best" among alternative options. Our true measure is taken by our ability to learn those lessons to be gained from each decision - whether "proper" or "improper" - and to push forward - always anticipating the next opportunity for choice as a welcome challenge upon which one builds the foundations of an interesting, exhilarating life.**

HARRIS, JEANETTE MARIANNE, writer; b. Berlin, Germany, Aug. 4, 1948; arrived in Canada, 1951; came to U.S., 1978; d. William Edward and Gerda Gisela (Adamaszek) H.; m. Peter William Harben, Apr. 22, 1978; children: Mark Peter, Victoria Elizabeth. BA, U. Toronto, Ont., Can., 1971, MA, 1973. Writer Camera Press, London, 1977-78; U.S. agt. Camera Press, N.Y.C., 1980-87; freelance writer, editor Butternut Books, Morris, N.Y., 1987—. Author: Canada: The Land and Its People, 1976, Mined It!, 1992, Mountain Magic, 1996, Salt Sisters, 1998; contbr. articles to jours. and mags. Pres. The Butternut Valley Arts & Crafts Ctr., 1992—.

HARRIS, JEFFREY, lawyer; b. Bklyn., Mar. 20, 1944; s. Herman and Pearl (Herman) H.; m. Joyce Rosa Meckler, June 22, 1975; 1 child, Daniela Rose. BS, NYU, 1965; JD, Syracuse U., 1968. Bar: N.Y. 1969, U.S. Supreme Ct. 1976, D.C. 1977, Va., 1990. Asst. U.S. atty. So. Dist. N.Y., U.S. Dept. Justice, N.Y.C., 1972-76; chief investigation rev. unit. U.S. Dept. Justice, Washington, 1976-77; dep. chief counsel U.S. Ho. of Reps., Korean Investigation, Washington, 1977-79; asst. dir. FTC, Washington, 1979-81; exec. dir. Atty. Gen.'s Task Force on Violent Crime, U.S. Dept. Justice, Washington, 1981; dep. assoc. atty. gen. U.S., Washington, 1981-83; sr. v.p. Capital Bank N.A., Washington, 1983-85; sr. v.p., counsel Capital Bancorp, Miami, Fla., 1983-85; ptnr. Sachs, Greenebaum & Tayler, Washington, 1985-90, Rubin, Winston, Diercks, Harris & Cooke, LLP, Washington, 1990—; instr. Advocacy Inst., U. Calif. Hastings Coll. Law, San Francisco, 1979-83; adj. asst. prof. George Washington U., Washington, 1980. Lt. (j.g.) USN, 1968-71. Named Meritorious Exec. Pres. of U.S.; recipient Spl. Commendation, Att. Gen. of U.S.; decorated Navy Commendation medal, Vietnam Cross of Gallantry. Mem. ABA. Office: Rubin Winston Diercks Harris & Cooke Sixth Fl 1155 Connecticut Ave NW Washington DC 20036

HARRIS, JEFFREY SAUL, physician executive, consultant; b. Pitts., Mar. 13, 1949; s. Aaron Wexler and Janet Mary (Wexler) Harris; m. Mary V. Anderson, Jan. 2, 1981; children: Sarah Ariel, Noah Aaron, Susannah Leia. BS in Molecular Biophysics/Biochemistry, Yale U., 1971; MD, U. N.Mex., 1975; MPH, U. Mich., 1982; MBA, Vanderbilt U., 1988. Diplomate Am. Bd. Preventive Medicine in Occupl. Medicine & Gen. Preventive Medicine & Pub. Health, Am. Bd. Emergency Medicine, Am. Bd. Medicine Quality, Am. Bd. Ind. Med. Examination; lic. Md., Calif., Tenn., Alaska. Gen. med. officer USPHS, Juneau, Alaska, 1976-78; clin. dir. S.E. Alaska Native Health Corp., Juneau, 1978-79; asst. to commr. Tenn. Dept. Health and Environment, Nashville, 1980-83; dir. health care mgmt. Northern Telecom Inc., Nashville, 1983-88; pres. HDM, Inc., Nashville, 1988-90; med. dir. Aetna Health Plans of Tenn., Nashville, 1990-91; leader nat. practice, health strategy Alexander & Alexander Cons. Group, San Francisco, 1991-94; chief prevention, health and disability officer Indsl. Indemnity, San Francisco, 1994-97; pres. J. Harris Assocs., Inc., Mill Valley, Calif., 1979—; pres., CEO MedFx, Inc., 1999—. Author: Strategic Health Management, 1994, Best Practices in Occupational Medicine, 1999; author, editor: Managing Employee Health Care Costs, 1992, Occupational Medicine Practice Guidelines: Evaluation and Management of Common Health Problems and Functional Recovery in Workers, 1997, Quick Reference to Practice Guidelines in Occupational Medicine, 1999, Managed Care in Occupational Medicine, 1998; author, co-editor: Manual of Occupational Health and Safety, 1992, 96, Health Promotion in the Work Place, 1994, Integrated Health Management, 1998; mem. editl. bd. Am. Jour. Health Promotion, 1985—, Occupl. Environment Med. Report, 1988—; contbg. editor JAMA, Am. Jour. Pub. Health, 1988—; contbr. articles to profl. jours. Fellow Am. Acad. Family Practice, Am. Coll. Occupl. Environ. Medicine (dir., chmn. practice guidelines com. 1992-98, Presdl. award 1996), Am. Coll. Preventive Medicine, Am. Coll. Med. Quality, Am. Bd. Ind. Med. Examiners. Avocations: skiing, running, playing music, painting, writing children's stories. Home: 386 Richardson Way Mill Valley CA 94941-4053 Office: J Harris Assocs Inc and MedFx 386 Richardson Way Mill Valley CA 94941-4053

HARRIS, JEFFREY SHERMAN, technology company executive; b. Boston, Aug. 18, 1944; s. Phillip Robert and Blanche Estell (Sherman) H.; children: Penny, Samantha. B.S. in Bus. Adminstrn, Boston U., 1970. Field rep. ARC, Boston, 1970-72; emergency med. services project dir. Health Planning Council Greater Boston, 1972-75; office emergency med. services program mgr. Mass. Dept. Public Health, Boston, 1975-76; exec. dir. Nat. Assn. Emergency Med. Technicians, Waltham, Mass., 1977-81; pres., chief exec. officer, dir. ComSystems Technologies Inc., Hudson, Mass., 1980-84; v.p. Media Bus. Service, Lowell, Mass., 1984-86, Hub Mail Advt., Boston, 1986-90; v.p., chief tech. officer Dickinson Direct, 1990-98; chief info. officer Chgo. Title-Market Intelligence, Hopkington, Mass., 1998—. Assoc. editor: The EMT Jour, 1977-80; mem. editorial bd.: Emergency Med. Services Jour, 1978-81. Br. dirs. and v.p. Jewish Cmty. Ctr. of Greater Boston. Mem. Nat. Assn. EMTs (sec. 1975-77, Nat. Leadership award 1980, A. Rogers Fox Founders award 1981), Mass. Assn. EMTs (founder, sec. 1973-75), Nat. Soc. EMT-Parametics (founder), Nat. Soc. EMT Instr./Coords. (founder), Nat. Soc. Emergency Med. Svc. Adminstrs. (founder). Office: Chgo Title-Market Intelligence 105 South St Hopkinton MA 01748-2206

HARRIS, JEREMY, mayor; s. Ann Harris; m. Ramona Sachiko Akui Harris. BA, BS in Marine Biology, U. Hawaii, 1972; M in Population and Environmental Biology and Urban Ecosystems, U. Calif., Irvine. Lectr. oceanography, biology Kauai C.C.; instr. on reef walks on Kauai U. Hawaii Sea Grant Program; del. Hawaii Constl. Conv., 1978; chmn. Kauai County Council; exec. asst. to Mayor Frank F. Fasi City and County of Honolulu, 1985-86, mng. dir. of Honolulu, 1986-94, mayor, 1994—. Named Pub. Adminstr. of Yr. Am. Soc. Pub. Adminstrn., 1993, 94; recipient Merit award Internat. Downtown Assn., others. Office: Office of the Mayor 530 S King St Rm 300 Honolulu HI 96813-3019

HARRIS, JEROME SYLVAN, pediatrician, pediatrics and biochemistry educator; b. N.Y.C., Feb. 27, 1909; s. Mark and Mary (Marcus) H.; m. Jacqueline Cato Hijmans, Oct. 23, 1958. A.B. summa cum laude, Dartmouth Coll., 1929; M.D. cum laude, Harvard U., 1933. Intern U. Chgo. Clinics, 1934; resident Boston Children's Hosp., 1935-36; mem. faculty Duke Sch. Medicine, Durham, N.C., 1937-79; J. Buren Sidbury prof. pediatrics, also prof. biochemistry Duke Sch. Medicine, 1950-79; chmn. dept. pediatrics Duke Med. Center, 1954-68; Cons. Nat. Bd. Med. Examiners, 1956-60; mem. human embryology and devel. study sect. NIH, 1959-63. Contbr. articles to profl. jours. Bd. dirs. Durham Child Guidance Clinic, 1950-54. Served to lt. col. M.C. AUS, 1942-46. Mem. Am. Soc. Clin. Investigation, Soc. Pediatric Research, Am. Acad. Pediatrics, Am. Pediatrics Soc., So. Soc. Pediatric Research, Phi Beta Kappa, Sigma Xi, Alpha Omega Alpha. Office: Duke Hospital Pediatrics Dept Durham NC 27710

HARRIS, JIM, state official. BA, Henderson State U., 1975. Photo features editor Hope Star, 1975-77; press sec. U.S. Congressman Ray Thornton, 1977-79; reporter Texarkana Gazette, 1979-84, regional editor, 1984-89, asst. city editor, 1989-94, city editor, 1994-95; dir. press ops. Office Gov. State of Ark., 1995—. Media rels. cons. Huckabee for U.S. Senate Campaign, 1992. Fax: 501-682-2614. Office: Office Gov State of Ark State Capitol Little Rock AR 72211

HARRIS, JOE FRANK, former governor; b. Cartersville, Ga., Feb. 16, 1936; s. Grover Franklin and Frances (Morrow) H.; m. Elizabeth Carlock Harris, June 25, 1961; 1 son, Joe Frank, Jr. BBA, U. Ga., 1958; LLD (hon.), Woodrow Wilson Coll. Law, 1981, Asbury Coll., 1983, Morris Brown Coll., 1983, LaGrange Coll., 1987, Mercer U., 1987. Sec.-treas. Harris Cement Products, Inc., Cartersville, 1958-79; pres. Harris Georgia Corp., Cartersville, 1979-83; mem. Ga. Gen. Assembly, 1965-83; gov. State of Ga., 1983-91; prof., Disting. Exec. fellow Ga. State U., Atlanta, 1993—. Bd. dirs. Univ. Sys. Ga., 1999—. Served with U.S. Army, 1958. Democrat. Methodist. Home: 712 West Ave Cartersville GA 30120-3441

HARRIS, JOEL B(RUCE), lawyer; b. N.Y.C., Oct. 15, 1941; s. Raymond S. and Laura (Greene) H.; m. Barbara J. Rous, June 13, 1965 (div.); 1 child, Clifford S.; m. Deborah Sherman, Apr. 1, 1986 (div.); children: Sydney Anne, Cassidy Raye. AB, Columbia U., 1963; LLB, Harvard U., 1966; LLM, U. London, 1967. Bar: N.Y. 1968, U.S. Dist. Ct. (so. dist.) N.Y. 1970, U.S. Ct. Appeals (2d cir.) 1970, U.S. Dist. Ct. (ea. dist.) N.Y. 1975, U.S. Supreme Ct. 1976, U.S. Ct. Appeals (3d cir.) 1980, U.S. Dist. Ct. (we. dist.) N.Y. 1981. Assoc. Simpson, Thacher & Bartlett, N.Y.C., 1967-70; asst. U.S. atty. So. Dist. N.Y., 1970-74, chief civil rights unit, 1973-74; assoc. Weil, Gotshal & Manges, N.Y.C., 1974-76, ptnr., 1976-86; ptnr. Thacher, Proffitt & Wood, N.Y.C., 1986—; chmn. litigation dept.; speaker, panelist, moderator confs. Contbr. articles to profl. jours. Knox Meml. fellow, 1966-67. Fellow Am. Bar Found.; mem. ABA (chmn. com. internat. litigation 1981-84, chmn. com. personal rights litigation 1984-87), N.Y. State Bar Assn. (mem. internat. law and practice sect., sect. chair 1997-98, mem. exec. com. 1990—, chmn. internat. dispute resolution com. 1990-93, chmn. seasonal meeting 1993, mem. exec. com. 1990—, sect. chair 1997, 98), Assn. Bar City N.Y., Inter-Am. Bar Assn., Fed. Bar Coun., Am. Soc. Internat. Law, Internat. Law Assn., Am. Judicature Soc. Home: 40 Prince St New York NY 10012-3426 Office: Thacher Proffitt & Wood 2 World Trade Ctr New York NY 10048-0203

HARRIS, JOHN CHARLES, agriculturalist; b. Fresno, Calif., July 14, 1943; s. Jack A. and Teresa Elizabeth (McManus) H.; m. Carole Lynn Glotz, Dec. 28, 1965. B.S., U. Calif.-Davis, 1965. Exec. v.p. Harris Farms Inc., Coalinga, Calif., 1968-81, pres., 1981—; sec., dir. Calif. Thoroughbred Breeders Assn., Arcadia, Calif., 1975—, Calif. Westside Farmers, Fresno; vice chmn., dir. Calif. Beef Council, Foster City, 1981-86; v.p. Calif. Thoroughbred Breeders Assn., 1986-88, pres., 1989-91, 96-97; dir. Pacific Legal Found., 1998—, Golden State Mus., 1998—; bd. dirs. Cattlemen's Beef Promotion and Research Bd., 1986, Nat. Cattlemen's Assn., 1986; chmn. Calif. Beef Council, 1984; chmn. bd. dirs. Bay Meadows Operating Co., 1992-98. Bd. dirs. St. Agnes Hosp., Fresno, vice chmn., 1993-94, chmn., 1994-96. 1st lt. U.S. Army, 1966-68. Mem. World Pres.'s Orgn., Rancheros Visitadores Club (Santa Barbara, Calif.), Chancellor's Club (U. Calif. at Davis), Jockey Club (N.Y.C.). Republican. Home: PO Box 188 Piedra CA 93649-0188 Office: Harris Farms Inc RT 1 Box 420 Coalinga CA 93210-9218*

HARRIS, JOHN EDWARD, lawyer; b. Mpls., Nov. 16, 1936; s. John Law and Harriet Comilla (Hunt) H.; m. Ruth Wilder Esty, Aug. 26, 1958; children—Jeffrey Langdon, Stowe John Wilder, Benjamin Wood. B.A. summa cum laude, Lawrence Coll., 1959; J.D., Harvard U., 1962. Bar: Minn. 1962, U.S. Dist. Ct. Minn. 1962, U.S. Tax Ct. 1963. Assoc. Faegre & Benson, Mpls., 1962-69, ptnr., 1970—, head, trusts, estates and found. group, 1974-97; trustee Ucross Found., Wyo., 1981-93, 97—. Contbr. articles to Notre Dame Planning Inst., 1976, 78. Bd. dirs. Meth. Health Care Minn., 1986-93; chmn. Meth. Hosp., St. Louis Park, Minn., 1979-81, bd. dirs., 1993-94; pres. West Met. Hosp. trustee Coun., Mpls., 1980-81; chmn. Minn. Coun. on Founds., Mpls., 1985-88; bd. dirs. Twin Cities RISE!, 1995—. Mem. ABA (chmn. com. on charitable trusts, real property and trust law sect. 1973-77, exempt orgns. com., tax section 1991—), Minn. Bar Assn. (chmn. probate and trust law sect. 1979-80, mem. study com. Minn. Nonprofit Corps. 1986-91, mem. nonprofit corps. com. 1998—), Phi Beta Kappa. Home: 5022 Bruce Pl Minneapolis MN 55424-1320 Office: Faegre & Benson 2200 Norwest Tower 90 S 7th St Ste 2200 Minneapolis MN 55402-3901

HARRIS, JOHN H., radiologist; b. Great Falls, Mont., Oct. 16, 1925; s. John Harold and Nancy Catherine (Hamilton) H.; m. Catherine Connell, Aug. 31, 1972; children: John H. III, Robert D. BSc, Dickinson Coll., 1948; MD, Jefferson Med. Coll., 1953; MSc, U. Pa., 1955, DSc, 1957. Diplomate Am. Bd. Radiology. Radiologist Carlisle (Pa.) Hosp., 1957-79; prof. radiology Mich. State U., East Lansing, 1979-80, U. Tex. Med. Sch., Houston, 1980—; assoc. prof. radiology Milton S. Hershey Med. Sch., Hershey, Pa., 1972-79; prof. radiology Jefferson Med. Coll., Phila., 1977-79; prof. emergency medicine U. Tex. Med. Sch., 1992—; adj. prof. radiology Baylor Coll. Medicine, Houston, 1985—. Author: Radiology of Emergency Medicine, 1994, Radiology of Acute Cervical Spine Trauma, 1996; editl. bd. Contemporary Diagnostic Radiology, Diagnostic Radiology, Current Problems in Diagnostic Radiology; cons. editor Skeletal Trauma, 1988—; assoc. editor Emergency Radiology. Mem. Fine Arts worship com. St. Luke's Meth. Hosp., Houston, 1989-92, chancel choir, 1981—. Fellow Am. Coll. Radiology (bd. chancellors 1976-79, vice chair bd. chancellors 1979-80, chair bd. chancellors 1980-82, pres. 1982-83), Am. Soc. Emergency Radiology (co-founder 1988, pres. 1988-90), Royal Australasian Coll. Radiologists (hon.); mem. Am. Acad. Orthop. Surgeons, Am. Coll. Emergency Physicians. Avocations: choral music, swimming, biking, tennis. Office: U Tex Med Sch 6431 Fannin St Houston TX 77030-1501

HARRIS, JOHN M., historian; b. Muncie, Ind., Aug. 8, 1944; s. James and Amy (Morris) H.; m. Jo Anna Halmbock, Dec. 19, 1964 (div. 1985); 2 children; m. Joan Ellen Hostetler, May 28, 1998. BA, Ind. U., 1966; MA, SUNY, Oneonta, 1969. Exhbns. coord., docent Children's Mus. Indpls., 1967-72; dir. Tippecanoe County Hist. Assn., Lafayette, Ind., 1972-87; from asst. dir. field svcs. to dir. local history svcs. Ind. Hist. Soc., Indpls., 1987—; mem. hist. markers adv. bd. Ind. Hist. Bur., Indpls., 1991—. Mem. Am. Assn. Mus., Am. Assn. State and Local History, Assn. Ind. Mus., Nat. Coun. Pub. History, Assn. Midwest Mus., Field Svcs. Alliance.

HARRIS, JOHN WALLACE, biology educator; b. Peoria, Ill., Aug. 28, 1941; s. Wallace Charles and Betty Jean (Cremeans) H.; m. Caroline Lee Edwards McKelvey, Mar. 31, 1979; stepchildren: Mary Catherine Kheil, John Edwards McKelvey, James Lawrence McKelvey. BS in Edn., Western Ill. U., 1963; AM, Ind. U., 1965, PhD, 1968. Asst. prof. Tenn. Tech. U., Cookeville, 1968-74, assoc. prof., 1974-80, dir. honors program, 1978-83, prof. biology, 1980—; exec. sec., treas. So. Regional Honors Coun., 1987-91, pres., 1984-85. Contbr. articles to profl. publs. Pres. Tenn. Tech. U. Faculty Senate, Cookeville, 1983-84. Fulbright Found. fellow, 1991-92. Mem. AAUP (pres. local chpt. 1971-72), Tenn. Acad. Sci. (treas. 1989—), Toastmasters (dist. gov. 1988-81, pres. local club 1971, Disting. Toastmaster award 1985), Lions (pres. Cookeville club 1995-96, Melvin Jones fellow 1998), Sigma Xi (pres. local chpt. 1976-77, 98—). Democrat. Methodist. Avocations: reading, travel. Office: Tenn Tech U Dept Biology Box 5063 Cookeville TN 38505

HARRIS, JOHN WILLIAM, physician, educator; b. Boston, Mar. 30, 1920; s. Ulysses Sylvester and Lillian (Dennett) H.; m. Stephanie Jean Bunting, Apr. 7, 1951; children: Wendy Alexandra, Alison Dennett, Stephen Bunting. B.S., Trinity Coll., Hartford, Conn., 1941; M.D., Harvard, 1944. Intern Boston City Hosp., 1944-45, resident, 1947-48; research fellow medicine Thorndike Meml. Lab., Harvard Med. Sch., 1948-51, research assoc., 1951-52; sr. instr. medicine Western Res. U., Cleve., 1952-54; asst. prof. Western Res. U., 1954-57, assoc. prof., 1957-62, prof., 1962—; hematologist, vis. physician Cleve. Met. Gen. Hosp., 1952—, assoc. dir. dept. medicine, 1967-81; attending physician VA Hosp., Cleve., 1953-58, sr. attending physician hematology, 1959—; cons. staff Lutheran Hosp., 1965—; mem. hematology study sect. NIH, 1962-66, chmn., 1983-85, mem. hematology tng. grants com., 1969-73; mem. com. blood and transfusion Nat. Acad. Scis.-NRC, 1963-65; chmn. Merit Rev. Bd. in Hematology, Med. Research Service, VA, 1977-80. Served to capt. U.S. Army, 1945-47. Recipient USPHS Research Career award, 1962, Martin Luther King, Jr. award for outstanding research in sickle cell anemia, 1972; Alfred Stengel Research fellow ACP, 1951-52; Markle scholar in medicine, 1955-60; named to Cleve. Med. Hall of Fame, 1998. Fellow ACP, Internat. Soc. Hematology (nat. counselor, Interam. div. 1986); mem. Am. Fedn. Clin. Research, Am. Soc. Clin. Investigation (past v.p.), Central Soc. Clin. Research, Soc. Exptl. Biology and Medicine, Am. Soc. Hematology (pres. 1981-82), Acad. Medicine Cleve., Assn. Am. Physicians, Phi Beta Kappa, Alpha Omega Alpha. Home: Judson Manor # 627 1890 E 107th St Cleveland OH 44106-2251 Office: 2500 Metrohealth Dr Cleveland OH 44109-1900

HARRIS, JOSEPH LAMAR, state official; b. Pensacola, Fla., Mar. 26, 1951; s. Joseph Erlis and Mazie Lois (Plant) H.; m. Elizabeth Gail Golden, Dec. 15, 1973; children: Heather Brooke, Brandon Lamar. AA in Bus., Pensacola Jr. Coll., 1971; BA in Acctg. magna cum laude, U. West Fla., 1973. CPA, Fla., Ala.; cert. govt. fin. mgr., govt. fin. officer. Staff acct. Touche Ross and Co., Atlanta, 1974-75; divsn. acct. Gulf Power Co., Pensacola, Fla., 1975; field auditor Audit Agy., HEW, Montgomery, Ala., 1975-77; budget analyst II Ala. Budget Office, Montgomery, 1977-82, budget analyst III, 1982-85, budget analyst IV, 1985-87; acting budget officer, dep. state budget officer State of Ala., Montgomery, 1987-88, dep. state budget officer, 1987-96; exec. dir. Ala. Bd. Pub. Accountancy, Montgomery, 1996—; bd. dirs. Ala. Gov.'s Legis. First Reading Com., Montgomery, 1984-96; bd. dirs. Ala. Bd. Pub. Accountancy, sec.-treas. 1989-94; chmn. state adv. group Ala. Mgmt. Improvement Program, Montgomery, 1987-89; mem. adv. coun. to govtl. acct. and auditor tng. program Auburn U., Montgomery, 1992—. Recipient Cert. of Appreciation, Office of the Gov. State of Ala., 1987. Mem. AICPA (mem. CPA exam. content oversight task force 1999—), Ala. Soc. CPAs (state legis. com. 1981—, Outstanding CPA in Govt. award 1997-98), Assn. Govt. Accts. (chpt. treas. 1975-77, chpt. programs dir. 1996-97, mem. chpt. scholarships com. 1997-98, programs com. 1998-99), Govt. Fin. Officers Assn. Ala. (legis. com. 1995-96), Ala. State Employees Assn., Nat. Assn. State Bds. Accountancy (govt. rels. com. 1990-93, strategic initiatives com. 1997-99, state bd. adminstrs. com. 1998-99). Mem. Assembly of God Ch. Avocations: hunting, sports card collecting. Home: 6032 Meridian Ln Montgomery AL 36117-2789 Office: Ala Bd Pub Accountancy 770 Washington Ave Ste 236 Montgomery AL 36104-3816

HARRIS, JOYCE FAYE, elementary education educator; b. Drummond, Okla., Feb. 22, 1912; d. David Samuel and Pearl (Joyce) Harris; m. Samuel Smith Kendrick, Aug. 8, 1939 (dec. Dec. 1944); 1 child, Patricia Joyce; m. John Henry Glass, Mar. 8, 1946 (dec. 1973); 1 child, William John; m. Theodore Ted Anderson, Oct. 14, 1979 (dec. Sept. 1989). Student, Sullins Coll.; BS, U. Okla., 1933. Tchr. Nome (Alaska) H.S., from 1935, Kodiak (Alaska) H.S., Halsey (Oreg.) Schs., Creslane (Oreg.) Elem. Sch., to 1976. Mem. DAR, Kappa Kappa Gamma. Republican. Avocations: studying and collecting antiques, reading, travel. Home: 205 Main St Drummond OK 73735-0155

HARRIS, JULES ELI, medical educator, physician, clinical scientist, administrator; b. Toronto, Ont., Can., Oct. 12, 1934; came to U.S., 1978; s. George Joseph and Ida Harris; m. Josephine Leikin; children: Leah, Daniel, Adam, Sheira, Robin, Naomi. MD, U. Toronto, 1959. Intern, then resident Toronto (Can.) Gen. Hsp., 1959-65; asst. prof. medicine M.D. Anderson Hosp. Med. Ctr., Houston, 1966-69; prof. medicine U. Ottawa (Ont.), 1969-78; prof. medicine, prof. immunology Rush Med. Coll., Rush U., Chgo., 1978—; dir. Rush Cancer Ctr., 1986-92, dir. Rush sect. med. oncology, 1978-93; mem. gov.'s adv. bd. for cancer control State of Ill., 1988—; chmn. bd. trustees Ill. Cancer Coun., Chgo., 1987-88; chmn. immunology devices panel FDA, 1995—. Author: Immunology of Malignant Disease, 1975; editor Prostaglandin Inhibitors in Tumor Immunology and Immunotherapy, 1994. Mem. internat. bd. govs. Ben Gurion U. of Negev, Beer-Sheva, Israel, 1986-95; pres. bd., chmn. sci. adv. com. Israel Cancer Rsch. Fund, Chgo. Fellow ACP, Royal Coll. Physicians Can. (cert. in internal medicine); mem. Am. Soc. Clin. Oncology (chmn. pub. rels. com. 1987-89), Univ. Club, Alpha Omega Alpha. Jewish. Office: Rush-Presbyn-St Luke's Med Ctr 1725 W Harrison St Ste 821 Chicago IL 60612-3863*

HARRIS, K. DAVID, state supreme court justice; b. Jefferson, Iowa, July 29, 1927; s. Orville William and Jessie Heloise (Smart) H.; m. Madonna Theresa Coyne, Sept. 4, 1948; children: Jane, Julia, Frederick. BA, U. Iowa, 1949, JD, 1951. Bar: Iowa 1951, U.S. Dist. Ct (so. dist.) Iowa, 1958. Sole practice Harris & Harris, Jefferson, 1951-62; dist. judge 16th Judicial Dist., Iowa, 1962-72; justice Iowa Supreme Ct., Des Moines, 1972-99, sr. justice, 1999—. Served with U.S. Amry, 1944-46, PTO. Mem. VFW, Am. Legion, Rotary. Roman Catholic. Avocation: writing poetry. Office: Iowa Supreme Ct State Capitol Bldg Des Moines IA 50319

HARRIS, KAREN, advertising executive. Exec. v.p., media dir. Grey Direct, N.Y.C. Office: Grey Direct 800 3rd Ave 15th Flr New York NY 10022-6286*

HARRIS, KATHERINE, state official; b. Key West, Fla., Apr. 5, 1957; m. Anders Ebbeson. Student, U. Madrid, 1978; BA in History, Agnes Scott Coll., 1979; MPA in Internat. Trade, Harvard U., 1996. Senator 24th dist. Fla. State Legislature, 1994-98; sec. of state State of Fla., 1999—; mem. banking and ins. com., regulated industries com., ways and means com., fin. and tax subcom., WAGES Targeted Econ. Devel. select com., vice chmn. govtl. reform and oversight com., chmn. commerce and econ. opportunities com. Fla. State Senate, 1996-98. Congl. intern U.S. Senate and U.S. Ho. of Reps., 1978; vice chmn. Sarasota County Legis. Del.; former mem. adv. coun. Mote Marine Lab.; mem. presdl. adv. coun. Women's Resource Ctr.; former bd. dirs. Sarasota County Arts Coun.; former mem. nominating and steering coms. Leadership Sarasota, Leadership Tampa; former vice chmn. bd. trustees Ringling Mus.; mem. nominating com. Pub. Svc. Commn.; mem. Supreme Ct. Gender Bias Commn.; vice chmn. for Fla. Am. Legis. Exch. Coun.; mem. arts and tourism com. Nat. Conf. State Legislators; alt. mem. energy com. So. Legis. Conf.; active Habitat for Humanity, New Coll., United Cerebral Palsy, Fla. Rep. Exec. Com. Recipient Disting. Leadership Alumni award Leadership Sarasota, 1994, Arts Advocacy award Sarasota County Arts Coun., 1995, Best Govt. Ofcl. award Sarasota Mag., 1995, Legislator of Yr. award Sarasota Opera, 1996, Ind. Funeral Dirs. of Fla., 1996, Fla. Optometric Assn., 1996, Legis. Leadership award Fla. Funeral Dirs. Assn., 1996, Legis. Appreciation award Dept. of Labor and Employment Security, 1996. Mem. Sarasota C. of C. (Disting. Leadership Alumni award 1994), Englewood C. of C., Charlotte C. of C., Venice C. of C., Jaycees. Presbyterian. Avocations: painting, skiing, skeet shooting, reading. Office: Fla Capitol PLO 2 Tallahassee FL 32399-0250 also: 3131 S Tamiami Trl Ste 101 Sarasota FL 34239-5101*

HARRIS, KATHERINE SAFFORD, speech and hearing educator; b. Lowell, Mass., Sept. 3, 1925; d. Truman Henry and Katherine (Wardwell) Safford; m. George Harris, Oct. 2, 1952; children: Maud White, Louise. BA, Radcliffe Coll., 1947; PhD, Harvard U., 1954. Rsch. assoc. Haskins Labs., New Haven, 1952-85, v.p., 1985—; prof. speech and hearing CUNY, N.Y.C., 1970—, Disting. prof., 1982—; active U.S./Israeli Speech Program Littauer Found., N.Y.C., 1986. Author: (with Borden and Raphael) Speech Science Primer, 1970, 3d edit., 1995, (with Baer and Sasaki) Phonatory Control, 1986. Nat. Inst. Deafness and Other Comm. Disorders grantee. Fellow AAAS, Acoustical Soc. Am., Am. Speech Hearing Assn., N.Y. Acad. Scis. Office: CUNY Grad Sch 33 W 42nd St New York NY 10036-8099

HARRIS, KATHLEEN MCKINLEY, writer; b. Wilmington, Del., Oct. 19, 1940; d. Howard Douglas and Eloise May (Haight) McKinley; m. Everett Wayne Harris, Aug. 14, 1969; children: Susannah McKinley, Elizabeth Eloise. BA in English, Middlebury Coll., 1962; MA in English, Case We. Res. U., 1964. Cert. secondary sch. tchr., Vt. Tchr. kindergarten Pierpont (Ohio) Elem. Sch., 1962-63; tchr. English, history Peoples Acad., Morrisville, Vt., 1964-67; tchr. English Lamoille Union H.S., Hyde Park, Vt., 1967-68; tchg. asst. U. Ill., Urbana, 1969-70; feature writer South County News and Suburban List, Shelburne, Vt., 1981; co-pub., co-editor Champlain Courier, Ltd., Vergennes, Vt., 1985-88; spkr. Resource Agts. Program Vt. Dept. Librs., 1988—; clk. Village Bookstore, Shelburne, 1989-94. Author: The Wonderful Hay Tumble, 1988; contbr. short story, poems, articles to profl. jours. Mem. Soc. Children's Book Writers and Illustrators, League Vt. Writers (sec. 1990-92, bd. dirs.), Vt. Hist. Soc., Charlotte Hist. Soc., Rokeby Mus. Episcopalian. Avocations: gardening, skiing, hiking, horsemanship, acting. Home: 30 Mutton Hill Dr Charlotte VT 05445-9577

HARRIS, KEVIN J., political science educator, consultant; b. Copperhill, Tenn., Oct. 11, 1968; s. Jimmy Joe and Frances Elizabeth (Caylor) H. AA, Young Harris Coll., 1989; BA, U. Ga., 1991, MPA, 1993. Intern So. States Energy Bd., Norcross, Ga., 1991; instr. Truett-McConnell Coll., Cleveland, Ga., 1993-95; asst. prof. Truett-McConnell Coll., Cleveland, 1995—; adj. faculty Truett-McConnell Coll., Epworth, Ga., 1993—; instr. Tri-County C.C., Murphy, N.C., 1997; advisor Phi Theta Kappa Honor Soc., 1995-97. Contbr.: Facets of Fannin, 1988. Del. 9th Dist. State Conv., 1988—; chmn. Fannin County Rep. Party, Blue Ridge, Ga., 1993-94, vice-chair, 1996—; mem. rules and bylaws com. 9th Dist. Rep. Party, 1999. Named to Outstanding Young Ams., 1996, 998. Mem. ASPA, So. Polit. Scis. Assn., Acad. Polit. Sci. Baptist. Avocations: reading, campaigning, community advocacy, UGA athletics. E-mail: kevin@truett.cc.ga.us. Home: PO Box 357 Blue Ridge GA 30513 Office: Truett McConnell Coll 100 Alumni Dr Cleveland GA 30528

HARRIS, LEON A., JR., writer; b. N.Y.C., June 20, 1926; s. Leon A. and Lucile (Herzfeld) H.; m. Jane Wolfe, Sept. 27, 1996; 1 child, Lee. Grad. cum laude, Phillips Acad., Andover, Mass., 1943; BA, Harvard U., 1947. Exec. v.p., gen. mgr. A. Harris & Co., Dallas, 1950-62. Author: (children's books) The Night Before Christmas In Texas, 1952, The Great Picture Robbery, 1963, Young France, 1964, Maurice Goes to Sea, 1968, Young Peru, 1969, The Russian Ballet School, 1970, The Moscow Circus School, 1970, Yvette, 1970, Behind the Scenes in a Department Store, 1972, Behind the Scenes in a Car Factory, 1972, Behind the Scenes of Television Programs, 1972, The Great Diamond Robbery, 1985; (adult non-fiction) The Fine Art of Political Wit, 1964, Only To God: The Extraordinary Life of Godfrey Lowell Cabot, 1967, Upton Sinclair: American Rebel, 1975; Merchant Princes, 1979; also articles to various publs., including Esquire, Town & Country, Gourmet, Smithsonian, Connoisseur, Wall Street Jour., European Travel & Life, Beaux Arts, N.Y. Mag., N.Y. Times, Good Housekeeping, McCalls, Art News, Harper's Bazaar, Ency. Americana, Cosmopolitan, Am. Heritage, Family Circle, Nat. Geographic Traveler, Passport; contbg. editor Town & Country mag., 1979-97. Mem. vis. com. mus. Harvard U.; mem. vis. com. classical art Boston Mus. Fine Art; mem. acquisitions com. Dallas Mus. Art; mem. nat. com. N.Y.C. Ballet Sch.; nat. bd. dirs. Critics Circle; trustee Dallas Hist. Soc. and Colophon. Served with USNR, 1944-46. Decorated Stella della Solidarieta Italiana. Mem. ASCAP. Clubs: Harvard, Century Assn. (N.Y.C.). Home and Office: 4300 Saint Johns Dr Dallas TX 75205-4335

HARRIS, LOUIS, public opinion analyst, columnist; b. New Haven, Jan. 6, 1921; s. Harry and Frances (Smith) H.; m. Florence Yard, June 16, 1943; children: Susan, Peter, Richard. A.B. in Econs., U. N.C., 1942. With Elmo Roper and Assocs., 1946-56, ptnr., 1954-56; chmn., CEO Louis Harris and Assocs., Inc. (marketing and pub. opinion research), N.Y.C., 1956-92; CEO LH Rsch. Inc., N.Y.C., 1992-94; cons. CBS News, 1962-68, ABC News Nat. Polling Day, 1971-72; dir. polling ABC News, 1976-80; columnist Washington Post, also Newsweek mag., 1963-68, Chgo. Tribune-N.Y. Daily News Syndicate, 1969-88, Creators Syndicate, 1988-92; dir. Time mag.-Harris Poll, 1969-72; guest analyst, commentator Nat. Pub. Radio, 1983-91; dir. Bus. Week-Harris Poll, 1982—; polled extensively in John F. Kennedy Presdl. campaign, 1960; mem. Kennedy Strategy Com., 1960; dir. Life Poll, 1969-71; faculty assoc. Columbia U., N.Y.C., 1953-64; adj. prof. polit. sci. U. N.C., 1964—; bd. dirs., mem. computation com. Donaldson, Lufkin & Jenrette, N.Y.C. Author: Is There a Republican Majority?, 1964, (with William Brink) The Negro Revolution in America, 1964, Black and White, 1967, Black-Jewish Relations in New York City: The Anguish of Change, 1973, Inside America, 1987, Americans and the Arts, No. VI: Nationwide Survey of Public Opinion, 1992, No. VII, 1996; also numerous articles. Chmn. bd. dirs. Am. Councils for Arts, 1975-82; chmn. Nat. Research Center Arts, 1971—; bd. dirs., v.p. Franklin and Eleanor Roosevelt Inst., 1983—; bd. dirs. Nat. Ctr. on Edn. and the Economy, 1987-97, Recruiting New Tchrs., 1987—, chmn., 1998—; hon. trustee Am. Archtl. Found., 1996—; exec. com. legal def. fund NAACP, 1990—; bd. dirs. First Book, 1995—, Get Am. Walking, 1998—, Youth Venture, 1997—. Served as officer USNR, World War II. Mem. Am. Assn. Pub. Opinion (dir.), Am. Sociol. Assn., Am. Statis. Assn., Am. Mgmt. Assn., Am. Mktg. Assn., Am. Polit. Sci. Assn., Fgn. Policy Assn. (bd. govs. 1986-91), Century Club. *To make those in power confront the facts is critically important for the sake of progress of any kind, but to get people with power to act upon the facts to better the lot of the human race is by far more important.*

HARRIS, LOUIS SELIG, pharmacologist, researcher; b. Boston, Mar. 27, 1927; s. Max Selig and Pearl (Oppochinski) H.; m. Ruth Irma Schaufus, Aug. 22, 1952; 1 child, Charles Allan. BA, Harvard U., 1954, MA, 1956, PhD, 1958. Sect. head, sr. rsch. biologist Sterling-Winthrop Rsch. Inst., Rensselaer, N.Y., 1958-66; lectr. in pharmacology Albany (N.Y.) Med. Coll., 1959-66; from assoc. prof. to prof. U. N.C., Chapel Hill, 1966-73; Harvey Haag prof. Med. Coll. Va./Va. Commonwealth U., Richmond, 1972—, chmn. pharmacology, toxicology dept., 1972-92, assoc. v.p. health scis., 1996—; acting assoc. dir. Nat. Inst. on Drug Abuse, Rockville, Md., 1987-88; Sterling Drug vis. prof., 1983; mem. com. on problems of drug dependence NAS/NRC, 1973-77; mem. Com. on Problems of Drug Dependence, Inc., 1977-93, chmn., 1990-92; hon. prof. Beijing Med. U., People's Republic of China, 1990—. Editor: (monograph) NIDA Monographs, Proceedings, Committee on Problems of Drug Dependence, 1979—; author chpts. in books. Recipient Hartung Meml. award U. N.C., 1981, Univ. Excellence award Med. Coll. Va./Va. Commonwealth U., 1984, Outstanding Faculty award, 1984, Nathan B. Eddy award Com. on Problems of Drug Dependence, 1985, Abe Wikler award Nat. Inst. on Drug Abuse, 1991, Gov.'s award on Drug Abuse Rsch., 1992, Presdl. medallion Va. Commonwealth U., 1993, Life Achievement awards in Sci. and Industry, 1997. Fellow Am. Coll. Neuropsychopharmacology, Coll. Problems Drug Dependence; mem. AAAS, AAUP, Am. Soc. Pharmacology and Exptl. Therapeutics, Am. Chem. Soc., Am. Assn. for Med. Sch. Pharmacology, Am. Pain Soc. (charter 1977), Am. Pharm. Assn., Am. Soc. for Clin. Pharmacology and Therapeutics, Assn. Harvard Chemists, Elisha Mitchell Sci. Soc., Internat. Narcotic Enforcement Officers Assn., Soc. for Neurosci., Internat. Soc. Biochem. Pharmacology, Internat. Soc. for Study of Pain, Collegium Internationale Neuro-Psychopharmacologicum, Va. Acad. Sci., Harvard Club Boston, Cosmos Club Washington. Achievements include research in field. Home: 7830 Rockfalls Dr Richmond VA 23225-1049 Office: Va Commonwealth U PO Box 980027 Richmond VA 23298-0027

HARRIS, LUCY BROWN, accountant, consultant; b. Ft. Smith, Ark., Feb. 25, 1924; d. Joseph Real and Lucy (McDonough) Brown; m. Clyde B. Randall, June 10, 1944 (div. Aug. 1970); children: Clyde B. III, Bradford, Sara, Lucy, Mark R.; m. Mack C. Harris, Aug. 1, 1980. Student, Holton Arms Jr. Coll., 1943, U. Mo., 1944; BA, U. Ark., 1970; grad., U. Tex., 1982. CPA. Comptroller Rebmar, Inc., Dallas, 1974-78; acctg. mgr. Republic Bank, Dallas, 1978-80; ptnr. Lucy B. Harris Ltd. Co., CPAs, Dallas, 1981—; cons. Discipleship Counseling Svcs., Dallas, 1987-90. Mem. Better Bus. Bur.; bd. dirs. Ethel Daniels Found., Dallas, 1987-90, NAWBO. Mem. AICPA, Nat. Assn. Women Bus. Owners, Tex. Soc. CPAs, CPA Club, Jr. League of Dallas, Brookhollow Golf Club, Kappa Alpha Theta. Episcopalian. Avocation: painting. Office: 3710 Rawlins St Ste 810 Dallas TX 75219-4237

HARRIS, LYNDON F., priest; b. Gaffney, S.C., June 3, 1961; s. Wallace Greer and Annie Laura (Murph) H.; m. Kirsten Whitney Rutherford, Apr. 19, 1986; 1 child, Margaret Kirsten. BA in Philosophy, Wofford Coll., 1983; MDiv, U. of South, 1990; postgrad., Gen. Theol. Sem., N.Y.C., 1995—. Ordained deacon Episcopal Ch., 1990, priest, 1991. Prodn. mgr. Milliken and Co., Spartanburg, S.C., 1983-87; asst. rector St. Alban's Episcopal Ch., Lexington, S.C., 1990-91, Episcopal Ch. of Advent, Spartanburg, 1991—; Episcopal chaplain Wofford Coll., Converse Coll., Spartanburg, 1991-95; interim rector St. Paul's Episcopal Ch., Spring Valley, N.Y., 1996—; chaplain St. Hilda's and St. Hughes Episcopal Sch., N.Y.C., 1996—; interim assoc. Grace Ch., N.Y.C., 1998—; coord. Jr. High Ministry, Diocese of Upper S.C., Columbia, 1990—, standing com., 1992—, pres., 1995, vice chair ecumenical commn., 1993—; tutor Gen. Theol. Sem., 1996—. Bd. dirs. Vols. Am., Spartanburg, 1993—; mem. human rels. group Shared Hope in People, 1992—; active Let's Stop the Violence. Recipient award for excellence in Bibl. studies Am. Bible Soc., 1990; Coll. of Preachers/Washington Nat. Cathedral fellow, 1994. Mem. Assn. Religion and Intellectual Life. Avocations: backpacking, scuba diving, amateur radio, Folk and Blues guitar, travel. Office: Gen Theol Sem 175 9th Ave New York NY 10011-4924

HARRIS, LYTTLETON TAZWELL, IV, property management-investment company executive; b. Baton Rouge, Aug. 7, 1940; s. Lyttleton Tazwell and Marjorie Fleming (Windsor) H.; m. Venita Walker VanCaspel, Dec. 26, 1987. BBA, U. Miss., Oxford, 1962; MS, La. State U., 1963. Product mgr. Scott Paper Co., Phila., 1968-71; mktg. mgr. Wm. B. Reily & Co., New Orleans, 1971-72; mktg. dir. Blue Plate Foods, Inc., New Orleans, 1972-74, Dallas Fed. Savs., 1974-77; v.p. First Magnolia Fed. Savs., Hattiesburg, Miss., 1977-81; pres. S.W. Mgmt. & Mktg. Co., Houston, 1982—; v.p. Inverview Pub. Co., Houston, 1984-86; mng. editor Money Dynamics Letter Pub. Co., Houston, 1985-91; gen. mgr. Diamond V Ranch of Bernardo, Tex., 1990—; mng. ptnr. Harris Investment Partnership, 1998—. V.p. Nat. Kidney Found. Miss., Jackson, 1980-82; bd. dirs. Nat. Kidney Found. S.E. Tex., Houston, 1983-88, Boy Scouts Am., Hattiesburg, 1980-82; vol. Big Bros. of Dallas, 1975-77; trustee Crystal Cathedral Ministries, 1998—, Northwood U., 1999—. With USAR, 1963-68. Mem. Inst. Real Estate Mgmt., Internat. Assn. Fin. Planning, Am. Mktg. Assn., Sales and Mktg. Execs. (pres. 1982), Nat. Gavel Soc., Nat. Congress of Patriotic Orgns., Soc. Colonial Wars (lt. gov. Tex. soc. 1997-98), Dep. Gov. Tex. Soc., 1998—, Mil. Order Stars and Bars, Order of Three Crusades, Huguenot Soc., Order Founders and Patriots of Am. (gov. Tex. chpt. 1987-91, gov. gen. 1992-94, Meritorious Svc. award 1990, Disting. Svc. award 1996), U. Miss. Alumni Assn., Sons of Confederate Vets., Soc. Ams. of Royal Descent, SAR, Sons of the Revolution (v.p. Tex. soc. 1997-98, pres. 1998—), Soc. of the War of 1812, Houston Racquet Club, Univ. Club, Sigma Alpha Epsilon, Delta Sigma Pi. Republican. Methodist. Avocations: snow skiing, international travel, genealogy. Office: Southwest Mgmt & Mktg 6524 San Felipe St Ste 102 Houston TX 77057-2611

HARRIS, MARCELITE JORDAN, retired air force officer; b. Houston, Jan. 16, 1943; d. Cecil Oneal and Marcelite Elizabeth (Terrell) Jordan; m. Maurice Anthony Harris, Nov. 29, 1980 (dec. Jan. 1996); children: Steven Eric, Tenecia Marcelite. BA, Spelman Coll., 1964; postgrad., Ctrl. Mich. U., 1973-75, crwa. State U., 1975-76, Chapman Coll., 1979-80; BS, U. Md., Okinawa, Japan, 1986. Tchr. Head Start, Houston, 1964-65; commd. 2d lt. USAF, 1965, advanced through grades to maj. gen., 1965-97; student Squadron officers Sch., 1975; with Hdqrs. USAF, Pentagon, 1975; comdr. 39 Cadet Squadron, USAF Acad., Colorado Springs, Colo., 1978, Air Refueling Wing, McConnell AFB, Kans., 1980, Avionics Maintenance Squadron, McConnell AFB, 1981, Field Maintenance Squadron, McConnell AFB, 1982; dir. maintenance Pacific Air Forces Logistics Support Ctr., Kadena Air Base, Japan, 1982; student Air War Coll., 1983; dep. chief maintenance Tech. Tng. Ctr., Keesler AFB, Miss., 1986, wing comdr., 1988; student Harvard U.Sr. Officers Course, 1988, Capstone Flag and Gen. Officers Course, 1990; vice comdr. Oklahoma City Air Logistics Ctr., Tinker AFB, 1990-97; dir. tech. tng. USAF, Randolph AFB, Tex., 1993-97; dir. of maintenance USAF, 1994, ret., 1997. Cabinet mem. United Way, Oklahoma City, 1991; mem. adv. bd. Salvation Army, Oklahoma City, 1991—; bd. dirs. U.S. Automobile Assn., 1993—, 5 Who Care, 1992, Urban League. Decorated Bronze star, D.S.M.; named one of Top 100 Afro-Am. Bus. and Profl. Women, Dollars and $ense Mag., 1989, named Most Prestigious Individual, 1991, One of Top 100 Most Influencial People, City News, N.J., 1997; recipient Ellis Island Medal of Honor award, 1996, Living Legacy award 1998. Mem. AAUW, Air Force Assn. (life), Tuskegee Airmen Inc. (life), Maintenance Officer Assn., Retired Officer Assn., Ret. Officer Assn., Delta Sigma Theta. *Life is a miracle, but you have to give it meaning, shape and value. Choose what you can contribute to make society better. My sister and I got our strength from our parents. We learned to keep trying until we succeeded. That's perseverance.*

HARRIS, MARGARET, pianist, conductor, composer; b. Chgo., 1943; d. William and Clara Harris. BS, Juilliard Sch. Music, 1964, MS, 1965. Am. mus. specialist, cons. Porgy and Bess State Theater of Opera and Ballet, Uzbekistan, 1995; music and artistic dir. United Negro Coll. Fund Chorale, N.Y.C., 1995—; adj. lectr. and prof. Bronx Cmty. Coll. of CUNY, 1991—; adjudicator, lectr. Unisys Symposium for African-Am. Composers Detroit Symphony Orch., 1993; keynote spkr. 30th anniversary conf. Mo. Arts Coun., 1995; music dir., founder New Millineum Chorale, N.Y.C., 1996. Debut as pianist at age 3; toured as child prodigy; debut with Chgo. Symphony Orch., 1953; condr., pianist Black New World ballet prodn.; toured Europe twice as mus. dir. Black New World and Negro Ensemble Co. N.Y.; debut Town Hall, 1970; pianist, condr. prodn. Hair; musical dir., condr. Two Gentlemen of Verona, Guys and Dolls; made debut as symphonic condr. with Grant Park and Chgo. Symphonies, 1971; soloist original piano concerto L.A. Philharmonic, 1972, 73; condr. St. Louis, Minn., San Diego, Detroit symphonies, L.A. Philharmonic, Wolf Trap Park, Opera Ebony, N.Y.C., 1977, Winston-Salem, N.C. Symphony, 1988; mus. dir. One More Time, Israel, Europe, N.Y.; mus. dir./pianist I Love New York, Europe, 1984; mus. dir. Amen Corner, Broadway, 1984; artist-in-residence Hillsborough Coll., Tampa, Fla., 1984; mus. dir., condr. nat. TV spls.; mus. dir., condr. Raisin on Broadway and nat. tour; exec./music dir. Newark Boys Chorus; panelist Nat. Endowment Arts, Nat. Opera Inst. Affiliate Artists, N.Y.C., Dame Knights of Malta; composer of musical (with Ruby Dee), 1988; former artistic dir., condr. N.Y. Boys Choir; vis. disting. prof. U. West Fla., 1989—; pres. Margaret R. Harris Enterprises; condr. Dayton Philharm., 1991; apptd. permanent artistic and music dir. Olympus Music Soc., N.Y.C., 1994; pianist European Concert tour, Germany, 1994; guest condr. Bklyn. Philharmonic, 1994; other compositions include David, Cycle of Psalms, Spiritual Suite, Stabat mater, Mass in A, the Lord's Prayer, We are D.C.'s Future, Christ is Alive Here, 1994; European concept tour as pianist, 1994; Am. cultural specialist for U.S.I.A., Porgy & Bess in Russian, 1995; numerous commissioned compositions for chorus, orch., voice and piano, 1994; commd. Inaugural Fanfare Fla. Symphony, 1998, Spriritual Suite for Piano, 1998. Exec. dir. Harlem Congregations for Cmty. Improvement Cultural and Performing Arts Programs, 1998; instr. Bedford Restoration Corp., 1998, African-Am. Leadership Forum of Westchester County, 1999; music dir., program coord. Applause Performing Arts Ctr., 1999. *It is imperative that we, as a people, instill the highest standards of literacy and morality in our youth, otherwise, our collective futures are doomed. Foundation, in all aspects, must be our "Battle Cry": Education for everyone.*

HARRIS, MARIA LOSCUTOFF, special education educator, consultant; b. Rahmet Abad, Iran, Jan. 25, 1940; came to U.S., 1949; d. Vasiliy Vasilivitch and Esfir Alexsevna (Samadouroff) Loscutoff; m. Bernard Harris, Sept. 30, 1972; children: William, Richard, Lynn, Clifford, Robert, Bernard, Peter, Steven, Barbara. AA, Sierra Coll., Rocklin, Calif., 1960; BS, San Francisco State U., 1963; MS, Manhattan Coll., 1985. Cert. in spl. edn. and field of dyslexia, N.Y., Calif. Tchr. bus. edn. Westmoor H.S., Daly City, Calif., 1963-66, Coll. San Mateo, Calif., 1964, 65, Amador Sch. Dist., Pleasanton, Calif., 1967-69; adminstrv. asst. LTV, Inc., Anaheim, Calif., 1969-71; office mgr. Western div. Ocean & Atmospheric Sci. Inc., Santa Ana, Calif., 1971-72; office mgr., asst. to adminstr. Ocean & Atmospheric Sci. Inc., Dobbs Ferry, N.Y., 1972-79; officer mgr., adminstr. Harris Sci. Svcs., Dobbs Ferry, 1979-84; reading and classroom tchr. Windward Sch., White Plains, N.Y., 1984-88; learning specialist Irvington (N.Y.) Union Free Sch. Dist., 1988—; cons., tutor Harris Sci. Svcs., Dobbs Ferry, 1993—; mem. Westchester Reading coun. Supporter, contbr. Midnight Run for Homeless, 1985—; vol. Census Bur., 1990, Dobbs Ferry, 1989. Mem. Orton Dyslexia Soc., Internat. Reading Assn., Kappa Delta Pi. Avocations: reading, cooking, travel, volunteer work. Home: 15 Overlook Rd Dobbs Ferry NY 10522-3209 Office: Irvington Union Free Schs 6 Dows Ln Irvington NY 10533-2102

HARRIS, MARILYN, retired academic administrator; b. N.Y.C.; d. Bernard and Rose (Block) Hochberg; m. Seymour J. Harris; children: Randall (dec.), April. AB summa cum laude, CUNY-Hunter Coll., 1945; MS, Iowa State U., 1947. Mem. faculty dept. math and stats. Hunter Coll., N.Y.C., 1946-48; sys. analyst, statistician market rsch. svcs. GE, N.Y.C., 1962-67; biostatistician comprehensive child care project Einstein Med. Sch., N.Y.C., 1967-69; asst. to dean, acting dir. computer ctr. Baruch Coll. CUNY, 1969-72; dir. data collection and evaluation office univ. mgmt. data Ctrl. Office, CUNY, 1972-74; dir. mgmt. info. sys. Bklyn. Coll., CUNY, 1974-79, dir. pers. svcs., 1979-85, asst. v.p. human resources and adminstrv. svcs., 1985-89, bd. dirs. Bklyn. Ctr. Performing Arts, 1982-89, chair seat campaign, 1984-86; Docent Pollock/Krasner House, East Hampton, L.I., 1995-97. Bd. dirs. Project Greenhope, 1988-93; vol. mgmt. cons. Women in Need, 1988-94, bd. dirs., 1989-92, sec. exec. com., 1990-92; bd. dirs. Women's City Club, 1990-97, active homeless project, 1989-91, mem. emergency task force, 1992-93, v.p. ops., 1993-94; active Womanspace of Gt. Neck, 1989, mem. exec. com.-at-large, 1990-94, mem. adv. bd., 1994-96; adv. bd. Omsbudservice of Nassau County, 1991—. Recipient Excellence award Art League Nassau County, 1994, Helen Nobel award of merit Nat. Art League, 1996, Gold medal 1st pl. in other media, 1996, Silver medal, 1997. Mem. Artists Network Great Neck (Hon. Mention awards), Artist Alliance of L.I., Phi Beta Kappa, Phi Kappa Phi, Pi Mu Epsilon. Home: 9 Knightsbridge Rd Great Neck NY 11021-4569

HARRIS, MARK, English educator, author; b. Mt. Vernon, N.Y., Nov. 19, 1922; s. Carlyle and Ruth (Klausner) Finkelstein; m. Josephine Horen, Mar. 17, 1946; children: Hester Jill, Anthony Wynn, Henry Adam. B.A., U. Denver, 1950, M.A., 1951; Ph.D., U. Minn., 1956; L.H.D. (hon.), Ill. Wesleyan U., 1974. Reporter Port Chester (N.Y.) Item, 1944, PM, N.Y.C., 1945, I.N.S., St. Louis, 1945-46; prof. English San Francisco State Coll., 1954-68, Purdue U., 1967-70; mem. faculty Calif. Inst. Arts, Valencia, 1970-73, Immaculate Heart Coll., Los Angeles, 1973-74, U. So. Calif., 1973-75, U. Pitts., 1975-80; prof. English Ariz. State U., Tempe, 1980—; Vis. prof. Brandeis U., 1963. Author: (novels) Trumpet to the World, 1946, City of Discontent, 1952, The Southpaw, 1953, Bang the Drum Slowly, 1956, Something About a Soldier, 1957, A Ticket for a Seamstitch, 1957, Wake Up, Stupid, 1959, The Goy, 1970, Killing Everybody, 1973, It Looked Like For Ever, 1979, Lying in Bed, 1984, Speed, 1990, The Tale Maker, 1994; (play) Friedman & Son, 1963; (non-fiction) Mark the Glove Boy, 1964, Twentyone Twice: A Journal, 1966, (autobiography) Best Father Ever Invented, 1976, Short Work of It: Selected Writing, 1979; Saul Bellow: Drumlin Woodchuck, 1980; editor abridged version of six vols. of Boswell's papers: The Heart of Boswell, 1981, Diamond, 1994; also screen plays, essays, reviews, articles, stories; subject of Norman Lavers book Mark Harris, 1978. Mem. San Francisco Art Commn., 1961-64. Served with AUS, 1943-44. Recipient award Nat. Inst. Arts and Letters, 1961, Profl. Achievement award U. Denver Alumni Assn., 1984; Fulbright prof. Japan, 1957; Ford Found. grantee, 1960; Guggenheim Found. fellow, 1965, 74; Nat. Endowment Arts grantee, 1966; numerous other invitations and awards. Office: Ariz State U Dept English Tempe AZ 85287 *I don't know if I have "present success." Success may lie in despising the usual ideas of success. I have been fortunate only. Success would mean enabling everyone else to be as fortunate. We must distribute the world's goods a great deal better than we do. We must focus not on gain, but on ending war. Only then can we even begin to think of such luxuries as "success."*

HARRIS, MARK L., neurologist; b. Oct. 15, 1954. BS, U.R.I., 1976; MD, Chgo. Med. Sch., 1982. Pres. Ga. Neurology Assn., Atlanta, 1995—. Mem. Am. Acad. Neurology. Office: 4500 N Shallowford Rd Ste 200 Atlanta GA 30338-6404

HARRIS, MARTIN HARVEY, aerospace company executive; b. N.Y.C., Mar. 14, 1932; s. Leo and Gertrude (Litt) H.; m. Patricia Ann Franklin, Apr. 27, 1970; children by previous marriage—Lori Kathryn, Barbara Ann. B of Aero. Engring., N.Y. U., 1953; MS in Systems Mgmt., U. So. Calif., 1973. With Curtis-Wright Corp., Woodbridge, N.J., 1952-53; ops. analyst Lockheed Martin Corp., Denver, 1957-58; dir. internat. programs Lockheed Martin Corp., Orlando, Fla., 1958-97; cons., 1997—. Contbr. articles to profl. publs. Trustee Aerospace Edn. Found., Air Force Meml. Found. Served with USAF, 1953-57; col. Res., 1958-81. Recipient Air Force Exceptional Service award, 1986. Mem. Air Force Assn. (nat. sec. 1971-76, dir. 1965—, nat. pres. 1984-86, chmn. bd. dirs. 1986—, recipient Gold Life Membership card 1988, named Nat. Man of Yr. 1972, Fla. Man of Yr. 1977, 79, 91), Am. Def. Preparedness Assn. (pres. Fla. Peninsula chpt. 1973-74, dir. 1968-80, nat. v.p. 1977-79), Ret. Officers Assn., Orlando Area C. of C., AIAA, Am. Helicopter Soc., Am. Mgmt. Assn., Res. Officers Assn. Patentee in field. Home: 15633 Vista Verde Dr Montverde FL 34756-3039

HARRIS, MATTHEW NATHAN, surgeon, educator; b. N.Y.C., Dec. 20, 1931; s. Saul and Deborah (Moskowitz) H.; m. Frances Wicentowski, June 27, 1954; children: Amy Rachel, Julie Rebecca, Daniel Charles. BA, NYU, 1952; MD, Chgo. Med. Sch., 1956. Diplomate Am. Bd. Surgery, Nat. Bd. Med. Examiners; lic. physician, N.Y. Intern Bellevue Hosp. Ctr., N.Y.C., 1956-57, resident in gen. surgery, 1957-58, 60-63; sr. clin. trainee in cancer USPHS, N.Y.C., 1963-64; instr. anatomy NYU, N.Y.C., 1966-68, dir. elective surg. anatomy, 1973-74; prof. surgery, dir. surg. oncology NYU Sch. Medicine, N.Y.C., 1979—; vis. surgeon Bellevue Hosp. Ctr.; attending surgeon Tisch Hosp.; cons. and lectr. in field.; cons. surgeon Manhattan V.A.

Hosp. Contbr. articles to Jour. ACS, Breast Disease, Cancer, Annals Surgery, Radiology, N.Y. State Jour. Medicine, Cancer Rsch., Surgery, Jour. Lab. Investigations, others. Capt. USAR, 1958-60, Korea. Chgo. Med. Sch. scholar, 1955. Fellow ACS (cancer liaison fellow, N.Y. state chmn.); mem. AMA, Am. Soc. Clin. Oncology, Am. Assn. Clin. Anatomists, Am. Radium Soc., N.Y. Cancer Soc., N.Y. Surg. Soc. (pres. 1991-92), N.Y. Med. Soc., N.Y. Met. Breast Cancer Group, Soc. Surg. Oncology, N.Y. Cancer Programs Assn., Inc., Pan-Am. Med. Soc., Soc. Cons. Armed Forces, 38th Parallel Med. Soc. (Korea), Pan Pacific Surg. Assn., Internat. Pigment Cell Soc., Assn. Cancer Edn., Assn. Academic Surgery, So. Alumni Bellevue Hosp., Chgo. Med. Sch. Alumni Assn., Alpha Omega Alpha, Sigma Xi, Beta Lambda Sigma. Achievements include research in cytologic evaluation breast diseases by stereoactic aspiration, malignant melanoma vaccine, primary surgical management malignant melanoma. Office: NYU Med Ctr 530 1st Ave New York NY 10016-6481

HARRIS, MELBA IRIS, secondary school educator, state agency administrator; b. Cullman, Ala., Aug. 8, 1945; d. Karl and Leona Christine (McDowell) Budweg; m. James Allen Harris, Apr. 17, 1965 (div. June 1981); 1 child, James Allen II. BS in Home Econs., U. Ala., 1970, MA in Elem. Edn., 1977, EdS, 1982; BS in Elem. Edn. magna cum laude, St. Bernard Coll., 1975. Instr. Cullman (Ala.) City Schs., 1966-68, Ft. Payne (Ala.) City Schs., 1974—; curriculum developer Ala. State Dept. Edn., Montgomery, 1987-89; aerospace edn. coordinator Ala. State Dept. Aeronautics, Montgomery, 1987-89. V.p. Ft. Payne Civettes, 1979. Recipient commendations Ala. Gov. George C. Wallace, 1985, 86, Gov. Guy Hunt, 1987, Ft. Payne City Coun., 1987, Ft. Payne City Bd. Edn., 1987, Civil Air Patrol Albertville Composite Squadron, 1987, Ala. State Bd. Edn., 1987, Ala. State Excellence in Edn. award Fed. Aviation Adminstrn., 1987, Stewart G. Potter award Nat. Aircraft Distbrs. and Mfrs. Assn., 1988, Nat. Frank G. Brewer Meml. Airospace Edn. award Civil Air Patrol, 1989, Aviation Edn. Excellence award Nat. Gen. Aviation Mfrs. Assn., 1989, NEWEST award NASA, 1995, Achievement in Edn. award Optimist Club, 1999; named A. Scott Crossfield Nat. Aerospace Educator of Yr., 1987, The Nat. Aerospace Edn. Tchr. of Yr., 1987; Christa McAuliffe fellow, 1987, Tchr. of Yr. Meml. award, 1991; named to Ala. Aviation Hall of Fame, 1991. Mem. NEA, NSTA, Ala. Edn. Assn. (state aerospace edn. coord. 1992—), Ft. Payne Edn. Assn. (pres. 1985-86), Air Force Assn. (life), Ala. Aviation Assn., Exptl. Aircraft Internat. (maj. achievement award 1988), Exptl. Aircraft Chpt. 683 (sec., treas. 1987, pres. 1988), Internat. Ninety-Nines, Inc., Kappa Delta Pi. Home: PO Box 681174 Fort Payne AL 35968-1613 Office: Wills Valley Sch 4111 Williams Ave NE Fort Payne AL 35967-3992

HARRIS, MERLE WIENER, college administrator, educator; b. Hartford, Conn., July 25, 1942; d. Irving and Leah (Glasser) Wiener; m. David R. Harris, June 23, 1963; children: Jonathan, Rebecca. BS, Cen. Conn. U., 1964, MS, 1973; EdD, U. Mass., 1988. Clk., edn. com. Conn. Gen. Assembly, Hartford, 1971-72; career edn. coordinator Bloomfield (Conn.) Pub. Schs., 1973-78; asst. to commr. Dept. of Higher Edn., Hartford, Conn., 1978-82, asst. commr., 1982-88, deputy commr., 1988-89; pres. Charter Oak State Coll., Newington, Conn., 1989—; exec. dir. Bd. for State Acad. Awards, Hartford, Conn., 1989—; interim pres. Cen. Conn. State U., 1995-96; cons. U.S. Dept. Edn. Career Edn., Washington, 1974; fellow Inst. for Ednl. Leadership, 1980; bd. dirs. Old State House, Conn. Literacy Vols., 1991-98, Conn. Humanities Coun., 1991-97; chmn. Joint Com. Ednl. Tech., 1991—. Mem. New Eng. Assn. Schs. and Colls., Am. Coun. on Edn. (commr. on ednl. credit and credentials 1995-98). Democrat. Jewish. Avocations: gardening, cooking, teaching.

HARRIS, MICHAEL GENE, optometrist, educator, lawyer; b. San Francisco, Sept. 20, 1942; s. Morry and Gertrude Alice (Epstein) H.; m. Dawn Block; children: Matthew Benjamin, Daniel Evan, Ashley Beth, Lindsay Meredith. BS, U. Calif., 1964, M in Optometry, 1965, D in Optometry, 1966, MS, 1968; JD, John F. Kennedy U., 1985. Bar: Calif., U.S. Dist. Ct. (no. dist.) Calif. Assoc. practice optometry Oakland, Calif., 1965-66, San Francisco, 1966-68; instr., coord. contact lens clinic Ohio State U., 1968-69; asst. clin. prof. optometry U. Calif., Berkeley, 1969-73, dir. contact lens extended care clinic, 1969-83, chief contact lens clinic, 1983—, assoc. clin. prof., 1973-76, asst. chief, then assoc. chief contact lens svc., 1970—, lectr., then sr. lectr., 1978—, vice chmn. faculty Sch. Optometry, 1983-85, 95—, prof. clin. optometry, 1984-86, clin. prof., 1986—, dir. residency program, 1993-95, asst. dean, 1994-95, assoc. dean, 1995—; John de Carle vis. prof. City U., London, 1984; vis. rsch. fellow U. New South Wales, Sydney, Australia, 1989; sr. vis. rsch. scholar U. Melbourne, Victoria, Australia, 1989, 92; pvt. practice optometry, Oakland, 1973-76; mem. ophthalmic devices panel, med. device adv. com. FDA, 1990—, interim chair, 1994; lectr., cons. in field; mem. regulation rev. com. Calif. State Bd. Optometry; cons. hypnosis Calif. Optometric Assn., Am. Optometric Assn.; cons. Nat. Bd. Examiners in Optometry, Soflens divsn. Bausch & Lomb, 1973—, Barnes-Hind Hydrocurve Soft Lenses, Inc., 1974-87, Pilkinton-Barnes Hind, 1987-94, Contact Lens Rsch. Lab., 1976—, Wesley-Jessen Contact Lens Co., 1977—, Palo Alto VA, 1980—, Primarius Corp., Cooper Vision Optics Alcon, 1980—; co-founder Morton D. Sarver Rsch. Lab., 1986. Editor current comments sect. Am. Jour. Optometry, 1974-77; editor Eye Contact, 1984-86; assoc. editor The Video Jour. Clin. Optometry, 1988—; cons. editor Contact Lens Spectrum, 1988—; author: Contact Lenses: Treatment Options for Ocular Disease, Contact Lenses for Pre & Post-Surgery; editor: Problems in Optometry, Special Contact Lens Procedures; Contact Lenses in Ocular Disease, 1990; mem. hon. internat. editl. bd. Contact Lens and Anterior Eye Jour.; contbr. chpts. to books, articles to profl. publs.; author various syllabi. Planning commr. Town of Moraga, Calif., 1986, vice-chmn., 1987-88, chmn., 1988-90; mem. Town Coun., Moraga, 1992—, vice mayor, 1994-95, mem. Medi-Cal. adv. planning commn., 1993-95, chair, 1994—, with Managed Care commn., 1995%, chair, 1996—; with City County Rels. Com., Contra Costa County, Calif.; founding mem. Young Adults divsn. Jewish Welfare Fedn., 1965—, chmn., 1967-68; commr. Sunday Football League, Contra Costa County, 1974-78; chmarer mem. Jewish Cmty. Ctr. Contra Costa County; founding mem. Jewish Cmty. Mus. San Francisco, 1984; Para-RAbbinic, Temple Isaiah, Lafayette, Calif., 1987, bd. dirs., 1990; life mem. Bay Area Coun. for Soviet Jews, 1976; bd. dirs. Jewish Cmty. Rels. Coun. Greater East Bay, 1979—, Campolindo Homeowners Assn., 1981-85; pres. student coun. John F. Kennedy U. Sch. Law, 1984-85. U. Calif. fellow, 1971; Calif. Optometric Assn. scholar, 1965, George Schneider Meml. scholar, 1964, Max Shapero Meml. lectr., 1995. Fellow Am. Acad. Optometry (diplomate cornea and contact lens sect., chmn. contact lens papers, mem. contact lens com. 1974—, vice chmn. contact lens sect. 1980-82, chmn. sect. 1982-84, immediate past chmn. 1984-86, chmn. jud. com. 1989—, chmn. bylaws com. 1989—), Assn. Schs. and Colls. Optometry (coun. on acad. affairs), AAAS, Prentice Soc. (pres.-elect 1994-96, pres. 1996—); mem. ABA, Assn. for Rsch. in Vision and Ophthalmology, Am. Optometric Assn. (proctor 1969—, cons. on hypnosis, mem. contact lens sect., mem. position papers com., mem. com. on ophthalmic stds., subcom. on testing and certification, cons. editor Jour.), Calif. Optometric Assn., Assn. Optometric Contact Lens Educators, Am. Optometric Found., Mexican Soc. Contactology (hon.), Nat. Coun. on Contact Lens Compliance, Internat. Soc. Contact Lens Rsch., Calif. State Bd. Optometry (regulation rev. com.), Calif. Acad. Scis., U. Calif. Optometry Alumni Assn. (life), Calif. Young Lawyers Assn., Contrac Costa Bar Assn., Mus. Soc., JFK U. Sch. Law Alumni Assn., Banjamin Ide Wheeler Soc. U. Calif., B'nai B'rith, Mensa, Robert Gardon Sproul Assn. U. Calif. Democrat. Office: U of Calif Sch of Optometry Berkeley CA 94720

HARRIS, MICHAEL JAMES, software engineer; b. Pocatello, Idaho, Feb. 6, 1951; s. James Vernon and Connie Rachel (Williams) H.; m. Colette Jilene Card, June 5, 1984; children: Gregory, Kristen, Jason, Jennifer, Jonathan, Connie. BS, U.S. Naval Acad., 1973; MSCS, Naval Postgrad. Sch., 1974. Commd. ens. USN, 1973, advanced through grades to lt., 1976, resigned, 1979; computer sci. instr. Brigham Young U., Provo, Utah, 1979-82; software engr. Eyring Rsch. Inst., Provo, 1982-84, Hewlett-Packard, Boise, Idaho, 1984-92, Word Perfect, Orem, Utah, 1992-98, Novell Inc., Orem, 1995-96, 97—, Datalogics, Orem, 1996; software engr., pres. HMC, Inc., Boise, 1979-84. Co-patentee software, printers. Republican. Mem. LDS Ch. Avocations: tennis, jogging, guitar, home remodeling, gardening. Home: 1396 N 725 W Orem UT 84057-5903

HARRIS, MILDRED STAEGER, retired broadcast executive; b. Newark, Oct. 18, 1917; d. Henry Ernest and Louise Sheffick Staeger; m. William Finlaw Harris, Oct. 20, 1945 (dec. Nov. 1963); children: Steven Alan, Sandra Louise, Douglas William. Prof. designation in bus. mgmt., UCLA, 1980. Mgr. fixed assets ABC, L.A., 1971-76, mgr. adminstrn., 1976-80, tech. mgr., 1980-85. Children's libr. counselor Kings County Literacy Coun., Hanford, Calif., 1990, bd. dirs., 1991—; coord. Am. Women in Radio and TV, L.A., 1979-84. Named Businesswoman of Yr., YWCA Coun., 1973; recipient Emmy award for Summer Olympics, NATAS, 1985. Mem. Calif. Sheriffs Assn., Literacy Vols. Am., Libr. of Congress. Avocations: history, language, reading, genealogy. Office: Kings Literacy Coun 505 W Cameron Hanford CA 93230

HARRIS, MILES FITZGERALD, meteorologist; b. Brunswick, Ga., Feb. 2, 1913; s. James Madison and Louise (Fitzgerald) H.; m. Marguerite Bertice Leonard, May 13, 1938; children: Ann Louise, Theresa Geraldine, Emily Leland. BSc in Meteorology, NYU, 1944, MSc in Meteorology, 1957. Weather observer U.S. Weather Bur., Macon, Ga., 1932-35, Savannah, Chattanooga,, Macon,, Washington, 1937-42; cadet/clk. South Atlantic Steamship Line, Savannah, 1935-37; meteorologist U.S. Weather Bur., Washington, 1944-45; hurricane forecaster U.S. Weather Bur., San Juan, P.R., 1945-48; spl. projects meteorologist U.S. Weather Bur., Washington, 1948-51, rsch. meteorologist, 1951-61, head editing and pub. br., 1961-66; phys. scientist, chief Sci. Info. Br. Environ. Sci. Svcs. Adminstrn., Washington, 1966-70; editor Mon. Weather Review, 1968-70; editor Am. Meteorol. Soc., Boston, 1970-83, ret., 1983; Editor, writer, cons. Earth Sci. Curriculum Project, Boulder, Colo., 1964-67. Author: Man Against Storm, 1962, Getting to Know the World Meterological Organization, 1966, Opportunities in Meteorology, 1972, Investigating the Earth, 1967-84, (with Marguerite L. Harris, Eleanor V. Spiller and Mary Carr) John Hale, A Man Beset by Witches, 1992; contbg. author Ency. Earth Scis., 1976. Mem. Am. Meteorol. Soc. Democrat. Congregationalist. Avocations: local history, writing and research on John Hale, The Salem Witchcraft Trials. Home: 40 Lothrop St Beverly MA 01915-5150

HARRIS, MILTON M., distributing company executive; b. San Francisco, Sept. 6, 1916; s. A.H. and Rebecca (Harris) H.; m. Lorraine D. Love, July 3, 1938; 1 child, Jerrold B. Ed. pub. schs. With Braun-Knecht-Heimann Co., San Francisco, 1933-60; v.p. Braun-Knecht-Heimann Co., 1951-60; (co. acquired by Van Waters & Rogers, Inc. (now Univar Corp.)), San Francisco, 1960; sr. v.p., gen. mgr. (co. acquired by Van Waters & Rogers, Inc. (now Univar Corp.)), 1960-61, pres., 1962-66, chmn., 1966-70, vice chmn., 1970—, also bd. dirs., 1970-88; dir. emeritus, 1989-95; bd. dirs. emeritus VWR Corp., Westchester, Pa. Mem. Bohemian Club (San Francisco), Desert Horizon Country Club (Indian Wells, Calif.). Home: 75-255 Saint Andrews Ct Indian Wells CA 92210-7603

HARRIS, NEIL, history educator; b. Bklyn., 1938; s. Harold and Irene Harris. AB, Columbia U., N.Y.C., 1958; BA, Cambridge U., Eng., 1960; PhD, Harvard U., 1965. From instr. to asst. prof. history Harvard U., Cambridge, Mass., 1965-69; assoc. prof. U. Chgo., 1969-72, prof., 1972-90, Preston and Sterling Morton prof. of history, 1990—, dir. Nat. Humanities Inst., 1975-77, chmn. dept. history, 1985-88; mem. adv. bd. Temple Hoyne Buell Ctr., Columbia, 1984-89; mem. adv. com. dept. architecture Art Inst. Chgo., 1982—; mem. Smithsonian Council, 1978-84, chmn. 1984-92; visiting prof. Yale U., 1974; dir. d'etudes Ecole des Hautes Etudes en Sci. Sociales, Paris, 1985. Author: Artist in American Society, 1966, Humbug: The Art of P.T. Barnum, 1970, Cultural Excursions, 1990, Building Lives, 1999; editor: Land of Contrasts, 1970, the WPA Guide to Illinois, 1983; bd. editors New Eng. Quar., 1982—; Winterthur Portfolio, 1978-80, 85—, Frederick Law Olmsted Papers, 1973, Am. Scholar, 1994—; mem. editorial adv. bd. History Today, 1978-86. Trustee H.F. DuPont Winterthur (Del.) Mus., 1978-87, Newberry Libr.; mem. Nat. Mus. Svcs. Bd., Washington, 1977-84; vis. com. J. Paul Getty Mus., 1995—; bd. dirs. Nat. Mus. Am. History, 1997—. Named Am. Coun. Learned Socs. fellow, 1972-73, NEH fellow, 1980-81, Guggenheim fellow, 1999-2000; Getty scholar, 1991, Nat. Mus. Am. Art scholar, 1995-96; Boucher lectr. Johns Hopkins U., 1971, Cardozo lectr. Yale U., 1974, Tandy lectr. Whitney Mus. Am. Art, 1982, Kemper lectr. Pitzer Coll., 1980, Buell lectr. Columbia U., 1993; recipient Joseph Henry medal Smithsonian Instn., 1991. Fellow Am. Acad. Arts and Scis.; mem. Am. Antiquarian Soc., Am. Coun. Learned Socs. (vice chmn. N.Y. 1978-89, chmn. 1989-93), Orgn. Am. Historians, Phi Beta Kappa (senator united chpts. 1985-97, vis. lectr. 1985-86). Home: 4950 S Chicago Beach Dr Chicago IL 60615-3207 Office: U Chgo Dept History 1126 E 59th St Chicago IL 60637-1580

HARRIS, NEISON, manufacturing company executive; b. St. Paul, Jan. 24, 1915; s. William and Mildred (Brooks) H.; m. Bette Deutsch, Jan. 25, 1939; children: Katherine, King, Toni. AB, Yale U., 1936. Founder Toni Home Permanent Co., 1936-46; pres. Toni div. Gillette Safety Razor Co., 1946-66; pres. Paper Mate div. Gillette Co.; pres., bd. dirs. Pittway Corp., Northbrook, Ill., 1959-84, chmn. bd., 1984—; chmn. bd., dir. Standard Shares, Inc. Named One of Ten Outstanding Young Men U.S., Jr. C. of C., 1948. Clubs: Standard, Lake Shore Country (Chgo.); Boca Rio Country (Boca Raton, Fla.). Office: Pittway Corp 333 Skokie Blvd Ste 114 Northbrook IL 60062-1680

HARRIS, NICHOLAS GEORGE, publisher; b. Salisbury, Eng., Sept. 8, 1939; s. George Ivan and Phyllis Dorothy (Porter) H.; m. Margaret Jane Darling, Feb. 3, 1968; children—Nicola, Gregory. Sales rep. Collins Pubs., London, 1963-67, Montreal, 1967-72; sales dir. Collins Pubs., Toronto, 1972; exec. v.p. Collins Pubs., 1973; pres. William Collins Sons & Co., Can. Ltd., 1974-87; chmn., pres. Collins Pubs. N.Am., 1986-87; mng. dir. McClelland & Stewart, 1988-89; pres. Wright Harris, Inc., 1990; v.p., gen. mgr. Grolier, Ltd., 1990-92; pres. Nick Harris Assocs., 1993—. Served to 1st lt. Brit. Army, 1958-63. Mem. Donalda Club (Toronto). Anglican. Office: 3080 Yonge St Ste 5000, Toronto, ON Canada M6N 3N1

HARRIS, PAMELA SUE, rehabilitation physician; b. Emporia, Kans., May 27, 1962; d. Thomas Lee and Janet Kaye (Dant) Fitzpatrick; m. Thomas Wayne Harris, Dec. 19, 1987; children: Emily Elizabeth, Bethany Elaine. BA with honors in Human Biology, U. Kans., 1984, MD, 1988. Diplomate Am. Bd. Phys. Medicine and Rehab. Resident U. Kans., 1988-92; assoc. med. dir. Bethany Rehab. Ctr., Kansas City, Kans., 1992-96; rehab. med. dir. Providence Med. Ctr./St. John Hosp., Kansas City, 1996-98; pvt. practice rehab. medicine Kansas City, 1992—. Fellow Am. Acad. Phys. Medcine and Rehab.; mem. AMA, Kans. Med. Soc., Kiwanis (chmn. internat. com. young children Priority One 1997-99, mem. internat. com., 1996-97, chmn. Kans. dist. 1994-97). Avocations: cross stitch, crafts, flower arranging.

HARRIS, PATRICIA LEE, engineering executive; b. Balt., Dec. 24, 1952; d. George Jesse and Vivian Elsa (Kernan) Steinbach; m. John Cummings Harris, Jan. 6, 1973; children: Kristin Elizabeth, Michael George. BS in Chemistry, U. Md., 1973; PhD in Chemistry, U. Pa., 1977. Mem. tech. staff AT&T Western Elec., Princeton, N.J., 1977-80; dept. chief, MOS semiconductor engrng. AT&T Western Elec., Allentown, Pa., 1980-84, engrng. mgr. MOS semiconductor engrng., 1984-86; dept. head hybrid integrated circuit devel. AT&T Bell Labs., Lawrence, Mass., 1986-90, dept. head frequency control products, 1990-91; divsn. mgr. network implementation engrng. AT&T, Bedminster, N.J., 1991-94, network v.p. engrng. svcs., 1994-96; network v.p. global transition team AT&T Bell Labs., Bedminster, 1998—; v.p. ops. devel. and tech. ARCOR Telecom., Frankfurt, Germany, 1997-98. Pres. ch. coun. Luth. Ch., Manchester, N.H., 1990-91; troop leader Girl Scouts U.S., Clinton, N.J., 1994—; swim meet referee YMCA, Flemington/Bernardsville, N.J., 1994—. Recipient Tribute to Women in Industry award YWCA, 1988, Catherine B. Cleary woman of the Yr. award AT&T, 1996. Mem. Sigma Xi, Phi Beta Kappa.

HARRIS, PATRICK DONALD, physiology educator; b. Nebraska City, Nebr., Mar. 30, 1940; s. Donald Wilson and Theresia Marie (Bierl) H.; m. Doris Jean, July 18, 1959; children: Donna Beth, Wesley Mark, Kennet Fulton. BSEE with honors, U. Mo., 1962, MSEE with honors, 1963; PhD in Physiology, Northwestern U., Evanston, Ill., 1967. Nat. Heart & Lung Inst. postdoctoral fellow dept physiology Sch. Medicine, Ind. U., Indpls., 1967-68; asst. prof. physiology Sch. Medicine U. Mo., Columbia, 1968-71, assoc. prof. Sch. Medicine, 1971-77, assoc. prof. Grad. Sch., 1974-77, prof. Sch. Medicine and Grad. Sch., 1977-81, investigator Dalton Rsch. Ctr., 1974-80, assoc. dir. Dalton Rsch. Ctr., 1980-81; vis. assoc. biomed. engrng. div. engrng. and applied scis. Calif. Inst. Tech., Pasadena, 1977-78; chmn. dept. physiology and biophysics Sch. Medicine, U. Louisville, 1981-94, dir. Ctr. Applied Microcirculatory Rsch., Health Scis. Ctr., 1986-94, prof., 1981—; pres. Micro-Med Inc., 1989—; spl. rsch. fellow Nat. Heart and Lung Inst., 1970-72; mem. nat. com. Commn. on Life Scis., NRC, 1984-90; sci. program cons. Nat. Heart, Lung and Blood Inst., 1972-93; mem. advanced tech. coun. Louisville Urban Area and Commonwealth of Ky., 1987-94; bd. dirs. Jewish Hosp. Heart & Lung Inst., 1990-94, chmn. sci. affairs com., 1990-94. Referee Jour. Microvascular Rsch., 1969-86, bd. editors, 1979-86; referee Anesthesia and Analgesia-Current Researches, 1970-74; bd. editors Proc. Soc. Exptl. Biol. Medicine, 1975-78; referee Am. Jour. Physiology, 1974—, bd. editors, 1986-93; referee Sci., 1979-84; bd. editors Microcirculation, 1980-85; referee Circulation Rsch., 1981-85, Jour. AMA, 1982-84, Hypertension, 1982-88; bd. editors Circulatory Shock, 1986-93; contbr. articles to profl. jours. Adult leader Boy Scouts Am., 1967-68, 75-84; vol. parole officer State of Mo., Columbia, 1974-81; bd. dirs. Ky. affiliate Am. Heart Assn., 1987-93; active MGC Cath. Ch., Louisville, 1981—, Cath. Archdiocese, Louisville, 1981—; coach, v.p. Daniel Boone Little League Baseball, 1973-77; mem. hosp. worship svc. program Interfaith Coun. Columbia, 1974-81; mem. athletic bd. Mother of Good Counsel ath. Ch., Louisville, 1982-86, chmn., 1982-84, mem. adult formation program, 1981—. Grantee Lilly Rsch. Labs., 1969-70, Nat. Inst. Gen. Med. Scis., 1969-71, Nat. Heart and Lung Inst., 1972-77, NIH, 1970-90, NSF, 1980-81, VA, 1984—, Merck Rsch. Inst., 1985, Am. Heart Assn., 1975-89, Humana Corp., 1986-90, Commonwealth Ctr. Excellence, 1987-94; recipient Rsch. Career Devel. award Nat. Heart and Lung Inst. Fellow Am. Heart Assn.; mem. IEEE (mem. exec. com. Columbia chpt. engrng. in medicine and biology group 1970-75), Microcirculatory Soc. (pres. V World Congress for Microcirculation 1987-91), European Soc. Microcirculation, Am. Physiol. Soc. (mem. program exec. com. 1984-90), Soc. Exptl. Biology and Medicine, Shock Soc., Assn. Chairpersons Depts. Physiology, Ky. Heart Assn. (mem. rsch. peer rev. com. 1981-91, bd. dirs. 1987-93), Jefferson County Med. Soc., Tau Beta Pi. Roman Catholic. Avocation: golf, bridge. Home: 9014 Billingsgate Pl Louisville KY 40242-2440 Office: Micro-Med Inc 4400 Breckenridge Ln Ste 413 Louisville KY 40218-4023

HARRIS, PAUL, sculptor; b. Orlando, Fla., Nov. 5, 1925. Student, U. N.Mex., New Sch. Social Research, Hans Hofmann Sch. Fine Arts. Fulbright prof. sculpture Universidad Catolica de Chile, 1961-62; later faculty San Francisco Art Inst., Calif. Coll. Arts and Crafts, Oakland; artist-in-residence Rinehart Sch. Sculpture, Md. Inst. Art, 1981, U. Ariz., Tucson, 1986; vis. critic, lectr. U.S.F.S. Ctrs., Valparaiso and Concepcion, Chile, 1962, Rinehart Sch. Sculpture, spring 1981, Md. Inst. Art, (9 times) 1963-86, U. Oreg., Eugene, 1968, Newark (N.J.) State U., 1970, Mont. State U., Bozeman, 1970, 74, State U. N.Mex., Las Cruces, 1971, Montclair (N.J.) State U., 1973, Commonwealth U. Va., 1975, 76, 95, Clemson U., 1975, Haverford Coll., 1977, Phila. Coll. Art, 1977, R.I. Sch. Design, 1977, U. Ariz., Tucson, 1986. Exhibited group shows, Mus. Modern Art, N.Y.C., 1958, 63, N.Y. World's Fair, 1965, Art Inst. Chgo., 1965, Md. Inst. Art, 1966, Mus. Contemporary Crafts, 1966, 73, São Paulo Bienal, 1967, Crocker Art Gallery Assn., Sacramento, 1968, Smithsonian Instn. Traveling Exhbn., 1969, also Phila. Inst. Art, San Francisco Mus. Art, N.J. State Mus., L.A. County Mus., 1968, 73, Brandeis U., A.C.A. Gallery, 1972, Contemporary Art Center Cin., 1973, Coll. Marin Galleries, 1974, JPL Gallery, London, Eng., 1975, Yellowstone Art Center, Billings, Mont., 1976, Renwick Gallery, Nat. Coll. Fine Arts, Washington, 1976-77, Falkirk Center, San Rafael, Calif., 1980, Transam. Bldg. Gallery, San Francisco, 1982, San Francisco Mus. Modern Art, 1983, Otis Art Inst. Parsons Sch. Design, 1984, Fendrick Gallery, 1984, William Sawyer Gallery, San Francisco, 1985, 93, Iannetti Lanzone Gallery, 1987, Meml. Union Art Gallery, U. Calif. Davis, 1988, Civic Arts Gallery, Walnut Creek, Calif., 1988, Contantine Grimaldis Gallery, Balt., 1988, 87, Gallery, San Francisco, 1989, Cologne (Germany) Art Fair, 1989, 92, 95, 97 Galerie Redmann, Berlin, 1990, 93, 94, Bolinas Mus., Calif., 1990, Wolk Gallery, St. Helena, Calif., 1993, 94, Oliver Art Ctr., Calif. Coll. Arts and Crafts, Oakland, Calif., 1993, Orlando (Fla.) History Mus., 1994; Sheldon Memorial Art Gallery, U Nebraska, 1996; Western book exhbt., San Francisco, 1996; The Woodson Art Museum, Wausaw, Wisconsin, 1997-98; one-man show, Poindexter Gallery, N.Y.C., 1957, 60, 63, 67, 70, Lanyon Gallery, 1965, Berkeley Gallery, 1965, William Sawyer Gallery, San Francisco, 1969, 71, 86 Galerie Thelen, Essen, 1970, San Francisco Mus. Art, 1972, U. Calif. at Santa Barbara, 1972, U. N.Mex., 1973, Ark. Arts Center, 1973, Loch Haven Art Ctr., Orlando, Fla., 1981, Stanford U. Art Mus. (Calif.), 1982, Greenville County Mus. Art (S.C.), 1982, Fuller Goldeen Gallery, San Francisco, 1983, William Sawyer Gallery, San Francisco, 1987, Iannetti-Lanzone Gallery, San Francisco, 1989, C. Grimaldis Gallery, Balt., 1989, Galerie Redmann, Berlin, 1990, 95, Michael Himovitz Gallery, Sacramento, 1993, Bolinas (Calif.) Mus., 1999, Fresno (Calif.) Art Mus., 1999; founder Wrongtree Press, 1973; collaborator (with Leni Alexander): on aspects of ballet A False Alarm on the Nightbell Once Answered-It Cannot Be Made Good, Not Ever; contbr. Art in Am. Illus. Torso (Dorothy Schmidt), 1974, Paul Harris (Dennis Leon, Harry Abrams, 1975); drawings for Pas d'Une, 1979; writer, drawings Phases of the Moon, 1995; design of book Motives and Cues by Marguerite Harris, 1993, lithgraphs Paradise: Variations, 1996; Paul Harris, drawings, 1998, sculpture, 1999. Recipient Longview Found. grant, 1960, Neallie Sullivan award, 1967; Tamarind fellow, 1969-70; named Miembro Academico de la Facultad de Bellas Artes Universidad Catolica de Chile, 1962; resident Macdowell Colony, 1977; grantee Lebovitz Fund, 1978; Guggenheim fellow 1979. Address: PO Box 930 Bolinas CA 94924-0930

HARRIS, PAUL LYNWOOD, aerospace transportation executive; b. Richmond, Va., May 30, 1945; s. Paul Lynwood Sr. and Marjorie (Southward) H.; m. Susan Lee, Sept. 20, 1969; children: Meredith Lynn, Joanna Lee. AA, Ferrum Coll., 1965; BS, U. Richmond, 1967. CPA, Va. Staff acct. Price Waterhouse & Co., Washington, 1967-71, sr. acct., 1971-73; v.p. fin. Universal Restoration Inc., Washington, 1973-76; treas. Hawker Siddely Aviation Inc., Washington, 1976-78; treas. Brit. Aerospace Inc., Herndon, Va., 1978-81, v.p. fin., 1981-86, sr. v.p. fin., 1986-88; fin. dir. Brit. Aerospace Comml. Aircraft, Hatfield, Eng., 1988-92; sr. v.p. adminstrn. Brit. Aerospace, Inc., Herndon, Va., 1992-93; sr. v.p., gen. mgr. Brit. Aerospace N.Am., Inc., Herndon, Va., 1993-99; mem. chief adminstrv. offices coun. Conf. Bd., 1993—. Bd. dirs. Reflectone, Inc., Cheshire Homes No. Va., Arlington, 1986, Washington Dulles Task Force, 1993—, Dulles Area Transport Assn., 1993-95; chmn. fin. com. United Christian Parish, Reston, Va., 1979. Mem. AICPA, Nat. Aviation Club (pres. 1995-96), Fin. Execs. Inst. Methodist. Home: 2525 Heath Pl Reston VA 20191-4224 Office: Brit Aerospace NAm Inc Ste 200 15000 Conf Ctr Dr Chantilly VA 20151-3819

HARRIS, PENELOPE CLAIRE, children's center administrator, consultant; b. Martinez, Calif., Aug. 20, 1952; d. John R. and Watrine (Spencer) H.; children: Sara A. Davidson, Rachel L. Harris. AA, Diablo Valley Coll., Pleasant Hill, Calif., 1973; BA, San Francisco State U., 1975; MA, Calif. State U., Hayward, 1993. Teaching credential, community colls. instr. credential, Calif. Tchr. spinning Albany (Calif.) Adult Sch., 1976; guest instr. U. Calif. Extension, Berkeley, 1978; tchr. Martinez Early Childhood Ctr., 1981-83, YWCA Child Care Ctr., Pacheco, Calif., 1986-87; co-dir. Martinez Parent Coop. Nursery Sch., 1983-87; program dir. YWCA of Contra Costa County, Pacheco, 1987-90; assoc. Internat. Child Resource Inst., Berkeley, 1988-92; dir. Escondido Children's Ctr., Stanford, Calif., 1990-92; coord. Sch. Age Parenting and Infant Devel. Program, Hayward, Calif., 1992—; teen pregnancy prevention coord. Helen Turner Children's Ctr., Hayward, Calif., 1995—, latchkey coord., 1998—; textile arts cons. Judy Chicago's Through the Flower Corp., Benecia, Calif., 1986-87; instr. Chabot Coll., Hayward, Calif., 1996-97. Bd. dirs. Through the Flower, Belen, N.Mex., 1999—. Mem. AAUW, Calif. Assn. Concerned with Sch. Age Parents, Calif. School-Age Consortium, Delta Kappa Gamma. Office: Helen Turner Children's Ctr 23640 Reed Way Hayward CA 94541-7326

HARRIS, PENNY SMITH, fundraising consultant; b. Old Town, Maine, Apr. 6, 1941; d. Owen Halbert and Louise Marion (Whitten) Smith; m. Parker Fred Harris, June 22, 1963 (div. 1992); children: Susan Leslie, Nancy Lynne. BS in Sociology, U. Maine, 1963; MS in Bus. Mgmt., Husson Coll., 1984. Social worker Elizabeth Lund Home, Burlington, Vt., 1964-65; pub. sch. tchr. Essex Junction, Vt.; asst. dir. devel., corp. support mgr. Maine Pub. Broadcasting Network, Bangor, 1985-89; dir. devel. Eastern Maine Healthcare, Bangor, 1989-94; dir. healthcare campaign N.E. Health, Rockland, Maine, 1994-97; sr. assoc. Copley Davenport Co., Inc., Wenham, Mass., 1997-98, M. Davenport Assocs., 1998—. Trustee Maine Pub. Broadcasting Corp., 1991-95, Maine Coast Artists, 1993—, U. Maine System, 1991—; mem. task force on campaign fin. Senator George Mitchell, Augusta, Maine, 1983; mem. All Am. City selection award jury Nat. Civil League, N.Y.C., 1987; bd. dirs. Greater Bangor United Way, 1990-93. Mem. LWV (pres. Bangor-Brewer chpt. 1979-81, state pres. 1982-85, nat. bd. dirs. 1986-88, sec. nat. bd. dirs. 1988-90, project dir. TV polit. debates Bangor 1982, project dir. Nat. Security and You Conf., Portland, Maine 1983), U. Maine Alumni Assn. (v.p. bd. dirs. 1991—), Greater Portland C. of C. Democrat. Methodist. Avocations: skiing, tennis, travel, running, biking. Home and Office: PO Box 2862 S Portland ME 04116-2862

HARRIS, PHILIP JOHN, engineering educator; b. Montreal, Que., Can., Mar. 22, 1926; s. Thomas Percival and Gladys Marion (Gillett) H.; m. Norma Joyce Maynard, May 23, 1953; children: Elizabeth Joyce Harris Richardson, Janet Constance. B.Sc., U. Man., 1948; M.Eng., McGill U., 1949, Ph.D., 1964. Structural designer Dominion Bridge Co. Ltd., Lachine, Que., 1949-51; chief civil engr. C.D. Howe Co., Ltd., Montreal, 1951-58; asst. prof. dept. civil engring. McGill U., Montreal, 1958-59, assoc. prof., 1959-73, prof. dept. civil engring., 1973-91, chmn. dept., 1977-84, bd. govs., 1975-82, prof. emeritus, 1993—; prof. dept. civil engring. McMaster U., Hamilton, Ont., 1991-95; cons. structural and found. engring., 1958-91; cons. engr., 1991-97. Contbr. articles to profl. jours. NRC Can. grantee, 1965-79; Natural Scis. and Engring. Research Council grantee, 1979-87. Fellow Can. Soc. Civil Engring., Engring. Inst. Can.; mem. ASCE (life). Anglican. Home and Office: 408 Sawnson Ct, Burlington, ON Canada L7R 4G6

HARRIS, PHILIP ROBERT, management and space psychologist; b. Bklyn., Jan. 22, 1926; s. Gordon Roger and Esther Elizabeth (Delahanty) H.; m. Dorothy Lipp, July 3, 1965 (dec. 1997). B.B.A., St. John's U., 1949; M.S. in Psychology, Fordham U., 1952, Ph.D., 1956; spl. student, NYU, 1948-49, Syracuse U., 1961. Lic. psychologist U. of State of N.Y., 1959, N.Y. Dir. guidance St. Francis Prep. Sch., N.Y.C., 1952-56; dir. student personnel, v.p. St. Francis Coll., N.Y.C., 1956-63; exec. dir. Assn. Human Emergency-Thomas Murray Tng. Program, 1964-66; vis. prof. Pa. State U., 1965-66; vis. prof., cons. Temple U.; sr. assoc. Leadership Resources Inc., 1966-69; v.p. Copley Internat. Corp., La Jolla, Calif., 1970-71; pres. Mgmt. and Orgn. Devel. Inc. (now Harris Internat. Ltd.), La Jolla, 1971—; edn. dir. Air/Space Am., 1988; sr. scientist Netrologic, Inc., La Jolla, Calif., 1990-93; rsch. assoc. Calif. Space Inst., U. Calif., San Diego, 1984-90; adj. prof. Pepperdine U., U. No. Colo.; acad. adv. Command Coll., Commn. on Peace Officers Stds. and Tng. State of Calif., Dept. Justice, 1986-94; past cons. Westinghouse, N.V. Philips, I.B.M., Computer Sci. Corp. Control Data, govt. agys.; chmn. bd. dirs. United Socs. in Space, Inc., 1993-97. Author: Effective Management of Change, 1976, Improving Management Communication Skills, 1978, Managing Cultureal Differences, 1979, 3d edit., 1991, 4th edit., 1996, New Worlds, New Ways, New Management, 1983, Managing Cultural Synergy, 1982, Management in Transition, 1985, Living and Working in Space, 1992, 2d edit., 1996, High Performance Leadership, 2d edit., 1994, New Work Culture, 1998; co-author: Transcultural Leadership, 1993, Developing Global Organizations, 1993, Multicultural Management 2000, 1998, Developing Global Organizations, 1993, Multicultural Law Enforcement, 1995; editor: Innovations in Global Consultation, 1980, Global Strategies in Human Resource Development, 1983; author (series) New Work Culture, 3 vols., 1994-98; co-editor Manging Cultural Differences Series Gulf Pubs., Houston, 1990—; mem. editl. bd. European Bus. Rev.; founding editor emeritus Space Governance Jour., 1993-98; contbr. 200 articles to profl. jours. V.p. Bklyn. Downtown Renewal Effort, 1957-59. Naemd to Gulf Pub. Author Hall of Fame, 1999; Fulbright prof. to India U.S. State Dept., 1962; NASA faculty fellow, 1984. Fellow AIAA (assoc.); mem. ASTD (Torch award 1975), Aviation Space Writers Assn. (journalism awards 1986, 88, 89, 93), World Bar Assn. (Space Humanitarian award1992), Nat. Space Soc., United Socs. in Space (dir. emeritus), Soc. for Human Performance in Extreme Environments, La Jolla Beach and Tennis Club. Independent. Home and Office: 2702 Costebelle Dr La Jolla CA 92037-3524

HARRIS, RALPH WILLIAM, religious journalist; b. Detroit; s. Charles and Georgia Alice (Stilwell) H.; m. M. Estelle Overton, Apr. 16, 1938; children: Carole Estelle, Sharon Beth Snyder. Diploma, Ctrl. Bible Inst., 1937, BA, 1961, MA, 1969. Pastor Faith Tabernacle, Clio, Mich, 1938-43; nat. youth leader Assemblies of God, Springfield, Mo., 1943-48; pastor Fremont-Tabernacle, Seattle, 1948-54; editor-in-chief sch. lit. Assemblies of God, Springfield, Mo., 1954-76, exec. editor Complete Biblical Libr., 1983-91; semi-ret.; editor in chief ch. sch. lit. Assemblies of God, Springfield, Mo., 1954-76. Author: (book) Now What, 1964, Spoken by the Spirit, 1973, Acts Today, 1994; producer column Assembly Lines, 1956-86; contbr. numerous articles to profl. jours. Founder Langston Neighborhood Watch, Springfield, 1983; ad hoc chmn. for Ozarks Crime Prevention Coun., Springfield, 1989; occasional column News-Leader, Springfield, 1993—. Named hon. mem. Evang. Press Assn. Avocation: directing more than 30 tours to Middle East. Home: 2322 E Langston St Springfield MO 65804-2648

HARRIS, RAYMOND JESSE, retired government official; b. Van Buren, N.Y., Dec. 28, 1916; s. Francis Elbert and Anna Marie (Selinsky) H.; m. Rosalba Emilia Prestianni, Jan. 7, 1950 (dec. 1989). A.B., Harvard U., 1940, postgrad., 1940-42; postgrad., U. Pa., 1952-54, 59-60. Corr. drafter U.S. State Dept., Washington, 1947; vice consul Am. consulate palermo, Italy, 1947-50, Munich, Germany, 1950-51; personnel technician, information officer City of Phila., 1952-59, administrv. asst. to water commr., 1959-79; ret., 1979; Republican committeeman 59th ward City of Phila., 1986-98. *As American vice consul in Sicily (1947-50), he wrote numerous reports on the political and economic affairs of that island at a time when Italy was being revived under the Marshal Plan. These reports were of much help to American authorities. Drawn to Philadelphia by municipal reform (1952), he became a public relations official, serving various mayors and city departments. Author of numerous reports, brochures for the public transit study committee (1963). This contributed to creation of the Southeastern Pennsylvania Transportation Authority. Also author of a book "The New City Government" (1955).* Served with USAAF, 1942-45; ETO. Named Water Dept. Supr. of Year, 1971, 72, 73, 76; recipient Ted Moses award Pa. Water Pollution Control Assn., 1978. Mem. Am. Water Works Assn., Archeol. Inst. Am., Amnesty Internat. USA, Nat. Trust Historic Preservation, Pa. Hist. Soc., Acad. Polit. Sci., Am. Anti-Vivisection Soc., Planetary Soc., Harvard of Phila. Club, Germantown Rep. Home: 275 W Tulpehocken St Philadelphia PA 19144-3209

HARRIS, RICHARD A., film editor. Works include: (films) Downhill Racer, 1969, Dusty and Sweets McGee, 1971, The Christian Licorice Store, 1971, The Candidate, 1972, Chandler, 1972, Catch My Soul, 1974, Smile, 1975, The Bad News Bears, 1976, Semi-Tough, 1977, The Bad News Bears Go To Japan, 1978, An Almost Perfect Affair, 1979, The Island, 1980, The Toy, 1982, The Survivors, 1983, Fletch, 1985, Tiger Town, 1985, The Golden Child, 1986, Wildcats, 1986, The Couch Trip, 1988, Fletch Lives, 1989, L.A. Story, 1991, The Bodyguard, 1992, Terminator 2: Judgement Day, 1991 (Acad. award nomination, Emmy nomination), True Lies, 1994 (Emmy nomination); (TV films) A Mother's Courage: The Mary Thomas Story, 1990, My Boyfriend's Back, 1990, Indictment: The McMartin Trial (Emmy award, Outstanding Individual Achievement in Editing for a Mini Series of a Spl. 1995, ADB Cable ACF award 1995). Office: care Lawrence Mirisch The Mirisch Agency 10100 Santa Monica Blvd Ste 700 Los Angeles CA 90067-4100*

HARRIS, RICHARD ANTHONY SIDNEY, trust company executive; b. Bklyn., Dec. 22, 1940; s. Stanley Sidney and Rose (Franquelli) H.; m. Sharon Lynne Harvey, Dec. 21, 1975 (div. 1998); 1 child, Aaron Nathaniel Graeme. Student St. John's U., Jamaica, N.Y., 1958-61. Adminstr. Harris Trust, N.Y.C., 1972—, trustee, 1972—; adminstr. Beehive Trading Co., Provo, Utah, 1980—, Aaron Reseda Med., Calif., 1976—; pres. Reseda Mgmt., 1976—, also dir.; pres. World Perspective, 1995—. Mem. Am. Assn. Individual Investors, Internat. Platform Assn., Heritage Found. Roman Catholic. Office: PO Box 1197 Simi Valley CA 93062-1197

HARRIS, RICHARD EUGENE VASSAU, lawyer; b. Detroit, Mar. 16, 1945; s. Joseph S. and Helen Harris; m. Milagros A. Brito; children: Catherine, Byron. AB, Albion Coll., 1967; JD, Harvard U., 1970; postdoctoral, Inst. Advanced Legal Studies, London, 1970-71. Bar: Calif. 1972. Assoc. Orrick, Herrington, Rowley & Sutcliffe, San Francisco, 1972-77; ptnr. Orrick, Herrington & Sutcliffe, San Francisco, 1978-98; pvt. practice Oakland, Ca., 1998—; faculty Calif. Tax Policy Conf., 1987, 95; spkr. univ., govtl. and profl. groups. Mem. Christian Edn. Bd., Piedmont (Calif.) Community Ch., 1983-86. Knox fellow Harvard U., 1970-71. Mem. ABA (urban state and local govt. sect. 1983-88, vice chmn. govt. liability com. 1982-84, antitrust law sect. state action com. 1981—, BOULDER task force 1983-84, internat. com. 1994—, litigation sect. corp. counsel com., subcom. chmn. 1980-82, 83—, vice chmn. 1982-83, tax litigation com. 1992—, co-chmn. Nat. Insts. Antitrust Liability 1983, 85, bus. law sect., SEC investigation atty.-client privilege waiver task force 1988, corp. counsel com., 1995—, conflicts of interest task force 1993-96, conflicts of interest com., 1996—, tax sect., state and local taxes com. 1989—, Ctr. for Profl. Responsibility ABA Ethics 2000 adv. group 1999—), Am. Law Inst. (cons. restatements of law unfair competition 1991-94, governing lawyers 1991-99, torts 1993—, agy. 1996—, trusts 1996—), Bar Assn. San Francisco (ethics com., 1980—).

HARRIS, RICHARD FOSTER, JR., insurance company executive; b. Athens, Ga., Feb. 8, 1918; s. Richard Foster and Mai Audli (Chandler) H.; m. Virginia McCurdy, Aug. 21, 1937 (div.); children: Richard Foster, Gaye Karyl Harris Law; m. Kari Melandso, Dec. 29, 1962. BCS, U. Ga., 1939. Bookkeeper, salesman 1st Nat. Bank, Atlanta, 1936-40; agt. Vol. State Life Ins. Co., Atlanta, 1940-41; asst. mgr. N.Y. Life Ins. Co., Atlanta and Charlotte, N.C., 1941-44; mgr., agt. Pilot Life Ins. Co., Charlotte and Houston, 1944-63; mgr., agt. bus. planning div.; city agy. Am. Gen. Life Ins. Co., Houston, 1963—; bd. dirs. Fidelity Bank & Trust Co., Houston, 1965-66, mem. bd. business devel., Sterling Bank, Upper Kirby Br., 1996. Chmn. fund drive Am. Heart Assn., Charlotte, Mecklenburg County, 1958-59, chmn. bd., 1959-61; gen. chmn. Shrine Bowl Promotion, Charlotte Shriners, 1955; v.p., bd. dirs. Myers Park Meth. Ch. Men's Class, 1956-59, bd. stewards, Charlotte, 1959-61; bd. dirs. Houston Polit. Action Com., 1982—; charter mem. Rep. Presdl. Task Force, pres., 1981-90; at large del. Rep. Nat. Convention Planning Platform, Houston, 1992; co-chmn. Christian Community Service Ctr., 1984-90; mem. First Tuesday Group, Houston, 1985—; tchr. Mens's Bible class St. John the Divine Ch., 1963-93; founder Episcopal High Sch., Houston, 1984. Recipient Pres.'s Cabinet award Am. Gen. Life Ins. Co., 1964-67, 69, 71, 77-83, Disting. Salesman award Charlotte Sales Exec. Club, 1955, 57-59, Bronze Medallion award Am. Heart Assn., 1959, Nat. Quality awards, 1965-92, The Rep. Presdl. Legion of Merit award, 1992; named Adm. of Tex. Nav. Gov. of Tex., 1989. Mem. Assn. Advanced Life Underwriters, Am. Soc. CLUs, Nat. Assn. Life Underwriters, SAR (Good Citizenship award 1991), Life Underwriters Polit. Action Com. (life), Houston Estate and Fin. Forum, English Speaking Union, Mensa Internat., Houston Assn. Life Underwriters, Lone Star Leaders Club, Tex. Leader's Round Table (life), Million Dollar Round Table (life), Tex. Assn. Life Underwriters, Am. Security Council (nat. adv. bd. 1979—), Houston Club, 100 Club, Deerwood Club, Forum Club of Houston, Pachyderm Club, Campaigner Club, Tex. Circle Club, Kiwanis (bd. dirs. 1979—), Masons (32 degree), Shriners, Sertoma (life, v.p. bd. dirs. Charlotte chpt.), Royal Order Jesters. Episcopalian. Home: 2701 Westheimer Rd Houston TX 77098-1243 Office: Am Gen Life Ins Co Wortham Tower 2727 Allen Pkwy Ste 104 Houston TX 77019-2100

HARRIS, RICHARD FOSTER, III, lawyer; b. Charlotte, N.C., Apr. 10, 1942; s. Richard Foster and Frances Virginia (McCurdy) H.; m. Jacqueline Kaplan; children—Richard Foster, IV, John Walter Rodney. A.B. in English, Duke U., 1964; J.D., U. N.C., Chapel Hill, 1967. Bar: N.C. 1967, U.S. Dist. Ct. (we. dist.) N.C. 1971, U.S. Ct. Appeals (4th cir.) 1973. Assoc. Eugene C. Hicks III, Charlotte, 1968-70; ptnr. Hicks, Harris & Sterrett and predecessor Hicks & Harris, Charlotte, 1970-81; sole practice, Charlotte, 1982—. Served with Air N.G., 1967-73. Mem. ABA, N.C. State Bar, N.C. Bar Assn. (Outstanding Young Lawyer award 1977, chmn. Young Lawyers Sect. 1977-78), Assn. Trial Lawyers Am., N.C. Acad. Trial Lawyers, Mecklenburg County Bar Assn. (chmn. young lawyers sect. 1976-77). Democrat. Presbyterian. Club: Myers Park Country (Charlotte). Home: 329 Cherokee Pl Charlotte NC 28207-2301 Office: 757B Providence Rd Charlotte NC 28207-2245

HARRIS, RICHARD JOHN, diversified holding company executive; b. Attleboro, Mass., July 19, 1936; s. John Francis and Lauretta Louise (Tharl) H.; m. Carole Mae St. Pierre, May 11, 1963; children—Mark Richard, Pamela Jean. Assoc. Sci. in Acctg., Bentley Coll., 1962. C.P.A., Mass., R.I. Mgmt. trainee Gen. Motors Corp., Wilmington, Del., 1962-65; mem. audit staff Price Waterhouse & Co., Providence, 1965-69; internat. controller metal and electronic products group Tex. Instruments, Inc., Attleboro, Mass., 1969-72; v.p., treas., dir. Nortek, Inc., Providence, 1972—. Served with USAF, 1954-58. Fellow Mass. Soc. C.P.A.s; mem. Am. Inst. C.P.A.s. Roman Catholic. Office: Nortek Inc 50 Kennedy Plz Ste 1700 Providence RI 02903-2360

HARRIS, RICHARD JOHN, social sciences educator; b. Belgrade, Minn., Apr. 5, 1948; s. Johnny Lee and Marjorie (Meyers) H.; m. Carolyn Besser (div. 1993); children: Karl, Mark; m. Juanita M. Gillette Firestone, Apr. 19, 1994. BA, Macalester Coll., 1971; MA, Cornell U., 1974, PhD, 1976. From asst. to assoc. prof. U. Tex., San Antonio, 1976—. Contbr. articles to profl. jours.; editor: The Politics of San Antonio: Community Progress and Power, 1983. Active Odyssey of the Mind, San Antonio Sch. Sys., 1994-95; mem. faculty adv. com. U. Tex. Sys., Austin, 1994-96; sec. gen. faculty U. Tex., 1991-96. Staff sgt. USAFR, 1969-74. Recipient cert. of achievement Black Legis. Caucus, U.S. Congress, 1996; postdoctoral fellow U. So. Calif., 1980-82. Mem. Am. Sociol. Assn., Population Assn. of Am., Am. Acad. Polit. and Social Scis., Southwestern Social Sci. Assn., Tex. Econ. and Demographic Assn. (bd. dirs.), Alpha Kappa Delta. Office: U Tex San Antonio Divsn Social & Policy Scis San Antonio TX 78249

HARRIS, RICHARD LEE, engineering executive, retired army officer; b. Bellevue, Pa., Dec. 26, 1928; s. Everett Lee and Marjorie Anna (Messer) H.; m. Patricia Ann Walton, Dec. 12, 1953; children: Sandra Jo, Carole Jill, William Walton, Robert Lee. B.S., U.S. Mil. Acad., West Point, N.Y., 1951; student, Army Engr. Sch., 1951, 59; M.S., MIT, 1956; grad., Oak Ridge Sch. Reactor Tech., 1957, Command and Gen. Staff Coll., 1963, Nat. War Coll., 1967. Designated sr. parachutist, nuclear reactor comdr. registered profl. engr., Pa., Tex. Commd. 2d lt. U.S. Army, 1951, advanced through grades to maj. gen., 1973; with (32d Engrs. Combat Bn.), 1951; co-comdr. (13th Engrs. Combat Bn., 7th Inf. Div.), Korea, 1952-53; res. engr. (Phila. Engrs. Dist.), 1953-54; engrs. supply officer Columbus Depot, 1954-55; tech. ops. officer AEC, N.Y.C., 1957-59; officer in charge (SM-1A Nuclear Power Plant), Alaska, 1960-62; with (U.S. STRIKE Command), 1963-65; bn. comdr. (20th Engrs. Combat Bn.), Vietnam, 1965-66; with Office Chief of Staff, U.S. Army, 1967-68, Hdqrs. U.S. Army Pacific, 1968-70; comdr. div. support command (1st Cav. Div.), Vietnam, 1970-71; asst. comdt. Army Engrs. Sch., 1971-73; dir. mgmt. info. systems Office Chief Staff Army, Hdqrs. Dept. Army, 1973-76; comdr. U.S. Army Tng. Center-Engr. and Ft. Leonard Wood, Mo., 1976-78; div. engr. North Central Engr. Div., 1978-80; ret., 1980; v.p. Radian Corp., Austin, 1980-93; ret., 1993. Decorated D.S.M., Legion of Merit with 4 oak leaf clusters, Bronze Star with 2 oak leaf clusters, Air medal with 4 numerals, Joint Services Commendation medal, Purple Heart. Fellow Soc. Am. Mil. Engrs.; mem. Assn. U.S. Army, Ret. Officers Assn., Nat. Soc. Profl. Engrs., Phi Kappa Phi. Home: 8817 Balcones Club Dr Austin TX 78750-3042

HARRIS, R(ICHARD) STEVEN, data processing executive, consultant, educator; b. Kansas City, Kans., Aug. 3, 1949; s. George Joseph and Bonnie Jean (Knecht) H.; m. Phyllis Lea Stopp, Aug. 29, 1970; children: April Lea, Steven Erhardt. BA magna cum laude, Knox Coll.; MS in Edn., Western Ill. U.; postgrad., Columbia Pacific U. Cert. secondary tchr., sch. guidance counselor, Ill.; cert. vocat. and tech. adult edn. tchr., Wis. Sci. tchr., counselor Brimfield (Ill.) High Sch., 1972-74, grad. of five factories, Galesburg, Ill., 1971-72, 74-80; plant mgr. Jacobson Barrel Corp., Milw., 1980-82; ind. systems cons. Milw. area, 1982-84; programmer Effective Mgmt. Systems, Milw., 1984-85; systems and programming tchr. Milw. Bus. Tng. Inst., 1985-86; programmer, customer support analyst, software package quality assurance specialist Systems For Profit, Inc., Milw., 1986-89; mgr. MIS Gendex Corp., Milw., 1989; ind. cons./contract programmer Milw., 1989-90, 91-92; staff analyst, cons. CAP Gemini Am., Milw., 1990-91; bus. math. systems and programming tchr. Milw. Area Tech. Coll., 1987-91; sr. systems and tech. cons. Chaney Systems, Inc., New Berlin, Wis., 1992-95; sr. cons., founder JoB Sys. LLC, Oak Creek, Wis., 1996—; ind. rep. Excel Comm., regional dir., regional tng. dir., 1999—. Pastor Covenant Apostolic Ch. Greater Milw. area, 1991—. Fellow Am. Prodn. and Inventory Control Soc. (fellow cert. inst. Milw. 1985-87); mem. Creation Sci. Soc. Milw. (program chmn. 1985-86), Creation Rsch. Soc. (life), Creation Social Sci. and Humanities Soc. (voting), Inst. Cert. Computer Profls. (cert. computer profl. with six specializations, cert. data processor, cert. bus., sci. and operating systems computer programmer, charter mem., voting mem.), Assn. Systems Mgmt. (cert. systems profl.), Soc. Data Educators (cert.), Phi Beta Kappa. Mem. Covenant Apostolic Ch. Avocations: swimming, bicycling, home bible study, research activities, teaching and pastoring ministry. Home and Office: 10853 S Nicholson Rd Oak Creek WI 53154-7015 *Personal philosophy: I believe in the Lord Jesus Christ as my Creator-God, Savior, Lord, and King. In all things we should prayerfully ask, "What would Jesus do?".*

HARRIS, RIVKAH, liberal arts educator; b. Mar. 18, 1928. BA, Lake Forest Coll., 1950; PhD, U. Chgo., 1954. Assoc. prof. religion Northwestern U., Evanston, Ill., 1973-78; assoc. prof. liberal arts Sch. Art Inst. Chgo., 1985—. Office: Sch Art Inst Chgo Liberal Arts Dept 37 S Wabash St Chicago IL 60603

HARRIS, ROBERT DALTON, history educator, researcher, writer; b. Jamieson, Oreg., Dec. 24, 1921; s. Charles Sinclair and Dorothy (Cleveland) H.; m. Ethel Imus, June 26, 1971. BA, Whitman Coll., Walla Walla, Wash., 1951; MA, U. Calif., Berkeley, 1953, PhD, 1959. Tchg. asst. U. Calif., Berkeley, 1956-59; instr. history U. Idaho, Moscow, 1959-61, asst. prof., 1961-68, assoc. prof., 1968-74, prof. history, 1974-86, prof. emeritus, 1986—. Author: (Book) Necker, Reform Statesman of Ancient Regime, 1979, Necker & Revolution of 1789, 1986. 1st lt., U.S. Army, 1942-46; Ballet Folk of Moscow, Idaho, (bd. dirs., 1971-73), Historian, First United Methodist Church, Moscow, Idaho, 1989—. Mem. Am. Hist. Assn., Am. Assn. of U. Prof. Democrat. Methodist. Avocations: social dancing, violinist. Home: 928 E 8th St Moscow ID 83843-3851

HARRIS, ROBERT LAIRD, minister, theology educator emeritus; b. Brownsburg, Pa., Mar. 10, 1911; s. Walter William and Ella Pearl (Graves) H.; m. Elizabeth Krugar Nelson, Sept. 11, 1937 (dec. 1980); children: Grace Sears, Allegra Smick, Robert Laird; m. Anne Paxson Krauss, Aug. 1, 1981. B.S. in Chem. Engring, U. Del., Newark, 1931; postgrad, Washington U., 1931-32; Th.B., Westminster Theol. Sem., 1935, Th.M., 1937; M.A. in Oriental Studies, U. Pa., 1941; Ph.D., Dropsie Coll., 1947. Ordained to ministry Presbyn. Ch. Am., 1936; instr. Faith Theol. Sem., Phila., 1937-43, asst. prof. Bibl. Exegesis, 1943-47, prof. Bibl. Exegesis, 1947-56; prof. Covenant Theol. Sem., St. Louis, 1956-81, dean, 1964-71, prof. emeritus, 1981—; vis. lectr. Wheaton Coll., Ill., 1957-61; prof. Winona Lake Summer Sch. of Theology, 1964, 66, 67, Near East Sch. Archaeology and Bible, Jerusalem, 1962; lectr. Japan, Korea, 1965, India, 1981, Australia, 1989; vis. prof. China Grad. Sch. Theology, Hong Kong, 1981, Freie Theologische Akademie, Giessen, Fed. Republic Germany, 1982-85, Tyndale Theol. Sem., Amsterdam, The Netherlands, 1986—, Bibl. Theol. Sem., Hatfield, Pa., 1992, J. Manoel Conceicao Presbyn. Sem., Sao Paulo, Brazil, 1995; moderator Presbyn. Ch. in Am., 1982. Author: Introductory Hebrew Grammar, 1950, Inspiration and Canonicity of the Bible, 1957, 2d ed., 1995, Man-God's Eternal Creation, 1971, You and Your Bible, 1990; editor: Theological Wordbook of the Old Testament, 2 vols., 1981, Leviticus in Expositor's Bible Commentary, Vol. 2, 1990; mem. editorial bd. New Internat. Version of Bible, 1965—, chmn., 1970-74; contbg. author various books. Trustee Bibl. Theol. Sem., Hatfield, Pa., 1985—. DuPont fellow U. Del., 1930-31; recipient first prize Zondervan Textbook Contest, 1955; Foxwell Lecture lectureship Tokyo Christian Theol. Sem., 1981. Mem. Soc. Bibl. Lit. and Exegesis, Evang. Theol. Soc. (pres. 1961), Tau Beta Pi, Phi Kappa Phi. Republican. Home: 9 Homewood Rd Wilmington DE 19803-3401 *In my ministry of over 60 years I have seen a distressing erosion of national morals and decency. But there has also been a counter-resurgence of evangelical faith. As part of this movement, I am gratified to have had a part in producing the New International Version of Bible.*

HARRIS, ROBERT M., college president. BA in Anthropology, U. Calif., Santa Barbara, 1970; MA with honors, U. Kans., 1973, PhD with honors, 1975. Life cert. cmty. coll. instr. spl. edn., counselor, supr., psychology instr., chief adminstr. Dir. Kansas state demographic studies U. Kans. Med. Ctr., United Way of Wyandotte County, 1973-75; sr. clin. rehab. psychologist Casa Colina Hosp. for Rehab. Medicine, Pomona, Calif., 1976; program mgr. Casa Colina Hosp. for Rehab. Medicine, Pomona, 1976-77; dist. specialist programs for students devel. disabilities Chaffey C.C., Alta Loma, Calif., 1977-79, dist. dir. spl. edn., 1981; acting assoc. dean student svcs. Chaffey C.C., Alta Loma, 1981, acting supt., pres., 1985, v.p., bus. and student svcs., 1985-86, v.p. student svcs., 1981-87; pres. Sacramento City Coll., 1987—; cons. and presenter in field. Contbr. articles to profl. publs. Bd. dirs. United Way, Sacramento, bd. chair 1998—. Named Affirmative Action Officer of Yr., 1980-81; doctoral fellow U. Kans., 1974-75; recipient various grants. Mem. Assn. of Calif. C.C. Adminstrs., Calif. C.C. Chief Student Svcs. Adminstrs. Assn. (v.p. southern sect.), Nat. Assn. of Student Pers. Adminstrs., Am. Psychol. Assn. (divsn. 22 rehab. psychology), Calif. Assn. of Post-Secondary Educators for the Disabled, Easter Seal Soc. of Superior Calif. (bd. dirs.). Office: Sacramento City Coll 3835 Freeport Blvd Sacramento CA 95822-1386

HARRIS, ROBERT NORMAN, advertising and communications educator; b. St. Paul, Feb. 11, 1920; s. Nathan and Esther (Roberts) H.; m. Paula Nidorf, May 2, 1992; children: Claudia, Robert Norman, Randolph B. B.A., U. Minn., 1940. A founder Toni Co., div. Gillette Co., 1940-55; exec. v.p. Lee King & Ptnrs., Chgo., 1955-60, Allen B. Wrisley Co., Chgo., 1960-62, North Advt., Chgo., 1962-72; pres. Robert Piguet, Ltd., Chgo., 1972-73, Westbrook/Harris, Inc., Chgo., 1973-77; exec. v.p., gen. mgr. Creamer Inc., Chgo., 1977-81; pres. The Harris Creative Group, Inc., 1981—; prof. advt. and mass communications San Jose State U. (Calif.), 1983-92. Bd. dirs. KTEH Pub. Broadcasting Sys. Found., San Jose, 1987—, CHM Villages Golf and Country Club CATV Sys., 1995—. Mem. NATAS, Am. Mktg. Assn., Am. Advt. Fedn., Am. Assn. Advt. Agys., Sons in Retirement (bd. dirs. 1986-90).

HARRIS, ROBERTA LUCAS, social worker; b. St. Louis, Nov. 13, 1916; d. Robert Joseph and Clara Louise (Mellor) Lucas; AB, St. Louis U., 1955, MSW, 1964; m. William F. Sprengnether Jr., Aug. 21, 1937 (dec. 1951); children: Robert Lucas, Madelon Sprengnether Littlejohn, Ronald John; m. Victor B. Harris, Sept. 13, 1955 (dec. June 1960). Field instr. Sch. Social Work St. Louis U., 1967-70; chief of domestic rels. City of St. Louis, 1966-86. Dir., Citizens' Housing Coun., 1956-60; del. to Community Family Life Clinic, 1957; dir. Landmarks Assn., 1957-63; pres. Compton Heights Improvement Assn., 1973, bd. dirs., 1994-96; hon. mem. Normandy Hist. Assn., 1995. NIMH grantee. Mem. NASW, Mo. Assn. Social Workers, Assn. Family Conciliation Cts. (dir. 1968-86), Greater St. Louis Probation and Parole Assn. (sec. 1976), St. Louis U. Sch. Social Svc. Alumni Assn. (sec. 1973), LWV (dir. 1956-61), Wednesday Club. Methodist. Home: 3137 Longfellow Blvd Saint Louis MO 63104-1609

HARRIS, ROGER CLARK, psychiatrist, consultant; b. Washington, Aug. 27, 1938; s. Lester Wilbur and Margaret Elizabeth (Gilligan) H.; m. Ann Marie Dorman, Sept. 22, 1962; children: Laura Colleen, Gregory Scott Henry. BS, U. Md., 1961; postgrad., U. Md., College Park, 1961-62; MD, U. Md., Balt., 1964-68. Diplomate Am. Bd. Med. Examiners, Am. Bd. Psychiatry and Neurology. Intern Washington Hosp. Ctr., 1968-69; resident in psychiatry U. Md. Med. Sch., 1969-72; staff psychiatrist Portsmouth (Va.) Psychiat. Ctr., 1972-73, Larry H. Dizmang and Assoc., Annapolis, Md., 1973-74; pvt. practice Annapolis, 1974-75; prin. Roger C. Harris Group Practice of Psychiatry and Assocs., Annapolis, 1975—; pres. Chesapeake Comprehensive Counseling Ctrs., Inc., Washington and Balt., 1988-96; co-founder Psychiatry Consultation Svc. of Baltimore City Police Dept., 1970-72; chief psychiatry svc. Anne Arundel Gen. Hosp., Annapolis, 1978-81; asst. clin. prof. psychiatry U. Md. Sch. Medicine, 1973—; acting dir. of outpatient clinic U. Md. Emergency Psychiat. Svcs., 1971-72, chief resident, 1971-72; primary founder psychiatry dept. Anne Arundel Gen. Hosp. Mem. Disability Rev. Bd. for Anne Arundel County, 1985-87, Orgn. of Physicians for Social Responsiblity, 1985—. Recipient Cert. Appreciation Arundel Lodge, Inc., Annapolis, 1988, Mitchell Scholarship, Alpha Tau Omega Social Fraternity, College Park, Md., 1960. Mem. Chesapeake Bay Psychiat. Soc., Am. Psychiat. Assn., Md. Psychiat. Soc., Anne Arundel County Med. Soc., Am. Group Psychotherapy Assn., Orthopsychiat. Assn., Epping Forest Boat Club, Young Foresters Orgn., Alpha Tau Omega (sec. 1958-60). Democrat. Presbyterian. Avocations: boating, swimming, body surfing, bodyboard surfing, classical music. Home: 212 Eareckson Ln Stevensville MD 21666-3040 Office: 1511 Ritchie Hwy Ste 201 Arnold MD 21012

HARRIS, ROGER J., mortgage company executive, entrepreneur; b. Chgo., Nov. 20, 1930; s. Stanley and Mary (Koba) Pokwinski; married, 1948 (div. Jan. 1970); 1 child, Linda; m. Betty J. Henry, Nov. 21, 1971. BS in Commerce, Roosevelt U., Chgo., 1956; postgrad., Loyola U. Law Sch., Chgo., 1959-62. Systems sales rep. Univac, Chgo., 1953-55; merchandising systems analyst Montgomery Ward, Chgo., 1956-62; cons. Haskins & Sells, Chgo., 1962-65; prin. A.T. Kearney, L.A., 1965-70; bus. cons. Roger J. Harris and Assocs., Inc., Calif. and Alaska, 1970—; chmn. bd. dirs., CEO Mortgage Co. Alaska; chmn. bd. dirs. MBI Corp.; conf. reader Am. Mgmt. Assn., L.A., 1970-82. Mem. Am. Soc. of Accts., Small Bus. Adminstrn. (chmn. score/ACE program 1990-91). Office: PO Box 210707 Anchorage AK 99521-0707

HARRIS, ROGERS SANDERS, bishop; b. Anderson, S.C., Feb. 22, 1930; s. Wilmot Louis and Sarah Elizabeth (Sanders) H.; m. Anne Marshall Stewart, Mar. 28, 1953; children: Katherine Anne, Frances Elizabeth, Rebecca Susan. *Wife Anne is the daughter of Katherine Keen Stewart and the late Rev. Dr. Marshall Bowyer Stewart. Anne and Rogers have three daughters: Katherine Anne Wood, wife of Michael David Wood, is a special education teacher in Spartanburg, South Carolina. Frances Elizabeth Harris, wife of James Taylor Jones, is a bio-statistician at the University of California in San Francisco. Rebecca Susan Brunson, wife of Michael E. Brunson, is a second grade teacher in Bamberg, South Carolina. Anne and Rogers have four grandchildren: Kristen Rebecca Wood, Jason Michael Wood, Sarah Katherine Wood, and Hannah Lynn Brunson.* BA, U. of South, 1952, MDiv, 1957, DD (hon.), 1986; D Ministry, Va. Theol. Sem., 1977, DD (hon.), 1986. Ordained deacon Episcopal Ch., 1957, priest, 1958, bishop, 1985. Vicar Grace Episcopal Ch., Ridge Spring, S.C., 1957-59, St. Paul's Episcopal Ch., Batesburg, S.C., 1957-59; rector Ch. of Good Shepherd, Greer, S.C., 1959-69, St. Christopher's Ch., Spartanburg, S.C., 1969-85; suffragan bishop Diocese of Upper S.C., Columbia, S.C., 1985-89; bishop Diocese of S.W. Fla., St. Petersburg, 1989-97; v.p. Province IV of Episcopal Ch., 1991-94, pres., 1994-97; mem. Presiding Bishop's Coun. of Advice, N.Y.C., 1994-97. Trustee U. of South, Sewanee, Tenn., 1985—; trustee, v.p. Bishop Gray Inn, Davenport, Fla., 1989-97. 1st lt. USMC, 1952-54, Korea. Mem. Order of Holy Cross (assoc.).

HARRIS, ROLAND ARSVILLE, JR., college official; b. Portsmouth, Va., July 25, 1930; s. Roland Arsville Sr. and Odelle (Thomas) H.; m. Helen Beatrice Johnson, Oct. 12, 1956; children: Roland Arsville III, Benjamin Christopher. BA, Paine Coll., 1971; MEd, U. Ga., 1972; PhD, U. Tenn., 1981. Enlisted U.S. Army, 1948, advance through grades to sgt. 1st class, 1968; from instr. to asst. prof. Knoxville (Tenn.) Coll., 1972-76, dir. institutional rsch. and planning, 1976-85, Title III coord., 2nd officer-in-charge, 1985-87, chief adminstrv. officer, 1987-88; exec. v.p., chief operating officer, 1995-96, acting pres., 1996-97; exec. dir. instnl. advancement Stillman Coll., Tuscaloosa, Ala., 1988-92. Hearing examiner U.S. Civil Svc. Merit award, Knoxville, 1985; mem. Tuscaloosa Tourism Adv. Com., 1989; loaned exec. United Way, Tuscaloosa, 1990, team capt., 1991. Mem. Am. Sociol. Assn., Optimists Internat., Phi Beta Sigma, Sigma Pi Phi. Democrat. Baptist. Avocations: reading, golf, travel, walking. Home: 802 Wildview Way Knoxville TN 37920-7605

HARRIS, RONALD DAVID, chemical engineer; b. Norman, Okla., Apr. 9, 1938; s. Loyd Ervin and Maurine Cora (Dill) H.; m. Judith Anne Wright, July 28, 1962 (div.); children: Todd David (dec.), Scott Howard, Susanna Katherine. B.Chem. Engring., Ohio State U., 1961, M.Sc., 1961; M.B.A., U. Cin., 1970; student, Chase Law Sch., Cin., 1970-71. Chem. engr. Procter & Gamble Co., Cin., 1961-62; process devel. group leader Procter & Gamble Co., 1964-71; mgr. food product devel. Clorox Co., Oakland, Calif., 1971-73; dir. R & D Clorox Co., Pleasanton, Calif., 1973-77; v.p. R & D Anderson Clayton Foods, Dallas, 1977-87; v.p. tech. Kraft Inc., Glenview, Ill., 1987-90; v.p. Kraft U.S.A. Tech., 1990-94; v.p. sci. rels. Kraft Foods, Inc., 1994-96; instr. Keller Grad. Sch. Mgmt., 1995—; assoc. dir. exec. edn., sr. lectr. Ohio State U., 1996-98. Trustee San Ramon Valley Unified Sch. Dist., 1977; mem. Richardson City Planning Commn., 1980-83, Richardson City Coun., 1983-87, Lake Forest Bldg. Rev. Bd., 1993—; bd. dirs. Richardson Symphony Orch., 1982-85, Heard Natural Sci. Mus., 1985-87, Richardson br. YMCA, 1984-87, 1st United Meth. Ch., Richardson, 1986-87, Chilled Foods Assn., 1988-94, 1st Presbyn. Ch., Lake Forest, 1988—; bd. dirs. Hull House Assn., 1988-96, vice chmn., 1993-96; mem. citizens adv. com. North Tex. Mcpl. Water Dist., 1980; mem. adv. com. doctorate in chemistry program U. Tex., Dallas, 1983-89; mem. adv. bd. dept. food sci. U. Minn., 1984-96; mem. adv. bd. dept. chem. engring. Ohio State U., 1991—, pres. Chem. Engring. Alumni Soc., 1998—; mem. adv. bd. Masters in Ops. and Tech. Ill. Inst. Tech., 1995—; mem. Leadership Richardson, 1984-87; life mem. Julian C. Hyer Youth Camp; mem. Littlefield Soc., U. Tex., Austin, 1991—. Officer U.S. Army, 1962-64. Named Disting. Alumnus, Ohio State U., 1992. Mem. Am. Chem. Soc., Inst. Food Technologists, Am. Oil Chemists Soc., Richardson C. of C. (1st v.p., dir., pres. 1982), Richardson Hist. Soc., Tex. Mcpl. League, Lake Forest Club, Lions (bd. dirs., pres. 1982-83, Tau Beta Pi, Phi Eta Sigma (past chpt. pres.), Phi Lambda Upsilon, Delta Mu Delta, Kappa Sigma (past chpt. pres., alumnus advisor 1996—). Patentee process for adsorbent bleaching oils, dry prepared fluffy frosting mixes. Home: 734 Jaeger St Columbus OH 43206-2109 Office: 618 Fisher Hall 2100 Neil Ave Columbus OH 43210

HARRIS, RONALD WILLIAM, commodities trader; b. Orange, Tex., Mar. 14, 1952; s. Harold Abraham Harris and Mary (Gaspar) Fohrman; m. Joan Fuetterer, Feb. 27, 1982 (div. July 1988); 1 child, Julie Ann. B in Fin., North Tex. State U., 1976; Securities Diplomas, Wall Street Inst., Salt Lake City, 1984. Registered broker. Broker Woodstock Commodities, Chgo., 1976-78, Fox Investment Group, Chgo., 1978—; TV commentator Commodity Update WCIV-TV, Chgo., 1982. Author: (commodity trading system) The Ron Harris Program, 1988. Tennis champion Chgo. Sun-Times Regional, Chgo., 1980, table tennis champion, So. Ill. U., Carbondale, 1971. Avocations: travel, racquetball, coaching children's sports. Office: Rosenthal-Fox Div 141 W Jackson Blvd Ste 1800A Chicago IL 60604-2982

HARRIS, ROY HARTLEY, electrical engineer; b. Madison, Ga., Dec. 17, 1928; s. Richard Paul and Florrie (Judd) H.; m. Margaret P. Pitman, Sept. 14, 1951; children: Kathryn, Audrey. BSEE, Ga. Inst. Tech., 1951; MEE, Poly. Inst. Bklyn., 1956. Sr. engr. Hazeltine Elec. Corp., Little Neck, L.I., N.Y., 1951-56; supr. Bell Telephone Labs., Burlington, N.C., 1956-64; guidance systems engring. mgr. Western Electric, Burlington, 1965-68, mgr. mil. systems engring., 1968-72; mgr. naval mil. engring. Western Electric, Winston-Salem, N.C., 1972-82; dir. govt. systems Western Electric, Greensboro, N.C., 1982-86; v.p. adv. tech systems AT&T, Greensboro, N.C., 1986-87; v.p. tech. service Triad Tech., Greensboro, 1987-88, pres., 1988—. Mem. indsl. adv. com. N.C. A&T U., Greensboro, 1983—, trustee, 1985-93; bd. dirs. Alamance Eldercare, 1993—, vice chmn., 1995, chmn., 1996-98. Fellow IEEE (bd. dirs. 1978-79, Engring. Mgr. of Yr. 1984); mem. Anak Soc. Ga. Tech., Nat. Security Indsl. Assn. (mem. ASW COM exec. com. 1983-86, mem. AAW COM exec. com. 1986-87), Rotary Internat., Omicron Delta Kappa, Phi Kappa Phi, Tau Beta Pi. Republican. Methodist. Club: Alamance Country (Burlington, N.C.).

HARRIS, ROY JAY, JR., editor, business journalist; b. St. Louis, Oct. 2, 1946; s. Roy Jay and Ruth Dorothy (Schofer) H.; m. Andrea McKenna (dec.); children: David McKenna Harris, Roy Jay Harris III. BS in Journalism, Northwestern U., 1968, MS in Journalism, 1971. Staff reporter The Wall Street Jour., Pitts., 1971-74; staff reporter The Wall Street Jour., L.A., 1974-88, dep. bur. chief, 1988-95; sr. editor CFO Mag., Boston, 1996—. With U.S. Army, 1969-70. Mem. Soc. Am. Bus. Editors and Writers, Soc. Profl. Journalists, Am. Soc. Bus. Press Editors. Office: CFO Mag 253 Summer St Fl 3 Boston MA 02210-1118

HARRIS, RUBY LEE, realtor; b. Booneville, Miss., Mar. 5, 1939; d. Carl Jackson and Gladys (Downs) Hill; m. Lee Kelly Harris, Apr. 21, 1962; children: Lee Kelly Jr., Bradford William. Student, N.E. Miss. Jr. Coll., Booneville, 1957-58, U. Ala., Tuscaloosa, 1958-59. Lic. real estate agt., Calif. Agt. Forest E. Olson, El Toro, Calif., 1974-76, Coldwell Banker, Mission Viejo, Calif., 1976-78, Associated Realtors, Mission Viejo, 1978—. Mem. Children's Home Soc. Calif., Mission Viejo, 1985-88, Boys and Girls Club Am., San Clemente, Calif., 1989-91, Capistrano, 1994-95; mem. election com. Orange County, Mission Viejo, 1974—. Mem. Nat. Assn. Realtors, Calif. Assn. Realtors, Saddleback Valley Bd. Realtors (bd. dirs. 1989). Republican. Avocations: bicycling, gardening. Office: Associated Realtors 25350 Marguerite Pkwy Ste B Mission Viejo CA 92692-2993

HARRIS, SALLY LEE, public relations coordinator; b. Saltville, Va., Nov. 29, 1945; d. Carl Howard and Barbara Harris. BS, Radford Coll., 1968, MS, 1975. English, Spanish tchr. Rural Retreat (Va.) H.S., 1968-72; reporter, columnist Smyth County News, Marion, Va., 1972-74; English tchr. Marion Sr. H.S., 1974-75; county editor Smyth County News, 1976-79; news editor The Gazette, Galax, Va., 1979-81; feature writer Roanoke (Va.) Times, 1981-84; pub. rels. coord. Va. Tech. Coll. Arts & Scis., Blacksburg, 1984—. Literacy vol., Blacksburg, 1985; reader to visually impaired WVTF Pub. Radio, Roanoke, 1986-88; vol. Montgomery County Christmas Store, Va., 1987-90; vol. Native Am. Village Explore Park, Roanoke, 1996. Mem. Nat. Fedn. Press Women, Va. Press Women (dist. dir.). Avocations: travel, music, Native American literature and studies, reading, fiction writing. Office: Va Tech 116 ASAB (0405) Blacksburg VA 24061

HARRIS, SCOTT BLAKE, lawyer; b. N.Y.C., June 18, 1951; s. Stanley Robert and Adele Jean (Ganger) H.; m. Barbara Straughn Harris, Aug. 5, 1978. AB magna cum laude, Brown U., 1973; JD magna cum laude, Harvard U., 1976. Bar: D.C. 1977, U.S. Ct. Appeals (D.C. cir.) 1978, U.S. Supreme Ct. 1983. Law clk. to presiding justice U.S. Dist. Ct., Washington, 1976-77; assoc. Williams & Connolly, Washington, 1977-84, ptnr., 1984-93; chief counsel Bur. Export Adminstrn., U.S. Dept. Commerce, Washington, 1993-94; chief internat. bur. FCC, 1994-96; ptnr. Gibson, Dunn & Crutcher, Washington, 1996-98; mng. ptnr. Harris, Wiltshire & Grannis LLP, Washington, 1998—; mem. adv. bd. Ctr. for Wireless Tech., Va. Tech. U., 1996—, Satellite Comms. Mag., 1996—, Time Domain Sys., Inc., 1999—, Critical Infrastructure Fund LLP, 1999—. Trustee Fed. Comms. Bar Assn. Found., 1997—. Mem. ABA (vice chair telecoms. com., sect. internat. law 1997—, co-chair 1999), Phi Beta Kappa. Home: 3409 Fulton St NW Washington DC 20007-1436 Office: Harris Wiltshire & Grannis LLP 1200 18th St NW Washington DC 20036-2506

HARRIS, SHELLEY FOLLANSBEE, proposal manager; b. Quantico, Va., Oct. 20; d. Lawrence Peyton and June Maynard (Trout) H. Student, Western Carolina U., 1967-69; BS in Fine Arts, Towson State U., 1974-75. Surgeon's asst. Drs. Bennett, Johnson & Eaton, P.A., Balt., 1979-82; pers. adminstr., human resources specialist Morino Assocs., Inc., Vienna, Va., 1983-88; pers. cons. Snelling & Snelling, Vienna, 1988-89; acct. exec. Forbes Assocs., Inc., Annandale, Va., 1989-90; sol. adminstr. legal affairs Electronic Data Sys. Corp., Herndon, Va., 1991-94; contract adminstr. Electronic Data Sys. Corp., Herndon, 1994-96; proposal mgr. govt. svcs. divsn. Govt. Industry Group, Herndon, 1997—. Vol. scuba instr. asst., EDS Mentor Program, In Touch-EDS Friends of Viet Nam Vets, emergency rm. vol. Reston Hosp.; active Walk for Wealth; cmty. rels. ambassador Bowl for Bus. Jr. Achievement; active Holiday LINCS family project, Holiday 1994-96. Recipient regional awards for paintings, regional and nat. awards for sales and mktg., also awards for community contbns. Mem. Artist's Equity. Episcopalian. Avocations: fine arts, painting, sculpting, printmaking, scuba diving. Home: 851 Dogwood Ct Herndon VA 20170-5446

HARRIS, SHERELLE DENISE, journalist, librarian; b. Great Lakes, Ill., May 14, 1965; d. James Henry and Rosie Lee (Harris) H. BA in Journalism, Columbia Coll., 1989; cert. in children's lit., Inst. Children's Lit., 1993; MS in Libr. and Info. Sci., Pratt Inst., 1995. Freelance journalist N.Y.C., 1992—; med. libr. NCI Advt., N.Y.C., 1996-97; young adult libr. South Norwalk (Conn.) Pub. Libr., 1997-99, dept. head children's libr., 1999—; staff reporter The Hour, Norwalk, Conn., 1997-99, corr., 1999—. Contbg. author to mags. and children's books. Fellow for poetry and lit. Conn. Urban Artist Initiative, 1999-01. Home: PO Box 7047 New York NY 10116-7047 Office: South Norwalk Pub Libr 10 Washington St Norwalk CT 06854

HARRIS, SIGMUND PAUL, physicist; b. Buffalo, Oct. 12, 1921; s. Nathan N. and Ida (Lebovitz) H.; m. Florence Katcoff, Sept. 19, 1948; 1 child, Roslyn. BA cum laude, SUNY, Buffalo, 1941, MA, 1943; postgrad., Yale U., 1943; PhD, Ill. Inst. Tech., 1954. Physicist Metall. Lab. U. Chgo., 1943-44; jr. scientist Los Alamos (N.Mex.) Nat. Lab., 1944-46; assoc. physicist Argonne Nat. Lab., Chgo., 1946-53; sr. physicist Tracer Lab., Inc., Boston, 1954-56; sr. research engr. Atomics Internat., Canoga Park, Calif., 1956-64; head physics sect. research div. Maremont Corp., Pasadena, Calif., 1964-66; from asst. prof. to full prof. L.A. Pierce Coll., Woodland Hills, Calif., 1966-86, prof. physics emeritus, 1986—; cons. Space Scis. Inc., Monrovia, Calif., 1968—. Author: Introduction to Air Pollution, 1973. Patentee method for measuring power level of nuclear reactor, apparatus for producing neutrons. Mem. Am. Nuclear Soc., Am. Assn. Physics Tchrs., Am. Phys. Soc., Phi Beta Kappa, Sigma Xi. Home: 5831 Saloma Ave Van Nuys CA 91411-3018 Office: 6201 Winnetka Ave Woodland Hills CA 91371-0001

HARRIS, STANLEY S., judge; b. Washington, Oct. 19, 1927; s. Stanley Raymond and Elizabeth (Sutherland) H.; m. Rebecca Ashley, Aug. 1, 1964; children: Scott Sutherland, Todd Ashley, Mark Ashley. BS, U. Va., 1951, JD, 1953. Bar: D.C. 1953, U.S. Supreme Ct. 1964. Assoc., then ptnr. Hogan & Hartson, Washington, 1953-70; judge Superior Ct. D.C., 1971-72, D.C. Ct. Appeals, 1972-82; U.S. atty. for D.C. Dept. Justice, 1982-83; judge U.S. Dist. Ct. D.C., 1983—, sr. judge, 1996—; mem. com. on criminal law Jud. Conf. U.S., 1988-94, chmn. com. intercircuit assignments, 1994—. Served with U.S. Army, 1945-47. Recipient Judiciary award Assn. Fed. Investigators, 1982. Mem. Bar Assn. D.C. (bd. dirs. 1970-72, Lawyer of Yr. award 1982, Disting. Career award 1996), Lawyer's Club of Washington (pres. 1998-99). Republican. Home: # 406 4982 Sentinel Dr Bethesda MD 20816-3579 Office: US Dist Ct US Courthouse 333 Constitution Ave NW Washington DC 20001-2802

HARRIS, STEPHEN ERNEST, electrical engineering and applied physics educator; b. Bklyn., Nov. 29, 1936; s. Henry and Anne (Alpern) H.; m. Frances Joan Greene, June 7, 1959; children—Hilary Ayn, Craig Henry. B.S., Rensselaer Poly. Inst., 1959; M.S., Stanford U., 1961, Ph.D., 1963. Mem. tech. staff Bell Telephone Labs., Murray Hill, N.J., 1959-60; coop. student Sylvania Electric Systems, Mountain View, Calif., 1961-63; prof. elec. engring. Stanford U., Calif., 1963-79, prof. elec. engring. and applied physics, 1979—, dir. Edward L. Ginzton Lab., 1983-88, Kenneth and Barbara Oshman prof., 1988—; chair Dept. Applied Physics, Stanford U., 1993-96. Recipient Alfred Noble prize ASCE, 1965, Curtis McGraw rsch. award Am. Soc. Engring. Edn., 1973, Davies medal for engring. achievement Rensselaer Poly. Inst., 1984, Einstein prize, 1991, optical Soc. Am. Teaching award, 1992, IEEE/LEOS Quantum Electronics award, 1994. Fellow Am. Assn. Advancement Sci., Am. Acad. Arts & Scis., IEEE (David Sarnoff award 1978), Optical Soc. Am. (Charles Hard Townes award 1985), Am. Phys. Soc.; mem. Nat. Acad. Engring., Nat. Acad. Scis. Office: Stanford Univ Edward L Ginzton Lab 450 Via Palou Mall Stanford CA 94305-4014

HARRIS, STEVEN BROWN, lawyer; b. 1947; s. Sam and Madelyn Harris; married; 2 children. BA with honors, Dartmouth Coll., 1969; LLB, George Washington U., 1973. Bar: D.C. 1974; U.S. Ct. Appeals 1974. With Time Inc., 1969-70; atty. Office of Gen. Counsel, Office of Econ. Opportunity, 1973-75, Legal Svcs. Corp., 1975-77; asst. gen. counsel Mcpl. Securities Rulemaking Bd., 1977-78; staff rep. Nat. Commn. for Rev. of Antitrust Laws and Procedures, 1979; legis. counsel Rep. Barbara Jordan, 1979, Senator Donald W. Riegle Jr., 1979-81; counsel U.S. Senate Com. on Banking, Housing and Urban Affairs, 1981-86, staff dir., chief counsel, securities subcommittee, 1986-88, chief counsel to full com., 1989-90, staff dir., chief counsel, 1990-94, minority staff dir., chief counsel, 1994—. Office: Banking Housing & Urban Affairs US Senate Commn 534 Dirksen Bldg Washington DC 20510

HARRIS, SYDNEY MALCOLM, retired judge; b. Toronto, Ont., Can., June 23, 1917; s. Samuel Aaron and Rose (Geldzaeler) H.; m. Enid Harriet Perlman, Nov. 9, 1949; children: Mark, David. BA, U. Toronto, 1939; Barrister-at-Law, Osgoode Hall, Toronto, 1942; LLB, York U., Toronto, 1991. Bar: Ont. 1942, created Queen's counsel 1962. Barrister, solicitor firm Harris & Rubenstein, Toronto, 1950-76; judge criminal div. Ont. Provincial Ct., Toronto, 1976-90; judge provincial divsn. Ont. Ct., Toronto, 1990-92; mem. Assessment Rev. Bd., 1993-99; dep. judge Small Claims Ct., 1993—. Pres. Canadian Jewish Congress, 1974-77. Recipient Centennial medal, 1967, Queen's Jubilee medal, 1977. Mem. Am. Judges assn., Can. Bar Assn., Provincial Judges Assn., Assn. of Ont. Land Surveyors (mem. exec. com. coun. and complaints rev. councillor 1995—). Home: 3303 Don Mills Rd Apt 2006, North York, ON Canada M2J 4T6

HARRIS, T. GEORGE, magazine editor; b. Simpson County, Ky., Oct. 4, 1924; s. Garland and Luna (Byrum) H.; m. Sheila Hawkins, Oct. 31, 1953 (dec. Jan. 1977); children: Amos, Anne, Crane, Gardiner; m. Ann Rockefeller Roberts, Mar. 3, 1979 (div. Apr. 1993); children: Clare, Joseph, Mary Louise and Rachel Pierson; m. Jeannie Pinkerton, Oct. 20, 1999; 1 child, A.T. Clancy. Student, U. Ky., 1946; BA, Yale U., 1949. Reporter Clarksville (Tenn.) Leaf-Chronicle, 1942; corr. Time, 1949-55; Chgo. bur. chief Time-Live-Fortune, 1955-58; San Francisco bur. chief Time-Life-Fortune, 1960-62; sr. editor Look mag., 1962-68; editor in chief Psychology Today mag., 1969-76, 88-90; founding editor, editor-in-chief Am. Health mag., AH Fitness Bull., 1980-90; cons. editor U. Calif., San Diego, 1993—; editor Harvard Bus. Rev., Boston, 1992-93, Spirituality & Health - The Soul Connection, 1996-98; BODYWATCH commentator PBS; bd. sci. advisors Inst. for the Advancement Health, ABC's 20-20 program.. Cons. editor Next, US, Runner, Somatics, Aware, Industry Week, Modern Maturity, Psychologie Heute mags., Addison-Wesley Pub. Co., Abby Press of Benedictine Order, Age Wave; editor-in-residence U. Calif.-San Diego; columnist Beyond Health. Bd. dirs. Am. Health Found., Nat. Vol. Ctrs., Rockefeller Bros. Fund; mem. med. adv. com. Nat. YMCA; regent Cathedral of St. John the Devine. Commd. 2d lt. on Bastogne battlefield, F.A., AUS, WWII. Decorated Bronze Star, Air medal with cluster; nominated Croix de Guerre; recipient Econ. Journalism prize U. Mo. Brotherhood award NCCJ, 1973, 85, Mag. of Yr. editing award Columbia U., Psychology Today, 1975, Am. Health, 1983, Am. Psychology Fedn. award for Lifetime Contbn., 1983, FMI-Esther Peterson award for nutrition edn., 1990, Centennial award APA, 1992, Disting. Svc. award Psychosomatic Soc., 1995, Nat. Fitness Leader award, '91 Dist. Svc. medal Inst. for Adv. Health; named Outstanding Young Man of Chgo., 1955, Ky. Col., Am. Fitness Leader, 1987; named to Ky. Hall of Fame. Mem. Yale Club (N.Y.C.), Century Assn., La Jolla Beach and Tennis Club, Phi Beta Kappa. Episcopalian. Home and Office: 8115 Paseo Del Ocaso La Jolla CA 92037-3140

HARRIS, TERRY ALLEN, associate principal; b. Grand Island, Nebr., Oct. 30, 1950; s. Farl Ross and Elizebeth Emma (Sommers) H.; m. Marsh Ann Leonard, Dec. 18, 1971; children: Bradley Allen, Rebecca Ann. BS in Geology, U. Mo., Rolla, 1972; MA in Sch. Adminstrn., N.E. Mo. State U., Kirksville, 1979; PhD in Sch. Adminstrn., St. Louis U., 1993. Cert. tchr. physics, geology and gen. sci., prin., supt., Mo. Physics tchr. Hazelwood East H.S., Florissant, Mo., 1974-88; asst. prif. Hazelwood Ctrl. H.S., Florissant, 1989-93; assoc. prin. Lafayette H.S., Ballwin, Mo., 1993—; adj. prof. Lindenwood U., St. Charles, Mo., 1998—. Troop leader Boy Scouts Am., Chesterfield, Mo., 1997—. Sgt. Army N.G., 1972-78. Mem. Nat. Assn. Secondary Sch. Prins., Phi Delta Kappa. Lutheran. Avocation: woodworking. Home: 1255 Somerset Field Dr Chesterfield MO 63005-1346 Office: Lafayette HS 17050 Clayton Rd Ballwin MO 63011-1792

HARRIS, THELMA LEE, data processing executive; b. Decatur, Ill., Mar. 21, 1932; d. Newell Elwood and Bessie Cecilia (Ewing) Shriver; m. Charles Fredrick Greeno, Nov. 25, 1952 (div. Mar. 1975); children: Thelma Lee Lewis, Charles Elwood, Jeffrey Alan, Philip Nathaniel; m. Bobby Joe Harris, May 12, 1979. AA in Bus. Mgmt., Cochise Coll., Sierra Vista, Ariz., 1986. Supr civilian pers. mgmt. U.S. Army, Munich, Germany, 1968-71; mil. pers. clk. U.S. Army, Ft. Leonardwood, Mo., 1971, sec., 1971-73, supr. ctrl. appointment sys., 1973-75; sec. U.S. Army, Ft. Huachuca, Ariz., 1975-76; mgmt. asst. manpower U.S. Army, various locations, 1976-82, mgmt. analyst, 1982-92; part-time computer operator Penmac Profl., Lebanon, Mo., 1994—; Contbr. articles to profl. jours.; editor Toastmaster newspaper, 1987-90. Den mother Cub Scouts/Boy Scouts Am., Munich, 1968-70, treas., 1970; vol. disaster relief ARC, 1997—. Mem. Fed. Employed Women (publicity chmn. 1975-76, newsletter author 1975-76), Toastmasters (charter mem., editor 1987-90). Roman Catholic. Avocations: knitting, crossword puzzles, singing, songwriting, reading.

HARRIS, THEODORE CLIFFORD, songwriter, music publisher; b. Lakeland, Fla., Aug. 2, 1937; s. Thomas Carl and Rhoda Keen (Sutton) H.; m. Jackie Ann Thompson, Dec. 20, 1967; children: Bradley Carlton, Joshua Chandler. Grad. high sch., Lakeland. Staff songwriter Silver Star Music, Nashville, 1958-62; co-owner Harbot Music, Nashville, 1965-67; owner Contention Music, Nashville, 1967-97; guest instr. U. Tenn., Nashville, 1975-76. Rec. artist country music field, 1958-66. Recipient 70 composer, pub. award, 1965-90, Named to the Nashville Songwriter's Assn. Internat. Hall of Fame, 1990. Mem. Country Music Assn. (bd. dirs. Nashville chpt. 1972-73), Nashville Songwriters Assn. Internat. Republican. Baptist. Avocations: fishing, metal detecting, lapidary arts.

HARRIS, THEODORE EDWARD, mathematician, educator; b. Phila., Jan. 11, 1919; s. Julius and Hazel (Rosenfield) H.; m. Constance Ruth Feder, June 29, 1947; children: Stephen Joel, Marcia Faye. Student, So. Meth. U., 1935-37; BA, U. Tex., 1939; MA, Princeton U., 1946, PhD, 1947; D of Tech. (hon.), Chalmers Inst. of Tech., Gothenburg, Sweden, 1989. With Rand Corp., 1947-66, chmn. dept. math., 1959-66; prof. math. U. So. Calif., 1966-89, prof. emeritus, 1989—; vis. asst. prof. UCLA, 1949-50; vis. assoc. prof. Columbia, 1953; vis. prof. Stanford U., 1963; lectr. U. So. Calif., 1989-97. Author: The Theory of Branching Processes, 1963; Editor: Annals of Math. Statistics, 1955-58. Served to maj. USAAF, 1942-45. Recipient Albert S. Raubenheimer disting. faculty award, 1985, disting. emeritus award U. So. Calif., 1990. Fellow AAAS, Inst. Math. Stats. (pres. 1966-67); mem. Am. Math. Soc., Nat. Acad. Scis., Phi Beta Kappa, Sigma Xi. Jewish. Fax: 213-740-2424. E-mail: THARRIS2MTHA.USC.EDU. Office: Univ So Calif Dept Math 1042 W 36th Pl DRB 155 Los Angeles CA 90007-5603

HARRIS, THOMAS L., public relations executive; b. Dayton, Ohio, Apr. 18, 1931; s. James and Leona (Blum) H.; m. JoAnn K. Karch, Apr. 14, 1957; children: James Harris, Theodore Harris. B.A., U. Mich., 1953; M.A., U. Chgo., 1956. Exec. v.p. Daniel J. Edelman Inc., Chgo., 1957-67; v.p. pub. rels. Neddham Harper & Steers, Chgo., 1967-72; pres. Foote Cone & Belding Pub. Rels., Chgo., 1973-78; pres. Golin-Harris Communications Inc., Chgo., 1978-89, also vice chmn.; adj. prof. Medill Sch. Journalism, Northwestern U., Evanston, Ill., 1987—; mng. ptnr. Thomas L. Harris & Co., Highland Pk., Ill., 1992—. Served with U.S. Army, 1953-55. Mem. Public Relations Soc. Am. Home: 241 Melba Ln Highland Park IL 60035-1904 Office: Thomas L Harris & Co 600 Central Ave Highland Park IL 60035-3211

HARRIS, THOMAS RAYMOND, biomedical engineer, educator; b. San Angelo, Tex., Feb. 19, 1937; s. Loyd Franklin and Rubye (Mitchell) H.; m. Alene Blythe Hawes; children: Calvin Thomas, Andrew Mitchell. B.S., Tex. A&M U., 1958, M.S., 1962; Ph.D., Tulane U., 1964; M.D., Vanderbilt U., 1974. Design engr. Standard Oil Co. Calif., 1958-60; mem. faculty Vanderbilt U., Nashville, 1964—; prof. biomed. engring. and chem. engring. Vanderbilt U., 1976—; assoc. prof. medicine Vanderbilt U. Sch. Medicine, 1980-85, prof. medicine, 1985—; dir. biomed. engring. program Vanderbilt U. Sch. Engring., 1977-88, chair dept. biomed. engring., 1988—; cons. in field. Author articles in field; mem. editorial bds. profl. jours. Served as 2d lt. AUS, 1958-59. Nat. Heart, Lung and Blood Inst. grantee; NSF grantee; Martha Washington Straus-Harry H. Straus Found. grantee; Barbara Ingalls Shook Found. grantee. Mem. Am. Physiol. Soc., Am. Inst. Chem. Engrs., Am. Soc. Engring. Edn., Am. Heart Assn. (sci. councils), Biomed. Engring. Soc. (pres. 1985-86), Soc. Engring. in Medicine and Biology, Microcirculatory Soc. Baptist. Office: Vanderbilt U Dept of Biomed Engring PO Box 1724 Nashville TN 37235*

HARRIS, VERA EVELYN, personnel recruiting and search firm executive; b. Watson, Sask., Can., Jan. 11, 1932; came to U.S., 1957; d. Timothy and Margaret (Popoff) H.; student U. B.C. (Can.), Vancouver; children—Colin Clifford Graham, Barbara Cusimano Page. Office mgr. Keglers, Inc., Morgan City, La., 1964-67; office mgr., acct. John L. Hopper & Assos., New Orleans, 1967-71; office mgr. Elite Homes, Inc., Metairie, La., 1971-73; comptroller Le Pavillon Hotel, New Orleans, 1973-74; controller Waguespack-Pratt, Inc., New Orleans, 1974-76; adminstrv. controller Sizzler Family Steak Houses of So. La., Inc., Metairie, 1976-79; dir. adminstrn. Sunbelt, Inc., New Orleans, 1979-82, sec., dir., 1980—; exec. v.p. Corp. Cons., Inc., 1980-83, pres., 1984-86; pres. Harris Personnel Resources, Arlington, Tex., 1986—, Harris Enterprises, Arlington, 1986—, Harris Personnel Resources Health Staff, Arlington, 1990—; exec. dir. Nat. Sizzler Franchise Assn., 1976-79. Mem. Am. Bus. Women's Assn., La. Assn. Personnel Consultants (treas. 1985-86), Indep. Recruiters Group, Soc. Exec. Recruiting Cons. (pres. 1997-99). Home: 4915 Arborgate Dr Arlington TX 76017-1049 Office: Harris Personnel Resources 1600 E Pioneer Pkwy Ste 340 Arlington TX 76010-6562

HARRIS, W. D., city housing inspector, small business owner; b. Natchez, Miss., Sept. 13, 1957; s. Julia Matthews Harris; m. Rosie B. Ford, Dec. 23, 1978; children: Demeshia, Shaneshia. BS in Tech. Edn., Alcorn State U., 1979. Former housing inspector City of Natchez, cmty. svcs. officer; owner Harris Video & Photography, Natchez; bd. dirs. Adams Jefferson Improvement Corp., Natchez. Mem. choir Milford Bapt. Ch., asst. min., 1981—; bd. dirs. Miss. Lou Crime Stoppers Orgn. 2d lt., U.S. Army combat engring., 1979-80, Va. Recipient Cmty. Svc. award Friends and Family, Natchez, 1996. Mem. NAACP, 100 Black Men United, Miss. Photography Club, Masons, Alpha Phi Alpha. Democrat. Baptist. Home: 38 Myrtle Dr Natchez MS 39120-2181

HARRIS, WALTER EDGAR, chemistry educator; b. Wetaskiwin, Alta., Can., June 9, 1915; s. William Ernest and Emma Louise (Humbke) H.; m. Phyllis Pangburn, June 14, 1942; children: Margaret Anne, William Edgar. BS, U. Alta., 1938, MS, 1939; PhD, U. Minn., 1944; DSc (hon.), U. Waterloo, 1987, U. Alta., 1991. Research fellow U. Minn., 1943-46; prof. analytical chemistry U. Alta., Edmonton, 1946-80; chmn. dept. chemistry U. Alta., 1974-79, chmn. Pres.'s Adv. Com. on Campus Revs., 1980-90. Author: (with H.W. Habgood) Programmed Temperature Gas Chromatography, 1965, (with B. Kratchovil) Chemical Separations and Measurements, 1974, Teaching Introductory Analytical Chemistry, 1974, An Introduction to Chemical Analysis, 1981, Risk Assessment, 1997, (with H.A. Laitinen) Chemical Analysis, 1975; contbr. numerous articles to profl. jours. Decorated Order of Can., 1998; recipient Outstanding Achievement award U. Minn., 1973; Govt. Alta. Achievement award, 1974. Fellow AAAS, Royal Soc. Can.; mem. Chem. Inst. Can. (Fisher Sci. Lecture award 1969, Chem. Edn. award 1975), Am. Chem. Soc., Sigma Xi. Home: 9212 118th St, Edmonton, AB Canada T6G 1T9 Office: Univ of Alta, Dept Of Chem, Edmonton, AB Canada T6G 2G2

HARRIS, WARREN LYNN, development engineer; b. Albuquerque, May 8, 1966; s. Jerry Dale and Viola Guadalupe (Gutierrez) H. BS, Ariz. State U., 1988. Programming mgr. I.P.C. Computer Svcs., Inc., Tempe, Ariz., 1985-89; software sys. engr. Intel Corp., Chandler, Ariz., 1990; dir. software R & D Pics, Inc., Tempe, 1990-91; dir. software R & D parics divsn. Ansoft Corp., Tempe, 1991-94; devel. engr. Ansoft Corp., Phoenix, 1994—. Mem. IEEE, Assn. for Computing Machinery, Mortar Bd., Golden Key, Upsilon Pi Epsilon. Avocations: racquetball, model building, chess, pool, Star Trek collecting. Office: Ansoft Corp 4949 W Phelps Rd Glendale AZ 85306-1426

HARRIS, WARREN WAYNE, lawyer; b. Houston, Nov. 5, 1962. BBA, U. Houston, 1985, JD, 1988. Bar: Tex. 1988, U.S. Ct. Appeals (5th cir.) 1989, U.S. Ct. Appeals (fed. cir.) 1995, U.S. Ct. Appeals (8th, 10th and 11th cirs.) 1996, U.S. Dist. Ct. (so., no., ea. and we. dists.) Tex. 1990, U.S. Supreme Ct. 1991; bd. cert. civil appellate law Tex. Bd. Legal Specialization. Briefing atty. Tex. Supreme Ct., Austin, 1988-89; ptnr. Porter & Hedges, L.L.P., Houston, 1989-96, Bracewell & Patterson, L.L.P., Houston, 1996—. Editor-in-chief: Houston Lawyer mag., 1991-92; assoc. editor: The Appellate Advocate, 1992-97; editor: Pocket Parts, 1993-95, The Appellate Lawyer, 1994-96. Fellow Tex. Bar Found. (co-chair dist. 4 nominating com. 1994—), Houston Bar Found., Houston Young Lawyers Found. (vice-chair 1996-98); mem. ABA (litigation sect. appellate practice com. 1990—, tort and ins. practice sect. appellate advocacy com. 1990—, chair-elect 1999—), State Bar Tex. (appellate sect. 1988—, coun. 1997—, pro bono com. chair 1997-99), State Bar Coll. (bd. dirs. 1994-95), State Bar Pro Bono Coll., Tex. Young Lawyers Assn. (bd. dirs. 1994-98, outstanding dir. 1995-96, Pres.'s award 1996-97), Houston Bar Assn. (Pres.'s award 1993-94, chair appellate practice sect. 1998-99, coun. appellate practice sect. 1993—), Houston Young Lawyers Assn. (pres. 1999—), Houston Lawyer Referral Svc. (trustee 1994-95), Stages Repertory Theatre (pres. 1994-95, bd. dirs. 1994-96, chair 1994-95, WineFest com. chair 1994-96), Order of Barristers, Order of Barons, Phi Delta Phi (life). Republican. Office: Bracewell & Patterson LLP 711 Louisiana St Ste 2900 Houston TX 77002-2781

HARRIS, WAYNE MANLEY, lawyer; b. Pittsford, N.Y., Dec. 28, 1925; s. George H. and Constance M. Harris; m. Diane C. Quigley, Sept. 30, 1978; children: Wayne, Constance, Karen, Duncan, Claire. LLB, Albany Law Sch., U. Rochester, 1951. Bar: N.Y. 1952, U.S. Supreme Ct. 1958. Ptnr. Harris, Chesworth & O'Brien (and predecessor firms), Rochester, N.Y., 1958—. Pres. Delta Labs., Inc. (non-profit environ. lab.) Adopt-A-Stream program, 1971—, Friends of Bristol Valley Playhouse Found., 1984-87, Monroe County Conservation Coun. Inc., 1956-61, v.p., 1984-87; v.p. Powder Mills Pk. Hatchery Preservation Inc., 1993-95, pres., 1995—. Served with combat inf., Germany, 1944-46. Decorated Bronze Star; recipient Sportsman of Yr. award Genesee Conservation League, Inc., 1960, Conservationist of Yr. award Monroe County Conservation Coun., Inc., 1961, Kiwanian of Yr. award, Kiwanis Club, 1965, Livingston County Fedn. of Sportsmen award, 1966, N.Y. State Conservation Coun. Nat. Wildlife Fedn. Water Conservation Conservationist of Yr. award, 1967, Rochester Acad. Sci. Hon. Fellowship award, 1970, Conservation award Nat. Am. Motors Corp., 1971, Meritorious Leadership in Civic Devel. award Rochester C. of C., 1972, Svc. award Rochester Against Intoxicated Drivers, 1989. Mem. ATLA, N.Y. State Trial Lawyers Assn., AIDA Reins. and Arbitration Soc., Indsl. Mgmt. Coun., Wild Turkey Fedn. Drafter 5 laws passed in N.Y. State. Home: 60 Mendon Center Rd Honeoye Falls NY 14472-9363 Office: Harris Chesworth & O'Brien 1820 East Ave Rochester NY 14610-1829

HARRIS, WESLEY L., aeronautics engineering educator; b. Richmond, Va., Oct. 29, 1941; s. William M. and Rosa P. (Minor) H.; m. Myrtle Ann Satterwhite, June 14, 1960 (div. Mar. 1985); children: Wesley Jr., Zelda, Marcus, Kamau, Kalomo, Eletha; m. Sandra Maria Butler, Sept. 2, 1985; 1 child, Tosha. B in Aeronautical Engring. with honors, U. Va., 1964; MA in Aeronautical Scis., Princeton U., 1966, PhD in Aeronautical Scis., 1968; LHD (hon.), Lane Coll., 1994; DEng (hon.), Milw. Sch. Engring., 1994; DSc (hon.), Old Dominion U., 1995. Fellow AIAA, Am. Helicopter Soc.; mem. AAAS, NAE, Am. Phys. Soc., Math. Assn. Am., Nat. Tech. Assn. Asst. prof. aerospace engring. U. Va., 1968-70; assoc. prof. physics Southern U., 1970-71; assoc. prof. aerospace engring. U. Va., 1971-72, dir. Office Minority Edn., 1975-78; assoc. prof. aeronautics & astronautics/ocean engring. MIT, 1973-79, assoc. prof. aeronautics and astronautics, 1980-81, prof. aeronautics & astronautics, 1981-85; mgr. computational methods Office Aeronautics & Space Tech. NASA HQs, 1979-80; dean sch. engring. U. Conn., Storrs, 1985-90; v.p. U. Tenn. Space Inst., Tullahoma, 1990-93; assoc. administr. Office of Aeronautics NASA HQ, Washington, 1993-96; prof. aeronautics and astronautics MIT, Cambridge, Mass., 1996—; mem. adv. groups Nat. Rsch. Coun. Commn. Engring. and Tech. Systems, Bd. Engring. Edn., Bd. Army Sci. and Tech., Air Force Studies Bd., Com. Aeronautical Techs.; mem. adv. com. NSF, U.S. Army Sci. Bd.; advisor univs.; nat. adv. com. dept. engring. Hampton U., 1989—. Author more than 100 tech. papers. Trustee Sci. Mus. Conn., 1985-90; bd. dirs. Conn. Pre-Engring. Program, Inc., 1986-90; adv. bd. dirs. Am. City Bank, Tullahoma, 1990-93; bd. vis. sch. engring. Duke U., 1991—; vis. com. dept. aeronautics and astronautics MIT, 1988-95, past vis. com. dept. mech. engring., 1985-88. Recipient Herbert S. and Jane Gregory Disting. Lectr. award Coll. Engring. U. Fla., 1992; named Milton Pikarsky Meml. lectr. CCNY Sch. Engring., 1990. Democrat. Avocation: squash. Office: MIT Dept Aeronautics 33-410 77 Mass Ave Cambridge MA 02139-4307

HARRIS, WHITNEY ROBSON, lawyer, educator; b. Seattle, Aug. 12, 1912; s. Olin Whitney and Lily (Robson) H.; m. Jane Freund Foster, Feb. 14, 1964; 1 child, Eugene Whitney. AB magna cum laude, U. Wash., 1933; JD, U. Calif., 1936; LHD (hon.), McKendree Coll., 1999. Bar: Calif. 1936, U.S. Supreme Ct. 1945, Tex. 1953, U.S. Ct. Mil. Appeals 1955, Mo. 1964. Pvt. practice L.A., 1936-42; trial counsel U.S. Chief of Counsel, Nuremberg, 1945-46; chief legal advice br. U.S. Mil. Govt. for Germany, 1946-48; prof. law So. Meth. U., 1948-54; staff dir. legal service and proc. Com. Orgn. Exec. Br. Govt., 1954; exec. dir. ABA, 1954-55; solicitor for Tex. Southwestern Bell Telephone Co., Dallas, 1955-63; gen. solicitor Southwestern Bell Telephone Co., St. Louis, 1963-65; pvt. practice St. Louis, 1965-89; arbitration judge, 1993—; sr. counselor Mo. Bar Assn., 1987; lectr. UCLA, Stanford U., Washington U., Wellesley Coll., U. Denver, Reed Coll., U. Wash., Claremont Coll., Boston Coll., Williams Coll., So. Meth. U., U. Mo., McKendrick Coll. Author: Family Law, 1953, Tyranny On Trial, 1954, 3d edit. 1999, Legal Services and Procedure, 1955; (with others) Law, Culture and Values, 1989; contbr. numerous articles to profl. jours. including Ency. Brit., 1954, The Internat. Lawyer, 1986, Washington U. Law Quar., 1987, U. Toledo Law Rev., 1992. Bd. govs. Winston Churchill Meml. and Libr., 1980—; trustee Nat. Jewish Ctr. Immunol. and Respiratory Medicine, 1980-90. Decorated Legion of Merit, Order of Merit Officer's Class (Germany), Medal of the War Crimes Commn. (Poland); named nat. outstanding fund raising vol. Nat. Soc. Fund Raising Execs., 1985. Mem. ABA (chmn. internat. law sect. 1953-54, chmn. adminstrv. law sect. 1960-61), Japan-Am. Soc. St. Louis (pres. 1978-80, Disting. Svc. award 1995), Naval War Coll. Found. (grad. level), Order of Coif, Phi Beta Kappa, Phi Kappa Psi, Delta Theta Phi. Established Jane and Whitney Harris Rsch. Libr. at Winston Churchill Meml. and Libr., Fulton, Mo., 1980, Jane and Whitney Harris Reading Rooms at St. Louis Country Day Sch., 1980, and at Washington U., 1985, Jane and Whitney Harris Ann. Rsch. Fellowship in Arthritis at Washington U. Sch. Medicine, 1989, Whitney Robson Harris collection on Third Reich at Washington U., 1980, Jane and Whitney Harris Ann. Lecture on Tropical Ecology at U. Mo. St. Louis, 1991, Jane and Whitney Harris Secret Garden at Mo. Botanical Garden, 1993, Jane and Whitney Harris Child Care Facility at Jr. League, St. Louis, 1994, Jane and Whitney Harris Anniversary Garden, Forest Park, St. Louis, 1999. Home: 2 Glen Creek Ln Saint Louis MO 63124-1505 *Tyranny leads to inhumanity, and inhumanity is death. Let us resolve that tyranny shall not extend its sway, nor war become its game—placing our faith in the cause of justice, in the freedom of man, and in the mercy of God.*

HARRIS, WILEY LEE, financial services executive; b. Lynchburg, Va., Jan. 15, 1949; s. Willie M. Harris; m. Thelma E. Thomas, June 28, 1991. BS in Indsl. Sociology, Yale U., 1971. Human resources trainee GE, Lynchburg, 1972-74; equal employment opportunity mgr. GE, 1974-77; human resources mgr. GE Info. Svcs. Co., Chgo., 1977-79, Rockville, Md., 1979-87; compensation mgr. GE Capital, Stamford, Conn., 1987—. Mem. NAACP, Lynchburg, 1980—. Recipient Civic Achievement award NAACP, Lynchburg, 1986, Employment Achievement, State of Va., Richmond, Va., 1980. Mem. Internat. Assn. for Employee Benefits, Am. Compensation Assn., Am. Soc. for Personnel Adminstrn. Republican. Office: GE Capital 260 Long Ridge Rd Stamford CT 06927

HARRIS, WILLIAM FRANKLIN, III, biologist, environmental science director and educator; b. Jacksonville, Fla., Sept. 27, 1942; m. Marilyn Wohlleber, 1966; children: James G., Steven F. BA, Wabash Coll., 1964; MS, U. Tenn., 1966, PhD in Botany, 1970. Rsch. ecologist Oak Ridge (Tenn.) Nat. Lab, 1970-73, rsch. group leader, 1973-76, sect. head, 1976-80; program dir. NSF, 1980-81, dep. divsn. dir., 1981-87, exec. officer, 1987-82, dep. asst. dir. biology, 1992-93; dir., prof. divsn. biology U. Tenn., Knoxville, 1993—. Recipient Presdl. Rank award U.S. Govt., 1992. Fellow AAAS; mem. Ecol. Soc. Am., Am. Inst. Biol. Sci. Achievements include federal agency and university administration, research in biological sciences, emphasizing temperate terrestrial ecosystems. Home: 810 Glensprings Dr Knoxville TN 37922-5223 Office: U Tenn M303 Walters Life Scis Bldg Knoxville TN 37996*

HARRIS, WILLIAM HAMILTON, orthopedic surgeon; b. Gt. Falls, Mont., Nov. 18, 1927; s. John H. and LaRue (Hamilton) H.; m. Johanna Alderfer, June 8, 1952; children: William Hamilton, Kristin, Jonathan, David. AB, Haverford (Pa.) Coll., 1947; MD, U. Pa., 1951. Intern U. Pa. Hosp., 1951-52; resident in orthop. surgery Children's Med. Ctr., Boston, 1955, Mass. Gen. Hosp., Boston, 1957, Royal Nat. Orthopedic Hosp., London, 1959-60; mem. faculty Harvard U. Med. Sch., 1960—, clin. prof. orthop. surgery, 1975—, Alan Gerry clin. prof. orthop. surgery, 1997—; orthop. surgeon Mass. Gen. Hosp., 1960—, chief hip implant surgery unit, 1974—; sr. lectr. MIT, Cambridge, 1969—. Contbr. more than 420 articles to various publs., chpts. to books. Capt. M.C., USAF, 1952-54. Fellow, Nat. Found., 1959-60, Sprague Found., 1960-61, Med. Found. Boston, 1961-64; Clementine Cope fellow Haverford Coll., 1947; traveling fellow Am. Orthop. Assn., 1965; recipient Kappa Delta award for Orthop. Rsch., 1970, 76. Mem. AMA, Internat. Hip Soc. (past pres., a founder), Hip Soc. (a founder, 1st pres. 1969), Am. Acad. Orthopedic Surgeons, Interurban Orthopedic Club, Mass. Med. Soc., Boston Orthopedic Club, Société Internationale de Chirurgie Orthopedique et de Tramatologie, Phi Beta Kappa, Alpha Omega Alpha. Home: 665 Concord Ave Belmont MA 02478-2027 Office: Mass Gen Hosp 32 Fruit St Boston MA 02114-2620

HARRIS, WILLIAM HAMILTON, academic administrator; b. Fitzgerald, Ga., July 22, 1944; m. Wanda Filmore; children: Cynthia, Bill. BA, Paine Coll., 1966; MA, Ind. U., 1967, PhD, 1973; LLD (hon.), Paine Coll., 1991. Instr. history Paine Coll., Augusta, Ga., 1967-69, pres., 1982-88; assoc. instr. history Ind. U., Bloomington, 1969-71, lectr. in history, 1972-73, asst. prof. history, 1973-77, acting affirmative action officer, 1977-78, assoc. prof. history, 1977-81, prof. history, 1981-82, dir. CIC Minorities Fellowship program, 1977-82, assoc. dean. grad. sch., 1979-82; pres. Paine Coll., 1982-88, Tex. So. U., Houston, 1988-93, Ala. State Univ., Montgomery, 1994—; vis. prof. history Ind. U., 1993-94; bd. dirs. Tex. Commerce Bank; mem. exec. com. Coun. Pres.'s Tex. Pub. Colls. and Univs., 1991. Author: Keeping the Faith, 1977, The Harder We Run, 1982. Bd. dirs. Augusta Jr. Achievement, 1983-86, Ga.-Carolina coun. Boy Scouts Am., 1986-88, Leadership Ala., 1996—, Am. Coun. on Edn., 1986-90, Montgomery Metro YMCA, Montgomery Area United Way, v.p.; bd. visitors Air Univ. of USAF; trustee Greater Houston Partnership, 1989-93, mem. exec. com., 1990-93; vice chmn. Coun. Pres. of Ala. Pub. Univs., 1995—; chmn. Ala. Coun. Coll. and Univ. Pres., 1997—. Am. Coun. Learned Socs. fellow, 1979-80, Fulbright professorship U. Hamburg, Germany, 1978-79, So. Fellowships Fund fellow, 1970-71; recipient Paine Coll. Alumni award, 1984-85; named Disting. Son of Fitzgerald Ga. Centennial Observance, 1996. Mem. Am. Coun. Edn. (bd. dirs. 1986-88), United Negro Coll. Fund, Inc. (bd. dirs. 1984-88, vice chmn. instl. and individual mems. 1986-88, chmn. 1988), Ednl. Testing Svc. (bd. trustees 1985-91, chmn. 1988), Lilly Endowment Inc., Open Fellowships, Assn. for Study of Afro-Am. Life and History (pres. 1986-89), Nat. Assn. Equal Opportunity in Higher Edn. (bd. dirs. 1985-88), Nat. Assn. Ind. Colls. and Univs. (bd. dirs.), Nat. Assn. Colls. and Schs. of United Meth. Ch. (mem. exec. bd.), Ind. U. Alumni Assn. (Disting. Alumni Svd. award 1991), Paine Coll., L.L.D., 1991, Montgomery Area C. of C. (bd. dirs.). Office: Ala State Univ Office of the Pres 915 S Jackson St Montgomery AL 36104-5732*

HARRIS, WILLIAM JAMES, JR., research administrator, educator; b. South Bend, Ind., June 17, 1918; s. William James and Elizabeth M. (Scott) H.; m. Ruth Laubinger, Aug. 26, 1944 (dec. 1977); children: June Elizabeth Sherren, William James III, Debbie Shafer Hayden, Britta Shafer Kreuger, Barkley Shafer.; m. Elizabeth Dotten Shafer, June 24, 1978. B.S. in Chem. Engring; M.S. in Engring, Purdue U., 1940, D.Engring. (hon.), 1978; Sc.D., M.I.T., 1948. Head ferrous alloys br. metallurgy div. Naval Research Lab., 1947-51; exec. sec. materials adv. bd. Nat. Acad. Sci.-NRC, 1951-54, exec. dir., 1957-60, asst. sec., planning div. engring., 1960-62; asst. to dir. Battelle Meml. Inst., 1954-57, asst. to v.p., 1962-67; asst. dir. tech. Columbus Labs., 1967-69; v.p. research and test dept. Assn. Am. Railroads, 1970-85; E.B. Snead and Disting. prof. transp. engring. Tex. A&M U., 1985-95; assoc. dir. Tex. Transp. Inst., 1987-95; sr. rsch. engr. TTI, 1995—; disting. prof. emeritus/Snead prof. emeritus Tex. A&M U., 1995-97; commr. Pres.'s Commn. on Critical Infrastructure Protection, 1997-98, sr. exec., 1998-99; cons. CIAO, 1999—; hon. prof. China Acad. Ry. Scis., 1987; pres. W. J. Harris, Inc., 1985-98; pres., chmn. bd. Piscataway Co., Accokeek, Md., 1958-63; mem. Nat. Exec. Res. Dept. Transp., 1983—; sr. tech. advisor UN Indsl. Devel. Orgn., 1987-91. Editor: (with others) Perspectives in Materials Research, 1963; contbr. (with others) articles to tech. publs. Mem. nat. materials adv. bd. Nat. Acad. Sci., 1967—, chmn., 1969-70; sec. Pres.'s Com. on Hwy. Safety, 1969; mem. high speed ground transp. adv. com. U.S. Dept. Transp., 1972-74, Md. Gov.'s Sci. Adv. Com., 1972-76, Md. Gov.'s Energy Council, 1974-76; pres. Moyoane Assn., 1951-53, 58; pres., chmn. bd. Alice Ferguson Found., 1966-68; chmn. exec. com., disting. profs. Tex. A&M U. Served to lt. comdr. USNR, 1941-45. Decorated Naval letter of commendation; recipient Disting. Svc. award (Carey award) Transp. Rsch. Bd., NRC, 1977, Roy Crum award for disting. rsch., 1989; Disting. Rsch. award Transp. Rsch. Forum, 1986; named R.R. Man of Yr., 1976; inducted into Cooperstown Conf. R.R. Hall of Fame, 1993, Batteile Meml. Inst. Transp. Hall of Fame, 1994. Fellow Am. Soc. Metals, ASME, Metall. Soc. (pres. 1970), Nat. Acad. Engring. (chair program com. 1995-98, chmn. audit com. 1982, fin. com. 1995-98); mem. Intelligent Transp. Sys. Am. (coord. coun. 1990-97, bd. dirs. 1997—, chmn. N.Am. steering com. 1993-95, chmn. clearinghouse and publ. speech com., world congress bd. dirs., Spl. award for Internat. Congress Leadership 1995), Am. Inst. Mining, Metall., and Petroleum Engrs. (dir. 1964-69, v.p. 1964-67, chmn. inst. metals divsn. 1960, Mathewson medal 1950), Engrs. Joint Coun. (bd. dirs. 1965-70, pres. 1968-70), Engring. Found. (chmn. rsch. conf. com. 1964-67, bd. dirs. 1968-70), Am. Ordnance Assn. (chmn. materials divsn. 1966-68), Nat. Security Indsl. Assn. (chmn. exec. planning com. 1965-67, chmn. rsch. and devel. adv. com. 1967-69), Transp. Rsch. Bd. (exec. com. 1977-85, 87-90, chmn. coun. 1989-95, emeritus TRB-ITS com.), Nat. Def. Transp. Assn. (life, chmn. com. on engring. tech.), Found. on Engring. Techs. (chmn. 1990-97), Internat. Heavy Haul Assn. (chmn. 1982-89), Sigma Xi, Alpha Sigma Mu, Tau Beta Pi, Phi Lambda Upsilon, Sigma Delta Chi. Home: 1200 N Nash St Apt 1140 Arlington VA 22209-3682

HARRIS, WILLIAM JOHN, retired management holding company executive, consultant; b. Hamilton, Ont., Can., Feb. 6, 1928; s. William Frederick and Leila Matilda (Rodway) H.; m. Grace Edna Paddock, Oct. 12, 1957; children: Jeffrey Louis, Susan Marie, Laura Ann. Student, Wash. U., St. Louis, 1949-51. Sales and advt. mgr. Tuckett Ltd. (subs. Imperial Tobacco), Hamilton, 1951-64; mktg. mgr. Imperial Tobacco div. Imasco Ltd., Montreal, Que., Can., 1965-75; corp. sec. Imperial Tobacco div. Imasco Ltd., Montreal, 1976-79; sr. v.p. Imasco Ltd., Montreal, 1980-89, ret., 1989; cons. in field, 1990—. Recipient Gold Medal award Assn. Can. Advertisers Inc., 1979. Roman Catholic. Avocations: music, gardening, carpentry, golf.

HARRIS, WILLIAM NORMAN, music educator; b. Washington, Sept. 8, 1952; s. Clarence Norman and Helen Lucy (Holsey) H. *Great Aunt Louvenia Norman, (paternal grandmother's sister, Aunt Lou) is one of the original founders of the black professional sorority Alpha Kappa Alpha (AKA) Alpha chapter at Howard University, Wash. DC. Also related to Lucious Henry Holsey (maternal grandfather's and mother's maiden name) one of the founders of Payne College, Augusta, GA.* BMEd, Millikin U., 1974; MA, various, 1987. Elem. gen. music tchr. Montgomery County Pub. Schs., Rockville, Md., 1974—; prodr., dir. spring musical theatre, Poolesville (Md.) Jr./Sr. High Sch., 1986-91; leader, tenor/baritone soloist St. John's Episc. Ch., Bethesda, Md., 1995, U. Md. Chorus; baritone soloist Montgomery Coll. Chorus, 1995. Former mem. Montgomery County Masterworks Chorus, U. Md. Chorus; actor, singer Montgomery Coll., Summer Dinner Theatre, Rockville, 1988, 89, 90; artistic dir., choral master Damascus (Md.) Theatre Co.; singer U.S. Postal Svc. (Black History Month's Observances) Hdqrs., Washington, 1986-88; dir. children's chorus for PYE Panda Earth Day Expo '90. Fellow NEA, Music Educators Nat. Conf.; mem. Phi Mu Alpha Sinfonia, Beta Theta chpt. (treas. 1972-74). Democrat. Methodist. Avocations: tour narrator for Tourmobile, Washington Sightseeing Shuttle Svc., interior decorating, white water rafting. Home: 19256 Misty Meadow Ter Germantown MD 20874-5367

HARRIS, WILLIAM VERNON, history educator; b. Nottingham, Eng., Sept. 13, 1938; naturalized; 1982; s. K. W. F. and Elizabeth (Sargent) H.; 1 child, Neil. B.A., Oxford U., 1961, M.A., 1964, D.Phil., 1968. Instr. history Columbia U., N.Y.C., 1965-68, asst. prof., 1968-71, assoc. prof., 1971-76, prof., 1976—, William R. Shepherd prof. history, 1995—, chmn. history dept., 1988-94; mem. adv. council Am. acad. in Rome, 1976—, resident, 1978, 82; dir. NEH summer seminars, 1979, 81; mem. Inst. Advanced Study, Princeton, N.J., 1970-71, 78; Gray lectr. Cambridge U., 1998. Author: Rome in Etruria and Umbria, 1971, War and Imperialism in Republican Rome, 1979, Ancient Literacy, 1989; editor: (series) Columbia Studies in the Classical Tradition, 1976—; The Imperialism of Mid-Republican Rome, 1984, The Inscribed Economy, 1993, The Transformations of Urbs Roma in Late Antiquity, 1999. NEH sr. research fellow, 1978; Guggenheim fellow, 1982-83, fellow Nat. Humanities Ctr., 1998; vis. fellow All Souls Coll., Oxford U., Eng., 1983. Fellow Soc. Antiquaries (London), Finnish Soc. Scis.; mem. Academia Europaea (fgn.), Archaeol. Inst. Am., Am. Philol. Assn., Am. Hist. Assn., Assn. Ancient Historians, Century Assn. Office: Columbia U 624 Fayerweather Hall New York NY 10027

HARRIS, WILLIAM WOLPERT, treasurer political action committee; b. St. Paul, Mar. 11, 1940; s. Irving Brooks and Rosetta (Wolpert) H.; m. Robie Heilbrun, 1968; 2 children. BA, Wesleyan U., 1961; PhD, MIT, 1977. Exec. Conley Electronics, 1961-63; exec. v.p. G. Barr Co., div. Pittway Corp., 1963-66; asst. to pres. North Advt., Inc., 1966; dir. Janus Films, Inc., 1966-77; asst. to dir. Fordham U. Ctr. for Communications, 1967-68; founder, exec. dir. Pub. Interest Communication Svcs., Inc., 1976-88; instr. urban media MIT, 1977; lectr. urban media Boston U. Met. Coll., 1974, 75, 78; adj. assoc. prof. media and communications policy Tufts U., 1981-82; vis. prof. sociology Wesleyan U., 1993; vis. prof. Brandeis U., 1997-98; founder, treas. KIDSPAC, 1981—; founder, pres. Children's Rsch. and Edn. Inst., Inc., 1984—; bd. dirs. Pittway Corp., Cylink Corp. Ind. producer documentaries; contbr. articles to profl. jours. Bd. dirs. Pittway Corp. Charitable Found.; v.p. The Harris Found.; pres. Irving Harris Found. Recipient Outstanding Children's Leader award Statewide Adv. Coun., Office for Children, Commonwealth of Mass., 1992, Spl. Pub. Recognition award, Mass. Psychol. Assn., 1990, Award for Disting. Contbn. to Child Advocacy, Am. Psychol. Assn., 1989, Dale Richmond award Am. Acad. Pediats., 1997; hon. DHL, Lesley Coll., 1988. Office: 80 Trowbridge St Cambridge MA 02138-3102

HARRIS, WILSON, psychiatrist, research scientist; b. Arroyo, P.R., Mar. 30, 1952; widower. Grad., S.W. Sch. Hypnotherapy, La.; PhD in Law, Columbia U., 1970, MD, 1972; ThD, Am. Bapt. Sem., W.Va., 1974. Co-dir., rsch. scientist, psychiatrist, tchr. U.S. Indsl. Rsch. Labs., Washington, 1972-78, 85—, legal cons., 1972-78, 85—; dir. World Industries Internat. Rsch. Facilities, Washington, 1982-90; pres. Nat. Cons. Network, Sacramento, Calif., 1993—; host Do It With Dr. Harris, TV and radio program, 1985—, DownTowners (variety show); staff Carolina Christian U., Linwood, N.C. Prodr. Open Forum, 1980-82; prodr. (musical TV program) Heaven's Paradise, 1994-96. Dir., founder Haven Home for Children, dir. childrens devel. programs; overseer United Full Gospel Ministries and Chs., Calif., state overseer, bishop; founder, dir. Children's Consortium Network for Rights in Am., 1988—; developer Shepherds House I Learn Inst. for Abused Children, Calif., 1996—. Recipient Charles Neville Humanitarian award, 1979, 84, 89, Piedmont Humanitarian award, 1985, 90, Nat. Journalist award Owens Sci. Acad. Collegiate Assn., 1995. Mem. Am. Guild Hypnotherapists, Am. Assn. Nutritional Counselors Therapists, Internat. Assn. Christian Pastoral Counselors, Am. Guild Variety Artists, Investigators, Reporters, Editors Assn., Am. Fedn. Fed. Investigators Reporters, Am. Soc. Rsch. Scientists, N.C. Assn. Christian Counselors Therapists (diplomate), Nat. Chaplains Assn. (juvenile officer). Democrat. Avocations: art, archeology, watersports, inventing, karate (7th degree black belt Tirakuando karate). Office: Nat Cons Network PO Box 340792 Sacramento CA 95834-0792

HARRISON, ALONZO, construction company executive; b. Forrest City, Ark., Aug. 16, 1952; s. Walter James and Doris Nell (Burnett) H.; children:

Aliah T., Aloha A. BA, Washburn U., 1974; postgrad., Harvard U., 1977; MPA, Kans. U., 1978; postgrad., U. Pa., 1980; MBFP, Dartmouth Coll., 1995; postgrad., Ga. Tech. U. Sys. engr. IBM, Topeka, Kans., 1974-75; pub. svc. employment mgr. Dept. Labor Svcs., Topeka, 1975-79; mgmt. coord. The Menninger Found., Topeka, 1979-84; pres., CEO H.D.B. Constrn., Inc., 1984—; fin. seminars instr.; mgmt., investment and tax cons; mem. adv. com. Gen. Motors Corp. Fairfax Constrn. Project, Kansas City, Kans., 1984-86; chmn. region regulatory fairness Bd. U.S. Small Bus. Assn. Contbr. articles to profl. jours. Fin. advisor Topeka Alcoholic Info. Ctr., 1977, White House Conf. Small Bus., 1995; mgr. Women's Slow Pitch Softball, 1974-78; sponsor Girls AAU Basketball, 1977-79; mem. E. Topeka Neighboorhood Improvement Assn., 1981-82, East Topeka Cmty. Devel. Bd., Shawnee County Cmty. Devel. Corp.; mem. adv. com. Kans. Dept. Transp., 1985-86; youth counselor Upward Bound Program, 1970-74; minority committeeman Dem. Party, 1979-82; mem. Cmty. Housing Resource Adv. Coun., Cmty. Resource Coun. Bank IV of Kans., 1993—, WIBW TV Adv. Coun., 1989-93. Recipient Cert. of Achievement, Harvard U., 1977, Outstanding Minority Bus. in Kans., award, 1987; named Outstanding Contractor, 1987, 89-91, Gov.'s Martin Luther King, Jr. Man of Yr., Kans., 1993, K.C. Small Bus. Person of Yr., SBA, 1998. Mem. Assn. Disadvantaged Bus. Enterprises (sec., treas.), Omega Psi Phi. Baptist.

HARRISON, ANGELA EVE, industrial company executive; b. Little Rock, Apr. 9, 1967; d. Stephen E. and Donie E. (Brown) H.; m. Petey King, Sept. 19, 1998. BA in Psychology, U. Ark., 1989. Clin. specialist Nutri-Sys., Little Rock, 1990-91; sec., trea. Welsco, Inc., Maumelle, Ark., 1991-94, pres., CEO, 1994—. Co-chairperson Humane Soc., Pulaski County, Ark., 1996-98. Recipient Ark. Bus. Exec. Yr. Ark. Bus., 1997, named Top 100 Women Ark., 1996, 97, 98, Top 500 Women Owned Cos. Working Women Mag., 1998, 99. Mem. Nat. Assn. Women Bus. Owners (Woman Bus. Owner of Yr., Ark chpt. 1998), Nat. Welding Supply Assn. (regional chmn. 1996—), Internat. Oxygen Mfg. Assn. (bd. dirs. 1996—), Young Pres.'s Assn. Avocation: golf. Office: Welsco Inc 9006 Crystal Hill Rd North Little Rock AR 72113-6693

HARRISON, BENJAMIN LESLIE, retired army officer; b. Trumann, Ark., July 23, 1928; s. Benjamin Leslie and Ruth Venetta (Blackshane) H.; m. Carolyn Wright Algee, Sept. 29, 1951; children: Benjamin Leslie, III, Laura Louise. BA, U. Miss., 1951; MA, U. Mo., Kansas City, 1963; MBA, Auburn U., 1969; grad., Advanced Mgmt. Program, Harvard U., 1971. Enlisted U.S. Army, 1946, commd. 2d lt., 1951, advanced through grades to maj. gen., 1977; served as troop comdr. and staff officer, various locations, 1951-73; dep. comdt. U.S. Army Command and Gen. Staff Coll., Ft. Leavenworth, Kans., 1973-76; dep. comdg. gen. U.S. Army Aviation Center and Ft. Rucker, Ala., 1976-77; dir. rev. officers edn. and tng. U.S. Army, Washington, 1977-78; comdg. gen. U.S. Army Adminstrn. Center and Ft. Benjamin Harrison, Ind., 1978-79; ret., 1979. Decorated D.S.M., Silver Star with oak leaf cluster; named to U. Miss. ROTC Hall of Fame, 1992, U.S. Army Aviation Hall of Fame, 1992. Home: 221 E 21st Ave Belton TX 76513-2017 *My philosophy of life: Work and study as though you are going to live forever; enjoy life as though you are going to die tomorrow.*

HARRISON, CAROL LOVE, fine art photographer; b. Washington, Mar. 4, 1950; d. Hunter Craycroft and Margaret Varina (Edwards) H.; m. Gregory Grady, Feb. 25, 1978; children: Olivia Love Harrison, Blake McGregor, Harrison Edwards. BS in Fgn. Svc., Georgetown U., 1973; MFA, U. Md., 1983. guest lectr. art George Mason U., 1986, 87, Shephard Coll.,1987, 96, No. Va. C.C., 1986; participant creative program Fairfax County Coun. of Arts, 1990-92; participant artist workshop program Va. Mus. Fine Arts, Richmond, 1988-89. One-woman shows include Rizzoli Internat. Bookstore and Gallery, Washington, 1982, Arnold and Porter, Washington, 1983, Covington and Burling, Washington, 1983, Crowell and Moring, Washington, 1984, Nat. Strategy Info. Ctr., Washington, 1984, Swidler and Berlin, Washington, 1985, Reynolds Minor Gallery, Richmond, Va., 1987, Peninsula Fine Arts Ctr., Newport News, Va., 1989, Georgetown U., Washington, 1994, Touchstone Gallery, 1999, Rockville Arts Place, 1999; exhibited in group shows, Art Gallery U. Md., Smithsonian Instn., Washington Women's Art Ctr., including Washington Project for Arts, 1981, Beijing Inst., 1985, Art Inst. Pitts., 1986, Mus. Contemporary Art, Washington, 1996, 98, 99, Dallas Mus. Art, 1997, Washington Arts Coun. Gallery, 1998 ; represented in permanent collections at Corcoran Gallery Art, Washington, Va. Mus. Fine Arts, Richmond, Arnold and Porter, Williams Cos., Tulsa, Covington and Burling, United Va. Bank, Touchstone Gallery, 1999, Mus. of Contemporary Art, Washington, 1999, Artscape, Balt., 1999; pub. in Antietam Rev., Washington Rev., Photo Rev., Washingtonian, Profiles, Kalliope; Honorarium, Fla. Dept. Cultural Affairs, 1998; represented by Reynolds Gallery. Vol. Our Lady of Victory Sch., Washington, 1995-96, Westminster Sch., Annandale, Va., 1996-98; mem. women's com. Nat. Symphony Orch., 1998—. Recipient honorarium Fla. Dept. Cultural Affairs, 1998, Cash award for black and white photography Westmoreland Art Nats., LaTrobe, Pa., 1998. Mem. Nat. Mus. Women in Arts (women's com. 1997—), Congl. Country Club, Langley Swim and Tennis Club. Episcopalian. Avocations: films, swimming, bicycling. Home and Office: 666 Live Oak Dr Mc Lean VA 22101-1569

HARRISON, CHARLES MAURICE, lawyer, former communications company executive; b. Anderson, S.C., Aug. 30, 1927; s. Emmitte Smallwood and Jessie Maysel (Hawkins) H.; m. Lorna Jean Tomalty, June 27, 1970; children: Suzanne Elizabeth, Linda Jean. AB, Marshall U., 1949; JD, W.Va. U., 1952. Bar: W.Va. 1952, D.C. 1958, N.Y. 1965, N.J. 1972. Legal asst. W.Va. Dept. Ins., Charleston, 1952-54; hearing examiner Pub. Svc. Commn., Charleston, 1954-57; atty. Chesapeake and Potomac Tel. Co., Washington and Charleston, 1957-64, Western Electric Co., N.Y.C., 1964-69; gen. atty., sec., treas. Bellcomm, Inc., Washington, 1969-71; asst. gen. counsel, asst. sec. Bell Tel. Labs., Murray Hill, N.J., 1971-75; gen. atty., sec. Bell Tel. Labs., 1975-76, sec., gen. counsel corp. matters, 1976-84; asst. sec., asst. gen. counsel AT&T Bell Labs, 1985-87; gen. atty. AT&T, Berkeley Heights, N.J., 1987-89; of counsel Ventantonio & Wildenhain, Warren, N.J., 1993—; bd. dirs. Somerset County C. of C. (chmn. 1990-92). Trustee Family Counseling Svcs. Somerset County, N.J., 1976-94, pres., 1978-81; chmn. R&D Coun. N.J., 1985-87, Bridgewater (N.J.) Commn. Substance Abuse, 1986-89, Bridgewater Mcpl. Facilities Commn., 1988-89, Bridgewater Twp. Alliance Com. on Alcoholism, 1989—; bd. dirs. Martin Luther King Youth Ctr., 1984-90, Somerset Alliance for Future, 1992, N.J. affiliate Am. Heart Assn., 1991-94, Somerset County Coalition on Affordable Housing, 1995—; bd. dirs., pres. Somerset Treatment Svcs., 1992—; mem. Bridgewater-Raritan Youth Svcs. Commn., chmn., 1989-90; mem. Bridgewater Planning Bd., 1989-94, chmn., 1992-94; mgmt. com. Ridewise Traffic Mgmt. Assn., 1992-96; mem. Somerset County Local Adv. Com. on Alcohol and Drug Abuse, 1992—, Bridgewater Twp. Operation (police-pub.) Cooperation, 1992—, 200 Club of Somerset County, 1990—; trustee Henderson Meml. Scholarship Fund, 1993—; mem. Twp. Coun., 1994—, coun. pres., 1996. With AC, U.S. Army, 1945-46, W.Va. Air N.G., 1955-57, UsAFR, 1955-62. Named Somerset County Citizen of Yr., 1996. Mem. Rotary (treas. Somerville 1995—). Republican. *Regardless of profession, career, occupation, or trade, success in life can only be achieved if a significant part of one's effort includes the gift of one's personal talent, energy, and time to his or her community. In this part of one's life, financial reward, public recognition, or even results, do not count as much as dedication and sincerity, but the opportunities for creativity and personal satisfaction are enormous.*

HARRISON, CHARLES WAGNER, JR., applied physicist; b. Farmville, Va., Sept. 15, 1913; s. Charles Wagner and Etta Earl (Smith) H.; m. Fern F. Perry, Dec. 28, 1940; children—Martha R., Charlotte J. Student, U.S. Naval Acad. Prep. Sch., 1933-34, U.S. Coast Guard Acad., 1934-36; BS in Engring., U. Va., 1939, EE, 1940; SM, Harvard U., 1942, M of Engring., 1952, PhD in Applied Physics, 1954; postgrad., MIT, 1942, 52. Registered profl. engr., Va. Engr. Sta. WCHV, Charlottesville, Va., 1937-40; commd. ensign U.S. Navy, 1939, advanced through grades to comdr., 1948; research staff Bur. Ships, 1939-41, asst. dir. electronics design and devel. div., 1948-50; research staff U.S. Naval Research Lab., 1944-45, dir.'s staff, 1950-51; liaison officer Evans Signal Lab., 1945-46; electronics officer Phila. Naval Shipyard, 1946-48; mem. USN Operational Devel. Force Staff, 1953-55; staff Comdg. Gen. Armed Forces Spl. Weapons project, 1955-57; ret. U.S. Navy, 1957; cons. electromagnetics Sandia Nat. Labs., Albuquerque, 1957-73; instr. U. Va., 1939-40; lectr. Harvard U., 1942-43, Princeton U., 1943-44; vis. prof. Christian Heritage Coll., El Cajon, Calif., 1976. Author: (with R.W.P. King) Antennas and Waves: A Modern Approach, 1969; contbr. numerous articles to profl. jours. Fellow IEEE (Electronics Achievement award 1966, best paper award electromagnetic compatibility group 1972); mem. Internat. Union Radio Sci. (commn. B), Electromagnetics Acad., Famous Families Va., Sigma Xi. Home: 2808 Alcazar St NE Albuquerque NM 87110-3516 *Research is like saving - if postponed until needed, it is too late to start. One should keep expanding his mind.*

HARRISON, CHRISTINE DELANE, educational administrator; b. Dearborn, Mich., July 22, 1947; d. Walter Frederick and Marguerite Elaine (Champagne) Hancock; m. Charles Richard Bashawaty, Aug. 31, 1968 (div. 1972); 1 child, Brett Charles; m. Andrew David Harrison, June 14, 1980; 1 child, Andrew David, II. BS, Ea. Mich. U., 1969. Cert. early elem. tchr., Mich. Tchr. Westland Schs., Mich., 1969-71, Dept. Army, Ansbach, Germany, 1971-72; prin. sec. chemistry dept. U. Mich., Ann Arbor, 1973-78; word processing mgr. Great Copy Co., Ann Arbor, 1978-79; dir., v.p. Great Lakes Sch., Madison Heights, Mich., 1979-92; v.p., adminstrn. asst., Good Herbs, Inc., 1992—. Editor: Thorne's Guide to Herbal Extracts, 1992, A Practical Guide to Herbal Extracts, 1995; editl. asst. Herbal Extracts, 1984; Bull. of Thermodynamics and Thermochemistry, 1973-78. Bd. dirs. Perry Nursery Sch., Ann Arbor, 1976-77. Recipient Prodn. award and Dedication award Los Feliz Apple Sch. Mem. Nat. Trust for Hist. Preservation, Greenpeace, Sierra Club. Avocations: reading, bicycling, aerobics, sailing. Office: Good Herbs Inc 1875 Woodslee Dr Troy MI 48083-2234

HARRISON, CLIFFORD JOY, JR., banker; b. Nashville, Feb. 21, 1925; s. Clifford Joy and Rosa Lee (Bennett) H.; m. Saralu Fondren, May 3, 1957; children: Julia Lee, Clifford Joy III, John Fondren. B.A., Vanderbilt U., 1949; postgrad., Law Sch., 1949-50, Nashville Sch. Law, 1950-53; LL.B., Stonier Grad. Sch. Banking, Rutgers, 1963; student, Advanced Mgmt. Program, Harvard U., 1975. With 3d Nat. Bank, Nashville, 1950-88; ret. vice chmn. in charge trust div., retail div. and mktg. 3d Nat. Bank, 1988; past pres. Estate Planning Coun.; past pres. trust divns. Tenn. Bankers Assn. Past pres. YMCA Found. Bd.; past chmn. bd. trustees Tenn. Nature Conservacy. 1st lt. USAAF, 1943-46. Decorated Air medal with oak leaf cluster. Mem. Exch. Club, City Club (past pres.), Belle Meade Country Club, Beta Theta Pi, Phi Alpha Delta. Episcopalian. Home: 102 Abbottsford Nashville TN 37215-2437

HARRISON, CONNIE DAY, cardiovascular clinical nurse specialist, nursing administrator, consultant; b. Baton Rouge, Aug. 10, 1956; d. Earl Newsom and Ethel Mae (Law) Day; m. James Victor Harrison, Dec. 18, 1976; children: Amy Elizabeth, Michael Earl. BSN, Southeastern La. U., 1981, MSN, 1992. RN, La., Tenn. Critical care staff nurse Baton Rouge Gen. Med. Ctr., 1981, Lane Meml. Hosp., Zachary, La., 1981-82; cardiovascular edn. coord. Baton Rouge Gen. Med. Ctr., 1982-91, cardiovascular case mgr., 1991-92, nursing case mgmt. coord., 1992-93, dir. care mgmt., 1993-94; mgr. resource and outcomes mgmt. Columbia/HCA Healthcare Corp., Nashville, 1994-96; quality cons. Vanderbilt U. Med. Ctr., Nashville, 1996-97, dir. quality resource svcs., 1997—; cons. on healthcare edn., resource and outcomes mgmt., quality mgmt., compliance with accreditation standards, 1984-94; mem. case mgmt. benchmarking team Sunhealth Alliance, Charlotte, N.C., 1992-94; lectr. nat. confs. on resource and outcomes mgmt., quality mgmt., care mgmt. across the continuum of care; rsch. on needs of elderly cardiac surgery patients and elderly congestive heart failure patients postdischarge. Author: (patient edn. manual) The Beat Goes on After Heart Surgery, 1986. Lobbyist, nursing adv. La. Nurses Assn., Baton Rouge, 1980-94. Grantee SunHealth Alliance, 1992. Democrat. Methodist. Avocations: fishing, biking, tennis, gardening. Home: 7269 Old Franklin Rd Fairview TN 37062-9161 Office: Vanderbilt U Med Ctr A 1223 Medical Center N Nashville TN 37232-2668

HARRISON, DANIEL GORDON, music educator, musician; b. Chappaqua, N.Y., Apr. 20, 1959; s. Thomas Collins and Marylou (Wright) H.; m. Anne Charlotte Turnburke, Dec. 29, 1981; children: Glenn Palmer, Theodore Brooks, Charlotte Collins. BA, Stanford U., 1981; PhD, Yale U., 1986. Vis. lectr. Yale Inst. Sacred Music, New Haven, Conn., 1986-87; assoc. prof. music U. Rochester, N.Y., 1987—; assoc. prof. music theory Eastman Sch. of Music, Rochester, 1987—; asst. organist St. Paul's Episcopal Ch., Rochester, 1990—. Author: (book) Harmonic Function in Chromatic Music, 1994 (Young Scholar award Soc. for Music Theory 1995); also contbr. to music theory jours. Vestryman St. Paul's Episcopal Ch., Rochester, 1995—. Mem. Music Theory Soc. N.Y. State (sec. 1997—), Soc. for Music Theory (publs. com. 1992-95), Am. Guild of Organists, Torch and Triangle (founding mem.). Avocations: cooking, model railroading, driving. Office: U Rochester 205 Todd Union Rochester NY 14627

HARRISON, DEBORAH LYNN, human service executive; b. Chgo., Apr. 1, 1959; d. David L. and Helen Patricia (Moran) Harrison; m. Michael S. Elliott, May 12, 1979 (div. Aug. 1991); 1 child, Colin M. BS in Bus., Ind. U., 1982. Swing mgr. McDonalds, South Bend, Ind., 1980; exec. dir. First United Methodist Day Care, South Bend, 1981-83, Boys and Girls Clubs St. Joseph County, South Bend, 1983-96, Boys & Girls Club Bloomington, Ind., 1996—; mem. profl. adv. com. Boys and Girls Clubs. Am., Streamwood, Ill., 1996—, M.I.S. task force and mktg. adv. coun., Atlanta, 1997—. Pres. St. Joseph County Youth Devel. Commn., South Bend, 1995-96; mem. Monroe County Prevention Coalition, 1996—; mem. Leadership Bloomington/Monroe County, 1997—. Mem. Monroe County Prevention Coalition, Boys and Girls Club Profls., United Way Assn. Agy. Dirs. Roman Catholic. Avocations: sports, music, literature.

HARRISON, DON EDMUNDS, oceanographer, educator; b. New Haven, Conn., Aug. 22, 1950; s. Don Edward Jr. and India Boozer Harrison. BA, Reed Coll., 1972; MS, Harvard U., 1973, PhD, 1977. Affilliate prof. U. Wash., Seattle, 1984—; oceanographer Pacific Marine Environ. Lab./Ocean Climate Rsch. Div., Seattle, 1984—; lectr. Harvard U., Cambridge, Mass., 1977-78; vis. prof. MIT, Cambridge, 1978-84. Mem. Am. Meterol. Soc., Oceanography Soc., Phi Beta Kappa. Office: NOAA PMEL OCRD 7600 Sand Point Way NE Seattle WA 98115-6349

HARRISON, DONALD CAREY, university official, cardiology educator; b. Blount County, Ala., Feb. 24, 1934; s. Walter Carey and Sovola (Thompson) H.; m. Laura Jane McAnnally, July 24, 1955; children—Douglas, Elizabeth, Donna Marie. B.S. in Chemistry, Birmingham So. Coll., 1954; M.D., U. Ala., 1958. Diplomate Am. Bd. Internal Medicine (cardiovascular disease). Intern, asst. resident Peter Bent Brigham Hosp., 1958-60; fellow in cardiology Harvard U., 1961, NIH, 1961-63; mem. faculty Stanford U. Med. Sch., 1963-86, chief div. cardiology, 1967-86, prof. medicine, 1971-86; chief cardiology Stanford U. Hosp., 1967-86, William G. Irwin prof. cardiology, 1972-86; sr. v.p., provost for health affairs U Cin. Med. Ctr., 1986—; prof. medicine, cardiology U. Cin. Coll. Medicine; CEO U. Cin. med. Ctr., 1995—; cons. to local hosps., industry and govt.; bd. dirs. Novoste, Inc., Heart Stent Inc., Pharm Products Devel., Inc., Uterine Muscle Dysfunction, Inc., Bioconcepts, Am. Heart Assn., U. Cin. Med. Assocs., Health Alliance of Greater Cin., Univ. Health Systems Consortium, Inc. Mem. editorial bd. Brit. Jour. Clin. Practice, 1993—; mem. editorial bd. Drugs, 1980—, Am. Jour. Cardiology, 1984—, Health, 1988—, Inpharma, 19926; contbr. articles to med. jours., chpts. to books. Served with USPHS, 1961-63. Fellow Interam. Soc. Cardiology (v.p. 1980-86), Am. Coll. Cardiology (mem. chmn., v.p. 1972-73, sec. 1969-70, trustee 1972-78), Am. Heart Assn. (fellow coun. circulation, clin. cardiology and basic sci., chmn. program com. 1972-76, nat. chmn. publs. com. 1976-81, pres.-elect 1980-81, pres. 1982-83); mem. Am. Soc. Clin. Investigation, Am. Fedn. Clin. Rsch., Am. Assn. Physicians, ACP, Assn. U. Cardiologists, Am. Clin. and Climatol Assn., Brit. Cardiac Soc., Acad. Medicine Cin., Assn. Acad. Health Ctrs. (past chmn.). Home: 9250 Old Indian Hill Rd Cincinnati OH 45243-3438 Office: U Cin Med Ctr ML 663 250 Health Professions Bldg Cincinnati OH 45267-0663

HARRISON, DONY, poet, writer, journalist, lecturer; b. Beaumont, Tex., June 20, 1943; d. Claude Albert and Vivian (Toups) Smart; divorced; 1 child, Roann Brown. GED, Angelina Jr. Coll., Lufkin, Tex. Adminstrv. exec., cons. various auto dealerships, Houston, 1969—; journalist Galveston (Tex.) Daily News; journalist, advisor Hope Jour., Dallas; journalist, advisor, bd. dirs. The Recovery Jour.; journalist, advisor Galveston County Jour.; journalist Jasper (Tex.) Newsboy; trainer quarter horses Beaumont and Jasper, Tex., 1953-70; counselor various hosps., Tex.; lectr. child abuse issues. Author: People, Places & Times, Where is the Love, All for the Love, Poems by an Ocean Angel, People, Places and Times; contbr. poetry to various anthologies, mags. Facilitation trainer Nat. Mental Health Assn., Houston; chpt. leader Nat. Multiple Sclerosis Assn., Houston and Galveston; vol. counselor Gulfcoast Mental Health-Mental Retardation Assn.; vol. Galveston Fine Arts Assn., Houston Mus. Fine Arts. Scholar United Ways, Woodland, Tex., 1989. Mem. Poet's Guild, Acad. Am. Poets, Nat. Libr. Poetry, Creative Arts and Sci. Assn., Poetry Soc. of Am., Sparrow Grass Poetry Forum. Roman Catholic. Avocations: softball, horseback riding, mountain biking, auto clubs, art. E-mail: poetdony@cs.com. Fax: 409 741-2527. Home and Office: 5017 Avenue R Galveston TX 77551-5280

HARRISON, EARL DAVID, lawyer, real estate executive; b. Bryn Mawr, Pa., Aug. 25, 1932; divorced; 1 child, H. Jason. BA, Harvard U., 1954; JD, U. Pa., 1960. Bar: D.C. 1960. Pvt. practice Washington; exec. v.p. Washington Real Estate Corp., Washington, 1986-94; pres. EDH Assocs., Inc., 1994—. Capt. U.S. Army, 1954-57. Decorated Order of Rio Branco (Brazil); Order of Merit (Italy). Mem. ABA, Internat. Coun. Shopping Ctrs., D.C. Bar Assn., Washington Assn. Realtors, Greater Washington Comml. Assn. Realtors, Nat. Assn. Realtors, Nat. Restaurant Assn., Met. Washington Restaurant Assn., Coun. Internat. Restaurant Brokers (v.p., gen. coun.), Harvard Club Nat. Press Club. Office: 1077 30th St NW Ste 706 Washington DC 20007-3829

HARRISON, EARL GRANT, JR., educational administrator; b. Media, Pa., Oct. 10, 1932; s. Earl Grant and Carol Rogers (Sensenig) H.; m. Jean Spencer Young, July 6, 1957; children: Colin Young, Dana How. BA, Haverford Coll., 1954, LLD (hon.), 1991; BDiv, Yale U., 1959; MA in Social and Philos. Founds. Edn., Columbia U., 1965. Instr. Religion and Philosophy Antioch Coll., 1956-58; dir. Coun. Religion Ind. Schs., N.Y.C., 1959-64; tchr. Bklyn. Friends Sch., 1964-65; dir. religious edn. William Penn Charter Sch., Phila., 1965-68; headmaster Westtown (Pa.) Sch., 1968-78; head of sch. Sidwell Friends Sch., Washington, 1978-98; bd. mgrs. Haverford Coll., 1973-85; chmn. bd. trustees Coun. Rel. Ind. Schs., 1976-78; mem. commn. ednl. issues Nat. Assn. Ind. Schs., 1979-85; chair Middle States Assn. Evaluation Vis. Team, 1983, 85, 88, 90, 93, 95, 97; group leader sch. delegation, China, 1984; mem. instl. rev. bd. Nat. Eye Inst., 1987—. Trustee Good Hope Sch., St. Croix, 1974-80, 82-88. Mem. The Headmasters Assn. (v.p. 1986-87), Country Day Headmasters Assn. (pres. 1992-93), Assn. Ind. Schs. Greater Washington (pres. 1989-90). Democrat. Avocations: tennis, travel.

HARRISON, EDWARD ROBERT, physicist, educator; b. London, Jan. 8, 1919; came to U.S., 1965; s. Robert and Daisy (White) H.; m. Photeni Marangas, June 23, 1945; children: John Peter, June Zoe. Student, Sir John Cass Coll., London U., 1937-40. With Atomic Energy Research Establishment, Harwell, Eng., 1948-64; vis. scientist CERN, Geneva, 1959-60; prin. scientist Rutherford High Energy Lab., Harwell, 1964-65; sr. rsch. assoc. Nat. Acad. Sci., Washington, 1965-66; prof. dept. physics and astronomy U. Mass., Amherst Coll., Mt. Holyoke, Smith, Hampshire Coll., 1966-96, head five coll. astronomy depts., 1973-74; vis. prof. Astronomy Ctr., U. Sussex, Eng., 1974, U. Va., Charlottesville, 1976; staff mem. Nat. Radio Astronomy Obs., 1976; vis. astronomer Carter Obs., N.Z., 1981; Disting. vis. scholar U. N.C., 1987, Disting. Univ. prof. physics and astronomy, 1987-96; adj. prof. U. N.Mex., 1996-98, U. Ariz., 1998—; lectr. various fgn. univs. Author: Cosmology: The Science of the Universe, 1981, Masks of the Universe, 1985, Darkness at Night: The History of a Cosmological Riddle, 1987; contbr. articles and book revs. to profl. jours. With Brit. Army, 1940-47. Named Disting. Univ. Prof. of Physics and Astronomy, U. Mass., 1986. Fellow Inst. Physics (Eng.), AAAS, Royal Astron. Soc., Am. Phys. Soc.; mem. Internat. Astron. Union, Am. Astron. Soc., Sigma Xi. Home: # 815 11 E Orange Grove Rd Tucson AZ 85704-5553

HARRISON, ELZA STANLEY, medical association executive; b. Akron, Ohio, Apr. 10, 1938; d. Marshall Clayton and Elsie Helen (Gaczlyi) Stanley; m. Ronald L. Davis, Feb. 4, 1961 (div. June 1979); children: Mark Davis, Lesley Davis; m. William Harrison II, May 29, 1989 (dec.). BA in English, U. Akron, 1963. Cert. assn. exec. Acting exec. dir., dir. pub. affairs, legis. rep. Med. & Chirurg. Facility, Balt., 1975-86; v.p. industry affairs Med. Mut. Liability Ins. Co., Hunt Valley, Md., 1986-87; exec. dir. Md. Dental Assn., Columbia, 1987—; bd. dirs. Md. Found. Dentistry for Handicapped, Columbia, Dental Assn. Co., Columbia; mem. bd. visitors Nat. Mus. Dentistry. Mem. Am. Soc. Assn. Execs., Am. Soc. Constituent Dental Execs., Md. Soc. Assn. Execs. (pres. 1985-86). Democrat. Episcopalian. Office: Maryland Dental Assn 6450 Dobbin Rd Columbia MD 21045-5824

HARRISON, ETHEL MAE, financial executive; b. Ft. Dodge, Iowa, June 11, 1931; d. Arthur Melvin and Grace Gwendolyn (Hall) Cochran; m. Cleo Arden Goss, June 17, 1951 (div. 1962); m. Clarence Hobert Harrison, Dec. 23, 1965 (dec. Feb. 1993). Dipl., Internat. Corres. Schs., Riverside, Calif., 1986. Tax preparer Goss Tax Svc., Riverside, 1953-61; tax preparer H & R Block, Inc., Riverside, 1972-84, supr./bookkeeper, 1974-79; owner, pres. Ethel Harrison's Tax Svc., Riverside, 1984—. Mem. NAFE, Riverside Tax Cons. Assn. (sec. 1988—), Am. Soc. Profl. and Exec. Women, Am. Inst. Profl. Bookkeepers, Soc. of Calif. Tax Profls., Nat. Assn. Tax Cons., Nat. Soc. Tax Profls., Nat. Assn. Tax Preparers, Inland Soc. Tax Cons., Nat. Taxpayers Union. Avocations: camping, fishing, photography, auto racing. Home and Office: 10460 Gramercy Pl Riverside CA 92505-1300

HARRISON, FAYE VENETIA, anthropologist, educator; b. Norfolk, Va., Nov. 25, 1951; d. James and Odelia Blount (Harper) H.; m. William Louis Conwill, May 17, 1980; children: Giles, L. Mondlane, Justin. AB, Brown U., 1974; MA, Stanford U., 1977, PhD, 1982. Asst. prof. anthropology U. Louisville, 1983-89; assoc. prof. U. Tenn., Knoxville, 1989-97; prof. anthropology, grad. dir. women's studies U. S.C., Columbia, 1998—. Assoc. editor Urban Anthropology, 1992—; cons. editor Women and Aging, 1990-96, Identities: Global Studies of Culture and Power, 1992—; editor: Black Folks in Cities Here and There, 1988, Decolonizing Anthropology, 1991, 2d edit., 1997, W.E.B. DuBois and Anthropology, 1992, American Anthropologist Contemporary Forum: Race and Racism, 1998, African-American Pioneers in Anthropology, 1999; mem. editl. com. Critique of Anthropology, 1995—, Annual Rev. Anthropology, 1995—; mem. editl. bd. U. Tenn. Press, 1996-97; mem. adv. com. Womanist Theory and Research; contbr. articles to profl. jours. Organizer Ky. Rainbow Coalition, Louisville, 1988-89; mem. Black Women Organized for Power, Louisville, 1984-86, Alliance Against Women's Oppression, Louisville, 1988-89; mem. adv. bd. Knoxville Roman Cath. Diocese's Justice, Peace, Integrity of Creation, 1996-97. Recipient Cert. of Merit, Phi Beta Kappa, 1993; Ford Found. fellow, 1987-88. Mem. Assn. Black Anthropologists (pres. 1989-91), Internat. Union Anthrop. and Ethnol. Scis. (co-chair commn. on anthropology of women 1993-98, 98—). Office: U SC Flinn Hall Columbia SC 29208

HARRISON, FRANK, former university president; b. Dallas, Nov. 21, 1913; s. Frank and Ruby (Davison) H.; m. Elsie Claire Redfearn, June 26, 1946; children—Frank, Susan Claire, James Redfearn. B.S., So. Methodist U., 1935; M.S., Northwestern U., 1936, Ph.D., 1938; M.D., U. Tex. Southwestern Med. Sch., 1956. Mem. faculty U. Tenn. med. units, Memphis, 1938-51, prof., 1946-51, chief div. anatomy, 1946-51; prof. anatomy U. Tex. Southwestern Med. Sch., Dallas, 1952-68, assoc. dean, 1956-68; asso. dean grad. studies U. Tex. at Arlington, 1965-68, acting pres., 1968-69, pres., 1969-72; pres. Health Sci. Ctr., San Antonio, 1972-85; dir. Inst. Biotech., 1985. Named Distinguished Alumnus So. Meth. U., 1971. Mem. Am. Assn. Anatomists, Am. Physiol. Soc., Tex. Philos. Soc., Biophys. Soc., IEEE, Soc. Exptl. Biology and Medicine, Phi Beta Kappa, Alpha Omega Alpha, Kappa Sigma, Alpha Kappa Kappa. Home: 4168 Valley Ridge Rd Dallas TX 75220-1924

HARRISON, GEORGE BROOKS, research engineer, retired career officer; b. Greenville, S.C., July 30, 1940; s. William Henry and Mary Carter (Ogburn) H.; m. Pennie Maria Jenkins, Nov. 29, 1963; children: Taylor Leigh, Todd Henry, Tracy Elizabeth. BS in Pub. Policy, USAF Acad., 1962; MBA, U. Pa., 1970. Cert. flight instr. single and multi-engine instrument glider (6000 accident-free flying hours, 540 combat hours). Commd. 2d lt. USAF, 1962, advanced through grades to maj. gen., 1989; fighter pilot, forward air contr. and instr. 557th and 436th Tactical Fighter Squadron, Florida and Vietnam, 1963-69; joint exercise planner U.S. Readiness Command, MacDill AFB, Fla., 1971-74; grad. Armed Forces Staff Coll., Norfolk, Va., 1974; ops. officer 13th and 25th Tactical Fighter Squadron, Udorn, Thailand, 1974-75; squadron comdr. 4485th Test Squadron, Eglin AFB, Fla., 1975-78; grad. Air War Coll., Montgomery, Ala., 1979; wing comdr. 479th Tactical Tng. Wing, Holloman AFB, N.Mex., 1982-86; chief joint ops. div. Orgn. of Joint Chiefs of Staff, Washington, 1984-86; dept. chief of staff, plans U.S. Air Forces in Europe, Ramstein AFB, Fed. Republic Germany, 1986-89; asst. chief of staff, studies and analyses Hdqrs. USAF, Washington, 1989-91; dep. chief of staff for ops. U.S. Air Forces in Europe, Ramstein AFB, 1991-92; comdr. Air Warfare Ctr., Eglin AFB, Fla., 1992-93; comdr. combined/joint task force USAF, S.W. Asia, 1993; comdr. Air Force Operational Test and Evaluation Ctr., Kirtland AFB, N.Mex., 1994-97; dir. rsch. ops. Ga. Tech Rsch. Inst., 1997—; mem. USAF Sci. Adv. Bd., Washington, 1998—; sponsor Mil. Ops. Rsch. Soc., 1989-91; U.S. del. NATO Adv. Group on Aerospace R&D, Paris, 1989-91; lectr. to mil., tech. and civic groups, 1982-95. Contbr. articles to mil. jours. Mem., lt. col. CAP, S.C., N.Mex. and Ga., 1978—; dist. commr. Boy Scouts Am., Fed. Republic Germany, 1986-89, coun. commr., 1991-92, exec. coun. N.M., 1995-97; exec. v.p., bd. dirs. Air Warrior Courage Found., 1998—; bd. dirs. Nat. Mus. Aviation, 1998—. Decorated D.S.M. with oak leaf cluster, D.F.C., Air medal with eleven oak leaf clusters, Legion of Merit with one oak leaf cluster, Def. Superior Svc. medal. Fellow Beta Gamma Sigma; mem. Order of Daedalians (flight capt. 1987-89), Air Force Assn., Quiet Birdmen. Baptist. Avocation: civilian flying. Office: Ga Tech Rsch Inst 400 10th St CRB 225 Atlanta GA 30318-5712

HARRISON, GEORGE HARRY, III (HANK HARRISON), publishing executive, author; b. Monterey, Calif., June 17, 1940; s. Edith Cooke; 1 child, Courtney Love. BA in Psychology, San Francisco State Univ., 1965; postgrad., Univ. London, 1978-81. Mgr. Grateful Dead (formerly Warlocks), Palo Alto, Calif., 1965-66; founder, counselor LSD rescue Inst. Contemporory Studies, San Francisco, 1967; pvt. practice counselor San Francisco, 1967-78; pub., founder Archives Press, San Francisco, 1979—; writer-in-residence Montalvo Ctr. Arts, Saratoga, Calif., 1974; founder Media Assocs., Los Altos, Calif., 1991—; presenter, expert witness, lectr. in field; co-owner Sacramento Equestrian Ctr., Riverglades, 1998; story cons. NBC prodn. The Search for the Unicorn Killer, 1999. Author: The Dead Trilogy, 1972-97, Quest for Flight, 1975, 2nd edit., 1995, The Cauldron and the Grail, 1992, Mysteries of the Grail, 1998, Ace of Cups The Grail in Tarot, 1998, Confessions of a Naked Beekeeper, 1996, The Stones of Ancient Ireland, 1996; contbr. VSD (Paris), San Francisco Oracle, The Berkeley Barb, The Ga. Straight and L.A. Free Press, Dragon's Quest, The Green Knight; editor emeritus Doctor Dobb's Jour.; tech., staff writer Info World, A Plus; Vancouver Magazine, radio, TV guest including Geraldo, Am. Jour., Inside Edition, Hard Copy, Maury Povitch Show, America's Most Wanted, Fox News Contribution, 1998; editor: Vancouver Mag., 1974-75, Las Vegas Sun, 1976-77, Jour. Psychedelic Drugs, 1967; contbg. editor High Times, 1996-97; prodr. (CD) Garcia: The Lost Concert, 1999. With USN Med. Corps., 1958-61. Rocky Mountain Writer's Conf. scholar, 1968, Frances Yates scholar Warburg Inst. Univ. London, 1981, Applied Materials Corp. scholar, 1984. Mem. Press Club, Ind. Pub. Assn., San Francisco Press Club, Las Vegas Press Club, Masons. Democrat. Avocations: motorcycle repair, horse breeding, dog breeding. E-mail: hank@arkives.com., hankskids@aol.com. Home & Office: PO Box 46 Wilton CA 95693-0046

HARRISON, GORDON RAY, engineering executive, consultant, research scientist; b. Wister, Okla., Dec. 14, 1931; s. Trannie Gordon and Isah Lee (Ray) H.; m. Barbara Ann Herndon, June 22, 1957; children: William Andrew, Melissa Leigh, Lori Jeanne, Amanda Ray. B.S. in Physics, U. Central Ark., 1952; M.S., Vanderbilt U., 1954, Ph.D., 1958. Sr. staff engr. and engring. mgr. Sperry Microwave, Clearwater, Fla., 1957-71; prin. research scientist to lab. dir. Engring. Expt. Sta., Ga. Inst. Tech., Atlanta, 1971-83; v.p. Electromagnetic Scis., Inc., Atlanta, 1983-91; ind. cons. tech., bus., 1991—. Contbr. chpt. to book, numerous articles to profl. jours. Fellow IEEE; mem. Soc. Microwave Theory and Techniques, Magnetics Soc., Mustang Club Am., Sigma Xi. Democrat. Methodist. Patentee microwave ferrimagnetic garnets. Office: Electromagnetic Scis Inc Box 7700 Norcross GA 30091-7700

HARRISON, GREGORY, actor; b. Avalon, Calif., May 31, 1952; s. Ed Harrison; m. Randi Oakes; children: Emma Lee, Lily Anne, Kate La Priel, Quinn Edgar. Studied at Estelle Harman Actors Workshop and with Lee Strasberg and Stella Adler. Co-founder Catalina Prodns. Performances include: (films) Fraternity Row, 1977, Razorback, 1984, North Shore, 1987, Body Chemistry II: Voice of a Stranger, 1992, Cadillac Girls, 1993, Hard Evidence, 1994, It's My Party, 1996; (star TV series) Logan's Run, 1977-78, Trapper John, M.D, 1979-86, The Family Man, 1990, FalconCrest, 1989, True Detectives, 1991, New York News, 1995; (mini-series) Centennial, 1978, Fresno, 1986; (TV films) Trilogy of Terror, 1975, The Gathering, 1977, The Best Place To Be, 1979, The Women's Room, 1980, Enola Gay, 1980, For Ladies Only, 1981, The Fighter, 1983, Seduced, 1985, Oceans of Fire, 1986, Hot Paint, 1988, Red River, 1988, Dangerous Pursuit, 1990, Angel of Death, 1991, Bare Essentials, 1991, Duplicates, 1992, Breaking the Silence, 1992, Split Images, 1993, A Family Torn Apart, 1993, Caught in the Act, 1993, Deadly Lessons, 1993, Sudden Fury, 1993, Robin Cook's Mortal Fear, 1994, Lies of the Heart: The Story of Laurie Kellogg, 1994, A Christmas Romance, 1994, A Dangerous Affair, 1995, Summer of Fear, 1996, When Secrets Kill, 1996, When Secrets Kill, 1997; (TV episodes) Barnaby Jones, M*A*S*H, Code R, Sisters, Touched By An Angel, 1996; (theatre) The Hasty Heart, 1981-82, Billy Budd, 1984, Picnic, 1986, The Promise, 1975, The Fantasticks, 1971, The Subject Was Roses, 1974, Carnal Knowledge, 1993, Child's Play, 1991, Paper Moon-The Musical, 1993, The Music Man, 1994, Steel Pier, 1997. With U.S. Army, 1969-71. Recipient Best New Actor award Dallas Film Festival, 1976.

HARRISON, GREGORY, public information officer; b. Jan. 24, 1966. Dep. comms. dir. to Senator John Ashcroft U.S. Senate, Washington, 1995—. Office: 316 Senate Hart Office Bldg Washington DC 20510-2504

HARRISON, HAROLD HENRY, physician, scientist, educator; b. Oak Park, Ill., Mar. 18, 1951; s. Orlow Harold and Wanda Odell (Olesczynski) H.; m. Brenda E. Naccari, 1993; children: Amelia, Margaret, Henry. BS in Biochemistry with honors, U. Ill., 1972; MD, U. Ill., Chgo., 1979, PhD, 1979. Diplomate Nat. Bd. Med. Examiners, Am. Bd. Pathology. Resident in internal medicine U. Ill. Hosps., Chgo., 1979-80; resident lab. medicine Northwestern U. Hosp., Chgo., 1980-83; asst. prof. U. Chgo. Med. Sch., 1984-92; asst. dir. clin. chemistry U. Chgo. Hosps., 1984-86, dir. spl. chemistry, toxicology and molecular pathology, 1986-90, dir. protein and genetic chemistry, 1990-92, staff physician, 1984-92; staff physician United Blood Svcs., Chgo., 1981-84; dir. clin. pathology, med. dir. Phoenix Labs., 1992-97, Genetrix, Inc., Scottsdale, Ariz., 1992-97; assoc. dir. Southwest Biomedical Rsch. Inst., Scottsdale, 1992-97; med. dir. S.W. Genetics and Lab. Medicine, Phoenix, 1997—, HEMEX Labs., Phoenix, 1997—, Quest Diagnostics, Teterboro, N.J., 1998—; chair workshop program Genetics Task Force Ill., Chgo., 1988; sr. clin. lectr. pathology Med. Sch., U. Ariz., Tucson, 1993—; lectr. in field. Contbr. articles to profl. publs. Adelmann Fund scholar, 1976, T. B. Sachs scholar, 1975, V. S. Yarros scholar, 1974, Edmund J. James scholar, 1969-72. Fellow Coll. Am. Pathologists (inspector 1992), Am. Soc. Clin. Pathologists; mem. Am. Coll. Med. Genetics, Am. Coll. Physician Execs., Am. Soc. Human Genetics, Am. Assn. Clin. Chemistry, Sigma Xi, Phi Eta Sigma. Achievements include discovery ofXRD image process, prealbumin Chicago, serum protein polymorphism M-158, low-Z expressor phenotype, CDGS diagnosis with 2DE-immunogloblin chain microheterogeneity and clonality analysis; research in clinical and genetic applications of two-dimensional electrophoresis. Office: U Ariz AMRI 3031 N Civic Plz Ste 228 Scottsdale AZ 85251

HARRISON, HENRY STARIN, real estate educator, entrepreneur; b. New Haven, June 19, 1930; s. Julius and Helen (Starin) H.; m. Minna Snyder, Apr. 16, 1960 (div. 1970); children: Julie, Eve; m. Ruth Lambert, May 30, 1976; children: Kate, H. Alex. BS in Econs., U. Pa., 1952; MA, Goddard Coll., 1974. Asst. to pres. Charlton Press, Derby, Conn., 1954-56; assoc. Harris Weissbuck Co., New Haven, 1956-57; pres. Harrison Appraisal Co., New Haven, 1958-90, H & R Ins. Agy., 1975-88, Health Care Mmgt. Co., 1964-86, The H2 Co., New Haven, 1986-95, H Squared Co., 1995—, A&A World Travel, New Haven, 1989-94; treas., v.p. Forms & Worms, Inc., 1989-97; pub. NAFFA, Inc., New Haven, 1985—; appraisal cons. Nat. Assn. Environ. Risk Auditors, Bloomington, Ind., 1989-94. Author: Houses, Houses, Houses, 1974, URAR-Illustrated Guide, 1975, Appraising Single Family Residences, 1978, Home Buying - The Complete Illustrated Guide, 1980, Small Income Property-Illustrated Guide, 1980, Small Income Property-Illustrated Guide, 1980, Dictionary of Real Estate Appraisal, 1982, Condominium-Illustrated Guide, 1984, Review Appraisers Handbook, 1987, Appraising Residences and Income Properties, 1989, ARIP Student Workbook, 1989, NAERA Environmental Manual, 1989, Environmental Risk Screening, 1990, Standards of Professional Appraisal Practice and Ethics, 1991, ARIP General Property Supplement, Real Estate Evaluation Illustrated Guide, 1993, Real Estate Principles and Practices Plus, 1994, Russian Appraisal Textbook, 1994, Advanced Appraisal Methods, 1994, Guide to New Haven, Connecticut, 1995; pub. Real Estate Valuation Mag., 1985—; also articles, book chpts., audio-visual materials; patentee Perpetual Birthday and Anniversary Reminder Calendar. Alderman City of New Haven, 1961-63; pres. Young GOP, New Haven, 1960, Real Estate Edn. Found., 1980—, Greater New Haven Arts Coun., 1989-91; trustee Goddard Coll., 1976-78. 1st lt. USAF, 1952-54. Recipient Real Estate Educators Assn. award, 1995. Fellow Am. Coll. Health Care Adminstrs. (award 1984); mem. Am. Inst. Real Estate Appraisers (pres. Conn. chpt. 1975-76, Profl. recognition award 1976, 78, MAI award 1980), Am. Soc. Appraisers (award 1987), Soc. Real Estate Appraisers (nat. vice gov. 1980), Columbia Soc. Appraisers (award 1959), Greater New Haven Real Estate Bd. (Realtor of Yr. award 1976, Educator of Yr. 1992), Lawn Club. Jewish. Avocations: water sports, travel. Home: Carriage House 315 Whitney Ave New Haven CT 06511-3772 Office: Harrison Cos Lowel Level 315 Whitney Ave New Haven CT 06511-3772

HARRISON, JAMES OSTELLE, ecologist; b. Harrison, Ga., June 17, 1920; s. James Drew and Marie (Mills) H.; m. Katherine Deal, Jan. 12, 1942 (div. 1970); m. Joyce Rape, Mar. 21, 1971; children: Michael James, Juliet. BA, Mercer U., 1949; MS, U. Ga., 1953; PhD, Cornell U., 1962. Assoc. entomologist United Fruit Co., Palmar Sur, Costa Rica, 1956-62; asst. prof. biology Mercer U., Macon, Ga., 1962-64, assoc. prof., 1964-67, prof., 1967-85, prof. emeritus, 1986—; columnist Macon Telegraph, 1976-80; editorial assoc. Seabreeze Mag., St. Simons Island, Ga., 1985-96; ecol. cons. Avland Devel. Co., Macon, 1970-71. Contbr. articles to profl. jours. Chmn. Area Water Quality Adv. Com., Macon, 1979-82, City Energy Adv. Com., Macon, 1979-80; pres. Ocmulgee Monument Assn., Macon, 1981-83. Capt. USAAF, 1942-47, North Africa, ETO. Mem. Nat. Audubon Soc., Nat. Wildlife Fedn. Republican. Baptist. Avocations: photography, hiking, camping, writing, travel. Home: 1179 Matthews Pl Macon GA 31210-3425 Office: Mercer U 1400 Coleman Ave Macon GA 31207-0003

HARRISON, JAMES WILBURN, gynecologist; b. Martin, Tenn., Mar. 23, 1918; s. Woodie and Georgia Harrison; m. Babs Wise Dudley, Jan. 29, 1948; children: James Wilburn Jr., James Michael, Babs Suzanne, Linda Denise. Student, U. Tenn., Martin, 1936-37, U. Tenn., Knoxville, 1937-38; MD, U. Tenn., Memphis, 1941; grad., U.S. Army Staff Coll., Ft. Leavenworth, Kans., 1972. Diplomate Am. Bd. Ob-gyn. Asst. resident Brooke Gen. Hosp., Ft. Sam Houston, Tex., 1947; chief surgery Station Hosp., Clark AFB, Philippines, 1948-49; resident, sr. resident Letterman Gen. Hosp., San Francisco, 1949-51; advanced through grades to col. U.S. Army, ret., 1954; chief staff St. Michael Hosp., Texarkana, Ark., Wadley Regional Med. Ctr., Texarkana, Tex., So. Clinic, Texarkana, Ark.; asst. clin. prof. ob.-gyn. U. Ark. Coll. Medicine, Little Rock. Chmn. Bowie County Child Welfare Bd.; mem. N.E. Tex. Mental Health Bd. Decorated Army Commendation medal, Legion of Merit. Fellow ACS (life), ICS (life), Am. Coll. Ob-gyn. (life), Assn. Mil. Surgeons U.S. (life), Tex. Soc. Ob-gyn. (life); mem. AMA (life), Tex. Med. Assn., Northridge Country Club (founding), Alumni Assn. U.S. Army Command and Gen. Staff Coll., Tri-State Med. Soc. (pres. 1960s), Am. Legion, AMA Sr. Phyicians, Tex. 50 Yr. Club. Methodist. Avocations: collecting, travel, military history. Home: 4009 Pecos St Texarkana TX 75503-2857

HARRISON, JEFFREY WOODS, poet, educator; b. Cin., Oct. 10, 1957; s. Robert Sattler and Anne Woods H.; m. Julia Wells, Nov. 28, 1981; children: William, Eliza. BA, Columbia U., 1980; MFA, U. Iowa, 1984. Rsch. asst. Phillips Collection, Washington, 1987; instr. Johns Hopkins U., Balt., 1989; lectr. George Washington U., Washington, 1990-93; writer in residence Phillips Acad., Andover, Mass., 1997—; vis. writer U. Md., College Park, 1991. Author: The Singing Underneath, 1988, Signs of Arrival, 1996; contbr. poetry to publs. Recipient Lavan Younger Poets award Acad. Am. Poets, 1989; Wallace E. Stegner fellow Stanford U., 1985-86, Amy Lowell fellow Harvard U., 1988-89, Ingram Merrill Found. fellow, 1988, 95 Nat. Endowment Arts fellow, 1992, John Simon Guggenheim Meml. Found. fellow, 1999. Home: 59 Highland Rd Andover MA 01810

HARRISON, JEREMY THOMAS, dean; b. San Francisco, Dec. 23, 1935; s. James Gregory and Agnes Johanna (Patrick) H.; m. Roseanne E. Thomas, Dec. 29, 1962 (dec. Oct. 1983); children: James, Amelia, Roseanne, Jeremy, Alexandra, Nadya, Rachel; m. Laura Ellen Marrack, Apr. 28, 1990; children: Robert, Peter, Paul, Philip. BS, U. San Francisco, 1957, JD, 1960; LLM, Harvard U., 1962. Bar: Calif. 1961, Hawaii 1987. Assoc. Brobeck, Phleger & Harrison, San Francisco, 1960-61; law clk. to assoc. justice U.S. Ct. Claims, Washington, 1962-63; lectr. law U. Ghana, Accra, 1963-64, U. Ife, Ibadan, Nigeria, 1964-66; prof. law U. San. Francisco, 1966-85; dean Sch. Law U. Hawaii, Honolulu, 1985-94; dean Detroit Coll. Law Mich. State U., East Lansing, 1996-98, prof. law, 1998—; vis. prof. law Haile Sellassie I U., Addis Ababa, Ethiopia, 1971-74, U. Hawaii, 1977-79; Elips Disting. prof. law Gadjah Mada U., Yogyakarta, Indonesia, 1995-96. Author: Cases and Materials on Evidence, Africa, 1967, Cases and Materials on Ethiopian Civil Procedure, 1974. Counsel citizen's panel Hawaii's Jud. Adminstrn., Honolulu, 1985-86; bd. dirs. Straub Found., Honolulu; pres. Pacific Health Rsch. Inst., Honolulu, 1993-95. Mem. ABA, Am. Bar Found., Calif Bar Assn., Hawaii Bar Assn., Internat. 3d World Legal Studies Assn. Office: Mich State U Detroit Coll Law 368 Law College Bldg East Lansing MI 48824-1300

HARRISON, JOHN ALEXANDER, financial executive; b. Lakeland, Fla., Jan. 22, 1944; s. William Henry and Aileen Helen (Jarvi) H.; m. Susan Leigh Smart, May 9, 1970; children: Kathryn Leigh, Jane Elizabeth. B.I.E. with highest honors, Ga. Inst. Tech., 1966; M.B.A. (J. Spencer Love fellow 1966-68), Harvard U., 1968. With Baxter Travenol Labs., Inc., Deerfield, Ill., 1968-78; v.p. fin. and adminstrn. internat. Baxter Travenol Labs., Inc., 1977-78; v.p. fin. Tiger Leasing Group, 1980-82, N.Am. Car Corp., subs. Tiger Internat., Inc., Chgo., 1978-81; pres. Tiger Fin. Services, Inc., 1981-82; exec. v.p. Merrill Lynch Leasing Inc., N.Y.C., 1982-85; mng. dir. Merrill Lynch Capital Markets, N.Y.C., 1982-87, real estate fin. group investment banking div., 1985-87; chief fin. officer U.S. Consumer Banking Group Citibank, N.A., N.Y.C., 1987-91; chief fin. officer and mng. dir. Fin. Security Assurance Holdings Ltd., N.Y.C., 1991—. Bd. dirs. Youth Guidance, Chgo., 1979-80. Mem. Harvard Bus. Sch. Club Chgo. (dir. 1970-71), Tau Beta Pi, Phi Kappa Phi, Phi Eta Sigma, Tau Kappa Epsilon. Office: Fin Security Assurance Holdings Ltd 350 Park Ave New York NY 10022-6022

HARRISON, JOHN CONWAY, state supreme court justice; b. Grand Rapids, Minn., Apr. 28, 1913; s. Francis Randall and Ethlyn (Conway) H.; m. Ethel M. Strict; children—Nina Lyn, Robert Charles, Molly M., Frank R., Virginia Lee. LLD, George Washington U., 1940. Bar: Mont. 1947, U.S. Dist. Ct. 1947. County atty. Lewis and Clark County, Helena, Mont., 1934-60; justice Mont. Supreme Ct., Helena, 1961-98, ret., 1998. Pres. Mont. TB Assn., Helena, 1951-54, Am. Lung Assn., N.Y.C., 1972-73, Mont. coun. Boy Scouts Am., Great Falls, Mont., 1976-78. Col. U.S. Army. Mem. ABA, Mont. Bar Assn., Kiwanis (pres. 1953), Sigma Chi. Home: 215 S Cooke St Helena MT 59601-5143

HARRISON, JOHN RAYMOND, foundation executive, retired newspaper executive; b. Des Moines, June 8, 1933; s. Raymond Harrison and Dorothy (Stout) Harrison Cohen; m. Lois Cowles, June 24, 1955 (div. Apr. 1981); children: Gardner Mark, Kent Alfred (dec.), John Patrick, Lois Eleanor; m. Mary Gee MacQueen, Sept. 5, 1981. Grad., Phillips Exeter Acad., 1951; AB, Harvard U., 1955, postgrad. Sch. Bus., 1955-56; DHL (hon.), Fla. So. Coll. With various papers throughout the U.S.; vice pres. N.Y. Times Co., ret.; chmn. Harrison Charitable Found., Atlanta; dir. Internat. Herald-Tribune, Paris, 1974-91. Bd. dirs. Ft. Pierce (Fla.)-St. Lucie County Indsl. Devel. Coun., 1959-62, Ft. Pierce Meml. Hosp., 1959-62, Lincoln Pk. Child Care Ctr., Ft. Pierce, 1959-62, Gainesville United Fund, 1965, Boys Club Gainesville, 1965, U. Fla. Found., 1967, YMCA Greater Lakeland, 1967-69, Human Rels. Coun. Lakeland, 1967-69, Boys Club Lakeland, ARC, 1967-69; trustee Robert H. Anderson Found., Ridge Sch., Bartow, Fla., High Mus., 1988-94; mem. Pres.'s Resources Coun. Wellesly (Mass.) Coll.; mem. bd. counsellors Fla. So. Coll., 1974; mem. bd. visitors Emory U., 1984, pres., 1986; trustee Westminster Schs., 1989-92, Kennesaw State Coll. Found.; mem. bd. councillors Carter Presdl. Ctr.; mem. bd. overseers Harvard U., 1995—. Recipient Pulitzer prize for editl. writing, 1965, Nat Headliners award for pub. svc. editl. writing, Nat. Headliners Club, 1972, Walker Stone award for editl. writing Scripps-Howard Found., 1974, 76, Silver Gavel award for pub. svc. editls. ABA, 1977, Sigma Delta Chi Bronze medal, 1970, 73. Mem. Greater Lakeland C. of C. (dir. 1966-67), Associated Harvard Alumni (dir. 1979-82), Spee Club, Hasty Pudding Inst. 1770 (grad. dir.), Capital City Club, Commerce Club, Knickerbocker Club, Harvard Club (N.Y.C., Boston, Ga. bd. dirs.), Kennebunk River Club, Piedmont Driving Club (Atlanta). Office: Harrison Charitable Found 2600 Peachtree Rd NW Apt 8 Atlanta GA 30305-3609

HARRISON, JOHN TODD, social studies teacher; b. July 1, 1969. BA in History and Education, College of William and Mary, 1991. Cert. secondary social studies tchr., Va. Tchr. Roanoke (Va.) city schs., 1991—; advanced placement U.S. govt. tchr. Roanoke, 1996—. E-mail:tharris2@ix.netcom.com. Home: 5133 Sugar Loaf Drive Roanoke VA 24018-2251

HARRISON, JONATHAN EDWARD, accountant, law enforcement consultant; b. Mobile, Ala., Dec. 23, 1975; s. Billy Ray and Eddie Ruth Harrison. Student, S.W. Ala. Police Acad., 1997, U. S. Ala. Dep. Mobile County Sheriff's Office, 1997—. With U.S. Army, 1996—. Scholar US Army ROTC, 1997. Mem. AICPA, Assn. Cert. Fraud Examiners, Acctg. Club, Beta Alpha Psi. Avocations: mountain biking, running, weight lifting, football, scuba diving. E-mail: jharrisonú1999@yahoo.com.

HARRISON, JOSEPH WILLIAM, state senator; b. Chgo., Sept. 10, 1931; s. Roy J. and Gladys V. (Greenman) H.; B.S., U.S. Naval Acad., 1956; postgrad. Ind. U. Law Sch., 1968-70; m. Ann Hovey Gillespie, June 9, 1956; children—Holly Ann, Tracy Jeanne, Thomas Joseph, Amy Beth, Kitty Lynne, Christy Jayne. Asst. to pres. Harrison Steel Castings Co., Attica, Ind., 1960-64, sales research engr., 1964-66, asst. sec., 1966-69, sec., 1969-71, v.p., 1971-84, dir., 1968-84, mem. Ind. Senate, 1966—, majority leader, 1980—. Mem. Attica Consol. Sch. Bd., 1964-66, pres., 1966-67. Served with USN, 1956-60. Mem. Am. Legion, Sigma Chi. Republican. Methodist. Lodges: Elks, Eagles. Home: 504 E Pike St Attica IN 47918-1524 Office: PO Box 409 Attica IN 47918-0409 also: State Senate State Capitol Indianapolis IN 46204

HARRISON, JULIA, councilwoman; b. Rochester, N.Y., June 10, 1920; d. Henry Hirsch (dec.) and Magdalena Hirsch; m. Joseph Harrison; children: Christopher, Susan Diane, Elizabeth. BA cum laude, Queens Coll., 1972. Chmn. Queens County new Dem. Coalition; dist. leader 26th Assembly Dist. Part A, 1972-83; N.Y. state assemblywoman 26th Dist., 1983-85; city councilwoman dist. 20 N.Y.C. Coun., 1986—; former mem. consumer affairs, internat. intergroup rels., spl. events and state legis. coms. N.Y.C. Coun., chairwoman aging com., mem. health, edn. and govt. operating coms. Mem. NAACP, Flushing Boys Club, Dem. Club Flushing, Whitestone and Col Point, Edward I. Lipsky Post Jewish War Vets. Office: 39-15 Main St Flushing NY 11354*

HARRISON, KENNY, Olympic athlete; b. Milw., Feb. 13, 1965. Grad., Kans. State U., 1988. Track & field athlete; winner silver medal Pan-Am Jr. Games, 1984; ranked No. 1 in world triple jump Track & Field News, 1990, 91; winner Goodwill Games, 1990; winner gold medal Olympic Summer Games, 1996. Office: c/o USA Track & Field Ste 140 1 RCA Dome Indianapolis IN 46225*

HARRISON, LOIS SMITH, hospital executive, educator; b. Frederick, Md., May 13, 1924; d. Richard Paul and Henrietta Foust (Menges) Smith; m. Richard Lee Harrison, June 23, 1951; children: Elizabeth Lee Boyce, Margaret Louise Wade, Richard Paul. BA, Hood Coll., 1945, MA, 1993; MA, Columbia U., 1946; LHD (hon.), Hood Coll., 1993. Counselor CCNY, 1945-46; founding adminstr., counselor, instr. psychology and sociology Hagerstown (Md.) Jr. Coll., 1946-51, registrar, 1946-51, 53-54, instr. psychology and orienta, 1954-56; registrar, instr. psychology, Balt. Jr. Coll., 1951-54; bus. mgr., acct. for pvt. med. practice Hagerstown, 1953—; trustee Washington County Hosp., Hagerstown, 1975-97; chmn. bd. Washington County Hosp., 1986—; mem. bd. Washington Couty Health Sys. Inc., 1997—; bd. dirs. Home Fed. Savs. Bank, Hagerstown, 1984—, chmn., 1997; chmn. acute care Health Sys. Bd., 1997—; chmn. bd. dirs. Home Fed. Savs. Bank, 1998; speaker ednl. panels, convs. hosp. panels and seminars. Author: The Church Woman, 1960-65. Trustee Hood Coll., Frederick, 1972—, chmn. bd., 1979—; mem. Md. Gov.'s Commn. to Study Structure and Ednl. Devel. Commn., 1971-75; pres. Washington County Coun. Ch. Women, 1970-72; appointee Econ. Devel. Commn., County Impact Study Commn. Bd.; bd. dirs. Md. Hosp. Assn., Md. Chs. United, 1975—; chmn. bd. dirs. Md. Hosp. Edn. Inst., 1988-98; mem. Christ's Reformed Ch., 1935—; pres. Ch. Consistory; chmn. Chesapeake Healthcare Forum, 1995—. Recipient Alumnae Achievement award Hood Coll., 1975, Washington County Woman of Yr. award, AAUW, 1984, Md. Woman of Yr. award, 1984, Md. Woman of Yr. award Francis Scott Key Commn. for Md.'s 350th Aniversary, 1984; named one of top 10 women Tri-State area, Herald-Mail Tri-State newspaper, 1990, Zonta Internat. Woman of Yr., 1994. Mem. Hagerstown C. of C. Republican. Home: 12835 Fountain Head Rd Hagerstown MD 21742-2748 Office: Washington Cty Hosp Off Chmn Bd Hagerstown MD 21740

HARRISON, MARION EDWYN, lawyer; b. Phila., Sept. 17, 1931; s. Marion Edwyn and Jessye Beatrice (Cilles) H.; m. Carmelita Ruth Deimel, Sept. 6, 1952; children: Angelique Marie (Mrs. Kevin B. Bounds), Marion Edwyn III, Henry Deimel. BA, U. Va., 1951; LLB, George Washington U., 1954, LLM, 1959. Bar: Va. 1954, D.C. 1958, Supreme Ct. 1958. Spl. asst. to gen. counsel Post Office Dept., 1958-60, assoc. gen. counsel, 1960-61, mem. bd. contract appeals, 1958-61; ptnr. firm Harrison, Lucey & Sagle (and predecessors), Washington, 1961-78, Barnett & Alagia, 1978-84; ptnr. Scott, Harrison & McLeod, 1984-86, Law Offices Marion Edwyn Harrison, Washington, 1986—; mem. coun. Adminstrv. Conf. U.S., 1971-78, sr. conf. fellow, 1984-88; mem. D.C. Law Revision Commn., 1975-92; lectr. Nat. Jud. Coll., Reno, 1979, La. State U. Law Sch., Aix-en-Provence, 1987, 89, Tulane U. Law Sch., Crete, 1997, Hoffstra U. Law Sch., Nice, 1999; adv. dir. NationsBank, N.A., 1987-93. Contbr. articles to profl. publs.; editor-in-chief Fed. Bar News, 1960-63; mem. editorial bd. Adminstrv. Law Rev., 1976-89. Trustee AEFC Pension Fund, Chgo., 1986-92; pres. Young Rep. Fedn. Va., 1954-55; mem. Va. Rep. Cen. Com., 1954-55; bd. visitors Judge Adv. Gen. Sch., Charlottesville, Va., 1976-78; chmn. Wolf Trap Assn., 1984-87; bd. dirs. Wolf Trap Found., 1984-88; pub. mem. USIA Insp. Mission, Argentina, 1971. Officer AUS, 1955-58. Decorated Commendation medal. Fellow Am. Bar Found. (life); mem. ABA (chmn. sect. adminstrv. law 1974-75, ho. of dels. 1978-88, bd. govs. 1982-86, chmn. com. on fgn. and internat. orgns. 1986-87, lawyers in govt. com. 1980-82), FBA (nat. coun. 1966-82), Inter-Am. Bar Assn., Bar Assn. D.C. (chmn. adminstrv. law sect. 1970-71, bd. dirs. 1971-72), George Washington U. Law Assn. (pres. 1974-77), Smithsonian Instn. (nat. bd. dirs. 1991-97), Federalist Soc., Soc. Mayflower Desc., Washington Golf and Country Club, Met. Club, Nat. Lawyers Club (Washington), Farmington Country Club (Charlottesville, Va.), Knight of Malta. Republican. Roman Catholic. Home: 4111 N Ridgeview Rd Arlington VA 22207-4617 also: 7222 E Gainey Ranch Rd Scottsdale AZ 85258-1529 Office: 1700 K St NW Ste 700 Washington DC 20006-3813 also: 107 Park Washington Ct Falls Church VA 22046-4519 also: Falkenstrasse 14, 8008 Zurich Switzerland

HARRISON, MARK ISAAC, lawyer; b. Pitts., Oct. 17, 1934; s. Coleman and Myrtle (Seidenman) H.; m. Ellen R. Gier, June 15, 1958; children: Lisa, Jill. AB, Antioch Coll., 1957; LLB, Harvard U., 1960. Bar: Ariz. 1961, Colo. 1991. Law clk. to justices Ariz. Supreme Ct., 1960-61; ptnr. Harrison,

Harper, Christian & Dichter, Phoenix, 1966-93, Bryan Cave, LLP, Phoenix, 1993—; adj. prof. U. Ariz. Coll. Law, 1995-97; nat. bd. visitors, 1996—. Co-author: Arizona Appellate Practice, 1966; editorial bd. ABA/BNA Lawyers Manual on Profl. Conduct, 1983-86; contbr. articles to profl. jours. Bd. dirs. Careers for Youth, 1963-67, pres., 1966-67; vice-chmn. Maricopa County Dem. Cen. Com., 1967-68, Ariz. Dem. Com., 1969-70, legal counsel, 1970-72; del. Dem. Nat. Conv., 1968; chmn. Phoenix City bond Adv. Commn., 1976-79; pres. Valley Commerce Assn., 1978; bd. dirs. Planned Parenthood of Cen. and No. Ariz., 1992-98, pres., 1995. Fellow Am. Bar Found., Am. Acad. Appellate Lawyers (pres. 1993-94); mem. ABA (chmn. commn. pub. understanding law 1984-87, standing com. profl. discipline 1976-84, chmn. 1982-84, chmn. coord. com. on professionalism 1987-89, com. on women in the profession, Michael Franck Profl. Responsibility award 1996), Assn. Profl. Responsibility Lawyers (pres. 1992-93), Maricopa County Bar Assn. (pres. 1970), Am. Bd. Trial Advocates, State Bar Ariz. (bd. govs. 1971-77, pres. 1975-76), Ariz. Bar Found. (pres. 1991), Am. Inns of Ct. (master, pres. Sandra Day O'Connor chpt. 1993-94), Nat. Conf. Bar Pres. (pres. 1977-78), Western States Bar Conf. (pres. 1978-79), Am. Judicature Soc. (exec. com. 1983-86, bd. dirs. 1983-87), Ariz. Civil Liberties Union, Harvard Law Sch. Assn. (nat. exec. oun. 1980-84), Am. Law Inst. (nat. coun., lawyers com. for human rights). Office: Bryan Cave Ste 2200 2 North Central Ave Phoenix AZ 85004

HARRISON, MICHAEL, opera company executive; b. Augusta, Ga., June 22, 1940; s. Oscar T. and Helen (Harrison) Smith; m. Patricia Arnell Ragusa, Oct. 7, 1989. BA, Vanderbilt U., 1962; postgrad., Yale U., 1962-64. Actor, singer Broadway, Regional Opera and Theatres, 1964-80; gen. dir. Providence Opera Theatre, 1979-81, Opera/Columbus, Columbus, Ohio, 1983-89, Balt. Opera Co., 1989—; pres. Harrison/Connor Consultants, L.A., 1981-83. Mem. Ctr. Club, Rotary, Md. Club. Episcopalian. Home: 208 E Cold Spring Ln Baltimore MD 21212-4701 Office: Balt Opera Co Inc 110 W Mount Royal Ave Baltimore MD 21201-5732

HARRISON, MICHAEL GREGORY, judge; b. Lansing, Mich., Aug. 4, 1941; s. Gus and Jean D. (Fuller) H.; m. Deborah L. Dunn, June 17, 1972; children: Abigail Ann, Adam Christopher, Andrew Stephen. AB, Albion (Mich.) Coll., 1963; JD, U. Mich., 1966; postgrad., George Washington U. Bar: Mich. 1966, U.S. Dist. Ct. (ea. and we. dists.) Mich. 1967. Asst. pros. atty. County of Ingham, Lansing, 1966-70, corp. counsel, 1970-76; judge 30th Jud. Cir. State of Mich., Lansing, 1976—; chief judge 30th Jud. Cir. State of Mich., Lansing, 1980-91; judge Ct. of Claims, 1979—; counsel Capital Region Airport Authority, Lansing, 1970-76, Ingham Med. Ctr., Lansing, 1970-76; chmn. Ingham County Bldg. Authority, Mason, Mich., 1971-76; adj. prof. Thomas M. Cooley Law Sch., Lansing, 1976—. Editor Litigation Control, 1996; contbr. chpt. to Michigan Municipal Law, Actions of Governing Bodies, 1980; contbr. articles to profl. jours. Mem. shared vision steering com. United Way-C. of C.; mem. adv. bd. Hospice of Lansing, 1989—; pres. Greater Lansing Urban League, 1974-76, Lansing Symphony Assn., 1974-76; chmn. Mid. Mich. chpt. ARC, Lansing, 1984-86; bd. dirs., sec. St. Lawrence Hosp., Lansing, 1980-88; bd. dirs. ARC Gt. Lakes Regional Blood Svcs., 1991-95, Lansing 2000, 1987—; mem. exec. bd. Chief Okemos coun. Boy Scouts Am.; mem. criminal justice adv. com. Olivet Coll.; hon. bd. dirs. Lansing Area Safety Coun.; mem. State Bar Bd. Commrs., 1993-96; mem. felony sentencing guidelines steering com., mem. caseflow mgmt. coordinating com., mem. juror use and mgmt. task force Mich. Supreme Ct. Recipient Disting. Citizens award Boy Scouts Am., Disting. Vol. award Ingham County Bar Assn., Disting. Alumni award Albion Coll. Fellow Am. Bar Found., Mich. Bar Found. (pres. 1991—); mem. ABA, Am. Judicature Soc. (bd. dirs. 1996—), Mich. Judges Assn. (treas. 1991, sec. 1992, 2d v.p. 1993, 1st v.p. 1994, pres. 1995), Nat. Conf. State Trial Judges (exec. com. 1991-94, vice-chmn. 1995-96, chmn. 1997-98), Country Club Lansing, Rotary. Republican. Congregationalist. Avocations: skiing, golf, tennis, travel, photography. Office: Cir Ct 407 N Cedar St Mason MI 48824

HARRISON, MICHAEL JAY, physicist, educator; b. Chgo., Aug. 20, 1932; s. Nathan J. and Mae (Nathan) H.; m. Ann Tukey, Sept. 1, 1970. A.B., Harvard, 1954; M.S., U. Chgo., 1956, Ph.D., 1960. Fulbright fellow and H. Van Loon fellow in theoretical physics U. Leiden, Netherlands, 1954-55; NSF fellow U. Chgo., 1957-59; research fellow math. physics U. Birmingham, Eng., 1959-61; asst. prof. Mich. State U., East Lansing, 1961-63; assoc. prof. Mich. State U., 1963-68, prof., 1968—, faculty grievance officer, 1972-73, dean Lyman Briggs Coll., 1973-81, adj. prof. community health scis., 1988-93, adj. prof. internal medicine and epidemiology, 1993—; vis. research physicist Inst. Theoretical Physics, U. Calif., Santa Barbara, 1980-81; with Air Force Cambridge Research Center, summer 1953, M.I.T. Lincoln Lab., summer 1954, RCA Sarnoff Lab., summers 1961-63; physicist Westinghouse Labs., summer 1956; cons. RCA Lab., 1961-64, United Aircraft Co., 1964-66, U.K. Atomic Energy Authority, Harwell Lab., summer 1960, Thailand project in Bangkok, Mich. State U.-AID, summer 1968; vis. research affiliate theoretical biology and biophysics, Los Alamos Nat. Lab., 1987-88. Contbr. articles to U.S., fgn. profl. jours. Am. Council on Edn. fellow U. Calif., Los Angeles, 1970-71. Fellow Am. Phys. Soc.; mem. AAUP (chpt. treas. 1966-67), N.Y. Acad. Scis., Harvard Club of Ctrl. Mich. (pres. 1988-93), Rotary, B'nai B'rith, Phi Beta Kappa, Sigma Xi. Jewish. Avocations: hiking, travel, photography. Home: 277 Maplewood Dr East Lansing MI 48823-4746 Office: Mich State U Physics Dept East Lansing MI 48824

HARRISON, MONIKA EDWARDS, business development executive; b. Waiblingen, Federal Republic of Germany, July 31, 1949; came to U.S., 1957; d. Donnie Everette and Irmgard (Weber) E. BA, Fla. State U., 1970, MS, 1977. Cabinet aide State Treas. Fla., Tallahassee, 1971-73; advisor to Pres. Fla. Senate, Tallahassee, 1973-74; legis. analyst U.S. Dept. Agr., Washington, 1975-76; dir. policy and planning U.S. Dept. Edn., Washington, 1976-85; dep. dir. Inst. Mus. Svcs., Washington, 1985-86; assoc. adminstr. U.S. SBA, Washington, 1986-89; assoc. dir. bus. devel. COLSA, Inc., Arlington, Va., 1989-92; assoc. adminstr. for small bus. devel. ctrs. U.S. SBA, Washington, 1992-93, assoc. adminstr. for bus. initiatives, 1993—; commr. Cen. European Small Bus. Enterprise Devel. Commn., 1992-95; lectr. George Mason U., Fairfax, Va., 1985-86. Recipient Sr. Exec. Svc. award U.S. SBA, 1992-95. Office: US SBA 409 3rd St SW Washington DC 20024-3212*

HARRISON, MOSES W., II, state supreme court justice; b. Collinsville, Ill., Mar. 30, 1932; m. Sharon Harrison; children: Luke, Clarence. BA, Colo. Coll.; LLB, Washington U., St. Louis. Bar: Ill. 1958, Mo. 1958. Pvt. practice, 1958-73; judge 3d Jud. Cir., Ill., 1973-79, 5th Dist. Appellate Ct., Ill., 1979-92; justice Ill. Supreme Ct., 1992—. Mem. ABA, Am. Judicature Soc., Ill. State Bar Assn. (former bd. govs.), Madison County Bar Assn. (former pres.), Tri-City Bar Assn., Met. St. Louis Bar Assn., Justinian Soc. Office: 333 Salem Pl Ste 170 Fairview Heights IL 62208

HARRISON, PATRICK WOODS, lawyer; b. St. Louis, July 14, 1946; s. Charles William and Carolyn (Woods) H.; m. Rebecca Tout, Dec. 23, 1967; children: Heather Ann, Heath Aaron. BS, Ind. U., 1968, JD, 1972. Bar: Ind. 1973, U.S. Dist. Ct. (so. dist.) Ind. 1973, U.S. Dist. Ct. Nebr. 1982, U.S. Supreme Ct. 1977. Assoc. Goltra, Cline, King & Beck, Columbus, Ind., 1972-73; ptnr. Goltra & Harrison, Columbus, 1973-78; pvt. practice Columbus, 1979-80; ptnr. Cline, King, Beck and Harrison, Columbus, 1980-85, Beck, Harrison & Dalmbert, Columbus, 1985—; Ind. Jud. Nominating Commn. nominee Ind. Supreme Ct., 1984. With U.S. Army, 1968-70. Fellow Ind. Trial Lawyers Assn. (bd. dirs. 1984—); mem. Am. Trial Lawyers Assn. Republican. Baptist. Avocation: golf. Home: 14250 W Mount Healthy Rd Columbus IN 47201-9309 Office: Beck Harrison & Dalmbert 320 Franklin St Columbus IN 47201-6732

HARRISON, RICHARD DEAN, minister, counselor; b. Gaffney, S.C., Oct. 15, 1952; s. Wiley H. and Georgia Ann (Earwood) H.; m. Sandra Kay Parris, Oct. 16, 1970; children: Kathryn Hope, Richard Dean Jr. BA, U. S.C., 1973, MAT, 1975; MDiv, So. Bapt. Theol. Sem., 1986, DMin, 1990. Ordained to ministry So. Bapt. Conv., 1985. Pastor English Bapt. Ch., Stephensport, Ky., 1985-87, Rehoboth Bapt. Ch., Gaffney, 1987-92; counselor Cherokee Mental Health and Counseling Ctr., Gaffney, S.C., 1992—; pastor Lando (S.C.) Bapt. Ch., 1997—. Chaplain Gaffney Jaycees, 1977-79, Asbury-Rehoboth Vol. Fire Dept., Gaffney, 1989—; bd. dirs. Piedmont Community Action Agy., Spartanburg, S.C., 1979-81. Mem. Breckinridge Bapt. Assn. (exec. com. 1985-87), Broad River Bapt. Assn. (exec. com., dir. Sunday sch. 1987-92). Home: 117 Stacy Dr Gaffney SC 29341-1433 Office: Cherokee Mental Health and Counseling Ctr 125 E Robinson St Gaffney SC 29340-2444

HARRISON, RICHARD WAYNE, lawyer; b. Marfa, Tex., June 23, 1944; s. George Willis and Mildred Irene (Rooks) H.; m. Teresa Green, Jan. 14, 1981; children: Michelle, Breck, Shawn, Victoria. AA with honors, Schreiner Inst., Kerrville, Tex., 1964; BBA, U. Tex.-Austin, 1966, JD, 1968. Bar: Tex. 1968, U.S. Dist. Ct. (ea. dist.) Tex. 1968, U.S. Dist. Ct. (so. dist.) Tex. 1973, U.S. Dist. Ct. (we. dist.) Tex. 1974, U.S. Supreme Ct. 1975, U.S. Ct. Appeals (5th cir.) 1977, U.S. Dist. Ct. (no. dist.) Tex. 1983, U.S. Ct. Fed. Claims, 1987. Ptnr. Florence & Harrison, Hughes Springs, Tex., 1968-69; sole practice Hughes Springs, Tex., 1969-73; asst. atty. gen. Atty. Gen.'s Office of Tex., Austin, 1973-74, chief tax div., 1974-76, spl. asst. atty. gen., 1976-78; ptnr. McGinnis, Lochridge & Kilgore, Austin, Tex., 1978-87, ptnr. Jones, Day, Reavis & Pogue, Austin, 1987-94; mng. ptnr. Harrison & Rial, L.L.P., Austin, 1994—. Precinct chmn. Cass County Dem. Com., 1969-73; pres. Hughes Springs Indsl. Found., 1970; Cass County chmn. Salvation Army, 1970-72; area coordinator Lloyd Bentsen for Senate Com., 1970; chmn. Hughes Springs United Fund Drive, 1972; mem. Austin Convocation Cursillo Steering Com., 1983-86, chmn., 1985-86; sr. warden St. Luke's-on-the-Lake Episcopal Ch., 1984. Fellow Tex. Bar Found.; mem. State Bar of Tex. (mem. fed. jud. com. 1980-83, bar jour. com. 1980-83), Travis County Bar Assn., Cass County Bar Assn. (past pres.), Schreiner Coll. Former Student Assn. (bd. dirs. 1985-88), trustee, treas. St. Andrews Episcopal Sch., Austin. Democrat. Clubs: Austin, Horseshoe Bay Country, Barton Creek Country. Lodge: Masons. Home: 1730 Camp Craft Rd Austin TX 78746 Office: Harrison & Rial LLP 410 Congress Ave Ste 100 Austin TX 78701-3620

HARRISON, ROBERT DREW, management consultant; b. Des Moines, May 17, 1923; s. Roland T. and Grace M. (Drew) H.; m. Evelyn Colonna Berkley, June 5, 1948 (dec. Nov. 1982); children: Nancy Berkley, Evelyn Lee, Roberta Drew, Adrienne Tipp; m. Suzanne Bien, Oct. 14, 1985. SB cum laude, Harvard, 1945, MBA with distinction, 1948. Mem. faculty Harvard Grad. Sch. Bus. Administrn., 1948-49; with John Wanamaker, Phila., 1949-87, mdse. exec., 1949-60, v.p., mdse. mgr., 1960-66, v.p. stores, 1966-67, exec. v.p., 1967-68, pres., chief exec. officer, 1968-78; vice chmn. John Wanamaker div. Carter, Hawley Hale Stores, Inc., Phila., 1978-87, cons., 1985-87; bd. dirs. Phila. Electric Co.; bd. dirs. Mut. Assurance, Phila., chmn., 1970-94; mng. ptnr. U.S. Golf Mgmt. Ptnrs. Bd. dirs. Phila. Urban Coalition, 1971-84, Ctrl. Phila. Devel. Corp. (formerly Old Phila. Devel. Corp.), Exec. Svc. Corps Delaware Valley, 1984-94; bd. dirs. Urban Affairs Partnership (formerly Greater Phila. Movement), 1983-87, co-chmn., 1974. Lt. (j.g.) USNR, 1943-46. Mem. Merion (Pa.) Golf Club, Merion Cricket Club. Home: 74 Parkridge Dr Bryn Mawr PA 19010-2259 Office: 259 N Radnor Chester Rd Ste 140 Radnor PA 19087-5256

HARRISON, ROBERT WILLIAM, zoologist, educator; b. Napoleon, Ohio, Nov. 3, 1915; s. Charles Foster and Goldie Della (Fahrer) H.; m. Marion Murlless Billings, May 30, 1943 (div. 1973); children: Suzanne Harrison Marchetti, Elizabeth A. Harrison Greene, Barbara A. Harrison DiOrio; m. Ruth Lightner Hastings, July 31, 1974 (div. Nov. 1980). AB, Oberlin Coll., 1938; postgrad., Springfield (Mass.) Coll., 1938-39; cert., Marine Biology Lab., Woods Hole, Mass., summer 1939, 41; MA, Wesleyan U., Middletown, Conn., 1941; MS, Yale U., 1942, PhD (Nat. Cancer Inst. rsch. fellow), 1949; cert., U.S. Naval War Coll., Newport, R.I., 1969, U.S. Naval Med. Sch. Asst. in biology Springfield Coll., 1938-39; asst. Wesleyan U., 1939-41, vis. assoc. prof., 1957; asst. in zoology Yale U., New Haven, 1941-42, 46-48, rsch. asst. pathology Med. Sch., 1942; instr. zoology U. R.I., Kingston, 1949-50, asst. prof., 1950-56, assoc. prof., 1956-65, prof., 1965-77; vis. extension prof. physiology R.I. Hosp. Sch. Nursing, Providence, 1966, 67, 70; prof. emeritus U. R.I., Kingston, 1977—, assoc. dean divsn. univ. extension, 1968-69, acting dean, 1969-70; acting chmn. dept. zoology U. R.I., 1974-75; cons. Crime Lab.; chmn. Faculty Senate, U. R.I., Kingston, 1963-64; advisor to health professions, 1970-74; vis. spl. instr. Brown U., 1958. Author: An Analysis of a Random Sample of Navy Air-Sea Rescues, 1945. d. dirs. Animal Rescue League So. R.I.; mem. Rep. Town Com. of South Kingstown, R.I., 1962-66, chmn. bipartisan com. on town adminstr. Town Coun., 1966; pres. Friends of U. R.I. Libr.; scoutmaster, commr. Boy Scouts Am.; choir Kingston Congl. Ch., 1952—. Cpl. Ohio N.G., 1932-41; lt. USNR, active duty, 1942-46; capt. USNR, Med. Svc. Corps, 1953-70, ret. AEC grantee, 1962; Physiol. Soc. rsch. fellow U. Ill., 1959. Mem. AAUP, AAAS, Am. Inst. Biol. Scis., R.I. Assn. Health, Phys. Edn. and Recreation (hon. life), N.Y. Acad. Scis., Am. Soc. Zoologists, Am. Coll. Sports Medicine, Fleet Res. Assn., Ret. Officers Assn., Am. Assn. Ret. Persons, Commodore Point Judith Yacht Club, South County Chamber Singers Club, Tavern Hall Club of Kingston, U.S. Sailing Assn., Sierra Club, Oberlin Coll. Heisman Club, Smithsonian Assocs., River Bend Athletic Club, YMCA South County, Yale Assn. R.I., U. R.I. Faculty Ctr. Assn. Congregationalist. Home: 40 Dockray St Wakefield RI 02879-3915 Office: U RI Dept Zoology Kingston RI 02881

HARRISON, ROSLYN SIMAN, lawyer; b. Phila., Mar. 6, 1935; d. Max and Stella (Shapiro) Siman: m. Saul E. Harrison, June 12, 1955 (div. Mar. 1990); children: Dana Lynn, Julia Anne, Michael E. BA summa cum laude, Bryn Mawr Coll., 1956; LLB with honors, Rutgers U., Newark, 1977. Bar: N.J. 1977, U.S. Dist. Ct. N.J. 1977, U.S. Ct. Appeals (3rd cir.) 1981, N.Y. 1985, U.S. Dist. Ct. (ea. dist.) N.Y. 1985, U.S. Dist. Ct. (so. dist.) N.Y. 1987, U.S. Supreme Ct. 1987, U.S. Dist. Ct. (ea. dist.) Pa. 1988, U.S. Ct. Appeals (fed. cir.) 1994. Tchr. history Longmeadow (Mass.) High Sch., 1957-59; instr. polit. sci. Webster Coll., Webster Groves, Mo., 1964-66; assoc. McCarter & English, LLP, Newark, 1977-85, ptnr., 1986—. Social Sci. Rsch. Coun. grantee, 1955. Mem. ABA, N.Y. State Bar Assn., Assn. Fed. Bar State of N.J., N.J. Bar Assn. (mem. curriculum adv. com. Inst. for Continuing Legal Edn. 1990-96, chmn. N.J. bar intellectual property law sect. 1993-95), N.J. Intellectual Property Law Assn. (chmn. copyright com. 1993, chmn. trademark com. 1994-95), Internat. Trademark Assn. (internat. com., meetings com.), Am. Arbitration Assn., John J. Gibbons Am. Inn. of Ct. (mem. com. 1993—). Office: McCarter & English LLP 4 Gateway Ctr 100 Mulberry St Newark NJ 07101-0652*

HARRISON, RUTH FEUERBORN, retired literature and writing educator; b. Garnett, Kans., Aug. 23, 1930; d. Vincent Herman and Mary Jane (Weaver) Feuerborn; m. Bryce Robert Howard, Sept. 14, 1949 (div. Aug. 1973); children: Sam Bryce Howard, Bryan Jeffrey Howard, Gregory Robert Howard; m. Frederick Charles Harrison, Sept. 13, 1973. BA in English, Portland State U., 1966, MA in English, 1968; PhD in Medieval Comparative Lit., U. Oreg., 1974. Asst. prof. English dept. Portland (Oreg.) State U., 1969-74; freelance editor, cons. Editing, Inc., 1974-77; textbook reviewer Prentice-Hall, 1974-77; adj. prof. English dept. Linfield Coll., McMinnville, Oreg., 1977-82; tech. writer, tech. editor Bendix (aka UNC Geotech), Grand Junction, Colo., 1983-87; adj. prof. English dept. Oreg. Coast C.C., Newport, Oreg., 1987-93; textbook reviewer Prentice-Hall, 1974-77; poetry workshop leader Moon Fish, Yachats (Oreg.) Lit. Festival, others. Author: (textbooks) Punctuation: A Programmed Text, 1969, English 101: Survey of English Literature, 1972, hist. booklet for Little Log Ch. Hist. Mus., Yachats, 1994, (collected poems) Bone Flute, 1996, (chapbook) Kicking Sand, 1999. Joint honor scholar, 1947; NEH grantee, 1981; grad. assistantships Portland State U., 1966-68, U. Oreg., 1968-69. Mem. NOW, Oreg. State Poetry Assn., South County Tuesday Writing Group, Acad. Am. Poets. Democrat. Avocations: herb garden, writing poetry. Home: 2710 NW Bayshore Loop Waldport OR 97394-9515

HARRISON, STEPHEN EARLE, manufacturing executive; b. Little Rock, May 25, 1941; s. Richard G. and Edwin R. (McDaniels) H.; m. Donie Evelyn Brown, Aug. 5, 1960; children: Stephen Brian, Angela Eve. Grad. high sch., Joe T. Robinson, Pulaski County, Ark. Purchasing Welsco Inc., Little Rock, 1959-64, corp. sec., 1964, corp. sec., treas., 1964-80, pres., 1980-85, owner, pres., CEO, chmn. bd., 1985-89, chmn. bd. and CEO, 1977-94; chmn. E'Meritous, 1996—; bd. dirs., a founder Airgas Inc., Del. 1st v.p. Ark. Purchasing Agt. Assn., 1964. Recipient Leonard Parker Poole Safety award Compressed Gas Assn., Washington, 1986, 93, Fleet award for safety, 1989, 91. Mem. Internat. Oxygen Mfg. Assn. (pres. 1975-76), Nat. Welding Supply Assn., Compressed Gas Assn. Avocations: tennis, hunting, boating. Office: Welsco Inc 9006 Crystal Hill Rd North Little Rock AR 72113-6693

HARRISON, THERESE WYKA, school nurse; b. Yonkers, N.Y., Oct. 14, 1954; d. Stanley Albert and Genevieve Veronica (Marczak) Wyka; m. James Gerard Harrison, May 27, 1978; children: James Gerard, Daniel Matthew, Dianne Leigh, Jessica Kaitlyn. BS in Psychology, Manhattan Coll., Riverdale, N.Y., 1979; BS in Nursing, Mercy Coll., Dobbs Ferry, N.Y., 1982. RN, N.Y., Conn. Staff nurse Richmond Children's Ctr., Yonkers, 1974-76, charge nurse, 1976-78, insvc. edn. instr., 1978-80; interdisciplinary team leader Richmond Children's Ctr., 1980-81, coord. insvc. edn., 1981-82, asst. DON, 1982-88; sch. nurse Whitby Sch., Greenwich, Conn., 1997—; pub. health nurse Dept. Health, Greenwich; decision mem. Mercy Coll. BSN scholarship com., 1982—. Author: Richmond Children Center Nursing Procedure Manual, 1980, Richmond Children Center Policy Manual, 1980, Richmond Children Center Nursing Pharmacology, 1980. Mem. elem. sch. bldg. level team Mt. Pleasant (N.Y.) Ctrl. Sch. Dist., 1994, chairperson edn. com., 1992-94, mem. transition steering com., 1993, chairpersoı. elem. schs. Holiday Craft Shoppe, 1994-96. Mem. Am. Nurses Assn., Nat. Assn. Edn. Young Children, N.Y. State Assn. Sch. Nurses, Ct. Nurse's Assn., Mercy Coll. Nursing Alumni Assn., Sigma Theta Tau (local treas. 1982-84). Avocations: swimming, reading, arts and crafts. Home: 573 Manhattan Ave Thornwood NY 10594-1309 Office: Old Greenwich Sch 285 S Beach Ave Greenwich CT 06870

HARRISON, THOMAS FLATLEY, lawyer; b. N.Y.C., Jan. 11, 1942; s. John P. and Mary F. (Flatley) H.; m. Lorraine Brereton, Aug. 16, 1969; children: John J., Jane C., Ann B., Peter T. AB, Holy Cross Coll., 1963; JD, Fordham U., 1966. Bar: N.Y. 1967, Ill. 1979, Ohio 1981, D.C. 1988, Conn. 1989. Asst. counsel N.Y.C. Dept. Rent and Housing, 1966-69; asst. atty. gen. N.Y. State Dept. Law, 1969-74; chief enforcement N.Y. region U.S. EPA, 1974-76, regional counsel Chgo., 1976-80; sr. corp. counsel B.F. Goodrich Co., Akron, Ohio, 1980-87; ptnr. Manatt, Phelps, Rothenberg & Evans, Washington, 1987-88; ptnr., co-chair environ. and land use dept. Day, Berry & Howard, Hartford, Conn., 1988—; faculty mem. various programs Practising Law Inst. Contbr. articles to profl. jours. Mem. 49th Assembly Dist., Rep. Orgn., N.Y.C., 1963-73, bd. govs., 1969-73; active Silver Lake, Ohio, Rep. Orgn., 1981-87; mem. REp. Town Com., Avon, Ct., 1991—, Inland Wetlands Commn., Avon, 1992-95, Bd. Fin. 1995—, Conn. Coun. on Environ. Quality, 1997—; mem. Conn. Small Bus. Compliance Adv. Panel, 1996—. Recipient Outstanding Performance award EPA, 1976. Roman Catholic. Home: 51 Briar Hill Rd Avon CT 06001-4007 Office: Day Berry & Howard City Place Hartford CT 06103-3499

HARRISON, THOMAS JAMES, electrical engineer, educator; b. Wausau, Wis., May 13, 1935; s. Glenn M. and A. Laura (Barclay) H.; m. Carol H. Harrison; children: Nancy E., Kristine A. BS in Elec. Enging, Carnegie Inst. Tech., 1957, MS in Elec. Enging, 1958; PhD, Stanford U., 1964. Registered profl. engr., Calif. Design engr. IBM, Poughkeepsie, N.Y., 1958-59; assoc. engr. IBM, Peekskill, N.Y., 1960; staff engr., adv. engr. IBM, San Jose, Calif., 1960-68; sr. engr. IBM, Boca Raton, Fla., 1968-78; mem. corp. tech. com. IBM, Armonk, N.Y., 1979; program mgr., mgr. advanced software enging. tech. IBM, Boca Raton, 1980-83; cons. acad. specialist Tallahassee, Fla., 1984-87; prof. elec. enging. Fla. A&M U., Fla. State U., Tallahassee, 1987—, chmn. elec. enging., 1988-95; mem. U.S. Nat. Com. for Internat. Electrotech. Commn., 1972-82; U.S. expert Internat. Orgn. Standardization Coms., 1975-84; mem. enging. com. U. Fla., 1972-87, Fla. Atlantic U., 1971-83; alternate mem. bd. dirs. Accreditation Bd. for Enging. and Tech., 1995—. Author, editor: Handbook of Industrial Control Computers, 1972, Minicomputers in Industrial Control, 1978; contbr. articles to tech. handbooks and jours. With AUS, 1959. Fellow IEEE, Instrument Soc. Am. (bd. dir. standards and practices bd. 1971-84, v.p. 1980-81, soc. pres. 1985-86), Am. Nat. Standards Inst. (standard mgmt. bds.), Am. Soc. Enging. Edn., Rotary, Sigma Xi, Tau Beta Pi, Delta Upsilon, Omicron Delta Kappa, Eta Kappa Nu, Phi Kappa Phi. Patentee analog-to-digital converters, sampling filter. Home: 1119 Cherry St Tallahassee FL 32303-6307 Office: Fla A&M U Fla State U Coll of Enging Dept Elec Enging 2525 Pottsdamer St Tallahassee FL 32310-6046

HARRISON, THOMAS L., advertising executive; b. Waynesboro, Pa., Aug. 19, 1947; m. Pamela S. Harrison. BS, Shepherd Coll., 1969; MS, W.Va. U., 1972. Profl. sales rep. Pfizer, Inc., Balt., 1974-76, dist. hosp. rep., 1976-78; mat. sales service mgr. Pfizer, Inc., N.Y.C., 1978-80; account executive Rolf Werner Rosenthal, Inc. Advt., N.Y.C., 1980-81; account supr. Rolf Warner Rosenthal, Inc. Advt., N.Y.C., 1981-83, v.p. account mgmt. supr., 1983-84, v.p., dir. client service, 1984-86; pres. Harrison & Star, Inc., N.Y.C., 1986—. Office: Harrison & Star 16 W 22d St Fl 12 New York NY 10010-5803*

HARRISON, WALTER ASHLEY, physicist, educator; b. Flushing, N.Y., Apr. 26, 1930; s. Charles Allison and Gertrude (Ashley) H.; m. Lucille Prince Carley, July 17, 1954; children: Richard Knight, John Carley, William Ashley, Robert Walter. B. Enging. Physics, Cornell U., 1953; M.S., U. Ill., 1954, Ph.D., 1956. Physicist Gen. Elec. Research Labs., Schenectady, 1956-65; prof. applied physics Stanford (Calif.) U., 1965—, chmn. applied physics dept., 1989-93; scientific adv. bd. Max Planck Inst., Stuttgart, Germany, 1989-92. Author: Pseudopotentials in the Theory of Metals, 1966, Solid State Theory, 1970, Electronic Structure and the Properties of Solids, 1980, Elementary Electronic Structure, 1999; editor: the Fermi Surface, 1960, Proceedings of the International Conference on the Physics of Superconductors, 1985, Proceedings of the International Conference on Materials and Mechanisms of High-Temperature Superconductivity, 1989. Guggenheim fellow, 1970-71; recipient von Humboldt sr. U.S. scientist award, 1981, 89, 94; vis. fellow Clare Hall, Cambridge U., 1970-71. Fellow Am. Phys. Soc. E-mail: walt@stanford.edu. Home: 817 San Francisco Ct Stanford CA 94305-1021 Office: Stanford U Dept Applied Physics Stanford CA 94305

HARRISON, WARREN, finance company executive; b. N.Y.C., Aug. 9, 1951; s. Abraham and Lorraine (Niss) H. BS in Econs., U. Pa., 1973; JD, U. Mich., 1976. Bar: N.Y. 1977. Assoc. Curtis, Mallet-Prevost, Colt & Mosle, N.Y.C., 1976-77, Ullman, Miller & Wrubel, N.Y.C., 1977-78; gen. ptnr. David J. Greene & Co., N.Y.C., 1979-81; spl. ltd. ptnr. L.F. Rothschild, Unterberg, Towbin, N.Y.C., 1981-84; sr. v.p. TSG Holdings, Inc., N.Y.C., 1985-87; gen. ptnr. David J. Greene & Co., N.Y.C., 1987-88; risk arbitrageur Steinhardt Ptnrs., N.Y.C., 1988-90; sr. v.p. Oscar Gruss & Son, N.Y.C., 1990-91; v.p. Fahnestock & Co., N.Y.C., 1991; sr. v.p. Cantor, Weiss & Friedner, N.Y.C., 1991—. Editor: The Situation Review, 1985. Mem. ABA, N.Y. State Bar Assn. Home: 1700 York Ave Apt 4A New York NY 10128-7819 Office: Cantor Weiss & Friedner 880 3rd Ave New York NY 10022-4730

HARRISON, WENDY JANE MERRILL, university official; b. Waterbury, Conn., Dec. 4, 1961; d. David Kenneth and Jane Joy (Nevius) Merrill; m. Aidan T. Harrison (div. Nov. 1998); children: Christopher, Charlotte. BA in Journalism, George Washington U., Washington, 1981; MBA in mgmt., Cornell U., 1992. Intern in edn. HEW, Washington, summer 1978, writer, summer 1979; rsch. asst. dep. health svcs. adminstrn. George Washington U., Washington, 1979-81; sec. Nat. Assn. Beverage Importers, Washington, 1981; account exec. Staff Design, Washington, 1982; adminstrv. aide Internat. Food Policy Rsch. Inst., Washington, 1983-86; program assoc. Acad. for Edni. Devel., Washington, 1986-87; pvt. practice cons. Washington, 1987-88; adminstrv. mgr. food and nutrition policy program Cornell U., Ithaca, 1988-92; cons. in mgmt. of med. practices Med. Bus. Mgmt., Ithaca, 1994-95; realtor Century 21 Alpha, 1995-97; compensation mgr. Santa Clara (Calif.) U., 1996-98; sr. compensation analyst Stanford (Calif.) U., 1998-99, dir. fin. and adminstrn. dept. comparative medicine, 1999—; cons., editor George Washington U., 1986; cons., rapporteur Internat. Food Policy Restaurant Inst., Washington and Copenhagen, Denmark, 1987; cons., adminstr. Hansell & Post, Washington, 1987-88, Cornell U., Washington and Ithaca, 1988. Sponsor Worldvision, Tanzania, 1988-91. George Washington U. scholar, 1979-81. Mem. AMA, Soc. for Human Resources Mgmt., Sigma Delta Xi (scholar 1980). Democrat. Episcopalian. Avocations: piano, hiking, swimming. Home: 1648 Notre Dame Dr Mountain View CA 94040-3641 Office: Stanford U Med Sch P305 MC5487 Stanford CA 94305

HARRISON, WILLIAM ALAN, judge, arbitrator; b. Detroit, Mar. 13, 1947; s. Roger Holmes and Grace Jane (Campbell) H.; m. Janet Ellan

Harrison, May 16, 1970; 1 child, Mark Campbell. BBA, U. Mich., 1969; JD, Wayne State U., 1974. Bar: Wash. 1974. Adminstrv. appeals judge Environ. Hearings Office State of Wash., Olympia, 1975—; arbitrator, 1984—. With USAR, 1970-76. Mem. ABA (exec. com. Nat. Conf. of Adminstrv. Law Judges 1993—), Wash. Athletic Club. Avocations: hunting, fishing. Office: Environmental Hearings Office PO Box 40903 Olympia WA 98504-0903

HARRISON, WILLIAM BURWELL, JR., banker; b. Rocky Mount, N.C., Aug. 12, 1943; s. William Burwell and Katherine (Spruill) H.; m. Anne MacDonald Stpehens, Dec. 7, 1985; children Katherine Adams, Anne Stephens. AB in Econs., U. N.C., Chapel Hill, 1966, spl. student in bus. adminstrn., 1966-67; Sr. Mgmt. Program, Harvard Bus. Sch., Vevey, Switzerland, 1979. Trainee Chem. Bank, N.Y.C., 1967-69, Mid-South corp. and corr. banking group, 1969-74, West Coast corp. and corr. banking group, 1974-76; dist. head, Western regional coord. Chem. Bank, San Francisco, 1976-78; regional coord., sr. v.p. Chem. Bank, London, 1978-82, sr. v.p., divsn. head Europe, 1982-83; exec. v.p. U.S. corp. divsn. Chem. Bank, N.Y.C., 1983-87, group exec. banking and corp. fin. group, 1987-90, vice chmn. instl. banking, 1990—; vice chmn. Global Bank, 1992—; vice chmn. Chase Manhattan Corp., N.Y.C., 1995—, pres., CEO, 1999—; bd. dirs. Freeport-McMoRan Copper & Gold, Inc., New Orleans, Dillard Dept. Stores, Little Rock; mem. bd. advisors N.C. Outward Bound Sch., Asheville; mem. Bretton Woods Com.; bd. trustees Carnegie Hall. Bd. dirs. United Cerebral Palsy of N.Y.C., Inc.; trustee Ctrl. Pk. Conservancy; mem. bd. visitors Kenan Flagler Bus. Sch.; mem. bd. overseers Sloan-Kettering Cancer Ctr., 1999—. Mem. Bankers Roundtable, The Blind Brook Club, Racquet Club, The Links Club, Round Hill Club, Nat. Golf Links of Am., The Field Club of Greenwich, Golf Club Purchase. Episcopalian. Avocations: athletics, travel.

HARRISON, WILLIAM OLIVER, JR., lawyer, small business owner; b. Corpus Christi, Tex., Oct. 16, 1945; s. William Oliver and Nell Betty (Anderson) H.; m. Cathy Lynn Williams, Dec. 1, 1984. BA, Tex. Christian U., 1967; JD, U. Tex., 1970. Atty. Wood, Burney, Nesbitt and Ryan, Corpus Christi, 1971-75; sole practice Corpus Christi, 1975-78; ptnr. Harrison, Stone and Jordan, Corpus Christi, 1978-84; state rep. Tex. House of Reps., 1979-81, 83-85; ptnr. Parkinson and Assocs., Austin, Tex., 1983—; sec., treas. CompuPrint, Inc., Austin, Tex., 1983-86, Cooper's Alley Restaurant and Saloon, Inc., Corpus Christi, 1983-86; pres. Lighthouse Bar and Grill Inc., Corpus Christi, 1984—, chmn., chief exec. officer, 1987—; ptnr. Heard Goggan Blair Williams and Harrison, Houston, 1984-88; sole practice, 1989—. Bd. dirs. Corpus Christi C. of C., Cerebral Palsy Found., 1982-83; selection chmn. Leadership Corpus Christi, 1981-82, adv. com., 1989-90; mem. steering com. Goals for Corpus Christi; mem. Corpus Christi Conv. and Tourist Bur., LWV, Leadership Corpus Christi Alumni, Govtl. Commn. on Efficiency and Economy, 1986; chmn. Long Range Planning Heart of Corpus Christi, 1989-90, Downtown Revitalization Dist., 1991-92; v.p. Regional Transit Authority, 1991, bd. dirs., 1990, chmn., 1991-95; mem. govtl. affairs com. C. of C., 1991, vice chmn., 1992, chmn., 1993. Cpl. U.S. Army, 1964-70. Named one of Outstanding Young Men of Am., U.S. Jaycees, 1978. Mem. ABA, Houston Bar Assn., County Bar Assn., Nat. Restaurant Assn., Tex. Restaurant Assn. Democrat. Mem. Disciples of Christ Ch. Avocations: sailing, reading. Office: 214 Bayridge Dr Corpus Christi TX 78411-1212

HARRISON, WILLIAM WRIGHT, retired banker; b. Kingston, N.Y., Aug. 6, 1915; s. James Burwell and Isabella (Clarke) H.; m. Janet Phillips, Apr. 6, 1940; children: Janet P. (Mrs. Richard Rea Hinch), Susan F. (Mrs. Glassell Slaughter Fitz-Hugh Jr.), William Wright Jr. Student, U. Va., 1933-34. With Va. Nat. Bank (formerly Peoples Nat. Bank Charlottesville), 1942-81, chmn., chief exec. officer, 1969-80, dir., cons., 1980-85; former chmn. Allied Bank Internat.; dir. Royster Co., Norfolk, Shennandoah Life Ins. Co.; chmn. Minbanc Capital Corp., Washington. Former chmn. Mcpl. Bond Commn., Norfolk; chmn. Va. Found. Ind. Colls.; bd. dirs. Gen. Hosp. Virginia Beach, pres.; bd. dirs. U. Va. Patent Found., Va. Opera, Old Dominion U. Rsch. Found., Gov.'s Commn. on Indsl. Devel.; trustee Norfolk Found., Ea. Va. Med. Sch. Found., Chrysler Mus., Norfolk; former bd. visitors U. Va.; former commr. Va. Port Authority. Mem. Norfolk C. of C. (pres. 1971). Episcopalian. Clubs: Princess Anne Country, Harbor. Home: 1104 Wythe Ln Virginia Beach VA 23451-3814

HARRISON-JOHNSON, YVONNE ELOIS, pharmacologist; b. Norfolk, Va., Apr. 29, 1939; d. Herman Hugo and Georgia Mae (Hall) Harrison; m. Melvin C. Johnson, Sept. 27, 1975. BS in Zoology, Howard U., 1959, MS in Pharmacology, 1970, PhD in Pharmacology, 1972. Rsch. asst. Wellcome Rsch. Lab., Tuckahoe, N.Y., 1964-69; rsch. assoc. Howard U., Washington, 1970-72; from biol. rsch. coord. to asst. v.p. R&D div. Hoffmann-La Roche Inc., Nutley, N.J., 1972-92; asst. to v.p. preclin. devel. Hoffmann-LaRoche Inc., Nutley, N.J., 1992-94; v.p. HHJ Cons Inc. R & D, Manalapan, N.J., 1995—; mem. cancer control intervention program rev. com. div. extramural activities NNCI, 1985-88. Contbr. articles to profl. jours. Recipient Black Achiever in Industry award N.Y. YMCA, 1974, Twin Tribute to Women in Industry award YWCA, 1975, Disting. Alumni award, 1983. Mem. AAAS, Am. Mgmt. Assn., Am. PHarm. Assn., Acad. Pharm. Scis. (com. on hon. members 1984-88), Am. Physiol. Soc., Am. Soc. for Pharmacology and Exptl. Therapeutics (nominating com. 1985, 91, chmn. subcom. on affirmative action 1987-89, chmn. subcom. on minorities 1989-91, profl. affairs com. 1985-91, subcom. on grad. recruitment in pharmacology 1988-92). Home: 101 Highland Ridge Rd Manalapan NJ 07726-8641

HARRISON-JONES, VIRGINIA M., federal government agency employee; b. Cheverly, Md., Oct. 14, 1954; d. John Emory and Josephine (Holiday) H. AA in Bus. Mgmt., Prince George's C.C., Largo, Md., 1986; BRE, Washington Saturday Coll., 1992, MRE, 1993. Ordained minister. Founder, dir. Kingdom of God Ministries; corr. clk. typist Passport Office Dept. of State, Washington, 1972-75; passport/visa clk. typist US Army Svc. Ctr. for Armed Forces Dept. of Army, Washington, 1975-77, passport agt./adminstrv. asst. Nat. Def. U., 1977-79, tng. coord. Automation Support Detachment, 1979-81; mgmt. asst. Mil. Pers. Command Dept. of Army, Alexandria, Va., 1981-82; mgmt. analyst Adj. Gen. Ctr. Dept. of Army, Washington, 1982-84, mgmt. analyst Cmty. and Family Support Ctr., 1984-89; mgmt. analyst Bur. Naval Pers. Dept. of Navy, Washington, 1989-97; founder, pastor Kingdom of God Ministries, 1993; supervising mgmt. analyst USMC Resource and Mgmt. Analysis Office, Arlington, Va., 1997—; speaker Seminars, Retreats, Radio Talk Program. Author: Wedding Vows for Christians, 1992, 1993. Founder, dir. Kingdom of God Ministries, 1993. Named Outstanding Club Pres., Toastmasters Internat., 1991. Mem. Toastmasters Internat. (Disting. toastmaster). Democrat. Avocations: traveling, reading. Home: 11006 Penny Ave Clinton MD 20735-3937 Office: US Marine Corps HQBN HQMC Resource/Mgmt Analysis Ofc Arlington VA 22214-5000

HARRISON-SCOTT, SHARLENE MARIE, elementary education educator; b. Fresno, Calif., Dec. 5, 1949; d. Philip B. and Geraldine Marie (Doucette) German; m. Russell Albert Harrison, Aug. 29, 1970 (div. June 1991); children: Nicholas Benjamin, Christopher Ryan; m. Jeffrey Brian Scott, Dec. 11, 1993. BA, Calif. State U., Fresno, 1971; cert. in libr. media tchg., Fresno Pacific Coll., 1996. Tchr. kindergarten Modesto (Calif.) City Schs., 1972-90, tchr., libr. K-6th grades, 1991—; master tchr. Demonstration Sch. for Calif. State, Stanislaus, Calif., 1974-76; instr. Fresno Pacific Coll., 1985-91, Ottowa U., Phoenix, 1990; cons. Archdiocese L.A., 1986-91; coord. K-6 libr. media tchr. Modesto City Schs., 1999—. Author: Bear Necessities, 1987-93. Recipient Disting. Educator in Tech. award Computer Using Educators Region VI, 1998. Mem. Am. Libr. Assn., Calif. Reading Assn. (symposia speaker 1989-93), Calif. Sch. Lib. Assn. (pres. 1997-98), Phi Delta Kappa, Omega Nu. Democrat. Roman Catholic. Avocations: gardening, decorating, antique collecting, snow skiing. Home: 3501 Sagewood Ct Modesto CA 95356-1724 Office: Bear Necessities PO Box 6492 Modesto CA 95355

HARRIS-STEWART, LUSIA, retired basketball player; b. Minter City, Miss., Feb. 10, 1955. Grad., Delat State, 1977. Basketball player Lady Statesmen; tchr. Ctrl. H.S., Ruleville, Miss., Greenwood (Miss.) H.S. Named to Basketball Hall of Fame, 1992; mem. 1st women's Olympic team, 1976, recipient Silver Medal, 1976, nat. championship AIAW, 1977; mem. AIAW Nat. Championship Team, 1975, 76, 77; recipient Gold medal Pan Am. Games, 1975. Office: care Basketball Hall Fame 1150 W Columbus Ave Springfield MA 01105-2532*

HARROD, HOWARD LEE, religion educator; b. Holdenville, Okla., June 9, 1932; m. Annemarie Nussbaumer; children: Lee Ann, Amy Ceil. BA, Okla. U., 1957; BD, Duke U., 1960; STM, Yale U., 1961, MA, 1963, PhD, 1965. Asst. prof. Howard U., 1964-66; assoc. prof. Drake U., 1966-68; prof. Vanderbilt U., 1968—, chair grad. dept. religion, 1972-75; lectr. Howard U., 1964, Drake U. Div. Sch., 1966, U. Mont., 1971, Vanderbilt U., 1989. Author: Mission Among the Blackfeet, 1971, The Human Center: Moral Agency in the Social World, 1981, Renewing the World: Plains Indian Religion and Morality, 1987, Becoming and Remaining a People: Native American Religions on the Northern Plains, 1995; (with others) Radical Theology: Phase Two, 1967; contbr. to: The Encyclopedia of Religion, 1987, Dictionary of Pastoral Care and Counseling, 1990, Encyclopedia of the American Indian, 1995, Harper's Dictionary of Religion, 1995; mem. editorial bd.: (series) Social World of Biblical Antiquity; newsletter editor Soc. for Study of Native Am. Religious Traditions; contbr. articles to religious jours. Scholar Drake U., 1966, NEH, 1967, Vanderbilt U., 1969, 70, 75, Am. Assn. Theol. Schs., 1971, 94; fellow Yale U., 1960-62, Rockefeller fellow, 1962-63, 88, fellow Vanderbilt U., 1981-82, 87-88, Am. Coun. Learned Socs., 1981-82. Office: Div Sch Vanderbilt U Nashville TN 37240

HARROD, LOIS MARIE, secondary school educator, poet; b. Dec. 7, 1942. Supr. creative writing N.J. Gov. Sch. of Arts; tchr. English high sch. Author: (poetry books) Every Twinge A Verdict, 1987, Crazy Alice, 1991, (chapbook) Green Snake Riding, 1994, Part of the Deeper Sea, 1997; contbr. poems to Am. Poetry Rev., The Carolina Quarterly, Southern Poetry Review, American Pen, Prairie Schooner, The Literary Rev., Zone 3, Green Mt. Rev. Fellow N.J. Coun. Arts, 1998. E-mail: lmharrod@worldnet.att.net.

HARROD, SCOTT, consulting manufacturing executive; b. Sandwich, Ill., Aug. 11, 1910; s. Fred and Hattie (Scott) H.; m. Doris Shearer, Sept. 10, 1938; children—Scott B., Frederick S. A.B. magna cum laude, Knox Coll., 1933. Tchr. math. Galva (Ill.) High Sch., 1933-36; investment analyst Lawrence Stern & Co., Chgo., 1936-38; asst. treas. Spiegel, Inc., Chgo., 1938-43, Bell & Howell Co., Chgo., 1946-49; treas. Bell & Howell Co., 1949-50, sec.-treas., 1950-55; dir.; sec.-treas. Bell & Howell Can., 1954, Three Dimension Co., Chgo., 1954-55; sec. DeVry Corp., Chgo., 1955; v.p. DITTO, Inc., Chgo., 1955-57; exec. v.p., gen. mgr. DITTO, Inc., 1957-58, pres., chief exec. officer, 1958-64; also dir.; exec. v.p., dir. H.M. Harper Co., 1965-66, pres., chief exec. officer, 1966-71; pres., dir. ITT Harper Inc., 1971-72; cons. ITT Tech. & Indsl. Products Group, 1972-74; cons. to mgmt. Anti Corrosive Metal Products Co., 1965-72; treas., dir. Nat. Lecture Bur., Inc., 1950-55; dir., v.p. Bell & Howell Co., 1962-64. Contbr. articles to profl. publs. Pres. Park Ridge (Ill.) Sch. Bd., 1953-56; trustee Knox Coll., 1961-64, 69-85, life trustee, 1985-98 . Served with USNR, 1943-46. Recipient Sec. of Navy Forrestal commendation. Mem. Fin. Execs. Inst. (life), Phi Beta Kappa, Beta Theta Pi, Univ. Club (Chgo.). Home: 21084 N Middleton Dr Kildeer IL 60047-8501

HARROLD, BERNARD, lawyer; b. Wells County, Ind., Feb. 5, 1925; s. James Delmer and Marie (Mounsey) H.; m. Kathleen Walker, Nov. 26, 1952; children—Bernard James, Camilla Ruth, Renata Jane. Student, Biarritz Am. U., 1945; A.B., Ind. U., 1949, LL.B., 1951. Bar: Ill. 1951. Since practiced in Chgo.; assoc., then mem. firm Kirkland, Ellis, Hodson, Chaffetz & Masters, 1951-67; sr. ptnr. Wildman, Harrold, Allen & Dixon, 1967—. Note editor: Ind. Law Jour, 1950-51; contbr. articles to profl. jours. Served with AUS, 1944-46, ETO. Fellow Am. Coll. Trial Lawyers, Acad. Law Alumni Fellows Ind. U. Sch. Law; mem. ABA, Ill. Bar Assn. (chmn. evidence program 1970), Chgo. Bar Assn, Law Club, Univ. Club, Order of Coif, Phi Beta Kappa, Phi Eta Sigma. Home: 809 Locust St Winnetka IL 60093-1821 Office: Wildman Harrold Allen & Dixon 225 W Wacker Dr Fl 28 Chicago IL 60606-1229 *I try to see people and events for what they really are, apply my talents, work hard, and pay attention to fairness.*

HARROLD, RONALD THOMAS, research scientist; b. Fulham, London, Eng., Apr. 4, 1933; came to U.S., 1963; s. John and Cicely Helen (Eddenden) H.; m. Ann Marie Whitley, Dec. 3, 1955; children: Lesley Ann, Linda Jane. BS, Chelmsford Coll. Tech., Eng., 1962, Twickenham Coll. Tech., Eng., 1955. Student apprentice Brit. Thomson-Houston Co., Willesden, London, Eng., 1950-55; lectr. radar tech. Army Sch. Electronics, Arborfield, Berkshire, Eng., 1955-57; devel. engr. English Electric Valve Co., Chelmsford, Essex, Eng., 1957-61; rsch. engr. Sylvania-Thorn Color TV Labs., Enfield, Middlesex, Eng., 1961-63; adv. rsch. scientist Westinghouse Sci. and Tech. Ctr., Pitts., 1963-96, cons., 1996—. Contbr. articles to profl. jours. Fellow IEEE (life); mem. Instn. Elec. Engrs., Oxford Athletic Club. Republican. Episcopalian. Achievements include 18 U.S. patents in field of vapour mist dielectrics, acoustic waveguide monitoring. Home: 4052 Benden Cir Murrysville PA 15668-1336 Office: Westinghouse Sci and Tech Ctr 1310 Beulah Rd Pittsburgh PA 15235-5098

HARROP, DIANE GLASER, shop owner, mayor; b. Lafayette, Ind., June 2, 1953; d. Donald Anthony and Mary Ophelia (Rohner) G.; m. Randolph Allen Harrop, Aug. 7, 1976; children: William Donald, Steven Randolph. BE, U. Kans., 1975. Researcher U. Kans. Speech Dept., Lawrence, 1973-75; clk., book designer Pruett Pub. Co., Boulder, Colo., 1975; debate coach, English tchr. Olathe (Kans.) High Sch., 1975-76; cash items teller Converse County Bank, Douglas, Wyo., 1976-79; owner, mgr. R-D Pharmacy & Books, Douglas, 1979—; mayor City of Douglas, 1989-91, councilmember, 1991-93; columnist Casper Star Tribune, 1993—; weekly columnist Douglas Budget Newspaper, 1994; appt. Wyo. Econ. Devel. and Stabilization Bd., 1991-97, vice chmn. 1994-96, chmn. 1996-97; grants chmn. Wyo. Cmty. Found. Bd. Creator original jewelry (silverwork 1st prize winner Wyo. State Fair 1978). First woman councilmember City of Douglas, 1987-89; gov's. appointee, 1st chmn. State Adv. Coun. on Innovative Edn., Wyo., 1991; bd. trustees pres. Converse County Hosp., 1998—, aux. charter pres., 1985; sec.-treas. Converse County Joint Powers Bd., 1987; bd. dirs. Nicolaysen Art Mus., 1987; mem. Wyo. Mcpl. League Legis. Com. (chmn. 1988—); mem., exhibitor Firearms Engravers Guild of Am., 1988, 89; moderator Congl. Ch.; Douglas chpt. pres. Wyo. Jaycee Women, 1984-85; mem. P.E.O. Sisterhood Chpt. N, 1983-84, Zonta Internat. (treas. 1982-83); pres. Friends of Wyoming State Fair, 1990—; bd. dirs. Ea. Wyoming Mental Health, 1991, Converse County United Way, 1993—; Wyo. adv. com. Dwight D. Eisenhower Math. and Sci. Grant, 1992; mem. parents adv. coun. Douglas H.S., 1994—; chmn. grants com. Wyo. Cmty. Found., 1996—; bd. trustees Converse County Meml. Hosp. Recipient Celebrate Literacy award Internat. Reading Assn. Wyo., 1988, Outstanding Community Svc. award Douglas C. of C., 1991, Apple for Edn. award Gov. Mike Sullivan, 1992, Kellogg Found. scholarship to Heartland Ctr. for Leadership Devel. Seminars, 1993; named one of Outstanding Young Women in Am., 1983-86. Mem. Mountains and Plains Booksellers (bd. dirs. 1992-94), Douglas C. of C., Am. Booksellers Assn., Nat. Fedn. Ind. Businesses, Kiwanis (Douglas chpt. sec. 1994-95, pres. 1996-97), Kiwanis (pres. 1996-97). Republican. Avocations: hand engraving, silversmithing, reading, writing, teaching. Office: R-D Pharmacy & Books 206 Center St Douglas WY 82633-2543

HARROP, WILLIAM CALDWELL, retired ambassador, foreign service officer; b. Balt., Feb. 19, 1929; s. George A. and Esther (Caldwell) H.; m. Ann G. Delavan, Aug. 22, 1953; children—Mark D., Caldwell, Scott N., George H. AB, Harvard U., 1950; postgrad., Grad. Sch. Journalism U. Mo., 1953-54; fellow, Woodrow Wilson Sch., Princeton U., 1968-69. Fgn. Service officer, 1954-93; vice consul Palermo, 1954-55; 2d sec. Rome, 1955-58; internat. relations officer Dept. State, 1958-63; 1st sec. Brussels, 1963-66; consul Lubumbashi, Congo, 1966-68; dir. Office Research for Africa, Dept. State, Washington, 1969; dep. chief mission Am. embassy, Canberra, Australia, 1973-75; U.S. ambassador to Guinea, 1975-77, dep. asst. sec. of state for Africa, 1977-80, ambassador to Kenya and Seychelles, 1980-83; insp. gen. Dept. State and Fgn. Service, 1983-86; ambassador to Zaire, 1987-91, Israel, 1992-93; ret., 1994; chmn. Am. Fgn. Svc. Assn., 1970-73, bd. dirs.; bd. dirs. Assn. for Diplomatic Studies and Tng., Am. Acad. Diplomacy. Served with USMCR, 1951-52. Recipient Dept. State Merit Service award, 1968, Presdl. Disting. Service award, 1985, State Dept. Disting. Service award, 1987. Mem. Am. Acad. Diplomacy (bd. dirs.), Washington Inst. Fgn. Affairs, Fly Club (Cambridge, Mass.), Met. Club (Washington), Chevy Chase (Md.) Club. Address: 3615 49th St NW Washington DC 20016-3214

HARROW, NANCY (MRS. JAN KRUKOWSKI), jazz singer, songwriter, editor; b. N.Y.C., Oct. 3; d. Benjamin and Frances (Kirschenbaum) H.; m. Jan Krukowski; children: Damon, Anton. BA, Bennington Coll. From copy editor to editor William Morrow & Co., N.Y.C.; editor Am. Jour., N.Y.C., 1972-73, editor-at-large, 1974—; vocalist Tommy Dorsey Orch., 1958; singer Jazz Gallery, Café Au Gogo, Mars Club, N.Y.C. and Paris, 1961-64, Cookery, Plaza Hotel, Upstairs at Cecil's, N.Y.C., 1975-76, Rachel's, Lush Life, Freddy's, Blues Alley, N.Y.C. and Washington, 1984-85; singer WDR Big Band, Cologne, Brussels, Holland, NYU Highlights in Jazz, Mazur Theatre, 1986; singer Jan Wallman's N.Y.C., 1987, 89, Stockholm Jazz Festival, 1988, Michael's Pub, 1990, Judy's Supper Club, The Salon, N.Y.C., 1995-96. Songwriter (John Lewis music) As Long As It's About Love, 1981, Distant Lover, 1981; composer (Raymond Patterson lyrics) A Little Blue, 1990, (Nancy Harrow music and lyrics) Sea Change, Secrets, Skeleton Trees, I'm Back, So Why Am I Surprised, 1991, 12 songs for the Lost Lady album, 1992-93, 21 songs for Maya the Bee, 1994, 96, 13 songs for The Marble Faun, 1996; recording artist (albums) Wild Women Don't Have the Blues, 1961, You Never Know, 1963, Anything Goes, 1979, rev., 1991, The John Lewis Album for Nancy Harrow, 1981, Two's Company: Nancy Harrow with Jack Wilkins, 1984, 91, You're Nearer, 1986, 98, Street of Dreams, 1990, The Beatles and Other Standards, 1990, Secrets, 1992, Lost Lady, 1994, The Marble Faun, 1999, The Adventures of Maya the Bee, 1999, puppet show, 1998, concert workshop, 1999. Address: 130 E End Ave New York NY 10028-7553

HARROWER, THOMAS MURRAY, electro-mechanical design engineer; b. Alloa, Scotland, Jan. 4, 1918; arrived in U.S., 1952; s. William and Sarah Osbourne Boyes (Murray) H.; m. Dora Adkin; children: Sheila Murray, Sandra Murray. BSEE, BSME, Royal Tech. Coll., Glasgow, Scotland, 1942. Sr. rsch. engr. Lockheed Missile & Space, Van Nuys, Calif., 1960-63; engr., scientist McDonnell Douglas Missile, Santa Monica, Calif., 1965-69; sales-mktg. engr. Whittaker Controls, Culver City, Calif., 1973-75; engring. adminstr. HTL Kinetics, Santa Barbara, Calif., 1981-82; sr. proposal specialist Whittaker, EGG-Spectrolab., Litton, So. Calif., 1982-85; staff engr. VSE Corp., 1991-94; ret., 1994. Author: The Sea Pirates of Singapore, Sudan, The Tenement, The Tenement Goes to War, The Deadly Metamorphis, John Harrower: Colonial, Glenmannan, King's Warlock, The Condottiere, Son of Vittorio, The Modernized Elizabethan Guide to a Winning Proposal, The Rules Will Kill You, Clydeside Lass, It Started in Belfast, Cambus, An Illustrated Anthology of African Art, (children's fiction) Zig and Zag, Wiggly-Woo, The Magic Carpet. With Brit. Territorial Forces, 1940-46. Mem. Masons. Republican. Avocations: writing historical and adventure fiction, how-to books. Home: 729 Ivywood Dr Oxnard CA 93030-3412

HARRYMAN, RHONDA L., education educator; b. Perry, Okla., Apr. 1, 1954; d. Otis Issac Jr. and Jeanette Roberta (Creacy) Shelley; m. Gilbert Wayne Harryman, Mar. 19, 1978. BS in Edn. cum laude, U. Ctrl. Okla., 1975, M in Spl. Edn., 1979; postgrad., Okla. State U., 1992—. Cert. learning disabilities, mentally handicapped, physically handicapped, emotional disturbance, elem. sch. adminstrs., Okla. Asst. workshop coord. for trainable mentally handicapped, physically handicapped Edmond (Okla.) ARC, 1974-76; instr. educable mentally handicapped, physically handicapped, emotionally disabled Edmond Pub. Schs., 1976-77, instr. spl. edn., emotionally disabled, educable mentally handicapped, physically handicapped, visually and hearing impaired, 1977-91; univ. coord., supr. practicums, instr. spl. edn. U. Ctrl. Okla., Edmond, 1992—; edn. advisor tchrs. undrepresented populations in Shawnee, Okla. Three Feathers Assn., Norman, Okla. 1983; pvt. teaching, parent counseling learning disabilities, 1982-87; instr. spl. edn. Okla. Christian U., 1992—, mem. tchr. edn. adv. coun.; co-moderator New Eng. Joint Conf. Specific Learning Disabilities, Boston, 1991; edn. rep. Okla. Joint Conf. Juvenile Justice; edn. del. Okla. Japan-Am. Grassroots Coun., Tokyo, 1991; conducted workshops, presented insvcs., speaker in field. Editorial rev. bd. Teaching Resources, Dayton, Ohio. Counselor Edmond Youth Advocacy Bd.; mem. Gov.'s Round Table on Edn. and Bus., Edmond Juvenile Crime Commn.; sponsor Ala-Teen, Boys Ranch Town. Named Okla. Tchr. of Yr. by Okla. State Dept. Edn., 1992. Mem. Orton Dyslexia Soc., Coun. Exceptional Child, Kappa Delta Pi. Home: 2104 Running Branch Rd Edmond OK 73013-6646 Office: U Ctrl Okla Dept Curriculum and Spl Education 100 N University Dr Edmond OK 73034-5207*

HARSANYI, JANICE, soprano, educator; b. Arlington, Mass., July 15, 1929; d. Edward and Thelma (Jacobs) Morris; m. Nicholas Harsanyi, Apr. 19, 1952; 1 son, Peter Michael. B.Mus., Westminster Choir Coll., 1951; postgrad., Phila. Acad. Vocal Arts, 1952-54. Voice tchr. Westminster Choir Coll., Princeton, N.J., 1951-63; chmn. voice dept. Westminster Choir Coll., 1963-65; lectr. music Princeton Theol. Sem., 1956-63; voice tchr. summer sessions U. Mich., 1965-70; artist-in-residence Interlochen Arts Acad., 1967-70; voice tchr. N.C. Sch. Arts, Winston-Salem, 1971-78; music faculty Salem Coll., 1973-76; condr. voice master classes, choral clinics various colls., 1954—; prof. voice Fla. State U., Tallahassee, 1978—; chmn. dept. Fla. State U., 1979-83. Concert singer, 1954—, debut, Phila. Orch., 1958; appearances with, Am., Detroit, Houston, Minn., Nat., Symphony of Air orchs., Bach Aria Group, 1967-68, maj. music festivals, U.S., 1960—; toured with, Piedmont Chamber Orch., 1971-78, concerts and recitals, in major U.S. cities, also in Belgium, Eng., Ger., Italy, Switzerland and Sweden; rec. artist, Columbia, Decca, CRI records. Mem. Nat. Assn. Tchrs. Singing, Music Tchrs. Nat. Assn., Coll. Music Soc., Riemenschneider Bach Inst., Sigma Alpha Iota, Pi Kappa Lambda. Home: 2116 Trescott Dr Tallahassee FL 32312-3332 Office: Florida State Univ Sch Music Tallahassee FL 32306

HARSANYI, JOHN CHARLES, economics educator; b. Budapest, Hungary, May 29, 1920; came to U.S., 1961; s. Charles and Alice H.; m. Anne Klauber, Jan. 2, 1951; 1 child, Tom Peter. Dr. Phil., U. Budapest, Hungary, 1947; MA, Sydney U., Australia, 1953; PhD, Stanford U., 1959; DSc (hon.), Northwestern U., 1989. Univ. asst. U. Budapest, Hungary, 1947-48; lectr. in econs. U. Queensland, Brisbane, Australia, 1954-56; vis. asst. prof. Stanford U., Calif., 1958; sr. fellow Australian Nat. U., Canberra, 1959-61; prof. econs. Wayne State U., Detroit, 1961-63; prof. bus. adminstrn. U. Calif., Berkeley, 1964-90, prof. emeritus, 1990—. Author: Essays on Ethics, Social Behavior and Scientific Explanation, 1976, Rational Behavior and Bargaining Equilibrium, 1977, Papers in Game Theory, 1982, (with Reinhard Selten) A General Theory of Equilibrium Selection in Games, 1988; editl. bd. Internat. Jour. Game Theory, Games and Econ. Behavior; contbr. numerous articles to profl. publs., 1953—. Co-recipient Nobel Prize in Econs., 1994; NSF grantee, 1963-85; fellow Ctr. Advanced Study in Behavioral Scis., Stanford, Calif., 1965-66. Fellow Econometric Soc., Am. Acad. Arts and Scis., Am. Econ. Assn. (disting.); mem. NAS. Office: U Calif Haas Sch Bus Berkeley CA 94720-1900

HARSHA, AMY BETH, elementary education educator; b. Moline, Ill., Feb. 4, 1956; d. Carl John and Joan Jane (Hedgcock) Anderson; m. David B. Harsha, June 4, 1977; children: Bradley David, Wesley Matthew. BS in Edn., Ill. State U., Normal, 1977; MEd, Tex. Wesleyan U., Ft. Worth, 1997. Cert. in elem. edn., kindergarten and reading. Tchr. 2d grade St. Padua Sch., Fargo, N.D., 1978-81; tchr. Chpt. One, Title One and Reading Recovery Arlington (Tex.) Ind. Sch. Dist., 1989—; adj. prof. reading Tex. Wesleyan U., Ft. Worth, 1998—. Founding assoc. editor Wesleyan Grat. Rev., 1997. Mem. choir and handbell choir St. Barnabas United Meth. Ch., Arlington, 1981—. Named Tchr. of Yr., Swift Elem. Sch., 1997; Cmty. Edn. Fund grantee Ft. Worth Star-Telegram, 1993, 94. Mem. PEO (pres. 1986-88), Delta Kappa Gamma, Kappa Delta Pi. Methodist. Avocations: music, especially choir and piano.

HARSHBARGER, RICHARD B., economics educator; b. Lafayette, Ind., May 6, 1934; s. Albert E. and Olive M. (Shambaugh) M.; m. Jane L. Newcomer, Aug. 24, 1958; children: Lisa, Jon. BS, Manchester Coll., 1956; MA, Ind. U., 1958, PhD, 1964. Fuels economist Tenn. Valley Authority, Chattanooga, 1958; econ. prof. Manchester Coll., North Manchester, Ind., 1960—; vis. prof. Pasadena (Calif.) Coll., 1968-69, Eastern Nazarene Coll., Quincy, Mass, 1977-78. Mem. Manchester (Ind.) Park Bd., 1972-76, Manchester Sch. Bd., 1972-76, Town Forum, 1986—, Indsl. Policy Com., North Manchester, 1990—; bd. dirs. Bethany Theol. Sem., Oak Brook, Ill.,

1987-92, Camp Mack, Milford, Inc., 1986-92; mem. fin. com. Wabash County Found., 1997—. Fellow NSF, 1958-59, grad. fellow Ind. U., 1956-58. Mem. Am. Econ. Assn., Midwest Econ. Assn., Ind. Acad. Social Sci. (dir. 1965-66), Ind. Econ. Forum (pres. 1973-74), Rotary (pres. 1979-80). Democrat. Mem. Ch. of Brethren. Home: 400 Kohser Ave North Manchester IN 46962-1019 Office: Manchester Coll Dept Econs North Manchester IN 46962

HARSHBARGER, SCOTT, law educator, state attorney general; b. New Haven, Dec. 1, 1941; s. Luther Henry and Marian (Masemore) H.; m. Judith Stephenson, July, 1988; children: Michael, Benjamin, Tenly, Cameron, Anne. BA, Harvard U., 1964, LLB, 1968. Bar: Mass. 1968. Assoc. Goodwin, Procter & Hoar, Boston, 1968-70; dir. Lawyers' Com., Boston, 1970-72; dep. chief counsel Mass. Defenders, Boston, 1972-75; chief pub. protection bur. Office Mass. Atty. Gen., Boston, 1975-78; chief counsel State Ethics Commn., Boston, 1978-80; assoc. Posternak, Blankstein & Lund, Boston, 1980-82; dist. atty. Middlesex County, Mass., Cambridge, 1983-91; atty. gen. Commonwealth of Mass., 1991-98; pres. bd. dirs. Justice Resources Inst., Boston, 1979-91; lectr. Boston U. Law Sch., 1980—; Hadley Prof. criminal justice and law Northeastern U. Coll. Criminal Justice, Boston, 1999—; mem. White House Conf. Aging. Mem. Boston Bar Assn. (chmn. urban affairs sect. 1980-82), Nat. Dist. Attys. Assn. (chmn. policy com. 1983-91), Nat. Assn. Attys. Gen. (chmn. health care task force, gen. criminal law com., pres.). Democrat. Mem. Ch. of Brethren. Office: Coll Criminal Justice Northeastern U 360 Huntington Ave Boston MA 02067*

HARSHFIELD, NEIL ALAN, sculptor, educator; b. Washington, Aug. 4, 1962; s. Robert Leslie and Jessie Helena (Day) Harshfield. BA, George Mason U., 1988; MFA, Tulane U., 1995. Tchg. asst. George Mason U., Fairfax, Va., 1989-91, Temple U., Phila., 1992; asst. fabricator Nat Coun. on Edn. for Ceramics Conf., Phila., 1993; tchg. asst. Pilchuck Glass Sch., Stanwood, Wash., 1994; asst. prof., glass shop technician, coord. Tulane U., New Orleans, 1994-98, gallery preparator Woldenberg Art Ctr., 1996—; asst. prof. sculpture Loyola U., New Orleans, 1998; freelance fabricator, engr., Phila., 1991-93, New Orleans, 1994—; adv., cons. Arts Coun. New Orleans, 1996—; instr. Urban Arts Tng. Program, New Orleans, 1997. Contbr. articles to profl. publs. Contbr. Arts Against AIDS, New Orleans, 1996, Contemporary Arts Ctr., New Orleans, 1996. Mem. Glass Art Soc., Internat. Sculpture Ctr. (Outstanding Sculpture award 1995). Avocations: gardening, cycling, photography. Home: 1039 Marengo St New Orleans LA 70115-2714

HARSHMAN, MARC, writer, poet, consultant; b. Union City, Ind., Oct. 1, 1950; s. William Leonard Harshman and Janice Louise Wells; m. Cheryl Ryan, Aug. 25 1976; 1 child, Sarah Jayne. BA in Religious Studies, Bethany (W.Va.) Coll., 1973; MA in Religion and the Arts, Yale U., 1975; MA in English, U. Pitts., 1978. Children's author, poet W.Va., 1975—; instr. composition and creative writing U. Pitts., 1978-79; instr. composition W.Va. N. C.C., Wheeling, 1979-82; cons. writing Moundsville, W.Va., 1983—; tchr. grades 5-6 Marshall County Schs., Moundsville, 1986-97; profl. storyteller, 1976—. Author: (poetry) Turning Out the Stones, 1983, (children's books) A Little Excitement, 1989, Snow Company, 1990, Uncle James, 1993, Only One, 1993, Moving Days, 1994, The Storm, 1995 (Smithsonian Notable award, Parent's Choice award 1995), All the Way to Morning, 1999; co-author: (with Bonnie Collins) Rocks in My Pockets, 1991; mem. editl. rev. W.Va. English Jour., 1996-98. Recipient Alumni Achievement award in lit. Bethany Coll., 1994, W.Va. Lit. Merit award W.Va. Libr. Assn., 1993; Ezra Jack Keats/Kerlan fellow Kerlan Collection/U. Minn., 1994. Mem. Soc. Children's Book Writers, Poets & Writers, Inc., W.Va. English Lang. Arts Coun. (Lang. Arts Tchr. of Yr. 1995), W.Va. Highlands Conservancy, Union Lit. Inst., Internat. Reading Assn., Sierra Club, Amnesty Internat. Avocations: gardening, hiking, music, travel, gerbils.

HARSHMAN, MILTON MOORE, sales and marketing professional; b. Sullivan, Ill., July 30, 1936; s. Paul Irving and Gladys Leland (Moore) H.; m. Marsha Sue Minor, July 23, 1965; children: Hilary A. Harshman, Stacy A. Harshman-Hoffman. Grad. H.S., Sullivan. V.p. sales, and engring. AGRI-FAB, Inc., Sullivan. Office: AGRI-FAB Inc 303 W Raymond St Sullivan IL 61951-1823

HARSHMAN, MORTON LEONARD, physician, business executive; b. Youngstown, Ohio, Apr. 21, 1932; s. Ben and Lllian (Malkoff) H.; m. Barbara Elmore, June 21, 1957; children—Beth, Melissa. B.S., Ohio State U., 1953, M.D., 1957. Charter diplomate Am. Bd. Family Practice. Intern Grant Hosp., Columbus, Ohio, 1957-58; practice medicine specializing in family practice Cin., 1960-92; v.p. med. staff Bethesda Hosp., 1974-75, pres., 1975-77; mem. staff Christ Hosp., Cin., Children's Hosp., Cin., Bethesda Hosp., Cin., Providence Hosp., Cin.; assoc. med. dir. Western-Southern Life Ins. Co., 1993—; pres. Pacific Isle Co.; pres., bd. dirs. Morton Harshman Inc., 880 Real Estate Co. Trustee Bethesda Hosp. and Deaconess Assn., 1972-79, Bethesda Hosp. Inc., 1991—, Cin. Chamber Orch., 1992—, Jewish Family Svc., 1997—. With USNR, 1958-60. Fellow Am. Coll. Family Practice; mem. AMA, Ohio Med. Assn., Cin. Acad. Medicine, Am. Acad. Family Practice, Ohio Acad. Family Practice, Southwestern Ohio Acad. Family Practice, Ky. Col. Assn., Phi Beta Kappa, Alpha Epsilon Delta, Phi Delta Epsilon (Cin.). Home: 2121 Alpine Pl Apt 904 Cincinnati OH 45206-3612 Office: Western Southern Life Ins Co 400 Broadway St Cincinnati OH 45202-3312

HART, ARTHUR ALVIN, historian, author; b. Tacoma, Feb. 13, 1921; s. Albert Arthur and Erma Lola (Maltby) H.; m. Novella D. Cochran, Feb. 26, 1944; children—Susanna, Robin, Catherine, Allison. B.A., U. Wash., Seattle, 1948, M.F.A., 1948; postgrad., Biarritz Am. U., Hans Hofmann Sch. Fine Arts, U. Calif., Berkeley; H.H.D. honoris causa, Coll. Idaho, 1985. Head art dept., chmn. div. fine arts Coll. Idaho, 1948-53; instr. art Colby Jr. Coll. Women, New London, N.H., 1953-54; head art dept., dir. adult edn. Bay Path Jr. Coll., Longmeadow, Mass., 1955-69; dir. Idaho Hist. Mus., Boise, 1969-75, Idaho Hist. Soc., 1975-86; lectr. Am. architecture Boise State U., 1970-86 ; mem. Boise Allied Arts Council, 1970-78, Idaho Historic Preservation Council, 1971-87, Boise Bicentennial Commn., 1975-76, Idaho Centennial Commn., 1985-90, Idaho Humanities Council, 1985-86; mem. adv. bd. Snake River Regional Studies Center, 1969—, Boise Redevel. Agy., 1986-87, Basque Mus. and Cultural Ctr., 1985—, Idaho Aviation Hall of Fame, 1990—. Author: Steam Trains in Idaho, 1971, Space, Style and Structure: Building in Northwest America, 1974, Fighting Fire on the Frontier, 1976, Historic Boise, 1979, The Boiseans: At Home, 1984, Idaho, Gem of the Mountains, 1985, Basin of Gold, 1986, Life in Old Boise, 1989, Camera Eye on Idaho: Pioneer Photography 1863-1913, 1990, Wings Over Idaho: An Aviation History, 1991, Boise Baseball: The First 125 Years, 1994, The Boise Children's Home, 1996, Barns of the West, 1996, The Arid Club, Its Life and Times, 1997, Centennial History of the Western Idaho Fair, 1897-1997, 1997; weekly columnist (newspaper) Idaho Statesman, 1970-95, Boise Weekly, 1995—. Mem. Mayor's Boise 2000 Com. Recipient Idaho Statesman Disting. Citizen award, 1973, Allied Arts Coun. award for hist. writing, 1972, Phoenix award for leadership in conservation Soc. Am. Travel Writers, 1982, Idaho Bar Assn. award, 1985, James C. Howland Urban Enrichment award, 1990, Preservationist award Idaho Hist. Preservation Coun., 1999. Mem. AIA (hon.), AAUP, Coll. Art Assn., Soc. Archtl. Historians (pres. No. Pacific Coast chpt. 1974-76), Am. Assn. Museums (mem. council 1980-82, pres. Western regional conf. 1979-81).

HART, CECIL WILLIAM JOSEPH, otolaryngologist, head and neck surgeon; b. Bath, Avon, Eng., May 27, 1931; came to U.S., 1957.; s. William Theodore Hart and Paulina Olive (Adams) Gilmer; m. Brigid Frances Molloy, June 15, 1957 (dec. Nov. 1984); children: Geoffrey Arthur, Paula Mary, John Adams; m. Doris Crystel Katharina Alm, Mar. 14, 1987; children: Kristen-Linnea Alm, Erik Alm, Britt-Marie Alm. BA, Trinity Coll., Dublin, Ireland, 1952, MB, BCH, BAO, 1955, MA, 1958. Diplomate Am. Bd. Otolaryngology. Intern Dr. Steevens Hosp., Dublin, Ireland, 1956, Little Co. Mary Hosp., Evergreen Park, Ill., 1957; mem. staff Little Co. Mary Hosp., 1958-59; resident in otolaryngology U. Chgo. Hosp. and clinic, 1959-62; instr. U. Chgo. Med. Sch., 1962-64, asst. prof., 1964-65; practice medicine specializing in otolaryngology Chgo., 1958—; mem. staff Northwestern Meml. Hosp., 1972-97, Rehab. Inst. Chgo., 1965-97, Children's Meml. Hosp., 1972-97, Little Co. of Mary Hosp., 1977-94, LaGrange (Ill.) Community Meml. Hosp., 1977-94, Loyola U. Med. Ctr., 1997—; tchg. assoc. Cleft Palate Inst., 1968, dir. otolaryngology, 1969-92; asst. prof. dept. otolaryngology-head and neck surgery Northwestern U. Med. Sch., 1965-75, assoc. prof., 1975-92, prof., 1992-97, prof. emeritus, 1997—; lectr. dept. otorhinolaryngology Loyola U., 1972, prof. otolaryngology, head and neck surgery, 1997—; med. adv. bd. So. Hearing and Speech Found., Nat. Inst. of Deafness and Other Communicative Disorders, 1989-95. Producer videos, movie; contbr. numerous articles to profl. jours. and mags.; also guest appearances various radio and TV talk shows. NIH fellow U. Chgo., 1962-63; NIH grantee, 1985-88. Fellow Am. Neurotology Soc. (pres. 1974-75, chmn. editorial review & publ. com. 1978-79, constn. and bylaws com. 1979-97), Am. Acad. Otolaryngology-Head and Neck Surgery (chmn. subcom. on Equilibrium 1980-86, computer com. 1987-90), ACS, Inst. Medicine Chgo., Soc. for Ear, Nose and Throat Advances in Children; mem. AMA, Brit. Med. Assn., Ill. State Med. Soc., Chgo. Med. Soc., Am. Cleft Palate Assn., Am. Council Otolaryngology, Am. Otological Soc., Chgo. Laryngological and Otological Soc. (v.p. 1975-76), Northwestern Clin. Faculty Med. Assn. (vice chmn. 1976-78, pres. 1979-81), Barany Soc., Royal Soc. Medicine, Irish Otolaryngological Soc., So. Hearing and Speech Found (med. adv. bd.), Chgo. Hearing and Balance Assn. (pres.), Sigma Xi. Roman Catholic. Avocations: travel, baroque music, symphony, opera, tennis. Office: Bldg 105 Rm 1870 2160 S 1st Ave Maywood IL 60153-3304

HART, C(HARLES) W(ILLARD), JR., zoologist, curator; b. Farmville, Va., Jan. 30, 1928; s. Charles Willard and Etta Catharine (Sawyer) H.; m. Margaret Waddell Gordon, Sept. 17, 1957 (div. Jan. 1958); m. Nancy Dabney Gardner, June 9, 1962. BA, Hampden-Sydney (Va.) Coll., 1949, BS, 1950; postgrad., Fla. State U., 1950-52, 53-54; MA, U. Va., 1951. Instr. biology Washington Coll., Chestertown, Md., 1954-55, Randolph Macon Woman's Coll., Lynchburg, Va., 1955-56; med. editor Smith, Kline & French Labs., Phila., 1956-58; editor sci. publs. Acad. Natural Scis., Phila., 1958-70, dir. water pollution studies, 1968-74; asst. to dir. Natural History Mus., Smithsonian Instn., Washington, 1974-79, curator dept. invertebrate zoology, 1979-92, dep. chmn., 1985-88, chmn. dept., 1988-91, rsch. scientist, curator, 1992-96, rsch. scientist emeritus, 1996—. Author: A Dictionary of the Non-Scientific Names of Freshwater Crayfishes, 1994; (with Janice Clark) An Interdisciplinary Bibliography of Freshwater Crayfishes from Aristotle Through 1987, 1989; editor: (with P. Holt and R. Hoffmann) The Distributional History of the Biota of the Southern Appalachians, Part I: Invertebrates, 1969, (with S.L.H. Fuller) Pollution Ecology of Freshwater Invertebrates, 1974, Pollution Ecology of Estuarine Invertebrates, 1979, (with Dabney G. Hart) The Ostracod Family Entocytheridae, 1974; contbr. numerous articles to profl. jours. Mem. Phila. Rep. City Com., 1966-68; bd. dirs. Archbold Ctr. for Tropical Rsch., Dominica, 1987-96. Fellow AAAS; mem. Am. Soc. Zoologists (com. on rsch. in systematic biology 1974-78), Crustacean Soc. (treas. 1981-85), Biol. Soc. Washington (editor Procs. Biol. Soc. Washington 1978-80, sec. 1986-88), Assn. Southeastern Biologists (editor ASB Bull. 1961-72, pres. 1970-71), Coun. Biology Editors (treas. 1968-71), Cosmos Club, Cosmos Club Found. (trustee 1998—), Phi Beta Kappa, Sigma Xi. Episcopalian. Avocations: web page design and maintenance, flying, sailing, jewelry design, cartography of Bermuda. Home: 6449 Walters Woods Dr Falls Church VA 22044-1424

HART, CHRISTOPHER ALVIN, lawyer; b. Denver, June 18, 1947; s. Judson Duncan and M. Murlee (Shaw) H.; 1 child, Adam Christopher. B.S. in Aerospace Engring., Princeton U., 1969, M.S. in Aerospace Engring., 1971; J.D., Harvard U., 1973. Bar: D.C. 1973, U.S. Dist. Ct. D.C. 1973, U.S. Ct. Appeals (D.C. cir.) 1973, U.S. Ct. Appeals (8th cir.) 1981, U.S. Supreme Ct. 1985. Assoc. Peabody, Rivlin & Lambert, Washington, 1973-76, Dickstein, Shapiro & Marin, Washington, 1979-81; gen. atty. Air Transport Assn., Washington, 1976-77; dep. asst. gen. counsel U.S. Dept. Transp., Washington, 1977-79; charter, prin. firm Hart & Chavers, Washington, 1981-90; mem. Nat. Transp. Safety Bd., 1990-93; dep. adminstr. Nat. Highway Traffic Safety Adminstrn., 1993-94; assoc. adminstr. for system safety Fed. Aviation Adminstrn., 1994—. Bd. dirs. Howard U. Hosp. Cancer Ctr., Washington, 1983-88, WPFW (Pacific Found.)-FM, 1984-90. Recipient Superior Performance award U.S. Dept. Transp., 1979. Mem. D.C. Bar (com. ethics 1983-89, mem. bd. profl. responsibility 1989-94), ABA, Nat. Bar Assn., Washington Bar Assn., Fed. Bar Assn., Fed. Communications Bar Assn., Lawyer-Pilots Bar Assn., Black Princeton Alumni (dir. N.Y.C. 1981-87). Democrat. Episcopalian. Home: 1612 Crittenden St NW Washington DC 20011-4218 Office: Fed Aviation Adminstrn 800 Independence Ave SW Washington DC 20591-0001

HART, CLIFFORD HARVEY, lawyer; b. Flint, Mich. Nov. 12, 1935; s. Max S. and Dorothy H. (Fineberg) H.; m. Alice Rosenberg, June 17, 1962; children: Michael F., David E., Steven A. AB, U. Mich., 1957, JD, 1960. Cert. civil trial advocate, Nat. Bd. Trial Advocacy. Bar: Mich. 1960, U.S. Dist. Ct. (ea. and we. dists.) Mich. 1962. Assoc. Stevens & Nelson, Flint, Mich., 1960-62; ptnr. White, Newblatt, Nelson & Hart, Flint, 1962-64; with Dean, Dean, Segar, & Hart, P.C., and predecessor firms Leitson, Dean, Dean, Segar & Hart, Dean, Dean, Segar, Hart & Shulman, P.C., Flint, 1965-95; Dean, Dean, Segar & Hart, P.C., 1995-97; pvt. practice Law Offices Clifford H. Hart, 1997—; adj. assoc. prof. Flint sch. mgmt. U. Mich., 1972—; lectr. Inst. Continuing Legal Edn., Mich.; lectr. Mich. Jud. Inst. Pres. Vis. Nurse Assn., Flint, 1967; pres. Temple Beth El, 1973-75; trustee United Way Genesee County, 1981—; chmn. bd. United Way Genesee County, 1990-91; sec. 1988-89, chmn. bd. dirs. Genesee County and Lapeer County, 1990-91; chair corp. adv. bd. U. Mich., Flint, 1988-93. Faculty mem. Inst. Continuing Legal Edn., Ann Arbor, Mich., 1984—. Fellow Mich. Bar Found., Roscoe Pound Found.; mem. ABA, Mich. State Bar Assn. (chmn. Negligence Law sect. 1981-82, rep. assembly 1975-81), Mich. Trial Lawyers Assn. (pres. 1977-78, lectr.), Genesee County Bar Assn. (pres. 1975-76), ATLA (bd. govs. 1979—, lectr., home office and budget com. 1980-84, 87-89, chair 1989-91, 98—, exec. com. 1984-85, 90-93, chmn. elections com. 1984-87, nat. parliamentarian 1990-91, nat. treas. 1991-92), Am. Judicature Soc., Nat. Bd. Trial Advocacy (cert. 1980, 85, 95). Democrat. Lodge: B'Nai B'rith (past pres.). Office: Genesee Tower 120 E 1st St Ste 1915 Flint MI 48502-1915

HART, CLYDE J., JR., federal agency administrator. BS in Polit. Sci. & History with honors, St. Peter's Coll.; JD, Cath. U. Am.; MS in Pub. Policy, George Washington U. Law clk. U.S. Dist. Ct., Washington, 1975-77; assoc. Akin, Gump, Hauer & Feld, Washington, 1977-80; trial atty. Office Gen. Counsel Interstate Commerce Commn., 1980-93, agy. mgmt. counsel, 1993-94; sr. Dem. counsel U.S. Senate Com. on Commerce, Sci. and Transp., 1994-98; adminstr. Maritime Adminstrn. U.S. Dept. Transp., Washington, 1998—; tchr. No. Va. C.C., U. Md. U. Coll., U. Va. With USAF. Mem. Washington Bar Assn., D.C. Bar Assn. Office: Dept Transp 400 7th St SW Washington DC 20590

HART, DANIEL ANTHONY, bishop; b. Lawrence, Mass., Aug. 24, 1927; s. John J. and Susan M. (Tierney) H. BSBA, Boston Coll., 1956; MEd, Boston State Coll., 1972; MDiv, St. John's Sem., Brighton, Mass., 1974. Ordained priest Roman Catholic Ch., 1953; asst. pastor Lynnfield, Mass., 1953-54, Wellesley, Mass., 1954-56, Malden, Mass., 1956-64; vice-chancellor (Archdiocese of Boston), 1964-70; asst. pastor Peabody, Mass., 1970-76; titular bishop of Tepelta, aux. bishop of Boston, 1976-95, regional bishop S. region, 1976-95, archdiocesan vicar for pastoral devel., 1976-85; bishop of Norwich Conn., 1995—; pres. Boston Senate of Priests, 1972-74; mem. exec. bd. Nat. Fedn. Priests' Councils, 1973-75. Address: 201 Broadway Norwich CT 06360-4328

HART, DAVID ROYCE, structural engineer; b. Waxahachie, Tex., Aug. 16, 1960; s. Royce Lafayette and Deloris Jeanene (Spencer) H.; m. Julie Kay Darnall, Mar. 14, 1987; children: Spencer David, Madison Kathleen. BSCE, Tex. A&M U., 1982. Registered profl. engr., Tex. Structural designer L.D. White Assoc. Inc., Ft. Worth, 1982-84; project engr. Intrex Assoc., Inc., Dallas, 1984-88, Albert H. Halff Assoc. Inc., Dallas, 1988-91; v.p. Turner Engrs. Inc., Dallas, 1991-98; prin. Hart, Gaugler & Assoc., Inc., Dallas, 1998—. Pres. North Park Toastmasters, Dallas, 1990; deacon Prestonwood Bapt. Ch., 1989—. Mem. Structural Engrs. Assn. Tex. (membership chmn. 1995-96). Republican. Avocations: woodworking, water sports. Office: Hart Gaugler & Assoc Inc Ste 231 5440 Harvest Hill Dallas TX 75230

HART, DONALD MILTON, automotive and ranching executive, former mayor; b. Bakersfield, Calif., Oct. 22, 1914; s. Thomas Jefferson and Sara L. Hart; m. Margaret Willene, May 31, 1940; children: Donna Carol, Nancy Elizabeth, Donald Milton. BA in Edn., U. Calif., Santa Barbara, 1938; MA in Pub. Svc., Calif. Poly. State U., San Luis Obispo, 1968. V.p. S.A. Camp Cos., San Joaquin Valley, Calif., 1946—, also bd. dirs.; mayor City of Bakersfield, Calif., 1968-81. Mem. Calif. Citizen Adv. Coun. Crime Prevention, 1955, Calif. Com. for the Handicapped, 1956-64, Calif. Bd. Edn., 1960-64, U.S. Pres.'s Com. Employment of Handicapped, 1960-70; commr. Bakersfield Police Dept., 1960-68; trustee Calif. State Colls., 1960-68; chmn. bd. trustees Calif. State Univs. and Colls., 1967-68; mem. alumni bd. dirs. U. Calif., Santa Barbara, 1961-66, chmn. scholarship fund drive, 1963-64; mem. Coordinating Coun. for Higher Edn. Calif., 1967-68, mem. master plan adv. com., 1971; past pres. Kern County Com. for the Handicapped, Kern County Employment of the Handicapped Com.; mem. adv. bd. Bakersfield Assn. for the Mentally Retarded. Capt. USAAF, 1942-46, CBI. Decorated knight Commendatore dell 'Ordine al Merito (Italy); recipient Humanitarian award Kern County Lions Club, 1951, Man of Yr. award Bakersfield chpt. Am. Legion, 1952, 80, award of merit Kern County Office Civil Def., 1953, Outstanding Svc. award Bakersfield Assn. Retarded Children, 1958, 63, award Kern County Com. for the Handicapped, 1959, Outstanding Svc. award Bakersfield Sr. Football Bowl, 1960, Outstanding Alumni award U. Calif., Santa Barbara, 1962, Silver Anniversary All-Am. Football award Sports Illus. mag., 1962, Benjamin Franklin award Saturday Evening Post, 1962, resolution Calif. State Bd. Edn., 1964, resolution Calif. State Legislature, 1964, recognition award Chinese Ying On Assn., 1965, cert. Calif. Assn. Phys. Health Edn. Recreation, 1965, Good Govt. award Jr. C. of C., 1966, award Calif. Coun. Fitness, 1966, Golden Apple award Calif. Elem. Sch. Adminstrs., 1966, Shrine award local chpt. Shriners, 1967, Sportsman of Yr. award, 1967, Humanitarian Pub. Svc. award Bd. Suprs., 1967, award Women's Press Club, 1968, Life Membership award Calif. PTA, 1970, Civil Svc. award Order of Eagles, 1972, Community Svc. award Bakersfield Advt. Club, 1972, award Fullerton C. of C., 1974, award Bakersfield Boys Club, 1975, award Kern Youth Employment Svc., 1976, medal of honor DAR, 1977, award Kern Hospice, 1978, Medal of Friendship award Govt. of Republic of China, 1978, Filipino Community award, 1980, award Phi Delta Kappa, 1980, award Bakersfield Community for Handicapped, 1980, Meritorius Svc. award Kern County Shrine Club, 1980, award Bakersfield Coll., 1980, resolution Kern County Bd. Suprs., 1980, Svc. award Bakersfield City Coun., 1981, Svc. award Americanism Ednl. League, 1982, John Brock award Calif. State U., 1990, award Afro-Am. Sr. Citizen Heritage Com., 1991, Columbian award Italian Heritage Dante Assn., 1991, Golden Deeds award Bakersfield Exchange Club, 1992, Beautiful Bakersfield Sr. Individual award Bakersfield C. of C., 1992; Paul Harris fellow Rotary; elected to U. Calif.—Santa Barbara Athletic Hall of Fame, 1961, Bob Elias Sports Hall of Fame, 1991; Donald M. Hart Day observed in City of Bakersfield, 1967; named to Hon. Order Ky. Col., 1979, Mayors Hall of Fame, 1995, Bakersfield City Coll. Hall of Fame, 1995; Don Hart Dr. dedicated at Calif. State U., Bakersfield, 1991. Hon. mem. Chinese Ying On Benevolent Assn. Internat.; mem. Bakersfield C. of C. (chmn. mil. affairs com. 1982, Disting. Svc. award 1969, award women's div. 1980), Elks (hon.). Home: 2308 Spruce St Bakersfield CA 93301-3327 Office: PO Box 1556 Bakersfield CA 93302-1556 *The only people to try to get even with are those who have helped you.*

HART, DONALD PURPLE, bishop; b. N.Y.C., Apr. 22, 1937; s. Donald Buell Hart and Ann Wentworth (Ayres) Herrick; m. Elizabeth Ann Howard, Sept. 8, 1962; children: Sarah, Thomas. BA, Williams Coll., 1959; B of Divinity, Episc. Div. Sch., Cambridge, Mass., 1962. Curate Ch. of the Redeemer, Chestnut Hill, Mass., 1962-64; priest-in-charge Good Shepherd Mission, Huslia, Alaska, 1964-69; diocesan staff Native Ministry, Anchorage, Alaska, 1969-73; rector St. Matthew's Ch., Fairbanks, Alaska, 1973-83, St. James Ch., Keene, N.H., 1983-86; bishop Diocese of Hawaii, Honolulu, 1986-94; asst. bishop Diocese of Conn., Hartford, 1995-96, Diocese of Md., Balt., 1997-98, Diocese of So. Va., 1998—. Chmn. St. Andrew's Priory Sch., Honolulu, 1986-94, Seabury Hall Sch., Makawao, Hawaii, 1986-94, St. John's Sch., Tumon Bay, Guam, 1986-94; bd. govs. Iolani Sch., Honolulu, 1986-94. Avocations: biking, hiking, jogging. Office: 112 N Union St Petersburg VA 23803*

HART, DOROTHY, actress, international affairs speaker; b. Cleve.; d. Walter C. and Mabel (Keister) H.; BA with honors, Flora Stone Mather Coll., Case-Western Res. U., 1948; 1 child, Douglas Hart. First woman from field of motion pictures to work on behalf of the UN. Starred in 24 movies including The Naked City, 1949, Gunfighters, 1949, Take One False Step, 1949, The Story of Molly X, 1950, Loan Shark, Down to Earth, I Was a Communist for the FBI, Outside the Wall, Raton Pass, Second Dawn, 1953; also many TV dramas including Omnibus, Suspense, Playhouse 90, Medallion Theatre (opposite Ronald Reagan) Studio One, Robert Montgomery Presents, Kraft Theater, Four Star Playhouse (opposite Charles Boyer); TV panel shows include Pantomine Quiz, Stump the Stars, 1954-64, I've Got a Secret, Take a Guess, To Tell the Truth, Girl Talk, 1969; portrait artist; apptd. U.S. observer UN Conf., Geneva; speaker Motion Picture Producers Assn., Zonta Internat., UN 10th anniversary, Am. Assn. UN; ofcl. hostess reception com. N.Y.C. Mayor's Gracie Mansion, 1958-64; active USO, United Theatrical War Activities Com., ARC, Vis. Nurses Assn., work for retarded children. Recipient Golden Key award for outstanding actress Screenplay Motion Pictures Arts and Scis. Mem. Kappa Alpha Theta. Author poetry and prose.

HART, DOUGLAS EDWARD, investment company executive; b. San Francisco, Mar. 1, 1953; s. George David and Jessica Wilbur (Ely) H.; m. Lydia Melville Day, June 24, 1978; children: Andrew Ely, Caroline Brayton. BSBA, Boston U., 1976. Ptnr. Marsh & Cunningham, Inc., Boston, 1985-88; pres. Penobscot Investment Mgmt. Co., Inc., Boston, 1988—; overseer Jackson Lab., Bar Harbor, Maine, 1985-88; overseer Plimoth Plantation, 1990-92, bd. trustee, 1992—, treas., 1996—. Treas., trustee Plimoth (Mass.) Plantation; trustee Children's Med. Ctr., Boston, 1986-89, Emma Willard Sch., Troy, N.Y., 1999—; chmn. gov. bd. Dana-Farber Marathan Challenge, Boston, Dana-Farber Marathon Challenge, 1996—; overseer Children's Hosp., Boston, 1989—; corporator Dedham Inst. for Savings, 1997—. Mem. Boston Econ. Club, Bohemian Club (San Francisco), Country Club (Brookline, Mass.), Union Boat Club (Boston). Avocations: boating, marathon running, photography. Office: Penobscot Investment Mgmt Co Inc 50 Congress St Ste 410 Boston MA 02109-4002

HART, EDWARD WALTER, physicist; b. Easton, Pa., Jan. 14, 1918; s. Abraham S. and Sara (Rosenstrauch) H.; m. Flori L. Feder, Dec. 11, 1940 (dec. 1976); children: Enid L. Boasberg, Lucinda Hart-Gonzalez; m. Joanne Kreider, Aug. 5, 1978. BS, CCNY, 1938; PhD, U. Calif., Berkeley, 1950. Physicist Theoretics Group U. Calif. Radiation Lab., Berkeley, 1946-51, Corp. R&D, Gen. Electric Co., Schenectady, N.Y., 1951-77; prof. mechanics and materials sci. Cornell U., Ithaca, 1977-88, prof. emeritus, 1988—; Battelle vis. prof. Ohio State U., Columbus, 1975; vis. prof. Tech. U. Braunschweig, West Germany, 1982. Contbr. articles to profl. jours. Pres. Schenectady Civic Ballet Co., 1960-63. With USN, 1940-45. Recipient Meritorious Civilian Svc. award USN, 1945, sr. U.S. Scientist award Alexander von Hunboldt Found., 1982. Fellow Am. Phys. Soc.; mem. ASME, AIME, Metallurigcal Soc. Home: 11 Highgate Cir Ithaca NY 14850-1429 Office: Cornell U Thurston Hall Ithaca NY 14853

HART, ELIZABETH ANN, surgical nurse supervisor; b. Cleve., Feb. 19, 1942; d. John and Josephine Nina (Howard) Soltesz; m. Raymond Lavern Hart, Apr. 5, 1964; children: Christopher Roy, Melissa Joy, Holly Noelle. Diploma, Mansfield Gen. Hosp., 1963. Cert. ACLS. Staff nurse Cleve. Met. Gen. Hosp., Cleve., 1963-64; asst. head nurse, staff nurse Morrow County Hosp., Mt. Gilead, Ohio, 1971-78; oper. rm. staff nurse Galion (Ohio) Community Hosp., 1964-71, 84-87; oper. rm. supr. Morrow County Hosp., Mt. Gilead, 1987—; mem. oper. rm. task force VHA. Elder Evangelical Friends Ch., Cardington, Ohio. Mem. Assn. Oper. Rm. Nurses (cert. oper. rm. nursing). Home: 3234 Township Road 124 Cardington OH 43315-9214

HART, ERIC MULLINS, finance company executive; b. Clanton, Ala., May 6, 1925; s. Eric and Myrtle (Mullins) H.; m. Joy Porter, May 16, 1953; children: Anne Porter, Eric Mullins. BS, U. Ala., 1946; grad., Harvard Advanced Mgmt. Program, 1970. With Internat. Paper Co., 1946-69, asst. to v.p.-treas., 1962-64, comptroller, 1964-69; treas. Red River Paper Mill,

Inc., 1964-69; fin. v.p. Lever Bros. Co., 1969-83, dir., 1969-83; dir. Unilever U.S. Inc., 1981-83, Macmillan, Inc., 1975-88; exec. in residence Columbia U. Bus. Sch., 1983-88. Trustee King Sch., Stamford, Conn., 1970-76. Mem. Union League Club (N.Y.C.), Lakewood Golf Club, Fairhope Yacht Club, Sigma Alpha Epsilon. Home: PO Box 1147 Point Clear AL 36564-1147

HART, FREDERICK MICHAEL, law educator; b. Flushing, N.Y., Dec. 5, 1929; s. Frederick Joseph and Doris (Laurian) H.; m. Joan Marie Monaghan, Feb. 13, 1956; children: Joan Marie, Ellen, Christiane, F. Michael, Margaret, Andrew, Brigid, Patrick. B.S., Georgetown U., 1951, J.D., 1955; LL.M., N.Y. U., 1956; postgrad., U. Frankfurt, Germany, 1956-57. Lectr., dir. food law program N.Y. U., N.Y.C., 1957-58; asst. prof. N.Y. U., 1958-59; prof. law Albany Law Sch., Union U., 1959-61, Boston Coll., 1961-66, Law Sch., U. N.Mex., Albuquerque, 1966—; dean Law Sch., U. N.Mex., 1971-79, acting dean, 1985-86; dir. Law Sch., U. N.Mex. (Indian Law Center), 1967-69; vis. prof. U. Calif., Davis, spring 1981; pres., chmn. bd. trustees Law Sch. Admission Test Council, 1974-76. Author: Forms and Procedures Under the Uniform Commercial Code, 1963, Uniform Commercial Code Reporter-Digest, 1965, Handbook on Truth in Lending, 1969, Commercial Paper Under the U.C.C, 1972, Student Guide to Secured Transactions, 1985, Student Guide to Sales, 1987; editor: Am. Indian Law Newsletter, 1968-70. Served to lt. USAF, 1951-53. Mem. ABA (law sch. accreditation com. 1986-93, skills tng. com. 1995-98, nominating com. 1987), Order of Coif, Phi Delta Phi. Roman Catholic. Home: 1505 Cornell Dr NE Albuquerque NM 87106-3703 Office: U NMex Sch Law 1117 Stanford Dr NE Albuquerque NM 87106-3721

HART, GURNEE FELLOWS, investment counselor; b. Chgo., Apr. 26, 1929; s. Percival Gray and Marguerite May (Fellows) H.; BA cum laude, Pomona Coll., 1951; MBA, Stanford U., 1955; vis. scholar, Jesus Coll., Cambridge, England, 1994-95; m. Marjorie Walker Leigh, Apr. 23, 1966. With Willis & Christy, Los Angeles, 1955-65; investment counsel Scudder, Stevens & Clark, Inc., L.A., 1965-67; with Scudder, Stevens & Clark, N.Y.C., 1967—, ptnr., 1972-85, mng. dir., 1985-94, adv. mng. dir., 1994—. Bd. dirs. Lincoln Center for the Performing Arts, Inc., 1981-86, N.Y. Philharmonic, 1974—, vice chmn., exec. com., 1976-96, trustee, 1988—; chmn. Friends of N.Y. Philharm., 1975-82; bd. dirs., v.p. Berkshire Farm Center and Svcs. for Youth, 1972-83; trustee Pomona Coll., 1982—; bd. dirs., treas. Am. Friends of Cambridge U., 1997—. Served to 1st lt., inf. U.S. Army, 1951-53; Korea. Decorated Bronze Star. Mem. St. Andrew's Soc. State of N.Y., Soc. Mayflower Desc., Century Assn., Univ. Club, Indian Harbor Yacht Club (Greenwich, Conn.), Phi Beta Kappa. Republican. Episcopalian. Home: 133 E 64th St New York NY 10021-7045

HART, HOLLY JOY, educational administrator; b. Milw., Dec. 19, 1943; d. Abraham Jacob Guequierre and June Mavis Reibold; m. James Wallace Heine, Aug. 13, 1967 (div. July 1983); children: Jennifer Joy, April Joy. BA in English & Edn., Lawrence U., 1966; MS in Counseling, U. Wis., Menomonee, 1988, EdS, 1990; PhD, U. Wis., Madison, 1996. Tchr. English Eau Claire (Wis.) Area Sch. Dist., 1967-72; adminstr. Cray Rsch., Chippewa Falls, Wis., 1983-85; instr. Chippewa Valley Tech. Coll., Eau Claire, Wis., 1985; counselor Eau Claire Area Sch. Dist., 1985-86; prin. Coop. Svc. Agy. #10, Chippewa Falls, 1986-91; dir. Eau Claire Area Sch. Dist., 1991—; cons. in field. Contbr. articles to profl. jours. Bd. dirs. Bolton Refuge house, Eau Claire, 1997—. Mem. ASCD, Nat. Assn.Secondary Sch. Prins., Assn. Wis. Sch. Adminstrs., Rotary. Avocations: classical music, reading, walking, hiking, needle work. Home: 2609 Marilyn Dr Eau Claire WI 54701 Office: Eau Claire Area Sch Dist 500 Main Eau Claire WI 54701

HART, HOWARD ROSCOE, JR., retired physicist; b. Fayetteville, N.C., Dec. 6, 1929; s. Howard Roscoe and Elisabeth Grattan (Stover) H.; m. Emily Sawyer, Mar. 1, 1958; children: Evelyn, Alice, Susan. B of Engring. Physics, Cornell U., 1952; MS, U. Ill., 1955, PhD, 1960. Engring. physicist E.I. duPont de Nemours & Co. Inc., Wilmington, Del., 1952-54; rsch. assoc. U. Ill., Urbana, 1960; physicist corp. R & D GE, Schenectady, N.Y., 1960-94, ret., 1995, cons., 1995—. Contbr. over 100 articles to jours. in field; patentee in field. Named Inventor of Yr., Intellectual Property Owners Assn., Washington, 1991. Fellow Am. Physical Soc. (sec.-treas. div. condensed matter physics 1981-85); mem. NAE, Am. Geophys. Union.

HART, JACK ROBERT, newspaper editor; b. Tacoma, Sept. 7, 1946; s. John Sebald Hart and Alice Agnes Hurlbut; m. Cherie Denise Boston, Dec. 20, 1968 (div. Oct. 1976); children: Joshua John, Aaron Lee, Jesse Robert. BA, U. Wash., 1968; PhD, U. Wis., 1975. Instr. U. Wis. Ctr. Sys., Janesville, 1970-71, Calif. State U., Northridge, 1971-74; assoc. prof. U. Oreg., Eugene, 1974-81; reporter Register-Guard, Eugene, 1980; reporter, editor The Oregonian, Portland, 1981-89, staff devel. dir., 1989-98, mng. editor, 1998—; site dir. Nat. Writers' Workshop, Portland, 1994-95, 98; columnist Editor & Pub. Mag., N.Y.C., 1987—; prof. Oreg. State U., Lewis and Clark Coll., U. Oreg., Portland State U., 1996—; spkr. at workshops in field; Ruhl tchg. fellow U. Oreg., 1988. Author: The Information Empire, 1978; contbr. articles to profl. jours. Mem. City of Portland Pesticide Adv. Coun., 1996-97. 2d lt. U.S. Army, 1968-71. Recipient Disting. Tchg. award Am. Soc. Newspaper Editors, 1980, Purple Shield, U. Wash., 1968. Mem. Soc. Profl. Journalists, Oreg. Fly Fisherman, Phi Beta Kappa. Office: The Oregonian 1320 SW Broadway Portland OR 97205

HART, JACK WAYNE, English language educator; b. Athens, Ohio, Mar. 15, 1943; s. Thomas Bernard and Cecelia Margerite (Leifheit) H.; m. Maxine Lona Herdman, July 7, 1945; children: Kay, Charlotte, Ursula, Edson. PhD, Ohio U., 1970. Prof. English U. Rio Grande, Ohio, 1970—, chmn. communicative arts dept., 1975-79. Author: (poetry books) One Eye Upon the Queen, 1976, Pretty Girls, 1995; editor: (lit. mag.) Ship of Fools, 1996-98. Presdl. elector Ind. Candidacy of Dick Gregory for Pres., 1968. Mem. Southeastern Medieval Assn., Ohio Gamefowl Breeder's Assn. Libertarian. Lutheran. Home: 39340 Rocksprings Rd Pomeroy OH 45769-9739 Office: U of Rio Grande Rio Grande OH 45674

HART, JAMES, member of Canadian parliament; b. Oct. 30, 1955; 2 children. Cert. broadcast announcing, Columbia Acad. Radio and TV, 1982; marine elec. trade qualifications, Can. Forces Fleet Sch., Halifax, N.S.; BS in Internat. Rels., Pacific Western U., 1998. Sales and mktg., 1978-82, broadcaster, 1982-89; acct. exec. Shaw Comm. Ltd., 1989-93; M.P. for Okanagan-Similkameen-Merritt Ho. of Commons, Can., 1993-97, M.P. for Okanagan-Coquihalla, 1997—; chief critic nat. def. and vet. affairs Reform Party, 1994-97, mem. Reform party of Can. shadow cabinet, 1997—, mem. priorities & planning com., 1997—, question period coord. for ofcl. opposition, 1997-98, chief critic justice, 1998, critic for nat. def., 1998. Author: Decline of the Canadian Armed Forces, 1993-98. Elected sch. trustee, Sch. Dist. 77, Summerland, B.C., Can., 1988-90, re-elected, 1990-93; founded and provided leadership as commdg. officer 902 Royal Can. Air Cadet Squadron, Summerland; past dir. Penticton (B.C.) C. of C. With Can. Armed Forces, 1973-78. Fax: (613) 992-7200 and (250) 770-4484. E-mail: hartj@parl.gc.ca, and jimhart@reform.ca. Website: www.reform.ca/hart. Office: House of Commons, Rm 920 Confederation Blvd, Ottawa, ON Canada K1A 0A6 and: 301 Main St Ste 203, Penticton BC Canada V2A 5B7

HART, JAMES FRANCIS, civil engineer; b. Cumberland, Md., May 2, 1965; s. Vincent Regan Hart and Maureen Hart Shipp. BSCE, Tex. A&M U., 1988; MBA, Baylor U., 1992. Design engr. Transoncis Inc., Ft. Worth, 1988-91; computer analyst PRC Inc., Alexandria, Va., 1992-93; sys. engr. EDS, Paramus, N.J., 1993-95; project leader EDS, Bangkok, 1996; project mgr. EDS, Flint, Mich., 1997-98, Troy, Mich., 1999—. Battalion chem. officer Mich. Nat. Guard, 1998—, ops. officer selective svcs. system, 1998—. mem. Tex. A&M Century Club, S.E. Mich. Tex. A&M Club (muster chmn. 1998). Republican. Roman Catholic. Avocations: skiing, volunteer work, reading. Office: EDS Premises Infrastructure Program Svc Delivery Mgmt 3310 West Big Beaver Troy MI 48084

HART, JAMES WARREN, university athletic director, restaurant owner, former professional football player; b. Evanston, Ill., Apr. 29, 1944; s. George Ezrie and Marjorie Helen (Karsten) H.; m. Mary Elizabeth Mueller, June 17, 1967; children: Bradley James and Suzanne Elizabeth (twins), Kathryn Anne. B.S., So. Ill. U., 1967. Quarterback St. Louis Cardinals Profl. Football Team, 1966-83, Washington Redskins Profl. Football Team, 1984; radio sports personality Sta. KMOX, 1975-84, Sta. KXOK, 1985-86; sports analyst Sta. WGN Radio, Chgo., 1985-89; athletics dir. So. Ill. U., Carbondale, 1988-99; assoc. chancellor for external affairs, 1999—; head coach So. Ill. Spl. Olympics, 1973—, Mo. Spl. Olympics, 1976-78; co-owner Dierdorf & Hart's Steak House (2 locations), St. Louis. Co-author: The Jim Hart Story, 1977. Gen. campaign chmn. St. Louis Heart Assn., 1974-88; hon. chmn. St. Louis Sr. Olympics, 1986-88; bd. dirs. Carbondale Conv. and Tourism Bur., Carbondale Main St. Com. Named Most Valuable Player in Nat. Football Conf., 1974, Most Valuable Player with St. Louis Cardinals, 1973, 75, 78, Man of Year St. Louis Dodge Dealers, 1975, 76, Man of Year Miller High Life, 1980, So. Ill. U. Sports Hall of Fame, 1978, Mo. Sports Hall of Fame, 1998; recipient Brian Piccolo Meml. Humanitarian award Nat. YMCA, 1981. Mem. AFTRA, Fellowship Christian Athletes, Nat. Football League Players Assn. (Byron White award 1976). Republican. Office: So Ill U 207 Anthony Hall Carbondale IL 62901-4312

HART, JAMES WHITFIELD, JR., retired corporate public affairs executive, lawyer; b. Greenwood, Fla., Dec. 20, 1935; s. James Whitfield Sr. and Lela (Cox) H.; m. Patricia Ann Landrum, Mar. 11, 1961; children: William Gordon, Melanie Ann. AA, Chipola Jr. Coll., 1956; JD, U. Ala., 1973. Bar: Ala. 1974, Colo. 1976; cert. flight instr. News dir., anchorman Sta. WTVY-TV, Dothan, Ala., 1958-60, Sta. WSFA-TV, Montgomery, Ala., 1960-62; exec. dir. Am. Petroleum Inst., Montgomery, 1962-75; mgr. pub. affairs Gulf Oil Corp., Atlanta, 1975-76; dir. pub. affairs Gulf Oil Corp., Denver, 1976-81; sr. dir. pub. affairs Gulf Oil Corp., Pitts., 1981-85; sr. v.p. Blue Cross/Blue Shield, Jacksonville, Fla., 1985-86; sr. v.p., gen. mgr. Hill & Knowlton, Denver, 1986-88; v.p. pub. affairs PanEnergy Corp., Houston, 1988-97; v.p. Duke Energy Corp., 1997-99; ret.; res. dir. pub. affairs Office Sec. Air Force, 1988-95; bd. dirs. Vita-Living, Inc.; chmn. interstate natural gas Am. Pub. Affairs Com., 1994. Mem. adv. bd. City of Sugar Land Airport; former pres. Ala. N.G. Assn. Brig. gen. USAFR, 1990-95. Decorated Disting. Svc. medal, Legion of Merit, Meritorious Svc. medal, Air Force Commendation medal; recipient Meritorious Svc. award and Disting. Svc. award State of Ala., Outstanding Young Man of Am. award U.S. Jaycees, 1965, Outstanding Pub. Rels. Practitioner award, 1991, Pub. Rels. Practitioner of Yr., 1996. Mem. ABA, Pub. Rels. Soc. Am., Tex. Pub. Rels. Assn. (bd. dirs., chmn. pub. affairs coun. 1996, pres. 1996, Gold Spur award 1999), Coun. Assn. Execs. (former pres.), Am. Petroleum Inst., Am. Gas Assn., Pub. Affairs Coun. (past chmn.), Res. Officers Assn. (life), Air Force Assn. (life), Tex. Coun. Econ. Edn. (bd. dirs.), Tex. Rsch. League (bd. dirs.), Forum Club Houston, Houston Club, Univ. Club Houston, Rotary, Sigma Delta Kappa (former chancellor). Baptist. Home: 7371 Cox Rd Bascom FL 32423-9411 Office: Duke Energy Corp 5400 Westheimer Ct Houston TX 77056-5310

HART, JAY ALBERT CHARLES, retired real estate broker; b. Rockford, Ill., Apr. 16, 1923; s. Jabez Waterman and Monty Evangeline (Burgin) H.; m. Marie D. Goetz, July 16, 1976; children: Dale M. (dec. 1995), Jay C.H. Student, U. Ill., 1941-42, U. Mo., 1942-43, U. Miami, 1952-56, Rockford Coll., 1961-62. Exec. v.p. Hart Oil Co., Rockford, Ill., 1947-94, pres., CEO, 1994—; pres. Internat. Svc. Co., Pompano Beach, Fla., 1952-58; v.p. Ispen Industries, inc., Rockford, 1958-61; owner Hart Realtors, Rockford, 1987-96, ret., 1996; pres. Rock Cut Corp., 1978—; sec. Intra World, Inc., 1981-83; lectr. in field; trustee, sr. analyst Anchor Real Estate Incestment Trust, Chgo., 1971-80. Author: Real Estate Buyers and Sellers Guide, 1961, (website) Armchair Adventures, 1998; paintings in pvt., pub. collections; illustrations in numerous publs. Dir. Winnebago County (Ill.) CD, 1975; dep. coord. Winebago County ESDA, 1976-86; chmn. Rock River chpt. ARC, 1973, nat. nominating com., 1971, disaster chmn. Illiana divsn., 1972-80; bd. counselors Rockford Coll., 1974-80; emergency coord. 9th Naval dist. M.A.R.S., USN, 1960-68, civilian adv. coun., 1968-78, Ill. area coord., 1986-87, lifetime assoc. mem., 1987; net ops officer 4th region Navy-Marine Corps MARS, 1988-89; office mgr. Citizens for Eisenhower, Chgo., 1952. With USAAF, 1943-46. Mem. Rockford Air Guild (pres. 1974, 76-77), Rockford Art Guild (dir.), Exptl. Amateur Radio Soc. (pres. 1960-80), Nat. Assn. Real Estate Appraisers, Soc. Indsl. and Office Realtors, Nat. Assn. Rev. Appraisers and Mortgage Underwriters, Nat. Assn. Realtors, Masons, Shriners, Univ. City Club, Phi Eta Sigma. Home and Office: Hart and Assocs 2406 East Ln Rockford IL 61107-1116

HART, JOHN, professional sports team executive; b. Tampa, Fla., July 21, 1948; m. Sandi DeVorak; 1 child, Shannon. Degree in History and Physical Edn., U. Cen. Fla., 1973. Minor league mgr. Montreal Expos, 1969—; minor league mgr. Balt. Orioles, third base coach, 1988; spl. assignment scout, interim mgr. Cleve. Indians, 1989-91, exec. v.p. and gen. mgr., 1991—. Named Major League Baseball Exec. of the Yr. The Sporting News, 1994, 1995. Office: Cleveland Indians Jacobs Field 2401 Ontario St Cleveland OH 44115-4003*

HART, JOHN, JR., behavioral neurologist, neuroscientist, educator; b. Balt., May 10, 1957; s. John Sr. and Julia Ann (Nowakowski) H.; m. Laura Simpson Phipps, Oct. 6, 1984; 1 child, John Michael. BA, Johns Hopkins U., 1979; MD, U. Md., 1983. Med. intern Union Meml. Hosp., Balt., 1983-84; resident in neurology Johns Hopkins Hosp., Balt., 1984-86, 95-96, fellow in cognitive neurology and neuropsychology, 1986-90, rsch. assoc., 1990-93, asst. prof. neurology, 1993—; assoc. mem. Zanvyl Krieger Mind/Brain Inst., Balt., 1990—. Contbr. articles to profl. jours. Recipient Hammond award in neurology U. Md., Balt., 1983, Clin. Investigator Devel. award NIH, 1994. Mem. Am. Acad. Neurology, Behavioral Neurology Soc., Soc. for Neurosci., N.Y. Acad. Scis. Office: Johns Hopkins Hosp Meyer 222 600 N Wolfe St Baltimore MD 21287-0005

HART, JOHN CLIFTON, lawyer; b. Chgo., Apr. 29, 1945; s. Clifton Edwin and Eleanor (Zielinski) H.; m. Dianne Lynn Wenzel, Jan. 18, 1969; children: David Clifton, Steven Philip, Kristin Dianne. BS, Loyola U., Chgo., 1967; postgrad. Northwestern U., 1967-69; JD, U. N.D., 1972. Bar: Minn. 1973, U.S. Dist. Ct. Minn. 1973, Tex. 1979, U.S. Dist. Ct. (no. dist.) Tex. 1979, U.S. Ct. Appeals (8th cir.) 1980, U.S. Ct. Appeals (5th cir.) 1980, U.S. Dist. Ct. (we. dist.) Tex. 1981, U.S. Dist. Ct. (ea. dist.) Okla. 1983, U.S. Dist. Ct. (ea. dist.) Tex. 1984, U.S. Supreme Ct., 1997. Ptnr. Robins, Zelle, Larson & Kaplan, Mpls., 1973-81; v.p. Gollaher & Hart, Dallas, 1981-84; pres. Hart & Engen, Dallas, 1984-87, pres. Hart & Assocs., 1987-88, mng. ptnr. S.W. regional office of Robins, Kaplan, Miller & Ciresi, 1988-93; ptnr. Cantey & Hanger, L.L.P., Dallas, 1993-98, ptnr. Brown, Herman, Dean, Wiseman, Liser & Hart, L.L.P., 1998—. Contbr. articles to profl. publs. Maj. USAF, 1969-73. Mem. ABA, State Bar Tex., Tex. Assn. Def. Counsel, Tarrant County Bar Assn., Fedn. Ins. and Corporate Counsel, Def. Rsch. Inst., Loss Exec. Assn. Republican. Lutheran. Office: Brown Herman et al LLP 306 W 7th St Ste 200 Fort Worth TX 76102-4905

HART, JOHN EDWARD, lawyer; b. Portland, Oreg., Nov. 21, 1946; s. Wilbur Elmore and Daisy Elizabeth (Bowen) H.; m. Bianca Mannheimer, Mar. 29, 1968 (div. 1985); children: Ashley Rebecca, Rachel Bianca, Eli Jacob; m. Serena Callahan, Nov. 9, 1991; 1 child, Katelyn Elizabeth. Student, Oreg. State U., 1965-66; BS, Portland State U., 1971; JD, Lewis and Clark Coll., 1974. Bar: Oreg. 1974, U.S. Dist. Ct. Oreg. 1974, U.S. Ct. Appeals (9th cir.) 1975. Ptnr. Schwabe, Williamson and Wyatt, Portland, 1973-92, Hoffman, Hart & Wagner, Portland, 1992—; adj. faculty U. Oreg. Dental Sch., 1987—; legal cons. Oreg. Chpt. Obstetricians, Gynecologists, Portland, 1985—, Am. Cancer Soc. Mammography Project, 1987—. Contbr. articles to profl. jours. Co-chmn. Alameda Sch. Fair, Portland, 1983. With U.S. Army, 1967-68. Mem. ABA, Am. Coll. Trial Lawyers, Am. Bd. Trial Advocates (pres. 1995) Am., Inns of Ct., Oreg. State Bar Assn., Oreg. Assn. Def. Counsel (pres. 1989), Multnomah Athletic Club. Democrat. Presbyterian. Avocations: jogging, weight lifting, outdoor activities. Office: Hoffman Hart & Wagner 1000 SW Broadway Ste 2000 Portland OR 97205-3072

HART, JOHN LEWIS (JOHNNY HART), cartoonist; b. Endicott, N.Y., Feb. 18, 1931; s. Irwin James and Grace Ann (Brown) H.; m. Bobby Jane Hatcher, Apr. 26, 1952; children: Patti Sue, Perri Ann. Ed. pub. schs. Free-lance cartoonist, 1954-58; commerical artist GE, Johnson City, NY, 1957-58; syndicated cartoonist, 1958—. Comic strip, B.C., nationally syndicated, 1958—, (with Brant Parker) The Wizard of Id, 1964—; collections include: Hey B.C., 1958, Hurray for B.C., 1958, Back to B.C., 1959, B.C. Strikes Back, 1961, What's New B.C., 1962, B.C.- Big Wheel, 1963, B.C. is Alive and Well, 1964, The King is a Fink, 1964, Take a Bow, B.C., 1965, The Wonderous Wizard of Id, 1965, B.C. on the Rocks, 1966, The Peasants are Revolting, 1966, B.C. Right On, 1967, B.C. Cave In, 1967, Remember the Golden Rule, 1967, There's A Fly in My Swill, 1967, The Wizard's Back, 1968, B.C., 1972, B.C. Cartoon Book, 1973. Served with USAF, 1950-53, Korea. Recipient Best Humor Strip awards, Nat. Cartoonists Soc., 1967-71; Reuben Award, Nat. Cartoonist Soc., 1969, named Outstanding Cartoonist of Year, 1968; Yellow Kid award, 1970; Internat. Congress Comics for best cartoonist, Lucca, Italy; Best Humor Strip award, French Comics Council, 1971; Public Service Award, NASA, 1972. Mem. Nat. Comics Council, Nat. Cartoonists Soc. Premiered nationally pub. cartoon in Sat. Eve. Post, 1954. Office: care Creators Syndicate 5777 W Century Blvd Ste 700 Los Angeles CA 90045-5677*

HART, JOHN P., archaeologist; b. West Chicago, Ill., Mar. 30, 1958; s. J. Paxton and Jean E. H.; m. Harriet J. Smith, Aug. 18, 1984; children: James A., Katherine E. BS, Stephen F. Austin State U., 1980; MS, Northeast La. U., 1982; PhD, Northwestern U., 1992. Registered profl. archaeologist. Sr. staff archaeologist GAI Cons., Inc., Monroeville, Pa., 1989-94; dir. cultural resources survey program N.Y. State Mus., Albany, 1994—, bur. chief anthropl. surgey, 1997—. Editor: Current Northeast Paleonthnobotany, 1999; contbr. articles to profl. jours. Office: NY State Mus Anthrop Survey 3122 Cultural Edn Ctr Albany NY 12230

HART, JOHN WILLIAM, theology educator; b. N.Y.C., Oct. 5, 1943; s. Thomas Esmond and Veronica Frances (Merz) H.; m. Jane Helen Morell, Aug. 16, 1975; children: Shanti, Daniel. BA, Marist Coll., 1966; STM, Union Theol. Sem., 1972, MPhil, 1976, PhD, 1978. Dir. Heartland Project, Midwestern Cath. Bishops, 1979-81; asst. prof. religious studies Mt. Marty Coll., Yankton, S.D., 1981-82; assoc. prof. religious studies Coll. of Great Falls (Mont.), 1983-85; prof. theology Carroll Coll., Helena, Mont., 1985—; vis. asst. prof. religion Howard U., Washington, 1978-79; dir., founder environtl. studies program Carroll Coll., 1997—; lectr. in field in 21 states in U.S., Brazil, Can., Italy, Switzerland, Eng., 1980—. Author: The Spirit of the Earth: A Theology of the Land, 1984, Ethics and Technology: Innovation and Transformation in Community Contexts, 1997; ghost author various ch. documents, 1979—; contbr. articles to profl. publs., chpts. to books. Del. Internat. Indian Treaty Coun., Geneva, 1987, 90, UN Internat. Human Rights Commn., Oxford Sems. in Sci. and Christianity, 1999—. Recipient Templeton Sci.-Religion award, 1995; Danforth Found. fellow, 1973-74; NEH grantee, 1985, 86; AAR/Lilly Tcgh. Scholar in Religion, 1997-98, Oxford Sci. and Christianity scholar, 1999—. Mem. Soc. Christian Ethics, Am. Acad. Religion. Democrat. Roman Catholic. Office: Carroll Coll Theology Dept Helena MT 59625 *Humanity has been entrusted with a most sacred task: a caring responsibility for all creation. The survival of the earth and of all life depends on our fulfillment of that responsibility.*

HART, JOSEPH H., bishop; b. Kansas City, Mo., Sept. 26, 1931. Ed., St. John Sem., Kansas City, St. Meinrad Sem., Indpls. Ordained priest Roman Catholic Ch., 1956; consecrated titular bishop of Thimida Regia and aux. bishop Cheyenne Wyo., 1976; apptd. bishop of Cheyenne, 1978. Office: Bishop's Residence Chancery Office PO Box 426 Cheyenne WY 82003-0426

HART, JOSEPH THOMAS CAMPBELL, lawyer; b. Orange, N.J., May 23, 1936; s. Maurice I. and Anne G. (Campbell) H. AB, Fordham U., 1958, JD, 1961. Bar: N.Y. 1962, U.S. Dist. Ct. (so. and ea. dists.) N.Y. 1966, U.S. Ct. Appeals (2d cir.) 1974, U.S. Ct. Appeals (5th cir.) 1983. Assoc. Dewey, Ballatine, Bushby, Palmer & Wood, N.Y.C., 1962-65; assoc. Fulton, Rowe, Hart & Coon, N.Y.C., 1965-71, ptnr., 1971—; sec. The G. Unger Vetlesen Found., N.Y.C., 1987, The Ambrose Monell Found., N.Y.C., 1994. Mem. Assn. of the Bar of the City of N.Y. Office: Fulton Rowe Hart & Coon One Rockefeller Plaza New York NY 10020

HART, KAREN ANN, advertising executive; b. Olean, N.Y., July 11, 1943; d. John Eugene and Lillian Lila (Gardner) H. BSN, D'Youville Coll., Buffalo, 1965. RN, Ohio, N.Y., Calif. Staff nurse, head nurse, supr. Montefiore Med. Ctr., Bronx, N.Y., 1965-77; nurse recruiter L.A. New Hosp., 1978-79, Midway Hosp., L.A., 1979-80; dir. nurse recruitment Akron (Ohio) City Hosp., 1980-87; exec. dir. Nat. Assn. Health Care Recruitment, Akron, 1987-96; sr. v.p. health care divsn. Bernard Hodes Advt., N.Y.C., 1996—. Contbr. articles to profl. jours. Recipient Women in Comm. award Women Aware Program, 1986. Mem. Nat. Assn. Health Care Recruitment (past officer, Disting. Mem. award 1986, 87), Northeastern Ohio Assn. Health Care Recruitment (past officer), Sigma Theta Tau. Democrat. Roman Catholic. Avocations: traveling, writing, reading, swimming. Home: 201 N Hawkins Ave Akron OH 44313-6425 Office: 555 Madison Ave New York NY 10022-3301

HART, KENNETH NELSON, lawyer; b. Providence, Jan. 13, 1930; s. Gerald Ellerbeck and Dorothy Naomi (Nelson) H.; m. Carol Lee Hourula, Oct. 1, 1957; children—Lindsey, Lowell, Allison, Stephanie, Abigail, Jessica, Kevin, Rebecca. A.B., Colby Coll., 1951; LL.B., Boston U., 1957. Bar: Mass. 1957, N.Y. 1961, U.S. Ct. Appeals (2d cir.) 1963, U.S. Ct. Appeals (6th cir.) 1965, U.S. Supreme Ct. 1969, U.S. Ct. Appeals (3d. cir., D.C. cir.) 1981, U.S. Ct. Appeals (8th cir.) 1981. Trial atty. antitrust div. Dept. Justice, 1957-61; ptnr. Donovan Leisure Newton & Irvine, N.Y.C., 1961-97, chmn. exec. com., 1986-89, chmn. litigation dept., 1995-97; ptnr. Orrick Herrington & Sutcliffe, N.Y.C., 1998. Mem. bd. overseers Colby Coll., 1991—. Served with USMC, 1951-53. Fellow Am. Coll. Trial Lawyers. Office: 120 Barnegat Rd Pound Ridge NY 10576-2115

HART, KITTY CARLISLE, arts administrator; b. New Orleans, Sept. 3, 1917; d. Joseph and Hortence (Holtzman) Conn; m. Moss Hart, Aug. 10, 1946 (dec. 1961); children: Christopher, Cathy. Ed. London Sch. Econs., Royal Acad. Dramatic Arts; DFA (hon.), Coll. New Rochelle; DHL (hon.), Hartwick Coll.; LHD (hon.), Manhattan Coll., Amherst Coll. Chmn. emeritus N.Y. State Council on the Arts. Former panelist: TV show To Tell the Truth; actress on stage and in films including The Marx Brothers A Night at the Opera, 1936; Broadway theatre appearance in On Your Toes, 1983-84; singer, Met. Opera, TV moderator and interviewer; author: (autobiography) Kitty, 1988; contbr. book revs. to jours. Assoc. fellow Timothy Dwight Coll. of Yale U.; bd. dirs. Empire State Coll.; formerly spl. cons. to N.Y. Gov. on women's opportunities; mem. vis. com. for the arts MIT. Recipient Nat. medal of Arts from Pres. Bush, 1991. Office: Arts Coun 915 Broadway Fl 8 New York NY 10010-7108*

HART, LARRY EDWARD, communications company executive; b. Deland, Fla., Jan. 28, 1945; s. Joseph Joshua Hart and Gladys Mary (Rodgers) Ludlow; m. Carol Lee Byer, July 17, 1972; children: Danielle Elizabeth, Christopher Randolph. BS in CIS, EE, Ohio State U., 1969. Cert. data educator. Assoc. aero. engring. GE, Cin., 1965-67; pres. COPAC, Inc., Columbus, Ohio, 1967-69; comm. cons. UNIVAC, Blue Bell, Pa., 1969-72; dir. mkgt. Tes Data System Corp., McLean, Va., 1973-81; dir. mktg. No. Telecom, Marlton, N.J., 1981-85; pres. Intelligent Network Mgmt., Trenton, N.J., 1985-88; v.p. and gen. mgr. sales and mktg. Digilog, Inc., A CXR Co., Montgomeryville, Pa., 1988-92; pres. Network Mgmt. Cons., Mt. Laurel, N.J., 1992-93; pres., CEO Mgmt. Systems Integrators, Inc., Mt. Laurel, N.J., 1993—; instr., presenter, writer in field. Big brother Big Bros. of Pa., Phila., 1978-81; hon. faculty Dept. Def. Computer Inst., 1980. Named Big Brother of Yr., Phila., 1970; recipient Outstanding Seminar Presentation award Nat. Comms. Forum, 1984, Capital award Nat. Leadership found., 1991. Republican. Presbyterian. Avocations: golf, tennis, bowling, soccer, gymnastics. Home: 4 E Coach Ln Mount Laurel NJ 08054-1348

HART, LEROY BANKS, financial software executive, real estate developer; b. Thompsontown, Pa., July 12, 1954; s. Bill and Helen (Lauver) H.; student Houghton Coll., 1975; m. Virginia Sattazahn, June 26, 1976; children: Peter, Timothy, Michael, Evan. BS Kutztown State U., 1976; postgrad. Pa. State U., 1978-79, St. Joseph's Coll., 1979-81. Acct. Security of Am. Life, Reading, Pa., 1976-78, EDP coordinator, 1978-80, asst. v.p., controller, 1981-82; exec. v.p. Eastern Software Corp., 1982-88; pres. Hart Fin. Svcs., 1982-84, 88—, ERA Ulrich Realty Co., 1990-97, Hart Software, Inc., 1990—. Trustee Zion Evang. Congl. Ch., 1978-84, Lakeside Evang. Congl. Ch., 1987-88, Evangelical Sch. Theology, 1991—, Twin Pines Camp, Conf. and Retreat Ctr., 1990—, Mohn's Hill Meml. Evang. Congl. Ch., 1994—. Fellow Life Office Mgmt. Assn. Home and Office: 5 Buck Run Mohnton PA 19540-1220

HART, LORING EDWARD, academic administrator; b. Bath, Maine, Sept. 22, 1924; s. Joseph Edward and Elizabeth (Hayes) H.; m. Marilyn Louise Cummings, Jan. 7, 1950; children: Ellen Louise, Matthew Cummings. BA, Bowdoin Coll., 1948; MA, U. Miami, 1951; PhD, Harvard U., 1961; Hon. degrees, Bowdoin Coll.; Hon. degree, Norwich U. Teaching fellow Harvard U., 1954-56; instr. English U. Ky., 1956-57; from asst. prof. to prof. Norwich U., Northfield, Vt., 1957-83, head dept. English, 1961-68, dean of faculty, 1968-69, v.p., dean, 1969-72, pres., 1972-82; assoc. dir. devel. campaign Bowdoin Coll., Brunswick, Maine, 1983-86; pres. St. Joseph's Coll., Standish, Maine, 1987-95. With armored inf. AUS, World War II, ETO. Decorated Bronze Star, Combat Inf. badge; recipient Outstanding Civilian Svc. award Air Force, Army. Mem. Phi Beta Kappa, Alpha Kappa Psi, Sigma Nu. Address: PO Box 13 Yarmouth ME 04096-0013

HART, MARIAN GRIFFITH, retired reading educator; b. Bates City, Mo., Feb. 5, 1929; d. George Thomas Leon and Beulah Winiferd (Hackley) Griffith; m. Ashley Bruce Hart, Dec. 23, 1951; children: Ashley Bruce Hart II, Pamela Cherie Hart Gates. BS, Cen. Mo. State Coll., 1951; MA, No. Ariz. U., 1976. Title I-chpt. I reading dir. Page (Ariz.) Sch. Dist.; Title I dir. Johnson O'Malley Preschool; dist. reading dir. Page Sch. Dist.; bd. dirs. Lake Powell Inst. Behavioral Health Svcs., sec., 1993-95, chmn. fin. com., 1995-96. Contbr. articles to profl. jours., childrens mags. Vol., organizer, mgr., instr. Page Cmty. Adult Literacy Program, 1986-91, Marian's Literacy Program, 1991-95; lifetime mem. Friends of Page Pub. Libr., sec. bd., 1990-91. Mem. Delta Kappa Gamma (pres. chpt. 1986-90, historian 1990-92, Omicron state coms., scholarship 1988-89, nominations 1991, Omicron State Comms. com. 1995-99, Tau chpt. nominations com. chair 1998), Beta Sigma Phi (pres. chpt., v.p. chpt., pvt. reading tutor 1997—). Home and Office: 66 S Navajo Dr PO Box 763 Page AZ 86040-0763

HART, MELISSA A., state senator; b. Pitts., Apr. 4, 1962; d. Donald P. and Albina Simone Hart. BA, Washington and Jefferson Coll., 1984; JD, U. Pitts., 1987. Pa. state senator, atty.; chmn. Sen. Fin. Com.; vice chmn. Sen. Urban Affairs & Housing Com.; bd. dirs. C.C. Allegheny County, Pitts. Cancer Inst., SWPA Vets. Home Adv. Coun. Bd. dirs. Vietnam Vets. Leadership Program; bd. trustees U. Pitts. Mem. Pa. Bar Assn., Allegheny County Bar Assn., North Suburban Builders Assn. Republican. Office: Pa State Senate State Capitol Harrisburg PA 17120

HART, MICKEY, rock musician; b. Sept. 11, 1943. Musician, recording artist, mem. The Grateful Dead, 1965—. Albums include Grateful Dead, 1967, Anthem of the Sun, 1968, Aoxomoxoa, 1969, Live/Dead, 1969, American Beauty, 1970, Blues for Allah, 1975, Terrapin Station, 1977, Shakedown Street, 1978, Go to Heaven, 1980, Dead Set, 1981, Reckoning, 1981, In the Dark, 1987, Built to Last, 1989, Infrared Roses, 1991, One from the Vault, 1991, Two from the Vault, 1992; solo albums include Rolling Thunder, 1972, Diga Rhythm Band, 1976, Apocalypse Now Sessions, 1980, Dafos, 1983, Yamantaka, 1983, Music to Be Born By, 1989, At the Edge, 1990, Honor the Earth Powwow-Songs, 1991, Supralingua, Planet Drum, 1991, Mickey Hart's Mystery Box, 1996; performed with others, including Jefferson Airplane, David Crosby, Jerry Garcia, Bob Dylan, Joan Baez; author: (with Fredric Lieberman) Planet Drum, 1992, (with Jay Stevens) Drumming at the Edge of Magic, 1992. Mem. bd. trustees Am. Folklife Ctr. Libr. Congress, 1999—. Named to Rock and Roll Hall of Fame, 1994. Office: care Dead Heads PO Box 1065 San Rafael CA 94915-1065 Address: Rykodisc Shetland Park 27 Congress St Salem MA 01970-5575*

HART, MILDRED, counselor; b. Ever, Ky., Apr. 7, 1937; d. Dewey Otis and Malta Virginia (Adams) Cooper; m. Joseph Paul Surace, Oct. 26, 1956 (dec. Jan. 1966); children: Marisa Surace Craig, Vincent, Angela, Stephen (dec. 1994); m. James Robert Hart, June 26, 1994. BS in Edn., Ohio State U., 1974, MA in Guidance-Counseling, 1976. Cert. elem. and secondary tchr., secondary prin., supr., Ohio; lic. profl. counselor, Ohio. Sec. H.G. Snyder & Assocs., accts., Columubus, Ohio, 1958-63; tchr. Columbus Pub. Schs., 1974-79, counselor, 1977—, chmn. student svcs. dept., 1985—; adjustor Bancohio Nat. Bank, Columbus, 1985-93. Author: (booklet) College Handbook for Independence High School Students, 1988. Leader Girl Scouts U.S., Columbus, 1969-73. Mem. NEA, Ohio State U. Alumni Assn., Nat. Honor Soc., Pi Lambda Theta (sec. Ctrl. Ohio chpt. 1985-93, treas. Ctrl. Ohio chpt. 1997—), Phi Kappa Phi. Democrat. Roman Catholic. Avocations: travel, reading, cooking, antiques. Home: 2328 Sedgwick Dr Columbus OH 43220-5431 Office: Independence High Sch 5175 Refugee Rd Columbus OH 43232-5352

HART, MILFORD E., psychotherapist, counselor; b. Cambridge, Mass., Apr. 10, 1945; s. I. Lester and Florence D. (Robinson) H.; divorced; children: Joaquin, Norma, Jeremy, Thomas, Katherine. BA, U. No. Colo., 1968, MA, 1992. Lic. profl. counselor, hypnotherapist; nat. cert. counselor. Real estate broker ERA Ken Rice, Aurora, Colo., 1980-83; practice psychotherapy, eye movement desensitization and reprocessing, hypnosis, critical incident stress mgmt., Greeley, Colo., 1992—; real estate broker ERA Questor Real Estate Corp., Aurora, 1984-85, pvt. real estate broker, Denver, 1985-89; instr. psychology Morgan C.C., Ft. Morgan, 1993—; fin. counselor CCCS, Greeley, Colo., 1989—; mem. adv. bd. Family Self-Suffeciency, Greeley, 1993-94. Author poems; contbr. articles to profl. jours. Mem. Weld County Dem. Com., Greeley, 1967-68; vol. United Farm Workers, Weld County, 1966-69, Cath. Comty. Svcs., Greeley, 1989—, Pro Bono Project of Weld County; area dir. women's program U.S. Slowpitch Softball Assn., Weld County, 1990-93; chair grievance com. Aurora Bd. Realtors; chair polit. affairs Greeley Bd. Realtors. Recipient John A. Love Book award U. No. Colo., 1968; grantee Cmty. Correction, 1993-94, Morgan C.C., 1994. Mem. ACA, Colo. Housing Counseling Coalition (v.p. 1994). Democrat. Avocations: reading, writing, camping, softball. Office: 800 8th Ave Ste 317 Greeley CO 80631-1190

HART, PAMELA HEIM, banker; b. Chgo., July 14, 1946; d. Gordon Theodore and Leah Almira (Gardner) Heim; m. William Richard Hart, July 8, 1972 (div. 1979); 1 child, Elizabeth Alyson. BA, DePauw U., 1968; MA in Tchg., Washington U., St. Louis, 1970; M in Mgmt., Purdue U., 1982. Chartered bank auditor; cert. bank compliance officer. Tchr. history University City (Mo.) H.S., 1969-74; tchg. asst. Purdue U., Hammond, Ind., 1980-82, guest faculty, 1983-84; auditor Continental Bank NA, Chgo., 1984-86, legal and regulatory compliance specialist, 1986-88, asst. auditor, 1988-92, sr. portfolio risk analyst, 1992-94; with asset securitization group Bank of Am. (formerly Continental Bank NA), Chgo., 1994-98; v.p. Capital Raising Products, Chgo., 1994-99, v.p. pvt. bank strategic planning and projects, 1999—. Trustee Forest Ridge Acad., Schererville, Ind., 1987-88; mem. vestry St. Paul Episc. Ch., Munster, Ind., 1982-92, jr. warden, 1998, 99; active LWV. Mem. Chartered Bank Auditors Assn., Chicagoland Compliance Assn. (bd. dirs., treas. 1987-88), Cert. Bank Compliance Officer Assn. (exam. com. mem. 1992-96), P.E.O. Avocations: needlework, travel, reading. Home: 8936 Southmoor Ave Hammond IN 46322-1808 Office: Bank of Am 231 S La Salle St Chicago IL 60604-1407

HART, PATRICIA ANNE, public health officer; b. Pitts., Dec. 7, 1954; d. Charles Richard and Dorothy Mary (Froehlich) Dagnall; m. James A. Hart III, July 23, 1988. BS in Environ. Sci., Rutgers U., 1976, MPH, 1987. Lic. health officer, sanitary inspector, N.J.; registered environ. health specialist, N.J. Sanitarian Burlington County Health Dept., Mt. Holly, N.J., 1977-78, Hunterdon County Health Dept., Flemington, N.J., 1978-80; sanitarian East Winsdor Twp. (N.J.) Health Dept., 1980-82, sr. sanitarian, 1982-84; health officer East Windsor Twp. (N.J.) Health Dept., 1989—; prin. sanitarian East Winsdor Twp. (N.J.) Health Dept., 1984-87; health officer West Winsdor Twp. (N.J.) Health Dept., 1987-89; sec. Hazardous Waste Adv. Coun., Trenton, N.J., 1982-89; mem. conflict resolution bd. Ctrl. Jersey Maternal and Child Health Consortium, New Brunswick, N.J., 1992—. Co-author: The Role of the Local Health Official in Hazardous Material Response, 1983. Co-chair Mercer Partnership for Cmty. Health, 1998—. Pub. Health Leadership scholar We. Consortium for Pub. Health, 1995-96; RADON coord. grantee Nat. Environ. Health Assn., 1994. Mem. APHA, N.J. Health Officers Assn. (mem. exec. com. 1999—), N.J. Pub. Health Assn., N.J. Environ. Health Assn., Mercer County Health Officers Assn. (v.p. 1995—). Office: East Windsor Twp Health Dept 16 Lanning Blvd Hightstown NJ 08520-1999

HART, PAUL VINCENT, JR., emergency and family medicine physician, inventor; b. Estherville, Iowa, Sept. 28, 1950; s. Paul Vincent and Florence Mary (Gehringer) H.; m. Susan Murphey, Sept. 27, 1989. BS, Iowa State U., 1972; MD, Creighton U., 1976. Diplomate Am. Bd. Emergency Medicine. Resident in gen. surgery U. Minn., Mpls., 1976-77; emergency physician Wheeling (W.Va.) Med. Ctr., 1977-79; pvt. practice family practice and emergency medicine, Kansas City, Kans., 1979-84, Westwood, Kans., 1985—; v.p. Organ Design & Mfg., Westwood, 1989—. Co-patentee liver assist devices. Mem. AMA, Am. Acad. Family Physicians. Republican. Roman Catholic. Home: 2813 W 51st St Westwood KS 66205-1748

HART, RICHARD BANNER, lawyer; b. Winston-Salem, N.C., Apr. 9, 1932; s. Samuel Bruce and Cordia M. (Lamb) H.; m. Jean Elizabeth Shinn, Apr. 28, 1956; 1 dau., Fabra. AB in Polit. Sci, U. N.C., Chapel Hill, 1957, JD, 1959. Bar: N.C. 1959, Tenn. 1970, U.S. Supreme Ct. 1991; CLU. Assoc. counsel Jefferson Standard Life Ins. Co., Greensboro, N.C., 1959-70; with NLT Corp. and Nat. Life and Accident Ins. Co., Nashville, 1970-73, asst. v.p., counsel, 1973-75, sec., counsel, 1975-84; v.p., sec., assoc. gen. counsel Am. Gen. Ins. Cos., Nashville, 1982-88; v.p., sec., gen. counsel Intereal Co., 1984-85; spl. counsel Bowne of Nashville, Inc., 1988-94, Richard B. Hart & Assocs., 1988—; lectr. in field; mem. adv. com. U.S. Dist. Ct. (middle dist.) Tenn. Civil Justice Reform Act 1990. Bd. editors U. N.C. Law Rev., 1958-59. Mem. budget com. Guilford County United Fund, N.C., 1968-69; mem. Guilford County Mental Health Assn., 1968-69; treas. Nashville Exch. Club Charities, 1987-88; trustee West End United Meth. Ch., 1998—. With U.S. Army, 1953-55. Mem. Assn. Life Ins. Counsel, Am. Corp. Counsel Assn. (pres., chmn. bd. dirs. Tenn. chpt. 1990-92), Am. Soc. Corp. Secs. (exec. com., pres. S.E. region 1979-81), Nashville Com. Fgn. Rels., English Speaking Union U.S. (bd. dirs. 1998—, pres. Nashville br. 1999—), Phi Delta Phi, Phi Kappa Sigma (nat. officer, exec. bd. 1971-77), Phi Kappa Sigma Ednl. Fund, Inc. (trustee 1997—), The Cumberland Club (Nashville), Exch. Club (Nashville) (bd. dirs. 1984-85), Univ. Club (Nashville). Home: 2815 Kenway Rd Nashville TN 37215-1903

HART, RICHARD NEVEL, JR., financial exective, consultant; b. Quincy, Mass., June 18, 1940; s. Richard N. and A. Carmel (Deady) H.; m. Monica Anne Rielly, July 22, 1967; children—Richard, Patricia, Michael, Daniel, John, Matthew. B.S. in Bus. Adminstrn, Boston Coll., 1962. With Peat, Marwick, Mitchell & Co. (C.P.A.'s), Boston, 1962-66; with Dunkin Donuts Inc., Randolph, Mass., 1966-90; v.p., treas. Dunkin Donuts Inc., 1978-90; pvt. practice fin. cons., 1991-93; treas. Boston Coll. H.S., 1993-94; CFO Kinetic Rehab. Instruments Inc., Hanover, Mass., 1994-95; pvt. practice fin. cons., 1995—. Trustee, chair fin. com. Aquinas Coll.; trustee, v.p. bd. City Hosp. of Quincy; bd. dirs. South Shore chpt. ARC Massachusetts Bay; bd. govs., chair fin. com. Quincy Coll. Mem. Fin. Execs. Inst., Mass. Soc. CPAs, Inst. Mgmt. Accts. Roman Catholic. Clubs: Neighborhood of Quincy, Boston Coll. Home and Office: 5 Amber Rd Hingham MA 02043-3401

HART, ROBERT GORDON, federal agency administrator; b. San Francisco, Dec. 28, 1921; s. Edwin and Ruth Graves (Thompson) H. Student, Am. Inst. Banking, 1939-41. Br. mgr. Bank of Kodiak, Alaska, 1942-46; folk art cons. Indsl. Rsch. Adv. Coun., Honolulu, 1950-51; mgr. So. Highlanders, Inc., N.Y.C., 1946-52; Southwestern rep. Indian Arts and Crafts Bd., Santa Fe, 1954-57; treas. Westbury Music Fair, Inc., 1957; dir. pub. rels. Constructive Rsch. Found., N.Y.C., 1958-59; editor, dir. publs. Bklyn. Mus., 1959-61; gen. mgr. Indian Arts and Crafts Bd., 1961-93; ret. Indian Arts and Crafts Bd., Dept. Interior, Washington, 1993; gen. mgr. Dept. Interior, Washington, 1961-93; pres. The Crafts Report Ednl. Fund, 1990; art and craft cons. Mus. Internat. Folk Art, Santa Fe, 1954-57; chmn. Fed. Inter-Departmental Agy. for Arts and Crafts, 1963-93; U.S. del. OAS for Reunion Technica des Artesanias. Author: How to Sell Handicrafts, 1953, Alaska, 1959. Bd. dirs. Bur. Occupational Extension Svcs., N.Y.C., N.Y. Elder Crafts-Corp., Year of Am. Craft, 1993; mem. nat. adv. bd. Foxfire Fund, Inc., 1981—; mem. nat. adv. editorial bd. The Crafts Report, 1983-93; pres. The Crafts Report Ednl. Fund., 1990. With AUS, 1943-45. Recipient N.Y. State Gov.'s award for outstanding svc., 1951; hon. fellow Am. Craft Coun., 1993. Mem. Conseil Internat. des Musées, Am. Assn. Museums, Am. Craftsman's Council, World Crafts Council, Am. Polit. Sci. Assn. Home: 4100 N Charles St Apt 808 Baltimore MD 21218-1025

HART, ROBERT LEE, English educator; b. Phila.; s. Harry F. and Marion (Smith) H.; m. Valerie J. Shroeder; children: Jeffrey R., Daniel P. BS, West Chester U., 1960; EdM, Temple U., 1970; EdD, Nova Southeastern U., 1993. English instr. U.S. Army Tng. Ctr., San Juan, P.R., 1960-62; English tchr. Clearview H.S., Mullica Hill, N.J., 1962-70; prof. English Gloucester County Coll., Sewell, N.J., 1970—; cons. in field, 1996—; collaborative learning cons. various confs., workshops, 1993—. Author: Write On!, 1976, Collaborative Learning, 1991, Writing With Computers, 1991. Mem. Rep. Nat. Com., 1995—; sec. Coll. Acad. Assembly, Gloucester County Col, 1996-98. Mem. Nat. Coun. Tchrs. English, Tchrs. English in the Two-Yr. Coll., Coll. Composition and Comm. Presbyterian. Avocations: photography, bicycling, walking, swimming, reading. Office: Gloucester County Coll 1400 Tanyard Rd Sewell NJ 08080-4222

HART, ROBERT M., lawyer; b. N.Y.C., Nov. 7, 1944; s. Charles John and Helen Ann (Hammond) H.; m. Dale Elizabeth McConaughy, Nov. 21, 1970; 3 children. BA, Marist Coll., 1966; JD, Duke U., 1969. Bar: N.Y. 1969, U.S. Ct. Appeals (2d cir.) 1970, U.S. Dist. Ct. (so. dist.) N.Y. 1979. Assoc. Donovan Leisure Newton & Irvine, N.Y.C., 1969-71, 74-77, London, 1972-73; ptnr. Donovan Leisure Newton & Irvine, N.Y.C., 1977-84, 88-94, Dorsey & Whitney, N.Y.C., 1984-88; sr. v.p., gen. counsel, sec. Alleghany Corp., N.Y.C., 1994—; dir., chmn. comp.com. Chgo. Title Corp., 1998—; sr. lectr. law Duke U., Durham, N.C., 1986—. Contbr. articles to profl. jours. Sr. Fellow Duke U., 1983—. Mem. ABA (securities regulation com. 1981—), N.Y. State Bar Assn., Assn. Bar City N.Y. (securities regulation com. 1979-82), Am. Law Inst. Office: Alleghany Corp 375 Park Ave New York NY 10152

HART, RODERICK P., communications educator, researcher, author; b. Fall River, Mass., Feb. 17, 1945; s. R. P. and Mary Claire (Sullivan) H.; m. Margaret Louise McVey, Aug. 27, 1966; children—Christopher, Kathleen. B.A., U. Mass., 1966; M.A., Pa. State U., 1968, Ph.D., 1970. Asst. prof., assoc. prof. Purdue U., West Lafayette, Ind., 1970-79; prof. U. Tex., Austin, 1979-83, Liddell prof. communications, prof. govt., 1983—. Author: Public Communication, 1975, 83, The Political Pulpit, 1977, Verbal Style and the Presidency, 1984, The Sound of Leadership, 1987, Modern Rhetorical Criticism, 1990, Seducing America, 1994; assoc. editor Human Communication Research, 1980-86, Quar. Jour. Speech, 1983—. Recipient Disting. Rsch. award, 1993. Fellow Internat. Communication Assn.; mem. Internat. Soc. Polit. Psychology, Ctr. for Study of Presidency, Speech Communication Assn. (chmn. research bd. 1981-84, ann. monograph award 1972, 74, 83, Woolbert Research award 1984). Democrat. Avocations: reading; athletics. Home: 1601 W Lynn St Austin TX 78703-3445 Office: U Tex at Austin Dept Speech Communication Jesse H Jones Communication Ctr Austin TX 78712*

HART, RONALD WILSON, radiobiologist, toxicologist, government research executive; b. Syracuse, N.Y., Mar. 23, 1942; s. Wilson and Annabell Hart. B.S., Syracuse U., 1967; M.S., U. Ill., 1970, Ph.D., 1971; postgrad. (Nat. Cancer Inst. trainee), Oak Ridge Nat. Lab., 1973. USPHS trainee, 1970-71; asst. prof. dept. radiology Ohio State U., Columbus, 1971-75; dir. radiation biology research div. Ohio State U., 1971-82, assoc. prof. depts. biology, biophysics, preventive medicine, 1976-78, asso. prof. pharmacology, medicinal chemistry dept. preventive medicine, 1977-78, dir. chem., biomed. environ. research group dept. preventive medicine, 1977-82, prof. depts. radiology, preventive medicine, pharmacology, medicinal chemistry, vet. pathobiology, 1978-82; dir. Nat. Center for Toxicological Research, Jefferson, Ark., 1980-92; Disting. scientist in residence Nat. Ctr. for Toxicol. Rsch., 1992—; disting. prof. U. Poona, India, 1978—, Cairo U., 1989—; disting. prof. carcinogenesis Guang Zhou Med. Coll., China, 1988—; adj. prof. U. Ark. for Med. Sci., 1980—, U. Tenn. Health Scis., 1983—; adj. prof. pharmacology Coll. Pharmacy, U. Ark., 1997—; cons. Oak Ridge Nat. Lab., 1971-75, Brookhaven Nat. Lab., 1975-78, Argonne Nat. Lab., 1975-78, EPA, 1976, 78, Am. Indsl. Health Council, 1978, PPG Industries, 1978, Informatics, 1978-80, FDA, 1980; mem. Nat. Acad. Scis./NRC Bd. on Toxicology and Environ. Health Hazards, 1976-82; mem. interagy. staff group Office Sci. and Tech. Policy Exec Office of Pres., 1982-85, chmn., 1983-85; chmn. bd. dirs. Ark. Sci. and Tech. Authority, 1983-84, mem., 1985-88; bd. dirs. TELESCAN, CyberAction Ltd., Wireless, Trilux Internet Group, E-Med Ltd., chem. Overseas Link; mem. adv. bd. PETROTECH, 1991-92, VoiceNet, 1998—, Fla. A&M U. Research Ctr., 1985—; bd. visitors Memphis State U., 1984-90; mem. adv. bd. Miss. State U., 1987-96; chair task force on risk assessment/risk mgmt. HHS, 1985, chmn. com. to coordinate environ., health and related programs, 1985-88, chmn. sci. panel Agent Orange working group, 1986-88, mem. USAF toxicology rev. panel, 1987; chmn. Intergovtl. Task Force on Tech. Transer, 1987-88, DHHS Task Force on Tech. Transfer, 1987-88; mem. Inter Govt. Commn. on Competitiveness, 1987-94; apptd. del. to U.S.-USSR Emerging Leaders Summit, chmn. Sci. and Tech. Commn., 1988; disting. adjunct prof. Moscow State U., 1989—, Guanzou (China) Med. U., 1988—, U. Udina, Italy, 1999—; chmn. Ark. Sch. for Math. and Sci. Found., 1997—. Contbr. chpts. to books, numerous articles to profl. jours. Recipient Hopkins award for grad. research, 1971; recipient Japanese Med. Assn. award, 1978; Karl-August-Forester award W. Ger., 1980, award of merit FDA, 1982, 85, 86, Sr. Exec. Service award, 1982, 84, 85; Superior Service award USPHS, 1983, Gov.'s Award Outstanding Service, State of Ark., 1985, Letter of Commendation, Pres. of U.S., 1985, Commr's Spl. Citation, FDA, 1987, Pres. Rank award for Meritorious Service, 1987, Superior Svc. award outstanding accomplishment Guangzhou Med. Coll., 1988, Bose medal Bose Inst., 1994; Internat. Union Against Cancer; named Syracuse U. Outstanding Alumnus, 1976. Fellow Gerontol. Soc., Am. Coll. Toxicology (past pres.), Risk Anal Soc., Am. Assn. Clin. Chemistry, AAAS (Am. Assn. for the Advancement of Sci.); mem. Radiation Research Soc., Biophys. Soc., Photochem. and Photobiol. Soc., Sr. Execs. Assn., Sigma Xi. Office: NCTR 3900 NCTR Rd Jefferson AR 72079-9501

HART, RUSS ALLEN, telecommunications educator; b. Seguin, Tex., June 30, 1946; s. Bevelly D. and Hattie V. (Reeh) H.; m. Judith Harwood, 1984 (div. 1986); m. Patricia Barrios, Mar. 22, 1987. BA, Tex. Tech. U., 1968; MA, U. Ariz., 1976; PhD, U. Wyo., 1984. Chief cinematographer, producer-dir. dept. med-TV-film, health sci. ctr. U. Ariz., Tucson, 1973-77; instr., coord. ednl. TV and cinematography U. Wyo., Laramie, 1977-81; assoc. prof., dir. biomed. communication Mercer U., Macon, Ga., 1981-84; prof., dir. instructional telecommunications Calif. State U., Fresno, 1984-92, prof., assoc. dir. computing, comm. and media svcs., 1992-95, prof., assoc. dir. Acad. Innovation Ctr., 1995-98, prof. mass comm., 1998—; condr. ednl. confs.; tech. cons. for distance edn. Contbr. articles to profl. jours. Served to capt. USAF, 1968-73. Recipient Cert. Merit, Chgo. Internat. Film Festival, 1975, 1st pl. INDY Indsl. Photography award, 1976, 2d pl. INDY Indsl. Photography award, 1975, Silver plaque Chgo. Internat. Film Festival, 1978, Winner of case study competition Internat. Radio and TV Soc., 1989, Bronze Telly award, 1992-93, 95, Crystal Shooting Star award, 1993, 94, Cine Golden Eagle award, 1994. Mem. Assn. for Ednl. Comms. and Tech. (rsch. session chmn. 1983), Am. Assn. Adult and Continuing Educators (mem. eval. task force 1986), Broadcast Edn. Assn., Health Sci. Comms. Assn. (mem. continuing edn. subcom. 1983), Biol. Photog. Assn. (film judge 1975), Alliance for Distance Edn. in Calif. (founding mem. 1991), Ednl. Telecom. Consortium of Ctrl. Calif. (founding mem. 1993), Phi Delta Kappa, Phi Kappa Phi. Office: Calif State U Mass Comm & Journalism Fresno CA 93740

HART, SHAROWN, educator; b. Charlotte, N.C., Jan. 31, 1974; d. Julius Vincent Morrison and Alma Kay Hart. BS, Lincoln U., Pa., 1996; MA, The Univ. of the Arts, Phila., 1997. Cert. elem. tchr., Pa. Rschr. The Walters Art Gallery, Balt., 1996; team leader, coord. youth ednl. sites Va. Commonwealth U. AmeriCorp, Richmond, Va., 1996—. Vol. Penn. Prison Soc., Phila., 1997, Sleighton Sch.-Lincoln U., 1995-96. Recipient Mus. Edn. award for outstanding rsch. in culture and diversity, 1997. Avocations: praying, poetry, reading.

HART, SIDNEY, physician; b. N.Y.C., Apr. 18, 1939; s. Henry William abd Sylvia (Rosenfeld) H.; m. Madeline Solomon, Apr. 28, 1968; children: Jared, Alexandra. AB, Columbia Coll., 1960; MD, Albert Einstein Coll. Medicine, 1964. Dimplomate Am. Bd. psychiatry and Neurology. Intern BMHC, Bronx, 1964-65; physician Peace Corps USPHS, Monrovia, Liberia, West Africa, 1965-67; asst. resident internal medicine BMHC, 1967-68, resident psychiatry, 1968-70, chief reisdent, 1970-71; clin. instr. psychiatry AECOM, Bronx, 1971-74, asst. clin. prof., 1974-81; lectr. psychiatry Yale Med. Sch., New Haven, Conn., 1978-94; coord. psychiat. edn., assoc. dir. dept. psychiatry Greenwich (Conn.) Hosp., 1978-89, dir. dept. psychiatry, 1990-95; psychiatric cons. dept. neurology, sr. supr. Liaison/Consultation Svc. Montefiore Hosp. & Med. Ctr., Bronx, 1978-80; supr. lisiaon/consultation svc., psychiatric cons. dept. neurology BMHC, Bronx, 1973-78. Liaison Psychosomatic Medicine fellow Montefiore Med. Ctr., Bronx, 1971-73. Fellow Am. Psychiat. Assn. (pres. CPS chpt. 1990-91); mem. Am. Psychosomatic Soc. (mem. coun. 1994-98), Am. Acad. Psychosomatic Medicine, Alpha Omega Alpha. Office: 2 1/2 Dearfield Dr Greenwich CT 06831-5335

HART, STANLEY ROBERT, geochemist, educator; b. Swampscott, Mass., June 20, 1935; s. Robert Winfield and Ruth Mildred (Standley) H.; m. Joanna Smith, Sept. 1, 1956 (div. Dec. 1978); 1 dau., Jolene Kaweah; m. Pamela Coulouras Shepherd, Nov. 4, 1980; children—Elizabeth Ann, Nathaniel Charles. BS, MIT, 1956, PhD, 1960; MS, Calif. Inst. Tech., 1957. Staff mem. Carnegie Instn., Washington, 1960-75; prof. dept. earth and planetary sci. Mass. Inst. Tech., Cambridge, 1975-89; sr. scientist Woods Hole (Mass.) Oceanographic Instn., 1989—, C.O. Iselin chair; mem. U.S. Nat. Com. for Geochemistry, 1973-76, chmn., 1975; mem. ocean crust panel Internat. Phase of Ocean Drilling, 1974-76; mem. U.S. nat. com. Internat. Geol. Correlations Program, 1974-76. Assoc. editor: Jour. Geophys. Rsch., 1966-68, Revs. of Geophysics, 1970-72, Geochimica et Cosmochimica Acta, 1970-76; editorial bd.: Physics of the Earth and Planetary Interiors, 1977-92, Earth and Planetary Sci. Letters, 1977-87, Chem. Geology, 1985—; contbr. articles in field to profl. jours. Fellow Geol. Soc. Am., Am. Geophys. Union (Harry H. Hess medal 1997), Geochem. Soc. (councillor 1981-83, v.p. 1983-85, pres. 1985-87, V.M. Goldschmidt award 1992), European Assn. Geochemistry; mem. NAS. Home: 53 Quonset Rd Falmouth MA 02540-1656 Office: Woods Hole Oceanographic Inst Dept Geology & Geophysics Woods Hole MA 02543 *I view science, the search for truth and understanding, as an infinitely long road: getting to the end is not as important as how we get there.*

HART, TERRY JONATHAN, communications executive; b. Pitts., Oct. 27, 1946; s. Jonathan Smith Hart and Lillian Dorothy (Zugates) Hart Pierson; m. Wendy Marie Eberhardt, Dec. 20, 1975; children: Amy, Lori. B of Mech. Engrng., Lehigh U., 1968, DEng (hon.), 1988; MS, MIT, 1969; MEE, Rutgers U., 1978. Mem. tech. staff AT&T Bell Labs., Whippany, N.J., 1968-69, 73-78, supr., 1984—, head cellular systems strategic planning, 1989—; astronaut NASA Johnson Space Ctr., Houston, 1978-84; captured solar maximum satellite NASA Johnson Space Ctr., 1984, div. mgr. Telstar 4 Satellite Program; pres. Loral Skynet, Bedminster, N.J., 1997—. Patentee in field. Served to lt. col. USAF Air N.G., 1969-90. Recipient N.J. Disting. Service medal, NASA Space Flight medal, Pride of Pa. medal. Mem. IEEE, Sigma Xi, Tau Beta Pi. Avocations: skiing; golf. Office: Loral Skynet 500 Hills Dr Rm 3a21 Bedminster NJ 07921-1538

HART, THOMAS HUGHSON, III, lawyer; b. Montgomery, Ala., Aug. 19, 1955; s. Thomas H. and Nora A. (McDonald) H.; m. Jane Elizabeth Morgan, Aug. 4, 1979; children: Morgan Elizabeth, Katherine MacDonald, Mary MacQuarrie, Teresa Jane, Thomas MacGregor. BA in Polit. Sci., Furman U., 1977; JD, U. S.C., 1980. Bar: S.C. 1980, U.S. Dist. Ct. S.C. 1981, U.S. Ct. Appeals (4th cir.) 1981, U.S. Ct. Appeals (11th cir.) 1982, U.S. Ct. Appeals (10th cir.) 1985, U.S. Supreme Ct. 1987, U.S. Ct. Appeals (8th cir.) 1990, U.S. Ct. Appeals (3d cir.) 1991, V.I., 1991. Assoc. Blatt and Fales, Barnwell, S.C., 1980-83; ptnr. Ness, Motley, Loadholt, Richardson & Poole, P.A., Barnwell, 1983-90, Brady, Hart & Jacobs, Christiansted, V.I., 1990-93; ptnr. Alkon, Rhea & Hart, Christiansted, 1993—. Editor S.C. Law Rev., 1978-80. Baruch scholar Furman U., Greenville, S.C., 1973-77; James Verner scholar U. S.C. Law Sch., 1978, Paul Cooper scholar, 1979. Mem. ABA, S.C. Trial Lawyers Assn. (bd. govs.), Assn. Trial Lawyers Am., S.C. Bar Assn., V.I. Bar Assn., Barnwell County C. of C. (bd. dirs.). Roman

Catholic. Home: 2 Boetzburg Christiansted VI 00820-4516 Office: 2115 Queen St Christiansted VI 00820-4835

HART, TIMOTHY RAY, lawyer, dean; b. Portland, Jan. 5, 1942; s. Eldon V. and Wanda J. (Hillyer) H.; m. Mary F. Barlow, Aug. 31, 1964 (div. Dec. 1975); children: Mark, Matthew, Marisa, Martin; m. Annette Bryant, Aug. 8, 1981. AA, San Jose City Coll., 1968; BA, San Jose State U., 1970; MA, Wash. State U., 1973; JD, San Joaquin Coll. Law, Fresno, Calif., 1983. Bar: Calif. 1983, U.S. Dist. Ct. (ea. dist.) Calif. 1983. Police officer City of Santa Clara, Calif., 1965-71; chief of police U. Idaho, Moscow, 1971-73; crime prevention officer City of Albany, Oreg., 1973-75; instr. criminal justice Coll. of Sequoias, Visalia, Calif., 1975-81, dir. paralegal dept., 1981-83, chmn., dir. adminstrn. justice div., 1983-88; assoc. dean instruction, 1988—; sole practice, Visalia, 1983—; apptd. dep. chief police City of Sanger (Calif.), 1996-97. Chair nonprofit com. Sanger Interagy. Youth and Comty. Svcs., Inc. With USAF, 1960-63. Mem. ABA, Calif. Bar Assn., Assn. Trial Lawyers Am., Assn. Criminal Justice Educators, Am. Criminal Justice Assn., Delta Phi. Mennonite. Home: 1012 W Hemlock Ave Visalia CA 93277-7435 Office: Coll of Sequoias 915 S Mooney Blvd Visalia CA 93277-2214

HART, VALERIE GAIL, writer; b. Detroit, May 6, 1936; d. Royal Allen and Elsa Adele (Freeman) Oppenheim; m. Robert Fredric Hart, Mar. 29, 1959; children: Alexandra H. Bosshardt, Gregory S., Katherine Hart. Student, U. Mich., 1954-59, Cité-Université, 1956-57, Cordon Bleu Cooking Sch., 1970. Tchr. Eng. Dexter (Mich.) Shc., 1958-59; co-owner Imports For the Trade, 1962-95; tchr. cooking, etiquette classes, 1965—; food writer, restaurant critic Daily Comml. recorded children's books for the blind, 1948; recorded books Univ. Miami Recording For The Blind, 1960-65; food editor Panax, 1977-82; editor ZAGAT, 1992, 95; author: The New Tradition Cookbook, 1988, A Trilogy of Children's Stories: Strangers, The Prize, The Table Tangles of Tommy and Ted, 1996, Very Special Occasions Cookbook, 1998; writer Social Mag.; food columnist Daily Comml., 1999; contbr. articles to mags. Tutor freshman Eng. blind pre-coll. students Lighthouse for the Blind, N.Y.C., 1959; leader Girl Scouts Am., Miami Beach, 1967-69; pres. sponsors Mus. Sci., 1975-77, tchr. cooking mus. benefit, 1975-79, past bd. trustees; pres. Parents' Assn. Ransom-Everglades Sch., 1976-77; bd. dirs. March of Dimes, 1976—, chair gourmet gala, 1980, 85; bd. dirs. Children's Psychiat. Ctr., 1980-95, Alee Acad.; chmn. judges kahlua bake-off contest FBO Project Newborn, 1986-97; chmn. auction, ball St. Francis Hosp., red ribbon day Dade County Schs. Healthy Foods Recipe Contest; tchr. cooking benefit Mt. Dora Ctr. For The Arts; mem. vestry, lay reader, chalice bearer All Souls' Episc. Ch., 1982-94. Inducted into Chaine des Rotisseurs, 1981; honored by Gastronome Mag., honored Outstanding Couple, Am. Cancer Soc., 1996; recipient Outstanding Woman award Miami Ballet Soc., 1985, 99. Mem. Surf Club, Mount Dora Yacht Club, Surfside Miami Beach. Republican. Episcopalian. Avocation: opera. Home: 6849 S Clayton St Mount Dora FL 32757-7024 Office: Downtowne Mount Dora dba Renaissance 411 N Donnelly St Mount Dora FL 32757-5598

HART, VIRGINIA WADE, elementary education educator; b. Rolla, Mo., Nov. 20, 1943; d. Clifford Neil and Nellie Z. (Jaggers) Wade; m. Edward F. Hart, Oct. 12, 1968 (div. June 1994); children: Edward S., Clifford T., James R., Deborah J., Sarah E. BA in Sociology, Mary Washington Coll., Fredricksburg, Va., 1965; MA in Elem. Edn., Adelphi U., Garden City, N.Y., 1973; MA in Reading, U. Ala., Birmingham, 1988, student, 1990. Cert. in elem. edn., reading, early childhood edn., Ala. Tchr. 1st grade Nassakegg Elem. Sch., Setauket, N.Y., 1966-68, Blue Point (N.Y.)-Bayport Schs., 1968-69; ednl. outreach Discovery Place Children's Mus., Birmingham, 1986-87; tchr. developmental kindergarten Hall Kent Elem. Sch., Birmingham, 1989-90, tchr. kindergarten, 1990-91, tchr. 2d grade, 1991—; clin. master tchr. U. Ala., Tuscaloosa, 1993—; mem. curriculum adv. com. Hoover Pub. Sch., 1989-91. Bd. dirs. Grace House Ministries, Fairfield, Ala., 1993-96. Mem. Internat. Reading Assn., Nat. Coun. Tchrs. English, Kappa Delta Pi, Delta Kappa Gamma Soc. Internat. Baptist. Office: Hall Kent Elem Sch 213 Hall Ave Homewood AL 35209-6530

HART, WILLIAM C., insurance underwriter, educator, writer; b. Orange, N.J., Jan. 6, 1947; s. William Gerard and Etchen (Alsberg) H.; m. Wendy Clarkson, Oct. 14, 1978 (div.); m. Charlotte R. Wagner, Oct. 7, 1989. AB, Fla. So. Coll., 1969; diploma, NYU, 1975; postgrad., Dale Carnegie Inst., 1994; profl. garden tng. program, Longwood Garden, Kennett Sq., Pa., 1976. Cert. land title profl. Land Title Inst. Va., 1991. Regional underwriter Chgo. Title Ins. Co., Dallas, 1980-83; sr. adv. title officer Lawyers Title Ins. Corp., New Brunswick, N.J., 1983-85; chief title officer Am. Title Ins. Co., Miami, Fla., 1985-92; chief title underwriter emeritus T.A. Title Ins. Co., Media, Pa., 1993-97; prin. Title Law Assocs., Phila., 1999—; lectr. N.J. Land Title Sch., Upsala Coll., East Orange, N.J., 1972, Land Title Sch., Austin, 1982, N.J. Lawyers Title Inst., Summit, 1984-85, Land Title Inst. Va., 1990, 91; instr. Neumann Coll. CLE Cert., 1995-97. Author: Standard Title Underwriting Practices, 1991, Creditors Rights and Title Insurance, Questionable Titles, Remedies & Extra-hazardous Risks, 1991, Title Insurance Underwriting Principles and Exception Language, 1992, Instructions as the Use of Title Insurance Endorsements, 1992, The Title Insurance Underwriting Process, 1994, New York Real Estate Law and Land Title Insurance, 1996; editor: New Jersey Titles Annotated, 1986. Mem. USGA (assoc.), Fraternal Order of Police (assoc.), Pa. Sheriffs Assn., N.J.Land Title Assn. (chmn. title officers com. 1987-88), Pa. Land Title Assn. (forms com. 1989-92, 94), Internat. Platform Assn., Eagle Lodge Country Club, World Affairs Coun. of Phila., Sigma Phi Epsilon. Republican. Avocations: martial arts (black belt), gardening, golf, stamp collecting, gardening. Home: 612 Boyer Rd Cheltenham PA 19012-1610 Office: T A Title Ins Co 2 Veterans Sq Media PA 19063-3186

HART, WILLIAM THOMAS, federal judge; b. Joliet, Ill., Feb. 4, 1929; s. William Michael and Geraldine (Archambeault) H.; m. Catherine Motta, Nov. 27, 1954; children: Catherine Hart Fornero, Susan Hart DaMario, Julie Hart Boesen, Sally Hart Collins, Nancy Hart McLaughlin. JD, Loyola U., Chgo., 1951. Bar: Ill. 1951, U.S. Dist. Ct. 1951, U.S. Ct. Appeals (7th cir.) 1954, U.S. Ct. Appeals (D.C. cir.) 1977. Asst. U.S. atty. U.S. Dist. Ct. (no. dist.) Ill., Chgo., 1954-56; assoc. Defrees & Fiske, 1956-59; spl. asst. atty. gen. State of Ill., 1957-58; assoc. then ptnr. Schiff, Hardin & Waite, 1959-82; spl. asst. state's atty. Cook County, Ill., 1960; judge U.S. Dist. Ct. Ill., 1982—; now sr. judge; mem. exec. com. U.S. Dist. Ct. (no. dist.) Ill., 1988-92; mem. com. on adminstrn. fed. magistrates sys., Jud. Conf. U.S., 1987-92, 7th cir. Jud. Coun., 1990-92; mem. edn. com. Fed. Jud. Ctr., 1994—. Pres. adv. bd. Mercy Med. Ctr., Aurora, Ill., 1980-81; v.p. Aurora Blood Bank, 1972-77; trustee Rosary H.S., 1981-82, 93-98; bd. dirs. Chgo. Legal Asst. Found., 1974-76. Served with U.S. Army, 1951-53. Decorated Bronze Starl named to Joliet/Will County Hall of Pride, 1992. Mem. 7th Cir. Bar Assn., Law Club, Legal Club, Soc. Trial Lawyers, Union League Club of Aurora, Ill. (hon.), Inn of Ct. Office: US Dist Ct No Dist Ill US Courthouse Rm 2246 219 S Dearborn St Chicago IL 60604-1702

HART-DULING, JEAN MACAULAY, clinical social worker; b. Bellingham, Wash.; d. Murry Donald and Pearl N. (McLeod) Macaulay; m. Richard D. Hart, Feb. 3, 1940 (dec. Mar. 1973); children: Margaret Hart Morrison, Pamela Hart Horton, Patricia L. Hart-Jewell; m. Lawrence Duling, Jan. 20, 1979 (dec. May 1992); children: Lenora Daniel, Larry, Jayne Munch. BA, Wash. State U., 1938; MSW, U. So. Calif., 1961. Lic. clin. social worker, Calif.; accredited counselor, Wash. Social worker Los Angeles County, 1957-58; children's svc. worker Dept. Children's Svcs., L.A., 1958-59; program developer homemakers svcs. project Calif. Dept. Children's Svcs., L.A., 1962-64; developer homemaker cons. position State of Calif., L.A., 1964-66; supr. protective svcs. Dept. Children's Svcs., L.A., 1966-67; dep. regional svc. adminstrn. Dept. Los Angeles County Children's Svcs., 1967-76; adminstr. Melton Home for Developmental Disability, 1985-86; pvt. practice pro bono therapy Calif. and Wash.; therapist various pro bono cases. Mem. Portals Com., L.A., 1974, Travelers Aid Bd., Long Beach, Calif. 1969. Recipient Nat. award work in cmty., spl. award for work with emotionally disturbed Com. for Los Angeles, 1974. Mem. AAUW, NASW, Acad. Cert. Social Workers, Calif. Lic. Clin. Soc. Workers, Wing Point Golf and Country Club (Bainbridge Island, Wash.). Republican. Congregationalist. Avocations: golf, bridge. Office: 7300 Quill Dr # 212 Downey CA 90242-2031

HARTE, ANDREW DENNIS, transportation company executive, travel agent; b. Bronx, N.Y., Jan. 23, 1946; s. Bernard and Gertrude (Romm) H. BA, CUNY-Hunter Coll., 1968; MS in Spanish, SUNY, New Paltz, 1975, MS in English, 1979; MA in French, NYU, 1975; MS in Reading, L.I. U., 1979. Cert. tchr., 48 states. Tchr. Hendrick Hudson Sch., Montrose, N.Y., 1968-69, Mahopac Schs., N.Y., 1969-70, Croton-Harmon Schs., N.Y., 1970-83; pres., owner Dominion Limousine Corp., Peekskill, N.Y., 1989—; mem. local com. N.E. Conf. on Tchg. Fgn. Langs., N.Y.C., 1979-83. Mem. Am. Assn. Tchrs. French (life), Am. Assn. Tchrs. Spanish and Portuguese (life), N.Y. State Assn. Fgn. Lang. Tchrs. (life, bd. dirs. 1983-86), Mensa (life), The Intertel Soc., Phi Delta Kappa (life, editor, historian). Avocations: foreign and domestic travel, language study, philately, reading, current events. Office: Dominion Limousine Corp PO Box 328 Peekskill NY 10566-0328

HARTE, CHRISTOPHER MCCUTCHEON, investment manager; b. Hanover, N.H., Nov. 20, 1947; s. Edward Holmead and Janet (Frey) H.; m. Kay Marie Wagenknecht, Feb. 11, 1984 (dec.); 1 child, William. BA, Stanford U., 1969; MBA, U. Tex., 1974. Assoc. McKinsey and Co., Inc., Dallas, 1974-76; dir. research and promotion Austin (Tex.) Am. Statesman, 1976-79; pvt. practice pub., communications, 1979-83; mem. advanced mgmt. devel. program Miami (Fla.) Herald, 1983-85; asst. to pres. newspaper div. Knight-Ridder Inc., Miami, 1985-86; pres., pub. Centre Daily Times, State Coll., Pa., 1986-89, Akron (Ohio) Beacon Jour., 1989-92; pres. Portland Press-Herald and Maine Sunday Telegram, 1992-94; chmn. Tex. Restaurant Card, Inc.; ptnr. Cerrito Ptnrs.; bd. dirs. Harte-Hanks, Inc., Wildfire Fire Equipment, Inc., Geokinetics, Inc., Hi-Port, Inc., Infosis Corp. Office: 75 Pearl St Ste 440 Portland ME 04101-4101

HARTE, HOUSTON HARRIMAN, marketing executive; b. San Angelo, Tex., Feb. 15, 1927; s. Houston and Caroline Isabel (McCutcheon) H.; m. Carolyn Esther Hardig, June 17, 1950; children: Houston Ritchie, David Harriman, Sarah Elizabeth. B.A., Washington and Lee U., 1950. Partner Snyder (Tex.) Daily News, 1950-52, editor, 1952-54; with Des Moines Register and Tribune, 1954-56; pres. San Angelo Standard, Inc., 1956-62; v.p. Express Pub. Co., San Antonio, 1962-66; pres. Express Pub. Co., 1966-72; chmn. bd. Harte-Hanks Communications, Inc., 1971-99. Pres., bd. dirs. San Angelo Symphony, 1960; v.p. Concho Valley coun. Boy Scouts Am., 1960-62; bd. vistors USAF Acad., 1965-69; bd. regents East Tex. State U., 1970-81; trustee Stillman Coll., 1976—, Washington and Lee U., 1981-92; chmn. bd. trustees Tex. Presby. Found., 1985-88. With USNR, 1945-46. Presbyterian. Office: Harte-Hanks Communications PO Box 269 San Antonio TX 78291-0269

HARTE, JOHN JOSEPH MEAKINS, bishop; b. Springfield, Ohio, July 28, 1914; s. Charles Edward and Ruth Elizabeth (Weisenstein) H.; m. Alice Eleanor Taylor, Oct. 14, 1941; children: Victoria Ruth, Joseph Meakins Jr., Judith Alice. AB, Washington and Jefferson Coll., 1936; DD (hon.), Washington & Jefferson Coll., 1954; STM, Gen. Theol. Sem., 1939, STD (hon.), 1955, D in Ministry, 1985; DD (hon.), U. South, 1955. Ordained to ministry Episc. Ch., 1939. Rector All Saints' Ch., Miami, Okla., 1939-41; curate Trinity Ch., Tulsa, 1941-42; rector St. George's Ch., Rochester, N.Y., 1942-43, All Saints' Ch., Austin, Tex., 1943-51; chaplain Episcopal students U. Tex., Austin; dean St. Paul's Cathedral, Erie, Pa., 1951-54; suffragan bishop Dioceses of Dallas, 1954-62; bishop Diocese of Ariz., 1962-80; bd. dirs. Citibank, Ariz., Gen. Conv. Episcopal Ch., 1952; chmn. St. Luke's Hosp., Tucson, 1962-80, St. Luke's Hosp. Med. Ctr., Phoenix, 1962-80; trustee Bloy Episcopal Sch. Theology; pres. Pacific Province, 1967-68. Author: Some Sources of Common Prayer, 1944, The Language of the Book of Common Prayer, 1945, The Title Page of the Book of Common Prayer, 1946, The Church's Name, 1958, The Elizabethan Prayer Book, 1959, The 1662 Prayer Book, 1962. Bd. dirs. Human Rights Commn. City of Phoenix, 1962-65. Named Man of Yr. NCCJ, Ariz., 1969, Anti-Defamation League, Ariz., 1975. Mem. Nat. Orgn. Episcopalians for Life (chmn., founder 1966—), Am. Legion, Beta Theta Pi. Lodges: Shriners (Imperial chaplain 1962-65), KT (Grand chaplain 1951-52), Masons. Office: 6300 N Central Ave Phoenix AZ 85012-1109

HARTENBACH, STEPHEN CHARLES, small business owner; b. St. Louis, Oct. 9, 1943. Student, Rockhurst Coll., 1961-62, St. Louis U., 1964-67. Salesman Revere Copper and Brass, N.Y.C., 1969-72; pres. Hartenbach Interiors, St. Louis, 1972-75; pres. and chmn. bd. dirs. Hartenbach Carpet and Gallery, St. Louis, 1975—. Alderman City of Sunset Hills, Mo., 1979-83, 87-89. 1st lt. U.S. Army, 1964-68. Mem. Am. Soc. Appraisers (assoc.), Regional Commerce and Growth Assn., Down St. Louis, Inc., Mo. Athletic Club, Elks. Republican. Roman Catholic. Office: 1408 Hanley Industrial Ct Saint Louis MO 63144-1916

HARTER, CAROL CLANCEY, university president, English language educator; m. Michael T. Harter, June 24, 1961; children: Michael R., Sean P. BA, SUNY, Binghamton, 1964, MA, 1967, PhD, 1970; LHD, Ohio U., 1989. Instr. SUNY, Binghamton, 1969-70; asst. prof. Ohio U., Athens, 1970-74, ombudsman, 1974-76, v.p., dean students, 1976-82, v.p. for adminstrn., assoc. prof., 1982-89; pres., prof. English SUNY, Geneseo, 1989-95; pres. U. Nev., Las Vegas, 1995—. Co-author: (with James R. Thompson) John Irving, 1986, E.L. Doctorow, 1990; author dozens of presentations and news columns; contbr. articles to profl. jours. Office: U Nev Las Vegas Office of Pres 4505 S Maryland Pkwy # 1001 Las Vegas NV 89154-1001

HARTER, DONALD HARRY, research administrator, medical educator; b. Breslau, Germany, May 16, 1933; came to U.S., 1940; naturalized, 1945; s. Harry Morton and Leonor Evelyne (Goldmann) H.; m. Lee Grossman, Dec. 18, 1960 (div. 1976); children: Kathryne, Jennifer, Amy, David; m. Rikki Horne, May 18, 1985 (div. 1986); m. Marjorie Brandt Dahlin, Oct. 12, 1990. AB, U. Pa., 1953; MD, Columbia U., 1957. Diplomate: Am. Bd. Psychiatry and Neurology. Intern in medicine Yale-New Haven Med. Center, 1957-58; asst. resident, then resident neurology N.Y. Neurol. Inst., 1958-61; guest investigator Rockefeller U., 1963-66; mem. faculty Columbia Coll. Physicians and Surgeons, 1960-75, prof. neurology and microbiology, 1973-75; vis. fellow Clare Hall, Cambridge, Eng., 1973-74; attending neurologist N.Y. Neurol. Inst., Presbyn. Hosp., 1973-75; Charles L. Mix prof. Northwestern U., 1975-85, Benjamin and Virginia T. Boshes prof. neurology, 1985-87, chmn. dept. neurology, 1975-87; chmn. dept. neurology Northwestern Meml. Hosp., Chgo., 1975-87; dir. rsch. scholars program Howard Hughes Med. Inst./NIH, Bethesda, 1989—; vis. sci. officer Howard Hughes Med. Inst., 1986-87, sr. sci. officer, 1987—; clin. prof. neurology George Washington U. Sch. Medicine and Health Scis., 1987—; mem. adv. com. on fellowships Nat. Multiple Sclerosis Soc., 1976-79, chmn., 1977-79, rsch. programs adv. com., 1989-94; mem. Nat. Commn. on Venereal Disease, HEW, 1970-72; mem. med. adv. bd. Am. Parkinson Disease Assn., 1976-90, Myasthenia Gravis Found., 1980-87; mem. sci. adv. coun. Nat. Amyotrophic Lateral Sclerosis Found., 1978-85; mem. bd. sci. counselors Nat. Inst. Dental Rsch. NIH, 1990-95, sr. sci. advisor Amyotrophic Lateral Sclerosis Assn., 1992—. Mem. editorial bd. Neurology, 1976-82, Anns. of Neurology, 1983-89; mem. adv. bd. Archives of Virology, 1975-81. Recipient Joseph Mather Smith prize Columbia U., 1970, Lucy G. Moses award, 1970, 72, Donald W. Mulder award The ALS Assn., 1998; Am. Cancer Soc. scholar, 1973-74; USPHS spl. fellow, 1963-66, Guggenheim fellow, 1973. Fellow AAAS, Infectious Diseases Soc. Am., Am. Acad. Neurology; mem. Am. Soc. Clin. Investigation, Am. Neurol. Assn., Am. Soc. Microbiology, Am. Assn. for History of Medicine, Am. Soc. Virology, Deutsche Gesellschaft für Neurologie (corr.), Royal Soc. Medicine (U.K.), Cosmos Club, Yale Club N.Y.C., Univ. Club Chgo., Univ. Club Washington, Phi Beta Kappa, Sigma Xi. Home: 3502 Preston Ct Chevy Chase MD 20815-5741 Office: Howard Hughes Med Inst 4000 Jones Bridge Rd Chevy Chase MD 20815-6789 also: Howard Hughes Med Inst 1 Cloister Ct Bethesda MD 20814-1460

HARTER, HUGH ANTHONY, foreign language educator; b. Columbus, Ohio, Dec. 13, 1922; s. Anthony Hugh and Georgiana (Hayes) H.; m. Driscilla Escher, Aug. 31, 1959 (div. 1961); m. Frances D. Reichman, Oct. 7, 1970; stepchildren: Ellen Berliner, Andrew Berliner, Nancy Berliner Rudolph. Student, Ohio Wesleyan U., 1940-41, Hamilton Coll., 1943, Ecole du Syndicat de la Haute Couture, Paris, 1947, NYU, 1975, New Sch. Social Research, 1975; B.A. cum laude, Ohio State U., 1947, Ph.D., 1959; M.A. cum laude, Mexico City Coll., U. Ams., 1951. Student teaching asst. Ohio State U., 1946-47, grad. teaching asst., 1951-53; asst. to prof. French Mexico City Coll., U. Ams., 1951; instr., asst. prof. Romance langs. Wesleyan U., Middletown, Conn., 1953-59; assoc. prof. Elmira Coll., 1959-60; Andrew Mellow postdoctoral fellow U. Pitts., 1960-61, spl. lectr., 1963-64, NDEA Insts. fellow, 1962, 63; assoc. prof. Chatham Coll., 1961-64, Loyola U., Chgo., 1964-66; prof. Ohio Westeyan U., Delaware, 1966-84; chmn. dept. Romance langs. Ohio Wesleyan U., Delaware, 1966-80, Robert Hayward prof. modern fgn. langs., 1976-84; dir. Internat. Inst. of Spain Ohio Wesleyan U., 1984-87, prof. emeritus; pres. Vitalicio, Fundacion Juan Ruiz, Segovia, Spain, 1971-86, Horizons for Learning, Delaware, Ohio, 1974—, Cursos Americanos e Internacionales, Segovia, 1986—; acct. Columbus Coated Fabrics Corp., Columbus, 1941-42; auditor European Post Exchange System, Bad Nauheim, Germany, 1948; co-owner John Anthony Studios, Columbus, 1954-64; v.p., dir. Von Mock Assocs., N.Y.C., 1969-70; spl. lectr. U. Catolica de Santa Maria, Arequipa, Peru, 1969; dir. Acad. Program in Segovia, 1969—. Author: Gertrudis Gomez de Avellaneda, 1981, Tangier and All That, 1993, reissue, 1997, D'Utah Beach aux Ardennes: Itiéraires 1944-1994, 1996; co-author: (with J. D. Mitchell) Staging a Spanish Classic: El hospital de los locos, 1990; translator, author: (most recent) Shattered Vision (Rabah Belamri), 1994, The Butts (Driss Chraïbi), 1983, Mother Comes of Age (Driss Chraïbi), 1983, Mother Spring (Driss Chraïbi), 1989, Past Tense (Driss Chraïbi), 1990, The Distant Friend (Claude Roy), 1990, Shadow of Paradise: Vicente Aleixandre, 1987; translator The Scavenger, 1962, Femmes/Hommes, 1977, Remembrance of a Time Just Past, 1993; translator, editor: A History of Spanish Literature, 1971; co-editor: (with Willis Barnstone) Riconoнete y Cortadillo, 1960, (with R.C. Allen, Jr.) A First Spanish Handbook for Teachers in Elementary Schools, 1961, A Second Spanish Handbook for Teachers in Elementary Schools, 1963; lyricist: More About the Pear Tree, The Death of the Soldier Guard, 1976. Bd. dirs. Centro Segovia, 1971-80; v.p. Delaware (Ohio) Heritage Inc., 1973-75, bd. dirs., 1975-78, pres., 1978-80; pres. Delaware Shakespeare Soc., 1980-81. Served with M.I. 3d Army, Normandy, No. France, then Air Transport Command, U.S. Army, ETO. Recipient medals of St. Calais, Vendome, Blois, Dombasle (France), Utah Beach, Avranches, Blois, St. Calais, Ouzouer, Dombasle, 1994, medaille d'Honneur of Confedn. Europeene des Anciens Combattants (France), 1992, 93; named Hon. Citizen City of Segovia, 1976; summer rsch. grantee Andrew Mellon Found., Morocco, 1973; spl. grantee Govt. of Morocco, 1975; spl. langs. grantee Mellon Mediterranean Studies, Algeria and Tunisia, 1977. Mem. AAUP, MLA, Am. Assn. Tchrs. Spanish and Portuguese, Authors' Guild, Coll. Lang. Assn., ASCAP, La Academia de San Quirce (Segovia corr.).

HARTER, LAFAYETTE GEORGE, JR., economics educator emeritus; b. Des Moines, May 28, 1918; s. Lafayette George and Helen Elizabeth (Ives) H.; m. Charlotte Mary Toshach, Aug. 23, 1950; children—Lafayette George III, James Toshach, Charlotte Helen. B.A. in Bus. Adminstrn, Antioch Coll., 1941; M.A. in Econs, Stanford, 1948, Ph.D., 1960. Instr. Menlo Coll., Menlo Park, Calif., 1948-50; instr. Coll. of Marin, Kentfield, Calif., 1950-60; prof. econs. dept. Oreg. State U., 1960-85, prof. emeritus, 1985—, chmn. dept., 1967-71; mem. panel arbitrators Fed. Mediation and Conciliation Svc., 1965-84, Oreg. Conciliation Svc., 1967-84; mem. Univ. Ctrs. for Rational Alternatives. Author: John R. Commons: His Assault on Laissez-faire, 1962, Labor in America, 1957, Economic Responses to a Changing World, 1972; editorial bd. Jour. Econ. Issues, 1981-84. Assoc. campaign chmn. Benton United Good Neighbor Fund, 1970-72, campaign chmn., v.p., 1972-73, pres., 1973-74, vice chmn.; pub. mem. Adv. Commn. on Unemployment Compensation, 1972, 73, chmn., 1974-78; Bd. dirs. Oreg. Coun. Econ. Edn., 1971-89; pub. mem. local profl. responsibilities Oreg. State Bar Assn., 1980-83; pub. mem. Oreg. Coun. on Ct. Procedures, 1985-93, bd. mem. Community Econs. of Corp., Community Econ. Stabilization Corp. Lt. comdr. USNR, 1941-46. Mem. AAUP, Am. Arbitration Assn. (pub. employment disputes panel 1970-92), Am. Western Econ. Assns., Indsl. Rels. Rsch. Assn., Am. Assn. for Evolutionary Econs., Oreg. State Employees Assn. (v.p. faculty chpt. 1972, pres. 1973), Am. Assn. Ret. Persons (pres. local chpt. 1992-93), Corvallis Retirement Village (fin. com., bd. dirs.). Democrat. Mem. United Ch. of Christ (moderator 1972, 73; mem. fin. com. Oreg. conf. 1974-82, dir. 1978-81, mem. personnel com. 1983-85). Home: 3755 NW Van Buren Ave Corvallis OR 97330-4952

HARTER, RALPH MILLARD PETER, lawyer, educator; b. Auburn, N.Y., Mar. 15, 1946; s. Donald Robert and Ruth (Ashdown) H.; m. Robin Ann Bampton, June 29, 1968 (div. Oct. 1994); m. Leslie J. Teague, Sept. 13, 1997; children: Robin Brooke, Donald Bampton. BA, Hobart Coll., 1968; JD, Cornell U., 1972. Bar: Pa. 1972, U.S. Dist. Ct. (ea. dist.) Pa. 1972, N.Y. 1981, U.S. Dist. Ct. (we. dist.) N.Y. 1981. Assoc. Duane, Morris & Heckscher, Phila., 1972-81, Harter, Secrest & Emery, Rochester, N.Y., 1981-83; ptnr. Goldstein, Goldman, Kessler & Underberg, Rochester, 1983-91, Sutton, DeLeeuw, Clark & Darcy, Rochester, 1991-94; mng. ptnr. Burke, Albright, Harter & Rzepka, LLP, Rochester, 1994—; educator elder law issues, right to die, ethics, trusts and estates issues. V.p., gen. counsel, bd. dirs. Otetiana council Inc., Boy Scouts Am., Rochester, 1982—; mem. various coms. Episcopal Diocesen and Ch., Phila. and Rochester, 1972—; chair bd. dirs. Episcopal Ch. Home, 1995—; bd. trustees Colls. of Seneca (Hobart & William Smith Colls.), 1987-96; bd. dirs. Allendale Columbia Sch., 1991-96; trustee Sigma Phi Ednl. Found., N.Y.C., 1990—. Served with USAR, 1969-75. Mem. ABA, N.Y. State Bar Assn. (various sects., lectr.), Pa. Bar Assn., Phila. Bar Assn., Monroe County Bar Assn., Nat. Acad. Elder Law Attys., Rochester Area C. of C. (United Way coms. 1984-96), Alzheimer's Disease and Related Disorders Assn. Inc. (pres., gen. counsel, bd. dirs. 1981—), Assn. of Adirondack Scout Camps (bd. dirs. 1986-93), Cornell U. Law Sch. Assn., Hobart Coll. Alumni Assn. and Alumni Council (pres. 1984-86), Hobart Coll. Statesmen Athletic Assn. (gen. counsel, bd. dirs. 1983—), Hobart Coll. Club of Rochester (pres. 1984—), The Genesse Valley Club (Rochester), Webhannet Golf Club (Kennebunkport, Maine), Delta chpt. Sigma Phi. Republican. Avocations: flyfishing, duck decoy carving, white water rafting, canoeing, golf. Home: Tuckaway Farm 98 Canfield Rd Pittsford NY 14534-9709 Office: Burke Albright Harter & Rzepka LLP 500 East Ave Ste 200 Rochester NY 14607-1912

HARTER, ROBERT DUANE, soil scientist, educator; b. Muskegon, Mich., July 6, 1936; s. Maurice Dale and Rachel Virginia (Baker) H.; m. Nancy Burt Bradshaw, Feb. 22, 1969; children: Carl William, Eric Dale, Laura Alden. BS in Agriculture, Ohio State U., 1961, MS, 1962; PhD, Purdue U., 1966. Asst. soil scientist Conn. Agrl. Expt. Sta., New Haven, 1966-68; assoc. rsch. scientist NYU, N.Y.C., 1968-69; asst. prof. soil chemistry U. N.H., Durham, 1969-75, assoc. prof., 1975-83, prof., 1983-99, prof. emeritus, 1999—; vis. prof. Pa. State U., State College, 1976, Agrl. U. of The Netherlands, Wageningen, 1983-84; vis. scientist Commonwealth Sci. and Indsl. Rsch. Inst., Adelaide, Australia, 1993-94. Assoc. editor Soil Sci. Soc. Am. Jour., 1988-93; editor: Absorption Phenomena, 1986; contbr. articles to profl. jours., chpts. to books. Elder Durham Evang. Ch., 1984-90, 91—; orgnl. leader 4-H Club, 1986-90. Fellow Soil Sci. Soc. Am. (chmn. soil chemistry divsn. 1982); mem. Am. Soc. Agronomy, Internat. Soil Sci. Soc. Baptist. Office: U NH Dept Natural Resources Durham NH 03824

HARTER, ROGER KARR, retired telecommunications executive; b. Normal, Ill., Dec. 12, 1923; s. Omar Newton and Helena (Karr) H.; m. Clair Phylis Caverly, Dec. 23, 1944; children: Deborah, Duncan, Malcolm, Penelope. BA, Swarthmore Coll., 1942; MA, Harvard U., 1948; postgrad., U. Mich., 1949-51. Staff asst. New Eng. Telegraph & Telephone, Boston, 1948-49; gen. staff asst. Mich. Bell Telephone & Telegraph, Detroit, 1949-51; gen. staff supr. AT&T, N.Y.C., 1951-58, Mich. Bell Telephone Co., Detroit, 1958-80. Chmn. bd. dirs. South Oakland Symphony Soc., Oak Park, Mich., 1960-62; pres. Southfield (Mich.) Symphony Soc.; state and regional pres. Navy League of U.S., Mich., 1975-80, nat. dir., 1975—; nat. dir. U.S. Naval Sea Cadet Corps, Washington, 1989-92. Col. USMC, 1942-75. Mem. VFW, Nat. Assn. Parliamentarians (registered parliamentarian, nat. dir. 1989-93), Am. Legion, Mich. State Assn. Parliamentarians (pres. 1994-96), Res. Officers Assn. (state pres. 1976), M.C. Res. Officers Assn. (chpt. pres.), Birmingham Power Squadron (charter), Mil. Inst. Windsor (charter), Marine Corps Assn., Fleet Res. Assn., Naval War Coll. Found., Naval Inst. Republican. Presbyterian. Avocations: sailing, traveling. Home: 1060 Puritan Ave Birmingham MI 48009-4637

HARTFORD, DOUGLAS BENNETT, university administrator; b. Balt., May 18, 1943; s. Winslow H. and Mary Haviland Hartford; m. Patricia L. Rathmann, Aug. 31, 1968; children: James G., Scott M. BS, St. Lawrence U., 1965; MS, Syracuse U., 1966; EdD, U. Northern Colo., 1976. Dir. news svcs. and alumni affairs U. Southern Colo., Pueblo, 1973-77; exec. dir. alumni assn. U. Calif., Davis, 1977-82, dir. of devel., 1982-86, spl. asst. to vice chancellor, 1986-87, dir. of planning giving, 1987-89; vice chancellor, external affairs Ind. U., South Bend, 1989-97; v.p. pub. affairs Met. State U., St. Paul, Minn., 1998—; univ. mktg. adv. team Ind. U., Bloomington, 1996-97; market rsch. adv. team Minn. State Colls. and Univs., St. Paul, 1998—. Contbr. articles to profl. jours. Dir. Fish Off Nat. Chamber Music Assn., South Bend, 1994-98, United Way, South Bend, 1994-97, C. of C., South Bend, 1989-97; pres. Granger Sunrise Rotary, 1995-96. 1st lt. U.S. Army, 1966-68. Mem. St. Paul Rotary. Avocations: skiing, photography, theatre. E-mail: doug.hartford@metrostate.edu. Home: 1292 Ingerson Rd Arden Hills MN 55112 Office: Met State U 700 East 7th St Saint Paul MN 55106

HARTFORD, MARGARET ELIZABETH (BETTY HARTFORD), social work educator, gerontologist, writer; b. Cleve., Dec. 12, 1917; d. William A. and Inez (Logan) H. BA, Ohio U., 1940; MS, U. Pitts., 1944; PhD, U. Chgo., 1962. Dir. youth svc. YWCA, Canton, Ohio, 1940-42; program cons. Intercultural Rels. Am. Svc. Inst., Pitts., 1943-48, exec. dir., 1948-50; prof. social work Case Western Res. U., Cleve., 1950-75; first dir. Sch. Gerontology U. So. Calif., L.A., 1975-77, prof. gerontology, social work, 1977-83, prof. emeritus, 1983—; instr. Claremont (Calif.) Adult Sch. Dist., 1983—, mentor/tchr. adult edn., 1990-95; instr. retirement Pasadena (Calif.) City Coll., 1983-84, Mt. San Antonio Coll., 1988-90; cons. pre-retirement, retirement planning to corps. and ednl. systems, various cities, 1980—; cons., lectr. 1970—; instr. gerontology/mental health Kaiser Permanente, 1997-99. Author: Groups in Social Work, 1973, (workbook) Making the Best of the Rest of Your Life, 1982, rev. edit., 1998, Leaders Guide to Making the Best of the Rest of Your Life, 1986; contbr. monthly column on successful aging Pomona Valley Cmty. Svcs. on Aging Newsletter, 1988—; contbr. numerous articles to profl. publs. Commr. human svcs. City of Clairmont, 1986-89, city coun. observer LWV, 1994-95; trustee Mt. San Antonio Gardens Retirement Com., 1985-92, sec., 1988-91; v.p. Mt. San Antonio Gardens Club Coun., bd. dirs. admissions com. 1996-99, nominating com. 1992-97, health svcs. com. 1996-98, chmn. task force on wellness/fitness, historian 1996-99; trustee Corp. Pilgrim Pl. Ret. Cmty., chmn. health and svcs. com., 1987-94, 96—; bd. dirs., trustee Vol. Assn. Rancho Santa Ana Bot. Gardens, 1991—; chmn. vol. pers. com., goals and evaluation com. St. Ambrose Episcopal Ch., Claremont, 1988—, mem. TRAM com., 1996—, chmn., 1998—, trail steward, 1999; chmn. bd. Friends of Claremont Srs., 1997—. Named Outstanding Contbn. to Social Work, Alumni Assn. Schs. Social Work U. So. Calif., 1984, Outstanding Contbr. Social Group Work, Com. Advancement of Group Work, Toronto, Ont., Can., 1985, Woman of Yr., Trojan Women U. So. Calif., 1976, Woman of Yr., YWCA of Pomona Valley, 1989, Vol. of Yr., L.A. County Coun. on Aging, 1990; recipient Dart award for Innovative Tchg., U. Soc. Calif., 1974, 1st pl. award at juried show Am. Assn. Chinese Brush Painting, 1987, 2nd pl. short story Sedona Writers Contest, Hon. Mention non-fiction, 1989, County Commr. Citation State of Calif. Ho. of Reps., Outstanding Contbn. award Mt. San Antonio Gardens Retirement Cmty., 1994, 99, Contbn. to Srs. award Pomona Valley Cmty. Svcs., 1994, Spl. Recognition award, Social Work, U. So. Calif., 1996, Jo Smith award for outstanding contbrs. to Claremont Srs., 1998, Mt. San Antonio Gardens award for svc., 1999. Fellow Gerontol. Soc. Am.; mem. AAUW, Nat. Assn. Social Workers (cert., nat. chmn. 1962-64, group work sect., chmn. Cleve. chpt. 1969-72), Am. Soc. Aging (chmn. program com. 1983-85, City of Claremont com. on aging 1983—, chmn. 1991, program chair 1985-94), Rembrandt Soc., Scripps Fine Arts Assn., Harvey Mudd Gallilio Soc. Episcopalian. Avocations: botanical gardens docent, birdwatching, watercolor painting, sculpturing, poetry writing. Home: 918 Harrison Ave Claremont CA 91711-4129

HARTFORD, SHAUN ALISON, pediatrics nurse, educator; b. Houston, Mar. 30, 1962; m. Mark M. Danney; children: Angela, Nicholas. BSN, U. Tex. Health Sci. Ctr., San Antonio, 1984, MSN, 1988. Cert. pediatric nurse Nat. Assn. Pediatric Nurse Practitioners and Nurses. Staff nurse, pediatrics Santa Rosa Health Care Corp., San Antonio, 1985-89; mem. faculty Sch. Profl. Nursing, Bapt. Health Sys., San Antonio, 1989—. Mem. Am. Diabetes Assn. (Patient Edn. award 1994, Champions for Life award 1996), Sigma Theta Tau.

HARTFORD, WILLIAM HENRY, magazine editor, writer, lecturer; b. Amityville, N.Y., Mar. 9, 1938; s. Harold John and Lillian May (Kattau) H.; m. Shari Elyse Green, June 1, 1980; children by previous marriage: Amy Joan, Christopher William. Student, Poly. Inst. N.Y.; BA in English Lit., Adelphi U., 1961, postgrad. Auto editor Popular Mechanics mag., N.Y.C., 1969-79, mng. editor, 1979-90. With USNR, 1955-63. Mem. Internat. Motor Press Assn. (pres. 1975-76). Home and Office: 380 Rector Pl Apt 17J New York NY 10280-1448

HARTGEN, VINCENT ANDREW, museum director, educator, artist; b. Reading, Pa., Jan. 10, 1914; s. William J. and Jane (Hadfield) H.; m. Frances Caroline Lubanda, July 6, 1940; children: David Thomas, Stephen Anthony. BFA, U. Pa., 1940, MFA, 1941; DFA (hon.), U. Maine, 1987. Traveling curator Anna Hyatt Huntington Exhbn. of Sculptures, 1937-39; dir. U. Maine Art Gallery; prof., head art dept. U. Maine, 1946-75, John H. Huddilston prof. art, 1962-82, John H. Huddilston prof. emeritus, 1983—, curator art collections, 1975-82; Art adviser Cultural Olympics, U. Pa., 1939-41; mem. Gov.'s Commn. Arts and Humanities, 1966-70. Works in collections including, Boston Mus. Fine Arts, Brooks Meml. Mus., Memphis, Howard U. Collection, John and Norma Marin Collection, Mus. Contemporary Arts, Houston, Wichita (Kans.) Art Mus., Butler Inst. ARts, Youngstown, Ohio, Everhart Mus., Scranton, Pa., U. Maine, Art Collection, Wadsworth Atheneum, Hartford, Smith, Colby colls., Reading (Pa.) Mus., Phoenix Art Mus., ITT Collection, Brandeis U., Elvejhem (Wis.) Mus., Kalamazoo Inst. Coll., Walker Art Inst., Mpls., Sheldon Swope Gallery, Terre Haute, Ind., one-man exhibits include Binet Gallery, N.Y.C., Md. Inst., Howard U., Everhart Mus., Claflin U., Coll. of Pacific, U. Idaho, Bermuda Art Assn., Chase Gallery N.Y., Farnsworth Mus., Rockland, Maine, State Dept. Art in the Embassies, Fifty Drawings Cen. Place Gallery, Bangor, Maine Art Gallery, 1992, U. Maine, 1994; also more than 150 throughout mus. and galleries in U.S. Trustee Haystack Mountain Sch. Crafts, Liberty, Maine, 1953-55. Served with U.S. Army, 1942-45. U. Pa. fellow; recipient BAID award, 1935, Soldier Art award, 1945; Audubon Artists award, 1950, Audubon Artists medal for creative aquarelle, 1965, Silver medal Audubon Artists, 1974, Distinguished Faculty award, 1965, Gov.'s Art award State of Maine, 1967, Franklin Mint Bicentiennial Medal Design award, 1972, U. Maine Alumni Black Bear award, 1974; named A Maine State Treasure State of Maine Dept. Edn., 1994. Mem. AAUP, Audubon Artists, Am. Watercolor Soc., Phi Kappa Phi. Home: 109 Forest Ave Orono ME 04473-1417 *To have lived, and to have seen such an incredible and beautiful world as this is to easeily understand my consummate joy in having been an artist and teacher for such a long life.*

HARTH, ERICA, French language and comparative literature educator; b. N.Y.C. B.A., Barnard Coll., 1959; M.A., Columbia U., 1962, Ph.D. in French, 1968. Instr. French, NYU, 1964-66; from instr. to asst. prof. Columbia U., 1967-71; lectr. Tel-Aviv U., Israel, 1971-72; asst. prof. Brandeis U., 1972-75, assoc. prof. French, 1975-85, prof. French and comparative lit., 1985-92, prof. humanities and women's studies, 1992—. NEH fellow, 1970; Am. Council Learned Socs. fellow, 1978, 1990, Bunting Inst. fellow, 1990, NEH fellow, 1989. Mem. MLA. Author: Cyrano de Bergerac and the Polemics of Modernity, 1970; Ideology and Culture in Seventeenth Century France, 1983, Cartesian Women: Versions and Subversions of Rational Discourse in the Old Regime, 1992; contbr. articles to profl. jours. Office: Brandeis U MS 024 Dept Romance & Languages Waltham MA 02254

HARTH, ROBERT JAMES, music festival executive; b. Louisville, June 13, 1956; s. Sidney and Teresa O. H.; m. Melanie Lynn Pope; 1 child, Jeffrey David Harth Curtis. B.A. in English, Northwestern U., 1977. Assoc. mgr. Ravinia (Ill.) Festival Assn., 1977-79; v.p., gen. mgr. Los Angeles Philharm. Assn., 1979-89, Hollywood Bowl, 1979-89; pres., chief exec. officer Aspen (Colo.) Music Festival and Sch., Music Assocs. of Aspen, Inc., 1989—. Office: Aspen Music Festival Sch 2 Music School Rd Aspen CO 81611-8500

HARTH, SIDNEY, musician, educator; b. Cleve., Oct. 5, 1929; s. Leonard and Anne (Dunnire) H.; m. Teresa Testa, July 7, 1949; children: Laura, Robert. Mus.B., Cleve. Inst. Music, 1947; studied with, Joseph Knitzer, Mishel Piastro, Georges Enesco. Assoc. prof. U. Louisville, 1953-58; faculty DePaul U., 1959-62; chmn. dept. music, A.W. Mellon disting. prof. Carnegie-Mellon U., Pitts., 1963-73; mem. faculty Aspen (Colo.) Music Festival, 1963-74; exchange artist Les Jeungesses Musicales de France, 1952; exchange artist internat. tours France, Corsica, North Africa, State Dept. tour Germany, 1952; with Mrs. Harth nat. tour, 1952; concertmaster Louisville Orch., 1953-58, Chgo. Symphony, 1959-62; condr. Evanston (Ill.) Orch., 1960-62; assoc. condr., concertmaster Los Angeles Philharm., 1973-79; chief guest condr. Jerusalem Symphony, 1975-77; music dir. Puerto Rican Symphony, 1977-79; condr. Can. Nat. Chamber Orch., 1979, 80; concertmaster N.Y. Philharm., 1980-81; orch. dir. Mannes Coll. of Music, 1981-84; condr., music dir. Northwest Chamber Orch., N.W. Chamber Orch., 1990-93; prof. SUNY, Stony Brook, 1981-82, Yale U., 1982—; prin. condr. Natal Symphony Orch., Durban, South Africa, 1994—; dir. orchestral activities Hartt Sch. Music, U. Hartford, 1991-93; prof. violin Wieniawski competition laureate, Poland, 1957; orch. dir., vis. prof. U. Houston, 1985; dir. orchestral studies Carnegie-Mellon U., Pitts., 1989-90; prin. condr. Natal Symphony, Durban, South Africa, 1994—. Ann. internat. tours including Yugoslavia, Poland, Belgium, Austria, Eng., USSR, Poland, Czechoslovakia, Romania, Switzerland, Holland., Vanguard, Iramac, Concert Hall Soc., Stradivari Records; contbr. articles to nat. mags. Recipient Ysaye medal; Wieniawske medal. Home: 135 Westland Dr Pittsburgh PA 15217-2538 Office: care Sheldon Soffer Mgmt 130 W 56th St New York NY 10019-3803

HARTH-BEDOYA, MIGUEL, conductor; b. Lima, Peru, 1968. Degree, Curtis Inst. Music, Juilliard Sch. Music dir. Eugene (Oreg.) Symphony Orch.; music dir., condr. N.Y. Youth Symphony Carnegie Hall; guest condr. N.Y. Philharm., L.A. Philharm., Florida Orch., Seattle Symphony, Colorado Symphony, Quebec Symphony, Auckland Philharmonia, New Zealand, Puerto Rico Symphony, Buenos Aires Philharmonia, Evansville Philharm. Orch., Ind., others; condr. Juilliard Orch. tour, France, 1993, Japan, 1995, St. Luke's Orch., 1995; founder, artistic dir. New Opera Co. Peru, Orquestra Filarmonica de Lima; mem. conducting faculty Juilliard Sch. Condr. (opera) Il Tutore Burlato, 1994, Italy, recording, 1995. Office: Eugene Symphony Orch 45 W Broadway Ste 201 Eugene OR 97401-3002

HARTIGAN, GRACE, artist; b. Newark, Mar. 28, 1922; d. Matthew A. and Grace (Orvis) H.; m. Robert L. Jachens, May 1941 (div. 1948); 1 son, Jeffrey A.; m. Robert Keene, Dec. 14, 1959 (div. 1960); m. Winston H. Price, Dec. 24, 1960 (dec. 1981). Student pvt. art classes. Dir. Md. Inst. Grad. Sch. Painting, 1965—. One-woman shows Tibor de Nagy Gallery, N.Y.C., 1951-55, 57-59, Vassar Coll. Art Gallery, 1954, Martha Jackson Gallery, N.Y.C., 1962, 64, 67, 70, U. Chgo., 1967, Gertrude Kasle Gallery, Detroit, 1968, 70, 72, 74, Robert Keene Gallery, Southampton, N.Y., 1957-59, Gres Gallery, Washington, 1960, U. Minn., 1963, William Zierler Gallery, N.Y.C., 1975—, C. Grimaldis Gallery, Balt., 1979, 81, 82, 84, 86, 87, 89, 90, 93, 95, 97, Hamilton Gallery, N.Y.C., 1981, Gruenebaum Gallery, N.Y.C., 1984, 86, 88, Kouros Gallery, N.Y.C., 1989, ACA Gallery, N.Y.C., 1991, 92, 94, 97, ACA Munich, 1996; exhibited in numerous group shows including Modern Art in U.S., 1955-56, 3d Internat. Contemporary Art Exhbn., 1957, 4th Internat. Art Exhbn., Japan, 1957, IV Biennial, Sao Paulo, 1957, New Am. Painting Show, Europe, 1958-59, World's Fair, Brussels, 1958, The Figure Since Picasso, Mus. Ghent, Belgium, Moca in Moca Chicago, Hand Painted Pop Moca L.A., Whitney Mus. Am. Art, N.Y.C., 1992-93; represented in permanent collections Mus. Modern Art, Walker Art Center, Whitney Mus. Am. Art, Art Inst. Chgo., Met. Mus. Art, Raleigh Mus., Providence Mus., Bklyn. Mus., Mpls. Mus., Albright-Knox Gallery, Buffalo, numerous others. Recipient Merit award for art Mademoiselle Mag., 1957, Nat. Inst. Arts and Letters purchase award, 1974. Address: 1701 1/2 Eastern Ave Baltimore MD 21231-2420

HARTJES, LAURIE BETH, pediatric nurse practitioner, woman's health nurse; b. Port Washington, Wis., July 17, 1956; d. Paul G. and Dorothy C. (Gilman) Davies; m. Thomas Lee Hartjes, June 12, 1982; children: Elizabeth, Julia. BS, U. Wis., 1978, MS, 1983. RN, Wis.; cert. PNP. Pub. health nurse Dept Health City of Milw., 1979-81; clin. instr. Rock Valley Coll., Rockford, Ill., 1982-83, Coll. Nursing U. Ill., Chgo., 1982-83; PNP Crusader Cen. Clin. Assn., Nat. Health Svc. site, Rockford, 1983-94, 95; clin. instr. Sch. Nursing U. Wis., Madison, 1984-94; clin. nurse specialist/PNP U. Wis. Children's Hosp., Madison, 1984-94; clin. asst. prof. U. Wis.-Madison Sch. Nursing, 1995—; naturalist U. Wis.-Madison Arboretum, 1995—. Contbr., cons. articles to profl. jours. Active Am. Heart Assn. (cert. CPR). Recipient Theodore Herfurth award 1978, Louise Troxel award; federal grantee 1977-78 and 1981-83. Mem. ANA (mem. coun. primary health care nurse practitioners), Nat. Assn. Pediatric Nurse Assocs. and Practitioners, Wis. Assn. Pediatric Nurse Assocs. and Practitioners (treas. 1990-93, fin. and adolescent health subcoms., WisTrec rep. 1997—), Wis. Nurses Assn., Sigma Theta Tau, Phi Kappa Phi. Home: 530 Linden Ct Verona WI 53593-1683

HARTKE, STEPHEN PAUL, composer, educator; b. Orange, N.J., July 6, 1952; s. George William Hartke, Jr. and Priscilla Nancy (Redfearn) Elfrey; m. Lisa Louise Stidham, Sept. 12, 1981; 1 child, Alexander Stidham. BA magna cum laude, Yale U., 1973; MA, U. Pa., 1976; PhD, U. Calif., Santa Barbara, 1982. Advt. mgr. Theodore Presser Co., Bryn Mawr, Pa., 1977-78; advt. and art dir. European Am. Music Corp., Clifton, N.J., 1978-79; ednl. dir. Carl Fischer Inc., N.Y.C., 1980; Fulbright prof. composition U. São Paulo, Brazil, 1984-85; prof. composition Sch. Music U. So. Calif., L.A., 1987—; vis. composer Coll. Creative Studies U. Calif., Santa Barbara, 1981-83, 85-87; composer-in-residence L.A. Chamber Orch., 1988-92. Composer: Caoine, 1980, Sonata-Variations for violin and piano, 1984 (Kennedy Friedheim award 1985), Oh Them Rats Is Mean In My Kitchen, 1985, Pacific Rim for orch., 1988, The King of the Sun, 1988, Symphony Number 2, 1990, Concerto for violin and orch., 1992, Wulfstan at the Millennium, 1995, The Ascent of the Equestrian in a Balloon, 1995, Sons of Noah, 1996, The Horse with the Lavender Eye, 1997, Piano Sonata, 1998, The Rose of the Winds, 1998; recordings on CRI, New World Records, ECM EMI record labels. Recipient Acad. award AAAL, 1993, Rome prize Am. Acad. in Rome, 1992, Stoeger award Lincoln Ctr. Chamber Music Soc., 1997; Composer-in-Residence grantee Nat. Endowment for Arts (1990, 91), Commn. grantee Koussevitzky Music Found., 1992, Fromm Found. Commn. grantee, 1994, Inst. for Am. Music Commn. grantee; Guggenheim fellow, 1997. Mem. Opera Am., Am. Mus. Ctr. Office: U So Calif Sch Music 308 University Park Los Angeles CA 90089-0851

HARTL, DANIEL LEE, genetics educator; b. Marshfield, Wis., Jan. 1, 1943; s. James W. and Catherine E. (Stieber) H.; m. Carolyn Teske, Sept. 5, 1964 (div. Apr. 1978); children: Dana Margaret, Theodore James; m. Christine Blazynski, July 23, 1980; 1 child, Christopher Lee. BS, U. Wis., 1965, PhD in Genetics, 1968. Postdoctoral fellow in genetics U. Calif., Berkeley, 1968-69; asst. prof. genetics and cell biology U. Minn., St. Paul, 1969-73, assoc. prof., 1973-74; assoc. prof. biol. scis. Purdue U., West Lafayette, Ind., 1974-78, prof., 1978-81; prof. genetics Washington U. Sch. Medicine, St. Louis, 1981-92, James S. McDonnell prof. genetics, head genetics dept., 1984-91, dir. divsn. biology and biomed. scis., 1986-89; prof. biology Harvard U., Cambridge, Mass., 1993—; mem. genetics study sect. NIH, Washington, 1976-80, mem. genetic basis of disease rev. com., 1983-87. Author: Principles of Population Genetics, 1980, 3d edit., 1997, Human Genetics, 1983, General Genetics, 1985, Primer of Population Genetics, 1988, Basic Genetics, 1988, Genetics, 1994, 2d edit., 1997, Essential Genetics, 1996; assoc. editor Ann. Revs. Inc., 1984-89, Molecular Biology and Evolution, 1983—, Molecular Phylogenetics and Evolution, 1993—, Molecular Ecology, 1993—, Genetics, 1977-85, BioSci., 1974-80, Theoretical Population Biology, 1975-81, Molecular Ecology, 1992—, Molecular Phylogenetics and Evolution, 1992—. Recipient Career Devel. award NIH, 1974-79. Mem. Genetics Soc. Am. (pres. 1989), Phi Beta Kappa. Office: 219 Biological Labs Harvard U 16 Divinity Ave Rm 295 Cambridge MA 02138-2020*

HARTL, JOHN GEORGE, film critic; b. Wenatchee, Wash., June 28, 1945; s. David and Georgiann (MacLean) H. BA in Journalism, U. Wash., 1967. Film critic Seattle Times, 1966—. Avocations: swimming, reading, camping. Office: Seattle Times PO Box 70 Fairview Ave N & John St Seattle WA 98111-0070*

HARTLE, ROBERT WYMAN, retired foreign language and literature educator; b. Kongmoon, China, Sept. 1, 1921; s. Jacob Everett and Margaret (Wyman) H.; m. Ann Dorothy Mordhorst, Jan. 5, 1980; 1 son, Robert Wyman, Jr.; children by previous marriage: Shirley Ann (Mrs. Jan McDaniel), John Wyman. BA, U. Tex., 1947, MA, 1947; AM, Princeton U., 1949, PhD, 1951. Instr. French Princeton U., 1950-53, asst. prof., 1953-60; assoc. prof. modern langs. U. Oreg., 1961-63; asst. prof. Romance langs. Queens Coll. (now CUNY-Queens Coll.), N.Y.C., 1960-61; prof., chmn. dept. Romance and Slavic langs. Queens Coll. (now CUNY-Queens Coll.), 1963-65, assoc. dean faculty, 1964-65, dean faculty, 1965-70, prof., 1972-87, prof. emeritus, 1987—, chmn. ad hoc legal affairs com., mem. univ. acad. senate, 1979-81, dir. PhD program in France, 1970-72, mem. senate; founder, dir. programs of study abroad, 1963-70; vis. prof. Inst. Liberal Arts, Emory U., 1985-93. Author: Index du vocabulaire du théâtre classique: Racine, 8 vols, 1956-64; transl. Tartuffe (Molière), 1963; contbr. articles on the iconography of Alexander the Great, 17th century French art and architecture, Hellenistic Art, 1955—; French translator Papers of Robert Morris, 1973-84; French cons. Papers of Thomas Jefferson, Princeton U. Press, 1986—. Bd. dirs. Am. Ctr. for Students and Artists, Paris, 1970-78. Decorated officer Ordre des Palmes Académiques (France), knight Order of Merit (Italy), officer's cross Order of Merit (Germany). Mem. MLA, AAUP (pres. chpt. 1975-80). Home: 1803 Westminster Way NE Atlanta GA 30307-1134

HARTLEY, ALAN HASELTON, lexicographer, stevedoring administrator; b. Duluth. Minn., Dec. 3, 1946; s. Alfred and Ann Hardy (Haselton) H.; m. Susan Beers Rice, June 21, 1969; two children. BA, Carleton Coll., 1969; MS, U. Wash., 1972. Geologist Exxon Minerals, Ely, Minn., 1969-70, 77; ranger Nat. Park Svc., Isle Royale, Mich., 1973-77; comml. fisherman Sivertson Fisheries, Duluth, Minn., 1974-80; stevedoring supt. Empire Stevedoring, Duluth, 1981-95, Rogers Terminal (Cargill), Duluth, 1995—; lexicographer Oxford Univ. Press, England, 1995—. Trustee Longshoremen's Pension and Welfare Funds, Duluth, Longshoremen's Tonnage Incentive Program Fund; parent rep. world langs. curriculum com. Duluth Pub. Schs. NSF fellow, 1970-72. Home: 119 W Kent Rd Duluth MN 55812-1152

HARTLEY, BOB, hockey coach; b. Hawesbury, Ont., Can., Sept. 7, 1960. Head coach Colo. Avalanche, 1998—. Office: care Colo Avalanche McNichols Arena 1635 Clay St Denver CO 80204*

HARTLEY, CARL WILLIAM, JR., lawyer; b. Carthage, Mo., Aug. 12, 1946; s. Carl William and Doris Eillene (Wilcox) H.; m. Martha Anderson Gouch (div. 1991); children: Zach, Jordan. BS, U. Fla., 1968, JD with High Honors, 1976. Bar: Fla. 1976, U.S. Dist. Ct. (so. dist.) Fla. 1976, U.S. Dist. Ct. (mid. dist.) Fla. 1980. Sales rep. Scott Paper Co., Miami, Fla., 1971-73; assoc. Grenbherg, Traurig et al., Miami, 1976-80; ptnr. Thomas Thomas Hartley & Spraker, Orlando, Fla., 1980-83, Holland & Knight, Orlando, 1983-85, Hartley, Wall & Norman, Orlando, 1985—. Editor U. Fla. Law Rev., 1976. Democrat. Methodist. Avocations: fishing, hunting, camping. Office: Hartley Wall & Norman PO Box 2168 Orlando FL 32802-2168

HARTLEY, CELIA LOVE, nursing educator, nursing administrator; b. Colfax, Wash., Oct. 25, 1935; d. Thomas Warren and Ella Marie (Kerkman) Love; m. Lawrence Dosser (div.); children: Laurie Denise Draper, Byron Garth Dosser; m. Gordon E. Hartley, Dec. 17, 1972. Diploma, Deaconess Hosp. Sch. Nursing, Spokane,, 1956; BSN, U. Wash., 1965, MSN, 1968. RN, Wash., Calif. Staff nurse Deaconess Hosp., Spokane, 1956-62; charge nurse Northgate Gen. Hosp., Seattle, 1963-65; hosp. supr. Stevens Meml. Hosp., Edmonds, Wash., 1965-66; prof. nursing Shoreline C.C., Seattle, 1967-73, dir. nursing edn., asst. div. chmn. health occupations, 1973-92; chair health sci. divsn. Coll. of the Desert, Palm Desert, Calif., 1992—; pres. Coun. on Nursing Edn. in Wash. State, 1992; adv. com. Antioch West and Seattle U., 1979-81, Nursing Edn. Com. Higher Edn. Coordinating Bd., 1990, Western Wash. U. Nursing, 1984, Seattle Pacific U. Nursing, 1992; other coms. various orgns., 1979—; presenter to profl. orgns., 1980—. Author: (with Janice Ellis) Nursing in Today's World; Challenges, Issues, and Trends, 1980, 2nd rev., 1984, 3rd rev., 1988, 4th rev., 1992, 5th rev., 1995, 6th rev., 1998, Managing and Coordinating Patient Care, 1991, 2nd rev., 1995; (with others) Fundamentals of Nursing, 1992; mem. editl. bd. Assoc. Degree Nurse, 1987-91, Jour. Nursing Edn., 1991—; contbr. articles to profl. publs. Mem. ANA, Nat. League of Nursing (bd. dirs. 1981-84, appeal panel Coun. AD Programs 1988-91, 95-98, chmn.-vice chmn. various com.), Wash. Constituent League (v.p. 1986-87, chmn. nominating com. 1984-85, chmn. membership com. 1985-86), Calif. Nursing Strategic Planning Com., Sigma Theta Tau. Methodist. Home: 53-760 Avenida Montezuma La Quinta CA 92253

HARTLEY, CORINNE, painter, sculptor, educator; b. L.A., July 24, 1924; d. George D. and Marjorie (Fansher) Parr; m. Thomas L. West, Sept. 3, 1944 (div. 1970); children: Thomas West III, Tori West, Trent West; m. Clabe M. Hartley, Aug. 27, 1973 (div. 1997). Attended, Chouinard Art Inst., L.A., 1942-44, Pasadena (Calif.) Sch. Fine Arts, 1952-54. Paste up artist Advt. Agy., L.A., 1944; fashion illustrator May Co., L.A., 1944-45; freelance fashion illustrator Bullock's, L.A., 1946-76; art tchr. Pasadena Sch. Fine Arts, 1965-71; pvt. art tchr., owner studio, Venice, Calif., 1971—; presenter art workshops; works pub. and distributed by Art in Motion, Prints and Cards, Vancouver, B.C., Can., 1990—. Gallery representation includes Dassin Gallery, L.A., 1981—, Legacy Gallery, Scottsdale, Ariz., 1989—, G. Stanton Gallery, Dallas, 1990—, Coda Gallery, Palm Desert, Calif., 1993—, Huntsman Gallery, Aspen, Colo., 1995—, Carol Kavanaugh Gallery, Des Moines, 1996—, Jones & Terwilliger Gallery, Carmel, Calif., 1997—, Lee Youngman Gallery, Calistoga, Calif., 1997—, Coda Gallery, Park City, Utah, 1997—, Terbush Gallery, Santa Fe, 1997—, Water Street Gallery, 1999. Recipient Purchase award Nat. Orange Show, San Bernardino, Honor award All City Art Festival, Barnsdall Park, L.A., Best of Show award Clumer Mus. Wash., 3d pl. award still life Calif. Art Club, others. Mem. Am. Acad. Women Artists, Calif. Art Club, Oil Painters Am. Republican. Avocation: singing in ch. choir. Studio: 411 N Venice Blvd Venice CA 90291-4534

HARTLEY, CRAIG SHERIDAN, mechanical and materials engineering educator; b. Quantico, Va., Dec. 9, 1937; s. Cleo Stancil and Velva Marie (Grayson) Bowers; m. Cornelia Margaret McMann, June 7, 1958; children: Margaret Ann, Katherine Jeanne, David Brian. BMetE, Rensselaer Poly. Inst., 1958; MS, Ohio State U., 1961, PhD, 1965; MFA, U. Fla., 1980. Registered profl. engr., Ala., Fla., La., N.Y. Project engr. USAF Materials Lab., WPAFB, Ohio, 1959-66; postdoctoral fellow NSF, 1965-66; prof. materials sci. and engring. U. Fla., Gainesville, 1966-80; chair materials sci. and engring. SUNY, Stony Brook, 1980-82; assoc. dean engring. La. State U., Baton Rouge, 1982-86; program dir. NSF, Washington, 1986-87; chair materials sci. and engring. U. Ala., Birmingham, 1987-90; dean engring. Fla. Atlantic U., Boca Raton, 1990-96; program dir. NSF, 1996-97; guest rschr. Nat. Inst. of Stds. and Tech., Gaithersburg, Md., 1997-98; program officer Dept. of Energy, Germantown, Md., 1998—; cons. Materials Cons., Inc., Gainesville, 1975-90, Brookhaven (N.Y.) Nat. Lab., 1980-82, NSF, Washington, 1987—. Contbr. articles to jours. Acta Metallurgica et Materialia, Exptl. Mechanics, Philos. Mag., Jour. Applied Physics. Pres. Gainesville Little Theatre, 1967-69, Fla. Theatre Conf., 1977-79. Capt. USAF, 1959-62. Grantee NSF, 1966-69, 82-85, Office of Naval Rsch., 1967-69, AEC, 1973-79, Nuclear Regulatory Commn., 1976-79, Army Rsch. Office, 1983-86. Fellow AAAS, ASM Internat.; mem. ASME, The Metall. Soc. (mining, metals and materials sect., chmn. edn. and profl. affairs com. 1990-92), Am. Soc. Engring. Edn., Soc. Exptl. Mechanics. Unitarian.

HARTLEY, DUNCAN, fundraising executive; b. Sept. 27, 1941; s. Harold Shephard and Catherine Carmichael (Hursley) H.; m. Adrienne Ashley, Aug. 19, 1971. BA, U. Mich., 1964; MA, Wayne State U., Detroit, 1966, PhD. Instr. English dept. Wayne State U., 1969-71; asst. prof. William Paterson Coll., 1971-74; adminstr. ednl. resources, chpt. liaison Young Pres.'s Orgn., N.Y.C., 1974-78; dir. planned giving Carroll Coll., Waukesha, Wis., 1978-80; dir. capital gifts Greater N.Y. Coun. Boy Scouts Am., N.Y.C., 1980-84; dir. individual giving, exec. dir. pres.'s coun. Meml. Sloan-Kettering Cancer Ctr., N.Y.C., 1984-96; assoc. dean of devel. and alumni affairs Sch. Medicine Case Western Res. U., Cleve., 1996—. Co-editor, author: The Sociology of the Arts, 1974. Mem. Princeton Club of N.Y., Audiophile Soc. Presbyterian. Avocation: audio equipment reviewing. Home: 310 E Stonebrooke Ct Chagrin Falls OH 44022-2100 Office: Case Western Res U Sch Medicine 10900 Euclid Ave Cleveland OH 44106-1712

HARTLEY, ELISE MOORE, theatrical milliner, costume designer; b. Salt Lake City, Mar. 11, 1953; d. Paul Caine and Elaine Mary (Harvey) Moore; m. Edward A. Hartley, Feb. 14, 1986. BFA in Theatre, Design, U. Utah, 1976. Protégée Patricia Zipprodt, N.Y.C., 1976; costumeiere Equity Libr. Theatre, N.Y.C., 1977-78; costumer, milliner Triad Amphitheatre, Salt Lake City, 1986; milliner Utah Opera, Salt Lake City, 1986-90; fashion design asst. Shari Alexander Design Firm, N.Y.C., 1978; design cons. First Presbyn. Ch. 202nd Gen. Assembly, Salt Lake City, 1990—; dir. Children's Camp Ministry and Program, Wasatch Acad., Mt. Pleasant, 1994, 95, 96, 97, 98 ; curator "A Celebration of Life", Premiere Presentation Children's Easter Art Show, 1998, House of the Lord, 1999. Milliner, costume designer for numerous prodns. including Endymion, 1976, Music Man, 1986, West Side Story, 1986; set designer Ceilidh, Ann Scottish Festival, Salt Lake City, 1989, 90, milliner Utah Opera prodns. including La Traviata, 1986, La Boheme, 1987, The Magic Flute, 1987, The Marriage of Figaro, 1988, Die Fledermaus, 1988, Rigoletto, 1989, Don Giovanni, 1989, The Tales of Hoffman, 1990; dresser Les Misérables, 1993. Deacon, Sun. sch. tchr., Bethel series tchr., mission bull. bd. artist and designer, First Presbyn. Ch., Salt Lake City, 1989-91, mem. Evangelism Com., 1990, 92, staff Small Group Coord., 1993-94, pastor nominating com., 1996-97; coord. Children's Ministries First Presbyn. Ch., 1996—. Theatre Guild scholar U. Utah, 1974; recipient Children's Ministry award 1st Presbyn. Ch., 1995. Avocations: com. svc. through ch., beadwork, embroidery, designing stuffed toys, dolls and puppets. Home: 446 Wall St Salt Lake City UT 84103-1751

HARTLEY, HAL, film director; b. Lindenhurst, N.Y., Nov. 3, 1959. BA with honors in Film, SUNY, Purchase, 1984. Film maker True Fiction Pictures, N.Y.C., 1984—. Writer, dir.: (feature films) The Unbelievable Truth, 1990, Trust, 1991, Simple Men, 1992, Amateur, 1994, Flirt, 1995 (short films) Dogs, The Cartographer's Girlfriend, (TV films) Surviving Desire, 1989, Theory of Achievement, 1991, Ambition, 1991. Office: True Fiction Pictures 39 W 14th St Ste 406 New York NY 10011-7489

HARTLEY, JAMES EDWARD, lawyer; b. Orange, N.J., Nov. 4, 1949; s. George and Carolyn (Stewart) H.; m. Judy Franklin, Mar. 1, 1986; 1 child, Jonathan. BA, U. Calif., Berkeley, 1971, JD, 1974. Bar: Colo. 1974, U.S. Dist. Ct. Colo. 1974, U.S. Ct. Appeals (10th cir.) 1975, U.S. Supreme Ct. 1981, U.S. Ct. Appeals (Fed. cir.) 1993. Assoc. Holland & Hart, Denver, 1974-80, ptnr., 1980—; adj. prof. Denver U. Law Sch., 1985-86. Co-author: Private Litigation Under Section 7 of the Clayton Act: Law and Policy, 1989, Antitrust Pitfalls in Outpatient Services, 1992; asst. editor: ABA Antitrust Law Jour., 1994-98. Mem. ABA (vice chair sect. 1 com. antitrust sect.), Nat. Health Lawyers Assn., Colo. Bar Assn., Denver Bar Assn., Order of Coif, Phi Beta Kappa. Home: 2540 Briarwood Dr Boulder CO 80303-6804 Office: Holland & Hart LLP 555 17th St Ste 3200 Denver CO 80202-3950

HARTLEY, KAREN JEANETTE, lawyer, mediator, state official; b. Oakland, Calif., Aug. 2, 1950; d. Samuel Louis and Jean Iris (Beven) Ostrow; m. Terry Van Hook, Aug. 29, 1970 (div. Mar. 1976); m. William Headley, Jan. 22, 1977 (div. Mar. 1988). BA in Psychology with highest honors, UCLA, 1972; DMin, Sch. of Theology, Claremont, Calif., 1976; JD cum laude, U. San Diego, 1982. Bar: Calif. 1982, U.S. Dist. Ct. (9th cir.), 1983, Hawaii 1991, Oreg. 1996; ordained to ministry, Meth. Ch., 1973. Intern to asst. United Meth. Ch., 1969-71; asst. minister St. Paul's United Meth. Ch., San Bernardino, Calif., 1973-74; assoc. minister Claremont United Meth. Ch., 1974-76; sr. minister Santee (Calif.) United Meth. Ch., 1977-79; clk. Calif. Supreme Ct., San Francisco, 1981; cons. Regional Dept. Edn., San Diego, 1979-81; assoc. atty. Duke, Gerstel, Shearer & Bregante, San Diego, 1983-84, Finley, Kumble, Wagner et al, San Diego, 1984-87; prin. atty., mediator Hartley & Assocs., San Diego, 1987-95, Eugene, Oreg., 1996-99; coord. pub. policy dispute resolution for human svc. agys. Oreg. Dept. Human Resources, Salem, 1999—; mediator San Diego Mediation Ctr., 1990-95; prof. negotiation and mediation, instr. Mediation Clinic U. Oreg. Sch. Law, Eugene, 1996-97; instr. constrn. law Lane C.C., Eugene, 1996-99. Mem. Oreg. Bar Assn., Lan County Bar Assn. Avocations: art, travel. Office: Oreg Dept Human Resources 500 Summer St NE Salem OR 97310

HARTLEY, ROBERT MILTON, internist, rheumatologist, medical director; b. Sarnia, Ont., Can., Feb. 2, 1951; s. Maurice Samuel and Dorene Mae (Johnston) H.; married June 8, 1996. AB magna cum laude, Harvard U., 1973, MD, 1977; MSc in Epidemiology and Biostats., London Sch. Hygiene & Tropical Medicine, 1981. Diplomate Am. Bd. Internal Medicine, 1980, Rheumatology, 1985, Nat. Bd. Med. Examiners. Intern, resident in internal medicine Peter Bent Brigham Hosp., Boston, 1977-80; rsch. fellow St. Thomas's Hosp., London, 1982; fellow rheumatology Brigham and Women's Hosp., 1982-84; assoc. dir. Brigham Internal Medicine Assocs., Boston, 1982-86; mgr., sr. cons., cons. Bain & Co., Boston, 1986-90; co-founder The Healthcare Mgmt. Coun., Inc., Boston, 1991; assoc. physician Brigham and Women's Hosp., Boston, 1982-86, 92—; v.p., med. dir. Quality Standards in Medicine, Inc., Boston, 1993-94; med. dir. Brookside Cmty. Health Ctr., Boston, 1994—; vis. physician, Waltham (Mass.) Hosp., cons. in medicine Brockton (Mass.) VA Hosp., attending physician West Roxbury (Mass.) VA Hosp., assoc. physician Brigham & Women's Hosp., 1982-86; instr. in medicine Harvard U. Med. Sch., 1982-86, 92—. Contbr. articles to profl. jours., chpt. to book; presenter in field. George Morris Piersol Tchg. and Rsch. scholar, ACP, 1985-86, Milbank Meml. Fund scholar 1980-85, Harvard Nat. scholar, 1969-77. Mem. ACP, Am. Coll. Physician Execs., Alpha Omega Alpha. Office: Brookside Cmty Health Ctr 3297 Washington St Jamaica Plain MA 02130-2655

HARTLEY, TERRY L., management consultant; b. Kawkawlin, Mich., Feb. 6, 1947; s. Robert John Hartley and Elizabeth Louise (Morrill) Trace; m. Lynn Helen Kitchen, July 5, 1969; children: Jill Ann, Jena Kaye, Lauren Nichole. BS, Ferris State Coll., Big Rapids, Mich., 1969; MBA, Cen. Mich. U., 1975. Terminal mgr. Ryder Truck Lines, Saginaw, Mich., 1974-79; corp. traffic dir. Ryder Truck Lines, Jacksonville, Fla., 1979-82; v.p. pricing Helms Express, Irwin, Pa., 1982-84; dir. pricing Con-Way Cen. Express, Ann Arbor, Mich.; mem. bd. govs. Mich. Trucking Assn., mem. motor carrier adv. com. Transp. div. Ill. Commerce Commn.; speaker in field. Contbr. articles to profl. jours. Republican. Presbyterian. Avocation: golfing. Office: Con Way Cen Express 4880 Venture Dr Ann Arbor MI 48108-9559

HARTMAN, BARRY DAVID, rabbi; b. Bronx, N.Y., Mar. 24, 1951; s. Gustave and Sarah (Taub) H.; m. Shoshana Turner, Oct. 8, 1975; children: Neshe Esther, Yehoshua Zev, Chava Frayde, Eliyahu Zvi, Aaron Pesach. BA, Yeshiva Coll., 1972; MS, Yeshiva U., 1975; MA, Long Island U., 1978. Ordained rabbi, 1976. Prin. Jewish Ctr. Mapleton Park, Bklyn., 1977-78; housing asst. N.Y.C. Housing Authority, 1978-79; rabbi Ahavath Achim Synagogue, New Bedford, Mass., 1979—; chaplain, mem. ethics com. St. Luke's Hosp., New Bedford, 1982—; bd. dirs. Ctr. for Jewish Culture, Southeastern Mass. U., North Dartmouth, 1982—, Jewish Fedn. New Bedford, North Dartmouth, 1979—, Providence Hebrew Day Sch., 1989-97, U. Mass., Dartmouth. Contbr. articles to publs. Bd. dirs. On Board Inc. Anti-Poverty Agy., New Bedford, 1982-85, U. Mass., North Dartmouth. Recipient Nat. Rabbinic Leadership award United Jewish Appeal, N.Y.C., 1990, Disting. Rabbinic Svc. award Coun. Jewish Fedns., N.Y.C., 1990, Appreciation award Am. Legion, New Bedford, Mass., 1996. Mem. Rabbinical Coun. Am., Vaad Harabonim of Mass. (v.p.), Rabbinic Ct. Justice, Am. Planning Assn., Rabbinic Alumni Yeshiva U., Vaad Harabanim of Mass. (pres.). Office: Ahavath Achim Synagogue 385 County St New Bedford MA 02740-4931 *I believe the best advice was stated by Micah: Do justice, love, mercy and walk humbly with God.*

HARTMAN, (HOWARD) CARL, newspaperman; b. Morris Twp., N.J., Jan. 9, 1917; s. Dennis and Ruth (Shavelson) H.; m. Josephine M. Troxell, Aug. 25, 1942; 1 dau., Jessica A. Student, George Washington U., 1932-33; A.B., Princeton, 1936; M.S. in Journalism, Columbia, 1942. Engaged in gold mining Calif., 1936-37; translator, publicity, copy boy, reporter various newspapers, 1937-40; fgn. editor Puerto Rico World-Jour., San Juan, P.R., 1940-41; reporter, rewrite man N.Y.C. News Assn., 1941; Washington corr. Jewish Telegraphic Agy., also Overseas News Agy., 1942-44; city editor Puerto Rico World-Jour., 1944; with Asso. Press, 1944—; assigned Asso. Press, N.Y.C., Madrid, Paris, Washington, Vienna, 1944-57; corr. Asso. Press, Budapest, Hungary, 1957-59; staff mem. Asso. Press, Frankfurt, 1959; corr. Asso. Press, Berlin, 1959-63, Bonn and European Econ. Affairs, 1963-67, Common Market and NATO, Brussels, 1967-78; European editor N.Y.C., 1978; reporter internat. econ. affairs AP World Services, Washington, 1978-96; arts and humanities, 1997—. Alternate Pulitzer travelling fellow, 1942. Mem. Berlin Fgn. Press Assn. (pres. 1960-61), Anglo-Am. Press Assn. Paris (dir. 1951, 56), Overseas Writers Club, Nat. Press Club, Phi Beta Kappa. Home: 1066 Thomas Jefferson St NW Washington DC 20007-3832 Office: Associated Press 2021 K St NW Fl 6 Washington DC 20006-1082

HARTMAN, CHARLES HENRY, nonprofit management consultant; b. Red Lion, Pa., Feb. 1, 1933; s. Earl Eugene and Jeannette (Kline) H.; m. Patricia A. Cooper, Aug. 3, 1956 (div. May 1974); children: Elizabeth Jean, Amy Joan; m. 2d Catherine M. Wheeler, June 7, 1975 (div. Aug. 1994); children: Eric Michael, Jennifer Leigh, David Wheeler, Scott Andrew. BS, Millersville U., 1954; MA, Mich. State U., 1958, EdD, 1962. Tchr. Hollidaysburg Pub. Schs., Pa., 1956-57; assoc. prof. Ill. State U., Normal, 1959-62; vis. lectr. edn. U. Wis., Madison, 1962-63, Milw., 1963-64; dir. edn. Automotive Safety Found./Hwy. Users Fedn., Washington, 1964-70; dep. adminstr. Nat. Hwy. Traffic Safety Adminstrn., U.S. Dept. Transp., Washington, 1970-73; pres. Motorcycle Safety Found., Irvine, Calif., 1973-84; also pres. Touchstone Mgmt. Svcs., Delta, Pa., 1984-88; exec. v.p. AAHPERD, Reston, Va., 1988-90; exec. dir. Am. Coll. Health Assn., Balt., 1990-98; pres. Nonprofit Orgn. Mgmt. and Consultation, 1998—; lead cons. York Nonprofit Mgmt. Devel. Ctr., 1998—; lectr. bus. adminstrn. Capitol Campus, Pa. State U., Middletown, 1987-88; dir. Nat. Safety Coun., Chgo., 1976-79, vice chmn. traffic conf., 1976-78; presdl. appointee Nat. Hwy. Safety Adv. Commn., Washington, 1977-80; gov.'s appointee Pa. Task Force on Alcohol and Hwy. Safety, 1981-82; vice chmn. Alliance for Traffic Safety, 1981-83, chmn. 1983-85; mem. policy commn. Hwy. Users Fedn.; cons. Nat. Assn. Women Hwy. Safety Leaders, Md. State Edn. Dept., 1969-70; bd. dirs. Lincoln Intermediate Unit #12, 1987-89, 91-93; speaker pub. meetings U.S. and abroad. Trustee Nat. Motorcycle Fund; pres. Howard County C. of C., Columbia, Md., 1985-87; sch. dir. Red Lion (Pa.) Area Schs., 1986—, also pres. sch. bd., 1988, 96, 97, 98, 99, v.p., 1989-95. With U.S. Army, 1954-56. Recipient Traffic Safety Educator of Yr. award Wis. Traffic Edn. Assn, 1972, Sec.'s award U.S. Dept. Transp., 1973; elected to Hall of Fame, Red Lion (Pa.) Area Sch. Dist., 1993. Fellow Am. Acad. Safety Edn. (pres. 1975-76); mem. NEA, Am. Soc. Assn. Execs. (vice-chmn. evaluation com. 1984-85, chmn. 1985-86), Soc. Automotive Engrs., Pres. Assn./Am. Mgmt. Assn., Am. Driver and Traffic Safety Edn. Assn., York 2000 Commn., Assn. for Advancement of Automotive Medicine, Pa. Sch. Bds. Assn., Phi Delta Kappa. Republican. Home and Office: 901 Delta Rd Red Lion PA 17356-1404

HARTMAN, DAVID GARDINER, actuary; b. Evanston, Ill., July 10, 1942; s. Fred E. and Martha Hartman; m. Katherine A. Holmes; children: Timothy, Andrew. Student, Ripon (Wis.) Coll., 1960-62; BBA, U. Mich., 1964, M in Actuarial Sci., 1965. Various positions Kemper Ins. Co., Chgo., 1966-71; mng. dir., sr. v.p., chief actuary Chubb & Son, Warren, N.J., 1971—. Elder New Providence (N.J.) Presbyn. Ch., 1973-75, 86-88; trustee Overlook Hosp., Summit, N.J., 1993—. Fellow Can. Inst. Actuaries, Casualty Actuarial Soc. (cert., v.p. 1985-86, pres. 1987-88); mem. Am. Acad. Actuaries (cert., v.p. 1983-85, pres.-elect 1992-93, pres. 1993-94), Internat. Actuarial Assn. (coun. mem. 1996-98), Actuarial Stds. Bd. (bd. dirs. 1996—, chair 1998—). Office: Chubb Group of Ins Cos 15 Mountain View Rd Warren NJ 07059-6795

HARTMAN, EARL KENNETH, writer; b. Chgo., Jan. 31, 1943; s. Ferdinand Frederick and Betty Marie (Sjerslee) H.; m. Linda Lee Griffin, July 10, 1981 (div. June 1988); m. Beatrice Gail Adams, Mar. 11, 1989. BA, Fla. Atlantic U., 1980, B of Edn., 1981. Promotion mgr., spl. issues editor Asheville (N.C.) Citizen-Times, 1966-67; reporter Shelby (N.C.) Daily Star, 1967; copy editor Palm Beach Post-Times, West Palm Beach, Fla., 1968-69; dist. exec. Boy Scouts Am., West Palm Beach, Fla., 1973-76, Albany, Ga., 1983-84; tchr., asst. dir. Unity Sch., Delray Beach, Fla., 1981-83; tchr. Tift County (Ga.) Bd. Edn., 1984-85; sr. reporter Island Reporter, Sanibel Island, Fla., 1985-87; free-lance writer Fort Myers, Fla., 1987—. Mem. Nat. Eagle Scout Assn. Avocations: photography. Home and office: 1210 Westfield Dr Fort Myers FL 33919-2244

HARTMAN, ELIZABETH DIANE, retired elementary education educator; b. Berlin Center, Ohio, Feb. 25, 1937; d. Keith Gayle and Edna Elizabeth (Blymiller) Renick; m. Lowell Lloyd Hartman, June 29, 1956; children: Deborah Kay, Dennis Lowell, Kathrine Sue. BS in Edn., Bowling Green State U., 1970, MEd, 1978. Cert. edn. profl. Substitute tchr. Genoa Area & Oak Harbor Schs., Ohio, 1966-70; dir. migrant sch. Genoa Area Schs., Clay Center, Ohio, 1969, elem. tchr., 1970-95; ret., 1995; rep. career edn. Penta County Vocat. Sch., 1980-90; prin.'s adv. bd. Allen Elem. Curtice, Ohio, 1989-94; adv. bd. educators Toledo Blade, 1992-93. Author poem. Organist, jr. choir dir. St. John Luth. Ch., Williston, Ohio, 1957-80, dir. bell choir, 1986-96; delivery person Mobile Meals, Genoa, 1988-94. Recipient Tchrs.'s in Am. Enterprise award Sohio, 1982-83; Educator of Yr., Consumer Econ. Edn. Assn. Ohio, 1989. Mem. Internat. Reading Assn. (vacationland coun., pres. 1982-83), Allenettes (past officer 1970—, chairperson United Way 1989-90), Delta Kappa Gamma (music chmn. 1990-94). Democrat. Lutheran. Avocations: music, golfing, boating, fishing, traveling.

HARTMAN, GEOFFREY H., language professional, educator; b. Germany, Aug. 11, 1929; came to U.S., 1946, naturalized, 1946; s. Albert and Agnes (Heumann) H.; m. Renee Gross, Oct. 21, 1956; children: David, Elizabeth. BA, Queens Coll., N.Y.C., 1949, LHD (hon.), 1990; PhD, Yale U., 1953. Mem. faculty Yale U., 1955-62; assoc. prof. English U. Iowa City, 1962-64, prof. English, 1964-65; prof. English Cornell U., Ithaca, N.Y., 1965-67; prof. English and comparative lit. Yale U., 1967—, Karl Young Prof., 1974-94, Sterling prof., 1994-97, prof. emeritus, 1997—; disting. vis. scholar George Washington U., 1998—; vis. lectr. and/or prof. U. Chgo., U. Wash., Hebrew U., Jerusalem, U. Zurich, Switzerland, Princeton U., NYU, Tel Aviv U., U. Konstanz, Germany; Clark lectr. Trinity Coll., Cambridge, 1983; Tamblyn lectr. U. Western Ont., 1983; Wellek lectr. U. Calif., Irvine, 1992, Tanner lectr. U. Utah, 1999; dir. Sch. Theory and Criticism, Dartmouth Coll., 1982-87, also sr. fellow. Author: The Unmediated Vision, 1954, Andre Malraux, 1960, Wordsworth's Poetry, 1964 (Christian Gauss award Phi Beta Kappa 1965), Beyond Formalism, 1970, The Fate of Reading, 1975, Akiba's Children, 1978, Criticism in the Wilderness, 1980, Saving the Text, 1981, Easy Pieces, 1985, The Unremarkable Wordsworth, 1987, Minor Prophecies, 1991, The Longest Shadow, 1996, The Fateful Question of Culture, 1997, A Critic's Journey, 1999; editor: Hopkins: A Collection of Critical Essays, 1966, Selected Poetry and Prose of William Wordsworth, 1970, Romanticism: Vistas, Instances, Continuities, 1973, Psychoanalysis and the Question of the Text, 1978, Shakespeare and the Questions of Theory, 1985, Bitburg in Moral and Political Perspective, 1986, Midrash and Literature, 1986, Holocaust Remembrance: The Shapes of Memory, 1993. Trustee English Inst., 1978-85; Revson project dir. Video Archive Holocaust Testimonies, Yale, 1982—. Served with AUS, 1953-55. Decorated chevalier Order of Arts and Letters govt. of France, 1997; recipient Disting. Alumnus award Queens Coll. CUNY, 1971, award Nat. Found. Jewish Culture, 1997, René Wellek prize Am. Assn. Comparative Lit., 1998, Disting. Scholar award Keats-Shelley Assn., 1998; Fulbright fellow U. Dijon, France, 1951-52, study fellow Am. Coun. Learned Socs., 1963, 79, Guggenheim fellow, 1969, 86, fellow Humanities Ctr. Wesleyan U., 1972, NEH, 1975, Inst. Advanced Studies Hebrew U., 1986, Inst. Humanities U. Calif., Irvine, 1989, Woodrow Wilson Internat. Ctr., 1995, Sackler Inst., U. Tel Aviv, 1997; assoc. fellow Ctr. Rsch. Philosophy and Lit. U. Warwick, Eng., 1993; Gauss seminarist Princeton U., 1968; Fulbright Disting. lectr., 1986, 87. Mem. Modern Lang. Assn. (exec. council 1977-80), Am. Acad. Arts and Scis. Home: 260 Everit St New Haven CT 06511-1309

HARTMAN, GEORGE EITEL, architect; b. Ft. Hancock, N.J., May 7, 1936; s. George Eitel and Evelyn (Ritchie) H.; m. Ann Burdick, May 22, 1965; children—Sarah, Joshua. B.A., Princeton, 1957, M.F.A., 1960. Registered architect, Md., Washington, Va. Pvt. practice architecture, 1964-65; ptnr. Hartman-Cox Architects, Washington, 1965—; Design critic Cath. U. Am., 1964-69, U. Md.; Kea Disting. prof. architecture N.C. State U., 1973-74, prof. architecture, 1977; chmn. adv. coun. Princeton U. Sch. Architecture, 1985-87; mem. architecture rev. panel Fgn. Bldg. Office, Dept. State, 1991—, mem. architecture adv. bd. Works include EURAM office bldg, Washington, Waterfront Center, Washington; Brewer residence, Chevy Chase, Md., Conant residence, Potomac, Md., Nat. Humanities Center, Raleigh, N.C., Nat. Permanent Bldg., Washington, 1001 Pennsylvania Ave, Washington; Folger Shakespeare Library, Washington, Immanuel Presbyn. Ch., McLean, Va., Sumner Sch., Washington, H.E.B. hdqrs., San Antonio, Market Square, Washington, Franklin Sq., Washington, Pa. Plaza, Washington, U.S. Embassy, Kuala Lumpur, Malaysia, Chrysler Mus., Norfolk, Va. Served to 2d Lt., F.A. AUS, 1957. Recipient Louis Sullivan award for architecture, 1972, 100 Nat., State and Local Design awards, 1967—; fellow Am. Acad. in Rome, 1977-78. Fellow AIA (pres. Washington chpt. 1975, chmn. nat. capitol com. 1976, chmn. nat. com. on design 1977, AIA Nat. Honor award 1970, 71, 81, 83, 89, 94, AIA Firm award 1988); mem. U.S. Commn. Fine Arts, Cosmos Club (pres. 1985). Home: 3525 Hamlet Pl Chevy Chase MD 20815-4822 Office: Hartman Cox Architects 1074 Thomas Jefferson St NW Washington DC 20007-3832

HARTMAN, HERBERT ARTHUR, JR., oncologist; b. Halstead, Kans., Aug. 8, 1947; s. Herbert Arthur and Margrete Laverne (Schroeder) H.; m. Cynthia Craig, Dec. 26, 1971; m. April Craig, Herbert Arthur III. BA in Chemistry, U. Kans., 1969, MD, 1973. Diplomate Am. Bd. Internal Medicine, Am. Bd. Med. Oncology. Resident internal medicine U. Nebr. Med. Ctr., Omaha, 1973-76, fellow in med. oncology, 1976-78; oncologist Radiologic Ctr. Inc., Omaha, 1978-79, Sole Proprietorship, Omaha, 1979-80, Oncology Assocs., Omaha, 1980—; chmn. dept. medicine Immanuel Med. Ctr., Omaha, 1988-90; clin. assoc. prof. internal medicine U. Nebr. Med. Sch., 1979—. Contbr. articles to med. jours. Pres. Nebr. Cancer Soc., 1991. Fellow Am. Coll. Physicians; mem. AMA, Am. Soc. Internal Medicine, Am. Soc. Clin. Oncology, Nebr. Med. Assn. (bd. dirs. 1989-95), Metro Omaha Med. Soc. (exec. com. 1987), N.Y. Acad. Scis., Mensa, Omaha C. of C. (bd. dirs. 1998—). Republican. Episcopalian. Avocations: tennis, personal finance, reading. Home: 6211 Chicago St Omaha NE 68132-2727 Office: Oncology Assocs PC Meth Cancer Ctr 8303 Dodge St Ste 225 Omaha NE 68114-4108

HARTMAN, JAMES AUSTIN, retired geologist; b. Lanark, Ill., Jan. 29, 1928; s. Llewelyn John and Gladys Mae (Doyle) H.; m. Zoe Marie Wiley, June 16, 1951 (dec. Dec. 1996); children: Victoria Lynn, Lester James; m. Annette Wiley Lee, June 9, 1997. BS, Beloit (Wis.) Coll., 1951; MS, U. Wis., 1955, PhD, 1957. Cert. petroleum geologist. Geologist Reynolds Jamaica (W.I.) Mines, Jamaica, W.I., 1951-53, Union Carbide Ore Co., Parimaribo, Surinam, 1956-57; various positions Shell Oil Co., New Orleans, 1957-86; cons. New Orleans, 1986-94; ret., 1994. Bd. mgmt. YMCA, Metairie, 1972-74; pres. Jefferson Com. for Better Schs., Metairie, 1961-63, pres. Westgate PTA, Kenner, La., 1964-65. With U.S. Army, 1946-47. Union Carbide Rsch. fellowship U. Wis., 1954-56. Mem. Am. Assn. Petroleum Geologists (hon., sec. 1981-83, Disting. Svc. award 1985), New Orleans Geol. Soc. (hon., 2d v.p. 1975-76, pres.-elect 1984-85, pres. 1985-86, Outstanding Mem. 1977), Gulf Coast Assn. Geol. Socs. (hon., v.p. 1987, pres. 1988), Sigma Xi. Republican. Episcopalian. Achievements include research in heavy minerals in Jamaican Bauxite, titanium mineralogy of Bauxites, petroleum geology. Home: 4512 Newlands St Metairie LA 70006-4138 also: 936 N Stygler Rd Gahanna OH 43230-2029

HARTMAN, JAMES THEODORE, physician, educator; b. De Ridder, La., June 13, 1925; s. George Bernhardt and Mary Gertrude (Moore) H.; m. Jean Ann Rinehart, Dec. 29, 1954; children: James Theodore, Thomas Moore, Martha Susan. B.S., Iowa State U., 1949; B.S.M., Northwestern U., 1949, M.D., 1952. Intern Charity Hosp. La., New Orleans, 1952-53; resident U. Mich. Hosp., Ann Arbor, 1953-57; registrar Nuffield Orthopedic Centre, Oxford (Eng.) U., 1957-58; instr. orthopedic surgery U. Mich., Ann Arbor, 1958-61; mem. staff Cleve. Clinic, 1961-68; chmn. dept. orthopedic surgery Cook County Hosp., Chgo., 1968-71; asso. prof. Northwestern U., Chgo., 1968-71; prof. Tex. Tech. U. Sch. Medicine, Lubbock, 1971-92, chmn. dept. orthopedic surgery, 1971-81, dean, 1981-88; dir. MEDNET project Tex. Tech. U. Sch. Medicine, 1989-92, dean emeritus, 1989—, prof. emeritus, 1992—; dir. Am. Bd. Orthopaedic Surgery, 1978-87. Author: Fracture Management: A Practical Approach, 1977; contbr. articles to profl. jours. Trustee Austin Presbyn. Theol. Sem., 1989-98. Served in AUS, 1943-46. Fellow ACS; Tex. Med. Assn., Am. Orthopaedic Assn. (v.p. 1991-92), Assn. Bone and Joint Surgeons, Clin. Orthopaedic Soc., Am. Acad. Orthopaedic Surgeons, Alpha Omega Alpha, Sigma Xi, Phi Delta Theta, Nu Sigma Nu.

HARTMAN, JEFFREY EDWARD, pastor; b. Nyack, N.Y., June 23, 1959; s. Edward Harold and Constance Ruth (Gibbs) H.; m. Cynthia Lynn Chason, Aug. 14, 1982; children: Joshua Jefferson, Jeremiah Jordan, Julia Lyndsay. BS, Liberty U., 1982; postgrad., Westminster Theol. Sem., 1984-87, Trinity Evang. Div. Sch., 1990, Yale U., 1999; MDiv, Princeton Theol. Sem., 1998. Ordained to ministry, 1985. Assoc. pastor Maranatha Bapt. Ch., Gainesville, Ga., 1982-84; pastor Christ Community Ch., Newfield, N.J., 1984—; baseball head coach Cumberland Christian Sch., Vineland, N.J., 1991-95; chaplain Newcomb Med. Ctr., Vineland, N.J., 1987—. Founder, editor, columnist: Newfield Neighbors newspaper, Newfield, N.J., 1988—; chaplain New Med. Ctr., Vineland, N.J., 1990—. Co-founder, bd. dirs. Compassion Crisis Pregnancy Cr., Clayton, N.J., 1986-90, chmn. bd. dirs. 1990-95. Recipient John Finley McLaren prize in Bibl. theology Princeton Theol. Sem., N.J., 1997. Office: Christ Community Ch 201 Salem Ave Newfield NJ 08344-9074 *What happens to you is not nearly as important as how you react to what happens to you.*

HARTMAN, JULIE MARIE, school psychologist; b. Columbus, Ohio, Sept. 10, 1959; d. Marvin Edward Jones and Betty Marie Arrowood Carter; m. Mark Edward Hartman, June 27, 1987; 1 child, Sarah Marie. BA cum laude, Ohio State U., 1981, MA, 1984. Nat. cert. sch. psychologist; cert. sch. psychologist, Ohio. Intern sch. psychologist Hilliard (Ohio) City Schs., 1984-85; sch. psychologist Muskingum Valley Ednl. Svc. Ctr., Zanesville, Ohio, 1985—. Editor (newsletters) The Parents' Press, 1993—, Classroom Communiqué, 1991—; contbr. article to Jour. Sch. Psychology. Mem. Muskingum County Parenting Coalition, Zanesville, 1992—. Recipient Ohio's BEST award, 1995; Ohio Dept. Edn. Tng. Ohio's Parents for Success grantee, 1991-97. Mem. ASCD, Nat. Assn. Sch. Psychologists, Ohio Sch. Psychologists Assn. (Best Practices award 1997), E. Ctrl. Ohio Sch. Psychologists Assn. (sec. 1997—). Lutheran. Avocations: playing piano, singing. Home: 7693 Godfrey Cir Reynoldsburg OH 43068-8110 Office: Muskingum Valley Ednl Svc Ctr 205 N 7th St Zanesville OH 43701-3791

HARTMAN, MARGARET J., biologist, educator, university official; b. Columbus, Ohio, Nov. 10, 1943; d. Herbert Joyce and Amabelle Bailey (Haller) H.; m. Robert G. Zahary, Jan. 6, 1990. BS, Calif. Poly. State U., 1966; MA, Oreg. State U., 1968, PhD, 1970. Mem. faculty Calif. State U., L.A., 1970—, prof. biology, 1980—, chmn. dept., 1977-81, asst. v.p. for acad. affairs, 1981-85, assoc. v.p. for acad. affairs faculty and adminstrn., 1986-93, provost, 1994—. Grantee Calif. State U., Boston Land Co., Gill Cattle Co., NIH. Mem. Phi Kappa Phi, Beta Beta Beta.

HARTMAN, MARY S., historian; b. Mpls., June 25, 1941; married. BA, Swarthmore Coll., 1963; MA, Columbia U., 1964, PhD, 1970. From instr. to asst. prof. Rutgers U., 1968-75; from assoc. prof. to prof. history Douglass Coll., Rutgers U., 1975—; dean Douglass Coll., Rutgers U., 1982-94; dir. Inst. for Women's Leadership Douglass Coll., 1994—; prof. Rutgers U., 1994—. Author: Clio's Consciousness Raised, 1974, Victorian Murderesses, 1978; editor: Talking Leadership: Conversations with Powerful Women, 1999. Office: 162 Ryders Ln New Brunswick NJ 08901-8555

HARTMAN, ROBERT LEROY, artist, educator; b. Sharon, Pa., Dec. 17, 1926; s. George Otto and Grace Arvada (Radabaugh) H.; m. Charlotte Ann Johnson, Dec. 30, 1951; children: Mark Allen, James Robert. BFA, U. Ariz., 1951, MA, 1952; postgrad., Colo. Springs Fine Arts Center, 1947, 51, Bklyn. Mus. Art Sch., 1953-54. Instr. architecture, allied arts Tex. Tech. Coll., 1955-58; asst. prof. art U. Nev., Reno, 1958-61; mem. faculty dept. art U. Calif., Berkeley, 1961—, prof., 1972-91, prof. emeritus, 1991—, chmn. dept., 1974-76; mem. Inst. for Creative Arts, U. Calif., 1967-68. One man exhbns. include, Bertha Schafer Gallery, N.Y.C., 1966, 69, 74, Santa Barbara Mus. Art, 1973, Cin. Art Acad., 1975, Hank Baum Gallery, San Francisco, 1973, 75, 78, San Jose Mus. Art, 1983, Bluxome Gallery, San Francisco, 1984, 86, U. Art Mus., Berkeley, 1986, Instituto D'Arte Dosso Dossi, Ferrara, Italy, 1989, Victor Fischer Galleries, San Francisco, 1991, Triangle Gallery, San Francisco, 1992, 93, 95, 97, 99, Augusta State U., 1998; group exhbns. include Richmond Mus., 1966, Whitney Mus. Biennial, 1973, Oakland Mus., 1976, San Francisco Arts Commn. Gallery, 1985 (award), Earthscape Expo '90 Photo Mus., Osaka, Japan, 1990, In Close Quarters, American Landscape Photography Since 1968, Princeton Art Mus., 1993, Facing Eden: 100 Years of Landscape Art in The Bay Area, San Francisco, 1995, Colorado Springs Fine Arts Ctr., 1998; represented in permanent collections, Nat. Collections Fine Arts, Colorado Springs Fine Arts Center, Corcoran Gallery, San Francisco Art Inst., Roswell Mus., Princeton Art Mus. U. Calif. humanities research fellow, 1980. Office: U Calif Dept Art Berkeley CA 94720

HARTMAN, ROBERT S., retired paper company executive; b. Chgo., Oct. 7, 1914; s. Edward A. and Blanche S. (Straus) H.; m. Betty Regenstein, Oct. 25, 1941; children: Ann, Ruth. Student, Northwestern U., 1933-34. Br. mgr. Draper & Kramer, Inc., 1937-41; pres. Arvey Corp., Chgo., 1957-85. Vice pres., bd. dirs. Chgo. Boys Clubs. Served with AUS, 1943-46. Mem. Chgo. Envelope Mfg. Assn. (pres. 1949-51), Envelope Mfg. Assn. Am. (dir. 1950-54). Clubs: Lake Shore Country (Glencoe, Ill.), Mayacoo Lakes (W. Palm Beach, Fla.). Home: 220 Woodley Rd Winnetka IL 60093-3739

HARTMAN, ROSEMARY JANE, special education educator; b. Gainesville, Fla., Aug. 24, 1944; d. John Leslie and Irene (Bowen) Goddard; m. Alan Lynn Gerber, Feb. 1, 1964 (div. 1982); children: Sean Alan, Dawn Julianne Silva, Lance Goddard; m. Perry Hartman, June 27, 1992. BA, Immaculate Heart Coll., 1967; MA, Loyola U., 1974. Cert. resource specialist. Tchr. L.A. Unified Schs., 1968-78; resource specialist Desert Sands Unified Sch. Dist., Palm Desert, 1978-83, Palm Springs Unified Schs., 1983-99. Co-author: The Twelve Steps of Phobics Anonymous, 1989, One Day At A Time in Phobics Victorious, 1992, The Twelve Steps of Phobics Victorious, 1993; founder Phobics Victorious, 1992. Mem. Am. Assn. Christian Counselors (charter), Internat. Platform Assn., Nat. Assn. of Christian Recovery, Anxiety Disorders Assn. Am. Office: Phobics Victorious PO Box 695 Palm Springs CA 92263-0695

HARTMAN, RUTH ANN, educator; b. Galion, Ohio, Aug. 18, 1938; d. Richard Lewis and Florence Evelyn (Ireland) Campbell; m. Richard Louis Hartman, Jan. 14, 1956; children: Jeffery Lee, Marsha Elaine, Jerry Steven. BS, Ohio State U., 1970; MEd, U. LaVerne, 1976, postgrad., 1985—; postgrad., U. Akron, 1977-85. cert. tchr., Ohio. Tchr. Willard (Ohio) City Schs., 1964-65; educator Mansfield (Ohio) City Schs., 1966—, home tutor, 1971-81, educator, 1977—, faculty advisory com., 1990-98, young authors coord., 1991-92, co-coord. career edn., 1991-97; cons. Ohio State U., Ashland (Ohio) Coll., Mt. Vernon (Ohio) Nazarene Coll., 1976—. Co-author: Handbook for Student Teachers, 1983; contbr. to Norde News. Mem NEA, Ohio Edn. Assn., North Cen. Ohio Tchrs. Assn., Mansfield Edn. Assn. Republican. Methodist. Avocations: reading, traveling, tennis, music. Home: RR 1 Plymouth OH 44865-9801 Office: Mansfield City Schs 1138 Springmill St Mansfield OH 44906-1525

HARTMAN-ABRAMSON, ILENE, adult education educator; b. Detroit, Nov. 8, 1950; d. Stuart Lester and Freda Vivian (Nash) Hartman; m. Victor Nikolai Abramson, Oct. 24, 1941. BA, U. Mich., 1972; MEd, Wayne State U., 1980, PhD in Higher Edn., 1990. Cert. continuing secondary tchr., Mich. Program developer and instr. William Beaumont Hosp., Royal Oak, Mich., 1972-74; vocat. counselor for emigres Jewish Vocat. Svc. and Cmty. Workshop, Detroit, 1974-81; program developer and cons. Detroit Psychiat. Inst., 1982; instr. for foreign students Oakland C.C., Farmington Hills, Mich., 1983-99, acad. coord. overseas info. program, 1995—; mem. adv. bd. Mich. Dept. Edn., Detroit, 1981; lectr. Internat. Conf. Tchrs. English to Speakers of Other Langs., 1981; guest presenter Wayne State U., Lawrence Tech. U., 1991, U. Mich. Anxiety Disorders Program, 1993; presenter rsch. presentations Nat. Coalition for Sex Equity in Edn., Ann Arbor, Mich.; presenter at seminar on learning anxiety Interdisciplinary Studies program Wayne State U., 1995; chair profl. stds. and measures com. Mich. Devel. Edn. Consortium, editor newsletter, 1997; mem. rehab. adv. coun. State of Mich.; guest lectr. med. edn./residency tng. initiatives Detroit Med. Ctr. Hutzel Hosp., Providence Hosp., Beaumont Hosp., Detroit Med. Ctr. Harper Hosp. Mem. editl. bd. Mensa Rsch. Jour.; contbr. articles to prof. jours. Mem. Internat. Assn. Med. Sci. Educators, Am. Anthropol. Assn., Am. Acad. on Physician and Patient, Am. Mensa (rsch. rev. com.). Jewish. Avocations: self-defense for women, dramatics, karate. Office: Oakland Community Coll 27055 Orchard Lake Rd Farmington Hills MI 48334

HARTMANIS, JURIS, computer scientist, educator; b. Riga, Latvia, July 5, 1928; came to U.S., 1950, naturalized, 1956; s. Martins and Irma (Liepins) H.; m. Ellymaria Rehwald, May 16, 1959; children: Reneta, Martin, Audrey. Student, U. Marburg, 1947-49; MA, U. Kansas City, 1951; PhD, Calif. Inst. Tech., 1955; LHD (hon.), U. Dortmund, Germany, 1995. Instr. Cornell U., Ithaca, N.Y., 1955-57; prof. Cornell U., 1965—, Walter R. Read prof. engring., 1980—, chmn. dept. computer sci., 1965-71, 77-82, 92-94; asst. prof. Ohio State U., 1957-58; rsch. mathematician Gen. Electric R&D Ctr., Schenectady, 1957-65; asst. dir. NSF for Computer and Info. Sci. & Engring., Arlington, Va., 1996-99. Author: (with R.E. Stearns) Algebraic Structure Theory For Sequential Machines, 1966; Feasible Computations and Provable Complexity Properties, 1978; editor: SIAM Jour. Computing; assoc. editor: Jour. Computer and Systems Scis, 1966—, Jour. Math. Systems Theory, 1966-89; co-editor: Springer-Verlag Lecture Notes in Computer Sci, 1973—. Recipient Turing award, 1993, B. Bolzano Gold medal, The Acad. of Scis. of Czech Republic, 1995. Fellow AAAS, Am. Acad. Arts Scis., Assn. Computing Machinery; mem. NAE, Am. Math. Soc., Assn. N.Y. Acad. Scis., Latvian Acad. Sci. (fgn.), Sigma Xi. Home: 324 Brookfield Rd Ithaca NY 14850-2008 Office: Cornell Univ Upson Hall Ithaca NY 14853

HARTMANN, DALE WALTER, librarian; b. May 12, 1932. BA in Edn., Concordia Tchrs. Coll., Seward, Nebr., 1954; MA in LS, U. Denver, 1957. Elem. tchr. Immanuel Luth. Ch., Kansas City, Mo., 1954-55; libr. Luther H.S. North, Chgo., 1955-65, Concordia Theol. Sem., Springfield, Ill., 1965-76, Concordia U., Irving, Calif., 1976—. Home: 2400 E Palm Ave Orange CA 92867 Office: Concordia U 1530 Concordia West Irvine CA 92612

HARTMANN, FREDERICK HOWARD, political science educator emeritus; b. N.Y.C., July 6, 1922; s. Frederick Herman and Grace (MacNamara) H.; m. Regina Lou Kiracofe, Dec. 26, 1943; children—Lynne Merry, Vicky Carol, Peter Howard. A.B., U. Calif. at Berkeley, 1943; M.A., Princeton, 1948, Ph.D., 1949; student, Grad. Inst. Internat. Studies, U. Geneva, Switzerland, 1947. Instr. politics Princeton, 1947; from asst. prof. to prof. polit. sci. U. Fla., 1948-66; dir. Inst. Internat. Relations, 1963-66; Alfred Thayer Mahan prof. maritime strategy U.S. Naval War Coll., 1966-88, prof. emeritus, 1988—, spl. acad. advisor, 1966-86; vis. prof. Wheaton (Mass.) Coll., part-time, 1966-69, Brown U., part-time, 1968-69, U.S. Naval War Coll., 1966-88, U. R.I., part-time, 1970-71, Tex. Tech U., 1974-75; vis. prof. polit. sci. U. Calif., Berkeley, 1979-80, Middle East Tech. U., Ankara, Turkey, 1988. Author: The Relations of Nations, 4th edit., 1973, 5th edit., 1978, 6th edit., 1983, Spanish edit., 1986, The Swiss Press and Swiss Foreign Affairs, 1960, Germany Between East and West, 1965, The New Age of American Foreign Policy, 1970, Naval Renaissance: The U.S. Navy in the 1980s (Chinese transl.), 1990; (with Robert L. Wendzel) To Preserve the Republic, 1985, Defending America's Security, 1988, America's Foreign Policy in a Changing World, 1994; editor: Basic Documents of International Relations, 1951, Readings in International Relations, 1952, World in Crisis, 4th edit., 1973; contbr. to: System for Educating Military Officers in the U.S., 1976, The Conservation of Enemies, 1981. U. Fla. rep. Fla. Bd. Control Com. Acad. Freedom, 1961-62; mem. Fulbright Nat. Selection Com., 1954-56; U.S. del. 4th Conf. Naval War Colls. Am., 1966, 6th Conf., 1970, 10th Conf., 1980, 12th Conf., 1985. Served to lt. (j.g.) USNR, 1943-46; capt. Res. Recipient Meritorious Civilian Service medal Dept. Navy, 1985; Fulbright research prof. U. Bonn, Germany, 1953-54; Rockefeller grantee, 1959; Exxon Corp. grantee, 1973. Mem. AAUP (pres. U. Fla. chpt. 1959-60, mem. nat. council 1963-66), Am. Polit. Sci. Assn., Internat. Studies Assn. (pres. New Eng. div. 1971-72), New Eng. Polit. Sci. Assn. (exec. com. 1982-84), Blue Key, Pi Sigma Alpha, Delta Phi Epsilon. Home: 8457 Twin Rocks Rd Granite Bay CA 95746-8123

HARTMANN, FREDERICK WILLIAM, newspaper editor; b. Wilmington, Del., Feb. 3, 1928; s. William and Louise (Askani) H.; m. Mary Lucille Nelson, Oct. 16, 1954; children: Michele Mary, Randi Lucille, Frederick Andrew, Eric William, Adam Nelson. BA, U. Del., 1951; postgrad., Am. U., 1952; MS, Columbia U. Grad. Sch. Journalism, 1953. Reporter AP, N.Y.C., 1954; dir. news and sports WDEL Radio, Wilmington, 1954-56; reporter Morning News, News-Jour. Co., Wilmington, 1956-60; asst. city editor Morning News, News-Jour. Co., 1961-62, city editor, 1962-64; city editor Morning and Evening Jour., 1964-67, met. editor, 1967-72, asst. to pres., 1972-74, dir. corp. mktg., 1974-75, exec. editor, 1975-80, v.p., 1977-80; mng. editor Fla. Times-Union, Jacksonville, 1980-83; exec. editor Times-Union/Jacksonville Jour., Jacksonville, 1983-88; exec. editor Times-Union, Jacksonville, 1988-98, ret., 1998; lectr. U. Del., 1971, 72; Pulitzer prize juror, 1981, 82. Mem. budget com. United Way of Del., 1973, 74; v.p. Brandywine Little League, 1973; bd. dirs. United Cerebral Palsy Assn. of Del., 1970-72. Served with AUS, 1946-48. Mem. Theta Chi. Home: 3852 McGirts Blvd Jacksonville FL 32210-4337

HARTMANN, GEORGE HERMAN, retired manufacturing company executive; b. N.Y.C., Nov. 6, 1927; s. George Dietrich Herman and Margaret Bertha (Winkler) H.; m. Anne Katharine Martin, July 9, 1960; children: Michael George, Steven Herman, Katharine Margaret, Elizabeth Anne. AB, Dartmouth Coll., 1949, MS in Mech. Engring, 1950. With Gen. Electric Co., 1950-70; v.p. mfg. Gen. Signal Corp., 1970-71; exec. v.p., then pres. GE Espanola, 1971-74; pres. Davol Co. (subs. Internat. Paper Co.), 1975-78, corp. v.p. human resources, then v.p. materials, 1979-80; pvt. investor, 1980-81; group v.p. Textron Inc., Providence, 1981-92; ret., 1992. Trustee R.I. Coun. Econ. Edn., 1977, vice chmn. 1983-92; trustee Am. Sch., Bilbao, Spain, 1972-74, chmn., 1973-74; trustee Joint Coun. Econ. Edn., 1986-91, Nat. Security Indsl. Assn., 1988-92, Calvin K. Kazanjian Econs. Found., Inc., 1996—; U.S. del. NATO Indsl. Adv. Group, 1989-92. Served to lt. USNR, 1955-60. Mem. NAM (dir. 1977-80), R.I. C. of C. (dir. 1977-78), Greater Providence C. of C. (dir. 1976-78), N.Y. Yacht Club, Cruising Club Am. (Parkinson Meml. Trophy for Transoceanic Passage 1993, 97). Republican.

HARTMANN, ROBERT ELLIOTT, manufacturing company executive, retired; b. Bklyn., Apr. 10, 1926; s. James and Edna Mae (Schroeder) H.; m. Anne Marie Mongiello, Feb. 15, 1948; children: Barbara Hartmann Kaszor, Donna Hartmann Dow. BS, Miami U., Oxford, Ohio, 1946. CPA, N.Y. Accountant Price, Waterhouse & Co., N.Y.C., 1948-57; mgr. financial accounting Air Products & Chemicals, Allentown, Pa., 1957-58; v.p. Alpha Portland Cement Co. div. Alpha Portland Industries, Inc., Easton, Pa., 1958-82; sec. Slattery Group, Inc. (formely Alpha Portland Industries, Inc.), Easton, 1962-89; sec., treas. Energy and Resource Recovery Corp., until 1982; sec., treas., dir. H.O.H. Corp., until 1982; bd. dirs. Moravian Book Shop, Inc., pres., until 1992. Bd. dirs. Bethlehem Area Moravians. Served to lt. Supply Corps USNR, World War II. Mem. Inst. Mgmt. Accts. (pres. Lehigh Valley chpt. 1973-74), Financial Execs. Inst. (treas. N.E. Pa. chpt. 1972-74), Am. Inst. C.P.A.s. Mem. Moravian Ch. Home: 285 East Bridle Path Rd Bethlehem PA 18017-3867

HARTMANN, ROBERT TROWBRIDGE, author, consultant; b. Rapid City, S.D., Apr. 8, 1917; s. Miner Louis and Elizabeth (Trowbridge) H.; m. Roberta Sankey, Jan. 17, 1943; children: Roberta H. Brake, Robert S. A.B., Stanford U., 1938. Reporter Los Angeles Times, 1939-41, 45-48, editorial and spl. writer, 1948-54, chief Washington bur., 1954-63; chief (Mediterranean and Middle East Bur.), 1963-64; FAO info. adviser Washington, 1964-65; editor Republican Conf. U.S. Ho. Reps., 1966-69; minority sgt.-at-arms U.S. Ho. Reps., 1969-73; chief staff to the Vice Pres., 1973-74; counsellor (with cabinet rank) to Pres. Gerald R. Ford, 1974-77; sr. research fellow Hoover Instn., Stanford U., 1977—; trustee Gerald R. Ford Found., 1981—; mem. staff 1st U.S. Ho. of Reps. Mission to Peoples' Republic of China, 1972. Author: Palace Politics, An Inside Account of the Ford Years, 1980. Asst. to permanent chmn. Rep. Nat. Conv., 1968, 72; bd. visitors U.S. Naval Acad., 1977-80. Served from ensign to lt. comdr. USNR, 1941-45, PTO; now capt. Res. ret. Recipient Sigma Delta Chi Distinguished Service award for Washington Corrs., 1957; Better Understanding citation English Speaking Union of U.S., 1958; Overseas Press Club citation for best articles on Latin Am., 1961; Freedoms Found. citation, 1963; Distinguished Eagle Scout award Boy Scouts Am., 1975; Reid Found. fellow Middle East, 1951. Mem. Navy League, Oceanic Ednl. Found., Hammer and Coffin Soc., Delta Chi, Sigma Delta Chi, Delta Sigma Rho. Mem. Ch. of Christ. Clubs: Nat. Press (Washington), Army and Navy (Washington), Capitol Hill (Washington); Mil. Order of the Carabao, Chevaliers du Tastevin; Country Club of St. Croix (V.I.). Home: 5001 Baltimore Ave Bethesda MD 20816-1607 *I'm not sure I have "achieved success" but I have had a very good life so far. The greatest evil in life is a lie, and the greatest blessings are love and laughter.*

HARTMANN, WILLIAM HERMAN, pathologist, educator; b. N.Y.C., Mar. 13, 1931. BA, Syracuse U., 1951; M.D., SUNY, 1955. Diplomate Am. Bd. Pathology. Exec. v.p. Am. Bd. Pathology, Tampa, Fla., 1993—; prof. pathology U. So. Fla., Tampa, 1993—. Office: Am Bd Pathology PO Box 25915 Tampa FL 33622-5915

HARTMANN, WILLIAM KENNETH, astronomy scientist; b. June 6, 1939; m. Gayle Harrison, Mar. 22, 1970; 1 child, Amy. BS in Physics, Pa. State U., 1961; MS in Geology, U. Ariz., 1965, PhD in Astronomy, 1966. Asst. prof. Lunar and Planetary Lab., U. Ariz., 1967-70; assoc. and sr. scientist IIT Research Inst., 1970-72; sr. scientist Planetary Sci. Inst., Sci. Applications Internat. Corp., Tucson, 1972-95, Planetary Sci. Inst., San Juan Rsch. Inst., 1995—; co-investigator 1971 Mariner 9 Mars Mission, 1971-72, Mars Observer Mission, 1991, Mars Global Surveyor Mission, 1996, Russian Mars 96 Mission; vis. assoc. prof. Inst. for Astronomy, U. Hawaii; affiliate faculty U. Hawaii at Hilo, 1990—, U. Ariz., 1993—; cons. Smithsonian Air and Space Mus., 1977; photog. cons. House Select Com. on Assassinations, 1978-79; mem. various coms. NASA, 1978—; co-organizer Kona Conf. on Origin of Moon, 1984; mem. com. on planetary exploration NRC, 1984-87. Author: Astronomy: The Cosmic Journey, 1978, last edit., 1993, Moons and Planets, 1972, 3d edit., 1992, Out of the Cradle, 1984, Cycles of Fire, 1987, The History of Earth, 1991, Mars Underground, 1997; co-author: The Grand Tour: A Traveller's Guide to the Solar System, 1981, last edit., 1993; co-editor: Origin of the Moon, 1986, Desert Heart, 1989; prin. editor: In the Stream of Stars: The Soviet-American Space Art Book, 1990; also numerous tech. articles to sci. publs. Co-winner 1965-66 Ninninger Meteorite award; Asteroid 3341 named Hartmann in honor of his rsch. on solar system evolution; recipient Carl Segan medal Am. Astron. Soc., 1997. Office: Planetary Sci Inst 620 N 6th Ave Tucson AZ 85705-8331*

HARTMETZ, WALTER JUDSON, library director; b. Wichita, Apr. 14, 1941; s. Gerald Jacob and Virginia Pate H.; m. Sherrie Karen Edwards, May 26, 1973; 1 child, Sean Edwards. BA, Wichita State U., 1969; MLS, Emporia State U., 1971. Libr. dir. Miami (Okla.) Pub. Libr., 1971-76, Cass County Pub. Libr., Harrisonville, Mo., 1976-78, North Kansas City (Mo.) Pub. Libr., 1978—. With U.S. Army, 1962-65. Mem. ALA, Mo. Libr. Assn., So. Pacific Hist. & Tech. Soc., Greater Kansas City Model Railroad Club (sec./treas. 1981—). Avocations: model railroading, woodworking. Office: North Kansas City Pub Libr 715 E 23d Ave North Kansas City MO 64116

HARTNESS, SANDRA JEAN, venture capitalist; b. Jacksonville Fla., Aug. 19, 1944; d. Harold H. and Viola M. (House) H. AB, Ga. So. Coll., 1969; postgrad., San Francisco State Coll., 1970-71; MA in Taxation, Golden Gate U., 1997. Researcher Savannah (Ga.) Planning Commn., 1969, Environ. Analysis Group, San Francisco, 1970-71; dir. Mission Inn, Riverside, Calif., 1971-75; developer Hartness Assocs., Laguna Beach, Calif., 1976—; ptnr. Western Neuro-Care Ctr., Tustin Calif., 1983-89; pres. Asset Svcs., Inc., 1981—. V.p., mem. bd. dirs. Evergreen Homes, Inc., 1986-90. Recipient numerous awards for community svc. Democrat.

HARTNETT, ELIZABETH A., trade association executive; b. Metuchen, N.J., June 28, 1952; d. John J. and Rita (Hackett) Kirwan; m. Raymond T. Hartnett, July 16, 1977; children: Kathleen E., John T. BS, Wheeling Coll., 1974. CPA, Pa. Jr. acct. Deloitte Haskins & Sells, Pitts., 1974-76; sr. acct. Deloitte Haskins & Sells, Washington, 1976-81, mgr., 1981-84; contr. Electronic Industries Assn., Washington, 1984-86, v.p. fin., 1986-98; contr. Am. Soc. Health Sys. Pharmacists, 1998—; treas. Electronic Industries Found., Washington, 1984-98. Mem. Am. Soc. Assn. Execs., Greater Washington Soc. Assn. Execs., Pa. Inst. CPA's, D.C. Inst. CPA's. Republican. Roman Catholic. Office: Am Soc Health Sys Pharmacists 7272 Wisconsin Ave Bethesda MD 20814

HARTNETT, JAMES PATRICK, engineering educator; b. Lynn, Mass., Mar. 19, 1924; s. James Patrick and Anna Elizabeth (Ryan) H.; m. Shirley Germaine Carlson, July 14, 1945 (div. 1969); children: James, David, Paul, Carla, Dennis; m. Edith Zubrin, Sept. 10, 1971. BS in Mech. Engring, Ill. Inst. Tech., 1947; MS, MIT, 1948; PhD, U. Calif., Berkeley, 1954. Engr. gas turbine div. Gen. Electric Co., 1948-49; rsch. engr. U. Calif., Berkeley, 1949-54; asst. prof. to prof. mech. engring. U. Minn., 1954-61; Guggenheim fellow, vis. prof. U. Tokyo, Japan, 1960; cons. ICA, Seoul, Korea, 1960; Fulbright lectr., cons. mech. engring. U. Alexandria, Egypt, 1961; H. Fletcher Brown prof. mech. engring., chmn. dept. U. Del., 1961-65; engring. cons., 1954-74; prof., head dept. energy engring. U. Ill., Chgo., 1965-74; dir. Energy Resources Ctr., 1974-98; sci. exch. visitor, Romania, 1969; vis. prof. Israel Inst. Tech., 1971; cons. Asian Inst. Tech., Bangkok 1977; 1st Dr. Arcot Ramachandran prof. heat transfer Indian Inst. Tech., Madras, 1995-96. Editor: Recent Advances in Heat and Mass Transfer, 1961; co-editor: Internat. Jour. Heat and Mass Transfer, 1960—, (with T.F. Irvine, Jr.) Advances in Heat Transfer, 1963—, Heat Transfer-Japanese Research, Soviet Research, 1971, Fluid Mechanics-Soviet Research, 1971; contbr. articles on heat transfer, fluid mechanics, energy to tech. jours. Mem. organizing com. and sci. coun. Internat. Centre Heat and Mass Transfer, Belgrade, Yugoslavia, 1969—; mem., sec. Ill. Energy Resources Commn., 1974-85; mem. sci. coun. Regional Center for Energy, Heat and Mass Transfer for Asia and Pacific, 1976—; sec. Midwest Univs. Energy Consortium, 1980—. Recipient Profl. Achievement award Ill. Inst. Tech. Alumni Assn., 1977; recipient Luikov medal Internat. Ctr. Heat and Mass Transfer, 1981; Japan Soc. for Promotion of Sci. fellow, 1987. Fellow ASME (Meml. award heat transfer divsn. 1969, 40th Anniversary award 1989, AIChE-ASME Max Jakob Meml. award 1989), Indian Nat. Acad. Engring., Japanese Soc. Mech. Engrs. (hon.); mem. Internat. Higher Edn. Acad. of Scis./Moscow (Disting. prof. 1997), Sigma Xi, Tau Beta Pi, Pi Tau Sigma. Address: Univ of Ill 1919 W Taylor St Chicago IL 60612-7246

HARTNETT, MAURICE A., III, judge; b. Dover, Del., Jan. 20, 1927; s. Maurice and Anna Louise (Morris) H.; m. Elizabeth Anne Hutchinson, Aug. 21, 1965; 1 child, Anne Elizabeth. *His ancestors, on his mother's side, include John Harris, who in 1720 founded Harris's Ferry, now Harrisburg, Pennsylvania. In 1665 John Winder came to Manokan section of Maryland from Virginia. In 1745 Captain John Morris emigrated to Somerset County, Maryland from Long Island, New York. Colonel Henry Ridgely, about 1657, emigrated to Ann Arundal County, Maryland. William Giles, in 1672, emigrated to Somerset County, Maryland. On his father's side, William Hartnett and Catherine McKinery immigrated from Ireland in 1853 and located in Kent County, Delaware. The Hartnett family engaged in the lumber business in Dover, Delaware for over 100 years* Student, Washington Coll.-Chestertown, Md., 1946-47; BS, U. Del.-Newark, 1951; postgrad. Georgetown U., 1951; JD, George Washington U., 1954; EdM, U. Del., 1956. Bar: Del. 1954, U.S. Dist. Ct. Del. 1957, U.S. Supreme Ct. 1959. Pvt. practice law, Dover, Del., 1955-76; exec. dir. Del. Legis. Ref. Bur., Dover, 1961-69; vice chancellor Del. Ct. Chancery, Dover, 1976-94, justice Del. Supreme Ct., 1994—; code revisor Del. Rev. Code Commn., 1961-72; commr. Nat. Conf. Com. Uniform State Laws, Chgo., 1962—, sec., exec. com., 1977-83; chmn. State Tax Appeal Bd., Wilmington, Del., 1973-76. Served with U.S. Army, 1945-46. Mem. ABA, Del. Bar Assn., Kent County Bar Assn. (pres. 1974), Am. Law Inst. Democrat. Home: 144 Cooper Rd Dover DE 19901-4926 Office: PO Box 476 Dover DE 19903-0476 Office: Delware Supreme Court 55 The Green Dover Wilmington DE 19903

HARTNETT, THOMAS ROBERT, III, lawyer, author; b. Sioux City, Iowa, July 19, 1920; s. Thomas R. and Florence Mary (Graves) H.; m. Betty Jeanne Dobbins, Mar. 3, 1943; children: Thomas Robert Joseph, Jeanine Elizabeth, Dennis Edward, Glenn Michael. Student, Trinity Coll., 1937-39; LLB, U. So. Calif., 1948. Bar: Tex. 1948, U.S. Dist. Ct. (no. dist.) Tex., 1949, U.S. Ct. Appeasl (5th cir.) 1954, (10th cir.) 1955, (11th cir.) 1983, U.S. Supreme Ct., 1957. Pvt. practice Dallas, 1948-88; of counsel Hartnett Law Firm, Dallas, 1988—. Author: The Root of the Whys on the Internet. With USAAF, 1939-45. Mem. State Bar Tex., Dallas Bar Assn. Republican. Roman Catholic. Home: 5074 Matilda St Apt 224 Dallas TX 75206-4268 Office: 4900 Thanksgiving Tower 1601 Elm St Dallas TX 75201-7254

HARTNETT, WILL FORD, lawyer; b. Austin, Tex., June 3, 1956; s. James Joseph and Emily (High) H.; m. Tammy Lynn Cotton, Dec. 7, 1996; 1 child, Will. BA, Harvard U., 1978; JD, U. Tex., 1981. Bar: Tex. 1981, U.S. Ct. Appeals (5th cir.) 1985, U.S. Supreme Ct. 1985; cert. in Estate Planning and Probate Law Tex. Bd. Legal Specialization. Assoc. Turner & Hitchins, Dallas, 1981-82; ptnr. The Hartnett Law Firm, Dallas, 1982—; bd. dirs. Tex. Guaranteed Student Loan Corp., Austin, 1987-90. Co-author: Annual Survey of Wills and Trusts, 1986. Mem. Tex. Ho. of Reps., 1991—; vice-chmn. House Jud. Affairs Com., 1995—. Fellow Am. Coll. Trust and Estate Coun., Tex. Bar Found.; mem. SAR, Dallas Bar Assn., Mensa, Harvard Club Dallas (bd. dirs., treas. 1983-95), Rotary. Republican. Roman Catholic. Home: 4722 Walnut Hill Ln Dallas TX 75229-6354 Office: The Hartnett Law Firm 4900 Thanksgiving Tower Dallas TX 75201

HARTON, JOHN JAMES, utility executive, consultant; b. Del Rio, Tex., Dec. 26, 1941; s. John Teague and Ara Velva (Boggs) H.; m. Dianne Voss, May 30, 1968; children: Angela Deanne, John Jay. BSEE, U. Ark., 1964, MSEE, 1965. With Ark. Power & Light Co., 1965-93; dir. corp. planning Ark. Power and Light Co., Little Rock, 1974-79; treas., asst. sec. Ark. Power & Light Co., 1979-81, v.p. fin. svcs., CFO, treas., asst. sec., 1981-91, v.p. adminstrn., asst. sec., 1991-93; dir. bus. planning and budgeting Entergy Svcs., Little Rock, 1993-95; coord. spl. products, cons. Entergy Power, 1995-97, cons., 1997—; instr. Pines Vocat.-Tech. Sch., Pine Bluff, Ark., 1966-68. Bd. dirs. Welsey United Meth. Ch., Pine Bluff, 1971; mem. bldg. com. St. James United Meth. Ch., Little Rock, 1980-91, trustee, 1985-87, vice chmn. fin. com. 1991-92, chmn. fin. com., 1993-94; treas. Savanna Estates Property Owners Assn., 1997-98. Mem. NSPE, Ark. Acad. Elec. Engrs. (bd. dirs. 1992-95, v.p. 1992-93, pres. 1993-94, sec.-treas. 1996—), Shriners, Quapaw, Ark. Consistory.

HARTONG, HENDRIK J., JR., transportation company executive. Chmn. bd. Air Express Internat. Office: Air Express Internat Corp 120 Tokeneke Rd Darien CT 06820-4825*

HARTRICK, JANICE KAY, lawyer; b. Baytown, Tex., Oct. 15, 1952. BA, Rice U., 1974; JD, U. Houston, 1976. Bar: Tex. 1977, La. 1980. With contracts sect. Texaco Corp., Houston, 1977-78; asst. gen. counsel Cities Exploration Co., Watson Oil Corp., Houston, 1978-79; sr. atty. Coastal Corp., Houston, 1979-87; chief counsel, v.p. Seagull Energy Corp., Houston, 1987-97; gen. counsel, sr. v.p. EEX Corp., Houston, 1997—. Contbg. editor Regulation of the Natural Gas Industry, 1980-84. Mem. adv. bd. Internat. Oil and Gas Ednl. Ctr., Southwestern Legal Found., co-chair 50th Inst. on Oil and Gas Law and Tax. Mem. ABA, Ind. Tex. Bar Assn., Houston Bar Assn. (oil, gas and mineral law sect. coun. mem. 1989-90), State Bar of Tex. (oil, gas and mineral law sect. Chair elect chmn. 1998-99, mem. coun. 1992—), La. Bar Assn., Southwestern Legal Found. 50th Inst. on Oil and Gas Law and Taxation (chmn.). Avocation: track. Office: EEX Corp 2500 Citywest Blvd Ste 1400 Houston TX 77042-3024

HARTSBURG, JUDITH CATHERINE, computer web programmer; b. Terre Haute, Ind., June 16, 1955; d. Ferris Lee and Mary Ann (Tully) Roberson; m. Donald Matthew Seprodi, Aug. 1, 1972 (div. Oct. 1994); children: Antoinette, Autumn, Jacob, Brooklyn; m. Joseph Wayne Hartsburg, Feb. 14, 1998. AA, Ivy Tech., 1990; grad., Dale Carnegie Course. Lic. property/casualty ins. agt.; notary public. Sec. Equifax, Oklahoma City, 1975-76; ins. clk. Northside Family Medicine, Del City, Okla., 1976; office mgr. Dick Clark Ins., Terre Haute, 1981, Simrell's, Terre Haute, 1981-85; ADC acctg. clk./typist V Vigo County Welfare, Terre Haute, 1985-86, head ADC acctg., clk./typist IV, 1986-87; purchasing agt. Bruce Fox, Inc., New Albany, Ind., 1987-88; acctg. mgr. Terre Haute Coke and Carbon, 1988-96, acting sec. bd. dirs., 1989; ptnr., owner Thistlehare; office mgr. Terre Haute (Ind.) Truck Ctr., 1996; internet programmer (webmaster) Advanced Microelectronics, Inc., Vincennes, Ind., 1997—; ptnr., owner Thistlehare; bookkeeper Seprodi Constrn., Terre Haute, 1989—; grad. asst. Dale Carnegie

Inst.; owner Take-A-Letter. Author employee manuals. Coach, Terre Haute Youth Soccer Assn., 1979-82, bd. dirs., 1979-82; player North Tex. Women's Soccer Assn., Plano, 1977-78. Recipient Dale Carnegie highest award for achievement. Mem. NAFE, AIPB, Am. Notary Assn., Profl. Bookkeepers Assn., Vigo County Taxpayers Assn. Democrat. Roman Catholic. Avocations: gardening, camping, sewing, piano. Home: PO Box 323 Sandborn IN 47578-0323

HARTSELL, HORACE ED, college president; m. Joyce Powell; 6 children. BS, U. Fla.; MS, Fla. Atlantic U.; D in Adminstrn. of Higher Edn., Auburn U. Founder East Ark. C.C.; with Broward C.C., Fla. Atlantic U.; pres. Pensacola Jr. Coll., 1990-98, pres. emeritus, 1999—; interim pres. Daytona Beach C.C., 1998—; vice-chair, chair Fla. Coun. of Pres.; mem. coun. Pres.'s Legis. com. Founder, mem. Leadership Fla. Named Bus. and Profl. Leader of Yr. Pensacola News Jour., 1983; recipient Disting. Life Svc. award Fla. Assn. of C.C., 1997, Adminstrn. Commn. award, 1997. Mem. Pensacola Area C. of C. (chmn.). Home: Daytona Beach Cmty Coll 1385 Salem Rd Minor Hill TN 38473 Office: Daytona Beach Cmty Coll PO Box 2811 Daytona Beach FL 32120

HARTSELL, SAMUEL DAVID, insurance agent; b. Aberdeen, Miss., Oct. 15, 1937; s. Walter Eugene and Clara Otis (Jennings) H.; m. Virginia McAden, June 14, 1959; children: Cynthia H. Jones, Susan H. Sexton. BS in Engring., Va. Polytech. Inst. & State U., 1959; MS in Fin. Svcs., The Am. Coll., 1984. CLU, ChFC; accredited estate planner; registered health underwriter. Ins. agt. Principal Mutual Life Ins Co, Birmingham, Ala., 1972-92; sales engr. U.S. Steel Corp., Birmingham, 1959-72. Contbr. articles to profl. jours. Named Man of Distinction, Shades Valley Sun newspaper, 1985. Fellow Life Underwriter Tng. Coun.; mem. Nat. Assn. Life Underwriters, Am. Soc. CLU's, Million Dollar Round Table.

HARTSFIELD, HENRY WARREN, JR., electronics company executive, retired astronaut; b. Birmingham, Ala., Nov. 21, 1933; s. Henry Warren and Alice Norma (Sorrell) H.; m. Judy Frances Massey, June 30, 1957; children: Judy Lynn, Keely Warren. BS, Auburn U., 1954; postgrad., Duke U., 1954-55, Air Force Inst. Tech., 1960-61; MS, U. Tenn., 1970; DSc (hon.), Auburn U., 1986. Commd. 2d lt. USAF, 1955, advanced through grades to col., 1974; assigned to tour with 53d Tactical Fighter Squadron USAF, Bitburg, Fed. Republic Germany, 1961-64; instr. USAF Test Pilot Sch., Edwards AFB, Calif., 1965-66; assigned to Manned Orbiting Lab. USAF, 1966-69; astronaut, NASA Lyndon B. Johnson Space Ctr., 1969-97, mem. support crew Apollo 16, Skylabs 2, 3, 4 missions, pilot STS-4; comdr. STS-41D, STS-61A, ret., 1977; civilian astronaut NASA; dep. dir. Flight Crew Ops. Directorate, 1987-89; dir. tech. integration and analysis Office Space Flight, NASA Hqrs., 1989-90; dep. dir. ops. space sta. projects Marshall Space Flight Ctr. NASA, 1990-91; mgr. man-tended capability phase Space Sta. Freedom Program, 1991-94; mgr. Internat. Space Sta. Ind. Assessment at Johnson Space Ctr., 1994-97; ret., 1998; dir. Houston ops. Raytheon Sys. Co., 1998—. In space: 483 hours. Decorated Meritorious Service medal, D.S.M. NASA, 1982, 88, Space Flight medal NASA, 1982, 84, 85; recipient Nat. Geog. White Space Trophy, 1973. Mem. Soc. Exptl. Test Pilots, Air Force Assn., Sigma Pi Sigma. Office: Raytheon Sys Co 2224 Bay Area Blvd Houston TX 77058-2008

HARTSHORN, TERRY O., health facility administrator; b. 1944. Adminstrv. sec. Centinela Valley Hosp., Inglewood, Calif., 1965-68, adminstrv. asst., 1969; adminstr., cons. Community Health Svc., USPHS, L.A., 1969-71; adminstr. Luth. Hosp. Soc. So. Calif., L.A., 1971-73, Moore-White Med. Clinic, L.A., 1973-76; chmn. Pacificare Health Systems, Inc., Cypress, Calif., 1977—; chmn., pres., CEO Pacificare Health Systems, Inc., Burbank, Calif., 1993—; chmn. bd., pres., CEO UniHealth Am., Inc., Burbank, 1993—. Office: Unihealth Am 3400 W Riverside Dr Fl 8 Burbank CA 91505-4673*

HARTSOCK, JANE MARIE, nurse, educator; b. Rock Island, Ill., Nov. 19, 1948; d. George Vincent and Patricia Anna (Holland) Woeber; m. Donald Lee Hartsock, Jan. 16, 1971; children: Cara Elizabeth, David Vincent. BS in Nursing, Marycrest Coll., 1977; MA, U. Iowa, 1982. Cert. oncology nurse, clin. nurse specialist. Head nurse U.S. Naval Hosp., Great Lakes, Ill., 1970-71; staff nurse Moline Pub. Hosp. (Ill.), 1971-72, instr. Sch. Nursing, 1977-87; nurse bone marrow transplant unit, U. Minn., 1987-92; instr. Mpls. C.C., 1988-92, Trinity Sch. Nursing, 1992-94; staff nurse oncology Trinity Med. Ctr., 1992—; assoc. prof. Trinity Coll. Nursing, 1994—; mem. adj. faculty Marycrest Internat. U., 1998. Contbr. chpt. in book. Song leader Blue Grass Ch., 1977-87. With USN 1970-72, maj. Nurse Corps USAR. Mem. AAUW, Am. Nurses Assn., Nurse Educators Assn. (pres. 1984-85), Oncology Nursing Soc, Internat. Platform Assn., Res. Officer Assn., Pioneer Club (Blue Grass, Iowa sec. 1983-87), Sigma Theta Tau (pres.). Home: 2035 43rd St Rock Island IL 61201-4913

HARTSOCK, LINDA SUE, educational and management association executive; b. St. Joseph, Mo., Feb. 20, 1940; d. Waldo Emerson and Martha (Skelkop) H. BS, Ctrl. Meth. Coll., Fayette, Mo., 1962; MEd, Pa. State U., 1965, EdD, 1971. Cert. assn. exec. Am. Soc. Assn. Execs. Tchr. Jr. High Sch. (North Kansas City (Mo.) Public Sch. System), 1962-63; sr. resident Pa. State U., 1963-64, asst. coordinator residence halls, 1964-65, residence hall coordinator, 1965-66, asst. dean women, 1966-68, asst. dean students, 1968-71; researcher Center for Study Higher Edn., 1971, dir. new student programs, 1971-72; nat. dir. program AAUW, 1972-76; exec. dir. Adult Edn. Assn., 1976-80; now chief exec. officer Integrated Options, Inc., assn., edn. and mgmt. svcs., Alexandria, Va.; designer tng. and ednl. programs for various orgns. and assn; v.p. fin. Com. for Full Finding Edn., 1979; mem. first adv. panel convened future directions of a learning soc. project Coll. Entrance Exam. Bd., 1978, mem. planning group for course-by-newspaper exam. project, 1979; bd. dirs. Coalition Adult Edn. Orgns., 1976; mem. White House Conf. on Aging Planning, 1979; mem. nat. adv. bd. Nat. Center Higher Edn. Mgmt. System Project to Develop a Taxonomy for the Field of Adult Edn., 1978; nat. adv. council on adult edn. Futures and Amendments Project, 1977; adv. Collection of Census Data, Nat. Center Ednl. Stats., 1977; mem. public policy com., program com. chmn. Adv. Council Nat. Orgns. to Corp. for Public Broadcasting, 1976; adv. devel. New Mediated Programs, Office Instructional Resources, Miami Dade Community Coll., 1976; mem. innovative awards com. Nat. Univ. Extension Assn., 1977; field reader U.S. Dept. Edn., 1981-83. Mem. editlr. bd. Off to Coll. mag, 1972-74 ; contbr. articles to profl. jours. Recipient Disting. Alumni award Central Meth. Coll., 1978. Mem. Am. Soc. Assn. Execs. (individual membership coun. 1979-81, edn. com. 1985-88, 92-94, univ. affairs commn. 1989-92, awards com. 1991), Washington Women's Forum (budget, program and exec. coms. 1978-82), Alumni Soc. Coll. Edn. Pa. State U. (bd. dirs., chairperson strategic planning com. 1986, Outstanding Alumni award). Office: Integrated Options Inc PO Box 10280 Alexandria VA 22310-0280

HARTSOE, JAMES RUSSELL, minister; b. Quarryville, Pa., Apr. 11, 1934; s. Russell E. and Laura Amanda H.; m. Mary Louise Eby, Dec. 18, 1955 (div. Sept. 1993); children: Alison, Judith. BS, Millersville State U., 1955; MDiv, Princeton Theol. Sem., 1961; postgrad., U. Minn., 1984-87. Ordained to ministry United Presbyn. Ch., 1961; Evang. Luth. Ch., 1988. Pastor Knox Presbyn. Ch., Cedar Rapids, Iowa, 1961-66; project coord. Pa. div. Am. Cancer Soc., Harrisburg, 1966-68; pastor West Hempfield Presbyn. Ch., Irwin, Pa., 1968-77; asst. pastor House of Hope Presbyn. Ch., St. Paul, 1977-78; interim pastor Bethel Luth. Ch., Hudson, Wis., 1988, Bethany Luth Ch., Mpls., 1990-91; pastor Christ English Luth. Ch., Mpls., 1991-93; devel. dir. St. Olaf Retirement Cmtys., 1993-95; visitation pastor Bethel Luth. Ch., Mpls., 1994—; exec. dir. Norwin Coun. of Chs., 1971-75. Bd. dirs. People, Inc., St. Paul, 1977-81. With USAF, 1957-58. Democrat. Home: 4430 Arden View Ct Arden Hills MN 55112-1945 *Life finds its deepest meaning in relationship—our relationship with God and with other people. In those relationship which are whole there is love.*

HARTSOUGH, GAYLA ANNE KRAETSCH, management consultant; b. Lakewood, Ohio, Sept. 16, 1949; d. Vernon W. and Mildred E. (Austin) Kraetsch; m. James N. Heller, Aug. 20, 1972 (div. 1977); m. Jeffrey W. Hartsough, Mar. 12, 1983; 1 child, Jeffrey Hunter Kraetsch Hartsough. BS, Northwestern U., 1971; EdM, Tufts U., 1973; MEd, U. Va., 1978, PhD, 1978. Vol. VISTA, Tenn., 1970-71; asst. tchr. Perkins Sch. for the Blind, Watertown, Mass., 1971-72; resource tchr. Fairfax (Va.) County Pub. Schs., 1972-76; asst. dir. ctr. U. Va., Charlottesville, 1976-78; sr. program officer Acad. for Edn. Devel., Washington, 1978-80; mng. cons. Cresap/Towers Perrin, Washington and L.A., 1980-86; pres. KH Consulting Group, L.A., 1986—; mem. nat. adv. coun. Northwestern U. Sch. Speech, Evanston, Ill., 1992—; cons. in field. Contbr. more than 20 articles to profl. jours. Co-founder L.A. Higher Edn. Roundtable, L.A., 1987-94; mem. nat. adv. coun., co-chair for Sch. of Speech Campaign $1 Billion, Northwestern U.; mem. Coun. 100 Northwestern U., 1999—. Recipient Outstanding Woman of Achievement award Century City C. of C., 1991. Mem. Orgn. Women Execs. (past pres., bd. dirs. L.A. 1986-95). Fax: 310-203-5419. E-mail: khcggak@aol.com. Home: 15624 Royal Ridge Rd Sherman Oaks CA 91403-4207 Office: KH Consulting Group 1901 Ave Of Stars Fl 18 Los Angeles CA 90067-6001

HARTSTEIN, SAM, educational administrator; b. N.Y.C., Aug. 6, 1921; m. Rachel Zimmerman, June 23, 1963; children: Gila, Jonathan. Tchrs. Diploma, Yeshiva U., 1941, BA, 1943, LHD (hon.), 1994; postgrad., New Sch. Social Rsch. Dir. pub. rels. Yeshiva U., N.Y.C., 1943-94; writer, producer films including: Faith and Learning, The Story of Yeshiva U.; vis. lectr. to various schs., profl. meetings, nat. orgns. Past pres. Met. Coll. Pub. Rels. Coun. Author: A Guide to Public Relations, 1970, Yeshiva U. Centennial film Building an American Tradition: Yeshiva University—The First Century, 1987 (Bronze medal, CASE); contbr. numerous articles to various publs. Past pub. rels. chmn. Jewish Cmty. Coun. Washington Heights-Inwood; mem. bd. edn. Yeshiva Rabbi Moses Soloveitchik; bd. dirs. YM & YWHA Washington Heights and Inwood. Recipient Gold medal Yeshiva U. Mem. CASE (Seasoned Sage award 1970, Centennial Celebration Spl. Events award 1997), Nat. Sch. Pub. Rels. Assn., Coll. Sports Info. Dirs. Am., Am. Jewish Pub. Rels. Soc. Home: 66 Overlook Terr New York NY 10040-3824 Office: Yeshiva U 500 W 185th St New York NY 10033-3201

HARTUNG, JAMES H., airport authority executive. Pres. Toledo-Lucas County Port Authority. Office: Toledo Lucas County Port Authority 1 Maritime Plz Toledo OH 43604*

HARTUNG, PATRICIA MCENTEE, therapist; b. Syracuse, N.Y.; d. James Henry and Frances Julia (Yehle) McEntee; m. Duane James Hartung, July 30, 1960; children: James Joseph, Tamara Ann, John Patrick, Jennifer Lynn. BS, LeMoyne Coll., 1957; MSW, Boston U., 1959. Diplomate Am. Bd. Examiners in Clin. Social Work; lic. social worker, Fla. Social worker Dept. of Pub. Welfare/Child Welfare Div., Bay Shore, N.Y., 1959-60, Dept. Pub. Welfare/Alcohol Rehab. Prog., Omaha, 1961; cons./social worker Carnegie Gardens Nursing Home, Melbourne, Fla., 1970-72; parent educator Brevard Community Coll., Cocoa, Fla., 1968-74; therapist Circles of Care, Rockledge, Fla., 1974-81; program dir. Circles of Care, Titusville, 1981-93, therapist, 1981—; adv. com. When Entering New Directions I, Cocoa, 1988-93; mem. Family Svc. Planning Team, Titusville, 1991-93. Mem. NASW, AAUW (Cen. Brevard chpt., v.p. membership 1991-93, pres. 1993-95),Acad. Cert. Social Workers. Democrat. Roman Catholic. Avocations: gardening, music, travel. Office: Circles of Care 6700 S US # 1 Titusville FL 32780

HARTUNG, ROLF, environmental toxicology educator, researcher, consultant; b. Bremen, Federal Republic Germany, Mar. 1, 1935; came to U.S., 1952, naturalized, 1958. BS in Wildlife Mgmt., U. Mich., 1960, MWM in Wildlife Mgmt., 1962, PhD in Wildlife Mgmt., 1964. Diplomate Am. Bd. Toxicology. Instr. in wildlife mgmt. U. Mich., Ann Arbor, 1963, lectr. in indsl. health, 1964, asst. prof. indsl. health, 1965-69, assoc. prof. environ. and indsl. health, 1969-73, prof. environ. toxicology, 1973-97, prof. emeritus, 1997—, chmn. toxicology program, 1974-80; com. or sub-com. mem. Nat. Acad. Scis., 1971-72, 79-97, Mich. Dept. Natural Resources, 1977-97; mem. Mich. Environ. Rev. Bd., 1982-86; mem. hazardous materials com. U.S. Congress Office Tech. Assessment, 1980-83; chmn. com. on environ. effects, transport and fate of sci. adv. bd. EPA, 1982-87, mem. exec. com. of sci. adv. bd., 1982-87. Editor, contbg. author: Environmental Mercury Contamination, 1972; assoc. editor Jour. Toxicology and Indsl. Health, 1984-87, Ency. of Toxicology, 1998; contbr. chpts. to books and articles to profl. jours. Recipient H. M. Wight award U. Mich., 1963; NSF fellow, 1960-64. Mem. Am. Indsl. Hygiene Assn., Mich. Indsl. Hygiene Assn., Soc. Environ. Toxicology and Chemistry, Soc. Toxicology, Wildlife Disease Assn., Wildlife Soc., Sigma Xi, Phi Sigma, Phi Kappa Phi. Home: 3125 Fernwood St Ann Arbor MI 48108-1955

HARTWELL, LELAND HARRISON, geneticist, educator; b. Los Angeles, Oct. 30, 1939; s. Majorie (Taylor) H.; m. Theresa Naujack. BS, Calif. Inst. Tech., 1961; PhD, MIT, 1964. Postdoctoral fellow Salk Inst., 1964-65; asst. prof. U. Calif., Irvine, 1965-67, assoc. prof., 1967-68; assoc. prof. U. Washington, Seattle, 1968-73, prof., 1973—; pres., dir. Fred Hutchison Cancer Rsch. Ctr., Seattle, 1997—; rsch. prof. Am. Cancer Soc., 1990—. Recipient Eli Lilly award, 1973, NIH Merit award, 1990, GM Sloan award, 1991, Hoffman LaRoche Mattia award, 1991, Gairdner Found. Internat. award, 1992, Simon Shubitz award U. Chgo., 1992, Brandeis U. Rosenstiel award, 1993, Sloan Kettering Cancer Ctr. Katherine Berkan Judd award, 1994, Genetics Soc. of Am. medal, 1994, MGH Warren Triennial prize, 1995, Keith Porter award Am. Soc. Cell Biology, 1995, Carnegie Mellon Dickson award, 1996, Louisa Gross Horwitz prize Columbia U., 1995, Albert Lasker Basic Med. Rsch. award Albert and Mary Lasker Found., 1998, Brinker Internat. award for basic sci. Susan G. Komen Breast Cancer Found., 1998, Disting. Alumni award Calif. Inst. Tech., 1999; Guggenheim fellow, 1983-84; Am. Bus. Cancer Rsch. grantee, 1983—; Am. Cancer Soc. scholar; laureate Passano Found., 1996. Mem. NAS, AAAS, Am. Soc. Microbiology, Am. Soc. Cell Biology, Genetics Soc. Am. (pres. 1990). Office: Fred Hutchinson Cancer Rsch Ctr 1100 Fairview Ave N Seattle WA 98109-1024

HARTWELL, STEPHEN, investment company executive; b. Phila., Apr. 10, 1915; s. Stephen Warren and Elizabeth (Thompson) H.; m. Elizabeth van Laer Speer, Feb. 21, 1946 (div. 1973); children: Stephen Warren II, Robert van Laer; m. Norma Bostick, Dec. 9, 1978. BS in Adminstrv. Engring., Lafayette Coll., 1936. Investment analyst Pa. Co. Banking & Trusts, 1936-41; procurement officer electronic equipment CAA, 1947-48; indsl. specialist AEC, 1948-49, chief progress and stats. sect., prodn. div., 1949-51, chief constr. engring. reports br., 1951-54; exec. v.p. Atomic Devel. Securities Co. (and successor cos.), 1954-68; v.p. Washington Mut. Investors Fund, Inc., 1968-81, pres., 1981-85, chmn., 1985—; pres. Washington Investment Advisers Inc., 1992—; chmn. Tax Exempt Bond Fund Md., Tax Exempt Fund Va., 1986-97, chmn. emeritus, 1997—; pres., bd. dirs. Colchester Corp., Woodbridge, Va., 1971—; chmn. WMIF Mgmt. Corp., Washington, 1986— Hartick LLC, 1997—; bd. dirs. Wentz Corp., Wilmington, Del., Oratec Corp., Herndon, Va., Johnston Lemon Group Inc.; trustee Amer-ibanc Investors Group, 1985-95. Mem. Fairfax County (Va.) Planning Commn., 1961-67, chmn., 196466; mem. No. Va. Regional Planning and Econ. Devel. Commn., 1963-64, Fairfax County Rep. Com., 1955-61, 66-70, 79-81; bd. govs. Gunston Hall Sch., Va.; active Mt. Vernon Life Guards, 1992—, chmn., 1998—; trustee Am. U., 1983-88, trustee emeritus, 1990—; trustee Woodlawn Found., 1983-89; trustee, treas. Found. for Middle East Peace, 1993—, Fairfax Hosp. Assn., 1986-93; trustee, treas. Inova Health Systems, 1987-96, chmn. investment and pension com., 1997—; chmn. Jefferson Hosp., Alexandria, Va., 1986-92; chmn. Virginia Coll. Bldg. Authority, Richmond, Va., 1994—; mem. Commonwealth Coun. Investment Advisers, 1998—. Maj. AUS, 1941-45. Mem. Washington Soc. Investment Analysts, SAR, Nat. Assn. Securities Dealers (dist. 10 com. 1968-71), Met. Club, Nat. Economists Club, Zeta Psi (trustee ednl. found. 1997—). Home: Riversedge PO Box 33 Mount Vernon VA 22121-0033 Office: AMA Bldg 1101 Vermont Ave NW Fl 12 Washington DC 20005-3583

HARTWICK, PATRICK JAMES, special education educator; b. Buffalo, Feb. 29, 1956; s. William Frederick and Mary Ann (Amatrano) H.; m. Christine Rita Brinkworth, Oct. 20, 1984; children: Alexandria, Jonathan. BS, Buffalo State Coll., 1978, MS, 1984; Ednl. Doctorate, W.Va. U., 1987. Permanent cert. in spl. edn. N-12, N.Y. Tng. coord., tchr. Niagara County A.R.C., Niagara Falls, N.Y., 1983-85; grad. asst. W.Va. U., Morgantown, 1985-87; ednl. cons. Mansfield (Conn.) Tng. Sch., 1987-88; edn. coord. New Medico Rehab. Ctr., Niskayuna, N.Y., 1988-90; asst. prof. SUNY, Geneseo, N.Y., 1990-93; assoc. prof., chair Daemen Coll., Amherst, N.Y., 1993—. Mem. CEC, Am. Assn. on Mental Retardation (treas. N.Y. state chpt. 1993-94, v.p. N.Y. state chpt. 1993-94, pres. N.Y. state chpt. 1995-96, regional rep. N.Y. state chpt. 1996-98), N.Y. State Assn. for Tchr. Educators. Avocations: golf, hiking, coaching soccer, basketball, research. Office: Daemen Coll 4380 Main St Amherst NY 14226-3544

HARTWICK, THOMAS STANLEY, technical management consultant; b. Vandalia, Ill., Mar. 19, 1934; s. William Arthur and Bernice Elizabeth (Daniels) H.; m. Alberta Elaine Lind, June 10, 1961; children: Glynis Anne, Jeffrey Andrew, Thomas Arthur. BS, U. Ill., 1956; MS, UCLA, 1958; PhD, U. So. Calif., 1969. Mgr. quantum electronics dept. Aerospace Corp., El Segundo, Calif., 1973-75, asst. dir. electronics research lab., 1975-79; mgr. electro-optical devel. lab. Hughes Aircraft Co. subs. Gen. Motors Corp., El Segundo, 1979-82, chief sci. advanced tactical programs, 1982-83; mgr. electro-optics research ctr. TRW Corp., Redondo Beach, Calif., 1983-86, mgr. microelectrics ctr., 1986-90, program mgr., 1990-96; chmn., bd. dirs. Laser Tech., Inc., Hollywood, Calif., 1990-94; cons. mem. U.S. Dept. Def. Adv. Group on Electronic Devices, Washington, 1977—, group C chmn., 1988-94; mem. Japan/U.S. Tech. Assessment Team, Washington, 1984; mem. Army Rsch. Labs. Adv. Bd., 1993-95; bd. dirs. 3D Tech. labs., Inc., IMEC, Inc., ARIES Tech., Inc.; chmn. Nat. Rsch. Coun. FAA Security, 1997—. Contbr. articles to profl. jours.; inventor FAR Infrared Laser, 1975. Mem. Am. Phys. Soc., Optical Soc. Am., (com. mem. 1976-79), Am. Def. Preparedness Assn. (dep. chmn. West Coast seminar 1987-88), mem. Nat. Res. Coun. Comm. Optical Sci and Engring., 1995—. Avocations: piano, sports.

HARTY, JAMES D., former manufacturing company executive; b. Bridgeport, Conn., Oct. 5, 1929; s. John S. and Catherine (Lee) H.; m. Margaret O'Connor, June 4, 1955; children—Shaun, Kevin, Maura, Megan. Degree in indsl. engring, U. Bridgeport, 1962. Analyst E.I. DuPont, 1947-51; prodn. control mgr. Sikorsky Aircraft, 1954-62; plant mgr. Stanley Works, 1962-68; corp. mgr. prodn. and inventory control ITT, 1968-70; corp. dir. mfg. projects Singer Co., N.Y.C., 1970-74; pres., chief operating officer Raymond Corp., Greene, N.Y., 1974-84; also dir. Raymond Corp., now ret.; owner, cons. J.D. Harty Assocs., Hilton Head Island, S.C., 1984-94. Mem. engring. tech. adv. com. and M.B.A. adv. bd. SUNY-Binghamton, mem. found.; mem. Sch. Bd. Found., Hilton Head Island, S.C. Served with U.S. Army, 1951-53. Recipient Corp. Leadership award MIT, 1987. Mem. Am. Mgmt. Assn. (Internat. Svc. award), Am. Prodn. and Inventory Control Soc. (past internat. v.p. edn. and rsch., Disting. Svc. award), Hilton Head Island Computer Club, Country Club of Hilton Head. Home: 4 Herring Gull Ln Hilton Head Island SC 29926-2655

HARTZ, DEBORAH SOPHIA, editor, critic; b. Plainfield, N.J., July 11, 1951; d. Sylvester and Margaret (Buschart) H.; m. Thomas McDonald July 24, 1971 (div. Dec. 1976). BA, U. Pa., 1973; MS, U. Wis., 1977. Asst. editor Whitney Communications Corp., N.Y.C., 1978-79; lifestyles editor News Dispatch, Michigan City, Ind., 1979-80; food editor, restaurant critic Daily Herald, Arlington Heights, Ill., 1980-88; editor in chief Cook's mag., Bridgeport, Conn., 88-90; food Editor Sun-Sentinel, Ft Lauderdale, Fla., 1990—; cons. newsletter, Cuisinart Corp., Greenwich Conn., 1985-88. Recipient Golden Carnation award, 1986, James Beard Journalism award. Mem. Am. Inst. of Wine and Food, Assoc. of Food Journalists; restaurant award com. for James Beard Found. Office: Sun-Sentinel 200 E Las Olas Blvd Ste 1000 Fort Lauderdale FL 33301-2293

HARTZ, JILL, museum director; b. Montreal, Que., Can., July 25, 1950. Undergrad. study, Oberlin U., 1969-71; MA in English Lang. and Lit. with honors, U. St. Andrews, Scotland, 1973; student, Cornell U., 1989-94. Mgr. Tompkins County Arts Coun., Ithaca, 1981-82, Grapevine Graphics, Ithaca, 1982-83; co-editor Grapevine Weekly Mag., Ithaca, 1983-84, Living Publs., Ithaca, 1984-86; coord. exhbns., asst. to dir. Herbert F. Johnson Mus. of Art, Cornell U., 1976-81; dir. pub. rels. and publs. Herbert F. Johnson Mus. of Art, Cornell U., Ithaca, 1986-93; asst. to chair, dept. of art Cornell U., Ithaca, 1993-94; coord. pub. rels. and spl. programs Coun. for the Arts, Cornell U., Ithaca, 1993-94; dir. comm. Arts & Scis. Devel. Office, U. Va., Charlottesville, 1994-97; interim dir. Bayly Art Mus., U. Va., Charlottesville, 1997, dir., 1997—; co-curator Agnes Denes exhbn., 1991-92, editor monograph; co-founder, ptnr. LunaMedia pub. rels. co., Ithaca, 1993-94. Mem. Am. Assn. Museums, Nat. Cultural Alliance. Fax: 804-924-6321. Office: Bayly Art Mus U Va Rugby Rd Charlottesville VA 22903*

HARTZ, LUETTA BERTHA, account executive; b. Sept. 29, 1947; d. Alfred Bernard Carl and Bertha Martha (Stauffer) Janz; m. James Patrick Hartz, Dec. 31, 1975 (dec. 1995). Student, Madison Bus. Coll., 1965-66. With Employers Ins. of Wausau, Wis., 1966-68; casualty rater Sentry Ins. Co., Stevens Point, 1968-70, casualty supr., 1970-71, casualty tranor, 1971-72, customer svc. corr., 1972-74, bur. technician, 1974-75; customer svc. and acctg. mgr. Sentry Ins. Co., Concord, Mass., 1975-79, personal lines property processing mgr., 1979-81, personal lines casualty processing mgr., 1981-83, comml. lines underwriting svcs. mgr., 1983-85, comml. lines ops. mgr., 1985-87; agt. Lewis P. Bither Ins. Agy., Inc., Tewksbury and Tyngsboro, Mass., 1988-90; acct. rep. Brewer & Lord LLP, Acton, Mass., 1990-98, acct. exec., 1998—. Campaign treas. Reps., county clk. candidate, Portage County, Wis., 1972. Mem. U.S. Golf Assn. (assoc.), Nat. Assn. Ins. Women, Mass. Assn. Ins. Women (Middlesex chpt. 1984-96), Maynard Country Club (bd. govs. 1984-86, 96-97). Roman Catholic. Home: 40 Drummer Rd Acton MA 01720-5202

HARTZ, RENEE SEMO, cardiothoracic surgeon; b. Bessemer Twp., Mich., Dec. 7, 1946; d. Rita Ann Semo; children: Tyler Joseph, Colin Wilson. BA, Western Mich. U., 1969; MD, Northwestern U., 1974. Diplomate Am. Bd. Surgery, Am. Bd. Thoracic Surgery. Intern pediatrics Children's Meml. Hosp., Chgo., 1974-75; intern gen. surgery Northwestern Meml. Hosp., Chgo., 1975-76, resident gen. surgery, 1976-79; chief resident cardiothoracic surgery Northwestern Meml. Hosp., 1979-81; instr. dept. surgery Northwestern U. Med. Sch., Chgo., 1978-81, assoc. in surgery, 1981-85; asst. prof. surgery med. sch. Northwestern U., Chgo., 1985-87, assoc. prof. surgery med. sch., 1987-92; prof. surgery, chief div. cardiothoracic surgery U. Ill. Hosp. & Clinics, Chgo., 1992-97; prof. surgery dept. surgery divsn. of cardiothoracic surgery Tulane U. Sch. of Medicine, New Orleans, La., 1997—; apptd. to Northwestern Meml. Hosp., Chgo., Children's Meml. Hosp., Chgo., VA Lakeside Hosp., Chgo., Evanston (Ill.) Hosp., Columbus Hosp., Chgo.; laser researcher Northwestern U. Med. Sch., 1984—, U. of Ill. Hosp., West Suburban Hosp., Ill. Masonic Hosp. Contbr. articles to profl. jours.; contbr. chpts. to Perioperative Cardiac Dysfunction II, 1985, General Thoracic Surgery, 1989, New Technology in Vascular Surgery, 1988. Mem. Am. Coll. Chest Physicians, Am. Coll. Surgeons, Am. Heart Assn., Am. Women's Med. Assn., Assn. for Acad. Surgery, Chgo. Heart Assn., Chgo. Surg. Soc., Ill. Surg. Soc., Laser Inst. Am., Soc. Thoracic Surgeons, Soc. Univ. Surgeons, Am. Assn. Thoracic Surgeons, Sigma Xi. Avocations: wind surfing, gourmet cooking, spending time with sons. Office: Tulane U Sch of Medicine 1430 Tulane Ave # Sl22 New Orleans LA 70112-2699*

HARTZ, STEVEN EDWARD MARSHALL, lawyer, educator; b. Cambridge, Mass., July 11, 1948; s. Louis and Stella (Feinberg) H.; m. Janice Lindsay, June 12, 1976. A.B. magna cum laude, Harvard Coll., 1970; J.D. U. Chgo., 1974. Bar: N.Y. 1975, U.S. Dist. Ct. (so. and ea. dists.) N.Y. 1975, Fla. 1979, U.S. Dist. Ct. (so. dist.) Fla. 1979, U.S. Ct. Appeals (2d cir.) 1975, U.S. Tax Ct. 1979, U.S. Ct. Appeals (5th cir.) 1979, U.S. Ct. Appeals (11th cir.) 1981, U.S. Supreme Ct. 1979, U.S. Dist. Ct. (mid. dist.) Fla. 1984. Assoc. Cleary, Gottlieb, Steen & Hamilton, N.Y.C., 1974-79; asst. U.S. atty. U.S. Dept. Justice, Miami, Fla., 1979-82, dep. chief criminal div., chief fraud and pub. corruption sect. 1981-82; sole practice, Miami, Fla., 1982-90; of counsel Akerman, Senterfitt & Eidson, P.A., Miami, 1980, ptnr./shareholder, 1991—; lectr. dept. English, U. Miami 1984, adj. assoc. prof., 1985-86. Co-author: Housing, A Community Handbook, 1973. Vol. atty. M.F.Y. Legal Services, N.Y.C., 1978. Recipient Dirs.' award U.S. Dept. Justice, 1981; Fulbright Hays scholar, 1970. Mem. ABA, Fla. Bar, Assn. Bar City N.Y., N.Y. State Bar Assn., Fed. Bar Assn., Dade County Bar Assn., Nat. Assn. Criminal Def. Lawyers, Phi Beta Kappa. Office: One Southeast 3rd Ave 28th Fl Miami FL 33131-4943

HARTZELL, ANDREW CORNELIUS, JR., lawyer, retired; b. Balt., Nov. 5, 1927; s. Andrew Cornelius and Mary Frances (Milholland) H.; m. Mary Leontine McPhillips, July 31, 1954; children: Andrew Cornelius III, Stephen

Carroll, Mary Leontine, James Francis, John Michael, Peter Milholland. B.A., Yale U., 1950, LL.B., 1953. Bar: N.Y. 1953, Ohio 1955, U.S. Supreme Ct. Law clk. Fed. Judge Irving R. Kaufman, N.Y.C., 1953-54; assoc. Thompson, Hine & Flory, Cleve., 1954-63, Debevoise, Plimpton, Lyons & Gates, N.Y.C., 1963-65; ptnr. Debevoise and Plimpton and predecessor firms, 1966-96, chmn. litigation dept., 1989-92, of counsel, 1996-98. Author: The Treacherous Snows, 1993; contbr. articles to legal jours. and to Antitrust Advisor, McGraw-Hill Pub. Co., 1971, 78; Note and Comment editor Yale Law Jour, 1952-53. Mem. bd. archtl. rev. Village of Scarsdale, N.Y., 1965-67; mem. Adv. Coun. on Environ. Conservation, 1986-90, chmn., 1987-89; mem. Sch. Facilities Adv. Com., 1988-90; bd. dirs. Friends of Scarsdale Parks, 1991—; Bd. Assessment Review, 1998—; Rep. candidate for Congress 18th dist. N.Y., 1994. With U.S. Army, 1946-48. Fellow Am. Coll. Trial Lawyers; mem. ABA, Union Internat. des Avocats. Roman Catholic. Clubs: Yale of N.Y., Town and Village (Scarsdale), Am. Alpine. Home: 7 E Woods Ln Scarsdale NY 10583-6401 Office: Debevoise & Plimpton 875 3rd Ave Fl 23 New York NY 10022-6256

HARTZELL, CHARLES R., research administrator, biochemist, cell biologist; b. Butler, Pa., Aug. 12, 1941; s. Charles R. and Ada Grace (Giles) H.; m. Marguerite K. Getty; children: Scott David, Amy Lynette. BS, Geneva Coll., 1963; PhD, Indiana U., 1967. Post-doctoral fellow Ind. U., Bloomington, 1967; rsch. fellow Commonwealth Sci. and Industry Rsch. Orgn., Melbourne, Australia, 1967-68; rsch. fellow, asst. rsch. prof. U. Wis., Madison, 1968-71; asst. prof. Pa. State U., University Park, 1971-75, assoc. prof., 1975-78; sr. rsch. scientist Alfred I. DuPont Inst., Wilmington, Del., 1978-80, dir. rsch., 1981-97; dir. rsch. Nemours Children's Clinics, Fla., 1987—; rsch. mgr. The Nemours Found., Jacksonville, 1987—; prof. pediatrics Jefferson Med. Coll., Phila., 1989—. Contbr. articles to profl. jours. NIH fellow, 1968-70; established investigator Am. Heart Assn., 1970-75. Mem. Am. Chem. Soc., Am. Soc. Biochemistry and Molecular Biology, Biophys. Soc., Am. Soc. Cell Biology, AAAS. Republican. Presbyterian. Avocations: ballroom dancing, music, carpentry, exercise. Office: The Nemours Found 807 Nira St Jacksonville FL 32207-8426 also: Nemours Children's Clinic PO Box 5720 Jacksonville FL 32247-5720

HARTZELL, IRENE JANOFSKY, psychologist; b. L.A. Vor-Diplom, U. Munich, 1961; *Irene Hartzell's parents are Leonard S. and Annelies Janofsky. Father Leonard S. Janofsky is founding partner of the law firm of Paul, Hastings, Janofsky & Walker and past president of the American Bar Association. Son Mark Adam Hartzell received a BA 1994 from University of California and an MFA 1998 Loyola Marymount University. He is an assistant video/film editor and member of the Screen Editors Guild in Los Angeles* BA, U. Calif., Berkeley, 1963, MA, 1965; PhD, U. Oreg., 1970. Lic. psychologist, Wash., Ariz. Psychologist Lake Washington Sch. Dist., Kirkland, Wash., 1971-72; staff psychologist VA Med. Ctr., Seattle, 1970-71, Long Beach, Calif., 1973-74; dir. parent edn. Children's Hosp., Orange, Calif., 1975-78; clin. psychologist Kaiser Permanente, Woodland Hills, Calif., 1979-94; clin. instr. dept. pediatrics U. Calif. Irvine Coll. Medicine, 1975-78. Author: The Study Skills Advantage, 1986; contbr. articles to profl. jours. Intern Oreg. Legislature, 1974-75. U.S. Vocat. Rehab. Adminstrn. fellow U. Oreg., 1966-67, 69. Mem. APA, Pi Lambda Theta.

HARTZELL, JOHN MASON, poet, service technician; b. Hardtner, Kans., Jan. 23, 1945; s. Kenneth and Freda Irene (Hamilton) H. AA in Nursing, Pratt County Jr. Coll., 1965; BA in Sociology, Southwestern Coll., 1973. Service technician Automacic Coin Machine Corp., Winfield, Kans., 1975—. Contbr. poetry to anthologies and profl. publs. Recipient numerous awards for poetry, including Nat. Libr. Poetry, Internat. Soc. Poets, Kans. Author's Club. Mem. VFW, Am. Legion, Kiwanis. Presbyterian. Avocations: collecting records, horseshoes, poetry. Home: 1434 E 1st Ave Winfield KS 67156-1808

HARTZLER, GENEVIEVE LUCILLE, physical education educator; b. Hammond, Ind., June 19, 1921; d. Lewis Garvin and Effie May (Orton) H. BS in Edn., Ind. U., 1944; MEd, U. Minn., 1948. Tchr. phys. edn. Griffith (Ind.) Pub. Schs., 1944-45, Northrup Collegiate Sch., Mpls., 1945-47; supr. student tchrs., 1947-79; tchr. phys. edn. Marquette (Mich.) Pub. Schs., 1948-50, Albion (Mich.) Pub. Schs., 1951-56; tchr. phys. edn. Jackson (Mich.) Pub. Schs., 1957-79, coord., project dir., tchr., coach, 1979-83; chair equity workshop Jackson Pub. Schs., 1979-83; chair various convs., 1964-70. Mem. Am. Heart Assn., Jackson, 1977-83; mem., chair Women in Mgmt., Jackson, 1981-83; mem. Bus. and Profl. Women, Jackson, 1980-90. Recipient Honor awards Young Woman's Christian Assn. and Mich. Divsn. Girls and Women's Sports. Mem. AAHPERD, NEA, Mich. Assn. Health, Phys. Edn. and Recreation (Honor award), Mich. Edn. Assn. (Women's Cultural award), Delta Kappa Gamma (Woman of Distinction award). Avocations: golf, swimming, travel, reading. Home: 703 Bay Meadows Cir Lady Lake FL 32159-2285

HARTZLER, GEOFFREY OLIVER, retired cardiologist; b. Goshen, Ind., Nov. 6, 1946; s. Robert Willis and Emma Irene (Blosser) H.; m. Lois Anne Kauffman, June 1967 (div. May 1983); children: Abigail, Christine, Amanda; m. Dorothy Eloise Arnn, July 1985. BA, Goshen Coll., 1968; MD with honors, Ind. U., 1972. Diplomate Am. Bd. Internal Medicine, Bd. in Cardiovascular Disease. Intern Mayo Grad. Sch. Medicine, Rochester, Minn., 1972-73; fellow in medicine Mayo Grad. Sch. Medicine, Rochester, 1973-74, fellow in cardiology, 1974-76; assoc. cons. internal medicine and cardiovascular disease Mayo Clinic, Rochester, 1976-77; instr. medicine Mayo Med. Sch. and Grad. Sch. Medicine, Rochester, 1976-79; cons. cardiovascular disease and internal medicine Mayo Clinic and Mayo Found., Rochester, 1977-80; dir. invasive diagnostic electrophysiology Mayo Clinic, Rochester, Minn., 1979-80; cardiologist Cardiovascular Cons., Inc., Kansas City, Mo., 1980-93; clin. prof. medicine U. Mo., Kansas City, 1985-95; cons. cardiologist Mid-Am. Heart Inst., Kansas City, 1980-95; dir. advanced angioplasty fellowship program St. Luke's Hosp., Kansas City, 1985-92, med. dir. cardiovascular clin. rsch. ctr. Mid-Am. Heart Inst., 1993-95; cons. Advanced Cardiovascular Systems, Inc., Santa Clara, Calif., 1983-95; past mem. editl. or rev. bd. Am. Jour. Cardiology, Jour. Am. Coll. Cardiology, Cath. and CV Diagnosis, others; co-founder Ventritex, Inc., Sunnyvale, Calif., 1985-88, Triax Internat., Inc., Lenexa, Kans., 1989-96; prin., bd. dirs. Kustom Signals, Inc., Lenexa, 1990-96, LMP Steel & Wire Co., Maryville, Mo., 1992—, Hartz Properties, Inc., Prarie Village, Kans., 1993—, Lett Electronics, Inc., Topeka, 1995-98, Intraluminal Therapeutics, Inc., Kansas City, Kans., 1997—. Contbr. articles to profl. jours., chpts. to books; made TV presentations to lay people on aspects of cardiology. Recipient KK Chen award, 1970, E.V. Allen scholarship, 1971, Osler award U. Miami, 1986, 1st Ann. Career Achievement award Cardiol. Rsch. Found., 1994. Fellow Am. Coll. Cardiology, Coun. on Clin. Cardiology of Am. Heart Assn., Soc. for Cardiac Angiography; mem. AMA, Mo. State Med. Assn., Jackson County Med. Assn., Am. Heart Assn., Alpha Omega Alpha. Avocations: music, motorcycling, reading, travel, business. Office: 2600 Verona Rd Shawnee Mission KS 66208-1266

HARTZLER, VICKY J., state legislator. Mem. Mo. Ho. of Reps., Jefferson City, 1998—. Address: 22804 E 299th St Harrisonville MO 64701-6320*

HARTZOG, WILLIAM W., retired military officer. BA in English, Citadel Mil. Coll. of S.C.; MA in Psychology, Appalachian State U.; grad., USMC Command and Staff Coll., U.S. Army War Coll. Commd. 2d lt. U.S. Army, 1963, advanced through grades to gen., 1994, ret., 1998; staff officer, team chief, then chief war plans divsn. Office of Dep. Chief of Staff for Ops. and Plans, U.S. Army, Washington, 1981-84; exec. officer Office of Comdg. Gen. U.S. Army Tng. and Doctrine Command, Ft. Monroe, Va., 1984-85; comdr. 197th Infantry Brigade, Ft. Benning, Ga., 1985-87; asst. commandant U.S. Army Infantry Sch., Ft. Benning, 1987-89; comdg. gen. 1st Infantry Divsn. and Ft. Riley, Ft. Riley, Kans., 1991-93; dep. comdr. in chief, chief of staff U.S. Atlantic Command, Norfolk, Va., 1993-94; comdg. gen. U.S. Army Tng. and Doctrine Command, Ft. Monroe, 1994-98. Decorated Def. Disting. Svc. medal with oak leaf cluster, Disting. Svc. medal with oak leaf cluster, Legion of Merit with 4 oak leaf clusters, Bronze Star medal with V device and oak leaf cluster, Purple Heart, Meritorious Svc. medal with oak leaf cluster.

HARVAN, ROBIN ANN, health professions educator; b. Paterson, N.J., July 24, 1955; d. Robert L. and Victoria A. (Martin) Muccio; m. Christopher Harvan, Oct. 22, 1977. AAS cum laude, Felician Coll., Lodi, N.J., 1976; BS, Montclair (N.J.) State Coll., 1979; EdM, Rutgers U., 1983, EdD, 1989. Registered med. lab. technician. Med. lab. technician Holy Name Hosp., Teaneck, N.J., 1976; sr. lab. technician Warner-Lambert Co., Morris Plains, N.J., 1976-79; curriculum project coord. Rutgers U. Vocat.-Tech. Project, Piscataway, N.J., 1982; dental office mgr. J.C. Harvan, Manalapan, N.J., 1979-84; adj. instr. Montclair State Coll., 1984; grad. teaching asst. Rutgers U. Grad. Sch. Edn., New Brunswick, N.J., 1984-85, affiliate asst. prof., 1985-89; asst. prof. dept. interdisciplinary studies U. Medicine and Dentistry N.J., Newark, 1985-91, assoc. prof. clin. interdisciplinary studies, 1991-95; assoc. dir. grad. program in allied health edn. Rutgers U. Grad. Sch. Edn. & U. Medicine and Dentistry N.J., Newark, 1985-89, dir. grad. program in health professions edn., 1989-95, chair dept. interdisciplinary studies, 1992-95; dir. Office of Edn. U. Colo. Health Sci. Ctr., Denver, 1995—; chairperson com. on continuing edn. Sch. Health Related Professions U. Medicine and Dentistry of N.J., Newark, 1991-95; mem. faculty devel. Sch. Health Related Professions U. Medicine & Dentistry N.J., Newark, 1992-95; mem. univ.-wide adv. com. on continuing edn. U. Medicine and Dentistry N.J., Newark, 1992-95; chair teaching com., chair bridge to future program, co-chair campus ctr. com. edn. U. Colo., Denver, 1995-98; chmn. edn. vision team U. Colo. Health Sci. Ctr., 1998—, chairperson tchg. com., 1995—; chairperson multicompetent practitioner task force U. Medicine and Dentistry N.J. Sch. Health-Related Professions, 1989-90, mem. task force on grad. edn., 1987-95, mem. task force on grading policy, 1987-89; ednl. cons. N.J. Dental Sch., 1992-95; ednl. specialist Nat. Assn. Trade and Tech. Sch. Accreditation Team, 1984-95. Contbr. articles to profl. jours., chpts. to books. Grantee N.J. Dept. Higher Edn., 1981-82, 86-88, 95-98; recipient Excellence award Rutgers U. Alumni Assn., 1990. Mem. Assn. Schs. Allied Health Profns. (Outstanding Poster award 1992, state chpts. com. 1988-95, ethics com. 1994—, chair ethics com. 1995—), Am. Soc. Med. Tech., Assn. Moral Edn. (honorable mention award 1991), Soc. Health and Human Values, Am. Soc. Clin. Pathologists (assoc.), N.J. Soc. Allied Health Profns. (pres. 1987-89, 94-95, editor newsletter 1983-85, chair publs. com., pub. rels. com. 1984-86), Kappa Delta Pi, Omicron Tau Theta. Avocations: doll artist, ceramist, crafts artist, botanical illustrator, graphic artist. Home: 3100 S Pleasant View Dr Castle Rock CO 80104-2856 Office: U Colo Health Scis Ctr/Office Edn Campus Box A075 Denver CO 80262

HARVARD, BEVERLY JOYCE BAILEY, protective service official; b. Macon, Ga., Dec. 22, 1950; d. Arcelious and Irene (Perkins) Bailey; m. Jimmy C. Harvard, 1972; 1 child: Christa. BA, Morris Brown Coll., 1972; MS, Ga. State U., 1980. Cert. FBI Nat. Acad. Police officer Police Bur. City of Atlanta, crime analysis officer Police Bur., exec. protection officer Police Bur., dep. chief of police, spl. asst. to commr. dept. pub. safety, dir. pub. affairs dept. pub. safety, chief of police, 1994—; commr. Commn. Accreditation for Law Enforcement Agys., 1991; bd. dirs. Met. Atlanta ARC, 1991, Coun. on Battered Women, 1991; trustee Leadership Atlanta, 1991; adv. bd. dir. Big Bros./Big Sisters, 1986—, Atlanta Victim/Witness Assistance Program, 1985—. Named Outstanding Atlantan, 1983, Alumna Yr., Morris Brown Coll., 1985, Bronze Woman Yr., Iota Phi Lambda, 1986, Woman Achiever Atlanta YWCA; recipient Trailblazer award for Law Enforcement City of Atlanta. Mem. Internat. Assn. Chiefs Police (tng. com. Ga. chpt.), Nat. Orgn. Black Law Enforcement (chmn. program), Bus. System Planning Team, Ga. State U. Alumni Assn. (bd. dirs. Atlanta chpt.), Delta Sigma Theta (parliamentarian). Office: Police Svcs City Hall 9th Fl 675 Ponce De Leon Ave NE Atlanta GA 30308-1829*

HARVEGO, EDWIN ALLAN, mechanical engineer; b. Vallejo, Calif., June 5, 1943; s. Edwin Simon and Bette Jean (Owens) H.; m. Lisa Ann Actis; children: Jessica Marie, Joshua Michael, Erin Alane, Deidre Denise. BSME, U. Calif., Berkeley, 1966, MSME, 1967. Registered profl. engr., Calif., Idaho. Sr. preliminary design engr. AiResearch Mfg. Co., L.A., 1967-72; sr. engr. Gen. Atomic, San Diego, 1972-76; sci. and engring. supr. EG&G Idaho, Inc., Idaho Falls, Idaho, 1976-80, br. mgr., 1980-84, sr. engring. specialist, 1984-91, tech. unit mgr., 1991-94; consulting engr., group leader Lockheed Martin Idaho Techs. Co., Idaho Falls, 1994—; course developer, tchr. internat. workshop, 1997. Author: (tech. publ.) Topics in Two-Phase Heat Transfer and Flow, 1978, (book chpt.) Nuclear Space Power Systems, 1987. Fellow ASME (chmn. nuclear heat exch. com. 1986-88, chmn. Idaho sect. 1989-90, chmn. nuclear engring. divsn. 1992-93, mem. energy conversion bd. 1993—, v.p. energy conversion group 1998—, rep. U.S. Nat. Com. World Energy Coun., 1998—). Achievements include development of Nuclear Regulatory Commission severe accident and fuel behavior codes at Idaho National Engineering Lab; development of advanced reactor concept for space and terrestrial applications; lead planning and analysis for loss-of-fluid test international test program; development of analysis methods for high-temperature gas-cooled reactor. Avocations: golf, rafting, skiing. Office: Lockheed Martin Idaho Techs Co 2525 N Fremont Idaho Falls ID 83415

HARVEY, ALBERT C., lawyer; m. Nancy Rutherford; children: Anne, Elizabeth. BS, U. Tenn., 1961, J.D., 1967. Asst. pub. defender Tenn. Supreme Ct.; asst. to pub. defender Shelby County, 1969-71; ptnr. Thomason, Hendrix, Harvey, Johnson & Mitchell, Memphis; instr. med. and dental jurisprudence U. Tenn., Memphis. Bd. editors Tennessee Law Review. Pres. Goodwill Boys Club, 1983-85; active YMCA, Arthritis Found., Citizens Assn. Memphis and Shelby County, Shelby County War Memls.; sr. warden of vestry Calvary Episcopal Ch. Maj. gen. USMCR, comdg. gen. 4th Marine div. Recipient Sam A. Myar, Jr. award Tenn. Bd. Law Examiners, 1978. Fellow Am. Bar Found. (life), Tenn. Bar Found. (pres. 1993-94); mem. ABA (bd. govs., ho. dels. charter mem. and coun. sect. litigation, young lawyers sect., fellow young lawyers divsn., com. on ethics and profl. responsibilty, ethics 2000 spl. com.), Am. Judicature Soc. (nat. bd. dirs.), Am. Bd. Trial Advocates (advocate), Tenn. Bar Assn. (bd. govs., pres. young lawyers conf.), Memphis Bar Assn. (v.p. 1989, pres. elect 1990, pres. 1991, pres. young lawyers divsn.), U. Tenn. Nat. Alumni Assn. (pres. Memphis chpt., nat. bd. govs.), Ctrl. Garden Area Assn. (pres.), Memphis Area C. of C. (pres. mil. affairs coun.), Navy League, Phoenix Club (1st v.p.), Kiwanis, University Club of Memphis (v.p.). Office: 1 Commerce Sq 29th Fl Memphis TN 38103

HARVEY, ALEXANDER, II, federal judge; b. Balt., May 3, 1923; s. Fred B. and Rose (Hopkins) H.; m. Mary E. Williams, Feb. 24, 1951; children: Elizabeth H., Alexander IV. BA, Yale U., 1947; LLB, Columbia U., 1950. Bar: Md. 1950. Assoc. Ober, William, Grimes & Stinson, Balt., 1950-66, ptnr., 1953-66; asst. atty. gen. Md., 1957-58; judge U.S. Dist. Ct. Md., 1966-86, chief judge, 1986-91; sr. judge U.S. Dist. Ct. Md., Balt., 1991—; mem. Gov.'s Com. To Study Blue Sky Law of Md., 1961; mem. character com. Ct. Appeals Md. for 8th Jud. Cir. Bd. dirs. Balt. Symphony Assn., 1966-68; pres., dir. Balt. Opera Guild, 1960; bd. dirs. Balt. Coun. Social Agys., 1957-63; trustee Ch. Home and Hosp., Balt., 1952-71. 1st lt. AUS, World War II, ETO. Mem. Am., Md., Balt. bar assns., Phi Beta Kappa. Episcopalian (vestry 1967-70). Home: 7300 Brightside Rd Baltimore MD 21212-1011 Office: US Dist Ct 101 W Lombard St Ste 404 Baltimore MD 21201-2626

HARVEY, ANDRE, sculptor; b. Hollywood, Fla., Oct. 9, 1941; s. Edmund H. and Jeanne C. (Bright) H.; m. Roberta R. Rush, Jan. 12, 1964. BA, U. Va., 1963. Sculptor Rockland, Del., 1971—. Exhbns. include: Images of Am. Exhbn., Moscow, London, Paris, The Internat. Ctr. for Wildlife Art, Gloucester, U.K., Nat. Sculpture Soc., N.Y.C., NSS Port of History Mus., Phila., Nat. Acad. of Design, N.Y.C., Tiffany & Co., N.Y.C., Nat. Audubon Soc., N.Y.C., Hunter Mus., Chattanooga, Brandywine River Mus., Chadds Ford, Pa., Gibbes Art Gallery, Charleston, S.C., Phila. Flower Show, Longwood Gardens, Kennett Square, Pa., Contemporary Sculpture at Chesterwood, Stockbridge, Mass., Palazzo Mediceo, Seravezza, Italy, others; selected pub. collections include: The Frederik Meijer Gardens, Grand Rapids, Mich., Brandywine River Mus., Chadds Ford, Pa., Botanic Garden Ctr. & Conservatory, Ft. Worth, Tex., MBNA Am., Wilmington, Del., Nature in Art Trust, Gloucester, U.K., U. Va., Charlottesville, Del. Art Mus., Wilmington, Greenville Mus., S.C., The Jockey Club, Washington, Crown Controls Corp., New Bremen, Ohio, others; specific bronze sculptures include: The Sunbathers, Gamecock: Floyd's Finest, The Phoenix, First Light, Helen, Chloe and Lucinda, Scent of Honeysuckle, Water's Edge, The Survivor, others. Recipient Joel Meissner award Nat. Sculpture Soc., N.Y.C., 1980, Tallix Foundry award, 1989. Fellow Nat. Sculpture Soc.; mem. Nature in Art Trust, Artist's Equity, Internat. Sculpture Ctr. Avocation: automobile preservation. Home: PO Box 8 Rockland DE 19732-0008

HARVEY, ARTHUR JOHN, landscape architect, golf course architect; b. Lansing, Mich., May 9, 1963; s. William Thomas and Marie Cornelia (Cook) H.; m. Kim Caswell Crosthwaite, Sept. 3, 1989 (div. Dec. 1996); 1 child, Kristen Marie; m. Caroline T. Thees, July 17, 1998. AS in Landscape Architecture Tech., Lansing C.C., 1985; B in Landscape Architecture with honors, Mich. State U., 1988. Golf course design and constrn. Robert Trent Jones, Sr., Montclair, N.J., Fort Lauderdale, Fla., 1988-85; golf course design and constrn. Roger Rulewich Group, L.L.C., Bernardston, Mass., 1995—, Long Valley, N.J., 1995—. Mem. Am. Soc. Landscape Architects, Am. Soc. Golf Course Archs., Golf Course Supt.'s Assn., U.S. Golf Assn., Oldsmobile Club Am. Republican. Roman Catholic. Avocations: golf, classic auto restoration, sketching, hiking, reading. Home: 491 Naughright Rd Long Valley NJ 07853 Office: Roger Rulewich Group LLC 160 Purple Meadow Rd Bernardston MA 01337-9662

HARVEY, AUBREY EATON, III, industrial engineer; b. Charlottesville, Va., Oct. 20, 1944; s. Aubrey Eaton Jr. and Jaquelin Ambler (Nicholas) H.; m. Elizabeth Dillard Pettit, June 6, 1964; children: Eleanor Taylor, Philip Ambler. BS, U. Ark., 1966; MA, U. Va., 1970; PhD, U. Ark., 1974. Asst. prof. indsl. engring. dept. Tex. A&M U., College Station, 1973-74; asst. prof. dept. systems analysis Miami U., Oxford, Ohio, 1974-78; analyst computer svc. Norfolk and Western Railway, Roanoke, Va., 1978-80, systems analyst computer svc., 1980-83; ops. rsch. analyst Norfolk (Va.) Southern Corp., 1983-90, sr. ops. rsch. analyst, 1991; rsch. assoc. Va. Polytech Inst. and State U., Blacksburg, 1991-93, rsch. scientist, 1993-94; sr. ops. rsch. analyst Rsch. Mgmt. Cons., Inc., McLean, Va., 1994-95; adv. knowledge engr. Elec. Data Systems Corp., Herndon, Va., 1995-99; sr. sys. analyst Elec. Data Systems Corp., Herndon, 1999—; cons. Ark. Dept. Labor, Little Rock, 1971-72, Ark. Health Systems Found., Little Rock, 1972-73; adj. faculty Va. Polytech Inst. and State U., 1980-85. Contbr. articles to profl. jours. Pres. U. Va. Law and Grad. Young Reps., Charlottesville, 1969; treas. Va. Young Reps., Richmond, 1970, 71. Mem. Inst. Ops. Rsch. and Mgmt. Scis., Inst. Indsl. Engrs. (divsn. dir. 1983-84), Disting. Svc. award 1985), Sigma Xi, Alpha Pi Mu, Omega Rho. Episcopalian. Achievements include development of a track quality index; developed a consensus measure; developed the immigration and naturalization svc. compensation expert system and attorney scheduling expert system. Home: 11019 Saffold Way Reston VA 20190-3804

HARVEY, BIRT, retired pediatrician, educator; b. Teheran, Iran, Nov. 24, 1928; five children. BA, Johns Hopkins U., 1948; MD, N.Y.U., 1952. Pvt. practice, 1958-88; prof. pediat. emeritus Stanford U., Palo Alto, Calif., 1995—; past sr. fellow Inst. Health, Policy Studies, U. Calif., San Francisco. Mem. Inst. Med. Nat. Acad. Scis. (emeritus), Am. Acad. Pediatrics (past pres.). E-mail: birtharvey@aol.com.

HARVEY, BRYAN LAURENCE, crop science educator; b. Newport, Gwent, Wales, U.K., Nov. 1, 1937; came to Can., 1948; s. Laurence W.J. and Irene E.D. (Stoneman) H.; m. Eileen Bernice Pfeifer, Sept. 24, 1961; children: Donald, James. BSA, U. Sask., 1960, MSc, 1961; PhD U. Calif.-Davis, 1964. Asst. prof. crop sci. U. Guelph, Ont., Can., 1964-66; from asst. prof. to prof. crop sci. U. Sask., Saskatoon, 1966—, head dept. crop sci. and plant ecology, 1983-94, head dept. horticulture, 1994-97, univ. coord. agrl. rsch., 1997—; dir. Crop Devel. Ctr., 1983-94, asst. dean Coll. Agr., 1980-83; vis. prof. U. Nairobi, Kenya, 1975; dir. accreditation Agr. Inst. Can., 1996—; chmn. Can. Expert Com. Grain Breeding, 1984-89, Can. Expert Com. on Plant gene resources, 1986-93, Can. Adv. Com. on Variety Registration, 1987-95, Can. Prairie Registration Recommending Com. for Grain, 1989-95, Can. Adv. Com. on Plant Breeders Rights, 1986—, Barley Devel. Coun., 1994-96, Can. Com. on Crops, 1996—, Can. Agrifood Rsch. Coun., 1993—. Developed 36 varieties of barley; contbr. articles to sci. jours. on plant genetics. Recipient Outstanding Svc. award Master Brewers of the Ams., 1996, Significant Sci. Contbn. award Can. Seed Trade Assn., 1997. Fellow Agrl. Inst. Can. (pres. 1994-95, Fellowship award 1990), Am. Soc. Agronomy, Crop Sci. Soc. Am.; mem. Assn. Faculties of Agr. Can. (pres. 1982-83), Barley Genetics Congress (pres. 1986-91, 96-2000), Am. Barley Workers (pres. 1970-74), Can. Seed Growers Assn. (hon. life), Sask. Seed Growers Assn. (hon. life), Rotary (pres. 1987-89). Office: U Sask, 204 Kirk Hall 117 Sci Pl, Saskatoon, SK Canada S7N 5C8

HARVEY, CALVIN REA, lawyer; b. Saxonburg, Pa., Sept. 25, 1943; s. Howard F. and Evelyn (Rea) H.; m. Patricia McCabe, May 30, 1987; children: Jesse F., Matthew N. AB, Washington and Jefferson Coll., 1965; JD, George Washington U., 1968. Bar: Pa. 1968. Ptnr. Buchanan Ingersoll P.C., Pitts., 1968—. Mem. ABA, Pa. Bar Assn., Alleghany County Bar Assn., Am. Coll. Real Estate Lawyers, Duquesne Club, Pitts. Field Club. Presbyterian. Home: 71 Fair Oaks Dr Pittsburgh PA 15238-1936 Office: Buchanan Ingersoll PC One Oxford Centre 301 Grant St Fl 20 Pittsburgh PA 15219-1410

HARVEY, CHRISTINE LYNN, publishing executive; b. Bklyn., Dec. 7, 1962. AS in Liberal Arts, Nassau C.C., 1982; BA in Comm. Arts, Adelphi U., 1985. Cert. EMT, 1983-86. Franchise mgr. N.Y. Daily News, Mineola, 1981-84; copywriter, vido prodr., 1984-85; pub. rels. assoc. King Features Syndicate, N.Y.C., 1986; account exec. Promotional Broadcasting Svc., Babylon, N.Y., 1986-87; sr. account mgr. L.I. Bus. News, Ronkonkoma, N.Y., 1987-91; sr. ptnr. Karen Saeger Assocs., Stony Brook, N.Y., 1990—; editor The Steuben News, Ridgewood, N.Y., 1992—; founder, pub., editor-in-chief New Living, Stony Brook, 1991—; pub. rels. cons. Am. Health Found., Valhalla, N.Y., 1994—; TV prodr./dir./host New Living Prodns., Stony Brook, 1997—; cofounder Fama/Harvey Prodns., S.I., N.Y., 1998; TV prodr. Outlook Mag., 1985; TV news reporter, field prodr. LI News Tonite, 1984. Mem. Stony Brook Runners and Walkers Club (pres., co-founder), Long Island Health and Fitness Assn. (founder, exec. dir. 1996—), Steuben Soc. of Am., Long Island Sports Commn. Avocations: running, swimming, cycling, hiking, golf. Office: New Living 1212 Route 25A Ste 1B Stony Brook NY 11790-1919

HARVEY, COLIN EDWIN, veterinary medicine educator; b. Reading, Berkshire, Eng., May 20, 1944; s. Edwin William Alexander and Marian (Heap) H.; m. Catherine Ellen Rein, May 24, 1969; children—Susan Victoria, Edwin Rein. B.V.Sc., F.R.C.V.S., Bristol U., Eng., 1966; M.A. (hon.), U. Pa., 1974. Intern, resident U. Pa. Sch. Vet. Medicine, Phila., 1966-69, from asst. prof. to assoc. prof., 1969-80, prof. surgery, 1980-92, prof. surgery, dentistry, 1992—, vice chair dept. clin. studies, 1996—; adj. prof. U. Pa. Sch. Dental Medicine, Phila., 1984—. Author: Veterinary Dentistry, 1985, Small Animal Surgery, 1990, Small Animal Dentistry, 1993; others; editor: Vet. Surgery, 1982-87, Jour. Vet. Dentistry, 1994—. Organizer, commr. Fairmount Soccer League, Phila., 1982-87. Recipient Simon award Brit. Small Animal Vet. Assn., 1983, Bourgelat award, 1994. Fellow Acad. Vet. Dentistry (charter, sec. 1987-89), Coll. Physicians Phila., Royal Coll. Vet. Surgeons; mem. AVMA, Am. Coll. Vet. Surgery (diplomate), Am. Vet. Dental Coll. (diplomate, charter, pres. 1990-92, Emily award 1993), Am. Vet. Dental Soc. (sec. 1985-89, Edn. and Rsch. award 1995), Internat. Vet. Ear, Nose and Throat Assn. (co-organiser), European Coll. Vet. Surgeons (diplomate). Avocations: reading; walking; watching. Home: 10 Llanfair Rd Apt 2 Ardmore PA 19003-2325 Office: U Pa Sch Vet Medicine 3900 Delancey St Philadelphia PA 19104-6010

HARVEY, CURRAN WHITTHORNE, JR., investment management executive; b. Balt., Dec. 23, 1928; s. Curran Whitthorne and Charlotte C. (Cromwell) H.; m. Marjorie Jo Simons, Apr. 23, 1955; children: Charlotte B., Curran Whitthorne III, Marjorie M., Roland S. B.Engring., Yale U., 1951; postgrad., Columbia U., 1951-52, Johns Hopkins U., 1959-61. Project mgr. Belock Instrument Co., College Point, N.Y., 1954-55; sr. sales engr. Ford Instrument Co. div. Sperry Rand Corp., 1955-59; sales mgr. aerospace div. Aeronca Mfg. Co., 1959-61; security analyst T. Rowe Price Assos., Inc., Balt., 1961-70; vice chmn. bd. T. Rowe Price Assos., Inc., 1974-80, chief operating officer, 1978-81, pres., 1980-84, chief exec. officer, 1981-84, dir., 1970-84; v.p., dir. T. Rowe Price New Horizons Fund, Inc., Balt., 1965-69; pres., dir. T. Rowe Price New Horizons Fund, Inc., 1969-78, chmn. bd., 1978-85; bd. govs. Investment Co. Inst., 1990-95; spl. ptnr. New Enterprise Assocs., 1984—; gen. ptnr. Spectra Enterprise Assocs., 1986—; bd. dirs. Comm. Sys. Tech., Photonic Sys. With USN, 1951-54. Mem. Yale Club (N.Y.C.), Elkridge Club (Balt.), Port Royal Club, Naples Yacht Club. Roman Catholic. Home: 1866 Circle Rd Baltimore MD 21204-6415

HARVEY, DANIEL RICHARD, minister; b. Franklin, Pa., Aug. 27, 1930; s. Richard H. and Dorothy E. (Winder) H.; m. Lois V. Meyers, Mar. 7, 1953; children: Deborah, Stephen, Rebecca, Timothy, Rachel. BA, John Brown U., 1952; postgrad., Moody Bible Inst., 1953-54, Burnside-Ott Aviation, 1970-71. Ordained to ministry Trans World Radio Ch., 1956. Pastor Christian and Missionary Alliance, Siloam Springs, Ark., 1949-52, Urbana, Ill., 1953-55; missionary Trans World Radio, various locations, 1956—; evangelist, 1992—; chaplain Guam Dept. Pub. Safety, Agana, 1975-82, Lakeland, Fla. Police Dept., 1991—; chmn. bd. dirs. Chaplaincy Corps, 1991-93; civilian chaplain USN, Agana, 1975-82; pres. adv. coun. Taccoa Falls (Ga.) Coll., 1996—. Bd. dirs. ARC, Agana, 1976-82. Named to Ancient Order of Chammori, Govt. of Guam, 1982; recipient citation Comdr. Naval Forces Marianas, USN, 1982. Home: 4818 Leisurewood Ln Lakeland FL 33811-1592 Office: Trans World Radio PO Box 8700 Cary NC 27512-8700

HARVEY, DONALD, artist, educator; b. Walthamston, Eng., June 14, 1930; s. Henry and Annie Dorothy (Sawell) H.; m. Elizabeth Clark, Aug. 9, 1952; children—Shan Mary, David Jonathan. Art tchrs. diploma, Brighton Coll. Art, 1951. Art master Ardwyn Grammar Sch., Wales, 1952-56; mem. faculty dept. art U. Victoria, B.C., Can., 1961-95; now prof. emeritus painting U. Victoria. One man exhbns. include, Albert White Gallery, Toronto, 1968, retrospective, Art Gallery of Victoria, 1968; represented in permanent collections, Nat. Gallery Can., Montreal Mus., Albright-Knox Mus., Seattle Art Mus. Mem. accessions com. Art Gallery of Victoria, 1969-72. Can. Council fellow, 1966. Mem. Royal Can. Acad. of Arts (full academician), Can. Group Painters, Can. Painters and Etchers. Home: 1025 Joan Crescent, Victoria, BC Canada V8S 3L3

HARVEY, DONALD FREDERICK, bishop; b. St. John's, Nfld., Can., Sept. 13, 1939; s. Robert J. and Elsie M. (Vaters) H.; m. Gertrude M. Hiscock, Oct. 31, 1964. BA, Meml. U. Nfld., 1984, MA, 1986; MDiv, Queen's Theol. Coll., 1986; DD (hon.), Huron Coll., 1996. Ordained deacon Anglican Ch. Can., 1963, ordained priest, 1964, consecrated bishop, 1993. Asst. priest Parish of Portugal Cove, Nfld., 1963-64; rector Parish of Twillingate, Nfld., 1964-65, Parish of King's Cove, Nfld., 1965-68, Parish of Happy Valley, Labrador, Can., 1968-73, Parish of Portugal Cove, 1973-76, Parish of St. Michael, St. John's, 1976-83; chaplain Univ. Chaplain, St. John's, 1983-89; dean Cathedral of St. John, St. John's, 1989-92; bishop Diocese of Eastern Nfld. and Labrador, St. John's, 1993—; sessional lectr. English Meml. U. of Nfld., St. John's, 1984-90; sessional lectr. theology Queen's Coll., St. John's, 1983-91. Chmn. Fedn. Sch. Bds., St. John's, 1975, Nfld. Pub. Librs. Bd., 1970-87. Mem. Rotary Club, Kiwanis (chmn. music festival 1985). Home: 22 Church Hill, Saint John's, NF Canada A1C 3Z9 Office: Anglican Diocesan Centre, 19 King's Bridge Rd, Saint John's, NF Canada A1C 3K4

HARVEY, DONALD JOSEPH, history educator; b. N.Y.C., Oct. 4, 1922; s. William Harold and Helen (Chiampou) H.; m. Jacqueline Rozendaal, June 11, 1955; 1 child, Nanette. B.A. cum laude, Princeton U., 1943; M.A., Columbia U., 1948, Ph.D., 1953; postgrad., U. Paris, 1950-51. Instr. Hunter Coll., CUNY, 1951-56, asst. prof., 1956-60, asso. prof., 1960-67, prof. history, 1967-84, emeritus, 1984—, chmn. dept. history, 1968-71; Reader/cons. univ. presses Yale, Cornell, State U. N.Y.; cons. Rockefeller Found. humanities fellowship program, 1974-78, Nat. Endowment for Humanities, 1977-85, Funk & Wagnall's, 1989-91; cons. on hist. TV series Sta. WGBH-TV, Boston, 1987. Author: (with E.M. Earle) Modern France, 1951, France Since the Revolution, 1968, (with W.O. Shanahan) Nationalism: Essays in Honor of Louis Snyder, 1981; assoc. editor: (with H. Rowen) Reviews in European History, 1973-79; contbr. articles to profl. jours. Served to capt., arty. AUS, 1943-46, ETO. Ford Found. fellow, 1954-55; Fulbright alternate, 1959-60. Mem. Am. Hist. Assn., Soc. for French Hist. Studies, AAUP, Phi Alpha Theta. Home: 666 Main St Apt 404 Winchester MA 01890-1959 Office: 695 Park Ave New York NY 10021-5024

HARVEY, DONALD PHILLIPS, retired naval officer; b. Geddes, S.D., Jan. 24, 1924; s. Ernest Lyle and Beryl (Phillips) H.; m. Deborah Stults, Dec. 13, 1952; children—Craig, Lynn, Reid, Anne. BS, U.S. Naval Acad., 1947; MA, MALD, Fletcher Sch. Law and Diplomacy, 1961. Commd. ensign U.S. Navy, 1947, advanced through grades to rear adm., 1973; service in Pacific, Atlantic, Bahrain, France and Japan; dir. Naval Intelligence, Washington, 1976-78; dir. program requirements TRW, Washington, 1978-89. Decorated DSM, Legion of Merit, Meritorious Service medal, Joint Commendation medal (2), Navy Commendation medal (2). Mem. U.S. Naval Inst., Nat. Mil. Intelligence Assn. (bd. dirs.), Assn. Former Intelligence Officers. Republican. Episcopalian. Home: 440 Island Circle Sarasota FL 34242-1940

HARVEY, DOUGLASS COATE, retired photographic company executive; b. Batavia, N.Y., Aug. 28, 1917; s. Homer A. and Dells S. Harvey; m. Elizabeth Kellas, June 27, 1942; children: Robert, Anne, Katharine, Douglass Coate Jr. BSME with highest distinction, Purdue U., 1939, DEng honoris causa, 1982. With Eastman Kodak Co., Rochester, N.Y., 1939-82; dir. corp. product devel. Eastman Kodak Co., 1970-73, v.p., gen. mgr. apparatus div., 1973-77; exec. v.p., gen. mgr. Eastman Kodak Co. (mgr. U.S. and Canadian photog. divs.), 1977-82; ret., 1982; also dir. Eastman Kodak Co.; dir. Tex. Instruments, Inc., 1982-88; commr. Monroe Co. Case Commn. Former trustee Alfred (N.Y.) Univ.; former mem. exec. bd. Otetiana (N.Y.) coun. Boy Scouts Am.; former chmn. bd. dirs. Rochester and Monroe County YMCA, also former mem. nat. bd. dirs.; ret. chmn. engring. adv. coun. Clarkson U., Potsdam, N.Y.; former mem. bd. mgrs. Meml. Art Gallery; trustee Internat. Mus. Photography, Adirondack Pk. Inst., Inc. Named Outstanding Mech. Engr., Purdue U., 1991. Mem. Nat. Acad. Engring., Optical Soc. Am., Photog. Soc. Am., Soc. Photog. Scientists and Engrs., Rochester Engring. Soc., Rochester C. of C., Nat. Security Indsl. Assn. (ret., trustee 1973-78), Rochester Country Club (former mem. bd. stewards), Genesee Valley Club, Lake George Club (Diamond Point, N.Y.), Rotary, Tau Beta Pi, Pi Tau Sigma. Republican. Home: 3155 East Ave Rochester NY 14618-3427

HARVEY, ELAINE LOUISE, artist, educator; b. Riverside, Calif., Mar. 1, 1936; d. Edgar Arthur and Emma Louise (Shull) Siervogel; m. Stuart Herbert Harvey, June 16, 1957; children: Kathleen Robin, Laurel Lynn, Mark Stuart. BA with highest honors, with distinction, San Diego State U., 1957. Cert. gen. elem. tchr., Calif. Tchr. Cajon Valley Schs., El Cajon, Calif., 1957, 58; free-lance artist El Cajon, 1975—; tchr. Athenaeum Sch. Music & Art, 1990—; juror various art exhbns., Calif., 1983—; lectr., 1984—; tchr. painting seminars, 1987—. Editor: Palette to Palate, 1986; contbr. The Artists Mag., 1987, 94, 96, 98, The New Spirit Watercolor, 1989, Calif. Art Rev., 1989, The Artists So. Calif., 1989, Splash, 1990, Splash II, 1992, Watercolor Techniques for Releasing the Creative Spirit, 1992, Collage Techniques, 1994, The Artistic Touch, 1994. Trustee San Diego Mus. Art, 1985, 86; vol. art tchr., San Diego area pub. schs., 1973-76; choral dir. Chapel of Valley United Meth., 1991—. Recipient Merit award La. Watercolor Soc., 1984, Arches Canson Rives award Midwest Watercolor Soc./Tweed Mus., Greenbay, Wis., 1984, Winsor Newton award Midwest Watercolor Soc./Neville Mus., Duluth, Minn., 1985, McKinnon award Am. Watercolor Soc. 1985, Creative Connection award Rocky Mountain Nat. Exhbn., 1986, 1st Juror's award San Diego Internat. Watercolor Exhbn., 1986, Dassler Mochs award Adirondacks Exhbn. of Am. Art, 1988, Arjomari/Arches/Rives award Watercolor West, Brea Cultural Ctr., 1990. Mem. Nat. Watercolor Soc. (bd. dirs. 1987-88, elected juror 1989), Watercolor West (bd. dirs. 1986-88, 94-98), West Coast Watercolor Soc. (pres. 1992-98), San Diego Watercolor Soc. (pres. 1979-80, chmn. internat. exhbn. 1980-81, Silver Recognition award 1986), San Diego Mus. Art Artists Guild (pres. 1985-86, bd. dirs. 1986-87, 90-94) Western Fedn. Watercolor Socs. (del. 1983-91), Rocky Mountain Nat. Watermedia Soc., Allied Artists Am., Grossmont Garden Club (Elson Creativity Trophy 1977, 79). Home and Studio: 1602 Sunburst Dr El Cajon CA 92021-1541

HARVEY, ELINOR B., child psychiatrist; b. Boston, Jan. 11, 1912; d. William and Florence (Maysles) H.; m. Donald K. Freedman, July 2, 1936; children: Peter, F. Kenneth. BS cum laude, Jackson Coll., 1933; MD, Tufts U., 1936. Diplomate Am. Bd. Psychiatry and Neurology, Nat. Bd. Med. Examiners. Intern New Eng. Hosp. Women and Children, Roxbury, Mass., 1936-37; resident Sea View Hosp., Staten Island, N.Y., 1937-39; adminstrv. and indsl. physician Assoc. Hosp. Svc. N.Y., 1939-41; house physician, resident Henry St. Settlement House, N.Y.C., 1939-41; pvt. practice Arlington, Va., 1941-43; pvt. practice as pediatrician Newport News, Va., 1943-46; clinician Westchester County Health Dept., White Plains, N.Y., 1947; pediatrician Arrowhead Clinic, Duluth, Minn., 1947-48; resident in psychiatry VA Hosp., Palo Alto, Calif., 1949-52; resident in child psychiatry child guidance clinic Children's Hosp. San Francisco, 1952-53, fellow in child psychiatry, 1953-54; pvt. practice as child and family psychiatrist Berkeley, Calif., 1954-68, Juneau, Alaska, 1968-77; instr. Am. U., Washington, 1941-43; clinician prenatal clinics Arlington County Health Dept., Arlington, 1941-43; clinician Planned Parenthood, Washington, 1941-43; mem. adv. com. emergency maternal and infant care program Children's Bur., Washington, 1942-48; instr. pediatrics schs. nursing Buxton and Riverside Hosps., 1943-46; consulting pediatrician Cmty. Hosp. & Clinic, Two Harbors, Minn., 1947-48; mem. courtesy staff Herrick Hosp., Berkeley, Calif., 1955-68, Bartlett Meml. Hosp., Juneau, 1968-77; cons. U.S. Bur. Indian Affairs Dept. Edn., Alaska, 1968-76, S.E. Regional Mental Health Clinic, Juneau, 1975-77, Mars & Kline Psychiat. Clinic and Hosp., Port-Au-Prince, Haiti, 1977-78, Navajo Area Indian Health Svc., Gallup, N.Mex., 1980—, Brookside Hosp., San Pablo, Calif., 1984—; instr. mental health and mental illness Alaska Homemaker-Home Health Aide Svcs., Juneau C.C., 1968-77; coord. State of Alaska Program Continuing Edn. Mental Health, 1974-76; clin. assoc. prof. dept. psychiatry and behavioral scis. U. Wash., Seattle, 1976-77; vol. child and family psychiatrist Bapt. Mission, Fermathe, Haiti, 1977-79; instr. child devel. Mars & Kline Psychiat. Clinic and Hosp., 1977-78; mem. hosp. staff Gallup (N.Mex.) Indian Med. Ctr., 1980—; cons. Brazelton neonatal behavioral assessment Navajo Area Indian Health Svc., 1982—, infant-parent program Brookside Hosp., 1984—; demonstrator, trainer Brazelton neonatal behavioral assessment scale Ctr. de Recursos Educatius per a Deficients Visuals a Catalunya, Barcelona, Spain, 1992; active Child Protection Agy., Juneau; mem. planning bd. Coordinated Child Care Ctr., Juneau; mem. grant writing com. of planning bd. Cmty. Mental Health Ctr., Juneau; presenter in field. Author: (with others) Annual Progress in Child Psychiatry and Child Development, 10th ann. edit., 1977, Expanding Mental Health Intervention in Schools, Vol. I, 1985, Psychiatric House Calls, 1988, The Indian Health Service Primary Care Provider, 1991; contbr. articles to profl. jours. Mem. comprehensive health planning coun. City and Borough of Juneau. Grantee NIMH, 1958-63. Fellow Am. Psychiat. Assn. (life), Am. Acad. Child and Adolescent Psychiatry (life, mem. task force Am. Indian children); mem. No. Calif. Psychiat. Assn. (Outstanding Achievement award 1996), Internat. Assn. Child Psychiatry, World Fedn. Mental Health, Internat. Assn. Circumpolar Health, Soc. Reproductive and Infant Psychology, Phi Beta Kappa. Home and Office: 1547 Buckeye Ct Pinole CA 94564-2124

HARVEY, ELIZABETH SCHROER, lawyer; b. Rockford, Ill., June 17, 1960; d. Philip Paul and E. Rebecca (Whisler) Schroer; m. Robert J. Harvey, July 27, 1985 (div. Nov. 1995). BA in History and Polit. Sci., U. Iowa, 1982; JD, So. Ill. U., 1986. Bar: Ill. 1986, U.S. Dist. Ct. (no. dist.) Ill. 1990, U.S. Dist. Ct. (cen. and so. dists.) Ill. 1995. Rsch. atty. Ill. Supreme Ct., Springfield, 1986-87; atty. Ill. Pollution Control Bd., Chgo., 1987-95; environ. atty. McKenna, Storer, Rowe, White & Farrug, Chgo., 1995—. Contbr. articles to profl. publs. Mem. Ill. State Bar Assn., Chgo. Bar Assn. (chmn. practice and procedure com. of environ. law sect. 1989-90), Environ. Law Inst., So. Ill. U. Law Alumni Assn., U. Iowa Alumni Assn. Presbyterian. Avocations: gardening, reading, walking, sports. Office: McKenna Storer Rowe White & Farrug 200 N Lasalle St Ste 3000 Chicago IL 60601-1019

HARVEY, EMILY DENNIS, art history educator; b. Alexandria, Va., Mar. 15, 1934; d. Lawrence and Eleanor Dennis; m. Dermot Harvey, Feb. 21, 1971; children: Samantha, Julian. BA, Vassar Coll., 1955; MA, NYU Inst. Fine Arts, 1968. Prof. art history Rockland C.C., Suffern, N.Y., 1980—, chair dept. art, 1990—; asst. dir. B.C. Mus., 1959-68, acting dir., 1969—; with Met. Mus. Art, Bklyn. Children's Mus., Hudson River Mus., N.Y.C. Dept. Cultural Affairs; founder, dir. Mus. Collaborative, 1970-73. E-mail: eharvey@sunyrockland.edu. Office: Rockland CC 145 College Rd Suffern NY 10901-3611

HARVEY, F. REESE, mathematics educator; b. Atlantic Beach, Fla., Feb. 7, 1941; married, 1969; 3 children. BS, MS, Carnegie-Mellon U., 1963; PhD in Math., Stanford U., 1966. Instr. math. U. Calif., Berkeley, 1966-68; from asst. prof. to assoc. prof. Rice U., Houston, 1968-73, prof. math., 1973—; mem. U.S. Nat. Com. Math., 1980-83; bd. govs. Inst. Math. and Its Applications, 1981-83; trustee Math. Sci. Rsch. Inst., 1983-89. Mem. Am. Math. Soc. Rsch. in complex analysis, partial differential equations and differential geometry. Office: Rice U Dept Math Houston TX 77251*

HARVEY, GEORGE EDWIN, communications company executive; b. Bromborough, Cheshire, Eng., June 10, 1938; came to Can., 1979.; s. Donald Jocelyn and Catherine (Abbott) H.; m. Janet Christine Moore, Aug. 10, 1963; children: Gavin Anthony, Rachel Josselyn. BA with honors in Econs., Leeds U., 1959. Sales rep. Burroughs Corp., Manchester, Eng., 1961-66; acct. mgr. Burroughs Corp., London, 1966-71, sales mgr., 1971-74; dir. fin. mktg. Burroughs Corp., Detroit, 1974-79; pres. Burroughs Can., Toronto, Ont., Can., 1979-82, ROLM Can., Toronto, 1982-86; v.p. world-wide mktg. ROLM Corp., Santa Clara, Calif., 1986-87; pres., chief exec. officer CNCP Telecommunications (then Unitel Communications Inc.), Toronto, 1987-93, also bd. dirs.; chmn. Unitel Comm., Toronto, 1993-94, vice chmn., 1995-96; pres. Bus. Svcs. Group AT&T Canada Long Distance Svcs., Toronto, 1996—; bd. dirs. Royal Ins. Co. Can. Bd. dirs. Tronto Symphony Orchestra, Jr. Achievement Can., Toronto. Lt. RASC, 1959-61. Clubs: Granite, St. George's Golf (Toronto); Fortitude, Old Cumberland #12 (master 1973-74). Home: 175 Cumberland St Ste 1609, Toronto, ON Canada M5R 3M9 Office: AT&T Can Long Distance Svcs, 200 Wellington St W, Toronto, ON Canada M5V 3G2*

HARVEY, GLENN F., association executive; b. Tarentum, Pa., May 10, 1940; s. Howard F. and Evelyn H.; m. Linda M. Herr, Mar. 19, 1960; children: Jeffrey Howard, Lisa Anne. B.S.Ed., Slippery Rock State Coll., 1961; M.Ed., Duquesne U., 1964; M.B.A., U. Pitts., 1975. Tchr. Fox Chapel Area Schs., Pitts., 1961-67; exec. dir. Instrument Soc. Am., Research Triangle Park, N.C., 1967-99. Mem. Am. Soc. of Assn. Execs., Coun. Engring. and Sci. Soc. Execs., Capital City Club (Raleigh). Republican. Office: Instrument Soc Am Po Box 12277 2421 Coley Forest Pl Raleigh NC 27612

HARVEY, JACK K., holding company executive; b. 1943. With Douglas County Bank & Trust Co., Omaha, 1960—; chmn. bd., exec. v.p. State Bank Holding Co., Omaha. Office: Great Western Bank 14545 W Center Rd Omaha NE 68144*

HARVEY, JACKSON, film producer; b. Orange, Calif., Feb. 1, 1958; s. John Albert and Sarah (Reed) H.; m. Diana Kavanikas. AB, U. So. Calif., 1981, cert. visual anthropology (hon.), 1981. Vice-pres. GCO Pictures, Inc., L.A., 1986-87; v.p. Cinema Plus, Inc., L.A., 1987-88; pres. Cinecraft Pictures, L.A., 1988—; producer motion pictures: Season of Fear, 1987, Witchtrap, 1988; assoc. producer: ...Bark Like a Dog, 1986, Night of the Demons, 1987; dir. plays Lessor Sawyer's Cricket, 1990, Puntilla and His Hired Man, 1990, Purgation, 1998; artistic dir. Artists in Action, L.A., 1988—. Author: (with Diana Karanikas Harvey) Dead Before Their Time, 1996, Neil Diamond-Biography, 1996, Barbra Streisand-Biography, 1997, Katharine Hepburn-Biography, 1998. Mem. U. So. Calif. Cinema TV Alumni Assn., U. So. Calif. Cinema Curiculus. Office: 333 S Beaudry Ave Fl 18 Los Angeles CA 90017-1466

HARVEY, JAMES GERALD, educational counselor, consultant, researcher; b. California, Mo., July 15, 1934; s. William Walter and Exie Marie (Lindley) H. BA Amherst Coll., 1956; MAT (fellow), Harvard U., 1958, MEd, 1962. Asst. to dean grad. sch. edn. Harvard U., Cambridge, Mass., 1962-66, dir. admissions, fin. aid, 1966-69; dir. counseling service U. Calif., Irvine, 1970-72; ednl. cons., Los Angeles, 1972—. Author: (ednl. materials) HARVOCAB Vocabulary Program, 1985—. 1st lt. USAF, 1958-61. Amherst Mayo-Smith grantee, 1956-57; UCLA Adminstrv. fellow, 1969-70. Mem. Am. Ednl. Research Assn., Nat. Council Measurement in Edn. Address: 1845 Glendon Ave Los Angeles CA 90025-4653

HARVEY, JAMES MATHEWS, JR., instructional media producer, columnist; b. Detroit, Dec. 5, 1964; s. James M. and Leotha (Frazier) H. BS, Troy State U., 1987. Media assoc. Ctr. for Environ. Rsch., Troy, Ala., 1987-88; producer, dir. Coop. Extension Svc. (became Coop. Extension Sys. 1995), Auburn, Ala., 1988—. Dir. videos including: Nature's Way, 1988, Red Drum: A Struggle for Survival, 1989, Pond Management, 1991; slide series including: Nature's Way, 1988, Beach Mice and Their Habitat, 1989; dir., editor Safety in the Logging Woods series, 1989-95, Forestry in Alabama, 1993, Small Business Resources Series, 1995, Adult Education Principles for Loggers, 1996, Multiple Use Management, 1996; assoc. producer, dir. Extension Today, 1990; assoc. producer satellite programs Principles of Parenting and State of Our Environment, 1991, White-Tailed Deer Management, 1991-92, Residential Landscaping, 1992, Small Business Resources, 1994, Wildlife Damage Management, 1995, Alabama Forest Resources Today, 1996; creator, producer Ala. 4-H Congress Video, 1990—, 4-H Performing Arts Video, 1993-94; prodr., dir. Street Trees and Sewing Update for Entrepreneurs, 1994, Tax Fraud Prevention, 1995, AU Presents, 1998; guest columnist The Messenger, 1993—. Mem. agrl. adv. com. Pike County H.S., Brundidge, Ala., 1983-95, pres. 1995—; bd. dirs. Pike County Agrl. Complex Bd. Mem. Assn. Ednl. Communications and Tech., Troy State U. Journalism Alumni Assn., So. Region Ext. Video Prodrs. Baptist. Avocations: music, movies, tennis, model trains. Office: Ala Coop Extension Sys Duncan Hall Anx Auburn AL 36849-5634

HARVEY, JOEL, chaplain, educator; b. Bklyn., Oct. 26, 1938; s. Abraham and Jenny (Miller) Smolensky; m. Patricia Moore, Mar. 21, 1970; children: Mical Sushil, Alexis Irina, Colin James. BA, Bklyn. Coll., 1968; AM, Adelphi U., 1969; PhD, Fla. State U., 1980; cert., Mercer Sch. Theology, 1984. Ordained to ministry Episcopal Ch. as deacon, 1984, as priest, 1985; diplomate Coll. Pastoral Supervsn. & Psychotherapy. Assoc. prof. Adelphi U., Garden City, N.Y., 1970-91, Episcopal chaplain, 1985-89; dir. pastoral care St. Mary's Hosp. for Children, Bayside, N.Y., 1987-97, St. John's Episcopal Hosp., 1997—; asst. chaplain St. John's Episcopal Hosp., Smithtown, N.Y., 1985-86; chaplain Village of St. John, Smithtown, 1985-86; spiritual dir. Youth Ministries Coun., Diocese L.I., 1986—; assoc. Community St. Mary, 1987—; lectr. George Mercer Sch. Theology, Garden City, N.Y., 1988—; mem. Cath. Fellowship of Episcopal Ch., 1989—. Fellow Am. Bd. Cert. Managed Care Providers, Am. Assn. Pastoral Counselors; mem. Coll. Chaplains, Assembly Episcopal Hosps. and Chaplains, Am. Assn. Coll. Profs., Sea Cliff Yacht Club (chaplain 1988—). Home: 12-17 119th St College Point NY 11356-1648

HARVEY, JOHN ADRIANCE, psychology and pharmacology educator, researcher, consultant; b. N.Y.C., Oct. 14, 1930; s. John Adriance Harvey and Paula Ann (Truhar) Oestreich; m. Rhoda S. Sadigur, Dec. 20, 1958; children—David Alexander, Andrew Martin, Michael Allen. A.B., U. Chgo., 1955, Ph.D., 1959. Research assoc. U. Chgo., 1959-61, asst. prof., 1961-67, assoc. prof., 1967-68; prof. psychology and pharmacology U. Iowa, Iowa City, 1968-88; prof. pharmacology and psychiatry, chief div. behavioral neurobiology Med. Coll. Pa. and Ea. Pa. Psychiat. Inst., Phila., 1988—; guest worker Maudsley Hosp., London, 1966-67; chmn. biopsychology rsch. rev. com. NIH, 1983-85; chmn. behavioral neurobiology rsch. rev. com. NIMH, 1986-90, mem. adv. panel; mem. extramural sci. adv. bd. Nat. Inst. on Drug Abuse, 1990—. Author: Behavioral Analysis of Drug Action, 1971; editor Jour. Pharmacology and Exptl. Therapeutics, 1990-98; contbr. numerous articles to profl. jours. Recipient Research Devel. award NIMH, 1963-68, Research Scientist award, 1969-74. Fellow APA (pres. divsn. 28 1984-85), Am. Coll. Neuropsychopharmacology; mem. Am. Soc. for Pharmacology and Exptl. Therapeutics (editl. adv. bd.), Soc. for Neurosci. (fin. com.), Soc. for Neurochemistry, European Soc. for Neurochemistry, Pavlovian Soc., Soc. for Biol. Psychiatry, Behavioral Pharmacol. Soc. (pres. 1996-98). Home: 1 Druim Moir Ct Philadelphia PA 19118 Office: MCP Hahnemann U Dept Pharmacology 3200 Henry Ave Philadelphia PA 19129-1137

HARVEY, JOHN COLLINS, physician, educator; b. Youngstown, Ohio, Sept. 11, 1923; s. J. Paul and Mary J. (Collins) H.; m. Adele Dillon, Nov. 26, 1949; children: Elizabeth V.R. (Mrs. Charles Yon), John Collins Jr., William Charles II, Amy L.R. (Mrs. L. F. Reese), Margaret J.B. (Mrs. Gregory Granitto). Grad., Phillips Exeter Acad., 1941; BS, Yale U., 1944; MD, Johns Hopkins U., 1947, MLA, 1968; MAS, Johns Hopkins, 1974; MA, St. Mary's U., 1975, PhD in Theology, 1988; DSc (hon.), Barry U., 1992. Diplomate: Am. Bd. Internal Medicine. Successively house officer, asst. resident, resident Osler Med. Service, Johns Hopkins Hosp., 1947-53, physician, 1953-73; successively instr., asst. prof., asso. prof., prof. medicine Johns Hopkins, 1953-73; prof. medicine Georgetown U., Washington, 1973-89, prof. medicine emeritus, 1989—; sr. rsch. scholar Kennedy Inst. of Ethics, Georgetown U., Washington, 1989—, Ctr. for Clin. Bioethics, Georgetown Med. Ctr., 1993—; Vis. prof. medicine U. Ibadan, Nigeria, 1964; hon. assoc. prof. medicine Guy's Hosp., London, 1973. Co-editor: Catholic Perspectives on Medical Morals, Catholic Studies in Bioethics; Contbr. articles to profl. publs. Mem. various local, state and nat. govt. med. adv. coms.; trustee Washington Home for Incurables; mem. med. adv. com. Sacred Congregation for Causes of Saints, Holy See, Vatican City. Col. (ret.) M.C., USAR. A. Blaine Brower Traveling fellow ACP to Guy's Hosp. London, 1956; sr. scholar Kennedy Inst. Ethics, Georgetown U., 1973-89. Fellow ACP (master), APHA; mem. AAAS, AMA, Am. Clin. and Climatol. Assn., Biophys. Soc., Johns Hopkins Soc. Scholars, Peripatetic Club, Tudor and Stuart Club (Balt.), Yale Club (N.Y.C.), Chevy Chase Club, Cosmos Club, Knights of St. Gregory, Knights of Malta, Phi Beta Kappa, Sigma Xi, Alpha Omega Alpha. Republican. Roman Catholic. Home: 12610 Three Sisters Rd Potomac MD 20854-6359 Office: Georgetown U Med Ctr Bldg D Ctr Clin Bioethics Rm 234 4000 Reservoir Rd NW Washington DC 20007-2145

HARVEY, JOHN GROVER, mathematics educator; b. Waco, Tex., Aug. 10, 1934; s. John Grover and Mary Inez (Davidson) H. AA, Navarro Jr. Coll., Corsicana, Tex., 1953; BS, Baylor U., 1955; MS, Fla. State U., 1957; PhD, Tulane U., 1961. Instr. math. U. Ill., Urbana, 1961-63, asst. prof., 1963-66; assoc. prof. math. U. Wis., Madison, 1966-75, prof., 1975—; prin. investigator Wis. R & D Ctr. for Cognitive Learning, Madison, 1968-78. Editor: Matching High School Preparation to College Needs: Prognostic and Diagnostic Testing, 1996; editor, contbg. author: Models for Technology Teacher Education in Mathematics, 1997; contbr. chpts. to books. Mem. Math. Assn. Am. (assoc. editor 1969-74, chmn. com. on testing 1988-93), Am. Ednl. Rsch. Assn., Nat. Coun. Tchrs. of Math., Wis. Math. Coun. (Disting. Math. Educator award 1993). Democrat. Lutheran. Home: 5606 Stadium Dr Madison WI 53705-4644 Office: U Wis Dept Math 480 Lincoln Dr Madison WI 53706-1325

HARVEY, JOHN HERTFORD, academic and athletics administrator, consultant; b. The Hague, The Netherlands, Nov. 9, 1935; came to U.S., 1939; s. Frederick Sailor and Alexandria Commins H.; m. Lois Anderson, Dec. 20, 1971 (div. 1995). BA in Philosophy, Coll. William and Mary, 1957, MEd in History, 1969; PhD in Higher Edn., Boston Coll., 1971. Tchr., coach Coll. William and Mary, Williamsburg, Va., 1964-69; acad. adminstr., coach Harvard U., Cambridge, Mass., 1970-80; tchr., coach, adminstr. Grinnell (Iowa) Coll., 1980-83; asst. prof., dir. athletics St. Mary's (Md.) Coll., 1983-89; dir. athletics Carnegie Mellon U., Pittsburgh, Pa., 1989—; cons. in field. Author: (with others) Organizational Management for Athletics, 1998; contbr. articles to publs. Active Big Bros. Assn., Boston, 1970-80, Nantucket (Mass.) Libr. Assn., 1992-99. Recipient So. Fellowship award Coll. William and Mary, 1957-58. Mem. NCAA (v.p. divsn. III, 1992-94, exec. com. 1992-95, chmn. coun. 1992-96, chmn. governance com. 1995-97), Nat. Assn. Basketball Coaches, Am. Assn. Health Phys. Edn. Recreation, Athletic Dirs. Assn. (divsn. III), Phi Beta Kappa, Omicron Delta Kappa. Episcopalian. Avocations: white water rafting, sports, music, fitness. E-mail: jh8dt@cmu.edu. Office: Carnegie Mellon U Pittsburgh PA 15213

HARVEY, JOSEPH EMMETT, construction executive; b. L.A., Dec. 4, 1951; s. Emmett Allan and Mary Summerall (Anderson) H. BA in Psychology with distinction, U. Hawaii, 1974; postgrad., U.S. Internat. U., 1975-76, San Diego State U., 1976-77. Program coord. Crisis House, El Cajon, Calif., 1975-79; ops. mgr. C.S. Goodale Co., San Diego, 1977-84; sales mgr. Dunn & Co., San Diego, 1985-89; constrn. mgr. Comml. Shelving,

Inc., Honolulu, 1989-92; constrn. exec. Skylights of Hawaii, Honolulu, 1992-97; pres. Harvey Bldg. Specialties, Inc., Kamuela, Hawaii, 1998—. Mem. Bldg Industry Assn., Constrn. Specifications Inst. (dir. 1994-96, asst. chair western region tech. com. 1994-95, awards chair 1995-97, Constrn. Document Technician cert. 1995, merit award 1993, Pacesetter award 1994), Hawaii Island Contractors Assn., Rotary (Svc. award 1993), Phi Beta Kappa. Avocations: yachting, skiing.

HARVEY, JOSEPH HOWARD, mathematics educator, musician; b. Miami, Fla., Oct. 29, 1957; s. William James Harvey and June Bernice Morris Whaley; m. Michele Dawn Manieri, May 27, 1989. BS summa cum laude, Trevecca Nazarene Coll., Nashville, 1979; MEd, U. South Fla., 1993. Cert. tchr. secondary math., Fla. Tchr. Princeton Christian Sch., Miami, 1981-83, Homestead Jr. H.S., Miami, 1983-84, Parrott Jr. H.S., Brooksville, Fla., 1984-86; tchr. Hernando H.S., Brooksville, 1986—, chair dept. math., 1999—; musical dir. Stage West, Richey Suncoast Theatre, Playhouse 19, 1990—; pianist First Bapt. Ch., Brooksville, 1986-98, deacon, sec., 1991-94; adj. prof. St. Leo Coll., 1995—, Pasco-Hernando C.C., 1996—; profl. pianist Norwegian Cruise Lines, 1986; featured pianist Avila Country Club, Tampa, Fla., 1996-97. Mem. Nat. Coun. Tchrs. Math., 1994—, Fine Arts Coun. Avocations: computer, composition of music, films, theatre. Home: 33257 Westwood Dr Ridge Manor FL 33523-9051 Office: Hernando HS 700 Bell Ave Brooksville FL 34601

HARVEY, JOSEPH PAUL, JR., orthopedist, educator; b. Youngstown, Ohio, Feb. 28, 1922; s. Joseph Paul and Mary Justinian (Collins) H.; m. Martha Elizabeth Toole, Apr. 12, 1958; children: Maryalice, Martha Jane, Frances Susan, Helen Lucy, Laura Andre. Student, Dartmouth Coll., 1939-42; MD, Harvard U., 1945. Diplomate: Nat. Bd. Med. Examiners. Intern Peter Bent Brigham Hosp., Boston, 1945-46; resident Univ. Hosp., Cleve., 1951-53, Hosp. Spl. Surgery, N.Y.C., 1953-54; instr. orthopedics Cornell Med. Coll., N.Y.C., 1954-62; mem. faculty Sch. Medicine, U. So. Calif., Los Angeles, 1962-92; prof. orthopedic surgery U. So. Calif., 1966-92, prof. emeritus, 1992—; chmn. sect. orthopedics Sch. Medicine, U. So. Calif., 1964-78; dir. dept. orthopedics U. So. Calif.-Los Angeles County Med. Center, 1964-79, mem. staff, 1979—. Editor-in-chief: Contemporary Orthopedics, 1978-96. Served to capt. AUS, 1946-48. Exchange orthopedic fellow Royal Acad. Hosp., Upsala, Sweden, 1957. Fellow Western Orthopedic Assn., Am. Acad. Orthopedic Surgery, A.C.S., Am. Soc. Testing Materials; mem. AMA, Calif. Med. Assn., Los Angeles County Med. Assn., Am. Rheumatism Assn., Am. Orthopedic Assn., Internat. Soc. Orthopedics and Truamatology. Club: Boston Harvard. Home: 432 Arlington Dr Pasadena CA 91105-2850 Office: 39 Congress St Pasadena CA 91105-3024

HARVEY, JUDITH GOOTKIN, elementary education educator, real estate agent; b. Boston, May 29, 1944; d. Myer and Ruth Augusta (Goldstein) Gootkin; m. Robert Gordon Harvey, Aug. 3, 1968; children: Jonathan Michael, Alexander Shaw. BS in Edn., Lesley Coll., Cambridge, Mass., 1966; MS in Edn., Nazareth Coll., Rochester, N.Y., 1987. Kindergarten tchr. Williams Sch., Chelsea, Mass., 1966-69; owner, tchr. Island Presch., Eleuthera, Bahamas, 1969-70; substitute tchr. Brighton Cen. Schs., Rochester, N.Y., 1985—; agt. The Prudential Rochester Realty, Pittsford, N.Y. Author, dir.: (play) The Parrot Perch, 1991. Bd. dirs. in charge pub. rels. George Eastman House Coun., mem. award steering com honoring Lauren Bacall, 1990, chmn. gala celebration honoring Audrey Hepburn, 1992, mem. steering com. honoring Ken Burns, 1995; mem. art in bloom steering com. for fashion show Meml. Art Gallery, 1994; co-chmn. Fashionata, Rochester Philharm. Orch., 1990; mem. steering com. of realtors Ambs. to Arts; mem. Parrot Players Acting Group, 1990—; mem. steering com. Reels and Wheels Antique Car Festival, 1995, 96; mem. pub. rels. com. Detroit Bloomfest, 1999. Mem. Chatterbox Club, Genesee Valley Club, Multimillion Dollar Producer's Club. Avocations: acting, directing, tennis, gardening, paddle tennis. Home: 30750 Ivyglen Ct Bingham Farms MI 48025-4624

HARVEY, KEIKO TAKEUCHI, telephone company executive; b. Ashiya, Hyogoken, Japan, Sept. 7, 1948; came to U.S., 1966; d. Toshio and Nobuko (Nakahara) T.; m. Gerald Christopher Harvey, May 5, 1972; children: Edward Peter, Emma Elizabeth. BSEE, Rutgers Coll., 1972; postgrad., Fuqua Sch. of Bus., 1987, U. Va., 1993, Leadership Am., 1998. Various engring. and mgr. positions N.J. Bell, Newark, 1972-83; various dir. positions Bell Atlantic, Newark, 1983-93, v.p. ctrl. and so. N.J. ops., 1993-95; v.p. network engring. and planning Bell Atlantic, Balt., 1995—; mem. The Scientific and Engring. Coun., Md. Acad. Scis., 1997-99. Commr. N.J. Commn. on Higher Edn., Trenton, N.J., 1994-95; pub. mem., bd. govs. Rutgers U., New Brunswick, N.J., 1992-97. Mem. Tau Beta Pi, Eta Kappa Nu. Office: Bell Atlantic 1 E Pratt St Ste 1 Baltimore MD 21202-1096

HARVEY, KENNETH RAY, professional football player; b. Austin, Tex., May 6, 1965. Student, Laney Coll., U. Calif. Linebacker Phoenix Cardinals, 1988-93, Wash. Redskins, 1994—. Selected to Pro Bowl, 1994, 95, 96, 97; tied for AFC lead in sacks (13.5), 1994. Office: c/o Washington Redskins Dulles Internat Airport PO Box 17247 Washington DC 20041-7247 also: 21300 Redskin Park Dr Ashburn VA 20147-6100*

HARVEY, KENNETH RICHARD, middle education educator, writer; b. Saugus, Mass., Jan. 27, 1958; s. Kenneth Henry and Edna Mary (DuLong) H. BA magna cum laude, Bowdoin Coll., 1980; MA in Spanish, Middlebury (Vt.) Coll., 1991. Tchr., chair dept. Chapel Hill-Chauncy Hall, Waltham, Mass., 1981-90; tchr., counselor Shady Hill Sch., Cambridge, Mass., 1990—; presenter, spkr. numerous confs. in field. Contbg. author: Other Voices, 1995, Mass. Rev., 1996, Nebr. Rev., 1996, Evergreen Chronicles, 1997, The Balt. Rev., 1998, others. Trustee Shady Hill Sch., Cambridge, 1995-98, co-leader S.E.E.D. seminar, 1994—; mem. adv. bd. Ensemble Theater Cmty. Sch., N.Y.C., 1988-92; vol. AIDS Action Com., Boston, 1993-95; mem. nat. S.E.E.D. project Wellesley (Mass.) Coll. Ctr. for Rsch. on Women, 1994—; theater adjudicator Ea. Mass. Assn. Cmty. Theaters, 1997; pres. bd. dirs. Winchester Unitarian Players, 1993-94; mem. Vokes Players, 1997—. Fellow Thomas J. Watson Found., 1980-81, Mass. Arts Coun., Boston, 1988; grantee Ortega y Gasset Found., Madrid, 1994. Mem. Gay and Lesbian Edn. Network. Democrat. Unitarian Universalist. Avocations: theater, book collecting. Home: 24 Slade St Belmont MA 02478-2228

HARVEY, LEIGH KATHRYN, lawyer; b. Abilene, Tex.; d. Jasper Elliott and Kathryn E. (McDaniel) H.; m. Bert Gubbels, Oct. 1983 (div. 1993). BA cum laude, U. Tex., 1971, JD, 1974. Bar: Tex. 1975. Asst. atty. City of San Angelo, Tex., 1974-77; asst. dist. atty. County of Fort Bend, Richmond, Tex., 1978; pvt. practice various cities, Tex., 1977—. Bd. dirs. Tom Green County Community Action Council, San Angelo, 1975-77, pres. 1976; vol. judge bd. advs. U. Tex. Law Sch., Austin, 1980; mem. Met. Austin 2000, 1982; mem. vestry St. Mary's Episcopal Ch., Lampasas, Tex., 1989-91; mem. Natural Resources Def. Coun., The Heritage Found., 1994-98; host for Jan Patterson Austin/Temple receptions Ct. Appeals 3rd cir., 1998. Keeton fellow U. Tex., 1997—; recipient Young Careerist award Dist. 7 Bus. and Profl. Women's Club, 1977, Cert. of Achievement Rep. Nat. Conv., 1998; named Guardian of the Wild Nat. Wildlife Fedn., 1998. Mem. ABA, Tex. Bar Assn. (legal forms com. manual for Real Estate Transactions rev. edit. 1986-92), Travis County Bar Assn., Bell Lampasas Mills County Bar Assn. (sr. citizen project 1986). Episcopalian. Office: PO Box 926 Lampasas TX 76550-0926

HARVEY, MORRIS LANE, lawyer; b. Madisonville, Ky., Apr. 22, 1950; s. Morris Lee and Margie Lou (Wallace) H.; divorced; children: Morris Lane Jr., John French, Laura Kathleen. BS, Murray State U., 1972; JD, U. Ky., 1974. Bar: Ill. 1975, U.S. Dist. Ct. (so. dist.) 1979. Assoc. Hanagan & Dousman, Mt. Vernon, Ill., 1975-77; ptnr. Feiger, Quindry, Molt & Harvey and successor firms, Fairfield, Ill., 1977-85; sole practice Fairfield, 1986-97, Mt. Vernon, 1997—; instr. Frontier C.C., Fairfield, 1977-79; spl. asst. atty. gen. State of Ill., Fairfield, 1977-82; Ill. pres. Woodman of World Life Inst. Soc., 1985-87; mem. nat. fraternal com., 1987-89, nat. legis. com., 1989-93, nat. jud. com., 1993-97. Recipient Outstanding Young Man Am. U.S. Jaycees, 1978, 81, 89. Mem. ABA, Ill. Bar Assn., Assn. Trial Lawyers Am., Ill. Trial Lawyers Assn., Am. Judicature Soc. Home: 3415 Westmont St Apt 7 Mount Vernon IL 62864-6274 Office: 2029 Broadway St Mount Vernon IL 62864-2910

HARVEY, NORMAN RONALD, finance company executive; b. Rahway, N.J., Aug. 17, 1933; s. George Henry and Jennie Louise (Proudfoot) H.; m. Gail Molitor, May 26, 1962; 1 dau., Anne. B.A. in Econs., Cornell U., 1955; M.B.A. in Investments, NYU, 1962. Security analyst Bankers Trust Co., N.Y.C., 1958-61, Anchor Corp., Elizabeth, N.J., 1961-64; dir. research Auerbach, Pollak & Richardson, N.Y.C., 1964-75; chief investment officer E.W. Axe & Co., Inc., Tarrytown, N.Y., 1975-82; sr. v.p., equity funds investment officer Merrill Lynch Asset Mgmt., Princeton, N.J., 1982—. Served to 1st lt. USAR, 1957-58. Corson Meml. scholar, 1951. Mem. N.Y. Soc. Security Analysts, N.Y. Assn. Bus. Economists, The Union League N.Y., Cherry Valley Country Club. Republican. Home: 39 Florence Ln Princeton NJ 08540-2631 Office: Merrill Lynch Asset Mgmt PO Box 9011 Princeton NJ 08543-9011

HARVEY, PATRICIA JEAN, educator, administrator, retired; b. Newman, Calif., Oct. 27, 1931; d. Willard Monroe and Marjorie (Greenlee) Clougher; m. Richard Blake Harvey, Aug. 29, 1965; children: G. Scott Floden, Timothy P. BA, Whittier Coll., 1966, MA, 1971. Resource specialist Monte Vista High Sch. and Whittier (Calif.) High Sch., 1977-98; dept. chair spl. edn. Whittier (Calif.) High Sch., 1982-94; ret., 1998. Author: (tchrs. manual) The Dynamics of California Government and Politics, 1970, 90; co-author: Meeting The Needs of Special High School Students in Regular Education Classrooms, 1988. Active Whittier Fair Housing Com., 1972; pres. Women's Aux. Whittier Coll., 1972-73, sec., 1971-72; historian Docian Soc. Whittier Coll., 1963-64, pres. 1965-66. Democrat. Episcopalian. Home: 424 E Avocado Crest Rd La Habra CA 90631-8128 Office: The Learning Advantage Ctr 13710 Whittier Blvd Ste 206 Whittier CA 90605-4407

HARVEY, PAUL, news commentator, author, columnist; b. Tulsa, Sept. 4, 1918; s. Harry Harrison and Anna Dagmar (Christensen) Aurandt; m. Lynne Cooper, June 4, 1940; 1 child, Paul Harvey. Litt.D. (hon.), Culver-Stockton Coll., 1952, St. Bonaventure U., 1953; LL.D., John Brown U., Ark., 1959, Mont. Sch. Mines, 1961, Trinity Coll. Fla., 1963, Parsons Coll., 1968; H.H.D., Wayland Bapt. Coll., 1960, Union Coll., 1962, Samford U., 1970, Howard Payne U., Tex., 1978, Sterling Coll., 1982; Degree (hon.), Rosary Coll., 1996. Announcer radio sta. KVOO, Tulsa; sta. mgr. Salina, Kans.; spl. events dir. radio sta. KXOK, St. Louis; program dir. radio sta. WKZO, Kalamazoo, 1941-43; dir. news and information OWI, Mich., Ind., 1941-43; news commentator, analyst ABC, 1944—; syndicated columnist Los Angeles Times Syndicate (formerly Gen. Features Corp.), 1954—; TV commentator, 1968. Author: Remember These Things, 1952, Autumn of Liberty, 1954, The Rest of the Story, 1956, You Said It, Paul Harvey, 1969, Our Lives, Our Fortunes, Our Sacred Honor; Album rec. Yesterday's Voices, 1959, Testing Time, 1960, Uncommon Man, 1962. Bd. dirs. John D. and Catherine T. MacArthur Found.; mem. bd. govs. Orchestral Assn. Chgo. Symphony Orch. Recipient citation DAV, 1949, 11 Freedoms Found. awards, 1952-76, radio award Am. Legion, 1952, citation of merit, 1955, 57, Cert. of merit VFW, 1953, Bronze Christopher's award, 1953, award of honor Sumter Guards, 1955, nat. pub. welfare services trophy Colo. Am. Legion, 1957, Great Am. KSEL award, 1962, Spl. ABC award, 1973, Ill. Broadcaster award, 1974, John Peter Zenger Freedom award Eagles, 1975, Am. of Year award Lions Internat., 1975,Outstanding Broadcast Journalism award, 1980, Gen. Omar N. Bradley Spirit of Independence trophy, 1980, Man of Yr. award Chgo. Broadcast Advt. Club, 1981, Golden Radio award Nat. Radio Broadcasters Assn., 1982, Best Speaking Voice award Am. Speech, Lang. and Hearing Assn., 1982, Horatio Alger award, 1983, Outstanding Broadcast Personality award Advt. Club Balt., 1984, Meritorius Svc. award Am. Acad. Family Physicians, 1984, Cert. of Appreciation Humane Soc. of U.S., 1985, Genesis award The Fund for Animals, 1986, Okla. Assn. Broadcasters award, 1987, Henry G. Bennett Disting. Svc. award Okla. State U., 1987, James Herriot award Humane Soc. U.S., 1987, Lowell Thomas award, 1989, Gold medal Internat. Radio & TV Soc., 1989, Others award Salvation Army, 1989, Journalism award Internat. Radio Festival, 1989, Marconi award Network Personality of Yr., 1989, 91, 96, 98, Dante award, 1990, William Booth award Salvation Army, 1990, Journalism award Chgo. Hall of Fame, 1990, Bd. of Dirs. award Nat. Religious Broadcasters, 1991, Great Am. Race Legend's award Interstate, 1991, Good Guy award Am. Legion, 1992, Outstanding Pub. Spkr. award Toastmasters Internat., 1992, Paul White award Radoi T.V. News Dirs., 1992, Peabody award 1993, 94, Spirit of Broadcasting award NAB, 1994, Silver award Am. Advertising Fedn., 1994, Hall of Fame award Broadcasting & Cable Mag., 1995, Am. Spirit award USAF, 1996, Lifetime Achievement award Radio Mercury, 1997, Lifetime Achievement award Gold Angel, 1998, Lifetime Achievement award Radio Mercury, 1997; elected to Okla. Hall of Fame, 1955, Nat. Assn. Broadcasters Hall of Fame, 1979; named Top Commentator of Yr. Radio-TV Daily, 1962, Laureate Lincoln Acad. of Ill., 1987 (Ill. highest honor); to Emerson Radio Hall of Fame, 1990, among 20th Century's Most Significant Americans George Mag., 1998. Mem. Washington Radio and Television Corrs. Assn., Aircraft Owners and Pilots Assn. Club: Chicago Press. Broadcasts and columns reprinted in Congressional Record 102 times. Office: 333 N Michigan Ave Ste 1600 Chicago IL 60601-4005

HARVEY, PETER MARSHALL, podiatrist; b. Lubbock, Tex., Nov. 12, 1941; s. Marshall and Betty (Compton) H.; BS, Tex. Tech. U., 1962; grad. Ill. Coll. Podiatric Medicine, 1966; m. Sue Kadane, Feb. 1, 1981; children by previous marriage—Jason, Jacob; stepchildren—Chris Robertson, Jill Robertson, Brent Robertson; m. Debby Williams, 1997; 1 stepchild, Cameron Rodriguez. Intern, Community Hosp., Lubbock, Tex., 1966-67; practice podiatry specializing in foot surgery, Wichita Falls, Tex., 1967—; bd. dirs. Podiatry Ins. Co. Am. Mem. Am. Podiatric Med. Assn. (Tex. del. to ho. of dels. 1985—), Tex. Podiatry Med. Assn. (dir. 1975—, pres. 1982-83, Svc. award 1978), Am. Coll. Foot and Ankle Surgeons (assoc.). PICA (chmn. claims com. 1984—). Republican. Fax: 940-723-4646. E-mail: mharvey@cyberstation.net. Office: 1612 10th St Wichita Falls TX 76301-4390

HARVEY, RAYMOND CURTIS, conductor; b. N.Y.C., Dec. 9, 1950; s. Shirley Nathaniel and Doris Louise (Walwin) H. BMus, MMus, Oberlin Coll., 1973; M. in Musical Arts, Yale U., 1978, D in Musical Arts, 1984. Choral dir. Northfield (Mass.) Mt. Hermon Sch., 1973-76; asst. conductor Des Moines Metro Opera, Indianola, Iowa, 1977-80; music dir. Tex. Opera Theater, Houston, 1978-80; Exxon/arts endowment conductor Indpls. Symphony, 1980-83; assoc. conductor Buffalo Philharmonic, 1983-86; music dir. Marion (Ind.) Philharmonic, 1982-86, Springfield (Mass.) Symphony, 1986-94, Fresno Philharm. Orch., 1993—; guest conductor Minn. Orch., 1991, 92, Detroit Symphony, 1990, 92, N.Y. Philharmonic, 1987, Atlanta Symphony, 1992, Louisville Orch., 1990, 93; Utah Symphony, 1993. Democrat. Methodist. Avocations: running, fitness. Office: Fresno Philharm Orch 2610 W Shaw Ave Ste 103 Fresno CA 93711-2767*

HARVEY, REBECCA SUZANNE, accountant, management consultant; b. Somerville, N.J., July 21, 1971; d. Ronald Glen H. and Susan Lynn (Hagenbuch) Gerwer. BS in Accounting, Susquehanna U., 1993. Asst. to acct. pay clk. Akzo Engring. Plastics, Neshanic Station, N.J., 1990; asst. to mgr. Wilson Color Inc., Neshanic Station, N.J., 1990-92, asst. to peronnel dir., 1993, acct., 1993-95; SAP R/3 fin. bus. analyst M.A. Hanna Color, Suwanee, Ga., 1995-97; cons. Grant Thornton, mgmt. cons., Phila., 1997—. Mem. Inst. Mgmt. Accts. Avocations: crafts, sewing, reading. Home: 2058 Maple Ave Apt D1-5 Hatfield PA 19440-1425 Office: Grant Thornton Mgmt Cons 2 Commerce Sq Philadelphia PA 19103-7044

HARVEY, RICHARD DIAMOND, psychology educator; b. Culver City, Calif., Sept. 17, 1968; s. Donald Lee Green and Tommie May Williams; m. Rueneaka Beth Mosley Baptiste Feb. 11, 1989 (div. Oct. 1994); children: Alexandra, Jessica; m. Kimberly Winona Hickerson, July 20, 1996; 1 child, Krystani. BA, Ctrl. State U., 1990; MA, U. Kans., 1992, PhD, 1995. Asst. instr. dept. psychology U. Kans., Lawrence, 1990-95; asst. prof. dept. psychology St. Louis U., 1995—; cons. Defrain, Mayer, Lee & Burgess, Kansas City, 1992-96, Ctr. for Application of Behavioral Scis., St. Louis, 1995—; dir. urban rsch. and analysis Metro Assocs. Inc., St. Louis, 1998—. Contbr. articles to profl. jours. Fellow Ctr. for the Application of Behavioral Scis., Ctr. for Orgnl. Learning and Renewal; mem. Am. Psychol. Assn., Soc. of Indsl./Organizational Psychology, Soc. of Minority Issues. Avocation: music. E-mail: harveyr@slu.edu. Office: Dept Psychology St Louis U 221 N Grand Blvd Saint Louis MO 63103

HARVEY, RONALD GILBERT, research chemist; b. Ottawa, Ont., Can., Sept. 9, 1927; came to U.S., 1948; s. Gilbert and Adeline (LeClair) H.; m. Helene H. Szpara, May 18, 1952; 1 child, Ronald Edward. BS in Biology, UCLA, 1952; MS in Chemistry, U. Chgo., 1956, PhD in Chemistry, 1960. Project leader Sinclair Research Labs., Harvey, Ill., 1956-58; instr. U. Chgo., 1960-63, asst.prof., 1964-68, assoc. prof., 1968-75, prof., 1975-97, prof. emeritus, 1997—; postdoctoral fellow Imperial Coll., London, Eng., 1963-64; cons. Nat. Cancer Inst., Washington, Farmacon Corp., Oakbrook, Ill., CIDAC, Palo Alto, Calif., 1978-80; OMNI Research Mayaguex, P.R., 1973-74, Nat. Inst. Environ. Health Sci., Washington, Am. Cancer Soc., Atlanta. Author: Polycyclic Aromatic Hydrocarbons Chemistry and Carcinogenesis, 1991, Polycyclic Aromatic Hydrocarbons, 1997; editor: Polycyclic Hydrocarbons and Carcinogenesis; mem. editl. bd. Polycyclic Aromatic Compounds; contbr. more than 420 articles to profl. jours. Recipient ISPAC award for rsch. in polycyclic hydrocarbon chemistry, 1995. Fellow Royal Chem. Soc., Am. Inst. Chemists; mem. Am. Chem. Soc., Am. Assn. Cancer Research, AAAS, Sigma Xi. Achievements include patents for synthesis of alpha-olefins, anti-androgen compounds. Home: 10550 Golf Rd Orland Park IL 60462-7420 Office: U Chgo Ben May Inst 5841 S Maryland Ave Chicago IL 60637-1463

HARVEY, SIMON, actor, writer; b. Tel Aviv, July 17, 1958; came to U.S., 1959; s. Eric and Esther (Tabori) S. BA, Columbia U., 1980; MFA, U. So. Calif., 1988. Actor television and theatre; freelance writer, 1980—. Appeared in TV on Munsters Today, 1989-90, Lifestories, 1990, Knots Landing, 1990, Parker Lewis Can't Lose, 1991, Reasonable Doubts, 1992, Beverly Hills 90210, 1992, Days of Our Lives, 1992, The Young and the Restless, 1992, 98, Friends, 1996, Timecop, 1997, The Drew Carey Show, 1997, Payne, 1999; mem. Free Shakespeare Co., Chgo., 1980-82, Players Workshop of Second City, Chgo., 1981-82, Kern Shakespeare Festival, Bakersfield, Calif., 1987, Utah Shakespeare Festival, 1988, Theater of N.O.T.E., L.A., 1990-92; appeared in L.A. Theater Prodns.; writer Frontiers Newsmag., 1994; author, performer: (play) Still Negative...After All These Years, 1998. Mem. SAG (awards nominating com. 1995, 97), AFTRA, AEA. Office: The Levin Agy 8484 Wilshire Blvd Ste 745 Beverly Hills CA 90211-3216

HARVEY, VIRGINIA ISHAM, curator, fiber artist; b. Hot Springs, S.D., July 5, 1917; d. Russell Raymond and Goldie Marguerite (Coles) Isham; m. William A Harvey, Aug. 27, 1937 (dec. Apr. 1994); children: William A Jr., Russell Wilson. Student, Mills Coll., Oakland, Calif., 1935-36, U. Wash., 1936-37, Cornish Sch. Arts, Seattle, 1955-59. Curator Textile Study Ctr., U. Wash., Seattle, 1958-78; cons. Tethers Unltd., Freeland, Wash., 1995—; workshop tchr., lectr. in field. Contbr. articles to profl. jours.; author books and monographs, including Macrame, The Art of Creative Knotting, 1967, Color and Design in Macrame, 1970, Techniques of Basketry, 1976, Threads in Action; exhbns. include N.W. Craftsman Exhbn., 1955-68, Calif. Palace of the Legion of Honor, San Francisco, 1957, Frye Mus., 1959, 60, 61, Contemporary Crafts Gallery, Portland, Oreg., 1961, Mus. History and Industry, Seattle, 1962, Mills Coll., 1963, 64, Kentucky Train, 1966, Mus. Contemporary Crafts, N.Y.C., 1966, Bainbridge Arts and Crafts Festival, 1965, Wash. State Mus., Olympia, 1967, Edmonds Arts and Crafts Festival, 1969, Grand Rapids (Mich.) Art Mus., 1970, Ea. Mich. U., 1973, Boise Mus. Art, 1974, Allied Arts of Tacoma, 1972, Peninsula Textile Exhibit, Port Townsend, 1979, Fiberworks, 1988, others. Panel mem. basketry symposium Wing Luke Mus., Seattle, 1988; judge weaving Skagit County Fair, 1989, 90. Recipient N.W. Craftsmen Exhbn. award, 1957, Rsch. award Pacific N.W. Arts and Crafts Fair, Bellevue, Wash., 1957, 64, Fiberworks award, 1988; Am. Crafts Coun. Hon. fellow, 1996. Mem. Seattle Weavers Guild (pres. 1956), Whidbey Weavers Guild, Pacific N.W. Needlarts Guild (hon.), N.W. Designer Craftsmen (hon.), PEO Sisterhood (rec. sec. 1951-54). Avocation: gardening.

HARVEY, WILLARD ALBERTSON, JR., writer, distribution company executive; b. Huntingdon, Pa., Dec. 20, 1931; s. Willard Albertson and Mary Elsie (LaMotte) H.; m. Jo Anne Feick, Feb. 6, 1954; children: Patricia Jo, Merrily Jo, Willard Louis. BA in Econs., Washington & Jefferson Coll., 1953. Sales clk. G.C. Murphy Co., Pitts., 1948-53; account mgr. Aluminum Co. Am., Pitts., 1953-93; mng. ptnr. NKP CAR, Cin., 1993—. Author: Cabooses of the Nickel Plate Road, 1992, Mikes of the Nickel Plate Road, 1995, Passenger Cars of the Nickel Plate Road, 1995, Railroads of the Ohio Valley, I, 1996, II, 1997; editor: NKPH & TS Mag. reprints, 1993, 94. Bible tchr. Anderson Hills United Meth. Ch., Cin., 1972—, choir mem., 1973—. Mem. Nickel Plate Hist. & Tech. Soc. (nat. sec., info. dir.), Cin. R.R. Club. Republican. Avocations: photography, model building, travel.

HARVEY, WILLIAM BRANTLEY, JR., lawyer, former lieutenant governor; b. Walterboro, S.C., Aug. 14, 1930; s. William Brantley and Thelma (Lightsey) H.; m. Helen Coggeshall, Dec. 30, 1952; children: Eileen L., William Brantley, III, Helen C., Margaret D., Warren C. AB in Polit. Sci., The Citadel, 1951, LLD (hon.), 1978; JD magna cum laude, U. S.C., 1955. Bar: S.C. 1955. Since practiced in Beaufort, S.C.; sr. ptnr. Harvey & Battey; mem. S.C. Ho. of Reps. from Beaufort County, 1958-74, chmn. rules com., mem. constl. revision com.; lt. gov. State of S.C., 1974-78; bd. dirs., past chmn. Carolina Motor Club (AAA); chmn. Assoc. Marine Inst.; bd. dirs., sec. Beaufort Marine Inst.; chmn. Beaufort County Transp. Com.; pres. S.C. Bar, 1986-87. Former commr. S.C. Dept. Hwys. and Pub. Transp.; former commr., vice chmn. S.C. Parks, Recreation and Tourism Commn.; mem. Coastal Caroline coun. Boy Scouts Am.; former mem., bd. dirs. Citadel Devel. Found.; bd. dirs. Boys and Girls Club of Beaufort, Lowcountry Habitat for Humanity, Mustard Seed Found. Mem. ABA, S.C. Bar Assn., Beaufort County Bar Assn., Rotary, Phi Beta Kappa, Kappa Alpha, Phi Delta Phi, Omicron Delta Kappa. Presbyterian (elder). Home: 501 Pinckney St Beaufort SC 29902-4739 Office: PO Box 1107 1001 Craven St Beaufort SC 29902-5577

HARVEY, WILLIAM J., religious service organization, religious publication editor. Exec. sec. Foreign Mission Bd. of Nat. Baptist Conv., USA, Phila., 1961—, editor Mission Herald, 1961—. Office: Foreign Mission Bd 701 S 19th St Philadelphia PA 19146-1801*

HARVEY GIBBS, JANE, graphic designer; b. Allentown, Pa., Sept. 21, 1965; d. Kenneth Lee and Margaret Louise Harvey; m. Anthony Gibbs, Feb. 22, 1989; children: Molly Marie and Katie Elizabeth (twins). BFA, Parsons Sch. Design, 1988. Graphic designer Towers Perrin, N.Y.C., 1986-88; mgr. elect. pub. sys. Iversen Assocs., N.Y.C., 1988-90; self employed N.Y.C., 1990-96; graphic designer Merck & Co. Inc., Whitehouse Station, N.J., 1996—. Home: 1825 Ferry St Easton PA 18042-3968 Office: Merck & Co Inc One Merck Dr PO Box 100 WS 20-27 Whitehouse Station NJ 08889-0100

HARVIE, CRAWFORD THOMAS, lawyer; b. N.Y.C., Mar. 28, 1943; s. William Mead and Barbara Adele (Johnson) H.; m. Iris Ruth Alofsin, June 10, 1972; children: Katherine, Edward. AB, Stanford U., 1965; LLB, Yale U., 1968; cert. advanced mgmt. program, Harvard U., 1992. Bar: N.Y. 1969. Assoc. Debevoise & Plimpton, N.Y.C., 1971-75; counsel TRW, Inc., Cleve., 1976-77, sr. counsel, 1978-79, asst. gen. counsel, v.p., 1980-83; v.p. law TRW Automotive, Cleve., 1983-90; v.p., assoc. gen. counsel TRW Inc., 1990-95; sr. v.p., gen. counsel Goodyear Tire and Rubber Co., Akron, Ohio, 1995—. Trustee Cleve. Inst. of Music, 1989—, Akron Art Mus., Cleve. Opera, Cleve. Coun. on World Affairs; bd. overseers Blossom Music Ctr. Mem. Am. Corp. Counsel Assn., Assn. of Gen. Counsel, Chief Legal Officer Roundtable-U.S., Assn. of Bar of City of N.Y. Home: 6537 Thornbrook Cir Hudson OH 44236-3552 Office: Goodyear Tire and Rubber Co 1144 E Market St Akron OH 44316-0002

HARVIE, J. JASON, administrative aide, private secretary; b. Seattle, Wash., Dec. 12, 1937; s. James Joseph Harvie and Betty Clair (Walton) Krussow; m. Maureen W.Y. Johnson, June 12, 1970 (div. Sept. 1980). Cert. Law Enforcement, U. Guam, Agana, 1973, Grad. Basic Police Acad., 1973, Advanced Police Technology, 1974; Diploma, San Francisco Police Acad., 1980. Police officer II Gov. of Guam/Dept. Pub. Safety, Agana, 1972-77; chief dept. safety and security U. Calif. Hastings/Coll. of Law, San Francisco, 1978-82; chief patrol officer San Francisco Parking Authority, 1982-84; aide H.E. Sheik Abdullah O. Mahdi, Pebble Beach, Calif., 1984-96. Decorated Navy Achievement medal USN; named Knight Chevalier, Grand

Knight/Police Hall of Fame, Miami, 1989; recipient Legion of Honor award Am. Police Hall of Fame, Miami, 1990. Mem. Am. Fedn. Police, Calif. Peace Officers Assn., Marine's Meml. Club, Am. Police Hall of Fame. Republican. Episcopalian. Avocations: bicycling, swimming, stamp collecting, reading. Home and Office: PO Box 1018 Pebble Beach CA 93953-1018

HARVIE, JAMES DUNCAN, nuclear regulator; b. Glasgow, Scotland, Jan. 21, 1945; arrived in Can., 1966; s. George Stein and Jessie McLennan (McLeod) H.; m. Marion Cunningham, Oct. 16, 1967; children: Derek, Lisa, Amber. BSc in Math., Glasgow U., 1966. Rschr. thermal hydraulics Atomic Energy Can., Ltd., Chalk River, Ont., Can., 1966-74; sr. project officer Atomic Energy Control Bd., Tiverton, Ont., Can., 1974-79; mgr. power reactors Atomic Energy Control Bd., Ottawa, Can., 1979-90, dir. gen. rsch. & safeguards, 1990-96, dir. gen. reactor regulation, 1996—. V.p. Cumbrae Sch. Dancing, Ottawa, 1980—. Avocations: sailing, cycling, soccer, golf. Office: Atomic Energy Control Bd, 280 Slater St, Ottawa, ON Canada K1P 5S9

HARVIEUX, ANNE MARIE, psychotherapist; b. St. Paul, Sept. 5, 1945; d. Walter Wallace and Magdalene C. (Rauer) H. BA, Mt. Mary Coll., Milw., 1970; MSW, U. Wis., Milw., 1979. Cert. ind. clin. social worker. Caseworker Washington County Dept. Social Svc., West Bend, Wis., 1970-72; social worker St. Michael's Hosp., Milw., 1972-74; adminstrv. asst. Family Hosp., Milw., 1974-82; dir. social svc. Beloit (Wis.) Meml. Hosp., 1982-87; dir. counseling svc. Beloit Clinic, 1987-92; dir. social svcs. N.W. Gen. Hosp., Milw., 1992-95; program adminstr. Childrens Hosp. of Wis. Sudden Infant Death Ctr., Milw., 1995—; mem. adv. bd. Credible Care, Janesville, Wis., 1987-92, Parkside Lodge Wis., Beloit, 1989-92. Bd. dirs. Waukesha (Wis.) Mental Health Assn., 1980-82; mem. women's exch., 1990-92, Family Violence Coun., Beloit, 1983-85, Rock County Mental Health Assn., Janesville, Wis., 1986, Beloit Teen Pregnancy Task Force, 1988-91; v.p. First Light Group Home, Beloit, 1984-87. Mem. NASW, Assn. for Social Work Adminstrs. in Health Care (pres. 1995-96). Home: 2744 Sandra Ln Waukesha WI 53188 Office: Childrens Hosp of Wis PO Box 1997 9000 W Wisconsin Ave Milwaukee WI 53226-3518 also: Inst Mental Health 14555 W National Ave New Berlin WI 53151-4494

HARVILL, MELBA SHERWOOD, university librarian; b. Bryson, Tex., Jan. 22, 1933; d. William Henry and Delta Verlin (Brawner) Sherwood; m. L. E. Harvill Jr., Feb. 2, 1968; children: Sherman T., Mark Roling. BA, North Tex. State Coll., 1954; MA, North Tex. State U., 1968, MLS, 1973, PhD, 1984. Tchr. Graham (Tex.) Ind. Sch. Dist., 1966-68; reference libr. Midwestern U., Wichita Falls, 1968-73; dir. librs. Midwestern State U., Wichita Falls, 1973—; presenter in field. Vol. Boy Scouts Am., Wichita Falls, 1969-74; vol. Wichita Falls Sr.-Jr. Forum, 1978—, mem. exec. bd. girls club, ways and means com., sec., asst. treas.; chmn. United Way, Midwestern State U., 1975-76; mem. talent coordinating com. Wichita Falls Centennial Celebration; mem. U. North Tex. Advancement Adv. Coun.; vol. Conv. and Vis. Bur., Lone Stars, 1993—; bd. dirs. YWCA Wichita Falls, 1987-94, pres. bd. dirs., 1989-91, 94-95; grad. Leadership Wichita Falls, 1990; pres. Southside Girls Club, 1997-98; auditor, budget com. chair Woman's Forum, 1997-99. Recipient Svc. award Sr.-Jr. Forum, Wichita Falls United Way Community Svc. award, 1975, Svc. award YWCA Bd. Dirs., 1991; named Met. BPW Woman of Yr., 1980. Mem. ALA, LWV (program v.p., pres. 1991-92), Tex. Libr. Assn. (mem. planning com., mem. membership com., mem. legis. com., mem. rsch. and grants com., chairperson dist VII, chairperson adminstrn. round table), Tex. Coun. State U. Librs. (sec.-treas. 1990-92), Wichita Falls Rotary North (sec. 1993-96), U. North Tex. Alumni Assn. (bd. dirs. 1992-94, 97—), Soroptimist Internat., Phi Alpha Theta, Pi Sigma Alpha, Phi Delta Phi, Gamma Theta Upsilon, Alpha Chi, Beta Phi Mu, Phi Delta Kappa. Democrat. Avocations: spectator sports, swimming, music, reading, travel. Home: 4428 BUS 287J Iowa Park TX 76367 Office: Midwestern State U 3410 Taft Blvd Wichita Falls TX 76308-2096

HARVILLE SMITH, MARTHA LOUISE, special education educator; b. Detroit, Sept. 28, 1958; d. Henry and Emma Jean (Campbell) H.; m. Russell Smith, May 1, 1993; 1 child, David-Akem. BA in Edn., Queens Coll., 1981, MS in Edn., 1986; postgrad., Columbia U., 1992. Cert. tchr. spl. edn., elem. tchr. N-6, sch. dist. adminstr., N.Y.; lic. asst. prin., N.Y. Caseworker Bur. of Child Welfare, Jamaica, N.Y., 1981-82; tchr. spl. edn. Pub. Sch. 46Q, Bayside Queens, N.Y., 1982-83, Pub. Sch. 213Q, Bayside Queens, N.Y., 1983-85; Pub. Sch. 153, Maspeth, 1986; gen. indsl. arts tchr. Ind. Sch. 227Q/Louis Armstrong East, Elmhurst, N.Y., 1985-89; spl. edn. tchr. Pub. Sch. 153, Bayside Queens, 1986; tchr. technology Ind. Sch. 227Q/Louis Armstrong East, Elmhurst, N.Y., 1990-91, 93-94; staff devel. specialist Cen. Bd. Edn., Bklyn., 1989-90; rsch. asst. Columbia U. Tchr.'s Coll., N.Y.C., 1991—; rsch. asst., intern Ctr. If Adaptive Tech., N.Y.C., 1991—; tech. cons. CSTIP project Tchrs. Coll. Columbia U. IUME Ctr.; computer tchr. Bd. Edn. Dist. 26, Bayside Queens, 1983-85; software evaluator, Bd. Edn., Bklyn., 1988-89; yearbook adv. Ind. Sch. 227Q, 1986-89; adj. lectr. Big Buddy Program at Queens Coll., Flushing, N.Y., 1989-90. Inventor in field; contbr. articles to profl. jours. Mem. exec. bd. Reach for Cultural Heights, 1992—; mem. Lincoln Ctr. Inst., 1984—; del. Citizen Amb. Program in Russia, 1995; dep. gov. Am. Biog. Rsch. Inst., 1995—. Recipient Svc. award Girl Scouts US, Jamaica, 1980. Mem. Coun. Exceptional Children, Queens Coll. Alumni, Edn. Adminstrn. Orgn. Columbia U., Queens Coll. Grad. Student Assn. (pres. 1988), Kappa Delta Pi. Avocations: theatre, drawing, reading, hobbies.

HARVIN, CHARLES ALEXANDER, III, state legislator, lawyer; b. Sumter, S.C., Feb. 7, 1950; s. Charles Alexander Harvin, Jr. m. Cathy Jane Brand; 1 child, Mary Franklin; Grad. in history and polit. sci. Baptist Coll., Charleston, S.C., 1972, Augusta Law Sch., 1976; hon. degree Sherman Chiropractic Coll., Spartanburg, S.C., 1979, Francis Marion Coll., 1986; LLD (hon.) Charleston So. Univ., 1988. Mem. S.C. Ho. of Reps., 1976—, asst. majority leader, majority whip, 1978-82, majority leader, 1982—, mem. ways and means com., vice chmn. rules com., majority leader Emeritus Ho. of Reps., S.C., 1987—. Pres. Bapt. Coll. Young Democrats, 1970-72; officer Charleston County Young Dems., 1971-72; chmn. 6th Congl. Dist. Young Dems., 1975-76; life mem. S.C. Young Dems.; chmn. Clarendon County Dem. Com.; vice chmn. S.C. Dem. Com., 1976-78, also mem. exec. com.; del. Dem. Nat. Conv., 1984; mem. S.C. Gov.'s Agr. Study Com.; U.S. Constn. Bicentennial Commn., 1985—; trustee S.C. Hall of Fame; vice chmn. alumni bd. Bapt. Coll., 1975-76; bd. visitors Clemson U., 1977-78, Med. Univ. S.C., 1986-87, Charleston So. Univ., 1988-90. Maj. USNG. Recipient Outstanding Service award Charleston County Young Dems., 1972, S.C. Young Dems., 1977; Disting. Service award S.C. Dem. Com., 1981; appreciation award S.C. Tech. Edn. Colls., 1981; Legislator of Yr. award S.C. Young Dems., 1982, S.C. Student Legislature, 1981, S.C. State Library Bd., 1982, S.C. Assn. for Deaf, 1985; award S.C. Council for Exceptional Children, 1982, S.C. Agrl. Community, 1982; Outstanding Legislator Service award United Parcel Service, 1984; Disting. Service award Bapt. Coll. of Charleston Alumni Assn., 1984, also numerous other awards and commendations. Mem. ABA, Am. Judicature Soc., S.C. Trial Lawyers Assn., Clarendon County Farm Bur., Clarendon County Hist. Soc. (v.p. 1983-84, pres. 1985-86), S.C. State Employees Assn., NAACP, Huguenot Soc. of S.C., First Families of S.C., Alpha Phi Omega (life). Lodges: Masons, Shriners. Office: South Carolina Ho of Reps PO Box 11867 Columbia SC 29211-1867

HARVIN, DAVID TARLETON, lawyer; b. Houston, Feb. 15, 1945; s. William Charles and Ruth Helen (Beck) H.; m. Sarah Ann Hartman, Apr. 21, 1973; children—Kimberly Kate, William Hartman, John Andrew. B.A., Yale U., 1967; J.D., U. Tex., 1970. Bar: Tex. 1970, U.S. Dist. Ct. (so. dist.) Tex. 1972, U.S. Dist. Ct. (ea. dist.) Tex. 1977, U.S. Dist. Ct. (no. dist.) Tex. 1979, U.S. Dist. Ct. (we. dist.) Tex. 1988, U.S. Ct. Appeals (5th cir.) 1971, U.S. Supreme Ct. 1977. Law clk. U.S. Ct. Appeals (5th cir.), 1970-71; assoc. Vinson & Elkins L.L.P., Houston, 1971-77, ptnr., 1977—. Trustee Episcopal Theol. Sem. of S.W., 1995—, Stehlin Found. for Cancer Rsch., 1986-96, The Kinkaid Sch., 1997—; vice chancellor Episcopal Diocese of Tex. Fellow Am. Coll. Trial Lawyers, Tex. Bar Found., Houston Bar Found.; mem. ABA, Houston County Club, Houston Ctr. Club. Home: 111 Maple Valley Rd Houston TX 77056-1007 Office: Vinson & Elkins LLP 1001 Fannin St Ste 3300 Houston TX 77002-6760

HARVITT, ADRIANNE STANLEY, lawyer; b. Chgo., May 15, 1954; d. Stanley and Maryln (Loye) H.; m. Donald Martin Heinrich, Aug. 27, 1977; children: Patrick Loye, Christina Marie. AB, U. Chgo., 1975, MBA, 1976; JD with honors, Ill. Inst. Tech., 1980. Bar: Ill. 1980, U.S. Dist. Ct. (no. dist.) Ill. 1980, U.S. Ct. Appeals (7th cir.) 1985, (9th cir.) 1988, U.S. Supreme Ct. 1985, Wis. 1993. Fin. analyst Bell & Howell Co., Chgo., 1976-77; trial atty. U.S. Commodity Futures Trading Commn., Chgo., 1980-83; assoc. Hannafan & Handler, Chgo., 1983-85; ptnr. Harvitt & Gekas, Ltd., Chgo., 1985-97, Harvitt & Assoc., Ltd., Milw., 1997-98; appt. pub. svc. spl. prosecutor Milw. County Dist. Atty.'s Office, 1998; v.p., assoc. gen. counsel Stephens Inc., Little Rock, 1999—; adj. prof. securities regulation U. Ark. Sch. of Law, Little Rock, Ark., 1999. Mem. Law Rev. Chgo.-Kent Coll. Law, 1979-80. Mem. ABA, Ill. Bar Assn. (article hon. mention 1982), Chgo. Bar Assn., Assn. Women Lawyers, U. Chgo. Alumni Assn. (svc. citation 1995, bd. govs. 1996-98), U. Chgo. Women's Bus. Group (v.p. 1988-90), U. Chgo. Women's Bd., Art Inst. Chgo. Avocations: skiing, swimming, scuba diving.

HARVUOT, CATHLEEN MARY, elementary education educator, principal; b. Cleve., June 16, 1951; d. Richard William and Josephine Mary (Shubiak) Vasicek; m. Clifford Allen Harvuot, July 25, 1987. BS in Elem. Edn., U. Akron, Ohio, 1973; MEd in Supervision of Instruction, Ohio U., 1978. Cert. elem. edn., spl. edn., nursery, and kindergarten tchr., N.Y., sch. adminstr., N.Y. Tchr. Cambridge (Ohio) City Schs., 1973-78; tchr. remedial reading East Muskingum Schs., New Concord, Ohio, 1978-81; tchr. 2d and 3d grades Englewood (N.J.) Schs., 1981-82; tchr. 1st grade Haworth (N.J.) Schs., 1982-83; tchr. spl. edn. Leonia (N.J.) Pub. Schs./Anna C. Scott Schs., 1983-85; tchr. 1st grade Ardsley (N.Y.) Unified Free Sch. Dist./Concord Rd. Sch., 1985-89, tchr. 2d grade, 1989-94; asst. prin. North Mianus Sch. Greenwich (Conn.) Pub. Schs., 1994-97; prin. Franklin Ave. Sch., Pearl River (N.Y..) Schs., Pearl River, N.Y., 1997—; cons. Bd. Coop. Svcs. of Westchester County for Social Studies, N.Y., 1986-90; ind. cons. for DMP math. program, Ardsley, 1987-89; maths. curriculum leader Ardsley Schs., 1988-89. Mem. ASCD, Nat. Assn. Elem. Sch. Prins., Nat. Coun. Tchrs. of Maths., Internat. Reading Assn. (pres., v.p. Muskingum chpt. 1980-81). Home: 2 Regis Ct Suffern NY 10901-3430

HARWARD, DONALD, academic official. V.p. acad. affairs Coll. Wooster, Ohio, until 1989; pres. Bates Coll., Lewiston, Maine, 1989—. Office: Bates Coll Office of Pres Lewiston ME 04240*

HARWELL, DAVID WALKER, retired state supreme court chief justice; b. Florence, S.C., Jan. 8, 1932; s. Baxter Hicks and Lacy (Rankin) H.; divorced; children: Robert Bryan, William Baxter. LL.B., J.D., U. S.C., 1958; HHD (hon.), Frances Marion U., 1987. Bar: S.C. 1958, U.S. Dist. Ct. S.C. 1958, U.S. Ct. Appeals 1964, U.S. Supreme Ct. 1961. Circuit judge 12th Jud. Ct. S.C., 1973-80; justice S.C. Supreme Ct., 1980-91, chief justice, 1991-94; ret., 1994; spl. counsel Nelson, Mullins, Riley and Scarborough. Mem. S.C. Ho. of Reps., 1962-73. Served with USNR, 1952-54. Mem. Am. Bar Assn., Am. Trial Lawyers Assn., S.C. Bar Assn., S.C. Trial Lawyers Assn. (Portrait and Scholarship award 1986). Presbyterian. Office: PO Box 2459 Myrtle Beach SC 29578-2459

HARWELL, EDWIN WHITLEY, judge; b. Ashland, Ala., June 4, 1929; s. William Thomas and Effie Belle (Whitley) H.; m. Olma Lillian Motes, Nov. 27, 1957. Student, Jacksonville State U., 1948-49; B.S., J.D., U. Ala., 1952. Bar: Ala. bar 1952. Practicing atty., 1954-71; circuit judge Anniston, Ala., 1971-77; city judge City of Oxford, 1977—; individual practice law, 1977—. Served with AUS, 1952-54. Mem. Ala. Bar Assn., Calhoun County Bar Assn. (past pres.), VFW, Ala. Mcpl. Judges Assn. (past pres.), United Comml. Travelers, Elk, Moose, Anniston Exch. (past pres.). Baptist. Home: 813 Blue Ridge Dr Anniston AL 36207-3328

HARWELL, WILLIAM EARNEST (ERNIE HARWELL), broadcaster; b. Washington, Ga., Jan. 25, 1918; s. Davis Gray Harwell; m. Lula Tankersley, Aug. 30, 1941; children: William Earnest, Jr., Gray Neville, Julie, Carolyn. AB, Emory U., 1940; LittD (hon.), Adrian Coll., 1985; LHD (hon.), No. Mich. Coll., 1990. Sports dir. Sta. WSB, Atlanta, 1940-43; announcer Atlanta Crackers, 1946-48, Bklyn. Dodgers, 1948-49, N.Y. Giants, 1950-53, Balt. Orioles, 1954-59, Detroit Tigers, 1960-91, 93—; announcer All-Star games, World Series, NBC, CBS Radio, pro football Balt. Colts, N.Y. Giants; broadcaster Master's golf tournament, NBC, 1942, 46. Author: Tuned to Baseball, 1985, Diamond Gems, 1991, The Babe Signed My Shoe, 1994; composer songs including I Don't Know Any Better, Move over Babe, Only a Fool, One-Room World, One Dream, Sing Every Song. With USMC, 1942-46. Recipient Lowell Thomas Broadcast award, 1985, Alvin Foon award Mich. Jewish Sports Hall of Fame, 1988, 90, Big Mac award Detroit News, 1989, Golden Compass award Campfire Inc., 1989, Life Directions Enrichment award, 1989, Nat. Lifetime Nat. Achievement award March of Dimes, 1991, Joe Louis award, 1991, Ken Hubbs Meml. award, 1991, Stanley Kresge award, 1994, U. Detroit Jesuit Magis award, 1995; inducted Baseball Hall of Fame, Cooperstown, 1981, Mich. Sports Hall of Fame, Emory U. Hall of Fame, Nat. Sportscasters and Sportswriters Hall of Fame, Am. Sportscasters Hall of Fame, Catch Hall of Fame, Ga. Broadcasters Hall of Fame, Nat. Radio Hall of Fame, 1998. Mem. ASCAP, Sigma Alpha Epsilon. Home: 25387 Witherspoon St Farmington Hills MI 48335-1367

HARWICK, BETTY CORINNE BURNS, sociology educator; b. L.A., Jan. 22, 1926; d. Henry Wayne Burns and Dorothy Elizabeth (Menzies) Routhier; m. Burton Thomas Harwick, June 20, 1947; children: Wayne Thomas, Burton Terence, Bonnie Christine Foster, Beverly Anne Carroll. Student, Biola, 1942-45, Summer Inst. Linguistics, 1945, U. Calif., Berkeley, 1945-52; BA, Calif. State U., Northridge, 1961, MA, 1965; postgrad., MIT, 1991. Prof. sociology Pierce Coll., Woodland Hills, Calif., 1966-95, pres. acad. senate, 1976-77, pres. faculty assn., 1990-91, chmn. dept. for philosophy and sociology, 1990-95, co-creator, faculty advisor interdisciplinary program religious studies, 1988-95; chmn. for sociology L.A. C.C. Dist., 1993-95. Author: (with others) Introducing Sociology, 1977; author: Workbook for Introducing Sociology, 1978. faculty rep. Calif. C.C. Assn., 1977-80. Alt. fellow NEH, 1978. Mem. Am. Acad. Religion, Soc. Bibl. Lit., Am. Sociol. Assn. Presbyterian. Home: 19044 Superior St Northridge CA 91324-1845

HARWICK, DENNIS PATRICK, lawyer; b. Nampa, Idaho, May 27, 1949; s. T. Dale and Lois L. (Patrick) H.; m. Rebecca Cowgill, May 10, 1980. BA, U. Idaho, 1971, JD, 1974. Bar: Idaho 1974, U.S. Dist. Ct. Idaho 1974. Legal officer Idaho Bank & Trust, Pocatello, 1974-79, v.p.-legal, Boise, 1979-85, spokesman, 1983-85, editor corp. newsletter, 1983-85; mem. adv. coun. U. Idaho Coll. Letters and Sci., 1986-90; exec. dir. Idaho State Bar and Idaho Law Found., Inc., 1985-90; exec. dir., CEO Washington State Bar Assn., 1990-97; pres. Kans. Lawyers Svc. Corp., 1998—; exec. dir. Kans. Bar Assn./Kans. Bar Found., Topeka, 1998—. Bd. dirs. Boise Philharm., 1984-89, v.p. adminstrn., 1985-87; chmn. Idaho Commn. U.S. Constl. Bicentennial, 1986-88; chmn. Idaho Bus. Week Program, 1984; treas. Idaho State Dem. Conv., 1980. Mem. ABA, Nat. Assn. Bar Execs. (mem. exec. com., pres. 1996-97), Nat. Conf. Bar Founds. (trustee), Idaho State Bar (examiner/grader 1975-90), Idaho Bankers Assn. (spokesman), Am. Inst. Banking (state chmn. 1982-83), Idaho Assn. Commerce and Industry (chmn. coms.), Boise Bar Assn., Bar Assn. Adminstrn., Phi Beta Kappa. Democrat. Clubs: Boise Racquet and Swim (bd. dirs. 1988-90, pres. 1990). Office: Kans Bar Assn PO Box 1037 Topeka KS 66601-1037

HARWICK, WAYNE THOMAS, economist; b. Oakland, Calif., Feb. 29, 1948; s. Burton Thomas and Betty Corinne (Burns) H. BA in Econs., Calif. State Univ., Northridge, 1970, MA in Econs., 1975; BA in Math., Calif. State Univ., L.A., 1983. Planner Ventura (Calif.) County Schs., 1975-76; labor market economist Calif. Employment Data Rsch., L.A., 1976-83; cost analyst TRW, Redondo Beach, Calif., 1983-88; engrng. specialist Northrop-Grumman, Pico Rivera, Calif., 1988-92, 96—; cost economist Aerojet, Azusa, Calif., 1992-94; sr. assoc. Mgmt. Consulting Rsch., Thousand Oaks, Calif., 1994-95; instr. Oxnard (Calif.) Coll., 1975-78; owner Industry Metrics, Torrance, Calif., 1995—; rep. Space Systems Cost Analysis Group for Northrop Grumman Corp.; spkr. in field. Bd. dirs. Homeowners Assn., Torrance, 1993-95, 97—. Mem. Soc. Cost Estimating Analysis (cert. cost analyst), Internat. Soc. Parametric Analysts (So. Calif. bd. dirs. 1997), World Affairs Coun. Lutheran. Avocations: weightlifting, swimming, applied mathematics, religious studies, astronomy. E-mail: harwick@mail.northgrum.com. Home: 4404 Spencer St Torrance CA 90503-2434 Office: Northrop Grumman Corp 8900 Washington Blvd Pico Rivera CA 90660-3765

HARWIT, MARTIN OTTO, astrophysicist, writer, educator, museum director; b. Prague, Czechoslovakia, Mar. 9, 1931; came to U.S., 1946, naturalized, 1953; s. Felix Michael and Regina Hedwig (Perutz) Haurowitz; m. Marianne Mark, Feb. 1, 1957; children: Alexander, Eric, Emily. B.A. in Physics, Oberlin Coll., 1951; M.A. in Physics, U. Mich., Ann Arbor, 1953; Ph.D. in Physics, Mass. Inst. Tech., 1960. NATO postdoctoral fellow Cambridge (Eng.) U., 1960-61; NSF fellow Cornell U., Ithaca, N.Y., 1961-62; asst. prof. astronomy Cornell U., 1962-64, asso. prof., 1964-68, prof., 1968-87, prof. emeritus, 1988—, chmn. dept. astronomy, 1971-76, co-dir. program for history and philosophy of sci. and tech., 1985-87; dir. Nat. Air and Space Mus. Smithsonian Instn., Washington, 1987-95; E.O. Hulburt fellow Naval Research Lab., Washington, 1963-64; Nat. Acad. Sci. exchange visitor Czechoslovak Acad. Sci., Prague, 1969-70; v.p., dir. Spectral Imaging Inc., Concord, Mass., 1971-77; external mem. Max Planck Soc., Inst. Radioastronomy, Bonn., W. Ger., 1979—; cons. NASA.; chair for space history Nat. Air and Space Mus., Smithsonian Instn., 1983; chmn. astrophysics mgmt. ops. working group, NASA, 1985-87. Author: Astrophysical Concepts, 1973, 2d edit. 1988, 3d edit., 1998 (transl. into Chinese 1981), (with N.J.A. Sloan) Hadamard Transform Optics, 1979, Cosmic Discovery-The Search, Scope and Heritage of Astronomy, 1981 (transl. into German and French 1982), (with the mus. staff) Treasures of the National Air and Space Museum, 1995, An Exhibit Denied: Lobbying the History of Enola Gay, 1996 (transl. into Japanese 1997). With U.S. Army, 1955-57. Recipient Alexander von Humboldt Found. sr. U.S. scientist award Max Planck Inst. Radioastronomy, 1976-77; NSF grantee, 1963-68; Research Corp. grantee, 1970-75; NASA grantee, 1965—; Air Force Cambridge (Mass.) Research Labs. grantee, 1969-74. Fellow AAAS, Am. Phys. Soc. (chmn. div. history of physics 1986-87, chmn. astrophysics div. 1988-89), Royal Astron. Soc.; mem. Soc. for History of Tech., Am. Astron. Soc. Home: 511 H St SW Washington DC 20024-2725

HARWOOD, BERNICE BAUMEL, artist, community volunteer; b. Bklyn., Mar. 6, 1923; d. Max and Mildred (Weinberger) Baumel; m. Daniel J. Harwood, Aug. 23, 1947; children: René Gordon, Felice Spodick. BS in Art Edn. cum laude, Hofstra U., Hempstead, N.Y., 1973; MS in Spl. Edn., Hofstra U., 1975; student, Ruth Leaf Studio, Douglaston, N.Y., 1980-87, Studio Camitzer, Valdottavo, Italy, 1983. Artist in residence Syossett (N.Y.) Sch. Dist., 1986; pres. Graphic Eye Gallery, 1986-87. One-woman shows at Calkins Gallery, Hofstra U., 1985, Graphic Eye Gallery, Port Washington, N.Y., 1989; exhibited in group shows at Norton Gallery Art, Profl. Artists Guild, West Palm Beach, Fla., Hutchins Gallery, C.W. Post U., Greenvale, N.Y., Albrecht Mus., St. Joseph, Mo., Monmouth (N.J.) Mus. Art, Foxhall Gallery, Washington, Elaine Benson Gallery, Bridghampton, N.Y., 1989, Daruma Gallery, Woodmere, N.Y., 1991, Boca Mus. Art, Fla., Nat. Mus. Am. Jewish Mil. History, Washington, 1999—, others; represented in pvt. collections including IBM, Bethlehem, Pa., Am. Stock Exchange, N.Y.C., Chase Manhattan (N.Y.) Bank, Sandoz, Nabisco; represented in permanent collection Queensborough C.C. Art Gallery, N.Y.; illustrator: Five Towns, 1962. Chairperson LWV, Woodmere, N.Y., 1957-61; v.p. Nat. Coun. Jewish Women, Lawrence, N.Y., 1976-81; committeewoman Dem. Party, Woodmere, 1962-84; mem. bd. advisors Nassau County Mus. Fine Art, Roslyn, N.Y., 1981-88. With U.S. Navy (WAVES), 1944-46. Recipient art awards including Sally Carson award Norton Gallery of Art, West Palm Beach, Fla., 1993, 2d prize Emily Lowe Gallery, Hofstra U., 1984, award of excellence Long Beach (N.Y.) Art League, 1987, hon. mention Profl. Artists Guild, Coral Springs (Fla.) Civic Ctr., 1997. Mem. Nat. Assn. Women Artists (juror 1988-90, Leila Sawyer award 1983), Nat. Mus. of Women in Art (charter, Washington), Fla. Watercolor Soc., Palm Beach County Cultural Coun, Womens Vet. Meml. (charter), Arlington Cemetary. Democrat. Jewish. Avocations: golf, reading, travel, music, theatre. Home: 41 Windsor Ln Boynton Beach FL 33436-6068

HARWOOD, BRIAN DENNIS, securities industry executive; b. London, Feb. 3, 1932; arrived Can., 1953; s. William Henry and Catherine Mary (O'Brien) H.; m. Diane Louise McLean, Sept. 1, 1988. Ed. pvt. schs., London. Fgn. exch. cashier Thos. Cook & Sons, London, 1949-50, 52-53; to br. mgmt. Bank of Montreal, Vancouver and Montreal, Can., 1953-62, 64-70; lending officer Security First Nat. Bank, L.A., 1963-64; with Canaccord Capital Corp (formerly L.O.M. Western Securities Ltd.), Vancouver, 1970—, exec. v.p., 1975-87, pres., chief oper. officer, 1987-94; vice chmn., 1994—; also bd. dirs. Canaccord Capital Corp (formerly L.O.M. Western Securities Ltd.), Vancouver; past chmn. Can. Investor Protection Fund, also bd. dirs. Sgt. Brit. Army, 1950-52. Mem. Investment Dealers Assn. Can. (bd. dirs., nat. and exec. coms. 1989-94), Vancouver Stock Exch. (bd. govs. 1985-94, vice chmn. 1989, chmn. 1991-93), Royal Vancouver Yacht Club, Vancouver Lawn Tennis Club, Terminal City Club. Avocations: boating, reading, walking, cycling. Office: Canaccord Capital Corp, 609 Granville St PO Box 10337, Vancouver, BC Canada V7Y 1H2*

HARWOOD, ELEANOR CASH, librarian; b. Buckfield, Maine, May 29, 1921; d. Leon Eugene and Ruth (Chick) Cash; B.A., Am. Internat. Coll., 1943; B.S., New Haven State Tchrs. Coll., 1955; m. Burton H. Harwood, Jr., June 21, 1944 (div. 1953); children—Ruth (Mrs. William R. Cline), Eleanor, James Burton. Librarian, Rathbun Meml. Library, East Haddam, Conn., 1955-56; asst. librarian Kent (Conn.) Sch., 1956-63; cons. to Chester (Conn.) Pub. Library, 1965-71. Served from ensign to lt. (j.g.) USNR, 1944-46. Mem. ALA, Conn. Libr. Assn., Chester Hist. Soc. (trustee 1970-72), D.A.V., Am. Legion, Am. Legion Aux., Soc. Mayflower Descs., Appalachian Mountain Club. Mem. United Ch. Author: (with John G. Park) The Independent School Library and the Gifted Child, 1956; The Age of Samuel Johnson, LLD, Remember When, 1987, (essay) Growing Up in Chester, 1993, Moosley Yours, 1996. Home: 10 Maple St # 255 Chester CT 06412-1316

HARWOOD, IVAN RICHMOND, pediatric pulmonologist; b. Huntington, W.Va., July 3, 1939. BA, Dartmouth Coll., 1961; MD, U. W.Va., 1965. Diplomate Nat. Bd. Med. Examiners; lic. physician, Calif., Can.; cert. Am. Bd. Pediatrics. Intern in pediatrics U. W.Va. Hosp., Morgantown, 1965-66; resident in pediatrics Yale-New Haven (Conn.) Hosp., 1966-68, sr. resident outpatient dept., 1968-69; chief pediatrics USAF Hosp. 3646, Del Rio, Tex., 1968-70; asst. prof. pediatrics U. Calif. Med. Ctr., San Diego, 1971-78, chief pediatric pulmonary div., 1972-93, dir. pediatric intensive care unit, 1972-78, assoc. adj. prof. pediatrics, 1978-86, prof., 1987—; mem. patient care rev. and numerous other coms. U. Calif. Med. Ctr., 1976—; co-dir. Cystic Fibrosis Ctr., San Diego, 1972-73, dir., 1973; mem. Cystic Fibrosis Young Adult Com., Atlanta, 1974-80, chmn., 1976-80, Cystic Fibrosis Ctr. Com., 1986-89, vice-chmn., 1990-94; mem. San Diego County Tuburculosis Control Bd., 1974-78; dir. Cystic Fibrosis Ctr. Children's Hosp. and Health Ctr., San Diego, 1995—; presenter, lectr. in field. Producer: (videos) Issues in Cystic Fibrosis Series; mem. rev. bd., CF Film, 1980; contbr. chpts. to books, and numerous articles to profl. jours. Mem. Air Quality Adv. Com., State of Calif., 1974-80; mem. Genetically Handicapped Persons Program Adv. Com., Calif., 1977-87; mem. adv. bd. Grossmont Coll. Inhalation Therapy Sch., San Diego, 1975-76; mem. inpatient adolscent adv. com., Mercy Hosp., 1982-85. U. Calif. fellow in pediatric cardiology, 1970-71; recipient 1st Prize Internat. Rehab. Film Library Competition, 1980. Mem. Calif. Med. Assn. (patient care audit com. 1975-78), Nat. Cystic Fibrosis Found. (mem. adv. com. 1976-80, planning ad hoc com. 1976-77, patient registry subcom. 1986-90), San Diego Found. for Med. Care (major med. rev. com. 1978-84), San Diego Lung Assn. (pediatric com. 1976-80, chmn. Project Breath-Easy 1976-78). Home: PO Box 431 Jamul CA 91935-0431 Office: Childrens Hosp 3020 Childrens Way San Diego CA 92123-4282

HARWOOD, JERRY, market research executive; b. Jersey City, June 19, 1926; s. Louis and Dorothy (Cohen) Horowitz; m. Ruthella Zimmerman, June 25, 1950; children: Robin Jill, Dean Brook. B.A. cum laude, L.I. U., 1949; M.A., NYU, 1953. Tech. instr. U.S. Bur. Census, 1950-51; v.p., assoc. research dir. Kenyon & Eckhardt Advt., N.Y.C., 1962-66; sr. v.p., dir. research Needham, Harper & Steers Advt., N.Y.C., 1966-73; sr. v.p., group research dir. Benton & Bowles Advt., N.Y.C., 1975-88; mktg. cons. Short Hills, NJ, 1988—; mem. Census Adv. Com., 1976-83; adj. assoc. prof. NYU Grad. Sch. Bus., 1984-85. Pres. Temple B'nai Jeshurun, 1980-82, Jewish Family Svc. of MetroWest, 1984-87, N.J. Jewish News, 1992-95; v.p. Mental

Health Assn. Essex County, 1992—; mem. Essex County Child Placement Rev. Bd., 1988—; bd. dirs. Am. Jewish Com., 1996—. Mem. Am. Mktg. Assn. (founder Effie awards, Advt. Effectiveness Awards Program, pres. N.Y.C. chpt. 1970-71, nat. v.p. pub. policy and issues 1973, nat. v.p. mktg. rsch. 1981-82, mem. editl. bd. 1992-98, chmn. Marketing Hall of Fame 1995—), Nat. Assn. Jewish Family and Children Agys. (pres. 1997-99, trustee HIAS 1997-98). Home and Office: 22 Athens Rd Short Hills NJ 07078-1312 *The individual who respects the rights, opinions and needs of others is the individual who manages his own life most productively and successfully.*

HARWOOD, JOHN J., journalist; b. Louisville, Nov. 5, 1956; s. Richard Lee and Beatrice (Mosby) H.; m. Frankie L. Blackburn, Feb. 16, 1985; children: Mary Jeanne, Leigh, Avery. AB in History, Econs., Duke U., 1978; Nieman fellow, Harvard U., 1989-90. State capital corr. to polit. editor to Washington corr. St. Petersburg (Fla.) Times, 1978-91; polit. editor, White House corr., congl. corr. Wall St. Jour., Washington, 1991—. johnharwood@news.wsj.com. Office: The Wall St Jour 1025 Connecticut Ave NW Washington DC 20036

HARWOOD, JULIUS J., metallurgist, educator; b. N.Y.C., Dec. 3, 1918; m. Naomi Beitner, 1941; children: Dane L., Gail A., Caren L., Rochelle. BS, CCNY, 1939; MS, U. Md., 1953; D of Engring. (hon.), Mich. Tech. U., 1986. Materials engr. U.S. Naval Gun Factory, 1940-46; metall. Off Naval Rsch., 1946-60; mgr. metall. sci. lab. Ford Motor Co., Dearborn, Mich., 1960-69, mgr. rsch. planning engring. and rsch. staff, 1969-71, dir. Material Sci. Lab, engring. and rsch. staff, 1971-83; prof. engring. Wayne State U., Detroit, 1984; pres. Ovonic Synthetic Material Co., Troy, Mich., 1984-87; pres. Harwood Cons., Orchard Lake, Mich., 1987—, West Bloomfield, Mich.; adj. prof. Wayne State U., Detroit, 1975. Contbr. articles to profl. jours. Fellow AAAS, Metall. Soc. (pres. 1973), Am. Soc. Metals (John H. Shoemaker award 1977), Engring. Soc. of Detroit (Gold Medal award 1983); mem. Am. Inst. Mining, Metall. and Petroleum Engrs. (pres. 1976, hon.), Am. Ceramic Soc. (Orton lectr. 1978), Nat. Acad. Engrs. Office: 5023 Pheasant Cv West Bloomfield MI 48323-2093

HARWOOD, MATTHEW DAVID, artist; b. Ft. Riley, Kans., Feb. 21, 1959; s. Michael Sullivan and Adele Theresa (Gomez) H.; m. Eileen Marie Taylor, Apr. 30, 1993. BArch cum laude, Va. Tech., 1983. Artist-in-residence Torpedo Factory Art Ctr., Alexandria, Va., 1984—; pres. Torpedo Factory Artists' Assn., Alexandria, 1992-94. One man show includes Target Gallery, 1998. Bd. mem. Friends of the Torpedo Factory, Alexandria, 1990-91, Old Town Bus. Assn., Alexandria, 1994, Alexandria Promotion Team, 1994; com. mem. Alexandria Mktg. Fund, 1994. Named Artist of the Yr., Friends of the Torpedo Factory, Alexandria, 1997. Office: Torpedo Factory Art Ctr 105 N Union St # 305 Alexandria VA 22314-3217

HARWOOD, RICHARD LEE, journalist, newspaper editor; b. Chilton, Wis., Mar. 29, 1925; s. Luther Milton and Ruby (Heath) H.; m. Beatrice Bottrell Mosby, Dec. 18, 1950; children: Helen, John, Richard, David. A.B., Vanderbilt U., 1950. Reporter Nashville Tennessean, 1947-52; Reporter Louisville Courier-Jour. and Times, 1952-61, Washington corr., 1961-65; nat. corr. Washington Post, 1966-68, nat. editor, 1968-70, asst. mng. editor, 1970-74, dep. mng. editor, 1976-88, ombudsman, 1988-92, editorial columnist, 1992—; v.p. Trenton Times Newspapers, 1974-76; lectr. U. Md., 1988—, Washington Coll., 1992—; exec. editor Literary House Press. Author: Lyndon, a Biography of L.B. Johnson; contbr. articles to nat. mags. Bd. dirs. Marine Corps Hist. Assn., 1987-91; bd. govs. Washington Coll., 1994—. Served with USMCR, 1942-46, PTO. Recipient citation Nat. Edn. Writers Assn., 1957; George Polk Meml. award L.I. U., 1967, 71; Distinguished Service medal Sigma Delta Chi, 1967, 71; Nieman fellow in Journalism Harvard U., 1955-56; Carnegie fellow in journalism Columbia U., 1965-66; sr. fellow Washington Coll., 1994—; named to Hall of Fame Soc. Profl. Journalists, 1997. Mem. Soc. Nieman Fellows (dir. So. chpt. 1959-61), A.C.L.U. (dir. Ky. 1959-61), Am. Polit. Sci. Assn. (citation 1960). Democrat. Clubs: Nat. Press, Fed. City, Cosmos (Washington). Office: care Washington Post 1150 15th St NW Washington DC 20071-0001

HARWOOD, STANLEY, retired judge, lawyer; b. N.Y.C., June 23, 1926; s. Benjamin and Hannah (Schwartz) H.; m. Deborah Weinerman, June 18, 1950 (dec. 1995); children: Richard, Ellen Harwood Jacobs, Michael, Jonathan; m. Cathleen Hamilton, May 25, 1997. AB, Columbia U., 1949, LLB, 1952. Bar: N.Y. 1954, U.S. Dist. Ct. (ea. and so. dists.) N.Y. 1956, U.S. Supreme Ct. 1960. Assoc. Benjamin Harwood, Bklyn., 1953-56; pvt. practice Levittown, N.Y., 1956-65; law clk. to justice N.Y. Supreme Ct., Mineola, 1961-65; justice N.Y. Supreme Ct., 1982-92, appellate divsn., 1987-92; ptnr. Mishkin, Miner, Harwood & Semel, Mineola, 1965-69, Shayne, Dachs, Stanisci & Harwood, Mineola, 1969-81, Bower & Gardner, N.Y.C., 1992-94; counsel Jaspan, Schlesinger, Silverman & Hoffman, 1994—. Mem. N.Y. State Assembly, 1966-72; chmn. Nassau County Dem. Com., 1973-81; commr. elections Nassau County Bd. Elections, 1976-81; bd. dirs. Nat. Conf. Christians and Jews, 1993—. With USNR, 1944-46. Mem. N.Y. State Bar Assn., Nassau County Bar Assn. (chmn. cts. com. 1971-73, chmn. pro bono com. 1988-90, bd. dirs. 1997—), Mill River Club. Jewish. Home: 2 Bull Calf Ln Centerport NY 11721-1669 Office: Jaspan Schlesinger Silverman & Hoffman 300 Garden City Plz Garden City NY 11530-3302

HARWOOD, VANESSA CLARE, ballet dancer; b. Cheltenham, Eng., 1947; emigrated to Can., 1951, naturalized, 1961; d. Peter G. and Hazel M. (Smith) H.; m. Hugh E. Scully, June 14, 1980; 1 child, Shannon. Grad., Nat. Ballet Sch. Can., 1964. Mem. corps Nat. Ballet Can., Toronto, 1965-67, soloist, 1967-70, prin. dancer, 1970-86; tchr. master class U. So. Fla., 1977; tchr. Dance Centre Toronto, 1981; artistic dir. Balletto Classico, 1989; artistic adviser Ballet Orlando, 1990; guest artist Australian Ballet, Sydney, 1977, Detroit Symphony, 1977, Chgo. Ballet, 1978, Dominion U., Norfolk, Va., 1978, Dutch Nat. Ballet, Amsterdam, 1979, Munich Opera, 1981, Universal Ballet, Seoul, Korea, 1985; ptnrs. include Godunov, Nureyev, Dowell, Augustyn, Jeffries, Norman, Bissell, Bujones, Schaufuss, Eagling; coach Wilson & McCall Ice Dance Team, Bronze medalists from Can., 1988 Olympics, Worlds '88, Budapest, Hungary; guest tchr. Parksville, B.C., 1986, 90; artistic asst. to dir. LeBal Theatre Plus Toronto, 1992; guest tchr. U.S., Can. Appeared in TV ballet spls. Encore! Encore!, Expo '86; staged and danced ballet Merry Widow, Dallas Opera, 1989, starred in Swan Lake, La Fille Mal Gardee, Romeo and Juliet, Sleeping Beauty, Giselle, La Sylphide, Nutcracker, Don Quixote, Cinderella; choreographed Stars on Parade Internat. Variety Club Conv., 1986, La Traviata for Hamilton Opera, 1989-90; choreographed, appeared Andre Chenier Can. Opera Co., 1988; acting debut (play) The Mousetrap, Kingston, Ont., 1989, film ballerina role Stepping Out, 1991, TV role Road to Avonlea, Due South. Bd. dirs. Theatre Plus Toronto, 1988-89, Toronto Arts Found., 1991—; v.p. Actors Fund of Can., 1991-96, pres. 1996—; del. Korean Dance Summit, 1995; mem. exec. coun. World Dance Alliance, 1995. Decorated officer Order of Can., 1984; recipient commemorative medal for 125th anniversary of Can. Fedn., 1992; Can. Coun. grantee, 1969. Mem. Can. Actors Equity, Assn. Can. TV and Radio Artists, World Dance Alliance. *If something is meant to be it will be, but achieved by work and perserverance.*

HASAN, AHMED ABDUL KASHEM, biomedical researcher, research scientist; b. Faridpur, Bangladesh, Jan. 7, 1955; s. Adeluddin Ahmed and Hamida Begum; m. Tahmina Ferdaus, Mar. 2, 1984; children: Jishan Adel, Joshua Adel. HSC, Dhaka (Bangladesh) Coll., 1973; MD Diploma with Honors, Moscow 2nd Med. Inst., 1980; PhD in Internal Medicine, Cardiology, Acad. Med. Scis., Moscow, 1986. splst.-cardiologist, Moscow, 1986; gen. practitioner internal medicine, Moscow, 1980; cardiologist, gen. med. practitioner Bangladesh Med. Coun., 1981. House physician Hosp. Inst. Internal Medicine Acad. Med. Scis., Moscow, 1980-82, staff cardiologist, fellow Hosp. Inst. Clin. Cardiology, 1982-86; cardiology cons. Dhaka, Bangladesh, 1986-87; postdoct., rsch. assoc. dept. biochemistry and thrombosis rsch. Temple U., Phila., 1987-91; rsch. asst., prof. dept. med. biochemistry Temple U. Sch. Medicine, Phila., 1991; rsch. investigator dept. internal medicine U. Mich. Med. Ctr., Ann Arbor, 1991-96, asst. rsch. scientist, asst. prof. dept. internal medicine, 1996—; founder, v.p., dir. rsch. Thromgen, Inc., Ann Arbor, 1995—; invited spkr. Gordon Rsch. Confs., Barga, Italy, 1997, Ventura, Calif., 1999, San Diego, 1999, others. Contbr. numerous articles to scientific and med. jours., chpts. to books including Jour. Biol. Chemistry, Procs. NAS, Blood, Thrombosis & Haemostasis, Biochemistry, Circulation; reviewer Am. Inst. Biol. Scis., Am. Nat. Acad. Scis. Mem. AHA (coun. on clin. cardiology 1986, coun. on thrombosis 1990), AAAS. Achievements include basic and clinical research in thrombosis, thrombolysis, heart failure, hypertension, role of kinin in blood pressure regulation and coronary circulation, cardiovascular pharmacology; development and clinical trials of cardiovascular medicines; development of cardiovascular drugs, new generation thrombolytic agent with salutary anti-thrombotic effect, peptide congeners of BK as possible pharmaceutics for regulation of BK elaboration on endothelial cell surface; research of clot formation and dissolution; inventor of Thrombostatin-a selective Thorombin receptor inhibitor, 1996; patents for non-invasive method of determination of functional parameters of left ventricle by rheocardiography, 1985, thrombus-targeted complexes of plasminogen activator and fibrin fragments, 1994, bradykinin analogs are selective thrombin inhibitors, 1995; Thrombostatins are selective inhibitor of Thrombin mediated vascular cell activation, 1997; discovered Cytokeratin I as vascular cell receptor for Kininogens. Avocations: travel, gardening, photography, reading, music. Home: 5940 Dexter Ann Arbor Rd Dexter MI 48130-9505 Office: Thromgen Inc 5692 Plymouth Rd Ann Arbor MI 48105-9522 also: U Mich Med Ctr MSRB III, Rm 5220B 1150 W Medical Center Dr Ann Arbor MI 48109-0726

HASAN, SYED EQBAL, environmental geologist, educator; b. Patna, Bihar, India, Apr. 15, 1939; came to U.S. 1973; s. Syed Mohammad and Heyat (Imam) H.; m. Faruukh Hasan, Jan. 26, 1968; children: Danish, Zeenat, Zeba. BS, Patna U., 1960; MS, Roorkee U., India, 1963; PhD, Purdue U., 1978. Jr. geologist Geol. Survey of India, Lucknow, 1965-70, sr. geologist, 1971-73; vis. asst. prof. Mich. Tech. U., Houghton, 1978, U. Ariz., Tucson, 1978-79; asst. prof., then assoc. prof. geology U. Mo., Kansas City, 1979-97, prof., 1997—, dir. Ctr. Environ. Studies, 1996—. Author: (textbook) Geology and Hazardous Waste Management, 1995. Fellow Geol. Soc. India (life), Geol. Soc. Am.; mem. Assn. Mo. Geologists, Assn. Engring. Geologists (chmn. Kansas City-Omaha sect. 1989-91), Internat. Assn. Engring. Geologists, Sigma Xi. Avocations: photography, tennis. Fax: (816) 235-5535. E-mail: hasans@umkc.edu. Office: Univ of Mo Dept Geosciences Kansas City MO 64110-2499

HASBROOK, A. HOWARD, aviation safety engineer, consultant; b. Trenton, N.J., July 15, 1913; s. Albert Howard and Mabel (Naar) H.; m. Christel Anna Schneider, 1938 (div. 1955); children: Barbara Elaine, Howard Richard Jay; m. Virginia Randolph Whiting, 1955. Grad. high sch., DuBois, Pa. Safety engr., Calif. Flight instr., engring. test pilot USAAF, 1942-45; agrl., charter, airline & test pilot, comml. flight examiner, 1945-50; assoc. dir. Av-CIR Cornell U., 1950-55, dir. Av-CIR and aviation crash injury rschr., 1955-60; chief crash safety, sr. rsch. scientist FAA Civil Aeromed. Inst., 1960-67, chief flight performance, sr. rsch. scientist, 1968-75; aviation safety cons., profl. engr., accident investigator, analyst & reconstructionist, rsch. pilot, engring. test pilot, flight instr., 1975—, also accident prevention counselor FAA, 1975—, assoc. prof. Embry-Riddle Aerospace U., 1982, expert witness in accident litigation. Presenter lectures/tech. papers before numerous orgns.; contbr. more than 200 tech. papers & reports to profl. jours. Served with U.S. Army, 1933-34. A. Howard Hasbrook sect. established in his honor by Wright State U. Med. Sch. Libr., 1990; recipient Flight Safety Found. award, 1958, Gen. Spruance award, 1970, Harry G. Mosely award, 1972; named to Ariz. Aviation Hall of Fame, 1992, OX5 Aviation Pioneers Hall of Fame, 1995; fellow in aerospace medicine, 1972. Fellow Aerospace Med. Assn. (Hasbrook award named in his honor); mem. Internat. Soc. Air Safety Investigators, Quiet Birdmen, OX-5 Aviation Pioneers, Nat. Forensic Ctr. Home and Office: Safety Engring & Rsch HC 30 Box 813 Prescott AZ 86305-7484

HASCHMANN, THOMAS EDWIN, social services agency administrator; b. Rochester, N.Y., July 31, 1948; s. Edwin Matthew and Myrtle Arline (Wentz) H.; m. Barbara Pilato, June 18, 1971; children: James David, Amy Joy, Matthew Charles, Jeffrey Thomas. BA, Roberts Wesleyan Coll., 1971. Asst. dir. Rochester (N.Y.) Teen Challenge, 1970-72; drug edn. counselor Rochester City Sch. Dist., 1972; outreach counselor Drug and Alcohol Coun., Rochester, 1972-74; program coord. Health Assn., Rochester, 1974-76; asst. planner Monroe County Mental Health, Rochester, 1976-77; contract mgr. N.Y. State Divsn. Substance Abuse, Rochester, 1977-79; regional supr. N.Y. State Office of Alcoholism and Substance Abuse Svcs., Rochester, 1979—. Bd. dirs. Jr. Achievement of Rochester; town leader Rep. Party, Henrietta, N.Y., 1996—; mem. overcoming disabilities investment team United Way, Rochester, 1996—. Named Outstanding Friend of Labor, AFL-CIO/United Way Cmty. Svcs. Group, 1987. Avocations: furniture refinishing, stringed instruments. Home: 64 Crystal Valley Overlook Rochester NY 14623-5206 Office: NY State Office Alcoholism and Substance Abuse 109 S Union St Fl 4 Rochester NY 14607-1858

HASE, DAVID JOHN, lawyer; b. Milw., Feb. 27, 1940; s. John Henry and Catherine Charlotte (Leekley) H.; m. Penelope Sue Pritchard, Sept. 2, 1964; children—Jeffrey David, Jennifer Anne, John Paul. AB, Dartmouth Coll., 1962; LLB, U. Wis., 1965. Bar: Wis. 1965, U.S. Dist. Ct. (ea. dist.) Wis. 1965, U.S. Ct. Appeals (7th cir.) 1971, U.S. Ct. Appeals (D.C. cir.) 1975, U.S. Ct. Appeals (9th cir.) 1989, U.S. Supreme Ct. 1975. Assoc. Grootemaat, Cook & Franke, Milw., 1965-67; ptnr. and shareholder Grootemaat, Cook & Franke, Milw., 1968-70; shareholder Cook & Franke S.C., Milw., 1970-73; legal counsel to gov. Wis., Madison, 1973-74; dep. atty. gen. State of Wis., Madison, 1974-76; assoc. Foley & Lardner, Milw., 1976-77, ptnr., 1977-94; shareholder Cook & Franke S.C., Milw., 1994—. Mem. Sch. Bd., Mequon, Wis., 1971-94, treas., 1973-75, pres., 1975-94. Mem. ABA. Democrat. Home: 2108 W Raleigh Ct Mequon WI 53092-5416 Office: Cook & Franke SC 660 E Mason St Ste 401 Milwaukee WI 53202-3877

HASEK, DOMINIK, professional hockey player; b. Pardubice, Czech Republic, Jan. 29, 1965. Goaltender Buffalo Sabres, 1992—. Recipient Lester B. Pearson award, 1997, Vezina Trophy, 1997. Office: Buffalo Sabres Marine Midland Arena One Seymour H Knox III Plaza Buffalo NY 14203*

HASELBUSH, RUTH BEELER, retired newspaper editor; b. Kansas City, Mo., July 19, 1922; d. Maxwell Newton and Mary Springer Beeler; m. Weber F. Trout, Aug. 15, 1942 (dec. May 1985); m. Willard C. Haselbush, May 22, 1988; children: Gregory, Jeffrey Trout. BA, U. Denver, 1946; postgrad., U. Kans., 1939, 40, 41, U. Wis., 1940. Editor Park Ridge Adv. Pioneer Press, Chgo., 1967-88; ret., 1988. Charter mem. Park Ridge (Ill.) Hist. Soc., 1971. Named Mem. of Yr., Park Ridge C. of C., 1980. Mem. DAR (sec. Colo. chpt. 1990-94, chaplain 1994-99), Denver Post Retirees, Denver Press Club, Soc. Profl. Journalists (sec., mem. chmn. Headline club 1974-76), Alpha Chi Omega (pres. 1956-57), U. Denver Alumni. Republican. Baptist. Avocations: gardening, oil painting, swimming, sewing, music. Home: 370 Forest St Denver CO 80220-5753

HASELEU, ROSEANN MARIE, medical/surgical nurse; b. Comfrey, Minn., Jan. 17, 1960; d. Leslie Ray and Neola Marie (Schunk) Amsden; m. Randy William Haseleu, May 9, 1981; children: Ashley Marie, Derek William, Brent Allen. ASN, Rochester (Minn.) Jr. Coll., 1981. Charge nurse Springfield Med. Ctr. Mayo Health Sys., 1981—; ambulance crew Springfield Ambulance Svc., 1981—; paramed. examiner, ins. Mpls., 1983—. Mem. HIV task force Brown County, New Ulm, Minn.; mem. charter com. City of Springfield, 1996—. Avocations: golf, watching sports. Home: 420 S Hoyt Ave Springfield MN 56087-1225

HASELKORN, ROBERT, virology educator; b. Bklyn., Nov. 7, 1934; s. Barney and Mildred (Seplowin) H.; m. Margot Block, June 23, 1957; children: Deborah, David. AB, Princeton U., 1956; PhD, Harvard U., 1959. Asst. prof. biophysics U. Chgo., 1961-64, assoc. prof., 1964-69, prof., chmn. dept., 1969-84, F.L. Pritzker Disting. Service prof. dept. molecular genetics and cell biology, 1984—; dir. Ctr. for Photochemistry and Photobiology, 1987—; chmn. bd. dirs. Integrated Genomics, Inc., Chgo., 1997—; cons. virology and rickettsiology study sect. USPHS, 1969-73; mem. sci. adv. bd. Sloan-Kettering Inst., 1978-79; mem. nitrogen fixation panel U.S. Dept. Agr., 1978-79; mem. panel sci. advs. UNIDO Internat. Ctr. for Genetic Engring. and Biotech., 1984-94, 97—; mem. recombinant DNA adv. com. NIH, 1991-95; adj. scientist Woods Hole Oceanographic Instn., 1994—. Editor: Virology, 1973—; mem. editl. bds. Molecular Microbiology, Biochemistry; contbr. to sci. jours. Recipient USPHS Rsch. Career Devel. award, 1963-69, Interstate Postgrad. Med. Assn. Rsch. award, 1967, Darbaker prize Bot. Soc. Am., 1982, Gregor Mendel medal in biol. scis. Acad. Scis. Czech Republic, 1996, Buzatti-Traverso lectr., CNR, Rome, 1997; Am. Cancer Soc. postdoctoral rsch. fellow ARC Virus Rsch. Unit, Cambridge, Eng., 1959-61, Guggenheim fellow Institut Pasteur, Paris, 1975, Sackler fellow Tel Aviv U., 1987. Fellow AAAS, Am. Acad. Arts and Scis. (chmn., midwest coun., v.p. 1993—); mem. NAS, Internat. Soc. Plant Molecular Biology (pres. 1987-89). Home: 5834 S Stony Island Ave Chicago IL 60637-2060 Office: U Chgo Dept Molecular Genetics and Cell Biology 920 E 58th St Chicago IL 60637-5415

HASELMANN, JOHN PHILIP, marketing executive; b. Summit, N.J., Feb. 25, 1940; s. John and Elizabeth Haselmann; divorced; children—Terri Lee, Karen Lynn, Guy Philip. BSEE, N.J. Inst. Tech., 1961; MBA in Indsl. Mgmt., Ops. Research and Mgmt. Sci., U. Pa., 1963. Asst. dir. Behavior Systems, Phila., 1961-63; prof. econs. Union Coll., 1964-66; mgr. mgmt. sci. div. Western Electric Co., Princeton, N.J., 1970-73; mgr. mktg. sci. div. AT&T Long Lines, Bedminster, N.J., 1974-78; pres., founder, chmn. of bd. Info. Mgmt. Group, Morristown, N.J., 1978-83; pres. Trinet Inc., Morristown, N.J., 1984-85; pres., founder, chmn. of bd. Entity Advt. and Graphics, Inc., Florham Park, N.J., 1986-88, Integrated Mktg. Svcs., Inc., Parsippany, N.J., 1989—; founder and exec. dir. Am. Employers Assn., Washington, 1989—; co-founder, vice chmn., exec. v.p., bd. dirs. TCI Comm. Mgmt. Corp., Parsippany, N.J., 1991-95; pres., founder, chmn. bd. Computer Tech. Integration, 1995—; guest lectr. on application of sci. to problems in mtkg. Columbia Grad. Sch. Bus., Sloan Sch. MIT, Wharton Grad. Sch. U. Pa. Author: Computers and Data Processing Applied to a Personnel Processing System as a Management Tool, 1963, How to Improve the Effectiveness of Your Advertising/Marketing/Sales Investment, 1987, How to Lower the Cost of Getting an Order and Increase Revenues through Improved Market Analysis and Sales Management, 1990. Mem. Am. Mgmt. Assn., Am. Soc. Assn. Execs., Am. Soc. Profl. Cons. Republican. Lutheran. Avocations: golf, sailing. Office: PO Box 128 Morristown NJ 07963-0128

HASELTINE, FLORENCE PAT, research administrator, obstetrician, gynecologist; b. Phila., Aug. 17, 1942; d. William R. and Jean Adele Haseltine; m. Frederick Cahn, Mar. 12, 1964 (div. 1969); m. Alan Chodos, Apr. 18, 1970; children: Anna, Elizabeth. BA in Biophysics, U. Calif., Berkeley, 1964; PhD in Biophysics, MIT, 1964-69; MD, Albert Einstein Coll. of Medicine, 1972. Diplomate Am. Bd. Ob-Gyn, Am. Bd. Reproductive Endocrinology. Asst. prof. dept. ob-gyn. and pediatrics Yale U., New Haven, 1976-82, assoc. prof. dept. ob-gyn. and pediatrics, 1982-85; dir. Ctr. for Population Research, Nat. Inst. Child Health and Human Devel. NIH, Bethesda, Md., 1985—; founder Haseltine System, Inc., Products for the Disabled, 1995—. Co-author: Woman Doctor, 1976, Magnetic Resonance of the Reproductive System, 1987; co-editor 25 books on reproductive scis. Bd. dirs. Older Women's League, 1998—, Am. Women in Sci., 1998—. Fellow AAAS (bd. dirs.); mem. Inst. of Medicine, Soc. Gynecol. Investigation, Soc. for Advancement Women's Health Rsch. (founder, bd. dirs.), Soc. Cell Biology. Office: NIH/NICHD Ctr Population Rsch 9000 Rockville Pike 6100/8B07 Executive Blvd Bethesda MD 20892*

HASELTINE, JAMES LEWIS, artist, consultant; b. Portland, Oreg., Nov. 7, 1924; s. William Ambrose and Clara Thusnelda (Scharpf) H.; m. Jane Winsberg, Nov. 14, 1948 (div. 1953); m. Margaret Ann Wilson, Aug. 15, 1955; children: Thomas, Jean, Kay, Suzanne, Angela. Student Ark. State Coll., 1943-44, Reed Coll., 1946-47, Mus. Art Sch., 1947, 1949, Art Inst. Chgo., 1947-48, Bklyn. Mus. Sch., 1950-51. Dir. Salt Lake Art Ctr., Salt Lake City, 1961-67; vis. lectr. art history U. Utah, Salt Lake City, 1964-65; exec. dir. Wash. State Arts Commn., Olympia, Wash., 1967-80; profl. artist, 1950—; panel mem. Nat. Endowment for the Arts, Washington, 1969-80; various art cons. positions, 1980—. Author: 100 Years of Utah Painting, 1965 (Mormon History Assn. award 1965). Paintings and prints represented in permanent collections Portland Art Mus., Oakland Art Museum, Mus. Art U. Oreg., Mus. Fine Arts U. Utah. Mem. search com. for pres. Evergreen State Coll., Olympia, 1984; trustee Portland Art Mus., 1953-55. Served with U.S. Army, 1943-46, ETO. Mem. Western Assn. Art Mus. (pres. 1964-66), Artists Equity Assn. (nat. dir. 1955-58, chmn. Oreg. chpt. 1953-55), Western States Arts Found. (bd. dirs. 1975-77), Brit.-Am. Art Assn. (trustee 1980-84). Home and Office: 3820 Sunset Beach Dr NW Olympia WA 98502-3542

HASELTON, RICK THOMAS, lawyer; b. Albany, Oreg., Nov. 5, 1953; s. Shirley (Schantz) H. AB, Stanford U., 1976; JD, Yale U., 1979. Chair Oreg. State Bd. Bar Examiners, 1988-89, bd. dirs., 1986-88; mem. adv. com. on rules of practice 9th Cir. Ct., 1991-93. Law clk. U.S. Ct. Appeals (9th cir.) Oreg., Portland, 1979-80; from assoc. to ptnr. Lindsay, Hart, Neil & Weigler, Portland, 1979-93; sole practice Portland, 1993-94; assoc. judge Oreg. Ct. Appeals, Salem, 1994—. Chair Multnomah County Legal Aid, Portland, 1985-86, bd. dirs., 1982-87. Mem. ABA, Oreg. Bar Assn., ACLU (cooperating atty. 1982-94), Phi Beta Kappa. Jewish. Office: 300 Justice Blvd Salem OR 97310

HASELWOOD, ELDON LAVERNE, education educator; b. Barnard, Mo., July 19, 1933; m. Joan Haselwood; children: Ann, Karen, Polly, Amy. BS in Edn., U. Omaha, 1960; MA in Libr. Sci., U. Denver, 1963; PhD, U. Nebr., 1972. Libr. Omaha Pub. Schs., 1960-61, Lewis Cen. Community Schs., Council Bluffs, Iowa, 1961-63; documents libr. U. Omaha, 1963-66; prof. dept. tchr. edn. U. Nebr., Omaha, 1966—, coord. ednl. tech. Coll. Edn., 1993—; cons. Nat. Park Svc., Omaha, 1978—. Cpl. U.S. Army, 1953-55. Mem. ALA (councilor 1988-91, excellence in teaching award 1987), Am. Assn. Sch. Librs., Mountain Plains Libr. Assn. (rep. 1999—), Nebr. Libr. Assn. (pres. 1981, meritorious svc. award 1983, Mad Hatter award 1998), Nebr. Ednl. Media Assn. (disting. svc. award 1993), Iowa Assn. Ednl. Media, Nebr. Libr. Commn. (commr. 1981-86). Home: 9919 Pasadena Ave Omaha NE 68124-3765 Office: U Nebr Kayser Hall # 208D Omaha NE 68182

HASEN, BURTON STANLEY, artist; b. N.Y.C., Dec. 19, 1921; s. Herman Harold and Mina (Leibowitz) H.; m. Mary Franz, Nov. 28, 1983. Student, Art Students League, 1940-42, 46, H. Hoffmann Sch. Fine Arts, 1947-48, Acad. dela Grande-Chaumiere, Paris, 1948-50; student (Fulbright grantee), Acad. delle Belle-Arti, 1959-60. tchr. Sch. Visual Arts, N.Y.C., 1953—, Mpls. Sch. Art and Design, 1966. One-man shows include T'Pandje Galerie, Belgium, 1981, Anita Shapolsky Gallery, 1987, 1992, 94, Gallery 1100-Niagara, Buffalo, 1993, Staller Ctr. for Arts, SUNY, Stony Brook, 1995, Hamilton Coll., Clinton, N.Y., 1996, Hugode Pagano gallery, N.Y.C., 1997, Nat. Jewish Mus., Washington, 1997; group shows include Mus. Modern Art, Paris, 1951, Whitney Mus. Am. Art, N.Y.C., 1964, Corcoran Gallery Art, Washington, 1959, Kresge Art Center, U. So. Ill., 1961, Krannert Art Mus.-U. Ill., Urbana, Am. Acad. Arts and Letters, N.Y.C., 1965, Berlin Acad. Arts, 1956, W.G. Picker Gallery, 1969, Colgate U., Hamilton, N.Y., 1969, Mus. Modern Art, N.Y.C., 1966, Met. Mus. Art, N.Y.C., 1952, Worcester (Mass.) Art Mus., 1968, Walker Art Center, Mpls., 1966, Bklyn. Mus., 1954, Artist Choice Mus., N.Y.C., NAD, N.Y.C., 1985, Anita Shapolsky Gallery, 1989, 90, 92, Neo Persona Gallery, 1989, 90, Rider Coll., 1992, Albright-Knox Mus., 1992, Islip Art Mus., 1992, Cleve. Inst. Art, 1993, Swiss Cultural Inst., 1993, David Anderson Gallery, Buffalo, 1993, Henry St. Settlement, N.Y.C., 1993, Sordoni Art Gallery, Wilkes-Barre, Pa., 1994, Nat. Acad., 1995, 96, 97, Alysia Duckler Gallery, Portland, 1996, Pagano Gallery, N.Y.C., 1997 ; represented in permanent collections Walker Art Center, Worcester Art Mus., Hampton Inst., CIBA-GEIGY Co., Bibliotheque Nationale, Paris, N.Y. Pub. Library, Princeton U., Columbia U., Mus. Fine Art, Portland, Maine, N.Y. Crestview Coll., Muhlenberg, Fine Prints Dept., SUNY, Buffalo, 1989, CCNY, Rider U., Lawrenceville, N.J., 1993, Islip Mus., East Islip, N.Y., Hamilton Coll., Clinton, N.Y., Nat. Jewish Mus., Washington; illustrator books, 1959-89, Beyond the Furies, 1985, Franklin Mint, Phila., 1991, Alea Mag., 1993, Newark Mus., 1993, Islip (N.Y.) Mus., 1994; archives include Smithsonian Mus. Am. Art, Centre Georges Pompidou, Musée d'Art Moderne, Paris. Served with AUS, 1942-46. Recipient Emily Lowe Found. Purchase prize, 1955; N.Y. Found. Arts grantee, 1990; Pollack Krasner fellow 1995-96. Mem. Nat. Acad. Design, Fulbright Alumni Assn. Office: 209 E 23rd St New York NY 10010-3901 *The motivating force of my life has been the desire to paint meaningful paintings that express my innermost feelings. Art for me is the exhilarating experience of discovering new worlds. Each work is a projection of myself* *into the cosmic universe. This compulsion to paint my fantasy has never faltered or been self-deceptive.*

HASEN-SINZ, SUSAN KATHERINE, state agency administrator, actress; b. LaGrange Park, Ill., Jan. 30, 1965; d. Hans and June Catherine (Huml) H.; m. Mark Thomas Sinz, Aug. 31, 1991; 1 child, Rachel Katherine. BA in Polit. Sci., Spanish, U. Ill., 1987; postgrad., Loyola U., Chgo. Actress Springfield (Ill.) Theatre Ctr., 1987—; mem. mgmt. staff Ill. Dept. Driver Svcs., Chgo., Gov.'s Office, Ill. Dept. Pub. Aid; mgr. employee svcs., divsn. chief Gov.'s Office Ill. Toll Hwy. Authority, Downers Grove; speaker various youth groups, 1985—; dance instr. YMCA, Springfield, 1987, counselor Miss Ill./USA Pageant, Arlington Heights, Ill., 1987; fellow adminstrv. hearings under Sec. of State Jim Edgar, Springfield, 1987—. Lead actress A Day in Hollywood-A Night in the Ukraine, 1987 (Best of Springfield award), 42d St., Ill., 1991—, Oklahoma, Ill., The Dance Factory, Chgo., A...My Name Is Still Alice, Chgo.; actress Manny, nat. tour A Christmas Carol, 1989, Joseph and the Amazing Technicolor Dreamcoat, Ill.; supporting actress Singin' in the Rain, Ill.; backup singer Kenny Rogers Christmas Tour, Ill.; actress, singer, dancer Jesus Christ Superstar, 1992; singer Miss Ill./USA Pageant, 1987; understudy Puttin On the Ritz, Ill., West Side Story, Ill. Active in drama ministry Hope Ch., Springfield; soloist Christ Ch. of Oak Brook, Ill., 1983—, leader youth group Koinonia; student del. Internat. Strategic Affairs Conf., N.Y.C., 1987—; mem. campaign staff Jim Edgar for Gov. Ill., 1991; judge Miss Teen Ill./U.S.A. Pageant; staff asst. Congressman Harris Fawell's Office; rep. for 13th dist. Ill.; vol., singer Salvation Army (youth adv. com.); committeewoman DuPage County Rep. Ctrl. Com., 1999. Recipient Miss Amity award Miss I.../U.S.A., 1986; scholarship winner Miss Illini contest. Mem. U. Ill. Alumni Assn. (named one of 100 top srs. at Champaign-Urbana campus 1986, named outstanding student 1986-87), Kappa Alpha Theta, Kappa Alpha Theta Alumni Assn. (chaplain, pres. standards com. 1986-87, songleader 1986-87). Home: 24 Sheffield Ln Oak Brook IL 60523-2359 Office: One Authority Dr Downers Grove IL 60515-1703

HASERICK, JOHN ROGER, retired dermatologist; b. Mpls., Sept. 23, 1915; s. Ernest B. and Addie (Swanson) H.; m. Jane Margaret Fleckenstein, May 10, 1941; children: John Roger, Jane. BA, Macalester Coll., 1937; MD, U. Minn., 1941, MS in Dermatology, 1946. Diplomate: Am. Bd. Dermatology (pres. 1975). Intern Ancker Hosp., St. Paul, 1940-41; resident in medicine Univ. Hosps., Mpls., 1941-42, resident in dermatology, 1945-46; pvt. practice Pinehurst, N.C., 1970-87; head dept. dermatology Cleve. Clinic, 1948-67; prof. Case Western Res. U., Cleve., 1967-70; clin. prof. medicine and dermatology Duke U., Durham, N.C., 1970-85; with Pinehurst Dermatology Clinic, 1970-87; clin. prof. dermatology U. Minn., 1997—. Contbr. 75 articles to med. jours.; Author: LE Primer, 1972. Mem. Vols. in Medicine, Martin County Med. Soc., Stuart, Fla., 1997—. Recipient Discovery award Dermatology Found., 1999. Fellow ACP; mem. AMA (Hektoen Silver award 1952), Am. Acad. Dermatology (pres. 1974), Am. Soc. Dermatopathology (pres. 1975, Founder's award 1996), N.C. Med. Assn., Am. Soc. Investigative Dermatology, Am. Dermatol. Assn., Yacht and Country Club (Stuart), Wolves Club (Pinehurst, pres. 1983). Discovered LE factor (antinuclear) in blood of patients with lupus erythematosus. Home: 4063 SE Fairway E Stuart FL 34997-6172

HASH, JOHN FRANK, broadcasting executive; b. Charlottesville, Va., Apr. 26, 1944; s. John Wendell and Lucy Virginia H.; m. Mary Virginia Muldrow, June 10, 1968; children: Rebecca, Katherine, Lauren. BA, Davidson Coll., 1966; MBA, U. Va., 1968. Various positions Gen. Mills, Mpls., 1968-76; pres. Love Broadcasting Co., Biloxi, Miss., 1976-95, Greenville TV, Inc., Gulfport, Miss., 1992—. Bd. dirs. Phillips Colls., Inc., Gulfport, Miss., 1989-91, Gulfport Sch. Bd., 1986-99, Miss. Gulf Coast Econ. Devel. Coun.; trustee Miss. Power Found. Episcopalian. Fax: (228) 864-1512. Office: Greenville TV Inc PO Box 8395 Gulfport MS 39506-8395

HASHE, JANIS HELENE, editor; d. James William and Arlene Florence (Houses) H. AA with honors, Cabrillo Coll., 1974; BA summa cum laude, San Francisco State, 1976; MA, San Jose State, 1982. Asst. editor Sunset Trade Publs., L.A., 1988-89, assoc. editor, 1989-90; editor Western Grocery News, L.A., 1990-95; sr. editor L.A. Parent Mag., Burbank, Calif., 1995—. Author: (radio play) A Knot in the Heart, 1990; writer essays. Vol. Braille Inst., L.A., 1988—; block capt. Crime Watch Catalina, L.A., 1990-91. Scholar Am. Assn. U. Women, 1972. Mem. Nat. Writers Union, New One-Act Theatre Ensemble (artistic dir., 1985-88, pres., bd. dirs. 1995—). Democrat. Buddhist. Office: L A Parent Mag 433 Irving Dr Burbank CA 91504-2408

HASHIMI, CAREN SUE, food service manager; b. Longview, Tex., Feb. 11, 1955; d. Keith C. and Patricia (Kuhn) Shaffer; m. Michael A. Grabner, Oct. 7, 1978 (div. Nov. 1989); m. Sayed R. Hashimi, Oct. 10, 1998. Grad. high sch., Ft. Wayne, Ind. Exec. mgr. Ponderosa, Ft. Wayne, 1972-79; gen. mgr. Sizzler Steak House, Ft. Wayne, 1980-83; mgr. Pizza Hut, Ft. Wayne, 1984-86; sr. mgr. Burger King, Ft. Wayne, 1986-87; mgr. Ponderosa, Ft. Wayne, 1987-88; gen. bus. mgr. Taco Bell, Inc., Grand Rapids, Mich., 1988—.

HASHIMOTO, CHRISTINE L., physician; b. Chgo., June 29, 1947; d. Shigeru and Kiyo (Sato) H. BA, Oberlin Coll., 1968; MD, Med. Coll. of Pa., 1973. Clin. instr. internal medicine, emergency medicine Med. Coll. and Hosp. of Pa., Phila., 1976-77; asst. prof. medicine Health Service Ctr. U. Colo., Denver, 1977-80, clin. asst. prof. medicine, 1980-87; staff physician emergency dept. St. Joseph Hosp., Denver, 1980-88, Rose Med. Ctr., Denver, 1988-91, Luth. Med. Ctr., Wheatridge, Colo., 1991—. Mem. Colo. Med. Soc., Denver Med. Soc., Am. Coll. Emergency Physicians. Office: Luth Med Ctr 8300 W 38th Ave Wheat Ridge CO 80033-6005

HASHIMOTO, JERRY SHIGERU, child psychologist; b. Cin., Apr. 21, 1949; s. James and Berniece Hashimoto. BA, Miami U., Oxford, Ohio, 1971; MSW, U. Denver, 1975, PsyD, 1986. Lic. clin. psychologist, Colo. Sch. social worker Adams County Sch. Dist., Westminster, Colo., 1975-76; child therapist Aurora (Colo.) Community Mental Health Ctr., 1976-84; treatment leader Denver Children's Home, 1985-86; psychologist Cherry Creek Sch. Dist., Aurora, 1986—; pvt. practice psychology Denver, 1988—; cons. in field; founder Origins Cons., Inc., Denver, 1989—. Mem. Colo. Adv. Com. on Edn. Gifted and Talented, Denver, 1990—; vice chmn. Asian Pacific Devel. Ctr., Denver, 1985; founding mem. Asian Human Svcs. Assn., Denver, 1972. Mem. Am. Psychol. Assn., Coun. for Exceptional Children, Asian Am. Psychol. Assn. Avocations: tennis, skiing, running, jazz. Office: Child Assocs 1220 S Parker Rd # 106 Denver CO 80231-2166

HASHIMOTO, KEN, dermatology educator; b. Niigata City, Japan, June 19, 1931; came to U.S., 1956; m. Noriko Sakai, Oct. 3, 1961; children: Naomi, Martha, Eugene, Amy. MD, Niigata U., 1955. Cert. Am. Bd. Dermatology, 1968, Dermatopathology, 1972. Asst. prof. dermatology Tufts U. Sch. Medicine, Boston, 1965-68; assoc. prof. medicine, anatomy U. Tenn., Memphis, 1968-70; prof. medicine, assoc. prof. anatomy U. Tenn., 1970-77, dir., dermatopathology, prof., 1975-77; prof., dir. dermatology, prof. anatomy Wright State U., Dayton, Ohio, 1977-80; chief, dermatology sect., dir. elec. microscopy lab. VA Med. Ctr., Dayton, 1977-80; dermatologist in chief Detroit Med. Ctr., 1987—; prof., chmn. dermatology Wayne State U., Detroit, 1980—; mem. dermatol. drugs adv. com. FDA. Fulbright scholar, 1956-59; participant med. investigatorship career devel. program VA, 1969-77. Mem. Am. Soc. Dermatopathology (pres. 1986-87), Nat. Bd. Med. Examiners, Japanese Soc. Investigative Dermatology (hon.), Memphis Dermatological Soc. (pres. 1973-74), Soc. Investigative Dermatology (v.p. 1980-81, chmn. program com. 1985-86), Soc. Francaise de Dermatologie et de Syphilographie (corr. 1989), Japanese Assn. Dermatology (hon.). Home: 7000 Warren Rd Ann Arbor MI 48105-9722 Office: Wayne State U Sch Medicine Dept Dermatology 540 E Canfield St Detroit MI 48201-1928

HASHIMOTO, KYOSUKE, investment company executive. Gen. ptnr. Brown Bros. Harriman & Co., N.Y.C. Office: Brown Bros Harriman & Co 59 Wall St New York NY 10005-2808*

HASHMI, SAJJAD AHMAD, business educator, university dean; b. India, Dec. 20, 1933; m. Monica Ruggiero; children: Serena, Jason, Shawn, Michelle. BA, U. Karachi, 1953, MA, 1956; PhD in Ins., U. Pa., 1962. Lectr. Ohio State U., Columbus, 1962-64; asst. prof. Roosevelt U., Chgo., 1964-66; prof. Ball State U., Muncie, Ind., 1966-83, chmn. dept. fin., 1973-83; Jones disting. prof., dean Sch. Bus., Emporia (Kans.) State U., 1983—; cons. and speaker to profl. ins. agts., Indpls., Louisville, Springfield, Ill.; tech. advisor Ind. Arts Commn.; vice chmn. bd. trustees Kans. Ins. Edn. Found.; bd.d irs. Blue Cross and Blue Shield of Kans.; appeared on TV and radio programs, testified before N.Y., Kans. and Ind. legis. coms. Author: Insurance is a Funny Business, 1972, Automobile Insurance, 1973, Contemporary Personal Finance, 1985, Make Every Second Count, 1989, Strategies for The Future, 1990; contbr. articles, revs., monographs to profl. publs. Named Prof. of Yr., Ball State U. Students, 1971, Outstanding Tchr. of Yr., Ball State U., 1970. Mem. Am. Risk and Ins. Assn., Midwest Fin. Assn., Fin. Mgt. Assn., Emporia C. of C., Beta Gamma Sigma, Sigma Iota Epsilon, Alpha Kappa Psi, Gamma Iota Epsilon, Phi Kappa Phi. Club: Emporia Country. Lodge: Rotary. Home: 2909 Lakeridge Rd Emporia KS 66801-5982 Office: Emporia State U Sch of Bus 1200 Commercial St Emporia KS 66801-5087

HASKAYNE, RICHARD FRANCIS, petroleum company executive; b. Calgary, Alta., Can., Dec. 18, 1934; s. Robert Stanley and Bertha (Hesketh) H.; m. Lee Mary Murray, 1958 (dec. 1993); m. Lois P. Heard, 1995. B.Comm., U. Alta., 1956; postgrad., U. Western Ont., 1968, LLD; LLD, U. Calgary, U. Alta. Chartered acct., Alta. With Riddell, Stead & Co., chartered accts., Calgary, 1956-60; corp. acctg. supr. to v.p. fin. Hudson's Bay Oil & Gas Co., Ltd., Calgary, 1960-73; compt. Canadian Arctic Gas Study Ltd., 1973-75; sr. v.p. to pres. Hudson's Bay Oil & Gas Co. Ltd., Calgary, 1975-81; pres., chief exec. officer Home Oil Co., Ltd., Calgary, 1981-91, also bd. dirs.; chmn. bd. NOVA Corp., Calgary, 1992-98; pres., CEO, bd. dirs. Interprovincial Pipe Line Co., 1987-91, Interhome Energy, 1989-91; bd. dirs. Fording Inc., Can. Imperial Bank of Commerce, Crestar Energy Inc., Alta. Energy Inc.; chmn. bd. TansAlta Corp., 1996-98, Trans-Can. Pipelines Ltd., 1998—, MacMillan Bloedel Ltd., 1996—. Chmn. bd. govs. U. Calgary, 1990-96. Awards Officer of the Order of Can., 1997. Fellow Fin. Execs. Inst.; mem. Calgary Petroleum Club (past pres.), Calgary Golf and Country Club, Earl Grey Golf Club, Ranchmen's Club, U. Calgary Chancellor's Club, The York Club, Libr. Club, Commerce Club, Alta Inst. Chartered Accts., Kappa Sigma. Office: 2030 Bankers Hall 855 2d St SW, Calgary, AB Canada T2P 4J8

HASKELL, ARTHUR JACOB, retired steamship company executive; b. Newark, Apr. 16, 1926; s. Isidore David and Elena (Greenbaum) H.: m. Amparo Serrano, Dec. 31, 1958 (div.); children: Amparo Rocio, Vincent Isidore, Joaquin Arthur; m. Marge Gibson, June 8, 1986. B.S., U.S. Naval Acad., 1947; profl. naval engr., MIT, 1953. Sr. procurement engr. Nat. Bulk Carriers, N.Y.C., 1956-62; asst. plant mgr. Western Gear Corp., Belmont, Calif., 1962-64; project engr. Matson Nav. Co., San Francisco., 1964-70, v.p., 1970-73, sr. v.p., 1973-91, ret., 1991; mem. marine bd. NRC, 1981-85; bd. mgrs. Am. Bur. Shipping, 1988-92; bd. dirs., budget officer Nat. Liberty Ship Meml. Bd. dirs. San Francisco Marine Exchange, 1975-78, v.p., 1976-77, pres., 1977-78. Served to comd. USN, 1947-56. Mem. Soc. Naval Architects and Marine Engrs. (chmn. No. Calif. sect. 1971-72, v.p. 1973-83, exec. com. 1977-80, 83-96, hon. v.p. for life 1983—, pres. 1989-91), Assn. for Preservation of Presdl. Yacht Potomac (bd. govs. 1984—, co-pres. 1993-99). Home: 287 Sheridan Rd Oakland CA 94618-2717

HASKELL, BARBARA, curator; b. San Diego, Nov. 13, 1946; d. John N. and Barbara (Freeman) H.; m. Leon Botstein; children: Clara Haskell Botstein, Maxim Haskell Botstein. BA, UCLA, 1969. Dir. UCLA Exptl. Arts Festival, 1966; asst. registrar Pasadena (Calif.) Art Mus., 1969, curatorial asst., 1970, asst. curator, 1970, assoc. curator, 1970-72, curator painting and sculpture, 1972-74, dir. exhbns. and collections, 1974; curator painting and sculpture Whitney Mus. Am. Art, N.Y.C., 1975—. Author: Arthur Dove, 1974, Marsden Hartley, 1980, Milton Avery, 1982, Blam! The Explosion of Pop, Minimalism and Performance 1958-64, 1984, Georgia O'Keefe: Works on Paper, 1985, Ralston Crawford, 1985, Charles Demuth, 1987, Donald Judd, 1988, Burgoyne Diller, 1990, Agnes Martin, 1992, Joseph Stella, 1994, also collection catalogs. Named Woman of Yr., Mademoiselle mag., 1973. Office: Whitney Mus Am Art 945 Madison Ave New York NY 10021-2701

HASKELL, BARRY GEOFFRY, communications company research administrator; b. Lewiston, Maine, 1941; s. George Raymond and Dorothy H.; m. Ann Kantrow, Sept. 13, 1964; children: Paul Eric, Andrew. AA, Pasadena City Coll., 1962; BSEE, U. Calif., Berkeley, 1964, MSEE, 1965, PhD, 1968. Electronics engr. Lawrence Livermore (Calif.) Lab., 1965; rsch. asst. Electronics Rsch. Lab. U. Calif., Berkeley, 1965-68; mem. tech. staff AT&T Bell Labs., Holmdel, N.J., 1968-76, head radio comm. rsch. dept., 1976-83, visual comm. cons., 1984-86, head visual comm. rsch. dept., 1987-95; head image processing rsch. dept. AT&T Labs., Middletown, N.J., 1996—; adj. prof. Rutgers U., New Brunswick, N.J., 1976-79, CCNY, 1983-84, Columbia U., N.Y.C., 1987, 93; negotiator Internat. Stds. Orgn., Am. Nat. Stds. Inst., Internat. Telecom. Union - Telecom Sector. Co-author: Image Transmission Tech., 1979, Digital Pictures, 1988, 2d edit., 1995, Digital Video—An Introduction to MPEG-2, 1996; contbr. articles to profl. jours.; patentee in field. Recipient Elec. Engring. Dept. Outstanding Alumnus award U. Calif., Berkeley, 1998; co-recipient Japan's Computer and Comm. prize, 1997; AT&T fellow, 1998. Fellow IEEE; mem. Phi Beta Kappa, Sigma Xi. Avocations: sailing, skiing, guitar playing. Office: AT&T Labs 100 Schultz Dr Red Bank NJ 07701-6750

HASKELL, BRENTON ERNEST, health facility administrator. MD with distinction, U. Alberta, Edmonton, Alberta, 1978; MS, Wright State U., Dayton, Ohio, 1985. Diplomate Am. Bd. Preventive Medicine. Regional aviation med. officer Civil Aviation Medicine, Toronto, Can., 1990-97; med. dir. occupl. health program Columbus (Ohio) Health Dept., 1997—. Office: 600W Spring St (Rear) Columbus OH 43215-2327

HASKELL, ELLERY BICKFORD, retired philosophy educator; b. Waltham, Mass., Sept. 15, 1911; s. Harold Cheney and Carrie Eleanor Cornwall (Dakin) H.; m. Grace Elizabeth Campbell, Apr. 5, 1941; children: Helen Jeanne Bosart, Richard Campbell. AB, Colgate U., 1933; postgrad., Yale Divinity Sch., 1933-35; BD, Colgate-Rochester Divinity Sch., 1936; MA in Am. History, U. Pa., 1945; PhD, U. Chgo., 1964. Ordained min. Bapt. Ch., 1937. Min. Spencer (N.Y.) Federated Ch., 1937-41, Emmanuel Bapt. Ch., Chester, Pa., 1941-45; prof. philosophy, dept. head Albright Coll., Reading, Pa., 1946-77, prof. emeritus, 1977—; part-time min., instr. First Bapt. Ch., Reading, 1946—. Pres., bd. dirs. World Affairs Coun., Reading, 1970-92, bd. dirs. emeritus, 1992—, leader Great Decisions group, 1996—; leader Peacemakers, 1985—. Democrat. Avocations: writing letters, fgn. policy, peace. Home: 25 Price Dr Topton PA 19562-1607

HASKELL, JOHN HENRY FARRELL, JR., investment banking company executive; b. N.Y.C., Jan. 24, 1932; s. John Henry Farrell and Paulette (Heger) H.; m. Francine G. Le Roux, June 30, 1955; children: Michael J., Christopher E., Diana F. T. BS, U.S. Mil. Acad., 1953; MBA with distinction, Harvard U., 1958. Assoc. Dillon, Read & Co., N.Y.C., 1958-61; mgr. European office Dillon, Read & Co., Paris, 1961-66; Dillon, Read & Co. (now Warburg Dillon Read LLC) Dillon, Read & Co., N.Y.C., 1964-75, mng. dir., 1975—; pres., CEO, The France Fund, Inc., 1986-89; bd. dirs. The Equitable Cos. Inc., The Equitable Life Assurance Soc. U.S., Pall Corp.; mem. adv. coun. Overseas Pvt. Investment Co., 1972-75. Bd. dirs. Belgian-Am. Ednl. Found.; pres. bd. trustees French Inst./Alliance Francaise. Decorated Legion of Honor, Ordre National du Merite France; recipient Presdl. Recognition award For Community Service, 1986. Mem. Coun. Fgn. Rels., French-Am. C. of C. (councillor), Assn. Grads. of U.S. Mil. Acad. (trustee 1984-87), Am. Soc. French Legion of Honor (bd. dirs., v.p.), Links Club, Univ. Club, Meadow Brook Club (Jericho, N.Y.), Bohemian Club (San Francisco), Eagle Springs Golf Club (Wolcott, Colo.). Home: 120 East End Ave New York NY 10028-7552 Office: Warburg Dillon Read LLC 299 Park Ave New York NY 10171-0026

HASKELL, MARGARET HOWARD, writer, psychotherapist; b. Boston, Apr. 28, 1923; d. Charles Pagelsen and Katherine Montague (Graham) Howard; m. Gordon Chipman Dewey, Feb. 6, 1943 (annulled); 1 child, Katherine Dewey (dec.); m. Dayton Ball, Nov. 10, 1952 (dec.); 1 child, Damon Howard Ball. AB, Radcliffe Coll., 1948; MA in English and Comparative Lit., Columbia U., 1952; MSW, Boston Coll., 1965. Lic. ind. clin. social worker Divsn. of Registration in Social Work, Commonwealth of Mass. Ednl. sec., editor of unsolicited fiction Cosmopolitan Mag., N.Y.C., 1952-54; pvt. practice literary agt. N.Y.C., 1954-57; clin. social worker Child Guidance Ctr., Lynn, Mass., 1965-67, VA Clinic, Lowell, Mass., 1968-87; mem. Harvard U., Harvard Inst. for Learning in Retirement, Cambridge, Mass., 1989—; co-chmn. poets' roundtable Harvard U., Harvard Inst. for Learning in Retirement, Cambridge, 1996—, chmn. anthology com., 1997-98; fieldwork instr. Boston U., 1969-77, Boston Coll., Newton, Mass., 1978; VA state-wide coord. Commonwealth of Mass. Commn. for Blind, 1980-82; VA social workers Consultation to St. Anne's Ch., Lowell, 1984-86; writer, critic, founder Writers' Workshop, Marblehead, 1996-98. Author of short stories and poems. Vol. Mass. Audubon Soc., Topsfield, Mass., 1993-95, Harvard U., Harvard Inst. for Learning in Retirement, Cambridge, 1995; active Friends of Abbot Pub. Libr., Marblehead, 1995—. Recipient Best of Show for Fiction award Marblehead Festival of Arts, 1992, Editor's award for poetic excellence Nat. Libr. of Poetry, Owings Mills, Mo., 1996. Fellow NASW, Acad. Cert. Social Workers, Harvard Club Boston, Club Small Gardens, Marblehead Yacht Club. Avocations: reading poetry and fiction, taking courses, sailing, gardening.

HASKELL, MOLLY, author; b. Charlotte, N.C., Sept. 29, 1939; d. John Haskell and Mary Clark; m. Andrew Sarris, May 31, 1969. BA, Sweet Briar Coll.; student, U. London, England, Sorbonne, Paris. Pub. rels. assoc. Sperry Rand; writer, editor French Film Office, New York; film critic Village Voice, Viva, New York Magazine, Vogue, 1969-74, 74-80; film reviewer "Special Edition" Pub. TV; film reviewer "All Things Considered" Nat. Pub. Radio; adj. prof. film Columbia U., New York, 1996; writer; artistic dir. Sarasota French Film Festival. Author: From Reverence to Rape: The Treatment of Women in the Movies, 1973, rev. edit., 1987, Love and Other Infectious Diseases: A Memoir, 1990, Holding My Own in No Man's Land, 1997; (plays) The Last Anniversary, 1990; contbr. articles and essays to jours. Recipient Nat. Bd. Review of Motion Pictures award, 1989, Chevalier de l'Ordre des Artes et des Lettres, 1989, Disting. Alumna award Stweet Briar Coll., 1994. Mem. Nat. Soc. of Film Festival Selection Critics, N.Y. Film Critics Circle, N.Y. Film Festival Selection Com., N.Y. Inst. for the Humanities, The Century Club, Phi Beta Kappa. Address: Georges Borchardt Inc 136 E 57th St New York NY 10022-2707

HASKELL, PAUL GERSHON, retired law educator; b. Boston, Mar. 31, 1927; s. David Israel and Leah (Paris) H.; m. Sarah Potter Evarts, Jan. 22, 1955; children: Peter, Thomas, John. AB, Harvard U., 1948, LLB, 1951. Bar: N.Y. 1952. Assoc. Kelley, Drye, Newhall & Maginnes, N.Y.C., 1951-56, White & Case, N.Y.C., 1956-59; asst. gen. counsel The Houston Corp., St. Petersburg, Fla., 1959-60; resident counsel, asst. treas. Ednl. Testing Service, Princeton, N.J., 1960-62; prof. law Georgetown U., Washington, 1962-67, Case Western Res. U., Cleve., 1967-79; prof. law U. N.C., Chapel Hill, 1979-83, Graham Kenan prof. law, 1983-91, William R. Kenan prof. law, 1991-98; ret., 1998. Co-author: Preface to Estates In Land and Future Interests, 1966, 2d edit., 1984; author: Preface to the Law of Trusts, 1975, Preface to Wills, Trusts and Adminstration, 1987, 2d edit. 1994, Why Lawyers Behave As They Do, 1998; contbr. articles to profl. jours. Bd. dirs. Cleve. Fair Housing Inc., 1967-70; trustee Harvard Club of Cleve., 1976-79. Served with USN, 1945-46. Am. Coll. Trust and Estate Counsel fellow. Mem. ABA (spl. com. to revise standards for legal edn. 1970-73, coun., sect. on legal edn. and admissions to bar 1973-76, standing com. on legal assts. 1976-80). Republican. Home: 1805 Rolling Rd Chapel Hill NC 27514-7505 Office: The Univ of NC Sch of Law Chapel Hill NC 27514

HASKELL, PETER ABRAHAM, actor; b. Boston, Oct. 15, 1934; s. Norman Abraham and Rose Veronica (Golden) H.; m. Ann Compton, Feb. 27, 1960 (div. 1974); m. Dianne Tolmich, Oct. 26, 1974; children: Audra Rosemary, Jason Abraham. BA, Harvard U., 1962; student, N.Y. Law Sch., 1982-83. Actor (films) Finnegans Wake, 1965, Legend of Earl Durand, 1972, Christina, 1974, Forty Days of Musa Dagh, 1982, Riding the Edge, 1987, Child's Play II, 1990, Child's Play III, 1991, Robot Wars, 1993; (TV series) Bracken's World, NBC, 1968-70, Rich Man Poor Man, Book II, ABC, 1976-77, Ryan's Hope, ABC, 1982-83, Search for Tomorrow, NBC, 1983-85, Rituals, Metromedia, 1985, The Law and Harry McGraw, CBS, 1987-88; (TV films) Love, Hate, Love, 1970, The Eyes of Charles Sand, 1972, Mandrake, 1977, The Cracker Factory, 1979, Christine Cromwell, 1990, Columbo, 1991, Maid for Each Other, 1992, Faces of Deception, 1993, Never Talk to Strangers, 1997. Wwith U.S. Army, 1954-56. Mem. SAG, AFTRA, Actors Equity. Democrat. Avocations: photography, skiing. Office: care Eric Klass 144 S Beverly Dr Ste 605 Beverly Hills CA 90212-3022

HASKELL, PRESTON HAMPTON, III, construction company executive; b. Birmingham, Ala., Oct. 6, 1938; s. Preston Hampton and Mary Wyatt (Rushton) H.; m. Joan Elizabeth Smith, June 9, 1961; children—Rushton H. Callaghan, Preston Hampton IV, Sally H. Singletary. BS in Engring., Princeton U., 1960; MBA, Harvard U., 1962. Registered profl. engr., Fla., Ala., S.C., Va. V.p. S.S. Jacobs Co., Jacksonville, Fla., 1962-65; pres. The Haskell Co., Jacksonville, Fla., 1965—; dir. Barnett Bank Jacksonville, 1978—. Chmn. Jacksonville Electric Authority, 1976-78; chmn., pres. United Way Jacksonville, 1982-85; chmn. Fla. Postsecondary Edn. Commn., Tallahassee, 1980-84; bd. dirs. Fla. Coun. of 100, 1984-88; bd. dirs., vice chmn. Am. Symphony Orch. League, 1990-95; bd. dirs. Jacksonville Symphony Assn., 1973—, pres., 1986-87; trustee Princeton U., 1996—; chmn. Cummer Mus. Art, 1996—, Design-Build Inst. Am., 1993-94. Recipient Top Mgmt. award Sales and Mktg. Execs., Jacksonville, 1978, Above and Beyond award United Way, 1987, Entrepreneur of Yr. award Inc. mag., 1989. Mem. NSPE, Fla. Engring. Soc., Soc. for Advancement Mgmt. (hon.), Jacksonville C. of C. (pres. 1979, Industrialist of Yr. award 1986), Soc. of Cincinnati, River Club (pres. 1984-85), Fla. Yacht Club, Timuquana Country Club, The Links. Republican. Episcopalian. Office: The Haskell Co Haskell Bldg Jacksonville FL 32231*

HASKELL, THOMAS LANGDON, history educator; b. Washington, May 26, 1939; s. Anthony Porter and Martha Averill (Bullock) H.; m. Dorothy Ann Wyatt, Aug. 27, 1966; children: Alexander Bullock, Susan Wyatt. BA, Princeton U., 1961; PhD, Stanford U., 1973. From instr. to prof. Rice U., Houston, 1970—, Samuel G. McCann prof. history, 1987—; vis. mem. Inst. Advanced Study, Princeton, N.J., 1978-79. Author: Emergence of Professional Social Science, 1977, Objectivity is Not Neutrality, 1998; editor: The Authority of Experts, 1984; co-editor: (with Richard Teichgraeber) The Culture of Capitalism, 1993; mem. bd. editors Jour. Am. History, 1983-86, Am. Hist. Rev., 1988-91; contbr. articles to profl. jours. Lt. USN, 1961-65. Guggenheim Found. fellow, 1986-87; fellow NEH, Rockefeller Found., Mellon Found., Am. Coun. Learned Socs. Mem. Orgn. Am Historians, Am. Hist. Assn. Office: Rice U Dept History Houston TX 77005-1892

HASKETT, DIANNE LOUISE, mayor, lawyer; b. London, Can., Mar. 4, 1955; d. Allan Douglas and Frances Shirley (Crone) H.; m. Jacek Kotowicz; 1 child, Annie. BA, U. Waterloo, Ont., Can., 1974; LLB, U. Western Ont., 1977; LLM, London Sch. of Econs., Eng., 1979. Lawyer Law Soc. of Upper Can., Ont., 1980—; v.p. London Urban Alliance on Race Rels. Contbr. articles to profl. jours. City councillor London City Coun., 1991-94, mayor, 1994—; founder Open Homes Can., London, 1992—; founding mem. London Citizens Com., 1980-84; v.p. Ark Aid Street Mission Inc., London, 1986-88. Grad. scholarship Rotary Internat., 1978-79. Mem. Law Soc. of Upper Can., Fedn. of Can. Municipalities Assn. (politician). Avocations: journalism, collecting antiques and rare books, reading, speech-making. Office: London City Hall, 300 Dufferin Ave, London, ON Canada N6A 4L9

HASKIN, J. MICHAEL, lawyer; b. Kansas City, Mo., Sept. 25, 1949; s. Harley V. and Geraldine E. (Porterfield) H.: m. Pamela J. Lutz, May 22, 1999. BA, Baker U., 1971; JD, U. Mo., 1976. Bar: Kans. 1976, Mo. 1987, U.S. Fed. Tax Ct., U.S. Supreme Ct. Ptnr., atty. Haskin, Hinkle, Slater & Snowbarger, Olathe, Kans., 1976-83, Dietrich, Davis, Dicus, Rowlands, Schmitt & Gorman, Kansas City, Mo., 1984-88; pres., atty. J. Michael Haskin, PA, Olathe, 1989—; bd. dirs., exec. com., The Assn. K-10 Corridor Devel., Inc., Lawrence, 1993-95. City councilman-at-large City of Olathe, 1989-93, mayor, 1993-95; mem., vice chmn., chmn. Stormwater Mgmt. Adv. Coun., Johnson County, Kans., 1989-95; bd. dirs. Olathe Pub. Libr., 1989-90, 93-95; bd. dirs. Hidden Glen Arts Festival, vice chmn., chmn., 1990—); mem. Mid-Am. Regional Coun. Perimeter Transp. Com., 1995—. Recipient Boss of Yr. award Johnson County Legal Secs. Assn., 1991-92, Cmty. Leadership award Olathe Area C. of C., 1992. Mem. Kans. Bar Assn., Mo.

Bar Assn., Olathe Rotary Club (bd. dirs., pres. 1981—, Paul Harris award 1992, Olathe Rotarian of Yr. 1995), Olathe Arts Alliance (pres. 1988), Kaw Valley Philological Soc. Republican. Methodist. Avocations: golfing, sailing. Office: PO Box 413 100 E Park St Ste 203 Olathe KS 66061-3463

HASKIN, LARRY ALLEN, earth and planetary scientist, educator; b. Olathe, Kans., Aug. 17, 1934; s. Harvard Glenn and Mary Virginia (Callaway) H.; m. Mary Anita Gehl, Dec. 21, 1963; children: Dierk Allen, Rachel Lee, Jean Marie. B.A., Baker U., 1955; Ph.D., U. Kans., 1960. Asst. prof. Ga. Inst. Tech., 1959-60; instr. U. Wis., Madison, 1960-61; asst. prof. U. Wis., 1961-65, asso. prof., 1965-68, prof. chemistry, 1968-73; cons. NASA, 1970-73, Argonne Nat. Lab., 1960-68; chief planetary and earth scis. div. NASA-JSC, 1973-76; prof. earth and planetary scis., chemistry Washington U., St. Louis, 1976-90, R.E. Morrow Disting. prof. earth and planetary scis., prof., 1986—, chmn. dept., 1976-90; mem. Mercury rev. panel NAS, 1970-71; mem. U.S. Nat. Com. on Geochemistry, 1975-78; mem. NASA Solar Sys. Exploration Com., 1983-87, mem. mgmt. coun., 1984-86, adv. com. Space and Earth Scis., 1985-88; mem. NRC Com. Planetary and Lunar Exploration, 1985-88, 97-99; mem. NASA Adv. Coun., 1988-90, Lunar and Planetary Rev. Panel, mem. cosmochemistry rev. panel, 1996-98. Recipient Exceptional Sci. Achievement award NASA, 1971; Guggenheim fellow Max Planck Inst. for Nuclear Physics, Heidelberg, Germany, 1966-67. Fellow The Meteoritical Soc., St. Louis Acad. of Sci.; mem. Am. Chem. Soc., Geochem. Soc. (v.p. 1985-87, pres. 1987-89), Am. Geophys. Union, AAAS, Phi Beta Kappa, Sigma Xi. Research on trace inorganic elements in meteoritic, lunar, martian, and terrestrial matter.

HASKINS, CARYL PARKER, scientist, author; b. Schenectady, Aug. 12, 1908; s. Caryl Davis and Frances Julia (Parker) H.; m. Edna Ferrell, July 12, 1940. Ph.B., Yale U., 1930; Ph.D., Harvard U., 1935; D.Sc., Tufts Coll., 1951, Union Coll., 1955, Northeastern U., 1955, Yale U., 1958, Hamilton Coll., 1959, George Washington U., 1963; LL.D., Carnegie Inst. Tech., 1960, U. Cin., 1960, Boston Coll., 1960, Washington and Jefferson Coll., 1961, U. Del., 1965, Pace U., 1974. Staff mem. rsch. lab. Gen. Electric Co., Schenectady, 1931-35; rsch. assoc. MIT, 1935-45; pres., rsch. dir. Haskins Labs., Inc., 1935-55; dir., founder Haskins Labs., Inc., Yale U., 1935—, chmn. bd., 1969-87; dir. E.I. du Pont de Nemours, 1971-81; research prof. Union Coll., 1937-55; pres. Carnegie Instn. of Washington, 1956-71, also trustee, 1949—; Asst. liaison officer OSRD, 1941-42, sr. liaison officer, 1942-43; exec. asst. to chmn. NDRC, 1943-44, dep. exec. officer, 1944-45; sci. adv. bd. Policy Council, Research and Devel. Bd. of Army and Navy, 1947-48; cons. Research and Develop. Bd., 1947-51, to sec. def., 1950-60, to sec. state, 1950-60; mem. Pres.'s Sci. Adv. Com., 1955-58, cons., 1959-70; mem. Pres.'s Nat. Adv. Commn. on Libraries, 1966-67, Joint U.S.-Japan Com. on Sci. Coop., 1961-67, Internat. Conf. Insect Physiology and Ecology, 1971-73; panel advisers Bur. East Asian and Pacific Affairs, Dept. State, 1966-68; mem. Sec. Navy Adv. Com. on Naval History, 1971-83, vice chmn., 1975-83. Author: Of Ants and Men, 1939, The Amazon, 1943, Of Societies and Men, 1950, The Scientific Revolution and World Politics, 1964; contbr. to anthologies and tech. papers.; editor: The Search for Understanding, 1967; Chmn. bd. editors: Am. Scientist, 1971-83 ; chmn. publs. com., 1971-83 . Trustee Carnegie Corp. N.Y., 1955-80, hon. trustee, 1980—, chmn. bd., 1975-80; trustee Rand Corp., 1955-65, 66-75, adv. trustee 1988—; fellow Yale Corp., 1962-77; regent Smithsonian Instn., 1956-80, regent emeritus, 1980—, mem. exec. com., 1958-80; bd. dirs. Council Fgn. Relations, 1961-75, Population Council, 1955-80; bd. dirs. Ednl. Testing Service, 1958-61, 67-71, chmn. bd., 1969-71; trustee Center for Advanced Study in Behavioral Scis., 1960-75, Thomas Jefferson Meml. Found., 1972-78, Council on Library Resources, 1965—, Pacific Sci. Center Found., 1962-72, Asia Found., 1960—, Marlboro Coll., 1962-77, Wildlife Preservation Trust Internat., Inc., 1976—, Nat. Humanities Center, 1977—; trustee Woods Hole Oceanographic Instn., 1964-73, mem. council, 1973—; bd. dirs. Franklin Book Programs, 1953-58; mem. Save-The-Redwoods League, 1943—, mem. council, 1955—; mem. vis. coms. Harvard, Johns Hopkins; bd. visitors Tulane U. Yale Corp. fellow, 1962-77; recipient Presdl. Cert. Merit U.S., 1948, King's medal for Service in Cause of Freedom Gt. Britain, 1948, Joseph Henry medal Smithsonian Inst., Centennial medal Harvard U., 1991. Fellow AAAS (bd. dirs. 1971-75), Am. Phys. Soc., Am. Acad. Arts and Scis., Royal Entomol. Soc., Entomol. Soc. Am., Pierpont Morgan Library; mem. NAS, Genetics Soc. Am., Washington Acad. Scis., Nat. Geog. Soc. (trustee 1964-84 , honorary trustee, 1984—, fin. com. 1972-85, com. on rsch. and exploration 1972—, exec. com. 1972-84), Royal Soc. Arts (Benjamin Franklin fellow), Faraday Soc., Met. Mus. Art, Am. Mus. Natural History (trustee 1973-89, bd. mgmt. 1973-89), Am. Philos. Soc. (councillor 1976-78, 81-83), Brit. Assn. Advancement Sci., Linnean Soc. London, Internat. Inst. Strategic Studies, Asia Soc., Japan Soc., Biophys. Soc., N.Y. Zool. Soc., N.Y. Acad. Scis., Audubon Soc., N.Y. Bot. Garden, P.E.N., Pilgrims, Phi Beta Kappa, Sigma Xi (nat. pres. 1966-68, dir. 1966-83), Delta Sigma Rho, Omicron Delta Kappa. Episcopalian. Clubs: Somerset (Boston), St. Botolph (Boston), Century (N.Y.C.), Yale (N.Y.C.), Mohawk (Schenectady), Metropolitan, Cosmos (Centennial award 1978, bd. mgmt. 1973-76), Lawn (New Haven). Home: 22 Green Acre Ln Westport CT 06880-5027 Office: Haskins Labs Inc 270 Crown St New Haven CT 06511-6695*

HASKINS, JAMES LESLIE, mathematics educator; b. St. Louis, Aug. 10, 1947; s. Delbert George and Betty Ann (Reese) H.; m. Laura Ann Placio, June 25, 1993; children: Todd M., Nathan E., Elizabeth M. BS in Applied Math. and Computer Sci., Washington U., St. Louis, 1969, MBA, 1983; MAT, Webster U., 1971; postgrad., St. Louis U., 1995—. Tchr. math. Desmet Jesuit H.S., St. Louis, 1969-70, John Burroughs Sch., St. Louis, 1970—; adj. prof. Washington U., St. Louis, 1982—, St. Louis U., 1994—; traveling team mem. Woodrow Wilson Found., Princeton, N.J., 1991—; instr. Command and Gen. Staff Officer Course USAR, St. Louis, 1991-94; bd. dirs. Martha Rounds Acad., St. Louis. Author: Algebra, 1990. Bd. dirs. Forsyth Sch., St. Louis, 1986-91, bldgs./grounds com., 1986—; credit com. chmn. Credit Union, St. Louis, 1989-96. Woodrow Wilson fellow, 1990. Mem. Nat. Coun. Tchrs. of Math., Mo. Coun. Tchrs. Math., Math. Educators Greater St. Louis (exec. bd. 1991—, pres. 1997), Beta Tau Sigma. Democrat. Presbyterian. Avocations: travel, sports, antiques. Home: 2857 Laclede Station Rd Saint Louis MO 63143-2809 Office: John Burroughs Sch 755 S Price Rd Saint Louis MO 63124-1899

HASKINS, MICHAEL DONALD, naval officer; b. Angels Camp, Calif., Sept. 8, 1942; s. Harold Marion and Dorothy (Ryan) H.; m. Joanne Mary Nesline, June 25, 1966; children: Eileen Lily, Julie Anne. BS, U.S. Naval Acad., 1966, postgrad., 1990; MA, Oxford U., Eng., 1975. Commd. ensign USN, 1966, advanced through grades to rear adm., 1992, instr. history of seapower Naval Acad., 1972, asst. plans/ops. officer cruiser destroyer group 12, 1975-78; adminstrv. officer, ops. officer, safety/NATOPS officer patrol squadron 45 USN, Jacksonville, Fla., 1975-80; tng. officer patrol wing 2 USN, 1980-81; exec. officer patrol squadron 22 USN, Barbers Point, Hawaii, 1981-82, commdg. officer patrol squadron 22, 1982-83, commdg. officer patrol squadron 1, 1983-84; current ops. officer 3d fleet USN, Ford Island, Hawaii, 1984-85; commdg. officer patrol squadron 31 USN, Moffett Field, Calif., 1985-86; dep. dir. chief of naval ops. exec. panel USN, Washington, 1986-88; comdr. patrol wing 1/task force 72 USN, Kami Seya, Japan, 1988-90; commandant midshipmen U.S. Naval Acad. USN, Annapolis, Md., 1990-92; comdr. Iceland Def. Force USN, Keflavik, 1992-94; comdr. Patrol Wings U.S. Atlantic Fleet USN, 1994-96; comdr. JTF 160, Guantanamo, Cuba, 1995; comdr. U.S. Naval Forces Japan USN, 1996-98; dep. commdr.-in-chief U.S. Naval Forces Europe, 1998—. Decorated Def. Superior Svc. medal with oak leaf cluster, Legion of Merit with gold star (2), Nat. Def. Svc. medal with bronze star, Meritorious Svc. medal with 3 gold stars, Armed Forces Expeditionary medal, Icelandic Order of the Falcon, Japanese Order of Sacred Treasure; Fulbright scholar U. La Plata, Argentina, 1966, Chief of NAval Ops. scholar U. Oxford, 1973. Office: Commander Naval Forces Psc 473 Box 12 FPO AP 96349-0051

HASKVITZ, ALAN PAUL, educational consultant, school educator; b. Mpls., Sept. 7, 1942; s. Harry and Rose (Portugal) H.; married, Apr. 1, 1970; children: Anna, Maxwell Harry. AA, Chaffey Coll., 1963; MS, Calif. State U., 1965; BE, Meml. Coll., St. John's, Newfoundland, 1972; MA, Calif. State U., L.A., 1970. Cert. secondaray tchr., adminstr., Calif.; cert. tchr., Ont., Newfoundland, N.Y.; cert. community coll. instr., Calif.; cert. audio-visual. Tchr. Cornwall (Ont.) Sch. Bd., Can., 1970-78; vice prin. Quest School for the Gifted, Oshawa, Ont., 1978-80; tchr. Corono (Calif.) Sch. System, 1980-81, Walnut (Calif.) Sch. Dist., 1987—; cons. Edn. Strategies, Alta Loma, Calif., 1981—; lectr. Calif. State U., 1970-89; pres.-elect Nat. Coun. for the Social Scis.; mem. Nat. Critical Thinking Com., Coun. of Chief State Sch. Officers, Nat. Assessment of Ednl. Progress, Nat. Responder Com. on Tchrs. and Schs., Constl. Rights Found., Western States Accreditation Commn., Cal Poly Master Tchr. Com. on Student Tng. Programs. Author: Resources for Social Studies Educators; syndicated automobile journalist The Car Family; contbr. numerous articles to profl. jours.; speaker to numerous orgns., meetings and confs. Commr. City of Rancho Cucamonga, 1986—; pres. United Counties Sports, Cornwall, 1980-84. Recipient Am.'s Profl. Best Tchr. award Learning mag., Heroes in Edn. award Reader's Digest, George Washington medal Freedom Found., Spirit of Edn. award NBC, Nat. Bicentennial Tchg. award Bicentennial Com., Presdl. award for environ. edn. Calif. Dept. Water Agencies, Cmty. award Walnut Valley Water Dist., Outstanding Citizen award L.A. County Supr., Outstanding Tchr. award, Christa MacAuliffe award, Nat. Coun. for Social Studies, 1992, Nation's Best Program, Nation's Outstanding Middle Sch. Tchr., Nat. Coun. for Social Studies, Agr. Tchr. of the Year, Baylor U., Calif. Ag. in Classroom, Robert Cherry Internat. Tchr. of the Year, Campbell's Tchrs. in Am. award, Disney Regional Winner, Busch Environ. Award, Nat. Garden award, Leavey award for Pvt. Enterprise Edn., Freedom Found., Calif. Water Environ. Edn. award Calif. Agy. for Water Edn., Calif. History Tchrs. of Yr., Daughters of Am. Colonies, numerous awards for sch. programs; named one of 100 Most Influential Educators in Am.; inductee Nat. Tchrs. Hall of Fame, 1997. Achievements include devel. of Reach Every Child and the Children's Speed Reading Record Holders. Avocations: writing, photography, automobiles, environment. E-mail: freealan@yahoo.com. Home: 9655 Carrari Ct Alta Loma CA 91737-1653

HASLAM, CHARLES LINN, aerospace executive, lawyer, educator; b. Birmingham, Ala., June 7, 1944; s. John Billups and Edmonia Berry (Henley) H.; m. Foley Ann Vickerman, May 30, 1981 (div. Aug. 1995); 1 child, Charles Linn. AB in Politics, Princeton U., 1965; cert., Coll. Europe, 1966; JD, Duke U., 1969. Asst. prof. Va. Poly. Inst. & State U., Blacksburg, Va., 1969-72; assoc. counsel, assoc. sec. AAUP, Washington, 1972-74; univ. counsel, adj. prof. law Duke U., Durham, N.C., 1974-77; gen. counsel U.S. Dept. Commerce, Washington, 1977-79; pvt. practice Washington, 1980-96; chmn., CEO Krug Internat. Corp., Houston, 1996-98; pres., CEO U.S. Transgenics, Inc., Washington, 1998—; sec. DDL Electronics, Inc., Newbury Park, Calif., 1995-96; chmn. Krug Internat. Ltd., London, 1996—. Democrat. Presbyterian. Avocation: aviation. Home: 4620 Sedgwick St NW Washington DC 20016-5614 Office: US Transgenics Inc 3050 K St NW Ste 205 Washington DC 20016

HASLAM, GERALD WILLIAM, writer, educator; b. Bakersfield, Calif., Mar. 18, 1937; s. Fredrick Martin and Lorraine Hope (Johnson) H.; m. Janice Eileen Pettichord, July 1, 1961; children: Frederick W., Alexandra R., Garth C., Simone B., Carlos V. BA, San Francisco State U., 1963, MA, 1965; PhD, Union Grad. Sch., 1980. Instr. English San Francisco State U., San Francisco, 1966-67; asst. prof. English Sonoma State U., Rohnert Park, Calif., 1967-70, assoc. prof. English, 1970-74, prof. English, 1971-97, emeritus prof. English, 1997—; adj. prof. Union Grad. Sch., Cin., 1984—, The Nat. Faculty, Atlanta, 1984—. Editor various anthologies; author various booklets, monographs, film scripts, (fiction) Okies: Selected Stories, 1973, Masks: A Novel, 1976, The Wages of Sin: Collected Stories, 1980, Hawk Flights: Visions of the West, 1983, Snapshots: Glimpses of the Other California, 1985, The Man Who Cultivated Fire and Other Stories, 1987, That Constant Coyote: California Stories, 1990, Condor Dreams and Other Fictions, 1994, The Great Tejon Club Jubilee, 1996, Manuel and the Madman, 1999, (non-fiction) Voices of a Place, 1987, Coming of Age in California, 1990, The Other California, 1990, The Great Central Valley: California's Heartland, 1993, Workin' Man Blues: Country Music in California, 1999. With U.S. Army, 1958-60. Creative Writing fellow Calif. Arts Coun., 1989; recipient Benjamin Franklin award, 1993, Bay Area Book Reviewers' Non-fiction award, 1994, Commonwealth Club medal for Calif., 1994, award of merit Assn. State & Local History, 1994; Fulbright sr. lectr., 1986-87, Josephine Miles award, 1990. Mem. Nat. Writers Union, Western Lit. Assn. (bd. dirs., past pres., Disting. Achievment award 1999), Calif. Studies Assn. (steering com., founding mem.), Calif. Hist. Assn., Calif. Tchrs. Assn., San Francisco State U. Alumni Assn. (life), Union Inst. Alumni Assn., Multi-Ethnic Lit. of U.S. (founding mem.), Robinson Jeffers Assn. (founding mem.), Sierra Club, The Nature Conservancy, Calif. Trout (founding mem.), Tulare Basin Archeology Group, Defenders of Wildlife, Common Cause. Roman Catholic. Avocations: bicycling, hiking, fishing. Office: Sonoma State U 1801 E Cotati Ave Rohnert Park CA 94928-3609*

HASLAM, JAMES A., III, petroleum sales executive; b. 1954. CEO and COO Pilot Corp., Knoxville. Office: Pilot Corp 5508 Lonas Rd Knoxville TN 37909-3221*

HASLAM, ROBERT THOMAS, III, lawyer; b. Taunton, Mass., May 4, 1946; s. Robert Thomas and Marcella Neale (Compton) H.; m. Mary Ashley Brayton, June 14, 1969; children: Laurel Ashley, Julia Compton. BS Aeronautics and Astronautics, MIT, 1968; JD, Hastings Coll., 1976. Bar: Calif., 1976. Atty., ptnr. Heller, Ehrman, Palo Alto, Calif., 1976—. Capt. USAF 1969-73. Mem. ABA (co-chair intellectual property sect. 1993—). Avocations: tennis, soccer. Home: 437 Chaucer St Palo Alto CA 94301-2202 Office: Heller Ehrman 525 University Ave Palo Alto CA 94301-1903

HASLANGER, PHILIP CHARLES, journalist; b. Menominee, Mich., May 11, 1949; s. Harry LeRoy and Agnes Gertrude (Seidl) H.; m. Rosemary Ann Raasch Carta, May 27, 1972 (div.); children: Brian David, Sarah Marie; m. Ellen Jean Reuter, Apr. 9, 1983; children: Michael Kenneth, Julia Jane. BA in Sociology, U. Wis., 1971, MA in Journalism, 1973. Mng. editor The Capital Times, Madison, Wis., 1973—. Author: Stories of Call, 1988. Mem. Nat. Conf. Editl. Writers (bd. dirs. 1993, 94, 97, sec. 1999), New Media Fedn. Roman Catholic. Avocations: reading, music, hiking. Home: 5409 Vicar Ln Madison WI 53714-3443 Office: The Capital Times 1901 Fish Hatchery Rd Madison WI 53713-1248

HASPEL, ARTHUR CARL, podiatrist, surgeon; b. Bklyn., May 18, 1945; s. Ephraim and Sophie (Rabinowitz) H.; m. Anna Kiperman, Feb. 2, 1969; children: Mark Steven, Alan Charles. BS, L.I. U., 1967; D of Podiatric Medicine, Ohio Coll. Podiatric Medicine, 1972. Cert. Am. Bd. Ambulatory Foot Surgery, Am. Bd. Quality Assurance and Utilization Rev. in Podiatric Medicine, Am. Podiatric Med. Specialties Bd. in Surgery and Podiatric Medicine, Am. Acad. Pain Mgmt. Practice medicine specializing in podiatry Chgo., 1972-77, Hallandale, Fla., 1977—, Miami Shores, Fla., 1990-96, Boca Raton, Fla., 1996—; lectr. in field. Author HMOs- Long Term Effects, 1986, (with others) Lions and Retinitis Pigmentosa, 1982, Procedural Podiatric Service Codes, 1986. Bd. govs. Hillel Community Day Sch., 1980-82; mem. land acquisition and devel. com. Beth Torah Congregation, 1986; active Am. Red Magen David for Israel (charter 1st v.p. South Broward profl. chpt. 1980, 1st v.p. 1980—, fin. sec. 1980—, southeastern U.S. steering com. 1980-82), Highland Lakes Homeowners Assn. Fellow Acad. Ambulatory Foot Surgery (trustee, 1984-89, 91-93, mem. profl. standards com., research and devel. com., seminars com., ins. com., pres. Region IX, 1981-85, sec.-treas. 1979-81, mem.-at-large 1978-79, mem. adv. bd. 1985—, seminar coordinator 1979-85, chmn. statewide referral service, coordinator continuing med. edn. State of Fla. 1979-85), Am. Assn. Hosp. Podiatrists, Am. Podiatric Circulatory Assn., Am. Soc. Podiatric Medicine; mem. Am. Coll. Foot and Ankle Surgeons, Fla. Podiatric Med. Assn. (pres. 1990-91, 1st v.p. 1989-90, v.p. 1988-89, treas. 1987-88, sec. 1986-87, exec. com. sec. 1986-87, exec. bd. 1986, chmn. banner com. 1981, 86, chmn. pub. health com., 1982, co-chmn. membership com., 1983, 84, 85, mem. sci. and surg. program com. 1984—, chmn. sunshine com. 1986, chmn. profl. standards rev. orgn. 1982), Broward County Podiatric Med. Assn. (co-chmn. legis. appreciation night 1979-81, sec. 1981-83, sec. May Day com., sec. continuing med. edn. cert., March of Dimes Walk-a-Thon, health fairs, ethical advt. com.), Am. Podiatric Circulatory Assn., Am. Podiatric Med. Assn., Ill. Podiatry Assn., Fla. Podiatric Med. Assn. (del. to Am. Podiatric Med. Assn. 1989-93), Am. Pub. Health Assn., Ohio Coll. Podiatric Medicine Alumni Soc., Hallandale C. of C., Lions (charter treas. Fla. community hearing bank 1979, treas. 1979-82, 83-85, pres. 1982-83, v.p. 1985-87, exec. dir. 1983-84, mem. exec. com. 1979-84, TV and radio liaison 1982-84, bd. dirs. Hallandale club 1978-80, treas. 1978-80, charter treas. dist. 35A for Retinitis Pigmentosa 1980, treas. 1980-82, mem. exec. com. 1980-82, co-chmn. state com. on deaf and hearing impaired, multiple dist. 35, sec. Fla. Lions deaf profject 1980-82), Optimists (soccer coach, tee ball coach), Kappa Tau Epsilon. Office: 1105 E Hallandale Beach Blvd Hallandale FL 33009-4431

HASS, JOSEPH MONROE, automotive executive; b. Syracuse, N.Y., July 28, 1955; s. Joseph Monroe and Susan Faith (Betts) H.; m. Lisa Michelle Palmer, Aug. 14, 1982. BS in Secondary Edn., Tenn. Temple U., 1977. Diesel mechanic Cummins Engines Tenn., Chattanooga, 1978-81; mgr. tng. Cummins Engines Tenn., Nashville, 1981-85; svc. fl. foreman Cummins Cumberland, Nashville, 1985-86, CompuChek technician, 1986-87, fleet systems support engr., 1987-89, tech. advisor, instr., 1989-90, dir. devel., 1990—. Mem. ASTD, Internat. Platform Assn., Am. Assn. Individual Investors, Citizens Against Govt. Waste, Exptl. Aircraft Assn. Avocations: music, sailing, carpentry, cycling, reading. Office: Cummins Cumberland 706 Spence Ln Nashville TN 37217-1190

HASS, MICHAEL SHEPHERDSON, architect; b. Rochester, N.Y., Apr. 7, 1944; s. Peter Stibolt and Harriet Frances (Shepherdson) H.; m. Joan Alexandra Barkhorn, June 25, 1966; children: Norah Katherine Hass Kelley, Claire Alexis. AB, Harvard Coll., 1965, MArch, 1968; Engr. Boukundig, Technische Hogeschool, Delft, Netherlands, 1969. Arch. Paul Rudolph, Arch., Boston, 1969-71, Haldeman/Goranson Assocs., Boston, 1971-73, Design Five, Cambridge, Mass., 1973-74; prin. ADD Inc, Archs., Cambridge, 1976—. Co-chmn. Boston Housing Commn., 1991-93. Recipient awards for arch. from AIA, Pitts. chpt., Nat. Soc. Indsl./Office Parks, Bldg. Owners and Mgrs. Assn., Progressive Architecture Mag., others. Mem. AIA, Boston Soc. Archs., Soc. Archs., Union Club (Boston), Maidstone Club (East Hampton, N.Y.). Avocations: swimming, squash, gardening, golf. Office: ADD Inc 80 Prospect St Cambridge MA 02139-2599

HASS, ROBERT L., writer, educator; b. San Francisco, 1941. Prof. Dept. English U. Calif., Berkeley. Author: (books of poetry) Sun Under Wood: New Poems, 1996, Human Wishes, 1989, Praise, 1979, Field Guide, 1973; co-translator vols. of poetry with Czeslaw Milosz including: Facing the river, 1995; author/editor essays and translation including: The Essential Haiku: Versions of Basho, Buson, and Issa, 1994, Twenthieth Century Pleasures: Prose on Poetry, 1984 (Nat. Book Critics Circle award). Bd. dirs. Internat. Rivers Network. Apptd. Poet Laureate of U.S., 1995; MacArthur "Genius" fellow; named Educator of the Yr., N.Am. Assn. on Environ. Edn., 1997. Email: bobhass@uclink4.berkeley.edu. Office: Steven Barclay Agy 321 Pleasant St Petaluma CA 94952*

HASS, ROBERT MICHAEL, editor; b. Phila., Jan. 10, 1947; s. Louis Herman and Selma (Levit) H. BA, Earlham Coll., 1968; MS in Edn., U. Pa., 1971. Cert. secondary English educator, reading specialist. Cmty. worker VISTA, Pueblo, Colo., 1968-70; tutorial coord. Pueblo Unified Sch. Dist., 1971-72; reading tchr. North Penn Sch. Dist., Lansdale, Pa., 1972-74; reading specialist Phila. Pub. Schs., 1974-77; asst. pub. rels. & devel. Santa Rosa (Calif.) Meml. Hosp., 1979-81; tchr. Mt. Tamalpais Primary Sch., Mill Valley, Calif., 1983-85; program asst. gifted/talented Sch. of Edn. U. Calif., Berkeley, 1985-89, sr. editor Grad. Sch. of Edn., 1989-97; pres. Hass & Assocs., Sonoma, Calif., 1997—. Mentor Berkeley High Sch., 1993-94; cellist numerous cmty. symphonies. Mem. Edn. Writers Assn., Phi Delta Kappa. Avocations: chamber music, gardening, meditation, ecology, cooking. Home: 19002 Olive Ave Sonoma CA 95476-5312 Office: Hass & Assocs Grad Sch of Edn PO Box 188 Sonoma CA 95476-0188*

HASSAN, AFTAB SYED, education specialist, author, editor; b. Lahore, Punjab, Pakistan, Apr. 20, 1952; came to U.S., 1976; s. Maqsud Syed and Saliha Akhtar Hassan. BSCE with distinction, U. Engring. and Tech., Lahore, 1973; postgrad. in aerodyns., Colo. State U., 1976; MS, George Washington U., 1977; PhD, Columbia Pacific U., 1985. Scientist in ocean, coastal and environ. engring. George Washington U., 1977-84; grad. tchg. asst. George Washington U., Washington, 1979-84, asst. prof., 1980-85; chmn. math. and sci. Emerson Prep. Inst., Washington, 1979-89; acad. coord. Ctr. for Minority Student Affairs Georgetown U. Med. Sch., Washington, 1983-87; v.p. Met. Acctg. Assocs., Washington, 1987-88; acctg. mgr. Washington Info. Group, 1988-91; owner Met. Acctg. and Rsch., Washington, 1988-91; sr. tech. editor and author Betz Pub. Co., Rockville, Md., 1991-94, designer new products, dir. sci. rsch., 1991-94, v.p. acad. devel. Williams and Wilkins Ednl. Svcs. div., 1994-96, v.p. acad. devel. Betz Sci. Rsch. div., 1994-96; v.p. acad. devel., strategic planning Metro Acad. Rsch., Washington, 1996—; adj. prof., clin. coord. Harlem Hosp. Ctr. Physicians Asst. program, The Sophie Dairs Sch. Biomed. Edn., 1998—. Author, dir. sci. rsch.: A Complete Preparation for the MCAT, 7th edit., 1996, Preparing for the D.A.T., 1992, Dental Admission Test--The Betz Guide, 1993, Optometry Admission Test--The Betz Guide, 1993, Problem Solving Software for the MCAT-Biological Sciences and Physical Sciences, 1994, Pharmacy College Admission Test--The Betz Guide, 1994, Allied Health Professions Admission Test--The Betz Guide, 1994, Veterinary Entrance Tests--The Betz Guide, 1995. Bd. dirs. Ctr. for Edn. Achievement, Charles R. Drew U. Medicine and Sci., Ebon Internat. Acad., Forsythe, Ga.; ednl. specialist Am. Physician Asst. Programs; curriculum advisor statewide programs for minority health professions State of Pa.; curriculum and ednl. specialist for ACCESS, statewide program at Priarie View (Tex.) A&M U. Recipient Merit award Nat. Assn. Chiefs of Police, Leaders in Cmty. Svc. award Am. Biog. Inst. 1990, Bell award Nat. Assn. Black Sch. Educators Found. Mem. ASCE, NSPE, Am. Soc. Engring. Edn., Am. Inst. Profl. Bookkeepers, Soc. Am. Mil. Engrs., Nat. Soc. Tax Profls., Nat. Coun. for Testing and Measurement, Nat. Law Enforcement Acad. (hon.), Nat. Assn. Advisors for Health Professions, Nat. Assn. Fgn. Student Advisors, Nat. Sci. Tchrs. Assn., Nat. Assn. Profl. Educators, Nat. Assn. Minority Med. Educators, Am. Ednl. Rsch. Assn., Soc. Tchrs. Family Medicine, N.Y. Acad. Scis., Soc. Competitive Intelligence Profls., Assn. Am. Med. Colls. (assoc.), Acad. Physician Assts. (assoc.). Avocations: exotic cooking, swimming, collecting currency. Address: Americian Soc Landscape Asso 636 I St NW Washington DC 20001-3736

HASSAN, FRED, pharmaceutical executive; b. Pakistan, Nov. 12, 1945; came to U.S., 1970; s. Syed Fida and Zeenat (Hussain) H.; m. Noreen Shah, Mar. 15, 1969. BS in Chem. Engring. with honors, U. London, 1967; MBA, Harvard U., 1972. Chem. engr., sales mgr. Dawood Corp., Lahore, Pakistan, 1967-70; sales rep. Richardson-Vicks, N.Y.C., 1970; project mgr., corp. planning Sandoz Pharms. Corp., East Hanover, N.J., 1972-74, chief ops. officer, 1984-86, CEO, 1987-89; mgr. planning Dorsey Labs. div. Sandoz Pharms. Corp., Lincoln, Nebr., 1974-76, dir. mktg., 1975-80; CEO Sandoz Pakistan, Karachi, 1980-83; exec. v.p. Am. Home Products, Madison, N.J., sr. v.p., 1995, exec. v.p., bd. dirs., 1995-97; pres. Wyeth Ayerst Labs., Madison, N.J., 1989-93; pres., dir., CEO Pharmacia & Upjohn, Inc.; group v.p. Sandoz Corp. (USA), N.Y.C., 1987-89; bd. dirs. Ex Lax, Inc., Huamacao, P.R. Mem. Alliance for Aging Rsch. (bd. dirs. 1987-89, 96—), Pharm. Mfrs. Assn. (bd. dirs. 1999). Office: Pharmacia & Upjohn Worldwide Headquarters 95 Corporate Dr Bridgewater NJ 08807

HASSAN, HOSNI MOUSTAFA, microbiologist, biochemist, toxicologist and food scientist, educator; b. Alexandria, Egypt, Sept. 3, 1937; came to U.S., 1961; s. Moustafa Hosni and Sania M. (El-Hariri) H.; m. Awatif El-Domiaty, July 12, 1961 (div. May 1983); children: Jehan, Suzanne; m. Linda C. McDonald, Dec. 16, 1992; 1 child, Nora Elizabeth. BSc, Ain Shams U., Cairo, 1959; PhD, U. Calif., Davis, 1967. Asst. prof. Cairo High Polytech. Inst., 1968-70, U. Alexandria, 1970-72; vis. prof. McGill U., Montreal, 1972-74; rsch. asst. prof. U. Maine, Orono, 1974-76; rsch. assoc. biochemistry Duke U. Med. Ctr., Durham, N.C., 1976-79; assoc. prof. McGill U. Med. Sch., Montreal, 1979-80; assoc. prof. N.C. State U., Raleigh, 1980-84, prof., 1984-93, prof., head microbiology dept., 1993—. Mem. editl. bd. Free Radicals in Biology and Medicine, 1984—; author: (chpts.) Enzymatic Basis of Toxicology, 1980, Biological Role of Copper, 1980, Advances in Genetics, 1989, Stress Responses in Plants, 1990, FEMS Microbiol. Reviews, 1994, Lung Biology Series, Vol. 15, 1997, others; author/co-author over 100 rsch. publs. fellow NIH, 1967, Fulbright sr. fellow, Paris, 1987-88; NIH-NSF grantee N.C. State U., 1982, 83-93. Fellow Am. Inst. Chemists, Sigma Xi; mem. Am. Soc. Biol. Chemists and Molecular Biology, Am. Soc. for Microbiology (pres.-elect and pres. N.C. chpt. 1993-95). Democrat. Achievements include discovery of the toxicity and mutagenicity of oxygen free radicals and the protective role of the antioxident enzymes superoxide dismutases and hydroperoxidases; the mechanism of regulation of the synthesis of the enzyme Mn-superoxide dismutase in bacteria. E-mail: hmhassan@mbio.ncsu.edu. Home: 2637 Freestone Ln Raleigh NC 27603-3950 Office: NC State U Microbiology Dept 4515 Gardner Hall Box 7615 Raleigh NC 27695-7615

HASSAN, LOIS MARY, English language educator; b. Detroit, May 20, 1949; d. Louis and Eleanor Garavaglia; m. Ernest Hassan, June 29, 1974; children: Lori Lynn, Ernest III. BA, U. Detroit, 1971; MEd, Wayne State U., 1974; M English, Ea. Mich. U., 1988. Cert. elem. and humanities tchr., Mich. Instr. study skills Schoolcraft Coll., Livonia, Mich.; grad. asst. in English Ea. Mich. U., Ypsilanti, 1986; instr. English Oakland Community Coll., Union Lake, Mich., 1988-89, Madonna Coll., Livonia, Mich., 1988-89, Siena Heights Coll., Southfield, Mich., 1988-89; instr. English Henry Ford Community Coll., Dearborn, Mich., 1982—, instr. devel. reading, writing, ESL basic skills. Contbr. articles to Pvt. Lives Pub. Voices. President's scholar U. Detroit. Mem. ASCD, Internat. Reading Assn., Nat. Coun. Tchrs. English, Mich. Reading Assn., Nat. Cath. Edn. Assn., Tchrs. of English of Second Langs. Home: 17703 Francavilla Dr Livonia MI 48152-3109

HASSEL, RUDOLPH CHRISTOPHER, English language educator; b. Richmond, Va., Nov. 16, 1939; s. Rudolph Christopher and Helen Elizabeth (Poehler) H.; m. Sedley Louise Hotchkiss, June 16, 1962; children: Bryan Christopher, Paul Sedley. BA, U. Richmond, 1961; MA, U. N.C., 1962; PhD, Emory U., 1968. English instr. Mercer U., Macon, Ga., 1962-65; asst. prof. Vanderbilt U., Nashville, 1968-73, assoc. prof., 1973-85, prof., 1985—; dir. grad. studies English dept. Vanderbilt U., 1974-81, dir. undergrad. studies, 1991; mem. exec. com. Folger Inst., Washington, 1986-95; cons. State of Tenn., Nashville, 1987-93; cons. for various univ. presses and profl. jours. Author: Renaissance Drama and the English Church Year, 1979, Faith and Folly in Shakespeare's Romantic Comedies, 1980, Songs of Death, 1987; contbr. articles to Shakespeare Quar. and others and poems to Vanderbilt Rev. and Arts and Letters. Mem. choir Christ Episcopal Ch., Nashville, 1974-95, outreach vol., 1974—, vestryman, 1980-83; vol. United Way, Vanderbilt U., 1980—, Habitat for Humanity. Woodrow Wilson Found. fellow, 1962; Emory U. fellow, 1965; Folger Libr. fellow, 1976; Am. Philol. Soc. fellow, 1986. Mem. MLA, Shakespeare Assn. Am., Malone Soc. New Variorum Editor, South Atlantic MLA, Christianity and Lit. Soc., Phi Beta Kappa, Omicron Delta Kappa. Avocations: biking, hiking, tennis, gardening, woodcrafting. Home: 107 Pembroke Ave Nashville TN 37205-3728 Office: Vanderbilt U PO Box 129B Nashville TN 37202-0129

HASSELHOFF, DAVID, actor; b. Balt., July 17, 1952; m. Catherine Hickland (div.); m. Pamela Bach; children: Taylor-Ann, Hayley Amber. television appearances include: (series) The Young and the Restless, 1975-82, Semi-Tough, 1980, Knight Rider, 1982-86; exec. prodr., star Baywatch, (NBC) 1989-90, (syndicated) 91—, Baywatch Nights, 1995—; (movies) Griffin and Phoenix: A Love Story, 1976, Pleasure Cove, 1979, The Cartier Affair, 1984, Bridge Across Time, 1985, Perry Mason: The Case of the Lady in the Lake, 1988, Knight Rider the Movie, 1988, Panic at Malibu Pier, 1989, Knight Rider 2000, 1990, Ring of the Muskateers, 1992, Avalanche, 1994, Gridlock, 1996, Nick Fury, 1997, Shaka Zulu: The Citadel, 1999, Diamond Hunters, 1999; films include: Starcrash, 1979, Starke Zeiten, 1988, W.B. Blue and the Bean, 1989 (also co-prodr.), The Final Alliance, 1989, Legacy, 1998; albums include Looking for Freedom, 1989 (Platinum), Crazy for You, 1991 (Gold), David, 1991 (Gold), Everybody's Sunshine, 1992 (Gold), You Are Everything, 1993 (Gold), Du, 1994, Best of David Hasselhoff, 1995, David Hasselhoff, 1995, Hooked on a Feeling, 1997; (video) Baywatch: Forbidden Paradise, 1995. Office: care Jan McCormack 11342 Dona Lisa Dr Studio City CA 91604-4315

HASSELL, LEROY ROUNTREE, SR., state supreme court justice; b. Aug. 17, 1955. BA in Govt. and Fgn. Affairs, U. Va., 1977; JD, Harvard U., 1980. Bar: Va. Former ptnr. McGuire, Woods, Battle and Boothe; now justice Supreme Ct. of Va.; former mem. Va. gen. assembly task force to study violence on sch. property. Former mem. adv. bd. Massey Cancer Ctr.; mem. policy com., former chmn. Richmond Sch. Bd., ; former bd. dirs. Richmond Renaissance, Inc., richmond chpt. ARC, Garfield childs Fund, Carpenter Ctr. for Performing Arts, St. John's Hosp., Legal Aid Ctrl. Va.; vol. Richmond Pub. Schs., Hospice vol.; bd. dirs. Va. State conf. of Christians and Jews; elected sch. bd. chmn. 4 terms. Recipient Liberty Bell award 1985, 86, Black Achievers award, 1985-86, Outstanding Young Citizen award Richmond Jaycees, 1987, Outstanding Young Virginian award Va. Jaycees, 1987; one of youngest persons to both serve on the Richmond Sch. Bd. and to serve as bd. chmn. Mem. Va. Trial Lawyers Assn., Assn. Trial Lawyers Am., Va. Assn. Def. Attys., Old Dominion Bar Assn., Va. Bar Assn. Office: Supreme Ct of Virginia PO Box 1315 Richmond VA 23218-1315

HASSELL, MARK JOSEPH, counselor; b. Newark, Dec. 5, 1960; s. Louis Desmond and Miriam Charlotte (Jones) H.; m. Dayna Martine Hollis, Oct. 12, 1985; children: Phillip Alexander, Adrienne Alexis. BS, U. Pitts., 1982, MEd, 1985. Sr. therapist Brighton Woods Treatment Ctr., Pitts., 1985-88; intake coord. St. Francis Med. Ctr., Pitts., 1988-91; counselor, cons. U. Pitts. Med. Ctr., 1991-97; mgr. ea. region Continental Airlines, Newark, 1997—. Mem. Employee Assistance Profl. Assn. (cert.). Avocations: running, computers.

HASSELL, PETER ALBERT, electrical and metallurgical engineer; b. Springfield, Mass., Aug. 8, 1916; s. Cornelius and Erica (Farkasch) H.; m. Elizabeth Heffner, July 11, 1941; children: Cornelius, Kenneth Joseph. Student, Case Sch. Applied Sci., 1935-38, Fenn Coll., 1940-41, U. Wis., 1946-48. Lab. technician Tocco Div., Ohio Crankshaft, Cleve., 1940-42; radar officer USN, USS Mindanao and Puget Sound Navy Yard, 1942-45; application engr. Allis Chalmers Mfg. Co., Milw., 1945-48, Lindberg Engring. Co., Chgo., 1948-51, Westinghouse Electric Co., Chgo., 1951-54; high freqency div. mgr., then asst. to pres. Ajax Magnethermic Corp. Warren, Ohio, 1954-83; retired, 1983; cons. Hassell Assocs., 1983-95; tech. adv. bd. Magnetic Processing Sys., Inc., 1994-97. Contbr. articles to profl. jours. and tech. papers. Recycle coord. Breckenridge Village, Willoughby, Ohio, 1989-91; mgmt. counselor SCORE/SBA, Willoughby, 1983-95; tech. cons. Ctr. Indsl. Heat Treating Processes, U. Cin., 1990-94; induction expert Teletech Resource Network, 1986—; active with Ret. Srs. Vol. Program; mem., chmn. Willoughby Clean City Commn.; trustee Seaman's Svc. Lt. USNR, 1945-53. Mem. ASM Internat., Am. Foundrymen's Soc. Unitarian. Avocations: sailing, iceboating, bicycling, cross country skiing., boomeranging. Home: 194 N Ridge Dr Willoughby OH 44094-5639

HASSELMAN, RICHARD B., retired transportation company executive; b. Jersey City, Nov. 28, 1926; s. Benjamin R. and Clara A. (Borchert) H.; m. Mildred E. Schaber, May 29, 1954; children: Richard Dwight, James Christopher. BME, Yale U., 1947; MBA, NYU, 1949. Student engr. N.Y. Central R.R., 1947-49, trainee, 1949-52, brakeman, 1952-53, signalman, freight agt., 1953; transp. insp. Eastern region Syracuse, N.Y., 1953-55; trainmaster Mowhawk div. Albany, N.Y., 1955-57; div. trainmaster Syracuse div., 1957; div. supt. Boston & Albany div. Springfield, Mass, 1957-59; dist. transp. supt. Western region Cleve., 1959-60; gen. supt. yards and terminals N.Y. Central System, N.Y.C., 1960-63; gen. mgr. Ind. Harbor Belt and Chicago River & Ind. R.R., Hammond, Ind., 1963; gen. mgr. No. Region N.Y. Cen. R.R., Detroit, 1964; gen. mgr. So. Region N.Y. Cen. R.R., Indpls., 1964-66; gen. mgr. Western Region N.Y. Cen. R.R., Cleve., 1967; asst. v.p. transp. N.Y. Central System, N.Y.C., 1967-68; v.p. transp. Penn. Central, Phila., 1968-76; pres. Ind. Harbor Belt RR, 1968-87; sr. v.p. ops. Consol. Rail Corp., Phila., 1976-89; transp. cons., 1989—. Home and Office: 5289 Ladyfinger Lake Rd Sanibel FL 33957-2436

HASSELMEYER, EILEEN GRACE, medical research administrator; b. Bklyn., May 23, 1924; d. Edwin Allen and Margaret Grace (Cody) H. RN, Bellevue Sch. Nursing, 1946; BS, NYU, 1954, MA, 1956, PhD, 1963. Mem. staff Pediatric Metabolic and Nutritional Rsch. Svc., NYU Children's Med. Svc., Bellevue Hosp., N.Y.C., 1946-56, study coord., 1951-56; rsch. nursing supr. Met. Hosp., N.Y.C., 1951; lectr. pediatric nutrition rsch. U. Tex. Sch. Nursing, 1952-53; nursing dir. nutritional rsch. studies Children's Hosp. of John Seely Hosp. (U. Tex. Med. Br.), Galveston, 1952-53; lectr. and nursing rsch. assoc. nutritional service pediatrics dept. Hosp. Infantile, Mexico City, 1953; nursing dir. rsch. unit Willowbrook State Sch., S.I., 1953-54; commd. USPHS, 1956, advanced through grades to asst. surgeon gen.-rear adm., 1989; ret.; nurse cons. Div. Nursing Resources, Bur. Med. Services, USPHS, Washington, 1956-59; prin. investigator Handling and Premature Infant Behavior project, NYU, N.Y.C., 1961-63; sr. nurse cons. Div. Nursing, Bur. State Svcs., USPHS, Washington, 1963; spl. asst. for prematurity Office of Dir., Nat. Inst. Child Health and Human Devel., Bethesda, Md., 1963-66; acting dir. perinatal biology and infant mortality program, extramural programs Office of Dir., Nat. Inst. Child Health and Human Devel., 1967-68, dir., 1969-74, asst. to dir. for perinatology, 1974-80; chief pregnancy and infancy br. Ctr. for Rsch. for Mothers and Children, 1974-79, acting chief clin. nutrition and early devel. br., 1979-80; assoc. dir. for sci. rev. Office of Dir., 1979-89; sec. asst. to dir. N.C. for Nursing Rsch., 1986-89; exec. dir. Uniform Svcs. U. Health Sci., Fed. Coll. Nursing Feasability Study Task Force, 1989-92; Annie W. Goodrich vis. prof. Yale U. Sch. Nursing, New Haven, 1968-69; asst. surgeon gen. USPHS, Dept. Health and Human Svcs., 1981-89, chmn. interagy. panel on sudden infant death syndrome, 1974-82, others. Contbr. articles to profl. jours. Recipient NICHD Recognition of Outstanding Performance, 1973, plaque for 25 yrs. dedicated svc., 1987, Chief Nurse Officer's medal USPHS, 1989; USUHS Commendable Svc. medal, 1990; USPHS Surgeon Gen.'s Cert. of Appreciation, 1990; HEW-USPHS Commendation medal, 1975; recipient Perinatal Research Soc. award, 1979; NYU Sch. Edn., Health, Nursing and Arts Professions Creative Leadership award, 1980; Achievement award Nat. Sudden Infant Death Syndrome Found., 1987, Eileen G. Hasselmeyer Disting. Sci. Achievement award Sudden Infant Death Syndrome Alliance, 1990; Outstanding Performance award NCNR, 1987, Meritorious Svc. medal HHS-USPHS, 1989; cert. appreciation NIH-NCNR, 1989; Nat. League for Nursing Commonwealth fellow, 1959-62; NIH fellow, 1962-63; Am. Nurses Found. grantee, 1962-63; State of Conn. Maternal and Infant Program grantee, 1969; Sigma Theta Tau research grantee, 1969-71; Yale U. Sch. Nursing developmental grantee, 1969; disting. alumnae award Bellevue Alumnae Assn., 1997. Mem. Am. Pediatric Soc., PHS Commd. Officers Assn., Bellevue Alumnae Assn.

HASSELMO, NILS, university official, linguistics educator; b. Kola, Sweden, July 2, 1931; came to U.S., 1958; s. A. Wilner and Anna Helena (Backlund) H.; m. Patricia June Tillberg, Oct. 25, 1958; children: Nils Peter, Michael Erik, Anna Patricia. Fil. mag., Uppsala U., 1956, Fil. lic., 1962, PhD (hon.), 1979; BA, Augustana Coll., Ill., 1957, DHL (hon.), 1995; PhD, Harvard U., 1961; LHD (hon.), North Park Coll. Theol. Sem., 1992. Asst. prof. Swedish Augustana Coll., Rock Island, Ill., 1958-59, 61-63; from assoc. prof. to prof. Scandinavian langs. and lit. U. Minn., Mpls., 1965-83, 88—, chmn. Scandinavian langs. and lit., 1970-73; dir. U. Minn. Ctr. for N.W. European Langs. and Area Studies, Mpls., 1970-73; assoc. dean U. Minn. Coll. Liberal Arts, Mpls., 1973-78; v.p. for adminstrn. and planning U. Minn., Mpls., 1980-83; sr. v.p. acad. affairs, provost U. Ariz., Tucson, 1983-88, prof. English and linguistics, 1983-88; pres. U. Minn., Mpls., 1988-97, Assn. Am. Univs., Washington, 1998—; vis. com. dept. Germanic langs. and lit. Harvard U., Cambridge, Mass., 1981-86; trustee Nat. Merit Scholarship Corp., 1992-97. Author: Amerikasvenska, 1974, Swedish America: An Introduction, 1976; editor: Perspectives on Swedish Immigration, 1978. Bd. dirs. Swedish Council Am., 1978—, Walker Art Ctr., 1989-95; mem. Gov.'s Task Force on Technology and Improvement of Employment, Minn., 1982-83; mem. bd. overseers Mpls. Coll. Art & Design, 1982-83; trustee Am. Scandinavian Found., 1992—. Served to sgt. Royal Signal Corps, Swedish Army, 1951-54. Fulbright-Hays fellow, 1968; decorated Royal Order of North Star Sweden, 1973; recipient King Carl XVI Gustaf's Bicentennial medal in Gold Sweden, 1976, Swedish-Am. of Yr. award Swedish Govt. and Vasa Order Am., 1991, Ellis Island medal of honor, 1993. Mem. MLA, Soc. for Advancement Scandinavian Study (pres. 1971-73), Linguistic Soc. Am., Vetenskaps-Societeten, Royal Gustavus Adolphus Acad., Swedish-Am. Hist. Soc. (chmn. bd. 1984-86), Nat. Assn. State Univs. and Land Grant Colls. (exec. com. Acad. Affairs Coun. 1986-88, chmn. coun. pres. and chancellors 1992-93, chair bd. 1994-95), Univ. Rsch. Assn. (trustee 1993-97).

HASSENBOEHLER, DONALYN, principal. Prin. McMain Magnet Secondary Sch.; evaluator FIRST grants U.S. Dept. Edn. Recipient U.S. Dept. Edn. Blue Ribbon award, 1990-91. Office: McMain Magnet Secondary Sch 5712 S Claiborne Ave New Orleans LA 70125-4908*

HASSENFELD, ALAN GEOFFREY, toy company executive; b. Providence, Nov. 16, 1948; s. Merrill Lloyd and Sylvia (Kay) H. B.A., U. Pa., 1970. Asst. to pres. Hasbro Industries, Inc., Pawtucket, R.I., 1969-72, v.p. internat. ops., 1972-78, v.p. mktg. and sales, 1978-80, exec. v.p., 1980-84, pres., 1984-89, chmn., chief exec. officer, 1989—. Bd. dirs. Foster Parents Plan, 1989—, Assn. Gov. Bds. Univs. and Colls.; trustee Miriam Hosp., 1984-93, Brown U., 1990, Bryant Coll., 1992; mem. adv. bd. Big Bros. of R.I., 1991; chmn. Right Now! Coalition, 1991—; chmn. Gov.'s Adv. Council on Refugee Resettlement, 1986; bd. overseers U. Pa. Sch. Arts and Scis., 1986—, Harvard U. Sch. Pub. Health, 1997; chmn. bd. overseers Brown U. Med. Sch., 1997; trustee R.I. and Southeastern New Eng. region, NCCJ, 1988, Deerfield Acad., 1996; bd. dirs. Jewish Fedn. R.I., 1989—, Bus. for Social Responsibility, 1994, Founds. Milken Families, 1993; hon. chmn. World Scholar Athlete Games, 1993, dir. The Jerusalem Found., 1995—, mem. dean council harvard U., 1995. With AFNG, 1967-73. Mem. R.I. Commodores (adm. 1991-98). Office: Hasbro Inc 1027 Newport Ave Pawtucket RI 02861-2500*

HASSERT, ELIZABETH ANNE, transportation executive; b. Joliet, Ill., July 28, 1956; d. Wilbur Clarence and Frances Romayne (McLaughlin) H. BA, St. Mary's Coll., Notre Dame, Ind., 1978. Dept. mgr. Lord & Taylor, Aurora, Ill., 1978-79, Oak Brook, Ill., 1979-80; account exec. Cast (N.Am.) Ltd., Rolling Meadows, Ill., 1980-82; sales mgr. Cast (UK) Ltd., London, 1982-83, Sofati Container (UK), Birmingham, Eng., 1983-84; account exec. Sea-Land Svc., Inc., Rolling Meadows, 1984-88, sales mgr., 1988-90, sales exec., 1990—. Recipient of CSX award of Excellence, 1993. Mem. Ocean Freight Agts., World Trade Club, Midwest Fgn. Freight Club, Hinsdale Jr. Women's Club, Detroit Ocean Freight Agy., St. Mary's Coll. Alumnae Assn. Republican. Roman Catholic. Avocations: needlepoint, cross country skiing, travel, gardening, cooking. Home: 625 N County Line Rd Hinsdale IL 60521-2406 Office: Sea-Land Svc Inc 3501 W Algonquin Rd Ste 600 Rolling Meadows IL 60008-3132

HASSETT, BRIAN THOMAS, administrator local chapter of United Way; b. Bronx, N.Y.. BA, Niagara U., 1976; MPA, U. R.I., 1977. Sr. v.p. United WAy Svcs., Richmond, Va., 1983-90; pres. United Way Ctrl. Mass., Worcester, 1990-95; pres., CEO Valley of the Sun United Way, Phoenix, 1995—; mgr. fam. bus., 4052 Kilanea Ptnrs. Mem. Greater Phoenix Leadership. Office: Valley of the Sun United Way 1515 E Osborn Rd # 10748 Phoenix AZ 85014-5318

HASSETT, EVA M., city commissioner. BA in Psychology with honors, Harvard U.; M in Pub. and Pvt Mgmt., Yale U. Assoc., mcpl. bond sales/pub. fin. CS 1st Boston (formerly 1st Boston Corp.), 1982-85; mgr. real estate investments Gen. Atlantic Corp., N.Y.C., 1985-86; sr. assoc. Greater Buffalo (N.Y.) Devel. Found., 1988-92; project dir. Buffalo Fin. Plan Commn., 1992-93; v.p., pub. policy and analysis Greater Buffalo Partnership, 1993; commr., adminstrn. and fin. City of Buffalo, 1994—. Vol. Leadership Buffalo, 1989; dir. BBB, Buffalo; mem. SUNY Buffalo Found.; mem. N.Y. State Atty. Grievance Com., 8th Judicial Dist.; mem. The Women's Group, Buffalo. Recipient Buffalo Bus. First 40 Under 40 award, 1993, Top 100 Influence People award, 1995. Office: City of Buffalo Commn Adminstrn & Fin 203 City Hall/65 Niagara Sq Buffalo NY 14202*

HASSETT, JOSEPH MARK, lawyer; b. Buffalo, May 1, 1943; m. Carol A. Melton, June 23, 1984; children: Matthew, Meredith. B.A. summa cum laude, Canisius Coll., 1964; LL.B. cum laude, Harvard U., 1967; M.A. with 1st class honors, Univ. Coll. Dublin, 1981, Ph.D., 1985. Bar: N.Y. 1967, D.C. 1970, U.S. Supreme Ct. 1976. Assoc. Hogan & Hartson, Washington, 1970-74, ptnr., 1974—; bd. trustees Canisius Coll. Author: Yeats and the Poetics of Hate, 1986; contbr. articles to profl. publs. Mem. ABA, D.C. Bar Assn. Home: 6035 Crimson Ct Mc Lean VA 22101-1818 Office: 555 13th St NW Washington DC 20004-1109

HASSETT, MARY RUTH, nursing educator; b. San Bernardino, Calif., July 20, 1944; d. Raymond Vernon and Mary Elizabeth (Rudolph) Mortorff; m. Roland Warren Coleman, Dec. 26, 1964 (div. Feb. 1977); 1 child, Timothy James Coleman; m. C. Michael Hassett, Feb., 1977; stepchildren: Deborah Kay Hassett Riffel, Vicki Lynn Hassett Ellis. BSN, Pacific Luth. U., 1971; M of Nursing, UCLA, 1974; PhD in Nursing, U. Tex., 1990. CNS, Kans.; cert. informatics nurse Am. Nurses Credentialing Ctr. Staff nurse med.-surg. Mercy Hosp., San Diego, 1964; charge nurse well-care unit Whittier (Calif.) Presbyn. Intercom. Hosp., 1964; staff nurse med.-surg. Tacoma (Wash.) Gen. Hosp., 1969-70; staff nurse oper. rm. & med.-surg. Providence Hosp., Washington, 1965; staff nurse oper. rm./PAR & med.-surg. Whittier Hosp., 1968-69; charge nurse oper. rm./PAR Beverly Hosp., Montebello, Calif., 1970-72; staff nurse mental health D.E. Brotman Meml. Hosp., Culver City, Calif., 1973-74; instr. psychiat. tech. Rio Hondo C.C., Whittier, 1974-75; instr. registered nursing Cypress (Calif.) Coll., 1975-77; prof., dir. grad. studies Ft. Hays State U., Hays, Kans., 1979-94, chair, prof. dept. nursing, 1994—; cons. sex and disability U. Calif.-San Francisco Sch. Medicine, 1976; cons. computer-based instrn. Kans. State Bd. Nursing, Topeka, 1992—. Contbr. book chpts.: Computer applications in nursing education and practice, 1992 (AJN award 1993), Procs. of Fourth Internat. Conf. on Nursing Use of Computers and Info. Sci., 1991; contbr. book abstracts: Dissertation Abstracts International, 1991, Procs. Fifth Internat. Conf. on Nursing Use of Computers and Info. Sci., 1994; contbr. articles to nursing jours.: script cons. (videotapes) Spiritual Care practicua, 1981. Chair bd. dirs. Comty. Day Care Ctr., Inc., Hays, 1981-82; chair com. on grants, rep. Care Network, Inc., Hays, 1986-88; mem. human resources devel. com. Kans. Dept. Social and Rehab. Svcs., Mental Health & Retardation Svcs., Topeka, 1991-92, co-chair Healthcare subcom. Hays Info., 1995-96. Dept. Health, Edn. & Welfare Mental Health Tng. grantee, 1976-78, grantee Ellis County, Kans., 1988, IBM, 1989-92, 90, U.S. Dept. Health & Human Svcs. Tng. grantee, 1992-95, Co-grantee Kans. Health Found., 1995-96. Mem. ANA (coun. for nursing systems and adminstrn., coun. nurse rschrs.), Nat. League for Nursing (coun. nursing informatics), Assn. for Devel. Computer-Based Instrnl. Sys. (interactive video-audio SIG chair 1992-94, bd. dirs. 1993-94, editl. rev. bd. 1994-95), Am. Med. Informatics Assn. (assoc., nursing informatics working group), Kans. State Nurse's Assn. (coun. on edn. 1985-87, steering com. 1986-88, pres. dist. 16 1986-88, editl. bd. 1992, 93, Excellence in Continuing Edn. award 1992). Republican. Mem. Assemblies of God. Avocations: computing, reading, dogs, art, swimming. Home: 2910 Roosevelt Ave Hays KS 67601-2033 Office: Ft Hays State U STH 122 C 600 Park St Bldg 1 Hays KS 67601-4099

HASSETT, ROBERT WILLIAM, lawyer; b. Franklin, Va., June 17, 1950; s. George Abe and Peggy Rita (Scher) H.; m. Lynn Ellen Shier, June 12, 1983; children: Laura, Elizabeth, Joe. B in Indsl. Engring., Ga. Inst. Tech., 1973; JD, U. Ga., 1976. Bar: Ga. 1976. Assoc. Garland Nuckles & Kadish, Atlanta, 1976-80; ptnr. Gort Hassett & Shannon, Atlanta, 1980-84, Rubin & Hassett, Atlanta, 1984-88, Hassett, Cohen, Beitchman & Goldstein, LLP, Atlanta, 1988—; chair multimedia fair Ind. Media Artists of Ga., 1995, membership chair, 1994-97, also bd. dirs.; bd. dirs., spl. events chmn. Ga. chpt. Internat. Interactive Comm. Soc., Atlanta, 1994-97; spkr. profl. confs. Contbr. articles to profl. jours. Mem. ABA (co-chair subcom. top level domain names 1998-99). Avocations: computers, multimedia, running. Website: www.internetlegal.com. E-mail: rob@internetlegal.com. Office: Hassett Cohen Beitchman & Goldstein LLP 990 Hammond Dr NE Ste 990 Atlanta GA 30328-5589

HASSETT, SULVIA ANN, educator; b. Greenfield, Mass., Feb. 21, 1935; d. Waldo Sylvanus and Rena May (Dean) Allen; m. John P. Hassett, Dec. 27, 1957; children: Julia, Kevin. BS in Edn., State Coll., 1957, MEd, 1973. Cert. tchr., Mass. Tchr. Greenfield (Mass.) Pub. Sch., Montaque (Mass.) Pub. Sch. Mem. Greenfield Area Television Exec. Bd., 1990-94; rep. state com. woman from 1st senatorial dist., 1988-99; vice dept. chair Western Mass. Rep. State Com.; past chair Rep. Town Com.; pres. Franklin County Rep. Women's Club, 1988-99; dist. rep. Franklin-Berkshire Dist. to Mass. Fedn. of Rep. Women's Clubs, 1988-90, alt. del. for Bush, Nat. Rep. Conv., 1988, mem. Mass. planning com., co-chmn. Mass. conv. registration com., 1980-97; sec., mem. Greenfield Sch. Com., sec., 1980-97; founder Friends of Greenfield Pub. Schs., 1993—. Recipient numerous grants. Mem. NEA (congl. contact team), Mass. Tchrs. Assn. (polit. action com.). Roman Catholic. Avocations: painting, tole wear, crafts. Home: 31 Lovers Ln Greenfield MA 01301

HASSETT, VALERIE JANE, interior architect; b. San Degia, Calif., Dec. 22, 1962; d. Roger John and Cecealia Virginia (Ceborich) H. Student, U. Tenn., 1982-86; BFA in Interior Design, Va. Commonwealth U., Richmond, 1988; MArch, Va. Poly. U., Alexandria, 1993. Registered profl. interior designer, Va.; cert. constrn. documents technologist. Interior architect Washington Area Transit Authority, 1988-90, 91-92, Prince William County Va. Govt., 1993-95, RTKL, Balt., 1995-97; instr. Mt. Vernon Coll. at Georgetown U., Washington, 1997-98; project mgr., head interior design dept. Sharadan, Behm, Eustice and Assocs. Ltd., Arlington, Va., 1997—. Mem. AIA (chair women in architecture com. No. Va. chpt. 1993-95), Internat. Interior Design Assn., Neighborhood Design Ctr. Balt. Avocation: paper making. Office: Sheridan Behm Eustice & Assocs 3440 Fairfax Dr Arlington VA 22201-4431

HASSFURDER, LESLIE JEAN, principal; b. Bedford, Ind., June 26, 1943; d. Don Bernell and Rose E. (Bridwell) Armstrong; m. M. Duane Wilson, June 17, 1965 (dec. Aug. 1986); children: Douglas Troy, Marisa Lynn; m. Steven Wayne Hassfurder, Mar. 19, 1988; step-children: Holly Renee, Lorrie Leigh. BS, Ind. U., 1965, MS, 1971; EdS, Ind.-Purdue U., Indpls., 1984. Cert. tchr. and prin., Ind. Elem. tchr. Fontana, Calif., 1965-67, Churubusco, Ind., 1967-69; dir. presch., Goshen, Ind., 1977-80; prin. Pittsboro Elem. Sch. (Ind.), 1980—; dir. summer library. Co-author: Energy Play, 1982, operettas for local schs. Mem. Internat. Reading Assn., Mortar Bd., Enomone, Pleiades, Phi Delta Kappa, Alpha Delta Kappa. Republican. Mem. Christian Ch. (Disciples of Christ). Office: Pittsboro Elem Sch North Meridian Pittsboro IN 46167

HASSID, SAMI, architect, educator; b. Cairo, Egypt, Apr. 19, 1912; came to U.S., 1957, naturalized, 1962; s. Joseph S. and Isabelle (Israel) H.; m. Juliette Mizrahi, June 29, 1941; children: Fred, Muriel. Diploma in architecture with distinction, Sch. Engring., Giza, Egypt, 1932; B.A. in Architecture with honors, U. London, Eng., 1935; M.Arch., U. Cairo, 1943; Ph.D. in Architecture, Harvard U., 1956. Tchr. Alexandria (Egypt) Tech. Sch., 1932-34; successively tchr., lectr., asst. prof. U. Cairo, 1934-56; prof. architectural theory and design U. Ein-Shams, Cairo, 1957; mem. faculty U. Calif., Berkeley, 1957—; prof. architecture U. Calif., 1964-79, prof. emeritus, 1979—; also assoc. dean U. Calif. (Coll. Environ. Design), 1977-83, faculty asst. to vice-chancellor for campus planning, 1980-85, dir. campus planning office, 1983-84; archtl. practice Cairo, 1932-57, Berkeley, 1957-85; from draftsman to sr. designer office Ali Labib Gabr (architect), Cairo, 1935-47; ptnr. Sami Hassid and Youssef Shafik, Cairo, 1947-57, Hassid and Kelemen, Berkeley, 1963-65. Author: The Sultan's Turrets, 1939, Architectural Construction Details, 1954, Development and Application of a System for Recording Critical Evaluations of Architectural Works, 1964, Architectural Education U.S.A, 1967, (with others) Innovations in Housing Design and Construction Techniques as Applied to Low-Cost Housing, 1969, Surface Materials in Architecture, 1970, Doctoral Studies in Architecture, 1971, Methods for the Development of Shipboard Habitability Design Criteria, 1974, Fire Safety in Buildings, A Course Offering Package, 1976, (with others) The Berkeley Campus Space Plan, 21 publs., 1981-83; Proc. Workshop on Seismic Upgrading of Existing Bldgs., NSF, 1982; prin. works include Hill House; student hostel, Am. U. Cairo, 1952. Commr. Calif. Bd. Archtl. Examiners, 1961-71. Fulbright grantee, 1954-56; recipient First prize Al-Chams Competition, Cairo, 1947, First prize San Francisco AIA Hdqrs. Competition, 1963. Fellow AIA; mem. Bldg. Research Inst., Assn. Collegiate Schs. Architecture. Democrat. Jewish (trustee temple; v.p. East Bay synagogue council 1970-71). Home: Sami Hassid FAIA 2851 Rockridge Dr Pleasant Hill CA 94523

HASSIG, GORDON L., automotive sales executive; b. Detroit, Aug. 28, 1920; s. Walter and Selma (Zehnder) H.; m. Doris J. Brooks, Feb. 21, 1948; children: Gail, Brigit. Student, Wayne State U., 1938-42, 46-47. Mem. sales staff IBM, Detroit, 1947; pres. Wayne (Mich.) Hall Dodge Co., 1948-95; ret. Wayne (Mich.) Hall Dodds Co. Commr. City of Huntington Woods, Mich., 1971-97, mayor pro tem, 1977-95; mem. Southeast Mich. Coun. on Govt., 1971-97; bd. dirs., pres. Huntington Woods Resident Assn., 1961-71. Lt.

comdr. USN, 1942-46. Decorated bronze star, 1944, 45, five battle stars, 1943-45. Republican. Lutheran. Avocations: civic activities, golf, gardening, church work. Home: 13157 Ludlow Ave Huntington Woods MI 48070-1411

HASSLEIN, GEORGE JOHANN, architectural educator; b. Los Angeles, Aug. 31, 1917; s. August Theodore and Lena (Matranga) H.; m. Neva B. Henderson, Oct. 13, 1945 (dec. Dec. 1963); children: Vaughn, Tracey; m. Marilyn L. Collins, Sept. 10, 1966 (dec. Dec. 1967). BArch, U. So. Calif., 1946. Registered architect, Calif. With Army Engrs., Costa Rica, 1942-44; archtl. designer firm Welton Becket (architect), Los Angeles, 1948-50; mem. faculty Calif. State Poly. Coll., San Luis Obispo, 1949—; prof., head dept. archtl. engring. Calif. State Poly. Coll., 1952-68, founding dean Sch. Architecture and Environ. Design, 1968-84, prof., 1984—; archtl. adviser bd. trustees Calif. State Univs. and Colls., 1961-84; mem. AID mission to Argentina, 1963; regent Roofing Industry Ednl. Inst., 1979—; mem. del. Archtl. Educators to Republic of China, 1979; commr. Calif. State Bd. Archtl. Examiners, 1961—, Western Assn. Sch. and Colls., 1980—. Recipient Achievement award L.A. C. of C., 1981; health, edn. and welfare travel grantee to Israel, 1965. Fellow AIA (Distinguished service award edn. 1971, Excellence in Edn. award 1977); mem. Am. Arbitration Assn., Scarab, Delta Phi Delta, Tau Sigma, Alpha Rho Chi. Office: Calif Poly State U Sch Architecture & Environ Design San Luis Obispo CA 93407 also: 2333 Helena St San Luis Obispo CA 93401-4511

HASSLER, DONALD MACKEY, II, English language educator, writer; b. Akron, Ohio, Jan. 3, 1937; s. Donald Mackey and Frances Elizabeth (Parsons) H.; m. Diana Cain, Oct. 8, 1960 (dec. Sept. 1976); children: Donald, David; m. Sue Smith, Sept. 13, 1977; children: Shelly, Heather. B.A. (Sloan fellow), Williams Coll., 1959; M.A. (Woodrow Wilson fellow), Columbia U., 1960, Ph.D., 1967. Instr. U. Montreal, 1961-65; instr. English Kent (Ohio) State U., 1965-67, asst. prof., 1967-71, assoc. prof., 1971-76, prof., 1977—, acting dean honors and exptl. coll., 1979-81, dir., 1973-83, coord. writing cert. program, 1986-91, chmn. undergrad. studies, 1987-91, dir. Wick Poetry Competition, 1987-91, coord. grad. studies, 1991—; sec. faculty senate Kent (Ohio State U., 1996—. Author: Erasmus Darwin, 1974, The Comedian as the Letter D: Erasmus Darwin's Comic Materialism, 1973, Asimov's Golden Age: The Ordering of an Art, 1977, Hal Clement, 1982, Comic Tones in Science Fiction, 1982, Patterns of the Fantastic, 1983, Patterns of the Fantastic II, 1984, Death and the Serpent, 1985, Isaac Asimov, 1991; mng. editor Jour. Extrapolation, 1986-87, co-editor, 1987-89, editor, 1990—; co-editor (with Sue Hassler) Letters of Arthur Machen and Montgomery Evans, 1923-1947, 1993, (with Clyde Wilcox) Political Science Fiction, 1997; adv. editl. bd. Hellas, 1988—; editl. bd. Paradoxa, 1994—. Co-chmn. Kent Am. Revolution Bicentennial Commn., 1974-77; deacon Presbyn. Ch., 1971-74, elder, 1974-77; sec. Kent State Faculty Senate, 1996—, chancellor's faculty adv. com., 1996—, univ. priorities and budget adv. coun., 1998—. Recipient J. Lloyd Eaton award Eaton Libr. Collection U. Calif., Riverside, 1993. Mem. Sci. Fiction Rsch. Assn. (treas. 1983-84, pres. 1985-86), Kiwanis (bd. dirs. 1974-76), Phi Beta Kappa (pres. 1983-84). Home: 1226 Woodhill Dr Kent OH 44240-2832

HASSON, JAMES KEITH, JR., lawyer, law educator; b. Knoxville, Tenn., Mar. 3, 1946; s. James Keith and Elaine (Biggers) H.; m. Jayne Young, July 27, 1968; 1 son, Keith Samuel. BA, Duke U., 1967, JD, 1970. Bar: Ga. 1971, D.C. 1971. Assoc. Sutherland, Asbill & Brennan, Atlanta, 1970-76, ptnr., 1976—; prof. law Emory U., Atlanta, 1976-94; dir. House-Hasson Hardware Co., Knoxville, 1971—. Editor Jour. Taxation; contbr. and editor articles to profl. jours. Chmn. Met. Atlanta Crime Commn., 1986-87, also trustee; trustee Reinhardt Coll., 1989—; mem. Atlanta Civilian Review Bd.; mem. Leadership Atlanta, 1981-82; mem. IRS Commr. exempt orgn. adv. group; chmn. bd. dirs. Foxfire Fund, 1988—. 1st lt. U.S. Army, 1970-71. Mem. ABA (com. chmn. 1983-85), Atlanta Bar Assn. (counsel 1977-80, Pres's. Disting. Svc. award 1980), Lawyers Club. Presbyterian. Home: 3185 Chatham Rd NW Atlanta GA 30305-1101 Office: Sutherland Asbill & Brennan 999 Peachtree St NE Ste 2300 Atlanta GA 30309-3996

HASSON, RAYMOND EDWARD, III, artist, writer; b. Columbus, Ohio, Oct. 13, 1946; s. Raymond Edward Jr. and Elsie Lucille (Offord) H.; m. Judith Ann Shabbott, Oct. 12, 1968; children: Geoffrey Randall, Mathew Francis, Christopher Jon. AA with high honors, Three Rivers Cmty. Tech. Coll., 1995; BA in Fine Art summa cum laude, Ea. Conn. State U., 1997. Enlisted USN, 1965, apptd. chief petty officer, 1978; instr. USN, Groton, Conn., 1965-90; dist. mgr. IC Systems Inc., Mpls., 1990-92; artist Pumpkin Hill Studio, Ledyard, Conn., 1996—; command career counselor USS U.S. Grant, Charleston, S.C., 1975-77; navigation instr. U. Va., Charlottesville, 1977-80. Exhibited in group shows at The Nude Show, North Woodstock, Conn., 1995, 33d Ann. Milford (Conn.) Green Fall Show, 1995, The Green Marble Coffee House, Westerly, R.I., 1996, 97, 98, Mystic (Conn.) Art Assn., 1996, 97, 98, Florence Griswold Mus., Old Lyme, conn., 1996, 97, Akus Gallery, Willimantic, Conn., 1997, Pfizer, Inc., Groton, Conn., 1997, Wood-Pawcatuck Watershed Assn., Carolina, R.I., 1997; represented in numerous personal and corp. collections; editor Ledyard Adventure Club newsletter, 1996—; contbr. articles to profl. jours. Recipient Artist-at-Work award Florence Griswold Mus., 1996, 97, 98. Mem. Mystic Art Assn. (artist-at-work coord. 1999, co-chair young-at-art exhibit 1998, 99), Omicron Delta Kappa. Avocations: hiking, woodworking, bird watching.

HASSOURI, HASSAN, neurologist; b. Feb. 13, 1943. MD, Tehran U., 1969. Resident in neurology NYU Med. Ctr., N.Y.C.; clin. asst. prof. neurology Allegheny U., Pitts.; pvt. practice Pitts. Home: 1514 Fox Chase Dr Pittsburgh PA 15143 Office: 1 Allegheny Sq Ste 206 Pittsburgh PA 15212-5323

HASSRICK, PETER HEYL, art historian; b. Phila., Apr. 27, 1941; s. Royal Brown and E. Barbara (Morgan) H.; m. Elizabeth Drake, June 14, 1963; children: Philip Heyl, Charles Royal. Student, Harvard U., 1962; BA, U. Colo., 1963; MA, U. Denver, 1969. Tchr. Whiteman Sch., Steamboat Springs, Colo., 1963-67; also bd. dirs. Whiteman Sch., Steamboat Springs; curator of collections Amon Carter Mus., Ft. Worth, 1969-75; dir. Buffalo Bill Hist. Ctr., Cody, Wyo., 1976-96, Georgia O'Keefe Mus., Santa Fe, N.Mex., 1996-97; dir., prof. art history Charles M. Russell Ctr. Study Art U. Okla., Norman, 1998—. Author: Frederic Remington, 1973, The Way West, 1977, (with others) The Rocky Mountains, 1983, Treasures of the Old West, 1984, (with others) Frederic Remington, The Masterworks, 1988, (with others) Frontier America, 1988, Charles M. Russell, 1989, (with others) Frederic Remington: A Catalogue Raisonne, 1996, Georgie O'Keeffe Mus., 1997. Office: U Oklahoma 520 Parrington Oval Rm 202 Norman OK 73019

HAST, ADELE, editor, historian; b. N.Y.C., Dec. 6, 1931; d. Louis and Kate (Miller) Krongelb; m. Malcolm Howard Hast, Feb. 1, 1953; children—David Jay, Howard Arthur. B.A. magna cum laude, Bklyn. Coll., 1953; M.A., U. Iowa, 1969, Ph.D., 1979. Rsch. assoc. Atlas Early Am. History Project, Newberry Library, Chgo., 1971-75; assoc. dir. Atlas Great Lakes Indian History Project, 1976-79, Hist. Boundary Data File Project, 1979-81; editor in chief Marquis Who's Who, Inc., Chgo., 1981-86; survey dir. Nat. Opinion Rsch. Ctr., U. Chgo., 1986-89; rsch. fellow Newberry Libr., Chgo., 1989-95, scholar in residence, 1995—; exec. editor St. James Press, Chgo., 1990-92; mng. editor Hist. Ency. of Chgo. Women U. Ill., Chgo., 1991-93, project dir., editor Hist. Ency. of Chgo. Women, 1993—; mem. faculty Newberry Libr. Summer Inst. Cartography, 1980. Author: Loyalism in Revolutionary Virginia, 1985; compiler: Iowa, Missouri, vol. 4 of Historical Atlas and Chronology of County Boundaries, 1788-1980, 1984; editor: International Director of Company Histories, vols. 3-5, 1991-92; assoc. editor: Atlas of Great Lakes Indian History, 1987; contbr. articles to profl. jours. Mem. profl. adv. grad. program pub. history Loyola U., 1986—; treas., bd. dirs. Chgo. Map Soc., 1980-91, 93-95; mem. New Trier Twp. H.S. Bd. Caucus, 1972-74; mem. acad. coun. Am. Jewish Hist. Soc., 1985—; pres. Chgo. Jewish Hist. Soc., 1980-81, bd. dirs., 1977—. Recipient Alumna of Yr. award Bklyn. Coll., 1984, Colonial Williamsburg Found. grantee-in-aid, 1975, Brit. Acad. rsch. fellow, 1979; Am. Coun. Learned Socs. grantee-in-aid, 1980; NEH rsch. grantee, 1985, 87, 93, 97-98. Fellow Royal Hist. Soc., Phi Beta Kappa, Kappa Delta Pi; mem. Am. Hist. Assn., Orgn. Am. Historians, Chgo. Area Women's History Conf. (sec., treas. 1994—, bd. dirs. 1990—), Caxton Club (coun. 1990-93).

HAST, MALCOLM HOWARD, medical educator, biomedical scientist; b. N.Y.C., May 28, 1931; s. Irving William and Rose Lillian (Berlin) H.; m. Adele Krongelb, Feb. 1, 1953; children: David Jay, Howard Arthur. B.A., Bklyn. Coll., 1953; postgrad., U. So. Calif., 1955-57; M.A., Ohio State U., 1958, Ph.D. (NIH fellow), 1961; CBiol, FIBiol, Gt. Britain, 1991. Instr. U. Iowa, 1961-63; NIH spl. fellow U. Iowa (Coll. Medicine), 1963-65, asst. prof., 1965-69; assoc. prof. otolaryngology-head and neck surgery Northwestern U. Med. Sch., Chgo., 1969-74, prof., 1974—, dir. research otolaryngology, 1969-93, prof. cell and molecular biology (anatomy), 1977—; prof. basic and behavioral scis. Northwestern U. Dental Sch., 1989—; assoc. med. staff Northwestern Meml. Hosp., 1969-90, health profl., 1990-93; rsch. assoc. zoology Field Mus. Natural History, 1995—; guest scientist Max Planck Inst. für Psychiatrie, 1976; vis. prof. Royal Coll. Surgeons Eng., 1980-86, U. Edinburgh, 1987; assoc. editor Clinical Anatomy, 1995—; mem. task force on new materials Am. Bd. Otolaryngology, 1969-77; dir. Ill. Soc. Med. Rsch., 1973-77; mem. Internat. Anat. Nomenclature Com., 1983-91; guest scientist Zoologisches Forchungsinstitut und Mus. A. Koenig, 1988; Brodel meml. lectr. Assn. Med. Illustrators, 1995; mem. Chgo. Clin. Ethics Programs. Contbr. articles to profl. jours., chpts. to books. Mem. adv. bd. Ctr. Deafness, 1977-80; bd. dirs. Cliff Dwellers Arts Found., 1979-82; trustee Wilmette Libr. Bd., 1982-83. Served with U.S. Army, 1953-55. NATO sr. fellow in sci. Oxford U., Eng., 1978; NIH rsch. grantee, 1964-84, 95—, NSF rsch. grantee, 1975-77, NEH grantee, 1995—; recipient Gould Internat. award, 1971, Disting. Alumnus award of Honor, Bklyn. Coll., 1977, Alumnus of Yr. award, 1984; Arnott demonstrator Royal Coll. Surgeons Eng., 1985. Fellow AAAS, Linnean Soc. London, Inst. Biology, Am. Speech-Hearing Assn., Royal Soc. Medicine; mem. AMA, AAUP (chpt. pres. 1977-82), Am. Physiol. Soc. (animal care and experimentation com. 1976-82), Am. Assn. Clin. Anatomists, Chgo. Laryngol. and Otol. Soc. (coun. 1988-89), Am. Soc. Mammalogists, Anat. Soc. Gt. Britain and Ireland, Am. Assn. History Medicine, Soc. Med. History Chgo., Amnesty Internat. (coord. Chgo. Health profls. group 1986-87), Am. Assn. Anatomists, Sigma Xi (chpt. pres. 1971-72), Sigma Alpha Eta. Rsch. on neuromuscular physiology, embryology and comparative anatomy of the larynx, history of medicine. Office: 303 E Chicago Ave Chicago IL 60611-3093

HASTAACCA, ALFREDO XAVIER, medical researcher; b. Medervalil, Kakala, Finland, May 25, 1925; came to U.S., 1929; s. Turi Jorgan Hastaacca and Marie Ruth Swenson; m. Halle Mande Peterson, Oct. 29, 1949; children: Halle Jr., Turison. BS in Agrl. Rsch., Wis. State Agrl. Extension, 1947; BA in Rsch., Washington U., St. Louis, 1951; M Chem. Studies, 1955; DS, Chem. Warfare Rsch. Inst., 1958. Internat. rschr. O.S.S., W.Va., 1957-67; dir. rsch. Space Probeing, White Sands, N.Mex., 1968-78; internat. rschr. CIA, W.Va., 1979-87; freelance rschr. Knox Instruments, Venice, Calif., 1987-93; rschr. Microspect, Inc., Issaquah, Wash., 1993-97; profl. witness San Rafael, Calif., 1997—. Avocation: research on Sweden's conquest of Finland.

HASTERT, (J.) DENNIS, congressman; b. Aurora, Ill., Jan. 2, 1942; m. Jean Kahl, 1973; children: Joshua, Ethan. BA, Wheaton Coll., 1964; MS, No. Ill. U., 1967. Tchr., coach Yorkville (Ill.) High Sch.; mem. Ill. House Reps., Springfield, 1980-86; mem. 100th-105th Congresses from 14th dist. Ill., 1987—, mem. commerce com.; mem. govt. reform and oversight com. 100th-106th Congresses from 14th dist. Ill. Lodge: Lions (Yorkville). Office: US Ho of Reps 2263 Rayburn Washington DC 20515-1314*

HASTIE, RONALD LESLIE, sales executive; b. Perry, Iowa, July 29, 1941; s. Leslie Hope and Leona Nadine (Verchio) H.; m. Patricia Louise Agee, Apr. 29, 1961; children: Lori Lynn, Lisa Lynn, Jennifer Lynn. Grad. pub. schs., Rippey, Iota. Salesman Standard Oil Co., Des Moines, 1960-70; sales mgr. Jewel Co., Perry, 1970-83; sr. ter. mgr. sales, water treatment specialist State Chem. Co., Boone, Iowa, 1983—. Mem. NRA, Sportsman Club. Republican. Avocations: ham radio, hunting, travel. Home: 221 Linn St Boone IA 50036-3733 Office: State Chem Co 3100 Hamilton Ave Cleveland OH 44114-3783

HASTINGS, ALBERT WALLER, English and journalism educator, consultant; b. St. Catharines, Ont., Can, Jan. 10, 1952; came to U.S., 1956; s. Graham Thomas and Anna Virginia (Waller) H.; m. Suzanne Kathleen Gillings, Jan. 12, 1985; children: Sara Beth, Emily Marie. AB in Biology, Brown U., 1974; MA in English, DePaul U., 1983; PhD in English, U. Wis., 1988. Staff writer Internat. Med. News Group, Rockville, Md., 1974-78; med. writer Sun-Sentinel, Ft. Lauderdale, Fla., 1978-79; bur. chief Med. Tribune, Chgo., 1979-82; freelance writer Chgo. and Madison, Wis., 1982-84; instr. U. Wis., Richland, 1988; asst. prof. English No. State U., Aberdeen, S.D., 1988-93; assoc. prof. English No. State U., Aberdeen, 1993-98, coord. dept. English and linguistics, 1996—, prof. English, 1998—; freelance ednl. and editl. cons., Aberdeen, 1993—. Bd. dirs. L. Frank Baum Festival, Aberdeen, 1996-97, chair edn. task force, 1995-97; mem. planning com. reading series S.D. Humanities Coun., Brookings, 1995—. Mem. MLA, Nat. Coun. Tchrs. English, Children's Lit. Assn. Democrat. Presbyterian. Avocations: camping, fishing, theater. Home: 1018 S Washington St Aberdeen SD 57401-7141 Office: No State U 1200 S Jay St Aberdeen SD 57401-7155

HASTINGS, ALCEE LAMAR, congressman, former federal judge; b. Altomonte Springs, Fla., Sept. 5, 1936; s. Julius C. and Mildred L. H.; 1 child. B.A., Fisk U., 1958; postgrad., Howard U. Sch. Law, 1958-60; J.D., Fla. A&M U., 1963. Bar: Fla. 1963. Mem. firm Allen and Hastings, Ft. Lauderdale, 1963-66; pvt. practice law Ft. Lauderdale, 1966-77; judge Cir. Ct. Broward County, Fla., 1977-79, U.S. Dist. Ct. (so. dist.) Fla., from 1979; mem. 103rd-106th Congress from 23d Fla dist., 1993—; mem. internat. rels. com., mem. sci. com.; adj. prof. criminal justice dept. Nova U.; lectr. So. Regional Council on Black Am. Affairs; lectr., cons. Internat. Juvenile Officers Assn., Peace Corps Vols. in Avon Park, Fla., 1966; legal counsel Community Action Migrant Program, Broward County Classroom Tchrs.; mem. Gov.'s Conf. on Criminal Justice, State of Fla.; lectr., cons. to elem. and secondary public and pvt. schs., chs., synagogues, social orgns., civic orgns., colls. and univs. in U.S.; co-propr. Tri-City News. Host TV program: Pride, Sta. WPLG; columnist: West Side Gazette. Atty. various civic assns., Broward County and State of Fla.; mem. Bi-Racial Adv. Commn., Broward County Personnel Adv. Commn.; sec. Fla. Council on Aging; chmn. Broward Youth Services Task Force; mem. State of Fla. Edn. Commn., Task Force on Crime, Democratic Exec. Com; candidate for Fla. Ho. of Reps., Fla. Senate, U.S. Senate, Fla. Public Service Commn.; bd. dirs. Urban League of Broward County, Child Advocacy, Inc., The Starting Place, Broward County Sickle Cell Anemia Found., Fla. Voters League, Broward County Council on Human Relations; trustee Mt. Hermon A.M.E. Ch., Ft. Lauderdale, Broward Community Coll., Bethune Cookman Coll. Recipient numerous awards and honors including; Humanitarian award Broward County Young Democrats, 1978; Citizen of Year award Zeta Phi Beta, 1978; Sam Delevoe Human Rights award Community Relations Bd. of Broward County, 1978; Glades Festival of Afro Arts award Zeta Phi Beta, 1981; named Man of Year, Com. Italian Am. Affairs, 1979-80; Judge Alcee Hastings Day proclaimed for City of Daytona Beach in his honor on Dec. 14, 1980. Mem. ABA (standing com. profl. discipline), Nat. Bar Assn. (Chmn.'s award 1981), Am. Trial Lawyers Assn., Fla. Bar Assn., U.S. Dist. Judges Council., A.M.E. Ch. Clubs: Elks, KP. Office: US Ho of Reps 2235 Rayburn Washington DC 20515-0923*

HASTINGS, DEBORAH, bass guitarist; b. Evansville, Ind., May 11, 1959; d. Mortimer Winthrop Hastings and Margaret Hooper (Smith) Zimmerman. Student music, U. Wis. Bass guitarist N.Y.C. and Madison, Wis., 1975—; freelance photographer Madison, 1976-81; band leader Bo Diddley, 1992—; founder A/Prompt Computer Telepromting Svcs., Inc., 1994—; featured bassist with Duck Dunn for Bush inauguration, performing with Billy Preston, Dr. John, Koko Taylor, Willie Dixon, Albert Collins, Joe Cocker, Carla Thomas, Eddie Floyd, Ron Wood, Steve Cropper, Bo Diddley, Jerry Lee Lewis, Chuck Berry, Joe Louis Walker; has also performed with Ben E. King, Little Anthony, Sam Moore, John Lee Hooker, Mick Fleetwood, Al Kooper, James Cotton; TV shows include Legends of Rock and Roll Live from Rome. Bass player TV shows Joan Rivers, 1987, Classsics of Rock and Roll, 1988, Gunslingers tour Live from the Ritz with Ron Wood & Bo Diddley, 1988, Live from the Ritz, 1989, Legends of Rock and Roll (live from Australia), Legends of Guitar from Seville, Spain, 1991, Showtime at the Apollo, 1992, N.Y. at Night, 1992; performed Into The Night, 1991 (TV show) Nashville Now, 1991, American Musicshop, 1991, Johnny Carson Show, 1990, Pat Sajak Show, 1990, Carla Thomas, 1991, Arts & Entertainment Revue, 1990, (Madison Sq. Garden) Tribute to John Lee Hooker, 1990, Richard Nader's 25th Anniversary Show, 1994, Conan O'Brien Show, 1996; recordings include Bo Diddley's Grammy Nominated Album "A Man Amongst Men", 1996; performer in concert video "A Man Amongst Men", 1996; tours in Europe, Australia and Japan; performed at inaugurations of Pres. George Bush, 1989, Pres. Bill Clinton, 1997; contbg. photographer: Photographers Market. Fundraiser, bassist polit. campaigns, Madison. Recipient numerous awards for pottery, award Arts Coun., Madison, Arts Coun., Ann Arbor, Mich.; played at Rock and Roll Hall of Fame Mus. Johnnie Johnson in Buenos Aires, Argentina. Mem. Musicians Union (local 802). Democrat. Avocations: computers, photography, graphics design, video. Office: Talent Cons Internat 1560 Broadway Ste 1308 New York NY 10036-1518

HASTINGS, DOC, congressman; b. Spokane, Wash., Feb. 7, 1941; m. Claire Hastings; 3 children. Student, Columbia Basin Coll., Ctrl. Wash. U. Mem. Wash. State Ho. of Reps., 1979-87; pres. Columbia Basin Paper & Supply, 1983-94; mem. 104th-106th Congress from 4th Wash. dist., 1994—; mem. ways and means com., rules com., energy and utilities com., agriculture com., judiciary com., constitution and elections com.; bd. dirs. Yakima Fed. Savings & Loan; chmn. Franklin County Republican Com., 1974-78. Office: US House Reps 1323 Longworth Bldg Washington DC 20515-4704*

HASTINGS, DONALD FRANCIS, actor, writer; b. Bklyn., Apr. 1, 1934; s. Charles Benedict and Hazel May (Kirk) H.; m. Noretta Kennedy, Dec. 29, 1956 (div. Feb. 1980); children: Jennifer, Julie Ann, Matthew; m. Leslie Denniston, June 7, 1980; 1 dau., Katharine Scott. Student pvt., pub. schs., N.Y. State. Appeared on network radio shows, 1940-53, including Cavalcade of Am; appeared in plays including Life With Father, 1941-43, I Remember Mama, 1944-45, On Whitman Avenue, 1946, Young Man's Fancy, 1947, Summer and Smoke, 1948; various TV shows, from 1947, including Captain Video, 1949-55, Studio One, 1955, Big Story, 1959, Chevrolet on Broadway, 1948, Edge of Night, 1956-60, As The World Turns, 1960—; author: scripts of As The World Turns, 1972-73, Guiding Light, 1974, 77, film Prisoner at Gilbert House, 1976. Mem. AFTRA, Screen Actors Guild, Actors Equity, Writers Guild-East. Roman Catholic. Office: RR 1 Box 131 Millerton NY 12546-9724

HASTINGS, DOUGLAS ALFRED, lawyer; b. Oak Park, Ill., July 28, 1949; s. Douglas A. and Elaine M. (Schramm) H.; m. Virginia Joslin, June 28, 1982; children: Corey, Douglas. BA, Duke U., 1971; MPA, Memphis State U., 1977; JD, U. Va., 1981. Bar: D.C. 1981. Assoc. dir. Inst. for Govt. Studies, Memphis State U., 1976-77; adminstrv. intern Fed. Exec. Inst., Charlottesville, Va., 1977-78; project coord. Assn. Acad. Health Ctrs., Charlottesville, 1978-80; cons. Shenandoah PSRO, Charlottesville, 1980-81; ptnr. Epstein Becker & Green, Washington, 1981—; vis. lectr. dept. health adminstrn. Duke U., Durham, N.C., 1985-90. Contbr. articles to profl. jours. Mem. ABA, Washington Coun. Lawyers, Am. Health Lawyers Assn. (bd. dirs. 1991—), Order of Coif, Phi Beta Kappa. Democrat. Unitarian. Avocations: karate, tennis, basketball, coaching. Home: 7525 Elba Rd Alexandria VA 22306-2504 Office: Epstein Becker & Green 1227 25th St NW Fl 7 Washington DC 20037-1156

HASTINGS, EDWARD WALTON, theater director; b. New Haven, Apr. 14, 1931; s. Edward Walton and Madeline (Cassidy) H. B.A., Yale, 1952; postgrad., Royal Acad. Dramatic Art, London, 1953, Columbia U., 1955-56. bd. dirs. Asian/Am. Theater Co., 1986, Arts Internat., 1987, Eugene O'Neill Found., 1993; guest instr. Shanghai Drama Inst., 1984. Dir. Australian premiere Hot L Baltimore, 1975, Shakespeare's People nat. tour, 1983, Nothing Sacred, Hong Kong, 1992, Come Back Little Sheba, Gogol Theatre, Moscow, 1995, Dial M for Murder nat. tour, 1995, others; exec. dir. Am. Conservatory Theatre, San Francisco, 1965-80, artistic dir., 1986-92; freelance dir., 1980-86. Served with U.S. Army, 1953-55. Mem. Coll. of Fellows of the Am. Theatre. Club: Elizabethan (New Haven). Office: Am Conservatory Theatre 30 Grant Ave San Francisco CA 94108-5800

HASTINGS, EDWIN H(AMILTON), lawyer; b. Yonkers, N.Y., Jan. 2, 1917; s. Edwin H. Jr. and Emily (Clark) H.; m. Mabel Hurst, July 12, 1941 (div. June 1957); children: Judy H. Hastings Johnson, Jill S. Hastings Cane; m. Suzanne Saul, July 1, 1957; 1 child, Andrew C. AB, Amherst Coll., 1938; LLB, Columbia U., 1941. Bar: N.Y. 1941, R.I. 1946, U.S. Dist. Ct. R.I. 1947, U.S. Ct. Appeals (1st cir.) 1950, Mass. 1951. Assoc. Larkin, Rathbone & Perry, N.Y.C., 1941-42, Tillinghast, Collins & Tanner, Providence, 1946-53; ptnr. Tillinghast Collins & Graham, Providence, 1953-96, Tillinghast Licht & Semonoff, Providence, 1996—; cons. ptnr. estate planning and adminstrn.; bar examiner State of R.I., 1968-74, chmn. of bd., 1971-74; chmn. com. on future of criminal law R.I. Supreme Ct., 1973-75; bar examiner U.S. Dist. Ct. R.I., 1981-84. Served to 1st lt. U.S. Army, 1942-46, 51-52, Korea. Mem. ABA, R.I. Bar Assn., Lawyers Alliance World Security. Baptist. Avocation: bird watching. Home: 210 Payton Ave Warwick RI 02889-5133 Office: Tillinghast Licht & Semonoff 1 Park Row Ste 1 Providence RI 02903-1288

HASTINGS, HAROLD MORRIS, mathematics educator, researcher, author; b. Dayton, Ohio, Nov. 21, 1946; s. Julius M. and Celia A. (Morse) H.; m. Gretchen E. Saalbach, June 2, 1968; children: Curtis, Matthew. BS, Yale U., 1967; MA, Princeton U., 1969, PhD, 1972. From instr. to assoc. prof. math. Hofstra U., N.Y., 1968-81, prof., 1981—, dept. chmn., 1985-90, 93-96, assoc. dean, 1990-93, chair dept. physics, 1999—; vis. assoc. prof. SUNY, Binghamton, 1974-75, U. Ga., Athens, 1978-79; prin. Hastings, Saalbach Assocs., Inc., Garden City, N.Y., 1983-96; prin. Prisma Med. Tech., 1999—; mem. working group on supercomputers NASA, Greenbelt, Md., 1985-90. Author: (with D. Edwards) Cech and Steenrod Homotopy Theory, 1974; editor: (with M. Kochen) Advances in Cognitive Sci., 1988, (with G. Sugihara) Fractals: A User's Guide for the Natural Scis., 1993, Fraktale: Ein Leitfaden für Anwender, 1996; contbr. articles to profl. jours. Patentee in field for computerized acoustic fetal monitor, ultrasonic tissue classification; research in fractals, mathematical biology, bio-medicine, algebraic topology. Pres., v.p. Garden City Lay Ecumenical Com., N.Y., 1983-93. Grantee NSF, 1977, 80, Woodrow Wilson Found., NAS. Mem. Am. Math. Soc., Assn. Computing Machinery, Soc. Math. Biology. Avocations: running, photography, music. Office: Hofstra Univ Adams 109 103 Hofstra Univ Hempstead NY 11549-1030

HASTINGS, JOHN WOODLAND, biologist, educator; b. Salisbury, Md., Mar. 24, 1927; s. Vaughan Archelaus and Kathrine (Stevens) H.; m. Hanna Machlup, June 6, 1953; children: Jennifer, David, Laura, Karen. BA, Swarthmore Coll., 1947; MA, Princeton U., 1950, PhD, 1951; MA, Harvard U., 1966. AEC postdoctoral fellow Johns Hopkins, 1951-53; instr. to asst. prof. biol. scis. Northwestern U., 1953-57; from asst. prof. to prof. biochemistry U. Ill. at Urbana, 1957-66; prof. biology Harvard, 1966-87, Paul C. Mangelsdorf prof. natural scis., 1987—; master Pforzheimer House, 1976-96; summer rsch. participant Oak Ridge Nat. Lab., 1958; vis. lectr. biochemistry Sheffield (Eng.) U., 1961-62; instr. physiology Marine Biol. Lab., Woods Hole, Mass., 1961-66, dir., 1962-66, dir. marine ecology, 1989-91, mem. corp., 1961, trustee, 1966-74, exec. com., 1968-74; guest prof. Rockefeller U., 1965-66, Inst. Biol. Phys. Chemistry Paris, 1972-73, U. Konstanz, Ger., 1979-80, Nat. Biology Inst., Okazaki, Japan, 1986, U. Munich, 1993; mem. panel molecular biology NSF, 1963-66, mem. adv. com. biology and medicine, 1968-71; com. postdoctoral fellowships chemistry Nat. Acad. Scis., 1965-67, com. photobiology, 1965-71, com. on phototherapy, 1971-73, com. on low frequency radiation, 1975-77; mem. Commn. Undergrad. Edn. in Biol. Scis., 1965-66; space biology com. NASA, 1966-71; biochemistry tng. com. Nat. Inst. Gen. Med. Scis., 1968-72; a founding mem., mem. internat. adv. bd. Marine Biol. Lab., Eilat, Israel, 1968—. Contbr. profl. jours. Served with USNR, 1944-45. Guggenheim fellow, 1965-66, NIH fellow, 1972-73, Yamada Found. fellow, Osaka, Japan, 1986; recipient Alexander von Humboldt prize, 1979, Humboldt fellow, 1993. Fellow AAAS, Am. Soc. Biol. Chemists, Biophys. Soc., Soc. Am. Microbiologists, Soc. Gen. Physiology (pres. 1963-65), Am. Acad. Arts and Scis., Soc. Chemi- and Bioluminescence (founding pres. 1994-98), Johns Hopkins Soc. Scholars. Home: 14 Concord Ave Cambridge MA 02138-2356 Office: 16 Divinity Ave Cambridge MA 02138-2020

HASTINGS, LAWRENCE VAETH, lawyer, physician, educator; b. Flushing, N.Y., Nov. 23, 1919; m. Doris Lorraine Erickson, Dec. 11, 1971. Student, Columbia U., 1939-40, student Law Sch., 1949-50; student, U. Mich. Engrng. Sch., 1942-43, Washington U., 1943-44, U. Vt., 1943; MD, Johns Hopkins U., 1948; JD, U. Miami, 1953. Bar: Fla. 1954, U.S. Supreme Ct. 1960, D.C. 1976; cert. Am. Bd. Legal Medicine. Intern U.S. Marine Hosp., S.I., N.Y., 1948-49; asst. surgeon, sr. asst. surgeon USPHS, 1949-52; asst. resident surgery Bellevue Hosp. Med. Ctr., 1951; med. legal cons., trial atty. Miami, Fla., 1953—; ptnr. Lawrence V. Hastings, P.A.; asst. prof. medicine U. Miami, 1964-70, lectr. law, 1966; past adj. prof. St. Thomas U. Law Sch., Miami, Fla. Contbr. articles to profl. publs. Bd. dirs. Miami Heart Inst.; past trustee Barry U., Miami; trustee Fla. Internat. U., 1979—. Served with AUS, 1943-46. Fellow Acad. Fla. Trial Lawyers, Am. Coll. Legal Medicine, Law-Sci. Acad. Found. Am.; mem. ABA, AMA, ATLA, Fla. Bar Assn., Dade County Bar Assn., Am. Acad. Forensic Scis., Fla. Med. Assn., Dade County Med. Assn., Fla. Bar (vice chmn. med. legal com. 1957, vice chmn. trial tactics com. 1963-65, chmn. steering com. trial tactics and basic anatomy seminars), Pitts. Inst. Legal Medicine, Johns Hopkins Med. and Surg. Assn., Pithotomy Club, Assn. Mil. Surgeons, U. Miami Law Alumni Assn. (pres. 1967), Acad. Psychosomatic Medicine, Fairbanks Ranch Country Club (Rancho Santa Fe, Calif.), Alpha Delta Phi, Phi Eta Sigma, Phi Alpha Delta. Roman Catholic. Clubs: Surf (bd. govs. 1976—, chmn. bd. 1980-82, pres. 1978-80), Com. 100, Indian Creek Country, Miami Beach, River of Jacksonville; N.Y. Athletic, Metropolitan, Princeton (N.Y.C.). Address: 9133 Collins Ave Miami FL 33154

HASTINGS, LEE L., secondary education educator. Secondary educator Westlake High Sch. Recipient Tchr. Excellence award Internat. Tech. Edn. Assn., 1992. Office: Westlake High Sch 3300 Middletown Rd Waldorf MD 20603-3705*

HASTINGS, L(OIS) JANE, architect, educator; b. Seattle, Mar. 3, 1928; d. Harry and Camille (Pugh) H.; m. Norman John Johnston, Nov. 22, 1969. B.Arch., U. Wash., Seattle, 1952, postgrad. in Urban Planning, 1958. Architect Boeing Airplane Co., Seattle, 1951-54; recreational dir. Germany, 1954-56; architect (various firms), Seattle, 1956-59, pvt. practice architecture, 1959-74; instr. archtl. drafting Seattle Community Coll., part-time 1969-80; owner/founder The Hastings Group Architects, Seattle, 1974—; lectr. design Coll. Architecture, U. Wash., 1975; incorporating mem. Architecta (P.S.), Seattle, 1980; pres. Architecta (P.S.), from 1980; mem. adv. bd. U. Wash. YWCA, 1967-69; mem. Mayor's Com. on Archtl. Barriers for Handicapped, 1974-75; chmn. regional public adv. panel on archtl. and engrng. services GSA, 1976; mem. citizens adv. com. Seattle Land Use Adminstrn. Task Force, from 1979; AWIU guest of Soviet Women's Con., 1983; speaker Pacific Rim Forum, Hong Kong, 1987; guest China Internat. Conf. Ctr. for Sci. and Tech. of the China Assn. for Sci. and Tech., 1989; mem. adv. com. Coll. architecture and urban planning U. Wash., 1993; mem. accreditation team U. Oreg. Coll. Architecture, 1991, N.J. Inst. Tech. Sch. Architecture, 1992; jurur Home of the Yr. ann. award AIA/Seattle Times, 1996. Design juror for nat. and local competitions, including Red Cedar Shingle/AIA awards, 1977, Current Use Honor awards, AIA, 1980, Exhibit of Sch. Architecture award, 1981; Contbr. to: also spl. features newspapers, articles in profl. jours. Sunset mag. Mem. bd. Am. Women for Internat. Understanding, del. to, Egypt, Israel, USSR, 1971, Japan and Korea, 1979, USSR, 1983; mem. Landmarks Preservation Bd. City of Seattle, 1981-83; mem. Design Constrn. Rev. Bd. Seattle Sch. Dist., 1985-87; mem. mus. con. Mus. History and Industry, 1987—; leader People to People del. women architects to China, 1990. Recipient AIA/The Seattle Times Home of Month Ann. award, 1968; Exhbn. award Seattle chpt. AIA, 1970; Environ. award Seattle-King County Bd. Realtors, 1970, 77,; AIA/House and Home/The American Home Merit award, 1971, Sp. Honor award Wash. Aggregates and Concrete Assn., 1993, Prize bridge Am. Inst. Steel Contrn., 1993; Honor award Seattle chpt. AIA, 1977, 83; Women Achievement award Past Pres. Assembly, 1983, Washington Women and Trading Cards, 1983; Nat. Endowment for Arts grantee, 1977; others; named to West Seattle High Sch. Hall of Fame, 1989, Woman of Achievement Matrix Table, 1994; named Woman of Distinction, Columbia River Girl Scout Coun., 1994. Fellow AIA (pres. Seattle chpt. 1975, pres. sr. coun. 1980, state exec. bd. 1975, N.W. regional dir. 1982-87, Seattle chpt. found. bd. 1985-87, Bursar Coll. Fellows 1989-90, Coll. of Fellows historian 1994—, internat. rels. com. 1988-92, vice chancellor 1991, chancellor 1992, Seattle chpt. medal 1995), Internat. Union Women Architects (v.p. 1969-79, sec. gen. 1985-89, del. UIA Congress, Montreal 1990), Am. Arbitration Assn. (arbitrator 1981—), Coun. of Design Professions, Assn. Women Contrs., Suppliers and Design Cons., Allied Arts Seattle, Fashion Group, Tau Sigma Delta, Alpha Rho Chi (medal). Office: The Hastings Group-Architects 603 Stewart St Ste 915 Seattle WA 98101-1264 *It is not the quantity but the quality of space that is important.*

HASTINGS, MARY LYNN, real estate broker; b. Carthage, N.Y., Jan. 16, 1943; d. Floyd Albert and Mary Frances (Schack) Neuroth; m. Ronald Anthony Casel, Nov. 28, 1963 (div. Nov. 1977); children: Mark, Steven, Glen; m. Charles F. Hastings, Apr. 27, 1991 (dec. 1998). Grad., Harper Method, Rochester, N.Y., 1961. Lic. real estate broker. Owner M.L. Salon, Rochester, N.Y., 1962-72; splty. tchrs.-aide Broward County, Ft. lauderdale, Fla., 1973-77; office mgr. Broward County Voter Registration, Margate, Fla., 1977-82; real estate salesperson Pelican Bay, Daytona Beach, Fla., 1982-84, broker, 1984—; broker, owner Mary Lynn Realty, Daytona Beach, Fla., 1989—. Mem. adv. bd. Dem. Club, Margate, 1977-82. Mem. NAFE, Nat. Assn. Realtors, Fla. Home Builders Assn., Nat. Home Builders Assn., Daytona Beach Home Builders Assn., Daytona Beach Bd. Realtors, Ft. Lauderdale Bd. Realtors, Nat. Assn. Women in Constrn. (v.p. 1988-89, pres.-elect 1989—, pres. 1990—), Sales and Mktg. Coun. Democrat. Episcopalian. Avocations: travel, round and square dancing, theater, real estate investments. Home: 112 Marsh Wren Ct Daytona Beach FL 32119 Office: Mary Lynn Realty 1301 Beville Rd Ste 20 Daytona Beach FL 32119-1503

HASTINGS, MELANIE (MELANIE JEAN WOTRING), television news anchor; b. Phila., May 9, 1955; d. Jean Athanase and Annabell (Snyder) Sayegh; m. Edmund Ross Wotring Jr., Apr. 19, 1980; children: Edmund Ross III, Allison Stewart. Attended, U. Nice, France, 1975; BA in Speech, Comm., U. Del., 1977. Anchor, reporter Sta. WOAY-TV, Oak Hill, W.Va., 1977-78, Sta. WSAZ-TV, Huntington, W.Va., 1978-79, 85-89, Sta. KTVI-TV, St. Louis, 1979-80; anchor ten o'clock news Sta. WTTV, Indpls., 1989-90; anchor (cable TV) NewsChannel 8, Washington, 1991—; anchor Sta. WDCA-TV, 1995-96. Mem. AFTRA, NATAS-DC, Am. Women in Radio and TV. Avocations: exercise, skiing. Office: 7600 D Boston Blvd Springfield VA 22153-3136

HASTINGS, RONNIE JACK, secondary school educator; b. Ranger, Tex., Apr. 8, 1946; m. Sylvia Louise Hastings, July, 1968; children: Dan, Chad. BS in Physics, Tex. A&M U., 1968, PhD in Physics, 1972. Tchg. asst. dept. physics Tex. A&M U., 1966-72, rsch. asst. Cyclotron Inst., 1968-70; regional sci. advisor U. Tex., Austin, 1972-73; tchr. physics and advanced math. Waxahachie (Tex.) H.S., 1973—, chmn. dept. sci., 1973-85, 97—, curriculum developer, coord., 1973-85, dir. computer svcs., 1975-88, chmn. sci. and math. depts., 1995-96; bd. dirs. nat. Ctr. Science Edn.; adj. asst. prof. dept. physics Tex. Woman's U., 1975-84; instr. Navarro Jr. Coll., 1975-84, 98; mem. Nat. Supercollider Edn. Consortium, 1989-91; mem. Tex. State Textbook Com. Secondary Edn., Secondary Sci., 1990, 91, 92; mem. biology sect., Tex. secondary sci. textbook com., 1990, chemistry sect. 1992, chmn. physics sect. , 1991; mem. Tex. Science Adv. Com., 1990, 91; instr., master tchr. Superconducting Supercollider's First Summer Inst. Physics and Physical Science Tchrs., 1993; v.p. Tex. Coun. Science Edn.; mem. edn. subcom. Com. Sci. Investigation of Claims of Paranormal; participant tchr. space program NASA; chair edn. pubs. task force Nat. Ctr. Science; presenter numerous seminars. Contbr. articles to profl. jours.; rsch. on dinosaur tracks, 1981—. Recipient Recognition of Achievement and Contributions to Science Edn. Tex. State Senate, 1988; named Waxahachie I.S.D. Tchr. of Yr. 1998, Region X T.O.Y. finalist, 1998. Mem. AAAS, Am. Assn. Physics Tchrs. (Excellence in Physics teaching award Tex. sect. 1988), Nat. Assn. Geology Tchrs. (pres. Tex. sect. 1987-88), Tex. Acad. Sci., Sci. Tchrs. Assn. Tex., North Tex. Skeptics (co-founder, pres. 1980-84, tech. advisor 1985—), Sigma Xi (Outstanding Secondary Schs. Tchr. award Tex. A&M chpt. 1986), Phi Kappa Phi, Sigma Pi Sigma. Office: Waxahachie High Sch 1000 Dallas Hwy N Waxahachie TX 75165

HASTINGS, STANLEY, librarian, organist; b. Vicksburg, Miss.; s. Richard Granbery Hastings and Charlotte Louise Stanley. AA, Hinds Jr. Coll., 1974; BS, U. So. Miss., 1977, MLS, 1986; studied organ with Elsie Hutto, Helen Ott, Marty Wheeler, Gulfport, Miss., 1980-95. Bookmobile libr. Hattiesburg (Miss.) Pub. Libr., 1976-77; libr. St. John H.S., Gulfport, 1977-86; head reference Biloxi (Miss.) Libr., 1986—; organist St. James Cath. Ch., Gulfport, 1982-85, St. Joseph Cath. Ch., Gulfport, 1984-85, St. Thomas Episcopal Ch., Diamonhead, Miss., 1985-87, Bethel Luth. Ch., Biloxi, 1988—. Mem. workshop/chorus Gulf Coast Opera Theatre, Biloxi, 1978-83; mem. Gulf Coast Cmty. Chorus, Biloxi, Gulfport, 1983-84. Mem. Miss. Libr. Assn. Democrat. Episcopalian. Avocations: working out, swimming, writing, genealogical research. E-mail: hastings@harrison.lib.ms.us. Office: Harrison County Libr Sys Biloxi 139 Lameuse St Biloxi MS 39501

HASTINGS, WILLIAM CHARLES, retired state supreme court chief justice; b. Newman Grove, Nebr., Jan. 31, 1921; s. William C. and Margaret (Hansen) H.; m. Julie Ann Simonson, Dec. 29, 1946; children—Pamela, Charles, Steven. B.Sc., U. Nebr., 1942, J.D., 1948; LHD (hon.), Hastings Coll., 1991. Bar: Nebr. 1948. With FBI, 1942-43; mem. firm Chambers, Holland, Dudgeon & Hastings, Lincoln, 1948-65; judge 3d jud. dist. Nebr., Lincoln, 1965-79; judge Supreme Ct. Nebr., Lincoln, 1979-88, chief justice, 1988-95; ret., 1995; bd. dirs. Nat. Conf. Chief Justices, 1989-91. Pres. Child Guidance Ctr., Lincoln, 1962, 63; v.p. Lincoln Community Coun., 1968, 69; vice chmn. Antelope Valley coun. Boy Scouts Am., 1968, 69; pres. 1st Presbyn. Ch. Found., 1968—; mem. Lincoln Parks and Recreation Adv. Bd. Served with AUS, 1943-46. Named to Nebr. Jaycee Hall of Fame, 1998. Mem. ABA, Nebr. Bar Assn. (George H. Turner award 1991, Pioneer award 1992), Am. Jud. Soc., Lincoln Bar Assn., Nebr. Dist. Judges Assn. (past pres.), Nat. Conf. Chief Justices (past bd. dirs.), Am. Judicature Soc. (Herbert Harley award 1997), Phi Delta Phi. Republican. Presbyterian (deacon, elder, trustee). Club: East Hills Country (pres. 1959-60). Home: 1544 S 58th St Lincoln NE 68506-1407

HASTINGS, WILMOT REED, lawyer; b. Salem, Mass., May 29, 1935; s. Abner Horace and Florence (Hylan) H.; m. Joan Amory Loomis, Aug. 30, 1958; children: W. Reed, Jr., Melissa H., Claire A. A.B. magna cum laude, Harvard U., 1957, LL.B. magna cum laude, 1961; postgrad., U. Paris, 1957-58. Bar: Mass. 1961. Law clk. Chief Justice Raymond S. Wilkins, Boston, 1961-62; assoc. firm Bingham, Dana & Gould, Boston, 1962-68; 1st asst. and dep. atty. gen. Mass., 1968-69; spl. asst. and exec. asst. to undersec. state, 1969-70; gen. counsel HEW, 1970-73; ptnr. Bingham, Dana & Gould, Boston and London, 1973-90; writer, 1990—. Home and Office: 180 Prentice Rd Worthington MA 01098-9590

HASTY, MICHAEL JOE, protective services official; b. June 9, 1959. AA, Maple Woods C.C., Kansas City, 1991; BA, Park Coll., 1993, M in Pub. Affairs, 1997. Patrolman Excelsior Springs (Mo.) Police Dept., 1981-84; pub. safety sge. Gladstone (Mo.) Pub. Safety, 1984—. E-mail: sgt213@aol.com. Home: 7241 N Myrtle Ave Gladstone MO 64119-1973

HASTY, WILLIAM GRADY, JR., lawyer; b. Canton, Ga., July 7, 1947; s. William Grady and Hazel Bonnie (Wyatt) H.; m. Linda Lacey Nichols, Aug. 9, 1969; children: William Grady III, Lauren Elise, Jeffrey Nichols. AA, Reinhardt Coll., 1967; BS, U. Ga., 1969; JD, Mercer U., 1974. Bar: Ga. 1974, U.S. Dist. Ct. (no. dist.) Ga. 1975, U.S. Ct. Appeals (11th cir.) 1975. bd. dirs. Bank of Canton, The Presdl. Roundtable. Chmn. Cherokee County Recreation Commn., 1975-85; charter mem. Leadership Cherokee County, 1987, steering com., 1988—; mem. Leadership Ga.; trustee Canton 1st United Meth. Ch., sec., exec. com.; bd. trustees Reinhardt Coll., Cherokee County Hosp. Authority, Northside Hosp., Cherokee; exec. bd. Cherokee Founder's Club; abd. dirs. Northsided Hosp., Cherokee. Named Outstanding Citizen Cherokee County Commr., 1986, 87. Mem. VFW, ATLA, Ga. Bar Assn., Canton Bar Assn., Blue Ridge Bar Assn., Trial Lawyers Assn. Ga., Phoenix Soc. Atlanta Canton Golf Club, Moose Club, Atlanta Track Club, Cherokee County C. of C., Commerce Club Atlanta. Avocations: tennis, running, fishing, hunting. Home: 1746 Cumming Hwy Canton GA 30114-8043 Office: William G Hasty Jr PC PO Box 1818 211 E Main St Canton GA 30114-2710

HASWELL, CARLETON RADLEY, banker; b. Milw., May 18, 1939; s. Clayton Lyman and Jane (Radley) H.; m. Almut Haberkamp, Dec. 10, 1966; children—Angela, Robin. B.S., Northwestern U., 1961; M.B.A., NYU, 1967. Chief internat. credit officer Chem. Bank, N.Y.C., 1963-87; dir. Chem. Internat. Inc., N.Y.C., 1981-86, Chem. Internat. Fin., N.Y.C., 1981-84; pres. Carleton Haswell Assocs., 1987—. Dir., United Givers, Wayne, N.J., 1980-83. Served with U.S. Army, 1961-63. Mem. Robert Morris Assocs. Isles Yacht Club Fla. Republican. $D. Home and Office: Villa 514 2645 W Marion Ave Punta Gorda FL 33950-5979

HATCH, CHARLES R., university dean. BS in Forest Mgmt., U. Mont., 1964; M in Forestry, Forest Mensuration, Oreg. State U., 1966; PhD in forest Mensuration/Stats., U. Minn., 1971. Grad. asst. Oreg. State U. Sch. Forstry, Corvallis, 1965-66; instr. U. Minn. Sch. Forestry, St. Paul, 1967-71; asst. prof. dept. forestry So. Ill. U., Carbondale, 1971-73; assoc. prof. Coll. Forestry, Wildlife and Range Scis., U. Idaho, Moscow, 1973-77, prof., 1977—, program dir. continuing edn. in forest ecology/silviculture, 1977-82, assoc. dean rsch., assoc. dir. forestry, wildlife, 1979-83, head dept. forest resources, 1987-89, assoc. dean rsch., internat. programs, dir. experiment sta., 1994-95, dean, 1995—; forestry advisor U.S. AID, New Delhi, India, 1983-87; chief of party forestry planning and devel. project Winrock Internat., Islamabad, Pakistan, 1989-94. Contbr. articles to profl. jours. Recipient Outstanding Svc. to Am. Embassy Cmty. award Am. Amb. to Pakistan. Recipient Outstanding Svc. award to Am. Embassy Cmty., Islamabad, Pakistan, 1993, 94. Mem. Mont. Druids, Gamma Sigma Delta, Sigma Xi, Xi Sigma Pi. Office: U Idaho Coll Forestry Wildlife & Range Scis Moscow ID 83844-1138*

HATCH, D. PATRICIA P., principal. Prin. Naubuc Sch. Recipient U.S. Dept. Edn. Elem. Sch. Recognition award, 1989-90, Women of the Year award Glastonbury Profl. Women. Office: Naubuc Sch 84 Griswold St Glastonbury CT 06033-1006*

HATCH, DAVID LINCOLN, sociology educator; b. Belmont, Mass., Oct. 2, 1910; s. Roy Winthrop and Bertha May (Roper) H.; m. Mary Alice Gies, Aug. 24, 1940; children—Charles Winthrop, Abby (Mrs. Joel S. Cleland), Faith Winslow (Mrs. William R. Mann), Elizabeth Ann (Mrs. Terry R. Dimmery). A.B., Dartmouth Coll., 1933; M.A., Montclair State Coll., 1934, Harvard U., 1948; Ph.D., Harvard U., 1949. Tchr. history and social studies pub. high schs. Madison, N.J., 1934-36, Summit, N.J., 1936-37, Montclair, N.J., 1937-40; instr. sociology Conn. Coll. for Women, New London, 1942-43; vis. lectr. sociology Clark U., Worcester, Mass., 1945-46; asst. prof. sociology U. Ky., Lexington, 1946-48; asso. prof. Syracuse (N.Y.) U., 1948-54; prof., head dept. history and sociology, dir. div. social sci. Madison Coll., Harrisonburg, Va., 1954-57; prof. U. S.C., Columbia, 1957—; acting chmn. dept. anthropology and sociology U. S.C., 1969-70, chmn. dept., 1970-73; vis. prof. Benedict Coll., Columbia.; Research cons. S.C. State Hosp., Columbia, 1962-64. Author: (with R. W. Hatch) The Story of New England, 1938, (with Mary G. Hatch) Under the Elms: Yesterday and Today, 1949; Contbr. (with Mary G. Hatch) numerous articles to profl. jours., popular mags. Mem. adv. bd. Le Domain Humain, London, Eng., 1964-76; mem. adv. council S.C. Desegregation Cons. Center, Columbia, 1968; mem. regional aging adv. com. Central Midlands Regional Planning Council, S.C. Fellow Am. Sociol. Assn. (chmn. com. on recruitment for S.C. 1964-67); mem. Soc. Sci. Study Religion, Nat. Council on Family Relations, Eastern Sociol. Soc., So. Sociol. Soc. (chmn. com. on teaching sociology 1958-60), S.C. Sociol. Assn. (pres. 1977-78). Home: 2420 Terrace Way Columbia SC 29205-2342

HATCH, DONALD JAMES (JIM HATCH), business leadership and planning executive; b. Live Oak, Fla., May 23, 1933; s. Albert James and Grace (Peeples) H.; m. Marilyn Blackmon Hatch, June 11, 1953; children: Rebecca, Melanie, Lynn, Donald J. Jr. BPE, U. Fla., 1955. Col. USMC, 1955-80; dir. Intelligence Systems System Planning Corp., Rosslyn, Va., 1980-86; advanced systems engr. RCA, Rosslyn, Va., 1986-88; advanced systems mktg. GE Aerospace, Arlington, Va., 1988-93; advanced systems bus. planning Martin Marietta, Arlington, Va., 1993-94; pres. Bus. Leadership and Planning, Jacksonville, Fla., 1994—. Author: Marine Corps Master Intelligence Plan, 1982. Recipient Bronze Star Sec. Navy, 1966, Legion of Merit Sec. Navy, 1970, 80, Gen. Mgrs. award GE Govt. and Comm. Sys., Camden, N.J., 1993. Mem. Marine Corps Cryptologic Assn. (pres.), Naval Cryptologic Vets. Assn., Armed Force Comm. Electronics Assn., U. Fla. Blue Key (Hall of Fame 1955), Nat. Mil. Intelligence Assn., Rotary. Episcopalian. Avocations: stamp collecting, gardening. Home: 15331 Cape Dr N Jacksonville FL 32226-1266

HATCH, EDWARD WILLIAM (TED HATCH), health care executive; b. Greenwich, Conn., Jan. 2, 1952; s. Denison Hurlbut and Louise (Bingham) H.; m. Jean Brummer, May 26, 1990. BA, Beloit Coll., 1974; MAHCA, George Washington U., 1978. Planning assoc. East Cen. Ill. Health Systems Agy., Champaign, 1978-81; mgr. planning & mktg. Evang. Health Systems, Oak Brook, Ill., 1981-82, coord. instl. planning & mktg., 1983-84; dir. mktg. Bethany Hosp., Chgo., 1985-86; v.p. planning Holy Family Hosp., Des Plaines, Ill., 1986-87; exec. dir. Behavioral Health Systems, Palos Heights, Ill., 1987-88, chief exec. officer, 1989-91; pres., CEO Behavioral Health Sys., Burr Ridge, Ill., 1991-94; phys. hosp. orgn. adminstr. Columbia Behavioral Health, Forest Park, Ill., 1996—. Contbr. articles to profl. jours. Mem. Am. Coll. Health Care Execs., Chgo. Health Execs. Forum (pres. 1989, sec. 1988, program chmn. 1987). Avocations: rollerblading, biking, bonsai, reiki. Office: CBHPO 8311 Roosevelt Rd Forest Park IL 60130-2529

HATCH, FREDERICK TASKER, chemicals consultant; b. Boston, Aug. 27, 1924; s. Frederick Southard and Beatrice (Tasker) H.; m. Virginia Weeks, Mar. 3, 1946; children: Daniel F., Daphne A., Deborah J., Douglas E. BA, Dartmouth Coll., 1944; MD, Harvard U., 1948; PhD, MIT, 1960. Diplomate Nat. Bd. Med. Examiners. Intern Roosevelt Hosp., N.Y.C., 1948-49; rsch. fellow Columbia U., N.Y.C., 1949-52; established investigator Am. Heart Assn./Mass. Gen. Hosp., Boston, 1960-65; sr. scientist, sect. leader Lawrence Livermore (Calif.) Nat. Lab., 1965-80, asst. assoc. dir., 1980-87, cons., 1987—; mem. lipid metabolism adv. com. Nat. Heart, Lung and Blood Inst., Bethesda, Md., 1968-73. Assoc. editor Lipids Jour., 1964-73; author chpts. in books; contbr. numerous articles to profl. jours. Sec. Land Conservation Task Force, Meredith, N.H., 1989-90, chmn. Hwy. Task Force, 1994—. Capt. USAR, 1952-55. Fellow Am. Inst. Chemists; mem. Am. Chem. Soc., Am. Soc. Biochemistry and Molecular Biology, Environ. Mutagen Soc., Arteriosclerosis Coun. of Am. Heart Assn. (exec. com. 1971-73). Avocations: tree farmer, skiing, hiking, biotechnology investing. Home and Office: 27 Pease Rd Meredith NH 03253-5506

HATCH, GEORGE CLINTON, television executive; b. Erie, Pa., Dec. 16, 1919; s. Charles Milton and Blanche (Beecher) H.; m. Wilda Gene Glasmann, Dec. 24, 1940; children: Michael Gene Zbar, Diane Glasmann Orr, Jeffrey Beecher, Randall Clinton, Deepika Hatch Avanti. AB, Occidental Coll., 1940; MA in Econs., Claremont Coll., 1941; HHD (hon.), So. Utah U., 1988. Pres. Comms. Investment Corp., Salt Lake City, 1945-95; chmn. Double G Comm. Corp., Salt Lake City, 1956—; dir. Republic Pictures Corp., Los Angeles, 1971-94; pres. Sta. KVEL, Inc., 1978-94; pres. Standard Corp., Ogden, 1993-98, Hatch Family LLC, 1998—; past mem. Salt Lake adv. bd. First Security Bank Utah; past chmn. Rocky Mountain Pub. Broadcasting Corp.; past chmn. bd. govs. Am. Info. Radio Network; past bd. govs. NBC-TV Affiliates. *George Hatch commenced his broadcast career as manager of KLO-AM in Ogden, Utah, in 1941. He served as chairman of Intermountain Radio Network, 1941-87, and constructed KALL-AM in Salt Lake City, Utah, in 1945, and KALL-FM, in 1968. He operated radio stations: KGHL-AM and KIDX-FM, Billings, KYSS-AM-FM, Missoula, KMON-AM, Great Falls, KOPR-AM, Butte, Montana; KGEM-AM and KJOT-FM, Boise, KUPI-AM and KQPI-FM, Idaho Falls, KLIX-AM, Twin Falls, Idaho; KULA-AM, Honolulu, Hawaii; WISH-AM-FM, Indianaplis, and WTHI-AM, Terre Haute, Indiana. He also operated television stations KUTV-TV, Salt Lake City, Utah; KARD-TV, Wichita, KSNT-TV, Topeka, Kansas; KTVJ-TV, Joplin, Missouri; and KGMB-TV, Honolulu, Hawaii. He co-founded Telecommunications, Inc., in 1968, and served as Vice-Chairman until 1980.* Past pres. Salt Lake Com. on Fgn. Relations; past mem. Utah Symphony Bd., Salt Lake City; mem., past chmn. and mem. Utah State Bd. Regents, 1964-85. Recipient Svc. to Journalism award U. Utah, 1966, silver medal Salt Lake Advt. Club, 1969, Disting. Svc. award Utah Tech. U., 1984, Disting. Utahan Centennial Yr. award Margaret Thatcher U.K., Utah Festival, 1996. Mem. Nat. Assn. Broadcasters (past pres., radio bd. dirs., ambassador to Inter-Am. mtgs. in Latin Am. 1962), Utah Broadcasters Assn. (past pres., Mgmt. award 1964, Hall of Fame award 1981), Salt Lake City Advt. Club (silver medal 1969), Phi Beta Kappa, Phi Rho Pi (life). Democrat. Avocations: hiking, rock art. Office: The Std Corp 1537 Chandler Dr Salt Lake City UT 84103-4220

HATCH, HAROLD ARTHUR, retired military officer; b. Avon, Ill., Dec. 29, 1924; s. Walter Samuel and Marie (Fennessy) H.; m. Mildred Jean Gehrig, Aug. 18, 1950; children—Sue, Sara, Sallie. B.S., Coll. William and Mary, 1962. Commd. 2d lt. U.S. Marine Corps, 1949, advanced through grades to lt. gen., 1981; div. asst. chief staff for logistics (3d Marine Div.), Okinawa, 1970-71; dep. chief staff Fleet Marine Force Pacific, Hawaii, 1971-74; dep. chief staff for installations and logistics Hdqrs. U.S. Marine Corps, Washington, 1977-84; ret. Decorated Legion of Merit, Bronze Star, Air Medal, Meritorious Service medal, Disting. Service medal. Republican. Presbyterian. Home: 8655 White Beech Way Vienna VA 22182-5056

HATCH, LYNDA SYLVIA, education educator; b. Portland, Oreg., Feb. 19, 1950; d. Marley Elmo and Undine Sylvia (Crockard) Sims. BA, Wash. State U., 1972; MS, Portland State U., 1975; EdD, Oreg. State U., 1984. Cert. tchr., Oreg. Tchr. 5th grade, outdoor sch. specialist Clover Park Sch. Dist. 400, Tacoma, 1971-72; tchr. 6th grade, outdoor sch. specialist Hillsboro (Oreg.) elem. Dist. 7, 1972-78; tchr. 6th grade, outdoor sch. specialist Bend (Oreg.)-La Pine Sch. Dist., 1978-82, elem. curriculum specialist, 1983-85, tchr. 4th grade gifted and talented, 1985-90; grad. teaching asst. Oreg. State U., Corvallis, 1982-84; asst. prof., assoc. prof. No. Ariz. U., 1991-99, chair instnl. leadership, 1997-98; Boeing disting. prof. sci. edn. Wash. State U., Pullman, 1999—; ednl. cons., tchr. workshops, 1973—; presenter workshop Soviet-Am. Joint Conf., Moscow State U., 1991, Meeting of Children's Culture Promoters, Guadalajara, Mex., 1994, and others; faculty Ariz. Journey Schs. for Math. and Sci. Tchg. Improvement; coord. Odyssey of the Mind, Bend, 1985-89, tchr.-mentor program for 1st-yr. tchrs., Beaverton, Oreg., 1982-83; presenter Social Edn. Assn. of Australia, 1997. Author: Pathways of America: Lewis and Clark, 1993, Pathways of America: The Oregon Trail, 1993, Pathways of America: The California Gold Rush Trail, 1994, Pathways of America: The Santa Fe Trail, 1995, Fifty States, 1997, U.S. Presidents, 1997, U.S. Map Skills, 1997, Human body, 1998, National Parks and Other Park Service Sites, 1999, Our National Parks, 1999; contbr. articles to profl. jours. Vol., leader, bd. dirs. Girl Scouts U.S., 1957—; elder First Presbyn. Ch., Bend, 1980—; vol. hist. interpretation High Desert Mus., Bend, 1987-91; docent Mus. No. Ariz.; pres. bd. dirs. The Arboretum at Flagstaff. Recipient Excellence in Teaching award Bend Found., 1985-86, 86-87; named Tchr. of Yr. Oreg. Dept. Edn., 1982; Celebration Teaching grantee Geraldine Rockefeller Dodge Found., 1989, 90, 91, 92, 93, 94, 95, EPA grantee, 1997-99, Eisenhower Math and Sci. Edn. Act grantee, 1997. Mem. NEA, Nat. Coun. Tchrs. Math., NSTA (internat. com.), Nat. State Tchrs. of Yr. (nat. pres. 1988-90), Oreg. Coun. Tchrs. Math. (bd. dirs. 1981-82), Oreg. Coun. Tchrs. English (bd. dirs. 1981-82), Ariz. Reading Assn. (bd. dirs.), Ariz. Sci. Tchrs. Assn., No. Ariz. Reading Coun. (exec. bd. 1991-92, 92-93), Ariz. State Early Childhood Assn., Nat. Coun. for Social Studies, Coun. for Elem. Sci. Internat. (bd. dirs. 1995-98, chair informal edn. com.), Internat. Reading Assn., Oreg.-Calif. Trails Assn., Nat. Sci. Edn. Leadership Assn., Assn. for Edn. of Tchrs. in Sci., Ariz. Assn. for Learning in and about the Environment, S.W. Oreg.-Calif. Trails Assn., Delta Kappa Gamma (1st v.p.), Phi Delta Kappa (found. rep. 1991-92, v.p. programs 1992-93, historian 1993-94, v.p. membership 1994-95), Golden Key Hon., Kappa Delta Pi (past chpt. counselor), others. Avocations: cross-country skiing, photography, hiking, crafts, gardening. Home: 845 SE Green Hill Rd Pullman WA 99163

HATCH, MARK BRUCE, software engineer; b. Lynn, Mass., July 20, 1959; s. Carroll Bruce and Claire Adelle (Sherys) H. BS, U. Mass., 1981; MS, U. Mass., Lowell, 1990. Cons. Bassook & Brisk, Wayland, Mass., 1988-90; dir. R&D Toltran Ltd., Lake Zurich, Ill., 1990-94; pres. Minisoft Systems Design, Lynn, Mass., 1994-98; sr. analyst/client server New England Computer, Wakefield, Mass.; dir. ops. Web Knowlogy, LLC, Wakefield, Mass.,

1998—; sr. software engr. One Core Fin. Network, Inc., Woburn, Mass., 1998—, OneCore.com, Woburn, Mass., 1998—; instr. computer sci. North Shore C.C., Lynn, Mass., 1988—. Mem. Internat. Asns. Machine Trans., Assn. Machine Trans. in Americas. Achievements include U.S. and fgn. patents for improved trans. system in the field of machine trans. based on a multi-lingual approach to computer analysis; design on a complete lang.-ing, multi-lingual machine trans. system, integrated client-server svcs. to implement translation techniques in an open systems environment. Home: 67 Mudge St Lynn MA 01902-1215 Office: OneCor.com Ste 2800 800 West Cummings Park Woburn MA 01801 also: One Core Fin Network Inc 800 W Cummings Park Woburn MA 01801

HATCH, MARY GIES, German language educator; b. Omaha, Feb. 17, 1913; d. Charles George and Jane Elizabeth (Sturman) Gies; m. David Lincoln Hatch, Aug. 24, 1940; children: Charles Winthrop, Mary Abby Hatch Cleland, Faith Hatch Mann, Elizabeth Ann Hatch Dimmery. AB, Vassar Coll., 1935; postgrad., U. Heidelberg, 1935; MA, U. Mich., 1937; PhD, Syracuse U., 1952. Tchr. Detroit pub. schs., 1937-38, Montclair (N.J.) High Sch., 1938-40, Dana Hall, Wellesley, Mass., 1940-42; prof. German Columbia (S.C.) Coll., 1960—, chmn. dept., 1963—. Editor newsletter S.C. Conf. on Fgn. Lang. Teaching; contbr. articles to profl. jours. Named Syracuse U. scholar 1952; Vassar fellow, 1935; Columbia Coll. rsch. grantee, 1964, So. Assn. rsch. grantee, 1968. Mem. MLA, Am. Assn. Tchrs. German, Am. Sociol. Assn., Southeastern Medieval Assn. (exec. coun.), Phi Beta Kappa. Home: 2420 Terrace Way Columbia SC 29205-2342 Office: Columbia Coll 1301 Columbia College Dr Columbia SC 29203-5949

HATCH, MICHAEL WARD, lawyer; b. Pittsfield, Mass., Nov. 19, 1949; s. Ward Sterling and Elizabeth (Hubbard) H.; m. Lisa Schilling, June 8, 1974; children: Stuart, Andrew, Gillian. AB in Econs., St. Lawrence U., 1971; JD, Yale U., 1974. Bar: Wis. 1974, N.Y. 1980. Ptnr., chmn. real estate group Foley & Lardner, Milw., 1974—. Mem. ABA, N.Y. State Bar Assn., Wis. Bar Assn., Milw. Bar Assn., Am. Coll. Real Estate Lawyers, Urban Land Inst., Nat. Multi Housing Coun., Mortgage Bankers Assn. Wis., Bldg. Owners and Mgrs. Assn., Local Initiatives Support Corp., Milw. Athletic Club, Town Club. Avocations: architecture, historic preservation. Office: Foley & Lardner 777 E Wisconsin Ave Ste 3800 Milwaukee WI 53202-5367

HATCH, MIKE, state attorney general; m. Patti Hatch; 3 children. BS in Polit. Sci. with honors, U. Minn., Duluth, 1970; JD, U. Minn., 1973. Commr. of commerce State of Minn., 1983-89; pvt. practice law; atty. gen. State of Minn., 1999—. Office: Minn Atty Gen's Office 102 State Capitol Saint Paul MN 55155*

HATCH, NATHAN ORR, university administrator; b. May 17, 1946; m. Julia Gregg; 3 children. AB summa cum laude, Wheaton Coll., 1968; AM, Washington U., 1972, PhD, 1974. Postdoctoral fellow Johns Hopkins U., 1974-75; from asst. prof. to prof. history U. Notre Dame, Ind., 1975-88, dir. grad. studies dept. history, 1980-83, assoc. dean Coll. Arts and Letters, dir. Inst. for Scholarship in the Liberal Arts, 1983-89, acting dean Coll. Arts and Letters, 1988-89, v.p. for grad. studies and rsch., 1989-96; prof. U. Notre Dame, 1989, provost, 1996—, Andrew V. Tackes prof. history, 1999—. Author: The Sacred Cause of Liberty: Republican Thought and the Millennium in Revolutionary New England, 1977, The Democratization of American Christianity, 1989 (Albert C. Outler prize Am. Soc. Ch. History 1989, 1989 Book prize Soc. for Historians of Early Am. Republic, co-winner John Hope Franklin Publ. prize Yale U. Press 1990); also articles; editor: The Professions in American History, 1988; co-editor: The Bible in America: Essays in Cultural History, 1982, Jonathan Edwards and the American Experience, 1988. Bd. dirs. United Way St. Joseph County, Ind., 1987-92; trustee St. Joseph's Med. Ctr., 1994, chair bd. trustees, 1997—; mem. nat. adv. bd. Salvation Army, 1997—; trustee Fuller Theol. Sem., 1998—. Recipient Paul Fenlon Teaching award U. Notre Dame, 1981; Am. Coun. Learned Socs. fellow, 1976, Fred Harris Daniels fellow Am. Antiquarian Soc., 1977, Charles Warren fellow Harvard U., 1977-78; grantee Lilly Endowment, 1979, Ind. Com. for the Humanities, 1981-82, NEH, 1981-85. Mem. Johns Hopkins Soc. Scholars, Am. Soc. Ch. Hist. (pres. 1993), Phi Beta Kappa. Office: U Notre Dame Office of the Provost Notre Dame IN 46556

HATCH, ORRIN GRANT, senator; b. Homestead Park, Pa., Mar. 22, 1934; s. Jesse and Helen (Kamm) H.; m. Elaine Hansen, Aug. 28, 1957; children: Brent, Marcia, Scott, Kimberly, Alysa, Jess. B.S., Brigham Young U., 1959; J.D., U. Pitts., 1962; LLD (hon.), U. Md., 1981; MS (hon.), Def. Intelligence Coll., 1982; LLD (hon.), Pepperdine U., 1990, So. Utah State U., 1990. Bar: Pa. 1962, Utah 1962. Ptnr. firm Thomson, Rhodes & Grigsby, Pitts., 1962-69, Hatch & Plumb, Salt Lake City, 1976; mem. U.S. Senate from Utah, 1977—, past chmn. labor and human resources com., chmn. Senate judiciary com., mem. subcom. on taxation, fin. com., senate Rep. policy com., com. on Indian affairs, fin. com.; mem. select com. on intelligence, 1997—. Author ERA Myths and Realities, 1983; contbr. articles to newspapers and profl. jours. Recipient Outstanding Legislator award Nat. Assn. Rehab. Facilities, Legislator of Yr. award Am. Assn. Univ. Affiliated Programs, Legis. Leadership award Health Profl. Assn., many others. Mem. Am., Nat., Utah, Pa. bar assns., Am. Judicature Soc. Republican. Mormon. Avocations: golf, poetry, piano playing, composer lyrics. *

HATCH, PAMELA H., state legislator. Mem. from dist. 100 Maine State Ho. of Reps., 1993-95, mem. from dist. 98, 1995—. Office: Maine Ho of Reps State Capitol Augusta ME 04330*

HATCH, ROSS RIEPERT, weapon system engineering executive; b. N.Y.C., Sept. 6, 1934; s. Aylmer Roscoe and Ebba (Riepert) H.; m. Phyllis Anne Hess, July 21, 1961; children: Robert Ross, Michael Aylmer. BS in Engring., U.S. Naval Acad., Annapolis, Md., 1956; MS in Engring. Electronics, U.S. Naval Postgrad. Sch., Monterey, Calif., 1964; MS in Fin. Mgmt., George Washington U., 1972. Commd. ensign USN, 1956, advanced through grades to capt., 1977, ret., 1985, dept. head destroyers, cruisers, icebreakers, 1956-71; commanding officer guided missile destroyer USS Semmes (DDG-18), Charleston, S.C., 1971-72; commanding officer guided missile cruiser USS Belknap (CG-26), Norfolk, Va., 1979-82; head missile br. Office of Chief Naval Ops., Washington, 1972-76; program mgr. Naval Sea Sys. Command, Washington, 1976-79; dir. combat sys. Naval Sea Sys. Command, 1982-85; strike/cruise missile program mgr. Applied Physics Lab.-Johns Hopkins U., Laurel, Md., 1985-96, asst. dept. head power projection dept., 1996-99. Editor procs. Precision Strike Tech. Symposium, 1990-98. Scout master Boy Scouts Am., 1972-75. Recipient Legion of Merit, Sec. of Navy, Arlington, Va., 1985; Hatch Outcrop Antartica named in his honor U.S. Bd. of Geographic Names, Washington, 1962. Mem. IEEE, Am. Soc. Naval Engrs., Precision Strike Assn. (bd. dirs. 1988—), U.S. Naval Inst. Republican. Episcopalian. Avocations: photography, studio art glass, computers, travel. Home: 9538 Helenwood Dr Fairfax VA 22032-2006

HATCH, STEVEN GRAHAM, publishing company executive; b. Idaho Falls, Idaho, Mar. 27, 1951; s. Charles Steven and Margery Jane (Doxey) H.; BA, Brigham Young U., 1976; postgrad. mgmt. devel. program U. Utah, 1981; m. Rhonda Kay Frasier, Feb. 13, 1982; children: Steven Graham, Kristen Leone, Cameron Michael, Landon Frasier, McKell Margery. Founder, pres. Graham Maughan Enterprises, Provo, Utah, 1975—, Internat. Mktg. Co., 1980—, Mcht. Acct. Svcs., 1996—; bd. dirs. Goldbrickers Internat., Inc., Net Solutions Internat. Inc. Sec., treas. Zions Estates, Inc., Salt Lake City, Kansas City, Mo. Eagle Scout Boy Scouts Am., 1970; trustee Villages of Quail Valley, 1984-88. Recipient Duty to God award, 1970; missionary France Mission, Paris 1970-72, pub. rels. dir. 1972. Mem. Provo Jaycees, Internat. Entrepreneurs Assn., Mormon Booksellers Assn., Samuel Hall Soc. (exec. v.p. 1979), U.S. C. of C., Provo C. of C. (chmn. legis. action com. 1981-82, mem. job svc. employer com.), Rotary (pres. Provo 1995-96, area rep. 1996-97). Republican. Mem. LDS Ch. Office: Graham Maughan Pub Co 50 E 500 S Provo UT 84606-4809

HATCH, WILDA GENE, broadcast company executive; b. Ogden, Utah, Nov. 28, 1917; d. Abraham Lincoln and Edris Alida (Toombs) Glasmann; m. George Clinton Hatch, Dec. 24, 1940; children: Michael Zbar, Diane G. Orr, Jeffrey B., Randall C., Deepika Ogsbury. BA, Stanford U., 1939; HHD (hon.), Weber State U., 1981. Pres. The Std. Corp., Ogden, 1955-93; v.p. Sta. KUTV, Salt Lake City, 1956-94. Pres. Women's State Legis. Coun., Salt Lake City, 1967-69; active LWV, Salt Lake City, 1965—. Democrat. Avocations: hiking, rock art, fishing. Home: 1537 Chandler Dr Salt Lake City UT 84103-4220

HATCHELL, SYLVIA, basketball coach; b. Gastonia, N.C., Feb. 28, 1952; m. Sammy Hatchell; 1 child, Van. B.Phys. Edn. cum laude, Carson-Newman Coll., 1974; MS, U. Tenn., 1975. Coach jr. varsity women's team U. Tenn.; head coach Francis Marion Coll.; head women's basketball coach U. N.C., Chapel Hill, 1986—; asst. coach U.S. World Univ. Games team, 1983, 85; ct. coach U.S. Olympic basketball try-outs, 1984, 92; basketball events taff Olympic Games, L.A., 1984; asst. coach U.S. team 1988 Olympic Games, Goodwill Games and World Championships; coach USA team World Univ. Games, Fukuoka, Japan, 1995, R. william Jones Cup, 1994. Named Nat. Coach of the Yr., USA Today, 1994, Coll. Sports Mag., 1994, Converse NAIA Reg. Coach of the Yr., 1986, AMFVoit Championship Coach, 1986, Coll. Basketball Coach of the Yr., Athletes Internat. Ministries, 1995, Carson-Newman Disting. Alumnus of the Yr., 1994; inductee Francis Marion U. Athletic Hall of Fame, 1993. Mem. Women's Basketball Coaches Assn. (pres. 1996-97, past bd. dirs.), Amateur Basketball Assn. of U.S. (women's games com.). *

HATCHER, BALDWIN, minister, educator; b. Chgo., Aug. 27, 1953; s. Willie James and Carmelethia (Hunt) H. BA, NYU, 1976; MDiv, Union Theol. Sem., N.Y.C., 1980. Ordained to ministry Bapt. Ch., 1980. Min. Sharon Bapt. Ch., N.Y.C., 1973-77, Greater Zion Hill Bapt. Ch., N.Y.C., 1979-87; tchr. N.Y.C. Bd. Edn., 1984—; min. Riker's Island Ho. of Detention for Men, N.Y.C., 1975; guest lectr. NYU, 1976; adj. lectr. Bronx Community Coll., 1982-83, Mercy Coll.; chaplain Terence Cardinal Cook Hosp., N.Y.C., 1985-87; panelist Black studies program Taconic Correctional facility, Mt. Kisco, N.Y. Vol. fund raiser Assn. for Help of Retarded Children, N.Y.C., 1990—. Nat. Fellowship Fund fellow, 1976-80; Roothbert Fund scholar, 1976; named Teacher of Yr. N.Y.C. Bd. Edn. Home: 790 Concourse Village W # 8-B Bronx NY 10451 *Oppression has many ramifications. Many times when a group of people are oppressed by a common enemy, they tend to oppress each other. However, those with scope never lose sight of the common enemy.*

HATCHER, CHARLES ROSS, JR., cardiothoracic surgeon, medical center executive; b. Bainbridge, Ga., June 28, 1930; s. Charles Ross and Vivian Elizabeth (Miller) H.; m. Phyllis Gregory Slappey, July 9, 1988; children by previous marriage: Marian Barnett Thorpe, Charles III. BS magna cum laude, U. Ga., 1950; MD cum laude, Med. Coll. Ga., 1954. Intern Johns Hopkins Hosp., Balt., 1954-55; resident in surgery Peter Bent Brigham Hosp., Boston, 1955-56; resident in surgery Johns Hopkins Hosp., 1958-62; prof. surgery, chief cardiothoracic surgery Emory U. Sch. Medicine, Atlanta, 1971-90, dir., chief exec. officer Emory Clinic, 1976-84; v.p. for Health Affairs, dir. Woodruff Health Scis. Ctr. of Emory U., 1984-96, dir. emeritus; chmn., CEO Emory HealthCare, 1995-96; bd. dirs. Healthdyne Info. Enterprises, Life of the South Corp., Japan Am. Soc. Capt. U.S. Army, 1956-58. Mem. ACS, Am. Coll. Cardiology (bd. govs. 1976-80), Am. Coll. Chest Physicians (bd. regents 1977-81, bd. govs. 1974-77), Am. Surg. Assn., So. Surg. Assn., Am. Assn. Thoracic Surgery, Soc. Thoracic Surgeons (pres. 1986-87), Am. Cancer Soc., So. Thoracic Surg. Assn. (pres. 1984), Johns Hopkins Soc. Scholars, Capital City Club, Piedmont Driving Club, Buckhead Club, Bainbridge Country Club, Rotary (bd. dirs. Atlanta club 1976-80), Phi Beta Kappa, Sigma Xi, Alpha Omega Alpha. Methodist. Contbg. author profl. publs. Home: 1105 Lullwater Rd NE Atlanta GA 30307-1245 Office: Emory U Woodruff Health Scis Ctr 1365B Clifton Rd NE # 6205 Atlanta GA 30322-1013

HATCHER, HERBERT JOHN, biochemist, microbiologist; b. Mpls., Dec. 18, 1926; s. Herbert Edmond and Florence Elizabeth (Larson) H.; m. Beverly J. Johnson, Mar. 28, 1953 (dec. July 1985); children: Dennis Michael, Steven Craig, Roger Dean, Mark Alan, Susan Diane, Laura Jean; m. Louise Fritsche Nelson, May 24, 1986; children: Carlos Howard Nelson, Kent Robert Nelson, Carolyn Louise Tyler. BA, U. Minn., 1953, MS, 1964, PhD, 1965. Bacteriologist VA Hosp., Wilmington, Del., 1956-57; microbiologist Smith, Kline, French, Phila., 1957-60, Clinton (Iowa) Corn Processing, 1966-67; microbiologist, biochemist Econs. Lab. Inc., St. Paul, 1967-84; biochemist EG&G Idaho Inc., Idaho Falls, 1984-90; co-owner B/CG Cons. Svcs., Idaho Falls, 1990—. Chmn. bd. edn. Cross of Christ Luth. Ch., Coon Rapids, Minn., 1974-76; pres. chpt. Aid Assn. Luths., Idaho Falls, 1986; pres.-elect St. Johns Luth. Ch., 1988, pres., 1989. With USNR, 1945-46. Avocations: skiing, hiking, camping, hunting, fishing.

HATCHER, JAMES MITCHELL, principal; b. Erwin, Tenn., Aug. 19, 1950; s. James Walter and Delorese Kathleen (Callahan) H.; m. Ernestine Buchanan, Nov. 18, 1967; 1 child, Christopher Scott. BS, East Tenn. State U., 1972, MEd, 1983; EdD in Edn. Adminstrn., 1994. Cert. tchr., adminstr. and supr., supt. of schs. Corrective therapist McGuire VA Hosp., Richmond, Va., 1973—; tchr. Unicoi County Bd. Edn., Erwin, 1973-84, prin., 1984—. Mem. Unicoi County Polit. Action Com., Erwin, 1973—, Tenn. Polit. Action Com., Nashville, 1973—, PTA, Erwin, 1982; deacon Bapt. Ch. Fellow Tenn. Edn. Assn., NEA; mem. Unicoi County Edn. Assn. (pres. 1981-82, negotiator 1979-83, rep. to Tenn. Edn. Assn. 1980-82), Unicoi County Prins. Assn. (v.p. Erwin chpt. 1986-87, pres. 1987-88). Avocations: golf, coaching baseball (Erwin Little League 1982-86), basketball, football. Home: 212 Railroad St Erwin TN 37650-3212 Office: Unicoi Elem Sch 300 Massachusetts Ave Unicoi TN 37692-9707

HATCHER, JOE BRANCH, executive search consulting company executive; b. Ft. Worth, July 28, 1936; s. W. Joe and Jessie Mae Hatcher; m. Irma Gail Collins, Apr. 18, 1957; children: Gregory Layne, Geoffrey Alan, Gailyn. BA, U. Wichita, 1960; MA, U. Kans., 1967, PhD, 1968. Mem. English lit. faculty Baker U., Baldwin City, Kans., 1966-74; asst. to pres. Park Coll., Kansas City, Mo., 1974-75; v.p. Albion (Mich.) Coll., 1976-81; pres. Hendrix Coll., Conway, Ark., 1981-91; vice chmn. 1st Comml. Bank, Little Rock, 1992-95, also bd. dirs., 1992-95; cons. Hatcher & Assocs., Conway, Ark., 1995—; of couns. AST/BRYANT, Conway, 1995—. Bd. dirs. Ark. Coun. for Econ. Edn. Mem. Conway C. of C. Methodist. Avocation: tennis. Office: 916 Heather Cir Conway AR 72032-9395

HATCHER, THOMAS FOUNTAIN, management consultant, publisher; b. Monroe, Mich., Dec. 26, 1931; s. Fountain H. and Cecilia E. (Boylan) H. m. Rosemary K. Downs, June 23, 1956; children: Mary Kathleen, Roberta Joan, Margaret Ann. BS, NYU, 1968. With Equitable Life Assurance Soc., N.Y.C., 1955-71, mgr. learning systems, 1968-71; owner Thomas Hatcher Assocs. Thomas Hatcher Assocs., Mpls., 1971-79; pres., owner Futures Unlimited, Inc., Mpls., 1979—; pres., CEO Profl. Publs., Mpls., 1988-90. Author: The Definitive Guide to Long Range Planning, 1981, 2d edit., 1988, Facilitator's Handbook for Planning, 1985. Mem. ASTD, Nat. Speakers Assn., Am. Soc. Profl. Cons. Roman Catholic. Home and Office: Futures Unlimited Inc 18525 Texas Ave Prior Lake MN 55372-3110

HATCHER, WAYNE, academic administrator; b. Waco, Tex., Apr. 25, 1951; s. Doris Mae (Nichols) Boucher; m. Martha N. Gustafson, June 4, 1971; children: Jennifer, Eric. BA, BS, Howard Payne U., 1973; MA, Baylor U., 1980; PhD, U. North Tex., 1995. From dir. residence hall to assoc. dean students Baylor U., Waco, 1973-78; regional mgr. Steaks of Tex., Dallas, 1978; asst. dean students Midwestern State U., Wichita Falls, Tex., 1979-80; sales mgr. Uni-Lab, Houston, 1980-81; assoc. dean students Midwestern State U., Wichita Falls, 1981-88; dean students Cameron U., Lawton, Okla., 1988-99; pres. student affairs Gordon Coll., Barnesville, Ga., 1999—. Contbr. chpts. in books. Bd. dirs. Am. Red Cross, Lawton chpt. treas. Mem. Christian Fam. Couns. Ctr., 1989-94, pres., 1995, ASJA, Nat. Student Pers. Adminstrs. (chair/coord. 1994-96, adult student coord. 1993-94), Okla. Coll. Student Pers. Assn. (exec. coun. 1993-95, pres. 1997-98). Office: Gordon Coll 419 College Dr Barnesville GA 30204

HATCHETT, EDWARD BRYAN, JR., state auditor, lawyer; b. Glasgow, Ky., Aug. 8, 1951; s. Edward Bryan and Leona Katherine (Azbill) H.; m. Judie Etta James, Aug. 3, 1973; children: Catherine Wade, Elizabeth Black, James Edward Bryan. BA, Centre Coll., Danville, Ky., 1973; JD, U. Louisville, 1976; diploma Nat. Grad. Trust Sch., Northwestern U., 1980; diploma Stonier Grad. Sch. Banking, U. Del., 1986; diploma Ky. Mgmt. Inst., Western Ky. U., 1988. Bar: Ky. 1976. Editorial asst. Dept. Agr., Washington, 1971; edn. rsch. asst. Ky. Legis. Rsch. Commn., Frankfort, 1972; law clk. Dept. Law, City of Louisville, 1973-76; pvt. practice Glasgow, 1978-88; v.p., trust officer New Farmers Nat. Bank, Glasgow, 1980-88, sec., 1986-88; asst. gen. counsel Ky. Dept. Fin. Instns., Frankfort, 1977, commr., 1988-94, dir. securities divsn., 1992-94; auditor pub. accts. Commonwealth Ky., 1996—; chmn. Ky. Fin. Instns. Bd., Frankfort, 1988-94; bd. dirs. Commonwealth Preservation Advs., Inc., Frankfort; pres. Barren County Bar Assn., Glasgow, 1988, Estate Planning Coun. So. Ky., Bowling Green, 1988. Gov.'s appointee Ky. Heritage Coun., Frankfort, 1985-88; pres. Mammoth Cave Area 4-H Found., Glasgow, 1981; lay reader Ch. of the Ascension, 1988—; elected Ky. Auditor of Public Accounts, 1995. Named nat. pub. speaking champion Future Farmers Am., 1970. Mem. N.Am. Securities Adminstrs. Assn., Nat. Assn. State Auditors, Controllers and Treasurers (bond com. 1997—), Nat. State Auditors Assn., Frankfort Rotary Club. Democrat. Episcopalian. Avocations: historical research, golf. E-mail: hatchett@apa1.aud.state.ky.us. Home: 454 Chinook Trl Frankfort KY 40601-1602 Office: 144 Capitol Ave Frankfort KY 40601-2831

HATCHETT, JOSEPH WOODROW, federal judge; b. Clearwater, Fla., Sept. 17, 1932; s. John Arthur and Lula Gertrude (Thomas) H.; children: Cheryl Nadine, Brenda Audrey. A.B., Fla. A. and M. U., 1954; J.D., Howard U., 1959; J.D. certificate mil. judge course, U.S. Naval Justice Sch., Newport, R.I., 1973. Bar: Fla. 1959, U.S. Ct. Appeals (5th and 11th cirs.). Pvt. practice Daytona Beach, 1959-66; asst. U.S. atty. Dept. Justice, Jacksonville, Fla., 1966-70; U.S. magistrate U.S. Cts., Jacksonville, 1971-75; justice Supreme Ct. Fla., Tallahassee, 1975-79; chief judge U.S. Ct. Appeals (5th cir.), Tallahassee, 1979-81, U.S. Ct. Appeals (11th cir.), Tallahassee, 1981-99; Cooperating atty. N.A.A.C.P. Legal Def. Fund, 1960-66; gen. counsel Masons of Fla., 1963-66; cons., mem. staff dept. urban renewal, Daytona Beach, 1963-66, spl. asst. to city atty., 1964; Mem. com. selection for Jacksonville Naval Res. Officer Tng. Corps, 1971. Contbr. articles to profl. jours. Mem. John T. Stocking Meml. Trust, med. sch. scholarships, 1961-66; Co-chmn. United Negro Coll. Fund of Volusia County, Fla., 1962; bd. dirs. Jacksonville Opportunities Industrialization Center, 1972-75. Served to 1st lt. AUS, 1954-56, Germany. Recipient Mary McCloud Bethune medallion for community service Bethune-Cookman Coll., 1965, medallion for human relations, 1975, Tampa Urban League Accolade, 1975, Postgraduate Achievement award Howard U., 1977. Mem. Am., Nat., Fla., Jacksonville, D. W. Perkins, Fed. bar assns., Am. Judicature Soc., Nat. Council Fed. Magistrates, V.F.W., Omega Psi Phi. Baptist (trustee). Club: Fla-Jax (Jacksonville) (Man of Year 1974). Office: US Ct Appeals 11th Circuit 110 E Park Ave Tallahassee FL 32301*

HATEM, MICHAEL THOMAS, child psychology educator; b. Methuen, Mass., Oct. 29, 1958; s. Herbert Joseph and Joan Marie (Kosloske) H. BA, Haverford Coll., 1982; MLA, Harvard U., 1986; PhD, U. Minn., 1995. Asst. prof. psychology Westbrook Coll. campus U. New Eng., Portland, Maine, 1994—. Contbr. short story: Swimming with Horses (Loft-McKnight award for fiction 1992-93). Mem. APA, Soc. for Rsch. in Child Devel. Roman Catholic. Avocations: exercise, reading, stamp collecting. Home: 9 Phillips Rd Falmouth ME 04105 Office: U New Eng Westbrook Coll campus 716 Stevens Ave Portland ME 04103-2693

HATFIELD, CHRISTIAN ANDREW, lawyer; b. Madison, Wis., June 6, 1965; s. Philip Mitchell and Julie Ann (Stockwell) H. BA, Reed Coll., 1990; MA LS, St. John's Coll., 1991; JD cum laude, Vt. Law Sch., 1994. Bar: Mass. 1995, U.S. Dist. Ct. Mass. 1996, U.S. Ct. Appeals (1st cir.) 1997, N.Mex. 1998, U.S. Dist. Ct. N.Mex. 1998, U.S. Ct. Appeals (10th cir.) 1999. Pvt. practice Boston, 1995-97; asst. atty. gen. Office of Atty. Gen., Boston, 1997-98; atty. Comeau, Maldegen, Templeman, Indall LLP, Santa Fe, 1998—; lt. gov. law student div. ABA, 1992-93. With U.S. Army, 1983-84. Home: 1753B Camino Corrales Santa Fe NM 87501

HATFIELD, ELAINE CATHERINE, psychology educator; b. Detroit, Oct. 22, 1937; d. Charles E. and Eileen (Kalahar) H.; m. Richard L. Rapson, June 15, 1982. BA, U. Mich., 1959; PhD, Stanford U., 1963. Asst. prof. U. Minn., Mpls., 1963-64, assoc. prof., 1964-66; asso. prof. U. Rochester, 1966-68, U. Wis., Madison, 1968-69; prof. U. Wis., 1969-81; now prof. U. Hawaii, Honolulu; chmn. dept. psychology U. Hawaii, 1981-83. Author: Equity: Theory and Research, 1978, Mirror, Mirror: The Importance of Looks in Everyday Life, 1986, Psychology of Emotions, 1991, Love, Sex and Intimacy, 1993, Emotional Contagion, 1994, Love and Sex: Cross-cultural Perspectives, 1996; contbr. articles to profl. jours. Recipient Disting. Scientist award Soc. Exptl. Social Psychology, 1993. Fellow APA; mem. Soc. Sci. Study of Sex (pres., Disting. Scientist award 1996, Alfred Kinsey award 1998). Home: 3334 Anoai Pl Honolulu HI 96822-1418 Office: U Hawaii 2430 Campus Rd Honolulu HI 96822-2216

HATFIELD, JACK KENTON, lawyer, accountant; b. Medford, Okla., Jan. 26, 1922; s. Loate L. and Cora (Walsh) H.; m. D. Ann Keltner, Dec. 5, 1943 (dec. Sept. 1988); children: Susan Kathryn Hatfield Bechtold, Sally Ann Hatfield Clark; m. K. Dean Walker, Aug. 7, 1997. BS in BA, Phillips U., Enid, Okla., 1947; BA, Phillips U., 1953; LLB, Oklahoma City U., 1954, JD, 1967. Bar: Okla. 1954; CPA 1954. Pvt. practice, Enid, Okla., 1954-58; with Dept. Interior, Tulsa, 1958-77; pvt. practice, Tulsa, 1977—. Mem. ABA, Okla. Bar Assn., Tulsa Co. Bar Assn., Am. Inst. CPA's, Okla. Soc. CPA's. Club: Petroleum. Avocations: photography, tennis. Home: 4013 E 86th St Tulsa OK 74137-2609 Office: 7060 S Yale Ave Ste 601 Tulsa OK 74136-5739

HATFIELD, JAMES ALLEN, theater arts educator; b. Marion, Ind., May 1, 1953; s. Frederick Marion and Mary Josephine (Murray) H.; m. Teresa Faye House, Mar. 28, 1977; 1 child, Edward Everett. BS, Ball State U., 1974, MA, 1975; PhD, Wayne State U., 1981. Asst. prof. Oakland U., Rochester, Mich., 1978-83; assoc. prof. Jackson (Miss.) State U., 1983-86; assoc. prof., chmn. theater dept. Butler U., Indpls., 1986-90; prof., dir. theater dept. U. Tex., Tyler, 1990—; bd. dirs. Opera South, 1984-86; mem. Performance evaluation com. Miss. Arts Commn., Jackson, 1983-86; vice-chair Tex. Kennedy Ctr./Am. Coll. Theatre Festival, 1992-95, state chair, 1996-99. Dir., designer: (operas) Lost in the Stars, 1987, The Marriage of Figaro, 1988, The Merry Widow, 1989, The Great Soap Opera, 1990; (plays) My Sister in This House, 1988 (Am. Coll. Theatre Festival nomination), Another Antigone, 1991 (Am. Coll. Theatre Festival N.E. Tex. Cert. of Excellence), The Doctor in Spite of Himself, 1991, Thymus Vulgaris, 1991, Antigone, 1992, Habeas Corpus, 1992, The Norman Conquests, 1992, Getting Married, 1993, Anatol, 1993, Old Times, 1993, La Ronde, 1994, As You Like It, 1994, You Never Can Tell, 1994, Oleanna (Am. Coll. Theatre Festival Critics Choice Cert. of Excellence), 1994, Oleanna, 1995, KC/ACTF Region VI Production, Later Life, 1995 The Heiress, 1995, 3 Courtelines, 1995, Lettice & Lovage, 1995, Best of Friends, 1996, Phaedra, 1996, Octavia, 1996, Mrs. Klein, 1996, A Midsummer Night's Dream, 1997, Love Letters, Ravenscroft, 1998, The School for Wives, 1998, Love Letters, 1998, Molly Sweeney, 1999, Indiscretions, 1999; (mus. theater prodns.) Candide, 1987, Sunday in the P George, 1988, Marry Me a Little, 1989 (Am. Coll. Theatre Festival Nomination), Two by Two, 1993, Candide, 1998. State chmn. Kennedy Ctr./Am. Coll. Theatre Festival, 1996-99; bd. govs. The Assn. for Theatre in Higher Edn., 1997-99. Recipient medal of excellence in lighting Am. Coll. Theatre Festival, 1978, Outstanding Tchg. award U. Tex. Chancellor's Coun., 1993, KC/ACYF Bronze medal for excellence in theatre, 1999. Mem. AAUP, Am. Fedn. Musicians, Assn. for Theatre in Higher Edn. (governing coun.), U.S. Inst. for Theatre Tech., Ind. Theatre Assn., Speech Communication Assn., Assn. Communication Adminstrn., Soc. Stage Dirs. and Choreographers, Tex. Ednl. Theatre Assn., Am. Alliance for Theatre and Edn., South West Theatre Assn. Avocations: photography, graphic design, sailing. Office: U Tex Dept Theater Sch Visual & Performing Art 3900 University Blvd Tyler TX 75701-6622

HATFIELD, JERRY LEE, plant physiologist, biometeorologist; b. Wamego, Kans., May 1, 1949; s. Virgil H. and Elsie L. (Fischer) H.; m. Patricia JoAnne Reigle, Sept. 1, 1968; children: Mark E., Andrew J. BS, Kans. State U., 1971; MS, U. Ky., 1972; PhD, Iowa State U., 1975. Biometeorologist U. Calif., Davis, 1975-83; plant physiologist USDA-Agrl. Rsch. Svc., Lubbock, Tex., 1983-89; lab. dir. Nat. Soil Tilth Lab., USDA-Agr. Rsch. Svc., Ames, Iowa, 1989—. Editor: Biometeorology and Integrated Pest management, 1982, Limitations to Plant Root Growth, vol. 19, Advances in Soil Science, 1992, Soil Biology: Impacts on Soil Quality, Advances in Soil Science, 1993, Crops Residue Management, Advances in

Soil Science, 1994, Sustainable Agriculture Systems, 1994, Utilization of Manure as a Soil Resource, Advances in Soil Science, 1998, Innovative Weed and Soil Management, Advances in Soil Science, 1998; mem. editl. bd. Advances in Soil Sci.; contbr. over 260 articles to profl. jours. Recipient Arthur S. Fleming award for outstanding svc. to fed. govt., 1997. Fellow Soil Sci. Soc. Am., Am. Soc. Agronomy (editor jour. 1989-95, editor-in-chief 1996—), Crop Sci. Soc. Am.; mem. Am. Geophys. Union, Am. Meteorol. Soc. (chair agrl./forest com. 1980-81, agrl. and forest meteorology com. 1999—), Indian Agrometeorol. Soc. (hon.), Soil & Water Conservation Soc. (program chair 1997-98, Pres. Leadership award 1998), Phi Kappa Phi. Republican. Avocations: reading, photography, landscaping. Office: USDA Agrl Rsch Svc Nat Soil Tilth Lab 2150 Pammel Dr Ames IA 50011-4420

HATFIELD, JULIE STOCKWELL, journalist, newspaper editor; b. Detroit, Mar. 22, 1940; d. William Hume and Ruth Reed (Palmer) Stockwell; m. Philip Mitchell Hatfield, Aug. 1, 1964 (div. 1979); children—Christian Andrew, Juliana, Jason David; m. Timothy Leland, Nov. 23, 1984; stepchildren—Christian Bourso, London Chamberlain. B.A., U. Mich, 1962. Staff reporter Women's Wear Daily, NYC, 1962-64; freelance feature writer Bath-Brunswick Times, Wis. State Jour., 1964-68, Quincy Patriot Ledger, Mass., 1968-77; freelance music critic, fashion editor Boston Herald, 1977-79; fashion editor Boston Globe, 1979-95, living/arts writer, 1995-96, soc. columnist, 1996—. Author: (with others) Guide to the Thrift Shops of New England, 1982. Recipient Lulu award Men's Fashion Assn., 1985, Atrium award for Outstanding WRiting on Fashion U. Ga., 1987, 92; Nat. Endowmend Arts grantee, 1973. Episcopalian. Avocation: piano. Office: Boston Globe Newspaper PO Box 2378 Boston MA 02107-2378

HATFIELD, LEONARD FRASER, retired bishop; b. Port Greville, N.S., Can., Oct. 1, 1919; s. Otto Albert and Ada (Tower) H. BA, King's-Dalhousie U., Halifax, N.S., 1940; MA, Dalhousie U., 1943; DD (hon.), U. Kings Coll., 1956, Atlantic Sch. Theology, 1985. Ordained deacon Anglican Ch. of Can., 1942, ordained priest, 1943; priest asst. All Sts. Cathedral, Halifax, 1942-46; rector Antigonish, N.S., 1946-51; asst. sec. council social service Anglican Ch. of Can., 1951-54, gen. sec., 1955-61; rector Christ Ch., Dartmouth, N.S., 1961-71, St. John's Ch., Truro, N.S., 1971-76; canon All Sts. Cathedral, Halifax, 1969; suffragan bishop of Nova Scotia, 1976-80; bishop of N.S. Halifax, 1980-84; chmn. Diocesan Council of N.S. Synod, corp. Anglican Diocesan Ctr.; chmn. Dean and Chpt. All Sts. Cathedral; organizing sec. Primate's World Relief and Devel. Fund; mem. Council of Chs. on Justice and Corrections; founding mem. Vanier Inst. Family, Ottawa; mem. Anglican Consultative Council; various coms. World Council Chs. and Gen. Synod; convenor Primate's Task Force on Ordination of Women to Priesthood; Anglican mem. and Can. rep. Internat. Bishops' Seminar, Rome, 1980. Author: He Cares, 1958, Simon Gibbons, 1987, Sammy-The Prince, 1990, Great Fun With Organists, 1995. Former chmn. bd. govs. King's Coll.; bd. dirs. Inst. Pastoral Tng. Atlantic Sch. Theology. Address: Site 31 Box O RR 3, Parrsboro, NS Canada B0M 1S0

HATFIELD, MARK ODOM, former senator; b. Dallas, Oreg., July 12, 1922; s. Charles Dolen and Dovie (Odom) H.; m. Antoinette Kuzmanich, July 8, 1958; children: Mark, Elizabeth, Theresa, Charles. AB, Willamette U., 1943; AM, Stanford U., 1948. Instr. Willamette U., 1949, dean students, assoc. prof. polit. sci., 1950-56; mem. Oreg. Ho. of Reps., 1951-55, Oreg. Senate, 1955-57; sec. State of Oreg., 1957-59, gov., 1959-67; U.S. senator from Oreg., 1967-97; chmn. appropriations com., energy and natural resources com., rules and adminstrn. com., joint printing com., joint libr. com., select com. Indian Affairs, Republican Policy Com.; chmn. Appropriations subcom. on transp. & related agencies. Author: Not Quite So Simple, 1967, Conflict and Conscience, 1971, Between A Rock and A Hard Place, 1976; co-author: Amnesty: The Unsettled Question of Vietnam, 1976, Freeze! How You Can Help Prevent Nuclear War, 1982, The Causes of World Hunger, 1982; co-author: What About the Russians, 1984, Vice Presidents of the United States 1789-1993, 1997. Lt. (j.g.) USN, 1943-45, PTO. Recipient over 100 hon. degrees. Republican. Baptist. Office: PO Box 8639 Portland OR 97207-8639

HATFIELD, PAUL GERHART, federal judge, lawyer; b. Great Falls, Mont., Apr. 29, 1928; s. Trueman LeRoy and Grace Lenore (Gerhart) H.; m. Dorothy Ann Allen, Feb. 1, 1958 (dec. Aug. 1992); children: Kathleen Helen, Susan Ann, Paul Allen. Student, Coll. of Great Falls, 1947-50; LL.B., U. Mont., 1955. Bar: Mont. bar 1955. Assoc. firm Hoffman & Cure, Gt. Falls, Mont., 1955-56, Jardine, Stephenson, Blewett & Weaver, Gt. Falls, 1956-58, Hatfield & Hatfield, Gt. Falls, 1959-60; chief dep. county atty. Cascade County, Mont., 1959-60; dist. ct. judge 8th Jud. Dist., Mont., 1961-76; chief justice Supreme Ct. Mont., Helena, 1977-78; U.S. Senator from Mont., 1978-79; U.S. dist. judge for Dist. of Mont., Gt. Falls, 1979-96; chief judge, 1990-96, sr. judge, 1996—; Vice chmn. Pres.'s Council Coll. of Great Falls. Author standards for criminal justice, Mont. cts. Served with U.S. Army, 1951-53. Korea. Mem. Am., Mont. bar assns., Am. Judicature Soc. Roman Catholic. Office: US Dist Ct US Post Office & Cthouse PO Box 1529 Great Falls MT 59403-1529*

HATFIELD, SAMUEL FAY, JR., retired military officer, construction consultant; b. Sumter, S.C., May 6, 1945; s. Samuel Fay and Mary Louise (Geddings) H.; m. Valerie Jean Widding, Dec. 31, 1964; children: John Michael, David Andrew. BSBA, U. Nebr., 1967; MS in Indsl. Mgmt., U. N.D., 1970. Securities and life ins. lic. Commd. 2d. lt. USAF, 1967, advanced through grades to col., 1990; registered rep. Fortis Investments, Inc., Torrance, Calif., 1990-91; project mgr. B-2 Div. Northrop Grumman Corp., Pico Rivera, Calif., 1991-94; sales mgr. Primerica Fin. Svcs., Longmont, Colo., 1994—; owner Java House, Louisville, Colo., 1995-97; substitute tchr. Dist. 50 Adams County, Westminister, Colo., 1996-97, St. Vrain Valley Sch. Dist., Longmont, Colo., 1996-98, Clark County Sch. Dist., Las Vegas, Nev., 1998-99; cons. PCI Group of Nev., Las Vegas, 1999—. Chmn., deacon Parkwood Bapt. Ch., Fairfax, Va., 1979; deacon 1st Bapt. Ch. Palos Verdes, Calif. 1987; v.p. Baywatch Home Owners Assn., San Pedro, Calif., 1992; assoc. pastor Front Range Cmty. Ch., Superior, Colo., 1995-98, clk., 1996-98; intern The Ch. at Green Valley Ranch, Henderson, Nev., 1998—. Mem. Nat. Contract Mgmt. Assn., Village Square Mchts. Assn. (treas. 1996-97). Republican. Avocations: racquetball, tennis, reading, hiking, golf. Home: 503 Elkhurst Pl Henderson NV 89012-4569

HATFIELD, STEVEN MICHAEL, data processing executive; b. Sept. 3, 1952. BS in Computer Info. Systems, Regis U., 1994, MS in Mgmt., 1996. Sr. systems analyst IBM, Boulder, Colo.; mgr. telecomms. DynCorp, Golden, Colo.; project mgr. (y2k) Analysts Internat., Denver, Colo. E-mail: shatfie@uswest.com. Office: Analysts Internat 5864 N Orchard Creek Cir Boulder CO 80301-5834

HATFIELD, SUSAN WILLIAMS, school psychologist, psychologist, consultant; b. Sioux City, Iowa, June 12, 1932; d. Keith Eugene Strange and Victorine Jessie (Williams) Strange Bridenbaugh; m. Robert Eugene Hatfield, Aug. 16, 1958 (div. Sept. 1973); children: Heidi Hatfield Fagerquist, Rex Hatfield. Student, Smith Coll., 1950-52; BA, U. N.Mex., 1955, MA, 1958; postgrad., U. Minn., 1974; EdD, U. S.D., 1976. Cert. sch. psychologist, Iowa. Camp swimming counselor Sioux Trails for Girl Scout Camp, Sioux City, 1951; grad. asst. in psychology U. N.Mex., Albuquerque, 1955-56; dist. dir. Sioux Trails Girl Scout Coun., Sioux City, 1958; part owner, mgr. Hatfield Apt. Bldg., Sioux City, 1958-68; psychologist Goodwill Industries, Sioux City, 1961-62; census taker, office worker U.S. Census Bur., Sioux City, 1970; life ins. agt. Bob Hatfield Ins. Co., Sioux City, 1970-73; psychologist Dr. Richard Satterfield, Sioux City, 1973-76; rsch. asst. U. S.D., Vermillion, 1974-76; pvt. practice Sioux City, 1976—; sch. psychologist Western Hills Area Edn. Agy., Sioux City, 1976-99; ret., 1999; cons. to lawyer, Sioux City, 1982; cons., psychologist Goodwill Industries, Sioux City, 1990-94, Vocat. Rehab. Dept., Sioux City, 1993—; workshop presenter U. N.Mex., Albuquerque, 1980; participant/dir. rsch. projects in reading, written lang., math. for sch. children. Contbr. papers to profl. jours. Mem. Jr. League, Sioux City, 1959-66, Found. Bd. for Family Planning, 1988—, Planned Parenthood of Greater Iowa, 1968—, St. Luke's Hosp. Aux., 1996—, PEO, Sioux City, 1955-73; bd. dirs. Sioux Trails Girl Scout Coun., Sioux City, 1959-62; vol., case aide for returnees from mental health instns. ARC, Sioux City, 1961-66; bd. dirs., v.p., regional rep. pres. Planned Parenthood, Sioux City, 1968-74, 84-97; bd. dirs., pres. Siouxland Drug Abuse Coun., Sioux City, 1974; Sunday sch. tchr. 1st Congl. Ch., Sioux City, 1964-68; leader Brownie troop, Girl Scout troop, Cub Scout troop, 1966-70; mem., chairperson Iowans for Med. Control of Abortion, Sioux City, 1968-73; mem., workshop presenter Women's Polit. Caucus, Sioux City, 1973-80; com. mem. for youth seminar Morgningside Coll., Sioux City, 1973; mem., precinct chairperson, del. Dem. Party, Sioux City, 1980-94. Mem. NOW, Nat. Assn. for Sch. Psychologists, Portfolio Club. Democrat. Unitarian. Avocations: swimming, reading, traveling, fine arts, cross country skiing. Home and Office: 17 Congress Ave Sioux City IA 51104-4053

HATFIELD, WILLIAM KEITH, minister; b. Detroit, Dec. 26, 1951; s. William Grant and Marquita (Ratliff) H.; m. Sharon Jean, Aug. 26, 1972; children: Sarah, Elisabeth, Matthew, Charity, Jonathan, Joshua. BA, Bapt. Bible Coll., 1976. Ordained to ministry Beacon Bapt. Ch., 1976. Assoc. pastor Brown Ave. Bapt. Ch., Springfield, Mo., 1974-76; pastor Bible Bapt. Ch., South Haven, Mich., 1976-79, Golden Gate Bapt. Ch., Tulsa, 1979-85, Charity Bapt. Ch., Tulsa, 1985—; prof. O.T. Survey Mingo Bible Inst., 1987—; mem. bd. advisors Moral Majority, Tulsa, 1981—; pres. Dynamics for Living, Inc. Author: Dynamics for Living, A Heart for God, When God Empties You; columnist Tulsa Tribune, 1983—; host Dynamics for Living radio program; host TV show Dynamics for Living, 1982-83, 85—. Spokesman Oklahomans for Life, 1983-85, Tulsans for Life, 1983-85. Republican. Home: PO Box 691050 Tulsa OK 74169-1050 Office: Charity Bapt Ch PO Box 691050 Tulsa OK 74169-1050 *Never view God through your circumstances, view your circumstances through God.*

HATGIL, PAUL PETER, artist, sculptor, educator; b. Manchester, N.H., Feb. 18, 1921; s. Peter and Katina (Karkadou) H.; m. Katherine Haritos. BS, Mass. Coll. of Art, 1950; MFA, Columbia U., 1951. Instr. art U. Tex., Austin, 1951-54, asst. prof., 1954-56, assoc. prof., 1956-67, prof., 1967-85, prof. emeritus, 1985—, design curator Archer M. Huntington Gallery Mus., 1965-68; vis. instr. Columbia U. (summer) 1958; designed and installed Tex. Pavilion Exhbn., N.Y. World's Fair; ccord. for Gov. John Connolly's Exhbn. of Art and Conf. on the Arts; aux. edn. officer Dist. 8 U.S. Coast Guard, 1965-74. Author: Establishing Residency in Greece, 1988, (autobiography) Apostolos, The Immigrant's Son, 1990; (book) Contemporary Encaustic Painting, 1994; contbr. numerous articles and papers to profl. jours.Internat. and Nat. exhbns. include: 42 annual faculty exhbns. U. Tex., Austin, 2d, 3d, 4th Internat. Invitational Exhbn. of Ceramic Art Smithsonian Mus., Washington, 2d, 3d and 7th Nat. Decorative Arts Exhbns., Wichita, Kans., Internat. Invitational Exhbn. of Ceramic Art Iowa State U., Ceder Rapids; in numerous nat. and internat. mus. and private collections including St. Paul's Luth. Ch., U. Tex. Bus. Administrn. Bldg., Huston Tillotson Coll., Seguin Luth. Coll., U. Tex. Faculty Club, U. Tex. Coll. Fine Arts, Woodlands Corp., Houston, Zapata Corp., Houston, Warren Cravens Corp., Houston, U.S. Mil. Ins. Corp., Harry Litwin Industries, Wichita, Kans., Coopers & Lybrand Corp., Houston, Cesar Design Inc., Cleve., Abilne (Tex.) 1st Nat. Bank, Tchr. Retirement Sys., Austin, FAA, Panama C.Z. With USAAF, 1943-45, PTO. Recipient Estelle Grey Meml. prize in art, Margaret Flowers prize in art, White Mus., San Antonio, Wolff and Marx prize in art, Dallas Mus. of Fine Arts; purchase prizes Dallas Mus. of Art, Laguan Gloria Mus. Austin; grantee U. Tex. Mem. Am. Hellenic Ednl. and Progressive Assn. (pres. Stephen F. Austin chpt. 312), , Am. Legion. Home: 2203 Onion Creek Pky Unit 7 Austin TX 78747-1648

HATHAWAY, CARL EMIL, investment management company executive; b. Boston, Aug. 12, 1933; s. Carl Barbour and Tekla (Neumaier) H.; m. Gail Humphries Oglee, Dec. 6, 1958 (div. Oct. 23, 1996); children: Brian Kent, Carl Nichols, Andrew Oglee; m. Martha Livingston, Jan. 1, 1999. B.A., Harvard U., 1955; M.B.A., Cornell U., 1959. With Morgan Guaranty Trust Co. N.Y., 1959-81, sr. v.p. pension investments, vice chmn. trust and investments dept., 1969-81; pres. Hathaway & Assocs. Ltd. (instl. investment mgmt.), Rowayton, Conn., 1981—, Hathaway Ptnrs., Inc., Rowayton, Conn., 1994—; corp. dir. Pacer Tech., Fountainhead Water. Served to lt. (j.g.) USNR, 1955-57. Clubs: Links (N.Y.C.), Blind Brook (Purchase, N.Y.), Tokeneke (Darien, Conn.), Harvard (Fairfield County, Conn.), Eastward Ho Country (Chatham, Mass.). Home: 526 Flax Hill Rd Norwalk CT 06854-2317 Office: Hathaway & Assocs Ltd Rowayton Ave Norwalk CT 06853

HATHAWAY, CARMRID GLASTON, sports association executive, real estate investor; b. Tarboro, N.C., Feb. 8, 1922; s. Carmrid Glaston and Estelle (Pittman) H.; m. Margaret Tryphena Deese (dec. Oct. 7, 1988), June 20, 1944; children: Pletcha Joyce, Carmrid Glaston III; m. Klara Dadmanesh, Sept. 30, 1994. Student, George Washington U., 1941-42, Naval Air Tng. Ctr., 1944; BS in Mil. Sci. and Bus. Adminstrn., U. Md., 1971. Lic. pilot, real estate, Md. Enlisted USN, 1942, advanced through grades to capt., 1965, ret., 1975; comdg. officer naval air sta. USN, Grosse Ile, Mich., 1967-69; comdg. officer naval tng. ctr. USN, Washington, 1972-75; pres. Harness Racing Inc., Suitland, Md., 1975—; chmn. bd. dirs. Activities Investments, Inc., Washington, Pre-Capital Specialties, Washington; adv. com. Md. Standardbred Race Fund; mem. Md. Racing Commn., 1984-85. Adv. com. Md. Racing Commn., 1984-85; mem. Md. Standard Bred Race Fund, 1984-85. Mem. Ret. Officers Assn., U.S. Trotting Assn., Standard Bred Breeders Md. (bd. dirs. 1980-), Standardbred Race Fund (adv. com), Md. Harness Horseman's Assn. (bd. dirs. 1979-), Cloverleaf Standard Bred Owners Assn., U. Md. Alumni Assn. Internat. Baptist. Club: Commd. Officers (Andrews AFB, Md. and Washington D.C.). Home: 205 Yoakum Pkwy Apt 1625 Alexandria VA 22304-3842 Office: Activities Investments Inc 3352 Upland Ter NW Washington DC 20015-2445

HATHAWAY, CHARLES E., academic administrator. BS in Physics, Tex. A&M U., 1958; PhD in Physics, U. Okla., 1965. Mem. faculty dept. physics Kans. State U., Little Rock, 1965-81; dept. head Kans. State U., 1971-81; dean Coll. Sci. and Engrng. U. Tex., San Antonio, 1981-86; v.p. acad. affairs Wright State U., 1986-93; chancellor U. Ark., Little Rock, 1993—. Founder, sr. editor Met. Univs.: An Internat. Forum. Mem. Ark. Sci. and Tech. Authority, 1995—. Woodrow Wilson fellow U. Okla. Mem. Ark. Sci. and Tech. Authority (chair). Office: U Ark Little Rock Office of Chancellor 2801 S University Ave Little Rock AR 72204-1000

HATHAWAY, DAVID ROGER, physician, medical educator, scientist; b. Lafayette, Ind., Jan. 8, 1948; s. Ralph Roger Hathaway and Marjorie Alice Friend; m. Elaine Mary Green, Aug. 3, 1974; children: Julia E., Alison S. AB, Ind. U., 1970, MD, 1975. Diplomate Am. Bd. Internal Medicine, Cardiovascular Diseases. Clin. asst. NHLBI/NIH, Bethesda, Md., 1977-79; intern Ind. U. Med. Ctr., Indpls., 1975-76, resident, 1976-77, chief resident, 1979-80, from asst. prof. to assoc. prof., 1980-86, prof., 1986-95, chief cardiovascular divsn., 1990-95, dir. Krannert Inst. Cardiology, 1990-95; exec. dir. cardiovasc. rsch. Bristol-Myers Squibb Pharm. Rsch. Inst., Princeton, N.J., 1995-96; v.p. Cardiovascular Drug Discovery Bristol-Myers Squibb Pharm. Rsch. Inst., Princeton, 1996—. Lt. comdr. USPHS, 1977-79. Fellow Am. Coll. Cardiology; mem. Am. Fedn. for Clin. Rsch. (pres. 1987-88), Am. Soc. for Clin. Investigation, Assn. Am. Physicians (sec. 1991-96, councillor 1996—), Assn. Univ. Cardiologists, Phi Beta Kappa, Alpha Omega Alpha. Achievements include patents for composition and method for delivery of drugs, method for preventing restenosis following reconfiguration of body vessels, hemostatic puncture closure device, method and apparatus for intravascular drug delivery. *

HATHAWAY, FRED WILLIAM, lawyer; b. Lewiston, Maine, Sept. 18, 1956; s. William Dodd and Mary Lee (Bird) H.; m. Lee Broadfoot, June 11, 1988; children: William Broadfoot, Benjamin Dodd. BA, Harvard U., 1979; JD, U. Maine, 1985. Bar: Maine 1985, D.C. 1986, U.S. Patent Office 1986, Virginia 1999. Assoc. Robbins & Laramie, Washington, 1985-90, Venable, Baetjer, Howard & Civiletti, LLP, Washington, 1990-95, Burns, Doane, Swecker & Mathis, LLP, Alexandria, Va., 1995—; adj. prof. Georgetown U. Law Ctr., 1998—. Vol. Community Children's Ministry, 1993-96. Mem. ABA (chair various coms., sub.-coms). Episcopalian. Avocations: rowing, basketball, carpentry. Office: Burns Doane Swecker & Mathis LLP 1737 King St Ste 500 Alexandria VA 22314-2756

HATHAWAY, LOLINE, zoo and botanic park curator; b. Whittier, Calif., June 27, 1937; d. Richard Franklin and F. Nadine (Applegate) H.; 1 child, Patrick Paul Kundtz. BA, Reed Coll., Portland, Oreg., 1959; PhD, Washington U., St. Louis, 1969. Instr. St. Louis U., 1966-68; curator of edn. Chgo. Zool. Soc., Brookfield, Ill., 1968-71; cons. on terrestrial biology Ryckman, Edgerly, Tomlinson & Assocs., St. Louis, 1972-75; marina mgr. Lake Piru (Calif.) Recreation Area, 1976-77; curator, dir. Navajo Nation Zool. and Botanical Park, Window Rock, Ariz., 1983—. Vice chmn., chmn. City of Santa Fe Springs (Calif.) Traffic Commn., 1979-83; mem. Navajo Estates Vol. Fire Dept., Yah-ta-hey, N.Mex., 1984-85; bd. dirs. Hathaway Ranch Mus., Santa Fe Springs, 1986-93, Gallup Cmty. Concerts Assn., 1994—; leader 4-H Club, 1989—; master gardener, 1997—. Mem. AAAS (vice chmn. S.W.-Rocky Mountain div. sci. edn. sect. 1983-84, chmn. 1984-85), AAUW (scholarship com. Gallup 1992—, bd. govs. 1997—), Am. Assn. Zool. Parks and Aquariums, Am. Assn. Bot. Gardens and and Arboretums, Assn. Living. Hist. Farms and Agr. Mus., Am. Inst. Biol. Scis., Sierra Club (Ozarks chpt. founder, bd. dirs., sec. Gt. Lakes chpt. 1963-72). Democrat. Home: 27 S LaChee PO Box 4172 Yatahey NM 87375-4172 Office: Navajo Nat Zool and Bot Pk PO Box 9000 Window Rock AZ 86515-9000

HATHAWAY, MICHAEL JERRY, personal care assistant, editor, publisher; b. El Paso, Tex., Sept. 20, 1961; s. Jerry Robert and Elsie Jane (Smith) H. Grad. high sch., St. John H.S., 1980. Pub. and editor Chiron Rev. Lit. Mag., St. John, Kans., 1982—; typesetter Great Bend (Kans.) Tribune, 1981-94, editor Localife, 1995; supported living asst. Sunflower Diversified Svcs., Great Bend, 1996-98. Author: (poetry) Inconspicuous, 1988, Excerpt, 1989, Stumbling Into Light, 1993, Ratboy, Etc., 1994. Chmn. Poetry Rendezvous, Great Bend, 1988-94; v.p. Great Plains Writers Assn., 1995, 97. Avocations: music, cats, piano, art. Home and Office: 702 N Prairie St Saint John KS 67576-1516

HATHAWAY, RICHARD DEAN, language professional, educator; b. Chillicothe, Ohio, Aug. 8, 1927; s. Dale and Edith (Hart) H.; m. Viola Hale, Apr. 16, 1978; children by previous marriage: Linda Hathaway Ellis, Bruce. AB summa cum laude, Oberlin Coll., 1949; AM, Harvard U., 1952; PhD, Western Res. U., 1964. Instr. English Oberlin Jr. H.S., 1949-50; chief interviewer U.S. Bur. of Census, Boston, 1952-53; exec. sec. New Eng. Fellowship of Reconciliation, Boston, 1953-55; instr. in English, Rensselaer Poly. Inst., Troy, N.Y., 1957-62; from asst. prof. to assoc. prof. SUNY, New Paltz, 1962-69; prof. SUNY, 1970—; assoc. prof. Millsaps Coll., Jackson, Miss., 1965-66. Author: Sylvester Judd's New England, 1981, The Henry James Scholar's Guide to Web Sites, 1997; (computer software) Text: A Program About Literature, 1990; contbr. articles to profl. jours. Chair legis. com. SCLC Poor People's Campaign, 1968. Served with USNR, 1945-46. Mem. MLA. Mem. Religious Soc. of Friends. Home: 11 Crescent Ln New Paltz NY 12561-2809 Office: SUNY New Paltz English Dept New Paltz NY 12561

HATHAWAY, ROBERT LAWTON, Romance languages educator; b. Fall River, Mass., Jan. 20, 1932; s. Wallace C. and Helen (Lawton) H.; m. Phyllis Ann Allen, July 21, 1969; stepchildren—Lisa P. Gustafson, Jeffrey H. Patterson. B.A., Williams Coll., 1953; M.S., Georgetown U., 1957; M.A., Brown U., 1963, Ph.D., 1969. Mem. faculty Colgate U., Hamilton, N.Y., 1964—; Drake prof. humanities Colgate U., 1989-94, rsch. prof. Spanish lit., 1994-97, emeritus prof., 1997—. Author: Love in the Early Spanish Theatre, 1975, Not Necessarily Cervantes, 1995; editor: The Villancicos from the Cancionero of Pedro Jimenez de Urrea (Logrono 1513), 1976, Jimenez de Urrea, Penitencia de amor (Burgos 1514), 1990, Granada Study Group, 1970, 75, 79, 83. Served with U.S. Army, 1953-55. NEH fellow-in-residence Harvard U., 1976-77. Mem. Cervantes Soc. Am., Assn. de Cervantistas. Office: Colgate U 215 Lawrence Hall Hamilton NY 13346-1398

HATHAWAY, RUTH ANN, chemist; b. Sidney, Ohio, Dec. 6, 1956; d. Earl Eugene and Mary Helen (Smith) Schmidt; m. Bruce Alan Hathaway, May 16, 1981. BS in Sci., Huntington Coll., 1979; postgrad., Purdue U., 1979-80. Instr. Harvey Mudd Coll., Claremont, Calif., 1981-82; head chemist So. Indsl. Products, Cape Girardeau, Mo., 1983-86; cons. Cape Girardeau, 1987-89; alterationist Patricks Cleaner, Cape Girardeau, 1988-89; lab. dir. Delta-Y Electric Co., Sedgewickville, Mo., 1989-91; quality control/quality assurance dir. Environ. Analysis South, Cape Girardeau, 1991-95; cons. Hathaway Cons., Cape Girardeau, 1995—. Editor: Safety Considerations in Microscale Lab, 1991; contbr. articles to profl. jours. Mem. exec. bd. dirs. NAACP, Cape Girardeau, 1986—; chmn. disaster com. ARC, Cape Girardeau, 1986-91; dir. S.E. Mo. Regional Sci. Fair, 1992—. Mem. Am. Chem. Soc. (divsn. environ. chem. health and safety 1989-98, local sect. nat. chemistry week coord., 1988—), Am. Inst. Chemists, Internat. Assn. Water Quality, S.E. Mo. Local Emergency Planning Com. (chmn. 1987-98). Republican. Home and Office: 1810 Georgia St Cape Girardeau MO 63701-3816

HATHAWAY, STANLEY KNAPP, lawyer; b. Osceola, Nebr., July 19, 1924; s. Franklin E. and Velma Clara (Holbrook) H.; m. Roberta Louise Harley, Nov. 26, 1948; children—Susan Garrett, Sandra D'Amico. A.B., U. Nebr., 1948, LL.B., 1950; LL.D., U. Wyo., 1975. Bar: Nebr. 1950, Wyo., 1950, U.S. Dist. Ct. Wyo., Nebr., Mont. 1950, U.S. Supreme Ct. 1964. Sole practice, Torrington, Wyo., 1950-66; gov. Wyo., 1967-75; assoc. Hathaway, Speight & Kunz, Cheyenne, Wyo., 1975—; dir. Apache Corp., Houston; county atty. Goshen County (Wyo.), 1955-62; gov. State of Wyo., 1967-75; sec. U.S. Dept. Interior, 1975. Served with USAAF, 1943-45. Decorated Air medals with 5 clusters. Mem. ABA, Wyo. State Bar Assn. Republican. United Episcopalian. Clubs: Masons (Cheyenne); Shriners (Rawlins, Wyo.). Office: Hathaway Speight & Kunz 2515 Warren Ave Cheyenne WY 82001-3113

HATHAWAY, WILLIAM DODD, federal agency administrator; b. Cambridge, Mass., Feb. 21, 1924; s. James Franklin and Charlotte Ann H.; m. Mary Lee Bird, Aug. 21, 1945; children: Susan Louise Boydston, Fred William. AB, Harvard U., 1949, JD, 1953; LLD (hon.), St. Joseph Coll., Alfred, Maine, 1973, U. Maine, 1974, St. Francis Coll., Biddeford, Maine, 1975, Colby Coll., 1976. Bar: Mass. 1953, Maine 1954, U.S. Dist. Ct. Maine 1954, U.S. Supreme Ct. 1965, D.C. 1980. Pvt. practice Lewiston, Maine, 1953-65; asst. county atty. Androscoggin County, Auburn, Maine, 1955-57; hearing examiner liquor commn. State of Maine, Augusta, 1957-61; mem. U.S. Ho. of Reps., Washington, 1965-72, U.S. Senate, Washington, 1973-79; atty. Patton, Boggs & Blow, Washington, 1979-90; commr. FMC, Washington, 1990-96, chmn., 1993-96; ret., 1996. Capt. USAF, 1942-46, ETO. Decorated Air medal, Purple Heart, Presdl. citation, Prisoner of War medal. Mem. ABA, Mass. Bar Assn., Maine Bar Assn., D.C. Bar Assn., Former Mems. in Congress (pres. 1991-92), Pathways Inc. (Auburn). Democrat. Episcopalian. Avocations: golf. Home: 6707 Wemberly Way Mc Lean VA 22101-1529*

HATHCOCK, JOHN EDWARD, vocalist; b. Memphis, Sept. 6, 1955. BA in Psychology, Memphis State U., (now U. Memphis), 1986; studied with Dr. David Williams, U. Memphis, 1992-97; studied with Ethel Maxwell, 1982-98. Singer, performer, composer opera and sacred classical music, vocal coach, 1999—; pres. Position Prodns., 1988-90; pres., founder Soaring Spirit Music, 1996—. Author: Seasons of Wonder, 1995; author poems; patentee in field; exec. prodr., vocal performer Grace: The Eternal Song. Mem. Bellevue Choir, 1991-92, Memphis Vocal Arts Ensemble, 1993, The Heritage Found. Recipient Mr. Wheelchair Am. award, 1990, Man of Yr. award Happi Internat. Talent, Trailblazer award City of Memphis, 1990. Mem. Gospel Music Assn. (profl.), Beethoven Club (dir. pub. rels. 1993), Internat. Platform Assn., Heritage Found., Internat. Soc. Poets. Baptist. Home: 4285 Powell Ave Memphis TN 38122-2634

HATHEWAY, ALSON EARLE, mechanical engineer; b. Long Beach, Calif., Nov. 15, 1935; s. Earle Miller and Carla (Barnhart) H.; m. Robin Lewis, Aug. 24, 1968; children: Jason Teale, Teale. BSME, U. Calif., Berkeley, 1959. Registered profl. engr., Calif. Engr. Boeing Aerospace Co., Seattle, 1959-60, Ford Aerospace Co., Newport Beach, Calif., 1960-66; mgr. Xerox Corp., Pasadena, Calif., 1966-72, Hughes Aircraft Co., Culver City, Calif., 1972-76, Gould Inc., El Monte, Calif., 1976-79; pres. Alson E. Hatheway Inc., Pasadena, 1979—; instr. U. La Verne, Calif., 1989—, indsl. seminars in optomechanics, 1986—. Editor: Procs. Structural Mechanics of Optical Systems II, 1987, Procs. Precision Instrument Design, 1989, Procs. Optomechanical and Precision Instrument Design, 1995, 97, Procs. Actuator Technology and Applications, 1996, 98; contbr. articles to profl. jours. Fellow Soc. Photo-Optical Instrumentation Engrs. (instr. 1987—, conf. chmn. 1987, 89, 91, 94, 96, 97, 98, 99, program chmn. 1990, 91, 96); mem. AIAA (sr., chmn. San Gabriel Valley sect. 1992-93), ASME, Am. Soc. Precision Engrs., Calif. Soc. Profl. Engrs. (treas. 1965-66), Optical Soc. So. Calif. (pres. 1986-87), Opto-Mech. Engrng. and Precision Instrument Design

Working Group (chmn. 1992—), Assn. Old Crows. Achievements include patents on optical scanner, precision transducer, micrometer tip cushion, and optical calibration target; findings on Optical Analog and optical constraint equations; development of Angstrom and Rubicon activators and Hector calibration standard. Home: 419 S Meridith Ave Pasadena CA 91106-3512 Office: 595 E Colorado Blvd Ste 400 Pasadena CA 91101-2018

HATHEWAY, JOHN HARRIS, advertising agency executive; b. Waterbury, Conn., Aug. 9, 1926; s. Fred Whipple and Louise (Wood) H.; m. Patricia Mary Flaherty, Sept. 24, 1955; children: John Harris, Geoffrey Mills, Sara Wood. AB, Dartmouth Coll., 1948; MBA, Amos Tuck, 1950. With Young and Rubicam Inc., N.Y.C., 1950-89, sr. v.p., mgmt. supr., 1968-74, sr. v.p., group dir., 1974-83, exec. v.p., group dir., 1983-87, exec. v.p., western regional dir., 1987-89, also dir.; bd. overseers Hanover Inn, N.H., 1968-78, 94—. Mem. editl. bd. Dartmouth Life, 1991—. Mem. Council of Alumni Dartmouth, 1968-90, mem. alumni awards com., 1982-86, chmn., 1986-90, chmn. pub affairs adv. com., 1990—; pres. Dartmouth Class 1948, 1994-98; assembly of overseers Dartmouth-Hitchcock Med. Ctr., 1996—; bd. dirs. Chappaqua Summer Sch. Program, Horace Greeley Ednl. Fund, 1978-85, Upper Valley Hostel, 1999—; dir. Friends of Hopkins and Hood, 1990—; mem. Diocesan Mission Com.; mem. com. Parents' Fund, U. Vt., 1981-86. Served with AUS, 1945-46. Recipient Alumni award Dartmouth Coll., 1980. Mem. Dartmouth Coll. of N.Y. Alumni Assn. (pres. 1965-66, bd. dirs. 1958-64, 67-70, 72-87), Waccabuc Country Club, Manchester (Vt.) Country Club, Hanover Country Club, Dartmouth Club Upper Valley (dir. 1994—), Phi Beta Kappa. Episcopalian (vestryman, warden). Home: 10 Buell St Hanover NH 03755-2416 Office: Young and Rubicam Inc 285 Madison Ave New York NY 10017-6486

HATHORNE, GAYLE GENE, musician, genealogical educator, writer; b. Concordia, Kans., Sept. 3, 1953; d. Richard and R. Virginia (Huscher) Hathorne; 1 child, Amanda Kimberly. BMusic, Manhattan Sch. Music, N.Y.C., 1976; Artist's Diploma, Karajan Akademie, Berlin Philharm. Orch., 1980; student, Mars Hill (N.C.) Coll., 1989-90, Blue Ridge C.C., Flat Rock, N.C., 1991, 92. Backstage hornplayer Bayreuth (Germany) Festival, 1977; 3d/1st solo hornist Stadt. Orch., Solingen, Germany, 1980-88; part-time faculty Blue Ridge C.C., 1989-92, genealogy instr., 1999—; pvt. horn tchr., Hendersonville, 1989—; substitute tchr. music and German, Henderson County Pub. Schs., 1988—. Sr. editor Tarheel Tattler, 1994-96, River Ramblings, 1994-96; editor Kuykendall Gazette, 1996-97; performer on CDs/cassettes. Nat. Fedn. Music Clubs nat. scholar, 1971. Mem. DAR (state pub. rels. N.C. Soc. 1997-99, organizing regent Abraham Kuykendall chpt. 1996), Children of Am. Revolution (organizing sr. pres. French Broad River Soc. 1992, state libr. 1996-98). Democrat. Avocations: genealogical research, photography, travel, writing, listening to opera. Home: 346 Stoney Mountain Rd Hendersonville NC 28791-2085

HATLEN, BURTON NORVAL, English educator; b. Santa Barbara, Calif., Apr. 9, 1936; s. Julius Herbert and Lillie (Torvend) H.; m. Barbara Karlson, Sept. 20, 1961 (div. Nov. 1982); children: Julia, Inger; m. Virginia Nees, Nov. 10, 1983. BA, U. Calif., Berkeley, 1958; MA, Columbia U., 1959, Harvard U., 1961; PhD, U. Calif., Davis, 1972. Asst. prof. English King Coll., Bristol, Tenn., 1961-62; instr. U. Cin., 1962-65; asst. prof. U. Maine, Orono, 1967-72, assoc. prof., 1972-81, prof., 1981—, chmn. dept. English, 1985-88; interim dean Coll. Arts and Humanities, 1996-97; dir. Nat. Poetry Found. Author: George Oppen: Man and Poet, 1981, (poems) I Wanted To Tell You, 1988; editor Sagetrieb, 1981—. Mem. MLA, Lang. and Thinking Inst. (assoc.). Democrat. Office: U of Maine Dept Of English Orono ME 04469

HATLEY-BRICKEY, LAEL ANN, university administrator; b. Pullman, Wash., Sept. 18, 1956; d. James Monroe and Betty Ann (Gillespie) Hatley; m. Randolph Avery Brickey Jr., Oct. 1, 1977; 1 child, James Randolph; 1 stepchild, Brandy. Student, Spokane Community Coll., 1975-76; BA, Wash. State U., 1994. With The Crescent, Spokane, Wash., 1976-77, Cowles Pub., Spokane, 1977, Keith's Music, Spokane, 1977-78, Myklebust's Clothing, Pullman, Wash., 1978, Wash. State U. Instructional Media Svc., Pullman, summer 1978; office asst. dept. parking svcs. Wash. State U., Pullman, 1978-82, telephone operator, 1982-84, program asst., 1984-87, program mgr. telecommunications, 1987-91, office ops. supr., 1991-97; owner small bus. ins. agy. Pullman; owner Melalueca, 1997—. V.p. Pullman Meml. Hosp. Found., 1986-88; sec. Ewartsville Grange, 1996—. Mem. NAFE, Grange (sec. 1998—), Jobs Daus., Xi Beta Epsilon (treas. 1987-88, sec. 1989-90, v.p. 1990-91). Avocations: creative writing, handwork, antiques, photography. Home: 3201 Wawawai Pullman Rd Pullman WA 99163-8640

HATSOPOULOS, GEORGE NICHOLAS, mechanical engineer, thermodynamicist, educator; b. Athens, Greece, Jan. 7, 1927; came to U.S., 1948, naturalized, 1954; s. Nicholas and Maria (Platsis) Hatzopoulos; m. Daphne Phylactopoulos, June 14, 1959; children: Nicholas, Marina. Student, Nat. Tech. U., Athens, 1945-47; BS, MS, MIT, 1949, ME, 1954, ScD, 1956; ScD (hon.), N.J. Inst. Tech., 1982; DHL, U. Lowell, 1991; DSc (hon.), N.J. Inst. Tech., 1982; D degree (hon.), Adelphi U., 1994. Instr. MIT, 1954-56, asst. prof. mech. engring., 1956-58, assoc. prof., 1959-63, sr. lectr. in mech. engring., 1963-90; mem. Corp. of MIT, Cambridge, 1992—; founder, CEO, chmn. bd. dirs. Thermo Electron Corp., Waltham, Mass., 1956—; mem. adv. bd. program tech. and econ. policy Kennedy Sch. Govt. Harvard U.; mem. Mass. Gov. William F. Weld's adv. coun. on econ. growth and tech., 1991-94, adv. coun. The Internat. Ctr. in N.Y., Inc., 1991—, exec. com. Nat. Bur. Econ. Rsch., 1989—; mem. vis. com. dept. mech. engring. MIT; mem. adv. com. Export Import Bank of U.S., 1993-94. Author: Principles of General Thermodynamics, 1965, Thermionic Energy Conversion, vol. 1, 1973, vol. 2, 1979; contbr. numerous articles to profl. jours. Trustee Maliotis Found., 1983—, Ctr. for Policy Rsch., Am. Coun. for Capital Formation, Congl. Econ. Leadership Inst., 1986-96; dir. NRC Bd. on Sci. Tech., Econ. Policy, 1991—; mem. Am. Bus. Conf., 1994—; chmn. Fed. Res. Bank Boston, 1988-89; Coll. Yr. in Athens, Inc., 1970—; tech. witness numerous Senate and Congl. hearings; bd. dirs. Concord Coalition, 1992—; overseer Boston Mus. Sci., 1993—. Recipient Am. Achievement Gold Plate award, 1961, Corp. Leadership award MIT, 1980, Master Entrepreneur, Inc. Mag. award, 1989, Businessperson of the Yr. award New Eng. Bus. Mag., 1989, Inventor of the Yr. award Boston Mus. Sci., 1990, Entrepreneurship award Internat. Ctr. in N.Y.C., 1991, Medallion for Entrepreneurship, Beta Gamma Sigma, U. Lowell, 1992, Award of Appreciation, Internat. Inst. Energy Conservation, 1989, Man of Yr. award Alpha Omega Coun., 1994, Environ. Bus. award for Industry, New Eng. Environ. Bus. Coun., Inc., 1994, Co. of Yr. award Boston Bus. Jour., 1994, Founders Tribute Internat. Inst. Energy Conservation, 1994, New Englander of Yr. award, 1995, Nat. Pub. Svc. award Am. Hellenic Inst., 1996, Golden Door award Internat. Inst. Boston, 1996, Heinz award (philanthropist) Teresa Heinz, 1996. Fellow IEEE, AIAA (assoc.), ASME (John Fritz medal New Eng. coun. 1996), Am. Soc. Metals (Disting. Life Membership award 1993), Nat. Acad. Engring. (councillor), Am. Acad. Arts and Scis.; mem. Comml. Club of Boston, Sigma Xi, Pi Tau Sigma (Gold medal award 1961). Greek Orthodox. Home: Tower Rd Lincoln MA 01773-3210 Office: Thermo Electron Corp PO Box 9046 81 Wyman St Waltham MA 02454-1229

HATSTAT, JUDY ANNE, nursing administrator; b. Laconia, N.H., Apr. 14, 1948; d. Boleslaw Henry and Phyllis Elizabeth (Varrell) Chernewski; m. Bruce John Hatstat, May 28, 1969; 1 child, Todd Channing. Diploma in practical nursing, David Hale Fanning Trade Sch., 1967; AS, Quinsigamond C.C., Worcester, Mass., 1972; BSN, Worcester State Coll., 1987; MSN, Anna Maria Coll., 1994. RN, Mass.; BLS, BCLS instr. Med.-surg. LPN staff nurse Worcester City Hosp., 1967-72, med.-surg. staff RN, 1972-74, surg. intensive care unit staff and charge nurse, 1974-81, adminstrv. coord., 1981-91; adminstrv. coord. Marlborough (Mass.) Hosp., 1991-93; med.-surg. clin. care coord. Health Alliance Leominster (Mass.) Hosp., 1994-95; adminstrv. coord. St. Vincent Hosp., Worcester, Mass., 1994—; nursing supr. Jewish Health Care Ctr., 1995-97; active Paxton Bd. Health. Mem. Ctrl. Mass. Nursing Consortium, Sigma Theta Tau. Home: 281 Pleasant St Paxton MA 01612-1406 Office: St Vincent Hosp 25 Winthrop St Worcester MA 01602

HATTAN, SUSAN K., legislative staff member; b. Lincoln, Nebr., Jan. 11, 1951; d. Hubert Curtis and Margaret Marie H. BA summa cum laude, Washburn U., 1973; MA with distinction, Am. U., 1977. Legis. aide to Senator Robert J. Dole, Washington, 1973-77; policy analyst, special asst. Adminstrn. of Food Safety and Quality Svc., Dept. Agrl., Washington, 1977-78; legis. dir. to Senator Nancy L. Kassebaum, Washington, 1978-89; minority staff dir., sub-committee on educ., arts and humanities Senate Com. on Labor and Human Resources, Washington, 1989-92, minority staff dir., 1993-94, staff dir., 1995-96; dep. staff dir. Senate Com. Health, Edn., Labor and Pensions, Washington, 1997—. Mem. Phi Kappa Phi, Zeta Tau Alpha. Office: Health Education Labor and Pensions Rm 835 Senate Hart Office Bldg Washington DC 20510

HATTEBERG, LARRY MERLE, photojournalist; b. Winfield, Kans., June 30, 1944; s. Merle Lawrence and Mary Dorothy (Early) H.; m. Judy Beth Keller, June 6, 1965; children: Sherry Renee, Susan Michelle. Student, Kans. State Tchrs. Coll., 1962-63, Emporia-Wichita State U., 1963-66. Photographer Sta. KAKE-TV, Wichita, Kans., 1963, photojournalist, 1966-67, chief photographer, 1967-81, assoc. news dir., 1981-87, exec. news dir., 1987-88, co-anchor 5 p.m. newscast, 1988-92; co-anchor Evening News broadcasts KAKE-TV, Wichita, Kans., 1992—; co-chmn. faculty Nat. Press Photographers TV Workshop, U. Okla., 1975—. Author: Larry Hatteberg's Kansas People,1991; developed Hatteberg's People series for TV, 1976. Served with USAR, 1966-72. Regional semi-finalist NASA Journalist-in-Spece Program; recipient Brotherhood award Kans. region NCCJ, 1995. Life mem. Nat. Press Photographers Assn. (Nat. TV News Photographer of Yr. award 1975, 77, Joseph Sprague award 1983, Joseph Costa award 1991). Office: 1500 N West St Wichita KS 67203-1323

HATTEN, WILLIAM SEWARD, manufacturing company executive; b. Chgo., Apr. 7, 1917; s. William Seward and Margaret (Ahearn) H.; m. Marjorie Popp, Dec. 29, 1939; 1 dau., Patricia Marie (Mrs. Dudley D. Pendleton III). B.A., Lawrence Coll., 1939; M.B.A., Northwestern U., 1944. Indsl. engr. Sears, Roebuck & Co., 1940-43; mgr. control div. Chgo. Ordnance Dist., 1943-45; owner Eskimo Ice Cream Co., Tucson, 1945-50; gen. mgr. Utica Knitting Co., N.Y., 1950-54; cons. Worden & Risberg, Phila., 1954-64; pres., chief exec. officer, dir. Clayton Mark & Co., Evanston, Ill., 1964-67; chmn. bd. Ken-Ray Brass Products, Inc., Vermont, Ill., 1964-67; pres., chief exec. officer, dir. Harper-Wyman Co., Hinsdale, Ill., 1967-69; exec. v.p. Warner Electric Brake & Clutch Co., Beloit, Wis., 1969-72; group v.p. engines and generators, dir. Kohler Co., Wis., 1973-80; pres. Hatten & Assocs., Lakeland, Fla., 1980—. Mem. Ill. C. of C., Chgo. Assn. Commerce and Industry, Am. Ordance Assn., N.A.M., Northwestern U. Grad. Bus. Alumni Assn., Am. Inst. Mgmt., Phi Delta Theta, Lone Palm Country Club (Lakeland, Fla.). Episcopalian. Clubs: Golf (Evanston), University (Evanston); Union League (Chgo.), Executives (Chgo.); Sheboygan Country, University (Milw.). Home: 4010 Cheverly Dr E Lakeland FL 33813-1207 Office: Hatten & Assocs 4010 Cheverly Dr E Lakeland FL 33813-1207

HATTENDORF, DIANE LYNN, principal; b. Joliet, Ill., Sept. 6, 1945; d. Marvin Albert and Mildred Emma (Vogt) Cappel; m. Ronald V. Hattendorf, July 6, 1968; children: Renee Lynn, Rachel Allison. BS in Edn., Concordia U., Seward, Nebr., 1966; MA in Edn., Governs State U., University Park, Ill., 1989, MA in Ednl. Adminstrn., 1995. Cert. tchr. elem. edn. K-9, adminstrn., Ill. Tchr. Zion Luth. Sch., Matteson, Ill., 1966-70; cons. Peotone (Ill.) Sch. Dist., 1976-79; tchr. Green Garden Elem. Sch., Frankfort, Ill., 1977-96, prin., 1996—; prin. Wilton Ctr. Elem. Sch., Manhattan, Ill., 1996—. Pres. Green Garden PTO, Frankfort, 1976-78; chmn. Bd. Edn., Immanuel Sch., Richton Park, Ill., 1992-94. Mem. Ill. Prins. Assn. (Excellence in Leadership 1997), Delta Kappa Gamma (Beta Omega chpt. legis. chmn. 1992-94). Lutheran. Home: 26544 S Center Rd Monee IL 60449-9416 Office: Peotone Sch Dist 207-U 9526 255th St Frankfort IL 60423-8012

HATTER, TERRY JULIUS, JR., federal judge; b. Chgo., Mar. 11, 1933. A.B., Wesleyan U., 1954; J.D., U. Chgo., 1960. Bar: Ill. 1960, Calif. 1965, U.S. Dist. Ct. 1960, U.S. Ct. Appeals 1960. Adjudicator Chgo., 1960-61; assoc. Harold M. Calhoun, Chgo., 1961-62; asst. pub. defender Cook County Chgo., 1961-62; asst. U.S. atty. No. Dist. Calif., San Francisco, 1962-66; chief counsel San Francisco Neighborhood Legal Assistance Found., 1966-67; regional legal svcs. dir. Exec. Office Pres. OEO, San Francisco, 1967-70; exec. dir. Western Ctr. Law and Poverty, L.A., 1970-73; exec. asst. to mayor, dir. criminal justice planning L.A., 1974-75; spl. asst. to mayor, dir. urban devel., 1975-77; judge Superior Ct. Calif., L.A., 1977-80; judge U.S. Dist. Ct. (cen. dist.) Calif., L.A., 1979-98, chief judge, 1998—; lectr. Police Acad., San Francisco Police Dept., 1963-66, U. Calif., San Diego, 1970-71, Colo. Jud. Conf., 1973; assoc. clin. prof. law U. So. Calif. Law Ctr., L.A., 1970-74, mem. bd. councilors; prof. law Loyola U. Sch. Law, L.A., 1973-75; mem. faculty Nat. Coll. State Judiciary, Reno, 1974. V.p. Northbay Halfway House, 1964-65; vice chmn. Los Angeles Regional Criminal Justice Planning Bd., 1975-76; mem. Los Angeles Mayor's Cabinet Com. Econ. Devel., 1976-77, Mayor's Policy Com., 1973-77, chmn. housing econ. and community devel. com., City Los Angeles, 1975-77, chmn. housing and community devel. tech. com., 1975-77; vice chmn. Young Dems. Cook County, 1961-62; chmn. bd. Real Estate Coop; bd. dirs. Bay Area Social Planning Coun., Contra Costa, Black Law Center L.A., Nat. Fedn. Settlements & Neighborhood Ctrs., Edn. Fin. & Governance Reform Project, Mexican Am. Legal Def. & Ednl. Fund, Nat. Health Law Program, Nat. Sr. Citizens Law Ctr., Calif. Law Ctr., L.A. Regional Criminal Justice Planning Bd.; mem. exec. com. bd. dirs. Constl. Rights Found; trustee Wesleyan Univ. Meth. Ch.; mem. bd. visitors U. Chgo. Law Sch. Mem. NAACP (exec. com., bd. dirs. Richmond chpt.), Nat. Legal Aid & Defender Assn. (dir., vice chmn.), L.A. County Bar Assn. (exec. com.), Am. Judicature Soc., Charles Houston Law Club, Phi Delta Phi, Order Coif. Office: US Dist Ct 312 N Spring St Los Angeles CA 90012-4703

HATTERSLEY-SMITH, GEOFFREY FRANCIS, retired government research scientist; b. London, Apr. 22, 1923; s. Wilfrid Percy Ashby and Ethel Mary (Willcocks) H.-S.; m. Maria Kefallinou, May 12, 1955; children: Kara Mary, Fiona Anastasia. Student, Winchester Coll., Eng., 1937-41; BA, Oxford U., Eng., 1948, MA, 1951, DPhil, 1956. Base leader Falkland Islands Dependencies Survey, 1948-50; def. sci. staff officer Def. Rsch. Bd., Ottawa, Ont., Can., 1951-73; prin. sci. officer Brit. Antarctic Survey, Cambridge, Eng., 1973-91; sec. Antarctic place names com. Fgn. and Commonwealth Office, London, 1975-91. Author: North of Latitude Eighty, 1974, Present Arctic Ice Cover, 1974, The History of Place Names in the Falkland Islands Dependencies, 1980, The History of Place Names in the British Antarctic Territory, 1991, Geographical Names in the Ellesmere Island National Park Reserve, 1998; editor: The Norwegian with Scott, 1984. Sub-lt. Royal Navy, 1942-46. Fellow Royal Soc. Can. (Acad. Scis.), Royal Geog. Soc. (Founder's Gold medal 1966), Arctic Inst. N. Am. (gov. 1963-66), Arctic Circle Club (pres. 1967-69), Arctic Club (pres. 1976), Antarctic Club (London) (com. mem. 1983-85). Avocations: polar history; gardening. Home: The Crossways, Cranbrook TN17 2AG, England

HATTERY, ROBERT R., radiologist, educator; b. Phoenix, Dec. 15, 1939; s. Robert Ralph and Goldie M. (Secor) H.; m. D. Diane Sittler, June 18, 1961; children: Angela, Michael. BA, Ind. U., 1961, MD, 1964; cert. in diagnostic radiology, Mayo Grad. Sch. Medicine, 1970. Diplomate Am. Bd. Radiology. Intern Parkland Meml. Hosp.-Southwestern Med. Sch., Dallas, 1964-65; fellow Mayo Clinic, Rochester, Minn., 1967-70, cons., 1970-81, chmn. dept. diagnostic radiology, 1981-86; instr. radiology Mayo Med. Sch., 1973-75, asst. prof. radiology, 1975-78, assoc. prof. radiology, 1978-82, prof. radiology, 1982—; chair Mayo Group Practice Bd., 1991-93; chmn. bd. govs Mayo Clinic, Rochester, 1994—. Author numerous jour. articles and abstracts, book chpts. Capt. USAF, 1965-67, Willford Hall Hosp., San Antonio. Fellow Am. Coll. Radiology; mem. Radiol. Soc. N.Am., Am. Roentgen Ray Soc., Soc. Computed Body Tomography (pres. 1982-83), Soc. Genitourinary Radiography (pres. 1986-88). Office: Mayo Clinic 200 1st St SW Rochester MN 55905-0002

HATTIN, DONALD EDWARD, geologist, educator; b. Cohasset, Mass., Nov. 16, 1928; s. Edward Arthur and Una Vestella (Whipple) H.; m. Marjorie Elizabeth Macy, July 15, 1950; children: Sandra Jane, Ronald Scott, Donna Jean. B.S., U. Mass., 1950; M.S., U. Kans., 1952, Ph.D. (Shell fellow), 1954. Asst. instr. geology U. Kans., 1950-52, instr., 1953-54; asst. prof. geology Ind. U., Bloomington, 1954-60; assoc. prof. Ind. U., 1960-67, prof., 1967-95, prof. emeritus, 1995—; asst. geologist Kans. Geol. Survey, 1952, research assoc., 1959-68, 70-74, 77-82, 86-87; vis. prof. Ernst-Moritz-Arndt U., Greifswald, German Dem. Republic, 1985; geologist Ind. Geol. Survey, 1957-58; cons. in field; mem. N.Am. Commn. on Stratigraphic Nomenclature, 1987-90, 91-94; vis. disting. prof. U. Kans., 1991. Author: Stratigraphy of the Wreford Limestone, 1957, Stratigraphy of the Carlile Shale, 1962, Stratigraphy of the Graneros Shale in Central Kansas, 1965, Stratigraphy and Depositional Environment of Greenhorn Limestone of Kansas, 1975, Upper Cretaceous Stratigraphy and Depositional Environments of Western Kansas, 1978, Stratigraphy and Depositional Environment of Smoky Hill Chalk, Niobrara Chalk, Western Kansas, 1982. Served to capt. USAFR, 1950-59, active duty, 1955-57. Recipient Erasmus Haworth Disting. Alumni honors in geology U. Kans., 1976, Alumni Disting. Tchg. award Coll. Arts and Scis. Ind. U., 1988, Disting. Tchg. and Mentoring award Grad. Sch. Ind. U., 1995; NSF grantee, 1975-77, 88-90, Geol. Soc. Am. grantee, 1975, Am. Chem. Soc. grantee, 1978-80, 84-86; NSF fellow, 1969. Fellow Geol. Soc. Am.; mem. Am. Assn. Petroleum Geologists (Outstanding Educator award Ea. sect. 1993), Soc. Econ. Paleontologists Mineralogists, Paleontol. Soc. Republican. Office: Ind U Dept Geol Scis Bloomington IN 47405

HATTIS, ALBERT DANIEL, business executive, retired educator, journalist; b. Chgo., Oct. 12, 1929; s. Robert E. and Victoria C. (Kaufman) H.; m. Fern Hollobow; children: Kim Allyson Hattis Mercer, Kay Arlene Hattis Draper, John Elmore, Michael Allen, Sharon Beth Cosgrove. BS with highest distinction, Northwestern U., 1948, postgrad. in bus. adminstrn., 1950, DD (hon.), 1968. Vice-pres., sec.-treas. Robert E. Hattis Engrs., Inc., Hattis Svc. Co., Inc. (sub. White Motor Corp. also sub. of REH Corp.), Deerfield, Ill., 1950-73; v.p., sec.-treas. Servbest Foods, Inc., Highland Park, Ill., 1973-78; A.C. Equipment Co., 1978-80, Prime Packing Co., Inc., Haitian Am. Meat & Provision Co. SA, Spanish-Am. Foods, Inc., 1973-78; pres., chief exec. officer Frigidmeats, Inc., Chgo., 1978-80; pres. Gits Enterprises, Inc., 1978-80, Double K Bar J Ranch, Inc., 1968—; prof. bus., holder Schwan Endowed Chair for Free Enterprise, S.W. State U., Marshall, Minn., 1981-89, ret. 1989; dir. S.W. Minn. Small Bus. Devel. Ctr., 1984-87, S.W. Minn. Homegrown Economy Local Cooperation Office, 1984-89; dir., fin. and adminstrn. Chlorine Free Products Assn., 1995-96; chmn. Minn. Small Bus. Procurement Adv. Coun., 1986-87. Exec. dir. The Lambs, Inc., Libertyville, Ill., 1980-81; trustee Orphans of the Storm Found., 1972-74, Cobblers Found., 1972-74; mem. adv. bd. Northwestern Psychiat. Inst., 1972-74; bd. dirs. Marshall Industries Found.; chmn. Marshall Planning Commn., 1982-85. Capt. USAF, 1946-48, 50-52. Mem. Assn. Pvt. Enterprise Edn., Internat. Coun. Small Bus., U.S. Assn. Small Bus. and Entrepreneurship, Minn. C. of C. (small bus. council 1984-87), Marshall Area C. of C. (bd. dirs. 1981-88), Beta Gamma Sigma. Lodges: Lions, Rotary. Syndicated columnist, broadcaster Straight Talk, 900 newspapers, 500 radio stas. Home and Office: 708 Ascot Ct Libertyville IL 60048-5238

HATTON, BRENDA SHIRLEY (LINDA WELLINGTON), writer, poet, songwriter; b. Winchester, Ky., Apr. 28, 1945; d. Benjamin Marion and Minnie (Rice) Huff; m. Wallace Glenn Hatton, Feb. 8, 1964; children: Carolyn, Sherry Lynn, Connie Gail and Ronnie Dale (twins). Student, Ea. Ky. U., 1995. Contbr. poems to books; singer (stage name Linda Wellington); gospel album There Stands Jesus, 1997; mem. His Music Group; own radio program. Mem. Ch. of God. Mem. Ky. Gospel Music Assn., Broadcast Music Inc., Internat. Platform Assn. Avocations: fishing, camping, singing, meeting people, discovering new places. Home: 1011 Bethel Rd Lancaster KY 40444-9737

HATTON, JANIE R. HILL, principal. Formerly prin. Milw. Trade and Tech. H.S.; dep. supt. Leadership Svcs., Milw., 1997—. Recipient Nat. Principal of the Year award Nat. Assn. Secondary Sch. Principals and Met. Life Ins. Co., 1993. Office: Leadership Svcs PO Box 2181 Milwaukee WI 53201-2181*

HATTON, STEPHEN BARTH, chemical company executive, information executive; b. Columbus, Ohio, Sept. 22, 1946; s. Willard Jay and Wanita Virginia (Thoman) H.; m. Maria del Rosario Otelina Guevara Hernández, Aug. 22, 1988; 1 child, Zoe Gabriela; child by previous marriage, Sophia Aletheia. BA, Wheaton Coll., 1968; student, Pa. State U., 1968-70; MBA, Ill. Inst. Tech., 1985. Rsch. editor, sr. rsch. editor Encyclopaedia Britannica, Chgo., 1971-73; programmer jr., programmer analyst Sears, Roebuck & Co., Chgo., 1974-76, system programmer, 1976-78, sr. tech. programmer, 1978-80; techniques and planning project mgr. Morton Salt/Morton Internat., Chgo., 1980-82, mgr. systems devel., 1982-87; data base adminstr. Corp./Morton Internat., Chgo., 1987-90, projects mgr., 1990-96, mgr. info. systems, bus. application, 1996—. Editor, author: Good Old Days, The Report, 1995. Mem. Infinium UserNet, Ohio Hist. Soc., Corp. Quality Soc., Soc. Biblical Lit., Phi Sigma Tau, Sigma Iota Epsilon. Office: Morton Internat 100 N Riverside Plz Chicago IL 60606-1596

HATTON, THURMAN TIMBROOK, JR., retired horticulturist, consultant; b. Bartow, Fla., Feb. 4, 1922; s. Thurman Timbrook Sr. and Pearl Catherine (Holliday) H.; m. Eileen Marie Snowber, Jan. 25, 1947 (dec. Jan. 1976); children: Mary, Nina, Alexa, Michele; m. Marilyn Mae Memory, July 12, 1979. BS, U. Fla., 1943, MS, 1949; PhD, Wash. State U., 1953. Teaching fellow U. Fla., Gainesville, 1948-49; asst. prof. U. P.R., Mayaguez, 1949-50; instr. Wash. State U., Pullman, 1950-53; extension specialist N.C. State U., Raleigh, 1953-55; investigations leader Market Quality Rsch. Lab. USDA, Miami, Fla., 1955-68; rsch. leader Export and Quality Improvement Unit USDA, Orlando, Fla., 1968-89; cons. Chuluota, Fla., 1989—; adj. prof. U. Fla., 1972-89; cons. Agrl. Rsch. Svc. USDA, Japan, 1974-86, Pub. Law 480 Projects, India and Pakistan, 1977, 81, 85, U.S. AID, India, 1982. Author 3 book chpts.; contbr. numerous articles to profl. jours. Bd. dirs. Am. Youth Exchange Program, Miami, 1962-68. Col. U.S. Army, 1943-48, ETO. Recipient rsch. award Fla. Fruit and Vegetable Assn., 1973, Exceptional Svc. award Fla. Citrus Packers, 1989, Award of Merit Fla. Citrus Commn., 1989. Fellow Am. Soc. for Hort. Sci.; mem. Fla. State Hort. Soc. (pres. 1988), Fla. Mango Forum (pres. 1963), InterAm. Soc. for Tropical Horticulture, Internat. Hort. Soc., Internat. Soc. for Citriculture, Sigma Xi. Achievements include development of maturity standards for Florida avacados, of a cold treatment for quarantine purposes in the export of grapefruit. Home and Office: PO Box 660068 Chuluota FL 32766-0068

HATZAKIS, MICHAEL, retired electrical engineer, research executive; b. Chania, Crete, Greece, Jan. 1, 1928; came to U.S., 1956; s. John and Poly (Lionakis) H.; m. Mary Giannickos, Sept. 29, 1955 (dec.); children: Michael Jr., Helene. BSEE, NYU, 1964, MSEE, 1967. Technician Radio Engring. Labs., Long Island City, N.Y., 1958-61; technician IBM T.J. Watson Rsch. Ctr., Yorktown Heights, N.Y., 1961-67, staff mem., 1967-76, mgr., 1976-88, IBM fellow, 1988-91; ret., 1991; dir. Microelectronics Inst. at Democritos, Athens, Greece, 1988—. Mem. NAE, IEEE (sr., Cledo Brunetti award 1987), Am. Vacuum Soc., Electrochem. Soc., Materials Rsch. Soc. Democrat. Greek Orthodox. Office: Microelect Inst NCSR Demokritos, PO Box 60228s, 153-10 Aghia Paraskevi Athens Greece

HAUBER, FREDERICK AUGUST, ophthalmologist; b. Pitts., July 3, 1948; s. Michael H. and Cecilia (Azinger) H.; m. Cathy Lu Rosellini, Aug. 3, 1981; children: Elizabeth Alexandra, Natalia Fredericka. BS in Microbiology cum laude, U. Pitts., 1970; MD, U. Tenn., 1974. Intern U. South Fla., Tampa, 1975, resident in ophthalmology, 1982; pvt. practice Pasco Eye Inst., New Port Richey, Fla., 1983—; asst. clin. prof. U. South Fla., Tampa, 1984—; rechr., spkr. in field, 1990—; cons. Optimed, Inc. Contbr. articles to profl. jours. Advisor health care cost containment com., Tarpon Springs, Fla., 1988; founder Pasco County Diabetes Assn.; mem. bd. counsellors U. Tampa. Fellow ACS, Am. Acad. Ophthalmology; mem. Southeastern U.S. Debate Soc. Achievements include patent for achromatic intraocular lens; first to insert glaucoma pressure regulator; development of binary optical intraocular lens, color vision eye chart system. Office: Pasco Eye Inst 5347 Main St New Port Richey FL 34652-2506

HAUBER, PATRICIA ANNE, educator; b. Phila., Feb. 16, 1953; d. Frederick Joseph and Dorothy Marie (Delaney) Hauber. AA, Montgomery County Community, Blue Bell, Pa., 1973; BS, Bloomsburg U., 1975; MEd, Lehigh U., 1985, elem. prin. cert., secondary prin. cert., 1990. Tchr. North Penn Sch. Dist., Lansdale, Pa., 1975-85; sci. coord., tchr. St. Jude Sch., Chalfont, Pa., 1985—. Instr., trainer ARC, CPR programs, Lansdale, Pa., 1979-90. Mem. AAAS, ASCD, Nat. Coun. Tchrs. Math., Nat. Sci. Tchrs. Assn., Pa. Sci. Tchrs. Assn., Pa. Assn. for Supervision and Curriculum Devel., Phi Delta Kappa. Democrat. Roman Catholic. Avocations: antiques, crafts. Home: 391 Huckleberry Ln Harleysville PA 19438-2334 Office: St Jude Sch 323 W Butler Ave Chalfont PA 18914-2329

HAUBOLD, SAMUEL ALLEN, lawyer; b. Watertown, S.D., July 29, 1938; s. Gustuv Herman and Leone Marjorie (York) H.; m. Caroline V. Thompson, Sept. 27, 1969; 1 child, Caroline A. BS in Engring., Northwestern U.; JD, Harvard U. Bar: Ill. 1966, N.Y. 1990, U.S. Dist. Ct. (no. dist.) Ill. 1966, U.S. Ct. Appeals (7th cir.) 1970, U.S. Ct. Appeals (9th cir.) 1979, U.S. Supreme Ct. 1974. Assoc. Kirkland & Ellis, Chgo., 1966, ptnr., 1972—; resident ptnr. Kirkland & Ellis Internat., London, 1994—. Served to lt. USN, 1960-63. Mem. ABA, Ill. Bar Assn., Internat. Bar Assn., Mid-Am. Club, Saddle and Cycle club (Chgo.), The Hurlingham Club (London). Presbyterian. Home: 40 S Eaton Pl, London SW1W 9JJ, England Office: Kirkland & Ellis Internat, Internat Fin Ctr, Old Broad St, London EC2N 1HQ, England

HAUBRICH, ROBERT RICE, biology educator; b. Claremont, N.H., May 4, 1923; s. Frederick William and Marion Norma (Rice) H. BS in Forestry, Mich. State U., 1949, MS in Zoology, 1952; PhD in Biology, U. Fla., 1957. Asst. prof. biology East Carolina U., Greenville, N.C., 1957-61, Oberlin (Ohio) Coll., 1961-62; asst. prof. biology Denison U., Granville, Ohio, 1962-64, assoc. prof. biology, 1964-67, prof. biology, 1968-88, chair dept. biology, 1968-69, alumni chair, 1983-89, prof. emeritus, 1988—; assoc. dir. Earlham Coll. Biol. Sta., Syracuse, Ind., 1967-72; mem. marine sci. edn. consortium Duke Marine Lab., Beaufort, N.C., 1983-88; libr. reader Marine Biol. Lab., Woods Hole, Mass., 1965—. Contbr. articles to profl. publs. Sgt. USAF, 1943-46. Fellow AAAS, Ohio Acad. Sci.; mem. Internat. Soc. History, Philosophy and Social Studies. Avocations: swimming, hiking. Home and Office: Denison U Dept Biology Granville OH 43023

HAUCH, VALERIE CATHERINE, historian, educator, researcher; b. Washington, May 20, 1949; d. Charles Christian and Ruthadele Bertha (LaTourrette) H.; life ptnr. Jacquelyn Farrow. BA in History, Kalamazoo Coll., 1971; MA in Medieval Studies, Western Mich. U., 1977; grad. cert. C.C. Teaching, U. St. Thomas, St. Paul, 1995. Social sci. analyst congl. rsch. svc. Libr. Congress, Washington, 1971-72; ind. contractor Minn. Hist. Soc., St. Paul, 1987-88, adminstrv. asst., 1990—; mus. asst. John H. Stevens House Mus., Mpls., 1990; teaching intern Normandale C.C., Bloomington, Minn., 1995; cmty. edn. tchr. Mpls. Pub. Schs., 1990—; instr. Minn. Sch. Bus., 1999—. Mem. Am. Hist. Assn., Am. Assn. Mus., Phi Beta Kappa. Home: 2609 Morgan Ave N Minneapolis MN 55411-1840

HAUCK, FREDERICK HAMILTON, retired naval officer, astronaut, business executive; b. Long Beach, Calif., Apr. 11, 1941; s. Philip and Virginia (Hustvedt) H.; m. Dolly Bowman, Aug. 27, 1962 (div.); children: Whitney Irene, Stephen Christopher; m. Susan Cameron Bruce, June 27, 1993. BS in Physics, Tufts U., 1962; MS in Nuclear Engring., MIT, 1966. Commd. ensign USN, 1962, advanced through grades to capt., 1983; pilot Attack Squadron 35, USS Coral Sea, 1968-70; instr. pilot Attack Squadron 42, Oceana, Va., 1970-71; test pilot Naval Air Test Ctr., Patuxent River, Md., 1971-74; ops. officer Carrier Air Wing 14, Miramar, Calif., USS Enterprise, 1974-76; exec. officer Attack Squadron 145, Wash., 1976-78; astronaut NASA, Houston, 1978-89; space shuttle pilot shuttle transp. system mission 7, 1983; space shuttle comdr. STS-51A, 1984; assoc. adminstr. for external rels. NASA, 1986; space shuttle comdr. STS-26, 1988; dir. Navy Space Systems (OP-943), Washington, 1989-90, ret., 1990; pres., CEO AXA Space (formerly Internat. Tech. Underwriters), Bethesda, Md., 1990—; mem. comml. space transp. adv. com. Dept. Transp., 1990-98, chmn. COMSTAC task group on Soviet entry into world space markets; mem. comml. programs adv. com. NASA, 1991-92, mem. mission rev. group on spacecraft salvage and repair, 1992; mem. panel on space launch industry U.S. Congress Office Tech. Assessment, 1994-95; chmn. NASA External Ind. Readiness rev. group for Second Hubble space Telescope Servicing Mission, 1995-97; mem. Nat. Rsch. Coun. Aeronautics & Space Engring. Bd., 1996—, com. internat. space sta. meteoroid/debris risk mgmt., 1995-97, chair space shuttle meteoroid/debris risk mgmt. com., 1997—; chair bd. overseers Schs. Arts and Scis., Tufts U. Co-author: An Analysis of the Salvage/Repair Market for Commercial Communications Satellites, 1993; contbg. author: The Greatest Adventure, 1995. Trustee Tufts U.; bd. govs. St. Albans Sch., 1989-95. Decorated Def. D.S.M. (2), Def. Superior Svc. medal, Legion of Merit, DFC, Air medal (9), Navy Commendation Medal with Gold Star and Combat V, NASA D.S.M., NASA medal for Outstanding Leadership, NASA Space Flight medal (3), Presdl. Cost Saving Commendation, AIAA Haley Space Flight award, Lloyd's of London Silver medal for meritorious svc., Am. Astronautical Soc. Flight Achievement award (2), Federation Aeronautique Internationale Yuri Gagarin Gold medal, Federation Aeronautique Internationale Komarov Diploma (2), Tufts U. Presdl. medal, Light on the Hill award, Delta Upsilon Disting. Alumnus award; named Navy's Outstanding Test Pilot for 1972. Fellow AIAA, Soc. Exptl. Test Pilots; mem. Assn. Space Explorers (v.p. 1991-93), Am. Astron. Soc. (bd. govs. 1997—), Early and Pioneer Naval Aviators Assn., Winter Harbor Yacht Club (Maine), Ocean Reef Club (Key Largo, Fla.). Office: AXA Space 4800 Montgomery Ln 11th Fl Bethesda MD 20814-3429

HAUCK, MADELINE (AGNES), special and adult basic education educator; b. Flushing, N.Y.; d. Frances and Loretta (Bethel) DeCarmine; m. Walter Hauck; children: Walter, Frank, Laura. BS in Elem. Edn., U. Bridgeport, Conn., 1969; MA in Spl. Edn., Fairfield (Conn.) U., 1978. Cert. spl. and adult edn. tchr., Conn.; cert. substitute tchr., Conn. Tchr. spl. edn. Kennedy Ctr., Inc., Bridgeport, 1972-94; tchr. adult basic edn. Bridgeport Bd. of Edn., 1972-94. Charter mem., v.p. Jr. Woman's Club, Fairfield, 1965; pres. Welcome Alumni Club, Fairfield, 1971; mem. Fairfield Woman's Club, 1976—, program chmn., 1987; dir.-at-large Fairfield Ch. housing for elderly, 1982—, nominating com., 1997, 98, decorating com., 1997, 98, 99. Recipient Recognition award Conn. State Fedn. of Coun. for Exceptional Children, 1992. Mem. Jaycees (Tchr. of Yr. 1979), Conn. Assn. Pub. Schs. Adult Educators. Roman Catholic. Avocations: gymnastics, theater, nutrition, swimming, book discussion. Home: 104 Roberton Xing Fairfield CT 06432-1162

HAUCK, MARGUERITE HALL, broadcasting executive; b. Bayside, N.Y., June 30, 1948; d. Carlyle Washington and Anzonette Marguerite (Asmussen) Hall; m. Harry Lennon, 1996. Student, Syracuse U., 1966-67; BA summa cum laude, Queens Coll., CUNY, 1974. Assoc. producer Animatic Prodns., Ltd., N.Y.C., 1968-72; mktg. analyst BBDO, Inc., N.Y.C., 1974-75, CBS, Inc., N.Y.C., 1975-76; dir. mktg. and research FM nat. sales, Radio div. CBS Radio, N.Y.C., 1976-85; dir. mktg. and research Christal Radio Sales div. Katz Communications, 1985-87; pres. Lennon Hall Antiques, Inc., 1986-94; v.p. research and mktg. Christal Radio Sales divsn., Katz Media, 1987-97; v.p., dir. sales mktg. KATZ Radio Group subs. of Chancellor Media, N.Y.C., 1997—. Author: The 321 Billion Dollar Market, 1981, The Mid-Day Myth Exploded, 1982; columnist, TV-Radio Age mag., 1982, 89. Bd. dirs. Queens Coll. Student Services Corp., 1973-74. Recipient Queens Coll. Disting. Service award, 1974. Home: 26 Gilbert St Northport NY 11768-3121 Office: KATZ Radio Group 125 W 55th St New York NY 10019-5369

HAUDENSCHILD, CHRISTIAN CHARLES, pathologist, educator, inventor; b. St. Gallen, Switzerland, May 3, 1939; came to U.S., 1972; s. Charles Haudenschild. MD, U. Basel, 1968. Diplomate Am. Bd. Pathology. Rsch. fellow, assoc. F. Hoffman-LaRoche Exptl. Medicine, Basel, Switzerland, 1968-72; rsch. assoc. Children's Hosp. Med. Ctr., Boston, 1973-74; rsch. assoc. in surgery and pathology Harvard U. Med. Sch., Boston, 1974-76, clin. instr. pathology, 1976-80; resident in pathology Boston City Hosp., 1974-76; asst. prof. pathology Boston U. Sch. Medicine, 1976-79; assoc. pathologist Mallory Inst. Pathology, Boston, 1977-92; assoc. prof. Boston U. Sch. Medicine, 1977-92, prof., 1982-92; assoc. vis. physician Boston City Hosp., 1977-92; adj. prof. pathology Boston U. Sch. Medicine, 1992—, Georgetown U., Washington, 1992-95; rsch. prof. pathology George Washington U. Sch. Medicine, Washington, 1992-95, prof. pathology and medicine, 1996—; cons. pathologist Boston VA Hosp., 1978-92; asst. vis. pathologist Univ. Hosp., Boston, 1986-92; hon. cons. prof. U. Studi, Siena, Italy, 1985; Disting. vis. scientist Armed Forces Inst. Pathology, Washington, 1992—; Disting. vis. prof. U. Utrecht, Netherlands, 1993—; head exptl. pathology dept. Holland Lab. ARC, Rockville, Md., 1992—. Contbr. articles to med. jours., chpts. to books; patentee in field. Recipient rsch. grants HEW, NIH, Nat. Heart, Lung and Blood Inst., Am. Heart Assn, 1978—. Mem. AMA, Am. Heart Assn. (fellow coun. on arteriosclerosis), Swiss Med. Soc., Am. Soc. for Cell Biology, Am. Assn. Pathologists, Internat. Acad. Pathology, Wash. Acad. Medicine. Office: Holland Lab ARC 15601 Crabbs Branch Way Rockville MD 20855-2736

HAUENSTEIN, GEORGE CAREY, life insurance executive; b. Hattiesburg, Miss., May 8, 1936; s. George Jacob Jr. and Earline (Allsup) J.; m. Marjorie Rutland, Aug. 27, 1960; children: Ruth Hauenstein Austin, George Jacob III. Student, Miss. State U., Starkville, 1954-56; BS, U. So. Miss., 1961. CLU. Prin. G. Carey Hauenstein & Assocs., Laurel, Miss., 1962—. Contbr. articles to numerous profl. publs.; spkr. profl. convs. and symposia. Mem. Jones County Econ. Devel. Authority, Laurel; bd. dirs. Miss. Easter Seal Found., 1966, Laurel Community Concert Assn., 1990—; chmn. dist. xi Am. Heart Assn. 1964-65; ruling elder Evang. Presbyn. Ch.; bd trustees French Camp Acad., U. So. Miss. Found., mem. estate planning coun. Served to Sgt. U.S. Marine Corps, 1956-58. Otho Smith fellow U. Miss., 1989; named to Hall of Fame The New England, 1982. Me. Nat. Assn. Life Underwriters, Am. Soc. CLU and CFC, Internat. Ins. Soc., Assn. for Advanced Life Underwriting, Miss. Estate Planning Coun., Miss. Assn. Life Underwriters (pres. 1964-65), Million Dollar Round Table (exec. com. 1986-90, pres. 1989), Miss. Chpt. CLU (dir. 1991). Avocations: scuba, hunting, fishing.

HAUENSTEIN, JILL PLEDGER HODGES, psychiatrist; b. Kingstree, S.C., Jan. 31, 1948; d. Marc E. and Margaret Pledger (Hodges) H.; m. Louis Rutledge Andrews, Jan. 9, 1982; stepchild, Mary Elizabeth Bull Andrews. BA, Columbia (S.C.) Coll., 1970; MD, Med. U. S.C., 1982. Resident in psychiatry Med. Coll. Ga., Augusta, 1982-86; pvt. practice Augusta, 1986—. Bd. dirs. Comfort House, Inc., Augusta, 1980-96, pres., 1992-93 ; trustee Columbia Coll., 1995—. Mem. AMA, Am. Psychiat. Assn., So. Psychiat. Assn., So. Med. Assn., Med. Assn. Ga. (assembly del. 1994-99), Ga. Psychiat. Physicians Assn. (trustee 1989-99, pres. 1996-97), Ctrl. Savannah River Area Psychiat. Assn. (trustee 1987-96, pres. 1988-89), Richmond County Med. Soc. (v.p. 1998, pres.-elect 1999). Episcopalian. Avocations: genealogy, travel, Celtic history and myth. Office: 2301 Wrightsboro Rd Augusta GA 30904-6219

HAUENSTEIN, KAREN, physician's assistant, critical care nurse; b. Brigham City, Utah, Jan. 18, 1963; d. DeWayne Edgar and Vaudis Jennie (Yates) H.; m. Donald Pope Arnett, Apr. 12, 1997; 1 adopted child, Cory Dee Arnett. Degree in nursing, Weber State U., Ogden, Utah, 1983; cert. physician asst., U. Utah, 1995. RN, Utah. Staff nurse Ecclesiastical Mission, Bolivia, S.Am., 1984-85, McKay Dee Hosp., Ogden, 1983-89; critical care registered nurse LDS Hosp., Salt Lake City, 1989-95; physician asst. Dr. William T. Graff, St. George, Utah, 1995-97, Utah Dept. Juvenile Corrections, St. George, 1996-97. Vol. Am. Cancer Soc., 1995—, Am. Heart Assn., 1994—. Sterling scholar Deseret News-Salt Lake City, 1980, acad. scholar Weber State U., 1983, Utah Bur. Rural Health, 1993. Fellow Am. Acad. Physician's Assts.; mem. AACN, Bus. and Profl. Women (Young Career Woman 1997), Elks. Avocations: children, animals, music, poetry, hiking. Home: PO Box 540 New Harmony UT 84757-0540 Office: Red Cliffs Fam Medicine 620 S 400 E Ste 105 Saint George UT 84770-3700

HAUFF, SARA JEANNETTE, newspaper editor; b. Allentown, Pa., Apr. 28, 1972; d. Edmund Guido and Harriet Kaye (Laudenslager) H. BA, U. Del., 1994. Mgr.-in-tng. Nine & Co., Willow Grove, Pa., 1994-95; reporter, editor The Free Press Upper Bucks Pub. Co., Quakertown, Pa., 1995—. Com. mem. Quakertown Cares Fund Dr., 1997. Mem. Pa. Soc. Newspaper Editors, Pa. Newspapers Pubs. Assn. (Deadlines Writing award 1996). Avocations: biking, aerobics, skiing. Office: The Free Press 312 W Broad St Ste 1 Quakertown PA 18951-1241

HAUG, EDWARD JOSEPH, JR., mechanical engineering educator, simulation research engineer; b. Bonne Terre, Mo., Sept. 15, 1940; s. Edward Joseph and Thelma (Harrison) H.; m. Carol Jean Todd, July 1, 1979; 1 child, Kirk Anthony. BSME, U. Mo., Rolla, 1962; MS in Applied Mechanics, Kans. State U., 1964, PhD in Applied Mechanics, 1966. Rsch. engr. Army Armaments Command, Rock Island, Ill., 1966-69; chief sys. analysis Army Weapons Command, Rock Island, Ill., 1970, chief sys. rsch., 1971-72, chief concepts and tech., 1973-76; prof. U. Iowa, Iowa City, 1976—, Carver Disting. prof., 1990—, dir. Ctr. for Computer Aided Design, 1983-95; dir. Nat. Advanced Driving Simulator and Simulation Ctr., 1992-98. Author 11 books on computer aided design and dynamics; editor 5 books; contbr. numerous papers to profl. jours. Capt. U.S. Army, 1966-68. Recipient Innovative Info. Tech. award Computerworld/Smithsonian Instn., 1989, Colwell Merit award Soc. Automotive Engrs., 1989. Fellow ASME (Design Automation award 1991, Machine Design award 1992), Am. Acad. Mechanics. Achievements include patents for Constant Recoil Automatic Cannon, and for Real-Time Simulation System. Home: 2440 County Rd 500 Bayfield CO 81122 Office: U Iowa Dept Mech Engring Iowa City IA 52242

HAUG, MARILYN ANN, reading and mathematics educator; b. Medford, Wis., Sept. 28, 1935; d. Michael and Mary Frances (Koestner) Zirngibl; m. Ernest Raymond Haug, Aug. 3, 1963; 1 child, Stephanie. BS in Edn., Alverno Coll., 1958. Cert. tchr., Wis., cert. reading tchr. Wis., cert. speech adjudicator Wis. High Sch. Forensics Assn. Tchr. South 55th St. Sch., Milw., 1958-78; reading tchr. Audubon Middle Sch., Milw., 1980-83; chpt. II reading/math. tchr. U.S. Grant Sch., Milw., 1984—; cooperating tchr. Alverno Coll., Milw., 1962-78; team chairperson, Middle Sch. coordinating com. Audubon Middle Sch., Milw., 1982-83; forensics coach Saint Mary's Sch., Elm Grove, Wis., 1989-92. Mem. NEA, ASCD, Wis. Edn. Assn., Milw. Tchrs. Edn. Assn., Nat. Coun. Tchrs. Math., Wis. Math. Coun., Internat. Reading Assn., Reading/Libr. Com., Writing to Reading Com., Math. Com. Avocations: reading, travel, music, art, forensics.

HAUGAARD, NIELS, pharmacologist; b. Copenhagen, Denmark, Feb. 25, 1920; came to U.S., 1940, naturalized, 1952; s. Gotfred C. and Karen L. (Pedersen) H.; m. Ella Elizabeth Shwartzman, June 22, 1947 (dec. Feb. 1980); children: David Gregory, Lisa Karen; m. Dorothy Tosi, 1983; children: Gregory, Kimberly, Pamela. Student, U. Copenhagen, 1938-40; A.B. with honors, Swarthmore Coll., 1942; Ph.D. in Biochemistry, U. Pa., 1949. Instr. U. Pa., Phila., 1949-52, asst. prof. rsch. medicine, 1952-54, asst. prof. pharmacology, 1954-60, assoc. prof., 1960-65, prof., 1965-87, emeritus prof., 1987—, mem. Med. Coun., 1972-75, chmn. Grievance Commn., 1986; mem. cardiovascular scis. study sect. NIH, 1978-82. Sect. editor: Chem. Abstracts, 1960-65; editorial bd.: Circulation Research, 1964-69, Molecular and Cellular Biochemistry, 1986—; contbr. articles to profl. jours. Mem. Bristol Twp. (Pa.) Sch. Bd., 1957-60. Guggenheim Found. fellow, 1952; Commonwealth Found. fellow, 1965. Mem. ACLU, Am. Soc. Biol. Chemists, Am. Soc. Pharmacology and Exptl. Therapeutics (editorial bd. jour. 1965-68). Rsch. on mechanism of hormone action, oxygen toxicity, mitochondrial metabolism, bladder function and metabolism. Office: Urology Rsch Lab Hosp Univ Pa Ravdin Courtyard Bldg Philadelphia PA 19104

HAUGAN, GERTRUDE M., clinical psychologist; b. New Richland, Minn.; d. Henry Albert and Ella Pauline (Gardson) H. BA, George Washington U., 1952, MA, 1956; PhD, U. Md., 1970. Lic. psychologist, D.C., Md. Research psychologist New Eng. Med. Ctr., Boston, 1959-62; intern clin. psychology Hall Psychiat. Inst., Columbia, S.C., 1968-69; fellow in pediatrics Sch. Medicine Johns Hopkins U., Balt., 1970-71; clin. psychologist adloescent program Devel. Services Ctr., Washington, 1971-72, chief children's unit, 1972-85; chief Devel Services Ctr., Washington, 1986-94; cons. in psychology Ea. Shore State Hosp., Cambridge, Md., 1969-71, in child psychology Ctr. for Spl. Edn., Annapolis, Md., 1972-76; instr. in child psychology Montgomery Coll., Rockville, Md., 1977-78. Contbr. articles to profl. jours. Mem. profl. adv. council Easter Seal Soc. for Disabled Children and Adults, Washington, 1987. Mem. APA, D.C. Psychol. Assn., Am. Assn. on Mental Retardation, Phi Beta Kappa. Home: 4720 S Chelsea Ln Bethesda MD 20814-3720

HAUGH, CLARENCE GENE, agricultural engineering educator; b. Spring Mills, Pa., Oct. 11, 1936; s. Clarence Glenn and Estella Jane (Baney) H.; m. Patricia Anne Breon, June 16, 1962; children: Amy Elizabeth Dodds, Jennifer Lea Ulsh, Mitchell Breon. BS in Agrl. Engring., Pa. State U., 1958; MS in Agrl. Engring., U. Ill., 1959; PhD, Purdue U., 1964. Registered profl. engr., Fla. Asst. prof. U. Fla., Gainesville, 1964-65; asst. prof. Purdue U., Lafayette, Ind., 1965-68, assoc. prof., 1968-72, prof., 1972-79; prof. Va. Poly. Inst. & State U., Blacksburg, 1979—; dept. head Va. Poly. Inst. & State U., 1979-86; mem. Nat. Engring. Accreditation Commn., 1985-90; trustee Chippokes Plantation, Surry, Va., 1980-91; cons. King Faisall U., Hofhuf, Saudi Arabia, 1984-86. Patentee in field; contbr. over 50 articles to profl. jours. Asst. scoutmaster Boy Scouts Am., Blacksburg, 1985-91; deacon, elder, trustee Covenant Presbyn. Ch., Lafayette, 1968-76; adminstrv. bd. Blacksburg Meth. Ch., 1979-82. Served as 1st lt. USAF, 1958-64. Republican. Methodist. Fellow Am. Soc. Agrl. Engrs. (bd. dirs. 1989-91, chmn. 12 tech. coms., Young Rschr. award 1976); mem. Am. Soc. Engring. Edn. (chmn. agrl. engring. sect. 1982-83), Inst. Food Technologists, Soc. Rheology, Internat. Soc. Agromaterials Sci. and Engring. (sci. bd. 1992—), Arnold Air Soc., Rotary, Masons, Shriners, Sigma Xi, Tau Beta Pi, Alpha Epsilon, Gamma Sigma Delta, Phi Tau Sigma, Alpha Zeta, Phi Beta Delta. Republican. Methodist. Lodges: Rotary, Masons, Shriners. Avocations: sailing, backpacking, collecting antiques. Home: 406 Murphy St Blacksburg VA 24060-2539 Office: Va Poly Inst & State U Dept Biol Sys Engring 314 Seitz Hall Blacksburg VA 24061

HAUGH, JOYCE EILEEN GALLAGHER, education educator; b. Ironton, Ohio, Sept. 3, 1937; d. Lawrence James and Frances Irene (Wilson) Gallagher; m. Charles R. Haugh, July 29, 1978; children: Kevin Charles, Maria Frances, Kateri Lynn. BS, Coll. St. Teresa, Winona, Minn., 1967; MEd, Ohio U., 1969; PhD, Loyola U. Chgo., 1975; ME/PD, U. Wis.-LaCrosse, 1984. Tchr. various schs., various locations, 1958-68; instr. psychology Coll. St. Teresa, Winona, Minn., 1969-72; v.p. student affairs, dean students Coll. St. Teresa, 1975-76; assoc. prof psychology St. Mary's Coll., Winona, 1976-82; assoc. prof. edn. St. Mary's Coll., 1982-86, prof. edn., 1986-95; prof. emeritus, 1995—, ind. beauty cons., edn. cons., 1995—, real estate cons., 1997—; ptnr. Real Estate Consultants Who Care, 1999—; co-chmn. dept. edn. St. Mary's Coll., 1986-87, dir. grad. program in counseling and psych. svcs., 1986-87, dir. grad. program in pastoral svc., 1986-88, others; adj. prof. U. Wis.-LaCrosse, 1985, Winona State U., 1988; mem. Cath. Schs. Acreditation Visitation Team, 1988; NAEYC validator, 1988-99. Franciscan cojourner, 1985—; chmn. continuing edn. com. Birthright, 1981, mem., 1980-99; eucharistic min. Cathedral of the Sacred Heart, 1981—, others; bd. dirs. Winona Day Care, Inc., 1991-95. NDEA fellow, 1968-69. Mem. ACA, Nat. Assn. for Edn. Young Children, Exch. Club Winona (treas. 1985-87, bd. dirs. 1985-90), Nat. Assn. of Realtors, Minn. Assn. of Realtors, Southeastern Minn. Assn. of Realtors, Psi Chi, Phi Delta Kappa, Kappa Delta Pi (counselor 1989-95), Delta Epsilon Sigma (pres. 1993-95). Roman Catholic. Home: 109 Rivers Ln Winona MN 55987-4111

HAUGH, LARRY DOUGLAS, statistics professor; b. Gary, Ind., June 11, 1944; s. William Edward and Mary Patricia (McFarland) H.; m. Jane Anne Booher, Aug. 21, 1966; children: Wendi Allyn, Joshua Douglas, Jeremy Alan. BA summa cum laude, Wabash Coll., 1966; MA in Math., U. Wis., 1967, MS in Stats., 1970, PhD in Stats., 1972. Asst. prof. stats. U. Fla., Gainesville, 1972-75; faculty assoc. IBM, Burlington, Vt., 1978-81; statistician Shell Research, Amsterdam, The Netherlands, 1981-82; prof. U. Vt., Burlington, 1975—; dir. statistics program, 1990—; lectr. in field, 1981—, U. Tenn., 1985-92; cons. in field. Assoc. editor Technometrics, 1981-86, Jour. Am. Statistics Assn., 1996—; editor Quality Engring., 1996—; co-editor book; mem. editl. bd. Quality Progress, 1992—; contbr. 7 chpts. to books, 63 articles to profl. publs., 87 proceedings. Recipient several rsch. grants including NIH, Nat. Inst. Occupl. Safety & Health, Nat. Inst. Disability & Rehab. Rsch., Fulbright-Hays, 1970-71; fellow Woodrow Wilson, 1966, NDEA, 1969-70; NSF trainee, 1966-67. Mem. Am. Statis. Assn. (chair com. on presentation awards 1980-81, chair quality and productivity sect. 1993, Presentation award 1977), Am. Soc. for Quality (sr.), Biometric Soc., Internat. Statis. Inst., Royal Statis. Soc. (chartered statistician). Office: U Vt 16 Colchester Ave Burlington VT 05401-1455

HAUGHEY, JAMES MCCREA, lawyer, artist; b. Courtland, Kans., July 8, 1914; s. Leo Eugene and Elizabeth (Stephens) H.; m. Katherine Hurd, Sept. 8, 1938; children: Katherine (Mrs. Lester B. Loo), Bruce Stephens, John Caldwell. Student, Deep Springs Coll., 1930-31; LLB, U. Kans., 1939. Bar: Kans. 1939, Mont. 1943. Landman Carter Oil Co., 1939-43; practice in Billings, Mont., 1943-98; ptnr. Crowley, Haughey, Hanson, Toole & Dietrich, 1950-86, counsel, 1986-98; ret. dir. Mont.-Dakota Resources Group Inc. One-man shows include, U. Kans., U. Mont., Mont. State U., Concordia Coll., Nebr., C.M. Russell Mus., Great Falls, Mont., Boise Mus. Art, Mont. State Mus., Helena, Sandzen Gallery, Bethany Coll., Luidsborg, Kans., Yellowstone Art Ctr., Billings, Mont., also numerous group shows. Pres. Rocky Mountain Mineral Law Found., 1957-58, trustee, 1955—; pres. Mont. Inst. Arts Found., 1965-67; pres. Yellowstone Art Center Found., 1969-71, trustee, 1964-81; mem. Mont. Ho. of Reps., 1960-64, Mont. Senate, 1966-70, senate minority leader, 1969-70. Recipient Gov.'s award for Arts, 1981. Fellow Mont. Inst. Arts (Permanent Collection award 1960), Am. Artists Profl. League; mem. ABA, Am. Coll. Real Estate Lawyers, Yellowstone County Bar Assn. (pres. 1960-61), U. Kans. Law Soc. (bd. govs. 1989-92), Am. Watercolor Soc. (Midwest v.p. 1978-82), N.W. Watercolor Soc. (life), Midwest Watercolor Soc., Kans. Watercolor Soc. (hon.), Mont. Watercolor Soc. (hon.), Phi Delta Theta, Phi Delta Phi. Republican. Episcopalian. Home: 2205 Tree Ln Billings MT 59102-2560 Office: Crowley Haughey Hanson Toole & Dietrich TransWestern Pla II 490 N 31st St Billings MT 59101-1256

HAUGHT, JAMES ALBERT, JR., journalist, newspaper editor, author; b. Reader, W.Va., Feb. 20, 1932; s. James Albert and Beulah (Fish) H.; m. Nancy Carolyn Brady, Apr. 22, 1958; children: Joel, Jacob, Jeb, Cassie. Student, Morris Harvey Coll., 1950-52; part-time, W.Va. State Coll., 1960-63. Apprentice printer Charleston Daily Mail, 1951-53; reporter Charleston Gazette, 1953—, varied positions as night and weekend city editor, music and film critic, govt., schs., suburban, religion and investigative reporter, 1970-82, assoc. editor, 1983-92, editor, 1992—. Author: Holy Horrors, 1990, Science in a Nanosecond, 1990, The Art of Lovemaking, 1992, Holy Hatred, 1994, 2000 Years of Disbelief, 1996; sr. editor (part-time): Free Inquiry mag., 1996—. Recipient award Headliners Club, 1971, 1st Ann. Consumer Writing prize Nat. Press Club, 1973, Nat. Hwy. Safety Writing award Uniroyal Tire Co., 1975, First Amendment award Sigma Delta Chi, 1977, Merit award ABA, 1977, Consumer Writing prize Nat. Press Club, 1979, 83, Spl. award Religion Newswriters Assn., 1980, Health Journalism award Am. Chiropractic Assn., 1981, 83, First Amendment award People for Am. Way, 1986, Nat. award for edn. reporting Edn. Writers Assn., 1989, Hugh M. Hefner First Amendment award Playboy Found., 1989, Benjamin Fine award for edn. reporting Nat. Assn. Secondary Sch. Prins., 1990. Democrat. Unitarian. Home: 15kh Lake Shore Dr Charleston WV 25313-3513 Office: Charleston Gazette 1001 Virginia St E Charleston WV 25301-2895

HAUGHT, WILLIAM DIXON, lawyer; b. Kansas City, Kans., June 12, 1939; s. Walter Dixon and Florence Louise (Rhoads) H.; m. Julia Jane Headstream, July 22, 1967; 1 dau., Stephanie Jane. B.S., U. Kans., 1961; LL.B., U Kans., 1964; LL.M., Georgetown U., 1968. Bar: Kans. 1964, Ark. 1971. Assoc. Stanley, Schroeder, Weeks, Thomas & Lysaught, Kansas City, Kans., 1968-70; ptnr. Wright, Lindsey & Jennings, Little Rock, 1970-91; pvt. practice Little Rock, 1991-95; ptnr. Haught & Wade, 1996—. Author: Arkansas Probate System, 1977, 5th ed. 1992, (with others) Probate and Estate Administration: The Law in Arkansas, 1983. Served to capt. USAR, 1964-68, Korea, Washington. Mem. ABA (coun. chmn. coms.), Am. Coll. Trust and Estate Counsel (regent, editor studies program, chmn. editl. bd., state chair), Internat. Acad. Estate and Trust Law, Am. Law Inst., Am. Counsel Assn., Ark. Bar Assn. (chmn. probate law sect. 1981-82, chmn. econs. of law practice com. 1982-84, chmn. agrl. law com. 1986-88), Ctrl. Ark. Estate Coun., Pulaski County Bar Assn., Ark. Bar Found., Country Club of Little Rock. Presbyterian. Office: Haught & Wade 111 Center St Ste 1320 Little Rock AR 72201-4405

HAUGHTON, JAMES GRAY, medical facility administrator, municipal health department administrator, consultant, physician; b. Panama City, Republic of Panama, Mar. 30, 1925; came to U.S., 1942, naturalized, 1953; s. Johnathan Antonio and Alice Eugeney (Gray) H.; m. Vivian Bruna Sodini, July 10, 1982; children—James Gray, Paula Yvette. B.A., Pacific Union Coll., 1947; M.D., Loma Linda U., 1950; M.P.H., Columbia U., 1962; D.Sc. (hon.), U. of Health Scis., Chgo. Med. Sch., 1971. diplomate Am. Bd.

Preventive Medicine. Intern Unity Hosp., Bklyn., 1949-50; fellow in abdominal surgery Unity Hosp., 1950-54; resident in preventive medicine N.Y.C. Health Dept., 1960-63, exec. med. dir., 1964-66; first dep. N.Y.C. Health Svcs. Adminstrn., 1966-70; exec. dir. Health and Hosps. Governing Commn. Cook County, Ill., 1970-79; v.p. Drew Postgrad. Med. Sch., Los Angeles, 1980-83; dir. Houston Dept. Health and Human Services, 1983-87; med. dir. Martin. Luther King Jr./Charles Drew Med. Ctr., L.A. Dept. Health Svcs., 1987-93; assoc. dean Drew U., 1989-93; prof. medicine Charles Drew U., 1987—, UCLA, 1987—; cons. AID Costa Rica Mission, 1982; adj. prof. adminstrv. scis. U. Tex. Health Sci. Ctr., Houston, 1984-87; mem. health svcs. com. Houston Red Cross, 1984-87; mem. Houston Mayor's Task Force on Aids, 1984-87; bd. dirs. Alan Gutmacher Rsch. Inst., 1985-91; AIDS cons. Regional Ministry Pub. Health, Santiago de Compostela, Spain, 1986; sr. investigator Digestive Diseases Ctr., L.A., 1987-91; AIDS med. adv. com. L.A. County Dept. Health Svcs., 1988-91, chair com. on access to health svcs., 1988-91, sr. health svcs. policy advisor, 1993-96, med. dir. pub. health programs & svcs., 1996—; mem. substance abuse coverage study com. Inst. Medicine NAS, 1988-90, study com. environ. justice, 1996-99; mem. Commn. Future Structure of VA Med. Care, 1990-91; com. study co-adminstrn. svc./rsch. programs of Alcohol, Drug Abuse and Mental Health Adminstrn. HHS, 1990-91; mem. nat. adv. com. AIDS Svcs. Program, Robert Wood Johnson Found., 1986-91, AIDS Prevention Program, 1987-91; mem. personal health svcs. planning com. L.A. County Dept. of Health Svcs., 1991-93; mem. AIDS adv. com. Alcohol, Drug Abuse, Mental Health Administrn., U.S. Dept. Health and Human Svcs., 1991-93, study com. ethical consideration managed care; bd. dirs. Local Health Officers, 1993—, mem. health info. syss. com., 1993—, co-chair personal health svcs. com., 1996—; bd. dirs. Local Initiative Health Authority L.A. County, 1996-97, Preventive Med. Residence Adv. Com., State Calif. Preventive Med. Residency Prog.; hosp. surveyor Consolidated Accreditation and Licensure Survey Program, Calif. Med. Assn./Joint Com. Accreditation Healthcare Orgn., 1992-96. Mem. editl. bd. Jour. Cmty. Health, 1990—, Jour. Pub. Health Policy, 1999—. Mem. Houston Clean City Commn., 1985-87. Lt. comdr. USN, 1956-58. Recipient Merit award N.Y.C. Pub. Health Assn., 1964, Humanitarian award Nat. Assn. of Health Svc. Execs., 1972, cert. meritorious svc. Health and Hosp. Governing Commn. Cook County, Ill., 1979, Merit award March of Dimes, 1987, Sanville lectureship U.C.L.A. Sch. of Pub. Health, 1992. Fellow Am. Coll. Preventive Medicine (v.p. 1976-78), Am. Pub. Health Assn. (governing council 1965-70, medicine/pub. health initiative, chair com. on pub. health edn. in medicine residencies 1994—, managed care task force 1997—, Rosenhaus award 1974); mem. AMA, Inst. Medicine Nat. Acad. Scis., Tex. Med. Assn. (sexually transmitted diseases com. 1984-87), L.A. County Med. Assn., Calif. Med. Assn., Health Care Assn. So. Calif. (med. adv. com. 1995—), L.A. Acad. Medicine. Democrat. Avocations: music; photography; swimming. Home: 4259 Palmero Dr Los Angeles CA 90065-4220 Office: 313 N Figueroa St Ste 227 Los Angeles CA 90012-2602

HAUGLAND, SUSAN WARRELL, education educator; b. Portland, Oreg., Aug. 29, 1950; d. George William and Commery Wallace (Coleman) Warrell; m. Jerry Lee Haugland, July 24, 1982; children: Charles, Michael. BS in Child Devel., Oreg. State U., 1972; PhD in Psychology, Saybrook Inst., 1976. Cert. family and consumer scis. Dir., head tchr. Lafayette Co-op Nursery Sch., Detroit, 1973-75; handicapped svcs. coord. OutWayne County Head Start, Wayne, Mich., 1975-76; asst. prof. child devel. Va. Poly. Inst. and State U., Blacksburg, 1976-79; prof. child devel. S.E. Mo. State U., Cape Girardeau, 1979-99; dir. Ctr. for Child Studies, Cape Girardeau, 1979-99, Kids Interacting with Devel. Software, Cape Girardeau, 1985—; chair Human-Environ. Studies, Cape Girardeau, 1990-93; judge Developmental Software Awards, 1991—, Child Mag. Awards, 1992—. Author: Helping Young Children Grow, 1980, Developmental Evaluations of Software for Young Children, 1990, Young Children and Technology: A World of Discovery, 1997, Haugland Developmental Software Scale, 1997, Haugland/Gertzog Developmental Scale for Web Sites, 1998; dept. editor Early Childhood Education Jour., 1992-94; mem. editl. bd. Jour. Computing in Childhood Edn.; contbr. numerous articles to profl. jours. Grantee numerous orgns.; recipient Gov.'s award for Teaching Excellence, 1996. Mem. Assn. for Childhood Edn. Internat., Nat. Assn. for Edn. Young Children, Nat. Assn. for Early Childhood Tchr. Educators, Tech. and Young Children Caucus (sec.), Nat. Assn. Family and Consumer Scis., Omicron Nu, Phi Kappa Phi. Democrat. Methodist. Avocations: reading, travel, cooking, bicycling. Office: Ctr for Child Studies SE Mo State U Cape Girardeau MO 63701

HAUK, A. ANDREW, federal judge; b. Denver, Dec. 29, 1912; s. A.A. and Pearl (Woods) H.; m. Jean Nicolay, Aug. 30, 1941; 1 dau., Susan. AB magna cum laude, Regis Coll., 1935; LLB, Cath. U. Am., 1938; JSD (Sterling fellow), Yale U., 1942. Bar: Calif. 1942, Colo. 1939, D.C. 1938, U.S. Supreme Ct. 1953. Spl. asst. to atty. gen., counsel for govt. antitrust div. U.S. Dept Justice, Los Angeles, Pacific Coast, Denver, 1939-41; asst. U.S. atty., Los Angeles, 1941-42; with firm Adams, Duque & Hazeltine, Los Angeles, 1946-52; individual practice law Los Angeles, 1952-64; asst. counsel Union Oil Co., Los Angeles, 1952-64; judge Superior Ct., Los Angeles County, 1964-66; U.S. dist. judge Central Dist. Calif., 1966—, chief judge, 1980-82, now sr. judge, chief judge emeritus; instr. Southwestern U. Law Sch., 1939-41; lectr. U. So. Calif. Law Sch., 1947-56; vice chmn. Calif. Olympic Com., 1954-61; ofcl. VIII Olympic Winter Games, Squaw Valley, 1960; Gov. Calif.'s del. IX Olympic Games, Innsbruck, Austria, 1964. Bd. dirs. So. Calif. Com. for Olympic Games. Served from lt. to lt. comdr., Naval Intelligence USNR, 1942-46. Recipient scroll Los Angeles County Bd. Suprs., 1965, 66, 75; Alumnus of Yr. Regis Coll., 1967; named to Nat. Ski Hall of Fame, 1975. Mem. Los Angeles County Bar Assn. (chmn. pleading and practice com. 1963-64, chmn. Law Day com. 1965-66), State Bar Calif. (corps. com., war work com. past vice-chmn.), ABA (com. criminal law sect.), Fed. Bar Assn., Lawyers Club Los Angeles, Am. Judicature Soc., Am. Legion, Navy League, U.S. Lawn Tennis Assn., Far West Ski Assn. (Nat. Sr. Giant Slalom champion 1954), Yale Law Sch. Assn. So. Calif. (dir., past pres.), Town Hall. Clubs: Yale of So. Calif. (dir. 1964-67), Newman; Valley Hunt (Pasadena); Jonathan (Los Angeles). Office: US Dist Ct US Courthouse 312 N Spring St Los Angeles CA 90012-4701*

HAUK, GARY H., associate director, discipleship and family group; b. Kingsport, Tenn., Dec. 24, 1950; s. Benjamin R. and Kathryn (Newbanks) H.; m. Brenda Kay Rhame, Aug. 21, 1971; children: Jennifer K., Benjamin G., Dori E. BA, Baylor U., 1972; MDiv, Southwestern Bapt. Theol. Sem., Ft. Worth, 1975; DMin, Phillips U., 1978. Ordained to ministry Bapt. Ch. 1975. Assoc. pastor 1st Bapt. Ch., Norman, Okla., 1975-78; sr. adult cons. Family Ministry, Nashville, 1978-82, mgr., family enrichment, 1982-92; dir. discipleship and family mag. dept. Bapt. Sunday Sch. Bd., Nashville, 1992-98; assoc. dir. discipleship and family group LifeWay Christian Resources (formerly Bapt. Sunday Sch. Bd.), Nashville, 1998—; min., Franklin, Tenn., 1975—. Author: Building Bonds Between Adults and their Aging Parents, 1985, Family Enrichment in Your Church, 1988. Mem. Evang. Christian Pub.'s Assn., So. Bapt. Assn. Family Ministry (pres. 1989-90), So. Bapt. Religious Edn. Assn. Southern Baptist. Avocations: boating, hiking, gardening, family. Home: 4276 Warren Rd Franklin TN 37067-4045 Office: LifeWay Christian Resources 127 9th Ave S Nashville TN 37203-0149

HAULENBEEK, ROBERT BOGLE, JR., government official; b. Cleve., Feb. 24, 1941; s. Robert Bogle and Priscilla Valerie (Burch) H.; m. Rebecca Marie Talley, Mar. 1, 1965; children: Kimberly Kaye, Robert Bogle III. BS, Okla. State U., 1970. Micro paleon. photographer Pan Am. Rsch. Co., Tulsa, 1966-67; flight instr. Okla. State U., 1970; air traffic control specialist FAA, Albuquerque, 1970-73, Farmington, N.Mex., 1973-78; flight svc. specialist FAA, Dalhart, Tex., 1978-80, Albuquerque, 1980—; staff officer CAP, Albuquerque, 1970-73, Farmington, 1974-78, advanced through grades to col., 1988, dir. ops. for hdqrs., 1981-86, 98—, N.Mex. Wing dep. commdr., 1986-88, N.Mex. Wing comdr., 1988-91, N.Mex. Wing dir. sr. programs, 1993-95, N.Mex. Wing. Ops. Staff, 1995—; mem. faculty Nat. Staff Coll., Gunter Air Force Sta., Montgomery, Ala., 1981-82; dir. South West Region Staff Coll., Albuquerque, 1986; mem. 1995 Nat. Air Traffic Control Facility of Yr. With U.S. Army, 1964-65. Recipient Meritorious Svc. award CAP, 1978, 81, 82, Lifesaving award, 1982, 95, Exceptional Svc. award, 1981, Disting. Svc. award, 1991. Mem. Exptl. Aircraft Assn., Nat. Assn. Air Traffic Specialists (facility rep. 1978-86, Nat. Transp. Safety Bd. rep. 1997-99), Nat. Assn. Flight Instrs., Aircraft Owners and Pilots Assn., Girl Scouts Am. (life). Republican. Presbyterian. Home: 5229 Carlsbad Ct NW Albuquerque NM 87120-2322

HAUM, BARBARA ROSE, artist, researcher; b. Frankfurt on Main, Germany, July 11, 1962; came to U.S., 1980; d. Herbert Nicolas and Ilse Marianne (Heinemann) H.; m. Henri Lustiger-Thaler, June 19, 1994; 1 child, Talia Lustiger-Thaler. BFA in Photography, Sch. Visual Arts, N.Y.C., 1985; MA, NYU, 1992, ArtsD, 1995. presenter in field. One-woman shows include Visual Arts Gallery, N.Y.C., 1985, Jewish Mus., Frankfurt, Germany, 1989, 91, Kommunale Gallery, Leinwandhaus, Frankfurt, 1992, Hebrew Union Coll., N.Y.C., 1993, Phila. Mus. Judaica, 1993, Congregation B'nai Jeshurun, N.Y.C., 1996, Dartmouth Coll., Hanover, N.H., 1996, Penny Liebmann Contemporary Art, N.Y.C., 1996; exhibited in group shows Akasaka Gallery, Tokyo, 1984, Paris Aduiovisuel Espace de Photo, 1987, Clocktower Gallery, N.Y.C., 1990, Women Photography, N.Y.C., 1990, 494 Gallery, N.Y.C., 1990, Hillwood Art Mus., 1994, Dooley Le Cappelaine, N.Y.C., 1992, Bronx (N.Y.) Mus. of the Arts, 1994, Casa Italia, N.Y.C., 1995, Photographic Resource Ctr., Boston, 1995, The Jewish Mus., San Francisco, 1997, Howard Greenberg Gallery, N.Y.C., 1997, Hebrew Union Coll., N.Y.C., 1997, The Broad St. Art Fair, N.Y.C., 1997, Raleigh Hotel, Miami, Fla., 1997, The Nat. Mus. of Women in the Arts, Washington, 1997, Steinbaum Krauss Gallery, N.Y.C., 1997; represented in permanent collections Photography Forum, Frankfurt, Mus. Modern Art of City of Paris, City of Frankfurt, Ma'yan Collection of Contemporary Women Artists, numerous pvt. collections; commissions include Congregation B'nai Jeshurun, N.Y.C.; contbr. art to jours. in field. Recipient Creativity award, cert. of distinction Art Direction Creativity Mag., 1990; Quadrille Ball Assn. scholar, N.Y.C., 1993-94. Jewish. Home: 183 Garfield Pl Brooklyn NY 11215-2105

HAUMSCHILD, MARK JAMES, pharmacist; b. West Bend, Wis., Apr. 6, 1951; s. James Harlow and Helen Marie (Bohn) H.; m. Mary Jo Snider, Oct. 15, 1976; 1 child, Ryan James. BA in Chemistry, Fla. Atlantic U., 1973; BS in Pharmacy, U. Fla., 1976; MS in Mgmt., U. South Fla., 1982; PharmD, Mercer U., 1984. Cert. nuc. pharmacist; cert. nutritional support pharmacist; cert. geriatric pharmacist. Continuing edn. instr. St. Petersburg (Fla.) Jr. Coll., 1977-81; staff pharmacist Morton F. Plant Hosp., Clearwater, Fla., 1976-78, nuclear pharmacy coordinator, 1978-83, clin. pharmacist, 1984-86, resident, 1984-85; ctr. mgr. Foster Infusioncare, St. Petersburg, 1986-88; gen. mgr. Healthinfusion Inc., St. Petersburg, 1988-95; pres. Pharm D. Cons., Largo, Fla., 1984—; regional dir. ops.-Fla. UPC Health Network, Clearwater, Fla., 1995-98; adj. instr. Coll. Pharmacy, U. Fla., Gainesville, 1980-86. Fellow Am. Soc. Cons. Pharmacists; mem. Am. Soc. Hosp. Pharmacists, S.W. Soc. Hosp. Pharmacists, Am. Pharm. Assn. (cert. in nuclear pharmacy), Soc. Nuclear Pharmacy, Am. Coll. Hosp. Adminstrs., S.W. Fla. Soc. Hosp. Pharmacists (cert. nuclear pharmacist), Beta Gamma Sigma, Phi Kappa Phi. Republican. Avocations: golf, walking, reading. Home: 12494 104th Ter Largo FL 33778-3407 Office: Rhone-Poulenc Rorer 12494 104th Terrace N Largo FL 33778-3407

HAUN, HENRY LAMAR, corrections department executive. BS in Edn., U. Utah, 1959; postgrad., Polton State Mental Hosp., San Bernardino, Calif., 1960-61. Dir. Kiwanis, Salt Lake City, 1961-65; fed. probation and parole officer U.S. Cts., Utah, 1978-83, supervising probation officer, 1983-89; chairperson Utah State Bd. of Pardons, 1989-97; exec. dir. Utah Corrections Dept., Murray, 1997—. Recipient J. A. Larson award State of Utah, citation Assn. of Parole Authorities Internat. Mem. U.S. Probational Alumni Assn., Utah State Corrections Assn., Commn. on Criminal and Juvenile Justice, Utah Sentencing Commn. Office: State of Utah Corrections Dept Ste 400 6100 S Fashion Blvd Murray UT 84107

HAUN, JAMES WILLIAM, retired food company executive, consultant, chemical engineer; b. Birmingham, Ala., Sept. 8, 1924; s. James Cecil and Eva (Walker) H.; m. Lucia Land, Sept. 6, 1946; children: James William, Lucy Margaret, Daniel Victor, Robert Paul. BSChemE, U. Tex., 1946, MS, 1948, PhD, 1950; grad. Advanced Mgmt. Program, Harvard U., 1961. Registered profl. engr. Instr. chem. engring. U. Tex., 1948-49; successively research engr., sr. research engr. and research group leader plastics div. Monsanto Chem. Co., 1950-56; with Gen. Mills, Inc., Mpls., from 1956; dir. corp. engring. Gen. Mills, Inc., from 1960, v.p., 1963-75, v.p. engring. policy, 1975-85, now ret.; mem. environ. engring. com. Sci. Adv. Bd. EPA, 1982-90; mem. food industry adv. com. U.S. Dept. Energy, 1978-81; mem. indsl. adv. council U. Minn. Inst. Tech.; dept. chem. engring. U. Calif., Berkeley, 1971-77; chmn. Internat. Centre for Industry and Environ., Paris and Nairobi, 1977-80; bd. dirs. World Environ. Center, N.Y.C., 1977-85. Author: Guide to the Management of Hazardous Waste, 1991. Bd. dirs. Center for Parish Devel., Chgo., chmn., 1980-85; bd. advisors U. Minn. Grad. Sch. Served with USMCR, 1942-45. Humble Oil & Refining Co. fellow U. Tex., 1949-51; named Engr. of Year Minn. Soc. Profl. Engrs., 1974. Fellow Am. Inst. Chem. Engrs. (emeritus); mem. NAM (dir., chmn. environ. quality com. 1973-79), C. of C. U.S. (com. on environ.), Sigma Xi, Omega Chi Epsilon, Phi Lambda Upsilon. Home: 1552 Wyldwood Ln NE Spring Park MN 55384

HAUN, JOHN DANIEL, petroleum geologist, educator; b. Old Hickory, Tenn., Mar. 7, 1921; s. Charles C. and Lydia (Rhodes) H.; m. Lois Culbertson, June 30, 1942. AB, Berea Coll., 1948; MA, U. Wyo., 1949, Ph.D., 1953. Registered profl. engr., Colo. Geologist Stanolind, Amoco, Vernal, Utah, 1951-52; v.p. Petroleum Research Corp., Denver, 1952-57; mem. faculty dept. geology Colo. Sch. Mines, Golden, 1955-80; prof. Colo. Sch. Mines, 1963-80, part time, 1980-85, emeritus prof., 1983—; cons. Barlow & Haun, Inc., Evergreen, Colo., 1957-90; cons. Potential Gas Agy., 1966-78, mem. com., 1978—; mem. adv. com. Colo. Water Pollution Control Commn., 1969-70; mem. adv. council Kans. Geol. Survey, 1971-76; del. Internat. Geol. Congress, Sydney, Australia, 1976; U.S. rep. Internat. Com. on Petroleum Res. Classification UN, N.Y.C., 1976-77; mem. oil shale adv. com. Office of Tech. Assessment, Washington, 1976-79, mem. U.S. natural gas availability adv. panel, 1983; mem. Colo. Oil and Gas Conservation Commn., 1977-87, vice-chmn., 1983-85, chmn. 1985-87; mem. energy resources com. Interstate Oil and Gas Compact Commn., 1978—; mem. exec. adv. com. Nat. Petroleum Coun., 1968-70, 79-89, mem. com. on unconventional gas sources, 1978-80; com. on Arctic oil and gas resources, 1980-81; mem. U.S. Nat. Com. on Geology Dept. Interior and NAS, 1982-89, chmn., 1985-87; mem. com undiscovered oil and gas resources, 19881-91, com. status and rsch. objectives in solid-earth scis.: critical assessment, 1988-92, Nat. Rsch. Coun.; del. Internat. Geol. Congress, Paris, 1980, Moscow, 1984; mem. Colo. Oil and Gas legis. com., 1993-94. Editor: The Mountain Geologist, 1963-65, Future Energy Outlook, 1969, Methods of Estimating the Volume of Undiscovered Oil and Gas Resources, 1975; asst. editor: Geologic Atlas of the Rocky Mountain Region, 1972; co-editor: Subsurface Geology in Petroleum Exploration, 1958, Symposium on Cretaceous Rocks of Colorado and Adjacent Areas, 1959, Guide to the Geology of Colorado, 1960; contbr. articles to profl. jours. Served with USCG, 1942-46. Recipient Disting. Svc. award Am. Assn. Petroleum Geologists, 1973, Mines medal Colo. Sch. Mines, 1995. Fellow Geol. Soc. Am., AAAS; mem. Am. Assn. Petroleum Geologists (editor 1967-71, pres. 1979-80, hon. mem. 1984, Sidney Powers Meml. award 1995), Am. Inst. Profl. Geologists (hon. mem., v.p. 1974, pres. 1976, exec. com. 1981-82, Ben H. Parker Meml. award 1983), Am. Geol. Inst. (governing bd. 1976, 79-82, sec.-treas. 1977-78, v.p. 1980-81, pres. 1981-82, Ian Campbell medal 1988, William B. Heroy Jr. award 1996), Rocky Mountain Assn. Geologists (sec. 1961, 1st v.p. 1964, pres. 1968, hon. mem. 1974), Soc. Econ. Paleontologists and Mineralogists, Am. Petroleum Inst. (com. exploration 1971-73, 78-88), Nat. Assn. Geology Tchrs., Wyo. Geol. Assn. (hon. life), Colo. Sci. Soc. (hon. life), Sigma Xi, Sigma Gamma Epsilon, Phi Kappa Phi. Home: 1238 Kerr Gulch Rd Evergreen CO 80439-9522

HAUPENTHAL, LAURA ANN, clinical psychologist; b. Rochester, N.Y., May 22, 1951; d. Carl Vincent and Helen (Hadden) H.; m. Alvin LaFrance Beers Jr., June 1, 1985. BS, No. Ariz. U., 1976, MA, 1977; EdD, U. No. Colo., 1979. Lic. psychologist, Colo., Calif. Lectr. Arapahoe Community Coll., Littleton, Colo., 1980; asst. prof. stress mgmt. U. No. Colo., Greeley, 1980; clin. psychologist Am. Med. Ctr., Denver, 1980-82, Anaheim (Calif.) Psychol. Assocs., 1986-87, Garden Park Med. Clinic, Inc., Anaheim, 1986-89, CIGNA Healthplans, Fountain Valley, Calif., 1986-88; psychol. cons. Irvine (Calif.) Internal Medicine Assocs., 1987-89; clin. psychologist Van Steenhouse and Assocs., Aurora, Colo., 1989-90, Colo. Family Ctr., Littleton, 1980-85, 90-93; pvt. practice clin. psychology Denver, 1993—; day camp counselor Rochester (N.Y.) Parks and Recreation, 1969; vol. counselor Marc Sch. for Handicapped, Mesa, Ariz., 1973, Cath. Social Svcs., Flagstaff, Ariz., 1976; counselor, house parent Our House, Inc., Greeley, 1977-78. Contbr. articles to profl. publs. Mem. Am. Acad. Behavioral Medicine (diplomate), Nat. Register Health Svc. Providers in Psychology, Am. Psychol. Assn., Colo. Psychol. Assn., Colo. Women Psychologists, Assn. Applied Psychophysiology and Biofeedback, Orange County Psychol. Assn., Am. Soc. of Psychiat. Oncology/AIDS. Avocations: skiing, yoga. Office: 6500 S Quebec St Ste 300 Englewood CO 80111-4674

HAUPIN, ELIZABETH CAROL, retired secondary school educator; b. East Orange, N.J., June 10, 1929; d. Edward M. and Edna (Wolverton) Bohsen; m. George W. Haupin, June 9, 1951; children: George, Linda, James, Robert. BA, Douglass Coll., Rutgers U., 1951; elem. cert., Newark State Coll., 1952; postgrad., Trenton (N.J.) State Coll. Cert. permanent English and Latin tchr., elem. endorsement, N.J. Elem. tchr. Bloomfield (N.J.) Bd. Edn., 1951-53; home tchr., East Brunswick, N.J.; elem. tchr. Pub. sch., Milltown, N.J., 1957-58; tchr. lang. arts Milltown (N.J.) Bd. Edn., 1970-92. Past moderator, bd. deacons, deacon Trinity Presbyn. Ch., East Brunswick, N.J., elder session, 1998; active local ch.; formerly active Girl Scouts USA; past pres., rec. sec. PTA. Recipient Outstanding Elem. Tchr. award, 1974. Mem. NEA, N.J. Edn. Assn., Middlesex County Ret. Educators Assn., Phi Beta Kappa (rep. Douglass alumnae coun.). Home: 32 Ellwood Rd East Brunswick NJ 08816-3003

HAUPT, EDWARD J., psychology educator; b. N.Y.C., Dec. 28, 1936; s. Edward and Wilma (Miller) H.; m. Mari-Lorraine Molenaar, Dec. 22, 1960 (div. Aug. 1981); children: Carl, Marcus, Jeremy. BS in Aero. Engring., U. Minn., 1959; PhD in Social Psychology, NYU, 1969. Math. statistician NIMH, Bethesda, Md., 1964-67; asst. prof. psychology Hampton (Va.) Inst., 1967-69; asst. prof. psychology Montclair State U., Upper Montclair, N.J., 1969-74, assoc. prof. psychology, 1974-99, prof., 1999—. Contbr. articles to profl. jours. Mem. APA, Assn. for Rsch. in Vision and Ophthlamology. E-mail: haupt@pilot.njin. Home: 400 Passaic Ave Nutley NJ 07110 Office: Montclair State U Dept Psychology Montclair NJ 07043-1624

HAUPT, H. JAMES, mechanical design engineer; b. Palmerton, Pa., Jan. 3, 1940; s. Harry C. and Mary L. (Patrick) H.; m. Betty S. Niemi, Sept. 5, 1970; children: Nadine R., Heather J. AAS, Broome Tech. Coll., 1964; BS, Ill. Inst. Tech., Chgo., 1971. Lic. profl. engr. Mech. engr. Argonne (Ill.) Nat. Lab., 1964—. Co-contbr. articles to profl. publs. AEC scholar, Washington, 1969. Mem. Am. Nuclear Soc., Ill. Profl. Engrs., Phi Theta Kappa, Tau Beta Pi. Republican. Roman Catholic. Avocation: golf. Home: 3215 Saddle Dr Joliet IL 60435-1142 Office: Argonne Nat Lab 9700 Cass Ave Bldg 310 Argonne IL 60439-4820

HAUPT, ROGER A., advertising executive. CFO Leo Burnett Co., Inc., Chgo., 99—. Office: Leo Burnett Co Inc 35 W Wacker Dr Chicago IL 60601-1648

HAUPTFUHRER, GEORGE JOST, JR., lawyer; b. Abington, Pa., Aug. 1, 1926; s. George Jost and Emilie (Schoenhut) H.; m. Barbara Barnes, Sept. 9, 1950; children: George Jost III, William Barnes. A.B., Harvard U. 1948; J.D., U. Pa., 1951. Bar: Pa. 1951. Assoc. Dechert Price & Rhoads, and predecessor, Phila., 1951-59; ptnr. Dechert Price & Rhoads, Phila., 1959-92, chmn., chief exec. officer, 1984-91, of counsel, 1992—; former bd. dirs. The West Co., Inc. Trustee emeritus Princess Grace Found., Abington Meml. Hosp.; chmn. adv. com. Joint State Govt. Commn. Commonwealth of Pa., 1982-93. Fellow Am. Bar Found.; mem. ABA (past chmn. real property, probate and trust law sect.), Pa. Bar (past chmn. real property, probate and trust law sect.), Phila. Bar (past chmn. probate and trust sect.), Order of Coif. Clubs: Pine Valley Golf, Union League, Roaring Gap, Johns Island, Huntingdon Valley Country, Harvard of Philadelphia, The Hon. Co. Edinburgh Golfers. Home: 1700 Old Welsh Rd Huntingdon Valley PA 19006-5838 Office: Dechert Price & Rhoads 1717 Arch St 4000 Bell Atlantic Tower Philadelphia PA 19103-2793

HAUPTLI, BARBARA BEATRICE, program administrator; b. Glenwood Springs, Colo., Sept. 20, 1953; d. Frederick James and Evelyn June (Rood) H.; m. Curtis Scott Bostian, July 4, 1992. BBA, Western State Coll., 1975. Contract specialist USA-TACOM, Warren, Mich., 1981-86; contract buyer Martin Marietta Orlando (Fla.) Aerospace, 1986; purchasing expediter Moog, Inc., Clearwater, Fla., 1986-89; subcontract adminstr. Olin Ordnance, St. Petersburg, Fla., 1989-91; sr. subcontract adminstr. Olin Ordnance, 1991-93; reimbursement specialist Tod. K. Allen, Inc., 1993-96; program mgr. Nat. Rsch. Tech. Contract Mfg., Tallahassee, 1997—. Avocations: reading, sailing, travel.

HAUPTMAN, HERBERT AARON, mathematician, educator, researcher; b. N.Y.C., Feb. 14, 1917; s. Israel and Leah (Rosenfeld) H.; m. Edith Citrynell, Nov. 10, 1940; children: Barbara, Carol Hauptman Fullerton. BS in Math., CCNY, 1937; MA, Columbia U., 1939; PhD, U. Md., 1955, PhD (hon.), 1985; PhD (hon.), CCNY, 1986, U. Parma, Italy, 1989, D'Youville Coll., 1989, Bar-Ilan U., Israel, 1990, Columbia U., 1990, Tech. U., Lodz, Poland, 1992, Queen's U., Kingston, Ont., Can., 1994, Niagara U., 1996. Statistician U.S. Census Bur., Washington, 1940-42; civilian instr. electronics and radar U.S. Army Air Force, Boca Raton, Fla., 1942-43, 46-47; physicist, mathematician Naval Rsch. Lab., Washington, 1947-70; mathematician Hauptman-Woodward Med. Rsch. Inst., 1970-72, exec. v.p., rsch. dir., 1972-85, pres., rsch. dir., 1985-87, pres., 1988—, also bd. dirs., 1972-94; prof. biophys. scis. SUNY, Buffalo, 1970—, prof. computer scis., 1992—; chmn. N.Y. State Inst. on Superconductivity, 1988—; mem. sci. adv. bd. BioCryst, 1989—; math. instr. U. Md., 1958-70; chmn. Inter Congress Symposium Direct Methods in Crystallography, Buffalo, 1976; pres. Assn. Ind. Rsch. Insts., 1979-80; mem. U.S. Nat. Com. for Crystallography, 1979-81, 82-85, 88, 89. Author: (with J. Karle) Solution of the Phase Problem., 1953, Crystal Structure Determination: The Role of the Cosine Seminvariants, 1972; editor: Dir. Methods in Crystallography, Proceeding of the 1976 Intercongress Symposium, 1978; contbr. chpts. to books, articles to profl. jours. Trustee Buffalo Gen. Hosp., 1990-96; chmn. communications com. Philos. Soc. Washington, 1966-67, corr. sec., 1967-69, pres., 1969-70. Served to lt. (jg.) USNR, 1943-46. Sr. fellow for travel, lectures and rsch. in Italy NATO, 1973; grantee NSF, 1972-92, grantee NIH, 1992—; recipient Belden prize (gold medal) in Math., 1935, RESA award in Pure Scis., 1959, Citizen of Yr. award Buffalo Evening News, 1986, Schoelkopf award Am. Chem. Soc., 1986, Gold Plate award Am. Acad. Achievement, 1986, Nat. Libr. Medicine medal, 1986, Law Sch. award Maimonides Chabad House, 1986, others, (with J. Karle) Patterson award, 1984, Nobel Prize in Chemistry, 1985; honoree Western New York Man of Yr. Buffalo C. of C., 1986, YMCA Dinner, 1986, 90th Nobel Ann. Dinner, 1991; inductee Nobel Hall Mus. Sci. and Industry, 1986, Townsend Harris Hall of Fame, 1989, U. Md. Alumni Hall of Fame; guest of honor Roswell Park Meml. Inst., 1985, YMCA Luncheon, 1986, others; invited guest Am. Nobel Convocation, 1987, 88, Weizmann Nat. Dinner, 1988, others. Fellow Washington Acad. Scis., Jewish Acad. Arts and Scis. (medal 1986); mem. AAAS, Am. Math. Soc., Am. Phys. Soc., Am. Crystallographic Assn. (mem. Fankuchen award com. 1988), Math. Assn. Am., U.S. Nat. Acad. Scis., Cosmos Club, Saturn Club (guest of honor 1985), Phi Beta Kappa, Sigma Xi (sec. Buffalo chpt. 1971-72). Avocations: stained glass art, swimming, hiking. Office: Hauptman Woodward Med Rsch 73 High St Buffalo NY 14203-1149

HAUPTMAN, LAURENCE MARC, history educator; b. N.Y.C., May 18, 1945; s. David and Frieda (Landesman) H.; m. Ruth Jacobs, May 23, 1970; children: Beth, Eric. BA, NYU, 1966, MA, 1968, PhD, 1971. From instr. to assoc. prof. SUNY, New Paltz, 1971-82, prof., 1982—; hist. cons. for Am. Indian nations including Mashantucket Pequot Tribal Nation of Conn., Oneida Nation of Wis., Seneca Nation of Indians, N.Y.; expert witness Senate select com. on Indian Affairs, U.S. Congress, 1990, House subcom. on interior and insular affairs, 1990; Alexander Flick lectr. in N.Y. history N.Y. State History conf., 1998. Author: The Iroquois and the New Deal, 1981, The Iroquois Struggle for Survival, 1986 (Notable Book of Yr. Choice mag.), Formulating American Indian Policy in New York State, 1988, The Iroquois Indians in the Civil War: From Battlefield to Reservation, 1993, Tribes & Tribulations, 1995, Between Two Fires: American Indians in the Civil War,

1995 (Notable Book of Yr. Choice mag.), Conspiracy of Interests: The Iroquois Dispossession and the Rise of New York State, 1999 (John Ben Snow Book prize); editor: Neighbors & Intruders, 1978, The Oneida Indian Experience: Two Perspectives, 1988, The Pequots in Southern New England, 1990, A Seneca Indian Sergeant in the Civil War, 1995, The Oneida Indian Journey: from New York to Wisconsin, 1998. Recipient Peter Doctor Meml. award Peter Doctor Fellowship Found. of Iroquois Indians, 1987, 98, NYS-UUP Award for Excellence in Teaching, 1991, Excellence in Rsch. award N.Y. State Bd. of Regents, 1992. Mem. Am. Hist. Assn., Orgn. Am. Historians, Western History Assn., Am. Soc. for Ethnohistory, N.Y. State Hist. Assn. Avocations: golf, travel. Home: 2 Sarafian Rd New Paltz NY 12561-3816

HAUPTMAN, MICHAEL, broadcasting company executive; b. Bklyn., Jan. 6, 1933; s. Hyman A. and Toba L. (Hershman) H.; m. Betty Holzman, Nov. 28, 1957; children: James, William. B.A., U. Vt., 1954. Program dir. Sta. WSTC, Stamford, Conn., 1960-61; prodn. mgr. Sta. WABC, N.Y.C., 1961-62; advt., promotion mgr. Sta. WABC, 1962-63; with Sta. WINS, N.Y.C., 1963-67, Sta. KYW-TV, Phila., 1967-68; mgr. mktg. services Westinghouse Broadcasting Co., N.Y.C., 1968-69; dir. retail mktg. ABC owned radio stas., N.Y.C., 1969-72; dir. planning ABC owned radio stas., 1972-73; v.p. ABC Radio, 1973-76, sr. v.p., 1976-81; v.p.-in-charge ABC Radio Enterprises, Inc., 1981-83; v.p. ABC Video Enterprises Inc., 1983-85; pres. Nat. Communications Corp., Cos Cob, Conn., 1985-89, 90—; pres. Physicians Radio Network div. Primark Corp., v.p. Health Info. Internat., 1989-90; pres. Group H Radio, Inc., 1992—. Address: 13 Carriage Rd Cos Cob CT 06807-1301

HAUPTMAN, WILLIAM, playwright; b. Wichita Falls, Tex., Nov. 26, 1942; s. Herman Ray and Arlene (Vanderhook) H.; m. Marjorie Erdreich, June 22, 1984; children: Sarah Olivia, Maxwell Lee. BFA in Drama, U. Tex., 1966; MFA in Playwriting, Yale U., 1973. Author: (plays) Shearwater, 1974, Heat, 1975, Domino Courts/Commanche Cafe, 1976 (Obie award distinguished playwriting 1978), Durango Flash, 1977, Big River, 1984 (Boston Theatre Critics' Circle award best new musical 1985, San Diego Theatre Critics' Circle award best new musical 1985, Tony award best musical book 1985), Gillette, 1986 (Los Angeles Drama Logue award distinguished playwriting 1986); (novel) The Storm Season, 1993; (stories) Good Rockin' Tonight and Other Stories, 1988 (Jesse Jones award best fiction Texas Inst. of Letters 1986); (teleplay) Denmark Vesey's Rebellion (Emmy award nomination, NAACP award, Freedom Foundation award); contbr. short stories to Playboy, Atlantic Monthly mags., The Best American Short Stories of 1982; contbr. articles to Atlantic Monthly, N.Y. Times. CBS Playwriting grantee, 1977, Nat. Endowment for the Arts grantee, 1977, Guggenheim Playwriting grantee, 1978. Mem. Writers Guild of Am. East, Dramatists Guild. Address: care Watkins Loomis Agency Inc 133 E 35th St New York NY 10016-3886*

HAUPTMANN, RANDAL MARK, biotechnologist; b. Hot Springs, S.D., July 6, 1956; s. Ivan Joy and Phyllis Maxine (Pierce) H.; m. Beverly Kay Suko, May 22, 1975; 1 child, Erich William. BS, S.D. State U., 1979; MS, U. Ill., 1982, PhD, 1984. Postdoctoral rschr. Monsanto Corp. Rsch., St. Louis, 1984-86; vis. rsch. scientist U. Fla., Gainesville, 1986-88; asst. prof. No. Ill. U., DeKalb, 1988-90, dir. plant molecular biology ctr., 1989-90; sr. rsch. scientist Amoco Life Sci. Techs., Naperville, Ill., 1990-94; comml. mgr. advanced tech. Seminis Vegetable Seeds, Woodland, Calif., 1994-98; gen. mgr. Ball Helix, West Chicago, Ill., 1998—. Author: (with others) Methods in Molecular Biology, 1990; contbr. articles to profl. jours. Mem. Internat. Assn. Plant Tissue Culture, Internat. Soc. Plant Molecular Biology, Am. Soc. Plant Physiologists, Tissue Culture Assn. (Virginia Evans award 1982), Sigma Xi, Gamma Sigma Delta. Republican. Office: Ball Helix 622 Town Rd West Chicago IL 60185-2614

HAUS, HERMANN ANTON, electrical engineering educator; b. Ljubljana, Slovenia, Aug. 8, 1925; came to U.S., 1948, naturalized, 1956; s. Otto Maxmilian and Helene (Hynek) H.; m. Eleanor Laggis, Jan. 24, 1953; children: William Peter, Stephen Christopher, Cristina Ann, Mary Ellen. Student, Technische Hochschule, Graz, 1946-48, Technische Hochschule, Vienna, 1948; BS, Union Coll., 1949; MS, Rensselaer Poly. Inst., 1951; ScD, Mass. Inst. Tech., 1954; DSc (hon.), Union Coll., 1989, Tech. U. Vienna, Austria, 1990, U. Gent, Belgium, 1994. Asst. to assoc. prof. MIT, Cambridge, 1954-62, prof. elec. engring., 1962-73, Elihu Thomson prof. elec. engring., 1973-87, inst. prof., 1987—; vis. prof. Technische Hochschule, Vienna, 1959-60, Tokyo Inst. Tech., 1980; vis. MacKay prof. U. Calif. at Berkeley, summer 1968; cons. Raytheon Co., 1956-91, Lincoln Labs., 1963—; mem. Nat. Acad. Scis. adv. panel, Radio Propagation Lab. Nat. Bur. Standards, 1965-67. Author: (with R.B. Adler) Circuit Theory of Linear Noisy Networks, 1959, (with L.D. Smullin) Noise in Electron Devices, 1959, (with P. Penfield, Jr.) Electrodynamics of Moving Media, 1967, Waves and Fields in Optoelectronics, 1984, (with J.R. Melcher) Electromagnetic Fields and Energy, 1989; mem. editorial bd. Jour. Applied Physics, 1960-63, Electronics Letters, 1965-73, Internat. Jour. Electronics, 1975-82. Recipient Pres.'s Nat. Medal of Sci., 1995, Frederic Ives medal Optical Soc. Am., 1994, Ludwig Wittgenstein prize Osterreichische Forschungsgemeinschaft, 1997; Guggenheim fellow, 1959-60, Fulbright scholar, 1985. Fellow IEEE, Am. Phys. Soc., Optical Soc. Am., Am. Acad. Arts and Scis.; mem. NAS, NAE, Sigma Xi, Eta Kappa Nu., Tau Beta Pi, Phi Delta Theta. Home: 3 Jeffrey Ter Lexington MA 02420-1307 Office: Mass Inst of Technology 77 Massachusetts Ave Rm 351 Cambridge MA 02139-4301

HAUS, RUTHANN ELIZABETH, geriatrics, community health nurse; b. Bklyn., Oct. 20, 1933; d. Carl Emmanuel and Lisa Marie (Larson) Lindfors; divorced; children: Lori Janine, David Craig, Michele Deanne. Diploma, New England Meml. Hosp., Stoneham, Mass., 1955; BS in Health Sci., Atlantic Union Coll., 1986; MPH, Loma Linda U., 1992. Head nurse, relief supr. Sunrest Nursing Home, Port Jefferson, N.Y., 1976-80; evening supr. Adventist Nursing Home, Livingston, N.Y., 1980-83; dir. staff devel., community health educator Adventist Health and Retirement Ctr., Livingston, 1983—; producer/radio talk show host Focus on Health, WHUC-AM, Hudson, N.Y., 1984-95. Outreach coord. Livingston Seventh-day Adventist Ch., 1989, 90; mem. nursing adv. coun. Columbia Greene C.C., chair nursing adv. coun., 1997-99. Recipient Outstanding Program award Am. Heart Assn., 1988, 90-93. Mem. APHA, Assn. Profls. in Infection Control and Epidemiology (bd. dirs. N.E. N.Y. chpt. 1990-94, pres.-elect 1992, pres. 1993, coord. coun. 1992—, rec. sec. 1994, 95), Am. Cancer Soc. (support group coord./facilitator 1995-98). Home: PO Box 531 Claverack NY 12513-0531

HAUSCHILD, DOUGLAS CAREY, optometrist; b. Manchester, Conn., Oct. 3, 1955; s. Vernon Francis and Barbara Gwendolyn (Rose) H.; 1 child, Chelsea Anna. BA in Biology magna cum laude, Wesleyan U., 1977; OD, New Eng. Coll. Optometry, 1981. Clinician Boston Eye Clinic, 1978-81; assoc. Drs. Todd, Todd & Hauschild, Hendersonville, N.C., 1981-84; owner, optometrist Weaverville (N.C.) Eye Assocs., 1984—, Asheville (N.C.) Eye Care Assocs., 1985—; clinician Walter Reed Army Med. Ctr., 1980, West Roxbury VA Med. Ctr., 1981, NEWENCO Pediatric/Geriatric Sply. Clinic, 1981; nominee Buncombe County Bd. of Health. Contbr. health articles to newsletters. Mem. Henderson County Bd. Health, 1983-85; actor Asheville Community Theatre, 1988—; instr. phys. edn. Evangel. Chapel Christian Acad., Asheville, 1985-86; mem. Bent Creek Bapt. Ch. Choir, Soloist; leader Bent Creek Bapt. Ch. Care Group, 1987-91; choir mem., soloist St. Eugene's Roman Cath. Ch., 1992—; mem. St. Eugene's Pastoral Coun., 1995—, chair, 1997-98. Fax: (828) 645-7279. E-mail: shapsight@msn.com. Mem. Am. Optometric Assn., So. Coun. Optometrists, N.C. State Optometric Soc., Mtn. Dist. Optometric Soc., Am. Pub. Health Assn., Lions (past pres.), KC, Elks, Beta Sigma Kappa, Delta Tau Delta. Republican. Avocations: photography, animal husbandry, gardening, theater, numismatics. Office: Weaverville Eye Assocs PO Box 1628 Weaverville NC 28787-1628

HAUSE, EDITH COLLINS, college administrator; b. Rock Hill, S.C., Dec. 11, 1933; d. Ernest O. and Violet (Smith) Collins; m. James Luke Hause, Sept. 3, 1955; children—Stephen Mark, Felicia Gaye Hause Friesen. B.A., Columbia Coll., S.C., 1956; postgrad. U. N.C.-Greensboro, 1967, U. S.C., 1971-75. Tchr. Richland Dist. II, Columbia, 1971-74; dir. alumnae affairs Columbia Coll., 1974-82, v.p. alumnae affairs, 1982-84, v.p. devel., 1984-89, v.p. alumnae rels., 1989-99, ret. 1999. Named Outstanding Tchr. of Yr., Richland Dist. II, 1974. Mem. Columbia Network for Female Execs., Council for Advancement and Support Edn., Nat. Soc. Fund Raising Execs., S.C. Assn. Alumni Dirs. (pres. 1996-98), S.C. Advocates for Women on Bds. and Commrs. (bd. dirs.). Republican. Methodist. Home: 92 Mariners Pointe Rd Prosperity SC 29127-7674

HAUSEL, WILLIAM DAN, economic geologist, martial artist; b. Salt Lake City, July 24, 1949; s. Maynard Romain and Dorthy (Clark) H.; children: Jessica Siddhartha, Eric Jason. BS in Geology, U. Utah, 1972, MS in Geology, 1974. Astronomy lectr. Hansen Planetarium, Salt Lake City, 1968-72; rsch. asst. U. Utah, 1972-74; tchg. asst. U. N.Mex., Albuquerque, 1974-75; project geologist Warnock Cons., Albuquerque, 1975; geologist U.S. Geol. Survey, Casper, Wyo., 1976-77; staff geologist Geol. Survey of Wyo., Laramie, 1977-81, dep. dir., 1981-91, sr. econ. geologist, 1991—; assoc. curator mineralogy Wyo. State Mus., Cheyenne, 1983-90; cons. Western Gold Exploration and Mining, Anchorage, 1988, 89, Chevron Resources, Georgetown, Mont., 1990, Fowler Resources, Phillipsburg, Mont., 1992, Bald Mountain Mining, U.S., 1993, A and E Diamond Exploration, Calif., 1993, Echo Bay Exploration, Diamond Exploration, U.S., 1994; instr. diamond exploration methods, U. Wyo., 1988, 94, Wyo. Geol. Assn., 1993, N.Am. Exploration, 1994, MK Gold, 1996; instr. (Grandmaster) WKU, 1998, JKI "open" Shorin-Ryu, 1998; state rep. JUKO-KAI Internat., Wyo., 1994; U.S. dir. open divsn., Shorin-Ryu Karate 1996, open divsn. head, Shorin-Ryu Karate and Kobudo (Juko-kai Internat.), 1997—; instr. martial arts dept. phys. edn., U. Wyo., 1995—, Campus Shorin-Ryu Karate and Kobudo Club. Author: Partial Pressures of Some Lunar Lavas, 1972, Petrogenesis of Some Representative Lavas, Southwestern Utah, 1975, Exploration for Diamondiferous Kimberlite, 1979, Gold Districts of Wyoming, 1980, Ore Deposits of Wyoming, 1982, Geology of Southeastern Wyoming, 1984, Minerals and Rocks of Wyoming, 1986, The Geology of Wyoming's Precious Metal Lode and Placer Deposits, 1989, Economic Geology of the South Pass Greenstone Belt, 1991, Economic Geology of the Cooper Hill Mining District, 1992, Mining History and Geology of Wyoming's Metal and Gemstone Districts, 1993, Geology Mining Districts and Ghost Towns of the Medicine Bow Mountains, 1993, Diamonds, Kimberlite and Lamproite in the United States, 1994, Pacific Coast Diamonds-An Unconventional Source Terrane, 1995, Economic Geology of the Seminoe Mountains Greenstone Belt, 1994, The Great Diamond Hoax of 1872, 1995, Geology and Gold Mineralization of the Rattlesnake Hills, Granite Mouontains, Wyoming, 1996, Copper, Lead, Zinc, Molybdenum and Associated Metal Deposits of Wyoming, 1997, Diamonds and Mantle Source Rocks in the U.S., with Special Emphasis on the Wyoning Craton, 1998, Water Training Techniques for Martial Artists, 1998; contbr. more than 350 articles to sci. and profl. jours. and contbr. to 5 books. Grantee NASA, 1981, Office of Surface Mining, 1979, U. Wyo., 1981-92, U.S. Geol. Survey Coop. Geol. Mapping Initiative, 1985-88, 98, Union Pacific Resources, 1991-94; recipient Pres.'s Cert. Excellence Am. Assn. Petroleum Geologists, 1992, Outstanding Contributions award Wyo. Geol Assn., 1992, Prospector's Best Friend award Rocky Mountain Prospector's Assn., 1998; named Laramie Lyceum Disting. Lectr., 1994, Disting. Lectr. U. Wyo., 1998; named to World Karate Union Hall of Fame, 1998, Millennium Hall of Fame, 1998. Mem. Wyo. Geo. Assn., Wyo. Profl. Geologists, U. Utah Geology Club (pres. 1969-71), Laramie Bushido Dojo Karate (pres. 1985-88), U. Wyo. Campus Shotokan Karate Club (instr. 1988-93), Shorin-Ryu Karate and Kobudo Club (U. Wyo. Campus headmaster 1993—), Juko-Kai Internat., Okinawan Karate Fedn. Avocations: karate (8th degree black belt hanshi), jujutsu and other martial arts (7 black belts inlcuding Juko-Kai Interat. Samurai and Juko-Kai Internat. Prof. Martial Arts), sketching. Home: 4238 Grays Gable Rd Laramie WY 82072-6911 Office: Geol Survey of Wyo PO Box 3008 Laramie WY 82071-3008 also: Shorin-Ryn Karate & Kobudo Club Univ Wyoming Box 3625 Wyoming Union Laramie WY 82071

HAUSELT, DENISE ANN, lawyer; b. Wellsville, N.Y., Oct. 12, 1956. BS, Cornell U., 1979, JD, 1983. Bar: N.Y. 1984, Ill. 1984, U.S. Dist. Ct. (we. dist.) N.Y. 1984, U.S. Bankruptcy Ct. 1984. Summer assoc. Wildman, Harrold, Allen & Dixon, Chgo., 1982; assoc. Nixon Hargrave Devans & Doyle, Rochester, N.Y., 1983-86; asst. counsel Corning (N.Y.) Inc., 1986-93, divsn. counsel, 1993-99, asst. gen. counsel, 1999—; Bd. dirs. So. Tier Legal Svcs., Bath, N.Y., 1986-89, Home Health Svcs., Inc., Corning, 1986—, 171 Cedar Arts Ctr., 1999—. Mem. Cornell Law Sch. adv. coun. Recipient Am. Jurisprudence Constl. Law prize, Cornell U., 1981, others. Mem. ABA, N.Y. State Bar Assn., Cornell Law Assn., Keuka Yacht Club. Republican. Avocations: sailing, skiing. Home: 164 Delevan Ave Corning NY 14830-3224 Office: Corning Inc Riverfront Plz MP-HQ-E2 Corning NY 14831

HAUSER, BERNICE WORMAN, inter-campus director; b. N.Y.C., Sept. 13, 1932; d. Aaron and Rose (Dunkel) Worman; m. A. Daniel Hauser, June 13, 1953; children:Mitchell Alan, Lisa Ann Hauser Pinero. BA cum laude, Hunter Coll., 1953, MS, 1956; MS in Adminstrn. and Supervision, CUNY, 1978. Tchr. Yonkers Pub. Schs., N.Y.C., 1953-54, N.Y. Pub. Schs., N.Y.C., 1954-60; primary sci. tchr., cons. Pub./Parochial/Ind. Schs., N.Y.C., 1960-72; tchr., primary sci. chair Walden Sch., N.Y.C., 1972-80, coord. student tchrs., 1980-88, curriculum cons., prin. sci. chair, 1988-91; asst. to headministress Horace Mann Sch., N.Y.C., 1991-93, dir. inter-campus acitivities, 1993—; cons. Scholastic Publs., N.Y.C., 1980—; bd. dirs. CUNY Pub.-Pvt. Schs. Partnership Coun. Author: How to Help Your Child at Home with Science, 1991, the Cat in the Hat Comes Back, 1997, You're the Apple of My Eye, 1998, (adoption issues) Am. Baby, 1984; primary corres. articles Tchr. Clearinghouse for Sci., 1987—; editor: Horace Mann Bull., 1993—; contbr. articles to Ind. Sch., Bull. of Sci. Tech & Soc., Parents League Bull., others. Mem. parks coun. Ctrl. Park Conservancy, 1970—; mem. Citizens Com. For Better N.Y., N.Y.C., 1980—; cons., speaker and writer Adoptive Parents Com., N.Y.C., 1975—; trustee, v.p., nominating chair Louis Wise Svcs. for Children, N.Y.C., 1976—. Recipient Impact II award Exxon, 1987, Jeremy Rifkin award NASTS, 1991; honoree United Jewish Appeal for Disting. Vol. Svc. to Louise Wise Svcs., 1998. Fellow Phi Delta Kappa; mem. AAUW, ASCD, Nat. Sci. Tchrs. Assn. (presenter 1985—), Nat. Assn. Ind. Schs., Nat. Assn. Sci. Tech. and Soc., Assn. Tchr. Ind. Schs. (program chairperson), N.Y. Assn. Ind. Schs. (liaison), Hunter Coll. High Sch. Alumni Assn. (past pres), Phi Beta Kappa, Epsilon Pi Tau, Cum Laude Soc. Avocations: indoor gardening, theater, opera, reading, writing. Office: Horace Mann Sch 231 W 246th St Riverdale NY 10471-3430

HAUSER, CHARLES NEWLAND MCCORKLE, newspaper consultant; b. Newton, N.C., Feb. 3, 1929; s. John Nathaniel and Charlotte (McCorkle) H.; m. Jane Ann Edwards, Dec. 29, 1956; children: David McCorkle, Susan Jane. AB, U. N.C., 1954; postgrad., Harvard U., 1968. Ordained elder United Presbyn. Ch. U.S.A., 1977. Washington corr. Charlotte (N.C.) Observer, 1961-62, Carolinas editor, 1962-65; fgn. corr. UPI, London, 1958-59, Paris, 1959-60; mng. editor Greensboro (N.C.) Daily News, 1965-66; exec. editor Greensboro News & Record, 1967-68; v.p., gen. mgr. Virginian-Pilot & Ledger Star, Norfolk, Va., 1969-73; v.p., exec. editor Providence Jour. and Evening Bull., 1973-89; cons., 1990—; lectr. Am. Press Inst., Reston, Va., 1969-89, U. R.I., 1987-90, U. N.C., 1991-92, Duke U., 1995—; bd. dirs. Sun Coast Media Group, Venice, Fla.; adj. assoc. prof. Brown U., Providence, 1981-84. With AUS, 1951-54. Decorated Bronze Star medal, Purple Heart. Mem. Am. Soc. Newspaper Editors, Alpha Tau Omega. Club: Nat. Press (Washington). Home and Office: 1031 Fearrington Post Pittsboro NC 27312-5503

HAUSER, CHRISTOPHER GEORGE, lawyer; b. Syracuse, N.Y., May 5, 1954; s. W. Dieter and Nancy (Keating) H. BA, Washington & Jefferson Coll., 1976; JD, Dickinson Sch. Law, 1979. Bar: Pa. 1979, U.S. Dist. Ct. (we. dist.) Pa. 1981, N.Y. 1987, U.S. Supreme Ct. 1992. Legal asst. Pa. Dept. of Justice, Harrisburg, 1978-79; assoc. McDowell, McDowell, Wick & Daly, Bradford, 1979-83; ptnr. McDowell, Wick, Daly, Gallup, Hauser, & Hartle and predecessor firm McDowell, McDowell, Wick & Daly, Bradford, 1983—; broker, owner Re/Max Alpine Sales, Ellicottville, N.Y., 1991-93; pres./owner Alpine Sales and Rental Mgmt., Inc., Ellicottville, N.Y., 1987-94; chmn. adv. bd. Office Econ. Cmty. Devel., Bradford, 1988—. Chmn. campaign Bradford Area United Way, 1984, v.p., 1987-89, pres., 1990-92; chmn. Downtown Bradford Revitalization Corp., 1986—; Bradford Parking Authority, 1986-94; pres. Alleghany Highlands coun. Boy Scouts Am., Falconer, N.Y., 1986-88; dir. Bradford Econ. Devel. Corp., 1987—, Exch. Club, 1989-91; sec., treas. Bradford Redevel. Authority, 1992-96, chmn., 1996—; active Bradford Area Citizens Adv. Com., 1992—; dir. Pa. Economy League, 1997—; dir., sec. Bradford Area Alliance, 1997—; bd. dirs. Rte. 219 Assn., 1996—; dir. Continental One Alliance. Recipient Outstanding Svc. award Bradford Area United Way, 1985, Silver Beaver award Allehany Highlands coun. Boy Scouts Am., 1990, Founder's award Order Arrow Boy Scouts Am., 1991, Cmty. Svc. award City of Bradford Office Econ. and Cmty. Devel., 1995; named Bus. Person of Yr. Bradford C. of C., 1986, One of Outstanding Young Men Am. U.S. Jaycees, 1983. Mem. N.Y. Bar Assn., Pa. Bar Assn., McKean County Bar Assn. (v.p. 1992-93, pres. 1994-96), Bradford Area Jaycees (pres. 1983-85), Pennhills Club (sec. 1985-90, 99—, pres. 1990-92), Bradford Club. Republican. Episcopalian. Home: 110 Congress St Bradford PA 16701-2228 Office: McDowell Wick Daly Gallup Hauser & Hartle PO Box 361 78 Main St Bradford PA 16701-2026

HAUSER, ELLOYD, finance company executive. CEO Solutran. Office: Solutran 3600 Holly Ln N Ste 60 Plymouth MN 55447-1286*

HAUSER, GEORGE, biochemist, educator; b. Vienna, Austria, Dec. 13, 1922; came to U.S., 1939.; s. Hans Joseph and Juliane Therese (Gleissner) H.; m. Louise Jean Russo, July 2, 1955. BS, Ohio State U., 1949; PhD, Harvard U., 1955. Mem. faculty Harvard Med. Sch., Boston, 1952-55, from rsch. assoc. to prof., 1955-93, prof emeritus, 1993—; from asst. biochemist to biochemist McLean Hosp., Belmont, Mass., 1957-93, sr. biochemist, 1993—; mem. editl. bd. Neurochem. Rsch; adv. and editl. bd. Jour. Neurochemistry, 1977-86, dep. ch ief editor, 1986-92; interim dir. Ralph Lowell Labs., McLean Hosp., Belmont, 1983-93; reviewer many sci. jours.; spl. cons. NIH, NSF. Co-editor: Inositol & Phosphoinositides: metabolism & metabolic regulation. Mem., treas. Dem. Ward Com., Newton, Mass., 1976—. With U.S. Army, 1943-48. Grantee Nat. Insts. Health, 1965-92, Nat. Sci. Found., 1980-82; fellow Japan Soc. for the Promotion of Sci., 1988. Mem. Biochem. Soc., Am. Soc. Biochemistry and Molecular Biology, Internat. Soc. Neurochemistry, Am. Soc. Neurochemistry (coun. 1983-87), Soc. Neurosci., Soc. Glycobiol. Democrat. Jewish. E-mail: george-hauser@hms.harvard.edu. Home: 47 Windermere Rd Auburndale MA 02466-2521 Office: McLean Hosp 115 Mill St Belmont MA 02478-9106

HAUSER, GUSTAVE M., cable television and electronic communications company executive; b. Cleve., Sept. 3, 1929; s. Abraham and Stella H.; m. Rita Abrams, June 10, 1956; children: Glenvil A., Patricia A. AB, Western Res. U., 1950; JD, Harvard U., 1953; LLM, NYU, 1957; diploma in law, U. Paris, 1958. Bar: Ohio 1953, N.Y. 1957. Instr. Harvard U. Law Sch., Cambridge, Mass., 1955-56; counsel internat. affairs Office Sec. Def., Washington, 1958-60; v.p. Gen. Telephone & Electronics Internat., N.Y.C., 1960-71; dir.-at-large U.S. Overseas Pvt. Investment Corp., Washington, 1968-77; exec. v.p. Western Union Internat., N.Y.C., 1971-73; pres., CEO Warner Cable Corp., N.Y.C., 1973-75, chmn., chief exec. officer, 1975-79; chmn., chief exec. officer Warner Amex Cable Communications, Inc., N.Y.C., 1979-83; chmn., CEO Hauser Comm., Inc., N.Y.C., 1983—; bd. dirs. Orion Network Sys., Inc., Washington, chmn., 1996-98. Author: A Guide to Doing Business in the European Common Market, 1960. Chmn., bd. dirs. Hauser Found., Inc., 1989—; trustee Steep Rock Land Trust, 1992—; trustee, mem. exec. com. The Mus. TV and Radio, 1992—; mem. exec. com. Harvard U., com. on univ. resources, 1997—. Served with AUS, 1953-55. Mem. Nat. Cable TV Assn. (dir. 1976-84, exec. com. 1978-84, vice chmn. 1983-84). Office: Hauser Comm 712 5th Ave New York NY 10019-4108

HAUSER, HARRY RAYMOND, lawyer; b. N.Y.C., July 12, 1931; s. Milton I. and Lillian (Perlman) H.; m. Deborah Marlowe, Aug. 6, 1954; children: Mark Jeffrey, Joshua Brook, Bradford John, Matthew Milton. AB, Brown U., 1953; JD, Columbia U., 1959. Bar: N.Y. 1959, Mass. 1963, Wash. 1972. Practice in N.Y.C., 1959-61, Boston, 1962—; atty. Sperry Rand Corp., 1959-61, Hotel Corp. Am., N.Y.C., 1961-62; v.p., sec., gen. counsel Hotel Corp. Am., 1962-70; mem. firm Gadsby & Hannah, 1971—. Life trustee Temple Israel, Boston; pres., dir. N. Bennett St. Sch.; trustee, gen. counsel The Boston Harbor Assn., Inc. Mem. ABA, N.Y. State Bar Assn., Mass. Bar Assn., D.C. Bar Assn., Internat. Bar Assn., Brown U. Club. Home: 1175 Chestnut St #2 Newton Upper Falls MA 02464-1336 Office: Gadsby & Hannah 225 Franklin St Boston MA 02110-2804

HAUSER, JOHN REID, electrical engineering educator; b. Advance, N.C., Sept. 19, 1938; s. Reid R. and Lillian (Sheek) H.; m. Ann Covington, June 15, 1962; children: John R. Jr., James W., Daniel R. BS, N.C. State U., 1960; MS, Duke U., 1962, PhD, 1964. Mem. tech. staff Bell Telephone Labs., Winston-Salem, N.C., 1960-62; rsch. engr. Rsch. Triangle Inst., Rsch. Triangle Pk., N.C., 1963-66; asst. prof. N.C. State U., Raleigh, 1966-68, assoc. prof., 1968-73, Disting. prof., 1983—, prof., 1973—; dir. Solid State Electronics Lab., N.C. State U., 1984—. Author: Fundamentals of Silicon Internal Devel. Tech., vol. II, 1968; contbr. over 125 articles to profl. jours. Recipient R.J. Reynolds Indsl. award for excellence N.C. State U., 1982. Fellow IEEE (Outstanding Engr. in N.C. award, 1978); mem. Am. Phys. Soc., Am. Soc. for Engring. Edn. Home: 6800 Phillips Ct Raleigh NC 27607-4924 Office: NC State U Dept of Elec Engring Raleigh NC 27695

HAUSER, JOHN RICHARD, marketing and management science educator; b. Scranton, Pa., Apr. 19, 1949; s. Jesse Ransberry and Muriel Florence (Myers) H.; m. Marija Danüte Eiva Hauser, June 9, 1979; children: Marius John, Aleksas Jonas, Rolandas Aras. SB in Elec. Engring., MIT, 1973, SM in Elec. Engring. and Civil Engring., 1973, ScD in Ops. Rsch., 1975. Asst. prof. mktg. and transp. Northwestern U., Evanston, Ill., 1975-80; assoc. prof. mgmt. sci. MIT, Cambridge, Mass., 1980-84; prof. mgmt. sci. MIT, Cambridge, 1984-89, Kirin prof. mktg., 1989—, head mktg. group, 1988—, co-dir. Internat. Ctr. Rsch. on Mgmt. of Tech., 1993—, rsch. dir. Ctr. for Innovation in Product Devel., 1997—; Marvin Bower fellow Harvard U., Cambridge, Mass., 1987-88; prin. Applied Mktg. Sci., Waltham, Mass., 1989—; vis. lectr. European Inst. Bus. Adminstrn., Fontainbleau, France, 1985; speaker, lectr. in field; expert witness in field; cons. in field. Author: Applying Marketing Management: Four Simulations, 1986, (with others) Essentials of New Product Management, 1986, Design and Marketing of New Products, 2nd edit., 1993, Enterprise: An Integrating Management Exercise, 1989; editor-in-chief Mktg. Sci., 1989-94; contbr. articles to profl. jours. NSF fellow, 1971-74; grantee in field. Mem. Am. Mktg. Assn. (segment chmn. educator's conf. 1978, 1st Pl. Thesis Supervision award 1981, Paul D. Converse award 1996), European Mktg. Acad., Inst. Mgmt. Sci. (1st Pl. Best Paper award 1982, 83, 93), Product Devel. and Mgmt. Assn., Tau Beta Pi, Eta Kappa Nu, Sigma Xi. Episcopalian. Avocations: sailing, skiing, basketball. Office: MIT E56-314 38 Memorial Dr Cambridge MA 02142-1347

HAUSER, JOYCE ROBERTA, marketing professional; b. N.Y.C.; d. Abraham and Helen (Lesser) Frankel; divorced; children: Mitchell, Mark, Ellen. BA, SUNY, 1976; PhD, Union Grad. Sch., 1987. Editor Art in Flowers, 1956-58; pres. Joyce Advt., 1958-65; ptnr. Hauser & Assocs., Pub. Rels., 1966-75; dir. broadcasting Bildersee Pub. Rels., 1973-75; pres. Hauser & Assocs., Inc., Pub. Rels., 1975-78; chief oper. ofnicer, pres. Hauser-Roberts, Inc., Pub. Rels./Mktg., N.Y.C., 1978-85; pres. Mktg. Concepts & Communications Inc., N.Y.C., 1985-92; moderator show Perceptions Sta. WEVD, 1975-77, Speaking of Health Sta. WNBC, 1977-89, 97 Health Line, Sta. WYNY, 1980-83, Conversations with Joyce Hauser, Sta. WNBC, 1975-86, What's on Your Mind, Sta. WYNY, 1983-84, Talk-Net, 1983-90; entertainment critic Sta. NBC, 1986-92; instr. Baruch Coll., CCNY, 1980-85; asst. prof. NYU, 1987—, prof. edn. 1992—. Sr. editor Art & Leisure News Svc., 1988—; editor-in-chief N.Y. State Comms. Annual, 1999—; contbg. editor Alive, 1976-77; author: Good Divorces, Bad Divorces: A Case for Divorce Mediation, 1995; contbr. articles to profl. jours. Mem. Citywide Health Adv. Coun. on Sch. Health, 1970-88, treas., 1980-92; mem. adv. bd. degree programs NYU Sch. Continuing Edn.; mediator/arbitrator Victim Svcs. Agy., 1986-87, Inst. Mediation and Conflict Resolution, 1985-86. Named one of 10 Top Successful Women, Cancer Soc., 1976, Tchr. of Yr., Zeta Beta Tau, 1989-90, one of 20 Women in Pub. Rels., 1981, Prof. of Yr. Sch. of Edn., 1999; recipient Professionalism award Sta. WNBC, 1980; John E. Wilson fellow, 1996-97. Mem. AFTRA, Nat. Assn. Scholars, Pub. Rels. Soc. Am., Am. Women in Radio and TV (corr. sec. 1973, chmn. coll. women in broadcasting 1974), Nat. Assn. Speech Communicators, Nat. Assn. Scholars, N.Y. State Speech Communicators (treas., v.p. 1996, pres. 1997), N.Y. State Comms. Assn. (editor annual 1998), Acad. Family Mediators, Soc. Profl. Dispute Resolutions, Drama Desk, Outer Critics Cir., N.Y. Press Club. Home: 115 E 82nd St New York NY 10028-0831

HAUSER, MICHAEL GEORGE, astrophysicist; b. Chgo., Dec. 3, 1939; s. Julius and Sylvia Ann (Gross) H.; m. Miriam Freedman, Sept. 11, 1960 (div. May 1977); children: Karen Celia (dec.), Gerald Paul; m. Deanna Grove, May 8, 1981. B.Engring. Physics with distinction, Cornell U., 1962; Ph.D. in Physics (NSF fellow), Calif. Inst. Tech., 1967. Instr. Princeton U., 1967-70, asst. prof. physics, 1970-72; sr. research fellow in physics Calif. Inst. Tech., 1972-74; head infrared astronomy group lab. for high energy astrophysics Goddard Space Flight Center, Greenbelt, Md., 1974-77; head sect. infrared astrophysics Lab. for Extraterrestrial Physics Goddard Space Flight Center, 1977-85, head infrared astrophysics br. Lab. Extraterrestrial Physics, 1985-87, head infrared astrophysics br. Lab. Astronomy and Solar Physics, 1987, chief Lab. Astronomy and Solar Physics, 1988-95; dep. dir. Space Telescope Sci. Inst., Balt., 1995—; mem. joint sci. working group Infrared Astron. Satellite, 1977-84; prin. investigator Diffuse Infrared Background Experiment, Cosmic Background Explorer, 1977-97; mem. NASA Space Sci. Adv. Com., 1994-97. Vice pres. PTA, Kensington (Md.) Jr. High, 1977-78, mem. exec. bd., 1978-79. Hon. Woodrow Wilson fellow, 1962; recipient NASA Exceptional Sci. Achievement medal, 1984, 91, John C. Lindsay Meml. award Godard Space Flight Ctr., 1986, Meritorious Exec. award Sr. Exec. Svc., 1993. Fellow Am. Phys. Soc.; mem. Am. Astron. Soc., AAAS, Internat. Astron. Union (v.p. commn. 21, 1991-94), Sigma Xi. Rsch., numerous publs. on elem. particle physics, astronomy, and cosmology. Office: Space Telescope Sci Inst 3700 San Martin Dr Baltimore MD 21218-2464

HAUSER, RAY LOUIS, research engineer, entrepreneur; b. Litchfield, Ill., Apr. 16, 1927; s. A. Vernon and Grace (Gregg) H.; m. Consuelo Wright Minnich, Sept. 2, 1951; children: Beth, Cynthia, Dewi, Chris. BS, U. Ill., 1950; M in Engring., Yale U., 1952; PhD, U. Colo., 1957. Registered profl. engr., Colo., safety engr., Calif. Sr. project engr. Conn. Hard Rubber Co., New Haven, 1950-52; rsch. staff U. Colo., Boulder, 1954-57; material tech. staff Martin Co., Denver, 1957-61; owner, mgr. Hauser Labs., Boulder, 1961-89; bd. dirs. Surface Solutions Inc., Boulder, ICAT Systems Inc., Phoenix; vis. lectr. U. Colo., Boulder, 1957-63. Pres. Boulder Civic Opera, 1971-72. Sgt. U.S. Army, 1952-54. Recipient U. Colo. medal, 1995. Fellow AAAS; mem. AIChE, Soc. Plastics Engrs. (bd. dirs. 1959-62), Assn. Cons. Chemists and Chem. Engrs. (bd. dirs. 1986), Am. Assn. Lab. Accreditors (bd. dirs. 1986-91), Rotary (bd. dirs. 1975-77). Home: 5758 Rustic Knolls Dr Boulder CO 80301-3029 Office: Hauser Inc 4750 Nautilus Ct Boulder CO 80301-3240

HAUSER, RICHARD ALAN, lawyer; b. Litchfield, Ill., Feb. 26, 1943; s. Melvin Henry and Helen Maxine (Roberts) H.; m. Carol E. Clampett, Jan. 2, 1965 (div. 1974); children: Jennifer Macey, Sarah Hampton; m. Karen Rollow Allen, July 26, 1977; children: Kristin Anne, Erica Christine, Alissa Marie. BS, U. Pa., 1965; JD cum laude, U. Miami, 1968. Bar: Fla., D.C. Law clk. U.S. Dist. Ct. Fla., Miami, 1968-70; asst. U.S. atty. Dept. Justice, Miami, 1970-71; atty. adviser Dept. Atty. Gen.'s Office Dept. Justice, Washington, 1971-73, asst. dir. Office of Policy Planning, 1974-75; assoc. counsel White House, Washington, 1973-74, dep. counsel to pres., 1981-86; pvt. practice Washington, 1975-81; ptnr. Baker & Hostetler, Washington, 1986—; chmn. Pennsylvania Ave. Devel. Corp., 1988-96; mem. Internat. Ctr. Settlement of Investment Disputes, 1986-94; chmn. bd. dirs. The Luther Inst., Washington; bd. dirs. Lutheran Brotherhood Mutual Funds. Recipient Spl. Asst. U.S. Atty. award for Superior Performance, Dept. Justice. Mem. Fla. Bar Assn., D.C. Bar Assn., Va. Bar Assn., Chevy Chase Club, Met. Club (bd. govs.), Econ. Club. Office: Baker & Hostetler 1050 Connecticut Ave NW Washington DC 20036-5304

HAUSER, RITA ELEANORE ABRAMS, lawyer; b. N.Y.C., July 12, 1934; d. Nathan and Frieda (Litt) Abrams; m. Gustave M. Hauser, June 10, 1956; children: Glenvil Aubrey, Ana Patricia. AB magna cum laude, CUNY Hunter Coll., 1954; D in Polit. Economy with highest honors, U. Strasbourg, France, 1955; Licence en Droit, U. Paris, 1958; student law sch., Harvard U., 1955-56; LLB with honors, NYU, 1959; LLD (hon.), Seton Hall U., 1969, Finch Coll., 1969, U. Miami, Fla., 1971, Colgate U., 1995. Bar: D.C. 1959, N.Y. 1961, U.S. Supreme Ct. 1967. Atty. U.S. Dept. Justice, 1959-61; pvt. practice N.Y.C., 1961-67; ptnr. Moldover, Hauser, Strauss & Volin, 1968-72; sr. ptnr. Stroock & Stroock & Lavan, N.Y.C., 1972-92, of counsel, 1992—; pres. The Hauser Found., N.Y.C., 1990—; Handmaker lectr., Louis Brandeis Lecture Series, U. Ky. Law Sch.; lectr. on internat. law Naval War Coll. and Army War Coll.; Mitchell lectr. in law SUNY, Buffalo; USIA lectr. constl. law Egypt, India, Australia, New Zealand; bd. dirs. The Eisenhower World Affairs Inst.; U.S. chmn. Internat. Ctr. for Peace in Middle East, 1984-92; bd. dirs. Internat. Peace Acad., 1990—, chair 1993—; U.S. pub. del. to Vienna follow-up meeting of Conf. on Security and Cooperation in Europe, 1986-88; mem. adv. panel in internat. law U.S. Dept. State, 1986-92, Am. Soc. Internat. Law Award to honor Women in Internat. Law; mem. Pacific Coun. on Internat. Policy, 1998—; bd. dirs. The Rand Corp. Contbr. articles on internat. law to profl. jours. U.S. rep. to UN commn. on Human Rights, 1969-72; mem. U.S. del. to Gen. Assembly UN, 1969; vice chmn. U.S. Adv. Com. on Internat. and Cultural Affairs, 1973-77; mem. N.Y.C. Bd. Higher Edn., 1974-76, Stanton Panel on internat. info., edn., cultural rels. to reorganize USIA and Voice of Am., 1974-75, Mid. East Study Gruop Brookings Inst., 1975, 87-88, U.S. del. World Conf. Internat. Women's Yr., Mexico City, 1975; co-chair Com. for Re-election Pres., 1972, Presdl. Debates project LVW, 1976, Coalition for Regan/Bush; adv. bd. Nat. News Coun., 1977-79; bd. dirs. Bd for Internat. Broadcasting, 1977-80, Catalyst, Internat. Peace Acad., The Aspen Inst., The RAND Corp., U.S. Coun. Germany; trustee, exec com. N.Y. Philharm. Soc.; trustee Lincoln Ctr. Performing Arts; adv. bd. Ctr. For Law and Nat. Security, U. Va. Law Sch., 1978-84; vis. com. Ctr. Internat. Affairs Harvard U., 1975-81, John F. Kennedy Sch. Govt., Harvard U., 1992—; dean's bd. advisor's Harvard Law Sch., 1996—, vice-chair, nat. co-chair univ. fund-raising campaign, 1997—; mem. bd. advisors Middle East Inst., Harvard U.; bd of visitors Georgetown Sch. Fgn. Svc., 1989-94; chmn. adv. panel Internat. Parlimentary Group for Human Rights in Soviet Union, 1984-86; mem. Lawyers Com. for Human Rights, 1995—; mem. spl. refugee adv. panel Dept. State, 1981; bd. fellows Claremont U. Ctr. & Grad. Sch., 1990-94; former trustee Internat. Legal Ctr., Legal Aid Soc. N.Y., Freedom House; mem. Lawyer's Comm. Human Rights, 1996—. Fulbright grantee U. Strasbourg, 1955; Intellectual Exch. fellow Japan Soc.; recipient Jane Addams Internat. Women's Leadership award, 1996, women in internat. law award Am. Soc. Internat. Law, 1995, Fulbright award for Fulbright Alumni, 1997. Fellow ABA (life, mem. standing coms. on law and nat. security 1979-85, standing com. on world order under law 1969-78, standing com. on jud. selection, tenure, compensation 1977-79, coun. sect. on ind. rights and responsibilities 1970-73, advisor bd. jour. 1973-78); mem. Am. Soc. Internat. Law (v.p. 1988—, mem. exec. com. 1971-76), Am. Fgn. Law Assn. (bd. dirs.), Am. Arbitration Assn. (past bd. dirs.), Ams. Soc. (bd. dirs. 1988—), Coun. Fgn. Rels. (bd. dirs.), Internat. Inst. for Strategic Studies (London, bd. dirs. 1994—), Am. Coun. on Germany, The Atlantic Coun. U.S., Friends of the Hauge Acad. Internat. Law (bd. dirs.), Assn. of Bar of City of N.Y., Catalyst (bd. dirs. 1989-96). Republican. Office: Stroock & Stroock & Lavan 180 Maiden Ln New York NY 10038-4925 also: The Hauser Found Office of Pres 712 5th Ave New York NY 10019-4108

HAUSER, SARA NOONEY, writer, educator; b. Jacksonville, Fla., Feb. 19, 1919; d. Austin Thomas and Camilla (Raulerson) Nooney; m. Thomas Allan Smith, Apr. 20, 1946 (dec. Aug. 1977); children: Thomas Allan Jr., Linda Smith Bates, Sean Patrick Smith; m. Elmer Leonard Hauser, June 19, 1978. BA, Fla. State U., 1941; MA, U. South Fla., 1972. Math. educator Duval County Schs., Jacksonville, Fla., 1941-46; librarian Brownsville Children's Libr., Bklyn., 1946-47; educator U.S. Navy Base, Port Lyautey, Morocco, 1948-53; media specialist Hillsborough County Schs., Plant City, Fla., 1954-79; established ctrl. media ctrs. in elem. schs., Plant City, 1956-60. Author: Scattered Leaves, 1994; contbr. feature articles to Lakeland (Fla.) Ledger, 1970-73. Mem. AAUW, DAR (registrar 1992—), Friendship Force (sec. 1992-93), Federated Woman's Club (treas. 1992-93), New Eng. Hist. Geneal. Soc., Fla. State Geneal. Soc., Alpha Chi Alpha, Delta Kappa Gamma. Avocations: travel, hiking, genealogy research. Home: 4444 Saxon Dr New Smyrna Beach FL 32169-4135

HAUSER, WILLIAM BARRY, history educator, historian; b. Washington, May 2, 1939; s. Philip Morris and Zelda Barnett (Abrams) H.; children: Benjamin Lester, Aaron Davidson, Zachary Barnett. SB in Math., U. Chgo., 1960; MA in East Asian Studies, Yale U., 1962, PhD in History, 1969. Lectr., asst. prof. U. Mich., Ann Arbor, 1967-69, 70-74; asst. prof. history U. Rochester, N.Y., 1974-77, assoc. prof. history, 1977-83, prof. history, 1983—, chmn. dept. history, 1979-85. Author: Economic Institutional Change in Tokugawa Japan, 1974, (with Jeffrey P. Mass) The Bakufu in Japanese History, 1985; contbr. articles and revs. to profl. publs. Fulbright-Hays fellow U.S. Dept. State, Osaka, Japan, 1964-66; NEH fellow, 1972-73, 82-83; Mellon Faculty fellow U. Rochester, 1977; Japan Found. fellow, 1976, 82. Mem. Assn. for Asian Studies (chmn. adv. com. Bibliography of Asian Studies 1984-96). Avocations: cooking; gardening. Home: 425 Westminster Rd Rochester NY 14607-3231 Office: U Rochester Dept History Rochester NY 14627

HAUSERMAN, JACQUITA KNIGHT, electricity company executive; b. Donaldsonville, Ga., Apr. 23, 1942; d. Lendon Bernard and Ressie Mae (Robinson) Knight; m. Mark Kenny Hauserman, July 8, 1978. BS in Math., U. Montevallo, Ala., 1964; M of Applied Tchg. in Math., Emory U., 1973; MBA in Fin., Ga. State U., 1978. Fin. analyst Cleve. Electric Illuminating Co., 1982-83, gen. supr. employment svc., 1983-85, sr. corp. planning advisor, 1985-86, dir. customer svc., 1986-88, v.p. adminstrn., 1988-90; v.p. customer svc. & comty. affairs Centerior Energy Corp., Independence, Ohio, 1990-93, v.p. customer support, 1993-95, v.p. bus. svcs., 1995-97; bd. dirs. Am. Store Industries, 1998—; ind. cons. Bd. trustees Benjamin Rose Inst., Cleve., John Carroll U., University Heights, Ohio, Bus. Volunteerism Coun.; bd. govs. Ohio Motorists Assn., Meridia Health System. Home: Centerior Energy Corp 29325 Bolingbrook Rd Pepper Pik OH 44124*

HAUSFELD, JAMES FRANK, executive director; b. Chgo., July 22, 1955; s. James J. and Geraldine M. (Nesladek) H.; 1 child, Laura Beth. BA in Fine Arts, Columbia Coll., 1976. Producer, cameraman Chgo. Bulls Basketball Team, 1976-77; media specialist Bell and Howell, Chgo., 1977-79; producer, dir. New Trier Technology Coop., Winnetka, Ill., 1979-94, exec. dir., 1994—, adminstr. in charge devel. high speed data and video network; mem. adv. coun. New Trier Technology Coop., Winnetka, 1995—; mem. State of Ill. Instnl. Tech. Adv. Coun., 1994—; mem. ind. video competition jury Chgo. Internat. Film Festival, 1979-86; freelance editor, cameraman On Location, Ltd., Chgo., 1983-90; freelance video editor, videographer Bougainville Prodns., 1991—. Producer, editor, dir.: (videotapes) North Suburban Spl. Edn. Dist.-One Child at a Time, 1984, The Pursuit of Excellence-Illinois Style, 1985, Social Service: A Committment to Caring, 1987, To Enrich Their Lives, 1989, Nazi Concentration Camps: an Eyewitness Account, 1990, Peer Helping: A Code of Friendship, 1992, Education and the Common Denominator: The Teacher, 1995, Abriendo Puertas: The Winnetka Schools Foreign Language Program, 1996, New Trier Technology Cooperative 1997 Institute Day: Thinking in the Future Tense, 1997; editor (videotapes) Perspectives on China, 1987, The Other Side of Summer: The Wrecking of Old Comiskey Park, 1993. Mem. Internat. TV Assn. Roman Catholic. Clubs: Argyle-Magnolia Glenwood Block (capt. 1985-89), Montrose Elite (Chgo.); BMG Music Service (Indpls.). Avocations: softball, darts, collecting music, attending Chgo. White Sox games. Home: 1431 W Argyle St Chicago IL 60640-3502 Office: New Trier Tech Coop 385 Winnetka Ave Winnetka IL 60093-4238

HAUSLER, WILLIAM JOHN, JR., microbiologist, educator, public health laboratory administrator; b. Kansas City, Kans., Aug. 31, 1926; s. William John and Clifton (McCambridge) H.; m. Mary Lois Rice, Apr. 19, 1949; children—Cheryl Kaye Johnson, Kenneth Randall, Eric Rice, Mark Clifton. AB in Microbiology, U. Kans., 1951, MA in Microbiology, 1953, PhD in Microbiology, Math., 1958. Diplomate Am. Bd. Med. Microbiology (chmn. 1979-82, Profl. Recognition award 1995). Asst. instr. U. Kans., Lawrence, 1951-56, rsch. asst., 1956-58; assoc. bacteriologist Iowa State Hygienic Lab., Iowa City, 1958-59, asst. dir., prin. bacteriologist, 1959-65, dir., 1965-95; dir. emeritus, 1995—; asst. prof. U. Iowa Coll. Medicine, Iowa City, 1959-66; assoc. prof. U. Iowa Coll. Medicine, 1966-90, prof., 1990—; assoc. prof. U. Iowa Coll. Dentistry, 1966-90, prof., 1990—; cons. to Iran WHO, 1969, U.S. EPA, 1970-72, CDC, 1965—, People's Republic China WHO, 1990, WHO Western Pacific Region, 1991, UNDP India, 1992; cons. to industry. Editor: Standard Methods for the Examination of Dairy Products, 1972, Manual Clinical Microbiology, 3d edit., 1980, 4th edit., 1985, 5th edit., 1991, Compendium of Methods for the Microbiological Examination of Foods, 1980, 2d edit., 1984, Diagnostic Procedures for Bacterial Mycotic and Parasitic Infections, 1981, Laboratory Diagnosis of Infections Diseases: Principles and Practice, 1988; co-editor: Topley & Wilson's Microbiology and Microbial Infections, 9th edit., 1997; mem. editl. bd. various profl. jours.; contbr. articles to profl. jours. Councilman City Govt., University Heights, Iowa, 1966-69; commr. Iowa Air Pollution Control Comm., 1967-74; mem. exec. com. Iowa Dept. Environ. Quality, 1974-80, Nat. Com. for Clin. Lab. Standards, bd. dirs., 1987-93. Lt. comdr. USNR, 1944-67. Recipient Henry Albert Meml. award Iowa Pub. Health Assn., 1974. Fellow APHA, Am. Acad. Microbiology (chmn. 1983-89, Profl. Recognition award 1995); mem. Am. Soc. Microbiology, Assn. State and Territorial Pub. Health Lab. Dirs. (pres. 1984-85, Lifetime Achievement award 1998), Sigma Phi Epsilon, Rotary (Paul Harris fellow). Avocations: photography; woodworking; wilderness backpacking. Home: 11 The Woods NE Iowa City IA 52240-7986 Office: U Iowa Hygienic Lab Oakdale Hall Iowa City IA 52242

HAUSMAN, ARTHUR HERBERT, electronics company executive; b. Chgo., Nov. 24, 1923; s. Samuel Louis and Sarah (Elin) H.; m. Helen Mandelowitz, May 19, 1946; children: Susan Lois, Kenneth Louis, Catherine Ellen. B.S. in Elec. Engring, U. Tex., 1944; S.M., Harvard U., 1948. Electronics engr. Engring. Research Assos., St. Paul, 1946-47; supervisory electronics scientist U.S. Dept. Def., Washington, 1948-60; now advisor, v.p., dir. research Ampex Corp., Redwood City, Calif., 1960-63, v.p. ops., 1963-65, group v.p., 1965-67, exec. v.p., 1967-71, exec. v.p., pres., chief exec. officer, 1971-83, chmn. bd., 1981-87, chmn. bd. emeritus, 1987—; chmn. tech. adv. com. computer peripherals Dept. Commerce, 1973-75; mem. Pres.'s Export Coun.; chmn. Subcom. on Export Adminstrn., 1984-88; bd. dirs. Drexler Tech. Inc., T.C.I. Inc., Vista Rsch. Inc., Calif.-Amplifier, Inc. Trustee United Bay Area Crusade.; mem. vis. com. dept. math. MIT; Bd. dirs. Bay Area Council. Served with USNR, 1944-54. Recipient Meritorious Civilian Service award Dept. Def. Mem. IEEE, Army Ordnance Assn. (dir. chpt. 1969-71), Am. Electronics Assn. (dir.). Clubs: Commonwealth of Calif.; Cosmos.

HAUSMAN, BRUCE, retired lawyer; b. N.Y.C., Mar. 4, 1930; s. Samuel and Vera (Kuttler) H.; m. Jeanne Epstein, June 8, 1952 (div. Oct. 1992); children: Robert Lloyd, Arlene; m. Amy Kadin, Dec. 12, 1992. BA, Brown U., 1951; MS, Columbia U., 1952; postgrad., N.Y. Law Sch., 1979. Bar: N.Y. 1980. Dir. Belding Real Estate Corp., Corticelli Real Estate Corp., 1960-63; pres., dir. Va. Dyeing Corp., 1962-64; div. mgr. M. Hausman & Sons, Inc. (named changed to Belding Hausman Fabrics Inc.), 1952-64; ptnr. Kastex Corp., L.A., 1964; regional sales mgr. Belding Heminway Co., Inc., 1965; pres., dir. contract knitting divsn. Mozzil Knits Inc., 1969-73; exec., adminstrv. officer apparel fabric divsn. Belding Heminway Co., Inc., N.Y.C., 1966-73, exec. asst. to chmn. bd., 1973-74, group pres. home furnishings divsn., 1975-79, corp. v.p., 1979; corp. counsel Belding Heminway Co., Inc., 1980-85; sr. vice chmn. Belding Heminway Co., Inc., N.Y.C., 1980-86, chmn. exec. com., 1981-86, cons., 1987-88, sr. v.p., 1988-92; ret., 1993; exec. adminstrv. head Belding Hausman Fabrics Inc., 1975-79; adminstrv. officer Va. Dyeing Corp., Belding Corticelli Fiberglass Fabrics Inc.; pres. M.K. Leasing Corp., 1974; mem. exec. com. Daltex Med. Scis., Inc., 1993, pres., CEO, 1995—. Bd. overseers Parsons Sch. Design, 1975-91; trustee, mem. exec. com. Beth Israel Med. Ctr., N.Y.C., 1976-93, hon. trustee, 1993—; trustee, mem. exec. com. Beth Israel Nursing Home, 1991-93, hon. trustee, 1994—. Named Man of Yr., Fabric Salesmens Guild, Inc., 1972. Mem. Textile Salesmen's Assn. (bd. govs., Man of Yr. award 1987), Textile Distbrs. Assn. (gov. 1979, v.p. 1982, sec. 1983-87), Am. Arbitration Assn., NCCJ (bd. dirs. 1974-88). *To maintain a high standard of ethics in dealing with others. To respect my fellow persons and treat them with dignity. To devote part of my life in helping others less fortunate than I.*

HAUSMAN, C. MICHAEL, lawyer, judge; b. Chgo., Oct. 4, 1940; s. Charles Martin and Evelyn (Partridge) H.; children: Laura, Sarah, Craig, Karen, Richard, Ronald, Charles, Ashley, Courtney Megan. BS, Marquette U., 1962, JD, 1967. Bar: Wis. 1967, U.S. Dist. Ct. (ea. dist.) Wis. 1967, U.S. Supreme Ct. 1972. Ptnr. Frisch, Dudek & Slattery, Ltd., Milw., 1967-88, Slattery & Hausman, Ltd., Waukesha, 1988—; mcpl. judge City of Delafield, Wis., 1983—; lectr. State Bar of Wis. Family Law Seminars, Am. Acad. Matrimonial Lawyers. Named Outstanding Young Man Brookfield (Wis.) Jaycees, 1975. Fellow Internat. Acad. Matrimonial Lawyers, Am. Acad. Matrimonial Lawyers (pres. Wis. chpt. 1988-89); mem. Assn. Trial Lawyers Am., Am. Arbitration Assn., Wis. Acad. Trial Lawyers, State Bar Wis., Milw. Jr. Bar Assn. (bd. dirs. 1969-71), Brookfield C. of C. (pres. 1977-78), Brookfield Rotary (pres. 1980-81). Avocations: fishing, hiking, stamp and coin collecting. Home: South 608 St Johns Dr Delafield WI 53018

HAUSMAN, GERALD ANDREWS, writer; b. Balt., Oct. 13, 1945; s. Sidney and Dorothy Emma (Little) H.; Loretta Ruth Wright, June 17, 1968; children: Mariah, Hannah. BA in English Lit., N.Mex. Highlands U., 1968. English and creative writing tchr. The Windsor Mt. Sch., Lenox, Mass., 1968-73; poet-in-residence Ctrl. Conn. State Coll., New Britain, Conn., 1973-74; freelance writer, editor, 1974-79; editor Sunstone Press, Santa Fe, 1980-84; English tchr. Santa Fe Prep. Sch., 1984-93; freelance writer, 1993-99. Author: Tunkashila, 1993, Kebra Nagast, 1998, Doctor Bird, 1998, The Story of the Blue Elk, 1998. Lit. arts coord. Berkshire Cmty. Arts Coun., Gt. Barrington, Mass., 1975. Named Poet-in-the-Schs. Mass. Coun. on the Arts and Humanities, 1972-74; recipient Aesop Accolade award Am. Folklore Soc., 1995, award Nat. Coun. for Social Studies, 1995. Mem. Soc. Children's Book Writers and Illustrators, Poets and Writers. Avocation: swimming. E-mail: ghausman@compuserve.com. Home: 12699 Cristi Way Bokeelia FL 33922

HAUSMAN, HOWARD, electronics executive; b. N.Y.C., July 4, 1945; s. Edward A. and Bella H.; m. Gloria Lynn; children: Lawrence Stuart, Bradley Russel. BSEE, Poly. Inst. N.Y., 1967, MSEE, 1971. Computer programmer Harry Kahn Assocs., Great Neck, N.Y., 1965-67; engr. Airborne Instruments Lab., Deer Park, N.Y., 1967-72; dept. head Miteq Inc., Hauppauge, N.Y., 1972-81; pres. Labred Electronics Corp., Bohemia, N.Y., 1981—; chief scientist Microphase Systems Inc., Hauppage, N.Y., 1992—; mem. tech. cons. com., v.p. local adv. counsel 1st supervisory dist. Bd. Coop. Ednl. Services, Suffolk County, N.Y., 1986—; cons. Arista Devices, Inc., Ronkonkoma, N.Y., 1974-81; prof. Hofstra U., Hempstead, N.Y., 1996, Polytech. U., Farmingdale, N.Y., 1978—. Contbr. articles to profl. jours. Mem. IEEE (sr.), AIAA (sr.), AAAS, Nat. Contracts Mgmt. Assn., N.Y. Acad. Scis., Am. Inst. Aeronautics and Astronautics (sr.). Home: 105 Hidden Ponds Cir Smithtown NY 11787-5229 Office: Labred Electronics Corp 80 Orville Dr Bohemia NY 11716-2534 *As we acquire more knowledge we realize how little we know. It is a very humbling experience that tends to limit our creativity. It is important that we realize the subliminal negative feedback effects inherent in our learning experience and conciously focus our energies on piercing the envelope of the psychologically comfortable known universe.*

HAUSMAN, JERRY ALLEN, economics educator, consultant; b. Weirton, W.Va., May 5, 1946; s. Harold H. and Rose (Hausman); m. Margaretta Stone, Dec. 21, 1968; children: Nicholas, Claire. A.B., Brown U., 1968; B.Phil., Oxford U., 1972, D.Phil., 1973. Mem. faculty MIT, Cambridge, 1973—, prof. econs., 1979—. Contbr. articles to profl. jours. Marshall scholar, 1970-72; recipient Frisch medal Econometrics Soc., 1980; John Bates Clark award Am. Econs. Assn., 1985. Office: MIT Dept Econs 77 Massachusetts Ave Dept Econs Cambridge MA 02139-4307

HAUSMAN, KEITH LYNN, hospital administrator, physical therapist; b. Cleve., Nov. 20, 1949; s. Harold Herbert and Betty (Reed) H.; 1 child, Sierra Dawn. BS, Loma Linda U., 1972, MA in Pub. Health, 1975. Lic. real estate broker; cert. flight instr. Acting adminstr. Thomas Rehab. Hosp., Asheville, N.C., 1976-77; pres. Marion County Hosp., Jefferson, Tex., 1977-81, Jellico (Tenn.) Community Hosp., 1981-91; health care cons., 1991—; pres. Premier Rehab., Inc., 1994—. Bd. dirs. Pvt. Indsl. Coun. SDA4, Tenn., 1989—. Fellow Am. Coll. Health Care Execs.; mem. Tenn. Hosp. Assn. (bd. dirs. 1991, pres. Mid-East dist. 1991), Campbell County C. of C. (bd. dirs. 1989-92). Republican. Seventh-Day Adventist. Home: PO Box 541 Jellico TN 37762-0541

HAUSMAN, STEVEN JACK, health science administrator; b. Phila., May 20, 1945; s. Leo and Bella Hausman. BA, U. Pa., 1967, MS, 1968, PhD, 1972. Postdoctoral fellow Inst. for Cancer Rsch., Phila., 1972-75; staff fellow Nat. Inst. on Aging, Balt., 1975-77; spl. asst. to assoc. dir. Nat. Inst. Arthritis, Metabolism and Digestive Diseases, Bethesda, Md., 1977-78, dir. etrs. program, 1978-86; dep. dir. extramural program Nat. Inst. Arthritis and Musculoskeletal and Skin Diseases, Bethesda, 1986-90, dep. dir., 1990—, dir. extramural program, 1997—. Mem. AAAS, Am. Assn. Immunologists, Soc. In Vitro Biology, Am. Chem. Soc., Am. Soc. for Cell Biology. Office: NIAMS-NIH Bldg 31 Rm 4C-32 31 Center Dr MSC2350 Bethesda MD 20892-2350

HAUSMAN, WILLIAM RAY, fund raising and management consultant; b. Bradford, Pa., Apr. 22, 1941; s. Raymond Harvey and Eleanor Janet (Freeman) H.; m. Rosalyn Schmidt, Aug. 16, 1963; children: Valerie Noelle, Stephanie Carol. AB, Wheaton Coll., 1963; MA, Trinity Evang. Div. Sch., 1966, DD (hon), 1981; postgrad., North Park Theol. Sem., 1968-69; EdM, Harvard U., 1977. Ordained to ministry Evang. Covenant Ch., 1971. Minister Christian edn. Glen Ellyn (Ill.) Covenant Ch., 1966-69; from registrar, dir. admissions to assoc. dean Trinity Evang. Div. Sch., Deerfield, Ill., 1969-80; pres. North Park Coll. and Theol. Sem., Chgo., 1980-86; from cons. to group mgr. Donald A. Campbell & Co., Inc., Chgo., 1986-94, v.p. ea. regional mgr., 1994—, sr. v.p., 1995—; bd. dirs. InTrust mag. Bd. dirs. Rockport Chamber Music Festival. Mem. Nat. Soc. Fund Raising Execs. (cert. 1989), Lehigh County Hist. Soc., Coun. Advancement and Support Edn., New Eng. Hist. Geneal. Soc. Office: Campbell & Co Eastern Regional Office 85 Eastern Ave Ste 305 Gloucester MA 01930-1869

HAUSNER, JERRY, electronic engineer, consultant; b. Bklyn., Jan. 17, 1938; s. Irving and Lee (Schneider) H.; m. Helene B. Hausner, Apr. 14, 1962; children: Joyce Fawn, Jeffrey Mitchell. BSEE, CCNY, 1960. Engr. Polarad Electronics Corp., Long Island City, N.Y., 1960-66; chief engr./product line mgr. Narda Microwave Corp., Hauppauge, N.Y., 1966-84; sr. rsch. specialist Logicon R & D Assocs., Albuquerque, 1984-96; v.p., scientific cons. Electro Sci. Applications, Albuquerque, 1996—; pres. Microwave Theory & Technique Chpt., L.I., N.Y., 1981-82, Albuquerque, 1986, gen. chmn. symposium, Albuquerque, 1992. Patentee in field; contbr. articles to Microwaves, 1977-79. Amb., City of Albuquerque, 1996. Recipient Rsch. Publs. award U.S. Navy Rsch. Lab., Washington, 1994. Mem. IEEE (sr.), N.Mex. Entrepreneurs Assn. (bd. dirs. 1995—, pres. 1998—). Achievements include design of specialized radar equipment for military and commercial applications; development of microwave integrated circuit technology and product line. Home: 12925 Manitoba Dr NE Albuquerque NM 87111-2947 Office: Electro Science Applications 2601 Wyoming Blvd NE Albuquerque NM 87112-1031

HAUSNER, JOHN HERMAN, judge; b. Detroit, Oct. 31, 1932; s. John E. and Anna (Mudrak) H.; m. Alice R. Kieltka, Aug. 22, 1959. Ph.B. cum laude, U. Detroit, 1954, M.A., 1957, J.D. summa cum laude, 1966. Bar: Mich. 1967, U.S. Ct. Appeals (6th cir.) 1968, U.S. Supreme Ct. 1971, U.S. Tax Ct. 1976, U.S. Ct. Claims 1976, U.S. Ct. Mil. Appeals 1976. Tchr. Detroit Pub. Schs., 1954, 56-59; tchg. fellow U. Cin., 1959-61; instr. U. Detroit, 1961-74; sole practice U. Detroit, Detroit, 1967-69; asst. U.S. atty. Detroit, 1969-73; chief asst. U.S. atty. ea. dist. Mich., 1973-76; judge 3rd Jud. Cir. Mich., Wayne County, 1976-94; ret. 3d Jud. Cir. Mich., Wayne County, 1994, 1994; lectr. Law Sch.; faculty adviser Nat. Jud. Coll., 1978-79. Author: Sebastian, The Essence of My Soul, 1982; contbr. articles to Detroit Advertiser. Active Civic Searchlight. Served with U.S. Army, 1954-56. Mem. Fed. Bar Assn. (mem. exec. bd. Detroit chpt. 1976-82), State Bar Mich., Mich. Retired Judges Assn., Blue Key, Alpha Sigma Mu. Republican. Home: 22433 Louise St Saint Clair Shores MI 48081-2034 also: 8420 E Desert Palm Tucson AZ 85730-4723

HAUSSERMANN, OSCAR WILLIAM, JR., lawyer, retired; b. Cambridge, Mass., Aug. 17, 1921; s. Oscar William and Eleanor (Drinker) H.; m. Mary Whitney, 1943 (div. 1951); children—William Burgess (dec.), Richard Hayward (dec.); m. Jean Saltonstall. B.A., Harvard U., 1942, LL.B., 1948. Bar: Mass. Ptnr. Ropes & Gray, Boston, 1949-93, of counsel, 1994—. Chmn. bd. govs. New Eng. Med. Ctr., Boston; v.p., bd. dirs. Sherrill House, Inc., Boston. Mem. Boston Bar Assn. Episcopalian. Club: Country (Brookline, Mass.). Home: 28 Fresh Pond Ln Cambridge MA 02138-4602 Office: of counsel Ropes & Gray 1 International Pl Boston MA 02110-2602

HAUVER, CONSTANCE LONGSHORE, lawyer; b. Abington, Pa., Oct. 9, 1938; d. Malcolm Rettew and Margaret Evans (Lyon) L.; m. Arthur R. Hauver, 1962 (div. Mar. 1979); 1 child, Sian; m. Giles Toll, 1990. BA with high honors, Swarthmore Coll., 1960; MA, UCLA, 1962; JD magna cum laude, U. Denver, 1967. Bar: Colo. 1968, U.S. Dist. Ct. Colo. 1968, U.S. Tax Ct. 1970. Libr. Friends Com. on Nat. Legis., Washington, 1960-61; lectr. U. Hawaii, Honolulu, 1963-64; assoc. Sherman & Howard, Denver, 1968-73, ptnr., 1973-91; vol. naturalist Lookout Mountain Nature Ctr., 1998—; mem. grievance com. Colo. Supreme Ct., 1981-86. Co-contbr. legal articles. Trustee Rocky Mountain Women's Inst., Denver, 1987-90, Swedish Med. Ctr. Found., Denver, 1978-85; bd. dirs. Women's Forum Colo. Inc., Denver, 1988-89, Girls Count, Denver, 1995—, pres., 1996-97. Recipient Athena award Alliance Profl. Women, 1987. Fellow Am. Coll. Probate Counsel; mem. Colo. Bar Assn. (chair probate and trust law sect. 1982-83), Denver Bar Assn. (del. to ABA Ho. of Dels. 1986-88), Rocky Mountain Estate Planning Coun. (pres. 1980-81). Democrat. Mem. Soc. of Friends. Avocations: mountain climbing, kayaking, skiing, reading.

HAVARD, BERNARD, theater producer; b. London, Sept. 5, 1941; came to U.S., 1977; m. Judith Capuzzi, Dec. 17, 1993. Adminstrv. dir. St. Laurence Ctr., Toronto, Ont., 1973-75; gen. mgr. Citadel Theatre, Edmonton, Alta., 1975-77; mng. dir. Alliance Theatre, Atlanta, 1977-82; producing artistic dir. Walnut St. Theatre, Phila., 1982—. Office: Walnut St Theatre 825 Walnut St Philadelphia PA 19107-5107*

HAVAS, PETER, physicist, educator; b. Budapest, Hungary, Mar. 29, 1916; came to U.S., 1941, naturalized, 1948; s. George G. and Irene (Harmos) H.; m. Helga Francis Höllering; children: Eva Catherine, Stephen Walter. Student, U. Vienna, 1937-38; Absolutorium, Technische Hochschule, Vienna, Austria, 1938; PhD, Columbia U., 1944. Rsch. fellow Institut de Physique Atomique, Lyon, France, 1938-41; lectr. in physics Columbia U., N.Y.C., 1941-45; instr. physics Cornell U., 1945-46; asst. prof. physics Lehigh U., Bethlehem, Pa., 1946-49; assoc. prof., 1949-54, prof., 1954-65; prof. physics Temple U., Phila., 1965-81; prof. emeritus, 1981—; mem. Inst. for Advanced Study, Princeton, N.J., 1953-54, Bohr Inst., Copenhagen, 1954, Argonne Nat. Lab., 1958; vis. prof. U. Göttingen, Germany, 1973; adj. prof. physics U. Pa., 1982-88, Utah State U., 1987-90. Mem. editl. bd. Acta Phys. Austriaca, 1968-76, Jour. Math. Physics, 1975-77, KINAM (mex.) 1979—; mem. editl. adv. bd. The Collected Papers of Albert Einstein, 1989-91. Guggenheim fellow, 1953-54. Fellow AAAS, Am. Phys. Soc., Soc. Gen. Relativity and Gravitation (internat. com. 1980-89), Acad. Scis. at Phila. (bd. dirs. 1983—). Rsch. on classical and quantum theories of radiation, theory of relativity, especially equations of motion, found. problems, math. physics, history and philosophy of physics. Office: Temple U Dept Physics Philadelphia PA 19122

HAVEKOST, DANIEL JOHN, architect; b. Fremont, Nebr., May 12, 1936; s. Alvin Deidrich and Magdalen (Osterman) H.; m. Patricia Jo Haney, June 6, 1959 (div. June 1983); children: Christopher, Karen; m. Sandra Schwendemann, Aug. 29, 1993. Lic. architect, Colo., Calif., Tex., N.D.; cert. Nat. Council Archtl. Registration Bds. Designer Papachristou & Assoc., Denver, 1959-61; architect Anshen & Allen, San Francisco, 1961-62; assoc. Hornbein & White, Denver, 1962-63; ptnr. Papachristou & Havekost, Denver, 1963-64; prin. Havekost & Assocs., Denver, 1964-71; pres. HWH Assocs., Inc., Denver, 1971-91, Havekost & Lee Architects P.C., Denver, 1991-95, Havekost & Assoc., P.C., 1996—; vis. lectr. U. Colo., Denver, 1969, 72, 82; sec., treas. Encore Devel. Corp., Denver, 1984-91. Prin. works include Encore Redevel. (AIA award 1985,86), Grant Street Mansion (Colo. Soc. Architects, AIA award 1979), Reverend's Ridge (Western Mountain Region AIA award 1973, Havekost Residence Western Mountain Region AIA award 1971). Bd. dirs. Denver Cmty. Design Ctr., 1968-72, Hist. Paramount Found., Denver, 1980-94, Hist. Denver, 1978-82; panel mem. Gen. Svcs. Adminstrn., Denver, 1978-79, mem. plan enforcement rev. and variation com., Denver, 1970-76. Served with USNR, 1954-62. Recipient Archtl. Excellence awards WOOD Inc., 1968-82, Honor award for Adaptive Re-use, Historic Denver, 1975, WOOD Design award Nat. Cattlemen's Hdqrs., 1982. Fellow AIA (pres. Denver chpt. 1978-81, chmn. Colo. chpt. govt. affairs com. 1984-91, pres. Colo. chpt. 1981-83, Colo. hist. preservation officer 1982—, recipient Fisher Traveling award of Colo. AIA Ednl. Fund 1988, excellence archtl. design award 1960). Avocations: skiing, tennis, drawing. Office: Havekost & Assocs PC 1121 Grant St Denver CO 80203-2301

HAVEL, JEAN EUGÈNE MARTIAL, author, educator; b. Le Havre, France, June 16, 1928; m. Anne Marie Luhr, Aug. 13, 1955 (dec. Jan. 22, 1977); children: Jean Guillaume, Frédérik, Sophie Mathilde, Ingrid Lucie. Licencié en Droit, U. Paris, 1950; diploma, Institut des Etudes Politiques, 1952; postgrad., Institut des Etudes Scandinaves, 1952-53, Doctorat ès Lettres, 1956. Part-time tchr. extension div. U. Stockholm, 1956-59; asst. prof. polit. sci. U. Montreal (Que.), Can., 1959-62; asst. prof. polit. sci. Laurentian U., Sudbury, Ont., Can., 1962-64, asso. prof., 1964-69, prof., 1969-93, prof. emeritus, 1995—. Author: Cours de Journalisme: La Rédaction, 1956, La Fabrication du Journal, 1957, Cent soixante-quinze ans de peinture et de sculpture en France, 1957, La Politique Suédoise du Logement de 1940 à 1957, 1957, Le Mouvement Socialiste Norvégien, 1958, Le Socialisme Danois, 1958, Le Socialisme Réformiste Modéré en Suéde, 2 vols., 1958, La Condition de la Femme, 1961; also Italian, Spanish transl.: Les Citoyens de Sudbury et la Politique, 1966, also English transl. Les Etats Scandinaves et l'Intégration èuropéenne, 2d edit., 1970, Habitat et Logement, 5th edit., 1985, Spanish, Chinese transls. La Finlande et la Suéde, 1978, Effacement de la Normandie?, 1998; contbr. chpts. to books and articles to profl. jours. Mem. Can. Polit. Sci. Assn. Home: 175 Boland Ave, Sudbury, ON Canada P3E 1Y1 *I write because I feel an inner urge to do it. I dream of a world of men and women who are both free and responsible. And I try to contribute, small steps by small steps, to build such a world. To be successful, I try to set up my contributions on the findings of the observers of human nature.*

HAVEL, RICHARD JOSEPH, physician, educator; b. Seattle, Feb. 20, 1925; s. Joseph and Anna (Fritz) H.; m. Virginia Johnson, June 28, 1947; children: Christopher, Timothy, Peter, Julianne. BA, Reed Coll., 1946; MS, MD, U. Oreg., 1949. Intern Cornell U. Med. Coll., N.Y.C., 1949-50; resident in medicine Cornell U. Med. Coll., 1950-53; clin. assoc. Nat. Heart Inst., NIH, 1953-54, research assoc., 1954-56; faculty Sch. Medicine, U. Calif., San Francisco, 1956—; prof. medicine Sch. Medicine, U. Calif., 1964—; assoc. dir. Cardiovascular Research Inst., 1961-73, dir., 1973-92; chief metabolism sect., dept. medicine, 1967-97 ; dir. Arteriosclerosis Specialized Center of Research, 1971-96 ; mem. bd. sci. counselors Nat. Heart, Lung and Blood Inst., 1976-80; chmn. food and nutrition bd. NRC, 1987-90. Contbr. chpts. to books, numerous articles to profl. jours.; editor: Jour. Lipid Research, 1972-75; co-editor: Adv. Lipid Res., 1991—; mem. editorial bd.: Jour. Biol. Chemistry, 1981-85, Jour. Arteriosclerosis, 1980—. Established investigator Am. Heart Assn., 1956-61, chmn. coun. on arteriosclerosis, 1977-79. With USPHS, 1951-53. Recipient Disting. Achievement award Am. Heart Assn., 1993, Bristol-Myers award for nutrition rsch., 1989, gold medal Charles U., Prague, Czech Republic, 1996. Fellow AAS (Theobald Smith award 1960); mem. NAS, Inst. Medicine NAS, Am. Acad. Arts and Scis., Am. Soc. Clin. Nutrition (McCollum award 1993), Assn. Am. Physicians, Am. Soc. for Clin. Investigation, Am. Inst. Nutritional Sci., Western Soc. Clin. Investigation (Mayo Soley award 1997), Phi Beta Kappa, Alpha Omega Alpha. Office: U Calif San Francisco Cardiovascular Rsch In San Francisco CA 94143-0130

HAVEL, RICHARD W., lawyer; b. Fairmont, Minn., Sept. 20, 1946; s. Thomas Earl and Elizabeth (Shiltz) H.; m. Arlene Havel, July 6, 1968; children: Stephanie, Derek. BA, Notre Dame U., 1968; JD, UCLA, 1971. Bar: Calif., U.S. Dist. Ct. (no., ea., cen. and so. dists.) Calif., U.S. Ct. Appeals (9th cir.). Atty. Shutan & Trost, L.A., 1971-80, Sidley & Austin, L.A., 1980—; instr. law U. Loyola, 1975-80; bd. govs. Fin. Lawyers Conf., 1991-94, 95-98, officer, 1998—; spkr., panelist Bankruptcy Litigation Inst., 1989-95, ALI-ABA, 1989, 90, 91; chmn. L.A. City Indsl. Devel. Authority, 1993-98, bd. dirs., 1998—. Contbr. articles to profl. jours. Trustee Jonsson/UCLA Cancer Ctr., 1998—. Fellow Am. Coll. Bankruptcy, 1997; mem. ABA, Calif. Bar Assn., L.A. County Bar Assn. (comml. law & bankruptcy sect. bankruptcy subcom. 1986-89, exec. com. 1987-90, lawyer assistance com. 1985—), UCLA Law Alumni Assn. (trustee 1996—). Office: Sidley & Austin 555 W 5th St Fl 40 Los Angeles CA 90013-1010

HAVELIWALA, HOZEFA Y.A., journalist, writer; b. Lahore, Pakistan, Feb. 6, 1971; came to U.S., 1971; s. Yoosuf and Maryam (Bengali) H. BA in Pub. Policy, Trinity Coll., 1992; MFA in Creative Writing, Emerson Coll., 1997. Journalist CBS Evening News with Dan Rather, N.Y.C., 1991-92, 96, CBS Dem. Nat. Conv., N.Y.C., 1992-96, CBS News Radio, N.Y.C., 1996-98; reporter Post Rev., Paramus, N.J., 1997-98; with 1st Amendment Press Internat., Ridgewood, N.J., 1998—. Office: 1st Amendment Pres Internat 38 E Ridgewood Ave Ste 217 Ridgewood NJ 07450-2902

HAVELKA, THOMAS EDWARD, secondary education educator; b. Wheeling, W.Va., July 10, 1947; s. Alfred and Marilyn Eleanor (Hays) H.; m. Susan Kay Wilson, June 16, 1973; children: Trevor Hays, Havaleh Ann. BFA, Ohio U., 1969, MusM, 1975; postgrad., Akron U., Ashland U., Cleve. State U. Cert. tchr., Ohio; national registered music tchr. M.E.N.C. Music instr., chmn. fine arts dept. Bellaire (Ohio) Bd. Edn., 1969-74; choir dir., chmn. music dept. Coshocton (Ohio) City Bd. Edn., 1975—; founder Coshocton City Schs., Arts Festival, 1985—; state rep. All Am. Youth Honor Musicians, Miami, Fla., 1970-90; asst. condr. All Am. Youth Honor Choir, 1970, 77-78, condr., 1980-90; adjudicator Internat. Choir Fest., Mexico City, 1978, Dulcimer Festival, Roscoe Village, Ohio, 1986-88, Show Choir Festival, Portsmouth, Ohio, 1986, Lander Coll., S.C. Composer: Piece for String Quartet, 1974, (choral) Offertorium from Missae Requiem Brevis, 1974, Bless Ye the God of All, 1975, Joseph's Lullaby, 1997, Peter's Praise, 1999. Mem. Big Bros./Big Sisters Assn., Columbus, 1970—; dist. exec., chmn. bd. Boy Scouts Am., Coshocton, 1979-80; sect. leader, asst. accompanist, asst. conductor Coshocton Community Choir, 1984—; active various theater groups, Coshocton and Wheeling, 1974—; singer St. Matthew's Episcopal Ch., Wheeling, W.Va., 1973-75; asst. organist Grace United Meth. Ch., Coshocton, 1986—; pres., bd. dirs. Ohio U. Sch. of Music Soc. of Alumni and Friends. Recipient awards from Mayors of Malaga, Spain, 1981, Agnani and Fuiggi, Italy, 1984 and Paris, 1985, Istra, USSR, 1989, award of Merit Coshocton City Schs., 1984. Mem. NEA, Ohio Edn. Assn., Ohio Music Edn. Assn. (asst. contest chmn., approved adjudicator in piano, voice, and choir, chmn. county membership com. 1977-78), Internat. Soc. for Music Edn., Internat. Fedn. for Choral Music, Am. Guild Organists, Am. Choral Dirs. Assn., Ohio Choral Dirs. Assn. (chmn. county membership com. 1978-79), Coshocton City Edn. Assn. (sec. 1984-85, 88-89), Music Educators Nat. Conf., Soc. Music Tchr. Edn., Kappa Kappa Psi, Phi Mu Alpha, Pi Kappa Lambda. Republican. Methodist. Avocations: travel, camping, backpacking, coin collecting. Home: 1628 Woodland Dr Coshocton OH 43812-3151 Office: Coshocton High Sch 1205 Cambridge Rd Coshocton OH 43812-2741

HAVEMANN, JOEL, projects editor; b. N.Y.C., 1943. BA in Math., Harvard U., 1965. Gen. assignment reporter Portland Oregonian, 1965-67; edn. reporter Chicago Sun-Times, 1967-73; budget reporter National Journal, 1973-78, dep. ed., 1978-83; econ. reporter L.A. Times, 1983-84, projects editor, 1984-90, Brussels bur. chief, 1990-93, DC projects editor, news editor, 1993—. Author: (book) Congress and the Budget, 1978. Office: Los Angeles Times/Wash Bur 1875 Eye St NW Ste 1100 Washington DC 20006-5421*

HAVEMANN, JUDITH MCINTOSH, reporter; b. Vinton, Iowa, June 26, 1944; d. Roy and Lola Leona (Miller) McI.; m. Joseph D. Nicol Jr., Apr. 16, 1962 (div. Dec. 1969); 1 child, Theresa L.; m. Joel Havemann, June 17, 1972; children: Anne E., Margaret R., William E. BA, Mich. State U., 1966. Reporter Jackson (Mich.) Citizen Patriot, 1965-66, Highland Park (Ill.) Herald, 1966-68, Chgo. Am., 1968-69, Chgo. Sun Times, 1969-73; reporter, editor Washington Post, 1973—. Pres. Nat. Child Rsch. Ctr., Washington, 1987-88. Recipient Nieman fellowship Harvard U., Cambridge, Mass., 1979-80. Methodist. Office: Washington Post 1150 15th St NW Washington DC 20071-0002

HAVEMANN, MICHAEL R., court administrator; b. San Francisco, Aug. 31, 1944. BA in Polit. Sci., Brigham Young U., 1969, MPA, 1972. Coord. criminal justice planning City Mgr.'s Office City of Phoenix, 1972-74, asst. ct. adminstr. Mcpl. Ct., 1975-78, ct. adminstr., 1978-83; mgmt. asst. planning and rsch. bur. Phoenix Police Dept., 1974-75; ct. exec. State of Utah 4th Jud. Dist., 1983-92; ct. adminstr. Las Vegas Mcpl. Ct., 1992—; mem. Ct. Exec. Devel. Program. Co-author: (study) Internal Audition in State Govt., 1972. Fellow Inst. Ct. Mgmt. (Nat. Ctr. State Cts.); mem. Nat. Assn. Ct. Mgmt. Office: Mcpl Ct City of Las Vegas City Hall 400 Stewart Ave Las Vegas NV 89101-2927*

HAVEN, RICHARD, English language educator; b. Bennington, Vt., Aug. 22, 1924; s. William LeRoy and Margaret Loring (Gilbert) H.; m. Josephine Ruth Corbishley, June 24, 1950 (dec. 1996); 1 child, Gillian Margaret. BA, Harvard U., 1950; B of Lit., Oxford U., England, 1954; PhD, Princeton U., 1958. Instr. English U. Mass., Amherst, 1953-58, asst. prof. English, 1958-63, assoc. prof. English, 1963-69, prof. English, 1969-86; free-lance cons. Mass.; vis. prof. English U. Pubjab, Pakistan, 1960-61. Author: Patterns of Conciousnes, 1969; co-editor: Samual Tayler Goleridge: A Bibliography, 1976; contbr. articles to profl. jours. Chair Sister City Com., Amherst, 1997—. Sgt. U.S. Army, 1943-46. Grantee Danforth Found., 1956-57, NEH, 1967-68, 70-71. Home: 3 Chadwick Ct Amherst MA 01002-2825

HAVEN, THOMAS EDWARD, lawyer; b. Oakland, Calif., Aug. 25, 1920; s. Thomas Comfort and Erminie (Sala) H.; m. Carol Mae Goeppert, Dec. 24, 1942 (dec. May 1978); children: Patricia Byrne, Charles E., Thomas A. BS, U. Calif., 1941; LLB, Stanford U., 1948. Law clk. to presiding justice U.S. Ct. Appeals (9th cir.), San Francisco, 1948-49; assoc. Pillsbury, Madison & Sutro, San Francisco, 1950-60, ptnr., 1961-85, adv. ptnr., 1986-90, ret. ptnr., 1991—. Served to lt. USNR, 1942-46, PTO. Mem. ABA, Am. Soc. Internat. Law, Bar Assn. San Francisco, Bankers Club, Foothills Swimming and Tennis Club. Republican. Office: Pillsbury Madison & Sutro PO Box 7880 San Francisco CA 94120-7880

HAVENS, CANDACE JEAN, planning consultant; b. Rochester, Minn., Sept. 13, 1952; d. Fred Z. and Barbara Jean (Stephenson) H.; m. Bruce Curtis Mercier, Feb. 22, 1975 (div. Apr. 1982); 1 child, Rachel; m. James Arthur Renning, Oct. 26, 1986; children: Kelsey, Sarah. Student, U. Calif., San Diego, Darmouth Coll., 1970-72, Am. U., Beirut, 1973-74; BA in Sociology, U. Calif., Riverside, 1977; MPA, Harvard U., 1994. Project coord. social svc. orgn. Grass Roots II, San Luis Obispo, Calif., 1976-77; planner City San Luis Obispo, 1977-86, city parking, spl. projects mgr., 1986-88; spl. asst. to city adminstr. City of San Luis Obispo, 1989, planning cons., mediator, 1991—; mgmt. rsch. specialist Bank of Boston, 1995-96; owner Office Suites, San Luis Obispo, Calif., 1997—, ADR Collaborative, 1997—. Past pres. Nat. Charity League, Riverside; mem. San Luis Obispo Med. Aux., 1986-93, San Luis Obispo Arts Coun., 1986—; pres. bd. dirs. San Luis Obispo Children's Mus., 1990-91, CFO, 1993; mediator in Newton (Mass.) Cts., 1996, San Luis Obispo, 1997. Mem. AAUW, Soc. Profls. in Dispute Resolution, Am. Inst. Cert. Planners, Toastmasters (sec. 1986-87, v.p. 1987-88, pres. 1989-90, treas. 1991-92), Am. Planning Assn., Mass. Assn. Mediation Profls. and Practitioners. Avocations: photography, running, arts, cooking, travel, languages. Office: 25 Hunnewell Ave Newton MA 02458-2214

HAVENS, CAROLYN CLARICE, librarian; b. Nashville, Sept. 11, 1953; d. Charles Buford and Iris Mae (Anderson) H.; m. Hilton Harris Huey, June 9, 1990; children: Heather Louise, Quentin Harris. AA, Sue Bennett Coll., 1973; BA in English, U. West Fla., 1974; MLS, U. Ky., 1981. Tchr. Escambia High Sch., Pensacola, Fla., 1974-75; salesperson Univ. Mall, Pensacola, 1975-77; libr. tech. U. Ky., Lexington, 1978-82; libr. Auburn (Ala.) U., 1982—. Contbr. articles to profl. jours. and newspapers; editorial bd.: A Dynamic Tradition, 1991. Bd. dirs. Nat. Kidney Found. Ala., Opelika, 1986-89; active Conscientious Alliance for Peace, Auburn, 1989—. Clergy and Laity Concerned, Atlanta, 1991—. Mem. ALA, Southeastern Libr. Assn., Ala. Libr. Assn., North Am. Serials Interest Group, Ala. Assn. Coll. and Rsch. Librs., Studio 218. Democrat. Methodist. Avocations: painting, writing, photography. Office: Auburn U Ralph Draughon Libr Auburn AL 36849-5606

HAVENS, CHARLES W., III, lawyer; b. Balt., Mar. 22, 1936; m. Lucille Bowman; children—Charles W. IV, Jessica Madaline. A.B., Franklin and Marshall Coll., 1958; LL.B., U. Va., 1961. Bar: D.C. 1961, Va. 1961, U.S. Supreme Ct. Assoc. Covington & Burling, Washington, 1961-66; spl. asst. to gen. counsel Dept. Def., Washington, 1966-67, spl. asst. to asst. sec. def., 1967-70; gen. counsel then pres. Reins. Assn. Am., Washington, 1970-81; ptnr. LeBoeuf, Lamb, Leiby & MacRae, Washington, 1981—. Contbr. articles to profl. jours. Mem. Fedn. Ins. and Corp. Counsel, Internat. Assn. Ins. and Corp. Counsel, AIDA Reins. and Ins. Arbitration Soc. (founding, bd. dirs.). Club: Metropolitan (Washington). Avocation: squash. Home: 4641 Garfield St NW Washington DC 20007-1026 Office: LeBoeuf Lamb Greene MacRae Ste 1200 1875 Connecticut Ave NW Washington DC 20009-5728

HAVENS, EDWIN WALLACE, manufacturing executive; b. Rockville Center, N.Y., Mar. 5, 1950; s. Edwin Wallace and Helen Marie (Lamb) H.; m. Maria Antonia Gorgone, Sept. 20, 1980; 1 child, Brian Patrick. BA, Hofstra U., 1973. Nat. svc. mgr. Garrard U.S.A., Plainview, N.Y., 1975-79; product mgr. TDK Electronics, Garden City, N.Y., 1979-83; tech. mgr. Fuji Photo Film, N.Y.C., 1983-84, Maxell Corp. Am., Moonachie, N.J., 1984-87; nat. sales mgr. SKC Am. Inc., East Rutherford, N.J., 1987-89; dept. mgr. SKC Am. Inc., Mount Olive, N.J., 1989-95, divsn. mgr., 1995-96, gen. mgr., 1996-98, dir., 1998—. Editor: Viewpoint, 1995; author: (comic strip) The Korea Side, 1987—. Acting Spring St. Mchts. Assn., Newton, N.J., 1994-97. Mem. Video Software Dealers Assn., Internat. Recording Media Assn. (bd. dirs. 1993—, mem. environ. com. 193—, mem. seminar com. 1993—, mem. statis. com. 1993—), Am. Mgmt. Coun. (mem. vision fund 1987—). Avocations: deep sea fishing, horseback riding. Office: SKC Am Inc 850 Clark Dr Budd Lake NJ 07828-4313

HAVENS, HARRY STEWART, former federal assistant comptroller general, government consultant; b. Little Rock, Dec. 18, 1935; s. Ralph Murray and Catherine Clara (Clark) H.; m. Frances Jones, June 12, 1960. BA in Econs. magna cum laude, Duke U., 1957; BA in Philosophy, Politics, Econs., Oxford U., England, 1959, MA, 1963. Economist U.S. Budget Bur., Washington, 1964-66, budget examiner, 1966-70, chief housing br., 1970-72, dep. dir. human resources divsn., 1972-74; chief income maintenance br. U.S. Office Mgmt. and Budget, Washington, 1972-74; dir. program analysis divsn. U.S. GAO, Washington, 1974-80, asst. comptroller gen., 1980-93; pvt. practice cons. Washington, 1993—; cons. Orgn. Econ. Coop. & Devel., Paris, 1993—, U.S. GAO, 1993-96, Supreme Soviet of Russian Fedn., 1992-93, State Duma of Russian Fedn., 1994; hon. councillor Atlantic Coun. U.S., 1995—. Contbr. articles to profl. jours.; contbr. book chpts. Rhodes scholar, 1957. Fellow Nat. Acad. Pub. Adminstrn. Home and Office: 4515 Neptune Dr Alexandria VA 22309-3129

HAVENS, KEITH CORNELL, artist; b. Mpls., Sept. 27, 1921; s. Lee Willard and Ruth Marguerite (Mallett) H.; m. Marian Gail Niggeler, Mar. 11, 1944; 1 child, Shelley Ross. Cert., Mpls. Sch. Art, 1949. Instr. drawing, painting and design Mpls. Sch. Art, 1949-58; assoc. prof. art Spl. Sch. Assoc. Arts, St. Paul, 1959-73; dir. studio classes Mpls. Sch. Art, 1949-58, instr. night sch. classes, 1949-58; co-founder, instr. Minnetonka Ctr. Art and Edn., Wayzata, Crystal Bay, Minn., 1950-70; dir. Twin Cities Theater Galleries, Mpls., St. Paul, 1952-72; architect's cons. Mpls. Sch. Art, 1956-58, designer spl. equipment, 1956-58; instr. watercolor painting St. Paul Sch. Art, 1958-59; judge Lutsen (Minn.) Art Fair, 1975, Mpls. Photo Club, 1975. Author: Fantanimals, 1980; paintings commd. by North Meml. Hosp., Robbinsdale, Minn., 1962, 63; exhibited in numerous one-man shows including Duluth Art Inst., 1994. Recipient 1st award Women's Club Art Show, 1952, 1st award-watercolor Minn. State Fair Art Exhibit, 1953. Avocations: gardening, photography, model building, painting.

HAVENS, LESTON LAYCOCK, psychiatrist, educator; b. Bklyn., July 31, 1924; s. Valentine Britton and Nellie Falk (Laycock) H.; m. Susan Elizabeth Miller, May 19, 1973; 1 child, Emily E.; children by previous marriage: Christopher W., Jeffry B. (dec.), Jennifer F., Sarah B. BA, Williams Coll., 1947; MD, Cornell U., 1952; MA (hon.), Harvard U., 1987; LHD, Mass. Sch. Profl. Psychology, 1993. Intern N.Y. Hosp., 1952-53, asst. resident internal medicine, 1953-54; resident, chief of service Mass. Mental Health Ctr., Boston Psychopathic Hosp., 1954-58, staff visit and asst. clin. dir., 1958-62, prin. investigator studies in visual word perception, 1960-66, program dir. psychiat. rehab. internship program, 1962-68, program dir. med. student teaching, 1964-81; asst. prof. psychiatry Harvard Med. Sch., Boston, 1963-64; asso. clin. prof. psychiatry Harvard Med. Sch., 1965-71, psychoanalyst, 1967—, prof. psychiatry, 1971—; Cargnegie vis. prof. humanities MIT, 1968; H. B. Williams traveling prof. Australian and New Zealand Coll. of Psychiatrists, 1975; chief psychiat. cons. Mass. Rehab. Commn., 1959-65; mental health adminstr. Region VI, Mass. Dept. Mental Health, 1968-69; dir. of residency tng. Cambridge Hosp., 1987-96, dir. edn., 1996—. Author: Approaches to the Mind, 1973, Participant Observation, 1977, Making Contact, 1986, A Safe Place: Laying the Groundwork of Psychotherapy, 1989, Coming to Life, 1993, Learning To Be Human, 1994; also articles. Served to 2d lt. AUS, 1944-46. Recipient H.C. Solomon award, 1977, Benjamin Rush award APA, 1995. Mem. Am. Psychiat. Assn., Soc. Biol. Psychiatry (A.E. Bennett award 1958), Mass. Soc. for Rsch. in Psychiatry (McCurdy prize 1962), Phi Beta Kappa, Alpha Omega Alpha. Home: 151 Brattle St Cambridge MA 02138-2243 Office: Cambridge Hosp 1493 Cambridge St Cambridge MA 02139-1099

HAVENS, MURRAY CLARK, political scientist, educator; b. Council Grove, Kans., Aug. 21, 1932; s. Ralph Murray and Catherine Clara (Clark) H.; m. Agnes Marie Scharpf, July 5, 1958 (dec. 1969); children: Colin Scott, Theresa Agnes; m. Carolyn Trost, May 5, 1997. B.A., U. Ala., 1953; M.A. (Woodrow Wilson fellow 1953-54), Johns Hopkins U., 1954, Ph.D., 1958. Postdoctoral fellow Brookings Instn., Washington, 1958-59; asst. prof. polit. sci. Duke U., 1959-61; from asst. prof. to prof. U. Tex., Austin, 1961-73; vis. lectr. U. Sydney (Australia), 1966; prof. polit. sci. Tex. Tech U., Lubbock, 1973—; chmn. dept. Tex. Tech U., 1975-83. Author: City Versus Farm?, 1957, The Challenges to Democracy, 1965, The Politics of Assassination, 1970, Assassination and Terrorism, 1975, Texas Politics Today, 1995; book rev. editor Jour. Politics, 1971-83; contbr. numerous articles to profl. jours. Served with AUS, 1954-56. Mem. Am. Polit. Sci. Assn., So. Polit. Sci. Assn., Southwestern Polit. Sci. Assn. (pres. 1983-84), AAUP, Phi Beta Kappa. Avocation: offshore sailing. Home: PO Box 41015 Lubbock TX 79409-1015 Office: Tex Tech Univ Dept Polit Sci Lubbock TX 79409-1015

HAVENS, OLIVER HERSHMAN, lawyer, consultant; b. Bradley Beach, N.J., July 19, 1917; s. Abram Vaughn and Sara Mildred (Atkinson) H.; m. Ervanna Josephine Cummings, Aug. 16, 1941 (div. 1976); children: Janice Patricia Havens Greer, Judith Ann Havens; m. Elizabeth Lewis Lykes, Nov. 13, 1976. B.A., Princeton U., 1939; J.D., Yale U., 1942. Bar: N.Y. 1947; conseil juridique, France, 1978. Assoc. Cahill Gordon & Reindel, N.Y.C., 1946-54, ptnr., 1955-82, ret., 1982; gen. counsel U.S. Golf Assn., 1985-88. Mayor Jupiter Island, Fla., 1988-93. Served to capt. U.S. Army, 1942-46. Mem. ABA. Republican. Episcopalian. Clubs: Baltusrol Golf (Springfield, N.J.); Island (Hobe Sound, Fla.); Seminole Golf (Juno, Fla.); Royal & Ancient Golf Club of St. Andrews (Scotland); Pine Valley (N.J.) Golf. Home: 2 Isle Rdg W Hobe Sound FL 33455-2504

HAVER, THOMAS M., publishing company executive; b. Somerville, N.J., Mar. 28, 1947. BS, Bates Coll., Lewisotn, Maine, 1969. Chmn. dept. math. Holbrook (Mass.) H.S., 197-—74; math. cons. McMillan Pub. Co., N.Y.C., 1976-79; sr. v.p., divsn. mgr. D.C. Heath & Co., Lexington, Mass., 1979-88; pres. William K. Bradford Pub. Co. Inc., Acton, Mass., 1988—. Mem. Am. Assn. Pubs. (exec. com.). Office: William K Bradford Pub Co 16 Craig Rd Acton MA 01720-5405*

HAVERLAND, MICHAEL ROBERT, architect; b. May 26, 1967. BA, Rice U., 1989, BArch, 1991; MArch, Yale U., 1994. Critic in archtl. design Yale U., New Haven, Conn., 1994-96; prin. Michael Haverland Design, N.Y.C. and New Haven, Conn., 1996—; dir. Yale Urban Design Workshop, New Haven, 1994—; asst. prof. Yale Sch. Architecture, New Haven, 1996—. Office: PO Box 205673 New Haven CT 06520-5673

HAVERLY, DOUGLAS LINDSAY, librarian, historian; b. Stamford, N.Y., Apr. 16, 1925; s. De Forest Ward and Amy Elizabeth (Lindsay) H. Student,

Albany Bus. Coll., 1948, Alfred U., 1948-49, Russell Sage Coll., 1950-52. With N.Y. State Libr., Albany, 1949-77; with Bur. Testing N.Y. State Dept. Edn., Albany, 1978-82; ret., 1982; pres., curator Donald C. Ringwald Marine Navigation Ltd., Albany, 1987—. With USN, 1943-54. Mem. Steamship Hist. Soc. (budget dir. 1973-76, bd. dirs. 1977-80, organizer Hudson Valley chpt. 1974, chmn. 1975-78, libr. 1990-93), Hudson River Maritime Ctr., Sons and Daus. of Pioneer Rivermen, Palatines to Am. (historian N.Y. chpt. 1991-95), Herkimer (N.Y.) Hist. Soc., Schoharie County Hist. Soc. (life), Clan Lindsay Assn. USA Inc. (charter), N.Y. Hist. Soc., Ulster County Geneal. Soc., Van Aken/Auken Newsletter. Avocation: genealogy. Home and Office: DC Ringwald Marine Nav Ltd 23 Wedgewood Dr Loudonville NY 12211-1940

HAVERTY, RAWSON, retail furniture company executive; b. Atlanta, Nov. 26, 1920; s. Clarence and Elizabeth (Rawson) H.; m. Margaret Middleton Munnerlyn, Aug. 25, 1951; children: Margaret Elizabeth, Jane Middleton, James Rawson, Mary Elizabeth, Ben Munnerlyn. B.A., U. Ga., 1941. With Haverty Furniture Co., Atlanta, 1941, 46—, sec., v.p., treas., pres., CEO, 1955-84, chmn. bd., mem. exec. com., 1984—; instr. credit and collection Sch. Retail Furniture Assn. Sch. for Execs., U. N.C., 1960, instr. credits, collections and market analyses, 1951; instr. br. stores Nat. Retail Furniture Sch. for Execs., U. Chgo., 1957—; chmn. bd. dirs. Bank South Corp., 1977-90. Former chmn. Met. Atlanta Rapid Transit Authority; former chmn. bd. trustees St. Joseph's Hosp.; pres. U. Ga. Alumni Soc., 1973-75, mem. exec. com., 1975—, chmn. loyalty fund, 1969-70, 70-71; past chmn. bd. trustees St. Joseph's Village; trustee Atlanta Arts Alliance, Westminster Sch., Atlanta, U. Ga. Found.; past pres. bd. sponsors Atlanta Art Sch.; life trustee High Mus. Art; life trustee High Point U., N.C.; former mem. Fulton Indsl. Authority; bd. dirs. Nat. Retail Fedn., Washington, Aquinas Ctr. of Theology at Emory U., Create Your Dream of Atlanta. Maj. AUS, 1942-46. Decorated Bronze Star medal, Order of Leopold, Croix de Guerre with palms (Belgium); named All Am. Mcht. in retail furniture industry, 1958, knight comdr. Order of St. Gregory the Great, 1990. Mem. Atlanta Retail Mchts. Assn. (past pres., dir.), Nat. Home Furnishings Assn. (past v.p., dir., Retailer of Yr. award 1980), Nat. Furniture Mfrs. Assn. (Johnny Shillngs award 1990), Nat. Retail Furniture Assn. (dir. 1952-69), Am. Retail Fedn., Atlanta Jr. C. of C. (hon. life), Assn. U.S. Army (past pres., adv. bd.), Atlanta C. of C., Piedmont Driving Club, Capital City Club, Ponte Vedra Club, Kiwanis, Sigma Alpha Epsilon. Roman Catholic. Home: 3740 Paces Valley Rd NW Atlanta GA 30327-3208 Office: Haverty Furniture Cos Inc 866 W Peachtree St NW Atlanta GA 30308-1123*

HAVEWALA, NOSHIR BEHRAM, chemical engineer; b. Bombay, India, Dec. 19, 1938; came to U.S. 1961; s. Behram Dadabhai and Piroja Fakirji (Todiwala) H.; m. Carol Jean Ames, Dec. 19, 1963; children: Zarine N. Andolino, Tonia N. Fletcher. BSChemE, Nagpur U., India, 1961; MSChemE, U. Maine, 1962; PhDChemE, N.C. State U., Raleigh, 1969. Product devel. engr. Kimberly Clark Corp., Munising, Mich., 1962-65; process engr. Corning (N.Y.) Inc., 1965-67, project mgr. bioengring., 1969-73, mgr. chem. engring., 1973-76, mgr. engring. svcs., 1976-80, mgr. chem. process tech., 1980-84, mgr. engring. rsch., 1984-98, dir. tech. strategy, 1998—; mem. ind. adv. group N.C. A&T State U., Greensboro, 1987-96. Contbr. articles to profl. jours., chpts. to books. Mem. AIChE (chair sessions on ceramic materials and fiber optics and microelectronic processing), Am. Chem. Soc., Am. Ceramic Soc., Soc. for Info. Display, Phi Kappa Phi. Achievements include patents for low temperature glasses, immobilized enzymes and for annealing of liquid crystal display glass. Home: 56 Overbrook Rd Painted Post NY 14870-9343 Office: Corning Inc HP-ME-02 Corning NY 14830-2425

HAVEY, FRANCIS POWERS, fund raising executive, lawyer; b. Milw., Mar. 27, 1928; s. Joseph David and Ethyl Sara Havey; m. Rita J. Wysocki, June 7, 1952; children: Roberta Mary, Paula Marie, Stephen Joseph, Patrick Francis, Mary Michelle, Lisa Marie. AB, Marquette U., 1950, JD, 1953. Bar: Wis. Pvt. practice law Milw., 1953—; sr. cons. Am. City Bur., Chgo., 1956-60; v.p. Fund Fulfillment Corp., Chgo., 1960-61, The Cosgriff Orgn., Omaha, Nebr., 1961-62; pres. Havey-Fund Raising Mgmt., Inc., Milw., 1962—, also chmn. bd.; founder, chmn. of bd. Fund-Raising 800, Inc., 1997. Mayor City of Greenfield, 1980-84; co-chmn. Dems. for Reagan, Wis., 1980. Mem. State Bar of Wis. Roman Catholic. Avocation: professional fundraising. Office: Havey Fund-Raising Mgmt Inc 8777 W Forest Home Ave Greenfield WI 53228-3499

HAVEY, J. MICHAEL, psychologist, educator; b. Madison, Ind., July 24, 1953; s. Merle Freeman and Dorothy Elizabeth (Waldon) H.; m. Kathy Jo Kratz, Oct. 22, 1977; children: Elizabeth Anne, Sarah Catherine. AB magna cum laude, Hanover (Ind.) Coll., 1975; MS in Edn., Ind. U., 1980; EdD, Ball State U., 1985. Lic. sch. psychologist, Ill., Ind.; lic. psychologist, Ind. Tchr. Southwestern H.S., Hanover, 1975-81; counselor Southeastern Career Ctr., Versailles, Ind., 1981-82; sch. psychologist Greater Lafayette (Ind.) Area Spl. Svcs., 1985-88; prof. psychology Ea. Ill. U., Charleston, 1988—; spl. edn. due process hearing officer Ill. State Bd. Edn., 1992-98. Contbr. articles to profl. jours. Mem. sch. Bd. Charleston Cmty. Sch. Dist., 1995—; chmn. work area on missions Wesley United Meth. Ch., Charleston, 1992-95, mem. adminstrv. coun., 1992-95. Mem. Nat. Assn. Sch. Psychologists, Ill. Sch. Psychologists Assn. (contbg. editor 1991—, governing bd. 1991-93), Internat. Sch. Psychologists Assn. Avocations: reading, biking. Home: 2607 Village Rd Charleston IL 61920-4235 Office: Eastern Illinois Univ Dept Psychology Charleston IL 61920

HAVICE, PAMELA ANN, maternal/women's health nurse, nurse educator; b. Ashland, Kans., Nov. 11, 1957; d. Gary Robert and Peggy Ann (Rolfs) Moore; m. William Havice, June 19, 1976; children: Brooke Ann, Briana Lea. BSN, Ft. Hays State U., 1980, MS in Counseling, 1984; PhD in Ednl. Leadership, Clemson U., 1999. Staff and charge nurse Hadley Regional Med. Ctr., Hays, Kans., 1981; asst. prof. Ft. Hays State U., Hays, 1980-96, dir. nursing continuing edn., 1986-96; grad. tchg. asst. Clemson U., 1997-99, vis. prof., 1999—; spkr. and pub. in field. Recipient citation Am. Diabetes Assn., 1987, 90; named Young Alumni of 1995, Ft. Hays State U. Mem. Nat. Assn. Student Pers. Adminstrs., Am. Assn. Adult Continuing Edn., Phi Kappa Phi, Sigma Theta Tau.

HAVIGHURST, CLARK CANFIELD, law educator; b. Evanston, Ill., May 25, 1933; s. Harold Canfield and Marion Clay (Perryman) H.; m. Karen Waldron, Aug. 28, 1965; children: Craig Perryman, Marjorie Clark. BA, Princeton U., 1955; JD, Northwestern U., 1958. Bar: Ill. 1958, N.Y. 1961. Assoc. Debevoise Plimpton Lyons & Gates, N.Y.C., 1958, 61-64; assoc. prof. law Duke U., Durham, N.C., 1964-68, prof., 1968-86; William Neal Reynolds prof. Duke U., 1986—; interim dean Duke U. Sch. of Law, 1999—; dir. Program on Legal Issues in Health Care Duke U., 1969-88; adj. scholar Am Enterprise Inst. Pub. Policy Rsch., 1976—; resident cons. FTC, Washington, 1978, Epstein, Becker & Green, Washington, 1989-90; scholar in residence Inst. Medicine of NAS, Washington, 1972-73, RAND Corp., Santa Monica, 1999. Author: Deferred Compensation for Key Employees, 1964, Regulating Health Facilities Construction, 1974, Deregulating the Health Care Industry, 1982, Health Care Law and Policy, 1988, 2d edit., 1998, Health Care Choices: Private Contracts as Instruments of Health Reform, 1995; editor Law and Contemporary Problems jour., 1965-70. Served with U.S. Army, 1958-60. Mem. Inst. Medicine of Nat. Acad. Sci., Order of Coif. Office: Duke U Sch Law PO Box 90360 Durham NC 27708-0360

HAVILAND, BANCROFT DAWLEY, lawyer; b. Yonkers, N.Y., May 13, 1925; s. Harold Bancroft and Dorothy (Dawley) H.; m. Dorothy MacFarland, Oct. 30, 1945; children: Lucy, William, Thomas, Amy. BA in Polit. Sci., U. Pa., 1947, LLB, 1949. Bar: N.Y. 1951, Pa. 1952. Gowen teaching fellow U. Pa. Law Sch., Phila., 1949-50; assoc. Donovan, Leisure, Newton & Irvine, Phila., 1950-51; assoc. Schnader, Harrison, Segal & Lewis, Phila., 1951-61, ptnr., 1961-90, ret., 1991. Trustee Westtown (Pa.) Friends' Sch., 1960-94, Media-Providence (Pa.) Friends' Sch., 1960-95; chmn. Westtown Sch. Com., 1988-93; commr. Rose Tree Soccer Club, Media, 1971-98, Aston Twp., Pa., 1954-61; justice of peace Middletown Twp., Pa., 1963-65. Lt. (j.g.) USN, 1943-45, PTO. Mem. ABA, Pa. Bar Assn., Phila. Bar Assn., Am. Judicature Soc., Order of Coif. Democrat. Soc. of Friends. Lodge: Lions. Avocations: woodworking, reading, gardening. Home: 344 S Old Middletown Rd Media PA 19063-4751 Office: Schnader Harrison Segal & Lewis 1600 Market St Ste 3600 Philadelphia PA 19103-7240

HAVILAND, DAVID SANDS, architectural educator, researcher, administrator; b. Rome, N.Y., Apr. 26, 1942; s. William Erwin and Barbara Hannon (Huguenin) H.; m. Kathleen Anne Kelly, July 8, 1983; children: Kelly Sands, Wallace Sands. BS, Rensselaer Poly. Inst., 1964, BArch, 1965, MArch, 1967. Rsch. asst., instr. Rensselaer Poly. Inst., Troy, N.Y., 1965-67, asst. prof. architecture, 1967-70, assoc. prof., 1970-79, prof., 1979—, dean Sch. of Architecture, 1980-90, v.p., student life, 1994—; cons. facilities planning and mgmt.; vis. prof. constrn. mgmt. and engring. U. Reading, U.K., 1990-96. Editor: The Architect's Handbook fo Profl. Practice, 12th edit., 1994; contbr. articles to profl. jours. Trustee Rensselaer Newman Found., 1975—, Howard and Bush Found. Recipient James L. Haecker award for disting. rsch. leadership, 1996, also numerous rsch. grants. Mem. AIA (hon., Inst. award 1989), N.Y. State Assn. Architects, Rensselaer Alumni Assn. Home: 63 Pinewoods Ave Troy NY 12180-4701 Office: Rensselaer Polytech Inst Off VP Student Life Troy Bldg 110 8th St Troy NY 12180-3522

HAVIR, BRYAN THOMAS, urban planner; b. Allentown, Pa., Feb. 9, 1963; s. Donald John and Ruth Mary (Schmoyer) H. BA in Polit. Sci., History, Pa. State U., 1985, MPA, 1990; cert. in Environ. Studies, Delaware Valley Coll., 1994; postgrad., U. Pa., 1994—. Planning intern City of Allentown, 1984-85; legal rschr. Pa. State U., University Park, 1985; enforcement officer zoning and code South Whitehall Twp., Allentown, 1985-86; asst. site planner Montgomery County Planning Commn., Norristown, Pa., 1986-87; asst. planner Mercer County Planning Bd., Trenton, N.J., 1987-88; planning dir., zoning code enforcement officer Warwick Twp., Jamison, Pa., 1988-90; coord. cmty. devel. Evesham Twp., Marlton, N.J., 1991-97; dir. cmty. planning Heritage Conservancy, Doylestown, Pa., 1997-98; asst. twp. mgr. Cheltenham Twp., Elkins Park, Pa., 1998—; sec. to bd. dirs. McCandless Opticians, Inc. Asst. scoutmaster Boy Scouts Am., Allentown, 1980—; mem. Lehigh County Hist. Soc.; bd. dirs. Bucks County Agrl. Land Preservation Bd., 1990; active Preservation N.J. Mem. Am. Planning Assn., Am. Soc. Pub. Adminstrn., Urban Land Inst., Ams. for Dem. Action, Pa. State U. Alumni Assn., Keystone Soc., Acad. Polit. Sci., Am. Inst. Cert. Planners, N.J. Bd. Profl. Planners, N.J. Assn. Planning and Zoning Adminstrs., Nat. Trust for Hist. Preservation, Pa. Land Trust Alliance, Nat. Eagle Scout Assn., Ranconcas Conservancy Watershed Assn., Heritage Conservancy. Democrat. Lutheran. Avocations: history, fgn. affairs, boating, auto racing, hockey. Fax: 215-887-1561. E-mail: township1@home.com. Home: 404 Old Farm Rd Wyncote PA 19095-2034 Office: Cheltenham Twp Adminstrn Bldg 8230 Old York Rd Elkins Park PA 19027-1589

HAVIS, ALLAN STUART, playwright, theatre educator; b. N.Y.C., Sept. 26, 1951; s. Mickey and Esther H.; m. Julia Fulton. BA, CCNY, 1973; MA, Hunter Coll., 1976; MFA, Yale U., 1980. Film animation tchr. Guggenheim Mus., N.Y.C., 1974-76; playwriting tchr. Dramatist Guild, N.Y.C., 1985-87, Ulster County C.C., Stoneridge, N.Y., 1985-88; prof. theatre, head playwriting program U. Calif.-San Diego, La Jolla, 1988—. Author: (novel) Albert the Astronomer, 1979, (plays) Morocco, 1986 (HBO award), Lilith, 1991, The Gift, 1998, (anthology) Plays by Allan Havis, 1989, A Daring Bridge, 1997, Ladies of Fisher Cove, 1997, Sainte Simone, 1997, (play) A Vow of Silence, 1996, (anthology) Plays by Allan Havis, 1997; editor, contbr.: American Political Plays of 1990's, 1998—. Dramaturg Young Playwrights Festival, N.Y.C., 1984, juror, 1993; juror N.J. Arts Coun., Trenton, 1987; panelist Theatre Communications Group, N.Y.C., 1987; juror McKnight Playwriting Fellowship, 1995; v.p. Literary Mgrs. and Dramaturgs of Am., So. Calif. region, 1995—. Playwriting fellow Nat. Endowment for the Arts, 1986, Rockefeller Found., 1987, Guggenheim Found., 1987-88; recipient New American Plays award Kennedy Ctr./Am. Express, Washington, 1988, Dramatists Guild/CBS award, 1995, HBO award, 1996. Democrat. Jewish. Avocations: tennis, motorcycles, racquetball, swimming, horseback riding. Office: Dept of Theatre Univ Calif-San Diego La Jolla CA 92093

HAVIS, LEE, executive director educational association; b. Riverdale, Md., Nov. 1, 1943. BS in Engring., U. Conn., 1965; B in Fgn. Trade, Am. Inst. for Fgn. Trade, Glendale, Ariz., 1966; JD, Cath. U. Am., 1973; MEd in Early Childhood Edn., U. Md., 1974; Cert. Montessori Tchr. Edn. (3-6), AERCO, 1976. Asst. prof. Peace Corps, U. Panama, Panama City, 1967-68; early childhood tchr. Edufax Early Learning Ctr., Bethesda, Md., 1970-71; substitute tchr. Prince George County (Md.) Schs., 1973-74; intern Montessori method (ages 2-6) Early Learning, Inc., Montgomery County, Md., 1976-77; dir. Campus Tutuoring, Largo, Md., 1975-78; founder, dir. Trust Tutoring, Silver Spring, Md., 1992—; exec. dir., founder Internat. Montessori Soc., Silver Spring, 1979—. Home and Office: Internat Montessori Soc 912 Thayer Ave Ste 207 Silver Spring MD 20910-4570

HAVIST, MARJORIE VICTORIA, librarian, educator; b. Johnstown, Pa., Nov. 6, 1931; d. Victor Dale and Lillie Mae (Bross) Mulhollen; m. George I. Melhorn, Aug. 8, 1953 (dec. Dec. 1962); children—Susan Lynn, Bradford George; m. Ewald Jack Havist, Aug. 7, 1969. B.S. in Edn., Bucknell U., 1953; M.L.S., U. Wash., 1966. Cert. librarian, Wash. Engr., Boeing Co., Seattle, 1955, 57-58; librarian Bellevue Community Coll., Wash., 1966-78; head librarian Seattle Central Community Coll., Seattle, 1978-80; dean library Skagit Valley Coll., Mt. Vernon, Wash., 1980-98, ret., 1998. Bd. dirs. ARC Skagit County, Mt. Vernon, 1982; loaned exec. United Way Skagit County, 1983-85, 89-90. Mem. ALA, Community Coll. Librarians and Media Specialists (pres. 1977-78), Community Coll. Library Dirs. Council (pres. 1981-82), Phi Theta Kappa. Republican. Lutheran. Office: Skagit Valley Coll 2405 E College Way Mount Vernon WA 98273-5821

HAVLICEK, FRANKLIN J., communications executive; b. N.Y.C., July 18, 1947; s. Raymond Joseph and Rosalia Maria (Zona) H.; m. Louise Sferrazza, Dec. 21, 1980. BA, Columbia U., 1968, JD, 1973, MA, 1977, MPhil, 1980; cert., Internat. Inst. Human Rights, Strasbourg, France, 1972. Bar: N.Y. 1974, U.S. Dist. Ct. (so. and ea. dists.) N.Y. 1974, U.S. Ct. Appeals (2d cir.) 1975, U.S. Supreme Ct. 1979, D.C. 1990. Atty. Battle & Fowler, N.Y.C., 1973-78; spl. advisor to Mayor of N.Y.C., 1978-82; ptnr. Seham, Klein, Zelman, N.Y.C., 1982-84; dir. labor rels. NBC, N.Y.C., 1984-88; v.p. indsl. rels. and environ. svcs. Washington Post, 1988-97; ind. cons. Washington, 1997—; adj. prof. Sch. Internat. & Pub. Affairs Columbia U., N.Y.C., 1978-88, Sch. Pub. Affairs, Am. U., Washington, 1997—; chmn. Sunnyside Found., 1981-91; legal advisor Internat. Monetary Fund, 1998—; adj. prof. Sch. Pub. Affairs, Am. U., 1999—. Editor: Collective Bargaining, 1979, Presidential Selection, 1982, Election Communications, 1984; contbr. numerous articles on law, govt., communications to mags., newspapers. Mem. chmn.'s task force in NLRB, Washington, 1976-77; exec. com. N.Y. Gov.'s Task Force in Schs. and Bus., 1986-88; counsel Vietnam Vets. Meml. Commn., 1982-85, State Commn. on Dioxin, 1983-85; candidate for U.S. Senate in N.Y., 1986; mem. U.S. U.S.S.R. Emerging Leaders Summit, 1988, 90; bd. dirs. World Affairs Coun., 1991—, Washington Performing Arts Soc., 1995—, Internat. Peace Acad., 1989-90, World Media Colloquium UNESCO, 1989; U.S. Tech. expert ILO, 1990; cons. to UN High Commr. for Human Rights in Bosnia, 1992; study grant on media and communications European Cmty., 1994. With U.S. Army, 1968-70. Ford Found. fellow, 1977; study grantee on media and comms. European Cmty., 1994. Mem. ABA, Assn. of Bar of City of N.Y., Am. Polit. Sci. Assn., Am. Acad. Polit. Sci., Czechoslovakian Soc. Arts and Scis., N.Y. Acad. Scis. Roman Catholic. Club: City N.Y. (trustee 1985-87). Avocations: tennis, running, climbing, films, architectural restoration. Home: 3364 Tennyson St NW Washington DC 20015-2443 Office: Washington Post Co 1150 15th St NW Washington DC 20071-0002

HAVLICEK, JOHN J. (HONDO HAVLICEK), former professional basketball player; b. Martins Ferry, Ohio, Apr. 8, 1940; s. Frank and Maudy H.; m. Beth Evans, June 17, 1967; children: Christopher, Jill. Student, Ohio State U., 1958-62. Basketball player Boston Celtics, NBA, 1962-78. Player Nat. Basketball Assn. All-Star Game, 1966-78; mem. Nat. Basketball Assn. Championship Teams, 1963-66, 68-69, 74, 76, NCAA Championship Team, 1960; named to Nat. Basketball Assn. 35th Anniversary All-Time Team, 1980, Sporting News All-America Second Team, 1962, All-NBA First Team, 1971-74, ALL-NBA Second Team, 1964, 66, 68-70, 75-76, NBA All-Defensive Second Team, 1969-71, NBA Finals MVP, 1974; inducted into Naismith Meml. Basketball Hall of Fame, 1983. Address: Naismith Mem Basketball Hall of Fame PO Box 179 1150 W Columbus Ave Springfield MA 01105*

HAVLICEK, SARAH MARIE, educator, artist, small business owner; b. N.Y.C., Jan. 29, 1950; d. Raymond Joseph and Rosalie Maria (Zona) Havlicek; m. william Gabriel Tortora, Sept. 16, 1972 (div. 1995); children: Nina-Gabrielle, Eva-Juliet. BS, NYU, 1972; MA, San Francisco State U., 1976. Cert. tchr., N.Y. Co-owner, mgr., instr. Sound Universe Inc., N.Y.C., 1972-74; customer rels. Chartered Bank, San Francisco, 1974-76, Standard Chartered Bank, N.Y.C., 1976-78; co-owner, mgr. Design Constrn. Co., N.Y.C., 1978-94; mgr. edn. Internat. Automotive Parts & Accessories Assn., Bethesda, Md., 1994-98; mgmt. cons., instrnl. technologist Soza Co., Ltd., Fairfax, Va., 1998—. Painting exhibits include Daughters, Patterns; poetry collections include Lines of Evidence, Coney Island Games, Quid Pro Quo, Air Circles. Mem. Internat. Platform Assn., Am. Soc. Assn. Execs. Avocations: roller blading, ice skating, bicycling, meditating. Home: Kenwood Pl 5301 Westbard Cir Apt 337 Bethesda MD 20816-1431 Office: 8550 Arlington Blvd Fairfax VA 22031

HAVLIN, JOHN LEROY, soil scientist, educator; b. Chgo., May 8, 1950; s. Joseph Leroy and Dorothy Jean (Williams) H.; m. Saundra Joyce Crowley, July 7, 1979; 1 child, Jonathon Cary. MS, Colo. State U., 1980, PhD, 1983. Asst. prof. U. Nebr., Scottbluff, 1983-85; asst. prof. Kans. State U., Manhattan, 1985-90, prof. dept. agronomy, 1990-96; prof., head soil sci. dept. N.C. State U., Raleigh, 1996—. Author Soil Fertility ad Fertilizers; contbr. articles to profl. publs., chpts. to book. Named Researcher of Yr. Nat. Fertilizer Solutions Assn., 1989; recipient Werner L. Nelson Rsch. award, 1991; Nat. Assn. Coll. Teachers of Agrl. Teacher Fellow, 1994. Mem. Am. Soc. Agronomy, Soil Sci. Soc. Am. (fellow 1995), Am. Soil and Water Conservation Soc., Sigma Xi, Phi Kappa Phi, Gamma Sigma Delta (Outstanding Tchr. award 1992). Republican. Presbyterian. Achievements include research in advancement of dryland soil and crop management technologies to improve productivity and profitability, crop rotation and tillage effects on soil organic matter and productivity, dryland fertilizer management, and precision farming. Home: 8709 Bluff Pointe Ct Raleigh NC 27615-4195 Office: Dept Soil Sci NC State U Raleigh NC 27695

HAVNER, KERRY SHUFORD, civil engineering and solid mechanics educator; b. Huntington, W.Va., Feb. 20, 1934; s. Alfred Sidney and Jessie May (Fowler) H.; m. Roberta Lee Rider, Aug. 28, 1954; children: Karen Elese Smith, Clark Alan, Kris Sidney. BSCE, Okla. State U., 1955, MS, 1956, PhD, 1959. Registered prof. engr., Okla. Stress analyst Douglas Aircraft Co., Tulsa, 1956; from instr. to asst. prof. civil engring. Okla. State U., Stillwater, 1957-62; sr. stress and vibration engr. Garrett Corp., Phoenix, 1962-63; sect. chief solid mechs. rsch. missile/space systems divsn. McDonnell-Douglas Corp., Santa Monica, Calif., 1963-68; lectr. civil engring. U. So. Calif., L.A., 1965-68; from assoc. prof. to prof. civil engring. N.C. State U., Raleigh, 1968-82, prof. civil engring. and materials sci., 1982-99, prof. emeritus, 1999—; sr. vis. dept. applied math. and theoretical physics U. Cambridge, 1981, 89. Author: Finite Plastic Deformation of Crystalline Solids, 1992; contbg. author: Mechanics of Solids, The Rodney Hill 60th Anniversary Volume, 1982; contbr. articles to Jour. Applied Math. and Physics, Jour. of Mechs. and Physics of Solids, Acta Mechanica, Procs. and Phil. Trans. Royal Soc., others; bd. editors Mechs. of Materials, Internat. Jour. Plasticity. 2d lt. U.S. Army, 1961, 1st lt. USAR. Rsch. grantee NSF, 1971, 74, 76, 78, 81, 83, 87, 91, 94; vis. fellow Clare Hall, 1981; recipient Melvin R. Lohmann medal Okla. State U., 1994. Fellow ASCE (sec. engring. mechs. divsn. 1983-85, chmn. 1987-88, chmn. engring. mechs. adv. bd. 1990-91, chmn. TAC-CERF awards com. 1991-94; assoc. editor Jour. Engring. Mechs. 1981-83), Am. Acad. Mechanics (assoc. editor Mechanics, 1991-97); mem. ASME, Soc. Engring. Sci., Soc. Indsl. and Applied Math., Sigma Xi. Democrat. Methodist. Achievements include research in theories and analyses of anisotropic hardening and finite deformation in crystalline materials, particularly metals. Home: 3331 Thomas Rd Raleigh NC 27607-6743 Office: NC State U Dept Civil Engring Box 7908 Raleigh NC 27695

HAVRAN, MARTIN JOSEPH, historian, educator, author; b. Windsor, Ont., Can., Nov. 12, 1929; came to U.S., 1956; s. Joseph W. and Helen (Bachinger) H.; m. Clara L. Kovacs, Aug. 30, 1958; 1 child, Justin M. PhB, U. Detroit, 1951; MA, Wayne State U., 1953; PhD, Case Western Res. U., 1957. Instr. history Kent (Ohio) State U., 1957-60, asst. prof., 1960-64, assoc. prof., 1964-68; assoc. prof. history U. Va., Charlottesville, 1968-72, prof., 1972—, chmn. dept. history, 1974-79, dir. Self-Study Program, 1984-86, sec. of gen. faculty, 1994-99; vis. assoc. prof. history Northwestern U., Evanston, Ill., 1967-68. Author: Catholics in Caroline England, 1962, England: Prehistory to Present, 1968, Life of Lord Cottington, 1973; editor: Readings in English History, 1967. Recipient Whittaker History prize Mich. Hist. Commn., 1953; Social Sci. Rsch. Coun. fellow, 1956-57; Govt. of Can. grantee, 1984. Fellow Royal Hist. Soc.; mem. Am. Cath. Hist. Assn. (pres. 1982), N.Am. Conf. on Brit. Studies (pres. 1979-81), Royal Stuart Soc., Ch. of Eng. Record Soc., Multicultural History Soc. Ont., Raven Soc., Torch Club (pres. 1993-94). Roman Catholic. Avocations: classical music, walking, gardening.

HAVRILCSAK, GREGORY MICHAEL, history educator; b. Uniontown, Pa., Feb. 18, 1951; s. Michael and Geneveve Anne (Satterfield) H.; m. Laura Ann Hart. BA, U. Mich., Flint, 1978; MA, Oakland U., 1989; postgrad., U. Va., 1995. Instr. history St. Mary's Sch., Swartz Creek, Mich., 1978-79, Riverside Mil. Acad., Gainesville, Ga., 1979-85, Notre Dame High Sch., Harper Woods, Mich., 1985-88, East Detroit Cmty. Schs., Eastpointe, Mich., 1986-91; instr. history Notre Dame High Sch., Harper Woods, Mich., 1991—, chmn. dept. social sci., 1996, debate and forensics coach, 1998—; dir. social studies learning ctr. L'Anse-Creuse Cmty. Schs., Mt. Clemens, Mich., 1986-89; adj. instr. history Monroe (Mich.) County C.C., 1988-94, Oakland C.C., Auburn Hills, Mich., 1989—; Monticello-Stratford Hall Plantation Summer Seminar for Tchrs., 1995; with Inst. on the Tchg. of Advanced Placement European History, St. Johnsbury Acad., Vt., 1992, Internat. Symposium on the War of 1812 on the Great Lakes, U. Windsor, 1988; radio host Havrilcsak's History, WSDS AM 1480, 1998—. Vol. Big Bros., Big Sisters, Macomb County, Mich., 1987-89. With USN, 1969-71. Named Outstanding Young Men of Am., U.S. Jaycees, 1980. Mem. Mich. Hist. Soc., Oakland U. Alumni Assn., U. Mich. Alumni Assn., Orgn. Am. Historians, Mich. C.C. History Assn., Ctr. Tchg. Mich. History, Phi Alpha Theta. Avocations: photography, traveling. Home: 15094 El Dorado Terr Warren MI 48093-3266 Office: Notre Dame High Sch 20254 Kelly Rd Harper Woods MI 48225-1287

HAW, BILL, association executive. Pres. Nat. Farms Inc., Kansas City, Mo. Office: National Farms Inc 1600 Genessee St Ste 846 Kansas City MO 64102-1079*

HAWE, DAVID LEE, consultant; b. Columbus, Ohio, Feb. 19, 1938; s. William Doyle and Carolyn Mary (Hassig) H.; m. Margret J. Hoover, Apr. 15, 1962; children: Darrin Lee, Kelly Lynn. Project mgr. ground antenna systems W.D.L. Labs., Philco Corp., 1960-65; credit mgr. for Western U.S., Am. Hosp. Supply Corp., Burbank, Calif., 1965-74; owner, mgr. Hoover Profl. Equipment Co., contract health equipment co., Guasti, Calif., 1974-75; pres. Baslor Care Services, owner convalescent homes, Santa Ana, Calif., 1975-80; pres. Application Assocs., 1980—; bd. dirs., chmn. bd. dirs. Xiron, Inc., 1984—; dir. Medisco Co., Casa Pacifica, Broadway Assocs. Bd. dirs. Santa Ana Community Convalescent Hosp., 1974-79, pres., 1975-79. With USN, 1954-56. Lic. real estate broker, Calif. Mem. Am. Vacuum Soc. Republican. Roman Catholic. Home: 18082 Hallsworth Cir Villa Park CA 92861-4503

HAWES, DOUGLAS WESSON, lawyer; b. West Orange, N.J., Nov. 17, 1932. BA, Principia Coll., 1954; JD, Columbia U., 1957; MBA, NYU, 1961. Bar: N.Y. 1958, U.S. Supreme Ct. 1961. Assoc., then ptnr. LeBoeuf, Lamb, Greene & MacRae L.L.P., N.Y.C., 1958—; adj. prof. law Vanderbilt U., 1972-74, NYU, 1976-89; bd. dirs. Bay State Gas Co., Hackensack Water Co., United Water Resources Inc. Contbr. articles to legal publs. Mem. ABA (exec. com. fed. regulation securities coms., pub. utility holding co., internat. securities matters sects.), N.Y. State Bar Assn., Bar Assn. City N.Y. (corp. law com.), Am. Law Inst., Internat. Faculty for Corp. and Capital Market Law. Home: 23 rue Ballu, 75009 Paris France Office: LeBoeuf Lamb Greene & MacRae LLP 125 W 55th St New York NY 10019-5369*

HAWES, NANCY ELIZABETH, mathematics educator; b. Phila., Oct. 28, 1944; d. Charles E. and Margaret M. (Cassel) H. BS in Edn., Millersville

(Pa.) State Coll., 1966; MAT, Purdue U., 1970; M.Div., Ea. Bapt. Theol. Sem., Phila., 1979. Ordained deacon A.M.E. Zion Ch., 1978, elder, 1980. Tchr. math. Penncrest High Sch./Rose Tree Media (Pa.) Sch. Dist., 1966-68; asst. pastor Wesley A.M.E. Zion Ch., Phila., 1975-82; pastor St. John A.M.E. Zion Ch., Bethlehem, Pa., 1982-88, Mt. Tabor A.M.E. Zion Ch., Avondale, Pa., 1988-90; assoc. pastor Wesley A.M.E. Zion Ch., Phila., 1990—; tchr. math. Upper Merion Area Sch. Dist., King of Prussia, Pa., 1968—; sponsor, Upper Merion Area High Sch. Math. Team, 1987—. Mem. Nat. Coun. Tchrs. Math., Math. Assn. Am., Pa. Coun. Tchrs. Math., Assn. Tchrs. Math. of Phila. and Vicinity. A.M.E. Zion Ch. Office: Upper Merion Area High Sch 435 Crossfield Rd King Of Prussia PA 19406

HAWES, SUE, lawyer; b. Washington, Mar. 30, 1937; d. Alexander Boyd and Elizabeth (Armstrong) H.; m. James E. Brodhead, June 21, 1963; children: William James Pusey Brodhead, Daniel Alexander Hawes Brodhead. BA, Sarah Lawrence Coll., 1959, MA, 1963; JD, Whittier (Calif.) Sch. of Law, 1983. Bar: Calif. 1988, U.S. Dist. Ct. (cen. dist.) Calif. 1990. Dancer and choreographer N.Y.C., Washington, Latin Am., Europe, 1959-62; instr., dir. dance program dept. theatre and phys. edn. Smith Coll., Northampton, Mass., 1963-65; instr. dept. dance UCLA, 1973-75; freelance script supr. L.A., 1976-80; prin. Law Office of Sue Hawes, L.A., 1988-96; ptnr., mem. RESULTS. Articles editor Whittier Law Rev., 1982-83. Active Santa Barbara Symphony League. Mem. AAUW, Results, State Bar Calif., Actors' Equity Assn. Democrat. Avocations: music, gardening, politics.

HAWES, WILLIAM KENNETH, communication educator; b. Grand Rapids, Mich., Mar. 6, 1931; s. William Kenneth and Cora Elizabeth (Tibble) H.; m. Ella Margaret Plant, Aug. 13, 1961 (dec. 1998); children: William III, Robert Ernest. AB, Eastern Mich. U., 1955; MA, U. Mich., 1956, PhD, 1960. Teaching asst. U. Mich., Ann Arbor, 1956-57; instr. English and speech Eastern Mich. U., Ypsilanti, 1956-60; asst. prof., mgr. KTCU Tex. Christian U., Ft. Worth, 1960-64; vis. assoc. prof., mgr. WUNC U. N.C., Chapel Hill, 1964-65; assoc. prof., mgr. KUHF U. Houston, 1965-76, prof., 1976—; admissions bd. Biomed. Program, Sch. Allied Health Scis., U. Tex. Health Sci. Ctr., Houston, 1974-95. Author: The Performer in Mass Media, 1976, American Television Drama, 1986, Television Performing, 1991, Ante La Cámara, 1993, Public Television: America's First Station, 1996; contbg. author: Understanding Radio, 1967, 85, La Radio: Une Carriere, 1970, Understanding Television, 1978, Television Station Management and Operations, 1989; editor: Pornography Cinema Community Standards, 1975, 82, 93; prodr., creator TV series including Video Workshop, 1967—; film guest Fed. Republic of Germany, 1981. With USAF, Mich. Air NG, 1949-54. Recipient Avery Hopwood award U. Mich., 1957; grantee U. Houston and/or NEH, 1982, 83, 86, 87, 91; named to U. Houston London Program, 1984, 94. Mem. Am. Film Inst. Home: Parc V-902 3600 Montrose Blvd Houston TX 77006-4658 Office: U Houston Sch of Comm Houston TX 77204-4072

HAWK, BEVERLY GALE, political scientist, educator; b. Fort Riley, Kans., Sept. 25, 1952; d. John Francis and Winsome (Beasley) H. BS in Polit. Sci., John Carroll U., 1975; MA in African Studies, Howard U., 1980; MA in Polit. Sci., U. Wis., Madison, 1983, PhD, 1988. Asst. prof. Colby Coll., Waterville, Maine, 1985-92, U. Ala., Birmingham, 1992—; planner State of Maine, Augusta, 1993. Editor: Africa's Media Image, 1992, Issue: A Jour. of Opinion, 1993—. Fulbright scholar U. Nairobi, 1993-94; Sloan Found. grantee, 1988-89, U.S. Dept. of Energy grantee, 1993, Speaker's grantee U.S. Info. Agy., 1994. Mem. Pi Mu Epsilon, Phi Beta Delta. Democrat. Avocation: collecting pens. Home: 8 Hazelwood Ave Waterville ME 04901-5736 Office: U Ala Birmingham Polit Sci and Pub Affairs Birmingham AL 53294

HAWK, CAROLE LYNN, insurance company executive, research analyst; b. Springfield, Ill., June 17, 1947; d. Warren Wesley and Mary June (Moore) Weiser; m. Charles Edward Hawk, Aug. 2, 1963; 1 child, Cynthia Jean Hawk-Lindzy. Student, Lincoln Land C.C., Springfield, 1970-75, Ind. U., South Bend, 1982-83. Cert. data processor, computer programmer, systems profl., assoc. in customer svc.; assoc. Ins. Regulatory Compliance. Systems analyst Office Ill. Sec. of State, Springfield, 1969-78; software specialist Clark Equipment Co., Buchanan, Mich., 1978-84; GC056 software analyst Contel Corp., Wentzville, Mo., 1984-87; tech. rsch. analyst The Horace Mann Cos., Springfield, 1988—. Mem., vol. interpreter Dana-Thomas House Found.; adult literacy tutor; active Friends of the Fox Theatre, St. Louis. Fellow Life Mgmt. Assn.; mem. Assn. Info. Tech. Profls. (sec. Capital chpt. 1993-94, exec. pres. 1995, pres. 1996), Ctrl. Ill. Life Mgmt. Inst. (co. rep. 1995-97), Toastmasters (sec. Horace Mann chpt. 1992, pres. 1993, gov. area 1 1994-95, gov. dist. C 1995-97, v.p. edn. 1997-98, v.p. pub. rels. 1998-99, v.p. edn. 1999—).

HAWK, CLARK WILLIAMS, mechanical and aerospace engineering educator; b. Berea, Ohio, Sept. 16, 1936; s. Harry Lyle and Catherine (Williams) H.; m. Julia Ann Milthaler, Nov. 7, 1959; children: Sandra Lynn Smith, Brian Clark. BSME, Pa. State U., 1958; MSME, Purdue U., 1968, PhD, 1970. Registered mech. engr., Calif., Ala. Project engr. Propulsion Lab., Wright-Patterson AFB, Ohio, 1958-59; project engr. Rocket Propulsion Lab., Edwards AFB, Calif., 1959-67, sect. chief, researcher, 1969-71, br., sect. chief, 1971-81; div. dir. Astronautics Lab., Edwards AFB, Calif., 1983-91; lectr. U. So. Calif., L.A., 1971; prof. mech. & aerospace engring., dir. Propulsion Rsch. Ctr. U. Ala., Huntsville, 1991—; mem. NRC Earth To Orbit Propulsion Options, Washington, 1991-92; mem. NRC Com. on Advanced Space Techs., Washington, 1992-98. Contbr. articles to profl. jours. Recipient Gilbert award Antelope Valley YMCA, 1982, Meritorious Svc. award L.A. County Bd. Edn., 1985, Cert. of Merit, L.A. Sch. Trustees Assn., 1985, Excellence award Air Force Space Div., 1986. Fellow AIAA (assoc. editor Jour. Propulsion and Power 1986-90); mem. NSPE, Pi Tau Sigma. Achievements include conceiving and creating LPIAG and SPIAG which brought together U.S. liquid rock engine and solid rocket motor manufacturers to solve problems of mutual concern; creation of JANNAF Rocket Nozzle Tech. Com. to establish a community of interest in carbon-carbon nozzle technology area. Home: 179 Stoneway Trl Madison AL 35758-8543

HAWK, DAWN DAVAH, secondary education educator; b. Dodge, Nebr., Apr. 14, 1945; d. Fred John and Marcella Martha (Kunes) Lerch; m. Floyd Russell Hawk, June 14, 1969. BAE, Wayne State Coll., 1967. Cert. tchr., Nebr., Iowa, Ariz. English tchr. Tekamah (Nebr.) Pub. Sch., 1967-69, West Lyon Community Schs., Inwood, Iowa, 1970-74, Norfolk (Nebr.) Cath. Schs., 1974-85; English tchr., libr. Beemer (Nebr.) Pub. Schs., 1969-70; English and reading tchr. San Manuel (Ariz.) Sch. Dist., 1986—; chair adaptive edn. dept. San Manuel (Ariz.) High Sch., 1992-93; tutor in field. Active Catalina Luth. Ch., Tucson. Recipient Cooper Found. award for excellence in teaching U. Nebr., 1983; NEH edn. grantee, 1987, 89, 91, 95; Ariz. Reading Assn. grad. scholar, 1995. Mem. NEA, Nat. Coun. Tchrs. English, Internat. Reading Assn., Ea. Pinal Lit. Coun., Ariz. English Tchrs. Assn., Tucson Area Reading Coun. (bd. advisors), San Manuel Tchrs. Assn. Republican. Avocations: reading, writing poetry, travelling, visiting museums, golf. Home: 3950 E Hawser St Trlr 5 Tucson AZ 85739-9537 Office: San Manuel HS PO Box 406 San Manuel AZ 85631-0406

HAWK, FLOYD RUSSELL, secondary school educator; b. Fresno, Calif., Oct. 7, 1945; s. Floyd Edward and Velma Irene (Lyon) H.; m. Dawn Davah Lerch, June 14, 1969. BA in Bus., Wayne State Coll., 1971. Cert. tchr. Ariz. Tchr. W. Lyon Pub. Schs., Inwood, Iowa, 1970-74, Norfolk (Nebr.) Cath. Schs., 1974-76, Madison (Nebr.) Pub. Schs., 1977-85, Young (Ariz.) Pub. Schs., 1985-86, San Manuel (Ariz.) High Sch., 1986--; state rep. Nat. Coaches Assn., Madison, Nebr., 1980-82; bd. dirs. Pinal County Adult Literacy, San Manuel. Mem. adv. bd. Multiple Sclerosis Soc.; mem. dist. 6 of Ariz. coord. We the People... NEH grantee, 1995. Mem. NEA, Ariz. Edn. Assn., Nat. Coun. Social Studies, Ariz. Bus. Edn. Assn., Ariz. Hist. Soc., Optimist Club (pres. 1972, lt. gov. 1973). Republican. Lutheran. Avocations: baseball, reading, teaching, church work. Office: San Manuel HS PO Box 406 San Manuel AZ 85631

HAWK, FRANK CARKHUFF, SR., industrial engineer; b. Bound Brook, N.J., Sept. 5, 1912; s. Frank Carkhuff and Martha Elizabeth (Maier) H.; m. Ruth H. Housel, June 6, 1937 (dec. Nov. 4, 1989); children: Frank Carkhuff III, Nancy Leigh Linky. BS in Indsl. Engring., Lehigh U., 1935. Registered profl. engr., Ohio. Application engr. York Ice Machinery Corp., N.Y.C., 1936-38; sales engr. Peerless of Am., Chgo., 1938-40, divsn. mgr., 1940-42; chief engr. applications Chrysler Airtemp, Dayton, Ohio, 1942-44; export refrigeration engr. Worthington Pump and Machinery, Harrison, N.J., 1944-46; sales mgr. Cecil Boling Co., N.Y.C., 1946-50; v.p. Brunner Mfg. Co., Utica, N.Y., 1950-57; gen. mgr. Bohn Aluminum & Brass Co., Danville, Ill., 1957-58; pres., owner Hawk Engring. Co., Barnegat, N.J., 1958—. Author: Industrial Refrigeration Manual, 1991; designer plastic mold cooler, 1963, automatic hot gas defrost system refrigeration, 1959-60, photo water cooler, 1948-49, bakery ingred water cooler, 1948. Dir. Navy League Coun., Long Branch, N.J., 1992. Recipient (2) Citations, Manhattan Project-Atom Bomb, U.S. Army, 1943. Mem. Am. Soc. Refrigeration Engrs., Refrigeration Svc. Engrs. Soc. (N.J. chpt.), U.S. Naval Inst., Shawnee Village Resort (pres., dir. 1979-93). Republican. Presbyterian. Home: 76 Pine Oak Blvd Barnegat NJ 08005-3104 Office: Hawk Engring Co 76 Pine Oak Blvd Barnegat NJ 08005-3104

HAWK, GEORGE WAYNE, retired electronics company executive; b. Warren, Ohio, Feb. 21, 1928; s. Oscar Wilmer and Morda Irene (Klingensmith) H.; m. Charline Hines Bond, Feb. 12, 1955; children: George Wayne, David James, John Robert. BS in Aero. Engring, Purdue U., 1951; MSME, U. So. Calif., 1955; postgrad., U. Tenn. Registered profl. engr., Ind. Asst. R & D officer gas dynamics facility Arnold Engring. Devel. Ctr., Tullahoma, Tenn., 1951-53; project engr. Hughes R & D Lab., Culver City, Calif., 1953-56; sr. rsch. engr. Goodyear Aircraft Corp., Akron, Ohio, 1956-57; with Moog Inc., East Aurora, N.Y., 1957-81, v.p. aerospace divsn., 1968-69, exec. v.p., dir., gen. mgr. controls divsn., 1969-76, exec. v.p., dir. pres. controls group, 1976-81; pres. G.W. Hawk Inc., 1981-86; pres., CEO Acme Electric Corp., 1986-91, chmn. bd. dirs., CEO, 1992-94; chmn. bd. dirs. Comptek Rsch. Inc., 1983-87, M.H.P. Machines, Inc., Buffalo, 1983-92; bd. dirs. Acme Electric Corp., Comptek Rsch., Inc., Century Jet Corp.; chmn. bd. dirs. B.I.S. Ptnrs., Western N.Y. Tech. Devel. Corp. Contbr. articles profl. jours.; patentee in field. Bd. dirs. Niagara Luth. Home; vice chmn. bd. dirs. Buffalo Philharm. Orch., lifetime dir.; past pres. Greater Niagara Frontier coun. Boy Scouts Am.; past chmn. bd., pres. Greater Buffalo Devel. Found.; bd. regents emeritus Canisius Coll.; bd. trustees, treas. Buffalo Gen. Hosp. Found.; past bd. dirs. Fluid Power Ednl. Found. With AUS, 1946-48; 1st lt. USAF, 1951-53. Inducted into Niagara Frontier Aviation Hall of Fame. Fellow AIAA (assoc.); mem. Air Force Assn. (pres. Larry D. Bell chpt. 1978), Navy League, Am. Def. Preparedness Assn., Nat. Fluid Power Assn. (past chmn. bd.), Nat. Conf. on Fluid Power (past conf. dir.) Buffalo C. of C. (past vice chmn.). Avocations: private pilot (twin engine-instrument), skiing, golf, fishing. Home: 1634 Hubbard Rd East Aurora NY 14052-3011

HAWK, PHILLIP MICHAEL, service corporation executive; b. Oklahoma City, June 14, 1939; s H. M. and Rosetta (Cross) H.; m. Nancy Batton, Aug. 13, 1966; children—Tabatha Lynn, Phillip Michael. BBA, U. Okla., 1961. Pub. rels. exec. Coca Cola Co., Dallas, 1961-63; salesman svc. Reynolds Metals Co., Dallas, 1963-65; corp. dir. mktg. Cole Pubs. Co., Dallas, 1965-71; sr. v.p. Club Corp. of Am., Dallas, 1972-90; CEO club acquisition and devel., pres. Interclub Corp., Blackwell, Tex., 1990—; CEO, Clubnet, Kingwood, Tex., 1990—; bd. dirs. Club Corp. Mex. Exec. v.p. United Golf Group, N.Y.C., 1998—. Republican. Avocation: golf. Office: 1525 Lakeville Dr Ste 126 Kingwood TX 77339-2069

HAWK, ROBERT DOOLEY, wholesale grocery company executive; b. Aug. 27, 1940; s. Henry Dooley and Loretta Elizabeth (Rutherford) H.; m. Sandra Lynn Winters, Dec. 30, 1963; 1 son, Robert Dooley. BBA, U. Okla., 1963; MBA, U. Tulsa, 1969. Buyer Hale Halsell Co., Tulsa, 1963-68, purchasing dir., 1968-72, asst. sec., treas., 1972-78, v.p. fin., sec., treas., 1978-86, pres., 1986-98, chmn., CEO; chmn. bd., CEO Hale-Halsell Co., Tulsa, 1997-98; bd. dirs. Git-N-Go, Inc., Foodland, Inc., Foodtown, Inc., Ark. Valley Distbn. Co., Inc., Sipes Food Markets Inc., Texoma Drug Sales Co. Inc., United Supermarkets, Inc., Fadler, Inc., Guaranty Nat. Bank, Tulsa, Curtis Equipment Co. Mem. Nat. Am. Wholesale Grocery Assn., Tulsa Better Bus. Bur., Cedar Ridge Country Club, Shadow Mountain Tennis, Masons. *

HAWKE, BERNARD RAY, planetary scientist; b. Louisville, Oct. 22, 1946; s. Arvil Abner and Elizabeth Ellen (Brown) H. B.S. in Geology, U. Ky., 1970, M.S., 1974; M.S., Brown U., 1977, Ph.D. in Planetary Geology, 1978. Geologist U.S. Geol. Survey, 1967-68; researcher U. Ky., 1972-74, Brown U., 1974-78; planetary scientist Hawaii Inst. Geophysics, U. Hawaii, Honolulu, 1978—; dir. NASA Pacific Regional Planetary Data Ctr., 1981—; prin. investigator NASA grants; assoc. dir. Hawaii Space Grant Coll. Author papers in field. Served with USAR, 1970-72. Decorated Bronze Star. Mem. Geochem. Soc., Meteoritical Soc., Am. Geophys. Union, Am. Chem. Soc., Geol. Soc. Am., Sigma Xi, Sigma Gamma Epsilon, Alpha Tau Omega. Republican. Office: U Hawaii SOEST Hawaiian Inst Geophysics Honolulu HI 96822

HAWKE, DEBORAH SUE, academic counselor; b. Woodland, Calif., Dec. 11, 1953; d. Fred Henry III and Harriett Grace (Kies) Abbott; children: Jamie Abbott, Robert Stewart. Student, Napa Jr. Coll., 1972-74, U. Calif., Davis, 1976—. Lic. real estate broker, Calif. Sec. Lucas, Landucci & Bick, Davis, 1974-75; sec. dept. sociology U. Calif., Davis, 1975-76, sec., advising asst. dept. psychology, 1976-84, acad. counselor sect. neurobiology, physiology and behavior, 1984—; mem. pers. adv. com. divsn. biol. sci. U. Calif., Davis, 1997—, mem. undergrad. student award com., 1997—; mem. steering com. Systemwide Acad. Advisor/Counselors Conf., Davis, 1987, 95; chair Execution for Agrl. and Environ. Scis. Coll. Celebration, 1993, 94; pres. Acad. Adv. Workshop, Davis, 1991, 92. Recipient Debbie Hawke Day award Undergrad. Physiology Club, Davis, 1989, Mem. of Month award Cross Court Athletic Club, 1990, Outstanding Acad. Advising award 1990, 96, 97, 98. Republican. Avocations: running, weight lifting, snow and water skiing, tennis. Home: 809 W Gibson Rd Woodland CA 95695-5013 Office: U Calif Sect Neurobiology Physiology & Behavior Davis CA 95616

HAWKE, ETHAN, actor; b. Austin, Tex., Nov. 6, 1970. Co-founder Malaparte Theatre Co. Performances include: (plays) Casanova, 1991, A Joke, The Seagull, 1992, Sophistry; (films) Explorers, 1985, Dead Poets Society, 1989, Dad, 1989, White Fang, 1991, Mystery Date, 1991, A Midnight Clear, 1992, Waterland, 1992, Alive, 1993, Rich in Love, 1993, Reality Bites, 1994, Quiz Show, 1994, Floudering, 1994, Before Sunrise, 1995; dir.: Straight to One, 1993. Office: Creative Artists Agy Inc 9830 Wilshire Blvd Beverly Hills CA 90212-1825*

HAWKE, JOHN DANIEL, JR., lawyer; b. N.Y.C., June 26, 1933; s. John Daniel and Olga (Buchbinder) H.; m. Marie Reddan, June 15, 1962 (dec. Mar. 1991); children: Daniel, Caitlin, Anne, Patrick. B.A., Yale U., 1954; LL.B., Columbia U., 1960. Bar: D.C. 1961, U.S. Supreme Ct. 1968. Law clk. to judge U.S. Ct. Appeals (D.C. cir.), Washington, 1960-61; counsel Select Subcom. on Edn., U.S. Ho. of Reps., Washington, 1961-62; assoc. Arnold & Porter, Washington, 1962-66, ptnr., 1967-75, 78-95; gen. counsel bd. govs. Fed. Res. System, Washington, 1975-78; under sec. for domestic fin. Dept. of Treasury, Washington, 1995-98, comptroller of the currency, 1998—; dir. Fed. Deposit Ins. Corp., Washington, 1998—; adj. prof. law Georgetown U., Washington, 1971-87; lectr. law Columbia U., N.Y.C., 1979; bd. advisers Morin Ctr. for Banking Law Studies, Boston U. Sch. Law, 1982—, lectr., 1984-88; mem. Shadow Fin. Regulatory Com., 1986-95; lectr. in field. Author: Commentaries on Banking Regulation, 1985; chmn. editorial adv. bd. Banking Policy Report, 1982-95; contbr. numerous articles to profl. jours., chpt. to book. Mem. Fed. City Coun., 1990-95; trustee Found. for Nat. Capital Region, 1992—; trustee Washington Opera, 1992-96; mem. Pres.'s Com. on the Arts and Humanities, 1996—. 2d lt. USAF, 1955-57. Mem. Fed. Bar Assn. (banking law com., chmn. 1976-78), Cosmos Club, Exchequer Club, Econ. Club, Yale Club, Vineyard Haven Yacht Club. Home: 3800 Harrison St NW Washington DC 20015-1926 Office: Comptroller of the Currency 250 E St SW Washington DC 20219-0001

HAWKE, PAUL HENRY, historian; b. Canton, Ohio, Mar. 9, 1958; s. Richard Carl and Sara (Hemming) H.; m. Gaynel O. Allen, May 2, 1987; children: Cailean Stewart, Angela Janette. BA in History, Geography, Hist. Preservation, Mary Washington Coll., 1982; postgrad., Temple U., 1983, U. Ark., 1984-85; MA in History and Heritage Preservation, Ga. State U., 1993. Park tech. Petersburg (Va.) Nat. Battlefield, 1978-81; intern Fredericksburg (Va.) and Spotsylvania Nat. Mil. Park, 1981-82; park ranger Independence Nat. Hist. Park, Phila., 1982-83; park historian Pea Ridge (Ark.) Nat. Mil. Park, 1983-85; historian Southeast Regional Office, Atlanta, 1985-95; S.E. coord. Am. Battlefield Protectio Program, Atlanta, 1991-95, Civil War sites adv. commn. staff, 1991-93; coord. Nat. Historic Landmarks Program, Atlanta, 1986-95; chief interpretation and resources mgmt. Shiloh (Tenn.) Nat. Mil. Park, 1995—. Co-author: Civil War Battlefield Guide, 1991; editor The Parapet: Newsletter of the Civil War, 1992—; asst. editor, author: Jour. of Civil War Fort Study Group, 1994. Water safety chmn. Am. Nat. Red Cross, Benton County, Ark., 1984-85, water safety instr., Canton, Ohio, 1975-80, Fredericksburg, Va., 1980-82, small craft safey inst., Benton County, Ark., 1984-85, Canton, 1975-80. Named Ky. Col., Gov. of Ky., 1992. Mem. Civil War Fortification Study Group (sec., treas.), Coast Def. Study Group, Assn. of Nat. Park Rangers, Assn. for Preservation of Civil War Sites, Nat. Trust for Hist. Preservation, Civil War Trust, Soc. of Mil. Historians. Avocations: swimming, travel, movies, military history, sports. Home: Rt 10 Box 128 5000 N Harper Rd Corinth MS 38834-7074 Office: Nat Park Svc Shiloh Nat Mil Park RR 1 Box 9 Shiloh TN 38376-9704

HAWKE, ROBERT DOUGLAS, retired state legislator; b. Gardner, Mass., July 20, 1932; s. Arthur Eugene Hawke and Gladys Emma (Waite) Sorton; m. Nancy Marie Moschetti, July 20, 1958; children: Linda, Cynthia, Heather, Dean, Mark. BA, Northeastern U., 1954; LLB, Boston U., 1956; MA, Fitchburg State U., 1970. Cert. tchr., Mass. Tchr. Murdock High Sch., Winchendon, Mass., 1956-66, Gardner (Mass.) High Sch., 1966-90; mem. Mass. Ho. of Reps., Boston, 1990-97. Trustee Heywood Hosp., Gardner, 1981—, Gardner Mus., 1980-83; mem. So. Gardner Hist. Soc., 1984—; mem. adv. bd. Mt. Wachusett C.C., Gardner, 1968-81; chmn. Gardner Rep. Com., Rep. City Com., 1966-76; area campaign coord. Reagan Com., North Ctrl. Mass., 1980-84. Named Citizen of Yr. Grange of Gardner, 1993, So. Gardner Hist. Soc., 1993, Legislator of Yr. award Worcester County League of Sportmen's Clubs, 1996. Mem. Nat. Rep. Legis. Assn., Nat. Conf. State Legislators, Polish Am. Citizens Club, Account Exec. for Greater Gardner C. of C., Eagles. Republican. Baptist. Avocations: reading, tennis, softball. Home: 162 Pearl St Gardner MA 01440-2357

HAWKE, ROBERT FRANCIS, dentist; b. Pasadena, Calif., Oct. 26, 1946; s. George Herbert and Mildred Estelle (Wood) H.; m. Emily Sue Wilkins, Aug. 17, 1973; 1 child, Kristen. BA, U. Ariz., 1969; DDS, Baylor U., Dallas, 1973. Assoc. B.J. Barber, Tucson, 1976-78; ptnr. Barber-Hawke, P.C., Tucson, 1978-87; pvt. practice Tucson, 1987—; bd. dirs., pres. Delta Dental Ariz., Phoenix, 1985-91. Mem. Tucson Bus. Alliance, 1981—, pres., 1983, 94, Comty. Auto Immune Deficiency Syndrome Adv. Coun., Tucson, 1987-90, Auto Immune Deficiency Syndrome Edn. Project, Tucson, 1988-90. Maj. U.S. Army. Fellow Am. Coll. Dentists, Internat. Coll. Dentists; mem. ADA (alt. del. 1988-92, del. 1994—, 14th dist. chmn. ADPAC 1995—), Ariz. State Dental Assn. (trustee 1988, v.p. 1991, pres.-elect 1992-93, pres. 1993-94, past pres. 1994-95), So. Ariz. Dental Soc. (bd. dirs. 1983-89, pres. 1987-88), Pierre Fauchard Acad., Rotary (Paul Harris fellow), Beta Beta Beta. Republican. Evangelical. Avocations: golf, jogging, tennis, racquetball, reading. Home: 6745 E Tivani Dr Tucson AZ 85715-3348 Office: 1575 N Swan Rd Ste 200 Tucson AZ 85712-4068*

HAWKE, ROGER JEWETT, lawyer; b. N.Y.C., July 2, 1935; s. John Daniel and Olga (Buchbinder) H.; m. Rose Marie Ferri, Aug. 15, 1964; children—Christopher, Allison, John. B.A. cum laude, Amherst Coll., 1956; LL.B., Columbia U., 1959. Bar: N.Y. 1960, U.S. Supreme Ct. 1976. Assoc. Donovan, Leisure, Newton & Irvine, N.Y.C., 1960, 62-65; asst. U.S. atty. U.S. Atty.'s Office, So. Dist. N.Y., N.Y.C., 1965-69; assoc. Brown & Wood, and predecessor firm Brown, Wood, Ivey, Mitchell & Petty, N.Y.C., 1969-71, ptnr., 1971—; arbitrator Nat. Assn. Securities Dealers. Acting village justice Village of Lloyd Harbor, N.Y., 1977-83, trustee, 1983—; police commr., 1983—, dep. mayor, 1983—. With U.S. Army, 1961-62. Mem. ABA, Assn. of Bar of City of N.Y., N.Y. Law Inst. (exec. com.), Am. Law Inst. Club: Lloyd Neck Bath (pres. 1981). Home: 405 W Neck Rd Huntington NY 11743-1621 Office: Brown & Wood LLP 1 World Trade Ctr Fl 54 New York NY 10048-0557

HAWKE, SIMON NICHOLAS, writer, educator; b. Sept. 30, 1951. Student, Am. U., 1969; BA in Comms., Hofstra U., 1974; MA in English and History, Western N. Mex. U., 1994. Instr. Pima C. C., Tucson, 1995-98, Elon Coll., Elon Coll., N.C., 1998, Guilford Tech. C.C., Jamestown, N.C., 1998—, N.C. A&T U., Greensboro, 1999—; guest faculty Milford Profl. Writers Conf., Telluride and Glenwood Springs, Colo., 1979, 80, 81, Colo. Mountain Coll., Glenwood Springs, 1980, Western New Mex. U., Silver City, 1994, U. Ariz., 1994. Author: (as Nicholas Yermakov) Jehad, 1984, The Ivanhoe Gambit, 1984, The Timekeeper Conspiracy, 1984, The Pimpernel Plot, 1984, The Zenda Vendetta, 1985, The Nautilus Sanction, 1985, The Khyber Connection, 1986, The Argonaut Affair, 1987, The Wizard of Fourth Street, 1987 (Locus Bestseller), The Dracula Caper, 1988, The Wizard of Sunset Strip, 1989, (as J.D. Master) Killer Steele, (as J.D. Masters) Jagged Steele, The Hellfire Rebellion, 1990, The Wizard of the Rue Morgue, 1990, The Cleopatra Crisis, 1990, To Stalk a Spectre, 1991, Samurai Wizard, 1991, The Wizard of Santa Fe, 1991, The Sixgun Solution, 1991, The Reluctant Sorcerer, 1992, The Nine Lives of Catseye Gomez, 1992, Sons of Glory, 1992, The Wizard of Camelot, 1993, The Romulan Prize, 1993 (N.Y. Times Bestseller), The Outcast, 1993, The Call to Battle, 1993, The Inadequate Adept, 1993, The Wizard of Lovecraft's Cafe, 1993, The Nomad, 1994, The Seeker, 1994, The Patrian Transgression, 1994, Blaze of Glory, 1995, The Broken Blade, 1995, The Whims of Creation, 1995 (nominated Best Book of Yr. Young Adult Libr. Svcs. Assn., one of Ten Best Books for Young Adults N.Y. Pub. Libr.), The Iron Throne, 1995, The Ambivalent Magician, 1996, War, 1996, The Last Wizard, 1997, numerous others; contbr. short fiction (as Nicholas Yermakov) to The Magazine of Fantasy and Sci. Fiction, Heavy Metal mag., Galaxy mag., Dragon mag., anthologies; co-author: (screenplays) Battlestar Galactica, Friday the Thirteenth, Friday the Thirteenth part II, III, IV Jason Lives, Predator 2. Named Colo. Writer of Yr., 1992;. E-mail: SimonHawke@aol.com.

HAWKEN, PATTY LYNN, retired nursing educator, dean of faculty; b. Wheaton, Ill., July 13, 1932; d. Leonard William and Betty (Stock) H. BSN, U. Mich., 1956; MSN, Case Western Res. U., 1962, PhD, 1970. Instr. U. Mich., Ann Arbor, 1956-57, Highland Hosp., Oakland, Calif., 1957-59; from instr. to assoc. prof., assoc. in adminstrn. Case Western Res. U., Cleve., 1960-71; assoc. prof. Emory U., Atlanta, 1971-72, prof., dir., 1972-74; dean, prof. U. Tex. Health Sci. Ctr. Sch. Nursing, San Antonio, 1974-97, ret., 1997. Contbr. articles to profl. jours. Bd. dirs. Wesley Cmty. Ctr., San Antonio, 1986, 89; mem. United Way Allocation Com., San Antonio, 1987; adv. com. Trinity U. Health Care Adminstrn., San Antonio, 1984-97, VA Dean's Com., San antonio, 1982-97. Recipient Nurse of Yr. award Tex. Nursing Assn., San Antonio chpt., 1985, Disting. Alumni award Case Western Res. U., 1991, U. Mich., 1995; named to Women's Hall of Fame. Mem. ANA (cabinet on edn. 1986-88), Nat. League Nursing (pres. 1989-91, Disting. Svc. award 1991), Am. Assn. Colls. of Nursing (com. on edn. 1986-88), Commns. Grads. Fgn. Nursing Schs. (trustee, pres. 1983-85), Am. Acad. Nursing (bd. govs. 1994-97), San Antonio 100 Club, Internat. Women's Forum (San Antonio pres. celebration, Hall of Fame 1994-97). Avocations: snorkeling, swimming. Home: 1826 Fallow Run San Antonio TX 78248-2000

HAWKES, CAROL ANN, university dean; b. N.Y.C.; d. Howard N. and Lavinia M. (Lally) H. B.A., Barnard Coll., 1943; M.A., Columbia U., 1944, Ph.D., 1949. Dir. acad. English liberal arts div. Katharine Gibbs Sch., N.Y.C., 1950-57; prof. English, chmn. dept. English and comparative lit. Finch Coll., N.Y.C., 1957-75; v.p. for ednl. affairs, dean of coll. Hartwick Coll., Oneonta, N.Y., 1975-80; pres. Endicott Coll., Beverly, Mass., 1980-87; dean Sch. Arts and Scis., Western Conn. State U., Danbury, 1987—; Trustee Norwich U., Hartwick Coll.; adv. bd. Harvard Sch. Dental Medicine. Author: Master's Degree Programs and the Liberal Arts College, 1968. Mem. MLA, LWV, Modern Humanities Rsch. Assn., Am. Assn. Higher Edn., Princeton Club (N.Y.C.), Columbia U. Club New Eng., Phi Beta Kappa. Office: Western Conn State U Sch Arts and Scis Danbury CT 06810

HAWKES, GLENN ROGERS, psychology educator; b. Preston, Idaho, Apr. 29, 1919; s. William and Rae (Rogers) H.; m. Yvonne Merrill, Dec. 18, 1941; children—Kristen, William Ray, Gregory Merrill, Laura. B.S. in Psychology, Utah State U., 1946, M.S. in Psychology, 1947; Ph.D. in

Psychology, Cornell U., 1950. From asst. prof. to prof. child devel. and psychology Iowa State U., Ames, 1950-66, chmn. dept. child devel., 1954-66; prof. human devel., rsch. psychologist U. Calif., Davis, 1966-89, prof. emeritus, 1990—, acad. coord. Hubert Humphrey fellowship program, 1990-97, assoc. dean applied econs. and behavioral scis., 1966-83, chmn. dept. applied behavioral scis., 1982-86, chmn. teaching div., 1970-72, prof. behavioral scis. dept. family practice, Sch. Medicine; acting dir. Internat. Programs, U. Calif., Davis, 1994-97; vis. scholar U. Hawaii, 1972-73, U. London, 1970, 80, 86; bd. dirs. Creative Playthings Inc., 1962-66. Author: (with Pease) Behavior and Development from 5 to 12, 1962; (with Frost) The Disadvantaged Child: Issues and Innovations, 1966, 2d edit., 1970; (with Schutz and Baird) Lifestyles and Consumer Behavior of Older Americans, 1979; (with Nicola and Fish) Young Marrieds: The Dual Career Approach, 1984. Contbr. numerous articles to profl. and sci. jours. Served with AUS, 1941-45. Recipient numerous research grants from pvt. founds. and govtl. bodies; recipient Iowa State U. faculty citation, 1965, Outstanding Service citation Iowa Soc. Crippled Children and adults, 1965, citation Dept. Child Devel., 1980, Coll. Agrl. and Environ. Scis., 1983; named hon. lt. gov. Okla., 1966. Home: 1114 Purdue Dr Davis CA 95616-1736 Office: U Calif Internat House 10 College Park Davis CA 95616-3607

HAWKES, KEVIN CLIFF, illustrator, author; b. Sherman, Tex., Aug. 28, 1959; s. Joseph Milton and Carma (Wiser) H.; m. Karen Perkes, Dec. 15, 1982; children: Spencer Morgan, Jessie Elizabeth, Ian David. BA, Utah State U., 1985. Graphic arts asst. Utah State U., Logan, 1983-85; animation asst. Xam! Inc., Midvale, Utah, 1985; photog. retoucher Gibby Studios, Ogden, Utah, 1985-86; clk. Booksmith, Boston, 1986-87; freelance illustrator, Waltham, Mass., 1987-90; illustrator children's books various pubs., Belmont, Mass., 1990—. Illustrator: By the Light of the Halloween Moon, 1993 (Golden Kite award), The Turnip, 1993 (Parents Choice award), The Librarian Who Measured the Earth, 1994 (Parents Choice award), Painting the Wind, 1996, My Little Sister Ate One Hare, 1996, Marven of the Great North Woods, 1997 (Nat. Jewish Book award), Boogie Bones, 1997, The Poombah of Badoombah, 1998, Imagine That! Poems of Never Was, 1998, Weslandia, 1999. Mem. Soc. Children's Book Writers and Illustrators. Avocations: bicycling, playing soccer, reading, gardening, painting furniture.

HAWKEY, G. MICHAEL, lawyer; b. Apr. 17, 1941; m. Frances Tripp, Feb. 27, 1971; children: Samuel, Eliza, MacKenzie. AB, Princeton U., 1963; postgrad., Columbia Bus. Sch., 1964; LLB, Cornell U., 1967. Bar: Mass. 1967. Ptnr. Sullivan and Worcester, Boston, Mettowee Valley Partnership, Vt.; lectr. Mass. Restaurant Assn. Author: The Union-Management Controversy Over Subcontracting and Plant Relocation, 1963. Bd. dirs. Pacific Internat. Inst., Lewiston, Idaho, 1992-97, St. Lukes Cancer Rsch. Found., Inc., Cork, Ireland, 1994-97; mem. N.Am. bd. Michael Smurfit Grad. Sch. Bus., Univ. Coll., Dublin, Ireland, 1994-98; trustee Maruzen Hawthorne Coll., Antrim, N.H., 1991-92; gov. Wianno Club, 1982-98; founder Sun Valley Properties, MeHowee Valley Partnership. Mem. Real Estate Fin. Assn. (bd. dirs. 1989-92), Sr. Execs. Club of Mass. Real Estate Fin. Assn., Mass. Conveyance Assn., Abstract Club, The Country Club (Brookline, Mass.). Avocations: golf, tennis, skiing, real estate development. Home: 26 Arlington Rd Wellesley MA 02481-6129 Office: Sullivan & Worcester 1 Post Office Sq Ste 2300 Boston MA 02109-2129

HAWKINS, ARMIS EUGENE, former state supreme court chief justice; b. Natchez, Miss., Nov. 11, 1920; s. Charles Mayfield and Lela (Hill) H.; m. Patricia Burrow, Aug. 20, 1948; children: Janice Hawkins Shrewsbury, Jean Ann, James Charles. Student, Wood Jr. Coll., 1938-39, Millsaps Coll., 1943; LL.B., U. Miss., 1947. Bar: Miss. 1947. Pvt. practice law Houston, Miss., 1947-51; dist. atty. 3d Cir. Ct. Dist. Miss., 1951-59; assoc. justice Miss. Supreme Ct., 1981-88, presiding justice, 1988-92, now chief justice, 1993-95. Served with USMC, 1942-46, PTO. Mem. ABA, Am. Judicature Soc., Miss. Trial Lawyers Assn., Miss. State Bar. Baptist. *

HAWKINS, AUDREY DENISE, academic administrator, educator; b. Marshall, Tex., Apr. 13, 1958; d. Oscar and Mattie D. Rand. BA in History magna cum laude, Wiley Coll., 1978; MEd in Guidance and Counseling, Prairie View A & M, 1979; postgrad., East Tex. State U., 1983, 92, 94, South Tex. Coll. Law, 1983-85. Cert. secondary social sci. tchr., Tex. Tchr. social studies Marshall (Tex.) Ind. Sch. Dist., 1979-80; counselor East Tex. Ednl. Opportunity Ctr., Longview, 1980-83, counselor, specialist fin. aid, 1988-92; aide law libr. South Tex. Coll. Law, Houston, 1983-84; asst. dir. fin. aid, instr. bus. law, constl. law Wiley Coll., Marshall, Tex., 1985-87; paralegal specialist EPA, Dallas, 1987-88; paralegal Devel. Planning and Rsch. Assocs., Dallas, 1987-88; asst. dir. Mach III/student support svcs. East Tex. State U., Commerce, 1992-94; dir. student svcs. Wiley Coll., Marshall, Tex., 1995-96; TRIO programs review panelist U.S. Dept. Edn., 1997, 98; transfer counselor Trinity Valley C.C., Athens, Tex., 1997—, dir. sch. rels., 1999—; dir. Ednl. Talent Search Program Paris (Tex.) Jr. Coll., 1994-95; participant numerous seminars, confs. Contbr. article to Women in Higher Edn., 1994. Mem. staff Nat. Student Leadership Congress, 1992; team liason vol. Honda Campus All-Star Challenge, 1996—. Mem. Tex. Assn. Student Spl. Svcs. Programs (pres. 1996-97), Tex. Assn. Student Fin. Aid Adminstrs., S.W. Assn. Student Assistance Programs, Phi Alpha Delta, Alpha Kappa Alpha, Alpha Kappa Mu. Democrat. Mem. Ch. Christ. Avocations: bowling, jogging, skating, travel. Home: 729 E Corsicana St Apt 527 Athens TX 75751-2626

HAWKINS, BARRY TYLER, author, mental health services professional; b. Seattle, June 28, 1943; s. Stuart Maxwell and Roberta (Mabry) H.; children: Kelly Ann, Renee Noel; m. Lorraine Joyce Pearson, May 29, 1976; children: Jeremy Allan, Aaron Stuart. BA with honors, U. Puget Sound, 1965; MDiv, Luth. Sch. Theol., 1969; STM, N.Y. Theol. Sem., 1973, PhD, 1986. Nat. cert. addiction counselor. Pastor Bethany Luth. Ch., Jamaica, N.Y., 1969-73; team leader Archdiocese Drug and Alcohol Prevention Program, N.Y.C., 1973-76; faculty, faculty chmn. Martin Luther H.S., Maspeth, N.Y., 1976-80; therapist St. Vincents Alcohol Program, Staten Island, N.Y., 1980-82; pastor Christ Luth. Ch., Newburgh, N.Y., 1982-89; dir. Crossroads at Mercy, Port Jervis, N.Y., 1989-91; dir. chem. dependency svcs. Orange County Dept. Mental Health, Goshen, N.Y., 1991—; pvt. practice Middletown, N.Y., 1992—; chmn. N.Y. State Alcohol Counselor Credentials Bd., Albany, 1986-92; pres. Mid-Hudson Alcohol and Substance Abuse Coalition, 1994—. Author: Puppet Master, 1993, Dark Medicine, 1996; editor: Orange County Democrat-Observer, 1996-97; contbr. articles and poems to profl. publs. including Best Poems of 1997, Best Poems of 1998. Recipient Hon. Mention award Writers Digest Nat. Writing Competition, 1994, Achievement award Nat. Assn. Counties, 1992-98, 3d Pl. award Nat. Open Poetry Competition, 1996. Mem. Nat. Assn. Alcohol and Drug Abuse Counselors, Nat. Assn. Prevention Profls., Amethyst Soc. (founder, chmn. 1994—), Mystery Writers Am., Am. Soc. Poets. Avocations: writing, running, computers. Office: Dept Mental Health PO Box 471 Goshen NY 10924-0471

HAWKINS, BRETT WILLIAM, political science educator; b. Buffalo, Sept. 15, 1937; s. Ralph C. and Irma A. (Rowley) H.; m. Linda L. Knuth, Oct. 31, 1974; 1 child, Brett William. A.B., U. Rochester, 1959; M.A., Vanderbilt U., 1962, Ph.D., 1964. Instr. polit. sci. Vanderbilt U., 1963; instr. in polit. sci. Washington and Lee U., 1963-64, asst. prof., 1964-65; asst. prof. U. Ga., Athens, 1965-68; asso. prof. U. Ga., 1968-70; asso. prof. U. Wis., Milw., 1970-71, prof., 1971—. Author: Nashville Metro, 1964, The Ethnic Factor in American Politics, 1970, Politics in the Metropolis, 2d edit, 1971, Politics and Urban Policies, 1971, The Politics of Raising State and Local Revenue, 1978, Professional Associations and Municipal Innovation, 1981; contbr. articles to profl. jours. Mem. Phi Beta Kappa, Iota of N.Y. Home: 5318 N Kent Ave Whitefish Bay WI 53217-5109 Office: U Wis Dept Polit Sci Milwaukee WI 53201

HAWKINS, BRIAN L., academic administrator, educator; b. Lafayette, Ind., Aug. 5, 1948; s. Robert H. and Majorie Joan (Bradley) H.; m. Lisa Ellen Herrick, Dec. 30, 1970; children: Timothy, Steven. BA, Mich. State U., 1970, MA, 1972; PhD, Purdue U., 1975. Asst. prof. U. Tex., San Antonio, 1975-76, asst. dean of bus., 1976-81; assoc. v.p. acad. affairs Drexel U., Phila., 1981-86, assoc. v.p. computing and telecommunications, 1984-86; v.p. Brown U., Providence, 1986—, spl. asst. to pres., assoc. provost acad. planning, 1990-92, v.p. acad. planning and adminstrn., 1992-96, sr. v.p. acad. planning and adminstrv. affairs, 1997-98; pres., CEO Educause, 1998—; trustee EDUCOM, Washington, 1986-90, chmn. bd., 1989-90. Author: Managerial Communication, 1981; editor: Managing & Organizing Info Resources on Campus, 1990, The Mirage of Continuity: Reconfiguring Academic Information Resources in the 21st Century, 1998. Bd. dirs. CAUSE, 1992-96. Office: Educause 4772 Walnut St Ste 206 Bolder CO 80301-2538*

HAWKINS, CORNELIUS L. (CONNIE), retired basketball player; b. Bklyn., July 17, 1942. Grad., U. Iowa, 1981. Basketball player Pitts. Rens, 1961, Harlem Globetrotters, 1963-64, 66-67, Pitts. Pipers, 1967, Minn. Pipers, 1968, Phoenix Suns, 1969-73, L.A. Lakers, 1973-75, Atlanta Hawks, 1975-76. Named to Basketball Hall of Fame, 1992, ABL Most Valuable Player, 1962, ABL All-Star Team, 1962, All-NBA 1st Team, 1970. Office: c/o Basketball Hall Fame 1150 W Columbus Ave Springfield MA 01105-2532*

HAWKINS, DAVID, philosophy and history of science, educator; b. El Paso, Tex., Feb. 28, 1913; s. William Ashton and Clara Thurston (Gardiner) H.; m. Frances Lothrop Pockman, Apr. 15, 1938; 1 child, Julie Elizabeth. BA, Stanford U., 1934, MA, 1936; PhD, U. Calif., Berkeley, 1940. Instr. Stanford (Calif.) U., 1940-41, U. Calif., Berkeley, 1941-43; asst. to dir. Los Alamos (N.Mex.) Nat. Lab., 1943-44, historian, 1944-46; assoc. prof. George Washington U., Washington, 1946-47; assoc. prof. U. Colo., Boulder, 1946-48, prof., 1948-78, Disting. prof., 1979—, prof. emeritus, 1982—; vis. prof. Coll. Edn., Queens U., 1989; dir. Elem. Sci. Study, Watertown, Mass., 1962-64; mem. Smithsonian Coun., Washington, 1969-75, adv. coun. on edn., 1986-88; co-dir. Mountain View Ctr. for Environ. Edn., Boulder, 1970-82. Author: The Language of Nature, 1964; The Informed Vision, 1974, The Science and Ethics of Equality, 1977, Project Y: The Los Alamos Story, 1947, 82; co-author: Science and the Creative Spirit, 1957, Science Education: A Minds on Approach, 1990; contbr. articles to profl. jours. Chmn. Colo. Humanities Coun., Boulder, 1971. Recipient Thomas Jefferson award U. Colo., 1967, Robert L. Stearns award, 1984; Humanist of Yr. award Colo. Endowment for Humanities, 1986; Coun. Learned Socs. fellow, 1952-53, Faculty fellow U. Colo., 1957-58, 68-69, Inst. for Advanced Study fellow, 1969-70, MacArthur fellow, 1981-86; Carnegie intern, 1952-53. Democrat. Avocations: mathematical invention, bricolage. Home: 511 Mountain View Rd Boulder CO 80302-5013 Office: U Colo Dept Philosophy Boulder CO 80309

HAWKINS, DAVID RAMON, psychiatrist, writer, researcher; b. Milw., June 3, 1927; s. Ramon Nelson and Alice-Mary (McCutcheon) H.; children: Lynn Ashley, Barbara Catherine. BS, Marquette U., 1950; MD, Med. Coll. Wis., Milw., 1953; PhD, Columbia Pacific U., 1995. Med. dir. North Nassau Mental Health Ctr., Manhasset, N.Y., 1956-80; dir. rsch. Brunswick Hosp., L.I., N.Y., 1968-79; pres. Acad. Orthomolecular Psychiatry, N.Y.C., 1970-80; dir. Inst. Spiritual Rsch., Sedona, Ariz., 1979-88, The Rsch. Inst., Sedona, 1988—; pres. Attractor Rsch., Sedona, 1989—, Veritas Pub., Sedona, 1995—; chmn. Inst. Advaned Theoretical Rsch., 1993—; guest lectr. U. Notre Dame, Harvard U., U. Mich., 1970-88, U. Calif., San Francisco, 1997; Landsberg lectr. U. Calif. San Francisco Med. Sch., 1997; guest on TV news and interview shows including McNeal-Lehrer, Barbara Walters, Today, 1972-76; chief of staff Mingus Mountain RTC, 1995; cons. psychiatrist MJL Hosp., Cottonwood, Ariz., 1995; cons. USN, Dept. Health Edn. Welfare, Congress. Author: (with Linus Pauling) Orthomolecular Psychiatry, 1973, Force vs. Power, 1995; contbr. articles to profl. jours. With U.S. Navy, 1945-46, PTO. Decorated knight Sovereign Order St. John of Jerusalem, Danish Crown; Rsch. grantee N.Y. State Dept. Mental Hygiene, annually, N.Y. State Legis., 1967-87; recipient Mosby Book award, 1953. Mem. AMA, APA, Ariz. Med. Soc., Ariz. Psychiat. Soc., Alpha Omega Alpha. Avocations: inventing, designing, woodcraft, dance, architecture. Office: Rsch Inst 151 Keller Ln Sedona AZ 86336-9748 *Our lives are created more by our vision of the future then they are by the details of our past.*

HAWKINS, DAVID ROLLO, SR., psychiatrist; b. Springfield, Mass., Sept. 22, 1923; s. James Alexander and Janet (Rollo) H.; m. Elizabeth G. Wilson, June 8, 1946; children: David Rollo Jr., Robert Wilson, John Bruce, William Alexander. B.A., Amherst Coll., 1945; M.D., U. Rochester, N.Y., 1946. Intern Strong Meml. Hosp., Rochester, 1946-48; Commonwealth Fund fellow in psychiatry and medicine U. Rochester, 1950-52; instr. psychiatry U. N.C. Sch. Medicine, 1952-53, asst. prof., 1953-57, asso. prof. psychiatry, 1957-62, prof., 1962-67; prof., chmn. dept. psychiatry U. Va. Sch. Medicine, 1967-77, Alumni prof. psychiatry, 1967-79, asso. dean, 1969-70; psychiatrist-in-chief U. Va. Hosp., 1967-77; prof. psychiatry Pritzker Sch. Medicine, U. Chgo., 1979-90, U. Ill., 1990—; clin. prof. psychiatry U. N.C., Chapel Hill, 1992—; dir. liaison and consultation svcs. dept. psychiatry Michael Reese Hosp., Chgo., 1979-87, chmn., 1987-92; assoc. attending physician N.C. Meml. Hosp., Chapel Hill, 1952-62, attending physician, 1962-67; cons. Watts Hosp., Durham, 1952-67, VA Hosp., Fayetteville, N.C., 1956-67, Eastern State Hosp., Williamsburg, Va., 1971—, VA Hosp., Salem. Va., 1969-79, mem. deans com., 1971-77; spl. rsch. fellow Inst. Psychiatry, U. London, 1963-64, Fogarty internat. rsch. fellow, 1976-77, U.S.-USSR and Romania health exch. fellow, 1978. Rev. editor Psychosomatic Medicine, 1958-70; assoc. editor Psychiatry, 1970-92. Mem. small grants com. NIMH, 1958-62; mem. nursing rsch. study sect. NIH, 1965-67; mem. Gov.'s Commn. Mental, Indigent and Geriatric Patients, 1968-72; mem. rsch. evaluation com. Va. Dept. Mental Hygiene and Hosps., 1970-73; mem. behavioral sci. test com. Nat. Bd. Med. Examiners, 1970-73. Served as capt. M.C., AUS, 1948-50. Fellow Am. Coll. Psychoanalysts (charter bd. regents 1979-81, treas. 1989-91, pres.-elect 1992, pres. 1994), Am. Psychiat. Assn.; mem. AAUP, Am. Psychosomatic Soc. (mem. coun. 1959), AMA, Group for Advancement Psychiatry (bd. dirs. 1987-89), Assn. Am. Med. Colls. (coun. acad. socs. 1973-78), Am. Psychoanalytic Assn., Am. Coll. Psychiatrists, AAAS, Va. Psychoanalytic Soc., Washington Psychoanalytic Soc., Chgo. Psychoanalytic Soc., N.C. Psychoanalytic Soc., Ill. Psychiat. Soc. (coun. 1981-82, pres.-elect 1987, pres. 1988-90), Soc. Neurosci., Am. Assn. Chmn. Depts. Psychiatry (sec.-treas. 1971-73, pres. 1974-75), Sleep Rsch. Soc., Nat. Bd. Med. Examiners (exam. com. 1983-87), Phi Beta Kappa, Sigma Xi, Alpha Omega Alpha. Address: 405 Deming Rd Chapel Hill NC 27514-3207

HAWKINS, DEBORAH CRAUN, community health nurse; b. Atlanta, Feb. 13, 1941; d. Adolph F. and Suzanne (Catchings) Spear; m. Hugh M. Hawkins Jr.; children: Kimberley Ann, Susan Elizabeth. BSN, U. Va., 1962, MS in Nursing, 1981; post-master's cert. family nurse pract., Va. Commonwealth U., 1999. Cert. in nursing adminstrn., advanced. Pub. health nurse supr. Va. Dept. Health, Charlottesville, 1975-85; pub. health nurse mgr. Va. Dept. Health, Culpeper, 1985-96. With Nurse Corps, USN, 1961-63, comdr. USNR. Mem. Va. Nurses Assn., Va. Pub. Health Assn., Sigma Theta Tau. Home: 2312 Banbury St Charlottesville VA 22901-1823

HAWKINS, EDWARD JACKSON, lawyer; b. Fall River, Mass., June 24, 1927; s. Edward Jackson and Harriet (Sherman) H.; children: Daniel, George, Robert, Harriet. Grad., Phillips Acad., Andover, Mass., 1945; AB summa cum laude, Princeton U., 1950; LLB magna cum laude, Harvard U., 1953. Bar: Ohio 1954, D.C. 1990. Assoc., ptnr. Squire, Sanders & Dempsey, Cleve., 1953-78; ptnr. Squire, Sanders & Dempsey, Cleve. and Washington, 1982-96, counsel, 1997—; chief tax counsel U.S. Senate Fin. Com., Washington, 1979-80, minority tax counsel, 1981; gen. chmn. Cleve. Tax Inst., 1969. Contbr. articles to profl. jours. With U.S. Army, 1945-46. Mem. ABA (vice chmn. govt. rels. tax sect. 1987-89), FBA, Ohio Bar Assn., D.C. Bar Assn., Phillips Acad. Alumni Assn. (alumni coun. 1967-70), Quadrangle Club. Democrat. Home: 6041 25th Rd N Arlington VA 22207-1206 Office: Squire Sanders & Dempsey PO Box 407 1201 Pennsylvania Ave NW Washington DC 20044

HAWKINS, EMMA B., humanities educator; b. Ardmore, Okla., July 28, 1946; d. Bernard C. and Occie E. (Morris) H. BA, Okla. Bapt. U., 1968; MDiv, Southwestern Bapt. Theol. Sem., 1976; MA, U. North Tex., 1990, PhD in English (Medieval), 1995. Instr. U. North Tex., Denton, 1990-95; lectr. Lamar U., Beaumont, 1995-97, asst. prof., 1997—; chair program and arrangements South Cen. Conf. on Christianity and Lit., 1999. Mng. editor Lamar Jour. Humanities; contbr. articles to profl. jours. Recipient Go the Extra Mile award, 1997. Mem. MLA (sec. Old and Mid. English sect. South Ctrl. chpt. 1997, chair Old and Mid Eng. sect. chpt. 1998), Tex. Medieval Assn., Conf. on Coll. Tchrs. English, South Ctrl. Conf. Christianity and Lit. (chpt. chmn. contemporary voices sect. 1999, exec. bd.), Phi Kappa Phi, Sigma Tau Delta. Office: Lamar U PO Box 10023 Beaumont TX 77710-0023

HAWKINS, FALCON BLACK, JR., federal judge; b. Charleston, S.C., Mar. 16, 1927; s. Falcon Black Sr. and Mae Elizabeth (Infinger) H.; m. Jean Elizabeth Timmerman, May 28, 1949; children: Richard Keith, Daryl Gene, Mary Elizabeth Hawkins Eddy, Steely Odell II. BS, The Citadel, 1958; LLB, U. S.C., 1963, JD, 1970. Bar: S.C. bar 1963. Leadingman electronics Charleston (S.C.) Naval Shipyard, 1948-60; salesman ACH Brokers, Columbia, S.C., 1960-63; from assoc. to sr. ptnr. firm Hollings & Hawkins and successor firms, Charleston, 1963-79; U.S. dist. judge Dist. of S.C., Charleston, 1979—, chief judge, 1990-93, sr. status, 1993—. Served with Mcht. Marines, 1944-45, with AUS, 1945-46. Mem. Jud. Conf. 4th Jud. Circuit, ABA, S.C. Bar Assn., Charleston County Bar Assn., Am. Trial Lawyers Assn., S.C. Trial Lawyers Assn., Carolina Yacht Club, Hibernian Soc. Charleston, Masons. Democrat. Methodist. Fax: (843) 579-1499. Office: Hollings Jud Ctr PO Box 835 Charleston SC 29402-0835

HAWKINS, FRANCIS GLENN, banker, lawyer; b. Jamesville, Mo., May 31, 1917; s. Ottas G. and Mary (Uhrig) H.; m. Virginia Mavis Saker, Jan. 18, 1947; children: Glenn Joseph, Russell Brian. A.B., S.W. Mo. U., 1938; M.A., Okla. State U., 1941; J.D., U. Tulsa, 1955. Reporter Monahans (Tex.) Express, 1938-39; trainee Montgomery Ward, Springfield, Mo., 1941-42; rsch. asst. Fed. Res. Bank, Kansas City, 1945-46; with Bank of Okla., Tulsa, 1946-82; sr. v.p., sr. trust officer, sr. v.p. charge bank ops. Bank of Okla., 1970-73, sr. v.p. charge adminstrv. svcs., 1973-77, sr. v.p., sr. trust officer, trust div., 1977-81, sr. v.p. and trust counsel, 1981-82; trust counsel, 1982-91; with Robinson, Boese, Orbitson & Lewis; pvt. practice, 1982-90. Trustee Tulsa Jr. Coll. Found., 1978-90. Capt. USAAF, 1942-45, ETO; lt. col. USAFR, ret. Decorated Air medal with oak leaf cluster, Bronze Star medal. Mem. Am. Inst. Banking (life, past chpt. pres.), Tulsa Estate Planning Forum (past pres.), Okla. Bankers Assn. (past pres. trust div.), Okla., Tulsa County bar assns., Tulsa C. of C., Pi Gamma Mu, Phi Alpha Delta. Home and Office: 4410 S Louisville Ave Tulsa OK 74135-2713

HAWKINS, HAROLD STANLEY, pastor, police chaplain, school director; b. Santa Ana, Calif., Oct. 16, 1927; s. Henry Jesse and Susan Brown (Young) H.; m. Paula Juanita Paeschke, Feb. 19, 1949; children: Bert Stanley, Harold Paul, Kathleen Faith Mummert. Grad., L.I.F.E. Bible Coll., 1950; cert., So. Bay Regional Police Acad., 1978; DD, Hawthorne Christian Sch./Coll., 1978. Pastor Internat. Ch. of the Foursquare Gospel, Redondo Beach, Calif., 1949-58, 69-97, Reséda, Calif., 1958-66; staff mem. Oral Roberts U., Tulsa, 1966-67; pastor Internat. Ch. of the Foursquare Gospel, Bell, Calif., 1967-69; chaplain Redondo Beach Police, 1978-98, res. police officer, 1978-88; master police chaplain L.A. Police Dept., 1988-92; dir. Camp Cedar Crest, Running Springs, Calif., 1961-81, Wings of Mercy, Santa Ana, 1966-70, Hawthorne (Calif.) Christian Schs., 1973-96. Mem. Redondo Beach Round Table, 1974—, pres. 1991-92; commr. Harbor Commn., Redondo Beach, 1982-92, planning commn., 1996—. With USN, 1944-46, World War II. Rotary (pres. 1982-83). Republican. Office: Internat Ch Foursquare Gospel 324 N Catalina Ave Apt 7 Redondo Beach CA 90277-2810 *We live in exciting days! President Clinton has been impeached and will be tried in the Senate. He will probably get off with censure. Polls show his popularity at an all time high. This show us that the morals of America are at an all time low. "Peace and safety, then cometh sudden destruction." Back to Biblical principals is answer.*

HAWKINS, J. MICHAEL, housing development administrator; b. Newport News, Va.; s. Jerry Morris and Patricia Gay Hawkins. BA, Coll. William and Mary, 1984; MPA, Old Dominion U., 1993. Dep. coord. emergency mgmt. City of Newport News, Va., 1984-85; ops. mgr. Pearle Vision Ctr., Hampton, Va., 1985-90; chief planner Office of Human Affairs, Newport News, 1991-92; home program coord. Newport News Redevel. and Housing Authority, 1992-94, mgr. home program, 1994-98; dir. programs and cmty. devel. Chesapeake Redevelopment and Housing Authority, 1998—. Mem. svc. team explorer program Boy Scouts Am., Newport News, 1994. Mem. Internat. City Mgmt. Assn. (affiliate), Am. Soc. Pub. Adminstrn. (Outstanding Svc. award Hampton Rds. chpt. 1995), Am. Planning Assn., Nat. Assn. Housing and Redevel. Ofcls., Pi Alpha Alpha. Avocation: music. Office: Newport News RHA PO Box 77 227 27th St Newport News VA 23607-3901

HAWKINS, JACK, JR., academic administrator; b. Mobile, Ala., Mar. 30, 1945; s. Jack Hawkins Sr. and Phoebe Jane (Proctor) Weiss; m. Ervetta Arnold, Jan. 22, 1966 (div. Apr. 1974); 1 child, Jack Arnold; m. Janice Grindley, Apr. 7, 1977; children: Katherine Brooke, Kelly Burns. AB, U. Montevallo, 1967, EdM, 1971; PhD, U. Ala., 1976. Tchr. Montevallo (Ala.) High Sch., 1967; edn. specialist U. Ala., Birmingham, 1971-72; exec. dir. Health Careers Coun. Ala. Sch. Health Related Professions, U. Ala., 1972-74, jr. coll. coord., instr., 1974-75, dir. student svcs., asst. prof., 1975-76, dir. student and pub. rels., assoc. prof., 1976-77, asst. dean., assoc. prof., 1978-79; pres. Ala. Inst. for Deaf and Blind, Talledega, 1979-89; chancellor Troy (Ala.) State U. System, 1989—; bd. dirs. Troy Bank and Trust Co., Edge Regional Med. Ctr. Co-author: Out of Silence and Darkness: The History of the Alabama Institute for Deaf and Blind, 1983; contbr. numerous articles to profl. jours. 1st v.p., bd. dirs. Ala. Inst. Deaf and Blind Found., 1980-89; trustee Am. Found. for Blind, N.Y.C., 1985—; mem. Gov.'s and Pres.'s Com. Employment of Handicapped, 1980—; bd. dirs. Ptnrs. of Americas, 1986—, Ala. Humanities Found., Birmingham, 1989—; state devel. chmn. Am. Heart Assn., 1989-90; v.p., mem. exec. bd. Boy Scouts Am., 1987—. Recipient Chmn.'s award Jefferson Health Found., Birmingham, Disting. Alumnus award U. Montevallo, 1985. Mem. Coun. Advancement and Support Higher Edn., Am. Legion, Captial City Club, Rotary, Phi Kappa Phi, Alpha Tau Omega, Omicron Delta Kappa, Phi Alpha Theta, Alpha Eta, Capital. Republican. Baptist. Avocations: family activities, golf, reading, hunting, college athletics. Home: 110 Mckinley Dr Troy AL 36081-4117 Office: Officer of the Chancellor University Ave Troy State U Troy AL 36082*

HAWKINS, JAMES DOUGLAS, JR., structural engineer, architect; b. Dallas, Jan. 29, 1959; s. James Douglas Sr. and Evelyn Carolyn (Roos) H.; m. Debra Anita Hewitt; 1 child, Olivia Hope. BArch, Tex. Tech. U., 1986, BSCE, 1986. Registered profl. engr. Landscape architect asst. New Leaf Environ. Systems, Ft. Worth, 1980-82; clk. Lone Star Gas Co., Dallas, 1983; architect asst. Al Cox, Architect, Dallas, 1984; technician Geotech Lab. Tex. Tech U., Lubbock, 1985; constrn. labor George Chadick, Dallas, 1987; structural engr. and architect U.S. Army Corps of Engrs., Jacksonville, Fla., 1988—. Co-author: Overton Revitalization, 1985. Vol. Habitat for Humanity, Jacksonville, 1988—. Mem. AIA, ASCE, Jacksonville Jaycees. Achievements include rehab. buildings for public housing and design development of residents following Hurricane Hugo; evaluation and design repairs following Hurricane Andrew. Home: 5533 Kilary Ct Jacksonville FL 32244-6252 Office: US Army Corps Engrs 400 W Bay St Jacksonville FL 32202-4410

HAWKINS, JAMES VICTOR, state official; b. Coeur d'Alene, Idaho, Sept. 28, 1936; s. William Stark and Agnes M. (Ramstedt) H.; m. Gail Ruth Guernsey, June 19, 1959; children—John William, Nancy Clare. BS, U. Idaho, 1959, D of Adminstrv. Sci., 1996; postgrad., Am. Savs. and Loan Inst., 1960-67, Pacific Coast Banking Sch., 1970—. Mgmt. trainee Gen. Telephone Co. of N.W., Coeur d'Alene, 1959-60; asst. mgr. First Fed. Savs. & Loan Assn., Coeur d'Alene, 1960-67; v.p., gen. mgr. Idaho S.W. Devel. Co., Boise, 1967-68; v.p., trust officer First Security Bank of Idaho, N.A., Boise, 1968-72; pres. Statewide Stores Inc., Boise, 1972-82; spl. projects adminstr. Lucky Stores Inc., 1982-84; pvt. practice fin. cons. Boise, 1984-87; dir. dept. commerce State of Idaho, Boise, 1987-96, ret., 1996; bd. dirs. Blue Cross of Idaho, Early Childhood Devel., State of Idaho. Bd. dirs., chmn. adv. bd. Coll. Bus. and Econs. U. Idaho; bd. dirs. Idaho Coun. Econ. Edn., Boise United Fund, Boise Art Assn.; pres., mem. U. Idaho Found.; exec. bd. Coun. State Community Affairs Agys.; bd. dirs., pres. Nat. Assn. State Devel. Agys.; mem. Indsl. Devel. Rsch. Coun.; mem. exec. com. Coun. State and Community Devel. Agys.; bd. dirs. Idaho Total Quality Inst.; chmn. Idaho R.R. Adv. Coun. Named Outstanding Young Idahoan Idaho Jr. C. of C., 1967; Eagle Scout. Mem. Am. Inst. Banking, Boise C. of C., U. Idaho Alumni Assn. (mem. exec. bd.), Elks, Coeur d'Aleue, Rotary, Crane Creek

Country Club, Arid Club (Boise), Phi Gamma Delta. Episcopalian. Home: 163 E Ridgeline Dr Boise ID 83702-6517

HAWKINS, JANICE EDITH, medical/surgical clinical nurse specialist; b. Greer, S.C., Sept. 12, 1950; d. Theron Gibson and Christine Edith (Bright) H. Diploma, Greenville (S.C.) Gen. Hosp. Sch. Nursing, 1971; BSN, Med. U. of S.C., 1974; MN, Emory U., 1977. RN, Ga.; CS; cert. nutrition support nurse. Staff nurse Emory U. Hosp., Atlanta, 1974-76; instr., staff nurse Med. U. of S.C., Charleston, 1978-79; instr. nursing edn., staff nurse Wilford Hall Med. Ctr. Lackland AFB, San Antonio, 1979-83; clin. nurse specialist med.-surg./nutrition support VA Med. Ctr., Decatur, Ga., 1983—; affiliate faculty BCLS Am. Heart Assn., 1989-97; BCLS instrn., trainer, 1997—; presenter in field. Contbr. chpts. to books and articles to profl. jours. Chairperson Ga. Nurses Polit. Action com., 1996—. Lt. col. USAFR, 1993—. Fellow Aerospace Med. Assn. (assoc., scientific program com.); mem. ANA (chairperson coun. clin. nurse specialists 1989-91, chairperson coun. nurses in advanced practice 1991-92, task force to delineate the substructure of the Congress Nursing Practice 1990-91), Nurses Orgn. Vets. Affairs, Am. Soc. Parenteral and Enteral Nutrition (nurses com., stds. com. 1988-90, 96-97, nominating com. 1992), Assn. Mil. Surgeons of the U.S., Res. Officers Assn., Ga. Soc. Parenteral and Enteral Nutrition (bd. dirs. 1992-94), Ga. Nurses Assn. (cabinet on govtl. affairs 1989-93, chairperson 1995-96, 5th dist. honoree 1989), Sigma Theta Tau. Home: 1750 Clairmont Rd # 21 Decatur GA 30033-4030

HAWKINS, JASPER STILLWELL, JR., architect; b. Orange, N.J., Nov. 10, 1932; s. Jasper Stillwell and Bernice (Ake) H.; m. Patricia A. Mordigan, Mar. 22, 1980; children: William Raymond, John Stillwell, Karen Ann, Jasper Stillwell III. B.Arch., U. So. Calif., 1955. Registered architect, Calif., Ariz., N.Mex. Founder, prin. Hawkins & Lindsey & Assocs., L.A., 1958-90, Hawkins Lindsey Wilson Assocs., L.A. and Phoenix, 1978-85; pres. Fletcher-Thompson Assocs., 1981-84; prin. Jasper Stillwell Hawkins, F.A.I.A., architect, Phoenix, 1990—; bd. visitors Nat. Fire Acad., 1978-80; bd. dirs. Nat. Inst. Bldg. Scis., 1976-85, chmn. bd. dirs., 1981-83, consultative council, 1978—; mem. com. protection of archives and records centers GSA, 1975-77; mem. archtl. adv. panel Calif. State Bldg. Standards Commn., 1964-70; mem. U.S. del. to UN Econ. Commn. for Europe Working Party on Bldg., 1978-84; mem. U.S. presdl. del. to Honduran Presdl. Elections, 1985; mem. com. standards and evaluation Nat. Conf. States on Bldg. Codes and Standards, 1971-74; mem. Am. Arbitration Assn., 1992—; trustee Underwriter's Labs., 1984—, mem. nat. coun. Archtl. Registration Bds., 1971—; participant and speaker numerous confs. Contbr. articles to profl. jours.; maj. works include Valley Music Theatre, L.A., Houston Music Theatre, Sundome Theatre and R.H. Johnson Ctr., Sun City West, Ariz., Bell Recreation Ctr., Sun City, U. Calif. at Irvine Student Housing, Oxnard (Calif.) Fin. Ctr., condominium devels., Lakes Club, Sun City. Mem. Nev. Gov.'s Commn. Fire Safety Codes, 1980-81, Pres. Reagan's Commn. on Housing, 1981-82, City of Phoenix ACDC Task Force, 1985-86, ACDC Aesthetics Commn., 1986-89, City of Phoenix Camelback East Village Planning Com., 1983-89; mem. fire rsch. panel Nat. Bur. Stds., 1978-81; chmn. NAS fire assessment rev. com., 1987-88, com. on analytical methods for designing bldgs. for fire safety, 1977-78; chmn. bldg. seismic safety coun. ind. rev. panel San Francisco War Meml. Opera House, 1995. Recipient design awards from Ariz. Rock Products Assn., Theater Assn. Am., Nat. Food Facilities, House and Home Mag., Practical Builders Mag., Am. Builders Mag., Nat. Inst. of Bldg. Sci. Inst. award, 1995, others. Fellow AIA (mem. codes and stds. com. 1970—, chmn. 1970-73, nat. liaison commn. with Assoc. Gen. Contractors 1969-70, chmn. nat. fire safety task force 1972-74, chmn. Calif. coun. AIA state code com. 1964-68, chmn. nat. conf. industrialized constrn. 1969-70, nat. com. bldg. industry coordination 1969-70, nat. rep. to Internat. Conf. Bldg. Ofcls. 1969, state Calif. AIA codes com. 1960-70, chmn. 1965-70, nat. AIA codes and stds. com. 1970-80, chmn. 1970-74, nat. crisis adv. com. 1988-89), 1976—; mem. ASCE (task force bldg. codes 1971-74), ASTM, Nat. Fire Protection Assn. (com. bldg. heights and areas 1965-72, chmn. 1968-72, fire prevention code com. 1974-76, bd. dirs. 1985-93, chmn. nat. model codes coordinating com. 1983-86, stds. coun. 1996—), Nat. Fire Acad. (bd. regents 1980-83), Nat. Bur. Stds. Fire (rsch. adv. com. 1979-82), Nat. Acad. Forensic Engrs., Ariz. C. of C. (policy com. 1983-84), Ariz. Biltmore Village Estates Homeowners Assn. (pres. 1981-83), Phoenix C. of C. (chmn. Water task force 1982-83). Office: 1158 E Missouri Ave Ste 220 Phoenix AZ 85014-2720

HAWKINS, JOELLEN MARGARET BECK, nursing educator; b. Harvey, N.D., Dec. 15, 1941; d. Charles Joel and Gertrude Adelaide (Waits) Beck; m. Charles Albert Watson, June 27, 1964 (div. 1978); children: John Charles, Andrew Bruce; m. David Gene Hawkins, Oct. 4, 1978. Student, Oberlin Coll., 1959-61; Diploma, Chgo. Wesley Meml. Hosp., Sch. of Nursing, 1964; BS in Nursing, Northwestern U., Chgo., 1964; MS, Boston Coll., 1969, PhD, 1977. Cert. women's health nurse practitioner. Staff nurse Sheboygan (Wis.) Meml. Hosp., 1964-65; instr., staff Boston Lying in Hosp., 1965-66, 68-69; staff nurse Brookline (Mass.) Vis. Nurse Assn., 1968, Guy's Hosp., London, 1968; campus nurse Roger Williams Coll., Bristol, R.I., 1969-70; instr. Salve Regina Coll., Newport, R.I., 1970-74; mem. faculty Roger Williams Coll., Bristol, 1974-75; prof. U. Conn., Storrs, 1978-83; asst., assoc. prof. Boston Coll., Chestnut Hill, Mass., 1975-78, prof., 1983—; women's health nurse practitioner Crittenton Hastings House, 1984—, U. Conn. Student Health Women's Clinic, 1978-83. Author, co-author over 31 books, including: Maternal-Newborn Nursing: Pretest Self-Assessment and Review, 1978, Clinical Experience in Collegiate Nursing Education: Selection of Clinical Agencies, 1981, Health Care of Women: Gynecological Assessment, 1982, Women and the Menopause, 1983, Nursing and the American Health Care Delivery System, 2d edit., 1985, Linking Nursing Education and Practice: Collaborative Experiences in Maternal Child Health, 1987, Dictionary of American Nursing Biography, 1988, Protocols for Nurse Practitioners in Gynecologic Settings, 3d edit., 1991, 4th edit., 1993, The Advanced Practice Nurse: Current Issues, 4th edit., 1996, Nurse-Social Worker Collaboration in Managed Care: A Model of Community Case Management, 1998; editor: Linking Nursing Education and Practice, 1987 (Book of Yr. award Am. Jour. Nursing 1988), Dictionary of American Nursing Biography, 1988, Clin. Excellence for Nurse Practitioners: The Internat. Jour. of NPACE, 1996—; contbr. numerous articles to profl. jours. and chpts. to books. Recipient Disting. Alumni award North H.S., 1989, Miriam Manisoff award Planned Parenthood Fedn. Am., 1997; named Nurse Practitioner of Yr. Am. Acad. of Nurse Practitioners, 1995. Fellow Am. Acad. Nursing; mem. ANA, Mass. Nurses Assn. (Disting. Nurse Rschr. award 1984, Lucy Lincoln Drown Nursing History award 1994), Internat. Coun. Women's Health, Nat. Acad. Practice, Am. Assn. for History Nursing (nominating chmn. 1989), Assn. Women's Health Obstetric and Neonatal Nurses, Sigma Theta Tau (Elizabeth Russell Belford Founder's award for excellence in edn. 1993). Democrat. Unitarian. Avocation: nursing history. Home: 151 Stanton Ave Auburndale MA 02466-3005 Office: Boston Coll Chestnut Hill MA 02467

HAWKINS, JOHN, writer; b. N.Y.C., May 15, 1941; s. Baseem and Valentine (Orfali) Trabulsi; m. Nadine Thomas, Nov. 6, 1971; 1 child, Robert Trabulsi. BS in Acctg. and Fin., CUNY, Bklyn., 1967. Cert. instr. NRA. Tax acct. Morris & McVeigh, N.Y.C., 1959-67; stockbroker Walston & Co., N.Y.C., 1967-71; self-employed various bus., N.Y.C., 1971-94; writer West Palm Beach, Fla., 1994—. Author: Bells of Revenge, 1995, Jack's Place, 1996. Mem. Am. Numismatic Assn. (life) Masons, Cedars of Lebanon.

HAWKINS, JOSEPH ELMER, JR., retired acoustic physiologist, educator; b. Waco, Tex., Mar. 4, 1914; s. Joseph Elmer and Maude Burke (Schlenker) H.; m. Jane Elizabeth Daddow, Aug. 24, 1939; children: Richard Spencer Daddow, Peter Douglas Huntington, James Marion Davis, William Alexander Parmley, Priscilla Ann (Mrs. Philip A. Leach). Student, Altes Realgymnasium, Munich, 1929-30; AB, Baylor U., 1933; postgrad., Brown U., 1933-34; BA in Physiology, U. Oxford, 1937, MA, 1966, DSc in Clin. Medicine, 1979; PhD in Med. Sci., Harvard U., 1941. Tchg. fellow in physiology Harvard Med. Sch., 1937-41, instr., 1941-45; asst. investigator Nat. Def. Rsch. Com.-Office Sci. Rsch. & Devel., Harvard U., 1941-43; spl. rsch. assoc. Harvard Psycho-Acoustic Lab., Cambridge, 1943-45; asst. prof. physiology Bowman Gray Sch. Medicine, Wake Forest Coll., 1945-46; rsch. assoc. neurophysiology Merck Inst. for Therapeutic Rsch., Rahway, N.J., 1946-56; assoc. prof. otolaryngology NYU Sch. Medicine, 1956-63; prof. physiol. acoustics U. Mich., Ann Arbor, 1963-84, prof. otolaryngology emeritus, 1984—; chmn. grad. program in physiol. acoustics U. Mich., 1969-81; assoc. dir. Kresge Hearing Rsch. Inst., 1979-82; disting. vis. prof. biology Baylor U., Waco, Tex., 1985-93; mem. NIH sensory diseases study sect., 1958-61, communicative disorders rsch. tng. com., 1965-69, communicative scis. study sect., 1975-79; mem. Nat. Libr. Medicine Communicative Disorders Task Force, 1977-79; lectr. Armed Forces Inst. Pathology, 1969-74; cons. various pharm. cos. Contbr. to: Ency. Brit., 1974, 86, 99; editor: (with M. Lawrence and W.P. Work) Otophysiology, 1973, (with S.A. Lerner and G.T. Matz) Aminoglycoside Ototoxicity, 1981; contbr. sci. articles to profl. jours. Pres. Fleming Creek Neighborhood Assn., Washtenaw County, Mich., 1973-74; mem. Bd. Edn., Cranford, N.J., 1958-61. Rhodes scholar Tex. and Worcester Coll., U. Oxford, 1934-37; USPHS spl. fellow Öronkliniken, Sahlgrenska Sjukhuset U. Göteborg, Sweden, 1961-63; NAS exch. lectr. to Yugoslavia and Bulgaria, 1977; Chercheur étranger de l'INSERM, Lab. d'Audiologie Expérimentale, U. Bordeaux II, 1978; recipient Disting. Achievement award Baylor U., 1982, City of Pleven, Bulgaria medal, 1982, U. Bordeaux medal, 1983, Humboldt Rsch. award for sr. U.S. scientists U. Würzburg, 1991, Hon. Citizen award, Bordeaux, 1991, Disting. Alumnus award Baylor U., 1996. Fellow AAAS, Acoustical Soc. Am.; mem. Am. Physiol. Soc., Assn. for Rsch. in Otolaryngology (award of merit 1985), Collegium Oto-rhino-laryngologicum Amicitiae Sacrum, Bárány Soc., European Workshop for Inner Ear Biology, Am. Assn. for History of Medicine, Am. Otol. Soc. (assoc.), Prosper Menière Soc. (hon., Gold medal for basic sci. 1998), Pacific Coast Oto-ophthalmol. Soc. (hon.), Connétablie de Guyenne (Bordeaux, assoc.), Phi Beta Kappa, Sigma Xi. Anglican. Democrat. Home: 4004 E Joy Rd Ann Arbor MI 48105-9609 Office: U Mich Med Sch Kresge Hearing Rsch Inst Ann Arbor MI 48109-0506 *Except in science, medicine, and technology, our bloody twentieth century has wantonly betrayed the promises and hopes of the nineteenth. With nationalisms and religious fundamentalisms, tribalisms and fanaticisms resurgent, and earth's ever-growing population exhausting her resources and fouling her air and water, if we are to expect better of the twenty-first we had better start now.*

HAWKINS, LAWRENCE CHARLES, management consultant, educator; b. Greenville County, S.C., Mar. 20, 1919; s. Wayman and Etta (Brockman) H.; m. Earline Thompson, Apr. 29, 1943; children: Lawrence Charles Jr., Wendell Earl. BA, U. Cin., 1941, BEd, 1942, MEd, 1951, EdD, 1970; AA (hon.), Wilmington Coll., 1979; LittD (hon.), Cin. Tech. and C.C.; LHD (hon.) Mt. St. Joseph Coll. Cert. sch. supt., Ohio. Elem./secondary tchr. Cin. Pub. Schs., 1945-52, sch. prin./dir., 1952-67, asst. supt., 1967-69; dean U. Cin., 1969-75, v.p., 1975-77, sr. v.p., 1977-83; vis. asst. prof. Eastern Mich. U., Ypsilanti, summers 1955-60; mem. Cincinnatus Assn., 1971-87; bd. dirs. Western and So. Life, 1990—; vice chair Student Loan Funding Corp., 1982—; mem. cmty. rels. panel Cin. Manors, 1979—, others; cons. U.S. Dept. Justice, Dept. Edn. Bd. dirs. exec. com. Ohio Citizens Coun. Health and Welfare, 1966-73; vice chair Ohio Valley Regional Med. Program, 1972-77, bd. trustees Cmty. Chest and Coun. Cin. Area Inc., 1970-72; bd. dirs. Wilmington (Ohio) Coll., 1980-90, Bethesda Hosp., Cin., 1980-90; trustee Children's Home of Cin., 1978-90, Coll. Mt. St. Joseph, 1989-93; pres., CEO Omni-Man, Inc., 1981-96; bd. dirs. Nat. Underground R.R. Freedom Ctr., 1994—; owner The L.C.H. Resource; vice chmn. Greater Cin. TV Ednl. Found., WCET-TV, 1983; co-chmn. Cin. area NCCJ 1980-87; nat. bd. dirs. Inroads, 1982-87. Served to lt. USAAF, 1943-45 (an original Tuskegee Airman). Recipient award of Merit, Cin.Area United Appeal, 1955, 73, cert. Pres.'s Council on Youth Opportunity, 1968, City Cin., 1968, Disting. Svc. citation Greater Cin. Nat. Conf. of Christians and Jews, 1988; named Great Living Cincinnatian Greater Cin. C. of C., 1989. Mem. NEA (life), ASCD, Am. Assn. Sch. Adminstrs. (convention spkr.), Nat. Congress Parents and Tchrs. (hon. life; chmn. com.), Phi Delta Kappa, Kappa Delta Pi, Kappa Alpha Psi, Sigma Pi Phi. Home: 3544 Sherbrooke Dr Cincinnati OH 45241-3831 Office: 3909 Reading Rd Cincinnati OH 45229-1605

HAWKINS, LINDA PARROTT, school system administrator; b. Florence, S.C., June 23, 1947; d. Obie Lindberg Parrott and Mary Francis (Lee) Evans; m. Larry Eugene Hawkins, Jan. 5, 1946; 1 child, Heather Nichole. BS, U. S.C., 1969; MS, Francis Marion Coll., 1978; EdS in Adminstrn., U. S.C., 1994. Tchr. J.C. Lynch High Sch., Coward, S.C., 1973-80; tchr. Lake City (S.C.) High Sch., 1980-89, coord. alternative program, 1989-90, asst. prin., 1990-94; assoc. prin. Lake City H.S., 1994-98, dir. tchr. evaluation & staff devel., 1998-99, dir. tech. and testing, 1999—; chair dept. bus. Lake City H.S., 1980-89; mem. Williamsburg Tech. Adv. Coun., Kingstree, S.C., 1985-90; mem. adv. coun. Florence-Darlington (S.C.) Tech., 1981-87; co-chair Pee Dee Tech Prep consortia steering com.; co-chmn. allied health adv. com., 1990-93; spkr., presenter leadership workshops. Editor: Parliamentary Procedure Made Easy, 1983; contbr. articles to profl. jours. State advisor Future Bus. Leaders of Am., Columbia, S.C., 1978-86; treas. S.C. State Women's Aux., 1983-93; sec.-treas. J.C. Lynch Elem. Sch. PTO. Named Outstanding Advisor S.C. Future Bus. Leaders of Am., 1985, Tchr. of Yr., S.C. Bus. Edn. Assn., 1988-89, Secondary Tchr. of Yr., Nat. Bus. Edn. Assn., 1989-90, Educator of Yr. S.C. Trade & Indsl. Edn. Assn., 1993, S.C. Asst. Prin. of Yr., 1995. Mem. Profl. Secs. Internat., Nat. Bus. Assn. (S.C. chpt. membership dir. 1986-89, so. region membership dir. 1989-92, secondary program dept. dir. 1991-92), S.C. Bus. Edn. Assn. (jour. editor 1985-86, v.p. for membership 1986-87, treas. 1987-88, pres. elect 1988-89, pres. 1989-90), Am. Vocat. Assn., S.C. Vocat. Assn. (parliamentarian 1985-86, v.p. 1989-90, treas. 1991-92), Internat. Soc. Bus. Educators, Lake City C. of C., Kappa Kappa Iota, Delta Kappa Gamma. Democrat. Baptist. Avocations: cross-stitching, reading, softball. Office: Florence County Sch Dist 3 PO Box 1389 Lake City SC 29560-1389

HAWKINS, LISA LYNNE, lawyer, municipal official; b. Washington, Mar. 15, 1971; d. Joseph Addison Jr. and Barbara Lynne (Brown) H. BA, Frostburg (Md.) State U., 1993; postgrad., Harvard U., 1995-96; JD, U. Calif., Berkeley, 1996. Bar: Md. 1996, D.C. 1998. Assoc. Patton Boggs, L.L.P., Washington, 1998—; polit. columnist Digital City Washington, Am. Online, Washington. Supervising editor Harvard Jour. on Legislation, Cambridge, Mass., 1995-96. Bd. dirs. Women Leadership Found., Washington, 1996-97; dir. fundraising Montgomery County (Md.) Young Dems., 1996-98; mem. city coun. Takoma Park, Md., 1997-98. Mem. ABA, Am. League of Lobbyists, Women in Govt. Rels., Bar Assn. D.C. Avocations: classic art, theater, mentoring. Office: Patton Boggs LLP 2550 M St NW Ste 400 Washington DC 20037-1350

HAWKINS, LORETTA ANN, secondary school educator, playwright; b. Winston-Salem, N.C., Jan. 1, 1942; d. John Henry and Laurine (Hines) Sanders; m. Joseph Hawkins, Dec. 10, 1962; children: Robin, Dionne, Sherri. BS in Edn., Chgo. State U., 1965; MA in Lit., Governor's State U., 1977, MA in African Cultures, 1978; MLA in Humanities, U. Chgo., 1998. Cert. tchr., Ill. Tchr. Chgo. Bd. Edn., 1968—; lectr. Chgo. City Colls., 1987-89; tchr. English Gage Park H.S., 1988—; Mem. steering com. Mellon Seminar U. Chgo., 1990; tchr. adv. com. Goodman Theatre, Chgo., 1992, mem. cmty. adv. coun., 1996—; spkr. in field. Author: (reading workbook) Contemporary Black Heroes, 1992, (plays) Of Quiet Birds, 1993 (James H. Wilson award 1993), Above the Line, 1994, Good Morning, Miss Alex; contbr. poetry, articles to profl. publs.; featured WTTW-Educate, 1996. Santa Fe Pacific Found. fellow, 1988, Lloyd Fry Found. fellow, 1989, Andrew W. Mellon Found. fellow, 1991, Ill. Arts Coun. fellow, 1993; Cmty. Arts Assistance Program Award grantee Chgo. Dept. Cultural Affairs; recipient Feminist Writers 3d pl. award NOW, 1993, Zora Neale Hurston-Bessie Head Fiction award Black Writer's Conf., 1993, numerous others; featured on WTTW-TV Educate, 1996. Mem. AAUW, Nat. Coun. Tchrs. English (spkr. conv.), Am. Fedn. Tchrs., Women's Theatre Alliance, Dramatists Guild of Am., Internat. Women's Writing Guild. Avocations: films, coins, reading, walking. Home: 8928 S Oglesby Ave Chicago IL 60617-3047 Office: Gage Park HS 5630 S RockwellAve Chicago IL 60629

HAWKINS, LORRAINE C., symphony musician; b. Tampa, Fla., July 7, 1944; d. Joe J. and Charlotte L. (Downall) Collins; m. Larry E. Hawkins, May 11, 1984; children: Cheryl L. Jones, Deborah L., Nobel, Aaron J. Wooten. Student, U. South Fla., 1967, 89—, U. Nebr., 1970-72, U. Tenn., 1977-79. Violoncellist Imperial Symphony Orch., Lakeland, Fla., 1984—; violoncellist Tampa Bay "Mostly Pops" Orch., in residence at U. Tampa, 1988-94; violoncellist Notables String Quartet, 1997—; musician Oak Ridge (Tenn.) Symphony Orch., 1973-80, Knoxville (Tenn.) Symphony Orch., 1978-79, U. South Fla. Symphony Orch., Tampa, 1982-83. Recipient Cert. of Parent Recognition, Shaw Elem. Sch., 1986, Cert. of Musical Achievement, 1986, 87; honored for Outstanding Achievement, James A. Haley Vet.'s Hosp., 1988. Home: 15503 Morning Dr Lutz FL 33549-3272

HAWKINS, MARY ELLEN HIGGINS (MARY ELLEN HIGGINS), former state legislator, public relations consultant; b. Birmingham, Ala.; student U. Ala., Tuscaloosa, 1945-47; m. James H. Hawkins, Feb. 13, 1960 (div., 1971); children: Andrew Higgins, Elizabeth, Peter Hixon. Congl. aide to several mems. U.S. Ho. Reps., 1950-60; art instr. Sumter County Schs., Americus, Ga., 1971-72; staff writer Naples (Fla.) Daily News, 1972-74; prin. Daniels-Hawkins, Naples, 1982-84; mem. Fla. Ho. of Reps., Tallahassee, 1974-94; vice chmn. BancFlorida Fin. Corp., Naples, 1979-91, chmn., 1991-93, pres., CEO, 1991-92, also bd. dirs. Columnist, contbr. articles to local newspapers. V.p. Naples Philharmonic, 1984-91; numerous offices Rep. Party of Ga., Americus, 1965-71. Recipient numerous awards for work in Fla. Legislature. Mem. Zonta Internat. Avocation: painting.

HAWKINS, MERRILL MORRIS, SR., college administrator; b. Maben, Miss., Mar. 19, 1914; s. Edgar Preston and Viola (Monts) H.; m. Carrie Lee Brabham, Dec. 22, 1946; children: Jane (Mrs. William L. Smith), Merrill Morris Jr. Student, Wood Jr. Coll., 1934-36; B.S., Miss. State U., 1944, M.S., 1950; Ed.D., U. Miss., 1960. Supt. schs. Centreville, Miss., 1953-56; critic tchr. Univ. High Sch., U. Miss., 1956-57; instr. edn. U. Miss., 1956-57; prof. dept. elementary and secondary edn. Miss. State U., State College, 1965-66; asst. dean Coll. Edn., 1966-68, asso. dean, 1968-70; dean Coll. Edn., dir. tchr. edn., 1970-79, dean emeritus, 1979—; v.p. devel. Wood Jr. Coll., 1979-92; asst. supt. schs. Vicksburg, Miss., 1957-60; supt., 1960-65. Served with AUS, 1941-43. Mem. Miss. Assn. Sch. Adminstrs. (past pres.), Starkville C. of C., Masons, Rotary Internat. (past pres., past dist. gov.), Phi Delta Kappa, Kappa Delta Pi, Phi Kappa Phi, Omicron Delta Kappa Blue Key. Home: 3 Tally Ho Dr Starkville MS 39759-2747 Office: PO Box 771 Mississippi State MS 39762-0771

HAWKINS, MICHAEL DALY, federal judge; b. Winslow, Ariz., Feb. 12, 1945; s. William Bert and Patricia Agnes (Daly) H.; m. Phyllis A. Lewis, June 4, 1966; children: Aaron, Adam. BA, Ariz. State U., 1967, JD cum laude, 1970; LLM, U. Va., 1998. Bar: Ariz. 1970, U.S. Ct. Mil. Appeals 1971, U.S. Supreme Ct. 1974. Pvt. practice law, 1973-77, 80-94; U.S. atty. Dept. Justice, Phoenix, 1977-80; judge U.S. Ct. Appeals (9th cir.), Phoenix, 1994—; mem. Appellate Cts. Jud. Nominating Commn., 1985-89. Staff editor: Ariz. State U. Law Jour, 1968-70. Mem. Ariz. Lottery Commn., 1980-83, Commn. on Uniform State Laws, 1988-93. Capt. USMC, 1970-73. Recipient Alumni Achievement award Ariz. State U., 1995. Mem. ABA, Maricopa County Bar Assn. (bd. dirs. 1975-77, 81-89, pres. 1987-88), State Bar of Ariz., Ariz. Trial Lawyers Assn. (bd. dirs. 1976-77, state sec. 1976-77), Phoenix Trial Lawyers Assn., Adminstrv. Conf. U.S. (pub. mem. 1985-94), Nat. Assn. Former U.S. Attys. (pres. 1989-90). Lutheran.

HAWKINS, NAOMI RUTH, nurse; b. Ft. Smith, Ark., Mar. 8, 1947; d. William Oscar and Sallie Inez (Reynolds) H. BS in Nursing, U. Cen. Ark., 1974. RN, Ark.; cert. pediatric nurse practitioner, Ark. Nurse practitioner Booneville (Ark.) Med. Clinic, 1975-78; lic. practical nurse Greenhurst Nursing Home, Charleston, Ark., 1967-73, RN, 1973-75; pediatric nurse practitioner Ark. Dept. Health, Paris, Ark., 1978—. Fellow Nat. Assn. Pediatric Nurse Assocs. and Practitioners; mem. Ark. Assn. Pediatric Nurse Assocs. and Practitioners, Am. Assn. Christian Counselors, Pub. Health Nurses Assn. Ark., Ark. State Employees Assn. Democrat. Baptist. Avocations: photography, counted cross stitch. Home: RR 2 Box 93 Charleston AR 72933-9418 Office: 102 E Academy St Paris AR 72855-4432

HAWKINS, PAMELA LEIGH HUFFMAN, biochemist; b. Washington, Oct. 7, 1950; d. Lauria Carl and Maryalice (Flinner) Huffman; m. James Lee Hawkins, Mar. 7, 1981 (div. Aug. 1993). BS in Biochemistry, Va. Polytech. Inst. & State U., 1972; MS in Biochemistry, Pa. State U., 1975. Sci. info. specialist Informatics, Inc., Rockville, Md., 1972; asst. rsch. scientist Union Carbide Corp., Tarrytown, N.Y., 1975; assoc. rsch. scientist Am. Hosp. Supply Corp., Gibbstown, N.J., 1976-78; rsch. scientist Am. Hosp. Supply Corp., Miami, Fla., 1978-85; R & D scientist Baxter Healthcare Corp., Miami, 1985-95, sr. rsch. scientist, 1993-95; prin. scientist Sigma Diagnostics, St. Louis, 1995—. Contbr. articles to profl. jours. Recipient Baxter Diagnostics Tech. award for Thromboplastin-IS, 1990, Baxter Internat. Tech. award, 1991. Mem. Internat. Soc. Thrombosis and Hemostasis, Am. Chem. Soc., Mortar Bd., Phi Sigma, Gamma Sigma Delta, Phi Lambda Upsilon. Lutheran. Achievements include U.S. and European patent for fresh blood (unfixed) hematology control, 3 U.S. and 1 European patents for improved extraction methods for preparing thromboplastin reagents, patent for thromboplastins for recombinent tissue factor, U.S. patent for thromboplastin reagents based on recombinent technology, production of thromboplastin IS, Innovin, various others. Office: Sigma Diagnostics 545 S Ewing Ave Saint Louis MO 63103-2991

HAWKINS, RICHARD ALBERT, medical educator, administrator; b. Greenwich, Conn., Mar. 27, 1940; s. Albert Rice and Florence Marie Elizabeth (Hansen) H.; m. Enriqueta Elias, May 9, 1964; children: Richard Alfred, Paul Andrés. BSc magna cum laude, San Diego State U., 1963; PhD, Harvard U., 1969; LHD (hon.), U. Phoenix, 1994. Rsch. fellow Metabolic Rsch. Lab. Radcliffe Infirmary, Oxford (Eng.) U., 1969-71; staff fellow in neurochemistry St. Elizabeth Hosp., Washington, 1971-72, NIMH/NIAAA sr. staff fellow in neurochemistry, 1972-74; chief phys. sci. br. FDA, Rockville, Md., 1974-76; assoc. prof. neurosurgery and physiology NYU Med. Ctr., N.Y.C., 1976-77; prof. anesthesia and physiology Pa. State U., Hershey (Pa.) Med. Ctr., 1977-88; prof., chmn. physiology and biophysics Herman M. Finch U. Health Scis./Chgo. Med. Sch., North Chicago, Ill., 1988-93, exec. v.p. acad. affairs, chief academic officer, 1993-98, pres. acad. affairs, 1999—; hon. prof. U. Valencia, Spain, 1989. Mem. editorial bd. Am. Jour. Physiology, Endocrinology and Metabolism; contbr. numerous articles to profl. jours. Recipient Meritorious Rsch. award Morris Parker Found., 1992. Fellow Am. Heart Assn.; mem. Am. Physiol. Soc., Am. Soc. Neurochemistry, Biochem. Soc., Soc. for Neurosci., Alpha Omega Alpha. Fax: (847) 578-3404. Home: 150 Brierfield Ct Lake Bluff IL 60044-1917 Office: Finch U Health Scis Chgo Med Sch 3333 Green Bay Rd North Chicago IL 60064-3037

HAWKINS, RICHARD MICHAEL, lawyer; b. Nevada City, Calif., July 23, 1949; s. Robert Augustus and Virginia June (Hawke) H.; m. Linda Lee Chapman, Sept. 27, 1975; child, Alexandra Michelle. BS in Math., U. Calif., Davis, 1971; JD, U. Calif., San Francisco, 1974; LLM in Taxation, U. Pacific, 1983. Bar: Calif. 1974, U.S. Dist. Ct. (ea. dist.) Calif. 1974, U.S. Dist. Ct. (no. dist.) Calif. 1982, U.S. Ct. Claims 1982, U.S. Tax Ct. 1982, U.S. Ct. Appeals (9th cir.) 1982, U.S. Supreme Ct. 1982. From assoc. to ptnr. Larue & Francis, Nevada City, 1974-76; ptnr. Larue, Roach & Hawkins, Nevada City, 1977-78; of counsel Berliner & Ellers, Nevada City; ptnr. Berliner, Spiller & Hawkins, Nevada City, 1981; sole practice Grass Valley, Calif., 1981—. Bd. dirs. 49ers Fire Dist., Nevada City, 1977-81, 89-98, asst. fire chief, 1981-83, fire chief, 1983-89. Mem. ABA, Calif. State Bar (cert. specialist in estate planning, trust and probate law 1990), Nevada County Bar Assn. (v.p. 1976), Order of Coif, Phi Kappa Phi. Republican. Roman Catholic. Avocations: bicycling, snow and water skiing, running, showing Morgan horses. E-mail: rhawk53@aol.com. Fax: (530) 272-7861. Home: 14762 Banner Quaker Hill Rd Nevada City CA 95959-8813 Office: 10563 Brunswick Rd Ste 2 Grass Valley CA 95945-7801

HAWKINS, ROBERT A., college administrator; b. Anabelle, W.Va., Aug. 21, 1924; s. Lawrence R. Hawkins and Grace O. (Lauer) Glover Hawkins; B.A., Abilene Christian Coll., 1948, M.A., 1967; Ed.D., Tex. Tech U., 1974; m. Nina Jo Milton, June 6, 1943; children: Paul C., Sheila Ann. Administr. youth camps, 1949-64; tchr., adminstr. Denver schs., 1953-56; instr. Abilene (Tex.) Christian Coll., 1965-68; instr., registrar Lubbock (Tex.) Christian Coll., 1968-74; dir. guidance Midland (Tex.) Coll., 1974-83, dir. testing, 1982-87, instr. behavioral and social sci. depts., 1974-87. Recipient Outstanding Tchr. award Lubbock Christian Coll., 1971. Mem. Am., Tex., Permian Basin personnel and guidance assns., Jr. Coll. Student Personnel Assn. Tex., Tex. Jr. Coll. Tchrs. Assn., Phi Kappa Phi, Alpha Chi. Author, translator: Bible Student's New Testament, New Century Testament; The Power of God, The Grace of Giving and Living; contbr. articles to profl. jours. Home and Office: Ste 3436 6110 W Pleasant Ridge Rd Arlington TX 76016-4307

HAWKINS, ROBERT B., think tank executive. Pres., CEO Inst. for Contemporary Studies, Oakland, Calif. Office: Inst for Contemporary Studies Latham Sq 1611 Telegraph Ave Ste 902 Oakland CA 94612*

HAWKINS, ROBERT GARVIN, management educator, consultant; b. Gower, Mo., Feb. 3, 1936; s. Floyd G. and Grace (Long) H.; m. Estelle Turcic, June 9, 1962; children: Paul R., Kenneth J. AB, William Jewell Coll., 1958; PhD, NYU, 1966. Cons. computer systems Equitable Life, N.Y.C., 1958-61; from instr. to prof. NYU, 1964-80, vice dean, prof., 1980-84; dean Sch. Mgmt. Rensselaer Poly. Inst., Troy, N.Y., 1984-92; dean Ivan Allen Coll. Ga. Inst. Tech., Atlanta, 1993-98; bd. dirs. James Investment Rsch., Inc., Alpha, Ohio, Petricca Industries, Inc., Pittsfield, Mass.; cons. in field. Co-author: Gold and World Power, 1965, U.S. in International Markets, 1976; editor: Economic Effects of MNCs, 1977; contbr. articles to profl. jours. Bd. dirs. Family and Children Svcs., Montclair, 1976-81, Troy Music Hall Assn., 1985-92, Japan-Am. Soc. of Ga., 1993-99. Sgt. Air NG, 1957-64. Named Outstanding Alumni, William Jewell Coll., 1979; grantee in field. Mem. Am. Econ. Assn., Am. Fin. Assn. (exec. sec. 1977-83), Acad. Internat. Bus. (pres. 1983-84, fellow 1981). Home: 1075 Sheridan Park NE Atlanta GA 30324-3261 Office: Ga Tech Ivan Allen Coll Atlanta GA 30332

HAWKINS, ROBERT LEE, health facility administrator; b. Denver, Feb. 18, 1938; s. Isom and Bessie M. (Hugley) H.; m. Ann Sharon Hoy, Apr. 28, 1973; children: Robert, Jeanne, Julia, Rose. AA, Pueblo Jr. Coll., 1958; BS, So. Colo. State Coll., 1965; MSW, U. Denver, 1967. Psychiat. technician Colo. State Hosp., Pueblo, 1956-58, 1962-63, occupl. therapist asst., 1964-65, clin. adminstr. psychiat. team, 1969-75, dir. cmty. svcs., 1975-92, supr. vol. services, 1975—, mem. budget com., 1975—; asst. supt. clin. svcs., 1992—; supt. Colo. Mental Health Inst., Pueblo, 1996—; counselor (part-time) Family Svc. Agy., Pueblo, 1968-69, exec. dir., 1969-70; mem. faculty U. So. Colo., 1968-75; ptnr. Human Resource Devel., Inc., 1970-75; mem. Nat. Adv. Com. on Instnl. Quality and Integrity, U.S. Dept. Edn., Washington, 1993—. Mem. Pueblo Positive Action Com., 1970; chmn. adv. bd. Pueblo Sangre de Cristo Day Care Center, 1969-72; chmn. Gov.'s So. Area Adv. Council of Employment Service, 1975-76, chmn. Pueblo's City CSC, 1976-77, Pueblo Cmty. Corrections, 1985-87, Pueblo Civil Svc. Commn., 1988—; commr. Pueblo Housing Authority, 1986—, Colo. Commn. Higher Edn., 1987—, USED Commn. for Ednl. Quality & Integrity, 1993—; mem. gov.'s. adv. com. Mental Health Stds., 1981—; mem. Colo. Juvenile Parole Bd., 1977; bd. dirs. Pueblo United Fund, 1969-74, pres., 1973; bd. dirs. Pueblo Community Orgn., 1974-76, Spanish Peaks Mental Health Center, 1976—, Neighborhood Health Center, 1977-79, Pueblo Community Corrections, 1983—, Pueblo Legal Svcs., 1983—, Girl Scouts USA, 1996—; mem. Pueblo Colo. 2010 Commn., 1994—, adv. com. YWCA, 1994—, Healthy Pueblo 2000 Task Force, 1993—. Bd. dirs. Posada Shelter for Homeless, 1990—, Boys Girls club, 1991—, ARC, 1994—, pres., 1994—, Colo. Common Cause, 1998—. With U.S. Army 1958-62. Mem. Nat. Assn. Social Workers (nominating com. 1973-76), ACLU (dir. Pueblo chpt. 1980—), NAACP, Broadway Theatre Guild. Democrat. Methodist. Mem. Kiwanis. Home: 220 Melrose Ave Pueblo CO 81004-1053 Office: Colo State Hosp 1600 W 24th St Pueblo CO 81003-1411

HAWKINS, ROBERTA ROSENTHAL, theater educator; b. L.A., Dec. 16, 1951; d. Robert and Mary Lu (Clayton) R.; m. Joseph Angelo Carter, Feb. 21, 1986; 1 child, Jessica Clayton. BA in English, U. Mass., 1973; MFA in Theatre Arts, Brandeis U., 1981. Cert. secondary tchr. Mass., N.Y., Calif. Tchr. English and drama Maynard (Mass.) H.S., 1973-76, J.F.K. Mid. Sch., Hudson, Mass., 1978-79; English dept. coord. dist. 6 mid. sch. N.Y.C., 1981-86; English, speech advisor Park West H.S., N.Y.C., 1986-90; chmn. dept. fine arts Rancho Verde H.S., Moreno Valley, Calif., 1991-96; adminstrv. dir. The Players' Conservatory, Riverside, Calif., 1996-98; stage dir. 13th St. Theatre, N.Y.C., 1983-86, various summer stock, off-off Broadway, 1974-86; singer/actor various roles; adj. prof. DeVry Inst. of Tech., 1997—, U. of Redlands, 1997-99. Prodr./dir. over 30 plays; actress/singer over 30 performances. Avocation: travel.

HAWKINS, WILLIAM E. N., newspaper editor; b. N.Y.C., Dec. 4, 1943; s. Frank Nelson and Lottie (Norton) H.; m. Diane Taylor, Apr. 1, 1967; children: William E.N. Jr., Geoffrey W.T. BA, Cornell U., 1966. Reporter Patriot-News, Harrisburg, Pa., 1968-73; reporter Balt. Evening Sun, 1973-78, city editor, 1978-83, asst. mng. editor, 1983-88; exec. editor The Herald-Sun, Durham, N.C., 1988—; v.p. The Durham Herald Co., 1994—. Mem. bicentennial adv. com. U. N.C., 1992-93. 1st lt. U.S. Army, 1966-68, Vietnam. Decorated Bronze Star. Mem. Am. Soc. Newspaper Editors, AP Mng. Editors, N.C. Press Assn. (bd. dirs. 1992-96), N.C. Press Found. (pres.), Soc. Profl. Journalists, Americal Divsn. Vets. Assn. Presbyterian. Avocation: skiing. Home: 7 Hartley Pl Durham NC 27707-2437 Office: The Herald-Sun 2828 Pickett Rd Durham NC 27705-5613

HAWKINS, WILLIS MOORE, aerospace and astronautical consultant; b. Kansas City, Mo., Dec. 1, 1913; s. Willis M. Hawkins and Elizabeth (Daniels) Hawkins Walter; m. Anita Stanfill, June 22, 1940 (dec. 1982); children: Nancy Gay, Willis M. III, James Walter. BS in Aero. Engring., U. Mich., 1937, ED (hon.), 1965; DSc (hon.), Ill. Coll., 1966. Registered profl. engr., Calif. Engring. trainee Grumman Corp., Bethpage, N.Y., 1936; sr. layout engr. Lockheed Corp., Burbank, Calif., 1937-49, chief, preliminary design, 1949-53; asst. gen. mgr., dir. engring. Lockheed Missiles & Space Div., Sunnyvale, Calif., 1953-61; gen. mgr., corp. v.p. Lockheed Space Div., Sunnyvale, 1961; corp. v.p. sci. and engring. Lockheed Corp., Burbank, 1962-63; asst. sec. R & D U.S. Army, 1963-66; sr. v.p. sci. and engring. Lockheed Corp., Burbank, 1966-74, corp. dir., 1972-80; sr. adv. Lockheed Corp., Calabasas, Calif., 1974-76, sr. v.p. aircraft, 1979-80, sr. advisor, 1980-95; pres. Lockheed Calif. Co., 1976-79; bd. dirs. George C. Marshall Inst., Washington. Contbr. numerous articles on nat. energy and trans. policy to profl. jours.; patentee in field. Mem., chmn. aero. and space engring. bd. NRC, 1960, chmn. aero. panel Naval Studies Bd., 1989-92; chmn. Army star study bd. Army Sci. & Tech. Com., Washington, 1988-91, Army strategic tech. com. 1989-91; mem. NASA Rsch. Coun., 1978-85; trustee Leelanau Ctr. for Edn., Glen Arbor, Mich., 1987—. Recipient Disting Civilian Svc. medal with oak leaf cluster U.S. Army, 1965-66, Disting. Pub. Svc. medal NASA, 1975, Nat. Medal of Sci. Pres. of U.S., 1988. Fellow AIAA (hon.), Royal Aero. Soc.; mem. NAE (various coms., founders lectr.), Nat. Aero. Assn. (Wright Bros. lectr. 1982, bd. dirs.), Tau Beta Pi. Republican. Avocation: flying. *

HAWKINSON, BRIAN PATRICK, professional association executive; b. El Paso, Tex., Mar. 3, 1956; s. Norman A. and Shirley M. Hawkinson; m. Deborah A. Duncan, Sept. 2, 1978; children: Erin C., Michael P. BBA, James Madison U., 1978; MBA, Va. Tech., 1995. Materials contr. Aminoil USA Inc., Denver, 1982-84; prodn. acct. Phillips Petroleum Co., Sidney, Mont., 1984-85; assoc. dir. N.E. region United Way of Am., Alexandria, Va., 1985-92, dir. nat. corp. rels., 1992-94; loan officer N.Am. Mortgage Co., Vienna, Va., 1994-96; dir. ctr. for pub. affairs mgmt. Pub. Affairs Coun., Washington, 1996—. Contbg. editor: Assessing, Managing and Maximizing Public Affairs Performance, 1997 (APEX award, 1998) ImPACT, 1996— (Best in the Bus. 1996). Vestry St. Luke's Episcopal Ch., Alexandria, 1995-97; bd. dirs. Waynewood Recreation Assn., Alexandria, 1997—. Capt. U.S. Army, 1978-82. Office: Public Affairs Coun 2033 K St NW Ste 700 Washington DC 20006-1002

HAWKINSON, GARY MICHAEL, financial services company executive; b. Chgo., Oct. 30, 1948; s. Roy G. and June M. (Miller) H.; m. Patricia Kaye Schlievert, Jan. 9, 1971; children: Kenneth, Christopher. BBA in Fin., U. Toledo, 1971; postgrad., U. Harvard, 1989. Various mgmt. and analytical positions Toledo Edison Co., 1972-79, asst. treas., asst. sec., 1979-86; treas. Centerior Energy Corp., Independence, Ohio, 1986-94, dir. govtl. affairs, 1995-98; dir. fin. and adminstrn. Parkwood Corp., Cleve., 1998—. Trustee Luth. Med. Ctr. Found. Served to 2d lt. U.S. Army, 1971-72. Mem. Cleve. Treas.'s Club (v.p. 1988-89, pres. 1989-90), Rotary. Avocations: skiing, sailing. Home: 26875 Kenley Ct Westlake OH 44145-1456 Office: Parkwood Corp 2829 Euclid Ave Cleveland OH 44115

HAWKINSON, THOMAS EDWIN, environmental and occupational health engineer; b. Worthington, Minn., Oct. 15, 1952; s. Robert Edwin and Vivian Julia (Foss) H.; m. Ann Elizabeth Koepsell, Aug. 14, 1977; children: Timothy, William, Elizabeth. BA in Chem., St. Olaf Coll., 1974; MS in Environ. Health, U. Minn., 1978. Cert. indsl. hygienist, cert. safety profl. Res. assoc. Indsl. Health Engr., Mpls., 1976-77; asst. teaching Univ. Minn., 1977-78; indsl. hygienist Medtronic, Inc., Mpls., 1978-86, corp. health environ. adminstr., 1986-93; safety and environ. engr. Gen. Mills, Inc., Mpls., 1993-97; mgr. environ. engring. and safety Yoplait-Colombo, Mpls., 1997-98, corp. mgr. safety and environ., 1998—; panel of advisors Minn. Safety Coun., 1986-89, bd. dirs., 1989-90. Mem. Am. Indsl. Hygiene Assn. (mem. upper Midwest local sect. 1988-89, chmn. local sects. coun. 1988-89, chmn. com. on tng. and edn. 1989-90), Am. Chem. Soc., Air and Waste Mgmt. Assn., Semiconductor Safety Assn. (dir. north ctrl. region 1989-97). Avocation: astronomy. Home: 825 Pineview Ln N Plymouth MN 55441-5750 Office: Gen Mills Inc 1 General Mills Blvd Minneapolis MN 55426-1348

HAWKS, JAMES WADE, county highway superintendent, county surveyor; b. Lexington, Nebr., Mar. 20, 1957; s. Glenn Emmett and C. Jo Anne (Warren) H.; m. Janelle Sue Kloepping, May 14, 1977; children: James Matthew Hawks, Nathaniel Thomas Hawks. AA, Mid Plains C.C., North Platte, Nebr., 1992; BS in Adminstrn., U. Nebr., Kearney, 1996; grad. student, U. of Nebraska, Kearney. Cert. govt. fin. mgr. Nebr. Safety Coun. Adv. Bd. Dawson county surveyors dept. Dawson County surveyor's/Engrs. Office, Lexington, 1980-87; engring. office mgr. Tagge Engring. Cons., North Platte, 1987-88; county surveyor, county hwy. supt. Lincoln county, North Platte, 1988—; adv. bd. Southeast Cmty. Coll., Milford; bd. dirs. Nebraskaland, Inc. Chmn. Lincoln County Sheriff's Merit Commn., North Platte, 1990-98. Mem. Profl. Surveyors Assn. of Nebr. (pres., chmn. exam workshop 1990—, bd. dirs. 1993—, v.p. 1995-97), Nat. Assn. of County Engrs., Nebr. Assn. of County Engrs., Surveyors and Hwy. Supts. (sec.-treas. 1994, v.p. 1995, pres. 1996), North Platte Sunrise Rotary, Sigma Beta Delta, Phi Theta Kappa. Republican. Lutheran. Avocations: hunting, fishing, reading, working. Home: 1601 Sunset Dr North Platte NE 69101-6418 Office: Lincoln County Surveyor 2010 Rodeo Rd North Platte NE 69101-2603

HAWLEY, ELLIS WAYNE, historian, educator; b. Cambridge, Kans., June 2, 1929; s. Pearl Washington and Gladys Laura (Logsdon) H.; m. Sofia Koltun, Sept. 2, 1953; children—Arnold Jay, Agnes Fay. B.A., U. Wichita, 1950; M.A., U. Kans., 1951; Ph.D. (research fellow), U. Wis., 1959. Instr. to prof. history North Tex. State U., 1957-68; prof. history Ohio State U., 1968-69; prof. history U. Iowa, 1969-94, prof. emeritus, 1994—, chmn. dept. history, 1986-89; hist. cons. Pub. Papers of the Presidents: Hoover, 1974-78. Author: The New Deal and the Problem of Monopoly, 1966, The Great War and the Search for a Modern Order, 1979, (with others) Herbert Hoover and the Crisis of American Capitalism, 1973, Herbert Hoover as Secretary of Commerce, 1981, Federal Social Policy, 1988, Herbert Hoover and the Historians, 1989; contbr. articles to profl. jours., essays to books. Investigator Project to Study Hist. in Iowa Pub. Schs., Iowa City, 1978-79; cons. Quad Cities hist. project Putnam Mus., Davenport, 1978-79. Served to 1st lt. inf. AUS, 1951-53. North Tex. State U. Faculty Devel. grantee, 1967-68, U. Iowa, 1975-76. Mem. Am. Hist. Assn., Orgn. Am. Historians, So. Hist. Assn., AAUP (mem. exec. coun. Iowa chapt. 1982-84), Iowa Hist. Soc. Democrat. Home: 2524 E Washington St Iowa City IA 52245-3724 Office: U Iowa Dept History Iowa City IA 52242

HAWLEY, FRANK JORDAN, JR., venture capital executive; b. Roanoke Rapids, N.C., Oct. 3, 1927; s. Frank Jordan and Mary (Miller) H.; m. Alethea Wood, Sept. 12, 1959; children: Frank J. III, Mark R., Andrew D., Stuart W., Alethea S. BS in Physics, U. N.C., 1949; MBA, Harvard U., 1955. Rsch. analyst Eaton & Howard, Inc., Boston, 1955-59; banking assoc. Lazard Freres, N.Y.C., 1959-64; portfolio mgr. Stein, Roe & Farnham, N.Y.C., 1964-69; exec. v.p. Laidlaw Coggeshall, Inc., N.Y.C., 1969-74; gen. ptnr. Foster Mgmt. Co., N.Y.C., 1974-82; mng. ptnr. Saugatuck Capital Co., Stamford, Conn., 1982—; chmn. bd. Morgan Products Ltd., Williamsburg, Va.; bd. dirs. United Linen Svcs., Inc., Landover, Md.; chmn. bd. dirs. Collision Team Am., Inc., Indpls, Ind. Vice pres., treas. New Canaan (Conn.) YMCA, 1981-85; trustee Chocorua Chapel Assn., Squam Lake, N.H.; bd. visitors U. N.C., Chapel Hill, 1990-94; trustee Kenan Inst. Pvt. Enterprise of U. N.C. Lt. (j.g.) USN, 1950-53, Korea. Mem. Links Club, Harvard Club (N.Y.C.), New Canaan Country Club, Mill Reef Club (Antigua), Bald Peak Club (N.H.), Phi Beta Kappa. Republican. Episcopalian. Avocations: tennis, fly fishing, hunting. Home: 613 Silvermine Rd New Canaan CT 06840-4325 Office: Saugatuck Capital Co 1 Canterbury Grn Stamford CT 06901-2032 also: Morgan Products Ltd 469 Mclaws Cir Williamsburg VA 23185-5645

HAWLEY, HAROLD PATRICK, educational consultant; b. Paducah, Ky., Jan. 8, 1945; s. Mathew Mark and Mae (Herndon) H.; m. Ann Dunbar, 1971 (div. 1982); Lucrecia Thomas, Aug. 27, 1983; children: Cherise, Charlotte. AA, Paducah Jr. Coll., 1965; BA, U. Ky., 1968; MS, Ind. U., New Albany, 1974; EdD, Ind. U., Bloomington, 1977; postgrad., Mary Baldwin Coll., 1988, Ala. A&M U., 1996. Liaison to adjutant gen. 5th army U.S. Army, Ft. Carson, 1970, Bien Hoa, Vietnam, 1969-70; English tchr. Southwestern Consol. Schs., Hanover, Ind., 1971-73; asst. prin. Whitewater Consol. Sch., Lyons, Ind., 1978-80; assoc. prof., dir. secondary edn. Birmingham (Ala.) - So. Coll., 1980-86, chmn. freshman seminar, 1984-86; 1988-95 Ga. Dept. Edn., Atlanta, 1988-95; evaluator So. Assn. Schs. and Colls., 1988—; ednl. cons. Ga. Dept. Edn., Atlanta, 1988-95; adj. prof. Ind. U., Bloomington, 1975-80, Samford U., 1980-84, Auburn U., 1987, U. Ala., Gadsen, 1984-85, Brenau U., Gainesville, Ga., 1988-96, Reinhardt Coll./Brenau Coll. Collaboration, 1995—, Ala. A&M U., 1999, univ. supr., 1996—; cons. Intervarsity Beach Project, 1982—, Ford Ednl. Found., Parker H.S., Birmingham, Ala., 1981-85, Christian Acad., Cornerstone, Baton Rouge, 1983-84, FCA, 1983, Happy Valley Elem., Fairview Elem. Schoolwide Project, 1995, Walker County Curriculum Specialist, 1995-96, Nicholas Soc., 1997—; tech. advisor Polk County Schoolwide Projects, 1995; ednl. cons. Ga. Dept. Edn., Atlanta, 1988-95; coord. 9th Dist. Schs. of Excellence, Ga., 1988-92; team leader sch. improvement teams Ga. Dept. Edn., Calhoun, 1995; numerous ESEA Instrnl. Confs., Ga., 1993-94; presenter ESEA Instrnl. Conf., Statesboro, 1994, Carrolton, Ga., 1995; dir. 1st State Remedial Edn. Conf., Lafayette, Ga., 1994; dir. 1st statewide instrnl. conf. ESEA, 1995-96, Lone Oak Edn. Svcs., 1998; participant Inst. for Comm. Seminars, Birmingham So. Coll., 1983-86; tech. advisor Floyd County Schoolwide Project, 1995—, Dade County Schoolwide Project, 1996; student tchr. supr. Covenant Coll., Chattanooga, 1996—; dir. Title I Northwest Ga. Instrnl. Conf., 1996; ednl. cons. Attention Deficit Disorder/HD, 1995—; dir. Lone Oak Edn. Svcs. 1999. Author: (with Don Manlove) Classroom Climate Teacher-Student Relations, Expectancy Effects, 1976; rsch. asst. (with Floyd Coppedge) Binford Middle School Project, Bloomington, Ind., 1976, Individual Instrn. Project, 1975, Lebanon High Sch. Project, 1975-76, Katherine Hamilton Rsch. Project, New Albany, Ind., 1974 (with Carol Lewis). Bd. dirs. Boys Club of Am., Paducah, Ky., 1963-65; tech. adv. Polk County Consolidated Schs., 1995-96, Dade County Consolidated Schs., 1995. Basketball scholar, 1965, attention deficit rsch. scholar univ. supr., Ala. A&M U., 1997—; Spenser grantee, 1981, Mellon grantee, 1985; grad fellow Okla. State Sch. Supt.,1975-77, Nat. Study Sch. Evaluation fellow Ind. U., 1977. Mem. Ga. Com. Leaders Assn., Internat. Platform Assn., Phi Delta Kappa. Avocations: jogging, basketball, camping. Home: 406 N Malone St Athens AL 35611-1567

HAWLEY, JOHN STRATTON, religious studies educator; b. Schenectady, N.Y., Aug. 27, 1941; s. Robert Charles and Elizabeth (Stratton) H.; m. Laura Shapiro, Sept. 28, 1974; 1 child, Nell. AB cum laude, Amherst Coll., 1963; MDiv. summa cum laude, Union Theol. Seminary, 1966; postgrad., Hebrew U., Jerusalem, 1966, Goethe Inst., 1969, U. Wis., 1971, U. Delhi, 1972; PhD, Harvard U., 1977. Tchr. St. George's Sch., Jerusalem, 1967-68; tchg. fellow Harvard Divinity Sch., Cambridge, Mass., 1971-72, 77; asst. prof. religion Bowdoin Coll., Brunswick, Maine, 1977-78; from asst. prof. to prof. Asian langs. U. Wash., Seattle, 1978-86; prof., chair dept. religion Barnard Coll., Columbia U., N.Y.C., 1986—; vis. assoc. prof. Grad. Theol. Union, 1982; vis. prof. depts. religion, Middle East langs., cultures Columbia U., 1984-86; dir. South Asia Nat. Resource Ctr., Columbia U., 1989-97, So. Asian Inst., 1989-95; mem. Ford Found. del. Am. scholars of South Asia to People's Rep. of China, 1986. Author: At Play with Krishna: Pilgrimage Dramas from Brindavan, 1981, paper, 1985, South Asian edit., 1992, Krishna, The Butter Thief, 1982, South Asian edit., 1989, Sur Das: Poet, Singer, Saint, 1984, Songs of the Saints of India, 1988; editor, co-editor: The Divine Consort: Radha and the Goddesses of India, 1982, paper, 1986, Saints and Virtues, 1987, Studying the Sikhs: Issues for North America, 1993, Fundamentalism and Gender, 1994, Sati, The Blessing and the Curse: The Burning of Wives in India, 1994, Devi Goddesses of India, 1996. Rockefeller Bros. Theol. fellow, 1963-64, Frank Knox fellow Harvard U., 1973-74, Roothbert fellow, 1976-77, Guggenheim fellow, 1985-86, others; NEH grantee, 1978, 82-85, 85-86, Smithsonian Travel grant to India, 1992-93, others. Mem. Am. Acad. Religion (chair Hinduism group 1978-82), Am. Oriental Soc., Assn. Asian Studies, Rajasthan Studies Group, Am. Soc. Study of Religion, Am. Com. South Asian Art, Phi Beta Kappa. Office: Barnard College Dept Religion New York NY 10027-9999

HAWLEY, JOHN W., military officer. BS in Chemistry, U. Wyo., 1969; grad., Squadron Officer Sch., 1974, Air Command and Staff Coll., 1975; M of Pub. Adminstrn., U. No. Colo., 1977; M of Mil. Arts and Scis., Army Command/Gen. Staff Coll., 1980. Commd. 2d lt. USAF, 1969, advanced through grades to maj. gen., 1996; staff officer air staff tng. program Air Force Mil. Pers. Ctr., Randolph AFB, Tex., 1976-77; F-4E pilot 309th Tactical Fighter Squadron, Homestead AFB, Fla., 1977-79; chief air def. divsn. U.S. Air Forces in Europe and U.S. Army Europe, Ramstein Air Base, West Germany, 1980-82; comdr. 512th Tactical Fighter Squadron, Ramstein Air Base, 1982-84; dep. chief tactical weapons divsn. Directorate of Operational Requirements, Hdqs. USAF, Washington, 1985-87; dep. comdr. F-16 ops., 401st Tactical Fighter Wing, Torrejon Air Base, Spain, 1987-88; comdr. 40th Tactical Group, Aviano Air Base, Italy, 1988-89; exec. officer to comdr. in chief U.S. Air Forces in Europe, Ramstein Air Base, 1990-92; asst. chief of staff offensive ops. divsn. Allied Air Forces Cen. Europe, Ramstein Air Base, 1990-92; comdr. 52d Fighter Wing, Spangdahlem Air Base, Germany, 1992-94; dir. Global Power programs Office of Asst. Sec. of Air Force for Acquisition, Washington, 1994-96; dir. requirements Hdqs. Air Combat Command, Langley AFB, Va., 1996-97; comdr. Aerospace Command and Control Agy., Hdqs. Air Combat Command, Langley AFB, 1998—. Decorated Def. Superior Svc. medal, Legion of Merit with oak leaf cluster, D.F.C. with 2 oak leaf clusters, Meritorious Svc. Medal with 3 oak leaf clusters. Office: ASC2A/CC Ste 216 130 Andrews Blvd Langley AFB VA 23665

HAWLEY, LINDA DONOVAN, advertising executive; b. Bryn Mawr, Pa., Nov. 1, 1946; d. John Donovan and Ann (Durnall) H. Diploma in advt., Charles Morris Price Sch. Advt., Phila., 1965. Sr. writer The Bulletin Co., Phila., 1968-72, The Advt. People, Inc., Bala Cynwyd, Pa., 1973-75, Elkman Advt. Co., Inc., Bala Cynwyd, 1975-77; sr. copywriter Mel Richman Inc., Bala Cynwyd, 1977-80; pres., creative dir. Hawley & Matthews Inc., Southeastern, 1980—; instr. Charles Morris Price Sch., Pa. State U. Pres. Soc. Hawley Family, Inc., 1998—; v.p. bd. Pa. Lupus Found., pres., 1993-94; mem. adv. bd. Joseph J. Peters Inst., 1991-93; house com. Hist. Waynesborough, Paoli, Pa. Recipient various advt. awards including Neographics award, 1970, Addy award, 1976, 93, Addy awards 2d Dist., 1980, Phila., 1981, 89, Charles Morris Price Sch. Disting. Alumni award, 1977, TRAC award, 1983, 84, Billy award, 1985. Mem. Phila. Club Advt. Women (pres. 1978-80), Phila. Women's Network (pres. 1983-84, dir. 1984-85), Soc. of Hawley Family, Inc. (pres. 1998—), Am. Advt. Fedn. (Pa. lt. gov. 1979-84, 87-88, lt. gov. 1990-92, 2d dist. sec. 1981-82, Crystal Prism award), TV and Radio Advt. Club, Phila. Advt. Club (bd. dirs.). Office: Hawley & Matthews Inc PO Box 964 Southeastern PA 19399-0964

HAWLEY, NANCI ELIZABETH, social services administrator; b. Detroit, Mar. 18, 1942; d. Arthur Theodore and Elizabeth Agnes (Fylling) Smisek; m. Joseph Michael Hawley, Aug. 28, 1958; children: Michael, Ronald, Patrick (dec.), Julie Anne. Pres. Tempo 21 Nursing Svcs., Inc., Covina, Calif., 1973-75; v.p. Profl. Nurses Bur., Inc., L.A., 1975-83; cons. Hawley & Assocs., Covina, 1983-87; exec. v.p. Glendora (Calif.) C. of C., 1984-85; dir. membership West Covina (Calif.) C. of C., 1985-87; exec. dir. San Dimas (Calif.) C. of C., 1987-88; mgr. pub. rels. Soc. for Advancement of Material and Process Engrs., Covina, 1988-92; small bus. rep. South Coast Air Quality Mgmt. Dist., 1992-94; bus. counselor Commerce and Trade Agy., Small Bus. Devel. Ctr., 1994; exec. v.p. Ontario (Calif.) C. of C., 1994-97; CEO, RMH Elec. Contractors, Colorado Springs, Colo., 1997-98; exec. v.p. Teen Resources, Inc., Colorado Springs, 1998; owner/CEO Hawley and Assoc. V.p. San-gabriel valley chpt. Women in Mgmt. Recipient Youth Motivation award Foothill Edn. Com., Glendora, 1987. Mem. NAFE, Colo. Assn. Nonprofit Orgns., Pub. Rels. Soc. Am., Soc. Nat. Assn. Publs., Am. Soc. Assn. Execs., Nat. Assn. Membership Dirs., Profl. Communicators Assn. So. Calif., Am. Birding Assn. (registrar), West End Bus. Assn. (pres. 1997—), Western Assn. Chamber Execs. (Spl. merit award for mag. pub. 1995), Kiwanis Internat. (sec. 1989-90, pres. West Covina 1990-91, Kiwanian of Yr. 1989), Rotary Internat. Avocations: reading, walking, painting, gardening. Fax: 719-596-2573. E-mail: nanmick58@AOL.com. Office: PO Box 6599 Colorado Springs CO 80934-6599

HAWLEY, PHILIP METSCHAN, retired retail executive, consultant; b. Portland, Oreg., July 29, 1925; s. Willard P. and Dorothy (Metschan) H.; m. Mary Catherine Follen, May 31, 1947; children: Diane (Mrs. Robert Bruce Johnson), Willard, Philip Metschan Jr., John, Victor, Edward, Erin (Mrs. Kevin Przybocki), George. BS, U. Calif., Berkeley, 1946; grad. advanced mgmt. program, Harvard U., 1967. With Carter Hawley Hale Stores, Inc., L.A., 1958-93, pres., 1972-83, chief exec. officer, 1977-93, chmn., 1983-93; bd. dirs. Weyerhaeuser Co. Trustee Calif. Inst. Tech., U. Notre Dame; chmn. L.A. Energy Conservation Com., 1973-74. Decorated hon. comdr. Order Brit. Empire, knight comdr. Star Solidarity Republic Italy; recipient Award of Merit L.A. Jr. C. of C., 1974, Coro Pub. Affairs award, 1978, Medallion award Coll. William and Mary, 1983, Award of Excellence Sch. Bus. Adminstrn. U. So. Calif., 1987, Bus. Statesman of Yr. award Harvard Bus. Sch., 1989, 15th ann. Whitney M. Young Jr. award L.S. Urban League, 1988; named Calif. Industrialist of Yr. Calif. Mus. Sci. and Industry, 1975. Mem. Calif. Retailers Assn. (chmn. 1993-95, dir.), Beach Club, Calif. Club, L.A. Country Club, Bohemian Club, Pacific-Union Club, Newport Harbor Yacht Club, Multnomah Club, Links Club, Phi Beta Kappa, Beta Alpha Psi, Beta Gamma Sigma. Office: 400 S Hope St Ste 1900 Los Angeles CA 90071-2801

HAWLEY, PHILLIP EUGENE, investment banker; b. Tecumseh, Mich., Dec. 9, 1940; s. Paul P. and Vadah Arlene (Lawhead) H.; m. Linda Darlene Miller, Feb. 14, 1957; children: Pierre Lee, Paul Marvin, Danny Parke, David Eugene, Martin Edward. Student in mgmt., Yale U., 1959-63; BSBA, Northwestern Coll., Tulsa, 1980. With Credit Bur. Ft. Myers (Fla.), Inc., 1956—; chmn. bd. dirs., regional mgr. Credit Bur. Internat. Corp., Ft. Myers, 1993—; pvt. investigator Transworld Investigators, Inc., 1964, now v.p.; mgr., founder real estate co. Gold Coast Devel. Corp., 1965, pres.; pres. Phillip Hawley Investment Banking Co.; bd. dirs. Caribbean Industries Internat. Corp., Future Investment Corp. Author: Law and It's Alternative to Chaos, 1958, The Happiest Man in the World, 1970, The Best Buys in Fort Myers, 1982. Named Outstanding Individual, Fla. Fedn. Young Reps., 1971; recipient Presdl. Sports award, 1979. Mem. Am. Collectors Assn. (scholar degree Collection Bus. Acad. 1994, fellow degree 1996), Fla. Collectors Assn. (Outstanding Spkr. 1967), Assn. Credit Bus. Am., Med.-Dental Hosp. Bus. Am., Fla. Assn. Mortgage Brokers, Fla. Assn. Pvt. Investigators, Am. Numismatic Assn., Gideons Internat., Collier-Lee Wrestling Assn. (co-founder, bd. dirs. 1974—). Mem. Nazarene Ch. Home: 6535 Winkler Rd Fort Myers FL 33919-8167 Office: Internat Collection Svc Inc 255 S Tamiami Trail Nokomis FL 34275

HAWLEY, RAYMOND GLEN, pathologist; b. Cambridge, Kans., Jan. 13, 1939; s. Pearl Washington and Gladys Laura (Logsdon) H.; m. Phyllis Ann Williams, Aug. 25, 1963; children: Bradford, Anthony, Douglas. BS, Kans. State U., 1961; MD, U. Kans., 1965. Intern Wesley Med. Ctr., Wichita, 1965-66; pathology resident Riverside Meth. Hosp., Columbus, Ohio, 1966-70; pathologist St. Joseph Hosp., Concordia, Kans., 1973-75, St. Joseph Med. Ctr., Wichita, 1975-82, Via Christi Regional Med. Ctr., Wichita, 1983—. Maj. U.S. Army, 1970-73. Fellow Am. Coll. Pathologists; mem. AMA, Am. Soc. Clin. Pathologists, Kans. Soc. Pathology (sec.-treas. 1989-99). Home: 1451 N Woodlawn St Wichita KS 67208-2428

HAWLEY, SANDRA SUE, electrical engineer; b. Spirit Lake, Iowa, May 7, 1948; d. Byrnard Leroy and Dorothy Virginia (Fischbeck) Smith; m. Michael John Hawley, June 7, 1970; 1 child, Alexander Tristin. BSEE, U. Dayton, 1981; BS in Math. and Stats., Iowa State U., 1970; MS in Stats., U. Del.,

1975. Rsch. analyst State of Wis., Madison, 1970-71; rsch. asst. Del. State Coll., Dover, 1972-73; asst. prof. math. and statis. Wesley Coll., Dover, 1974-81, chmn. dept. math. and computer sci., 1978-80; elec. engr. Control Data Corp., Bloomington, Minn., 1982-85; sr. elec. engr. Custom Integrated Circuits, 1985-89; sr. lead engr. Cardiac Pacemakers, Inc., 1989-90; mgr. Tech. Rosemount Inc., 1990-94; prin. cons. Tri-Ess, Mpls., 1994—. Contbr. articles to profl. jours. Elder Presbyn. Ch. U.S.A., 1975—, mem. session Oak Grove Presbyn. Ch., Bloomington, 1985-88; moderator Presbytery of Twin Cities Areea, 1996, chair Presbytery Coun., 1994, chair Coun. United Action, 1989-92, adminstrv. comm., 1989-91, com. on ministry, 1998—, commr. to Synod of Lakes & Prairies, 1990, Gen. Assembly Coun., 1992-98, com. on coun., 1992, commr. Gen. Assembly, 1991, chair Nat. Ministries divsn. Gen. Assembly, 1992-98. NSF scholar U. Dayton, 1981. Mem. IEEE, Soc. Women Engrs. Office: Tri-Ess 7724 W 85th St Minneapolis MN 55438-1382

HAWN, GOLDIE, actress; b. Washington, Nov. 21, 1945; d. Edward Rutledge and Laura (Steinhoff) H.; m. Gus Trinkonis, May 16, 1969 (div.); m. Bill Hudson (div.); children: Oliver, Kate Garry, Wyatt Russell. Student, Am. U. Profl. dancer, 1965; profl. acting debut in Good Morning, World, 1967-68; mem. company TV series Laugh-In, 1968-70; appeared in TV spl. Pure Goldie, 1971; films include: The One and Only Genuine Original Family Band, 1968, Cactus Flower, 1969 (Acad. award best supporting actress 1969), There's A Girl In My Soup, 1970, $, 1971, Butterflies Are Free, 1971, The Sugarland Express, 1974, The Girl from Petrovka, 1974, Shampoo, 1975, The Duchess and the Dirtwater Fox, 1976, Travels with Anita, 1978, Foul Play, 1978, Seems Like Old Times, 1980, Lovers and Liars, 1981, Best Friends, 1982, Swingshift, 1984, Overboard, 1987, Bird on a Wire, 1989, Deceived, 1991, Housesitter, 1992, Death Becomes Her, 1992, Crisscross, 1992, The First Wives Club, 1996, Everyone Says I Love You, 1996; exec. producer and star films Private Benjamin, 1980, Protocol, 1984, Wildcats, 1986, My Blue Heaven (co-exec. prodr. only), 1990, Something to Talk About, 1995 (exec. prodr. only), The Out of Towners, 1999, Town and Country, 1999; host TV spl. Pure Goldie, 1970, Goldie Hawn Special, 1978, Goldie and Liza Together, 1980, Goldie and Kids: Listen to Us!, 1982. Office: care ICM Ed Limato 8942 Wilshire Blvd Beverly Hills CA 90211-1934*

HAWORTH, CHARLES RAY, lawyer; b. Little Rock, June 23, 1943; s. Clarence Frederick and Vinita Leona (Bowers) H.; m. Nancy Anne Patterson, Aug. 16, 1970; 1 child, Alan. BA, U. Tex., 1965, JD, 1967. Bar: Tex. 1967, U.S. Dist. Ct. (no. dist.) Tex. 1968, U.S. Dist. Ct. (we. and so. dists.) Tex. 1988, U.S. Dist. Ct. (ea. dist.) Tex. 1989, U.S. Ct. Appeals (5th cir.) 1968, U.S. Ct. Appeals (11th cir.) 1982, U.S. Supreme Ct. 1971; bd. cert. civil trial law Tex. Bd. Legal Specialization. Law clk. U.S. Ct. Appeals (5th cir.), Houston, 1967-68; assoc. Coke & Coke, Dallas, 1968-71; prof. law Washington U. Sch. Law, St. Louis, 1971-79; ptnr. Johnson & Gibbs, Dallas, 1979-85, Andrews & Kurth, Dallas, 1985-92; mng. ptnr. Scott, Douglass, Luton & McConnico, L.L.P., Dallas, 1992-95; ptnr. Owens, Clary & Aiken, L.L.P., Dallas, 1995—; vis. prof. U. Va. Sch. Law, Charlottesville, 1975-76, U. Tex. Sch. Law, Austin, 1977; cons. Dept. Justice, Washington, 1978. Editor: Congress and the Courts, 1977; contbr. numerous articles to profl. jours. Bd. dirs. Dallas Opera, 1991—. Grantee Dept. of Justice, 1978. Mem. Tex. Bar Assn. (bus. cts. com. 1989, adminstrn. justice com. 1982-85, 89-92), City Club Dallas, Tower Club. Republican. Avocation: fishing. Office: Owens Clary & Aiken LLP 2400 Bank One Ctr 1717 Main St Ste 2400 Dallas TX 75201-4672

HAWORTH, DALE KEITH, art history educator, gallery director; b. Denver, Sept. 8, 1924; s. Murle Calvin and Hildur Elizabeth (Lindquist) H.; m. Ruth Anne Cushing, July 25, 1948 (div. 1980); children: Brooke Karen, Leah Anne, Nicholas Cushing; m. Karen Friedmann Beall, Dec. 31, 1983. BS in Edn., Washington U., 1950, MA, 1951; PhD, U. Iowa, 1960. Instr. art history Washington U., St. Louis, 1951-53, fellow in charge of exhbns., 1954-56; instr. art history Beloit (Wis.) Coll., 1953-54, U. Iowa, Iowa City, 1957-60; prof. art history Carleton Coll., Northfield, Minn., 1960-77, 79—, dir. exhbns., 1979—, now prof. emeritus; acting chief, prints and photographs div. Libr. Congress, Washington, 1977-79; vis. prof. art history U. Pa., Phila., 1961, 63, U. Minn., Mpls., 1970-71, 73-74; vis. prof. humanities Internat. Christian U., Tokyo, 1990; vis. scholar art history Doshisha U., Kyoto, Japan, 1983, 94; cons. Kress Found., Ohio, 1964; mem. com. for developing advanced placement exam. in history of art Coll. Bd., 1991-93; reader, table leader art history Ednl. Testing Svc., 1990-93. Contbr. articles to profl. jours. V.p. Northfield Arts Guild, 1964-66, pres. Northfield Parents Council, 1970. Served as staff sgt. USAC, 1943-46, PTO. Fulbright scholar, 1956-57, 1962; research grantee HEW, 1967-68; vis. scholarship U.S. Friendship Commn., 1983. Mem. Archeol. Inst. Am., Sch. Am. Rsch., Coll. Art Assn., Midwest Art History Soc. (bd. dirs. 1968-7). Avocation: drawing.

HAWORTH, DANIEL THOMAS, chemistry educator; b. Fond du Lac, Wis., June 27, 1928; s. Arthur Valentine and Mary Lena (Wattawa) H.; m. Mary Hormuth, Dec. 27, 1952; children: Daniel G., M. Judith, Steven T. BS, U. Wis., Oshkosh, 1950; MS, Marquette U., 1952; PhD, St. Louis U., 1959. Nuclear chemist Bur. of Ships, Washington, 1952-53; research chemist All-Chalmer Mfg. Co., Milw., 1958-60; instr. chemistry Marquette U., Milw., 1955, from asst. prof. to assoc. prof., 1960-68, prof., 1968—. Contbr. numerous articles to profl. jours.; patentee in field. Served as cpl. U.S. Army, 1953-55. Recipient Pere Marquette award for teaching excellence Marquette U., 1971, Nicolos Salgo Outstanding Tchr. award, 1971. Mem. Am. Chem. Soc. (emeritus), N.Y. Acad. Scis., Wis. Acad. Arts/Scis./Letters, Sigma Xi (emeritus). Roman Catholic. Avocation: philately. Home: 3483 N Frederick Ave Milwaukee WI 53211-2902 Office: Marquette Univ Dept Chemistry PO Box 1881 Milwaukee WI 53201-1881

HAWORTH, GERRARD WENDELL, office systems manufacturing company executive; b. Alliance, Nebr., Oct. 9, 1911; s. Elmer R. and Lulu (Jones) H.; m. Dorcas A. Snyder, June 22, 1938 (dec.); children: Lois, Richard, Joan, Mary, Julie; m. 2d Edna Mae Van Tatenhove, Feb. 5, 1979. A.B., Western Mich. U., 1937; M.A., U. Mich., 1940. Tchr. Holland High Sch., Mich., 1937-48; founding chmn. Haworth Inc., Holland, Mich., 1948—. Office: Haworth Inc 1 Haworth Ctr Holland MI 49423-9570

HAWORTH, JAMES CHILTON, pediatrics educator; b. Gosforth, Eng., May 29, 1923; emigrated to Can., 1957, naturalized, 1972; s. Walter Norman and Violet Chilton (Dobbie) H.; m. Eleanor Marian Bowser, Oct. 18, 1951; children—Elizabeth Marian, Peter Norman James, Margaret Jean, Anne Ruth. M.B., Ch.B, U. Birmingham, Eng., 1945, M.D., 1960. House physician Birmingham Gen. and Children's Hosps., 1946-47; fellow Cin. Children's Hosp., 1949-50; house physician Hosp. for Sick Children, London, 1951; pediatric registrar Alder Hey Children's Hosp., Liverpool, Eng., 1951-52; sr. registrar Sheffield Children's Hosp., 1953-57; pediatrician Winnipeg (Man., Can.) Clinic, 1957-65; asst. prof. dept. pediatrics U. Man., 1965-67, assoc. prof., 1967-70, prof., 1970-94, head dept. pediatrics, 1979-85, senate mem., 1985-90, prof. human genetics, 1987-94, prof. emeritus, 1994—; mem. active staff Health Scis. Centre-Children's, 1957-93; cons. staff St. Boniface Hosp., 1974-93; hon. staff Health Sci. Ctr., 1993—. Contbr. numerous articles to profl. jours. Served with Royal Naval Vol. Res., 1947-49. Fellow Royal Coll. Physicians (Can., London), Can. Coll. Medical Geneticists (hon.); mem. Canadian Soc. Clin. Investigation, Am. Acad. Pediatrics, Am. Pediatric Soc., Soc. Pediatric Research, Canadian Pediatric Soc., Midwest Soc. Pediatric Research. Home: 301 Victoria Crescent, Winnipeg, MB Canada R2M 1X8 Office: Childrens Hosp Dept Pediatrics, 678 William Ave, Winnipeg, MB Canada R3E 0W1*

HAWORTH, LAWRENCE LINDLEY, philosophy educator; b. Chgo., Dec. 14, 1926; s. Lawrence Lindley and Ruth Ethyl (Johnson) H.; children: Lawrence Lindley III, Ruth Ellis. BA with highest distinction, Rollins Coll., 1949; MA, U. Ill., 1950, PhD (Univ. fellow), 1952. Asst. prof. U. Ala., 1952-54, asst. dean, 1953-54; asst. prof. Purdue U., 1954-59, assoc. prof., 1959-65; prof. philosophy U. Waterloo, Ont., Can., 1965-96, disting. prof. emeritus, 1996—; dir. Ctr. for Soc., Tech. and Values U. Waterloo, 1984-86, chmn. dept. philosophy, asso. dean grad. studies, assoc. dean computing and rsch., 1967-70, 88-89. Author: The Good City, 1963, Decadence and Objectivity, 1977, Autonomy, 1986, Value Assumptions in Risk Assessment, 1991, A Textured Life: Empowerment and Adults with Developmental Disabilities, 1999; contbr. articles to profl. jours. Served with AUS, 1945-46. Purdue U. rsch. fellow, 1956, 59, 64; U. Waterloo rsch. fellow, 1967, 68, 69, 70; Can. Coun. leave fellow, 1971-72; Can. Coun. rsch. grantee, 1973-75, 81-83, 85-87, Social Sci. and Humanities Rsch. Coun. leave fellow, 1985-86, rsch. grantee 1981-84, 85-87, 91—. Fellow Royal Soc. Can.; mem. Canadian Philos. Assn., Phi Beta Kappa. Office: U Waterloo, Dept Philosophy, Waterloo, ON Canada N2L 3G1

HAWORTH, MICHAEL ELLIOTT, JR., investor, former aerospace company executive; b. Pitts., Dec. 18, 1928; s. Michael E. and Margarett (Thomas) H.; m. Elizabeth Jean Evans, Dec. 20, 1949; children: Michael Elliott III, Jean Evans. Student, U. Ala., 1946-50; B.S., Samford U., 1958. Gen. mgr. Haworth Engring. & Mfg. Co., Birmingham, Ala., 1954-56; chief contract negotiator U.S. Army Ordnance, Birmingham, 1956-61; dir. procurement Kennedy Space Center NASA, 1961-67; v.p., sec. Hayes Internat. Corp., Birmingham, 1967-86, pres., chief exec. officer, 1986-88, also bd. dirs.; pvt. investor, 1989-99. Life mem. Bapt. Med. Ctr.-Montclair Aux. With Q.M. Corps, U.S. Army, 1952-54. Mem. Am. Def. Indsl. Assn. (life, chpt. pres. 1969-71, 82-85), Nat. Aerospace Svcs. Assn. (dir. 1971-74, chmn. 1972-73), Coun. Def. and Space Industry Assns. (vice chmn. 1973-74, chmn. 1974-75), Nat. Contract Mgmt. Assn. (bd. dirs. Birmingham area chpt. 1976-78, lifetime cert. profl. contracts mgr.), Birmingham Urban League (dir. 1971-75), Phi Gamma Delta, Birmingham Country Club, The Club, Rotunda Club. Methodist. Home: 4805 Mill Springs Cir Birmingham AL 35223-1682

HAWORTH, RICHARD G., office furniture manufacturer; b. 1942. With Haworth Inc., Holland, Mich., chm. bd., 1975—. Office: Haworth Inc 1 Haworth Ctr Holland MI 49423-9570

HAWORTH, RICHARD THOMAS, geophysicist, science director; b. Wirksworth, Eng., May 24, 1944; s. Bertram and Eleanor (Buxton) H.; m. Wilma Haworth, Sept. 13, 1969; children: Neil, Mark. BSC with honors in Physics with Geology and Math, Durham U., 1965; PhD in Geophysics, Cambridge U., 1968. Rsch. mgr., rsch. sci. Bedford Inst. Oceanography-Atlantic Geosci. Ctr. of Geological Survey of Can., Dartmouth, N.S., Can., 1968-83; chief geophysicist Brit. Geological Survey, 1983-90; dir. gen. sedimentary and marine geosci. br. Geological Survey of Can., Ottawa, 1990—; faculty dept. geology dept. civil engring. Nottingham U., U.K.; external examiner Leeds, Newcastle, London Univs.; faculty appointment advisor London, Liverpool and Oxford Univs.; grad. student supr. Dalhousie, McGill Univs.; mem. gen. com. Internat. Sedimentology Cong., 1990; mem. program com. Internat. Assn. Geodesy, 1989; numerous overseas projects including Bahrein, China, Sudan, Spain, Turkey. Contbr. numerous articles to profl. jours., symposia; reviewer pubs. in field. Derbyshire County Exhibition scholar, Shell postgraduate scholar in geophysics. Fellow Royal Astron. Soc., Geol. Assn. Can. (program chmn. 1980), Geol. Soc. London (coun. 1985-88, v.p. 1986-88, adv. editor jour. 1985—), Geol. Soc. Am.; mem. Am. Geophysical Union. Avocations: choral singing, tennis, cycling. Office: Geological Survey of Canada, 601 Booth St, Ottawa, ON Canada K1A 0E8

HAWPE, DAVID VAUGHN, newspaper editor, journalist; b. Pikeville, Ky., Feb. 4, 1943; s. Chester and Betty Frances (Fletcher) H.; m. Linda Shadoin, Aug. 13, 1966; children: Christopher Fidler, Jonathan Bragdon. AB in Journalism, U. Ky., 1965; postgrad. (Nieman fellow), Harvard U., 1974-75. Reporter, editor AP, Lexington and Louisville, 1965-67; editorial writer St. Petersburg Times, Fla., 1967-69; various positions Courier-Jour., Louisville, 1969-78, mng. editor, 1979-87; editor Courier-Jour., 1987—; city editor Louisville Times, 1978-79; tchr. Appalachian studies Harvard U., spring 1975; tchr. Appalachian studies and journalism U. Louisville, U. Ky. Served with USAR, 1966-73. Named to Ky. Journalism Hall of Fame, 1994, U. Ky. Hall Disting. Alumni, 1995. Mem. Am. Soc. Newspaper Editors, AP Mng. Editors, Ky. Press Assn. (pres. 1990, 96-97). Democrat. Presbyterian. Office: Courier-Jour Co 525 W Broadway St Louisville KY 40202-2206

HAWRYLUK, CHRISTINE JOANNE, school nurse; b. Balt., June 19, 1964; d. John and Alexandra S. Hawryluk. BSN, Rutgers U., Camden, N.J., 1986; sch. nurse cert., Trenton (N.J.) State Coll., 1990, MEd in Health Edn., 1994. Cert. EMT, CPR instr. Emergency rm. nurse Zurbrugg Meml. Hosp., Riverside, N.J., 1986-93; sch. nurse Cinnaminson (N.J.) Mid. Sch., 1991—. Contbr. articles to profl. jours. Vol. Samaritan (N.J.) Hospice, 1995-96. Recipient Burlington County Sch. Nurse of Yr. award, 1998. Mem. Nat. Sch. Nurses Assn., N.J. Sch. Nurses Assn., N.J. Edn. Assn., Burlington County Sch. Nurses Assn., Cinnaminson Edn. Assn., Palmyra Ambulance Assn. (life; publicity chmn. 1986-95, 2d lt. 1990-93, 95, trustee 1994).

HAWRYLUK, RICHARD JANUSZ, physicist; b. Mansfield, Eng., June 7, 1950; came to U.S., 1952; s. Michal and Jozefa H.; m. Mary Katherine McMahon, Feb. 7, 1976; children: David, Kevin. BS, MIT, 1972, MS, 1972, PhD, 1974. Dep. dir. Princeton Plasma Physics Lab., 1974—; cons. Lincoln Lab., Lexington, Mass., 1970-74, 79. Contbr. over 100 articles to profl. jours. and conf. proceedings. Recipient Disting. Assoc. award Dept. of Energy, 1995, Kaul Found. prize for excellence in plasma physics rsch. and technology, 1996. Fellow Am. Phys. Soc. (Excellence in Plasma Physics award 1988). Achievements include research on heating and confinement of Tokamak plasmas and electron beam lithnography. Office: Princeton Plasma Physic Lab PO Box 451 Princeton NJ 08544-0451

HAWS, HALE LOUIS, medical consultant; b. Anaheim, Calif., June 15, 1923; s. Lloyd Albert and Nancy Jean (Hale) H.; m. Jo Ann Penn Haws; children: Kathleen Seghiere, Jay B., Jerald L. BA, Pepperdine Coll., 1947; MD, UCLA, 1958. Diplomate Med. Bd. Calif., Am. Bd. Preventive Medicine, Bd. Life Ins. Medicine. Intern Gorgas Hosp., Canal Zone, 1958-59; pvt. practice L.A., 1959-60; plant med. dir. Chrysler Corp., Commerce, Calif., 1960-71; physician, surgeon Narcotic Control, Dept. Corrections, L.A., 1961-75; v.p. med. svcs. Pacific Mut. Life Ins. Co., Newport Beach, Calif., 1962-81; consulting med. dir. Calif., 1981—; dir. Best Life Assurance Co. of Calif., Irvine, 1981-97; med. adv. bd. Equifax Svcs., Inc., Atlanta, 1977-81; spkr. in field. Mem. Church of Christ. Recipient Cert. of Appreciation, Selective Svc. Sys., 1975; scholar Kaiser Family Found., 1957. Fellow Am. Coll. Preventive Medicine, Am. Coll. Angiology, Am. Coll. Occupl. and Environ. Medicine, Am. Geriatrics Soc.; mem. Am. Acad. Ins. Medicine, Am. Coun. Life Ins., Calif. Scholastic Soc. (life), Pepperdine Alumni Assn. (dir. 1968-70). Avocations: art collecting, classic/antique autos, continuing medical education, reading, gardening. E-mail: haleyboy@aol.com. Home: 5268 Royal Canyon Ln Paradise CA 95969-6683

HAWS, KARL WAYNE, physician, consultant; b. Miami, Okla., Dec. 30, 1961; s. Charles Leroy and Doris Ellen H. AA in Phys. Edn., Northeastern Okla. A & M Jr. Coll., Miami, 1982; BS in Biology, East Ctrl. U., 1985; DO, Okla State U., 1990. Diplomate Am. Bd. Family Practice. Physician Cooper Family Medicine, Springdale, Ark., 1993—. Fellow Am. Acad. Family Physicians; mem. AMA, Am. Osteo. Assn., Am. Osteo. Acad. Sports Medicine, Am. Coll. Occupl. and Environ. Medicine, Am. Coll. Sports Medicine, Ark. Osteo. Med. Assn., Ark. Acad. Family Physicians. Avocations: physical fitness, baseball, bicycling, skiing. Office: Cooper Family Medicine PA 307 S Thompson St Springdale AR 72764-4240

HAWTHORNE, FRANK HOWARD, lawyer; b. Hope Hull, Ala., Sept. 16, 1923; s. William Blackwell and Bessie Louise (Greene) H.; m. Esther Rae Wille, Feb. 26, 1952; children: Frank Howard, Raymond James, Mary Jule Burleson. Student, Vanderbilt U., 1943-44; BS, Auburn U., 1946; JD, U. Ala., 1949. Bar: Ala. 1949. Instr. Auburn U., 1946, U. Ala., 1946-49; ptnr. Balch & Bingham, Montgomery, Ala., 1949-93, Hawthorne, Hawthorne and Vance, L.L.C., Montgomery, $D, 1994—. Author: Kissin Kin and Lost Cousins, 1989. Chmn. adv. bd. Salvation Army, 1968-70, life mem., 1989—; mem. adv. coun. Coll. Bus., Auburn U., 1973-76, 78-81, 90-94, chmn., 1977; past chpt. chmn. Nat. Found.; bd. dirs. Montgomery Pub. Libr., 1968-74, Goodwill Industries, 1982—. Served to 2d lt. USAAF, 1943-45; 1st lt. USAF, 1951-52. Recipient Srs. of Achievement award, 1998. Mem. ABA (mem. resolutions com. 1959-60, tax com. 1987—), Ala. Bar Assn. (grievance com. 1961-62, chmn. legis. com. 1972, chmn. legis. liaison com. 1983-84), Montgomery County Bar Assn., Auburn U. Nat. Alumni Assn. (exec. com. 1957-59), Pioneers of Montgomery (pres. 1972), The Thirteen, Montgomery C. of C. (treas. 1973, v.p. 1974, pres. 1975), Omicron Delta Kappa, Pi Kappa Phi (nat. historian 1954-56, nat. chancellor, mem. nat. coun. 1954-64, bd. dirs., pres. Pi Kappa Phi Properties 1966-70), Phi Alpha Delta. Episcopalian. Clubs: Com. of 100 (bd. of control 1968-71); Montgomery Auburn (past pres. 1957). Lodge: Kiwanis. Home: 3382 Thomas Ave Montgomery AL 36111-1428 Office: Bell Bldg Ste 1100 207 Montgomery St Montgomery AL 36104-3537

HAWTHORNE, MARION FREDERICK, chemistry educator; b. Ft. Scott, Kans., Aug. 24, 1928; s. Fred Elmer and Colleen (Webb) H.; m. Beverly Dawn Rempe, Oct. 30, 1951 (div. 1976); children: Cynthia Lee, Candace Lee; m. Diana Baker Razzaia, Aug. 14, 1977. BA, Pomona Coll., 1949; PhD (AEC fellow), U. Calif. at Los Angeles, 1953; DSc (hon.), Pomona Coll., 1974; PhD (hon.), Uppsala U., 1992. Rsch. assoc. Iowa State Coll., 1953-54; rsch. chemist Rohm & Haas Co., Huntsville, Ala., 1954-56, group leader, 1956-60; lab. head Rohm & Haas Co., Phila., 1961; prof. chemistry U. Calif., Riverside, 1962-68, UCLA, 1968—; Univ. prof. U. Calif. System, 1998—, 1998—; vis. lectr. Harvard U., 1960; vis. prof. U. Tex., Austin, 1974, Harvard, 1968; mem. sci. adv. bd. USAF, 1980-86, NRC Bd. Army Sci. and Tech., 1986-90; disting. vis. prof. Ohio State U., 1990; mem. dir.'s external adv. bd. divsn. M, Los Alamos (N.Mex.) Nat. Lab., 1991-94; lectr. in field. Editor-in-chief: Inorganic Chemistry, 1969—. Decorated Meritorious Svc. medal USAF, 1986; recipient Chancellors Research award, 1968, Herbert Newby McCoy award, 1972, Am. Chem. Soc. award in Inorganic Chemistry, 1973, Glenn T. Seaborg medal, 1997, Tolman Medal award, 1986, Nebr. sect. Am. Chem. Soc. award, 1979, Disting. Service in the Advancement of Inorganic Chemistry award Am. Chem. Soc., 1988, Disting. Achievements in Boron Sci. award, 1988, Bailar medal, 1991, Polyhedron Medal and prize, 1993, Chem. Pioneer award Am. Inst. Chemists, 1994, Willard Gibbs medal Am. Chem. Soc., 1994, Internat. award in Polyhedral Borane Chemistry, Internat. Com. on Boron Chemistry, 1996; named sr. scientist Alexander von Humboldt Found., Inst. Inorganic Chemistry U. Munich, 1990-96, Centenary lectr. Royal Soc. Chemistry, London, 1998; Sloan Found. fellow, 1963-65, Japan Soc. Promotion Sci. fellow, 1986; named Col. Confederate Air Force, 1984. Fellow AAAS; mem. U.S. Nat. Acad. Scis. (award in chem. scis. 1997), Am. Acad. Arts and Scis., Göttingen Acad. Scis. (corr. mem.), Aircraft Owners and Pilots Assn., Cosmos Club, The Internat. Soc. for Neutron Capture Therapy for Cancer (mem. exec. com. 1992—, pres. 1996—), Sigma Xi, Alpha Chi Sigma, Sigma Nu. Home: 3415 Green Vista Dr Encino CA 91436-4011

HAWTHORNE, MARK R., investigator, educator; b. San Francisco, Nov. 21, 1951; s. Richard E. and Barbara L. Hawthorne; m. Sheila Y. Laughridge, Sept. 18, 1977; children: Andrew J., Ashley D. AA, San Francisco C.C., 1977; BA, Golden Gate U., 1981, MPA, 1998. Sr. dep. sheriff San Francisco Sheriff's Office, 1972-78; police officer San Francisco Police Dept., 1978-84, crime scene investigator, 1984—, coord. mentor program, 1996—; instr. City Coll., San Francisco, 1986—, San Francisco Police Regional Tng. Acad., 1990—; guest lectr. U. San Francisco Law Sch., 1997-98; chair blood com. San Francisco Police Dept., 1996—. Author: First Unit Responder, 1998. Sgt. U.S. Army Nat. Guard, 1970-76. Fellow Internat. Assn. for Identification (cert. sr. crime scene analyst, cert. latent print examiner, past pres. Calif. divsn. 1995-96), Fingerprint Soc. Eng.; mem. Calif. Assn. Criminal Justice Educators, Pi Alpha Alpha. Home: 1314 Plymouth Ave San Francisco CA 94112 Office: San Francisco Police Dept Rm 577-16 850 Bryant St San Francisco CA 94112

HAWTHORNE, NIGEL BARNARD, actor; b. Coventry, U.K., Apr. 5, 1929; s. Charles Barnard and Agnes Rosemary (Rice) H. Student, Christian Bros. Coll., Cape Town, S. Africa, 1945; MA (hon.), Sheffield U., 1987, Leicester U.; LittD (hon.), Hertfordshire U., 1992, MA (hon.). Appeared in plays As You Like It., U.S. tour, 1974, Shadowlands, (Broadway) 1990-91 (Tony award for best actor 1991, Outer Cir. Critics award for best actor 1991, Olivier award nomination for best actor 1991), The Madness of George III, U.S. tour, 1993 (Olivier award for best actor 1992, Evening Standard award for best actor 1992, Time Out's Readers award for best actor 1992, Plays and Players Mag. award for best actor 1992); (films) Firefox, 1982, Ghandi, 1982, The Chain, 1985, Demolition Man, 1993, The Madness of King George, 1994 (Oscar nominee for Best Actor 1995, BAFTA award for best actor 1996), Richard III, 1995, Inside, 1995, Twelfth Night, 1995, Murder in Mind, 1996, Amistad, 1997, The Object of My Affection, 1997, Madeline, 1997, A Reasonable Man, 1999, The Clandestine Marriage, 1999, The Big Brass Ring, 1999, The Winslow Boy, 1999, Tarzan, 1999; (TV series) Yes, Prime Minister, 1979-88 (BAFTA best actor light entertainment award 1981, 82, 86, 87, Broadcasting Press Guild TV award for best actor 1980), The Fragile Heart, 1996 (BAFTA award for best actor 1997); TV appearances include: Yes Prime Minister, 1982, Barchester Chronicles, 1984, Mapp & Lucia, 1986, The Trials of Oz, 1991, The Miser, 1988, Stanley and Livingstone, 1997, others; prodr. Murder in Mind, 1997, At Sachem Farm, 1998; TV guest appearance Dad's Army, 1968. Recipient Tony award, 1990, Olivier award, 1992, Evening Standard award, 1992, Gold medal Nat. Arts Club, 1996; named Comdr. Brit. Empire, 1987. Avocations: gardening, writing, swimming, tennis. Office: Ken McReddie, 91 Regent St, London W1R 7TB, England*

HAWTHORNE, TIMOTHY ROBERT, direct response advertising and communications company executive; b. Evanston, Ill., June 29, 1950; s. John and Marjie Phyllis (Horner) H.; 1 child, Jessica Hope. BA cum laude, Harvard U., 1973. Editor, producer Sta. WCCO-TV, Mpls., 1973-78; field producer Sta. KYW-TV, Phila., 1978-80; pres., founder Producer/Writer Network, Newtown, Pa., 1980-82; v.p. prodn. Teleimage, Inc., Phila., 1982-83; pres. Hawthorne Prodns., Phila., Los Angeles and Fairfield, Iowa, 1983—; co-founder, pres. Fairfield TV, 1984-86; pres. Hawthorne Communications, Inc., Fairfield, 1986—. Producer, writer, dir.: (TV series) Real People, That's Incredible, Ripley's Believe It Or Not, Entertainment Tonight, 1979-85. Dir. Fairfield Cultural Soc., 1985-87; mem. Pres. Soc. Maharishi Internat. U., Fairfield, 1984—. Named Iowa/Nebr. Entrepreneur of Yr., 1996. Mem. Dirs. Guild Am., Nat. Info. Mktg. Assn. (founding mem., bd. dirs.), Direct Mktg. Assn., Fairfield C. of C. Avocations: travel, skiing. Home: 1825 Okra Blvd Fairfield IA 52556-8709 Office: Hawthorne Dir Inc 300 N 16th St Fairfield IA 52556-2604*

HAWTHORNE, VICTOR MORRISON, epidemiologist, educator; b. Glasgow, Scotland, June 19, 1921; came to U.S., 1978; s. John Morrison and Isabel Stuart (Crowe) H.; m. Jean Christie Mackenzie, Aug. 19, 1948; children—Hilary June, Wendy Victoria, Jean Rosalind. MB ChB, U. Glasgow, 1951, MD, 1962, DSc (hon.), 1996; diploma, Scottish Coun. for Health Edn., 1976. Sr. lectr. dept. epidemiology U. Glasgow, 1967-78, sr. research fellow dept. community medicine, 1978-91; cons. physician Nat. Health Service, Glasgow Health Bd., 1966-78; coordinator Scottish MMR services Nat. Health Service Scotland, 1970-78; prof. epidemiology U. Mich., Ann Arbor, 1978-91, chmn. dept., 1978-86, prof. dept. family practice, 1982-91, prof. epidemiology emeritus, 1991—; chmn. epidemiology study sect. NIH, Bethesda, Md., 1979-83, active, 1979-93; chmn. kidney disease adv. com. Mich. Dept. Pub. Health, Lansing, 1979-95, mem. chronic disease adv. com., 1979; chmn. Continuing Med. Edn./Pub. Health Consortium Mich., 1987—; hon. dir. Bayer Rsch. unit Royal Coll. Physicians of Edinburgh, 1987-93, hon. cons. Royal Coll. Physicians of Edinburgh Diabetes Register, 1989—. Author: First Aid For Medical Students, 1978, Tuberculosis, Respiratory and Cardiovascular Risks of Dying in the West of Scotland, 1985; contbr. articles to profl. jours. Served to capt. British Army, 1941-46. Recipient Bronze medal U. Helsinki, 1985; Victor Hawthorne: Young Investigator Rsch. Award Program established in his honor Mich. Dept. Pub. Health, 1986. Fellow Royal Coll. Physicians and Surgeons of Glasgow, Royal Coll. Physicians of Edinburgh, Faculty of Pub. Health Medicine, Soc. Antiquaries of Scotland, Am. Coll. Epidemiology. Mem. Ch. of Scotland. Avocations: sketching; gardening. Office: Univ Mich Sch Pub Health Dept Epidemiology 109 Observatory St Ann Arbor MI 48109-2029

HAWTHORNE, SIR WILLIAM (REDE), aerospace and mechanical engineer, educator; b. May 22, 1913; s. William and Elizabeth H.; ed. Trinity Coll., Cambridge, M.I.T.; m. Barbara Runkle, 1939; 1 son, 2 daus. Devel. engr. Babcock & Wilcox Ltd., 1937-39; sci. officer Royal Aircraft Establishment, 1940-44; with Brit. Air Commn., Washington, 1944; dep. dir. engine research Ministry of Supply, 1945; assoc. prof. mech. engring. MIT, 1946, George Westinghouse prof. mech. engring., 1948-51, Jerome C. Hunsaker prof. aero. engring., 1955-56; master Churchill Coll., Cambridge, 1968-

83, now fellow; Hopkinson and ICI prof. applied thermodynamics U. Cambridge, 1951-80, head dept. engring., 1968-73; chmn. Home Office Sci. Adv. Council, 1967-76, Adv. Council Energy Conservation, 1974-79; dir. Cummins Engine Co., Inc., 1974-86, dir. Dracone Devels. Ltd. Bd. govs. Westminster Sch., 1956-76. Recipient U.S. Medal of Freedom, 1947, Royal medal Royal Society, 1982, R. Tom Sawyer award ASME, 1992. Fellow AIAA (hon.), ASME (hon.), Royal Soc., Royal Acad. Engring.; mem. NAE (fgn. assoc.), NAS (fgn. assoc.). Office: Churchill Coll, Cambridge England also: 19 Chauncy St Cambridge MA 02138-2549

HAWVER, DENNIS ARTHUR, psychological consultant; b. Millbury, Ohio, Apr. 9, 1940; s. Carl Fullerton and Frances Jewell (Renick) H.; m. Anne M. Augustyn, 1961 (div. Oct. 1974); children: Timothy, Laura, Derek; m. Judith M. Anderson, Jan. 28, 1977. B.A., U. Akron, 1964, M.A., 1965; Ph.D., Temple U., 1970. Dir. research Temple U., Phila., 1964-70, instr. Grad. Sch., 1968-70, internal cons., 1964-70; mng. ptnr. Cardall Assocs., Princeton, N.J., 1970-72; nat. program dir. The RHR Inst., N.Y.C., 1972-80; pres. The Hawver Group, N.Y.C. and Princeton, 1980—; pres. Princeton chpt. Inst. Mgmt. Cons., chmn. of Leadership Devel. Com. of the C of C; Author: How to Improve Your Negotiating Skills, 1983; contbr. to bus. and profl. jours.; developer research and tng. programs; internat. cons. in exec. identification and devel. and bus. negotiations. Mem. Am. Psychol. Assn., Soc. Indsl. and Organizational Psychology, Internat. Assn. Applied Psychology, Inst. Mgmt. Cons. (CMC), Soc. Assessment Systems Practitioners, Internat. Personnel Mgmt. Assn. Assessment Council. Office: The Hawver Group 2 Research Way Princeton NJ 08540-6628

HAX, ARNOLDO CUBILLOS, management educator, industrial engineer; b. Santiago, Chile, Aug. 9, 1936; came to U.S., 1961; s. Egon and Adela (Cubillos) H.; m. Neva Mimica, Jan. 28, 1962; children: Andrew, Neva. Degree in Indsl. Engring. with highest honors, Cath. U. Chile, Santiago, 1960; MS in Insdl. Engring., U. Mich., 1963; PhD in Ops. Rsch., U. Calif., Berkeley, 1967. Asst. prof. math. Sch. Engring., Cath. U. Chile, 1960-61, dir., assoc. prof. Ops. Rsch., 1963-65; asst. specialist Ops. Rsch. Ctr. U. Calif., Berkeley, 1965-67; mgmt. cons. ops. rsch. Arthur D. Little, Inc., Cambridge, Mass., 1976-70; lectr. Bus. Sch. Harvard U., Boston, 1970-72; assoc. prof. Sloan Sch. Mgmt., MIT, Cambridge, 1972-76, prof., 1976—, Alfred P. Sloan prof., 1985—, dep. dean, 1987-90; Thomas Henry Carroll Ford Found. vis. prof. bus. Harvard Bus. Sch., 1993-94; indsl. engr. Chilean Inst. Steel, Santiago, 1960-61; lectr. linear programming Centro Interam. de Ensenanza de Estadistica, Santiago, 1963-65; cons. ops. rsch. and stats. CADE, Santiago, 1963-65; cons. stategic planning processes Digital Equipment Corp., Motorola, GM, Citibank, Westinghouse Electric, others in U.S., Europe, Mex., S.Am., Can.; Ford Found. vis. prof. bus. sch. Harvard U., 1993-94. Co-author: (with D. Candea) Production and Inventory Management, 1984 (Inst. Indsl. Engrs.-Joint Pubs. Book of Yr. award 1985), (with N. Majluf) The Strategy Concept and Process: A Pragmatic Approach, 1991, Strategic Management: An Integrative Perspective, 1984; author: (with others) Manuale di Gestione della Produzione, 1975, Studies in Management Science, Vol. 1, Logistics, 1975, Modern Trends in Logistics Research, 1976, Applied Mathematical Programming, 1977, Conflicting Objectives in Decisions, 1977, Handbook of Operations Research, 1978, Studies in Operations Management, 1978 (also editor), Disaggregation: Problem in Manufacturing and Service Organizations, 1979, Applications of Management Science, Vol. 1, 1981, The Management Handbook, 1981, Implementation of Stategic Planning, 1982, Production Handbook, 1987; editor: Readings in Strategic Management, 1984, Planning Strategies That Work, 1987; strategic mgmt. editor Interface jour., 1981—; former editor Ops. Rsch. jour., Naval Rsch. Logistics Quar.; contbr. numerous articles to profl. jours. and publs. Thomas Henry Carroll Ford Found. vis. prof. bus. Harvard U. Bus. Sch., Cambridge. Mem. Inst. Mgmt. Scis., Ops. Rsch. Soc., Am. Inst. Indsl. Engrs., AAAS, Am. Inst. Decision Scis., Vineyard Haven Yacht and Tennis Club, Alpha Pi Mu. Home: 242 Otis St Newton MA 02465-2525 Office: MIT Sloan Sch Mgmt 50 Memorial Dr Cambridge MA 02142-1347*

HAXO, FRANCIS THEODORE, marine biologist; b. Grand Forks, N.D., Mar. 9, 1921; s. Henry Emile and Florence (Shull) H.; m. Judith Morgan McLaughlin, Apr. 15, 1961; children: John Frederick, Barbara, Philip, Francis Theodore, Aileen. B.A., U. N.D., 1941; Ph.D., Stanford U., 1947. Teaching, research asst. Stanford U., 1941-44, acting instr., 1943; research asst. Calif. Inst. Tech., 1946; research asso. Hopkins Marine Sta., Pacific Grove, Calif., 1946-47; from instr. to asst. prof. plant physiology Johns Hopkins U., 1947-52; mem. faculty U. Calif. Scripps Inst. Oceanography, La Jolla, 1952-88; prof. biology U. Calif. Scripps Inst. Oceanography, 1963-88; prof. emeritus, 1988—; chmn. marine biology dept. U. Calif. Scripps Inst. Oceanography, 1960-65, chmn. marine biology research div., 1960-77; instr. marine botany Marine Biol. Lab., Woods Hole, Mass., 1949-52, 70; vis. faculty botany U. Calif. at Berkeley, 1957, U. Wash. Marine Lab., Friday Harbor, 1963. Abraham Rosenberg fellow Stanford, 1945. Fellow AAAS, San Diego Zool. Soc.; mem. Am. Soc. Photobiology, Phycological Soc. Am., Western Soc. Naturalists, Internat. Phycological Soc., Phi Beta Kappa, Sigma Xi. Spl. rsch. photosynthesis, plant pigments, physiology of algae. Home: 6381 Castejon Dr La Jolla CA 92037-6933

HAXTON, DAVID, computer graphics educator, computer animator, photographer; b. Indpls., Jan. 6, 1943; s. John Laird and Dorothy Margaret (Peters) H.; m. Kay Elizabeth Keller, Feb. 8, 1969. BA, U. South Fla., 1965; MFA, U. Mich., 1967. Prof. computer graphics William Paterson Coll., Wayne, N.J., 1974-95, U. Ctrl. Fla., Orlando, 1995—. One-man shows include: Sonnabend Gallery, N.Y.C., 1979, 80, 81, 83, Paris, 1978, Mus. Modern Art, N.Y.C., 1978, Rosa Esman Gallery, N.Y.C., 1986; group shows include: Whitney Mus. Am. Art, N.Y.C., 1979, 81, 83, Rosa Esman Gallery, N.Y.C., 1986, Anne Plumb Gallery, N.Y.C., 1987, Ringling Art Mus., Sarasota, Fla., 1987; represented in permanent collections, Mus. Modern Art, N.Y.C., Whitney Mus. Am. Art, N.Y.C., Denver Art Mus., Australian Mus. Art. Recipient awards for computer animation direction Gold Plaque award Chgo. Internat. Film Festival, 1988, 89, Art Dream award Siggraph Film and Video Show, 1988, Nat. Computer Graphics Assn. 2d award, 1989, Siggraph Animation Screening award, 1990, NCGA Video Show 3rd award, 1991, 1st pl. award Alias Desing Competition, 1991, Siggraph Electronic Theater award, 1992, Pri Ars Electronica award, 1993, UN Cabinet D'Amateurs Cinematheque Francaise, Films, 1995, Siggarph Animation Screening Rm. award, 1997; N.Y. Coun. on Arts grantee, 1977-78, Nat. Endowment for Arts grantee, 1978-79; Individual Artist fellow, 1979-80; Nat. Computer Graphics Assn. faculty student, 1992, 2d prize award, 1991. Office: U Ctrl Fla Art Dept Orlando FL 32789

HAY, ALLAN STUART, chemist, educator; b. Edmonton, Alta., Can., July 23, 1929; s. Stuart Lumsden and Verna Emila (Hodgins) H.; m. Janet Mary Keck, Dec. 15, 1956; children: Randall, Bruce, Lauren, Susan. B.Sc., U. Alta., Edmonton, 1950, M.Sc., 1952; Ph.D., U. Ill., Urbana, 1955; D.Sc. (hon.), U. Alta., 1987. Research chemist Gen. Electric Co., Schenectady, N.Y., 1955-67, mgr. chem. lab., 1968-81, mgr. chem. labs., 1982-87; prof. chem. dept. McGill U., Montreal, 1987—, Tomlinson chair, 1997. Contbr. articles to acad. jours.; multiple patentee in field. Recipient Internat. award Soc. Plastics Engrs., 1975, Achievement award Indsl. Rsch. Inst., 1984, Chem. Pioneer award Inst. Chemists, 1985. Fellow AAAS, Royal Soc. of London, N.Y. Acad. of Sci., Royal Soc. Chemistry; mem. Am. Chem. Soc. (Carothers award 1985). Avocation: philately. E-mail: ch19@musica.mcgill.ca. Home: 5015 Glencairn Ave, Montreal, PQ Canada H3W 2B3 Office: McGill U Dept Chemistry, 801 Sherbrooke St W, Montreal, PQ Canada H3A 2K6

HAY, BETTY JO, civic worker; b. McAlester, Okla., June 6, 1931; d. Duncan and Kathryn Myrtle (Albert) Peacock; m. Jess Thomas Hay, Aug. 3, 1951; children: Deborah Hay Spradley, Patricia Lynn Daibert. BA, So. Meth. U., 1952. Bd. dirs. White House Preservation Fund, 1980-87, Nat. Parents as Tchrs., 1991-94; bd. dirs. Nat. Mental Health Assn., 1978-87, pres., 1986, mem. fin. com. and child adolescent com., 1978-79, mem. resource devel. com., 1980-83; v.p. fundraising Mental Health Assn. Tex., 1980, bd. dirs., 1974-90, pres., 1983-84; bd. dirs. Mental Health Assn., Dallas County, 1972-88, pres., 1981-82; bd. dirs. United Way Met. Dallas, 1983-94, treas., 1989; bd. dirs. Assn. Higher Edn. North Tex., 1980-82, vice chmn., 1982-83, chmn., 1984-85; mem. adv. bd. Sch. Social Work, U. Tex., Arlington, 1983-94; mem. Nat. Commn. on Children, 1989-92, Dallas Coun. on World Affairs, Woman's Div., March of Dimes Aux., 1982—; bd. dirs. Baylor Coll. Dentistry, 1987-94. mem. exec. com., 1989, vice chmn., 1992; mem. Tex. Commn. on Children and Youth, 1994-95; pres. Tex. Mental Health Found., 1982—; many past involvements in charitable orgns. Address: 7236 Lupton Cir Dallas TX 75225-1737

HAY, DENNIS LEE, lawyer; b. L.A., Feb. 18, 1958; s. Frank Henry, Jr. and Kyoko (Sukuya) H.; m. Kerry Lynne Hatfield, Aug. 11, 1984; children: Michelle, Jason, Katheryne. BS in Fin., San Jose State U., 1984; JD, U. Honolulu, 1988. Bar: Calif. 1989. Law clk. Legal Aid Soc. of Alameda Co., Hayward, Calif., 1985-87, Cohn, Becker & Jacquint, Hayward, Calif., 1987; law clk. Souza, Coats, McInnis, Mehlhaff & Hay, Tracy, Calif., 1987-89, assoc. counsel atty., 1989-92; ptnr. Mehlhaff & Hay, Tracy, Calif., 1992—; judge pro tem San Joaquin Superior Cts.; prof. law U. Honolulu Law Sch., Modesto, Calif., 1990—. Mem. ABA, Calif. Bar Assn., San Joaquin County Bar Assn. (chairperson bus. litig. sect. com. 1997-98). Republican. Presbyterian. Avocations: drag racing, horse back riding, raquetball. Office: Mehlhaff Hay & Adrejko PO Box 1129 1011 Parker Ave Tracy CA 95376-3933

HAY, DICK, artist, educator; b. Cin., Nov. 19, 1942; s. Richard Walter and Evelyn (Crosby) H.; m. Nancy Carder, June 1964; 1 child, richard Carder. BFA, Ohio U., 1964; MFA, Alfred (N.Y.) U., 1966. Prof. art Ind. State U., Terre Haute, 1966—; lectr. in more than 80 univs. worldwide. Exhibited works in more than 200 exhbns. in U.S., Japan, Can., Russia, Latvia, Korea; works in maj. collections, including Pushkin Mus., Russia, Riga (Latvia) Mus. Art, Byung-Tak Woo Pub. Collection, Korea, Sea of Japan Collection, Butler Inst. Art,. Recipient Caleb Mills Disting. Tchg. award Ind. State U., 1988; Arts Endowment grantee, 1997-98. Mem. Nat. Coun. on Edn. for the Ceramic Arts (pres. 1978-80). Home: 2108 W 340 Brazil IN 47834 Office: Ind State U Terre Haute IN 47809

HAY, ELIZABETH DEXTER, embryology researcher, educator; b. St. Augustine, Fla., Apr. 2, 1927; d. Isaac Morris and Lucille (Lynn) H. AB, Smith Coll., 1948; MA (hon.), Harvard U., 1964; ScD (hon.), Smith Coll., 1973, Trinity Coll., 1989; MD, Johns Hopkins U., 1952, LHD (hon.), 1990. Intern in internal medicine Johns Hopkins Hosp., Balt., 1952-53; instr. anatomy Johns Hopkins U. Med. Sch., Balt., 1953-56, asst. prof., 1956-57; asst. prof. Cornell U. Med. Sch., N.Y.C., 1957-60; asst. prof. Harvard Med. Sch., Boston, 1960-64, Louise Foote Pfeiffer assoc. prof., 1964-69, Louise Foote Pfeiffer prof. embryology, 1969—, chmn. dept. anatomy and cellular biology, 1975-93; prof. dept. cell biology, 1993—; cons. cell biology sect. NIH, 1965-69; mem. adv. coun. Nat. Inst. Gen. Med. Sci., NIH, 1978-81; mem. sci. adv. bd. Whitney Marine Lab., U. Fla., 1982-86; mem. adv. coun. Johns Hopkins Sch. Medicine, 1982—; chairperson bd. sci. counselors Nat. Inst. Dental Rsch., NIH, 1984-86; mem. bd. sci. counselors Nat. Inst. Environ. Health Sci., NIH, 1990-93. Author: Regeneration, 1966; (with J.P. Revel) Fine Structure of the Developing Avian Cornea, 1969; editor: Cell Biology of Extracellular Matrix, 1981, 2d edit., 1991; editor-in-chief Developmental Biology Jour., 1971-75; contbr. articles to profl. jours. Mem. Scientists Task Force of Congressman Barney Frank, Massach, 1982-92. Recipient Disting. Achievement award N.Y. Hosp.-Cornell Med. Ctrl. Alumni Coun., 1985, award for vision rsch. Alcon, 1988, Excellence in Sci. award Fedn. Am. Socs. Exptl. Biology. Mem. Soc. Devel. Biology (pres. 1973-74, E.G. Conklin award 1997), Am. Soc. Cell Biology (pres. 1976-77, legis. alert com. 1982—, E.B. Wilson award 1989), Am. Assn. Anatomists (pres. 1981-82, legis. alert com. 1982—, Centennial award 1987, Henry Gray award 1992), Am. Acad. Arts and Scis., Johns Hopkins Soc. Scholars, Nat. Acad. Sci., Inst. Medicine, Internat. Soc. Devel. Biologists (exec. bd. 1977), Boston Mycol. Club. Home: 14 Aberdeen Rd Weston MA 02493-1733 Office: Harvard Med Sch Dept Cell Biology 220 Longwood Ave Boston MA 02115-5701

HAY, GEORGE ALAN, law and economics educator; b. N.Y.C., Feb. 4, 1942; s. George N. and Marjorie H. (Prote) H. BS, Le Moyne Coll., 1963; MA, Northwestern U., 1967, PhD, 1969. From asst. to assoc. prof. econs. Yale U., New Haven, 1967-74; dir. econs. antitrust div. U.S. Dept. Justice, Washington, 1973-79; prof. law and econs. Cornell U., Ithaca, N.Y., 1979-92, Edward Cornell prof. law, prof. econs., 1992—; vis. prof. law U. Sydney, 1992. Contbr. articles on antitrust to profl. jours. Fulbright scholar Oxford U., 1984-85. Mem. ABA, Am. Econ. Assn., Assn. Am. Law Schs. (chmn. antitrust sect. 1985-87). Office: Cornell Law Sch 214 Myron Taylor Hall Ithaca NY 14853-4901

HAY, GEORGE AUSTIN, actor, producer, director, musician, artist; b. Johnstown, Pa., Dec. 25, 1915; s. George and Mary Louise (Austin) H. BS, U. Pitts., 1938; postgrad., U. Rochester, 1939; MLitt, U. Pitts., 1948; MA, Columbia U., 1948. dir. Jr. League hosp. shows, N.Y.C., 1948-53. *As a kind of legacy from his physician and surgeon father, Austin Hay has enjoyed a regimen of lifelong healthfulness. In his impressionable youth, he became markedly inspired by knowing two young local figures: an obscure endlessly exuberant, surprisingly skilled, astonishingly agile, indefatigable teacher in his own home town--by the name of Gene Kelly; and a lanky assistant to a prestidigitator in a neighboring small town--unknown Princeton student, James Stewart. To a youngster, all this exemplified magical adventureland. Manifestly from such extraordinary early influences, a career in theater and movies followed. Through ensuing halcyon times, friendships continued with notables in the field, among them, "the most trusted man in America", television's Walter Cronkite, in whose home and yacht, on Martha's Vineyard, Austin Hay has been welcomed. In a lively saga of effort to broaden horizons and enhance quality of life, it is an enriching venture to strive for excellence in a variety of disciplines, to persevere as well as serve in different fields of creative endeavor. Being born on Christmas day, He helps nurture in a joyous way a wondrous continuing ethic of faith, integrity, and healthful living.* Producer, dir. off-Broadway prodns., 1953-55; motion picture casting dir. for Dept. Def. films, Astoria Studios, N.Y., 1955-70, motion picture producer-dir., U.S. Dept. Transp., Washington, 1973—, Office Presdl. Personnel, The White House, 1993—; group exhbns. of paintings and sculpture include, Lincoln Ctr., N.Y.C., 1965, Parrish Art Mus., Southampton, N.Y., 1969, Carnegie Inst., 1972, Duncan Galleries, N.Y.C., 1973, Bicentennial Exhbn. Am. Painters, Paris, 1976, Chevy Chase Gallery, 1979, Watergate Gallery, 1981, Le Salon des Nations a Paris, 1983; rep. permanent collections, Met. Mus. Art, N.Y.C., Library Congress, also, pvt. collections; bibliog. reference to works pub. in History of Internat. Art, 1982; author, illustrator: Seven Hops to Australia, 1945, The Moving Image, A Career in Pictures, 1990; Dir.: Bicentennial documentary Highways of History, 1976; dir.: film World Painting in Museum of Modern Art, 1972; Composer: Rhapsody in E Flat for piano and strings, 1950; writer: TV program Nat. Council Chs., 1965; Broadway appearances include: What Every Woman Knows, 1954; original Broadway run of Inherit the Wind, 1955-57; created role of Prof. Fiveash in premiere of The Acrobats, White Barn Theater, Westport, Conn., 1961; feature films include: Murder, Inc., 1960, Pretty Boy Floyd, 1960, The Landlord, 1970, Child's Play, 1971, Chekhov's The Bet, 1978, Being There, 1980, No Way Out, 1986, Her Alibi, 1988, The Distinguished Gentleman, 1992, Guarding Tess, 1994, Contact, 1997; TV appearances include Am. Heritage, 1961, Americans-A Portrait in Verses, 1962, Naked City, 1962, U.S. Steel Hour, 1963, Another World, 1965, Edge of Night, 1968, As the World Turns, 1969, Love Is a Many-Splendored Thing, 1972, The Adams Chronicles, 1976, A Woman Named Jackie, 1991; piano soloist in concerts and recitals, 1937; performer Cruise Ship, Europe, 1938; author, illustrator: The Arts Scene; entrepreneur in mgmt. of property, portfolio of stocks and bonds; contbr. articles to periodicals. Apptd. time adv. panel, pres.'s coun. Coll. William and Mary; mem. World Affairs Coun., Am. Archtl. Found.; bd. govs., trustee Hist. Home of Pres. James Monroe; mus. donor Am. doctor's office turn-of-century period preservation; bd. dirs. Washington Film Coun. With AUS, 1942-46, PTO. Recipient Loyal Svc. award Jr. League, 1953, St. Bartholomew's Silver Leadership award, 1966, Gold medal Accademia Italia, 1980, Smithsonian Instn. Pictorial award, 1982; Fed. Govt. Honor award in recognition 40 yrs. dedicated svc., 1995; subject of biog. work: Austin Hay, Adventures of a Christmas Child, 1970. Mem. NATAS, AFTRA, SAG, Am. Artists Profl. League, Allied Artists Am., Internat. Bach Soc., Beethoven Soc. (bd. dirs.), Nat. Soc. Arts and Letters (bd. dirs.), Music Libr. Assn., Nat. Symphony Orch. Assn., Actors Equity Assn., Nat. Assn. Investors, Nat. Trust Hist. Preservation, SAR, Nat. Parks and Conservation Assn., Shakespeare Oxford Soc., St. Andrew's Soc., Victorian Soc. (bd. dirs.), Cambria County Hist. Soc., Am. Philatelic Soc., Am. Mus. Moving Image, Jimmy Stewart Mus. (Indiana, Pa.), English Speaking Union (bd. dirs.), Nat. Arts Club (N.Y.C.), Players Club (N.Y.C.), Nat. Travel Club, Columbia U. Club, Nat. Press Club, Arts Club of Washington, Classic Car Club Am., Nat. Naval Med. Command, Sigma Chi, Phi Mu Alpha. Home: 2022 Columbia Rd NW Washington DC 20009-1352 Office: US Dept Transp 400 7th St SW Washington DC 20590-0001 also: Hay Ave Johnstown PA 15902

HAY, HOWARD CLINTON, lawyer; b. Portland, Maine, Apr. 16, 1944; s. Willis and Ruth (Clark) H.; m. Carol Anne Newsome, Dec. 21, 1968; children: Mark, David, Scott. AB (with distinction), Duke U., 1966; JD magna cum laude, U. Mich., 1969. Bar: U.S. Supreme Ct. 1977, Calif. 1970. Law clerk U.S. Ct. Appeals, Boston, 1970; atty. NLRB; ptnr. Paul, Hastings, Janofsky & Walker, Costa Mesa, Calif., 1971—; program chmn. Certificate in Employee Rels. Law; instr. U. S.C. Grad. Sch. Bus. Editor Mich. Law Review; contbr. articles to profl. jours. Mem. State Bar Calif. (exec. com. labor and employment sect.), Calif. Bar Assn. Office: Paul Hastings Janofsky & Walker 695 Town Center Dr Fl 17 Costa Mesa CA 92626-1924

HAY, JESS THOMAS, retired finance company executive; b. Forney, Tex., Jan. 22, 1931; s. George and Myrtle Hay; m. Betty Jo Peacock, 1951; children: Deborah Hay Spradley, Patricia Hay Daibert. BBA, So. Meth. U., 1953, JD magna cum laude, 1955. Bar: Tex. Assoc. Locke, Purnell, Boren, Laney & Neely, 1955-61, partner, 1961-65; pres., chief exec. officer Lomas Fin. Corp., Dallas, 1965-69, chmn. bd., chief exec. officer, 1969-94; chmn. bd., chief exec. officer, trustee Lomas & Nettleton Mortgage Investors, 1969-92; chmn., CEO Capstead Mortgage Corp. (formerly Lomas & Nettleton), 1985-91; bd. dirs. Trinity Industries, Inc., Exxon Corp., Viad Corp., SBC Comm. Inc.; chmn. HCB Enterprises Inc. Former mem. Dem. Nat. Com., also former nat. fin. chmn.; former chmn. bd. regents U. Tex. Sys.; former mem. Dallas Citizens Coun., Dallas Assembly; mem. Greater Dallas Planning Coun.; mem. WWII Meml. Adv. Bd.; bd. dirs. Tex. Rsch. League, North Tex. Food Bank, Child Care Partnership Dallas, Dallas County Hist. Found.; chmn. bd. Tex. Found. for Higher Edn.; trustee Southwestern Med. Found. Recipient Disting. Service award Assn. Governing Bds. of Univs. and Colls., 1987. Mem. ABA, Dallas Bar Assn., Tex. Bar Assn., Am. Judicature Soc., Newcomen Soc. N.Am., U.S. C. of C. Methodist. Home: 7236 Lupton Cir Dallas TX 75225-1737 Office: 2200 Ross Ave Ste 4300 Dallas TX 75201-2787

HAY, LEROY E., school system administrator. BA in Secondary English Edn., SUNY, Cortland, 1966; MA in Theatre, U. Conn., 1971, 6th-yr. cert. in adminstrn., 1977, PhD in Secondary Edn., 1978. Tchr. English, Marcellus (N.Y.) High Sch., 1966-68; tchr. English, Manchester (Conn.) High Sch., 1968-89, chmn. dept., 1983-89, interim. vice prin., 1988-89; asst. supt. schs. East Lyme (Conn.) Pub. Schs., 1989-92, acting supt., 1990; supt. schs. Windsor Locks (Conn.) Pub. Schs., 1992-93; asst. supt. schs. Wallingford (Conn.) Pub. Schs., 1993—; founding faculty mem. MS program in edn. innovation and tech. Walden U., 1994—; adj. instr. Boston Coll., 1987—, U. Conn., Sacred Heart U., Bridgeport, Conn., Manchester C.C. cons. on English teaching Granby (Conn.) Pub. Schs., 1988; mem. English adv. bd. Conn. Dept. Edn., 1987-90; mem. adv. bd. Conn. Inst. for Tchr. Evaluation, 1987-89; mem. Presdl. Scholars Commn., 1983-84; grant reviewer U.S. Dept. Edn.; mem. nat. adv. bd. Project 6 Found., Nat. Ctr. for Innovative Ednl. Media., 1987-93. Author: (with Richard Zboray) Complete Communication Skills, 1992; contbg. author: The Shape of Things to Come: Employment and Higher Education to the Year 2000, 1988; editor: (with Arthur Roberts) Curriculum For the New Millennium, 1988, 2d edit., 1994; mem. editorial adv. bd. Edn. Digest, 1984-86; contbr. articles to profl. publs. Mem. Conn. Gov.'s Commn. on Equity and Excellence in Edn., 1984-85, Congl. Task Force on Merit Pay, 1984; judge Birmingham Internat. Ednl. Film Festival, 1984. Named Nat. Tchr. of Yr., 1983, Disting. alumnus SUNY at Cortland and U. Conn. Mem. ASCD (bd. dirs. 1990—, exec. coun. 1996-99, pres.-elect 1999—), nat. conv. adv. com. 1990-92), Conn. ASCD (bd. dirs. 1988-90, v.p. 1990-92, pres. 1992-94), World Future Soc., U. Conn. Alumni Assn., Phi Delta Kappa. Home: 33 Risley Rd Vernon CT 06066-5924 Office: Wallingford Pub Schs 142 Hope Hill Rd Wallingford CT 06492-2254

HAY, RICHARD LE ROY, geology educator; b. Goshen, Ind., Apr. 29, 1926; s. Edward Le Roy and Angela H.; m. Barbara J. Herbert, Dec. 13, 1956; 1 child, Randall E.; m. Lynn Simonds, July 14, 1973. BS, Northwestern U., 1946, MS, 1948; PhD, Princeton U., 1952. Asst. prof. geology La. State U., Baton Rouge, 1955-57; asst. prof. to prof. geology and geophysics U. Calif., Berkeley, 1957-83; Ralph E. Grim prof. geology U. Ill., Urbana-Champaign, 1983-97; geologist U.S. Geol. Survey, intermittently 1948-84. Author: Geology of the Olduvai Gorge, 1976. Recipient Arnold Guyot award Nat. Geog. Soc., 1978. Fellow AAAS, Geol. Soc. Am. (Kirk Bryan award 1978), Mineral. Soc. Am., Calif. Acad. Sci. Home: 4320 N Alvernon Way Tucson AZ 85718-6180

HAY, ROBERT DEAN, retired management educator; b. LaPorte, Ind., Nov. 17, 1921; s. Carl Roy and Almetta (Diedrich) H.; m. Margaret B. Appelman, 1944; children—Sue Ann, Carol Lynn, Taj Margaret. B.S., U. Okla., 1949, M.B.A., 1950; Ph.D., Ohio State U., 1954. C.P.A., Okla. Mem. faculty U. Ark., Fayetteville, 1949-90, mem. emeritus, 1990—; prof. mgmt. U. Ark., 1959-86, Univ. prof., 1986-90. Author: (with F. Broyles) Athletic Administration, 1979, (with Ed Gray and Paul Smith) Business and Society, 1989, Strategic Management in Non-Profit Organizations, 1990; also 10 other books. Served with USAAF, 1942-47. Mem. Am. Bus. Communications Assn., Acad. Mgmt., Case Rsch. Assn., other profl. orgns. Office: Univ Ark Mgmt Dept Fayetteville AR 72701

HAY, ROBERT PETTUS, history educator; b. Eagleville, Tenn., Oct. 23, 1941; s. Ira James and Alice Elizabeth (Pettus) H.; m. Carla Jean Humphrey, Dec. 31, 1966. BS with highest honors, Middle Tenn. State U., 1962; PhD, U. Ky., 1967. Instr. history Middle Tenn. State U., Murfreesboro, 1964; lectr. history U. Ky., 1966-67, instr. history Sch. Edn.'s Nat. Def. Edn. Act Inst., 1967; asst. prof. history Marquette U., Milw., 1967-71, assoc. prof., 1971—, asst. chmn. dept., 1975, chmn. dept., dir. grad. study, 1975-79. Assoc. history editor USA Today, 1980—; contbr. numerous articles and commentaries to hist., popular and profl. jours., book reviewer numerous publs.; author poetry and chpts. in books. Mem. Milw. County Zool. Soc., Milw. Art Mus., Friends of Milw. County Pub. Mus., Tenn. State Mus. Assn., Colonial Williamsburg Found., Friends of John F. Kennedy Libr. Found., Art Inst. Chgo., Habitat for Humanity Internat. U.S. Com. for UNICEF, Brookfield Civic Ctr. Farmers' Market Assn.; adv. coun. Bradley Inst. Dem. & Pub. Values, 1988-89; dir's. cir. Patrick & Beatrice Haggerty Mus. Art, Middle Tenn. State U. Found.; life mem. pres.'s coun. Marquette U.; life mem. U. Ky. Fellows; rsch. grantee Marquette U., 1968, grantee Bradley Inst. Democracy & Pub. Values, 1989; summer faculty fellow Marquette U., 1969, 73. Commd. Ky. Col., 1980, Woodrow Wilson fellow, 1962-63, 65-66, NDEA fellow, 1962-65, NEH fellow, 1969-70. Mem. AAUP, Orgn. Am. Historians (life), Am. Soc. for 18th Century Studies, So. Hist. Assn. (life), Soc. Historians Early Am. Rep. (life), Tenn. Hist. Soc. (life), Am. Cath. Hist. Assn. (life), Milw. County Hist. Soc. (life), Ky. Hist. Soc. (life), Filson Club (life), Am. Hist. Assn. (life), Milw. Met. Historians Assn., East. Tenn. Hist. Soc. (life), Nat. Trust Hist. Preservation, West Tenn. Hist. Soc. (life), Inst. Early Am. History and Culture, Ctr. for Study of Presidency, Wis. Assn. Promotion of History, Waukesha County Hist. Soc. (life), Wis. Club, Helfaer Recreation Ctr., Atlanta Track Club, Phi Alpha Theta, Pi Gamma Mu. Democrat. Roman Catholic. Avocations: running, gardening, poetry, weight-lifting, basketball. Home: 2146 Laura Ln Waukesha WI 53186-2858 Office: Marquette U PO Box 1881 Dept History Milwaukee WI 53201-1881

HAY, SUSAN STAHR HELLER, museum curator; b. Mpls., Oct. 12, 1938; d. John Lewis and Suzanne Wallace (Finley) Heller; m. Edwin J. Anderson (div.); 1 child, Fletcher Scott Anderson; m. Edward Merrill Hay, July 20, 1984. BA in French Linguistics, Cornell U., 1960; MA in French Lit., Brown U., 1963; MA in Am. Civilization, U. Pa., 1981. From curatorial asst. to mus. curator Nat. Hist. Park, Phila., 1976-78; editor W. B. Saunders Co., Phila., 1978-79; asst. mng. editor Am. Quar., 1979-80; teaching fellow U. Pa., Phila., 1980-81; curatorial asst. costume and textiles Phila Mus. Art, 1981-82, asst. curator costume and textiles, 1982-85; curator costume and textiles Mus. Art R.I. Sch. Design, Providence, 1985—; lectr. and presenter papers in field. Contbr. articles to profl. jours. Past v.p., trustee Coggeshall Farm Mus., Bristol, R.I.; past trustee Smith's Castle Historic Site, Wickford, R.I. Cooper-Woods Meml. Travel Study grant English Speaking Union,

1978. Mem. Am. Assn. Mus., Costume Soc. Am. Textile Soc. Am., Ctr. Internat. d'Etudes des Textiles Anciens., Tex. Soc. Am. (ea. rep. bd. trustees). Home: 108 Davis St Rehoboth MA 02769-1604 Office: RI Sch Design Mus Art 224 Benefit St Providence RI 02903-2723

HAYAKAWA, KAN-ICHI, food science educator; b. Shibukawa, Gumma, Japan, Aug. 12, 1931; came to U.S., 1961, naturalized, 1974; s. Chyogoro and Kin (Hayakawa) H.; m. Setsuko Maekawa, Feb. 18, 1967. *Grandparents are late Kurasaburo (son of a cottage school teacher, descendant of over 15 generations of Buddhist priests) and Wasa. Godfather is late Chyotaro Harizuka, founder of Japanese sericulture college education. Brothers are Nagao, a retired labor union leader, and Jiro, a professor emeritus at Waseda University. Sister Kiyoko (Mrs. Kazuo Watanabe), is ailing. Setsuko's parents are the late Takuji, a physician, and Kou Maekawa, one of the first registered nurses in Japan. Her brother is Makotoo Maekawa.* BS, Tokyo U. Fisheries, 1955; PhD, Rutgers U., 1964. Bar: N.J., N.Y. Rsch. fellow Canners' Assn. Japan, 1955-60; asst. prof. food sci. Rutgers U., New Brunswick, N.J., 1964-70; assoc. prof. food sci. Rutgers U., 1970-77, prof. food engring., 1977-82, Disting. prof. food engring., 1982-99; counsel, corp. sec. Nitto Permacel Corp.; OAS vis. prof. U. Campinas, Brazil, summers 1972, 73, vis. prof., 1994; cons. to food processing cos.; organizer, chmn., participant NSF sponsored U.S.-Japan Coop. Conf., Tokyo, 1979; lectr. Industry R&D Inst. and Nat. Taiwan U., 1982, Wuxi Inst. Light Industry, China, 1986, Tokyo U. of Fisheries, 1992. Co-editor: Heat Sterilization of Food, 1983. Contbr. articles to books, profl. jours. and encys.; developer new math methods for predicting safety of food processes; found theoretical and exptl. theorems on heat and mass transfer in biol. material with or without strain--stress formation. Rsch. grantee USPHS, 1966-73, Nabisco Found., 1975-76, NSF, 1981-82, travel grantee NSF, 1972, Rutgers Rsch. Found., 1977, rsch. grantee Advanced Food Tech. Ctr., 1985-89, John von Neumann Nat. Supercomputer Ctr., 1989-90, Pitts. Nat. Supercomputer Ctrs., NSF, 1990-97, Cray Rsch. Inc., 1993-95, U.S. Army Natick R&D Ctr., 1992-94, USDA, 1994-98. Fellow Inst. Food Technologists; mem. AAAS, Am. Inst. Chem. Engrs., ASHRAE (life, chmn. tech. com. on thermophys. property values of food 1981-85, mem. com. 1981-96), Am. Soc. Agrl. Engrs., Can. Inst. Food Sci. and Tech., Sigma Xi. Home: 631 Lake Dr Princeton NJ 08540-5634 Office: Rutgers U Dept Food Sci 65 Dudley Rd New Brunswick NJ 08901-8520

HAYASAKI, YOSHI, coach. B, Univ. Washington, 1971; M, Univ. Ill., 1973. Asst. coach Univ. Ill., 1971-73, coach, 1974-92, program dir., 1993-96, head coach, 1997—; coaching staff 1988 Summer Olympics, Seoul, U.S. head coach 1989 Golden Sands Internat., Bulgaira, head coach 1986 Moncado Cup, Havana, Cuba, head coach 1985 USA World Univ. Games, head coach 1984 Coca-Cola Internat., London, coach U.S. Olympic Festival, 1978, 85. Recipient USA All-Around Champion, 1968, 69, NCAA All-Around Champion, 1970, 71, Big Ten Coach of Yr., Nat. Coach of Yr. Office: Univ Ill Athletic Dept 1700 S 4th St Champaign IL 61820-6941

HAYASHI, ALAN T., mathematics educator; b. Honolulu, Mar. 10, 1954; s. Harold T. and Sally S. (Nakamoto) H.; married. BSc, AB, U. Calif., Riverside, 1975; postgrad., Ohio State U., 1983-84. Cert. secondary tchr., single subject teaching and community coll. instr.'s credentials, Calif. Tchr., coach boys track and girls basektball Jurupa Jr. High Sch., Jurupa Unified Sch. Dist., Riverside, Calif., 1976-79; tchr. math., coach acad. decathlon and knowledge bowl Channel Islands High Sch., Oxnard (Calif.) Union High Sch. Dist., 1979-91; instr. Oxnard Coll., Ventura County C.C. Dist., 1989—, dept. chmn., 1995, 98; casino dealer Harrah's Hotel & Casino, Stateline, Nev., 1980-81; teaching asst., instr. Ohio State U., Columbus, 1983-84; mathematician Pacific Missile Test Ctr., U.S. Dept. Def., Point Mugu, Calif., 1990; textbook reviewer Calif. Dept. Edn., 1981, 89; statistician Channel Islands High Sch. football team, 1980-92; asst. dir. summer inst. Calif. State Math. Project/Tri-County Math Project, 1996, co-dir., 1997-99. Contbg. author: Prentice-Hall Interactive Math Program, 1998. Newsletter editor Internat. Rels. Coun. Riverside, 1975-77. Recipient Chpt. Outstanding Tchr. award Calif. Mini-Corp., 1991-92, Tandy Tech. scholar nat. semi-finalist, 1990-91; named Tchr. of Yr., Calif. Scholastic Fedn. chpt., 1989, Channel Islands H.S. Tchr. of Yr., 1983, Oxnard Coll. Acad. Senate Treas., 1994, 97; NSF fellow, 1981, 82, Calif. Math Project/Tri-County Math Project fellow, 1994, sr. fellow, 1995, TCMP Leadership Network fellow, 1995—. Mem. NEA, Math. Assn. Am., Nat. Coun. Tchrs. Math., U. Calif.-Riverside Alumni Assn., Calif. Fedn. Tchrs., Ventura County Math. Coun. (bd. dirs. 1998—). Office: Oxnard Coll 4000 S Rose Ave Oxnard CA 93033-6699

HAYASHI, HAJIME, immunologist; b. Gifu, Japan, Aug. 26, 1927; came to U.S., 1955.; s. Sho and Masao Hayashi; m. Takeko Kochi, Dec. 21, 1962; children: Masako, Keiko. Diploma in veterinary medicine, Gifu U., 1948; BS, Mich. State U., 1957, MS, 1959, PhD, 1961. Grad. asst. Mich. State U., East Lansing, 1959-61; assoc. Henry Ford Hosp., Detroit, 1961-69; dir. immunology Henry Ford Hosp., 1969—; assoc. prof. Case Western Res. U., Cleve., 1994—. Contbr. articles to profl. jours. Recipient Difco award APHA, 1981, Disting. Career award Henry Ford Med. Assn., 1997. Fellow Am. Acad. Microbiology; mem. AAAS, APHA, Am. Soc. Histocompatibility Immunogenetics, Am. Soc. Microbiology (pres. Mich. br. 1991-92), Microscopy Assn. Am., Internat. Soc. Analytical Cytology, Soc. Leukocyte Biology, Soc. In Vitro Biology, N.Y. Acad. Scis., Transplantation Soc. Mich. (bd. dirs. 1994—), United Network for Organ Sharing, Gt. Lakes Transplantation Assn. (bd. dirs. 1987—), Mich. State U. CNS Alumni Assn. (bd. dirs. 1991—, pres. 1996-97), Sigma Xi. Achievements include research in immunology of organ transplatation and AIDS. Home: 13322 Borgman Ave Huntington Woods MI 48070-1006 Office: Henry Ford Hosp 2799 W Grand Blvd Detroit MI 48202-2689

HAYASHI, MITSUHIKO, retired physics educator; b. Okazaki, Aichi Pref, Japan, Sept. 3, 1930; s. Katsuzo and Rakuko (Morita) H.; m. Etsuko Ito, Oct. 18, 1964; children: Mayura, Nao. BS, Nagoya (Japan) U., 1958, MS, 1960; PhD, Tokyo Inst. Tech., 1971. Rsch. assoc. Nagoya U., 1960-70, asst. prof., 1970-75, assoc. prof., 1975-76; prof. Toyama (Japan) Med. and Pharm. U., 1976-96, prof. emeritus, 1996—; lectr. Kinjo Women's Coll., Nagoya, 1962-73, Toyama U., 1985-90; cons. Noritake China Co., Nagoya, 1973-76; vis. scientist U. Wash., Seattle, 1980-81, 82, Tech. U. Denmark, Lyngby, 1986; guest prof. Delft U. Tech., The Netherlands, 1987. Author: Introductory Physics, 1966, Ultrafine Particles 1984; contbr. articles to profl. jours. Supporting mem. Asia Health Inst., Nisshin, Japan, 1978—, Yamabato Home for Disabled, Makinohara, Japan, 1980—. Mem. Phys. Soc. Japan, Am. Phys. Soc. Presbyterian. Avocation: concerts. Home: 831-2758 Kitayama Obata, Moriyama-ku Nagoya 463-0011, Japan

HAYASHI, TERU, zoologist, educator; b. Atlantic City, Feb. 12, 1914; s. Andrew Tetsuji and Shizuka H.; m. Sarah Darlington Rexon, Sept. 22, 1943; children: Curt, Tesa, Tomi, Tuck; m. Sarah Dixon Browne, May 15, 1970. BS, Ursinus Coll., 1938, ScD (hon.), 1992; student, U. Pa., 1939; PhD, U. Mo., 1943; ScD (hon.), Ursinus Coll., 1991. Instr. physics USAAF-ASTP program, 1943- 44; instr. zoology U. Mo., 1944-45, research asso. zoology, 1945-46; mem. faculty Columbia, 1946-67, prof. zoology, 1958-67, chmn. dept. zoology, 1963-67; prof., chmn. dept. biology Ill. Inst. Tech., Chgo., 1967-79; sr. scientist Papanicolaou Cancer Research Inst., Miami, Fla., 1980-85; prof. emeritus dept. biochemistry U. Miami, 1984—; vis. prof. Japan Soc. Promotion Sci., 1974; Mem. NRC. Author articles in field.; Editor: Subcellular Particles; co-editor: Molecular Architecture in Cell Physiology. Trustee Marine Biol. Lab., Woods Hole, Mass., 1968—. Recipient award Ill. Acad. Sci., 1978, Alexander von Humboldt award, 1979; Fulbright and Guggenheim fellow Denmark, 1954-55; Fulbright fellow Germany, 1975. Mem. Soc. Gen. Physiologists (pres. 1962-63), Am. Inst. Biol. Scis., Am. Physiol. Soc., Harvey Soc., Am. Soc. Cell Biology, AAAS, Biophys. Soc., Japan Soc. Cell Biology. *

HAYASHI, TETSUMARO, English and American literature educator, author; b. Sakaide City, Japan, Mar. 22, 1929; came to U.S., 1954, naturalized, 1969; s. Tetsuro and Shieko (Honjyo) H.; m. Akiko Sakuratani, Apr. 14, 1960; 1 son, Richard Hideki. BA, Okayama (Japan) U., 1953; MA, U. Fla., 1957, Kent State U., 1959; PhD, Kent State U., 1968. Assoc. dir. Culver-Stockton Coll. Libr., Canton, Mo., 1959-63; instr. English Kent State U., Ohio, 1965-68; prof. English Ball State U., Muncie, Ind., 1977-93; dir. Steinbeck Rsch. Inst., 1981-93; vis. grad. prof. Kwassui Women's Coll., Japan, 1993-96; v.p., grad. prof. English Yasuda Women's U., Hiroshima, Japan, 1996—. Author: Sketches of American Culture, 1960, John Steinbeck: A Concise Bibliography, 1967, Arthur Miller Criticism, 1969, Robert Greene Criticism, 1971, Shakespeare's Sonnets: A Record of 20th Century Criticism, 1972, Index to Arthur Miller: Criticism, 1976; editor: A Looking Glass for London and England (Thomas Lodge, Robert Greene), An Elizabethan Text, 1970, (with Richard Astro) Steinbeck: The Man and His Work, 1971, John Steinbeck: A Dictionary of His Fictional Characters, 1976; Steinbeck's Literary Dimension, 1973, series II, 1991, A Study Guide to Steinbeck: A Handbook of His Major Works, 1974, 79, 93; also 21 other books, 21 monographs; founder, editor-in-chief: Steinbeck Quar., 1968-93, Steinbeck Monograph Series, 1970-93. Rotary Internat. jr. fellow U. Fla., 1957, Folger sr. fellow, 1972; grantee Am. Philos. Soc., 1975, 81, Am. Coun. Learned Socs., 1976, Bernard Boyd Meml. Found., 1986, Lyndon B. Johnson Found., 1987, other founds. Mem. MLA, Am. Lit. Assn., Shakespeare Assn. Am., Internat. John Steinbeck Soc. (co-founder, pres.). Home: C/O Richard Hayashi 1376 N Claridge Way Carmel IN 46032-8309

HAYCOCK, CHRISTINE ELIZABETH, medical educator emeritus, health educator; b. Mt. Vernon, N.Y., Jan. 7, 1924; d. John B. and Madeline (Sears) H.; m. Sam Moskowitz, July 6, 1958 (dec. Apr. 1997). SB, U. Chgo., 1948; MD, SUNY, Bklyn., 1952; MA in Polit. Sci., Rutgers U., 1981. RN, N.J.; diplomate Am. Bd. Surgery. Intern Walter Reed Army Med. Ctr., Washington, 1952-53; resident in surgery St. Barnabas Med. Ctr., Newark, 1954-58, St. John's Episcopal Hosp., Bklyn., 1958-59; pvt. practice Newark, 1959-68; asst. prof. surgery, N.J. Med. Sch. U. Med. and Dentistry N.J.-N.J. Med. Sch., Newark, 1968-75; assoc. prof. surgery, N.J. Med. Sch. UMDNJ, Newark, 1975-89, prof. clin. surgery, 1989-92; prof. emeritus, 1992—; chief GYN Clinic, VA Hosp., East Orange, N.J. Trauma Soc.; pres. Med. Amature Radio Coun., 1981, bd. dirs. (Coun. award 1978); editorial bd. Jour. N.J. Med. Soc., 1979-95, The Physician and Sports Medicine, 1975—, The Main Event, 1987; adv. com. N.J. Phys. Conditioning of the Police Tng. Commn., 1984-96. Editor: Trauma and Pregnancy, 1985, Sports Medicine for the Athletic Female, 1980; contbr. articles to profl. jours. Chmn. bd. Essex County chpt. Am. Cancer Soc., West Orange, N.J., 1978-79, bd. mgrs., Livingston, N.J., 1962—, hon. life mem., 1992. With U.S. Army, 1947-86, col. Res. ret. Recipient Outstanding Alumnae award Bloomfield Coll., 1971, Res. Forces Achievement award, 1974, Distinguished Lecturer award Downstate Med. Ctr., 1976, Dr. Frank L. Babbott Meml. award SUNY Alumni Assn., 1982, Pres. Honor citation, N.J. Assn. Phys. Edn. and Health Tchrs., 1982, Presdl. Citation, N.J. Assn. for Health, Phys. Edn. and Recreation, 1984, Med. Bd. Svc. award Newark City Hosp., 1986, Bertha Van Hoosen award Am. Med. Women's Assn., 1997; grantee Abbott Labs, 1981-82. Fellow ACS (hon., life, N.J. com. on trauma 1970-91), Am. Coll. Sports Medicine (trustee 1978-80), Photog. Soc. Am. (chmn. video/motion picture divsn. 1993-95); mem. AMA, Am. Med. Women's Assn. (bd. dirs. 1976-86, pres. 1980, hosp. assn. com. 1985—, Silver Medallion award 1980), Zonta Internat., Assn. Women Surgeons (treas. 1989-91, chair found. com. 1991-95, sec. 1995—, Disting. Surgeon award 1990), N.J. Women's Assn. (pres. 1976, treas. 1989-92, Woman of Yr. 1987), Amateur Radio Relay League. Republican. Avocations: photography, dog training, sports, collecting elephants, amateur radio. Home: 361 Roseville Ave Newark NJ 07107-1721

HAYCOCK, KENNETH ROY, educator, consultant, administrator; b. Hamilton, Ont., Can., Feb. 15, 1948; s. Bruce Frederick T. and Doris Marion P. (Downham) H.; m. Sheila Tripp, Jan. 28, 1990. BA, U. Western Ont., 1968, diploma in edn., 1969; specialist cert., U. Toronto, Can., 1971; MEd, U. Ottawa, Can., 1973; AMLS, U. Mich., 1974; EdD, Brigham Young U., 1991. Tchr., dept. head Glebe Collegiate Inst., Ottawa, 1969-70, Col. By Secondary Sch., Ottawa, 1970-72; cons. Wellington County Bd. Edn., Guelph, Ont., 1972-76; coord. libr. svcs., supr. instrn. Vancouver (Can.) Sch. Bd., 1976-84, acting mgr., elem./secondary edn., 1984-85, dir. instrn., head program svcs., 1985-89, 91-92; prin. Waverley Elem. Sch., 1989-91; prof., dir. Sch. Libr., Archival and Info. Studies U. B.C., Vancouver, 1992—; instr. univs. and colls.; pres. Ken Haycock and Assocs., Inc. Editor Tchr. Libr.; author various books; contbr. articles to profl. jours. Trustee Guelph Pub. Libr., 1975-76; trustee West Vancouver Sch. Bd., 1993—, chair, 1994-97. Recipient award Beta Phi Mu, 1976, Queen Elizabeth Silver Jubilee medal, 1977. Fellow Can. Coll. Tchrs.; mem. ALA (coun. 1995-99, exec. bd., 1999—), ASCD (urban curriculum leaders 1985-92, internat. panel 1990-94), IFLA (Internatl. Federation of Libr. Assns. and Institutions, section on Edn. and Trng.), 1997—, AASL (pres. 1997-98, Baker and Taylor Disting. Svc. award 1996), Can. Sch. Libr. Assn. (pres. 1974-75, Margaret B. Scott award of merit 1979, rsch. award 1984, 95, Disting. Sch. Adminstr. award 1989), B.C. Sch. Libr. Assn. (Ken Haycock Profl. Devel. award named in his honor 1984, Disting. Svc. award 1989), Ont. Libr. Assn., Can. Libr. Assn. (pres. 1977-78, Outstanding Svc. award 1991), Assn. for Libr. and Info. Sci. Edn. (sec. coun. dean and dirs. 1993-96), B.C. Libr. Assn., Ont. Libr. Assn., Internat. Assn. Sch. Librarianship (dir. N.Am. chpt. 1993-95, exec. dir. 1995—), Coun. for Can. Learning Resources (pres. 1995-98), Phi Delta Kappa (young leaders panel 1980). E-mail: ken.haycock@ubc.ca. Home: 5118 Meadfeild Rd, West Vancouver, BC Canada V7W 3G2 Office: U BC Sch Libr Arch and Info, Studies, 831-1956 Main Mall, Vancouver, BC Canada V6T 1Z1

HAYDANEK, RONALD EDWARD, lawyer and consultant; b. Chgo., Apr. 4, 1932; s. Edward J. and Rose (Hustoles) H.; m. Dorothy E. Mehalek, Nov. 17, 1956; children: Mary Jo, RaeJean (dec. Jan. 1994), Mark, Thomas, Beth Ann. BA, Ill. Benedictine Coll., 1954; MS in Indsl. Rels., Loyola U., Chgo., 1955, JD, 1959. Bar: Ill. 1959, D.C. 1974, Pa. 1976. Exec. asst. to pres. Ill. Benedictine Coll., Lisle, 1959-65; adminstrv. ptnr. Mayer, Brown & Platt, Chgo., 1965-73, Arnold & Porter, Washington, 1973-75, Schnader, Harrison, Segal & Lewis, Phila., 1975-94. Editor: Model Accounting Systems, 1977, Lawyer Advertising, 1980. Chmn. Hinsdale Community Relations Bd., Ill., 1965-68; trustee Benet Acad., Lisle, 1971-73. Served with USN, 1955-56. Recipient Alumnus of Yr. award Ill. Benedictine Coll., 1966. Fellow Found. for Econ. Edn., Coll. Law Practice Mgmt.; mem. ABA (chmn. econs. of law practice sect. 1985-87), Pa. Bar Assn., Phila. Bar Assn., Ill. Bar Assn., D.C. Bar Assn., Assn. Legal Adminstrs., Union League (Chgo.). Avocations: golf, tennis, swimming, skiing. ronúhaydanek@shsl.com. Home: 322 Harbour Dr 303A Naples FL 34103-4095 Office: Schnader Harrison Segal 1600 Market St Ste 3600 Philadelphia PA 19103-7240

HAYDAR, ZIAD RAFIC, geriatrician; b. Oct. 14, 1962. BS, Am. U. Beirut, 1983, MD, 1987. Resident in family practice Med. U. S.C., Charleston, 1991-94; postdoctoral fellow Johns Hopkins U., Balt., 1994-96; asst. chief geriatrics Baylor Health Care Sys., Dallas, 1997—. Avocations:sr.haydar@baylordallas.edu. Home: 16218 Red Cedar Trail Dallas TX 75248 Office: 4004 Worth Dallas TX 75246-1607

HAYDEL, RAYMOND, computer animation artist; b. Apr. 17, 1957. BFA in Drawing, U. Tex., San Antonio, 1987; MFA in Drawing, U. Idaho, 1991; AA in Computer Animation, Art Inst. Dallas, 1997. Bus. graphics artist U. Idaho, Moscow, 1989-91, fine arts instr., 1991-92; computer animation instr. Art Inst. Dallas, 1997—. Home: # 1520 8620 Park Ln Dallas TX 75231

HAYDEN, CARLA, library director. BA, Roosevelt U., 1973; MA in Libr. and Info. Sci., U. Chgo., 1977, PhD, 1987. Children's and young adult libr. Chgo. Pub. Libr., 1973-81; libr. svcs. coord. Mus. Sci. and Industry, Chgo., 1982-87; mem. faculty Sch. Libr. and Info. Sci., Pitts., 1987-91; chief libr. Chgo. Pub. Libr., 1991-93; dir. Enoch Pratt Free Libr., Balt., 1993—; adj. prof. U. Md., College Park, 1995—; faculty mem. L.I. U., N.Y., 1994, Columbia U., N.Y.C., 1990, 91. Contbr. numerous articles to profl. jours. Bd. dirs. Chesapeake Bay Trust, Md., Md. African Am. Mus. Corp., Goucher Coll., Md., Franklin and Eleanor Roosevelt Inst. and Libr., N.Y.C., Kennedy Krieger Inst., Balt., Md. Hist. Soc., Nat. Aquarium, Balt., U. Pitts. Sch. Info. Scis. Named Libr. of Yr., Libr. Jour., 1995, Md.'s Top 100 Women, 1996; recipient Legacy of Literacy award DuBois Cir., 1996, Andrew White medal Loyola Coll. Balt., 1997, Pres.'s medal Johns Hopkins U., 1998. Mem. ALA, Pub. Libr. Assn., Md. Libr. Assn. Office: Enoch Pratt Free Library 400 Cathedral St Baltimore MD 21201-4401

HAYDEN, DOLORES, author, architect, educator; b. N.Y.C., Mar. 15, 1945; d. J. Francis and Katharine (McCabe) H.; m. Peter Horsey Marris, May 18, 1975; 1 child, Laura Hayden Marris. BA, Mt. Holyoke Coll., 1966; diploma in English studies, Cambridge (Eng.) U., 1967; LHD (hon.), Mt. Holyoke Coll., 1987; MArch, Harvard U., 1972; diploma in English studies, Cambridge (Eng.) U., 1977; MA (hon.), Yale U., 1991. Registered architect. Lectr. U. Calif., Berkeley, 1973; assoc. prof. MIT, Cambridge, 1973-79; prof. UCLA, 1979-91, Yale U., New Haven, 1991—; Registered Arch., Conn.;. Author: Seven American Utopias, 1976, The Grand Domestic Revolution, 1981, Redesigning the American Dream, 1984 (award for outstanding publ. in urban planning Assn. Collegiate Schs. of Planning 1986), The Power of Place: Urban Landscapes as Public History, 1995 (Assn. Am. Pubs. award), Playing House, 1998; also articles (Best Feature Article award Jour. Am. Planning Assn. 1994). Guggenheim fellow, 1981, Rockefeller Humanities fellow, 1980, ACLS/Ford fellow, 1989, Nat. Endowment for the Humanities fellow; recipient Notable Book award ALA, 1984, Radcliffe Grad. Soc. medal, 1991, Preservation award L.A. Conservancy, 1986, Vesta award Woman's Bldg., L.A., 1985, Design Rsch. award Nat. Endowment for the Arts, Feminist scholarship in the arts. Mem. Am. Studies Assn., Orgn. Am. Historians, Am. Planning Assn. (Diana Donald award 1987, various awards L.A. and Calif. chpts.), Urban History Assn. (dir. 1991-93). Avocations: travel, poetry. E-mail: dolores.hayden@yale.edu. Office: Yale Univ Sch Architecture PO Box 208242 180 York St New Haven CT 06511-4804

HAYDEN, GARY THOMAS, contract management director; b. Jan. 10, 1949. BA in Econs., U. Pittsburgh, 1974; MBA, Pepperdine U., 1983. Purchasing mgr. Hughes Aircraft Co., Newport Beach, Calif., 1978-84; material mgr. GM Hughes Electronics, Fullerton, Carlsbad, Calif., 1985-92; dir. procurement Univ. of Pittsburgh, 1993-98, dir. contract mgmt., 1998—. E-mail: gth1@pitt.edu. Home and Office: 2528 Cathedral of Learning Pittsburgh PA 15260

HAYDEN, HARROLD HARRISON, information company executive; b. Cin., Jan. 16, 1942; s. Harold Richard and Blanche Marie (Sargent) H. BA, Millikin U., Decatur, Ill., 1964; MA, DePaul U., Chgo., 1970. Dir. mktg. tng. Automatic Electric, Northlake, Ill., 1968-70; dir. Universal Tng. Co., Wilmette, Ill., 1970-80; pres. Performance Achievement Group, Chgo., 1980-85; v.p. Lead Mgmt. Service, Chgo., 1985-90, Qualified Lead Systems, Chicago Heights, Ill., 1990—; pres. Intramark, Chicago Heights, Ill., 1992-94, chmn., 1995-97; pres. Pace Airline Svcs. USA, Chgo., 1994-97; exec dir. Internat. Meetings Inst., 1997—. Author: (multimedia package) Successful Telephone Selling, 1979, Santa Fe Railroad Data, 1975, Best Ill. award, 1975; editor Secrets of Successful Telemarketing, 1985. Mem. Ohlmstead Hist. Soc., Riverside, Ill., 1985; bd. dirs. 44th Ward Bus. Com., Chgo,. 1985-86; exec. mgr. British Consortium, 1989-91; bd. dirs. North Park Village, 1993-96; bd. dirs. Ill. Acad. Criminology, 1996—; vols. v.p. Am. Police Ctr. & Mus., 1996—. Recipient award Best Condo Bldg., Northside Real Estate Bd., Chgo., 1985. Mem. Am. Mgmt. Assn. (spkr. 1979-85), Pine Point Ski Club, Simply Singles (CEO). Avocations: sailing, skiing. Office: Internat Meetings Inst One World Trade Ctr 2400 Merchandise Mart Chicago IL 60654

HAYDEN, JOHN OLIN, English literature educator, author; b. Los Angeles, Dec. 18, 1932; s. John Ellsworth and Norah Elizabeth (Bussens) H.; m. Mary Kathleen Garland, Dec. 18, 1965; children—Michael, John, Mark, Ann. BA, U. Calif.-Santa Barbara, 1958; MA, Columbia U., 1959, PhD, 1965. Asst. prof. U. Colo., Boulder, 1964-66; assoc. prof. English lit. U. Calif.-Davis, 1966-75, prof. English lit., 1975-94, prof. emeritus, 1994—. Author: Romantic Reviewers, 1969, Polestar of the Ancients, 1979, William Wordsworth and the Mind of Man, 1993, Why the Great Books are Great, 1998; editor: Sir Walter Scott, 1970, Wordsworth: The Poems, 1977, Wordsworth: The Prose, 1988, Wordsworth: Selected Poetry, 1994. Served with USAF, 1951-55. E. J. Noble Found. fellow Columbia U., N.Y.C., 1959-61; fellow NEH, 1971, Am. Council Learned Socs., 1984. Democrat. Roman Catholic. Avocation: numismatics. Home: 25199 Carlsbad Ave Davis CA 95616-9434 Office: U Calif English Dept Davis CA 95616

HAYDEN, JOSEPH A., JR., lawyer; b. Newark, Apr. 2, 1944; s. Joseph A. and Mary (Giblin) H.; m. Donna Heinrich, Aug. 26, 1967; children: Kathryn Elizabeth, Patrick Joseph; m. Katharine Jackson Sweeney, July 19, 1987. Student, Boston Coll., 1966; JD magna cum laude, Rutgers U., 1969. Bar: N.J. 1969, U.S. Dist. Ct. N.J. 1969, N.Y. 1981. Law sec. to chief justice N.J. Supreme Ct., Trenton, 1969-70; dep. atty. gen. organized crime and spl. prosecution sect. Div. Criminal Justice, Atty. Gen.'s Office, Trenton, 1970-73; pvt. practice Newark, Hoboken and Weehawken, N.J., 1973—. Mem. editl bd. N.J. Law Jour., 1998—. Counsel to Essex County Dems., 1976-80; mem. adv. com. U.S. Dist. Ct. N.J. Named Top Lawyer N.J. Monthly mag., 1997. Fellow Am. Coll. Trial Lawyers, Am. Bar Found.; mem. FBA (trustee 1996-99), N.J. State Bar Assn. (prosecutorial and jud. appointment com. 1992-97, trustee 1998-99), Assn. Criminal Def. Lawyers N.J. (trustee 1985—, founder, 1st pres.), Ct. of Appeal Lawyers 3rd cir. (adv. com.), Fed. Bar Assn. (program chair 1998-99). Democrat. Avocations: running, recreational basketball, skiing. Home: 811 Hudson St Hoboken NJ 07030-5003 Office: Hayden & Silber 1500 Harbor Blvd Weehawken NJ 07087-6732

HAYDEN, JOSEPH PAGE, JR., company executive; b. Cin., Oct. 8, 1929; s. Joseph Page and Amy Dorothy (Weber) H.; m. Lois Taylor, Dec. 29, 1951; children: Joseph Page III, William Taylor, John Weber, Thomas Richard. B.S. in Bus, Miami U., Oxford, Ohio, 1951; student, U. Cin. Law Sch., 1952; DL (hon.), Miami U., 1986. With mobile home div. Midland-Guardian Co., Cin., 1952-61; v.p. Midland-Guardian Co., 1954-60; pres., chief exec. officer, dir. Midland Co., Cin., 1961-80; chmn. bd., CEO, dir. Midland Co., 1980-98, chmn. exec. com., bd. dirs., 1998—; bd. dirs. Firstar Corp., Cin. Mem. bus. adv. com. Miami U., Oxford, Ohio; mem. pres.'s council Xavier U., Cin.; bd. trustees Miami U. Found. Mem. Bankers Club, Met. Club (Cin., Ohio), Comml. Club (Ohio), Boca Bay Pass Club (Fla.), Lemon Bay Golf (Fla.), Useppa Island Club (Fla.), Sigma Chi. Clubs: Queen City, Hyde Park Golf and Country, University (Cin.); Boca Grande (Fla.). Office: 7000 Midland Blvd Amelia OH 45102-2608

HAYDEN, NEIL STEVEN, communications company executive; b. Bronx, N.Y., May 23, 1937; s. Aaron Alexander and Selma (Turtletaub) H.; m. Elaine Charlotte Lawson, July 3, 1960 (div. 1975); children: Stephanie, Jennifer, Aaron II; m. Carolyn Sue Carper, May 8, 1975 (div. 1985); m. Ellen Maxine Sulcov, Feb. 4, 1990. Student, U. Fla., 1955-58; student, U. Miami, Fla., 1958. With copy staff Miami Herald, 1958; reporter Albany Herald, 1959, Hickory Daily Record, Hickory, N.C., 1959-60; editor The Jackson Herald, Jefferson, Ga., 1960-62; editor, publ. The Hartwell Sun, Hartwell, Ga., 1962-67; publ. Athens Banner-Herald & The Daily News, Athens, Ga., 1967-72; pres., publ. Huntington Herald-Dispatch & Huntington Advertiser, Huntington, W.Va., 1972-76, Statesman and Capital Jour., Salem, Oreg., 1976-79, Courier-Post, Camden, N.J., 1979-80, The Bulletin, Phila., 1980-82; pres., chief operating officer Herald Examiner, Hearst Community Newspapers, L.A., 1982-84; pres. AD/SAT, Inc., N.Y.C., 1984-92, Capital Devel. Assocs., Inc., Fair Lawn, N.J., 1992—; pres., CEO Agora, Inc., Balt., 1993—; pres. Mktg. & Pub. Assocs., Ltd., Fair Lawn, 1993—. Bd. dirs. World Affairs Council Phila.; bd. dirs. Police Athletic League; mem. Phila. Orchestra Council; bd. dirs. Phila. Conv. & Visitors Bur.; mem. Greater Phila. Partnership; mem. adv. bd. Haddonfield (N.J.) Symphony Soc. Mem. Am. Newspaper Publs. Assn., Am. Soc. Newspaper Editors; Nat. Newspaper Assn., Advt. Counc. Newspaper Com., Am. Coun. on Edn. for Journalism and Mass Communications; Women in Communications, Inc., Calif. Newspaper Publs. Assn., Greater Phila. C. of C. (bd. dirs.), Newsletter Pub. Assn. Home: 749 Rivenwood Rd Franklin Lakes NJ 07417-1443 Office: Mktg & Pub Assocs Ltd 23-00 State Rt 208 Fair Lawn NJ 07410-1558

HAYDEN, RAYMOND PAUL, lawyer; b. Rochester, N.Y., Jan. 15, 1939; s. John Joseph and Orpha (Lindsay) H.; m. Suzanne Saloy, Sept. 1, 1962; children—Thomas Gerard, Christopher Matthew. BS in Marine Transit, SUNY Maritime Coll., 1960; LLB, Syracuse U., 1963. Bar: N.Y. 1963, U.S. Ct. Appeals (2d cir.) 1963, U.S. Dist. Ct. (ea. and so. dists.) N.Y. 1964, U.S. Supreme Ct. 1967. Assoc. Haight Gardner Poor & Havens, N.Y.C., 1963-70; asst. gen. counsel Commonwealth Oil Co., N.Y.C., 1970-71; ptnr. Hill Rivkins & Hayden LLP, N.Y.C., 1971—. Mem. Coll. Coun., SUNY Maritime Coll., 1977-98, chmn., 1983-98; mem. adv. coun. Tulane U. Admiralty Law Inst. Served as lt. (j.g.) USNR, 1960-70. Mem. ABA (chmn. standing com. on admiralty and maritime law 1982-86), Maritime Law Assn. U.S. (chmn. com. on admissions 1974-82, exec. com. 1988-91, membership sec. 1996-98, 2nd v.p. 1998—), India House Club, Brookville Country Club (N.Y.). Office: Hill Rivkins & Hayden LLP 90 West St New York NY 10006-1039

HAYDEN, RICHARD MICHAEL, investment banker; b. Balt., July 31, 1945; s. Richard Taylor and Cecelia (Hense) H.; m. Susan Frances Margolies, June 4, 1978. A.B., Georgetown U., 1967; M.B.A., U. Pa., 1969. Assoc. Goldman, Sachs & Co., N.Y.C., 1969-73, v.p., 1974-80, gen. ptnr., 1980-98, adv. dir., 1999—; bd. dirs. Witco Corp. With USNG, 1968-73. Mem. Quogue Field Club, Quogue Beach Club, Union Club (N.Y.C.), Links Club, River Club, The Hurlingham Club, Vanderbilt Racquet Club, Queens Club, Harbour Club, Phi Beta Kappa. Republican. Episcopalian. Office: Goldman Sachs Internat, Peterborough Ct 133 Fleet St, London EC4A 2BB, England

HAYDEN, RON L., library director; b. San Pedro, Calif., Dec. 24, 1948; s. Larnie Alphonsis and Myrtie Louise (Pilcher) H.; m. Marilee Ann Brubaker, May 30, 1971 (dec. June 1978); m. Susan Ann Huffman, Jan. 1, 1982. AA, Golden West Coll., 1969; BA, Long Beach State U., 1972; MLS, Fullerton U., 1974. Reference sr. libr. Huntington Beach (Calif.) Libr., 1975-79, pub. svc. libr., 1979-86, libr. dir., 1986—; liason Libr. Patrons Assn., Huntington Beach, 1986—. Author: Collection Development Library Journal, 1979. Recipient Award of Excellence Calif. S.W. Recreation Park Conf., 1990. Mem. ALA (Libr. in Media award, Best of Show award 1990), Calif. Libr. Assn., Friends Libr., So. Calif. Tennis Assn., Rotary (bd. dirs., vocat. chmn. 1988—). Avocations: tennis, running, reading. Office: Huntington Beach Libr 7111 Talbert Ave Huntington Beach CA 92646*

HAYDEN, SPENCER JAMES, management consultant; b. N.Y.C., Sept. 18, 1922; s. Thomas Churchill and Anna May (Forshay) H.; B.S., St. John's Coll., 1942; M.A., Columbia U., 1946; Ph.D., Fordham U., 1951; m. Erica Bannister, Feb. 18, 1950; children—Lisa, Christopher, Robert, Wendy. Cons., Booz, Allen & Hamilton, Genoa, Italy and N.Y.C., 1957-61; v.p., sec. Richardson, Bellows, Henry & Co., Inc., N.Y.C., 1961-63; pres. Spencer Hayden Co., Inc., Hopewell Junction, N.Y., 1963—; prof. mgmt. Rensselaer Poly. Inst., 1967-70; mng. dir. Smith Bros., Ravenel Investment Bankers, Southport, Conn., 1987—. trustee Knickerbocker Hosp., N.Y.C., 1963-70. Served to lt. USAAF, 1942-45. Mem. Am. Inst. Indsl. Engrs., Am. Soc. for Microbiology, Am. Psychol. Assn., AAAS. Clubs: Union League (bd. govs. 1980—), Engrs., Columbia U. (N.Y.C.). Author: Solving the Problems of International Operations, 1970. Home: Creamery Rd Hopewell Junction NY 12533 Office: Spencer Hayden Co Inc 48 Creamery Rd Hopewell Junction NY 12533-5208

HAYDEN, VERN CLARENCE, financial planner; b. Endicott, N.Y., Jan. 24, 1937; s. Clarence Butch and Ruth (Storm) H. BA, Wheaton Coll., 1959; postgrad., NYU, 1960, U. Oreg., 1963, Am. U., 1966, U. So. Calif., 1967. Cert. Fin. Planner. Pvt. practice San Rafael, Calif., 1970-83; cons. Am. Express, Firemens Fund, San Rafael, 1979, 80; workshop speaker IBM, Pitney Bowes, Champion Internat., Texaco, 1980—. Author: Money Use It or Lose It, 1980, The Process of Financial Counseling, 1981, How to Build Using Seminars, 1988, The Hayden Investment Matrix, 1990; contbg. editor, weekly columnist TheStreet.com.; contbr. articles to profl. jours.; regular guest on CNBC's Money Club; contbg. editor, weekly columnist TheStreet.com. Bd. regents Coll. Fin. Planning, Denver; chmn. Nat. Endowment for Fin. Edn.; bd. dirs., bd. stds. for cert. fin. planners; chmn. legacy and planned giving So. Conn. Am. Cancer Soc. With USAF, 1962-68. Mem. Internat. Assn. Fin. Planning (pres. 1975, founding pres. Westchester/Rockland, N.Y. 1987, pres. 1989), Registry Fin. Planning Practitioners, Inst. Cert. Fin. Planners (bd. govs., bd. standards and practices), IBCFP. Republican. Avocations: handball, racquetball, reading, travel, writing. Office: 830 Post Rd E Westport CT 06880-5222

HAYDEN, WILLIAM ROBERT, lawyer; b. Chgo., May 22, 1947; s. Robert George and Dorothy (Honan) H.; m. Carol Ann Brock, Aug. 12, 1978; 1 child, Nathaniel. BA, Kans. State U., 1969; JD with honors, George Washington U., 1972. Bar: D.C. 1973, U.S. Dist. Ct. D.C. 1975, U.S. Ct. Appeals (D.C. cir.) 1975, Ariz. 1978, U.S. Dist. Ct. Ariz. 1978, U.S. Ct. Appeals (9th cir.) 1979, U.S. Ct. Appeals (10th cir.) 1997. Mem. gen. counsel's staff NLRB, Washington, 1973-75; assoc. O'Donoghue and O'Donoghue, Washington, 1975-78; assoc. Snell and Wilmer, Phoenix, 1978-82, ptnr., 1982—. Contbg. editor: Developing Labor Law, 1974, Employment Discrimination Law, 1989. Mem. ABA (labor and employment law sect.), Nat. Panel; Am. Arbitration Assn. (employment dispute resolution), Ariz. Bar Assn. (exec. com., past chmn. labor and employment law sect. 1984-89, employment civil jury instructions com.), Maricopa County Bar Assn., D.C. Bar Assn., Ariz. C. of C. (employee rels. subcom.). Avocations: tennis, softball, skiing. Office: Snell and Wilmer 1 Arizona Ctr Phoenix AZ 85004

HAYDOCK, MICHAEL DAMEAN, building and code consultant, writer; b. Schenectady, N.Y., Sept. 3, 1940; s. Louis and Olive Ann (Keenan) H.; m. Elizabeth Knouse, Dec. 18, 1993. AA, U. of State of N.Y., Albany, 1974, BA, 1975. With bldg. dept. City of Schenectady, 1965-70, bldg. insp., 1970-71; zoning adminstr. Town of Niskayuna, N.Y., 1971-80; bldg. insp. City of Poughkeepsie, N.Y., 1980-86; bldg. commr. City of Albany, 1986-95; instr. Empire State Coll., 1995—; instr. in code enforcement State of N.Y., 1986—, Empire State Coll., 1995—; instr. Marist Coll. Ctr. for Lifetime Studies, 1999. Contbr. articles to Nat. Bldg. Ofcls. and Code Adminstr. mag., 1983—, Dutchess County Hist. Soc. Yearbook, 1986, Bermuda Maritime Mus. Quar., 1993-97, The Artilleryman, 1994, Army Times, 1995-98, Mil. History, 1996-97, Am. History, 1996-98, World War II Mag., 1999, Confrontation-The Lit. Jour. L.I. U., 1998, Buffalo Spree, 1996, Many Waters, 1996, Air Force Times, 1996-98, Echoes, 1998, VFW Mag., 1998, Am. Heritage of Invention & Technology, 1998; author: City Under Siege: The Berlin Blockade and Airlift, 1948-49, 1999; scriptwriter: As it Happend-The Berlin Airlift, 1998, In Search of History-Forgotton Wars, 1999. With U.S. Army, 1959-62. Mem. N.Y. State Firefighting and Code Enforcement Pers. Standards and Edn. Commn. (1982-95), Bldg. Ofcls. and Code Adminstrs. Internat. (chpt. pres. 1995—), N.Y. State Bldg. Ofcls. Conf. (pres. Capital Dist. area 1988-89, state pres. 1995-96), Am. Legion, VFW, Authors Guild, Rotary, Univ. Club Albany.

HAYDOCK, WALTER JAMES, banker; b. Chgo., Dec. 14, 1947; s. Joseph Albert and Lillian V. (Adeszko) H.; student Harvard Bus. Coll., 1969-71, Daily Coll., 1971-73; BS in Acctg., DePaul U., 1976; m. Bonnie Jean Thompson, Aug. 22, 1970; children: Nicole Lynn, Matthew Michael. Computer operator, jr. programmer Pepper Constrn. Co., Chgo., 1972-73; input analyst Continental Bank, Chgo., 1973-76, data control supr., 1976-79, corporate fixed asset adminstr., 1979-83, properties systems analyst, 1983-87, props. sr. systems supr., 1987-91, unit chief conversions Fed. Deposit Ins. Corp., 1992-93, info. security specialist, 1993-96; data security mgr. U. Ill. at Chgo., 1996—; pres. Wal-Bon., Inc.; distbr. Lic. Disney Character Mdse. Mem. Southwest Suburban Bd. Realtors. Home: 14129 Somerset Ct Orland Park IL 60467-1142 Office: 809 S Marshfield Ave # 1000 Chicago IL 60612-4305

HAYDU, JOHN N., psychic counselor; b. Wilmington, N.C., Feb. 24, 1959; s. George Haydu and Veronica (Haydu) Herman; m. Elizabeth Conley, Nov. 3, 1983 (div. Mar. 1985); m. Daisy Elizabeth Silva; children: Michale Renegar. Student, Daytona Beach C.C., 1979. Spiritualist minister Cassadaga (Fla.) Spiritualist Ch., 1980—; psychic counselor Cassadaga Spiritualist Ctr.; pers. reader Daytona Beach C.C., Dade-Duval-Sanford Police Dept.; appeared in radio and TV programs. Author: Development of Mediumship, 1994. Pres. Golden Dawn Spiritualist Ch., Cassadaga. E-mail: johnhaydu@usa.net. Home: 1080 Marion St Cassadaga FL 32706-0151

HAYEK, CAROLYN JEAN, retired judge, former church administrator; b. Portland, Oreg., Aug. 17, 1948; d. Robert A. and Marion L. (DeKoning) H.; m. Steven M. Rosen, July 21, 1974; children: Jonathan David, Laura Elizabeth. BA in Psychology, Carleton Coll., 1970; JD, U. Chgo., 1973. Bar: Wash. 1973. Assoc. Jones, Grey & Bayley, Seattle, 1973-77; sole practice law Federal Way, Wash., 1977-82; judge Federal Way Dist. Ct., 1982-95; ret., 1995; task force mem. Alternatives for Wash., 1973-75; mem. Wash. State Ecol. Commn., 1975-77; columnist Tacoma News Tribune Hometown Sect., 1995-96. Bd. dirs. 1st Unitarian Ch., Seattle, 1986-89, vice chair 1987-88, pres. 1988-89; ch. adminstr. Northlake Unitarian Universalist Ch.; den leader Cub Scouts Mt. Rainier coun. Boy Scouts Am., 1987-88, scouting coord., 1988-89; bd. dirs. Twin Lakes Elem. Sch. PTA. Recipient Women Helping Women award Federal Way Soroptimist, 1991, Martin Luther King Day Humanitarian award King County, 1993, Recognition cert. City of Federal Way Diversity Commn., 1995. Mem. AAUW (co-pres. Kirland-Redmond br., br. pres. 1978-80, 90-92, chmn. state level conf. com. 1986-87, mem. diversity com. 1991-98, state bd. mem. 1995-97, dir. ESL project), ABA, Wash. Women Lawyers, Wash. State Bar Assn., King County Dist. Ct. Judges Assn. (treas., exec. com. 1990-91, 92-93, com. chmn., chair and rules com. 1990-91, 92-94), Elected Wash. Women (dir. 1983-87), Nat. Assn. Women Judges (nat. bd. dirs., dist. bd. dirs. 1984-86, chmn. rules com. 1988-89, chmn. bylaws com. 1990-91), Fed. Way Women's Network (bd. dirs. 1984-87, 88-91, 95-97, pres. 1985, program co-chair 1989-91, co-editor newsletter), Greater Fed. Way C. of C. (dir. 1978-82, sec. 1980-81, v.p. 1981-82), Sunrise Rotary (com. svc. chair, bd. dirs., membership com., Federal Way chpt. 1991-96, youth exch. officer 1994-95), Washington Women United (bd. dirs. 1995-97), Unitarian Universalist Women's Assn. (chair bylaws com. 1996), Eliot Inst. (bd. dirs. 1996—, vice chmn. 1998-99, bd. chair 1999—), Plaza on State Owners Assn. (bd. dirs. 1997—, pres. 1997-99).

HAYEK, SALMA, actress; b. Coatzacoalcos, Veracruz, Mexico, Sept. 2, 1968; d. Sami Hayek Domingues and Diana H. Television work includes: Teresa, 1989, The Sinbad Show, 1993, Roadracers, 1994, The Hunchback, 1997. Films include Mi Vida Loca, 1993, Four Rooms, 1995, Desperado, 1995, Fair Game, 1995, From Dusk Til Dawn, 1996, Fled, 1996, Fools Rush In, 1997, Follow Me Home, 1997, Breaking Up, 1997, The Velocity of Gary, 1998, The Faculty, 1998, 54, 1998, Dogma, 1999, Wild Wild West, 1999, Shiny New Enemies, 2000, Frida, 2000. *

HAYES, ALICE BOURKE, university official, biology educator; b. Chgo., Dec. 31, 1937; d. William Joseph and Mary Alice (Cawley) Bourke; m. John J. Hayes, Sept. 2, 1961 (dec. July 1981). BS, Mundelein Coll., Chgo., 1959; MS, U. Ill., 1960; PhD, Northwestern U., 1972; DSc (honoris causa), Loyola U., Chgo., 1994; HHD (honoris causa), Fontbonne Coll., 1994; LHD (honoris causa), Mount St. Mary Coll., 1998. Researcher Mcpl. Tb San., Chgo., 1960-62; faculty Loyola U., Chgo., 1962-87, chmn. dept., 1968-77, dean natural scis. div., 1977-80, assoc. acad. v.p., 1980-87, v.p. acad. affairs, 1987-89; provost, exec. v.p. St. Louis U., 1989-95; pres. U. San Diego, 1995—; mem. space biology program NASA, 1980-86; mem. adv. panel NSF, 1977-81, Parmly Hearing Inst., 1986-89; del. Bot. Del. to South Africa, 1984, to People's Republic China, 1988, to USSR, 1990; reviewer Coll. Bd. and Mellon Found. Nat. Hispanic Scholar Awards, 1985-86; bd. dirs. Pulitzer Pub. Co., Scripps Bank, Loyola U. Chgo., Cath. Charities, San Diego Found., San Diego Hist. Soc., Old Globe. Co-author books; contbr. articles to profl. publs. Campaign mem. Mental Health Assn. Ill., Chgo., 1973-89; trustee Chgo.-No. Ill. divsn. Nat. Multiple Sclerosis Soc., 1981-89, bd. dirs., 1980-88, com. chmn., sec. to bd. dirs., vice chmn. bd. dirs.; trustee Regina Dominican Acad., 1984-89, Civitas Dei Found., 1987-92, Rockhurst Coll., Loyola U., Chgo., San Diego Found.; trustee St. Ignatius Coll. Prep. Sch., bd. dirs., 1984-89, sec., vice chmn.; bd. dirs. Urban League Met. St. Louis, St. Louis Sci. Ctr., 1991-95, Cath. Charities St. Louis, 1992-95, St. Louis County Hist. Soc., 1992-95, Cath. Charities San Diego, 1996—, San Diego Hist. Soc., 1996—, Old Globe Theater, 1996—, also trustee. Named to Teachers' Hall of Fame Blue Key Soc.; fellow in botany U. Ill., 1959-60; fellow in botany NSF, 1969-71; grantee Am. Orchid Soc., 1967; grantee HEW, 1969, 76; grantee NSF, 1975; grantee NASA, 1980-85. Mem. AAAS, AAUP (corp. rep. 1980-85), Am. Assn. for Higher Edn., Am. Assn. Univ. Adminstrs. (mem. program com. nat. meeting 1988), Am. Soc. Gravitational and Space Biology, Assn. Midwest Coll. Biology Teachers, Am. Soc. Plant Physiology, Bot. Soc. Am., Am. Inst. Biol. Scis. Acad., Chgo. Network, Soc. Ill. Microbiologists (edn. com. 1969-70, Pasteur award com. 1975, pub. rels. com. 1974, chair speakers' bur. 1974-79), Chgo. Assn. Tech. Socs. (acad. liaison 1982-85, awards com. 1984-89), Am. Coun. on Edn. (corp. rep. higher edn. panel), Ctr. Rsch. Librs. (nominating com. 1986), North Ctrl. Assn. Colls. and Schs. (cons., evaluator Commn. on Higher Edn. 1984-95, commr.-at-large 1988-94), Mo. Women's Forum Club, Sigma Xi, Delta Sigma Rho, Sigma Delta Epsilon, Phi Beta Kappa, Alpha Sigma Nu. Roman Catholic. Office: U San Diego 5998 Alcala Park San Diego CA 92110-2429

HAYES, ALLENE VALERIE FARMER, government executive; b. Washington, Sept. 23, 1958; d. Thomas Jonathan and Allena V. (Joyner) Farmer; m. Thomas Gary Hayes; children: Tommia Chanel, Alle Victoria. Student, Richmond Coll., London, 1980; BA, Clark U., 1980; cert., U. Oxford, Eng., 1981; M.L.S., U. Md., 1986. Libr. asst. NUS Corp., Gaithersburg, Md., 1981-82; cataloger Libr. of Congress, Washington, 1982-84, copyright specialist, 1984-85; congl. fellow Ho. of Reps. Com. on D.C., Washington, 1985—; English tutor, writer Natural Motion, Washington, 1983-84; intern, archivist Howard U., Washington, 1985; intern Libr. Congress Intern Program, 1991-92. Compiler: Single Mother's Resource Directory, 1984. Compiler, editor: Policy Research, 1985. Author booklet: D.C. Statehood Issue, 1986. Mem. U. Md. College Park Black Women's Coun., 1984, NAACP; vol. Congl. Black Caucus Found., Washington, 1985. Recipient Fgn. Study award Am. Inst. for Fgn. Study, 1981; Congl. Black Caucus fellow, 1985. Mem. ALA, Libr. of Congress Profls. Assn., Daniel A.P. Murray Afro-Am. Culture Assn. of Libr. of Congress (mem. exec. bd., newsletter editor, pres. 1994—), D.A.P. Murray African Am. Culture Assn. (pres. 1994-96),Delta Sigma Theta (tutor 1986). Avocations: travel; writing; dance; drama; tennis. Home: 1120 K St NE Washington DC 20002-7110 Office: Libr of Congress 101 Independence Ave SE Washington DC 20540-0002

HAYES, ANDREW WALLACE, II, consumer products company executive; b. Corning, Ark., Aug. 21, 1939; s. Andrew Wallace and Helen (Latimer) H.; m. Sandra Smith, Dec. 28, 1963; children: Andrew Wallace III, Helen Cathleen, Benjamin Bailey. AB, Emory U., 1961; MS, Auburn U., 1964, PhD, 1967. Diplomate Am. Bd. Toxicology, Am. Bd. Forensic Medicine, Am. Bd. Forensic Examiners; cert. nutrition specialist. NIH postdoctoral fellow, rsch. assoc. div. toxicology Vanderbilt U. Sch. Med., Nashville, 1966-68; asst. prof. dept. microbiology U. Ala., Tuscaloosa, 1968-71, assoc. prof. dept. microbiology, 1971-75, prof. depts. microbiology and biochemistry, 1975; assoc. prof. dept. pharmacology and toxicology U. Miss. Med. Ctr., Jackson, 1975-76, prof. dept. pharmacology and toxicology, 1976-80, program dir. NIEHS tng. program in environ. toxicology, 1977-80; dir. toxicology rsch. Rohm and Haas Co., Spring House, Pa., 1980-84; dir. regulatory affairs, agrl. chemicals (worldwide) Rohm and Haas Co., Phila., 1984; corp. toxicologist RJR Nabisco Inc., Winston-Salem, N.C., 1984; corp. toxicologist, dir. biochem. and biobehavioral rsch., Bowman Gray Tech. Ctr. R.J. Reynolds Tobacco Co., Winston-Salem, N.C., 1984-86, corp. toxicologist, group dir. biochem. and biobehavioral rsch., 1986-87, corp. toxicologist, v.p. biochem. and biobehavioral rsch., 1987-92; prof. Bowman Gray Sch. Medicine Wake Forest U., Winston-Salem, 1992; v.p. corp. product integrity The Gillette Co., Boston, 1993—; faculty risk assessment summer sch., 1990, 92, 94, 96, 98; vis. sr. scientist biochemistry dept. Cen. Vet. Lab., New Haw, Weybridge, Surrey, Eng., 1977; disting. lectr. U. Calif., 1979; vis. prof. dept. vet. pub. health Tex. A&M U., 1979—; rsch. prof. dept. physiology and biophysics Sch. Dentistry, Temple U., 1981-84, Phila. Coll. Pharmacy and Sci., 1982-84, dept. medicine and toxicology program Duke U., 1986—, dept. pharmacology and toxicology Med. Coll. Va., 1987—, Sch. Vet. Med., Va. Poly. Inst., 1988—, Sch. Pub. Health U. Mass, Armherst, 1994—; dept. pharmacology and toxicology Sch. Medicine, U. Louisville, 1997—; mem. faculty Wayne State U., 1987; collaborator Interlab. Collaborative Study for Aflatoxin B1, FDA, 1977, Aflatoxin Check Sample Survey, Internat. Agy. Rsch. on Cancer, 1978; mem. Target Organ Toxicity Conf. Steering Com., 1978-88, Panel on Equivalent Safety Concept of Maritime Hazardous Materials, Nat. Materials Adv. Bd., NAS, 1979-82, Safe Drinking Water Com., Bd. Toxicology and Environ. Health Hazards, NAS, 1979-81, Environ. Health Scis. Rev. Com. NIEHS, 1981-85, sci. program com. Internat. Congress Toxicology, 1982-83, Testing Task Group, CMA, 1981-84, Chem. Systems Lab. Toxin Def. Group Rev. Panel, U.S. Army, 1982, TDB/CIS User Assessment Panel Life Scis. Rsch. Office, FASEB, Bethesda, Md., 1982; alt. del. Internat. Union Toxicology, 1982-83; advisor U.S. Army Med. Command, 1982-84; del. Internat. Union Toxicology, 1984-86; cons. Walter Reed Army Inst. Rsch., 1984-86; mem. selection com. Immunotoxicology Found., 1986, Commn. on Comm., Internat. Union Toxicology, 1986-89, program com. Toxilogy Forum, 1986-87, toxicology adv. bd. Raven Press, N.Y.C., 1982-96; mem. external adv. bd. La. Inst. Toxicology, 1996—; bd. dirs. Toxicology Edn. Found., 1997—; mem. sci. adv. bd. Inst. In Vitro Scis., 1997—; mem. commn. strategic devel. INTOX, 1997—. Author: Mycotoxin Teratogenicity, 1981; editor: Toxicology of the Eye, Ear and Other Special Senses, 1985, Extrapolation of Dosimetric Relationships for Inhaled Particles and Gases, 1989, Prinicples and Methods of Toxicology, 3d edit., 1994, Human and Experimental Toxicology, 1993—; co-author: Loomis's Essentials of Toxicology, 4th edit., 1996; co-editor: Target Organ Toxicity Series, 1989—; founding editor Comments of Toxicology, 1986—; assoc. editor Regulatory Toxicology and Pharmacology, 1986—, Toxicology and Applied Pharmacology, 1980, editor, 1981-86, mem. editl. bd., 1978-80; mem. editl. bd. Archives Environ. Contamination and Toxicology, 1987—, Environ. Toxin Series, 1987-95, Toxicology, 1978-83, Jour. Toxicology and Environ. Health, 1979—, Food and Chem. Toxicology, 1987—; mem. editl. coun. Toxicon, 1980-90; contbr. articles to profl. jours., chpts. to books. Mem. adv. coun. Auburn U., 1987-97, dept. environ. health Harvard Sch. Pub. Health, 1997—, nat. coun. Fla. Coll., 1980-97; trustee Am. Assn. for Accreditation of Lab. Animal Care, Chgo., 1984-89; bd. dirs. Join Hands-The Health and Safety Alliance, 1995—, Fla. Coll., 1998—. Named Exec. of Yr. Winston-Salem chpt. Profl. Secs. Internat., 1989-90; recipient cert. of merit, EPA, 1981, Rsch. Career Devel. award NIH, 1973-78. Fellow Acad. Toxicological Scis. (bd. dirs. 1993—), Inst. Biology; mem bd. dir., Ctrs for Alternatives to animal testing, 1995—, mem. External adv. bd., Inst. Toxicology, 1996—; mem. Soc. Toxicology (co-chmn. tech. com. 1978, chmn. 1978-79, pres. Mid-Atlantic chpt. 1983-84, v.p. mech. sect., 1981-82, 82-83, animals in rsch. com. 1996-99, chmn. 1998-99, bd. dirs. toxicology edn. found. 1996—, pres. 1998—), Am. Soc. Pharmacology and Exptl. Therapeutics (chmn. com. on environ. pharmacology 1981-82, coun. sect. toxicology), Am. Chem. Soc. (com. on chemistry and pub. affairs task force on TSCA Interagy. Testing Com.'s Preliminary List of Chem. Substances, 1977-80), Am. Soc. for Nutritional Scis., Am. Soc. for Microbiology (environ. microbiology com. 1975-76), Internat. Union Pharmacology (sect. on toxicology), Internat. Soc. Regulatory Toxicology and Pharmacology, Sigma Xi. Mem. Ch. of Christ. Avocation: fishing. Office: The Gillette Co Corp Product Integrity Prudential Towers Bldg Boston MA 02199

HAYES, ARTHUR HULL, JR., physician, clinical pharmacology educator, medical school dean, business executive, consultant; b. Highland Park, Mich., July 18, 1933; s. Arthur Hull and Florence Margaret (Gruber) H.; m. Barbara Anne Carey, July 16, 1960; children: Arthur Hull III, Elizabeth, Katherine. AB magna cum laude, U. Santa Clara, 1955, D in Pub. Svc. (hon.), 1980; MA, Oxford U., 1957; postgrad., Georgetown U., 1957-60; MD, Cornell U., 1964; LLD (hon.), St. John's U., 1983; DSc (hon.), N.Y. Med. Coll., 1983. Diplomate Am. Bd. Clin. Pharmacology. Intern in medicine N.Y. Hosp., N.Y.C., 1964-65; resident in cardiology N.Y. Hosp., 1967-68; assoc. prof. pharmacology, asst. prof. medicine, assoc. dean Cornell U. Med. Coll., N.Y.C., 1968-72; prof. pharmacology and medicine, chief div. clin. pharmacology Pa. State Coll. Medicine, Hershey (Pa.) Med. Center, 1972-81; U.S. commr. food and drugs, asst. surgeon gen. USPHS, Rockville, Md., 1981-83; provost, dean N.Y. Med. Coll., 1983-86, prof. medicine, pharmacology and community and preventive medicine, 1983—; pres., CEO EM Pharms., Inc., Hawthorne, N.Y., 1986-91; pres. MediSci. Assocs., Inc., New Rochelle, N.Y., 1991—; trustee U.S. Pharmacopeial Conv., 1980-81, 85—, pres., 1985-90; bd. dirs. Cadbury-Schweppes, Stamford, Conn., Synergen, Inc., Denver, Myriad Genetics, Inc., Salt Lake City, Food and Drug Law Inst., Washington; chmn. Coun. Family Health, N.Y.C.; chmn. Medic Alert Found., Inc., Turlock, Calif., 1991-93; prin. Ctr. Excellence in Govt. Contbr. articles to profl. jours.; mem. editorial bd. Rational Drug Therapy, Clin. Pharmacology and Therapeutics, Med. Advt. News, Jour. Clin. Pharmacology, Today's Therapeutic Trends, Pharmaceutical Medicine, Prescriber's Newsletter, World Pharm. Report. Bd. dirs. Peace Found., N.Y.C.; bd. regents Santa Clara (Calif.) U.; mem. coun. overseers L.I.U. Coll. Pharmacy. Served as capt. M.C. U.S. Army, 1965-67. Decorated Knight of Holy Sepulchre (comdr.); recipient Foch medal Govt. of France, 1953; Recipient Nobili medal U. Santa Clara, 1955, Good Physician award Cornell Med. Coll., 1964, Faculty Devel. award Pharm. Mfrs. Assn. Found., 1968, Bronze medallion seal award Dept. Health and Human Services, 1982, Disting. Pub. Service award Dept. Health and Human Services, 1983, Founders Day award Lebanon Valley Coll., 1983, Henry Elliot Disting. Svc. Clin. Pharacology award; Rhodes scholar, 1955; Danforth fellow, 1955; NIH fellow, 1960-62. Fellow ACP, N.Y. Acad. Medicine, Am. Soc. Clin. Pharmacology and Therapy (Henry Elliot Disting. Svc. Clin. Pharacology award 1993), Am. Coll. Cardiology, Royal Soc. Medicine, Coll. Physicians Phila., Am. Coll. Chest Physicians, Acad. Pharm. Scis., Am. Acad. Pharm. Physicians; mem. AMA, Am. Soc. Pharmacology and Exptl. Therapeutics, Am. Soc. Clin. Pharmacology and Therapeutics (pres. 1980-81), Am. Pharm. Assn. (hon.), Am. Fedn. Clin. Rsch., N.Y. Acad. Sci., Harvey Soc., Med. Soc. State N.Y., Assn. Am. Med. Colls. (coun. of deans, council acad. socs.), Phi Beta Kappa, Sigma Xi, Alpha Sigma Nu, Alpha Omega Alpha. Roman Catholic (permanent deacon). Lodge: KC, Knights of Malta. Office: MediScience Associates 71 Elk Ave New Rochelle NY 10804-4212*

HAYES, BERNARDINE FRANCES, computer systems analyst; b. Boston, June 29, 1939; d. Robert Emmett and Mary Agnes (Tague) H. BA in Edn., St. Joseph Coll., 1967; MA in Urban Affairs and Pub. Policy, U. Del., 1973, PhD in Pub. Policy, 1978. Elem. tchr. St. Dominick Sch., Balt., 1960-63; tchr. sci., math. and art St. Mary's Sch., Troy, N.Y., 1963-65, Our Lady Queen of Peace Sch., Washington, 1965-68, St. Patrick Sch., Richmond, Va., 1968-69, St. Peter Cathedral Sch., Wilmington, Del., 1969-71; planner health and social svcs. Model Cities Program, Wilmington, 1971-72; dir. rsch. Del. State Dept. Mental Health, Wilmington, 1972-75; dir. planning and evaluation Mental Health, Mental Retardation Svcs., West Chester, Pa., 1976-78; instr. Boston U., 1978; divsn. dir. Sys. Archs., Inc., Randolph, Mass., 1979-81; group mgr. Unisys Corp., Cambridge, Mass., 1981-97; sr. computer scientist Computer Sci. Corp., Cambridge, 1997—; cons. in field; pres., founder Hayes Assocs., a comm. firm, 1989—; developer Project Helplink, 1990-92; instr. Radcliffe Seminars, Cambridge, 1994—; self-cultivation instr. YUANTI Health and Sci., 1998—; cert. instr., dir. edn. Yuanji Sci. Found., 1998—. Contbr. numerous articles to profl. jours. Bd. sec. Model Cities, 1969-70; chairperson bd. State Svc. Ctr., Wilmington, 1972-75; mem. Human Rels. Commn., Washington, 1965-68; co-chmn. State-wide Coalition for Human Svcs., Del., 1972-74; activist Vietnam protest, Del., 1970-74, Civil Rights Movement, 1965—, numerous polit. campaigns, 1972—; alt. del. Mass. Dem. Conv., 1985; bd. v.p. Women's Action for Nuc. Disarmament, Arlington, Mass., 1982-91, fin. com. chmn., 1983-85, 88-90, treas., 1988-90, chmn. polit. action com., 1983-84, dir. nat. voter registration campaign, 1984; active Mondale for Pres., 1984, John Kerry for Senator, Mass., 1984, Clinton for Pres., 1992, Studds for Congress, 1992; del. Com. for an Enduring Peace, Soviet Peace Commn., Moscow, 1987; trustee Mass. Assn. for the Blind, 1989—, Children's Justice Ctrs., Tulsa, 1994—; coord. Women's Acad. Group, 1995—; instr. adn dir. edn. (sci. and med.) YUANJI; cert. instr. 1997—; dir. edn. Yuanji Sci. Found., 1998—. Fellow NSF, 1966. Mem. NAACP, NOW, Women's Inst. Housing and Econ. Devel. (bd. dirs. 1985-88), Boston Mus. Fine Arts. Roman Catholic. Avocations: fiction writing, photography, philately. Home: 49 Crane Rd Quincy MA 02169-2621

HAYES, BONAVENTURE FRANCIS, priest; b. Buffalo, Nov. 8, 1941; s. Carl Milford and Louise Christine (Kolb) H. BA in Philosophy, St. Bonaventure U., 1964; MA in Semitics, Cath. U. Am., 1972, Licentiate in Sacred Theology, 1972; MLS, SUNY, Buffalo, 1988. Joined Franciscan Order, Roman Cath. Ch., 1961, ordained priest, 1967. Lectr. Christ The King Sem., Allegany, N.Y., 1968-70; from asst. prof. to assoc. prof., libr. dir. Christ The King Sem., East Aurora, N.Y., 1976—; archivist Holy Name Province, Franciscan Order, N.Y.C., 1988—; various adv. bds. 1982—. Contbr. articles to profl. jours. Mem. Am. Theol. Libr. Assn., Western N.Y. Cath. Libr. Assn. (pres. 1989-91), Cath. Bibl. Assn., Soc. Bibl. Lit., Cath. Libr. Assn. (nat. exec. bd. 1991-97, v.p., pres.-elect 1997-99, pres. 1999—), Beta Phi Mu. Republican. Home and Office: Christ the King Sem Libr 711 Knox Rd East Aurora NY 14052-9444

HAYES, BYRON JACKSON, JR., retired lawyer; b. L.A., July 9, 1934; s. Byron Jackson and Caroline Violet (Scott) H.; m. DeAnne Saliba, June 30, 1962; children: Kenneth Byron, Patricia DeAnne. Student, Pomona Coll., 1952-56; BA magna cum laude, Harvard U., LLB cum laude, 1959. Bar: Calif. 1960, U.S. Supreme Ct. 1963. Assoc., McCutchen, Black, Verleger & Shea, L.A., 1960-68, ptnr., 1968-89; ptnr. Baker & Hostetler, 1990-97, ret., 1998. Trustee L.A. Urban Found., 1996—, CFO, 1998—; trustee L.A. Ch. Extension Soc. United Meth. Ch., 1967-77, pres., 1974-77, chancellor ann. conf. Pacific and S.W., 1979-86, dir. 1010 devel. corp., 1993—, v.p., 1995—; Dir., pres. Pacific and S.W. United Meth. Found., 1978-84. Named Layperson of yr. Pacific and S.W. Ann. Conf., United Meth. Ch., 1981, recipient Bishop's award, 1992. Mem. ABA, Am. Coll. Mortgage Attys. (regent 1984-93, pres. 1993-94), Calif. Bar Assn., Los Angeles County Bar Assn. (chmn. real property sect. 1982-83), Toluca Lake Property Owners Assn. (sec. 1990-94), Pomona Coll. Alumni Assn. (pres. 1984-85), Lakeside Golf Club. Office: Baker & Hostetler 600 Wilshire Blvd Fl 12 Los Angeles CA 90017-3212

HAYES, CAROL JEANNE, physical education educator; b. Cambridge, Mass., Apr. 18, 1942; d. Joseph Raymond and Gertrude Marie (Poitras) Boudreau; m. James Anthony Hayes, Oct. 24, 1964 (wid. Mar. 1978); children: James Anthony, Sharon Marie. BSEd, Boston State Coll., 1963, MEd, 1978, postgrad., 1980; postgrad., Boston State Coll./Salem State, 1986—. Cert. CPR and first aid provider. Phys. edn./health instr. Wilmington (Mass.) Pub. Schs., 1963-65, 72—; part-time phys. edn. tchr. Concord (Mass.) Pub. Schs., 1968-69; trainer Spl. Olympics participants, Wilmington, 1983-86; Little League mgr., LExington, 1974-76; bike safety com. Wilmington Police Dept., 1983-85; coord. After Sch. Tournaments, North Intermediate Sch., Wilmington, 1986-91; mem. adv. coun. Woburn St. Sch., 1992—, mem. crisis team, 1993—. Author: (curriculum) Elementary/Adaptive/Kindergarten, 1986. Badge counselor Boy Scouts Am., Lexington, 1978-84; vol./minister of comfort St. Brigid, 1978—, care eucharistic minister, 1993—; mem. Lexington Hist. Soc.; coord. Heart Week Activities for Intermediate Students, 1990—; others. Mem. AAHPERD, NEA, Wilmington Tchrs. Assn. (exec. bd. 1972, bargaining team 1992, greivance com. 1991, pres. 1995—), Mass. Tchrs. Assn., Mass./AHPERD. Roman Catholic. Avocations: travel, reading, golf, swimming. Home: 9 Farmcrest Ave Lexington MA 02421-7112 Office: Wilmington Pub Schs Wilmington MA 01887

HAYES, CHARLES, religious organization executive, clergyman; b. Chgo., Aug. 4, 1950; s. Charles and Doris Yvonne (Davis) H.; children: Tammy, Beverly, Christine, Crystal, Enda. Degree in Theology, Emmaus Bible Sch., 1977; AA in Data Processing, Kennedy King Coll., 1982, AS in Acctg., 1985; BA, Chgo. State U., 1986; AA in Bus. Mgmt., Ctr. Degree Studies, Scranton, Pa., 1988; MS in Libr. Sci., Chgo. State U., 1996. Lic. minister; cert. libr. media specialist. Instr. Kennedy King Coll., Chgo., 1980-82; asst. coll. libr. city colls. Chgo., 1985-86; agt. IRS, Chgo., 1986; assoc. pastor St. Mary's Missionary Bapt. Church, Chgo., 1980—; nat. pres. Christians Taking Action, Inc., Chgo., 1983—; libr., lectr. Olive-Harvey Coll., Chgo., 1997—; bd. dirs. Organized Urban Resource, Inc., Chgo. Contbr. articles to profl. jours. Recipient Recognition award Ch. Christ, 1977, Appreciation award U.S. Com. for UNICEF, 1985, Internat. World Leaders award. Democrat. Baptist. Avocations: horticulture, aquariums.

HAYES, CHARLES AUSTIN, economic development executive, consultant; b. Norlina, N.C., Nov. 4, 1946; s. Clarence Holt and Eleanor Mitchell (Spain) H.; m. Janet Perkinson McDougald, Mar. 7, 1998; 1 child, Elizabeth Warren; stepchildren: Grant Levi Perkinson, Anna Stewart Perkinson. BSBA, East Carolina U., 1972, MA in Edn., 1974. Cert. econ. developer. Instr. in bus. Isothermal Community Coll., Forest City, N.C., 1972-73, Wilson (N.C.) Tech. Coll., 1973-74; county mgr., indsl. developer Warren County, Warrenton, N.C., 1974-78; prin. Warrenton Ins. & Real Estate, 1978-86; pres. Moore County Econ. Devel. Corp., Pinehurst, N.C., 1986-96; pres., CEO Rsch. Triangle Regional Partnership, N.C., 1996—; adj. faculty mem. Sandhills Community Coll., 1987-96. Author: Managing Financial and Marketing Rural Economics Development. Adv. bd. Cape Fear Area Consortium of Small Bus. Tech. and Devel. Ctr.; mem. friends of children com. Bapt. Children's Home, 1986-96; ex officio dir. Pinehurst Area Conv. and Vis. Bur., 1988-96. With U.S. Army, 1968-69, Vietnam. Recipient Disting. Svc. award, Warren County, N.C., 1977. Mem. Internat. Devel. Rsch. Coun., N.C. Indsl. Assn. (pres. 1978-79), Am. Econ. Devel. Coun., So. Indsl. Devel Coun., Sandhills C. of C. (ex officio), Pinehurst Country Club, Rotary (Sandhills, N.C.) (bd. dirs. 1989-96. Avocations: tennis, golf, reading, traveling. E-Mail: chayes@researchtriangle.org. Office: Research Triangle Regional Partnership PO Box 80756 Raleigh NC 27623-0756

HAYES, CHARLES LAWTON, insurance company executive, holding company executive; b. Cherryville, N.C., Nov. 8, 1927; s. Charles Lafayette and Alma D. Hayes; m. Joyce Williams, Oct. 7, 1950; children: Charles Gregory, Joy and Jill (twins). B.S., U. N.C., 1949. C.P.A., Md. With Monumental Life Ins. Co. subs. Monumental Corp., Balt., 1949-68; sr. v.p. Monumental Life Ins. Co. subs. Monumental Corp., until 1968; sec.-treas. Monumental Corp., 1968-83; dir. fin. Dome Corp., subs. Johns Hopkins U. and Health System, Balt., 1985-88; contr. Sheppard T Powell Assocs., Balt., 1988-94; assoc. VR Bus. Brokers, Md., 1994—. Former trustee Western Md. Coll.; former chmn. and bd. dir. Jr. Achievement of Met. Balt., Inc. Served with USNR, 1945-46. Fellow Life Office Mgmt. Assn.; mem. Phi Beta Kappa, Beta Gamma Sigma. Office: 8775 Cloudleap Ct Ste 231 Columbia MD 21045-3058

HAYES, CLAUDE QUINTEN CHRISTOPHER, research scientist; b. N.Y.C., Nov. 15, 1945; s. Claude and Celestine (Stanley) H. BA in Chemistry and Geol. Sci., Columbia U., 1971, postgrad., 1972-73; postgrad., N.Y. Law Sch., 1973-75; JD, Western State Law Sch., 1978. Cert. community coll. tchr. earth scis., phys. sci., law, Calif. Tech. writer Burroughs Corp., San Diego, 1978-79; instr. phys. scis. Nat. U., San Diego, 1980-81; instr. bus. law, earth scis. Miramar Coll., 1978-82; sr. systems analyst Gen. Dynamics Convair, 1979-80, advanced mfg. technologist, sr. engr., 1980-81; pvt. practice sci. and tech. cons. Calif., 1979—; instr. phys. sci., phys. geography, bus. law San Diego Community Coll. Dist., 1976-82, 85-90; U.S. Dept. Def. contractor Def. Nuclear Agy., Strategic Def. Initiative Agy., USAF, Def. Advance Rsch. Projects Agy., 1986—, U.S. Army, 1991—; adj. prof. phys. chemistry San Diego State U., 1986-87; bus. and computer sci. def. rsch. contractor to Maxwell Labs., Naval Ocean Sys. Ctr.; tech. cons. Pizza Hut, Inc., Carts of Colo., Smiths Industries. Contbr. articles to profl. jours.; patentee in field. Mem. Am. Chem. Soc., N.Y. Acad. Sci., Am. Inst. Aero. and Astronautics, Princeton Columbia Barnard Club. Avocations: travel, technical, ancient history, art, people. Home and office: 3737 3rd Ave Apt 308 San Diego CA 92103-4133

HAYES, COLLEEN BALLARD, writer, photographer; b. Kansas City, Mo.; d. Charles Richard and Mary Frances (Ballard) Hayes. *Searching for family descended from direct ancestors, including Sir John Spencer's daughter, Mary, sister and co-heir of Princess Diana's ancestor; PhilaDelphia Lee Ludwell; Mary Queen of Scots; and Col. Thomas Ballard who, circa 1660, established himself at Virginia's Middle Plantation (later, Williamsburg). Ballard was speaker of the House of Burgesses, lawyer and member of the Governor's Council (equivalent to England's House of Lords). Descendant Larkin Ballard married Elizabeth Gaines, making Colleen Ballard twice descended from Sir John Gaines (Games) of Brecon, Wales, whose ancestor, Sir Dafyyd Gam, died at the Battle of Agincourt, France, fighting for his friend King Henry V.* BA in English, U. Kans., 1972. Assoc. editor, reporter Johnson County Sun newspapers, Johnson County, KS, 1967-68; editor, writer press releases and pub. rels. Met. Plan Agy., 1968-70; writer speeches, Freedom of Info. and other letters for Pres. U.S., U.S. Sens., U.S. Reps., midwest govs., EPA, 1972-82. Contbr. articles to Elle Mag., Travel-Holiday, Country Inns Mag., Archtl. Digest publs., The Boston Globe, The Phila. Inquirer, Chgo. Tribune, L.A. Times, The Balt. Sun, and more than 70 others. Published photography to illustrate her articles in the foregoing, as well as both in Odyssey, San Francisco Examiner, The Denver Post, Christian Science Monitor, The Detroit News, The Orlando Sentinel, St. Petersburg Times, St. Louis Post Dispatch, San Jose Mercury News, N.Y. Daily News, The Plain Dealer, Chicago Sun-Times, Des Moines Register, Richmond (VA) Times-Dispatch, Women's Sports and Fitness, The Calgary Herald, numerous others in U.S. and Can. Travelled world-wide on writing assignments.; co-author: Anthology Am. Holidays; contbr. numerous nat. and regional poetry anthologies; Nat. Scholastic Mag. (recipient writing award), Mo. Hist. Rev., numerous others; lead in drama prodns. at regional theaters and Topeka Civic Theater; commentator on WIBW-TV, performed role of Medea on WIBW-TV, guest interviewer KCUR-FM, others. Recipient 1st prize Bethany Coll. Creative Writing Award, numerous others; Key to City of St. Joseph, Mo.; Commissioned to Hon. Order Ky. Cols.; winner of City and regional Tennis awards. Mem. Jackson County Historical, Quantrill Historical, Pony Express Historical and St. Andrew Scottish Socs., Woodside Racquet Club. Avocations: history, international and adventure travelling, lap swimming, tennis, golfing. E-mail: bcolin77@hotmail.com., bballard7@yahoo.com. Address: PO Box 40133 Shawnee Mission KS 66204

HAYES, CONSTANCE J., pediatric cardiologist; b. Cortland, N.Y., July 16, 1937; d. John Burns and Anna Marie (McGuire) H.; m. Edward William Lewison, Nov. 8, 1980. RN, BS, Coll. St. Rose, 1959; MD, Loyola U., Chgo., 1965. Diplomate Am. Bd. Pediatrics, Am. Bd. Pediatric Cardiology, Nat. Bd. Med. Examiners. Resident in pediat. St. Vincent's Hosp., N.Y.C., 1965-68; fellow in pediat. cardiology Columbia U., N.Y.C., 1968-71, assoc. pediat. coll. p. & s., 1971-72, asst. prof. clin. pediat., 1972-80, assoc. clin. prof. pediat., 1980-99, prof. clin. pediat., 1999—. Contbr. articles to profl. jours. Fellow Am. Acad. Pediatrics, Am. Coll. Cardiology; mem. Am. Heart Assn., N.Y. Heart Assn., Pediatric Cardiology Soc. Greater N.Y. (pres. 1987-88). Office: Columbia Presbyn Med Ctr 3959 Broadway New York NY 10032-1537

HAYES, DAVID JOHN ARTHUR, JR., legal association executive; b. Chgo., July 30, 1929; s. David J.A. and Lucille (Johnson) H.; m. Anne Huston, Feb. 20, 1963; children—David J.A. III, Cary. A.B., Harvard U., 1952; J.D., Ill. Inst. Tech.-Kent Coll. Law, 1961. Bar: Ill. Trust officer, asst. sec. First Nat. Bank of Evanston, Ill., 1961-63; gen. counsel Ill. State Bar Assn., Chgo., 1963-66; asst. dir. ABA, Chgo., 1966-68, div. dir., 1968-69, asst. exec. dir., 1969-87, v.p., 1987-88, assoc. exec. v.p., 1989-90, sr. assoc. exec. v.p., 1990, exec. dir., 1990-94, exec. dir. emeritus, 1994—; exec. dir. Naval Res. Lawyers Assn., 1971-75; asst. sec. gen. Internat. Bar Assn., 1978-80, 90—, Inter-ABA, 1984—. Contbr. articles to profl. jours. Capt. JAGC, USNR. Fellow Am. Bar Found. (life); mem. Ill. State Bar Assn. (ho. of dels. 1972-76), Nat. Orgn. Bar Counsel (pres. 1967), Chgo. Bar Assn., Michigan Shores Club. Home: 908 Pontiac Rd Wilmette IL 60091-1349 Office: ABA 750 N Lake Shore Dr Chicago IL 60611-4403

HAYES, DAVID MICHAEL, lawyer; b. Syracuse, N.Y., Dec. 2, 1943; s. James P. and Lillie Anna (Wood) H.; m. Elizabeth S. Tracy, Aug. 26, 1972; children: Timothy T., AnnElizabeth S. AB, Syracuse U., 1965; LLB, U. Va., 1968. Bar: Va. 1968, N.Y. 1969. Assoc. Hiscock & Barclay, Syracuse, 1968-72; asst. gen. counsel Agway Inc., Syracuse, 1972-81, gen. counsel, sec., 1981-87, v.p., gen. counsel, sec., 1987-92, sr. v.p., gen. counsel, sec., 1992—; adj. prof. law Syracuse U. Coll. Law; former chmn. Nat. Coun. of Farmer Coops. Legal Tax and Acctg. Com. Bd. dirs., former pres. Boys and Girls Club of Syracuse. With Army N.G., 1968-74. Fellow N.Y. Bar Found.; mem. ABA, Onondaga County Bar Assn. (pres. 1998), N.Y. State Bar Assn. (ho. of dels.), Va. State Bar, Century Club, Skaneateles Country Club. Democrat. Office: Agway Inc PO Box 4933 Syracuse NY 13221-4933

HAYES, DAVID VINCENT, sculptor; b. Hartford, Conn., Mar. 15, 1931; s. David Vincent and Adelaide (Brown) H.; m. Julia Moriarty, June 22, 1957; children—David Matthew, Brian James, Mary Judith, John Mark. AB, U. Notre Dame, 1953; MFA, Ind. U., 1955. Vis. lectr. visual and environ. studies Harvard U., 1972-73; regent U. Hartford, 1992-94. One man shows include Ind. U., 1955, Wesleyan U., Middletown, Conn., 1958, Mus. Modern Art, 1959, Willard Gallery, N.Y.C., 1961-64, 66, 69, 71, U. Notre Dame-Ind. U., 1963, Root Art Center, Clinton, N.Y., 1963, Galerie David Anderson, Paris, France, 1966, Columbus (Ohio) Mus., 1974, Martha Jackson Gallery, N.Y.C., 1974, Everson Mus., Syracuse, N.Y., 1975, DeCordova Mus., Lincoln, Mass., 1977, Springfield (Mass.) Mus., 1978, SUNY, Albany, 1978, Dartmouth Coll., 1979, Amherst Coll., 1979, Nassau County (N.Y.) Mus., 1979, Saratoga Performing Arts Center, Sarasota Springs, N.Y., 1980, Old State House, Hartford, 1981, Shippee Gallery, N.Y.C., 1984, 86, Elaine Benson Gallery, Bridgehampton, N.Y., 1993, Anderson Gallery, Buffalo, 1994, Prudential Ctr., Boston, 1996, U. New Haven, 1997, Orlando City Hall, Boca Raton Mus., 1998; numerous group shows, 1959—; represented in permanent collections Mus. Modern Art, Guggenheim Mus., Carnegie Inst., Hirshhorn Mus., Washington, U. Notre Dame, Mus. Fine Arts, Houston, Wadsworth Atheneum, Hartford, Addison Gallery Am. Art, Andover, Mass., Currier Gallery Art, Manchester, N.H., Williams Coll., Dartmouth Coll., Harvard U., Hartwood Acres, Pitts., Hartford Pub. Library, Snite Mus., Notre Dame, Ind., Western Mich. U., Kalamazoo, U. Hartford, others. Regent, U. Hartford, Conn., 1992-96. Recipient Logan medal Art Inst. Chgo., 1960; Fulbright research grantee, 1961; Guggenheim fellow, 1961; grantee Nat. Inst. Arts and Letters, 1965. Mem. Sculptors Guild N.Y. (bd. dirs. 1994—).

HAYES, DEBRA TROXELL, family nurse practitioner; b. Highland, Ill., Oct. 11, 1952; d. Robert E. and Marilyn M. (Schwend) Troxell; m. Jay F. Hayes, May 31, 1985; children: Amy Myers, Eric Myers. Diploma, Graham Hosp. Sch. Nursing, 1973; BSN, Sangamon State U., Springfield, Ill., 1985; MS, U. Ill., Chgo., 1995. RN, Ill.; cert. family nurse practitioner. Staff and relief charge nurse, head nurse Mason Dist. Hosp., Havana, Ill., 1973-77; staff and relief charge nurse, nursery charge nurse Graham Hosp., Canton, Ill., 1979-85; nurse coord. problem pregnancy program Cath. Social Svcs., Peoria, Ill., 1985-86; nurse clinician Oncology Hemtalogy Assocs., Peoria, 1986-95; FNP Coleman Clinic, Ltd., Canton, Ill., 1995—. McFarland scholar Mason Dist. Hosp., 1970, Illinois Farm Bur. Nurse Practitioner scholar, 1993-94. Mem. ANA, Ill. Nurses Assn., Ill. NP Coun., Ill. Rural Health Assn.$d, Oncology rsing Soc. Home: 9526 W Lake Lancelot Dr Mapleton IL 61547-9723

HAYES, DENNIS EDWARD, geophysicist, educator; b. St. Joseph, Mo., Oct. 3, 1938; s. William Franklin and Gertrude Margaret (Lorson) H.; m. Leslie Eve Price, May 17, 1978; children—Jennifer, Katharine, Elizabeth, Élan. B.S.E. summa cum laude, Kans. U., 1961; Ph.D., Columbia U., 1966. Research asso. Columbia U., 1966-71, sr. research asso., 1971-74, asso. prof., 1974-77, prof. geophysics, 1977—, chmn. dept. geol. scis., 1989-94, 97—; chmn. exec. com. Arts and Scis. faculty, 1994-96; assoc. dir. Lamont-Doherty Geol. Obs., 1978-81, 84—; deputy dir. edn. Lamont-Doherty Obs. Columbia U., 1998—; mem. ocean scis. bd. and polar rsch. bd. NAS; mem. adv. panel to earth scis. divsn. NSF, polar programs divsn., ocean scis. divsn.; vis. prof. Stanford U., 1981; mem. IOC Commn. on Non-living Resources, Joint Oceanographic Insts. for Deep Earth Sampling Planning Commn., 1977-87; mem. Univ. Nat. Oceanog. Lab. Sys. coun., 1991—. Editor books including Antarctic Oceanology II, 1972, Marine Geophysics of S.E. Asia, I and II, 1978, 83, Marine Geology/Geophysics of the Circum-Antarctic, 1991; contbr. numerous articles to profl. jours. Recipient Haworth Disting. Alumni Honors in Geology Kans. U., 1977; NSF fellow, 1961-65; John Simon Guggenheim fellow, 1980-81. Fellow Am. Geophys. Union, Geol. Soc. Am.; mem. Soc. Exploration Geophysicists, Am. Assn. Petroleum Geologists, Tau Beta Pi. Home: 6 Century Rd Palisades NY 10964-1503 Office: Lamont-Doherty Geol Obs Palisades NY 10964 *I believe maintaining one's personal integrity may be the single most important ingredient in a successful and satisfying career.*

HAYES, DENNIS JOSEPH, library director; b. Jersey City, N.J., Jan. 17, 1934; s. Thomas and Clara (Williams) H. BS, St. Peter's Coll., Jersey City, 1956; MLS, Rutgers U., 1958; student, Jersey City State Coll., 1958-60. Cert. profl. libr., N.J. With Jersey City Pub. Libr., 1951—, dep. dir., 1985, libr. dir., 1986-90, supr. tech. svcs., 1991-92, libr. dir., 1992—. Mem. Jour. Squ. Adv. and Action Com., Jersey City; area coord. Hudson County Librs., Jersey City, 1983. Mem. ALA, N.J. Libr. Assn., Hudson County Libr. Asn. (past pres.), Jersey City Suprs.' Assn. (past pres.), Kiwanis (Jersey City chpt.). Democrat. Roman Catholic. Home: 74 Tonnele Ave Jersey City NJ 07306-5409 Office: Jersey City Free Pub Libr 472 Jersey Ave Jersey City NJ 07302-3456*

HAYES, DEREK CUMBERLAND, banking executive, lawyer; b. Toronto, Ont., Can., Sept. 27, 1936; s. Charles Walter and Phyllis (Cumbel) H.; m. Susan Howard Bennett, July 13, 1963; children—Sean, Kate, Stewart. B.A., U. Toronto, 1958; LL.B., 1961; LL.M., U. London, 1965. Bar: Called to Ont. bar 1963. Solicitor firm McCarthy & McCarthy, Toronto, 1963-67; lawyer Massey-Ferguson Ltd., Toronto, 1967-71; sec. Massey-Ferguson Ltd., 1977-80; v.p., gen. counsel, sec. Shell Can. Ltd., Toronto, 1980-84; gen. counsel, sr. v.p. Canadian Imperial Bank of Commerce, 1984-94; exec. v.p., gen. counsel, 1994—; sr. solicitor T. Eaton Co. Ltd., Toronto, 1971-73; legal adviser Govt. of Tanzania, 1973-74. Bd. dirs. Opera Hamilton, 1993—, Toronto Symphony Orchestra, 1995—; mem. provost's com. Trinity Coll., 1995—. Mem. Law Soc. Upper Can., Can. Bar Assn. Club: Univ. (Toronto). Office: Commerce Ct N, Toronto, ON Canada M5L 1A2

HAYES, DONALD PAUL, JR., elementary and secondary education educator; b. Boston, Aug. 30, 1947; s. Donald P. and Grace E. (Moore) H.; m. Deborah J. Moore, July 15, 1978; children: Erin Eliza, Heather Alice, Jill Melina. AB, Salem State Coll., 1969; MEd with high distinction, Rivier Coll., 1992. Cert. tchr., prin., Mass. Tchr. E.N. Rogers Sch., Lowell, Mass., 1969-70, H.J. Molloy Sch., Lowell, 1970-78, Bartlett Sch., Lowell, 1978-81; founding tchr. McDonough City Magnet Sch., Lowell, 1981-95; tchr. Lowell H.S., 1995—, mem. curriculum frameworks com., 1995-99; founding tchr. The Latin Lyceum at Lowell H.S.; cons. Yonkers (N.Y.) Pub. Schs., 1986-87, Ft. Worth Ind. Sch. Dist., 1994; program dir. 1st ann. Micro-Soc. Conf., N.Y.C., 1993; founder, mem. Micro-Soc. Consortium; publs. mgr. 2nd Ann. Micro-Soc. Conf., Pepperrell, Mass., 1994. Author, coord., developer Micro-Soc. Pub. Strand Curriculum, 1981-95; author, developer Micro-Soc. history curriculum for grade 9; author: Locke Family Genealogy Supplement I, 1979, Historic Andover, 1971, Guide to Andover History, 1976; mem. adv. bd. Equity, Choice, 1986-94, New Schools, New Communities, 1994-96; co-author: The Micro-Society School, 1992; editor: Locke Sickle and Sword, 1972—. Sec. Locke Family Assn., Rye, N.H., 1971—; asst. dir. Samuel Parris Archaeol. Excavation, 1970-73; active Andover (Mass.) Hist. Commn., 1974-78; pres. Andover Hist. Soc., 1976-78, 1st Parish Unitarian Universalist Ch., Chelmsford, Mass., 1992-93. Recipient Award of Appreciation, Airflow Club of Ami, 1998, Locke Family Assn., 1980, 97, Andover Hist. Soc., 1978, Town of Andover, 1976, 78. Mem. Nat. Assn. Tchrs. of History, Airflow Club Am. (v.p. 1994-98), Piscataqua Pioneers (chaplain 1995-96, v.p. 1996—), New England Hist. Geneaol. Soc., Soc. Automotive Historians, Sons Union Vets. of Civil War (patriotic instr., sr. vice commdr. 1997-98). Mem. Unitarian Universalist Ch. Avocations: antique cars, historical research. Home: 102 Crooked Spring Rd North Chelmsford MA 01863-2307 Office: Lowell High Sch 50 Father Morissette Blvd Lowell MA 01852-1050

HAYES, EDWARD LEE, religious organization administrator; b. Modesto, Calif., Sept. 26, 1931; s. George Lester and Sylvia (Utzinger) H.; m. Marilyn Elizabeth Bjorklund, July 31, 1954; children: Carla Hayes Strickfaden, Darryl, Bryan. BA in Social Sci., Westmont Coll., 1953; ThM in Bibl. Studies, Dallas Theol. Sem., 1957; postgrad., Calif. State U., L.A., 1962-65, Iliff Theol. Sem., Denver, 1962-65; PhD in Higher Edn. Adminstrn., U. Denver, 1966. Ordained to ministry Bapt. Ch., 1957. Min. to youth Reinhardt Bible Ch., Dallas, 1954-57; asst. prof. ch. edn. Biola U., La Mirada, Calif., 1957-60; min. edn. First Bapt. Ch., Montebello, Calif., 1958-61; prof., acad. dean Denver Sem., 1960-79, pres., 1993-97, pres. emeritus, 1997—; exec. dir. Mt. Hermon (Calif.) Assn., 1979-92; cons. Scripture Press Pub. Co., 1963-73; lectr. in field. Author: Words To Live By, 1968, The Focused Life, 1986, The Church, 1999. Pres. PTA, Littleton, Colo., 1975-77; trustee Westmont Coll., Santa Barbera, 1973—. Grantee Lilly Found., Assn. Theol. Schs., 1968, Rsch. grantee Assn. Theol. Schs., 1976. Mem. Evang. Theol. Soc., Assn. Governing Bds. Republican. Avocations: art, horticulture, music, travel. Office: Denver Sem PO Box 10000 Denver CO 80250-9099

HAYES, EDWIN JUNIUS, JR., business executive; b. Brockton, Mass., July 20, 1932; s. Edwin Junius and Edith Franklin (Miller) H.; m. Brenda Storrs, Apr. 19, 1958; children: Bradford, Jonathan, Christopher. A.B., Dartmouth Coll., 1954, M.B.A., 1955; cert., U. Manchester (Eng.) Inst. Sci. and Tech., 1972. Various mgmt. positions Gen. Mills, 1955-67; product group mgr. Quaker Oats Co., Chgo., 1967-69; dir. mktg. Quaker Oats Ltd. (U.K.), London, 1969-72; v.p. internat., mng. dir. Quaker Oats Ltd. (U.K.), 1972-76; v.p. internat. William Underwood Co., Boston, 1976-77; exec. v.p. William Underwood Co., 1977-79; pres., chief exec. officer M. Grumbacher, Inc., N.Y.C., 1979-85; prin. and dir. Center for Concept Development Inc., N.Y.C., 1985-88, 1992—; pres., chief executive officer Diethelm and Keller (USA) Ltd., 1988-92, Delta Tech. Coatings, Inc., 1988-92; dir. Norfra Shipping Co. Mem. exec. adv. bd. Rutgers U., Newark; advisor Nat. Art Edn. Assn.; dir. Art and Craft Material Inst. Mem. Art and Craft Material Inst. (bd. dirs.), Nat. Maritime Mus. Greenwich (Eng.), Delta Upsilon. Office: Ctr for Concept Devel 33 State Rd Princeton NJ 08540-1304

HAYES, ELIZABETH LAMB, biology educator; b. Portland, Oreg., Aug. 5, 1940; d. Clyde Chester and Helen (Penni) Lamb; m. Robert William Hayes; children: Andrew Chester, Margaret Elizabeth Anne, Jennifer Eleanor Carlotta. BA, Marylhurst Coll., Oswego, Oreg., 1962; postgrad., So. Ill. U., 1962-63, U. Wis., Milw., 1965, 66; MS, Marquette U., 1965. Rsch. assoc. Marquette U., Milw., 1966; mem. faculty Cardinal Stritch Coll., Milw., 1965-66, Milw. Area Tech. Coll., 1966-68; assoc. prof. biology U. Wis., Fond du Lac, 1968—. Contbr. articles to profl. jours. Pres. Fond du Lac Sch. Bd., 1988-91, bd. dirs., clk., 1986, 87, 92-95. Marquette Univ. fellow, grad. scholar, 1963-65; Univ. Ctr. Sys. grantee U. Wis., 1991, 95, Undergrad. Tchr. Improvement grantee, 1992, grantee Choices of Northeastern Wis., 1993, 94, AAUW Fond du Lac br., 1997, Teens for Women in Sci. Seminar, 1997, Soroptimist Internat. of Fond du Lac, 1997; faculty fellow U. Wis. Mem. AAUW (pres. 1975-77, Postsecondary State Educator award, Post-Secondary Wis. Women Leaders in Edn. award Wis. State divsn. 1988-89, Fond du Lac br. 1988-89), AAAS, Am. Inst. Biol. Scis., Soroptimist Internat., Round Table. Episcopalian. Avocation: tennis. Office: U Wis Fond Du Lac 400 Campus Dr Fond Du Lac WI 54935-2950

HAYES, ELVIN ERNEST, retired basketball player; b. Rayville, La., Nov. 17, 1945. Grad., U. Houston, 1968. Basketball player San Diego Rockets, 1968-71, Houston Rockets, 1971-72, 81-83, Balt. Bullets, 1972-74, Capital Bullets, 1973-74, Washington Bullets, 1974-78. Named to Basketball Hall of Fame, 1989, All-NBA 1st Team, 1975, 77, 79, All-NBA 2d Team, 1973, 74, 76, NBA All-Defensive 2d Team, 1974, 75, NBA All-Rookie Team, 1969; record-holder single season most minutes played by rookie, 1969, NBa Finals single-game record most offensive rebounds, 1979; recipient Coll. Player of Yr. sporting News, 1968, All-Am. 1st Team, 1967, 68, All-Am. 2d Team, 1966. Home: 252 Piney Point Rd Houston TX 77024-7325 Office: c/o Basketball Hall Fame 1150 W Columbus Ave PO Box 179 Springfield MA 01101-0179*

HAYES, ERNEST M., podiatrist; b. New Orleans, Jan. 21, 1946; s. Ernest M. and Emma Hayes; m. Bonnie Ruth Beigle, Oct. 16, 1970. B.A., Calif. State U., Sacramento, 1969; B.S., Calif. Coll. Podiatric Medicine, San Francisco, 1971, D.P.M., 1973. Diplomate Am. Coun. Cert. Podiatric Physicians and Surgeons. Resident in surg. podiatry Beach Community Hosp., Buena Park, Calif., 1973-74, dir. residency program, 1974-75; practice podiatry, Anaheim, Calif., 1974-80, Yreka, Calif., 1980-95, Machias, Lubec and Calais, Maine, 1995—; surg. privledges Down East Cmty. Hosp., 1997—; sr. clin. instr. So. Calif. Podiatric Med. Center, Los Angeles, 1975-78; vice chmn. podiatry dept. Good Samaritain Hosp., Anaheim, Calif., 1978-79; mem. med. staff Mercey Med. Ctr., Mt. Shasta, Calif., CEO, Siskiyou Foot Group, Yreka, 1980-95; pres. Down East Podiatry, 1996—. Bd. dirs. Little Bogus Ranches Home Owners Assn., 1981-83, pres., 1983-84. Fellow Nat. Coll. Foot Surgeons; mem. Am. Assn. Podiatric Physicians and Surgeons, Kiwanis. Baptist. Home: PO Box 424 Machias ME 04654-0424

HAYES, GEORGE J., retired neurosurgeon; b. Washington, 1918. MD, Johns Hopkins U., 1943. Diplomate Am. Bd. Neurol. Surgery. Intern Johns Hopkins Hosp., 1944; fellow neurosurgeon Lahey Clinic, Boston, 1944-46; chief neurosurgery svc. Walter Reed Gen. Hosp., Washington, 1947-49, 50-51, 55-66; fellow neurosurgery Duke Hosp., 1949-50; chief neurosurg. svc. Brooke Army Hosp., Ft. Sam Houston, Tex., 1953-55; dir. profl. svc. Office Svc. Gen. Dept. Army, 1966-68; prin. dep. asst. sec. def. health & environment Office Sec. Def., 1971-74; clin. prof. neurosurgery George Washington U. Mem. ACS, Inst. Medicine-NAS, Am. Assn. Neurol. Surgeons.

HAYES, GEORGE NICHOLAS, lawyer; b. Alliance, Ohio, Sept. 30, 1928; s. Nicholas John and Mary Irene (Fanady) H. BA, U. Akron, 1950; MA, Western Res. U., 1953, LLB, 1955. Bar: Ohio 1955, U.S. Dist. Ct. Alaska 1957, U.S. Ct. Appeals (9th cir.) 1958, Alaska 1959, U.S. Supreme Ct. 1964, Wash. 1972. Mcpl. ct. prosecutor, asst. county prosecutor Portage County, Ravenna, Ohio, 1955-57; asst. U.S. atty. Fairbanks and Anchorage, Alaska, 1957-59; dep. atty gen. State of Alaska, Anchorage, 1959-62; dist. atty. 3d Jud. Dist., Anchorage, 1960-62; atty gen. Juneau, Alaska, 1962-64; spl. counsel to Gov. on earthquake recovery program State of Alaska, Washington, 1964; stockholder Delaney, Wiles, Hayes, Gerety & Ellis, Inc. and predecessor, Anchorage, 1964-92, of counsel, 1992. Mem. ABA, Wash. State

Bar Assn., Alaska Bar Assn, Ohio Bar Assn., Anchorage Bar Assn. Democrat. Office: Delaney Wiles Hayes 1007 W 3rd Ave Anchorage AK 99501-1917

HAYES, GERALD JOSEPH, lawyer; b. Bronx, N.Y., July 24, 1950; s. James Joseph and Gladys (Guest) H.; m. Diane Elizabeth Willoughby, July 21, 1984; children: Erin Jane, Thomas Joseph, Cara Elizabeth. BA, U. Mass., 1972; JD, U. Miami, 1978. Bar: N.Y. 1979, U.S. Dist. Ct. (so. dist.) N.Y. 1979. Assoc. Baker & McKenzie, N.Y.C., 1978-85, ptnr., 1985—, mng. ptnr., 1995, 97, mem. policy com., 1997—; mem. Bus. Coun. for UN, 1990-95. Nat. alumni adv. bd. U. Miami Sch. Law, 1992—. Mem. ABA (atomic energy com. publ utility law sect. 1983, vice chair internat. tort & ins. law com., tort & ins. practice sect. 1997—), Assn. Bar City N.Y. (com. on nuclear tech. and law 1979-82, 85-88, com. on ins. law 1983-84), Nat. Assn. Ins. Commrs. (adv. com. on internat. law 1989-90), Nat. Risk Retention Assn. (govt. affairs com.). Office: Baker & McKenzie 805 3rd Ave New York NY 10022-7513

HAYES, J. MICHAEL, lawyer; b. St. Louis, Dec. 10, 1946; s. Frank J. and Louise J. (Lough) H.; m. Vicky J. Verbocy, May 27, 1972; children: Thomas K., James M. BS summa cum laude, SUNY, Brockport, 1973; JD, SUNY, Buffalo, 1976. Bar: N.Y. 1977, U.S. Dist. Ct. (we. dist.) N.Y. 1977. Assoc. Smith, Murphy & Schoepperle, Buffalo, 1977-79, Tenney, Smith & Scott, Buffalo, 1979-82, Terry D. Smith, Buffalo, 1982-86; ptnr. Smith, Keller, Hayes & Miner, Buffalo, 1986-94; pvt. practice Buffalo, 1994—. Office: 69 Delaware Ave Rm 1111 Buffalo NY 14202-3805

HAYES, JACK IRBY, historian; b. Danville, Va., Aug. 13, 1944; s. Jack Irby and Minnie Lee (Conner) H.; m. Bernadine Joy Arnn, June 5, 1966; children: Emily Wilson, Julia Arnn. BS in History, Hampden-Sydney Coll., 1966; MA in History, Va. Poly. Inst. and State U., 1968; PhD in History, U. S.C., 1972; BS in Bus., Averett Coll., 1987. Dir. continuing edn. U. S.C., Columbia, 1972-74; asst. prof. history Averett Coll., Danville, 1974-77, assoc. prof., 1977-82, prof., 1982-90, W.C. Daniel prof. history and polit. sci., 1990—, chmn. dept. history, 1976—; adj. prof. grad. sch. Va. Poly. Inst. and State U., Blacksburg, 1977-79; archival cons. Dibrell Bros., Inc., Danville, 1990-91. Author: A History of Averett College, 1984, Dan Daniel and the Persistence of Conservatism in Virginia, 1997. Jud. ethics adv. com. Commonwealth Va., 1999—. Grantee Va. Found. for Humanities and Pub. Policy, Charlottesville, 1976-87, Commn. on Bicentennial of U.S. Constn., Washington, 1989, 90; Westmoreland Davis Meml. Found. fellow, 1967-68, Seminar for Hist. Adminstrs. fellow, Colonial Williamsburg, Va., 1967, Louis P. Jones fellow, U. S.C., 1998; named one of Outstanding Young Men of Am., 1977. Mem. So. Hist. Assn., Assn. for Preservation of Va. Antiquities (life), Kiwanis (lt. gov. div. 2 capital dist. 1991-92, pres. Danville club 1989), So. Assn. Colls. and Schs. (mem. re-accreditation com. 1986-99), German Club Danville. Avocations: running, tennis. Home: 245 Linden Dr Danville VA 24541-3523 Office: Averett Coll 420 W Main St Danville VA 24541-3612

HAYES, JACQUELINE CREMENT, real estate broker and developer; b. Chgo., Aug. 12, 1941; d. John and Lottie (Czech) Crement; m. Larry G. Hayes, Mar. 4, 1972 (div. Dec. 1978). BA in Mgmt., DePaul U., 1977. Lic. real estate broker, Ill. Bldg. mgr. LaSalle Bank Bldg., Chgo., 1978-80; v.p., gen. mgr. The Hayman Co., Chgo., 1981-83; pres. Jacqueline Hayes & Assoc., Chgo., 1983—; ptnr. The Retail Group, Chgo., 1986-93; panelist retail planning seminar Dept. Planning, City of Chgo., 1988, steering com. River North urban design plan, 1987-89, pedestrian count, 1989, Streeterville urban design plan, 1990-95, Downtown Framework Plan, 1990-95; mem. mentorship program Woman of Destiny, 1992-93. Docent Chgo. Archtl. Found.; mem. Burnham Park Planning Bd., Chgo.; bd. dirs., mem. exec. com., v.p., chmn. planning, zoning and urban design, chmn. civc affairs, chosen mem. of last decade, 1999, spokesperson Greater North Michigan Ave. Assn., Chgo., 1986—; mem. adv. coun. Friends of Downtown, 1987-89; bd. dirs. Cactus Theatre, 1990-92; bd. dirs., mem. franchising task force, chmn. nominating com. Lawson House YMCA, 1993—; liaison to real estate com. Streeterville Orgn. of Active Residents. Named Broker of Yr. Chgo. Sun-Times, 1986, one of Top Businesswomen Crain's Chgo. Bus., 1990-91, Woman of Destiny, 1990-92, one of 100 Women Who Make a Difference Today's Chgo. Woman, 1995; recipient Cert. of Leadership, YWCA of Met. Chgo., 1997. Mem. NAFE, Internat. Coun. Shopping Ctrs., Comml. Real Estate Orgn. (bd. dirs., v.p., chmn. membership 1986-89), Am. Biol. Inst. (rsch. bd. advisors, Disting. Leadership award), Chgo. Real Estate Exec. Women (bd. dirs., sec., mentorship program 1988-95), Chgo. Assn. Commerce and Industry (mem. govt. affairs com.), Urban Land Inst., River North Assn., Met. Planning coun. (mem. bus. leaders for transp. com.), Women in Planning and Devel., Women in Retail Leasing (founder 1993), Lambda Alpha (bd. dirs., sec. 1994, v.p. edn. 1995, v.p. programs 1996, pres. 1997, mem. of Yr. 1995). Office: Jacqueline Hayes & Assocs 155 N Harbor Dr Ste 301 Chicago IL 60601-7386

HAYES, JACQUELINE M., geriatrics nurse; b. Worcester, Mass., June 25, 1936; d. Romey I. and Leona L. (Brown) Sweet; m. James G. Hayes, Oct. 11, 1971; children: Michael J., Daniel E. Diploma, Burbank Hosp. Sch. Nursing, 1959; BS, Framingham State Coll., 1974; MS in Nursing, Anna Maria Coll., 1988. RN, Mass.; cert. gerontol. nurse. Clin. dir. nursing edn. Marlboro (Mass.) Hosp., asst. dir. nursing; staff devel. coord. Belmont Home, Worcester; mgmt. minutes questionaire nurse Westboro Nursing Ctr., 1995—. Mem. ANA (cert. nursing adminstr.), Mass. Nurses Assn. (dist. bd. dirs., mem. cabinet in nursing ethics, cabinet on continuing edn.), Sigma Theta Tau Internat. Home: 70 Londonderry Rd Grafton MA 01519-1502

HAYES, JANET GRAY, retired business manager, former mayor; b. Rushville, Ind., July 12, 1926; d. John Paul and Lucile (Gray) Frazee; A.B. Ind. U., 1948; M.A. magna cum laude, U. Chgo., 1950; m. Kenneth Hayes, Mar. 20, 1950; children: Lindy, John, Katherine, Megan. Psychiat. caseworker Jewish Family Service Agy., Chgo., 1950-52; vol. Denver Crippled Children's Service, 1954-55; vol. Adult and Child Guidance Clinic, San Jose, 1958-59; mem. San Jose (Calif.) City Council, 1971-75, vice-mayor, 1973-75, mayor, 1975-82; co-chmn. com. urban econs. U.S. Conf. Mayors, 1976-78, co-chmn. task force on aging, mem. sci. and tech. task force, 1976-80, bd. trustees, 1977-82; bd. dirs. League Calif. Cities, 1976-82, mem. property tax reform task force, 1976-82; chmn. State of Calif. Urban Devel. Adv. Com., 1976-77; mem. Calif. Commn. Fair Jud. Practices, 1976-82, client-community relations dir. Q. Tech., Santa Clara, Calif., 1983-85, bus. mgr. Kenneth Hayes MD, Inc., 1985-88; pres. bd. trustees San Jose Mus. Art, 1987-89; founder, adv. bd. Calif. Bus. Bank, 1982-85. Mem. Dem. nat. campaign com., 1976; mem. Calif. Dem. Commn. Nat. Platform and Policy, 1976; del. Dem. Nat. Conv., 1980; bd. dirs. South San Francisco Bay Dischargers Authority; chmn. Santa Clara County Sanitation Dist.; mem. San Jose/Santa Clara Treatment Plant Adv. Bd.; chmn. Santa Clara Valley Employment and Tng. Bd. (CETA); past mem. EPA Aircraft/Airport Noise Task Group; bd. dirs. Calif. Center Rsch. and Edn. in Govt., Alexian Bros. Hosp., 1983-92; bd. dirs., chmn. adv. council Public Tech. Inc.; mem. bd. League to Save Lake Tahoe, 1984—. AAUW Edn. Found. grantee. Mem. Assn. Bay Area Govts. (exec. com. 1971-74, regional housing subcom. 1973-74, regional housing subcom. 1973-74), LWV (pres. San Francisco Bay Area chpt. 1968-70, pres. local 1966-67), Mortar Bd., Phi Beta Kappa, Kappa Alpha Theta.

HAYES, JANICE CECILE, education educator; b. St. Paul, May 25, 1941; d. Robert E. Osgard and Elizabeth (Scheer) Olin; m. Dean Anthony Hayes, Dec. 14, 1938; children: Erin Elizabeth, Kara Lyn. AA, Itasca Jr. Coll., Coleraine, Minn., 1961; BS, U. Minn., Mpls., 1963; MEd, Middle Tenn. State U., Murfreesboro, 1967, DA, 1973. Tchr. rsch. program Kinesthetic, Auditory & Visual Devel. Program, Lake Forest, Ill., 1963-65; tchr. Lake Forest (Ill.) Sch. System, 1963-65, Murfreesboro (Tenn.) City Sch. System, 1965-66; prof. edn. Mid. Tenn. State U., Murfreesboro, 1973—; edn. coms. to pub. sch. sys., 1975—; reviewer Sch. Libr. Jour., N.Y., 1985—; mem. task force on implementing tchr. edn. in Tenn. State Dept. Edn., Nashville, 1989-94; bd. Concerned Faculty and Adminstrv. Women, Murfreesboro, 1984-88, 92-94; nat. appeals bd. Nat. Coun. for Accreditation of Tchr. Edn. Co-author: Beginning Teaching Handbook, 1988, Bridges to Strength: Tea-Ael Mentor Teacher, 1989, Establishing a Mentoring Program for Beginning Teachers, An Administrator's Guide, 1989, Attitude, Attitude, Attitude (grade 6-9), 1992, (grade 3-6), 1993, 94—, (grade K-3), 1997. Mem. adv. bd. June Anderson Women's Ctr., 1998—. Mem. MTSU Edn. Assn. (pres. 1998-99, bd. trustees 1994—, exec. com. 1997-98), Tenn. Edn. Assn. (bd. dirs. 1989-92, 94-98, disting. tchr. 1989, bd. Dept. Higher Edn., editor Success Stories 1997), Kappa Delta Pi (faculty rep. 1976-98), Phi Delta Kappa (past historian, bd. dirs.), Gamma Beta Phi, Delta Kappa Gamma. Democrat. Presbyterian. Avocations: traveling, reading, outdoor activities. Office: Mid Tenn State U PO Box 535 Murfreesboro TN 37133-0535

HAYES, JOHN EDWARD, broadcasting executive; b. Niagara Falls, N.Y., Sept. 14, 1941; s. John H. and Margaret (Wilson) H.; m. Jean Wheeler, Jan. 1, 1964; children: John Jr., Janice. BS in Broadcasting, U. Fla., 1963. State capital bur. chief Sta. WTVJ-TV, Miami, 1963-67; exec. asst. Fla. Dept. Consumer Svcs., 1967-71; state capitol bur. chief Sta. WTVT-TV, Tallahassee, 1971-77; asst. news dir. Sta. WTVT-TV, Tampa, Fla., 1977-79; news dir. Sta. WBRC-TV, Birmingham, Ala., 1979-82, Sta. KNTV-TV, San Jose, Calif., 1982-83; v.p., gen. mgr. Sta. KLAS-TV, Las Vegas, Nev., 1983-87; gen. mgr. Sta. WIVB-TV, Buffalo, 1987-89; pres. Jour. Broadcasting of Charlotte (N.C.) Co., 1989-92; v.p. TV Providence Jour. Co., 1992-97; pres., CEO, Raycom Media Inc., Montgomery, Ala., 1997—. Recipient Nat. Headliners award Headliners Club, 1973, Emmy award TV Acad. Arts and Sci., 1982, Alumnus of Distinction award U. Fla., 1998. Mem. Nat. Assn. Broadcasters, TV Bur. Advertisers, NBC Affiliates and CBS Alliance Group. Methodist. Avocation: golf. Office: Raycom Media Inc 201 Monroe St Montgomery AL 36104-3735

HAYES, JOHN FRANCIS, lawyer; b. Salina, Kans., Dec. 11, 1919; s. John Francis and Helen (Dye) H.; m. Elizabeth Ann Ireton, Aug. 10, 1950; children: Carl Ireton, Ann Chandler. A.B., Washburn Coll., 1941; LL.B., 1946. Bar: Kans. 1946, Mo. 1987. Pvt. practice Hutchinson, Kans., 1946—; dir. Gilliland & Hayes, P.A. (and predecessors), 1946—; mem. Commn. Uniform State Laws, 1975—; bd. dirs. Cen. Bank and Trust Co., Hutchinson, United Group of Funds, Cen. Fin. Corp., Waddell & Reed Funds, Inc. Mem. Kans. Ho. of Reps., 1953-55, 67-79, majority leader, 1975-77. Served as capt. AUS, 1942-46. Fellow Am. Bar Found., Am. Coll. Trial Lawyers; mem. Hutchinson C. of C. (pres. 1961), Kans. Assn. Def. Counsel (pres. 1972-73), Internat. Assn. Def. Counsel. Republican. Home: 31 Pawnee Dr Hutchinson KS 67502-2981 Office: 20 W 2nd Ave Fl 2 Hutchinson KS 67501-5246 also: 1211 Penntower Bldg 3100 Broadway St Kansas City MO 64111-2406 also: PO Box 49406 200 N Broadway St Ste 300 Wichita KS 67202-2324

HAYES, JOHN FREEMAN, architect; b. Media, Pa., June 16, 1926; s. James Alfred and Katharine Stoddard (Williams) H.; m. Anne Gitt Fox, Apr. 5, 1952; children—John Fox, Thomas Freeman, Anne Clarke. Grad., Haverford Sch., 1944; B.Arch., U. Pa., 1950. With various cos., 1954-60; partner Hayes & Hough (Architects), Phila., 1960-95; sr. cons. Blackney Hayes Architects, Phila., 1995—. Pres., The Carpenters Co. of the City and County of Phila., 1993. Served with USNR, 1944-46; served with USAF, 1951-53. Fellow Am. Inst. Architects. Episcopalian. Clubs: Martins Dam, Phila. Curling. Office: Blackney Hayes Architects 105 S 12th St Philadelphia PA 19107-4809

HAYES, JOHN M., writer, sculptor, photographer; b. May 21, 1922. BA, Butler U., 1948. Writer, sculptor, photographer, Balt., 1979—. E-mail: hayesaw@hotmail.com. Home: 1409 Kirkwood Rd Baltimore MD 21207

HAYES, JOHN PATRICK, electrical engineering and computer science educator, consultant; b. Newbridge, Ireland, Mar. 3, 1944; s. Patrick Joseph and Christine (Duggan) H.; m. Joan Benson, June 7, 1969; children: Thomas, Michael. BE in Elec. Engring., Nat. U. Ireland, Dublin, 1965; MS in Elec. Engring., U. Ill., 1967, PhD in Elec. Engring., 1970. Systems engr. Royal Dutch Shell Co., The Hague, The Netherlands, 1970-72; asst. prof. elec. engring. and computer sci. U. So. Calif., L.A., 1972-77, assoc. prof., 1977-82; prof. U. Mich., Ann Arbor, 1982—; cons. to various orgns., 1972—. Author: Computer Architecture and Organization, 1978, 3d edit., 1998, Digital System Design and Microprocessors, 1984, Hierarchical Modeling for VLSI Circuit Testing, 1990, Layout Minimization for CMOS Cells, 1992, Introduction to Digital Logic Design, 1993; contbr. articles to profl. jours. Fellow IEEE (assoc. editor jour. 1989-94); mem. Assn. Computing Machinery (assoc. editor jour. 1978-81), Sigma Xi. Office: U Mich Dept Elec Engring & Computer Sci Ann Arbor MI 48109

HAYES, JOHN PATRICK, retired manufacturing company executive; b. Manistee, Mich., May 9, 1921; s. John David and Daisy (Davis) H.; m. Margaret Barbara Butler, Apr. 12, 1947; children—John Patrick, Timothy Michael. BS, U. Detroit, 1947. With Nat. Gypsum Co., 1947-90, group v.p., 1970-75, pres., 1975-90, chmn. bd., chief exec. officer, 1983-90, also bd. dirs. Served to 1st lt. AUS, 1942-45. Mem. Brook Hollow Golf Club (Dallas). *

HAYES, JOHN ROBERT, health care executive, psychiatrist; b. Shelbyville, Ind., Mar. 18, 1948; s. Robert Earl and Betsy Ross (Fleming) H.; children from previous marriage: Daniel Ian, Mary Elizabeth; m. Barbara Marie Ryan, June 11, 1988; 1 child, Abigail Jane. BA in Zoology, Ind. U., 1970, MD, 1973. Diplomate Am. Bd. Psychiatry and Neurology. Intern in internal medicine Mayo Clinic, Rochester, Minn., 1973-74, resident in psychiatry, 1974-76; staff cons. in psychiatry Scott and White Clinic and Meml. Hosp., Temple, Tex., 1977-81; consultation-liaison psychiatrist Ind. U. Sch. Medicine, Indpls., 1981-83, dir. divsn. consultation liaison psychiatry, 1983-88; dir. med. psychiatry St. Vincent Hosps. and Health Care Ctrs., Indpls., 1988-90, dir. acad. affairs, 1991-95, v.p. for acad. and devel. affairs, 1996, sr. v.p. for the delivery sys., 1996-98, interim pres., 1998; CEO Seton Health Corp. of Ind., 1998; exec. dir. Eli Lilly and Co., Indpls., 1998—; part-time emergency rm. physician Cmty. Meml. Hosp., Spring Valley, Minn., 1975-76; lectr. dept. psychiatry Tex. A&M U., Temple, 1979-81; asst. prof. medicine Ind. U., 1981-84, asst. prof. psychiatry and medicine, 1984-88, clin. asst. prof. psychiatry and medicine, 1988—; bd. dirs. Pediat. Urgent Care Ctr., 1995-97; mem., sec., bd. dirs. Family Practice Technologies, Inc., 1995—. Contbr. articles to profl. jours. Co-pres. Southeastern Minn. Childbirth Edn. Assn., 1976; bd. dirs. Indpls. Met. YMCA Camp, 1981-84, chmn., bd. dirs., 1984, dir. for Psychiatry, Am. Bd. of Famlty Practice, 1990-95; bd. dirs. St. Vincent Found., 1999—, Chartwell Midwest Ind., 1996-98, Ind. U./Moi U. Kenya Project, 1998—. Recipient Man of Yr. award Flat Rock River YMCA, 1985, Svc. Recognition award Indpls. Met. YMCA, 1986. Fellow Am. Acad. Psychosomatic Medicine (mem. edn. directorate 1984-91, mem. nominating com. 1986-87, mem. long range planning com. 1986-87, mem. exec. coun. 1987-90, mem. ethics and stds. com. 1987-88, 90-91, mem. program com. 1987-91, program chmn. for nat. meeting 1988-89, rep. to nat. consultation/liaison psychiatry consortium 1988, chmn. budget and fin. com. 1989-93, v.p. 1992-93, pres.-elect 1993-94, pres. 1994-95, gov. 1996—), Am. Psychiat. Assn. (mem. com. consultation/liaison psychiatry 1985, cons. to com. consultation liaison psychiatry and primary care edn. 1990, 91, Nancy C.A. Roeske Cert. Recognition award 1992); mem. AMA del. to sect. on med. schs.), Am. Coll. Psychiatrists, Am. Coll. Physician Execs., Am. Coll. Healthcare Execs., Am. Soc. Psycho-Oncology/AIDS (mem. organizing group 1987), Am. Psychosomatic Soc., Ind. State Med. Assn., Ind. Psychiat. Soc. (program chmn. 1985-87, mem. exec. coun. 1986-87, mem. ethics com. 1989—, acting chmn. 1989-90), Indpls. Med. Soc., Internat. Coll. Psychosomatic Medicine., Blue Key, Alpha Omega Alpha. Presbyterian. Avocations: gardening, music, golf, fly fishing. Office: St Vincent Hosp & Health Care Ctr Lilly Corp Ctr Indianapolis IN 46285

HAYES, JOHN T., lawyer, accountant; b. Chgo., Oct. 9, 1927; s. Frank D. and Mildred G. (McEvoy) H.; m. Dolores J. Donahue, Aug. 21, 1954; 1 child, Virginia M. O'Sullivan. BS in Commerce, Loyola U., 1952; JD, I.I.T.-Chgo. Kent Coll. Law, 1960. Bar: Ill. 1960; CPA, Ill. Ptnr. Arthur Young & Co., Chgo., 1952-85; of counsel Schiff, Hardin & Waite, Chgo., 1985—; bd. dirs. Erikson Inst., Chgo.; adj. prof. Loyola U., Chgo., 1961-71; mem. com. planned giving Art Inst. Chgo., 1985—. mem. editl. bd. Estate Planning Mag., N.Y.C., 1975—; mem. charitable adv. bd. Trusts and Estates Mag., N.Y.C., 1995—; contbr. articles to profl. jours., chpts. to book. Bd. dirs. Kohl Children's Mus., Wilmette, Ill., 1992—, Grover Hermann Found., Chgo., 1992—. Pvt. 1st class USA, 1946-47. Mem. Chgo. Estate Planning Coun. (disting. svc. award 1995), Chgo. Bar Assn., Chgo. Athletic Assn., Ill. State Bar Assn., Ill. CPA Soc. Avocations: reading, chess, opera. Home: 444 Wagner Rd Northfield IL 60093-2922 Office: Schiff Hardin & Waite 233 S Wacker Dr Ste 7200 Chicago IL 60606-6473

HAYES, JOYCE MERRIWEATHER, secondary education educator; b. Bay City, Tex., Aug. 29, 1943; d. Calvin and Alonia (Harris) Merriweather. BS, Wiley Coll., Tex., 1967; postgrad., U. N.Y., Stony Brook, 1968; MS in Guidence Counseling, Ea. Mich. U., 1974; postgrad., Mercy Coll., 1991-92, Ea. Mich. U., 1991-92; MEd, U. Detroit, 1992. English tchr. Terrance Manor Mid. Sch., Augusta, Ga., 1968-69, Longfellow Jr. H.S., Flint, Mich., 1969-81; English tchr. No. H.S., Flint, 1981—, chmn. English dept., 1992—; English and speech tchr. Jordan Coll., Flint, 1989-91; adult edn. tchr. Mott Adult H.S., Flint, 1978-80, on-state content stds. com.; presenter workshops in field. Composer 3 gospel songs. Vol. Second Ward City Coun., Flint, 1989, Cmty. Coun., Flint, 1992-93, Cmty. Wide Assn. Coun., Flint, 1993; intercessory prayer warrior, 1995—; area dir. Home Ministry new mem. class tchr., Grace Emmanuel Bapt. Ch., co-coord. spl. svc. for Nat. Coun. Tchr. of Eng. Conv. Detroit, 1997. Mem. NEA, Nat. Coun. Tchrs. English (chair workshops 1992-93, mem. nominating com. 1994), Mich. Edn. Assn., United Tchrs. of Flint (in-svc. com., Flares-English tchrs.), Nat. Sorority Phi Delta Kappa (xinas advisor, del. to conf. 1999, past pres., advisor Gamma Delta chpt.). Home: 621 Thomson St Flint MI 48503-1942

HAYES, JUDY DIANE, medical/surgical and ophthalmological nurse, nursing administrator; b. Atlanta, Mar. 17, 1961; d. Coley Walter and Cloreece (Markham) H. Student, Tift Coll., Forsyth, Ga., 1979-81; BSN, Med. Coll. Ga., 1983. Camp nurse Camp Pinnacle Woman's Missionary Union of Ga., Atlanta; staff nurse postpartum Piedmont Hosp., Atlanta, staff nurse preceptor med.-surg. unit, 1984-91, charge nurse on med.-surg. unit, 1991—; vol. missionary nurse to Rio de Janeiro, 1985, to Mombassa, Kenya, 1988. Vol. missionary nurse to Panama, 1993, Belice, 1997. Mem. Nat. Bapt. Nursing Fellowship (v.p. Ga. chpt. 1991, pres.-elect 1992, pres. Ga. chpt. 1993-95, chmn. nominating com. 1996—), Sigma Theta Tau.

HAYES, KEVIN GREGORY, university administrator; b. Jamestown, N.Y., May 14, 1941; s. Francis Joseph and Mary Blanche (Driscoll) H.; m. Marilyn Jane Dougherty, Dec. 7, 1968; children: Tracy Lynn, Brendan Paul. AA in Humanities, Jamestown C.C., 1966; BA in English, Allegheny Coll., 1968; MA in Journalism, Pa. State U., 1974; EdD, Okla. State U., 1995. Broadcaster James Broadcasting Co., Jamestown, 1959-63, 65-66; program dir. Regional Broadcasters, Meadville, Pa., 1966-69; asst. radio-TV editor Pa. State U., University Park, 1969-71, assoc. publs. editor, 1971-75, publs. editor, 1975-80, asst. dir. agrl. comm., 1980-83, interm dir., 1983-84; info. specialist, chief of party Swaziland Cropping Systems Rsch. and Extension Tng. Project, 1984-87; asst. dir. agrl. comms. Pa. State U., University Park, 1987-88; prof., head agrl. com., Divsn. of Agrl., Okla. State U., Stillwater, 1988-94, prof., distance edn. coord., 1994-99, asst. dean grad. coll., 1997-98, dir. agrl. coms. svcs., 1999—. Author: On Coming Home, 1979, Distance Learning Policies in Postsecondary Education, 1996. With U.S. Army, 1963-65. Recipient Pioneer ACE award Agrl. Communicators in Edn., 1976. Mem. KC (grand knight 1990-92, dist. dep. 1992-97, state advocate 1997-99, state treas. 1999—), Phi Kappa Phi (treas. chpt. 24 1998-99), Kappa Tau Alpha, Epsilon Sigma Phi. Democrat. Roman Catholic. Avocations: creative writing, photography, woodworking, gardening. Home: 1123 S Mansfield Dr Stillwater OK 74074-1506 Office: Okla State U 437 Agr Admin Bldg Stillwater OK 74078-6031

HAYES, LARRY B., lawyer; b. Atlanta, Oct. 4, 1939; s. Luther F. and Ruby (Thomas) H.; m. Rebecca Thomason, Feb. 12, 1959; children: Laura Alison, Lawrence Bruce. BS in Pharmacy, U. Fla., 1962; JD, St. Mary's U., 1977. Bar: Tex. 1978, U.S. Dist. Ct. (no. dist.) Tex. 1979, U.S. Ct. Appeals (5th cir.) 1979; cert. personal injury trial law, Tex. Trial counsel Windle Turley PC, Dallas, 1978-82; ptnr. Ware & Hayes, Dallas, 1982-83; sr. trial atty. Green, Hayes & Ryan, Dallas, 1983-86; ptnr. Cantey & Hanger, Ft. Worth, 1986—. Mem. Tex. Bar Assn., Tex. Assn. Def. Counsel, Def. Rsch. Inst., Tarrant County Bar Assn., Tarrant County Civil Trial Lawyers Assn., Ridglea Country Club, Phi Delta Phi. Home: 3455 Mist Hollow Ct Fort Worth TX 76109-3112 Office: Cantey & Hanger 2100 Burnett Plaza 801 Cherry St Ste 2100 Fort Worth TX 76102-6898

HAYES, MARY ANN, social studies educator; b. Princeton, Ind., Sept. 25, 1941; d. John W. and Mozelle Scott; m. Donald L. Hayes, Aug. 18, 1963; 1 child, Elizabeth Ann. BA, U. Evansville, Ind., 1963; MLS, Ind. U., 1968. Tchr. Greater Jasper (Ind.) Schs., 1963—; dept. chair social studies Jasper H.S., 1990—. Alt. del. Rep. Nat. Conv., Kansas City, Mo., 1976; treas. North Dubois, Raintree Girl Scout Coun., 1995-98; pres. Dubois County Hist. Soc., 1997—; troop leader Girl Scouts, 1991—; v.p. Dubois County Mus. Inc., 1998—. Recipient Appreciation award Raintree Girl Scout Coun., Evansville, 1996. Mem. NEA, Ind. State Tchrs. Assn., Jasper Classroom Tchrs. Assn., Jasper Bus. and Profl. Women's Club (Woman of Yr. 1979), Jasper Bus. and Profl. Women's Club (pres. 1974-76, Woman of Yr. 1979), Dubois County Hist. Soc. (v.p. 1979-97), Psi Iota Xi (pres. 1971-72, pres. Aux. 1982-84). Republican. Presbyterian. Avocations: history, archaeology. Office: Jasper HS 1600 Saint Charles St Jasper IN 47546-9210

HAYES, MARY ESHBAUGH, newspaper editor; b. Rochester, N.Y., Sept. 27, 1928; d. William Paul and Eleanor Maude (Seivert) Eshbaugh; m. James Leon Hayes, Apr. 18, 1953; children: Pauli, Eli, Lauri Le June, Clayton, Merri Jess Bates. BA in English and journalism, Syracuse U., 1950. With Livingston County Republican, Geneseo, N.Y., summers, 1947-50, mng. editor, 1949-50; reporter Aurora Advocate, Colo., 1950-52; reporter-photographer Aspen Times, Colo., 1952-53, columnist, 1956—, reporter, 1972-77, assoc. editor, 1977-89, editor in chief, 1989-92, contbg. editor, 1992—; tchr. Colo. Mountain Coll., 1979, Aspen corr. Reuters, 1997—. *At age 8, Mary Eshbaugh and her brother, John Paul, were photographed for a third-grade textbook, Adventures in Science, published by Allyn and Bacon. Fascinated with the book project, Mary decided to follow that formula and become a writer, using real people in photographs. She followed her dream of becoming a writer and today her award-winning feature stories and profiles appear in newspapers and magazines. She has written a cookbook, Aspen Potpourri, featuring residents and their recipes and photographs. Her history book, The Story of Aspen, features photographs of Aspen residents with their stories.* Author, editor: The Story of Aspen, 1996; contbg. editor: Destinations Mag., 1994-97, Aspen Mag., 1996—; editor: Aspen Potpourri, 1968, rev. edit., 1990. Mem. Nat. Fedn. Press Women (1st prizes in writing and editing 1976-80, 1st prize Aspen Potpourri rev. 1990, 1st prize Story of Aspen 1996, 1st prize in adv. photography 1998), Colo. Press Women's Assn. (writing award, 1974, 75, 78-85, sweepstakes award for writing 1977, 78, 84, 85, 91-93, 2d place award 1976, 79, 82, 83, 94, 95, Woman of Achivement 1986), Aspen Cmty. Ch. Photographer. Home: PO Box 497 Aspen CO 81612-0497 Office: Box E Aspen CO 81612

HAYES, MARY PHYLLIS, savings and loan association executive; b. New Castle, Ind., Apr. 30, 1921; d. Clarence Edward and Edna Gertrude (Burgess) Scott; m. John Clifford Hayes, Jan. 1, 1942 (div. Oct. 1952); 1 child, R. Scott. Student, Ball State U., 1957-64, Ind. U. East, Richmond, 1963; diploma, Inst. Fin. Edn., 1956, 72, 76. Teller Henry County Savs. and Loan, New Castle, 1939-41, loan officer, teller, 1950-62, asst. sec., treas., 1962-69, sec., treas., 1969-73, corp. sec., 1973-84; v.p., sec. Ameriana Savs. Bank (formerly Henry County Savs. and Loan), New Castle, 1984-91; exec. sec. Am. Nat. Bank, Nashville, 1943-44; corp. sec. Ameriana Fin. Svcs., 1984-91. Treas. Henry County Chpt. Am. Heart Assn., New Castle, 1965-67, 76-87, vol. Indpls. chpt. 1980—; membership sec. Henry County Hist. Soc., New Castle, 1975-90; sec. Henry County chpt. ARC, New Castle, 1976-91; elected mem. Found. Inst. Fin. Edn., 1991—; mem. Internat. Platform Assn., 1974—, Woman's Club 1992—; vol. Ind. Basketball Hall of Fame, 1993—. Mem. Inst. Fin. Edn. (sec.-treas. East Ctrl. Ind. chpt. 1973-91), Ind. League Savs. Insts. (25 Yrs. award 1975, 40 Yrs. Cert. award 1988), Internat. Platform Assn., Henry County Hist. Soc. (mem. sec.), Altrusa (past officer, bd. dirs. New Castle chpt.), PEO (past chaplain, sec., past pres. 1994-95), Woman's Club, New Castle Henry County C. of C., Guyer Opera House Guild, Art Ctr. of Henry County, Psi Iota Xi (past sec.-treas.). Mem. Christian Ch. Avocations: music, travel, history, swimming.

HAYES, MAXINE DELORES, physician; b. Nov. 29, 1946; children: Leon Williams, Kevin Williams. AB in Biology, Spelman Coll., 1969; MD, SUNY

Buffalo, 1973; MPH, Harvard U., 1977. Intern pediat. Vanderbilt Hosp., Nashville, 1973-75; resident Children's Hosp., Boston, 1975-76; dir. Divsn. Parent-Child Health Svcs., Olympia, Wash., 1988-90; asst. sec. Divsn. Parent-Child Health Svcs., Olympia, 1990-93; asst. sec. Cmty. and Family Health, Olympia, 1993—, acting health officer, 1998—; pres. Assn. Maternal and Child Health Programs, Washington, 1995-97; nat. program dir. Robert Wood Johnson Child Health Initiative, 1994-97. Recipient Outstanding Contbns. in Field of Pub. Health award Wash. State Pub. Health Assn., 1994, Guardian of Women's Health award Aradia Women's Health Ctr., 1996. Fellow Am. Acad. Pediatrics; mem. APHA. Avocations: opera, art, science. Office: Cmty and Family Health PO Box 47830 Olympia WA 98504-7830

HAYES, MICHAEL, artist, editor; b. Chgo., July 23, 1946; d. Alva Michel and Elizabeth (Rosse) H.; m. Mitchell Jay Berg, Jan. 7, 1954. Student, Art Inst., Chgo., Inst. Design Ill. Inst. Tech.; BFA, Cooper Union Sch. Art & Arch. Artist: works exhibited in 10 one-person shows in N.Y. Galleries ; group shows include Galerie in Loft, Munich, Germany, 1985, Fratten Galerie Andere Zeichen, Berlin, 1985, Am. Cultural Ctr., Brussels, 1986, Atlantic Gallery, N.Y., Met. Mus. of Art, Cornelia St. Cafe, N.Y.; works are also included in private collections in U.S., U.K., Germany, Greece and Japan; columnist for Diversion Travel Planner, articles appeared in other art mags. including Fairlanes and First Mag., 1982-86. Home and Studio: 398 Columbia Ave Cliffside Park NJ 07010-2112

HAYES, MICHAEL ERNEST, psychotherapist, educator; b. N.Y.C., June 28, 1943; s. Raphael and Evelyn (Kaminier) H.; m. Agnes Beatrix Praetorias, May 9, 1967 (div. May 1970); m. Suellen Carroll Croteau, May 16, 1974; children: Elizabeth Carroll Croteau, Sarah Emily English Hayes. AB, Lawrence U., 1965; MA, U. Mich., 1966, MSW, 1969, PhD, 1972. Lic. clin. social worker; bd. cert. diplomate in clin. social work. Asst. prof. cmty. leadership and devel. Springfield (Mass.) Coll., 1972-73; asst. prof. social work U. N.H., Durham, 1973-76; vis. prof. social work U. So. Maine, Portland, 1976-77; assoc. prof. tchg. and adminstrn. Marywood Coll., Dunmore, Pa., 1977-81; assoc. dean arts & sci. U. New Haven, 1981-85; supr. med. social work Vis. Nurse of New Haven, 1985-87; psychotherapist Cmty. Health Care Plan, Branford, Conn., 1987-92; clin. mgr. TeamWorks for Adults Elmcrest Psychiat. Inst., Portland, Conn., 1992-96; dir. dual diagnosis program Stonington Inst., North Stonington, Conn., 1996—; pvt. practice psychotherapist, 1976—. Mem. NASW, Coun. on Social Work Edn., Porsche Club Am., Delta Tau Delta. Avocations: tennis, swimming, photography, reading. Office: PO Box 620 Guilford CT 06437-0620

HAYES, NEIL JOHN, lawyer; b. N.Y.C., Nov. 16, 1951; s. John T. and Marion G. (Watson) H.; m. Rebecca A. Wisner, Dec. 8, 1985. BA, Villanova U., 1973; JD, Stetson U., 1981. Bar: Fla. 1982, U.S. Dist. Ct. (so. and mid. dists.) Fla. 1982, U.S. Supreme Ct. 1986. Detective Mt. Laurel (N.J.) Police Dept., 1974-79; law clk. to chief judge Fla. 5th Dist. Ct. Appeals, Daytona Beach, 1982-83; assoc. Jones & Foster P.A., West Palm Beach, Fla., 1983-88, Bobo, Spicer & Ciotoli, West Palm Beach, 1988-89; pvt. practice West Palm Beach, 1989—. Assoc. editor Stetson U. Law Rev., 1981. Mem. ABA, Fla. Bar Assn., Palm Beach County Bar Assn., Palm Beach County Claims Assn., Fla. Def. Lawyers Assn., Tuscawilla Club. Roman Catholic. Avocations: motorcycling, aviation, photography. Home: 8733 Marlamoor Ln West Palm Beach FL 33412-1614 Office: 4365 Northlake Blvd Palm Bch Gdns FL 33410-6253

HAYES, PATRICIA ANN, health facility administrator; b. Binghamton, N.Y., Jan. 14, 1944; d. Robert L. and Gertrude (Congdon) H. BA in English, Coll. of St. Rose, 1968; PhD in Philosophy, Georgetown U., 1974. Tchr. Cardinal McCloskey High Sch., Albany, N.Y., 1966-68; teaching asst. Georgetown U., Washington, 1968-71; instr. philosophy Coll. of St. Rose, Albany, 1973-75, instr. bus., spring 1981, adminstrv. intern to acad. v.p., 1973-74, dir. admissions, 1974-78, dir. adminstrn. and planning, 1978-81, v.p. adminstrn. and fin., treas., 1981-84; pres. St. Edward's U., Austin, Tex., 1984-98; exec. v.p., COO Seton Healthcare Network, Austin, 1998—. Bd. dirs. Sta. KLRU Pub. TV. Roman Catholic. Office: Seton Med Ctr 1201 W 38th St Austin TX 78705-1006

HAYES, PAUL ROBERT, special education educator; b. Shelby County, Ind., Apr. 30, 1939; s. J. Robert and Evelyn Hayes; m. Rhoda Stuenkel, 1979; children: Robert, Susan, Adam. AB, Franklin Coll., 1964; MS, Ind. U., 1967, Ed specialist degree, 1973. Tchr. Southwestern Sch. Dist., Shelbyville, Ind., 1964-67; prin. Noble Twp. Sch., St. Paul, Ind., 1967-72, Woodstock (Ill.) Cmty. Sch. Dist., 1972-80; supt. Sandoval (Ill.) Sch. Dist., 1980-83; prin. Macomb (Ill.) Sch. Dist., 1983-93; instr., grad. field experience supr. Western Ill. U., Macomb, 1994—; evaluator of new public schs. State Bd. of Edn., 1989-93, 94. Editor: Allying the Arts in Education, 1987. Founding bd. mem. Habitat for Humanity, Macomb, 1995—; chairperson, mem. Wesley Day Care Ctr., Macomb, 1993—; mem., com. chair Lions Club, Macomb, 1990—. Recipient Assoc. award Ill. State Bd. of Edn., 1992, Mem. award, 1994. Mem. Nat. Assn. of Elem. Prins. (fellowhip 1984, 85, 87), Coun. for Exceptional Children, Ill. Asn. of Sch. Adminstrs., Internat. Reading Assn. Avocations: travel, community service, gardening, bear hunting, archeology. Office: Western Ill Univ Special Edn Dept Macomb IL 61455

HAYES, PAULA FREDA, government official; b. Providence, Apr. 5, 1950; d. Ario Louis and Elena Marguerite (Gentile) Freda; m. Robert J. Hayes, Sept. 6, 1975; children: Brendan Michael, Lauren Ann. BA magna cum laude, R.I. Coll., 1972; MPA, Maxwell Sch., Syracuse U., 1973. Criminal Justice planner City of Syracuse (N.Y.), 1973-75, asst. crime control coordinator, 1975-77; supervisory grants specialist Nat. Endowment Arts, Washington, 1977-78; criminal justice program analyst Dept. Justice, Washington, 1978-79, program mgr. arson discretionary grant program, 1979-80, sr. mgmt. analyst, 1980-81; dir. legis. and analysis div. Office of Insp. Gen., Dept. Agr., Washington, 1982-89, asst. inspector gen. for policy devel. and resources mgmt., 1989—. Roman Catholic. Office: USDA Office Insp Gen Stop 2310 1400 Independence Ave SW Washington DC 20250

HAYES, RANDALL L., environmental organizer, lecturer; b. East Liverpool, Ohio, July 11, 1950; s. Harold and Beverly J. (Ulbright) H. BA, Bowling Green State U., 1973; MA in Environ. Planning, San Francisco State U., 1983. Truck driver, bartender, 1973-79, carpenter, furniture mover, 1976-79; film producer Four Corners Films, 1979-84; pres., mem. bd. dirs. Rainforest Action Network, San Francisco, 1984—; bd. dirs. Reef Relief, Key West, Fla., Forest Trends. Producer documentary films The Cracking of Glen Canyon Dam: With Edward Abbey and Earth First, 1981, The Four Corners: A National Sacrifice Area?, 1983; contbr. chpts. to books. Mem. bd. advisors Alliance for a Paving Moratorium, Am. Comms. Project., Earth Island Inst., Ecol. Coun. Ams., Environ. Bamboo Found., Fair Trade Coalition, Green Corps, Japan Tropical Forest Action Network, Mangrove Action Project, Media Prodn. Group, Pro Forest Found., Rainforest Info. Ctr., numerous others; mem. adv. com. Nat. Ctr. for Econ. Alternatives: Index of Environ. Trends Project, Rainbow Coalition. Recipient award for best student documentary Acad. Motion Picture Arts and Scis., 1983, Golden Eagle CINE Golden Eagle, 1983, Silver medal Houston Internat. Film Festiva, 1983; Sterling China Citizens scholar, 1968. Mem. Coral Forest, Earth Island Inst., Friends of the Earth, Green Seal, Natural Resource Def. Coun., World Rainforest Movement, Sierra Club. Office: Rainforest Action Network 221 Pine St Ste 500 San Francisco CA 94104-2740

HAYES, RICHARD DONALD, architect; b. Evanston, Ill., Dec. 6, 1954; s. Joseph P. and Florence A. (Balmes) H.; m. Bessie Athene Gallanis, May 27, 1995. BArch with honors, Ill. Inst. Tech., 1981. Registered arch., Ill. Arch. Thomas Jon Rosengren, Inc., Evanston, 1981-83; project arch. Holabird & Root, Chgo., 1983-94; project mgr. VOA Assocs., Inc., Chgo., 1994-95; sr. project mgr. A. Epstein and Sons Internat., Inc., Chgo., 1995—. Project mgr. Ill. Bell Telephone Co. switching station, 1988 (story in Progressive Architecture 1990), Ameritech Svcs. data ctr., 1991-93, Amoco Corp. plz. redevel., 1992-94, ABN-AMRO Svcs. data ctr. expansion, 1994-95, Rose Hulman Inst. Tech. student union addition, 1994-95, Hyatt Regency 800-room hotel, 1996-97. Adv. bd. Nat. Vietnam Vets. Art Mus., Chgo., 1996-99. Mem. AIA (real estate com. 1988-92), Assn. for Project Mgrs., U.S. Sailing Assn., BMW Car Club of Am. Home: 979 Cherry St Winnetka IL 60093-2412 Office: A Epstein and Sons Internat Inc 600 W Fulton St Chicago IL 60661-1199

HAYES, RICHARD JOHNSON, association executive, lawyer; b. Chgo., May 25, 1933; s. David John Arthur and Lucille Margaret (Johnson) H.; m. Mary R. Lynch, Dec. 2, 1961; children: Susan, Richard, Jr., John, Edward. B.A., Colo. Coll., 1955; J.D., Georgetown U., 1961. Bar: Ill. 1961. Assoc. firm Barnabas F. Sears, Chgo., 1961-63, Peterson, Lowry, Rall, Barber and Ross, Chgo., 1963-65; staff dir. Am. Bar Assn., Chgo., 1965-70; exec. dir. Internat. Assn. Def. Counsel, Chgo., 1970—; instr. various legal programs, 1966—; pres. Heritage Resource Mgmt. Group, 1997—, Tri Star Corp., 1997—; dir. nat. jury innovations program Internat. Assn. Def. Counsel, Chgo., 1998—; dir. Def. Counsel Trial Acad., 1973—; exec. dir. Nat. Pre-Suit Mediation, 1991—. Editor: Antitrust Law Jour., 1969-71. 1st lt. USAR, 1955-57. Mem. ABA (chmn. various coms. 1977—), Ill. Bar Assn., Chgo. Bar Assn., Jr. Bar (chmn. 1965), Am. Soc. Assn. Execs., Chgo. Soc. Assn. Execs., Nat. Conf. Lawyers and Ins. Cos. (bd. dirs. 1983—), Rotary/One (Chgo.), Tower Club (Chgo.), Monroe Club (Chgo.), Met. Club (Chgo.), Mich. Shores Club (Wilmette, Ill.). Clubs: Rotary/One (Chgo.), Tower (Chgo.); Mich. Shores Club (Wilmette, Ill.). Home: 1920 Thornwood Ave Wilmette IL 60091-1403 Office: One N Franklin Ste 2400 Chicago IL 60606

HAYES, RICHARD L., government executive; b. Mar. 14, 1945; s. Laurence and Lossie Mae (Dixon) H.; 1 child, Kathy. BA, Case-Western Res. U., 1972; M of Regional Planning, Cornell U., 1976, PhD, 1977. Youth employment coord. Kinsman Opportunity Ctr., 1968; program specialist Coun. for Econ. Opportunities, 1968-69; dir. comty. svcs. dept. human resources City of Cleve., 1969-70, dir. Cleve. Area Manpower Planning Coun., 1970-72; sr. rsch. asst. Hill House Rehab. Ctr., Inc., 1973; rsch. specialist, project dir. Coll. Human Ecology Cornell U., 1973-74; sr. rschr. Mathematica Policy Rsch., Inc., 1974-78; program analyst, cons. office of sec. U.S. Dept. of Labor, Washington, 1978-79, spl. asst. to sec. of labor, 1979-81; founder, pres. The Policy Rsch. Group, Inc., 1981-83; dir. social and econ. studies divsn. SRA Corp., 1983-85; dir. info. mgmt. program Nat. Gov.'s Assn., 1985-93; dep. asst. sec. occupational safety and health adminstrn. U.S. Dept. of Labor, Washington, 1993-95, sr. advisor, asst. sec. for policy and budget, 1995—; mem. Project on EPA Priorities: Allocating Resources Based on Risk, Nat. Acad. Pub. Adminstrn.; mem. environ. stats. subcom. Nat. Adv. Coun. Environ. Policy and Tech., U.S. EPA, co-chair, 1991-93, mem. environ. measures and chem. accident and prevention com., 1991-93, mem. pollution prevention measurements subcom., 1991-93; cons. Comty. Action Against Addiction, Inc., 1973; adj. asst. prof. dept. city and regional planning Cornell U., 1981-82, vis. asst. prof. dept. city and regional planning, 1976-78. Contbr. articles to profl. publs. Recipient EPA award for exemplary assistance, 1991, Nat. Scholastic Art award, 1962-64, Exhibit award, East Aurora, N.Y., 1963, Women's Advt. League award, 1963, Cleve. Home Furnishing Design award, 1962; Cornell U. fellow, 1975-76, Am. Soc. Planning Ofcls.-Ford Found. fellow, 1973-75; Nat. Scholastic Art scholar, 1964. Home: 3908 Jocelyn St NW Washington DC 20015-1906 Office: Small Business Adm 409 Third St SW Washington DC 20416-0002

HAYES, ROBERT (ROBIN HAYES), congressman; b. Concord, N.C., Aug. 14, 1945; m. Barbara; children: Winslow, Bob. BS in History, Duke U., 1967. Businessman Concord, 1967—; mem. U.S. Congress from 8th N.C. dist., 1999—; current owner, operator of Mt. Pleasant Hosiery Mill; other bus. ventures include Arctic So. Turbines, Mack Sales of Birmingham, Colville Environ. Svcs., Palmer Mt. Farms (hwy. contractor) and Central Motor Lines. In Ho. Reps. serves on Coms. on Agr., Armed Svcs., Resources. Has been chosen to serve in House Leadership as an asst. whip. Elected mem. Concord Bd. Aldermen, 1978; elected 1992 to N.C. Ho. Reps., where he served as majority whip. Under former Gov. Jim Martin, served on the Wildlife Resources Commn., Coun. on Drug Abuse and as chmn. Cabarrus County Drug Task Force, Prison Fellowship in N.C. Nominated 1996 as Rep. candidate for gov. of N.C. Mem. 1st Presbyn. Ch. Concord. Chosen as Legislator of Yr. by Nat. Rep. Legislator's Assn., 1996. Office: 130 Cannon HOB Washington DC 20515*

HAYES, ROBERT BRUCE, former college president, educator; b. Clarksburg, W.Va., Nov. 15, 1925; s. Bruce and Ruby (Hitt) H.; m. Ruth Harrison, July 19, 1947 (dec.); children: Steven, Ruthann, Mark; m. Kathleen Peters. Student, Fairmont (W.Va.) State Coll.; BA, Asbury Coll., Wilmore, Ky., 1950; MEd, U. Kans., 1956, EdD, 1960. Tchr., prin. elem. and secondary schs. Kans., 1951-57; chmn. dept. edn. and psychology Asbury Coll., Wilmore, Ky., 1957-59; dir. tchr. edn. Taylor U., Upland, Ind., 1959-65; dean Coll. Edn. Marshall U., Huntington, W.Va., 1965-74; pres. Marshall U., 1974-83; prof. edl. adminstrn. Coll. Edn., Marshall U., 1983-90; exec. v.p. Warner So. Coll., Lake Wales, Fla., 1991-92; interim dean coll. bus. Marshall U., Huntington, W.Va., 1992-93; coord. accreditation Marshall U., Huntington, 1993-95, pres. emeritus, 1992-95; provost Marshall U., 1996-97, 99—; interim v.p. Cmty. & Tech. Coll., 1995-97; mem. W.Va. Adv. Com. Tchr. Edn., 1965-74; dir. Twentieth St. Bank. Editor, contbr.: 1966 Yearbook of Assn. Student Teaching. Bd. dirs. Cabell-Wayne United Way, 1981; chmn. bd. Green Acres, 1983; commr. Cabell County (W.Va.), 1983-88. Served with USMCR, 1944-46. Recipient Green Acres award for contbn. to mentally retarded, 1972, Golden Knight award Nat. Mgmt. Assn., 1981. Mem. Huntington Area C. of C. (dir. 1974-83), Phi Delta Kappa, Kiwanis. Methodist. Home: 347 Bradley Foster Dr Huntington WV 25701-9451 Office: Marshall U Office Huntington WV 25755-2310

HAYES, ROBERT EMMET, retired insurance company executive; b. Los Angeles, Nov. 21, 1920; s. Robert and Marion Verbeck (Weatherwax) H.; m. Alice McCarthy, June 26, 1943; children: Kathleen Byers, Joanne, Marianne Frank, Robert Emmet Jr., Janet Gheer, Philip. A.B., Loyola U., Los Angeles, 1941. Group ins. rep. Aetna Life Ins. Co., N.Y., Conn., Calif., Oreg., 1941-46; co-pilot Matson Nav. Co., San Francisco, 1946-47; employee benefit cons. Cosgrove & Co., Los Angeles, 1947-57; v.p. Marsh & McLennan, Inc., Los Angeles, 1957-62, Equitable Life Assurance Soc., N.Y.C., 1962-67; sr. v.p., group nat. accounts Met. Life Ins. Co., N.Y.C., from 1967; now ret. Served with USN, 1941-45. Home: 18670 Polvera Dr San Diego CA 92128-1122

HAYES, ROBERT FRANCIS, lawyer; b. Boston, Jan. 1, 1941; s. Robert Francis and Miriam Frances (Comfrey) H.; m. Nancy Hite Roach, Apr. 26, 1969; children: Robert Francis III, Katherine M., Rebecca C. AB, Harvard U., 1962, JD, 1965. Bar: Mass. 1965. With Ropes & Gray, Boston, 1966—. Trustee Thayer Acad., Braintree, Mass., 1985-96; dir. Jordan Hosp., Inc., Plymouth, Mass., 1984—; trustee, dir. Duxbury (Mass.) Beach Reservation, Inc., 1986—. Office: Ropes & Gray One International Pl Boston MA 02110

HAYES, ROBERT HERRICK, technology management educator; b. Wakeeney, Kans., July 17, 1936; s. Daniel Frank and Ruth Dee (Herrick) H.; m. Priscilla Jane Alden, Aug. 25, 1963; children: Melissa, Jonathan, Michelle. BA, Wesleyan U., 1958; MS, Stanford U., 1962, PhD, 1966; AM (hon.), Harvard U., 1973. Prof. Harvard U., Boston, 1966-91, Caldwell prof. bus. adminstrn., 1991—; sr. assoc. dean, 1992-98; bd. dirs. Helix Tech. Corp., Mansfield, Mass., Perkin-Elmer Corp., Norwalk, Conn. Co-author: Restoring our Competitive Edge, 1984 (Assn. Am. Pubs. award 1984), Dynamic Manufacturing, 1988, Manufacturing Renaissance, 1995, Strategic Operations, 1996. Trustee Wesleyan U., Middletown, Conn., 1985-88. Recipient McKinsey award 1980, 81, 82, Outstanding Alumnus award Wesleyan U., 1983. Avocations: sailing, reading, travelling. Office: Harvard Bus Sch Soldiers Fld Boston MA 02163-1317

HAYES, ROBERT MAYO, university dean, library and information science educator; b. N.Y.C., Dec. 3, 1926; s. Dudley Lyman and Myra Wilhelmina (Lane) H.; m. Alice Peters, Sept. 2, 1952; 1 son, Robert Dendrou. BA, UCLA, 1947, MA, 1949, PhD, 1952. Mathematician Nat. Bur. Standards, Washington and Los Angeles, 1949-52; mem. tech. staff Hughes Aircraft Co., 1952-54; head applications group Nat. Cash Register Co., 1954-55; head bus. systems group Magnavox Co., 1955- 60; pres. Advanced Information Systems, Inc., Los Angeles, 1960-64; v.p., sci. dir. Electrada Corp., Los Angeles, 1960-64; lectr. dept. math. UCLA, 1952-64, prof. library and info. sci., 1964-91, dean, 1974-89, dean emeritus, 1989—, dir. Inst. Libr. Rsch., 1965-70; prof. emeritus, 1991—; vis. lectr. Am. Univ., 1959, U. Wash., 1960-62; Windsor lectr. U. Ill., 1970; vis. prof. U. NSW, 1979, 93, Tsukuba U., 1987, Nankai U., 1987, Loughborough U., 1989, Keio U., Japan, 1994, Khazar U., Azerbaijan, 1995; mem. adv. com. White House conf. Libr. and Info. Svcs., 1979; v.p. Becker & Hayes, Inc., 1969-73, 93-96; cons. On Line Computer Libr. Ctr., 1990-94. Author: Strategic Management for Academic Libraries, 1993; co-author: Introduction to Information Storage and Retrieval: Tools, Elements, Theory, 1963, Handbook of Data Processing for Libraries, 2d edit., 1974, Strategic Management for Public Libraries, 1996; U.S. regional editor Problems in Info. Storage and Retrieval, 1959-63; editor Info. Scis. Series, 1963-75; mem. editorial bd. Libr. Info. Sci. Rsch., 1978—. Recipient Profl. Achievement award UCLA Alumni Assn., Beta Phi Mu award ALA, 1st Tezak award U. Zagreb, 1990. Mem. ALA (pres. info. sci. and automation div. 1969), Am. Soc. Info. Sci. (pres. 1962-63, nat. lectr. 1968, Award of Merit 1993), Am. Math. Soc., Assn. for Computing Machinery (assoc. editor jour. 1959-69, nat. lectr. 1969), Phi Beta Kappa, Sigma Xi. Club: Cosmos. Home: 3943 Woodfield Dr Sherman Oaks CA 91403-4239 Office: UCLA 405 Hilgard Ave Los Angeles CA 90095-9000

HAYES, ROGER MATTHEW, deputy sheriff; b. Youngstown, Ohio, May 27, 1943; s. Roger and Edith (Wellendorff) H.; m. Carolyn Starr; children: Troy, Trent, Todd. BA, Columbia Coll., 1992; postgrad., U. Colo.; MA, Regis U., 1996. Dep. sheriff Arapahoe County (Colo.) Sheriff Dept., 1986—. Past pres. Arapahoe County Rep. Men's Club; pres. Fraternal Order of Police, Arapahoe County, Colo., West Metro Found.; mem. mil. acad. selection com. U.S. Senator William Armstrong, Denver, 1982, White House Adv. Team, Reagan/Bush, Denver, 1982; pres. West Metro Fire Found. Sgt. USMC, 1963-66, Vietnam. Recipient medal of Merit Air Force Assn., Washington, 1984. Mem. Am. Soc. Pub. Adminstrs., Am. Sociol. Assn. Avocation: golf. Home: 9883 W Progress Pl Littleton CO 80123-2177

HAYES, SAMUEL E., JR., state agency administrator. BS, Pa. State U., MS. Mem. Pa. Ho. of Reps., 1970-92, served at majority leader and whip; sec. of agr. Commonwealth of Pa. Served with U.S. Army, 5 yrs., Vietnam. Decorated Bronze Star; recipient numerous awards including Lawmaker of Yr. award Pa. Retailers Assn., Man of Yr. award Pa. Rural Electric Coops., Livestock Hall of Fame award, Barn Raiser award Pa. Farm Bur. Mem. VFW, Am. Legion. Office: Commonwealth of Pa Dept of Agr 2301 N Cameron St Harrisburg PA 17110-9408

HAYES, SAMUEL LINTON, III, business educator; b. Phila., Feb. 23, 1935; s. Samuel L. and Ann Walsh (Barclay) H.; m. Barbara Frances Lloyd, Dec. 21, 1963; children: Elizabeth Ann, Susan Lloyd, Judith Linton. AB, Swarthmore Coll., 1957; MBA with distinction, Harvard U., 1961, DBA, 1966. Asst. prof. bus. adminstrn. Columbia U., N.Y.C., 1965-68; assoc. prof. Columbia U., 1968-70; vis. assoc. prof. Harvard U., Cambridge, Mass., 1970-72; prof. Harvard U., 1972-75, Jacob Schiff prof. investment banking, 1975—; chmn. faculty Research and Mgmt. Ctr. Harvard U., Vevey, Switzerland, 1979-81; cons. in field; bd. dirs. Tiffany & Co., Eaton Vance Mut. Funds, Kobrick Funds. Mem. editorial bd. Harvard Bus. Rev., 1976-84, Harvard Bus. Sch. Press, 1986-89; contbr. articles to profl. jours. Mem. Mass. Fin. Adv. Bd., 1976-87, chmn., 1978-87; trustee Swarthmore Coll., 1983-94, 96—, New Eng. Conservatory, 1989—; hon. dir. Nat. Scoliosis Found. With USN, 1957-59. Mem. Fin. Mgmt. Assn., Am. Guild Organists, Harvard Club (N.Y.C.), Dedham Polo Club. Office: Harvard U Sch Bus Cumnock Hall 300 Boston MA 02163

HAYES, SAMUEL PERKINS, social scientist, educator; b. South Hadley, Mass., Jan. 28, 1910; s. Samuel Perkins and Agnes Hayes (Stone) H.; m. Alice Mary Cable, Mar. 25, 1937; children—Susan, Jonathan. A.B., Amherst Coll., 1931, L.H.D., 1966; Ph.D., Yale U., 1934; postgrad. (fellow Social Sci. Research Council), U. Chgo., 1937-38. Asst. psychology Yale U. Inst. Human Relations, 1931-34; instr. psychology Mt. Holyoke Coll., 1934-37; faculty dept. econs. Sarah Lawrence Coll., 1938-40; market research Young & Rubicam, Inc., N.Y.C., 1940-42; various positions U.S. govt. in, Washington, Algiers, London, Scandinavia, (mainly for Fgn. Econ. Adminstrn. and State Dept.), 1942-45, 48-51; assoc. dir. mktg. and research div. Dun & Bradstreet, Inc., N.Y.C., 1945-48; chief Spl. Tech. and Econ. Mission, Indonesia, 1951-52; asst. dir. Mut. Security Agy., Far East, 1952-53; dir. Found. for Research on Human Behavior, 1953-60; lectr. econs. U. Mich., 1955-57, prof. econs., 1959-62; dir. Ctr. for Research on Econ. Devel., 1961-62; pres. Fgn. Policy Assn., 1962-74; dir. N.Y. regional office Campaign for Yale, 1974-76; asso. Devel. Alternatives Inc., 1981-85; cons. UNESCO, 1954-58, President's Task Force on Fgn. Econ. Assistance, 1961, Peace Corps, 1961-62, World Bank, 1976-82, U.S. AID, 1978, U.S. Ho. of Reps. Com. on Agr., 1979-81; sr. specialist East-West Center, Honolulu, 1968; resident scholar Villa Serbelloni, Italy, 1971. Author: Measuring the Results of Development Projects, 1959, An International Peace Corps, 1961, Evaluating Development Projects, 1966, The Beginning of American Aid to Southeast Asia, 1971; editor: (with others) Some Applications of Behavioral Research, 1957; contbr. articles to profl. publs., also chpts. to books. Mem. Am. Econ. Assn., Amateur Chamber Music Players, Cosmos Club, Phi Beta Kappa, Sigma Xi, Chi Phi. Democrat. Home: 80 Cedar St Apt 331 Branford CT 06405-3698

HAYES, SCOTT BIRCHARD, raw materials company executive; b. Washington, Apr. 2, 1926; s. Webb C. II Hayes and Martha Baker; m. Dorothy Walter, Oct. 27, 1951; children: Scott B. Jr., James W., Timothy W., Michael S. BS, Yale U., 1950. Sr. v.p. Pickands Mather & Co., Cleve., 1953-87, ret., 1987. Bd. dirs., v.p. Hayes Presdl. Ctr., Fremont, Ohio, 1965, pres., 1987—; trustee Ohio Hist. Soc., 1993-96. With USN, 1944-46. Mem. AIME, Am. Iron and Steel Inst., Am. Foundrymen's Soc., Tavern Club, Kirtland Country Club, Union Club (Cleve.) (pres. 1985-87). Avocations: golf, tennis, squash, fishing. Home: PO Box 1070 Boca Grande FL 33921-1070

HAYES, SHERRILL D., religious organization administrator. Asst. to the pres. Warner Southern Coll., Lake Wales, Fla. Office: Warner Southern Coll 2700 US Hwy 27N #5 Lake Wales FL 33853

HAYES, SHIRLEY ANN, special education educator; b. Lindsay, Calif., June 15, 1955; d. Clarence Berwine and Betty Francis (Matthews) Fox; m. Darren Wayne Hayes, Feb. 11, 1990; children: Norman Tony Whited Jr., Samuel Hayes, James Hayes. AA, Porterville Jr. Coll., Calif., 1982; BA, Calif. State U., Bakersfield, 1984; specialist credential, Fresno (Calif.) Pacific Coll., 1985. Resource specialist cert. Teaching asst. Porterville Developmental Ctr., 1977-84, tchr. of severly handicapped, 1984—. Sec. PTA, West Pubnam Sch., Porterville, 1992. Mem. Edn!. Svc. Profl. Orgn. (chair 1990), Calif. State Employees Assn. (bargaining unit rep. 1990—). Avocations: artist, cooking, antique car restoration. Home: PO Box 8624 Porterville CA 93258-8624 Office: Porterville Devel Ctr PO Box 2000 Porterville CA 93258-2000

HAYES, STEPHEN KURTZ, author; b. Wilmington, Del., Sept. 9, 1949; s. Ira Maurice and Carolyn (Kurtz) H.; m. Rumiko Urata, Apr. 14, 1980; children: Reina Emily, Marissa Christine. BA, Miami U., Oxford, Ohio, 1971. Ordained Tendai sect Japanese Esoteric Buddhist priest, 1991. Author: The Ninja and Their Secret Fighting Art, 1981, Ninjutsu: Art of the Invisible Warrior, 1984, The Mystic Arts of the Ninja, 1985; Ninja: Spirit of the Shadow Warrior, Vol. I, 1980, Warrior Ways of Enlightment, Vol. II, 1981, Warrior Path of Togakure, Vol. III, 1983, Legacy of the Night Warrior, Vol. IV, 1984, Wisdom from the Ninja Village of the Cold Moon, 1984, Ninja Realms of Power, 1986, Tulku, 1985, Ancient Art of Ninja Warfare, 1988, Lore of the Shinobi Warrior, 1989, Action Meditation, 1992, Enlightened Self-Protection, 1992. Bd. mem. Tibetan Cultural Ctr.; founder Stephen K. Hayes' Quest Ctr. for Martial Arts Tng., 1996. Named to Black Belt Hall of Fame, Black Belt. mag., 1985. Mem. Tibetan Med. Inst. (life), Togakure Ryu Ninjutsu (10th degree black belt), To-Shin Do (founder, 1997). Home: PO Box 326 Bellbrook OH 45305-0326 Office: PO Box 291947 Dayton OH 45429-0947

HAYES, STEPHEN MATTHEW, librarian; b. Detroit, Sept. 30, 1950; s. Matthew Cleary and Evelyn Mary (Warren) H. BS in Psychology, Mich. State U., 1972; MLS, Western Mich. U., 1974; MS in Adminstrn., U. Notre Dame, 1979. Cons. Western Mich. U., Kalamazoo, 1974; libr. U. Notre Dame, Ind., 1974-76, ref. and pub. documents libr., 1976-84; libr. Bus. Svcs. Libr., 1984—. Author/contbr.: What is Written Remains: Historical Essays on the Libraries of Notre Dame, 1994; editor: Environmental Concerns, 1975; contbr.: Depository Library Use of Technology: A Practitioner's Perspective, 1993. Recipient Rev. Paul J. Foik award, 1998. Mem. AAUP,

ALA (govt. documents roundtable 1978—, chair 1987-88, chair pubs. com. 1989-91, coord. com. on access to info. 1989-90, 93-95, exec. bd. dirs. 1988-91, awards com. 1991-93, chair Godort orgn. com. 1991-93, bus. ref. and svc. sect. 1994—, bus. & adult ref. roundtable 1995—, edn. com. 1996—, resolution com. 1997—), Assn. Pub. Data Users (census com., steering com. 1987-96), Indigo (fed. rec. commn. chair 1992-93, apptd. depository libr. coun. to pub. printer 1994-97). Roman Catholic. Home: PO Box 6032 South Bend IN 46660-6032 Office: U Notre Dame 313 College Bus Adminstr Bl Notre Dame IN 46556-5646

HAYES, TIMOTHY GEORGE, lawyer, consultant; b. New London, Conn., June 27, 1954; s. George Melen and Lauretta C. (Bresnahan) H.; m. Barbara Joan White, Jan. 27, 1983; children: Laura Katherine, Kevin Michael. BS, Fla. State U., 1976, MS, 1977; JD, Stetson Coll. Law, 1982. Bar: Fla. 1982, U.S. Dist. Ct. (mid. dist.) Fla. 1983. Legis. aide Fla. State Rep. George H. Sheldon, Tallahassee, 1978-79; assoc. Alice K. Nelson, P.A., Tampa, Fla., 1982-83; ptnr. Cotterill, Gonzalez & Hayes, Lutz, Fla., 1983-84, Cotterill, Gonzalez, Hayes & Grantham, Lutz, 1984-88; sr. ptnr. Hayes & McClelland, Lutz, 1988-90, Hayes, Winick & Albrechta, Lutz, 1990-91, Hayes & Albrechta, P.A., Lutz, 1991-93, Hayes & Assocs., Lutz, 1993—. V.p. Hillsborough County Young Dems., Tampa, 1978, pres., 1979; bd. dirs. Tampa Bay Commuter Rail Authority, Tampa, 1990-97, Pasco County Econ. Devel. Coun., New Port Richey, Fla., 1990-92, Ctrl. Pasco Coalition, Land O' Lakes, Fla., 1991-95, Pasco Food Bank, 1996—, Sunshine Youth Soccer Assn., 1997—; bd. dirs., coach Ctrl. Pasco United Soccer Assn., 1995—, pres., 1996-98; mem. Tampa-Orlando High-Speed Transp. Study Task Force, 1992-94; mem. adv. bd. Pasco-Hernando C.C., 1994-95; bd. dirs., v.p. Heritage Park Found., 1997—. Named Outstanding Young Man in Am. by Jaycees, 1980; recipient Sam Walton Bus. Leader award, 1998. Mem. ABA (real property, probate and trust law sect.), Fla. Bar Assn. (environ. and land use law sect., real property, probate and trust law sect.), Hillsborough County Bar Assn. (environ. and land use law sect.), Land O' Lakes C. of C. (v.p. 1988-89, pres. 1991-92, chmn. bd. 1992-93, bd. dirs. 1995—). Roman Catholic. Avocations: soccer, bicycling, camping, gardening. Office: Hayes & Assocs 21859 State Road 54 Ste 200 Lutz FL 33549-6986

HAYES, WILBUR FRANK, biology educator; b. Rhinelander, Wis., Nov. 10, 1936; s. Wilbur Mead and Evelyn (Stritesky) H.; m. Dawn Olivia Waldorf, July 21, 1979 (div. Feb. 1991); stepchildren: Lynn, Robert, Dana, Richard, Gary, Kevin. BA, Colby Coll., 1959; MS, Lehigh U., 1961, PhD, 1965. Postdoctoral fellow Yale U., New Haven, 1965-67; asst. prof. biology Wilkes Coll., Wilkes-Barre, Pa., 1967-71, assoc. prof., 1971—; vis. prof. Northea. U., Boston, 1987-88. Contbr. articles to profl. jours. Chmn. bd. dirs. Northea. Pa. chpt. Am. Heart Assn., Wilkes-Barre, 1986-87. Mem. Soc. for Integrative and Comparative Biology, Pa. Acad. Sci., Microscopy Soc. Am., Sigma Xi (pres. Wilkes Coll. chpt. 1976-77, sec.-treas. 1984-87, 88-91). Republican. Congregationalist. Avocations: downhill skiing, photography, travel, colonial American history. Home: 47 Stanley St Wilkes Barre PA 18702-2308 Office: Wilkes U Dept Biology Wilkes Barre PA 18766

HAYES, WILLIAM ALOYSIUS, economics educator; b. Chgo., June 25, 1920; s. John and Stella (Ahern) H.; m. Joan Leahy, Aug. 22, 1953; children—Mary, Joseph, William, Anne, Patrick, Margaret, John, Teresa. A.B., DePaul U., 1942; M.A., Cath. U. Am., 1948, Ph.D., 1952. Instr. econs., asst. prof., asso. prof. DePaul U., Chgo., 1950-60; prof. econs. DePaul U., 1960—, chmn. dept., 1959-67. Exec. bd. Nat. Cath. Social Action Conf., pres., 1962; bd. dirs. Adult Edn. Centers, Chgo. Mem. Am. Econ. Assn., Cath. Econ. Assn. (exec. council, pres. 1968), AAUP, Blue Key, Beta Gamma Sigma, Pi Gamma Mu. Home: 10600 S Leavitt St Chicago IL 60643-3130 *I try to be the type of person that I would like each one of my children to be as they develop into and through their adult years.*

HAYES, WILLIAM MEREDITH, pilot, retired career officer; b. San Antonio, Mar. 28, 1947; s. Oscar Junior and Mary Kathern (Leuthart) H.; m. Beverly Jeanne Lowe, May 20, 1972; children: Loren Elaine, Colin Meredith. BA, Western Ky. U., 1971. Cert. naval aviator, airline transport pilot FAA. Commd. ensign USCG, 1973, advanced through grades to capt., 1994; asst. ops. officer USCG Base, Honolulu, 1973-74; pub. affairs officer USCG Air Sta., Mobile, Ala., 1975-78; tng. officer USCG Group/Air Sta., Corpus Christi, Tex., 1978-81; head Falcon jet tng. USCG Aviation Tng. Ctr., Mobile, 1981-87; air ops. officer USCG Air Sta., Miami, Fla., 1987-92; exec. officer USCG Air Sta., Elizabeth City, N.C., 1992-94; commdg. officer USCG Activities, San Diego, 1994-97; chief office of ops. 8th C.G. Dist., New Orleans, 1997; pilot Humana, Inc., Louisville, Ky., 1997—; bd. dirs. USO, San Diego, Armed Svcs. YMCA, San Diego; mem. mil. adv. coun. C of C,. San Diego, 1994—. Contbr. articles to profl. jours. Recipient Humanitarian Svc. medal USCG, Corpus Christi, 1978, Commendation medal USCG, Miami, 1992, Achievement medal USCG, Elizabeth City, 1994, Meritorious Svc. medal, 1997. Mem. Amateur Radio Relay League, Delta Tau Delta (life mem., chpt. v.p. 1969-70). Byzantine Catholic. Avocations: surfing, fishing, sailing, amateur radio, golf. Home: 2420 Napoleon Blvd Louisville KY 40205-2011 Office: 8th CG Dist 1180 Standiford Ct Louisville KY 40213-2019

HAYFLICK, LEONARD, microbiologist, cell biologist, gerontologist, educator, writer; b. Phila., May 20, 1928; s. Nathan Albert and Edna (Silbert) H.; m. Ruth Louise Heckler, Oct. 3, 1954; children: Joel, Deborah, Susan, Rachel, Anne. BA in Microbiology and Chemistry, U. Pa., 1951, MS in Med. Microbiology, 1953, PhD in Med. Microbiology and Chemistry, 1956. McLaughlin rsch. fellow in infection and immunity, dept. microbiology U. Tex. Med. Br., Galveston, Tex., 1956-58; assoc. mem. Wistar Inst. Anatomy and Biology, Phila., 1958-68; asst. prof. rshc. medicine U. Pa., Phila., 1966-68; prof. med. microbiology Stanford (Calif.) U. Sch. Medicine, 1968-76, senator-at-large, Basic Med. Scis., 1970-73, chmn. gen. rsch. support grant com., 1972-74; sr. research cell biologist Children's Hosp., Oakland, Calif., 1976-81; prof. zoology, prof. microbiology and immunology U. Fla., Gainesville, 1981-87, dir. Ctr. for Gerontol. Studies, Coll. Liberal Arts and Scis., 1981-87; prof. anatomy, cell biology and aging sect. U. Calif. Sch. Medicine, San Francisco, 1988—; mem. subcom. on mycoplasmataceae Internat. Com. Bacteriol. Nomenclature, 1965-78; mem. steering com. cell and devel. biology film program MIT, 1970-73; chmn. Calif. State Com. Health White Ho. Conf. Aging, 1971-72, Calif. state rep., 1972; Nat. Cancer Planning Com. Nat. Cancer Inst., NIH, 1972; chmn., adult devel. and aging rsch. and tng. com. Nat. Inst. Child Health and Human Devel., NIH, 1972-73; non-resident fellow Inst. Higher Studies, Santa Barbara, Calif., 1973—; mem. Argonne Nat. Lab. rev. com. biol. and med. rsch. div. Argonne Nat. Lab., 1973-76; mem. rsch. adv. com. Tchrs. Ins. and Annuity Assn. Am.-Coll. Retirement Equities Funds, N.Y.C., 1974-80; founding mem. Nat. Adv. Coun. on Aging, Nat. Inst. on Aging, NIH, Bethesda, Md., 1975; cons. Office of Dir. Nat. Cancer Inst., Bethesda, 1963-74; vis. scientist Ctr. for Aging Weizmann Inst. Sci., Rehovoth, Israel, 1980, 86; mem. adv. bd. Internat. Exchange Ctr. Gerontology, Fla. Univ. System, Tampa, 1982-86; mem. jury for Sandoz prize in gerontology and geriatrics, 1985-89; bd. dirs. Ctr. for Climacteric Studies, Inc., Gainesville, 1985-88; expert cons. various coms. U.S. Congress, vis. prof. Oita Med. U., Japan, 1991-95, U. Parma, Italy, 1991, Kurume U. Med. Sch., Japan; lectr. in field. Author: How and Why We Age, 1996; editor: Biology of the Mycoplasmas, 1969, Handbook of the Biology of Aging, 1977; sr. editor Biol. Scis. Microfiche Collection Info. on Gerontology and Geriatric Medicine Univ. Microfilms Internat., Ann Arbor, Mich., 1984-98; editor-in-chief Exptl. Gerontology, 1984-98; asst. editor In Vitro jour. Tissue Culture Assn., 1969-75; editor biol. scis. sect. Jour. Gerontology, 1975-80; assoc. editor Cancer Rsch., 1972-80; mem. editorial bd. Jour. Bacteriology, 1964-72, Jour. Virology, 1967-70, Infection and Immunity jour., 1968-78, Exec. Health Report, 1970—, Mechanisms of Aging and Devel., 1972—, Gerontology and Geriatrics Edn., 1980—, A Revista Portuguesa de Medicina Geriatrica, 1987—; mem. adv. com. Bergey's Manual of Determinative Bacteriology, 1965-78; bd. dirs., mem. editorial bd. Bollettino Dell Instituto Sieroterapico Milanese, Archivo de Microbiologia ed Immunologia, Milan, Italy, 1968—; contbr. numerous articles in field to profl. jours. Staff sgt. U.S. Army, 1946-48. Recipient Samuel Roberts Noble Found. Rsch. Recognition award, 1984; co-recipient Sandoz prize Internat. Assn. Gerontology, 1991, Biomed. Scis. & Aging award U. So. Calif., 1974, Rsch. Recognition award Samuel Roberts Noble Found., 1984; Karl-Forster lectr. Acad. Sci. and Lit., Mainz, Germany, 1983, Hoffman-LaRoche lectr. Waksman Inst. Microbiology Rutgers U., 1984, Wadworth Meml. Fund lectr. Rush-Presbyn.-St. Luke's Med. Ctr., Chgo., 1984, hon. lectr. Rosenfield Program Pub. Affairs Grinnell Coll., 1989, invited speaker Sandoz lectrs. in Gerontology, Basle, Switzerland, 1986, 92, numerous other lectureships U.S.A., Can. and Europe, 1970—, Career Devel. award Nat. Cancer Inst., NIH, 1962-70, Lifetime Achievement award Soc. In Vitro Biology, 1996. Fellow AAAS, Gerontol Soc. Am. (program and awards com. 1972-77, chmn., exec. com. biol. scis. sect. 1972-74, com. on internat. rels. 1980-82, pub. policy com. 1980-82, pres. 1982-83, ann. Robert W. Kleemeier award 1972, Brookdale award 1980); mem. Am. Soc. for Microbiology, Tissue Culture Assn. (hon., trustee 1966-68, program com. 1970, mem. coun. 1972-74, v.p. 1974-76, pres. Calif. chpt. 1971-73), Soc. for Exptl. Biology and Medicine (councillor 1984-88), Assn. for Advancement of Aging Rsch. (adv. coun. 1970-71), Am. Aging Assn., Am. Cancer Soc. (virology and cell biology study sect. 1974-76), Internat. Assn. Microbiol. Standardization (sec. cell culture com. 1963-73, chmn. 1985—, mem. coun. 1987-89), Internat. Orgn. for Mycoplasmology (Presdl. award 1984), Am. Gerontol. Soc. (v.p., coun. 1972-74, 81-83, program com. 1977-79, bd. dirs. 1981-83), Am. Fedn. Aging Rsch. (bd. dirs., exec. com., rsch. adv. com. 1981—, chmn. study sect. 1987—, v.p. 1988—, Leadership award 1983), Fedn. Am. Socs. for Exptl. Biology, Aging Prevention Rsch. Found. (sci. adv. bd. dirs.), Am. Assn. for Cancer Rsch., Am. Soc. Pathologists, Calif. Found. for Biomed. Rsch., Am. Longevity Assn. (sci. adv. bd. dirs. 1981—), Western Gerontology Assn. (coun. 1972-74, bd. dirs. 81-83), Internat. Assn. Gerontology (mem. Am. exec. com. 1972-75, treas., exec. com. 1985-89, co-recipient Sandoz award gerontology 1991), Found. on Gerontology (sci. adv. bd. 1985—), Soc. Medicine and Natural Sci., Ukrainian Acad. Med. Scis. (fgn., academician 1991), French Biol. Soc. (fgn.). Office: U Calif 36991 Greencroft Close PO Box 89 The Sea Ranch CA 95497-0089

HAYGOOD, PAUL M., lawyer; b. Baton Rouge, La., Oct. 30, 1942. AB, La. State U., 1964; LLB, Harvard U., 1967. Bar: La. 1968. Law clk. to Hon. Alvin B. Rubin U.S. Dist. Ct. (ea. dist.) La., 1967-68; atty. Correro, Fishman, Haygood, Phelps, Weiss, Walmsley & Casteix, L.L.P., New Orleans; special lectr. corp. fin. Tulane Law Sch., 1973; sr. legis. asst. and counsel to U.S. Sen. J. Bennett Johnston, 1973-75; mem. jud. coun. Supreme Ct. La., 1987-89. Pres. Coun. For a Better La., 1990-91, New Orleans Bur. Govtl. Rsch., 1994-96. Fellow Am. Bar Found., Am. Coll. Trust and Estate Counsel; mem. ABA, New Orleans Bar Assn., La. State Bar Assn. (sec.-treas. corp. law sect. 1972-73, 79-80, vice chmn. corp. law sect. 1980-81, chmn. corp. law sect. 1981-82, chmn. corp. and bus. laws com. 1992—, examiner corp. law bar admissions com. 1977-82, bd. govs. 1985-86), La. State Law Inst. (coun. mem. 1984-90), La. Bankers Assn. (bank counsel com. 1988-90), Omicron Delta Kappa. Address: Bank One Ctr 46th Fl 201 Saint Charles Ave New Orleans LA 70170-1000*

HAYHURST, JAMES FREDERICK PALMER, career and business consultant, inspirational speaker, writer; b. Toronto, May 24, 1941; s. W. Palmer and Jean E. (Hunnisett) H.; m. Susan Ebbs, Oct. 17, 1964; children: Cindy, Jim, Barbara. H.B.A., U. Western Ont., 1963. Brand man Procter & Gamble, Toronto, 1963-66, exec. v.p., 1975-82; pres. Hedwyn Communications Inc., Toronto, 1983-86; chmn. Saatchi & Saatchi Compton Hayhurst, Toronto, 1983-86; owner Wyldwyn Holdings Ltd., Toronto, 1986—; pres. The Hayhurst Career Ctr., Toronto, 1988—, The Right Mountain Crew, 1994—. Author: The Right Mountain, 1996. Chmn. Outward Bound Can., 1985-87; founding co-chmn. Trails Youth Initiatives. Mem. Toronto Golf Club, Olde Fla. Golf Club (Naples), Caledon Mountain Trout Club. Office: Wyldwyn Holdings Ltd, 378 Fairlawn Ave, Toronto, ON Canada M5M 1T8 *True success is the attainment of purpose without compromising your core values.*

HAYLLAR, BEN, city finance director; b. Phila., Sept. 30, 1946; married; 2 daus. BA in Liberal Arts, U. Pitts., 1967, MA in Elizabethan and Jacobean Theater, 1969, PhD in Comm., 1985; completed exec./mgmt. devel. program, Carnegie-Mellon U., 1985. Cert. Govt. Fin. Mgr., 1995. Assoc. prof. comm. C.C. Allegheny County, Pa., 1969-77; sr. asst. exec. sec. to mayor City of Pitts., 1977-85; v.p., divsn. mgr. met. banking Equibank, 1985-89; dir. fin. City of Pitts., 1989-93, City of Phila., 1993—; bd. mem. Phila. Facilities Mgmt. Corp., 1993—, Pa. Conv. Ctr. Authority, 1993—; bd. mem., exec. com. Phila. Indsl. Devel. Corp., 1993—; bd. mem., commr., Phila. Planning Commn., 1993—; bd. mem., sec. Pitts.-Allegheny County Pub. Auditorium Authority, 1992-93; bd. mem., treas. Pitts. Equipment Leasing Authority, 1989-93; bd. mem., sec.-treas. Pitts. Water & Sewer Authority, 1989-93; bd. mem. Pitts. Countywide Corp., 1989-93; pub. info. cons. govt. study commn., City of Pitts., 1972-74; reporter Pitts. Forum, 1970-75. Author: The Image of Lyndon Baines Johnson: The Journalist's Role in the Making of a Public Image, 1972; contbr. numerous articles to mags.; contbg. writer Pitts. Mag., 1972-77. Mem. negotiating com., del. Allegheny Labor Coun., Am. Fedn. Tchrs. Local 2067, 1971-77; mem. Three Rivers Shakespeare Festival bd., 1980-83; mem. econ. devel. com. Allegheny Conf. on Cmty. Devel., 1983-84; mem. adv. com. on housing for homeless people in Pitts. and Allegheny County, 1984-86; chair mayor's com. on accessibility for the handicapped, Pitts., 1980-86. Mem. Assn. Govt. Accts., Govt. Fin. Officers Assn. (spkr. nat. convs. 1994, 95, 96, mem. standing com. on govtl. debt and fiscal policy 1996). Fax: (215) 568-1947. Office: Office of Director of Finance 1330 Mcpl 1401 Jfk Blvd Philadelphia PA 19102-1617*

HAYMAN, HARRY, association executive, electrical engineer; b. Lewistown, Pa., Mar. 20, 1917; s. Sidney and Nettie (Hirsch) H.; m. Edith Harriet Levitz, Mar. 18, 1946; children: Gail A., Beth (Mrs. Stanley Truman), Sidney F., Stuart A. BS, NYU, 1938; postgrad., George Washington U., 1947-50. Engr. FCC, Washington, 1940-54; pres., gen. mgr. radio sta. WPGC, Morningside, Md., 1954-55; project mgr. U.S. Navy and FAA, Washington, 1956-60; program mgr. NASA project Apollo, Washington, 1960-71; chmn. IEEE Computer Soc., Washington, 1965; exec. sec. IEEE Computer Soc., N.Y.C., 1971-82; dir. confs. and tutorials IEEE Computer Soc., Silver Spring, Md., 1982-89, coord. robotics and automation div., 1988—. Vice pres. Nat. Childrens Center, 1960; pres. Henryton State Hosp. Assn., 1970, 74; Bd. dirs. D.C. Assn. Retarded Children, 1956-70, pres. Washington chpt., 1953-55; pres. Gt. Oaks Aux., 1975-78. Served with USNR, 1944-46. Recipient Apollo Achievement award 1969. Mem. IEEE (treas. Computer Soc. Internat. Conf. 1970, treas. Internat. Conf. on Computer Comm. 1972, spl. asst. to chmn. Conf. on Computer Comm. 1974, coord., treas. Internat. Conf. on Robotics and Automation 1980-96). Home: 3037C Exeter E Boca Raton FL 33434 Office: 1201 Elm Grove Cir Silver Spring MD 20905-7020

HAYMAN, RICHARD WARREN JOSEPH, conductor; b. Cambridge, Mass., Mar. 27, 1920; s. Fred Albert and Gladys Marie (Learned) H.; m. Maryellen Daly, June 25, 1960; children: Suzanne Marie, Olivia Kathryn. D Hum. (hon.), Detroit Coll. Bus., 1980. Freelance composer, arranger 20th Century Fox, Warner Bros., MGM, Universal Film Studios; music arranger, dir. Vaughn Monroe Orch. records and TV show, N.Y.C., 1945-50; chief arranger Arthur Fiedler and Boston Pops Orchestra, 1950-95; mus. dir. Mercury Record Corp., N.Y.C., 1950-65, Time-Mainstream Records, N.Y.C., 1960-70; prin. pops condr. Detroit Symphony Orchs.; prin. pops condr., McDonnell Douglas chair St. Louis; prin. pops condr. Birmingham (Ala.), Hartford (Conn.), Calgary (Can.), Grand Rapids (Mich.) Symphony Orch., London (Ont., Can.) Orch. Composer: No Strings Attached, Dansero, Skipping Along, Carriage Trade, Serenade to a Lost Love, Olivia, Suzanne, Freddie the Football; recorded and released 50 C.D. recordings on Naxos Internat. Records with Richard Hayman and His Symphony Orch., 1991—. Recipient Best Instrumental Record award Sta. WERE, Cleve., 1963, Best TV Comml. Jingle award Nat. Acad. Rec. Arts and Scis., (N.Y.C.), 1960; star dedicated to him on Hollywood Blvd Walk of Fame. Mem. Nat. Acad. Rec. Arts and Scis., ASCAP, Am. Fedn. Musicians. Roman Catholic. Office: Richard Hayman Prodns 784 Us Highway 1 Ste 22B No Palm Beach FL 33408-4411 also: St Louis Symphony Orch 718 N Grand Blvd Saint Louis MO 63103-1011

HAYMOND, PAULA J., psychologist, diagnostician, hypnotherapist; b. Warsaw, Ind., Sept. 29, 1949; d. George Milton and Phyllis (Freeman) H. BA, Butler U., 1971, MS, 1973; EdD, Ind. U., 1982. Lic. psychometrist, Ind.; lic. psychologist, Tex. Sr. asst. psychology dept. Butler U., Indpls., 1970-71; behavioral clinician I psychology dept. Ind. Boys Sch., Plainfield, 1973-75, behavioral clinician II diagnostic unit, 1975-78; behavioral clinician II diagnostic unit Ind. Girls Sch., Indpls., 1978-80; human factors cons. Lund Cons. Inc., N.Y.C., 1981-82; adminstr. DePelchin Children Ctr./Bayou Pl., Houston, 1982-85; diagnostician Larry Ppollock PhD & Assoc., Houston, 1985-88; ptnr. Montrose Psychotherapy P.C., Houston, 1988—; CEO Noah's House, Houston, 1998—; biofeedback therapist Teresa A. Atkinson RPT, Houston, 1989-91; psychology supr. Larry Pollock PhD & Assocs., Houston, 1990-91; presenter S.W. Women's Conf., Houston, 1990, 5th Internat. Congress on Ericksonian Approaches to Hypnosis and Psychotherapy, 1992; seminar instr. Inst. Group and Family Psychotherapy, Moscow, Russia, 1994. Presenter U. Tex. Dental Sch., Houston, 1990, 91. Mem. APA, AACD, Am. Soc. Clin. Hypnosis, Nat. Bd. Crt. Clin. Hypnotherapists, Biofeedback Soc. Tex., Exec. and Profl. Assn. Houston (bd. dirs., comty. affairs com. 1993-96, bd. trustees 1996-98), Delta Delta Delta, Kappa Kappa Kappa. Avocations: camping, creative writing, golf. Office: Montrose Psychotherapy PC 812 Hawthorne St Houston TX 77006-3902

HAYNER, HERMAN HENRY, lawyer; b. Fairfield, Wash., Sept. 25, 1916; s. Charles H. and Lillie (Reifenberger) H.; m. Jeannette Hafner, Oct. 24, 1942; children: Stephen, James K., Judith A. BA, Wash. State U., 1938; JD with honors, U. Oreg., 1946. Bar: Wash. 1946, Oreg. 1946, U.S. Dist. Ct. Wash. 1947, U.S. Ct. Appeals (9th cir.) 1947. Asst. U.S. atty. U.S. Dept. Justice, Portland, Oreg., 1946-47; atty. City of Walla Walla, Wash., 1949-53; ptnr. Minnick-Hayner, Walla Walla, 1949—; mem. Wash. State exec. bd. U.S. West, Seattle, 1988-95. Regent Wash. State U., Pullman, 1965-78; dir. YMCA, Walla Walla, 1956-67. Lt. col. Infantry, 1942-46. Decorated Bronze Star medal and four Battle Stars; recipient Disting. Svc. award Jr. C. of C., 1951, Wash. State U. Alumni award, 1988. Fellow ABA, Am. Coll. Trust & Estate Counsel; mem. Wash. State Bar Assn., Walla Walla County Bar Assn. (pres. 1954-55), Walla Walla C. of C. (merit award 1977, dir. 1973-88), Rotary (pres. 1956-57), Walla Walla Country Club (pres. 1956-57). Republican. Lutheran. Avocations: golf, photography. Home: PO Box 454 Walla Walla WA 99362-0013 Office: Minnick-Hayner PO Box 1757 Walla Walla WA 99362-0348

HAYNES, CALEB VANCE, JR., geology and archaeology educator; b. Spokane, Wash., Feb. 29, 1928; m. Elizabeth Hamilton, Jan. 11, 1954 (div. 1991); 1 child, Elizabeth Anne.. Student, Johns Hopkins U., 1947-49; degree in geol. engring., Colo. Sch. Mines, 1956; PhD, U. Ariz., 1965. Mining geology cons., 1958-60; sr. project engr. Am. Inst. Research, Golden, Colo., 1956-60; sr. engr. Martin Co., Denver, 1960-62; geologist Nev. State Mus. Tule Springs Expedition, 1962-63; research asst. U. Ariz., Tucson, 1963-64, asst. prof. geology, 1965-68, prof. geoscis., anthropology, 1974—, Regents prof., 1991—; assoc. prof. So. Meth. U., Dallas, 1968-73, prof., 1973-74. Served with USAF, 1951-54. Guggenheim fellow 1980-81, Smithsonian sr. post doctoral fellow, 1987 ; grantee NSF, Nat. Geographic Soc., others. Fellow AAAS, Geol. Soc. Am. (Archeol. Geology award 1984); mem. Nat. Acad. Sci., Am. Quaternary Assn. (pres. 1976-78), Soc. Am. Archaeology (Fryxell award 1978), Sigma Xi. Office: U Ariz Dept Anthropology Tucson AZ 85721

HAYNES, DOUGLAS MARTIN, physician, educator; b. N.Y.C., Jan. 25, 1922; s. Daniel Hagood and Courtenay (Collins) H.; m. Elizabeth B. Johnson, June 17, 1961; children: Douglas Marshall, Lewis Daniel. BA, BS, So. Meth. U., 1943; MD, Southwestern Med. Coll., 1946; MA, Louisville Presby. Theol. Sem., 1989, ThM, 1994. Diplomate: Am. Bd. Obstetrics and Gynecology (assoc. examiner). Intern in pathology Parkland Meml. Hosp., Dallas, 1946-47; resident obstetrics and gynecology Parkland Meml. Hosp., 1949-52; asst. prof. obstetrics and gynecology U. Tex. Southwestern Med Sch., 1952-55; asso. prof. obstetrics and gynecology U. Louisville Sch. Medicine, 1955-57, prof., 1957-87, prof. emeritus, 1987—, chmn. dept., 1957-69; interim dean U. Louisville Sch. Medicine (Sch. of Medicine), 1969-70, dean, 1970-72. Author: Medical Complications During Pregnancy, 1969; Contbr. articles to med. jours. Served to capt., M. C. AUS, 1947-49. Fellow Am. Gynec. and Obstet. Soc.; mem. Am. Coll. Obstetricians and Gynecologists, A.C.S., Central Assn. Obstetricians and Gynecologists (v.p. 1977-78), So. Med. Assn., Phi Beta Kappa, Phi Chi, Delta Chi, Alpha Omega Alpha, Phi Kappa Phi. Democrat. Episcopalian. Home: 5204 Tomahawk Rd Louisville KY 40207-1643

HAYNES, GARY ALLEN, photographer, journalist, newspaper editor; b. Beloit, Kans., Jan. 25, 1936; s. Blair W. and Evelyn H. (Allen) H.; children by previous marriage: Stephanie L., Philip A., Emily L.; m. Audrey M. Edwards. BS in Journalism, Kans. State U., 1957. Staff photographer Salina (Kans.) Jour., 1957; photographer UPI, Detroit, 1958; mgr. picture bur. UPI, Phila., 1959-62, Atlanta, 1962-63; spl. projects photographer UPI, N.Y.C., 1964; mgr. picture bur. UPI, L.A., 1964-68; photographer Internat. Olympic Photo Pool, Tokyo, 1964; mgr. div. newspictures UPI, Chgo., 1968-70; asst. to mng. editor newspictures UPI, N.Y.C., 1970-71; asst. picture editor N.Y. Times, N.Y.C., 1971-74; photo editor San Francisco Examiner, 1974; dir. graphic arts Phila. Inquirer, 1974-95, asst. mng. editor; with Photography weekly column, syndicated by Knight Newspapers (later Knight-Ridder), 1976-87; cons. N.Y. Times, 1996—; photographer NASA Photo Pool, 1962-63; spkr., del. USA-USSR Photo Summit, Moscow, 1990, Washington, 1991. Contbg. photographer: (book) Four Days, 1963, A Week at Kansas State, 1988; picture editor: Assignment America, 1972, A Day In the Life of California, 1989; judge W.R. Hearst photojournalism competition, San Francisco, 1986-88; lectr. photography and photo editing, Am. Press Inst., Reston, Va., 1987-96, The New Sch., 1991, Internat. Ctr. Photography, New York, 1990, U. Arts, Phila., 1989-91, Kansas State U., Manhattan, 1989-99, Temple U., Phila., 1992. Capt. Adj. Gen. Corps, U.S. Army, 1957-58. Recipient 1st pl. award Look mag. Sports Photo Contest, 1962, 1st and Best of Show awards The White House News Photographers Assn., 1962, Photo awards World Press Photo, 1st and 3d pl. gen. news, 1963, Sweepstakes award Atlanta Press Assn., Sweepstakes 1st and 3rd pl. awards Gen. News, 1964, Judges Spl. award for newspaper picture editing, 1979, best use of photos in newspaper zoned edit NPPA/Pictures of Yr. Competition, Silver medal mag. photo editing Soc. Newspaper Design, 1988, Pictures of Yr. 18th Ann. Competition 1st pl. spot news, 1st pl. feature, 1st pl. gen. news. Mem. Nat. Press Photographer's Assn., Sigma Delta Chi. Home: 234 Pine St Philadelphia PA 19106-4314

HAYNES, GARY ANTHONY, archaeologist; b. Long Beach, Calif., Sept. 30, 1948; s. Ellsworth Wallace and Martha Louise (Ryan) H. BA, U. Md., 1970; MA, Cath. U. Am., 1978, PhD, 1981. Vis. asst. prof. anthropology Cath. U. Am., Washington, 1981; assoc. prof. lectr. George Washington U., Washington, 1982; research assoc. anthropology dept. Smithsonian Inst., Washington, 1981-85; asst. prof. anthropology U. Nev., Reno, 1985-88, assoc. prof. anthropology, 1988-95, prof. anthropology, 1995—, chair dept., 1998—; founder, vice-chmn. bd. Hwange Rsch. Trust, 1987—. Author: Mammoths, Mastodonts and Elephants, 1991; contbr. articles to profl. jours. Active Scientist Exchange Acad. Scis. U.S. Nat. Research Council, 1987. Smithsonian Inst. fellow, 1980; grantee Nat. Geog. Soc., 1981-88, 91, Leakey Found., 1990, 91, IREX, 1995; Fulbright sr. scholar Subsaharan Africa Rsch. Program, 1993. Mem. Soc. Am. Archaeology (Fryxell com. chmn. 1986-89), Am. Quaternary Assn., Soc. Vertebrate Paleontology, Zimbabwe Sci. Assn., Am. Geophys. Union. Office: Dept Anthropology U Nev Reno Reno NV 89557*

HAYNES, J. NEAUELL, clergyman, bishop. Bishop Ch. of God in Christ for Northeast Tex. Office: Ch of God in Christ 6743 Talbot Pkwy Dallas TX 75232-3316*

HAYNES, JOHN MABIN, retired utilities executive; b. Albany, N.Y., Apr. 22, 1928; s. John Mabin and Gladys Elizabeth (Phillips) H.; m. Marion Enola Hamilton, Apr. 7, 1956; children: John David, Douglas Hamilton, Robert Paul. B.S., Utica Coll., Syracuse U., 1952. Accountant Price Waterhouse & Co., N.Y.C., Syracuse, N.Y., 1953-61; successively auditor, adminstrv. asst., asst. treas., treas., treas. and v.p., sr. v.p. Niagara Mohawk Power Corp., Syracuse, 1961-88; past pres., chmn., dir. N.Y. Bus. Devel. Corp., Syracuse; past dir., pres. N M Uranium, Inc.; past dir., treas. Canadian Niagara Power Co. Ltd.; past treas. Moreau Mfg. Co., St. Lawrence Power Co.; past treas. Empire State Power Resources, Inc.; past dir. and treas. Beebee Island Corp.; past bd. dirs. treas. Opinac Investments Ltd., Opinac Energy Ltd., Opinac Holdings Ltd.; past mng. dir. Niagara Mohawk Fin. N.V. Mem. Westhill Cen. Sch. Bd. Edn., 1968-73, pres., 1969-71; treas. Henderson County Humane Soc., 1989-90. With AUS, 1945-47. Mem. Nat. Assn. Accountants (past dir.), Am. Gas Assn. (fin. com.), Fin.

Execs. Inst. Clubs: Bond of Syracuse (past dir.), Masons. Home: 3108 Cove Loop Rd Hendersonville NC 28739-8870

HAYNES, KAREN SUE, university president, social work educator; b. Jersey City, July 6, 1946; d. Edward J. and Adelaide M. (Hineson) Czarnecki; m. James S. Mickelson; children: Kingsley Eliot, Kimberly Elizabeth, David. AB, Goucher Coll., 1968; MSW, McGill U., 1970; PhD, U. Tex., 1977. Cons. Inst. Nat. Planning, Cairo, 1977-78; asst. prof. Ind. U., Indpls., 1978-81, assoc. prof., 1981-85; prof. social work U. Houston, 1985-95, dean, 1985-95, pres., 1995—; pres. Ind. Coalition Human Services, Indpls., 1984-85. Author: Sage Publications, 1984; Longman, 1986, 91, 93, 96, Springer, 1989, also articles. Mem. Nat. Assn. Social Workers, Council Social Work Edn., Internat. Assn. Schs. Social Work, Nat. Alliance Info. and Referral (pres. 1983-87), Leadership Houston, 1986, Leadership Tex., 1990, Leadership Am., 1996. Avocation: poetry. Office: U Houston-Victoria 2506 E Red River St Victoria TX 77901-4450

HAYNES, MARGARET ELIZABETH, English educator; b. Oak Ridge, Tenn., June 11, 1947; d. Sherwood Kimball and Pauline Julia (MacBride) H.; m. Adi Wang, June 11, 1977 (div. Oct. 1992); children: Erin Alda, Sherwood Hayner; m. Bruce Edward Froelich, Aug. 30, 1996; stepchildren: David Forrest, Courtney Lynne, Ashleigh Marie. BA in French, Mount Holyoke Coll., 1969; MAT, John Hopkins U., 1972; MA, So. Ill. U., 1979; PhD in Interdisciplinary Arts/Letters, Mich. State U., 1989. English instr. Kodak Co., Taipei, Taiwan, 1976-78; English lectr. Fu-jen U., Hsinchu, Taiwan, 1976-77, Soochow U., Shihlin, Taiwan, 1977-78; reading coord. Internat. English Inst., Nashville, 1983-85; assoc. prof. English divsn. Delta Coll., Univeristy Center, Mich., 1988—. Author, editor (with others): Second Language Reading and Vocabulary Development, 1993. Program com. Unitarian-Universalist Ch., Midland, 1992—; mem. Merian's Friends, 1997-98; mem. strategic planning diversity com. Midland Pub. Schs., 1991-93. Mem. Tchrs. of English to Spkrs. of Other Langs. (nominating com., 1997—). Avocations: folk dance and contra dance, reading, parenting. E-mail: mehaynes@alpha.delta.edu. Home: 10 Brown Ct Midland MI 48640 Office: English Divsn Delta Coll University Center MI 48710

HAYNES, MOSES ALFRED, physician; b. Guyana, Nov. 17, 1921; came to U.S., 1947, naturalized, 1955; s. Milton Alphonso and Charlotte Mildred (Alleyne) H.; m. Hazel Louise Edgecombe, July 1, 1951; 1 child, Theresa Sue (Mrs. Larry Law). B.S., Columbia U., 1951; M.D., State U. N.Y., 1954; M.P.H., Harvard U., 1963. Intern St. John's Episcopal Hosp., Bklyn., 1954-55; physician USPHS Indian Hosp., Cheyenne Agy., S.D., 1955-59; asst. prof. community medicine U. Vt., 1959-64; asso. prof. Sch. Pub. Health, Johns Hopkins, 1966-69; prof. preventive and social medicine and pub. health UCLA, 1969-77; asso. dean Drew Postgrad. Med. Sch., Los Angeles, 1969-77; chmn. dept. community medicine Drew Postgrad. Med. Sch., 1969-74, acting dean, 1975-76, dean, pres., 1979-86; dir. Drew/Meharry/Morehouse Consortium Cancer Ctr., 1986-90; pres. SECON Inc., 1977-79; vis. prof. Med. Coll., Trivandrum, Kerala, India, 1964-66; mem. cancer support rev. com. Nat. Cancer Inst. Chmn. health task force Urban Coalition, 1968-69; mem. Pres.'s Com. Health Edn., 1972; exec. dir. Nat. Med. Assn. Found., 1968-69; mem. adv. com. Nat. Ctr. Health Stats., 1974-76; mem U.S. Preventive Svcs. Task Force, 1985-86; mem. bd. sci. counselors, divsn. cancer prevention and control Nat. Cancer Inst., 1989-93, chmn., 1991-93; bd. dirs. Ptnrs. for Prevention, 1991-92; mem. adv. bd. Fogarty Internat. Ctr., 1992-93. With USPHS, 1955-59. Fellow Am. Coll. Preventive Medicine, (pres. 1983-85); fellow AAAS; mem. Inst. Medicine of Nat. Acad. Sci. (internat. health bd., com. human rights 1986-89), Inst. Medicine (council 1983-86), Alpha Omega Alpha. Home: 29249 Firthridge Rd Palos Verdes Peninsula CA 90275-4713 *Being is more important than doing.*

HAYNES, PETER LANCASTER, utility holding company executive; b. Ellsworth, Maine, July 8, 1939; s. Charles A. and Hazel G. (Giles) H.; m. Judith A. Bates, Aug. 26, 1961; children: Jeffrey, Timothy, Christopher. BS, U. Maine, 1961; MBA, Cornell U., 1963. Registered profl. engr. Mass., Vt. V.p. switched svcs. New Eng. Telephone, Boston, 1978-83, v.p. mktg., 1983-85; pres., CEO Nynex Enterprises, N.Y.C., 1985-90, Quality Logistics Mgmt., Inc., Bedford, N.Y., 1991-92, Consumers Water Co., Portland, Maine, 1992-99. Trustee Portland Symphony, Maine Med. Ctr.; chmn., bd. govs. Boys and Girls Club Am., Atlanta. Mem. Cornell Club N.Y., Woodlands Club. Home: 98 Starboard Reach Yarmouth ME 04096-6158 Office: PO Box 7650 Three Canal Plaza Portland ME 04112-7650

HAYNES, R. MICHAEL, lawyer; b. Safford, Ariz., Oct. 3, 1940; s. Rodman and Angeline (Fragale) H.; m. Anne Marie de Almeida, Aug. 15, 1972; 1 child, Michelle Chloe. BA, Rutgers U., 1963, JD with honors, 1968. Bar: N.Y. 1969, N.J. 1977, D.C. 1992, U.S. Dist. Ct. (so. and ea. dists.) N.Y. 1973, U.S. Ct. Appeals (2d cir.) 1973, U.S. Supreme Ct. 1973, U.S. Dist. Ct. N.J. 1977, U.S. Dist. Ct. D.C. 1992. Assoc. Cooper, Ostrin, DeVargo & Ackerman, N.Y.C., 1968-69; asst. dist. atty., dep. chief rackets bur. N.Y. County Dist. Atty.'s Office, N.Y.C., 1969-74; exec. asst. dist. atty. spl. narcotics Prosecutor's Office, N.Y.C., 1974-76; asst. U.S. atty. Dist. N.J., Newark, 1976-79; minority counsel Com. on Small Bus., U.S. Senate, Washington, 1979-81; chief counsel Com. on Small Bus., U.S. Senate, 1981-86; gen. counsel Nat. Assn. Small Bus. Investment Cos., Washington, 1986-90; pvt. practice of law, 1990—; adj. prof. L.I. U., 1975-76; instr. N.Y. State Commn. Investigation, 1974-75, Atty. Gen.'s Adv. Inst., Dept. Justice, 1978-79; counsel White House Conf. on Small Bus., 1980. Advisor Washington Internat. Sch. Mock Trial Team, 1991-95. Recipient Atty. Gen.'s Spl. Achievement award, 1977. Mem. ABA (chmn. SBIC subcom. small bus. com. 1986-89), Fed. Bar Assn. (chmn. small bus. com. fin. insts. and economy sect. 1988-89), U.S. C. of C. (small bus. coun. 1987-89), SEC Govt. Bus. Forum on Capital Formation (exec. com. 1988-89). Republican. Office: 3509 Idaho Ave NW Washington DC 20016-3151 *The law holds everyone equally accountable, but requires of a lawyer a higher duty to honor the principles that the law prescribes while at the same time serving the people whom it governs. To that end, a lawyer must insure that the law itself remains just and fair and that those who make and enforce the law do so with integrity.*

HAYNES, THOMAS MORRIS, philosophy educator; b. Waukesha, Wis., Oct. 24, 1918; s. George Albert and Lois (Morris) H.; m. Jane Louise Riggs, Sept. 12, 1942; children: Christopher Thomas, Jonathan Marshall, Carolyn Martha. AB, Butler U., 1941; PhD, U. Ill., 1949. Indsl. engr. RCA, Indpls., 1942-44; research and devel. engr. P.R. Mallory, Indpls., 1944-46; U. Ill. postdoctoral fellow Faculty Law U. Paris, 1949-50; instr. philosophy U. Ill., 1950-51; research asst. U. Ill. (Coll. of Law), 1950-51; instr. philosophy Lehigh U., 1952-54, asst. prof., 1954-61, asso. prof., 1961-69, prof., 1969-83, prof. emeritus, adj. prof., 1983-91; founder, pres. World-Sense, Inc.; dir. World-Sense Dialogue. Mem. AAUP, Am. Philos. Assn., N.Y. Acad. Scis., Environ. Def. Fund, World Wildlife Fund, Natural Resources Def. Coun., The Wilderness Soc., Rodale Inst., Nat. Wildlife Fedn. (assoc.), The Nature Conservancy, The Costeau Soc., Worldwatch Libr., Union Concerned Scientists (sponsor), Amnesty Internat., Nat. Trust for Historic Preservation, Woodrow Wilson Internat. Ctr. for Scholars (assoc.), Phi Beta Kappa, Phi Kappa Phi. Home: 175 W North St Apt 427A Nazareth PA 18064-1435 Office: World Sense Inc PO Box E Bethlehem PA 18015-0427*

HAYNES, TODD, film writer, producer, director; b. L.A., Jan. 2, 1961; s. Allen E. and Sherry Lynne (Semler) H. BA in Art and Semiotics with honors, Brown U., 1985. Co-founder Apparatus Prodns., N.Y.C., 1987-91. Writer, dir., prodr. (films) The Suicide, 1978, Assassins: A Film Concerning Rimbaud, 1985, Superstar: The Karen Carpenter Story, 1987 (Golden Gate award 1987), Poison, 1990 (Grand Jury prize Best Feature Sundance Film Festival 1991, Critics award Locarno and Portugal Internat. Film Festivals), Dottie Gets Spanked, 1993 (Grand Jury prize Best Film USA Film Festival 1994), Safe, 1995 (Dir.'s Fortnight Cannes Film Festival 1995, Best Ind. Film Seattle Film Festival 1995). Office: Bronze Eye Prodns 525 Broadway Rm 701 New York NY 10012-4411*

HAYNES, ULRIC ST. CLAIR, JR., university dean; b. Bklyn., June 8, 1931; s. Ulric St. Clair and Ellaline (Gay) H.; m. Yolande Toussaint, Sept. 20, 1969; children: Alexandra, Gregory. BA, Amherst Coll., 1952; JD, Yale U., 1956; LLB (hon.), Ind. U., 1981, John Jay Coll., 1981, Fisk U., 1982, Ala. State Coll., 1982; JD, Butler U., 1988. Exec. asst. N.Y. State Dept. Commerce, Albany, 1956-57; adminstrv. officer UN European Office, Geneva, 1959-60; asst. to rep. Ford Found., Lagos, Nigeria, Tunis, Tunisia, 1960-63; asst. officer in charge Moroccan affairs Dept. State, Washington, 1963; officer in charge Southwest Africa and High Commn. Ters. Affairs Dept. State, 1963-64; mem. NSC staff White House, 1965-66; pres. Mgmt. Formation Inc., N.Y.C., 1966-70; sr. v.p., ptnr. Spencer Stuart and Assocs. Mgmt. Consultants, N.Y.C., 1970-72; v.p. for mgmt. devel. Cummins Engine Co., Columbus, Ind., 1972-74; v.p. for Mid-East and Africa Cummins Engine Co., 1974-77; ambassador to Algeria Am. Embassy, Algiers, 1977-81; v.p. internat. bus. planning Cummins Engine Co., 1981-83; acting pres. SUNY/Coll. at Old Westbury, 1985-86; pres. AFS Intercultural Programs, N.Y.C., 1986-88; cons. N.Y.C., 1989-91; exec. dean Hofstra U. Sch. Bus., Hempstead, N.Y., 1991-96; exec. dean univ. internat. rels. Hofstra U., Hempstead, N.Y., 1996—; bd. dirs. HSBC Bank USA, Pall Corp., ReliaStar Life Ins. Co. N.Y., INNCOM Internat., Inc. Contbr. articles to profl. publs. Mem. selection com. Henry Luce Found. Asian Scholars Program; mem. Middle East adv. com. Human Rights Watch. Root-Tilden scholar; John Hay Whitney scholar. Mem. Coun. Fgn. Rels., Coun. Am. Ambs., Yale Club of N.Y.C., The Pilgrims of the U.S. Democrat. Episcopalian. Home: 19 Threepence Dr Melville NY 11747-3408 Office: Hofstra U Sch Bus Hempstead NY 11550

HAYNES, WILLIAM FORBY, JR., retired internist, cardiologist, educator; b. Newark, June 6, 1926; s. William Forby and Grace (Brien) H.; BS, U.S. Mcht. Marine Acad., 1946; AB, Princeton U., 1950; MD, Columbia U., 1954; postgrad. La Salle U., 1997—; m. Constance Simpson, July 2, 1960; children: William, Suzanne, David; m. Aline Linehan James, Aug. 25, 1984. Intern, St. Luke's Med. Center, N.Y.C., 1954-55, resident, 1957-59, N.Y. Heart Assn. fellow in cardiology, 1959-60; practice medicine specializing in internal medicine, cardiology, Princeton, N.J.,a 1960-97, ret., 1997; asst. prof. medicine Robert Wood Johnson Med. Sch., 1972—; sr. attending internal medicine Princeton Med. Ctr., 1960-89, ret., hon. staff, 1997—; lectr. on spirituality and med. practice, 1982—. Author: A Physician's Witness to the Power of Shared Prayer, 1990, Minding the Whole Person: Cultivating a Healthy Lifestyle from Youth Through the Senior Years, 1994; contbr. articles to profl. jours. Served as ensign USNR, 1944-46, to lt., M.C., 1955-57. Diplomate Am. Bd. Internal Medicine (subcert. in cardiovascular diseases), Nat. Bd. Med. Examiners. Recipient Archbishop Theodore McCarrick award for Disting. Svc., 1997. Fellow ACP, Am. Coll. Cardiology, Am. Coll. Chest Physicians; mem. Am. Heart Assn. (fellow coun. clin. cardiology), Mercer County Heart Assn. (v.p. 1970, trustee 1964-76, Cardiologist of Yr. 1995), Third Order of St. Francis, Univ. Cottage Club Princeton, Princeton U. Alumni Coun. for Athletics, Princeton Officers Soc., Princeton U. Friends of Swimming (pres. 1975-87), U.S. Masters Swimming Assn. (top ten), Univ. Cottage Club, Nassau Club. Republican. Episcopalian. Co-inventor GI String for detecting intestinal bleeding, 1960. Home: 6 Skyfield Dr Princeton NJ 08540-7403 Office: 281 Witherspoon St Princeton NJ 08540-3210

HAYNES, WILLIAM J(AMES), II, lawyer; b. Waco, Tex., Mar. 30, 1958; s. William James and Caroline (Bynum) H.; m. Margaret Frances Campbell, Aug. 21, 1982; children: William James III, Sarah Insley, Taylor Bynum. BA, Davidson Coll., 1980; JD, Harvard U., 1983; LLD (hon.), Stetson U., 1999. Bar: N.C. 1983, Ga. 1989, D.C. 1990. Law clk. to Hon. James B. McMillan U.S. Dist. Ct. N.C., Charlotte, 1983-84; assoc. Sutherland, Asbill & Brennan, Washington, 1989; spl. asst. to gen. counsel Dept. Def., Washington, 1989-90; gen. counsel Dept. Army, Washington, 1990-93; ptnr. Jenner & Block, Washington, 1993-96; v.p., assoc. gen. counsel Gen. Dynamics Corp., Falls Church, Va., 1996-98; gen. counsel Gen. Dynamics Marine Group, 1997-98; ptnr. Jenner & Block, Washington, 1999—. Capt. U.S. Army, 1984-88. Mem. ABA, N.C. Bar Assn., D.C. Bar Assn., Ga. Bar Assn., Army-Navy Club. Presbyterian. Avocation: tennis. Office: Jenner and Block 601 13th St NW Washington DC 20005*

HAYNIE, THOMAS POWELL, III, physician; b. Hearne, Tex., Aug. 9, 1932; s. Thomas Powell, Jr. and Sue Cummings (Gibson) H.; m. Bette Flossel, Mar. 10, 1956; children: David Powell, Amy Cummings, Sue Cummings, Garner Powell. Student, U. South, Sewanee, Tenn., 1949-51, U. Tex., Austin, 1951-52; M.D., Baylor U., 1956. Diplomate: Am. Bd. Internal Medicine, also Sub-Bd. Med. Oncology, Am. Bd. Nuclear Medicine. Intern, then resident in internal medicine U. Mich. Med. Center, Ann Arbor, 1956-60; instr. U. Mich. Med. Center, 1960-62; asst. prof. medicine, dir. nuclear med. service U. Tex. Med. Br., Galveston, 1962-65; assoc. prof. medicine U. Tex.-M.D. Anderson Cancer Ctr., Houston, 1965-75; prof. U. Tex.-M.D. Anderson Hosp. and Tumor Inst., Houston, 1975-95, James E. Anderson prof. nuclear medicine, 1988-95, prof. emeritus of nuclear medicine, 1995—, chief sect. nuclear medicine, 1967-84, chmn. dept. nuclear medicine, 1984-93, head dept. internal medicine, 1977-84; adj. prof. radiology Baylor Coll. of Medicine, Houston, 1996—; pres. Am. Coll. Nuclear Medicine, 1993-94; cons. in field. Author articles in field, chpt. in books; editor Jour. Nuclear Medicine, 1985-89. Mem. AAAS, ACP, AMA, Am. Coll. Nuclear Physicians, Am. Coll. Nuclear Medicine, Radiol. Soc. N.Am., Am. Thyroid Assn., Assn. Univ. Radiologists, Soc. Nuclear Medicine, Tex. Med. Assn., Tex. Assn. Physicians in Nuclear Medicine, Am. Coll. Radiology, Sigma Xi, Phi Gamma Delta, Doctor's Club. Episcopalian. Office: 1515 Holcombe Blvd Houston TX 77030-4009

HAYNIE, TONY WAYNE, lawyer; b. Houston, Sept. 26, 1955; m. Mary E. Steward, Sept. 1, 1978. BA, U. Okla., 1978; postgrad., Boston U., Heidelberg Br., Fed. Republic Germany, 1980-81; JD, U. Tulsa, 1984; MBA, Okla. State U., 1993. Bar: Okla. 1985, U.S. Dist. Okla. 1985, U.S. Ct. Appeals (10th cir.) 1987, U.S. Ct. Appeals (5th cir.) 1992, U.S. Ct. Appeals (7th and D.C. cirs.) 1998, U.S. Supreme Ct. 1990. Assoc. Conner & Winters, Tulsa, 1984-90, ptnr., 1991-92, shareholder, 1992—; pres., CEO The Colonneh Co., Tulsa, 1991—; arbitrator N.Y. Stock Exch., 1991—; trustee Transvoc, Inc., 1995—, pres. bd. trustees, 1998-99. Adv. bd. mem. Tulsa Area United Way, 1998—. 1st lt. U.S. Army, 1978-82. Mem. ABA (sect. bus. law and litig., chair subcom. on expert witness on trial evidence com. of litig. sect. 1991-94), Am. Inns of Ct. (barrister Hudson-Hall-Wheaton chpt. 1996—), Okla. Bar Assn., Okla. Bar Found., Tulsa County Bar Assn., Tulsa County Bar Found., Phi Delta Phi. Democrat. Methodist. Office: Conner & Winters 3700 1st Place Tower 15 E 5th St Tulsa OK 74103-4391

HAYNSWORTH, ROBERT F., JR., anesthesiologist; b. El Paso, Tex., Aug. 11, 1954. MD, U. Tex., Houston, 1981. Cert. in anesthesiology, specialty in pain mgmt. Flex intern Tex. Tech. U. Health Sci. Ctr., Lubbock, 1981-82, resident in anesthesiology, 1982-84, chief resident in anesthesiology, 1983-84; fellow in pain mgmt. U. Tex. S.W. Med. Sch., Dallas; attending anesthesiologist Baylor U., Tex., assoc. attending; clin. dir. Baylor Pain Mgmt. Ctr. Office: 618 Clara Barton Blvd Ste 1 Garland TX 75042-5731

HAYO, GEORGE EDWARD, management consultant; b. L.A., Nov. 2, 1934; s. George Edward Hayo Sr. and Esther Marie (Goodman) Arthur; m. Nixie Joanne Hunt, Aug. 4, 1956; children: Michael Edward, Kenneth Marvin, Michelle Virginia. BS in Applied Math., Calif. State U., 1960; MBA in Mgmt., U. Denver, 1968. Cert. mgmt. cons. Mathematician U.S. Naval Civil Engring. Lab., Port Hueneme, Calif., 1961-63; corp. systems planner No. Natural Gas Co., Omaha, 1963-66; asst. to pres. C.A. Norgren Co., Littleton, Colo., 1966-68; sr. staff cons. Emerson Electric, St. Louis, 1968-71; dir. adminstrn. Fisher Radio, N.Y.C., 1971-72; v.p., dir. The Emerson Cons., N.Y.C., 1973-87; pres. The Hayo Cons., Albuquerque, 1988—; arbitrator Am. Arbitration Assn., N.Y., 1985—. Contbr. articles to profl. jours. Mem. Inst. Mgmt. Cons., Am. Inst. Plant Engrs., Am. Prodn. and Inventory Control Soc. Avocations: running, sailing, golf. Home and Office: The Hayo Cons 536 Stagecoach Rd SE Albuquerque NM 87123-4123

HAYON, ELIE M., chemist, educator; b. Cairo, Egypt, May 15, 1932; came to U.S., 1965; s. Mayer E. and Regina (Cohen); m. Nina Mokady, 1982; 1 child, Rona. B.Sc., U. Strathclyde, Glasgow, Scotland, 1954; Ph.D., Durham U., Newcastle-upon Tyne, Eng., 1957. Brit. Empire Cancer Research fellow Kings Coll., Newcastle-upon Tyne, 1957-58, Brookhaven Nat. Lab., Upton, N.Y., 1958-60, Cambridge (Eng.) U., 1960-62, Centre Nuclear Studies, Saclay, France, 1963-65; head phys. chemistry Natick (Mass.) Labs., 1966-75, Gen. Foods Corp., Tarrytown, N.Y., 1976-78; dean grad. studies and research, prof. chemistry Queens Coll., City U.N.Y., 1978—. Contbr. articles to profl. jours. Mem. numerous profl. assns. in U.S. and U.K. Home: 240 E 82nd St New York NY 10028-2703 Office: 6 Einstein St, Ra'ananna Israel

HAYS, CINDY SHELTON, fundraising company executive; b. Mayfield, Ky., Aug. 20, 1949; d. William Edward III and Mary (Hadfield) Shelton; m. Paul Hays, July 4, 1984. BA, U. Miss., 1971; cert. in European studies, Inst. Am. Univs., Aix-en-Provence, France, 1971. Exec. dir. Young Rep. Nat. Fedn., Washington, 1971-84; campaign cons. CSM, Memphis, 1972-84; real estate agt. Poplar Pike, Inc., Memphis, 1973-84; v.p. TelAc, Inc., Arlington, Va., 1984-91; pres. JL Gourmand, Inc., Alexandria, Va., 1991-94, The Hays Group, Washington, 1994—; internat. cons. Internat. Rep. Inst., Washington, 1990-94; cons. Civic Dem. Alliance, Czech Republic, 1994; internat. election observer Bulgaria, 1990, 91, Albania, 1991-92, Kuwait, 1992, Azerbaijan, 1998; bd. dirs. Bus. Info. Network, 1999. Editor: East European Democratic Campaign Manual, 1991; contbr. articles to various telecom. newsletters and periodicals. Mem. exec. com. Young Rep. Nat. Fedn., 1976-82, Austrian-Am. Alliance Benefit, Washington, 1997-98; mem. ctrl. com. D.C. Rep. Com., 1984-88; mem., chmn. house tour Capitol Hill Restoration Soc., Washington, 1985; mem. Leadership Memphis, 1981—, Leadership Washington, 1997—; mem., pres. The Charter 100, 1986—. Named Young Rep. of Yr., Tenn. Young Reps., 1981, Realtor Assoc. of Yr., Tenn. Assn. Realtors, 1982. Mem. Women of Washington. Methodist. Avocations: reading, golf, antiquing. Home: 147 12th St SE Washington DC 20003-1420

HAYS, DAVID ARTHUR, theater producer, stage designer; b. N.Y.C., June 2, 1930; s. Mortimer and Sarah (Reich) H.; m. Lenore Landau, Dec. 28, 1954; children: Julia Carrie, Daniel Edward. AB magna cum laude, Harvard U., 1952; MFA (tchg. fellow), Boston U., 1955; postgrad., Yale Drama Sch., 1953-54; LHD (hon.), Gallaudet Coll., 1975; ArtsD (hon.), Wesleyan U., Middletown, Conn., 1986; DFA (hon.), Conn. Coll., 1992; DHL (hon.), Manhattanville Coll., 1997, Emerson Coll., 1998. tchr. stage designing NYU, 1961-62, Boston U., 1963; asst. prof. Columbia U., 1964-65, Conn. Coll., 1971—; guest lectr. English Harvard U., 1977, 79; tech. adviser Kabuki tour U.S., Japan, 1960; vis. com. on performing arts Harvard bd. overseers; cons. George Balanchine N.Y. State Theater, 1963; designer Mummer's Theater, Oklahoma City, 1960. Apprentice Brattle Theatre, Cambridge, Mass., 1949-52; designer stock theatres, Green Mansions, N.Y., 1954, Tanglewood, Mass., 1955; off-Broadway prodns. The Iceman Cometh, 1956, Cradle Song, 1955, Children of Darkness, 1958, Endgame, 1958, The Quare Fellow, 1958, Our Town, 1959, The Balcony, 1960, Desire Under the Elms, 1963; Broadway prodns. including Night Circus, 1957, The Innkeepers, 1955, Long Day's Journey into Night, 1956, Tenth Man, 1959, Roman Candle, 1960, All the Way Home, 1960, Love and Libel, 1960, Sunday in New York, 1961, Gideon, 1961, Strange Interlude, 1963, A Family Affair, 1962, Look, We've Come Through, 1961, No Strings, 1962, In the Counting House, 1962, Lorenzo, 1963, A Murderer Among Us, 1964, Marco Millions, 1964, The Last Analysis, 1964, The Changeling, 1964, Tartuffe, 1964, Peterpat, 1964, Hughie, 1964, The Diamond Orchid, 1965, Drat the Cat, 1965, Mrs. Dally, 1965, UTBU, 1966, Dinner at Eight, 1966, We Have Always Lived in the Castle, 1966, Yerma, 1966, The Goodbye People, 1968, The Miser, 1969, Two By Two, 1970, The Gingerbread Lady, 1970, Platinum, 1978, Bring Back Birdie, 1981, Kingdoms, 1981, Scarlett, Tokyo, 1970, Gone With the Wind, London, 1972, N.Y.C. Opera prodns., St. Joan, 1959, The Cradle Will Rock, 1960, Met. Opera prodns., Susannah, 1965, La Boheme, 1966; designer, Shakespeare Festival prodns., Hamlet, Stratford, Conn., 1958, A Mid-Summer Night's Dream, 1958, Romeo and Juliet, 1959, A Winter's Tale, 1958, Murder in the Cathedral, 1965, N.Y.C. Ballet; prodns. Pastorale, 1958, The Masquers, 1957, Stars and Stripes, 1959, Native Dancers, 1959, Episodes, 1959, Panamerica, 1960, Liebeslieder Waltzer, 1960, Electronics, 1961, Midsummer Night's Dream, 1962, Bugaku, 1963, The Chase, 1963, Irish Fantasy, 1964, Divertimento No. 15, 1966; staff designer prodns., Vivian Beaumont Theatre, Lincoln Center, A Cry of Players, 1969; designer Dance Theare of Harlem prodns. Dance Theatre of, Bugaku, 1974, Spiritual Suite, 1976; dir. prodns. include Four Saints in Three Acts, Nat. Theatre of Deaf, 1976; playwright prodns.: The Wooden Boy, Nat. Theatre of Deaf, 1979, (with others) Parzival, From the Horse's Mouth, 1982; author: (book) Light on the Subject, 1988, (with son, Daniel) My Old Man and The Sea, 1995; artistic dir., founder Nat. Theatre of the Deaf, 1967—. Panelist N.Y. State Coun. on Arts, 1970-75, NEA, 1977-79, 94; bd. dirs. Sholem Aleichem Found., N.Y.C. Fulbright grantee to Old Vic London, 1952-53, Ford Found. grantee to design an ideal theatre, 1959-61; recipient Obie awards for The Quare Fellow, 1958, Obie awards for The Balcony, 1960, Critic's Poll Best Designer award for No Strings, 1962, Ann. award New Eng. Theater Conf., 1967, Ann. Nat. Gov. award, 1992, Alumni award Boston U., 1980, 94, U. Conn., 1987, Harvard Arts award, 1999. Mem. PhiBeta Kappa, Sociètè Nautique de Casablanca, Century Assn., Harvard Club. Holder passage record for small boat sailing from Africa to N.Y., 1963; 1st ocean passage catboat, 1980; Feller trophy for ocean dinghy passage, 1980; Cape Horn passage in 25' sloop Sparrow, 1985. Address: PO Box 235 Chester CT 06412-0235

HAYS, E. EARL, youth organization administrator; b. Uniontown, Kans.; s. Earl Loren and Avis Marie (Mccollum) H.; m. Betty Ann Frigo, Nov. 21, 1966. BA, Whittier Coll., 1962; MA, Ottawa U., 1993; PhD, Pacific Western U., 1993. Dir. pub. rels., fin., dist. exec. Boy Scouts Am. L.A. Area Coun., 1962-71; asst. dir. exploring Boy Scouts Am. Nat. Coun., North Brunswick, N.J., 1971-73; dir. fin. svcs. Boy Scouts Am. Golden Empire Coun., Sacramento, 1973-75; dir. field svc. Boy Scouts Am. Santa Clara County, San Jose, Calif., 1975-77; scout exec., CEO Boy Scouts Am. Clinton Valley Coun., Pontiac, Mich., 1977-82, Boy Scouts Am. Grand Canyon Coun., Phoenix, 1982—. *E. Earl Hays has more than 36 years progressively responsible experience as a professional Scouting Executive. While Chief Executive Officer in Phoenix, Arizona, youth membership has grown by 84%, ranking among the top 12 out of 328 local councils nationwide. Honored as a member of the Chief Scout Executive's Winners' Circle for Balanced Youth Membership Growth (54,080 youth members), Sound Fiscal Operations, Quality Program, and as a National Quality Council. In 1996-1997, he received the Ansel Adams Mountain Portrait Award for Endowment Development, and the Excellence in Marketing the Scouting Program award from the Western Region Boy Scouts of America.* Bd. dirs. Pontiac Oakland Symphony, 1980-82; pres. United Way Exec. Dirs. Assn., Phoenix, 1984-85. Fellowship honor Boy Scouts Am., 1991, James E. West fellow, 1994. Mem. Ottawa U. Alumni Assn. (bd. dirs. 1995-98), Nat. Eagle Scout Assn. (life, Disting. Eagle Scout 1998), Rotary (pres. Pontiac 1982, bd. dirs., sec.) Phoenix 100 Club (Paul H. Harris fellow). Democrat. Lutheran. Avocations: travel, music, reading, scuba, golf. Office: Grand Canyon Coun 2969 N Greenfield Rd Phoenix AZ 85016-7715

HAYS, GARRY D., academic administrator. Pres. U.S. Internat U., San Diego, 1992—. Office: US Internat Univ Office of President 10455 Pomerado Rd San Diego CA 92131-1799*

HAYS, HERSCHEL MARTIN, electrical engineer; b. Neillsville, Wis., Mar. 2, 1920; s. Myron E. and Esther (Marquardt) H.; E.E., U. Minn., 1942; grad. student U. So. Calif., 1947; children—Howard Martin, Holly Mary, Diane Esther, Willet Martin Hays II. Elec. engr. City of Los Angeles, 1947-60; pres. Li-Bonn Corp. Served as radio officer, 810th Signal Service Bn., U.S. Army, 1942-43; asst. signal constrn. officer, E.T.O., 1943-45, tech. supr. Japanese radio systems, U.S. Army of Occupation, 1945-46; mem. tech. staff, Signal Corps Engring. Labs., U.S. Army, 1946; col. U.S. Army, ret. Signal Officer Calif. N.G. 1947-50. Registered profl. engr. Calif. Mem. Eta Kappa Nu, Pi Tau Pi Sigma, Kappa Eta Kappa. Republican. Episcopalian. Home: 603 Alhambra Rd Venice FL 34285-2502

HAYS, HOWARD H. (TIM HAYS), editor, publisher; b. Chgo., June 2, 1917; s. Howard H. and Margaret (Mauger) H.; m. Helen Cunningham, May 27, 1947 (div. Dec. 1988); children: William, Thomas; m. Susie Gudermuth, Sept. 1992. BA, Stanford U., 1939; LLB, Harvard U., 1942. Bar: Calif. 1946. Spl. agt. FBI, 1942-45; reporter San Bernardino (Calif.) Sun, 1945-46; asst. editor Riverside (Calif.) Daily Press, 1946-49, editor, 1949-65, editor, co-pub., 1965-83, editor, pub., chief exec. officer, 1983-88, editor, chmn., chief exec. officer, 1989-92, chmn. bd., 1992-97, chmn. emeritus, 1997—; Mem. Pulitzer Prize Bd., 1976-86; mem. AP Bd., 1980-89, vice chmn. 1988-89. Bd. visitors John S. Knight Fellowships for Profl. Journalists, Stanford U., 1983-98; mem. nat. com. Washington U. Sch. of Art, 1992—. Recipient Dist. award Calif. Jr. C. of C., 1951; named Pub. of Year Calif. Press Assn., 1968. Mem. Calif. Bar Assn., Am. Soc. Newspaper Editors (dir. 1969-76, pres. 1974-75), Stanford Alumni Assn. (dir. 1970-74), Internat. Press Inst. (chmn. Am. com. 1971-72, mem. exec. bd. 1977-83), Am. Press Inst. (bd. dirs. 1973—, chmn. 1978-83), New Directions for News (bd. dirs. 1987-92),

Nature Conservancy Calif. (bd. dirs. 1982-86). Home: 3724 Utah Pl Saint Louis MO 63116-4831

HAYS, JAMES FRED, geologist, educator; b. Little Rock, July 10, 1933; s. Orren Lee and Virginia (Russell) H.; m. Diane Lee Huntoon, Dec. 22, 1956; 1 dau., Lee Anne. A.B., Columbia U., 1954; M.S. (NSF fellow), Calif. Inst. Tech., 1961; Ph.D., Harvard U., 1966. Geologist U.S. Geol. Survey, 1961; guest investigator Geophys. Lab., Carnegie Instn. of Washington, 1965; Soc. Fellows jr. fellow Harvard U., 1963-66, asst. prof. geology, 1966-69, assoc. prof., 1969-72, prof., 1972-84, chmn. dept. geol. scis., 1981-82; dir. div. earth scis. NSF, 1982-87, sr. sci. advisor, 1987-91, dir. earth scis. div., 1991-95; cons. NASA Astronaut Tng. Program, 1969-73; mem. NASA Lunar Sample Analysis Planning Team, 1973-76, chmn. Lunar and Planetary Rev. Panel, 1978-81; prin. investigator Apollo Lunar Sample Program; vis. prof. chemistry and geology Ariz. State U., 1978-79; adminstrs. bd. Harvard and Radcliffe Colls., 1976-78; mem. Harvard Ctr. for Earth and Planetary Physics, 1970-84, sci. adv. bd. Mt. St. Helens Nat. Volcanic Monument, 1983-87, adv. com. on mining and minerals rsch. Dept. Interior, 1983-85, Working Group for U.S.-Peoples' Republic of China Agreement for Cooperation in Earth Scis., 1982-87, Space Grant Rev. Panel NASA, 1992-95; NRC com. on Rsch. Opportunities and Priorities for EPA, 1995-97; exec. sec. Pres.'s Com. on Nat. Medal Sci., 1987-91; vis. scholar U. Ariz., 1997—. Assoc. editor: Nature of the Solid Earth, 1970, Jour. Geophys. Research, 1978-80, 83-85. Served to capt. USNR, 1954-59. Recipient Presdl. Rank award U.S. Govt., 1994; NSF grantee, 1974-82, NASA grantee, 1971-82. Fellow AAAS (councilor 1989-92), Geol. Soc. Am. (councilor 1988-91), Mineral. Soc. Am.; mem. Am. Geophys. Union, Geol. Soc. Washington, Potomac Geophys. Soc., Am Ornithologists Union, Naval Res. Assn., Harvard Club (N.Y.C. and Washington), Cosmos Club, Phi Beta Kappa, Sigma Xi. Rsch. and publs. on exptl. petrology and geochemistry. Home: 3381 W Foxes Den Dr Tucson AZ 85745-5107

HAYS, JOHN ALAN, military officer, construction company executive; b. West Frankfort, Ill., Oct. 16, 1940; s. John D. and Henrietta (Allen) H.; m. Shirley Ann Shelton, Feb. 6, 1965; children: John B., Andrea Lynn. BA, Governors State U., University Park, Ill., 1990. Commd. 2nd lt. inf. Ill. Army N.G., 1962-65, advanced through grades to brig. gen., 1993, infantry platoon leader, 1962-67, rifle co. exec. officer Co. A, 3rd Bn., 130th Inf., 1967-68, tactical officer Ill. Officer Candidate Sch., hdqrs., 1968-70, brigade chem. officer hdqs., 1970-72, rifle co. comdr., 1972-75, staff intelligence officer, 1975-77, ops. and tng. officer hdqrs., 1977-81, inf. bn. exec. officer hdqrs., 1981-83, inf. bn. comdr. hdqrs., 1983-86, mil. support officer, 1986-87, tng. officer, 1987-88, dep. dir. plans, ops., tng. and mil. support, 1989, chief plans, ops. and tng., 1989, dir. plans, ops. tng. and mil. support, 1989-93, dep. STARC comdr., state area comdr., 1992—. Decorated Legion of Merit, Meritorious Svc. medal with 2 oak leaf clusters, Army Commendation medal with 3 oak leaf clusters, Army Achievement medal, Army Res. Components Achievement medal with silver oak leaf cluster, Nat. Def. Svc. medal, Armed Forces Res. medal with 2 hour glass devices, Army Svc. Ribbon, Expert Infantryman Badge. Mem. N.G. Assn. of U.S., N.G. Assn. of Ill., Governors State U. Alumni Assn.

HAYS, JOHN TENNYSON, III, import, export company executive; b. Sullivan, Ind., June 29, 1940; m. Susan Lucinda Brown; 2 children. BA summa cum laude, Wabash Coll., 1962; student, Edinburgh (Scotland) U., 1960-61; MBA, Harvard U., 1964. Trainee Esso SA Petrolera Argentina, Buenos Aires, 1964-67; fin. mgr., dir. Exxon Corp., Asunción, Paraguay, 1967-69; area fin. mgr. Exxon Corp., Kingston, Jamaica, 1969-70; mgr. spl. projects First Nat. Bank Boston, 1970-71; treas. Chrysler Corp. Group, Argentina, 1971-73, dir. fgn. mktg., 1973-75; exec. dir. Banco Intercambio Regional, COMEXBIR, Buenos Aires, 1975-79; pres., CEO Ten Tola Trading, Panama, Argentina, U.S., 1980—; coord., mng. dir. Paraguay Aluminios, Asunción, 1980-83, coord., ptnr. mgr., 1983-84; founder, pres. Coffees of Hawaii, Inc., Honolulu, Molokai, 1984-90; pres. Ikatu Coffee, Honolulu, 1987—; dir. Bank USA NA, Kihei, Hawaii, 1991-92; exec. dir. Integrated Coffee Tech., Inc., Honolulu, Molokai, 1995-96, JLD Merchandise & Investment Bank, Kailua, Hawaii, 1998—; coord., ptnr. Asunción, Paraguay and Western Pacific, 1983-84; coord., mng. dir., Paraguay Aluminios, Paraguay, 1980-83. Active St. Andrew's Cathedral, Honolulu. Mem. Internat. Coffee Orgn. (charter, expert panel), Hawaii Coffe Assn. (charter dir.), Hawaii Coffee Growers' Assn. (charter, exec. dir. 1991), Downtown Exchange Club, Full Gospel Bus. Men's Fellowship Internat., Travelers' Century Club, Mensa, Intertel, Ala Wai Boat Club, Outrigger Canoe Club, Honolulu Rowing Club (pres.), Phi Beta Kappa. Episcopalian. Avocations: reading, painting, photography, gardening, golfing. E-mail: coffeeh@aloha.net. Office: PO Box 1855 Honolulu HI 96805-1855

HAYS, MARGUERITE THOMPSON, physician; b. Bloomington, Ind., Apr. 15, 1930; d. Stith and Louise (Faust) Thompson; m. David G. Hays, Feb. 4, 1950 (div. 1975); children: Dorothy Adele, Warren Stith Thompson, Thomas Glenn. A.B. cum laude, Radcliffe Coll., 1951; postgrad., Harvard U. Med. Sch., 1954; M.D., UCLA, 1957; Sc.D. (hon.), Ind. U., 1979. Diplomate Am. Bd. Internal Medicine, Am. Bd. Nuclear Medicine. Intern UCLA Sch. Medicine, 1957-58, resident, 1958-59, 61-62, USPHS postdoctoral trainee, 1959-61, USPHS postdoctoral fellow, 1963-64, asst. prof. medicine, 1964-68; asst. prof. medicine SUNY-Buffalo, 1968-70, asst. prof. biophys. sci., 1968-74, assoc. prof. medicine, 1970-76, clin. assoc. prof. nuclear medicine, 1973-77; asst. chief nuclear medicine VA Med. Ctr., Wadsworth, Calif., 1967-68; chief nuclear medicine Buffalo VA Med. Ctr., 1968-74, assoc. chief of staff for research, 1971-74; dir. med. research service VA Central Office, Washington, 1974-79; asst. chief med. dir. for research and devel. VA Central Office, 1979-81; chief of staff Martinez VA Med. Ctr., Calif., 1981-83; prof. radiology Sch. Medicine U. Calif., Davis, 1981-93, prof. medicine and surgery, 1983-91, assoc. dean, 1981; clin. prof. diagnostic radiology and nuclear medicine Stanford U. Sch. Medicine, 1990—; assoc. chief of staff for research Palo Alto VA Med. Ctr., Palo Alto, 1983-97, staff physician, 1997—; vis. rsch. scientist Euratom, Italy, 1962-63; chmn. radiopharm. adv. com. FDA, 1974-77; co-chmn. biomedicine com. Pres.'s Fed. Coun. on Sci., Engring. and Tech., 1979-81; mem. rsch. restructuring adv. com. Va. R&D Office, 1995-96, chair task group to restructure R&D Career Devel. Program, 1996—; chmn. coop. studies evaluation com., Med. Rsch. Svc., VA, 1990-93; mem. sci. rev. and evaluation bd. Health Svcs. Rsch. and Devel. Svc., VA, 1988-91, chmn. career devel. com., 1991—, chmn. career devel. com. Rehab. Rsch. and Devel. Svc., 1997—. Rsch. grantee VA, 1968—. NIH grantee, 1964-71. Fellow ACP; mem. Soc. Nuclear Medicine (chmn. publs. com., trustee, v.p. 1983-84), Am. Thyroid Assn. (bd. dirs. 1993-96), Endocrine Soc., Western Assn. Physicians, Western Soc. for Clin. Investigation. Home: 270 Campesino Ave Palo Alto CA 94306-2912 Office: 3801 Miranda Ave Palo Alto CA 94304-1207

HAYS, MARY KATHERINE JACKSON, civic worker; b. Flora, Miss.; d. Rufus Lafayette and Ada (Collum) Jackson; m. Halbert Puffer Oliver, Aug. 9 1927 (dec. 1934); m. Donlad Osborne Hays, Aug. 30, 1937. Student, U. Miss., 1925-26, Millsaps Coll., 1926-27, 43-44; grad., Clark Bus. Sch., 1934; student, Columbia U., 1935; student, Strayer Bus. Coll., 1951. Sec. to pres. McCullough Box and Crate Co., Pharr, Tex., 1934-36; sec. to field supr. Miss. Unemployment Compensation Commn., 1936-37; rep. Homes of Tomorrow, 1940 N.Y. World's Fair; sec. to head interior design Lord & Taylor, N.Y.C., 1940; sales dept. Knabe Piano Co., N.Y.C., 1941-43. Active, Little Theatre, Wilkes Barre, Pa., 1937-39; charter mem., incoroporator Conf. State Socs., Washington, 1952; vol. worker Am. Cancer Soc., Washington, 1957; mem. Center City Residnets Assn., Phila., 1956; mem. women's com. Nat. Symphony Assn., vol. worker USO, 1945-48, mem. symphony sustaining com. drives, 1957; mem. women's com. Corcoran Gallery Art, Wasington, 1957-62; mem. Pierce-Warwick Adoption Assn. of Washington Home for Foundlings; vol. Washington Heart Assn., 1959-66; mem. Nat. Capital Area chpt. United Ch. Women, 1957-72; mem. D.C. Episcopal Home for Children, 1961-86, D.C. Salvation Army Aux., 1962—. Mem. Miss. State Soc. D.C. (sec. 1950-53), Miss. Women's Club D.C., DAR (chpt. regent 1972-74, vice chair D.C. com. celebration Washington's birthday 1972-76, state libr. 1974-76, state officers club 1976—), UDC (chpt. historian 1982-84, 86—, chaplain 1984-86), Johnstone Clan Am. (exec. coun. 1976-81, nat. chair membership com. 1976-81), First Families of Miss., Women's Club of Flora, Miss., The Washington Club. Episcopalian. Home: 200 Dominican Dr Apt M 201 Madison MS 39110-8630

HAYS, MYRNA MANTEL, educational association administrator, fashion consultant; b. Bowling Green, Ohio, Mar. 8, 1939; d. Ora Vernon and Vita (Eishen) Mantel; m. Peter L. Hays, Sept. 14, 1963; children: Melissa, Eric, Jeffrey. BS, Bowling Green State U., 1961; MA, Ohio State U., 1963. Editor, writer U. Calif., Davis, 1966-67, exec. dir. faculty assn., 1979—; tchr., dir. Discovery Pre-Sch., Davis, 1975-77; image cons. Beauty for All Seasons, Davis, 1985-92; fashion cons. CMCE Custom Fashions, Davis, 1987—, area dir., 1988-94; legis. coord. Coun. Univ. Calif. Faculty Assn., Davis, 1992—. Bd. dirs. PTA, Davis, 1967-87, pres., 1981-83; co-chair county sch. bd. campaign State Supr. Pub. Instrn., Davis, 1985. Home and Office: 1129 Fordham Dr Davis CA 95616-0926

HAYS, OTIS EARL, JR., writer. BA, U. Ark., 1938; grad. study journalism, Northwestern U., 1945-46. Prof. journalism Henderson State Coll., 1946-48, U. Tulsa, 1948-51; fgn. svc. officer USIA, Washington, 1966-75; freelance author Pierce City, Mo., 1975—. Intelligence officer U.S. Army, 1941-45, 51-66. Home and Office: Rt 3 Box 464 Pierce City MO 65723

HAYS, PAUL LEE, JR., insurance company executive; b. Hays, Kans., Jan. 11, 1950; s. Paul Le Roy Sr. and Doris Jean (Cotten) H.; m. Gladys Sue Johnson, Mar. 14, 1971; children: Ryan Lee, Rachel Alison. BSBA, Ft. Hays U., 1971. Flight instr. Jayhawk Aviation, Topeka, 1973; prodn. test pilot Cessna Aircraft Co., Wichita, Kans., 1973-75; ins. sales Prudential Ins. Co., Wichita, Kans., 1975-77, Am. Gen. Life, Wichita, Kans., 1977-78, Am. Fidelity Assurance Co., Wichita, Kans., 1978-80, C.A. Langhoffer and Assoc., Wichita, Kans., 1980-83; mgr. Capitol Agy., Overland Park, Kans., 1983—; agt's coun. Hanover Ins., Overland Park, 1992-97. Contbr. articles to profl. jours. Corp. sec. Abudant Life Assembly of God, Lenexa, Kans., 1993-98. Mem. Nat Assn. Life Underwriters (Nat. Sales Achievement award 1977, Nat Quality award 1977), Nat. Assn. Profl. Ins. Agts., Kans. Assn. Ins. Agts., Internat. Assn. Fin. Planners. Avocations: flying, traveling. Office: Capitol Agy PO Box 678 Shawnee Mission KS 66201-0678

HAYS, RICHARD SECREST, minister; b. Warren, Ohio, Feb. 1, 1951; s. Robert Collins and Sarah Lewis (Secrest) H.; m. Paula Jeanne Barron, Dec. 27, 1975; children: Elizabeth Anne, Andrew Paul. AB, Lafayette Coll., Easton, Pa., 1973; postgrad., U. Edinburgh, Scotland, 1973-74; MDiv, Pitts. Theol. Sem., 1976. Ordained to ministry Presbyn. Ch. (USA), 1976. Student asst. to chaplain Lafayette Coll., Easton, 1971-73, Edgewood Presbyn. Ch., Pitts., 1975-76; pastor Rockford (Ohio) Presbyn. Ch., 1976-87, First Presbyn. Ch., Waverly, Ohio, 1987—; exec. sec. Rockford C. of C., 1985-87; jour. clk. Maumee Valley Presbytery, Findlay, Ohio, 1986-87; gen. assy. commr. Presbyn. Ch. (USA), Hartford, 1982, Albuquerque, 1996, Charlotte, 1998; moderator Scioto Valley Presbytery, 1998-99. Recipient David Fowler Atkins prize, Lafayette Coll., 1973. Mem. Pike County C. of C. Democrat. Office: First Presbyn Ch 122 E North St Waverly OH 45690-1146 *When the burdens of ministry get heavy, I remember the words of a trusted mentor, "What the people need is someone to love them". That reminds me that if God loves me and I love the people, then the people will grow to love God.*

HAYS, RICK F., public policy executive; b. St. Joseph, Mo., Oct. 27, 1952; s. William Andy and Alma LaVonne (Temple) H.; m. Jane Reid, Aug. 16, 1975; children: Matthew Patrick, Benjamin Reid, Lara Elizabeth. BS in Journalism, U. No. Colo., 1973. Editor Town & Country News, Greeley, Colo., 1973-74; pub. relations rep. Mountain Bell, Greeley, 1974-77; pub. relations supr. Mountain Bell, Tucson, 1977-79; pub. relations mgr. Mountain Bell, Denver, 1979-83; dir. regional pub. rels. US WEST Comm., Boise, Idaho, 1984-96; v.p. Mont. US WEST Comm., Helena, 1996—; mem. mktg. com. Boise Area Econ. Devel. Coun., 1987-96; chair Idaho Bus. Week, 1991; chair edn. com. IACI, 1993-94; exec. com. Idaho Sch. Improvement Com., 1993-95. Coach Capital Youth Soccer, 1986-93; mem. strategic com. Idaho Edn. Project, 1990-91; mem. exec. bd. Ada County United Way, Boise, 1991-94; active Schs. 2000, 1992-95; mem. ecumenical comm. Cath. Ch., 1990-95; mem. bd. Gateway Econ. Devel. Coun., 1998—; mem. Mont. Gov.'s Ambs., 1997, mem. bd., 1999—; chmn. Mont. Gov.'s Workforce Investment Bd., 1999—; mem. president's coun. Carroll Coll., 1998—; mem. nat. adv. bd. Burns Telecom. Ctr., Bozeman, Mont., 1997—. Recipient award Idaho Assn. Supervision and Curriculum Devel., 1990; named Outstanding Young Man, 1992. Mem. Pub. Rels. Soc. Am. (bd. dirs. 1988-92). Roman Catholic. Avocations: photography, golf, antiques. Office: US WEST Comm 441 N Park PO Box 1716 Helena MT 59624-1716

HAYS, ROBERT, actor; b. Bethesda, Md., July 24, 1947. Student, Grossmont Coll., San Diego State U. Mem. Old Globe Theatre. Appeared in films, including Airplane, 1980, Take This Job and Shove It, 1981, Some Summer Day, Airplane II, 1982, Utilities, Trenchcoat, 1983, Scandalous, 1984, Cat's Eye, 1985, Honeymoon Academy; co-star (TV show) Angie, also appeared in The Love Boat, Laverne and Shirley, Most Wanted, California Gold Rush, Will Rogers: Champion of the People.

HAYS, ROBERT GLENN, journalism educator; b. Carmi, Ill., May 23, 1935; s. Lewis Earl and Margaret Elizabeth (White) H.; m. Mary Elizabeth Corley, Dec. 21, 1957; children: Alan Gregory, David Robert. BS in Journalism, So. Ill. U., 1961, MS in Journalism, 1972, PhD, 1976. Reporter Granite City (Ill.) Press-Record, 1961-63; pub. rels. writer So. Ill. U., Carbondale, 1963-66, alumni publs. editor, 1966-71; rschr., asst. scientist Ill. Bd. Natural Resources/Conservation, 1971-73; primary campaign mgr. Paul Simon for Congress, Ill., 1974; asst. prof. journalism Sam Houston State U., Huntsville, Tex., 1974-75; assoc. prof. journalism U. Ill., Urbana, 1975-86, 87—; chair mass comm. dept. S.E. Mo. U., Cape Girardeau, 1986-87; mem. lit. rev. panel Jour. Applied Comms., 1990—, manuscript rev. bd., 1992—; editor rsch. sect. ACE Quar., 1978-80; assoc. editor Jour. Correctional Edn., 1969-70. Co-author: G-2: Intelligence for Patton, 1971, new edit., 1999; author: Country Editor, 1974, State Science in Illinois, 1980, A Race at Bay, 1997; editor: Early Stories From the Land, 1995; contbr. articles to profl. jours. Mem. steering com. Champaign County (Ill.) ACLU, 1992-95; dep. registrar Champaign County Clk. Office, 1988-91. With U.S. Army, 1955-57. Mem. Internat. Assn. Agrl. Communicators in Edn. (vice chair tchg. divsn. 1991-93, Rsch. Excellence award 1993, Tchg. Excellence award 1994), Assn. Edn. in Journalism and Mass Comm., Investigative Reporters and Editors, Rsch. Soc. Am. Periodicals, Ill. Press Assn., Soc. Profl. Journalists. Democrat. Home: 2314 Glenoak Dr Champaign IL 61821-6220

HAYS, ROBERT WILLIAM, communications consultant, educator, writer; b. Atlanta, Oct. 17, 1925; s. Calvin Samuel and Elizabeth (Green) H.; m. Rebecca Copeland, June 15, 1950; children: Michael, David, William. Student, Duke U., 1943-44; AB summa cum laude, Presbyn. Coll. S.C., 1947; MEd, Emory U., 1957. Comml. mgr. Sta. WSFT-AM, Thomaston, Ga., 1947-48, Sta. WLBG, Clinton, S.C., 1948; co-owner Clinton Plastic Co., 1948-49; instr. English So. Tech. Inst. (now So. Polytechnic State U.), Chamblee, Ga., 1950-51; supr. of tng. course devel. Lockheed Aircraft Corp., Marietta, Ga., 1951-52; asst. prof. So. Tech. Inst. (now So. Polytechnic State U.), Chamblee, Ga., 1952-57; head English dept. So. Tech. Inst. (now So. Polytechnic State U.), Marietta, 1953-73, assoc. prof., 1958-60, prof., 1960-85, prof. emeritus, 1985—; cons. in communications, Marietta, 1965—, Mid. East, summer 1968-70. Author: Pacific Parodies, 1947, Principles of Technical Writing, 1965, Practically Speaking in Business, Industry and Government, 1969, Guide to Technical Writing, 1970, (with others) Getting Your Message Across, 1981; published many poems; contbr. numerous articles to profl. jours. Mem. adv. bd. Salvation Army, Marietta, 1996—. Served to lt. (j.g.) USNR, 1943-46. Hixson fellow Kiwanis, 1996; recipient Arthur Williston award, 1967, Internat. Tech. Communications Conf. Honor, 1980, 83, Cmty. Svc. award King Ctr., 1994, 95. Fellow Soc. for Tech. Communication (life, Disting. award 1993); mem. Assn. for Bus. Communication. Home: 3360 Trickum Rd Marietta GA 30066-4683

HAYS, RONALD JACKSON, career officer; b. Urania, La., Aug. 19, 1928; s. George Henry and Fannie Elizabeth (McCartney) H.; m. Jane M. Hughes, Jan. 29, 1951; children: Dennis, Michael, Jacquelyn. Student, Northwestern U., 1945-46; B.S., U.S. Naval Acad., 1950. Commd. ensign U.S. Navy, 1950, advanced through grades to adm., 1983; destroyer officer Atlantic Fleet, 1950-51; attack pilot Pacific Fleet, 1953-56; exptl. test pilot Patuxent River, Md., 1956-59; exec. officer Attack Squadron 106, 1961-63; tng. officer Carrier Air Wing 4, 1963-65; comdr. All Weather Attack Squadron, Atlantic Fleet, 1965-67; air warfare officer 7th Fleet Staff, 1967-68; tactical aircraft plans officer Office Chief Naval Ops., 1969-71; comdg. officer Naval Sta., Roosevelt Roads, P.R., 1971-72; dir. Navy Planning and Programming, 1973-74; comdr. Carrier Group 4, Norfolk, Va., 1974-75; dir. Office of Program Appraisal, Sec. of Navy, Washington, 1975-78; dep. and chief staff, comdr. in chief U.S. Atlantic Fleet, Norfolk, Va., 1978-80; comdr. in chief U.S. Naval Force Europe, London, 1980-83; vice chief naval ops. Dept. Navy, Washington, 1983-85; comdr. in chief U.S. Pacific Command, Camp H.M. Smith, Hawaii, 1985-88; pres., chief exec. officer Pacific Internat. Ctr. for High Tech. Rsch., Honolulu, Hawaii, 1988-92; tech. cons., 1992—. Decorated D.S.M. with 3 gold stars, Silver Star with 2 gold stars, D.F.C. with silver star and gold star, Legion of Merit, Bronze Star with combat V, Air Medal with numeral 14 and gold numeral 3, Navy Commendation medal with gold star and combat V. Baptist. Home and Office: 869 Kamoi Pl Honolulu HI 96825-1318

HAYS, RUTH, lawyer; b. Fukuoka, Japan, Sept. 20, 1950; d. George Howard and Helen Jincy (Mathis) H. AB, Grinnell Coll., 1972; JD, Washington U., 1978. Bar: Mo. 1978. Law clk. U.S. Ct. Appeals (8th cir.), St. Louis, 1978-80; assoc. Husch & Eppenberger, St. Louis, 1980-87, ptnr., 1987—. Articles editor Urban Law Annual, 1977-78. Bd. dirs. Childhaven, St. Louis, 1982-93, pres. 1987-88. Olin fellow Monticello Coll. Found., St. Louis, 1975-78; recipient Spl. Svc. award Legal Svs. Ea. Mo., 1993. Mem. ABA, Mo. Bar Assn., Bar Assn. Met. St. Louis, Employee Benefits Assn. (pres. 1995), Order of Coif, Phi Beta Kappa. Office: Husch & Eppenberger 100 N Broadway Ste 1300 Saint Louis MO 63102-2789

HAYS, SARAH W., federal judge. Magistrate judge U.S. Dist. Ct. (we. dist.) Mo., Kansas City, 1992—. Office: 811 Grand Blvd Rm 445 Kansas City MO 64106-1904

HAYS, STEELE, retired state supreme court judge; b. Little Rock, Mar. 25, 1925; s. L. Brooks and Marion (Prather) H.; m. Peggy Wall, July 12, 1980; children from previous marriage: Andrew Steele, Melissa Louise, Sarah Anne. B.A., U. Ark., 1948; J.D., George Washington U., 1951. Bar: Ark. 1951. Adminstrv. asst. to Congressman Brooks Hays, 1951-53; practice in Little Rock, 1953-79; mem. firm Spitzberg, Mitchell & Hays, 1953-79; circuit judge 6th Jud. Circuit Ark., Little Rock, 1969-70; judge Ark. Ct. Appeals, 1979-81; assoc. justice Ark. Supreme Ct., 1981-95; ret., 1995; chmn. Bd. Law Examiners, 1968-70. Mem. Ark. com. U.S. Civil Rights Commn.; del. Presbyn. Ch. Consultation on Ch. Union, 1968-70; trustee Presbyn. Found.; chancellor Episcopal Diocese of Ark. Mem. Ark. Bar Assn. (past sec.-treas.), Sigma Chi, Delta Theta Phi. Home: 12 Deerwood St Conway AR 72032-6113

HAYS, THOMAS CHANDLER, holding company executive; b. Chgo., Apr. 21, 1935; s. Marion C. and Carolyn (Reid) H.; m. Mary Ann Jergens, June 8, 1958; children: Thomas, Michael, Paul, Jennifer. BS, Calif. Inst. Tech., 1957, MS, 1958; MBA with high distinction, Harvard U., 1963. Ops. rsch. analyst Lockheed Corp., L.A., 1963-64; ops. rsch. analyst Andrew Jergens Co. (formerly Am. Brands, then Fortune Brands 1997—), Cin., 1964-70, v.p. product mgmt., 1970-76, v.p. mktg., 1976-78; exec. v.p. Andrew Jergens Co. (formerly subs. Am. Brands, then Fortune Brands 1997—), Cin., 1978; pres., CEO Andrew Jergens Co. (formerly subs. Am. Brands), Cin., 1979-80; v.p. mktg. Am. Tobacco Co. (former subs. Am. Brands, then Fortune Brands 1997—), 1980-81, exec. v.p., 1981-85, pres., 1985-87, pres., COO, 1985-86, CEO, 1986-87, chmn., 1987-88, also bd. dirs.; chmn. Fortune Brands Internat. Corp., 1988-90; v.p. Fortune Brands, Inc. (formerly Am. Brands, Inc.), Old Greenwich, Conn., 1984-85; v.p. tobacco, 1985-87; pres., COO Fortune Brands, Inc. (formerly Am. Brands, Inc.), Old Greenwich, Conn., 1988-94, chmn., CEO, 1995—, also bd. dirs., 1981—, chmn. exec. com., 1996—; bd. dirs. ACNielsen, Gallaher Ltd. Trustee Andrew Jergens Found., The Devereux Found.; bd. dirs. Fairfield County Cmty. Found. 1st lt. USAF, 1958-62. Baker scholar Harvard U., 1963. Mem. Southwestern Area Commerce and Industry Assn. (bd. dirs.), Amb. Roundtable, Bus. Roundtable, Conf. Bd. and Econ. Club, Cin. Country Club, Darien Country Club, Bel Air Bay Club, Tokeneke Club, brd. trustees, Deveraux Found.

HAYS, THOMAS S., medical educator, medical researcher; b. Winter Haven, Fla., Dec. 20, 1954; married:. BS in Zoology, U. N.C., 1976, PhD in Cell Biology, 1985. Rsch. asst. dept. zoology U. N.C., Chapel Hill, 1975-76; rsch. asst. dept. biol. scis. Duke U., Durham, N.C., 1976-79; asst. instr. quantitative and analytical microscopy Marine Biol. Lab., Woods Hole, Mass., 1981-83; asst. instr. optical microscopy U. Calif., Santa Cruz, 1982; postdoctoral fellow dept. molecular, cellular and devel. biology U. Colo., Boulder, 1985-89; asst. prof. dept. genetics and cell biology U. Minn., St. Paul, 1989-95, assoc. prof. dept. genetics and cell biology, 1995—; external reviewer NSF, 1989—. Reviewer Jour. Cell Biology, Jour. Biol. Chemistry, Molecular Biology of the Cell, Molecular Cellular Biology, Proceedings Nat. Acad. Sci. USA, Cell Motility and the Cytoskeleton, Jour. Cell Sci., Genetics; contbr. articles to profl. jours. Founders scholar Marine Biol. Lab., 1980; H.V. Wilson fellow U. N.C., R.J. Reynolds fellow, 1983; Postdoctoral fellow NIH, 1985-88; recipient Basil O'Connor Scholar award March of Dimes, 1993, Established Investigator award Am. Heart Found., 1996; Tng. grantee NIH, 1991-95, grantee, 1995—; Rsch. Tng. grantee NSF, 1991-95; March of Dimes grantee, 1995—. Mem. Am. Soc. Cell Biology, Genetics Soc. Am. Office: U Minn Biol Sci Ctr Rm 250 1445 Gortner Ave Saint Paul MN 55108-1095*

HAYS, WILLIAM GRADY, JR., corporate financial and bank consultant; b. Covington, Ga., July 9, 1927; s. William Grady and Ella Maude (Wofford) H.; m. Emily Ann Holcombe, Aug. 1, 1954; children: Woodfrin Grady, Steven Gregory, William Danfield. B.S., U. Ga., 1949; M.Litt., U. Pitts., 1950. Pres. First So. Corp., Atlanta, 1955-57; v.p. Comml. Trust Co., 1957-59; pres., chief exec. officer Comml. Acceptance Corp., 1959-74; fin. cons. William G. Hays & Assocs., Inc., 1974—; cons., chief exec. officer N.Am. Acceptance Corp., 1974—; cons. Kaleidoscope, Inc., 1979—, Speir Ins. Agy., Inc., 1982—; CEO United Am. Fin. Corp., Knoxville, Tenn., 1983—; cons. Banque Nationale De Paris, Nat. Westminister Bank, PLC, United Bank of Kuwait, PLC, Security Pacific Nat. Bank, First Nat. Bank of Boston; trustee Beacon Fin. Group, Inc., 1986; cons. Micro Mart, Inc., 1987; examiner World Bazzar Franchise Corp., 1992; spl. master Hannover Corp. Am., 1991; spl. agt. Diversified Growth Corp., 1989; trustee Internat. Trading Inc., 1993, Aledo Fin. Svcs., Inc., 1985. Contbr. articles to profl. jours. Mem. Kappa Delta Pi. Republican. Presbyterian. Clubs: Cherokee Town and Country, Univ. Yacht. Home: 2755 Normandy Dr NW Atlanta GA 30305-2822 Office: William G Hays & Assocs Inc 1422 W Peachtree St NW Ste 218 Atlanta GA 30309-2940

HAYTAIAN, GARABED (CHUCK), state legislator; b. N.Y.C., Jan. 28, 1938; s. David and Zakia (Vaniskhian) H.; m. Joan Harriett Mardenly, 1961; children: David Ned, Debra Lucy Snyder, Darrell Charles. BS, U. Ala., 1961. Elec. engr. Am. Machine & Foundry, 1961-62, Grumman Aircraft Engr. Corp., 1962-66; pres. Mardenly Cleaners & Sons, Inc., 1966-82; mktg. dir. east coast L. Robert Kimball & Assoc., 1982-86; exec. cons. Group Tech. Inc., 1986-90; bus. adminstr. Hovanian Armenian Sch., 1990; mktg. dir. Superior Graphics, Inc., 1990—; freeholder Warren County, N.J., 1976-81; assemblyman dist. 23 N.J. State Assembly, 1982—; chmn. N.J. State Rep. Party, 1995—; minority whip N.J. State Assembly, 1984-85, asst. minority leader, 1985-86, majority leader, 1986-89, minority leader, 1990-92, spkr., 1992—. Recipient disting. svc. award Sussex County Edn. Assn., 1990, disting. citizen award Boy Scouts Am., 1988, ten year svc. award Am. Cancer Soc., 1984; named freshman assemblyman of yr. Nat. Assn. Counties, 1982, legis. of yr., 1983. Bd. dirs. Warren County C.C., 1988—; trustee Centenary Coll., 1988—. Mem. Hackettstown C. of C., Tall Cedars Lebanon, Masons. Office: 28 W State St Ste 300 Trenton NJ 08608*

HAYTHE, PAMELA FLEMING, secondary education educator; b. N.Y.C., Dec. 8, 1969; d. Thomas Madison and Sabine (Cailliau de Gaulle) H. BA in Social Anthropology cum laude, Harvard U., 1993; MA in English and Edn., Columbia U., 1996. With Noonan/Russo Comm., N.Y.C., 1993-94; tchr. English, Seward Park H.S., N.Y.C., 1996—. Mem. Harvard Club, Phi Delta Kappa. Republican. Episcopalian. Avocations: volunteering, inter-personal psychology, writing for fun. Home: 210 E 75th St Apt 4A New York NY 10021-2974 Office: Seward Park HS 350 Grand St New York NY 10002-4629

HAYTHORNTHWAITE, ROBERT MORPHET, civil engineer, educator; b. Whitley Bay, Eng., May 5, 1922; came to U.S., 1953, naturalized, 1964; s. William and Doris (Morphet) H.; m. Beatrice Mary Swift, Mar. 29, 1952; children: Richard Swift, Jennifer Anne, Susan Mary, Sheila Margaret. *His wife, Mary, has completed 45 years as a physician in Britain and the U.S. His son, Richard, studied librarianship with the Commonwealth of Pennsylvania and has been working with newspaper and book publishers in Illinois and Pennsylvania. His daughter, Jennifer, a clinical psychologist, is an associate professor in the department of psychiatry at Johns Hopkins University. His daughter, Susan, left Price Waterhouse and is an Independent consultant on computerized management systems. His daughter, Sheila, is an engineer at ADA Technologies in Denver researching power plant emission control technologies.* B.Sc., Durham U., 1942, London U., 1945; Ph.D., London U., 1952; M.S., Brown U., 1953, M.A., 1957. Registered profl. civil engr., Pa. Sci. officer Bldg. Research Sta., Watford, Eng., 1942-47; lectr. Sheffield U., 1947-53; instr. to asso. prof. Brown U., 1953-59; prof. engring. sci. U. Mich., 1959-67; prof. engring. mechanics Pa. State U., 1967-79, head dept., 1967-74; dean Coll. Engring. Tech., Temple U., Phila., 1979-81, prof. engring. sci., 1979-96, prof. emeritus, 1996—; vis. prof. Cambridge U., 1961, Manchester U., 1965-66, Lehigh U., 1974-75; cons. to Council Grad. Schs. U.S., Detroit Tank Arsenal, Engrs. Council for Profl. Devel., NASA, NSF. *Robert Haythornthwaite was founder and first president of the American Academy of Mechanics and continuously active in that organization during the 28 years since its inception. After 54 years in research laboratories and universities, he is now concentrating primarily on privately funded research in the field of theoretical and applied mechanics.* Editor Proc. of the 3d U.S. Nat. Congress Applied Mechanics, 1958, Mechanics, 1972, 73, 88-97; contbr. articles to profl. jours. Commonwealth Fund fellow, 1950. Fellow ASCE (tech. editor jour. engring. mechanics div. 1967-70, chmn. engring. mechanics div. 1966-67, rsch. prize 1963), Am. Acad. Mechanics (pres. 1969-71, Disting. Svc. to Theoretical and Applied Mechanics medal 1996, pub. Mechanics jour. 1997—, conf. procs., 1999); mem. ASME, Am. Soc. Engring. Edn. (chmn. mechanics div. 1966-67), Sigma Xi, Tau Beta Pi (faculty adviser Pa. Beta chpt. 1968-79). Home: 313 Wellington Ter Jenkintown PA 19046-3831

HAYUNGA, MARY ANN, women's health nurse; b. Bklyn., May 1, 1948; d. John and Theresa (Grombliniak) Mendelewski; m. Eugene Hayunga, Dec. 11, 1971; children: Christina, Joseph, Michael, Robert. Diploma, Bklyn. Meth. Hosp., 1967; BS, Empire State Coll., 1977; MPH, Johns Hopkins U., 1984. Classroom and clin. instr. Albany (N.Y.) Vocat. Sch., 1975-76; childbirth educator CEA, Kensington, Md., 1980-83; supr. pediatric and surg. specialities Kaiser Permanente, Kensington, 1987-89; clin. instr., adj. prof. maternal/child health and med.-surg. nursing Montgomery Coll., 1992—; mem. nursing faculty Kaplan Ednl. Svcs., 1997—. With (Nurse Corps) U.S. Army Res., 1974—. Mem. APHA, Polish Legion Am. Vets. Home: 10603 Wheatley St Kensington MD 20895-2623

HAYUTIN, DAVID LIONEL, lawyer; b. Phoenix, Apr. 19, 1930; s. Henry and Eva (Gaines) H.; m. Lee June Rodgers, June 15, 1951. A.B., U. So. Calif., Los Angeles, 1952, J.D., 1958. Bar: Calif. 1958. Assoc. Pillsbury Madison & Sutro LLP and predecessor firms., Los Angeles, 1958-67, ptnr., 1967—; bd. dirs. Asahi Bank of Calif. Author: Distributing Foreign Products in the United States, 1988, revised edit., 1993; assoc. editor So. Calif. Law Rev.; contbr. legal articles to profl. jours. Served to lt. (j.g.) USN, 1952-55. Mem. ABA, Internat. Bar Assn., Calif. Bar Assn., Maritime Law Assn., Mountaingate Country Club. Republican. Avocations: opera; golf. Office: Pillsbury Madison & Sutro LLP 725 S Figueroa St Los Angeles CA 90017-5524

HAYWARD, CHARLES WINTHROP, retired railroad company executive; b. Andover, Mass., May 30, 1927; s. Harry W. and Myrtle (Trommer) H.; m. Barbara Burns, Nov. 4, 1952; children: Patricia, John, Paul, Laura, Lee, Linda. BS, U.S. Mil. Acad., 1950; MBA, Syracuse U., 1957. Commd. 2d lt. U.S. Army, 1950, advanced through grades to col., 1968; served in Korea and Vietnam; ret., 1975; budget officer Nat. RR Passenger Corp., Washington, 1976-82, v.p. fin., chief fin. officer, 1982-93; ret., 1993; pres., chmn. bd. dirs. Chgo. Union Sta. Co., 1986-93; bd. dirs. Washington Terminal Co. Mem. Fin. Execs. Inst. (chpt. bd. dirs. 1982-90, pres. 1990-91). Avocations: golf, raising Angus cattle. *

HAYWARD, EDWARD JOSEPH, lawyer; b. Springfield, Mo., Dec. 4, 1943; s. Joseph Hunter and Rosemary (Barber) H.; m. Ellinor Duffy, Aug. 30, 1968; children: Jeffrey, Stephen, Susan. Student, U. d'Aix Marseille, Aix-en-Provence, France, 1963-64; AB, Stanford U., 1965; JD magna cum laude, Harvard U., 1971. Bar: N.Y. 1972, Minn. 1980. Assoc. Cleary, Gottlieb, Steen & Hamilton, N.Y.C. and Brussels, 1971-74, Oppenheimer Wolff & Donnelly, Brussels, 1975-79; ptnr. Oppenheimer Wolff & Donnelly, Mpls., 1978—; pres. Twin Cities Fgn. Trade Zone Inc., Mpls., 1983-84. Chmn. legis. com. Minn. World Trade Assn., Mpls., 1984-87. Served to capt. U.S. Army, 1965-68. Mem. ABA, Minn. Bar Assn. (councillor internat. law sect. 1983—, sec. 1986-88, vice chmn. 1988-89, chmn. 1989-90), French-Am. C. of C. (bd. dirs. 1983—, pres. 1985-87, 96—,. nat. sec. 1988—), German-Am. C. of C. (bd. dirs. 1994—), Dist. Export Coun. (chmn. 1996—). Republican. Presbyterian. Avocations: languages, sports. Home: 6625 W Shore Dr Minneapolis MN 55435-1528 Office: Oppenheimer Wolff & Donnelly 45 S 7th St Ste 3400 Minneapolis MN 55402-1609

HAYWARD, FREDRIC MARK, social reformer; b. N.Y.C., July 10, 1946; s. Irving Michael and Mildred (Feingold) H.; m. Ingeborg Beck, Aug. 18, 1971 (div. 1974); 1 child, KJ. BA, Brandeis U., Waltham, Mass., 1967; MA, Fletcher Sch. Law & Diplomacy, Medford, Mass., 1968, MALD, 1969. Exec. dir. Men's Rights, Inc., Boston, 1977—; vis. lectr. Tufts U., Medford, Mass., 1979; lectr. in field; conductor workshops in field; mem. adv. bd. Ctr. for Men's Studies, 1988-93; host, prodr. The SacraMENshow; founder Nat. Coalition Just Draft; co-founder Free Men Boston, Children's Rights Coun. Sacramento; co-founder, exec. dir. The Fathers' Symposium, 1996—. Author 3 published anthologies; contbg. editor: The Liberator, Forest Lake, Minn., 1988-89; contbg. writer Spectator, Berkeley, Calif., 1988—; contbr. articles to profl. jours. Farrell fellowship on Men, 1989; Fletcher Sch. Law and Diplomacy fellow, 1967-69; recipient award of Excellence Nat. Coalition of Free Men, 1993, W.A.V.E award, 1995. Mem. Nat. Congress for-Men (bd. dirs. 1981-90), Am. Fedn. TV and Radio Artists, Men. Internat. (bd. dirs. 1982-86). Office: Mr Inc PO Box 163180 Sacramento CA 95816-9180

HAYWARD, PATRICIA CARROLL, university administrator; b. Balt., Aug. 10, 1942; d. Benjamin Edward and Barbara Sparks (Broemmelsiek) Carroll; m. Robert Louis Hayward, Dec. 30, 1964. BA in Biology, Goucher Coll., 1964; MS, Fla. State U., 1972, PhD, 1985. Lab. technician Fla. State U., Tallahassee, 1964-70, coord. intro biology, 1970-83, dir. Office of Sci. Tchg., 1983-93, assoc. dean Coll. Arts and Scis., 1993-95, asst. v.p. acad. affairs, 1995-98, assoc. v.p. acad. affairs, 1998—. Contbr. articles to profl. jours. Founding mem. Univ. Mus. Assocs., Tallahassee, 1986—; bd. dirs. Tallahassee Symphony Orch., 1986-93, pres., 1987-90. Recipient grant NSF, 1984-95, grant Fla. Dept. Edn., 1983-93, grant U.S. Dept. Edn., 1986-88, grant NIH, 1991-93, grant Fla. Game and Freshwater Fish, 1991-92. Mem. Capital Women's Network, Club at Univ. Ctr. Democrat. Episcopalian. Avocations: hiking, reading, travel. Home: 3305 Charleston Rd Tallahassee FL 32308-9202 Office: Fla State Univ 212 Westcott Bldg Tallahassee FL 32308

HAYWARD, THOMAS ZANDER, JR., lawyer; b. Evanston, Ill., Apr. 21, 1940; s. Thomas Z. and Wilhelmina (White) H.; m. Sally Madden, June 20, 1964; children: Thomas Z., Wallace M., Robert M. BA, Northwestern U., 1962, JD, 1965; MBA, U. Chgo., 1970. Bar: Ill. 1966, Ohio, 1966, U.S. Dist. Ct. (no. dist.) Ill. 1966, U.S. Supreme Ct. 1970. Assoc. Defrees & Fiske, Chgo., 1965-69, ptnr., 1969-81; ptnr. Boodell, Sears, Giambalvo & Crowley, Chgo., 1981-87; ptnr. Bell, Boyd, Lloyd, Chgo., 1987—. Trustee Northwestern U., 1980-84, 97—; bd. dirs. Ill. Continuing Legal Edn., 1987-92, Chgo. area Found. for Legal Svcs., 1983—. Recipient Northwestern U. Alumni Svc. award, 1973. Mem. ABA (ho. of dels. 1984—, fed. jud. com. 1993-97, bd. govs. 1998—), Ill. State Bar Assn., Chgo. Bar Assn. (pres. 1983-84). Republican. Presbyterian. Clubs: Chicago, Casino, Barrington Hills Country (pres. 1985-87). Home: 8 W County Line Rd Barrington IL 60010-2613 Office: Bell Boyd & Lloyd 3 1st Nat Plz 70 W Madison St Ste 3300 Chicago IL 60602-4284

HAYWOOD, ANNE MOWBRAY, pediatrics, virology, and biochemistry educator; b. Balt., Feb. 5, 1935; d. Richard Mansfield and Margaret (Mowbray) H. BA in Chemistry, Bryn Mawr Coll., 1955; MD, Harvard U., 1959. Cert. Am. Bd. Pediatrics. Intern pediatrics U. Calif. Med. Ctr., San Francisco, 1959-60; postdoctoral fellow biochemistry dept. Columbia U., N.Y.C., 1961-62; postdoctoral fellow div. biology Calif. Inst. Tech., Pasadena, 1960-61, 62-64; asst. prof. microbiology, microbiology dept. Northwestern U. Med. Sch., Chgo., 1964-66, Yale U. Med. Sch., New Haven, 1966-73; resident pediatrics U. Wash., Seattle, 1974-75, pediatric infectious disease fellow, 1975-76; pediatric infectious disease fellow Vanderbilt U., Nashville, 1976-77; assoc. prof. pediatrics and microbiology U. Rochester, N.Y., 1977—; vis. asst. prof. Rockefeller U., N.Y.C., 1971-72; vis. scientist biophysics unit Agrl. Rsch. Coun., Cambridge, Eng., 1972-74, Inst. for Immunology and Virology, U. Zürich (Switzerland), 1987; vis. assoc. prof. dept. zoology U. Calif., Davis, 1986. Co-author: Practice of Pediatrics, 1977, Infections in Children, 1982, Liposome Letters, 1983, Practice of Pediatrics, 1987, Molecular Mechanisms of Membrane Fusion, 1988, Membrane Fusion, 1991, Encyclopedia of Human Biology, 1991, 2d edit., 1997, Cell and Model Membrane Interactions, 1991. Fogarty Internat. Ctr. Sr. fellow NIH, 1987, European Molecular Biology Orgn. fellow, 1973-74, NIH Spl. fellow, 1971-73, Am. Cancer Soc. Postdoctoral fellow, 1960-62; Harvard Med. Sch. scholar, 1955-59, Harriet Judd Sartain scholar, 1955-59, N.Y. Alumnae scholar Bryn Mawr Coll., 1951-55. Mem. Biophys. Soc., Am. Soc. for Biochem. and Molecular Biology, Infectious Diseases Soc. Am. Democrat. Office: U Rochester Med Ctr PO Box 777 Rochester NY 14642-8777

HAYWOOD, B(ETTY) J(EAN), anesthesiologist; b. Boston, June 1, 1942; d. Oliver Garfield and Helen Elizabeth (Salisbury) H.; m. Lynn Brandt Moon, Aug. 29, 1969 (div. Aug. 1986); children: Kaylin, Kris Lee, Kelly, Kasy R. BSc, Tufts U., 1964; MD, U. Colo., 1968; MBA, Oklahoma City U., 1993; Grad., Air War Coll., 1997. Intern Wilford Hall AFB, San Antonio, Tex., 1968-69; resident in pediatrics U. Ariz., Tucson, 1971-72, resident in anesthesiology, 1972-74; dir. anesthesia dept. Pima County Hosp., Tucson, 1975-76; staff anesthesiologist South Community Hosp., Oklahoma City, 1977—; staff anesthesiologist Moore (Okla.) Mcpl. Hosp., 1981-94, chief of anesthesia, 1990-94; staff anesthesiologist St. Anthony Hosp., Oklahoma City, 1982—; instr. dept. anesthesia U. Okla. Health Sci. Ctr., Oklahoma City, 1999—; chief of ethics com. S.W. Med. Ctr., 1996. Bd. dirs. N.Am. South Devon Assn., Lynnville, Iowa, 1978-86; mem. med. com. Planned Parenthood Okla., 1992—. Col. USAFR, 1968—. Mem. AMA, NAFE (co-dir. Oklahoma City chpt. 1996—), World South Devon Assn. (U.S. rep. 1985, 88), Tufts U. Alumni Assn. (rep.), Chi Omega (treas. 1963-64). Republican. Presbyterian. Avocations: skiing, sailing. Home: 6501 Hunting Hill Ln Oklahoma City OK 73116-3523

HAYWOOD, BRUCE, retired college president; b. York, Eng., Sept. 30, 1925; came to U.S., 1951, naturalized, 1957; s. Joseph Edgar and Eva (Street) H.; m. Isona Gretchen Shelley, June 21, 1947; children—Anne Margaret, Elizabeth Shelley. Student, U. Leeds, Eng., 1947-48; B.A., McGill U., 1950, M.A., 1951; Ph.D., Harvard, 1956. Mem. faculty Kenyon Coll., 1954, prof. German lit., 1960-63, dean coll., 1963-67, provost, 1967-80; pres. Monmouth (Ill.) Coll., 1980-94; ret., 1994. Author: The Veil of Imagery, 1959. Served with Brit. Army, 1943-47. Mem. Am. Assn. Tchrs. of German. Home: 1885 Cornelia Rd Galesburg IL 61401-1423

HAYWOOD, H(ERBERT) CARL(TON), psychologist, educator; b. Taylor County, Ga., July 2, 1931; s. Howard Chapman and Rosebud (Smith) H.; m. Nancy Patricia Roberts, Oct. 5, 1951 (div. Mar. 1971); children: Carlton, Terence, Elizabeth, Kristin; m. Dona June Wooldridge Tapp, Sept. 6, 1993. A.B., San Diego State Coll., 1956, M.A., 1957; Ph.D., U. Ill., 1961. Mem. faculty George Peabody Coll. (merged with Vanderbilt U. 1979), Nashville, 1962-93; Alexander Heard disting. svc. prof., 1993-94; prof. psychology George Peabody Coll. (merged with Vanderbilt U. 1979), Nashville, 1969-93, prof. spl. edn., 1975-79, prof. emeritus, 1994—, dir. mental retardation research tng. program, 1968-70; dir. Inst. Mental Retardation and Intellectual Devel., 1970-73, Office Research Adminstrn., 1974-76, John F. Kennedy Center Research Edn. and Human Devel., 1971-83; prof. neurology Vanderbilt U. Sch. Medicine, 1971-93; prof. psychology and edn., dean grad. sch. edn. & psychology Touro Coll., N.Y.C., 1993—; vis. prof. U. Toronto, 1965-66; sr. fellow Vanderbilt Inst. Pub. Policy Studies, 1983-88; chmn. Nat Mental Retardation Research Center Dirs., 1979-82; adv. bd. Ill. Inst. Developmental Disabilities, Chgo., 1970-78, Eunice Kennedy Shriver Center Mental Retardation, Waltham, Mass., 1973-80, Tenn. Dept. Mental Health, 1964-92 ; mem. nat. child health and human devel. council NIH, 1983-88; cons. President's Com. on Mental Retardation, 1968-73; mem. sci. rev. com., health research facilities br., div. edn. and research facilities NIH, 1967-71. Author: (with Brooks and Burns) Bright Start: Cognitive Curriculum for Young Children, 1992; editor: Brain Damage in School Age Children, 1968, Social Cultural Aspects of Mental Retardation, 1970, (with Begab and Garber) Prevention of Retarded Development in Psychosocially Disadvantaged Children, 1981, (with J.R. Newbrough) Living Environments for Developmentally Retarded Persons, 1981, (with D. Tzuriel) Interactive Assessment, 1992, (with S. Friedman) Developmental Follow-Up: Domains, Concepts, and Methods, 1994; editor Am. Jour. Mental Deficiency, 1969-79; mem. editl. bd. Jour. Abnormal Child Psychology, 1973-89, Contemporary Psychology, 1982-85, Acta Paedologica, 1983-87, Jour. Mental Deficiency Rsch., 1984—, Internat. Rev. Rsch. in Mental Retardation, 1982-97; contbr. articles on child devel., motivation, cognitive edn., and mental retardation to profl. jours. Served with USN, 1950-54. Fellow Am. Assn. Mental Retardation (v.p. psychology 1975-77, 1st v.p. 1978-79, pres. 1980-81), Am. Psychol. Assn. (pres. Div. 33 1978-79, mem. Council of Reps. 1980-82); mem. Internat. Assn. Cognitive Edn. (pres. 1988-92), Soc. Research Child Devel., Inst. Medicine, Psychonomic Soc. Democrat. Episcopalian. Office: Touro Coll 350 5th Ave Ste 1700 New York NY 10118-1799 *Dominant values include enthusiasm for scholarship, equal parts of dedication to science for its own sake and concern for social progress, and the conviction that self-concern and self-seeking constitute the most dangerous threat to the collective goals of humanity. The future lies in education designed to stretch minds and develop processes of critical thought rather than to impart job-oriented skills.*

HAYWOOD, JOHN WILLIAM, JR., engineering consultant; b. Savannah, Ga., Mar. 10, 1955; s. John William Sr. and Elizabeth (Williams) H.; m. Carol Johnice Staton, Jan. 15, 1976 (div. 1985); children: Venus Roshone, Maurice Antonio. BS in Mech. Engring. Tech. cum laude, Savannah State Coll., 1979; MS in Tech. summa cum laude, Pitts. State U., 1980. Aircraft foreman Grumman Aircraft Corp., Savannah, 1977-80; sr. mfg. engr. Superior Accessories Co., Parsons, Kans., 1980-81; sr. mech. engr. Martin Marietta Aerospace, Orlando, Fla., 1981-85; mem. tech. staff Rockwell Internat., Duluth, Ga., 1985-86; sr. mfg. engr. Boeing Airplane Co., Wichita, Kans., 1986-87; engring. cons. Sverdrup Tech. Inc., Elgin FB, Fla., 1987-90; pvt. practice engring. cons. Raritan, N.J., 1990-92; pvt. practice contract engring. Savannah, Ga., 1992—; cons. TP Cons., Oakland, N.J., 1990-91; mgr. environ. and indsl. engring. N.J. Inst. Tech., Newark, 1991-92; safety cons. N.Am. Contract Engring. Svcs., Tigard, Oreg., 1993-94; environ. mgr. Chatham County Dept. of Pub. Health, Savannah, Ga., 1995-96; cons. engr. HCI, Savannah, 1996—. Contbr. numerous articles to profl. jours. Teacher Macedonia Bapt. Ch., Savannah, 1991—; mentor Ramah Jr. Acad., Savannah, 1991—. With USAF, 1973-77. Mem. AIAA, Am. Soc. Safety Engrs., Inst. Indsl. Engrs., Soc. Mfg. Engrs. Republican. Home and Office: 1809 Vassar St Savannah GA 31405-3864

HAYWOOD, L. JULIAN, physician, educator; b. Reidsville, N.C., Apr. 13, 1927; s. Thomas Woodly and Louise Viola (Hayley) H.; m. Virginia Elizabeth Paige, Dec. 3, 1953; 1 child, Julian Anthony. BS, Hampton Inst., 1948; MD, Howard U., 1952. Intern St. Mary's Hosp., Rochester, N.Y., 1952-53; resident L.A. County Hosp., 1956-58; fellow cardiology White Meml. Hosp., 1959-61; traveling fellow U. Oxford, Eng., 1963; instr. medicine Loma Linda (Calif.) U., 1960-61, asst. prof., 1961-73, assoc. clin. prof., 1973-82, clin. prof., 1982—; asst. prof. medicine U. So. Calif., 1963-67, assoc. prof., 1967-76, prof., 1976—; past dir. comprehensive sickle cell ctr. Los Angeles County/U. So. Calif. Med. Ctr., dir. ECG Dept., 1996—, past dir. coronary care unit, physicians tng. program (Regional Med. Programs), 1970-75; cons. Los Angeles County Coroner, Indsl. Accident Bd. Calif., Health Care Tech. Divsn., USPHS, Nat. Heart and Lung Inst.; past mem. cardiology adv. com. divsn. heart and vascular diseases; bd. dirs., pres. Sickle Cell Diseases Found.; mem. Armed Forces Epidemiol. Bd., 1996—; pres. U. So. Calif. Salerni Collegium, 1997-98. Contbr. articles profl. jours.; Mem. editorial bds.: Jour. Nat. Med. Assn. Past pres., hon. mem., bd. dirs. Am. Heart Assn. Greater L.A., 1989—. With M.C. USNR, 1954-56. Recipient award of merit Los Angeles County Heart Assn., 1968, 69, 73, 75, Disting. Alumnus award Howard U., 1982, Louis B. Russel award Am. Heart Assn., 1988, Merit award, 1991, Heart of Gold award Am. Heart Assn./Greater L.A. Affiliate, 1989, Dedicated Svc. award, 1991, 93, award of Achievement in Rsch., 1994, 20th Anniversary Founder's award Assn. Black Cardiologists, 1994, Disting. Svc. award Howard U. Sch. Medicine, 1996; J.B. Johnson Meml. lectr., 1975, 88; honoree Internal Medicine sect. Nat. Med. Assn., 1988; named Alumnus of Yr.-at-Large, Hampton U., 1993. Fellow ACP, AAAS, L.A. Acad. Medicine, Am. Coll. Cardiology, Am. Heart Assn. (coun. on clin. cardiology, coun. on atherosclerosis, exec. com. coun. on epidemiology, long range planning com., dir., past sec., v.p. Greater L.A. affiliate, pres.); mem. AMA, AAUP, Am. Fedn. Clin. Rsch., Western Soc. Clin. Investigation, Assn. Advancement Med. Instrumentation, Nat. Med. Assn. (Charles Drew Med. Soc.), N.Y. Acad. Scis., Hampton Inst. Alumni Assn. (past pres. L.A. chpt.), Med. Faculty Assn. U. So. Calif. Sch. Medicine (past pres.), Assn. Physicians L.A. County Hosp. (pres. 1991—), Western Assn. Physicians, Fedn. Am. Scientists, Assn. Black Cardiologists (Walter Booker Innovation award 1990), Assn. Acad. Minority Physicians (councilor, pres.-elect 1992-93, pres. 1993-94), Alpha Omega Alpha, Am. Coll. Physicians (Laureate award So. Calif. Region I 1997). E-mail: Jhaywood.usc.hsc.edu. Home: 3551 Lowry Rd Los Angeles CA 90027-1433 Office: LA County/U So Calif Med Ctr Box 305 1200 N State St Los Angeles CA 90033-1029

HAYWOOD, NORCELL DAN, architect; b. Bastrop, Tex., Jan. 23, 1935; s. Roy and Amandie (Green) H.; children: Micheal Obershan, Natalie D., Nan D., David N. BArch, U. Tex., 1960. Registered architect, Ala., La., S.C., Tex., Iowa, La., Fla., Calif.; cert. Nat. Coun. Archtl. Registration Bds.; lic. interior designer, Tex. Instr. Prairie View (Tex.) A&M U., 1960-61; city planner City of Austin, Tex., 1961-62; architect apprentice Eugene Wurasch Architects, Austin, 1962-63; architect-in-tng. O'Neil Ford & Assocs., San Antonio, 1963-68; pres. N.D. Haywood and Assocs., San Antonio, 1968-71, Haywood Jordan McCowan SAT, Inc., San Antonio, 1971—; v.p. Haywood Jordan McCowan of Dallas, Inc., 1974-94; pres. Haywood Jordan McCowan of Dallas, Inc., San Antonio, 1994—; chmn. Haywood Jordan McCowan SAT, Inc., 1996—, Haywood Jordan McCowan Dallas, Inc., 1996—; vice-chmn. Tex. Bd. Archtl. Examiners, Austin, 1991-93, mem., 1993-97. Prin. works include 2d Bapt. Ch., 1969 (merit design award 1970), St. Paul Square redevel., 1977 (merit design award 1979), Student Union Bldg. U. Tex., Dallas, 1981 (merit design award 1983), Frank E. Hornsby Apts., San Antonio, Ebenezer Child Devel. Ctr., Austin. Mem. devel. bd. U. Tex., Austin, 1990—; past commr. Bexar County Housing Authority; former mem. San Antonio Bd. Rev. for Hist. Dists. Landmarks; mem. Tex. Gov.'s Leadership Coun.; bd. mem. Builder's Square Alamo Bowl; del. White House Sub-Com. on Small Bus., 1995. Recipient merit design award Stock Exch. Club, San Antonio, 1973, Conservation award San Antonio Conservation Soc., 1976, Trail Blazer award Bank of Am., 1997, Outstanding Texans at Large award Tex. Legis. Black Caucus, 1997. Mem. AIA, Soc. Am. Mil. Engrs., Guild for Religious Architecture, Nat. Orgn. for Minority Architects (founder), Tex. Soc. Architects, Minority Architects Tex. and La. (past pres.), Greater San Antonio C. of C. (bd. dirs. U. Health Sys. and East Area Coun.), Dallas C. of C., Coun. Ednl. Facilities Planners Internat., Alamo C. of C., Southside C. of C., Mexican-Am. C. of C., NAACP (life), U. Tex.-Austin Ex-Student Assn. (life), U. Tex.-Austin President's Club (life), San Antonio Ex's U. Tex., Masons, Alpha Phi Alpha (life). Baptist. Avocations: ranching, fishing, the arts, youth mentoring, travel. Home: PO Box 200378 San Antonio TX 78220-0378 Office: Haywood Jordan McCowan SAT Inc 1221 S Ww White Rd San Antonio TX 78220-3425*

HAYWOOD, THEODORE JOSEPH, physician, educator; b. Monroe, N.C., Feb. 13, 1929; s. Jesse Beman and Mary (McDonald) H.; m. Nancy Hume Ferguson, Dec. 21, 1959; children: Elizabeth Linscott, Keene McDonald, Mark Shepard. B.S., The Citadel, 1948; M.D., Vanderbilt U., 1952. Diplomate: Am. Bd. Pediatrics, Am. Bd. Allergy and Immunology. Pvt. practice allergy Houston, 1958—; mem. staff Tex. Children's Hosp., 1958—, mem. active staff Pediatrics, 1963—; mem. faculty Baylor U. Coll. Medicine, 1958—, clin. assoc. prof. pediatrics and allergy, 1977—, clin. asst. prof. microbiology & immunology, 1970—. Served with M.C. AUS, 1955-57. Fellow Am. Coll. Allergists, Am. Acad. Allergy and Immunology, Am. Acad. Pediatrics; mem. Sigma Xi. Republican. Episcopalian. Club: River Oaks Country (Houston). Home: 2923 Ferndale Pl Houston TX 77098-1117 Office: McGovern Allergy & Asthma Clinic 4710 Bellaire Blvd Ste 200 Bellaire TX 77401-4505

HAYWORTH, JOHN DAVID, JR., congressman, sportscaster, commentator, broadcaster; b. High Point, N.C., July 12, 1958; s. John David and Gladys Ethel (Hall) H.; m. Mary Denise Yancey, Feb. 25, 1989; children: Nicole Irene, Hannah Lynne, John Micah. BA in Speech and Polit. Sci., N.C. State U., 1980. Sports anchor, reporter Sta. WPTF-TV, Raleigh, N.C., 1980-81, Sta. WLWT-TV, Cin., 1986-87; sports anchor Sta. WYFF-TV (formerly Sta. WFBC-TV), Greenville, S.C., 1981-86, Sta. KTSP-TV, Phoenix, 1987-94; congressman, Ariz. U.S. House Reps., Washington, D.C., 1995—, mem. ways and means com., mem. budget com.; radio commentator; play-by-play broadcaster. Dist. committeeman Ariz. Rep. Com., Scottsdale, 1988-89; bd. dirs. Am. Humanics Found., Ariz. State U., Tempe, 1991-92; chmn. Scout-A-Rama, Theodore Roosevelt coun. Boy Scouts Am., 1991-92. Recipient honor roll award Atlantic Coast Conf., 1977, Young Am. award Unharrie coun. Boy Scouts Am., 1979, Friend of Edn. award Sch. Dist. Greenville County, 1985, Sch. Bell/Friend of Edn. award S.C. Dept. Edn., 1985. Mem. Rotary (bd. dirs. Phoenix 1989-90). Baptist. Avocations: reading, distance running, Bible study, public speaking, television trivia. Office: US House Reps 1023 Longworth Bldg Ofc Bldg Washington DC 20515-0306*

HAZAN, MARCELLA MADDALENA, author, educator, consultant; b. Cesenatico, Italy, Apr. 15, 1924; d. Giuseppe and Maria (Leonelli) Polini; m. Victor Hazan, Feb. 24, 1955; 1 child, Giuliano. Dr. in Natural Scis., U. Ferrara, 1952, Dr. in Biology, 1954. Researcher Guggenheim Inst., 1955-58; prof. math. and biology Italian State schs., 1963-66; founder Sch. of Italian Cooking, N.Y.C., 1969-94, Marcella Hazan Sch. of Classic Italian Cooking, Bologna, Italy, 1976-94, Master Classes in Classic Italian Cooking, Venice, Italy, 1986-98; pres. Hazan Classic Enterprises, Inc., 1978—. Author: The Classic Italian Cookbook, 1973, More Classic Italian Cooking, 1978, Marcella's Italian Kitchen, 1986, Essentials of Classic Italian Cooking, 1992, Marcella Cucina, 1997. Roman Catholic. Fax: (941) 387-0183. Address: 122 Gulf of Mexico Dr # 109 Longboat Key FL 34228

HAZARD, CHRISTOPHER WEDVIK, international business executive; b. N.Y.C., Aug. 9, 1943; s. Herbert Ray and Ellen Clausine (Wedvik) H.; m. Sally Grace Woodruff, Sept. 1, 1966; children: Mark Alexander, Julie Lynne. BA, Ohio State U., 1965; MPA, U. Colo., 1973; postgrad., U. Pa., The Wharton Sch. Officer USAF, 1965-86; near east region dir. ops. Def. Security Assitance Agy., Washington, 1982-86; exec dir. internat. mktg. United Def. Ltd. Partnership, Arlington, Va., 1986—. Pres. M. Vernon Citizens Assn., Alexandria, Va., 1984-85; mem., 1982—. Recipient Def. Superior Svc., Sec. of Def., 1986, Joint Svc. Achievement, Dept. of Def., 1984; decorated Air Force Meritorious Svc. medal. Avocations: international affairs, historic preservation, skiing, sailing, gardening. Home: 9399 Mt Vernon Cir Alexandria VA 22309-3218

HAZARD, GEOFFREY CORNELL, JR., law educator; b. Cleve., Sept. 18, 1929; s. Geoffrey Cornell and Virginia (Perry) H.; m. Elizabeth O'Hara; children: James G., Katherine W., Robin P., Geoffrey Cornell III. BA, Swarthmore Coll., 1953, LLD (hon.), 1988; LLB, Columbia U., 1954; LLD (hon.), Gonzaga U., 1985, U. San Diego, 1985, Ill. Inst. Tech., 1990, Repubblica Italiana, 1998. Bar: Oreg. 1954, Calif. 1960, Conn. 1982, Pa. 1994. Assoc. Hart, Spencer, McCulloch, Rockwood & Davies, Portland, Oreg., 1954-57; exec. sec. Oreg. Legis. Interim Com. Jud. Adminstrn., 1957-58; assoc. prof. law, then prof. U. Calif., Berkeley, 1958-64; prof. law U. Chgo., 1964-71; prof. law Yale U., 1971-94, prof. mgmt., 1979-83, acting dean Sch. Orgn. and Mgmt., 1980-81, Sterling prof. law, 1986-94; trustee prof. U. Pa., Phila., 1994—; mem. Adminstrv. Conf. U.S., 1971-78; jud. conf. U.S. com.

on rules practice and procedure, 1994—. Author: (with D.W. Louisell, C. Tait and W. Fletcher) Pleading and Procedure, 1972, 7th edit., 1994, Research in Civil Procedure, 1963, (with F. James and J. Leubsdorf) Civil Procedure, 4th edit., 1992, Ethics in the Practice of law, 1978, (with W. W. Hodes) Law of Lawyering, 2d edit., 1990), (with S. Koniak and R. Cramton) Law and Ethics of Lawyering, 2d edit., 1994, (with M. Tanruffu) Am. Civil Procedure, 1994; editor: Law in a Changing America, 1968, (with D. Rhode) Legal Profession: Responsibility and Regulation, 1985, 3d edit., 1994; contbr. articles to profl. jours. Served with USAF, 1948-49. Fellow Am. Bar Found. (exec. dir. 1964-70, rsch. award 1986), Am. Acad. Arts and Scis.; mem. ABA (cons. code jud. conduct 1970-72, reporter stds. jud. adminstrn. 1971-77, reporter model rules of profl. conduct 1978-83), Am. Law Inst. (reporter restatement of judgments 1973-81, dir. 1984-99), Nat. Legal Aid and Defender Assn., Inst. Jud. Adminstrn., Am. Judicature Soc., Selden Soc., Pa. Bar Assn., Calif. State Bar, Conn. Bar Assn., Assn. Bar City N.Y., Phi Beta Kappa. Episcopalian. Avocations: tennis, history.

HAZARD, MARGARET LOUISE (PEGGY HAZARD), management consultant; b. Bryn Mawr, Pa., June 26, 1960; d. James Edgerton and Ann (Davin) H.; m. Robert Harris Levin, June 19, 1996; 1 child, Isabel Pannell. BA in Mgmt., U. Pa., 1982; postgrad., Cornell U., 1995-96, Harvard U., 1997. Product dir. Polo Ralph Lauren, N.Y.C., 1983-85; dir. merchandising and design Warnaco, Bridgeport, Conn., 1983-85; dir. spl. programs Shubert Theatre, New Haven, 1988-90; dir. mktg. Arts Connection, N.Y.C., 1991-93; nat. exec. dir. Plays for Living, N.Y.C., 1993-97; pres. Creative Mgmt. Solutions, 1997-98; exec. dir., cons. Simmons Assocs., New Hope, Pa., 1998—; bd. dirs. Kopeyia Ghana Sch. Fund, N.Y., Sickle Cell Anemia Advocs. for Rsch. and Empowerment, N.Y., Figure Skating in Harlem, N.Y., Ctr. for Safety in the Arts, N.Y. Recipient Women in Leadership award New Haven, 1989, Phillips award Swarthmore H.S., 1978, Best Practices in Diversity award U.S. Glass Ceiling Commn., 1995, 96, 97, Chase Racial Harmony and Diversity award, 1995, 96, 97; named to Nat. Register of Commended Scholars, 1977-78; St. Elmo scholar, St. Elmo Club, Phila., 1978-82. Mem. Women in Health Mgmt., Women in Fin. Devel., Planned Parenthood Spkrs. Bur., N.Y. Women's Agenda. Avocations: squash, traveling, reading, sailing, cooking.

HAZARD, ROBERT CULVER, JR., hotel executive; b. Balt., Oct. 23, 1934; s. Robert Culver and Catherine B. H.; m. Mary Victoria Cranor, Jan. 2, 1981; children by previous marriage: Alicia W., Letitia A., Robert Culver, III, Thomas E.J., Anne. BA cum laude, Woodrow Wilson Sch., Princeton U., 1956; postgrad., Johns Hopkins U., U. Denver. Mktg. rep. IBM Corp., Denver, 1959-68; with Am. Express Co., 1968-74, v.p. exec. accounts, 1973-74; CEO Best Western Internat., 1974-80; CEO, retired chmn. Choice Hotels Internat., Silver Spring, Md., 1980-96; chmn. Creative Hotel Assocs., Phoenix, 1996—. Capt. USAF, 1956-59. Recipient Man of Yr. award Motel Brokers Assn. Am., 1976, Silver Plate award Hospitality mag., 1979, Albert E. Koehl award HSMA, 1992, Cecil B. Day Hospitality award AAHOA, 1993, Silver Plate award Lodging Hospitality Mag., 1995. Mem. Am. Hotel and Motel Assn. Office: Creative Hotel Assocs 6001 Montrose Rd Ste 1040 Rockville MD 20852*

HAZEKAMP, PHYLLIS WANDA ALBERTS, library director; b. Chgo.; d. John Edward and Mary Ann (Demski) Wojciechowski. BA, De Paul U., 1947; MSLS, La. State U., 1959; postgrad., Santa Clara U., U. Chgo. Cert. tchr., Calif., Ariz. Libr. Agrl. Experiment Sta., U. Calif., Riverside, 1959-61; tech. libr. Lockheed Tech. Libr., Palo Alto, Calif., 1962-63; asst. law libr. Santa Clara (Calif.) U. Law Sch., 1963-72; libr. dir. Carmelite Seminary, San Jose, Calif., 1973-78; reference libr. San Jose State U., 1978-79; libr. dir. SAI Engrs., Santa Clara, 1980-81, Palmer Coll. Chiropractic, San Jose, 1981-90; libr. dir. Camp Verde (Ariz.) Community Libr., 1990-98, retired, 1998—; mem. Cultural Commn., Santa Clara, 1968-72; pres. Santa Clara Art Assn., 1973-74; cons. various librs.; lectr. in field. Bd. dirs. Camp Verde Art Coun., 1994—; bd. dirs., spkr. House of Ruth, 1995—; bd. elders Montezuma Chapel, 1995-98. Mem. Kiwanis Internat., Ladies Guild Montezuma Chapel. Avocations: writing articles, painting, teaching, giving talks to groups.

HAZEL, JAMES R. C., JR., small business owner, civic volunteer; b. Sturgis, Ky., Oct. 11, 1940; s. James R.C. Hazel Sr. and Lucille Vivian (Brumfield) Palmer; m. Donna Jean Wideman, July 8, 1960; children: Juliee Teresa Hazel Norman (dec.), James R.C. III. AA, Kellogg Community Coll., 1990; grad., E.K. Williams Profl. Mgmt. Sch. With family auto svc. sta., 1952-64, mgr., 1964; pres., owner Jim Hazel's CITCO 76 Svc. and Auto Parts Store, Battle Creek, Mich.; mem. adv. bd. Auto Wares, Inc.; bd. dirs. Battle Creek Community Found. Active S.W. Mich. coun. Boy Scouts Am., 1970—, vice chmn., 1987-93; bd. dirs. Sherman Lake Y Ctr., 1990—, v.p., 1996; chmn. Battle Creek Cmty. Leadership Acad., 1985—; bd. dirs. Art Ctr. Battle Creek, 1985-88; chairperson small bus. div. fund drive United Arts Coun., 1987; mem. adv. bd. United Way; sponsor Youth to Sweden Hockey Tournament, 1979; charter mem. Y-Ctr., co-chmn. capital campaign, 1999; charter mem. Binder Park Zoo; sponsor, patron various civic orgns.; mem. adv. com. youth initiates program W.K. Kellogg Found., 1989. Named Dealer of Yr., Pure Oil Co., 1967, Super Citizen, City of Battle Creek, 1989, Scene Mag. Man of Yr., 1997; recipient Silver Beaver award Boy Scouts Am., 1983, George award Battle Creek Enquirer, 1988; Carnation Cmty. Svc. award Battle Creek Vol. Bur., 1985, Vol. of Yr. award, 1998; Small Bus. of Yr. award 1992, 1st Ann. Pride award Harper Creek Schs., 1992, Book of Golden Deeds award Exch. Club, 1994, Disting. Citzen award Calhoun Area Vocat. Ctr., 1989, Calhoun County Intermediate Sch., 1994. Mem. Mich. Svc. Sta. Dealers Assn. (bd. dirs. 1980-90, vice chairperson polit. action com.), Mich. Auto Parks Assn. (bd. dirs. 1989—), Battle Creek C. of C. (charter, vice chmn. 1986-89, chmn. Leadership Acad., Small Bus. of Yr. award 1992), Ducks Unltd., Rotary (bd. dirs. Battle Creek chpt. 1992—, Red Rose award 1998, Paul Harris fellow 1999), Optimists (life, sec., treas. Harper Creek Club 1979, Achievement in Edn. award 1989), Masons, Shriners. Avocations: photography, backpacking, reading, travel. Home: 6695 E Dr N Battle Creek MI 49014-8558 Office: Jim Hazel's Unocal 76 Svc 14301 Beadle Lake Rd Battle Creek MI 49014-8213

HAZEL, JOSEPH ERNEST, geology educator, stratigrapher; b. Caruthersville, Mo., July 7, 1933; s. Joseph and Pearl Irene (Hall) H.; m. Marilyn Mae Pate, Aug. 11, 1956; children: Joseph, James, Jonathan. BA, U. Mo., 1956, MA, 1960; PhD, La. State U., 1963. NRC postdoctoral fellow Harvard U., 1963-64; rsch. geologist U.S. Geol. Survey, Washington, 1964-83, chief paleontologist, 1973-78; rsch. assoc. Amoco Prodn. Co., Tulsa, 1983-86; Campanile prof. geology La. State U., Baton Rouge, 1986—, chmn. dept. geology and geophysics, 1990-94; chmn. Internat. Rsch. Group, Ostracoda, 1985-88; cons. Govt. Japan, 1985. Co-editor: Biostratigraphy, 1977; contbr. numerous articles to profl. jours., book chpts. Lt. U.S. Army, 1956-58. Recipient Meritorious Svc. award Dept. Interior, 1980; Humble Oil fellow, 1961-63. Mem. Soc. Econ. Paleontologists and Mineralists, Paleontol. Soc. Am., Geol. Soc. Am., Internat. Paleontol. Union, Brit. Micropaleontol. Assn. Avocations: genealogy. Office: La State U Dept Geology And Geoph Baton Rouge LA 70803

HAZEL, JOSEPH PATRICK, law educator; b. 1933. STL, Gregorian U., Rome, 1960; MEd, U. Loyola, Chgo., 1968; JD, U. Tex., 1971. Bar: Tex. 1971. Briefing atty. Ct. Criminal Appeals, Austin, Tex., 1971-72; assoc. Gibbins & Spivy, Austin, 1872-76; pntr. Spivey, Hazel & Grigg, Austin, 1976-78; of counsel Spivey, Grigg, Kelly & Knisely, Austin, 1978-87; Tiny Gooch prof. trial practice U. Tex., Austin, 1984—; lectr. U. Tex., 1975-78, adj. prof., 1978-84. Editor The Advocate. Mem. State Bar Tex., Barristers, Order of Coif. Office: U Tex Sch Law 727 E Dean Keaton Austin TX 78705-3224*

HAZEL, MARIANNE ELIZABETH, educational administrator; b. Bellefonte, Pa., Mar. 14, 1967; d. Joseph Edward and Patricia (Rumberger) H. BS, Pa. State U., 1990, MEd, 1995, MS, 1998. Cert. reading specialist; cert. adminstrn.; cert. curriculum and instrn. Tchr. 1st grade Carroll County Pub. Schs., Westminster, Md., 1991-97; elem. asst. prin.. reading supr. Conewago Valley Sch. Dist., New Oxford, Pa., 1997—. Mem. ASCD, Nat. Coun. Tchrs. Math., Internat. Reading Assn., Pa. Sch. Bds. Assn., Pa. Assn. Fed. Program Coordinators, Pa. State U. Alumni Assn., We. Md. Coll. Alumni Assn., Pi Lambda Theta, Phi Delta Kappa. Home: 15 Segovia Ct Hanover PA 17331-8994

HAZELETT, S(AMUEL) RICHARD, mechanical engineer; b. Cleve., July 24, 1923; s. Clarence William and Ruth Hazelett. BA, Oberlin Coll., 1965; MA, U. Tex., 1969, Boston U., 1973. Registered profl. engr., Vt. rsch. engr. Hazelett Strip-Casting Corp., Colchester, Vt., 1950—. Editor: Einstein Myth and the Ives Papers, 1979; contbr. articles to profl. jours.; patentee in metall. machinery. Sgt. USMCR, 1943-46. Mem. ASME. Jewish. Office: Hazelett Strip Casting Corp PO Box 600 Colchester VT 05446-0600 *Intellectualizing about religion is a toboggan-slide to perdition, right? Wrong!.*

HAZELTINE, BARRETT, electrical engineer, educator; b. Paris, Nov. 7, 1931; came to U.S., 1932; s. L. Alan and Elizabeth (Barrett) H.; m. Mary Frances Fenn, Aug. 25, 1956; children—Michael B., Alice W., Patricia F. BSE, Princeton U., 1953, MSE, 1956; PhD, U. Mich., 1962; ScD (hon.), SUNY, Stony Brook, 1988. Registered profl. engr., R.I. Asst. prof. engring. Brown U., 1959-66, assoc. prof., 1966-72, prof., 1972—; asst. to dean Brown U. (The Coll.), 1962-63, asst. dean, 1968-74, assoc. dean, 1974-93; Robert Foster Cherry chair for disting. teaching Baylor U., 1991-92; prof. U. Botswana, 1993; lectr., vis. prof. U. Zambia, Lusaka, 1970-71; -76-77; vis. prof. U. Malawi-Poly., Blantyre, 1980-81, 83-84, 88-89, Africa U. Mutare, Zimbabwe, 1996-97; asst. to mgr. rsch. labs., space and info. sys. divsn. Raytheon Co., 1964-65, cons., 1965-67; cons. R.I. Utilities Commn., 1977-80, others. Author: Introduction to Electronic Circuits and Applications, 1980, Appropriate Technology; Tools, Choices and Implications, 1998; editor: The Weaver. Trustee Stevens Inst. Tech. Recipient award for excellence in instrn. Western Electric, 1968; grantee NSF, Dept. Edn.; grantee Met. Life Ins. Ednl. Found.; Fulbright fellow 1988-89, 93. Mem. IEEE (sr., chmn. Providence sect. 1971-72), Providence Engring. Soc. (pres. 1977-78), Am. Soc. Engring. Edn., Sigma Xi, Tau Beta Pi. Congregationalist (deacon). Clubs: Providence Art, Providence Review. Achievements include patents for color recognition system. Home: 60 Barnes St Providence RI 02906-1502 Office: Brown U Div Engring Providence RI 02912

HAZELTINE, JOYCE, state official; b. Pierre, S.D.; m. Dave Hazeltine; children: Derek, Tara, Kirk. Student, Huron (S.D.) Coll., No. State Coll., Aberdeen, S.D., Black Hills State Coll., Spearfish, S.D. Former asst. chief clk. S.D. Ho. of Reps.; former sec. S.D. State Senate; sec. of state State of S.D., Pierre, 1987—. Adminstrv. asst. Pres. Ford Campaign, S.D.; Rep. county chmn. Hughes County S.D.; state co-chair Phil Gramm for Pres., 1996. Mem. Nat. Assn. Secs. of State (exec. bd., pres.), Women Execs. in State Govts. (bd. dirs.). Office: Sec of State's Office 500 E Capitol Ave Ste 204 Pierre SD 57501-5070

HAZELTON, ASTOR MILLER, artist; b. Feb. 19, 1924; d. Henry O. Miller and Rose Bottoms; m. James J. Hazelton, Apr. 10, 1959; 1 child, John Henry. BA, Calif. State Long Beach, 1974. One-woman shows include Orange County Adminstrn. Bldg., 1989, Costa Mesa Playhouse, 1989, Costa Mesa Sr. Ctr. Gallery, 1990, Brookhurst Cmty. Ctr. Gallery, Anaheim, Calif., 1992, Newport Beach City Hall Exhibit, 1992, Coastline Cmty. Office Bldg., 1993, Newport Beach City Libr., 1993, Showcase Gallery, 1995; exhibited in group shows at Jewel Ct. Ann. Fine Arts, 1987, Orange County Fair, 1988, CMAL Orange County Centennial Show, 1989 (Best of Show), Coastline Cmty. Coll. Artist Ann. Show, 1989, 15th Cypress Ann. Open, 1990 (Juror's Spl. award), CMAL Jewel Ct. Show, 1991, Orange County Fair, 1992, Art-A-Fair, Laguna Beach, Calif., 1993, 96, 93 Shades of Pastel, Huntington Beach Arts Assocs. Show, 1995, La Fond Gallery, Pitts., 1995, Artist's Eye, 1995, 97. Mem. Orange County Fine Arts, Inc. Avocations: travel, weight lifting, swimming. Home and Studio: 8431 Castilian Dr Huntington Beach CA 92646

HAZELTON, CATHERINE LYNETTE, elementary school educator; b. Augusta, Ga., Jan. 27, 1969; d. James Allen Hazelton and Dearia Ann (Ratliff) Davis. BA in Edn., N.C. Ctrl. U., 1991. Cert. elem. edn. tchr., N.C. Office mgr., enrichment coord. N.C. Ctrl. U., Durham, 1988-94; tchr. Guilford County Schs., Greensboro, N.C., 1991—; cons., workshop presenter, facilitator, assessor N.C. Tchg. Fellows Program, Raleigh, 1991—. Mem. N.C. Assn. Educators, Guilford County Assn. Edns. Avocations: reading, writing poetry, listening to music, tutoring. Office: Guilford County Schs Bessemer Elem 918 Huffine Mill Rd Greensboro NC 27405-6238

HAZELTON, JUANITA LOUISE, librarian; b. Glendale, Calif., June 12, 1942; d. James Chester and Eddith Pearl (Henson) McChain; m. Merrill Edward Hazelton, Apr. 27, 1968; children: Larry Scott, James Edward. BA in Arts and Letters, U. Oreg., 1964; MLS, U. Tex., 1970; tchg. cert., Tex. Woman's U., 1984. Cert. county libr., 1997. Librarian Dallas Pub. Libr., 1966-69; libr. asst. Austin Coll., Sherman, Tex., 1974-75; tchr., librarian Gunter (Tex.) Ind. Sch. Dist., 1984-94; librarian Plano (Tex.) Pub. Libr., 1994-95; libr. dir. Van Alstyne (Tex.) Pub. Libr., 1995—; tech. com. Gunter Ind. Sch. Dist., 1994; campus devel. com. Van Alstyne Ind. Sch. Dist., 1997, campus devel. com., 1998—; A-V com., ad hoc planning coord. N.E. Tex. Libr. Sys., Garland, Tex., 1997-98. Author: Telling Our Stories-Texas Family Secrets, 1997 (Gold Star award 1997); columnist Bookshelf, 1995—. Den leader, adv. coun. Cub Scouts, Gunter, 1984-88; club leader, adv. coun. 4-H, Gunter, 1988-95. Named Bus. Citizen of Yr. Van Alstyne C. of C., 1998. Mem. Tex. Libr. Assn., Toastmasters Internat., Van Alstyne Genealog. Assn., Tex. Storytelling Assn. Republican. Mem. Ch. of Christ. Avocations: collecting kachinas and folk tales, amateur storytelling, computers, geneaology, writing poetry and family history. E-mail: vanalstynepl@texoma.net. Office: Van Alstyne Pub Libr PO Box 629 117 N Waco Van Alstyne TX 75495

HAZELTON, PENNY ANN, law librarian, educator; b. Yakima, Wash., Sept. 24, 1947; d. Fred Robert and Margaret (McLeod) Pease; m. Norris J. Hazelton, Sept. 12, 1971; 1 dau., Victoria MacLeod. BA cum laude, Linfield Coll., 1969; JD, Lewis and Clark Law Sch., 1975; M in Law Librarianship, U. Wash., 1976. Bar: Wash. 1976; U.S. Supreme Ct. 1982. assoc. law libr., assoc. prof. U. Maine, 1976-78, law libr., assoc. prof., 1978-81; asst. libr. for rsch. svcs. U.S. Supreme Ct., Washington, 1981-85, law libr., 1985; law librarian U. Wash., Seattle, 1985—, prof. law, 1985—; tchr. legal rsch., law librarianship, Indian law; cons. Maine Adv. Com. on County Law Librs., Nat. U. Sch. Law, San Diego, 1985-88, Lawyers Cooperative Pub., 1993-94. Author: Computer Assisted Legal Research: The Basics, 1993; contbr. articles to legal jours. Recipient Disting. Alumni award U. Wash., 1992. Mem. ABA (sect. legal edn. & admissions to bar, chair com. on librs. 1993-94, vice chair 1992-93, 94-95), Am. Assn. Law Schs. (com. law librs. 1991-94), Law Librs. New Eng. (sec. 1977-79, pres. 1979-81), Am. Assn. Law Librs. (cert., program chmn. ann. meeting 1984, exec. bd. 1984-87, v.p., pres.-elect 1989-90, pres. 1990-91, program co-chair Insts. 1983, 95), Law Librs' Soc. Washington (exec. bd. 1983-84, v.p., pres.-elect 1984-85), Law Librs. Puget Sound, Wash. State Bar Assn. (chair edit. adv. bd. 1990-91), Wash. Adv. Coun. on Librs., Westpac. Office: U Wash Marian Gould Gallagher Law Libr 1100 NE Campus Pkwy Seattle WA 98105-6617

HAZELWOOD, JOHN A., lawyer; b. July 9, 1938; s. Clark John Adam and Katherine (Kletzsch) H.; m. Anne Messinger, Aug. 17, 1964; children: Katherine, Sara, Robin. BA, Yale U., 1960; JD, U. Mich., 1963; LLM in Taxation, NYU, 1964. Bar: Wis. 1963, U.S. Dist. Ct. (ea. dist.) Wis. 1964, U.S. Ct. Appeals (7th cir.) 1965, U.S. Tax Ct. 1965. Assoc. Quarles & Brady, Milw., 1964-70, ptnr., 1971—, ptnr.-in-charge bus. tax group, 1979-89; vis. prof. corp. taxation U. Wis., 1971; dir., sec. 7 pvt. corps. Bd. dirs., chmn. bd. Zool. Soc. Milw., 1987-89; civilian participant joint civilian orientation conf. Dept. Def., 1990. Contbr. articles to legal jours. Chmn. PBS affiliate TV auction, 1976; assoc. fellow Pierson Coll., Yale U., 1986—. Mem. ABA, Wis. Bar Assn. (chair bd. tax sect. 1989-90), Yale Alumni Assn. (Wis. rep., bd. govs. 1986-89), Milw. Athletic Club (Iron Man champion 1992), Yale Club (N.Y.C.). Office: Quarles & Brady LLP 411 East Wisconsin Ave Milwaukee WI 53202-4497*

HAZEN, DEAN SCOTT, meteorologist; b. Columbus, Ohio, June 30, 1961; s. Claude B. Jr. and Joan Marilyn Hazen; m. Tammy A. Evans, Aug. 1, 1981. BS, Fla. State U., 1983; MS, U. Okla., 1988. Commd. 2d lt. USAF, 1983, advanced through grades to capt., 1987; weather officer 363d Tactical Fighter Wing, Shaw AFB, S.C., 1983-85, 8th Tactical Fighter Wing, Kunsan Air Base, Republic of Korea, 1985-86; staff meteorologist Air Force Astronautics Lab., Air Force Flight Test Ctr., Edwards AFB, Calif., 1988-92; staff meteorologist 45th Space Wing, Kennedy Space Ctr., Cape Canaveral, Fla., 1992-94; resigned, 1994; sci. and ops. officer Nat. Weather Svc., Pocatello, Idaho, 1994—; instr. Cerro-Coso C.C., Edwards AFB, 1990-92. Contbr. articles to profl. jours. Mem. Portneuf Valley Cmty. Adv. Panel, Pocatello, 1995—; trustee Portneuf Dist. Libr., 1998—. Mem. Am. Meteorology Soc. (sec. Ea. Idaho chpt. 1996-97, treas. 1998—), Nat. Eagle Scout Assn. Avocations: hiking, home brewing, camping, golf. Office: Nat Weather Svc 1320 Beechcraft Ave Pocatello ID 83204-7446

HAZEN, ELIZABETH FRANCES, retired special education educator; b. Lamar, Colo., May 27, 1925; d. Otis Garfield and Cora B. (Baker) McDowell; children: H. Ray, Bobby D., Anita K. Iezza, Gloria G. Gill. AA, Lamar Jr. Coll., 1946; BS in Edn., Southwestern Okla. U., 1967, MS in Edn., 1969; postgrad., Ea. Ky. U., 1983. Cert. speech-hearing therapist, reading specialist, learning and behavior disorders, Ky. Elem. tchr. Granada (Colo.) Sch., 1946-51, South Ctrl. Elem. Sch., Lamar, Colo., 1951-52; lead tchr. Tom Thumb Pre-Sch., Ellsworth AFB, S.D., 1961-62; math. and sci. tchr. Elk City (Okla.) Elem. Sch., 1966-67; beginning speech tchr. Sayer Jr. Coll., Okla., 1967-68; speech and hearing therapist Burns Flat (Okla.) Schs., 1967-69, Maconaqueh Sch. Corp., Bunker Hill, Ind., 1969-72; reading specialist Myers Mid. Sch., Louisville, Ky., 1972-76; tchr. Core Westport Jr. H.S., Louisville, 1977-79, chmn. Core dept., 1978-79; learning disabled resource tchr. Jeffersontown H.S., Louisville, 1979-80, Waggoner Mid. Sch., Louisville, 1980-81, Westport Mid. Sch., Louisville, 1981-94; ret., 1994; chmn. exceptional children's edn. dept. Westport Mid. Sch., Louisville, 1983-91; speech and hearing therapist Burns Flat (Okla.) Bd. Edn., 1967-69. Bd. dirs. Westport Middle Schs. PTA/Student Assn., 1989-90. Named Outstanding Tchr. of Disadvantaged, State of Okla., 1969. Mem. NEA (ret.), Ky. Mid. Sch. Assn., Ky. Edn. Assn. (ret.), Ky. Ret. Tchrs. Assn., Jefferson County Tchrs. Assn. Home: 1207 McVey Rd Sedalia MO 65301-8869

HAZEN, PAUL MANDEVILLE, banker; b. Lansing, Mich., 1941; married. BA, U. Ariz., 1963; MBA, U. Calif., Berkeley, 1964. Asst. mgr Security Pacific Bank, 1964-66; v.p. Union Bank, 1966-70; chmn. Wells Fargo Realty Advisors, 1970-76; with Wells Fargo Realty Advisors, San Francisco, 1979—, exec. v.p., mgr. Real Estate Industries Group, 1979-80, mem. exec. office Real Estate Industry Group, 1980, vice-chmn. Real Estate Industries Group, 1980-84, pres., chief oper. officer Real Estate Industries Group, 1984—, also dir. Real Estate Industries Group, 1984—; pres., treas. Wells Fargo Mortgage & Equity Trust, San Francisco, 1977-84; with Wells Fargo & Co., San Francisco, 1978—, from exec. v.p. to vice-chmn., pres., chief operating officer, 1978-95, chmn, CEO, 1995—, chmn. bd. dirs.; trustee Wells Fargo Mortgage & Equity Trust; bd. dirs. Pacific Telesis Group. Office: Wells Fargo Bank NA 420 Montgomery St San Francisco CA 94104-1298

HAZEN, ROBERT MILLER, research scientist, musician; b. Rockville Centre, N.Y., Nov. 1, 1948; s. Dan Francis and Dorothy Ellen (Chapin) H.; m. Margaret Hindle, Aug. 9, 1969; children—Benjamin Hindle, Elizabeth Brooke. BS, SM, MIT, 1971; PhD, Harvard U., 1975. NATO fellow U. Cambridge, Eng., 1975-76; rsch. sci. Geophys. Lab., Carnegie Instn., Washington, 1976—; Robinson prof. earth sci., George Mason U. Trumpeter with numerous ensembles including Nat. Symphony, Boston Symphony, N.Y. Opera, Met. Opera, Washington Opera, Royal Ballet, Am. Ballet Theatre, Orchestre de Paris, also recordings; author: Comparative Crystal Chem., 1982, Music Men, 1987, The Breakthrough, 1988, Science Matters, 1990, Keepers of the Flame, 1991, New Alchemist, 1993; The Sciences, 1995, Why Aren't Black Holes Black?, 1997; contbr. numerous articles to sci. publs. Recipient Deems Tayor award ASCAP, 1989. Fellow AAAS, Mineral. Soc. Am. (editor, Mineral. Soc. Am. award 1982, council); mem. Am. Geophys. Union, Am. Chem. Soc. (Ipatief prize 1985), History of Sci. Soc., Internat. Guild Trumpeters, Sigma Xi, Phi Lambda Upsilon. Avocations: doubles volleyball; ballroom dancing; Am. art. Office: Geophys Lab 5251 Broad Branch Rd NW Washington DC 20015-1305

HAZEN, VINCENT ALLAN, painter, printmaker; b. Casper, Wyo., Sept. 4, 1967; s. Claude Allan and Charla Jean (Gates) H. BA with honors, Anderson (Ind.) U., 1990; MFA, U. Notre Dame, Ind., 1995. Asst. prof. art Chadron (Nebr.) State Coll., 1995—. Avocations: entomology, field and stream sports, backpacking. Home: 15541 Hwy 385 Chadron NE 69337-9361 Office: Chadron State Coll Art Dept 1000 Main St Chadron NE 69337-2667

HAZEN, WILLIAM HARRIS, finance executive; b. Salem, Mass., Jan. 6, 1931; s. Julius Elijah and Dorothy (Harris) H.; m. Judith Ettl, Feb. 22, 1959; children: Cordelia, Alexes. A.B., Bowdoin Coll., 1952; J.D., Harvard U., 1958. Bar: N.Y. 1959. With firm Pell, Butler, Hatch, Curtis & LeViness, N.Y.C., 1959-61; exec. asst. to N.Y. supt. banks, 1962-64; with J.W. Seligman & Co., N.Y.C., 1964-68, partner, 1969-80, mem. mng. com., 1981-96, mng. dir., 1981—; pres., chief exec. officer Seligman Securities, Inc., N.Y.C., 1981-83, 89-93, J. & W. Seligman Trust Co., 1983-95; v.p. Seligman Mut. Funds, 1969-81, Tri-Continental Corp., N.Y.C., 1969-81. Mem. bd. overseers Bowdoin Coll., 1981-93, pres., 1992-93, trustee, 1993—. Lt. USNR, 1952-55, Korea. Mem. Heights Casino Club, N.Y. Yacht Club, The Angler's Club of N.Y. Congregationalist. Home: 55 Remsen St Brooklyn NY 11201-4112 Office: 100 Park Ave New York NY 10017-5516

HAZLEHURST, GEORGE EDWARD, physician; b. Jackson, Tenn., Dec. 29, 1928; s. George Edward and Alicia (Davidge) H.; m. Aud Staumo, Oct. 17, 1964; children: Anne Garrard, Edward, Rolf, Alicia. BS, U. Tenn., 1951, MD, 1954. Diplomate Am. Bd. Surgery. Intern Confederate Meml. Med. Ctr., Shreveport, La., 1955, resident, 1956-57, 59-62; physician Stevens Clinic Hosp., Welch, W.Va., 1962-64, Jackson-Madison County Gen. Hosp., Jackson, Tenn., 1965—. Capt. U.S. Army, 1957-59. Mem. AMA, Tenn. Med. Assn., Soc. Am. Gastrointestinal Endoscopic Surgeons, Am. Soc. for Gastrointestinal Endoscopy, Am. Coll. Gastroenterology. Office: 620 Skyline Dr Jackson TN 38301-3923

HAZLEHURST, ROBERT PURVIANCE, JR., lawyer; b. Spartanburg, S.C., Jan. 7, 1919; s. Robert Purviance and Lottie Lee (Nicholls) H.; m. Mary Kierulff, Feb. 20, 1947 (dec. July 1971); children: Ellen Hazlehurst Courtney, Charlotte Hazlehurst Leonesio, Anne Hazlehurst Goldberg; m. Dorothy Wilson Deemer, Jan. 7, 1972. A.B., Princeton U., 1940; LL.B., Yale U., 1947. Bar: N.J. 1947. Since practiced in Newark and Morristown; ptnr. Pitney, Hardin, Kipp & Szuch, 1952-89; Bd. dirs. Princeton Fund, 1966-71, chmn. ann. giving campaign, 1967-68. Sec., trustee Greater Newark Hosp. Devel. Fund; trustee Kent Pl. Sch., Summit, N.J., 1960-70; trustee, v.p. Silver Hill Found., New Canaan, Conn., 1973-85; trustee United Hosps. Newark, 1958-73, pres., 1970-73. Served to capt. USAAF, 1942-45. Clubs: Short Hills (N.J.), Nassau (N.J.). Home: 38 Sinclair Ter Short Hills NJ 07078-1714

HAZLETON, RICHARD A., chemicals executive; b. 1941. Pres., ceo Dow Corning Corp, Midland, Mich., 1965—, chmn., CEO. Office: Dow Corning Corp PO Box 994 Midland MI 48686-0001*

HAZLETT, PAUL EDWARD, realtor, information systems executive; b. Gallipolis, Ohio, Dec. 10, 1937; ž. Vickers James and Wilma (Dickey) H.; m. Lynn Todd; 1 child, Esther. BBA, Cleve. State U., 1964. Real estate agt., Ohio. Freight sales N.Y. Cen., Cleve., 1964-66; with computer systems dept. Honeywell, Inc., Cleve., 1966-75; investment real estate Cleve., 1975-78; mgr. Fairview Gen. Hosp., Cleve., 1978-96; realtor Middleburg Heights, Ohio, 1995—; adj. faculty Cuyahoga C.C., Cleve., 1977-95; cons. in field; real estate agt., Cleve. Bd. mgrs. West Side YMCA, 1987-95. Avocations: jogging, racquetball. Home: 6987 Big Creek Pkwy Middleburg Heights OH 44130-4902 Office: 7087 Pearl Rd Middleburg Heights OH 44130-7812

HAZLITT, DONALD ROBERT, artist; b. Stockton, Calif., Jan. 6, 1948; s. Hilbert Alexander and Margaret E. (Jackson) H.; m. Josephine G. McIntyre, Aug. 14, 1987 (div. 1998); children: William Alexander, Angela Destiny. AA Art, San Joaquin Delta Coll., 1969; BA Art, Sonoma State Coll., 1971; M Art, Calif. State U., 1977. Artist in residence San Joaquin Delta Coll., Stockton, Calif., 1977; vis. artist, instr. Corpus Christi (Tex.) State U., 1981; vis. artist Columbia U., N.Y.C., 1981, asst. prof., 1982—; drawing instr. Long Island U., Bklyn., 1986; drawing instr. L.I. U., Bklyn., 1986; vis. artist Loft Calle Isidro, Cadaques, Spain, 1996, Tex. A&M U.,

Corpus Christi, 1996; juror Scholastic Nat. Art awards, N.Y.C., 1982; mem. com. Artist Talk on Art, N.Y.C., 1977-78. Contbr. articles to profl. jours. Recipient art award Bank of Am., Stockton, Calif., 1967, Internat. Achievement award Stockton Arts Commn., 1982; award Scudder Found., Princeton, N.J., 1970. Mem. Coll. Art Assn., Van Cortlandt Golf Club (champion 1989), Bklyn. Marine Dunes Golf Club. Democrat. Presbyterian. Avocations: golf, body building. Home: 182 Nevins St Brooklyn NY 11217-2600

HAZUDA, HELEN PAULINE, sociologist, educator; b. San Francisco, Oct. 20, 1943; d. Alexander William and Dolores Underwood (Green) H.; children: Ann Elizabeth Richter, Sean. BA in Sociology and Philosophy, Incarnate Word Coll., 1965, MA in Edn. and History, 1968; PhD in Sociology, U. Tex., 1975. Asst. prin. Incarnate Word H.S., San Antonio, 1967-71; discipline head for curriculum, instrn., dir. bilingual edn. Our Lady the Lake U., San Antonio, 1976-79; asst. prof. clin. medicine in medicine and psychiatry U. Tex. Health Sci. Ctr., San Antonio, 1980-88, assoc. prof. medicine dept. medicine and psychiatry, 1988-96, prof. medicine dept. medicine and psychiatry, 1996—; del. Gov's White House Conf. Children and Youth, Austin, 1970; admissions com. med. sch. U. Tex. Health Sci. Ctr., San Antonio, 1986-91, med. humanities curriculum planning com., 1989-91, tech. adv. panel for clin. and epidemiological rsch., 1991—; faculty mem. Ctr. Ethics and the Humanities in Health Care, 1992—, assoc. dir. Med. Humanities Course, 1997-98, Instnl. Rev. Bd., 1998—; doctoral dissertation com. Sch. Nursing, 1992-93, adj. asst. prof. medicine and psychiatry, 1979-80; lectr. Incarnate Word Coll., San Antonio, 1971-72; cons. San Luis Valley Health and Aging Study/U. Colo. Health Sci. Ctr., Denver, 1992—; mem. nat. adv. panel RMC Rsch. Corp., 1977-81; mem. ad hoc study section NIH, 1988, mem. clin. applications and prevention adv. com. divsn. epidemiology and clin. applications Nat. Heart, Lung and Blood Inst., 1991-94, chair behavioral medicine working group, 1993-94, task force on rsch. in epidemiology and prevention cardiovascular disease, 1993-94; reviewer grants and proposals; mem. working group on epidemiology of hypertension in Hispanic-Ams., Native Ams., and Asian/Pacific Islanders-Ams., 1993-94; co-chair NHLBI Conf. socioeconomic status and cardiovascular health and disease, 1995; cons. McDonnell-Douglas Automation Co., St. Louis, 1969-78, Devel. Assocs., 1975-77; speaker and presenter in field. Contbr. articles to profl. jours. Panelist San Antonio Cmty. Symposium on the Changing Role Women in Personal and Profl. Life, 1976; resource person Leadership San Antonio, 1976; co-chair Working Women in Am.: Where Are They and Why are They There?, 1976-77; judge Hobby Middle Sch. Sci. Fair, San Antonio, 1984, John Jay H.S. Sci. Fair, San Antonio, 1987, Alamo Area Regional Sci. Fair, San Antonio, 1987; alumnae bd. dirs. Incarnate Word H.S., San Antonio, 1986-89; pledge vol. Womens Faculty Assn., San Antonio, 1991. U.S. Seminar on the Epidemiology and Prevention Cardiovascular Disease fellow, Lake Tahoe, Calif., 1983; instl. rsch. grantee U. Tex. Health Scis. Ctr./Hogg Found. for Mental Health, Austin, 1981-82; grantee Am. Heart Assn., 1983-84, Morrison Trust Found., 1986-87, NIH, 1979—, Nat. Cancer Inst., 1985-89. 03880391 Sociol. Assn., Soc. for Behavioral Medicine, Am. Diabetes Assn., Soc. for Epidemiol. Rsch., Am. Heart Assn. (mem. coun. on cardiovasc. epidemiology), Am. Soc. Bioethics and Humanities, Gerontol. Soc. Am., Acad. Behavioral Medicine Rsch., Gerontol. Soc. Am., Phi Kappa Phi, Kappa Gamma Phi, Alpha Chi, Alpha Lambda Delta. Avocations: hiking, horseback riding, reading, travel, music. Office: U Tex Health Sci Ctr Dept Medicine/Epidemiology 7703 Floyd Curl Dr San Antonio TX 78284-6200

HAZZARD, MARY ELIZABETH, nurse, educator; b. Evansville, Ind., Mar. 2, 1941; d. John Waven and Lucille Elizabeth (Theobold) H.; 1 child, Mary Lucille. BSN, Nazareth Coll., 1963; AM, NYU, 1965, PhD, 1970; family nurse practitioner, U. Tenn., 1997. Cert. min.; cert. family nurse practitioner. Staff nurse Caldwell County War Meml. Hosp., Princeton, Ky., 1962, staff nurse supr., 1963, 65; asst. nurse St. Joseph's Hosp., Louisville, 1962-63; teaching fellow NYU, 1966, instr., 1966-68; nursing sister-in-charge Meru (Kenya) Dist. Hosp., 1966; asst. prof. U. Va. Sch. Nursing, Charlottesville, 1968-70, assoc. prof., 1970-74, dir. learning resources, 1971-74; assoc. prof. Sangamon State U., Springfield, Ill., 1974-79; prof. Western Ky. U., Bowling Green, 1979-99; prof. emeritus, 1998; prof. Nat. U., LaJolla, Calif., 1998—; head dept. nursing Western Ky. U., Bowling Green, 1979-96; adj. assoc. prof. U. Ky., Lexington, 1983-94; curriculum cons. MacMurray Coll., Jacksonville, Ill., 1978, U. Louisville, 1981; pres. So. Coun. on Collegiate Edn. in Nursing, 1993-95; nurse practitioner Cmty. Health Care Plus, Brownsville, 1997-98, St. Vincent DePaul Med. Clin. Homeless, San Diego, 1998—. Author: Review of Med-Surg Nursing, 1976, Nursing Outline Series: Critical Care Nursing, 1978; also articles; mem. edit. rev. bd. Health Care for Women Internat., 1984—. Pres. So. Coun. on Collegiate Edn. in Nursing, 1993-95. Fellow Am. Acd. Nursing; mem. ANA, Ky. Nurses Assn. (pres. 1986-87), Ky. League for Nursing (bd. dirs. 1980-83), Ky. Acad. Sci., Ky. Assn. Baccalaureate and Higher Degree Programs (sec. 1986-87), Ky. Cols., Sigma Theta Tau, Pi Lambda Theta. Democrat. Roman Catholic. Office: Nat U 11255 N Torrey Pines Rd La Jolla CA 92037

HAZZARD, SHIRLEY, author; b. Sydney, Australia, Jan. 30, 1931; d. Reginald and Catherine (Stein) H.; m. Francis Steegmuller, Dec. 22, 1963 (dec. Oct. 1994). Ed., Queenwood Sch., Sydney, to 1946. With Combined Services Intelligence, Hong Kong, 1947-48, U.K. High Commr.'s Office, Wellington, N.Z., 1949-50, UN (Gen. Service Category), N.Y.C., 1952-62; Boyer lectr., Australia, 1984, 88. Author: Cliffs of Fall and Other Stories, 1963; novel The Evening of the Holiday, 1966; fiction People in Glass Houses, 1967; novel The Bay of Noon, 1970; History Defeat of an Ideal: A Study of the Self-Destruction of the United Nations, 1973; novel The Transit of Venus, 1980, History Countenance of Truth, 1990; contbr. short stories to New Yorker mag. Trustee N.Y. Soc. Library. Recipient 1st prize O. Henry Short Story awards, 1976, Lit. award Nat. Inst. Arts and Letters, 1966; Guggenheim fellow, 1974; recipient Nat. Book Critics Circle award for Fiction, 1981. Fellow Royal Soc. Lit.; mem. AAAL (Natl. Acad. of Arts and Letters), Nat. Arts and Scis., Century Club (N.Y.C.). Address: 200 E 66th St New York NY 10021-6728

HAZZARD, WILLIAM RUSSELL, geriatrician, educator; b. Ann Arbor, Mich., Sept. 5, 1936; s. Albert Sidney and Florence Bernice (Woolsey) H.; m. Ellen Bennett Friedman, June 10, 1961; children: Susan Lovejoy Roque, Russell Holden, Rebecca Cornell Oliver, Daniel Bennett. AB, Cornell U., 1958, MD, 1962. Diplomate Am. Bd. Internal Med. Resident in internal medicine U. Wash. Sch. Med. and Affiliated Hosps., Seattle, 1966-67, fellow in endocrinology and metabolism, 1965-66, 67-69; from instr. to prof. medicine U. Wash., Seattle, 1969-82, dir. Northwest Lipid Rsch. Clinic, 1972-78; investigator Howard Hughes Med. Inst., U. Wash., Seattle, 1972-80; prof. medicine, assoc. dir. dept. medicine Johns Hopkins Med. Instns., Balt., 1982-86, dir. ctr. on aging, 1983-86; prof., chmn. dept. internal med. Bowman Gray Sch. Medicine of Wake Forest U., Winston-Salem, N.C., 1986-98; dir. J. Paul Sticht Ctr. on Aging of Wake Forest U., Winston-Salem, N.C., 1987-97; sr. adv. J. Paul Ctr. On Aging of Wake Forest U., 1998—. Editor: Principles of Geriatric Medicine and Gerontology, 1984, 89, 93, 99; contbr. over 100 articles to jours. in field. Lt. USNR, 1963-65. Fellow ACP; mem. Inst. Medicine of NAS, Am. Geriatrics Soc. (bd. dirs. 1988—, pres. 1993), Assn. Profs. Medicine, Gerontol. Soc. Am. (chmn. clin. med. sect. 1984), Am. Heart Assn. (Coun. on Arterosclerosis), Am. Fedn. Clin. Rsch. (mem. emeritus), Am. Soc. Clin. Investigation (mem. emeritus), Assn. Am. Physicians, AM. Clin. and Climatol. Assn., Nat. Inst. on Aging (aging rev. com. 1990-94, Geriatric Medicine Acad. award 1980). Avocations: gardening, conservation and nature study, music, athletics. Home: 970 Arbor Rd Winston Salem NC 27104-1040 Office: Wake Forest U Sch Medicine Dept Internal Medicine Med Center Blvd Winston Salem NC 27157-1207*

H'DOUBLER, FRANCIS TODD, JR., surgeon; b. Springfield, Mo., June 18, 1925; s. Francis Todd and Alice Louise (Bemis) H'D; m. Joan Louise Huber, Dec. 20, 1951 (dec. Dec. 1983); children—Julie H'Doubler Thomas and Sarah H'Doubler Muegge (twins), Kurt, Scott; m. Marie Ruth Duckworth, Jan. 18, 1986. Student, Washington U., St. Louis, 1943, Miami U., Oxford, Ohio, 1943-44; B.S., U. Wis., 1946, M.D., 1948. Intern Milw. Hosp., 1948-49; resident in surgery U.S. Naval Hosp., Oakland, Calif., 1950-51; practice medicine specializing in alternative medicine Springfield, Mo., 1952—; mem. courtesy staff St. John's Hosp., Springfield, L.E. Cox Hosp., Springfield; bd. dirs. Union Planters Bank. Active Singing Doctors; chmn. fundraising drive YMCA, 1960-61, Sch. Bond and Tax Levy Com., 1958, Greene County Rep. Com., 1974-75; past bd. trustees Shriners Hosps., past chmn. spinal cord injury com., past chmn. rsch. com., past chmn. long range planning com., emeritus mem. rsch. com.; mem. Commn. to Reapportion Mo. Senate, 1971, Rep. State Fin. Com., 1972-75, steering com. Wilson's Creekl Battlefield Nat. Park, 1951-61, pres.'s adv. coun. Sch. Ozarks, Point Lookout, Mo., 1975-89; trustee Cottey Coll., Nevada, Mo., past bd. chmn.; bd. trustees Forest Inst. With USNR, 1943-46, 49-51. Decorated Bronze Star with V, Purple Heart with oak leaf cluster; recipient Disting. Service award Mo. Jaycees, 1959; Humanitarian award S.W. Mo. Drug Travelers Assn., 1971; named Young Man of Yr., City of Springfield, 1959. Fellow Am. Coll. Nuclear Medicine (founder's group); mem. AMA, Greene County Med. Assn., Mo. Med. Soc., Southwestern Surg. Congress, Mo. Surg. Assn., Soc. Nuclear Medicine, Am. Thyroid Assn., Springfield Jr. C. of C. (past pres.), Springfield C. of C., DAV, VFW, SAR, Am. Legion, Green Gang (co-founder), Sigma Nu (Outstanding Alumnus nat. award 1980), Nu Sigma Nu. Presbyterian. Club: Hickory Hills Country. Lodges: Mason (33 deg.), Shriners (imperial potentate 1980-81), Red Cross of Constantine, Order DeMolay Legion Honor (hon.), Royal Order Scotland. Home: 2445 E Melbourne Rd Springfield MO 65804-5207 Offfice: 1900 S National Ave Ste 2900 Springfield MO 65804-2276

HE, GUANG SHENG, research scientist; b. Yingkou, China, Jan. 13, 1941; came to U.S., 1986; s. Kwei-Wu and Chung-Kuay (Li) He; m. Lan Huang, Feb. 1, 1970; 1 child, Katherine. Grad., Changchun (China) Inst. Optics, 1963. Jr. rsch. scientist Beijing Electronics Inst., 1963-65; sr. scientist Shanghai (China) Inst. Optics & Fine Mechanics, 1965-86; sr. rsch. scientist Photonics Rsch. Lab., SUNY, Buffalo, 1987—; sr. rsch. sci. photonics rsch. lab. Laser Photonics Tech., Inc., Amherst, N.Y., 1990-95; invited lectr. prof. various univ., China, 1980-86. Co-author: Laser Physics, 1975, Design and Technology of Lasers, 1979, Introduction of Nonlinear Optics, 1987, Laser Nonlinear Optics, 1995. Home: 107 Sundown Trl Williamsville NY 14221-2220 Office: SUNY Photonics Rsch Lab Dept Chemistry Buffalo NY 14260

HE, PINGNIAN, physiologist, researcher; b. Tianjin, China, Aug. 12, 1951; d. Deqian He and Congmin Wang; m. Jingchun Xu, Feb. 2, 1978 (dec. May 1998); children: Amy J. Xu, Maria M. Xu. MD, Tianjin Med. Coll., 1982; PhD, U. Calif., Davis, 1990. Resident Tianjin Med. Coll., 1982-84; postgrad. rschr. U. Calif., Davis, 1984-89, postdoctoral rsch. physiologist, 1990-92, asst. rsch. physiologist, 1992-99, assoc. rsch. physiologist, 1999—; peer reviewer N. A. peer rev. com. Am. Heart Assn., Calif., 1997—. Editl. reviewer Am. Jour. Physiol., 1996—, Microvascular Rsch., 1996—, Microcirculation, Rev. Annual Biomed. Engring. Recipient Travel award for new investigator, Fifth World Congress Microcirculation, 1991; Prin. Investigator Rsch. grantee NIH, 1996—, Nat. Am. Heart, 1996—. Mem. Am. Physiol. Soc., Microcirculatory Soc. (chmn. mem. com. 1998—, Grega-Zacharkow Young Investigator award 1989). E-mail: pnhe@ucdavis.edu. Office: Dept Human Physiology Sch Medicine U Calif One Shields Ave Davis CA 95616

HEACOCK, DONALD DEE, social worker; b. Anthony, Kans., Feb. 21, 1934; s. C.W. and Thelma Olive (Hilton) H.; m. Margaret Newberry, Sept. 4, 1953; children: Teresa Ellen, Mark Dee. AB, Washburn U., 1956; BD cum laude, United Sem., 1959; MSW, Barry Coll., 1971, Thd. Slidell Baptist Seminary, 1999. Ordained priest Episcopal Ch., 1965; diplomate in clin. social work. Parish minister St. John's Ch., Clinton, Mich., 1961-66; chaplain, Margarita, Canal Zone, 1966-69; tchr. Christ Ch. Acad. Secondary Sch., Colon, Panama, 1966-69; counselor South Fla. Neighborhood Youth Corp., Miami, 1969-70; chief social service, instr. pediatric comprehensive health care program U. Miami, 1971-72; asst. dir. Alpha House, Dade County, Fla. and field supr. Barry Coll., 1972-73; marriage and family therapist Psychiatric Assocs., Shreveport, La., 1973-75; pvt. practice social work, Shreveport, 1975—; dir. Holy Cross Child Placement Agy., Inc., 1984; lectr. sociology Centenary Coll., 1981-88. With USAF, 1959-61. Mem. Am. Assn. Marriage and Family Therapy, Nat. Assn. Social Workers, Acad. Cert. Social Work, Phi Kappa Mu, Phi Gamma Mu. Lodge: Masons. Home: 748 Thora Blvd Shreveport LA 71106-1824 Office: 910 Pierremont Rd Ste 356 Shreveport LA 71106-2063

HEACOCK, PHILLIP KAGA, aerospace executive; b. Danville, Ill., Nov. 20, 1938; s. Earl Rice and Helen Irene (Kaga) H.; m. Barbara J. Ryan, Sept. 2, 1995; children: Nancy Michelle, Phillip Eric. BSME, U. Ill., 1961; MBA in Mgmt., George Washington U., 1968; disting. grad., Air War Coll., 1978. Commd. 2d lt. USAF, 1961, advanced through grades to col.; action officer Hdqrs. USAF, The Pentagon, Washington, 1970-72; exec. officer to comdr. Air Force Comm. Command, Richards Gebour AFB, Mo., 1972-74; comdr. 1913 Comm. Group, Langley AFB, Va., 1974-77; chief communications div. Pacific Command Hdqrs., Honolulu, 1978-80; dir. readiness Air Force Communications Command Hdqrs., Scott AFB, Ill., 1980-82; comdr. 1931st Comms. Wing, Elmendorf AFB, Alaska, 1982-84; comdr Space Comm. Div., Peterson AFB, Colo., 1984-86; dist. mgr. Harris Corp., Colorado Springs, Colo., 1987-93; dir. Harris Corp., Alexandria, Va., 1993—. Decorated Legion of Merit, Def. Superior Svc. medal. Mem. Nat. Security Indsl. Assn. (vice chair space com. 1989-91, 94-96, pres. Rocky Mountain chpt. 1991-93, v.p. 1989-91). Avocations: skiing, scuba diving, jogging. Home: 815 Green St Alexandria VA 22314-4212 Office: 1201 E Abingdon Dr Ste 300 Alexandria VA 22314-1420

HEAD, CHRISTOPHER ALAN, lawyer; b. Buffalo, Nov. 28, 1951; s. Alan S. and Mary Ellen (Carrig) H.; m. Kathleen Rosemarie Meosky, Aug. 22, 1976; children: Matthew, David, Maribeth, Sally, Thomas, Susan. BA, Canisius Coll., 1974; JD, U. Akron, 1977. Bar: Ohio 1977, N.Y. 1978, U.S. Dist. Ct. (we. dist.) N.Y. 1979. Adminstr. contracts Comptek Research Inc., Buffalo, 1977-78, corp. counsel, 1978-82, gen. counsel, 1983-85, v.p., gen. counsel, 1985—, now exec. v.p., gen. counsel; corp. counsel Barrister Info. System Corp., Buffalo, 1982-83; trustee St. Mary of the Cataract Ch. Mem. ABA, N.Y. State Bar Assn., Erie County Bar Assn., Niagara Frontier Corp. Counsel Assn. (pres. 1984-85). Democrat. Roman Catholic. Home: 3311 Calvano Dr Grand Island NY 14072-1072 Office: Comptek Rsch Inc 2732 Transit Rd Buffalo NY 14224-2523

HEAD, EDWARD DENNIS, bishop; b. White Plains, N.Y., Aug. 5, 1919; s. Charles W. and Nellie (O'Donahue) H. Student, Cathedral Coll. Columbia U., St. Joseph's Sem., Dunwoodie, Yonkers, N.Y.; M.A., N.Y. Sch. Social Work, 1948. Ordained priest Roman Catholic Ch., 1945; formerly tchr. Notre Dame Coll., S.I., N.Y.; asst. pastor Sacred Heart Ch., Bronx, St. Roch's Ch., S.I.; with Cath. Charities Office Archdiocese of New York, 1947-66; exec. dir. Cath. Charities, 1966-70; aux. bishop of New York, 1970-73, bishop of Buffalo, 1973-94, bishop emeritus of Buffalo, 1994—; Chmn. health affairs com. U.S. Cath. Conf. Office: Chancery Office 795 Main St Buffalo NY 14203-1215*

HEAD, ELIZABETH, lawyer; b. Rochester, Minn., Dec. 17, 1930; d. Walter Elias and Ruth Winnogene (Evesmith) Bonner; m. C.J. Head, Dec. 30, 1950; 1 child, Alison Elizabeth. BA, U. Chgo., 1949, JD, 1952. Bar: Ill. 1952, Calif. 1955, N.Y. 1958, U.S. Supreme Ct. 1963, D.C. 1978. Atty. Nat. Labor Rels. Bd., Washington, 1953-54; assoc. Johnston & Johnston, San Francisco, 1954-56; atty. Aminoil Inc., San Francisco, 1956-57; teaching assoc. Law Sch. Columbia U., N.Y., 1957-58; assoc. Skadden Arps, N.Y., 1958-60; atty. The Coca-Cola Corp., N.Y., 1961-65; assoc. Kaye Scholer, N.Y., 1965-72, ptnr., 1973-82; ptnr. Hall & Estill, Tulsa, 1983-87; vis. fellow antitrust analysis Fed. Energy Regulatory Commn., Washington, 1987-89; gen. counsel Columbia U., N.Y.C., 1989-97. Trustee Philbrook Mus., Tulsa, 1983-87, Mary Baldwin Coll., Staunton, Va., 1983-87. Mem. ABA (standing com. on dispute resolution 1983-90), Assn. of Bar of City of N.Y. (non-profit orgns. com. 1989-90, chair 1992-95, health law com. 1997—), Century Assn., Order of Coif, Phi Beta Kappa. Avocations: travel, music, art, theatre. Office: 303 E 57th St # 47F New York NY 10022-2947

HEAD, GLENN OAKES, investment company executive; b. Peoria, Ill., Aug. 16, 1925; s. Glenn L. and Helen (Oakes) H.; m. Carol Head, Nov. 13, 1954; children: Kathryn, Glenn, Marcia, Leslie Head Smith, Linda Head Flanagan. AB, U. Ill., 1946. Asst. gen. mgr., actuary Farm Bur. Life of Iowa, Des Moines; v.p., actuary, dir. U.S. Life Ins. Co., N.Y.C.; chmn. First Investers Consol. Corp., N.Y.C. Elected mem. Madison (N.J.) Bd. Edn., 1963, pres., 1964; mayor Madison, N.J., 1971. Fellow Soc. Actuaries. Avocation: commercial pilot. Office: First Investors Consol Corp 95 Wall St 23d Fl New York NY 10005-4201*

HEAD, GREGORY ALAN, mechanical engineer, consultant; b. Dallas, Mar. 2, 1955; s. A. Lee and Georgia M. Head. BSME, Brigham Young U., 1981; MS in Engring. Mgmt., U. Alaska, Anchorage, 1988; postgrad., U. Tex., Arlington, 1990-98. Registered profl. engr., Tex. Engr. tech. Hercules Aerospace, Inc., Salt Lake City, 1978-79, LTV Aerospace Inc., Dallas, 1979-80; engr. Hercules Aerospace Inc., Sale Lake City, 1980-82, CMH-Vitro, Anchorage, 1982-84; petroleum engr. Arco Alaska, Anchorage, 1984-87; cons. FAH World Wide Photographers, Anchorage and Dallas, 1987—; sr. v.p. systems divsn. D.C. Systems, Denton, Tex., 1988-94; pres. D.C. Systems, Sanger, 1994—; cons. Alaska Mountaineering Assn., Anchorage, 1990—; capt. Arctic Adventurers, 1988-98. Author: Arctic Lands and Uses, 1989, Missionary, Ch. of Jesus Christ of Latter Day Saints, Washington, 1975-77; mem. Mountain Rescue Team, Anchorage, 1989-96; emergency med. technician State of Alaska, 1987-97. Named Photographer of the Yr., FAH Worldwide Photo, Inc., 1990. Mem. ASME, Nat. Geog. Soc., Nat. Assn. Pvt. Enterpreneurs, Am. Soc. Profl. Photographers, Brigham Young U. Football Alumni Assn., Suzuki Moto Cross Team. Republican. Avocations: international expeditionary hiking, mountain/rock climbing, enduro motor bike racing, civic activities, international travel. Office: DC Systems Tex Bolivar Indsl Pk 8280 FM 455 W Chapman Dr Sanger TX 76266-2634

HEAD, HAYDEN WILSON, JR., judge; b. Sherman, Tex., Nov. 12, 1944; s. Hayden W. Head and Marshall (Elmore) Skinner. Student, Washington and Lee U., 1962-64; B.A., U. Tex., 1967, LL.B., 1968. Bar: Tex. Assoc. Head & Kendrick, Corpus Christi, Tex., 1968-69, 1972-76, ptnr., 1976-81; judge U.S. Dist. Ct. (so. dist.) Tex., Corpus Christi, 1981—. Lt. JAGC, USNR, 1969-72. Fellow Tex. Bar Found.; mem. State Bar Tex. Office: US Dist Ct 521 Starr St Fl 2 Corpus Christi TX 78401-2349

HEAD, HENRY BUCHEN, physician; b. Evanston, Ill., Nov. 24, 1933; s. Jerome Reed and Jean Helen (Milne) H.; divorced; children: Elizabeth, Catherine, Heather, Henry, Alexander. BA, Amherst Coll., 1955; MD, Northwestern U., 1959; MS, U. Minn., 1964. Intern Phila. Gen. Hosp., 1959-60; assoc. Northwestern U. Med. Sch., Chgo., 1965-93; attending physician Northwestern Meml. Hosp., Chgo., 1965-93, Smith County Meml. Hosp., Carthage, Tenn., 1993-96; locum tenens, 1996—. Contbr. papers to profl. publs. Maj. U.S. Army Med. Corps, 1967-69. Internal Medicine fellow Mayo Clinic, Rochester, Minn., 1960-63, Gastroenterology fellow Northwestern U. Med. Sch., 1963-65; decorated Bronze Star. Fellow Am. Coll. Physicians. Avocations: fishing, travel, hunting.

HEAD, IVAN LEIGH, law educator; b. Calgary, Alta., Can., July 28, 1930; s. Arthur Cecil and Birdie Hazel (Crockett) H.; m. Barbara Spence Eagle, June 23, 1952; children: Laurence Allan, Bryan Cameron, Catherine Spence, Cynthia Leigh; m. Ann Marie Price, Dec. 1, 1979. BA, U. Alta., 1951, LLB, 1952; LLM, Harvard U., 1960; LLD (hon.), U. Alta., 1987, U. West Indies, 1987, U. Western Ont., 1988, U. Ottawa, 1988, U. Calgary, 1989, Beijing U., 1990, St. Francis Xavier U., 1990, U. Man., 1991, U. Notre Dame, 1991, Carleton U., 1996. Bar: Alta. 1953; Queen's Counsel, Can. Practiced in Calgary, 1953-59; partner firm Helman, Barron & Head, 1955-59; fgn. service officer Dept. External Affairs, Ottawa, Kuala Lumpur, 1960-63; prof. law U. Alta., 1963-67; asso. counsel to Minister of Justice, Govt. of Can., 1967-68, spl. asst. to prime minister of Can., 1968-78; pres. Internat. Devel. Research Centre, Ottawa, 1978-91; prof. law, dir. Liu Centre for the study of global issues U. B.C., Vancouver, Can., 1991—; sr. fellow Salzburg Seminar; bd. dirs. Acad. Ednl. Devel. Author: International Law, National Tribunals and the Rights of Aliens, 1971, On a Hinge of History, 1991, The Canadian Way, 1995; editor: This Fire Proof House, 1967, Conversation with Canadians, 1972; contbr. articles to profl. jours. Trustee Internat. Food Policy Rsch. Inst., 1979-88; mem. Ind. Commn. on Internat. Humanitarian Issues, 1983-87. Decorated officer Order of Can.; officer Grand Cross, Order of The Sun (Peru); Chief Justice's medallist U. Alta. Law Sch.; Frank Knox Meml. fellow Harvard Law Sch., 1959-60. Mem. Internat. Law Assn., Can. Council Internat. Law, Can. Inst. Internat. Affairs, Am. Soc. Internat. Law, Law Soc. Alta., Inter-Am. Dialogue. Anglican. Home: 2343 Bellevue Ave, West Vancouver, BC Canada V7V 1C9 Office: U BC, Faculty Law, Vancouver, BC Canada V6T 1Z1

HEAD, JAMES W., III, geological sciences educator; b. Richmond, Va., Aug. 4, 1941. BS, Washington and Lee U., 1964, DSc, 1995; PhD, Brown U., 1969. With Bellcomm, Inc., Washington, 1968-72; interim dir. Lunar Sci. Inst., Houston, 1973-74; asst. prof. rsch. Brown U., Providence, 1973-74, assoc. prof. rsch., 1975-74, assoc. prof., 1975-80, prof. geol. scis., 1980—; vis. assoc. Calif. Inst. Tech., Pasadena, 1990-91; prof. Universidad Complutense, Madrid, 1997. Contbr. chpts. to books, more than 300 articles to profl. jours. Recipient medal for exceptional sci. achievement NASA, also pub. svc. medal; award Alpha Circle of Omicron Delta Kappa, 1990. Fellow AAAS, Am. Geophys. Union, Geol. Soc. Am., Meteoritical Soc.; mem. Am. Astron. Soc., European Geophys. Soc. Office: Brown U Box 1846 Dept Geo-Scis Providence RI 02919

HEAD, JOHN FRANCIS, JR., distributing company executive; b. N.Y.C., May 29, 1920; s. John Francis Head and Pauline DeLamar; m. Jacqueline; children: John III, Paula, Andrew. BSBA, U. Ga., 1942. Sales mgr. Dun & Bradstreet, Atlanta, 1946-70; chmn. bd. Head Distbg. Co., Atlanta, 1970—, pres., 1970-93. Capt. C.E., U.S. Army, 1942-45, ETO. Mem. Nat. Assn. Tobacco Distbrs. (v.p. fin. 1982-90), Nat. Candy Wholesalers Assn. (bd. dirs. 1984-90), So. Whole Distbr. Assn. (chmn. bd. 1988-90), Am. Wholesale Marketers Assn. (bd. dirs.), Georgian Club. Republican. Presbyterian. Office: Head Distbg Co 4820 N Church Ln Smyrna GA 30080-7210

HEAD, JONATHAN FREDERICK, cell biologist; b. Syracuse, N.Y., Nov. 23, 1949; s. Arthur Everard and Lillian Myrtle (Hendra) H.; m. Priscilla Catherine Tambone, July 28, 1984; 1 child, Catherine Elizabeth. BS in Zoology, Syracuse U., 1971; MA in Biology, Bklyn. Coll., 1977; PhD in Biology, Fordham U., 1985. Rsch. asst. Naylor Dana Inst. Disease Prevention/Am. Health Found., Valhalla, N.Y., 1974-78, Cornell U. Med. Coll., N.Y.C., 1978; rsch. asst. Mt. Sinai Sch. Medicine, N.Y.C., 1978-84, rsch. assoc., 1984-86, rsch. asst. prof., 1986-87; dir. tumor cell biology Ctr. Clin. Scis./Internat. Clin. Labs., Nashville, 1986-89; pres. Mastology Rsch. Inst., Baton Rouge, 1989—; dir. R&D Med. Thermal Diagnostics, Baton Rouge, 1995—; adj. asst. prof. Tulane U. Sch. Medicine, New Orleans, 1989—; adj. prof. Delta State U., Cleveland, Miss., 1992—; researcher and lectr. in field of cancer. Contbr. articles, abstracts and chpts. to sci. publs. Mem. State of La. Adoption Cmty. Adv. Bd., 1992-95. Mem. AAAS, Am. Assn. Cancer Rsch., Am. Soc. Clin. Oncology, Soc. Biol. Therapy, European Soc. Med. Oncology. Methodist. Home: 6144 Hagerstown Dr Baton Rouge LA 70817-3917 Office: Mastology Rsch Inst 8221 Kelwood Dr Baton Rouge LA 70806-4802

HEAD, LOUIS ROLLIN, surgeon; b. Madison, Wis., Apr. 8, 1924; s. Jerome R. and Jean (Milne) H.; m. Emily Johnson, Sept. 15, 1951; children: Emily, Julia, Marjorie, Mary, Anne, Louis, Frederic. AB, Amherst Coll., 1945; MD, Johns Hopkins U., 1952. Diplomate Am. Bd. Surgery, Am. Bd. Thoracic Surgery. Intern Northwestern U. Hosp., Chgo., 1952-53; resident in gen. surgery U. Chgo., 1953-57; fellow in thoracic surgery Northwestern U., 1957-58; fellow in cardiac surgery St. Vincent's Charity Hosp., Cleve., 1958-60; assoc. in surgery Northwestern U. Med. Sch., Chgo., 1960-88; field rep. The Joint Commn. on Accreditation of Healthcare Orgns., Oakbrook Terrace, Ill., 1990-95, assoc. dir. standards interpretation, 1995-97; pvt. practice Evanston, Ill., 1997—. Contbr. over 30 articles to profl. jours. 1st lt. USAF, 1942-45, Italy. Rsch. grantee John Hartford Found., N.Y., 1963-71. Fellow Am. Assn. Cardiac and Thoracic Surgery, Ill. Thoracic Surg. Soc., Chgo. Surg. Soc.; mem. Air Force Escape and Evasion Soc. (life). Republican. Anglican. Avocations: tennis, fishing. Home: Apt 2-South 1107 Lake St Evanston IL 60201-4147 Office: 524 W Diversey Pkwy Chicago IL 60614-1610

HEAD, MARY MAE, elementary education educator; b. Branson, Mo., Apr. 9, 1963; d. Thomas Edwin and Evelyn Jean (Hazell) H. BS in Computer Sci., Sch. of Ozarks, Point Lookout, Mo., 1989. Asst. computer lab., libr. aide Hollister (Mo.) Elem. Sch., 1989—. Sunday sch. tchr. Hollister

Presbyn. Ch., 1979—. Avocations: bible study, prayer. Office: Hollister Elem Sch 119 Myrtle Ave Hollister MO 65672-5461

HEAD, PATRICK JAMES, lawyer; b. Randolph, Nebr., July 13, 1932; s. Clarence Martin and Ellen Cecelia (Magirl) H.; m. Eleanor Hickey, Nov. 24, 1960; children: Adrienne, Ellen, Damian, Maria, Brendan, Martin, Sarah, Daniel, Brian. A.B. summa cum laude, Georgetown U., 1953, LL.B., 1956, LL.M. in Internat. Law, 1957. Bar: D.C. 1956, Ill. 1966. Assoc. John L. Ingolsby (and predecessor firm), Washington, 1956-64; gen. counsel internat. ops. Sears, Roebuck & Co., Oakbrook, Ill., 1964-70; counsel midwest ter. Sears, Roebuck & Co., Skokie, Ill., 1970-72; v.p. Montgomery Ward & Co., Inc., Washington, 1972-76; v.p., gen. counsel, sec. Montgomery Ward & Co., Inc., Chgo., 1976-81; v.p., gen. counsel FMC Corp., Chgo., 1981-96; ptnr. Altheimer E. Gray, Chgo., 1997—; bd. visitors Northwestern Law, 1988-91. Mem. Chgo. Crime Commn.; bd. regents Georgetown U., Washington, 1981-87; bd. visitors Georgetown Law Sch., 1992—. Mem. ABA, D.C. Bar Assn., Chgo. Bar Assn., Am. Law Inst. Democrat. Roman Catholic. Clubs: Met. (Washington); Chgo, Internat. Office: Altheimer & Gray 10 S Wacker Dr Fl 36 Chicago IL 60606-7407

HEAD, SHANE EVERETT, animal nutrition company executive, consultant; b. Brookfield, Mo., Aug. 30, 1966; s. Gary Wayne and Bonnie Sue H.; m. Danielle Christine Sergent, Jan. 12, 1991; children: Gavin Lucas, Kaitlan Christine. BS, N. Ctrl. Mo. State. Sales rep. Ricketts Farm Svc., Salisbury, Mo., 1986-96; cons. Cargill, Inc., Mpls., 1996—; sales rep. Purina Mills, St. Louis, 1995; chmn. Bd. Pub. Works, Salisbury. Avocations: hunting, golfing, fishing, sports. E-mail: sehead@cvalley.net. Home: 109 Melody Ave Salisbury MO 65281

HEAD, WILLIAM CARL, lawyer, author; b. Columbus, Ga., Mar. 4, 1951; s. Louis Bernice and Betty June (Vickery) H.; m. Sandra Earle, Sept. 3, 1972 (div. 1979); m. Kathleen Crenshaw, Aug. 8, 1981 (div. 1988); 1 stepchild, Stephanie A. Hansen; m. Kris L. Foreman, Feb. 14, 1990; children: Lauren Ansley, Shelby Jordan. BA cum laude, U. Ga., 1973, JD, 1976. Bar: Ga. 1976, U.S. Dist. Ct. (mid. dist.) Ga. 1976, U.S. Ct. Appeals (5th and 11th cirs.) 1979, S.C. 1990. Ptnr. Galis, Timmons, Andrews & Head, Athens, Ga., 1977-79, Andrews & Head P.C., Athens, 1979-82; pvt. practice Athens, 1982-85; ptnr. McDonald, Head, Carney & Haggard, Athens, 1985-88; real estate developer Athens, 1979-88; regent, co-founder Nat. Coll. DUI Def., Inc. Author: The Georgia DUI Trial Practice Manual, 1998, Handling License Revocations and Suspensions in Georgia, 1993, Georgia DUI Trial Practice, 1998; co-author: 101 Ways to Avoid A Drunk Driving Conviction, 1991. Pres. Joseph Henry Lumpkin Found., Inc., Athens, 1979; chmn. Bridge the Gap seminar, Atlanta, 1980. Awardee Athens-Clarke Heritage Found. Inc., Athens, 1983. Mem. ABA, Ga. Bar Assn., S.C. Bar Assn., Assn. Trial Lawyers Am., Ga. Trial Lawyers Assn., Def. Drinking Drivers Network (founder), Order of Barristers, U. Ga. Pres.'s Club. Democrat. Presbyterian. Home: 6115 Spalding Bluff Ct Norcross GA 30092-4540 Office: 750 Hammond Dr NE Ste 12-100 Atlanta GA 30328-6135

HEAD, WILLIAM CHRISTOPHER, military officer, health care administrator; b. Clarksville, Tenn., Apr. 24, 1944; s. Asbury Jefferson and Dorothy Lillian (Brown) H.; children: Sara Christine, William Christopher Jr.; m. Gwendolyn Marie More, Jan. 16, 1999. BSBA, U. Tenn., Knoxville, 1967; MHA, Duke U., 1969. Commd. 2nd lt. USAF, 1967, advanced through grades to col., 1990; asst. adminstr. USAF Hosp., Homestead AFB, Fla., 1969-72; adminstr. USAF Clinic, Greenham Common, U.K., 1972-74; asst. adminstr. USAF Regional Hosp., Lakenheath, U.K., 1974-77; instr. Sch. Health Care Scis., Sheppard AFB, Tex., 1977-79; health sys. planner Office of Surgeon Gen., Bolling AFB, 1979-80; health sys. analysis Air Force Med. Svc. Ctr., Brooks AFB, Tex., 1980-82; chief med. sys. divsn. Sch. Health Care Scis., Sheppard AFB, 1982-86; adminstr. 325th Med. Group, Tyndall AFB, Fla., 1986-89, 1st Med. Group, Langley AFB, Va., 1989-91; dir. health care support Office of Command Surgeon, Langley AFB, 1991-92, 92-94; command surgeon Hdqrs. Air Combat Command (Provisional), Langley AFB, 1992; dep. command surgeon Hdqrs. Air Combat Command, Langley AFB, 1994-95; dep. comdr. 96th Med. Group, Eglin AFB, Fla., 1995—. Mem. cmty. adv. bd. Bay Med. Ctr. Panama City, Fla., 1986-89; mem. regional adv. bd. Am. Hosp. Assn., Chgo., 1982-85; bd. dirs. Young Execs. Healthcare Bus., Wichita Falls, Tex., 1982-86; bd. govs. Career Decision, Inc., 1993-94. Fellow Am. Coll. Healthcare Execs. (nominating com. 1995-98, chmn. bd. policy com. 1996-97, chmn. 1994-95, immediate past chmn. 1995-97, chmn.-elect 1993-94, chmn. credentialing task force 1993-94, fin. com. chmn. 1993-94, gov. dist. VIII 1989-93, strategic planning com. 1988-89, gov. dist. VI 1985-86, regional adv. bd. Region 7 1982-85, regent-at-large 1982-85, many other coms., Fed. Excellence in Healthcare Leadership award 1996, Regent's Sr. Level Healthcare Exec. award 1997, 99); mem. Am. Hosp. Assn., Fla. Hosp. Assn., Tex. Hosp. Assn. Assn. Mil. Surgeons U.S. (Outstanding Fed. Svc. Adminstrs. award 1995, Ray E. Brown award 1986, Young Fed. Healthcare Adminstr. award 1984), Fla. Hosp. Assn., L.R. Jordan Healthcare Mgmt. Soc., Emerald Coast Healthcare Execs. Forum, Healthcare Adminstrs. of Tidewater, Royal Soc. Health, Air War Coll. Alumni Assn. (life), Interagy. Inst. for Fed. Health Care Execs., Duke U. Health and Hosp. Adminstrn. Alumni Assn., Profl. Soc. Svcs. Inc. (bd. govs., chmn. 1993-94), Northwest Fla. Track Club, Omicron Delta Kappa (pres. 1967), Kappa Alpha (pres. Pi chpt. 1965-67). Methodist. Avocations: scuba diving, travel, fine dining, classical music, running. Home: 119 Lake Lorraine Circle Shalimar FL 32579-1619 Office: 96 Medical Group 307 Boatner Rd Ste 114 Eglin AFB FL 32542-1391

HEAD, WILLIAM IVERSON, SR., retired chemical company executive; b. Tallapoosa, Ga., Apr. 4, 1925; s. Iverson and Ruth Britain (Hubbard) H.; m. Mary Helen Ware, June 12, 1947; children: William Iverson, Connie Suzanne Head Toohey, Alan David. BS Ga. Inst. Tech., 1949; D of Textile Engring. (hon.), World U., 1983; PhD in Indsl. Mgmt., Columbia Pacific U., 1988. Textile engr. Tenn. Eastman Co., Kingsport, 1949-56, quality control-mfg. sr. textile engr., 1957-67, dept. supt., 1968-74; supt. acetate yarn dept., mem. bus. team, chems. div. Eastman Kodak Co., Kingsport, 1975-85; info. officer U.S. Naval Acad., 1983-97; mem. adv. bd., rsch. assoc. Point One Adv. Group, Inc., 1988—. Patentee textured yarns tech. in U.S., Great Britain, Fed. Republic of Germany, Japan and France. Capt. USNR, 1943-83. Decorated Navy Commendation medal, Selective Svc. System Meritorious Svc. medal, 1980. Mem. Internat. Soc. Philos. Enquiry (pers. cons. 1978-79, v.p. 1979-80, sr. rsch. fellow and internat. pres. 1980-85, diplomate and trustee 1986—, chmn. bd. trustees 1987—, Whiting Meml. award 1993), Prometheus Soc., Internat. Platform Assn., Naval Res. Assn., Assn. Naval Aviation, Mil. Order World Wars, Res. Officers Assn. (pres. Tenn. dept. 1981-82, nat. councilman 1991-98, nat. coun. steering com. 1993-97), Ret. Officers Assn., VFW, Mensa (pres. Upper East Tenn. 1976-79), Sons of Revolution, Internat. Legion of Intelligence. Unitarian. Home and Office: 4035 Lakewood Dr Kingsport TN 37663-3374

HEAD, WILLIAM PACE, historian, educator; b. Miami, Oct. 15, 1949; s. Downer Pace and Ella Marguerite (Crittenden) H.; m. Randee Lynne Geiger, June 6, 1975; children: Matthew Brian, Evan Zachery. AS Bus., Miami-Dade C.C., 1969; PhD History, Fla. State U., 1980, BA History, 1971; MA History, U. Miami, 1974. Asst. prof. history U. Ala., Huntsville, 1981-84; historian USAF, Robins AFB, Ga., 1984—; chief Office of History WR-ALC USAF, 1996—; adj. prof. history Fla. State U., Tallahassee, 1980-81, Macon (Ga.) State Coll., 1985—, Mercer U., 1985-92, Ga. Mil. Coll., 1986-94; site dir. Ala. Heritage Festival, Ala. Humanities Coun., Huntsville, 1981; hist. advisor WMAZ-TV Robins at Fifty, 1991, Ga. Pub. TV, The State of War: Ga. in WWII, Atlanta, 1994. Author: America's China Sojourn, 1983, Yenan, 1983, Reworking the Workhorse: The C-141B, 1984 (Best in AF 1985), Every Inch a Soldier, 1995 (Best in AF 1996); co-author, editor: Plotting a True Course: Reflections on Strategic Attack Theory and Doctrine, the Post-World War II Experience, 1999; co-author: Time Capsule: A History of Robins AFB, 1936-96, 1997; editor Tet Offensive, 1996, Looking Back at the Vietnam War, 1993, Eagle in the Desert, 1996, Weaving A New Tapestry: Asia In The Post Cold War World, 1999; assoc. editor Asia, Jour. of Third World Studies, 1985-98. Mem. Houston County Dem. Com. Coun., Warner Robins, Ga., 1990—; active little league baseball and basketball, Warner Robins City League, 1992—; hist. judge, Ga. Hist. Day/Ga. Humanities Coun., Atlanta, 1988—. Recipient Spl. Commendation award Ala. State Senate, Huntsville, 1986, Air Force Spl. Achievements award, 1994; Fla. State U. grad. fellow, 1977. Mem. Assn. Third World Studies (nom. com. chmn. 1989-98), Ga. Assn. Historians (pubs. com. 1984—), Assn. Asian Studies, Soc. Mil. History, Soc. Hist. Fed. Govt., Phi Kappa Phi. Democrat. Methodist. Avocations: golf, travel, tennis, sports. Home: 111 Chantilly Dr Warner Robins GA 31088-6329 Office: USAF-Warner Robins ALC 955 Robins Pky Robins AFB GA 31098-2423

HEAD, WILLIS STANFORD, music educator, performer; b. Memphis, June 21, 1953; s. Willis Lockhart and Mildred (Garrard) H. B in Music Edn., Ark. State U., 1975, M in Music Edn., 1980. Percussion instr. Dixie Music Camp, Jonesboro, Ark., 1972-81; timpanist Tupelo (Miss.) Symphony Orch., 1973-74, N.E. Ark. Symphony, Jonesboro, 1974-81; band dir. Mammoth Spring (Ark.) High Sch., 1975-77; percussionist Memphis Symphony and Little Symphony, 1981—, "Artists in Schs.", Memphis, 1985—; bd. dirs. Lindenwood Percussion Studio, Memphis, 1980—; lectr. Mid-South Bible Coll., Memphis, 1982—; percussion instr. Shelby State Community Coll. Memphis, 1984—; percussion cons. Harding Acad., Memphis, 1985—, Osceola (Ark.) High Sch., 1986—, Millington (Tenn.) High Sch., 1987—; timpanist Jackson (Tenn.) Symphony Orch. Mem. Percussive Arts Soc. (sec. treas. 1977-78), Nat. Assn. Recording Arts and Scis., Phi Mu Alpha Sinfonia Frat., Kappa Delta Pi. Home: 652 S Prescott St Memphis TN 38111-4325 Office: Lindenwood Percussion Studio 2400 Union Ave Memphis TN 38112-4318

HEAD-HAMMOND, ANNA LUCILLE, retired secondary education educator; b. Providence, Ky., Dec. 16, 1924; d. Nathaniel A. and Nora D. (Martin) Rinehammer; m. Robert F. Head, Oct. 24, 1940 (wid. Apr. 1981); 1 child, Robert N. Head; m. Arthur G. Hammond, Aug. 24, 1995. BS, Oakland City U., Ind., 1955; MS, Ind. State Coll., 1964. Tchr. Princeton (Ind.) H.S., 1955-64; instr., Oakland City U., 1964-77; owner, operator mobile home ct., Providence, 1973-78; real estate salesperson, appraiser Ball Real Estate, Providence, 1973-89; appraiser Frontier Properties, Okeechobee, Fla., 1973-89. Elected mem. Providence City Coun., 1972-73; adv. coun. Gulfstream Agy. on Aging, West Palm Beach, 1986-87; coun. mem. Cen. Fla. Regional Planning Coun., 1988-89. Mem. AAUW, Elks, Habitat for Humanity, Hospice, Alpha Phi Gamma. Republican. Presbyterian. Avocations: swimming, golf, walking. Home: 622 Delgado Ave Lady Lake FL 32159-8768

HEADLEE, RAYMOND, psychoanalyst, educator; b. Shelby County, Ind., July 27, 1917; s. Ortis Verl and Mary Mae (Wright) H.; m. Eleanor Case Benton, Aug. 24, 1941; children—Sue, Mark, Ann. A.B. in Psychology, Ind. U., 1939, A.M. in Exptl. Psychology, 1941, M.D., 1944; grad., Chgo. Inst. Psychoanalysis, 1959. Diplomate: Am. Bd. Psychiatry and Neurology (examiner 1964—). Intern St. Elizabeth's Hosp., Washington, 1944-45; resident in psychiatry St. Elizabeth's Hosp., 1945-46; resident in psychiatry Milw. Psychiat. Hosp., 1947-48, pres. staff, 1965-70; practice medicine specializing in psychiatry and psychoanalysis Elm Grove, Wis., 1949—; clin. asst. prof. psychiatry Med. Coll. Wis., 1958-59, clin. asso. prof., 1959-62, clin. prof., 1962—, chmn. dept. psychiatry, 1963-70; prof. psychology Marquette U., 1966-76; Bd. dirs. Elm Brook (Wis.) Meml. Hosp., 1969-71. Author: (with Bonnie Corey) Psychiatry in Nursing, 1949, I Think, Therefore I Know, 1996; contbr. numerous articles to profl. jours. 1st lt. Ft. Knox Armored Med. Rsch. Lab., AUS, 1945, to col. USPHS. Fellow Am. Psychiat. Assn. (life), Am. Coll. Psychiatry (emeritus); mem. State Med. Soc. Wis. (editorial dir. 1971-77), Wis. Psychiat. Assn. (pres. 1971-72), Milw. Club. Home and Office: 4535 N 92nd St Apt S308 Milwaukee WI 53225-5415 *My life story represents a gradual and often difficult transition from the puritan ethic, which got me into this book, to a lighter style of living. This is what the Germans call Lebenskünstler.*

HEADLEY, KATHRYN WILMA, secondary education educator; b. Grand Rapids, Mich., Mar. 10, 1940; d. William L. and Kathryn (Mekkes) H. BA, Hope Coll., 1967; MEd, Grand Valley Univ., 1981. Cert. tchr., Mich. Missionary Reformed Ch. in Am., N.Y.C., summers 1959-64; various ch. positions Ottawa Reformed Ch., West Olive, Mich., 1956—, Bible day camp dir., 1979-92; tchr. lang. arts/phys. edn. Jenison Pub. Schs. (Mich.), 1967—, head coach girls basketball, volleyball, 1967-78, head coach girls track, softball, 1967-73, head coach girls bowling, 1973-78, class advisor, 1983-90; numerous other sch. activities; coach girls soccer, basketball Borculo Christian Sch., Mich., 1981-88. Bd. dirs. Ottawa County Tchrs. Credit Union, Grand Haven, Mich., 1978-90, 94—, v.p., 1984-88. Mem. Mich. Edn. Assn. (rep.), NEA, Jenison Edn. Assn. (rep.), Mich. High Sch. Athletic Assn. (ofcl.), Hope Coll. Alumni Assn., Mich. Christian Endeavor Bd., Delta Kappa Gamma. Mem. Reformed Ch. in Am. Home: 9111 96th Ave RR 1 Zeeland MI 49464 Office: Jenison Pub Schs 2140 Bauer Rd Jenison MI 49428-9539 *Personal philosophy: After a life threatening experience following a 1982 surgery...I believe in the following quote, "I asked God for all things that I might enjoy life. He gave me life that I might enjoy all things." Each morning I wake up thanking God for another day and I try to make it a masterpiece.*

HEADLY, GLENNE AIMÉE, actress; b. New London, Conn., Mar. 13, 1959. Mem. of ensemble Steppenwolf Theatre. Appeared on stage in Curse of Starving Class, Balm in Gilead, Arms and the Man; films: Making Mr. Right, 1987, Nadine, 1987, Dirty Rotten Scoundrels, 1988, Paperhouse, 1989, Dick Tracy, 1990, Mortal Thoughts, 1991, Mr. Holland's Opus, 1995, Sgt. Bilko, 1995, Two Days in the Valley, 1996, Breakfast of Champions, 1998, Babe II, 1998; TV miniseries: Lonesome Dove, 1989 (Emmy nomination for best supporting actress); TV films include Seize the Day, 1986, And the Band Played on, 1994, Bastard Out of Carolina, 1996 (Emmy nomination for best supporting actress), E.R., 1996, Pronto, 1997, My Own Country, 1998, Winchell, 1998. Recipient three Joseph Jefferson awards for best supporting actress, Chgo.; named Best Newcomer Theatre World Award Com., N.Y. Office: Internat Creative Mgmt 8942 Wilshire Blvd Beverly Hills CA 90211-1934

HEADRICK, DANIEL RICHARD, history and social sciences educator; b. Bay Shore, N.Y., Aug. 2, 1941; s. William Cecil and Edith (Finkelstein) H.; m. Rita Koplowitz, June 20, 1965 (dec. 1988); children: Isabelle, Juliet, Matthew; m. Kate Ezra, Aug. 23, 1992. B, Lycée de Garcons, Metz, France, 1959; BA, Swarthmore Coll., 1962; MA, Johns Hopkins U., 1964; PhD, Princeton U., 1971. Instr. history Tuskegee (Ala.) Inst., 1968-71, asst. prof., 1971-73, assoc. prof., 1973-75; assoc. prof. social scis. Roosevelt U., Chgo., 1975-82, prof., 1982—; Author: Ejercito y Politica, 1981, The Tools of Empire, 1981, Tentacles of Progress, 1988, The Invisible Weapon, 1991, The Earth and Its Peoples, 1997. Coll. Tchrs. fellow NEH, 1983-84, 88-89, Guggenheim fellow, 1994, Sloan fellow, 1998; recipient Faculty Achievement award Burlington No. Found., 1988, 92. Mem. Am. Hist. Assn., World History Assn. (exec. com. 1991—), Soc. for History Tech. (exec. com. 1992—). Home: 5483 S Hyde Park Blvd Chicago IL 60615-5827 Office: Roosevelt U Univ Coll 430 S Michigan Ave Chicago IL 60605-1301

HEADRICK, THOMAS EDWARD, lawyer, educator; b. East Orange, N.J., June 28, 1933; s. Lewis Barnard and Marian Elizabeth (Rogers) H.; m. Mary Margaret Shontz, June 27, 1957; children—Trevor, Todd. B.A., Franklin and Marshall Coll., 1955; B.Litt., Oxford (Eng.) U., 1958; LL.B., Yale U., 1960; Ph.D., Stanford U., 1975. Bar: Conn. 1960, Calif. 1962. Asst. dir. Ansonia (Conn.) Redevel. Agy., 1959-60; law clk. to justice Wash. State Supreme Ct., Olympia, 1960-61; assoc. firm Pillsbury, Madison & Sutro, San Francisco, 1961-64; mgmt. cons. Emerson Cons., London, 1964-66, Baxter, McDonald & Co., Berkeley, Calif., 1966-67; asst. dean Stanford U. Law Sch., 1967-70; v.p. acad. affairs Lawrence U., 1970-76; dean law sch. U. at Buffalo, 1976-85, prof. law, 1976—, interim dean arts and letters faculty, 1990, disting. svc. prof., 1993—, provost, 1995-99, sr. counselor to pres., 1999—; cons. Nat. Endowment for Humanities, NSF; legal commentator Sta. WKBW-TV, 1978-80. Author: The Town Clerk in English Local Government, 1962; co-editor Law and Policy, 1988-92. Mem. Law and Soc. Assn., Phi Beta Kappa. Office: University at Buffalo 562 Capen Hall Buffalo NY 14260-0101

HEAFEY, EDWIN AUSTIN, JR., lawyer; b. Oakland, Calif., Nov. 1, 1930; s. Edwin Austin Sr. and Florence (Jochim) H.; married; children: Ryan, Matthew, Alison. AB, U. Santa Clara, 1952; LLB, Stanford U., 1955. Bar: Calif. 1955, U.S. Dist. Ct. (no. and cen. dists.) Calif. 1955, U.S. Supreme Ct. 1984. Sr. ptnr. Crosby, Heafey, Roach & May, Oakland, 1955—; instr. law U. Calif., Berkeley, 1963-78; bd. fellows Georgetown Law Sch. Author: California Trial Objections, 1967, 6th edit., 1998. Trustee U. Santa Clara. Fellow Am. Bd. Trial Advs. (life, sr., past pres.); mem. ATLA, Am. Bar Found., Am., Calif. Trial Lawyers Assn., Am. Coll. Trial Lawyers, Calif. Bar Assn., Alameda County Bar Assn., San Francisco Bar Assn., Internat. Soc. Barrister, Claremont Country Club, Pacific Union Club. Office: Crosby Heafey Roach & May Profl Corp PO Box 7936 4 Embarcadero Ctr 19th Fl San Francisco CA 94111-4106 also: Crosby Heafey Roach & May Profl Corp 1999 Harrison St PO Box 2084 Oakland CA 94604-2084 also: Crosby Heafey Roach & May Profl Corp Ste 2200 700 South Flower St Los Angeles CA 90017-4209 also: Ste 3870 2049 Century Park East Los Angeles CA 90067

HEAGARTY, MARGARET CAROLINE, pediatric physician; b. Charleston, W.Va., Sept. 8, 1934; d. John Patrick and Margaret Caroline (Walsh) H. BA, Seton Hill Coll., 1957; BS, W.Va. Sch. Medicine, 1959; MD, U. Pa., 1961; DSc honoris causa, Iona Coll., 1989. Diplomate: Am. Bd. Pediatrics. Intern Phila. Gen. Hosp., 1961-62; resident in pediatrics St. Christopher's Hosp. for Children, Phila., 1962-64; dir. pediatric ambulatory care services N.Y. Hosp.-Cornell Med. Ctr., N.Y.C., 1969-78; dir. pediatrics Harlem Hosp. Ctr. Columbia U., N.Y.C., 1978—, prof. pediatrics Coll. Physicians & Surgeons, 1987—; cons. Dept. HEW Promotion of Child Health, Washington; mem. Com. Community Oriented Primary Care Inst. Medicine, Washington; mem. Robert Wood Johnson Found. Program for Prepaid Managed Health Care, 1984; mem. governing council Inst. Medicine, Nat. Acad. Scis., 1986. Author: Changing the Medical Car System-Report of an Experiment, 1974, Medical Sociology: A Systems Approach, 1975, Child Health: Basics for Primary Care, 1980. Grantee Commonwealth Found., 1981, Robert Wood Johnson Found., 1983, Ctr. for Disease Control, 1985, Health Rsch. and Svc. Adminstrn., 1988, Nat. Inst. Allergy/Infectious Disease, 1988. Fellow Inst. Medicine (steering group for nat. forum on future of children and their families 1987—); mem. Ambulatory Pediatric Assn. (pres. 1976-77), Soc. Pediatric Research, Am. Pediatric Soc., Am. Acad. Pediatrics (com. on hosp. care 1988—), Assn. Pediatric Program Dirs., Nat. Bd. Med. Examiners. E-mail: mheagarty@aol.com. Home: 2520 Kingsland Ave Bronx NY 10469-6108 Office: Columbia U-Harlem Hosp Ctr 506 Lenox Ave New York NY 10037-1802

HEAGY, THOMAS CHARLES, banker; b. Fresno, Calif., Jan. 4, 1945; s. Clarence H. and Ruth (Geer) H.; m. Regina Victoria Polk, Apr. 12, 1980 (dec. Oct. 1983); m. Linda Anne Hutton, Jan. 10, 1987. BA in Physics, U. Chgo., 1967, MBA with honors, 1970; MSc in Fin., London Sch. Econs., 1970. Dep. mgr. mgmt. scis. First Nat. Bank Chgo., 1970-75; chmn. bd., chief exec. officer South Shore Nat. Bank, Chgo., 1975-80; exec. v.p. Exchange Nat. Bank Chgo., 1980-90; vice chmn. LaSalle Nat. Bank, 1990—, LaSalle Nat. Corp., 1990—; CFO ABN AMRO N.Am., 1996—. Bd. dirs. Chgo. Symphony, 1995—, The Regina V. Polk Scholarship Fund, Chgo., 1983—, Mus. Contemporary Art, Chgo., 1994—, Chgo. Music and Dance Theater, 1994—; vis. com. Oriental Inst., U. Chgo., 1988—; mem. The Renaissance Soc., 1989—; governing bd. Chgo. Assn. Commerce and Industry, 1991—, Chgo. ctrl. area com., 1996—; endowment com. Am. Rsch. Ctr. Egypt, 1996—. Home: 4939 S Greenwood Ave Chicago IL 60615-2815 Office: LaSalle Nat Bank 135 S Lasalle St Fl 5 Chicago IL 60603-4174

HEAL, GEOFFREY MARTIN, economics educator; b. Bangor, Wales, Apr. 9, 1944; s. Thomas John and Gwen Margaret (Owen) H.; children: Bridget, Natasha. BA first class, Cambridge U., 1966, PhD, 1969. Dir. studies Christs Coll., Cambridge U., 1967-73; prof. econs. Sussex U., Brighton, Eng., 1973-81, head dept. econs., 1976-81; mng. editor Rev. Econ. Studies, London, 1973-78; dir. Economists Adv. Group, London, 1975-80; prof. Essex U., Colchester, Eng., 1981-83; exec. dir. Fin. Telecommunications, London, 1984-89; prof. Grad. Sch. Bus., Columbia U., N.Y.C., 1983—; sr. vice dean Grad. Sch. Bus. Columbia U., 1991-94; Fulbright prof. U. Siena, Italy, 1997; Paul Garret prof. pub. policy and corp. responsibility Columbia U., N.Y.C., 1995—; cons. U.K. Dept. Energy, London, 1973-76, U.S. Dept. Energy, Washington, 1976-78, OPEC Sec. Gen., Vienna, Austria, 1979-81, OECD, Paris, 1994, Global Environ. Facility, World Bank, 1994. Author: The Theory of Economic Planning, 1973, Public Policy and the Tax System, 1976, Economic Theory and Exhaustible Resources, 1979, Linear Algebra and Linear Economics, 1980, The Evolving International Economy, 1987, Oil in the International Economy, 1991, The Economics of Exhaustible Resources, 1993, Sustainability: Dynamics and Uncertainty, 1998, Valuing the Future, 1998, Topological Methods in Social Choice, 1998, The Economics of Increasing Returns, 1998. Grantee NSF, NOAA, Sloan Found. Fellow Econometric Soc., Royal Soc. Arts. Home: 400 W 119th St Apt 13H New York NY 10027-7149 Office: Columbia Univ Bus Sch Uris Hall New York NY 10027

HEALD, BRUCE DAY, English and music educator, historian; b. Boston, June 5, 1935; s. Henry M. and Muriel D. (Day) H. m. Helen Peaslee, May 21, 1960; children: William Forristall III, Craig, Eric Bentley, Allyson Kaye. A.A., Boston U., 1956; B.S. in Music Edn., Lowell State U., 1959; M.A., Columbia Pacific U., 1984, Ph.D., 1985. Supr. music Ashland-Meredith Union 2, Meredith, N.H., 1959-65; dir. music, lectr. fine arts Belknap Coll., Center Harbor, N.H., 1963-65; dir. bands Plattsburgh (N.Y.) City Schs., 1969-70; supr. music Inter-Lakes Sch. Dist., Meredith, 1965-69, dir. music edn., 1970-77; dir. instrumental music Kennebunk (Maine) High Sch., 1977-79; prodn. mgr. Annalee Mobilitee Dolls, Meredith, 1979-81; lectr. English and journalism Moultonborough Acad., 1981-86; dir. music Congl. Ch., Laconia, N.H., 1985-86; chair English dept. Holy Trinity Sch., Laconia, 1987—; mentor Columbia Pacific U., 1986—; instr. music N.H. Coll., Manchester, 1988—; historian Weirstimes Pub. Co., 1992—; lectr. English lit. Plymouth State Coll., 1995-97, lectr. U.S. history, 1998—. Author: Follow the Mount, 1968, 70, 93, 97, Postmaster of the Lake, 1971, Mail Service on the Lake, 1980, Steamboats in Motion, 1984, New Hampshire Learnin' Days, 1987, Boats 'n Ports I and II, 1989, Landmarks and Legacy, 1990, The Boston See Party, 1991, Reminisce the Valley, 1992, Shadows in the Window, 1995, Images of America: Meredith, 1996, Images of America: The Lakes Region of New Hampshire, 1996, vol. I and II, 1998, Images of America: The Upper Merrimack to Winnipesaukee by Rail, 1997, Images of America: Boats and Ports in Lake Winnipesaukee, vol. I and II, 1998, Images of America: The White Mountains Region by Rail, 1999, Image of America: Plymouth State College, 1999; composer: Kennebunk Concert March, The Hills of Old N.H., Moultonboro Concert March, Cascades, Trilogy. Commr. Parks and Playgrounds, Meredith, 1966-69; selectman Town of Meredith, 1971-76; pres. Lake Winnipesaukee Hist. Soc. Served with USMC, 1954-62. Mem. Nat. Catholic Edn. Assn., Masons, Order Eastern Star. Republican. Home: PO Box 1052 Meredith NH 03253-1052 Office: Holy Trinity Sch Laconia NH 03246

HEALD, DARREL VERNER, retired Canadian federal judge; b. Regina, Sask., Can., Aug. 27, 1919; s. Herbert Verner and Lottie (Knudson) H.; m. Doris Rose Hessey, June 30, 1951; children: Lynn, Brian. B.A., U. Sask., 1938, LL.B., 1940. Bar: Called to Sask. bar 1941. Partner firm Noonan, Embury, Heald, Molisky and Gritzfeld, Regina, until 1964; atty. gen. and provincial sec. Province Sask., 1964-71; MLA for Lumsden dist. Sask. Legislative Assembly, Regina, 1964-71; judge trial div. Fed. Ct. Can., Ottawa, Ont., 1971-75; judge Fed. Ct. Appeal, Ottawa, 1975-94. Served with RCAF, 1941-45. Home: 44 Aleutian Rd, Ottawa, ON Canada K2H 7C8

HEALD, MORRELL, humanities educator; b. Oak Park, Ill., July 16, 1922; s. Howard Leslie and Helen (Morrell) H.; m. Barbara Legg, June 25, 1949; children—David M., Seth G., Sarah H. A.B., Yale U., 1946, A.M., 1947, Ph.D., 1951. Instr. history Yale, 1950-53; mem. faculty Case Inst. Tech., 1953-68, asso. prof. history, 1958-68, chmn. dept. humanities and social studies, 1959-62; prof. Am. studies Case Western Res. U., 1968-82, Samuel B. and Virginia C. Knight prof. humanities, 1982-88, prof. emeritus, 1988—, chmn. div. spl. interdisciplinary studies, 1971-78, 79-82; vis. prof. Am. history Indian Inst. Tech., Kanpur, 1966-67; dir. Armington Research Program on Values in Children, 1978-80, chmn. adv. com., 1978-82. Author: The Social Responsibilities of Business: Company and Community, 1900-1960, 1970, Japanese edit., 1974, 2d edit., 1988, Transatlantic Vistas: American Journalists in Europe, 1900-1940, 1987; (with Lawrence S. Kaplan) Culture and Diplomacy: The American Experience, 1977; co-editor: The Aims and Organization of Liberal Studies, 1966. Vice pres. Cleveland Heights Your Schools Com., 1962, pres., 1965; Pres. of the First Ward Democratic Club,

Cleveland Heights, 1962; mem. Cleve. Heights Landmarks Commn., 1987—. Served with AUS, 1943-45, ETO. Mem. Soc. for History of Am. Fgn. Rels., Western Res. Hist. Soc. (publs. com. 1981-89), Phi Beta Kappa. Episcopalian. Home: 2219 Demington Dr Cleveland OH 44106-3320

HEALEY, DAVID LEE, investment company executive; b. Pomona, Calif., Dec. 13, 1950; s. Robert Lincoln Sr. and Bernice (Mayes) H.; m. Barbara Petty, June 24, 1995; children: Paul Marcus, Elaina Rose. BS, U. Tulsa, 1978, postgrad. in law, 1979-80; cert., N.Y. Inst. Fin., 1980. Sales mgr. Magnavox, Tulsa, 1978-80; dir. tng. First State Fin., Tulsa, 1980-81; asst. v.p. Prudential-Bache Securities, Tulsa, 1981-86, E.F. Hutton, Tulsa, 1986-91, Paine Webber, Inc., Tulsa, 1991—; sales cons., Tulsa, 1981—. Judge Miss Teen USA pageant, 1984; chair endowment fund adv. com. Tulsa YWCA. Sgt. USAF, 1974-78. Mem. Internat. Assn. Fin. Planners (bd. dirs. 1984), Toastmasters Internat. (speakers bur.). Republican. Baptist. Avocations: computer programming, antique car restoration, public speaking. Home: 3269 Riverside Dr Apt 240 Tulsa OK 74105-1836 Office: Paine Webber 321 S Boston Ave Ste 1010 Tulsa OK 74103-3324

HEALEY, DEBORAH LYNN, education administrator; b. Columbus, Ohio, Sept. 15, 1952; d. James Henry and Marjorie Jean Healey; 1 child, Jesse Healey Winterowd. BA in German/Religion, Queen's U., 1974; MA in Linguistics, U. Oreg., 1976, PhD in Edn., 1993. Instr. Lane C.C., Eugene, Oreg., 1976-77; instr., materials developer Rogue C.C., Ashland, Oreg., 1977-79; instr. Chemeketa C.C., Salem, Oreg., 1979-80; instr., computer ops. English Lang. Inst. Oreg. State U., Corvallis, 1979-85, 88-93; instr., computer ops. Yemen-Am. Lang. Inst., Sana'a, Yemen, 1985-88; programmer, cons. Internat. Soc. for Tech. in Edn., Eugene, 1989-91; coord. instr. English Lang. Inst. Oreg. State U., Corvallis, 1993-95, tech. coord., 1995-99, dir., 1999—; Macintosh support Computer-Enhanced Lang. Instrn. Archive, 1993—; computer cons. in field. Author: (book) Something To Do On Tuesday, 1995; co-author: (chpts.) A Handbook for Language Program Administrators, 1997, CAL Environments Research, Practice and Critical Issues, 1999; editor, author Computer-Assisted English Lang. Learning Jour., 1990-98; co-editor (ann. publ.) CALL Interest Sect. Software List, 1990—; co-author (software) The House, At The Zoo, 1993. Mem. TESOL (interest sect. chair 1992-92), Oreg. TESOL (newsletter editor 1981-84), Nat. Assn. Fgn. Student Advisors-Assn. Internat. Educators, Am. Ednl. Rsch. Assn., Computer Assn. Lang. Instrn. Consortium. Avocations: language learning, traveling, music, reading. Office: ELI Oreg State Univ 301 Snell Hall Corvallis OR 97331-8515

HEALEY, EDWARD HOPKINS, architect; b. Dubuque, Iowa, Jan. 3, 1925; s. George Beach and Marian (Hopkins) H.; m. Alice Letitia Dawson, Sept. 11, 1954; children: Susan Healey Toussaint, Carolyn Healey Olson, Ellen Hopkins Healey. BS in Architecture, U. Ill., 1950; cert., Ecoles D'Art Americaines, Fountainbleau, France, 1950. Registered architect, Iowa, Ill., Wis., Minn. Ptnr. Brown & Healey, Architects, Cedar Rapids, Iowa, 1953-60, Brown, Healey & Bock, Architects and Engrs., Cedar Rapids, 1960-81; pres. Brown, Healey & Bock, Architects, Planners, Interior Designers, Cedar Rapids, 1981-90, Brown, Healey, Stone & Sauer, Architects, Planners, Interior Designers, Cedar Rapids, 1990-95. Del. The White House Conf. on Libraries and Info. Svcs., Washington, 1979, 91; pres. profl. adv. bd. dept. architecture Iowa State U., Ames, 1981-82; pres. East Cen. Regional Library Bd., Cedar Rapids, 1981-84; mem. Iowa Library Commn., Des Moines, 1987-90, chmn., 1987-89; bd. dirs. Iowa Cultural Affairs Adv. Coun., Des Moines, 1987-89; trustee Linn County Hist. Mus., 1990—, pres., 1995-96; trustee Brucemore, 1983-89. Fellow AIA (Iowa medal of Honor 1996, pres. Iowa chpt. 1965-66); mem. ALA, Nat. Coun. Archtl. Registration Bds. (bd. dirs. 1975-77), Literary Club (sec. 1980-86, pres. 1987-88). Avocations: sailing, swimming. Home: 2500 White Eagle Trl SE Cedar Rapids IA 52403-1548 Office: Brown Healey Stone & Sauer Architects PC 800 1st Ave NE Cedar Rapids IA 52402-5002

HEALEY, FRANK HENRY, retired research executive; b. Worcester, Mass., Oct. 5, 1924; s. Frank H. and Elizabeth (MacGillivray) H.; m. Loretta Marguerite Finnigan, June 5, 1948; children: Steven Allan, Elaine Elizabeth, Frank Henry. A.B., Clark U., 1947, Ph.D., 1949. Asst. prof. chemistry Lehigh U., Bethlehem, Pa., 1949-56; with Lever Bros. Co., Edgewater, N.J., 1956-88, v.p. research and devel., 1964-73, research v.p., 1973-78, v.p. research and engring., 1978-80, research v.p., dir., 1968-88; pres. Lever Research Inc., Edgewater, 1982-88. Served to lt. (j.g.) USN, 1943-46. Mem. Indsl. Rsch. Inst. (pres. 1977-78, bd. dirs. 1972-79), Assn. Rsch. Dirs., Am. Chem. Soc., Dirs. Indsl. Rsch., Am. Oil Chemists Soc., Soap and Detergent Assn. (steering com. tech. and materials divsn.), Ridgewood Country Club (sec. 1981-82, bd. dirs. 1990-94), Hobbyists Unlimited (v.p. 1994-95, pres. 1996). Home: 255 W Ridgewood Ave Ridgewood NJ 07450-3629

HEALEY, JOHN G., human services organization executive; b. Pitts., Mar. 24, 1938; s. Martin A. and Mary (Gaughan) H. B.A., St. Fidelis Coll., Herman, Pa.; M.A., Capuchin Coll., Washington; LHD (hon.), Southeastern Mass. U., 1987; HHD (hon.), Providence Coll., 1988; LLD (hon.), Northeastern U. Law Sch., 1988; PhD (hon.), Bridgewater State Coll., 1989; LLD (hon.), Notre Dame Coll., N.H., 1992, Old Dominion U., 1993; D Pub. Svc. (hon.), Westfield State Coll., Mass., 1992. Ordained priest, Roman Cath. Ch., 1966, laicized, 1969. Exec. dir. Freedom From Hunger, 1969-74; program officer Ctr. for Commnity Change, Washington, 1974-77; country dir. Peace Corps, Lesotho, 1977-81; exec. dir. Amnesty Internat., N.Y.C., 1981-93; exec. producer Conspiracy of Hope Tour, 1986, Human Rights Now! World Tour, 1988; producer Desde Chile, Un Abrazo a la Esperanza (concerts) Santiago, 1990; pres. Action Ctr. for Human Rights; bd. dirs. Internat. Voluntary Service, 1970-74; chair Internat. Devel. Conf., 1971; charter mem. Inst. Food and Devel., San Francisco, 1975. Recipient Merton award Merton Ctr., Pitts., 1976, MTV Disting. Svc. awrad, 1986, Internat. Rock "Elvis" award, 1989, Madison award Phila. Soc. Profl. Journalists, 1989, Global Cedar Rapids award, 1990, Sean MacBride award Irish Am. Unity Conf., 1991, Billboard music award Bill Graham Assn., 1991, recognition Irish Am. mag., 1991, Martin Luther King, Jr. Spirit award House of Blues, L.A., 1996; named Person of Week, ABC Nightly News, Peter Jennings, 1988; subject of profile U.S. News & World Report, 1991. Address: 451 1st St SE Washington DC 20003-1827*

HEALEY, MYRON DANIEL, actor; b. Petaluma, Calif., June 8, 1923; s. Robert Daniel and California Myrtle (Penney) H.; m. Dorothy Ann Pemberton, Dec. 26, 1944 (div. June 1949); 1 child, Christine Ann Healey Dickerson; m. Elizabeth Mary D'Errico, Dec. 3, 1966 (div. Sept. 2, 1970); 1 child, Mikel Derrica. U.S. Army Coll. Tng. Cert., East Cen. Tchrs. Coll., 1943. Freelance actor, writer, dialogue dir., drama coach, Hollywood, Calif., N.Y.C., Bombay, Honolulu, Manila, 1941—; dir. Santa Monica (Calif.) Theater Guild, 1949. Author: (tng. manual) Info. Officers Guide, 1955; screenwriter: Colorado Ambush, 1951, Texas Lawman, 1951. Capt. USAFR, 1943-46, ETO. Decorated Air medal with Cluster. Mem. Screen Actors Guild, AFTRA, Writers Guild of Am. West, Am. Film Inst. Avocations: photography, archtl. design, swimming, cycling, camping.

HEALEY, ROBERT WILLIAM, school system administrator; b. Charleston, Ill., Sept. 29, 1947; s. William Albert and Ruth M. (Wiedenhoeft) H.; m. Sharon Barbara Grande, Aug. 7, 1982; children: William Robert, Steven Anthony. BS in Elem. Edn., Ea. Ill. U., 1970, MS in Ednl. Adminstrn., 1972; EdD in Curriculum and Supervision, No. Ill. U., 1977. Cert. elem. teaching K-9, gen. adminstrv. K-12, Ill. Prin. Glidden Elem. Sch., De Kalb, Ill., 1972-74, Lincoln Elem. Sch., De Kalb, 1974-83, Littlejohn Elem. Sch., De Kalb, 1983-84, Littlejohn and Cortland Elem. Schs., De Kalb, 1984-85; prin., dist. coord. testing and evaluation Jefferson Elem. Sch., De Kalb, 1986-96; dir. personnel DeKalb Sch. Dist., 1996—; dir. Title I Elem. and Secondary Edn. Act., Pre-Sch. Base Line Program, 1972-74; dir. gifted edn. Bd. Edn. Negotiating Team, 1974-81, coordinator dist. testing and evaluation, 1981-84, coordinator spl. edn., 1984-86; mem. adv. bd. Evanston (Ill.) Educators Computer Software, 1983—; dir. testing DeKalb Sch. Dist. 428, 1986—; treas. No. Ill. Commn. for Gifted Edn., Oakbrook, 1980-82; mem. various elem. sch. planning and program councils, De Kalb, 1973—; coordinator numerous sch. programs, De Kalb, 1973—; leader numerous workshops DeKalb, 1976-85; sec. De Kalb Sch. Bd. Study com. on sch. lunch programs, 1976-77; cons. Scholastic Testing Service, 1980-83; chmn. dist. reading com., De Kalb, 1986—. Coordinator 10 yr. study of student achievement in DeKalb Schs., 1980-83; author numerous presentations, 1975-84; revisor DeKalb School District Parent Handbook, 1986; contbr. articles to profl. jours; inventor multi-purpose table and stage. Chmn. Task Force I DeKalb Sch. Dist., 1973-75; treas. No. Ill. Planning Commn., 1980-82; active Supts. Task Force on Spl. Edn., DeKalb, 1976-79, Mayor's Commn. DeKalb Planning Commn. for Yr. of Child, DeKalb, 1979, Dist. Computer Com., DeKalb, 1980-83, Dist. Revenue and Donations Com., 1980-83, Ill. PTA. Recipient Disting. Program award Nat. Assn. for Tchr. Educators, Chgo., 1978; named Citizen of Day, Sta. WLBK, De Kalb, 1983; Reading is Fundamental grantee Lincoln Sch., 1980-83, Ill. Ctr., 1980-83, Ill. Arts Coun., Littlejohn Sch., 1984, Jefferson Sch., 1986; named master, Ill. Adminstrs. Acad., 1995. Mem. NEA (life), ASCD, NAESP (Nat. Disting. Prin. award representing Ill. 1995), Ill. Prins. Assn. (Prin. of Yr. award 1995, Herman Graves award 1998), Ill. Assn. for Supervsion and Curriculum Devel., Soc. Am. Inventors, Ill. Coun. Gifted Edn. Avocations: swimming, computer, home improvement. Office: De Kalb Cmty Unit Sch Dist 901 S 4th St Dekalb IL 60115

HEALTON, BRUCE CARNEY, data processing executive; b. Montebello, Calif., Oct. 22, 1955; s. Donald Carney and Doris May (Kubler) H.; m. Deborah Louise Stevens, Nov. 26, 1977; children: Alexander Carney, Michaela Shawn. BA of Bus., Western Ill. Univ., 1977; Cert. Brokerage Ops., N.Y. Inst. of Fin., 1986. Programmer Westinghouse Learning Corp., Iowa City, 1977-78; contract programmer Cutler-Williams, Mpls., 1978-79; programmer/analyst Northwest Computer Svcs., Mpls., 1979-81; cons. Cytrol, Edina, Minn., 1981-90; cons./pres. Elegant Tech. Solutions, Brooklyn Park, Minn., 1990—; treas. Minn. Joint Computer Conf., Mpls., 1990-91, asst. treas., 1989-90. Mem. IEEE (cons. software com. 1989-90), Assn. for Computing Machinery, Twin Cities (sec. 1987-89, chmn. 1993-96, past chmn. 1997—). Office: Elegant Tech Solutions 8480 Yates Ave N Minneapolis MN 55443-2186

HEALY, ALICE FENVESSY, psychology educator, researcher; b. Chgo., June 26, 1946; d. Stanley John and Doris (Goodman) Fenvessy; m. James Bruce Healy, May 9, 1970; 1 dau., Charlotte Alexandra. AB summa cum laude, Vassar Coll., 1968; PhD, Rockefeller U., 1973. Asst. prof. psychology Yale U., New Haven, 1973-78, assoc. prof. psychology, 1978-81; assoc. prof. psychology U. Colo., Boulder, 1981-84, prof. psychology, 1984—; rsch. assoc. Haskins Labs., New Haven, 1976-80; mem. com. NIMH, Washington, 1979-81; co-investigator rsch. contract USAF, U. Colo., 1985-86; prin. investigator rsch. contract U.S. Army Rsch. Inst., U. Colo., 1986—, Naval Tng. Systems Ctr., 1993-94; rsch. grant prin. investigator U.S. Army Rsch. Office, U. Colo., 1995—, NASA, 1999—. Co-author: Cognitive Processes, 2d edit., 1986; editor: Memory and Cognition, 1986-89, (with S.M. Kosslyn and R.M. Shiffrin) From Learning Theory to Connectionist Theory: Essays in Honor of William K. Estes, Vol. I, 1992, From Learning Processes to Cognitive Processes: Essays in Honor of William K. Estes, Vol. II, 1992, (with L.E. Bourne Jr.) Learning and Memory of Knowledge and Skills: Durability and Specificity, 1995, Foreign Language Learning: Psycholinguistic Studies on Training and Retention, 1998; assoc. editor Jour. Exptl. Psychology, 1982-84; contbr. more than 120 articles to profl. jours. and chpts. to books. Recipient Sabbatical award James McKeen Cattell Fund, 1987-88; NSF Rsch. grantee, 1977-86, Spencer Found. Rsch. grantee, 1978-80. Fellow APA (exec. com. divsn. 3 1989-92, chair membership com. 1992-93), AAAS (nominating com. 1988-91, chair 1991, chair-elect psychology sect. 1994, chair psychology sect. 1995-96, retiring chair psychology sect. 1996-97), Soc. Exptl. Psychologists; mem. Psychonomic Soc. (governing bd. 1987-92, publs. com. 1989-93), Soc. Math. Psychology, Rocky Mountain Psychology Assn. (pres.-elect 1993-94, pres. 1994-95, past pres. 1995-96), Cognitive Sci. Soc., Soc. for Applied Rsch. in Memory and Cognition, Univ. Club, Phi Beta Kappa, Sigma Xi. Avocation: French pastries. Home: 840 Cypress Dr Boulder CO 80303-2820 Office: U Colo Dept Psychology PO Box 345 Boulder CO 80309-0345

HEALY, BARBARA ANNE, insurance company executive, financial planner; b. Chgo., May 21, 1951; d. William James Healy and Eileen Mary (Dooley) Dashiell; m. Joel Feldman, June 25, 1991. BA, No. Ill. U., 1973; MBA, DePaul U., 1976. Cert. fin. planner. Dept. head, instr. St. Benedict High Sch., Chgo., 1973-76; account rep. Xerox Corp., Chgo., 1976-78, mktg. specialist, 1978-79, high volume sr. sales exec., 1979-81; western dist. mgr. McGraw Hill, N.Y.C., 1981-82; fin. planner United Resources Ins. Service, Torrance, Calif., 1982-83, sales mgr., 1983-85, exec. v.p., 1985-86; regional v.p. United Resources Ins. Service, Foster City, Calif., 1986-89; v.p., nat. mktg. dir. Met. Life Resources (formerly United Resources Ins. Svcs.), Phoenix, 1990—; Tempe, Ariz.; instr. Trenton Coll., Riverside, Ill., City Coll. Chgo., Northeastern Ill. U., Chgo., Prairie State Coll., Chicago Heights, 1976-81. Author: Financial Planning for Educators, 1987; contbr. articles to prof. jours.; speaker in field. Mem. Internat. Assn. Fin. Planners, Inst. Cert. Fin. Planners, Registry Fin. Planning Practitioners, Nat. Council Fin. Edn. Republican. Roman Catholic. Avocations: flying, skiing, scuba diving, horse back riding. Home: 20791 W Chartwell Dr Lake Zurich IL 60047-8542 Office: Met Life Resources 426 N 44th St Phoenix AZ 85008-6508

HEALY, BERNADINE P., physician, educator, federal agency administrator, scientist; b. N.Y.C., Aug. 2, 1944; d. Michael J. and Violet (McGrath) Healy; m. Floyd Loop, Aug. 17, 1985; children: Bartlett Anne Bulkley, Marie McGrath Loop. AB summa cum laude, Vassar Coll., 1965; MD cum laude, Harvard Med. Sch., 1970. Diplomate Am. Bd. Med. Examiners, Am. Bd. Cardiology, Am. Bd. Internal Medicine (bd. dirs. 1983-87); lic. physician, Md., Ohio. Intern in medicine Johns Hopkins Hosp., Balt., 1970-71, asst. resident, 1971-72; staff fellow sect. pathology Nat. Heart, Blood & Lung Inst., NIH, Bethesda, Md., 1972-74; fellow cardiovascular div. dept. medicine Johns Hopkins U. Sch. Medicine, Balt., 1974-76, fellow dept. pathology, 1975-76, asst. prof. medicine and pathology, 1976-81, assoc. prof. medicine, 1977-82, asst. dean postdoctoral programs and faculty devel., 1979-84, assoc. prof. pathology, 1981-84, prof. medicine, 1982-84; dean Coll. Med. and Pub. Health Johns Hopkins U. Sch. Medicine, 1995—, prof. internal medicine, physiology, 1995—; active staff medicine and pathology Johns Hopkins Hosp., 1976—, dir. CCU, 1977-84; dep. dir. Office Sci. and Tech. Policy Exec. Office of Pres., White House, Washington, 1984-85; chmn. Rsch. Inst. The Cleve. Clinic Found., 1985-91, sr. health and sci. policy advisor, 1994-95; dean Med. Sch. Ohio State U., 1995-97; dir. NIH, Bethesda, Md., 1991-93; vice-chmn. Pres.' Coun. Advisers on Sci. and Tech., 1990-91; mem. Spl. Med. Adv. Group, Dept. Vet.'s Affairs, 1990-91, chmn. adv. panel for Basic Rsch. for 1990s, office Tech. Assessment, 1990-91, mem. NHLBI Task Force on Atherosclerosis, 1990; mem. Vis. Com. Bd. Overseers Harvard Med. Sch. and Sch. of Dental Medicine, Boston, 1986-91; councillor Harvard Med. Alumni Assn., 1987-90; mem. Nat. Adv. Bd. Johns Hopkins Ctr. for Hosp. Fin. and Mgmt., 1987-91; mem. Bd. Overseers Harvard Coll., 1989—; chmn. Office of Tech. Assessment Panel New Devels. in Biotech., U.S. Congress, 1986-87; mem. U.S.-Brazil Panel on Sci. and Tech., 1987; mem. White House Sci. Coun., 1988-89; cons. Nat. Heart, Lung and Blood Inst., NIH, 1976-91, mem. Adv. Com. to Dir., NIH, 1986-91; chmn. steering com. Post-CABG Clin. Trial, 1987-91; bd. dirs. Medtronic, Inc., Mpls., Nat. City Corp., Cleve., Nova Pharms., Balt.; mem. adv. bd. Bayer Fund for Cardiovascular Rsch., N.Y.C., 1987-89; trustee Edison BioTech. Ctr., Cleve., 1990—; chmn. Ohio Coun. on Rsch. and Econ. Devel., 1989-91; Editl. cons. numerous jours.; abstract reviewer; editl. bd. Jour. Cardiovascular Medicine, 1980-91, Am. Jour. Medicine, 1986-91, Am. Jour. Cardiology, 1981-82, Circulation, 1981—, Jour. Am. Coll. Cardiology, 1982-84; contbr. articles to profl. jours. Matthew Vassar scholar, 1962-65, Harvard Nat. scholar, 1965-70; Eloise Ellery fellow, 1965-66, Stetler Rsch. fellow, 1976-77; recipient Nat. Bd. Ann. award for Medicine, Med. Coll. Pa., 1983. Mem. Am. Fedn. Clin. Rsch. (pres. 1983-84), Am. Heart Assn. (award 1983-84, 90, pres. 1988-89, fellow coun. on Clin. Cardiology, Coun. on Circulation, dir. 1983-84), Am. Coll. Cardiology (bd. govs. 1979-82), ACP, Assn. Am. Med. Colls., Internat. Acad. Pathology, Am. Med. Women's Assn., Assn. for Women in Sci., Am. Soc. Clin. Investigation, Am. Bd. Internal Medicine (bd. govs. 1986—), Inst. Medicine, NAS, Johns Hopkins U. Soc. Scholars, Phi Beta Kappa, Alpha Omega Alpha. Office: Ohio State Univ Coll Medicine 254 Meiling Hall 370 W 9th Ave Columbus OH 43210-1238*

HEALY, DANIEL THOMAS, secondary education educator; b. Wenona, Ill., May 25, 1930; s. Timothy John and Helen Ann (Duller) H.; m. Beverly Ann Imm, Oct. 1, 1966; 1 child, Owen Jay. AA, Fresno (Calif.) City Coll., 1972; BS, Calif. State U., Fresno, 1974; MA, Azusa (Calif.) Pacific U., 1980. Farmer Wenona, 1948-58; mgr. Garfield Grain Elevator, Wenona, 1958-66; supt. Cargill Inc., San Joaquin, Calif., 1966-69; educator Redlands (Calif.) Unified Sch. Dist., 1974—; advisor Future Farmers of Am., Redlands High Sch., 1974-88; leader Osage Livewires 4-H Club, Wenona, 1950-55. Performer on nat. TV, movies including Hero and Hot Shots II, appearances as Pres. Bush celebrity look-alike, 1990—. Sgt. U.S. Army, 1953-54. Fellow Am. Legion (life mem.), Elks (life). Roman Catholic. Office: Orangewood High Sch 515 Texas St Redlands CA 92374-3071

HEALY, DONALD EUGENE, JR., special education educator, consultant; b. Chgo., Sept. 27, 1953; s. Donald E. Sr. and Ida Belle (Mackey) H.; m. Katherine Sue Witty, June 14, 1975; children: Caitlin, Ian. BS in Edn., Ill. State U., 1975, MS in Edn., 1979; EdS, Western Ill. U., 1984; PhD, U. Iowa, 1992. Cert. adminstv. and tchg. elem. edn. and spl. edn., Ill., Iowa. Spl. edn. tchr. Black Hawk Area Spl. Edn. Ctr., E. Moline, Ill., 1977-80, asst. prin., 1980-86; elem. tchr. Ericsson Sch., Moline, Ill., 1986-91; elem. prin. Willard Sch., Moline, 1992-96; owner, dir. H.E.A.L.Y. Consulting, Rock Island, Ill., 1995—; asst. prof. Mary Crest Internat. U., Davenport, Iowa, 1996-97; asst. prof. spl. edn. dept. Western Ill. U., Macomb, 1997—; cons. Ill. State Bd. Edn., Springfield, 1996—, Grant Basic Intensive Elem., Rock Island, 1998, Chgo. Pub. Schs., 1998—, Regional Offices Edn., Moline, Annawan, Ill. Writer, dir. (ednl. video) The Syndrome of Autism, 1990. Event dir. Miss. Valley Spl. Olympics, Moline, 1976-96. Spl. Olympic scholar Chgo. Park Dist. Spl. Olympics, 1972-75. Mem. ASCD, Coun. Exceptional Children, Ill. Quad City C. of C. (mem. com.), Phi Delta Kappa (Outstanding Doctoral Dissertation award 1995). Roman Catholic. Avocations: gourment cooking, creative writing, Greco-Roman culture, reading, internet. E-mail: DE-Healy@wiu.edu. Home: 2227 26th St Rock Island IL 61201 Office: Western Ill U 3561 60th St Moline IL 61265

HEALY, GEORGE WILLIAM, III, lawyer, mediator; b. New Orleans, Mar. 8, 1930; s. George William and Margaret Alford H.; m. Sharon Saunders, Oct. 26, 1974; children: George W. IV, John Carmichael, Floyd Alford, Hyde Dunbar, Mary Margaret. BA, Tulane U., 1950, JD, 1955. Bar: La. 1955, U.S. Supreme Ct. 1969. Assoc. Phelps, Dunbar, Marks, Claverie & Sims, New Orleans, 1955-58; ptnr. Phelps Dunbar, 1958-95, of counsel, 1996—; mem. U.S. del. Comité Maritime Internat., Tokyo, 1969, Lisbon, 1985, Paris, 1990, Sydney, 1994, titulary mem. Mem. planning com. Tulane U. Admiralty Law Inst., dir. World Trade Ctr., 1993—; dir. New Orleans Pro Bono Project, 1995-97. Fellow Am. Bar Found., Am. Coll. Trial Lawyers, Maritime Law Assn. U.S. (mem. exec. com. 1984-87, 2d v.p. 1988-90, 1st v.p. 1990-92, pres. 1992-94), La. Bar Found.; mem. New Orleans Bar Assn. (pres. 1992), Def. Rsch. Inst., La. Assn. Def. Counsel, New Orleans Assn. Def. Counsel, Com. Maritime Internat. Am. Found. (dir. 1990—), New Orleans Bar Assn. Inn of Ct. (master), Boston Club, La. Club, Stratford Club, Plimsoll Club, Recess Club (pres. 1978), Pinfeathers Hunting Club, New Orleans Lawn Tennis Club, Propeller Club, Mariners Club. Republican. Episcopalian. Fax: (504) 568-9130; e-mail: healyg@phelps.com. Home: 6020 Camp St New Orleans LA 70118-5902 Office: 400 Poydras St New Orleans LA 70130-3245

HEALY, GWENDOLINE FRANCES, controller; b. Brighton, Sussex, Eng., Nov. 25, 1940; came to U.S., 1971, naturalized, 1995; d. Frank William Barnes and Violet May (Kelly) Billingham; m. John Francis Healy, Sept. 1, 1972; children: Robert Charles, Jennifer Diane. BA, Brighton (Eng.) Poly. Inst., 1958. Acct. Comstock Internat., N.Y.C., 1972-73, Burgdorff Realtors, Summit, N.J., 1973-75; artist Athens, 1976-79; acct. Temple B'nai, Morristown, N.J., 1985-88; contr. W.H. Collins, Inc., Whippany, N.J., 1988—; dir. mktg. Healy Fin. Svcs., Morristown, 1989—. Leader MCC Commerce, Morristown, 1994-95; mem. Morristownship Task Force, 1995. Mem. Morris County Mental Health Assn. (sec.-treas. 1995-97, pres. 1997—), Daus. Brit. Empire (past treas. J. Elliot Langstaff chpt.), Internat. Platform Assn. Republican. Avocations: art, writing, music, theater, reading. Office: Healy Fin Svcs PO Box 16 Convent Station NJ 07961-0016

HEALY, HAROLD HARRIS, JR., lawyer; b. Denver, Colo., Aug. 27, 1921; s. Harold Harris and Lorena (Isom) H.; m. Elizabeth A. Debevoise, May 24, 1952; 1 son, Harold Harris III. A.B., Yale U., 1943, LL.B., 1949. Bar: N.Y. 1949, U.S. Supreme Ct 1957. Exec. asst. to U.S. atty. gen., Washington, 1957-59; mem. Debevoise & Plimpton, N.Y.C., 1959-89; resident ptnr. Debevoise & Plimpton, Paris, 1964-67; of counsel Debevoise & Plimpton, N.Y.C., 1989-92; Mem. Am. adv. council Ditchley Found., 1972—; bd. dirs. Legal Aid Soc., 1968-89, chmn., 1975-79, pres.'s coun., 1989—. Bd. dirs. Met. Opera Guild, 1975—, Acad. Am. Poets, 1993-94; nat. coun. Glimmerglass Opera, 1992—; adv. dir. Met. Opera Assn., 1986-95; trustee Vassar Coll., 1977-86. Capt. F.A., AUS, 1943-46, ETO. Decorated Bronze Star medal. Mem. ABA (mem. coun. sect. of internat. law and practice 1987-90), N.Y. State Bar Assn., Assn. Bar City of N.Y. (sec. 1959-61), Am. Law Inst., Order of Coif, Am. Soc. Internat. Law (mem. exec. coun. 1977-80), Internat. Law Assn., Internat. Bar Assn., Union Internationale des Avocats (pres. 1979-81), Am. Coll. Investment Counsel, Coun. Fgn. Rels., Pilgrims U.S., Yale Law Sch. Assn. (exec. com. 1974-82, v.p. 1980-82), Century Assn., Univ. Club, Travellers Club, Met. Club, Cercle de L'Union Interalliée, Phi Beta Kappa, Zeta Psi, Phi Delta Phi, Chevalier de la Legion d'Honneur. Republican. Episcopalian. Home: 1170 5th Ave New York NY 10029-6527 Office: Debevoise & Plimpton 875 3rd Ave Fl 23 New York NY 10022-6256

HEALY, JAMES BRUCE, cooking school administrator, writer; b. Paterson, N.J., Apr. 15, 1947; s. James Burn and Margaret Mercy (Patterson) H.; m. Alice Fenvessy, May 9, 1970; 1 child, Charlotte Alexandra. BA, Williams Coll., 1968; PhD, The Rockefeller U., 1973. Mem. faculty Inst. Advanced Study, Princeton, N.J., 1973-75; J.W. Gibbs instr. physics Yale U., New Haven, Conn., 1975-77, research affiliate, 1977-80; dir. Healy-Lucullus Sch. French Cooking, New Haven, 1978-80, Boulder, Colo., 1980—; cons. Claudine's, Denver, 1985-86; vis. instr. Salem (Mass.) State Coll., 1984, and various culinary schs. Author: Mastering the Art of French Pastry, 1984, The French Cookie Book, 1994; contbr. articles and revs. on restaurants and cooking to mags. and profl. jours. Mem. Internat. Assn. Cooking Profls. (cert.), Confederation Nationale des Patissiers, Glaciers, et Confiseurs de France. Methodist. Home and Office: Healy-Lucullus Sch French Cooking 840 Cypress Dr Boulder CO 80303-2820

HEALY, JAMES CASEY, lawyer; b. Washington, Feb. 19, 1956; s. Joseph Francis Jr. and Patricia Ann (Casey) H.; m. Kelly Anne Quinn, Nov. 4, 1995; 1 child, Caitlin Quinn. BS, Spring Hill Coll., 1978; JD, Emory U., 1982. Bar: Ga. 1983, Conn. 1983, U.S. Dist. Ct. Conn. 1984, U.S. Tax Ct. 1984, U.S. Supreme Ct. 1987. Assoc. Gregory and Adams PC, Wilton, Conn., 1982-87, ptnr., 1988-89, mng. ptnr., 1990-94; v.p. Gregory and Adams PC, Wilton, 1995—; spl. counsel Wilton Police Commn., 1986-98; mem. Parks and Recreation Commn., 1991—, sec., 1991-93, chmn., 1997—; corporator Ridgefield Bank, 1997—. Bd. dirs. Mark Lavin Meml. Offshore Med. and Safety Found., Empire, Mich., 1987-97, Village Market Inc., 1988-90; chmn. leadership giving program United Way, 1991; bd. mgrs. Wilton Childrens. Ctr., 1996-98; mem. athletic fields subcom. of bldg. com. Wilton H.S., 1998-99; active various charity and athletic orgns. Mem. ABA, State Bar Ga., State Bar Conn. (exec. com., planning and zoning sect. 1992-94, 98—), Am. Planning Assn., Stamford/Norwalk Regional Bar Assn. (law office mgmt. com. 1994-96, co-chmn. land use com. 1996—, real estate broker's contract com. 1997-98), Wilton C. of C. (bd. dirs. 1994-96), Silver Spring Country Club. Republican. Roman Catholic. E-mail: jhealy@gregoryandadams.com. Office: Gregory and Adams 190 Old Ridgefield Rd Wilton CT 06897-4023

HEALY, JANE ELIZABETH, newspaper editor; b. Washington, May 9, 1949; d. Paul Francis and Connie (Maas) H.; children: Randall, Kevin. BS, U. Md., 1971. Copy clk. N.Y. Daily News, Washington, 1971-73; met. reporter Orlando (Fla.) Sentinel, 1973-81, editorial writer, 1981-83, chief editorial writer, 1983-85, assoc. editor, 1985-92; mng. editor, 1993—. Recipient Pulitzer Prize, Columbia U., 1988, Sigma Delta Chi Disting. Service award, 1988. Mem. Am. Soc. Newspaper Editors. Office: Orlando Sentinel 633 N Orange Ave Orlando FL 32801-1349*

HEALY, JOSEPH FRANCIS, JR., lawyer, arbitrator, retired airline executive; b. N.Y.C., Aug. 11, 1930; s. Joseph Francis and Agnes (Kett) H.; m. Patricia A. Casey, Apr. 23, 1955; children: James C., Timothy, Kevin,

Cathleen M., Mary, Terence. BS, Fordham U., 1952; JD, Georgetown U., 1959. Bar: D.C. 1959. With gen. traffic dept. Eastman-Kodak Co., Rochester, N.Y., 1954-55; air transp. examiner CAB, Washington, 1955-59; practiced in Washington, 1959-70, 80-81; asst. gen. counsel Air Transport Assn. Am., 1966-70; v.p. legal Eastern Air Lines, Inc., N.Y.C. and Miami, Fla., 1970-80; ptnr. Ford, Farquhar, Kornblut & O'Neill, Washington, 1980-81; v.p. legal affairs Piedmont Aviation, Inc., Winston Salem, N.C., 1981-84, sr. v.p., gen counsel, 1984-89, ret., 1989; sr. v.p., gen. counsel Trans World Airlines Inc., Mt. Kisco, N.Y., 1993-94. Mem. bd. visitors Sch. Law Wake Forest U., 1988-96. 1st lt. USAF, 1952-54. Mem. FBA, Am. Arbitration Assn. (mem. nat. panel arbitrators 1989—), Nat. Aero. Assn., Internat. Aviation Club (Washington), Univ. Club (Washington), Beta Gamma Sigma, Phi Delta Phi. Home: 104 Overlink Ct Lynchburg VA 24503-3200

HEALY, KIERAN JOHN PATRICK, lighting designer, consultant; b. London, June 6, 1957; came to U.S., 1980; citizen of Ireland.; s. Denis Finbarr and Dawn Josephine (O'Hannigan) H.; m. Debra Leslie Liebling, Jan. 6, 1990; children: Conor Thomas, Tighe Joseph. Student, Isleworth Polytechnic, Middlesex, Eng., 1975-76. Lighting designer The Who, 1976-80, The Rolling Stones, 1980; v.p. Showlites, L.A., 1980-81; freelance lighting designer various TV prodns., 1982-89; dir. photography Design Ptnrs., Inc., Hollywood, Calif., 1989-97; lighting designer, owner Spotlight Design Inc., Agoura Hills, Calif., 1997—. Lighting designer for TV programs, including Live Aid, ESPY Awards, Arsenio Hall, Gracelands in Africa, The Tonight Show, Whose Line Is It Anyway, other spls. Mem. Nat. Acad. Cable Programming (ACE nomination 1988), Acad. TV Arts and Scis. (Emmy nominations 1984, 87, 89, 92, 94), BECTU (British Film Union). Roman Catholic. Avocations: collecting antiques, fine art and books, films, sailing, Irish history and genealogy, reading. Office: Spotlight Design Inc 2775 Triunfo Canyon Rd Agoura Hills CA 91301-3425

HEALY, MARY (MRS. PETER LIND HAYES), singer, actress; b. New Orleans, Apr. 14, 1918; d. John Joseph and Viola (Armbruster) H.; m. Peter Lind Hayes, Dec. 19, 1940 (dec. Apr. 1998); children: Peter Michael, Cathy Lind. Student parochial schs., New Orleans; hon. degree, St. Bonaventure U. With 20th Century Fox, Hollywood, Cal. Author: Twenty-five Minutes from Broadway, 1961; pictures and others, 1937-40; Broadway prodns. Around the World, 1943-46; (with husband) TV series Inside U.S.A, 1949, Peter and Mary Show, Star of the Family, 1952, Peter Lind Hayes Radio show, CBS, 1954-57; Broadway prodn. Who Was That Lady, 1957-58, Peter Lind Hayes show, ABC-TV, 1958-59, Peter and Mary, ABC-Radio, 1959—, Peter and Mary in Las Vegas; TV-film; Star (with husband) WOR radio show, 6 yrs; TV film series Fin. Planning for Women; (with husband) Film The 5000 Fingers of Dr. T, 1953; Appeared in: (with husband) Film Peter Loves Mary, 1960, When Television Was Live, 1975; films: You Ruined My Life, 1986, Looking To Get Out with Jon Voight, 1985. Roman Catholic. Club: Pelham Country. Home: 3538 Pueblo Way Las Vegas NV 89109-3339

HEALY, MAUREEN, marketing executive. Mgr. direct mktg. United Parcel Svc., Atlanta. Office: United Parcel Svc 55 Glenlake Pkwy NE Atlanta GA 30328-3498*

HEALY, NICHOLAS JOSEPH, lawyer, educator; b. N.Y.C., Jan. 4, 1910; s. Nicholas Joseph and Frances Cecilia (McCarthy) H.; m. Margaret Marie Ferry, Mar. 29, 1937; children: Nicholas, Margaret Healy Parker, Rosemary Healy Bell, Mary Louise Healy White, Donall, Kathleen Healy Hamon. AB, Holy Cross Coll., 1931; JD, Harvard U., 1934. Bar: N.Y. 1935, U.S. Supreme Ct. 1949. Pvt. practice N.Y.C., 1935-42, 48—; mem. Healy & Baillie (and predecessor law firms), 1948—; spl. asst. to atty. gen. U.S., 1945-48; tchr. admiralty law NYU Sch. Law, 1947-86, adj. prof., 1960—; Niels F. Johnsen vis. prof. maritime law Tulane Maritime Law Ctr., 1986; vis. prof. maritime law Shanghai Maritime Law Inst. (now Shanghai Maritime U.), 1981, 86, 88. Contbr. chpts. on admiralty to Ann. Survey Am. Law, 1948-87; author: (with Sprague) Cases on Admiralty, 1950, (with Currie) Cases and Materials on Admiralty, 1965, (with Sharpe) Cases and Materials on Admiralty, 1974, 3rd edit., 1998, (with Sweeney) The Law of Marine Collision, 1998; editor: Jour. Maritime Law and Commerce, 1980-90, mem. bd. editors, 1969-79, 91—; assoc. editor: American Maritime Cases; mem. bd. dirs. Il Dirittimo Marittimo; contbr. to Ency. Brit. Chmn. USCG Adv. Panel on Rules of the Road, 1966-72; mem. permanent adv. bd. Tulane Admiralty Law Inst. Lt. (s.g.) USNR, 1942-45. Fellow Am. Coll. Trial Lawyers; mem. ABA (ho. of dels. 1964-66), N.Y. State Bar Assn., Assn. of Bar of City of N.Y., N.Y. County Lawyers Assn., Maritime Law Assn. U.S. (pres. 1964-66), Assn. Average Adjusters U.S. (chmn. 1959-60), Com. Maritime Internat. (exec. coun. 1972-79, v.p. 1985-91, hon. v.p. 1991—), Ibero-Am. Inst. Maritime Law (hon.). Home: 132 Tullamore Rd Garden City NY 11530-1139 Office: Healy & Baillie 29 Broadway Fl 27 New York NY 10006-3293

HEALY, PATRICIA COLLEEN, social worker; b. Denver, Aug. 24, 1935; d. Cecil John and Gracia Maude (Walker) Schulte; m. John Patrick Healy III, Aug. 3, 1957 (div. Jan. 1972); 1 child, Sean Patrick. BA, Sacred Heart Coll., Wichita, 1957; MSW, U. Kans., 1983; postgrad., Wichita State U., 1974, 75, 89, Emporia (Kans.) State U., 1990, U. Kans., 1998. Lic. specialist clin. social worker, Kans.; cert. in spinal cord injury medicine. Proofreader Wichita Pub. Co., 1953; clk. typist Nat. Sales, Inc., Wichita, 1954-58, Dept. of Army, Ft. Leavenworth, Kans., 1958-60, Air Force, McConnell AFB, Kans., 1962-63; clk., typist VA Regional Office, Wichita, 1963-66; self-employed typist Wichita, 1966-70; ward clk., typist VA Regional Office and VA Med. Ctr., Wichita, 1970-73; vets. benefits counselor VARO, Wichita, 1973-83; social worker VA Med. Ctr., Wichita, 1983—. Author filmstrip, columns, book revs., feature stories and poetry. Former mem. Ctrl. Plains AAA Coun. on Aging; bd. dirs. Ind. Living Ctr. South Ctrl. Kans., 1990-96. Mem. Clin. Social Work Fedn., Paralyzed Vets. Am. (assoc., Eddy L. Sutton award 1992, Spinal Cord Injury Svcs. award 1997, Sunflower subchpt. Assoc. Mem. of Yr. award 1998), Kans. Profl. Grant Assn., Wichita Assn. of Visually Handicapped (bd. dirs. 1989-92), Kans. Authors Club. Roman Catholic. Avocations: writing, reading, photography, music, knitting and sewing. Office: VA Med Ctr 5500 E Kellogg Dr Wichita KS 67218-1607

HEALY, PHYLLIS M. CORDASCO, school social worker; b. Newark, Oct. 2, 1939; d. Carl and Mae (Serafina) Cordasco; married, Dec. 22, 1966. BA, Caldwell Coll., 1978; MS, Columbia U. Sch. Social Work, 1981; MA, Fairleigh Dickinson U., 1989. Cert. social worker, N.Y.; sch. social work specialist; diplomate in clin. social work; qualified clin. social worker; lic. clin. social worker, N.J. Social worker United Cerebral Palsy of North Jersey, East Orange, 1982-84, Cerebral Palsy Assn. Middlesex County, Edison, N.J., 1984-85; sch. social worker, mem. presch. child study team Newark Bd. Edn., 1985-92, social svcs. coord. N.J. Goodstarts prog. curr. svcs., 1992-96; sch. social work specialist Newark Bd. Edn., Office of Early Childhood, 1996—; cons. in field. Founding mem. sr. citizen ctr. Borough of Caldwell, mem., past chair rent review bd. Recipient Alumna of Yr. award Caldwell Coll., 1985-86, Marion award, 1991, Veritas award, 1999. Mem. AAUW (legis. chair 1982-84), Nat. Assn. for the Edn. of Young Children, Acad. Cert. Social Workers, Coun. for Exceptional Children (N.J. divsn. early childhood pres. 1992-94, Mideast regional coord. for the internat. divsn. for early childhood 1994-98), Caldwell Coll. Alumni Assn. (scholar chair 1982-87), Columbia U. Alumni Assn. Roman Catholic. Home: Westover House 519 Bloomfield Ave Caldwell NJ 07006-5550 Office: Newark Pub Schs 2 Cedar St Newark NJ 07102-3015

HEALY, SONDRA ANITA, consumer products company executive; b. 1939; married; 3 children. BFA, Goodman Sch. Drama, 1963; MA, Nat. Coll., 1964. Owner, chair Turtle Wax, Chgo., 1973—. Office: Turtle Wax 5655 S. 73rd Ave Chicago IL 60638*

HEALY, SONYA AINSLIE, health facility administrator; b. Sudbury, Ont., Can., Apr. 7, 1937; came to U.S., 1949; d. Walter B. and Wilma A. Scott; m. Richard C. Healy, Jr., Dec. 16, 1961. Diploma, Good Samaritan Hosp., West Palm Beach, Fla., 1958; student, U. Mass., 1963-64, NYU, 1964-66; BS, Boston U., 1969, MS in Med.-Surg. Nursing, 1974. Various staff nursing, charge nurse positions, suprs., med.-surg. and obstet. nursing, 1958-69; chmn. jr.-sr. teaching team Sch. of Nursing Melrose (Mass.) Wakefield Hosp., 1969-73; asst. dir. nurses Boston State Hosp., 1973-74; asst. dir., DON Mt. Zion Hosp. and Med. Ctr., 1974-75; asst. dir. patient care svcs., DON St. Elizabeth's Hosp., Boston, 1975-80, St. Joseph's Hosp., Nashua, N.H., 1980-82; adminstr. U. Calif. Med. Ctr., San Diego, 1982-91, corp. chief nursing officer, 1991, assoc. dir. hosp. and clinics, dir. patient care svcs., 1982-93; cons. health care Noyes & Assocs. Ltd., Bainbridge Island, Wash., 1993—; mem. acad. affairs com., bd. trustees U. San Diego; clin. assoc. Ul. San Diego, 1984—; mem. adj. faculty San Diego State U.; mem. clin. faculty UCLA Sch. of Nursing; presenter in field. Author: The 12-hour Shift: Is It Viable?-Nursing Outlook, 1984, (handbook) Human Resource Management Handbook, 1987, Human Resources Management Handbook, 1987, Nursing Economics, 1989; mem. editl. adv. bd. dirs. OR Nurse Today, 1989-96; editl. rev. Nursing Economics; contbr. articles to profl. jours. Mem. ASNSA (nominations com. 1978, cert.), Am. Orgn. of Nurse Execs. (bd. dirs. 1990-92, by laws com. 1990-92), Mass. Soc. of Nursing Svcs. Adminstrs. (pres. pres. 1977), Calif. Soc. of Nursing Svc. Adminstrs. (task force on orgns. program com. 1984-85, bd. dirs. 1985-87, mem. com. 1987-88, long range planning com.), San Diego Dirs. of Nurses (sec. 1982-83, pres. 1988-89), Sigma Theta Tau (Zeta Mu chpt.). Avocations: reading, golfing. *

HEALY, STEVEN MICHAEL, accountant, city official; b. Chgo., July 20, 1949; s. Daniel Francis and Angelina (Massino) H. BA, U. Ill., Chgo., 1971; MBA, Dominican U., 1984. Br. mgr. Assocs. Capital Co., Chgo., 1971-74; credit analyst Motorola, Inc., Schaumburg, Ill., 1974-76; office mgr. Triple "S" Steel Corp., Franklin Park, Ill., 1976-79; accounts payable supr. Zenith Electronics, Chgo., 1979-84; supr. acctg. Village of Oak Park, Ill., 1984-86; bus. analyst Cablevision of Chgo., Oak Park, 1986-87; dir. fin. Village of Maywood, Ill., 1988-91; dir. fin., treas. City of DeKalb, Ill., 1991-93; dir. fin. Village of Cahokia, Ill., 1993—. Mem. Friends of Oak Park Libr., Friends of the Conservatory, Oak Park Village Players Group, Cahokia Econ. Devel. Commn.; bd. dirs. Oak Park Employees Credit Union; treas. Cahokia Assn. for the Tricentennial. Mem. Nat. Soc. Pub. Accts., Nat. Govt. Fin. Officers Assn., Ill. Govt. Fin. Officers Assn., U. Ill. Alumni Assn., Dominican U. MBA Alumni Assn. (founder, soc. com. 1984—), Oak Park Area Jaycees, Rotary Club of St. Clair Valley (chair, sec.), Cahokia C. of C., Cath. Alumni Club, Village Oak Park Chess Club (pres. 1984-86), Maywood Rosary, Kishwaukee Sunrise Rotary, Cahokia Kiwanis Club. Avocations: participation sports, reading, travel, writing, chess. Home: 2013 Oak Tree Ln Cahokia IL 62206-1408 Office: 103 Main St Cahokia IL 62206-1019

HEALY, THERESA ANN, former ambassador; b. Bklyn., July 14, 1932; d. Anthony and Mary Catherine (Kennedy) H. BA, St. John's U., 1954, LLD (hon.), 1985. cons. Office of Freedom Info., 1997—. Tchr. elem. and secondary schs. N.Y.C., 1951-55; with U.S. Fgn. Svc., 1955-94, amb. to Sierra Leone, 1980-83; with Ctr. for Internat. Affairs, U. South Fla., Tampa, 1983-84; faculty Nat. Def. U., Washington, 1984-86; with pers. and mgmt. policy bur. U.S. Dept. State, 1986-92; with Office of Freedom of Info., 1992-94; ret., 1994. Mem. Am. Fgn. Svc. Assn., Diplomatic and Consular Officers Ret., Fng. Svc. Club. Roman Catholic. Home: 6800 Fleetwood Rd Apt 1002 Mc Lean VA 22101-3610

HEALY, WALTER F. X., lawyer; b. N.Y.C., Sept. 15, 1941; s. Walter Patrick and Helen Theresa (Fischer) H.; BA, St. Joseph's Coll., Yonkers, N.Y., 1963; LLB, Fordham U., 1966; m. Margaret O'Hanlon, Nov. 26, 1966; 1 child, Katherine Healy Burrows. Bar: N.Y. 1967, Pa. 1980, U.S. Ct. Appeals (9th cir.) 1983; assoc. Dewey, Ballantine, Bushby, Palmer & Wood, N.Y.C., 1966-76; corp. counsel Singer Co., N.Y.C., 1976; corp. sec., dep. gen. counsel Studebaker-Worthington, Inc., N.Y.C., 1976-79; v.p., gen. counsel UGI Corp., Valley Forge, Pa., 1979-84; ptnr. Windels, Marx, Davies & Ives, N.Y.C., 1984—. Mem. ABA, Assn. Bar City of N.Y., N.Y. Athletic Club. Avocations: squash, basketball, theatre. Office: Windels Marx Davies & Ives 156 W 56th St Fl 23 New York NY 10019-3867

HEALY, WILLIAM CHARLES, electrical engineer; b. Mpls., Aug. 19, 1950; s. Donald Edward and Helen Francis (Norton) H.; m. Linda Lee O'Dell, June 5, 1976. BSEE, S.D. State U., 1972. Registered profl. engr., Iowa, Nebr., Ill., S.D., Kans. Asst. engr. Atlantic Richfield Co., East Chgo., Ind., 1973-76; assoc. project engr. IBP, Inc., Dakota City, Nebr., 1976-77; project engr. IBP, Inc., Dakota City, 1977-84, sr. project engr., 1984-88, dir. elec. engring., 1988—. Mem. NSPE, IEEE, Internat. Assn. Elec. Inspectors, Instrument Soc. Am. Avocations: computers, golf. Home: 108 Parkview Dr South Sioux City NE 68776-3815 Office: IBP Inc 800 Stevens Port Dr Ste 711 Dakota Dunes SD 57049

HEANEY, DOROTHY PHELPS, nurse, nursing administrator; b. Elmer, N.J., Apr. 8, 1963; d. Joseph Francis and Dorothy Ruth (Andrews) Phelps; m. Bradley George Heaney, June 8, 1985. AS in Nursing, Gloucester County Coll., Sewell, N.J., 1984. Nursing asst. Pine Crest Nursing Home, Sewell, 1982-84, staff nurse, 1984, charge nurse, 1984-85; charge nurse Le Havre Convalescent Hosp., Menlo Park, Calif., 1985-86, dir. staff devel., 1986-87, asst. dir. nursing, 1986, dir. nursing, 1986-87; dir. nursing Hillhaven Convalescent Hosp., Menlo Park, 1987-90, Brookside Convalescent Hosp., San Mateo, Calif., 1990-92; owner, mgr. Friendly Vending, 1992-93; legal nurse cons., skilled nursing/geriatric care Mountain View, Calif., 1993—; med., legal cons., 1997—. Avocations: skiing, bowling, quiltmaking, hiking. Home: 12672 Larchmont Ave Saratoga CA 95070-3906

HEANEY, GERALD WILLIAM, federal judge; b. Goodhue, Minn., Jan. 29, 1918; s. William J. and Johanna (Ryan) H.; m. Eleanor R. Schmitt, Dec. 1, 1945; children—William M., Carol J. Student, St. Thomas Coll., 1935-37; BSL, U. Minn., 1938, LLB, 1941. Bar: Minn. 1941. Lawyer securities div. Dept. of Commerce Minn., 1941-42; mem. firm Lewis, Hammer, Heaney, Weyl & Halverson, Duluth, 1946-66; judge U.S. Ct. Appeals (8th cir.), 1966-88, sr. judge, 1989—. Mem. Dem. Nat. Com. from Minn., 1955; Bd. regents U. Minn., 1964-65. Served from pvt. to capt. AUS, 1942-46. Mem. ABA, Minn. Bar Assn., Am. Judicature Soc. Roman Catholic. Office: US Ct Appeals 8th Cir US Courthouse & Federal Bldg 315 W 1st St Duluth MN 55802-1302*

HEANEY, SEAMUS JUSTIN, poet, educator; b. Mossbawn, County Derry, No. Ireland, Apr. 13, 1939; s. Patrick and Margaret H.; m. Marie Devlin, 1965; children: Michael, Christopher, Catherine. B.A., Queen's U., Belfast, 1961; postgrad., St. Joseph's Coll., Belfast, 1961-62; Ph.D. (hon.), Queen's U., Belfast. Tchr. St. Thomas's Secondary Sch., Belfast, No. Ireland, 1962-63; lectr. St. Joseph's Coll. Edn., Belfast, 1963-66, Queen's U., Belfast, 1966-72; free-lance writer, 1972-75; lectr. Carysfort Coll., 1975-81; Boylston visiting prof. rhetoric and oratory Harvard U., 1982—; prof. poetry Oxford U., 1989-94. Author: Eleven Poems, 1965, Door into the Dark, 1969, Death of a Naturalist, 1966 (Somerset Maugham award 1967, Cholmondeley award 1968), Wintering Out, 1972, North, 1975 (W.H. Smith award, Duff Copper prize), Stations, 1975, Bog Poems, 1975, Field Work, 1979, Poems: 1965-75, 1980, Preoccupations: Selected Prose 1968-78, 1980, Sweeney Astray: A Version from the Irish, 1984, Station Island, 1984, The Haw Lantern, 1987 (Whitbead award), The Government of the Tongue, 1988, The Place of Writing, 1990, New Selected Poems, 1966-78, 1990, (play) The Cure at Troy (A Version of Sophocles' Philoctetes), 1991, Seeing Things, 1991, (Oxford lectures) The Redress of Poetry, 1995, The Spirit Level, 1996; ed. poetry anthologies. Recipient Eric Gregory award, 1966, Faber Meml. prize, 1968, Irish Acad. Letters award, 1971, Denis Devlin Meml. award, 1973, Am.-Irish Found. award, 1975, E.M.Forster award Nat. Inst. Arts and Letters, 1975, Bennett Award, 1982, Premio Mondello (Internat. Poetry prize) Mondello Found., Palermo, Sicily, 1993, Nobel Prize for Literature, 1995. Mem. Royal Dublin Soc. (hon. life), Am. Acad. Arts and Letters (fgn. hon.), Am. Acad. Arts and Scis. (hon. life), Irish Acad. Letters. Office: Harvard U Dept English Cambridge MA 02138*

HEANEY-HUNTER, JOANN CATHERINE, theology educator; b. N.Y.C., Oct. 19, 1957; d. Thomas Brendan and Joan Marie (Buchan) Heaney; m. Gregory S. Hunter, Apr. 21, 1979; children: Beth, Kate. BA, St. John's U., N.Y.C., 1978, MA, 1981; PhD, Fordham U., N.Y.C., 1988. Asst. dir. fin. aid St. John's U., N.Y.C., 1978-83, prof. theology, 1987—; doctoral fellow Fordham U., N.Y.C., 1983-87; advisor Nat. Conf. Cath. Bishops, Washington, 1988-91, Sacramental Practice Com., L.I., N.Y., 1993—. Co-author: Christian Marriage: Theological/Pastoral Perspective, 1996, Christian Marriage: Pastoral Handbook, 1998; author: (edn. program) Unitas: A Process of Marriage Formation, 1997. Mem. sch. bd. St. Aidan Sch., Williston Park, N.J., 1990-95, pres. sch. bd., 1995, pres. PTO, 1992-94. Grantee Mems. of Fadica, Washington, 1995-98. Mem. Cath. Theol. Soc. Am., Coll. Theology Soc. Democrat. Roman Catholic. Avocations: music, running, sailing, theatre. Home: 177 Banbury Rd Mineola NY 11501-1518 Office: St Johns U 8000 Utopia Pkwy Jamaica NY 11432-1343

HEAP, JAMES CLARENCE, retired mechanical engineer; b. Trinidad, Colo.; s. James and Elsie Mae (Brobst) H.; m. Alma Mae Swartzendruber. Registered profl. engr., Wis. Sr. mech. engr. Cook Electric Research Lab, Morton Grove, Ill., 1955-56; assoc. mech. engr. Argonne (Ill.) Nat. Lab., 1956-66; sr. project engr. Union Tank Car Co., East Chicago, Ind., 1966-71; sr. engr. Thrall Car Mfg. Co., Chicago Heights, 1971-77; research design engr. Graver Energy Systems, Inc., East Chicago, Ind., 1977-79; mech. cons. design engr. Pollak & Skan, Inc., Chgo., 1979-83, ret., 1983; cons. mech. design and stress analysis, 1965-83. Author: Formulas for Circular Plates Subjected to Symmetrical Loads and Temperatures, 1966; contbr. tech. papers to profl. jour.; patentee in field. Served with USAF, 1946-47. Mem. ASME, Christian Businessmen's Com. U.S., The Gideon's Internat. Home: 1406 Ashton Ct Goshen IN 46526-4679 *Personal philosophy: To assist and encourage others as ascertained through the perseverance by the fortitude and guidance of my "Savior Jesus Christ".*

HEAP, SYLVIA STUBER, civic worker; b. Clifton Springs, N.Y., Sept. 25, 1929; d. Stanley Irving and Helen (Hill) Stuber; BA cum laude, Bates Coll., 1950; postgrad. U. Conn. Sch. Social Work, 1952-54, Boston U. Sch. Social Work, 1953-54, SUNY, Brockport, 1979, SUNY-Potsdam, 1980, MS in Adult Edn., Syracuse U., 1989; m. Walker Ratcliffe Heap, June 9, 1951; children: Heidi Anne, Cynthia Joan, Walker Ratcliffe III. Dir. Y-Teens, YWCA, Holyoke, Mass., 1950-51; social group worker West Haven (Conn.) Community House, 1951-54; program dir. YWCA, Ann Arbor, 1954-55, part-time, 1955-59; mem. adv. bd. div. continuing edn. Jefferson Community Coll., 1965—, chmn. adv. bd., 1968-98; pres. Jefferson County Med. Soc. Aux., 1971-72; bd. dirs. St. Lawrence Valley Ednl. TV, 1973-83, sec., 1976-80, treas., 1980-82; v.p., 1982-83, dir. Chem. People Project, 1983; bd. dirs. Watertown Lyric Theatre, 1973-83; bd. dirs. N.Y. State Med. Soc. Aux., 1974-85, 2d v.p. bd., 1979-80; fitness instr. Jefferson Community Coll., Watertown, 1977-86; chmn. health projects N.Y. State Med. Soc. Aux., 1981-85. Named Citizen of Yr. Greater Watertown C. of C., 1975, Friend of Community Colls. N.Y. State Bd. Trustees, 1988. Mem. AAUW, Friends of Pub. TV, Coll. Women's Club Jefferson County, Phi Beta Kappa. Unitarian Universalist. (UN office envoy 1978—, St. Lawrence dist. envoy 1992—).

HEAPHY, JANIS D., newspaper executive; b. Kalamazoo, Oct. 10, 1951; d. Elvin Julius and Margaret Louise (Throndike) Olson; m. Douglas R. Dern, Aug. 15, 1980 (div. Nov. 1985); m. Robert Thomas Heaphy, Feb. 11, 1989; 1 child, Tanner. BS, Miami U., 1973, MEd, 1976. Tchr. Edgewood Jr. High Sch., Seven Mile, Ohio, 1973-75; acct. exec. L.A. Times, 1976-79, L.A. Mag., 1979-82; mgr. L.A. Omni Mag., 1982-86; sr. acct. exec. L.A. Times, 1986-87, ea. mag. mgr., 1987-89, nat. advt. mgr., 1989-92, retail advt. mgr., 1992—; sr. v.p., advt./mktg. L.A. Times, L.A.; now pub. Sacremento Bee. Co-editor: Secrets of the Master Sellers, 1987. Mem. Advt. Club L.A. Avocations: home decorating, reading, swimming, music. Office: Sacramento Bee McClatchy Newspapers 2100 Q St Sacramento CA 95852

HEAPHY, JOHN MERRILL, lawyer; b. Escanaba, Mich., Apr. 27, 1927; s. John Merrill and Catherine R. (Feeney) H.; m. Martha Jean Knowles, Nov. 16, 1951; children—John Merrill III, Catherine Jean Heaphy DeThorne, Barbara H. Murphy. B.A., U. Mich., 1950; J.D., Wayne State U., 1953. Bar: Mich. 1954. Atty. office of gen. counsel HEW, Washington, 1954-57; ptnr. Vandeveer & Garzia, P.C. and predecessor firms, Detroit, 1958-86, pres. firm, 1986-92, of counsel, 1992—. Served with USNR, 1945-46. Fellow Am. Coll. Trial Lawyers; mem. ABA, Internat. Assn. Def. Counsel, Mich. Bar Assn., Delta Theta Phi, Alpha Sigma Phi. Republican. Home: 14650 N Desert Rock Dr Tucson AZ 85737-7135 Office: Vandeveer & Garzia PC 333 W Fort St Fl 1600 Detroit MI 48226-3148

HEAPS, MARVIN DALE, food services company executive; b. Boone, Iowa, June 26, 1932; s. Donald and Mary Isabel (Robson) H.; m. Martha Coleman Davis, July 4, 1957; children—Mitchell, Matthew, Martha. B.A. in Econs, Whitworth Coll., 1953; postgrad., George Washington U., 1957; M.B.A. (Achievement scholar), U. Pa., 1959. Asso. McKinsey & Co. (mgmt. cons.), Washington, Geneva and N.Y.C., 1960-66; dir. service systems engrng. Automatic Retailers of Am., Phila., 1967; v.p. Automatic Retailers of Am., 1968; sr. v.p. ARA Svcs., Inc., Phila., 1969-71; pres. ARA Food Svcs. Co., 1971-75; exec. v.p. ops. ARA Svcs., Inc., 1975-77, pres., chief operational officer, 1977-81; pres./chief exec. officer Marvin D. Heaps Assos., Inc., 1981—; bd. dirs. Morse/Diesel Internat., Inc., Adult Communities Total Svc., chmn., 1997—; cons. to Office Edn., HEW; mem. food svc. industry adv. com. Exec. Office Pres., 1969—. Bd. dirs. Whitworth Coll., U. Arts; chmn. Salvation Army, ACE, Inc.; chmn. ACTS, Inc. Lt. USN, 1955-59. Mem. Conf. Bd., Am. Mgmt. Assn., Soc. Personnel Adminstrn., Assn. Internat. Devel., Nat. Automatic Mdse. Assn. (dir.), Wharton MBA Alumni Club. Republican. Presbyterian (elder). Clubs: Metropolitan (Washington); Union League (Phila.). Home and Office: 301 Elm Ave Swarthmore PA 19081-1431

HEARD, (GEORGE) ALEXANDER, retired educator and chancellor; b. Savannah, Ga., Mar. 14, 1917; s. Richard Willis and Virginia Lord (Nisbet) H.; m. Laura Jean Keller, June 17, 1949; children: Stephen Keller, Christopher Cadek, Francis Muir, Cornelia Lord. A.B., U. N.C., 1938, LL.D., 1968; M.A., Columbia U., 1948, Ph.D., 1951, LL.D., 1965; 25 other hon. degrees. U.S. Govt. service in depts. Interior, War and State, 1939-43; research asso. bur. pub. adminstrn. U. Ala., 1946-49; research asso. Inst. Research in Social Sci., U. N.C., 1950-51, research prof., 1952-58; asso. prof. polit. sci. U. N.C., 1950-51, prof. polit. sci., 1952-63, dean Grad. Sch., 1958-63; prof. polit. sci. Vanderbilt U., 1963-85, chancellor, 1963-82. Author: (asst. to V.O. Key, Jr.) Southern Politics in State and Nation, 1949, (with Donald S. Strong) Southern Primaries and Elections, 1950, A Two-Party South?, 1952, The Costs of Democracy, 1960, rev. edit., 1962, The Lost Years in Graduate Education, 1963, Made in America: Improving the Nomination and Election of Presidents, 1991, Speaking of the University: Two Decades at Vanderbilt, 1995; editor and contbr.: State Legislatures in American Politics, 1966; editor, contbr. (with Michael Nelson) Presidential Selection, 1987. Chmn. Pres.'s Commn. on Campaign Costs, 1961-62; spl. adviser to Pres. U.S. on campus affairs, 1970; Dir. Citizens' Research Found., 1958-71, pres., 1968-71; mem. U.S. Adv. Commn. Intergovtl. Relations, 1967-69, Trustee Ford Found., 1967-87, chmn., 1972-87; trustee Robert A. Taft Inst. Govt., 1973-76, Ctr. for Study of Presidency, 1988-91; chmn. Task Force on So. Rural Devel., 1974-77; public trustee Nutrition Found., 1976-82; mem. council Rockefeller U., 1977-82; mem. Commn. on U.S. Policy Toward So. Africa, Fgn. Policy Study Found., 1979-85. Lt. USNR, 1943-46. Mem. Internat. Polit. Sci. Assn., Am. Polit. Sci. Assn. (v.p. 1962-63), So. Polit. Sci. Assn. (pres. 1961-62), Assn. Am. Univs. (dir. council fed. relations 1969-70, v.p. 1973-74, pres. 1974-75), Council on Fgn. Rels., Cosmos Club (Washington), Belle Meade Country Club (Nashville), Century Assn. (N.Y.C.), Oglethorpe Club (Savannah), Sigma Alpha Epsilon. Episcopalian. Home: 2100 Golf Club Ln Nashville TN 37215-1224 Office: Vanderbilt U 401 Kirkland Hall Nashville TN 37240

HEARD, EDWIN ANTHONY, banker; b. N.Y.C., Oct. 31, 1926; s. Edwin Anthony and Frances Weaver (Taylor) H.; m. Phyllis Marie Gregory, Dec. 18, 1948; children: Elizabeth Gregory, Edwin Anthony III. A.B., Princeton U., 1948; grad., Advanced Mgmt. Program, Harvard U., 1966. V.p. Irving Trust Co., N.Y.C., 1960-71; treas. U.S. Trust Co., N.Y.C., 1971-73, exec. v.p., 1973-76, vice chmn., 1976-89; pres. Excelsior Income Shares, Inc., 1989-92, also bd. dirs. Trustee Trinity Episcopal Sch. Corp. With USNR, 1944-46. Mem. Belle Meade Country Club (Nashville), Bond Club (N.Y.C.). Home: 3901 Harding Rd Nashville TN 37205-1837 Office: Excelsior Income Shares Inc 114 W 47th St New York NY 10036-1510

HEARD, JAMES HENRY, lawyer, educator; b. Woburn, Mass., Sept. 28, 1940; s. James Henry Heard and Thelma Mae Bailey; m. Deloris Heard, Sept. 2, 1978; children: Patrick, Malcolm, Anthony. BS, Boston State Coll., 1963; MAT, U. Chgo., 1968; JD, DePaul U., 1974. Bar: Ill. 1975, U.S. Dist. Ct. (no. dist.) Ill. 1975, U.S. Supreme Ct. 1975. Chmn. social sci. Bloom Twp. H.S., Chgo. Heights, Ill., 1965-70; prof. of history Prarie State Coll., Chgo. Heights, 1970-71; prof. of history Harold Washington Coll., Chgo., 1971—, chmn. social scis. dept., 1980-85, 90—; chmn. faculty coun. Harold

Washington Coll., 1993—; dean applied scis. Kennedy-King Coll., Chgo., 1985-90; arbitrator Cook County Cir. Cts., Chgo., 1975—; coord. common ground projects Harold Washington Coll., Chgo., 1995—. Contbr. to book and profl. jours.; chorister Kennedy King Coll. Comty. Chorus, 1985—. Cantor St. Thomas the Apostle Ch., Chgo., 1985—; chmn. of adv. bd. Ill. Infant Mortality Project, 1980-85; chmn. bd. dirs. New City Health Ctr., Chgo., 1980-90. Named Educator of Yr., Comty. Coll. Assn. of Ill. and U. Mich. Consortium, 1995, Disting. Prof. Harold Washington Coll., 1995, Most Disting. Advisor, Phi Theta Kappa Internat. Honor Soc., Jackson Miss. chpt., 1995; recipient award Chgo. Urban League, 1985, Osterman Outstanding Svc. award City of Chgo., 1996. Mem. Comty. Colls. Humanities Assn. Avocations: music appreciation, running, reading.

HEARD, RONALD ROY, motion picture producer; b. Denver, Oct. 3, 1947; s. John Arthur and Louise Marie (Smith) H.; m. Kim Widing Aug. 12, 1967 (div. 1969). BS, Colo. State U., 1969; postgrad., U. Colo., 1969-72, U. Paris/Sorbonne, 1964-65. Prodn. design/stage mgr. The Rolling Stones, London, 1969-99; property/set dresser Universal Studios, Universal City, Calif., 1978-79, Warner Bros. Studios, Burbank, Calif., 1979-80; producer stage plays Hollywood, 1980-85; music video cons. L.A., 1984—; corres. CBS Network News, Chgo., 1971-72; writer/photographer UPI/Nat. Geographic/Denver Post, 1969-73; ptnr. Silver Screen Ptnrs. II and III, L.A., 1986—; CEO, pres. Radio Safari, 1991—; pres. Brightstar Entertainment dba Liberty Tree Studios, 1994—; owner Yankee Pride Ent., North Hollywood, Calif., 1986—, LAPD Police Cmty. rep. 1995-95, LAPD Citizen Tagger Task Force, 1995. Exec. com. Dem. Party, Larimer County, Colo., 1972-79; Dem. candidate for Ho. of Rep., 1972, 76. Named honorary citizen of S.D. by Gov. Richard Kneip, 1972, Rock and Roll Hall of Fame. Mem. Am. Film Inst., Smithsonian Instn., Statue of Liberty/Ellis Island Cen. Commn., Rock and Roll Hall of Fame. Democrat.

HEARD, WILLIAM T., automotive executive; b. Columbus, Ga., Sept. 8, 1934; s. William Tillman Sr. Heard; m. Sara Bolin; children: Bill III, Edward. BA, Auburn U., 1956. With Muscogee Motor Co.; prin. Bill Heard Chevrolet (formerly Muscogee Motor Co.); CEO Bill Heard Enterprises Inc. (formerly Bill Heard Chevrolet). Pres. Boys Club, Jr. Achievement, United Way Columbus, Coll. Coll. Found.; treas., chmn. fin. com. Columbus Mus.; chmn. Columbus Olympic Fund Raising Found.; mem. 1st Presbyn. Ch. of Columbus, past chmn. bd. deacons. Named Disting. Alumnus of Auburn U. Coll. Bus., 1994. Mem. Rotary, C. of C. (pres.). Office: Bill Heard Enterprises, Inc PO Box 6749 Columbus GA 31917-6749*

HEARIN, WILLIAM JEFFERSON, newspaper publishing company executive; b. Mobile, Ala., Aug. 27, 1909; s. William Jefferson and Mary Lou (Ludington) H.; m. Emily Staples Van Antwerp, July 2, 1981; 1 child, Ann Bartlett Hearin. PhD (hon.), U. Mobile, 1994, Spring Hill Coll., 1996. Classified and retail advt. solicitor Mobile News-Item, 1927-32; retail advt., solicitor, retail advt. mgr., nat. advt. mgr., circulation mgr., advt. dir., bus. mgr. Mobile Press Register, 1932-44, gen. mgr., exec. v.p., 1944-65, co-pub., 1965-70, pub. pres., 1970-92, chmn., 1992—, also dir; chmn. Miss Press Register, Pascagoula, Energy South, Inc.; bd. dirs. Am.'s Jr. Miss, Cmty. Found. So. Ala., Sr. Bowl Com., U. So. Ala. Found.; trustee Hearin/Chandler Found.; bd. dirs. South Ala. Bank. Bd. dirs. United Fund, YMCA; former mem. nat. adv. bd. Salvation Army, Jr. Achievement; former regent Spring Hill Coll. Named Hon. Col. Salvation Army, 1974, Lion of Yr. Lions Club, 1975, Mobilian of Yr., 1977; recipient Others award Salvation Army, Melvin L. Jones Fellowship award Lions Club, 1995. Mem. Newspaper Assn. Am., So. Pubs. Assn., Mobile Area C. of C. (past pres.), Sigma Delta Chi. Office: Mobile Press Register Inc 304 Government St PO Box 2488 Mobile AL 36652-2488*

HEARLE, DOUGLAS GEOFFREY, public relations consultant; b. N.Y.C., Apr. 7, 1933; s. Douglas G. and Regina Irene (Booth) H.; m. Mary Elizabeth Hogan, July 13, 1957; children: Douglas, Christopher, Matthew. B.A., Iona Coll., 1954, M.B.A., 1970. Reporter-editor N.Y. Jour.-Am., N.Y.C., 1954-63; pub. relations mgr. Borden Inc., N.Y.C., 1963-66; account exec. Hill & Knowlton, N.Y.C., 1966-70, v.p., 1970-73, sr. v.p., 1973-80, exec. v.p., 1980-86, vice chmn., 1989-90, also bd. dirs.; founder, pres. Douglas G. Hearle & Co., N.Y.C., 1993—; pres. John W. Hill Found., N.Y.C., 1980-86; founder, pres. Douglas G. Hearle & Assoc., Inc., N.Y.C., 1986-89; pres., CEO Carl Byoir & Assocs., N.Y.C., 1990-92; adj. prof. Iona Coll., 1982-84, Coll. New Rochelle, 1996—, Fordham U., 1998-99; disting. lectr. Ball State U., 1981, U. Tex., 1984. V.p. Bd. Edn., Pelham, N.Y., 1972-78; v.p. N.Y. Newspaper Reporters Assn., 1961-63; mem. exec. coun. Boy Scouts Am., 1967-69; vice chmn. bd. trustees Coll. New Rochelle, 1989-95; bd. dirs. The Roper Ctr., U. Conn., 1990—. Recipient Disting. Service award Asean P.R. Congress, Jakarta, Indonesia, 1981; recipient Citizen of Yr. award Pelham Men's Club, 1978, Five Most Respected award by PR Week, 1988, All Star award Inside PR Mag., 1992. Mem. Silurians, N.Y. Newspaper Reporters Assn., Asia Soc., Internat. C. of C., Pelham Country Club, Sky Club of N.Y. Republican. Roman Catholic. Home: 254 Cliff Ave Pelham NY 10803-2220 Office: PO Box 480 Pelham NY 10803-0480

HEARLE, EDWARD F.R., retired management consultant; b. Pasadena, Calif., Apr. 21, 1931; s. John R. and Kathleen W. (Brathwaite) H.; m. Patricia Ann Woodbridge, Dec. 23, 1958; children: Kevin C., Keith W., Jeffrey R. AB, Occidental Coll., 1952; MPA, UCLA, 1954. Cert. mgmt. cons. Inst. Mgmt. Consulting. Asst. to city adminstr. City of Covina, Calif., 1956-59; analyst The Rand Corp., Santa Monica, Calif., 1959-65; dir. Griffenhagen Kroeger, San Francisco, 1965-66; office dir. U.S. Govt., Washington, 1966-67; sr. v.p. Booz Allen & Hamilton, Washington, 1967-92; ret.; cons. UN, N.Y., 1964-70. Co-author: A Data Processing System for State and Local Governments, 1963. Pres. Westminter Presbyn. Retirement Corp., Lakeridge, Va., 1985-92; dir. Jacksonville Symphony Assn., 1998, Jacksonville Cmty. Coun., Inc., 1998, Trinity Internat. Found., 1998, vice chair, 1998 . With U.S. Army, 1954-56. Home: 13845 Fiddlers Point Dr Jacksonville FL 32225

HEARN, CHARLES LEE, petroleum reservoir engineer; b. Nashville, May 22, 1935; s. Charles Aubrey and Florence Rebecca (Conner) H.; m. Lerma Loula Engberg, July 21, 1962; children: Robert Aubrey, Lerma Rebecca. B in Engring., Vanderbilt U., 1957; PhDChemE, Rice U., 1963. Registered profl. engr., Okla. Rsch. engr. Cities Svc. Oil Co., Tulsa, 1963-67, rsch. mgr., 1967-73, chief reservoir engr., 1973-81, engring. cons., 1981-85; tech. coord. Occidental de Colombia, Bogota, 1985-88; sr. engring. cons. Occidental Petroleum, Bakersfield, Calif., 1988-95; sr. staff engr. Occidental of Qatar, Doha, 1995-97, ret., 1997; petroleum reservoir engring. cons., 1997—. Contbr. more than 15 articles to profl. jours. Patentee in field. Mem. Soc. Petroleum Engrs. Achievements include contributions to petroleum reservoir description and numerical reservoir simulation.

HEARN, GEORGE, actor; b. St. Louis, MO, June 18, 1934; m. Mary Harrell (div.), 1 child, David; m. Susan Babel (div.); m. Dixie Carter, 1978 (div.); m. Leslie Simons, 1985. B.S. Philosophy, Southwestern U. numerous stage appearances, including: The Changing Room, 1973, An Almost Perfect Person, 1977, Sweeny Todd, 1979 (Broadway), 1980 (tour of U.S. cities, Emmy award - PBS broadcast), I Remember Mama, 1979, Watch on the Rhine, 1980, A Doll's Life, 1982, La Cage aux Folles, 1983 (Broadway, Tony award, 1984), 1986 (London, Olivier award), Sunset Boulevard, 1993-95 (Broadway, Tony award, 1995); TV appearances include: The Silence, 1975, The Adams Chronicles, 1976, Sanctuary of Fear, 1979, A Piano for Mrs. Cimino, 1982, False Arrest, 1991, Fire in the Dark, 1991, Johnny's Golden Quest, 1993 (voice only), Deadly Secret: The Robert Bierer Story, 1993, Daisy-Head Mayzie, 1994 (voice only), Murder She Wrote; films include: See You in the Morning, 1989, Sneakers, 1992, The Vanishing, 1993, The Pagemaster, 1994 (voice only), Annie: A Royal Adventure, 1995, (voice) All Dogs Go to Heaven 2, 1996, The Devil's Own, 1997, Barney's Great Adventure, 1998. Office: care Paradigm Talent Agency c/o Clifford Stevens 200 W 57th St Ste 900 New York NY 10019-3211*

HEARN, GEORGE HENRY, lawyer, steamship corporate executive; b. Bklyn., July 4, 1927; s. Henry G. and Grace A. (Flaherty) H.; m. Cecelia Anne Philbin, June 28, 1952; children—Annemarie Jude, Margaret Mary, George Henry. B.A., St. Francis Coll., 1950; student, Fordham U. Sch. Bus. Adminstrn., 1948; LL.B., St. John's U., 1954. Bar: N.Y. 1955, U.S. Supreme Ct. 1960, D.C. 1965. Jr. ptnr. Haight, Gardner, Poor and Havens (specializing admiralty matters), N.Y.C., 1954-61; mem. CAB, 1961-64; commr. Fed. Maritime Commn., 1964-75; maritime adminstr. Govt. Sultanate of Oman, 1975-80; counsel to firm Hill, Rivkins, Carey, Loesberg & O'Brien (specializing in maritime and transp. law), N.Y.C., 1977-82; exec. v.p. Waterman Steamship Corp., N.Y.C., 1982—; lectr. transp. Georgetown U., Am. U., Tulane U., St. Francis Coll. Contbr. articles to profl. jours. Dist. commr. Boy Scouts Am., 1958—, mem. N.Y.C. coun., 1958-61; chmn. Kings County speakers com. for 1960 presdl. election of John F. Kennedy; vice chmn. com. nationalists and intergroup rels. N.Y. State Dem. Com., 1960—; pres. Fleet Week Found., 1990—. Served with USNR, World War II, PTO. Recipient Disting. Svc. award U.S. Jr. C. of C., 1958, Man of Yr. awards N.Y. Freight Forwarders and Brokers Assn., 1968, Man of Yr. award Cathedral Club of Bklyn., 1974. Mem. D.C. Bar Assn., Fed. Bar Assn., Maritime Adminstrv. Bar Assn., Maritime Law Assn., Soc. Maritime Arbitrators, U.S. Maritime Assn. Port of N.Y. and N.J. (pres.), India House (bd. govs.), Adminstrv. Conv. U.S., St. Patrick's Soc. Bklyn. (past pres.), Am. Com. Italian Migration (rec. sec. Bklyn. divsn.), KC. Home: 78 Roxbury Rd Garden City NY 11530-2622 also: 110 Baldwin Ave Point Lookout NY 11569 Office: 1 Whitehall St New York NY 10004-2109 also: 1000 16th St NW Washington DC 20036-5705

HEARN, JOHN PATRICK, biologist, educator; b. Limbdi, India, Feb. 24, 1943; s. Hugh Patrick and Cynthia Ellen (Nicholson) H.; m. Margaret Ruth McNair, Sept. 30, 1967; children: Shaun, Karina, Bruce, Adrian, Nicholas. BS, Univ. Coll., Dublin, Ireland, 1966, MSc, 1968; PhD, Australian Nat. U., Canberra, 1972. Lectr. in zoology Strathmore Coll., Nairobi, Kenya, 1967-69, head biology dept., dean sci., 1968-69; rsch. scholar zoology dept. Australian Nat. U., 1969-72; scientist med. rsch. coun. reproductive biology unit U. Edinburgh, Scotland, 1972-79; prof. in reproductive biology Univ. Coll., London, 1979-95; dir. Wellcome Labs. of Comparative Physiology, Inst. Zoology Zool. Soc. London, 1979-80, dir. sci., 1980-87; prof. dept. physiology Med. Sch. U. Wis., Madison, 1990-96; dir. Wis. Regional Primate Rsch. Ctr., 1990-96; prof., sr. cons. scientist WHO, Geneva, Switzerland, 1997—; cons. scientist WHO, Geneva, 1978-79; mem. coun. NIH Nat. Ctr. Rsch. Resources, 1995—, NAS Inst. for Lab. Animal Resources, 1991—; mem. tech. adv. com. Contraceptive Devel. Orgn., 1990—. Author, editor: Reproduction in New World Primates, 1983, Advances in Animal Conservation, 1985, Reproduction and Disease in Captive and Wild Animals, 1988, Conservation of Primates Studies in Biomedical Research, 1995. Recipient Bolliger award Australian Mammal Soc., 1972; fellow Inst. Biology, 1980. Fellow Zool. Soc. London (sci. medal 1983); mem. Am. Soc. Primatology, Soc. for Study of Reproduction, Soc. for Study of Fertility, Primate Soc. Gt. Britain (Osman-Hill medal 1986), Internat. Primatol. Soc. (pres. 1984-88). Avocations: gymnasium, running, conservation. Office: WHO, CH-1211, 27 Geneva Switzerland*

HEARN, JOYCE CAMP, retired state legislator, educator, consultant, business owner, lobbyist; b. Cedartown, Ga., d. J.C. and Carolyn (Carter) Camp; m. Thomas Harry Hearn (dec.); children: Theresa Hearn Potts Bailey, Kimberly Ann Johnson, Carolyn Lee Becker. Student, U. Ga.; BA, Ohio State U., 1957; postgrad. U. S.C. Former high sch. tchr.; dist. mgr. U.S. Census, 2d Congl. Dist., 1970; mem. S.C. Ho. of Reps., 1975-89, asst. minority leader, 1976-78, 86-89; chmn. commn. alcohol beverage control, 1989-91; pres., cons. Hearn & Assocs., Columbia, S.C., 1995—. Mem. Richland County Planning Commn., 1974-76; bd. dirs. Meml. Youth Ctr. and Stage South; chmn. Sexual Assault Awareness Week; vice chmn. Dist. Republican Com., 1968; Rep. chmn. 2d Congl. Dist., 1969; Rep. chmn. Richland County, 1972; del., platform com. Rep. Nat. Conv., 1980, 84; moderator Kathwood Bapt. Ch., 1979-80, former asst. Sunday Sch. tchr.; bd. dirs. Small Bus. Devel. Ctr. S.C., Columbia Coll. Bd. Vis., Columbia Urban League, Fedn. of Blind; trustee Columbia Mus. Art; apptd. to Alcohol Beverage Control Bd., 1989, apptd. chmn. commn., 1990-92, commr., 1991-94; bd. dirs. Lupus Found., 1990—; chair nat. adv. com. Occupational Safety and Health, 1980-88. Recipient Outstanding Citizen award Columbia Rape Coalition, 1977, Disting. Service award Claims Mgmt. Assn. S.C., 1977, Nat. Fedn. Blind S.C., 1978, Columbia Urban League, 1983, MADD, 1985, Outstanding Legislator of Yr. award Alcohol and Drug Abuse Assn., 1980, Retarded Citizens Assn., 1982, S.C. Rehab. Assn., 1984, S.C. Assn. of Deaf, 1987, Legislator of Yr., Fedn. of Blind, 1988, Disting. Legislator, DAV, 1989; Honoree, Easter Seals, 1989; numerous other awards. Mem. Nat. Order of Women Legislators (v.p., pres.), Order of the Palmetto, S.C. Women's Club, Columbia Women's Club (bd. dirs.), Larkspar Garden Club.

HEARN, RUBY PURYEAR, foundation executive; b. Winston-Salem, N.C., Apr. 13, 1940; c. Mahlon Tasher H. and Ruby Mae (Hamilton) Puryear; m. Robert W. Hearn, Dec. 30, 1961; children: Janna E., Jennifer L. B.A., Skidmore Coll., 1960; M.S., Yale U., 1964, Ph.D., 1969. Postdoctoral rsch. assoc. Yale U., New Haven, 1968-69; dir. content devel. Children's TV Workshop, 1972-76; program officer Robert Wood Johnson Found., Princeton, N.J., 1976-80, sr. program officer, 1980-82, v.p., 1983-96, sr. v.p., 1996—. Trustee Meharry Med. Coll., 1981-86; bd. overseers Dartmouth Med. Sch., 1986-92. Recipient Outstanding Alumnae award Skidmore Coll., 1972. Fellow Yale Corp.; mem. AAAS, ABA (pub. mem. accreditation com. 1980-82), Inst. Medicine, Ambulatory Pediatric Assn., Periclean Honor Soc. Home: 7 Saint Johns Rd Baltimore MD 21210-2121 Office: Robert Wood Johnson Found PO Box 2316 Princeton NJ 08543-2316*

HEARN, THOMAS K., JR., academic administrator; b. Opp, Ala., July 5, 1937; s. Thomas H. Hearn; m. Laura Walter; children: Thomas K., William Neely, Lindsay. B.A. summa cum laude, Birmingham-So. Coll., 1959; B.D., Baptist Theol. Sem., 1963; Ph.D. (NDEA fellow), Vanderbilt U., 1965. Instr. Birmingham-So. Coll., summers 1964-65; asst. prof. Coll. William and Mary, 1965-68, assoc. prof., 1968-74; prof. philosophy U. Ala., Birmingham, 1974-83, chmn. dept. philosophy, 1974-76, dean Sch. Humanities, 1976-78, v.p. Univ. Coll., 1978-83; pres. Wake Forest U., Winston-Salem, N.C., 1983—. Contbr. articles to profl. jours. Recipient Thomas Jefferson Teaching award, 1970; summer grantee Nat. Found. Humanities, 1967; summer fellow Council Philos. Studies, 1968; fellow Coop. Program in Humanities, 1969-70; faculty summer grantee Coll. William and Mary, 1970, 72, 73. Mem. AAUP, So. Soc. Philosophy, Psychology (exec. council 1974-77 Jr. award), Soc. Philosophy Religion (pres. 1974-75), Am. Philos. Assn., David Hume Soc., Newcomen Soc. N.Am., Phi Beta Kappa, Omicron Delta Kappa, Phi Kappa Phi. Home: 1000 Kearns Ave Winston Salem NC 27106-5824 Office: Wake Forest U Office of the Pres PO Box 7226 Winston Salem NC 27109-7226*

HEARNE, BARBRA M., foundation administrator; b. Austin, Tex., June 8, 1969; d. Woodie and Marie Hart Miller; m. Lewis C. Hearne, Jr., Mar. 11, 1995. BA, Tex. So. U., 1995; MA, U. St. Thomas, 1998. Asst. pub. affairs coord. HEB Grocery Co., Houston, 1995-97; employment cons. ETC, Houston, 1997; dist. mgr. Am. Diabetes Assn., Houston, 1998—. Mem. Internat. Assn. Bus. Comm., Am. Mktg. Assn., Soc. Profl. Journalists, Pub. Rels. Soc. Am. Avocations: skiing, rollerblading, cycling, reading novels. E-mail: bhearne@diabetes.org. Home: 13915 Carrington Ln Cypress TX 77429 Office: Am Diabetes Assn 2400 Augusta Ste 420 Houston TX 77057

HEARNE, CAROLYN FOX, art, history educator, artist, art museum director; b. Brownwood, Tex., June 15, 1945; d. Marshal D. and Lena May (Parson) Fox; m. Roy Nicholas Hearne, Apr. 14, 1968; children: Jason Nicholas, Angela Della. BA in Spanish, Art, So. Meth. U., 1967; MA in Fine Arts, U. Tex., Tyler, 1985. Astrology lady, commls. K-BUY Radio, Ft. Worth, 1970-71; decorator, exec. dir. Holiday Inns, Inc., Houston, 1971-73; exec./bilingual sec. Kennecott Copper Corp., Houston, 1973-74; owner Fox-Hearne Studio, Kilgore, Tex., 1977—; art/music, history tchr. LeTourneau U., Longview, Tex., 1988—; dir. Longview Art Mus., 1997—; co-chmn. LeTourneau Fine Arts Week, Longview, 1992—; demonstreator, lectr. mus. and art groups, Longview and Tyler, 1979—; judge East Tex. art groups, Longview, Kilgore, and Henderson, 1990—; invited participant Master Artists Workshop, L.I. U., 1990. Prin. works include book cover, Gory Days, 1987, bronze sculpture, Frontier Spirit, 1983 (Citation 1983), sculpture for dedication, Gussie Nell Davis, 1983, commnd. A Race Against Time, 1978 (Spl. award 1978), model for catalogue, TV commls. for Strictly Petites, 1987—; exhbns. incl. Tex. Art Gallery, 1990-92. Bd. dirs. Kilgore Hist. Preservation Found., Kilgore, 1989—, past sec., past pres.; chmn. art fest Kilgore Improvement and Beautification Assn., 1981-86; chmn. Kilgore Civic Ball, 1980; decorator Jr. League Charity Ball, Longview, 1992; pres. Kilgore Garden Club, 1982-83; chmn. Theatre Restoration Kilgore, 1989-92; life mem. Tex. PTA, 1978—; bd. dirs., 1st v.p. Longview Art Mus., 1994—, exhbns. and acquisitions chmn., 1995-97. Recipient 5 Citation awards East Tex. Classics, 1981, Outstanding Achievement award Artitudes mag., 1989. Mem. East Tex. Fine Arts Assn. (pres. 1981-83, Top Citation award 1984), Tex. Fine Arts Assn., LeTourneau Faculty Orgn., Coterie Club (pres. 1990). Republican. Presbyterian. Avocations: singing, gardening, cooking, cross-stitching, volunteer work. Home: 8 Briar Ln Kilgore TX 75662-2201 Office: LeTourneau Univ Mobberly Ave PO Box 7001 Longview TX 75607-7001

HEARNE, GEORGE ARCHER, academic administrator; b. Tampa, Fla., Oct. 31, 1934; s. William Duncan and Marguerite Estelle (Archer) H.; m. Jean May Helmstadter, June 9, 1956; children: Diana Leslie, George Harrison. BA, Bethany Coll., 1955; MDiv, Yale U., 1958; MA, Ill. State U., 1968; HHD (hon.), Culver-Stockton Coll., 1986; LLD, Bethany Coll., 1997. Min. Arlington Christian Ch., Jacksonville, Fla., 1958-59; dir. admissions Eureka (Ill.) Coll., 1960-70, v.p. student devel., 1970-73, dean admissions and student devel., 1973-77, dean admissions and coll. rels., 1977-82, v.p. coll. rels., 1982-84, exec. v.p., 1984-85, pres., 1985—. Bd. dirs. Christian Ch., Ill., Wis. and Ind., 1985—, Higher Edn. divsn. Christian Ch., St. Louis, 1985; pres. Eureka Bd. Edn., 1967-76; active various cmty. drives. Mem. Assoc. Colls. Ill. (bd. dirs. 1985—), Fedn. Ill. Ind. Colls. and Univs. (bd. dirs. 1985—), Coun. for Advancement and Support of Edn., Coun. Ind. Colls., Coun. of Pres. (higher edn. div.). Lodge: Rotary. Avocations: reading, music, antiques, golf. Office: Eureka Coll 300 E College Ave Eureka IL 61530-1500

HEARNE, STEPHEN ZACHARY, minister, educator; b. Burlington, N.C., Jan. 18, 1952; s. Stephen Thomas and Diana (Zachary) H.; m. Mary Gay Jaundrill, Dec. 31, 1974; children: Stephen Zachary Jr., David Phillip. BA in Religion, Elon (N.C.) Coll., 1976; MDiv, Southeastern Bapt. Theol. Sem., Wake Forest, N.C., 1979, ThM in New Testament, 1981; postgrad., Yale U., 1983, So. Bapt. Theol. Sem., 1990; DMin, Erskine Theol. Sem., 1996. Ordained to ministry So. Bapt. Ch., 1978. Interim minister Berea United Ch. of Christ, Elon Coll., N.C., 1975-77; minister of edn. Hocutt Meml. Bapt. Ch., Burlington, N.C., 1977-81; instr. (part-time) Tech. Coll. of Alamance, Haw River, N.C., 1978-81; campus minister North Greenville Coll., Tigerville, S.C., 1981-87; religion prof. North Greenville Coll., 1981-93; chaplain, dir. in-svc. guidance Anderson (S.C.) Coll., 1993-96; dir. admissions Gardner-Webb Sch. Divinity, Boiling Springs, N.C., 1996—, asst. prof. religion, 1996—; dir. Bapt. Student Union, Tigerville, 1981-85; conf. leader various chs., North Greenville Coll. faculty, 1984-88; elected faculty marshal, 1988-89. Contbr. articles, papers, dictionary entries to various religious publs. Chief Tigerville Vol. Fire Dept., 1982-88; asst. v.p. Tigerville Dem. precinct orgn., 1989-90; mem. Faith & Order Commn. Nat. Coun. Chs. Recipient faculty mini-grants, 1983, 85; Burlington-South Boston Ministerium Award, Elon Coll., 1976. Mem. S.C. Acad. Religion, Nat. Assn. Bapt. Profs. Religion, S.C. Bapt. Hist. Soc. Avocations: family outings, hunting, golf, reading, fishing. Home: 5 Crystal Springs Rd Apt 261 Greenville SC 29615-3182 Office: Gardner-Webb U Sch Divinity PO Box 327 Boiling Springs NC 28017-0327

HEARN-HAYNES, THERESA, lawyer; b. Chgo., Feb. 27, 1954; d. Gustia L. and Johnnie Hearn; m. Emil P. Haynes, Dec. 20, 1985 (dec. Apr. 1990); children: Dominique, Ashley, Alexis; m. William Ivory Murphy, 1993; 1 child, William Myles Murphy. BS, U. Ill., 1975; MS, U. Iowa, 1980; JD, South Tex. Coll. Law, 1986; postgrad. in mediation tng., A.A. White Dispute Resolution Inst., 1997. Ordained to ministry, Ch. of Yahvah Ala Hay, 1991. Pvt. practice Spring, Tex., 1986—, gubernatorial candidate for Tex., 1989—; specialist pub. interest law, excessive taxation, unconstnl. statutory and case law, pub. corruption, 1989—. Author: 20th Century Slavery in America, How to Stop Homeowner Association Abuse, 1999. Chairperson Senatorial dist. 18, Fort Bend County, Tex., 1988; v.p. Southside Comty. Improvement Assn., Houston, 1985; active African-Am. Legal Def. Fund, 1994; bd. dirs. Harris County Coop. Resources, 1994; dist. supt. for state of Tex., Ch. of Yahvah Ala Hay. Named Hon. Tuskegee alumni, 1994. Mem. Trial Lawyers of Am., Landowners Assn. (bd. dirs. 1984—), Wild Heather Civic Club. Avocations: singing, dancing, teaching, sewing, jogging. Office: PO Box 1495 Spring TX 77383-1495

HEARN-YOUNGBLOOD, PEGGY ELAINE, organist; b. New Orleans, May 24, 1922; d. Henry Otto and Jessie Edna (Pierce) Hearn; m. Stephen Gilbert Youngblood, 1941 (dec. 1996); 1 child, Mark. *Mrs. Hearn-Youngblood and son Mark are moving to Natchitoches, Louisiana, the oldest town in the Louisiana Purchase, and Mark's birthplace. Husband Steve passed away on April 9, 1996.* Student, Southeastern La. Coll., 1945; BS, Mary Washington Coll., 1945-46; postgrad., Southwestern Sem., Ft. Worth, 1951; studied voice with Elizabeth Wasor, N.Y.C. Tchr. pub. schs., Natchitoches, La., 1946-47, Cloutierville and Gorham, La., 1952-53; profl. accompanist Northwestern La. U., Natchitoches, 1948-49, Southwestern Sem. Music Sch., 1955-61; choir dir. Poplar Springs Drive Bapt. Ch., Meridian, Miss., 1950-51; accompanist Oglethorpe U., Atlanta, 1963-65; accompanist, soloist 2d Ponce de Leon Bapt. Ch., Atlanta, 1961-90; organist Northside Park Bapt. Ch., Atlanta, 1989—; accompanist music sch., 1952-61. Mem. Robert Shaw Chorus, Repertory Opera Co., Atlanta, 1989—. Home: 3428 Regalwoods Dr Atlanta GA 30340-4020 Office: Northside Park Bapt Ch 1877 Howell Mill Rd NW Atlanta GA 30318-2512

HEARON, SHELBY, writer, lecturer, educator; b. Marion, Ky., Jan. 18, 1931; d. Charles Boogher and Evelyn Shelby (Roberts) Reed; m. William Halpern, Aug. 19, 1995; children from previous marriage: Anne Rambo, Reed Hearon. BA, U. Tex., 1953. Disting. vis. prof. U. Ill., Chgo., 1993, Colgate U., 1993, U. Miami, 1994, U. Mass., Amherst, 1994-96, Middlebury Coll., 1996—. Author: (novels) Armadillo in the Grass, 1968; The Second Dune, 1973; Hannah's House, 1975; Now and Another Time, 1976; A Prince of a Fellow, 1978; Painted Dresses, 1981; Afternoon of a Faun, 1983; Group Therapy, 1984; A Small Town, 1985, Five Hundred Scorpions, 1987, Owning Jolene, 1989, Hug Dancing, 1991, Life Estates, 1994, Footprints, 1996; also short fiction, articles, book revs.; mem. editl. bd. American Literary Rev. Pres. Tex. Inst. Letters, 1980; chair lit. panel Tex. Commn. on Arts, 1980; mem. lit. panel N.Y. Council on Arts, 1985. Recipient NEA/PEN Syndication prizes, 1984-85, 87-88. Lit. award Am. Acad. Arts and Letters, 1990; Guggenheim fellow, 1982, Nat. Endowment Arts fellow, 1983; Ingram Merrill grant, 1987. Mem. PEN, Authors Guild, Poets & Writers Inc., Tex. Inst. Letters (Fiction award 1973, 78), Associated Writing Programs. Democrat. Presbyterian. Home: 246 S Union St Burlington VT 05401-4514

HEARST, (GERALD) GARRISON, professional football player; b. Lincolnton, Ga., Jan. 4, 1971. Student, Ga. State U. Running back Phoenix Cardinals, 1993, Arizona Cardinals, Phoenix, 1994-95, Cin. Bengals, 1996, San Francisco 49ers, 1997—. Recipient Doak Walker award, 1992; named running back The Sporting News coll. All-Am. 1st team, 1992. Office: c/o San Francisco 49ers 4949 Centennial Blvd Santa Clara CA 95054-1229*

HEARST, GEORGE RANDOLPH, JR., publishing executive, diversified ranching and real estate executive; b. San Francisco, July 13, 1927; s. George and Blanche (Wilbur) H.; m. Mary Thompson, Apr. 23, 1951 (dec. Dec. 1969); children: Mary, George Randolph III, Stephen T., Erin; m. Patricia Ann Bell, Nov. 30, 1969 (div. Nov. 1985). Pvt. bus., 1946-48; staff Los Angeles Examiner, 1948-50, San Francisco Examiner, 1954-56; with Los Angeles Evening Herald-Express, from 1956, bus. mgr., 1957, pub., from 1960; pub. Los Angeles Herald-Examiner, from 1962; v.p. Hearst Corp., 1977—; also dir. Trustee Hearst Found. Served with USNR, 1945-46; with AUS, 1950-54. Mem. V.F.W. Clubs: Burlingame Country, Jonathan, California, Riviera.

HEARST, JOHN EUGENE, chemistry educator, researcher, consultant; b. Vienna, Austria, July 2, 1935; came to U.S., 1938; s. Alphonse Bernard and Lily (Roger) H.; m. Jean Carolyn Bankson, Aug. 30, 1958; children: David Paul, Leslie Jean. B.E., Yale U., 1957; Ph.D., Calif. Inst. Tech., 1961; D.Sc. (hon.), Lehigh U., 1992. Postdoctoral rschr. Dartmouth Coll., Hanover, N.H., 1961-62; prof. chemistry U. Calif., Berkeley, 1962-95; prof. emeritus U. Calif., 1996—, Miller rsch. prof., 1970-71; founder, dir. HRI Rsch. Inc., 1978—; sr. rsch. scientist Lawrence Berkeley Lab., 1980—, dir. divsn. chem. biodynamics, 1986-89; founder, sr. cons. Advanced Genetics Rsch., Inc., Oakland, Calif., 1981-84; founder, dir. Steritech Inc., Concord, Calif., 1992-

96; founder, dir., v.p. new sci. opportunities Cerus Corp., Concord, 1992—; Disting. lectr. Purdue U., 1986; Merck Centennial lectr. Lehigh U., 1992, Robert A. Welch Found. lectr., 1992-93; cons. Codon, Inc., 1993-97. Author: Contemporary Chemistry, 1976. editor: General Chemistry, 1974; exec. editor Nucleic Acids Rsch., 1990-93; inventor, patentee in field. Bd. dirs. U. No. Calif., 1993-95. Recipient NSF sci. profl. devel. award, 1977-78; John Simon Guggenheim fellow, 1968-69, European Molecular Orgn. sr. fellow, 1973-74. Mem. AAAS, Am. Chem. Soc., Biophys. Soc., Am. Soc. Biol. Chemists, Am. Soc. for Photobiology (coun., pres. elect 1990-91, pres. 1991-92, Rsch. award 1994), Am. Phys. Soc. Home: 101 Southampton Ave Berkeley CA 94707-2036 Office: Cerus Corp 2525 Stanwell Concord CA 94520*

HEARST, RANDOLPH APPERSON, publishing executive; b. N.Y.C., Dec. 2, 1915; s. William Randolph and Millicent (Willson) H.; m. Catherine Campbell, Jan. 12, 1938 (div. Apr. 1982); children: Catherine, Virginia, Patricia, Anne, Victoria; m. Maria C. Scruggs, May 2, 1982 (div. Oct. 1986); m. Veronica de Uribe, July, 1987. Student, Harvard U., 1933-34. Asst. to editor Atlanta Georgian, 1934-38; asst. to pub. San Francisco Call-Bull., 1940-44, exec. editor, 1947-49, pub., 1950-53; asso. pub. Oakland Post-Enquirer, 1946-47; pres., dir., chief exec. officer Hearst Consol. Publs., Inc. and Hearst Pub. Co., Inc., 1961-64; pres. San Francisco Examiner, 1972—; dir. The Hearst Corp., 1965—, chmn. exec. com., 1965-73, chmn., 1973—; Dir. Hearst Found., 1945—, pres., 1972—; dir. Wm. Randolph Hearst Found., 1950—. Dir., trustee Hearst Corp.; pres., dir. Hearst Found.; pres. William Randolph Hurst Found. Served as capt., Air Transport Command USAAF, 1942-45. Roman Catholic. Clubs: Piedmont Driving (Atlanta); Burlingame Country, Pacific Union. Office: Hearst Corp 959 8th Ave New York NY 10019-3795*

HEARST, ROSALIE, philanthropist, foundation executive; b. Oklahoma City, Mar. 7; d. Mathis O. and Audell Bertha (Clary) Wynn; m. George Randolph Hearst, Sr., July 16, 1958. Student, Oklahoma City Coll., UCLA. Hearst rep. U.S. Senate Youth Program; pres. George Randolph Hearst Meml. Found. for Diabetic Edn.; pres. Rosalie Hearst Ednl. Found.; bd. dirs. Elvirita Lewis Found; life mem. Eisenhower Med. Ctr., Pathfinders, Tiempo de Los Ninos, Desert Hosp. Aux., Desert Press Club, Coll. of the Desert Aux., Internat. Orphans; bd. dirs. Pathfinder's Ranch Boys' Club; past bd. dirs. numerous charitable orgns.; trustee emeritus The Bob Hope Cultural Ctr.; coord. Officers' Wives Vol. Svcs. Dibble Gen. Hosp., Palo Alto; coord. Am. Women's Vol. Svcs. Sawtelle Hosp. L.A.; created Rosalie and George Hearst Fellowship in Ophthalmology U. Calif Berkeley. Named Woman of Yr. City of Hope, 1971, Disting. Woman Northwood Inst. Midland, Mich., 1988; recipient award for Lifetime Achievement in Community Service Palm Springs Women's Press Club. Home: 550 Camino Del Sur Palm Springs CA 92262-6010

HEART, SANDY See HORNER, SANDRA MARIE GROCE

HEART, TRACY, therapist, counselor; b. La Jolla, Calif., Mar. 25, 1961; d. Palmer and Sandra Lee (Sweeney) Osborn. BA in Psychology, Lewis & Clark Coll., 1983, MA in Counseling Psychology, 1992. Practicum and contract therapist Luth. Family Svcs., Portland, Oreg., 1991-92; on-call therapist Ryles Ctr. for Evaluation & treatment, Portland, 1992-93; triage, intake therapist Network Behavioral Health, Portland, 1993—, Ceres Behavioral Health, Portland, 1995-97; counselor Tigard, Oreg., 1995—; instr., spkr. Portland C.C., 1996-97. Mem. Am. Counseling Assn. Avocation: singing. Office: 6970 SW Sandburg St Ste 340 Portland OR 97223-8039

HEARTFIELD, THAD, judge; b. 1940. Student, Notre Dame U., 1959-60, Southwest Tex. Jr. Coll., 1960; BA, St. Mary's U., 1962, JD, 1965. Asst. dist. atty. Jefferson County, 1965-66; assoc. Weller, Wheelus & Green, 1966-69; city atty. Beaumont, 1969-73; ptnr. O'Brian, Richards & Heartfield, 1973-77, Crutchfield, DeCordova, Brocato & Heartfield, 1981-85; dir. Lower Neches Valley Authority, 1983-94; dist. judge U.S. Dist. Ct. (ea. dist.)Tex., 1995—. adv. dir. St. Elizabeth Hosp., 1992-94. Office: US Dist Ct PO Box 949 Beaumont TX 77004-0949*

HEARTT, CHARLOTTE BEEBE, university official; b. N.Y.C., Nov. 12, 1933; d. Stacey Kile and Charlotte Beebe; BA, Wellesley Coll., 1954; m. William Hollis Peirce, 1954; children: Daniel Converse, William Kile; m. Stephen Heartt, 1962; children: Thomas Beebe, Sarah Lincoln. Intern Office of V.p. Richard Nixon, Washington, 1953; asst. in Computing Numerical Analysis Lab. U. Wis., Madison, 1954-56; dir. fund raising Boston Arts festival, 1961; sec. to dean coll. rels. Radcliffe Coll., Cambridge, Mass., 1961-62; sec. to chmn. dept. city planning Harvard U., Cambridge, 1962; Fulbright program adviser, study abroad adviser Brandeis U., 1966-71, dir. office internat. programs, 1971-75, dir. found. and corp. rels., 1976-79; dir. corp. rels., asst. dir. devel. Smith Coll., Northampton, Mass., 1979-81, dir. devel., 1981-95, dir. prin. gifts, 1995-98; ind. cons., 1999—. Mem. Commonwealth Task Force on the Open Univ., 1973; bd. dirs. Coun. on Internat. Ednl. Exch., 1973-77, mem. exec. com., 1975-77; bd. dirs. Boston Area Seminar for Internat. Students, 1973-76. Mem. Sect. on U.S. Study Abroad (nat. sec., regional rep. 1972-74), Nat. Assn. Fgn. Student Affairs (nat. commr. liaison), Nat. Assn. Women Deans, Adminstrs. and Counselors (internat. students and programs com. 1974-76), Nat. Soc. Fund Raisers, Coun. for Advancement and Support Edn.; mem. adv. com. New England Colls. Fund, 1981-95; trustee Berkshire Sch., 1989-98, trustee emerita, 1999—; bd. dirs. Hampshire Cmty. United Way, 1996—. Home: 11 Carver Rd Wellesley MA 02481-5351

HEATER, WILLIAM HENDERSON, retired psychology educator; b. Webster Groves, Mo., May 12, 1928; s. Elsor and Mary Eliza (Henderson) H.; m. Mary Ellen Fischbach, Jan. 22, 1955; children: John William, Susan Elizabeth Salinas, David Julius. BA, Denison U., 1950; MDiv, Union Theol. Sem., 1953; PhD, Mich. State U., 1967. Asst. min. Fort Street Presbyn. Ch., Detroit, 1953-56; min. 1st Bapt. Ch., Nitro, W.Va., 1956-59, Owosso, Mich., 1959-64; instr. psychology Lansing (Mich.) C.C., 1966-69, chmn. social sci. dept., 1969-86, prof., 1986-93; vis. scholar U. Mich., 1991. Mem. Lansing Bd. Edn., 1978-89, v.p., 1979, 80, 88, pres., 1981, 86, 87; bd. dirs. Econ. Crisis Ctr., East Lansing. Recipient Excellence in Tchg. award United Ch. of Christ Gen. Synod, 1989. Mem. Torch Club Internat. Democrat. Mem. United Church of Christ. Avocations: travel, hiking, stained glass, gardening, numismatics. Home: 2025 Cogswell Dr Lansing MI 48906-3610

HEATH, ALICE PRIVÉ, women's health nurse, educator; b. Burlington, Vt.; d. Joseph Alfred and Carmen (O'Kane) Privé; children: Jeanne Marie, Brian, Erin. AA in Nursing, Hillsborough Community Coll., 1973; BSN, San Jose State U., 1980; MS, U. Calif., San Francisco, 1985; cert. in theol. studies, Grad. Theol. Union, Berkeley, 1997; postgrad. in Ethics., U. So. Calif., 1998—. RN, Calif. Staff nurse labor and delivery Bapt. Hosp., Pensacola, Fla.; staff nurse labor and delivery, maternity, newborn units Mills Meml. Hosp., San Mateo, Calif.; staff, charge nurse labor and delivery Alexian Bros. Hosp., San Jose, Calif.; staff developer, perinatal clin. specialist Santa Clara Valley Med. Ctr., San Jose; ACLS, BCLS instr., regional trainer AHA neonatal resuscitation; electronic fetal monitoring princs. and practices instr. Vol. coord. BCLS instr. program of the AHA, USS Abraham Lincoln Carrier. Linda Lee Miller rsch. scholar. Mem. Assn. of Women's Health, Obstetrics and Neonatal Nursing (sect. legis. chair 1993-95), Bay Area Soc. of Health, Edn. and Tng., Sigma Theta Tau (nominating com. chair 1979-80).

HEATH, BERTHANN JONES, education administrator; b. Dallas, May 4, 1938; d. James Lafayette and Allie Mae (Hudson) Jones; m. John William Heath, Jr., July 14, 1963 (div. 1975); 1 child, John William, III. BS cum laude, Pepperdine U., 1959; MS, UCLA, 1960. Cert. nat. family and consumer scientist. Tchr., dept. chair L.A. Unified Sch. Dist., 1960-69, dist. resource tchr., 1972-75; counselor L.A. H.S., 1968-72; regional supr., home econs. edn. L.A. Regional Office Calif. State Dept. Edn., 1975-85; program mgr., sch.-to-career transition San Diego City Schs., 1985—; trustee Consumer Credit Counselors of San Diego and Imperial Counties, Calif., 1986—; mem. adv. com. Calif. State Dept. Edn. Home Econs. and Health Careers, Sacramento, 1985—; mem. articulation team SDUSD and San Diego C.C.s, 1987—. Contbr. to curriculum guides, pamphlets and leaflets. V.p. San Diego chpt. The Links, Inc., 1995-97; presenter TV-8 Looks at Learning and Inside San Diego, 1985-95. Recipient Appreciation/Commendation award Calif. Dept. Edn., 1987, Nat. Gourmet Cook award Nat. Assembly, Links, Inc., 1996, Fin. Literacy Program Svc. award Consumer Credit Counselors of San Diego and Imperial Counties, 1996, Am. Assn. Family and Consumer Scis. Nat. Leader of Yr. award, 1998; named Woman of Distinction, Women, Inc., 1999. Mem. Am. Vocat. Assn. (bylaws chair F&CS ed. divsn. 1993-97), Nat. Assn. Local Suprs. of Family and Consumer Scis. (pres. 1992-93), Am. Vocat. Assn. (mem. policy and planning com. 1991-97), Calif. Assn. F&CS (mem. San Diego chpt., chair secondary edn. 1985-95, state chair edn. com. 1989-90, ex-officio mem. articulation com. 1989-96, Leader of the Yr. award 1998), So. Calif. Biotech. Consortium (founding 1994-96), Alpha Rho Tau, Delta Sigma Theta, Kappa Omicron Nu, Phi Delta Kappa. Avocations: traveling, recipe experimentation, writing, elder care research and development. Office: San Diego Unified Sch Dist Instructional Media Ctr 2441 Cardinal Ln San Diego CA 92123-3799

HEATH, CHARLES DICKINSON, lawyer, telephone company executive; b. Waterloo, Iowa, June 28, 1941; s. George Clinton and Dorothy (Dickinson) H.; m. Carilyn Frances Cain, June 3, 1972. B.B.A., U. Iowa, 1962, J.D., 1966; M.B.A., U. Ariz., 1963. Bar: Iowa 1966, Pa. 1969, Ind. 1970, U.S. Supreme Ct. 1971, Wis. 1973, Ariz. 1975, Mich. 1979, Fla. 1979, Calif. 1989. Asst. gen. counsel Kohler Co. (Wis.), 1973-79; securities and tax counsel Kellogg Co., Battle Creek, Mich., 1979-81; assoc. gen. counsel Universal Telephone Inc., Milw., 1981-89, also corp. sec., 1987-89; atty. Century Telephone Enterprises, Inc., LaCrosse, Wis., 1989—.

HEATH, DOUGLAS EDWIN, geography educator; b. Beverly, Mass., Dec. 3, 1948; s. Arnold Currier and Gladwyn Lorraine (Blackwell) H.; m Ellen Rosemary Morris, June 5, 1971; 1 child, Laura Ellen. BS in Geology, Bucknell U., 1971; MA in Geography, Syracuse U., 1974, PhD in Geography, 1978. Prof. Northampton C.C., Bethlehem, Pa., 1977—. Contbr. articles to profl. jours, including: Jour. Geography, Profl. Geographer, Jour. of the Water Pollution Control Fedn. Mem. Assn. Am. Geographers, Nat. Coun. for Geographic Edn. (Disting. Tchg. Achievement 1983), Nat. Assn. Geosci. Tchrs, Sierra Club, Nat. Resources Def. Coun., Omicron Delta Kappa. Democrat. Unitarian. Avocations: backpacking, photography. Home: 516 Sherwood Rd Ho Ho Kus NJ 07423-1513 Office: Northampton CC 3835 Green Pond Rd Bethlehem PA 18020-7568

HEATH, DWIGHT BRALEY, anthropologist, educator; b. Hartford, Conn., Nov. 19, 1930; s. Percy Leonard and Luise (Hosp) H.; 1 child, David Braley (dec.). AB in Social Rels., Harvard U., 1952; PhD in Anthropology, Yale U., 1959. Mem. faculty Brown U., 1959—, prof. anthropology, 1970—; dir. Ctr. for Latin Am. Studies, 1984-87, 88-89; vis. prof., U.S. and abroad, cons. in field. Author: A Journal of the Pilgrims at Plymouth, 1963, 86, Land Reform and Social Revolution in Bolivia, 1969, Historical Dictionary of Bolivia, 1972, Contemporary Cultures and Societies of Latin America, 1965, 74, 2d edit., 1988, Cross-Cultural Approaches to the Study of Alcohol, 1976, Alcohol Use and World Cultures, 1980, Cultural Factors in Alcohol Research and Treatment of Drinking Problems, 1981, International Handbook on Alcohol and Cultures, 1995, Drinking Occasions, 1999; contbr. articles to profl. jours. With AUS, 1952-54. Grantee Nat. Acad. Scis., 1974, Am. Philos. Soc., 1972, Social Sci. Research Council, 1958, Doherty Found., 1956-57, Nat. Inst. Alcohol Abuse and Alcoholism, 1976-81. Mem. AAAS, Am. Anthrop. Assn., Am. Ethnol. Soc., Am. Soc. Ethnohistory, Royal Anthrop. Inst., L.Am. Studies Assn. Office: Brown U Dept Anthropology PO Box 1921 Providence RI 02912-1921

HEATH, FRANK BRADFORD, dentist; b. Houston, Dec. 11, 1938; s. Robert Bradford and Maudie H. (Sweeney) H.; m. Heide J.M. Schmidt, Aug. 20, 1965; children: Dirk Alan, Shannon Erika, Kent Bradford. BA, Sam Houston State U., 1961; DDS, U. Tex., Houston, 1965. Pvt. practice dentistry, Houston, 1967—. Served as capt. U.S. Army, 1965-67. Fellow Acad. Gen. Dentistry, Acad. Dentistry Internat.; mem. ADA, Houston Dist. Dental Soc., Tex. Dental Assn., Delta Tau Delta, Xi Psi Phi. Republican. Methodist. Home: 12904 W Shadow Lake Ln Cypress TX 77429-5907 Office: 12337 Jones Rd Ste 322 Houston TX 77070-4845

HEATH, GARY BRIAN, manufacturing firm executive, engineer; b. Pueblo, Colo., Nov. 5, 1954; s. William Sidney Heath and Eleanor Aileen (Mortimer) Svedman, (stepfather) Donald Svedman; m. Francine Marie Tamburelli, Apr. 28, 1990. BSME, U. So. Colo., 1979; MBA, U. Phoenix, 1984. Engr. ADR Ultrasound Corp., Tempe, Ariz., 1979-81; sr. engr. Technicare Ultrasound, Englewood, Colo., 1981-83; engring. mgr. COBE Labs., Inc., Lakewood, Colo., 1983-89; dir. mfg. COBE BCT, Inc., Lakewood, 1989-96, v.p. mfg., 1996—; Patentee fluid flow transfer device, pressure diaphragm for fluid flow device. Mem. Soc. Mfg. Engrs., Soc. Plastics Engrs. Avocations: skiing, fishing, reading, weight training. Home: 7 Mule Deer Trl Littleton CO 80127-5790 Office: COBE BCT INC 1201 Oak St Lakewood CO 80215-4409

HEATH, GEORGE ROSS, oceanographer; b. Adelaide, Australia, Mar. 10, 1939; s. Frederick John and Eleanora (Blackmore) H.; m. Lorna Margaret Sommerville, Oct. 5, 1972; children: Amanda Jo, Alisa Jeanne. BSc, Adelaide U., 1960, BSc with honors, 1961; PhD, U. Calif., San Diego, 1968. Geologist S. Australian Geol. Survey, Adelaide, 1961-63; asst. prof. oceanography Oreg. State U., Corvallis, 1969-72, assoc. prof., 1972-75, prof., dean, 1978-84; assoc. prof. oceanography U. R.I., Narragansett, 1974-77, prof., 1977-78; dean U. Wash., Seattle, 1984-96, prof., 1984—, dean emeritus, 1996—; pres., exec. dir. Monterey Bay Aquarium Rsch. Inst., Moss Landing, Calif., 1996-97; mem. bd. oceans and atmosphere Nat. Assn. State Univs. and Land Grant Colls., 1982-96, co-chmn. exec. com., 1992-93; chmn. legis. com. Commn. on Food, Environment and Renewable Resources, 1994-96; chmn. bd. ocean sci. and policy NRC, 1984-85, mem. bd. radioactive waste mgmt., 1982-90; bd. govs. Joint Oceanographic Instns., Inc., 1978-96, chmn., 1982-84; v.p. sci. com. on oceanic rsch. of Internat. Coun. of Sci. Unions, 1984-90; chmn. performance assessment peer rev. panel Waste Isolation Pilot Plant, 1987-98; bd. dirs. Monterey Bay Aquarium Rsch. Inst.; mem. found. com. Coll. Marine Sci. and Fisheries, Sultan Qaboos U., Muscat, Sultanate of Oman, 1994—; mem. adv. panel Odyssey, 1990—; environ. analyst Sta. KIRO-TV, Seattle, 1993; bd. govs. Consortium for Oceanographic Rsch. & Edn., 1994-98, chmn., 1996-98; bd. govs. Seattle Aquarium Soc., 1998—. Contbr. articles to profl. jours. Recipient Fulbright award, 1963. Fellow AAAS, Geol. Soc. Am., Am. Geophys. Union; mem. Oceanography Soc. Home: 3857 50th Ave NE Seattle WA 98105-5235 Office: U Wash Sch Oceanography PO Box 357940 Seattle WA 98195-7940

HEATH, GLENN EDWARD, planner; b. Kirkwood, Mo., Feb. 28, 1958; s. Glenn Anderson and Dorothy Elizabeth (Tonn) H.; m. Deanna Shunnarah, Aug. 26, 1989. AA, Edison CC., 1981; BA, Goddard Coll., 1985; MS, Fla. Inst. Technology, 1988. Cert. Am. Inst. Cert. Planners. Intern Caloosa Nature Ctr., Ft. Myers, Fla., 1985; student asst. Marine Resources Coun. East Fla., Melbourne, 1986-87; from intern to sr. planner Southwest Fla. Regional Planning Coun., North Ft. Myers, 1987—. Co-author: Indian River Lagoon Management Study, 1987, Southwest Florida Regional Hurricane Evacuation Study Update, 1987, 91, 95, Charlotte Harbor National Estuary Program Nomination Document, 1995. Mem. Am. Planning Assn. Democrat. Avocations: comic book collecting, tropical fish, military history, nature study, birding. Office: Southwest Fla Regional Planning Coun 4980 Bayline Dr Fort Myers FL 33917-3909

HEATH, JAMES EDWARD, physiology educator, retired; b. Evansville, Ind., May 3, 1935; s. Max Levy and Mae Blossom (McNutt) H.; m. Maxine Shoemaker, Apr. 2, 1955; children: Cynthia Maxine, Pamela Diane, Jessica Scott. BA, UCLA, 1957, MA, 1958, PhD, 1962. Asst. prof. physiology U. Ill., Urbana, 1964-67, assoc. prof. physiology, 1967-72, prof. physiology, 1972-75, 75-95, head dept. physiology, 1976-82, prof. emeritus, 1995—; prof., dept. chmn. U. Fla., Gainesville, 1974-75; cons. evaluator North Ctrl. Assn., 1978-95; vis. scholar U. Tex., Austin, 1996—. Editor Physiol. Zoology, 1975-92, Jour. Thermal Biology, 1975—; mem. editl. bd. Ann. Rev. Physiology, 1980-85; contbr. over 100 articles to profl. jours. NSF, NIH grantee; Fulbright fellow, 1986-87. Fellow AAAS; mem. Am. Physiol. Soc., Ecol. Soc. Am. (editl. bd. 1972-76), Soc. Ichthyology and Herpetology, SAR, SCV, Descs. of War 1812. Avocations: sailing, guitar, model railroading. E-mail: jheath@tstar.net. Home: RR 1 Box 217 Buchanan Dam TX 78609-9734 Office: U Ill Dept Physiology 405 S Goodwin Ave Urbana IL 61801-3702

HEATH, JAMES LEE, food science educator, researcher; b. Monroe, La., Dec. 6, 1939; s. James Lee and Alodi (Blank) H.; m. Mary Alice Noble, Dec. 25, 1960. B.S., La. State U., 1963, M.S., 1968, Ph.D., 1970. Asst. prof. food sci. U. Md., 1970-74, asso. prof., 1974-79, prof., 1979—. Editor Md. Poultry, 1976-78; assoc. editor Poultry Sci. Jour., 1980-95; contbr. articles to profl. publs. Officer U.S. Army, 1963-65. Recipient research and service awards, 1979, Alumni award for research, 1981, Alumni award for teaching. Mem. Poultry Sci. Assn. (award 1979), Am. Inst. Biol. Scis., Inst. Food Tech., World's Poultry Congress, Sigma Xi (sec. Md. chpt. 1976-77, pres. chpt. 1977-78), Gamma Sigma Delta (pres. 1987-88, award for excellence in teaching), Alpha Zeta. Home: 6224 86th Ave New Carrollton MD 20784-2704 Office: U Md Dept Poultry Sci College Park MD 20742

HEATH, JEFFREY A., executive recruiter; b. Kent, Washington, Sept. 30, 1950; s. Harold Herbert and Charlotte (Mitchell) H.; m. Karen Sue Bradley, Sept. 12, 1982. BS in Psychology, Manhattan Coll., 1975; MBA in Finance, Pace U., 1978. Various mgmt. positions Lafayette Radio Corp., Syosset, N.Y., 1972-77; sales mgr. U.S. JVC Corp., Elmwood Park, N.J., 1977-79; nat. corp. adminstr. U.S. JVC Corp., Elmwood Park, 1979-81; pres. Mgmt. Recruiters Internat., N.Y.C., 1981—. Bd. dirs. New Castle Conservation Bd., Chappaqua, N.Y., 1984—. Mem. Psi Chi. Republican. Home: 9 Crystal Spring Rd Chappaqua NY 10514-1412 Office: 295 Madison Ave Fl 36 New York NY 10017-6304

HEATH, JEFFREY DALE, minister; b. Fayetteville, N.C., Oct. 31, 1962; s. Norman W. and Eula M. (Oakley) H.; m. Beth Landing, June 30, 1985; children: Sarah Beth, Jeffrey Scott, Sonya Lea. BA, Bob Jones U., 1985, MA, 1989, DMin, 1991. Ordained to ministry Bapt. Ch., 1985. Tchr. Trinity Christian Sch., Greenville, N.C., 1985-87; assoc. pastor, adminstr. Grace Ch., Greenville, 1985-92, pastor, 1992—. Mem. Nat. Assn. Ch. Bus. Adminstrs., Greenville C. of C. Republican. Home: 420 Lee St Greenville NC 27858-8657 Office: Grace Ch 3551 Charles Blvd Greenville NC 27858-9609

HEATH, JEROME BRUCE, information systems educator; b. East Chicago, Ind., Nov. 12, 1939; s. King Ralph and Doris Lois (Young) H.; m. Joan M. Wall, Aug. 20, 1960 (div. Aut. 1990); children: Linda, Deej, Lisa, Dean; m. Valerie May Meyers, Jan. 6, 1991. BA, Monmouth Coll., 1962; MBA, U. Minn., 1985; PhD, U. Hawaii, 1997. Environ. engr. Waldorf Paper, St. Paul, 1970-76; chem. engr. Combustion Equip., Fridley, Minn., 1976-80; project engr. EKA, Raissio, Appleton, Wis., 1980-83; computer coord. Nat. Coll., St. Paul, 1988-90; mem. faculty Metro State U., St. Paul, 1990-93, Hawaii Pacific U., Honolulu, 1993-97, North Seattle C.C., 1997—; computer trainer Access, Honolulu, 1993-97; reviewer Idea Group Pub., Hershey, Pa., 1997—. Author textbook: Structured Program Design, 1993; contbr. article, poem and chpt. to profl. publs. Vice chair Lino Lakes (Minn.) Planning and Zoning Bd., 1978-80. Honeywell fellow, 1984. E-Mail: heathj@hawaii.edu.

HEATH, JINGER L., cosmetics executive; b. 1952. Homemaker, 1973-81; part-time interior decorator, cons. Dallas, 1981; chmn. bd. Beauticontrol Cosmetics Inc., Carrollton, Tex., 1981—. Office: Beauticontrol Cosmetics Inc 2121 Midway Rd Carrollton TX 75006-5039*

HEATH, JOSEPHINE WARD, foundation administrator; b. San Jose, Calif., Sept. 5, 1937; d. James Hugh and Adella Johanna (Paetsch) Ward; m. Stratton Rollins Heath Jr.; children: Stratton, Kristin Heath-Colon, Joel. BS, Ea. Oreg. State U., 1959; MS, U. Wis., 1960. Commr. Boulder (Colo.) County, 1982-90; tchg. fellow John F. Kennedy Sch. of Govt., Harvard U., Cambridge, Mass., 1991; spl. asst. to the dir. White Ho. Office of Nat. Svc., Washington, 1993; pres. Jurismonitor, Boulder, 1993-95; tchr., project liberty John F. Kennedy Sch. Govt., Harvard U., Cambridge, 1994—; pres. The Cmty. Found., Boulder, 1995—; tchr. Bad Kreuznoch, Germany, 1966-67, El Paso, Tex., 1963-64, Appleton, Wis., 1961-62; regional dir. ACTION, Denver, 1977-79. Editor: Alternative Work Patterns, 1977. Candidate U.S. Senate, Colo., 1992, 1990; commr. Met. Baseball Stadium Dist., Maj. League Colo. Rockies, 1991—; county commr. Boulder County, 1982-90; co-founder Women's Found. of Colo., 1987; trainer for elected offcls. in Ctrl. Europe, 1994—. Recipient Eagle award Colo. Rural Housing Authority, 1990; named Torch Bearer Olympic Torch Run, 1996, Pacesetter for the Environ. Daily Camera, 1990; inducted to YWCA Civic award Hall of Fame 1999. Mem. Internat. Women's Forum (bd. dirs. 1986-89), Women's Forum of Colo. (pres. 1991), Women of the West Mus. (founding bd. mem. 1996—). Democrat. Avocations: skiing, hiking, sports. Home: 2455 Vassar Dr Boulder CO 80303-5728 Office: The Cmty Found 2060 Broadway St Ste 380 Boulder CO 80302-5281

HEATH, MARIWYN DWYER, writer, legislative issues consultant; b. Chgo., May 1, 1935; d. Thomas Leo and Winifred (Brennan) Dwyer; m. Eugene R. Heath, Sept. 3, 1956; chilren: Philip Clayton, Jeffrey Thomas. BJ, U. Mo., 1956. Mng. editor Chemung Valley Reporter, Horseheads, N.Y., 1956-57; freelance writer, platform spkr., editor Tech. Transls., Dayton, Ohio, 1966—; cons. Internat. Women's Commn., 1975-76; ERA coord. Nat. Fedn. Bus. and Profl. Women's Clubs, 1974-82, 92—; polit. and mgmt. coms. ERAmerica, 1976-82, exec. dir., 1982-88; pres. Miami Valley Regional Transit Authority, 1986-88; chair Regional Transit Coalition, 1991-94. Author: 75 Years and Beyond-BPW/USA, 1994. Active Gov. Ohio Task Force Credit for Women, 1973, Ohio Womens Commn., 1990-98, vice-chair, 1993-96, chair, 1996-98; midwest regional adv. com. SBA, 1976-82; task force Women Ohio Bicentennial Commn., 1999—; pres. Dayton Pres. Club, 1973-74; chmn. Ohio Coalition ERA Implementation, 1974-75; appt. joint civilian orientation conf. U.S. Dept. Def., 1988. Recipient Legion of Honor award Dayton Pres. Club, 1987, Keeper of Flame award Ohio Sec. of State, 1990; named one of 10 Outstanding Women of World Soroptimist Internat., 1982; named to Ohio Womens Hall of Fame. Mem. AAUW (dir. Dayton 1965-72, Woman of Yr. award Dayton 1974), Nat. Fedn. Bus. and Profl. Womens Clubs (pres. Dayton 1967-69, Ohio 1976-77, nat. polit. action com. 1985-98, chmn. 1988-98), Miami Valley Mil. Affairs Assn. (bd. dirs.), Ohio Women (v.p. 1983-86, bd. dirs. 1977-89), Assn. Women Execs., Women in Comm. Republican. Roman Catholic. Address: 10 Wisteria Dr Dayton OH 45419-3451

HEATH, MICHELE CHRISTINE, botany educator; b. Bournemouth, England, Sept. 22, 1945; arrived in Can., 1971; d. Percy and Winifred Iris Lily (Downes) Roy; m. Ian Brent Heath, Sept. 23, 1967; 1 child, Lorraine. BSc in Botany with honors, U. London, 1966, PhD in Plant Pathology, 1969. Postdoctoral fellow dept. plant pathology U. Ga., 1969-71; postdoctoral fellow dept. botany U. Toronto, Ont., Can., 1971-72, from lectr. to assoc. prof. botany dept., 1972-81, prof., 1981—; chair programme com. 6th Internat. Congress Plant Pathology, Montreal, 1993. Co-author: Ultrastructure of Rust Fungi, 1979; mem. editorial bd. Caryologia, 1979-83, Phytopathology 1982-84, assoc. editor, 1991-93; sr. editor Physiol. & Molecular Plant Pathology, 1982-89; contbr. sci. articles to profl. jours. and chpts. to books. Recipient Huxley Meml. medal Imperial Coll., 1979; Steacie Meml. fellow Nat. Scis. and Engring. Rsch. Coun. Can., 1982. Fellow Royal Soc. Can., Am. Phytopathol. Soc. (sr. editor APS press 1988-91, soc. awards and honors com. 1992-96, vice chair 1994, chair 1995); mem. Can. Phytopathol. Soc. (nominating com. 1979-80, disease and pathogen physiology com. 1987-96, chair 1988-96, v.p. 1993-94, pres.-elect 1994-95, pres. 1995-96, Gordon Green award 1984). Avocations: lapidary arts, painting, horse riding. Office: U Toronto Botany Dept, 25 Willcocks St, Toronto, ON Canada M5S 3B2

HEATH, PETER LAUCHLAN, philosophy educator; b. Milan, May 9, 1922; came to U.S., 1962; s. Philip George and Olga (Sinclair) H. BA with honors, Magdalen Coll., Oxford, Eng., 1942. Asst. prof. U. Edinburgh, Scotland, 1946-58; assoc. prof. U. St. Andrews, Scotland, 1958-62; prof. philosophy U. Va., Charlottesville, 1962-95, prof. emeritus, 1995—. Author/commentator: The Philosopher's Alice, 1974; editor: On the Syllogism (A. de Morgan), 1966; translator: Science of Knowledge (J.G. Fichte), 1970, System of Transcendental Idealism (F.W.J. Schelling), 1978, others. Capt. Brit. Army, 1942-46, ETO. Mem. Lewis Carroll Soc. N.Am. (pres. 1976-8). Avocations: book collecting, golfing. Home: 808 Winston Ter Charlottesville VA 22903-1637 Office: U Va Dept Philosophy 521 Cabell Hall Charlottesville VA 22901

HEATH, PRESTON, clergy member, religious organization administrator; b. Dec. 21, 1963; m. Iris Marie Turner Heath; children: Connie Marie Heath Bradshaw, Preston Gerome Heath, Jr. Student, East Carolina U. Dir. Ministry Council of the Pentecostal Free Will Baptist Ch., Dunn, N.C.; gen. supt. The Pentecostal Free Will Bapt. Ch., Inc., Dunn, N.C., 1996—; bible instr. Heritage Bible Coll., 1982—; conv. spkr. Office: The Pentecostal Bapt Ch Inc PO Box 1568 Dunn NC 28335-1568*

HEATH, RICHARD EDDY, lawyer; b. N.J., Nov. 15, 1930; s. W. Eddy and Dorothy (Brown) H.; m. Beth M., June 17, 1955; children: Ellen Louise, David Montgomery, Karen Elizabeth, Deborah Anne. BA cum laude, Swarthmore Coll., 1952; LLB cum laude, Harvard U., 1955. Bar: N.Y., Fla. Teaching fellowship Harvard Law Sch., Cambridge, Mass., 1955-56; assoc. Hodgson and Russ, Buffalo, N.Y., 1956-61, ptnr., 1961—; bd. dirs. IDEX Corp., Northbrook, Ill., Cliffstar Corp., Dunkirk, N.Y. Trustee Children's Hosp., Buffalo, 1975-98; trustee U. at Buffalo Found., 1966-89, sec., 1976—. Recipient Walter P. Cooke award U. Buffalo, 1978.

HEATH, RICHARD MURRAY, retired hospital administrator; b. Amanda, Ohio, Sept. 24, 1927; s. Cecil E. and Mary Eva (Murray) H.; m. Charlene Wilson, June 4, 1948; children: Jenifer Sue, Janet Lynn. BS in Edn, Wilmington (Ohio) Coll., 1949; MS in Social Adminstrn, Case Western Res. U., 1953; MS in Hosp. Adminstrn, Northwestern U., 1958. Adminstr. Orient (Ohio) State Hosp., 1956-61; asst. supt. Colo. State Hosp., 1961-72; dir. instl. services N.Y. State Dept. Mental Hygiene, 1972-77; dir. Mohawk Valley Psychiat. Centers, 1977-93; ret., 1993; project dir. NIMH grants; survey cons. Joint Commn. Accreditation of Hosps. Author articles in field. Served with USNR, World War II. Recipient Kleber award N.Y. State Assn. for Blind, 1976. Mem. NASW (charter), Assn. Mental Health Adminstrs. (pres. 1970, gov. region II 1986-89, Peipenbrink award 1992), Am. Coll. Healthcare Execs., Masons, Scottish Rite (32 degree).

HEATH, RICHARD RAYMOND, investment executive; b. La Junta, Colo., June 22, 1929; s. Perry Stanford and Genevieve Anabelle (Whitney) H.; m. Arlene Newbrow, Nov. 3, 1961. BA in Econs., U. Colo., 1951, LLB, 1954. Bar: Colo. 1954, Calif. 1957, Ark. 1973. Mem. firm Neyhart & Grodin, San Francisco, 1957-66; dep. Peace Corps dir. Ivory Coast, 1966-68, dir., 1968-69; Peace Corps dir. Mali, 1969-72; dir. Ark. Dept. Fin. and Adminstrn.; also chief fiscal officer, commr. revenues State of Ark., mem. gov.'s cabinet, 1972-77; dir. San Francisco Internat. Airport, 1977-81; v.p., dir. mktg. AIS, Inc., 1981-84; exec. v.p., chief fin. officer United Bank, San Francisco, 1984-85; chmn., chief exec. officer Nat. Bus. Resources Inc., 1985-87; ptnr. Hakman & Co., Investment Bankers, 1987—; chmn., CEO Podarok Internat., Inc., 1993—; chmn., pres. Heath Mgmt. Svcs., 1994—; chmn., CEO 1st Calif. Bus. and Indsl. Devel. Corp., United Bus. Ventures; bd. dirs. V-Ray Imaging, Inc.; vice chmn. Multi-State Tax Commn., 1973-74, chmn., 1976-77, mem. exec. com., 1974-77; del. Conf. State Bar Dels. Bd. dirs., treas. San Francisco Midsummer Mozart Fet., 1985--; mem. nat. bd. dirs. Coalition for a Dem. Majority, 1973-76; chmn. bd. dirs. FORUM; mem. conservative caucus nat. Tax Limitation Com., 1980--; mem. rep. presdl. task force Rep. nat. Com., 1980-91. Mem. State Bar Calif., San Francisco Bar Assn. (past chmn. indsl. accident com.), San Francisco Lawyers Club, Am., Calif. trial lawyers assns., San Francisco Planning and Urban Renewal Assn., Nat. Parks Assn., Calif. Applicants Attys. Assn. (v.p.). Clubs: Little Rock Racquet, San Francisco Tennis (gov.), Rotary Internat., World Trade. Home: 461 Yerba Buena Ave San Francisco CA 94127-2127 Office: Hakman & Co 1350 Old Bayshore Hwy Ste 300 Burlingame CA 94010-1812

HEATH, ROGER CHARLES, state senator, writer; b. Franklin, N.H., Jan. 21, 1943; s. Everett M. and Madeline (White) H. BS, No. Ariz. U., 1966. Tchr. pub. schs., N.H., Ariz., N.Y., 1966-69; mgr. E.M. Heath Stores, Inc., N.H., Ariz., N.Y., 1969-73, now dir., treas., 1969-73; mem. N.H. Ho. of Reps., 1979-84; mem. N.H. Senate, 1984-92, chmn. ways and means com., 1985-87, asst. majority whip, 1988-92; asst. dir. Gov.'s Office Energy and Cmty. Svc., Concord, 1992-97. Author: The Policital Spectrum, The Language of Politics, 1978; contbr. articles to nat. mags. Chmn. natural resources com. N.H. Rep. Platform Com., 1983; vice chmn. N.H. Pub. Radio Adv. Bd., Concord, 1981-84; commr. Ednl. Commn. of States, 1985-87; del Coun. of State Govts., Eastern Regional Conf., 1985, Coun. of State Govts. Environ. Task Force; commr. Atlantic States Marine Fisheries Commn.; chmn. Christa McAuliffe Planetarium Commn., 1989-92. Mem. Nat. Coun. State Legislatures, Am. Legis. Exch. Coun. (membership coord., chmn. nat. task force on edn. 1985-92), Nat. Conf. State Legislatures (internat. trade com.), Internat. Assn. for Energy Econs., Gun Owners N.H. (bd. dirs., v.p. 1980-84), Mead Wilderness Base High Adventure Program (adv. com.), Winnipesaukee Sportsmen's Club (bd. dirs. 1980-87), Masons. Avocations: early home restoration, fishing, hunting, taurine.

HEATH, ROSS BRADLEY, consulting company executive; b. Geneva, Ill., June 26, 1959; s. Donald Jeremiah Heath and Louise Zalithea (Taylor) H. BA in English, Augustana Coll., 1982; MS in Tech. Mgmt., U. Md., 1996. Mng. dir. J.G. Van Dyke & Assocs., Alexandria, Va., 1992—. Mem. City of Alexandria Commn. on Aging, 1989-92. Grantee Andrew Mellon Found., 1979; recipient award of Merit City of Alexandria Commn. on Aging, 1993, Cert. of Recognition City of Alexandria, 1993. Mem. Toastmasters (pres. 1998—, Schweitzer award 1998). Avocation: public speaking. E-mail: ross.heath@mindspring.com. Home: 6301 Stevenson Ave #913 Alexandria VA 22304 Office: JG Van Dyke & Assocs Inc 5510 Cherokee Ave Ste #300 Alexandria VA 22312

HEATH, THOMAS CLARK, lawyer; b. Sarasota, Fla., Feb. 6, 1948; s. Roy Fulmer and Ruby (Clark) H.; m. Marsha Robert Hubbard, June 26, 1971 (div. Dec. 1977); m. Anne Frances Wilson, Sept. 6, 1980; 1 child, Benjamin. BSBA, U. Fla., 1970, JD, 1973. Bar: Fla. 1973, U.S. Dist. Ct. (so. dist.) Fla. 1976, U.S. Ct. Appeals (11th cir.) 1976. Assoc. Howell, Kirby, Montgomery et al, Ft. Lauderdale, Fla., 1973-75, Carey, Dwyer, Cole, Selwood & Bernard, Ft. Lauderdale, Fla., 1975-81; ptnr. Hainline, Billing, Cochran & Heath, Ft. Lauderdale, Fla., 1981-85; ptnr. Billing, Cochran, Heath, Lyles & Mauro, Ft. Lauderdale, Fla., 1985—, West Palm Beach, Fla., 1985—. Fellow Am. Bd. Trial Advocacy (charter); mem. Am. Assn. Hosp. Attys., Assn. Trial Lawyers Am., Trial Attys. Am., Fla. Defense Lawyers Assn. Avocations: fishing, hunting. Office: Billing Cochran Heath et al 888 SE 3rd Ave Ste 301 Fort Lauderdale FL 33316-1159

HEATHCOCK, CLAYTON HOWELL, chemistry educator, researcher; b. San Antonio, Tex., July 21, 1936; s. Clayton H. and Frances E. (Lay) H.; m. Mabel Ruth Sims, Sept. 6, 1957 (div. 1972); children: Cheryl Lynn, Barbara Sue, Steven Wayne, Rebecca Ann; m. Cheri R. Hadley, Nov. 28, 1980. BSc, Abilene Christian Coll., Tex., 1958; PhD, U. Colo., 1963. Supr. chem. analysis group Champion Paper and Fiber Co., Pasadena, Tex., 1958-60; asst. prof. chemistry U. Calif.-Berkeley, 1964-70, assoc. prof., 1970-75, prof., 1975—, chmn., 1986-89; chmn. Medicinal Chemistry Study Sect., NIH, Washington, 1981-83; mem. sci. adv. coun. Abbott Labs., 1986—. Author: Introduction to Organic Chemistry, 1976; editor-in chief Organic Syntheses, 1985-86, Jour. Organic Chemistry, 1989—; contbr. numerous articles to profl. jours. Recipient Alexander von Humboldt U.S. Scientist, 1978, Allan R. Day award, 1989, Prelog medal, 1991, Centenary medal Royal Soc. Chemistry, 1995. Mem. AAAS, Am. Acad. Arts and Scis., Am. Chem. Soc. (chmn. divsn. organic chemistry 1985, Ernest Guenther award 1986, award for creative work in synthetic organic chemistry 1990, A.C. Cope scholar 1990), Nat. Acad. Scis., Royal Soc. Chemistry (Centenary medal 1995), Am. Soc. Pharmacology. Home: 5235 Alhambra Valley Rd Martinez CA 94553-9765 Office: U Calif Dept Chemistry Berkeley CA 94720

HEATHERLEY, JAMES LAWRENCE, psychologist, educator; b. Ft. Worth, Nov. 21, 1946; s. Gordon Inez and Katherine Elizabeth (Eddins) H.; m. Elinor Parent, June 1968 (div. July 1974); 1 child, Charlotte Kelly; m. Melody Ann Jones, July 21, 1982. AAS, Tarrant County Jr. Coll., Ft. Worth, 1972; student, North Lake C.C., Irving, Tex., 1988, U. Tex., Arlington, 1972-89, Parker Coll. Chiropractic, Dallas, 1989; BA, Amber U., Garland, Tex., 1997, MA Candidate, 1997-99; PhD Candidate, Honolulu U., 1998-99. Registered radiol. technologist. Paramedic Ray Crowder, Ft. Worth and Detroit, 1968-76; instr., tutor radiation physics and tech. Parker Coll. Chiropractic and Southwestern Med. Sch., Dallas, 1989; merchandiser Walt Disney World, Buena Vista, Fla., 1990; real estate broker Ft. Worth and Orlando, Fla., 1986-93; spl. tutor St. John's Sch., Ennis, Tex., 1998; tchr. Mesquite (Tex.) Ind. Sch. Dist., 1998—, Ferris (Tex.) Ind. Sch. Dist., 1998—; fed. mediator All About Taxes, Ferris, 1993—; radiol. technologist multiple hosps., clinics, physician's offices, Arlington, Tex., Bryan, Tex., Dallas, Ft. Worth, Kissimmee, Fla., Orlando, St. Cloud, Fla., 1972-92; practicum, intern Richland Coll., Dallas, 1998-99. Contbr. poetry to profl. jours. Pres. Rolling Meadows Cmty. Civic Action League, Arlington, 1969-74. With USN, 1968, Vietnam. Recipient Am. Poet's award, 1998. Mem. ACA, Tarrant County Soc. Radiol. Technologists (sec. pro-tem 1974), Nat. Assn. Student Nurses, Tex. Assn. Student Nurses, Am. Chiropractic Assn., Mason (steward master of ceremonies 1987—), Scottish Rite (med. officer 1987—, Golden Trowel award 1989), York Rite (knighthood 1987—), DeMolays, Order Eastern Star. Avocations: art, music, research, outdoors, history.

HEATHERLEY, MELODY ANN, nursing administrator; b. Dallas, Apr. 15, 1957; d. Harold Ray and Barbara Ann (Roebuck) Jones; m. James Lawrence Heatherley, July 21, 1982. BSN, U. Tex., Arlington, 1979; MBA in Mgmt., Amber U., Garland, Tex., 1997. RN, Tex., Fla. Surg. nurse St. Paul Hosp., Dallas, 1979, Mesquite (Tex.) Meml. Hosp., 1979-80; charge nurse All Saints Hosp.-Main, Ft. Worth, 1980-87; house supr., charge nurse All Saints Cityview Hosp., Ft. Worth, 1987-88; staff nurse ICU, critical care coord. Hosp. Corp. Am. Med. Plz. Hosp., Ft. Worth, 1986-89; staff nurse ICU, CCU Harris Meth. Hurst, Euless, Bedford, Bedford, Tex., 1989-91; staff nurse rehab. unit Harris Meth. HEB, Bedford, 1991; charge nurse surg. ICU, cardiovascular recovery Humana Hosp.-Lucerne, Orlando, Fla., 1991-93, relief house supr., 1991-93; divsn. supr. nursing adminstrn. St. Paul Med. Ctr., Dallas, 1993-94; adminstrv. supr Baylor Med. Ctr. Ellis County, Waxahachie, Tex., 1994-97; data output specialist, mgr. Baylor U. Med. Ctr., Dallas, 1997-98; dir. quality improvement & assurance Baylor SurgiCare & Texas Surgery Ctr., 1998—. Mem. AACN, ANA, NAFE, Assn. Rehab. Nurses, Tex. Orgn. Nurse Execs., Tex. Nurses Assn., Dallas Area Helathcare Quality Assn. Episcopalian. Avocations: scuba diving, travel, counted cross-stitch, ceramics, crochet. Office: Baylor SurgiCare & Tex Surgery Ctrs 3920 Worth St Dallas TX 75246-1683

HEATHERTON, TODD FREDERICK, psychology educator; b. Lethbridge, Alta., Can., Feb. 9, 1961; came to U.S., 1989; s. Frederick George and Marlene Ernestine Sandercock; m. Patricia Ryrie Dickson, June 24, 1989; children: Sarah Grace Ryie, James Frederick Dickson. BSc, U. Calgary, Alta., 1984; MA, U. Toronto, 1986, PhD, 1989. Rsch. assoc. Case Western Res. U., Cleve., 1989-90; asst. prof. Harvard U., Cambridge, Mass., 1990-94; assoc. prof. Dartmouth Coll., Hanover, N.H., 1994—; internat. spkr. Mind Matters Seminar, Los Altos, Calif., 1995-98. Editor: Can Personality Change?, 1994; author: Losing Control, 1994; assoc. editor Psychology of Addictive Behaviors, 1994-98. McLean family fellow Dartmouth Coll., Hanover, 1998. Mem. APA, Am. Psychology Soc., Soc. Personality and Social Psychology (exec. 1990—). Office: Dartmouth Coll 6207 Gerry Hall Hanover NH 03755-3549

HEATON, CHARLES LLOYD, dermatologist, educator; b. Bryan, Tex., May 8, 1935; s. Homer Lloyd and Bessie Blanton (Sharp) H. BS, Tex. A&M U., 1957; MD, Baylor U., 1961; MA (hon.), U. Pa., 1973. Diplomate Am. Bd. Dermatology. Intern Jefferson Davis Hosp., Houston, 1961-62; resident Baylor U., 1962-65; sr. attending physician Phila. Gen. Hosp., 1965-69, chief of svc., 1970-77; mem. dept. dermatology U. Pa. Sch. Medicine, 1966-78; assoc. prof. dermatology U. Pa., 1973-78; assoc. prof. dermatology U. Cin., 1978-85, prof., 1985—, interim dir. dept. dermatology, 1998. Author: Audiovisual Course in Venereal Disease, 1972, (with D.M. Pillsbury) Manual of Dermatology, 1980; contbr. 35 articles to profl. jours., 12 chpts. to books. Served to lt. comdr. USPHS, 1965-67. Fellow ACP, AAD, Coll. Physicians of Phila.; mem. AMA, Soc. Investigative Dermatology, Am. Venereal Disease Assn., Am. Dermatol. Assn., Royal Soc. Medicine (London), Cin. Dermatol. Soc., Alpha Omega Alpha. Home: 5534 E Galbraith Rd Apt 25 Cincinnati OH 45236-2840 Office: U Cin Coll Coll Medicine Dept Dermatology 231 Bethesda Ave Cincinnati OH 45219-0523

HEATON, DEBBIE ANN, mental health services worker; b. El Paso, Tex., Jan. 28, 1959; d. Joe Harrison and Patricia Ann (Major) Williams; m. Donald Esplin Heaton, Aug. 10, 1978 (div. Aug. 1981); 1 child, Marsha Camille. BSBA, Chadwick U., 1993; BS, La Salle U., 1995, M Health Svcs. Mgmt., 1997. Cert. substance abuse counselor, Ariz., behavioral therapist, domestic violence therapist. Receptionist Gallup (N.Mex.) Animal Hosp., 1980-82; clk. Allsup's, Gallup, 1983-85; security guard Giant Refinery, Gallup, 1985-86; asst. mgr. Circle K, Thatcher, Ariz., 1986-87; asst. house mgr. Graham/Greenlee Counseling, Safford, Ariz., 1987-89; adult case mgr. Southeastern Behavioral Health Svcs., Willcox, Ariz., 1989-96; adult mental health case mgr. Ariz. Physicians IPA, Safford, 1996—. Recipient Case Mgmt. Svc. award U. Ariz. Divsn. Rehab. Svcs., 1995. Mem. Assn. Social Work Mgrs., Nat. Assn. Case Mgmt. (conf. workshop presenter 1996), Internat. Women's Writers Guild. Avocations: horseback riding, writing, animal assisted therapy, raising dogs, collecting classical movies. Home: 3405 S Sage Trl Thatcher AZ 85552-5176

HEATON, JANET NICHOLS, artist, art gallery director; b. Miami, Fla., May 27, 1936; d. Wilmer Elwood and Katherine Elizabeth (Rodgers) Nichols; m. Wendell Carlos Heaton, Apr. 14, 1956; children: Benjamin Nichols Heaton, Nancy Elizabeth Breedlove. Student, Fla. State U., 1954-56. Artist Heaton's Studio & Gallery, Lake Park, Fla., 1976—, dir., 1979—. One woman show Comercia Bank Trust, Palm Bch. Gardens, Fla., 1999; Exhibited in group shows at Leigh Yawkey Woodson Art Mus., Wausau, Wis., 1988-89, 91-93, 95-97, 99, Norton Gallery Art, West Palm Beach, Fla., 1989, 92, Mt. Kenya Safari Club, Kenya, East Africa, 1989, 92, Prestige Gallery, Toronto, Can., 1989, Kimball Art Ctr., Park City, Utah, 1990-91, Grand Cen. Gallery, N.Y.C., 1990, Gallery Fine Arts, Ft. Myers, Fla., 1990, Cornell Fine Art Mus., Winter Park, Fla., 1990, Cen. Park Zoo Gallery, N.Y.C., 1991, The Art League Marco Island, Fla., 1993, 96, Washington State Hist. Soc. Mus., Tacoma, 1993, Old Sch. Sq. Cultural Arts Ctr., Delray Beach, Fla., 1993, 94, The Salmagundi Club, N.Y.C., 1994, J.N. Bartfield Galleries, N.Y.C., 1994, Pt. Royal Gallery, Naples, Fla., 1994, Brookfield Zoo, Chgo., 1994, Ward Mus. Wildfowl Art, Salisbury, Md., 1995, Easton (Md.) Waterfowl Festival, 1995, Sarasota (Fla.) Visual Art Ctr., 1995, Shenandoah Art Ctr., North Wainsboro, Va., 1996, Village Gallery, Venice, Fla., 1997, The Hiram Blauvelt Art Mus., Oradell, N.j., The Mus. of Hounds and Hunting, Leesburg, Va., 1997, Nat. Arts Club Grand Gallery, N.Y.C., 1997, Fort Hayes Met. Edn. Ctr., Columbus, Ohio, 1997, Nat. Arts Club, N.Y.C., 1997, Leigh Yawkey Woodson Art Mus., Wausau, 1997, Wendell Gilley Mus., Southwest Harbour, Maine, 1996, Tampa (Fla.) Mus. Art, 1998, Village Gallery, Venice, Fla., 1998, 99, Disney's Animal Kingdom, Orlando, 1998, Smithsonian Instn.'s Conservation & Rsch. Ctr. & Noah's Network, Front Royal, Va., 1998, 99, Comercia Bank Trust, Palm Bch. Gardens, 1998, The Nature Gallery, West Boylston, Mass., 1998, Mus. Sci. and Scpace Transit Planetarium, Miami, 1998, Ambleside Gallery, Groose Points, Mich., Bigfork Art & Cultural Ctr., Bigfork, Mont., 1998, Holland and Holland Function, N.Y.C., 1999, Leigh Yawkey Woodson Art Mus., Wausau, Wis., 1999, John L. Wehle Gallery at Genesee County Mus., Mumford, Fla., 1999, Cleve. Mus. Natural Hist., Cleve., 1999; numerous others; numerous traveling exhbns., 1994—; represented in permanent collections Leigh Yawkey Woodson Art Mus., State House, Nairobi, Kenya, PGA Nat., Palm Beach Gardens, Fla., also numerous pvt. collections; subject numerous art jours.; represented by J.N. Bartfield Gallery, N.Y.C. Mem. Soc. Animal Artists (signature), Pastel Soc. Am. (signature), Fla. Watercolor Soc. (signature), Outdoor Writers Assn. Am., Catherine Lorillard Wolfe Art Club (signature). Avocation: photography. Home: 11680 Lake Shore Pl No Palm Beach FL 33408-3204 Office: Heatons Studio and Gallery 1169 Old Dixie Hwy Lake Park FL 33403-2311

HEATON, PATRICIA, actress; b. Cleve., Mar. 4, 1959; d. Chuck and Pat Heaton; m. David Hunt, 1992; children: Sam, John. BA in Theater, Ohio State U., 1980. Actress playing Debra Barone on Everybody Loves Raymond CBS-TV, 1996—. Appearances include (TV series) Room for Two, 1992-93, Someone Like Me, 1994, Women of the House, 1995, (TV episodes) Alien Nation, 1989, thirtysomething, 1990, (TV movie) Shattered Dreams: The Charlotte Fedders Story, 1990, (films) Beethoven, 1992, Memoirs of an Invisible Man, 1992, The New Age, 1994, Space Jam, 1996, (stage) The Johnstown Vindicator, 1987, Don't Get God Started, 1987-88. Agent's office: Internat Creative Mgmt 8942 Wilshire Blvd Beverly Hills CA 90211-1934

HEATON-MARTICORENA, JEAN, early childhood educator; b. Equality, Ill., Feb. 27, 1933; d. Lytle and Loretta (Drone) Mossman; m. Fred T. Heaton, June 10, 1954 (div. Dec. 1979); children: Fred T., Laura, Sheri; m. Michael Marticorena, Mar. 14, 1987. BS in Home Econs., Southern Ill. U., 1955, MS in Edn., 1958; PhD in Child Devel., Early Childhood Edn, Fla. State U., 1971. Cert. secondary educator Ill., Fla., Calif. Tchr. Corham (Ill.) High Sch., 1955-57; rsch. asst. Southern Ill. U., Carbondale, 1957-58; tchr. Jefferson High Sch., Tampa, Fla., 1958-60, Hamilton Jr. High Sch., Oakland, Calif., 1960-61; prof. San Francisco State U., 1961-94; ednl. cons. Dept. Home and Cmty. Devel., U. Monrovia, Liberia, 1982, Calif. State Dept. Edn., 1974-76; mem. adv. bd. Skyline Coll., 1973—, coord. Study Tours; presenter at profl. confs. Recipient Meritorious Performance award SFSU, 1986 and 1989. Mem. Infant/Toddler Consortium San Francisco Bay Area (exec. com. 1988-93), San Francisco/San Mateo Child Care Consortium (exec. com. 1987-93), Calif. Coun. on Children and Youth (exec. com. Region II 1982-90), San Francisco Assn. for Edn. Young Children (pres. 1990-92), AAUW (exec. com. San Mateo br. 1981-83, exec. bd. San Carlos br. 1996—), Child Care Coord. Coun. of San Mateo County (adv. com. 1995—, bd. dirs. 1997—, exec. com. 1997—), Family Forum '96 (chair planning com. 1996), Pi Lambda Theta, Omicron Nu.

HEATWOLE, MARK M., lawyer; b. Pitts., Jan. 28, 1948; s. Marion Grove and Phyllis Adelle (Leiter) H.; m. Sarah Ann Collier, Dec. 30, 1970; children: Mary Phyllis, Elizabeth Collier, Anna Bell. BA, Washington and Lee U., 1969, JD, 1972. Bar: Ill. 1972, U.S. Dist. Ct. (no. dist.) Ill. 1972, U.S. Ct. Appeals (7th cir.) 1977, U.S. Supreme Ct. 1980, U.S. Tax Ct. 1987. Assoc. Chadwell & Kayser, Ltd., Chgo., 1972-79, ptnr., v.p., 1979-89; ptnr. Winston & Strawn, Chgo., 1990—. Mem. 1st ward Rep. com. on candidates Lake Forest (Ill.) Caucus, 1985-88, chmn., 1987-88; vice-chmn. Lake Forest Caucus, 1989-90, chmn. 1990-91; mem. session Lake Forest Presbyn. Ch., 1978-84, chmn. ch. and society com., 1980; bd. dirs. Lyric Opera Chgo. Guild, 1976—, treas., 1980-81, v.p., 1981-82, chmn. fund-raising, 1986; bd. dirs. Lake Forest Symphony, 1987-91, Rehab. Inst. Chgo. Enterprises, 1991—, Gorton Community Ctr., 1982-88, vice chmn., 1986; chmn. bd. Gorton Community Ctr. Found., 1986-89; trustee Barat Coll., 1982-85, The Admiral, Chgo., 1988—, Allendale Assn., 1991—. Mem. ABA (mem. anti-trust com. young lawyers sect. 1978-81, continuing legal edn. com. 1978-79, com. on civil practice and procedure antitrust sect. 1980, bus. law sect. 1986—, patent trademark and copyright sect. 1990—), Chgo. Bar Assn. (chmn. profl. responsibility com. young lawyers sect. 1977-78, mem. exec. com. 1978-79, bd. dirs.), Computer Law Assn., Nat. Assn. Bond Lawyers, Shoreacres Club, Econ. Club Chgo., Winter Club, Law Club. Republican. Office: Winston & Strawn 35 W Wacker Dr Ste 4200 Chicago IL 60601-1695

HEBB, MALCOLM HAYDEN, physicist; b. Marquette, Mich., July 21, 1910; s. Thomas Carlyle and Evelyn Shewell (Hayden) H.; m. Marion Elizabeth Evers, May 8, 1943. B.A., U. B.C., 1931, D.Sc. (hon.), 1963; postgrad., U. Wis., 1931-34; Ph.D., Harvard, 1936. Instr. physics Harvard, 1936-37; Harvard Sheldon travelling fellow to U. Utrecht, 1937-38; instr. physics Duke, 1938-42; anti-submarine devices Harvard Underwater Sound Lab., Nat. Def. Research Com., 1942-45; physicist research lab. Sharples Corp., 1945-49; research asso. Gen. Electric Co., 1949-51, mgr. gen. physics research dept., 1951-68, physicist, 1968-75; Vis. com. physics Tufts U., 1967; mem. council Harvard Found., 1958-63; vis. com. elec. engring. Princeton, 1959-71. Recipient Gov. Gen. Medal B.C., 1931. Fellow Am. Phys. Soc.; mem. Netherlands Phys. Soc., Sigma Xi. Clubs: Mohawk, Mohawk Golf. Home: 1600 E Crooked Lake Dr Eustis FL 32726-5720 Office: Gen Electric Co Research Lab Schenectady NY 12345

HEBDA, LAWRENCE JOHN, data processing executive, consultant; b. East Chicago, Ind., Apr. 9, 1954; s. Walter Martin and Barbara (Matczynski) H.; m. Cynthia Ruta Aizkalns, June 17, 1978. BS, Purdue U., 1976; MBA, U. Iowa, 1983. Cert. data processor. Programmer Inland Steel Co., East Chicago, 1976-77; data analyst Deere & Co., Moline, Ill., 1977-82, systems analyst, 1982-83, project mgr., 1983-84, dealer systems cons., 1984-85, corp. planning analyst, 1985-87, systems edn. adminstr., 1987-88, telecommunications analyst, 1988; info. systems sr. cons. Hewitt Assocs., Lincolnshire, Ill., 1988-93, MIS bus. mgr., 1994-97, mgr. software distbn./oper. sys., 1997—; instr. computer sci. dept. Coll. Lake County Ill., 1996—. Mem. Nat. Rep. Congl. Com., 1982-85; charter mem. Rep. Presdl. Task Force, 1980; chmn. pastoral coun. Roman Cath. Ch., 1994-95. Recipient Cert. Recognition, Nat. Rep. Congl. Com., 1982-85, Presdl. Achievement award Rep. Nat. Com., 1984. Mem. Data Processing Mgmt. Assn., Am. Legion, Internat. Platform Assn., DAV Comdr.'s Club, King's Men Religious Orgn. (v.p. 1985, pres. 1986-87), Toastmasters (assoc. area gov. 1983-84). Roman Catholic. Club: Toastmasters Internat. (assoc. area gov. 1983-84). Home: 306 Spring Ln Vernon Hills IL 60061-2123 Office: Hewitt Assocs 100 Half Day Rd Lincolnshire IL 60069-3242

HEBEL, DORIS A., astrologer; b. Chgo., Jan. 1, 1935; d. Erich and Anna Dorothea (Hircy) H.; m. Leon L. Bram, Apr. 29, 1961 (div. Dec. 1973); 2 children. Libr. Campbell-Mithun, Chgo., 1958-61, Kenyon & Eckhardt, Chgo., 1961-64; pres. Astro-Technic Forecasting, Chgo., 1965—. Author: Contemporary Lectures, 1975, Celestial Psychology, 1985; contbr. various articles in astrological jours. and magazines. Mem. Am. Fedn. Astrologers (life), Nat. Coun. for Geocosmic Rsch. (life, nat. bd. dirs. 1975-80), Nat. Astrol. Soc., Assn. for Astrol. Networking, Internat. Soc. for Astrol. Rsch. Avocations: reading, singing, walking, metaphysical subjects, arts. Home and Office: 151 N Michigan Ave Apt 1001 Chicago IL 60601-7543

HEBELER, HENRY KOESTER, retired aerospace and electronics executive; b. St. Louis, Aug. 12, 1933; s. Henry and Viola O. (Koester) H.; m. Mirriam Robb, Aug. 12, 1978; children by previous marriage: Linda Ruth, Laura Ann. BS in Aero. Engring., MIT, 1956, MS, 1956, MBA, 1970. Gen. mgr. rsch./engring. Boeing Aerospace Co., Seattle, 1970-72, pres., 1980-85; v.p. bus. devel. The Boeing Co., Seattle, 1973-74, exec. coun. and corp. v.p. planning, 1988-89; pres. Boeing Engring. & Constrn. Co., Seattle, 1975-79, Boeing Electronics Co., Seattle, 1985-87; bd. dirs. Microelectronics and Computer Tech. Corp.; mem. fusion panel Ho. of Reps., 1979-81, energy rsch. adv. bd. Dept. Energy, 1980-81, task force on internat. industry Def. Sci. Bd., 1982-84, adv. com. nat. strategic materials and minerals program U.S. Dept. Interior, 1986—. Patentee in field. Bd. govs. Sloan Sch., MIT, 1980-84; bd. visitors Def. Systems Mgmt. Coll., Ft. Belvoir, Va. Recipient Mead prize for aero. engrs., 1956; Kuljian humanities award, 1954; Sperry Gyroscope fellow, 1956; Sloan fellow M.I.T., 1970. Mem. AIAA, Nat. Aeros. Assn., Assn. of U.S. Army, Armed Forces Commn. and Electronics Assn. (bd. dirs.), Aviation Hall of Fame, Ala. Space and Rocket Ctr. (sci. and adv. com. 1980-85), Nat. Space (bd. govs. 1980-85), Meridian Valley Country Club. Home and Office: 24600 140th Ave SE Kent WA 98042-5160

HEBENSTREIT, JAMES BRYANT, agricultural products executive, bank and venture capital executive; b. Long Beach, Calif., Mar. 8, 1946; s. William Joseph and Jean (Stark) H.; m. Marilyn Bartlett, Aug. 23, 1986. AB, Harvard U., 1968, MBA, 1973. Pres. Terra-Light div. Butler Mfg. Co., Boston, 1980-82, Capital for Bus., Inc. (SB/C, venture capital affiliate Commerce Bancshares), St. Louis and Kansas City, Mo., 1982-87; sr. v.p. fin., CFO Commerce Bancshares, Inc., Kansas City, 1985-87, bd. dirs., 1987—; pres. Bartlett and Co., Kansas City, 1992—. Lt. USNR, 1968-71. Home: 1016 W 58th St Kansas City MO 64113-1133 Office: Bartlett & Co 4800 Main St Kansas City MO 64112-2510*

HEBER, RUTH R., psychologist, consultant; b. Lodz, Poland, June 27, 1935; came to U.S., 1957; d. Moses Zwi and Ryna (Glucklich) Borenstein; m. Jacob Heber, 1955 (div. 1982); children: Ron, Sheldon, Lorraine; m. Lawrence Walter Kullman, 1987. BA in Psychology, CUNY, 1972; MS in Ednl. Psychology and Guidance, Yeshiva U., 1974, PhD in Devel. Psychology, 1979. Lic. psychologist, N.Y. Staff psychotherapist North Suffolk Mental Health Ctr., N.Y., 1980-82; supervising psychologist, clinic and program coord. Creedmoor Psychiat. Ctr., N.Y., 1982-88; dir. East Side Consultation Ctr., N.Y.C., 1988—; adj. asst. prof. psychology Queens Coll., CUNY; cons., lectr. Humanistic Psychology Ctr., N.Y., 1983-93; lectr. psychiatry Mt. Sinai Sch. Medicine, CUNY, 1990-9 5, asst. clin. prof., 1995—; supr. psychiat. residents Mt. Sinai Med. Ctr., N.Y.C., 1989—; adj.

prof. The Union Inst. Grad. Sch. Cin., 1991—; participant, supr. Holocaust Survivors Treatment Program, 1993—; pvt. practice; presenter, guest spkr., workshop leader. Mem. APA (program chmn. humanistic psychology divsn. 1988-89, treas. 1989-92, pres. 1993-94, 95—), Am. Group Psychotherapy Assn., Ea. Group Psychotherapy Assn., N.Y. State Psychological Assn. (disaster/crisis response network 1993-95, colleague assistance program com. 1992—), Assoc. Alumni Mt. Sinai Med. Ctr., Phi Beta Kappa, Psi Chi, Kappa Delta Pi, Delta Phi Alpha. Avocations: art, literature, travel. Office: 200 E 33rd St Apt 4I New York NY 10016-4826

HEBERLING, TIMOTHY ALAN, information systems engineer; b. Portsmouth, Va., Sept. 3, 1955; s. Donald Anthony and Phyllis Elaine (McMillan) H.; m. Judith Ann Tohill, June 13, 1992; children: Ellen, Ben, Hanna. Student, James Madison U., 1973-74; BS in Computer Sci., Va. Tech., 1986. Commd. 2nd lt. USAF, 1986, advanced through grades to capt., 1990; law enforcement specialist USAF, Hampton, Va., 1975-79; entry controller USAF, Chievres, Belgium, 1979-82; security police flight chief USAF, Enid, Okla., 1982-83; comms.-computer officer Air Force Hdqts., Washington, 1987-91; info. systems officer Def. Info. Systems, Reston, Va., 1991-94; sr. systems adminstr. The White House, Washington, 1994-96; ret. USAF, 1995; sr. info. systems engr. Mitretek Systems, McLean, Va., 1996-97; tech. mgr. Am. Online Internat Svcs., Sterling, Va., 1997—; cons. WebVisor, Leesburg, Va., 1996—. Blood drive coord. Def. Info. System Agy., Reston, 1991-94. Decorated various Air Force medals. Mem. Microsoft Sitebuilders. Home: 19553 Herndon Ct Leesburg VA 20175-6759 Office: Am Online Internet Svcs 22080 Pacific Blvd Sterling VA 20166-9304

HEBERT, BLISS EDMUND, opera director; b. Faust, N.Y., Nov. 30, 1930; s. Wilfrid Joseph and Merle Addasah (Bliss) H. B.A., Syracuse U., 1951, M.Mus., 1952; piano pupil of, Robert Goldsand, Simone Barrere, Lelia Gousseau. Gen. mgr. Washington Opera Soc., 1960-63; guest dir. Juilliard Sch., 1975-76; mem. faculty Boston U., 1952-53, U. Wash., 1969. Stage dir., Met. Opera, N.Y.C., 1973-75, N.Y. City Opera, 1963-75, Santa Fe Opera, 1957—; dir. opera companies of, San Francisco, 1963, Houston, 1964, Seattle Opera, 1967, Toronto, 1972, San Diego, 1970, Vancouver, B.C., 1969, Ft. Worth, 1966, Washington, 1959, Cin., 1968, Portland, Oreg., 1969, Caramoor Festival, Katonah, N.Y., 1966, La Gune Festival, 1968—, New Orleans, 1970, Balt., 1972, Tulsa, 1975, Miami, Fla., 1975, Charlotte, N.C., 1975, Dallas, 1977, Shreveport, La., 1977, Chgo., 1983, Montreal, 1984, Boston, 1984, Cleve., 1988, Opera Nothern Ireland, 1988, Virginia Opera, 1991, Opera Mexico City, 1993, Austin Opera, 1993, Florentine Opera, Milw., 1994; rec. artist, Columbia records; as stage dir. for Igor Stravinsky's major operas under his conducting. Served AUS, 1954-56. Mem. Lambda Chi Alpha, Phi Mu Alpha. Office: care John S Miller 801 W 181st St Apt 20 New York NY 10033-4518

HEBERT, CHRISTINE ANNE, educator; b. Waltham, Mass., Aug. 31, 1953; d. Alfred Lionel and Virginia Eugenia (Nogas) Mellor; m. Dennis Armand Hebert, Dec. 18, 1976; 1 child, Kirsten Erica. BS in Early Childhood Edn., Wheelock Coll., Boston, 1975; MS in Spl. Edn., Coll. William and Mary, Williamsburg, Va., 1985; postgrad., Old Dominion U., 1996—. Cert. elem. tchr., learning disabled, emotional disturbances. Title I aide Fryeburg (Maine) Pub. Schs., 1975-76; title I tutor Conway (N.H.) Pub. Schs., 1976-77; presch. tchr. Elmendort AFB, Anchorage, 1978-80; counselor, caregiver Intermission/Parent Resource Ctr., Anchorage, 1980-81; residential counselor Group Home for MR Adults, Bridton, Maine, 1983-84; tchr. learning disabled Norfolk (Va.) Pub. Schs., 1985-90, tchr. elem., 1990—, lead tchr. sci., 1992—, tchr. magnet sch. math. and sci., 1995—, sci. tchr. specialist, 1998—; tutor Learning Resource Ctr., Virginia Beach, Va., 1986-89; inclusion tchr., 1993-95; mem. NASA Tchr. Enhancement Inst., summers 1994, 97; nat. instrnl. leader Activities for Integration of Math. and Sci., 1997—. Recipient Norfolk Sch. Bell award, 1994-95; faculty scholar Coll. William and Mary, 1984-85; AT&T fellow Va. Sci. Mus., 1997. Mem. ASCD, NSTA, Nat. Coun. Tchrs. Math., Optimists (pres. Bayside chpt. 1996-97), Kappa Delta Pi.

HEBERT, DONNA MARIE, food product executive; b. Worcester, Mass., June 20, 1951; d. Charles George and Lena Marie (Diliddo) Olson; m. Raymond Louis Hebert, June 17, 1972; children: Wendy Ann, Daniel Raymond. Student, Quinsigamond C.C., Worcester, 1969-70, Assumption Coll., Worcester, 1970-72. Sales person F.W. Woolworth, Worcester, 1967-69; rschr. State Mut. Life Ins., Worcester, 1969-70; bus. office pers. Assumption Coll., Worcester, 1970-73; pres. Stage Stop Candy, Ltd., Dennis Port, Mass., 1982-96, treas., 1996—. Treas. troop 82 Boy Scouts Am., South Dennis, Mass., 1988-93; Eucharistic Min.; mem. southside Civic Assn.; bd. dirs. Dennis Salute to Scouting Breakfast. Recipient Bronze Pelican, Diocesan Scout Office, Fall River, 1990. Mem. Dennis C. of C. (bd. dirs., mem. nominating com., mem. govt. affairs com.), Cape Cod Pers. Assn., New Eng. Retail Confectioners Assn., Cape Cod Human Resources Assn. Roman Catholic. Avocation: traveling. Office: Stage Stop Candy Ltd 411 Main St Dennis Port MA 02639-1308

HEBERT, LEO PLACIDE, physician; b. Houma, La., Oct. 27, 1940; s. Leo Placide and Ethel (Trosclair) H.; m. Carolyn Mae St. Amant, Aug. 2, 1969; children: Anne-Marie, Catherine, Elizabeth (dec.), Leo, Maria, Julie. BS, U. Southwestern La., 1963; MD, La. State U., New Orleans, 1965. Lic. physician, La. Physician, internist in pvt. practice Thibodaux, La., 1971—; chief of staff Thibodaux Hosp., 1978. Mem. com. of 100, La. State U. Sch. Medicine. Capt. USAF, 1966-68. Mem. Am. Soc. Internal Medicine, La. Med. Soc., LaFourche Parish Med. Soc., U. Southwestern La. Alumni Assn., U. Southwestern La. Found., Ragin Cajun Club-U. Southwestern La., Phi Kappa Phi, Alpha Omega Alpha. Roman Catholic. Avocations: amateur radio, music, pets, tennis, roses. Office: 1101 Audubon Ave Thibodaux LA 70301-4957

HEBERT, ROBERT D., academic administrator; b. Abbeville, La., Nov. 14, 1938; married. BA, U. Southwestern La., 1959; MA, Fla. State U., 1961, PhD, 1966. Asst. prof. history Miss. State U., 1962-69, assoc. prof. history, 1969-76; prof. McNeese State U., 1976—, v.p. acad. affairs, 1980-87, pres., 1987—. Office: McNeese State U Office of Pres Lake Charles LA 70609

HECHE, ANNE, actress; b. Aurora, Ohio, May 25, 1969; d. Donald Heche. Appearances include (film) An Ambush of Ghosts, 1993, The Adventures of Huck Finn, 1993, A Simple Twist of Fate, 1994, Milk Money, 1994, I'll Do Anything, 1994, The Wild Side, 1995, Pie in the Sky, 1995, Walking and Talking, 1996, The Juror, 1996, Volcano, 1997, Donnie Brasco, 1997, Wag the Dog, 1997, I Know What You Did Last Summer, 1997, Return to Paradise, 1998, Six Days Seven Nights, 1998, Psycho, 1998, The Third Miracle, 1999; (TV movies) O Pioneers!, 1992, Girls in Prison, 1994, If These Walls Could Talk, 1996, Wild Side, 1996 (TV series) Another World, 1988-92, Murphy Brown, 1991-92, (TV spls.) Soap Opera Digest, 1989, The 16th Ann. Daytime Emmy Awards, 1989, (stage) Getting Away with Murder, 1991-92. Recipient Emmy award Another World. •

HECHLER, DAVID SAMUEL, journalist; b. N.Y.C., Jan. 9, 1950; s. Ira Jesse and Marilyn Enid (Eisen) H.; m. Diana Kahl Munger, Apr. 23, 1988; children: Jeffrey, Peter. BA in English, Grinnell Coll., 1972; MA in Teaching English, Brown U., 1974; MS in Journalism, Columbia U., 1984. Tchr. Sacramento (Calif.) Country Day Sch., 1974-80, Marello Prep. High Sch., Santa Cruz, Calif., 1980-81; freelance writer Santa Cruz (Calif.) Express, 1982-83; stringer The N.Y. Times, 1984-87; journalist major newspapers and mags., 1984—; lectr. on incest The New Sch. Social Rsch., N.Y.C., 1993; lectr. on child abuse various seminars; Prudential fellow for Children and the News Columbia U. Sch. of Journalism, 1995-96. Author: The Battle and the Backlash: The Child Sexual Abuse War, 1988; contbr. articles to The Wall Street Jour., Dallas Life mag., The N.Y. Times, Columbia Journalism Rev., 1984—, others. Bd. dirs. Nat. Assn. Counsel for Children, 1999—, College Horizons, 1988—; tutor Harlem tutorial program, 1984-85; mentor Columbia U. Grad. Sch. Journalism, 1987-90. Recipient The Sevellon Brown award Columbia U. Grad. Sch. Journalism, 1984; grantee Fund for Investigative Journalism, 1985, 92.

HECHLER, ELLEN ELISSA, elementary education educator; b. Detroit, May 20, 1954; d. Mark and Rose (Rifkin) H. BS, Wayne State U., 1976, MEd, 1980, EdD in Curriculum and Instrn., 1995. Math. tchr. Detroit Pub. Schs., 1977—; presenter workshops in field. Author: (book) A Mathematical Word Search Puzzle Book, 1996, Real-Life Experiences Using Classified Ads, 1997, (card game) Mental Math, 1991, Mental Math Series II, 1992, mental math elem. series, 1997, mental math Spanish edit., 1997; developer in field. Bd. dirs. Orgn. for Rehab. Through Tng., Southfield, 1980—. Recipient scholarship Stephen Bufton Meml. Educators Fund, 1992-93. Mem. ASCD, Detroit Area Coun. Tchrs. of Math. (pres. 1988-89), Mich. Coun. Tchrs. of Math. (exec. bd. dirs. 1980-90, presenter workshops), Nat. Coun. Tchrs. of Math. (presenter workshops), Nat. Coun. Suprs. Math., Mich. Assn. Computer Users in Learning, Southwest Ont. Math. Educators (presenter workshops), Am. Bus. Women's Assn. Avocations: ceramics, taking videos, craft shows. Office: MidMath PO Box 2892 Farmington Hills MI 48333-2892

HECHLER, KEN, state official, former congressman, political science educator, author; b. Roslyn, N.Y., Sept. 20, 1914; s. Charles Henry and Catherine Elizabeth (Hauhart) H. *Grandfather George Hechler emigrated from Germany in 1854, enlisted with Union infantry at Parkersburg, West Virginia, wounded at Antietam and discharged at Wheeling, West Virginia. Great Uncle John Hechler captured at Chickamauga, died in Andersonville Prison. Father University of Missouri graduate, managed Clarence H. Mackay's 600 acre farm estate on Long Island, elected to numerous Republican county offices and President of Board of Education, secretary-treasurer of New York Guernsey Breeders' Association, bank president. Mother was a school teacher in St. Louis County, elected to numerous Republican county offices on Long Island, noted raiser and exhibitor of Chrysanthemums.* AB, Swarthmore Coll., 1935; AM, Columbia U., 1936, PhD, 1940; LittD (hon.), U. Charleston, 1988; HHD (hon.), W. Va. Inst. Tech., 1988. Lectr. govt. Barnard Coll., Columbia Coll., N.Y.C., 1937-41; research asst. to Judge Samuel I. Rosenman, 1939-50; research asst. on Pres. Roosevelt's pub. papers, 1939-50; sect. chief Bur. Census, 1940; personnel technician Office Emergency Mgmt., 1941; adminstrv. analyst Bur. of Budget, 1941-42, 46-47; spl. asst. to Pres. Harry S. Truman, 1949-53; research dir. Stevenson-Kefauver campaign, 1956; adminstrv. aide Senator Carroll of Colo., 1957; mem. 86th-94th Congresses from 4th W.Va. dist., 1959-77; sec. of state State of W.Va., 1985—; mem. Sci. and Tech. Com. 86th to 94th Congresses from 4th W.Va. Dist., chmn. Energy (Fossil Fuels) Subcom.; mem. Joint Com. on Orgn. of Congress, 1965-66, NASA Oversight Subcom. (U.S. Congress); asst. prof. politics Princeton U., 1947-49; prof. polit. sci. Marshall U., Huntington, W.Va., 1957, 82-84; sec. of state State of W.Va., 1984—; sci. cons. U.S. House Com. on Sci. and Tech., 1978-80; radio, TV commentator Sta. WHTN, Huntington, 1957-58, Sta. WWHY, 1978; adj. prof. polit. sci. U. Charleston (W.Va.), 1981; keynote spkr. Harry Truman lecture ser. USAF Acad., 1995; lectr. Harry S. Truman Libr., George C. Marshall Found., Washington & Lee U. Law Sch., 1996, Harry S. Truman Coll. of Chgo., 1997, Southern Ilinois Univ., 1998, Mid Ga. Coll., Appalachian State U., Ill. Wesleyan, Ill. State U., 1999. *Only Congressman to march with Martin Luther King in Selma, Alabama. First Congressman sponsoring legislation to limit coal dust and provide strict safety standards in Federal Coal Mine Health and Safety Act of 1969. Fought against corruption in coal union, risked life to campaign for Jock Yablonski, insurgent candidate later murdered. Crusaded against strip mining and mountain top removal of coal. Helped mobilize secretaries of state and attorneys general in 33 states to limit campaign spending. Led campaign to more fairly appraise and tax West Virginia natural resources owned by out-of-state corporations. Cracked down on West Virginia political corruption.* Author: Insurgency: Personalities and Politics of the Taft Era, 1940, The Bridge at Remagen, 1957, rev. edit., 1998, West Virginia Memories of President Kennedy, 1965, Toward the Endless Frontier, 1980, The Endless Space Frontier, 1982, Working with Truman, 1982, rev. edit., 1996; weekly columnist Cabell Record, Hampshire Rev., Elk River and Little Kananha News, W.Va. Hillbilly, 1990—. Bd. dirs. W.Va. Humanities Coun., 1982-84; del. Democratic Nat. Conv., 1964, 68, 72, 80, 84. Served to maj. AUS, 1942-46; served to col. Res. Decorated Bronze Star; named W.Va. Son of Yr., W.Va. State Soc. of D.C., 1969, W.Va. Speaker of Yr., W.Va. U., 1970; recipient Conservation award Nat. Audubon Soc., 1973, Mother Jones award W.Va. Environ. Coun., 1995; subject of biography by Dr. Charles H. Moffat, Ken Hechler: Maverick Public Servant, 1987; Smithsonian Instn. lectr. on 50th Anniversary of Pres. Truman, 1985; elect. to W. Va. St. Democratic Exec. Comm., 1998. Mem. Am. Polit. Sci. Assn. (assoc. dir. 1953-56), Civitan, Am. Legion, VFW, DAV, Judson Welliver Soc. of Presdl. Speech-Writers. Democrat. Episcopalian. Lodge: Elks. Home: 101-B Greenbrier St Charleston WV 25311 Office: State Capitol 1900 Kanawha Blvd E Ste 157-k Charleston WV 25305-0770

HECHT, ALAN DANNENBERG, insurance executive; b. Balt., Aug. 31, 1918; s. Lee I. and Miriam (Dannenberg) H.; m. Margaret R. Moses, June 27, 1943 (dec. Nov. 1, 1984); children: Stephen Lee, Nancy H., Elizabeth Ann; m. Marcia Levin Oberfeld, Dec. 8, 1985. BS, Johns Hopkins U., 1940, M Liberal Arts, 1976. CLU, 1951. Solicitor Travelers Ins. Co., 1945-60; partner Hecht-Schoenfeld Ins. Agy., 1960-62; merged and formed Wolman-Hecht-Schoenfeld, Inc., 1962, v.p., 1962-64; v.p. Wolman-Hecht, Inc., 1964-91, pres., 1971-92, chmn., 1992; v.p. Tongne Brooks & Co., Inc. (merged with Wolman-Hecht, Inc.), 1992-95; founder, pres. Alan D. Hecht & Co., Inc., 1966—; gen. agt. Sunamerica Life Ins. Co. Am. and other cos., Balt., 1960—; assoc. Ins., Inc., Balt., 1995—; pres. Balt. Estate Planning Coun., 1978-79; tchr. CLU econs. and fin. Johns Hopkins U., 1954-81; mem. faculty dept. econs. Mount St. Mary's Coll., Emmitsburg, Md., 1981-84; past bd. graders Am. Coll. Life Underwriters. Pres. Balt. Jewish Council, 1971-73; life and qualifying mem. Million Dollar Round Table, 1985, mem. resolutions com., 1976; bd. dirs. Balt. chpt. Am. Jewish Com., pres., 1958-60, former mem. nat. exec. com.; trustee Sinai Hosp. of Balt., 1959-68. Served to 1st lt. AUS, 1941-45. Recipient Nat. Quality award Nat. Assn. Life Underwriters; Nat. Sales Achievement award; Szold award Temple Oheb Shalom Brotherhood, 1980; George S. Robertson award Balt. Life Underwriters Assn., 1981. Mem. Soc. Fin. Svc. Profls. (CLU, ChFC, dir. 1957—, nat. sec. 1962-63, pres. 1964-65, Helen Hottenbacher award Balt. chpt. 1991), Omicron Delta Kappa, Pi Delta Epsilon. Jewish (pres. congregation 1968-70, past dir.). Home and Office: 111 Hamlet Hill Rd Apt 312 Baltimore MD 21210-1521 *With some background in economics, I believe that we can improve our life and environment only by greater productivity. Each person should accept responsibility for finishing assigned tasks at every level, no matter how menial or unimportant that task may seem.*

HECHT, ALAN JAY, cardiologist; b. 1958. BS, Northwestern U., 1979, MD, 1981. Resident internal medicine Mt. Sinai Med. Ctr., N.Y.C., 1982-84, fellow cardiology, 1984-86, physician; pvt. practice cardiology Mt. Sinai Hosp. Vol., N.Y.C., 1987—; clin. instr. Mt. Sinai Med. Ctr., N.Y.C. Fellow Am. Coll. Cardiology; mem. AHA, ACP. Office: 994 5th Ave New York NY 10028-0100

HECHT, ANTHONY EVAN, poet; b. N.Y.C., Jan. 16, 1923; s. Melvyn Hahlo and Dorothea (Holzman) H.; m. Patricia Harris, Feb. 27, 1954 (div. 1961); children: Jason, Adam; m. Helen D'Alessandro, June 12, 1971; 1 child, Evan Alexander. BA, Bard Coll., 1944, DLitt (hon.), 1970; MA, Columbia U., 1950; LHD (hon.), Georgetown U., 1981, Towson State U., 1983, U. Rochester, 1987, St. John Fisher Coll., 1989. Tchr. Kenyon Coll., 1947, State U. Iowa, 1948, NYU, 1949, Smith Coll., 1956-59; assoc. prof. English, Bard Coll., 1961; faculty U. Rochester, 1967; John H. Deane prof. poetry and rhetoric, 1968; Hurst prof. Washington U., fall 1971; vis. prof. Harvard U., 1973, Yale U., 1977; faculty Salzburg Seminar in Am. Studies, 1977; univ. prof. Georgetown U., 1985-93; cons. in poetry Libr. of Congress, 1982-84; trustee Am. Acad. in Rome, 1983—; Andrew Mellon lectr. fine arts Nat. Gallery Art, 1992; Rockefeller Found. resident Villa Serbelloni, Bellagio, Italy, 1993. Author: A Summoning of Stones, 1954, The Seven Deadly Sins, 1958, A Bestiary, 1960, The Hard Hours (Brit. Poetry Book Soc. choice 1967, Miles Poetry award Wayne U., Pulitzer Prize 1968), 1968 (Russell Loines award Nat. Inst. Arts and Letters), Millions of Strange Shadows, 1977, The Venetian Vespers, 1979, Obbligati: Essays in Criticism, 1986, The Transparent Man, 1990, Collected Earlier Poems, 1990, The Hidden Law: The Poetry of W.H. Auden, 1993, On the Laws of the Poetic Art, 1995, The Presumtions of Death, 1995, Flight Among the Tombs, 1996, A Gehenna Florilegium, 1998; contbr. intro. to The New Cambridge Shakespeare Edit. of The Sonnets, 1996; co-author, co-editor: Jiggery Pokery, 1967; translator: (with Helen Bacon) Seven Against Thebes (Aeschylus), 1973; editor: The Essential Herbert, 1987. Recipient Prix de Rome, 1950, Brandeis U. Creative Arts award, 1965; Guggenheim fellow, 1954, 59; Hudson Rev. fellow, 1958; Ford Found. fellow, 1960; Rockefeller Found. fellow, 1967; Fulbright prof. Brazil, 1971; recipient Bolligen prize, 1983, English Speaking Union award, 1981, Charles Kellogg award Bard Coll., 1982, Eugenio Montale award for Poetry, 1983, Harriet Monroe award, 1987, Ruth B. Lilly award, 1988, Aiken Taylor award The Sewanee Rev., 1989, Dorothy Tanning award for poetry, 1997; NEA grantee, 1989. Fellow Acad. Am. Poets (hon., chancellor 1971-95); mem. Nat. Inst. Arts and Letters, Am. Acad. Arts and Scis., Century Assn., Phi Beta Kappa. Home: 4256 Nebraska Ave NW Washington DC 20016-2130

HECHT, DONN, songwriter, screenwriter, agent; b. Pitts., Apr. 18, 1930. *Donn Hecht is one of the first New Wave writers who became a major force in establishing "crossover" composition techniques which defied stylistic confinement of music to traditional commercial categories. The crossover movement entered mainstream in the late 1950's when his melding of traditional Country, Popular, and B-Flat Blues served to catapult the late Patsy Cline to legendary star status. Recognized by many writers, artists and producers to follow, including Paul McCartney, John Lennon, Charlie Rich, the music soon gave birth to a new music category: New Country. In 1980 he established DHO (Donn Hecht Organization) for international marketing representation of music properties.* Creative works include: (compositions) Walking After Midnight, Snowbound, Night Train, La Mirada, Cry Not for Me, The Touch of His Hand, The Sermon On The Mount, Rock Bottom, So Dear to My Heart, Never No More, Spring is Gone, Without Your Love, Theme for Billie, I Took the Blues Out of Tomorrow, In the Country, The Battle of Chavez Ravine, Downgrade, I'm Satisfied, Poet's Love Letter, Philosophy, One-By-One, Fingerprints, Who Am I?, Nothing But Love, Half Past Midnight, The Theme from the Raisin Tree, Once Upon a Star, Save a Place in Your Heart for Me, I Was Only Teasing You, Who Knows, As Long As I Have You, I Never Got Over You, More and More and More, I'll Still Be in Love with You, All Those Teardrops, I've Cried, Until, With Love Everything Will be Right, It's Funny What Love Can Do, Because I Just Can't Take It, That's What Love Means to Me, I Don't Want No Heartaches, It All Depends on You, Pills, Pills, Pills, Why Are You Leaving Me, Well That's Love, Day By Day, Zombie Woman, One Short of Living, Together, Too Much Month for the Money Blues, Sho Ya' Right, Misery, (recs.) The Patsy Cline Story, 1977, I Remember Patsy, 1978, All My Best, 1979, Unstoppable, 1982, Come Down from the Hills, 1984, The Trinity Session, 1989, The Chase, Garth Brooks, 1992-94 (No. 1 Best Seller Billboard Top Country Albums Chart), Greatest Hits (Patsy Cline), 1992-93 (No. 1 Best Seller Billboard Top Country Catalogue Albums), (motion picture soundtracks) Coalminer's Daughter, 1980, Sweet Dreams, 1986, (TV series) Wise Guy, 1989-99, Diamonds and Chicken Soup, Clear and Present Danger, Your Ring is Off My Finger (but Still Around My Heart), (song) Hawaii Five-O, Alice in Wonderland, Millenuim II, The Pretenders, Women O the Night, Celine, Theme for Holiday in Spain, Hello Bed, I Guess I'll Just Be Moving On, Looking for Mr. Right; contbr. articles to profl. jours. Home: 1602 Alton Rd Miami Beach FL 33139-2421

HECHT, FREDERICK, physician, researcher, author, educator, consultant; b. Balt., July 11, 1930; s. Malcolm and Lucile Burger (Levy) H.; m. Irene Winchester Duckworth, Aug. 29, 1953 (div. 1977); children: Frederick Malcolm, Matthew Winchester, Maude Bancroft, Tobias Ochs; m. Barbara Kaiser McCaw, May 29, 1977; children: Kerrie Kristine, Brian Stuart. Student, U. Paris, 1950-51; BA, Dartmouth Coll., 1952; student, Boston U., 1955-56; MD, U.Rochester, N.Y., 1960. Lic. physician, Oreg., Ariz., Nev., Kans.; diplomate Am. Bd. Pediatrics. Intern Strong Meml. Hosp., Rochester, N.Y., 1960-61, resident, 1961-62; resident U. Wash. Hosp., Seattle, 1962-64, asst. in pediatrics, med. genetics, 1962-64, instr. pediatrics, med. genetics, 1962-65; asst. in pediatrics U. Rochester, 1960-62; prof. pediatrics U. Oreg., Portland, 1965-78; founder, pres., dir. S.W. Biomed. Rsch. Inst., Scottsdale, Ariz., 1978-89; founder, pres. Hecht Assocs. Inc., Jacksonville, Fla., 1989—; prof. zoology Ariz. State U., Tempe, 1978-89; prof. ob-gyn. U. Nev., Reno and Las Vegas, 1983-89; dir. molecular medicine Children's Mercy Hosp., Kansas City, Mo., 1990-91; prof. medicine U. Mo., Kansas City, 1990-91; founder, dir. div. molecular medicine Children's Mercy Hosp., Kansas City, Mo., 1990-91; vis. prof. cytogenetics and molecular genetics Adelaide Children's Hosp., North Adelaide, South Australia, 1992; assoc. prof. faculty medicine Lab. de Génetique Moleculaire des Cancers Humains, l'Université de Nice, France, 1992—; bd. dirs. Youth Law Ctr., San Francisco ; prof. med. U. Mo., Kansas City, 1990-91. Author: Fragile Sites on Human Chromosomes, 1985; editor: Trends and Teaching in Medical Genetics, 1977; mem. editorial bd. Am. Jour. Human Genetics, Cancer Genetics and Cytogenetics; contbr. over 600 articles to profl. jours. Sgt. M.I. Corps, U.S. Army, 1952-55. NIH grantee, 1968—, USPHS grantee, 1968-89; recipient Pediatric Rsch. award Ross Labs., 1970; Royal Soc. Medicine traveling fellow, London, 1971-73. Mem. Am. Pediatric Soc., Am. Soc. Human Genetics (bd. dirs.), Am. Acad. Pediatrics (charter mem. genetics sect. 1990), Soc. Pediatric Rsch., Western Soc. Pediatric Rsch. (bd. dirs.), Nat. Found. Jewish Genetic Diseases. Jewish. Avocations: writing, publishing nonfiction, fiction and poetry; gardening. Office: Hecht Assocs Inc 4134 Mcgirts Blvd Jacksonville FL 32210-4362

HECHT, HAROLD ARTHUR, orchidologist, chiropractor; b. St. Louis, Mo., Apr. 30, 1921; s. William Frederick and Myrtle Regina (Hugo) H.; m. Barbara Evelyne Ross, Nov. 19, 1942. D Chiropractic Medicine, Logan Coll. Sole practice St. Louis, 1942-95, orchidologist, 1950—; judge Orchid Digest Corp., 1959; internat. lectr., photographer in field radiotelephone engr., 1942. Contbr. articles to profl. jours. Mem. World Orchid Cong. (founding com. 1954), Mid-Am. Orchid Cong. (founder, pres. 1959, judge 1968), Am. Orchid Soc. (grand jurist, judge 1968), Mark Twain Orchid Soc. (pres. 1966, 90), Mo. Orchid Soc. (pres. 1959), European Orchid Congress (USA com. 1967). Republican. Avocations: philatilist, numismatist, amateur radio operator, antiquary.

HECHT, IRENE MARGRET, lawyer; b. Edmonton, Alta., Can., Dec. 2, 1956; came to U.S., 1964; d. Erich Ernst and Auguste (Schindler) H. BA in Speech Comm. magna cum laude, U. Wash., 1977, JD with honors, 1980. Bar: Wash., 1980. Assoc. Keller Rohrback, Seattle, 1980-85; ptnr. Keller Rohrback LLP, Seattle, 1986—. Mem. Internat. Assn. Def. Counsel, Rainier Club. Avocations: hiking, climbing, travel. Office: Keller Rohrback LLP 1201 3rd Ave Ste 3200 Seattle WA 98101-3052

HECHT, LEE, software company executive; b. Phila., May 11, 1942; s. Hymen Nathan and Anne Rosalee (Brodsky) H.; 1 dau., Kimberley Kenney. M.S. in Physics, U. Chgo., 1965, M.B.A. (NDEA fellow), 1969. Teaching asst. physics, research asst. U. Chgo., lectr. physics, 1966-67; applied maths. U. Chgo. (Sch. Bus.), 1967-69, policy studies, 1973-80; chmn., pres., chief exec. officer Phoenix-Hecht Inc. (computer services co.), Chgo., 1968-75, dir., 1968-76; pres., chief exec. officer Phoenix-Hecht Cash Mgmt. Services Inc., Chgo., 1973-75, chmn. bd., 1973-76; pres., chief exec. officer, chmn. Kenwood-Pacific Corp., San Francisco, 1973-82; dir. Holloway Mgmt. Group, Ltd., Chgo., 1973-82; chmn. Holloway Mgmt. Group, Ltd., 1976-82, Kenwood Group, San Francisco, 1977-82; chief exec. officer Teknowledge, Inc., Palo Alto, Calif., 1981-88, chmn., 1982-88; pres., chief exec. officer Middlefield Group Inc., 1981-91, Middlefield Capital Corp., 1981-86; dir. Digital Pathways Inc., Palo Alto, Calif., 1976-82, 89, chmn., 1994-96; chmn. Kenwood Group Inc., 1978-82; dir. Cimflex Teknowledge Corp., 1989-91; chmn., pres., chief exec. officer Modernsoft., Inc., Palo Alto, 1989-97; mng. ptnr. Salent LLC, 1997—; vis. lectr. bus. adminstrn. U. Calif., Berkeley, 1975-77; vis. lectr. mgmt. Stanford U., 1976; v.p. Nat. Vidiograph Inc. (motion picture prodn.), Berkeley, 1975-77; dir. U.S. Home Corp., Houston, 1985-86. Mem. Econ. Address: Salent LLC 555 Bryant St Ste 374 Palo Alto CA 94301-1704

HECHT, MARIE BERGENFELD, retired educator, author; b. N.Y.C., Oct. 21, 1918; d. Frank Falle and Marie (Trommer) Bergenfeld; BA, Goucher Coll., 1939; MA, New Sch. for Social Research, 1971; m. Morton Hecht, Jr., Dec. 17, 1937 (div.); children: Ann (Mrs. David Bloomfield), Margaret, Laurence, Andrew. Tchr. Am. history Mineola High Sch., Garden City Park, N.Y., 1960-80. Mem. Am. Hist. Assn., Orgn. Am. Historians. Author (with Herbert S. Parmet): Aaron Burr: Portrait of an Ambitious Man, 1967; Never Again: A President Runs for a Third Term, 1968; John Quincy Adams: A Personal History of An Independent Man, 1972; The Women, Yes, 1973; Beyond the Presidency: The Residues of Power, 1976; Odd Destiny: The Life of Alexander Hamilton, 1982, The Church on the Hill, 1987. Address: 5 Hewlett Pl Great Neck NY 11024-1605

HECHT, MARJORIE MAZEL, editor; b. Cambridge, Mass., Dec. 21, 1942; d. Mark and Theresa (Shuman) Mazel; m. Laurence Michael Hecht, July 2, 1972. B.A. cum laude, Smith Coll., 1964; postgrad., London Sch. Econs., 1964-65; M.S.W, Columbia U., 1967. Dir. Forest Neighborhood Service Ctr., N.Y.C., 1967-70, Wiltwyck Sch. for Boys, Bronx Center, N.Y., 1970-73; mng. editor Fusion Mag., Washington, 1977-87, 21st Century Sci. & Technol. Mag., Washington, 1987—; sci. editor Exec. Intelligence Rev., Washington, 1997—. Co-author: Beam Defense: An Alternative to Nuclear Destruction, 1983 (Aviation and Space Writers award 1983); editor: Colonize Space! Open the Age of Reason, 1985, The Holes in the Ozone Scare: The Scientific Evidence That the Sky Isn't Falling, 1992. Press rep. LaRouche Campaign, N.Y.C., 1984. Democrat. Jewish. Avocation: astronomy. Office: 21st Century Sci & Technol Mag PO Box 16285 Washington DC 20041-6285

HECHT, NATHAN LINCOLN, state supreme court justice; b. Clovis, N.Mex., Aug. 15, 1949; s. Harold Lee and Mary Loretta (Byerly) H. BA, Yale U., 1971; JD cum laude, So. Meth. U., 1974. Bar: Tex. 1974, D.C. 1975, U.S. Dist. Ct. D.C. 1975, U.S. Dist. Ct. (no. and we. dists.) Tex. 1976, U.S. Ct. Appeals (D.C. cir.) 1975, U.S. Ct. Appeals (5th cir.) 1976, U.S. Supreme Ct. 1979. Law clk. to judge U.S. Ct. Appeals (D.C. cir.), 1974-75; assoc. Locke, Purnell, Boren, Laney & Neely, Dallas, 1976-80, ptnr., 1981; dist. judge 95th Dist. Ct., Dallas, 1981-86; justice Tex. 5th Dist. Ct. Appeals, 1986-89, Texas Supreme Ct., Austin, 1989—. Contbr. articles to profl. jours. Bd. visitors So. Meth. U., Dallas, 1984-87; trustee Children's Med. Found., Dallas, 1983-89; bd. dirs. Children's Med. Ctr. North, Dallas, 1985-89; elder Valley View Christian Ch., Dallas, 1981—. Lt. USNR, 1971-79. Named Outstanding Young Lawyer of Dallas, Dallas Assn. of Young Lawyers, 1984. Fellow Tex. Bar Found., Am. Bar Found.; mem. ABA, Dallas Bar Assn., D.C. Bar Assn., Am. Law Inst. Republican. Avocations: piano, organ, jogging, bicycling. Office: Tex Supreme Ct PO Box 12248 201 West 14th Room 104 Austin TX 78711

HECHT, SUSAN ELIZABETH, consulting executive; b. Houston, Jan. 26, 1942; d. Clarence Herbert and Mildred Bertie (Turner) Vogt; m. William Herbert Hecht, July 21, 1960; children: Herbert William, Timothy Paul, James Christian. Student, Rice U., 1959, Washington U., St. Louis, 1960, U. Okla., 1964. V.p. Hecht, Spencer & Assocs., Washington, 1985—; sec. Washington adv. coun. Luth. Ch.-Mo. Synod, Washington, 1987—; chairperson commn. on orgns. Luth. Ch.-Mo. Synod, St. Louis, 1987—. Contbr. Luth. Witness mag., 1989; photographer high sch. football recruiting films, 1980-87. Office mgr. Nixon for Pres., Jefferson City, Mo., 1968; del. office George Bush for Pres., Washington, 1988; mem. White House transition team, 1988-89; mem. pres.'s adv. coun. Concordia Sem., St. Louis, 1987-91, Concordia Theol. Sem., Ft. Wayne, Ind., 1986-91. Recipient Miles Christi award Concordia Theol. Sem., 1989. Republican. Home: 2228 Aryness Dr Vienna VA 22181-3046 Office: 499 S Capitol St SW Ste 501 Washington DC 20003-4019

HECHT, WILLIAM DAVID, accountant; b. N.Y.C., Nov. 7, 1941; s. Adolph J. and Lillian (Shore) H.; m. Francine Rosen, Aug. 22, 1964; children: Peter, Dana, Allison. BS in Acctg., Queens Coll., 1962; JD, Bklyn. Law Sch., 1971; LLM in Taxation, NYU, 1974. Bar: N.Y. 1972. Ptnr., mem. mgmt. com. M.R. Weiser & Co. LLP, CPAs, N.Y.C., 1964—; mem. faculty Found. Acctg. Edn., N.Y.C.; lectr. in field. Contbr. articles to CPA Jour. Mem. ABA, AICPA, N.Y. State Soc. CPAs, N.J. State Soc. CPAs, N.Y. State Bar Assn. Republican. Jewish. Avocations: skiing, basketball. Home: 8 Tutor Pl East Brunswick NJ 08816-3658 Office: MR Weiser & Co LLP CPAs 399 Thornall St Edison NJ 08837-2236

HECHT, WILLIAM F., electric power industry executive; b. 1943. BSEE, Lehigh U., 1964, MSEE, 1970. Engr. Pa. Power & Light Co., Allentown, 1964-68, project engr., 1968-72, sr. project engr., 1972-75, mgr. distbn. planning, 1975-76, exec. dir. corp. energy planning coun., 1976-78, mgr. systems planning, 1978-84, v.p. systems power, 1984-87, v.p. mktg., 1987-90, exec. v.p., 1990-93, CEO, chmn., pres., 1993—. Office: PP&L Resources Inc 2 N 9th St Allentown PA 18101-1139*

HECHTMAN, HOWARD, financial analyst; b. N.Y.C., Sept. 1947; s. Charles and Pauline (Barmatz) H.; m. Marsha Louise Garwin, Dec. 19, 1976 (div. 1984). BS, Bklyn. Poly. U., 1968; MS in Physics, Adelphi U., 1970, MBA in Mgmt. with distinction, 1972. Grad. teaching asst. physics Computer Ctr. Adelphi U., Garden City, N.Y., 1970-72; from asst. to assoc. analyst N.Y.C. Transit Authority, 1973—. Capt. N.Y. State Guard. Named Patron of Arts Soc. for Theater Arts Resources, 1989-90; recipient Cert. of Merit Rep. Nat. Com., 1990. Mem. Soc. Am. Mil. Engrs., Civil Svc. Tech. Guild (del. 1994-99), Poly U. Alumni Assn. (alumni bd. dirs. 1978—, life dir. 1996—). Office: NYC Transit Authority MOW Finance Rm 1261 370 Jay St Ste 1 Brooklyn NY 11201-3817

HECK, ALBERT FRANK, neurologist; b. Balt., Oct. 9, 1932; s. Albert Franklin and Dorothy Mary (Jirsa) H.; divorced; children: Albert William, Karl Andrew, Robert Conrad, Paul Christopher. A.B., Johns Hopkins U., 1954; M.D., U. Md., 1958. Diplomate: Am. Bd. Psychiatry and Neurology. Intern Mercy Hosp., 1958-59; NIH fellow in neurology U. Md., Balt., 1959-62; faculty, instr. to prof. U. Md., 1964-77; prof., chmn. dept. neurology U. Tenn. Center for Health Scis., Memphis, 1977-82; dir. neurosci. program U. Tenn. Center for Health Scis., 1978-82; prof. neurology W. Va. U., 1982—; vis. prof. Medezinische Hochschule Hannover, W. Ger., 1973-74. Contbr. writings to profl. publs. Served with M.C. U.S. Army, 1962-64. Recipient jr. investigator award NIH, 1965, U.S. sr. scientist award, 1973; Humboldt Found. prize Fed. Republic Germany, 1973-74. Fellow Am. Acad. Neurology, ACP; mem. Am. Neurol. Assn., Stroke Council of Am. Heart Assn., Internat. Coll. Angiology, Alpha Omega Alpha. Condr. research in field. Home: 325 Southpointe Dr Charleston WV 25314-2486 Office: 1218 Virginia St E Charleston WV 25301-2909

HECK, CHARLES RALPH, university dean; b. Dec. 13, 1948. MBA, Embry-Riddle U., 1988; EdD, Nova U., Ft. Lauderdale, Fla., 1992. Instr., pers. mgr. Dept. of Defense, Fort Rucker, Rome, Ga.; asst. prof. bus. Floyd Coll., Rome; chair dept. bus. Alderson-Broaddus Coll., Phillipi, W. Va.; divsn. dean Mashall U., Huntington, W. Va. E-mail: drflyboy@aol.com. Home: 2028 Harris Way Russell KY 41169-1760

HECK, DEBRA UPCHURCH, information technology, procurement professional; b. Valparaiso, Fla., Nov. 4, 1956; d. Robert P. and Sallaine S. (Sledge) Upchurch; m. Robert J. Heck, May 31, 1980; children: Andrew W., Jennifer A. BS in Math., Purdue U., 1978, MS in Mgmt., 1980. Analyst mgmt. sci. Monsanto Corp. Mgmt. Sci., St. Louis, 1980-81; sys. analyst Monsanto Agr. Group, St. Louis, 1981-82, sr. sys. analyst, 1982-84; sr. analyst mgmt. sci. Monsanto Polymer Products Group, St. Louis, 1984-86; total quality fundamentals instr. Monsanto Co., St. Louis, 1985-86; project mgr. Monsanto Chem. Co., St. Louis, 1986-88; group leader Monsanto Corp. MIS, St. Louis, 1988-92, sr. group leader, 1992-95; info. tech. dir. Monsanto Bus. Svcs.-Fin., St. Louis, 1995-96; info. tech. dir. Monsanto Bus. Svcs.-Fin. & Procurement, St. Louis, 1996, dir. strategic sourcing, procurement strategic initiatives, 1997—. Trustee, chair fall gathering, doubles, social com. Ethical Soc., St. Louis, 1982—; mem. sci. adv. com., PTO bd. Parkway Sch. Dist., St. Louis, 1992—; vol. St. Louis Assn. for Retarded Citizens, 1978-85. Mem. Nat. Assn. Purchasing Mgmt., Human Resource Sys. Profls., Leadership Am. Alumni (award 1994). Avocations: travel, sports, friends, family. Office: Monsanto Co 800 N Lindbergh Blvd Saint Louis MO 63167-0001

HECK, HENRY D'ARCY, toxicologist; b. Bryn Mawr, Pa., Apr. 18, 1939; s. Harold Joseph and Lydia Suzanne (Holt) H.; m. Mercedes Casanova, Dec. 21, 1984; children: Katherine (Mrs. Daniel Troy), Julia, John Schmitz, Lara (Mrs. Daniel King). AB, Princeton U., 1962; PhD, Northwestern U., 1966. Asst. prof. chemistry U. Calif., Berkeley, 1968-72; chemist Stanford Rsch. Inst., Menlo Park, Calif., 1972-77; scientist Chem. Ind. Inst. Toxicology, Research Triangle Park, N.C., 1977-85, sr. scientist, 1985-99; adj. assoc. prof. U. N.C., Chapel Hill, 1983-99, Duke U., Durham, N.C., 1987-99. Assoc. editor: Fundamental and Applied Toxicology, 1986-1991, editor-in-chief, 1991-97. Fellow NSF, NIH, EMBO, 1963-68; mem. AAAS, Am. Chem. Soc., N.C. Soc. Toxicology (pres. 1995-96), Soc. Toxicology (Frank Blood award 1983, Inhalation Toxicol. Paper of Yr. award 1987, 93). E-mail: casaheck@beaufortco.com. Home: 101 Halcyon Cv Washington NC 27889-7901

HECK, JAMES BAKER, university official; b. Columbus, Ohio, Aug. 26, 1930; s. Arch O. and Frances (Agnew) H.; m. Jo Ann Gatton, Nov. 18, 1950; children: Janice M., Judith L., J. Jeffrey. BS in Edn., Ohio State U., 1953, MA (Nat. Def. Edn. Act fellow), 1961, Ph.D., 1967. Comml. sales engr. Ohio Bell Telephone Co., Dayton, 1955-57; tchr. Ohio Pub. Schs., Dayton, 1957-59; sch. counselor Ohio Pub. Schs., 1959-60; instr. Ohio State U., 1960-63, asst. to dean Coll. Edn., 1963-66, asst. dean faculties, rsch. assoc. Coll. Edn., 1966-67, assoc. dean faculties, asst. prof. edn., 1967-68; prof., dean Coll. Edn. U. Del., Newark, 1968-71; prof., dean, dir. Mansfield campus Ohio State U., 1971-78; dean regional campus affairs U. South Fla., 1978-81, assoc. v.p. acad. affairs, dean regional campus affairs, 1981-84, prof., assoc. v.p. acad. affairs, dir. office of tech., 1984-86, prof., dean Sch. Extended Studies & learning techs., gen. mgr. pub. broadcasting Sta. WUSF-TV/FM, WSFP-TV/FM, spl. asst. to provost, dir. office tech., 1986-90; prof., gen. mgr. Sta. WUSF-TV/FM, 1990—, Sta. WSFP-TV/FM, 1990-96; mem. bd. adminstrv. reps. USF Pub. Broadcasting, 1999—; asst. state supr. for guidance service Ohio Dept. Edn., 1962-63; Am. Coun. on Edn. fellow in academic adminstrn. U. Ill., 1965-66; evaluator Nat. Coun. for Accreditation Tchr. Edn., 1972-78; mem. planning com. Nat. Conf. Br. and Regional Campus Adminstrs., 1973-82, chmn., 1972, 80; chmn. planning com. Am. Council Edn. Acad. Fellows Working Reunion, 1972, 79, 85; vice chmn. Am. Coun. Edn. Coun. Fellows, 1980-81, chmn., 1981-82, exec. com., 1980-83, chmn. SE Region Conf., 1988, mem. alumni rels. com.; cons., lectr. in field. Co-author: Counseling: Selected Readings, 1962, Educational Administration: Selected Readings, 1965, 2d edit., 1971, Analysis of Educational Change in Ohio Public Schools, 1968; also numerous articles, monographs, papers, book revs., abstracts in field. Gen. chmn. Mansfield Area United Way campaign, 1975, bd. dirs., 1976-78, v.p., 1977, 78; bd. dirs. Mansfield Symphony Orch., 1972-78, pres., 1978; bd. dirs. Rsch. for Better Schs., Inc., 1968-71, pres., 1970-71; mem. Kiwanis Club of Mansfield, 1971-78, bd. dirs., 1974-78; mem. citizens adv. com. Richland County Regional Planning Commn., 1973-74, bd. dirs., 1975-78, v.p.; mem. Manpower Adv. Coun. Richland and Morrow Counties, 1977-78; trustee Hillsbrough County Hosp. Authority, Tampa, Fla., 1980-84, Tampa Heart Ctr., 1982-84; sec.-treas., 1983-84; mem. Leaderhip Tampa, 1982-83, Leadership Tampa Alumni, 1983—, Leadership Tampa Bay, 1992—; mem. Tampa-Hillsborough Cable adv. com., 1984-92, vice chmn., 1987-88, chmn., 1988-92; instl. rep. PBS and Nat. Pub. Radio, Am. Pub. TV Stas. 1986—, Legis. adv., APTS, 1995—; market fund adv. com. CPB, 1996; steering com. Higher Edn. Telecomm. Consortium, 1995—; steering com., pub. broadcasting joint licensee Consortium, 1996—; bd. dirs. Fla. Pub. Broadcasting Svc. Inc., 1986—, chair Long Range Planning Com., 1988-93, treas., 1991-93, vice chair, 1993-95, chair, 1995-97, chair programs and ops. com., 1993-95, exec. com. 1991-99; bd. dirs. Program Resources Group, 1993—, exec. com., 1995—, vice-chair, sec., 1995—; mem. Palma Ceia United Meth. Ch., 1980—, chair coun. on ministries, 1985-86, chair pipe organ com., 1985-91, chair adminstrv. bd., coun., 1987-89, 93-98; mem. pastor parish com., 1990-92, 96-98, chair, 1992; mem. Master Chorale of Tampa Bay, 1983—; bd. dirs. Chorale Masterworks Festival, Inc., 1987—, v.p., 1991-93, chair and pres., 1993-95, 97-99; bd. dirs. So. Ednl. Comms. Assn., 1986-97, mem. budget and fin. com., 1989-91. bd. dirs. Nat. Edn. Telecom. Assn., 1997—, long range planning coun. 1997-98. With USAF, 1953-55; USAFR, ret. 1973. Mem. Assn. Higher Edn. (life), Ohio State U. Assn. (life), Nat. Univ. Continuing Edn. Assn. (instnl. rep., bd. dirs. region III, mem. honors and awards com. 1986-90), Greater Tampa C. of C. (chmn. emergency preparedness task force 1991-94), Civitan (club founding pres. 1980-89), Phi Delta Kappa (life), Kappa Delta Pi, Phi Kappa Phi. Office: WRB 219 4202 Fowler Ave Tampa FL 33620

HECK, MELODY ANN, library director; b. Kewanee, Ill., July 8, 1957; d. Edwin and Helen M. Nelson; m. Michael Robert Heck, Feb. 25, 1984; children: David M., Holly Ann Elizabeth. Cert. libr. tech. asst., Black Hawk Coll., 1996. Staff librarian Galva (Ill.) Pub. Libr., 1975-84, asst. dir., 1984-96, libr. dir., 1996—. Mem. ALA, Ill. Libr. Assn. Avocations: reading, needlework. Office: Galva Pub Libr Dist 120 NW Third Ave Galva IL 61434

HECK, RICHARD T., tree farmer; b. Madison, Ind., Sept. 16, 1924; s. Richard Charles and Virginia (Tevis) H.; m. Ruth Irwin Heck, June 27, 1948; children: Richard Gregory, Rebecca Jeanne. Student, Admiral Farragut Naval Acad., Pine Beach, N.J., 1942-43, Hanover Coll, 1947-48. Tree farmer Hanover, Ind., 1943—. Vol. firefighter, 1946—; mem. arson investigation team Jefferson County, Ind., 1983-90, Hanover Twp. Vol. Fire Co., 1956—; trustee Hanover Coll., 1991—. With USN, 1944-54, WWII, Korea. Named to Hon. Order of Ky. Cols., 1971; named Ind. Outstanding Tree Farmer, Ind. Tree Farm Commn., 1983, Nat. Outstanding Tree Farmer Am. Forest Found., 1984, Good Steward award Nat. Arbor Day Found., 1984, North Cen. Region Outstandng Tree Farmer, 1984, Ind. Conservationist of Yr., Ind. Dept. Natural Resources, 1985, Forest Conservationist of the Yr. Ind. Wildlife Fedn., 1987. Mem. Soc. Am. Foresters (hon.), Nat. Forestry Assn. (life), Ind. Foresty and Woodland Owners Assn. (bd. dirs. 1984-95, Ind. state tree farm com. 1984—), NRA (life), Ind. Vol. Firemans Assn. (life), Nat. Muzzle Loading Rifle Assn. (life), Nat. Eagle Scout Assn., Soc. Ind. Pioneers, Am. Legion, Wahpanipe Muzzle Loading Rifle Club, Connor Prairie Rifles Club, Masons, Elks. Republican. Presbyterian. Avocations: hunting, fishing, hiking, collecting Indian artifacts, competitive muzzle loading shooting. Address: 163 Clemmons St Hanover IN 47243-9660

HECKART, EILEEN, actress; b. Columbus, Ohio, Mar. 29, 1919; d. Leo Herbert and Esther (Stark) Purcell; m. John Harrison Yankee Jr., June 26, 1943; children: Mark Kelly, Philip Craig, Luke Brian. BA, Ohio State U., 1942, LHD (hon.), 1981; postgrad., Am. Theatre Wing, 1944-48; LLD, Sacred Heart U., Bridgeport, Conn., 1973; DFA (hon.), Niagara U., 1981. Broadway plays include Voice of the Turtle, 1944, Brighten the Corner, 1946, They Knew What They Wanted, 1948, Stars Weep, 1949, The Traitor, 1950, Hilda Crane, 1951, In Any Language, 1953, Picnic, 1953, Bad Seed, 1955 (Tony nomination), A View From the Bridge, 1956, Dark at the Top of the Stairs, 1958 (Tony nomination), Invitation to a March, 1960 (Tony nomination), Everybody Loves Opal, 1961, Family Affair, 1962, Too True to Be Good, 1963, And Things That Go Bump in the Night, 1965, Barefoot in the Park, 1965-66, You Know I Can't Hear You When the Water's Running, 1967, The Mother Lover, 1968, Butterflies Are Free, 1969 (Tony nomination), Veronica's Room, 1973, The Effect of Gamma Rays on Man-in-the-Moon Marigolds, 1971, Remember Me, 1975, Mother Courage and Her Children, 1975, Mrs. Gibbs in Our Town, 1976, Elemosynary, 1987, Northeast Local, 1995; one-woman shows: Eleanor, 1976, Ladies at the Alamo, 1977, Margaret Sanger-Unfinished Business, 1989, The Cemetery Club, 1990, Love Letters, 1991, Driving Miss Daisy, 1991; movies include Miracle in the Rain, Bad Seed (Oscar nomination), Bus Stop, Hot Spell, Daily Citation, 1956 (Oscar nomination, Drama Critics award), My Six Loves, 1962, Up the Down Staircase, 1966, Save Me a Place at Forest Lawn, 1967 (Emmy award), No Way to Treat a Lady, 1968, Butterflies Are Free, 1972 (Acad. award, Straw Hat award 1973, 75, 77), Zandy's Bride, 1974, The Hiding Place, 1975, Burnt Offerings, 1975, Wedding Band, 1975 (Emmy nomination), Heartbreak Ridge, 1986, The Cemetery Club, 1990, Love Letters, 1990, Driving Miss Daisy, 1991, The First Wives Club, 1996; TV movies, 1947—; TV series Trauma Center, Annie McGuire, 1988-89, Partners in Crime, Mary Tyler Moore Show, 1976, 77 (2 Emmy nominations), Back Stairs at the White House, 1979 (Emmy nomination), FDR's Last Year, 1987, The Cosby Show, 1987 (Emmy nomination), (daytime show) One Life to Live, 1987 (Emmy nomination), Love and War (Emmy award, Guest Actress - Comedy Series, 1994), The Five Mrs. Buchanans, 1994. Recipient Outer Circle award, 1953, Daniel Blum award, 1953, Sylvania TV award, 1954, Donaldson award, 1955, Hollywood Fgn. Press award, 1956, March of Dimes award, 1970, Aegis award, 1970, Ohio State U. Centennial award, 1970, Gov.'s award of Ohio, 1977, Ohiana Libr. award, 1978, Emmy award, 1994, Lichtenberg award Pi Beta Phi, 1994; named to Theatre Hall of Fame, 1995. Mem. Pi Beta Phi.

HECKEL, JAMES JOHN, library director; b. Denver, May 23, 1942; s. Henry and Molly Heckel; m. Pamela Smith; 1 child, Garth. BA, U. Colo., 1965; MA, U. Denver, 1969. Dir. cmty. svcs. Boulder (Colo.) Pub. Libr., 1969-78; asst. dir. Loveland (Colo.) Pub. Libr., 1978-80; collection mgr. Lewis and Clark Libr., Helena, Mont., 1980-87, dir., 1988; dir. Gt. Falls (Mont.) Pub. Libr., 1988—. Columnist Ind. Record newspaper; contbr. articles to profl. jours. Bd. dirs. Sta. KGPR, pub. radio, Gt. Falls, 1993-96, Cable Seven, Gt. Falls, 1994—, Ctr. for the Book, Helena and Washington, Paris-Gibson Mus. Art, 1990-93. Mem. ALA, Mont. Libr. Assn. (chmn. intellectual freedom com. 1994-95, pres. 1997, Pat Williams Intellectual Freedom award 1996), Mountain Plains Libr. Assn., Mountain Plains User Group (pres. 1990-93), Preservation Cascade, ACLU (bd. dirs. Mont. 1997—), NAACP, Rotary. Avocations: mountain biking, hiking, skating, reading, film. E-mail: jheckel@orion.mtlib.mtgf.org. Office: Gt Falls Pub Libr 301 2d Ave N Great Falls MT 59404

HECKEL, JOHN LOUIS (JACK HECKEL), aerospace company executive; b. Columbus, Ohio, July 12, 1931; s. Russel Criblez and Ruth Selma (Heid) H.; m. Jacqueline Ann Alexander, Nov. 21, 1959 (div. 1993); children: Heidi, Holly, John; m. Linda Holleran, Aug. 1, 1994. BS, U. Ill., 1954; PhD with honors, Nat. U. San Diego, 1984. Div. mgr. Aerojet Divs., Azusa, Calif., 1956-70, Seattle and Washington, 1956-70; pres. Aerojet-Space Gen. Co., El Monte, Calif., 1970-72, Aerojet Liquid Rocket Co., Sacramento, 1972-77; group v.p. Aerojet Sacramento Cos., 1977-81; pres. Aerojet Gen., La Jolla, Calif., 1981-85; chmn., chief exec. officer Aerojet Gen., 1985-87; pres., chief operating officer GenCorp., Akron, 1987-94, also bd. dirs.; bd. dirs. WD-40 Corp., Advanced Tissue Sci., Inc., San Diego, Applied Power Inc., Milw. Bd. dirs. Applied Power Corp., Milw., San Diego Econ. Devel. Corp., 1983-86, Akron Regional Devel. Bd., Akron Gen. Hosp., Summit County United Way; pres. Summit Edn. Partnership Found., Akron. Recipient Disting. Alumni award U. Ill. Alumni Conv., 1979. Fellow AIAA (assoc.); mem. Aerospace Industries Assn. Am. (gov. 1981), Navy League U.S., Am. Def. Preparedness Assn., San Diego C. of C. (bd. dirs.).

HECKEL, RICHARD WAYNE, metallurgical engineering educator; b. Pitts., Jan. 25, 1934; s. Ralph Clyde and Esther Vera (Zoerb) H.; m. Peggy Ann Simmons, Jan. 3, 1959 (dec. Apr. 1998); children—Scott Alan, Laura Ann Rowe. BS in Metall. Engrng., Carnegie Mellon, 1955, MS, 1958, PhD, 1959. Sr. research metallurgist E.I. duPont de Nemours & Co., Wilmington, Del., 1959-63; prof. metall. engrng. Drexel U., Phila., 1963-71; head dept. metall. engrng. and materials sci. Carnegie Mellon, Pitts., 1971-76; pres., prof. emeritus metall. & materials engrng. Mich. Tech. U., Houghton, 1976—. Contbr. articles to profl. jours. Served as 1st lt. Ordnance Corps, U.S. Army, 1959-60. Recipient Lindback Teaching award Drexel U., 1968; Research award Mich. Tech. U., 1985. Fellow ASM Internat. (life; Bradley Stoughton Young Tchr. of Metallurgy award 1969, Phila. Ednl. Achievement award 1967); mem. The Metals, Minerals and Materials Soc., Am. Welding Soc. (Adams Meml. mem. 1966), Am. Soc. Engrng. Edn., Sigma Xi, Omicron Delta Kappa, Tau Beta Pi, Phi Kappa Phi, Alpha Sigma Mu. Address: 1281 Hickory Ln Houghton MI 49931-1609 Office: Mich Tech U Dept Metall & Materials Engrng Houghton MI 49931

HECKELMANN, CHARLES NEWMAN (CHARLES LAWTON), author, publishing consultant; b. Bklyn., Oct. 24, 1913; s. Edward and Sophia (Hodum) H.; m. Anna M. Auer, Apr. 17, 1937; children: Lorraine Heckelmann Kane, Thomas Edward. B.A. maxima cum laude, U. Notre Dame, 1934. Sports feature writer Bklyn. Eagle, 1934-37; editor-in-chief Cupples & Leon, N.Y.C., 1937-41, Popular Library, N.Y.C., 1941-58; v.p. Popular Library, 1953-58; pres., editor-in-chief Monarch Books, Inc., N.Y.C., 1958-65; mng. editor, rights dir. David McKay, N.Y.C., 1965-68; sr. editor Cowles Book Co., N.Y.C., 1968-71; sr. editor, rights dir. Hawthorn Books, N.Y.C., 1971-72; editor-in-chief Hawthorn Books, 1972-75, v.p., 1972-75; book editor Nat. Enquirer, 1975-78. Author: Vengeance Trail, 1944, Lawless Range, 1945, Six-Gun Outcast, 1946, Deputy Marshal, 1947, Guns of Arizona, 1949, Let The Guns Roar, 1950, Two-Bit Rancher, 1950, Outlaw Valley, 1950, Danger Rides the Range, 1950, Fighting Ramrod, 1951, Hell In His Holsters, 1952, The Rawhider, 1952, Hard Man With A Gun, 1954, Bullet Law, 1955, Trumpets in the Dawn, 1958, The Big Valley, 1966, The Glory Riders, 1967, Writing Fiction for Profit, 1968, Stranger from Durango, 1971, Return to Arapahoe, 1980, Wagons to Wind River, 1982; books and stories adapted for motion pictures Deputy Marshal, 1949; Stranger from Santa Fe, 1947, Frontier Feud, 1948; author (pen name Charles Lawton): Clarkville's Battery, 1937, Ros. Hackney, Halfback, 1937, The Winning Forward Pass, 1940, Home Run Hennessey, 1941, Touchdown to Victory, 1942, Jungle Menace, 1937. Life mem. Nat. Cowboy Hall of Fame and Western Heritage Ctr. Mem. Cath. Writers Guild of Am. (pres. 1949-52), Western Writers of Am. (v.p. 1955-57, pres. 1964-65), Torch Club of Boca Raton (bd. dirs.). Home: 10634 Greentrail Dr S Boynton Beach FL 33436-4918 *Life, as I view it, is a series of milestones that periodically challenge our faith and will to succeed. It does not really matter if we don't pass each test. What is important, however, is to maintain a firm commitment to push ahead toward our goal.*

HECKENKAMP, ROBERT GLENN, lawyer; b. Quincy, Ill., June 29, 1923; s. Joseph Edward and Ethel E. (Requet) H.; m. Jean E. Duker, June 22, 1946 (dec. 1983); children: Gae Kelly, Joy Heckenkamp-Roate; m. Wilma E. Dobbs, Nov. 15, 1985. BS, Quincy Coll., 1947; JD, DePaul U., 1949. Bar: Ill. 1949, U.S. Dist. Ct. (cen. and so. dists.) Ill. 1949, U.S. Ct. Appeals (7th cir.) 1952, U.S. Supreme Ct. 1965. Sr. ptnr. Heckenkamp, Simhauser, Ward & Zerkle, Springfield, Ill. Fellow Am. Coll. Trial Lawyers (com. chmn. 1983-86), Internat. Acad. Trial Lawyers; mem. ABA, Ill. State Bar Assn. (pres. 1980-81), Sangamon County Bar Assn., Assn. Trial Lawyers Am., Ill. Trial Lawyers Assn. (pres. 1977-78). Soc. Trial Lawyers. Avocations: hunting, fishing. Home: 60 Yacht Club Rd Springfield IL 62707-9525 Office: Heckenkamp Simhauser Ward & Zerkle West Mezzanine Hilton Hotel 7th & Adams Springfield IL 62701

HECKER, GEORGE SPRAKE, lawyer; b. St. Louis, Jan. 20, 1922; s. Harold Frederick and Leona (Sprake) H.; m. Susan Strickler Niekamp, Mar. 18, 1960; children: Susan Darcy, Gilbert Cox (dec.), Edward Niekamp. BA magna cum laude, Amherst Coll., 1943; LLB, Yale U., 1949. Bar: Mo. 1949, U.S. Dist. Ct. (ea. dist.) Mo., U.S. Ct. Appeals (8th and 9th cirs.), U.S. Supreme Ct. From assoc. to ptnr. Shepley, Kroeger, Fisse & Ingamells, St. Louis, 1949-67; ptnr. Shepley, Kroeger, Fisse & Hecker, St. Louis, 1967-68, Shepley, Kroeger & Hecker, St. Louis, 1969-71; ptnr. Bryan, Cave, McPheeters & McRoberts, St. Louis, 1971-95, of counsel, 1995—; chmn. 22d jud. circuit com. Mo. Supreme Ct., 1971-74. Bd. dirs. Independence Ctr., 1981—, Barnard Free Skin and Cancer Hosp., 1951—, Nat. Alliance for Mentally Ill, 1979-84, pres., 1979-81, Mo. Coalition Alliances for Mentally Ill, 1992-96, pres., 1993-96; mem. gen. bd. German Am. Heritage Soc., 1992—, pres., 1992-94, chmn., 1995—; bd. trustees St. Louis County Mental Health Mil. Bd., 1993—; mem. Mo. Gov.'s McBride Commn. on Mental Health, 1995. Mem. ABA, Bar Assn. St. Louis (v.p. 1958-59), Phi Beta Kappa, Noonday Club, St. Louis (Mo.) Country Club. Republican. Episcopalian. Office: Bryan Cave 1 Metropolitan Sq Ste 3600 Saint Louis MO 63102-2750 Home: 1 McKnight Place Saint Louis MO 63124

HECKER, LAWRENCE HARRIS, industrial hygienist; b. Detroit, July 14, 1944; s. Joseph and Rose Vivian (Harris) H.; m. Phyllis Rosalind Cohen, June 29, 1966; children: Charles Aaron, David Alan. BA in Geography and Chemistry, Wayne State U., 1965, MS in Indsl. Hygiene, 1967; MS in Air Pollution, U. Mich., 1969, PhD of Indsl. Health, 1972. Cert. indsl. hygienist Am. Bd. Indsl. Hygiene. Asst. prof. indsl. and environ. health U. Mich., Ann Arbor, 1972-78; mgr., dir. corp. indsl. hygiene Abbott Labs., North Chgo., Ill., 1978-94; dir. corp. health and safety regulatory affairs Abbott Labs., North Chgo., 1994—; cons. Ann Arbor, 1970-78, Northbrook, Ill., 1996—; chief chemist, ind. hygienist Environ. Health Labs. Franklin, Mich., 1966-68; lab. technician Wayne State U., Detroit, 1964-66. Contbr. numerous articles to profl. jours. Mem. AAAS, APHA, ASTM, Am. Acad. Indsl. Hygiene, Am. Chem. Soc., Am. Conf. Govtl. Indsl. Hygienists, Am. Indsl. Hygiene Assn. (bd. dirs. 1983-86), Air Pollution Control Assn., Assn. for Advancement of Med. Instrumentation, Internat. Stds. Orgn. (U.S. del. Geneva, convener tech. com. 194, working group 11, mem. working groups 12 and 15, liaison to ISO tech. com. 210 working group 4), Chem. Mfrs. Assn. (mem. occupl. safety and health com., mem. OSHA legis. group), Ethylene Glycol Panel, Ethylene Oxide Industry Coun. (bd. dirs. 1980—, vice chmn. of bd. and exec. com. 1982-95), Halogenated Solvents Industry Alliance, Health Industry Mfrs. Assn., Orgns. Resource Councillors (mem. respirator com., chairperson respiratory study task force, mem. risk assessment task force, mem. permissible exposure limit adv. com. task force, mem. Tb task force, chairperson latex rubber task force, mem. pvc task force), Remote Sensing of Atmosphere (mem. Nat. Inst. for Sci. and Tech. com.), Pharm. Mfrs. Assn., Pharm. Safety Group, Bus. Coun. on Indoor Air (bd.

dirs.), Nat. Assn. Mfrs. (mem. occupl. safety and health com., mem. occupl. safety and health steering com., mem. ergonomics com., mem. chem. safety com. 1992—), Sigma Xi. Home and Office: 3823 Russett Ct Northbrook IL 60062-4263 Office: Abbott Labs 200 Abbott Park Rd Bldg Apt 52 Abbott Park IL 60064-6212

HECKER, MARGO JOAN, editor, writer; b. Glendive, Mont., Nov. 17, 1955; d. Peter P. and Veronica P. (Boltz) H.; div.; Leah, Rebecca, Brendan Ryan. BA in Journalism, U. N.D., 1978. News editor Turtle Mountain Star, Rolla, N.D., 1978-80; reporter Williston (N.D.) Herald/Williston Basin Oil Reporter, 1980-84; news editor Williston Daily Herald, 1984-87, mng. editor, 1988-95; editor Telluride (Colo.) Times Jour., 1995-96, Dunn County News, Menomonie, Wis., 1997—. Recipient Best Pub. Edited by Entrant award Nat. Fedn. Press Women, 1987, Best Column award, 1987. Mem. Williston Bus. & Profl. Women (Young Careerist award 1984), Williston Rotary. Roman Catholic. Avocations: hiking, antiques, writing. Office: Dunn County News 710 Main St E # Menomonie WI 54751-2615

HECKER, MICHAEL HANNS LOUIS, retired electrical engineer, speech scientist; b. Hamburg, Germany, Mar. 30, 1936; came to U.S., 1948; s. Hanns Ewald Hecker and Wilhelmine (Corinth) Klopfer; m. Elizabeth Ann Bowen, Sept. 3, 1960 (div.); 1 child, Serena Suzanne; m. Dorothy Louise Dunlap, Mar. 12, 1971. BSEE with honors, Northeastern U., 1959; MSEE, MIT, 1961; PhD in Speech & Hearing Scis., Stanford U., 1974. Sr. rsch. engr. Bolt Beranek and Newman Inc., Cambridge, Mass., 1964-67, SRI Internat., Menlo Park, Calif., 1967-95; cons. forensic acoustics, Los Altos, Calif., 1967-98; retained by White House during Watergate investigation to examine presdl. tapes; sci. cons. Nat. Commn. Rev. Fed. & State Laws Relating to Wiretapping & Electronic Surveillance, 1974-76. Author: Speaker Recognition, 1971; co-editor: Speech Evaluation in Psychiatry/Medicine, 1981; contbr. articles to profl. jours., chpts. to med. books. 1st lt. U.S. Army, 1962-64. NIH grantee, 1982-88. Mem. Eta Kappa Nu, Tau Beta Pi, Sigma Xi. Achievements include studies of speech changes related to emotional states, psychological stress, and neurologic disorders; developed methods of speech analysis to assess behavioral risk for coronary heart disease.

HECKER, WILLIAM FULHAM, JR., architect; b. Opelousas, La., Apr. 18, 1961; s. William F. and Catherine Ann (Mayne) H.; m. Frederica White, June 4, 1994. BArch, La. State U., Baton Rouge, 1984. Registered architect, Colo. Ala., Ga. Intern architect Frank T. Colby-Architect, Lafayette, La., 1983, Barton & Thweat Inc., Baton Rouge, 1984-86; inter/project architect Morgan Assocs., Denver, 1986-88; porject architect Architects South, Inc., Birmingham, Ala., 1988-89; accessible design specialist Evan Terry Assocs., Birmingham, 1989-92; accessible design cons. Hecker Design Ltd., Birmingham, 1992—; expert witness, cons. U.S. Dept. Justice, Washington, 1994—; guest instr. Harvard Grad. Sch. Design, Cambridge, 1992; workshop instr. IBM Corp., 1991; cons. in field. Primary author: Americans with Disabilites Act Facilities Compliance Workbook, 1992; editl. adv. bd. Am. with Disabilities Act Compliance Guide, 1995—. Vol. access specialist Ind. Living Ctr., Birmingham, 1992—. Mem. AIA (chpt. newsletter editor 1988-90, Pres.'s award 1990, Ala. coun. bd. dirs. 1989-90, leader accessibility task force 1997—), Kiwani (bd. dirs. 1995-98). Episcopalian. Avocations: martial arts, fishing, photography. Office: Hecker Design Ltd PO Box 59706 Birmingham AL 35259-9706

HECKERLING, AMY, film director; b. Bronx, May 7, 1954; m. Neal Israel. Grad., NYU, 1975; fellow, Am. Film Inst. directing program, 1975. Dir. films including (short film) High Finance, Getting It Over With, Fast Times at Ridgemont High, 1982, Johnny Dangerously, 1984, National Lampoon's European Vacation, 1985, Look Who's Talking Too, 1990, Clueless, 1995; screenwriter, dir. Look Who's Talking, 1989; co-exec. prodr., dir. Look Who's Talking Now, 1993; dir. (TV) Twilight Zone, 1986, (series) Fast Times at Ridgemont High; film appearance in Into the Night, 1985; author: (with Pamela Pettler) The No-Sex Handbook, 1990. *

HECKERT, PAUL CHARLES, sociologist, educator; b. May 30, 1929; s. Paul Kester and Clara Belle (Plessinger) H.; m. Sara Mae Raezer, Sept. 6, 1952; children: Paul Andrew, Druann Maria, Daniel Alex, Nathanael Alan, Diane Manette. A.B., Catawba Coll., 1951; B.D., Lancaster Theol. Sem., 1954; M.S., Cornell, 1959, PhD., 1964. Ordained minister United Ch. of Christ, 1954. Missionary United Ch. of Christ, Honduras, 1954-60; clergyman of various Methodist chs. N.Y., 1960-64; assoc. prof. sociology, also chmn. dept. Catawaba (N.C.) Coll., 1964-68, prof., 1968-72; also chmn. joint dept. sociology with Livingstone Coll. Salisbury, N.C.; chmn. dept. sociology Frostburg (Md.) State U., 1972-87, prof., 1987-94; participant Prison Visitation and Support Visitor, 1995—; del. Rowan Coop. Christian Ministry, 1968-72; mem. leadership devel. com. Pa. West Conf., United Ch. of Christ, 1973-78. Bd. dirs. Salisbury Rowan Cmty. Svc. Coun., 1971-72. Served with AUS, 1948-50. Ford fellow, summer 1968, NASA/ASEE summer faculty fellow, 1969, 77, AEC summer faculty fellow, 1973. Contbr. book revs. to profl. jours. NEH grantee 1975, 79, 83, 86. Mem. AAAS, Am. Sociol. Assn., Rural Sociol. Soc., Alleghany County Ret. Tchrs. Assn. (mem. chmn. 1997, pres.-elect 1998, pres. 1999), Phi Kappa Phi, Alpha Kappa Delta, Sigma Delta Pi, Delta Tau Kappa. Home: 13 N Woodlawn Ave Cumberland MD 21502-7254

HECKLER, FREDERICK ROGER, plastic surgeon; b. N.Y.C., Mar. 7, 1942; s. Frances George; children: Jeremy, Michael, Adrienne, Lauren. Student, Tufts U., 1959-62, MD, 1966. Diplomate Nat. Bd. Med. Examiners, Am. Bd. Surgery, Am. Bd. Plastic Surgery with qualification in surgery of the hand. Intern in surgery U. Chgo. Med. Ctr., 1966-67; resident in gen. surgery Tufts New Eng. Med. Ctr., Boston, 1967-69; fellow in surgery Malmo (Sweden) Gen. Hosp., 1969-70; resident in plastic surgery Wilford Hall USAF Med. Ctr., San Antonio, 1973-75; fellow in hand surgery Denver Gen. Hosp., 1976-77; chief surgery USAF Hosp., Taiwan, 1976-77; asst. prof. surgery U. Miss. Med. Ctr., Jackson, 1977-79, chief divsn. plastic surgery, 1979-82; dir. divsn. plastic surgery Allegheny Gen. Hosp., Pitts., 1982—; clin. assoc. prof. plastic surgery U. Pitts. Sch. Medicine, 1982—; active med. staff Miss. Cripple Children's Treatment and Tng. Ctr., Miss., 1981-82; dir. cleft palate clinic Allegheny Gen. Hosp., Pitts., 1982-88; attending physician St. Margaret Meml. Hosp., Pitts., 1984-89, Montefiore Hosp., Pitts., 1986-89, Divine Providence Hosp., Pitts., 1991—, North Hills Passavant Hosp., Pitts., 1993; cons. med. staff Harmarville Rehab. Ctr., Inc., Pitts., 1985; cons. in plastic surgery VA Hosp., Pitts., 1993—, Miss. Meth. Rehab. Ctr., Jackson, 1977-82, VA Hosp., Jackson, 1977-82; dir. burn unit U. Miss. Med. Ctr., Jackson, 1979-82, co-dir. hand surgery svc., 1979-82; mem. med. staff Miss. Crippled Children's Treatment and Tng. Ctr., Jackson, 1981-82; presenter in field. Contbr. numerous articles to profl. publs., chpts. to books; assoc. editor Jour. Plastic and Reconstructive Surgery. Lt. col. USAF, 1972-76. Mem. AMA, ACS, Am. Soc. Plastic and Reconstructive Surgeons, Am. Assn. Plastic Surgeons, Assn. Mil. Plastic Surgeons, Soc. Air Force Clin. Surgeons, Am. Burn Assn., Internat. Soc. for Burn Injuries, Am. Cleft Palate Assn., Plastic Surgery Rsch. Coun., Am. Soc. for Surgery of Hand, Am. Assn. Hand Surgery, Royal Soc. Medicine, Assn. Acad. Chmn. of Plastic Surgery, Lipolysis Soc. N.Am., Allegheny County Med. Soc., Pa. Med. Soc., Ohio Valley Plastic Surg. Soc., Pitts. Surg. Soc. Office: Allegheny Gen Hosp 320 E North Ave Pittsburgh PA 15212-4756

HECKLER, JOHN MAGUIRE, stockbroker, investment company executive; b. Meriden, Conn., Nov. 11, 1927; s. George Ernest and Mary Catherine (Maguire) H.; m. Sheryl Jean Bills, Nov. 30, 1985; children: Belinda West Mulliken, Alison Anne Heckler-Haensler, John Maguire. AB, Fairfield U., 1951; postgrad. Fordham U., 1951-53, Harvard U., 1953-54. Exec. Maguire Homes, M. W. Maguire, 1954-62; instl. salesman Harris Upham & Co., Boston, 1962-68; resident mgr. Middendorf, Colgate & Co., Boston, 1968-70; founder, chmn., CEO Boston Instl. Svcs., Inc., 1971-92; chmn. Spur Publs., Inc., 1989-94; founder, chmn., CEO Independence Instl. Securities & Co., L.P., Middleburg, Va., 1994-97; mng. dir. Independence Instl. divsn. Moors & Cabot, Inc., Boston, 1998—; del. White House Conf. on Small Bus., 1995; mem. N.Y. Stock Exch., 1970-93. Campaign asst. Congressman Bradford Morse, 1960. With USCG, 1945-47. Republican. Episcopalian. Clubs: Harvard (Washington), Piedmont (Va.) Hunt. Home and Office: Foxleigh Zulla Rd Middleburg VA 20118-1772

HECKLEY, TERESA JOANN, health facility administrator; b. Blue Earth, Minn., May 8, 1956; d. Milton and Kathryn (Grise) Rauenhorst; m. Gregg Heckley, June 28, 1986; children: Laura Ann, Nicole Kristina. BS, Coll. St. Teresa, 1978; MS in Nursing, U. S. Fla., 1990. Cert. critical care registered nurse, advanced cardiac life support instr., basic cardiac life support instr. Staff nurse Tampa Gen. Hosp., 1978-79; staff nurse intensive care Vets. Hosp., Tampa, Fla., 1979-86, nurse mgr. surgery unit, 1986-89, nurse mgr. coronary care unit, 1989—; nurse mgr. emergency rm. Vets. Hosp., Tampa, 1997—. Mem. Am. Assn. Critical Care Nurses, Sigma Theta Tau, Phi Kappa Phi.

HECKLINGER, RICHARD E., ambassador; b. Syracuse, N.Y.; m. Carol Pratt. Grad., St. Lawrence U.; JD, Harvard U.; grad. in advanced internat. studies, Johns Hopkins U. Joined Fgn. Svc., Dept. State, Washington, 1967—, prin. dep. asst. sec. for econ. and bus. affairs, sr. advisor and exec. asst. to under sec. for econ. affairs; dep. chief mission U.S. Mission to OECD; dep. asst. sec. for European and Can. affairs Dept. State, sr. insp. Office Insp. Gen., advisor to under sec. for polit. affairs, dir. Internat. Energy Policy Office; acting dep. asst. sec. for internat. affairs Dept. Energy, Washington; amb. to Thailand, Am. Embassy, Bangkok. Office: Dept State Am Ambassador to Thailand Washington DC 20521-7100*

HECKMAN, CAROL A., biology educator; b. East Stroudsburg, Pa., Oct. 18, 1944; d. Wilbur Thomas and Doris (Betts) H. BA, Beloit (Wis.) Coll., 1966; PhD, U. Mass., Amherst, 1972. Rsch. assoc. Yale U. Sch. Medicine, New Haven, 1973-75; staff mem. Oak Ridge (Tenn.) Nat. Lab., 1975-82; adj. assoc. prof. U. Tenn.-Oak Ridge Biomed. Grad. Sch., 1980-82; assoc. prof. Bowling Green (Ohio) State U., 1982-86, prof. biology, 1986—; cons. NSF, Washington, 1977-80, NIH, Rockville, Md., 1996-98; dir. EM facility Bowling Green State U., 1982—; NSF trainee, Amherst, 1967-70. Contbr. articles to profl. jours., chpts. to books. Internat. Cancer Rsch. Tech. fellow Internat. Union Against Cancer, 1980, Heritage Found. fellow, 1982, guest rsch. fellow, Uppsala, Sweden, 1989-90; grantee NSF, 1981-84, 90-92, NIH, 1987-88, 98—. Mem. AAAS, Am. Soc. Cell Biology, Microscopy Soc. Am., N.W. Ohio Microscopy (sec.-treas. 1986-90, pres. 1990-94), Soc. In Vitro Biology, Ohio Drug Devel. (pres. 1993—), Ohio Acad. Sci., Sigma Xi. Episcopalian. Achievements include research evaluation and developement of in vitro anticarcinogens. Home: 861 Ferndale Ct Bowling Green OH 43402 Office: Bowling Green State U Dept Biol Scis Bowling Green OH 43403

HECKMAN, CAROL E., judge; b. Clinton, Iowa, Oct. 18, 1952; children: Tyler, Ethan. BA magna cum laude, Lawrence Univ., Wis., 1974; JD magna cum laude, Cornell Law Sch., 1977. Bar: N.Y., U.S. Supreme Ct., U.S. Tax Ct., U.S. Dist. Ct. (we. dist.) N.Y. Law clk. to Chief Judge John T. Curtin U.S. Dist. Ct. (we. dist.) N.Y., Buffalo, 1977-79, asst. U.S. atty., 1981-85, magistrate judge, 1992—; trial atty. Dept. of Justice, Civil Rights Div., D.C., 1979-81; assoc. Albrecht, Maguire, Heffern & Gregg, P.C., Buffalo, 1985-86, ptnr., 1986-89; ptnr. Lippes, Kaminsky, Silverstein, Mathias & Wexler, Buffalo, 1989-92; mem. adv. com. for adminstrv. office U.S. Cts. Bd. dirs. Children's Hosp. Buffalo, 1995-97; mem. steering com., trustee Coun. CGF Hosp., 1997—; mem. adv. coun. Cornell U. Law Sch. Recipient Farley prize in philosophy Lawrence Univ., Fraser prize for outstanding scholarship and character Cornell Law Review, Achievement award N.Y. State Women's Bar Assn., 1992. Mem. Nat. Assn. Women Judges, Fed. Magistrate Judges Assn. (sec. 1996-97, treas. 1997-98, 2d v.p.), Erie County Bar Assn., Women's Bar Assn. of the State of N.Y., Women Lawyers of We. N.Y., N.Y. State Bar Assn., Nat. Assn. of Women Judges. Office: US Courthouse 68 Court St Rm 418 Buffalo NY 14202-3405

HECKMAN, GARY WALTER, military career officer; b. Des Moines; m. Sally Mitchell; children: Wendy, Ryan, Benjamin. BA in Edn., U. No. Iowa, 1972; MPA, Troy State U., 1981; grad., Air Command and Staff Coll., 1981, Armed Forces Staff Coll., 1984, Air War Coll., 1989; M in Nat. Security and Strategic Studies, Naval War Coll., 1992; grad., Harvard U., 1995. Commd. 2d lt. USAF, 1973, advanced through grades to brig. gen., 1997; with 21st Tactical Airlift Squadron USAF, Clark Air Base, The Philippines, 1974-76; Spectre gunship instr., flight examiner 16th Spl. Ops. Squad USAF, Hurlburt Field, Fla., 1976-79; with readiness analysis and iniatives group hdqrs. USAF, Washington, 1979, with airlift forces divsn. hdqrs.; plans officer 1st Spl. Ops. Wing and 2nd Air Divsn. USAF, Hurlburt Field, Fla., 1980; force plans staff officer hdqrs. U.S. European Command USAF, Stuttgart, Germany, 1984-87; with 23rd Air Force, Air Force Spl. Ops. Command USAF, Hurlburt Field, 1987-89; dep. dir. programming and policy Mil. Airlift Command USAF, Scott AFB, Ill., 1989-91; chief mobility, tng. and spl. ops. requirements divsn. USAF; commdr. 16th Spl. Ops. Group USAF, Hurlburt Field, 1994-96; assessment dir. later dir. of resources USAF; dir. Ctr. for Force Structure, Resources, Requirements U.S. Spl. Ops. Command, MacDill AFB, Fla., 1996—. Decorated Legion of Merit with one oak leaf cluster, Def. Meritorious Svc. medal, Meritorious Svc. medal with three oak leaf clusters, Air medal, Joint Svc. Commendation medal, Air Force Commendation medal, Air Force Achievement medal. Office: US Spl Ops Command Tampa FL 33621

HECKMAN, HENRY TREVENNEN SHICK, steel company executive; b. Reading, Pa., Mar. 27, 1918; s. H. Raymond and Charlotte E. Shick H.; AB, Lehigh U., 1939; m. Helen Clausen Wright, Nov. 28, 1946; children: Sharon Anita (dec.), Charlotte Marie. Advt. prodn. mgr. Republic Steel Corp., Cleve., 1940-42, editor Enduro Era, 1946-51, account exec., 1953-54, asst. dir. advt., 1957-65, dir. advt., 1965-82; partner Applegate & Heckman, Washington, 1955-56; advt. mgr. Harris Corp., 1956-57. Permanent chmn. Joint Com. for Audit Comparability, 1968-93; chmn. Media Comparability Coun., 1969-83; chmn. indsl. advertisers com. Greater Cleve. Growth Assn., 1973-76; chmn. publs. com. Lehigh U., 1971-76; pres.'s adv. coun. Ashland Coll., 1966-76; advt. adv. council Kent State U., 1976-81; exec. com. Cleve. chpt. ARC, 1968-74; mem. Republican Fin. Exec. Com., 1966-87; coord. adv. coun. pub. svcs. campaign Employer Support for Guard and Res., 1973-83, 90—. Comdr. USNR, 1942-46, 51-53; Korea. Named to Advt. Effectiveness Hall of Fame, 1967; named Advt. Man of Yr., 1969; recipient G.D. Crain, Jr. award, 1973; Disting. Alumnus award Lehigh U., 1979; elected to Cleve. Graphic Arts Council Hall of Distinction, 1981. Mem. Indsl. Marketers Cleve. (past pres., Golden Mousetrap award 1968), Bus. Mktg. Assn. (pres. 1968-69, Best Seller award 1966, Hall of Fame, 1973), Assn. Nat. Advertisers (chmn. shows and exhibits com. 1966-74, dir. 1969-72), Am. Iron and Steel Inst. (com. chmn. 1961-69), Steel Svc. Ctr. Inst. (advt. adv. com. 1965-77), New Eng. Soc., Western Res. Soc., SAR (pres. 1979, Archibald Willard award 1996), Ohio Soc. SAR (Hub Scott award 1995), Mil. Order World Wars (comdr. 1980), Early Settlers, Cleve. Advt. Club (pres. 1961-62, Hall of Fame 1980), Ctr. for Mktg. Comm. (chmn. bd. 1965), Internat. Platform Assn., Pi Delta Epsilon. Clubs: Cheshire Cheese (pres. 1982), Cleve. Grays (trustee 1980-82), Cleve. Skating. Home: 6000 Nob Hill Dr Apt 401 Chagrin Falls OH 44022-3358

HECKMAN, JAMES JOSEPH, economist, econometrician, educator; b. Chgo., Apr. 19, 1944; s. John Jacob and Bernice Irene (Medley) H.; m. Lynne Pettler, 1979; children: Jonathan Jacob, Alma Rachel. AB in Math. summa cum laude (Woodrow Wilson fellow), Colo. Coll., 1965; MA in Econs., Princeton U., 1968, PhD in Econs. (Harold Willis Dodds fellow), 1971; MA, Yale U., 1989. Lectr. Columbia U., 1970-71, asst. prof. econs., 1971-73, assoc. prof., 1973-74; assoc. prof. econs. U. Chgo., 1973-76, prof., 1976—, Henry Schultz prof. of econ., 1985-95, Henry Schultz Disting. Svc. prof., 1995—, prof. econs. Harris Sch. Pub. Policy, 1990—; rsch. assoc. Nat. Bur. Econs. Rsch., 1970-77, sr. rsch. assoc., 1977-85, 87—; A. Whitney Griswold prof. econs., 1988-90, Sterling prof., 1990; prof., dept. stats. Yale U., New Haven, 1990; dir. Ctr. for Program Evaluation Harris Sch. Pub. Policy U. Chgo., 1991—, dir. Econs. Rsch. Ctr. Dept. Econs., 1997—; Irving Fisher prof. econs. Yale U., 1984; treas. Chgo. Econ. Rsch. Assocs.; rsch. assoc. Econs. Rsch. Ctr.-NORC, 1985—; cons. in field; cons. Chgo. Urban League, 1978-86; mem. status Black Ams. com. NRC; JAE lectr. Yale U., 1997; Marschak lectr. Econometric Soc., 1997; Woytinsky lectr. U. Mich., 1999, Harris lectr. Harvard U., 1995, Wildavsky lectr. U. Calif. (Berkeley), 1999; sr. rsch. fellow Am. Bar Found., 1991—; Ruth and Seymour Harris lectr. Kennedy Sch., 1995; hon. prof. U. Tucuman, Argentina, 1998. Editor Jour. Polit. Economy, 1981-87, Evaluating a Job Training Program: Empirical and Methodological Lessons, 1997, Evaluation Social Programs, 1997; assoc. editor Jour. Econometrics, 1977-83, Jour. Labor Econs., 1983—, Econs. Revs., 1987—, Rev. of Econs. and Statistics, 1994—, Jour. Econ. Perspectives, 1989-96, Labor Econs., 1992—; author: (with B. Singer and G. Tsiang) Lecture Notes on Longitudinal Analysis, 1994; editor: (with B. Singer), Longitudinal Analysis of Labor Market Data, 1985, (with E. Leamer) Handbook of Econometrics, Vol. 5, Incentives in Govt. Bureaucracies: A Study of Performance Standards And Their Effects, The Economic Approach to Program Evaluation; Am. editor Rev. Econ. Studies, 1982-85; contbr. articles to profl. jours. Founding faculty and curriculum com. U. Chgo. Harris Sch. Pub. Policy. Recipient L. Benezet Alumni prize Colo. Coll., 1985; fellow J.S. Guggenheim Found., 1978-79, Social Sci. Rsch. Coun., 1977-78, Ctr. for Advanced Study in Behavioral Scis., 1978-79. Fellow Am. Bar Found. (sr., rsch. affiliate 1989-91), Econometric Soc., Am. Acad. Arts and Scis., Nat. Acad. Scis.; mem. Am. Econ. Assn. (John Bates Clark medal 1983), Midwest Econs. Assn. (pres.-elect 1996-97, pres. 1997-98), Am. Statis. Assn., Indsl. Rels. Rsch. Assn., Econ. Sci. Assn. (founder), Phi Beta Kappa. Home: 4807 S Greenwood Ave Chicago IL 60615-1913 Office: U Chgo Dept Econs 1126 E 59th St Chicago IL 60637-1580

HECKMAN, JEROME HAROLD, lawyer; b. Washington, June 7, 1927; s. Morris and Pauline (German) H.; m. Margot Resh, June 16, 1948 (div. Oct. 1977); children: Eric Stephen, Carey Eugene; m. Ilona Ely Grenadier, Jan. 2, 1986. BSS, Georgetown U., 1948, LLB, 1953, JD, 1967. Bar: D.C. 1953, U.S. Supreme Ct. 1965. Assoc. Dow, Lohnes & Albertson, Washington, 1954-59, ptnr., 1959-62; sr. ptnr. Keller and Heckman, Washington, 1962—; gen. counsel Soc. of Plastics Industry Inc., N.Y.C., Washington, 1954—, Broadcasting Publs. Inc. Mag., Washington (co. sold to L.A. Times), 1968-87, Disposables Assn. Inc. (now named Internat. Nonwovens and Disposables Assn.), 1958-67. Contbr. articles to profl. jours. Chmn. regional Rep. com., Md., 1966-72; pres. Plastics Acad., 1995-97. Named to Hall of Fame of Plastics Industry, 1987; recipient Spes Hominum award, Nat. Sanitation Found., 1987. Mem. ABA, Bar Assn. D.C., George Town Club, Woodmont Country Club, Phi Delta Phi. Avocations: golf, tennis. Office: Keller & Heckman 1001 G St NW Ste 500 Washington DC 20001-4545

HECKMAN, PATRICIA A., geriatrics nurse, educator; b. St. Anne, Ill., Jan. 9, 1937; d. Alton E. and Dorine M. (Martin) Brouillette; m. Eugene A. Heckman, Oct. 10, 1970; children: Alyssa Gifford, Jeralyn LeMay, Kerry Heckman, Alicyn Heckman. Diploma, St. Mary's Sch. Nursing, Kankakee, Ill., 1957; student, St. Joseph's Coll., North Windham, Maine, 1990. Cert. in gerontol. nursing. Staff nurse Manteno (Ill.) State Hosp., 1961-76; DON Americana Healthcare Ctr., Kankakee, 1980-81, staff devel. coord., 1986-89; clin. instr. Kankakee Area Career Ctr., Bourbonnais, Ill., 1981-85; instr. nursing Kankakee Community Coll., 1985—. Home: 6740 S State Route 1 Saint Anne IL 60964-5268

HECTOR, BRUCE JOHN, lawyer; b. Newark, Feb. 18, 1950; s. Henry Francis and Doris Mary (Campbell) H.; m. Carol Ann Seely, Aug. 10, 1974. BA in English, Coll. of the Holy Cross, 1971; JD, NYU, 1974. Bar: N.J. 1974, U.S. Dist. Ct. N.J. 1974, N.Y. 1976, U.S. Dist. Ct. (ea. and so. dists.) N.Y. 1976, U.S. Ct. Appeals (4th cir.) 1977, U.S. Ct. Appeals (3d cir.) 1981. Assoc. Podvey & Sachs, Newark, 1974-75, Hill, Rivkins et al, N.Y.C., 1975-81; atty. Becton Dickinson & Co., Franklin Lakes, N.J., 1981-87, sr. atty., 1987-91; assoc. gen. counsel Becton Dickinson & Co., Franklin Lakes, 1992—; lectr. in field. Contbr. articles to profl. publs. Leader explorer law post Boy Scouts Am., Glen Rock, N.J., 1985-88; lectr. environ. law Hazardous Waste Expo '87, Chgo., HWAC Ann. Meeting, Washington, 1988, N.J. Environ. Expn., 1988, 90, Inside Superfund Conf., Washington, 1989-90, Calif. Inst. Bus. Law, 1991-92, others. Mem. Maritime Law Assn. U.S. (proctor in admiralty 1981—), Am. Corp. Counsel Assn., N.J. State Bar Assn., N.J. Corp. Counsel Assn. (bd. dirs. 1995-97, v.p., sec. 1997—), Am. Soc. Microbiol. Democrat. Roman Catholic. Avocations: jazz and classical guitar. Fax: (201) 848-9228. Home: 170 Gramercy Pl Glen Rock NJ 07452-2310 Office: Becton Dickinson & Co 1 Becton Dr Franklin Lakes NJ 07417-1880

HECTOR, HENRY JOSEPH, state commission administrator; b. Chgo., July 8, 1939. BA, U. Dubuque, 1961; MA, Columbia U., 1967, M in Internat. Affairs, 1970, EdD. Dir. planning and evaluation Fla. Bd. Regents, Tallahassee, 1979-86; dep. commr. Ind. Commn. on Higher Edn., Indpls., 1986-90; exec. dir. Ala. Commn. on Higher Edn., Montgomery, 1990—. Mem. ARC; bd. dirs. Montgomery YMCA; mem. steering com. Nat. Post-Secondary Edn. Coop. Mem. Rotary. Office: Ala Commn on Higher Edn PO Box 302000 Montgomery AL 36130-2000

HECTOR, LOUIS JULIUS, lawyer; b. Fort Lauderdale, Fla., Dec. 11, 1915; s. Harry Howard and Grace Elizabeth (Kellerstrass) H.; m. Dorothy Anne Dooley, Aug. 12, 1950 (dec. 1973); children: Denis Howard, Dorothy Anne, William Frederic, Louis Julius; m. Nancy Bean Hilles, Dec. 11, 1976. BA, Williams Coll., 1938; postgrad., Christ Church Oxford (Eng.) U., 1939; LLB, Yale U., 1942. Atty. Dept. Justice, Washington, 1942-43; asst. to under sec. Dept. State, 1944; pvt. practice Miami, 1946-47; pres. Hector Supply Co., Miami, 1948-56; mem. CAB, 1957-59; sr. ptnr. Steel, Hector & Davis, Miami, 1959—. Trustee emeritus U. Miami, Rockefeller U., Nat. Humanities Ctr., 1985-91; dir. emeritus Chamber Music Soc. Lincoln Ctr., 1987—; chmn. Lucille P. Markey Charitable Trust, 1983-97 . Served with OSS. Mem. Am. Acad. Arts and Scis. Home: One Grove Isle Dr # 809 Miami FL 33133-6530 Office: 200 S Biscayne Blvd Miami FL 33131-2310

HEDAHL, GORDEN ORLIN, theatre educator, university dean; b. Minot, N.D., Jan. 2, 1946; s. Chester Owen and Delores May (Johnson) H.; m. Kathleen Josephine Sawin, Sept. 2, 1967 (div.); children: Marc Oscar, Melissa Ann; m. Jean Louise Loudon, Dec. 31, 1983. BS, U. N.D., 1968, MA, 1972; PhD, U. Minn., 1980. Postdoctoral fellow Purdue U., West Lafayette, Ind., 1981-82; chmn. dept. theater and dance U. Wis., Whitewater, 1970-89, assoc. dean Coll. Arts, 1989-90, acting assoc. vice chancellor, 1991-92; dean Coll. Arts. and Scis. U. Wis., River Falls, 1998—; dean Coll. Liberal Arts U. Alaska, Fairbanks, 1993-98; acad. planner U. Wis. System, 1990-91; bd. dirs. Edward Albee Prince William Sound Theatre Conf., Fairbanks Shakespeare Theatre, Fairbanks Summer Arts Festival. Author: (plays) Tall Tales and True, 1976, The Brothers Grimm, 1977, Land of the Rising Sun, 1979, Trolls and Other Fjord Folk, 1983, Andersen's Storybook, 1986, The Magic of Oz, 1987, African Folk Tales, 1989, Tell Me a Story, 1992; editor: Guide to Curriculum Planning in Classroom Drama and Theatre, 1989. Recipient Roseman Excellence in Teaching award U. Wis. System, Whitewater, U. Wis. Mem. Am. Coun. of Colls. of Arts and Scis., Am. Alliance for Theatre and Edn., Internat. Coun. of Fine Arts Deans, Theatre in Higher Edn. Lutheran. E-mail: gorden.o.hedahl@uwrf.edu.

HEDBERG, PAUL CLIFFORD, broadcasting executive; b. Cokato, Minn., May 28, 1939; s. Clifford L. and Florence (Erenberg) H.; m. Juliet Ann Schubert, Dec. 30, 1962; children: Mark, Ann. Student, Hamline U., 1959-60, U. Minn., 1960-62. Program dir. Sta. KRIB, Mason City, Iowa, 1957-58, Sta. WMIN, Mpls., 1959; staff announcer Time-Life broadcast Sta. WTCN-AM-TV, Mpls., 1959-61, Crowell Collier Sta. KDWB, St. Paul, 1961-62; founder, pres. Sta. KBEW, Minn., 1963-81; founder, owner Sta. KQAD and KLQL-FM, Luverne, Minn., 1971-88; co-founder Sta. KMRS, KKOK-FM, Morris, Minn., 1956-94; pres. Sta. KMRS-AM, KKOK-FM, Morris, Minn., 1974-94; founder, pres. Courtney Clifford Inc., Mpls., 1977-79; founder, owner Market Quoters Inc., Blue Earth, 1974-96; pres. Complete Commodity Options Inc., Blue Earth, 1977-91; pres., owner Sta. KEEZ-FM, Mankato, Minn., 1977-92; founder, pres. Sta. KUOO-FM, Spirit Lake, Iowa, 1984—; owner Sta. KRIB and KLSS-FM, Mason City, Iowa, 1984-97; owner, pres. Sta. KAYL-AM-FM, Storm Lake, Iowa, 1990—; founder, chmn., CEO Hedberg Broadcasting Group; pres. KLGA AM-FM, Algona, Iowa, 1993—; founder, CEO Hedberg Broadcasting Group, Blue Earth, 1976—; pres. KSOU AM-FM (formerly KVDB-KTSB-FM), Sioux Center, Iowa, 1996—; bd. dirs. Minn. Good Roads, v.p., 1976-79, pres., 1979-81; bd. dirs. Blue Earth Indsl. Svcs. Corp., pres., 1970-76; dir. Spirit Lake Industries; mem. affiliates bd. NBC Radio Network, 1990-95, chmn., 1991-95; pres. CEO Arnolds Park (Iowa) Amusement Park, 1990-95; founder KUQQ-FM, Spirit Lake-Milford, Iowa, 1996, KIHK-FM Rock Valley, Iowa, 1997. Mem. Iowa Gt. Lakes Airport Commn., 1986-92; bd. dirs. Pavek Mus. Wonderful Wireless, St. Louis Park, Minn., 1987—. Recipient Disting. Service award Blue Earth Jaycees, 1971. Mem. Nat. Assn. Broadcasters (bd. dirs. 1985-89, 93-95), Minn. Assn. Broadcasters (radio bd. dirs. 1975-86, v.p. 1980-81, pres. 1983-84), Minn. AP Broadcasters (pres. 1966, bd. dirs. 1976-78), Iowa Lakes C. of C. (bd. dirs. 1985-86), Blue Earth C. of C. (pres. 1967, Leadership Recognition award 1967), Gredeh L.C. (founder 1995—), Masons, Shriners. Lutheran. Home: 4400 Gulf Shore Blvd N Naples FL 34103-2216 Office: Grebdeh LC PO Box 606 Naples FL 34106-0606

HEDBRING, CHARLES, computer consultant, writer; b. Wadsworth, Ohio, July 26, 1945; s. Olle S. and Margaret (Dickers) H. BA, Northwestern U., Evanston, Ill., 1969; MS, SUNY, Geneseo, 1974; EdS, Vanderbilt U., 1975; EdD, Columbia U., 1982. nat. and internat. cons. Rsch. grantee N.Y.C. Bd. Edn., 1983-87; award Assn. of Gifted and Talented, 1979, Computer Software award Nat. Assn. Schs., 1990. Avocations: computers, sports, piano, guitar, motorcycles. Home and Office: 310 Riverside Dr Apt 1712 New York NY 10025-4106

HEDDEN, GREGORY DEXTER, environmental science educator, consultant; b. Louisville, Sept. 13, 1919; s. Thomas Clark and Gladys (Dexter) H.; m. Genevieve Groves, Sept. 9, 1950; children—Thomas Dexter, James Jeffrey. B.S. in Chemistry and Meteorology, U. Chgo., 1942, cert. in meteorology, 1943, S.M., 1950, Ph.D. in Phys.-Organic Chemistry, 1951. Asst. to dir. Inst. Air Weapons, U. Chgo., 1951-54; research chemist DuPont Co., Wilmington, Del., 1954-59; tech. dir. Trionics, Madison, Wis., 1959-62; pres. Madison Research, 1962-65; dir. Wis. Tech. Services, 1966-69; prof. environ. scis., dir. sea grant adv. services U. Wis., Madison, 1969-83. Contbr. articles to profl. jours. Patentee in field. Served to capt. USAAF, 1942-46. Recipient New Product award Indsl. Research, 1963, award of honor Underwater Mining Inst., 1981, spl. award Gov. of Wis., 1983, Disting. Service award U. Wis. Sea Grant Inst., 1983; U.S. Rubber Co. fellow U. Chgo., 1950. Fellow AAAS, Am. Inst. Chemists; mem. Am. Chem. Soc., Wis. Acad. Sci., Arts and Letters, Tech. Transfer Soc., Kiwanis, Sigma Xi. Republican. Home: 4410 Travis Ter Madison WI 53711-1402

HEDDEN, KENNETH FORSYTHE, chemical engineer; b. Glendale, Calif., Aug. 13, 1941; s. Marion William and Pauline (Forsythe) H.; m. Ann Ellen Young, Jan. 26, 1963 (div. 1990); children: Randolph, Stephen, William; m. Suzanne A. Whitlock, Feb. 10, 1990. BS, U. Calif., Berkeley, 1963; PhD, U. Calif., Davis, 1968; M in Pub. Adminstrn., U. Ga., 1980. Registered profl. engr., sanitarian, specialist microbiologist. Research fellow Tufts U. Med. Sch., Boston, 1968-70; research assoc. Purdue U., Lafayette, Ind., 1970-72; lab. supr. Anheuser-Busch, Inc., Lafayette, 1972-75; sanitary engr. U.S. Army Environ. Hygiene Agy., Aberdeen (Md.) Proving Ground, 1975-78, EPA, Athens, Ga., 1978-83; chem. engr. Environ. Monitoring Systems Lab. EPA, Las Vegas, Nev., 1983-88; environ. engr. Warner Robins Air Logistics Ctr., Robins AFB, Ga., 1988-94, environ. chemist, 1994—. Contbr. articles to profl. jours. Col. USAR. Mem. Conf. Fed. Environ. Engrs., Sigma Xi, Alpha Chi Sigma. Republican. Baptist. Avocations: gardening, bowling, stamp collecting, woodworking, black powderguns. Home: 1736 Hwy 49 Fort Valley GA 31030-9233 Office: WR-ALC/TIELC 420 2nd St Ste 100 Robins AFB GA 31098-1640

HEDFORS, BO, company executive. Pres., CEO N.Am. operation br. Ericsson Inc., Richardson, Tex., 1994-95, pres., CEO, 1995—. Office: Ericsson Inc 740 E Campbell Rd Richardson TX 75081-6718*

HEDGE, ARTHUR JOSEPH, JR., corporate executive; b. Hudson County, N.J., Sept. 19, 1936; s. Arthur Joseph and Mary Cecelia (Kieran) H.; m. Julie Norton Dahm, Apr. 15, 1961; children: Arthur Joseph III, Peter Michael, Gregory Carlton. BS, St. Peter's Coll., Jersey City, 1960; MS, MIT, 1973. Several mktg. postions Data Processing divsn. IBM, N.Y.C., 1960-68; sr. mktg. mgr. Data Processing divsn. IBM, Chgo., 1968-70; br. mgr. Data Processing divsn. IBM, N.Y.C., 1970-73; dir. mktg. practices Data Processing divsn. IBM, White Plains, N.Y., 1973-74; regional mgr. Data Processing divsn. IBM, Chgo., 1974-77; v.p. mgmt. svcs. Data Processing divsn. IBM, White Plains, 1977-80, v.p. Real Estate and Constrn. divsn., 1980-85, pres. Real Estate and Constrn. divsn., 1985-87, IBM v.p. and pres. Real Estate and Constrn. divsn., 1987-88; IBM v.p. Corp. Real Estate and Constrn. divsn. IBM, Stamford, Conn., 1988-90, v.p. environ. affairs, 1990-93; pres., CEO, bd. dirs. Kroll Environ. Enterprises Inc. subs. Kroll Assocs., Stamford, 1993-97; chmn. Jannon Holdings, LLC, Stamford, 1997—; mem. adv. bd. Wharton Real Estate Ctr., Phila., 1988-94. Mem. vis. com. Harvard U. Grad. Sch. Design, Cambridge, 1985-91, Chgo. Crime Commn., 1974-77, Urban Gateways Exec. Com., Chgo., 1974-77, Conn. Bus. and Industry Assn. Exec. Com., Hartford, 1989-92, trustee, 1988-92; chmn. Bd. Regents Fairfield (Conn.) Coll. Prep. Sch., 1978-84; chmn. bd. dirs. White Plains Hosp. Ctr., 1985-92, trustee, bd. dirs., 1978—; chmn. bd. trustees Am. Festival Theatre, Stratford, Conn., 1988-93; trustee Coun. for Arts, White Plains, 1982-89, The Presbyn. Hosp. N.Y.C., 1993—; bd. dirs. N.Y. and Presbyn. Hosps., Inc., 1996—; vice chmn. HealthStar Network, 1996-97, chmn., 1998. Alfred P.Sloan fellow MIT, 1972-73. Mem. Westchester County Assn. (vice-chmn. 1989-92, trustee bd. dirs. 1986-96), Southwestern Area Commerce and Industry Assn. of Conn. (bd. dirs. 1992—), Conn. Golf Club (bd. dirs. 1980-85). Roman Catholic. Avocations: golf, reading, the arts. Office: Jannon Holdings LLC 5 High Ridge Park Stamford CT 06905-1332

HEDGE, JEANNE COLLEEN, computer programmer; b. Scottsburg, Ind., May 30, 1960; d. Paul Russell and Barbara Jean (Belshaw) H. BS in Environ. Health, Purdue U., 1983. Chemistry and health physics technician Marble Hill Nuclear Generating Sta., Pub. Svc. Ind., Madison, 1983-84; radiation protection asst. Pub. Svc. Electric and Gas Co., Hancock's Bridge, N.J., 1984-85, radiation protection technician, 1985-89, engr., 1989-90, lead engr., 1990-91, sr. staff engr., 1991-95, sr. staff health physicist, 1995-97; prin. health physicist Zion (Ill.) Generating Sta. Com Ed, 1997-98; software developer LIDP Cons. Svcs., Woodbridge, Ill., 1998—; mem. People to People Internat. Citizen Amb. Exch., People's Republic of China, 1988; del. Internat. Environ. Conf., Moscow, 1994. Mem. NOW, Am. Nuclear Soc., Health Physics Soc. Office: LIDP Cons Svcs 3590 Hobson Rd Woodridge IL 60517

HEDGEPETH, JOHN M(ILLS), aerospace engineer, mathematician, engineering executive; b. Southern Pines, N.C., June 29, 1926. BS, Purdue U., 1948; MS, Va. Polytech. U., 1958; PhD in Applied Math., Harvard U., 1962. Rsch. engr. Nat. Adv. Com. Aeronaut., 1948-52, sect. head dynamics and aeroelasticity, 1952-57, br. head structural mechanics, 1957-60; dept. mgr. structures and materials Martin Marietta Corp., 1961-63, dep. dir. engring., 1963-67; v.p. engring Astro Rsch. Corp., Santa Barbara, Calif., 1967-72, pres., 1972-83; pres. Digisim Corp., Santa Barbara, Calif., 1983—. Fellow AIAA; mem. NAE, Internat. Acad. Astronautics. Office: Digisim Corp 202 E Pedregosa St Santa Barbara CA 93101-1051

HEDGES, DONALD WALTON, lawyer; b. Kansas City, Mo., May 24, 1921; s. Byron C. and Irma (McCleary) H.; m. Mary Elizabeth Mancill, Jan. 29, 1944 (div.); children: Judith Elizabeth, Donna Louise, Byron C. III, Steven M.; m. Diane Scheid, Jan. 15, 1965; children: Scott Andrew, Hillary Carson. Student, Principia Coll., 1939-40; BS, U. Pa., 1943, LLB, 1947; D. Bus. Sci. (hon.), Webber Coll., 1947. Bar: Pa. 1949, U.S. Ct. Appeals (3d cir.) 1979, U.S. Dist. Ct. (ea. dist.) Pa. 1949. Law clk. to chief justice Horace Stern Pa. Supreme Ct., 1948-49; mem. firm Mancill, Cooney, Semans & Hedges, 1949-64; ptnr. Wolf, Block, Schorr & Solis Cohen, Phila., 1965-82, Obermayer, Rebmann, Maxwell & Hippel, Wayne, Pa., 1986-88; pvt. practice law Wayne, Pa., 1989—; dir. Servotronics, Inc. Trustee Atwater Kent Mus. Served as lt. (j.g.) Air Force, USNR, 1943-46. Decorated Distinguished Flying Cross, Air medal. Mem. ABA, Pa. Bar Assn., Phila. Bar Assn., Juristic Soc. Phila., Beta Theta Pi. Episcopalian. Clubs: Union League (Phila.); Sharswood Law (U. Pa.), Merion Cricket. Home: 538 Whitford Hills Rd Exton PA 19341-2050

HEDGES, EDITH RITTENHOUSE, nutrition and home economics educator; b. Oakland, Calif., Mar. 15, 1937; d. Lloyd Lee and Florence Muriel (McCurdy) Rittenhouse; m. Frank Hill Hedges III, Dec. 16, 1967. BS in Nutrition/Dietetics, U. Nev., Reno, 1960; MS in Nutrition Rsch., U. Wis., 1962; postgrad., Purdue U., 1971-75, U. Ill., 1975-78. Rsch. asst., cmty. nutritionist U. Wis., Madison, 1960-62; nutritionist Nat. Sch. Lunch program USDA Regional Office, N.Y.C., 1962-64; nutritionist, home economist Am. Friends Svc. Com., Mex., 1964-66; instr. English pub. secondary sch., Tonatico, Mex., 1965-66; from instr. to asst. prof. Eastern Ill. U., Charleston, 1966-93, prof. emeritus, 1993—; cons. nutritionist Coles County Mental Health Dept., 1982-85, 97. Mem. exec. bd. Coles County Arts Coun., Charleston, 1990—. Recipient Rehab. Achievement award Mercy Hosp. Rehab. Ctr., Urbana, Ill., 1987; named Woman of Achievement Women's Studies Coun., Eastern Ill. U., 1994, Outstanding Vol. Docent, Tarble Art Ctr., 1984, 85, 86. Mem. LWV, Soc. Nutrition Edn., Am. Assn. Family Consumer Svcs., Eastern Ill. U. Annuitants Assn., Zonta (chair various coms.), Handweavers Guild Am. (prs. local guild 1983-85), Coalition of Citizens with Disabilities in Ill., Phi Delta Kappa. Quaker. Avocations: photography, watercolors, camping, birdwatching. Home: 21324 E County Road 400N Charleston IL 61920-9077

HEDGES, HARRY GEORGE, computer scientist, educator; b. Lansing, Mich., Oct. 7, 1923; s. Charles William and Elsie (Frost) H.; m. Mary J. Corbishley, June 14, 1944 (dec.); children—Susan, Martha; m. Kamla J. King, July 24, 1988. B.S., Mich. State U., 1949, Ph.D., 1960; M.S., U. Mich., 1954. Electronics engr. USAF Wright Air Devel. Center, Dayton, Ohio, 1949-51; research asso. U. Mich., 1951-54; instr. Mich. State U., East Lansing, 1954-60; asst. prof. Mich. State U., 1960-63, asso. prof., 1963-69, prof., chmn. dept. computer sci., 1969-84, prof. emeritus, 1988—; sr. staff assoc. NSF, 1984-88, head Office Cross-Disciplinary Activities, 1988-92, program dir. undergrad. edn., 1992, program dir. exptl. & integrative activities, 1993—; dir. Nat. Electronics Conf., Inc., 1968-75. Tech. editor: Analysis of Discrete Physical Systems, 1967; mem. Computer Sci. Bd, 1973-84; chmn., 1974-75. Chmn. Selective Service Bd. 264, Lansing, 1970-76. Served with AUS, 1943-46, PTO. NSF sci. faculty fellow, 1960. Mem. Am. Soc. Engring. Edn. (chmn. N.Central sect. 1968-69), IEEE (dir. 1967-69, treas. 1969, vice chmn. 1973, chmn. 1974, Southeastern Mich. sect.). Home: 4331 Embassy Park Dr NW Washington DC 20016-3607

HEDGES, KAMLA KING, library director; b. Covington, Va.; d. John Wilton and Rhoda Alice (Loughrie) K.; m. Harry George Hedges, July 24, 1988. AB, Coll. of William and Mary, 1968; MLS, Vanderbilt U., 1969. Law and legis. reference libr. Conn. State Libr., Hartford, 1969-74; dep. law libr. Steptoe and Johnson, Washington, 1974-78; law libr. Wilkinson, Cragun and Barker, Washington, 1978-83; corp. libr. The Bur. of Nat. Affairs, Inc., Washington, 1983-94, dir. libr. rels., 1995—. Compiler: (directories) BNA's Directory of State and Federal Courts, Judges, Clerks, 1995, BNA's State Administrative Codes and Registers, 1995; contbr. chpt. to law manual. Mem. Am. Assn. Law Librs. (exec. bd. dirs. 1984-87), Spl. Libr. Assn. Episcopalian. Home: 4331 Embassy Park Dr NW Washington DC 20016-3607 Office: Bur Nat Affairs Inc 1231 25th St NW Washington DC 20037-1197

HEDGES, MARK STEPHEN, clinical psychologist; b. Chgo., Feb. 15, 1950; s. Norman T. and Doris Mae (Walters) H.; BS, Purdue U., 1972; MA, U. S.D., 1974, PhD, 1977; m. Janice Finnie, Aug. 16, 1975; children: Anna, Miriam. Psychology intern Western Mo. Mental Health Ctr., Kansas City, 1975-76; dir. children and adolescent svcs., psychologist Northeastern Mental Health Ctr., Aberdeen, S.D., 1977—; chmn. Northeastern Area Local Interagency Team. Mem. adv. bd. S.D. Mental Health Planning and Coord. Adv. Coun. Mem. APA, S.D. Assn. Sch. Psychologists, CASSP (co-chairperson Aberdeen area), Phi Beta Kappa, Psi Chi, Phi Kappa Phi. Methodist. Office: Northeastern Mental Health Ctr 703 3rd Ave SE Aberdeen SD 57401-4508

HEDGES, RICHARD HOUSTON, epidemiologist, lawyer; b. Louisville, July 16, 1952; s. Houston and Frances Ruth (Zemo) H.; m. Donna Jean Hough. BA, U. Ky., 1974; MA, Ea. Ky. U., 1975, MPA, 1983; PhD, U. Ky., 1986; JD, Capital U. Law, 1994. Bar: Ohio 1995. Rehab. specialist Commonwealth of Ky., Somerset, 1976-81; chief health planner Commonwealth of Ky., Frankfort, 1981-82; asst. prof. U. Ky., Lexington, 1985-87; rsch. assoc. dept. med. behavioral sci. U. Ky. Coll. Medicine, Lexington, 1982-85; program adminstr. Rollman Psychiat. Inst., Cin., 1987-88; asst. prof. Ohio U., 1988-92, assoc. prof., 1992—; assoc. law Garry Hunter, LPA, Athens, Ohio, 1997-98; ptnr. Thomas & Hedges LLP, 1998-99; sole practice, 1999—; asst. city atty. City of Nelsonville, Ohio, 1997—, city pros., 1997—; dir. divsn. on aging Ohio U. Health Promotion and Rsch., 1990-92, MHA Grad Prog. Coord., 1995-96; bd. dirs. Washington County Mental Health and Addiction Recovery, 1998-99. Contbr. articles to profl. jours. Mem. Athens County Domestic Violence Task Force, Athens County Victim's Assistance Adv.; treas. Athens County Heart Assn.. 1998. Fellow NIMH, 1984-86. Mem. ABA, ATLA, APHA, Ohio Acad. Trial Lawyers, Healthcare Fin. Mgmt. Assn., Am. Coll. Health Care Execs., Nat. Health Lawyers Assn., Nat. Employment Lawyers Assn., Ohio State Bar Assn., Ohio Employment Lawyers Assn., Pi Sigma Alpha, Phi Delta Phi. Democrat. Episcopalian. Fax: 592-3424. Avocations: backpacking, volleyball, bicycling, sailing. Home: RR 2 Box 14 Belpre OH 45714-9702 Office: Ohio Univ 11 E Washington St Athens OH 45981-0040 also: Ste 306 Wes Banco Bldg Marietta OH 45750

HEDGES, RONALD J., federal judge; b. 1952. BA, U. Md., 1974; JD, Georgetown U., 1977. Bar: N.J. 1977. Law sec. to Hon. Richard J. Hughes, U.S. Supreme Ct., 1977-78; assoc., then ptnr. McCarter & English, Newark, 1978-86; magistrate judge for N.J., U.S. Magistrate Ct., Newark, 1986—. Office: King Fed Bldg-US Courthouse 50 Walnut St Rm 2042 Newark NJ 07102-3506

HEDIEN, COLETTE JOHNSTON, lawyer; b. Chgo., 1939; d. George A. and Catherine (Bugan) Johnston; m. Wayne E. Hedien; 3 children. BS with honors, U. Wis., 1960; JD, DePaul U., 1981. Bar: Ill. 1981. Tchr. Sch. Dist. 39, Wilmette, Ill., 1960-63, Tustin (Calif.) Pub. Schs., 1964-66; extern law clk. to judge Chgo., 1980, U.S. Atty.'s Office, Chgo., 1980; pvt. practice Northbrook, Ill., 1981—; atty. Chgo. Vol. Legal Svcs.; mem. Chgo. Appellate Law Com., 1982-83, chmn., 1987-88; chmn. Northbrook Planning Commn., 1984-89; founder Am. Women of Surrey (Eng.), 1975-77; founding dir. U. Irvine Friends of Libr., 1965-66; guidance vol. Glenbrook High Sch., 1984-89; trustee Village of Northbrook, 1989—; mem. Women's Bd. Field Mus. Bd. dirs. Ill. Project for Spl. Needs Children, 1998—. NSF scholar, 1962. Mem. ABA (com. on real property), Ill. Bar Assn., Chgo. Bar Assn., North Shore Panhellenic Assn. (rep. 1989—), Phi Kappa Phi, Kappa Alpha Theta (bd. dirs.).

HEDIEN, WAYNE EVANS, retired insurance company executive; b. Evanston, Ill., Feb. 15, 1934; s. George L. and Edith P. (Chalstrom) H.; m. Colette Johnston, Aug. 24, 1963; 3 children. BSME, Northwestern U., 1956, MBA, 1957. Engr. Cook Electric Co., Skokie, Ill., 1957-64; bus. mgr. Preston Sci., Inc., Anaheim, Calif., 1964-66; security analyst Allstate Ins. Co., Northbrook, Ill., 1966-70, portfolio mgr., 1970-73, asst. treas., 1973-78, v.p., treas., 1978-80, sr. v.p., treas., 1980-83, exec. v.p., chief fin. officer, 1983-85, vice chmn., chief fin. officer, 1986, pres., 1986-89, chmn., 1989-94; chmn. The Allstate Corp., 1993-94, also bd. dirs.; retired, 1994. Mem. adv. coun. Kellogg Grad. Sch. Mgmt., Northwestern U.; bd. dirs. The PMI Group, Inc., Field Mus. Natural History, Morgan Stanley Dean Witter Funds. Mem. Comml. Club Chgo. Office: WEH Assocs 5750 Old Orchard Rd Ste 430 Skokie IL 60077-1061

HEDINE, KRISTIAN EINAR, lawyer; b. Whitefish, Mont., July 14, 1956; s. Duane Rodney and Edna Louise (Welz) H.; m. Kathy Ilene Schirmer, Apr. 14, 1984; 1 child, Kjirsten Dayle; 1 stepchild, Jarred P. BS in Psychology, U. Wash., 1978; JD, U. Kans., 1982. Bar: Wash. 1982, U.S. Dist. Ct. (ea. dist.) Wash. 1982, U.S. Bankuptcy Ct. (ea. dist.) Wash. 1982, U.S. Ct. Appeals (9th cir.) 1994. Intern Reese & Baffney P.S., Walla Walla, Wash., 1981-82; assoc. Reese, Baffney, Schrag & Siegel, P.S., Walla Walla, 1982-86; ptnr. Reese, Baffney, Schrag, Siegel & Hedine, P.S., Walla Walla, 1986-95, Reese, Baffney, Schrag & Hedine, P.S., Walla Walla, Wash., 1995-98; dir. legal affairs HighSpeed.Com, LLC, Walla Walla, Wash., 1998—; dep. city atty. City of Walla Walla, 1982—; bd. dirs. bankruptcy sect. Fed. Bar Assn. Ea. Dist.; spl. dist. counsel Wash. State Bar Assn., 1989—. Bd. dirs. Exchange Club of Walla Walla, 1986-87, Walla Walla Block Watch Com., 1984-94, Milton-Freewater (Oreg.) Planning Commn., 1998—. Mem. ABA, Fed. Comm. Bar Assn., Bankruptcy Ct. Ea. Dist. Wash. (local rules adv. com.), Elks. Avocations: skiing, motorcycling, water skiing, fishing, racquetball. Office: HighSpeed Com LLC 1520 Kelly Pl Ste 201 Walla Walla WA 99362

HEDKE, RICHARD ALVIN, gifted education educator; b. Evanston, Ill., Aug. 27, 1940; s. Alvin C. and Leona Amanda (Kieper) H.; m. Carol Ann Bormet, July 21, 1962; children: Deborah, Kristen. BS in Elem. Edn., Concordia U., 1968, MA in Curriculum and Instrn., 1975; postgrad., No. Ill. U., 1980—, Nat. Lewis U., 1980—, Gov.'s State U., 1980—. Cert. K-9 tchr., Ill. Classroom tchr., athletic dir. Immanuel Luth. Sch., Kingston, N.Y., 1962-65, St. Paul Luth. Sch., Addison, Ill., 1965-67, St. Peter Luth. Sch., Schaumburg, 1967-74; classroom tchr. Schaumburg Twp. Dist. 54 Schs., 1974-79, 97—, tchr. gifted students, 1979-97; vis. summer sch. instr. High Sch. Dist. 214, Ill., 1983-86, gifted students math. and sci. Dist. 20, 1987; mem. grad. adv. com. Concordia U., 1984-85; dir. future studies summer program High Sch. Dist. 214; presenter various confs. including Nuts 'N Bolts Confs. No. Ill. Planning Commn. for Gifted Edn., 1979-87, Ill. State Gifted Conf., 1980; adj. faculty Aurora U., 1990, 91, 92, 93. Author gifted students curriculum Dist. 54, 1979-98. Mem. long-range planning action com. Project Horizon, 1987-90; mem. sch. leadership team, 1999—. Mem. NEA, Nat. Assn. Gifted Children (mem. future studies subcom., visual and performing arts subcom., presenter Mid-Winter Conf. 1986), Nat. Coun. Tchrs. Math. (presenter ann. meeting 1982, 96, 98, regional meeting 1989, Far West meeting 1990, 97, 99, southeastern regional meeting 1997, Math. on the Rim Conf. 1997, Whistler, B.C., western regional meeting 1991, 93, 99), Ill. Coun. Tchrs. Math. (presenter ann. meeting 1981, 83, 84, 86, del. to Japan 1988, Outstanding Math. Educator), Ill. Coun. Gifted, Ill. Sci. Tchrs. Assn., Ill. Edn. Assn., Schaumburg Edn. Assn., World Future Soc. Avocations: photography, community theater acting and singing, traveling. Home: 614 Berkshire Ct Schaumburg IL 60193-3004 Office: Dist 54 Gifted Program 520 E Schaumburg Rd Schaumburg IL 60194-3510

HEDLER, KENNETH BRUCE, journalist; b. San Bernardino, Calif., June 29, 1955; s. Herbert Roland and Julia (Barahl) H. AA, Coll. of the Desert, 1975; student, Calif. State U., Fresno, 1975-76; BA, Calif. State U., Fullerton, 1978. Reporter Palo Verde Valley Times, Blythe, Calif., 1984-86; reporter, bus. editor The Union, Grass Valley, Calif., 1986-89; copy editor Appeal-Democrat, Marysville, Calif., 1989-92; bus., agr. reporter Imperial Valley Press, El Centro, Calif., 1992-93; reporter Mobile Homes Courier, Hemet, Calif., 1993-94; copy editor Adams/Green Industry Pub., Cathedral City, Calif., 1994-95; staff writer Elsinore Valley Sun-Tribune, Lake Elsinore, Calif., 1996-97; reporter Kingman Daily Miner, Ariz., 1997—; stringer AP, L.A., Phoenix and Sacramento, 1985-89. Treas. Comms. Workers Am., Grass Valley, Calif., 1988-89. Mem. Soc. Profl. Journalists, Desert Press Club (bd. dirs. 1995-96, editor newsletter). Avocations: hiking, travel, reading.

HEDLEY, DAVID VAN HOUTEN, investment banker; b. West Chester, Pa., Dec. 21, 1945; s. David Hartas and Helen (Peveril) H.; BA, Upsala Coll., 1968; m. Michele Michaels, Sept. 9, 1967; children: David Van Houten III, Melissa Michele, Peter Caleb. With investment banking div. E.F. Hutton & Co., Inc., N.Y.C., 1968-80; mng. dir., dir. utility fin. Shearson/Am. Express Inc., N.Y.C., 1980-85, corp. dir., 1984-85, also bd. dirs. 1984-85; mng. dir. utility fin. Drexel Burnham, Lambert, 1985-90, corp. fin. exec. commn., 1989-1990, mng. dir. utility fin. Donaldson, Lufkin & Jenrette, Inc., 1990—. Trustee Morristown-Beard Sch., 1979-90, chmn. 1985-88; active Pete Dawkins for U.S. Sen. Fin. Com.; mem. Rep. Congl. Com., 1989—; pres. Park Ave. Club, 1990-95; co-founder Park Ave. Found., 1990—; trustee Pine Manor Coll., 1992-95. With Army N.G., 1970-76. Mem. N.Y. Soc. Security Analysts. Club: Morris County Golf, Edgartown Yacht, Essex Hunt, Cornell Club. Home: 10 Morgan Ct Morristown NJ 07960-6992 also: Katama Rd Edgartown MA 02539 Office: Donaldson Lufkin & Jenrette Inc 277 Park Ave New York NY 10017-2016

HEDLEY-WHYTE, JOHN, anesthesiologist, educator; b. Newcastle-upon-Tyne, Eng., Nov. 25, 1933; came to U.S., 1960, naturalized, 1965; s. Angus and Nancy (Nettleton) H.-W.; m. Elizabeth Tessa Waller, Sept. 19, 1959. Student, Harrow Sch., 1947-52; B.A. (Rothschild scholar Clare Coll.), Cambridge U., 1955, M.B., 1958, M.A., 1959, M.D., 1972; A.M. (hon.), Harvard U., 1967. House surgeon St. Bartholomew's Hosp., London, 1958-59; resident in anesthesia Mass. Gen. Hosp., 1960-62, hon. anesthetist, 1977—; clin. asst. anesthesia Harvard U., 1961-63, instr., 1963-65, clin. asso., 1965-67, asso. prof., 1967-69, prof., 1969-76, 1st David S. Sheridan prof. anaesthesia and respiratory therapy, 1976—; prof. dept. health policy and mgmt. Harvard U. Sch. Pub. Health, 1988—; chmn. faculty seminar in health and medicine Harvard U., 1975-76; anesthetist-in-chief Beth Israel Hosp., Boston, 1967-88; chmn. com. on research Beth Israel Hosp., 1976-82; cons. in field; mem. tech. adv. bd. on med. devices tech. Am. Nat. Standards Inst., 1973-83; U.S. del. Internat. Electrotech. Commn., 1989-91, 92—; leader U.S. del. Internat. Orgn. Standardization, Geneva, 1973-89, chmn. com. TC 121, SC 3 on anaesthetic and respiratory equipment, 1978—. Author: Respiratory Care, 1965, Applied Physiology of Respiratory Care, 1976, Continuous Anesthesia Vapor Monitoring, 1990, Operating room and Intensive Care Alarms and Information Transfer, 1992; contbr. articles to profl. jours. Recipient Hichens prize St. Bartholomew's Hosp., London, 1957. Fellow ACP (life), Am. Soc. Testing and Materials (hon., chmn. com. F29 1983-89, Merit award 1994); mem. Am. Physiol. Soc., Abernethian Soc. (past pres.), Am. Soc. Anesthesiologists (chmn. com. mech. equipment 1977-82, chmn. com. on equipment and standards 1982-84), Mass. Soc. Anesthesiologists (pres. 1973-74), Am. Soc. Pharmacology and Exptl. Therapeutics, Roxbury Soc. Med. Improvement (libr. 1970-88, sec.-treas. 1988—), Mass. Med. Soc. (coun. 1975-78), Fairhaven Preservation Assn. (chmn. 1990—), Boodle's Club, The Country Club, Somerset Club, Harvard Club of Boston, Vicarage Club. Democrat. Episcopalian. Achievements include discovery that human blood has a constant relative solubility for oxygen. Home: PO Box 649 Concord MA 01742-0649 Office: VA Med Ctr 1400 VFW Pkwy West Roxbury MA 02132-4927

HEDLUND, BARBARA SMITH, musician, educator, music publisher; b. Orlando, Fla., Apr. 11, 1951; d. John Gerald and Marie Elizabeth (Shaulis) Smith; m. Ronald W. Hedlund, Nov. 12, 1974; 1 child, Alexander. BM magna cum laude, Phila. Music Acad., 1983. Prin. cellist N.J. Symphony, Newark, 1978-83, NEPA Philharm., Scranton/Wilkes Barre, Pa., 1978-84; prin. and quartet cellist Westfield (N.J.) Symphony, 1983-84; substitute cellist N.Y. Philharm., 1980-83; prin. cellist Ill. Symphony, Springfield, 1984-91, Champaign-Urbana (Ill.) Symphony, Ill., 1984—, Opera Ill., Peoria, 1988—; prof. music Ill. Wesleyan U., Bloomington, 1986-94; prin. cellist Danville (Ill.) Symphony, 1995—; mem. cello faculty Wilkes (Pa.) Coll.; vis. prof. cello U. Ill., Urbana, 1985-90; arts adminstr. Wesleyan Faculty Recital Series, 1986-94, Ill. Chamber Orch., 1985-91, Virtuoso Obbligato Publs., 1994, Orch. Leitung and Kammermusik Coord. Klassisches Music Festival, 1991-97; co-dir. Springfield Summer Strings, 1995. Soloist with orchs. include Opera Theater of St. Louis, N.W. Symphony, Chgo., Wesleyan Civic Orch., Purdue U. Symphony; solo recitals include appearances at Met. Opera Gala, Charleston, Ill., Smith Music Hall, U. Ill.-Urbana, Nat. Soc. Arts & Letters, Springfield, Tarbel Arts Ctr., Charleston, Sandwich (Ill.) Opera House, Springer Cultural Ctr., Champaign, Ill., Esterhazy Palace, Eisenstadt, Austria, 1992, 95, 1997, Aspen Music Festival, 1982, 91; appeared in Broadway shows including Fiddler on the Roof, Porgy and Bess, Shenandoah, Annie, Cats, Oklahoma, Beatlemania, My Fair Lady, Peter Pan and others; recordings include popular sound tracks, albums, live performances, radio and TV commmls.; editor and pub.: The Virtuoso Obbligato Collection, 1994—; pub. Musi Celli Publications, 1994—; contbr. articles to profl. jours.; tours include Music of Andrew Lloyd Webber, Phantom of the Opera, Shirley Bassey Orch. Adoption search buddy Adoptees Liberty Movement, Ill., N.Y., N.J., 1981—; founder and adminstr. Baroque Artists of Champaign-Urbana, 1996—; bd. dirs. Champaign-Urbana Symphony, 1986-94; parent vol. Coop. Nursery Sch., Urbana, 1986-87, Yankee Ridge Elem. Sch., 1992-94; vol. Urbana Nursing Home, 1966-99. Mem. Am. Fedn. Musicians, Chgo. Cello Soc., Internet Cello Soc., Am. String Tchrs. Assn. Home and Office: Music Pub Prodn Offices 505 Eliot Dr Urbana IL 61801-6727

HEDLUND, DENNIS M., film company executive; b. Hedley, Tex., Sept. 3, 1946; s. John J. and Jeanne (Dwyer) H.; m. Pearl Lee. BS in Bus. Adminstrn., U. Tex., 1968. Performer radio and TV various stas., S.W. and far west U.S., 1972-77; v.p. Allied Artists, N.Y.C., 1977-80; pres., founder Kultur Internat. Films, West Long Branch, N.J., 1980—; creator White Star Films, 1990; founder, distbr. Duke Motorsports, 1997—. Creator orig. tv prodns.: Roger Miller King of the Road, Jackie Mason An Equal Opportunity Offender, Talk Radio, Swoops on Hoops, Baby Love, George Jones

Golden Hits. Appted. by Gov. Whitman vice-chair N.J. Pub. Broadcasting Authority, Trenton. Served to capt. USMC, 1968-72, Vietnam. Mem. Friars Club (mem. admissions com.). Avocations: sailing, scuba diving, collecting classic cars. Office: Kultur/White Star/Duke Video 195 Highway 36 West Long Branch NJ 07764-1304

HEDLUND, JAMES LANE, retired psychologist, educator; b. L.A., Aug. 1, 1928; s. Clarence Ardel Hedlund and Bertha Merilla (Lane) Johnson; m. Doris Ellen Martinsen, Aug. 19, 1950; children—Ann Lane, Carey Ellen. B.A., State U. Iowa, 1950, M.A., 1951, Ph.D., 1953. Dir. clin. psychology intern tng. Walter Reed Army Hosp., Washington, 1959-63; psychology cons. Office Surgeon Gen. U.S. Army, Washington, 1963-66; chief biomed. stress research div. U.S. Army Med. Research and Devel. Comand, Washington, 1966-69; dir. computer support Mil. Psychiatry Walter Reed Med. Ctr., Washington, 1969-71; prof. Mo. Inst. Psychiatry U. Mo.-Columbia, 1971-90, prof. emeritus, 1990—, dir. Mo. Inst. Psychiatry, 1980-90; cons. Mo. Dept. Mental Health, Jefferson City, 1971-90, Va. Dept. Mental Health, Richmond, 1982, Naval Submarine Med. Rsch. Labs., Groton, Conn., 1981-82, R.I. Dept. Mental Health, Providence, 1979. Contbr. articles to profl. jours. Decorated Commendation medals with two oak leaf clusters, Legion of Merit. USPHS fellow 1951-52. Fellow Am. Psychol. Assn., Phi Beta Kappa. Home: 820 Pacific Ave Cayucos CA 93430-1624

HEDLUND, PAUL JAMES, lawyer; b. Abington, Pa., June 26, 1946; s. Frank Xavier and Eva Ruth (Hoffman) H.; m. Marta Louise Brewer, Dec. 7, 1985; children: Annemarie Kirsten, Brooke Ashley, Tess Kara. BSME, U. Mich., 1968; JD, UCLA, 1973. Bar: Calif. 1973, D.C. 1994, U.S. Dist. Ct. (ctrl. dist.) Calif. 1977, U.S. Dist. Ct. (ea. dist.) Calif. 1991, U.S. Dist. Ct. (no. dist.) N.Y. 1994, U.S. Patent and Trademark Office 1978, U.S. Ct. Appeals (9th cir.) 1994, U.S. Supreme Ct. 1997. Staff engr. So. Calif. Edison, L.A., 1968-70; ptnr. Hedlund & Samuels, L.A., 1974-88, Kananack, Murgatroyd Baum & Hedlund (and predecessor firms), L.A., 1988-92; shareholder Baum, Hedlund, Aristei, Guilford & Downey (and predecessor firms), L.A., 1993—; lectr. in field. *Paul Hedlund has spent the last 26 years fighting for individual's rights as a plaintiffs' lawyer. With involvement in complex issues of multi-district litigation and choice of law analysis, he aggressively sued huge corporations in protecting victims' rights in general and commercial aviation, tractor-trailer, bus and train accident litigation. His extensive academic and work background in mechanical and nuclear engineering formed the foundation for his licensing as a patent attorney which led to concentrating in mass transportation accident litigation. His most recent achievement is arguing a case of a highspeed police pursuit (Lewis v. Sacramento County) before the U.S. Supreme Court.* Mem. Bar. Assn. D.C., Consumer Attys. Calif., L.A. County Bar Assn. Office: Baum Hedlund Aristei Guilford & Downey 12100 Wilshire Blvd Ste 950 Los Angeles CA 90025-7114

HEDLUND, RONALD, baritone; b. Mpls., May 12, 1934; s. Cyril and Mildred H.; m. Barbara Smith, Nov. 12, 1974; children: Eric, Alexander. BA, Hamline U.; MusM, Ind. U. Mem. faculty dept. music U. Ill., 1970-74, 83—; bass soloist, instr. classical music seminar Eisenstadt and Vienna, Austria; singing voice cons. Carle Clinic Speech Ctr., Urbana, 1994—. Appeared throughout U.S. including opera cos. of San Francisco, Chgo., Houston, Miami, Seattle, Dallas, Ft. Worth, Phila., Washington, Omaha, Santa Fe, Lake George, Boston, N.Y.C. Opera, Met. Opera Nat. Co., New Orleans, Spoleto Festival, Edinburgh Festival, Vancouver Opera, Conn. Opera, Aspen Festival, R.I. Opera, Chgo. Opera Theater, Opera Theatre St. Louis, Utah Opera, Peoria Civic Opera, Ill. Opera Theatre; soloist with numerous orchs., recitals throughout U.S. Served with USNR, 1958-63. Office: String Soc Artists 505 Eliot Dr Urbana IL 61801-6727

HEDLUND, RONALD DAVID, academic administrator, researcher, educator; b. Joliet, Ill., June 16, 1941; s. Henry Gustav and Betty Marie (Nelson) H.; m. Ellen Louise Parrish, Aug. 22, 1964; children: Karen Marie, David Peter. BA, Augustana Coll., 1963; MA, U. Iowa, 1964, PhD, 1967. Asst. prof. U. Wis., Milw., 1967-73, assoc. prof., 1973-77, dir. social sci. rsch. facility, 1978-80, prof., 1977-89, assoc. dean of rsch. Grad. Sch., 1980-89; vice provost of rsch., prof. U. R.I., Kingston, 1989-96, acting dean grad. sch., 1995-96; vice provost rsch. and grad. edn., prof. Northeastern U., Boston, 1996—; co-chair rsch. network R.I. Partnership Sci. & Tech., Providence, 1990-93; bd. dirs. Econ. Innovation Ctr., Newport, R.I.; mem. R.I. legis. commn. on creating high-tech jobs and Univ. Contbr. numerous articles to profl. jours. Mem. Kingston Fire Dist. Study Com., 1990. NSF grantee, 1967, 77, 84, 95, Ford Found. grantee, 1985. Mem. Am. Polit. Sci. Assn., Internat. Polit. Sci. Assn., Nat. Coun. Univ. Rsch. Adminstrs., Midwest Polit. Sci. Assn. (exec. coun. 1987-90), Soc. of Rsch. Adminstrs., Southern Polit. Sci. Assn., Western Polit. Sci. Assn. Lutheran. Avocation: gardening. Office: Northeastern U 112 Hayden Hall Huntington Ave Boston MA 02115

HEDMAN, JANICE LEE, business executive; b. Elmhurst, Ill., Feb. 7, 1938; d. George Marion Hickman and Vera Beryl (Olsen) Sample; m. Daryl F. Hedman, Aug. 29, 1971 (div. Aug. 1983); children: Kevin G., Gregory Scott, Danny L., Shelly L. Wolanski-Bannon. Student, U. Puget Sound, 1970, Tacoma (Wash.) Community Coll., 1980. Head teller Puget Sound Nat. Bank, Tacoma, 1970-75; real estate agt. Shorewood Realty, Gig Harbor, Wash., 1975-80; mktg. rep. Western Fin. Planning, Inc., Tacoma, 1981-83; co-owner Schatz Avant Garde, Gig Harbor, 1984-86; asst. mgr. Classic Restaurant, Gig Harbor, 1984; co-owner Hedman Enterprises, Gig Harbor, 1976-93; owner, property mgr. Hedman Enterprises, 1993—; v.p. adminstrn. Teardrop Am., Inc., Wenatchee, Wash., 1986-90; pres. Teardrop N.W. Inc., Wenatchee, 1988-90; co-owner J&R Mktg., Wenatchee, 1989-90; mktg. specialist John L. Scott, Inc., Tacoma, Wash., 1991—; sr. mktg. rep. R & D, Excel Telecom., Gig Harbor, 1996—. Asst., Women's Task Force, Tacoma, 1980-81; asst. in fund raising events Am. Cancer Soc., 1992—. Mem. Epsilon Sigma Alpha (pres. 1980-81, v.p. 1981-82). Home and Office: PMB 235 5114 Pt Fosdick Dr NW # E Gig Harbor WA 98335-1735

HEDREEN, GUY MICHAEL, art educator; b. Dallas, Dec. 12, 1958; s. Richard Castle and Elizabeth Ann (Petrie) H.; m. Elizabeth Perce McGowan, Dec. 31, 1985; children: Elizabeth Rose, George Zschamisch. AB, Pomena Coll., 1981; MA, Bryn Mawr Coll., 1983, PhD, 1988. Asst. prof. art Middlebury (Vt.) Coll., 1989-90; asst. prof. art William Coll., Williamstown, Mass., 1990-97, assoc. prof. art, 1997—; vis. asst. prof. classics Franklin Coll., Lancaster, Pa., 1988-89. Author: Silens in Attic Black-Figure Vase-Painting, 1992; contbr. articles to profl. jours. Whiting fellow Bryn Mawr Coll., 1987-88, fellow Am. Acad. in Rome, 1993-94, NEH postdoctoral fellow, 1997—. Mem. Archaeological Inst. Am., Coll. Art Assn. Office: Williams Coll Dept Art Lawrence Hall Williamstown MA 01267

HEDREN, PAUL LESLIE, national park administrator, historian; b. New Ulm, Minn., Nov. 12, 1949; s. Thomas Harry and Muriel Mary (Kunz) H.; m. Janeen Margaret Wolcott, June 19, 1974 (div. 1997); children: Ethne Olivia, Whitney Elizabeth. BA, St. Cloud State Coll., 1972. Park ranger, historian Ft. Laramie (Wyo.) Nat. Hist. Site, 1971-76; historian Big Hole Nat. Battlefield, Wisdom, Mont., 1976-78; chief ranger, historian Golden Spike Nat. Hist. Site, Brigham City, Utah, 1978-84; supt. Fort Union Trading Post Nat. Hist. Site, Williston, N.D., 1984-97, Niobrara/Mo. Nat. Scenic Riverways, O'Neill, Nebr., 1997—. Author: First Scalp for Custer, 1980, With Crook in the Black Hills, 1985, Fort Laramie in 1876, 1988 (Best Book of 1988 Wyo. State Hist. Soc.); editor: Campaigning with King, 1991 (Merit award State Hist. Soc. Wis. 1991), The Great Sioux War 1876-77, 1991, Traveler's Guide to the Great Sioux War, 1996; contbr. articles to profl. jours. Bd. dirs. Conv. and Vis. Bur., Williston, 1984-96, pres., 1994-96. Mem. Co. Mil. Historians, Western History Assn. (mem. coun. 1990-93). Avocations: writing, lecturing on Am. western history. Office: Niobrara/Mo NSR PO Box 591 O'Neill NE 68763-0591

HEDRICK, BASIL CALVIN, state agency administrator, ethnohistorian, educator, museum and multicultural institutions consultant; b. Lewistown, Mo., Mar. 17, 1932; s. Truman Bloice and M. LaVeta (Stice) H.; m. Anne Kehoe, Jan. 19, 1957 (div. 1979); 1 dau., Anne Lanier Hedrick Caraker; m. Susan Elizabeth Pickel, Oct. 2, 1980. A.B., Augustana Coll., Rock Island, Ill., 1956; MA, U. Fla., 1957; PhD, Inter-Am. U., Mex., 1965; cert., U. Vienna, Strobl, Austria, 1956. Asst. prof., assoc. prof., prof. So. Ill. U., Carbondale, 1967-74, asst. dir. Univ. Mus., 1967-70, dir. Univ. Mus. and Art Galleries, 1970-77, dean internat. edn., 1972-74; asst. dir. Ill. Div. Mus., Springfield, 1977-80; prof. history U. Alaska, Fairbanks, 1980-88, dir. U. Alaska Mus., 1980-88, founder, dir. internat. affairs, 1985-87; founder, dir. Div. Mus., Archaeology and Publs. State of Mich., Lansing, 1988-91; multicultural cons., 1991—; dir. mktg., cons. Rosalie Whyel Mus. Doll Art, Bellevue, Wash., 1991—; Fulbright sr. lectr., Brazil, 1972; mem. nat. register adv. panel, Ill., 1977-80; mem. Alaska Coun. on Arts, Anchorage, 1983-85; chmn. Fairbanks Hist. Preservation Commn., 1982-88; mem. Alaska Land Use Coun.; bd. dirs. Alaska Hist. Preservation Found., 1986-88; mem. Gov.'s Revitalization Task Force, Lansing, Mich., mem. ethnic coun., Mich., 1988-89; bd. dirs. East King County Visitors Bur., 1993—, officer, 1997—; officer, bd. dirs. Wash. Mus. Assn., 1993—. Author: (with others) A Bibliography of Nepal, 1973, (with Carroll L. Riley) The Journey of the Vaca Party, 1974, Documents Ancillary to the Vaca Journey, 1976, (with C.A. Letson) Once Was A Time, a Wery Good Time: An Inquiry into the Folklore of the Bahamas, 1975, (with J.E. Stephens) In the Days of Yesterday and in the Days of Today: An Overview of Bahamian Folkmusic, 1976, It's A Natural Fact: Obeah in the Bahamas, 1977, Contemporary Practices in Obeah in the Bahamas, 1981; compilations and collections, 1959-69; editor: (with J. Charles Kelley and Riley) The Classic Southwest: Readings in Archaeology, Ethnohistory and Ethnography, 1973, (with J. Charles Kelley and Riley) The Mesoamerican Southwest: Readings in Archaelogy, Ethnohistory and Ethnology, 1974, (with Riley) Across the Chichimec Sea, 1978, (with others) New Frontiers in the Archaeology and Ethnohistory of the Greater Southwest, 1980, Trans. of Ill. Acad. Sci., 1979-81, (with Susan Pickel-Hedrick) Ethel Washington: The Life and Times of an Eskimo Dollmaker, The Role of the Steamboat in the Founding and Development of Fairbanks, Alaska, 1986, (with Susan Savage) Steamboats on the Chena, 1988; co-editor: Led Zeppelin live, 1993, 94, 97, Beautiful Children, 1996; author and editor of various other publications; contbr. articles to profl. jours. Chmn. Goals for Carbondale, 1972; active various local state, nat. polit. campaigns. Mem. NMA (bd. dirs. 1989-91), Am. Assn. Mus. (leader accreditation teams 1977—, sr. examiner), Ill. Archaeol. Soc. (pres. 1973-74), Mus. Alaska, Assn. Sci. Mus. Dirs., Midwest Mus. Conf. (treas. 1977-80), Western Mus. Assn., Wash. Mus. Assn. (bd. dirs. 1994—, v.p. 1995-97, pres. 1997—), BD Arts (bd. dirs. 1995-96), Phi Kappa Phi. *Pragmatism has been the ruling factor in both my personal and professional life. I have never assumed that anything is immutable and, therefore, I have rarely been overly surprised or disappointed in changes which have occurred. In our rush to succeed and excel, we often forego the realities of daily life in order to attempt the literally impossible. The better rule is, to adapt to reality without losing ethical and moral principle. Relax and learn.*

HEDRICK, FLOYD DUDLEY, retired government official, author; b. Lynchburg, Va., Jan. 19, 1927; s. Silas Dudley and Alice (Stowe) H.; m. Rachel Conelia Childress, May 27, 1950; children: Susan Kaye, Alice Rae. Grad., Va. Comml. Coll., 1948, Advanced Mgmt. Program, Harvard, 1971; PhD, U. Ctrl. Calif., 1981. Purchasing agt., supt. stores Trailways, Inc., 1947-65; v.p. purchasing Macke Co., Washington, 1966-72; pres. subsidiary Atlantic Supply Co., Hyattsville, Md., 1967-72; chief procurement and supply div. Library of Congress, Washington, 1973-97; mem. Inter-Agy. Procurement Policy Com., 1973-89, Inter-Agy. Metrecation Com., 1976-93; Pres. Lynchburg chpt. Fed. and State Credit Unions, 1956-57. Author: Purchasing Management in the Smaller Company, 1971, Purchasing for Owners of Small Plants, 1976, 79; assoc. editor: Purchasing Handbook, 1973, 81. Served with USNR, 1944-46, 50-52. Mem. Am. Mgmt. Assn. (purchasing planning coun. 1969-92, editor Mgmt. Handbook 1981, named to Wall of Fame 1982), Nat. Assn. Purchasing Mgmt. (v.p. 1972-73, chmn. orgn. and planning com., Disting. Svc. award 1976, J. Shipman gold medal 1986), Purchasing Mgmt. Assn. Washington (pres. 1969-70), Isaak Walton League (v.p. Lynchburg 1957), Masons (32d degree). Club: Mason (32 deg.). Home: 3824 King Arthur Rd Annandale VA 22003-2209

HEDRICK, HAL CLEMONS, company executive; b. Jacksonville, Fla., 1945. BA magna cum laude, U. Redlands, 1967; JD, Duke U., 1970. Atty. Ford Motor Co., 1970-79; asst. corp. sec. The LTV Corp., Cleve., 1979—. Mem. ABA, Ohio Bar Assn., Tex. Bar Assn., Mich. Bar Assn., Omicron Delta Kappa. Office: LTV Corp 200 Public Sq Cleveland OH 44114-2301*

HEDRICK, HUNT R(ANDOLPH), JR., sportswear company official; b. Danville, Va., Sept. 23, 1956; s. Hunt Raldolph and Dorothy Louise Hedrick; 1 child, Hunt Randolph III. BBA, BS, James Madison U., 1979. Dir. purchasing Clearwater (S.C.) Finishing Inc., 1988-90; spl. purchasing agt. Converse Inc., North Reading, Mass., 1990-94; sr. devel. mgr. The Stride Rite Corp., Lexington, Mass., 1994-98; dir. material sourcing Fila Sports Inc., Peabody, Mass., 1998—, Biella, Italy, 1998—. Avocations: golf, photography, scuba diving, kayaking, skiing. E-mail: h-hedrick@hotmail.com. Home: 17 Bowman St Lexington MA 02421 Office: Fila Sports Inc 83 Pine St Peabody MA 01690

HEDRICK, JERRY LEO, biochemistry and biophysics educator; b. Knoxville, Iowa, Mar. 11, 1936; s. Harvard L. and Dorothy E. (Hardin) H.; m. Karel J. Harper, June 22, 1957; children: Michael L., Kerry L., Benjamin A., Kimberly L. B.S., Iowa State U., 1958; Ph.D., U. Wis., 1961, postgrad., 1961-62; postgrad., U. Wash., 1962-65. Asst. prof. U. Calif.-Davis, 1965-68, assoc. prof., 1968-74, prof. biochemistry, 1974—, chmn. dept., 1982-84, assoc. dean grad. studies, 1998—; sabbatical leave Hakkaido U., Sapporo, Japan, 1985-86, 89, 96; U. Calif. exch. scientist, Hokkaido U., 1989; vis. sr. scientist Mitsubishi-Kasei Inst. of Life Scis., Machida, Japan, 1989. Recipient Guggenheim Found. award: John Simon Guggenheim fellow, Cambridge U., Eng., 1971-72; grantee NIH, NSF, USDA, 1966—. Mem. AAAS, Am. Soc. Biol. Chemists, Am. Chem. Soc., Soc. Study Reprodn., Am. Soc. Cell Biology, Sigma Xi. Home: 25280 Carlsbad Ave Davis CA 95616-9434 Office: U Calif Sect Molecular Cellular Bio 1 Shields Ave Davis CA 95616*

HEDRICK, JOAN DORAN, writer; b. Balt., May 1, 1944; d. Paul Thomas and Jane (Connorton) Doran; m. Travis K. Hedrick, Aug. 26, 1967; children: Jessica, Rachel. AB, Vassar Coll., 1966; PhD, Brown U., 1974. Instr. Wesleyan U., Middletown, Conn., 1972-74, asst. prof. English, 1974-80; prof. history Trinity Coll., Hartford, Conn., 1994—, also dir. women's studies program, 1987-98; vis. asst. prof. Trinity Coll., Hartford, 1980-81, vis. assoc. prof., 1981-82. Author: Solitary Comrade: Jack London and His Work, 1982, Harriet Beecher Stowe: A Life, 1994 (Pulitzer Prize for biography 1995); editor: The Oxford Harriet Beecher Stowe Reader, 1999. Mem. MLA, Am. Studies Assn., Orgn. Am. Historians, Soc. Am. Historians. Office: Trinity College Dept of History 300 Summit St Dept Of Hartford CT 06106-3186

HEDRICK, JOHN O., railroad executive; b. Sellersville, Pa., Sept. 16, 1944; s. John O. and Ruth Moyer H.; m. Patricia Marie Lott, Jan. 13, 1968; children: Sharon Kathleen Hedrick Busby, Michael Bryan. BS, NYU, 1966; MA, U. Ga., 1986. Lic. pvt. pilot. Various mgmt. positions So. Railway Co., Atlanta, 1966-74; pres. Pullman Palace Dining Co., Atlanta, 1974-77; realtor Doster Realty Co., Monroe, Ga., 1977-81; exec. dir. Catskill Rail Com., Stamford, N.Y., 1981-85; prin. cons. PTSI Transp., Bryn Mawr, Pa., 1985-90; gen. mgr. Western Md. Scenic R.R., Cumberland, Md., 1990-92, Railway Engring. Assocs., Balt., 1992-93; cons., project mgr. PTSI Transp., Bryn Mawr, Pa., 1992-93; gen. mgr., exec. dir. W.Va. State Rail Authority, Moorefield, 1993—; adv. mem. W.Va. Infrastructure and Jobs Devel. Coun., Charleston, 1995—; bd. dirs. Ft. Mill Rdge Civil War Trenches Found., Romney, W.Va. Contbr. articles to profl. jours. Mem. The Lexington Group, Am. Assn. of State Hwy. and Transp. Ofcls. (standing com. on rail transp.), Am. Assn. Railroad Supts., N.Am. Operating Rules Assn. Home: 117 Highland Ave Petersburg WV 26847-1707 Office: WVa State Rail Authority 120 Water Plant Dr Moorefield WV 26836

HEDRICK, JOYCE ANN CORYELL, educational support services professional; b. Washington, Sept. 12, 1943; d. Donald Edward and Myra Virginia (Thompson) Coryell; m. Donald Souder Hedrick, Aug. 29, 1964; children: Christina Elaine, Timothy Jomo. BS, James Madison U., 1965; postgrad., George Washington U., 1966-67; Masters Equivalent, James Madison U., 1970; MDiv, Ea. Bapt. Theol. Seminary, Phila., 1983; postgrad., Ea. Mennonite U. Lic. minister Franconia Mennonite Conf.; cert. secondary sch. tchr., Va., Md. Mem. math. faculty Woodrow Wilson H.S., Fishersville, Va., 1965-66, Belt Jr. H.S., Wheaton, Md., 1970-71; mem. faculty of math.; social sci., history Christopher Dock Menno H.S., Lansdale, Pa., 1968, 75-77; exec. sec. Franconia Mennonite Conf. Mission Commn., Souderton, Pa., 1984-85; adminstr. Mennonite Historians of Ea. Pa., Souderton, 1985-88; ch. planter Kona Mennonite Ministries, Kailua-Kona, Hawaii, 1988-91; mem. math. faculty Ea. Mennonite U., Harrisonburg, Va., 1994-96, asst. dir. Learning Ctr., 1993—, dir. student disability support svcs., 1997—; ch. devel. cons. Franconia Conf. Mission Commn., 1985-88; bus. cons. Village Bazaar, Harrisonburg, 1992-99; cons. in edn., spkr. in field. Author: (booklets) Meeting Learning Needs at Eastern Mennonite University, 1996; editor: (book) History of Salem Mennonite Church, 1996; editor: (jours.) MHEP Newsletter, 1985-88, AAUW Harrisonburg Inside Track, 1992-94; contbr. articles to profl. jours.; reviewer book revs. in field. Gifted program evaluator North Penn Sch. Dist., Lansdale, 1974-75, tutor, 1973-75; treas. Am. Women's Assn., Nairobi, Kenya, 1972-73, 71-73. Grantee U.S. Dept. Edn., Va. Dept. Edn., Va. Dept. Rehab. Svcs., 1994, Am. Mus. Assn., 1986, Pa. State Hist. Commn., 1987, Ea. Mennonite U., 1997. Mem. AAUW (v.p. 1994-96), Am. Assn. Christian Counselors, Am. Coll. Counseling Assn., Am. Counseling Assn., Assn. on Higher Edn. and Disabilities in Va., Assn. on Higher Edn. and Disabilities, Children and Adults with Attention Disorders, Phi Delta Kappa. Avocations: needlework, quilting, indoor and outdoor gardening, internat. travel and hosting. Fax: (540) 432-4977. Office: Ea Mennonite Univ 1200 Park Rd Harrisonburg VA 22802-2404

HEDRICK, KIRBY L., petroleum company executive. Pres., CEO Phillips Gas Co., Houston, Tex., 1986-94; sr. v.p. refining, mktg. and transp. Phillips Petroleum Co., Bartlesville, Okla., 1994-97; exec. v.p. Upstream Phillips Petroleum Co., 1997—. Office: Phillips Petroleum Co 17 Phillips Bldg Bartlesville OK 74004*

HEDRICK, LARRY WILLIS, airport executive; b. Newton, Kans., Dec. 23, 1939; s. A.C. and Goldie (Kerns) H.; m. Nancy Cashin, July 21, 1962; children: Christina, Kathleen, Thomas. BL, U. LaSalle, Chgo., 1973. Lic. airport mgr., Mass. Airport mgr., dir. civil def. Newton City-County Airport, 1966-73; airport mgr. Barnes Mcpl. Airport, Mass., 1973-77, Niagara Falls Internat. Airport, 1977-81, Greater Buffalo (N.Y.) Internat. Airport, 1981-87; appointed airport adminstr. Pt. Columbus Internat. Airport, Columbus, Ohio, 1987-91; appointed exec. dir. Columbus Airport Authority, 1991—; founding bd. mem. Airline Passengers of Am., 1987; guest speaker various univs. and airport confs. Bd. dirs. Greater Columbus Conv. and Visitors Bur., 1992; past squadron commdr. CAP Kans. Wing. With USN, 1958-62. Mem. Am. Assn. Airport Execs. (accredited 1973, nat. sec. 1982, treas. bd. dirs. 1983, 1st v.p. 1985, 2d v.p. 1984, nat. pres. 1986-87, Disting. Svc. award 1994), Nat. Fire Protection Assn. (airport industry's only rep.), Mass. Airport Mgmt. Assn. (pres. 1975-76). Lic. pilot and instrument technician. Office: Columbus Airport Authority 4600 Internat Gtwy Columbus OH 43219

HEDRICK, LOIS JEAN, retired investment company executive, state official; b. Topeka, Kans., Jan. 25, 1927; d. Arthur Lenard and Nellie Cecelia (Johnson) Lungstrum; m. Clayton Newton Hedrick, Apr. 26, 1949; 1 dau., Carol Beth. Cert., Strickler's Bus. Coll., 1947; student Washburn U., Topeka, 1980-83. Staff sec. Kans. State Senate, Topeka, 1946-65; co-owner Hedrick's Market, Topeka, 1953-67; exec. sec. to sr. legal counsel Security Benefit Life Ins. Co., Topeka, 1963-73; asst. corp. sec. Security Mgmt. Co., Topeka, 1973-92, Security Distbrs. Inc., SBL Planning Inc., SBL Fund, Security Action Fund, Security Equity Fund, Security Investment Fund, Security Ultra Fund, Security Bond Fund, Security Cash Fund, Security OmniFund, Security Tax-Exempt Fund, Security Benefit Group, Ins., Security Mgmt. Co.; mem. Kans. Adv. Coun. on Aging, 1990-93; mgmt. cons. United Way of Greater Topeka, 1981-89 , mem. pub. relations staff, 1982—, rep. precinct woman. Organizer, chmn. Topeka Crime Blockers, 1976—; vol. fundraiser Am. Heart Assn., Stormont-Vail Hosp. Expansion, 1976-77; chmn. Plant a Tree for Century III, 1976; mem. Greater Topeka Career Edn. Com., 1981—; staff sec., fundraiser Christian Rural Overseas Program, 1951, staff sec. USAF Supply Depot, 1951-53; vol. community and various hosps. Named Woman of Year, Am. Bus. Women's Assn., 1970; Sec. of Yr., Profl. Secs. Inc., 1975. Mem. Greater Topeka C. of C. (chmn. edn. com. 1981—, ambassador chmn. high sch. honors banquet, 1982—), Adminstrv. Mgmt. Soc. (dir., pres. 1976—). Republican. Home: 1556 SW 24th St Topeka KS 66611-1329

HEDRICK, STEVE BRIAN, psychotherapist; b. Orlando, Fla., Aug. 23, 1958; s. David Warrington and June (Nicholson) H.; 1 child, Stephen. BA, U. Ctrl. Fla., 1980, MA, 1988. Lic. mental health counselor, marriage and family therapist, Fla. Child devel. worker Seagrave, Orlando, 1985-86; deinstitutionalization case mgr. Mental Health Svcs. Orange County, Orlando, 1986-88; family therapist, mental health counselor Green House Family Counseling Ctr., Orlando, 1988-92, PruCare of Orlando, 1993-97, Charter Hosp. Tampa Bay, Fla., 1997-98, Charlee Family Care Svcs., Orlando, Fla., 1998—. Mem. ACA, Am. Mental Health Counselors Assn., Fla. Mental Health Counselors Assn., Fla. Assn. Counseling and Devel., Ctrl. Fla. Assn. Marriage and Family Therapy, Internat. Assn. Marriage and Family Counselors, Am. Assn. Marriage and Family Therapy (clin. mem.). Democrat. Avocations: reading, dancing, tennis, beach, travel. Office: Charlee Family Care Svcs 11875 High Tech Ave Ste 200 Orlando FL 32817

HEDRICK, TERRY ELIZABETH, psychologist, researcher; b. July 23, 1948. PhD, U. Mo., 1976; postdoctoral studies, Northwestern U., 1976-77. Asst. prof. psychology Kent (Ohio) State U., 1977-79; staff assoc. in employment policy Brookings Inst., Washington, 1979; dir. Tng. Inst., U.S. Office Govt. Affairs, Washington, 1988-94, asst. comptroller gen. for program evaluation, 1994-95; ret. VOl. sci. adv. com. CFIDS Assn. Am., 1997—. E-mail: lgvm@prodigy.com. Home and Office: PO Box 340 Cobb Island MD 20625

HEDRICK, WALLY BILL, artist; b. Pasadena, Calif., 1928; s. Walter Thomas and Velma Laurel (Thurman) H. Student, Otis Art Inst., Los Angeles, 1947, Calif. Coll. Arts and Crafts, 1954; B.F.A., Calif. Sch. Fine Arts, 1955; MA, San Francisco State U., 1958. Instr. San Francisco State U., 1958-59, Calif. Sch. Fine Arts, 1960-64, Art Inst. San Francisco, 1964-70, San Francisco Acad. Art, 1971, San Jose State U., 1972-73, Indian Valley Coll., 1974—; instr. summer session Art. Inst. San Francisco, 1978; instr. U. Calif., Davis, 1984, 86. One-man shows include Pasadena (Calif.) Arts Ctr., 1950, M.H. de Young Meml. Mus., San Francisco, 1955, Calif. Sch. Fine Arts, San Francisco, 1956, Oakland (Calif.) Mus., 1958, Isaacs Gallery, Toronto, Can., 1961, New Mission Gallery, San Francisco, 1963, San Francisco Art Inst., 1967, Sonoma Satte Coll., Calif., 1968, 63 Bluxome St., San Francisco, 1975, Gallery Paule Anglim, San Francisco, 1982, 84, 89, 90, Emanuel Walter Gallery, 1985, Atholl McBean Gallery, 1985, Natsoulas-Novelozo Gallery, Davis, Calif., 1989, Mills Coll. Art Gallery, 1994, Gallery Paule Anglim, 1994, Calif. Mus. of Art, 1999; group exhbns. include Pasadena Art Mus., L.A. County Mus. Art, 1953, San Francisco Mus. Modern Art, 1954, 57, 60, 66, Santa Barbara Mus. Modern Art, 1956, Mus. Modern Art, N.Y.C., 1959, 76, Calif. Palace Legion Honor., 1961, San Francisco Art Inst., 1962, San Francisco Mus. Art, 1962, 66, Norton Simon Mus. Art, Pasadena, 1962, Richmond (Calif.) Art Ctr., 1964, Calif. State U. Sonoma, Rhonert Park, 1968, Dallas Mus. Fine Arts, 1974, Wadsworth Antheneum, Hartford, Conn., 1975, San Francisco Mus. Modern Art, 1977, Gallery Paule Anglim, San Francisco, 1981, 83, 86, 92, South Market Cultural Ctr., 1982, Columbus (Ga.) Mus. Arts and Scis., 1984, Sheldon Meml. Art Gallery, U. Nebr., Licoln, 1984, Chgo. Internat. Arts Expo., 1984, Old Waterhouse Cabaret, Oakland, 1985, Arts Coun. San Mateo County, Belmont, Calif., 1985., Emanuel Walter Gallery, 1985, Atholl McBean Gallery, 1985, Newport Harbor Art Mus., Newport Beach., Calif., 1986, L.A. County Mus. Art, 1986-87, Mus. Contemporary Art, Chgo., 1986-87, Natsoulas Novelozo Gallery, 1990; group exhibitions include Gallery Paule Anglim, San Francisco, 1992, ACGI Gallery, Berkeley, Calif., 1993, The Crocker Mus., Sacramento, 1994, The Oakland Mus., Calif., 1994, San Francisco Art Inst., 1994, Richmond Art Ctr., Calif., 1995, San Francisco Women Artists Gallery, 1995, Whitney Mus. Am. Art, N.Y.C., 1995, Walker Art Ctr., Mpls., 1996, M.H. de Young Meml. Mus., 1996; represented in permanent collections, Aldrich Mus. Contemporary Art, Ridgefield, Conn., Mus. Modern Art, N.Y.C., Smithsonian Instn., San Francisco Mus. Modern Art, City and County San Francisco, L.A. County Mus. Art, Laguna (Calif.)

Mus., Mus. Contemporary Art, Ridgefield, Conn., Oakland Mus., Calif. State U. Sonoma, U. Calif. San Francisco. San Francisco Art Commn., San Francisco Art Inst., San Francisco Internat. Airport, Univ. Art Mus., Berkeley, Calif., Mills Coll., Oakland; represented by Gallery Paule Anglim. Served with AUS, 1950-52. Recipient Adeline Kent award, 1985, Golden Bear award Calif. State Fair, 1990, merit award, 1991, award of excellence, 1996; grantee Nat. Endowment Arts, 1962, 82, 93, Marin Arts Coun.-Bucks Found., individual artist grantee San Francisco Found., 1985-86, Adolph and Esther Gottlieb Found. grantee, 1997, Pollack-Krasner Found. grantee, 1999. Office: PO Box 94 Bodega CA 94922-0094

HEDRICK, WYATT SMITH, pharmacist; b. Roswell, N.Mex., Sept. 28, 1951; s. Wyatt Smith and Roberta Walker (Stuart) H. BS in Pharmacy, U. N.Mex., 1974; MS in Hosp. Pharmacy, U. Houston, 1978. Registered pharmacist, N.Mex., Tex. Pharmacy intern St. Mary's Hosp., Roswell, N.Mex., 1973, Ea. N.Mex. Med. Ctr., Roswell, 1973-74, U-SAVE Drug, Roswell, 1974-75; pharmacy resident U. Tex. Med. Br. Hosps., Galveston, 1977-78; staff pharmacist Meml. Gen. Hosp., Las Cruces, N.Mex., 1978, Columbia Med. Ctr. West, El Paso, Tex., 1978—. Mem. Am. Soc. Health-Sys. Pharmacists, Tex. Soc. Health-Sys. Pharmacists, El Paso Area Soc. Health-Sys. Pharmacists. Avocations: reading, traveling, physical fitness. Home: 1028 Quinault Dr El Paso TX 79912-1223

HEDSTROM, CORA ZALETEL, public relations director; b. Des Moines, Jan. 31, 1961; d. Joseph Henry and Myrtle Douglas (Bunch) H.; m. Randy Lee Shown, June 23, 1984 (div. June 1994); children: Clinton, Tyler; m. Bradley Lynn, June 29, 1996. BS, Emporia State U., 1983, MA, 1985; postgrad., U. Kans., 1997—. Reporter The Emporia (Kans.) Gazette, 1985-87; from corp. copywriter to mktg. comm. specialist Security Benefit Group, Topeka, Kans., 1987-89; from news bur. dir. to dir. univ. rels. Emporia State U., 1989—; dir. pub. rels. Nat. Tchrs. Hall of Fame, Emporia, 1991—; dist. VI bd. dirs. Coun. Advancement and Support of Edn., 1996-98, mem. comm. on comms., 1998—; mem. nat. comm. com. Honor Soc. Phi Kappa Phi, 1995—. Pres. bd. dirs. Emporia Main St., 1995-96; state comm. com. Am. Heart Assn., Topeka, 1993-96. 1996 Olympic torch bearer. Mem. Am. Assn. State Colls. and Univs. (nat. PIO adv. bd. 1993—). Republican. Roman Catholic. Avocations: antiques, all sports, reading, traveling, writing. Home: 1110 W 18th Ave Emporia KS 66801-5648 Office: Emporia State U 1200 Commercial St Emporia KS 66801-5087

HEDSTROM, MITCHELL WARREN, banker; b. Buffalo, Apr. 14, 1951; s. Eric Leonard and Eloise (Herrick) H.; m. Zoe C. Dyson, Apr. 28, 1990. BS, Northeastern U., Boston, 1975; MS, MIT, 1977. Acct. officer Citibank, N.A., N.Y.C., 1978-80; sr. acct. officer Citibank, N.A., 1980-82, asst. v.p., 1982-84, v.p., 1984—, restructuring com., 1989-95, chmn. bank adv. com. for Panama, Sudan and Senegal, 1993-95; sr. risk mgr. pvt. banking group Citibank Switzerland, Geneva, 1996-97; group portfolio mgr. pvt. banking group, N.Y.C., 1998—. Mem. Coun. on Fgn. Rels., Coral Beach and Tennis Club. Episcopalian. Office: Citibank NA 399 Park Ave 5th Fl New York NY 10022-4611

HEDSTROM, SUSAN LYNNE, maternal women's health nurse; b. Dowagiac, Mich., Jan. 17, 1958; d. Clinton J. and Gloria Anna (Hyink) Moore. ADN, Southwestern Mich. Coll., 1978. RN cert. maternal-newborn, Mich., Ind., Calif., Ga., Fla. Staff nurse obstetrics unit Lee Meml. Hosp., Dowagiac, Mich., 1979-81, Meml. Hosp., South Bend, Ind., 1981-90; with MRA Staffing Systems, Inc., Ft. Lauderdale, Fla., 1990-93; staff nurse traveler MUSC, Charleston, S.C., 1990-91; nurse Desert Hosp., Palm Springs, Calif., 1991, Ind. U. Hosp., Indpls., 1992, Valley Med Ctr., Fresno, Calif., 1992; staff nurse post partum/nursery Tallahassee Meml. Regional Med. Ctr., 1993-95, asst. head nurse post partum, 1995—. Mem. Am. Women's Health, Obstetrics and Neonatal Nurses. Office: Tallahassee Meml Reg Hosp Magnolia Dr & Miccosukee Rd Tallahassee FL 32308

HEDVIG, MICHAEL ELLIOTT, management consultant; b. Urbana, Ill., Oct. 12, 1960; s. Thomas Ivan and Eleanor Barbara (Herson) H.; m. Marilyn Deborah King, June 14, 1998. BA, Calif. State U. Northridge, 1984; BBA, Nat. U., 1992; MSBA, Tex. A&M, 1994. Mgmt. intern Army Material Command, Texarkana, Tex., 1993-94; logistician Army Corps of Engrs., Seattle, 1994-95; contract adminstr. Weapons Divsn. Naval Air Warfare Ctr., Point Mugu, Calif., 1995-96; contract adminstr. Naval Facilities Engring. Command, Port Hueneme, Calif., 1996-97, Xontech, Inc., Van Nuys, Calif., 1997-98; publicity intern Warren Cowan and Assocs., L.A., 1999—. Mem. Nat. Contract Mgmt. Assn. (publicity chair 1996-97). Avocations: sailing, travel, aircraft restoration, cooking. Office: Naval Facilities Engring NCBC Code 27 Bldg 41 Port Hueneme CA 93043

HEEBNER, ALBERT GILBERT, economist, banker, educator; b. Phila., Mar. 7, 1927; s. Albert and Julia (Zwada) H.; m. Dorothy Mae Kiler, Aug. 16, 1952. AB, U. Denver, 1948; AM, U. Pa., 1950, PhD, 1967. Instr. econs. Coll. of Wooster, Ohio, 1950-52; with Phila. Nat. Bank subs. CoreStates Fin. Corp, 1952-87, economist, 1960-87, asst. v.p., 1961-64, v.p., 1964-70, sr. v.p., 1970-73, exec. v.p., 1973-83; exec. v.p., chief economist CoreStates Fin. Corp., Phila., 1983-87; Disting. prof. econs. Eastern Coll., St. Davids, Pa., 1987-97; lectr. fin. Wharton Sch., U. Pa., 1968-69; spl. asst. to chmn. Coun. Econ. Advisers, Washington, 1971-72; vis. prof. econs. Swarthmore (Pa.) Coll., 1976; adj. prof. econs. Ea. Coll., St. Davids, Pa., 1982; chmn. econ. adv. com. Am. Bankers Assn., 1978-80; bd. dirs. Nat. Bur. Econ. Rsch., 1983-85, Global Interdependence Ctr., vice chmn., 1992—; bd. dirs. Market Street Fund, Inc., 1989—. Author: Negotiable Certificates of Deposit: The Development of a Money Market Instrument, 1969; contbr. Econ. Policy Survey of Nat. Assn. Bus. Econ.; author articles on fin. and econ. subjects. Served with USNR, 1945-46. Recipient Alumni Cmty. Svc. award N.E. H.S., Phila., 1995; named to N.E. H.S. Phila., Wall of Fame, 1996. Fellow Nat. Assn. Bus. Econs. (pres. 1975-76); mem. Am. Econ. Assn., Conf. Bus. Econs. (chmn. 1987-88), Union League Phila., World Affairs Coun. of Phila., Sunday Breakfast Club. Presbyterian. Home: 2 Etienne, Arbordeau Devon PA 19333 *I have always striven for excellence in everything that I undertake-reaching for the highest standards of which I am capable, not just meeting requirements. While I like to think that I have earned my way, I am deeply indebted to key people who encouraged me, mentored me, and steered me to opportunities. Thus, I do not see my career as a solo venture.*

HEEBNER, DAVID K., career officer; b. Feb. 15, 1945. Commd. officer U.S. Army, advanced through grades to lt. gen., 1997—. Office: US Army 201 Army Pentagon Washington DC 20310-0201

HEEFNER, WILLIAM FREDERICK, lawyer; b. Perkasie, Pa., July 8, 1922; s. Russell Edgar and Lydia Victoria (Spielman) H. BA, Ursinus Coll., 1942, LLD, 1975; LLB, Temple U., 1949. Bar: Pa. 1951. Assoc. Curtin & Heefner, Morrisville, Pa., 1951-66, sr. partner, 1966-93, of counsel, 1993—; bd. dirs. William Penn Savings & Loan Assn., Morrisville; founder, dir. 1st County Bank, Doylestown, Pa., 1995—. Bd. dirs. Bedminster Twp. Planning Commn., 1961-94, sec., 1961-90; treas. Bucks County Dem. Com., 1966-90; treas. Bucks County Dem. Com., 1966-90, bd. dirs., 1969—; v.p., treas., chmn. fin. com. Ursinus Coll., 1976-90, pres. bd. dirs., 1990-97; pres., trustee Mercer Mus. and Spruance Libr., 1974-90, 91—; pres. Fonthill Trust and Mus.; bd. dirs. Bucks County Conservancy (now Heritage Conservancy), 1976—, Pa. Hist. and Mus. Commn., 1989-95, Bucks County Hist. Soc., 1990—. 1st lt. inf. AUS, 1942-46. Decorated Purple Heart; recipient Henry Chapman Mercer awd. for contrib. to Bucks Co. heritage, 1998. Fellow Am. Bar Found.; mem. ABA, Pa. Bar Assn. (mem. ho. dels. 1971-79, mem. bd. govs. 1976-79, chmn. law office econs. and mgmt. com. 1972-73), Bucks County Bar Assn. (pres. 1965-66), Met. Club (N.Y.C.), Symposium Club, Rotary Internat. (Paul Harris fellow 1996), Phi Alpha Delta. Lutheran. Home: 555 Old Bethlehem Rd Perkasie PA 18944-3825 Office: Curtin and Heefner 250 N Pennsylvania Ave Morrisville PA 19067-1104

HEEGER, ALAN JAY, physicist; b. Sioux City, Iowa, Jan. 22, 1936; s. Peter J. and Alice (Minkin) H.; m. Ruthann Chudacoff, Aug. 11, 1957; children: Peter S., David J. BA, U. Nebr., 1957; PhD, U. Calif., Berkeley, 1961; hon. degree, U. Mons, Belgium, 1993; D in Tech. honoris causa, Linköping (Sweden) U., 1996; PhD honoris causa, Abo Akademie, Turku, Finland, 1998; DHL honoris causa, U. Mass., 1999. Asst. prof. U. Pa., Phila., 1962-64; assoc. prof. U. Pa., 1964-66, prof. physics, 1966-82; prof. physics U. Calif., Santa Barbara, 1982—, dir. Inst. for Polymers and Organic Solids, 1983—; pres. UNIAX Corp., Santa Barbara, 1990-94, chmn. bd., 1994—; dir. Lab. for Rsch. on Structure of Matter, U. Pa., 1974-81, acting vice provost for rsch., 1981-82; Morris Loeb lectr. Harvard U., 1973. Editor-in-chief Synthetic Metals jour.; contbr. sci. articles to profl. jours. Recipient John Scott medal City of Phila., 1989, Oliver P. Buckley prize; Alfred P. Sloan fellow, Guggenheim fellow, Balzan prize for the sci. of new materials Balzan Found., Italy and Switzerland, 1995; govt. grantee. Fellow Am. Physics Soc. (Buckley prize for solid stae physics 1983). Patentee in field. Office: U Calif Dept Physics Santa Barbara CA 93103 also: UNIAX Corp 6780 Cortona Dr Santa Barbara CA 93117-3022

HEEKIN, MARY ANN, oncology social worker; b. Cin., July 22, 1953; d. Herbert Joseph and Anna Jean (Hilberg) H.; children: John Patrick, Megan Hilberg, Anna Kathleen. BA in History with honors, Otterbein Coll., 1986; MSW, U. Cin., 1993. Lic. Ind. Social Worker. Acct. coord. Miner Raymond Assn., Cin., 1987-89; oncology social worker Cancer Family Care, Cin., 1996—; co-facilitator Wellness Cmty., Cin., 1997—. Parent campaign coord. Springer Sch., Cin., 1990; co-founder, past pres. bd. dirs., trustee First Step Home Inc., Cin., 1991-98; vol. mediator Aring Inst. Beech Acres, Cin., 1993—; mem. cornerstone leadership com. Summit Country Day Sch., Cin., 1995, chair ann. alumni fund campaign 1997; trustee, treas. Transitions, Newport, Ky., 1997—. Recipient Sesquisentennial Disting. Alumna award Otterbein Coll., 1997. Mem. NASW (Jane Addams award 1993), Social Work Oncology Group, Acad. Family Mediators, Women's City Club, Phi Alpha Theta. Republican. Roman Catholic. Avocations: divorce mediation, family preservation. Office: Cancer Family Care 7162 Reading Rd Ste 1201 Cincinnati OH 45237-3847

HEEKIN, VALERIE ANNE, telecommunications technician; b. Santa Monica, Calif., Nov. 7, 1953; d. Edward Raphael and Jane Eileen (Potter) H. AA, L.A. Valley Coll., 1980; BS magna cum laude, Calif. Baptist Coll., 1987. Telecommunications technician Pacific Bell Co., N. Hollywood, Calif., 1971—; pres. Odyssey Adventures, Inc., Stevenson Ranch, Calif., 1987—, Countryside Properties, Inc., Stevenson Ranch, 1995—. Pres. Parkwood Sylmar Homeowners Assn., 1981-89; activist civil rights. Republican. Roman Catholic. Avocations: flying, boating, water skiing, hiking, photography, travel. Office: Odyssey Adventures PO Box 221477 Newhall CA 91322-1477

HEELAN, PATRICK AIDAN, philosophy educator; b. Dublin, Ireland, Mar. 17, 1926; s. Matthew Henry and Pauline (Beirens) H. Student, Belvedere Coll., 1938-42; BA, Univ. Coll., Dublin, 1947, MA, 1948; PhD, St. Louis U., 1952; STL, Jesuit Theol. Faculty, Dublin, 1959; student, Princeton U., 1960-62; PhD, U. Louvain, 1964. Ordained priest Soc. Jesus, Roman Catholic Ch., 1958; lectr. math. physics Univ. Coll., Dublin, 1964-65; research asso. Dublin Inst. Advanced Studies, 1952-54, 64-65; asst. prof. philosophy Fordham U., 1965-67, asso. prof., 1967-70; prof. philosophy, chmn. dept. SUNY at Stony Brook, 1970-74, acting v.p. liberal studies, 1975-77, v.p. liberal studies, 1977-79, prof. philosophy, 1979-92, dean humanities and fine arts, 1990-92; exec. v.p. Georgetown U., Washington, 1992-95, William Gaston prof. philosophy, 1995—; external appraiser philosophy and arts and scis. programs U. Western Ont., Lowell U., John Carroll U., San Diego State U. Author: Quantum Mechanics and Objectivity, 1965, Space-Perception and Philosophy of Science, 1983. Fulbright fellow, 1960-62; NSF sr. fellow, 1983. Mem. AAAS, Am. Cath. Philos. Assn. (coun. 1973-75), Ctr. for Integrative Edn. (coun. 1972-74), Am. Philos. Assn. (program com. Ea. sect. 1975, nominating com. 1988), Philosophy Sci. Assn., Brit. Soc. Philosophy Sci., Soc. Phenomenology and Existential Philosophy, N.Y. Acad. Scis., Internat. Orgn. for Hermeneutics and Sci., Phi Beta Kappa, Sigma Xi. Address: 3612 O St NW Washington DC 20007-2615 Office: Georgetown Univ Philosophy Dept 234 New North Washington DC 20057

HEEN, WALTER MEHEULA, retired judge, political party executive; b. Honolulu, Apr. 17, 1928; s. Norma K. Tada; 1 child, Cameron K. BA in Econs., U. Hawaii, 1953; JD, Georgetown U., 1955. Bar: Hawaii 1955, U.S. Dist. Ct. Hawaii 1955. Dep. corp. counsel Honolulu, 1957-58; territorial ho. of reps., 1958-59; mem. State Ho. Reps., 1959-64; state senator, 1966-68; mem. Honolulu City Coun., 1969-72, chair, 1972-74; state dist. ct. judge, 1972-74, state cir. ct. judge, 1974-78; U.S. atty. U.S. Dist. Hawaii, 1978-80, U.S. dist. ct. judge, 1981; assoc. judge State Intermediate Ct. Appeals, 1982-94; ret., 1994. Past pres. Honolulu Hawaiian Civic Club; precinct club pres. Dem. Party, 1956-72; vice chmn. Oahu Dem. County Com., 1956-62, chmn., 1962-64; del. State Dem. Party Conv., 1956-70. Recipient Lei Hulu Mamo award, 1992; named Outstanding Young Man of the Yr., 1962. Mem. Native Hawaiian Bar Assn. (dir. 1994—). Avocations: photography, fishing, surfing, golf, family activities. Office: 777 Kapiolani Blvd Honolulu HI 96813-5211

HEER, EDWIN LEROY, insurance executive; b. American Falls, Idaho, Aug. 19, 1938; s. Edwin Frederick and Kathryn Irene (Franks) H; m. Jacquelin S. Jefford, May 23, 1960 (div. Mar. 1978); 1 child, Kevin Jack; m. Judith Lee Overton-Jones, Jan. 2, 1980. BS, U. Alaska, 1963; MBA, St. Mary's U. Tex., San Antonio, 1976. Asst. actuary Aetna Life & Casualty Co., Hartford, Conn., 1963-68; assoc. actuary Ins. Co. of N.Am., Phila., 1968-72; asst. v.p. USAA, San Antonio, 1972-78; v.p., corp. actuary W.R. Berkley Corp., Greenwich, Conn., 1978-91; sr. v.p., chief corp. actuary W.R. Berkley Corp., Conn., 1991—; bd. dirs. Union Std. Ins. Co., Dallas, Carolina Casualty Ins. Co., Jacksonville, Fla., Great Divide Ins. Co., Scottsdale, Ariz., Nautilus Ins. Co., Scottsdale, Ariz., ACADIA Ins. Co., Portland, Maine, Berkley Risk Mgrs., Inc., Rasmussen Agy., Inc., Somerset, N.J., Berkley Care Network, Inc., Greensboro, N.C., Hartford, Conn., FICO Ins. Co., Bethesda, Md., Berkley Regional Ins. Co., St. Louis, Chesapeake Bay Property and Casualty Ins. Co., Richmond, Va., Nautilus Ins. Co., Scottsdale, Ariz. Fellow Casualty Actuarial soc.; mem. Am. Acad. Actuaries, Soc. Chartered Property Casualty Underwriters (cert.). Republican. Lutheran. Avocations: fishing, travel, birding. Home: 44 Strawberry Hill Ave Stamford CT 06902-2632 Office: W R Berkley Corp 165 Mason St Greenwich CT 06830-6608

HEER, EWALD, engineer; b. Friedensfeld, Germany, July 28, 1930; s. Johannes and Lilli Friedericke (Jauch) H.; came to U.S., 1956. Diploma Archtl. Enginring., Sch. Hamburg, 1953; B.S., CUNY, 1959; M.S., Columbia U., 1960, C.E., 1962; Dr Enginrg. Sc. magna cum laude, Tech. U., Hannover, Fed. Republic Germany., 1964; m. Hannelore M. Oehlers, Jan. 26, 1952; children: Thomas Ewald, Eric Martin. Engr. Hinz Architects, Hamburg, Fed. Republic Germany, 1952-55; design engr. Hewitt Robins Co., N.Y.C., 1956-59; rsch. engr. Weidlinger Cons., N.Y.C., 1959-62, McDonnell Douglas, St. Louis, 1964-65; rsch. mgr. GE, Phila., 1965-66; rsch. mgr. Jet Propulsion Lab., Pasadena, Calif., 1966-70, program mgr. advanced studies, 1971-76, dir. rsch. program autonomous systems and space mechanics, 1976-84, pres. Heer Assocs., Inc., 1984—; program mgr. Lunar exploration office NASA, Washington, 1970-71; adj. prof. U. So. Calif., 1973-84, dir. Inst. Technoecon. Studies, 1978-84. Author: Operation Systems-Humans-Intelligence-Machines, 1998. Fellow ASME; assoc. fellow AIAA; mem. ASCE, IEEE, Am. Mgmt. Assn., Internat. Fedn. Theory Machines and Mechanisms, Sigma Xi. Editor: Remotely Manned Systems, 1973, Robots and Manipulator Systems I & II, 1977, Machine Intelligence and Autonomy for Aerospace Systems, 1988, Mechanism and Machine Theory; contbr. articles to profl. jours. Home: 5329 Crown Ave La Canada Flintridge CA 91011-2807 Office: 4800 Oak Grove Dr Pasadena CA 91109-8001

HEER, NICHOLAS LAWSON, Arabist and Islamist educator; b. Chapel Hill, N.C., Feb. 8, 1928; s. Clarence and Jean Douglas (MacAlpine) H. B.A., Yale U., 1949; Ph.D., Princeton U., 1955. Transl. analyst Arabian Am. Oil Co., Saudi Arabia, 1955-57; asst. prof. Stanford U., Calif., 1959-62; vis. lectr. Yale U., New Haven, 1962-63; asst. prof. Harvard U., Cambridge, Mass., 1963-65; assoc. prof. U. Wash., Seattle, 1965-76; prof. Near Eastern langs. and civilization U. Wash., 1976-90, prof. emeritus, 1990—; chmn. dept. Near Eastern langs. and civilization U. Wash, 1982-87; Middle East curator Hoover Instn., Stanford, Calif., 1958-62. Editor: Tirmidhi: Bayan al-Farq, 1958, Jami: Al-Durrah al-Fakhirah, 1981, Islamic Law and Jurisprudence: Studies in Honor of Farhat J. Ziadeh, 1990; translator: Jami: The Precious Pearl, 1979. Mem. Am. Oriental Soc., Middle East Studies Assn., Am. Assn. Tchrs. of Arabic (treas. 1964-76, pres. 1981, dir. 1982-84). Home: 1821 10th Ave E Seattle WA 98102-4214 Office: U Wash Dept Near Ea Langs & Civ PO Box 353120 Seattle WA 98195-3120

HEERENS, JOSEPH ROBERT, lawyer; b. Park Ridge, Ill., Aug. 9, 1962; s. Joseph Allen and Priscilla Joan (Pearson) H.; m. Anne Elizabeth Heerens, Sept. 14, 1991. BA, DePauw U., 1984; JD, Ind. U., 1987. Bar: Ind. 1987, U.S. Ct. Appeals (7th cir.) 1990. Assoc. Wooden McLaughlin & Sterner, Indpls., 1987-90; sr. law clk. Ind. Ct. Appeals, Indpls., 1990-92; from staff atty. to assoc. gen. counsel Marsh Supermarkets LLC, Indpls., 1992—, asst. sec., bd. dirs., 1996—; bd. dirs. S.D. Isle Sportswear, Indpls. Vice chmn. bd. dirs. Am. Heart Assn., Indpls., 1994-96, chmn. bd. dirs., 1996—; co-chmn. com. Newman for Prosecutor, Indpls., 1992-94; active United Way Leadership Series, Indpls., 1991-92; bd. dirs. Rep. for Ind., Indpls., 1992. Mem. ABA, Ind. Bar Assn., Indpls. Bar Assn. Presbyterian. Avocations: reading, home renovation, basketball, golf. Home: 14494 Stephanie St Carmel IN 46033-8641 Office: Marsh Supermarkets LLC 9800 Crosspoint Blvd Indianapolis IN 46256-3350

HEERENS, ROBERT EDWARD, physician; b. Evanston, Ill., July 2, 1915; s. Joseph and Karen (Larsen) H.; m. Martha Virginia Lysne, Aug. 21, 1943; children—Kisti Lyn, Martha Jill, Nancy Ann, Robin Jan, Sara Bryce. A.B., Kalamazoo Coll., 1938; postgrad., U. Ala. Med. Sch., 1939, 41; M.D., Northwestern U., 1944. Diplomate Am. Bd. Family Practice. Intern U.S. Naval Hosp., Great Lakes, Ill., 1943-44, resident, 1946-47; gen. practice medicine Rockford, Ill., 1947—; pres. med. staff Swedish-Am. Hosp.; mem. staffs St. Anthony, Rockford hosps.; clin. assoc. prof. family medicine Rockford Sch. Medicine, also dir. ind. studies, mem. exec. com.; mem. admissions com. U. Ill. Coll. Medicine, 1970—, promotions com., 1973-75, mem. Senate Med. Ctr., 1975-77, also mem. acad. council, mem. adv. com. on family practice. Bd. dirs. Rockford Community Chest, 1954-60, Vis. Nurse Assn.; pres. Winnebago Tb Assn., 1960-61, Winnebago County Bd. Health, 1961-69; mem. Rockford Community Devel. Com.; mem. Community Action Com., 1969-71; pres. Northwestern Area Agy. on Aging, 1991-93. Served with M.C., USN, 1942-47. Recipient Disting. Svc. award Pub. Health Winnebago County Health Dept., 1997, Ill. Govs. award Unique Achievement, 1992. Mem. Am. Acad. Family Physicians (Ill. del. to congress of dels. 1959-71, mem. pub. relations com. 1967-74, chmn. pub. relations com. 1971-74, bd. dirs. 1970-73, exec. com. 1972-73, v.p. 1974), Ill. Acad. Gen. Practice (pres. 1958), AMA, Ill. Med. Soc. (chmn. pub. relations com. 1961-62, Pub. Svc. award 1994), Winnebago County Med. Soc. (v.p. 1965, pres. 1966), Rockford C. of C. (pres. 1962, chmn. edn. com.), Phi Beta Phi. Home: 5664 Spring Brook Rd Rockford IL 61114-5553

HEERMANN, DALE FRANK, agricultural engineer; b. Scribner, Nebr., Mar. 2, 1937; s. Frank H. and Esther M. (Bock) H.; m. Betty Marie Tuchenhagen, July 21, 1957; children: Sara Heermann Buchleiter, Philip, Laura Heerman Langford. BS in Agrl. Engring., U. Nebr., 1959; MS in Agrl. Engring., Colo. State U., 1964, PhD, 1968. Instr. Colo. State U., 1965-68; engr. Agrl. Research Service, USDA, Ft. Collins, Colo., 1968-80; research leader Agrl. Research Service, USDA, Ft. Collins, 1980—; cons. Rainbird, Glendora, Calif., 1973-75, Valmont Industries, Valley, Nebr., 1984-85. Author numerous sci. jours., 1967-85 (Outstanding Paper awards 1968-85). Chmn. accountability com. Pourde Ri, Ft. Collins, 1981-85; bd. dirs. South Ft. Collins Sanitation Dist. Recipient Scribner Native Son award Scribner C. of C., 1996, sr. scientist award USDA-Agrl. Rsch. Svc., Outstanding No. Plains Area, 1996, Fed. Tech. Leadership award, 1997. Fellow Am. Soc. Agrl. Engrs. (bd. dirs. 1974-76); mem. Irrigation Assn. (program com., Man of Yr. 1985), Colo. State Alumni Assn. (Alumnus Hon. award 1988, Fed. Energy and Mgmt. award 1994), Soil and Water Conservation Soc., Am. Soc. Agronomy, Soil Sci. Soc. Am., U.S. Com. Irrigation and Drainage. Lutheran. Home: 4780 Hogan Dr Fort Collins CO 80525-3732 Office: USDA-ARS AERC-Colo State U Fort Collins CO 85023

HEESCHEN, DAVID SUTPHIN, astronomer, educator; b. Davenport, Iowa, Mar. 12, 1926; s. Richard George and Emily (Sutphin) H.; m. Eloise St. Clair, June 11, 1950; children: Lisa Clair, David William, Richard Mark. BS, U. Ill., 1949, MS, 1951; PhD, Harvard U., 1954; ScD (hon.), W.Va. Inst. Tech., 1974, New Mex. Inst. Tech., 1989. Instr. Wesleyan U., Middletown, Conn., 1954-55; lectr., rsch. assoc. Harvard U., 1955-56; scientist Nat. Radio Astronomy Obs., 1956-77, sr. scientist, 1977-92; emeritus, 1992—; dir. Nat. Radio Astronomy Obs., 1962-78; rsch. prof. astronomy U. Va., 1980-92; Karl Jansky lectr., 1993; cons. NASA, 1960-61, 68-72, Univs. Space Rsch. Assn., 1996—, Nat. Radio Astronomy Obs., 1997-98. Contbr. sci. jours. G.R. Agassiz fellow Harvard Obs., 1953-54; Recipient Disting. Public Svc. award NSF, 1980, Alexander von Humboldt Sr. Scientist award 1985. Fellow AAAS; mem. NAS, Am. Acad. Arts and Sci., Am. Philos. Soc., Am. Astron. Soc. (v.p. 1969-71, pres. 1980-82), Internat. Astron. Union (v.p. 1976-82), Internat Sci. Radio Union.

HEESE, WILLIAM JOHN, music publishing company executive; b. N.Y.C., June 4, 1936; s. William Theodore and Anna Maria (Bissinger) H.; m. Charlotte Anne Schlosser, Feb. 11, 1961; children: William, Philip, Peter. Student, Bronx C.C., 1971, Sch. for Visual Arts, 1972. Clk. Music Dealers Svc., Inc., N.Y.C., 1953-60; salesman Hansen Publs., N.Y.C., Miami Beach, Fla., 1960-61; mgr. sales Shapiro, Bernstein & Co., Inc., N.Y.C., 1961-69; mgr. ea. sales M.C.A. Music (divsn. Music Corp. Am.), N.Y.C., 1970-74; v.p. sales Carl Fischer, Inc., N.Y.C., 1974—. Dir. Scott Tower Housing Co., Inc., 1970-80, pres., v.p., sed.; dir. Our Lady of Angels Ch., 1978-82, pres. Parish Coun.; dir. Vets. Little League, mgr., coach, 1976-88; dir. East Coast Conf. Baseball League, 1989-91, mgr., coach sr. divsn., 1989-90; mgr., coach Unltd. Age Baseball Team, Westchester Baseball Assn., 1991-93. With Army N.G., 1959-65. Mem. KC, N.Y. State Sch. Music Assn., Westchester County Sch. Music assn., Music Pubs. Assn. (sec. 1982-84, dir. 1980-84, 88-92, 95—, treas. 1985-87), Music Educators Nat. Conf., Retail Print Dealers Assn. Republican. Home: 1 Fountain Ln Scarsdale NY 10583-4654

HEESTAND, DIANE ELISSA, educational technology educator, medical educator; b. Boston, Oct. 9, 1945; d. Glenn Wilson and Elizabeth (Martin) H. BA, Allegheny Coll., 1967; MA, U. Wyo., 1968; edn. specialist, Ind. U., 1971, EdD, 1979. Asst. prof. communication Clarion (Pa.) State Coll., 1971; asst. prof. learning resources Indiana U. of Pa., 1971-72; asst. prof. communication U. Nebr. Med. Ctr., Omaha, 1972-74; assoc. prof. learning resources Tidewater Community Coll., Virginia Beach, Va., 1975-78; ednl. cons. U. Ala. Sch. Medicine, Birmingham, 1978-81; dir. learning resources, assoc. prof. med. edn. Mercer U. Sch. Medicine, Macon, Ga., 1981-88; asst. dean ednl. devel. and resources Ohio U. Coll. Osteopathic Medicine, 1989-90; assoc. prof. clin. med. edn., dir. biomed. communications U. So. Calif. Sch. Medicine, L.A., 1990-95, acting chair dept. med. edn., 1992-95; prof., dir. office ednl. devel. U. Ark. for Med. Scis., Little Rock, 1995—; cons. Lincoln (Pa.) U., summer, 1975; vis. fellow Project Hope/China, Millwood, Va., summer, 1986. Author (teleplay) Yes, 1968 (award World Law Fund 1968); producer, dir. (slide tape) Finding a Way, 1980 (1st Pl. award HESCA 1981, Susan Eastman award 1981). Rsch. sect. chair So. Group on Ednl. Affairs, 1998—. Grantee Porter Found., 1984, Ark. Dept. Higher Edn., 1996-97, UAMS Spl. Devel., 1997-99. Mem. Health Scis. Comm. Assn. (bd. dirs. 1982-86, pres.-elect 1987-88, pres. 1988-89, Spl. Svc. award 1990), Assn. Ednl. Comm. and Tech. (pres. media design and prodn. div. 1985-86), Assn. Biomed. Comm. Dirs. (bd. dirs. 1993-95), Soc. of Dirs. of Rsch. in Med. Edn., Generalists in Med. Edn. (steering com. 1998—, chair-elect 1998-99). Republican. Unitarian Universalist. Avocations: tennis, gardening.

HEFFELFINGER, DAVID MARK, optical engineer; b. Ft. Worth, Jan. 10, 1951; s. Hugo Wagner and Betty Lu (Graf) H.; m. Gail Patricia Lindsay, Dec. 10, 1995; children: Jakob, Leon, Stacy. MS in Physics, Wayne State U., 1984. Project scientist GM Rsch. Lab., Warren, Mich., 1978-90; grad. rsch. asst. Wayne State U., Detroit, 1982-84; engring. dept. mgr. Bio-Rad Labs., Hercules, Calif., 1990-98; dir. engring. Biometric Imaging, Mountain View, Calif., 1998—. Contbr. articles to Jour. Applied Physics, Bull. Am. Phys. Soc., Biotechniques; patentee in field. Recipient Vaden Miles award Wayne State U., 1982. Mem. AAAS, Internat. Soc. Optical Engring., Optical Soc. Am. Achievements include research in laser ablation and photoacoustic interactions, laser scanning and imaging. Office: Biometric Imaging 1025 Terra Bella Ave Mountain View CA 94043-1829

HEFFERAN, COLIEN JOAN, economist; b. Mpls., May 13, 1949; d. Bernard and Rosemary Arnsdorf; m. Hollis Spurgeon Summers, Oct. 14, 1987; 1 child, Margaret Vimont Summers. BS, U. Ariz., 1971; MS, U. Ill., 1974, PhD, 1976. Asst. prof. Pa. State U., University Park, 1975-79; econ., rsch. leader Agrl. Rsch. Svc., USDA, Hyattsville, Md., 1979-88; adminstr. Coop. State Rsch., Edn. and Ext. Svc., 1988—; adj. prof. U. Md., University Park, 1982-88; chmn. Ctr. for Family, Washington, 1985-87; vis. fellow Australian Nat. U., Canberra, NSW, 1989-91. Mem. editl. bd. Jours.-Family Econ. Issues, 1987—. Recipient Outstanding Citizen award U. Ariz., 1985, Outstanding Alumni award U. Ill., 1986. Mem. Am. Econ. Assn., Am. Coun. on Consumer Interests. Democrat. Roman Catholic.

HEFFERNAN, JAMES ANTHONY WALSH, English language and literature educator; b. Boston, Apr. 22, 1939; s. Roy Joseph and Kathleen (Walsh) H.; m. Nancy Coffey, June 27, 1964; children: Virginia, Andrew. AB cum laude, Georgetown U., 1960; PhD, Princeton U., 1964. Instr. English U. Va., 1963-65; asst. prof. English Dartmouth Coll., Hanover, N.H., 1965-70, assoc. prof., 1970-76, prof., 1976—, chmn. dept. English, 1978-81, Frederick Sessions Beebe prof. in art of writing, 1997—; cons. Mt. Holyoke, 1986, PMLA, 1986-87, Johns Hopkins U., 1987, NYU, 1987, 89, U. Press New Eng., 1987, U. Press Chgo., 1988, NEH, 1988, 90, Rutgers U., 1988, U. Md., 1988, Vanderbilt U., 1989, Barnard Coll., 1992; dir. summer seminar English romantic lit. and visual arts NEH/Dartmouth Coll., Hanover, 1987, 89; spkr. various seminars. Author: Wordsworth's Theory of Poetry: The Transforming Imagination, 1969, The Re-Creation of Landscape: A Study of Wordsworth, Coleridge, Constable and Turner, 1985, Museum of Words: The Poetics of Ekphrasis from Homer to Ashbery, 1993; co-author: Writing: A College Handbook, 4th edit., 1994, Writing: A Concise College Handbook, 1st edit., 1996; editor: Space, Time, Image, Sign: Essays on Literature and the Visual Arts, 1987, Representing the French Revolution: Literature, Historiography and Art, 1992; contbr. articles to profl. jours. Trustee Vermont Acad., 1992—. Woodrow Wilson fellow, 1960-61, Franklin Murphy, Jr. fellow, 1961-62, R.K. Root fellow, 1962-63, Dartmouth Coll., 1968-69, NEH fellow, 1991; grantee Dartmouth Coll., 1971, 74, 87, NEH, 1984, 87, 89. Mem. MLA (evaluator essays, presenter, del. various convs.), Assn. Literary Scholars and Critics (coun. 1996—). Office: English Dept Dartmouth College Hanover NH 03755

HEFFERNAN, JAMES VINCENT, lawyer; b. Washington, Oct. 6, 1926; s. Vincent Jerome and Hazel Belle (Wiltfong) H.; m. Virginia May Adams, June 26, 1954; children: David V., Douglas J., Alan P., Margaret L., Thomas A. AB, Cornell U., 1949, JD with distinction, 1952. Bar: D.C., 1953, Md., 1959, U.S. Ct. Claims, 1955, U.S. Tax Ct., 1953, U.S. Supreme Ct., 1958. Assoc. Sutherland, Asbill & Brennan, Washington, 1952-59, ptnr., 1959—; adj. prof. Georgetown U., Washington, 1978-79. Contbr. articles on tax subjects to profl. jours. Served with USN, 1945-46. Mem. ABA, Bar Assn. of D.C., Order of Coif, Phi Alpha Delta. Democrat. Roman Catholic. Clubs: Metropolitan (Washington); Kenwood Golf and Country (Bethesda, Md.). Lodge: KC. Home: 5216 Falmouth Rd Bethesda MD 20816-2913 Office: Sutherland Asbill & Brennan 1275 Pennsylvania Ave NW Ste 1 Washington DC 20004-2415

HEFFERNAN, JOHN WILLIAM, retired journalist; b. Stockbridge, Hants., Eng., Oct. 21, 1910; came to U.S., 1946; s. John and Alice Ann (Edwards) H.; m. Edith Curry, Dec. 10, 1948 (dec. Aug. 1990); 1 stepchild, Anthony Edward; m. Martha Powell Hensley, Apr. 25, 1992. Student, Clarks Coll., Eng., 1924-26. Sub-editor Central News, London, 1929-34; sub-editor Press Assn., London, 1934-36, sports reporter, 1936-39; fgn. corr. Reuters, N.Y.C., 1946; fgn. corr. at UN, N.Y.C., 1946-57; chief corr. Reuters, Washington, 1957-76; ret., 1976. Pres. Gasparilla Island Conservation and Improvement Assn., Boca Grande, Fla., 1994; bd. dirs. Gasparilla Island Bridge Com., 1966-67. Maj. Brit. Army, 1941-46. Decorated Comdr. Order of Brit. Empire, 1969. Mem. Nat. Press Club (pres. 1969), UN Corr. Assn. (pres. 1956), Overseas Press Club. Avocations: golf, swimming. Home: PO Box 687 Boca Grande FL 33921-0687

HEFFERNAN, NATHAN STEWART, retired state supreme court chief justice; b. Frederic, Wis., Aug. 6, 1920; s. Jesse Eugene and Pearl Eva (Kaump) H.; m. Dorothy Hillemann, Apr. 27, 1946; children: Katie (Mrs. Howard Thomas), Michael, Thomas. BA, U. Wis., 1942, LLB, 1948; postgrad. in bus., Harvard U. Sch. Bus. Adminstrn., 1943-44; LLD (hon.), Lakeland Coll., 1995; LLD, U. Wis., 1999. Bar: Wis. 1948, U.S. Dist. Ct. (we. dist.) Wis. 1948, U.S. Dist. Ct. (ea. dist.) Wis. 1950, U.S. Ct. Appeals (7th cir.) 1960, U.S. Supreme Ct. 1960. Assoc. firm Schubring, Ryan, Peterson & Sutherland, Madison, Wis., 1948-49; practice in Sheboygan, Wis., 1949-59; partner firm Buchen & Heffernan, 1951-59; counsel Wis. League Municipalities, 1949; research asst. to gov. Wis., 1949; asst. dist. atty. Sheboygan County, 1951-53; city atty. City of Sheboygan, 1953-59; dep. atty. gen. State of Wis., 1959-62; U.S. atty. Western Dist. Wis., 1962-64; justice Wis. Supreme Ct., 1964—, chief justice, 1983-95; lectr. mcpl. corps., 1961-64, appellate procedure and practice U. Wis. Law Sch., 1971-83; faculty Appellate Judges Seminar, Inst. Jud. Adminstrn., NYU, 1972-87; former mem. Nat. Council State Ct. Reps., chmn., 1976-77; ex-officio dir. Nat. Ctr. State Cts., 1976-77, mem. adv. bd. appellate justice project; former mem. Wis. Jud. Planning Com.; chmn. Wis. Appellate Practice and Procedure Com., 1975-76; mem. exec. com. Wis. Jud. Conf., 1978—, chmn., 1983; pres. City Attys. Assn., 1958-59; chair Citizens Panel on Election Reform; co-chair Equal Justice Coalition. Wis. chmn. NCCJ, 1966-67; past exec. bd. Four Lakes Coun., Boy Scouts Am.; gen. chmn. Wis. Dem. Conv., 1960, 61; mem. Wis. Found.; bd. dirs. Inst. Jud. Adminstrn.; visitors U. Wis. Law Sch., 1970-83, chmn., 1973-76; past mem. corp. bd. Meth. Hosp.; former curator Wis. Hist. Soc., curator emeritus, 1990; trustee Wis. Meml. Union, Wis. State Libr., William Freeman Vilas Trust Estate; v.p. U. Wis. Meml. Union Bldg. Assn.; former deacon Conglist. Ch. Lt. (s.g.) USNR, 1942-46, ETO, PTO. Recipient Disting. Svc. award NCCJ, 1968, Ann. Disting. Svc. award Wis. Mediation Assn., 1995, Lifetime Achievement award Milw. Bar Assn., 1995, Disting. Svc. award Dem. Party Sheboygan County, 1995; Disting. Jud. fellow Marquette U. Law Sch., 1996. Fellow Am. Bar Found. (life), Inst. for Jud. Adminstrn. (hon., bd. dirs., mem. faculty seminar); mem. ABA (past mem. spl. com. on adminstrn. criminal justice, mem. com. fed.-state delineation of jurisdiction, jud. adminstrn. com. on appellate ct., com. appellate time standards), Am. Law Inst. (life, adv. com. on complex litigation), Wis. Bar Assn. (chmn. Wis. bar com. study on legal edn. 1995-96, hon. chmn. Equal Justice Coalition 1997—, Goldberg award for disting. svc.), Dane County Bar Assn., Sheboygan County Bar Assn., Am. Judicature Soc. (dir. 1977-80, chmn. program com. 1979-81), Wis. Law Alumni Assn. (bd. dirs., Disting. Alumni Svc. award 1989), Nat. Conf. Chief Justices (bd. dirs.), Nat. Assn. Ct. Mgmt., Order of Coif, Iron Cross, U. Club (Madison, Wis.), Phi Kappa Phi, Phi Delta Phi. Clubs: Madison Lit. (pres. 1979-80); Harvard (Milw.); Harvard Bus. Sch. (Wis.). Home: 17 Thorstein Veblen Pl Madison WI 53705

HEFFERNAN, PATRICIA CONNER, management consultant; b. N.Y.C., Oct. 11, 1946; d. Arthur S. and Catherine (Center) Conner; m. John Joseph Heffernan, Sept. 13, 1969 (dec. June 1996). BA, U. Va., 1968; MBA, Suffolk U., 1980. Cert. mgmt. cons. Office mgr. Wobbly Barn, Killington, Vt., 1968-72; bus. mgr. Woodstock Country Sch., Vt., 1972-74; assoc. dean Vt. Law Sch., Royalton, Vt., 1974-83; mgmt. cons. Heffernan & Assocs., Killington, 1982-87; mgmt. cons., v.p. Sandage Inc., Burlington, Vt., 1987-92; mgmt. cons., ptnr. Mktg. Ptnrs., Inc., Burlington, 1992—; Vt. del. White House Conf. on Small Bus.; mem. region 1 adv. coun. SBA. Mem. Vt. Gov.'s Commn. on Women; bd. dirs. Rutland Regional Med. Ctr., 1986-91, New Eng. Bus. for Social Responsibility, 1990-93; trustee, pres. Killington Mountain Sch., 1978-85; mem. Killington Planning Commn., 1975-87, Killington Zoning Bd., 1979-84, Vt. Epilepsy Assn., 1977—, Vt. Telecom. Commn., Vt. Econ. Devel. Adv. Coun.; mem. vt. steering com. for ACE Nat. Identification Program for Women in Higher Edn., 1978-83. Named Outstanding Leader, Vt. YWCA, 1985, Woman of Yr., Vt. Bus. and Profl. Women Found., 1986, Woman in Bus. Adv., SBA, 1993. Mem. Inst. Mgmt. Cons. (v.p. New Eng. region, nat. bd. dirs. 1991-93), Nat. Assn. Women Bus. Owners, Vt. Bus. Assn. for Social Responsibility (bd. dirs., pres. 1991—), Womwn Bus. Owners Vt. (founder, bd. dirs. 1983—, pres. 1984-86). Office: Mktg Ptnrs Inc 176 Battery St Burlington VT 05401-5296

HEFFERNAN, PETER JOHN, state official; b. Hartford, Conn., Feb. 19, 1945; s. Kenneth F. and Vivian (Lacourse) H. m. Rosemary Margaret Eagan, May 29, 1971; children: Peter John, Matthew Paul. BA, Providence Coll., 1967; MBA, George Washington U., 1971. Adminstrv. resident Waltham (Mass.) Hosp., 1970-71, asst. dir., 1971-74, v.p. adminstrn. and gen. svcs., 1974-78, exec. v.p., 1978-86; pres., chief exec. officer Cardinal Cushing Gen. Hosp., Brockton, Mass., 1986-87; regional v.p. Weatherby Health Care, Norwell, Mass., 1987-90; regional adminstr. health svcs. div. Mass. Dept. Correction, Jamaica Plain, 1990—; co-preceptor health care adminstrn. George Washington U., 1977; mem. faculty evening div. Stonehill Coll., 1990—. Mem. instructional conf. coun. New Eng. Hosp. Assembly Inc., 1976; bd. dirs. Waltham Boys Club, 1977, Hosp. Svcs. of New Eng., 1980-83. USPHS trainee, 1967-70. Fellow Am. Coll. Hosp. Adminstrs.; mem. Health Care Mgmt. Assn. Mass., ACHE Regents Adv. Council, 1994—, Lions. Roman Catholic. Home: 352 Mayflower Cir Hanover MA 02339-2119 Office: Mass Dept Correction Health Svcs Divsn PO Box 317 Medfield MA 02052-0317*

HEFFLEY, JAMES DICKEY, nutrition counselor; b. Collinsville, Tex., Jan. 12, 1941; s. Floyd F. and Bessie C. (Dickey) H.; m. Betty E. Dozier, Dec. 22, 1963; children: James M., Jon R., David D., Sara E., Anna C. BS, Abilene Christian U., 1964; PhD, U. Tex., 1970. Cert. clin. nutritionist. Rsch. asst., then rsch. assoc. Clayton Found. Bich. Inst., Austin, Tex., 1965-74; lab. supr. Ctr. for Better Health, Austin, 1984—; dir. Nutrition Counseling Svc., Austin, 1974—; cons. Tex. Sch. for Blind, Austin, 1972-74, Tex. Gov.'s Commn. on Aging, Austin, 1976. Contbr. articles to profl. jours. Mem. Internat. Acad. Nutrition and Preventive Medicine (pres. 1994-98), Internat. and Am. Assn. Clin. Nutritionists (pres. 1991-95), Clin Nutrition Cert. Bd. (chmn. 1996—). Office: Nutrition Counseling Svc 3913 Medical Pky Ste 101 Austin TX 78756-4016

HEFFLINGER, LEROY ARTHUR, agricultural manager; b. Omaha, Feb. 14, 1935; s. Leroy William and Myrtle Irene (Lampe) H.; m. Carole June Wickman, Dec. 23, 1956; children: Dean Alan, Andrew Karl, Roger Glenn, Dale Gorden. BS in Fin., U. Colo., 1957. Mgr. Hefflinger Ranches, Inc., Toppenish, Wash., 1963-97; pres. Hefflinger Ranches, Inc., 1973—; bd. dirs. Hop Adminstrv. Com., Portland, Oreg., 1980-86; trustee Agr. and Forestry Edn. Found., Spokane, Wash., 1988-94, vice chmn., 1993-94; mem. adv. bd. Ctrl. Bank, Toppenish, Wash., 1995—. Vestryman, bd. dirs. St. Michael's Ch., Yakima, Wash., 1969-74; mem. capital campaign com. Heritage Coll., Toppenish, 1990-91; bd. dirs. Am. Hop Mus., 1997—. Capt. USAF, 1958-63. Mem. Hop Growers Am. (past pres. 1982-95, bd. dirs.), Hop Growers Wash. (past treas. 1978-83, bd. dirs.), Beta Theta Pi. Republican. Episcopalian. Avocations: scuba diving, cross-country skiing, golf, photography, antique guns. Office: Hefflinger Ranches Inc PO Box 47 Toppenish WA 98948-0047

HEFFNER, RICHARD DOUGLAS, historian, educator, communications consultant, television producer; b. N.Y.C., Aug. 5, 1925; s. Albert Simon and Cely (Bender) H.; m. Anne de la Vergne, Dec. 14, 1946; m. Elaine Segal, July 30, 1950; children: Daniel Jason, Charles Andrew. A.B., Columbia U., 1946, M.A. (Mitchell fellow), 1947. Teaching asst. history U. Calif. at Berkeley, 1947-48; instr. Am. history Rutgers U., 1948-50, univ. prof. communications, pub. policy, 1964—; lectr. history Columbia, 1950-52; prof. history Sarah Lawrence Coll., 1952-53; dir. pub. affairs WNBC-TV, N.Y.C., 1955-57; dir. programs Met. Ednl. TV Assn., N.Y.C., 1957-59; editorial cons. CBS, Inc.; mem. editorial bd., dir. spl. projects CBS-TV Network, 1959-61; v.p., gen. mgr. ednl. TV Channel 13 WNET, N.Y.C., 1961-63; pres. Richard Heffner Assocs., Inc., N.Y.C., 1964—; mem. program adv. bd. Teleprompter Corp.; dir. commn. on campaign costs 20th Century Fund, 1968-69; dir. study of TV's environ. messages Ford Found., 1970-72; chmn. bd. classification and rating adminstrn. Motion Picture Assn. Am., 1974-94. Producer-moderator: The Open Mind, NBC-TV, 1956-59, Channel 13, N.Y.C., 1973—; moderator-host Nat. Ednl. TV series People and Politics, 1964; exec. editor-host WPIX-TV From the Editor's Desk, 1981-86; author: A Documentary History of the United States, 1952; editor: Democracy in America, 1956. Mem. exec. com. and vice chmn. bd. N.Y.C. Police Found.; chmn. judiciary com. on cameras in the cts. N.Y. State, 1987-89. Sr. fellow Freedom Forum Media Studies Ctr., N.Y.C., 1994-95. Mem. AAAS, Acad. Motion Picture Arts and Scis., Am. Hist. Assn., Nat. Assn. Ednl. Broadcasters, Phi Beta Kappa. Club: Century. Home: 90 Riverside Dr New York NY 10024-5306 Office: 301 E 57th St New York NY 10022-2900

HEFFRON, HOWARD A., lawyer; b. N.Y.C., Oct. 3, 1927; s. Jack and Sophie (Malkin) H.; m. Stella Meller, July 4, 1946; children: James, Robert, Nancy. A.B., Columbia U., 1948; LL.B., Harvard U., 1951. Bar: N.Y. State 1953, D.C. 1953. Practiced law N.Y.C. and Washington, 1953-58, 61-66, 69-77, 79—; asst. U.S. atty. So. Dist. N.Y., 1953-57; first asst. tax div. and asst. dep. atty. gen. Dept. Justice, Washington, 1958-61; chief counsel Fed. Hwy. Adminstrn., Dept. Transp., Washington, 1967-69; dir. Office Rail Public Counsel, Washington, 1977-79; prof. law U. Wash., Seattle, 1965-67; cons. Pres.'s Commn. on Law Enforcement and Adminstrn. of Justice, Washington, 1965-66, Nat. Commn. on Product Safety, Washington, 1969-70. Author: Federal Consumer Safety Legislation, 1970. Served with U.S. Army, 1946-47.

HEFFRON, MICHAEL EDWARD, software engineer, computer scientist; b. Battle Creek, Mich., Dec. 18, 1949; s. Michael Richard and Maxine Beverly (Piper) H.; m. Louella Mae Thompson, Apr. 12, 1969; children: Karen, Jennifer. BS in Computer Sci., Ariz. State U., 1986; MS in Computer Sci., Colo. Tech. U., 1998. Engring. asst. Motorola, Inc., Scottsdale, Ariz., 1977-81; calibration lab. supr. ADR Ultrasound, Tempe, Ariz., 1982-83; engring. aide Motorola, Inc., Scottsdale, 1983-86; v.p. CyberSoft, Inc., Tempe, Ariz., 1986-90; engr. Injection Rsch. Specialists, Inc., Colorado Springs, Colo., 1990-91; software devel. mgr. Injection Rsch. Specialists Co. div. Pacer Industries, Colorado Springs, 1991-92; sr. systems engr. Computer Data Systems Inc., Rockville, Md., 1992-93; software engr. Coergon, Inc., Boulder, Colo., 1993-95, Loral Comm. Systems (purchased by Lockheed Martin 1996), Colorado Springs, Colo., 1995-96, Lockheed Martin, Colorado Springs, 1996-97; sr. software engr. L-3 Comms. Corp. (formerly Lockheed Martin Wideband Sys.), Colo. Springs, 1997—. Patentee in field. Served with USAF, 1970-77. Mem. IEEE, Assn. Computing Machinery, Soc. Reliability Engrs. Republican. Pentecostal Ch. Office: L-3 Comms Corp 1150 Academy Park Loop Ste 240 Colorado Springs CO 80910-3716

HEFFRON, WARREN A., medical educator, physician; b. St. Louis, Nov. 7, 1936; s. Willard Page H. and Alma Alberta Revington; m. Rosalee Bowdish, June 10, 1961; children: Kimberly, Wanda, Kara, Arthur. AB, U. Mo., 1958, MD, 1962. Diplomate Am. Bd. Family Practice (pres. 1998—). Rotating intern U. Calif., Orange, 1962-63; physician Hosp. Castaner (P.R.), 1966-68; resident internal medicine U. N. Mex., Albuquerque, 1968-71, asst. prof., chief divsn., 1971-76; assoc. prof., asst. chair Family Committee and Emergency Medicine, Albuquerque, 1976-82, prof., chmn., 1982-93; chief med. staff U. N. Mex. Hosp., Albuquerque, 1993—; bd. dirs. Am. Acad. Family Physicians, Am. Bd. Family Practice; dir. family Med. Residency Program, Albuquerque, 1971-82; vis. prof., cons. Dept. Cmty. Health, Punjab, India, Christian Med. Coll., Punjab U., Ludihiana; prof. Dept. Family and Cmty. Medicine, Albuquerque, 1993—; various internat. vis. professorships. Contbr. numerous articles to profl. jours. Mem. free clinic Albuquerque Rescue Mission. Lt. comdr. USPHS, 1964-66. Recipient Recognition award Am. Med. Assn. Physicians, 1971, 74, 77, 80, 83, 86, 89, 92, 95, N. Mex. Family Physician of the Yr. award, 1990. Mem. N. Mex. Am. Acad. Family Physicians (pres. 1985, N. Mex. Family Dr. of Yr. award, chpt. svc. award 1988), N. Mex. Med. Soc. (pres. 1996-97, Robbins award Cmty. Svc. 1981), Soc. Tchrs. of Family Medicine (bd. dirs., treas. 1997, Smilkstein award for internat. family medicine edn. 1998), Christian Med. and Dental Soc. (bd. dirs. 1998—). Methodist. Home: 2406 Ada Pl NE Albuquerque NM 87106-2550

HEFLEY, JOEL M., congressman; b. Ardmore, Okla.; s. J. Maurice and Etta A. (Anderson) H.; m. Lynn Christian, Aug. 25, 1961; children: jana, Lori, Juli. BA, Okla. Baptist U., 1957; MS, Okla. State U., 1963. Exec. dir. Community Planning and Research, Colorado Springs, Colo., 1966-86; mem. Colo. Ho. of Reps., 1977-78, Colo. Senate, 1979-86, 100th-104th Congresses from 5th Colo. dist., 1987—; mem. armed svcs. com., mem. natural resources com., mem. small bus.-SBA com., mem. nat. security com., mem. stds. of offcl. conduct. Republican. Baptist. Clubs: Rotary, Colorado Springs Country. Office: Ho of Reps 2230 Rayburn Bldg Washington DC 20515-0605

HEFLIN, HOWELL THOMAS, former senator, lawyer, former state supreme court chief justice; b. Poulan, GA, June 19, 1921; s. Marvin Rutledge and Louise D. (Strudwick) H.; m. Elizabeth Ann Carmichael, Feb. 23, 1952; 1 son, Howell Thomas. AB, Birmingham So. Coll., 1942; JD, U. Ala., 1948, LLD (hon.); LLD (hon.), U. No. Ala., Samford U., Tuskegee U., Del. Law Sch., Widener Coll., Troy State U., Ala. Christian Coll., Tuskegee U., Livingston U., Ala. A&M U., Ala. State U., Stillman Coll.; DHH (hon.), Birmingham So. Coll., 1980; DHL (hon.), Talledega Coll. Bar: Ala. 1948. Practiced in Tuscumbia; sr. ptnr. firm Heflin, Rosser and Munsey; chief justice Supreme Ct. Ala., 1971-77; chmn. Nat. Conf. Chief Justices, 1976-77; mem. U.S. Senate from Ala., Washington, 1979-97; mem. judiciary com., agr. com.; Ala. A&M U.; bd. dirs. Meth. Pub. House, 1952-64; lectr. U. Ala., 1946-48, U. North Ala., 1948-52; Tazewell Taylor vis. prof. law Coll. William and Mary, 1977. Mem. Ala. Edn. Commn., 1957-58; chmn. Colbert County A.R.C., 1950; Ala. field dir. Crusade for Children, 1948; pres. Ala. Com. Better Schs., 1958-59; chmn. Tuscumbia Bd. Edn., 1954-64, Ala. Tenure Commn., 1959-64; pres. U. Ala. Law Sch. Found., 1964-66; co-chmn. NCCJ, Tri-Cities area, 1949-70; chmn. Brotherhood Week; bd. dirs., v.p. Nat. Center for State Cts., 1975-77; trustee Birmingham So. Coll.; hon. pres. Troy State U. Served to maj. USMC, 1942-46. Decorated Silver Star, Purple Heart; recipient Ala. Citizen of Yr. award Ala. Cable TV Assn., 1973, 82; Outstanding Alumnus award U. Ala. and Birmingham So. Coll., 1973; Herbert Lincoln Harley award Am. Judicature Soc., 1973; Justice award, 1981; Ala. Citizen of Year award Ala. Broadcasters Assn., 1975; mem. Ala. Acad. Honor; named Outstanding Appellate Judge in U.S., ATLA, 1976; recipient Highest award Am. Judges Assn., 1975, Thomas Jefferson award Ala. Press Assn., 1979; Inst. Human Relations award, 1980; Silver Chalice award Am. Council on Alcoholism, 1980; Disting. Am. award Nat. Football Found. and Hall of Fame; Warren E. Burger award Inst. Ct. Mgmt.; Leadership award Am. Security Council, 1985-96; Disting. Svc. award Nat. Ctr. State Cts.; Leadership award Southeastern Soc. Am. Forresters, 1986, Taxpayers Hall of Fame, 1987, Patriotic Civilian award U.S. Army, 1987, Henry Jackson Senatorial Leadership award, 1987, Golden Plow award Am. Farm Bur., Outstanding Svc. to Sci. award Nat. Bio-med. Rsch. Assn., 1992, Werner Von Braun award Nat. Sci. Coun., 1992; named Progressive Farmer's 1993 Man of Year in Agr., Disting. Svc. award Nat. Rural Electric Coop. Assn, Helen Keller, Outstanding Public Svs. award Am. Found. for Blind, 1996, Nat. Public Svs. award, Am. Heart Assn., 1996, John B. Medarie award, Am. Def. Assn., 1996, Charles Dickens Soc. Lit. award, 1996, Disting. Svc. award NASA, 1996, appreciation award U.S. Army Space and Strategic Def. Commands, 1996, Nat. Achievement award Nat. Contact Mgmt. Assn., 1998, Human Rels. award Ala. Edn. Assn., 1998, Thomas Jefferson award Am. Bd. Trial Advs., 1998, Ala. Common Cause Citizen of the Century award. Fellow Internat. Acad. of Law and Scis., Internat. Acad. Trial Lawyers, Internat. Soc. Barristers, Am. Coll. Trial Lawyers; mem. Ala. Bar Assn. (pres. 1965-66), Colbert County Bar Assn. (past pres.), Ala. Bar Found. (past pres.), Am. Judicature Soc. (v.p. 1977-79), Ala. Law Sch. Alumni Assn. (past pres.), Ala. Trial Lawyers Assn. (pres.), Nat. Assn. Biomedical Rsch. Assn. (Outstanding Pub. Svc. award, Nat. Veterans award), VFW, Am. Legion, 40 and 8, DAV, Third Marine Div. Assn., Order of Coif, Omicron Delta Kappa, Phi Delta Phi, Tau Kappa Alpha, Lambda Chi Alpha. Methodist. Office: PO Box 228 Tuscumbia AL 35674-0228

HEFLIN, MARTIN GANIER, foreign service officer, international political economist; b. Oklahoma City, July 5, 1932; s. Martin Henry and Eugenia Marie (Gabel) H.; m. Sydney Daffin Lewis, Nov. 24, 1954; children—Martin Hays, Stephanie Anne Heflin Pace. B.A., U. Okla., 1954, M.A., 1957; postgrad., U. Redlands, 1955, U. Tex., 1958-59. Vice consul U.S. Consulate, Ponta Delgada, Portugal, 1960-62, U.S. Consulate Gen., São Paulo, Brazil, 1962-64; 2d sec. U.S. Embassy, Tokyo, Japan, 1964-68; prin. officer U.S. Consulate, Sapporo, Japan, 1968-71; fgn. affairs officer U.S. Dept State, Washington, 1971-74; consul, econ. and commerce U.S. Consulate Gen., São Paulo, 1974-76; dir. U.S. Trade Ctr. U.S. Dept. Commerce, São Paulo, 1976-78; counselor econ. and comml. affairs U.S. Embassy, New Delhi, India, 1979-83; minister-counselor, sr. Fgn. Service; prin. officer U.S. Consultate Gen., Monterrey, Mexico, 1983-87; sr. fellow Ctr. for Study of Fgn. Affairs, Fgn. Service Inst., Dept. State, 1987-89; mng. dir. The Naiad Corp., 1990—. Served to 1st lt. USAF, 1954-56. Mem. Am. Fgn. Service Assn., Am. Legion, Phi Delta Theta. Roman Catholic. Avocations: golf; photography. Home: 4411 NW 12th Pl Gainesville FL 32605-5500

HEFNER, CHRISTIE ANN, publishing and marketing executive; b. Chgo., Nov. 8, 1952; d. Hugh Marston and Mildred Marie (Williams) H. BA summa cum laude in English and Am. Lit., Brandeis U., 1974. Freelance journalist, Boston, 1974-75; spl. asst. to chmn. Playboy Enterprises, Inc., Chgo., 1975-78, v.p., 1978-82, bd. dirs., 1979—, vice chmn., 1986-88, pres. 1982-88, COO, 1984-88, chmn., CEO, 1988—; bd. dirs. Playboy Found.-Playboy Enterprises, Inc., Ill. chpt. ACLU, Mag. Pubs. Assn. Bd. dirs. Nat. Coalition on Crime and Delinquency, Goodman Theatre, Chgo., Brandeis U., Rush-Presbyn.-St. Lukes Med. Ctr. Recipient Agness Underwood award L.A. chpt. Women in Communications, 1984, Founders award Midwest Women's Ctr., 1986, Human Rights award Am. Jewish Com., 1987, Harry Kalven Freedom of Expression award ACLU, Ill., 1987, Spirit of Life award City of Hope, 1988, Eleanor Roosevelt award Internat. Platform Assn., 1990, Will Rogers Meml. award Beverly Hills C. of C. and Civic Assn., 1993. Mem. Brandeis Nat. Women's Com. (life), Com. of 200, Young. Pres. Orgn., Chgo. Network, Voters for Choice, Phi Beta Kappa. Democrat. Office: Playboy Enterprises Inc 680 N Lake Shore Dr Fl 15 Chicago IL 60611-4455

HEFNER, HUGH MARSTON, editor-in-chief; b. Chgo., Apr. 9, 1926; s. Glenn L. and Grace (Swanson) H.; m. Mildred M. Williams, June 25, 1949 (div.); children: Christie A., David P.; m. Kimberley Conrad, July 1, 1989; children: Marston G., Cooper B. BS, U. Ill., 1949. Subscription promotion writer Esquire mag., 1951; promotion mgr. Pubs. Devel. Corp., 1952; circulation mgr. Children's Activities mag., 1953; chmn. bd. HMH Pub. Co. Inc. (now Playboy Enterprises, Inc.), 1953-88; editor-in-chief Playboy mag., from 1953; pres. Playboy Clubs Internat., Inc., 1959-86; editor, pub. VIP mag., 1963-75, Oui mag., 1972-81. Occasional film appearances include History of the World, Part I, 1981, The Comeback Trail, 1982, Beverly Hills Cop II, 1987. Served with AUS, 1944-46. Recipient 1st Amendment Freedom award B'nai B'rith Anti-Defamation League, L.A., 1980, Internat. Pub. award Internat. Press Directory in London, 1997; ; named Man of Yr. Mag. Industry Newslsetter, 1967; named to Pub. Hall of Fame, 1989; honored with Hugh M. Hefner chair in study of Am. film U. So. Calif. Sch. Cinema/TV, 1996. Office: Playboy Enterprises Inc 9242 Beverly Blvd Beverly Hills CA 90210-3732*

HEFNER, JAMES A., academic administrator; b. Brevard, N.C.. BBA, N.C. A&T U., 1961; MA in Econs., Atlanta U., 1962; PhD in Econs., U. Colo., 1971. Tchr. econs. Atlanta U., Clark Coll., Fla. A&M U.; prof. econs., chmn. dept. econs. and bus. adminstrn. Morehouse Coll., also holder Charles E. Merrill chair; provost Tuskegee (Ala.) U.; pres. Jackson State U.; now pres. Tenn. State U., Nashville, 1991—; vis. rsch. assoc. Harvard U., Princeton U., U. Wis.; econ. and bus. cons. to numerous pvt. and pub. orgns. Co-author and/or co-editor: Black Employment in Atlanta, Public Policy for the Black Community: Strategies and Perspectives; contbr. articles to profl. jours. Bd. dirs. Am. Coun. on Edn., Am Assn. State Colls. and Univs.; trustee ACT. Recipient NAFEO Achievement award in rsch. Mem. Mensa, Phi Beta Kappa, Phi Kappa Phi. Office: Tenn State U 3500 John A Merritt Blvd Nashville TN 37209-1500*

HEFNER, JOHN, principal. Principal Fruitvale Jr. H.S. Recipient Blue Ribbon award U.S. Dept. Edn., 1990-91. Office: Fruitvale Jr HS 2114 Calloway Dr Bakersfield CA 93312-2706*

HEFNER, PHILIP JAMES, theologian; b. Denver, Dec. 10, 1932; s. Theodore Godfred and Elizabeth Helen (Mittelstadt) H.; m. Neva Lamae White, May 25, 1956; children: Sarah Elizabeth, Martha White, Julia Margaret, Rebecca Mittelstadt. BA, Midland Luth. Coll., 1954, LHD, 1982; BD, Chgo. Luth. Theol. Sem., 1959; MA, U. Chgo., 1961, PhD, 1962; DD, Luther Coll., 1994. Ordained min., United Luth. Ch. in Am., 1962. Assoc. prof. systematic theology Hamma Div. Sch., Springfield, Ohio, 1962-64; prof. systematic theology Luth. Theol. Sem., Gettysburg, Pa., 1964-67; prof. systematic theology Luth. Sch. Theology, Chgo., 1967—, dir. grad. studies, 1979-88; dir. Chgo. Ctr. Religion and Sci., 1988—; vis. prof. Japan Luth.

Theol. Coll. and Sem., Tokyo, 1982, 96, Inst. fuer Theologie, Technologie, Naturwissenschaft, Munich, Germany, 1994; rsch. lectr. Human Scis. Rsch. Coun., Republic of South Africa, 1988; disting. vis. scholar Okla. scholar leader enrichment program U. Okla., 1991; lectr. religion Chautauqua Instn., 1991; mem. Human Genome Core Group project NIH, 1991-94; Hein-Fry nat. lectr. Evang. Luth. Ch. in Am., 1996; lectr. Vatican Conf. on Evolution and Faith, Rome, 1996; Am. Sci. Affiliation lectr., 1997—. Author: Faith and The Vitalities of History, 1966, Promise of Teilhard, 1970, The Human Factor: Evolution, Culture, Religion, 1993 (translated Japanese), Natur, Weltbild, Religion, 1995; co-author: Defining America, Christian Dogmatics; editor Zygon: Jour. of Religion and Sci., 1989—; dept. editor religion and sci. Religion in Geschichte und Gegenwart, 4th edit., 1993—; editorial assoc. Dialog: A Theol. Jour., 1982—; bd. cons. Jour. Religion, U. Chgo., 1995—; contbr. numerous articles to profl. jours. Mem. U.S.A. Luth.-Reformed Coordinating Com., 1992—; mem. adv. bd. Templeton Found. Humility Theology, 1997—. Fulbright scholar U. Tübingen, 1954-55; Rockefeller Found. Doctoral fellow, 1960-62, Russell fellow Ctr. for Theol. and Natural Scis., 1985; recipient Franklin Fry award for Scholarship, Luth. Brotherhood, 1977-78, Susan Colver Rosenberg award U. Chgo., 1963, Templeton Found. Book prize, 1995; Nobel lectr. Gustavus Adolphus Coll., 1987. Fellow Inst. on Religion in an Age of Sci. (pres. 1979-81, 84-87), Ctr. for Advanced Study in Religion and Sci. (grantee 1985), Soc. for Values in Higher Edn.; mem. AAAS (mem. judging panel, Sci. and Human Freedom award 1993-95), Am. Acad. Religion (chmn. cons. on theology and sci. group 1988-93), Internat. Luth./Reformed Dialogue, 1993-97, Soc. Midland Authors. Office: Luth Sch Theology 1100 E 55th St Chicago IL 60615-5199 *The greatest challenge facing humans today is fashioning adequate ways of living in the context of contemporary technology. It will require all the resources we can muster. Traditional Christian faith has the resources to help meet this challenge, but they must be retrieved and articulated in dramatically new ways.*

HEFNER, W. G. (BILL HEFNER), former congressman; b. Elora, Tenn., Apr. 11, 1930; s. Emory James and Icie Jewel (Holderfield) H.; m. Nancy Louise Hill, Mar. 23, 1952; children: Stacye, Shelly. Grad. high sch. Mem. 94th-105th Congresses from 8th N.C. dist., Washington, D.C., 1975-98; leadership adv. group mem., mem. appropriations com., subcom. on mil. constrn. (ranking mem.), subcom. on nat. security, leader on textile trade issues; former owner Sta. WRKB radio, Kannapolis, N.C. Former profl. entertainer with Harvesters Quartet; former performer weekly gospel show, Sta. WXII-TV, Winston-Salem, N.C.; also appeared on Sta. WBTV, Charlotte, N.C., Sta. WRAL-TV, Raleigh, N.C., Sta. WGHP-TV, High Point, N.C., Sta. WBTW-TV, Florence, S.C. Mem. bd. visitors U.S. Mil. Acad., 1982—; mem. Dem. Congl. campaign com. Address: 411 Brown's Creek Rd Guntersville AL 35976*

HEFTER, LAURENCE ROY, lawyer; b. N.Y.C., Oct. 13, 1935; s. Charles S. and Rose (Postal) H.; m. Jacqulyn Maureen Miller, June 13, 1957; children—Jeffrey Scott, Sue-Anne. B.M.E., Rensselaer Poly. Inst., 1957, M.S. in Mech. Engring., 1960; J.D. with honors, George Washington U., 1964. Bar: Va. 1964, N.Y. 1967, D.C. 1973. Instr. Rensselaer Poly. Inst., Troy, N.Y., 1957-59; patent engr. Gen. Electric Co., Washington, 1959-63; sr. patent atty. Atlantic Research Corp., Alexandria, Va., 1963-66; assoc. firm Davis, Hoxie, Faithfull & Hapgood, N.Y.C., 1966-69; mem. firm Ryder, McAulay & Hefter, N.Y.C., 1970-73, Finnegan, Henderson, Farabow, Garrett & Dunner, LLP, Washington, 1973—; professorial lectr. trademark law George Washington U., 1981-90; mem. adv. com. U.S. Patent and Trademark Office, 1988-92, Trademark Rev. Commn., 1986-89. Mem. ABA (chmn. patent office affairs com. patent, trademark and copyright sect. 1976-80, unfair competition com. 1980-81, governing com. franchise forum 1994-97), N.Y. State Bar Assn., D.C. Bar Assn., Va. Bar Assn. (dir. patent, trademark and copyright sect. 1976-78), Internat. Bar Assn. (chmn. trademark com. 1986-90), Am. Patent Law Assn. (chmn. trademark com. 1979-81, dir. 1981-84), U.S. Trademark Assn. (dir. 1982-84), Order of Coif, Alpha Epsilon Pi. Home: 6904 Loch Lomond Dr Bethesda MD 20817 Office: 1300 I St NW Washington DC 20005-3314

HEFTLER, THOMAS E., lawyer; b. Jersey City, 1943. AB, Princeton U., 1965; JD cum laude, NYU, 1968. Bar: N.Y. 1968. Mem. Stroock & Stroock & Lavan LLP, N.Y.C. Office: Stroock & Stroock & Lavan LLP 180 Maiden Ln New York NY 10038-4925

HEFTMANN, ERICH, biochemist; b. Vienna, Austria, Mar. 9, 1918; came to U.S., 1939; s. Salomon and Rosa (Seifert) H.; m. Lily Rubin (div. 1966); children: Rex, Lisa, Erica; m. Brigitte Hedwig Sander, Mar. 14, 1968; children: Karen, David. BS, NYU, 1942; PhD, U. Rochester, 1947. Cert. Clin. Chemist. Biochemist USPHS, Boston, 1947-48, NIH, Bethesda, Md., 1948-63; biochemist USDA, Pasadena, Calif., 1963-70, Berkeley, Calif., 1970-83; editor Jour. of Chromatography, Amsterdam, The Netherlands, 1983—. Author (books) Biochemistry Steroids, 1960, Steroid Biochemistry, 1970, Chromatography of Steroids, 1976; editor (books) Chromatography, 1961, 67, 75, 83, 92, Modern Methods of Steroid Analysis, 1973. Recipient Humboldt Prize German Govt., 1975. Fellow AAAS; mem. Am. Chem. Soc., Am. Soc. of Biol. Chemists. Home: PO Box 928 Orinda CA 94563-0818

HEGARTY, GEORGE JOHN, university president, English educator; b. Cape May, N.J., July 20, 1948; s. John Joseph and Gloria Anna (Bonelli) H.; m. Joy Elizabeth Schiller, June 9, 1979. Student, U. Fribourg, Switzerland, 1968-69; BA in English, LaSalle U., Phila., 1970; Cert., Coll. de la Pocatiere, Que., Can., 1970; postgrad., U. Dakar, Senegal, 1970, Case Western Res. U., 1973-74, U. N.H., 1976; MA in English, Drake U., 1977; cert., U. Iowa, 1977; DA, Drake U., 1978; Cert., UCLA, 1979, U. Pa., 1981. Tchr. English, Peace Corps vol. College d'Enseignment General de Sedhiou, Senegal, 1970-71; tchr. English Belmore Boys' and Westfields High Schs., Sydney, Australia, 1972-73; teaching fellow in English Drake U., Des Moines, 1974-76; mem. faculty English Des Moines Area Community Coll., 1976-80; assoc. prof. Am. lit. U. Yaounde, Cameroon, 1980-83; prof. Am. lit. and civilization Nat. U. Cote D'Ivoire, Abidjan, 1986-88; dir. ctr. for internat. programs and svcs. Drake U., Des Moines, 1983-91; prof. grad. program intercultural mgmt. Sch. for Internat. Tng., The Experiment in Internat. Living, Brattleboro, Vt., 1991-93; provost, prof. English Teikyo Loretto Heights U., Denver, 1992-94; pres., prof. English, Teikyo Westmar U., Le Mars, Iowa, 1994-95; program dir. Am. degree program Taylor's Coll., Malaysia, 1996-97; v.p. academic affairs, prof. English Teikyo Loretto Heights U., Denver, 1997—; acad. specialist USIA, 1983-84; workshop organizer/speaker Am. Field Svcs., 1986; cons. Coun. Internat. Ednl. Exch., 1986; evaluator Assn. des Univ. Partiellment Entierément de Langue Francais, 1987, Iowa Humanities Bd., 1990-91, USAID's Ctr. for Univ. Coop. and Devel., 1991; cons. in field. Book reviewer African Book Pub. Record, Oxford, Eng., 1981—, African Studies Rev., 1990—; host, creator TV show Global Perspectives, 1989-91; exhibitor of African art, 1989—; contbr. articles to profl. jours. Commr. Des Moines Sister City Commn., 1984-87, 91; bd. dirs. Iowa Sister State Com., 1988-91; pres. Chautauqua Park Nat. Hist. Dist. Neighborhood Assn., 1991; bd. dirs. Melton Found., 1994-95. Drake U. fellow, 1971-72, 74-76; Nat. Endowment for Humanities grantee, 1981; Fulbright grantee, USIA, 1980-83, 86-88. Mem. Am. Assn. Pres. Ind. Colls. and Univs., NAFSA: Assn. Internat. Educators (sectional chmn. region VI 1986-87, Vt. rep. 1992), Assn. Internat. Edn. Adminstrs., Inst. Internat. Edn. Avocations: collecting non-western art, travel, swimming, writing.

HEGARTY, MARY FRANCES, lawyer; b. Chgo., Dec. 19, 1950; d. James E. and Frances M. (King) H. BA, DePaul U., 1972, JD, 1975. Bar: Ill. 1975, U.S. Dist. Ct. (no. dist.) Ill. 1976, U.S. Supreme Ct. 1980. Ptnr. Lannon & Hegarty, Park Ridge, Ill., 1975-80; pvt. practice, Park Ridge, 1980—; dir. Legal Assistance Found. Chgo., 1983—. Mem. revenue study com. Chgo. City Coun. Fin. Com., 1983; mem. Sole Source Rev. Panel, City of Chgo., 1984; pres. Hist. Pullman Found., Inc., 1984-85; apptd. Park Ridge Zoning Bd., 1993-94. Mem. Ill. State Bar Assn. (real estate coun. 1980-84), Chgo. Bar Assn., Women's Bar Assn. Ill. (pres. 1983-84), NW Suburban Bar Assn., Park Ridge Women Entrepreneurs, Chgo. Athletic Assn. (pres. 1992-93). Democrat. Roman Catholic. Office: 301 W Touhy Ave Park Ridge IL 60068-4204

HEGARTY, THOMAS JOSEPH, academic administrator, history educator; b. Boston, Dec. 6, 1935; s. Thomas John and Abigail Barbara (Dunlap) H.; m. Louisa Ivanova, May, 1959; children: Alton Dunlap, Allison McAndrew (Mrs. Christopher Eck). A.B., Harvard U., 1957, A.M., 1958, Ph.D., 1965; cert., Inst. Ednl. Mgmt. Harvard U., 1973. Asst. prof. history and history of ideas Brandeis U., Waltham, Mass., 1962-67; assoc. prof. history, chmn. Soviet and East European studies program Boston U., 1967-71; assoc. prof. history, dean grad. studies Boston State Coll., 1971-78; prof. history, v.p. provost SUNY-Potsdam, 1978-82; v.p. acad. affairs Butler U., Indpls., 1982-88, prof. history, 1982-89; sr. cons. Am. Assn. State Colls. and Univs., 1988-89; provost, prof. history U. Tampa, Fla., 1989—; assoc. Russian Research Ctr., Harvard U., 1968-72. Mem. Tampa Bay Coun. on Fgn. Rels., 1989—; bd. dirs. Internat. Ctr., Indpls., 1983-85, Park-Tudor Sch., 1983-88; mem. 1000 Friends of Fla., 1990—. Fellow Ford Found., 1957-61. Mem. Indpls. Coun. World Affairs (bd. dirs. 1988), Indpls. Com. on Fgn. Rels., Am. Assn. State Colls. and Univs., Resource Ctr. for Planned Change, Greater Tampa C. of C., Greater Tampa World Affairs Coun. (pres. 1992—), Japan-Am. Soc. Cen. Fla. Inc. (bd. dirs. 1990, chair edn. coun. 1993), Greater Tampa Internat. Trade Coun., Rotary, Harvard Club of West Cen. Fla., Lit. Club of Indpls., Tampa Club (mem. com. 1990—), Fla. Humanities Coun., Phi Beta Kappa (bd. dirs. Alpha of Ind. chpt. 1986—), Phi Kappa Phi, Phi Alpha Theta. Office: U Tampa Box B Tampa FL 33606-1490

HEGEDÜS, ZOLTÁN LOUIS, retired chemist, researcher; b. Hódmezővásárhely, Hungary, Mar. 29, 1927; came to U.S., 1956; s. Lajos Hegedüs and Rozália (Rákosi) Kékesi; m. Evelyn Russ, 1961 (dec. Nov. 1965); m. Kathryn Marie Stewart, Jan. 23, 1971. BSChemE, Budapest (Hungary) U. Tech., 1951; MS in Organic Chemistry, U. Pa., 1964; postgrad., Northeastern U., Boston, 1971-78. Lab. dir. Csepel Oil Refinery, Budapest, 1951-52; asst. prof. U. Veszprém, Hungary, 1952-54; chemist Ctrl. Oil Quality Control Lab., Budapest, 1954-56; rsch. chemist ARCO, Phila., 1957-61, U. Pa., Phila., 1961-64, Harvard Med. Sch., Boston, 1965-83; rsch. assoc. Beth Israel Hosp./Harvard Med. Sch., Boston, 1983-93. Contbr. numerous articles to profl. jours. Democrat. Calvinist. Achievements include discovery of blood plasma soluble melanins (rheomelanins), blood plasma soluble lipofuscins, patent for motor fuel compositions. Office: Beth Israel Deaconess Med Ctr 330 Brookline Ave Boston MA 02215-5400

HEGEL, CAROLYN MARIE, farmer, farm bureau executive; b. Lagro, Ind., Apr. 19, 1940; d. Ralph H. and Mary Lucile (Rudig) Lynn; m. Tom Lee Hegel, June 3, 1962. Student pub. schs., Columbia City, Ind. Bookkeeper Huntington County Farm Bur. Co-op, Inc., Ind., 1959-67, office mgr., 1967-70; twp. woman leader Wabash County (Ind.) Farm Bur., Inc., 1970-73, county woman leader, 1973-76; dist. woman leader Ind. Farm Bur., Inc., Indpls., 1976-80, 2d v.p., bd. dirs., 1980—, chmn. women's com., 1980—, exec. com., 1988—; farmer Andrews, Ind., 1962—; dir. Farm Bur. Ins. Co., Indpls., 1980—, exec. com., 1988; spkr. in field. Women in the Field columnist Hoosier Farmer mag., 1980—. Mem. rural task force Great Lakes States Econ. Devel. Commn., 1987-88, Ind. Farm Bur. Svc. Co., 1980—; bd. dirs. Ind. farm Bur. Found., Indpls., 1980—, Ind. Inst. Agr., Food and Nutrition, Indpls., 1982—, Ind. 4-H Found., Lafayette, 1983-86; mem. Ind. Rural Health Adv. Coun., 1993-96; com. mem. Hoosier Homestead Award Cert. Com., Indpls., 1980—; organizer farm divsn. Wabash County Am. Cancer Soc. Fund Dr., 1974; Sunday sch. tchr., bd. dir. children's activities Bethel United Meth. Ch., 1965—, pres. Bethel United Meth. Women, Lagro, 1975-81; bd. dirs. N.E. Ind. Kidney Found., 1984—, Nat. Kidney Found. of Ind., 1985-89, v.p., 1986—; active Leadership Am. Program, 1988. Named one of Outstanding Farm Woman of Yr. Country Woman Mag., 1987; recipient State 4-H Home Econs. award Ind. 4-H, 1960. Mem. Women in Comm., Inc., Ind. Agrl. Mktg. Assn. (bd. dirs. 1980-94), Producers Mktg. Assn. (bd. dirs. 1980-94), Am. Farm Bur. Fedn. (midwest rep. to women's com. 1986-93), Ind. Rural Health Assn. (bd. dirs. 1998—, exec. com. 1999, treas. 1999). Republican. E-mail: chegel@iquest.net. Home: 3330 N 650 E Andrews IN 46702-9616 Office: Ind Farm Bur Inc PO Box 1290 225 S East St Indianapolis IN 46202-4058

HEGEMAN, GEORGE DOWNING, microbiology educator; b. Glen Cove, N.Y., Aug. 31, 1938; s. George Downing and Bonnie (Blair) H.; m. Sally Lorraine Lofgren, Aug. 26, 1961; children: Susan Elizabeth, Adrian Daniel. AB, Harvard U., 1960; PhD, U. Calif., Berkeley, 1965. Instr. bacteriology and immunology U. Calif., Berkeley, 1965, asst. prof. bacteriology, 1966-72; assoc. prof. microbiology Ind. U., Bloomington, 1972-79, prof. microbiology, 1979—; sr. fellow Ind. Inst. for Cellular and Molecular Biology, 1984—; mem. sci. adv. bd. BioTrol, Inc., Mpls., 1985-90; mem. basic energy scis. adv. com. U.S. Dept. of Energy, 1989-93. Mem. editorial review bd. Applied & Environmental Microbiology, 1984-97, J. Bacteriol. 1989-97; patentee in field; contbr. articles to profl. jours. Pres. Monroe County Health Bd., 1996—. USPHS fellow, 1962-66; grantee USPHS, NSF. Fellow Am. Acad. Microbiology; mem. AAAS, Am. Soc. Microbiology, Am. Soc. Biochemistry and Molecular Biology, Soc. for Indsl. Microbiology, Forest Resources Assn. (past pres., v.p.). Avocations: beekeeping, forest resource activities. Office: Ind U Biology Dept Bloomington IN 47405

HEGER, HERBERT KRUEGER, education educator; b. Cin., June 15, 1937; s. J. Herbert and Leona (Krueger) H.; m. Thyra Cleek. AS, Ohio Mechanics Inst., 1956; BS, Miami U., 1962, MEd, 1965; PhD, Ohio State U., 1969. Tchr. Marshall Jr. High Sch., Pomona, Calif., 1962-63; tchr. math. Mt. Healthy High Sch., Ohio, 1963-66; grad. asst., grad. assoc. Miami U.-Ohio State U., 1966-69; dir. Environ. Studies Center Central State U., Wilberforce, Ohio, 1968-69; asst. prof. U. Ky., 1969-75; assoc. dir. Louisville Urban Edn. Center, 1971-75; vis. prof. Sch. Profl. Studies, Pepperdine U., 1975-78; dir. student teaching U. Tex., San Antonio, 1975-77, coordinator curriculum and instrn., 1977-78; assoc. prof. edn. Whitworth Coll., Spokane, Wash., 1978-82, chmn. dept., 1978-79, dean Grad. Sch., 1979-82; prof. edn. U. Tex., El Paso, 1982-99, prof. emeritus, 1999—; cons. in field. Contbr. articles to profl. jours. Mem. Am. Ednl. Rsch. Assn., Nat. Soc. Study Edn., Phi Delta Kappa. Republican. Disciples of Christ. Home: PO Box 2008 Ruidoso NM 88355

HEGGEN, ARTHUR WILLIAM, insurance company executive; b. Eureka, Calif., Aug. 9, 1945; s. Arlo Murray and Edna Marie (Nelson) H.; m. Betty Louise Roddy, Nov. 21, 1970; children: Cherilyn, Christopher. BS in Indsl Adminstrn., Acctg., Iowa State U., 1967. CPA, Iowa, Fla.; CPCU, FLMI, AIAF. Audit staff mgr. Ernst & Whinney, Des Moines, 1971-84; sr. v.p., treas. Am. Bankers Ins. Co., Miami, Fla., 1984-96, exec. v.p., 1996—. Bd. dirs. Metro Dade YMCA, Miami; pres. Iowa Ptnrs. of the Yucatan, Des Moines, 1984; pres., treas. Des Moines Hearing Speech Ctr., 1976-82. Capt. USMC, 1967-70, Vietnam. Fellow Life Mgmt. Inst.; mem. AICPA, Soc. CPCU, Fla. Inst. CPAs, Ins. Acct. & Fin. Office: Am Bankers Ins Group 11222 Quail Roost Dr Miami FL 33157-6543

HEGGEN, IVAR NELSON, lawyer; b. Tulsa, Sept. 22, 1954; s. Ivar George Lewis and Marley L. (Whitson) H.; m. Caroline Ann Driscoll, Dec. 20, 1976 (div. 1980); children: Kristin Dominique. BS, Charter Oaks Coll., 1979; JD cum laude, U. Houston, 1983. Bar: Tex. 1983, U.S. Ct. Appeals (5th cir.) 1987, U.S. Ct. Appeals (11th cir.) 1994; cert. in personal injury and civil trial law Tex. Bd. Legal Specialization and Nat. Bd. Trial Advocates. Assoc. Dibrell & Greer, Galveston, Tex., 1983-86, Schmidt & Matthews, Houston, 1986-87, Hornbuckle & Windham, Houston, 1987-89; pvt. practice, Houston, 1989—. Mem. ABA, Tex. Bar Assn., Coll. of State Bar Tex., Houston Bar Assn., Tex. Trial Lawyers Assn. (lectr.), Order of the Baron. Avocations: theater, music. Home: 422 W 15th St Houston TX 77008-4122 Office: 2211 Norfolk 820 Houston TX 77098

HEGINBOTHAM, JAN STURZA, sculptor; b. Flushing, N.Y., Dec. 8, 1954; d. Herman and Evelyn (Cantor) Sturza; m. Donald Wesley Heginbotham, Aug. 3, 1975. BA in Art Edn., U. Md., 1975; pvt. study, Boris Blai, Phila., 1976-78; MFA, Am. U., 1992. Tchr. sculpture workshops Landen Sch., Bethesda, Md., 1985-97, Arlington County, Va., 1993, Holy Family Coll., Phila., 1985, Columbia Union Coll., Takoma Park, Md., 1987; workshop coord. Arlington (Va.) Art Ctr., 1986-90, 93; sculpture teaching asst. Am. U., 1990-92, vis. artist, 1998; lectr. Salisbury State U., 1999. Solo exhbns. include Cannon Rotunda, U.S. Congress, Washington, 1985, Holy Family Coll., Phila., 1985, Essex (Md.) C.C., 1986, Staunton (Va.) Fine Art Assn., 1989, McCrillis Gardens Gallery, Bethesda, Md., 1990, Am. U., Washington, 1992; group shows include Perry House Gallery, Alexandria, Va., 1997, Lexington Art Ctr., Ky., 1997, Art Inst. Gallery, Salisbury, Md., 1999, U. Va., Charlottesville, 1999, Raab Gallery, Phila., 1999, Brookside Gardens Cons., Wheaton, Md., 1999. Active pub. commn. Montgomery County Pub. Schs., Rockville, Md., 1988, funded commn. proposals Md. Nat. Capital Pk. and Planning Commn., Silver Spring, 1987, 91, Montgomery Pub. Schs., 1985. Recipient Orion Nova award Allied Artists of Am., 1982, Mems. and Assocs. award Allied Artists of Am., 1986, Mayor of Washington award, 1981; merit scholar Scottsdale (Ariz.) Artist's Sch., 1987, Graduate Sculptors award Am. Univ., 1992; fellow Am. U., 1990-92. Mem. Washington Sculptors Group. Avocations: reading, photography, bicycling, yoga. Home: 2022 Upper Lake Dr Reston VA 20191-3645

HEGSTED, DAVID MARK, nutritionist; b. Rexburg, Idaho, Mar. 25, 1914; married; 2 children. AM, Harvard U., 1962; DSc, U. Idaho, 1986. Asst. biochemist U. Wis., 1936-41; rsch. chemist Abbott Labs, 1941-41; instr. to prof. nutrition Harvard U., Sch. Pub. Health, 1942-78; adminstr. Human Nutitional Ctr. USDA, 1978-82; emeritus prof. nutrition New England Regional Primate Rsch. Ctr., 1982—; cons. Columbian Govt., Inst. Inter-Am. Affairs, Peru; chmn. food and nutrition bd. Nat. Acad. Sci., Nat. Rsch. Coun.; mem. various exptl. coms. WHO, UN, 1960—. Editor Nutritional Review, 1968-78. Recipient Eleanor Naylor Dana award Am. Health Found., Bristol-Myers Squibb award. Mem. NAS, AAAS, Am. Dietetic Assn. (hon. mem.), Am. Chemical Soc., Am. Inst. Nutrition (pres. 1972-73, Osborne-Mendel award 1965, Conrad Elvejhem award 1979). Home: One Pine Hill Dr Southborough MA 01772

HEGSTROM, WILLIAM JEAN, mathematics educator; b. Macomb, Ill., Oct. 21, 1923; s. Carl William and Thelma (Canavit) H. Student Western Ill. U., 1941-42; B.Sc., Rutgers U., 1949, Ed.M. 1952; MA in Teaching, Purdue U., 1964; postgrad. U. Fla., 1961, Fla. Atlantic U., 1965-68; EdD, U. Miami, 1971; m. Grace Ann Paladino, May 3, 1944; children: Elizabeth Louise, William Jean II, Jean (Mrs. Carl Zimbro). Tchr. jr. h.s., South Plainfield, N.J., 1949-52, high sch., Bernardsville, N.J. 1952-54, Oak St. Sch., Bernard's Twp., N.J., 1954-55, high sch., Summit, N.J., 1955-58, jr. h.s., Delray Beach, Fla, 1958-65; chmn. math. dept. John I. Leonard H.S., Lake Worth, Fla., 1965-68, dir. Palm Beach County rsch. project, 1966-68; adj. prof. Fla. Atlantic U., 1965-69, assoc. prof., 1969-70; counselor coord. John Leonard Adult Ctr., Lake Worth, 1965-68; supr. rsch. and evaluation Palm Beach County Sch. Bd., West Palm Beach, Fla., 1970-74; adj. prof. Palm Beach Jr. Coll., 1981-88, Palm Beach Atlantic Coll., 1984-86, asst. prof., 1986-87; Palm Beach Atlantic Coll., 1984-87; cons. math. prof. Palm Beach County Sch. Bd., 1985-87, ret., 1987. With USAAF, 1942-46. Mem. NEA, Nat. Assn. Investors Corp., Am. Assn. Individual Investors, Phi Delta Kappa. Contbr. articles to profl. jours. Home: 225 NE 22nd St Delray Beach FL 33444-4221

HEGYELI, RUTH INGEBORG ELISABETH JOHNSSON, pathologist, government official; b. Stockholm, Aug. 14, 1931; came to U.S., 1963; d. John Alfred and Elsa Ingeborg (Sjogren) Johnsson; m. Andrew Francis Hegyeli, July 2, 1966 (dec. June 1982). BA in Scis., U. Toronto, 1958, MD, 1962. Intern Toronto Gen. Hosp., 1962-63; sr. rsch. pathologist Battelle Meml. Inst., Columbus, Ohio, 1967-69; med. officer Nat. Heart and Lung Inst., 1969-73; chief program devel. and evaluation Nat. Heart, Lung and Blood Inst., Bethesda, Md., 1973-76, acting dir. office program planning, 1975-76, asst. dir. internat. relations, 1976-86, assoc. dir. internat. rels., 1986—; mem. sci. adv. bd. Giovanni Lorenzini Found., Inc., N.Y.C., Milan, 1982—, Lorenzini Rsch. Found. Coordinating editor Jour. Soviet Research in Cardiovascular Diseases, 1979-86. Editor: Christopher Columbus Commemorative Book on Discovering New Worlds in Medicine, 1992, also 10 sci. books. Contbr. poetry to nat. anthologies. Bd. dirs. Coun. on Geriatric Cardiology, chmn. internat. com.; nat. adv. bd. Nat. Mus. Women in Arts. Named Hon. Mem. Eagle Tribe of Haida Indians, Queen Charlotte Islands, B.C., Can., 1961; nat. adv. bd. Nat. Mus. Women in the Arts; recipient Outstanding Scientist award Battelle Meml. Inst., Columbus, Ohio, 1966, German Friendship award German Ministry Rsch. and Tech., 1988, Nicolaus Copernicus medal Academica Medica, 1988, Superior Svc. award, HEW, 1975, DHHS, 1991; inductee Internat. Poetry Hall of Fame, 1997. Fellow Acad. Medicine, Toronto; mem. Am. Soc. Artificial Internal Organs, N.Y. Acad. Scis., Acad. Am. Poets, World Literary Acad., Fed. Exec. Alumni Assn. (policy issues com.). Republican. Avocations: poetry, fiction writing; non-fiction writing; art; music. Home: 24301 Hanson Rd Gaithersburg MD 20882-3501

HEGYVARY, SUE THOMAS, nursing school dean; b. Dry Ridge, Ky., Nov. 28, 1943. BSN, U. Ky., 1965; MN, Emory U., 1966; PhD in Sociology, Vanderbilt U., 1974. Asst. prof. nursing and sociology Rush U., 1972-74, assoc. prof. med. nursing, chair dept., 1974-77; asst. prof. sociology Rush U. Med. Coll., 1977-80; prof. nursing, assoc. v.p., assoc. dean nursing Coll. Nursing, Rush U., Rush Presbyn.-St. Luke's Med. Ctr., 1977—; assoc. prof. sociology Med. Coll. Rush U., 1980-98, dean emeritus, prof., 1998—; dean, prof. Sch. Nursing U. Wash., Seattle, 1986-98; mem. health care adv. com. Rep. Jennifer Dunn, 1993-96; vis. com. Bd. 50 Emory U. Sch. Nursing, Atlanta, 1990-92; mem. adv. panel outcomes rsch. Nat. Ctr. Nursing Rsch. NIH, 1990-91; external mem. Five Yr. Review com. Coll. Nursing U. Ky., 1989-90; mem. govtl. affairs com. Am. Assn. Colls. Nursing, 1988-92; chair planning com. Wash. State Conf. Nursing Shortage, 1989; mem. Wash. State Commn. Nursing, 1989; mem. adv. com. Child Devel. & Mental Retardation Ctr. U. Wash., 1986—; mem. task force nursing shortage Seattle Area Hosp. Coun., 1987-88; vis. prof., ann. lectr. Sch. Nursing U. Va., Charlottesville, 1988; vis. prof. U. Oulu, Finland, 1985; site visitor accreditation schs. nursing Nat. League Nursing, 1977-80; cons. VA Hosp., Miami, Fla., 1968-69, Vanderbilt U., Nashville, 1971-72, Area Health Edn. Sys., Rockford, Ill., 1975, Western Interstate Commn. Higher Edn., Denver, 1975, Andrews U., Berrian Springs, Mich., 1976, dept. nursing studies Nat. Hosp. Inst., Utrecht, The Netherlands, 1976-80, Haukeland Sykehaus, Bergen, Norway, 1976-77, Sch. Nursing Marquette U., Milw., 1977, Wayne State U., Detroit, 1978, Cath. U. Leuven, Belgium, 1980, Walter Reed Army Med. Ctr., Washington, 1979-83, Dalhousie U. Sch. Nursing, Halifax, N.S., 1981, U. Minn., Mpls., 1988, U. Mo., Columbia, 1992. Editl. adv. bd. Nursing Policy Forum, 1995-96; editl. cons. Nursing Care Guide Pfizer Corp., 1993; editl. bd. Jour. Nursing & Health, 1993—, Nursing Adminstrn. Quarterly, 1988—; mem. manuscript review panel Jour. Nursing Quality Assurance, 1986—, Nursing Outlook, 1983—, Jour. Rsch. Nursing & Health, 1981—, Nursing Rsch., 1979-89; contbr. chpts. to books and articles to profl. jours. Mem. ANA, Am. Acad. Nursing, Sigma Theta Tau. Office: U Wash Sch NursingDean's Office PO Box 357266 Seattle WA 98195-7260

HEIBERG, ELVIN RAGNVALD, III, civil engineer, army officer; b. Schofield Barracks, Hawaii, Mar. 2, 1932; s. Elvin R. and Evelyn (Lytle) H.; m. Kathryn Louise Schrimpf, June 16, 1953; children: Kathryn Anna, Walter Dodge, Elvin Ragnvald IV, Kay Louise. B.S., U.S. Mil. Acad., 1953; M.S.C.E., MIT, 1958; M.A. in Govt, George Washington U., 1961, M.S. in Adminstrn, 1971. Registered profl. engr., La. Commd. 2d lt. U.S. Army, 1953, advanced through grades to lt. gen., 1984; svc. in Korea, 1954-55; co. comdr. Germany, 1961-62; faculty U.S. Mil. Acad., 1965-68; bn. comdr. Vietnam, 1968-69; detailed to Exec. Office of Pres., 1969-70, staff positions in Pentagon, 1971-74; dist. engr. C.E. New Orleans, 1974-75; div. engr. C.E. Ohio River, 1975-78; engr. U.S. Army-Europe, 1978-79; dir. civil works Washington, 1979-82; dep. chief of engrs., 1982-83; program mgr. Army Ballistic Missile Def. Orgn., Washington, 1983; v.p. Permanent Internat. Assn. Nav. Congresses., 1983-87; chief engrs. U.S. Army, Washington, 1984-88; bd. dirs. Stone Webster, Inc. Pres. Stratford-on-the-Potomac Citizens Assn., 1972-73; mem. Mississippi River Commn., 1975-78, Ohio River Commn., 1975-78. Decorated D.F.C., 2 D.S.M., Silver Star, 3 Legion of Merit medals, Comdr., Belgian Order of Crown, 1985, Grand Comdr., Brazilian Order of Mil. Merit, 1986; recipient Meritorious Svc. award Office Emergency Preparedness, 1970. Mem. ASCE, NSPE, Soc. Am. Mil. Engrs. (v.p. 1986-87, pres. 1987-88), Permanent Internat. Assn. Navigations Congresses (internat. v.p. 1983-87), Nat. Acad. Engring. Methodist. Office: Heiberg Assocs Inc 10715 Harley Rd Mason Neck VA 22079 *Engineering is a profession which demands much but gives much, and does not tolerate major errors. An Army officer's calling also demands much but gives much, and the contribution to a strong United States defense helps insure peace. Both these professions require a deep understanding of people, and my twin careers are built on insuring top performance.*

HEIBERG, ROBERT ALAN, lawyer; b. St. Cloud, Minn., June 29, 1943; s. Rasmus Adolph and Irene (Shaffer) H.; m. Sharon Ann Olson, Aug. 2, 1969; children—Eric Robert, Mark Alan, Maren Ann. B.A. summa cum laude, U. Minn., 1965, J.D. summa cum laude, 1968. Bar: Minn. 1968. Law clk. to assoc. justice Minn. Supreme Ct., 1968-69; assoc. Dorsey & Whitney, Mpls., 1969-73; ptnr. Dorsey & Whitney, 1974—; instr. Law Sch., U. Minn., 1968-72, instr. legal assts. program, 1972-77. Articles editor Minn. Law Rev., 1967-68. Mem. adv. com. U. Minn. Legal Assts. Program, 1977-84, bd. visitors Law Sch., 1991-96. Mem. ABA (sect. real property, probate and trust law), Minn. Bar Assn. (chmn. com. on legal assts. 1979), Hennepin County Bar Assn., Am. Rose Soc. (accredited judge 1996), Order of Coif, Phi Beta Kappa. Republican. Lutheran. Home: 4510 Wooddale Ave Minneapolis MN 55424-1137 Office: Dorsey & Whitney Pillsbury Ctr South 220 S 6th St Ste 2200 Minneapolis MN 55402-1498

HEICHEL, GARY HAROLD, crop sciences educator; b. Park Falls, Wis., Nov. 9, 1940; s. Harold H. and Bernice I. (Comp) H.; m. Iris Fehl Martin, Apr. 24, 1988. BS, Iowa State U., 1962; MS, Cornell U., 1964, PhD, 1968. Asst. plant physiologist Conn. Agrl. Expt. Stat., New Haven, 1968-73, assoc. plant physiologist, 1973-76, plant physiologist, 1976; plant physiologist USDA Agrl. Rsch. Svc., St. Paul, 1976-90, acting rsch. leader, 1988-90; head agronomy dept. U. Ill., Urbana, 1990-95, interim head plant pathology dept., 1994-95, head crop scis. dept., 1995—; adj. prof. agronomy U. Minn., 1976-90; program mgr. USDA Competitive Rsch. Grants Office, 1981. Contbr. chpts. to books, articles to profl. jours. Pres., mem. adminstrv. bd. Cheshire, Conn. United Meth. Ch., 1973-76, v.p. Cheshire Land Trust, 1975-76. Named Civil Servant of Yr., Twin Cities Fed. Exec. Bd., St. Paul, 1984. Fellow AAAS (chair sect. 0 1997-98), Crop Sci. Soc. Am. (pres. 1991-92, award 1987), Am. Soc. Agronomy (exec. com. 1990-92, pres. north ctrl. sect. 1991-93, pres. 1997-98), Am. Soc. Plant Physiologists (trustee 1988-90), Urbana Rotary (bd. dirs. 1997-99). Avocations: classical music, reading, hiking, gardening. Office: U Ill Dept Crop Scis 1102 S Goodwin Ave AW-101 Urbana IL 61801-4730

HEICK, LEON JOSEPH, data processing executive; b. New England, N.D., May 14, 1944; s. Joseph Philiph and Frances (Bosepflug) H.; m. Alicia Marie Finneman, July 13, 1968; children: Brent, Royce, Travis. BS in Bus. Adminstrn., U. Mary, Bismarck, N.D., 1991, BS in Acctg., 1998. Computer operator North Ctrl. Data Corp., Mandan, N.D., 1968-69, computer programmer, 1970-71, programming mgr., 1972-78, sys. mgr., 1979-83, asst. gen. mgr., 1984—, mgr. multi million dollar offshore software devel. projects, 1991—; dir. Project Back Home Coop, Mandan, 1994—, Rural Electric and Telephone Credit Union, Bismarck, N.D., 1993—. Singer No. Lights Barbershop Chorus, Bismarck, 1991-93; active ch. choir. With U.S. Army, 1965-67, Vietnam. Mem. Am. Legion, KC, Elks, Amvets. Avocations: singing, guitar playing, golf, hunting, fishing. Office: North Ctrl Data Corp PO Box 728 Mandan ND 58554-0728

HEIDBREDER, GAIL, architect, educator; b. Balt., Jan. 20, 1941; d. Gerald August and Ora Henderson (Longley) H.; children: Laura Temple Lundin, John Temple. BA, Stanford U., 1966, postgrad., 1975-78, 93—. Registered architect, Calif. With various firms, 1969-85; owner Gail Heidbreder, AIA-Architect, Porterville, Calif., 1985—; instr. architecture, constrn. CADD and computer animation, Coll. of Sequoias, Visalia, Calif., 1990—. Mem. AIA. Avocations: horse training, stockpacker. Office: Coll of Sequoias 915 S Mooney Blvd Visalia CA 93277-2214

HEIDE, HANS DIETER, JR., accountant; b. Johnson City, N.Y., June 2, 1968; s. Hans Dieter and Concetta Marie (Puzo) H. BS in Acctg., SUNY, Binghamton, 1992, BA in History, 1992; MS in Taxation, SUNY, Albany, 1993; postgrad., SUNY, Buffalo, 1996. Tax cons. Ernst & Young LLP, Syracuse, N.Y., 1994-95; sr. tax specialist KPMG Peat Marwick LLP, Albany, N.Y., 1995-96; profl. acct. IBM Corp., Endicott, N.Y., 1997-98; rsch./fin. analyst IBM Corp., Armonk, N.Y., 1998-99; profl. acct. IBM gf, 1999—. Legis. assoc. Office Majority Leader N.Y. State Assembly, Albany, 1992, rsch. asst. Office Oversight Analysis & Investigation, 1992, rsch. analyst Office Thomas Libous, 1993, legis. aide Office Glenn Warden, 1993; chpt. advisor Round hill DeMolay, 1989—; dep. region advisor Ctrl. Region N.Y. State DeMolay, 1995—. Mem. Masons. Republican. Roman Catholic. Avocations: reading, weightlifting. Home: 206 Squires Ave Endicott NY 13760-2939 Office: IBM Corp 1701 North St Endicott NY 13760-5598

HEIDE, JOHN WESLEY, engineering executive; b. Chgo., Sept. 14, 1946; s. Frederick Bernard Heiner-Heide and Eleanor Francis (Tuttle) Heide; m. Patricia Ann Lynn, Aug. 5, 1967 (div. Jan. 1973); children: John Wesley, Joseph Edward. AA, Phoenix Jr. Coll., 1972; BS, Ariz. State U., 1975. Quality assurance engr. Tex. Instruments, Dallas, 1969-70, ITT Courier, Tempe, Ariz., 1975-79; sr. project engr. GTE Comms., El Paso, 1979-83, Telxon Corp., Houston, 1983-87; engring. mgr. United Techs., Niles, Mich., 1987-91, Automotive Industries, Midland, Tex., 1991-94; divsn. quality assurance mgr. Pec Golden Triangle Plastics, El Paso, Tex., 1994-95; indsl. engring. mgr. Elcom, Inc., El Paso, Tex., 1995—, UFE, Inc., El Paso, Tex., 1997; quality assurance mgr. United for Excellence Inc., El Paso, 1997-99; TQM mgr. Dayco Inc., El Paso, 1999—; instr. engring. Houston C.C., 1984-85. Author: Reflections, 1990, Scan-It, 1991, A Step Beyond the Fog, 1992, How Cheap Is Cheap, 1993. Candidate for mayor, El Paso, 1980, 82, 84; candidate for State Rep., Berrien Springs, Mich., 1990. With USMC, 1965-69, Vietnam. Mem. NSPE, Soc. Plastics Engrs., Inst. Indsl. Engring. (v.p. 1982-83), Soc. Mfg. Engrs. (sr.), Am. Soc. Quality Control. Republican. Lutheran. Avocations: European travel, genealogy, stamp and coin collecting. Fax: 915-860-2116. Home: 10732 Chert El Paso TX 79924 Office: Dayco Industrial Divsn Ste 200 12134 Esther Lama El Paso TX 79936

HEIDE, KATHLEEN MARGARET, criminology educator, psychotherapist; b. Englewood, N.J., May 25, 1954; d. Victory Hillary and Eleanor (Mulhearn) H. BA in Psychology, Vassar Coll., 1976; MA in Criminal Justice, SUNY, Albany, 1978, PhD in Criminal Justice, 1982. Lic. mental health counselor, Fla.; diplomate Nat. Bd. for Clin. Hypnotherapists; cert. practitioner level So. Inst. Neurolinguistic Programming; lic. psychotherapist Ctr. for Mental Health. Asst. prof. criminology U. South Fla., Tampa, 1981-87, assoc. prof., 1987-94, prof., 1994—; paper presenter in field to profl. assns. Author: Why Kids Kill: Child Abuse and Adolescent Homicide, 1992, Young Killers: The Challenge of Juvenile Homicide, 1998; mem. editl. bd. Homicide Studies, 1996—; assoc. editor Internat. Jour. Offender Therapy and Comparative Criminology, 1995—. Bd. dirs. Hillsborough County Sexual Abuse Treatment Ctr., Tampa, 1983-87, Hillsborough County Crisis Ctr., 1982-87, Hillsborough Constituency for Children, 1994—. Recipient tchg. award Golden Key, 1993, award So. Sunshine Video Festival, 1995. Mem. APA, Am. Soc. Criminology, Acad. Criminal Justice Scis., Homicide Rsch. Working Group, Tampa Bay Assn. for Women Psychotherapists (pres. 1997-98). Avocations: swimming, boating. Office: U So Fla Dept Criminology 4202 E Fowler Ave Tampa FL 33620-9951

HEIDELBAUGH, NORMAN DALE, veterinary medicine educator, consultant, author, inventor; b. Phila., July 29, 1927; s. Milton Harold and Claire Agnus (Dale) H.; m. Judith Sweet Voss, Feb. 16, 1963; children: Clark Hayden, Todd Milton, Lynn Ruth. VMD, U. Pa., 1954; M in Pub. Health, Tulane U., 1958; SM, MIT, 1963, PhD, 1970. Diplomate Am. Coll. Vet. Preventive Medicine; charter diplomate splty. epidemiology; Diplomate Am. Bd. Vet. Pub. Health. Commd. USAF, 1954; vet. officer various locations worldwide; advanced through grades to col., 1972; chief food sci. Lyndon B. Johnson Space Ctr., NASA, Houston, 1970-74; USAF rep. Dept. Def. Research-Devel.-Test and Evaluation Program, Washington, 1974-77; retired USAF, 1977; prof. vet. pub. health Tex. A&M U., College Station, 1977-92, head dept., 1978-90, prof. food sci. and tech., 1977-92; prof. emeritus Tex. A&M U., Coll. Station, Tex., 1994—; mem. vis. com. MIT, Cambridge, 1977-84, cons. UN Devel. Program, N.Y.C., 1979-82; mem. NRC Nat. Acad. Scis., 1984-86. Contbr. 125 articles to profl. jours. Mem. nat. adv. com. on meat and poultry insp., USDA, Washington, 1980-92; archives vol. George Bush Presdl. Libr., 1997—. Decorated Legion of Merit with 2 Oak Leaf Clusters, USAF; named Tex. Scientist of Yr. Air Force Assn., 1966; Underwood-Prescott meml. lectr. MIT, 1974; recipient Skylab award NASA, 1979. Scroll of Appreciation, U.S. Army Europe and 7th Army, 1984-92; grantee numerous orgns. and govt. Mem. AVMA, (sci. program com. 1982-86, coun. on rsch. 1986-90, XII Internat. Vet. Cong. award 1992), Inst. food Technologists, Am. Assn. Food Hygiene Vets. (pres. 1983-84, Vet. of Yr. 1986). Office: Tex A&M U Coll Vet Medicine Dept Vet Anat & Pub Health College Station TX 77843-4458

HEIDELBERGER, KATHLEEN PATRICIA, physician; b. Bklyn., Apr. 13, 1939; d. William Cyprian and Margaret Bernadette (Hughes) H.; m. Charles William Davenport, Oct. 8, 1977. B.S. cum laude, Coll. Misericordia, 1961; M.D. cum laude, Woman's Med. Coll. Pa., 1965. Intern Mary Hitchcock Hosp., Hanover, N.H., 1965-66, resident in pathology, 1966-70; mem. faculty U. Mich., Ann Arbor, 1970—, assoc. prof. pathology, 1976-79, prof., 1979—. Mem. Am. Soc. Clin. Pathologists, U.S.-Can. Acad. Pathology, Soc. for Pediatric Pathology, Coll. Am. Pathologists. Office: U Mich Box 0054 Dept of Pathology UH 2G/332 Ann Arbor MI 48109

HEIDEMANN, MARY ANN, community planner; b. Detroit, Feb. 17, 1950; d. O.K. and Mary Elizabeth (Berry) Rodewald; m. Karl Werner, June 19, 1982; children: Heather Lisa, Karl Kristoffer. BA in Archtl. History, Reed Coll., Portland, Oreg., 1970; postgrad., U. Pa., Phila., 1972-75; MA in Pub. Adminstrn., U. Wis., 1985, PhD in Land Resources, 1989. Profl. cmty. planner, Mich.; lic. residential builder, Mich. Apprentice Paolo Soleri, Architect, Scottsdale, Ariz., 1970-71; staff planner Jack McCormick & Assocs., Devon, Pa., 1972-74; natural resource planner Brown County Planning Commn., Green Bay, Wis., 1976-78; planning cons. Champ, Parish, Raasch, De Pere, Wis., 1978-80; policy analyst U.S. EPA, Chgo., 1980-81; cmty. svc. specialist Wis. Dept. Natural Resources, Madison, 1981-85; chief environ. analysis Wis. Dept. Transp., Madison, 1985-86; project mgr. Wade-Trim/Impact, Taylor, Mich., 1987-88; owner, prin. planner Mary Ann Heidemann & Assocs., Rogers City, Mich., 1988-97; v.p., planning group mgr. Wade-Trim Engring., 1997—; lectr. U. Wis., Green Bay, 1977-78; asst. prof. Kans. State U., Manhattan, 1975-76; exec. dir. East Mich. Environ. Action, West Bloomfield, 1986-87; adj. prof. Lake Superior State U., Sault Ste. Marie, 1988—; mem. planner lic. bd. Gov. State Mich., Lansing, 1990-94. Founding mem. Bay Renaissance, Green Bay, 1979-80; mem. Orion Twp. Planning Commn., Mich., 1986-87; county commr. Presque Isle County Bd., Rogers City, Mich., 1992-93; bd. dirs. Presque Isle Harbor Assocs., 1993-96; elder Westminster Presbyn. Ch., 1997—. Dean Webster Meml. scholar Reed Coll., Portland, Oreg., 1968-69; fellow NEH, San Diego, 1978. Mem. AAUW, Am. Inst. Cert. Planners (planning exam. com. 1992), Am. Planning Assn., Mich. Soc. Planning Ofcls. (tng. workshop instr.), Harmony Choraleers, Mich. Historic Preservation Network, Presque Isle Lighthouse Assn. Democrat. Avocations: singing, swimming, bicycling, poetry writing, local history. Office: PO Box 879 Indian River MI 49749-0879

HEIDEMANN, ROBERT ALBERT, chemical engineering educator, researcher; b. St. Louis, Aug. 31, 1936; emigrated to Can., 1968; s. William Joseph and Gladys Emilie (Digman) H.; m. Linda Bea Szold, June 9, 1968; children: David, Douglas. B.Sc. in Chem. Engring., Washington U., St. Louis, 1958; Sc.D., Washington U., 1966. Asst. prof. chem. engring. Drexel Inst. Tech., Phila., 1963-68; assoc. prof. U. Calgary (Alta.), 1968-77, prof., 1977—, head dept. chem. and petroleum engring., 1981-92; vis. prof. Tech. U. Denmark, 1986-87; cons., 1982—. Co-author: (with A.A. Jeje and M.F. Mohtadi) Properties of Fluids and Solids, 1984; contbr. articles to profl. jours. Fellow Chem. Inst. Can.; mem. Canadian Soc. Chem. Engrs., Am. Inst. Chem. Engrs., Am. Chem. Soc., Am. Soc. Engring. Edn., Assn. Profl. Engrs., Geologists and Geophysicists of Alta., Tau Beta Pi. Home: 6212 Dalmarnock Crescent NW, Calgary, AB Canada T3A 1H2 Office: U Calgary, 2500 University Dr NW, Calgary, AB Canada T2N 1N4

HEIDEN, CHARLES KENNETH, former army officer, metals company executive; b. Detroit, July 7, 1925; s. Carl William and Elsie Mae (Langley) H.; m. Nancy Earle Gray, June 7, 1949; 1 son, Charles Gray. B.S., U.S. Mil. Acad., 1949; M.S. in Mech. Engring, U. Mich., 1957; grad. mgmt. execs. program, U. Pitts., 1971. Registered profl. engr., Ky. Enlisted U.S. Army, 1943, commd. 2d lt., 1949, advanced through grades to maj. gen., 1977; services in Panama, France, Korea and Vietnam; dep. dir. ops. Nat. Mil. Command Center, Joint Chiefs of Staff, 1973-74; dir. enlisted personnel U.S. Mil. Personnel Center, Washington, 1974-76; comdr. U.S. Army Mil. Personnel Center, 1977-80; comdg. gen. U.S. Army Tng. Ctr., Ft. Dix, N.J., 1980-81; pres., dir. Montel Metals Inc., 1981-83; pres., dir. Cedar Lake Lodge Inc., La Grange, Ky., 1985-86, chmn. bd. dirs., 1986-98; chmn. emeritus Cedar Lake Lodge Inc., La Grange, 1998—; cons. Computer Simulation, 1987-98; chmn. bd. dirs. Cedar Lake, Inc., La Grange, 1994-98, chmn. emeritus, 1998—. Bd. dirs. Park Glen Heights Assn., Annandale, Va., 1974-76; pres. Our Saviour Luth. Ch., Arlington, Va., 1974-76; mem. code enforcement bd. City Jeffersontown, Ky., 1998—. Decorated D.S.M., D.F.C., Legion of Merit with 3 oak leaf clusters, Air medal with 10 oak leaf clusters, Joint Services Commendation medal, Army Commendation medal with 2 oak leaf clusters, Meritorious Service medal with oak leaf cluster; Cross of Gallantry with silver star Vietnam; recipient Pace award Office Sec. Army, 1963. Mem. Armed Forces Relief and Benefit Assn. (dir. 1977-81), West Point Alumni Assn., Am. Legion, U.S. Army War Coll. Alumni Assn. Home: 10500 Brookhill Ct Louisville KY 40223-3475

HEIDER, JON VINTON, retired lawyer, corporate executive; b. Moline, Ill., Mar. 1, 1934; s. Raymond and Doris (Hinch) H.; m. Barbara L. Bond, Dec. 27, 1960 (div.); children: Loren P., John C., Lindsay L.; m. Mary R. Murray, Jan. 27, 1984. AB, U. Wis., 1956; JD, Harvard U., 1961; grad., Advanced Mgmt. Program, 1974. Bar: Pa. 1962, U.S. Dist. Ct. (ea. dist.) Pa. 1962, U.S. Ct. Appeals (3d cir.) 1962, U.S. Supreme Ct. 1991. Assoc. Morgan Lewis & Bockius, Phila., 1961-66; counsel Catalytic, Inc., Phila., 1966-68, Houdry Process & Chem. Co., Phila., 1968-70; counsel chems. group Air Products & Chems., Inc., Valley Forge, Pa., 1970-75, asst. gen. counsel, 1975-76, assoc. gen. counsel, 1976-78; gen. counsel Air Products & Chems., Inc., Allentown, Pa., 1978-80; v.p. corp. affairs, sr. adminstrv. officer-Europe, Air Products Europe, Inc., London, 1980-83; v.p. corp. devel. Air Products & Chems., Inc., 1983-84; v.p., gen. counsel BF Goodrich Co., Akron, Ohio, 1984-88, sr. v.p., gen. counsel, 1988-94, exec. v.p., gen. counsel, 1994-98; ret., 1998. Trustee Bluecoats, Inc.; mem. distbn. m. Charles E. and Mabel M. Ritchie Meml. Found. Lt. USNR, 1956-58. Mem. ABA, Am. Law Inst., Assn. Gen. Counsel, Blossom Music Ctr. Bd. Overseers, Sisler McFawn Found. (distbn. com.), U. Wis. Found., Portage Country Club, Rolling Rock Club, Key Biscayne Yacht Club.

HEIDISH, LOUISE ORIDGE-SCHWALLIE, transportation specialist, marketing professional; b. Cin., May 21, 1938; d. Leslie Jacob and Louise (Oridge) Schwallie; m. William Edward Heidish, Sept. 2, 1961; children: Sara Louise Heidish-Hurst, Amy Jean. BA in History, Denison U., 1960; MA in History, Miami U., Oxford, Ohio, 1962; MS in Urban Studies, Ala. A&M U., 1994. Secondary tchr. Fox Chapel Sch. Dist., Pitts., 1962-69; part-time instr. U. Ala., Huntsville, 1976-78; substitute history tchr. City of Huntsville Schs., 1977-79; dir. comm. svcs. Heidish Enterprises, Huntsville, 1979-83; transp. specialist City of Huntsville, 1981—; regional 5 state coord. AAUW and NEH, Huntsville, 1981-83. Author: Biography: Alexander Long 1816-86, 1962, Marketing Ride Sharing, 1994; co-editor: Glimpses into Antebellum Homes, Huntsville, AL, 1999. Mem., project chair, bd. dirs. Huntsville Symphony Orch. Guild, 1974—; bd. dirs. Huntsville-Madison County Sr. Ctr., 1980-86, sec. 1981, v.p. 1982, pres. 1983; bd. dirs. Huntsville High Sch. PTA, 1983-88, v.p. 1985-86, pres. 1986-88; com. chmn. Panoply of the Arts Festival, Huntsville, 1985-87; mem. adv. bd. women's studies U. Ala., Huntsville, 1998—; mem. adv. bd. capital campaign Fantasy Playhouse, 1998—; publicity chair Huntesville-Madison County Libr. Benefit, 1999. Mem. AAUW (local pres. 1979-81, state v.p. 1981-83, regional coord. 1981-83, Outstanding Local Svc. award 1999), Pub. Rels. Coun. No. Ala. (newsletter editor 1993, conf. treas. 1994, coun. treas. 1995, coun. sec. 1996, v.p. profl. devel. 1997, v.p. membership 1998, 99), S.E. Assn. for Commuter Transp. (regional conf. chair 1995, chpt. treas. 1996, 97), Kappa Kappa Gamma (alumnae officer, local pres., regional officer 1958—, Outstanding Kappa Kappa Gamma Svc. award 4 state region 1997). Presbyterian. Avocations: community arts volunteering, reading, swimming. Office: Pub Transp City Huntsville 100 Church St SW Huntsville AL 35801-4908

HEIDRICK, ROBERT LINDSAY, management consultant; b. Kansas City, Mo., June 8, 1941; s. Gardner W. Sr. and Eileen (Lindsay) H.; m. Deborah Nissen, June 26, 1971 (div.); 1 child, Lindsay T.; m. Raynelle Falkenau, Aug. 4, 1984; stepchildren: Kimberley A. Ransom, Stephen H. Ransom. BA, Duke U., 1963; MBA, U. Chgo., 1971. Vice pres. Am. Hosp. Supply Corp., Evanston, Ill., 1963-75, v.p. Dietary Products div., 1971-75; v.p. Spriggs and Co., Chgo., 1975-77; pres. Robert Heidrick Assocs. Inc., Chgo., 1977-82, The Heidrick Ptnrs. Inc., Chgo., 1982-98; ptnr. Heidrick & Struggle, Chgo., 1998—. Bd. dirs. Glenwood Sch. for Boys, Chgo., 1982-92; trustee Duke U., 1989-90, Golden Apple Found., 1992-95; chmn. state crusade Am. Cancer Soc., 1992-94, chmn. income devel., 1994-95, 2d vice chmn., 1995-97, chmn., 1997—. Mem. Duke U. Alumni Assn. (bd. dirs. 1981-90, pres. 1988-89), Glen View Club, Chgo. Club, Firestone Country Club, Econ. Club Chgo., Chgo. Commonwealth Club, Comml. Club. Office: Heidrick & Struggle 233 S Wacker Dr Ste #7000 Chicago IL 60606-2806*

HEIDT, RAYMOND JOSEPH, insurance company executive; b. Bismarck, N.D., Feb. 28, 1933; s. Stephen Ralph and Elizabeth Ann (Hirschkorn) H.; BA, Calif. State U., San Jose, 1963, MA, 1968; PhD, U. Utah, 1977; m. Joyce Ann Aston, Jan. 14, 1956; children: Ruth Marie, Elizabeth Ann, Stephen Christian, Joseph Aston. Claims supr. Allstate Ins. Co., San Jose, Calif., 1963-65; claims mgr. Gen. Accident Group, San Francisco, 1965-69; owner, mgr. Ray Heidt & Assocs., Logan, Utah, 1969-76; v.p. claims Utah Home Fire Ins. Co., Salt Lake City, 1976—; with Utah State U., 1970-76; dir. Inst. for Study of Pacifism and Militarism; vice-chmn. Benton County Parks and Recreation Bd., 1987-90. Active Kennewick Hist. Preservation Commn., 1989-90, 1st chmn., 1989-90, Magna Area Coun., 1992, pres. 1993-94; bd. trustees, sec. treas. Utah Ethnic and Mining Mus., 1994—. With U.S. Army, 1952-57. Decorated Bronze Star. Mem. Southeastern Wash. Adjusters' Assn. (pres. 1988-90), Utah Claims Assn. (pres. 1977-78), Lions, Am. Legion. Mormon. Republican. Home: 1715 W Flamingo Ave Apt #50 Nampa ID 83651-1669

HEIDT-DUNWELL, DEBRA SUE, vocational education educator; b. Liberty, N.Y., Oct. 28, 1952; d. Charles William and Lillian Lorraine (Ball) H. AA, Sullivan County Community Coll., Lock Sheldrake, N.Y., 1972; BS, SUNY, Oneonta, 1974, MS in Edn., 1979. Cert. permanent math. tchr., provisional elem. tchr., N.Y. High sch. tchr. math. Downsville (N.Y.) Cen. Sch., Oneonta Cen. Sch.; tutor Sullivan County Community Coll.; cons. tchr. related skills for vocat. programs Sullivan County Vocat.-Tech. Ctr., Liberty, fin. aid adminstr. LPN program; conf. presenter in field; rschr. Hudson Valley Faculty Portfolio Assessment. Contbr. poetry to various publs. Recipient Golden Poet award World of Poetry Press, 1986-91. Mem. ASCD, AAUW, AMTNYS, AMS, SSMA, Sullivan Reading Coun., Nat. Coun. Tchrs. Math., Am. Vocat. Assn., Nat. Coun. Tchrs. English, Internat. Reading Assn., Am. Poetry Assn. (Poet of Merit award 1989), Kappa Delta Pi, Delta Kappa Gamma (Tau chpt).

HEIENS, RICHARD ALLEN, education foundation executive; b. Alton, Ill., Aug. 6, 1940; s. Richard Alvin Heiens and Dorthey Verleen (Johnson) Depew; m. Gabriella Maria Sau, July 20, 1963; children: Marina, Deborah, Richard, Michael. BBA, Washington U., 1974; PhD, Kennedy-Western U., 1990. Social worker ARC, Republic of Vietnam, 1968-69, Munich, German Democratic Republic, 1969-70; internal auditor ARC, St. Louis, 1970-74; bus. mgr. ARC, Miami, 1974-76, asst. div. mgr., 1976-78, dep. mgr., 1978-82, exec. dir., 1982-85; exec. dir. Archdiocese Edn. Found., Miami, 1985-87, Our Lady of Lourdes Acad. Found., Miami, 1987—; pres. South Fla. Crack Ctrs., Inc., Miami, 1986—. Decorated Cross of Gallantry (Vietnam); recipient U.S. Civilian Service in Vietnam medal, 1969. Mem. Nat. Soc. Fund Raising Execs. (cert.). Republican. Roman Catholic. Lodge: Rotary (Miami). Avocations: golf, tennis. Office: Lourdes Acad Found 5525 SW 84th St Miami FL 33143-8398

HEIFETS, LEONID, microbiologist, researcher; b. Russia, Jan. 5, 1926; came to U.S., 1979; s. Boris and Luba Heifets; m. Seraphima Apsit, Jan. 1955 (div. July 1978); children: Michael, Herman. MD, Med. Inst., Moscow, 1947, PhD, 1953; DSc, Acad. Med. Scis., Moscow. Asst. prof. Med. Inst., Arkhangelsk, Russia, 1950-54, assoc. prof., 1954-57; lab. dir. Mechnikov Rsch. Inst., Moscow, 1957-69; sr. rschr. Inst. for Tb, Moscow, 1969-78; rsch. fellow Nat. Jewish Hosp., Denver, 1979-80; lab. dir. Nat. Jewish Ctr., Denver, 1980—; asst. prof. Colo. U., Denver, 1980-86, assoc. prof., 1986-92, prof. microbiology, 1992—; mem. com. on bacteriology Internat. Union Against Tb, Paris, 1986—. Author: Effectiveness of Vaccination, 1968, Clinical Mycobacteriology (Clinics in Laboratory Medicine), 1996; author, editor: Drug Susceptibility, 1991; assoc. editor Internat. Jour. Tuberculosis; contbr. articles to profl. jours. Mem. Am. Soc. Microbiology. Avocations: hiking, snowshoeing, photography, history. Office: Nat Jewish Med Rsch Ctr 1400 Jackson St Denver CO 80206-2761

HEIFETZ, ALAN WILLIAM, federal judge; b. Portland, Maine, Jan. 15, 1943; s. Ralph and Bernice (Diamon) H.; m. Nancy Butler Stone, Aug. 11, 1968; children: Andrew Stone, Peter Stone. A.B., Syracuse U., 1965; J.D., Boston U., 1968. Bar: Maine 1968, Mass. 1968, U.S. Dist. Ct. Mass. 1969, U.S. Supreme Ct. 1972. Assoc. Chayet and Flash, Boston, 1968-70; trial atty. ICC, Washington, 1970-72, counsel to chmn., 1972-78, adminstrv. law judge, 1978-80; adminstrv. law judge Fed. Labor Relations Authority, Washington, 1980-82; chief adminstrv. law judge Dept. HUD, Washington, 1982—; mem. forum faculty Am. Arbitration Assn., Washington, 1983; mem. faculty Nat. Jud. Coll., U. Nev., Reno, 1988-94; mem. Adminstrv. Conf. U.S., 1986-95; mem. Forum U.S. Adminstrv. Law Judges, v.p., 1986-87, pres., 1987-89; mem. exec. com. Fed. Adminstrv. Law Judges Conf., 1982-90; jurist-in-residence The John Marshall Law Sch., 1995. Contbr. articles to profl. jours. Mem. Fallsmead Civic Assn. (Md.). Mem. ABA, Potomac Tennis Club. Home: 23 Infield Ct N Potomac MD 20854-5506 Office: Dept of Housing & Urban Devel 409 3rd St SW Ste 320 Washington DC 20024-3212

HEIGHAM, JAMES CRICHTON, lawyer; b. Sheffield, Eng., Feb. 9, 1930; came to U.S., 1940; s. Clement and Vida (Crichton) H.; m. Katherine Little, Feb. 24, 1962; children: Thomas K. Blake, Susan Blake, Christopher J. AB, Harvard U., 1951, LLB, 1954. Bar: Mass. 1954, U.S. Supreme Ct. 1970. Assoc. Choate, Hall & Stewart, Boston, 1957-59, 62-65, ptnr., 1966-97; asst. U.S. atty. Dept. of Justice, Boston, 1960-61; ret. ptnr. Choate, Hall & Stewart, Boston, 1997—; spl. asst. atty. gen. Commonwealth of Mass., Boston, 1968. Chmn. Planning Bd., Belmont, Mass., 1980-94, Capital Budget Com., 1980-94, chmn. fin. com., 1997—. 1st lt. USMC, 1954-57, lt. col. USMC ret. Mem. ABA, Mass. Bar Assn., Boston Bar Assn. Home: 62 Orchard St Belmont MA 02478-3510 Office: Choate Hall & Stewart 53 State St Exchange Pl Boston MA 02109

HEIGHT, DAVID JOSEPH, consumer products executive, lawyer; b. Glendale, Calif., Oct. 24, 1952; s. Lewis Henry Jr. and Mary Virginia Height; m. Maike Oberwelland, Aug. 2, 1991; 1 child, Paul Stephen. BS in Bus. Adminstrn., Regis U., 1982; JD, Am. Coll. Law, Anaheim, Calif., 1997. Lic. pvt. pilot. Nat. sales mgr. Banner Distbn. Co., Denver, 1971-78; dist. sales mgr. Nat. Silver, L.A., 1978-79; sales rep. M&M/Mars, Hackettstown, N.J., 1979-83; v.p. Banker Nicholls, Denver, 1983-84; regional mgr. Storck USA, LP divsn. August Storck KG, Chgo. and Berlin, 1985-90; regional dir. CCVentures divsn. Rich Food Products, Buffalo, 1990-91; nat. sales mgr. Bee Internat., San Diego, 1991-92; pres. Height Cons. Group, Chgo., 1992—; trustee Catherine Cook Sch., Chgo. Author: (pamphlet) Aviation Theft and How to Prevent, 1982. Mem. Ill. C. of C. Republican. Roman Catholic. Avocations: reading, history, travel, photography. Home: 436-A E North Water St Chicago IL 60611 Office: Height Cons Group 436-A E North Water St Chicago IL 60611

HEIKEN, JAY PAUL, physician; b. N.Y.C., Aug. 31, 1952; s. Martin and Sylvia (Fisher) H.; m. Barbara Ellen Rayburn, Dec. 11, 1976 (div. 1982); m. Francine J. Rosen, Apr. 29, 1990; 1 child, Lauren M. BA, Williams Coll., 1974; MD, Columbia U., 1978. Intern Emory U. Hosp., Atlanta, 1978-79; resident in radiology Columbia-Presbyn. Med. Ctr., N.Y.C., 1979-82; fellow abdominal radiology Mallinckrodt Inst. Radiology, St. Louis, 1982-83; asst. prof. Washington U. Sch. Medicine, St. Louis, 1983-87, assoc. prof., 1988-93, prof., 1993—; dir. abdominal imaging and co-dir. body computed tomography Mallinckrodt Inst. Radiology, St. Louis; mem. Washington U. Cancer Ctr. Author, editor: Manual of Clinical Magnetic Resonance Imaging, 1986, 2nd edit., 1991, Computed Body Tomography with MRI Correlation, 3rd edit., 1998; contbr. articles to profl. jours. Mem. AMA, Radiol. Soc. N.Am., Am. Roentgen Ray Soc., Am. Coll. Radiology, Greater St. Louis Soc. Radiologists, Soc. Computed Body Tomography, Internat.

Soc. Magnetic Resonance in Medicine, Soc. Gastrointestinal Radiologists, Assn. Univ. Radiologists. Avocations: skiing, tennis, softball, wine tasting. Home: 1801 Aston Way Chesterfield MO 63005-4579 Office: Mallinckrodt Inst Radiology 510 S Kingshighway Blvd Saint Louis MO 63110-1076

HEIKER, VINCENT EDWARD, information systems executive; b. St. Louis, Apr. 21, 1942; s. Anthony E. and Muriel E. (Evans) H.; m. Sheryl Ann Bunevac, Sept. 13, 1969; children: Stacie Marie, Vincent Edward. Student, St. Louis U., 1960-62; BS in Systems & Data Processing with honors, Washington U., St. Louis, 1972; MBA, So. Ill. U., 1974. Cert. data processor, systems profl. Russian interpreter U.S. Army Security Agy., 1962-65; from asst. sales mgr. to product line mgr. Emerson Elec. Co., St. Louis, 1966-73; systems analyst Mallinckrodt, Inc., St. Louis, 1973-74; dir. MIS Permaneer Corp., St. Louis, 1974-77; info. systems mgr. Boise Cascade Corp., St. Louis, 1977-83; MIS dir. The Sunmark Cos., St. Louis, 1983-87; v.p. MIS Payless Cashways, Inc., Kansas City, Mo., 1988-89; v.p. systems devel. Foxmeyer Drug Co., Carrollton, Tex., 1989-92; exec. cons. Just Tech. Assocs., 1993; v.p. MIS APS Holding, Inc., 1993—; career counselor, speaker. Reviewer EDP books; contbr. articles to profl. jours. Bd. dirs., chmn. mktg. com. Dallas Chamber Orch., 1991-93. With AUS, 1962-65. Mem. Mensa. Republican. Avocations: jazz, science fiction. Home: 1402 Saint Francis Ln Flower Mound TX 75028-8302 Office: APS Inc Ste 700 15710 John F Kennedy Blvd Houston TX 77032-2366

HEIKES, KEITH, science administrator; b. 1957. With Ralsten Purina, Chilicothe, Mo., 1978-81, Kabsu, Inc., Manhattan, Kans., 1981-90; with Noba Inc., Tiffin, Ohio, 1990—, now COO; v.p. internat. programs 21st Century Genetics; with Coop. Resources Internat., Shawano, Wis. Office: Coop Resources Internat 100 MBC Dr Shawano WI 54166*

HEIL, KATHLEEN ANN, librarian; b. Easton, Penn., Sept. 22, 1949; d. Peter J. and Emily Elizabeth (Miller) H.; m. John Edward Zampier, Aug. 21, 1971; children: Kirsten Lynn, Heather Ann. BS, Millersville State U., 1971; MLS, U. Md., 1987. Librarian Caroline County Sch. System, Denton, Md., 1971-73; library asst. Meml. Hosp., Easton, Md., 1973-76; grants admistr. Talbot County Public Library, Easton, 1976-80; cons. U. Md. Ctr. on Aging, College Park, 1979-84; grand adminstr. Somerset County Pub. Library, Princess Anne, Md., 1980-82; librarian U. Md., Solomons, Md., 1983—; sec. Talbot County Interagency Council, Easton, Md., 1977-79, sec. U. Md. Sys. Libarary Dirs., 1996-97. *Kathleen Heil has over 25 years experience in school, medical, public, special &academic librarianship. She is experienced in administration, grant administration, bid specification, collection development, long & short term planning, community liaison, consulting, instruction, marketing, and computerization as well as general library services such as reference, interlibrary loan, scheduling, and audiovisual services. She has published articles on automation projects - planning and implementation and conversion from one system to another, reprint file collections, Chesapeake Bay resources. Collection development and library automation have been the main thrust of her work and research. Her goal is meeting community needs most efficiently and effectively.* Contbr. articles to profl. jours. Pres. Calvert H.S. Band Boosters, Prince Frederick, Md., 1990-91; sec. South Middle Sch. Music Supporters, Lusby, Md., 1988-89, 92-93; lay leader Olivet United Methodist Ch., Lusby, 1984-91, 98—; leader-disciple Olivet-Solomons Charge, Lusby, 1996—. Recipient Curve Bar Girl Scouts, Easton, Penn., 1967. Mem. Internat. Assn. of Aquatic and Marine Sci. Librs. and Info. Ctrs. (treas. 1996-98). Avocations: gardening, costume design, choir. Home: 12963 Ottawa Dr Lusby MD 20657-3255 Office: UMCES Chesapeake Biol. Lab 1 William St Solomons MD 20688

HEIL, MARY RUTH, former counselor; b. Westerville, Ohio, June 8, 1921; d. George Walter and Bertha Ellen (Shrodes) H. BS in Edn., Ohio State U., 1944; MEd, Wayne State U., 1956; cert. advanced study, Western Carolina U., 1987; cert. theol. edn., U. South, 1987. Cert. counselor, tchr., Ohio, Ky., Mich., Fla., N.C. Tchr. 7th grade Cheshire (Ohio) Sch., 1942-43; tchr. biology, English Ohio Soldiers' and Sailors' Orphans' Home, Xenia, 1943-47; tchr. 7th grade Lakeview High Schs., Winter Garden, Fla., 1947-48; tchr. English, journalism Pine Mountain (Ky.) Settlement Sch., 1948-49; field and established camp dir. Columbus (Ohio) and Franklin County Girl Scouts, 1949-50; tchr. Mary Lyon Jr. High Sch., Royal Oak, Mich., 1950-56, 57-62, Coston Secondary Modern Girls' Sch., Greenford, Middlesex, Eng., 1956-57; tchr. English West Henderson High Sch., Hendersonville, N.C., 1962-65, guidance counselor, 1965-86. Chmn. Mayor's Com. Employment of Handicapped, Hendersonville, 1972-74; v.p. Mountain Ramparts Health Planning Bd., Asheville, N.C., 1972-76, Western Carolina Health Systems Agy. Bd., Morganton, N.C., 1976-82; bd. dirs., sec., com. chmn., Henderson County Dispute Settlement Bd., 1989-95; exec. com., bd. dirs. Western Carolina Presbyn. Retirement Com., 1987-94; active Henderson County Coun. Women, Hendersonville, 1994-96, treas.; mem.-at-large Pisgah coun. Girl Scouts U.S., 1994-98, chair fund devel. com., 1995-98, exec. com., 1997-98; bd. dirs. Henderson County Coun. on Aging, 1998—, chair nom. com., 1999. Named Civitan Citizen of Yr. Civitan Club, Hendersonville, 1986, Woman of Achievement Hendersonville, Bus. and Profl. Women's Club, 1978; recipient award Galludent U., Washington, 1986, Thanks Badge, Pisgah coun. Girl Scouts U.S., 1998, Cert. of Appreciation, Pisgah coun. Girl Scouts U.S., 1998; named to Hon., Order Ky. Cols., 1988. Mem. NEA, ACA, Royal Oak Edn. Assn. (pres. 1954-56), N.C. Assn. Educators (pres. dist. 1970-72), Henderson County Mental Health Assn. (bd. dirs. 1965-74), Alpha Delta Kappa (N.C. 1st v.p. 1978-80, state pres. 1980-82, S.E. region grand v.p. 1987-89), Kappa Delta Pi. Democrat. Episcopalian. Avocations: golf, bowling, raising Irish Setters, classical music. Home: RR 6 Box 137 Hendersonville NC 28792-9428

HEILBORN, GEORGE HEINZ, investments professional; b. Cologne, Germany, Feb. 27, 1935; came to U.S., 1941; s. Walter and Christine (Spiegel) H.; m. Phyllis Dorothy Ehrhardt, Sept. 30, 1972; children: Stephanie, Allison. BA, Northwestern U., 1956; AM, Harvard U., 1958. With Thompson Ramo Wooldridge Products Co., El Segundo, Calif., 1958-60; project mgr. Electronics div. Gen. Mills, Mpls., 1960-61, Philco Corp., Willow Grove, Pa., 1961-63; pres., chmn. Info. Processing Systems, Inc., Hackensack, N.J., 1963-92; pres. G.H. Heilborn & Co., Inc., 1992—; bd. dirs. Continental Info. Sys. Corp. Mem. bd. vis. Coll. Arts and Scis., Northwestern U., 1992—, alumni regent, 1997—; mem. grad. sch. alumni coun. Harvard U., 1993—, chmn., 1996-98; trustee Family Counseling Svc., Ridgewood, N.J., 1992-95; mem. fin. and investment com. Children's Aid and Family Counseling, N.J., 1996—. Mem. Computer Dealers and Lessors Assn. (founding mem. 1971, pres. 1980-82, chmn. 1982-84), Equipment Leasing Assn. Am., U.S.-USSR Trade and Econ. Coun., N.Y. Acad. Scis., Harvard Club of N.Y. Home: 385 Knollwood Rd Ridgewood NJ 07450-4814 Office: G H Heilborn & Co Inc One University Plz Hackensack NJ 07601

HEILBRON, DAVID M(ICHAEL), lawyer; b. San Francisco, Nov. 25, 1936; s. Louis H. and Delphine A. (Rosenblatt) H.; m. Nancy Ann Olsen, June 21, 1960; children—Lauren Ada, Sarah Ann, Ellen Selma. B.S. summa cum laude, U. Calif., Berkeley, 1958; A.B. first class, Oxford U., Eng., 1960; LL.B. magna cum laude, Harvard U., 1962. Bar: Calif. 1962, U.S. Dist. Ct. (no. dist.) Calif. 1963, U.S Ct. Appeals (9th cir.) 1963, U.S. Ct. Appeals (D.C. cir.) 1972, U.S. Ct. Appeals (8th cir.), 1985, U.S. Ct. Appeals (1st cir.) 1987, U.S. Ct. Appeals (10th cir.) 1988, U.S. Ct. Appeals (7th cir.) 1988, U.S. Ct. appeals (11th cir.) 1988, U.S. Dist. Ct. Nev. 1982, U.S. Dist. Ct. (cen. dist.) Calif. 1983, U.S. Supreme Ct. 1988, U.S. Ct. Appeals (3rd cir.) 1992, (6th cir.), 1995, U.S. Ct. Appeals (2d cir.) 1998, U.S. Ct. Appeals (5th cir.) 1998. Assoc. McCutchen, Doyle, Brown & Enersen, San Francisco, 1962-69; ptnr. McCutchen, Doyle, Brown & Enersen, 1969—, mng. ptnr., 1985-88; vis. lectr. appellate advocacy U. Calif., Berkeley, 1981-82, 82-83. Bd. trustees Golden Gate U., 1993-97, vice chair, 1995-97; bd. dirs. San Francisco Jewish Cmty. Ctr., 1974—, Legal Aid Soc., 1974-78, Legal Assistance to Elderly, San Francisco, 1980, San Francisco Renaissance, 1982—; pres. San Francisco Sr. Ctr., 1972-75; co-chmn. San Francisco Lawyers' Com. for Urban Affairs, 1976. Rhodes scholar. Fellow Am. Bar Found.; mem. ABA, Am. Coll. Trial Lawyers, Am. Arbitration Assn. (bd. dirs. 1986—, adv. coun. No. Calif. chpt. 1982—, chmn. 1987, jud. coun. 1986-88, exec. bd. 1994—, instr. and panelist arbitrator tng. programs), Am. Acad. Appellate Lawyers, State Bar Calif. (chmn. com. cts. 1982-83, bd. govs. 1983-85, mem. commn. on discovery 1984-86, pres. 1985-86), Calif. Acad. Appellate Lawyers, Bar Assn. San Francisco (chmn. conf. dels. 1975-76, pres. 1980). Democrat. Clubs: Calif. Tennis. Office: McCutchen Doyle Brown & Enersen 3 Embarcadero Ctr San Francisco CA 94111-4003

HEILBRON, JOHN L., historian; b. San Francisco, Mar. 17, 1934; s. Louis Henry and Delphine A. (Rosenblatt) H.; m. Patricia Ann Lucero, Mar. 25, 1959 (dec. Dec. 1993); m. Alison Margaret Browning, May 28, 1995. AB, U. Calif., Berkeley, 1955, MA, 1958, PhD, 1964; Laurea in Philosophy honoris causa, U. Bologna, 1988. Asst. dir. Sources for History of Quantum Physics, Berkeley and Copenhagen, 1961-64; asst. prof. history, philosophy of sci. U. Pa., Phila., 1964-67; asst. prof. history U. Calif., Berkeley, 1967-71, assoc. prof., 1971-73, prof., 1973-94, dir. Office for History of Sci. and Tech., 1973-94, class of 1936 prof. history and history of sci., 1985-94, editor Hist. Studies in Phys. Scis., 1980-94, vice chancellor, 1991-94, prof. emeritus, 1994; Andrew Dickson White prof. at large Cornell U., 1984-90; chmn. Acad. Senate Berkeley div. U. Calif., 1988-90; sr. rsch. fellow Worcester Coll., Oxford and Oxford Mus. for the History of Sci., 1997—. Author: H.G.J. Moseley, The Life and Letters of an English Physicist, 1887-1915, 1974, (with P. Forman and S. Weart) Physics circa 1900: Personnel, Funding and Productivity of the Academic Establishments, 1975, (with W. Shumaker) John Dee on Astronomy, 1978, Electricity in the 17th and 18th Centuries: A Study of Early Modern Physics, 1979; Historical Studies in the Theory of Atomic Structure, 1981, Elements of Early Modern Physics, 1981, (with R.W. Seidel and B.R. Wheaton) Lawrence and his Laboratory: Nuclear Science in Berkeley, 1931-61, 1981, (with B.R. Wheaton) Literature on the History of Physics in the 20th Century, 1981, (with Wheaton) An Inventory of Published Letters to and from Physicists, 1982, Physics at the Royal Society during Newton's Presidency, 1983, The Dilemmas of an Upright Man: Max Planck as Spokesman for German Science, 1986, (with E. Crawford and R. Ullrich) The Nobel Population, 1901-1937: A Census of Nominees and Nominators for the Prizes in Physics and Chemistry, 1987, (with Seidel) A History of the Lawrence Berkeley Laboratory, vol. 1: Lawrence and His Laboratory, 1990, Weighing Imponderables and Other Quantitative Science Around 1800, 1993, Geometry Civilized: History, Culture, Technique, 1998, The Sun in the Church: Cathedrals as Solar Observatories, 1999; editor: Benjamin Franklin's Briefe von der Elektrizität, 1983, (with T. Frängsmyr and R. Rider) The Quantifying Spirit in the 18th Century, 1990. Mem. Internat. Acad. History of Sci., History of Sci. Soc. (Sarton medalist), Brit. Soc. History of Sci., Am. Acad. Arts and Scis., Am. Philos. Soc., Royal Swedish Acad. Scis. (fgn.). Home: April House, Shilton near Burford OX18 4AB, England Office: Oxford Mus History of Sci, Broad St, Oxford OX1 3A2, England

HEILBRONER, ROBERT LOUIS, economist, author; b. N.Y.C., Mar. 24, 1919; s. Louis and Helen (Weiller) H.; m. Joan Knapp (div.); children—Peter, David; m. Shirley E. T. Davis. B.A., Harvard U., 1940; Ph.D., New Sch. Social Research, 1963; LL.D., LaSalle Coll., Ripon Coll., L.I. U., Wagner Coll., SUNY, Purchase, New Sch. for Social Rsch. Norman Thomas prof. emeritus New Sch. for Social Research, 1972—; lectr. univ., bus. and labor groups. Author: Future as History, 1960, Great Ascent, 1963, Limits of American Capitalism, 1966, Between Capitalism and Socialism, 1970, The Making of Economic Society, rev. edit., 1989, (with James Galbraith) The Economic Problem, rev. edit., 1990, The Worldly Philosophers, rev. edit., 1999, Between Capitalism and Socialism, 1970, An Inquiry into the Human Prospect, rev. edit., 1980, Business Civilization in Decline, 1976, Beyond Boom and Crash, 1978, Marxism: For and Against, 1980, (with Lester Thurow) Five Economic Challenges, rev. edit., 1987, Economics Explained, rev. edit., 1987, The Nature and Logic of Capitalism, 1985, The Essential Adam Smith, 1986, Behind the Veil of Economics, 1988, 21st Century Capitalism, 1993, Visions of the Future, 1995, (with William Millberg) The Crisis of Vision in Modern Economic Thought, 1996, Teachings from the Worldly Philosophy, 1996, also many articles and brochures in field. Chmn. bd. Town Sch., N.Y.C., 1963-73, Council Econ. Priorities, 1973-79. Served to 1st lt. U.S. Army, World War II. Decorated Bronze Star; recipient 1st prize Gerald Loeb award for disting. bus. and fin. journalism U. Mo. Sch. Journalism, 1979, UCLA Grad. Sch. Mgmt., 1984, 87; Guggenheim fellow, 1983; named first scholar of yr., N.Y. Coun. for Humanities, 1994. Fellow AAAS; mem. Am. Econ. Assn. (exec. com. 1972, v.p. 1983-84), Assn. for an Evolutionary Economy (Vedlen-Commons award 1993), N.Y. Coun. for the Humanities (Scholar of Yr. 1994), Phi Beta Kappa. Office: New Sch Social Rsch 66 W 12th St New York NY 10011-8603

HEILBRUN, CAROLYN GOLD, English literature educator; b. East Orange, N.J., Jan. 13, 1926; d. Archibald and Estelle (Roemer) Gold; m. James Heilbrun, Feb. 20, 1945; children: Emily, Margaret, Robert. B.A., Wellesley Coll., 1947; M.A., Columbia U., 1951, PhD, 1959; DHL (hon.), U. Pa., 1984, Bucknell U., 1985, Russell Sage Coll., 1987, Smith Coll., 1989, Berea Coll., 1991, New Sch. for Social Rsch., 1993, Lewis and Clark Coll., 1993, Pace U., 1996, Brown U., 1997; D.F.A. (hon.), Rivier Coll., 1986; DHL, Lewis and Clark U., 1993; DFA, U. St. Thomas, 1994. Instr. Bklyn. Coll., 1959-60; instr. Columbia U., N.Y.C., 1960-62, asst. prof., 1962-67, assoc. prof., 1967-72, prof. English lit., 1972—; Avalon Found. prof. humanities Columbia U., 1986-93; prof. emerita Columbia U., N.Y.C., 1986-93; vis. prof. U. Calif., Santa Cruz, 1979, Princeton U., N.J., 1981, Yale Law Sch., 1989. Author: The Garnett Family, 1961, Christopher Isherwood, 1970, Towards Androgyny, 1973, Reinventing Womanhood, 1979, Writing a Woman's Life, 1988, Hamlet's Mother and Other Women, 1990, The Education of a Woman: The Life of Gloria Steinem, 1995, The Last Gift of Time, 1997, Collected Stories by Amanda Croos, 1997; 12 novels as Amanda Cross, 1964 (recipient Nero Wolfe award 1981—). Guggenheim fellow, 1966; Rockefeller fellow, 1976; Sr. Rsch. fellow NEH, 1983; recipient Alumnae Achievement award Wellesley Coll., 1984, award of excellence Grad. Faculty of Columbia Alumni, 1984. Mem. MLA (pres. 1984), Mystery Writers Am. (exec. bd. 1982-84), Phi Beta Kappa. Office: Ellen Levine Literary Agy 15 E 26th St Ste 1801 New York NY 10010-1505

HEILBRUN, JAMES, economist, educator; b. N.Y.C., Dec. 13, 1924; s. Maurice L. and Hortense (Unger) H.; m. Carolyn Gold, Feb. 20, 1945; children: Emily, Margaret, Robert. B.S., Harvard Coll., 1945; M.A., Harvard U., 1947; PH.D., Columbia U., 1964. Asst. economist Prentice Hall Inc., N.Y.C., 1947-50; econ. analyst Chase Manhattan Bank, N.Y.C., 1951-55; instr. Columbia U., N.Y.C., 1961-65, asst. prof. econs., 1965-70; assoc prof. econs. Fordham U., Bronx, 1970-74, prof., 1974-97, prof. emeritus, 1997—; research dir. Harlem Devel. Project, Columbia U., 1967-68. Author: Real Estate Taxes and Urban Housing, 1966, Urban Economics and Public Policy, 1973, 3d edit., 1987, (with Charles M. Gray) Economics of Art and Culture, 1993. Served with USN, 1944-46. Fellow Com. on Urban Econs., 1960-61; fellow Ford Found., 1969-70; UCLA resident scholar, 1978. Mem. Am. Econ. Assn., Nat. Tax Assn., Regional Sci. Assn., Am. Real Estate Urban Econs. Assn., Assn. Cultural Econs. Home: 151 Central Park W New York NY 10023-1514

HEILES, CARL EUGENE, astronomer, educator; b. Toledo, Sept. 22, 1939; children: Tod Scott, Katrina Marie. B in Engring. Physics, Cornell U., 1962; PhD in Astronomy, Princeton U., 1966. Asst. prof., then assoc. prof. U. Calif., Berkeley, 1966-69, astronomy prof., 1970—; rsch. astronomer Arecibo (P.R.) Obs., 1969-70; vis. fellow Joint Inst. for Lab. Astrophysics, Boulder, Colo., 1989-90. Recipient Dannie Heineman prize in astrophysics Am. Astron. Soc., 1989. Mem. NAS, Am. Acad. Scis., Calif. Acad. Scis. Office: U Calif Dept Astronomy Berkeley CA 94720-3411*

HEILICSER, BERNARD JAY, emergency physician; b. Bklyn., Jan. 19, 1947; s. Murray and Esther (Dubrow) H.; m. Marcia Cherry, June 2, 1976; children: Micah, Seth, Jacob. BA, SUNY, Binghamton, 1968; MS, Hahnemann Med. Coll., Phila., 1971; DO, Coll. Osteo. Medicine/Surgery, Des Moines, 1976. Diplomate Am. Bd. Emergency Medicine. Instr. anatomy and physiology U. Pa. and Hahnemann Med. Coll., Phila., 1971-73; staff physician Va. Inst. Tech., Blacksburg, 1977-78; asst. prof. emergency medicine Chgo. Coll. Osteo. Medicine, 1979; emergency physician St. Margaret Hosp., Hammond, Ind., 1979-83, Michael Reese Med. Ctr., Chgo., 1989-91, Ingalls Hosp., Harvey, Ill., 1983—; project med. dir. South Cook County Emergency Med. Svc., Harvey, 1984—; mem. faculty Chgo. Osteo. Med. Ctr., 1987—; faculty trauma nurse specialist St. James Hosp., Chicago Heights, Ill., 1980—; preceptor nurse practitioners Purdue U., Hammond, 1981—; fellow MacLean Ctr. Clin. Med. Ethics, U. Chgo., 1993-94; chmn. ethics com., hosp. med. ethicist Ingalls Hosp., Harvey, Ill., 1994—; cons. The Nat. Bd. Osteo. Med. Examiners, Harvey, 1994—, ethics com. Am. Coll. Osteo. Emergency Physicians, 1997—; chmn. disaster com. Ill. Region 7 Emergency Med. Svcs./Trauma, 1997—. Vol. fireman Flossmoor (Ill.) Fire Dept., 1985—, Matteson (Ill.) Fire Dept., 1980—. Fellow Am. Coll. Emergency Physicians; mem. Am. Osteo. Assn., Nat. Assn. Emergency Med. Svcs. Physicians, Am. Coll. Osteo. Emergency Physicians (ethics com. 1996—), Nat. Assn. Emergency Med. Technicians, Prehosp. Care Providers Ill., Sigma Sigma Phi. Jewish. Avocations: running, basketball. Office: Ingalls Hosp One Ingalls Dr Harvey IL 60426

HEILIG, MARGARET CRAMER, nurse, educator; b. Lancaster, Pa., Jan. 17, 1914; d. William Stuart and Margaret White (Snader) Cramer; m. David Heilig, June 1, 1942 (dec. 1998); children: Judith, Bonnie, Barbara. BA in Psychology, Wilson Coll., 1935; MSW, U. Pa., 1940; AAS in Nursing Delaware County C.C., 1970. Registered nurse. Caseworker Children's Bur., Lancaster, Pa., 1935-37, Phila., 39-42; group worker Ho. of Industry Settlement Ho., Phila., 1937-39; curriculum chmn. Upper Darby Adult Sch. (Pa.), 1958-68; health asst., camp mother Paradise Farm Camp, Downington, Pa., 1960-70, camp nurse, 1970-78, infirmary dir., 1978-86; med. surg. nurse Crozer-Chester Med. Ctr., Chester, Pa., 1970; out-patient nurse Maternal Infant Care, Chester, 1971; coll. nurse Delaware County C.C., Media, Pa., 1971-76, dir. health svcs., 1976-84, health cons., 1984—, writer bi-weekly health newsletter Life Lines, 1973—, Health Svcs., 1988—, mem. spkrs. bur., 1975-93, asst. dir. health fair, 1979—; cons. Coll. Health Svc. for Middle States Evaluation, 1988. Author: First Aid Booklet, 1976; also articles and columns in health field. Nurse for health screening children's program Tyler Arboretum, Media, 1982-93, Update on Personal Health, Broadmeadows Women's Prison, 1973, 82; former leader Delaware County Council Girl Scouts U.S.; clk. Lansowne Friends Meeting, 1987-91, active newsletter, 1990-94; mem. Upper Darby Recreation Bd., 1956-58, Upper Darby Adult Sch. Bd., 1956-68, curriculum chmn., 1958-68; provider host home for fgn. exchange students, 1965-75; participant Audubon Ann. Bird Count, 1970—; coord., dir. Bi-Ann. Soc. of Friends Ch. Retreat, 1970-92; ARC Speakers' Bur.-AIDS; tchr. Beginning Birding course Del. County C.C.; bd. dirs. Ret. Sr. Vol. Program Del. County, 1991-97. Recipient Ollie B. Moten award Am. Coll. Health Assn., 1987, Disting. Nursing Alumni award Del. County C.C., 1995; inducted into Legion of Honor Chapel of Four Chaplains, 1980; honored by dedication Park Area on Campus Del. County C.C.; team leader homeless advocacy, Upper Darby, Pa., 1990-98; vol. Coun. Bd. Tyler Arboretum, 1989-94. Mem. ANA, Pa. Nurses Assn., Delaware County Nurses Assn. (membership chmn. 1977-78), Southeastern Pa. Coll. Health Nurses Assn. (co-founder, pres. 1983-85), Middle Atlantic Coll. Health Assn., Delaware Valley Soc. for Adolescent Health, Family Svc. Assn. Delaware County (bd. dirs. 1989-91), LWV, Women's Internat. League for Peace and Freedom (bd. dirs. Del. county group 1998—), Brandywine Conservance, Tour Guide, Phila., Historic Area, Arch St Friends,1994. Quaker. Avocations: birding, piano and choral music, nature walking, handicrafts (craft participant Pa. Renaissance Faire 1985—, writer health and safety column in Shire Chronicle for participants, 1993-96). Home and Office: 605 Mason Ave Drexel Hill PA 19026-2429

HEILIG, WILLIAM WRIGHT, coal and manufacturing company executive; b. Phila., Jan. 24, 1940; s. Alois Bube and Anna Marguerite (Wright) H.; m. Louise Fay Hamon, July 31, 1971; 1 dau., Elizabeth Anne. A.B. with dept. honors in econs, Hamilton Coll., 1962; M.B.A., U. Pa., 1964. C.P.A., Pa.; chartered fin. analyst. Auditor, mgmt. cons. Coopers & Lybrand, Phila. and Bermuda, 1964-70; asst. treas. Berwind Corp., Phila., 1970-75; treas. Berwind Corp., 1975-80, v.p., treas., 1981—. Mem. The Merion Cricket Club. Republican. Presbyterian. Clubs: Phila. Treasurers, Union League (Phila.). Home: 924 Winding Ln Media PA 19063-1656 Office: 3000 Centre Sq W Philadelphia PA 19102-2174

HEILIGENSTEIN, CHRISTIAN E., lawyer; b. St. Louis, Dec. 7, 1929; s. Christian A. and Louisa M. (Dixon) H.; children: Christie; m. Liselotte Warbanoff, Feb. 6, 1981. BS in Law, U.Ill., 1953, JD, 1955. Bar: Ill. 1956, U.S. Dist. Ct. (so. dist.) Ill. 1956, U.S. Ct. Appeals (7th cir.) 1956, U.S. Dist. Ct. (cen. dist.) Ill. 1960, U.S. Supreme Ct. 1978. Assoc. Listeman & Bandy, East St. Louis, Ill., 1955-61; sole practice Belleville, Ill., 1962-84; ptnr., pres. Heiligenstein & Badgley, Belleville, 1984-98; pres. C.E. Heiligenstein, P.C., Belleville, 1998—; chair audit com. Magna Group, Inc., 1994-98; bd. dirs. Union Planters Corp., Union Planters Bank NA, 1998—. Recipient Alumni of Month award U. Ill. Law Sch., 1982. Mem. Ill. State Bar Assn., Internat. Acad. Trial Lawyers (bd. dirs. 1991-97), St. Clair County Bar Assn., St. Louis Bar Assn., Inner Circle Advs., Am. Bd. Trial Advs. (nat. bd. dirs. 1992, pres. St. Louis, So. Ill. region 1993), Am. Acad. Profl. Liabilities Attys. (Nat. bd. dirs., 1990-99), ATLA (bd. govs. 1985-87), Ill. Trial Lawyers Assn. (bd. mgrs. 1975-88, pres. 1989), Mo. Athletic Club, Beach Club (bd. dirs. 1996, v.p. 1998). Democrat. Home: 5200 Turner Hall Rd Belleville IL 62220-5628 Office: Heiligenstein & Badgley 30 Public Sq Belleville IL 62220-1693

HEILMAN, CARL EDWIN, lawyer; b. Elizabethville, Pa., Feb. 3, 1911; s. Edgar James and Mary Alice (Bechtold) H.; m. Grace Emily Greene, Nov. 29, 1934 (div. 1952); children: John Greene, Elizabeth Greene; m. Claire Virginia Phelps, Oct. 10, 1952 (dec. June 1990); m. Marie Wilmot Russ, Nov. 23, 1990. *Carl's son John Heilman, Lafayette College 1964, PhD New York University 1973, professor of Political Science at Auburn University, became interim dean of Auburn's College of Liberal Arts in 1998. John's wife Ursula for many years taught German at Auburn. Their son David, graduated from Harvard College in 1995, is an analyst with Credit Suisse First Boston Technology Group in Palo Alto, California, working on mergers and acquisitions in the information technology industry. Their daughter Catherine, graduated from Wellesley College in 1998, is an investment banking analyst with Merrill Lynch in New York City, specializing in leveraged buyouts.* BA, Lafayette Coll., Easton, Pa., 1932, MA, 1933; JD magna cum laude, U. Pa., 1939. Bar: N.Y. 1940, Pa. 1940, Mass. 1973, U.S. Supreme Ct. 1960. Tchr. English Easton High Sch., 1934-36; assoc. Dwight, Harris, Koegel & Caskey, N.Y.C., 1939-42; atty. OPA, Washington, 1942-43, N.Y. Gov.'s Commn. to Investigate Workmen's Compensation Law, N.Y.C., 1943-44; assoc. Dewey, Ballantine, Bushby, Palmer & Wood, N.Y.C., 1944-59, ptnr., 1959-73; counsel to firm Csaplar & Bok, Boston and San Francisco, 1973-90; trustee Upsala Coll., East Orange, N.J., 1970-73. Fellow Am. Bar Found., mem. ABA, Nat. Trust for Hist. Preservation, Order of Coif. Republican. Episcopalian. Home: 5850 Meridian Rd Apt 508A Gibsonia PA 15044-9683

HEILMAN, E. BRUCE, academic administrator; b. La Grange, Ky., July 16, 1926; s. Earl Bernard and Nellie (Sanders) H.; m. Betty June Dobbins, Aug. 27, 1948; children: Bobbie Lynn, Nancy Jo, Terry Lee, Sandra June, Timothy Bruce. BS, Vanderbilt U., 1950, MA, 1951; PhD, Peabody Coll., 1961; postgrad., U. Tenn., U. Omaha, U. Ky.; LLD (hon.), Wake Forest U., 1967, Ky. Wesleyan Coll., 1980, James Madison U., 1986, U. Richmond, 1986; DHum. (hon.), Campbell Coll., 1971; LLD; LHD (hon.), Bridgewater Coll., 1991; DHL, DPS, Campbellsville Coll., 1995. Instr. bus. Peabody Coll., Vanderbilt U., 1950-51, bursar, 1957-60, adminstrv. v.p., 1963-66; instr. accounting Belmont Coll., Nashville, 1951-52; auditor Albert Maloney Co., Nashville, 1951-52; asst. prof. accounting, bus. mgr. Ky. Wesleyan Coll., 1952-54; treas. Georgetown (Ky.) Coll., 1954-57, Georgetown (Ky.) Coll. (Louisville Housing Project), 1954-57; coordinator higher edn. and spl. schs. Tenn., 1960-61; v.p., dean Ky. So. Coll., Louisville, 1961-63; prof. ednl. adminstrn. Peabody Coll. Vanderbilt U., Nashville, 1963-66; pres. Meredith Coll., Raleigh, N.C., 1966-71; pres. U. Richmond, Va., 1971-86, chancellor, 1986—, chancellor, interim chief exec. officer, 1987-88; bd. dirs. Cooperating Raleigh Colls., 1967-71; cons. indsl. studies in edn. and adminstrn., 1954—; dir., cons. long range planning confs. Fund Advancement Edn., 1960—; cons. acad. Ednl. Study Task, 1964-65; mem. Wake County-Raleigh City Sh. Merger Study Com., 1969; adv. com. N.C. Dept. Pub. Instrn., 1970; bd. dirs. Fidelity Bankers Life Ins. Co., A.H. Robins Co., Richmond, Ctrl. Fidelity Bank, Fidelity Fed. Savs. Bank, Bapt. Theol. Sem., Richmond; mem. adv. bd. Sta. WLEE Radio-TV; chmn. Cardinal Savs. and Loan Assn., Fast Fox, Inc., Office Am., Richmond, Direct Med. Inc., Cordell Med., Va. Escrow & Title co. The Phoenix Corp.; trustee, chmn. bd. advisors, mem. exec. com., devel. coms. Campbellsville (Ky.) Coll; instnl. cons. adv. bd. Paine Webber, Inc. Author: (with others) Sixty College Study, 1954; also booklets and articles. Chmn. blood com. for edn. ARC, 1971; mem. Nashville Urban Renewal Coordinating Com., 1965-66; ann. giving chmn. for N.C. Peabody Coll. Vanderbilt, U., 1970-72; mem. Friends of HOME, 1974—; chmn. trustee orientation com. N.C. Bapt. Conv., 1961; mem. edn. commn. So.

Bapt. Conv.; mem. bd. advisors Bapt. Hosp. Sch. Nursing, Nashville, 1956-60, 64—; mem. com. Met. Gen. Hosp. Sch. Nursing, 1965-68; mem. Federated Arts Coun. Richmond, 1975—, Robert Lee coun. Boy Scouts Am., 1975—; mem. devel. adv. bd. Va. Ctr. Performing Arts, 1980; bd. dirs. Bill Wilkerson Speech and Hearing Ctr., Nashville, 1963-64, Bapt. Theology Sem., Richmond, 1964, N.C. Symphony, United Fund Wake County, 1968-71, N.C. Mental Health Assn., 1969-71, Wake County Mental Health Assn., 1969-71, Va. Thanksgiving Festival, 1972, Richmond Pub. Libr., Richmond chpt. NCCJ, Ba. Inst. Sci. Rsch., 1971—, Leadership Metro Richmond, 1980—, Maymont Found., 1996—, Metro Bank, 1996—, chmn. of bd., 1997—; hon. dir. Richmond Ballet, 1971; bd. govs. United Givers Fund Richmond, 1971; trustee Inst. Mediterranean Studies, 1972—, E.R. Patterson Ednl. Found., 1972—, U. Richmond, 1973-86; bd. govs. Marine Corps. Assn., 1990; pres. Marine Mil. Acad., 1964, exec. v.p. bd., 1979—, chmn. bd. trustees, 1994, chmn. bd. trustees, 1994—, bd. dirs. USMC Def. Bat., Chairman, Marine Corps. U. bd. of trustees, Quantico, Va., Nat. Def. Univ. Found., So. Sem. Found., Bapt. Theol. Sem., Richmond, Va.; mem. adv. bd., chmn. devel. com., bd. dirs. Marine Hist. Found.. Served with USMCR, 1944-47. Recipient award Owensboro (Ky.) Jr. C. of C., 1953; Agrl. and Industry Service award U. Nashville, 1961; Outstanding Civic and Ednl. award Raleigh, 1970; Distinguished Salesman award Richmond, 1972, Disting. Alumni award Campbellsville Coll. and Peabody Coll. Vanderbilt U., Distinguished Citizen of Oldham County (Ky.) award, Va. Assn. Future Farmers Am. award, 1976, Disting. Citizen award Meredith Coll., 1977; named Ky. Col., 1969; Paul Harris Rotary fellow, 1970; Reverse Exchange Eisenhower fellow to Peoples Rep. of China, 1987; named Hon. Pres. Sino-Am. Cultural Soc., 1988. Mem. Internat. Assn. Univ. Pres.'s (N. Am. council 1976—), Nat. Fedn. Bus. Officers, Nat. Fedn. Bus. Officers Cons. Service, So. Assn. Colls. Women (pres. 1969), Nat. Soc. Lit. and the Arts, So. Univ. Conf., Sino Am. Soc. (hon. pres.), Am. Council Edn., Tenn. Edn. Assn., Ky. Ednl. Buyers Assn., Am. Assn. Pres.'s Ind. Colls. and Univs., Ky. Assn. Acad. Deans, Peabody Alumni Assn. Vanderbilt U. (exec. com), Nat., So. assns. coll. and univ. bus. officers, Assn. Governing Bds. Univs. and Colls., Coll. and Univ. Personnel Assn., Internat. Platform Assn., Nashville, Raleigh, Richmond, Va. chambers commerce, Nat. Assn. Ind. Colls. and Univs., Navy League U.S., Marine Corps League, Council Ind. Colls. in Va. (pres. 1974-76), Va. Found. Ind. Colls., Assn. Va. Colls., Assn. So. Bapt. Colls. and Schs. (pres. 1976), N.C. Found. Ch.-Related Colls., Assn. Am. Colls., So. Assn. Colls. and Schs. (trustee 1977), Phi Beta Kappa, Pi Omega Pi, Kappa Phi Kappa, Kappa Delta Pi, Delta Pi Epsilon, Omicron Delta Kappa, Beta Gamma Sigma, Lambda Chi Alpha (Achiever award 1993), Va. Bapt. Hist. Soc., English-Speaking Union, Newcomen Soc. N. Am. Democrat. Baptist (deacon). Clubs: Rotary (Raleigh) (bd. advisers Raleigh 1966-71), Execs. (Raleigh) (v.p., dir. 1971), City (Raleigh); Downtown (Richmond); The Club, Forum. Home: 4700 Cary Street Rd Richmond VA 23226-1703 Office: President's Office University of Richmond Richmond VA 23173

HEILMAN, PAMELA DAVIS, lawyer; b. Buffalo, July 2, 1948; d. George Henry and Natalie (Maier) Davis; m. Robert D. Heilman, June 27, 1970. AB, Vassar Coll., 1970; JD, SUNY, Buffalo, 1975. Bar: N.Y. 1976, Fla. 1980. Assoc. Hodgson, Russ, Andrews, Woods & Goodyear, Buffalo, 1975-84, ptnr., 1984—. Bd. dirs. United Way Buffalo, 1985-97, vice chmn., 1989-92, chair, 1993—, gen. campaign chair, 1992; bd. dirs. D'Youville Coll. Ctr. for Women in Mgmt., Buffalo, 1985-90. Mem. ABA, N.Y. State Bar Assn. (vice chmn., exec. com., sect. on internat. law and practice 1988-90), Fla. Bar Assn., Erie County Bar Assn. Office: Hodgson Russ Andrews Woods & Goodyear LLP One M&T Plz Buffalo NY 14211-1638

HEILMAN, ROBERT EDWARD, mechanical engineer; b. Hammond, Ind., Sept. 23, 1961; s. Robert Guthrie and Jane Eleanor (Tangerman) H.; m. Kimberly Kay Lewis, Dec. 14, 1984 (div. 1987); m. Ginger Sue Thompson, Oct. 29, 1994; children: Robert Joseph, Kelly Elizabeth. BS in Mech. Engring., Ohio State U., 1984. Mfg. engr. Ambox Inc., Houston, 1984-89; engr. Weatherford, Houston, 1990; CAD operator Atlas Bradford, Houston, 1991; design engr. Dril-Quip, Houston, 1991-97, Cameron Inc., Houston, 1997—. Active Big Bros./Big Sisters Houston, 1990—; chmn. advancement, com. mem. troop 1453 Boy Scouts Am., Houston, 1994—. Named Big Brother of Yr. Big Bros./Big Sisters Houston, 1995. Mem. ASME (assoc.). Republican. Avocations: skydiving, flying. Home: 6111 Valkeith Dr Houston TX 77096-4608 Office: Cameron Inc 13013 Northwest Fwy Houston TX 77040-6305

HEILMAN, THOMAS LEWIS, educational administrator; b. Pitts., Nov. 8, 1943; s. Clarence Lysle and Elsie Mae (Thomas) H.; m. Susan Aubrey Rawl, Aug. 29, 1987; children: Rebecca Aubrey Heilman, Jessica Lewis Heilman. BS, Juniata Coll., 1966; MA, Cen. Mich. U., 1981; PhD, Tex. A&M U., 1988. Cert. med. technologist. Lab. microbiologist Maury County Hosp., Columbia, Tenn., 1972-75; instr., med. lab. tech. Laredo (Tex.) C.C., 1975-77; program dir., med. lab. tech. Halifax C.C., Weldon, N.C., 1977-82, Tex. Southmost Coll., Brownsville, 1982-87; assoc. prof. med. tech. King Abdulaziz U., U. Ala. at Birmingham, Jeddah, Saudia Arabia, 1987-88; program evaluation specialist Houston C.C., 1988-90; dean instrn. and student svcs. Coll. of Health Scis., Roanoke, Va., 1990-93; chmn. health occupations and phys. edn. Shoreline C.C., Seattle, 1993-96; dean of instrn. Anson C.C., Polkton, N.C., 1996—. Pres. Anson County Arts Coun., Wadesboro, N.C., 1997—; lighting designer Sneydsboro, A Ripple on the River, 1996—, Anson County Cultural Players, Wadesboro, N.C., 1997; singer various civic and profl.choruses, Pitts., Houston, Roanoke, 1966-96. Mem. Nat. Assn. Instrnl. Adminstrs., Wadesboro Rotary. Lutheran. Avocations: camping, choral singing, philately, community theatre, visual performing arts. Office: Anson Comm Coll PO Box 126 Polkton NC 28135-0126

HEILMANN, CHRISTIAN FLEMMING, corporate executive; b. Penang, Malaysia, Apr. 26, 1936; came to U.S., 1977; s. Poul Bent and Hedvig Buchwald (Moller) H.; m. Marilyn Mildred Harter, July 9, 1959 (div. 1973); children: Christian Philip, Nicholas John, Claire Marie; m. 2d, Judith Lucy Tucker, Sept. 15, 1973; children: Per Flemming, Niels Henrik. M.A., Cambridge (Eng.) U., 1957. Mng. dir., CEO Metal Box South Africa Ltd., Johannesburg, 1970-77; trustee Nat. Devel. and Mgmt. Found. South Africa, 1970-75; v.p. Continental Can Co., Stamford, Conn., 1977-78; pres. Continental Group Europe, Brussels, Belgium, 1978-80, Continental Diversified Industries, Stamford, Conn., 1980-81; exec. v.p., chief adminstrv. officer Continental Group, Inc., Stamford, 1982-84; dir., pres., CEO Am. Can Can. Inc. (name changed to Onex Packaging Inc. 1986), Rexdale, Ont., 1984-89; N.Y. rep. Dansk Samvirke, 1996; chmn., CEO Brockway Standard, Inc., Atlanta, 1989-94, dir. and chmn. of adv. bd., Whitlock Packaging Co., Oklahoma, 1998— ret., 1994; mem. adv. coun. U. Toronto Bus. Sch., 1985-92; bd. dirs. Porter Chadburn, Inc., Omaha, Porter Chadburn PLC, London, O'Shaughnessy Funds, Inc. U.S. rep. Nat. Olympic Com. Denmark, 1994-96; attaché Danish Sports Orgn. for the Disabled 1996 Paralympic Games in Atlanta; bd. dirs. Am. Friends of Cambridge U., 1996—; mem. Cornell U. Coun., 1996—; bd. dirs. Jacob Riis Settlement House, N.Y.C., 1996—; trustee Am. Scandinavian Found., 1997—. Apptd. Knight of the Order of Dannebrog, Denmark, 1998. Mem. Danish-Am. Soc. (bd. dirs. 1990—, pres. 1996—), Danish Am. C. of C. (bd. dirs. 1995—), Greenwich Country Club.

HEILMEIER, GEORGE HARRY, electrical engineer, researcher; b. Phila., May 22, 1936; s. George C. and Anna I. (Heineman) H.; m. Janet S. Faunce, June 24, 1961; 1 dau., Elizabeth. BEE, U. Pa., 1958; MS in Engring., Princeton U., 1960, MA, 1961, PhD, 1962; DEngring (hon.), Stevens Inst. Tech., 1995, Technion, Israel Inst. Tech., 1997. With RCA Labs., Princeton, N.J., 1958-70; dir. solid state device rsch. RCA Labs., 1965-68, dir. device concepts, 1968-70; White House fellow, spl. asst. to sec. def. Washington, 1970-71; asst. dir. def. rsch. and engring. Office Sec. Def., 1971-75; dir. Def. Advanced Projects Agy., 1975-77; v.p. rsch., devel. and engring. Tex. Instruments Inc., 1978-83, sr. v.p., chief tech. officer, 1983-91; pres., CEO Bell Comm. Rsch., Livingston, N.J., 1991-96, chmn., CEO, 1997, chmn. emeritus, 1997—; adv. group on electron devices Office Undersec. of Def., 1989—; bd. dirs. TRW, Compaq Computer Corp., Automatic Data Processing; mem. bd. trustees MITRE Corp., 1993—; mem. Pres.'s Com. on Nat. Medal of Sci., 1992-94; mem. U.S. Adv.Coun. on Nat. Info. Infrastructure, 1994—; mem. Def. Sci. Bd., 1979—; sci. adv. bd. Nat. Security Agy., 1992—; mem. Los Alamos Nat. Security Adv. Bd., 1988—; vis. com. MIT, 1988—, Sch. Engring., 1989—. Mem. vis. com. MIT, 1988—, Sch. Engrig., 1989—. Mem. vis. com. MIT, Sch. Engring. and Applied Sci. of U. Pa. Recipient IR-100 New Product award Indsl. Rsch. Assn., 1968-69, Disting. Civilian Svc. award U.S. Sec. Def., 1975, 77, Arthur Fleming award U.S. Jaycees, 1974, Nat. medal of Sci., NSF, 1991, Indsl. Rsch. Inst. medal, 1993, Tech. Leader of Yr. award Industry Week, 1994. Fellow IEEE (David Sarnoff award 1976, Outstanding Achievement award Dallas chpt. 1984, Philips award 1985, Founder's award 1986, Japan Computers and Comm. prize 1990, Pres. Nat. Medal of Sci. 1991, Medal of Honor 1997), Am. Acad. Arts and Scis. John Scott award for sci. achievement 1996); mem. NAE (Founders award 1992), U. Pa. Alumni Assn., Princeton U. Grad. Alumni Assn., Sigma Xi, Tau Beta Pi, Eta Kappa Nu (Outstanding Young Engr. in U.S. award 1969, Vladimir Karapetoff Eminent Mem. award 1993). Office: Telcordia Tech Inc 445 South St Morristown NJ 07960-6454*

HEILNER, ALEXANDER JOHN, photographer, educator, artist; b. Mount Kisco, N.Y., Apr. 10, 1971; s. John Lauren and Mary Beth (Verlinde) H. BA, Princeton U., 1993; MFA, Sch. Visual Arts N.Y.C., 1998. Freelance artist N.Y.C., 1993—; freelance photographer Bklyn., 1993-94, San Francisco, 1994-96; lectr. Hudson River Mus., Yonkers, N.Y., 1993. Dir. (video) Feeling Spacial, 1996; exhibited photographs New American Landscapes, 1996, Landscapes: Presence, 1997, Interior Views: New Digital Photographs, 1998; designer website You Are Here, 1997. Avocations: music, skiing, cartography, psychology, relativity. Home and Office: 237 E 17th St Apt 120 New York NY 10003-3664

HEILOMS, MAY (MRS. SAMUEL HEILOMS), artist; naturalized U.S. citizen, 1932; d. Mark A. and Eugenie (Mogilensky) Levinson; m. Samuel Heiloms, June 12, 1938. Student, Hunter Coll., 1929, Art Students League. Adviser Ford Found. Program in Humanities, 1958, 59; invited juror exhbn. Am. Acad. Arts and Letters. Exhibited paintings, Pa. Acad., Bklyn. Mus., Cleve. Mus., Denver Mus., Silvermine Guild, Butler Inst. Am. Art, Nat. Acad., Nat. Arts Gallery, Mexico Mus. Fine Arts, Okla. City Mus., others, one-man shows, Monmouth Guild, 1960, Bennett Coll., 1961, Silvermine Guild Conn., Jeanette Nessler Gallery, N.Y.C., East Central State Mus., Okla., Cortland Art Center, N.Y., Paducah Art Guild, Ky., Warder Pub. Library, Springfield, Ohio, Five Corners Library, Hudson Gallery, N.Y.C., Muhlemberg Library, N.Y., Mus. Fine Arts, Mexico City, Nat. Mus. Sports, N.Y.C., Loeb Center, N.Y. U., 1979, 80, Custom House Twin Towers Gallery, N.Y.C., 1980, 81, others, also univs. and colls., traveling shows, Cleve. Mus. Art, Allbright Art Gallery, Buffalo, Dallas Mus. Art, Corcoran Gallery, Rochester Meml. Art Gallery, Columbia Mus. Art, also Lisbon, Portugal, Naples, Italy, Athens, Greece, Brussels, Belgium, also, Museo De Bellas Artes, Buenos Aires, Argentina, paintings permanent collections, Phila. Mus. Art, Samuel S. Fleisher Meml. Art Found., Ludwig Bowman Collection, Collectors of Am. Art, Norfolk Mus. Art, Safed State Mus., Israel, Bat Yam Museum, Israel, Okla. City Mus., Denny Collection, Kenny Internat. Found., also pvt. collections. Recipient prize for oil Jersey City Mus., 1950, 51, 59, 63, 1st prize, medal, 1956, prize Painters and Sculptors N.J., 1952, 55, 75, Bocour prize, 1958, prize for oil, 1960, 62, prize Bklyn. Soc. Artists, 1957, Atwood Klinger prize for abstract oil Nat. Assn. Women Artists, 1954, Patricia Murphy prize, 1958, E. Morse Genius prize for watercolor, 1960, M. Grumbacher prize oil, 1961, Sarah E. Good prize oil, 1962, Bainbridge prize watercolor, 1963, prize watercolor Bklyn. Soc. Artists, 1958, Nat. Soc. Painters in Casein, prize casein, 1962, prize, 1967, 70, 73, prize for oil Painters and Sculptors N.J., 1964, prize for watercolor Nat. Assn. Women Artists, 1966, M.H. Steiglitz prize Nat. Soc. Painters in Casein, 1966, prize (oil) Am. Soc. Contemporary Artists, 1967, 68, 71, 80, Windsor Newton prize, 1980, prize for acrylic Nat. Soc. Painters in Casein and Acrylic, 1974, memorabilia on microfilm Archives Am. Art, memorabilia on microfilm Smithsonian Instn., prize for oil Painters and Sculptors N.J., 1975, prize for oil Nat. Arts, 1975, 76, Bocour prize for oil Bergen County Mus., 1982, prize for oil Allied Artists, 1983, Emily Lowe award for oil Audubon Artists, 1988, Silver medal of honor for oil, 1990, prize for oil Allied Artists, 1993. Fellow Royal Acad. Arts (Eng.); mem. Am. Painters and Sculptors (dir.), Painters and Sculptors N.J. (hon. life pres.), Audubon Artists (v.p., Stephen Hirsch Meml. award Prize for Oil, 1987), Painters in Casein (dir.), Artists Equity, Nat. Assn. Women Artists, Bklyn. Soc. Artists, Casein Soc., Allied Artists (officer exec. bd.), Watercolor Soc. Ala., Am. Soc. Contemporary Artists (1st v.p.), Knickerbocker Artists, Silvermine Guild, N.Y. Soc. Women Artists (chmn. membership com.), Art Students League, Manhattan Gallery Group, Am. Soc. Contemporary Artists (Simmons award 1984, 1st prize for oil 1985). Studio: 4125 W Cherrywood Ln Milwaukee WI 53209-1003 *My aim, my goal, is to bring beauty, joy, a kindly understanding by sharing my observations, my philosophy, by painting with my heart and mind.*

HEIM, DIXIE SHARP, family practice nurse clinician; b. Kansas City, Kans., Feb. 28, 1938; d. Glen Richard and Freda Helen (Milburn) Stanley; m. Theodore Eugene Sharp, Aug. 12, 1960 (dec. Apr., 1972); children: Diane Yvonne Price, Andrew Kirk, Bryan Scot; m. Roy Bernard Heim, June 14, 1979. Diploma nursing, St. Luke's Hosp. Sch. Nursing, Kansas City, Mo., 1959; family practice nurse clinician, Wichita State U., 1974. Cert. advanced registered nurse practitioner, Kans. Nurse surgical ICU Staff Kaiser Found. Hosp., San Francisco, 1959-61; operating room supr. St. Luke's Hosp., Kansas City, Mo., 1962-63; emergency room, operating room supr. Lawrence (Kans.) Meml. Hosp., 1963-72; nurse clinician various doctors, Lawrence, 1973-81; nursing supr. spl. projects St. Francis Hosp. and Med. Ctr., Topeka, Kans., 1981-94; primary health care giver Health Care Access, Lawrence, 1992-94; nurse practitioner Dr. Glen Bair, Topeka, 1990-94; advanced registered nurse practitioner Dr. Jerry H. Feagan, Topeka, 1994, McLouth (Kans.) Med. Clinic, 1994—, Jefferson County Meml. Hosp., Winchester, Kans., 1995-96; family practice nurse practitioner Robert E. Jacoby II., M.D., Topeka, 1996—; preceptor nurse practitioner program U. Kans., 1993—; primary health care provider Jefferson County Law Enforcement Ctr., Oskaloosa, Kans., 1995—. V.p. Am. Bus. Women. Assn. Lawrence chpt., 1969, sec. 1968; vol. Children's Hour, Lawrence, 1965-72, Comty. Resource for Career edn., 1975-76; adv. bd. E. Ctrl. Kans. Econs. Opportunity Corp., Lawrence, 1993-95; mem. Rep. Women Douglas County, Lawrence, 1994—. Recipient Nursing the Heart of Health Care award Kaiser Permanente, 1994. Mem. ANA, Kans. State Nurses Assn. (v.p. 1958, chairperson fund raising campaign 1994, bd. dirs. 1996). Address: 540 Arizona St Lawrence KS 66049-2100 Office: Mathew Bohm MD 901 SW Garfield Ave Topeka KS 66606-1670

HEIM, KATHRYN MARIE, psychiatric nurse, author; b. Milw., Sept. 29, 1952; d. Lester Sheldon Wilcox and Laura Dora (Corpie) Wilcox Sears; m. Vincent Robert Gouthro, June 30, 1970 (div. 1976); 1 child, Robert Vincent; m. George John Heim, Sept. 17, 1977 (div. 1988). AS in Nursing, Milw. Area Tech. Coll., 1983; BS in Nursing, NYU, 1986; MS in Mgmt., Cardinal Stritch Coll., 1988; PhD in Human Behavior, Newport U., 1997. Cert. psychiatric and mental health nurse, AMA. Staff geriatric nurse Clement Manor, Greenfield, Wis., 1983; nurse, health educator Milw. Boys Club, 1983-84; nurse mgr. Milw. County Mental Health Complex, Milw., 1984—, mem. gero-psychiat. inpatient adv. com., 1986-87; RN Psychiat. Acute Care Day Hosp., 1992—; mem. nursing rsch. com. Milwaukee County Mental Health Complex, 1986-93; research on loneliness as it relates to mental health, 1989-92. Mem. wellness task force Milw. County Mental Health Complex, 1988-89, chairperson sensory deficit com. Geropsychiatry, 1989-90; active Boy Scouts Am., Milw., 1978-80. Mem. ANA (cert. gerontol. nurse), NAFE (network dir. Milw. chpt. 1982-92), Wis. Nurses Assn., NYU Alumni Assn., Cardinal Stritch Alumni Assn. (class rep. 1986-88), Milw. Area Tech. Coll. Alumni Assn. Avocations: yoga, jogging, reading, writing, dancing. Home: 226 N 63rd St Milwaukee WI 53213-4137 Office: Milw County Mental Health 9455 W Watertown Plank Rd Milwaukee WI 53226-3559

HEIMAN, DEBORAH REID, medical and legal consultant, rehabilitation consultant; b. Sharon, Pa., June 25, 1950; d. Harold and Jo Anne (Offie) Reid; m. Ronald T. Heiman, July 24, 1994. Student, Youngstown (Ohio) State U., 1969, Edinboro (Pa.) State U., 1974; diploma, Jameson Meml. Hosp., New Castle, Pa., 1981; BSN, Pa. State U., 1990, MEd in Health Edn., 1996. Cert. in med.-legal issues. Coord. ambulatory surgery UPMC Horizon, Farrell, Pa., 1981-90; owner, mgr. Med. Legal Cons., Hermitage, Pa., 1989—; dir. med. mgmt. Essex Rehab., Pitts., 1995—; dir. health and safety ednl. svcs. Ergonomics and Safety Technology, Inc., Pitts., 1996—.

HEIMAN, GROVER GEORGE, JR., magazine editor, author; b. Galveston, Tex., July 26, 1920; s. Grover George and Rose Mary (Ulch) H.; m. Virginia D. Williamson, Feb. 14, 1942 (dec.); children: Virginia, Grover, Deborah, Richard. Student, Lee Coll., 1937-40, U. Tex., 1940-41; B.S. in Commerce cum laude, U. So. Calif., 1959. With USAAF, 1941-45; News reporter Corsicana (Tex.) Daily Sun, 1945-47; commd. 2d lt. USAAC, 1942; advanced through grades to col. USAF, 1963; spl. asst. to USAF Chief of Staff, Pentagon, Washington, 1959-63; chief of info. Allied Air Forces So. Europe, Naples, Italy, 1963-66; chief mags. and booksdiv. Dept. Def., Pentagon, 1966-68; ret., 1968; mng. editor Armed Forces Mgmt. mag., Washington, 1968-70; assoc. editor Nation's Business mag., Washington, 1970-76, industry editor, 1976-78, mng. editor, 1978-80, editor, 1980-82, editor emeritus, 1982—; chmn. Naples Dependent Schs. bd., 1964-65. Author: (with Rutherford Montgomery) Jet Navigator, 1959, Jet Tanker, 1961, Jet Pioneers, 1963, (with Virginia Myers) Careers For Women In Uniform, 1971, Aerial Photography, 1973. Decorated Legion of Merit. Mem. Jet Pioneers Am., Nat. Press Club, Beta Gamma Sigma. Roman Catholic.

HEIMANN, JOHN GAINES, investment banker; b. N.Y.C., Apr. 1, 1929; s. Sidney M. and Dorothy V.B. (Gainesburg) H.; m. Margaret E. Fechheimer, Dec. 2, 1956 (div.); children: Joshua Gaines, Eliza Faith; m. Maria Cristina Anzola, Oct. 17, 1989. BA in Econs., Syracuse (N.Y.) U., 1950; LLD (hon.), St. Michael's Coll., 1979. V.p. Smith, Barney & Co., N.Y.C., 1955-66; sr. v.p., dir. E.M. Warburg, Pincus & Co., Inc., N.Y.C., 1967-75; N.Y. State supt. banks, 1975-76, N.Y. State commr. housing and community renewal, 1976-77; compt. of the currency Washington, 1977-81; co-chmn. exec. com. Warburg, Paribas, Becker, N.Y.C., 1981-82; dep. chmn. A.G. Becker Paribas Inc., Paribas Internat., 1982-84; vice chmn. Merrill Lynch Capital Markets, N.Y.C., 1984-91; chmn. exec. com. Europe/Middle East Merrill Lynch, London, 1988-90; chmn. global fin. instns. group office of chmn. Merrill Lynch & Co. Inc., N.Y.C., 1991-99; chmn. Fin. Stability Inst. of the Bank for Internat. Settlements, N.Y.C., 1999—; chmn. Merrill Lynch Internat. Bank, ML Capital Markets Bank Ltd., dir.; chmn. Fin. Svcs. Coun.; mem. exec. com. Inst. Internat. Fin.; chmn. Fed. Fin. Instns. Exam. Coun., 1979-81, Comml. Reinvestment Task Force, 1978-81, 20th Century Task Force on Internat. Debt Crisis; mem. Depository Instns., Deregulation Com., 1980-81; spl. advisor to Gov. on Commn. Banking, Ins. and Fin. Reform; lectr. Harvard U., Yale U., Columbia U., U. Calif., NYU; mem. adv. bd. sch. mgmt. Fishman-Davidson Ctr. for Study of Svc. Sector; chmn. Brit-N.Am. com.; trustee Nat. Policyss Assn.; vice chmn., chmn. securities subcom. Am. Banking and Securities Assn. of London; chmn. N.Y. State Supt.'s Adv. Com. on Transnat. Banking Instns., 1981; co-chmn. Derivatives Policy Group; mem. Fed. Res. Bank of N.Y.'s Internat. Capital Markets Adv. Com.; mem. adv. com. on fin. svcs. Dept. U.S. Treasury; mem. Prep for Prep; trustee The Urban Assembly; mem. governing coun. Ctr. for Study of Fin. Instns.; mem. adv. coun. Ctr. for Econ. Policy Rsch. Bd. dirs., treas. Group of Thirty; bd. dirs. Am. Ditchley Found., Citizens Com. for N.Y.C., Mcpl. Art Soc. of N.Y.; mem. N.Y.C. Housing Partnership, Citizens Com. for Affordable Housing; trustee Hampshire Coll.; mem. adv. bd. Wharton Sch.; bd. dirs. Arthritis Found., N.Y.; mem. Citizens Com. for N.Y. C., bd. dirs., Inst. Internat. Fin.; mem. adv. coun. Ctr. for Econ. Policy Rsch.; mem. Coun. Fgn. Rels., Mcpl. Art Soc. N.Y., bd. dirs. Named Housing Man of Yr. Nat. Housing Conf., 1976; recipient Bank Adminstrn. Key for Disting. Svc., 1980, Alexander Hamilton award Treasury Dept., 1981, Brotherhood award NCCJ, 1986, Pacesetter award Nat. Assn. Bank Women, Inc., 1986. Mem. Nat. Policy Assn. (vice chmn.), Fgn. Rels. Coun. Democrat. Club: F Street (Washington). Office: Fin Stability Inst 33 Liberty St New York NY 10045

HEIMANN-HAST, SYBIL DOROTHEA, language arts and literature educator; b. Shanghai, May 8, 1924; came to U.S., 1941; d. Paul Heinrich and Elisabeth (Halle) Heimann; m. David G. Hast, Jan. 11, 1948 (div. 1959); children: Thomas David Hast, Dorothea Elizabeth Hast-Scott. BA in French, Smith Coll., 1946; MA in French Lang. and Lit., U. Pitts., 1963; MA in German Lang. and Lit., UCLA, 1966; diploma in Spanish, U. Barcelona, Spain, 1972. Cert. German, French and Spanish tchr., Calif. Assoc. in German lang. UCLA, 1966-70; asst. prof. German Calif. State U., L.A., 1970-71; lectr. German Mt. St. Mary's Coll., Brentwood, Calif., 1974-75; instr. French and German, diction coach Calif. Inst. of Arts, Valencia, 1977-78; coach lang. and diction UCLA Opera Theater, 1973-93, ret., 1993, lectr. dept. music, 1973-93; interviewer, researcher oral history program UCLA, 1986-93; dir., founder ISTMO, Santa Monica, Calif., 1975—; cons. interpreter/translator L.A. Music Ctr., U.S. Supreme Ct., L.A., J. Paul Getty Mus., Malibu, Calif., Warner New Media, Panorama Internat. Prodn., Sony Records, 1986—; voice-over artist; founder, artistic dir. Westside Opera Workshop, 1986-94. Author of poems. Mem. KCET Founder Soc. UCLA grantee, 1990-91. Mem. AAUP, MLA, SAG, AFTRA, KCET Founder Soc., Sunset Succulent Soc. (v.p., bd. dirs., reporter, annual show chmn.), German Am. C. of C., L.A. Avocations: performing arts, literature, history, plants, designing and knitting sweaters. Home and Office: 1022 17th St Apt 7 Santa Monica CA 90403-4339

HEIMARCK, GREGORY JAMES, psychoanalyst, child psychiatrist; b. Chgo., Feb. 9, 1935; s. Theodore and Valfried Margaret (Hegge) H.; m. Claire Adrienne Gunderson, Sept. 1, 1956; children: Kaia, Tamara, Brita, Heather. BA cum laude, St. Olaf Coll., 1956; MD, Columbia U., 1960. Cert. psychoanalysis, 1970. Residency psychiatry and child psychiatry Columbia U., N.Y.C., 1963-67; staff psychoanalyst Columbia Psychoanalytic Ctr, N.Y.C., 1972—; instr. clin. psychiatry Columbia U., N.Y.C., 1973-81; adj. assoc. prof. psychiatry & religion Union Theological Sem., N.Y.C., 1978-81; asst. prof. clinical psychiatry Columbia U., 1981—; cons. child psychiatry Mary Bassett Hosp., Cooperstown, N.Y., 1967-68; vis. lecturer Mayo Clinic, Rochester, Minn., 1978. Sponsor Graphic Arts Coun. N.Y., 1986—; friend Bklyn. Acad. Music, 1988—. Capt. USAF, 1961-63. Mem. Am. Psychiat. Assn. (life), Am. Psychoanalytic Assn. (assoc., discussant), Internat. Psychoanalytic Assn., Assn. Psychoanalytic Medicine. Avocations: gardening, poetry, sailing. Home: 190 Leonia Ave Leonia NJ 07605-1639 Office: Gregory Heimarck 132 E 64th St New York NY 10021-7349

HEIMBERG, MURRAY, pharmacologist, biochemist, physician, educator; b. Bklyn., Jan. 5, 1925; s. Gustav and Fannie (Geller) H.; children by previous marriage: Richard G., Steven A.; m. Anna Frances Langlois Knox, July 12, 1964; stepchildren: Larry M. Knox, David S. Knox. BS, Cornell U., Ithaca, N.Y., 1948, MNS, 1949; PhD in Biochemistry (NIH fellow), Duke, 1952; MD, Vanderbilt U., 1959. NIH Postdoctoral fellow in biochemistry Med. Sch. Washington U., St. Louis, 1952-54; research asso. physiology Med. Sch. Vanderbilt U., 1954-59, asst. prof. to prof. pharmacology, and asst. prof. medicine, 1959-74; prof., chmn. dept. pharmacology, prof. medicine U. Mo., 1974-81; prof. and chmn. dept. pharmacology, prof. medicine, endocrinology and metabolism U. Tenn., Health Sci. Ctr., Memphis, 1981-96; Van Vleet prof. pharmacology U. Tenn., Memphis, 1986-96; Disting. prof. pharmacology and medicine U. Tenn., 1996—; Cons. NSF, NIH; cons., established investigator Am. Heart Assn.; attending physician U. Tenn. Hosps.; dir. lipid metabolism clinic U. Tenn. Med. Group. Contbr. numerous articles to profl. jours. Served with inf., AUS, 1943-45, ETO. Decorated Purple Heart, Bronze Star; recipient Lederle Med. Faculty award; research grantee. Fellow AAAS; mem. Am. Soc. Biol. Chemistry and Molecular Biology, Am. Soc. Pharmacology and Exptl. Therapeutics, Endocrine Soc., Am. Heart Assn., Am. Diabetes Assn., So. Soc. Clin. Investigation. Home: 105 Devon Way Memphis TN 38111-7711 Office: U Tenn Dept of Pharmacology 100 Crowe 874 Union Ave Memphis TN 38103-3514

HEIMBERGER, EDWARD ALBERT See ALBERT, EDDIE

HEIMBOLD, CHARLES ANDREAS, JR., pharmaceutical company executive; b. Newark, May 27, 1933; s. Charles Andreas and Mary Joseph (Corrigan) H.; m. Monika Astrid Barkvall, Sept. 22, 1962; children: Joanna, Eric, Leif, Peter. B.A. cum Laude, Villanova U., 1954; LL.B. cum laude, U. Pa., 1960; LL.M., NYU, 1966; postgrad., Hague Acad. Internat. Law, 1959. Bar: N.Y. 1962. Assoc. Milbank, Tweed, Hadley & Mc Cloy, 1960-63; staff atty. Bristol-Myers Squibb Co., N.Y.C., 1963-70, dir. corp. devel., 1970-73, v.p. planning and devel., 1981-84, sr. planning and devel., 1981-84; pres., health care group, 1984-88, pres., health care group and sr. v.p. planning and devel., 1988-89, dir., 1989; exec. v.p. Bristol-Myers Squibb Co., N.Y.C., 1989-92, pres., 1992—, pres. and CEO, 1994—; chmn., CEO, 1995—; bd. dirs. Mobil Corp. Trustee U. Pa., Am. Mus. Natural History; bd. dirs.

Phoenix House; chmn. bd. overseers U. Pa. Law Sch. With USN, 1954-57. Mem. Assn. Bar of City of N.Y., Riverside Yacht Club, River Club, Causeway Club. Home: Leeward Ln Riverside CT 06878-2409 Office: Bristol Myers Squibb Co 345 Park Ave New York NY 10022-6000*

HEIMBURGER, ELIZABETH MORGAN, psychiatrist; b. Atlanta, Apr. 23, 1932; d. Henry Durand and Lillian Elizabeth (Palmour) Morgan; div.; children: Elizabeth Morgan Whitaker, Homer Aggie Whitaker III, Margaret Diane Heimburger, Richard Ames Heimburger Jr., Katherine Durand Heimburger. BS, Ga. State U., 1963; MD, Med. Coll. Ga., 1967. Diplomate Am. Bd. Psychiatry and Neurology. Intern in internal medicine Med. Coll. Ga., Augusta, 1967-68, resident in gen. psychiatry, 1968-70; fellow in child and adolescent psychiatry U. Tex., Galveston, 1970-72; asst. prof. dept. psychiatry U. Tex. Med. Br., Galveston, 1972-73, assoc. prof., dir. residency tng., 1980-87; asst. prof., assoc. prof., dir. psychosomatic svcs. U. Mo. Sch. Medicine, Columbia, 1973-80, clin. assoc. prof. dept. psychiatry, 1987-97; pvt. practice specializing in adolescent psychiatry Columbia, 1987-97, Atlanta, 1997—; examiner Am. Bd. Psychiatry and Neurology, Chgo., 1977—; specialist, site visitor residency rev. Coun. Grad. Med. Edn., Washington, 1983—; exec. bd. Am. Assn. Dirs. Psychiat. Residency Tng., 1982-90; exec. coun. Tex. Psychiat. Soc., Austin, 1983-86; dir. confs., workshops on orgnl. and group dynamics. Editorial cons. bd. Am. Psychiat. Assn. Press., Inc., Washington,1 987-90; contbr. articles, scholarly papers to profl. publs. Bd. dirs. Mental Health Assn., Galveston, 1984-87, YMCA, Columbia, 1987-89. Grantee NIMH, 1978-80, 80-83. Fellow Am. Psychiat. Assn.; mem. Am. Soc. Adolescent Psychiatry, Am. Assn. Child and Adolescent Psychiatry (com.), A.K. Rice Inst. (bd. dirs. 1979-85, pres. Cen. States Ctr. 1979-88, bd. dirs. 1979-95), Am. Horticulture Soc. Episcopalian. Avocations: gardening, fitness, needlepoint. Home and Office: 686 Montana Rd NW Atlanta GA 30327-1536

HEIMBURGER, IRVIN LEROY, retired surgeon; b. Tsinan, China, Sept. 28, 1931; came to U.S., 1934; s. LeRoy Francis and Margaret Coleman (Smith) H.; m. Marcia Jean Enlow, June 30, 1963; children: Angela R., Jeffrey L., Christian I., Jenny E. BA, Drury Coll., 1953; MD, Vanderbilt U., 1957. Diplomate Am. Bd. Surgery, Am. Bd. Thoracic Surgery. Intern Vanderbilt U. Hosp., Nashville, 1957-58; resident in surgery Ind. U. Hosp., Indpls., 1958-63; thoracic fellow Leeds (Eng.) U. Hosp., 1963-64; from instr. to clin. assoc. prof. Ind. U. Med. Ctr., Indpls., 1964-80; med. staff St. Mary Med. Ctr., Evansville, Ind., 1966—, Deaconess Hosp., Evansville, Ind., 1966—. Contbr. articles to profl. jours. Pres. Vanderburgh County Med. Soc., Evansville, Ind., 1977-78. Fellow ACS (pres. Ind. chpt. 1977-78); mem. Cen. Surg. Assn., Internat. Cardiovascular Soc., Soc. Thoracic Surgeons, Midwest Surg. Soc.

HEIMERT, ALAN EDWARD, humanities educator; b. Oak Park, Ill., Nov. 10, 1928; s. Ewald W. And Gertrude (Hilbert) H.; m. Arline Ireland Grimes, Oct. 20, 1962; children: Andrew Jackson, Larisa Louise. AB, Harvard U., 1949, PhD, 1960; MA, Columbia U., 1950. Instr English, history and lit. Harvard U., Cambridge, Mass., 1959-60, asst. prof. English, 1961-65, assoc. prof., 1965-69, Powell M. Cabot prof. Am. lit., 1969—, prof. history and lit., 1996—, master Eliot House, 1968-91, chmn. dept. English, 1972-76; mem. Inst. Advanced Study Princeton (N.J.) U., 1960-61; vis. assoc. prof. history U. Calif., Berkeley, 1967; Lee Kuan Yew disting. visitor and lectr. Nat. U. Singapore, summer 1986; elected mem. Emmanuel Coll., Cambridge, Eng., 1986. Author: (with Reinhold Niebuhr) A Nation So Conceived, 1964, Religion and the American Mind: from the Great Awakening to the Revolution, 1966; editor: (with Perry Miller) The Great Awakening, 1967, (with Andrew Delbanco) The Puritans in America, 1985. Served to sgt. AUS, 1952-55. Mem. MLA, Am. Studies Assn., Am. Antiquarian Soc., South African Inst. for Race Rels. (hon. life). Home: 4 Robinson Cir Winchester MA 01890-3755 Office: Harvard U 572 Eliot Mail Ctr Cambridge MA 02138-7551

HEIMLICH, HENRY JAY, physician, surgeon; b. Wilmington, Del., Feb. 3, 1920; s. Philip and Mary (Epstein) H.; m. Jane Murray, June 3, 1951; children: Philip, Peter, Janet and Elisabeth (twins). B.A., Cornell U., 1941, M.D., 1943; D.Sc. (hon.), Wilmington Coll., 1981, Adelphi U., 1982, Rider Coll., 1983; DSc (hon.), Alfred U., 1993. Diplomate: Am. Bd. Surgery, Am. Bd. Thoracic Surgery. Intern Boston City Hosp., 1944; resident VA Hosp., Bronx, 1946-47, Mt. Sinai Hosp., N.Y.C., 1947-48, Bellevue Hosp., N.Y.C., 1948-49, Triboro Hosp., Jamaica, N.Y., 1949-50; attending surgeon div. surgery Montefiore Hosp., N.Y.C., 1950-69; dir. surgery Jewish Hosp., Cin., 1969-77; prof. advanced clin. scis. Xavier U., Cin., 1977-89; assoc. clin. prof. surgery U. Cin. Coll. Medicine, 1969-78; pres. Heimlich Inst.; mem. Pres.'s Commn. on Heart Disease, Cancer and Stroke, 1965; pres. Nat. Cancer Found., 1963-68, bd. dirs., 1960-70; founder Heimlich Inst. Found. Author: Postoperative Care in Thoracic Surgery, 1962, (with M.O. Cantor, C.H. Lupton) Surgery of the Stomach, Duodenum and Diaphragm, Questions and Answers, 1965; also; contbr. chpts. to books; numerous articles to med. jours.; Producer: films Esophageal Replacement with a Reversed Gastric Tube (awarded Medaglione Di Bronzo Minerva 1961), Reversed Gastric Tube Esophagoplasty Using Stapling Technique, How to Save a Choking Victim: The Heimlich Maneuver, 1976, 2d edit., 1982, How To Save a Drowning Victim: The Heimlich Maneuver, 1981, Stress Relief: The Heimlich Method, 1983; video: Dr. Heimlich's Home First Aid Video, 1989 (Vira award 1989); mem. editorial bd.: films Reporte's Medicos. Bd. dirs. Community Devel. Found., 1967-70; bd. dirs. Save the Children Fedn., 1967-68, United Cancer Council, 1967-70. Served to lt. (s.g.) USNR, 1944-46. Recipient Lasker award for Pub. Svc., Lasker Found., 1984, China-Burma-India Vets. Assn. Amercanism award, 1988; 1st recipient Heimlich Humanitarian award Spirit of Am. Festival, 1994; Heimlich Inst. established in perpetuity by Deaconness Assns., Inc. Fellow ACS (chpt. pres. 1964), Am. Coll. Chest Physicians, Am. Coll. Gastroenterology; mem. Soc. Thoracic Surgeons (founding mem.), AMA (cons. to jour.), Cin. Soc. Thoracic Surgery, N.Y. Soc. Thoracic Surgery, Soc. Surgery Alimentary Tract, Am. Gastroent. Assn., Pan Am. Med. Assn., Collegium Internat. Chirurgiae Digestive, Central Surg. Assn. Developer Heimlich Operation (reversed gastric tube esophagoplasty) for replacement of esophagus; inventor Heimlich chest drain valve, Heimlich Micro-Trach (HMT) for COPD, emphysema and cystic fibrosis; developer Heimlich Maneuver to save lives of victims of food choking and drowning and prevents and overcomes asthma attacks (listed in Random House, Oxford Am. and Webster dictionaries); developer Computers for Peace, a program to maintain peace throughout world and A Caring World. Office: Heimlich Inst Deaconess Hosp 311 Straight St Cincinnati OH 45219-1018 *I have never been satisfied with existing methods and seek to simplify and improve them. After devising an operation for replacement of the esophagus, I became aware that with one such discovery I could help more people in a few weeks than in my entire lifetime as a surgeon in the operating room. The Heimlich Maneuver, which saves thousands of choking and drowning victims as well as asthmatics annually, confirmed this realization. My ultimate goal is to avoid needless death and promote well-being for the largest number of people by establishing a philosophy that will eliminate war and promote a caring world. Seeking to find a cure for cancer, AIDS, and Lyme disease through malariotherapy.*

HEIMLICH, RICHARD ALLEN, geologist, educator; b. Elizabeth., N.J., Aug. 8, 1932; s. Simon William and Sidnie W. (Simon) H.; m. Charlee Marcus, July 23, 1961; children: Steven A., John P. B.S., Rutgers U., 1954; M.S., Yale U., 1955, Ph.D. (J.D. Dana scholar 1956), 1959. Mem. faculty Kent (Ohio) State U., 1961—, prof. geology, 1970—, chmn. dept., 1976-92. Author: Field Guide: Southern Great Lakes, 1977, Field Guide: The Black Hills, 1980; also papers and articles. Served with Ordnance Corps AUS, 1959-60. Grantee NSF, 1967-69, 69-71, Los Alamos Nat. Lab., 1979, 80, U.S. Dept. Edn., 1979-92. Fellow Geol. Soc. Am.; mem. Am. Inst. Profl. Geologists, No. Ohio Geol. Soc., Sigma Xi. Home: 1596 Woodway Rd Kent OH 44240-5914 Office: Kent State U Dept Geology Kent OH 44242

HEIN, DAVID, religion educator; b. Balt., Oct. 2, 1954; s. Charles L. and Ruth Zeller (Giese) H. BA, U. Va., 1976, PhD, 1982; MA, U. Chgo., 1977. English master Blue Ridge Sch., Dyke, Va., 1982-83; asst. prof. religion Hood Coll., Frederick, Md., 1983-89; assoc. prof. religion Hood Coll., Frederick, 1989-94, prof. religion, 1994—, chair dept. religion and philosophy, 1988—; vis. prof. S.D. State U., Brookings, 1989; vis. lectr. Coll. William and Mary, Williamsburg, Va., 1994; mem. archives adv. com. Episcopal Diocese of Md., Balt., 1995—. Co-author: Essays on Lincoln's Faith and Politics, 1983; editor: A Student's View of the College of St. James, 1988, Readings in Anglican Spirituality, 1991; mem. editl. bd. Md. Hist. Mag., 1991-95, Anglican and Episcopal History, 1991—; contbr. articles to profl. jours. Trustee St. Paul's Sch., Brooklandville, Md., 1996—. Recipient Milo P. Jewett prize U. Chgo., 1977. Laughlin award for tchg., scholarship and svc. Hood Coll., 1997; English-Speaking Union scholar Oxford (Eng.) U., 1975; fellow-in-residence U. of the South, Sewanee, Tenn., 1997. Mem. Am. Soc. Ch. History, Hist. Soc. of the Episcopal Ch., Omicron Delta Kappa. Episcopalian. Home: 305 Grove Blvd Frederick MD 21701-4812 Office: Hood Coll 401 Rosemont Ave Frederick MD 21701-8575

HEIN, FRITZ EUGEN, engineer, consultant, architect; b. Bruex, Czechoslovakia, Mar. 25, 1926; came to U.S., 1956; s. Friedrich and Maria (Lehner) H.; m. Gertraud Marie Conrad, Dec. 28, 1954; children: Carmen, Wolfgang. Student, O.v. Miller, Munich, 1953. Registered architect, Bavaria, Wis.; registered profl. engr., Wis. Architect, engr. U. Wuerzburg, 1953-56; design engr. USN, Great Lakes, Ill., 1956-60; dir. of design USN, Washington and Madrid, 1971-79; facilities engr. U.S. Army, Karlsruhe, Fed. Republic of Germanay, 1979-82; chief engr. C.E., 1984-88; project mgr. C.E., Frankfurt, Fed. Republic of Germany, 1982-84; pvt. practice cons. Naples, Fla., 1988—. Author: Drydock Launch Facilities, 1961, Guide to Airborne Sound Control, 1971, Design Manual DM 1 & 18, 1974, Navy Civil Engineer, 1977, The Military Engineer, 1980. Bd. dirs. Bldg. Rsch. Adv. Bd., Washington, 1976-79; advisor Camp David constrn. modifications White House, Washington, 1962. Decorated D.S.M.; recipient Appreciation award U.S. Asst. Sec. of Def., 1976. Mem. ASTM (com. Washington chpt. 1976-79), Am. Nat. Metric Coun., Acoustial Soc. Am., Joint U.S./Spain Mil. Group, Contamination Control Assn. Achievements include development of air to ground missiles, 1945; design of the Geodesic Dome for the New South Pole Station; introduction of cogeneration power plants in U.S.; conception of a launch facility at equatorial sites which was executed in Kourou by European Space Agy. Home: 9701 Raven Wing Dr Chesterfield VA 23832-3860 Office: Wettersteinplatz 2, 81547 Munich Germany

HEIN, HERMAN AUGUST, physician; b. Olin, Iowa, July 30, 1936; s. Herman Fredrick and Marie Meta (Reyelts) H.; m. Carol Rae Bergquist, Aug. 31, 1958; children: Tracey, Paul. BA, Wartburg Coll., 1959; MD, U. Iowa, 1963. Diplomate Am. Bd. Pediatrics. Instr. Univ. of Tex. Coll. of Medicine, Dallas, 1964-65; pediatrician, pvt. practice Dubuque, Iowa, 1968-73; dir. Iowa Statewide Perinatal Care Program, Iowa City, 1973—; asst. prof. Univ. of Iowa Coll. of Medicine, Iowa City, 1973-76, assoc. prof., 1976-81, prof., 1981—; spl. cons. Iowa Dept. Pub. Health, Des Moines, 1990—. Med. cons. SIDS Alliance, Des Moines, 1996—; apptd. to Nat. Commn. to Prevent Infant Mortality, Washington, 1987-93. Recipient Nat. Unsung Hero award Newsweek Mag., 1988. Fellow Am. Acad. Pediatrics, Am. Pediat. Soc.; mem. Iowa Med. Soc. Independent. Lutheran. Avocations: golf, cooking. Office: Dept Pediatrics 200 Hawkins Dr Iowa City IA 52242-1009

HEIN, JOHN WILLIAM, dentist, educator; b. Chester, Mass., Sept. 29, 1920; s. Rudolf Jacob and Mercedes Viola H.; m. Jeannette Marie BeVier, Dec. 16, 1944. BS, Am. Internat. Coll., 1941; DMD, Tufts U., 1944; PhD, U. Rochester, 1952; AM (hon.), Harvard, 1962; DSc (hon.), Am. Internat. Coll., 1979, Tufts U., 1993. Student instr. oral pathology Tufts Coll. Dental Sch., 1943-44; head div. dental research U. Rochester, 1948-52, sr. fellow dental research, 1949-52, instr. pharmacology, 1951-53, asst. prof. dental research, 1952-55, asst. prof. pharmacology, 1954-55, chmn. dept. dentistry and dental research, 1952-55; instr. anatomy and physiology Eastman Sch. Dental Hygiene, 1950-55, lectr. dental research, 1953-55; research specialist Bur. Biol. Research, Rutgers U., 1955-59; dental dir. Colgate Palmolive Co., 1955-59; prof. preventive dentistry, dean Sch. Dental Medicine, Tufts U., 1959-62; dir. Forsyth Dental Center, 1962-91; prof. dentistry Harvard Dental Sch., 1962-67. Trustee Am. Internat. Coll., 1960-76. Served to capt. AUS, 1942-47. Fellow AAAS, Internat. Coll. Dentists (regent 1967-72, pres. U.S. 1975-76, internat. pres. 1983-84); mem. ADA, Mass. Dental Soc. (pres. 1964-65), Internat. Assn. Dental Research (treas. 1978-82), Am. Assn. Dental Research (treas. 1985-88), Am. Acad. Dental Sci., New Eng. Dental Soc. (hon. pres. 1978), Am. Soc. Dentistry for Children, Assn. Ind. Research Insts. (1st v.p. 1980, pres. 1981-83), Royal Soc. Medicine (hon.), Sigma Xi, Omicron Kappa Upsilon, Delta Sigma Delta. Club: Wellesley. Home and Office: 3 Bridge St Medfield MA 02052-1503

HEIN, KAREN KRAMER, pediatrician, epidemiologist; b. N.Y.C., Feb. 2, 1944; d. Irving W. and Ruth (Eisenberg) Kramer: m. Ralph Dell, Aug. 28, 1983; children: Ethan, Molly. BA, U. Wis., 1966; B of Med. Sci., Dartmouth Med. Sch., 1968; MD, Columbia U., 1970. Intern Bronx Mcpl. Hosp., Bronx (N.Y.) Mcpl. Hosp. Ctr., 1970; resident Bronx (N.Y.) Mcpl. Hosp. Ctr., Bronx, 1971-73; dir. adolescent AIDS program Montefiore Med. Ctr., N.Y.C., 1987-94; prof. pediatrics Albert Einstein Coll. Medicine, N.Y.C., 1991-94, prof. epidemiology and social medicine, 1993-94, clin. prof. pediatrics, epidemiology and social medicine, 1995-98; exec. officer Inst. Medicine NRC, Washington, 1995—; pres. William T. Grant Found., N.Y.C., 1998—, 1998—; cons. N.Y.C. Dept. Health, 1980-85, N.Y.C. Bd. Edn., 1987-93; bd. dirs. Dartmouth Med. Sch., Hanover, N.Y. Author: AIDS: Trading Fears for Facts Consumer Reports Books, 1989; contbr. articles to profl. jours. Named Outstanding Physician, Dept. Health and Human Svcs., 1989, Adminstrs. Citation award, 1993. Fellow Am. Bd. Pediatrics; mem. Am. Pediatric Soc., Soc. for Pediatric Rsch., Am. Acad. Pediatrics, Soc. for Adolescent Medicine (pres. 1992-93). Office: William T Grant Found 570 Lexington Ave Fl 18 New York NY 10022-6837 also: William T Grant Found 570 Lexington Ave New York NY 10022-6837

HEIN, LAURIE SNOW, artist, educator; b. Lakewood, N.J., Feb. 23, 1949; d. Lawrence Parlin and Jeanne Marion)Opdyke) Snow; m. William L. Casey (div.); 1 child, Shannon; m. Robert Carl Hein, Dec. 13, 1976; children: Karl, Caryn, Kristin, Lauren. Student, Columbus Coll. Art & Design, 1967-68, Enterprise State Coll., 1969-70, Palm Beach Jr. Coll., 1970-71. Instr. art Delray (Fla.) Elem. Sch., 1974; owner, ptnr. Casey & Jolly Gallery, Palm Beach, Fla., 1974-76, instr., portrait artist, 1974-88; instr. workshops Duluth (Ga.) Art Club, 1991, 95, DeKalb County (Ga.) Art, 1993; illustrator, fine artist ARTS Unique, Cooksville, Tenn., 1993—; instr. Everglades Club, Palm Beach, 1990—, Lost Tree Village, North Palm Beach, Fla., 1991—, Hope Sound Art Club, Jupiter, Fla., 1995, Symbionic Gallery, Stuart, Fla., 1995—; lectr. workshops Portrait Soc. Atlanta, 1997; commd. artist Reminiscence Gallery, Lake Worth, Fla., 1972-74; instr. oil painting Graham Ingels Studio, 1973-79; presenter workshops Gwinnet County (Ga.) Coun. of Art, 1993, pvt. classes, Atlanta, 1995. Group shows include Ann Arbor State Street, Winter Park Art Festival, Gasparilla Art Festival, Naples (Fla.) Nat. Art Festival; represented in permanent collections Chgo. Tribune, Powers Crossroads, Ga. Baptist. Mem. Am. Soc. Portrait Artists, Washington Soc. Portrait Artists, Atlanta Portrait Soc., Palm Beach Watercolor Soc. (v.p. 1995), Soc. Classical Realism. Avocations: raising haflinger horses, art festivals, gardening. Home and Studio: 5219 Melaleuca Ln Lake Worth FL 33463-5205

HEIN, LEONARD WILLIAM, accounting educator; b. Forest Park, Ill., Feb. 17, 1916; s. Harry Christian and Clara Antoinette (Klein) H.; m. Akemi Kishi, Feb. 28, 1981. B.S.C., Loyola U., Chgo., 1952; M.B.A., U. Chgo., 1954; Ph.D. (U. Calif. at Los Angeles Bus. Sch. Alumni Assn. fellow, Univ. fellow, Ford Found. fellow), U. Calif. at Los Angeles, 1962. C.P.A., Ill. With San. Dist. Chgo., 1941-56; asst. prof. accounting Calif. State U. at Los Angeles, 1956-59, asso. prof. accounting, 1959-65, prof. accounting, 1965—, coordinator program bus. info. systems, 1956-73, asst. dean grad. studies, 1963-72; Mem. nat. panel arbitrators Am. Arbitration Assn., 1972—. Author: Introduction to Electronic Data Processing for Business, 1961, Quantitative Approach to Managerial Decisions, 1967, Contemporary Accounting and the Computer, 1969, The British Companies Acts and the Practice of Accountancy, 1844-1962, 1978; Contbr. articles to profl. jours. Served with USNR, 1942-45. Mem. Am. Inst. C.P.A.'s, Am. Accounting Assn., Calif. Soc. C.P.A.'s, Beta Gamma Sigma, Beta Alpha Psi, Alpha Kappa Psi, Phi Kappa Phi. Home: 1225 N Granada Ave Alhambra CA 91801-1154 Office: Calif State U 5151 State University Dr Los Angeles CA 90032-4226

HEIN, TODD JONATHAN, accountant; b. Encino, Calif., May 11, 1960; s. Walter Adolph Jr. and Valerie Wynann (Phipps) H.; m. Jennifer Loomis, Jan. 5, 1991; 1 child, MacKenzie James. BA in Econs., UCLA, 1982; cert. in fin. planning, U. So. Calif., 1987. CPA, Calif., CFP, CLU. Account analyst Exec. Life Ins. Co., L.A., 1983; acct. Satriano & Young, L.A., 1983-85; personal acct. Barron Hilton; pres. Hilton Hotels Corp., Beverly Hills, Calif., 1985-86; acct. Gursey, Schneider & Co., L.A., 1987-88; sr. acct. Gursey, Schneider & Co., LLP, L.A., 1996-98; v.p. Hein Fin. Svcs., Inc., L.A., 1988-89; spl. agt. Northwestern Mut. Life, Woodland Hills, Calif., 1989-96; sr. acct. Gursey, Schneider & Co., LLP, L.A., 1996-98; sr. staff accountant Engel, Kalvin, McMillan & Kipper, LLP, L.A., 1998-99; sr. staff acct. Sher, Sherr, Gelb & Co., Sherman Oaks, Calif., 1999—. Life Underwriter Tng. Coun. fellow. Mem. AICPA, Calif. Soc. CPAs, Soc. Fin. Svc. Profls., Inst. Cert. Fin. Planners,Sierra Club. Avocations: hiking, reading, tennis, golf, gardening. Office: Sher Sherr Gelb & Co 15060 Ventura Blvd Ste 300 Sherman Oaks CA 91403

HEINDEL, NED DUANE, chemistry educator; b. Red Lion, Pa., Sept. 4, 1937; s. Penrose Horace and Dorothy May (Strayer) H.; m. Linda Clarella Heefner, Aug. 26, 1959. B.S., Lebanon Valley Coll., Annville, Pa., 1959; D.Sc. (hon.), Lebanon Valley Coll., 1985; M.S., U. Del., 1961, Ph.D., 1963; postdoctoral studies, Princeton U., 1964; DSc (hon.), Albright Coll., 1993. Instr. chemistry U. Del., 1962-63; asst. prof. chemistry Ohio U., Ironton, 1964-65, Marshall U., Huntington, W. Va., 1964-66; asst. prof. to assoc. prof. chemistry Lehigh U., Bethlehem, Pa., 1966-73, H.S. Bunn prof., 1973—, dir. Ctr. Health Scis., 1980-88; prof. nuclear medicine Hahnemann Med. U., Phila., 1971—; cons. Pa. State Police Crime Lab., Bethlehem, 1975-88; cons. safety program J.T. Baker Chem. Co., Phillipsburg, N.J., 1978-83; regional lectr. Mid. Atlantic region Sigma Xi. Author: Iron, Armor and Adolescents, 1982; editor: Chemistry of Radiopharmaceuticals, 1978; contbr. numerous articles to profl. jours. Trustee Keystone Jr. Coll., LaPlume, Pa., 1975-90, Ctr. for History of Chemistry, Phila., 1982—, Nat. Found. for History of Chemistry, Phila., 1988—. Recipient Alumni Assn. award Lebanon Valley Coll., 1971; fellow NSF, 1963-64; recipient numerous rsch. grants. Mem. Am. Chem. Soc. (councilor, bd. dirs., pres. 1994, Harry and Carol Mosher award 1995), Royal Soc., Soc. Nuclear Medicine, Am. Assn. Pharm. Scientists, Sigma Xi. Republican. Methodist. Home: 200 Hexenkopf Rd Easton PA 18042-9570 Office: Dept Chem Lehigh U Bethlehem PA 18015

HEINDL, CLIFFORD JOSEPH, physicist; b. Chgo., Feb. 4, 1926; s. Anton Thomas and Louise (Fiala) H. B.S., Northwestern U., 1947, M.S., 1948; A.M., Columbia U., 1950, Ph.D., 1959. Sr. physicist Bendix Aviation Corp., Detroit, 1953-54; orsort student Oak Ridge Nat. Lab., 1954-55; asst. sect. chief Babcock & Wilcox Co., Lynchburg, Va., 1956-58; research group supr. Jet Propulsion Lab., Pasadena, Calif., 1959-65, mgr. research and space sci., 1965—. Served with AUS, 1944-46. Mem. AIAA, Am. Nuclear Soc., Health Physics Soc., Planetary Soc., Am. Phys. Soc. Home: 179 Mockingbird Ln South Pasadena CA 91030-2047 Office: 4800 Oak Grove Dr Pasadena CA 91109-8001

HEINDL, MARY LYNN, magazine editor; b. Ridgway, Pa., Aug. 10, 1937; d. Linus Michael and Hildur Johanna Josephine (Johnson) H. BA in English, U. Pitts., 1966. Office mgr. Std. Svc., Inc., Pitts., 1956-63, J.C. Keaney & Sons, Inc., Pitts., 1964-67; exec. dir. Pitts. chpt. AIA, Pitts., 1967-74; asst. exec. dir. Builders Assn. of Metro Pitts., 1975-81; coord. practice devel. Peat Marwick Mitchell, Pitts., 1982; adminstr. CADD tng. Val-Mark Cos., Pitts., 1982-83; mgr. inpex Expositions, Pitts., 1984-85; exec. dir. Western Pa. Restauant Assn., Pitts., 1985-87; editor Dynamic Bus. SMC Bus. Couns., Pitts., 1987—. 2nd v.p. Music for Mt. Lebanon Inc., 1997. Named Western Pa. Media Advocate of Yr. U.S. SBA, 1992; recipient Seldon Hale award Nat. Assn. of Home Builders, 1976. Mem. Am. Soc. Assn. Execs., Am. Inst. Archs. (hon.), Altrusa Internat. (pres. 1978). Republican. Roman Catholic. Avocations: music, gardening, swimming, literature. Home: 651 Shady Dr E Pittsburgh PA 15228-2300 Office: SMC Bus Couns 1400 S Braddock Ave Ste A Pittsburgh PA 15218-1263

HEINDL, PHARES MATTHEWS, lawyer; b. Meridian, Miss., Dec. 14, 1949; s. Paul A. and Leila (Matthews) H.; m. Linda Ann Williamson, Sept. 21, 1985; children: Lori Elizabeth, Jesse Phares, Jared Matthews. BS in Chem. Engring., Miss. State U., 1972; JD, U. Fla., 1981. Bar: Fla. 1981, Calif. 1982, U.S. Dist. Ct. (cen. dist.) Calif. 1983, U.S. Dist. Ct. (mid. dist.) Fla. 1983; bd. cert. civil trial lawyer Fla. Bar. Assoc. Lafollette, Johnson et al, L.A., 1982-83, Sam E. Murrell & Sons, Orlando, Fla., 1983-84; pvt. practice Orlando, Fla., 1984-93, Altamonte Springs, Fla., 1993—; bd. cert. civil trial lawyer. Precinct coord. Freedom Coun., Orlando, 1986; pres. Friends of the Wekiva River, 1998. Mem. Fla. Bar Assn., Calif. Bar Assn., Seminole County Bar Assn. (pres. civil trial sect. 1998), ATLA, Christian Legal Soc. (past pres. Ctrl. Fla.), Fla. Acad. Trial Lawyers (Eagle mem.), Workers Compensation Rules Com. Republican. Avocation: kayak racing. Home: 2415 River Tree Cir Sanford FL 32771-8334 Office: 222 S Westmonte Dr Ste 208 Altamonte Springs FL 32714-4269

HEINDL, WARREN ANTON, law educator, retired; b. Chgo., Dec. 2, 1922; s. Anton T. and Louise (Fiala) H.; m. Margaret Carriger, July 11, 1958. Student, Morton Jr. Coll., 1941-43; LL.B., Chgo.-Kent Coll. Law, 1947, LL.M., 1948; B.S., Northwestern U., 1949. Bar: Ill. bar 1947. Practiced in Chgo., 1951-65; mem. faculty Chgo.-Kent Coll. Law, 1948-69, asst. prof., 1951-65, asso. prof., 1965-69; prof. law Ill. Inst. Tech., Chgo., 1969-94, prof. emeritus, 1994—. Fellow Chgo.-Kent Honor Council; mem. Am., Ill. bar assns., Soc. Kent Honor Men, Delta Mu Delta. Home: 508 Selborne Rd Riverside IL 60546-1629 Office: Ill Inst Tech Sch Law Chicago IL 60616*

HEINE, LEONARD M., JR., investment executive; b. N.Y.C., Nov. 14, 1924; s. Leonard Max and Elise (Frey) H.; m. Sandra Fleming, Oct. 14, 1966; children; Michael Kenneth, Nancy Ellen, Thomas Charles, Christopher Altman. BS in Econs., U. Pa., 1948. Salesman Lehman Bros., N.Y.C., 1952-58; sales mgr. Rothschild, N.Y.C., 1958-62; gen. ptnr. R.J. Buck & Co., N.Y.C., 1962-70; pres., founder, chmn. Mgmt. Asset Corp., Westport, Conn., 1970-90; investment mgr., chmn., pres. LMH Fund Ltd., 1983—; pres. Heine Mgmt. Group, Inc., 1983—; chmn., pub. Weston (Conn.) Voice. Treas. Weston Pub. Libr., 1980-81; trustee St. Mary's Hosp., Preservation Found., Palm Beach, Fla.; bd. dirs. Fairfield Home Elderly; nat. commr. Anti-Defamation League; bd. dirs. Intracoastal Health Sys., West Palm Beach, Fla.; trustee Albert Einstein Coll. Medicine's Soc. Founders. With U.S. Army, 1943-46. Decorated Purple Heart. Mem. Am. Soc. Profl. Cons., Birchwood Country Club (Westport), U. Pa. Club (N.Y.C.), Palm Beach Country Club (Fla.). Republican.

HEINECKE, DEBORAH ANN, pediatrics nurse; b. Marcos, Tex., Sept. 8, 1954; d. Casimir J. and Mary L. (Trunk) Bosak; m. James A. Heinecke, June 19, 1976. Diploma, Mercy Hosp. Sch. of Nursing, Pitts., 1972-74; BSN, Duquesne U., 1986, MSN in Nursing Adminstrn., 1994; MS in Human Resource Mgmt., LaRoche Coll., 1994. RN, Pa.; cert. neonatal intensive care nurse. Staff nurse Mercy Hosp., Pitts., 1974-80; staff nurse, asst. nurse mgr. neonatal ICU Magee Women's Hosp., Pitts., 1981-87; nurse coord. Pediatric Nursing Specialists, Pitts., 1988-89; staff nurse neo-natal ICU Magee-Women's Hosp., Pitts., 1989-91; case coord. ventilator assisted children/home program Children's Hosp. of Pitts., Pitts., 1991-98; case mgr. Highmark Blue Cross/Blue Shield, Pitts., 1998-99; exec. dir. Three Rivers Family Hospice, Pitts., 1999—. Mem. Nat. Assn. Neonatal Nurses, Three Rivers Assn. Neonatal Nurses (former sec.), Sigma Theta Tau (former chair mentoring Epsilon Phi chpt.). Home: 243 Meredith St Pittsburgh PA 15210-3946

HEINECKEN, ROBERT FRIEDLI, art educator, artist; b. Denver, Oct. 29, 1931; s. Friedli Wilhelm and Mathilda Louise (Moehl) H.; m. Janet Marion Storey, Jan. 7, 1955 (div. 1980); children—Geoffrey Robert, Kathé Marie, Karol Leslie. AA, Riverside Coll., 1951; BA, UCLA, 1959, MA, 1960. Vis. faculty Harvard U., 1972, San Francisco Art Inst., 1970, Art Inst. Chgo., 1970; Vis. faculty Internat. Museum Photography, Rochester, N.Y., 1967, SUNY, Buffalo, 1969; prof. art UCLA, 1960-90, prof. emeritus dept. art, 1990—, with oral history program, 1997—. One-man shows include Light Gallery, N.Y.C., Witkin Gallery, N.Y.C., Pasadena Art Mus., Focus Gallery, San Francisco, Madison (Wis.) Art Ctr., Friends of Photography Gallery, Carmel, Calif., Internat. Mus. Photography, Foto

Forum, Universitat Kassel, Gallery Min, Tokyo, Art Inst. of Chgo.; exhibited in group shows at Mus. Modern Art, N.Y.C., Whitney Mus., N.Y.C., Nat. Gallery Can., Ottawa, Camden Arts Ctr., London; represented in permanent collections Internat. Mus. Photography, Rochester, Mus. Modern Art, N.Y.C., Fogg Art Mus., Cambridge, Mass., San Francisco Mus. Art, Oakland (Calif.) Mus. Art, Libr. of Congress, Washington, Pasadena Mus. Art; represented by Pace/MacGill Gallery, N.Y.C., Archive at Ctr. for Creative Photography, U. Ariz. Trustee Friends of Photography, Carmel, 1974-75. Served with USMCR, 1953-57. Guggenheim fellow, 1975; Nat. Endowment for Arts grantee, 1977, 81, 86. Mem. Soc. for Photog. Edn. (chmn. bd. dirs. 1970-72). Office: 1801 W Wabansia Ave Chicago IL 60622-1334

HEINEKEN, FREDERICK GEORGE, biochemical engineer; b. Chgo., Oct. 22, 1939; s. Frederick W.G. Heineken and Marie Helene Faber Heineken; divorced; 1 child, Christopher P. BS, Northwestern U., 1962; PhD, U. Minn., 1966. Sr. biochem. engr. Monsanto, St. Louis, 1966-71; postdoctoral fellow U. Colo., Denver, 1972-74, rsch. assoc., instr., 1974-76; sr. project engr. Cobe Labs., Lakewood, Colo., 1977-79, dept. head, 1979-81, therapy scientist, 1981-84; cons. Heineken & Assocs., Potomac, Md., 1985—; program dir. NSF, Washington, 1985—. Trustee 1st Universalist Ch., Denver, 1980-83, vice-moderator, 1984. Recipient Young Investigator award, NIH, 1974. Mem. AIChE, AAAS, Am. Chem. Soc. (councilor 1990—), Assn. for Advancement of Med. Instrumentation, Am. Soc. for Artificial Organs, St. Louis Ski Club (pres. 1971). Home: 7908 Turncrest Dr Potomac MD 20854-2772 Office: NSF Engring 4201 Wilson Blvd Arlington VA 22230-0001

HEINEL, ROBERT STEVEN, social services administrator; b. Detroit, Feb. 10, 1943; s. Steve J. and Hazel M. (Cupples) H. BA, Wayne State U., 1971; MSW, Mich. State U., 1985. Cert. social worker, Mich. Program dir. regional office U.S. Dept. Vets. Affairs, Detroit, 1972-77; vets. counselor Grand Traverse County, Traverse City, Mich., 1979-87; instr. Mich. State U., East Lansing, 1988-90; dir. vets. affairs Livingston County, Howell, Mich., 1991—. Newspaper columnist Veterans Corner, 1994—. Mem. Consortium on Aging, Human Svcs. Coun., Livingston County, 1991—. With U.S. Army, 1965-68. Mem. NASW, Internat. Soc. Study Traumatic Stress, Am. Legion, Vietnam Vets. Am., Nat. Assn. County Vets. Svc. Officers, Phi Kappa Phi, Phi Alpha. Avocations: motorcycle touring, swimming, writing. Office: Livingston County Vets Affairs 2300 E Grand River Ave Howell MI 48843-7585

HEINEMAN, ANDREW DAVID, lawyer; b. N.Y.C., Nov. 5, 1928; s. Bernard and Lucy (Morgenthau) H. BA, Williams Coll., 1950; LLB, Yale U., 1953. Bar: N.Y. 1953. Assoc. Proskauer Rose Goetz & Mendelsohn, N.Y.C., 1953-63; ptnr. Proskauer Rose LLP, N.Y.C., 1963—. Pres., chmn. bd. dirs. Ernest and Mary Hayward Weir Found., N.Y.C., 1969-87, trustee Mt. Sinai Hosp. Med. Sch. and Med. Ctr., 1976—, Williams Coll., 1980-95, Abelard Found., 1976-96; Asphalt Green, 1992-96; bd. dirs. Jewish Home and Hosp. for Aged, 1967—, vice chmn. bd. dirs., 1992, chmn. bd. dirs. 1993-97; exec. asst. Citizens for Kennedy and Johnson, N.Y.C., 1960; mem. N.Y. Gov.'s Commn. on Minorities in Med. Schs., 1982. Mem. Yale Law Sch. Assn. N.Y. (pres. 1970-73), Yale Law Sch. Alumni Assn. (v.p. 1973-76, exec. com.). Office: Proskauer Rose LLP 1585 Broadway New York NY 10036-8200

HEINEMAN, BEN WALTER, corporation executive; b. Wausau, Wis., Feb. 10, 1914; s. Walter Ben and Elsie Brunswick (Deutsch) H.; m. Natalie Goldstein, Apr. 17, 1935; children: Martha Heineman Pieper, Ben Walter. Student, U. Mich., 1930-33; LLB, Northwestern U., 1936; LLD (hon.), Lawrence Coll., 1959; LL.D. (hon.), Lake Forest Coll., 1966, Northwestern U., 1967; LHD, DePaul U., 1986. Bar: Ill. 1936. Pvt. practice law and govt. svc. Chgo., Washington, Algiers, 1936-56; chmn. bd. dirs. Four Wheel Drive Auto Co., 1954-57; chmn. C. & N.W. Ry. Co., 1956-72; founder, former chmn., CEO Northwest Industries, Inc., 1968-85; dir., chmn. exec. com., bd. dirs. 1st Nat. Bank, Chgo.; chmn. orgn. com. First Chgo. Corp., 1965-86; Chmn. White House Conf. to Fulfill These Rights, 1966, Pres.'s Task Force on Govt. Orgn., 1966-67, Pres.'s Commn. Income Maintenance Programs, 1967-69. *Ben Walter Heineman was a auxiliary foreign service officer in 1943. He was vice charirman of the North African Economic Board in 1943 and a member of General Eisenhower's civil affairs staff in Algeirs the same year.* Life trustee U. Chgo.; chmn. Ill. Bd. Higher Edn., 1962-69; trustee, mem. investment com. Savs. and Profit Sharing Fund Sears Roebuck Employees, 1966-71; trustee, mem. exec. com., chmn. audit com. Rockefeller Found., 1972-78; life dir. Lyric Opera, Chgo.; life trustee Orchestral Assn.; sustaining fellow Art Inst. Chgo., 20th century acquisition com.; trustee emeritus The Corning (N.Y.) Glass Mus. Fellow ABA, AAAS, Am. Bar Found. (life); mem. Am. Law Inst. (life), Ill. Bar Assn., Chgo. Bar Assn., Ephraim Club (Wis.), Yacht Club, Mid-Am. Club, Chgo. Club, Wayfarers Club, Std. Club (life), Quadrangle Club, Comml. Club (life), Carlton Club, Order of Coif, Phi Delta Phi (hon.). Office: 180 E Pearson St Apt 4304 Chicago IL 60611-2171

HEINEMAN, BENJAMIN WALTER, JR., lawyer; b. Chgo., Jan. 25, 1944; s. Benjamin Walter and Natalie (Goldstein) H.; m. Jeanne Cristine Russell, June 7, 1975; children: Zachary R., Matthew R. B.A. magna cum laude, Harvard U., 1965; B.Letters, Balliol Coll., Oxford U., Eng., 1967; J.D., Yale U., 1971. Bar: D.C. 1973, U.S. Supreme Ct. 1973. Reporter Chgo. Sun Times, 1968; law clk. Assoc. Justice Potter Stewart U.S. Supreme Ct., 1971-72; staff atty. Center for Law and Social Policy, 1973-75; with Williams Connolly and Califano, Washington, 1975-76; exec. asst. to sec. HEW, Washington, 1977-78, asst. sec. for planning and evaluation, 1978-79; partner Califano, Ross & Heineman, Washington, 1979-82, Sidley & Austin, Washington, 1982-87; sr. v.p., gen. counsel, sec. Gen. Electric Co., Fairfield, Conn., 1987—. Author: The Politics of the Powerless: A Study of the Campaign Against Racial Discrimination, 1972, Memorandum for the President: A Strategic Approach to Domestic Affairs in the 1980's, 1981; editor-in-chief: Yale Law Jour., 1970-71. Rhodes scholar, 1965-67. Mem. Phi Beta Kappa. Office: General Electric Co 3135 Easton Tpke Fairfield CT 06431-0001*

HEINEMAN, DAVID, state official; b. Falls City, Nebr., May 12, 1948; s. Jean Trevers and Irene Larkin H.; m. Sally Ganem, 1977. BS, U.S. Mil. Acad., 1970. Sales rep. Procter & Gamble, 1976-77; campaign mgr. Daub for Congress, 1977-78; dep. dir. Policy Rsch. Office, Nebr., 1979; dir. Nebr. State Rep. Exec. Com., 1979-81; chief of staff to Congressman Daub, 1983-88, office mgr. for Congressman Berenter, 1990-94; city councilman City of Fremont, Nebr., 1990-94; state treas. State of Nebr., 1995—. Decorated Army Commendation medal; recipient Outstanding Rep. Vol. award Douglas County Rep. Party, 1976, Outstanding Young Am. award Jaycees, 1980. Office: Treasurer's Office PO Box 94788 Lincoln NE 68509-4788*

HEINEMAN, GREGORY LYLE, government agency administrator; b. Omaha, Jan. 18, 1955; s. Lyle August and Patsy Lou (Kessinger) H.; m. Debbra J. Deming, Aug. 21, 1982; children: Marypat, Katherine, Emily. BA, U. Nebr., 1977. Claims rep. SSA, Chgo., 1978-81; field rep. SSA, Evergreen Park, Ill., 1981-84; ops. supr. SSA, Chgo., 1984-86; claims rep. SSA, Grand Island, Nebr., 1986-89; ops. supr. SSA, Lincoln, Nebr., 1989-90; asst. dist. mgr. SSA, Grand Island, 1990-93; field office mgr. SSA, Norfolk, Nebr., 1993—. Chmn. Norfolk Interagy. Coun., 1997—; bd. dirs. Prairie Hills Girl Scout Coun., Columbus, Nebr., 1997—. Mem. Kansas City Social Security Mgmt. Assn. (treas. 1996—, area rep. 1992-96). Avocations: computerized football rankings, golf, horse racing. Office: SSA 208 N 5th St Norfolk NE 68701-4095

HEINEMAN, HEINZ, chemist; b. Berlin, Aug. 21, 1913; came to U.S., 1938; s. Felix and Edith (Boehm) H.; m. Elaine Patricia Silverman, Feb. 12, 1948 (dec. Dec. 1993); children: Susan Carol, Peter Michael; m. Barbara A. Tenenbaum, Apr. 23, 1995. PhD, U. Basel, Switzerland, 1938. Sect. chief Houdry Process Corp., Marcus Hook, Pa., 1948-57; dir. chem. and engring. rsch. M.W. Kellogg Co., N.Y.C., 1958-69; rsch. mgr. Mobil R & D Co., Princeton, N.J., 1969-78; disting. scientist Lawrence Berkeley Lab., U. Calif., Berkeley, 1978—; cons. Mobil R & D Co., Catalytica Assocs. Founding editor Catalysis Revs., 1968—; contbr. articles to profl. jours. Mem. Adult Sch. Bd., Princeton, 1968-72, Flood Control Commn., Princeton, 1970-75, Gov.'s Coun. for Rsch., N.J., 1976-78. Recipient Disting. Scientist award U.S. Dept. Energy, 1976, H.H. Lowry award, 1993. Mem. NAE, AIChE (Disting. Lectr. award), Am. Chem. Soc. (Indsl. and Engring. Chemistry award 1972), Internat. Congress Catalysis (pres. 1960-64), Catalysis Soc. N.Am. (E.J. Houdry award 1974), Spanish Acad. Sci. (hon.), Catalysis Club Phila. Avocations: music; photography. Home: 4600 Connecticut Ave NW Apt 206 Washington DC 20008-5702 Office: Lawrence Berkeley Lab 1250 Maryland Ave SW Washington DC 20024-2141

HEINEMAN, PAUL LOWE, consulting civil engineer; b. Omaha, Oct. 24, 1924; s. Paul George and Annie L. (Lowe) H.; m. Gloria Nixon; children by previous marriage: Karen E., John F., Ellen F. Student, U. Omaha, 1942-43; B.S.C.E., Iowa State U., 1945, M.S., 1948. Registered profl. engr. Mo., Calif., N.Y., Kans., 25 other states and Republic of Colombia. Instr. Iowa State U., 1946-48; designer, project mgr. Howard, Needles, Tammen & Bergendoff (Cons. Engrs.), Kansas City, Mo., 1948-64; ptnr. Howard, Needles, Tammen & Bergendoff (Cons. Engrs.), 1965-86; exec. v.p. Howard, Needles, Tammen & Bergendoff Internat., Inc., Kansas City, 1967-84, pres., v.p. subs., 1983-86; bd. dirs., sec.-treas. emeritus The Road Info. Program. Served with C.E. USNR, 1945-46. Fellow ASCE, Am. Cons. Engrs. Coun., Inst. Traffic Engrs.; mem. NSPE, Am. Ry. Engring. Assn., Am. Concrete Inst., Am. Arbitration Assn., Engrs. Club (Kansas City). Presbyterian (elder 1958—). Home and Office: 2 J St Lake Lotawana MO 64086-9749

HEINEMANN, HEINZ, chemist, educator, researcher, consultant; b. Berlin, Aug. 21, 1913; came to U.S., 1938; s. Felix and Edith (Boehm) H.; m. Elaine Patricia Silverman, Feb. 12, 1948 (dec. Dec. 1993); children: Susan Carol, Peter Michael; m. Barbara A. Tenenbaum, Apr. 23, 1995. Diploma, U. Berlin, 1935; PhD, U. Basel, Switzerland, 1937. Rsch. chemist Danciger Oil & Refineries, Pampa, Tex., 1940-41, Attapulgus Clay Co., Phila., 1941-48; sect. chief Houdry Process Corp., Marcus Hook, Pa., 1948-57; dir. chem. & engring. rsch. M.W. Kellogg Co., N.Y.C., 1957-69; mgr. catalysis rsch. Mobil R & D Corp., Princeton, N.J., 1969-78; disting. scientist Lawrence Berkeley Lab., U. Calif., 1978—; lectr. in chem. engring. U. Calif., Berkeley, 1979-90; pres. Internat. Congress on Catalysis, 1956-60; cons. numerous chem. and petroleum cos., 1978—. Editor Catalysis Revs. jour., 1966-86; author 130 publs. on catalysis and fuel chemistry; contbr. 6 chpts. to books. Mem. Flood Control Commn. Princeton Twp., 1970-75, Gov's. Adv. Coun. Rsch., Trenton, N.J., 1976-78; dir. Princeton Art Assn. Recipient Phila. Catalysis Soc. award, 1976, Disting. Scientist award U.S. Dept. Energy, 1978, Homer H. Lowry award U.S. Dept Energy, 1994; Advances in Catalysis Chemistry II symposium held in his honor, Salt Lake City, 1982. Fellow AAAS; mem. Am. Chem. Soc. (Indsl. & Engring. Chem. award 1972, numerous offices), Catalysis Soc. N.Am. (Applied Catalysis award 1975), Nat. Acad. Engring., Internat. Congress Catalysis (pres. 1956-60). Achievements include over 50 patents in field; invention of and participation in commercialization of 16 industrial processes. Home: 4600 Connecticut Ave NW Apt 206 Washington DC 20008-5702 Office: Lawrence Berkeley Lab 1250 Maryland Ave SW Washington DC 20024-2141

HEINEMANN, LARRY C., writer; b. Chgo., Jan. 18, 1944; s. John Hubert and Dorothy Heinemann; m. Edith Jane, Apr. 27, 1968; children: Sarah Catherine, Preston John. BA, Columbia Coll., 1971; AA, Kendall Coll., 1966. Tchr. Columbia Coll., Chgo., 1971-86; writer-in-residence U. Mass., Boston, 1991-98; writer-in-residence Northwestern U., Evanston, Ill., spring 1996, U. So. Calif., L.A., fall 1996. Author: Close Quarters, 1977, Paco's Story, 1986, Cooler by the Lake, 1992; contbr. articles to numerous mags. Bd. dirs. City Chgo. Adv. Com. Vets. Affairs, 1988-90, Nat. Vets. Legal Svcs. Project, 1990, My Lai Peace Park Project, Madison, Wis., 1995—. Sgt. U.S. Army, 1966-68, Vietnam. Recipient Bronze Star U.S. Army, Vietnam, 1967, Nat. Book award Nat. Book Found., 1987, Carl Sandburg award Chgo. Pub. Libr. Assn., 1987, Fiction award Soc. Midland Authors, 1987; fellow NEA, 1982, 86, Guggenheim, N.Y.C., 1988-89, Steinberg/Pen U. Pa., 1989; Regent's scholar U. Calif., Davis, spring 1995. Buddhist. Office: care Ellen Levine Lit Agy 15 E 26th St #1801 New York NY 10010

HEINEN, JAMES ALBIN, electrical engineering educator; b. Milw., June 23, 1943; s. Albin Jacob and Viola (DeBuhr) H. BEE, Marquette U., 1964, MS, 1967, PhD, 1969. Registered profl. engr., Wis. Data analyst Med. Sch. Marquette U., Milw., 1963, teaching asst. elec. engring. dept., 1964-65, 65-66, research asst., 1966, NASA trainee, 1966-69, research assoc. Provost's Office, 1970, asst. prof. and grad. adminstr., 1971-73, assoc. prof., chmn. elec. engring. dept., 1973-76, assoc. prof., 1976-80, prof. elec. engring. and computer sci., 1980-87, prof., dir. grad. studies elec. and computer engring., 1987-95, prof. elec. and computer engring., 1995—, dir. signal processing rsch. ctr., 1990—; cons. in field. Contbr. numerous articles and revs. on elec. engring. and computer sci. to profl. jours. Recipient Outstanding Engring. Tchr. award Marquette U., 1979, Teaching Excellence award Marquette U., 1985. Mem. IEEE (various coms., tech. reviewer Trans. Automatic Control 1969—, Trans. Circuits and Systems Soc. 1980—, Signal Processing Soc. 1980—, sr. mem., Meml. award Milw. sect. 1981, assoc. editor Trans. Circuits and Systems 1983-85, assoc. editor Trans. Indsl. Electronics 1996—), Am. Soc. Engring. Edn., Sigma Xi, Tau Beta Pi, Eta Kappa Nu (Most Oustanding Elec. Engring. Tchr. in U.S. award 1974), Pi Mu Epsilon, Alpha Sigma Nu. Home: 8200 W Menomonee River Pky Wauwatosa WI 53213-2537 Office: Marquette U Haggerty Hall Rm 298 PO Box 1881 Milwaukee WI 53201-1881

HEINEY, JOHN WEITZEL, former utility executive; b. Lancaster, Pa., Nov. 9, 1913; s. George and Gertrude G. (Weitzel) H.; m. Betty M. Horn, Apr. 12, 1941. B.S. in Bus. Adminstrn, Lehigh U., 1935. With various subsidiaries Am. Water Works Co., 1935-41, 46-60; pres., chief exec. officer, dir. Indiana Gas Co., Inc., Indpls., 1960-73; chmn. bd., chief exec. officer Indiana Gas Co., Inc., 1973-78, chmn. bd., 1978-84; pres., dir. Ohio River Pipe Line Corp., 1964-73, chmn. bd., 1973-78; pres., chmn. Gen. Assurance Services, Ltd., 1975-84. Bd. dirs. United Fund Greater Indpls., 1960-77; bd. dirs. Community Hosp. Indpls., 1968-73, 75-81, chmn., 1972-73; bd. dirs., chmn. Community Hosps. Found., 1983-89. Served to lt. col., inf. AUS, 1941-46. Decorated Bronze Star medal; named Sagamore of Wabash, Gov. of Ind., 1997. Mem. Am. Gas Assn. (past chmn. spl. com. on consumer affairs, 1st vice chmn. 1968, chmn. 1969, dir. Disting. Svcs. award com. 1975), Ind. Gas Assn. (past pres. and dir.), Inst. Gas Tech. (trustee 1965, chmn. bd. trustees 1968), Internat. Gas Union (mem. council and bur. 1973-75), Ind. C. of C. (dir. 1973-80), Newcomen Soc. N.Am., Beta Theta Pi. Club: Meridian Hills Country.

HEINICKE, PETER HART, computer consultant; b. Madison, Wis., Mar. 26, 1956; s. Herbert Raymond and Janet Louise (Hart) H.; m. Karen Sue Michel, May 30, 1992; 1 child, Jeremiah Peter. BA in Physics, Washington U., St. Louis, 1977, MA in Math., 1977; MA in Physics, Princeton U., 1980; MS in Computer Sci., ITT, Chgo., 1985. Programmer, analyst Princeton (N.J.) Plasma Physics Lab, 1977-79; systems analyst Encoth, Princeton, 1978-79, Internat. Harvester, Melrose Park, Ill., 1980, Fermi Nat. Accelerator Lab., Batavia, Ill., 1981-89; pres. Precision Computer Methods, Inc., Geneva, Ill., 1989-92; bd. dirs. CIM/DNC, Inc. McHenry, Ill., 1979; cons. Rutgers U., New Brunswick, N.J., 1979, Dept. of Energy, Washington, 1979, Internat. Harvester, Melrose Park, 1981-83, Abbot Labs., Abbot Park, Ill., 1983, Digital Equipment Corp., Maynard, Mass., 1985, Avco Everett Rsch. Lab., Everett, Mass., 1986, Lawrence Livermore Lab., Livermore, Calif., 1987, Reuters Info. Tech., Inc., Oak Brook, 1991—, Design Tech., Westmont, Ill., 1987—, The Board Room, Inc., Tinley Park, Ill., 1992—, Environ. Waste Svcs., Elburn, Ill. Author: (software) Tinytach, 1990, EWSMS, 1995; contbr. articles to profl. jours. Treas. African Crusade Ministry, Inc. Warrenville, Ill., 1991-95, Faith Luth. Ch., Geneva, Ill., 1995-98. Compton fellow Washington U., St. Louis, 1974-77, NSF Grad. fellow, Princeton, N.J., 1977-79; Nat. Merit scholar, St. Louis, 1974-77. Mem. IEEE, Am. Physical Soc., Digital Equipment Users Soc., Assn. Computing Machinery, Fellowship Cos. for Christ Internat., Am. Assn. Individual Investing. Republican. Lutheran. Avocations: travel, reading, hiking, swimming.

HEINICKE, RALPH MARTIN, consultant; b. Hickory, N.C., Sept. 3, 1914; s. Martin John and Lydia Sophia (Kurth) H.; m. Sarah Anne Hall, July 31, 1944; 1 child, Mark. BS, Cornell U., 1936; PhD, U. Minn., St. Paul, 1950. Agr. chemist Shell Oil Co., N.Y.C., 1939-43; tech. advisor Jintan-Dolph, Osaka, Japan, 1962-86; assoc. faculty U. Hawaii, Honolulu, 1950-86; chemist Pineapple Rsch. Inst., Honolulu, 1950-55; dir. rsch. Dole Co., Honolulu, 1955-72; v.p. Biol. Control Systems, Honolulu, 1981-86; pres. Biotech. Resources Inc., Clarksville, Ind., 1990-94; cons. Morinda, Inc.; cons. various drug cos., 1972—; cons. on the xeronine-sys. Inventor, patentee on xeronine; inventor, patentee on herve toxin insecticide. Master sgt. U.S. Army, 1942-45, CBI. Democrat. Avocations: music, writing, philosophy, new theory of physics. E-mail: ralph-m-h@juno.com. Home: Biotechnology Resources Inc. 1124 Rostrevor Cir Louisville KY 40205-1742

HEININGER, S(AMUEL) ALLEN, retired chemical company executive; b. New Britain, Conn., June 13, 1925; s. Alfred D. and Erma Geraldine (Kline) H.; m. Barbara Ashenfelter Griffith, June 16, 1948 (dec. Oct. 6 1994); children: Janet, Kathryn, Kenneth, Keith; m. Margot Morgan Danis, Nov. 27, 1998. A.B., Oberlin Coll., 1948; M.S., Carnegie Inst. Tech., 1951; D.Sc., 1952. Research chemist Monsanto Chem. Co., Dayton, Ohio, 1952-56, group leader, 1956-58; project mgr. devel. dept. Organic Chems. div. Monsanto Chem. Co., St. Louis, 1958-59, mgr. fine chems. intermediates and market exploration sect., 1959-65, dir. comml. devel., 1965-67, dir. food and fine chems., 1967-71, dir. corp. plans and devel., 1971-74; gen. mgr. plasticizers div. Monsanto Indsl. Chems. Co., St. Louis, 1974-76; dir. corp. research lab. Monsanto Chem. Co., St. Louis, 1977, v.p. research and devel., 1977-79., v.p. corp. plans and bus. devel., 1980-86, v.p. resource planning, 1986-90; retired, 1990. Contbr. articles to profl. jours.; U.S., fgn. patentee in field. Alderman, City of Warson Woods (Mo.), 1961-65, police commr., 1967-71, trustee St. Louis Sci. Ctr., 1997—, Repertory Theatre, 1998—. Served to lt. USNR, 1943-46. Mem. Am. Chem. Soc. (pres.-elect 1990, pres. 1991), Indsl. Rsch. Inst. (pres. 1987-88), Soc. Chem. Industry, N.Y. Acad. Scis., U.S./Mex. Found. (bd. dirs.), Old Warson Country Club, Creve Coeur Racquet Club. Republican. Episcopalian. Office: 20 S Central Ave Ste 100 Clayton MO 63105-1715

HEINKE, REX S., lawyer; b. Harrisburg, Ill., June 9, 1950; s. William Richard and Versa Lee (Bradley) H.; m. Margaret Ann Nagle, May 6, 1978; children: William Rex, Meghan Bradley. BA, U. Witwatersrand, Johannesburg, Republic of South Africa, 1971; JD, U. Columbia, 1975. Bar: Calif. 1975. Ptnr. Gibson, Dunn & Crutcher, L.A., 1983—. Office: Gibson Dunn & Crutcher 333 S Grand Ave Ste 4400 Los Angeles CA 90071-3197

HEINKE, WARREN E., social services administrator; b. Salem, Oreg., Jan. 26, 1943; s. Edward Carl and Charlotte Marie (Jensen) H.; m. Mariel Margaret Seefeldt, July 21, 1973; children: Erik Jens, David William, Jill Margrethe. BA in Polit. Sci. with honors, U. Oreg., 1965; MA in Polit. Sci., U. Wis., 1968, cert. in Russian area studies, 1968, MSSW, 1970. Lic. clin. social worker, Ill. Social worker II, III Wis. Divsn. Cmty. Svcs., Fond du Lac, 1970-79; supr. II Wis. Divsn. Cmty. Svcs., Wisconsin Rapids, 1979-82; regional exec. dir. Children's Home & Aid Soc. Ill., Rockford, 1982—. Mem. 7th St. Area Devel. Coun., Rockford, 1995-97. Mem. NASW (statewide nominations com. 1997-99, leadership identification com., dist. program com. 1994-95), Foster Family Based Treatment Assn. (chmn. Ill. chpt. 1996-98, vice chmn. 1995-96, nat. conf. presenter St. Louis, 1996, Toronto, 1997, Mpls., 1999), Child Welfare League Am. (regional conf. presenter Sioux Falls, S.D., 1975, Indpls. 1976). Democrat. Lutheran. Avocations: playing the bassoon and piano, gardening. Home: 2203 Oxford St Rockford IL 61103-4162 Office: Childrens Home & Aid Soc 910 2d Ave Rockford IL 61104

HEINLE, ROBERT ALAN, physician; b. Tarentum, Pa., Oct. 26, 1933; s. Edward William and Mary Alice (Purvis) H.; B.S., U. Pitts., 1955, M.D., 1959; m. Barbara Klimeck, Aug. 23, 1958; children—Richard, Jeffrey, Ronald, Robert, Thomas, Timothy. Intern, U. Pitts. Health Center, 1959-60, resident, 1962-65; research fellow in medicine Peter Bent Brigham Hosp., 1965-67; research asso. in medicine Harvard Med. Sch., 1967-68; asst. prof. medicine U. Rochester (N.Y.) Med. Sch., 1968-71, asso. prof., 1971-75, clin. asso. prof., 1975—; dir. cardiovascular lab. Genesee Hosp., Rochester, 1975—; sr. asso. physician Strong Meml. Hosp., Rochester, 1975—; cons. Am. Heart Jour., 1973—; NIH research fellow, 1965-68. Bd. dirs. Blue Cross in Rochester, Blue Shield in Rochester. Served with U.S. Army, 1960-62. Fellow ACP, Am. Coll. Cardiology; mem. Am. Heart Assn., AMA, Am. Fedn. Clin. Research, Rochester Individual Practice Assn. (dir.), Phi Beta Kappa, Omicron Delta Kappa, Alpha Omega Alpha. Republican. Roman Catholic. Home: 415 Warren Ave Rochester NY 14618-4319 Office: 224 Alexander St Rochester NY 14607-4002

HEINLEN, DANIEL LEE, alumni organization administrator; b. Columbus, Ohio, Nov. 16, 1937; s. Calvin Xenophon and Charlotte Elizabeth (Lanman) H.; m. Roberta Bishop, Mar. 20, 1966 (div. 1975); m. Gelene Vogel Kozlowski, June 17, 1978; children: Stephanie Heinlen, Kate Kozlowski Isler, Amy. BS in Social Work, Ohio State U., 1960. Youth program dir., extension dir. YMCA, Pitts., 1960-65; field dir. Alumni Assn., Ohio State U., Columbus, 1965-67, assoc. dir., 1967-73, dir. alumni affairs, 1973-92; pres., CEO Ohio State U. Alumni Assn., Inc., Columbus, 1992—; sec. Alumni Assn. Bd., Columbus, 1973—; pub. mag. Alumni Assn., Ohio State U., 1973—; ex-officio trustee Ohio State U. Found.; mem. presdl. search com. Ohio State U., 1990, 97; trustee Coun. for Advancement and Support of Higher Edn., Washington,1986-88, 90-94, chmn., 1992-93; chmn. 75th anniversary Colloquium, Columbus, 1988, chmn. ann. assembly alumni track, 1988, chmn. ann. assembly, 1990; chmn. Mgmt. Inst. for Alumni Assn. Execs., Chgo., 1996, pres. coun., 1994-96, bd. dirs., 1988-96; chmn. U. ProNet, Inc., Palo Alto, Calif., 1996—; chmn. alumni dirs. Big Ten, 1973, 84, 93; mem. Ohio State U. Pres.'s Coun., 1990-97; bd. dirs. River Road Hotel Corp., 1992—. Author chpts. in books. Exec. com. NW Ordinance U.S. Constn. Bicentennial Comnn., Ohio, 1986-88; bd. dir. Non-profit Mailers Fedn., Wash., 1985-88; mem. OSU Com. on Student Fin. Aids, Columbus, 1973—, Newcomen Soc. N.Am., 1975-90, 93—. Recipient Ohio State U. Coll. of Social Work Disting. Svc. award, 1996; named Hon. Trustee Easter Seal Rehab. Ctr. of Ctrl. Ohio, Columbus, 1988-92; D.L. Heinlen award for univ. advocacy named in his honor Ohio Sate U. Alumni Assn., Inc., 1995. Mem. Rotary (bd. dirs. Columbus Club 1986, v.p. 1987-89, pres. 1989-90), Univ. Club (bd. dirs., 2nd v.p. 1985-88, 94-95, 1st v.p. 1996), Faculty Club (mem. bd. control 1978-80, pres.-elect 1999), Kit Kat, Golden Key Nat. Honor Soc. (hon. mem.). Avocation: tennis. Home: 2981 E Powell Rd Lewis Center OH 43035-9517 Office: Ohio State U Alumni Assn Inc 2200 Olentangy River Rd Columbus OH 43210-1061

HEINLEN, RONALD EUGENE, lawyer; b. Delaware, Ohio, May 28, 1937; s. Carl Elwood and Evelyn Lucille (Scott) H.; m. Mary Pauline Turney, Dec. 28, 1955; children: James Michael, Deborah Lynn, Robert Christopher. AB, Harvard U., 1959, JD, 1962. Bar: Ohio 1962. Assoc. Frost & Jacobs, Cin., 1962-69, ptnr., 1969—; lectr. Tax Inst. NYU. Contbr. articles to profl. jour. Trustee Cin. Nature Ctr., 1986-95. Fellow Am. Soc. Hosp. Attys.; mem. ABA, Ohio State Bar Assn., Cin. Bar Assn. (chmn. tax sect.), Cin. Country Club, University Club. Office: Frost & Jacobs 2500 PNC Ct 201 E 5th St Ste 2500 Cincinnati OH 45202-4182

HEINRICH, BERND, biologist, educator; b. Bad Polzin, Germany, Apr. 19, 1940; came to U.S., 1950, naturalized, 1958; s. Gerd Hermann and Hildegard Maria (Bury) H. BA, U. Maine, 1964, MS, 1966; PhD in Zoology, UCLA, 1970. Teaching and research asst. UCLA, 1966-70; asst. prof. entomology U. Calif., Berkeley, 1971-75; assoc. prof. U. Calif., 1975-78, prof., 1978-80; prof. biology U. Vt., Burlington, 1980—. Author: Bumblebee Economics, 1979, Insect Thermoregulation, 1981, In a Patch of Firewood, 1984, One Man's Owl, 1987, Ravens in Winter, 1989, The Hot-Blooded Insects, 1993, A Year in the Maine Woods, 1994, The Thermal Warriors, 1996, The Trees in My Forest, 1998, Mind of the Raven, 1999; co-author: Biology, 1979; contbr. numerous articles to sci. jours. Recipient Winship and Rutstrums Author's awards, 1984, 95; Guggenheim fellow, 1976-77, von Humboldt fellow, 1988-89. Fellow AAAS; mem. Am. Ornithological Union, Sigma Xi. Office: U Vt Dept Biology Marsh Life Science Bui Burlington VT 05405

HEINRICH, RANDALL WAYNE, lawyer, investment banker; b. Houston, Nov. 29, 1958; s. Albert Joseph Sr. and Beverly June Earles; m. Linda Carol Cheek, June 6, 1993; children: Angela Leigh, Conrad Randall. BA, Baylor U., 1980, postgrad., 1981; postgrad., Rice U., 1981-82; JD, U. Tex., 1985. Bar: Tex. 1985. Assoc. Baker & Botts, Houston, 1985-87, Chamberlain, Hrdlicka, White, Williams & Martin, Houston, 1987-91, Norton & Blair, Houston, 1991-92; of counsel Gillis & Slogar, Houston, 1992—; mng. dir.

Baytree Investors, Houston, 1993—. Mem. dirs.' circle Houston Grand Opera, 1991, The Arts Symposium, 1991, Center Stage, Alley Theater, Houston, 1992-93, Houston Entrepreneurs' Forum, 1990-91; bd. dirs. The Cadre, 1991-92; pres. Exchange Club of Bayou City, 1992-93. Mem. ABA (YLD securities law com. 1993-95, vice chmn. 1994-95), NASD Pool Securities Arbitrators, Am. Arbitration Assn. (mem. nat. panel neutrals), Houston Bar Assn., Forum Club Houston, Phi Delta Theta. Republican. Baptist. Home: 4318 Saint Michaels Ct Sugar Land TX 77479-2986 Office: Gillis & Slogar 1000 Louisiana St Ste 6905 Houston TX 77002-5014

HEINRICHS, TIMOTHY ARNOLD, family practice physician; b. Coldwater, Ohio, Sept. 26, 1953; s. Robert William and Lucille (Wenning) H.; m. Mary Alice Kahlig, Aug. 25, 1979; children: Renee, Laura, Charlotte, Elizabeth. BA in Psychology, Wright State U., 1981, MD, 1986. Diplomate Am. Coll. Forensic Examiners, Am. Acad. Family Practice. Intern, then resident Miami (Ohio) Valley Hosp., 1986-89; pvt. practice Celina, Ohio, 1989-98, Coldwater, Ohio, 1998—; coroner County of Mercer, Celina, 1989—; owner Heinrichs Farm, Celina, 1989—. Mem. Am. Acad. Family Practice, Thoroughbred Owners and Breeders Assn. Republican. Home: 6712 Erastus Durbin Rd Celina OH 45822

HEINS, ESTHER, botanical artist, painter; b. Bklyn., Nov. 10, 1908; d. Israel and Margaret (Brown) Berow; m. Harold Heins; Sept. 8, 1929 (dec. 1987); children: Marilyn, Judith Leet. BS in Edn., Mass. Coll. Art, 1929. Freelance artist Boston, 1930-60; bot. artist, illustrator plant introductions Arnold Arboretum, Boston, 1960—. Contbr. bot. illustrations to profl. jours.; one-woman shows include Graham Arader Gallery, N.Y.C., Harvard Radcliffe Hilles Libr., Arnold Arboretum, Boston Pub. Libr., Schlesinger Libr., Cambridge, Mass.; group shows include Hunt Inst. for Bot. Documentation, Pitts., Arnold Arboretum, Munich, Germany, Smithsonian, Washington, Oakland, Calif., others; represented in permanent collections at Mus. Fine Arts, Boston, Hunt Inst. for Bot. Documentation, Schlesinger Libr., Radcliffe Coll., Arnold Arboretum, Boston Pub. Libr., Fogg Mus., Cambridge, and numerous others in pvt. collections; illustrator, contbr. essay: (book) Flowering Trees and Shrubs: The Botanical Paintings of Esther Heins, 1987; illustrator many covers Jour. AMA. Mem. Guild of Natural Sci. Illustrators. Avocations: attending concerts of Boston Symphony, gardening. Home and Studio: 8 Mitchell Rd Marblehead MA 01945-1130

HEINS, JOHN, publishing executive. Pres., CEO Parents Mag., N.Y.C., 1994—, Gruner & Jahr USA Pub., N.Y.C. Office: Gruner & Jahr USA Pub 375 Lexington Ave New York NY 10017-5514*

HEINS, MARILYN, college dean, pediatrics educator, author; b. Boston, Sept. 7, 1930; d. Harold and Esther (Berow) H.; m. Milton P. Lipson, 1958; children: Rachel, Jonathan. A.B., Radcliffe Coll., 1951; M.D., Columbia U., 1955. Diplomate Am. Bd. Pediatrics. Intern, N.Y. Hosp., N.Y.C., 1955-56; resident in pediatrics Babies Hosp., N.Y.C., 1956-58; asst. pediatrician Children's Hosp. Mich., Detroit, 1959-78; dir. pediatrics Detroit Receiving Hosp., 1965-71; asst., assoc. dean student affairs Wayne State U. Med. Sch., Detroit, 1971-79; assoc. dean acad. affairs U. Ariz. Med. Coll., Tucson, 1979-83, vice dean, 1983-88, prof. pediatrics, 1985-88. Author: (with Anne M. Seiden) Child Care/Parent Care, 1987; mem. editorial bd. Jour. AMA, 1981-91; contbr. articles to profl. jours. Bd. dirs. Planned Parenthood So. Ariz., 1983, pres., 1988-89, Ariz. Ctr. for Clin. Mgmt.,1991—, Nat. Bd. Med. Examiners, 1983-88; mem. adv. bd. So. Ariz. Women's Fund, 1992—, Ariz. State Hosp., 1985-88. Recipient Alumni Faculty Service award Wayne State U., 1972, Recognition award, 1977, Women on the Move Achievement award YWCA Tucson, 1983, Tuscon women of Vision award Weizmann Inst., 1997, pres.'s disting. svc. award Ariz. Med. Assn., 1997; mem. Ariz. Ctr. Clin. Mgmt. 1990—. Home: 6530 N Longfellow Dr Tucson AZ 85718-2416

HEINS, SISTER MARY FRANCES, educational administrator, nun; b. Galveston, Tex., Nov. 12, 1927; d. George and Rosella (Eckenfels) H. BA, Dominican Coll., 1954; MEd, Lamar U., 1973. Joined Dominican Sisters, Roman Cath. Ch., 1946. Tchr. parochial schs. Tex. and Calif., 1948-68; tchr., head sci. dept., asst. prin. Kelly H.S., Beaumont, Tex., 1968-80; co-prin., then prin. St. Pius X H.S., Houston, 1980-84; tchr., head sci. dept. O'Connell Jr. H.S., Galveston, 1984-86; prin. O'Connell H.S., Galveston, 1989-97; tchr., adminstrv. asst., computer coord., sci. fair coord. Galveston Cath. Sch., 1986-89, tchr., 1997—; mem. Goals for Beaumont Edn. task force Beaumont C. of C., 1979-80. Mem. interfaith com. Galveston Hist. Found., 1990; mem. ch. involvement com. City-wide Conf. on Youth Violence; participant Galveston Historical Foundations Annual Home Tours, Annual Home and Garden Show benefitting the Animal Shelter. Recipient O'Connell Booster of Yr. award, 1995-96; named one of the Top 50 Tchrs. in the City, 1998. Mem. Nat. Cath. Edn. Assn., Nat. Assn. Tchrs. Math., Lamar U. Alumni Assn., World Future Soc., Sci. Tchrs. Assn. Tex. (Outstanding Tchr. 1980), Galveston C. of C. (mem. edn. com. 1990-91), Galveston Garden Club (2nd v.p.), Delta Kappa Gamma (chpt. achievement award 1990, 97, pres. 1988-90, 97). Democrat. Roman Catholic. Avocations: needlepoint, word puzzles, reading, collecting owls, collecting apples. Home: 4307 Avenue N 1/2 Galveston TX 77550 Office: Galveston Cath Sch 2601 Ursuline Ave. Galveston TX 77550-4398

HEINSEN, LINDSAY, newspaper editor; b. Berwyn, Ill., May 6, 1950; d. Henry Arthur and Mabel Scott (Witt) H. BA in French Lit., U. Ill., 1972, postgrad., 1972-76. Features editor D Mag., 1977-80; home and design editor Dallas Morning News, 1980-81, arts editor, 1981-89; freelance writer and editor Dallas, 1989-92; fine arts editor Houston Chronicle, 1992—. Recipient Matrix award for Best Mag. Feature in Dallas, 1978; James scholar. Mem. Kappa Tau Alpha, Phi Kappa Phi. Office: Houston Chronicle 801 Texas St Houston TX 77002-2996*

HEINTZ, CAROLINEA CABANISS, retired home economics educator; b. Roanoke, Va., Jan. 19, 1920; d. Luther Bertie and Emblyn Bird (Jennings) Cabaniss; m. Howard Elmer Smith, Dec. 19, 1942 (div. Aug. 1975); children: Emblyn Davis, Cynthia Shannon, Cheryl Peterson, Melyssa Sexton; m. Raymond Walter Heintz, May 21, 1977; 1 stepchild, James. BS in Home Econ. Edn., U. Ala., Tuscaloosa, 1941; vocat. home econ. degree, Montevallo Coll., 1941. Cert. vocat. home econs. tchr. Swimming instr. Camp Mudjekeewis, Centerlovel, Maine, summer 1940; home econs. tchr. Roanoke Pub. Schs., 1941-43; dietitian U. Va., Charlottesville, 1943; nutrition edn. specialist Liberty Health Ctr. Svcs., Liberty Center, Ohio, 1974-80; home economist Dayton Hudson Dept. Store, Toledo, 1980-84; splty . food instr., continuing edn. U. Toledo, 1984-85; pres., mem. Greater Toledo Nutrition Coun., 1966-98; bd. dirs. Sunset House Aux., pres. 1999—. Spkr. United Way, Toledo, 1965-90; founder, pres. Mobile Meals Toledo, Inc., 1968-71, mem. adv. bd., 1988-95, bd. dirs., chmn. pub. rels., 1997-99, Spirit of Mobile Meals award, 1998; affiliate mem. Arts Commn., Toledo, 1976-77; chmn. Saphire Ball, Toledo Symphony Orch., Toledo Opera, 1978; adminstrv. coord. Feed Your Neighbor program Met. Chs. United, Toledo, 1979-86; deacon Collingwood Presbyn. Ch., 1969-71, elder, 1972-74, 77-79, trustee, 1984-86, elder, clk. of session, 1991-94, elder, 1997-99, stewardship chmn., 1996-97, del. to Maumee Valley Presbytery, 1991-99; mem. steering com. Interfaith Hospitality Network, 1992-94, bd. dirs., 1993-94; alt. del. Gen. Assembly Presbyn. Ch. U.S.A., 1993, del.-commr., 1994. Recipient Woman of Toledo award St. Vincent Hosp. and Med. Ctr. Guild, 1967, 80, Outstanding Community Svc. award United Way, 1987, Henry Morse vol. award, Greater Toledo award United Way, 1998, runner-up Nat. Vol. of the Year award Project Meal Found., Reynolds Metal Co., 1998. Mem. AAUW (bd. dirs. 1974-76, 94-96, 97-98, chmn. mem. gourmet group 1966-99, edn. found. chmn. 1994-96, book sale chmn. 1998, nominating com. chmn.), Ohio Med. Aux. (1st v.p. 1973-74), Aux. Acad. Medicine (pres. 1967-68, chmn. ed. gourmet group 1966-99, Health Care award 1974), Indian Trails Garden Club (pres. 1997-98), Sigma Kappa (various alumni offices). Republican. Avocations: volunteering, gourmet cooking, traveling, entertaining, bridge. Home: 3407 Bentley Blvd Toledo OH 43606-2860

HEINTZ, JOHN EDWARD, lawyer; b. Bronxville, N.Y., Dec. 12, 1948; s. Howard Theodore and Ruth Janet (Brodhead) H.; m. Lynn Ann Ohman, June 21, 1980; children: Eric John, Jennifer Ann. BA, Cornell U., 1970; MPA, Princeton U., 1974; JD, NYU, 1977. Assoc. Covington & Burling, Washington, 1977-86; shareholder Popham, Haik, Schnobrich & Kaufman, Ltd., Washington, 1986-91; ptnr. Howrey & Simon, Washington, 1991—. Contbr. articles to profl. jours. Democrat. Avocations: sailing, swimming, tennis. Office: Howrey & Simon 1299 Pennsylvania Ave NW Ste 1 Washington DC 20004-2420

HEINTZ, JOSEPH E., financial services company executive. CFO, KPMG LLP, N.Y.C. Office: KPMG LLP 345 Clark Ave New York NY 10154*

HEINTZ, MARY ETHEL, business owner; b. N.Y.C., Aug. 27, 1943. Owner, bookkeeper, paralegal, tax preparer Services, Etc., Englewood, Fla., 1983—. Coord. Police Athletic League, Englewood, 1992-93. Mem. Englewood C. of C. Home and Office: 935 N Boundary Rd Englewood FL 34223-2312

HEINY, JAMES RAY, lawyer; b. Albert Lea, Minn., Oct. 7, 1928; s. Albin James and Lola Marguerite (Keig) H.; m. Wava Jeanine Isaacson, Sept. 2, 1951 (dec. 1980); children: Jon Carl, Jane Ellen Heiny Smith, Ann Elizabeth Heiny Hohenshell, Thomas James; m. Norma Lou West, July 24, 1982. BA, Grinnell Coll., 1950; JD, U. Iowa, 1953. Bar: Iowa 1953. Assoc. Westfall, Laird & Burington, Mason City, Iowa, 1955-58; ptnr. Laird, Heiny, McManigal, Winga, Duffy & Stambaugh, Mason City, 1958—. Pres. Good Shepherd Geriatric Ctr., Inc., Mason City, 1960-72; bd. dirs. YMCA, Mason City, 1972-75; pres. Luth. Social Svcs. Iowa FODN, 1987—. With U.S. Army, 1953-55. Mem. ABA, Iowa State Bar Assn. (bd. govs. 1986-91), Cerro Gordo County Bar Assn. (pres. 1976). Republican. Avocations: amateur radio, bird watching, sports. Home: 2040 Hunters Ridge Dr Mason City IA 50401-7500 Office: Laird Heiny McManigal Winga Duffy & Stambaugh 300 Norwest Bank Bldg Mason City IA 50401

HEINZ, E(DWARD) RALPH, neuroradiologist, educator; b. Cleve., Sept. 8, 1929; s. Edwin George and Gail (Reeve) H.; m. Ann McCardle, June 19, 1976; children: Tad, Christopher, Dana, Lindsey. AB, W.Va. U., 1951; MD, U. Pa., Phila., 1955. Diplomate Am. Bd. Radiology, 1963. Intern Phila. Gen. Hosp., 1955-56; resident in internal medicine U. Calif., San Francisco, 1958-59; NIH fellow in neuroradiology Neurol. Inst. Columbia U., N.Y.C., 1962-67; asst. prof. radiology Emory U., Atlanta, 1964-66, assoc. prof. radiology, 1967; assoc. prof. radiology Yale U., New Haven, 1967-69; prof., chmn. radiology U. Pitts., 1969-77, prof. radiology, 1977-78; chief divsn. neuroradiology Duke U. Hosp., Durham, N.C., 1978—; prof. radiology Duke U., Durham, N.C., 1978—; mem Com. A, Neurol. Scis. Rsch. & Tng. Com., Nat. Inst. Neurol. Diseases and Stroke NIH, Bethesda, Md., 1966-79, mem. Neurol. Disorders Program Project Com., 1975-79. Editor: Clinical Neurosciences Part 4 Neuroradiology, 1984; assoc. editor Archives of Neurology, 1975-80; contbr. over 150 articles to profl. publs. concerning angiography, myelography, computed tomography, and magnetic resonance applications to diagnostic neuroradiology. Sr. asst. surgeon USPHS, 1956-58. Fellow Am. Coll. Radiology; mem. Am. Soc. Neuroradiology (v.p. 1975-76), Am. Soc. Pediat. Neuroradiology (founding), Durham-Chapel Hill Torch Club. Republican. Achievements include development of Cl-2 spinal fluid puncture used in neuroradiology. Office: Duke Univ Hosp Box 3808 Erwin Rd Durham NC 27710

HEINZ, JOHN PETER, lawyer, educator; b. Carlinville, Ill., Aug. 6, 1936; s. William Henry and Margaret Louise (Denby) H.; m. Anne Murray, Jan. 14, 1967; children: Katherine Reynolds, Peter Lindley Murray. AB, Washington U., St. Louis, 1958; LLB, Yale U., 1962. Bar: D.C. 1962, Ill. 1966, U.S. Supreme Ct. 1967. Teaching asst. polit. sci. Washington U., St. Louis, 1958-59, instr., 1960; asst. prof. Northwestern U. Sch. Law, Chgo., 1965-68, assoc. prof., 1968-71, prof., 1971-88, Owen L. Coon prof., 1988—, dir. program law and social scis., 1968-70, dir. rsch., 1973-74, prof. sociology, 1987—; affiliated scholar Am. Bar Found., Chgo., 1974—, vis. scholar, 1975-76, exec. dir., 1982-86, disting. research fellow, 1987—. Author: (with A. Gordon) Public Access to Information, 1979, (with E. Laumann) Chicago Lawyers, 1982, rev. edit., 1994, (with E. Laumann, R. Nelson, R. Salisbury) The Hollow Core, 1993; contbr. articles to profl. jours. Served to capt. USAF, 1962-65. Grantee NIMH, 1970-72, NSF, 1970, 78-81, 84-86, 94-97, CNA Found., 1972, Am. Bar Found., 1974—, Russell Sage Found., 1978-80. Fellow Am. Bar Found.; mem. Law and Soc. Assn. (Harry Kalven prize for disting. research 1987), Am. Polit. Sci. Assn., ABA. Home: 525 Judson Ave Evanston IL 60202-3083 Office: Northwestern U Sch Law 357 E Chicago Ave Chicago IL 60611-3059

HEINZ, RONEY ALLEN, civil engineering consultant; b. Shawano, Wis., Dec. 29, 1946; s. Orville Willard and Elva Ida (Allen) H.; m. Judy Evonne Olney, Oct. 30, 1965. BSCE, Mont. State U., 1973. Surveyor U.S. Army Corps Engrs., Seattle, 1966-73; civil engr. Hoffman, Fiske, & Wyatt, Lewiston, Idaho, 1973-74, Tippetts-Abbott-McCarthy-Stratton, Seattle, 1977-79; asst. editor Civil Engring. Mag. ASCE, N.Y.C., 1974-77; constrn. mgr. Boeing Co., Seattle, 1979-83; owner, gen. mgr. Armwavers Ltd., South Bend, Wash., 1983—; pres. Great Walls Internat. Inc., Elma, Wash., 1993-95, Heinz Internat., Inc., 1995—, Interocean Mgmt. Svcs., Inc., Republic of Panama, 1998—; mem. dams and tunnels del. to China, People to People Internat., Spokane, 1987; mem. U.S. com. on Large Dams. Asst. editor Commemorative Book Internat. Congress on Large Dams, 1987; contbr. articles to profl. publs., including Civil Engring. Mag., Excavator Mag., Internat. Assn. for Bridge and Structural Engring., Japan Concrete Inst., others. Dir. Canaan Christians Fund, Aberdeen, 1993—; bd. dirs. Seaman's Ctr., Aberdeen, Wash., 1990—. Recipient First Quality award Asphalt Paving Assn. Wash., 1991. Mem. ASCE (sec. met. sect. 1975-76, assoc. mem. forum), ASTM (Student award 1973), USCOLD. Republican. Lutheran. Achievements include management of first commercial installation worldwide of sediment control by water jets, of development of first private harbor and container terminal in Panama in Manzanillo Bay, Colon. Office: Armwavers Ltd PO Box 782 South Bend WA 98586-0782

HEINZ, TERESA F., foundation administrator; m. John Heinz (dec.); m. John Kerry. BA in Romance Langs., Lit., U. Witwatersrand, Johannesburg, South Africa; grad., U. Geneva, 1963; PhD (hon.), Beloit Coll., Wis., Bank ST. Coll. Edn., N.Y., Drexel U., Pa., Med. Coll. Pa. Cons. UN Trusteeship, N.Y.C.; chmn. Heinz Family Found., Pitts., Howard Heinz Endowment; trustee Vira I. Heinz Endowment; endowed creation of professorship environ. mgmt. Harvard Bus. Shc., chair environ. policy John F. Kennedy Sch. Govt.; vice chair Environ. Def. Fund; past mem. external adv. bd. Inst. Biospheric Studies, Yale U.; mem. adv. bd. Earth Comm. Office; founder Second Nature; co-founder, bd. dirs. Alliance to End Childhood Lead Poisoning; trustee Winslow Found.; bd. dirs. Carnegie Corp., Family Comm.; trustee emeritus Brookings Inst.; bd. dir. trustee Phillips Exeter Acad., St. paul's Sch., Georgetown U.; co-founder Nat. Coun. Families TV. Founding mem., co-chair Congl. Wives Soviet Jewry; trustee governing bd. Yale Art Gallery; mem. trustees coun. Nat. Gallery Art; bd. dirs. Carnegie Inst., Pitts., OVATION. Avocations: art collecting. Office: Heinz Family Offices Ste 619 1201 Pennsylvania Ave NW Washington DC 20004-2401*

HEINZ, WALTER ERNST EDWARD, retired chemical executive; b. Milw., Jan. 3, 1920; s. Paulina and William (Krueger) H.; m. Gayle Virginia Hillegeist, Mar. 29, 1946; children: Richard Lee, Jenny Lee, Paula Stel; m. Bonnie M. Giltner, Sept. 5, 1987. BS, U. Wis., 1942, MS, 1948. Chemist, then sect. leader Celanese Chem. Co., Corpus Christi, Tex., 1948-62; tech. mgr. Ticona Polymerwerke, Celanese/Hoechst Joint Venture, Kelsterbach, W. Ger., 1962-64; market devel. mgt. Celanese Plastics Co., Newark, 1964-65; mgr. formed plastic products Celanese Plastics Co., Clark, N.J., 1965-66; tech. and prodn. mgr. Celanese Plastics Co., Greer, S.C., 1966-69; dir. devel. Celanese Chem. Co., Inc., Corpus Christi, 1969-83; tchr. organic chemistry Del Mar Coll. Served as aviator USN, 1942-46. Mem. Am. Inst. Chem. Engrs., Alpha Chi Sigma. Republican. Presbyterian. Holder 30 patents in field. Office: PO Box 9077 Corpus Christi TX 78469-9077

HEINZ, WILLIAM DENBY, lawyer; b. Carlinville, Ill., Nov. 26, 1947; s. William Henry and Margaret (Denby) H.; children: Kimberly, Rebecca, Elizabeth; m. Catherine Lamb Heinz. BS, Millikin U., 1969; JD, U. Ill., 1973. Bar: Ill. 1973, U.S. Dist. Ct. (no. dist.) Ill. 1974, U.S. Ct. Appeals (3d cir.) 1982, U.S. Ct. Appeals (5th cir.) 1973, U.S. Ct. Appeals (7th cir.) 1976, U.S. Supreme Ct. 1979. Law clk. to judge U.S. Ct. Appeals (5th cir.), Tuscaloosa, Ala., 1973-74; assoc. Jenner & Block, Chgo., 1974-80, ptnr., 1980—; mem. faculty NITA, 1981—; adj. prof. Northwestern U. Sch. Law, 1995—; bd. visitors U. Ill. Coll. Law, 1990-93, pres.'s coun. U. Ill.; bd. dirs. Legal Aid Bur., Chgo. Bd. dirs. Met. Family Svcs. Chgo. Recipient Disting. Grad. award U. Ill. Coll. Law, 1995. Fellow Am. Coll. Trial Lawyers; mem. ABA, Ill. Bar Assn. (civil practice and procedure sect. coun., com. on liaison with Ill. ARDC), Chgo. Bar Assn. (jud. evaluation com. 1990-93), ARDC Ill. Profl. Responsibility Inst., Cribbett Soc., U. Ill. Coll. Law, Legal Club (bd. dirs. 1998—), Westmoreland Country Club. Home: 920 Pawnee Rd Wilmette IL 60091-1345 Office: Jenner & Block 1 E Ibm Plz Fl 46 Chicago IL 60611-7693

HEINZERLING, LARRY EDWARD, communications executive; b. Elyria, Ohio, Aug. 28, 1945; s. Lynn Louis and Agnes Corinne (Dengate) H.; m. Sharyn Lee Jorgensen, Jan. 11, 1969 (div. 1985); children: Jesse, Kristen, Benjamin; m. Sieglinde Wolf, Aug. 1, 1985 (dec. Mar. 1998); stepchildren: Andreas Klohnen, Eva Klohnen. BA in Polit. Sci., Journalism, Ohio Wesleyan U., 1967; MA in Internat. Journalism, Ohio State U., 1969. Reporter AP, Columbus, Ohio, 1969-71; corr. AP, Lagos, Nigeria, 1971-74; bur. chief AP, Johannesburg, South Africa, 1974-78; mng. dir. AP, Frankfurt, Germany, 1978-83; dir. world services AP, N.Y.C., 1983-87; dep. dir. AP World Svc., N.Y.C., 1987—, also spl. asst. to AP pres. News coverage includes: coverage West Africa including Sahel drought, 1971-74, coverage Soweto riots, Mozambique independence, Angola, Rhodesia (now Zimbabwe). Trustee Ohio Wesleyan U., 1993-96, Bancroft, Inc., 1993-97, Bancroft Schs. and Cmtys., 1997—. Recipient Headliners award Headliners Club, Atlantic City, 1977, AP reportorial Performance award Mng. Editors, N.Y.C., 1977; nominated for Pulitzer Prize, 1976. Mem. Phi Delta Theta. Roman Catholic. Avocations: foreign affairs, history, philosophy, science. Office: AP 50 Rockefeller Plz New York NY 10020-1605

HEIRD, JAMES C., agricultural studies educator; b. Blount County, Tenn.. BS in Agr., U. Tenn., 1970, MS in Agr., 1971; PhD in Agr., Tex. Tech. U., 1978. Livestock and horse specialist N.C. State U., Raleigh, 1972-76; horse specialist Tex. Tech. U., Lubbock, 1976-86; tching. coord. equine sci. program Colo. State U., Fort Collins, 1986-89, acting dean, Coll. Agrl. Scis., 1991-92, interim dean, Coll. Bus., 1993-94, assoc. dean/dir. acad. programs, Coll. Agrl. Scis., 1989—. Office: Colorado State Univ College of Agrl Sciences Fort Collins CO 80523*

HEIRMAN, DONALD NESTOR, training engineering company executive, consultant; b. Mishawaka, Ind., Aug. 16, 1940; s. Chester J. and Agnes M. Heirman; m. Lois M. Heirman. BSEE, Purdue U., 1962, MSEE, 1963. Mem. tech. staff, then disting. mem. tech. staff AT&T Bell Labs., Holmdel, N.J., 1963-83; mem. tech. staff Am. Bell, Holmdel, 1983-84; supr. AT&T Info. Systems, Holmdel, 1984-88; mgr. global product compliance dept. AT&T Bell Labs., Holmdel, 1989-1996, Lucent Technologies Inc., 1996-97; adj. prof., sr. rsch. scientist, assoc. dir. wireless EMC Ctr. for Study of Wireless EMC, U. Okla., 1997—; course dir. Ctr. for Profl. Advancment, East Brunswick, N.J., 1988—; mem. exec. com. U.S. Nat. Com. IEC, 1995—; U.S. tech. expert subcoms. (SC) A, E and G, Internat. Spl. Com. on Radio Interference (CISPR), 1986—; sec. SC A, 1998—; chmn. SC A WG1, 1998—; chmn. Am. Nat. Stds. Inst. Accredited Stds. Com. C63 Subcoms. 1 and 5, 1986—; adj. prof. U. Okla., 1997—, sr. rsch. scientist, assoc. dir. wireless EMC. Author of tech. papers on electromagnetic compatibility (EMC), 1973—. Cmdr. USNR, 1963-85, ret. Named Disting. Mem. Tech. Staff, AT&T Bell Labs., 1982. Fellow IEEE (stds. bd. 1990—, vice chmn., 1998—, Centennial medal 1984, Disting. Svc. award 1993, Charles Proteus Steinmetz award 1996-97); mem. IEEE Electromagnetic Compatibility Soc. (bd. 1981-93, 97—, pres., treas., chmn. stds. com. 1982—, v.p. for stds. 1997—, Laurence G. Cumming award 1986, Stoddart award 1995). Office: DON HEIRMAN CONSULTANTS 143 Jumping Brook Rd Lincroft NJ 07738-1442

HEISE, MARILYN BEARDSLEY, public relations company executive; b. Cedar Rapids, Iowa, Feb. 26, 1935; d. Lee Roy and Angeline Myrtle (Knudson) Beardsley; m. John W. Heise, July 9, 1960; children: William Earnshaw, Steven James, Kathryn Kay Benninghoff. BA, Drake U., 1957. Account exec. The Beveridge Orgn., Chgo., 1958-60; editor, pub. The Working Craftsman mag., Northbrook, Ill., 1971-78; columnist Chgo. Sun-Times, 1973-78; pres. Craft Books, Inc., Northbrook, 1978-84; v.p. Sheila King Pub. Rels., Chgo., 1984-87, Aaron D. Cushman, Inc., Chgo., 1987-88; pres. Creative Cons. Assocs., Inc., Glencoe, Ill., 1989—, Heartfelt Charity Cards, 1991—; mem. adv. panel Nat. Crafts Project, Ft. Collins, Colo., 1977; mem. adv. panel and com. Nat. Endowment for Arts, Washington, 1977; mem. editl. adv. bd. The Crafts Report, Seattle, 1978-86. Recipient achievement award Women in Mgmt., 1978. Mem. Pub. Rels. Soc. Am. (accredited). Office: Heartfelt 540 Frontage Rd Northfield IL 60093-1250

HEISE, MICHAEL RICHARD, law educator; b. Chgo., Mar. 30, 1960; s. Richard A. Sr. and Clair Anne (Fogarty) H.; m. Dawn Michelle Chutkow, July 30, 1988; children: Nicole, Matthew. AB, Stanford U., 1983; JD, U. Chgo., 1987; PhD, Northwestern U., 1990. Assoc. Rudnick & Wolfe, Chgo., 1990; sr. cousnel Office for Civil Rights, U.S. Dept. Edn., Washington, 1991; chief of staff Office of Sec., U.S. Dept. Edn., Washington, 1991-92; rsch. fellow Hudson Inst., Washington, 1992-94; asst. prof. law Ind. U. Sch. Law, Indpls., 1994—. Home: 4969 Woodfield Dr Carmel IN 46033-9424 Office: Ind U Sch Law 735 W New York St Indianapolis IN 46202-5222

HEISER, ARNOLD MELVIN, astronomer; b. Bklyn., Feb. 9, 1933; s. Hyman Samuel and Sadie (Kretchmer) H.; m. Vivian Carol Jacobs, June 6, 1964; children—Naomi Elizabeth, David Alan. AB, Ind. U., 1954, MA, 1956; PhD, U. Chgo., 1961. Rsch. asst. Ind. U., 1954-56; rsch. fellow U. Chgo., 1956-61; asst. prof. physics and astronomy Vanderbilt U., Nashville, 1961-66, assoc. prof., 1966-99, prof. emeritus, 1999—; dir. A.J. Dyer Obs., 1972-86; H. Shapley vis. prof. Am. Astron. Soc., 1969—. Subscriptions editor Comms. of the Internat. Amateur-Profl. Photoelectric Photometry, 1993—; contbr. articles to profl. jours. Mem. Am. Astron. Soc., Internat. Astron. Union, Tenn. Acad. Sci., Sigma Xi. Home: 6132 Gardendale Dr Nashville TN 37215-5602 Office: Vanderbilt Univ A J Dyer Observatory Nashville TN 37235

HEISER, CHARLES BIXLER, JR., botany educator; b. Cynthiana, Ind., Oct. 5, 1920; s. Charles Bixler and Inez (Metcalf) H.; m. Dorothy Gaebler, Aug. 19, 1944; children—Lynn Marie, Cynthia Ann, Charles Bixler III. A.B., Washington U., St. Louis, 1943, M.A., 1944; Ph.D., U. Calif. at Berkeley, 1947. Instr. Washington U. St. Louis, 1944-45; assoc. botany U. Calif. at Davis, 1946-47; mem. faculty Ind. U., Bloomington, 1947—; prof. botany Ind. U., 1957—, Disting. prof., 1979-86, disting. prof. emeritus, 1986—. Author: Nightshades, The Paradoxical Plants, 1969, Seed to Civilization, The Story of Man's Food, 1973, The Sunflower, 1976, The Gourd Book, 1979, Of Plants and People, 1985. Guggenheim fellow, 1953; NSF Sr. Postdoctoral fellow, 1962; recipient Pustovoit award Internat. Sunflower Assn., 1985. Mem. Am. Soc. Plant Taxonomists (pres. 1967, Asa Gray award 1988), Bot. Soc. Am. (Merit award 1972, pres. 1980), Soc. Study Evolution (pres. 1974), Internat. Assn. Plant Taxonomy, Soc. Econ. Botany (pres. 1978, Disting. Econ. Botanist 1984), Nat. Acad. Scis., Phi Beta Kappa, Sigma Xi. Rsch., numerous publs. on systematics flowering plants, natural and artificial hybridization, origin cultivated plants. Home: 1018 E Southdowns Dr Bloomington IN 47401-6091

HEISER, JANET DOROTHY, physical education educator; b. Myerstown, Pa., Mar. 4, 1947; d. H. Paul and Dorothy A. (Sands) Shirk; m. S. Joseph Heiser, Feb. 28, 1970; children: Kelly Jo, Kori Jan, Kasey Jo. BS in Health and Phys. Edn., Pa. State U., 1969; M in Phys. Edn. and Health, West Chester U., 1972. Tchr. Ea. Lebanon County Sch., Myerstown, 1969—; dept. chmn. Ea. Lebanon County Sch., 1990—. Mem. worship com. United Ch. of Christ of Schaefferstown. Mem. AAHPERD, Lancaster-Lebanon HPERD (member-at-large), Lebanon County Ednl. Honor Soc. Avocations: running, reading. Home: 738 W Main St Schaefferstown PA 17088 Office: Ea Lebanon County Schs 60 Evergreen Dr Myerstown PA 17067-2611

HEISER, ROLLAND VALENTINE, former army officer, foundation executive; b. Columbus, Ohio, Apr. 25, 1925; s. Rudolph and Helen Cecile H.; m. Gwenne Kathleen Duquemin, Feb. 26, 1949; children: Helen Heiser Sanford, Charlene Heiser Wolff. BS, U.S. Mil. Acad., 1947; MS in Internat. Affairs, George Washington U., 1965. Commd. 2nd lt. U.S. Army, 1947; advanced through grades to lt. gen., 1976; army planner Washington, 1973-74; comdr. 1st Armored divsn. Germany, 1974-75; chief of staff U.S. Army Europe, 1975-76; chief of staff U.S. European Comd., 1976-78, ret., 1978;

pres. New Coll. Found., Sarasota, Fla., 1979—. Decorated D.S.M. with oak leaf cluster, Def. Superior Svc. medal, Legion of Merit (3), Bronze Star, others. Mem. Sarasota Com. 100, Retired Officers Assn., Sarasota County C. of C., Ret. Officers Sarasota (past pres., dir.), Masons. Republican. Episcopalian. Home: 4104 Las Palmas Way Sarasota FL 34238-4532 Office: New Coll Found 5700 N Tamiami Trl Sarasota FL 34243-2146

HEISER, WALTER CHARLES, librarian, priest, educator; b. Milw., Mar. 16, 1922; s. Walter Matthew and Lauretta Katherine (Kopmeier) H. AB, St. Louis U., 1945, AM, 1947, STL, 1955; MSLS, Cath. U. Am., 1959. Joined S.J., Roman Cath. Ch., 1940, ordained priest, 1953. Latin tchr. St. Louis U. High Sch., 1947-50; divinity libr. Saint Louis U., St. Louis, 1955—; mem. faculty dogmatic and systematic theology St. Louis U. Div. Sch., 1966-92; ret.; cons. catalog Cath. supplement Wilson Sr. High Sch. Libr., 1968-77. Rev. editor Theology Digest, 1963—. Mem. Cath. Libr. Assn. Home: 3601 Lindell Blvd Saint Louis MO 63108-3301 Office: 3650 Lindell Blvd Saint Louis MO 63108-3302

HEISERER, ALBERT, JR., automotive educator, small business owner; b. Bklyn., Nov. 28, 1937; s. Albert Charles and Alice (Bonin) H.; m. Rosemarie E. Pollinger, May, 17, 1958; children: Albert A., Alicia R., Lawrence H. AAS Auto & Diesel Tech., SUNY, Farmingdale, 1957; BA in Biology & Math., Dowling Coll., 1975; postgrad., CUNY, 1976-77. Cert. tchr., N.Y. Tech. researcher Fairchild Engine Div., Deer Park, N.Y., 1957-59; owner, operator A&A Shell, Williston Park, N.Y., 1959-65; tractor trailer driver United Parcel Svc., Maspeth, N.Y., 1965-72; teaching asst. Dowling Coll. Marine Sci. Program, Oakdale, N.Y., 1973; student tchr. Wilson Tech.-B.O.C.E.S., Lindenhurst, N.Y., 1977; automotive & diesel tchr. Middle Country Sch. Dist., Centereach, N.Y., 1977-88; owner, pres. Personal Mechanic, Ronkonkoma, N.Y., 1983-87; freelance religious writer Ronkonkoma, N.Y., 1987—; adj. prof. Suffolk Community Coll., Selden, N.Y., 1988—. Contbr. articles to mags. Chmn., organizer Meals on Wheels, 1982-87; pres., organizer Fish of Ronkonkoma, 1975—, Aid Assn. for Luth., 1986—; v.p. C. of C.; mem. Shepherds Inn Soup Kitchen, 1986—, all Lake ronkonkoma. With USCGR, 1954-62, USCGA, 1977-82, USCG MBO, capt. 1965-97. Recipient Eleanor Roosevelt Community Svc. award, Gov. Cuomo N.Y. 1985, Mid. Country Cen. Sch. Dist. award 1986, 87. Mem. Nassau-Suffolk Counselors Assn., Suffolk Co. Vocat. Educators Assn., N.Yl. State United Tchrs. Assn., NRA, Am. Assn. Christian Councillors, Am. Legion. Republican. Methodist. Avocations: organizing programs for the disadvantaged & handicapped. Home and Office: 17 Peter Rd Ronkonkoma NY 11779-4316

HEISLER, BARBARA SCHMITTER, sociology educator; b. Heidelberg, Germany, Dec. 17, 1940; came to U.S., 1961; d. Bernhard and Gudrun (Löffler) Epple; m. Philippe C. Schmitter, May 6, 1962 (div. 1979); children: Monika Schmitter, Marc Schmitter; m. Martin Heisler. PhD, U. Chgo., 1979. Postdoctoral fellow Duke U., Durham, N.C., 1979-80; asst. prof. sociology SUNY, Buffalo, 1980-81; assoc. prof. sociology Cleve. State U., 1982-89; prof. sociology Gettysburg (Pa.) Coll., 1989—. Contbr. articles to profl. jours. Rsch. fellow German Marshall Fund, Washington, 1990; rsch. grantee Evang. Luth. Ch. Am., 1995. Mem. Am. Sociol. Assn. (officer polit. sociology sect. 1996—). Avocations: tennis, skiing. Office: Gettysburg College Dept Sociology Gettysburg PA 17325

HEISLER, ELWOOD DOUGLAS, hotel executive; b. Wilmington, Del., June 29, 1935; s. Elwood Dean and Laura Matilda (Hutchison) H.; B.A., Mich. State U., 1957; postgrad. Johns Hopkins U., 1979—. Asst. mgr. Kents Restaurants, Atlantic City, 1957; mgr. Korean Mil. Adv. Group Officers' Club and Housing Office, Tague, 1958-59; innkeeper Treadway Inns Corp., N.Y., Mass., Colo., Ohio, Va., Del., 1960-68, Holiday Inns, Inc., Lansing and Troy, Mich., 1969-77; gen. mgr. Quality Inns, Inc., Towson, Md., 1977-89; gen. mgr. Quality Stes. Hotel, Mt. Laurel, N.J., 1989-94; gen. mgr. Accor Hotels, Windsor Locks, Conn., 1994—. Mem. SAR, St. George's Soc. of Balt., Soc. of Sons of St. George of Phila., German Soc. of Md., German Soc. of Pa., L'Amicale-Soc. Francaise de Balt., Welsh Soc. Phila., St. David's Soc. N.Y., St. Andrew's Soc. Conn., St. David's Soc. Conn., Conn. Lodging and Attractions Assn., German Soc. (N.Y.C.), Rittenhouse Family Assn., Supreme Ct. Hist. Soc., Hist. Soc. of Delaware, Md. Hist. Soc., Nantucket Hist. Assn., Burlington County N.J. Hist. Soc., Md. Retired Officers Assn., sec. Md. state adv. coun. Future Bus. Leaders of Am./Phi Beta Lambda; bd. dirs. Gunpowder Youth Camps, Inc.; mem. Balt. Coun. on Fgn. Affairs, Ea. Shor Soc. of Balt. (v.p.), Nat. Cathedral Assn., Md. Press Club (1st v.p.). Served to 1st lt. U.S. Army, 1957-59. Named Top Ten Innkeeper Holiday Inns Internat., 1975; Md. Bus. Person of Yr., Future Bus. Leaders of Am., 1981, Bus. Person of Yr. nat. chpt., 1981, award of Merit Balt. County C. of C., 1982, Paul Harris fellow Rotary Found., 1983, Outstanding Svc. award Md. Future Bus. Leaders of Am., 1984, Balt. Mayor's Citation, 1984. Mem. Am. Hotel and Motel Assn., N.J. Hotel and Motel Assn., Hotel Sales Mgmt. Assn., Balt. County C. of C. (v.p.), St. George Soc. of N.Y., Univ. Club, Towson Rotary Club (pres.), Advt. Balt. Club. (bd. govs.), Balt. Yacht Club, Liederkranz Club, Williams Club (N.Y.C.). Republican. Congregationalist. Author manual for resort ops., 1965; author: The Rising Sun of the Japanese Hotel Industry, 1980. Home and Office: Motel 6 PO Box 250 Windsor Locks CT 06096

HEISLER, HAROLD REINHART, management consultant; b. Chgo.; s. Harold Reinhart and Beulah Mary (Schade) H.; B.M.E., U. Ill., 1954. Mgmt. cons. Ill. Power Co., Decatur, 1954-96, mem. Nuclear Power Group, Inc., Argonne (Ill.) Nat. Lab., 1955-57; chmn. fossil fuel com., West Central region FPC, Chgo., 1966-68; chmn. evaluation com. Coal Gasification Group, Inc., 1971-75; chmn. Decatur Marine Inc., 1964-66; dir. Indsl. Water Supply Co., Robinson, Ill., 1975-77; pub. speaker in field; mem. Ill. Gov.'s Fuel and Energy Bd., 1970, Ill. Commerce Commn. Fuel and Energy Bd., 1971-75, Ill. Energy Resources Commn. Coal Study Panel, 1976-79, evaluation com. of kilngas process, 1976-80; mem. power plant productivity com. Ill. Commerce Commn., 1977-79; mem. com. on nuclear power plant constrn. Inst. Nuclear Power Ops. Mem. ASME, Nat., Ill. socs. profl. engrs., U. Ill. Alumni Assn., Sigma Phi Delta. Conceptual designer power plant sites and recreational lakes, Baldwin and Clinton, Ill. Home: 2350 W Main St Decatur IL 62522-1853 Office: Ill Power Co 500 S 27th St Decatur IL 62521-2200

HEISLER, QUENTIN GEORGE, JR., lawyer; b. Jefferson City, Mo., June 30, 1943; s. Quentin George and Helen (Reynolds) H.; m. Susan Davis, Jan. 24, 1970; children: Sarah, Thomas, Margaret. AB magna cum laude, Harvard U., 1965, JD, 1968. Bar: Ill. 1968, U.S. Dist. Ct. (no. dist.) Ill. 1969, Fla. 1977. Assoc. McDermott, Will & Emery, Chgo., 1968-69, 70-75, ptnr., 1975—; legal counsel Office Minority Bus. Enterprise, Dept. Commerce, Washington, 1969-70; mem. adv. bd. Entrepreneurship Inst., Chgo. Co-author: Working With Family Businesses, 1995; gen. editor: Trust Administration in Illinois, 1979. Chmn. Winnetka Caucus, Ill., 1983; mem. Winnetka Bd. Edn., 1985-89; trustee Hadley Sch. for the Blind, Winnetka; bd. govs. Winnetka Cmty. House. Fellow Am. Coll. Trust and Estates Counsel; mem. ABA, Chgo. Coun. Estate Planning, Univ. Club, Harvard Club (bd. dirs. Chgo. chpt. 1984-95, pres. bd. 1989-91), Skokie Country Club (Glencoe, Ill.). Office: McDermott Will & Emery 227 W Monroe St Ste 3100 Chicago IL 60606-5096

HEISLER, STANLEY DEAN, lawyer; b. The Dalles, Oreg., Jan. 11, 1946; s. Donald Eugene and Roberta (Van Valkenburgh) H. BA, Willamette U., 1968, JD, 1972. Bar: Oreg. 1972, U.S. Ct. Claims 1972, U.S. Tax Ct. 1972, U.S. Ct. Appeals (9th cir.) 1972, D.C. 1973, U.S. Ct. Appeals (fed. cir.) 1973, U.S. Ct. Mil. Appeals 1973, N.Y. 1985, U.S. Supreme Ct. 1985. Assoc. Heisler & Van Valkenburgh, The Dalles, 1973-74; ptnr. Heisler, Van Valkenburgh & Coats, The Dalles, 1975-81, Heisler & Heisler, The Dalles, 1982-84, Cohen & Shalleck, N.Y.C., 1985-88, Phillips, Nizer, Benjamin, Krim & Ballon, N.Y.C., 1988-91, Squadron, Ellenoff, Plesent, Sheinfeld & Sorkin, N.Y.C., 1991-94; mng. ptnr. Shays & Kemper, LLP, N.Y.C., 1994-98, Shays, Rothman, & Heisler, LLP, N.Y.C., 1999—. Speechwriter Sec. of State Tom McCall, Salem, 1965, Gov. Tom McCall, Salem, 1966-68; speechwriter, legis. asst. U.S. Senator Bob Packwood, Washington, 1969-73; vice chmn. Pres.'s Air Quality Adv. Bd., Washington, 1973-76. Mem. ABA, N.Y. State Bar Assn., Assn. of Bar of City of N.Y., Arlington Club, Univ. Club (N.Y.C. and Portland, Oreg.), Soc. Mayflower Descs., Soc. of the Descs. Washington's Army at Valley Forge, Soc. for the Promotion of Hellenic Studies (London), Edmund Rice (1638) Assn. Republican. Home: 400 E 77th St Apt 8J New York NY 10021-2342 Office: Shays Rothman & Heisler LLP 276 5th Ave New York NY 10001-4509

HEISS, FREDERICK WILLIAM, political science educator, public administrator, policy researcher; b. Kansas City, Mo., Mar. 3, 1932; s. William and Sophia Else (Schmid) H.; m. Patricia Jane Stark, June 19, 1958 (div. May 1982): children: William Frederick, Scott Evan, Kerrel Kae; m. Carol Mae Knox, Jan. 9, 1983; 1 child, Brac Seaton. BSBA, U. Denver, 1958; MPA, U. Colo., 1968, PhD, 1973. Adminstr. City and County Denver, 1958-70; asst. prof. U. Colo., Boulder, 1973-78, assoc. prof., 1978-85; dir. Denver Urban Obs. U. Colo., Denver, 1970-82, dir. MPA grad. program, 1982-85; chmn. dpet. pub. adminstrn. Va. Commonwealth U., Richmond, 1985-91, prof., 1991—; dir. met. study Nat. Acad. Pub. Adminstrn., Washington, 1974-76; dir. sci. tech. NSF, Denver, 1976-78, nat. chmn. sci. and tech. transfer, 1977-78; cons. U.S. Civil Svc. Commn., Utah, 1975; dir. Capital Area Study and Program, Richmond, 1987-93; vis. prof. Huanghe U., Henan, China, 1989. Author: Urban Research and Urban Policy, 1975; contbr. articles to profl. jours. Keynote speaker League of Women Voters, Denver 1975, Pres. Carters Urban Conf., Denver, 1977; dir. regional governance Capital Area Assembly, Richmond, 1990-94. With Air Corps, USN, 1953-55, Korea. Grantee HUD, 1972-83, Dept. of Energy, 1979-82. Fellow Beta Theta Pi; mem. ASPA. Avocations: sailing, skiing, fishing. Home: 14198 Mill Creek Dr Montpelier VA 23192-2837 Office: Va Commonwealth U Dept Polit Sci & Pub Admin 923 W Franklin St Richmond VA 23284-9008 Address: 655 Kiowa Rd Lyons CO 80540-8211

HEISS, HARRY GLEN, archivist; b. Fort Smith, Ark., Jan. 3, 1953; s. Fred William and Mary Kathryn (Hall) H. BA, U. Ark., 1975, MA, 1984; archives cert., Western Wash. U., 1979. Archives intern Oreg. State Archives, Salem, 1979; asst. archivist Smithsonian Instn. Archives, Washington, 1980-85; archivist Nat. Air and Space Mus., Washington, 1985-87, Jefferson Nat. Expansion Meml., Nat. Pk. Svc., St. Louis, 1988-91, Libr. Congress, Washington, 1991—. Recipient Spl. Achievement award Nat. Pk. Svc., 1990. Mem. Soc. Am. Archivists, Soc. S.W. Archivists, Mid-Atlantic Archives Conf., D.C. Archivists. Democrat. Avocations: family history, bicycle touring, camping. E-mail: hhei@loc.gov. Home: PO Box 594 Arlington VA 22216-0594 Office: Libr Congress Manuscript Divsn LM-130 First & Independence Ave SE Washington DC 20540-4682

HEISS, RICHARD WALTER, former bank executive, consultant, lawyer; b. Monroe, Mich., July 8, 1930; s. Walter and Lillian (Harpst) H.; m. Nancy J. Blum, June 21, 1952; children: Kurt Frederick, Karl Richard. BA, Mich. State U., 1952; LLB, Detroit Coll., 1963, LLD (hon.), 1982; LLM, Wayne State U., 1969; cert., Stanford U. Exec. Program, 1979. Bar: Mich. 1963, U.S. Dist. Ct. (federal dist.) Mich. 1963. Asst. trust officer Mfrs. Nat. Bank of Detroit, 1960-62, trust officer, 1962-66; v.p., trust officer Mfrs. Nat. Bank Detroit, 1966-68, v.p., sr. trust officer, 1968-75, 1st v.p., sr. trust officer, 1975-77, sr. v.p., 1977-89, exec. v.p., 1989-92, sr. cons.; vice chair Detroit Coll. Law Found., 1995—; pres., CEO, Mfrs. Nat. Trust Co. Fla., 1984-88, chmn. bd., 1988-92; lectr. Inst. Continuing Legal Edn., Procknow Grad. Sch. Banking, U. Wis., Southwestern Grad. Sch. Bank, Am. Bankers Assn., Banking Sch. South; chmn. mem. exec. com. Trust Mgmt. Seminar, 1980; expert witness fiduciary law, 1993—. Mem. Legal-Fin. Network, Cmty. Found. S.E. Mich.; bd. dirs. Hist. Trinity, Inc., 1992—; trustee Detroit Coll. Law at Mich. State U., pres., 1983-94; pres. Mich. State U. Bus. Sch. Alumni Bd., 1983; mem. allocation and evaluation com. United Way S.E. Mich., 1989-92. 1st lt. AUS, 1952-57. Fellow State Bar Mich. Found.; mem. Mich. Bar Assn., Am. Bankers Assn. (pres. 1981, exec. com. trust divsn., pvt. banking com. 1984-89, investment adv. com. 1984-89), Mich. Bankers Assn. (chmn. trust divsn. exec. com. 1975), Detroit Golf Club (bd. dirs., pres. 1983), Mich. Srs. Golf Assn. (bd. govs. 1994—), Club of Seabrook Island, Delta Chi, Sigma Nu Phi. Republican. Lutheran. Home and Office: 30684 Sudbury Ct Farmington Hills MI 48331

HEISSER-METOYER, PATRICIA, psychologist, organizational consultant; b. L.A., May 15, 1946. BA in Psychology, Calif. State U., L.A., 1966; PhD; U. Calif., Irvine, 1976. Clin. psychology fellow UCLA Neuro-Psychiat. Inst., Westwood, Calif., 1971-72; sr. staff psychologist Cedar-Sinai Med. Ctr., L.A., 1972-84; dir. clin. tng., asst. prof. Antioch U., Marina del Rey, Calif., 1993—; cons. Xerox, IBM, among others, 1984-92, Fed. Emergency Mgmt. Agy., L.A., 1992-94, Musicians Assistance Program, L.A., 1995-96, Internat. Ho. of Blues, 1994-96, L.A. County Dept. Mental Health, Dept. Labor, Internat. Tng. Cons., Washington, 1966-69, exec. admin., Affirmative Action Screen Actors Guild, 1998—. Mem. APA, NAACP, L.A. Jazz Soc. (bd. dirs., dir. contbns. and devel.), Am. Mgmt. Assn., Alpha Kappa Alpha. Avocations: playwright, producer, radio personality, media consultant. Office: Antioch U 13274 Fiji Way Marina Del Rey CA 90292

HEISTAD, DONALD DEAN, cardiologist; b. Chgo., Apr. 2, 1940; m. Sandra J.; children: Wendy, Dean. BS, U. Ill., 1959; MD, U. Chgo., 1963. Asst. prof. medicine U. Iowa Coll. Medicine, Iowa City, 1970-73, assoc. prof. medicine, 1973-76, prof. medicine, 1976—, prof. pharmacology, 1987—; dir. cardiovascular divsn. U. Iowa Coll. Medicine, 1995—; bd. dirs. Iowa Ctr. on Aging; mem. sci. bd. Sarnoff Endowment for Cardiovasc. Sci.; chair acad. adv. bd. Pfizer Vis. Professorship Program. Editor: Cerebral Blood Flow: Effects of Nerves, 1982, Arteriosclerosis, Thrombsis, and Vascular Biology, 1999—; assoc. editor: Hypertension, 1989-93, Circulation Rsch., 1980-85; contbr. more than 380 papers to profl. jours. and chpts to books. Pres. U. Iowa Faculty Senate, Iowa City, 1980-81; vice-chair coun. on circulation Am. Heart Assn., 1994-96. Capt. U.S. Army, 1967-70. Recipient Irving S. Wright award Stroke Coun., 1976, Harry Goldblatt award Coun. for High Blood Pressure Rsch., 1980, Merit award, 1987, Disting. Lecture award Coun. on Thrombosis, Disting. Alumni award U. Chgo., 1991, Novartis award Coun. High Blood Pressure Rsch., 1997, Wiggers award Am. Physiol. Soc., 1999. Fellow Coun. for High Blood Pressure Rsch., Am. Soc. for Clin. Investigation, Assn. Am. Physicians, Coun. for Geriatric Cardiology, Assn. Univ. Cardiologist (sec.-treas. 1998—), Am. Physiol. Soc. (chair cardiovascular sect. 1995-96); mem. Internat. Soc. and Fedn. Cardiologists (chair arteriosclerosis coun.), Am. Heart Assn. (chair coun. on circulation). Democrat. Office: U Iowa Coll Medicine Dept Medicine Iowa City IA 52242

HEISTAND, ANITA MAY, writer; b. Chardon, Kans., Apr. 26, 1934; d. Alvin Corwin and Vera May (Hachenberg) Brown; m. Kenneth Wesley Heistand, Oct. 19, 1951; children: Kenneth Bruce, Rebecca Dell, Janette Elaine. Author articles to Kans. Mag., Reader's Digest, Harris' Farmers' Almanac, Ozark Mountaineer, Kansas City Star; writings included in anthologies: Christmas in the Ozarks, 1993, Legacy of Love, 1995, God's Vitamin C for the Christmas Spirit, 1996, Southeast Kansas, Land of Discovery, 1995. Mem. Kans. Authors Club (pres. dist. 3 1995—), Joplin Writers Guild (past pres.), Pittsburg Christian Writers (past pres.). Republican. Baptist. Home: 10250 SE 100th St Galena KS 66739

HEIT, IVAN, packaging equipment company executive; b. Phila., Sept. 16, 1946; s. Julius and Sylvia (Kantor) H.; m. Joanne Bernard, Oct. 5, 1968; children: Brad Eric, Scott Harris, Mark Alan. BA in English, Pa. State U., 1968. Store mgr. Cameo Stores Inc., Phila., 1968-70; territory mgr. Lester Brooks Assocs., Pitts., 1970-73; dept. mgr. Garrett-Buchanan Co., Phila., 1973-76, div. mgr., 1980-83; pres. Flex-Packaging Systems Inc., Camden, N.J., 1976-80; regional mgr. Allied Automoation Inc., Dallas, 1983-85, mktg. mgr., 1985-87, mktg. dir., 1987-90; v.p. sales and mktg. Arpac Corp., Schiller Park, Ill., 1990-96; global v.p. sales & mktg. Indsl. Dynamics Co., Ltd., Torrance, Calif., 1996-97; pres. Kayat Engring. Corp., Edgewater, Fla., 1997-98; v.p. bus. devel. Am. Packaging Capital, Inc., Danville, Calif., 1998—; guest lectr. St. Joseph's U., Phila., 1980-85; guest instr. U. Wis. Sch. of Mgmt., Madison. Mem. adv. bd. Spring Garden Coll., Phila., 1983-85; asst. dist. commr. Boy Scouts Am., Pitts., 1983; pres. Cherry Hill (N.J.) Eastern Little League, 1985; mgr. YMCA Athletic Program, Plano, Tex., 1986-87. Served with USCG, 1968. Mem. Inst. Packaging Profls. USA (profl. chmn. plastics in packaging tech. com. 1984-85, chmn. Greater Phila. chpt. 1981-84), Soc. Packaging and Handling Engrs. (profl.). Democrat. Jewish. Avocations: athletics, gardening.

HEITKAMP, HEIDI, state attorney general; b. Breckenridge, Minn.; m. Darwin Lange; children: Alethea Lange, Nathan Lange. BA, U. N.D., 1977; JD, Lewis and Clark Coll., 1980. Intern asst. Environ. Study Conf., Washington, 1976; legis. intern N.D. Legis. Coun., Bismarck, 1977; exec. dir. Northwestern Environ. Def. Ctr., Portland, 1978-79; rsch. asst. Nat. Resources Law Inst., Portland, 1979; atty. enforcement divsn. EPA, Washington, 1980-81; asst. atty. gen. Office of N.D. State Tax Commr., Bismarck, 1981-85, adminstrv. counsel, 1985-86, tax commr., 1986-92; atty. gen. State of N.D., Bismarck, 1993—; del. Am. Coun. Young Polit. Leaders, UK Internat. Def. Conf., 1988; trustee Fedn. Tax Adminstrs., 1991; presdl. appointee trade and environment policy adv. com. Office of Trade Reps., 1996. N.D. State Crusade chmn. Am. Cancer Soc., 1988—. Recipient Young Achiever award Nat. Coun. Women, 1987; named One of 20 Young Lawyers Making a Difference, ABA Barrister mag., 1990; Toll fellow Coun. State Govts., 1986. Mem. Nat. Assn. Atty. Gens. Office: Attorney General State Capitol 600 E Boulevard Ave Dept 125 Bismarck ND 58505-0040*

HEITLER, GEORGE, lawyer; b. N.Y.C., Sept. 3, 1915; s. John J. and Celia (Zeichner) H.; m. Florence A. Posner, Apr. 21, 1940; children: James B., Richard S. BS, Columbia U., 1936, JD, 1938. Bar: N.Y. 1938, Ill. 1962. Asso. firm Cutler, Wilson & McMahon, N.Y.C., 1938-40; spl. asst. to David L. Podell; counsel to Hays, Podell & Schulman, N.Y.C., 1940; asso. atty. firm Coughlan & Russell; also mng. agt. and asst. sec. Central Manhattan Properties, Inc., N.Y.C., 1940-43; chief clk., legal adviser rents and claims bd. 4th Service Command, U.S. Army, 1943-45; engaged as bus. exec., also house counsel various comml. orgns., 1946-57; asst. sec., staff counsel Blue Cross Assn., N.Y.C., 1957-60; corporate sec., staff counsel Blue Cross Assn., 1960-61; v.p., sec. Chgo., 1961-71; sr. v.p., corporate sec., gen. counsel, 1971-81; sr. v.p., legal counsel Nat. Blue Shield Assn., 1978-81; counsel to Kaye, Scholer, Fierman, Hays & Handler, N.Y.C., 1981-85; spl. adviser Dept. Labor, also speaker and panelist. Author articles. Mem. Am., Chgo. bar assns., Assn. Bar City N.Y. Home: 6700 Gulf Of Mexico Dr Longboat Key FL 34228-1337

HEITMAN, GREGORY ERWIN, state official; b. Lewiston, Idaho, June 7, 1947; s. Elmer William and Carmelita Rose Ann (Kinzer) H.; m. Phyllis Ann Pryor, Sept. 25, 1982. BS in Math., U. Idaho, 1969, MBA, 1971; student, Wash. State U., 1965-67. Student communications dir. Assoc. Students U. Idaho, Moscow, 1970-72, advisor, apt. mgr. dept. housing, 1971-72; traffic fatality analyst Idaho Dept. Transp., Boise, 1973-74; ops. mgr. Region IV Health & Welfare State of Idaho, Boise, 1974-78, supr. computer svcs., div. environ. in health and welfare, 1978-85; coord. field svcs., program dir. Idaho Ctr. for Vital Stats. and Health Policy, Boise, 1985—; acting dir. Idaho Ctr. for Health Statistics, Boise, 1988-89, spl. asst. program and policy devel., 1989—; mem. med. records adv. com. Boise State U., 1987—, cons., lectr. 1987—. Active various charitable orgns.; precinct committeeman Dem. of Latah County, 1972; election day coord. Ada County, 1986; vol. Am. Cancer Soc., 1990, Easter Seals, 1992, Arthritis Found., 1996. Mem. Idaho Pub. Health Assn., Assn. Vital Records and Health Statistics, Idaho Pub. Employees Assn., Assn. Govt. Employees. Roman Catholic. Avocations: bowling, card collecting. Home: 1762 E Summerridge Dr Meridian ID 83642-5586 Office: Idaho Vital Stats PO Box 83720 Boise ID 83720-3720

HEITMAN, SUSAN MARIE, artist; b. Detroit, Aug. 16, 1954; d. William and Lillian (Slager) Kobos; m. Roger Melvin Heitman, Sept. 18, 1976; 1 child, Brenda Jean. BFA, Ea. Mich. U., Ypsilanti, 1988, MA, 1995. Artist Plymouth, Mich., 1995—. Exhibited in group shows at Ann Arbor (Mich.) Art Ctr., 1995-97, Detroit Artists Mkt., 1995-97, Ann Arbor Women Painters, 1995-99, The New Regionalism, 1996-98, Jackson Area Show, 1997 (Merit award), State of Arts, Saginaw Twp., Mich., 1997, Ctrl. Mich. U. Art Gallery, Mt. Pleasant, 1997, Soumi Internat. Collection Art/Design, Hancock, Mich., 1997, First Internat. Open WomanMade Gallery, Chgo., 1998, National Women Made Gallery, Chgo., 1998, Bonifas Fine Arts Ctr., Escanaba, Mich., 1998, Beyond the Surface Nat., Paint Creek Ctr. for the Arts, Rochester, Mich., 1999, Sisson Gallery, Dearborn, Mich., 1999, Nat. Women in Art Exhibit, Wallace Smith Gallery, Oakland C.C., Farm Hills, Mich., 1999. Coord. crafts Northville (Mich.) Christian Assembly, 1997, tchr. crafts, 1995-96. Recipient Exceptional Merit award Ella Sharp Mus., Jackson, Mich., 1997; grad. fellow Ea. Mich. U., 1994-95. Mem. Detroit Artists Mkt., Ann Arbor Art Assn., Ann Arbor Women Painters (co-chairperson 1995—, co-chairperson exhibits 1997, 98—, chair exhibits 1998—, Merit award 1996), Paint Creek Ctr. Arts. Mem. Assembly of God. Avocations: gardening, travel, gourmet cooking, reading, web surfing. Home: 5303 Napier Rd Plymouth MI 48170-5033

HEITMANN, GEORGE JOSEPH, business educator, consultant; b. N.Y.C., Nov. 27, 1933; s. Frederick Charles and Henrietta (Boesl) H.; m. Marian Kingsley, Sept. 3, 1960; children: James, Noel, Peter. AB, Syracuse U., 1956; MA, Princeton U., 1960, PhD, 1963. Prof. mgmt. sci. Pa. State U., University Park, 1958-93, chmn. dept., 1978-87, dir. internat. programs Coll. Bus. Adminstrn., 1989-93; chmn. dept. acctg., bus. and econs., dean internat. programs Muhlenberg Coll., Allentown, Pa., 1994—; econ. advisor Ministry of Planning and Devel., Govt. of Libya, Tripoli, 1964-66; cons. energy policy staff Exec. Office of Pres., Washington, 1968-70; vis. lectr. Universität zu Köln, Cologne, Fed. Republic of Germany, 1974; vis. prof. Ruhr Universität, Bochum, Fed. Republic of Germany, 1970, 74, 77, W.Va. U., Morgantown, 1975, Shanghai Inst. Mech. Engring., Peoples Republic of China, 1985; cons. Helsinki Inst. Bus. Econs., Finland, 1980; Pa. State U. resident advisor U. West Indies, Kingston, Jamaica, 1987-89. Contbr. articles to profl. jours. Served as 1st lt. U.S. Army, 1957. Mem. Am. Econ. Assn., Am. Statis. Assn., Internat. Inst. Forecasters, Inst. Mgmt. Sci., Decision Scis. Inst., Phi Beta Kappa. Home: 930 S 24th St Allentown PA 18103-3706 Office: Muhlenberg Coll Ettinger Bldg Allentown PA 18104-5586*

HEITSCH, LEONA MASON, artist, writer; b. Pontiac, Mich., Jan. 6, 1931; d. Russell Leonard and Margaret M. (Arnold) Mason; m. Charles Weyand Heitsch, July 5, 1952; children: Russell, Carrie, Grace, Charles, Irene. *13 generations back, Catalina Trico, a Walloon born in Paris, arrived to Albany, New York in 1623 with her husband Joris Rapleje. One of the weavers who developed the trico knit. Catalina's words were saved in history: "I lived in Albany 3 years, all which time ye Indians were all as quiet as lambs and came and traded with all ye freedom imaginable." She died a widow at age 84 in 1669 on Long Island where she kept her garden. She had 150 descendants. Her outlook is treasured.* BA in chemistry, U. Mich., 1952. Edn1. asst. Spl. Sch. Dist., St. Louis County, Mo., 1969-81; commentator Sta. KUMR, Rolla, Mo., 1996-99. *Actively works with and supports diverse groups to encourage a swelling of literary and artistic endeavor to the children of our world. She seeks to teach that the kind of pleasure which can be known in reverence for all life, gentle observation of the infinite wonders of the universe, sharing with neighbors, and the process of living simply and honestly is exciting and rewarding. Thanks to teacher Dorothy McCannon for early inspiration and impetus.* Author: (pvt. printing) Echoes of the Ridge, 1985, Get Him to St. Louis, 1983; contbr. poetry, articles to various publs. Sec., activist Mo. Assn. Children with Learning Disabilities, St. Louis, 1973-75; fundraising, writing Friends of Foster-Dolbeer Farm, Walled Lake, Mich., 1996—; contbg. poet Wis. Breastfeeding Coalition, Lac du Flambeau, 1996—. Recipient honorable mention Mo. Writers Week award for poetry, 1992, 94, grand prize Artists Embassy Internat., San Francisco, 1997, Editors Challenge award Internat. Soc. Authors and Artists, Abilene, Tex., 1997. Mem. St. Louis Poetry Soc., Rolla Area Writers Guild. Avocations: fruit growing, nature study, genealogy, swimming. Home: HC 1 Box 66 Bourbon MO 65441-9305 Office: Ridge Orchards HC 1 Box 66 Bourbon MO 65441-9305

HEITSCHMIDT, RODNEY KEITH, rangeland ecologist; b. Hays, Kans., Oct. 28, 1944; s. Harold W. and Wilma I. (Sigle) H.; m. Judy S. Thompson, Nov. 27, 1944; children: Jason K., Dustin L. BS, Ft. Hays State U., 1967, MS, 1968; PhD, Colo. State U., 1977. Prof. Tex. Agrl. Expt. Sta., Vernon, 1977-90; rsch. leader USDA Agrl. Rsch. Svc., Miles City, Mont., 1990—. Past pres. Vernon Youth Soccer League, Kid League Baseball, Boys Club, Vernon Ind. Sch. Dist. Adv. Bd., Wilbarger County United Way, Booster Club, Wilbarger County Ag Workers; active First United Meth. Ch. Capt. USAF, 1969-74. Mem. Soc. for Range Mgmt. (dir. 1996-99, dir. Tex. sect. 1988-91, pres. No. Great Plains sect. 1997, mem. activities com. 1980, mem. Outstanding Rangeman com. 1981-83, mem. R & D com. 1984-86, grazing mgmt. session chmn. 1983, 85, 90, 91, assoc. editor Jour. Range Mgmt.

1987-91, mem. fin. com. 1995-97), Am. Inst. Biol. Scis., Ecol. Soc. Am., Coun. for Agrl. Sci. and Tech., Hillcrest Country Club (bd. dirs.), Lions Club, HCCC Mens Golf Assn., Phi Kappa Phi, Beta Beta Beta. Methodist. Home: 1116 S Merriam Ave Miles City MT 59301-4923 Office: USDA Ft Keogh Livestock & Range Rsch Lab RR 1 Box 2021 Miles City MT 59301-9200

HEITZ, EDWARD FRED, freight traffic consultant; b. Chgo., May 18, 1930; s. Fredo and Hildur (Olson) H.; m. Gaymae Woodrow Heitz, Apr. 28, 1960; children: Merry, Ted. Student, Northwestern U., Chgo., 1950-55. Registered I.C.C. practitioner. Supr. transp. rsch. Internat. Minerals and Chem. Corp., Chgo., 1946-58; asst. freight traffic mgr.-rate rsch. C.&.N.W.Ry., Chgo., 1958-64; traffic mgr. U.S. Dept. Agriculture, Washington, 1964-78; agriculture transp. analyst Fed. R.R. Adminstrn., Washington, 1978-82; freight traffic cons. Falls Church, Va., 1982-96; ret., 1996; participant with Am. Arbitration Assn. in program applying arbitration techniques to settlement of class action insur. claims for first time, 1998—. Commr. Boy Scouts Am., Fairfax County, Va., 1974-77; chmn. Community Action Agy. County of Fairfax, 1975-77; v.p. Coun. of Fairfax PTAs, 1975; deacon Arlington Ch. of Christ, Falls Ch. Ch. of Christ; mem. Fairfax Com. of 100. *In my techinical work, I found that a problem properly defined is a problem solved, or on the way to a rational solution. The same approach to social and civic problems has brought good benefits with one addition: Define what's important.*

HEITZ, JAMES W., anesthesiologist, internist; b. Balt., Oct. 22, 1963; s. James Wade and Barbara Jean (Johnson) H. BA, Vassar Coll., 1985; MD, U. Md., 1989. Diplomate Am. Bd. Internal Medicine, Am. Bd. Anesthesiology, Nat. Bd. Med. Examiners. Intern then resident in internal medicine Pa. Hosp., Phila., 1989-92; auxiliary staff physician Albert Einstein Med. Ctr., Phila., 1991—; staff physician, divsn. emergency svcs. Pa. Hosp., 1992-93; anesthesia resident U. Pa., Phila., 1993-96; staff anesthesiologist St. Agnes Med. Ctr., Phila., 1996—; contbr. to Com. for ReCertification, Am. Bd. Internal Medicine, Phila., 1995-99. Mem. ACP, AMA, Am. Soc. Anesthesiologists. Office: St Agnes Med Ctr Dept Anesthesiology 1900 S Broad St Philadelphia PA 19145-2304

HEIZER, EDGAR FRANCIS, JR., venture capitalist; b. Detroit, Sept. 23, 1929; s. Edgar Francis and Grace Adelia (Smith) H.; m. Molly Bradley Hunt, June 17, 1952; children: Linda Heizer Seaman, Molly Hunt, Edgar Francis III. BS, Northwestern U., 1951; JD, Yale U., 1954. Bar: Ill. 1954; CPA, Ill. Mem. audit and tax staff Arthur Andersen & Co., Chgo., 1954-56; fin. analyst Kidder, Peabody & Co., Chgo., 1956-58; mgmt. cons. Booz, Allen & Hamilton, Chgo., 1958-62; asst. treas., mgr. venture capital divsn. Allstate Ins. Co., Northbrook, Ill., 1962-69; chmn., founder, CEO Heizer Corp., a venture capital & bus. devel. co., Chgo., 1969-85; venture capitalist Tucker's Town, Bermuda, 1985—; bd. dirs. Needham & Co., N.Y., Material Sci. Corp., Elk Grove Village, Ill., Bermuda Commodities Exch., Hamilton, Chesapeake Energy Corp., Oklahoma City, Okla.; mem. adv. bd. Kellogg Sch. Mgmt., Northwestern U.; chmn. Heizer Ctr. for Entrepreneurship at Kellogg Sch. Mgmt. Chmn. task force on capital formation for White House Conf. on Small Bus., 1978-80. Mem. Nat. Venture Capital Assn. (founder, 1st pres., chmn.), Nat. Assn. Small Bus. Investment Cos., Delta Upsilon (chmn. bd. dirs. 1985-88, chmn. ednl. found. 1990-98). Republican. Presbyterian. Clubs: Chgo. Curling, Shoreacres, Econ. of Chgo., Coral Beach and Tennis, Mid-Ocean; Riddells Bay Golf (Bermuda). Home: 28 S Shore Rd, Tuckers Town HS 02, Bermuda also: 261 Bluffs Edge Dr Lake Forest IL 60045-3301

HEIZER, IDA ANN, retired real estate broker; b. Oxford, Colo., Mar. 14, 1919; d. Albert Henry and Ella (Engbrook) Ordener; m. Donald Heizer, Apr. 7, 1947; children: Robert John. Diploma, Brown's Bus. Coll., 1939; student Otero Jr. Coll., 1946-47, U. So. Colo., 1962; grad. Realtors Inst., Nat. Assn. Real Estate Bds., 1972. Cert. closer real estate, cert. residential specialist. Clk., Montgomery Ward Co., LaJunta, Colo., 1935-37; bookkeeper Colo. Bank & Trust Co., LaJunta, 1937-38; cashier/bookkeeper Fox Theatre, LaJunta, 1939-40; clk. Civil Service, LaJunta, 1940-45; steno/abstractor Deaf Smith Abstract Office, Hereford, Tex., 1948-50; sec. Otero County Agt. Office, Rocky Ford, Colo., 1953-55; real estate broker Pueblo Realty & Service Co., Inc., Colo., 1958-86; ret., 1988. Mem. Pueblo Bd. Realtors, Nat. Assn. Real Estate Appraisers, Nat. Assn. Realtors, Colo. Assn. Realtors, Women's Council Realtors, Daus. of the Republic Tex., Beta Sigma Phi. Home and Office: 331 Van Buren St Pueblo CO 81004-1807

HEIZER, RUTH BRADFUTE, philosophy educator; b. Knoxville, Tenn., Oct. 8, 1933; d. George Archibald and Margaret Eleanor (Smith) Bradfute; m. James Lee Heizer, Aug. 3, 1956; children: John Philip, Mark Russell, Virginia Ruth. BA, Baylor U., 1954; MRE, So. Baptist Theol. Sem., 1957; MA, U. Ky., 1965; PhD, Ind. U., 1971; postgrad., Oxford (Eng.) U., 1980-81, 89. Tchr. Jefferson County Pub. Schs., Louisville, 1956-58; secondary tchr. Gallatin County Pub. Schs., Warsaw, Ky., 1959-60, 61; teaching assoc. dept. philosophy Ind. U., Bloomington, 1965-67; from instr. to assoc. prof. Georgetown (Ky.) Coll., 1967-83, prof., 1983-95, prof. emeritus, 1996—, chair dept. philosophy, 1981-93; vis. prof. philosophy Baylor U., Waco, Tex., 1979, 84; tchr. oral English Jiangnan U., Wuxi, China, summers 1990, 91, Yantai U., China, summer 1994, Inst. for Advanced Qualification of Workers of Edn., Kazan, Russia, summer, 1995; prof. Moscow Bapt. Theol. Sem., 1996-98. Author: Bradfute Beginnings, 1988; co-author: Women, Philosophy, & Sport, 1983, Contemporary Essays on Greek Ideas, 1987. Deacon Faith Bapt. Ch., Georgetown. Recipient NEH summer stipend, 1973. Mem. AAUW, Am. Philos. Assn., So. Soc. Philosophy and Psychology, Ky. Philos. Assn. (pres. 1973-74), Bapt. Assn. Philosophy Tchrs. (pres. 1988-89), Omicron Delta Kappa (Baylor Woman of Merit award 1980). Republican. Avocations: photography, fgn. travel, teaching ESL. Home: 7231 Wellswood Ln Knoxville TN 37909-2436

HEJDUK, JOHN QUENTIN, dean, architect; b. N.Y.C., July 19, 1929; s. John and Mary (Renzler) H.; m. Gloria-Maria Fiorentino, Sept. 8, 1951; children: Rafael, Renata. Student, Cooper Union Sch. Arch., 1950; B.S., U. Cin., 1952; M.A., Harvard Grad. Sch. Design, 1953. Chmn. dept. arch. Cooper Union, 1964-75; dean Cooper Union (Sch. Architecture), 1975—; pvt. practice architecture N.Y.C., 1966—. Fellow Royal Soc., FAIA. Home: 5721 Huxley Ave Bronx NY 10471-2240 Office: Cooper Union Sch Architecture Cooper Sq New York NY 10003-7120

HEJTMANEK, DANTON CHARLES, lawyer; b. Topeka, July 22, 1951; s. Robert Keith and Bernice Louise (Krause) H.; m. Julie Hejtmanek; 1 child, Brian J. BBA in Acctg., Washburn U., 1973, JD, 1975. Bar: Kans. 1976, U.S. Dist. Ct. Kans. 1976, U.S. Tax Ct. 1976. Ptnr. Schroer, Rice, Bryan & Lykins, P.A., Topeka, 1975-86, Bryan, Lykins & Hejtmanek, P.A., Topeka, 1986—. Mem. ABA (rep. young lawyers Kans. and Nebr.), ATLA, Kans. Bar Assn. (pres. young lawyers 1985), Kans. Trial Lawyers Assn., Sertoma (pres. 1983, internat. pres. 1998-99). Republican. Presbyterian. Avocations: snow skiing, travel. Home: 2800 SW Burlingame Rd Topeka KS 66611-1316 Office: Bryan Lykins & Hejtmanek PA 222 SW 7th St Topeka KS 66603-3734

HELANDER, BRUCE PAUL, artist; b. Great Bend, Kans., Jan. 27, 1947; s. Amos Louis and Carmen Marie (Seoane) H.; children: Klee, Camila. BFA, R.I. Sch. Design, 1969, MFA, 1972. With R.I. Sch. Design, Providence, 1970-79, dir. extension programs, 1977-78, provost, 1978-79; pub., editor Art Express mag., N.Y.C. and Providence, 1980-82; dir., pres. Helander Gallery, Palm Beach, Fla., 1982-95; collage commns. for New Yorker Mag., Nations Bank Helander Gallery, Miami, Fla., 1989-90; dir., pres. Helander Gallery, N.Y.C., 1989-94; with Hollywood Film Inst., L.A., 1995; collage commns. for Miami New Times, City Link Mag., Palm Beach Times Mag., Red Herring Mag., 1998; set designer Irving Berlin, Puttin' on the Ritz, Pope Theatre, Manalapan, Fla.; art critic Marquis of Distinction, London, Palm Beach mag, Clematis mag., Palm Beach Times. One-man shows O.K. Harris Gallery, Birmingham, Mich., 1991, Lorenzo Rodriguez Gallery, Chgo., Martine Caulier Gallery, Paris, Peder Bonnier Gallery, N.Y.C., 1994, Marisa del Re Gallery, N.Y.C., 1995, 97, C.G. Rein Gallery, Mpls. and Scottsdale, 1998, Mus. of Art, Ft. Lauderdale, Fla., Virtual Gallery, Los Gatos, Calif., 1998, Regency Fine Art, Atlanta, 1998, Geo. Contemporary Fine Arts Gallery, San Diego, 1998, Addi Gallery, Maui, Hawaii, 1998; permanent collections include Guggenheim Mus., San Jose Mus., Akron Mus., Vassar Coll. Mus., Kemper Mus. Fine Arts, Met. Mus. Art, Phila. Mus. Art, Chgo. Art Inst., Norton Mus., Smithsonian Instn., Albany Mus., Butler Art Inst., Youngstown, Ohio, L.A. County Mus. Art, Albright-Knox Mus. Buffalo, Bklyn. Mus., San Francisco Mus. of Modern Art, Pa. Acad. Fine Art, The White House, Washington, Abergs Mus., Stockholm. Bd. dirs. Fla. Repertory Theatre, Palm Beach, 1989-92, Armory Sch., West Palm Beach, 1986-88, 96—, ARt in Pub. Places City of West Palm Beach; provost, v.p. acad. affairs R.I. Sch. Design, Providence, 1978-81; commr. Archtl. Rev. Bd. Town of Palm Beach; artistic bd. Palm Beach County Sch. of the Arts Found., 1995—. Fellow NEA, 1975. Mem. 308 Club (pres. West Palm Beach chpt. 1984-94).

HELANDER, ROBERT CHARLES, lawyer; b. Chgo., Oct. 30, 1932; s. William Eugene and Grace Pauline (Pedderson) H.; m. Betty Jane Vinson, Apr. 8, 1961; children—Diana Chaffin, Alexander Christian, Nicholas Charles. B.A., Amherst Coll., 1953; J.D., Harvard U., 1956, P.M.D., 1971. Bar: D.C. 1956, Ill. 1956, N.Y. 1979, U.S. Supreme Ct. 1960. Practice law Chgo., 1956-62; Amherst fellow in Middle East, 1960-61; mem. firm Helander, Farmanfarmaian & Ghany, Tehran, Iran, 1962-65; assoc. gen. counsel Internat. Basic Economy Corp., Lima, Peru, 1965-68; v.p. Internat. Basic Economy Corp., 1968-71; v.p. devel. and adminstrn., gen. counsel IBEC, N.Y.C., 1971-73; group v.p. and pres. IBEC, 1973-76; ptnr. firm Jones, Day, Reavis & Pogue (Surrey & Morse), N.Y.C., 1976-93; ptnr., LLP Kaye, Scholer, Fierman, Hays & Handler, N.Y.C., 1993—. pres. Accion Internat., 1978-88; chmn. Pan Am. Soc., 1979-88, Am. Fund for Ind. Univs., 1987—, Fund for Multinat. Mgmt. Edn., 1981-91; bd. dirs. Internat. Law Inst., 1975, Ams. Soc., 1982—, Univ. Andes Found., 1983—, Near East Found., 1977—, Bolivarian Soc., 1980—, IESA Found., 1991—, Internat. Coun. Escuela Superior Adminstrn. de Negocios, 1999—. Named Comendador, Orden del Sol (Peru). Fellow Am. Bar Found. (life); mem. ABA (chmn. inter-Am. law com. of sect. internat. law and practice 1978-83, editor-in-chief Inter-Am. Legal Materials 1983-91, del to Inter Am. Bar Assn.), Assn. of Bar of City of N.Y. (inter-Am. affairs com.), Inter-Am. Bar Assn., Am. Fgn. Law Assn., Coun. Fgn. Rels., Carnegie Coun., Century Club. Republican. Episcopalian. Home: 3 Mountainview Dr Mountainside NJ 07092-2510 Office: 425 Park Ave New York NY 10022-3506

HELANDER, TERRILL WEBB, educational psychologist; b. Pasadena, Calif., Apr. 11, 1958; d. Allen Paul and Dorothy Winder (Cannon) Webb; m. Wayne Richard Helander, June 27, 1982; children: Margaret, Thomas, David, Andrew. BA, Pitzer Coll., Claremont, Calif., 1980; MA, Calif. State U., Northridge, 1982; PhD, U. So. Calif., L.A., 1990. Lic. ednl. psychologist, Calif. advanced pupil pers. credential. Sch. psychologist Hacienda-La Puente (Calif.) Unified Sch. Dist., 1982-89, Placentia (Calif.) Unified Sch. Dist., 1989-91; pvt. practice Pasadena, Calif., 1990—; cons. Young & Healthy, Pasadena, 1991—; clin. assoc. prof. Grad. Sch. Psychology Fuller Theol. Sem., 1996—; advisor dist. adv. com. Claremont (Calif.) Unified Sch. Dist., 1994-95; supr. interns Pasadena Mental Health Ctr., 1990-91; presenter workshop on stress Orange County Dept. Edn., 1991. Mem. Pasadena Symphony Jrs., 1985-87; bd. mem. B'nai Simcha Presch., Arcadia, Calif., 1991; sch. vol. Parent Faculty Assn., Condit Elem. Sch., Claremont, 1994—. Recipient award Harry Steele Found., 1978. Republican. Avocations: writing, gardening, travel, tennis, crafts. Office: Youth & Healthy 325 S Oak Knoll Ave Pasadena CA 91101-3418

HELART, AUGUST MARVIN, state agency administrator. Law degree, LaSalle Ext. U., 1972. Ct. reporter U.S. Dist. Ct., Denver, 1965; clk. U.S. Dist. Ct., Cheyenne, Wyo., 1968-78; chief dep. clk. U.S. Dist. Ct., Nev., 1979-81; clk. U.S. Dist. Ct., So. Ill., 1982; ct. reporter State Dist. Ct., Wyo., 1990-94; asst. chief clk. Ho. of Reps., Cheyenne, 1995-96, chief clk., 1997—. Mem. Fed. Ct. Clk. Assn. (pres. 1986, Angie award 1987), Elks, Masons, Shriners. Home: 102 E Carlson St Cheyenne WY 82009 Office: Ho of Reps State Capitol Cheyenne WY 82002

HELBERG, SHIRLEY ADELAIDE HOLDEN, artist, educator; b. Solvay, N.Y.; d. Isaac Edgar and Gladys Evelyn (Tucker) Holden; m. Burton Edward Helberg; children: Keir Holm, Kristin Vaughan, Kecia Tucker Lau, Kandace Holden Mead, Kraig Brownlee. *Shirley Holden-Helburg's mother's ancestors came to Swansea, MA, 1623. Her father's Canadian ancestors, Margaret Cripps and Williamson Holden, came to Canada, 1831. Ancestor and Revolutionary War pensioner, Ezra Barker's daughter, Olive, and husband, Edy Mason, came by ox-cart in 1812 to Sennett, NY. Son, Edwin, and wife had daughter, Flora Mason. Flora's marriage to Willard Case, Civil War veteran, produced seventeen children, one of whom was Bertha Case, who married Oliver Tucker. Their child, Gladys, married I. Edgar Holden. Daughter Shirley has five grandchildren, Heather and Amanda Mead of Martha's Vineyard and Meredith, Olivia, and Neil Helberg of York, Pa.* BE, Johns Hopkins U., 1969; MFA, Md. Inst. Art, 1975. Tchr. various schs., N.J. and Pa., Manchester (Pa.) Pub. Schs., 1965-84, Balt. City Schs., 1988-92; demonstration tchr. Balt. City Schs., O'Donnel Heights Sch., 1992. One-woman shows include U. Va. Charlottesville, 1974, Cayuga Mus. Art and History, Auburn, N.Y., 1974, Hist. Soc. York Mus., Pa., 1977, York Coll., 1984, Country Club York; represented in permanent collections Pres. Richard Nixon; author poems. Bd. dirs. York (Pa.) Arts Coun., 1964-66. Named Outstanding Tchr. Northeastern Sch. Dist. Bd. Edn. Mem. NEA, Nat. League Am. Pen Women (Pa. State art chmn. 1972-74, pres. Pa. orgn. 1974-76, nat. scholarship chair 1976-98, registrar 1986-88, 5th v.p. 1988-90, Disting. Svc. award 1978, 80, 82, 84, 86, 88, 90, 92, Disting. Achievement award 1988, 94), Pa. State Edn. Assn., Internat. Platform Assn., Harrisburg Art Assn., York Art Assn., Pa. Watercolor Sco., Johns Hopkins Faculty Club. Republican. Methodist. Home: 5433 Pigeon Hill Rd Spring Grove PA 17362-9804 also: 727 S Ann St Baltimore MD 21231-3402

HELBERT, CLIFFORD L., graphic designer, journalism educator; b. Miles City, Mont., May 3, 1920; s. L. Roy and M. Mae (Stevenson) H.; 1944; children: Susan M., Thomas F., David P., Louise M., Anne R. PhB, Marquette U., 1948, AM, 1955. Supt. Marquette U. Press, 1947-51, asst. bus. mgr., 1951-55, bus. mgr., 1955-61; mem. faculty Coll. Journalism, Marquette U., 1947-84, prof., 1964-84, prof. emeritus, 1984—, dean coll., 1965-71; newspaper designer, 1951—, mag. designer, 1951—, book designer, 1947—, cons. in field, 1951—. Editor: Printing Progress a Mid-Century Report, 1959; also contbr.: Harpers Ency. Sci. Served to 1st lt. AUS, 1942-46. Named Internat. Craftsman of Year, 1961; recipient Andrew Hamilton award Marquette U., 1962; Benjamin Franklin award Graphic Arts Assn. Wis., 1966; Benjamin Franklin award Milw.-Racine Club of Printing House Craftsmen, 1981; fellow Internat. Newspaper Advt. Exec. Assn., 1963. Fellow Royal Soc. Art (London), Printing Hist. Soc. (London, Eng.), Am. Printing History Assn., Midwest Amateur Printers, Miniature Book Soc., Gutenberg Gesellschaft, Alpha Sigma Nu, Kappa Tau Alpha, Sigma Delta Chi, Alpha Delta Sigma. Home: PO Box 97 Milwaukee WI 53201-0097 Office: Studio 405 133 W Pittsburgh Ave Milwaukee WI 53204-1460

HELBURN, ISADORE B., arbitrator, mediator, educator; b. Cin., Aug. 14, 1938; s. I.B. and Jeanette (Greenburg) H.; m. Judith Dee Horwitz, Aug. 21, 1960; children: Graham D., Robin L. Holt. BS with honors, U. Wis., 1960, MS, 1962, PhD, 1966. Mem. faculty U. Tex., Austin, 1968-97, prof. indsl. relations Grad. Sch. Bus., 1979-92; contract prof. Area Estudios de Postgrado, U. Carabobo, Valencia, Venezuela, summer 1974; mem. arbitration panels Fed. Mediation and Conciliation Service, 1972—, Am. Arbitration Assn., 1974—, Nat. Mediation Bd., 1983—. Author: (with others) Total Group Productivity Motivation in Business, 1961, Progress Sharing at American Motors, 1964, Manpower, Employment and Income, A Statistical Profile of Texas, 1969, Public Employer-Employee Relations in Texas: Contemporary and Emerging Developments, 1971, (with others) Local Option Recognition and Bargaining: The Texas Fire Fighter and Police Experience, 1976; contbr. articles to profl. jours. and chpts. to books. Served to capt. U.S. Army, 1966-68. Recipient Jack G. Taylor Teaching Excellence award U. Tex., Austin, 1970. Mem. Nat. Acad. Arbitrators, Indsl. Rels. Rsch. Assn. Jewish. Home: 5914 Highland Hills Dr Austin TX 78731-4057

HELD, AL, artist, educator; b. N.Y.C., Oct. 12, 1928. Ed., Art Students League, N.Y.C., Academie de la Grande Chaumiere, Paris. Prof. art Yale U., New Haven, Conn., 1962-78, adj. prof. painting, 1978—. One-man shows: Andre Emmerich Gallery, N.Y.C., 1965, 67, 68, 70, 72, 73, 75, 76, 78, 79, 80, 81, 82, 84-92, 95, 96, 97, Stedelijk Mus., Amsterdam, 1966, Inst. Contemporary Art. of U. Pa., Phila., 1968, Contemporary Arts Mus., Houston, 1968, San Francisco Mus. Art, 1968, Corcoran Gallery Art, Washington, 1968, Whitney Mus., N.Y.C., 1974, Inst. Contemporary Art, Boston, 1978, Robert Miller Gallery, N.Y.C., 1980, 82, 87, 90, 94, also in Zurich, Amsterdam, Suttgart, London, Toronto, Stockholm, Bottrop, others including Donald Morris Gallery, Birmingham, 1971, 74, 77, 83, 88, Richard Gray Gallery, Chgo., 1984, Pace Editions, N.Y.C., 1984, Krannert Art Mus., U. Ill., 1993; group shows include: Whitney Mus., Kansas City Art Inst., Milw. Art Mus., Mus. Contemporary Art, Chgo., U. Tex.-Austin Art Mus., Minn. Mus. Art, Met. Mus. Art, N.Y., Nat. Gallery, Berlin, Albright-Knox Art Gallery, Buffalo, Kunstmuseum, Basel, Kunsthaus, Zurich, Rose Art Mus., Branoeis, Fogg Art Mus., Cambridge, High Mus. Art, Atlanta, numerous others; represented in permanent collections: Whitney Mus., Mus. Modern Art, N.Y.C., San Francisco Mus. Art, Cleve. Mus. Art, Dallas Mus. Fine Arts, Nat. Gallery Berlin, others including Hirshhorn Mus. and Sculpture Garden, Washington; stained glass at Washington nat. Airport; co-founder: Brata Gallery, N.Y.C., 1956. Contbr. articles to profl. jours. Recipient Logan medal Art Inst. Chgo., 1964, Jack I. and Lillian L. Poses Brandeis U. Creative Arts award painting medal, 1983. Office: c/o Robert Miller 41 E 57th St New York NY 10022-1908*

HELD, BARBARA KAY, pediatric nurse; b. Sandusky County, July 23, 1938; d. Kenneth M. and Mary Elizabeth (Bower) Stokes; m. Donald J. Held, Jan. 3, 1960; children: Elizabeth Marie, Theodore Joseph, John Merl. Student, Capital U., 1956-57; diploma, Riverside Hosp. Sch. Nursing, 1965. Cert. PALS. Team leader, pediatrics Riverside Hosp., Toledo; nurse, emergency rm. Riverside Hosp., ret.; presenter in field. Mem. Riverside Alumni Assn. (pres. 1990—).

HELD, EDWIN WALTER, JR., lawyer; b. Jacksonville, Fla., Feb. 14, 1947; m. Leslie Edwards, Aug. 18, 1974; children: Kimberly M., Eric E. BSBA, U. Fla., 1970; JD, Stetson U., 1973. Bar: Fla. 1973, U.S. Dist. Ct. (mid. dist.) Fla. 1973, U.S. Ct. Appeals (11th cir.) 1973. Assoc. Fischette, Parrish & Owen, Jacksonville, 1973-75; mem. Fischette, Parrish, Owen & Held, Jacksonville, 1975-90, Fischette, Owen & Held, Jacksonville, 1990-97, Fischette, Owen, Held & McBurney, Jacksonville, 1997—. Founding dir., bd. dirs. Jewish Cmty. Alliance, Jacksonville, 1990. Mem. Comml. Law League Am. (exec. con. bankruptcy and insolvency sect. 1990—, chmn. sect. 1997-98). Democrat. Avocations: boating, skiing, tennis, fishing, golf. Office: Fischette Owen Held & McBurney 1301 Riverplace Blvd Ste 1916 Jacksonville FL 32207-9024

HELD, GEORGE, English educator; b. White Plains, N.Y., Jan. 28, 1935; s. Carlysle and Janet Beulah (Maugans) H.; m. Jean Stuart Reinecke, June 20, 1958 (div. Aug. 1967). BA, Brown U., 1958; MA, U. Hawaii, 1962; PhD, Rutgers U., 1967. Instr. English Kamehameha Sch., Honolulu, 1958-64; tchg. asst. Rutgers U., New Brunswick, N.J., 1965-66; from asst. prof. to assoc. prof. English Queens Coll., Flushing, N.Y., 1967—. Bd. mem., co-editor South Fork Natural History Soc. newsletter, 1988—; co-editor The Ledge Poetry Jour., 1991—. Fulbright lectr., 1973-76. Mem. Assn. Literary Scholars & Critics. Avocations: writing poetry, gardening, bird watching. Home: 285 W 4th St New York NY 10014-2222

HELD, GEORGE ANTHONY, architect; b. Paterson, N.J., Sept. 4, 1949; s. George William and Carmella (De Negri) H.; m. Patricia Anne Corrado, Sept. 5, 1976; children: Nicole, Ryan. BS in Archtl. Tech., N.Y. Inst. Tech., 1972, BArch, 1977. Registered profl. architect, N.J., N.Y., R.I.; registered planner N.J. Architect intern Gerard J. Oakley, AIA, Teaneck, N.J., 1972-76; ptnr. Aybar Partership, Ridgefield, N.J., 1976-88; owner George A. Held, AIA & Assocs., Clifton, N.J., 1988—. Mem. Clifton Econ. Devel. Assistance Commn., 1994, vice chmn., 1998, mem. Clifton Zoning Task Force; mem. Clifton Beautification Com., 1997. Mem. AIA, N.J. Soc. Architects (dir. 1984-86), Architects League N.J. (dir. 1982-86, sec. 1986-88, Dirs. award 1985, 88, Vegliante award 1986, Firm award 1999). Roman Catholic. Home: 47 Westview Rd Wayne NJ 07470-6253 Office: George A Held AIA & Assocs 457 Crooks Ave Clifton NJ 07011-2151

HELD, JOE ROGER, veterinarian, epidemiologist; b. L.A., June 23, 1931; s. Edward Samuel and Carmen Antoinette (Planas) H.; m. Carolyn Ann Friderich, May 26, 1956; children: Lisa Held Doseff, Robert Joseph, Leslie Held Clark, Teresa Held Johnson. AA, Pasadena City Coll., 1950; BS, U. Calif., Davis, 1953, DVM, 1955; MPH, Tulane U., 1959. Lic. veterinarian, Calif. Pvt. practice Pasadena, Calif., 1957-58; various positions USPHS, 1959-72; dir. div. rsch. svcs. NIH, Bethesda, Md., 1972-84; asst. surgeon gen. USPHS, Bethesda, 1975-84; dir. Pan Am. Zoonoses Ctr., Buenos Aires, 1984-87; coord. vet. pub. health Pan Am./WHO, Washington, 1987-89; v.p. primate ops. Charles River Labs., Arlington, Va., 1989-91, dir. Washington office, 1991; dir. Lab. Animal Health Svcs. of Microbiol. Assocs., Rockville, Md., 1992-96; ret. Lab. Animal Health Svcs. of Microbiol. Assocs., Rockville, 1996; cons., Arlington, 1991—; chmn. AID Rinderpest Biosafety Commn., Washington, 1991; mem. USDA, APHIS panel on sci. and tech., Washington, 1987-91; mem. Pew Health Profl. Com. adv. panel on vet. medicine, Durham, N.C., 1991. Contbr. over 70 publs. to scientific jours. Rear adm. USPHS, 1955-84. Recipient Outstanding Svc. medal Uniformed Svcs., Univ. Health Sci., Bethesda, 1985. Mem. AAAS, Am. Vet. Med. Assn. (alt. del. 1981-84, Charles River prize 1984, XII Internat. Vet. Congress prize 1989), Am. Vet. Epidemiology Soc. (pres. 1990-93, K.F. Meyer award 1982), Assn. Mil. Surgeons of U.S. (chmn. vet. med. sect. 1977, McCallam award 1990), Am. Assn. for Lab. Animal Sci., Am. Assn. for World Health, NIH Alumni Assn. (pres. 1991-93), Am. Coll. Lab. Animal Medicine (hon.). Home: 1300 Crystal Dr Apt 505 Arlington VA 22202-3234

HELD, LILA M., art appraiser; b. Cleve., Oct. 5, 1925; d. Mark and Edythe H. (Dobrin) Bloomberg; m. Jacob Herzfeld, Oct. 20, 1946 (div. 1964); children: Garson, Michael; m. Merle Donald Held, Feb. 19, 1966 (dec. 1997); children: Joanne, Barbara. Student, Coll. William and Mary, 1945-46, Ohio State U., 1943-44, Case Western Res. U., 1944-45; postgrad., Case Western Res. U., 1962-66; student, Akron U., 1960-61; BS in Art Edn., Kent State U., 1961-62; M in Valuation Sci., Lindenwood Coll., 1989. Instr. art Canton (Ohio) YMCA, 1965, Beachwood (Ohio) Bd. Recreation, 1967-68; substitute tchr. art, art history Cleveland Heights, Ohio, 1967-68; freelance artist, writer, researcher, 1940—; art cons., appraiser Art Consultants Assocs., Englewood, Colo., 1985—; curatorial aid Denver Art Mus., 1985-89; fine arts appraiser, Cleve., 1989—. Works exhibited in museums and galleries in Cleve., Akron, Richmond, Va., St. Louis; speaker in field; judge at numerous art shows. Mem. Cleve. Artists Found.; mem. Akron (Ohio) Art Mus., Butler Inst. of Am. Art, Cleve. Mus. Natural History, Western Res. Hist. Soc., Toledo Mus. of Art; sec. Coun. of Cleve. Ctr. of Contemporary Art; active Continuing Edn. Assn. Case-Western Res. U., Allen Meml. Art Mus. Mem. Am. Soc. Appraisers (sr. mem., cert. in fine arts), Cleve. Mus. Art, Cleve. Ctr. for Contemporary Art (vol.), Contemporary Art Soc. of Cleve. Mus. of Art, Nat. Coun. Jewish Women, Ohio Contemporary Glass Alliance, Art Alliance for Contemporary Glass, Temple Mus., Mus. of Am. Folk Art, Allbright-Knox Mus. (Buffalo, N.Y.). Avocations: reading, travel, theatre, music, literature. Home and Office: 13800 Shaker Blvd Apt 804 Shaker Heights OH 44120

HELD, NANCY B., perinatal nurse, lactation consultant; b. Winchester, Mass., Sept. 4, 1957; d. Ann and Laurence Babine; m. Lew Held, May 22, 1976; children: David, Jessica. BSN, NYU, 1979; MS, U. Calif., San Francisco, 1992. Cert. Internat. Bd. Lactation Cons. Examiners. Labor/delivery nurse Pascack Valley Hosp., Westwood, N.J., 1979-83; obstetrics educator Drs. Pinski, Wiener & Grasso, Westwood, N.J., 1982-85; ob/gyn office nurse Drs. Power Hagbom Holter & Clark, San Francisco, 1986-87; asst. to dir. maternity svcs. Women's Health Assn., Greenbrae, Calif., 1987-89; perinatal edn. and lactation ctr. clin. coord. Calif. Pacific Med. Ctr., San Francisco, 1989-99; owner North Bay Lamaze, 1988-96; co-owner Health Designs, San Rafael, 1997-98, Day One, LLC, San Francisco, 1999—; speaker and cons. in field. Recipient Founders Day award, NYU. Fellow Am. Coll. Childbirth Educators; mem. Assn. Women's Health Obstetric and Neonatal Nursing (spkr. nat. con. 1993, nat. rsch. utilization team 1993), Am. Soc. Psychoprophylaxis (chpt. co-pres.), Nurses Assn. of Am. Coll. Ob/Gyn, Internat. Childbirth Educators Assn., Internat. Lactation Cons. Assn., Sigma Theta Tau.

HELDER, BRUCE ALAN, metal products executive; b. Grand Rapids, Mich., July 1, 1953; s. Harry Martin and Margaret (Ditmar) H.; m. Arlene

Faye Docter, May 29, 1975; children: Amanda Joy, David Ryan, Joel Brent, Jonathan Bruce, Brandon Michael. Student, Calvin Coll., 1972-73, Grand Valley State Coll., Allendale, Mich., 1974. Lic. realtor assoc.; cert. media specialist. Indsl. sales rep. Newman Communications, Inc., Grand Rapids, 1971-81; v.p. sales and mktg. Best Metal Products Co., Grand Rapids, 1981—; pres. Venture Property Mgmt. Co. Mem. Real Estate Bd. Grand Rapids. Republican. Mem. Christian Reformed Ch. Home: PO Box 88153 Grand Rapids MI 49518-0153 Office: Best Metal Products Co PO Box 888-440 Grand Rapids MI 49588-8440

HELDER, DAVID ERNEST, artist, educator; b. Seattle, Feb. 4, 1947; s. Reinard Wright and Maxine Edda (Spiva) H.; m. Sallye Ann Giles, Aug. 7, 1976; 1 child, Julian Oliver. AA, Yuba Coll., Marysville, Calif., 1966; BA in Sculpture, Calif. Coll. Arts and Crafts, Oakland, 1969, MFA, 1971; MA in Aesthetic Edn., Stanford U., 1975. Aesthetic edn. and art direction cons. U. Mpls. Super Computer Inst., 1988—. San Francisco Arts Festival, 1980, Stamford (Conn.) Art Assn., 1988, Exhibited in solo shows at Wake Gallery, Cape Town, South Africa, 1972, Margaret Jensen Gallery, San Francisco, 1976, Park Gallery, San Francisco, 1977, Lyle Tuttle Gallery, San Francisco, 1979, Jaymark Gallery, San Francisco, 1981, Kristi Phippen Gallery, Modesto, Calif., 1999, Running Wild Gallery, Murphys, Calif., 1998, Lynne White Running Wild Gallery, Kristi Phippen Gallery, Modesto, Calif., 1999; group shows include San Diego Art Inst., 1988, Alligator Gallery, San Francisco, 1988, Helio Gallery, N.Y.C., 1991, Rayco Gallery, San Francisco, 1991, North East Juried Exposition, Mass., 1993, Running Wild Gallery, Murphys, Calif., 1995, 98. Address: PO Box 54 Hanalei HI 96714 Also: Lynne White Running Wild Gallery 466A Main St Murphys CA 95247

HELDER, JAN PLEASANT, JR., lawyer; b. Marysville, Calif., Jan. 18, 1963; s. Jan Pleasant Sr. and Roleane Phylis (Harrison) H.; m. Barbara Irene Loring, July 14, 1990; children: Russell Wright, Zachary Allen, David Grant. BA in Econs., Calif. State U., Sacramento, 1986; JD, Georgetown U., 1989. Bar: Mo. 1989, U.S. Dist. Ct. (we. dist.) Mo. 1989, Kans. 1990, U.S. Dist. Ct. Kans. 1990, U.S. Ct. Appeals (10th cir.) 1994, U.S. Tax Ct. 1994. Exec. asst. to pres. Sacramento Trade Exch., 1983-84; legis. asst. Calif. Postsecondary Edn. Commn., Sacramento, 1985-86; assoc. Spencer, Fane, Britt & Browne, Kansas City, Mo., 1989-94; assoc. Sonnenschein Nath & Rosenthal, Kansas City, Mo., 1994-96, ptnr., 1996—; judge pro tem City of Prairie Village (Kans.) Mcpl. Ct.; bd. dirs. Edn., Inc., bd. sec., 1994-95; bd. dirs. Young Audiences, vice pres., 1997-98, vice chmn., 1999—. Bd. editor Bus. Torts Reporter, 1996—. Chair Calif. State Student Assn., Sacramento and Long Beach, 1984-85; mem. Leadership Mo., Jefferson City, 1992; mem. Centurions Leadership Program, 1993-95, mem. steering com., 1994-95. Pursuit of Worthwhile Endeavors scholar Calif. State U., Sacramento, 1982. Mem. ABA (vice-chair bus. torts subcom., bus. and corp. litigation com., bus. sect. 1993-95, task force on Litigation Reform, chair bus. torts subcom. 1995—, co-chair, Task Force on Year 2000 Legislation, 1999—), co-chair, Task Force on Litigation Reform and Rule Revision, 1999—; Nat. Inst. Trial Advocacy (western regional 1993), Mo. Bar Assn., Kans. Bar Assn., Kansas City Met. Bar Assn., Johnson County Bar Assn., Greater Kansas City C. of C. (chair subcom. on labor and jud. 1990-91, fed. affairs com. 1989—), Ross T. Roberts Inn Ct. (barrister 1991-92). Republican. Presbyterian. Avocations: jazz and classical and choral music, golf, tennis, running, politics. Home: 2216 W 63rd St Shawnee Mission KS 66208-1903 Office: Sonnenschein Nath & Rosenthal 4520 Main St Ste 1100 Kansas City MO 64111-7700

HELDMAN, JAMES GARDNER, lawyer; b. Cin., Mar. 7, 1949; s. James Norvin and Jane Marie (Gardner) H.; m. Wendy Maureen Saunders, Sept. 3, 1978; children: Dustin A., Courtney B. AB cum laude, Harvard U., 1971; JD with honors, George Washington U., 1974. Bar: D.C. 1975, U.S. Dist. Ct. (D.C. dist.) 1975, U.S. Ct. Appeals (D.C. cir.) 1975, U.S. Supreme Ct. 1980, Ohio 1981. Assoc. Perazich & Kolker, Washington, 1974-79, Wyman, Bautzer, Kuchel & Silbert, Washington, 1979-81; assoc. Strauss & Troy, Cin., 1981-83, ptnr., 1984—. Mem. ABA, Ohio State Bar Assn., Cin. Bar Assn. Avocations: tennis, platform tennis, swimming. Office: Strauss & Troy The Fed Res Bldg 150 E Fourth St Cincinnati OH 45202-4018

HELDMAN, LOUIS MARC, newspaper publisher and executive; b. Cin., Apr. 29, 1949; s. Richard Kaichen and Anne (Schwartz) H.; m. Terry Lynn Redford, June 27, 1981; children: Diana Redford, Nicholas Redford. BA, Ohio State U., 1972; postgrad. program for mgmt. devel., Harvard U., 1988. Reporter Detroit Free Press, 1972-79, bus. editor, 1979-81; mng. editor The News-Sentinel, Ft. Wayne, Ind., 1981-83; asst. mng. editor Miami (Fla.) Herald, 1983-85, dep. mng. editor, 1986-89; dir. 25/43 project Knight-Ridder Inc., Miami, 1989-91; exec. editor, sr. v.p. Tallahassee Democrat, 1991-95; pres., pub. Centre Daily Times, State College, Pa., 1996—. Bd. dirs. Chamber of Bus. Industry Centre County, 1996—, Friends of the Palmer Mus. of Art, 1996-99, Centre County Cmty. Found., 1997—, United Way Centre County, 1997—, Second Mile, 1997—, Downtown State Coll. Partnership, 1997—. Recipient Pulitzer prize (staff), 1983; named One of 100 Most Influential Bus. Leaders, Pa. Bus. Ctrl., 1997, 98, 99. Mem. Newspaper Assn. Am., Pa. Newspaper Pubs. Assn. (bd. dirs. 1998—). Office: Centre Daily Times PO Box 89 State College PA 16804-0089

HELDMAN, PAUL W., lawyer, grocery store company executive. BS, Boston U., 1973; JD, U. Cin., 1977. Bar: Ohio 1977. Assoc. Beckman, Lavercombe & Well, 1977-82; atty. The Kroger Co., Cin., 1982-86; sr. atty. Kroger Co., Cin., 1986-87, sr. counsel, 1987-89, v.p., gen. counsel, 1989-92; v.p., sec., gen. counsel The Kroger Co., 1992-97, sr. v.p., sec., gen. counsel, 1997—. Office: The Kroger Co 1014 Vine St Ste 1000 Cincinnati OH 45202-1100

HELDRETH, LEONARD GUY, English educator, university official; b. Shinnston, W.Va., Apr. 8, 1939; s. Orie Guy and Grace Louise (Myers) H.; m. Lillian Ruth Marks, June 18, 1964; children: Randall Thomas, Terrence Lon. BS in Physics, W.Va. U., 1962, MA in English, 1964; PhD in English, U. Ill., 1973. Abstractor, editor Nat. Coun. Tchrs. of English Eric Clearing House, Urbana, 1968-70; instr. dept. English No. Mich. U., Marquette, 1970-73, asst. prof. dept. English, 1973-76, assoc. prof., 1976-81, prof., 1981—, head. dept. English, 1988-91, 92-98, interim dean Coll. Art and Sci., 1991-92, assoc. dean, 1994—; mem. adv. bd. Jour. Popular Film and TV; mem. devel. bd. No. Mich. U., 1997—; mem. editl. bd. No. Mich. U. Press. Reviewer movies Sta. WNMU-FM Radio, Marquette, 1983-89; reviewer video cassettes Marquette Monthly newspaper, 1988—; contbr. articles to profl. jours. Pres. Urbana-Champaign Community Theatre, 1968-69. Recipient Distinguished Faculty award No. Mich. U., Marquette Mich., 1987, Research Grants No. MIch. U., Marquette Mich., 1983, 1984, 1987. Mem. Internat. Assn. for the Fantastic in the Arts (sec. 1990-95), Popular Culture Assn. (area chair fantasy and sci. fiction), Mich. Assn. Depts. English (treas., sec. 1989-98), Sci. Fiction Rsch. Assn., Mich. Coun. Humanities (bd. dirs. 1989-93), Univ. Club No. Mich. U. Home: 367 E Hewitt Ave Marquette MI 49855-3711 Office: No Mich U English Dept Marquette MI 49855

HELDRICH, ELEANOR MAAR, publisher; b. Hagerstown, Md, Nov. 4, 1929; d. Richard and Sara (Mish) Maar; m. Frederich Joseph Heldrich; children: Sarah, Susan, Frederick, Philip. Grad. high sch., Balt. Editor Federated Garden Clubs of Md., Balt., 1975—; pub., founder Prospect Hill Press, Balt., 1981—, Prospect House, Balt., 1996—. Pres. Beautiful Balt., Inc., 1985-89. Recipient Publ. award Nat. Coun. State Garden Clubs, 1984, 86. Mem. Pub. Mktg. Assn., Mid-Atlantic Pubs. Assn., Internat. Assn. Ind. Pubs. (com. small mag. editors and pubs.), Movable Book Soc., Md. Assn. for Dyslexic Youth and Adults.

HELDRICH, PHILIP JOSEPH, English educator, academic administrator, writer; b. Chgo., Nov. 6, 1965; s. Gerard Charles and Constance (Bellisario) H.; m. Christine Neill, June 15, 1993. BA, U. Calif., San Diego, 1988; MA, Kans. State U., 1993; PhD, Okla. State U., 1997. Tchg. asst. Kans. State U., Manhattan, 1990-93; tchg. assoc. Okla. State U., Stillwater, 1993-97; asst. prof. English Emporia (Kans.) State U., 1997—; dir. Bluestem Press, 1998—. Contbr. poems, short stories, and articles to profl. and lit. jours.: fiction editor Cimmaron Rev., 1994—, Midland Rev., 1995-96, Touchstone Rev., 1992-93; editor-in-chief Midland Rev., 1995-96; editl. asst. SUNY-James Fenimore Cooper edit. of The Spy, 1994-96; gen. editor (newsletter) The Englelight, Okla. State U., 1995-96; editor Flint Hills Rev., 1998—. Clinton Keeler fellow, Okla. State U., 1997; recipient Paul Klemp Renaissance Studies award, Okla. State U., 1996, Janemarie Luecke Meml. prize in poetry, 1996, Edward Jones Milton Textual Studies award, 1995, Janemarie Luecke Meml. prize in feminist studies, 1995, 2d place award in fiction Okla. State Univ., 1995, 1st place award in fiction, Kans. State U., 1993, 1st prize Coun. on Nat. Lits. award in fiction, 1998, honorable mention award in fiction Karamu mag., 1997, Herman Swafford Fiction award Potpourri Mag., 1999. Mem. MLA, Am. Culture Assn. (regional chair), Southwest Popular and Am. Culture Assns. (v.p. 1998—, regional chair ann. conf.). Office: Emporia State U Divsn English 1200 Commercial St Emporia KS 66801-5087

HELENIUS-LAPORTE, SUSAN ANN, elementary education educator; b. Concord, Mass., June 10, 1952; d. Lauri Eino and Marion Helen Toivonen; m. Allan Earl Helenius, Aug. 26, 1972 (dec. Jan. 1996); children: Ryan Helenius, Ross Helenius, Lauren Helenius; m. Robert Paul LaPorte Jr., Dec. 20, 1997; children: Joseph LaPorte, Thomas LaPorte. BS in Edn., Framingham State, 1974; M in Edn., Lesley Coll., 1997. Cert. elem. tchr., Mass., reading tchr. Title I reading tchr. Hudson (Mass.) Pub. Schs., 1975-76; tchr. grade 4 St. Michael's Elt. Sch., Hudson, 1976-77; reading asst. Westford (Mass.) Pub. Schs., 1993-96; reading specialist Carlisle (Mass.) Pub. Schs., 1996—. Mem. Internat. Reading Assn., Mass. Reading Assn., Mass. Tchrs. Assn., Reading Recovery Coun. N. Am. E-mail: susan850@aol.com. Office: Carlisle Pub Schs 83 School St Carlisle MA 01741

HELFAND, EUGENE, chemist; b. Bklyn., Jan. 8, 1934; s. Saul and Helen (Stern) H.; m. Sondra Ruth Yoskowitz, Nov. 17, 1957; children: Robin Hope, Dawn Alisa, Russ Daniel. BS summa cum laude, Poly. Inst. Bklyn., 1955; MS, Yale U., 1957, PhD, 1958. Mem. tech. staff AT&T Bell Labs., Murray Hill, N.J., 1958-60, supr. chem. computations group, 1960-83, disting. mem. tech. staff, 1983-96; cons. Lucent Techs., Bell Labs., Murray Hill, 1996—; adj. prof. Yeshiva U., N.Y.C., 1960-62, Poly. Inst. Bklyn., 1963-64; mem. panel on polymer sci. and engring. NRC, 1979-81. Contbr. articles to profl. jours. Guggenheim Meml. Found. fellow Stanford U., 1969-70. Fellow Am. Phys. Soc. (chmn. divsn. high polymer physics 1987-88, prize 1989); mem. Am. Chem. Soc., Soc. of Rheology, Soc. Info. Display, Sigma Xi, Phi Lambda Upsilon. Achievements include research in theory of polymers, colloids and liquid crystal displays. Office: Lucent Techs Bell Labs PO Box 636 New Providence NJ 07974-0636

HELFEN, SPENCER JON, lawyer; b. L.A., Aug. 4, 1961; s. Edward A. and Betty F. Helfen. BA summa cum laude, UCLA, 1984, MA, 1984; JD, U. Calif., Berkeley, 1987. Bar: Calif. Assoc. Gendel, Raskoff, Shapiro & Quittner, L.A., 1987-91; assoc. Murphy, Weir & Butler, L.A., 1991-95, shareholder, 1996—. Co-author manual: Up the Down Staircase--Failed Real Estate Partnerships, 1995. Mem. State Bar Calif., Beverly Hills Bar Assn. (com. chair 1995-97, bd. govs. 1997—), Nat. Eagle Scout Assn. (life), UCLA Alumni Assn. (life), U. Calif. Berkeley Alumni Assn. (life), Phi Beta Kappa. Avocations: American and Californian modern art.

HELFER, MICHAEL STEVENS, lawyer; b. N.Y.C., Aug. 2, 1945; s. Robert Stevens and Teresa (Kahan) H.; m. Ricki Rhodarmer Helfer; children: David, Matthew, Lisa. BA summa cum laude, Claremont Men's Coll., 1967; JD magna cum laude, Harvard U., 1970. Bar: D.C. 1971. Law clk. to chief judge U.S. Ct. Appeals D.C., 1970-71; asst. counsel subcom. on constl. amendments Senate Judiciary Com., 1971-73; assoc. Wilmer, Cutler & Pickering, Washington, 1973-78, ptnr., 1978—, mem. mgmt. com., 1990-98, chmn., 1995-98; professorial lectr. George Washington U. Law Sch., 1982; bd. dirs. 1st Cmty. Bankshares, Inc., Houston. Trustee Legal Aid Soc. D.C., 1983-95, pres., 1990-92; v.p., bd. dirs. Lawyers for Children Am., Inc., 1995—. Fellow Am. Bar Found.; mem. Am. Law Inst. Democrat. Home: 1336 31st St NW Washington DC 20007-3347 Office: 2445 M St NW Washington DC 20037-1435

HELFER, RICKI TIGERT, banking and finance consultant; b. N.C., Feb. 4, 1945; m. Michael S. Helfer; 1 child, Matthew. BA with honors, Vanderbilt U.; MA, U. N.C.; JD with honors, U. Chgo. Law clk. to hon. John Minor Wisdom U.S. Ct. Appeals; counsel to Jud. Com. U.S. Senate, Washington, 1978-79; assoc., ptnr. Leva, Hawes, Symington, Martin and Oppenheimer, 1979-83; sr. counsel internat. fin. Treasury Dept., Washington; chief internat. lawyer Fed. Reserve Bd., 1985-92; ptnr. Gibson, Dunn & Crutcher, Washington, 1992-94; chmn. FDIC, Washington, 1994-97; nonresident sr. fellow The Brookings Inst., Washington, 1998—; bd. govs., chmn. audit com. Phila. Stock Exch., 1997—; cons. internat. banking and fin. regulation. Bd. dirs. Girl Scouts U.S., 1995—; mem. vis. com. U. Chgo. Law Sch., 1989-92, 94-97. Mem. ABA (former chair internat. banking and fin. com.), Am. Law Inst., Coun. Fgn. Rels., Washington Fgn. Law Soc. (past pres.). Office: The Brookings Inst 1775 Massachusetts Ave NW Washington DC 20036-2188

HELFERT, ERICH ANTON, management consultant, author, educator; b. Aussig/Elbe, Sudetenland, May 29, 1931; came to U.S., 1950; s. Julius and Anna Maria (Wilde) H.; m. Anne Langley, Jan. 1, 1983; children: Claire L., Amanda L. BS, U. Nev., 1954; MBA with distinction, Harvard U., 1956, DBA, 1958. Newspaper reporter, corr., Neuburg, Fed. Republic of Germany, 1948-52; rsch. asst. Harvard U., 1956-57; asst. prof. bus. policy San Francisco State U., 1958-59; asst. prof. fin. and control Grad. Sch. Bus. Adminstrn., Harvard U., 1959-65; internal cons., then asst. to pres., dir. corp. planning Crown Zellerbach Corp., San Francisco, 1965-78, asst. to chmn., dir. corp. planning, 1978-82, v.p. corp. planning, 1982-85; mgmt. cons., San Francisco, 1985—; co-founding dir., chmn. Modernsoft, Inc.; mem. Dean's adv. coun. San Francisco State Bus. Sch., sch. fin. Golden Gate U.; bd. dirs., past chmn. and pres. Harvard U. Bus. Sch. No. Calif.; trustee Saybrook Inst. Author: Techniques of Financial Analysis, 1963, 10th ed. 2000, Valley of the Shadow, 1997, Valuation, 1966, (with others) Case Book on Finance, 1963, Controllership, 1965; contbr. articles to profl. jours. Exch. student fellow U.S. Inst. Internat. Edn., 1950; Ford Found. doctoral fellow, 1956. Mem. Assn. Corp. Growth (past pres., bd. dirs. San Francisco chpt.), Inst. Mgmt. Cons., Commonwealth Club, Phi Kappa Phi. Roman Catholic. Home: 111 W 3rd Ave Apt 401 San Mateo CA 94402-1521 Office: 1777 Borel Pl Ste 508 San Mateo CA 94402-3514

HELFGOTT, ROY B., economist, educator; b. Bklyn., Oct. 27, 1925; s. Moses N. and Dorothy A. (Levine) H.; m. Gloria Wolff, July 4, 1948; 1 son, Daniel Andrew. BS in Social Sci, City Coll., N.Y., 1948; MA, Columbia U., 1949; PhD, New Sch., 1957. Rsch. dir. N.Y. coat bd. Internat. Ladies Garment Workers Union, N.Y.C., 1949-57; indsl. rels. analyst Wage Stblzn. Bd., N.Y.C., 1952; economist N.Y. Met. Regional Study, 1957-58; asst. prof. econs. Pa. State U., University Park, 1958-60; rsch. dir. Indsl. Rels. Counselors, N.Y.C., 1960-66, 67-68; adj. assoc. prof. Baruch Coll., 1961-68; indsl. devel. officer UN, N.Y.C., 1966-67; head UN mission, Lower Mekong Basin, 1967; disting. prof. econs. N.J. Inst. Tech., Newark, 1968-93; disting. prof. econs. emeritus N.J. Inst. Tech., 1993—; cons. Orgn. Resources Counselors, Inc., N.Y.C., 1968—; pres. Indsl. Rels. Counselors, Inc., N.Y.C. Author: Computerized Manufacturing and Human Resources, 1988, Labor Economics, 1974, 2d edit., 1980; co-author: Industrial Planning, 1969, Management, Automation and People, 1964, Made in New York, 1959. Served with AUS, 1944-46, ETO. Decorated Bronze Star with Oak Leaf Cluster, Combat Inf. badge; fellow Inter-Univ. Inst. Social Gerontology, Berkeley, Calif., 1959; sr. Fulbright rsch. scholar U.K., 1955-56. Mem. Am. Econ. Assn., Indsl. Rels. Rsch. Assn., Met. Econ. Assn. (pres. 1978-79), Phi Beta Kappa.

HELFMAN, CAROLYN RAE, middle school educator; b. Dallas, July 15, 1941; d. Alfred Sallinger and Hermine Rita Morgenstern; m. Kenneth Harvey Helfman, Aug. 10, 1963 (div. June 1980); children: Theresa, Daniel, Kory. BA, Washington U., St. Louis, 1963; MEd in Counseling, U. North Tex., 1992. Tchr. Richardson (Tex.) Ind. Sch. Dist., 1963-64; homebound tchr. Garland (Tex.) Ind. Sch. Dist., 1970-71; tchr. Hockaday Sch., Dallas, 1971-84, 88-98, asst. head mid. sch., 1993-96, head mid. sch., 1996—; mktg. mgr. Omniplan Architects, Dallas, 1984-88. Mem. bd. dirs. devel. com. Temple Emanu-El, Dallas, 1998—; bd. dirs. Anti Defamation League, Dallas, 1996—. Mem. AAUW, ASCD, Nat. Mid. Sch. Assn., Ind. Schs. Assn. of S.W. (mem. adv. planning com. 1995—, mem. evaluation team 1998), Phi Delta Kappa. Jewish. Home: 5116 Meadowcreek Dr Dallas TX 75248 Office: Hockaday Sch 11600 Welch Rd Dallas TX 75229

HELFORD, PAUL QUINN, communications educator, academic administrator; b. Chgo., June 27, 1947; s. Norman and Eleanor (Kwin) H.; m. Leslie Gale Weinstein, July 11, 1971; children: Ross Michael, Benjamin Keith. BA, U. Ill., 1969; MA, Northeastern Ill. U., 1977. Cert. tchr., Ill., Oreg., Ariz. Tchr. John Hersey H.S., Arlington Heights, Ill., 1969-73; freelance writer Mill Valley, Calif., 1973-75; mgr., program dir. Sta. KOZY-TV, Eugene, Oreg., 1976-88, mktg., sales, and program dir. Group W Cable, 1984-88; prodr., with mktg. Northland Broadcasting, Flagstaff, Ariz., 1989-91; lectr. cinema and broadcasting No. Ariz. U., Flagstaff, 1989—, acad. coord. for instrnl. TV, 1995-97, dir. Native Am. video workshops, 1997—, dean Sch. Comm., 1999—; dir. Native Am. Video Workshops, 1991—, Flagstaff Festival of the Arts Film Festival, 1992, No. Ariz. U. Instrnl. TV Programming, 1994—; writer New Times, Phoenix, 1992, Flagstaff Live!, 1996—. Writer, prodr. Paul Helford's Hollywood Oldies, 1976-81, In Review, 1981, Live from the Fair, 1981-85, Group W Cable Minutes, 1984-85, Bad Horror and Sci. Fiction, 1985 (Award for Cable Excellence 1986), KOZY movie promotional spots 1976-88 (Award for Cable Excellence 1984, 88, CLIO award nomination 1988, 1989); contbr. articles to profl. jours. Recipient CLIO award 1984, 86, Cable Mktg. Grand award, 1981, 85. Mem. Nat. Assn. Cable Programmers. Avocations: hiking, camping, biking, movies. Office: No Ariz Univ Sch Comm Box 4131 Flagstaff AZ 86011

HELFRICH, THEODORA THOMPSON, spanish educator, academic administrator; b. Passaic, N.J., May 27, 1947; d. Donald William and Maryanna (Norton) Thompson; m. Robert William Helfrich, June 22, 1984; 4 stepchildren; 1 foster child. BA, Newton (Mass.) Coll. SacredHeart, 1969; MA, Middlebury Coll., 1971. Cert. tchr. and adminstr., Mass. Tchr. Brockton (Mass.) H.S., 1971—; head dept. fgn. langs. Brockton Pub. Schs., 1994—. Avocations: reading, travel, ethnic food. Home: 69 Thaxter St Hingham MA 02043 Office: Brockton HS 470 Forest Ave Brockton MA 02301

HELFRICH, THOMAS STOUGH, healthcare company executive; b. Ft. Wayne, Ind., Mar. 7, 1947; s. Donald Leroy and Elaine Elenore (Stough) H.; m. Mary Ann Mead, June 19, 1971; children: Julie, Jennifer, Thomas. AB in Zoology, Ind. U., 1970, BS in Optometric Sci., 1971, DO, 1973. Pvt. practice optometry St. Louis, 1973-96; dir. profl. svcs. Am. Home Vision, Inc., St. Louis, 1996—; clin. investigator Wesley-Jessem Inc., Chgo., 1974-76, Syntex Corp.-Optical, Phoenix, 1977-79. Pres. Tazewell County chpt. Am. Cancer Soc., Pekin, Ill., 1974. Mem. Am. Optometric Assn., Mo. Optometric Assn., St. Louis Optometric Soc., Heart of Am. Contact Lens Soc. Avocations: golf, racquetball, bridge. Home: 827 Woodcove Ct Chesterfield MO 63017-1743 Office: American Home vision Inc Ste 208 1030 Woodcrest Terrace Dr Creve Coeur MO 63141-5003

HELFRICK, EDWARD W., state legislator; b. Pottsville, Pa., Mar. 11, 1928; s. Edward and Elizabeth Rosenberger Helfrick; m. Rose Helfrick, 1952; five children. Grad. high sch., 1945. State rep. dist. 107 Pa. Ho. of Reps., 1977-80; state senator dist. 27 Pa. State Senate, 1981—; chmn. game and fisheries com. Pa. State Senate; mem. Gov.'s Task Force on Drunken Driving. Mem. Am. Legion, VFW, K.C., Elks, Eagles, Moose. Office: Pa State Senate State Capitol Harrisburg PA 17120*

HELGANZ, BEVERLY BUZHARDT, counselor; b. Tampa, Fla., June 7, 1941; d. M. O. Buzhardt and Jeanne M. Buzhardt Crabb; m. Charles F. Helganz Jr., June 26, 1964 (dec. Dec. 1977). AA, Jacksonville U., 1962, BA, 1974; MEd, U. North Fla., 1993. Lic. mental health counselor; nat. cert. counselor. Customer contact So. Bell, Jacksonville, Fla., 1959-66, supr., 1966-80, staff mgr., 1980-91; assessment counselor Charter Hosp., Jacksonville, 1995; sr. counselor River Region Human Svcs., Jacksonville, 1995-96; family link counselor Youth Crisis Ctr., Jacksonville, 1996—; past pres. Am. Bus. Women's Assn., Jacksonville, 1969-70. Mem. women's aux. U. Med. Ctr., Jacksonville, 1994-98; 1st v.p. Aux. Hospice of N.E. Fla., Jacksonville, 1994—; panel mem. foster care citizen's rev. bd. 4th Jud. Cir. Ct., Jacksonville, 1993—; docent Mus. Sci. and History, 1993—; past pres. Jacksonville Alumnae Panhellenic Assn., 1982; bd. dirs. N.E. Fla. Coun. on Alcoholism and Drug Abuse, 1997; mem. Jacksonville Mus. Contemporary Art. Recipient Merit award Am. Bus. Women's Assn., 1966, Woman of Yr. award, 1969, Honor Ring Alumnae's cert of merit Zeta Tau Alpha, 1975, 76, Girl of Yr. award Beta Sigma Phi. Mem. ACA, Fla. Mental Health Counselors Assn., N.E. Fla. Mental Health Counselors Assn., Mental Health Assn., Telephone Pioneers of Am. (life), Pilot Club Jacksonville (bd. dirs., past pres.), Club Continental, Phi Kappa Phi. Avocations: collecting penguins, films, fine dining, art/museums. Home: 5000 San Jose Blvd Apt 97 Jacksonville FL 32207-7687

HELGASON, SIGURDUR, mathematician, educator; b. Akureyri, Iceland, Sept. 30, 1927; came to U.S., 1952; s. Helgi and Kara (Briem) Skulason; m. Artie Gianopulos, June 9, 1957; children: Thor Helgi, Anna Loa. Student, U. Iceland, 1946, D honoris causa, 1986; MS, U. Copenhagen, 1952, D honoris causa, 1988; PhD, Princeton U., 1954; D honoris causa, Uppsala U., 1996. C.L.E. Moore instr. MIT, Cambridge, 1954-56, asst. prof. math., 1960-61, assoc. prof. math., 1961-65, prof. math., 1965—; lectr. Princeton (N.J.) U., 1956-57; Louis Block asst. prof. math. U. Chgo., 1957-59; asst. prof. Columbia U., 1959-60; vis. mem. Inst. Advanced Study, Princeton, 1964-66, 74-75, 83-84, 98, Mittag-Leffler Inst., 1970-71, 95. Author: Differential Geometry, Lie Groups and Symmetric Spaces, 1978, Groups and Geometric Analysis, 1984, Geometric Analysis on Symmetric Spaces, 1994, Radon Transform, 1999; editor Progress in Math., 1980-86, Perspectives in Math. Academic Press, Cambridge, 1985—; contbr. articles to profl. jours. Decorated Major Knight's Cross of Icelandic Falcon, 1991; recipient Jessen diploma Danish Math. Soc., 1982, Gold medal U. Copenhagen, 1951; Guggenheim fellow, 1964-65. Mem. Am. Acad. Arts and Scis., Royal Danish Acad. Scis. and Letters, Icelandic Acad. Scis., Am. Math. Soc. (Steele prize 1988). Avocations: music, photography. Office: MIT 77 Massachusetts Ave Dept Math Cambridge MA 02139-4307

HELGATH, SHEILA FAY, environmental company executive; b. Lebanon, Oreg., July 17, 1949; d. Paul Kruger and Edna Fay Sherwood H. BS in Botany, Wash. State U., 1971, MS in Forestry and Soils, 1974; PhD in Forest Mgmt., U. Wash., 1984. Rsch. analyst USFS/U. Alaska, Juneau, 1980-85; legis. analyst Alaska State Senate, Juneau, 1985-91; tech. advisor Corp. Nacional Forestal/Peace Corps, Santiago, Chile, 1991-93; environ. mgr. Savia Internat., Seattle, 1994-98; spl. projects advisor Banco Axial, São Paulo, Brazil, 1998—. Internat. editor Women in Nat. Resources, 1998-99. Avocations: outdoor activities, reading, swimming. Fax: 206-784-6004. E-mail: shelgath@nwlink.com. Office: Banco Axial 918 N 67th St Seattle WA 98103

HELGELAND, BRIAN, film director, writer, producer; b. Providence, RI, 1961. Writer (screeplays) A Nightmare on Elm Street 4: The Dream Master, 1988, 976-EVIL, 1988, Highway to Hell, 1992, Assassins, 1995, Conspiracy Theory, 1997, The Postman, 1997; writer, co-prodr. L.A. Confidential (N.Y. Film Critics Circle award 1997, Boston Soc. of Film Critics award 1997, Broadcast Film Critics Assn. award, 1997, Acad. award 1998, Fla. film Critics award 1998, Writers Guild of Am. award 1998); dir. Payback, 1999, Sin Eater, 1999. also: DGA 7920 Sunset Blvd Los Angeles CA 90046*

HELGERSON, JOHN WALTER, lawyer; b. Cleve., Aug. 27, 1938; s. Floyd G. and Evelyn Ann (Wilder) H.; m. Dorothy Elizabeth Hart, Dec. 5, 1984, children from previous marriage: Heidi Wilder, Holly Ward. A.B., Wittenberg U., 1960; J.D., Yale U., 1963. Bar: Ohio 1963. Assoc., Porter Wright Morris & Arthur, Columbus, Ohio, 1963-93, ret. 1993, ptnr., 1968—; ret. 1993; bd. dirs. Bry-Air, Inc., Sunbury, Ohio; mng. dir. Windsong Ltd., Grenada; chmn. lawyers div. United Way, 1979. Served to capt. USAR, 1963-70. Mem. Blue Key, Phi Gamma Delta, Pi Sigma Alpha, Pi Delta Epsilon, Tau Pi Phi, Capital Club, Grenada Yacht Club. Republican. Unitarian. Avocations: sailing; scuba diving, travel, power boating, deep sea fishing. Home: PO Box 26, Saint George's Grenada

HELGERSON, RICHARD, English literature educator; b. Pasadena, Calif., Aug. 22, 1940; s. Donald Theodore and Viola Dolores (Huss) H.; m. Marie-

Christine David, June 8, 1967; 1 child, Jessica. BA, U. Calif., Riverside, 1963; MA, Johns Hopkins U., 1964, PhD, 1970. Prof. English Coll. Notre-Dame d'Afrique, Atakpamé, Togo, 1964-66; asst. prof. English U. Calif., Santa Barbara, 1970-76, assoc. prof., 1976-82, chair dept. English, 1989-93, prof. English, 1982—, faculty rsch. lectr., 1998; vis. prof. Calif. Inst. Tech., Pasadena, 1987-88; chair Huntington (Calif.) Libr. Rsch. Rev., 1986-87; faculty rsch. lectr. U. Calif., Santa Barbara, 1998. Author: The Elizabethan Prodigals, 1976, Self-Crowned Laureates, 1983, Forms of Nationhood, 1992 (James Russell Lowell prize MLA, Brit. Coun. prize in humanities); contbr. numerous articles to profl. jours. Fellow Woodrow Wilson Found., 1963-64, NEH, 1979-80, Huntington Libr., 1984-85, Guggenheim Found., 1985-86, Folger-NEH, 1993-94, NEH, 1998-99, U. Calif. Pres.'s fellow, 1998-99. Mem. MLA (exec. com. English renaissance div. 1988-92), N.Am. Conf. on Brit. Studies, Renaissance Soc. Am., Spenser Soc. Am. (pres. 1988), Shakespeare Assn. Am., Western Humanities Conf. (exec. com. 1988-91). Democrat. Home: 334 E Arrellaga St Santa Barbara CA 93101-1106 Office: U Calif Dept English Santa Barbara CA 93106

HELGERSON, STEVEN DALE, epidemiologist, educator; b. Centralia, Wash., Oct. 31, 1946; s. Stanford Donald and Blanche Irene (Dean) H.; m. Linda Elizabeth Ortmeyer, Nov. 22, 1967; 1 child, Brandon Elizabeth. BS with honors, U. Puget Sound, 1968; MA in Biomed. History, U. Wash., 1971, MD, 1973, MPH, 1980. Diplomate Nat. Bd. Med. Examiners; cert. pub. health and preventive medicine Am. Bd. Preventive Medicine. Psychiatry resident U. Wash. Affiliated Hosps., 1973-74; preventive medicine resident U. Wash. Sch. Pub. Health and Cmty. Medicine, 1976-80; clin. instr. pub. health Sch. Medicine Oreg. Health Scis. U., 1980-82; clin. asst. prof. U. Wash.-Sch. Pub. Health and Cmty. Medicine, 1983-84, clin. assoc. prof. epidemiology, 1990; asst. clin. prof. epidemiology and pub. health Yale U. Sch. Medicine, 1985, assoc. clin. prof. epidemiology, 1986; lectr. U. Ariz. Sch. Medicine, 1987-89; pvt. practice Epidemiology for Action, 1997—; assoc. clin. prof. epidemiology and health svcs. W. Wash. Sch. Pub. Health & Cmty. Medicine, 1999—. Contbr. chpts. to books and articles to profl. jours. Capt. USPHS, 1974-96. Fellow Am. Coll. Preventive Medicine; mem. AMA, APHA, Am. Assn. for the History of Medicine, Commd. Officers Assn., Phi Kappa Phi, Phi Sigma. Office: Epidemiology for Action Ste 408 500 Union St Seattle WA 98101

HELGESON, DUANE MARCELLUS, retired librarian; b. Rothsay, Minn., July 2, 1930; s. Oscar Herbert and Selma Olivia (Sateren) H.; B.S., U. Minn., 1952. Librarian, Chance-Vought Co., Dallas, 1956-59, System Devel. Corp., Santa Monica, Calif., 1959-62, Lockheed Aircraft, Burbank, Calif., 1962-63, C.F. Braun Co., Alhambra, Calif., 1963-74; chief librarian Ralph M. Parsons Co., Pasadena, Calif., 1974-79; pres. Mark-Allen/Brokers-in-Info., Los Angeles, 1976-80; phys. scis. librarian Calif. Inst. Tech., Pasadena, 1980-84; corp. librarian Montgomery Watson, Pasadena, 1985-94, ret. 1994. mem. adv. bd. Los Angeles Trade Tech. Coll., 1974-79, U. So. Calif. Library Sch., 1974-79. Served with USAF, 1952-54. Mem. Spl. Libraries Assn. (chmn. nominating com. 1974). Co-editor: (with Joe Ann Clifton) Computers in Library and Information Centers, 1973. Home: 2706 Ivan Hill Ter Los Angeles CA 90039-2717

HELGESON, JOHN PAUL, plant physiologist, researcher; b. Barberton, Ohio, July 25, 1935; s. Earl Adrian and Marguerite (Dutcher) H.; m. Sarah Frances Slater, June 10, 1957; children: Daniel, Susan, James. AB, Oberlin Coll., 1957; PhD, U. Wis., 1964. NSF postdoctoral fellow Dept. of Chemistry, U. Ill., Urbana, 1964-66; from asst. to prof. botany and plant pathology U. Wis., Madison, 1966—; plant physiologist USDA Argl. Rsch. Svc. plant disease resistance unit, Madison, 1966-90, rsch. leader, 1990—; program dir. USDA, Washington, 1982-83; vis. scientist Lab. of Cell Biology, Versailles, France, 1985-86. Lt. USAF, 1957-60. Mem. Bot. Soc. Am., Am. Phytopathol. Soc., Internat. Soc. Plant Molecular Biologists, Am. Soc. Plant Physiologists. Achievements include development of tissue culture procedures for studying interactions of plants and fungi, of somatic hybridizations to obtain new disease resistances in plants. Office: USDA Plant Disease Resistnc Rsch Unit U Wis Madison Dept Plant Pathology Madison WI 53706

HELINGER, MICHAEL GREEN, mathematics educator; b. Syracuse, N.Y., Feb. 5, 1947; s. Harley George and Marion Irene (Green) H.; m. Susan Jessie McRae, Apr. 13, 1974 (div. Feb. 1987). BS with distinction, Clarkson U., Potsdam, N.Y., 1968; MS, Rensselaer Poly. Inst., Troy, N.Y., 1969. Instr. Clinton Community Coll., Plattsburgh, N.Y., 1969-73, asst. prof., 1974-86, assoc. prof. math., 1987—; life ins. agt. William LaCount Assocs., Franklin United Life, Plattsburgh, 1980-84; owner, mgr. Sue's Beauty Salon, Plattsburgh, 1984; pres., treas. Helinger Rentals, Inc., Plattsburgh, 1976—; owner B&M Firewood Co., 1990-92; gen. contractor, 1993—; mem. acad. affairs com. Clinton C.C., 1970-72, 75—, chmn., 1971-72, 86-90, 92-97, gen. edn. com., 1990-92, chmn., 1990-92, student retention com., 1993—, calendar com., 1995-96; dir. C.C.C. Annual Math. Scholar Contest, 1994—; presenter at confs. in field. Vol. Clinton Correctional Facility, Dannemora, N.Y., 1971-75, 88—; apptd. ministerial servant Jehovah's Witnesses, 1991-99, elder Jehovah's Witnesses, 1999—/. Recipient Cert. of Appreciation, Clinton Correctional Facility, Dannemora, 1989, 92, 99. Mem. Math. Assn. Am., N.Y. State Math. Assn. 2-Yr. Colls. (certs. of appreciation 1993-97), Math. League (team founder, coach 1984—, mem. state com. for Math. League exam. 1992—), Ski Club (advisor 1985—), Pi Mu Epsilon. Avocations: collecting art, antiques, coins, skiing, tennis. Home: 20 Riley Way Peru NY 12972-4950 Office: Clinton C C Plattsburgh NY 12901

HELINSKI, DONALD RAYMOND, biologist, educator; b. Balt., July 7, 1933; s. George L. and Marie M. (Naparstek) H.; m. Patricia G. Doherty, Mar. 4, 1962; children—Matthew T., Maureen G. BS, U. Md., 1954; PhD in Biochemistry, Western Res. U., 1960; postdoctoral fellow, Stanford U., 1960-62. Asst. prof. Princeton (N.J.) U., 1962-65; mem. faculty U. Calif., San Diego, 1965—, prof. biology, 1970—, chmn. dept., 1979-81, dir. Ctr. for Molecular Genetics, 1984-95, assoc. dean Natural Scis., 1994-97; mem. com. guidelines for recombinant DNA research NIH, 1975-78. Author papers in field. Mem. Am. Soc. Biol. Chemists, Am. Soc. Microbiology, AAAS, Am. Acad. of Arts and Scis., Am. Acad. Microbiology, Nat. Acad. Scis. Office: U Calif Ctr for Molecular Gen 9500 Gilman Dr La Jolla CA 92093-5003

HELIOFF, ANNE GRAILE, painter; b. Liverpool, Eng.; d. Max and Frances Elizabeth (Beilenson) H.; m. Benjamin Michael Hirschberg. Student, Columbia U., Art Students League, N.Y.C. mem. U.S. del. 5th Congress Internat. Assn. Art, Tokyo, 1966, invitation Woodstock Artists Assn., 1994; dir. exhbns. including 50 Yrs. of Woodstock Art (N.Y.), N.Y. State Tri-Centennial, 1959, dir. N.Y. State dedication show Lighthouse for Blind, N.Y.C. One-woman shows include Capricorn Gallery, N.Y.C., 1966-69, Phoenix Gallery, N.Y.C., 1972, 74, 76, 82, 85, Woodstock (N.Y.) Artists Assn., 1988; group exhbns. include Milch Gallery, N.Y.C., 1939-40 (Paintings of Yr. 1946), Pepsi-Cola Nat. travelling shows to major mus., U.S., 1947, Nat. Gallery Art, Washington, Pa. Acad. Ann, Art U.S.A., also bicentennial exhbn., 6 Americans in France traveling show, 1976, Mus. in Florence and Naples, Italy; slide show Am. Art 6th Congress Internat. Assn. Art, Helsinki, finland. Recipient Silver medal Albany (N.Y.) Mus. Art and Sci., 1957; Homer Boss scholar, 1939, Y. Kuniyoshi scholar and asst., 1940-45. Mem. Arista, Woodstock Artists Assn. (life, past dir.), Art Students League (past dir.), Am. Soc. Contemporary Artists (past dir., awards in oil, watercolor and acrylic), Nat. Assn. Women Artists, N.Y. Soc. Women Artists (past dir.), Archives of Am. Art, Smithsonian Mus. Address: 340 W 28th St New York NY 10001-4732

HELLAND, GEORGE ARCHIBALD, JR., management consultant, manufacturing executive, former government official; b. San Antonio, Nov. 28, 1937; s. George Archibald and Ruth (Gorman) H.; m. Josephine Howell, June 9, 1962 (div. 1989); children: Jane Elizabeth, Thomas Gorman; m. Antonia Scott Day, Nov. 24, 1990. BS in Mech. Engring., U. Tex., 1959; MBA with distinction, Harvard U., 1961. Registered profl. engr., Tex. With Cameron Iron Works, Inc., Houston, 1961-77, asst. sales mgr., 1963, dist. sales mgr., 1964, dist. sales mgr., U.K., Africa, 1965, product mgr., 1966, plant mgr., Leeds, Eng., 1967, mgr. oil tool products, 1968, v.p., 1969-75, exec. v.p., 1975-77; with Weatherford Internat., Inc., Houston, 1977-79; v.p. Weatherford Internat., Inc., 1977, pres., CEO, dir., 1978-79; pres. McEvoy Oilfield Equipment Co. (name changed to Sii McEvoy div. Smith Internat., Inc. 1980), Houston, 1979-85; pres. McCall Industries, Inc., Houston, 1986-87, bd. dirs.; gen. mgmt. cons., 1987-90; dep. asst. sec. of energy for export assistance U.S. Dept. Energy, Washington, 1990-93; v.p. Dreser Industries, Inc., Houston, 1993-97; sr. assoc. Cambridge Energy Rsch. Assocs., 1997—; pres. Lockwood Corp., Gering, Nebr., 1986-87; chmn. bd. dirs. SIE Internat., Inc., Ft. Worth; prin. Innova Ptnrs., 1988-90. Bd. dirs. Jr. Achievement Internat., Briarwood Sch., Houston; trustee S.W. Rsch. Inst.; mem. exec. com. Jr. Achievement of S.E. Tex.; trustee Eurasia Found., Washington. Recipient Five Outstanding Young Texans award Tex. Jr. C. of C., 1972; named Outstanding Young Houstonian Houston Jr. C. of C., 1972; Disting. Grad. Sch. Engring. U. Tex., 1977. Mem. ASME, Am. Inst. Mining, Metall. and Petroleum Engrs., Am. Petroleum Inst. (bd. dirs.), Inst. Gas Engrs. (U.K.), Tex. Soc. Profl. Engrs., Am. Wellhead Equipment Assn. (pres. 1967), Petroleum Equipment Suppliers Assn. (pres. 1976-77), Houston C. of C., Tau Beta Pi, Phi Eta Sigma, Pi Tau Sigma, Sigma Nu, Friars Soc. Presbyterian. Home and Office: 2622 W Lane Dr Houston TX 77027-4914

HELLAND, SHERMAN M., author; b. Racine, Wis., Nov. 16, 1913; s. Severin and Marie Kutinka (Fyhrie) H.; m. Rose Martha Steuck, Aug. 12, 1939; children: Mary, Sandra, Karen, Harold. Mgr. retail meats C&W Haummersen, Racine, Wis., 1933-35; sales area developer George A. Hormel Co., Austin, Minn., 1936-51; mgr. bus. analysis U.S. Govt., Richmond, Va., 1951-53; sales mgr., beef grader Donner Packing Co., Milw., 1953-54; supr. chain store meat Godfrey Co., Waukesha, Wis., 1954-55, purchaser, merchandiser select beef and lamb, 1956-57, with, 1958-76; cons. agr., livestock, breeding feeding, merchandising retail meat, 1991—. Author: Hoofs, Amen, 1978, E. Coli Kills--Wake Up or Die, 1997. Pres. Old Jr. Club of Milw. County, 1980. With USN, 1945. Mem. Am. Legion (chpt. pres. 1981-82). Republican. Lutheran. Avocations: flying, hunting, golf, fishing, philosophy. Home and Office: 5020 S 55th St Apt 303 Greenfield WI 53220-5370

HELLAWELL, ROBERT, law educator; b. Long Island, N.Y., Jan. 24, 1928; s. Edwin V. and Nora D. (Mahoney) H.; m. Jane Buck, June 16, 1951; 1 child, Kathleen Abbott. AB, Williams Coll., 1950; LLB, Columbia U., 1953. Bar: N.Y. 1954, Ohio 1955. Law clk. U.S. Circuit Ct. judge, 1953-54; with firm Jones, Day, Cockley & Reavis, Cleve., 1954-61; ptnr. Jones, Day, Cockley & Reavis, 1961; atty., adviser formation Peace Corps, 1961; dir. projects in Peace Corps, Tanganyika, 1961-63; dep. assoc. dir. Peace Corps, 1963-64; assoc. prof. law Columbia Law Sch., N.Y.C., 1964-67, prof. law, 1967-89, Wilber Friedman prof. emeritus, 1989—, vice dean, 1973-76, acting dean, 1976-77, dir. African Law Center, 1971-77, co-dir. Investment Negotiation Center, 1973-82, dir. Center for Law and Econs., 1978-79; vis. prof. U. Ghana, 1969; cons. admiralty law UN Commn. Internat. Trade Law, 1971. Co-author: Taxation of Business Enterprises, 1987, Taxation of Transnational Transactions, 1989; editor: United States Taxation and Developing Countries, 1980; co-editor: Competition in International Business, 1981, Negotiating Foreign Investments, 1982; notes editor: Columbia Law Rev, 1952-53. Bd. dirs. Internat. Law Inst., Georgetown U., 1973-85. With AUS, 1946-48, Korea. Mem. Delta Kappa Epsilon, Phi Delta Phi. Home: 410 Heron Pt Chestertown MD 21620-1679 Office: Columbia Law Sch New York NY 10027

HELLBUSCH, LESLIE CARL, neurosurgeon; b. Columbus, Nebr., Nov. 25, 1945; s. Carl Ludwig and Dora Lily Hellbusch; m. Joan Marie Swanson, May 28, 1988; children: Jeffrey, Laurie, Nicholas, Sarah. BS, U. Nebr., 1968; MD, Northwestern U., 1972. Diplomate Am. Bd. Neurol. Surgery, Am Bd. Pediat. Surgery. Intern Evanston (Ill.) Hosp., 1972-73; resident in neurosurgery Baylor Coll. Medicine, Houston, 1973-77; pvt. practice neurosurgery Omaha, 1977—; chmn. neurosurgery Meth. Hosp., Omaha, 1981-85, 90-91; vice-sect. chief sect. neurosurgery U. Nebr. Med. ctr., Omaha, 1994—, clin. assoc. prof. surgery, 1987-98, clin. prof. surgery, 1998—; tng. dir. resident physicians Meth. Hosp., Children's Hosp., 1994—; presenter in field. Contbr. articles to profl. jours. Trustee Children's Hosp., Omaha, 1990-95; bd. dirs. Heartland Equine Therapeutic Riding Acad., 1989-92, v.p., 1990-91, pres. 1992. Mem. AMA, Am. Acad. Pediatrics, Am. Assn. Neurol. Surgeons, Nebr. Med. Assn. (alt. del. 1980-90, del. 1991-98, clin. affairs com. 1996-98), Met. Omaha Med. Soc., Iowa-Midwest Neurosurg. Soc., Omaha-Midwest Med. Soc., Nebr. Acad. Neurologists and Neurosurgeons, Rocky Mountain Neurosurg. Soc., Phi Beta Kappa, Phi Eta Sigma, Theta Nu. Avocations: jogging, skiing, coaching soccer. Fax: (402) 298-9253. Home: 109 S 92d St Omaha NE 68114 Office: Midwest Neurosurgery PC 111 N 84th St Omaha NE 68114

HELLEINER, GERALD KARL, economics educator; b. St. Pölten, Austria, Oct. 9, 1936; s. Karl Ferdinand and Grethe (Deutsch) H.; m. Georgia Stirrett, Aug. 16, 1958; children—Jane Leslie, Eric Noel, Peter David. BA, U. Toronto, 1958; PhD, Yale U., 1962; LLD (hon.), Dalhousie U., 1988; DLitt (hon.), U. W.I. Asst. prof. Yale U., 1961-65; assoc., then prof. U. Toronto, 1965-98, prof. emeritus, disting. rsch. fellow Ctr. Internat. Studies, 1998—; dir. Econ. Rsch. Bur., Dar es Salaam, Tanzania, 1966-68; vis. fellow Inst. Devel. Studies, 1971-72, 75, Queen Elizabeth House, Oxford, 1979. dir. Econ. Rsch. Bur., Dar es Salaam, Tanzania, 1966-68; vis. fellow Inst. Devel. Studies, Sussex, 1971-72, 75, Queen Elizabeth House, Oxford, 1979. Rsch. coord. Group of 24; bd. dirs., chmn. bd. trustees Internat. Food Policy Rsch. Inst., 1988-94; bd. dirs. North-South Inst., 1976-92, chmn., 1990-92; bd. dirs. Internat. Devel. Rsch. Ctr., 1985-91, Econ. and Social Rsch. Found., African Capacity Bldg. Found. Guggenheim fellow, 1971-72. Fellow Royal Soc. Can.; mem. Royal Econs. Assn., Can. Econs. Assn., Can. Assn. Study Internat. Devel., Am. Econs. Assn., Soc. Internat. Devel., North-South Roundtable, Can. African Studies Assn. Office: 150 Saint George St, Toronto, ON Canada M5S 3G7

HELLENBRAND, SAMUEL HENRY, lawyer, diversified industry executive; b. N.Y.C., Nov. 11, 1916; s. Louis H. and Fannie (Cohen) H.; children: Kathy Noreen, Linda Caryn. LL.B., Bklyn. Law Sch. St. Lawrence U., 1941, LL.M., 1942. Bar: N.Y. 1942. With N.Y. Central R.R., 1942-68, atty., asst. to gen. atty., tax atty., 1947-52, gen. tax atty., 1952-56, dir. taxes finance dept., 1956-63, v.p. planning and devel., 1963-64, v.p. real estate, 1964-68; v.p. indsl. devel. and real estate Penn Central Co., 1968-70, v.p. real estate and taxes, 1970-71; pres. Pa. Co., 1970-71; v.p. exec. asst. to pres., dir. real estate affairs ITT, 1971-81; chmn. fin. com., vice-chmn. AMTRAK, 1982-90; of counsel Law Offices Kathy H. Rocklen, N.Y.C., 1993—. Mem. ABA, Assn. Bar City N.Y. Home: 177 E 75th St New York NY 10021-3230

HELLER, ABRAHAM, psychiatrist, educator; b. Claremont, N.H., Mar. 17, 1917; s. David and Rose Heller; m. Lora S. Levy, June 16, 1957; 1 child, Judith Rose. BA, Brandeis U., 1953; MD, Boston U., 1957. Diplomate Am. Bd. Med. Examiners, Am. Bd. Psychiatry and Neurology. Resident in psychiatry U. Colo., Denver, 1958-61; chief in-patient psychiatry Denver Gen. Hosp., 1961-65, asst. dir. psychiat. services, 1965-70, assoc. dir. psychiat. services, 1970-73, dir., community mental health services, 1970-72; chief psychiatry, dir. community mental health ctr. Newport (R.I.) Hosp., 1973-77; clin. assoc. prof. psychiatry Brown U., Providence, 1973-77; prof. psychiatry, community health Wright State U., Dayton, Ohio, 1977-91, vice chmn. dept., 1980-91, prof. emeritus, 1991—. Fellow Am. Psychiat. Assn., Am. Orthopsychiat. Assn., Am. Assn. for Social Psychiatry. Jewish. Home: 1400 Runnymede Rd Dayton OH 45419-2924 Office: Wright State U Sch Medicine Dept Psychiatry PO Box 927 Dayton OH 45401-0927

HELLER, ADAM, chemist, researcher; b. Cluj, Romania, June 25, 1933; came to U.S., 1962; s. Ephraim and Blanche (Nissel) H.; m. Ilana Grossbard, July 26, 1956; children: Ephraim, Jonathan. MSc, Hebrew U., 1957, PhD, 1961; D honoris causa, Uppsala U., Sweden, 1991. Postdoctoral rsch. assoc. U. Calif., Berkeley, 1962-63; mem. tech. staff Bell Labs., Murray Hill, N.J., 1963-64, 75-77, GTE Labs., Bayside, N.Y., 1964-70; mgr. exploratory rsch. GTE Labs., Waltham, Mass., 1970-75; head electronic materials rsch. dept. AT&T Bell Labs., Murray Hill, 1977-88; prof. chem. engring. U. Tex., Austin, 1988—; lectr. in field; adv. bd. Nat. Renewable Energy Lab., Golden, Colo., 1987-93, Basic Energy Scis. Dept. Energy, 1993-96; adj. prof. Brandeis U., Waltham, 1972-75, CUNY, 1968-88; vis. prof. Coll. de France, Paris, 1982; lectr. UCLA, 1984, Weizmann Inst., Israel, U. Guelph, Ont., Can., 1984, Tel-Aviv U., 1987; guest prof. Coll. de France. Editor: Semiconductor Liquid Junction Solar Cells, 1977, Inorganic Resists, 1982; contbr. articles to profl. jours.; patentee in field. Recipient Battery Divsn. award 1978, Grahame award Phys. Electrochemistry divsn. 1987, Vittorio De Nora-Diamond Shamrock award 1988, Am. Chem. Soc. award 1994, Faraday medal Royal Chem. Soc. (London), 1996, De Nora Gold medal The Electrochem. Soc., Chemistry of Materials award Am. Chem. Soc. Fellow AAAS, Electrochem. Soc.; mem. NAE, Internat. Soc. Electrochemistry, Internat. Union Pure and Applied Chemistry (assoc., com. photochemistry), U.S. Nat. Acad. Engring. Jewish. Achievements include research in electron conduction in chemically modified redox-enzymes, biosensors, environmental photo-catalysis, lithium batteries, liquid lasers, electronic materials. Home: 5317 Valburn Cir Austin TX 78731-1144

HELLER, AL, marketing consultant, business journalist. BA in Comms., Queens Coll., 1972; MBA in Mktg., Fordham U., 1977. Mng. editor Disclosure Record, Floral Park, N.Y., 1973-76; asst. pub. rels. dir. Fordham U., N.Y.C., 1977-81; contbg. writer and editor Venture, N.Y.C., 1982-84; assoc. editor Chain Store Age Supermarkets, N.Y.C., 1982-83; sr. editor Discount Store News, N.Y.C., 1983-86; exec. editor Drug Store News and Drug Store News for the Pharmacist, N.Y.C., 1986-93; editor-in-chief Supermarket HQ Quar., N.Y.C., 1990-93, Nonfoods Mdsg., N.Y.C., 1993-96; pres. Al Heller Editl. Svcs., 1996—; screening judge Jesse Neal awards Am. Bus. Press, N.Y.C., 1993-95. Author: Selling into Home Depot, 1997, Category Management in the Mass Market: Best Practices, 1998; co-author: The Passive Solar Dome Greenhouse Book, 1979. With USCG Res., 1969-75. Mem. Soc. Profl. Journalists, Nat. Writers Union. Avocations: writing, sports, photography, reading. Office: Al Heller Editl Svcs 28 Warren Dr Syosset NY 11791-6328

HELLER, ARTHUR, advertising agency executive; b. Bklyn., Mar. 14, 1930; s. Max and Tecla (Jacobs) H.; m. Phyllis Olarsch, Dec. 25, 1954; children: Todd, Tracy. B.A., Bklyn. Coll., 1951, M.A., 1952. Speech and speech correction tchr. N.Y.C. Bd. Edn., 1951-55; v.p., assoc. media dir., media analysis and planning Benton & Bowles, Inc., 1955-66; with Ted Bates & Co., N.Y.C., 1966—; v.p., media dir. Ted Bates & Co., 1966-69, v.p., assoc. dir. media-program dept., 1969-71, sr. v.p., 1971—, also account dir., 1974-78; sr. v.p., dir. media-programming-mktg. services Griffin Bacal Inc., N.Y.C., 1978-82, exec. v.p., 1982-97, also bd. dirs.; pres. Heller Mktg. & Comms.; former dir. media programming worldwide, former gen. mgr. Griffin Bacal Can. Served with AUS, 1952-54. Mem. Radio and TV Research Council, Actors Equity Assn., Internat. Radio and TV Soc.

HELLER, AUSTIN NORMAN, chemical and environmental engineer; b. Elizabeth, N.J., Aug. 18, 1914; s. Samuel Sidney and Bessie (Rosenfield) H.; m. Frances Sandler, Mar. 21, 1943; children: Richard David, Susan Starr. AB in Chemistry, Johns Hopkins U., Balt., 1938; MS, Iowa State U., 1941. Diplomate Am. Acad. Environ. Engrs. Emeritus. Rsch. asst. environ. sci. Rutgers U., New Brunswick, N.J., 1935-38, 39; chemist, bacteriologist Wallace and Tiernan Co., Belleville, N.J., 1942; rsch. assoc. dept. civil engring. N.Y.U. Coll. Engring., N.Y.C., 1946-48; supr. indsl. waste devel. sect., coord. long range planning Allied Chem. Corp., N.Y.C., 1948-61; dep. chief tech. assistance br. Air Pollution div. USPHS, Cin., 1961-66; cons. E.F. Drew and Co., Boonton, N.J., 1946-48; U.S. del. OECD, Sci. Div., Air Pollution Rsch. Survey Techniques Group, Paris, 1962-66, Surgeon Gen., Belgian Govt., 1965, Royal Commn. for Air Purification, Govt. Sweden, 1965; pres. Austin N. Heller, Inc., Annapolis, Md., 1977-88, cons. 1991-92; environ. adv. com. Fed. Energy Adminstrn., Washington, 1973-75; adj. prof. engring. Cooper Union Coll., 1966-67; mem. adv. coun. dept. chem. engring. Princeton (N.J.) U., 1967-70; adj. assoc. prof. environ. Columbia U.,. Contbr. articles to profl. jours. Trustee Engirng. Index, Inc., N.Y.C., 1969-72; expert testimony Pres. Nixon's Adv. Bd. on Water Pollution and Ocean Dumping, Washington, 1974; commr. Dept. Air Resources, N.Y.C., 1966-70; sec. Dept. Natural Resources and Environ. Control, Dover, Del., 1970-73; exec. dir. N.Y. State Coun. Environ. Advisers, N.Y.C., 1973-75; asst. adminstr. conservation U.S. Energy R&D Adminstrn., Washington, 1975-76. Lt. USN, 1942-46, PTO; lt. comdr. USN Rsch. Res., 1948-61. Recipient Cert. of award corp. planning seminar Am. Mgmt. Assn., N.Y.C., 1960, Engring. award ASME, N.Y.C., 1967, 15th Ann. Honor award N.Y. State Soc. Profl. Engrs., N.Y.C., 1968, Humanitarian award Children's Asthma Rsch. Inst. N.Y.C., 1969; Wallace and Tiernan rsch. fellow Iowa State U., Ames, 1940-41. Fellow APHA, Am. Chem. Soc., Am. Inst. Chemists; mem. Am. Inst. Chem. Engrs., Am. Water Works Assn. (life), Air and Waste Mgmt. Assn. (bd. dirs. 1960-63, 67-70), Fedn. Water Pollution Control Assn. (life), N.Y. Acad. Sci., Masons. Republican. Jewish. Achievements include patents for Cyclic Method for Removal of Impurities from Coke Over Tar by Water Washing, Recovery of Phenolics from Industrial Wastes, Process for Production of High Grade Naphthalene and Preparation of B-Naphthol from Acidic Waters Therefrom, Solvent Dephenolization of Aqueous Solutions; development of the use of process research and development as a primary method to solve industrial waste problems in chemical and allied industries at a profit; first use of a telemetry/computer system to measure, on a continuous basis, the air quality of urban atmospheres. Home and Office: 85 Manresa Dr Rm 223 Annapolis MD 21401-5878

HELLER, DANIEL ROBERT, investment banker, portfolio manager; b. Washington, Mar. 23, 1950; s. Lester Harry and Adele (Ravsky) H. BA, U. Md., 1972; MA, Catholic U. Am., 1976. Project mgr. Nat. Dist. Atty.'s Assn., Washington, 1973-75; theatre mgr. Catholic U., Washington, 1975-82; dir. devel. Provincetown (Mass.) Playhouse, 1982-84; computer mgr. Tandy Corp., Washington, 1984-91; investment advisor Prudential Securities, Washington, 1992-95; CFO Computer Ctr. Electronics, Kensington, Md., 1995-98; sr. v.p. investment bankingm sr. portfolio mgr. Strategic Assets, Inc., 1997-98; sr. v.p., CFO, dir. rsch. Bethesda Ptnrs., L.P., 1998—; investment advisor Summer Opera Theatre Co., Washington, 1993—; bd. dirs. Br. Am. Bus. Coun., Washington. Author: Structure and Efficiency Models for District Attorney Offices, 1973, 2d edit., 1974, 3d edit., 1975; photographer (book) 1915, The Cultural Moment, 1991. Bd. dirs. Project SHARE, Washington, 1993—, Summer Opera Theatre Co., Washington, 1993—, Am. Opera Scholarship Soc. Mem. Am. Opera Scholarship Soc. (bd. dirs.), Internat. Brotherhood Knights of the Vine, City Tavern Club. Republican. Roman Catholic. Avocations: theatre, opera, antiques, sailing, yachting. Home: 2912 Wilton Ave Silver Spring MD 20910-1219 Office: Strategic Assets Inc 7201 Wisconsin Ave Ste 700 Bethesda MD 20814-4810

HELLER, DEAN, state official; b. Castro Valley, Calif., May 10, 1960; m. Lynne Brombach, children: Hilary Anne, Harrison Clark, Andrew Dean. BS with honors, USC. Former mem. Ways & Means & Carson City Rep. Cent. Committee; former Rep. Assembly Caucus, former Nev. St. Assembly; former sr. cons. Bank of Amer.; former stockbroker, broker, trader Pac Stock Exchange; chief dep. Ofc. of St. Tex.; sec. of state State of Nev., Carson City, 1995—; Bd. dirs. Western Nev. Community Coll. Found, Boys & Girls Club. Natl. Assn. Sec. Dealers, Boy Scouts, Natl. Assn. Sec. of State. Home: 110 Plantation Dr Carson City NV 89703-5410 Office: Sec of State 101 N Carson St Ste 3 Carson City NV 89701-4786

HELLER, DOROTHY, artist; b. N.Y.C., June 15, 1926; d. Samuel and Rebecca (Cohn) H. Studied with, Hans Hofman, N.Y.C., 1942. One-woman shows include Tibor de Nagy Gallery, N.Y.C., 1953, Galerie Facchetti, Paris, 1955, Pondexter Gallery, N.Y.C., 1956, 57, East Hampton Gallery, N.Y.C., 1963, Betty Parsons Gallery, N.Y.C., 1972, 76, 78, U. Pa., 1976, Cathedral St. John the Divine, N.Y.C., 1976; exhibited in group shows Denver Art Mus., 1953, Whitney Mus. Ann., 1957, Mus. Modern Art Traveling Show, 1963, Betty Parsons Gallery, 1972-81, U. Calif. Art Mus., 1974, Met. Mus. Art, N.Y.C., 1979, Otis Art Inst., 1979, Bklyn. Coll. Art Gallery, 1990; represented in permanent collections Met. Mus. Art, N.Y.C., U. Calif. Art Mus., Berkeley, Cornell U., Johnson Mus., Ithaca, N.Y., Wadsworth Atheneum, Hartford, Conn., Smithsonian Instn. Archives, Washington, Zimmerli Mus., New Brunswick, N.J., Alexandria (La.) Mus., Auburn (Ala.) U., Whitney Comm., N.Y.C., Chase Manhattan Bank, N.Y.C., numerous others. Recipient Internat. Woman of Yr. award, 1976.

HELLER, EDWIN, lawyer; b. N.Y.C., Dec. 8, 1929; s. Joseph and Gizela H.; m. Dorothy L. Killgrew, Mar. 5, 1958; children: Dana, William. BA, Cornell U., 1950; LLB, Harvard U., 1954. Bar: N.Y. 1955. Teaching fellow Harvard U. Law Sch., 1956-57; ptnr. firm Fried, Frank, Harris, Shriver & Jacobson, N.Y.C., 1957-96, of counsel, 1996—. Office: Fried Frank Harris et al 1 New York Plz Fl 22 New York NY 10004-1980*

HELLER, FRANCIS H(OWARD), law and political science educator emeritus; b. Vienna, Austria, Aug. 24, 1917; came to U.S., 1938, naturalized, 1943; s. Charles A. and Lily (Grunwald) H.; m. Donna Munn, Sept. 3, 1949 (dec. Dec. 1990); 1 child, Denis Wayne. Student, U. Vienna, 1935-37; JD, U. Va., 1941, MA, 1941, PhD, 1948; DHL (hon.), Benedictine Coll., 1988. Asst. prof. govt. Coll. William and Mary, 1947; asst. prof. polit. sci. U. Kans., Lawrence, 1948-51; assoc. prof. U. Kans., 1951-56, prof., 1956-88, Roy A. Roberts prof. law and polit. sci., 1972-88, emeritus, 1988—, asso. dean Coll. Liberal Arts and Scis., 1957-66, assoc. dean of faculties, 1966-67, dean, 1967-70, vice chancellor for acad. affairs, 1970-72; vis. prof. Inst. Advanced Studies, Vienna, 1965, U. Vienna Law Sch., 1985, 97, Trinity U., Tex., 1992. Author: Introduction to American Constitutional Law, 1952, The Presidency: A Modern Perspective, 1960, The Korean War: A 25-Year Perspective, 1977, The Truman White House, 1980, Economics and the Truman Administration, 1982, USA: Verfassung und Politik, 1987, NATO: The Founding of the Alliance and the Integration of Europe, 1992, The Kansas State Constitution: A Reference Guide, 1992, The United States and the Integration of Europe, 1996. Mem. Kans. Commn. on Constl. Revision, 1957-61, Lawrence City Planning Commn., 1957-63, ednl. adv. commn. U.S. Army Command and Gen. Stagg Coll., 1969-72; bd. dirs. Harry S. Truman Libr. Inst., 1988-96, v.p., 1962-96; bd. dirs. Benedictine Coll., chmn., 1971-79; mem. nat. adv. coun. Ctr. for Study of Presidency, 1991-97. 1st lt. arty. AUS, 1942-47, capt. 1951-52, maj. USAR, ret. Decorated Silver Star, Bronze Star with cluster; recipient Career Teaching award Chancellor's Club, 1986, Silver Angel award Kans. Cath. Conf., 1987, Disting. Svc. citation U. Kans., 1998. Mem. Am. Polit. Sci. Assn. (exec. council 1958-60), Order of Coif, Phi Beta Kappa, Pi Sigma Alpha (mem. nat. council 1958-60). Home: 3419 Seminole Dr Lawrence KS 66047-1622 Office: U Kans Sch Law Green Hall Lawrence KS 66044-7577

HELLER, FREDERICK, retired mining company executive; b. Detroit, May 6, 1932; s. Robert and Lois (Mouch) H.; m. Catherine C. Flynn, Mar. 26, 1955 (div.); m. Rosamund Clifford, July 10, 1964 (div.); children: Thomas M., John G., Cynthia R. BA, Harvard U., 1954. With Hanna Mining Co., Cleve., 1957-87; v.p. sales Hanna Mining Co., 1973-76; sr. v.p. sales and transp. Hanna Mining Co., Cleve., 1976-81, sr. v.p. mktg., 1981-84; sr. v.p. sales and mktg. M.A. Hanna Co., Cleve., 1984-87. Trustee, exec. com. Cleve. Inst. Art, 1977-82; trustee, fin. com. McGregor Home, 1978-86. With U.S. Army, 1954-56. Mem. Mountain Oyster Club. Republican. Episcopalian. Home: 4825 N Camino Sumo Tucson AZ 85718-7403

HELLER, HANES AYRES, lawyer; b. New Orleans, Mar. 10, 1940; s. John Roderick and Susie Mae (Ayres) H.; BA, Yale U., 1962; LLB, Harvard U., 1965; m. Patricia R. Hawkins, Oct. 19, 1996; children: Hanes Ayres, Lee McGavock. Bar: N.Y. 1966. Assoc. firm Dewey, Ballantine, Bushby, Palmer & Wood, N.Y.C., 1965-68; atty. CPC Internat. (now Bestfoods), Englewood Cliffs, N.J., 1968-76, div. counsel Best Foods div., 1976-78, assoc. gen. counsel, 1978-80, gen. counsel N.Am. div., 1980-82, v.p., gen. counsel, 1982-84; asst. gen. counsel CPC Internat., 1982-87, dep. gen. counsel, 1987-95, v.p. legal affairs, 1995-97, v.p., gen. counsel, sec., 1997—. Mem. ABA, N.Y. State Bar Assn., Assn. Bar City N.Y. Home: 3 Lenape Dr Montville NJ 07045-9722 Office: Best Foods Internat Plz Englewood Cliffs NJ 07632

HELLER, H(EINZ) ROBERT, financial executive; b. Cologne, Germany, Jan. 8, 1940; s. Heinrich and Karoline (Hermann) H.; m. Emily Mitchell, Dec. 5, 1970; children: Kimberly, Christopher. MA in Econs., U. Minn., 1962; PhD, U. Calif., Berkeley, 1965. Instr. U. Calif., Berkeley, 1965; assoc. prof. econs. UCLA, 1965-71; prof. U. Hawaii, Honolulu, 1971-74; chief fin. studies div. Internat. Monetary Fund, Washington, 1974-78; sr. v.p., dir. internat. econ. rsch. Bank of Am., San Francisco, 1978-86; mem., bd. govs. Fed. Res. System, Washington, 1986-89; exec. v.p. VISA Internat., San Francisco, Calif., 1989-91; pres., CEO VISA, U.S.A., San Francisco, 1991-93; exec. v.p., chief adminstrv. officer Fair, Isaac and Co., San Rafael, Calif., 1994—, also bd. dirs.; bd. dirs. Fair, Isaac and Co., Plus Sys. Inc., Interlink, Merchant Bank Svcs. Corp., Bay Area Coun., San Francisco, First Am. Automotive, BMW of N.Am., Inc., mem. adv. bd.; vice-chmn. Fed. Fin. Instns. Examination Coun., 1988-89; mem. Nat. Adv. Coun. Internat. Monetary and Fin. Policies, 1987-89, U.S. Coun. Internat. Bus., N.Y.C., 1979—; trustee World Affairs Coun., 1990-96; mem. adv. bd. Nat. Ctr. Fin. Svcs., U.Calif., Berkeley, 1984-90, Ctr. Fin. Sys. Rsch., Ariz. State U., Tempe, 1989, Inst. Internat. Edn., San Francisco, 1989; mem. Bay Area Internat. Forum, 1989, Bay Area Coun., 1992; dir. Am. Inst. Contemporary German Studies, Johns Hopkins U., Washington, 1989; dir. Wharton Fin. Instns. Ctr., U. Pa., 1989—. Author: International Trade, 1968, rev. edit. 1973, International Monetary Economics, 1974, The Economic System, 1972, Japanese Investment in the U.S., 1974; mem. editorial bd. Jour. Money, Credit and Banking, 1975-83, Internat. Trade Jour., 1985-88. mem. Bankers Club of San Francisco, Royal Econ. Soc., Am. Econ. Assn., Western Econo. Assn. (exec. bd. 1977-81), San Francisco Yacht Club, Tiburon Peninsula Club. Avocations: sailing, skiing. Office: Fair Isaac and Co 120 N Redwood Dr San Rafael CA 94903-1958

HELLER, IRA LOUIS, research executive; b. Hauppauge, N.Y., Aug. 22, 1966; s. Bernard Milton and Amy Helene (Rubenstein) H.; m. Marta Helen Tyrlick, Sept. 1, 1990. BS in Advtg., U. Fla., Gainesville, 1988. Prodn. mgr. Keystone Pub., Orlando, Fla., 1988-89; sales asst. Time Warner Comm., Orlando, 1989-92, rsch. coord., 1992-95, rsch. supervisor, 1995-97, rsch. mgr., 1997—; mem. Tapscan Cable Users Adv. Com., Birmingham, Ala., 1995-. Mem. Ad 2 Greater Orlando (edn. chair 1993-94, v.p., treas. 1994-95, pres. 1995-96, immed. past pres. 1996-, treas. nat. divsn. 1996-97, 97-98, Dist. Pres. of the Yr. award 1995-96), Orlando Advt. Fedn. (bd. dirs. 1996-98, treas. 1997-98, pres. 1998-99; Dist. and Nat. Pres. of Yr. 1998-99). Avocations: science fiction, sports, classic era cinema. Office: Time Warner Comm 2251 Lucien Way Ste 200 Maitland FL 32751-7039

HELLER, JACK ISAAC, lawyer; b. Passaic, N.J., July 12, 1932; s. Aaron and Ruth (Brown) H.; m. Naomi Heller, Mar. 8, 1959; children—Michael Adam, Daniel Noah, Rafael Gustav. AB, U. Chgo., 1952; LLB, Columbia U., 1958. Teaching fellow, research asst. internat. program in taxation Harvard Law Sch., 1958-61; sr. tax adviser OAS, Washington, 1961-62; tax economist Latin Am. Bur., U.S. AID, 1962-65; with Office Gen. Counsel, AID, 1965-66; legal adviser AID, Brazil, 1966-67, asst. dir., 1967-68; dir. Office of Devel. Programs, Latin Am. Bur., AID, 1969-72; atty., mgr. spl. projects Office Gen. Counsel, Gen. Electric Co., 1972-74; pvt. practice Washington, 1974—; ptnr. Heller & Rosenblatt, Washington, 1991—; co-dir. programs in Latin Am. U. Ill. Coll. Law, 1975-80, spl. programs in China, 1982-86; sr. v.p., gen. counsel, dir. Fund for Democracy and Devel.; pres. Pan Am. Devel. Found. Author: Tax Incentives for Industry in Less Developed Countries, 1963. Served with AUS, 1953-55. Home: 3431 Porter St NW Washington DC 20016-3125 Office: Heller & Rosenblatt 1501 M St NW Washington DC 20005-1700

HELLER, JAMIE GALE, editor, lawyer; b. Bronx, N.Y., Mar. 8, 1967; d. Lawrence Arthur and Barbara Sue (Martin) H.; m. Jed Weissberg. BA in Govt., Dartmouth Coll., 1989; JD, Yale U., 1994. Bar: Conn. 1994, N.Y. 1996. Reporter Rutland (Vt.) Herald, 1989-90, Conn. Law Tribune, Hartford, 1990-91, Smart Money, N.Y.C., 1995-96; law clk. to Judge José Cabranes U.S. Ct. Appeals (2d cir.), New Haven, 1994-95; mng. editor TheStreet.com, N.Y.C., 1996-97, exec. editor, 1997—. Office: TheStreet.com 2 Rector St New York NY 10006-1819

HELLER, JANET RUTH, English language, writing and literature educator; b. Milw., July 8, 1949; d. William Charles and Joan Ruth (Pereles) H.; m. Michael Alexander Krischer, June 13, 1982. Student, Oberlin Coll., 1967-70; BA, U. Wis., 1971, MA, 1973; PhD, U. Chgo., 1987. Coord. writing program U. Chgo., 1976-81, lectr. creative writing, 1981-82; instr. English No. Ill. U., DeKalb, 1982-88; asst. prof. English Nazareth Coll., Kalamazoo, 1989-90, Grand Valley State U., Allendale, Mich., 1990-97, Albion Coll., 1998; asst. prof. English Dept. Western Mich. U., 1999—. Author: Coleridge, Lamb, Hazlitt, and the Reader of Drama, 1990; editor: Primavera Jour., 1974-82; contbr. articles to profl. jours.; commd. poem and display by Friends of Poetry, Kalamazoo, 1990-91. Recipient award Friends of Poetry, 1989. Mem. MLA (reg. del. 1985-87), Midwest MLA, Mich. Coll. English Assn. (campus rep., membership coord. 1990—, sec.), Nat. Coun. Tchrs. English, N.Am. Soc. Study of Romanticism, Soc. Study of Midwestern Lit. Democrat. Jewish. Avocations: hiking, birdwatching, canoeing, biking, gardening. E-mail: janet.heller@wmich.edu. Office: Western Mich Univ English Dept Sprau Tower Kalamazoo MI 49008

HELLER, JOHN L., II, food products executive; b. Galesburg, Ill., Jan. 23, 1953; s. John L. and Wilma (Medows) H.; m. Brenda June Baxter, Nov. 17, 1972 (div. 1995); children: Holly Renee, Kelly Susanne; m. Shirley D. Parrish, Sept. 27, 1997. Sales rep. H&K Electric Supply, Inc., Chillicothe, Mo., 1971-73, Schwan Sales Enterprises, Inc., Chillicothe, 1973-79; sales mgr. Schwan Sales Enterprises, Inc., Aurora, Mo., 1979-81; nat. promotions mgr. Schwan Sales Enterprises, Inc., Marshall, Minn., 1981-86; pres. ABar Assocs., Inc., Marshall, 1986-89, ADCO Sales Advt. and Cons. Firm, Marshall, 1989-90; sales mgr. food svc. div. Cookies Food Products, Inc., Wall Lake, Iowa, 1989-90; regional sales mgr. Tony's Food Svc. divsn. Schwan's Sales Enterprises Inc., Blue Springs, Mo., 1990-93; regional dir. Zartic, Inc., Blue Springs, 1993-95, Redi-Foods, Inc., Blue Springs, Mo., 1995-97; Eastern Poultry Dist., Inc., 1997—. Mem. Blue Springs C. of C. Republican. Baptist. Avocations: hunting, fishing, boating, golf. Home: 2331 NE Springbrook St Blue Springs MO 64014-1403 Office: Eastern Food Products Inc 1700 W 40 Hwy Ste 104 Blue Springs MO 64015-4646

HELLER, JOHN RODERICK, III, lawyer, business executive; b. Harrisburg, Pa., Aug. 14, 1937; s. John Roderick and Susie May (Ayres) H.; children: Elizabeth, Carolynn, John. AB summa cum laude, Princeton U., 1959; AM in History, Harvard U., 1960, JD magna cum laude, 1963. Bar: D.C. 1964. Assoc. Wilmer, Cutler & Pickering, Washington, 1963-65, 68-71, ptnr., 1971-82, of counsel, 1982-85; spl. asst. to dir. for India, AID, New Delhi, 1966-67; regional legal adviser for Pakistan AID, 1967-68; pres. Bristol Compressors, Inc., Va., 1982-85; pres., dir. NHP, Inc., 1985-97, also bd. dirs.; chmn. WMF Group, Inc., Washington, 1997—; bd. dirs. Auto-Trol Tech. Corp., Federal City Coun.; chmn. Civil War Trust, WETA; prof. law George Washington U., 1976-81. Author: The Confederacy Is On Her Way Up the Spout: Letters to South Carolina 1861-64, 1992, An Upcountry Chronicle, 1998. Recipient Meritorious Honor award U.S. Dept. State, 1967. Mem. ABA, Am. Soc. Internat. Law, Soc. of Cin., Met. Club (Washington). Presbyterian. Office: WMF Group 2445 M St NW Ste 460 Washington DC 20037-1435

HELLER, JOSEPH, writer; b. Bklyn., May 1, 1923; s. Isaac and Lena H.; m. Shirley Held, Sept. 3, 1945 (div. 1984); children: Erica Jill, Theodore Michael; m. Valerie Humphries, 1987. BA, NYU, 1948; MA, Columbia U., 1949; MA Fulbright scholar, Oxford U., 1949-50. Instr. English Pa. State U., 1950-52; advt. writer Time mag., N.Y.C., 1952-56, Look mag., N.Y.C., 1956-58; promotion mgr. McCall's, N.Y.C., 1958-61; tchr. fiction and dramatic writing Yale U., U. Pa.; disting. prof. English CUNY, N.Y.C., until 1975. Author: (novels) Catch-22, 1961, Something Happened, 1974, Good as Gold, 1979, God Knows, 1984 (Prix Interallie France 1985, Prix Medicis Etranger France 1985), Picture This, 1988, Closing Time, 1994, Love, Dad and Other Stories, 1997, Best of Playbou Fiction, 1997, As Good As Gold, 1997, Now & Then: From Coney Island to Here, 1998; (plays) We Bombed in New Haven, 1968, Catch-22: A Dramatization, 1971, Clevinger's Trial, 1973, (with Speed Vogal) No Laughing Matter, 1986; screenwriter (films) Sex and the Single Girl, 1964, Dirty Dingus Magee, 1970; contbr.: (TV drama) Of Men and Women, 1972. Served to lt. USAAF, World War II. Nat. Inst. Arts and Letters grantee in lit., 1963. Office: care Simon & Schuster 1230 Ave of Americas New York NY 10020-1513*

HELLER, JOSEPH, health professional; b. Tarnopol, Poland, June 15, 1940; came to U.S., 1956; s. Simon and Hinda (Kaufman) H. BS in Math., Calif. Inst. Tech., 1962. Group supr. Jet Propulsion Lab., Pasadena, Calif., 1962-71; pres. Rolf Inst., Boulder, Colo., 1972-78; founder, pres. Hellerwork, Mt. Shasta, Calif., 1979—. Author: Bodywise, 1986. Office: Hellerwork 406 Berry St Mount Shasta CA 96067-2548

HELLER, JULES, artist, writer, educator; b. N.Y.C., Nov. 16, 1919; s. Jacob Kenneth and Goldie (Lassar) H.; m. Gloria Spiegel, June 11, 1947; children: Nancy Gale, Jill Kay. AB, Ariz. State Coll., 1939; AM, Columbia U., 1940; PhD, U. So. Calif., 1948; DLitt, York U., 1985. Spl. art instr. 8th St. Sch., Tempe, Ariz., 1938-39; dir. art and music Union Neighborhood House, Auburn, N.Y., 1940-41; prof. fine arts, head dept. U. So. Calif., 1946-61; vis. asso. prof. fine arts Pa. State U., summers 1955, 57; dir. Pa. State U. (Sch. Arts), 1961-63; founding dean Pa. State U. (Coll. Arts and Architecture), 1963-68; founding dean Faculty Fine Arts York U., Toronto, 1968-73; prof. fine arts Faculty of Fine Arts, York U., 1973-76; dean Coll. Fine Arts, Ariz. State U., Tempe, 1976-85; prof. art Coll. Fine Arts, Ariz. State U., 1985-90; prof. emeritus, dean emeritus, 1990—; vis. prof. Silpakorn U., Bangkok, Thailand, 1974, Coll. Fine Arts, Colombo, Sri Lanka, 1974, U. Nacional de Tucumán, Argentina, 1990, U. Nacional de Cuyo, Mendoza, Argentina, 1990; lectr., art juror; Cons. Open Studio, 1975-76; mem. vis. com. on fine arts Fisk U., Nashville, 1974; co-curator Leopoldo Méndez exhbn. Ariz. State U., Tempe, 1999. Printmaker; exhibited one man shows, Gallery Pascal, Toronto, U. Alaska, Fairbanks, Alaskaland Bear Gallery, Visual Arts Center, Anchorage, Ariz. State U., Lisa Sette Gallery, 1990, Centro Cultural de Tucumán, San Miguel de Tucumán, 1990; retrospective exhbn. Ariz. State U., Tempe, 1999; exhibited numerous group shows including Canadian Printmaker's Showcase, Pollack Gallery, Toronto, Mazelow Gallery, Toronto, Santa Monica Art Gallery, L.A. County Mus., Phila. Print Club, Seattle Art Mus., Landau Gallery, Kennedy & Co. Gallery, Bklyn. Mus., Cin. Art Mus., Dallas Mus. Fine Arts, Butler Art Inst., Oakland Art Mus., Pa. Acad. Fine Arts, Santa Barbara Mus. Art, San Diego Gallery Fine Arts, Martha Jackson Gallery, N.Y.C., Yuma Fine Arts Assn., Ariz., Toronto Dominion Centre, Amerika Haus, Hannover, Fed. Rep. Germany, U. Md., Smith-Andersen Galleries, Palo Alto, Calif., Grunewald Ctr. Graphic Arts, L.A., Univ. So. Fla., Tampa, Sheldon Meml. Gallery, Lincoln, Nebr., Santa Cruz (Calif.) Mus., Drake U., Iowa, Bradley U., Ill., Del Bello Gallery, Toronto, Honolulu Acad. Fine Arts; represented in permanent collections, Nat. Mus. Am. Art Smithsonian Instn., Washington, Long Beach Mus. Art, Library of Congress, York U., Allan R. Hite Inst. of U. Louisville, Ariz. State U., Tamarind Inst., U. N.Mex., Zimmerli Mus. Rutgers U., N.J., Can. Council Visual Arts Bank, also pvt. collections; author: Problems in Art Judgment, 1946, Printmaking Today, 1958, revised, 1972, Papermaking, 1978, 79; co-editor: North American Women Artists of the Twentieth Century, 1995, Codex Méndez, 1999; contbg. artist: Prints by California Artists, 1954, Estampas de la Revolución Mexicana, 1948; illustrator: Canciónes de Mexico, 1948; author numerous articles. Adv. bd. Continental affairs com. Americas Soc., 1983-86. With USAAF, 1941-45. Can. Coun. grantee; Landsdowne scholar U. Victoria; Fulbright scholar, Argentina, 1990. Mem. Coll. Art Assn. (Disting. Teaching of Art award 1995), Authors Guild, Internat. Assn. Hand Papermakers (steering com. 1986—), Nat. Found. Advancement in the Arts (visual arts panelist 1986-90, panel chmn. 1989, 90), Internat. Assn. Paper Historians, Internat. Coun. Fine Arts Deans (pres. 1968-69), So. Graphics Coun. (printmaker emeritus 1999). Home: 6838 E Cheney Dr Paradise Valley AZ 85253-3525

HELLER, KENNETH JEFFREY, physicist; b. Port of Spain, Trinidad, Nov. 7, 1943; s. George M. and Florence (Gelb) H.; m. Patricia Margaret Autry, Sept. 29, 1972. BA, U. Calif., Berkeley, 1965; PhD, U. Wash., 1973. Physicist Naval Rsch. Lab., Corona, Calif., 1965; tchr. U.S. Peace Corps, Nigeria and Kenya, 1966-68; rsch. asst., teaching asst. U. Wash., Seattle, 1968-73; rsch. assoc., lectr. U. Mich., Ann Arbor, 1973-78; asst. prof. U. Minn., Mpls., 1978-82, assoc. prof., 1982-86, prof., 1987—, chair senate edn. policy com., 1993-95, mem. consultative com., 1993-95, dir. undergrad. studies Sch. of Physics and Astronomy, 1992-98, assoc. head Sch. Physics and Astronomy, 1998—, chair pres.'s com. on tchg. and learning, 1993-95, Morse alumni prof., 1997—; mem. users exec. com. Fermilab, Batavia, Ill., 1984-86, 98—, bd. overseers, 1988-92; trustee Univs. Rsch. Assn., 1985-88, 94. Editor: High Energy Spin Physics, 1988, 94; contbr. articles to profl. jours.; editor procs. Fellow Am. Phys. Soc. (chair forum on edn. 1999—), Am. Assn. Phys. Tchrs. (chair grad. edn. com.), Symposium of High Energy Spin Physics (internat. adv. com. 1988-96), Acad. Disting. Tchrs. Achievements include discovery of large polarization in high energy particle production technique for the precise measurement of hyperon magnetic moments; application of the quark model to understand the mechanism for polarized particle production technique of spin transfer to high energy hyperons; first observation of tan neutrino interactions. Office: U Minn Sch Physics & Astronomy Minneapolis MN 55455

HELLER, LOIS JANE, physiologist, educator, researcher; b. Detroit, Jan. 4, 1942; d. John and Lona Elizabeth (Stockmeyer) Skagerberg; m. Robert Eugene Heller, May 21, 1966; children: John Robert, Suzanne Elizabeth. BA, Albion Coll., 1964; MS, U. Mich., 1966; PhD, U. Ill., Chgo., 1970. Instr. med ctr. U. Ill., Chgo., 1969-70, asst. prof., 1970-71; asst. prof. U. Minn., Duluth, 1972-77, assoc. prof., 1977-89, prof., 1989—. Author: Cardiovascular Physiology, 4th edit., 1997; contbr. numerous articles to profl. jours. Mem. Am. Physiol. Soc., Am. Heart Assn., Soc. Exptl. Biology and Medicine, Internat. Soc. Heart Rsch., Sigma Xi. Avocation: birding. Home: 311 Halsey St Duluth MN 55803-2535 Office: Univ Minn Sch of Medicine Duluth MN 55812

HELLER, MARY BERNITA, psychotherapist; b. Roland, Iowa, Feb. 11, 1934; d. Casper and Blanche (Hanson) Stenberg; m. John R. Heller, June 7, 1958; children: Kristen, Jonathan, Kathryn. BA, St. Olaf Coll., 1956; MSW, Fordham U., 1970. Cert. social worker, N.Y.; bd. cert. diplomate in social work. Psychiatric social worker Beloit Children's Home, Ames, Iowa, 1957-58; caseworker Luth. Community Svcs., N.Y.C., 1958-59, Soc. Seamen's Children, Staten Island, N.Y., 1971-75; psychiatric social worker Staten Island Mental Health, 1971-75; psychotherapist Mid-Hudson Cons. Ctr., Wappinger Falls, N.Y., 1976-94; pvt. practice Poughkeepsie, N.Y., 1977—; psychotherapist Windsor Counseling Group, New Windsor, N.Y., 1989—; supr. Luth. Community Svcs., N.Y.C., 1987—. Bd. dirs. Children;s Home of Poughkeepsie, 1983-88, Seafarers and Internat. House, N.Y.C., 1990-96; mem. candidacy com. Met. N.Y. Synod, N.Y.C., 1986-94, v.p., 1992—; mem. coun. Hudson Valley Philharm., Poughkeepsie, 1983-88. Fellow Am. Orthopsychiat. Assn.; mem. NASW, Acad. Cert. Social Workers. Democrat. Lutheran. Avocations: alpine skiing, plants. Home: 24 Thornwood Dr Poughkeepsie NY 12603-4633 Office: 55 Wilbur Blvd Poughkeepsie NY 12603-3424

HELLER, MARYELLEN, special education educator; b. Mt. Kisco, N.Y., Apr. 9, 1957; d. Michael Joseph and Ellen Agnes (O'Grady) Romano; m. Robert Edward Heller, Dec. 22, 1979; children: Kerry, Rob, Kathleen. BA Psychology, Elem. Edn., Spl. Edn., Coll. of New Rochelle, 1979; MS Reading, Western Conn., 1989. Second grade tchr. St. Patrick's Grammar Sch., Yorktown, N.Y., 1979-82; art instr. Newtown (Conn.) Continuing Edn., summer 1992; resource rm. tchr. City Hill Mid. Sch., Naugatuck, Conn., 1992-93, spl. edn. tutor, 1993; reading cons. Community Scch., Prospect, Conn., 1993-94; reading specialist Broadview Mid. Sch., Danbury, Conn., 1994—; lang. arts specialist Roberts Ave. Sch., Danbury, Conn., 1995—; art instr. Southbury (Conn.) Parks and Recreation, 1992; dried flower instr. for adults, Newtown Adult Edn., 1992; profl. devel. instr. Community Sch., Prospect, Conn., 1994, Danbury Schs., Conn., 1995; reading cons. Broadview Mid. Sch., 1996-97; resource room tchr. Danbury H.S., 1997-98, reading specialist, 1999—. Pageant dir. Sacred Heart Ch., Southbury, 1991-94, CCD tchr., 1992-94; PTA program dir. Pomperaug Elem. Sch., Southbury, 1991-92; com. to select a site for group home for mentally retarded adults, Town Bd. of Somers, N.Y., 1978-79. Mem. Conn. Edn. Assn., Danbury Tchrs. Assn., ACES Alternat. Edn. Ctr. Avocations: watercolors, pen and ink drawing, arts and crafts, jogging, stenciling, reading. Home: 75 Stonegate Dr Southbury CT 06488-2671 Office: Danbury High Sch Clapboard Ridge Rd Danbury CT 06810-6021

HELLER, PAUL, medical educator; b. Komotau, Czechoslovakia, Aug. 8, 1914; came to U.S., 1946, naturalized, 1948; s. Alfred and Elsa (Hoenig) H.; m. Alice H. Florsheim, Aug. 3, 1946 (dec. Jan. 15, 1987); children—Thomas Allen, Carol Elizabeth; m. Anna Novak, June 15, 1989. M.D., Charles U., Prague, Czechoslovakia, 1938. Instr. biochemistry Prague, 1935-37; intern, then resident Beth Israel and Montefiore hosps., N.Y.C., 1946-48; physician Group Health Assocs., Washington, 1948-51, VA Hosp., Omaha, 1952-54; dir. research West Side VA Hosp., Chgo., 1954-67; chief med. service West Side VA Hosp., 1967-69; prof. medicine U. Ill. Coll. Medicine, 1963—; sr. med. investigator VA, 1969-87; cons. hematologist Presbyn.-St. Luke's Hosp., MacNeal Meml. Hosp.; Mem. adv. bd. Am. Cancer Soc., Chgo. Leukemia Research Found.; cons. USPHS. Author research papers, chpts. in books.; Editorial bd.: Yearbook of Medicine, Jour. Lab. Clin. Medicine, Blood. Recipient Middleton award for med. research, 1975; Esther Langer award for cancer research, 1980; Disting. Faculty award U. Ill., 1981. Fellow ACP, AAAS; mem. Central Soc. Clin. Research, Am. Assn. Immunologists, Assn. Am. Physicians, Am., Internat. socs. hematology. Imprisoned in German concentration camps, 1939-45. Home: 1522 Dobson St Evanston IL 60202-3720 Office: 820 S Damen Ave Chicago IL 60612-3728

HELLER, PAUL MICHAEL, film company executive, producer; b. N.Y.C., Sept. 25, 1927; s. Alex Gordon and Anna (Rappaport) H.; children: Michael Peter, Charles Paul. Student, Drexel Inst. Tech., 1944-45; BA, Hunter Coll., 1950. Freelance scenic designer N.Y.C., 1952-61, film producer, 1961—; instr. NYU, N.Y.C., 1964-66; prodn. exec. Warner Bros., 1970-71; pres. Paul Heller Prodns. Inc., Beverly Hills, Calif., 1973—. Producer over 30 films including David and Lisa, 1962, Enter the Dragon, 1973, First Monday in October, 1981, Withnail and I, 1987, My Left Foot, 1989, The Lunatic, 1990. Founding mem. Com. 100, Am. Film Inst. Served with U.S. Army. Recipient spl. award Nat. Assn. Mental Health. Mem. Dirs. Guild Am., Screen Actors Guild, Actors Equity Assn., Acad. Motion Pictrue Arts and Scis., Brit. Acad. Film and TV Arts (bd. dirs.), Hearst Castle Preservation San Simeon (bd. dirs.), Lotos Club (N.Y.C.). Home and Office: 1666 N Beverly Dr Beverly Hills CA 90210-2316

HELLER, PEGGY OSNA, psychotherapist, poetry therapist; b. Bklyn., Nov. 21, 1936; d. Charles S. and Miriam (Mendelson) Freundlich; m. Eugene Paul Heller, Aug. 3, 1957 (div. 1986); children: Elise Karen, Meredith Leslie. BA, Bklyn. Coll., 1958; MSW, Cath. U. Am., 1983; PhD, Pacific Western U., 1995. Diplomate Acad. Cert. Social Workers (lic. clin. social worker); registered clin. poetry therapist. Speech correction tchr. N.Y.C. Bd. Edn., 1958-60; program dir., instr., writer test courses Stanley H. Kaplan Edni. Ctrs., N.Y.C., Washington, 1959-81; clin. social worker D.C. Therapy Group, Washington, 1983-85; bibliotherapist Psychiat. Inst. Washington, 1985-87; pvt. practice, poetry therapist, psychotherapist Potomac, Md., 1985—; lectr. Create Ctr. for Therapy, Growth and Tng., Bethesda, Md., 1984-92, Cath. U. Am., Washington, 1984-89, Lesley Coll., Cambridge, Mass., 1992, Fla. Internat. U., Miami, 1992; poetry therapy cons. Mt. Vernon Hosp., Alexandria, Va., 1987-90, Dominion Hosp., Falls Church, Va., 1990-92, Psychiat. Inst., Washington, 1992-95; dir. Nat. Ctr. Poetry Therapy Edn., 1993—, Poetry Therapy Tng. Inst., 1995;co-dir. Wordsworth Ctr. Growth & Healing, 1997—. Mem. editl. staff Jour. Poetry Therapy, 1986—, Jour. Arts in Psychotherapy, 1988—; contbr. articles to profl. jours. Former program dir. Beverly Farms PTA, Potomac, Md., Hoover Cmty. Sch., Potomac; founder Last Friday Playreading Club, Potomac, 1983—. Mem. NASW, Am. Group Psychotherapy Assn., Nat. Assn. Poetry Therapy (pres. 1991-93, Disting. Svc. award 1993), Nat. Assn. Poetry Therapy Found. (v.p. 1993-96, pres. 1996-97), Nat. Fedn. Biblio/Poetry Therapy (treas. 1987-97), Bibliotherapy Round Table (treas. 1984—), Greater Washington Soc. Clin. Social Work, Mensa. Avocations: theatre, walking, swimming. Home and Office: 7715 Whiterim Ter Potomac MD 20854-1775

HELLER, PHILIP, lawyer; b. N.Y.C., Aug. 12, 1952; s. Irving and Dolores (Soloff) H.; divorced; 1 child, Howard Philip. Attended, Harvard Coll.; BA summa cum laude, Boston U., 1976, JD, 1979. Bar: Mass. 1979, N.Y. 1980, U.S. Ct. Appeals (1st, 2nd and 9th cirs.) 1980, U.S. Supreme Ct. 1983, Calif. 1984, U.S. Dist. Ct. (all dists.) Calif., U.S. Dist. Ct. (ea. and so. dists.) N.Y., U.S. Dist. Ct. Mass. Law clk. to judge Cooper So. Dist. N.Y., N.Y.C., 1979; ptnr. Fagelbaum & Heller LLP, L.A. *At age 13, obtained nearly perfect scores on the college entrance examination, skipped high school, was admitted to college at age 14. Attended Harvard College and Boston University. Graduated as University Professors' Scholar from Boston University with a BA, summa cum laude, 1976. Received his JD from Boston University School of Law in 1979 and is admitted to practice in New York, Massachusetts and California. Mr. Heller was a partner in one of the largest law firms in California prior to starting his own firm with Jerold Fagelbaum. Mr. Heller's practice is comprised primarily of complex civil litigation matters with an emphasis in securities and antitrust law.* Mem. ABA (litigation sect.), Calif. Bar Assn., L.A. County Bar Assn. E-mail: bestlawyers@worldnet.att.net. Fax: 310-286-7086. Office: Fagelbaum & Heller LLP 2049 Century Park E Ste 2050 Los Angeles CA 90067-3168

HELLER, REINHOLD AUGUST, art educator, consultant; b. Fulda, Hesse, Germany, July 22, 1940; came to U.S., 1949; s. Friedrich Leonhard and Brigitte Hermine (Schuler) H.; m. Vivian Faye Hall, June 11, 1966; children: Frederik Andreas, Erik Reinhold. Student, George Washington U., 1958-59; B.S., St. Joseph's Coll., 1963; M.A., Ind. U., 1966, Ph.D., 1968. Asst. prof., prof. U. Pitts., 1968-78; prof. U. Chgo., 1978—; acting dir. Smart Gallery, U. Chgo., 1983-86; cons., guest curator Nat. Gallery of Art, Washington, 1972,78. Author: Edvard Munch: The Scream, 1973, Munch: His Life and Work, 1984, Hildegard Auer: Ein Verlangen Nach Kunst, 1987, Am. edit., 1989, Toulouse-Lautrec: Painter of Montmartre, 1997; (catalogue) The Art of Wilhelm Lehmbruck, 1973, The Earthly Chimera and the Femme Fatale, 1981, Brücke: German Expressionist Prints from the Granvil and Marcia Specks Collection, 1988, Art in Germany from 1909 to 1936: From Expressionism to Resistance: The Marvin and Janet Fishman collection, 1990, Lyonel Feininger: Awareness, Recollection and Nostalgia, 1992, Stark Impressions: Graphic Prodns. in Germany, 1919-1933, 1994, Gabrielle Münter: The Years of Impressionism, 1905-1920, 1997. Am. Coun. Learned Socs. and Social Sci. Rsch. Coun. fellow, 1966-68, Fulbright fellow, 1966, Guggenheim fellow, 1975-76; Eisenmann Found. rsch. grantee, 1988-89. Mem. Coll. Art Assn., German Studies Assn., Modern Language Assn. Office: U Chgo Dept Art Hist 5540 S Greenwood Ave Chicago IL 60637-1506

HELLER, RICHARD H., writer, editor, book critic, publisher; b. Yonkers, N.Y., Oct. 16, 1924; s. Otto and Mary (Cohen) H.; m. Sonja Mentikov; 1 son, Matthew. A.B. cum laude, Syracuse U., 1948. Editor, also editorial dir. Sterling Group, N.Y.C., 1954-62; editor Dell Pub. Co.; also editorial dir. Dell Mags., N.Y.C., 1962-68; v.p., editor-in-chief Pyramid Books, N.Y.C., 1968-72; pres., editor, pub. Heller & Son, Inc., New Rochelle, N.Y., 1972-82; columnist and book critic Gannett Westchester Newspapers, 1976-81; dir. mktg. Macmillan Pub. Co., 1979-80. Author: Who's Who in TV, 1967, The Adventure Book, 1976; Editor: The President Speaks, 1964, The Life and Death of Robert F. Kennedy, 1968. Served with USMC, 1941-43. Mem. Am. Soc. Mag. Editors, Nat. Book Critics Circle, Sigma Delta Chi, Sigma Alpha Mu. Club: Dutch Treat.

HELLER, ROBERT MARTIN, lawyer; b. N.Y.C., Feb. 12, 1942; s. Philip B. and Mildred S. (Friedman) H.; m. Amy S. Wexler, July 11, 1965; children: David B., Pamela L. BA, Columbia U., 1963, LLB, 1966. Bar: N.Y. 1967, D.C. 1992, U.S. Dist. Ct. (so. and ea. dists.) N.Y. 1970, U.S. Ct. Appeals (2d cir.) 1967, U.S. Supreme Ct. 1976. Law clk. to judge U.S. Ct. Appeals (2d cir.), N.Y.C., 1966-67; atty. adviser to commr. FTC, Washington, 1967-69; asst. to mayor for housing, city planning, transp. and model cities, sec. to cabinet City of N.Y., 1971-73; ptnr. Kramer Levin Naftalis & Frankel LLP, N.Y.C., 1974—, mng. ptnr., 1991-94; adj. prof. architecture Columbia U., 1975-77; bd. visitors Columbia Law Sch., 1992—. Bd. govs. Hebrew Union Coll./Jewish Inst. Religion, 1996—; pres. bd. dirs. 1056 Fifth Ave. Corp., 1994-96; officer Union Am. Hebrew Congregations, 1997—, mem. joint commn. on social action, 1992—; trustee Rabbi Marc H. Tanenbaum Found. James Kent scholar; Harlan Fiske Stone scholar. Mem. ABA, N.Y. State Bar Assn., Assn. of Bar of City of N.Y. (com. on antitrust and trade regulation 1996—), Phi Beta Kappa. Avocations: aerobic walking, photography. Home: 1056 5th Ave New York NY 10028-0112 Office: Kramer Levin Naftalis & Frankel LLP 919 3rd Ave New York NY 10022-3902

HELLER, RONALD GARY, manufacturing company executive, lawyer; b. N.Y.C., May 29, 1946; s. Max and Lucy (Weinwurm) H.; m. Joyce R. Mueller, May 29, 1969; children—Caren, Amy, Beth. B.A., CCNY, 1967; postgrad., U. Wis. Law Sch., 1967-68; J.D., Fordham U., 1972. Bar: N.Y. Assoc. Cahill Gordon & Reindel, N.Y.C., 1972-77; asst. sec. Cluett, Peabody & Co. Inc., N.Y.C., 1977-81, sec., 1981-86, v.p., sec., gen. counsel, 1986-87; asst. gen. counsel Ingersoll-Rand Co., Woodcliff Lake, N.J., 1988—, sec., 1991—. Served with USAR, 1969-75. Mem. Am. Soc. Corp. Secs.

HELLER, RONALD IAN, lawyer; b. Cleve., Sept. 4, 1956; s. Grant L. and Audrey P. (Lecht) H.; m. Shirley Ann Stringer, Mar. 23, 1986; 1 child, David Grant. AB with high honors, Univ Mich., 1976, MBA, 1979, JD, 1980. Bar: Hawaii 1980, U.S. Ct. Claims 1982, U.S. Tax Ct. 1981, U.S. Ct. Appeals (9th cir.) 1981, U.S. Supreme Ct. 1992; Trust Ter. of Pacific Islands 1982, Republic of Marshall Islands 1982; CPA, Hawaii. Assoc. Hoddick, Reinwald, O'Connor & Marrack, Honolulu, 1980-84; ptnr. Reinwald, O'Connor & Marrack, Honolulu, 1984-87; stockholder, bd. dirs. Torkildson, Katz, Fonseca, Jaffe & Moore, Honolulu, 1988—; adj. prof. U. Hawaii Sch. Law, 1981; arbitrator ct.-annexed arbitration program First Cir. Ct., State of Hawaii; author, instr. Hawaii Taxes. Bd. dirs. Hawaii Women Lawyers Found., Honolulu, 1984-86, Hawaii Performing Arts Co., Honolulu, 1984-93; mem. panel. of arbitrators Am. Arbitration Assn.; named NFIB Hawaii Oustanding Sml. Bus. Vol. of 1998. Actor, stage mgr. Honolulu Community Theatre, 1983-87, Hawaii Performing Arts Co., Honolulu, 1982-87. Fellow Am. Coll. Tax Counsel; mem. AICPA (mem. coun. 1994-96), ABA, Hawaii State Bar Assn. (chair tax sect. 1997-98, chair state and local tax com. 1994-95), Hawaii Soc. CPAs (chmn tax com. 1985-86, legis. com. 1987-88, bd. dirs. 1988-98, pres. 1994-95), Hawaii Women Lawyers. Office: Torkildson Katz 700 Bishop St Fl 15 Honolulu HI 96813-4187

HELLER, STANLEY MARTIN, accountant; b. N.Y.C., Mar. 27, 1938; s. Joseph and Anna (Yahm) H.; m. Phyllis Gerry Kittler, Dec. 24, 1998; children—Sharon Li, Nancy Jean, Jeffrey Todd. B.B.A., CCNY, 1960; postgrad. St. John's U., 1965-66. C.P.A., N.Y., Fla. With Mfrs. Hanover Trust Co., N.Y.C., 1955-57; staff acct., auditor Joseph J. Bloom & Co., CPAs, Henry Sherman & Co., CPAs, Kipnis & Karchmer, CPAs, all N.Y.C., 1960-66; asst. controller Stern Bros. div. Allied Stores, N.Y.C., 1966-69; controller Gaylords Nat. Corp., N.Y.C., 1969-70; treas. Elwood Environ. Industries Ltd., East Northport, N.Y., 1970-73; dir. acctg. Unishops, Inc., Jersey City, 1973-75; treas. J.Z. Sales Corp., Plainview, N.Y., 1974-75; mng. ptnr. Heller & Martakis, CPAs, Commack, N.Y., 1975-79; pvt. practice acctg., Commack, 1980-85; resident ptnr. Suffolk County Office, Israeloff, Trattner & Co., CPAs, Hauppauge, 1986-90; exec. v.p., shareholder, dir. Peare & Heller CPAs, PC, Hauppauge, 1990—; dir. Dentistry Research & Designers, Inc., Basic Systems Hardware, Inc. Mem. adv. com. to exec. bd. Queens County Republican Com.; chmn. bd. dirs. Whitestone Rep. Club, 1969-70; treas. East Northport Jewish Ctr., 1974-75; mgr., coach Larkfield Little League, 1975-79; mem. Suffolk County Boy Scouts Am.; steering com. Disting. Citizens Award Dinner, 1976-79, Man of Yr. com., 1993; trustee bd. dir. Long Island MS Soc., 1995—. Mem. Am. Soc. Appraisers (dir. Long Is. Chpt., 1998), Am. Inst. CPAs, N.Y. State Soc. CPAs (pres. Suffolk chpt. 1980-81, bd. dirs. 1982-84, Profl. Achievement Registry 1984), Nat. Conf. CPA Practitioners (bd. dirs. L.I. chpt.), Inst. Bus. Appraisers, Rotary, Huntington C. of C. Office: Peare & Heller CPAs 525 Townline Rd Hauppauge NY 11788-2829

HELLER, TERRY L(YNN), English literature educator, writer; b. Geneseo, Ill., Feb. 3, 1947; s. Rollin G. and Betty (Ragan) H.; m. Linda Mary Marchand, June 7, 1969; 1 child, Gabriel A. AB, North Cen. Coll., 1969; AM, U. Chgo., 1970, PhD, 1973. Vis. asst. prof. U. Mo., St. Louis, 1973-74; Fulbright lectr. U. Turin, Italy, 1974-75; prof. English Coe Coll., Cedar Rapids, Iowa, 1975—. Author: The Delights of Terror, 1987, The Turn of the Screw, 1989; author short stories; editor: The Country of the Pointed Fir and Other Fiction by Sarah Orne Jewett, 1996. NEH summer fellow, 1995, 1977, Danforth Found. fellow, 1980—, Andrew Mellon Found. fellow U. Kans., 1982. Mem. AAUP, Modern Lang. Assn., Midwest Modern Lang. Assn., Sci. Fiction Rsch. Assn. Office: Coe Coll Dept of English 1220 1st Ave NE Cedar Rapids IA 52402-5008

HELLERMAN, LEO, retired computer scientist and mathematician; b. Bklyn., Feb. 8, 1924; s. Azriel and Rebecca (Hellerman) H.; children: David Seth, Lisa Beatrice Hellerman Kopchik, Daniel Asa. BEE, CCNY, 1946; PhD, Yale U., 1958. Patent examiner U.S. Patent Office, Washington, 1948-50; engr. IBM, Poughkeepsie, N.Y., 1956-73, 75-82, Böblingen, Fed. Republic Germany, 1974, Kingston, N.Y., 1983-87; ret., 1987; lectr. Fachtagung Struktur und Betrieb von Rechensystemen, Braunschweig, Fed. Republic Germany, 1974. Contbr. articles to profl. jours. Mem. Am. Math. Soc., Math. Assn. Am., Sigma Xi. Achievements include patent for logic performing device; development of first algebraic symbol manipulation program, of first statistical design of electronic circuits; a theory of computational work, of moment free methods for processing discrete distributions. Home: 1 Feller Rd Rhinebeck NY 12572-2307

HELLERSTEIN, ALVIN KENNETH, judge; b. N.Y.C., Dec. 28, 1933; s. Max and Rose (Lichtenstein) H.; m. Mildred Markow, June 29, 1936; children—Dina, Judith, Joseph. A.B., Columbia U., 1954, LL.B., 1956. Bar: N.Y. 1956, U.S. Ct. Appeals (2d cir.) 1960, U.S. Supreme Ct. 1964, U.S. Ct. Appeals (D.C. cir.) 1978, U.S. Ct. Appeals (3d and 9th cirs.) 1980, U.S. Ct. Appeals (10th cir.) 1981, U.S. Ct. Appeals (1st cir.) 1985, U.S. Ct. Appeals (8th cir.) 1996. Ptnr. Stroock & Stroock & Lavan, N.Y.C., 969-98, retired, 1998—; judge U.S. Ct. Dist. Ct. (so. dist.) N.Y., 1998—; lectr. Am. Law Inst., Practicing Law Inst.; hearing officer student demonstration disciplinary proc. Columbia U., 1987; former chmn. com. on improving civil litigation U.S. Ct. Appeals (2d cir.), mem. com. civil appeals mgmt. plan. Contbr. articles to profl. jours. Past chmn. Bd. Jewish Edn. Served to capt. JAGC, U.S. Army, 1957-60. Fellow Am. Bar Found. (life); mem. ABA, Assn. Bar City N.Y. (past chmn. com. on judiciary 1992-95, past exec. com., past chmn. com. on fed. cts., past com. on securities regulations, past com. profl. and jud. ethics), Fed. Bar Found. (past chmn., past pres.), N.Y. State Bar Assn. Democrat.

HELLERSTEIN, NINA SALANT, French literature and language educator; b. N.Y.C., Mar. 29, 1946; d. Allan and Martha (Cantor) Salant; m. Walter Hellerstein, Aug. 31, 1970; children: Michael, Margaret. BA, Brown U., 1968; MA, U. Chgo., 1969, PhD, 1974. Adj. asst. prof. Baruch Coll. CUNY, N.Y.C., 1974-75; vis. asst. prof. Vassar Coll., Poughkeepsie, N.Y., 1975-76; instr. Rosary Coll., River Forest, Ill., 1976-78, Roosevelt U., Chgo., 1976-78; asst. prof. U. Ga., Athens, 1978-83, assoc. prof. French literature and language, 1983-92, prof., 1992—, acting head dept. Romance langs., 1992-3. Author: Mythe et Structure Dans Les 'Cing Grandes Odes', 1990; mem. editorial bd. South Atlantic Rev., 1990-93, 97—; contbr. articles to profl. jours. Grantee Ford Found., 1968-72, U. Ga., 1982, 91, 97. mem. MLA, MADD, Am. Assn. Tchrs. French, Paul Claudel Soc. (v.p. 1978-79, sec.-treas. 1979-80, pres. 1981-82), Handgun Control, Inc., Societe Paul Claudel, Assn. des Amis de la Fondation St. John Perse. Jewish. Avocations: travel, cooking, reading. Office: U Ga Dept Romance Langs Athens GA 30602

HELLIE, RICHARD, Russian history educator, researcher; b. Waterloo, Iowa, May 8, 1937; s. Ole Ingeman and Mary Elizabeth (Larsen) H.; 1 son, Benjamin; m. Shujie Yu, Feb. 26, 1998. BA, U. Chgo., 1958, MA, 1960, PhD, 1965; postgrad., U. Moscow, 1963-64. Asst. prof. Rutgers U., 1965-66; asst. prof. Russian history U. Chgo., 1966-71, assoc. prof., 1971-80, prof., 1980—, dir. Ctr. for East European, Russian and Eurasian Studies, 1997—. Author: Muscovite Society, 1967, Enserfment and Military Change in Muscovy, 1971 (Am. Hist. Assn. Adams prize 1972), Slavery in Russia 1450-1725, (Laing prize U. Chgo. Press 1985, Russian translation in new post-Soviet format Kholopstvo v Rossii, 1450-1725, 1998), 1982, The Russian Law Code (Ulozhenie) of 1649, 1988; editor: The Plow, the Hammer and the Knout: An Economic History of Eighteenth Century Russia, 1985, Ivan the Terrible: A Quarcentenary Celebration of His Death, 1987, The Frontier in Russian History, 1993, Kholopstvov Rossii 1450-1725, Moscow, 1998, The Economy and Materials Culture of Russia 1600-1725, 1999; editor quat. jour. Russian History. Fgn. area tng. fellow Ford Found., 1962-65, Guggenheim fellow, 1973-74, fellow NEH, 1978-79; grantee NEH, 1982-83, summer, 1988, NSF, 1988-90, Bradley Found., 1988-91. Mem. PEN, Nat. Hist. Soc., Am. Soc. Legal History, Am. Assn. Advancement Slavic Studies (editorial bd. Slavic Rev. 1979-81), Econ. History Assn., Jean Bodin Soc., Historians Early Modern Europe, Soc. for Peasant History, Assn. for Comparative Econ. Studies, Nat. Assn. Scholars. E-mail: hell@midway.uchicago.edu. Home: 5807 S Dorchester Ave Apt 13E Chicago IL 60637-1729 Office: U Chgo Dept History 1126 E 59th St # 78 Chicago IL 60637-1580

HELLIWELL, THOMAS MCCAFFREE, physicist, educator; b. Minneapolis, Minn., June 8, 1936; s. George Plummer and Eleanor (McCaffree) H.; m. Bernadette Egan Busenberg, Aug. 9, 1997. BA, Pomona Coll., 1958; PhD, Calif. Inst. Tech., 1963. Asst. prof. physics Harvey Mudd Coll., Claremont, Calif., 1962-67, assoc. prof., 1967-73, prof., 1973—, chmn. dept. physics, 1981-89, chair of faculty, 1990-93, Burton Bettingen prof. physics, 1990—. Author: Introduction to Special Relativity, 1966; author papers in field of cosmology, gen. relativity and quantum theory. Sci. faculty fellow NSF, 1968. Mem. Am. Assn. Physics Tchrs., AAAS. Avocations: singing, hiking. Office: Harvey Mudd Coll Dept of Physics 301 E 12th St Claremont CA 91711-5901

HELLMAN, ARTHUR DAVID, law educator, consultant; b. N.Y.C., Dec. 9, 1942; s. Charles and Florence (Cohen) H. BA magna cum laude, Harvard U., 1963; JD, Yale U., 1966. Bar: Minn. 1967, U.S. Ct. Appeals (3d cir.) 1976, U.S. Ct. Appeals (9th cir.) 1979, U.S. Supreme Ct. 1980, Pa., 1985. Law clk. to assoc. justice Minn. Supreme Ct., 1966-67; asst. prof. William Mitchell Coll. Law, St. Paul, 1967-70, U. Conn. Sch. Law, West Hartford, 1970-72; vis. asst. prof. U. Ill. Coll. Law, Champaign, 1972-73; dep. exec. dir. Commn. on Revision Fed. Ct. Appellate System, Washington, 1973-75; assoc. prof. U. Pitts. Sch. Law, 1975-80, prof., 1980—; supervising staff atty. U.S. Ct. Appeals (9th cir.), San Francisco, 1977-79; vis. assoc. prof. U. Pa. Sch. Law, Phila., fall 1979; lectr. jud. confs., judges' seminars, 1976—; cons. various law firms, 1979—; faculty mem. Practicing Law Inst. Program on Fed. Appellate Practice, N.Y.C., 1984; planner Nat. Conf. Empirical Research in Judicial Adminstrn., Tempe, Ariz., 1988; gen. editor U.S. Ct. Appeals 9th Cir. Project Improvements in Judicial Adminstrn.., 1987-91; prin. investigator intercir. conflicts study Fed. Jud. Ctr., 1990; faculty mem. Fed. Jud. Ctr. Nat. Workshop for Judges of U.S. Cts. of Appeals, 1993; mem. evaluation com. U.S. Ct. Appeals (9th cir.), 1999—. Author: Laws Against Marijuana-The Price We Pay, 1975, Restructuring Justice-The Innovations of the Ninth Circuit and the Future of the Federal Courts, 1990; editor: Major Cases in First Amendment Law: Freedom of Speech, the Press, and Assembly, 1984; bus. editor: Yale U. Law Jour.; gen. editor: 9th Cir. Project on Improvements in Jud. Adminstrn., 1987-91; prin. researcher Fed. Jud. Ctr. study of intercircuit conflicts pursuant to Jud. Improvements Act of 1990. Mem. liaison task panel on psychoactive drug use/misuse Pres.'s Commn. on Mental Health, 1977-78; conferee Pound Conf., 1976, The Future and the Courts Conf., 1990; conferee Nat. Conf. on State-Fed. Jud. Relationships, 1992. Fellow Am. Bar Found.; mem. ABA (subcom. on stds. of com. appellate staff attys., jud. adminstrn. divsn., future of cts. com. 1992—, conferee Nat. Conf. on State-Fed. Jud. Rels. 1992, conferee summit on civil justice improvements 1990), Pa. Bar Assn. (discovery rules com. 1995—), Am. Law Inst., Supreme Ct. Hist. Soc., Am. Judicature Soc. (drafting com. project on jud. election campaigns, bd. dirs. 1985-89, justice reform com. 1992—, chair civil justice reform subcom. 1993-95, chair civil justice reform com. 1995—, invited witness hearing subcom. cts. and intellectual property house jud. com. jud. reform act 1997). Office: U Pitts Law Sch Pittsburgh PA 15260

HELLMAN, F(REDERICK) WARREN, investment advisor; b. N.Y.C., July 25, 1934; s. Marco F. and Ruth (Koshl) H.; m. Patricia Christina Sander, Oct. 5, 1955; children: Frances, Patricia H., Marco Warren, Judith. BA, U. Calif., Berkeley, 1955; MBA, Harvard U., 1959. With Lehman Bros., N.Y.C., 1959-84, ptnr., 1963-84; exec. mng. dir. Lehman Bros., Inc., N.Y.C., 1970-73; pres. Lehman Bros., Inc., 1973-75; ptnr. Hellman Ferri Investment Assocs., 1981-89, Matrix Ptnrs., 1981—; chmn. Hellman & Friedman LLC, San Francisco; bd. dirs. DN & E Walter, Levi Strauss & Co., Il Fornaio (Am.) Corp., Franklin Resources, Inc., Sugar Bowl Corp., PowerBar, Inc., Young & Rubicam Holdings, Inc.,; chmn. Hellman & Friedman, LLC; hon. trustee The Brookings Inst. Chmn. bd. trustees The San Francisco Found. Mem. Bond Club, Piping Rock Club, Century Country Club, Pacific Union Club. Office: Hellman & Friedman LLC 1 Maritime Plz Fl 12 San Francisco CA 94111-3404

HELLMAN, HERBERT MARTIN, lawyer; b. Spring Valley, N.Y., Aug. 4, 1943; s. Leon and Gertrude (Schwartz) H.; m. Reva Gaines, Dec. 26, 1965 (div. Aug. 1974); 1 child, Adam D.; m. Monica Deliso, Nov. 6, 1975; 1 child, Andrew D. BA, U. Ariz., 1966; JD, U. Tulsa, 1969. Bar: Okla. 1969, D.C. 1969, N.Y. 1971, U.S. Dist. Ct. (so. dist.) N.Y. 1972, U.S. Dist. Ct. (ea. dist.) N.Y. 1972. Trial atty. FTC, Washington, 1969-70; assoc. Weil, Gotshal & Manges, N.Y.C., 1970-78; sr. atty. J.C. Penney & Co., Inc., N.Y.C., 1978-80; v.p. R.H. Macy & Co., Inc., N.Y.C., 1980-84, sr. v.p., gen. counsel, 1984-93, group sr. v.p., gen. counsel, 1993-94; pres. Hampton Comml. Properties, Sagaponack, N.Y., 1994—. Editor U. Tulsa Law Rev. Recipient Appreciation award Nat. Retail Merchants Assn., N.Y.C., 1985. Mem. ABA (sec. corp. banking and bus. law 1984—), Assn. of Bar City N.Y. (com. on corp. law depts. 1984—), N.Y. State Bar Assn. (task force on simplification 1984—), Retail Industry Trade Action Coalition (mem. steering com. 1984—). Office: R H Macy & Co Inc 151 W 34th St New York NY 10001-2180 Address: PO Box 322 Sagaponack NY 11962-0322

HELLMAN, MARTIN EDWARD, retired electrical engineering educator; b. N.Y.C., Oct. 2, 1945; m. Dorothie Hellman. BEE magna cum laude, NYU, 1966; MSEE, Stanford U., 1967, PhD, 1969. Rsch. staff IBM's Watson Rsch. Ctr., 1968-69; faculty elec. engring. MIT, 1969-71; faculty Stanford (Calif.) U., 1971-96, prof. emeritus, 1996—, assoc. chmn. elec. engring. dept., chmn. elec. engring. grad. admissions, assoc. dean grad. studies; com. mem. Nat. Rsch. Coun., 1994-96; disting. lectr. Internat. Assn. Cryptologic Rsch., 1999. Co-editor: Breakthrough: Emerging New Thinking, 1988; editor Jour. Cryptology; contbr. articles to profl. jours.; patentee in field. Recipient Disting. Contbns. to Consumer Protection award Calif. State Psychol. Assn., 1978, Pioneer award Electronic Frontier Found., 1994, Nat. Computer Sys. Security award, 1996, Franklin Inst.'s Levy medal, 1997. Fellow IEEE (bd. govs. info. theory group 1975-80, chmn. 1979 Info. Theory Workshop, assoc. editor Transactions on Comm., Info. Theory Group's Best Paper award 1978, Donald G. Fink award 1981, Centennial medal 1984). Avocations: people, soaring, hiking. *

HELLMAN, PETER STUART, technical manufacturing executive; b. Cleve., Oct. 16, 1949; s. Arthur Cerf and Joan (Alburn) H.; m. Alyson Dulin Ware, Sept. 18, 1976; children: Whitney Ware, Garrettson Stuart. BA, Hobart Coll., 1972; MBA, Case Western Res. U., 1984. V.p. Irving Trust Co., N.Y.C., 1972-79; fin. planning assoc. Standard Oil Co., Cleve., 1979-82, mgr. fin. planning, 1982-84, dir. ops. analysis, 1984-85, asst. treas., 1985-86, treas., 1986-87, gen. mgr. crude oil supply and trading, 1987-89; v.p., treas. TRW Inc., Cleve., 1989-91, exec. v.p., CFO, 1991-94, asst. pres., 1994-95, pres., COO, bd. dirs., 1995—; bd. dirs. Arkwright Mut. Ins. Co., U.S. West, Inc. trustee The Cleve. Zool. Soc., Ctr. Families and Children; mem. vis. com. Case Western Res. U. Weatherhead Sch. Mgmt. Mem. Com. on Fgn. Rels. of the Cleve. Coun. of World Affairs, Soc. Automotive Engrs. Office: TRW Inc 1900 Richmond Rd Cleveland OH 44124-3760

HELLMAN, SAMUEL, radiologist, physician, educator; b. N.Y.C., July 23, 1934; s. Henry Sidney and Anna (Egar) H.; m. Marcia Sherman, June 30, 1957; children: Jeffrey Richard, Deborah Susan. B.S. magna cum laude, Allegheny Coll., 1955, D.Sc. (hon.), 1984; M.D. cum laude, SUNY, Syracuse, 1959, DSc (hon.), 1993; M.S. (hon), Harvard U., 1968. Med. intern Beth Israel Hosp., Boston, 1959-60; asst. resident radiology Yale Sch. Medicine and Grace-New Haven Hosp., 1960-62, postdoctoral fellow radiotherapy and cancer research, 1962-64; postdoctoral fellow Inst. Cancer Research and Royal Marsden Hosp., London, Eng., 1965-66; asst. prof. radiology Yale Sch. Medicine, 1966-68; assoc. prof. radiology Harvard Med. Sch., 1968-70; dir. Joint Center for Radiation Therapy, 1968-83, assoc. prof., chmn. dept. radiation therapy, 1971, prof., chmn. dept., 1971-83, also Alvan T. and Viola D. Fuller-Am. Cancer Soc. prof.; physician-in-chief Meml. Sloan Kettering Cancer Ctr., 1983-88, Benno Schmidt chair in clin. oncology, 1983-88; dean div. biol. sci. and Pritzker Sch. Medicine, v.p. for Med. Ctr. U. Chgo., 1988-93, Pritzker Prof., 1988-93, Pritzker Disting. Svc. Prof., 1993—; chmn. bd. sci. counselors divsn. cancer treatment Nat. Cancer Inst., 1980-84; bd. govs. Argonne Nat. Lab., 1990-93; trustee Brookings Inst., 1992—; bd. dirs. Varian Med. Systems Inc. Contbr. numerous articles to med. jours. Trustee Allegheny Coll., 1979-98, chmn. bd. trustees, 1987-93. Recipient Rosenthal award for cancer research, 1980, meadal City of Paris, 1986, award for Outstanding Contbns. to Cancer Care, Assn. Community Cancer Ctrs., 1993. Fellow AAAS; mem. Am. Radium Soc., Am. Soc. Therapeutic Radiologists (pres. 1983, Gold medal 1991), Am. Coll. Radiology, Assn. Univ. Radiologists, Am. Soc. Clin. Oncology (David A. Karnovsky lectr. 1994, pres. 1986), Am. Assn. Cancer Rsch., Am. Soc. Hematology, Am. Cancer Soc., Assn. Am. Physicians, Inst. Medicine NAS, Soc. Chmn. Acad. Radiology Depts., N.Y. Acad. Scis., Phi Beta Kappa, Sigma Xi, Alpha Omega Alpha. Home: 4950 S Chicago Beach Dr Chicago IL 60615-3207 Office: U Chgo Divsn Biol Scis 5841 S Maryland Ave Chicago IL 60637-1463

HELLMANN, DAVID BRUCE, medical educator; b. Louisville, Mar. 2, 1951. BA magna cum laude, Yale U., 1973; MD, Johns Hopkins U., 1977. Diplomate Am. Bd. Internal Medicine, Am. Bd. Rheumatology; lic. physician, Calif., Md. Intern, resident Johns Hopkins Hosp., Balt., 1977-80; fellow in rheumatology/clin. immunology U. Calif., San Francisco, 1980-82, asst. clin. prof. medicine, 1982-86; chief Moffitt Arthritis Clinics Johns Hopkins U., Balt., 1984-86, acting chief divsn. rheumatology/clin. immunology, 1989-96, May Betty Stevens prof., 1996—, dep. dir. dept. medicine, 1986-94, acting dir. dept. medicine, 1994-95, exec. vice chmn. dept. medicine, 1995—, med. dir. Faculty Practice Ctr., 1991-93, dir. Osler Med. Housestaff Tng. Program, 1992—, Mary Betty Stevens Prof. Medicine, 1996—; assoc. physician-in-chief Johns Hopkins Hosp., Balt., 1986-94, acting physician-in-chief, 1994-95; lectr. in field. Assoc. editor Medicine, 1993—; co-author: Rheumatology Committee, MKSAP II, 1995—; reviewer Jour. Rheumatology, Arthritis and Rheumatism, Western Jour. Medicine, Medicine, Jour. Clin. Investigatoin, Jour. of AMA; contbr. articles to profl. jours. Chmn. profl. edn. com. Md. chpt. Arthritis Found., 1991, 92, 93, 94. Recipient Kaiser Award for excellence in teaching U. Calif.-San Francisco, 1986, Cert. of Distinction in Teaching, 2d Yr. Med. Sch. Class, 1986, Profl. Edn. award Md. chpt. Arthritis Found., 1991, Disting. Svc. award for profl. edn., 1993, Faculty Teaching award Osler Med. Housestaff, 1992, Johns Hopkins Minority Faculty Assn. award, 1993; Henry Strong Denison scholar, 1975. Fellow ACP (gov. 1998—), Am. Coll. Rheumatology; mem. Assn. Program Dirs. Internal Medicine, Internat. Network for Study of the Systemic Vasculitides, Alpha Omega Alpha. Office: Johns Hopkins Univ 1830 E Monument St Ste 9030 Baltimore MD 21205

HELLMER, LYNNE BEBERMAN, education educator; b. Nome, Alaska, Sept. 26, 1947; d. Max and Elizabeth Forrer (Chapman) Beberman; divorced; children: Joshua Max, Lucas Andrew. BS, Eastern Illinois U., 1970; MEd, U. Ill., 1997. Tchr. Effingham (Ill.) Schs., 1970-72; personnel officer U. Ill., Urbana, 1972-81, tng. dir., 1981-93, dir. human resource devel., 1993—; pres. Univ. Clearinghouse, Champaign, 1992—; founder Biennial Conf. for Working Women, 1984—. Bd. dirs. Coll. and Univ. Pers. Assn. Found., 1998—. Recipient Nat. Achievement award for creativity Coll. and Univ. Pers. Assn., 1985-86, Outstanding Svc. and Leadership award Coll. and Univ. Pers. Assn. Midwest, 1991, Optimas award Workforce mag., 1996; named Most Valuable Cmty. Leader, Ill., Student Soc. for Pers., 1989. Mem. Coll. and Univ. Pers. Assn. (sec., treas. Midwest region 1988-89; editor Midwest News 1988-92, chair 1993-94, Creative Achievement and Publ. award 1998). Avocation: musician. Home: 910 W Green St Champaign IL 61821-3941 Office: U Ill Ste 204 505 E Green St Champaign IL 61820-5723

HELLMERS, NORMAN DONALD, historic site director; b. New Orleans, Feb. 3, 1944; s. Leonard H. and Meta J.C. (Wegener) H.; m. Patricia I. O'Brien, May 29, 1966; children: Jennifer I., Jeffrey N. BA, Concordia U., River Forest, Ill., 1966; postgrad., U. Iowa, 1966-67, La. State U., 1968. Writer, photographer Nebr. Game and Pks. Commn., Lincoln, 1969-71; ranger nat. pks. various locations, 1972-73; dist. naturalist Shenandoah Nat. Pk., Luray, Va., 1973-76; chief interpretation Grand Portage (Minn.) Nat. Monument, 1976-81; supt. Lincoln Boyhood Nat. Meml., Lincoln City, Ind., 1981-90, Lincoln Home Nat. Hist. Site, Springfield, Ill., 1990—. Lutheran. Avocations: photography, music.

HELLMUTH, GEORGE FRANCIS, architect; b. St. Louis, Oct. 5, 1907; s. George W. and Harriet M. (Fowler) H.; m. Mildred Lee Henning, May 24, 1941; children: George William, Nicholas Matthew, Mary Cleveland, Theodore Henning, Daniel Fox. BArch, Washington U., 1928, MArch, 1930; Steedman traveling fellow, 1931; diploma, Ecole des Beaux Arts, Fontainebleau, France. Founder Hellmuth, Yamasaki & Leinweber, 1949-55, Hellmuth, Obata & Kassabaum, 1955-78, HOK Internat., Inc., 1977-86; numerous offices including, St. Louis, N.Y.C., San Francisco, Dallas, Washington, Tokyo, Japan, Kuwait City, Kuwait, Berlin, Kansas City, Mo.,

Tampa, Fla., Los Angeles, Hong Kong and London; pres. Bald Eagle Co., Gladden, Mo.; co-founder Hellmuth Dunn Inc., Hellmuth Dunn and Co., St. Louis, 1994—; chmn. St. Louis Landmarks and Urban Design Commn., 1950-70; co-founder Hellmuth Dunn Inc., Designers and Mfrs. of Dinner and Decorative Wares. Prin. archtl. works include: King Saud U., Riyadh, Saudi Arabia; King Khaled Internat. Airport, Riyadh; (outside U.S.) Nile Tower, Cairo, Egypt, U. West Indies, Trinidad, Spanish Honduras secondary sch. system, Am. Embassy, El Salvador, Am. embassy housing, Cairo, Canadian medium and maximum prisons, Taipei World Trade Ctr., Taiwan, Housing for Royal Saudi Naval Forces, Saudi Arabia, Military Secondary Schools, Saudi Arabia, Air Def. Command Hdqtrs. Complex, Saudi Arabia, Burgan Bank Hdtrs., Kuwait, Asoka Dev., Kuala Lumpur, Chesterton Retail Mall, U.K.; prin. archtl. works include: (U.S.) Nat. Air and Space Mus., Washington, Marion Fed. Maximum Security Prison, (Ill.), IBM Advanced systems Lab, Los Gatos, Calif., Dallas/Ft. Worth Regional Airport, U. Wis. Med. Center, Madison; Internat. Rivercenter, New Orleans; SUNY Health Scis. Complex, Buffalo, The Galleria/Post Oak Center, Houston, E.R. Squibb Co, Lawrenceville, N.J., McDonnell Planetarium, St. Louis, Dow Research and Devel. Facility, Indpls.; Commonwealth P.R. Penal System; Duke U. Med. Center, Durham, N.C.; Lubbock Regional Airport, (Tex.), Lambert-St. Louis Internat. Airport, St. Louis, D.C. Courthouse, St. Louis U. Sch. Nursing, No. Ill. U. Library, Mobil Oil Hdqtrs., Fairfax, Va., Cities Service Research Ctr., Tulsa, Marriott Corp. Hdqtrs., Bethesda, Md., McDonnell Douglas Automation Ctr., St. Louis, Moscone Conv. Ctr., San Francisco, Piers 1. 2. 3., Boston, Clark County Dentention Ctr., Las Vegas, Nev., Pillsbury Research and Devel. Facility, Mpls., Saturn Automotive Facility, Tenn., Burger King World Hdqrs., Miami, Exxon Research and Egrning. Ctr., Clinton, N.J., Incarnate Word Hosp., St. Louis, Kellogg Co. Hdqrs., Battle Creek, Mich., Fleet Ctr., Providence, Phillips Point, West Palm Beach, Fla., Sohio Corp. Hdqrs., Cleve., Lincoln Tower, Miami, 2000 Pennsylvania Ave., Washington, Providence Park, Fairfax, Va., Tower One, Houston, Griffin Tower, Dallas, ARCO Tower, Denver, Levi's Plaza, San Francisco, Southwestern Bell Telephone Hdqrs., St. Louis, Met. Life Bldg., St. Louis, Burger King Hdqrs., Miami, Fla., Saturn Automotive Facility, Tenn., Living World Edn. Ctr., St. Louis Zoo, BP Hdqrs, London, U. Ala.-Birmingham Hosp., Univ. Hosp. at St. Louis U., Mo., Saint Louis Galleria Expansion, 801 Grand Office Bldg., Des Moines, Moore Bus. Forms Hdqrs., Lake Forest, Ill., The Fla. Aquarium, Tampa, Fed. Reserve Bank Mpls., Fed. Reserve Bank Cleve., Jacobs Field, Cleve., Oriole Park at Camden Yards, Balt., NYU Replacement Hosp., N.Y.C., Northwestern Meml. Replacement Hosp., Chgo., U.S. EPA Environ. Rsch. Facility, Research Triangle Park, N.C., Thomas F. Eagleton U.S. Courthouse, St. Louis, Exxon Corp. World Hdqs., Irving, Tex., Huangpu Dist. Master Plan, Shanghai, Hongkong Stadium, Victoria, Hong Kong, Fukuoka (Japan) Internat. Airport Terminal, Sendai (Japan) Internat. Airport Terminal, many other indsl. and bus. corporate hdqrs., research centers. Designated knight Sovereign Mil. Order of Malta in U.S.A. Fellow AIA (First Honor award 1956). Home: 5 Conway Ln Saint Louis MO 63124-1279 Office: One Met Sq 211 N Broadway Saint Louis MO 63102-2733 *My aims and objectives focused on a single thought that persisted over a lifetime, i.e., to make a significant contribution to the embellishment of man's environment, using the skills best suited to my talents, and coordinating and directing the abilities of other professionals.*

HELLMUTH, GEORGE WILLIAM, architect; b. Detroit, Nov. 21, 1942; s. George Francis and Mildred Lee (Henning) H.; m. Camille Byrns Carmody, Feb. 20, 1965; children—George, Holly, Julie, Emily. B.A. in Architecture, Yale U., 1964; M.B.A., Eastern N.Mex. U., 1969; B.Arch., CCNY, 1979. Sr. prin. Hellmuth, Obata & Kassabaum, Washington, 1971—. Served to capt. USAF, 1965-69. Mem. AIA. Roman Catholic. Club: Sky (N.Y.C.). Home: 9819 Quail Run Ct Fairfax Station VA 22039-2818 Office: Hellmuth Obata & Kassabaum PC 3223 Grace St NW Washington DC 20007-3614

HELLMUTH, JOHN S., healthcare executive; b. Springfield, Ohio, Aug. 6, 1953; s. Andrew Link and Mary Helen (Quinlan) H.; m. Deborah Lynn De Zorzi, May 27, 1959; children: Patrick John, Heather Ann. BBA, U. Notre Dame, 1995. Pres. Ryan Diagnostics, Inc., Naperville, Ill., 1986—. Home: 929 Spindletree Ave Naperville IL 60565

HELLMUTH, THEODORE HENNING, lawyer; b. Detroit, Mar. 28, 1949; s. George F. and Mildred Lee (Henning) H.; m. Laurie Kincaid, May 29, 1970; children: Elizabeth Ann, Theodore Henning, Sara Marie. BA, U. Pa., 1970; JD cum laude, U. Mo.-Columbia, 1974. Bar: Mo. 1974, U.S. Dist. Ct. (ea. dist.) Mo. 1974, U.S. Ct. Appeals (8th cir.) 1978. Assoc., then ptnr. Armstrong Teasdale LLP, St. Louis, 1974—. Author: Missouri Real Estate, 1985, 2d edit., 1998, Lease Audits: The Essential Guide, 1994; editor Distressed Real Estate Law Alert, 1987-88, Litigated Commercial Real Estate Document Reports, 1987-95. Mem. ABA (vice-chmn., chmn. litigation and dispute resolution com. real property and probate sect. 1991-95, mng. book editor real property and probate sect. 1998—), Am. Coll. Real Estate Lawyers (chmn. alternative dispute resolution com. 1993-96), Order of Coif. Office: Armstrong Teasdale LLP 1 Metropolitan Sq Ste 2600 Saint Louis MO 63102-2740

HELLUMS, JESSE DAVID, chemical engineering educator and researcher; b. Stamford, Tex., Aug. 19, 1929; s. John V. and Fannie May (Beauchamp) H.; m. Marilyn Biel, July 13, 1957; children—Mark William, Jay David. B.S., U. Tex., 1950, M.S., 1957; Ph.D., U. Mich., 1960. Registered profl. engr., Tex. Process engr. Mobil Oil Co., Beaumont, Tex., 1950-54; mem. faculty Rice U., Houston, 1960—; prof. chem. engring. Rice U., 1968—, dir. biomed. engring. lab., 1968-80, chmn. dept., 1969-75, dean engring., 1980-88; A.J. Hartsook prof., 1987—; adj. prof. Baylor U. Coll. Medicine, 1966—, U. Tex. Med. Sch., 1977—; NSF sci. faculty fellow Cambridge (Eng.) U., 1967-68; vis. prof. Imperial Coll., London, 1973-74, U. Tsukuba, Japan, 1995; vis. scholar U. Calif., San Diego, 1988; spl. vis. prof. Tokyo Inst. Tech., 1989, 98; eminent scientist Inst. Phys. & Chem. Rsch., Japan, 1997. Author papers in field. Served to 1st lt. USAF, 1954-56. Recipient Rsch. award NIH, 1986, Rsch. award Biomed. Engring. Soc., 1993. Fellow AIChE; mem. AAAS, AAUP, Nat. Acad. Engring., Am. Heart Coun. Thrombosis, Am. Inst. Med. Biol. Engrs. (founding fellow), Am. Chem. Soc., Am. Soc. Artificial Internal Organs, Microcirculation Soc., Soc. Rheology, Internat. Soc. Oxygen Transport to Tissue, Biomed. Engring. Soc. (sr. mem.). Home: 2202 Albans Rd Houston TX 77005-1520 Office: Rice Univ Biomed Eng Lab PO Box 1892 Houston TX 77251-1892

HELLWIG, EILEEN MARIE, critical care nurse; b. New Orleans, July 28, 1961; d. Nelson Joseph and Esperanza (Figaroa) H. Student, U. New Orleans, 1980-81; AS, La. State U., 1982; BSN, U. South Ala., 1992, MSN, 1994. Charge nurse med./srug. Jo Ellen Smith Med. Ctr., New Orleans, 1982-84; charge nurse ICU/CCU Jo Ellen Smith Med. Ctr., 1984-89, critical care instr., 1989-90, clin. coord. critical care, 1991-94; nursing instr. La. State U., Our Lady of Holy Cross Coll., 1994—; charge nurse ICU, CCU Meadowcrest Hosp., Gretna, 1994—. Mem. Am. Assn. Critical Care Nurses, Golden Key, Alpha Theta Epsilon, Phi Kappa Phi.

HELLY, WALTER SIGMUND, engineering educator; b. Vienna, Austria, Aug. 22, 1930; came to U.S., 1938, naturalized, 1944; s. Edward and Elizabeth (Bloch) H.; m. Dorothy Oxman, Mar. 4, 1956; 1 dau., Miranda. B.A., Cornell U., 1950; M.S., U. Ill., 1954; Ph.D., Mass. Inst. Tech., 1959. With Sylvania Electric Co., Waltham, Mass., 1954-56; sr. engr. Melpar Co., Boston, 1956-59; mem. tech. staff Bell Telephone Labs., N.Y.C., 1959-62; sr. engr. Port of N.Y. Authority, 1962-65; prof. ops. research Poly. Inst. N.Y., 1966—; cons. on traffic flow. Author: Urban Systems Models, 1975; Book rev. editor: Jour. Ops. Research, 1970—; Contbr. articles to profl. jours. Mem. Ops. Research Soc. Am. (past chmn. transp. sci. sect.). Home: 91 Central Park W New York NY 10023-4600 Office: 333 Jay St Brooklyn NY 11201-2907

HELLYER, CONSTANCE ANNE (CONNIE ANNE CONWAY), writer, musician; b. Puyallup, Wash., Apr. 22, 1937; d. David Tirrell and Constance (Hopkins) H.; m. Peter A. Corning, Dec. 30, 1963 (div. 1977); children: Anne Arundel, Stephanie Deak; m. Don W. Conway, Oct. 12, 1980. *Father David Tirrell Hellyer (1913-) is a physician, author ("Your Child and You", " At the Forest's Edge"), and founder of Northwest Trek Park in Washington. Mother Constance Hopkins Hellyer (1914-), a devoted partner to her husband's medical and philanthropic work, has also contributed to Tacoma cultural life. Husband Don Wesley Conway (1930-) is a jazz saxophonist, graphic designer, and founder of String of Pearls band (album, "Makin' Whoopee!"). Daughter Anne Arundel Corning (1965-), a University of Chicago graduate, is a writer and classical singer in Seattle. Daughter Stephanie Corning Cunningham (1969-) is an attorney in Tacoma, Washington.* BA with honors, Mills Coll., 1959. Grader, rschr. Harvard U., Cambridge, Mass., 1959-60; rschr. Newsweek mag., N.Y.C., 1960-63; author's asst. Theodore H. White and others, N.Y.C., 1964-69; freelance writer, editor Colo., Calif., 1969-75; writer, editor Stanford (Calif.) U. Med. Ctr., 1975-79; comm. dir. No. Calif. Cancer Program, Palo Alto, 1979-82, Stanford Law Sch., Palo Alto, 1982-97; mgr., vocalist, pianist String of Pearls Band, 1991—, co-leader China tour, 1999. *As editor of "Stanford Lawyer" for sixteen years, Constance Hellyer wrote and/or edited more than 40 articles. She previously assisted authors Arthur T. Hadley with "Power's Human Face," Theodore H. White with "Making of the President, 1964," and Rudolph Moos with "Environment and Utopia." A long-time classical performer, she took up jazz and pop in her forties and is now pianist and female vocalist of String of Pearls, the Bay Area swing and jazz octet she manages with husband Don Conway. The group has recorded an album ("Makin' Whoopee!") and has performed in China.* Founding editor (newsletters) Insight, 1978-80, Synergy, 1980-82, Stanford Law Alum, 1992-95; editor (mag.) Stanford Lawyer, 1982-98; contbr. articles to profl. jours. and mags. Recipient silver medal Coun. for Advancement and Support Edn., 1985, 89, award of distinction dist. VII, 1994. Mem. No. Calif. Sci. Writers Assn. (co-founder, bd. dirs. 1979-93), Phi Beta Kappa. Democrat. Avocations: singing, piano. Home: 2080 Louis Rd Palo Alto CA 94303-3451

HELLYER, TIMOTHY MICHAEL, protective services officer; b. Chgo., Nov. 30, 1954; s. William Al and Dotha Helen (Bucknum) H.; m. Nancy Ruth O'Donnell, Nov. 29, 1986; children: Jennifer Lynn, Allyson Jean. Student, So. Ill. U., 1985-86. Cert. firefighter III; cert. paramedic. Firefighter/paramedic Palatine (Ill.) Fire Dept., 1980—; instr. CPR, Chgo. Heart Assn., 1976—; pres. N.W. Assn. Provider Emergency Med. Svcs. Sys., 1989-92; mem. No. Ill. Critical Stress Debriefing Team. Deacon Palatine Presbyn. Ch., 1989-92; mem. comm. coun. Sch. Dist. 300, 1993—, mem. Year Round Sch. com., 1998-99; mem. improvement team Westfield Cmty. Sch., 1993—. Named Firefighter of the Yr., Jaycees of Palatine, 1987. Mem. Prehosp. Care Providers Ill. (bd. dirs. 1990), St. Francis Hook and Ladder Soc., Ill. Profl. Firefighters Assn., Smithsonian Instn., Nat. Trust Historic Preservation, Nat. Geographic Soc., U.S. Naval Inst., Nat. Space Soc. Republican. Presbyterian. Avocations: collecting Disney memorabilia, gardening, model railroading. Home: 1600 Kensington Dr Algonquin IL 60102-5104 Office: Palatine Fire Dept 39 E Colfax St Palatine IL 60067-5297

HELM, DEWITT FREDERICK, JR., consultant, professional association administrator; b. Charlotte, N.C., Apr. 24, 1933; s. DeWitt Frederick Sr. and Blanche Buchanan (DeBusk) H.; divorced; children: DeWitt Frederick III, Mary McNair Helm Bishop; m. Joyce Claire Williams, May 18, 1991. BS in History, Davidson (N.C.) Coll., 1956. Mgr. advt. Vick Chem. Co., N.Y.C., 1956-63; mgr. consumer products Pfizer, Inc., N.Y.C., 1963-66; mgr. consumer product acquisition and devel. A.H. Robins Co., Richmond, Va., 1966-69; exec. v.p. Miller Morton Co., Richmond, 1969-72, pres., 1972-81; pres. Miller Morton of Can. Ltd., 1969-81; sr. v.p. Jack Morton Prodns. Inc., Washington, 1981-84; exec. v.p. Assn. Nat. Advertisers, Inc., N.Y.C., 1984, pres., 1984-93, also bd. dirs.; mng. ptnr. DH Assocs., Palm City, Fla., 1994—, The Advt. Partnership LLC, N.Y.C., 1996—. Deacon, elder Presbyn. Ch., United Meth. Ch., 1990; bd. dirs. Nat. Tobacco Festival, Richmond, 1977-81, Traffic Audit Bur., N.Y.C., 1984-93. With U.S. Army, 1956-58. Mem. Consumer Healthcare Products Assn. (bd. dirs., exec. com. 1972-80, chmn. 1973-75), Coun. Better Bus. Burs. (bd. dirs. 1989-93), Am. Advt. Mus. (founding dir., nat. bd. 1987—), Smithsonian Instn.'s Ctr. for Advt. History (adv. bd. 1989—), Advt. Coun. (bd. dirs., treas. 1984-93), Advt. Rsch. Found. (bd. dirs. 1984-93), World Fedn. Advertisers (bd. dirs., mgmt. com. 1984-93), Media-Advt. Partnership for Drug-Free Am. (mgmt. bd.), and others. Clubs: Wintergreen (Va.); Sky, Metropolitan (N.Y.C.), Harbour Ridge (Fla.).

HELM, DONALD CAIRNEY, hydrogeologist, engineer, educator; b. Yokohama, Japan, Mar. 26, 1937; s. Nathan Teal and Rebecca Forsyth (Cairney) H.; m. Usha Monica Sundari Muliyil, Dec. 1961 (div.); m. Karen Emily Reed, Sept. 3, 1982; 1 child, Rebecca Bernice Vera. AB in Math. cum laude, Amherst Coll., 1959; MDiv in Theology, Hartford Sem. Found., 1962; postgrad., Colo. Sch. Mines, 1962-63, 64-65; MS in Geol. Engring., U. Calif.-Berkeley, 1970, PhD in Civil Engring., 1974. Registered profl. engr., Australia, U.S.A. Vol. in rural devel. Mitraniketan Project, Kerala State, India, 1963-64; hydraulic engr. U.S. Geol. Survey, Portland, Oregon, 1965-68, Berkeley, Calif., 1968-69; research hydrologist U.S. Geol. Survey, Sacramento, 1969-78, Las Vegas, Nev., 1991-93, Carson City, Nev., 1993-96; research physicist Lawrence Livermore Nat. Lab., U. Calif., 1978-84, ret. 1990, group leader, geohydrology and environ. studies group, 1981-84; prin. research scientist Geomechanics Div. Commonwealth Sci. and Indsl. Research Orgn. (CSIRO), Melbourne, Australia, 1984-92, ret. 1992, hydraulics group leader, 1984-86, chmn. selection com. for hiring research scientists, 1986, rep. to Research Officers Assn., 1986-87, mem. ex-officio divisional staff cons. com., 1986-87; rsch. hydrogeologist Nev. Bur. Mines and Geology U. Nev., Reno, Las Vegas, 1989-98; vis. rsch. scientist Nev. Bur. Mines and Geology U. Nev., Reno, 1989-92; chief Las Vegas Office, 1989-93; prof. geology U. Nev., Reno, 1992-98, adj. prof., 1998—; Massie prof. civil engring. Morgan State U., Balt., 1996—; instr. U.S. Geol. Survey Advanced Groundwater Sch., Denver, 1972-78, UNESCO Internat. Workshop on Land Subsidence, Mexico City, 1979, Pacific Sch. Religion, Berkeley, Calif., 1982, courses on subsidence for various mining cos., Western Australia, 1985, for U.S. Geol. Survey rsch. hydrologists, Tucson, 1987; advisor, mem. nat. steering com. Geothermal Subsidence Rsch. Program, U.S. Dept. Energy, 1976-84; vis. sr. rsch. scientist State Elec. Commn. Victoria, Australia, 1982-83, U.S. Bur. Reclamation, Phoenix, 1984; mem. subcom. on math. modeling of subsidence NSW Dept. Mineral Resources, 1984-86; internat. exch. scientist from Australia to Inst. Soil and Rock Mechanics, Acad. Sinica (Chinese Acad. Sci.), Wuhan, 1988, to dept. civil engring. U. Colo., Boulder, 1990; mem. grad. faculty joint CSIRO-James Cook U. program in rock engring., 1989-90, dept. geol. scis. U. Nev., Reno, 1990-98, hydrology/hydrogeology program, 1991-95, hydrol. scis. program, 1995-98, dept. civil engring., 1994-98, dept. geosci. U. Nev., Las Vegas, 1992-93; coord. multi-agy. rsch. project on subsidence of the Las Vegas Valley, 1989-91; mem. nat. liaison com. between ASCE, Geol. Soc. Am. and Assn. Engring. Geologists, 1997—. Contbr. articles to sci. jours., chpts. to books. Co-chmn. New Eng. Student Christian Movement, 1958-59; mem. high sch. com. Am. Friends Service Com., Salem Oreg., 1966-68; bd. dirs. Ctr. Theology and Natural Scis., Grad. Theol. Union, Berkeley, Calif., 1981-84, Montessori Sch. Council, Melbourne, 1986-87; mem. Md. Tributary Team for Protecting the Chesapeake Bay, 1998—. Recipient Bennet-Tyler award in systematic theology, 1962, Award for Outstanding Pub. Paper of Yr. Disciplines of Environ. and Engring. Geology from Assn. Engring. Geologists, 1994, Cert. of Appreciation Chinese (Taiwanese) Inst. of Civil and Hydraulic Engring. Com. of Geotech. Engring., 1992; Innaugural occupant of U.S. Dept. Energy's Samuel P. Massie Chair of Excellence in Environ. Disciplines, Morgan State U., 1996—. Fellow Geol. Soc. Am., Inst. Engrs. Australia (Coll. Civil Engrs.); mem. NSPE, ASTM (com. solid waste disposal), AAUP, AAAS, ASCE, ASME, Am. Geophys. Union, Am. Water Resources Assn., Assn. Engring. Geologists, Assn. Geoscientists for Internat. Devel., Nat. Water Well Assn., N.Y. Acad. Scis., Internat. Soil Mechanics and Found. Engring., Internat. Assn. Engring. Geology, Internat. Soc. Rock Mechanics, Nev. Water Resources Assn., Md. Soc. Profl. Engrs. (pres. Balt. chpt., Md. bd. dirs.), SAR, Outlook Club. Mem. Soc. of Friends. Home: 1413 Bolton St Baltimore MD 21217-4202 Office: Morgan State U Dept Civil Engring Baltimore MD 21251

HELM, JOHN LESLIE, mechanical engineer, company executive; b. Red Wing, Apr. 10, 1921; s. Leslie Cornell and Dora (Mcguigan) H.; m. Nancy Ellen Molle, May 15, 1954; children: John Leslie, Juli-Ann, Catherine Marie. BSME, Columbia, 1943, MS, 1944; postgrad. in nuclear engring., U. Conn., 1956-57. Registered profl. engr., N.Y. Asst. in mech. engring. Columbia U., 1943-44; process engr. Metals Disintegrating Co. unit of Manhattan Project, Elizabeth, N.J., 1944-45; project engr. Aero Manuscripts Inc., 1945-46; staff engr. ctrl. engring. dept. Gen. Foods Corp., White Plains, N.Y., 1946-52; with Gen. Dynamics Corp., Groton, Conn., 1952-74; spl. tech. asst. S5W USS Skipjack Nuclear Propulsion Plant; project mgr., chief engr. S5G Narwal Propulsion plant; spl. tech. asst. Office of Pres. Electric Boat divsn. Gen. Dynamics Corp., 1965-72; gen. mgr. Gen. Dynamics Energy Sys., 1972-74; founder, pres., CEO Proto-Power Mgmt. Corp., Groton, 1974-82; also dir.; pres., CEO Proto-Power corp. subs. of Killmorgen Corp., 1982-89; dir. Electronic Assocs., Inc., West Long Branch, N.J., 1983-89; founder, pres., CEO Transplex Inc., 1990—. Mem. Groton Bd. Edn., 1967-77, chmn., 1976-77; mem. State of Conn. Nuclear Adv. Coun., 1996—. Recipient citation for work on Manhattan Project, War Dept., 1945. Mem. ASME, Shonnecosset Yacht Club, Off Soundings Club, Princeton Club, Thames Club, N.Y. Yacht Club, Theta Tau. Republican. Roman Catholic. Home: 116 Tyler Ave Groton CT 06340-5923 Office: North Stonington Profl Ctr Routes 2 & 184 North Stonington CT 06359

HELM, KLAUS F., dermatology educator; b. Vienna, Austria, Dec. 23, 1959; s. Frederick and Juta (Sakk) H.; m. Jan. M. McAllister, Aug. 14, 1993. BA, U. Rochester, 1981, MD, 1985. Assoc. prof. Pa. State U. Hershey Med. Ctr., 1996—, asst. prof. dermatology, 1991-96. Author: Atlas of Differential Diagnosis in Dermatology, 1998. Office: Pa State U Geisinger Health System Hershey Med Ctr Hershey PA 17033

HELM, LEWIS MARSHALL, public affairs executive; b. Riverdale, Md., Sept. 9, 1931; s. William P. and Selma S. (Snyder) H.; m. Alice L. Kupferman, Sept. 12, 1953. AA in Comms., Am. U., 1957, MS in Pub. Rels., 1979; grad., U.S. Army War Coll., 1977. Newspaper reporter Wichita (Kans.) Eagle, 1950-51, Washington Times-Herald, 1951-54; press asst. Republican Nat. Com., 1954-55; dir. pub. rels. Plumbing Fixture Mfrs. Assn., Washington, 1956-59, Home Mfrs. Assn., 1961-63; pub. rels. cons., 1959-60, 64-68; info. dir. Citizens for Nixon, 1968; asst. to sec. U.S. Dept. Interior, Washington, 1969, dep. asst. sec. mineral resources, 1969-72; asst. sec. for pub. affairs HEW, Washington, 1973-76; pres. Capital Counselors, Inc., Washington, 1976-86; govt. rels. and mktg. cons., 1987—; commr. Washington Suburban Sanitary Commn., 1991-95, vice-chair, 1992-93, chair, 1993-94; instr. econs. Cath. U. Am., 1974; assoc. lecturing prof. polit. sci. George Washington U., 1980; commentator Sta. WAMU-FM, Washington, 1995—; adj. prof. Montgomery Coll., 1996-97; adj. instr. Coll. Journalism, U. Md., 1998—, MBA program Johns Hopkins U., 1999—. Co-author: Informing the People: A Public Affairs Handbook, 1981. Exec. dir. Sr. Army Res. Comdrs. Assn., 1987—; mem. Soc. of the Cin. in the State of Va.; mem. adv. bd. Vietnam Vets. Inst., 1993-96; bd. dirs. Mid-Atlantic region Audubon Naturalist Soc., 1995-97. Brig. gen. USAR, 1984-88. Decorated Legion of Merit with oak leaf cluster; recipient Meritorious Service medal Dept. Interior, USPHS and Dept. Army, Spl. citation for distinguished service Sec. HEW.

HELM, PHALA ANIECE, physiatrist; b. Ft. Worth, 1931. MD, U. Tex., Dallas, 1966. Diplomate Am. Bd. Phys. Medicine and Rehab. Intern Baylor U. Med. Ctr., Dallas, 1966-67, resident in phys. med. and rehab., 1967-70; mem. staff Parkland Meml. Hosp., Dallas, 1973—; prof. physiatry U. Tex. S.W. Med. Ctr., Dallas, 1973—. Mem. ABA, Am. Diabetes Assn., Am. Acad. Phys. Medicine and Rehab., Am. Congress Phys. Medicine and Rehab. Office: U Tex Southwestern Med Ctr Sprague Clin Sci Bld CS1104 5323 Harry Hines Blvd Dallas TX 75235-9055*

HELM, TERRY ALLEN, telecommunications consultant; b. Dallas, Jan. 26, 1951; s. Fred Lee and Jean (Patrick) H.; 1 child from previous marriage: Heather Brooke; m. Norma B. Martinez Deuane, 1995; 1 child, Allen Alexander. BA, U. Tex., 1974; M of Info. Mgmt., Washington U., St. Louis, 1991, M of Telecommunications Mgmt., 1993. Registered mem. Cherokee Nation. Data ctr. mgr. Southwestern Bell Telephone Co., Austin, Tex., 1974-78; computer systems mgr. Southwestern Bell Telephone Co., St. Louis, 1978-81, tech. support mgr., 1981-84, cons., 1984-94; mgr. data architecture Southwestern Bell Corp., Mexico City, 1994-96; project leader Tech. Infrastructure, Dallas, 1996—; sales assoc. Coldwell Banker Real Estate, Des Peres, Mo., 1989—; environ. com. Washington U. EDI Roundtable. Author: A History of the (Norman) Helme Family, 1987. Vice chair adm. bd. Kirkwood United Meth. Ch., 1990-92; v.p. cmty. devel. Jaycees, Garland, Tex., 1997—. Mem. IEEE, SAR, Mid-West VM Users Group (pres. 1983-84), United Meth. Men (pres. 1986-87), Sons of the Revolution (capt. color guard 1993—, membership chmn. 1993—), Soc. Descs. of Washington's Army at Valley Forge, Soc. Colonial Wars, Soc. of the War of 1812, Sons of Union Vets., Sons of Confederate Vets., Magna Charta Barons, Cherokee Nation, U. Tex. Ex-student Assn. (pres. 1987-88), Amdahl Users Group (speaker 1984-85), NetWare Users' Group, Jaycees. Avocations: genealogy, historical research, fishing, running, mountain climbing. Home: 338 Wildbriar Dr Garland TX 75043-2920 Office: 6301 Colwell Blvd Rm 215 Irving TX 75039-3131

HELM, THOMAS KENNEDY, JR., retired lawyer; b. Louisville, Ky., Sept. 16, 1918; s. Thomas Kennedy and Elizabeth Tebbs (Nelson) H.; m. Nell Hoge, Jan. 2, 1943,children: T. Kennedy III, Peyton Randolph, Hunt Chouteau. BA, Washington & Lee U., 1940; JD, U. Louisville, 1942. Assoc. Stites & Harbison Attys., Louisville, Ky., 1941-53; ptnr. Stites & Harbison Attys., Louisville, 1953-88, mng. ptnr., 1975; of counsel Stites & Harbison Attys., 1989—; bd. dirs. Griffin Chem. Co., Louisville, Marwood, Inc., Louisville, Frame House Galleries, Louisville, Whayne Supply Co., Louisville. Author: Kentucky Airport Law and Management, 1989. Chmn. bd. Ky. Country Day Sch., Louisville. Comdr. USCG Aux. Capt. AUS Res., 1942-46. Mem. Gen. Soc. Colonial Wars (gov. gen. 1990-93). Avocations: boating, woodworking, photography. Home: 321 Mockingbird Hill Rd Louisville KY 40207-1852

HELMAN, ALFRED BLAIR, retired college president, education consultant; b. Windber, Pa., Dec. 25, 1920; s. Henry E. and Luie (Pritt) H.; m. Patricia Ann Kennedy, June 22, 1947; children: Harriet Ann Helman Hill, Patricia Dawn Helman Magaro. AB magna cum laude, McPherson Coll., 1946, DD, 1956; MA, U. Kans., 1947, postgrad., 1948-51; LLD, Juniata Coll., 1976; LHD, Bridgewater Coll., 1977, Ind. U., 1981; HHD, Manchester Coll., 1986. Ordained to ministry Ch. of Brethren, 1942; pastor Newton, Kans., 1944-46, Ottawa, Kans., 1946-54; pastor First Ch. of Brethren, Wichita, Kans., 1954-56; faculty Ottawa U., 1947- 48, 51-54, chmn. div. social scis., 1952-54; faculty U. Kans., 1951-54, Friends U., 1955-56; pres. Manchester (Ind.) Coll., 1956-86, pres. emeritus, 1986—; chmn. com. on higher edn. Ch. of Brethren, 1965-67, 76-78, nat. moderator, 1975-76, mem. rev. and evaluation com., 1983-85, mem. denominational structure rev. com., 1989-91, mem. pension bd. restructure com., 1986-87; trustee McPherson Coll., 1951-56, chmn., 1955-56; trustee Kans. Found. Pvt. Colls. and Univs., 1955-56; pres. Ind. Conf. Higher Edn., 1960-61; mem. policy bd. dept. higher edn. Nat. Coun. Chs. of Christ Am., 1960-71; mem. pres.'s adv. com. Nat. Assn. Intercollegiate Athletics, 1966-70; mem. exec. com. Ind. Coun. Chs., 1960-62, bd. dirs., 1992-94; bd. dirs. Independent Colls. and Univs. of Ind., 1977-83, 84-86, chmn., 1978-79, 85-86; chmn., interim pres. Coun. Protestant Colls. and Univs., 1967, bd. dirs., 1961-69; bd. dirs. Ctrl. States Coll. Assn., 1965-77, chmn., 1968; pres. Assoc. Colls. of Ind., 1970-72, bd. dirs., 1956-86; mem. commn. on religion in higher edn. Assn. Am. Colls., 1968-71; bd. dirs. CTB, Inc., 1977-92. Author articles on religion and higher edn. Mem. IAUP-UN Commn. on Arms Control Edn., 1991—. Named Sagamore of Wabash, Gov. of Ind., 1980, Ky. Col., Gov. of Ky., 1964; recipient Outstanding Local Citizen award, 1972, Sparks-Jones award Associated Colls. Ind., 1977, Legion of Honor award Kiwanis Club North Manchester, 1976; elected to Ind. Acad., 1987. Mem. Soc. Historians of Am. Fgn. Rels., Internat. Assn. Univ. Presidents (mem. steering com. N.Am. coun. 1982-84), Ind. Assn. Ch.-Related and Ind. Colls. (pres. 1966-67), Am. Assn. Higher Edn., Am. Acad. Polit. and Social Sci., Nat. Assn. Ind. Colls. and Univs. (bd. dirs. 1983-84), Ind. Acad. Social Scis., Ind. Hist. Assn., Allen County/Ft. Wayne Hist. Soc., Ft. Wayne Rotary (Paul Harris fellow), Columbia Club (Indpls.), Univ. Club (Chgo.), Wabash Country Club (Ind.), Quest Club (mem. bd. govs. 1988-90, 92-94, 97—), Fortnightly Club, Phi Beta Kappa, Phi Alpha Theta, Pi Sigma Alpha, Pi Kappa Delta, Tau Kappa Alpha (hon.).

HELMAN, GERALD BERNARD, government official; b. Detroit, Nov. 4, 1932; s. Leo and Ann (Glassman) H.; m. Dolores Hammel, May, 1953; children: Ruth Leea, Deborah Gayle, David Robert. AB, U. Mich., 1953, LLB, 1956. Bar: Mich. 1956. Rsch. asst. U. Mich., 1955; intelligence rsch. specialist Dept. State, 1957; econ. consular officer Dept. State, Milan, Italy,

1958; polit. officer Dept. State, Vienna, Austria, 1960-62; econ. officer Dept. State, Barbados, 1962-63; fgn. affairs officer Dept. State, Washington, 1963-68; polit. mil. affairs officer, counselor U.S. Mission to NATO, Brussels, Belgium, 1968-73; dep. dir. NATO-Atlantic polit. mil. affairs U.S. Mission to NATO, Washington, 1974-76; dir. UN polit. affairs U.S. Mission to NATO, 1976-77; dep. asst. sec. Bur. Internat. Orgn. Affairs, 1977-79; U.S. ambassador to UN Orgns. in Europe, 1979-81; dep. and sr. advisor to undersec. for polit. affairs Dept. State, Washington, 1982-91, cons. on Internat. and Telecomm. matters, 1991-92; v.p. Ellipso, Inc., 1992—; bd. dirs. Internat. Small Satellite Ogrn. Woodrow Wilson fellow Princeton U., 1973. Jewish. Home: 2900 Maplewood Pl Alexandria VA 22302-2424

HELMAN, ROBERT ALAN, lawyer; b. Chgo., Jan. 27, 1934; s. Nathan W. and Esther (Weiss) H.; m. Janet R. Williams, Sept. 13, 1958; children: Marcus E., Adam J., Sarah E. Student, U. Ill., 1951-53; BSL, Northwestern U., 1954, LLB, 1956. Bar: Ill. 1956. Asso. firm Isham, Lincoln & Beale, Chgo., 1956-64, ptnr., 1965-66; ptnr. firm Mayer, Brown & Platt, Chgo., 1967—; bd. dirs. No. Trust Corp., The No. Trust Co., Zenith Electronics Corp., Dreyer's Grand Ice Cream Corp., Chgo. Stock Exch., Brambles USA, Inc.; vis. com. U. Chgo. Law Sch. Co-author: Commentaries on 1970 Illinois Constitution, 1971; assoc. editor Northwestern U. Law Rev., 1955-56; contbr. articles to legal jours. Mem. Chgo. Fin. Rsch. and Adv. Com.; chmn. Citizens' Com. on Juvenile Ct., Cook County, 1969-81; pres. Legal Assistance Found., Chgo., 1973-76; chmn. vis. com. Northwestern U. Law Sch., 1989-92; bd. dirs. United Charities Chgo., 1967-73; trustee Brookings Instn., Chgo. Coun. Fgn. Rels., Aspen Inst., 1986-92, Museum of Contemporary Art. Mem. ABA, Chgo. Bar Assn., Am. Law Inst., Chgo. Coun. Lawyers, Legal Club Chgo., Law Club Chgo., Comml. Club, Chgo. Club, Cliffdwellers Club, Mid-Day Club, Econs. Club, Point O'Woods Country Club (Mich.), Order of Coif. Home: 4950 S Chicago Beach Dr Chicago IL 60615-3207 Office: Mayer Brown & Platt 190 S La Salle St Ste 3100 Chicago IL 60603-3441

HELMAN, STEPHEN JODY, lawyer; b. Houston, Dec. 14, 1949; m. Gail Stevenson, 1974; children: Kimberley Brooke, Courtney Elizabeth, Caitlin Rebecca. BA in Spanish and Religion, So. Meth. U., 1971; postgrad., Perkins Sch. Theology, 1971-73; JD with honors, U. Tex., 1978. Bar: Tex., 1978; cert. estate planning and probate law, 1987. Assoc. Graves, Dougherty, Hearon & Moody, Austin, Tex., 1978-85, ptnr., shareholder, 1985-93; ptnr. Osborne, Lowe, Helman & Smith, L.L.P., Austin, Tex., 1993—; exam commr. in estate planning and probate law, Tex. Bd. Legal Specialization, 1990-94. Contbr. articles to profl. jours. Fellow Am. Coll. Trust and Estate Counsel (mem. profl. standards com. 1990-93); mem. ABA (mem. real property, probate, and trust law sects.), Coll. of the State Bar of Tex., State Bar Tex. (mem. real property, probate and trust law sects.), Travis County Bar Assn. (mem. probate and estate planning sect., pres. 1991-92, dir. 1989-92, ex-officio dir. 1992-93), Order of Coif. Avocations: nature photography, hiking. Office: Osborne Lowe Helman & Smith LLP 301 Congress Ave Ste 1900 Austin TX 78701-4041

HELMAR-SALASOO, ESTER ANETTE, literacy educator, researcher; b. Subiaco, W.A., Australia, Oct. 26, 1956; came to U.S., 1987; d. Harald R. and Liana M. (Kikas) H.; m. Lembit Salasoo, Jan. 2, 1988; children: Imbi, Markus, Kristjan. BA, U. W. Australia, Perth, Australia, 1977; Diploma in Edn., U. W. Australia, Perth, 1978; MS, SUNY, Albany, 1988; postgrad. studies in Edn., 1989—. Tchr. English, lit. Pub. Schs. W. Australia, 1978-85; ESL tchr. Tuart Coll., W. Australia, 1986; teaching asst. SUNY, Albany, 1988, rsch. asst., 1989-90; cons. Nat. Javits Project for Lang. Arts Rsch., Washington, 1992. Author: (reports) A National Study of States' Roles in Choosing Reading and Literature for Second Language Learning, 1993. Home: 2280 Berkley Ave Schenectady NY 12309-2726

HELMBOLD, NANCY PEARCE, classical languages educator; b. Abilene, Tex., Dec. 16, 1918; d. George Alfred and Bess (Hall) Pearce; m. William Clark Helmbold, July 27, 1958 (dec. 1969); 1 child, Alexandra Katherine. A.B., U. Tex.-Austin, 1939; M.A., U. Calif.-Berkeley, 1953, Ph.D., 1957. Asst. prof. Mt. Holyoke Coll., South Hadley, Mass., 1957-59; vis. asst. prof. U. Oreg., Eugene, 1961-63; asst. prof. U. Chgo., 1963-70, assoc. prof., 1970-83, prof., 1983—. Mem. editl. bd. Classical Philology, 1966—. Served to lt. (j.g.) USN, 1943-46. Mem. Am. Philol. Assn. Democrat. Club: Chgo. Classical (pres. 1981-83). Office: U Chgo 1050 E 59th St Chicago IL 60637-1559

HELMER, CAROL A., psychologist, school psychologist; b. Newport News, Apr. 24, 1946; d. Frederick Otto and Phyllis Amelia (Calf) Helmer; 1 child, Shannon Helmer Ducey. BA, Roanoke Coll., Salem, Va., 1967; MS, Radford U., Va., 1968; PhD, Hofstra U., 1985. Lic. psychologist, N.Y. Tchr. math. Brentwood (N.Y.) pub. schs., 1968-70, psychologist, 1970-72; psychotherapist Bi-County Cons. Ctr., Amityville, N.Y., 1970-78; psychologist BOCES II, Patchogue, N.Y., 1972-73, Middle Country Schs., Centereach, N.Y., 1973—; psychotherapist North Shore Cons., Smithtown, N.Y., 1978-82; pvt. practice psychology Coram, N.Y., 1986—; supr. interns, Hofstra U., 1980—, Adelphi U., 1985-86, Queens Coll., 1986-87, St. John's U., 1987—. Bd. dirs. Community House, Centreach, 1986-87. Redford U. grad. assistantship, 1967-68. Mem. APA (cert. in treatment of alcohol and other psychoactive substance user disorders), EMDRIA, N.Y. State Psychol. Assn. (pres. sch. divsn. 1994), Suffolk County Psychol. Assn. (sch. psychology com. chmn., exec. bd. mem. 1990-94), Rotary. Avocations: reading, gardening, swimming, walking, film/movie buff. Office: 1 Freemont Ln Coram NY 11727-3234

HELMER, M(ARTHA) CHRISTIE, lawyer; b. Portland, Oreg., Oct. 8, 1949; d. Marvin Curtis and Inez Bahl (Corwin) H.; m. Joe D. Bailey, June 23, 1979; children: Tim Bailey, Bill Bailey, Kim Easton. BA in English magna cum laude, Wash. State U., 1970; JD cum laude, Lewis & Clark Coll., 1974; LLM in Internat. Law, Columbia U., 1998. Bar: Oreg. 1974, U.S. Supreme Ct. 1975, U.S. Ct. Appeals (9th cir.) 1975. Assoc. Miller Nash, Portland, 1974-81, ptnr., 1981—; mem. Oreg. Bd. Bar Examiners, Portland, 1978-81; del. 9th Cir. Jud. Conf., 1984-87, mem. exec. com., 1987-90. Author: Arrest of Ships, 1985. Mem. ABA, Oreg. Bar (mem. bd. govs. 1981-84, treas. 1983-84), Maritime Law Assn., Internat. Bar Assn., Pacific N.W. Internat. Trade Assn. (bd. dirs., mem. exec. com.), Multnomah Athletic Club, Phi Beta Kappa. Avocations: antiques, travel, fashion. Office: Miller Nash 111 SW 5th Ave Ste 3500 Portland OR 97204-3699

HELMERICH, HANS CHRISTIAN, oil company executive; b. Tulsa, Okla., Sept. 4, 1958; s. Walter Hugo III and Peggy Josephine (Varnadow) H.; m. Lea Calhoon, Aug. 23, 1980; children: Isaac Breaker, Shelby Kate, Maxim Rainer, Sunday Lane, Hailey Beth. BA in Govt., Dartmouth Coll., 1981; cert. program mgmt. devel., Harvard U., 1985. Asst. to the pres. Helmerich & Payne, Inc., Tulsa, 1981-85, v.p., 1985-87, exec. v.p., dir., 1987, pres., chief operating officer, Dec., 1987—; chief exec. officer, 1989; bd. dirs. Atwood Oceanics, Inc., Fed. Res. Bank of Kansas City, 1996—. Commr. Tulsa Devel. Authority, 1986-87; bd. dirs. Hillcrest Med. Ctr. Assocs., Tulsa, 1982—, Gilcrease Mus. Assn., Tulsa, 1983—, Tulsa Area Unit Way, 1984—, Young Pres.'s Orgn., Inc., 1988—, Tulsa Boys' Home, 1990—; trustee Okla. Futures, Oklahoma City, 1987—, Fuller Theol. Sem., 1989—; dir. Indian Nations Coun., Tulsa, 1994, Okla. Heritage Assn., 1995—. Home: 2955 S Rockford Rd Tulsa OK 74114-5324 Office: Helmerich & Payne Inc 1579 E 21st St Ste 4 Tulsa OK 74114-1398

HELMETAG, STEVEN CHARLES, recording industry executive; b. West Lafayette, Ind., Dec. 19, 1961; s. Charles Hugh and Ruth Judith (Crispin) H.; m. Katherine Marie Bohusch, June 2, 1990; 1 child, Bernard Urban. BS, Villanova U., 1983; MBA, Drexel U., 1985. Cert. Am. Mgmt. Assn.; cert. small bus. mgmt. U. Pa. Program dir. WKVU, Villanova, Pa., 1982-83; supr. mktg. comm. AAMCO Transmissions, Bala Cynwyd, Pa., 1983-85; retail mgr. 8th St Music, Phila., 1985-94; project mgr. Disc Makers/Audio and Video Labs., Pennsauken, N.J., 1994—; CD-Rom team leader Disc Makers/Audio and Video Labs., Pennsauken, 1996—, customer svc. mgr., 1998—; on-air personality WZZD Radio, Lafayette Hill, Pa., 1986-87. Author, artist (video soundtrack) Slide-Aerobics, 1993, Nature Conservancy/Eastern Shore, 1994, (audio rec.) The Be Three "Get Organized", 1995. Recipient cert. achievement Roland Corp./U.S., L.A., 1992. Mem. Hist. Soc. Pa., Phila. Area New Media Assn. Home: 4804 Ogle St Philadelphia PA 19127-1905 Office: Disc Makers 7905 N Route 130 Pennsauken NJ 08110-1402

HELMHOLZ, AUGUST CARL, physicist, educator emeritus; b. Evanston, Ill., May 24, 1915; s. Henry F. and Isabel G. (Lindsay) H.; m. Elizabeth J. Little, July 30, 1938; children: Charlotte C.K. Colby, George L., Frederic V., Edith H. Roth. A.B., Harvard Coll., 1936; student, Cambridge U., 1936-37; Ph.D., U. Calif., Berkeley, 1940; Sc.D. (hon.), U. Strathclyde, 1979. Instr. physics U. Calif.-Berkeley, 1940-43, asst. prof., 1943-48, assoc. prof., 1948-51, prof., 1951-80, emeritus, 1980—, chmn. dept., 1955-62; rsch. physicist Lawrence Berkeley Lab., 1940—; mem. Vis. Scientist Program, 1966-71; governing bd. Am. Inst. Physics, 1964-67. Recipient Citation U. Calif., Berkeley, 1980; Berkeley fellow, 1988—, Guggenheim fellow, 1962-63. Fellow Am. Phys. Soc.; mem. AAAS, Am. Assn. Physics Tchrs., AAUP, Phi Beta Kappa, Sigma Xi. Home: 28 Crest Rd Lafayette CA 94549-3349 Office: U Calif Dept Physics Berkeley CA 94720

HELMHOLZ, R(ICHARD) H(ENRY), law educator; b. Pasadena, Calif., July 1, 1940; s. Lindsay and Alice (Bean) H.; m. Marilyn P. Helmholz. AB, Princeton U., 1962; JD, Harvard U., 1965; PhD, U. Calif., Berkeley, 1970; LLD, Trinity Coll., Dublin, 1992. Bar: Mo. 1965. Prof. law and hist. Washington U., St. Louis, 1970-81; prof. law U. Chgo., 1981—; Maitland lectr. Cambridge U., 1987. Author: Marriage Litigation, 1975, Select Cases on Defamation, 1985, Canon Law and the Law of England, 1987, Roman Canon Law in Reformation England, 1990, Spirit of Classical Canon Law, 1996. Guggenheim fellow, 1986; recipient Von Humboldt rsch. prize, 1992. Fellow Brit. Acad. (corr.), Am. Acad. Arts and Scis., Medieval Acad. Am.; mem. ABA, Am. Soc. Legal History (pres. 1992-94), Selden Soc. (v.p. 1984-87), Univ. Club, Reform Club. Home: 5757 S Kimbark Ave Chicago IL 60637-1614 Office: U Chgo Law Sch 1111 E 60th St Chicago IL 60637-2776

HELMICK, D.O., protective services official. A.Police Sci., Yuba (Calif.) Coll.; BA, Golden Gate U.; grad., FBI Nat. Inst. State trooper Calif. Hwy. Patrol, Sacramento, 1969-75, liaison to legis., spl. rep., 1975-86; comdr. coastal divsn. Calif. Hwy. Patrol, San Luis Obispo, 1986-89; dep. commr. Calif. Hwy. Patrol, Sacramento, 1989-95, commr., 1995—. Office: Calif Highway Patrol PO Box 942898 Sacramento CA 94298-0001*

HELMICK, RAYMOND GLEN, priest, educator; b. Arlington, Mass., Sept. 7, 1931; s. Raymond Glen and Alice Cecilia (Clancy) H. BA, Boston Coll., 1956, MA in philosphy, 1957; lic. philosphy, Weston Coll., 1957; lic. theol., Hochschule St. Georgen, Frankfurt, 1964. Joined Jesuit Order, 1949, ordained priest Roman Cath. Ch., 1963. Assoc. dir. Ctr. for Human Rights & Responsibilities, London, 1973-79, Inst. Soc. Rsch., London, 1973-79; found., co-dir. Ctr. of Concern for Human Dignity, London, 1979-81; sr. assoc. Conflict Analysis Ctr., Washington, 1982—; prof. of conflict resolution Boston Coll., 1984—; exec. comm. U.S. Interreligious Comm. for Peace in the Middle East, Seattle, 1987—, adv. bd. Organ. for Human Rights in Iraq, Boston, 1992—. Author: (with Richard Hauser) A Social Option, 1975, La Question Libanaise Selon Raymond Edde, 1990. Mediation No. Irish conflict, 1972-81, 92—, Kurdish conflict, 1973-81, 87—, Lebanese conflict, 1982—, Israeli-Palestinian conflict, 1986—, Balkan conflict, 1995—. Democrat. Roman Catholic. Office: Boston Coll Chestnut Hill MA 02467

HELMKE, (WALTER) PAUL, mayor, lawyer; b. Bloomington, Ind., Nov. 24, 1948; s. Walter P. and Rowene Mary (Crabill) H.; m. Deborah Jane Andrews, Aug. 23, 1969; children: Laura Andrews, Kathryn Elizabeth. BA with highest honors, Ind. U., 1970; JD, Yale U., 1973. Bar: Ind. 1973, Fla. 1982. Lawyer Helmke Beams Boyer Wagner, Ft. Wayne, Ind., 1973-87; mayor City Ft. Wayne, 1988—; asst. county atty. Allen County, Ft. Wayne, 1974-87; pres. Nat. Rep. Mayors and Local Ofcls. Orgn., 1993; pres. U.S. Conf. of Mayors, 1997—. Chmn. Allen-Wells chpt. ARC, Ft. Wayne, 1985-87; candidate for Rep. nomination 4th U.S. Congl. Dist.-Ind., 1980; Rep. nominee for U.S. Senate, Ind., 1998; bd. dirs. Nat. League of Cities, 1995-97, chair pub. safety and crime prevention com., 1995. Recipient J.C. Gallagher prize Law Sch. Yale U., New Haven, Conn., 1972. Mem. Ind. Assn. Cities and Towns (pres. 1996-97). Republican. Lutheran. Home: 1215 Korte Ln Fort Wayne IN 46807-2920 Office: Office of the Mayor City-County Bldg Rm 900 1 E Main St Fort Wayne IN 46802*

HELMLE, RALPH PETER, computer systems developer, manager; b. Detroit, Sept. 12, 1962; s. Ronald and Ingeborg (Kalb) H. BSME, Lawrence Tech. U., 1987; MS in Sys. Engring., Oakland U., Rochester, Mich., 1991. Registered profl. engr., Mich. Student designer Kent-Moore Stamping & Fabrication, Detroit, 1978-79; hardware tool and process engr. Fisher Body divsn. GM Corp., Warren, Mich., 1979-82; indsl. sys. engr. Fisher Guide divsn. GM Corp., Troy, Mich., 1982-85; site personal computer adminstr. Delphi Interior and Lighting Sys., GMC, Troy, Mich., 1985-96; sector PC deployment mgr. Delphi Automotive Sys., Troy, 1996-97; mgr. global desktop processes GM Info. Sys. and Svcs., Detroit, 1998—. Mem. Lambda Iota Tau. Home: 11584 Adams Dr Warren MI 48093-1137 Office: GM Info Sys and Svcs 1155 Brewery Park Blvd Detroit MI 48207-2668

HELMREICH, JONATHAN ERNST, history educator; b. Brunswick, Maine, Dec. 21, 1936; s. Ernst Christian and Louise Bertha (Roberts) H.; m. Martha Anne Schaff, Aug. 22, 1959 (div. 1978); children—Anne Linden, Dana Louise, Douglas Ernst Folger; m. Nancy L. Ross, Feb. 21, 1979. B.A. magna cum laude, Amherst Coll., 1958; M.A., Princeton, 1959, Ph.D., 1961; postgrad. (Fulbright grantee), Free U. of Brussels, 1961-62. Teaching asst. Princeton, 1961; asst. prof. Allegheny Coll., Meadville, Pa., 1962-66; asso. prof. Allegheny Coll., 1966-72, prof., 1972—, dean of instrn., 1966-81. Author: Belgium and Europe: A Study in Small Power Diplomacy, 1976, Gathering Rare Ores: The Diplomacy of Uranium Acquisition, 1943-54, 86, U.S. Relations with Belgium and the Congo, 1940-60, 98 (with others) Rebirth: A History of Europe since World War II, 1st ed. 1992, 2nd ed. 1999; contbr. articles to profl. publs. Mem. Pa. Trial Judge Nominating Commn. for Crawford County, 1973-75; Pres., bd. dirs. United Housing Corp. of Meadville, Fairview Housing Corp. of Meadville; bd. mem. United Way at Western Crawford County, 1996-99. Mem. Am. Hist. Assn., Crawford County Hist. Soc., Phi Beta Kappa, Pi Gamma Mu, Phi Alpha Theta. Democrat. Methodist. Club: Rotarian. Home: 370 Jefferson St Meadville PA 16335-1457

HELMREICH, WILLIAM BENNO, sociology educator, consultant; b. Zurich, Switzerland, Aug. 25, 1945; came to U.S., 1946; s. Leo and Charlotte (Preiss) H.; m. Helaine Phyllis Gewirtz, June 28, 1970; children: Jeffrey, Joseph, Deborah. BA, Yeshiva U., 1967; MA, Washington U., St. Louis, 1970, PhD, 1971. Vis., lectr., postdoctoral fellow Yale U., 1972-73; prof. dept. sociology CCNY, Grad. Ctr. CUNY, 1973—; chmn. bd. Byron Rsch. and Consulting, Great Neck, N.Y., 1976—. Author: Wake Up, Wake Up to Do the Work of the Creator, 1976 (Book of Month Club award 1977), The Things They Say Behind Your Back, 1982, Against All Odds, 1992 (Nat. Jewish Book award), 7 other books; editor: Issues in Contemporary Society, 1991. Pres. North Shore Hebrew Acad., Great NEck, 1980-90, v.p. bd., 1991—. Recipient award NEH, 1972, 78, Outstanding Young Man of Am. award Jaycees of Am., 1977; Woodrow Wilson fellow, 1970-71, Spencer Found. fellow, 1979. Mem. Am. Sociol. Assn. Avocations: tennis, travel, chess, reading. Office: CCNY Dept Sociology 138th St and Convent Ave New York NY 10031

HELMRICH, JOEL MARC, lawyer; b. Bklyn., Apr. 15, 1953; s. William and Edna (Steigman) H.; m. Barbara Ellen Richter, Sept. 2, 1984; children: Joshua David, Rachel Marysa. BS, Cornell U., 1975, MBA, 1976; JD, Syracuse U., 1979. Bar: Pa. 1979, U.S. Dist. Ct. (we. dist.) Pa. 1979. Assoc. Tucker Arensberg, P.C., Pitts., 1979-86; shareholder Tucker Arensberg, Pitts., 1986-99; ptnr. Meyer, Unkovic & Scott, LLP, Pitts., 1999—. Mem. Pa. Bar Assn., Allegheny County Bar Assn., Comml. Law League Am., Am. Bankruptcy Inst., Rolling Hills Country Club, Cornell Club. Avocations: golf, tennis. Office: Unkovil & Scott LLP 1300 Oliver Bldg Pittsburgh PA 15222-2304

HELMS, BYRON ELDON, associate director of research, biology and physiology administrator; b. Pitts., June 2, 1951; s. John Donald and Evelyn Marie (Wilson) H.; m. Gale Ann Barbarine Helms, Jan. 23, 1976 (div. Mar. 13, 1978); m. Shari Elisa Besterman Helms, Sept. 16, 1978; children: Brandon, Thomas, Nicholas. Ba in English, Duquesne U., Pitts., 1974. Field underwriter N.Y. Life Ins., Pitts., 1974; asst. legal adminstr. Eckert, Seamans, Cherin & Mellott, Pitts., 1974-77; legal adminstr. Hayward, Cooper, Straub & Cramer, Toledo, 1977-78; adminstr., Cell Biology and Physiology U. Pitts. Sch. Medicine, 1978-95; assoc. dir. U. Ill. at Chicago, Chgo., 1995—; P-30 adminstr. Nat. Inst. Child Health and Human Devel., Washington, 1978-94; dir., treas., bd. govs. Faculty Club U. Pitts., 1985-94; charter mem., officer Duquesne U. Arts and Sci. Alumni Assn., Pitts., 1992-94; dir., bd. mgmt. South Hills YMCA, Pitts., 1994-97; tax acct. H&R Block, 1995—. Editor: University of Pittsburgh Financial System Overview, 1986. Longhouse officer YMCA Indian Guide Program, Pitts., 1987-93; mgmt. officer YMCA Trailblazer Program, Pitts., 1991-96; unit coord. United Way, Pitts., 1978-94; mgr., coach Mt. Lebanon (Pa.) Baseball Assn., 1989-94. Recipient Honor award, 1993 Sy Lerner Meml. award, 1994, South Hills YMCA, Pitts., Cmty. Svc. award United Way, Pitts., 1994. Mem. Soc. Rsch. Adminstrs., Nat. Coun. Univ. Rsch. Adminstrs., Am. Mgmt. Assn., Islam Grotto Mystic Order of Veiled Prophets of Enchanted Realm, Grand Lodge of Pa., Crafton Lodge. Republican. Lutheran. Avocations: manage and coach baseball, soccer, football, basketball. Home: 912 Royal Blackheath Ct Naperville IL 60563-2304 Office: Univ of Illinois at Chicago Office Rsch Svcs 1737 W Polk St Chicago IL 60612-7224

HELMS, CHARLES MILTON, medical educator, consultant; b. Cambridge, Mass., May 5, 1942; s. James Thoburn and Alice Francis (Cooke) H.; m. Lelia Meredith Biggs, June 26, 1966; children: Emily (dec.), Wesley, Bethany, Timothy. AB, Cornell U., 1964; PhD, U. Rochester, 1969, MD, 1971. Resident Mass. Gen. Hosp., Boston, 1971-73; rsch. assoc. NIH, Bethesda, 1973-76; prof. U. Iowa, Iowa City, 1976—; fellow Robert Wood Johnson Health Policy Fellowship Program, Washington, 1985-86; mem. nat. vaccine adv. com. U.S. HHS, 1992-96; mem. adv. com. immunization practices Ctr. Disease Control and Prevention, 1997—. Contbr. articles to profl. jours. and chpts. to books. Bd. dirs. Goodwill Industries Internat., Inc., 1987-93, 94-98, chmn., 1995-97. Med. officer USPHS, 1973-76. Fellow ACP (Laureate award 1997), Infectious Diseases Soc. Am. (chmn. pub. policy com. 1993-97). Methodist. Office: U Iowa Coll Medicine 200 Hawkins Dr Iowa City IA 52242-1009

HELMS, J. LYNN, former government agency administrator; b. DeQueen, Ark., Mar. 1, 1925; s. Frank and Mamie (Johnson) H.; m. Lorraine Bisgard, Mar. 16, 1947; children: Loralyn, Jon, Carole, Zack. Dir. mktg. and sales N. Am. Aviation Co., Columbus, Ohio, 1956-62; group v.p. Bendix Corp., Ann Arbor, Mich., 1962-70; pres. Norden div. United Technologies Corp., Norwalk, Conn., 1970-74, Piper Aircraft Corp., Lock Haven, Pa., 1974-81; chmn. bd. Piper Aircraft Corp., 1978-81; adminstr. FAA, Washington, 1981-83; dir. Birchminster Industries. Served to lt. col. USMC, 1944-55. Decorated Air medal with oak leaf cluster. Fellow AIAA; mem. Soc. Exptl. Test Pilots.

HELMS, JESSE, senator; b. Monroe, NC, Oct. 18, 1921; s. Jesse Alexander and Ethel Mae (Helms) H.; m. Dorothy Jane Coble, Oct. 31, 1942; children: Jane (Mrs. Charles R. Knox), Nancy (Mrs. John C. Stuart), Charles. Student, Wingate (N.C.) Jr. Coll., Wake Forest Coll. City editor Raleigh (N.C.) Times, 1941-42; news and program dir. Sta. WRAL, Raleigh, 1948-51; adminstrv. asst. to U.S. senators Willis Smith and Alton Lennon, 1951-53; exec. dir. N.C. Bankers Assn., 1953-60; exec. v.p., vice chmn. Capitol Broadcasting Co., Raleigh, 1960-72; U.S. senator from N.C., 1973—; chmn. Agriculture, Nutrition and Forestry subcom. on Mktg., Inspection & Product Promotion, Com. on Fgn. Relations; mem. Rules & Adminstrn. Com., Republican Policy Com.; chmn. bd. Specialized Agrl. Publs., Inc., Raleigh, 1964-72; mem. Raleigh City Council, 1957-61. Bd. dirs. N.C. Cerebral Palsy Hosp., Durham, United Cerebral Palsy N.C., Wake County Cerebral Palsy and Rehab. Center, Raleigh, Camp Willow Run, Littleton, N.C.; former trustee Campbell Coll., Wingate Coll., Meredith Coll., John F. Kennedy Coll. Served with USNR, 1942-45, World War II. Recipient Freedoms Found. award for best TV editorial, 1962, for newspaper article, 1973, So. Bapt. Nat. award for Service to mankind, 1972; Gold medal VFW; Conservative Congressional award, 1976; Liberty award Am. Econ. Council, 1978; Disting. Public Service award Public Service Research Council, 1978; Watchdog of Treasury award; Guardian of Small Bus. award; named Man of Yr. Women for Constl. Govt., 1978; Legislator of Yr. award Nat. Rifle Assn., 1978, Taxpayer's Best Friend award Nat. Taxpayer's Union, 1993; other awards. Republican. Baptist (deacon). Clubs: Rotary (past pres. Raleigh), Raleigh Executives (past pres.), Masons (32 degree). Office: US Senate 403 Dirksen Senate Bldg Washington DC 20510*

HELMS, MICKY, engineering executive; b. Oklahoma City, July 25, 1934; d. John Talbert and Lora V. (Lyons) Kelly; m. Jimmie A. Helms, July 14, 1953; children: Kelly Janine, James Michael, Jennifer Ann. AS, Midland (Tex.) Coll., 1975. Engring. technician TU Electric, Midland, 1958-92; corp. sec., treas. Helms and May Engring, Inc., Midland, 1992—. Mem. Dachshund Club of Am. Avocations: breeding and showing wirehaired dachshunds and basset hounds, painting, photography. Home: 1909 W County Road 140 Midland TX 79706-6975 Office: Helms and May Engring Inc 2500 N Big Spring St Ste 280 Midland TX 79705-6675

HELMS, RICHARD MCGARRAH, international consultant, former ambassador; b. St. Davids, Pa., Mar. 30, 1913; s. Herman H. and Marion (McGarrah) H.; m. Julia Bretzman Shields, Sept. 8, 1939 (div. 1968); 1 son, Dennis J.; m. Cynthia McKelvie, 1968. B.A., Williams Coll., 1935. Staff corr. UP, Europe, 1935-37; mem. staff Indpls. Times Pub. Co., 1937-42; with CIA, 1947-73, dep. dir., then dir., 1965-73; ambassador to Iran, 1973-76; internat. cons., 1977-97; pres. Safeer Co., Washington, 1977-97. Served with OSS USNR, 1942-46, ETO. Recipient Career Service award Nat. Civil Service League, 1965, Disting. Intelligence medal, 1973, Nat. Security medal, 1983. Mem. Phi Beta Kappa. Office: 4649 Garfield St NW Washington DC 20007-1026

HELMS, ROBERT BRAKE, economist, research director; b. Mobile, Ala., Jan. 12, 1940; s. Osburn Charles and Julia May (Moore) H.; m. Sharon Gay Schliebe, Aug. 8, 1964; children—Elissa Lynelle, Julianne Nanette. B.S. in Agrl. Adminstrn., Auburn U., 1962; M.A. in Econs., UCLA, 1966, Ph.D. in Econs., 1973. Asst. prof. Loyola Coll., Balt., 1971-74; dir. health policy studies Am. Enterprise Inst., Washington, 1974-81, resident scholar, dir. health policy studies, 1990; dep. asst. sec. planning and evaluation/health HHS, Washington, 1981-84, acting asst. sec. planning and evaluation, 1984-86, asst. sec. for planning and evaluation, 1986-89; exec. dir. Am. Pharm. Inst., 1989-90; chmn. Sec.'s Task Force on Hosp. Deregulation, Washington, 1981-83, Sec.'s Task Force on Drug Reimbursement, Washington, 1983-85; mem. White House Working Group on Health Policy and Econs., Washington, 1984-85; mem. steering com. Health Policy Agenda Am. People, Chgo., 1984-88; mem. working party on social policy OECD, Paris, 1984-89. Author: Natural Gas Regulation, 1974; editor: Drug Development and Marketing, 1975, The International Supply of Medicines, 1980, Drugs and Health, 1981, American Health Policy: Critical Issues for Reform, 1993, Health Care Policy and Politics: Lessons From Four Countries, 1993, Health Care Reform: Competition and Controls, 1993, Competitive Strategies in the Pharmaceutical Industry, 1996, Medicare in the Twenty-first Century: Seeking Fair and Efficient Reform, 1999. Served to capt. U.S. Army, 1962-64. Republican. Lutheran. Avocations: tennis, travel, internet. Home: 1404 Foggy Glen Ct Silver Spring MD 20906-2092 Office: Am Enterprise Inst 1150 17th St NW Washington DC 20036-4603

HELMS, VERNON LAMAR, telecommunications executive; b. Nov. 8, 1948. BA, Wake Forest U., 1971, MA, 1975; MDiv, So. Theol. Sem., 1987. Sr. mgmt. Bell South, Atlanta, 1987—. Vol. music dir. Chapel, Big Canoe, 1996—. E-mail: lamarhelms@mindspring.com. Home: 747 Big Canoe Big Canoe GA 30143

HELMS GUBA, LISA MARIE, nursing administrator; b. Sioux City, Iowa, Nov. 24, 1962; d. Dean Edward and Betty Lou Victora (Guenther) H. BA in Nursing, Carroll Coll., Helena, Mont., 1986; postgrad., Calif. State U., Sacramento, 1990-92; MSN, Incarnate Word Coll., 1996. Cert. pediatric nurse. Enlisted U.S. Army, 1981, advanced through grades to capt., 1990; nurse U.S. Army, San Francisco, 1986-90, Calif. Nat. Guard, San Francisco, 1990-92, Rio Linda (Calif.) Union Sch. Dist., 1990-92; enlisted USAF, 1992; mem. A.F. Nurse Corps Wilford Hall Med Ctr., Lackland AFB, Tex., 1992-

96; asst. nurse mgr. and critical care aeromed. transp. team nurse dir. Malcolm Grow Hosp., Andrews AFB, Md., 1996—; deployed to Guantanamo Bay, Cuba, July to Oct. 1994 for Operation Sea Signal, Operation Safe Haven; provider med. care to Haitian/Cuban migrants. Vol. Big sister/Big brother program United Way. Decorated Humanitarian Svc. medal, Army Commendation medal, Air Force Commendation medal. Mem. AACN, Emergency Nurses Assn., Nat. Assn. Flight Nurses. Roman Catholic.

HELMSING, FREDERICK GEORGE, lawyer; b. Mobile, Ala., Dec. 30, 1940; s. Joseph Herman and Mary Gertrude (Zimlich) H.; m. Margaret Sue Oswalt, Mar. 22, 1969; children: Frederick George, Joseph Guy, Margaret Sue. BS in Acctg., Spring Hill Coll., 1963; JD, U. Ala., 1965; LLM in Taxation, NYU, 1967. Bar: Ala. 1965, Fla. 1989. Assoc. Gallalee, Denniston & Edington, Mobile, 1966-76; ptnr. Helmsing, Lyons, Sims & Leach, Mobile, 1976—; instr. U. South Ala., Mobile, 1969-78; instr. law U. Ala., Mobile, 1982. Active Mobile Estate Planning Coun.; Dem. chmn. 1st Congl. Dist. Campaign, 1976. Mem. ABA (mem. civil and criminal tax penalties com.), Ala. State Bar Assn. (chmn. tax sect. 1979-80), Mobile County Bar Assn. (treas. 1969), Mobile Bar Assn., Mobile Area C. of C. (mem. taxation and world trade coms.), Navy League U.S., Athelstan Country Club. Roman Catholic. Home: 240 Ridgelawn Dr E Mobile AL 36608-2417 Office: Helmsing Lyons Sims & Leach 200 LaClede Bldg 150 Government St Mobile AL 36602-3114

HELMSLEY, LEONA MINDY, hotel executive; b. N.Y.C.; m. Harry B. Helmsley, Apr. 8, 1972 (dec. Jan., 1997). Vice pres. Pease & Elliman, N.Y.C., 1962-69; pres. Sutton & Towne Residential, N.Y.C., 1967-70; sr. v.p. Helmsley Spear, N.Y.C., 1970-72, Brown, Harris, Stevens, N.Y.C., 1970-72; pres., CEO, chmn. bd. Helmsley Hotels, Inc., N.Y.C., 1980—. Named Woman of Yr. N.Y. Council Civic Affairs, 1970; named Woman of Yr. Town & Country Condos & Coops., 1981; recipient Service award Ort Sch. Engring., 1981, Profl. Excellence award Les Dames d'Escoffier, 1981, Spl. Achievement award Sales Execs. Club N.Y., 1981, Woman of Yr. award Internat. Hotel Industry, 1982. Home: 36 Central Park S New York NY 10019-1600 Office: Helmsley Hotels Inc 230 Park Ave New York NY 10169-0005

HELMSTETTER, CHARLES EDWARD, microbiologist; b. Newark, Oct. 18, 1933; s. Charles Edward and Elsa Simpson (Taylorson) H.; m. Wendy Lee; children—Charles Edward, Michael Frederick, Lee Grisetti. B.A., Johns Hopkins U., 1955; M.S., U. Mich., 1956, U. Chgo., 1957; Ph.D., U. Chgo., 1961. Scientist NIH, Bethesda, Md., 1961-63; USPHS fellow U. Copenhagen, 1963-64; scientist Roswell Park Meml. Inst., Buffalo, 1964-89, dir. dept. exptl. biology, 1974-89; prof. biol. scis. Fla. Inst. Tech., Melbourne, 1989—. Contbr. articles to sci. jours.; mem. editorial bd.: Jour. Bacteriology, 1970-76, 80-86. Recipient Selman A Waksman award Theobald Smith Soc., 1970; yearly NIH grantee, 1965—. Mem. AAAS, Am. Soc. Microbiology, Am. Soc. Biol. Chemists, Sigma Xi. Home: 854 Hawksbill Island Dr Melbourne FL 32937-3850 Office: Fla Inst Tech Dept of Biol Scis Melbourne FL 32901

HELMUTH, LES N., fund raising executive, non-profit consultant; b. Mattoon, Ill., July 19, 1955; s. Noah B. and Edna L. (Miller) H.; m. Sylvia Jean Clymer, Dec. 16, 1978; children: Aubrey Diane, Mary Caitlin. BA in Music, Ea. Mennonite U., 1978. Dir. alumni and ch. rels. Ea. Mennonite U., 1978-83; dir. devel. Spokane (Wash.) Symphony Orch., 1983-85, Ea. Mennonite H.S., Harrisonburg, Va., 1985—; cons. Devel. Systems Internat., Inc., Frederick, Md., 1997—. Bd. dirs. Rotary, Harrisonburg, 1993-96, Highland Retreat Camp, Bergton, Va., 1993—. Mem. Nat. Soc. Fund Raising Execs. (cert., pres. 1998), Harrisonburg-Rockingham County C. of C., Nat. Com. on Planned Giving, Va. Ind. Schs. Devel. Coun. Mennonite. Avocations: music, golf, tennis, travel. Home: 3158 Rawley Pike Harrisonburg VA 22801-9082 Office: Ea Mennonite HS 801 Parkwood Dr Harrisonburg VA 22802-2416

HELMUTH, NED D, financial planner; b. Kokomo, Ind., Mar. 24, 1928; s. Dewey J. and Mildred C. (Norton) H.; m. Arlene J. Schwartz, Oct. 5, 1952 (div. 1971); children: Pamela M. Jones, Michael J., Gretchen L.; m. S. Patricia Broadhurst Tautfest, Jan. 4, 1973; 1 child, Carol E. Green. BS in Mktg., Ind. U., 1952; MS in Fin. Services, Am. Coll., 1981. Cert. fin. planner; chartered fin. cons.; chartered life underwriter. Agt. Equitable Life Assurance Soc., Houston, 1952-53, Lafayette, Ind., 1953-58; agt. Nat. Life Ins. Co., Lafayette, 1958—; prin. Ned D Helmuth Fin. Svcs., Lafayette; nat. trustee Life Underwriters Tng. Council, Washington, 1975-78. Author: The Client Approach-A Quality Method of Selling, 1963, There's No Fun Like Work, 1989. Bd. dirs. South Side Cmty. Ctr., Lafayette, 1955-57, Lafayette Urban MInistry, 1975-78, Big Bros./Big Sisters, Lafayette, 1981-83, Million Dollar Round Table Internat. Found., 1990-93; life mem. Million Dollar Round Table; mem. adv. bd. Salvation Army, Lafayette, 1985-88; trustee Family Svcs., Inc., Lafayette, 1991-93; vol. Network Ind. U. Found. Cpl. U.S. Army, 1946-48, Korea. Named Underwriter of Yr. Lafayette Assn. Life Underwriters, 1972, Hoosier Underwriter of Yr. Ind. State Assn. Life Underwriters, 1972. Mem. Nat. Assn. Life Underwriters, Am. Soc. CIU's (bd. dirs., v.p. 1965-68), Am. Inst. Cert. Fin. Planners, Hoosier Hills Estate Planning Coun., Phi Gamma Delta, Rotary Club. Avocations: jogging, tennis, old Porsches. Home: 612 Winslow Farm Dr Bloomington IN 47401-4590 Office: Ned D Helmuth Fin Svcs Bank One Bldg 201 Main St Ste 1000 Lafayette IN 47901-1275 also: 7037 S Tamiami Trl Sarasota FL 34231-5552 also: 4325 E 3rd St Bloomington IN 47401-5551

HELMUTH, PHILIP ALAN, tax consultant; b. Alhambra, Calif., Dec. 29, 1965; s. Melvin I. and Elsie (Borkholder) H. Student, MiraCosta Coll., 1985-89, Palomar Coll., 1989-90. Data entry operator Melco Bus. Svc., Vista, Calif., 1980-83, bookkeeper, 1983-91, ptnr., tax cons., 1992-95, owner, 1995—; bookkeeper Underwater Schs. of Am., Oceanside, 1985-86; owner, notary pub. Vista, 1987—; owner Melco Bus. Svcs., Vista, 1995—; registered rep. H.D. Vest Fin. Svcs. Mem. Nat. Notary Assn. (com. mem. editl. adv. com. 1990-93, pub. image com. 1990-93), Nat. Assn. Enrolled Agts., Calif. Soc. Enrolled Agts. (Palomar chpt. dir. 1995-96, 2d v.p. 1996-98), Escondido Grad. Spokesman Club (sec. 1991-92, pres. 1992-93, treas. 1993-95). Avocations: singing, collecting compact discs, reading history, science fiction. Office: Melco Bus Svc Ste 102 410 S Santa Fe Ave Vista CA 92084-6163

HELOISE, columnist, lecturer, broadcaster, author; b. Waco, Tex., Apr. 15, 1951; d. Marshal H. and Heloise K. (Bowles) Cruse; m. David L. Evans, Feb. 13, 1981. B.S. in Math. and Bus, S.W. Tex. State U., 1974. Owner, pres. Heloise, Inc. Asst. to columnist mother, Heloise, 1974-77, upon her death took over internationally syndicated column, 1977; author: Hints from Heloise, 1980, Help from Heloise, 1981, Heloise's Beauty Book, 1985, All-New Hints from Heloise, 1989, Heloise: Hints for a Healthy Planet, 1990, Heloise from A to Z, 1992, Household Hints for Singles, 1993, Hints for All Occasions, 1995; contbg. editor Good Housekeeping mag., 1981, Speaker for the House; co-founder, 1st co-pilot Mile Pie in the Sky Balloon Club. Mem. Good Neighbor Coun. Tex.-Mex.; sponsor Nat. Smile Week. Recipient Mental Health Mission award Nat. Mental Health Assn., 1990, The Carnegians Good Human Rels. award, 1994. Mem. AFTRA, SAG, Women in Comm. (Headliner 1994), Tex. Press Women, Internat. Women's Forum, Women in Radio and TV, Confrerie de la Chaine des Rotisseurs (bailli San Antonio chpt.), Ordre Mondial des Gourmets De'Gustateurd de U.S.A., Death Valley Yacht and Racket Club, Zonta. Home: PO Box 795000 San Antonio TX 78279-5000 Office: care King Features Syndicate 235 E 45th St New York NY 10017-3305

HELPER, LEE, public relations executive. Pres. Bender, Helper Impact, L.A. Office: Bender Goldman & Bender 11500 W Olympic Blvd Ste 655 Los Angeles CA 90064-1597*

HELPERN, DAVID MOSES, shoe corporation executive; b. Boston, Nov. 14, 1917; s. Myron Earl and Rose H.; m. Charlotte Cooper, May 2, 1943 (dec. 1948); children: David Moses, Elizabeth; m. Joan Marshall Gruen, Aug. 14, 1960. AB, Harvard U., 1938, postgrad., 1940. Chmn. bd. Joan & David Helpern, Inc., N.Y.C., 1948—; chmn. Suburban Shoe Stores, Inc., Cambridge, Mass., 1948—; cons. Melville Shoe Corp., N.Y.C., 1966-67; mem. overseers' com. on univ. resources Harvard U., 1993—. Mem. Harvard Coll. com. on univ. resources, 1993—; vis. com. Harvard Grad. Sch. Edn., 1998—; bd. mem. Boston Latin Sch. Found. Recipient Coty award, 1978. Mem. Fashion Footwear Assn. N.Y. (founder, steering com., vice-chmn. 1988-93, chmn. 1993-94, Lifetime Achievement award 1996), Nat. Shoe Retailers Assn. (dir. 1966-69), Harvard Club. Democrat. Jewish. Home: 1010 Memorial Dr Cambridge MA 02138-4859 Office: Joan and David Helpern Inc 4 W 58th St New York NY 10019-2515 also: 1935 Revere Beach Pkwy Everett MA 02149-5922

HELPERN, JOAN (JOAN MARSHALL), designer, business executive; b. N.Y.C., Oct. 10, 1926; d. Edward and Ethel (Tilzer) Marshall; m. David M. Helpern, Aug. 14, 1960; children—David M., Elizabeth Joan. BA, Hunter Coll., N.Y.C., 1947; MA, Columbia U., 1948; postgrad., Harvard U., 1960-67. Psychologist, author, educator, lectr., 1948-68; pres., CEO, chief designer Joan and David (footwear, sportswear, accessory design/mfg.), N.Y.C., 1968—; fashion designer, pres. Joan Helpern Designs, Inc., N.Y.C. Author: Guidance of Children in the Elementary Schools. Recipient Coty award Am. Design, 1978, FFANY Footwear Designer award, 1992, Fairchild Footwear Designer award, 1992, Fairchild Hall of Fame award, 1993, Michelangelo Footwear Design award, 1993, Female Bus. Owners award, 1993-94, Athena award Hunter Coll., 1996; Columbia U. grantee, 1947-48; named one of 50 Leading Female Entrepreneurs of World, 1998, 50 Leading Bus. Women of World, Working Woman, 1995, 96, 97, 98. Mem. Com. of 200 (founding mem.). Office: 4 W 58th St New York NY 10019-2515

HELPERT-NUNEZ, RUTH ANNE, clinical social worker, psychotherapist; b. Rosebud, Tex., Jan. 7, 1956; d. Otto Henry and Lorene Margaret (Hoelscher) Helpert; m. J.W. Will Nunez. BS with high honors in Social Work, U. Tex., Austin, 1978, MS in Social Work, 1981. Lic. master social worker-advanced clin. practitioner; lic. marriage and family therapist, Tex. Student intern Child Protective Svcs. Tex. Dept. Human Svcs., Austin, 1978; child protective svcs. specialist Tex. Dept. Human Svcs., Killeen and Belton, 1979-80; grad. student intern Austin Child Guidance Ctr., 1981; caseworker Heart of Tex. Region Mental Health Mental Retardation, Waco, Tex., 1981-83; child protective svcs. specialist Tex. Dept. Human Svcs., Austin, 1983-84; caseworker DayGlo Family Treatment program Austin-Travis County Mental Health Mental Retardation Ctr., 1984-88; therapist, clin. social worker Anthony W. Arden, Ph.D & Assocs., Bryan, Tex., 1989-90, Thomas Edwards, Ph.D., P.C., Bryan, 1990-95; therapist/clin. social worker Brazos Valley Cmty. Action Agy.-Family Health Svcs.: Psychology Svcs., Bryan, 1996-98; contract svcs. provider Bryan, 1998—; therapist. clin. social worker Los Hermanos Ranch, Bryan, 1998—; clin. vol. Scotty's House Child Advocacy Ctr., 1992—; field instr. U. Houston Grad. Sch. Social Work, 1995-96. Bd. dirs. Toy Libr., College Station, Tex., 1989; mem. spkrs. bur. Child Advocacy Resource and Edn. Coalition, 1989-92, v.p., 1991. Mem. NASW (diplomate, qualified clin. social worker, chmn. Brazos Valley unit 1990-94, bd. dirs. Tex. chpt. 1990-94, exec. com. 1993-94, chmn. profl. stds. com. 1993-94), Acad. Cert. Social Workers, Phi Kappa Phi, Phi Theta Kappa. Democrat. Avocations: handbuilding pottery, gardening, Renaissance music, playing recorder. Home: 10004 Edge Cut Off Rd Hearne TX 77859-9322 also: Los Hermanos Ranch Broach Rd Bryan TX 77808

HELPHAND, BEN J., actuary; b. Columbus, Nebr., Feb. 2, 1915; s. David and Bess (Krupinsky) H.; m. Bessie H. Stine, Sept. 16, 1937; 1 child, Cathy Dee. Student, U. Nebr., 1932-35; B.A., U. Iowa, 1936, M.A., 1937. Actuarial asst. Pacific Mut. Life Ins. Co., Newport Beach, Calif., 1937-42; v.p., actuary Pacific Mut. Life Ins. Co., 1947-80; corp. actuary Best Life Assurance Co., Irvine, Calif., 1980-87; actuary Dept. Ins. State S.C., Columbia, 1946-47. Served to maj. USAAF, 1942-46. Fellow Soc. Actuaries (bd. govs.); mem. actuarial clubs Pacific States (past pres.), Los Angeles (past pres.), Am. Acad. Actuaries, Sigma Xi. Home: 1321 Keel Dr Corona Del Mar CA 92625-1238

HELPPIE, CHARLES EVERETT, III, financial consultant; b. Highland Park, Mich., Feb. 1, 1952; s. Charles Everett and Patricia Elizabeth (Cote) H.; m. Vali Renée Terhune, July 29, 1972. Student, Ea. Mich. U., 1970-73. Sales rep., sales mgr. Mich. Autosonics, Inc., Ann Arbor, 1972-74; mgr. World Wide Movers, Inc., Ypsilanti, Mich., 1973; sales rep. Godfrey Moving & Storage Co., Ann Arbor, 1974-78; account exec. Merrill Lynch Pierce Fenner & Smith, Detroit, 1978-83, E. F. Hutton, Ann Arbor, 1983-87; asst. br. mgr. Shearson Lehman Hutton, Ann Arbor, 1987-90; fin. cons. Shearson Lehman Bros., Detroit, 1991-92; investment exec. Paine Webber, Inc., Farmington Hills, Mich., 1992-99, br. office ins. coord., 1993—; accounts v.p. Paine Webber, Inc., Farmington Hills, 1999—. Artist and engr. auto. models including MPC World Champion, 1977 (1st Pl. 1977). Campaign worker Dem. Com., Ypsilanti, 1965-71; organizer Anti-War Workshops, Ypsilanti, 1968-70; pres., organizer Fin. Svcs. Softball League, Detroit, 1979-83; mem. Colonial Leadership Coun., Boston. Mem. Am. Funds Group (All-Am. Team), Nameless Nat. Luminaries (founder, chartered), Detroit Tigers Fantasy Camp (chartered), Key and Kite Club, Aim Summit Club (chmns. coun. 1992—), Franklin Group of Funds, Paine Webber Premium Producers Guild, Paine Webber Preservation Planning Inst. Avocations: model car building and collecting, automobile and auto racing photography, baseball. Office: Paine Webber Inc 32300 Northwestern Hwy Ste 150 Farmington Hills MI 48334

HELPRIN, MARK, author; b. N.Y.C., June 28, 1947; s. Morris A. and Eleanor (Lynn) H.; m. Lisa Kennedy, June 28, 1980; children: Alexandra Morris, Olivia Kennedy. AB, Harvard U., 1969, AM, 1972; postgrad., Magdalen Coll., Oxford (Eng.) U., 1976-77. Sr. fellow Claremont Inst. Study of Statesmanship and Polit. Philosophy. Author: A Dove of the East and Other Stories, 1975, Refiner's Fire, 1977, Ellis Island and Other Stories, 1981, Winter's Tale, 1983, Swan Lake, 1989, A Soldier of the Great War, 1991, Memoir from Antproof Case, 1995, A City in Winter, 1996, The Veil of Snows, 1997; contbg. editor The Wall Street Jour. Mem. Coun. on Fgn. Rels.; adviser in def. and fgn. rels. Rep. presdl. nominee Robert Dole. Served with Israeli Army and Air Force, 1972-73. Recipient Prix de Rome, Am. Acad. and Inst. Arts and Letters, 1982, Nat. Jewish Book award, 1982; sr. fellow Hudson Inst. Fellow Am. Acad. in Rome.

HELQUIST, PAUL M., chemistry educator, researcher; b. Duluth, Minn., Mar. 5, 1947; s. Paul O. and Marie E. (Parent) H.; m. Christie M. Wick, June 11, 1970; children: Sandra Ann, Kristina Ann. BSc, U. Minn., Duluth, 1969; MSc, Cornell U., 1971, PhD, 1971; PhD honoris causa, U. Uppsala, Sweden, 1988. Postdoctoral fellow Harvard U., Cambridge, Mass., 1973-74; asst. prof. SUNY, Stony Brook, 1974-80, assoc. prof., 1980-84, prof., 1984-86; prof. U. Notre Dame, Ind., 1986—, chmn. dept. chemistry and biochemistry, 1988-93; mem. exam. bd. Ednl. Testing Svc., Princeton, N.J., 1989-98; cons. Proctor and Gamble Pharms., 1990—. Author: Synthetic Organic Chemistry: Modern Methods and Strategy, 1989. Recipient Cat-acosinos Cancer Rsch. award, 1979; grantee NIH, 1977—, NSF, 1979—; Am.-Scandinavian Found. fellow, 1982. Mem. Am. Chem. Soc. (instr. 1981—, Exceptional Achievement award 1991). Avocations: foreign languages, classical music, model building, amateur astronomy. Office: U Notre Dame Dept Chemistry & Biochemistry Notre Dame IN 46556

HELSABECK, ERIC H., emergency physician; b. Winston-Salem, N.C.; s. Charles Robert and Ruth Haigler H.; m. Judy Ann Hinkleman; children: Keith, Graham. BS, U. N.C., 1971, MD, 1975. Intern Wilson Meml. Hosp., Johnson City, N.Y., 1975-76, resident in family practice, 1977-78; pvt. practice Bath, N.Y., 1978-82; staff emergency physician Randolph Hosp., Asheboro, N.C., 1983—. Mem. Am. Coll. Emergency Physicians, N.C. Med. Soc. Home: 1607 Brevard Dr Asheboro NC 27203-4105

HELSLEY, ALEXIA JONES, archivist; b. Louisville, Ky., Sept. 9, 1945; d. George Alexander and Evelyn (Masden) J.; m. Terry Lynn Helsley, Oct. 11, 1969; children: Cassandra Keiser, Jacob Henry. BA in History, Furman U., 1967; MA in History, U. S.C., 1974; cert., Modern Archives Inst., Washington, 1978, S.C. Exec. Inst., Columbia, 1995. Archival asst. S.C. Dept. Archives and History, Columbia, 1968-69, archivist I, 1969-72, asst. reference archivist, 1972-76, supr. reference and rsch., 1976-88, dir. pub. programs divsn., 1988-96, dir. edn., 1996—; historian Am. Lodging Resources, Inc. Author: Harbison: an Historical Sketch, 1986, First Baptist Church of Irmo: Historical Overview, 1992, Researching Family History: A Workbook, 1992, 96, The 1840 Revolutionary Pensioners of Henderson County, North Carolina, 1996, Unsung Heroines of the Carolina Frontier, 1997, Silent Cities: Cemeteries and Classrooms, 1997, South Carolina's African American Confederate Pensioners, 1923-1925, 1998; co-author: The Many Faces of Slavery-Documents from S.C. Dept. of Archives and History, 1999, S.C. Court Records, 1993, The Changing Face of S.C. Politics, 1993, African American Genealogical Research, 1997; contbr. articles to profl. jours. Chair social and recreation com. Harbison Cmty. Assn., Columbia, S.C., 1984-89; trustee S.C. Hall of Fame, Myrtle Beach, 1988-96; vice-chair Columbia Quincentennial Commn. S.C., 1989-93; pres. Richland Sertoma, Columbia, 1998—. Recipient Willie Parker Peace History Book award, 1997; named to Hon. Order of Ky. Cols. Mem. Henderson County Geneal. and Hist. Soc. (charter, v.p. 1998), Pace Soc. Am. (bd. dirs.), Joseph McDowell Nat. Soc. DAR, Soc. Am. Archivists (chair reference, access, outreac sect. 1981-83), S.C. Hist. Assn., Pace Soc. Am. (bd. dirs.). Baptist. Home: 1 Northpine Ct Columbia SC 29212-2911 Office: SC Dept Archives History 8301 Parklane Rd Columbia SC 29223-4905

HELSON, HENRY BERGE, publisher, retired mathematics educator; b. Lawrence, Kan., June 2, 1927; s. Harry and Lida G. (Anderson) H.; m. Ravenna W. Mathews, June 12, 1954; children—David M., Ravenna A., Harold E. AB, Harvard U., 1947, PhD, 1950; Sheldon travelling fellow, Warsaw and Wroclaw (Poland), 1947-48. Lectr. U. Uppsala, Sweden, 1950-51; instr., then asst. prof. math. Yale, 1951-55; mem. faculty U. Calif. at Berkeley, 1955—, prof. math.; retired, 1993; vis. prof. Swedish univs., spring 1962, U. Paris, Orsay, France, 1966-67, U. Sci. and Tech., Kumasi, Ghana, spring 1969, U. du Languedoc, Montpellier, France, 1971-72, Marseille, France, fall 1976; vis. prof. Indian Statis. Inst., Calcutta, spring 1980. Author: Invariant Subspaces, 1964, Harmonic Analysis, 1983, The Spectral Theorem, 1986, Linear Algebra, 1990, Honors Calculus, 1992, Calculus and Probability, 1998. Mem. Soc. Friends; treas. Friends Com. on Legis. Calif., 1989-95. Home: 15 The Crescent Berkeley CA 94708-1701

HELSPER, JAMES THOMAS, surgical oncologist, researcher, educator; b. Mpls., Mar. 29, 1924; s. Salvius John and Gretchen Louise (Gleissner) H.; m. Mildred Ann Belinsky, June 11, 1951 (div. Aug. 1972); children: James Thomas Jr., Richard Scott, Paige Carla; m. Carolyn Marie Harrison, Dec. 26, 1975; 1 child, Brian Harrison Helsper. BS, St. Vincent Coll., 1945; MD, Jefferson Med. Coll., 1947; postgrad., U. Pa., 1949-50. Lic. physician, Calif., N.Y., N.J., Fla., Mass. Intern Med. Ctr., Jersey City, N.J., 1947-48, residency, 1948-49; resident in surgery U.S. Naval Hosp., Portsmouth, Va., 1951-52; chief resident in surgery Queens Gen. Hosp., N.Y., 1952-53; asst. resident in surgery Meml. Ctr. for Cancer and Allied Diseases, N.Y.C., 1953-54, spl. fellow head and neck svc., 1954, sr. resident in surgery, 1955-57; surg. staff Huntington Meml. Hosp., Pasadena, Calif., Kenneth Norris Jr. Cancer Hosp.; attending surgeon L.A. County U. So. Calif. Med. Ctr.; assoc. clin. prof. surgery U. So. Calif. Sch. Medicine, L.A., prof. clin. surgery, 1996—; head melanoma site team U. So. Calif. Comprehensive Cancer Ctr., L.A.; mem. head and neck site team U. So. Calif. Comprehensive Cancer Ctr.; asst. clin. prof. surgery Loma Linda (Calif.) U. Sch. Medicine; chmn. tumor bd. L.A. County Gen. Hosp., 1963, 70, 81-82; cancer liaison fellow Am. Coll. Surgeons L.A. County/USC Med. Ctr., Norris Cancer Hosp.; head melanoma site team U. So. Calif. Comprehensive Cancer Ctr., L.A., head and neck site team. Capt. USNR. Mem. AMA, ACS (bd. govs. 1994), Am. Cancer Soc. (Calif. divsn., L.A. county unit chmn. profl. edn. com., 1965-67, v.p. for program 1967-69, 84—. pres. elect 1969-70, 85-86, pres. 1970-71, 86-87, chmn. nom. com. 1971-72, Calif. divsn. chmn. profl. edn com. 1974-75, mem. profl. edn. com. 1971-76, mem. bd. dirs. 1967—, mem. pub. info. com. 1969-71, mem. Macomber Legacy Com. 1975-82, mem. rsch. com. 1987-88, named Man of The Year 1991), Am. Fedn. Clin. Oncologic Socs., Am. Radium Soc., Am. Soc. Clin. Oncology, Calif. Med. Assn. (mem. com. on cancer), Calif. Med. Assn. (mem. com. on cancer), N.Y. Acad. Medicine, L.A. County Med. Assn. (mem. com. on cancer, jr. sect. pres. 1966), L.A. Surg. Soc., L.A. Acad. Medicine, Pasadena Med. Soc., Internat. Union Against Cancer (mem. sci. com.), Pan-Pacific Surg. Assn., Soc. Surg. Oncology (James Ewing Soc.), Soc. Head and Neck Surgeons (pres. 1988-89), Flying Physicians Assn., The Adventurer's Club, Quiet Birdmen. Avocations: flying, photography, sailing. Home: 580 Arbor St Pasadena CA 91105-1536 Office: care Norris Cancer Hosp 1441 Eastlake Ave Los Angeles CA 90033-1048

HELSTAD, ORRIN L., lawyer, legal educator; b. Ettrick, Wis., Feb. 9, 1922; s. Albert J. and Martha H. (Gimse) H.; m. Charlotte Dart Ankeney, June 26, 1954. Student, U. Wis., La Crosse, 1940-42; B.S., U. Wis., Madison, 1948, LL.B., 1950. Bar: Wis. 1950. Research assoc. Wis. Legis. Council, 1950-61; assoc. prof. law U. Wis., Madison, 1961-65; prof. U. Wis., 1965-85; assoc. dean U. Wis. (Sch. Law), 1972-75, acting dean, 1975-76, dean, 1976-83, dean emeritus, 1985—, prof. emeritus, 1985—; mem. consumer advisory council Wis. Dept. Agr., 1970-72; vice chmn. Wis. Supreme Ct. com. on the State bar, 1977; mem. Fed. Jud. Nominating Commn. Western Dist. Wis., 1979-83. Contbr. articles to law revs.; co-author, editor: Wisconsin Uniform Comml. Code Handbook, 1965, 1971. Recipient Disting. Svc. award Wis. Law Alumni Assn., 1991. Fellow Am. Bar Found.; mem. State Bar Wis., ABA (council sect. on local govt. law 1975-79), Wis. Bar Assn., Dane County Bar Assn., Am. Judicature Soc. Unitarian. Home: 8 Sebring Ct Madison WI 53719-3521

HELSTEDT, GLADYS MARDELL, vocational education educator; b. Forest City, Iowa, May 7, 1926; d. Gordon Ingeman and Pearl Gertrude (Hauan) Field; m. Lowell Lars Helstedt, Aug. 26, 1950; children: Mardell Lynn, David Lowell, Marilee Pearl, Marcia Kay. AA, Waldorf Coll., 1945; BS, Mankato State U., 1969. Bus. tchr. Crystal Lake (Iowa) H.S., Crystal Lake, Iowa, 1945-47; parish sec. St. Paul's Lutheran Ch., Mpls., 1949-51; bus. tchr. Sioux Valley High Sch., Lake Park, Iowa, 1969-70, Radcliffe (Iowa) High Sch., 1970-76; activity dir. Marinuka Manor Care Ctr., Galesville, Wis., 1976-79; bus. tchr. Galesville High Sch., 1979-80; asst. dir. Ret. Sr. Vol. Program, Whitehall, Wis., 1981-83; coord., instr. Western Wis. Tech. Inst., La Crosse, 1984; sr. instr. Tex. State Tech. Coll., Sweetwater, 1985-92; ret., 1992. Dir. music Salem Luth. Ch., Roscoe, Tex., 1985-90. Mem. Philos. Edn. Orgn. (pres. 1982-84), Tex. State Tech. Coll. Women (sec. 1991-92), Bus. Profls. Am. (advisor 1986-92). Avocations: plants, dolls, music, travel, knitting. Home: 570 Quant Ave N Lakeland MN 55043-9545

HELSTERN, LINDA LIZUT, university administrator, poet; b. Phila., Aug. 21, 1948; d. Otto Henry and Harriet Lucile (Stillwell) Lizut; m. Richard Andrew Helstern, Aug. 21, 1977; 1 child, Amina Katherine. BA, Hamline U., 1970; MA, U. N.Mex., 1995; postgrad., So. Ill. U., 1994—. Libr. asst. N.Mex. State Libr., Santa Fe, 1970-71; tchg. asst. dept. English U. N.Mex., Albuquerque, 1971-72; advt./pub. rels. profl. The Barbers, Hairstyling for Men, Mpls., 1972-73; receptionist Leo J. Shapiro & Assocs., Chgo., 1973; devel. asst. Am. Diabetes Assn., Chgo., 1974-75; youth coord. Nat. Multiple Sclerosis Soc., Chgo., 1975-76; comms. mgr. Trans Union Sys. Corp., Chgo., 1976-77; project mgr. Shawnee Design Studio, Carbondale, Ill., 1977-79; project developer coal miner's respiratory disease program Shawnee Health Svc. and Devel. Corp., Carbondale, 1979-81; corp. devel. asst. Coal Rsch. Ctr. So. Ill. U., Carbondale, 1982-86, pub. info. specialist Coll. Engring., 1986-91, asst. to dean for external affairs Coll. Engring., 1991—. Author: (song cycle) Unity Chamber Concert Series, 1993; rschr. TV documentary for Sta. KRWG-TV, 1977; writer, editor: (slide film) Governor's Task Force on the Future of Illinois, 1979; contbr. poetry and essays to anthologies. Pres. Jackson County LWV, Carbondale, 1983-87; dir. Girl Scout Day Camp, Carbondale, 1991. Finalist Poetry Book Competition, Carnegie Mellon U. Press, 1993, hon. mention Poetry Competition, Bay Guardian, 1994; competitive residency fellow Vallecitos Retreat/Witter Bynner Found., 1994. Mem. MLA, Western Lit. Assn., Assn. for Study of Am. Indian Lits., Soc. for Study of Multi-Ethnic Lits. of U.S., Assn. for Study of Lit. and Environment, African Lit. Assn., Shakespeare Assn. Am., Coun. for Advancement and Svc. to Edn. Home: 289 Egret Lake Rd Carbondale IL 62901-8232 Office: So Ill U Coll Engring MC6603 Carbondale IL 62901-6603

HELSTROM, CARL WILHELM, electrical engineering educator; b. Easton, Pa., Feb. 22, 1925; s. Carl Wilhelm H.; m. Barbro Elisabet Dahlbom, Oct. 13, 1956; children: Lars Vilhelm, Nils Stefan. BS in Engring Physics, Lehigh U., 1947; MS in Physics, Calif. Inst. Tech., 1949, PhD in Physics, 1951. Adv. mathematician Westinghouse Rsch. Labs, Pitts., 1951-66; prof. U. Calif.-San Diego, La Jolla, 1966-91, prof. emeritus, 1991—. Author: Statistical Theory of Signal Detection, 1968, Quantum Detection and Estimation Theory, 1976, Probability and Stochastic Processes for Engineers, 1991, Elements of Signal Detection and Estimation, 1995. With USNR, 1944-46. Recipient Quantum Comm. award, 1996. Fellow IEEE (editor Trans. on Info. Theory jour. 1967-71, Centennial medal 1984), Optical Soc. Am.; mem. Phi Beta Kappa. Office: U Calif San Diego Elec & Computer Engring La Jolla CA 92093-0407

HELTNE, PAUL GREGORY, museum executive; b. Lake Mills, Iowa, July 4, 1941; s. Palmer Tilford and Grace Katherine (Hanson) H.; children—Lisa, Christian. B.A., Luther Coll., Decorah, Iowa, 1962; Ph.D., U. Chgo., 1970. Asst. prof. Johns Hopkins U., Balt., 1970-82; dir. Chgo. Acad. Scis., 1982-91, pres., 1991-99, prof. emeritus, 1999—; cons. WHO, Am. Petroleum Inst. Author, editor: Neotropical Primates: Status and Conservation, 1976, Lion-Tailed Macaque, 1985, Science Learning in the Informal Setting, 1988, Understanding Chimpanzees, 1989, Chimpanzee Cultures, 1994. Trustee Balt. Zool. Soc., 1972-82. Mem. Am. Assn. Mus. (edn. task force, accreditation site visitor), Assn. Sci. Mus. Dirs. (sec.-treas. 1986-96), Am. Primatol. Soc., Internat. Primatology Soc., Am. Zool. Soc., Soc. for Study Evolution, Systematic Zoology Soc., Assn. Sci. and Tech. Ctrs. Office: Chgo Acad Scis 2060 N Clark St Chicago IL 60614-4713

HELTON, ARTHUR CLEVELAND, advocate, lawyer; b. St. Louis, Jan. 24, 1949; s. Arthur Cleveland Sr. and Marjorie Jane (Russell) H.; m. Jacqueline Dean Gilbert, May 14, 1982. AB, Columbia Coll., 1971; JD, NYU, 1976. Bar: N.Y. 1977, U.S. Dist. Ct. (so. and ea. dists.) N.Y. 1977, U.S. Ct. Appeals (2d cir.) 1978, U.S. Ct. Appeals (1st cir.) 1980, U.S. Ct. Appeals (4th and 9th cir.) 1988, U.S. Ct. Appeals (5th, 7th and 11th cir.) 1989, U.S. Ct. Appeals (3d cir.) 1994, U.S. Supreme Ct. 1980. Assoc. appellate counsel Legal Aid Soc., N.Y.C., 1976-79; assoc. Mailman & Rutheizer, N.Y.C., 1979-82; dir. refugee project Lawyers Com. Human Rights, N.Y.C., 1982-94; dir. migration programs, forced migration projects Open Soc. Inst., N.Y.C., 1994—; adj. prof. law NYU, 1986-99. Contbr. articles to profl. jours. Recipient Pub. Svc. award Law Alumni Assn. NYU, 1987; grantee The German Marshall Fund, The Ford Found. Fellow Am. Bar Found.; mem. Coun. Fgn. Rels., ABA (co-chmn. immigration and nationality law com. sect. internat. law and practice, coord. com. on immigration law 1997—), Internat. Bar Assn., Assn. Bar N.Y.C. (chmn. com. on immigration and nationality law 1982-85, legal assistance com. 1985-88, civil rights com. 1988-91, internat. human rights com. 1991-94, internat. law com. 1995-98, adminstrv. law com. 1999—), Pub. internatl. imm., naturalization, and customs. Home: 245 7th Ave Apt 10B New York NY 10001-7301 Office: Open Soc Inst 400 W 59th St New York NY 10019

HELTON, BILL D., utilities company executive. B of Elec. Engring., Tex. Tech. U. Registered profl. engr. Fin. v.p. Southwestern Pub. Svc., 1983-86, v.p. corp. svcs., 1986-87, exec. v.p., 1987-89, COO, 1989-91, CEO, 1991—; chmn. bd., CEO New Century Energies; chmn. bd., mem. Cheyenne Light, Fuel and Power Svc. Co., Pub. Svc. Co.; bd. dirs. Edison Electric Inst., Assn. Electric Cos. of Tex., Pub. Edn. and Bus. Coalition. Mem. campaign cabinet, bd. trustees Mile High United Way; bd. trustees Denver Area coun. Boy Scouts of Am. Mem. IEEE, Western Stock Show Assn., Rotary Club Denver. Office: 1225 17th St Denver CO 80202

HELTON, KIM, coach; b. Pensacola, Fla., July 28, 1948; married; children: Clay, Tyson. Univ. Fla., 1970. Coach Eastside H.S., Gainesville, Fla., 1970-71; grad. asst. Univ. Fla., 1972, offensive line coach, 1973-78; offensive coord. Univ. Miami, 1979-82; offensive line coach Tampa Bay Buccaneers, 1983-86, Houston Oilers, 1987-89, L.A. Raiders, 1990-92; head coach Univ. Houston, 1993—. Named Conf. USA Coach of Yr., 1996. Office: Univ Houston Athletic Dept 3100 Cullen Blvd Houston TX 77204*

HELTON, LUCILLE HENRY HANRATTIE, academic administrator; b. Ft. Worth, Mar. 2, 1942; d. P.D. and Virginia (Clark) Henry; m. Wayne Hanrattie, June 26, 1965 (div. Apr. 1986); children: Clark, Chris; m. William M. Helton, Jr., Mar. 19, 1988. BA, So. Meth. U., 1964; MEd, U. Pitts., 1968; cert. in adminstrn., William Paterson Coll., 1984; cert. in mid-mgmt., Tex. Christian U., 1987. Cert. elem. tchr. N.J., Pa., Tex. Nat. field sec. Kappa Kappa Gamma Sorority, Columbus, Ohio, 1964-65; elem. tchr. Pitts. Bd. Edn., 1965-69; co-dir, chmn. dept. maths. Assn. Children with Learning Disabilities Sch., Pitts., 1969-72; tchr. elem., secondary, gifted and remedial and home instrn. programs West Milford (N.J.) Bd. Edn., 1976-84; prin., exec. dir. Hill Sch., Ft. Worth, 1984—; mem. exec. bd. Tex. Assn. Non-pub. Schs. Mem. ASCD, Tex. Ind. Sch. Consortium, Learning Disabilities Assn. Am., Leadership Tex., Coalition for Spl. Needs Students, Orton Dyslexia Soc., Forum Ft. Worth, Rotary (bd. dirs.). Democrat. Methodist. Avocations: reading, biking, traveling, nature. Office: Hill Sch of Ft Worth 4817 Odessa Ave Fort Worth TX 76133-1640

HELTON, MAX EDWARD, minister, consultant, religious organization executive; b. Conasauga, Tenn., Nov. 24, 1940; s. Herman Marshall and Nellie Gladys (Haddock) H.; m. Jean Bateman, June 8, 1962; children: Elaine, Melanie, Crista, Becky. BA, Tenn. Temple U., 1963; DD (hon.), Hyles-Anderson Coll., 1973. Ordained minister Bapt. Ch., 1963. Sr. pastor Koolau Bapt. Ch., Kaneohe, Hawaii, 1964-71; exec. v.p. Hyles-Anderson Coll., Crown Point, Ind., 1971-77; sr. pastor Grace Bible Ch., White Plains, N.Y., 1977-83, West Park Bapt. Ch., Bakersfield, Calif., 1983-86; founder/pastor outreach program Grace Bapt. Ch., Glendora, Calif., 1986-88; pres. Motor Racing Outreach, Harrisburg, N.C., 1988—. Author: Thirty Qualities of Leadership, 1975, Beyond the Checkered Flag, 1996; contbr. articles to profl. jours.; keynote speaker Commonwealth Youth Day, Cayman Brac, B.W.I., 1964. Dep. sheriff Lake County (Ind.) Sheriff Dept., Crown Point, 1974-77; mem. adv. bd. legis. N.Y., Albany, 1980-82, sch. bd. Bakersfield Christian Sch. Dist., 1985-86; bd. dirs. N.C. Racing Hall of Fame Mus., Sports Outreach Am. Recipient Bill France Excellence award, 1992, Mike Rich award, 1993. Mem. Internat. Sports Coalition, Conservative Bapt. Assn. (cons. 1983—, chmn. fellowship com. 1985-87), Nat. Assn. for Stock Car Auto Racing, Championship Auto Racing Teams. Republican. Avocations: stock car racing, basketball. Office: Motor Racing Outreach Hwy 29 Harrisburg NC 28075-9402 *Of all the investments in the world, none are as valuable as people. Only people will last forever.*

HELTON, TERRY L., city administrator; b. Kansas City, Mo., May 15, 1945; s. Lloyd L. and R. Geraldine (Clark) H.; m. Donna Jo Drake, Jan. 21, 1967. AA, Mo. So. State Coll., Joplin, 1967, BA in Polit. Sci., 1969; MBA, U. No. Iowa, 1976. Owner, CEO Screen Printing and Design, Inc., Waterloo, Iowa, 1976-85; councilman, mayor pro-tem City of Evansdale, Iowa, 1979-82; city clk., econ. devel. City of Evansdale, 1985-87; city coord. City of Vinton, Iowa, 1987-89; city adminstr. City of Hermann, Mo., 1990-97, City of Bolivar, Mo., 1997—; chmn. bd. dirs. Mcpl. Gas Commn. of Mo., Columbia, Mo. Joint Mcpl. Electric Utility Commn., Columbia, Mo. Assn. Mcpl. Utilities, Columbia, Meremac Regional Planning Comm., Rolla. 1st lt. USAF, 1969-72, Vietnam. Decorated Air medal USAF, Air Force Wings, Rep. of Vietnam, Vietnam Honor Tng. medal. Republican. Methodist. Avocations: golf, fishing, hunting. Home: 1583 Hwy 32 Bolivar MO 65613-7315 Office: City of Bolivar 345 S Main Ave Bolivar MO 65613-2052

HELVESTON, EUGENE MCGILLIS, pediatric ophthalmologist, educator; b. Detroit, Dec. 28, 1934; d. Eugene McGillis and Ann (Fay) H.; m. Barbara Hiss, June 15, 1959; children: Martha Hiss, Lisa Hiss. B.A., U. Mich., 1956, M.D., 1960. Intern St. Joseph Hosp., Ann Arbor, Mich., 1960-61; resident Ind. U. Hosps., Indpls., 1961-66; dir. pediatric opthalmology Ind. U. Sch. Medicine, Indpls., 1967—, asst. prof., 1967-72, assoc. prof., 1972-76, prof., 1976—, chmn., 1981-83; dir. sect. pediatric ophthalmology Ind. U. Sch. Medicine, 1967—; fellow in opthalmology Wilmer Inst., Balt., 1966-67. Author: Pediatric Ophthalmology Practice, 1973, Atlas of Strabismus Surgery, 4th edit., 1993, Strabismus: A Decision Making Approach, 1994; chief editor; Am. Orthoptic Jour., 1976-82; contbr. articles to profl. jours. Mem. med. adv. bd. Project Orbis, 1989—. Kellogg scholar, 1959; grantee Heed scholar Heed Found., Chgo., 1966; recipient Outstanding Heed Fellow award, 1975. Fellow ACS, Am. Acad. Ophthalmology, Am. Orthoptic Coun. (pres. 1976-80), Am. Assn. Pediat. Ophthalmology and Strabismus (pres. 1990), Internat. Strabismus Assn. (sec.-treas.). Office: Ind U Sch Medicine 702 Rotary Cir Indianapolis IN 46202-5133

HELVEY, JULIUS LOUIS, II, finance company executive; b. Boise, Idaho, May 21, 1931; s. Julius Louis and Adeline (Jonasson) Turpin; m. Barbara June Ellis, Aug. 29, 1959; children: Janet E., Julius Louis III, Jennifer S., Mary A., Rebecca E. B.S., U.S. Naval Acad., 1953; M.B., Stanford U., 1959. C.P.A., Calif. Auditor, audit supr. Touche, Ross & Co., San Francisco, 1959-65; fin. v.p. Golden West Fin. Corp., Oakland, Calif., 1965-67, sr. v.p., 1973-88, group sr. v.p., 1988-96, exec. v.p., 1996—; audit mgr. Touche Ross & Co., San Francisco, 1967-73. Scoutmaster Boy Scouts Am., Lafayette,Calif., 1975-77. Served to lt. USN, 1953-57. Mem. Am. Inst. C.P.A.s, Calif. Soc. C.P.A.s, U.S. Naval Acad. Alumni, Satnford Alumni ASsn., Stanford Bus. Sch. Club. Republican. Men. Ch. of Jesus Christ of Latter-day Saints. Club: Stanford Bus Sch. Office: Golden West Fin Corp 1901 Harrison St Fl 6 Oakland CA 94612-3588

HELWIG, ARTHUR WOODS, chemical company executive; b. St. Louis, Feb. 1, 1929; s. Gunther Albert and Emma (Schumacher) H.; m. Evelyn Morgan, July 10, 1954; children: Paul, Katherine, Elizabeth, Mary. BS ChemE, U. Mo.-Rolla, 1950, ChemE (hon.), 1966; MS ChemE, U. Ill., 1952. Process engr. Ethyl Corp., Baton Rouge, 1952-53, econs. engr., 1953-56, supr., 1956-59, gen. supt., 1959-64; dir. planning Ethyl Corp., Baton Rouge and Richmond, Va., 1964-74; v.p. planning Ethyl Corp., Richmond, 1974-94; ret.; bd. dirs. Solite Corp., Richmond, Albemarle Corp. Trustee Sci. Mus. Va., Richmond, 1987—, chmn., 1992, pres. Found., 1984-87. Mem. Va. Inst. Marine Sci. (marine scis. devel. coun. 1994—), Met. Richmond C. of C. (bd. dirs. 1986), Engrs. Club Richmond (v.p. 1987—, pres. 1988-89). Methodist. Home: 8911 Highfield Rd Richmond VA 23229-7756

HELZ, GEORGE RUDOLPH, chemistry educator, research center director; b. Silver Spring, Md., Mar. 4, 1942; married, 1970; 1 child. AB, Princeton U., 1964; PhD in Geochemistry, Pa. State U., 1971. From asst. prof. to assoc. prof. U. Md., College Park, 1970-84, prof. chemistry, 1984—; dir. Md. Water Resources Rsch. Ctr., 1990—; mem. disinfectants chem. subcom. NAS-NRC, 1978; vis. prof. Stanford U., 1983-84, Cox vis. prof., 1998-99; sr. vis. fellow Manchester (Eng.) U., 1989-90. AAAS Environ. fellow, 1988. Mem. Am. Chem. Soc. (chmn. geochem. divsn. 1985), Am. Geophys. Union, Geochem. Soc. (treas. 1975-78), Geol. Soc. Am., Geol. Soc. Washington (pres. 1996). Achievements include research in aqueous geochemistry; geochemistry of mineral deposits; environmental chemistry; fate of pollutants in estuaries. Office: Univ of Maryland Water Resoures Research Ctn 3101 Chemistry Bldg College Park MD 20742

HELZER, JAMES DENNIS, hospital executive; b. Fresno, Calif., Apr. 27, 1938; s. Alexander and Katherine (Scheidt) H.; m. Joan Elaine Alinder, Feb. 25, 1967; children: Amy, Rebecca. B.S., Fresno State Coll., 1960; M.Hosp. Adminstrn., U. Iowa, 1965. Adminstrv. asst. Twilight Haven, Fresno, Calif., 1960-61, adminstr. resident, 1964-65; asst. adminstr. U. Calif. Hosps. and Clinics, San Francisco, 1965-68; asst. adminstr. Fresno Community Hosp., 1968-71, exec. adminstr., 1971-82, pres., chief exec. officer, 1982-91; pres., chief exec. officer Community Hosps. Cen. Calif., 1982-91, cons., 1991-95; adminstr. Veterans Home of Calif., Yountville, Calif., 1995—. Served with U.S. Army, 1961-63. Fellow Am. Coll. Hosp. Adminstrs.; mem. Am., Calif. hosp. assns. Presbyterian. Club: Rotary. Home: Veterans Home of Calif PO Box 6 Yountville CA 94599-0006

HEMAN, ROBERT JEROME, JR., printing company executive, association executive; b. Lowell, Mass., Nov. 15, 1926; s. Robert Jerome and Ethyl Bein (Pentz) H.; m. Constance Anne Bodwell, Sept. 18, 1954; children: Roberta, Dawn, Kevin. Student, Suffolk U., 1947-48, Suffolk Law Sch., 1948-50, Worcester Poly. Inst., 1957. Supr., quality control and quality assurance David Clark Co., Worcester, 1956-60; mgr., quality control and quality assurance Harrington & Richardson, Inc., Worcester, 1960-64; dir., quality control and quality assurance Gardner and Am. Optical Corp., Southbridge, Mass., 1964-75; gen. mgr. Acme Blue Print Co., Inc., Worcester, 1975-85, pres. and owner, 1985-92; cons. to pres. Acme Blue Print Co., 1992—. Pres. bd. trustees Worcester Pub. Libr., 1987-95; corporator Worcester Art Mus.; mem. Worcester City Beautification Com., 1991—, Target Worcester, 1991—. With USN, 1943-46, PTO. Mem. DAV (life), VFW (life), Elks (life, Elk of Yr. 1985-86, chpt. pres., state pres., editor Mass. Elks News 1982-86, Grand Lodge activities com., spl. rep.), Am. Legion (life, rep. to Grand Lodge), Connie Heman. Roman Catholic. Avocations: stamp collecting, coin collecting, traveling. Home: 143 Lovell St Worcester MA 01603-2554 Office: Acme Blue Print Co 102 1/2 Grove St Worcester MA 01605-2629

HEMANN, PATRICIA A., federal judge; b. 1942. BA summa cum laude, U. Ill., 1964; JD summa cum laude, Cleveland Marshall Coll. Law, 1980. Law clk. to hon. William K. Thomas U.S. Dist. Ct. (no. dist.) Ohio, 1980-82; assoc. Hahn Lowser & Parks, 1982-93; magistrate judge U.S. Dist. Ct. (no. dist.) Ohio, Cleve., 1993—; summer intern strike force organizad crime divsn. U.S. Dept. Justice, Cleve., 1979; mem. vis. com., hon. trustee Cleveland Marshall Coll. Law. Mem. ABA, Fed. Bar Assn., Nat. Assn. Women Judges (membership chair dist. 7), Ohio Women's Bar Assn., Greater Cleve. Bar Assn. (trustee). Fax: (216) 522-2000. Office: US Dist Ct No Dist Ohio 414 US Courthouse 201 E Superior Ave NE Cleveland OH 44114

HEMANN, RAYMOND GLENN, research company executive; b. Cleve., Jan. 24, 1933; s. Walter Harold and Marsha Mae (Colbert) H.; m. Lucile Tinnin Turnage, Feb. 1, 1958; children: James Edward, Carolyn Frances; m. Pamela Lehr, Dec. 18, 1987. BS, Fla. State U., 1957; postgrad., U.S. Naval Postgrad. Sch., 1963-64, U. Calif., Los Angeles, 1960-62; MS in Systems Engring., Calif. State U., Fullerton, 1970; MA in Econs., Calif. State U., 1972; cert. in tech. mgmt., Calif. Inst. Tech., 1990. Comml., glider and pvt. pilot. Aero. engring. aide U.S. Navy, David Taylor Model Basin, Carderock, Md., 1956; analyst Fairchild Aerial Surveys, Tallahassee, 1957; research analyst Fla. Rd. Dept., Tallahassee, 1957-59; chief Autonetics divsn. N.Am. Rockwell Corp., Anaheim, Calif., 1959-69; v.p., dir. R.E. Manns Co., Wilmington, Calif., 1969-70; mgr. Avionics Design and Analysis Dept. Lockheed-Calif. Co., Burbank, 1970-72; mgr. Advanced Concepts divsn. Lockheed-Calif. Co., 1976-82; gen. mgr. Western divsn. Arinc Research Corp., Santa Ana, 1972-76; dir. Future Requirements Rockwell Internat., 1982-85, dir. Threat Analysis, Corp. Offices, 1985-89; pres., CEO Advanced Systems Rsch., Inc., 1989—; adj. sr. fellow Ctr. Strategic and Internat. Studies, Washington, 1987—; bd. dirs. Fla. State U. Rsch. Found., 1995—; bd. dirs. Assn. Mgmt. Svc. Inc.; bd. dirs., pres. Associated Aviation, Inc., 1980-96; chmn. adv. coun. Coll. Engring. Fla. State U./Fla. A&M U., 1995; cons. to dir. Ctrl. Intelligence, Nat. Intelligence Coun., Nat. Air Intelligence Ctr., Inst. Def. Analyses, Battelle Meml. Inst., Ctr. Strategic and Internat. Studies; sec., bd. dirs. Calif State U., Fullerton, Econs. Found.; mem. naval studies bd. panels NAS, 1985—, Arms Control Working Group; chmn. indsl. panel Nat. Labs. Infrastructure Study, Office Sec. Def., 1995; chmn. indsl. panel Future Dirs. Mil. Aeronautics Study, 1996; asst. prof. ops. analysis dept. U.S. Naval Postgrad. Sch., Monterey, Calif., 1963-64, Monterey Peninsula Coll., 1963; instr. ops. analysis Calif. State U., Fullerton, 1963, instr. quantitative methods, 1969-72; program developer, instr. systems engring. indsl. rels. ctr. Calif. Inst. Tech., 1992-96; lectr. Brazilian Navy, 1980, U. Calif., Santa Barbara, 1980, Yale U., 1985, Princeton U., 1986, U.S. Naval Postgrad. Sch., 1986, Ministry of Def., Taiwan, Republic of China, 1990; Calif. Inst. Tech. Assocs., 1992—; mem. exec. forum Calif. Inst. Tech., 1991—. Contbr articles to profl. jours. and new media. Chmn. comdr.'s adv. bd. CAP, Calif. Wing; reader Recording for the Blind, 1989—. With AUS, 1950-53, Operation Blue Jay. Syde P. Deeb scholar, 1956; recipient honor awards Nat. Assn. Remotely Piloted Vehicles, 1975, 76; named to Hon. Order Ky. Cols., 1985. Fellow AAAS, AIAA (assoc.); mem. IEEE, Ops. Rsch. Soc. Am., Air Force Assn., N.Y. Acad. Scis., Assn. Old Crows., L.A. World Affairs Coun., Phi Kappa Tau (past pres.). Episcopalian. Office: Advanced Sys Rsch Inc 33 S Catalina Ave Ste 202 Pasadena CA 91106-2426

HEMBERGER, GLEN JAMES, university band director, music educator; b. Boulder, Colo., Jan. 18, 1962; s. James Frank and Jacqueline Ann (Kent) H.; m. Linda Dawn Thomas, June 3, 1989. BME, U. Colo., 1985, MMus, 1989. Dir. bands Thornton (Colo.) Sr. High Sch., 1985-87; grad. asst. U. Colo. Bands, Boulder, 1987-89; assoc. dir. bands, mem. music edn. faculty U. R.I., Kingston, 1989-92; assoc. dir. bands Okla. State U., Stillwater, 1992-97; doctoral conducting assoc. U. North Tex., 1997-99; dir. bands Southeastern La. U., 1999—; clinician R.I. Music Educators' State Conv., 1992, summer music camp U. Wis., 1993, 99, Chinese Armed Police Band, Beijing, 1996, 97, Melbourne, Brisbane & Sydney, Australia, 1997, Nat. Taiwan U. Wind Orch., Taipei and Hong Kong, 1996, Beijing Band Dirs. Assn., 1996, 97, U. S.D. Band Festival, 1996; guest condr. high schs., honor bands, clinics, 1984—, USCG Band, R.I. Jr. High All-State Band, Comty. Bands., 1991—, Okla. Mozart Internat. Music Festival, 1995, 96, Norwegian Band Championships, Hamar, 1999; founder So. New Eng. H.S. Honor Band, 1991. Contbr. articles to profl. jours.; presenter in field. Mem. Olympic All-Am. Marching Band, L.A., 1984. Mem. Coll. Band Dirs. Nat. Assn. (mem. jour. staff, nat. athletic band adv. coun., clinician nat. conv. 1995, 97), Internat. Assn. Jazz Educators, Music Educators Nat. Conf., World Assn. for Symphonic Bands and Ensembles, Okla. Music Educators Assn. (clinician state conv. 1995, jazz ensemble performance 1997), Phi Mu Alpha Sinfonia, Kappa Kappa Psi, Tau Beta Sigma, Pi Kappa Lambda. Home: 100 Heritage Ln Denton TX 76201-1925 Office: Southeaster Louisianna Univ Box 815 Hammond LA 70402-0001

HEMBREE, HUGH LAWSON, III, diversified holding company executive; b. Ft. Smith, Ark., Nov. 16, 1931; s. Raymond N. and Gladys (Newman) H.; m. Sara Janelle Young, Sept. 1, 1956; children—Hugh Lawson IV, Raymond Scott. B.S. in Bus. Adminstrn, U. Ark., 1953, J.D., 1958. In middle mgmt. Ark.-Best Freight Inc., Fort Smith, 1958-61, dir. finance, 1961-65, v.p., 1965-67; pres., dir. Ark.-Best Corp., Fort Smith, 1967-73, chmn. bd., chief exec. officer, 1973-88; owner, chmn. bd.; mng. ptnr. Sugar Hill Interests; chmn. exec. com. Mchts. Nat. Bank; bd. dirs. Okla. Gas and Electric, Oklahoma City; adv. dir. Arkwright Mut. Ins. Co.; chmn., bd. dirs. Trans States Lines; pres. Kiamichi Leasing Co., Ft. Smith; mem. adv. bd. Arkwright Ins. Dallas. Sec. Fort Smith/Sebastian County Joint Planning Commn., 1959-72; Ark. past chmn. Radio Free Europe Program; past chmn. devel. council, mem. dean's adv. com. Sch. Bus., U. Ark., past chmn. exec. com. univ. devel. assn.; past mem. Sebastian County Regional Park Commn.; past mem. Democratic Central Com. Ark.; past pres. Westark area council Boy Scouts Am., 1985-88, asst. treas. Nat. Exec. Bd. Boy Scouts Am., 1985-88, treas., 1988-92, chair pension investments retirement trust; past area pres., mem. exec. com. South Central region; past Chmn. Ark.-Okla. Livestock and Ednl. Found.; chmn. fund raising program U. Ark., 1973-74; past trustee John Brown U., Siloam Springs, Ark., U. Ark. Found.; trustee U. Ark., chmn. bd. trustees Razorback Found. Served to capt. USAF, 1953-55. Recipient Silver Antelope award Boy Scouts Am., 1967, Silver Beaver award, 1969, Silver Buffalo award, 1990, Distinguished Svc. Awd., UA Med. Svcs., 1998, Comm. Svc. Awd., Sam Walton Coll. of Bus., Univ. of Ark., 1998, Svc. Awd. from Razorback Found., 1998; Ark. Leadership and Community Svc. award, 1970, 75, Citation of Disting. Alumnus, U. Ark., 1977, Cmty. Svc. award Razorback Found., 1998, Outstanidng Svc. Alumnus, U. Ark. Coll. of Bus., 1998; named Ark. Outstanding Young Man of Yr., Ark. Jaycees, 1967; James E. West fellow Boy Scouts, Baden Powell fellow Boy Scouts. Mem. World Pres's. Orgn., World Bus. Orgn., Nat. Assn. of Devel. Orgns. (chmn. adv. com. 1969-72), Ark. C. of C. (1st v.p. 1970-73, pres. 1973, 86-87, dir. 1972-74), Ft. Smith C. of C. (pres. 1970-73, 86), Nat. Young Presidents Orgn., World Presidents Orgn., Ark. Alumni Assn. (dir., mem. bldg. com., vice chmn. bd. trustee), Am. Trucking Assn., Nat. Assn. Mfrs. (dir. 1976, regional v.p. 1973-75, regional dir. 1976-77), Ark. Arts Center, Scabbard and Blade, Ark. Bus. Coun., Kissing Camels Golf Club (Colorado Springs), El Paso Club (Colorado Springs), Sigma Alpha Epsilon, Beta Gamma Sigma, Phi Eta Sigma, Delta Theta Phi, Alpha Kappa Psi. Episcopalian (vestryman). Clubs: Masonss (32 deg.), Shriners, Ft. Smith Hardscrabble Country and Town, Fianna Hills Country (Ft. Smith), Garden of the Gods (Colorado Springs), Kissing Camels Golf (Colorado Springs). Home: PO Box 10233 Fort Smith AR 72917-0233 Office: Sugar Hill Farms Inc PO Box 10233 Fort Smith AR 72917-0233

HEMBREE, JAMES D., retired chemical company executive; b. Morris, Okla., Feb. 27, 1929; s. James D. and Mary Eleanor H.; m. Joyce Pickrell, Aug. 25, 1951; Victoria Lee Stilwell, Alex James, Kent Douglas. B.S.Ch.E., Okla. State U., 1951; M.S.Ch.E., U. Mich., 1952. Dir. mktg. inorganic chems. Dow Chem U.S.A., Midland, Mich., 1968-78, gen. mgr. designed products dept., 1976-78, v.p., 1978-80, group v.p., 1980-83; pres., chief exec. officer Dow Chem. Can., Sarnia, Ont., 1983-86; ret., 1986; bd. dirs. Endless Youth Products Inc., Las Vegas. Home and Office: 4620 Jupiter Dr Salt Lake City UT 84124-3900

HEMELESKI, JOHN PETER, retired academic administrator; b. Orange, N.J., Nov. 5, 1927; s. William Joseph and Susan (Mulherin) H.; m. Barbara Ann Eash, May 5, 1962; children: Amy, Patricia, Barbara, Karen, John, William, Thomas. BA in Communications and Journalism, U. Denver, 1950. Editor weekly newspapers Colo. and, N.Mex., 1950-52; fin. investigator Dun & Bradstreet, Inc., East Orange, N.J., 1953-59; supr. pub. rels. The Newark Mus., 1959-63; assoc. dir. pub. rels. Newark Coll. of Engring., 1963-75; acad. adminstr. N.J. Inst. Tech., Newark, 1963-91; cons. to non-profit orgns., 1965-75. Court appointed mem. Juvenile Rels. Coun., Essex County, N.J., 1975-80; implementator Gov.'s N.J. Pride Mobile Mus. and Jersey Jubilee, 1984-88; fundraiser United Way, and other cmty. orgns., N.J., 1985-88; organization first merit badge workshop between univ. and scouting orgns., 1978—. With U.S. Army, 1945-47, ETO. Recipient Cert. of Appreciation, N.J. Assn. Tchrs. of English, 1969. Mem. Pub. Rels. Soc. Am. (chmn. juried competitions, exec. com., ednl. instns. sect., nominating chmn., accreditation chmn. N.J. chpt., dir., governing bd., sec., treas. 1972-83), Nat. Assn. Accts., Am. Coll. Pub. Rels. Assn., Internat. Am. Bus. Communicators. Avocations: railroad history, model railroads, croquet, horses, dogs. Home: 126 Parkview Dr Bloomfield NJ 07003-2936

HEMENWAY, DAVID, public health educator; b. N.Y.C., Mar. 14, 1945; s. Henry Harold and Marjorie Sophie (Wilson) H.; m. Nancy Lou Williams, Sept. 12, 1969; 1 child, Brett Turner. BA, Harvard Coll., 1966; MA, U. Mich., 1967; PhD, Harvard U., 1974. Mgmt. intern Office of Sec. Defense, Arlington, Va., 1967-68; Washington corres. Consumers Union, Washington, 1969; asst. prof. Boston U., 1973-75; prof. Harvard Sch. Pub. Health, Boston, 1975—; dir. Harvard Injury Control Rsch. Ctr., Boston, 1997—; chmn., injury prevention coun. Nat. Assn. for Pub. Health Policy, S. Burlington, Va., 1988-98. Author: Industrywide Voluntary Product Standards, 1975, Monitoring and Compliance, 1985, Prices and Choices, 1993, Guns and the Constitution, 1995. Injury Rsch. fellow Pew Found., 1986, sr. Soros fellow, 1998—; Robert Wood Johnson investigator, 1998—. Mem. APHA, Am. Econ. Assn., Am. Coun. Consumer Interests, Assn. for Pub. Policy Analysis and Mgmt., Am. Soc. for Health Svcs. Rsch. Avocations: modeling, tennis. Home: 28 Adams St Brookline MA 02446-3168 Office: Harvard Sch Pub Health 677 Huntington Ave Boston MA 02115-6096

HEMENWAY, ROBERT E., academic administrator, language educator; b. Sioux City, Iowa, Aug. 10, 1941; s. Myrle Emery and Katharine Leone (Cook) H.; m. Marilyn Wickstrom, June 16, 1962 (div. 1970); children: Gina, Jeremy; m. Mattie Fenter, May 12, 1972 (div. 1980); children: Robin, Karintha, Matthew, Langston; m. Leah Renee Hattemer, Dec. 19, 1981; children: Zachary, Arna. BA, U. Nebr., Omaha, 1963; PhD, Kent (Ohio) State U., 1966. Asst. prof. English U. Ky., Lexington, 1966-68; assoc. prof. Am. studies U. Wyo., Laramie, 1968-73; prof. U. Ky., Lexington, 1973-86; dean arts and scis. U. Okla., Norman, 1986-89; chancellor U. Ky., Lexington, 1989-95, U. Kans., Lawrence, 1995—; dean Gov.'s Scholar's Program, Ky., 1984-86. Author: Zora Neale Hurston, 1977 (Best Biography of 1977 award Soc. Midland Authors 1978, Rembert Patrick prize Fla. Hist. Soc. 1978). Mem. Gov.'s Task Force on Literacy, Okla., 1987-89; bd. dirs. Okla. H.S. Sci. and Math., Oklahoma City, 1985-86, Coun. Colls. Arts and Scis., 1987-89. NEH fellow, 1974-75. Mem. MLA, Am. Studies Assn. (nat. coun.), South Atlantic Assn. Depts. English (pres. 1984-85). Lutheran. Avocation: duplicate bridge. Office: Univ Kansas Office of the Chancellor 230 Strong Hall Lawrence KS 66045-1500*

HEMENWAY, STEPHEN JAMES, record producer, author; b. San Gabriel, Calif., Aug. 26, 1955; s. Glenn Stephen and Patricia Ann (Reese) H.; (div. 1983); children: April Lynn, Stacie Michelle, Ashley Renee; m. Terri Lynn McAlister, Apr. 19, 1997. AS, Chaffey Coll., Alta Loma, Calif., 1981. Rec. artist Phil Good Records, Ontario, Calif., 1978-80; songwriter Airing Music, Ontario, Calif., 1979-84; prod. Brass Star Records, Chino Hills, Calif., 1984—; publisher Brass Star Music, Chino Hills, Calif., 1988—; music arranger Brass Star Records, Chino Hills, 1984—; promoter Games and Entertainment Unlimited, Chino Hills, 1987—; songwriter/publisher

Broadcast Music, Inc., 1988-95; pres., music arranger Brass Star Records; chmn., CEO Slouch & Friends, Inc., 1996—. Actor, artist, prodr. Plays, Music, 1968—; music arranger A Chino Hills Christmas, Regina; prodr. Don't Let Your Dreams Slip Away, 1996; author: (children's series) The Slouch in the Couch, 1998. Dep. sheriff, L.A. County, 1978. Republican. Roman Catholic. Avocations: music, movies, football, fishing, camping. Office: # E 309 4195 Chino Hills Pkwy Chino Hills CA 91709

HEMING, CHARLES E., lawyer; b. N.Y.C., Mar. 1, 1926; s. Charles E. and Lucile (Wolf) H.; m. Olga Landeck, Sept. 21, 1949 (div.); children—Michael, Lucy, Amanda; m. Barbara Krueger Meisel, Jan. 1, 1990. Grad., Phillips Acad., Andover, 1944; A.B., Princeton U., 1948; LL.B., Columbia U., 1950. Bar: N.Y. 1950, U.S. Dist. Ct. (so. dist.) N.Y. 1951, U.S. Supreme Ct. 1954, U.S. Tax Ct. 1968, U.S. Ct. Appeals (2d cir.) 1962. Ptnr. Wormser, Kiely, Galef & Jacobs, LLP, N.Y.C., 1982—. Trustee Village of Scarsdale, N.Y., 1972-76. Served with USNR, 1944-46. Fellow Am. Bar Found., Am. Coll. Trust and Estate Counsel, N.Y. State Bar Found. (pres.); mem. ABA (ho; of dels.), N.Y. State Bar Assn. (pres. 1986-87), Assn. of Bar of City of N.Y. (past chmn. com. lectures and continuing edn., com. trusts estates surrogate's cts.), Amateur Ski Club of N.Y. (past pres.). Office: Wormser Kiely Galef & Jacobs LLP 711 3rd Ave New York NY 10017-4014

HEMINGWAY, RICHARD WILLIAM, law educator; b. Detroit, Nov. 24, 1927; s. William Oswald and Iva Catherine (Wildfang) H.; m. Vera Cecilia Eck, Sept. 12, 1947; children: Margaret Catherine, Carol Elizabeth, Richard Albert. B.S. in Bus, U. Colo., 1950; J.D. magna cum laude (J. Woodall Rogers Sr. Gold medal 1955), So. Meth. U., 1955; LL.M. (William S. Cook fellow 1968), U. Mich., 1969. Bar: Tex. 1955, Okla. 1981. Assoc. Fulbright, Crooker, Freeman, Bates & Jaworski, Houston, 1955-60; lectr. Bates Sch. Law, U. Houston, 1960; assoc. prof. law Baylor U. Law Sch., Waco, Tex., 1960-65; vis. assoc. prof. So. Meth. U. Law Sch., 1965-68; prof. law Tex. Tech U. Law Sch., Lubbock, 1968-71, Paul W. Horn prof., 1972-81, acting dean, 1974-75, dean ad interim, 1980-81; prof. law U. Okla., Norman, 1981-83, Eugene Kuntz prof. oil, gas and natural resources law, 1983-92, Eugne Kuntz prof. emeritus oil, gas & natural resources law, 1992—. Author: The Law of Oil and Gas, 1971, 2d edit., 1983, lawyer's edit., 1983, 3d edit., 1991, West's Texas Forms (Mines and Minerals), 1977, 2d edit., 1991, 85; contbg. editor various law reports, cases and materials. Served with USAAF, 1945-47. Mem. Tex. Bar Assn., Scribes, Order of Coif (faculty), Beta Gamma Sigma. Lutheran. Home: Apt 518 5000 Old Shepard Pl Plano TX 75093

HEMINGWAY, W(ILLIAM) DAVID, banker; b. L.A., Apr. 28, 1947; s. Donald William and Donna (Laws) H.; m. Gay Etta Jorgensen, Apr. 15, 1977; children: Ryan, Jonathan, Jamon. BA, Brigham Young U., 1971; MBA, U. Utah, 1973. Sr. v.p. Zions First Nat. Bank, Salt Lake City, 1982-84, exec. v.p., 1984—; pres. Internat. TV Network, 1986-88; bd. dirs. Nev. State Bank, Las Vegas, Murdock Travel, Inc., Salt Lake City; dir. Fed. Agrl. Mortgage Corp., Washington, 1994—. Candidate Utah Legislature, Salt Lake City, 1974; mem. Electorial Coll., Salt Lake City, 1976, Utah adv. bd. to U.S. Civil Rights Commn., Salt Lake City, 1976—. Mem. Utah State Money Mgmt. Coun. (elected chmn. 1991), Utah Bankers Assn. (bd. dirs. 1992-94, vice chmn. 1994-95, chmn. 1995-96). Republican. Mormon. Office: Zions First Nat Bank 1 S Main St Salt Lake City UT 84111-1909

HEMKE, FREDERICK L., music educator, university administrator; b. July 11, 1935; s. Fred L. and May H. (Rowell) H.; m. Junita Borg, Dec. 26, 1959; children: Elizabeth Hemke Shapiro, Frederic John Borg. Premiere prix, Cons. Nat. de Musique, Paris, 1956; BS in Music Edn., U. Wis., Milw., 1958; MusM in Music Edn., Eastman Sch. of Music, Rochester, N.Y., 1962; DMA in Musical Arts, U. Wis., 1975. Chmn. dept. preparatory wind and percussion Sch. of Music Northwestern U., Evanston, Ill., 1962-75; chmn. dept. music performance and studies Sch. of Music Northwestern U., Evanston, 1962-94, prof. of music (saxophone), 1963—, sr. assoc. dean, 1994—; faculty athletics rep. Northwestern U., Big 10 Conf., NCAA; cons. La Voz Corp., Sun Valley, Calif., So. Music Co., San Antonio, The Selmer Co., Elkhart, Ind. Instrumental soloist (recordings) The American Saxophone, Music for Tenor Saxophone, Allan Pettersson, Symphony No. 15 (with Stockholm Philharmonic); Quintet for String Quarter & Saxo-Warren Benson, Concerto-Ross Lee Finney; author: The Early History of the Saxophone, Hemke Saxophone Series. Recipient Excellence in Teaching award Northwestern U. Alumni Assn., Music Alumni Achievement award, U. Wis., Milw.; grantee: Nat. Endowment for the Arts. Mem. Ill. Music Educators Assn., Pi Kappa Lambda, Kappa Kappa Psi, Phi Mu Alpha Sinfonia (past province gov.). Office: Northwestern U Sch of Music 1965 S Campus Dr Evanston IL 60208

HEMLEY, EUGENE ADAMS, trade association executive; b. Bklyn., Feb. 20, 1918; s. Benjamin and Fannie (Gottlieb) H.; m. Charlotte McClure, Dec. 22, 1948; children: Philip, Paul, Anne, Margaret. BEE, U.S. Naval Acad., 1940; MS in Internat. Affairs, George Washington U., 1968. Served as midshipman USN, 1936-40, commd. ensign, 1940, advanced through grades to capt., 1959, ret., 1970; elec. officer USS Nashville, 1940-43; engring. officer USS Seadragon, 1944; exec. officer USS Greenling, 1945; comdg. officer USS Bang, 1951, USS Taconic, 1961-62, USS Northampton, 1965-66; dir. fleet comm. divsn. Office Chief of Naval Ops., 1958-61, dep. dir. info. systems divsn., 1968-70; comdg. officer U.S. Naval Comm. Sta., Japan, 1962-65; dept. head U.S. Naval War Coll., 1967-68; dir. mgmt. info. systems Nat. Girl Scout Orgn., N.Y.C., 1970-74; computerization mgr. Nat. Coun. on Internat. Trade Documentation (name changed to The Internat. Trade Facilitation Coun.), N.Y.C., 1974-84, assoc. dir., 1984-85, exec. dir., 1985-92, hon. dir., 1992—; pres. Feda Realty Corp., 1993—; U.S. bus. adviser meetings UN Econ. Commn. for Europe, 1982-92, cos., 1992. Editor: Cardis Stds. Manual, 1981. Mem. Citizens nominating com. Town of Scarsdale, 1982-83. Decorated Silver Star. Mem. U.S. Naval Inst., Naval Acad. Alumni Assn. (v.p. N.Y. chpt. 1982-83, pres. 1984-85, trustee 1985—), Naval Order U.S. (vice cmdr. N.Y. chpt. 1997—), Squadron A Assn., Internat. C. of C. (electronic data interchange working group and incoterms panel of experts 1991-92). Clubs: N.Y. Yacht, Scarsdale Town, Westchester County Tennis (v.p. 1983-84, pres. 1985-87). Home and Office: 20 Cohawney Rd Scarsdale NY 10583-2227

HEMLOW, JOYCE, language and literature educator, author; b. Liscomb, N.S., Can., July 30, 1906; d. William and Rosalinda (Redmond) H. B.A., Queen's U., Kingston, Can., 1941, M.A., 1942; A.M., Harvard U., 1944; Ph.D., Radcliffe Coll., 1948; LL.D., Queen's, 1967, Dalhousie U., 1972. Mem. faculty McGill U., 1945—, Greenshields prof. English lit. and lang., 1965—, prof. emerita, 1975—. Author: The History of Fanny Burney, 1958 (James Tait Black Meml. book prize for best biography in U.K., also Gov. Gen. Can. medal for academic non-fiction 1958, Rose Mary Crawshay prize Brit. Acad. 1960); editor: Journals and Letters Fanny Burney (Madame d'Arblay), 12 vols., Fanny Burney: Selected Letters and Journals, 1986, 87. Guggenheim fellow, 1951-52, 66-67; recipient Disting. Achievement award Radcliffe Coll., 1969. Fellow Royal Soc. Can.; mem. Johnsonians, Internat. Assn. Univ. Profs. English, Phi Beta Kappa.

HEMMER, JAMES PAUL, lawyer; b. Oshkosh, Wis., Mar. 28, 1942; s. Joseph John and Margaret Louise (Nuernberg) H.; m. Francine M. Chamallas, June 4, 1967; children—James, Christopher, Sarah. A.B. summa cum laude, Marquette U., 1964; LL.B., Harvard U., 1967. Bar: Ill. 1967. Assoc. Bell, Boyd & Lloyd, Chgo., 1967-74, ptnr., 1975—, mng. ptnr., 1990-93; adj. prof. law Marquette U., 1985-86, Chgo. Kent Coll. Law, 1991-93; lectr. Ill. Inst. Continuing Legal Edn.; bd. dirs. Sanford Corp., Constrn. Projects Mgmt. Inc., Holco Corp. Mem. Kenilworth (Ill.) Sch. Dist. 38 Bd. Edn., v.p. 1985-87, pres. 1987-89, Kenilworth Citizens Adv. Caucus; bd. dirs. Joseph Sears Sch. Devel. Fund. Wickersham fellow; Fulbright scholar. Mem. ABA, Ill. Bar Assn. (editor banking and comml. law newsletter), Alpha Sigma Nu, Phi Theta Psi, Phi Sigma Tau, Sigma Tau Delta. Clubs: University, Law, Legal (Chgo.); Kenilworth. Contbr. articles to legal jours.

HEMMER, PAUL EDWARD, musician, composer, broadcasting executive; b. Dubuque, Iowa, Oct. 12, 1944; s. Andrew Charles and Elizabeth Marie (Goerdt) H.; m. Janet T. Demmer, Feb. 7, 1970; children: Michelle, Steven. BS in Music Edn., U. Wis., Platteville, 1966. Program dir. Sta. WDBQ-AM, Dubuque, Iowa, 1967-73; ops. dir. Sta. WDBQ-AM, Dubuque, 1973-93; leader Paul Hemmer Orch., Dubuque, 1967-96; pres. KGRR-FM, Dubuque, 1995—; co-owner Dukes Place Jazz Club, 1999—. Composer: (musical comedies) Get the Lead Out, 1976, Joe Sent Me!, 1978, Key City Komedy Company, 1981, Steamboat Comin', 1991, Hero's to Dubuque, 1998, Sketches from a Drawing Room, 1996; appeared in film Field of Dreams, 1989. Named Citizen of Yr., Dubuque Telegraph-Herald, 1976. Mem. Internat. Radio Broadcasters Idea Bank, Rotary. Roman Catholic. Home: 2375 Simpson St Dubuque IA 52003-7720 Office: KGRR 2115 Jfk Rd Dubuque IA 52002-3817

HEMMERLE, DAVE CHRIS, missionary; b. Allentown, Pa., Nov. 21, 1972; s. Robert George and Dorothy Joan (Heimbach) H. BS in Biology, Lafayette Coll., 1994; cert., Ednl. Svcs. Internat., Alhambra, Calif., 1994. Tchr. Sch. # 43, Sevastopol, Crimea, Ukraine, 1994-95; missionary Disciple Makers, State College, Pa., 1995—. Republican. Presbyterian. Avocations: golf, tennis, jogging, wine, reading. Home and Office: Disciple Makers 1927 W Liberty St Allentown PA 18104-5054

HEMMING, BRUCE CLARK, microbiologist; b. Pocatello, Idaho; s. Parley Lynn and Vernetta (Clark) H.; m. Caroline McDaniel, May 20, 1973; children: Eric M., Heidi, Heather, Crystal Lynn, Keri Lynn. BS in Microbiology, Brigham Young U., Provo, Utah, 1974, MS in Biochemistry, 1977; PhD in Plant Pathology, Mont. State U., Bozeman, 1982. Staff rsch. assoc. dept. chemistry Brigham Young U., 1977-78; sr. rsch. biologist molecular biology Monsanto Co., St. Louis, 1982-84, rsch. specialist plant molecular biology, 1984-89, project leader biocontrol crop protection, 1989, sr. rsch. specialist crop protection, 1989-91; pres. Microbe Inotech Labs., Inc., 1991—; chmn. regional com. USDA, Washington, 1986-89, mem. tech. subcom. on biocontrol expt. sta. com. on policy, 1987-89; panel mem. Nat. Rsch. Coun. Briefing, Washington, 1987; disting. guest lectr. Coll. Sci. Utah State U., Logan, 1989. Author: Methods in Enzymology, 1979; co-editor: Iron Chelation in Plants and Soil Microorganisms, 1993; mem. editorial bd. Biology of Metals, Springer-Verlag, 1988-91. Troop committeeman Boy Scouts Am., Manchester, Mo., 1985. Mem. AAAS, Am. Phytopath. Soc., Am. Chem. Soc., Am. Soc. Microbiology, Nat. Registry of Environ. Profls. Achievements include development of first microbial recombinant marker system tested in U.S. environment. Office: Microbe Inotech Labs Inc 12133 Bridgeton Sq Bridgeton MO 63044-2616

HEMMING, VAL G., university dean; b. Rexburg, Idaho, July 9, 1937; m. Alice Bell Hemming; children: Heidi, Julie, Jill, Patrick. BA in Entomology, U. Utah, 1962; MD, U. Utah Coll. Medicine, 1966. Diplomate Am. Bd. Pediatrics, Nat. Bd. Med. Examiners. Commd. 2d lt. USAF, 1965, advanced through grades to col.; pediatric intern U. Utah Affiliated Hosps., 1966-67; resident physician in pediatrics Wilford Hall USAF Med. Ctr., Lackland AFB, Tex., 1968-70; staff pediatrician USAF Hosp., Wiesbaden, West Germany, 1970-74; chmn., dir. pediatric residency tng. David Grant USAF Med. ctr., Travis AFB, Calif., 1976-80; assoc. prof. dept. pediatrics Uniformed Svcs. U. Health Scis., Bethesda, Md., 1980-84, prof. dept. pediatrics, 1984-87, prof., chmn. dept. pediatrics, 1987-95, from interim dean to dean F. Edward Hebert Sch. Medicine, 1995—; splty. cons. in pediatrics to Air Force Surgeon Gen., 1983-90; ret., 1990; cons. in pediatrics to the asst. sec. for health affairs Dept. of Def., 1988-91; adv. coun. Nat. Inst. of Child Health and Human Devel. Contbr. numerous articles to profl. jours. Mem. Am. Acad. Pediatrics, Am. Pediatric Soc., Infectious Disease Soc. of Am., Western Soc. for Pediatric Rsch., Pediatric Infectious Disease Soc., Lancefield Soc., Internat. AIDS Soc., Am. Soc. for Microbiology. Office: Uniformed Svcs U of Health Scis 4301 Jones Bridge Rd Bethesda MD 20814-4799*

HEMMING, WALTER WILLIAM, business financial consultant; b. Vineland, N.J., Oct. 2, 1939; s. Percy A. and Marguerite E. (Smith) H.; m. Shirley L. Derocher, June 10, 1961; children: Cynthia, Catherine, Walter Jr. BS, Syracuse U., 1961. CPA, N.Y., N.H. Prin. Arthur Young & Co., Stamford, Conn., 1961-72; contr. Coca-Cola Bottling Co. N.Y., Hackensack, N.J., 1972-78; exec. v.p., chief oper. officer KW Inc., Manchester, N.H., 1978-81; exec. v.p. fin. and adminstrn., chief fin. officer Coca-Cola Bottling Co. N.Y., Greenwich, Conn., 1981-86, Coca-Cola Bottling Plants of Maine, South Portland, 1987-88; gen. ptnr. Pleasant Ave. Assocs., 1988—, H&H Assocs., 1989—; v.p. bus devel. Coca-Cola Bottling Co. No. New Eng., Bedford, N.H., 1989; prin. Hemming Assocs., 1989—; treas. Island Approaches, Sunset, Maine, 1991—; also bd. dirs., Island Approaches, Sunset, Maine; mem. fin. rev. com. Coca-Cola Bottlers Assn., Atlanta, 1985-89; treas. N.H. Soft Drink Assn., Manchester, 1979-81; mem. exec. com., audit com., chmn. audit com. Centerpoint Bank, 1990-94, chmn. exec. com., 1995-96; bd. dirs. Cmty. Bankshares, Inc., mem. audit com., 1996-97; bd. dirs. Centrix Bank & Trust, mem. exec. com., audit com., chmn. audit com., 1999—. Treas. Clinton (Conn.) United Meth. Ch., 1969-72, Jesse Lee Meth. Ch., Ridgefield, Conn., 1974-77; treas. Hollis (N.H.) Congl. Ch., 1981, 92-95, asst. treas., 1982-92, deacon, 1988-92, trustee, 1997—. Mem. AICPA, N.H. Soc. CPAs, N.Y. Soc. CPAs, Rotary Internat., Fin. Execs. Inst. Republican. Avocations: tennis, gardening. Home: PO Box 610 Brookline NH 03033-0610 Office: Hemming Assocs 74 Northeastern Blvd Unit 11 Nashua NH 03062-3142

HEMMINGER, PAMELA LYNN, lawyer; b. Chgo., June 29, 1949; d. Paul Willis and Lenore Adelaide (Hennig) H.; m. Robert Alan Miller, May 14, 1979; children: Kimberly Anne, Jeffrey Ryan, Eric Douglas. BA, Pomona Coll., 1971; JD, Pepperdine U., 1976. Tchr. Etiwanda (Calif.) Sch. dist., 1971-74; law clerk Gibson Dunn & Crutcher, Newport Beach, Calif., 1974-76; assoc. Gibson Dunn & Crutcher, L.A., 1976-84, ptnr., 1985—. Contbg. author Sexual Harassment, 1992, Employment Discrimination Law, 1993; contbr. articles to profl. jours. Mem. comparable worth task force Calif., Sacramento, 1984, Pepperdine U. Sch. of Law Bd. Visitors, 1990—, Calif. Law Revision Commn., 1998-99. Named alumnus of yr. Pepperdine Sch. Law, 1996. Mem. L.A. County Bar Assn. (chair, labor and employment sect. 1996-97), Calif. C. of C. (employment rels. com. 1984—), Calif. Law Revision Commn., 1998-99. Republican. Lutheran. Office: Gibson Dunn & Crutcher 333 S Grand Ave Ste 4400 Los Angeles CA 90071-3197

HEMMINGHAUS, ROGER ROY, energy company executive, chemical engineer; b. St. Louis, Aug. 27, 1936; s. Roy Geroge and Henrietta E.M. (Knacht) H.; children: Sheryl Ann, Susan Lynn, Sally Ann; m. Dorotyh O'Kelly, Aug. 18, 1979; children: R. Patrick, Kelley Elizabeth, Roger Christian. Student, Purdue U., 1954-56; B.S. in Chem. Engring., Auburn U., 1958; grad. cert., Bettis Reactor Engring., Pitts., 1959; postgrad., La. State U., 1963-66. Various tech. and mgmt. positions Exxon Co. U.S.A., Baton Rouge, 1962-66, Benicia, Calif., 1967-70, Houston, 1970-76; refinery gen. mgr. C.F. Industries, East Chicago, Ind., 1976-77; pres. Petro United Inc., Houston, 1977-80; v.p. planning United Gas Pipe Line, Houston, 1980-82, United Energy Resources, Houston, 1982-84; v.p. corp. planning and devel. Diamond Shamrock Corp. (name changed to Maxus Energy Corp., 1987), Dallas, 1984-85, past exec. v.p.; pres. Diamond Shamrock Refining & Mktg., San Antonio, 1985—; chmn., dir., former CEO UltraMar Diamond Shamrock, Inc., San Antonio; dir. InterFirst Bank, San Antonio. Adviser Jr. Achievement, Baton Rouge, 1956-66; pres. congregation Lutheran Ch., Baton Rouge, 1965, Moraga, Calif., 1969; chmn. indsl. div. United Crusade, Solano County, Calif., 1970; assoc. gen. chmn. United Way, Tex. Gulf Coast, 1983-84. Served to lt. USN, 1958-62. Mem. Am. Chem. Soc., Am. Inst. Chem. Engrs., Naval Architects and Marine Engrs., Am. Petroleum Inst., San Antonio C. of C. (dir.), Tau Beta Pi, Phi Lambda Upsilon, Phi Kappa Phi, Kappa Alpha. Clubs: Fair Oaks Country; Plaza, Petroleum (San Antonio). Office: UltraMar Diamond Shamrock Inc PO Box 696000 San Antonio TX 78269-6000*

HEMMINGS, PETER WILLIAM, orchestra and opera administrator; b. London, Apr. 10, 1934; s. William and Rosalind (Jones) H.; m. Jane Frances Kearnes, May 19, 1962; children: William, Lucy, Emma, Rupert, Sophie. Grad., Gonville and Caius Coll., Cambridge, England, 1957; LLD (hon.), Strathclyude U., Glasgow, 1978. Clk. Harold Holt Ltd., London, 1958-59; planning mgr. Sadlers Wells Opera, London, 1959-65; gen. adminstr. Scottish Opera, Glasgow, 1962-77; gen. mgr. Australian Opera, Sydney, 1977-79; gen. dir. L.A. Music Ctr. Opera, London, 1984—; gen. mgr. New Opera Co., London, 1956-65; dir. Royal Acad. Music; gen. cons. Compton Verney Opera Project. Lt. Brit. Signal Corps, 1952-54. Deocrated Order Brit. Empire. Fellow Royal Scottish Acad. Music, Royal Acad. Music (hon.); mem. Am. Friends of Sadlers Wells (pres. 1994—), Opera Am. 9vice chmn.), Garrick Club (London), Royal Opera House Covent Garden (bd. dirs. 1999—). Anglican. Home: 775 S Madison Ave Pasadena CA 91106-3831 Office: LA Music Ctr Opera 135 N Grand Ave Los Angeles CA 90012-3013

HEMMINGS, ROBERT LESLIE, chemical engineer; b. Edmonton, Alberta, Canada, May 2, 1940; s. Charles and Phyllis (Jackson) H.; m. Micheline D.; children: Robert, Isabelle, Richard. BSChemE, U. Alberta, 1962; diploma, Imperial Coll Sci. & Tech., London, 1965; PhDChemE, U. London, 1965. Registered profl. engr., Ont., Que., Can., N.H. From rschr. to mgr. engring. Atomic Energy Can. Ltd., Montreal, Canada, 1965-78; v.p. Canatom Inc., Montreal, 1978-81, London Nuclear Svcs., Niagara Falls, N.Y., 1981-86; Columbia, S.C., 1981-86; v.p. Canatom Corp., Columbia, S.C., 1986-90; prin. process engr. Chem-Nuc. Sys. Inc., 1990-92; dir. process demonstration Rust Internat., Clemson Tech. Ctr., Anderson, S.C., 1992-94; dir. process technology Raytheon Engrs. and Constructors, Birmingham, Ala., 1994-99; head bldgs. and processes Internat. Thermonuclear Exptl. Reactor Program, Naka, Japan, 1999—. Mem. AIChE., Am. Chem. Soc., Am. Nuclear Soc., Nat. Soc. Profl. Engrs.. Avocations: golf, fishing, reading, opera, computer. Home: 1932 River Haven Ln Hoover AL 35244-1264

HEMOND, ROLAND A., professional baseball team executive; b. Central Falls, R.I., Oct. 26, 1929; m. Margaret Quinn, 1958; children—Susan, Tere, Robert, Jay, Ryan. Past dir. player personnel Chgo. White Sox, past exec. v.p., gen. mgr., spl. asst. to pres. and chmn., 1985-86; cons. commr. of Baseball, N.Y.C., 1986-87; formerly with Boston/Milw. Braves, Calif. Angels.; exec. v.p., gen. mgr. Baltimore Orioles, 1987-95; now sr. exec. vp baseball operations Arizona Diamondbacks, Phoenix. Served in USCG. Named The Sporting News Major League Exec. of Yr., 1972, 89, Major League Exec. of Yr. UPI, 1983, Am. League Exec. of Yr. UPI, 1989. Address: 1332 W Edgemont Ave Phoenix AZ 85007-1117

HEMP, RALPH CLYDE, retired reinsurance company executive, consultant, arbitrator, umpire; b. Fresno, Calif., Sept. 9, 1936; s. Ralph Edward and Mabel Alice (Knox) H.; m. Mary Ann Corley, Aug. 25, 1962; children—Ralph Kenneth, Laura Elizabeth. B.A., San Diego State U., 1961; J.D., Western States U., Santa Ana, Calif., 1971. Office mgr. Crawford & Co., L.A., 1961-67; regional claims mgr. Olympic Ins. Co., L.A., 1967-68; sr. v.p. Leatherby Ins. Co., Fullerton, Calif., 1968-76; pres. North Am. Co., Greenwich, Conn., 1976-86; chmn. Mt. Eagle Cos., Whitefish, Mont., 1986—. Republican. Avocations: hunting; fishing; golf; skiing. Home: PO Box 1971 Whitefish MT 59937-1971 Office: Mt Eagle Cos PO Box 1971 Whitefish MT 59937-1971

HEMPEL, FRED, federal government administrator; b. Nashville, Feb. 25, 1942. BS, Vanderbilt U., 1964; M in Civil Engring., W.Va. U., 1971. Regional dir. Fed. Hwy. Adminstrn., Denver, 1978-83; regional dir. office of environ. programs Fed. Hwy. Adminstrn., Washington, 1983-84; asst. divsn. adminstr. Fed. Hwy. Adminstrn., Balt., 1984-88; Ohio divsn. adminstr. Fed. Hwy. Adminstrn., Columbus, 1988-95; Calif. divsn. adminstr. Fed. Hwy. Adminstrn., Sacramento, 1995-96; dir. corp. mgmt. Fed. Hwy. Adminstrn., Washington, 1996—. Mem. Registered Profl. Engrs. Tenn. Office: Fed Hwy Adminstrn Program Quality Coord 400 7th St SW Washington DC 20590*

HEMPEL, JOHN P., mathematics educator; b. Salt Lake City, Oct. 14, 1935; s. Edgar W. and Emma B. (Johnson) H.; m. Edith Froese-Gertzen, Sept. 1, 1965; 1 child, Kristian J. BS, U. Utah, 1957; MS, U. Wis., 1959, PhD, 1962., Asst. prof. Fla. State U., 1962-63; asst. prof. Rice U., Houston, 1964-69, assoc. prof., 1969-76, prof., 1976—; with Inst. Advanced Study, 1971-72; vis. assoc. prof. U. Utah, 1976; vis. prof. U. Mich. 1980-81, U. B.C., 1987-88. Postdoctoral fellow Inst. Advance Study, 1963-64. Mem. Math. Sci. Rsch. Inst. Office: Rice University Dept Math PO Box 1982 6100 South Main Houston TX 77251

HEMPENIUS, GERALD EDWARD, real estate broker; b. Chgo., Sept. 6, 1934; s. John Garrett and Jessie Fern Hempenius; m. Patricia A. Woodcock, Jan. 28, 1955; children: Sharyl Lynn Hempenius Britt, Jeffrey Alan. BS, Whittier Coll., 1956; MS, NYU, 1957. Cert. Comml. Investment Mem. Nat. Assn. Realtors, Grad. Realtors Inst., Exchange Mktg. Specialist, Cert. Hotel Adminstr. Store mgr. J.C. Penney, various cities, Calif., 1957-75; real estate agt. Gold Coast Realty, Morro Bay, Calif., 1976-77; real estate broker, owner Com-Spec Properties, Inc., San Luis Obispo, Calif., 1977—, cons., 1986—; pres., bd. dirs. Calif. Lodging Industry Assn., Sacramento, 1984-88; mem. conf. com. Calif. Hotel and Motel Assn. and Forte Hotels Calif., 1991-96. Bd. dirs. Visitors and Conf. Bur., San Luis Obispo, 1991-96. Mem. Citizen Amb. Program, Seattle, 1996. Mem. Nat. Assn. Realtors, Nat. Coun. Exchangors, Nat. Assn. Counselors, Calif. Assn. Realtors, Morro Bay C. of C. (pres., bd. dirs. 1980-86), Rotary (pres. 1990, Paul Harris fellow 1984, Rotarian of Yr. award 1984). Republican. Avocations: golf, travel. Office: Com-Spec Properties Inc 1422 Monterey St Ste A-201 San Luis Obispo CA 93401-2954

HEMPERLY, REBECCA SUE, publishing manager; b. Reading, Pa., June 17, 1966; d. Kenneth Jay and Ann Rebecca (Riehl) H. BA, Wheaton Coll., 1988; MA, Emerson Coll., 1992. Editl. asst. Coll.-Hill Press/Little, Brown, Boston, 1988-90; editl. asst. Little, Brown and Co., Boston, 1990, contracts coord., 1990-92, asst. mgr. contracts, 1992-96, mgr. contracts, 1996-98; paralegal WGBH Ednl. Found., Boston, 1998-99, pub. contracts cons., 1998-99; client svcs. mgr. Databas Publ. Group, 1999—; del. 1st Amendment Congress, 1997; spkr. rights and permissions Assn. Am. Pub., Washington, 1996; mem. diversity task force Little, Brown and Co., Boston, 1993-98. Contbr. essays: The Book Group Book, 2d edit., 1995, Teaching Contemporary Theory to Undergraduates, 1995. Team capt. AIDS walk-a-thon Little, Brown and Co./AIDS Action Com., Boston, 1995, 96, 97; phone coord. GLOW, Watertown, Mass., 1989-98; mem. Rails to Trails Conservancy, 1995—. Mem. Women in Publishing, Nat. Writers' Union, Bookbuilders of Boston, Phi Beta Kappa (scholar 1988). Avocations: gardening, cycling, karate, photography.

HEMPFLING, GREGORY JAY, mechanical engineer; b. Terre Haute, Ind., Sept. 7, 1961; s. John G. and Sandra (Sutton) H. BSME, Rose-Hulman Inst. Tech., Terre Haute, Ind., 1983; M in Engring. Mgmt., George Washington U., Washington, 1991. Asst. engr. Cherne Contracting Corp., New Washington, Ind., 1983-84; engr. I Newport News Shipbuilding, 1984-86; engr. II Newport News (Va.) Shipbuilding, 1986-89, engring. supr., 1989-93, engring. dept. mgr., 1994-95, LPD-17 design mgr., 1995-96, Electric Boat br. mgr., 1996-97; sr. program mgmt. Allied Signal, Inc., Tempe, Ariz., 1997-98; mgr. program planning and control Allied Signal, Inc., 1998—; chmn. Industry Rels. Com. (ea. Va. sect.), 1990-92. Mem. ASME (chmn. industry rels. com. 1990-92, rep. Peninsula Engring. Coun. 1992-93), SAE (Marine Vehicle Systems panel 1989-97), Soc. Naval Architects and Marine Engrs., Am. Mgmt. Assn., Naval Submarine League, Program Mgmt. Inst. Avocations: golf, beach volleyball, tennis. Home: 10327 E Acacia Dr Scottsdale AZ 85259-8664 Office: Allied Signal Inc M/S 1233R 1300 W Warner Rd Tempe AZ 85284-2896

HEMPHILL, JAMES S., investment management executive, financial advisor; b. Richmond, Va., Sept. 13, 1956; s. John Mickle and Marie Jeanne (de Kiewiet) H.; m. Amy Guise, Oct. 16, 1993; children: John Reagan, Katharine Guise. BA with high honors, Swarthmore Coll., 1978. CFP, CLU. Legal asst. Schnader, Harrison, Phila., 1978; stockbroker, 2d v.p. Shearson/Am. Express, Media, Pa., 1978-84; asst. v.p. Merrill Lynch, Media, 1984-90; pres. TGS Fin. Advisors, Media, 1990—. Bd. dirs. Suburban Music Sch., Media, 1993—, chmn. capital campaign, 1995-96, v.p., 1996-97, pres., 1997-99; rsch. dir. Joachim for Congress, Havertown, Pa., 1982; founder Third Thursday Wine Club, Media, 1993—; commr. Media Sports League, 1985-86. Mem. Internat. Assn. for Fin. Planning. Republican. Avocations: travel, wine appreciation. Office: TGS Financial Advisors 103 Chesley Dr Media PA 19063-1757

HEMPHILL, JEAN HARGETT, college dean; b. Pollocksville, N.C., Aug. 21, 1936; d. Robert Franklin and Frances (Hill) Hargett; m. Raymond Arthur Hemphill, Feb. 28, 1964; 1 child, Gerald Franklin. BS, East Carolina U., 1958; MEd, U. Nev.-Las Vegas, 1968; student N.C. State U.,

1993. Sec.-treas. Five Points Milling Co., Inc., New Bern, N.C., 1968-77; instr. Craven C.C., New Bern, 1973-80, dean service techs., 1980—; mem. New Bern-Craven County Tech. Prep, steering com. New Bern-Craven County Sch., 1990-95; mem. Craven County Sch. to Work Steering Com., 1996—; supr. rep. curriculum improvement project N.C. C.C. Sys., 1992-96; mem. Craven County Schs. Sch.-to-Work Curriculum Com., 1996—. Scholarship chmn. continuing edn. div. Woman's Club, New Bern, 1981—, treas. continuing edn. div., 1986—. Mem. N.C. Assn. C.C. Instrnl. Adminstrs., Phi Kappa Phi. Democrat. Methodist. Office: Craven Community Coll 800 College Ct New Bern NC 28562-4900

HEMPHILL, JOHN MICHAEL, neurologist; b. Vernon, Tex., Aug. 6, 1947; s. Gipson Franklin and Floy Marie (Huntley) H.; m. Caroline Anne Frazzitta, Sept. 13, 1975; children: Kate, Ryan. BA, Baylor U., 1969, MD, 1974. Diplomate Am. Bd. Psychiatry and Neurology, Am. Bd. Pediatrics. Rockefeller fellow Div. Sch. Harvard U., 1972-73; fellow Johns Hopkins Med. Instns., Balt., 1974-80, asst. prof., 1980-81; neurologist Savannah (Ga.) Neurol. Assocs., 1981-93; med. dir. Ga. Neurol. Inst., 1993—; clin. asst. prof. Mercer Sch. Medicine, Macon, Ga., 1991—; clin. assoc. prof. neurology Med. Coll. Ga., Augusta, 1993—; chmn. dept. medicine Meml. Med. Ctr., Savannah, 1990-91, dir. neurol. edn., 1993—, v.p. rehab. svcs., 1994—. Bd. dirs. Savannah Symphony, 1991—, pres., 1996—. Fellow Am. Acad. Pediatrics, Am. Acad. Neurology; mem. Child Neurology Soc., The Chatham Club, Savannah Yacht Club, Secession Golf Club, Oglethorpe Club, Savannah Golf Club. Republican. Episcopalian. Avocations: golf, piano, symphony music. Office: Ga Neurol Inst 4600 Waters Ave Savannah GA 31404-6702

HEMPHILL, NORMA JO, special event planning and tour company executive; b. Enid, Okla., Nov. 25, 1930; d. Wyatt Warren and Wanda Markes (Parker) Stout; m. Benjamin Robert Hemphill, June 21, 1952; children: Susan Colleen, Robert Gary. Student, Okla. State U.; BA, U. Calif., Berkeley, 1955. Former acct. Better Bus. Bookkeeping, Lafayette, Calif.; tchr., Head Start tchr. Chino (Calif.) Elem. Sch., 1966-68; pres., founder Calif. Carousel and Carousel Tours, Lafayette, 1972—; spkr. in field; cons., dir. various orgns. Past bd. dirs. PTA, Moraga, Calif., Lafayette; bd. dirs. Children's Home Soc., Upland, Calif., 1965-69; past demonstation tchr. Presbytery of Bay Area, San Francisco; past supt. 1st Presbyn. Ch., Oakland, Calif., elder, 1977—, trustee, 1980; mem. hon. adv. com. Festival of Lake, Oakland, 1982; bd. govs. Goodwill Industries, 1978-79; founder, chmn. Joint Svc. Clubs Foster Children's Ann. Christmas Party; bd. dirs. William Penn Mott Jr. Visitors Ctr., Presidio of San Francisco Nat. Park, 1997-99. Named Person of Yr. award Advt.-Mktg. Assn. East Bay, 1978; co-recipient Event of Yr. award, Am. Pub. Rels. Assn., 1984. Mem. Lake Merritt Breakfast Club (Oakland, spl. events com., bd. govs., named Citizen of Community 1992), Lake Merritt Inst. (hon.), Soroptomist (very important women honor roll Diablo Valley 1990, keynote speaker 1991), Pi Beta Phi (bd. dirs., spl. events com. Contra Costa County chpt., Founder's Day speaker at U. Calif.-Berkeley, 1993). Avocations: travel, reading, arts, hiking, designing. Office: Calif Carousel & Carousel Tours PO Box 537 Lafayette CA 94549-0537

HEMPLEMAN, BARBARA FLORENCE, archivist; b. Bellevue, Pa., Mar. 3, 1925; d. Warren Wilson and Florence Permelia (Firth) Hampe; m. David William Hempleman, Aug. 4, 1956; children: Warwick, Terence. BA, Coll. of Wooster, 1947; MA, NYU, 1953; MLS, Atlanta U., 1973. Dir. Christian edn. Calvary Reformed Ch., Reading, Pa., 1951-52; libr. asst. Duke U., Durham, N.C., 1957-59; asst. prof. history Warren Wilson Coll., Asheville, N.C., 1948-51, 54-56, 66-69; libr. dir. Warren Wilson Coll., Asheville, N.C., 1978-86, archivist, 1986-98, adj. prof. women's history, 1983-96; vis. prof. libr. sci. Emory U., Atlanta, 1973-74; adj. prof. libr. sci. Atlanta U., 1973, 78, reference libr., 1974-78. Contbr. numerous articles to Owl and Spade mag. Bd. dirs. YWCA, Asheville, 1978-79; libr. developer, adminstr. Black Mountain (N.C.) Correctional Ctr. for Women, 1997—. Nat. Assn. Fgn. Student Affairs grantee, 1975. Mem. Women's History Club Asheville (historian 1996-97). Democrat. Presbyterian. Avocations: travel, reading.

HEMPSTEAD, GEORGE H., III, lawyer, diversified company executive; b. 1943. BBA, St. Johns U., 1965, LLB, 1967. Bar: N.Y. 1968, D.C. 1979. Atty. antitrust div. U.S. Dept. Justice, Washington, 1967-70; with Simpson, Thacher & Bartlett, N.Y.C., 1970-74; gen. counsel Burmah Oil, Inc., N.Y.C., 1974-76; asst. gen. counsel Hanson Industries Inc., Iselin, N.J., 1976-78; sr. coord. coun. ICI Am. Inc., Wilmington, Del., 1978-81; dir., v.p. sec., gen. counsel Hanson Industries, Iselin, 1982-96; assoc. dir. Hanson PLC, London and NYSE, 1990-96; chmn. bd. trustees Christian Brother Acad., 1993-95, Lincroft, N.J.; sr. v.p. law, sec. Millennium Chemicals Inc., 1996—; bd. suprs. Suburban Propane LLP, 1996-99. Office: Millennium Chemicals Inc PO Box 7015 230 Half Mile Rd Red Bank NJ 07701-5683

HEMPSTONE, SMITH, JR., diplomat, journalist; b. Washington, Feb. 1, 1929; s. Smith and Elizabeth (Noyes) H.; m. Kathaleen Fishback, Jan. 30, 1954; 1 dau. Student, George Washington U., 1946-47; BA with honors, U. of South, 1950, LittD (hon.), 1969; Nieman fellow, Harvard U., 1964-65. Rewrite man AP, Charlotte, N.C., 1952; with Nat. Geog. mag., Washington, 1954; reporter Louisville Times, 1953, Evening Star, Washington, 1955-56; fgn. corr. Africa, Asia, Europe and Latin Am. for Chgo. Daily News, 1960-66; fgn. corr. Washington Evening Star, 1966-69, assoc. editor, 1970-75; exec. editor Washington Times, 1982-84, editor-in-chief, 1984-85; nationally syndicated newspaper columnist, 1970-89, ambassador to Kenya, 1989-93; diplomat in residence U. of the South, Sewanee, Tenn., 1993, Va. Mil. Inst., Lexington, 1994; Fellow Inst. Current World Affairs, 1956-60. Author: Africa, Angry Young Giant, 1961, Rebels, Mercenaries and Dividends-The Katanga Story, 1962, Rogue Ambassador, 1997; (novel) A Tract of Time, 1966, In the Midst of Lions, 1968; editorial bd.: Nieman Reports, 1965-73. Alumni trustee U. South, 1974-78; bd. govs. Inst. Current World Affairs, 1974-78. Recipient Fgn. Corr. award Sigma Delta Chi and Overseas Press Club. Mem. Chevy Chase Club (Md.), Met. Club (Washington), Explorers Club (N.Y.C.). Episcopalian. Home and Office: 7611 Fairfax Rd Bethesda MD 20814-1313

HEMRY, JEROME ELDON, lawyer; b. Kirksville, Mo., July 22, 1905; s. U.S.G. and Rose M. (Plumb) H.; m. Martha L. Langston, Aug. 1, 1934; children: Jerome Louis, Kenneth Marshall. A.B., Oklahoma City U., 1926; J.D., U. Okla., 1928; LL.M., Harvard U., 1929. Bar: Okla. 1928. Partner Hemry & Hemry, Oklahoma City, 1931-82, of counsel, 1983—; prof. law Central Okla. Sch. Law, 1931-41; dean, prof. law Langston U., 1948-49; dir., counsel Am. Gen. Life Ins. Co. Okla., 1959-79; pres., gen. counsel Gen. Constrn. Corp., 1941-45; legislative counsel Okla. Chain Store Assn., 1941-44; Mem. Bd. Conf. Claimant's Okla. Ann. Conf.; treas. Oklahoma City S. Dist. Contbr. articles legal jours. Bd. dirs. Family and Children's Service, 1939-56. Mem. Okla. Assn. Mcpl. Attys. (pres. 1956-57), Am., Okla. bar assns., Order of Coif, Phi Delta Phi, Lambda Chi Alpha. Methodist (pres., counsel trustees). Clubs: Lions (Oklahoma City), Men's Dinner (Oklahoma City). Home: 2255 NW 55th St Oklahoma City OK 73112-7716 Office: 401 N Hudson Ave Oklahoma City OK 73102-3433

HEMRY, LARRY HAROLD, former federal agency official, writer; b. Seattle, Jan. 4, 1941; s. Harold Bernard and Florence Usborne (Achilles) H.; m. Nancy Kay Ballantyne, July 10, 1964 (div. Apr. 1976); children: Rachel Dalayne, Aaron Harold, Andrew LeRoy. BA, Seattle Pacific Coll., 1963; postgrad., Western Evang. Sem., Portland, Oreg., 1969, 70. Ordained to ministry Free Meth. Ch., 1968. Clergyman Free Meth. Ch., Vancouver, B.C., Can., 1963-64, Mt. Vernon, Wash., 1968-69; clergyman Colton (Oreg.) Community Ch., 1969-71; edit clk. Moody Bible Inst., Chgo., 1964-66; pres., founder Bethel Enterprises, Colton, 1969-71; immigration insp. U.S. Immigration and Naturalization Svc., Sumas, Wash., 1972-96. Author, historian: Some Northwest Pioneer Families, 1969, The Hemry Family History Book, 1985; author: An Earnest Plea to Earnest Christians, 1969. chmn. com. to establish and endow the James A. Hemry meml. scholarship fund Seattle Pacific U., 1975. Fellow Seattle Pacific U. (Centurians Club); mem. The Nature Conservancy, The Sierra Club, The Audubon Soc. Avocations: camping, nature study, woodcarving. Home: PO Box 532 Sumas WA 98295-0532

HEMSING, JOSEPHINE CLAUDIA, public relations professional for performing arts; b. Paris, France, June 5, 1953; d. Albert E. and Esther (Davidson) H.; m. Daniel F. Cameron, Sept. 22, 1990. Student, Sorbonne U. de Paris, 1972-73; BA, Sarah Lawrence Coll., 1974; postgrad., CUNY, 1982—. Dep. dir. distbn. ASCAP, N.Y.C., 1975-81; assoc. dramaturg and festival coordinator Städtische Bühnen Freiburg, Fed. Republic Germany, 1981-82; publicity asst. Audrey Michaels Pub. Relations, N.Y.C., 1983; publicity assoc. N.Y. Philharmonic, N.Y.C., 1984-85; publicist The Carson Office, N.Y.C., 1985-89; founder, dir. Hemsing Assocs., Inc., N.Y.C., 1989—. Mem. prodn. staff for New Russian Chamber Orch., N.Y.C., 1976-79, Encompass Music Theatre, N.Y.C., 1978-79, Wallgraben Theater on Tour, U.S.A., 1980, Rodger Hess Prodns., N.Y.C., 1982, John Hart Assoc., N.Y.C., 1982, Peter Witt Players Prodns., N.Y.C., 1982-83, numerous Broadway and off-Broadway shows including How I Got That Story, 1982, Twice Around the Park, 1983, Diary of a Madman, 1989; NBC-TV documentary Missiles Go Home, 1981; numerous published translations. Democrat. Home: 401 E 80th St Apt 29K New York NY 10021-0654 Office: 401 E 80th St Apt 14H New York NY 10021-0654 also: Hemsing Internat care Mary Louise Stott, 21 rue Chevert, 75007 Paris France

HEMSTREET, MARK S., hotel executive; b. Portland, Oreg., Mar. 15, 1950. Pres. Shilo Inns, Shilo Mgmt. Co., Portland, 1974—. Office: Shilo Inns 11600 SW Corby Dr Portland OR 97225

HENARD, ELIZABETH ANN, controller; b. Providence, Oct. 9, 1947; d. Anthony Joseph and Grace Johanna (Lokay) Zorbach; m. Patrick Edward Mann, Dec. 18, 1970 (div. July 1972); m. John Bruce Henard Jr., Oct. 19, 1974; children: Scott Michael, Christopher Andrew. Student, Jacksonville (Fla.) U., 1966. Sec. So. Bell Tel.&Tel., Jacksonville, 1964-69; office mgr. Gunther F. Reis Assocs., Tampa, Fla., 1969-71; exec. sec. Ernst & Ernst, Tampa, 1971-72; exec. sec. to pres. Lamalie Assocs., Tampa, 1972-74; exec. sec. Arthur Young & Co., Chgo., 1975; adminstrv. asst. Irving J. Markin, Chgo., 1975; contr., v.p., corp. sec. Henard Assocs., Inc., Dallas, 1983-92; real estate agt. Coldwell Banker Residential Real Estate, Tampa, 1999—. Mem. Dallas Investors Group (treas. 1986-91), Tampa Palms Country Club. Republican. Roman Catholic. Avocations: photography, crafts, golf, reading. Home: 15350 Amberly Dr Apt 3414 Tampa FL 33647-1634

HENBEST, JON CHARLES, accountant, consultant; b. Ill., May 29, 1969; s. Lawrence James and Barbara Lynne (Berry) H.; m. Christine Louise Maloney, July 11, 1992; 1 child, Ethan Samuel. AS, Ocean County Coll., 1989; BS, NYU, 1991. Acct. Withum, Smith & Brown, Princeton, N.J., 1991-95; cons. WS&B Cons. Group, Princeton, 1996—. Mem. Pine Beach (N.J.) Civic Assn., 1993-94; bd. dirs. Operation Friendship of Am., Toms River, 1984-95, treas., bd. dirs., 1994-95; founder, treas. Leukemia Benefit Found., Pine Beach, 1993—. Mem. AICPA, N.J. Soc. of CPAs. Republican. Presbyterian. Avocations: gardening, bicycling, carpentry. Office: WS&B Cons Group Inc 100 Overlook Ctr Princeton NJ 08540-7814

HENBEST, ROBERT LEROY, retired bank and insurance company executive; b. Elmira, N.Y., Aug. 25, 1923; s. Edmund James and Helen Mae (Yost) H.; m. Grace Edith Rowley; children: Judith H. Bayer, Jacqueline Lee, William H., R. Theodore E. Student, Lycoming Coll., 1943, Elmira Coll., 1950, 52, U. Conn., 1951, U. Hartford, 1953; cert., Wharton Bus. Sch., 1955. Ins. mgr. Henbest Ins. Svc., Elmira, 1941-42, 45-47; pres. Henbest & Morrisey, Inc., Elmira, 1945-89; bank dir. Elmira Savs. Bank, 1987-89; ret., 1989. Chmn. Chemung County Safety Orgn.; worked for United Fund; mem. Nat. Soaring Mus., Nat. Warplane Mus., Clemens Ctr. Performing Arts, Arnot Art Gallery, North Presbyn. Ch., trustee; vol. Ret. Sr. Vol. Program, Medicare/Medicaid Assistance Program, claims counselor Courier Arnot-Agden Med. Ctr. 6; treas. Thursday Morning Musicales; mem. Torch Internat.; Blood Bank vol. ARC. Maj. USAF, 1943-45, WWII, USAF Res., 1945-66, ret. 1966. Decorated DFC, Air Medal with four oak leaf clusters, Presdl. citation with oak leaf cluster, Euro/Meditteranean Theatre Ribbon, with four battle stars. Mem. Chemung County Ins. Agts. Assn. (pres. 1958), Am. Legion, Curtis Wright Air Force Assn., Profl. Ins. Agts. Assn., Ind. Agts. Assn., Chemung C. of C., 15th Air Force Assn., 451st Bomb Group Assn., Masons, Nat. Warplane Mus. (falcon). Republican. Home: 12 Roricks Glen Pky Elmira NY 14905-1966 Office: WH Ins Agy Inc 112 Baldwin St Elmira NY 14901-3025

HENCE, JANE KNIGHT, designer; b. Pitts., June 27, 1937; d. Luther and Doris (Ayers) Knight; m. Carleton Campbell Hence, May 12, 1962 (div. 1975); children: Kyle Fitz-Randolph Hence, Maxson Bentley Hence, Juliellen Hence Casey. Grad., Emma Willard Sch., Troy, N.Y., 1955; student, Skidmore Coll., Saratoga Springs, N.Y., 1955-58; Grad., Traphagen Sch. of Design, N.Y.C., 1960; student, Yale U., 1986-90, R.I. Sch. of Design, 1988-91. Owner various bus. ventures including Bed and Breakfast, catering bus., free-lance interior design, 1982—; owner, prin. JKH Design, 1989—; consulting assoc. and designer Michael McKinley & Assocs., Stonington, Conn., 1993—; mem. Westerly Sch. Facilities Com., Westerly, R.I., 1993-96, Westerly Sch. Bldg. Com., 1992-93; mem. Bd. S.E. Mus., Brewster, N.Y., 1970-74. Designer over 38 bldgs. in New Eng., 1987-99; co-designer more than 40 bldgs. in R.I. and Conn., 1989-99; painter various media in collections in Midwest, South, N.Y. and New Eng. Avocations: travel, reading, opera, theatre. Office: Rockbound Haversham Rd Westerly RI 02891 also: 946 Burgundy New Orleans LA 70116

HENCKE, PAUL GERARD, editor, writer, broadcaster; b. St. Louis, Oct. 4, 1927; s. Richard and Louise (Dierkes) H.; widowed, 1975; children: Thomas, John, Christopher, Mary, Andrew, Joseph, James; m. Jeannye Thornton, Sept., 1976; children: Matthew, Maximillian. BS, St. Louis U., 1950. Mag. and newspaper writer, freelancer St. Louis Globe-Dem., Nations' Bus. mag., Washington, St. Louis, 1947-53; assoc. editor Kiplinger Washington Letter, 1966-74; editor weekly newsletter U.S. News & World Report, Washington, 1974-85; editor newsletters Nat. Inst. Bus Mgmt., N.Y.C., Alexandria, Va., 1985-94; editor Phillips Pub. Internat., 1994-96. Broadcaster: NBC, 1977-79, Nat. Pub. Radio, 1979-80; broadcaster, commentator CBS, 1981—; co-editor: Dear NASA: Please Send Me A Rocket; contbr. numerous mag. and newspsper features. With USCG, 1945-47. Mem. AFTRA, Nat. Press Club. Roman Catholic. Home: 6315 Naval Ave Lanham MD 20706-3528

HENDEE, JOHN CLARE, university research educator; b. Duluth, Minn., Nov. 12, 1938; s. Clare Worden and Mary Myrtle (Parker) H.; m. Marilyn R. Riley; children: John Jr., James, Landon, Joy, Joni, Jared. BS in Forestry, Mich. State U., 1960; MF in Forestry Mgmt., Oreg. State U., 1962; PhD in Forestry, Econs. and Sociology, U. Wash., 1967. With USDA Forest Svc., 1961-85; with timber mgmt. dept. Waldport and Corvallis, Oreg., 1961-64; fire rsch. forester Pacific S.W. Forest Experiment Sta., Berkeley, Calif., 1964; recreation rsch. unit leader Pacific N.W. Forest Expt. Sta., Seattle, 1967-76; legis. affairs staff Washington, 1977-78; asst. sta. dir. Southeastern Forest Experiment Sta., Asheville, N.C., 1978-85; dean Coll. Forestry, Wildlife, and Range Sci. U. Idaho, Moscow, 1985-94, prof. forest resources and resource recreation and tourism, 1985, dir. wilderness rsch. ctr., 1994—; dir. Idaho Forest, Wildlife and Range Experiment Sta., 1985-94; mem. affiliate faculty in forestry U. Wash., Seattle, 1968-76; vice chmn. for sci. 4th World Wilderness Congress, 1987. Co-author: Wildlife Management in Wilderness, 1978, Introduction to Forests and Renewable Resources, 6th edit., 1994; sr. co-author: Wilderness Management, 1978, rev. 2d edit., 1990; founding mng. editor Internat. Jour. of Wilderness, 1995; contbr. numerous articles to profl. jours. Bd. dirs. WILD Found.; active Boy Scouts Am. Recipient Spl. Merit award Keep Am. Beautiful, 1972, Nat. Conservation Achievement award Am. Motors, 1974, Spl. award for Wilderness Rsch. and Edn. Nat. Outdoor Leadership Sch., 1985, Merit award USDA-Forest Service, 1979, 80, 85, Lifetime Achievement award Am. Soc. Pub. Adminstrn., 1988; Fed. Congl. fellow, Washington, 1976-77. Mem. Am. Forestry Assn., Nat. Assn. Profl. Forestry Schs. and Colls. (chmn. western div. 1987-89), Wildlife Soc., Soc. Am. Foresters (edn. and communication working group chmn. 1986-89). Avocations: backpacking, hiking, skiing, hunting, fishing. Office: Univ Idaho Wilderness Research Center Moscow ID 83843

HENDEE, WILLIAM RICHARD, medical physics educator, university official; b. Owosso, Mich., Jan. 1, 1938; s. C.L. and Alvina M. H.; m. Jeannie Wesley, June 16, 1960; children: Mikal, Shonn, Eric, Gareth and Gregory (twins), Lara and Karel (twins). B.S., Millsaps Coll., Jackson, Miss., 1959; Ph.D., U. Tex., 1962; DSc (hon.), Millsaps Coll., Jackson, Miss., 1988. Diplomate Am. Bd. Radiology, Am. Bd. Health Physics. AEC fellow Nat. Reactor Testing Sta., Idaho Falls, Idaho, 1960; asst. prof., then assoc. prof. physics Millsaps Coll., 1962-65, chmn. dept., 1964-65; instr. Miss. State U. (extension), 1963; asst. prof., then assoc. prof. radiology (med. physics) U. Colo. Med. Center, 1965-73, prof., 1974-85, chmn. dept., 1978-85; mem. staff VA Hosp., Denver, 1970-85, Mercy Hosp., 1971-85, Denver Gen. Hosp., 1971-85, Beth Israel Hosp., 1974-85; v.p. sci. and tech. AMA, Chgo., 1985-1991; prof. radiology, biophysics, radiation oncology, bioethics Med. Coll. Wis., Milw., 1991—, clin. prof. radiology and biophysics, 1985-91, sr. assoc. dean, v.p., 1991—, dean grad. sch., 1995—; prof. bioengring. Marquette U., 1993—; vis. lectr. Oak Ridge Assoc. Univs., 1964; adj. prof. radiology Northwestern U. Sch. Medicine, 1986-91. Contbr. articles to profl. jours. Served with USMC, 1957-62. Recipient Disting. Alumnus award Millsaps Coll., 1967, Disting. Svc. award Nat. Wildlife Fedn., 1990, Wright Langham Meml. award U. Ky., 1991; Gilbert X-ray fellow, 1960-62, summer fellow NSF, AEC; campus assoc. Danforth Found. Fellow Am. Coll. Radiology, Am. Inst. Med. and Biol. Engring. (pres. 1998-99); mem. AAAS, Health Physics Soc. (chmn. coms., Elda E. Anderson award 1972), Am. Assn. Physicists in Medicine (pres. 1976-77, Robert S. Landauer Meml. award 1977, William D. Coolidge award 1989), Nat. Wildlife Fedn. (Disting. Svc. award 1990), Soc. Biomed. Engring., (sr. mem.), Soc. Nuclear Medicine (pres. 1980-81, Benedict Cassen Meml. award 1984), Am. Acad. Home Care Physicians (Disting. Svc. award 1991), Omicron Delta Kappa, Theta Nu Sigma. Office: Med Coll Wis 8701 W Watertown Plank Rd Milwaukee WI 53226-3548

HENDERSHOT, CAROL MILLER, physical therapist; b. Lancaster, Pa., July 24, 1959; d. Richard Horace and Joan Marie (Nonnenmocher) Miller; m. Richard A. Hendershot, Dec. 29, 1989; 1 child, Scott Michael. BS in Physical Therapy, Quinnipiac Coll., 1981. Staff phys. therapist Easter Seal Rehab. Ctr., Lancaster, 1981-85, phys. therapy dept. head, 1986-89; staff phys. therapist Community Hosp. of Lancaster, 1985-86, Guilds' Sch. & Neuromuscular Ctr., 1990—. Dir. publicity and pub. rels. Lancaster Dist. United Meth. Women, 1988-89, chmn. ch. and soc. com., 1987, 88, mem. chancel choir, 1981-89, mem. adminstrv. bd., 1975-88; trustee Audubon Pk. United Meth. Ch., 1990-93, mem. chancel choir 1990-92, mem. staff parish rels. com. 1993-94, mem. Jubilee Bell Choir, 1990—; dir. Bethlehem and Joy Bells Handbell Choirs, 1994-96, Jubilee Handbell Choir, 1996—. Mem. Neuro-Devel. Treatment Assn., Lancaster County Visiting Nurse Assn. (mem. profl. adv. com. 1987-89), Beta Beta Beta. Democrat. Methodist. Avocations: sewing, music, cooking, needlework, gardening, stamping. Home: 6007 W Hopi Ct Spokane WA 99208-9046

HENDERSON, ALBERT JOHN, federal judge; b. Canton, Ga., Dec. 12, 1920; s. Albert Jefferson and Cliffie Mae (Cook) H.; m. Jenny Lee Medford, Feb. 24, 1951; children—Michael John, Jenny Lee. LL.B., Mercer U., 1947. Bar: Ga. bar 1947. Practiced law Marietta, Ga., 1948-60; judge Juvenile Ct. Cobb County, Ga., 1953-60, Superior Ct. Cobb County, 1961-68, U.S. Dist. Ct. for No. Dist. Ga., Atlanta, 1968-76; chief judge U.S. Dist. Ct. for No. Dist. Ga., 1976-79; judge U.S. Circuit Ct. of Appeals for 5th Circuit, 1979-81; judge U.S. Circuit Ct. Appeals for 11th Circuit, 1981-86, sr. judge, 1986—; asst. solicitor gen. Blue Ridge Jud. Circuit, 1948-52. Chmn. Cobb dist. Atlanta council Boy Scouts Am., 1964. Served with AUS, 1943-46. Fellow Am. Bar Found.; mem. ABA, FBA, Am. Judicature Soc., State Bar Ga., Atlanta Bar Assn., Cobb Jud. Bar Assn., Lawyers Club Atlanta, Old War Horse Lawyers Club. Office: US Ct Appeals 11th Circuit 56 Forsyth St NW Atlanta GA 30303-2205*

HENDERSON, ALBERT KOSSACK, publishing company executive, dairy executive, consultant; b. Phila., July 9, 1938; s. Harry Brinton, Jr. and Beatrice (Conford) H.; m. Tamara Ann McCormick, Feb. 14, 1968; children—Christopher Findley, Theodore Leon. Mus.B., Ithaca Coll., 1960; postgrad., N.Y. U. Editorial asst. Hearst Headline, 1960-62; asst. sales mgr. Royal McBee, 1960-64; editor Johnson Reprint Corp., 1964-69; gen. mgr., v.p., treas. Brit. Book Centre, Inc., N.Y.C., 1969-77; dir. Pergamon Press, Inc., v.p., treas., 1971-77; exec. v.p., dir. Newman Grove Creamery Co., Nebr., 1977-81; dir. publs. Am. Solar Energy Soc., N.Y.C., 1981-83; pres. Henderson Assoc. Cons., Bridgeport, Conn., 1980—, Chess Combination, Inc., Bridgeport, 1984—; editor Pub. Rsch. Quar., 1994—; exec. sec. Com. for Preservation Academic and Sci. Info. Resources. Co-chairperson adv. panel for sci. publs. Found. for Internat. Sci. Coop., 1990-92. Mem. Am. Soc. Info. Sci., Soc. Scholarly Publs., Council Biology Editors. Home: Box 2423 Noble Sta Bridgeport CT 06608-0423

HENDERSON, ANGELO B., journalist; m. Felecia Henderson; 1 child, Grant. Journalist, dep. bur. chief Wall Street Jour., Detroit. deacon Hartford Meml. Bapt. Ch., Detroit. Recipient Pulitzer prize for Feature Writing, 1999. Office: c/o Wall Street Jour Det Bur 500 Woodward Ave Ste 1950 Detroit MI 48226*

HENDERSON, ARNOLD GLENN, architect, educator; b. Shawnee, Okla., Nov. 10, 1934; s. Henry Glenn and Pearlalee H.; m. Beatriz Eugenia Chavez Escandon; children: Eric Neal, Alex Jon. B.Arch., U. Okla., 1961, B.S. in Archtl. Engring, 1961; M.S. in Architecture, Columbia U., 1964. Asst. prof. architecture U. Ill., Urbana, 1964-68; assoc. prof. U. Okla., 1968-73, prof., 1973—; disting. lectr. U. Okla., Norman, 1984, 88; pvt. practice architecture Norman, Okla., 1975—. Author: Document for an Anonymous Indian, 1974, The Surgeon General's Collection, 1976, (with others) Architecture in Oklahoma, 1978, (with others) The Point Riders Great Plains Poetry Anthology, 1982; co-editor: (with others) Point Riders Press, 1974—; painting exhbns. in Ind., Ill., Okla., La., Wyo., Ark., Kans., Ala., Colo., Tex. and London; author of poetry. Chmn. Norman Housing Authority, 1972-77; mem. Hist. Preservation and Landmark Commn., Guthrie, Okla., 1979-81. Served with U.S. Army, 1953-55. Grantee NSF, Nat. Endowment Arts, AIA, Okla. Arts Coun., Okla. Humanities Com., Graham Found. for Advanced Studies in the Fine Arts. Fellow AIA (award of excellence 1976); mem. Vernacular Architecture Forum, Nat. Trust Hist. Preservation, Okla. Hist. Soc. (Shirk Meml. award 1991), Soc. Archl. Historians, Sigma Tau. Democrat. Episcopalian. Home: 1208 Barkley Ave Norman OK 73071-4812 Office: U Okla Coll Arch Norman OK 73019

HENDERSON, ARVIS BURL, data processing executive, biochemist; b. Abilene, Tex., Oct. 24, 1943; s. Arvis Vernon and Aubra Lee (Patton) H.; m. Mary Ann Pickett, Mar. 17, 1966 (div. Sept. 1983); 1 child, Michelle Rene; m. Jo Nell Hartsell, July 2, 1985 (div. May 1996); m. Sherry Belyeu, May 23, 1997 (div. Jan. 1999). AA, San Angelo Coll., 1964; BA, U. Tex., 1966; MAS, So. Meth. U., 1969; PhD, U. Tex. Health Sci. Ctr., 1976. Postdoctoral fellow U. Tex., Austin, 1976-80; dir. rsch. lab. Instrumentation Specialities Co., Lincoln, Nebr., 1980-81; asst. prof. pediatrics U. Tex. Health Sci. Ctr., Houston, 1981-84; dir. sci. computing S.W. Found. for Biomed. Rsch., San Antonio, 1984-91; assoc. v.p. info. tech. U. Tex., San Antonio, 1991-96; vice provost for computing and info. tech. U. Tex., Arlington, 1996—; mem. strategic leadership coun. U. Tex., 1997—; co-prin. investigator Students' Work Consortium, 1997—. Contbr. articles on biomed. research to profl. jours., chpts. to books. Chmn. Alamo Area Quality Workforce Planning Com., 1990-92; active Class XII Gov. Exec. Devel. Program, 1993; reader North Tex. Taping and Radio for the Blind, 1999—. Recipient Research Service award NIH, 1976-79; fellow U. Tex., 1976-80, Clayton Found. Biochemistry Inst., 1980. Mem. NIH spl. study sect. 9, Data Processing Mgmt. Assn., Assn. Systems Mgmt., Assn. for Computing Machinery. Republican. Baptist. Avocation: photography. Home: 2719 Golden Creek Ln #407 Arlington TX 76006 Office: U Tex PO Box 19118 Arlington TX 76019-9118

HENDERSON, BRUCE WINGROVE, insurance executive; b. Balt., Feb. 20, 1946; s. Wilmer Paul and Margaret Virginia Henderson; m. Karen Todd, Sept. 14, 1968; 1 child, Katie Anne. BA in History, U. Balt., 1968. Sr. acct. exec. Conn. Gen. Life Ins. Co., Hartford, 1970-89; asst. v.p. Seabury & Smith, Indpls., 1989—. Author: (trademark for employee benefits plan design) Health Age/Actual Age Plan, 1994. Vol. Dayspring Ctr., Indpls., 1995. With USN, 1969-70. Mem. Soc. of Mary, Nat. Ind. Health Underwriters Assn., Ind. Astron. Soc., Am. Legion, Nat. History Honor Soc., U. Balt. (parliamentarian). Republican. Roman Catholic. Avocations: golf, telescope viewing. Home: 9009 Cloud Bay Ct Indianapolis IN 46236-9172

HENDERSON, CHARLES BROOKE, research company executive; b. Washington, Mar. 13, 1929; s. Robert Neel and Dorothy (Brooke) H.; m. Elizabeth Ann Carter, June 6, 1954; children: Katherine, Roger, Sally. BS,

Purdue U., 1950; SM in Chem. Engring, MIT, 1952. With Atlantic Research Corp., Alexandria, Va., 1954-88; dir. research and tech. Atlantic Research Corp., 1971-76, v.p., 1976-80, sr. v.p., 1980-88, also dir.; chmn. bd. dirs. Arctech Inc., 1988-92. Active Boy Scouts Am., 1965-69, Girl Scouts U.S.A., 1969-71; treas. Loudoun Symphony, 1993-97, bd. dirs., 1993—; bd. dirs. Loudoun Arts Coun., 1997—. Named Nat. Capital Outstanding Young Engr., 1961, One of Maj. Innovators, Tech. Mag., 1981. Fellow AIAA (assoc.); mem. Am. Chem. Soc., Combustion Inst., Sigma Xi. Patentee in field.

HENDERSON, CHARLES R., major general United States Air Force. BS, U. Tenn., 1969; grad., Squadron Officer Sch., Maxwell AFB, Ala., 1973; MS in Mgmt., Ctrl. Mich. U., 1976; student, Air Command and Staff Coll., Maxwell AFB, Ala., 1982, Indsl. Coll. Armed Forces, Ft. Lesley J. McNair, Washington, 1986. Commd. 2d lt. USAF, 1969, advanced through grades to maj. gen., 1997; pilot trainer Various AFBs, 1970-77; from mfg. quality assurance officer to asst. dir. quality mfg. and quality assurance Aero. Systems Divsn. USAF, Wright AFB, Ohio, 1978-81; from instr. pilot to flight comdr. 28th Bombardment Squadron USAF, Robins AFB, Ga., 1982-83; from ops. office to comdr. 23d Bombardment Squadron USAF, Minot AFB, N.D., 1983-86; mil. asst. to asst. dep. undersec. defense, acting asst. dep. dir. strategic aero. and theater nuclear forces USAF, Washington, 1987-89; vice comdr. to comdr. 28th Bombardment Wing USAF, Ellsworth AFB, S.D., 1989-91; chief nuclear ops. and command and control divsn. ops. dir. Joint Chiefs of Staff, Washington, 1991-93; from comdr. AF wings to commdg. gen. Task Force Op. Provide Comfort USAF, Incirlik AB, Turkey, 1993-96; dep. dir. ops. requirements, dep chief of staff plans, ops. Hdqrs. USAF, Washington, 1996-97; dir. command and control, dep. chief of staff air, space ops Hdqs. USAF, Washington, 1997; dir. plans and policy Hdqs. U.S. Strategic Command USAF, Offut AFB, Omaha, Nebr., 1998—. Decorated Legion of Merit with oak leaf cluster, Defense Superior Svc. medal with two oak leaf clusters, Meritorious Svc. medal with two oak leaf clusters, Air Force Commendation medal with oak leaf cluster. Office: USAF Strategic Air Command 901 Sac Blvd Ste 2E10 Offutt A F B NE 68113

HENDERSON, CHARLES WILLIAM, health and medical publishing executive; b. Fitzgerald, Ga., July 20, 1949; s. Ashton Leven Henderson Jr. and Frances Ethel Fortson. Cert. in health and WCI, Emory U., 1971; BA in Journalism and Mass Comms., U. Ga., Athens, 1971. Exec. editor Business Atlanta Mag., Atlanta, 1971; columnist Atlanta Mag., 1972; writer Atlanta Jour./Constitution, Atlanta, 1972; staff corr. Bur. Nat. Affairs, Inc., Washington, 1973-74; editor-pub. Buckhead Atlanta, 1975-76; dir. cmty. affairs divsn. City of Atlanta Dept. Cmty. and Human Devel., 1976-77; dir. pub. rels. and comms. Nat. Bank of Ga., Atlanta, 1977; publicist New World Pictures, L.A., Atlanta, 1977, TriStar Pictures, L.A., Atlanta, 1977-79; v.p. TriStar Studios, L.A., Atlanta, 1979; exec. v.p., exec. prodr. Henderson-Crowe Prodns., Inc., Atlanta, 1980-84; publisher, editor-in-chief C.W. Henderson, Publisher, Atlanta, 1984—; featured spkr. Internat. Newsletter Conf., Washington, 1996. Editor-in-chief: (periodicals) AIDS Weekly, 1985—, AIDS Weekly Plus, 1985—, Cancer Weekly, 1988—, Cancer Rschr. Weekly, 1988—, Cancer Biotech. Weekly, 1988—, Vaccine Weekly, 1993—, Blood Weekly, 1993—, TB Weekly, 1993—, Health Letter on the CDC, 1994—, Gene Therapy Weekly, 1994—, Disease Weekly, 1994—, Hepatitis Weekly, 1995—, Malaria Weekly, 1995—, Antiviral Weekly, 1996—, Immunotherapy Weekly, 1996—, Emerging Pathogen Weekly, 1996— (interactive database) NewsFile, 1996—; publisher (annual book) AIDS Therapies, 1988—, Tuberulosis and Airborne Disease Weekly, 1997—, Malaria and Tropical Disease Weekly, 1997—, World Disease Weekly Plus, 1997—, Transplant Weekly, 1998—, Herpes Viruses Weekly, 1998—, Alzheimer's Disease Weekly, 1998—, Angiogenesis Weekly, 1998, Health Letter on the NCI, 1999—, Health Letter in the NIH, 1999—. Cited by Billboard Mag. as Co-Founder First Nationwide Video Music Programming on Cable TV, 1980; cited by Arbitron TV Ratings as exec. producer of Highest Rated Syndicated Musical Variety Program 0f 1984; cited by USA Today as One of Six Who Made a Difference on the Impact of AIDS, 1985; cited by N.Y. Times as World's Largest Producer Weekly Health Info., 1995; recipient Eagle Scout award Boy Scouts Am., 1963, Fiftieth Anniversary award Order of the Arrow, 1964, WSB Radio Good Egg award, 1978, Top Pub. Rels. Mktg. Campaign award News Analysis Inst. Over 100 Club, 1979, Thriving Pub. Citation, Forbes Mag., 1995; named Atlantan of Week, 1978; cited by Chgo. Tribune as pub. of pioneering weekly med. newsletters, 1997. Mem. AP, Internat. AIDS Soc., Assn. for Continuing Med. Edn., Newsletter Publishers Assn., U. Ga. Alumni Assn., Journalism Alumni Assn. of the Univ. of Ga., Soc. Profl. Journalists, Phi Kappa Theta. Home and Office: CW Henderson Publisher PO Box 5528 Atlanta GA 31107-0528

HENDERSON, CONNIE CHORLTON, city planner, artist and writer; b. Cedar Rapids, Iowa, July 16, 1944; d. Robert Brown and Lorraine Madeline (Marquardt) Chorlton; m. Dwight Franklin Henderson, Dec. 24, 1966; 1 child, Patricia. BA, Anderson U., 1966; MA in Edn., St. Francis Coll., Ft. Wayne, Ind., 1972; MPA, U. Tex. San Antonio, 1987. Art coord. Ft. Wayne Comty. Schs., 1966-67; art tchr. East Allen County Schs., New Haven, Ind., 1968-71, 74-79; instr. Manchester Coll., N. Manchester, Ind., 1971-72; rsch. assoc. Tremar Real Estate Rsch., San Antonio, 1983-84; planning asst. (vol.) City of San Antonio, Tex., 1985-88; planner I City of San Antonio, 1988-89, project mgmt. specialist, 1990, conservation edn. coord., 1990-91; Planner II San Antonio Water System, 1990-96, water edn. coord., 1996-97, spl. events. coord., 1998—; docent (vol.) San Antonio Mus. Assn.; rsch. mgr. N. San Antonio C. of C., 1988. Artist: numerous paintings and fiber sculptures in juried and invitational shows, 1966-80; poetess: (2d prize Iowa Poetry Day Assn., 1961). Bd. dirs. Tex. Soc. to Prevent Blindness, San Antonio, 1981-83; v.p. U. Tex. at San Antonio Women's Club, 1981-82, pres. 1983-84; mem. San Antonio Conservation Soc., 1985—, mem. Assistance League of San Antonio, 1988—, liason Thrift House, San Antonio, 1995-96; co-pres. River Gardens Family and Friends, 1993-94, sec., 1995-96. Mem. Am. Planning Assn. (cert. planner, asst. dir. San Antonio sect. 1990, dir., 1991-93, Am. Water Works Assn., Univ. of Tex. at San Antonio Alumni Assn. Avocations: travel, reading, landscape design, swimming, mus. visits. Home: 2410 Shadow Cliff St San Antonio TX 78232-4010 Office: San Antonio Water System PO Box 2449 San Antonio TX 78298-2449

HENDERSON, D. AUSTIN, computer scientist; b. London, Ont., Can., Jan. 25, 1943; came to U.S., 1966; s. Dugald Austin and Nancy (Gilbert) H.; m. Lynne Ellen McHugh, Aug. 29, 1981; children: Kimberly, Mark, Brooke. Honors BSc in Math. and Sci., Queen's U., Kingston, Ont., 1965; MS in Computer Sci., U. Ill., 1967; PhD in Elec. Engring., MIT, 1975. Rsch. asst. computation structures and programming MIT, Cambridge, 1967-75; cons. on computer graphics and networks MIT Lincoln Lab., Lexington, 1968-75; cons. computer graphics and applications programmin Bolt Beranek and Newman Inc., Cambridge, 1970-75, computer scientist, 1975-78; mem. rsch. staff Xerox Palo Alto (Calif.) Rsch. Ctr., 1978-86; PARC-EuroPARC liaison Rank Xerox Cambridge (Eng.) EuroPARC, 1987-89; v.p. Fitch Richardson Smith, Worthington, Ohio, 1989; area mgr. design, use and shared spaces Sys. Scis. Lab., Xerox Palo Alto Rsch. Ctr., 1989-90; mgr. user interface architecture Xerox Corp., Palo Alto, 1990-94; user experience architect advanced tech. group Apple Computer, Inc., Cupertino, Calif, 1994-95, mgr. user experience lab., 1995-96, mgr. discourse architecture lab. Apple Rsch. Labs., 1996-97; prin. Pliant Rsch., Berkeley, Calif., 1997—, Rivendel Consulting & Design, Inc., La Honda, Calif., , 1997—. ontbr. articles to profl. jours.; patentee in field. em. Assn. Computer Machinery Spl. Interest Group on Computer Human Interaction (vice chair 1988-89, co-chair 1989-91, 91-93, past chair 1994-95, conf. chair 1985, disting. svc. award 1995). Avocations: kayaking, tennis, hiking, canoeing, photography. Home and Office: 8115 La Honda Rd PO Box 334 La Honda CA 94020-0334

HENDERSON, DAN FENNO, lawyer, law educator; b. Chelan, Wash., May 24, 1921; s. Joe and Edna (Fenno) H.; m. Carol Drake Hardin, Sept. 14, 1957; children: Louis, Karen, Gail, Fenno. AB, Whitman Coll., 1944, LLD, 1983; AB, U. Mich., 1945; JD, Harvard U., 1949; PhD in Polit. Sci, U. Calif., Berkeley, 1955. Bar: Wash. 1949, Korea 1954, Japan 1955, Calif. 1956. Movie, radio censor U.S. Dept. Def., Japan, 1946-47; teaching asst. polit. sci. dept. U. Calif., Berkeley, 1949-51; atty. firm Little, LeSourd, Palmer & Scott, Seattle, 1951-52; instr. ext. div. U. Calif., Berkeley, 1952-54; atty. firm Graham James & Rolph, San Francisco, 1955-57; ptnr. Graham James & Rolph, Tokyo, 1957-62; prof. law, dir. Asian Law Program U. Wash. Sch. Law, 1962-91; prof. law Hastings. Coll. U. Calif., San Francisco, 1991—; ptnr. firm Adachi, Henderson, Miyatake and Fujita, Tokyo, 1973-91; of counsel Graham and James/Riddell Williams, Seattle, 1990-97; vis. prof. law Harvard U., 1968-69, Monash U., Melbourne, Australia, 1979, Cambridge (Eng.) U., 1980, U. Melbourne, 1988, Beijing U., 1988, Erasmus U., The Netherlands, 1989, Duke U., 1990, U. Calif., Hastings, 1991, Washington U., St. Louis, 1993, U. Tokyo, 1994, U. Hawaii, 1999; cons. Asia Found., 1967-92, Battelle Inst., 1969-92. Author: Conciliation and Japanese Law, 1965, The Constitution of Japan, Its First Twenty Years, 1969, Foreign Enterprise in Japan, 1973, Village Contracts in Tokugawa, Japan, 1975, Law and Legal Process in Japan, 2d edit., 1988, Civil Procedure in Japan, 1981, 2d edit., 1985; contbr. articles to profl. jours. Trustee Seattle Art Mus., 1975-95, Blakemore Found., 1998—; overseer Whitman Coll., 1985—. Served to lt. AUS, 1943-46. Investment fellow Am. Soc. Internat. Law, 1962-64. Mem. Internat. Acad. Comparative Law, Internat. Acad. Comml. and Consumer Law, Am. C. of C. Japan (past sec., dir.), Japanese-Am. Soc. Legal Studies (pres.), Am. Assn. Comparative Study of Law (dir.), Hastings 65 Club, Bohemian Club (San Francisco), Rainier Club, Univ. Club (Seattle), Tokyo Lawn Tennis Club. Home: 530 McGilvra Blvd E Seattle WA 98112-5048 Office: Hastings Law Coll 200 McAllister St San Francisco CA 94102-4707

HENDERSON, DEE WURSTEN, dean; b. Preston, Idaho, Feb. 24, 1938; s. Chester A. and Bernice Wursten Henderson; m. Norma Mae Nelson, Sept. 13, 1961 (div. June 1995); m. Mary C. Black, Oct. 30, 1997; children: Dee II, John N., David N., Ruth N. Assoc., Ricks Coll., 1962; BS, Brigham Young U., 1963, MS, 1964; PhD, Am. U., 1972. Cert. Meyers-Briggs Type Indicator, Wilson Devel. Instruments, Schutz Devel. Instruments. Asst. dir. Grad. Sch. USDA, Washington, 1964-76; prof. Brigham Young U., Provo, Utah, 1976-89; acting dir. Grad. Sch. USDA, Washington, 1984-85; dir., prof. Calif. State U., Fresno, 1985-87; exec. cons. World Bank, Washington, 1988-89; gov.'s exec. cabinet, dir. human resources for state Wash. State Govt., Olympia, 1989-93; dir. Fed. Exec. Inst., Charlottesville, Va., 1993-94; asst. dir., exec. Office of Pers. Mgmt., Washington, 1994-95; dean profl. studies Richard Stockton Coll., Pomona, N.J., 1996—. Editor: (book) Revolution of Ideals, 1967; co-author: (book) Success Oriented Supervision, 1972; bd. editors: Pub. Adminstrn. Rev., 1993-98. Chmn. bd. Utah State Youth Corrections, Salt Lake City, 1983-84, vice chmn. bd., 1981-82; co-author, clk. Ala. Clk. of House, Birmingham, 1991. With USAR, 1960-66. Recipient Outstanding Contbn. to Edn. award Govt. Somalia, 1987, Profl. Svc. award Inst. Bus. Adminstrn. and Tech., 1998. Mem. Am. Soc. Pub. Adminstrn. (chair Brown Law Nat. award 1995, selection com., pub. svc. awards), Nat. Assn. State Pers. Execs. (exec. coun., pres.-elect, Outstanding Svc. award 1993). Mormon. Avocations: music, basketball, fishing, hiking. E-mail: hendersd@pollux.stockton.edu. Home: 522 Forrest Brook Dr Absecon NJ 08201 Office: Richard Stockton Coll NJ Pomona NJ 08240-0195

HENDERSON, DEIRDRE HEALY, interior decorating, leasing company executive; b. Chgo., Nov. 10, 1942; d. Laurin Hall and Patricia (Kelly) H.; m. Duncan Yeandle, Sept. 27, 1969; children: Allison Dow, Duncan Dylan. AA, Briarcliff Coll., 1962; BA, Conn. Coll., New London, 1964. Editorial asst. Commerce Clearing House, San Francisco, 1964-65; tchr. Harris Sch., Chgo., 1966-67; stockbroker Dominick and Dominick, E.F. Hutton, Chgo., 1968-70; ptnr. Park West Interiors, Chgo., 1976-88; founder, pres. Franklin and Copley, Ltd., Chgo., 1987-98; coord. gun control com. San Francisco Gen. Hosp. Trauma Found., 1998—; V.p., bd. mem., Com. for Handgun Control, Chgo., 1976-84, organizer G.A. Ranney for U.S. Senate, Donald Haider for Mayor, Chgo., 1985-87. Trustee Chgo. Hist. Soc., 1990-93, Westover Sch., Middlebury, Conn., 1990-96; officer, bd. dirs. Women's Bd. Rehab. Inst., Chgo., 1973-85, Women's Bd. Rush-Presbyn., St. Luke's Hosp., Chgo., 1973-84; mem. steering com. U. Chgo. Women's Bd., Field Mus. Women's Bd., 1989-93, Antiquarian Soc. of the Art Inst.; mem. events com. Coro No. Calif., 1997—, San Francisco Gen. Hosp. Found., 1998—. Mem. Chgo. Hist. Soc. Guild (officer, bd. dirs., chmn. 1985-93), Chgo. Acad. of Scis. (bd. dirs. 1984-93), Chgo. Found. for Edn. (bd. dirs. 1985-92), Friends of Lincoln Park (bd. dirs. 1985-92), Seven Seas Cruising Assn. (transatlantic sailor), Woman's Athletic Club (officer bd. dirs. 1975-81), Friday Club (officer bd. dirs. 1985-91), Children's Theatre Assn., Calif. Tennis Club, San Francisco Golf Club. Episcopalian. Avocations: tennis, sailing, golf, photography, biking.

HENDERSON, DONALD AINSLIE, public health educator; b. Lakewood, Ohio, Sept. 7, 1928; s. David Alexander and Grace Eleanor (McMillan) H.; m. Nana Irene Bragg, Sept. 1, 1951; children: Leigh Ainslie, David Alexander, Douglas Bruce. BA, Oberlin (Ohio) Coll., 1950, DSc (hon.), 1978; MD, U. Rochester (N.Y.), 1954, DSc (hon.), 1977; MPH, Johns Hopkins U., 1960; LLD (hon.), Marietta (Ohio) Coll., 1978; DSc (hon.), U. Ill., 1979, U. Md., 1980; MD (hon.), U. Geneva, 1977—; LHD (hon.), SUNY, 1981, Johns Hopkins U., 1994, Towson State U., 1994; DSc (hon.), Yale U., 1986, Albany Med. Coll., 1989, Lafayette Coll., 1991, U. Mo., 1992. Diplomate: Am. Bd. Preventive Medicine. Intern, then resident Mary Imogene Bassett Hosp., Cooperstown, N.Y., 1954-55, 57-59; chief epidemic intelligence service Center Disease Control, USPHS, Atlanta, 1955-57; chief surveillance sect. Center Disease Control, USPHS, 1960-66; chief med. officer smallpox eradication WHO, Geneva, 1966-77; dean Johns Hopkins U. Sch. Hygiene and Pub. Health, 1977-90; assoc. dir. Office Sci. and Tech. Policy, Exec. Office Pres. of U.S., Washington, 1991-93; dep. asst. sec. HHS, Washington, 1993-94; sr. sci. advisor Dept. Health and Human Svcs., HHS, 1994-95; prof. Johns Hopkins U. Sch. Pub. Health, Balt., 1995-97; dir. Hopkins Ctr. Civilian Biodefense Studies, 1998—. Contbr. articles to med. jours. Decorated Commendation medal; recipient Ernest Jung prize, 1976, award Govt. India-Indian Soc. Malaria and Other Communicable Diseases, 1975, Rosenhaus Internat. award for excellence, 1975, George MacDonald medal London Sch. Hygiene and Tropical Medicine, Royal Soc. Tropical Medicine and Hygiene, 1976, Health medal Govt. Afghanistan, 1976, Spl. Albert Lasker Pub. Health Svc. award WHO, 1976; Pub. Welfare medal Nat. Acad. Scis., 1978, Joseph C. Wilson award in internat. affairs, 1978, James D. Bruce Meml. award, 1978; Outstanding Alumnus award Delta Omega, 1980; Disting. Alumnus award Johns Hopkins U., 1982; Internat. Merit award Gairdner Found., 1983; Albert Schweitzer Internat. prize for medicine, 1985; Nat. Medal Sci., 1986; Richard T. Hewitt award Royal Soc. Medicine, 1986, Charles Dana Found. award for Pioneering Achievemnt in Health, 1986; Japan prize in Preventative Medicine, 1988, Health medal 1st Grade People's Republic China, 1988, Medal of Abnegation Uruguay, 1988, Honor award Pan Am. Health Orgn., 1990, Health for All medal WHO, 1990, Abraham Lilienfeld award Am. Coll, Epidemology, 1991, Award of Excellence Ronald McDonald Children's Charities, 1992, Surgeon Gen.'s medallion USPHS, 1992, City of Medicine award, Durham, N.C., 1993, Waltor Reed medal Am. Soc. Tropical Medicine and Hygiene, 1993, Merit award Nat. Coun. Internat. Health, 1993; hon. fellow London Sch. Tropical Medicine and Hygiene, 1993, Paul Harris fellow Rotary Internat., 1993, Gold medal Albert B. Sabin Found., 1994, John Stearns award N.Y. Acad. of Medicine, 1995, Oswaldo Cruz Gold medal of merit Govt. of Brazil, 1995, John Stearns award N.Y. Acad. Medicine, 1995, Soc. citation Infectious Diseases Soc. Am., 1996, Edward Jenner medal Royal Soc. Medicine (U.K.), 1996, named Burroughs Wellcome Vis. Prof., 1996. Fellow Nat. Acad. Arts and Scis., Am. Acad. Pediatrics (hon.), Royal Coll. Physicians U.K. (hon.); mem. Inst. Medicine Nat. Acad. Scis., Am. Pub. Health Assn., Internat. Epidemiol. Assn., Royal Coll. Physicians Edinburgh (Eng.), Royal Soc. Tropical Medicine and Hygiene, Indian Soc. Malaria and Other Communicable Diseases. Home: 3802 Greenway Baltimore MD 21218-1825 Office: Johns Hopkins U Sch Pub Health Candler Bldg Ste 850 Baltimore MD 21202

HENDERSON, DONALD BERNARD, JR., lawyer; b. Birmingham, Ala., June 27, 1949; s. Donald B. and Pauline V. (Szulinski) H.; m. Ruth Ann Jeffers, Sept. 12, 1981. BS, U. Ala., 1971, JD, 1974; LLM in Taxation, NYU, 1976. Bar: Ala. 1974, N.Y. 1983. Ptnr. Sirote and Permutt, Birmingham, 1976-83; sr. assoc. Mound, Cotton and Wollan, N.Y.C., 1983-85; ptnr. Kroll & Tract, N.Y.C., 1985-88, LeBoeuf, Lamb, Greene & MacRae, L.L.P., N.Y.C., 1988—; lectr. Birmingham chpt. Am. Coll., Bryn Mawr, Pa., 1977-82; dir. Nat. Integrity Life Ins. Co., Jackson Nat. Life Ins. Co. N.Y., SunLife Assurance Co. N.Y., John P. Woods Co., Inc.; counsel to Bronxville Planning Bd. Contbr. articles to profl. jours. Pres. Lenox Hill Dem. Club, N.Y.C., 1989-90; mem. Ala. State Dem. Com., 1978-83, N.Y.C. Community Bd. Number 8, 1987-88, Republican Club of Bronxville. Mem. ABA, N.Y. Bar Assn., Ala. Bar Assn. (sec. tax sect. 1982-83). Home: 108 Midland Ave Bronxville NY 10708-3206 Office: LeBouf Lamb Greene & MacRae LLP 125 E 55th St New York NY 10022-3502

HENDERSON, DOUGLAS, museum director; b. Elizabeth, N.J., Feb. 23, 1945; s. James and Effie (Douglas) H.; m. Barbara Jean Moore, June 15, 1965; children: Melissa Koenig, Laura Henderson, Kyle Henderson. BSBA, U. Denver, 1967, MS, 1969. Tchr. Madison (Wis.) Pub. Schs., 1969-74; tchr., adminstr. Sevastopol Pub. Schs., Sturgeon Bay, Wis., 1975-78; fundraiser Blair Acad., Blairstown, N.J., 1978-88; dir. devel. Wayland Acad., Beaver Dam, Wis., 1988-92; mus. dir. Door County Maritime Mus., Sturgeon Bay, 1993—. Chmn. Sturgeon Bay Waterfront Design Rev. Bd., 1994-98. Mem. Sturgeon Bay Rotary (bd. dirs. 1992—).

HENDERSON, DOUGLAS BOYD, lawyer; b. Pitts., Sept. 21, 1935; s. Arthur G. and Mildred E. (Rickenbach) H.; m. Olivia Lauer, July 6, 1957; children: Scotland Weaver, Keith Arthur, Heather Alice Atkinson. BS in Indsl. Engring., Pa. State U., 1957; JD with honors, George Washington U., 1963. Bar: Va. 1962, D.C. 1963. Mfs. agt. firm Arthur G. Henderson & Assos., Pitts., 1957-59; patent agt. Swift & Co., Washington, 1959-62; law clk. to Hon. Donald E. Lane U.S. Ct. Claims, Washington, 1962-63; assoc. Irons, Birch, Swindler & McKie, Washington, 1963-65; founding ptnr. Finnegan, Henderson, Farabow, Garrett & Dunner (and predecessors), Washington, 1965—; adv. coun. U.S. Ct. Fed. Claims, 1982—; mem. legal adv. bd. Martindale-Hubbell/LEXIS, 1996—. Author: Third Party Practice in the United States Court of Claims or Two's Company, Three's A Crowd, 1976; contbr. articles to legal jours. Bd. advisors George Washington U. Law Sch., 1991-97. Mem. ABA (coun. patent, trademark and copyright law sect. 1981-85, chair patent divsn. 1980-81), Internat. Bar Assn., Va. Bar Assn., Va. State Bar, D.C. Bar, Fed. Cir. Bar Assn. (founder 1985, bd. dirs. 1985-86, 96—, mem. jud. selection com. 1990—), Bar Assn. D.C. (chmn. Ct. Appeals for Fed. Cir. Com. 1982-83, chmn. patent, trademark and copyright law sect. 1974-75, chmn. Ct. of Claims com. 1973-74, bd. dirs. 1975-76, trustee rsch. found. 1980-81), U.S. Ct. Fed. Claims Bar Assn. (founder 1987, bd. dirs. 1987-90), ITC Trial Lawyers Assn. (founder 1984), U.S. C. of C. (chmn. patent, trademark and copyright coun. 1980-82), Am. Intellectual Property Law Assn., Internat. Trademark Assn., Patent Office Soc., Am. Arbitration Assn., Intellectual Property Owners Assn., Capital Soc., Burning Tree Club, Univ. Club, Club at Franklin Sq. (mem. bd. govs. 1990-95), Congl. Country Club, Tournament Players Club at Avenel, Christian Legal Soc., Supreme Ct. Hist. Soc., Phi Gamma Delta, Delta Theta Phi. Presbyterian (elder 1980-82). Home: 10 Beman Woods Ct Potomac MD 20854-5481 Office: Finnegan Henderson Farabow Garrett & Dunner LLP 1300 I St NW Fl 6-8 Washington DC 20005-3315

HENDERSON, DWIGHT FRANKLIN, dean, educator; b. Austin, Tex., Aug. 14, 1937; s. Ottis Franklin and Leona (Bady) H.; m. Connie Chorlton, Dec. 24, 1966; 1 dau., Patricia Ross. BA, U. Tex., 1959, MA, 1961, PhD, 1966. Assoc. prof. Ind. U., Ft. Wayne, 1966-68, chmn. dept. history, 1968-71, assoc. prof. history, 1971-80, chmn. arts and scis., 1971-76, dean arts and letters, 1976-80, acting chancellor, 1978-79; prof. history, dean Coll. Social and Behavioral Scis. U. Tex., San Antonio, 1980—, acting v.p. acad. affairs, 1986-87. Author: Private Journals of Georgiana Gholson Walker, 1963, Courts for a New Nation, 1971, Congress, Courts, and Criminals, 1985. Bd. dirs. Ft. Wayne Philharm. Orch., 1973-74, Pub. Transp. Corp., Ft. Wayne, 1975-77, Vis. Nurse Assn., San Antonio, 1989-94, 95-96, Vis. Nurse Assn. Hospice South Tex., 1996—, Employment Network, 1990-96. With AUS, 1962-64. Tex. Soc. Colonial Dames fellow, 1964-65, 65-66; Ind. U. fellow, 1968, 70, 72, Fulbright U.S.-German Internat. Edn. Adminstrs. Program, 1993. Mem. Orgn. Am. Historians, So. Hist. Assn., Tex. Assn. Deans of Liberal Arts and Scis. (bd. dirs. 1992—, v.p. 1994, pres. 1995-97), Delta Sigma Rho, Phi Alpha Delta. Home: 2410 Shadow Cliff St San Antonio TX 78232-4010 Office: U Tex Coll Social & Behavioral Sci San Antonio TX 78285

HENDERSON, FLORENCE (FLORENCE HENDERSON BERNSTEIN), actress, singer; b. Dale, Ind., Feb. 14, 1934; d. Joseph and Elizabeth Elder H.; m. Ira Bernstein, Jan. 9, 1956 (div.); children: Barbara, Joey, Robert Norman, Elizabeth; m. John Kappas, Aug. 4, 1987. Attended, St. Francis Acad., Owensboro, Ky; studied at, Am. Acad. Dramatic Arts. Broadway and stage debut in Wish You Were Here, 1952; on tour in Oklahoma!, 1952-53, at N.Y.C. Ctr., 1953, Fanny, 1954, The Sound of Music, 1961, in revival of Annie Get Your Gun, 1974; appeared in The Great Waltz, Los Angeles Civic Light Opera Assn., 1953, on Broadway in The Girl Who Came to Supper, 1963, in revival of South Pacific, 1967, in revival The Sound of Music, Los Angeles Civic Light Opera Assn., 1978, Bells are Ringing, Los Angeles Civic Light Opera Assn., 1979; appeared in Oldsmobile indsl. shows, 1958-61; actress: (movies) Song of Norway, 1970, Shakes The Clown, 1991, Naked Gun 33 1/2: The Final Insult, 1994, The Brady Bunch Movie, 1995; appeared on TV in Sing Along, 1958, The Today Show, 1959-60, The Brady Bunch, 1969-74, The Brady Bunch Hour, 1977, The Brady Girls Get Married, 1981, A Very Brady Christmas, 1988, The Bradys, 1990, Fudge-A-Mania, 1995, (host) Bradymania, 1993; numerous other TV appearances include The Love Boat, 1976, 83, The Brady Brides, 1981, Hart to Hart, 1981, Fantasy Island, 1981, 83, Alice, 1983, Murder She Wrote, Dean Martin TV Series; hostess Country Kitchen; appeared in TV spl. Just a Regular Kid; guest appearances It's Garry Shandling's Show, Wil Shriner Show, Jay Leno Family Spl.; first female host of The Tonight Show; writings, A Little Cooking, A Little Talking, and A Whole Lotta Fun. Recipient Sarah Siddons award. Office: William Morris Agy care Rick Hersh 151 El Camino Dr Beverly Hills CA 90212*

HENDERSON, FREDA LAVERNE, elementary education educator; b. Parker County, Tex., June 18, 1939; d. Johnnie C. and Golda Arlene (Porter) Holbrooks; m. Ronald S. Henderson, Apr. 12, 1958; children: Ronald Kevin, Kelly Doyle, Chetley Brian, Terry Dean. AA, Am. Inst. Art, 1960; BEd, U. Colo., 1991; MEd, Lesley Coll., 1997. Pvt. tchr. art, Calhan, Colo., 1981-86; elem. tchr. art Ellicott Schs., Colo., 1987-90, tchr. chpt. I, 1991-96; classroom tchr. Ellicott Schs., 1996—. Sec. Ellicott Sch. PTA; chmn. High Sch. Booster Club, 1979-80; active vol. activities, 1964-79. Home: 1975 Buck Rd Calhan CO 80808-8515 Office: Ellicott Schs # 22 350 S Ellicott Hwy Calhan CO 80808-8838

HENDERSON, GARY ALLEN, computer scientist, educator, consultant; b. Indpls., Apr. 8, 1953; s. John Alvin and Alpha Mae (Garner) H.; m. Leslie Carol Robinson, Jan. 11, 1988; children: Electra Bynoe, Taylor Joy. BS, Ind. U., 1976. Sr. ptnr. Electronic Mail Corp., L.A., N.Y.C., 1978; pres. Comms. Rsch. Labs., N.Y.C., 1979-82; lectr. artificial intelligence NYU, N.Y.C., 1982-93; lectr. Hunter Coll., N.Y.C., 1982-86, New Sch. for Social Rsch., N.Y.C., 1983-84; pres. Computer Help Inc., N.Y.C., 1989—; speaker Am. Inst. for Profls., N.Y.C., 1988-89; computer sci. lectr. various charitable orgns. Author: Computer Systems Design, 1983; editor: Multi-National Information Systems Jour., 1982-83, Help News, 1989—; programmer: Image Conversion System, 1987, Telex Forwarding System, 1989; contbr. articles to profl. jours. Mem. IEEE, N.Y. Acad. Scis.

HENDERSON, GEORGE, educational sociologist, educator; b. Hurtsboro, Ala., June 18, 1932; s. Kidd Large and Lula Mae (Crawford) H.; m. Barbara Ann Beard, Aug. 9, 1952; children: George, Michele, Faith, Lea, Joy, Lisa, Dawn. Student, Mich. State U., 1950-52; B.A., Wayne State U., 1957, M.A., 1959, Ph.D. in Ednl. Sociology, 1965. Caseworker Ch. Youth Service, Detroit, 1957-59; social economist Detroit Housing Commn., 1960-61; community services dir. Detroit Urban League, 1961-63; program dir. Mayor's Com. for Detroit Youth, 1963-64; asst. dir. delinquency control tng. center Wayne State U., 1964-65; asst. dir. intercultural relations Detroit Public Schs., 1965-66, asst. to supt., 1966-67; assoc. prof. sociology and edn. U. Okla., 1967-69, Sylvan N. Goldman prof. human relations, 1969—, prof. edn., assoc. prof. sociology, 1969—, David Ross Boyd prof. human relations, 1987—, Regents' prof. human rels., 1989—, chmn. dept. human relations, 1969-95, dean Coll. of Liberal Studies, 1996—; vis. prof. sociology Langston U., 1969-70; disting. vis. prof. U.S. Air Force Acad., 1980-81; cons. in field. Author: Foundations of American Education, 1970, Teachers Should Care, 1970, America's Other Children, 1971, To Live in Freedom, 1972, Education for Peace, 1973, Human Relations, 1974, Human Relations in the Military, 1975, A Religious Foundation of Human Relations, 1977, Introduction to American Education, 1978, Understanding and Counseling Ethnic Minorities, 1979, Police Human Relations, 1981, Transcultural Health Care, 1981, Physician-Patient Communication, 1981, The Human Rights of Professional Helpers, 1983, The State of Black Oklahoma, 1984, Psychosocial Aspects of Disability, 1984, Mending Broken Children, 1984, College Survival for

Student Athletes, 1985, International Business and Cultures, 1987, Understanding Indigeneous and Foreign Cultures, 1989, Values in Health Care, 1991, Social Work Interventions, 1994, Cultural Diversity in the Workplace, 1994, Migrants, Immigrants and Slaves, 1995, Human Relations Issues in Management, 1996, Our Souls to Keep, 1999. Recipient Outstanding Achievement award Human Rels. Assn., 1975, Human Rels. award Met. Human Rels. Commn. Nashville, 1979, Okla. Dept. of Mental Health award. Mem. AAUP, ACD, Am. Sociol. Assn., Nat. Assn. Human Rights Works, Assn. Black Sociologists, Inter-Univ. Seminar on Armed Forces and Soc., Internat. Soc. Law Enforcement and Criminal Justice Instrs., Am. Assn. High Edn. (Black Caucus award for Ednl. Svc. 1993), Golden Key, Omicron Delta Kappa, Delta Tau Kappa, Phi Kappa Phi, Kappa Alpha Psi. Democrat. Baptist. Home: 2616 Osborne Dr Norman OK 73069-5031 Office: 1700 Asp Ave Norman OK 73072-6407

HENDERSON, GEORGE ERVIN, lawyer; b. Pampa, Tex., June 7, 1947; s. Ervin L. and Elizabeth (Yoe) H.; m. Linda L. Dalrymple, Aug. 22, 1970; children: Andrew, Elizabeth. BA, Tex. Christian U., 1969; JD, Yale U., 1972. Bar: Tex. 1972, U.S. Dist. Ct. (so. dist.) Tex. 1974, U.S. Dist. Ct. (we. dist.) 1978. Assoc. Fulbright & Jaworski, Houston and Austin, 1972-79; ptnr. Fulbright & Jaworski, Austin, 1983—, Sneed & Vine, Austin, 1979-82; adj. instr. law U. Tex., Austin, 1983-85. Contbr. articles to profl. jours. Mem. S. Tex. Youth Soccer Assn. Rules Com., 1993-99, Greater Austin Soccer Coalition, 1995-98. Capt. USAR, 1972-78. Mem. ABA, State Bar of Tex. (chmn. corp. banking and bus. law sect. 1983, coun., chmn. corp. banking and bus. law sect. 1985-88), Tex. Assn. Bank Counsel (pres. 1985-86), Travis County Bar Assn. (bankruptcy law sect., chmn. 1988-89, vice-chmn. 1997-98), San Antonio Bankruptcy Bar Assn., Uniform Comml. Code Com., Austin Yacht Club, Capital Soccer Club (pres. 1993-95). Office: Fulbright & Jaworski 600 Congress Ave Ste 2400 Austin TX 78701-3271

HENDERSON, GEORGE MILLER, foundation executive, former banker; b. Indpls., Aug. 19, 1915; s. Ben Wymond and Verlinda (Miller) H.; m. Janice Himmelwright, Sept. 2, 1952; children: Donna, Bonnie, Heather, Randall, Darcy. Student, Harvard U., 1960. With S.H. Kress & Co., 1933-36; fire control supr. U.S. Forest Svc., Zig Zag, Oreg., 1936-42; asst. mgr. fgn. trade dept. Portland C. of C., 1946-47; with 1st Nat. Bank Oreg., Portland, 1947-80, v.p., 1953-62, sr. v.p., 1962-71, exec. v.p., 1971-80; pres. Oreg. Ind. Coll. Found., 1980-94. Chmn. Portland Aviation Commn., 1950-51, Oreg. Pks. Commn., 1956-86, Columbia Basin Export-Import Conf., 1961-62; pres. Rose Festival Assn., 1953-54, Family Counseling Svc., 1959-60, Pacific Internat. Livestock Exposition, 1965-67; chmn. woorld brotherhood banquet NCCJ, 1963; bd. dirs. Ind. Coll. Funds Am., 1980-94, Nature Conservancy, 1987-90. Mem. Oreg. Bankers Assn. (pres. 1962), Assn. Res. City Bankers, Pacific Northwestern Ski Assn. (pres. 1947-48), Pacific N.W. Trade Assn. (pres. 1964-65), Arlington Club, Multnomah Club, Cascade Club. Home: 7255 SW Bent Park Dr Portland OR 97225

HENDERSON, GLADYS EDITH, retired social welfare examiner; b. Black River, N.Y., Jan. 17, 1928; d. Lynn Bruce and Ina Marion (Carey) Scott; m. Vern V. Leeder, May 4, 1947 (dec. Oct. 1950); children: Linda Leeder McCarthy, Thomas Leon. AS in Criminal Justice, Jefferson C.C., 1977; BA in Pub. Justice, SUNY, Oswego, 1979. Sec.-receptionist Delavan Warehouse, Syracuse, N.Y., 1968-69; self employed cosmetologist Black River, 1970-74; receptionist N.Y. State DEC, Watertown, 1979-80; social welfare examiner Jefferson County Dept. Social Svcs., Watertown, 1980-90, ret., 1990. Author of poetry. Sec. Civil Svc. Employees Assn., Watertown, 1986-89; Sunday sch. tchr. Watertown Bapt. Temple, 1981-99, treas. ladies' group, 1993-97. Recipient Pres.' award for lit. excellence Nat. Authors Registry, 1996, 98; inductee Internat. Poetry Hall of Fame. Mem. Black River Valley's Writers Club (treas. 1997-99). Republican. Avocations: antiques and collectibles, crochet, embroidery, writing. Home: 432 Glenn Ave Watertown NY 13601-1825

HENDERSON, HAROLD RICHARD, JR., lawyer, labor relations executive; b. Washington, Nov. 5, 1942; s. Harold Richard and Channie (Catlett) H.; m. Franzine Moore, Dec. 31, 1965; children: Kimberly Michele, Jessica Nicole, Harold R. III. BS, Mich. State U., 1972; JD, Harvard U., 1976; grad Exec. Program, Stanford Grad. Sch. Bus., 1988. Bar: D.C. 1976, U.S. Dist. Ct. D.C. 1977, U.S. Ct. Appeals (D.C. cir.) 1977, U.S. Supreme Ct. 1985. Assoc. Morgan Lewis & Bockius, Washington, 1976-80; asst. gen. counsel Amtrak, Washington, 1980-82, dep. gen. counsel, 1982-84, gen. counsel, 1984-86, v.p. law, 1986-91; exec. v.p. labor rels., chmn. mgmt. coun., exec. com. NFL, N.Y.C., 1991—. Bd. dirs. Rosemont Daycare Ctr., Washington, 1978-92, Children's Hosp. Nat. Med. Ctr., Washington, 1987—; adv. bd. dirs. N&S Rwy., 1993—. Mem. ABA, Nat. Bar Assn., N.Y. Bar Assn., Com. Rlwy. and Airline Labor Lawyers, Am. Assn. R.R. (legal affairs com.), N.Y. City Bar Assn. (sports law com.). Baptist. Avocations: outdoor sports, photography. Home: 10504 Samaga Dr Oakton VA 22124-1627 Office: NFL 280 Park Ave New York NY 10017-1216*

HENDERSON, HARRIET, librarian; b. Pampa, Tex., Nov. 19, 1949; d. Ervin Leon and Hannah Elizabeth (Yoe) H. AB, Baker U., 1971; MLS, U. Tex., 1973. Sch. libr. Pub. Sch. System, Pampa, Tex., 1971-72; city libr. City of Tyler, Tex., 1973-80, City of Newport News, Va., 1980-84; dir. librs. and info. svcs. City of Newport News, 1984-90; dir. Louisville Free Pub. Libr., 1990-97; dir. Montgomery County (Md.) Pub. Librs., 1997—; del. White House Conf. Librs. and Info. Svcs.; bd. dirs. Tex. Libr. Systems Act Adv. Bd., 1979-80, Peninsula Womens Network, Newport News, 1983-85; mem. Leadership Louisville, 1991-97, Alliant Health System Adult Oper. Bd., 1991-97; mem. adv. com. dept. edn. Spalding U., 1991-95; diaconate Hidenwood Presbyterian Ch., Newport News, 1983-85; del. White House Conf. Librs. and Info. Svcs., 1991. Recipient Tribute to Women in Bus. and Industry, Peninsula YWCA, Newport News, 1984. Mem. ALA, Ky. Libr. Assn. (chair pub. libr. sect. 1995, Outstanding Pub. Libr. Svc. award 1997), Va. Libr. Assn. (chmn. legis. com. 1981-84, v.p. 1985, pres. 1986), Pub. Libr. Assn. (v.p. 1998—). Office: Montgomery County Pub Librs Office of Dir 99 Maryland Ave Rockville MD 20850-2330

HENDERSON, HELENA NAUGHTON, legal association administrator; b. New Orleans, Mar. 19, 1956; d. John Francis and Helen Naughton; div.; children: William Henry Henderson, Kevin Richard Henderson. BS in Psychology, Harvard U., 1976, Newcomb Coll, 1978; postgrad., Tulane U., 1990—. Exec. dir. New Orleans Bar Assn.; chair Subcom. to Establish La. Women's Commn. on Policy and Rsch., 1998-99, Juvenile Law Conf. for La., 1999. Bd. dirs. La. Ctr. for Law-Related Edn., New Orleans, 1992—, New Orleans Police Found., 1996—, Voices for Children, 1997—, Voice for Children, 1997—. Mem. ABA (assoc.), Am. Soc. Assn. Execs., Nat. Assn. Bar Execs. (chair strategic planning com. 1996-98), Nat. Ctr. for Nonprofit Bds. Office: New Orleans Bar Assn 228 Saint Charles Ave Ste 1223 New Orleans LA 70130-2643

HENDERSON, JAI, museum director. Exec. dir. Calif. Afro-Am. Mus., L.A. Office: Calif Afro-Am Mus Expedition Park 600 State Dr Los Angeles CA 90037-1267*

HENDERSON, JAMES ALAN, engine company executive; b. South Bend, Ind., July 26, 1934; s. John William and Norma (Wilson) H.; m. Mary Evelyn Kriner, June 20, 1959; children: James Alan, John Stuart, Jeffrey Todd, Amy Brenton. AB, Princeton U., 1956; Baker scholar, Harvard U., 1961-63. With Scott Foresman & Co., Chgo., 1962; chmn., CEO Cummins Engine Co., Inc., Columbus, 1995; staff mem. Am. Rsch. & Devel. Corp., Boston, 1963; faculty Harvard Bus. Sch., 1963; asst. to chmn. Cummins Engine Co., Inc., Columbus, Ind., 1964-65; v.p. mgmt. devel. Cummins Engine Co., Inc., Columbus, 1965-69, v.p. personnel, 1969-70, v.p. ops., 1970-71, exec. v.p., 1971-75, exec. v.p., COO, 1975-77, pres., 1977-94, pres., CEO, 1994-95; chmn., CEO, 1995—; also bd. dirs. Cummins Engine Co., Inc., Columbus; bd. dirs. Cummins Engine Found., Inland Steel Ind., Chgo., Ameritech, Chgo., Rohm and Haas Co., Phila., Landmark Comm., Norfolk; mem. policy com. The Bus. Roundtable, Washington; mem. The Bus. Coun., Washington. Author: Creative Collective Bargaining, 1965. Chmn. exec. com., trustee Princeton U., 1986-92; pres. bd. trustees Culver Ednl. Found. Presbyterian. Home: 4228 N Riverside Dr Columbus IN 47203-1121 Office: Cummins Engine Co Inc Box 3005 MC 60912 Columbus IN 47202-3005

HENDERSON, JAMES RONALD, industrial real estate developer; b. Columbus, Nebr., Dec. 2, 1947; s. Bill and Roeburta (Hamrick) H.; m. Jamey Lee Blevins, June 30, 1972 (div. Mar. 1993); children: Benjamin James, Katrin Lee, Joseph Marion. BSBA, Okla. State U., 1970. Commd. 2d lt. USAR, 1970, advanced through grades to maj., 1987, ret., 1992; appraiser Dorchester Cos., Tulsa, 1970-72; devel. mgr. Wolf Point Properties, Tulsa, 1972-82; v.p. Mager Mortgage Co., Tulsa, 1972-78; mktg. dir. Tulsa Port of Catoosa, Okla., 1987-89; pres. J. Ronald Henderson Real Estate, Tulsa, 1978—, Henderson Exploration Co., Tulsa, 1982—; mng. dir. Wolf Point Indsl. Pky. Owners Assn., Tulsa, 1984—. Organizer, incorporator Tulsa Charity Fight Night, Inc., 1993; organizer N.E. Okla. Econ. Devel. Assn., 1988. Maj. USAR ret. Mem. Nat. Assn. Indsl. and Office Pks. (pres. Tulsa chpt. 1990), Propeller Club Port of Catoosa (pres. 1987). Southern Baptist. Avocations: backpacking, history, geology. Office: Henderson Cos 1643 E 15th St Tulsa OK 74120-6044

HENDERSON, JANICE ELIZABETH, law librarian; b. N.Y.C., Dec. 22, 1952; d. James and Adeline M. (Fitzgerald) H. BA in Psychology, Hunter Coll., 1974; MS in Spl. Edn., CUNY, 1979; MS in Library Sci., Pratt Inst., 1980; JD, Bklyn. Law Sch., 1986. Law librarian Morgan, Lewis & Bockius, N.Y.C., 1977-83; reference librarian Weil, Gotshal & Manges, N.Y.C., 1983-85; law librarian Tenzer, Greenblatt et. al., N.Y.C., 1985-86, Robinson, Silverman et. al., N.Y.C., 1986-88, Kirkland & Ellis, N.Y.C., 1991-93; assoc. law libr. prof. CUNY Law Sch., N.Y.C., 1989-91; dir. libr. svcs. Epstein, Becker & Green, P.C., 1993-98; dir. profl. devel. and libr. svcs. Baker & McKenzie, 1998—; assoc. adj. prof. Sch. Libr. and Info. Sci., St. John's U., N.Y.C., 1990-93. Book reviewer Legal Info. Alert newsletter, 1984-86. Mem. Am. Assn. Law Librs., Law Libr. Assn. Greater N.Y. (advt. mgr. 1986-89, bd. dirs. 1989-90, mem. MCLE com. 1990-92, co-chair 1992-94, v.p. 1995-96, pres. 1996-97, immediate past pres. 1997-98. Democrat. Roman Catholic. Home: PO Box 020196 Brooklyn NY 11202-0196

HENDERSON, JOE H., lawyer, mediator, arbitrator, college dean; b. Pangburn, Ark., Apr. 14, 1936; s. John H. and Nancy L. (Johnston) H.; m. Marian Jones, July 31, 1965 (div. Feb. 1978); 1 child, James H.; m. Linda Gaye Bertucelli, Mar. 21, 1981; stepchildren: Jason, Daniel. BA in Pub. Adminstrn., Calif. State U., Sacramento, 1960; JD, Lincoln U., 1968. Bar: Calif. 1971. Budget and mgmt. analyst Sacramento County, 1960-64; asst. dir. pub. works Marin County, San Rafael, Calif., 1964-66; asst. city mgr. City of Santa Rosa (Calif.), 1966-71; dean sch. of law Empire Coll., Santa Rosa, 1989-97; pvt. practice Santa Rosa, 1971-97; arbitrator, mediator, 1972—. Recipient 1 of 7200 Best Attys. in U.S. award Steven Naifeh & Gregory White Smith, 1987. Mem. Nat. Acad. Arbitrators. Avocation: fishing. Fax: 707-573-1322. E-mail: joehh@sonic.net. Office: PO Box 463 Santa Rosa CA 95402-0463

HENDERSON, JOHN BROWN, economist; b. Glasgow, Scotland, Jan. 3, 1918; came to U.S., 1950, naturalized, 1956; s. John Brown and Mary (Kerr) H.; m. Joanna Baxter, Sept. 10, 1954; children—Mary Joanna, Margaret Brown, Elizabeth Campbell, John Stalker Kerr. M.A., U. St. Andrews, Scotland, 1939; student, King's Coll., Cambridge (Eng.) U., 1939-40; Ph.D., Harvard, 1956; LLD (hon.), U. St. Andrews, 1988. Lectr. polit. economy U. St. Andrews, 1946-52; vis. prof. Union Coll., Schenectady, 1950-51; tutor econs. Harvard, 1954-56; economist Fed. Res. Bank N.Y., 1956-60; Andrew Wells Robertson prof. econs. Allegheny Coll., Meadville, Pa., 1960-66; internat. economist Joint Econ. Com., U.S. Congress, 1966-68; dep. asst. sec. for econ. affairs Dept. Commerce, 1968-70; dir. econ. studies div. Bur. Labor Statistics, Dept. Labor, 1970-72; chief econs. div. Congl. Research Service, Library of Congress, 1972-75, sr. specialist in price econs., 1975-85; pres. Univ. St. Andrews Am. Found., 1986-92. Mem. Meadville Charter Commn., 1965. Served to flight lt. RAF, 1941-46. Home: 4119 27th Rd N Arlington VA 22207-5116

HENDERSON, JOHN DREWS, architect; b. St. Louis, July 30, 1933; s. Russell Dewey and Hazel Agnes (Drews) H.; m. Barbara Lee Beckman, June 25, 1955; children: Susan Lee, John Beckman. BArch, U. Ill., 1956. Registered architect, Calif., Nat. Coun. Archtl. Registration Bds. With Delawie, Macy & Henderson, San Diego, Calif., 1966-77, Macy, Henderson & Cole, AIA, San Diego, 1977-86; pres. John D. Henderson, FAIA, 1986—. Mem. San Diego Hist. Sites Bd., 1972-78, Gaslamp Quarter Task Force, 1976-78, Gaslamp Quarter Coun., 1984-86; mem. City Mgr.'s Com. for Seismic Retrofit for Older Bldgs., 1986-92; bd. dirs. Hist. Am. Bldgs. Survey Found., 1984-86; Calif. Hist. Bldgs. Code Safety Bd., 1976-96; apptd. by Gov. of Calif. to State Hist. Resources Commn., 1990-94, reapptd., 1994-98, 98-02, chmn. 1992-93, chmn. Calif. Heritage Found. com. 1993—; Calif. advisor Nat. Trust Hist. Preservation, 1975-78; chmn. adv. bd. Hist. Am. Bldgs. Survey, 1976-78; bd. dirs. Gaslamp Quarter Found., 1984-86. Lt. USN, 1956-59. Recipient Hist. Preservation awards from City San Diego, San Diego Hist. Soc., San Diego chpt. and Calif. Coun. AIA, La Jolla Women's Club, Am. Assn. State and Local History, Am. Inst. Planners, Save Our Heritage Orgn., Rancho Santa Fe Assn. Fellow AIA (officer, dir. local chpt. 1969-73, chpt. pres. 1972, editor guidebooks 1970, 76, state bd. dirs. 1971-73, nat. hist. resources com. 1974-76, 78, Calif. regional rep. 1976-78); mem. San Diego Archtl. Found. (bd. dirs. 1984-86, 89-91, emeritus 1999—), San Diego Hist. Soc. (officer, bd. dirs. 1975, pres. 1975), San Diego History Campaign (exec. com. 1981-86), Coronado Men's Golf Club. Republican. Presbyterian. Home and Office: John D Henderson FAIA 4879 Academy St San Diego CA 92109-3460

HENDERSON, KAREN LECRAFT, federal judge; b. 1944. BA, Duke U., 1966; JD, U. N.C., 1969. Ptnr. Wright & Henderson, Chapel Hill, N.C., 1969-70, Sinkler, Gibbs & Simons, P.A., Columbia, S.C., 1983-86; asst. atty. gen. Columbia, 1973-78; sr. asst. atty. gen., dir. of spl. litigation sect., 1978-82, deputy atty. gen., dir. of criminal div., 1982; judge U.S. Dist. Ct. S.C., Columbia, 1986-90, U.S. Ct. Appeals (D.C. cir.), Washington, 1990—. Apptd. Dist. Ct. Adv. Com. Mem. ABA (litigation sect. and urban, state and local government law sect.), N.C. Bar Assn., S.C. Bar (government law sect., trial and appellate practice sect., fed. judges assn.). Office: US Ct Appeals DC Cir US Courthouse 333 Constitution Ave NW Washington DC 20001-2802*

HENDERSON, KENNETH ATWOOD, investment counseling executive; b. Watertown, Mass., Oct. 18, 1905; s. Charles William and Anna Lyons (Atwood) H.; BS, Harvard U., 1926; m. Elizabeth Berry Marshall, June 10, 1944 (dec. March 1994); 1 child, Caroline Marshall. With fgn. dept. Brown Bros. & Co., Boston, 1926-30; analyst Weil McKey & Co., Boston, 1931; salesman, engr. home and comml. heating dept. Standard Oil Co. N.J., Boston, 1932-36; investigator Raymond E. Bell, Inc., N.Y.C., 1936; analyst, editor Poor's, Babson Park, Wellesley, Mass., 1937; investment counsellor Cromwell & Cabot, Inc., Boston, 1937-42, 46-50; sr. v.p. John P. Chase, Inc., Boston, 1950-74; pvt. practice investment counselling, Waban, Mass., 1975—; dir., treas. Henniker Crutch Co. Active investment, fin. coms. 2d Ch., Newton, Mass. Served to comdr. USNR, 1942-46. Fellow Harvard Travellers Club (hon.); mem. Boston Security Analysts Soc., Bond Analysts Soc. of Boston, Public Utility Analysts Boston, Am. Alpine Club (hon., hon. treas., Angelo Heilprin award 1982), Can., London alpine clubs, Harvard Mountaineering Club, Harvard Travellers Club (fellow, hon. mem., trustee of permanent funds), Explorers Club (medalist New England chpt.), Appalachian Mountain Club (hon.), Mountain Guides Assn. (hon.), Res. Officers Assn., Ret. Officers Assn., Mil. Order of the World Wars (perpetual mem.), 10th Mountain Divsn. Assn. (hon.). Author: Handbook of American Mountaineering, 1942; New England Canoeing Guide, 1965, 68, 71; editor: Appalachia, 1947-55; contbr. articles Am. Alpine Jour., Appalachia, Alpine Jour., others. Home: 29 Agawam Rd Waban MA 02468-1302

HENDERSON, LENNEAL JOSEPH, JR., political science educator; b. New Orleans, Oct. 27, 1946; s. Lenneal Joseph and Marcelle (Heno) H. A.B., U. Calif. at Berkeley, 1968, M.A., 1969, Ph.D., 1976; postgrad. in Sci., tech. and pub. policy, George Washington U. Asst. dean students, asst. prof. govt. St. Mary's Coll., Calif., 1969-71; dir. ethnic studies, asst. prof. govt. U. San Francisco, 1971-75; prof. Morgan State U., Balt., 1975—; asst. dean Sch. of Mgmt. John F. Kennedy U., Martinez, 1974-75; also lectr. polit. sci. Morgan State U., Balt.; asso. dir. research Joint Center Polit. Studies, Washington, 1977-78; pub. adminstrn. fellow U.S. Dept. Energy, 1978-79; lectr. urban studies Inst. Urban Studies U. Md., College Park; for U.S. State Dept. in, Somalia, Tanzania and Nigeria, South Africa, Swaziland, India; prof. Sch. Bus. and Public Adminstrn., Howard U., 1979-87; v.p. sci. and tech. Ronson Mgmt. Corp., Alexandria, Va., 1986-88; prof., head dept. polit. sci., dir. Bur. Pub. Adminstrn. U. Tenn., Knoxville, 1988-89; Disting. prof. govt. and pub. adminstrn., sr. fellow, Henry C. Welcome fellow William Donald Schaefer Ctr. for Pub. Policy, U. Balt., 1989—; vis. prof. polit. sci. Xavier U., New Orleans, 1970, Howard U., Washington, 1971, 75-76; instr. Ottawa U. of Kans., Ipoh, Penang, Malaysia and Hong Kong, 1997; vis. faculty city and regional planning dept. U. Calif., Berkeley, 1974-75; cons. Booz-Allen Pub. Adminstrn. Services, Inc., 1973-74, Shepard Assos., 1973-74, Morrison & Rowe, Inc., 1974, Dukes, Dukes & Assos., 1974-75; mem. U.S. del. Energy and Human Habitat Conf., EEC, Ottawa, Can., 1977; part-time faculty Fielding Inst., Santa Barbara, Calif., 1991—; lectr. USIA Tour, Namibia, Kenya, Ehiopia, Australia; spkr. internat. consulting seminar, Fielding Inst., Czech Republic, 1994. Editor: Black Political Life in the U.S, 1972; mem. editorial bd. Bureaucrat; contbr. articles to profl. jours. Pres., bd. dirs. Children and Youth Service Agy. of San Francisco, 1974-75; chmn. local reviewing com. San Francisco County Campaign for Human Devel., 1973-74; pres. San Francisco Youth Assn., 1964-65; mem. regional task force on open space Assn. of Bay Area Govt., 1973-75; pres., bd. dirs. African Am. Hist. and Cultural Soc., Inc., 1975-76; chmn. Mayor's Citizen Adv. Com. for Washington, 1981, Mayor's Budget Adv. Com., Washington, 1983; bd. dirs. Youth Svcs. Internat., Inc., 1998; apptd. Md. Commn. on African Am. History and Culture; bd. trustees Cath. Charities of the Archdiocese of Balt. Recipient Disting. Faculty award Howard U., 1984, Outstanding Faculty award, 1986; Calif. State fellow, 1969-71; Urban Affairs fellow, 1969-70; fellow Moton Center Ind. Studies, summer 1978; Nat. Assn. Schs. Public Affairs and Public Adminstrn. fellow U.S. Dept. Energy, 1978-79; research fellow Rockefeller Found.; research asso. Harvard U.; NRC postdoctoral fellow Johns Hopkins U. Sch. Advanced Internat. Studies, 1983-84; Kellogg nat. fellow, 1986. Mem. Am. Polit. Sci. Assn., Am. Soc. Pub. Adminstrn., AAAS, Western Govtl. Research Assn., Internat. Personnel Mgmt. Assn., Am. Social and Behavioral Sci. Assn. Independent. Roman Catholic. Home: 4530 Mustering Drum Ellicott City MD 21042-5949 Office: U Balt William D Schaefer Ctr Pub Policy 1304 Saint Paul St Baltimore MD 21202-2713 *Service is the heart of my life. Its demands hold me to the highest humanitarian ideals. Its standards teach me the value of mistakes made right. Without service, humanity falls below the lowest of life forms; for all animals serve God's purpose. So service will continue to lead me to others; to their needs, hopes, desires. And, as I fulfill these needs, hopes, desires, I fulfill my own.*

HENDERSON, MADELINE MARY (BERRY) (BERRY HENDERSON), chemist, researcher, consultant; b. Merrimac, Mass., Sept. 3, 1922; d. Burton B. and Irene R. (Murphy) Berry; m. Richard S. Henderson, Nov. 5, 1957; children: Anne M., Matthew R., Katherine M., Laura J. AB in Chemistry, Emmanuel Coll., Boston, 1944; MPA, Am. U., Washington, 1977. Chemist E.I. DuPont, Gibbstown, N.J., 1944-45, MIT, Cambridge, Mass., 1946-52; info. specialist Battelle Meml. Inst., Columbus, Ohio, 1953-55; rsch. assoc. NSF, Washington, 1956-62; computer specialist Nat. Bur. Standards, Washington, 1964-79; cons. Bethesda, 1980—; chmn. Gordon Rsch. Conf. on Sci. Info. Problems, 1972. *Madeline Henderson has been identified as a pioneer of information science for her early work in developing improved methods for handling scientific and technical information resources. Particularly, she participated in efforts to identify the semantic content of indexing terms, and to encode chemical structural formulas. More recently, as an independent consultant, she has guided managers of Federal and private-sector information systems in incorporating information processing standards into their operational procedures, and continues to advocate the development and appropriate use of such standards.* Author, co-author, editor books on info. sci.; co-author, author papers, articles on info. sci., standards, and libr. automation. Dept. of Commerce Sci.-Tech. fellow, 1971-72; Am. U. Key Exec. scholar, 1975-77. Fellow AAAS (sec. sect. info. scis. 1978-85); mem. Am. Chem. Soc., Am. Soc. Info. Sci. (mem. publs. com. 1983-87, chmn. pub. affairs com. 1987-89, Watson Davis award 1989), Pi Alpha Alpha (nat. honor soc. pub. adminstr.). Office: 30072 Cross Woods Dr Mechanicsville MD 20659-6122

HENDERSON, MARK GORDY, lawyer; b. Berkeley, Calif., Feb. 21, 1954; s. John Nelson and Shirley Belle (Queen) H.; m. Elizabeth Andrea Fulmer, June 24, 1978; children: Emily MacCaughey, James Ellis. BA, U. of the Pacific, 1976, JD, 1981, LLM in Bus. and Tax, 1985. Bar: Calif. 1981, U.S. Ct. Appeals (9th cir.) 1985, U.S. Dist. Ct. (ctrl. dist.) Calif. 1988, U.S. Dist. Ct. (ea. dist.) Calif. 1992; cert. specialist in estate planning, trust and probate law. Ptnr. Hiroshima, Jacobs & Roth, Sacramento, 1981-91; pvt. practice law Davis, Calif., 1991—. Exec. dir. Citizens Who Care, Inc., Davis. Mem. Calif. State Bar Assn. (estate planning, trust and probate law sect.), Yolo County Bar Assn., Order of the Coif. Office: PO Box 73914 Davis CA 95617

HENDERSON, MARSHA ROSLYN THAW, clinical social worker; b. San Antonio, Dec. 31, 1946; d. Eugene and Ann (Pokloff) Thaw; m. Thomas Jay Henderson, July 14, 1976; 1 child, Ashley Erin. BA, U. Houston, 1968, MSW, 1973. Lic. clin. social worker, Calif.; diplomate Am. Bd. Examiners in Clin. Social Work. Intake worker St. Joseph's Mid Houston Community Mental Health Ctr., 1968-69; caseworker II, Tex. Rsch. Inst. Mental Scis., Houston, 1969-71; pvt. practice, Houston, 1971-73; psychiat. social worker Intercommunity Child Guidance Ctr., Hawaiian Gardens, Calif., 1974-75; clin. social worker Family Guidance Ctr., Buena Park, Calif., 1975-77; pvt. practice, Laguna Hills, Calif., 1976—; exec. dir. Adoption Info. and Resource Ctr., 1997; art therapy workshops Calif. State U., L.A., 1977, U. Calif., Irvine, 1980; ct. apptd. 730-731 child custody evaluator; adj. faculty Grad. Sch. Social Work, U. So. Calif., Irvine, 1998—. Med. social work Mission Hosp. Regional Med. Ctr., Mission Viejo, Calif., 1998—. Mem. NASW, Acad. Cert. Social Workers, Calif. Soc. for Clin. Social Worker, Am. Adoption Congress, Calif. Forensic Mental Health Assn., Child Sexual Abuse Network. Avocations: art, music, sailing, travel. Office: 25301 Cabot Rd Ste 114 Laguna Hills CA 92653

HENDERSON, MARY LOUISE, civic worker; b. Windsor, Ont., Can., Apr. 24, 1928; came to U.S., 1932; d. Kenneth Charles and Florence McGie (Morton) Campbell; m. Ernest Flagg Henderson III, Dec. 31, 1953; children: Ernest Flagg IV, Roberta C. BA, Bard Coll., 1950. V.p. Ruse & Urban, Inc., advt., Detroit, 1950-53; v.p., bd. dirs. Henderson House Am., Sudbury, Mass., 1969—. Pres. Wellesley (Mass.) Friendly Aid Assn., 1970-75, Newton (Mass.) Wellesley Hosp. Aid, 1980-82, 88-89; co-founder, exec. com. mem. Wellesley Community Ctr., 1972, pres., 1983-85; bd. dirs., mem. exec. com. Norumbega Coun. Boy Scouts Am., 1974-95, pres., 1989-91; mem. exec. com. Knox Coun. Boy Scouts Am., 1995—; trustee Newton-Wellesley Hosp., 1982—, mem. exec. com., 1990-96; bd. dirs., mem. exec. com. Greater Boston adv. bd. Salvation Army, 1985—; mem. nat. adv. bd. Officers Tng. Sch. Salvation Army, 1994—; bd. dirs. Newton-Wellesley Vis. Nurse Assn., 1974—; corporator Boston Bio-Med. Inst., 1990—; mem. corp. Ptnrs. Healthcare Sys., 1999—, also others. Mem. Mensa, Am. Needlepoint Guild (founder, pres. Mass. chpt. 1974-77, bd. dirs. 1974—, nat. historian 1989—). Republican. Episcopalian. Avocations: travel, reading, needlepoint. Home: 171 Edmunds Rd Wellesley MA 02481-1331

HENDERSON, MAUREEN MCGRATH, medical educator; b. Tynemouth, Eng., May 11, 1926; came to U.S., 1960; d. Leo E. and Helen (McGrath) H. MB BS, U. Durham, Eng., 1949, DPH, 1956. Prof. preventive medicine U. Md. Med. Sch., 1968-75, chmn. dept. social and preventive medicine, 1971-75; assoc. epidemiology Johns Hopkins U. Sch. Hygiene and Pub. Health, 1970-75; prof. epidemiology and medicine U. Wash. Med. Sch., 1975-96, prof. emeritus epidemiology and medicine, 1996—, asst. v.p. and assoc. v.p. health scis., 1975-81, head cancer prevention rsch. program Fred Hutchinson Cancer Rsch. Ctr., 1983-94; mem. Nat. Inst. Environ. Health Scis. Adv. Coun., 1994-97; chmn. epidemiology and disease control study sect. NIH, 1969-82; chmn. clin. trial rev. com. Nat. Heart Lung and Blood Inst., 1975-79; mem. Nat. Cancer Adv. Bd., 1979-84; mem. bd. Robert Wood Johnson Health Policy Fellowship, 1989-93; bd. on radiation effects rsch. NRC, 1991-97, mem. com. on rsch. priorities for airborne particulate matters, 1998—; chmn. safety of silicone breast implants Inst. Medicine, 1998. Assoc. editor jour. Cancer Rsch., 1987-88; mem. editorial bd. Jour. Nat. Cancer Inst., 1988—; mem. editorial adv. bd. Cancer Detection and Prevention, 1992—. Recipient John Snow award Am. Pub. Health Assn., 1990; Luke-Armstrong scholar, 1956-57; John and Mary Markle scholar acad. medicine, 1963-68. Mem. Inst. Medicine of NAS (coun. 1981-85), Am.

Coll. Epidemiology, Assn. Tchrs. Preventive Medicine (pres. 1972-73), Soc. Epidemiol. Rsch. (chmn. 1969-70), Internat. Epidemiol. Assn. (exec. officer 1971-76), Internat. Coun. Cancer Rsch. (sci. adv. bd. 1989-92), Am. Epidemiol. Soc. (pres. 1990-91), Nat. Rsch. Coun. (mem. com. on rsch. priorities for airborne particulate matters 1998—, mem. report rev. com. 1996—). Home: 5309 NE 85th St Seattle WA 98115-3915

HENDERSON, MELFORD J., epidemiologist, molecular biologist, chemist; b. Birmingham, Ala., Dec. 28, 1950; s. Robert Burton and Rena Henderson; 1 child, Erica. Student, NYU Dental Sch., 1977-79; BS, Bishop Coll., Dallas, 1972; MA, Johns Hopkins U., 1976; MPH, Yale U., 1984. Ordained minister. Research assoc. Bishop Coll., 1972-73; rsch. assoc. Sch. of Pharmacy U. Md., Balt., 1976-77; microbiologist Torigian Labs., Queens, N.Y., 1979-81; pub. health analyst internat. program cardiovascular diseases NIH, Bethesda, Md., 1984; epidemiologist/analyst Task Force on Black and Minority Health, Bethesda, Md., 1985—; epidemiologist D.C. Govt., D.C. Health Dept., 1985-88, U.S. Govt., Agy. for Health Care Policy and Rsch., 1990; epidemiologist, sr. rsch. assoc. Prospect Assocs., 1989; epidemiologist, program ofcl. U.S. Dept. HHS; program ofcl. Mayor's Health Policy Coun. D.C. Govt. Author 7 scholarly sci. publs. Recipient numerous awards in chemistry and pub. health; NIH fellow, 1973-76, USPHS fellow, 1982-84, rsch. fellow Assn. Black Cardiologists, 1984-85. Mem. APHA, Md. Pub. Health Assn., Blacks in Govt., Soc. for Epidemiol. Rsch., Assn. Black Cardiologists, Beta Kappa Chi.

HENDERSON, MICHAEL HOWARD, artist, educator; b. Dallas, Aug. 30, 1958; s. Ralph Howard and Barbara Ruth Henderson. BFA, U. North Tex., 1983, MFA, 1986; postgrad., Whitney Ind. Study Program, N.Y.C., 1986-87. Vis. lectr. Princeton (N.J.) U., 1994; adj. faculty mem. Tex. Christian U., Ft. Worth, 1995; vis. asst. prof. U. Tex., Arlington, 1996; adj. instr. Navarro Coll., Corsicana, Tex., 1997-98, Tarrant County Jr. Coll., Ft. Worth, 1998-99, Brookhaven Coll., Dallas, 1998-99; lectr. in painting U. Tex., Dallas, 1999—; part-time instr. Hill Coll., Hillsboro, Tex., 1993-95; co-dir. Gray Matters, Dallas, 1996-97. One-man shows at alternate Gallery, Dallas, 1985, Artists Space, N.Y.C., 1990, Gray Matters, 1995, 97, John Michael Kohler Art Ctr., Sheboygan, Wis., 1997; exhibited in group shows at Chatauqua (N.Y.) Inst., 1984, D-Art Visual Ctr., Dallas, 1984, Theater Gallery, Dallas, 1984, Ark. Art Ctr., Little Rock, 1985, Arts Warehouse, Austin, Tex., 1986, Brown-Lupton Gallery, Tex. Christian U., Ft. Worth, 1986, 500X Gallery, Dallas, 1986, Soho Ctr. for Visual Arts, N.Y.C., 1987, Laguna Gloria Art Mus., Austin, 1989, Visual Arts Ctr. of Alaska, Anchorage, 1990, B4A Gallery, N.Y.C., 1990, Clocktower Gallery, N.Y.C., 1990, MMC Gallery Marymount Manhattan Coll., N.Y.C., 1991, Gray Matters, 1992, Lynn Goode Gallery, Houston, 1992, TZ'Art and Co. Gallery, N.Y.C., 1994, Islip Art Mus., East Islip, N.Y., 1995, Galeria de Arte Plastica Contemporania, Guatemala City, Guatemala, 1996, Diverse Works, Houston, 1996, Ft. Worth Contemporary Art Ctr., 1998, Webb Gallery, Waxahachie, Tex., 1998, McKinney Ave. Contemporary, Dallas, 1999, Hallwalls, Buffalo, N.Y., 1999, Arlington Mus. of Art, 1999; prodr. video Videokronografy, 1996. Grantee Artists Space, 1987, Pollock Krasner Found., 1989; tchg. fellow U. North Tex., 1984-88. Mem. Coll. Art Assn. E-mail: mhhndrsn@aol.com. Home: 512 Sunnyside Ave Dallas TX 75211

HENDERSON, MILTON ARNOLD, professional society administrator; b. Chattanooga, June 22, 1922; s. Milton Arnold and Margaret (Rawlings) H.; m. Joyce Crowder (dec. Nov. 13, 1977); children: George, Linda, Philip.; m. Betty Ann Harnage, Aug. 20, 1982. B.S., Northwestern U., 1948. Asst. sales mgr. Coca-Cola Bottling Co., Savannah and Macon, Ga., 1948-54; with Gideons Internat., Chgo., 1954-63, field rep., 1954-55, promotion mgr., 1955-56; with Gideons Internat., Nashville, 1964—, exec. dir., 1956-87, exec. dir. emeritus, 1987—. Editor The Gideon Mag. and Gideon Info. Bull., 1956-87; author: Sowers of the Word, a 95-Year History of The Gideons International, 1899-1994, 1995. 1st lt. USAAF, 1942-46; capt. USAF, 1951-52. Recipient Community Leader of Am. award, 1969, Personalities of the South award, 1975, Disting. Alumnus award Howe Mil. Sch., Ind., 1985. Mem. Am. Mgmt. Assn., Nashville City Club. Republican. Presbyterian. Home: 2524 Stones River Ct Nashville TN 37214-1425 Office: 2900 Lebanon Rd Nashville TN 37214-2509

HENDERSON, NANCY GRACE, marketing and technical documentation executive; b. Berkeley, Calif., Oct. 23, 1947; d. John Harry and Lorraine Ruth (Johnson) H. BA, U. Calif., Santa Barbara, 1969; MBA, U. Houston, 1985; teaching credential, UCLA, 1971. Chartered fin. analyst. Tchr. Keppel Union Sch. Dist., Littlerock, Calif., 1969-72, Internat. Sch. Prague, Czechoslovakia, 1972-74, Sunland Luth. Sch., Freeport, Bahamas, 1974-75; tchr., dept. head Internat. Sch. Assn., Bangkok, Thailand, 1975-79; exec. search Diversified Human Resources Group, Houston, Tex., 1979-82; data processing analyst Am. Gen. Corp., Houston, 1982-83, personnel and benefits dept., 1983-85, investment analyst, 1985-86, equity security analyst/quantitative portfolio analyst, 1986-87; dir. mktg. and communications Vestek Systems Inc., San Francisco, 1987-90, dir. technical publs., 1990—; tchr. English as Second Language program Houston Metro. Ministries, 1980-81. Pres., bd. dirs. Home Owners Assn., Walnut Creek, Calif., 1988-90; tchr. English to refugees Houston Metro Ministries, 1982; exec. dir. Internat. Child Abuse Prevention Found., 1989; ch. choir, session, fundraising and com. chmn. Presbyn. Ch.; active Crisis Hotline, 1978-79, 92-93; dir. project Working in Networks for Good Shelter, 1993-95. Named a Notable Woman of Tex., 1984-85. Mem. Assn. for Investment Mgmt. and Rsch., Toastmasters (pres. Houston chpt. 1983, v.p. 1982-83). Avocations: tennis, skiing, backpacking, canoeing, photography, writing short stories and essays. Office: Vestek Systems 388 Market St Ste 700 San Francisco CA 94111-5347

HENDERSON, NATHAN H., bishop. Bishop Ch. of God in Christ, Houston. Office: Ch of God in Christ Laws Meml 4807 Wayne St Houston TX 77026*

HENDERSON, PAUL BARGAS, JR., economic development consultant, educator; b. McKees Rocks, Pa., Nov. 20, 1928; s. Paul Bargas and Viola Mae (Mullins) Henderson; m. Betty D. Langewisch, Aug. 25, 1951; children: Keith, Karen, Laura. B.S. in Mech. and Indsl. Engring., Washington U., St. Louis, 1948, M.S. in Bus. Adminstrn., 1950; Ph.D. in Indsl. Econs., MIT, 1960. Asst. for mgmt. U.S. Navy Bur. Ordnance, Washington, 1950-58; mgr. sys. tech. Westinghouse Electric Corp., Pitts., 1960-67; program mgr. United Aircraft Corp., Hartford, Conn., 1967-68; dir. data services Allis-Chalmers Corp., Milw., 1968-74; v.p. Fed. Res. Bank N.Y., N.Y.C., 1974-77, sr. v.p., 1977-82, sr. adviser, 1982-84; bank ops. cons. N.Y.C., 1984—; econ. devel. cons. in Russia, chmn. Sierra Caucasus Corp., 1990—; exec. dir. United Meth. Econ. Devel. Initiative in Kazakstan, 1996—; asst. prof. econs. Sierra Nevada Coll., Incline Village, Nev., 1997—; bd. dirs. Direct Svcs., Inc., Found. for Ednl. Field Svcs. Author: (with E.M. Heigler) Library Automation, 1970, Electronic Funds Transfers and Payments: The Public Policy Issues, 1987; inventor in field. Office: 525 Spencer Way Incline Village NV 89451-8304 *There is a recurring necessity to induce change as the basis for comparative advantage: neglect makes it a matter of survival. There is also a constant and greater necessity to sustain existing operations: quality and efficiency depend on repetition. Anticipated change is thus compatible with stable management. Change for survival, and managers capable of inducing it, must be transitory for both are incompatible with sustained organizational success.*

HENDERSON, PETER HARRY, non-profit organization administrator; b. Balt., Jan. 2, 1960; s. Harry Elmont Jr. and Faye Agnes (Irish) H.; m. Laura Nell Smith, Sept. 30, 1989; children: Christopher Allen, Geoffrey Lancaster. BA, John Hopkins U., 1982, PhD, 1993; M in Pub. Policy, Harvard U., 1984. Presdl. mgmt. intern U.S. Dept. Housing & Urban Devel., Washington, 1984-86; assoc. ICF Inc., Vienna, Va., 1989-90; rsch. officer Nat. Assn. Housing & Redevel. Officials, Washington, 1994-96; study dir. NRC, Washington, 1996—. Office: NRC 2101 Constitution Ave NW Washington DC 20418-0007

HENDERSON, RALPH HALE, physician; b. N.Y.C., Mar. 5, 1937; s. Ralph Ernest and Clifford West (Sellers) H.; m. Ilze Sarma, May 21, 1966. AB, Harvard U., 1959, MD, 1963, MPH, 1970, M.Pub. Policy, 1972. Intern, then resident in internal medicine Boston City Hosp., 1963-65; joined USPHS, 1965, capt., 1973-81, asst. surgeon gen., 1981-90; svc. in USPHS, U.S. and West Africa, 1965-69; lectr. USPHS, 1995; asst. chief venereal disease br., state and cmty. svcs. divsn. Ctrs. Disease Control, Atlanta, 1972-73; dir. venereal disease control divsn. Bur. State Svcs., 1973-76; program mgr. expanded program on immunization WHO, Geneva, 1977-78, dir. expanded program immunization, 1979-89, asst. dir. gen., 1990-98, spl. advisor to dir. gen., 1998-99; Lilly lectr. Royal Coll. Physicians, 1989; lectr. disting. lecture series Baylor Coll. Medicine, 1995. Contbr. to med. publs. Trustee Dermatology Found., 1975-77. Recipient Commendation medal USPHS, 1969, Meritorius Svc. medal, 1984, Disting. Svc. medal, 1990, Donald MacKay Meml. medal Royal Soc. Tropical Medicine and Hygiene, 1990, Internat. Child Survival award U.S. Com. UNICEF and the Task Force for Child Survival and Devel., 1992, Ann. Pub. Health Forum award London Sch. of Hygiene and Tropical Medicine, 1994. Mem. Am. Coll. Preventive Medicine. Home: 1098 McConnell Dr Decatur GA 30033 Office: care WHO, 1211 Geneva 27, Switzerland

HENDERSON, RICHARD MARTIN, retired chemical engineer; b. Winston-Salem, Dec. 12, 1934; s. Billy Martin and Marion Lucille (Dunn) H.; m. Patricia Lucille Green, Dec. 27, 1958 (div. 1978); children: Marian Patricia, Richard Martin; m. Janice Lee Ferris, Apr. 3, 1981. BBA, Wake Forest U., 1957. Cert. quality engr. Jr. chem. engr. R.J. Reynolds Tobacco Co., Winston-Salem, 1957-58, asst. chem. engr., 1958-65, product devel. group leader, 1965-66, devel. sect. head, 1966-80, div. mgr., 1981-98; ret., 1998. Pres. Y Men's Club of Winston-Salem, 1989, Moravian Music Found., Winston-Salem, 1983; active United Way of Forsyth County, 1958—, Winston-Salem Arts Coun., 1958—. With Signal Corps, U.S. Army, 1960-61. Recipient Merit award, Moravian Music Found., 1984; Ky. Col. Mem. Am. Soc. for Quality Control (founding dir./sr. mem.), Forsyth Country Club. Republican. Moravian. Achievements include patents for the method of and apparatus for automatically analyzing the degradation of processed leaf tobacco, for the method and apparatus for automatically determining the stem content of baled tobacco, for the method and apparatus for automatically determining the basis weight and moisture content of paper and paper-like substance, for the method and apparatus for automatically sampling a material and transporting it from one location to another remote location. Home: 717 Mitch Dr Winston Salem NC 27104-5127 Office: RJ Reynolds Tobacco Co 401 N Main St Winston Salem NC 27101-3818

HENDERSON, R(ICHARD) WINN, physician; b. Gainesville, Fla., Oct. 3, 1948; s. William P. and Lillian June (Rudd) H.; m. Maureen Skudlarek, 1972 (div. 1985); 1 child, Heather Ann; m. Wanda Joyce Crittenden, Apr. 13, 1997. AB, Lagrange Coll., 1968; MD, U. Ala., 1972. Diplomate Am. Bd. Family Practitioners, Am. Bd. Emergency Medicine. Intern in family practice St. Elizabeth's Med. Ctr., Dayton, 1972-73; resident in aerospace medicine Brooks AFB, 1973; mem. courtesy staff, clin. instr. emergency dept. UTMRCH, Knoxville, Tenn., 1976-78; staff emergency physician, dir. emergency physicians Morristown (Tenn.) Hamblen Hosp., 1978-82; staff emergency physician, chmn. emergency dept. St. Mary's Med. Ctr., Knoxville, 1983-84; staff emergency physician Meth. Med. Ctr., Oak Ridge, Tenn., 1984-85; dir. East Tenn. Med./Acute Care Clinic, 1985-90; counselor, rschr. in addiction medicine Kennedy Ctr., Morgantown, W.Va., 1990-92; dir. The Recovery Group, Knoxville, 1992—; examiner FAA, 1982-90; internat. radio talk show host Share Your Mission, 1998—. Author: The Cure of Addiction, 1991, Doctor's Don't Lie, 1993, The 12 Steps (Explained and Revised), 1995, Forever Lovers, 1997, The Four Questions, 1998; radio host Share Your Mission, 1998—. Founder The Destiny House, 1998. Maj. USAF, 1973-76. Mem. Am. Assn. Christian Counselors, Am. Soc. Addiction Medicine. Avocation: sculpting, painting. Office: The Recovery Group 4301 Washington Pk Knoxville TN 37917-2509

HENDERSON, RICKEY HENLEY, professional baseball player; b. Chgo., Dec. 25, 1958. With minor league baseball clubs, 1976-79; with Oakland Athletics, 1979-84, 89-93, 94-95, N.Y. Yankees, 1985-89, Toronto Blue Jays, 1993-94, San Diego Padres, 1996-98, New York Mets, 98-. Winner Am. League Gold Glove, 1981; named Most Valuable Player, American League, 1990, Am. League All-Star team, 1980, 82-88, 90-91. Sporting News Am. League All-Star Team, 1981, 85, 90, Sporting News Am. League Silver Slugger Team, 1981, 85, 90, Sporting News Silver Shoe award, 1982, Sporting News Golden Shoe award, 1983, Am. Championship Series MVP, 1989. Holds major league record for stolen bases in one season (130), 1982, for most stolen bases in career; player World Series 1989, 90, 93. Office: New York Mets 123-10 Roosevelt Ave Flushing NY 11368

HENDERSON, RITA ELIZABETH, literary agent, journalist; b. Bitburg, German, Mar. 7, 1964; came to U.S., 1964; d. Walter Wanzley and Lola Bell (Boles) H.; adopted children: Christopher Allan Jackson, Kayla Elizabeth Octavia Davis. AAS, Camden County Coll., Blackwood, N.J., 1984; BS, Glassboro (N.J.) State Coll., 1987. Owner Henderson Lit. Representation, Sicklerville, N.J., 1994—; real estate agt. Weichert Realtors, Medford, N.J., 1998—. Author: The Boyz II Men Success Story: Defying the Odds, 1995; entertainment writer The N.Y. Amsterdam News, 1991-95, The Phila. Tribune, 1993-95. Democrat. Roman Catholic. Avocations: music, archery, antique collecting, baseball, computers. Office: Weichert Realtors 107 Taunton Blvd Medford NJ 08055-3400

HENDERSON, ROBB ALAN, minister; b. Wilkes Barre, Pa., Mar. 21, 1956; s. Robert Alan and Mary (Gallup) H.; m. Norma Jean Davis, Nov. 26, 1994; children: Jason Allyn, Gareth Kent. BA in Theology, King's Coll., Wilkes Barre, 1981; MDiv, Lancaster Theol. Sem., 1985; D Ministry, Bethany Theol. Sem., 1990. Ordained to ministry United Meth. Ch. as deacon, 1986, as elder, 1988; ordained into So. Episc. Ch., 1997. Pastor Luzerne (Pa.) United Meth. Ch., 1985-88, Carverton United Meth. Ch., Wyoming, Pa., 1988—, St. Paul's United Meth. Ch., Scranton, Pa., 1993-94; owner R&R Bus Line, Luzerne, 1990—; chmn. interreligious and ecumenical affairs com. Coun. of Chs., 1989—; bd. dirs. Wyoming Valley Coun. of Chs.; safety dir., dispatcher First Class Coach Co., St. Petersburg, Fla. Chaplain Mt. Zion Vol. Fire Dept., Mt. Zion, Harding, Pa.; mem. Wilkes Barre Dist. Coord. Coun., 1988—. Mem. Masons (chaplain Kingston lodge 1989), Irem Temple. Home and Office: 1257 Murray St Forty Fort PA 18704

HENDERSON, ROBERT EARL, mechanical engineer, educator, consultant; b. Olean, N.Y., Nov. 1, 1935; s. Kenneth Peter and Marion (Nichols) H.; m. E. Annalee Rosenswie, Aug. 10, 1957 (dec. July 20, 1994); children: Gregory Dwight, Michael Edwin, Lori Elizabeth; m. Mary J. Ball, Dec. 28, 1996 . BS, Pa. State U., 1958, MS, 1962; PhD, Cambridge (Eng.) U., 1973. Aerodynamicist McDonnel Aircraft Corp., St. Louis, 1958-59; rsch. asst., asst. prof., assoc. prof. engring. rsch. Applied Rsch. Lab., Pa. State U., 1959-73, assoc. prof. mech. engring., 1973-79, prof., 1979-91, prof. emeritus, 1991—, cons., 1991-95; chief sci. Noesis, Inc., 1995—; assoc. dir. Garfield Thomas Water Tunnel, 1980-82, head dept. fluid dynamics and turbomachinery, 1983-89, asst. dir. applied sci. div., 1990-91. Contbr. articles to profl. jours. Recipient Disting. Performance award Applied Research Lab., Pa. State U., 1981. Fellow ASME, AIAA (assoc.); mem. Am. Soc. Naval Engrs., Sigma Xi, Pi Mu Epsilon. Home: 4715 N Dittmar Rd Arlington VA 22207-4312 Office: 4200 Wilson Blvd Ste 900 Arlington VA 22203-1800

HENDERSON, ROBERT EDWARD, research institute director; b. Kokomo, Ind., Feb. 28, 1925; married, 1952; 6 children. BA, Carleton Coll., 1949; MA, U. Mo., 1951, PhD in Physics, 1953. Instr. physics U. Mo., 1951-53; exptl. engr. Allison divsn. GM Co., 1953-56, supr. applied physics, 1956-58, rsch. mgr. applied sci., 1958-66, mgr. exptl. rsch., 1966-69, dir. rsch., 1969-73; chmn. sci. adv. bd. Ind. Ctr. Adv. Rsch., Inc., 1970-83, exec. dir., 1973-78, pres., 1978-82; pres. Tech. Devel. Corp., 1982-83; dir. S.C. Rsch. Authority, Columbia, 1983-96; ret., 1996; mem. com. on solar energy for heating and cooling of bldgs. Bldgs. Rsch. Adv. Bd., NAS; advisor Aero. Sys. divsn. Divsn. Adv. Group, Dept. Air Force; prof. Sch. Engring. and Tech., Purdue U., West Lafayette; prof. dept. radiology Ind. U. Sch. Medicine, adj. prof. Sch. Pub. and Environ. Affairs; pres. Ind. Sci. and Engring. Found., 1982. Fellow AIAA; mem. Am. Phys. Soc., Solar Energy Soc., Sigma Xi. Achievements include research in energy conversion. E-mail: henderso@scra.org. Office: 225 Pebble Creek Rd Columbia SC 29223-3114*

HENDERSON, ROGENE FAULKNER, toxicologist, researcher; b. Breckenridge, Tex., July 13, 1933; d. Philander Molden and Lenoma (Rogers) F.; m. Thomas Richard Henderson II, May 30, 1957; children: Thomas Richard III, Edith Jeanette, Laura Lee. BSBA, Tex. Christian U., 1955; PhD, U. Tex., 1960. Diplomate Am. Bd. Toxicology. Research assoc. U. Ark. Sch. Med., Little Rock, 1960-67; from scientist to sr. scientist and group supr. chemistry and toxicology Lovelace Inhalation Toxicology Research Inst., Albuquerque, 1967—; mem. adv. com. Burroughs Wellcome Toxicology Scholar award, 1987-89, NIH toxicology study sect., 1982-86, Nat. Inst. Environ. Health Scis. adv. coun., 1992-95, EPA scientific adv. bd. environ. health commn., 1991-95. Assoc. editor Toxicology Applied Pharmacology, 1989-95, Jour. Exposure Analysis and Environ. Epidemiology, 1991-95; contbr. articles to profl. jours. Named Woman on the Move YWCA, Albuquerque, 1985; grantee NIH, 1958-60, 1960-62, 1986—. Mem. AAAS, NAS (bd. on environ. studies and toxicology 1998—), Am. Chem. Soc. (chmn. ctrl. N.Mex. sect. 1981), Soc. Toxicology (pres. Mountain-West Regional chpt. 1985-86, pres. inhalation specialty sect. 1989—), N.Y. Acad. Scis., Nat. Acad. Scis. (com. toxicology 1985-98, chair 1992-98, com. epidemiology of air pollution 1983-85, com. biol. markers 1986—, com. on risk assessment methodology 1989-92). Presbyterian. Home: 5609 Don Felipe Ct SW Albuquerque NM 87105-6765 Office: Lovelace Inhalation Toxicology Research Inst PO Box 5890 Albuquerque NM 87185-5890

HENDERSON, RONALD, police chief; b. St. Louis, Dec. 24, 1947. A in Criminal Justice, Florissant (Mo.) Valley C.C.; grad. exec. strategic mgmt. program, Sr. Mgmt. Inst. for Police, Boston, 1992; student, Dignitary Protection Sch., Washington, 1994. appointee Mo. Emergency Response Commn.; program dir. St. Louis Met. Police Dept. Intern Program; initiated New Year's Eve safety campaign. Several divsns. including vice-narcotics, internal affairs St. Louis Police Dept., patrolman, sgt., lt. col., comdr. bur. of patrol support, 1970-92, chief, 1995—; bd. dirs. St. Louis Cath. Charities. Recipient Robert Lamb Jr. Humanitarian award Nat. Orgn. of Black Law Enfocement Officers, 1997. Office: Met Police Dept 1200 Clark Ave Saint Louis MO 63103-2801*

HENDERSON, SALATHIEL JAMES, minister, clergy; b. Key West, Fla., June 15, 1944; s. James Joseph and Merlice Yvone (McIntosh) H.; m. Mary Louise Henderson, June 28, 1969; children: Salathiel James II, Shane Jamal. Diploma, LaSalle Extension U., 1977; AA, St. Leo Coll., 1987, BA, 1988. Ordained to ministry Bapt. Ch. 1989. Deacon Antioch Bapt. Ch., Hampton, Va., 1980-87, assoc. min., 1987—; vol. chaplain Hospice unit VA Med. Ctr., Hampton, Va., 1987—; substitute tchr. Hampton City Schs., 1991-95, adminstrv. asst., 1995—; sr. fed. supply cataloger Mason & Hanger Svcs., Inc., NASA/Langley AFB, Va., 1988-91; dir. Christian Edn., Antioch Bapt. Ch., 1986—, mem. fin. com., 1984-94, spiritual advisor Youth Usher Bd., 1984-90, sec. Ministerial Staff, 1991-94; dir. Bereavement Ministry, Antioch Bapt. Ch., Hampton, 1988—; cubmaster Cub Scouts Am., Antioch Bapt.-Hampton, 1990-95; chartered scouting rep. Antioch Bapt., 1995—; sec. Hampton Ministers' Coalition, 1992-94; v.p. Ministers' Coalition for Hampton & Vicinity, 1994-98, pres., 1999—. Mem. Hampton U. Min.'s Conf., 1990—; co-chmn. publicity com. Peninsula United Clergy Coun., 1994-96; vol. Am. Heart Assn., 1992—. With USAF, 1962-85. Mem. NAACP (mem. cmty. coordination com. Hampton br. 1997-98, chmn. religious affairs 1999—, grad. Hampton Neighborhood Coll. 1999), DAV (life), Am. Assn. Christian Counselors, Masons. Democrat. Home and Office: 607 Allendale Dr Hampton VA 23669-1621 *As one views society in its present state, and before an attempt is made to criticize the actions and values of the future generation (tomorrow's leaders) it is essential and imperative to carefully scrutinize today's grotesque situations. I believe our future leaders have many goals, with every hope of attaining them (if afforded the opportunity), but it is necessary that they also have acceptable role models as examples. Not just any role model, but one who institutes integrity, while propelling a greater force toward pride, trustworthiness and a genuine love for justice to all of God's Children!.*

HENDERSON, SCOTT, jazz guitarist; b. West Palm Beach, Fla., Aug. 26, 1954; s. Charles and Geneva (Mavity) H. Guitarist Jean Luc Ponty, L.A., Chick Corea, L.A., Joe Zawinul, L.A.; co-band leader Tribal Tech, L.A.; guitar instr. Musicians Inst., L.A.; columnist Guitar World mag., N.Y.C. Author: (videos) Jazz Fuzion Improvisation, Melodic Phrasing; bandleader albums: Spears, Dr. Hee, Nomad, Tribal Tech., Illicit, Face First, Reality Check, Dog Party, Tore Down House. Named Best Jazz Guitarist, Guitar Player mag., 1991, Best Blues Album award, 1995, Best Jazz Guitarist, Guitar World mag., 1992.

HENDERSON, SCOTTIE YVETTE, researcher; b. Shiprock, N.Mex., Oct. 3, 1968; d. David and Carmen Henderson. AS, No. N.Mex. C.C., Espanola, 1988; BA, U. Calif., Santa Cruz, 1992; postgrad., U. Wash., 1994—. Student rschr. Minority Biomed. Rsch. Support/Minority Access to Rsch. Ctrs, Santa Cruz, 1990-92; environ. rschr. Eight No. Indian Pueblo Couns., San Juan Pueblo, N.Mex., 1992; rschr. Minority Internat. Rsch. Tng., U. Calif. at Santa Cruz, Patagonia, Argentina, 1994; tchr. Rurals Girls in Sci. Program, Seattle, summer 1997; mentor Savanah (Ga.) State U., summer 1997. Regents scholar U. Calif., Santa Cruz, 1989, Navajo Nation scholar Navato Nation, U. Calif., 1989, U. Wash., 1994; Danforth-Compton fellow U. Wash., Seattle, 1994, NIH predoctoral fellow NIH, U. Wash., 1998—. Fellow Am. Indian Sci. and Engring. Soc. (sci. judge 1991); mem. Am. Naturalist, Soc. for Integrative and Comparative Biology, Soc. for the Advancement of Chicanos and Native Ams. in Sci., Student Coalition for Diversity in the Scis. Office: Univ Wash Dept Zoology Box 351800 Seattle WA 98195-1800

HENDERSON, SKITCH (LYLE RUSSELL CEDRIC), pianist, conductor; b. Birmingham, Eng., Jan. 27, 1918; m. Ruth Einsiedel; children: Heidi, Hans. Studied piano with Malcolm Frost, Roger Aubert; conducting with Albert Coastes, Fritz Reiner; theory with Arnold Schoenberg, Ernest Toch. Founder, dir. N.Y. Pops, N.Y.C., 1983—. Performed with area bands, theater orchs., with film and radio studios, West Coast, 1939-40; piano soloist, condr. Crosby, Sinatra radio shows, 1946; on tour with own dance band, 1947-48, radio work, 1949-51; pianist, condr., music dir. NBC, N.Y.C., from 1951, including Tonight Show; guest condr., N.Y. Philharmonic, Minn. Symphony, others, TV appearances; founder, music dir. N.Y. Pops Orch., 1983—; pops. dir. Fla. Orch.; past pops dir. Va. Symphony Orch., Louisville Orch. With RAF, 1940-41; USAAF, 1941-45. Address: c/o The NY Pops attn: Jennifer DeBard 881 7th Ave Ste 903 New York NY 10019-3210*

HENDERSON, STANLEY DALE, lawyer, educator; b. Monona, Iowa, June 17, 1935; s. Leon Gilbert and Iva Elizabeth H.; m. DeArliss Garretson, June 15, 1957; children: Lesli Kara, Heidi Elizabeth, Holly Ann. A.B., Coe Coll., 1957; postgrad. (Woodrow Wilson fellow), Cornell U., 1957-58; postgrad., U. Chgo. Law Sch., 1958-59; J.D., U. Colo., 1961. Bar: Colo. 1961, Va. 1973. Law clk. U.S. Dist. Ct., Denver, 1961-62; mem. firm Williams and Zook, Boulder, Colo., 1962-64; mem. faculty U. Wyo. Coll. Law, 1964-69; prof. law U. Va. Law Sch., Charlottesville, 1970; F.D.G. Ribble prof. law U. Va. Law Sch., 1976—; vis. prof. law Ind. U., 1974, Harvard Law Sch., 1978-79, Pepperdine U., 1992-93. Author: (with Dawson and Harvey) Contracts, (with Meltzer) Labor Law. Contbr. articles to profl. jours. Mem. Va. State Bar, Am. Law Inst., Am. Arbitration Assn., Order of Coif, Phi Beta Kappa, Phi Kappa Phi. Democrat. Presbyterian. Home: 1615 King Mountain Rd Charlottesville VA 22901-3003 Office: U Va Sch Law Charlottesville VA 22901

HENDERSON, STEPHEN KEITH, academic administrator; b. Covington, Ky., Oct. 24, 1954; s. Charles Harmon and Vonice Esta (Farley) H.; m. Robin Louise Shupe, May 14, 1978; children: Elizabeth, Kathleen, Abigail, Emily, Claire. BS, Vanderbilt U., 1976; ThM, Dallas Theol. Sem., 1980, postgrad., 1987. Teaching asst. Dallas Theo. Sem., Dallas, 1980-83; pastor Believers Fellowship, Houston, 1983-87, Fellowship BIble Ch., Greenville, S.C., 1988-92; adminstr. Council on Bible Manhood & Womanhood, Wheaton, Ill., 1992—, Siloam Christian Sch., Easley, S.C., 1994-99; pastor Munich Internat. Cmty. Ch., 1999—; adv. bd. Piedmont Women's Ctr., Greenville, S.C., 1989—. Editor: CBMW News, 1994-97. Mem. Evangelical Theol. Soc., Assn. Christian Schs. Internat., Internat. Fellowship Christian Sch. Adminstrs. Home: 1000 Windermere Ct Easley SC 29642-8362

HENDERSON, STEPHEN PAUL, lawyer; b. Oakland, Calif., July 14, 1949; s. Carl Edward and Esther Minnie (Miller) H.; m. Josephine Ann Bartlett. BA, Wash. State U., 1971; JD, U. Oreg., 1974; LLM, NYU, 1978.

Bar: Oreg. 1974, U.S. Ct. Mil. Appeals 1978, U.S. Tax Ct. 1979, U.S. Ct. Appeals (9th cir.) 1979, U.S. Ct. Appeals (6th cir.) 1990, U.S. Supreme Ct. 1979. Atty. GE Credit Corp., Providence, 1979-81; dept. counsel GE, Schenectady, N.Y., 1981-83; operation counsel GE, Atlanta, 1983-86, divsn. counsel, 1987-89; divsn. counsel GE Aircraft Engines, Cin., 1990-97; gen. counsel GE Engine Svcs., Inc., Cin., 1998—. Editor U. Oreg. Law Rev., 1972-73. Nat. Merit scholar, 1967. Mem. ABA, Oreg. Bar Assn., Ohio Bar Assn., Cin. Bar Assn., Corp. Counsel Assn. of Atlanta Bar Assn., Fed. Bar Assn., Horseshoe Bend Country Club, Phi Beta Kappa, Phi Kappa Phi, Phi Eta Sigma. Republican. Episcopalian. Office: GE 1 Neumann Way # F17 Cincinnati OH 45215-1915

HENDERSON, THELTON EUGENE, federal judge; b. Shreveport, La., Nov. 28, 1933; s. Eugene M. and Wanzie (Roberts) H.; 1 son, Geoffrey A. B.A., U. Calif.-, Berkeley, 1956, J.D., 1962. Bar: Calif. 1962. Atty. U.S. Dept. Justice, 1962-63; assoc. firm FitzSimmons & Petris, 1964, assoc., 1964-66; directing atty. San Mateo County (Calif.) Legal Aid Soc., 1966-69; asst. dean Stanford (Calif.) U. Law Sch., 1968-76; ptnr. firm Rosen, Remcho & Henderson, San Francisco, 1977-80; judge U.S. Dist. Ct. (no. dist.) Calif., San Francisco, 1980-90, 98—, chief judge, 1990-97; asso. prof. Sch. Law, Golden Gate U., San Francisco, 1978-80. Served with U.S. Army, 1956-58. Mem. ABA, Nat. Bar Assn., Charles Houston Law Assn. Office: US Dist Ct US Courthouse PO Box 36060 San Francisco CA 94102*

HENDERSON, THOMAS HENRY, JR., lawyer, legal association executive; b. Birmingham, Ala., Feb. 4, 1939; s. Thomas Henry and Edna (Green) H.; m. Elaine Dauphin (div. 1983); children: Ashley, Michelle; m. Paulette Maehara, June 1988. BSBA, Auburn U., 1961; JD, U. Ala., 1966; LLM, Nat. Law Ctr., George Washington U., 1987. Bar: D.C. 1970, Ala. 1966. Trial atty. organized crime and racketeering sect. U.S. Dept. Justice, Washington, 1966-70, dep. sect. chief mgmt. labor sect., 1970-73; dep. chief counsel, subcom. on adminstrn. practice and procedure U.S. Senate, Washington, 1973-74; dep. sect. chief mgmt. and labor sect. Dept. Justice, Washington, 1974-76, chief pub. integrity sect., 1976-80, sr. counsel criminal div., 1980-83; bar counsel D.C. Ct. Appeals, Washington, 1983-87; exec. dir. ATLA, Washington, 1988—. Columnist Bar Counsels Page, Washington Lawyer mag., bi-monthly, 1983-87. Pres. Christmas in April, Washington, 1986-87. Mem. Am. Soc. Assn. Execs. (bd. dirs. 1994-97, vice chair 1997-98), Omicron Delta Kappa. Avocations: golf, skiing, fitness, outdoor adventure. Home: 6698 Glenbrook Rd Chevy Chase MD 20815-6515 Office: ATLA 1050 31st St NW Washington DC 20007-4409

HENDERSON, WILLIAM CHARLES, editor; b. Phila., Apr. 5, 1941; s. Francis Louis and Dorothy Price (Galloway) H. B.A., Hamilton Coll., 1963; postgrad., Harvard U., 1963, U. Pa., 1965-66. Assoc. editor Doubleday & Co., N.Y.C., 1972-73; pub. Pushcart Press, Wainscott, N.Y., 1972—; sr. editor Coward, McCann & Geohagan, Inc., N.Y.C., 1973-75; cons. editor Harper & Row Inc., 1976—; guest lectr. Harvard U., summer 1974, Sarah Lawrence Coll., U. Rochester, summers 1978, 87; lectr. Columbia U., 1978-80, Princeton U., 1984, 86, 87, Johns Hopkins U., 1989, Radcliffe Pub. Course, 1989; mem. nat. adv. bd. Center for the Book Library of Congress, 1979; pres. Pushcart Found. Author: His Son: A Child of the Fifties, 1981, The Kid That Could, 1990, Her Father, 1995; editor, pub.: The Publish It Yourself Handbook, 1973, The Pushcart Prize: Best of the Small Presses, 1976—; editor: Rotten Reviews, 1986, Minutes of the Lead Pencil Club, 1996. Recipient Author award N.J. English Tchrs. Assn., 1972; Newsboy award Horatio Alger Soc., 1973; Carey-Thomas award, 1978. Mem. P.E.N., The Lead Pencil Club (founder). Home and Office: Pushcart Press PO Box 380 Wainscott NY 11975-0380

HENDERSON, WILLIAM DARRYL, army officer, writer; b. Trail, B.C., Can., Aug. 26, 1938; came to U.S., 1953; s. William Roland and Flora (McCallum) H.; m. Marilyn Jean Rapp, Nov. 1964 (div. 1981); children: Gregory, Timothy; m. Mary Ann Gutman, Dec. 6, 1985. Student, U. Vienna, Austria, 1959-60; BA in Polit. Sci., Stanford U., 1961; PhD in Internat. Rels. and Comparative Politics, U. Pitts., 1970; honor grad., Comd. and Gen. Staff Coll., 1974; postgrad., Nat. War Coll., 1982. Commd. 2d lt. U.S. Army, 1961, advanced through grades to col., 1988; writer San Francisco Examiner, 1990; writer, cons. Can. Govt., Ottawa, 1991-92; appointed presdl. commr. Women in the Armed Forces, Washington, 1992—; asst. prof. U.S. Mil. Acad., West Point, N.Y., 1972; mil. corr. San Francisco Examiner, 1991. testified Senate and House Armed Svcs. Com., 1993. Author: Why the Viet Cong Fought, 1979, Cohesion, The Human Element in Combat, 1985, The Hollow Army, 1990; included in book of Best Newspaper Editorials for 1990-91; contbr. articles to profl. jours. Decorated Legion of Merit, Bronze Star, Purple Heart, Combat Infantryman's Badge. Home and Office: 19880 Lark Way Saratoga CA 95070-6420

HENDERSON, WILLIAM EUGENE, education educator; b. Miami, Fla., Sept. 9, 1947; s. William Bartow and Evelyn Mildred (Stansell) H. BA in Polit. Sci., Acctg., U. South Fla., 1967; MS in Guidance, Counseling, Barry U., 1971, EdS in Sch. Psychology, 1976, MBA in Mgmt., Fin., 1981; postgrad., Fla. State U., Northwestern U., U. Miami. Cert. tchr., prin., sch. psychologist, Fla. From tchr. to subject area coord. Miami-Dade County Pub. Schs., Miami, 1968-83, asst. prin., 1983-89, assoc. intern prin., 1989—; adj. prof. Nova U., Ft. Lauderdale, Fla., 1983-90, Barry U., Miami Shores, Fla., 1987—; assessment cons. Fla. Dept. Edn., Tallahassee, 1979-83, Ednl. Testing Svc., Princeton, N.J., 1981-82. Author: S.O.S. Sourcebook, 1985; author curriculum materials; editor, curriculum reviewer Harcourt Brace Jovanovich, Orlando, Fla., 1985-86. Named Outstanding Econs. Educator Fla. Coun. Econ. Edn., 1981, 82, 93, Outstanding Secondary Social Studies Tchr. Dade County Coun. Social Studies, 1982. Mem. Nat. Coun. Social Studies, Coun. Exceptional Children (chair region II, sec. asst. prin. 1998—, Oustanding Expceptional Student Edn. Adminstr. 1988), Fla. Assn. Sch. Adminstrs., Assn. for Supervision and Curriculum Devel., Dade Assn. for Sch. Adminstrs., Phi Alpha Theta. Office: North Miami Sr H S 800 NE 137th St Miami FL 33161-3243

HENDERSON, WILLIAM J., postmaster general; b. June 16, 1947; 2 children. Grad., U. N.C. With U.S. Postal Svc.; postmaster, divsn. gen. mgr. U.S. Postal Svc., Greensboro, N.C.; v.p. employee rels. U.S. Postal Svc., chief mktg. officer, sr. v.p., chief operating officer, 1994-98, postmaster gen., CEO, 1998—. With U.S. Army. Recipient Roger W. Jones award for Exec. Leadership Am. U., 1998, John Wanamaker award U.S. Postal Svc., 1997. Office: US Postal Svc 475 Lenfant Plz SW Rm 2340 Washington DC 20260-1531

HENDIN, DAVID BRUCE, literary agent, author, consultant, numismatist; b. St. Louis, Dec. 16, 1945; s. Aaron and Lillian (Karsh) H.; m. Jeannie Luciano, Oct. 4, 1985; children: Sarah Tsvia, Benjamin Judah, Alexander Jacob. BS in Biology Edn, U. Mo., 1967, MA in Journalism, 1970. Sr. v.p., editorial dir., pub. United Media Inc., N.Y.C., 1970-93; clin. prof. off campus U. Mo. Sch. Journalism, 1971-86; pres. Pharos Books, 1992-3, DH Literary, Inc., Nyack, N.Y., 1993—; adj. lectr. Columbia U. Sch. Journalism, 1974-76; numismatist Joint Sepphoris Excavation, 1985-88. Author: Everything You Need to Know About Abortion, 1971, The Doctor's Save-Your-Heart Diet, 1972, Death As a Fact of Life, 1973, 1984, Save Your Child's Life, 1973, 86, The Life Givers, 1975, Guide to Ancient Jewish Coins, 1975, The World Almanac Whole Health Guide, 1977, The Genetic Connection, 1978, Collecting Coins, 1979, Guide to Biblical Coins, 1987, 96; mem. editorial bd. Israel Numismatic Jour., 1992-96, Publs. Bd. Union of Am. Hebrew Congregations, 1993. Bd. dirs. Holyland Conservation Fund, 1973-83; v.p. Council Advancement Sci. Writing, 1975-84; trustee Scripps-Howard Found., 1978-87, Kinsey Inst., 1985-92, Mus. Cartoon Art, 1986-92, Found. Nyack Pub. Sch. Edn., 1998—; chmn. numis. com. The Jewish Mus., 1980-85; mem. adv. com. Sch. Journalims, U. Fla., 1991-97. Recipient award merit Am. Assn. Blood Banks, 1972, Claude Bernard Sci. Journalism award, 1972, cert. commendation Am. Acad. Family Physicians, 1973, Med. Journalism award AMA, 1973, Blakeslee award Am. Heart Assn., 1973, Book of Yr. award Am. Med. Writers Assn., 1977, Best Column award Numismatic Literary Guild, 1993, Ben Odesser Judaic Literary award 1997. Fellow Am. Numismatic Soc.; mem. Coun. for Advancement Sci. Writing, Am.-Israel Numismatic Assn. (v.p. 1979-85), Kappa Tau Alpha, Sigma Alpha Mu. Office: PO Box 990 Nyack NY 10960-0990

HENDL, WALTER, conductor, pianist, composer; b. West New York, N.J., Jan. 12, 1917; s. William and Ella (Wittig) H.; m. Barbara Heisley; 1 dau by previous marriage, Susan. Pvt. study piano with, David Saperton; with, Clarence Adler, 1934-37; pvt. study conducting with, Fritz Reiner; faculty, Sarah Lawrence Coll., 1939-41, Curtis Inst. Music, 1937-41; MusD (hon.), Cin. Coll. Music, 1954; LHD (hon.), Edinboro U. Pa., 1990. Dir. Eastman Sch. Music, Rochester, N.Y., 1964-72; prof. conducting D'Angelo Sch. Music Mercy Hurst Coll., Erie, Pa., 1990-94. Active as condr. and pianist, Berkshire Music Center, 1941-42, asst. condr., pianist, N.Y. Philharmonic 1945-49, mus. dir., Dallas Symphony, 1949-58, Chautauqua (N.Y.) Symphony Orch., 1953-74, asso. condr., Chgo. Symphony Orch., 1958-64, mus. dir., Ravinia (Ill.) Festival, 1959-63; orchestral dir., Erie (Pa.) Philharm., 1976-89, condr. emeritus, 1989—; guest condr. in Europe, USSR, S. Am., Japan, Asia; also recs.; composer: Broadway prodn. Dark of the Moon, 1945, A Village Where They Ring No Bells, Loneliness (recipient Alice M. Ditson award, Columbia 1953).

HENDLER, NELSON HOWARD, physician, medical clinic director; b. N.Y.C., Aug. 15, 1944; s. Albert and Winifred (Siff) H.; m. Lee Meyerhoff, Oct. 20, 1974; children: Samuel, Alexander, Lindsay, Josepha. BA, Princeton U., 1966; MD, U. Md., 1972, MS, 1974. Diplomate Am. Bd. Psychiatry and Neurology. Resident in psychiatry Johns Hopkins Hosp., Balt., 1975; asst. prof. neurosurgery sch. medicine Johns Hopkins U., 1975—; owner, clin. dir. Mensana Clinic, Stevenson, Md., 1978—; assoc. prof. physiology sch. dental surgery U. Md., 1986—; pres. Pyramid Farms Crayfish Inc., Cambridge, Md.; chmn. bd. M.D. Pain Clinics, 1997—; bd. dirs. Mensana Diagnostics Corp., Columbia Bank, 1994-96, Nat. Heritage Life Ins. Co., 1993-95. Author: Diagnosis and Non-Surgical Management of Chronic Pain, 1981; (with others) Coping with Chronic Pain, 1979; editor Diagnosis and Treatment of Chronic Pain, 1982; contbr. 51 articles and 29 chpts. to books and profl. jours.; co-patentee direct current motor protector, 1972. Bd. dirs. Md. Mental Health Assn., Balt., 1976-78, Balt. Zool. Soc., 1978-85; bd. dirs. Am. Orgn. Rehab. through Tng., 1983—, pres. Balt. chpt.; bd. dirs. Am. Technion Soc., 1980-92, pres. Balt. chpt. Falk fellow Am. Psychiat. Assn., 1975. Fellow Acad. Psychosomatic Medicine; mem. Am. Inst. Stress (v.p. 1978-89), Internat. Soc. for Study of Pain, Am. Pain Relief Found. (bd. dirs. 1997—), Israeli Pain Soc. (hon.), Princeton U. Alumni Assn. Md. (bd. dirs., pres.), Princeton Club N.Y.C., Suburban Club, Safari Internat. Club, Loch Raven Skeet and Trap Club. Republican. Jewish. Avocations: bird hunting, skeet and trap shooting, fishing, record big game hunter. Office: Mensana Clinic 1718 Greenspring Valley Rd Stevenson MD 21153-0642

HENDLER, ROSEMARY NIELSEN, business owner, digital artist; b. Sydney, Australia, Oct. 18, 1946; came to U.S., 1954, naturalized, 1970; d. Robert Stanley McFarlane and Joyce Elizabeth (Annetts) Nielsen; m. Joel Arnold Hendler, June 1, 1977; 1 child, Stewart Maxwell. BA, U. Calif., Berkeley, 1968; postgrad., Acad. Art San Francisco, 1974-76, UCLA, 1985-87. Buyer linens Breuners Home Furnishings, Oakland, Calif., 1969-71; buyer textiles Liberty House, San Francisco, 1971-73, Bullock's, Palo Alto, 1973-75; graphic artist Montclarion Pubs., Oakland, 1975-77; pres., owner Cordeaux River Trading Co., L.A., 1986-93; owner, ptnr. Hendler Graphics, Orinda, Calif., 1995—. Advisor (CD-ROM) Visionary Stampede, Multimedia Project, San Francisco; exhibited computer art in numerous one-woman shows, 1994, 95, 96, 97, 98, 99. Bd. dirs. docent coun. L.A. County Mus. Art, 1981—; VIP hostess Olympic Games, L.A., 1984; bd. dirs. Young Audiences, L.A., 1985-87; exec. bd. Orinda Arts Coun., 1991—, pres., 1993-94; mem. art guild Oakland Mus., 1991—; mem. task force Arts and Cultural Coun. of Contra Costa County, 1994—; mem. exec. bd. Metro. Transi Authority, L.A.; mem. pilot Arts Docent Program touring art in all stas. for pub. and schs. Recipient Design award Levi Strauss, 1975, Honorable Mention awrd Manhattan Arts Internat., 1996, others. Mem. NAFE, Nat. Assn. Local Arts Agys., Nat. Assn. Desktop Pubs., Calif. Assn. Local Arts Agys., Jr. League L.A., Costume Coun., L.A. County Mus. Art, Lamorinda Arts Alliance, Artists in Tech., Orinda C. of C. Republican. Office: PO Box 2922 Big Bear Lake CA 92315-3425

HENDLEY, ASHLEY PRESTON, JR., clinical social worker; b. Tyler, Tex., Sept. 15, 1938; s. Ashley Preston Sr. and Theresa Marie (Parenti) H.; m. Vivian Janis Rodriguez, June 24, 1960 (div. Jan. 1977); children: Gerald Michael, Ashley Preston III, William Loy, Brian Matthew; m. Ann Louise Cherry, Dec. 29, 1984. BA in Comparative Sociology, U. Puget Sound, 1979; MSW, U. Wash., 1983. Cert. social worker, Wash. Clin. instr. U. Wash., Seattle, 1985—; cons., bd. dirs. Pierce County AIDS/HIV Adv. Bd., Tacoma, Wash., 1989—. Contbr. articles to profl. jours. Cons., bd. dirs. Children's Indsl. Home, Tacoma, 1989—; cons. City of Tacoma Sr. Svcs., 1983—; guardian ad Litem Superior Ct. State of Wash., County of Pierce, Tacoma, 1990-92. With U.S. Army, 1956-76, Vietnam. Mem. Am. Assn. Spinal Cord Injury Psychologists and Social Workers (assoc. editor 1988-94). Roman Catholic. Avocations: photography, cultural anthropology, hiking, cross country skiing. Home: 10501 Idlewild Rd SW Tacoma WA 98498-5608 Office: VA Puget Sound Health Care System American Lake Divsn Tacoma WA 98493

HENDLEY, DAN LUNSFORD, retired university official; b. Nashville, Apr. 26, 1938; s. Frank E. and Mattie (Lunsford) H.; m. Patricia Fariss, June 18, 1960; children: Dan Lunsford, Laura Kathleen. B.A., Vanderbilt U., 1960; grad., Stonier Grad. Sch. Banking, Rutgers U., 1969; postgrad., Program Mgmt. Devel., Harvard, 1972. With Fed. Res. Bank Atlanta, 1962-73, v.p., officer in charge Birmingham br., 1969-73; v.p., exec. v.p. AmSouth Bancorp, 1973-77; exec. v.p. First Nat. Bank Birmingham, 1976-77, pres., 1977-79, chmn. bd., chief exec. officer, 1979-83; pres., chief operating officer Am South Bank, N.A., 1983-90, also dir.; v.p. bus. affairs Samford U., Birmingham, Ala., 1991-94; ret., 1994. Trustee Children's Hosp., Samford U. With Tenn. Air N.G., 1961-67. Mem. Kiwanis, Mountain Brook Club, Shoal Creek Club, The Club. Baptist. Home: 3258 Dell Rd Birmingham AL 35223-1318

HENDLEY, EDITH DI PASQUALE, physiology and neuroscience educator; b. N.Y.C., Sept. 5, 1927; d. Michael and Rose (Parillo) Di Pasquale; m. Daniel Dees Hendley, Apr. 21, 1952; children: Jane Alice, Joyce Louise, Paul Daniel. AB, Hunter Coll. City N.Y., 1948; MS, Ohio State U., 1950; PhD, U. Ill., Chgo., 1954. Instr. U. Chgo., 1954-56; asst. lectr. U. Sheffield, Eng., 1956-57; instr., rsch. assoc. Johns Hopkins U. Sch. Medicine, Balt., 1963-72; sr. investigator Friends Med. Sci. Rsch. Ctr., Balt., 1972-73; from assoc. prof. to prof. U. Vt. Coll. Medicine, Burlington, 1973-94; prof. emeritus, 1994—. Co-author 6 books; contbr. articles to profl. jours. Rsch. grantee NIH, 1974-95, NSF, 1986-98, Vt. affiliate Am. Heart Assn., 1982-3, The Sugar Assn. Inc., 1984-85. Mem. AAAS, Am. Physiol. Soc., Am. Soc. Pharmacology and Exptl. Therapeutics, Soc. for Neurosci. (exec. com., treas. Vt. chpt. 1978-84), Assn. for Women in Sci. (treas. 1972-74, exec. com., long-range planning com. 1974-76). Avocations: music, opera, theatre, cinema. Home: 10 Highland Ter S Burlington VT 05403-7601 Office: U Vt Coll Medicine Dept Molecular Phys Bi Burlington VT 05405

HENDLEY, W. CLARK, academic provost; b. Tulsa, Sept. 2, 1943; s. William C. and Alice L. Hendley; m. Noreen Hendley, Aug. 7, 1976; children: William Clark III, J. Andrew, Megan Hendley Monarez, Jennifer H., Frederick, Floyd Kastner, Brian D. Kastner, David P. Kastner, Evan C. Kastner. BA, So. Meth. U., 1965; MA, U. Tex., 1966, PhD, 1970. Dir. of pace U. Mo., Kansas City, 1986-89, asst. dean, 1986-89, assoc. dean, 1989-92; dean Bridgewater (Mass.) State Coll., 1992-95; provost Coll. of St. Benedict/Saint John's U., St. Joseph, Minn., 1995—. Fellowship Am. Coun. of Edn., 1989-90. Office: Acad Affairs CSB St Josephs U Saint Joseph MN 56374

HENDRA, BARBARA JANE, public relations executive; b. Watertown, N.Y., July 14, 1938; d. Frederick R. and Irene J. H. BA, Vassar Coll., 1960. Publicity dir. Fawcett World Library, N.Y.C., 1961-69; v.p., dir. publicity and pub. relation Pocket Books-Simon & Schuster, N.Y.C., 1969-77; corp. dir. publicity and pub. relations Putnam Pub. Group, N.Y.C., 1977-79; pres. Barbara J. Hendra Assocs., Inc., N.Y.C., 1979-91, The Hendra Agy. Inc, Bklyn., 1991—; adj. prof. NYU, 1981. Contbg. author: Trade Book Marketing, 1983, The Encyclopedia of Publishing, 1995. Mem. Pubs. Publicity Assn. (bd. dirs. 1977-81, pres. 1979-81), Publicity Club N.Y., Soc. Profl. Journalists, Women's Media Group, Book Critics Cir., Vassar Club, Regency Whist Club. Home: 140 Sterling Pl Brooklyn NY 11217-3307 Office: The Hendra Agy Inc 142 Sterling Pl Brooklyn NY 11217-3307

HENDREN, DEBRA MAE, critical care nurse; b. Belle Fourche, S.D., Apr. 27, 1959; d. Clyde Leslie and Kathryn Ann (Daughters) F.; m. Anthony Ray Martinez, May 21, 1983 (div.); m. Cecil B. Hendren, Nov. 21, 1992. AD, Casper Coll., 1987, cert. EMT, 1990; BSN, U. Phoenix, 1997, MSN, 1999. RN, Colo., Wyo.; CCRN. Nurse Wyo. Med. Ctr., Casper, North Suburban Med. Ctr. (formerly Humana Hosp. Mountain View), Thornton, Colo.; nurse Swedish Med. Ctr., Englewood, Colo., charge nurse ICU, 1993-96; asst. nurse mgr. North Suburban Med. Ctr., Thornton, Colo., 1996-97; dir. ICU/CCU North Suburban Med. Ctr., Thornton, 1997—, dir. ICU/CCU and med. telemetry, 1997—. Mem. Wyo. Nurses Assn., Colo. Nurses Assn., AACN, Sigma Theta Tau Soc. Home: 5168 E 126th Ct Thornton CO 80241-3001

HENDREN, JIMM LARRY, federal judge; b. 1940. BA, U. Ark., 1964, LLB, 1965. With Little & Enfield, 1968-69; pvt. practice Bentonville, Ark., 1970-77, 79-92; chancellor, probate judge Ark. 16th Chancery Dist., 1977-78; chief judge U.S. Dist. Ct. We. Dist., Ark., 1997—. Served to lt. comdr. JAGC, USN, 1965-70, USNR, 1970-83. Mem. ABA, Ark. Bar Assn. Office: US Dist Ct PO Box 3487 Fayetteville AR 72702

HENDREN, JO ANN, small business owner; b. Maryville, Tenn., Feb. 26, 1935; d. Sidney W. and Myra (Hutto) Burns; m. R. Neil Southern, July 17, 1954, (div. Mar. 1973); children: Robert Neil Jr., Joel Burns, Myra Ann; m. James E. Hendren (June 10, 1976). Student, Va. Intermont, Bristol, 1952-53; student in home econs., U. Tenn., 1953-54. Asst. mgr. Hallmark Cards & Gifts, Maryville, 1977-84; owner, mgr. Hideaway Cottages, Townsend, Tenn., 1980—; gov. task force Tourism and the Arts, 1986-87. Bd. dirs. Blount County Hist. Trust, 1986-88; mem. Friends of Christy, the Musical, 1995, 96. Mem. Townsend C. of C., Blount County C. of C., Nature Conservancy. Republican. Episcopalian. Avocations: nature walks, bridge, reading, entertaining small groups of friends. Home and office: 102 Oriole Ln Maryville TN 37803-6524

HENDREN, LINDA SUE, secondary education educator; b. Bethany, Mo., Aug. 16, 1953; d. Ira I. and Twillia Melseen (Melson) Turner; m. Joel Tenney Hendren, May 25, 1975; children: Julie, Beth. BS in Edn., N.W. Mo. State U., Maryville, 1975, MS in Edn., 1996. Cert. tchr. home econs. and English, Mo. Tchr. home econs. Cainsville (Mo.) R-1 Sch., 1975-80; tchr. English North Harrison R-III Sch., Eagleville, Mo., 1985-97, tchr., tech. coord., 1997—; chmn. Career Ladder Com., Eagleville, 1993-97. Recipient Mo. Incentive grants Mo. Dept. Edn., 1995, 96. Methodist. Avocations: reading, camping, computers. Home: 14901 E State Highway O Blythedale MO 64426-9114 Office: North Harrison R-III Sch 12023 Fir St Eagleville MO 64442-8180

HENDREN, MERLYN CHURCHILL, investment company executive; b. Gooding, Idaho, Oct. 16, 1926; d. Herbert Winston and Annie Averett Churchill; student U. Idaho, 1944-47; B.A. with honors, Coll. of Idaho, 1986. m. Robert Lee Hendren, June 14, 1947; children—Robert Lee, Anne Aleen. With Hendren's Furniture Co., Boise, 1947-69; co-owner, v.p. Hendren's Inc., Boise, 1969-87, pres. 1987—. Bd. dirs. Idaho Law Found., 1978-84; chmn. Coll. of Idaho Symposium, 1977-78, mem. adv. bd., 1981—; bd. dirs. SW Idaho Pvt. Industry Council, 1984-87; pres. Boise Council on Aging, 1959-60, mem. adv. bd., 1986—; mem. Gov.'s Commn. on Aging, 1960, Idaho del. to White House Conf. Aging, 1961; trustee St. Luke's Regional Hosp., 1981-92; mem. adv. bd. dirs. Boise Philharm. Assn., Inc., 1981—, Ballet Idaho; bd. dirs. Children's Home Soc. Idaho, 1988; founding pres. Idaho Congl. Award Program, 1993—; sustaining mem. Boise Jr. League. Mem. Boise C. of C. (bd. dirs. 1984-87), Gamma Phi Beta. Episcopalian. Home: 3504 Hillcrest Dr Boise ID 83705-4503 Office: PO Box 9077 Boise ID 83707-3077

HENDREN, ROBERT LEE, JR., academic administrator; b. Reno, Oct. 10, 1925; s. Robert Lee and Aleen (Hill) H.; m. Merlyn Churchill, June 14, 1947; children: Robert Lee IV, Anne Aleen. BA magna cum laude, Coll. Idaho, LLD (hon.); postgrad., Army Univ. Ctr., Oahu, Hawaii. Owner, pres. Hendren's Inc., 1947—; pres. Albertson Coll. Idaho, Caldwell, 1987—; bd. dirs. 1st Interstate Bank Idaho. Trustee Boise (Idaho) Ind. Sch. Dist., chmn. bd. trustees, 1966; chmn. bd. trustees Coll. Idaho, 1980-84; bd. dirs. Mountain View coun. Boy Scouts Am., Boise Retail Merchants, Boise Valley Indsl. Found., Boise Redevel. Agy., Ada County Marriage Counseling, Ada County Planning and Zoning Com.; chmn. bd. Blue Cross Idaho. Recipient Silver and Gold award U. Idaho, Nat. award Sigma Chi. Mem. Boise C. of C. (pres., bd. dirs.), Idaho Sch. Trustees Assn., Masons, KT, Shriners, Rotary (Paul Harris fellow). Home: 3504 Hillcrest Dr Boise ID 83705-4503 Office: Albertson Coll Idaho 2112 Cleveland Blvd Caldwell ID 83605-4432

HENDRICK, ARNOLD J., game designer; b. Syracuse, N.Y., July 14, 1950; s. Douglas B. and Helen E. (Cooley) H.; children: Heather Hartig, Brian Hartig. BA in History, Wesleyan U., Middletown, Conn., 1972. Game developer, designer Simulations Publs., Inc., N.Y.C., 1972; freelance game designer, 1973-74; from designer to exec. dir. Milgamex, Wayland, Mass., 1975-78; pub. dir. Heritage USA, Dallas, 1979-82; game designer Coleco Industries, West Harford, Conn., 1983-85; sr. game designer, prodr. MicroProse Software, Hunt Valley, Md., 1985-95; sr. game designer Interactive Magic, Research Triangle Park, N.C., 1995-98; sr. producer Kesmai Corp, Charlottesville, Va., 1998—. Designer: (hist. miniatures games) Surface Warship, 1968, 1944, 1968, T-34, 1972, Ancient Armies, 1976, Sword & Spear, 1976, (hist. boardgame) Trireme, 1979, (fantasy miniatures game) Knights & Magick, 1980, (fantasy boardgame) Demonlord, 1981, (sci. fiction boardgames) Star Viking, 1981, Grav Armor, 1982, Barbarian Prince (Origins award best fantasy boardgame 1982), (fantasy role-playing game) Swordbearer, 1983, (computer simulation games) Gunship, 1986 (Computer Gaming World mag. Action Game of Yr., Computer Gaming World mag. Hall of Fame), F-19 Stealth Fighter, 1987 (Origins award best mil. computer game, Software Pubs. Assn. Best Computer Simulation award Computer Gaming World mag. Hall of Fame), M1 Tank Platoon, 1989 (Computer Gaming World mag. Mil./Strategy Game of Yr., Computer Gaming World mag. Hall of Fame), Silent Service II, 1990, iM1A2 Abrams, 1997, (computer strategy games) Pirates!, 1987 (Origins award for best fiction/fantasy computer game, Computer Gaming World mag. Action Game of Yr., Computer Gaming World mag. Hall of Fame), Red Storm Rising, 1988, (computer role-playing game) Darklands, 1992. Mem. Computer Game Developers Assn.

HENDRICK, DIANE GOZA, psychiatric nurse; b. Ft. Payne, Ala., Nov. 15, 1958; d. Charles Wayland and Doris Addie (Dixon) G.; m. Jeff Skidmore, June 1, 1981 (div. June 1991); 1 child, Jeffry Andrew; m. John P. Hendrick, Feb. 14, 1992; stepchildren: Jon, Jeff. AS, Cleveland (Tenn.) State C.C., 1991. Psychiat. nurse John P. Hendrick, MD, Chattanooga, 1991—; pschiat. cons. Home Health Care, Cleveland, 1992-98. Mem. Beta Sigma Phi (pres. Xi Gamma Theta 1997-98). Republican. Episcopalian. Avocation: art, reading, walking on beach. Office: John P Hendrick MD 105 Lee Pkwy Ste 7 Chattanooga TN 37421-6708

HENDRICK, GEORGE, English language educator; b. Stephenville, Tex., Mar. 30, 1929; s. Hoyt and Bessie Lea (Sears) H.; m. Willene Lowery, Jan. 21, 1955; 1 dau., Sarah. B.A., Tex. Christian U., 1948, M.A., 1950; Ph.D., U. Tex., 1954. Mem. English faculty S.W. Tex. State U., 1954-56, U. Colo., 1956-60; prof. Am. studies J.W. Goethe U., Frankfurt, Germany, 1960-65; prof. U. Ill., Chgo., 1965-67; prof. U. Ill., Urbana, 1967-99, spl. curator Univ. Libr., 1994-97. Author: Katherine Anne Porter, 1965, Henry Salt: Humanitarian Reformer and Man of Letters, 1977, Remembrances of Concord and the Thoreaus, 1977, (with Fritz Oehlschlaeger) Toward the Making of Thoreau's Modern Reputation, 1980, (with Willene Hendrick) On the Frontier: Dr. Hiram Rutherford, 1981, Thoreau Amongst Friends and Philistines, 1982, (with Margaret Sandburg) Ever the Winds of Chance, 1983, the Selected Letters of Mark Van Doren, 1987; (with Willene Hendrick) Katherine Anne Porter, rev. edit., 1988, Fables, Foibles, and Foobles, 1988, The Savour of Salt: A Henry Salt Anthology, 1989, To Reach Eternity: The Letters of James Jones, 1989, (with Willene Hendrick) Ham Jones, Antebellum Soutern Humorist: An Anthology, 1990, (with Willene Hendrick and Fritz Oehlschlaeger) Salt's Life of Thoreau, 1993, More Rootabagas,

1993, (with Willene Hendrick) Billy Sunday and Other Poems, 1993 (with Nancy Romero) Literary Treasures of the University Library, 1995, (with Willene Hendrick) Selected Poems of Carl Sandburg, 1996, (with Nancy Romero and Maarten van de Guchte) Alvin Langdon Coburn and H.G. Wells: The Photographer and the Novelist, 1997. Grantee Am. Coun. Learned Socs., Ford Found., NEH. Mem. MLA, James Jones Soc. (pres. 1991-92). Office: U Ill English Dept English Dept 608 S Wright St Urbana IL 61801-3613

HENDRICK, HAL WILMANS, human factors educator; b. Dallas, Mar. 11, 1933; s. Harold Eugene and Audrey Sarah (Wilmans) H.; m. Mary Francis Boyle; children: Hal L., David A., John A. (dec.), Jennifer G. BA, Ohio Wesleyan U., 1955; MS, Purdue U., 1961, PhD, 1966. Cert. profl. ergonomist; bd. cert. forensic examiner. Asst. prof. U. So. Calif., L.A., assoc. prof., 1979-86; exec. dir. Inst. of Safety and Systems Mgmt., U. So. Calif., L.A., 1986-87; prof., dean Coll. of System Sci., U. Denver, 1987-90; prof. U. So. Calif., 1986-95; prof. emeritus U. So. Calif., L.A., 1995—; prin. Hendrick and Assocs., 1996—; pres. Bd. Cert. in Profl. Ergonomics, 1992-94. Author: Behavioral Research and Analysis, 1980, 2d edit., 1989, 3rd edit., 1990; editor 10 books; contbr. articles to profl. jours. Lt. col. USAF, 1956-76. Fellow APA, Am. Psychol. Soc., Human Factors Ergonomics Soc. (pres. L.A. chpt. 1986-87, pres. Rocky Mountain chpt. 1989-90, 95-96); mem. Internat. Ergonomics Assn. (pres. Geneva 1990-94, immediate past pres. 1994-97, sec. gen. 1987-89, exec. com. 1984—, U.S. rep. 1981-87), Ergonomics Soc. (U.K.), Soc. for Indsl. and Orgnl. Psychology. Democrat. Avocations: travel, camping, hiking, reading, fishing. Home and Office: 7100 E Crestline Ave Englewood CO 80111-1600

HENDRICK, HOWARD H., state government administrator; b. Oklahoma City, Dec. 22, 1954; s. Robert Alexander and Geneva (Woodlee) H.; m. Tracy Elizabeth Williams, July 1, 1977; children: Chelsey Elizabeth, Cally Victoria, Christiana Juliet, Hudson Hamlin. BS in Acctg., So. Nazarene U., 1977; JD, U. Okla., 1980, MBA, 1980. Bar: Okla. 1980, U.S. Ct. Claims 1981, U.S. Tax Ct. 1981, U.S. Dist. Ct. (we. dist.) Okla. 1981, U.S. Dist. Ct. (no. dist.) Okla. 1984, U.S. Supreme Ct. 1984; CPA, Okla. Clk., intern, assoc. Speck, Philbin, Fleig, Trudgeon & Lutz, P.C., Oklahoma City, 1977-81; pvt. practice, Bethany, Okla., 1981-84; ptnr. Thom & Hendrick, P.C., Oklahoma City, 1984-93, of counsel, 1994-98; mem. Okla. Senate, 1986-98; pvt. practice, Howard H. Hendrick, P.C., Oklahoma City, 1994-98; exec. dir. Okla. Dept. Human Svcs., 1998—; adj. prof. So. Navarene U., Bethany, 1979-87; gov.'s legis. appointee Early Childhood Intervention Interagy. Coord. Coun., Oklahoma City, 1987-98; pres. pro tempore's appointee Okla. State Pension Commn., 1988-94, Okla. legislator Justice Pub. Safety & Consumer Affairs Com. So. Legislators Conf., 1988; chmn. Okla. Rep. Party Platform Com., 1988; health care com. Nat. Conf. of State Legislatures, 1993-98; health care task force Am. Legis. Exch. Coun., 1991-98. Asst. minority floor leader Okla. State Senate, 1989-92, minority floor leader, 1993-94; chmn. adv. bd. Children's Convalescent Ctr., Inc., Bethany, 1986; mem. Christian life bd. Bethany First Nazarene Ch., 1986—, chmn., 1986-89; mem. adv. bd. Mercy Hospice, 1992—, Deaconess Hosp. Found., 1995—; mem. Okla. Rep. Party State Com., 1987-98, Oklahoma City Pub. Sch. Round Table, 1991-98; mem. bd. visitors U. Okla. Sch. Bus., 1991-96; bd. mem. Putnam City Schs. Found., 1997—; chmn. fin. com., mem. bd. Nazarene Theol. Sem., Kansas City, Mo., 1997—. Mem. ABA, Okla. Bar Assn., Okla. Soc. CPAs, Bethany C. of C. (Bethany Hall of Fame 1994), Kiwanis (internat. pres. collegiate Kiwanis Internat. 1976-77, pres. Bethany chpt. 1981), Order of the Coif, Phi Alpha Delta, Phi Beta Lambda (named Nat. Mr. Future Bus. Exec. 1977). Republican. Avocations: playing basketball, golf, reading. Office: 4301 NW 63rd St Ste 103 Oklahoma City OK 73116-1504

HENDRICK, IRVING GUILFORD, dean, education educator; b. L.A., Aug. 30, 1936; s. Guilford and Ingeborg Johanna (Eid) H.; m. Sandra Lee Scheer, Aug. 16, 1958 (dec. Aug. 1994); children: Julie Lynn, Maralene Ayn, Stephanie Lee; m. Linda DeSoucey Scott, 1996. AB, Whittier Coll., 1958, MA, 1960; EdD with honors, UCLA, 1964. Asst. prof. edn. U. Mich., Flint, 1964-65; asst. prof. edn. U. Calif., Riverside, 1965-69, assoc. prof. edn., 1969-75, prof. edn., 1975—, chair dept. edn., 1970-75, assoc. dean Sch. of Edn., 1975-83, dean Sch. of Edn., 1987-98, asst. vice chancellor of devel., 1998—; mem. com. on planning & budget U. Calif. Sys., 1985-87, vice-chair com. on planning & budget, 1986-87, chair subcom. on pvt. devel. activities, 1986-87, chair, 1987-88; mem. subject A com. U. Calif.-Riverside, 1966-68, vice-chair con. on ednl. policy, 1972-73, mem. com. on courses, 1969-71, chair, 1972-73, mem. com. on coms., 1973-74, mem. acad. planning com., 1973-75, chair acad. planning com., 1974-75, mem. budget com. resources sect., 1984-87, chair budget com. resources sect. 1984-87, mem. adv. com., 1974-75, 85-87, mem. highlander awards com., 1967-71, search com. for dean of grad. divsn., 1974, chair com. on faculty devel., 1977-78, learning handicapped credential programs, 1984—, chair exec. vice chancellor search com., 1985, acad. program planning rev. bd. sub-com. on organized rsch., 1986, pres.'s com. on profl. edn., 1988-89, pres.'s budget adv. com., 1987, chair adv. com. on instrnl. tech., 1994—; chancellor's rep. citizen's adv. com. Univ. Area Comty. Plan, Riverside, 1982-83; profl. day spkr. Internat. Sch. Theology, 1985; adv. com. assembly com. on econ. devel. and new techs. State of Calif., 1983-85; proposal reviewer intermediate sch. coll. readiness program Calif. State U., 1986; chair campaign com. to re-elect Dale Holmes County Supt. of Schs., Riverside County, 1990; cons. Riverside County Commn. on Future of Edn., 1993; mem. com. accreditation Calif. Commn. on Tchr. Credentialing, 1995-90, chair, co-chair, 1995-97; presenter papers at numerous profl. meetings. Author: Academic Revolution in California, 1968, Development of a School Integration Plan in Riverside, California: A Hisotry and Perspective, 1968, Public Policy Toward the Education of Non-white Minority Group Children in California, 1848-1970, 1975, The Education of Non-Whites in California, 1848-1970, 1977, California Educations, 1980; co-editor: (with Reginald L. Jones) Student Dissent in the Schools, 1972; contbr. articles to profl. jours.; contbr. book revs. to profl. jours. including History of Edn. Quar., Pacific Hist. Rev., Calif. History, So. Calif. Quar., Jour. Ednl. Adminstrn. and History. Mem. Am. Ednl. Rsch. Assn. (divsn. F editl. com. 1981-82, co-chair divsn. F program ann. program com. 1983-85, chair nominating com. divsn. F 1977, 79, sec. divsn. F 1976-78), Am. Hist. Assn. (Pacific Coast br.), Calif. Coun. on Edn. of Tchrs. (bd. dirs. 1989-93, chair programs com. fall 1991 conf.), Coun. for Exceptional Children (com. on history of individual differences 1985, cons. on oral history project, guest reviewer of manuscripts), History of Edn. Soc. (program com. 1986, nominating com. 1981-82), Nat. Soc. for Study of Edn. (com. on expansion of soc. activities 1972), Pacific Coast History of Edn. Soc. (program chair 1985), So. Assn. of Schs. and Colls. (sr. coll. commn., on-site visitation com. Walden U. 1980), Western Assn. Schs. and Colls. (sr. coll. commn., on-site visitation com. mem. various univs.), Phi Delta Kappa (historian, mem. exec. com. Riverside chpt. 1976-78). Democrat. Lutheran. Achievements include research in history of education, specifically the history of teacher education and education of minority groups, as well as extension of public school's mission to include responsibility for education and training of learning disabled and mentally retarded children. Avocations: tennis, running. Office: U Calif Sch of Edn Riverside CA 92521

HENDRICKS, CHRIS, publisher. Pres., pub. Nando Media, Raleigh, N.C. Office: Nando Media 127 W Hargett St Ste 406 Raleigh NC 27601-1351*

HENDRICKS, DEBORAH J., medical/surgical and oncological nurse; b. Wood River, Ill., Aug. 28, 1953; d. Albert O. and Bennie Jean (Muffet) Downs; m. Melvin L. Hendricks, July 24, 1971; children: Cristi Ann, Kevin John. ADN, Lewis & Clark Community Coll., Godfrey, Ill., 1983; BSN, McKendree Coll., Lebanon, Ill., 1989. BCLS. Staff nurse in medicine and oncology St. Joseph's Hosp., Alton, Ill.; staff nurse, bone marrow transplant Barnes Hosp., St. Louis, per diem nurse in medicine and bone marrow transplant, preceptor, bone marrow transplant coord. Mem. Oncology Nursing Soc.

HENDRICKS, DONALD DUANE, librarian; b. Flint, Mich., Nov. 3, 1931; s. Edgar F. and Marion (Scoble) H.; m. Mary Jean Elrich, Feb. 17, 1951; children—Phillip, Scott, Randall. A.B., U. Mich., A.M. in L.S, 1955; Ph.D., U. Ill., 1966. With Detroit Pub. Libr., 1955-57; head libr. Owosso Pub. Libr., Mich., 1957-60, Millikin U., 1960-63; dir. librs. Sam Houston State Univ., 1966-70; dir. S. Central Regional Med. Libr. Program, Dallas, 1970-78, U. Tex. Health Sci. Ctr. Libr., 1971-78; dir. Earl K. Long Libr., U. New Orleans, 1978, dean library services, 1981-89, reference libr., 1989-92; mgr. Mandeville br., St. Tammany Parish Libr. System, 1993-96; libr. Slidell Br. Delgado C.C., La., 1996—; cons. in field. Author: Centralized Processing and Regional Library Development, 1970, also monographs, articles.; co-Author: Resources of Texas Libraries, 1968, Centralized Processing and Regional Library Development—The Midwestern Regional Library System, 1970, The Louisiana State Library Processing Center: An Evaluation, 1971, Medical Libraries, Needs and Services, 1972. Grantee U.S. Office Edn., 1965. Mem. ALA, Bibliog. Soc. (London), Bibliog. Soc. Am. Club: Grolier (N.Y.C.). Home: 61324 Brittany Dr Lacombe LA 70445-2818 Office: Delgado C C 320 Howze Beach Rd Slidell LA 70458-8515

HENDRICKS, EDWARD DAVID, speaker, educator, consultant; b. Bridgeport, Conn., July 29, 1946; s. James Lyons and Dorothy (James) H.; m. Elizabeth Mary Jessop, Sept. 14, 1968; children: Maureen, David. BS, BA, U. N.C., Charlotte, 1975; MA, SUNY, Albany, 1976. Cert. assn. exec. Contracts adminstr. Eutectic Corp., Flushing, N.Y., 1969-70; contracts adminstr. Interroyal Corp., N.Y.C., 1970-71, regional sales mgr., 1971-72; dir. tech. assistance project Conn. Justice Commn., Hartford, 1976-78; dir. Fairfield County Criminal Justice Planning Commn., Stratford, Conn., 1978-79; dir. adminstrn. ACME, Inc., N.Y.C., 1979-81, v.p., 1981-88, pres., 1988-96; pres. Inst. of Mgmt. Cons., N.Y.C., 1990-92, Coun. Consulting Orgns., N.Y.C., 1989-92, Found. for Excel in Cons. and Mgmt., N.Y.C., 1989-92, Edward D. Hendricks & Assocs., 1995—; dir. ctr. corp. edn. Sacred Heart U., 1999—; bd. dirs. Profl. Svcs. Coun., Washington, N. Am. Mgmt. Coun., N.Y.C.; steering com. UNDP/ILO Ea. Europe Project, Geneva, 1990-95; keynote speaker Escort Internat. Conf., Sofia, Bulgaria, 1990; faculty mem. Leadership Studies Program, Sacred Heart U., 1998—. Author: Student Rights and Responsibilities, 1973, An Insider's Guide To Consulting Success, 1997, Successful Business Networking, 1998, Back on the Right Track, 1999; contbg. author: A History of Consulting, 1987, The Role of Associations, 1990. Campaign coord. James Martin for Congress, Charlotte, 1973; internat. adv. com. mem. U.S. Dept. Commerce, 1994—; treas. Big Bros./Sisters of Fairfield County, Bridgeport, Conn., 1976-78; bd. dirs. United Way of Fairfield County, 1978; permanent deacon Roman Cath. Ch. With USCG, 1965-69. Elected Student Body Pres. U.N.C., Charlotte, 1975; recipient Hon. Mention award NSF, 1972, Acad. Fellowship SUNY, Albany, 1975-76. Fellow Am. Soc. Assn. Execs. (dir. 1991-96); mem. Tri-State Profl. Spkrs. Assn. (treas. 1995-96), N.Y. Soc. Assn. Execs. (pres., bd. dirs. 1986-92, Outstanding Assn. Exec. 1995), Disabled Am. Vets., Mensa, Inst. Mgmt. Cons. (bd. dirs. N.Y. chpt. 1996—). Avocations: speaking, counselling, various sports. Office: 354 Anton St Bridgeport CT 06606-2119 *Luck is not solely a matter of chance. Luck is what happens when opportunity collides with persisitence plus preperation. If you continue learning and continue striving, opportunity will find you.*

HENDRICKS, FLORA ANN, former case manager, former special education educator; b. Cape Girardeau, Mo., Apr. 3, 1955; d. James Philbert and Bessie Geraldine (Mason) Joyce; m. Norman Harold Hendricks, Oct. 5, 1985; stepchildren: Theresa Lynn Ramirez, David Lane Hendricks. BS in Edn., S.E. Mo. State U., 1978; student, U. Mo., 1994. Lifetime cert. tchr., Mo. Warehouse and prodn. line worker Procter and Gamble Corp., Jackson, Mo., summer 1973-78; tchr. spl. edn. I and II Poplar Bluff (Mo.) Regional Ctr., 1979-83; social svc. worker Jefferson County divsn. Family Svcs., Hillsboro, Mo., 1983; case mgr. I, II, III St. Louis Regional Ctr., 1983-94. Mem. Baby Boomer's Club, St. Luke's United Meth. Ch., civic activities vol., 1988-89, vol. ch. nursery, 1988-89; co-chair K-WG AAUW Diversity Book Group, 1997-99; visitor vol. St. Luke's United Meth. Ch., RCF, Nursing Homes. Mem. NAFE, S.E. Mo. State U. Alumni Assn. Democrat. Methodist. Avocations: reading, camping, personal computer. Home: 6339 Treeridge Trl Saint Louis MO 63129-4640

HENDRICKS, GILBERT L., III, physiologist, researcher; b. Richmond, Va., 1959; s. Gilbert L. Jr. and Ina Mae Hendricks. BS in Biology, Pa. State U., 1981, BS in Microbiology, 1984, MS in Physiology, 1989, PhD in Physiology, 1994. Surg. technician Lewistown (Pa.) Hosp., 1982-85; grad. rsch. asst. Pa. State U., University Park, 1987-94; postdoctoral rsch. scientist Biotech. Inst., University Park, 1995-96; advisor to MS candidates Pa. State U., 1993-94, instr. U.S.-AID Egypt project, 1994. Contbr. articles to profl. jours. Mem. SAR, Gamma Sigma Delta. Methodist. Achievements include development of assay to measure hormone production by leukocytes; determined corticotropin releasing factor (CRF) stimulates adrenocorticotropic hormone by chicken leukocytes, identified macrophage as primary leukocyte responsible for immune adrenocorticotropic hormone production. Avocation: basketball.

HENDRICKS, J(AMES) EDWIN, historian, educator, consultant, author; b. Pickens, S.C., Oct. 19, 1935; s. J.E. and Cassie (Looper) H.; m. Sue James, June 28, 1958; children—James, Christopher, Lee. B.A., Furman U., 1957; M.A., U. Va., 1959, Ph.D., 1961. Vis. prof. history U. Va., Charlottesville, summer 1961; asst. prof. history Wake Forest U., Winston-Salem, N.C., 1961-66, assoc. prof., 1966-75, prof., 1975—; chmn. Dept. of History, 1995—; dir. Hist. Preservation Program Wake Forest U., Winston-Salem, N.C., 1973—; vis. prof. history U. Tex.-El Paso, summer 1965; preservation cons.; vis. dir. Mus. Albermarle, Elizabeth City, N.C., summer 1975; dir. Preservation Field Sch., summers 1983-86, 88-90, 92—. Author: (with others) Liquor and Anti-Liquor in Virginia, 1619-1919, 1967; Charles Thomson and the Making of a Nation, 1729-1824, 1979; editor, contbg. author: Forsyth, The History of a County on the March, 1976; author: Wake Forest University School of Law: One Hundred Years of Legal Education, 1994. Trustee Hist. Bethabara; pres. Hist. Winston, 1979; chmn. Winston-Salem/Forsyth County Hist. Dists. Commn., 1978-79; pres. Wachovia Hist. Soc., 1983-87. Served with U.S. Army, 1958-59. Recipient R.J. Reynolds research leave, 1973, 87; Am. Philos. Soc. research grantee, 1969, 70. Mem. N.C. Lit. and Hist. Assn. (pres. 1980-81), Hist. Soc. N.C., Soc. Historians Early Am. Republic, Nat. Trust Hist. Preservation, others. Democrat. Baptist. Lodges: Kiwanis (pres. 1987-88), Torch (pres. Winston-Salem 1987-88). Office: Wake Forest U Dept History PO Box 7806 Winston Salem NC 27109-7806

HENDRICKS, JAMES POWELL, artist; b. Little Rock, Aug. 7, 1938; s. Leland Fuller and Christia Beatrice (Powell) H.; m. Betty Jean Fleming, Nov. 6, 1960 (div. 1977); children—Elizabeth Jane, Valerie Lee; m. Marcia Reed-Hendricks, 1978. B.A., U. Ark., 1962; M.F.A., U. Iowa, 1964. Instr. art State U. Iowa, 1962-64, Mt. Holyoke Coll., 1964-65; mem. faculty U. Mass., Amherst, 1965—; prof. art U. Mass., 1977—, dir. undergrad. programs in art, 1968-71, dir. grad. programs art, 1974-77; vis. artist Seoul Inst. of the Arts, Korea, 1986, Portland Sch. Arts, Maine, 1985, San Diego State U., 1986, Internat. Artist Colony, Ctr. Contemporary Visual Arts, Prilep, Macedonia, 1994. One-man exhbn., Nat. Air and Space Mus., Smithsonian Instn., fall 1969, Hudson River Mus., Yonkers, N.Y., 1970, U. Mass., Amherst, 1971-78, French and Co. Gallery, N.Y.C., 1972, Warren Benedek Gallery, N.Y.C., 1974, Helen Shlien Gallery, Boston, 1980, 82, 84, Smith Coll., Northampton, Mass., 1983, 84, SUNY-Oswego, 1983, Deerfield Acad., Mass., 1984, Portland Sch. Art, 1985, Space Art Gallery, Seoul, 1986, Mus. Fine Arts, Springfield, Mass., 1986, Slater-Price Fine Arts Gallery, N.Y.C., 1989, 90, Ark. Arts Ctr., Little Rock, 1993, Anderson Gallery, 1993, Art Gallery at Macedonia, Skopje, 1994, Westwood Gallery, Inc., N.Y.C., 1996, Hart Gallery, Northampton, Mass., 1996; group exhbns. include, Nat. Gallery Art, 1970, Nat. Air and Space Mus., 1976, 4th Internat. Biennial, Medellin, Colombia, 1981, Assemblage/Collage Exhbn. Seoul Inst. of Arts, Korea, in conjunction with World Olympics Arts Festival, 1988, Joy Moos Gallery, Miami, Fla., 1991, Vesti-dane Gallery, Scottsdale, Ariz., 1997; comms. include: Nat. Gallery Art, NASA, cover for Time mag., 1971, 2 album covers for Neuma Records, fall 1991; cover commn. for The Mass. Rev., Vol. XXXVII, No. 4, Winter, 1997. Named Ark. Traveler, 1971. Office: U Mass Art Dept Amherst MA 01003

HENDRICKS, JOHN S., broadcast executive; b. 1952. Gov. rels. dir. U. Ala., Huntsville, 1972-73; corp. rels. dir. U. Maryland, College Park, 1973-78; chmn., CEO The Disney Channel Discovery Comm., Inc., Bethesda, Md., 1982—. Mem. Am. Assn. Univ. Cons. Office: Discovery Comm Inc 7700 Wisconsin Ave Bethesda MD 20814-3578*

HENDRICKS, KENNETH, wholesale distribution executive. CEO, chmn. ABC Supply, Beloit, Wis. Office: ABC Supply One ABC Pkwy Beloit WI 53511-4466*

HENDRICKS, LEONARD D., emergency medicine physician, consultant; b. Chgo., Feb. 29, 1952; s. Leonard D. and Edith V. (Elliott) H.; m. Gail Williams, Aug. 26, 1989. BS in Engring., U. Ill., 1974; MD, U. Wis., 1979. Diplomate Am. Bd. Emergency Medicine, Am. Bd. Forensic Examiners, Am. Bd. Forensic Medicine, Am. Bd. Psychol. Specialties, Am. Acad. Experts in Traumatic Stress subsplty. cert. in forensic traumatology, Am. Bd. Quality Assurance and Utilization Review Physicians with subsplty. cert. in risk mgmt., Am. Bd. Managed Care Medicine. Med. dir. Cuyahoga County Corrections Facility; emergency physician Meridia Huron Hosp., East Cleveland, Ohio; asst. dir. emergency medicine Kaiser Permanente Hosp., Parma, Ohio; emergency physician Western Res. Care System, Youngstown, Ohio; dir. emergency medicine St. Joseph Riverside Hosp., Warren, Ohio; med. dir. emergency medicine Allen Meml. Hosp., Oberlin, Ohio; pres., CEO Avatar Healthcare Svcs.; med dir. urgent care/emergency dept. Peoples Hosp., Mansfield, Ohio; med. dir. emergency dept. Lodi Cmty. Hosp.; cons. Friedman, Domiano and Smith Law Firm, Cleve., Newman & Boyer Law Form, Chgo., Jaffe & Hough Law Firm, Phila.; regional physician mgr. Birman & Assocs.; instr. emergency medicine Case Western Res. U., Cleve., Northeastern Ohio U., Rootstown; instr. ACLS, Am. Heart Assn.; instr. advanced trauma life support ACS; instr. pediatric ALS, neonatal resuscitation, Am. Acad. Pediatrics. Fellow Am. Bd. Forensic Examiners, Am. Coll. Medicine, Am. Coll. Emergency Physicians, Am. Acad. Experts in Traumatic Stress; mem. Am. Coll. Physician Execs., Soc. Acad. Emergency Medicine.

HENDRICKS, MIRIAM JOAN, English educator; b. Johnson City, Tenn., Mar. 15, 1939; d. Lowell Wilson and Claudia Helen (Hatchett) Kinkead; m. John Pendleton Hendricks, Dec. 4, 1976. BS, East Tenn. State U., 1962, MA, 1975. Cert. tchr., Tenn. Fed. credit union clk. Tenn. Gas Transmission, Houston, 1960-61; hostess TransWorld Airlines, Inc., L.A., 1962-75; tchr. English Johnson City Pub. Schs., 1975—; mem. libr. adv. com. Science Hill H.S., Johnson City, 1994—; mem. so. assocs. leadership com., 1995-97. Vol. March of Dimes, Blountville area, 1991-99. Mem. NEA, Nat. Coun. Tchrs. English, Tenn. Edn. Assn., Johnson City Edn. Assn. Christian Ch. Avocations: reading, genealogy, boating, handwork, gardening. Office: Science Hill High Sch 1509 John Exum Pkwy Johnson City TN 37604-3826

HENDRICKS, RANDAL ARLAN, lawyer; b. Kansas City, Mo., Nov. 18, 1945; s. Clinton H. and Edith T. (Anderson) H.; m. Suann Rose, June 1, 1965 (div. 1976); children: Kristin Lee, Daehne Lynn; m. Jill Edith Duke, Mar. 22, 1982; 1 child, Bret Larson-Hendricks. Student, U. Mo.-Kansas City, 1963-65; BS with honors, U. Houston, 1968, JD with honors, 1970. Bar: Tex. 1970, U.S. Dist. (so. dist.) Tex. 1970, U.S. Tax Ct. 1985. Assoc. Baker & Botts, Houston, 1970-71; pvt. practice, Houston, 1971—; ptnr. Hendricks Sports Mgmt., Houston, 1977-81; pres. Hendricks Mgmt. Co., Inc., Houston, 1981—. Author: Inside the Strike Zone, 1994. Dir. profl. div. Excellence Campaign, U. Houston, 1971; bd. dirs. Cypress Creek Christian Ch., Spring, Tex., 1979-85; expert witness U.S. Senate Subcom. on Antitrust and Monopoly, 1972; mem. pub. adv. com. Houston/Harris County Sports Facility, 1995-96. Mem. Houston Bar Assn., Assn. Reps. Profl. Athletes (bd. dirs. 1978-88, mem. at large 1978-79, treas. 1979-80, v.p. 1980-81, pres. 1981-82, chmn. ethics com. 1978-80, chmn. baseball com. 1981-88), Sports Lawyers Assn. (bd. dirs. 1992—), Order of Barons (chancellor 1969-70), Phi Kappa Phi, Phi Delta Phi. Home: 20802 Highet Pl Tomball TX 77375-7042 Office: 400 Randal Way Ste 106 Spring TX 77388-8908

HENDRICKS, STANLEY MARSHALL, II, executive recruiter, consultant; b. Richmond, Ky., Nov. 15, 1952; s. Stanley Marshall and Margaret Cathleen (Cox) H.; m. Sara Jane Sargent, Aug. 9, 1975; children: Stanley M. III, Elizabeth Jean. BS, Ind. State U., 1976; post baccalaureate degree, Ind. U. Northwest, 1984. Cert. personnel cons. Assoc. A.R. Massena & Assocs., Merrillville, Ind., 1976-77; co-founder, owner Nat. Recruiting Svc., Dyer, Ind., 1977—. Council mem. Ind. State U., Terre Haute, 1983-88; pres. Ind. State U. Alumni Coun.; elder, trustee Immanuel Presbyn. Ch., Schererville, Ind., 1978—. Mem. Assn. Iron and Steel Engrs., Nat. Assn. Pers. Cons., Fabricating Mfrs. Assn., Iron and Steel Soc., Ind. Soc. Chgo., Am. Tube Assn., Internat. Tube Assn., Ind. State U. Alumni Assn. (v.p., coun. pres.), Order of Omega (hon.), Rotary (pres., bd. dirs., Paul Harris fellow, asst. dist. gov.), Sycamore Club N.W. Ind. (bd. dirs. 1984—), Tri-Town Optimist Club (charter), Phi Gamma Delta (housing corp. Iota Sigma chpt.). Avocations: flying, woodworking, scuba diving, swimming. Home: 301 Blickview Dr Schererville IN 46375-2372

HENDRICKS, WILLIAM LAWRENCE, theology educator; b. Butte, Mont., Mar. 10, 1929; s. Homer V.H. and Ruby E. (Jennings) H.; m. Lois Ann Lindsey, June 4, 1951; 1 child, John Lawrence. BA, Okla. Bapt. U., 1951; M Div, Southwestern Bapt. Theol. Sem., 1954, ThD, 1958; MA, U. Chgo., 1965, PhD, 1972; LHD, Campbell U., 1994. Ordained to ministry Bapt. Ch., 1950. Assoc. min. Immanuel Bapt. Ch., Wichita, Kans., 1949-50; min. South Bapt. Ch., Dodson, Tex., 1954-57; prof. theology Southwestern Bapt. Theol. Sem., Ft. Worth, 1957-78; prof. theol. and philosophy Golden Gate Bapt. Theol. Sem., Mill Valley, Calif., 1979-84; prof. theology, dir. doctoral studies So. Bapt. Theol. Sem., Louisville, 1984-94; dir. Ctr. for Religion and the Arts, sr. prof. Theology, 1995-96; dir. Baptist studies, lectr. theology Brite Divinity Sch., Ft. Worth, Tex., 1996-99. Author: A Theology for Aging, 1986, A Theology for Children, 1980, The Doctrine of Man, 1977, Pascal and Fenelon, 1980; (play) The Harrowing of Hell, 1977. Recipient Alumni award Okla. Bapt. U., 1985, Meritorious Service in Christian Higher Edn. award Okla. Bapt. U., 1985, Outstanding Alumni Achievement award, 1986, Festschrift award Bapt. Reflections on Christianity and the Arts, 1997; named Disting. Alumnus Southwestern Bapt. Theol. Sem., 1989. Mem. Am. Acad. Religion (pres. S.W. region), Soc. Biblical Lit., Pacific Coast Theol. Soc., Commn. on Religious Studies (pres. S.W. region). Democrat. Office: Brite Divinity Sch TCU Box 298130 Fort Worth TX 76129

HENDRICKSON, ANITA ELIZABETH, biology educator; b. LaCross, Wis., Feb. 20, 1936; d. Walter V. and Alno (Larkin) Schnell; m. Morris N. Hendrickson, June 8, 1957; children: Lisa, Karin, Gordon. BA, Pacific Luth. Coll., 1957; PhD, U. Wash., Seattle, 1964. Instr. anatomy Northwestern Med. Sch., Chgo., 1964-65; rsch. assoc. Children's Meml. Hosp., Chgo., 1964-65; rsch. instr. dept. biol. structure U. Wash., Seattle, 1965-67; instr. dept. ophthalmology U. Wash., 1967-69, asst. prof. dept. ophthalmology, 1969-73; affiliate/assoc. prof. dept. ophthalmology Reg. Primate Ctr./U. Wash., 1972—, 1973-81; affiliate Child Devel. & Mental Retardation Ctr., U. Wash., 1975; prof. dept. opthalmology U. Wash., 1981-97, prof. dept. biol. structure, 1984—, chair dept. biol. structure, 1994—, adj. prof. ophthalmology, 1997—; vis. assoc. prof. neuropathology Harvard Med. Sch., Boston, 1975-76; adj. assoc. prof. dept. psychology U. Wash., 1975-78; mem. NIH VisB study section, 1976-80. Editorial bd. Jour. of Neurosci., 1982-88, Investigative Ophthalmology, 1977-82, Vision Research, 1990-95; contbr. articles to profl. jours. Dolly Green rsch. grantee, 1981; named Alumnus of the Yr., Pacific Luth. U., 1982. Mem. AAAS, Am. Assn. Anatomists, Soc. for Neurosci. (mem. nat. coun. 1982-86), Internat. Soc. for Eye Rsch., Assn. for Rsch. in Vision and Ophthalmology (prog. chmn. 1983-84, trustee 1993—), Cajal Club. Home: 1029C NE 120th St Seattle WA 98125-5003 Office: Univ of Washington Dept Biol Structure PO Box 357420 Seattle WA 98195-7420*

HENDRICKSON, BRUCE CARL, life insurance company executive; b. Holdrege, Nebr., Apr. 4, 1930; s. Carl R. and Ruth E. (Bosserman) H.; m. Carol Schepman, June 12, 1952; children: Julie, Mark Bruce. B.A., U. Nebr., 1952. C.L.U., chartered fin. cons. Sr. agt. Prin. Mut. Life Ins. Co., Holdrege, 1950—. Bd. govs. Central Nebr. Tech. Community Coll.; mem. Nebr. Edn. Commn. of States, Nat. Hwy. Safety Advisors Com.; elder United Presbyterian Ch., Holdrege; pres. Holdrege City Council, 1979-86; pres. Phelps County Community Found.; trustee U. Nebr. Found.; moderator Cen. Nebr. Presbytery, Presbyn. Ch. USA, 1986-88; dir. Nebr. Art Collection Found., 1996. Served with USNR, 1953-56. Bruce Hendrickson Week declared by Gov. of Nebr., 1975; recipient Distinguished Alumni Achievement award U. Nebr., 1977, Disting. Svc. award Nebr. State Assn. Life Underwriters, 1998. Mem. Nat. Assn. Life Underwriters (pres. 1975-76), Assn. Advanced Life Underwriting, Am. Soc. C.L.U.s., Life Underwriters Polit. Action Com. (chmn. 1989), Life Underwriters Tng. Council (trustee 1979-82), Million Dollar Round Table, Phi Kappa Psi. Republican. Clubs: Rotary (Holdrege), Holdrege Country (Holdrege); Am. Legion, Elks. Office: Prin Fin Group PO Box 765 Holdrege NE 68949-0765

HENDRICKSON, CHRIS THOMPSON, civil and environmental engineering educator, researcher; b. Oakland, Calif., Mar. 31, 1950; s. Harold Thompson and E. Jean (Loomis) H.; m. Kathleen Devine, May 28, 1977; children: Andrew, Thomas, Peter. BS, MS, Stanford U., 1973; PhB, Oxford U., 1975; PhD, MIT, 1978. Asst. prof. Carnegie-Mellon U., Pitts., 1978-83, assoc. prof., 1983-87, prof., 1987—; assoc. dean Carnegie Inst. Tech., 1991-96, Duquesne Light Co. prof. Engring., 1996—, head dept., 1996—. Author: (with others) Transportation Investment and Pricing Principles, 1984, Project Management for Construction, 1989, Knowledge-based Process Planning for Construction and Manufacturing, 1989, Computer Integrated Building Design, 1993; editor Jour. Transp. Energy; contbr. articles to profl. publs. Bd. mem. St. Edmund's Acad., Pitts. Recipient C.E. Ladd Rsch. award Carnegie Inst. Tech., 1979; Rhodes scholar, 1973. Mem. ASCE (com. chmn. 1983—, chmn. urban transp. divsn. 1989-90, Huber Rsch. award 1989, Masters Transp. Engring. award 1994), Am. Econ. Assn., Transp. Rsch. Bd. (com. chmn. 1989-96), Phi Beta Kappa, Tau Beta Pi. Home: 6933 Rosewood St Pittsburgh PA 15208-2638 Office: Carnegie Mellon U Pittsburgh PA 15213-3890

HENDRICKSON, CONSTANCE MARIE MCRIGHT, chemist, consultant; b. Baton Rouge, June 7, 1949; d. Clifton Eugene and Evelyn Marie (Watson) McRight; m. William Harwell Hendrickson, Dec. 28, 1971; children: Charles Douglas (dec.), David Gillis, Emily Elizabeth Marie. BA, La. Tech. U., 1971; PhD, La. State U., 1975; MEd, U. North Tex., 1984. Cert. profl. chemist. NIH rsch. fellow Johns Hopkins U., Balt., 1975-78; clin. chemistry fellow Sch. Medicine U. Ala., Birmingham, 1978-79; temporary asst. prof. Tex. Wesleyan Coll., Ft. Worth, 1980-81; chief chemist Rockwood Systems Corp., Dallas, 1981-82; dir., owner Ar'Kon Cons., Dallas, 1982—; dir. environ. tech. program Brookhaven Coll., Dallas, 1994-97; chair Nat. Certification Commn. for Chemists and Chem. Engrs., 1992-94. Inventor high expansion foams. Fellow Am. Inst. Chemists (chair nat. cert. commn. for chemists and chem. engrs., pres. elect 1996-97, pres. 1998—); mem. Am. Chem Soc. (local chair 1987-88, treas. chem. mktg. and econs. divsn. 1990—), N.Y. Acad. Scis., Nat. Panel Consumer Arbitrators (sr.). Democrat. Avocations: fossil hunting, folk music, fiddling, zither. Home: 802 S Jefferson St Irving TX 75060-5355 Office: PO Box 171087 Irving TX 75017-1087 also: 1213 Stewart Dr Irving TX 75061-7354

HENDRICKSON, ELIZABETH ANN, retired secondary education educator; b. Bismarck, N.D., Oct. 21, 1936; d. William Earl and Hilda E. (Sauter) Hinkel; m. Roger G. Hendrickson, Apr. 18, 1960; 1 child, Wade William. BA, Jamestown Coll., 1958; postgrad., U. Calif., Davis, 1962, Calif. State U., Sacramento, 1964, U. San Diego, 1985-88, Ottawa U., 1986-88. Cert. tchr., Calif. Tchr. Napoleon (N.D.) High Sch., 1958-59, Kulm (N.D.) High Sch., 1959-61, Del Paso Jr. High Sch., Sacramento, 1961, Mills Jr. High Sch., Rancho Cordova, Calif., 1961-97; ret., 1997. Mem. NEA, AAUW, Calif. Assn. for Gifted, Calif. Tchrs. Assn., Calif. Ret. Tchrs. Assn., Folsom Cordova Ret. Tchrs. Assn. (sec.), Sacramento Area Gifted Assn., Soroptimists (news editor Rancho Cordova 1985, sec. 1986). Democrat. Lutheran. Home: 2032 Kellogg Way Rancho Cordova CA 95670-2435

HENDRICKSON, HARVEY SIGBERT, retired accounting educator; b. Mpls., July 23, 1928; s. Sigbert and Hilma M. (Johnson) H.; m. Rosanne C. Maddy, Aug. 18, 1962; children: Mary, Erik, Elise. BBA, U. Minn., 1957, MBA, 1962, PhD, 1963. CPA, Minn. (ret.). Instr. U. Minn., Mpls., 1958-61, vis. assoc. prof., 1969; asst. prof. acctg. SUNY, Buffalo, 1963-68; assoc. prof. acctg. Fla. State U., Tallahassee, 1968-69; asst. dir. exams. AICPA, N.Y.C., 1970-72; chmn. fin., acctg. div. Fla. Internat. U., Miami, 1972-77, prof. acctg., from 1972; now ret.; acad. acctg. fellow Office Chief Acct., SEC, Washington, 1980-81; cons. acctg., fin. reporting, and budgeting, expert witness, Miami, 1973—. Author: (with others) The Accounting Primer, 1972; editor: Relevant Accounting Concepts and Applications: The Writings and Contributions of C. Rufus Rorem, 1991, Carl Thomas Devine's Essays on Accounting Theory: A Capstone, 1999; editor: (with others) The Accounting Sampler, 1967, 72, 76, 86; mem. editorial bd. The Acctg. Rev., 1976-82, book rev. editor, 1984-87; contbr. articles to profl. jours. Active Dade County Pub. Schs., mem. South Area adv. com. 1973-76, chmn. 1973-74; bd. dirs. South Fla. Assn. Accts. Pub. Interest, 1976-80, chmn. 1976-77. Sgt. U.S. Army, 1951-52, Korea. Ford Found. predoctoral fellow, 1961-62, Arthur Andersen and Co. Found. doctoral dissertation fellow, 1961-63; Haskins and Sells Found. scholar, 1957. Mem. AICPA; Am. Acctg. Assn. (SEC liaison com. 1981-83, 85-86, chmn. S.E. region exec. planning com. 1977-82, chmn. 1978-79), Fin. Execs. Inst. (pres. South Fla. chpt. 1991-92, sec. 1988-92, bd. dirs. 1988-96), Beta Alpha Psi, Beta Gamma Sigma. Democrat. E-mail: hendrick@fiu.edu. Home: 7865 SW 158 Terr Miami FL 33157-2330 Office: Fla Internat U Sch Acctg Miami FL 33199

HENDRICKSON, JEROME ORLAND, trade association executive, lawyer; b. Eau Claire, Wis., July 25, 1918; s. Harold and Clara (Halverson) H.; student Wis. State Coll., 1936-39; J.D., U. Wis., 1942; m. Helen Phoebe Harty, Dec. 27, 1948 (dec. Oct. 1988); children—Jaime Ann, Jerome Orland. Bar: Wis., 1942, U.S. Supreme Ct., 1955; sole practice, Eau Claire, 1946; sales and advt. mgr. Eau Claire Coca-Cola Bottling Co., Inc., 1947-48; exec. sec. Eau Claire Community Chest, 1948-49; in charge dist. office Am. Petroleum Inst., Kansas City, Mo., 1950-53, Chgo., 1953-55; exec. dir. Nat. Assn. Plumbing-Heating-Cooling Contractors, 1955-64; sec. Joint Apprentice Text, Inc., 1955-64; exec. v.p. Cast Iron Soil Pipe Inst., Washington, 1964-74; pres. Valve Mfrs. Assn., McLean, Va., 1975-80; exec. v.p. Plumbing and Piping Industry Coun., Inc., 1981-90, ret. Treas., Wis. Community Chest, 1948-49. Treas., All-Industry Plumbing & Heating Modernization Com., 1956-57; co-sec. Joint Industry Program Com., 1958-64. Served to lt. USNR, 1943-46. Mem. ABA, Wis. Bar Assn.,, Am. Soc. Assn. Execs., Washington Soc. Assn. Execs., Wis. State Soc. Washington (pres. 1966-68), Nat. Conf. Plumbing-Heating-Cooling Industry (chmn. 1967-69), NAM, U. Wis. Alumni Assn., U. Wis. Law Sch. Alumni Assn. Washington (pres. 1970-74), C. of C. of U.S., Gamma Eta Gamma (pres. Upsilon chpt. 1941-42). Episcopalian. Mason (32 deg., Shriner). Clubs: Washington Golf and Country, Internat. (Washington). Home and Office: 4621 33rd St N Arlington VA 22207-4407

HENDRICKSON, KENT HERMAN, university administrator; b. Radcliffe, Iowa, Mar. 4, 1939; s. Herman Oliver and Minnie Ida (Dubberke) H.; m. Rosemary Lee Bergeson, Sept. 12, 1960 (div. 1981); children: Justin K., Susan K.; m. Ellen J. Waite, Mar. 26, 1994 (div. Dec. 1995). BS in History, Iowa State U., 1961; MALS, U. Mich., 1964. Assoc. dir. for tech. svcs. U. Nebr. Librs., Lincoln, 1964-70, dean of librs., 1985-95, assoc. vice chancellor info. svcs., 1995—; mgr. west coast operations Richard Abel Co., Beaverton, Oreg., 1970-74; v.p. corp. opers. Blackwell N.Am. Inc., Beaverton, Oreg., 1975-79, v.p., 1980-81; assoc. univ. libr. U. Ariz. Libr., Tucson, 1981-85, acting asst. univ libr. for pub. svcs., 1982-84, dir. ctrl. svcs., 1984-85; mem. Nebr. Conf. on Libr. and Info. Svcs., 1991; mem. adv. com. on integrated postsecondary edn. data system Nat. Ctr. for Edn. Statistics, 1990-93; mem. rsch. librs. adv. com. Online Computer Libr. Ctr. Inc., 1990-96, chair, 1992-93. Contbr. articles to profl. jours.; mem. editorial bd. U. Nebr. Press, 1990-95. Trustee AMIGOS, 1984-85; mem. info. systems and comm. com. U. Nebr.-Lincoln, 1988—, mem. acad. planning com., 1988-93, mem. adv. com. to Sheldon Art Gallery, 1985—, mem. adv. com. to computing resource ctr., 1987—, mem. campus wide campaign for health and human svcs., 1986-87, vice chair, 1986, chair, 1987; bd. dirs. Great Plains Network, 1999—. Mem. Assn. Rsch. Librs. (stats. com. 1989-92, chair 1991-92, mem. mgmt. com. 1992-96, chair 1993-96, chair office mgmt. svcs. adv. com. 1993-96, mem. collection devel. com. 1986-88, bd. dirs. 1993-96), Assn. Coll. and Rsch. Librs. (mem. exec. com. univ. librs. sect. 1992-95, chair pre-conf. planning com. 1992, chair univ. librs. stds. rev. com. 1986-89, chair acad. librs. stats. com. 1986-89), OCLC Users Coun. (mem. fin. com. 1991-92, v.p./pres.-elect 1992-94), U. Nebr. Coun. on Librs., Nebr. State Libr. Commn. (mem. strategic planning task force 1987-88). Office: U Nebr-Lincoln University Libraries Lincoln NE 68588-0496

HENDRICKSON, ROBERT FREDERICK, pharmaceutical company executive; b. Cambridge, Mass., Jan. 5, 1933; s. Charles H. and Ruth E. (Bjorklund) H.; m. Virginia H. Emery, Apr. 27, 1963; children: Karen, Susan, Douglas. A.B. in Econs. magna cum laude, Harvard U., 1954, M.B.A., 1958. Engaged in prodn. planning, internat. div. Internat. Latex Corp., Dover, Del., 1958-61; mgr. prodn. planning and control Merck Sharp & Dohme, West Point, Pa., 1961-66; dir. long-range planning Merck Sharp & Dohme, 1966-68, exec. sec. new products com., 1968-69, dir. prodn. planning and control, 1969-71, dir. ops., 1971-72, v.p. ops., 1972-80; sr. v.p. Merck & Co., Inc., Rahway, N.J., 1981-85; sr. v.p. mfg. and tech. Merck & Co., Inc., Rahway, 1985-90, ret., 1990; mfg. cons., 1990—; bd. dirs. Liposome Co. Inc., Cytogen, Inc., Unigene, Inc., Envirogen, Inc.; trustee Carrier Found., 1992—. Bd. dirs. Lenape Valley Mental Health Found., 1972-80, pres., 1976-77; trustee N.J. State Safety Coun., 1980-90. With AUS, 1954-56. Mem. North Pa. C. of C. (bd. dirs. 1974-77), Pharm. Mfg. Assn. (chmn. prodn. and engring. sect. 1980-81), NOW Legal, Def. and Edn. Fund (bd. dirs. 1987-93), N.J. State C. of C. (bd. dirs. 1985-90), N.J. Coun. for the Humanities (trustee 1992-96). Presbyterian. Home and Office: 204 Gallup Rd Princeton NJ 08540-7306

HENDRICKSON, WILLIAM GEORGE, business executive; b. Plainview, Minn., May 31, 1918; s. Clarence and Hildegarde (Heaser) H.; m. Virginia M. Price, Sept. 1, 1942; children: Robert, Thomas, Donald, Julie Ann. BS, St. Mary's Coll., Winona, Minn., 1939; MS, U. Detroit, 1941; PhD, U. Wis., 1946; D Humanities, St. Mary's U., Winona, Minn., 1991. Scientist Wis. Alumni Research Found., Madison, 1946-54, dir. devel., 1954-61; v.p. Ayerst Labs. div. Am. Home Products Corp., N.Y.C., 1961-67, exec. v.p., 1967-69; group v.p. Am. Home Products Corp., N.Y.C., 1969-80; chmn. emeritus bd. St. Jude Med., Inc., St. Paul; bd. dirs. emeritus Rsch. Corp. Techs., Tucson, chmn. bd. dirs. IntelliNet, Naples, Fla. Mem. Am. Chem. Soc., N.Y. Acad. Scis., Country Club N.C., Royal Poinciana Golf Club, Sigma Xi. Republican. Roman Catholic.

HENDRIE, JOSEPH MALLAM, physicist, nuclear engineer, government official; b. Janesville, Wis., Mar. 18, 1925; s. Joseph Munier and Margaret Prudence (Hocking) H.; m. Elaine Kostell, July 9, 1949; children: Susan Debra, Barbara Ellen. BS, Case Inst. Tech., 1950; PhD, Columbia U., 1957. Registered profl. engr., N.Y., Calif. Asst. physicist Brookhaven Nat. Lab., Upton, N.Y., 1955-57, assoc. physicist, 1957-60, physicist, 1960-71, sr. physicist, 1971-97, chmn. steering com., project chief engr. high flux beam reactor design and constrn., 1958-65, acting head exptl. reactor physics div., 1965-66, project mgr. pulsed fast reactor project, 1967-70, assoc. head engring. div., dept. applied sci., 1967-71, head, 1971-72, chmn. dept. applied sci., 1975-77, spl. asst. to dir., 1981-96; dir. Entergy Ops., Inc., 1987-95; dir. Houston Industries, Inc., Houston Lighting & Power Co., 1985-96; dep. dir. licensing for tech. rev. U.S. AEC, 1972-74; chmn. U.S. Nuclear Regulatory Commn., Washington, 1977-79, 81, commr., 1980, mem. adv. com. on enforcement policy, 1984-85; lectr. nuclear power plant safety MIT, Ga. Inst. Tech., Northwestern U., summers 1970-77; cons. radiation safety com. Columbia U., 1964-72; mem. adv. com. reactor safeguards AEC, 1966-72, chmn., 1970; U.S. mem. sr. adv. group on reactor safety standards IAEA, 1974-78; mem. nat. rsch. coun. com. Internat. Cooperation in Magnetic Fusion, 1983-85; cons. AEC, Nuclear Regulatory Commn., 1974-75, GAO, 1975-77, Electric Power Rsch. Inst., 1982, various nuclear utilities, 1981—. Mem. editorial adv. bd. Nuclear Tech, 1967-77. Served with AUS, 1943-45. Recipient E.O. Lawrence award, 1970, George C. Laurence Pioneeering award Am. Nuclear Soc., 1998; decorated comdr. Order of Leopold II (Belgium), 1982. Fellow Am. Nuclear Soc. (dir. 1976-77, v.p. 1983-84, pres. 1984-85), ASME; mem. IEEE, Nat. Acad. Engring., Am. Phys. Soc., ASTM (com. on rsch. and tech. planning 1985-90), Am. Concrete Inst., Inst. Nuclear Power Operation (adv. coun. 1984-90), Nat. Soc. Profl. Engrs., Sigma Xi, Tau Beta Pi. Achievements include research and publications on physics nuclear reactors, nuclear power plant safety, engineering design reactors, electrical power transmission, chem. physics nitrogen dissociation process, structure oxygen molecule. Office: Brookhaven Nat Lab Upton NY 11973

HENDRIX, BONNIE ELIZABETH LUELLEN, elementary school educator; b. Corry, Pa., July 21, 1942; d. Francis Wilson and Frances (Welch) Luellen. BEd, Anderson Coll., 1965; MEd, Berry Coll., 1986. 1st grade tchr. Madison County Bd. Edn., Anderson, Ind.; kindergarten tchr. Walker County Bd. Edn., LaFayette, Ga., 1994—, spl. instrn. asst., 1998—, spl. edn. tchr., 1999—; mentor tchr. Continuous Quality Instructions Sys; pvt. practice piano tchr. Active community and ch. orgns. Mem. NEA, ASCD, PAGE, Ga. Assn. Edn., Walker Assn. Edn. Home: 76 Old Trion Rd La Fayette GA 30728-3714

HENDRIX, JOHN WALTER, lieutenant general United States Army. BS in Elec. Engring., Ga. Tech. U., 1966; student infantry advanced course, U.S. Army Infantry Sch., Ft. Benning, Ga., 1969-70; student fixed wing aviator course, U.S. Army Aviation Sch., Ft. Stewart, Ga., 1970-71; MA in History, Mid. Tenn. State U., 1974; student, U.S. Army Command & Staff Coll, Ft. Leavenworth, Kans., 1977-78, U.S. Army War Coll., Carlisle Barracks, Pa., 1983-84. Commd. 1st. lt. U.S. Army, 1966, advanced through grades to lt. gen., 1997; instr. Mt. Ranger Camp, Company D U.S. Army Infantry Sch., Fort Benning, Ga., 1966-67; comm. officer to comdr. 1st Battalion, 101st Airborne Divsn. U.S. Army, Vietnam, 1967-68; air officer ops. to S-1 (pers.) 1st Battalion 101st Airborne Divsn. U.S. Army, Vietnam, 1968-69, commander Co. D. 1st Battalion,, 1969; evaluation officer CSA Evaluation Directorate U.S. Army, Ft. Hood, Tex., 1971-72; asst. prof. mil. sci. Mid. Tenn. State U., Murfreesboro, 1972-74; S-3 (ops.), 2d brigade, 5th infantry divsn. (mechanized) U.S. Army, Ft. Polk, La., 1978-79; comdr. 2d battalion, 13th infantry, 8th infantry divsn. U.S. Army Europe, Germany, 1980-83, comdr. 2d brigade, 8th infantry divsn., 1987-89; asst. divsn. comdr. 1st armored divsn. U.S. Army Europe and 7th Army Desert Shield/ Desert Storm, Saudi Arabia, 1990-91; exec. to Supreme Allied Comdr. Europe Supreme hdqtrs. Allied Powers Europe, Brussels, 1991-92; commanding gen. U.S. Army Infantry Ctr. Ft. Benning then 3d Infantry Divsn. (mechanized, Fort Stewart, Ga., 1996-97; commanding gen. V Corps U.S. Army Europe and Seventh Army, Europe, 1997—. Decorated Defense Disting. Svc. medal, Disting. Svc. medal with oak leaf cluster, Silver Star with oak leaf cluster, Legion of Merit with 3 oak leaf clusters, Bronze Star medal with V device with 3 oak leaf clusters, Defense Meritorious Svc. medal, Meritorious Svc. medal with 4 oak leaf clusters, Air Medals, Army Commendation medal with 5 oak leaf clusters. Office: Office of Commanding Gen V Corps US Army Europe and Seventh Army APO AE 09014

HENDRIX, JON RICHARD, biology educator; b. Passaic, N.J., May 4, 1938; s. William Louis and Velma Lucile (Coleman) H.; m. Janis Ruth Rouhselange, Nov. 24, 1962; children—Margaret Susan, Joann Ruth, Amy Therese. B.S., Ind. State U., 1960, M.S., 1963; Ed.D., Ball State U., 1974. Sci. supr. Sch. Town of Highland, Ind., 1960-71; instr. Ind. U., Gary, 1968-69; assoc. prof. biology Ball State U., Muncie, 1972-80, prof., 1980—; cons. Ind. Dept. Pub. Instrn., 1967-71, Ctr. for Values and Meaning, 1971—; mem. Ind. Sci. Edn. Adv. Bd., Dept. Pub. Instrn., 1967-71. Author: The Wonder of Somehow, 1974, The Wonder of Someplace, 1974, The Wonder of Sometime, 1974, Becomings: A Parent Guidebook for In-Home Experiences with Nine to Eleven Year Olds, 1974, Becomings: A Clergy Guidebook for Experiences with Nine to Eleven Year Olds and Their Parents, 1974; contbr. articles to profl. jours. Recipient Outstanding Young Educator award Highland Jr. C. of C., 1968, Outstanding Faculty award in edn. Ind. U. N.W. Campus, 1970, Outstanding Teaching Faculty award Ball State U., 1982, Ball State U. fellowship, 1971-73, Hon. Mem. award Nat. Assn. Biology Tchrs., 1992, Outstanding Undergrad. Sci. Tchr. in Nation, Soc. of Coll. Sci. Tchrs./Kendall Mgmt., 1997; named Ind. Prof. of Yr., Coun. for Advancement and Support of Edn./Carneige, 1997. Fellow Ind. Acad. Sci.; mem. Nat. Sci. Suprs. Assn. (dir. 1969-71), Ind. Sci. Suprs. Assn. (pres. 1968-69), AAUP, Assn. Suprs. and Curriculum Devel., Nat. Biology Tchrs. Assn. (bd. dirs. 1986, 91—), Nat. Sci. Tchrs. Assn. (life), Nat. Soc. Coll. Sci. Tchrs. (undergrad. tchg. award 1997), Central Assn. Coll. Biology Tchrs., Hoosier Assn. Sci. Tchrs. Inc. (bd. dirs. 1968-71), Ind. Assn. Tchr. Educators, Ind. Assn. Suprs. and Curriculum Devel., Ind. Biology Tchrs. Assn., Kappa Delta Pi, Phi Delta Kappa, Sigma Xi. Home: 8800 W Eucalyptus Ave Muncie IN 47304-9365 Office: Ball State U Dept Biology Muncie IN 47306

HENDRIX, LYNN PARKER, lawyer; b. McCook, Nebr., Apr. 24, 1951; s. Jack Hall and Betty Lee (Parker) H.; m. Theresa Louise Zabawa, June 19, 1976; children: Paige Ashley, Parker Jerome, Pierce Reid. BSEE, U. Nebr., 1973, JD with distinction, 1978. Bar: Nebr. 1978, U.S. Dist. Ct. Nebr. 1978, Colo. 1979, U.S. Dist. Ct. Colo. 1979, U.S. Ct. Appeals (10th cir.) 1993, Wyo. 1993, Mont. 1995, U.S. Patent Office, 1994. Surveyor Nebr. Dept. Roads, McCook, 1973; constrn. adminstr. Commonwealth Electric Co., Lincoln, Nebr., 1974; cons. engr. Commonwealth Electric Co., Lincoln, 1975; instr. U. Nebr., Lincoln, 1974-75; law clk. Nebr. Atty.-Gen., Lincoln, 1976-77; assoc. Holme Robert & Owen, LLP, Denver, 1978-83; ptnr. Holme Robert & Owen, Denver, 1984—. Editor-in-chief Nebr. Law Rev., 1977-78, exec. editor, 1976-77; contbr. articles to profl. jours. Sec., bd. dirs. Girls Club Denver, 1984-90, Girls Inc. of Metro Denver, 1992-94; trustee Rocky Mountain Minn. Law Found. Mem. ABA, Colo. Bar Assn., Mont. Bar Assn., Nebr. Bar Assn., Wyo. Bar Assn., S.E. Law Club (pres. 1990-91), Meridian Golf Club, Tau Beta Pi, Sigma Tau (pres.), Eta Kappa Nu. Home: 8125 S Glencoe Ct Littleton CO 80122-3876 Office: Holme Roberts & Owen LLP 1700 Lincoln St Ste 4100 Denver CO 80203-4541*

HENDRIX, RONALD WAYNE, physician, radiologist; b. St. Louis, June 4, 1943; s. Arthur W. and Lida (Martin) H.; m. Miriam Jensen, June 14, 1969. AB, Wash. U., St. Louis, 1965, MD, 1969. Diplomate Am. Bd. Nuclear Medicine, Am. Bd. Radiology. Intern Wash. U., Barnes Hosp., St. Louis, 1969-70; resident U. Chgo., 1970-73, fellow in nuclear medicine, 1973-74; staff radiologist Symmes Hosp., Arlington, Mass., 1976-77; asst. prof. radiology Northwestern U. Med. Sch., Chgo., 1977-84, assoc. prof. radiology, 1984—; attending physician Northwestern Meml. Hosp., Chgo., 1977—, chief, musculoskeletal radiology, 1977—; dir. radiology Rehab. Inst. of Chgo., 1986—. Contbr. articles to profl. jours.; contbg. author to several books. Pres. LaSalle St. Ch., 1982-84, treas., 1984-86, chmn. fin. com., 1986-92. Lt. comdr. USN, 1974-76. Mem. Radiol. Soc. of N.Am., Am. Roentgen Ray Soc., Assn. of U. Radiologists, Am. Coll. Radiology, Internat. Skeletal Soc. Office: Northwestern Meml Hosp 710 N Fairbanks Ct Chicago IL 60611-3013

HENDRIX, SHERMAN SAMUEL, biology educator, researcher; b. Bridgeport, Conn., June 1, 1939; s. Claude Smith and Olga (Kovachik) H.; m. Carol Ann Seibel, June 10, 1961; children: Marc, Robin. BA, Gettysburg Coll., 1961; MS, Fla. State U., 1964; PhD, U. Md., 1972. Instr. biology Gettysburg (Pa.) Coll., 1964-70, asst. prof., 1970-77, assoc. prof., 1977-90, prof., 1990—, chmn. dept., 1985-90, 97—. Contbr. articles to Jour. Parasitology, Zeitschrift für Parasitenkunde, Proc. Helminthological Soc. Washington, Jour. Helminthological Soc. Washington, Fisheries Bull. Bd. dirs. United Way Adams County, Gettysburg, 1983-86. Interam. fellow in tropical medicine NIH, 1973. Mem. Am. Soc. Parasitologists, Helminthological Soc. Washington (pres. 1984, editl. bd. 1985-93, editor jours. 1993-98. Anniversary award 1998), Pa. Acad. Sci. (pres. 1990-92, Lifetime Achievement award 1998), Wildlife Diseases Assn., Am. Malacological Union. Lutheran. Achievements include research on aquatic animal parasites. Office: Gettysburg Coll Dept Biology Gettysburg PA 17325

HENDRIX, STEPHEN C., financial executive; b. Phila., Feb. 24, 1941; s. Houston W. and Helen Hendrix; children: Kimberly, Jeffrey, Julie. BA, Tex. Christian U., 1964; M in Internat. Svc., Am. U., 1966; MBA, Ohio State U., 1972. Jr. officer U.S. Dept. State, AID, Washington, 1967-68; mgr. mktg. adminstrn. Amecom divsn. Litton Industries, College Park, Md., 1968-70; mgr. fin. and planning internat. divsn. Anchor Hocking Corp., Lancaster, Ohio, 1970-73; bank rels. mgr. E.I. Dupont de Nemours & Co., Wilmington, Del., 1973-78; corp. treas. mgr. SmithKline Beckman Corp., Phila., 1978-79, asst. treas. domestic, 1979-82, asst. treas. internat., 1982-87, v.p., asst. treas. internat., 1987-89; v.p., treas. SmithKline Beecham Corp. (formerly SmithKline Beckman Corp.), Phila., 1989-91; treas. Armstrong World Industries, Lancaster, Pa., 1993-96; cons. AstraZeneca, Wayne, Pa., 1997—. Contbr. articles to profl. jours. Mem. AIMR, Fin. Execs. Inst., Nat. Assn. Corp. Treas. (bd. dirs.). Office: AstraZeneca 1910 SwedesFord Rd Malvern PA 19355

HENDRIX, SUSAN CLELIA DERRICK, civic worker; b. McClellanville, S.C., Jan. 19, 1920; d. Theodore Elbridge and Susan Regina (Bauknight) Derrick; m. Henry Gardner Hendrix, June 5, 1943; children: Susan Hendrix Redmond, Marilyn Hendrix Shedlock. BA, Columbia Coll., 1941; MA, Furman U., 1961; EdD (hon.) Columbia Coll., 1985. Cert. tchr., S.C. Tchr. Whitmire Pub. Schs., 1941-43, Greenville Pub. Schs., S.C., 1944-46, 58-63, dir. Reading clinic, 1965-68; counselor Greenville Pub. Schs., 1963-65; supr. Greenville County Sch. Dist., S.C., 1965-68, dir. pub. rels., 1968-83; grad. instr. Furman U., 1967-69; cons. Nat. Seminar on Desegregation, 1973. Author: (with James P. Mahaffey) Teaching Secondary Reading, 1966; Communicating With the Community, 1979, History of Robert Morris Class, 1995; editor: Communique, 1968-83; mem. United Meth. Conf. editl. and revision com. Book of Discipline, 1996; contbr. articles to profl. jours. and mags. Trustee Columbia Coll., 1958-70; chmn. Greenville County Rehab. Bd., S.C., 1974-76; vice chmn. bd. Jr. Achievement, Greenville, 1978-79; mem, S.C. Commn. on Women, Columbia, 1979-88, chmn., 1982-88; pres. United Meth. Women, Buncombe St. Ch., Greenville, 1956-57; mem. adminstrv. bd. Buncombe St. Ch., 1968—, bd. trustees, 1980-88, lay del. to S.C. Ann. Conf., 1986—; mem. United Meth. Ch. Southeastern Jurisdictional Coun. on Ministries, 1984-88; chmn. S.C. Conf. Coun. on Ministries United Meth. Ch., 1980-88, del. gen. conf., 1980, 84, 88, 92; mem. S.C. Conf. Commn. Comm., 1995-97; chmn. S.C. Conf. Budgeting Task Force, 1996-97; mem. Columbia Coll. Strategic Planning Com., 1996-97; mem. Bd. Global Ministries United Meth. Ch., 1972-80, mem. commn. study of ministry, 1984-92, mem. gen. ch. coun. ministries, 1988-96, mem. gen. conf. agys. staff and site location com., 1988-96, rschr. missions project, West Africa, 1986, chmn. com. legis., 1992-96, chmn. com. on inter-agency legis, 1992-96, mission agy. site location com., 1993-96, structure com., 1992-96. Recipient Medallion Columbia Coll., 1980, Alumnae Disting. Svc. award Columbia Coll., 1983, Disting. Achievement award Women's History Week, Greenville, 1984, S.C. Woman of Achievement award, 1988. Mem. S.C. PTA (life), Columbia Coll. Alumnae Assn. (life), Democratic Women, S.C. Women in Govt. (bd. dirs. 1985-87), Alpha Delta Kappa (pres. 1970-72, 90-91). Home and Office: 309 Arundel Rd Greenville SC 29615-1303

HENDRIXSON, PETER S., lawyer; b. Wilmington, Del., Apr. 9, 1947; s. Philip Roe and Betty Jane (Schillo) H.; m. Carolyn Hodge Ford, June 14, 1969; children: Julie Elise, Bradley Scott. BA, Northwestern U., 1969; JD magna cum laude, Harvard U., 1972. Bar: Minn. 1973, U.S. Dist. Ct. Minn. 1973, U.S. Supreme Ct. 1978. Law clerk U.S. Ct. Appeals, Boston, 1972-73; assoc., ptnr. trial dept. Dorsey & Whitney, Mpls., 1973—, chair trial dept., 1989-93, chair trial and adminstrv. group, 1994—, mgmt. com., 1994—. Editor, officer Harvard Law Review, 1970-72. Treas. Fraser for Mayor Com., Mpls., 1983-95; bd. govs. Children's Theatre, Mpls., 1987-92; various positions Mayflower Congl. Ch.; bd. dirs. La Creche Early Childhood Ctrs., Mpls., 1990-98, Children's Home Soc., St. Paul, 1990—, Guthrie Theater, 1995—. Mem. Minn State Bar (chair anti-trust law sect. 1992-93), Phi Beta Kappa. Democrat. Congregationalist. Office: Dorsey & Whitney 220 S 6th St Ste 2200 Minneapolis MN 55402-1498

HENDRY, ANDREW DELANEY, lawyer, consumer products company executive; b. N.Y.C., Aug. 9, 1947; s. Andrew Joseph and Virginia (Delaney) H.; 1 child, Robert. AB in Econs., Georgetown U., 1969; JD, NYU, 1972. Bar: N.Y. 1973. Va. 1981, Mich. 1984, Pa. 1987. Assoc. Battle and Fowler, N.Y.C., 1972-79; sr. corp. and fin. atty. Reynolds Metals Co., Richmond, Va., 1979-82; sr. staff counsel Burroughs Corp., Detroit, 1982-83, assoc. gen. coun., 1983-86, dep. gen. counsel, 1986-87; v.p. legal affairs Unisys Corp, Blue Bell, Pa., 1987-88, v.p., gen. counsel, 1988-91; sr. v.p., gen. counsel, sec. Colgate-Palmolive Co., N.Y.C., 1991—. Bd. dirs. Youth Power (formerly Just Say No Internat.), Oakland, Calif., 1994—; dir., chmn., corp. adv. bd. Nat. Legal Aid & Def., Washington, 1992—. With JAGC USAF, 1973. Mem. ABA (corp. gen. counsel, com. chmn. 1996-98, standing com. on substance abuse, com. on corp. laws), Am. Law Inst., Am. Corp. Counsel Assn. (pres. Mich. chpt. 1985, bd. dirs. emeritus N.Y. chpt., chmn. nat. pro bono com. 1985-88), N.Y. Athletic Club. Office: Colgate-Palmolive Co 300 Park Ave New York NY 10022-7499

HENDRY, ARCHIBALD WAGSTAFF, physics educator; b. Darvel, Ayrshire, Scotland, Nov. 18, 1936; came to U.S., 1962; s. William and Maggie (Noble) H.; m. Jeanette Marie Brown, June 20, 1964; children: Diana Marie, Andrew William, Gordon Austin. BSc, Glasgow (Scotland) U., 1958, PhD, 1962. Rsch. assoc. U. Calif., San Diego, 1962-64; sr. sci. officer Rutherford

Lab. Oxford (Eng.) U., 1964-67; rsch. asst. prof. U. Ill., Urbana, 1967-69; asst. prof. Ind. U., Bloomington, 1969-72, assoc. prof., 1972-76, prof. physics, 1976—, assoc. dean for budget, 1985-88. Contbr. articles to sci. jours. Rsch. grantee Dept. Energy, 1970-95; recipient Pres.' award for excellence in tchg., 1993. Mem. AAUP, Am. Assn. Physics Tchrs., Sigma Xi (treas. local chpt.). E-mail: hendry@indiana.edu. Office: Ind U Physics Dept Bloomington IN 47405

HENDRY, ROBERT RYON, lawyer; b. Jacksonville, Fla., Apr. 23, 1936; s. Warren Candler and Evalyn Marguerite (Ryon) H.; children by previous marriage: Lorraine Evalyn, Lynette Comstock, Krista Ryon; m. Janet LaCoste. BA in Polit. Sci., U. Fla., 1958, JD, 1963. Bar: Fla. 1963. Assoc. Harrell, Caro, Middlebrooks & Whiltshire, Pensacola, Fla., 1963-66; assoc. Hewlliwell, Melrose & DeWolf, Orlando, Fla., 1966-67, ptnr., 1967-69; ptnr., pres. Hoffman, Hendry, Parker & Smith and predecessor Hoffman, Hendry & Parker, Orlando, 1969-77, Hoffman, Hendry & Stoner and predecessor, Orlando, 1977-82, Hendry, Stoner, Sims & Sawicki, Orlando, 1982-88, Hendry, Stoner, Townsend Sawicki & Brown, 1988-92, Hendry, Stoner, Sawicki & Brown, 1992—. Author: U.S. Real Estate and the Foreign Investor, 1983; contbr. articles to profl. jours. Mem. Dist. Export Coun., 1977-91, vice chmn., 1981, chair, 1995—, mem. nat. steering com., 1997—; bd. dirs. World Trade Ctr. and predecessor, Orlando, 1979-89, pres., 1980-82, 84; chmn. Fla. Gov.'s Conf. on World Trade, 1983; chmn. Fla. coun. on internat. edn., 1993-96; mem. internat. fin. and mktg. adv. bd. U. Miami Sch. Bus., Fla., 1979-90, Commn. on Internat. Edn., 1986-88; mem. Metro Orlando Internat. Bus. Coun., 1994-96, Metro Orlando Internat. Affairs Commn., 1995—, Fla. Econ. Summit, 1996—; mem. internat. trade and econ. devel. bd. and audit com. Enterprise, Fla., 1997—; chmn. Fla. Trade Grant Review Panel, 1998—. Lt. U.S. Army, 1958-60, capt. Army N.G., 1960-70. Mem. Fla. Coun. Internat. Devel. (bd. dirs. 1972-85, chmn. 1977-79, adv. bd. 1985-95, chmn. emeritus, 1991—, vice chair 1995-96, chair 1996-98), Fla. Bar (bd. cert. internat. lawyer 1999—, vice chmn. internat. law com. 1974-75, chmn. com. 1976-77, mem. exec. coun. internat. law sect. 1982—, original internat. law certification com. 1998—), Fla. Assn. Voluntary Agys. for Caribbean Action (bd. dirs. 1987—, pres. 1989-91, past pres. 1991—), Orange County Bar Assn. (treas. 1971-74), Soc. Internat. Bus. Fellows, Brit.-Am. C. of C. (bd. dirs., sec. 1984-85), Swiss Am. C. of C. (sec. Fla. chpt. 1996—), Univ. Club. Office: Hendry Stoner Sawicki Et Al 200 E Robinson St Ste 500 Orlando FL 32801-1956

HENDRY, TED, umpire; b. Oregon City, Oreg., Aug. 31, 1940. Student, Al Somers Sch., Oreg. State U., Portland. Former umpire Am. Assn., Northwest League, Calif. League, Tex. League; umpire maj. league baseball Am. League, N.Y.C., 1978—; with Umpires Union, Phila. With U.S. Army. Office: Am League 350 Park Ave New York NY 10022 also: Umpires Union 1735 Market St Philadelphia PA 19103

HENELY, GERALDINE JOSEPHINE, medical/surgical nurse; b. Spencer, Iowa, Apr. 12, 1950; d. Gerald Joseph and Rita Clara (Becker) Henely; children: Jillian Christine, Christopher Andrew. Diploma in nursing, St. Joseph Mercy Sch. Nursing, Sioux City, Iowa, 1971; BS in Health, Coll. St. Francis, Joliet, Ill., 1984; BSN, U. Phoenix, 1988; cert., Command & Gen. Staff Coll., 1992; M in health scis., Health Svcs. Adminstrn., 1995. RN, Ariz.; cert. oper. rm. nurse; cert. RN first asst. Operating rm. nurse St. Joseph Hosp., Sioux City, Iowa, 1971-74; operating rm. nurse St. Joseph Hosp., Phoenix, 1974-88, staff nurse cardiovascular operating rm., 1988-96, asst. charge nurse cardiovascular surgery, 1996-97; home health nurse Phoenix, 1997—. Lt. col. Ariz. N.G., 1981. Mem. Assn. Operating Room Nurses (preceptor). Home: 1645 W Weldon Ave Phoenix AZ 85015-5524

HENEMAN, ROBERT LLOYD, management educator; b. Mpls., Jan. 17, 1955; s. Herbert G. Jr. and Jane R. Heneman; m. Renee Brausch, Sept. 9, 1989. BA, Lake Forest Coll., 1977; MA, U. Ill., 1979; PhD, Mich. State U., 1984. Personnel specialist Pacific Gas & Electric Co., San Francisco, 1979-80; assoc. prof. Mgmt. Ohio State U., Columbus, 1984—, dir. grad. programs in labor and human resources. Author: (books) Merit Pay, 1992, Staffing Organizations, 1994. Mem. ch. coun. Holy Trinity Luth. Ch., Columbus. Mem. Acad. of Mgmt. (exec. com. human resource divsn. 1988-93, program chair 1992-93, divsn. chair 1994-95), Am. Compensation Assn. (rsch. com. 1992-93, edn. com. 1993-94, acad. ptnr. network, 1997—, cert. program fac., 1992—), Phi Kappa Phi, Sigma Iota Epsilon, Psi Chi. Home: 4815 Lytfield Dr Dublin OH 43017-2174

HENES, DONNA, celebration artist, ritualist, writer; b. Cleve., Sept. 19, 1945; d. Nathan and Adelaide (Ross) Trugman. Student, Ohio State U., 1963-66; BS, CCNY, 1971, MS in Art Edn., 1972. Prodr. series pub. participatory celebratory events in parks, museums and univs. 100 cities in 9 countries, 1970—; designer Olympic Medalist Tickertape Parade, N.Y.C., 1984; ednl. cons. New Wilderness Foundation, N.Y.C., 1985; judge Jane Addams Peace Assn. Children's Book Award, N.Y.C., 1983-89; ritual cons. Mama Donna's Tea Garden. Author, designer: Dressing Our Wounds in Warm Clothes, 1982, Noting the Process of Noting the Process, 1977, Celestially Auspicious Occasions, 1996; author, performer (CD) Reverence to Her: Part I Mythology, the Matriarchy & Me, 1998; pub., editor quar. Always in Season: Living in Sync with the Cycles; author (with others): Peace: Piece by Piece; editor: Celebration News, 1986-92; internationally syndicated columnist; contbr. numerous articles to profl. jours. Co-founder, pres. STAND (Stand Together Affirmative Neighborhood Devel.), N.Y.C.; composer Chants for Peace/Chance for Peace, Sta. WNYC, first peace message in space, 1982. Fellow Nat. Endowment for Arts, 1982, interarts, 1983, N.Y. Found. for Arts, 1986, 90; grantee N.Y. State Coun. on Arts, N.Y.C. State Bicentennial Commn., Com. for Visual Arts, Money for Women, Beard's Fund, Jerome Found., Ctr. for the Media Arts; recipient Citation award Mayor of N.Y.C. David Dinkins. Mem. Internat. Ctr. for Celebration (bd. dirs., co-founder). Avocations: dancing, travel, reading, walking, swimming.

HENEY, JOSEPH EDWARD, environmental engineer; b. Brockton, Mass., Feb. 22, 1927; s. John J. and Nellie A. (Byrnes) H.; m. Frances McElroy, Feb. 22, 1955; children: Mary, John, Edward, Stephen. BS, Northeastern U., 1952; MS in Sanitary Engring., Harvard U., 1954; DEng (hon.), Northeastern U., 1990. Diplomate Am. Acad. Environ. Engrs. With Camp, Dresser & McKee, Inc., Boston, 1950—, chmn. bd. dirs. emeritus. Trustee, mem. nat. coun. Northeastern U.. Fellow ASCE, Am. Cons. Engrs. Coun.; mem. Boston Soc. Civil Engrs. (hon.), Am. Water Works Assn., New England Water Works Assn., New England Water Environ. Assn., Inter-Am. Assn. San. Engrs. Home: 26 Winthrop Rd Hingham MA 02043-3533 Office: Camp Dresser & McKee Inc 1 Cambridge Ctr Ste 11 Cambridge MA 02142-1603*

HENEY, LYSLE JOSEPH, III, pharmacist; b. Somerville, N.J., Aug. 3, 1955; s. Lysle Joseph Jr. and Arthemise Ann (Wystrach) H.; m. Carol Ann Platz, June 13, 1976; children: Jason Scott, Matthew Ryan, Lisa Kristine. AAS, Middlesex C.C., Edison, N.J., 1977; BS in Pharmacy, Drake U., 1978. Registered pharmacist, Iowa, Mo., Kans., Okla., N.J. Pharmacist May's Drug, Joplin, Mo., 1978-79; pharmacist, mgr. May's Drug, Wichita, 1979-81, Revco Corp., Wichita, 1981, Rite-Aid Corp., Millville, N.J., 1981—. Mem. ch. coun. St. Paul's Luth. Ch., Millville, 1988-91; mem. com. Troop 5, Boy Scouts Am., Millville, 1990—. Mem. APHA, Am. Pharm. Assn. Home: 917 Sassafras St Millville NJ 08332-3366 Office: Rite-Aid Corp PO Box 3165 Harrisburg PA 17105-3165

HENG, DONALD JAMES, JR., lawyer; b. Mpls., July 12, 1944; s. Donald James and Catharine Amelia (Strom) H.; m. Kathleen Ann Bailey, Sept. 2, 1967; 1 child, Francesca Remy. BA cum laude, Yale U., 1967; JD magna cum laude, Minn., 1971. Bar: Calif. 1971, U.S. Dist. Ct. (no. dist.) Calif. 1971, U.S. Ct. Appeals (9th cir.) 1971. Assoc. Brobeck, Phleger & Harrison, San Francisco, 1971-73, ptnr., 1978-90; atty.-adviser Office Internat. Tax Counsel, Dept. Treasury, Washington, 1973-75; pvt. practice law San Francisco, 1990—; lectr., writer on tax-related subjects. Note and comment editor Minn. Law Rev., 1970-71. Co-recipient award for outstanding performance Am. Lawyer Mag., 1981; Fulbright scholar, Italy, 1967-68. Mem. ABA, Calif. Bar Assn., Oakland Mus. Assn. (pres. 1985-87, bd. dirs. 1983-89), Mus. Soc. San Francisco, Fine Arts Mus. (bd. dirs. 1989-90), Order Coif. Republican. Congregationalist. Office: 388 Market St Ste 500 San Francisco CA 94111-5313

HENG, GERALD C. W., lawyer; b. London, Mar. 6, 1941; came to U.S., 1964; s. Chong-Kwai and York-Choo (Eng); m. Eileen B-Y Tang; 1 child, Sharmaine. BS with honors, Harvard U., 1967; LLM in Taxation, Boston U., 1985; LLB, London U., 1973; JD, Suffolk U., 1983. Tchr. Malay and English langs. Ministry of Edn., Malaysia and Singapore, 1959-60; adminstr. hosp. and health Ministry of Health, Malaysia and Singapore, 1960-64; Fulbright fellow, scholar Inst. Internat. Edn., N.Y.C., 1964-69; atty. Heng Assocs., London, 1973-83; ptnr. Heng Assocs., Brookline, Mass., 1983—. Contbr. articles to newspapers including Boston Globe, Singapore Mirror, Boston Mag. and community newspapers. Com. mem. internship program Sch. Theology, Boston U., 1987; founding sponsor Civil Justice Found., 1987—; campaign vol., amb. Elliot L. Richardson for U.S. Senate, Boston, 1984. Mem. ABA, ATLA, Asian-Am. Lawyers Assn., Internat. Assn. Asian Ams. (pres. Boston chpt. 1981—), Boston Bar Assn. (specialist on internat. trade and human rights 1987—, gen. law practice and coms.), Mass. Acad. Trial Attys. Avocations: travel, hiking, horseback riding, sailing, golf. E-mail: gcwebheng@gis.net. Home and Office: 19 Lillian Rd Framingham MA 01701-4820

HENG, SIANG GEK, communications executive; b. Singapore, Singapore, Dec. 4, 1960; came to U.S., 1984.; m. G.J. Sturgis, 1991. BSEE with honors, Nat. U. Singapore, 1983; MSEE in Computer Engring., U. So. Calif., 1985; MS in Engring. Mgmt., Nat. Technol. U., 1993. Rsch. engr. Nat. Univ. Singapore, 1983-84; sys. mgr. LimCom Corp., L.A., 1985-87; fin. planner N.Y. Life Ins. Co., L.A., 1987-88; mem. tech. staff AT&T Bell Laboratories, Holmdel, N.J., 1988-96; sr. mem. tech. staff AT&T, N.J., 1996—; freelance computer and comm. cons., N.J., 1987-94. Contbr. articles to profl. jours.; patentee in field. Avocations: step aerobics, swimming, weightlifting, reading, music. Office: AT&T Rm C5-2C03 200 Laurel Ave S Middletown NJ 07748

HENG, STANLEY MARK, national guard officer; b. Nebraska City, Nebr., Nov. 4, 1937; s. Robert Joseph Sr. and Margaret Ann (Volkmer) H.; m. Sharon E. Barrett, Oct. 10, 1959; children: Mark, Nick, Lisa. Student, Command and Gen. Staff Coll., 1969, Nat. Def. U., 1979; BA, Doane Coll., 1987. Commd. adj. Nebr. N.G., 1966, advanced through grade to maj. gen., 1966-87; adj. Nebr. Mil. Dept., Lincoln, 1966-77, adminstrv. asst., 1978-86; adj. gen., dir. emergency mgmt. State of Nebr., Lincoln, 1987—. Mem. N.G. Assn. U.S., N.G. Assn. Nebr. (exec. sec. 1967-71, Svc. award 1970), Adj. Gens. Assn., Am. Legion. Democrat. Mem. United Ch. of Christ. Avocations: softball, basketball, running. Office: Mil Dept 1300 Military Rd Lincoln NE 68508-1051

HENGSTLER, GARY ARDELL, publisher, editor, lawyer; b. Wapakoneta, Ohio, Mar. 23, 1947; s. Luther C. and N. Delphine (Sims) H.; m. Linda K. Spreen, Mar. 8, 1969 (div. Aug. 1986); children: Dylan A., Joel S.; m. Laura M. Williams, Dec. 15, 1986. BS, Ball State U., 1969; JD, Cleve. State U., 1983. Bar: Ohio 1984, U.S. Dist. Ct. (no. dist.) Ohio 1984. Assoc. Blaszak, Schilling, Coey & Bennett, Elyria, Ohio, 1984-85; editor The Tex. Lawyer, Austin, 1985-86; news editor ABA Jour., Chgo., 1986-89, editor, pub., 1989—. Home: 834 N Arlington Hts Rd Arlington Heights IL 60004-5666 Office: ABA Jour 750 N Lake Shore Dr Chicago IL 60611-4403

HENICK, HENRY CHRISTOPHER, lobbyist; b. May 12, 1956. Student, U. Miss., 1974-78; BA, Georgetown U., 1993. Exec. dir. Reagan-Bush '84, Jackson, Miss., 1984; so. polit. dir. Rep. Nat. Com., Washington, 1987-91; exec. dir. Rep. Govs. Assn., Washington, 1991-95; ptnr. Barbour Griffith & Rogers, Washington, 1995—. Fellow Harvard U. Inst. Politics, 1995. Office: Barbour Griffith & Rogers 10th Fl 23755 Pennsylvania Ave NW Washington DC 20004-2404

HENIG, ROBIN MARANTZ, journalist; b. Bklyn., Oct. 3, 1953; d. Sidney S. and Clare (Stern) Marantz; m. Jeffrey R. Henig, June 17, 1973; children: Jessica, Samantha. BA, Cornell U., Ithaca, N.Y., 1973; MSJ, Northwestern U., Evanston, Ill., 1974. Assoc. editor Comprehensive Therapy Mag., Chgo., 1974-75; asst. editor, writer The New Physician Mag., Chgo., 1975-77; asst. mng. editor The Blue Sheet, Washington, 1977-78; features and news editor Bio Science Mag., Washington, 1978-80; freelance writer Takoma Park, Md., 1980—. Author: How A Woman Ages, 1985, The Myth of Senility, 1988, Being Adopted, 1993, A Dancing Matrix, 1994, The People's Health, 1997. Science Writer fellow Marine Biol. Lab., 1990. Mem. Am. Soc. Journalists and Authors (pres. D.C. chpt. 1992-94, June Roth award for Med. Writing 1993, 94, Author of the Yr. 1994), Nat. Assn. Sci. Writers (bd. dirs. 1999—), The Authors Guild, D.C. Sci. Writers Assn. (bd. dirs. 1996-97). Jewish. Avocations: reading, tap dancing.

HENIG, SUZANNE, retired educator, writer, editor; b. N.Y.C., Jan. 12, 1936; d. Samuel G. and Gicia (Gottesdiener) Henig. BA, NYU, 1957, MA, 1961, PhD, 1968. V.p. Am. Heritage Soc., Washington, 1975-80; editor Va. Woolf Quar., San Diego, 1976-79; pres. India Expo, San Diego, 1976-81; mng. dir. Aeolian Press, San Diego, 1976—; pres. Genesis Prodns. of Hollywood, San Diego, 1990—. Editor Internat. Jour. Medicine, 1996; contbr. articles to profl. jours. V.p. N.Y. Young Reps., N.Y.C., 1953-54. Recipient Thomas Wolfe award for poetry NYU, 1957; grantee ACLS, Leopold Schepp Found., Am. Philos. Soc. Home: 4082 Carmel Springs Way San Diego CA 92130-2275

HENIGSON, ANN PEARL, freelance writer, songwriter, lyricist; b. N.Y.C., Jan. 20, 1946; d. Leo and Lillian Shires; m. David Henigson, Oct. 23, 1988 (dec. July 1993); stepchildren: Helaine, Kenneth, Keith. Student, U. Miami, Fla., 1964-68, Miami-Dade Jr. Coll. Author: (song/poem) American Flag, 1986, pub. in Congressional Record, 1990, Dreamin' Reality, 1986, Parents, 1986, Miss Liberty, 1986, Eternal Love, 1986, (Looking at You) Face of Love, 1986, Book Without a Cover, 1986, 8 Days of Hanukkah, 1986, Songwriter, 1986, Hanukkah Sing Along, 1988, Oh Baby, Oh Baby, 1991, Hold Me Tight, 1995, Democracy, Democracy, (Freedom, Freedom) 1995, and numerous others; (cartoons/drawings) Ducks/Birds, 1988. Activist, lobbyist; candidate bd. govs. State of Fla., (non-attorney) 1993; 1st female usherette Temple Israel of Greater Miami High Holy Day Svcs.; mem. Civic League Miami Beach, 1976-89; patron Temple Emanu-El Cultural Series, 1989-90; mem. Friends of Bass Mus., 1991; del. nat. Dem. party, 1970s. Mem. ASCAP, Soc. Profl. Journalists, Quill and Scroll, Toastmasters Internat. (named competent toastmaster), Tiger Bay Club, 1974-91, Sigma Delta Chi. Avocations: football, baseball, stamp collecting, travel, designing jewelry.

HENIKOFF, LEO M., JR., academic administrator, medical educator; b. Chgo., May 9, 1939; m. Carole E. Andersen; children from previous marriage: Leo M. III, Jamie Sue. MD with highest honors, U. Ill., Chgo., 1963. Diplomate Am. Bd. Pediat., Am. Bd. Pediat. Cardiology. Intern Presbyn.-St. Luke's Hosp., Chgo., 1963-64, resident, 1964-66, fellow in pediatric cardiology, 1968-69; clin. instr. U. Ill. Coll. Medicine, Chgo., 1964-66; clin. instr. pediatrics Georgetown U. Med. Sch., Washington, 1966-68, clin. asst. prof., 1968; asst. prof. U. Ill. Coll. Medicine, Chgo., 1968-71; asst. prof. pediat. Rush Med. Coll., Chgo., 1971-74, assoc. prof., 1974-79, asst. dean admissions, 1971-74, assoc. dean student affairs, 1974-76, assoc. dean med. scis. and svcs., 1976-79, acting dean v.p. med. affairs, 1976-78, prof. pediatrics, prof. medicine, 1984—; v.p. inter-instl. affairs Rush-Presbyn.-St. Luke's Med. Ctr., Chgo., 1978-79, pres., 1984—; pres., CEO; trustee Rush-Presbyn.-St. Luke's Med. Ctr., Chgo., 1984—; dean and v.p. med. affairs Temple U. Sch. Medicine, Phila., 1979-84, prof. pediat. and medicine, 1979-84; pres. Rush U., Chgo., 1984—; adj. attending Presbyn.-St. Luke's Hosp., 1969, asst., 1970-72, assoc., 1973-76, sr. attending, 1977-79, 84—; staff Temple U. Hosp., 1979-84; assoc. staff St. Christopher's Hosp. for Children, 1979-84; mem. Ill. Coun. of Deans, 1977-79; vice chmn. Chgo. Tech. Pk., 1984-85, 86-87, chmn., 1985-86, 87-88; chmn. bd. dirs. Mid-Am. Health Programs, Inc., 1985—; bd. dirs. Harris Trust and Savs. Bank, Harris Bankcorp. Inc.; chmn. bd. dirs. Rush North Shore Health Svcs., 1988—, Rush/Copley Health Care Sys. Inc., 1988—. Contbr. chpts. to books, articles to profl. jours. Bd. dirs. Fishbein Found., 1975-79, Chgo. Regional Blood Program, 1977-79, Sch. Dist. 69, 1974-75, Johnston R. Bowman Health Ctr. for Elderly, 1984—; mem. bd. mgrs. St. Christopher's Hosp. for Children, 1979-84; mem. bd. govs. Temple U. Hosp., 1979-84, Heart Assn. S.E. Pa., 1979-84; trustee Episc. Hosp., 1983-84, Otho S.A. Sprague Meml. Inst., 1984—; mem. adv. bd. Univ. Village Assn., 1984—; mem. exec. com. Gov.'s Build Ill. Com., 1985—. Lt. comdr. USPHS, 1964-68, Res. 1968—. Recipient Roche Med. award, 1962, Mosby award, 1963, Raymond B. Allen Instructorship award U. Ill. Coll. Medicine, 1966, also Med. Alumni award, 1988, Phoenix award Rush Med. Coll., 1977. Fellow Am. Acad. Pediat., Inst. Medicine Chgo., Coll. Physicians Phila., Am. Coll. Physicians Execs.; mem. Assn. Am. Med. Colls. (chmn. nominating com. 1980, mem. coun. deans 1977-84, mem. audit com. 1984), Coun. Tchg. Hosps. (adminstrv. bd. 1987-90), Pa. Med. Sch. Deans Com., AMA (mem. coun. on ethical and jud. affairs 1984-88), Pa. Med. Soc., Philadelphia County Med. Soc., Assn. Acad. Health Ctrs. (bd. dirs. 1988-94, chmn.-elect 1991-92, chmn. 1992-93), Alpha Omega Alpha (chmn. nat. nominating com. 1981-90, nat. dir. 1979-90, pres. 1989-90), Omega Beta Pi, Phi Eta Sigma, Phi Kappa Phi. Office: Rush-Presbyn-St Luke's Med Ctr 1653 W Congress Pkwy Chicago IL 60612-3833

HENINGER, GEORGE ROBERT, psychiatry educator, researcher; b. L.A., Nov. 15, 1934; s. Owen P. and Rachel (Cannon) H.; m. Julie Hawkes, June 27, 1957; children: Steven, Catharine, Karen, Brian. BS, U. Utah, 1957, MD, 1960. Diplomate Am. Bd. Psychiatry and Neurology. Intern Boston City Hosp., 1960-61; resident in psychiatry Mass. Mental Health Ctr., 1961-63, chief resident, 1963-64; clin. assoc., clin. neuropharmacology rsch. ctr. St. Elizabeth's Hosp. NIMH, Washington, 1964-65; program specialist, office of dir. NIMH, Bethesda, Md., 1965-66; asst. prof. psychiatry, assoc. chief rsch. ward Yale U., New Haven, 1966-71, assoc. prof., 1971-76, chief rsch. ward, 1971-78, prof. clin. psychiatry, 1976-78, prof. psychiatry, dir. Abraham Ribicoff Rsch. Facilities, 1978-93, assoc. chmn. rsch. dept. psychiatry, 1988-93, dir. lab. clin. and molecular neurobiology, 1993—; cons. NIMH, 1975-86, 88-94, NIH, 1987, McGill U., 1989, VA, 1990-94, Nat. Rsch. Coun. Can., 1991-93, Nat. Inst. Aging, 1992-93, Wellcome Trust, 1992-94, Pfizer Inc., Merck, Sharp & Dohme, Inc., The Upjohn Co., Hoffman La Roche, Inc., Burroughs Wellcome Co., Bristol-Meyers Co., Squibb Corp., Kali DuPhar, Inc.; bd. sci. advisors, Neurogen Corp. REviewer manuscripts Archives Gen. Psychiatry, Am. Jour. Psychiatry, Psychiatry Rsch., Biol. Psychiatry, Jour. Affective Disorders, Jour. Clin. Psychopharmacology, Life Scis., Neurochemistry Internat., Psychiatry, Schizophrenia Bull., Psychoneuroendocrinology, Jour. AMA. Sr. asst. surgeon USPHS, 1964-66. Recipient Rsch. Sci. Devel. award Type II, NIMH, 1971, 1st prize Anna Monika Found., 1995; grantee NIMH, 1971, 74, 77, 82, 85, 89, 91. Fellow Am. Coll. Neuropsychopharmacology, Am. Psychiat. Assn.; mem. AAAS, Am. Psychopath. Assn., Soc. Neurosci., Soc. Biol. Psychiatry, Psychiat. Rsch. Soc., N.Y. Acad. Scis., Conn. Psychiat. Soc., Sigma Xi, Phi Kappa Phi, Alpha Omega Alpha. Avocation: running. Office: Yale U 34 Park St New Haven CT 06511

HENINGER, SIMEON KAHN, JR., English language educator; b. Monroe, La., Oct. 27, 1922; s. Simeon Kahn and Elsye (Lieber) H.; m. Irene Callen, July 16, 1957; children—Dale Callen, Kathryn Leigh, Philip Ward, Polly Elizabeth, Simeon Kahn III; m. Dorothy Cooper Langston, May 30, 1971. B.S., Tulane U., 1944, B.A., 1947, M.A., 1949; B.Litt. (Fulbright scholar), Oxford (Eng.) U., 1952; Ph.D., Johns Hopkins U., 1955. Instr. Duke U., Durham, N.C., 1955-57, asst. prof., 1957-62, assoc. prof., 1962-65, prof., 1965-67; prof. English U. Wis.-Madison, 1967-71; chmn. dept. U. Wis., Madison, 1968-70; prof. English U. B.C., Vancouver, Can., 1971-82; disting. prof. English and comparative lit. U. N.C., Chapel Hill, 1982—. Author: A Handbook of Renaissance Meteorology, 1960, Touches of Sweet Harmony, 1974, The Cosmographical Glass, 1977, Sidney and Spenser: The Poet as Maker, 1989, Proportion Poetical: The Subtext of form in the English Renaissance, 1994; editor: Thomas Watson, The Hekatompathia, 1964, Edmund Spenser, Poetry, 1970, Edmund Spenser, Shepheardes Calender, 1979, Kalendar of Sheepehards, 1979, Framing Fact and Fiction: Perspective in Early Modern England, 1992; asst. editor Modern Language Notes, 1953-55; mem. editorial bd. Duquesne Studies in Lang. and Lit., 1976-93, Renaissance and Reformation, 1976-93, Spenser Studies, 1977-93, Studies in English Lit., 1978-93, John Donne Jour., 1982-93, Huntington Libr. Quar., 1982-86, Spenser Newsletter, 1986-92, Studies in Philology, 1987-93, ANQ: A Quarterly Jour., 1988-93; contbr. articles to profl. jours. Exec. sec.-treas. Southeastern Renaissance Conf., 1958-67; mem. Nat. Shakespeare Anniversary Com., 1963-64; mem. ctrl. exec. com. Folger Inst. Renaissance and 18th Century Studies, 1982-92. Capt. USAAF, 1943-46. Folger Library fellow, 1961, Guggenheim fellow, 1962-63, Southeastern Inst. Medieval and Renaissance Studies fellow, 1967, Huntington Library fellow, 1970-71, 81, Killam Sr. fellow, 1975-76, Folger Inst. fellow, 1984, Ariz. Ctr. for Medieval and Renaissance Studies fellow, 1990. Mem. MLA, ACLU, Renaissance Soc. Am. (adv. coun. 1958-68, 75-80), Spenser Soc. (adv. coun. 1977-80, 86-90, pres. 1988-89), Milton Soc. (adv. coun. 1980-83), Medieval Acad. Am., Phi Beta Kappa. Home: 505 Lakeshore Ln Chapel Hill NC 27514-1731

HENINGTON, C. DAYLE, retired economist; b. Bartlett, Tex., Mar. 2, 1931; s; s. Clarence William and Ora (Robbins) H.; m. Julianne, Mar. 12, 1983. BA in Econs., U. Nebr., 194. Enlisted USAF, 1951, commd. 1st lt., 1952, advanced through grades to maj., 1971, ret., 1971; adminstrv. asst. Congressman W.R. Poage, Washington, 1971-77; sr. v.p. Chgo. Mercantile Exch., 1977-92; cons. San Antonio, Tex., 1992—. Democrat. Unitarian. Home: 10955 Wurzbach Rd Apt 104 San Antonio TX 78230-2537

HENINGTON, DAVID MEAD, library director; b. El Dorado, Ark., Aug. 16, 1929; s. Bud Henry and Lucile Check (Scranton) H.; m. Barbara Jean Gibson, June 2, 1956; children—Mark David, Gibson Mead, Paul Billins. BA, U. Houston, 1951; MS in L.S., Columbia U., 1956. Young adult libr. Bklyn. Pub. Libr., 1956-58; head lit. and history dept. Dallas Pub. Libr., 1958, asst. dir., 1962-67; dir. Waco (Tex.) Pub. Libr., 1958-62, Houston Pub. Libr., 1967-95. Served with USAF, 1951-55. Council on Library Resources fellow, 1970-71; recipient Liberty Bell award Houston Bar Assn., 1976. Mem. ALA, AIA (hon. mem. Tex. chpt.), Am. Mgmt. Assn., Tex. Libr. Assn. (Libr. of Yr. 1976, Disting. Svc. award 1993), Philos. Soc. Methodist. Home: 6225 San Felipe St Houston TX 77057-2809

HENISCH, HEINZ KURT, retired physics educator; b. Neudek, Czechoslovakia, Apr. 21, 1922; came to U.S., 1963; s. Leo and Fanny (Soicher) H.; m. Bridget Ann Wilsher, Feb. 6, 1960. BSc, U. Reading, Eng., 1942, PhD, 1949, DSc, 1979. Lectr. U. Reading, 1948-63; prof. physics Pa. State U., University Park, 1963-93, prof. history of photography, 1979-93, prof. emeritus, 1993—. Author 13 books in his fields; founder, editor Materials Rsch. Bull., 1966-94, History of Photography, 1977-90; contbr. over 165 articles to profl. jours. Fellow Inst. for Arts and Humanistic Studies, Am. Phys. Soc., Royal Photography Soc., Am. Photographic History Soc. Avocations: writing, piano. Home: 346 Hillcrest Ave State College PA 16803-3416

HENKE, MICHAEL JOHN, lawyer, educator; b. Evansville, Ind., Aug. 3, 1940; s. Emerson Overbeck and Beatrice Alice (Arney) H.; m. Leni Edith Anderson, Mar. 20, 1966; children: Blake, Paige, Britt. BA summa cum laude, Baylor U., 1962, LLB, 1965; LLM, NYU, 1966. Bar: Tex. 1965, D.C. 1967. Assoc. Covington & Burling, Washington, 1966-73; assoc. Vinson & Elkins, Washington, 1974-76, ptnr., 1976—; adj. prof. U. Va. Law Sch., 1988-94, 96—; chmn. pro bono adv. com. Legal Aid Soc., D.C., 1990-96, trustee, 1992—, chmn. ways & means com., 1997—; mem. Washington adv. coun. Baylor Washington Program, 1989-92; mem. sesquicentennial coun. of 150 Baylor U., 1993-95. Author: (with others) Petroleum Regulation Handbook, 1980, Natural Gas Yearbook, 1995; mem. editl. adv. bd. Nat. Gas Mag., 1992-97, Best Lawyers in America, 1989—, Best Lawyers in Washington, 1997, Worlds Leading Competition and Antitrust Lawyers, 1997—, World's Leading Litigation Lawyers, 1997—; contbr. articles to profl. jours. Founder, chmn. Old Presbyn. Meeting House Day Care Ctr., Alexandria, Va., 1970-74. Mem. ABA (chmn. energy antitrust subcom. litigation sect. 1987-88, vice chmn. energy litigation com. 1988-89, chmn. 1989-92, chmn. ann. fall meeting 1993, divsn. dir. 1993-95, co-chmn. audiotaping & videotaping com. 1995-96, co-chmn. ins. coverage litigation com. 1996-98, coun. mem. 1998—), D.C. Bar Assn., Tex. Bar Assn., Coll. State Bar Tex., Baylor U. Alumni Assn. (bd. dirs. 1994-98), Met. Club, Belle Haven Country Club, Farmington Country Club (Charlottesville). Democrat. Avocations: skiing, tennis, backpacking. Home: 310 Charles Alexander Ct Alexandria VA 22301-1500 Office: Vinson & Elkins 1455 Pennsylvania Ave NW Fl 7 Washington DC 20004-1013

HENKE, SHAUNA NICOLE, police dispatcher, small business owner; b. San Bernardino, Calif., Oct. 25, 1966; d. Gary Duane and Pamela Denyne (Duke) H. BA, U. San Francisco, 1988. Cert. police officer std. and tng. dispatcher, Calif.; internat. telecommunicator instr. tng. cert. Assn. Pub. Safety Comm. Ofcls. Pub. rels. dir. Sta. KUSF Radio, San Francisco, 1986; theater and recreational asst. Hamilton Field Recreation, Novato, Calif., 1986-89; morning asst., newswriter Sta. KTID Radio, San Rafael, Calif., 1987-88; dispatcher Warren Security, San Rafael, Calif., 1988-89; pub. safety dispatcher Twin Cities Police Dept., Larkspur/Corte Madera, Calif., 1989-94; family svc. worker Head Start, Bogalusa, La., 1994-95; police dispatcher Mandeville (La.) Police Dept., 1995-96, Bogalusa (La.) Police Dept., 1996—; co-owner Time After Time Designs. Mem. St. Matthew's Episcopal Churchwomen. Mem. Assn. Pub. Safety Officials Internat., Marin Emergency Dispatchers Assn. (hon. bd. dirs.), S.E. La. Dispatcher's Assn. (press info. officer Washington parish), La. Indian Heritage Assn. Office: Bogalusa Police Dept 202 Arkansas Ave Bogalusa LA 70427-3810

HENKEL, CYNTHIA LEIGH, elementary education educator; b. Cape Girardeau, Mo., July 15, 1960; d. Donald Gene and Doris Jo (Keaton) Lewis; m. Robert Revere Henkel, Mar. 21, 1987. BS in Edn., U. Mo., 1982; postgrad., NOVA. Cert. elem. tchr., Mo., N.Mex., Tex. Elem. tchr. Eldon (Mo.) Sch. Dist., 1982-84, Clark County Schs., Las Vegas, Nev., 1986-89; tchr. kindergarten and elem. grades, Pyongtaek (Republic of Korea) Am. Elem. Sch., 1989-90; tchr. Osan Am. Elem. Sch., Republic of Korea, 1990-91; elem. tchr. Alamogordo, N.Mex., 1995-98, N.E. Ind. Sch. Dist., San Antonio, 1998—; tchr. summer sch. Muckleshoot Indian Reservation, Auburn, Wash., 1985.

HENKEL, KATHRYN GUNDY, lawyer; b. West Columbia, Tex., Oct. 16, 1952; d. Louis Ory Jr. and Patricia Dolores (Fields) Gundy. BA cum laude, Rice U., 1973; JD cum laude, Harvard U., 1976. Bar: Tex. 1976, U.S. Dist. Ct. (no. dist.) Tex. 1982, U.S. Ct. Appeals (5th cir.) 1994, U.S. Tax Ct. 1981, U.S. Supreme Ct. 1983; bd. cert. estate planning and probate law, Tex. Bd. Legal Specialization. Ptnr. Hughes & Luce, L.L.P., Dallas, 1982—. Author: Estate Planning and Wealth Preservation: Strategies and Solutions, 1997; mem. editl. bd. Estate Planning mag. Mem. adv. coun. Cmtys. Found. Tex. Inc., 1982—; mem. planned giving com. Dallas Symphony Orch., 1987—; mem. planned giving adv. com. Children's Med. Ctr., Dallas; bd. dirs., chmn. bd. advisors to found. com. Dallas Opera. Fellow Am. Coll. Trust and Estate Counsel; mem. ABA (vice chair sect. real property, probate and trusts com. on generation-skipping transfers 1992-95, chair sect. of taxation com. on estate and gift taxes 1993-95, coun. dir. sect. taxation 1996-99, co-chair sect. real property, probate and trust law estate planning study com. on law reform), State Bar Tex. (chair sect. taxation 1992-93), Dallas Bar Assn. (past chair sect. taxation), Tex. Bar Found. Roman Catholic. Avocations: reading, travel. Home: 1717 Main St Ste 2800 Dallas TX 75201-7342 Office: Hughes & Luce LLP 1717 Main St Ste 2800 Dallas TX 75201-4685

HENKEL, WILLIAM, financial services executive; b. Mineola, N.Y., June 19, 1941; s. William and Joan (Oakes) H.; m. Joan Henkel (div.); children: Jon, Jeffrey, Jennifer, James, Jay; m. Alice O'Brien; 1 child, Jessica. BS, St. Lawrence U., 1963. Account exec. Merrill Lynch, N.Y.C., 1965-70, various staff, mgmt. and mktg. positions, 1977-82; v.p. quality assurance and policy planning pvt. client group Merrill Lynch, Plainsboro, N.J., 1987-95, 1st v.p., sr. dir. market planning group, 1995—; presdl. advance rep. White House, Washington, 1970-72, dir. presdl. advance, 1972-75, 84-86, spl. asst. to pres., 1982-84, dep. asst. to pres., 1984-86, asst. to pres., 1986-87; dep. asst. sec. Dept. Commerce, Washington, 1975-77. Republican. Office: Merrill Lynch Pvt Client Group PO Box 9014 Princeton NJ 08543-9014

HENKEN, BERNARD SAMUEL, clinical psychologist, speech pathologist; b. Everett, Mass., May 30, 1919; s. Issac Edward and Sarah B. (Shatzman) H.; m. Charlotte Popovsky, Dec. 20, 1953; children: Karen Beth, Donna Michele. *His talented wife Charlotte Henken gave birth to two daughters. The oldest daughter is Karen Beth Henken. She has an MBA from Stanford Business School and after graduating from Bowdoin College was on a Fulbright Scholarship in Japan for a year. Her husband Stephen Kahn is was a few years ago vice-president of Borland Industry. The youngest daughter is Donna Michele Henken, who is an assistant district attorney in the Manhattan, New York office and has had extensive experience as a prosecuting attorney. Her husband Eric Bernstein is an active attorney in the United States attorney's office in New York State. Karen has 2 children, Rachel and Joshua; Donna has two children, Margo and Jeremy.* Student, Boston Coll., 1938-41; BS, Harvard U., 1947; MS, Purdue U., 1950; D. Sci. in Psychology, Calvin Coolidge Coll., 1955. Lic. psychologist, cert. sch. psychologist, cert. rehab. counselor, lic. speech pathologist, Mass.; diplomate Am. Assn. Clin. Counselors. Psychologist Carney Hosp., Boston, 1950-51; dir. speech pathology, psychologist Audiology Ctr., Lynn, Mass., 1951-56; psychologist, chief clin. counseling svcs. Brusch Med. Ctr., Cambridge, Mass., 1956-80; speech pathologist Mass. Gen. Hosp., Boston, 1951-52; speech pathologist, sch. psychologist Everett Pub. Schs., 1955-85; psychologist Rescue Inc., 1959-71, v.p., 1972-74; psychologist, clin. counselor North Shore Children's Hosp., Salem, Mass., 1966-74; psychologist Medford (Mass.) Pediatric Assocs., 1974-94; prof. psychology Calvin Collidge Coll., Boston, 1958-69; lectr. psychology Lawrence Meml. Hosp., Medford, Mass., 1975-77, univ. extension courses Harvard U., 1960-68; psychologist Alfano Med. Inst., Melrose, Mass., 1956-64; guest lectr. Duke U. Med. Ctr., 1965, 72; co-chair symposium on clin. counseling and medicine Tufts U., 1974. Contbr. articles to profl. jours.; creator Henken Operator Safety Evaluation Technique; editor Clin. Counseling Bulletin, 1970-84. Cpl. M.C. U.S. Army, 1942-45, PTO. With MC U.S. Army, 1942-45. Cpl. M.C., U.S. Army, 1943-45, PTO. Mem. APA (charter mem. divsn. of psychotherapy), Am. Coll. Counselors (cert. forensic psychology), Nat. Assn. Sch. Psychologist Assn. (nat. cert. in sch. psychology), Am. Coll. Counselors, Mass. Speech and Hearing Assn. (treas. 1957-59), Am. Assn. Clin. Counselors (pres. 1959-63), Mass. Sch. Psychologists Assn. (pres. 1972-74). Republican. Jewish. Avocations: sports, music. Home and Office: 118 Waverly Ave Melrose MA 02176-4217

HENKIN, JOSHUA HERBERT, novelist, educator; b. N.Y.C., Mar. 7, 1964; s. Louis and Alice (Hartman) H. BA, Harvard Coll., 1987; MFA, U. Mich., 1993. Asst. editor Tikkun Mag., 1987-89; lectr. creative writing U. Mich., Ann Arbor, 1992-93, tchr. ind. fiction writing workshops, 1995—; adj. prof. creative writing U. Mich., 1994-95. Author: (novel) Swimming Across the Hudson, 1997, (short fiction) Getting By, 1992, Spitting Image, 1992 (nominated Pushcart prize 1992), Postcards, 1993, Juggling, 1993, Fuki's Blues, 1993, Congregants, 1993, The Fastest Animal in the World, 1994, What My Father Looked Like, 1995. Witness, 1995; contbr. essays and revs. Roy W. Cowden Meml. fellow creative writing, 1992, James fellow novel-in-progress, 1996; recipient Thomas Hoopes Prize, 1987, Fiction prize Playboy, 1992, Syndicated Fiction award PEN, 1992, Avery & Julie Hopwood award major essay, 1992, award major short fiction, 1992, award major novel, 1993. Democrat. Jewish. Home and Office: 809 E Kingsley St Apt 1 Ann Arbor MI 48104-1274

HENKIN, LEON ALBERT, mathematician, educator; b. Bklyn., Apr. 19, 1921; s. Ascher and Rose (Goldberg) H.; m. Ginette Potvin, Sept. 8, 1950; children: Paul Jacques, Julian David. AB, Columbia U., 1941; MA, Princeton U., 1942, PhD, 1947; DS (hon.), U. Ill., Chgo., 1995. Mathematician, Manhattan Dist. Project, 1942-46; Henry B. Fine instr., Frank Jewett postdoctoral fellow Princeton, 1947-49; from asst. prof. to asso. prof. math. U. So. Calif., 1949-53; faculty U. Calif.-Berkeley, 1953-91, prof. math., 1958-91, prof. emeritus, 1991—, chmn. dept., 1966-68, 83-85; vis. prof. Dartmouth Coll., 1960-61; Fulbright rsch. scholar, Amsterdam, The Netherlands, 1954-55, Technion, Haifa, Israel, spring 1979; Guggenheim fellow, mem. Inst. Advanced Study, Princeton, 1961-62; vis. fellow All Souls Coll., Oxford (Eng.) U., 1968-69; vis. scholar U. Colo., 1975, U. de Paris VII, 1987; Disting. vis. prof. Mills Coll., 1990-95. Author: La Structure Algebrique des theories Mathématique, 1955, (with others) Retracing Elementary Mathematics, 1962, Cylindric Algebras, Part I, 1971, Part II, 1985, Cylindric Set Algebras, 1981 also articles. Mem. U.S. Commn. on Math. Instrn., 1978-83, 88—, chmn., 1981-82. Fellow AAAS (coun. del. for math. sect.); mem. Nat. Coun. Tchrs. Math., Assn. Symbolic Logic (pres. 1962-64), Am. Math. Soc. (coun. 1962-64), Math. Assn. Am. (Chauvenet prize 1964, Yueh-Gin Gung and Dr. Charles Y. Hu award 1990), Can. Math. Soc., Assn. for Women in Math., Nat. Assn. Math., ACLU (bd. dirs. Berkeley chpt. 1964-66), Phi Beta Kappa (vis. lectr. 1993-94), Sigma Xi. Home: 9 Maybeck Twin Dr Berkeley CA 94708-2037 Address: Univ of CA-Berkeley Dept Of Mathematics Berkeley CA 94720-3840

HENKIN, ROBERT IRWIN, neurobiologist, internal medicine, nutrition and neurology educator, scientific products company executive, taste and smell disease physician; b. L.A., Oct. 5, 1930; s. William and Ida Mildred (Scher) H.; m. Marsha Lynn Jacobs, May 15, 1964 (div. Jan. 1982); children: Amanda Joan, Michael Jonathan, David Gorman, Joshua Adam, Elizabeth Madeline, Hannah Deborah. AB cum laude, U. So. Calif., 1951; MA, UCLA, 1953, PhD, 1956, MD, 1959. Intern in medicine U. Calif. Hosp., L.A., 1959-60; resident in medicine Jackson Meml. Hosp., U. Miami (Fla.), 1960-61; commd. officer USPHS, 1961, advanced through grades to sr. surgeon, resigned, 1975; rsch. assoc. Nat. Inst. Mental Health, NIH, Bethesda, Md., 1961-63, sr. investigator, 1963-69; chief sect. on neuroendocrinology Nat. Heart and Lung Inst., NIH, Bethesda, Md., 1969-75; dir. Ctr. Molecular Nutrition and Sensory Disorders Georgetown U. Med. Ctr., Washington, 1975-85, assoc. prof. pediatrics and neurology, 1975-82, dir. Taste and Smell Clinic, 1985—, prof., 1982—; pres., CEO Sialon Corp., Washington, 1987—; cons. Campbell Soup Co., 1969-74, USDA/NIH, 1975—, Hooker Chem. Co., Buffalo, 1976-77, Washington Conf. for Zinc, 1985—, Florasynth, N.Y.C., 1986-91, Squibb Pharm. Co., N.Y.C., 1986-87. Author: Zinc, 1975; contbr. articles to profl. jours.; patentee saliva, taste diagnostics, wound healing protein, drugs to treat taste/smell disorders. Recipient Vicennial medal Georgetown U., 1984; Atwater Kent fellow UCLA, 1957, Giovanni de Chiris Sci. award, 1998; grantee Dept. Def., USDA, NIH and various NIH insts., 1969—. Fellow Am. Coll. Nutrition; mem. Biophys. Soc. (charter), Am. Physiol. Soc., Am. Soc. of Nutrition, Am. Soc. Clin. Nutrition, Am. Fedn. Med. Rsch., Am. Soc. Clin. Investigation, Composers Guild Am., Cosmos Club, Phi Beta Kappa, Sigma Xi (nat. lectr. 1984-87, Giovanni de Chivo Sci. award 1998). Avocations: tennis, running, skiing. Fax: 202-364-9727. Home: 6601 Broxburn Dr Bethesda MD 20817-4709 Office: Ctr Mol Nutrn/Sensory Disorders Taste and Smell Clin 5125 Macarthur Blvd NW # 20 Washington DC 20016-3300

HENKLE, JAMES L., industrial designer; b. Cedar Rapids, Iowa, Mar. 13, 1927; s. Elmer E. and Helen Cecile (Black) H.; m. Dorothy Eleanor Shirley, Sept. 7, 1957; 1 child, Gregory Lee. BA, U. Nebr., 1949; Cert. in Indsl. Design, Pratt Inst., 1951. Designer Dave Chapman Indsl. Design, Chgo., 1952-53; tchr. design U. Okla., Norman, 1953-90; furniture designer Norman. Chmn. gallery com. Firehouse Art Ctr., Norman, 1990—. With USN, 1944-45. Recipient Purchase award Ark. Art Ctr., 1975. Mem. Okla. designer Crafdtsmen (v.p.). Democrat. Home and Office: 2719 Hollywood Ave Norman OK 73072-6731

HENLE, PETER, retired economic consultant, arbitrator; b. N.Y.C., Feb. 12, 1919; s. James and Marjorie (Jacobson) H.; m. Theda W. Ostrander, Aug. 25, 1941; children: Michael G., James M., Paul J. B.A., Swarthmore Coll., 1940; M.A., Am. U., 1947. Mem. rsch. staff, asst. dir. rsch. Am. Fed. Labor, Washington, 1946-55; asst. dir. rsch. AFL-CIO, Washington, 1955-61; chief economist Bur. Labor Stats., U.S. Dept. Labor, Washington, 1961-71; dep. asst. sec. U.S. Dept. Labor planning, evaluation research, 1977-79; sr. specialist Labor Congl. Research Service, Library of Congress, Washington, 1972-77; econ. cons., arbitrator Arlington, Va., 1979-92. Contbr. articles to profl. jours. Chmn. Arlington County (Va.) Manpower Planning Council, 1975-77; trustee Arlington County Employees Retirement System, 1985-89. With AUS, 1941-42; with USAAF, 1942-45. Recipient Disting. Achievement award U.S. Dept. Labor, 1968; Brookings Instn. fed. exec. fellow, 1971-72. Mem. Nat. Acad. Arbitrators, Indsl. Rels. Rsch. Assn. Address: 3411 N Woodrow St Arlington VA 22207-4417

HENLEY, ARTHUR, author, editor, television consultant; b. Rockaway Beach, N.Y., Sept. 9, 1921; s. Nathan Siegel and Theresa (Hohauser) H.; m. Janet Radskin, June 3, 1950; children: Eric, Kenneth. Engr. Assoc., Pratt Inst., 1944; BA, CCNY, 1969. Tech. writer Fairchild Camera Co., 1944-45; TV program cons., 1960—; mem. faculty NYU, 1969-70; mental health cons., Nat. Assn. Mental Health Keynoter, coll. lectr. Radio writer, producer shows Bob & Ray, Make Up Your Mind, 13 by Henley; others; also writer advt. jingles; TV producer Kate Smith Show, Make Up Your Mind, Broadway Open House; TV writer, producer, also indsl. films, others; mag. contbr. Ladies Home Jour., McCalls, Family Health, Public Affairs Com., N.Y. Times, Sat. Eve Post, others, 1961—; author: The Mathematics of Humor, 1948, Demon In My View, 1966, Make Up Your Mind, 1967, Yes Power, 1969, The Right to Lie, 1970, Schizophrenia, 1971, revised edit. 1987, What Other Child-Care Books Don't Tell You, 1972, The Complete Alibi Handbook, 1972, The Difficult Child, 1973, How to Be a Perfect Liar, 1978, Don't Be Afraid of Cataracts, 1978, Don't be Afraid of Cataracts, rev. edit., 1983, Phobias The Crippling Fears, 1987, paperback edit., 1988, Lily & Joel: A Novel of Life, Love and Audio Tapes, 1992, Talking Book and Braille edit., 1994; contbr. to anthologies How to Write for Pleasure and Profit, You and Your Mind, Treasury of Tips for Writers, How to Write Television Comedy, Tools of the Writer's Trade; editor: Interdisciplinary Communications Program, Smithsonian Inst., 1975. Cons. med. editor: Globe Communications, 1976-79; columnist Brides Mag, 1970. Recipient Russell Sage Found. award., TV-Radio Mirror Gold medals (2).; work included in U. Wyo. Am. Heritage Ctr. Mem. Am. Soc. Journalists and Authors, Nat. Assn. Sci. Writers, PEN, AFTRA. Club: Nat. Press. Home: 73-37 Austin St Forest Hills NY 11375-6219 Office: A H Prodns 175 5th Ave Ste 2462 New York NY 10010-7703 *If I have learned anything from living it is that a static life is no life at all while a life of change without direction is only half a life.*

HENLEY, DON, singer, drummer, songwriter; b. Linden, Tex., 1948; m. Sharon Summerall, May 20, 1995. Drummer with band Eagles, L.A., performer in numerous albums including The Eagles, 1972, Desperado, 1973, On the Border, 1974, One These Nights, 1975, Hotel California, 1976, The Long Run, 1979, Hell Freezes Over, 1994; solo performer, singer, composer albums I Can't Stand Still, 1982, Building the Perfect Beast, 1985 (Grammy award for song The Boys of Summer), The End of Innocence, 1989, Actual Miles: Henley's Greatest Hits, 1995; songs include Dirty Laundry, 1982, Long Way Home, I Will Not Go Quietly, New York Minute, If Dirt Were Dollars, Little Tin God, The Heart of the Matter. Active So. Poverty Law Ctr., Walden Woods Project. Office: care Lisa Barbaris Geffen Records 9130 W Sunset Blvd West Hollywood CA 90069-3110*

HENLEY, ERNEST JUSTUS, chemical engineering educator, consultant; b. Sept. 30, 1926. BS, U. Del., 1950; D Engring. Sci., Columbia U., 1953. Asst. prof. nuclear and chem. engring. Columbia U., N.Y.C., 1953-59; prof. chemistry and chem. engring. Stevens Inst. Tech., Hoboken, N.J., 1959-64; chief of party Aid Mission, Rio de Janeiro, 1964-66; prof. chem. engring. U. Houston, 1964—; founder, bd. dirs. Maxxim Med., St. Petersburg, Fla.; bd. dirs. Henley Healthcare, Sugar Land, Tex., Procedyne Corp., New Brunswick, N.J.; tech. cons.; founding dir. Rai Rsch., 1953—. Office: U Houston Dept Chem Engring Houston TX 77204-0001

HENLEY, ERNEST MARK, physics educator, university dean emeritus; b. Frankfurt, Germany, June 10, 1924; came to U.S., 1939, naturalized, 1944; s. Fred S. and Josy (Dreyfuss) H.; m. Elaine Dimitman, Aug. 21, 1948; children: M. Bradford; Karen M. B.E.E., CCNY, 1944; Ph.D., U. Calif. at Berkeley, 1952. Physicist Lawrence Radiation Lab., 1950-51; research assoc. physics dept. Stanford U., 1951-52; lectr. physics Columbia U., 1952-54; mem. faculty U. Wash., Seattle, 1954—; prof. physics U. Wash., 1961-95; prof. emeritus, 1995—; chmn. dept. U. Wash., 1973-76, dean Coll. Arts and Scis., 1979-87, dir. Inst. for Nuclear Theory, 1990-91; assoc. dir. Inst. for Nuclear Theory U. Wash., 1991—; rschr., author numerous publs. on symmetries, nuclear reactions, weak interactions and high energy particle interactions; chmn. Nuclear Sci. Adv. Com., 1986-89. Author: (with W. Thirring) Elementary Quantum Field Theory, 1962, (with H. Frauenfelder) Subatomic Physics, 1974, 2nd edit. 1991, Nuclear and Particle Physics, 1975. Bd. dirs. Pacific Sci. Ctr., 1984-87, Wash. Tech. Ctr., 1983-87; trustee Associated Univs., Inc., 1989—, chmn. bd., 1993-96. Recipient sr. Alexander von Humboldt award, 1984, T.W. Bonner prize Am. Physics Soc., 1989, Townsend Harris medal CCNY, 1989; F.B. Jewett fellow, 1952-53, NSF sr. fellow, 1958-59, Guggenheim fellow, 1967-68, NATO sr. fellow, 1976-77. Fellow AAAS (chmn. physics sect. 1989-90), Am. Phys. Soc. (chmn. div. nuclear physics 1979-80, pres. 1992), Am. Acad. Arts and Scis.; mem. NAS, Sigma Xi. Office: Univ Wash Physics Dept PO Box 351560 Seattle WA 98195-1560

HENLEY, JOSEPH OLIVER, manufacturing company executive; b. Sikeston, Mo., June 25, 1949; s. Fred Louis and Bernice (Chilton) H. m. Jane Ann Rhodes, Aug. 21, 1971. BSBA, U. Mo., 1972; MBA, Mich. State U., 1973. Ops. analyst Midland-Ross, Inc., Cleve., 1974, prodn. control mgr., 1974-75; engring. systems mgr. Cameron-Waldron div., Somerset, N.J., 1989-95, prodn. control mgr., 1976-77; prodn. planning and mfg. systems mgr. ICM div. Massey Ferguson, Inc., Akron, Ohio, 1977-78; sr. audit specialist mfg. United Techs. Corp., Hartford, Conn., 1978-82; mfg. control systems mgr. UT Diesel Systems div., Hartford, Conn., 1983-84, materials mgr., 1983-84, internal cons., 1984-86; inventory mgr. Pratt & Whitney Aircraft div., Hartford, Conn., 1986-89, mgr. sychronous mfg., 1989-95; dir. mfg. Case Corp., Racine, Wis., 1996—. With Army N.G., 1970-72. Mem. Nat. Assn. Purchasing Mgmt., Am. Prodn. and Inventory Control Soc., Assn. for Mfg. Excellence (N.E. region bd. dirs.), Beta Gamma Sigma, Sigma Iota Epsilon, Omicron Delta Epsilon. Presbyterian. Home: 11 Sprucewood Ct Racine WI 53402-5316 Office: Case Corporation 700 State St Racine WI 53404-3392

HENLEY, LILA JO, school social worker, consultant, retired; b. Winter Haven, Fla., Feb. 9, 1936; d. Harold James and Hazel Louise (Collier) Selman; m. James Wilson Henley, Jr., Feb. 2, 1968; 1 child, Joy Selman. BA, Tenn. Temple U., 1961; MSW, Ind. U., Indpls., 1967; EdD, Nova U., 1988. Lic. clin. social worker, Ga. Social worker Douglas County Dept. Family Svcs., Douglasville, Ga., 1961-62, Cobb County Dept. Family Svcs., Marietta, Ga., 1963-66; dir. mental health Cobb County Health Dept., Marietta, 1967-68; social worker Atlanta Pub. Schs., 1969-93, retired, 1993—; cons. Garden Terr. Nursing Home, Douglasville, 1968-70, various ch. youth groups, Douglasville, 1973—. Adv. bd. State of Ga. Sch. Social Work, 1970-85; vol. Mental Health Assn., 1970-73. Mem. NEA, NASW, Acad. Cert. Social Workers, Nat. Guild of Hypnotists, Parent Teacher Assn. Baptist. Avocations: bowling, golf, swimming, painting, collecting Precious Moments. Home: 6240 River Ridge Dr Douglasville GA 30135

HENLEY, RICHARD JAMES, health facility administrator; b. Wroclaw, Poland, May 31, 1956; came to U.S., 1959; s. Henry and Lidia (Alper) Horczak. BA and MA summa cum laude, CCNY, 1978. Asst. to v.p. fin. Mt. Sinai Med. Ctr., N.Y.C., 1978-80, dir. fin. planning, 1980-81, assoc. dir. fin., 1982-84, dir. fin. profl. svcs., 1984-85; v.p. fin., treas. Vassar Bros. Hosp., Poughkeepsie, N.Y., 1985-92, sr. v.p. for adminstrn., treas., 1992-97; exec. v.p., treas. Vassar Bros. Hosp., Poughkeepsie, 1997—; treas. VBH Corp., Poughkeepsie, 1986—, Vassar Bros. Hosp. Found., 1986—, VBH Ins. Co., Ltd., 1988-90, pres., 1991—, Riverside Diversified Svcs., Inc., 1986-92, pres., 1992—, Riverside Mgmt. Svcs., Inc., 1986-92, pres., 1992—; treas. Hudson Valley Home Care, Inc.; pres. HealthServe, LLC; exec. adminstr. Physicians Network, P.C. Contbr. articles to profl. jours. Treas. Bardavon 1869 Opera House, Poughkeepsie, 1986-91, Family Svcs. Dutchess County, Poughkeepsie, 1987-88, Samuel F. B. Morse Hist. Site, 1998—; pres. Hudson Terr. Owners' Corp., Poughkeepsie, 1987-88. Fellow Am. Coll. Healthcare Execs., Healthcare Fin. Mgmt. Assn. (nat. chmn. elect 1998-99, nat. chmn. 1999-2000, nat. treas. 1997-98, nat. sec. 1996-97, nat. dir. 1994-96, nat. chmn. 1999—, cost effectiveness award 1979-80, William G. Follmer Merit award 1986, Robert H. Reeves Merit award 1989, Fredric T. Muncie Mert award 1991, Medal of Honor award 1994). Office: Vassar Bros Hosp 45 Reade Pl Poughkeepsie NY 12601-3947

HENLEY, ROBERT LEE, school system administrator; b. Aug. 7, 1934; m. Patricia J. Ellis; 3 children. BA, Washington U., St. Louis, 1957, MEd, 1958; EdD, U. Mo., 1967. Tchr., counselor, pers. office, bus. mgr., asst. supt. Mehlville Sch. Dist., St. Louis, 1958-75; supt. schs. Independence (Mo.) Pub. Schs., 1975-93; asst. prof. U. Mo., Kansas City, 1991—; cons. in field; instr. various colls. & univs., St. Louis and Columbia, 1975—. Trustee Andrew Drumm Inst., Independence, 1980—; bd. dirs. Am. Cancer Soc., Independence, 1978—; adv. com. Kansas City Arts Ptnrs. Program, 1990—. Recipient Community Leader award Comprehensive Mental health Svcs., Jackson County, Mo., 1983, Disting. Svc. award Mo. chpt. Am. Assn. on Mental Deficiency, 1983, Outstanding Educator award State of Mo., 1985, Innovation in Edn. award Nat. Ctr. for Ednl. Computing, 1985-86, Exec. Educator 100 award Exec. Educator Mag., 1987, Sch. Adminstr. award Kennedy Ctr./Alliance for Arts Edn., Washington, 1988, Disting. Svc. award Am. Assn. Sch. Adminstrs., 1993; named Mo. Supt. of Yr., 1992. Mem. Am. Assn. Sch. Adminstrs., Mo. Assn. Sch. Adminstrs. (exec. com. 1988—, Robert L. Pearce award 1991, Disting. Svc. award 1993), Jackson County Sch. Adminstrs. Assn. (pres. 1981), Mid-Am. Assn. Sch. Supts., Met. Sch. Study Group (pres. 1985-86), Independence C. of C. Office: Independence Sch Dist 1231 Windsor St Independence MO 64055-1151*

HENLEY, TERRY LEW, computer company executive; b. Seymour, Ind., Nov. 10, 1940; s. Ray C. and Barbara Marie (Cockerham) H.; children: Barron Keith, Troy Grayson, Walker Reed; m. Jennifer L. Baldwin, Sept., 1991. BS, Tri-State U., 1961; MBA, Loyola U., 1980, D of Psychology, 1982. R & D engr. Halogens Rsch. Lab. Dow Chem. Co., Midland, Mich., 1961-63; lead process engr., polymer plant Dow Chem. Co., Bay City, Mich., 1964; supt. bromide-bromate plants Dow Chem. Co., Midland, 1964-68; nat. sales mgr. Ryan Industries, Louisville, 1968-70; internat. sales mgr. Chemineer, Inc., Dayton, Ohio, 1970-77; cons. mktg. Xenia, Ohio, 1977-78; pres. Med-Systems Mgmt., Inc., Dayton, 1978—, Medconnect Ltd., 1994—, Statis. Outcome Rsch. Corp., 1994—; chmn. United Telemgmt. Inc., Dayton, 1991—; pres. MedStrategy Consultants, 1997—. Author: Chemical Engineering, 1976; contbr. articles to profl. jours.; patentee in field. Mem. ASTM (com.), AIChE, Am. Hosp. Assn., Computer Based Patient Record Inst., Internat. Graphoanalysis Soc., Radiology Bus. Mgmt. Assn., Am. Nat. Std. Inst. (X12 health ins. com.), Am. Med. Peer Rev. Assn., Am. Mgmt. Assn., Med. Group Mgmt. Assn., Ohio Handwriting Analysts Assn., Soc. for Ambulatory Care Profls., Healthcare Fin. Mgmt. Assn., Assn. Electronic Healthcare Transactions, Data Interchange Stds. Assn., Inc., U.S. C. of C. (telecomm. infrastructure rsch. task force, health and benefits policy com., Civic award 1990), Am. Med. Info. Assn., Freedom in Medicine Found. Home: 278 N Childrens Home Rd Troy OH 45373-8653 Office: Med-Systems Mgmt Inc 7812 Mcewen Rd Dayton OH 45459-3910

HENLEY, VERNARD WILLIAM, banker; b. Richmond, Va., Aug. 11, 1929; s. Walter Abraham and Mary Ellen (Crump) H.; m. Pheriby Christine Gibson, June 14, 1958; children: Vernard William, Wade Gibson, Adrienne Christine. B.S., Va. State Coll., 1951; LHD, Va. State U., 1992. Teller, cashier Mechanics & Farmers Bank, Durham, N.C., 1951-52, 54-58; v.p. Consol. Bank & Trust Co., Richmond, 1958-71; pres., trust officer Consol. Bank & Trust Co., from 1971; chmn. bd., chief exec. officer, trust officer J. Sargeant Reynolds Community Coll. Edn. Found., Inc., 1984-92; chmn. bd., CEO Consol. Bank & Trust Co., Richmond, 1983—; bd. govs. Consumer Adv. Coun., Fed. Res. Bd., 1979-83; mem. Deferred Compensation Bd., 1982-87; bd. dirs. Retail Mchts. Assn. Greater Richmond, 1986; mem. Joint. Subcom. to study Capital Area Water Authority, Commonwealth of Va., 1994. Mem. Downtown Devel. Commn., 1984-85, gen. vocat. edn. adv. council Richmond Pub. Schs., 1975-78; dist. commr. Robert E. Lee council Boy Scouts Am., 1964-69; vice chmn. adv. com. Vol. Service Bur., 1964-69; asst. treas. Richmond chpt. ARC, 1968-69; bd. mgmt. North br. YMCA Met. Richmond, 1975-79; commr. Va. Housing Devel. Authority, 1972-83, chmn., 1980-83; bd. dirs. Richmond Community Hosp., 1970-83, Inst. Bus. and Community Devel., 1966-69, Richmond Met. Authority, 1966-69, Human Services Planning div. United Way Greater Richmond, 1970-72, Church Hill Econ. Devel. Corp., 1971-75, Central Ednl. TV, 1971-81, Richmond Meml. Hosp., 1970, Children's Hosp., 1975-85, Richmond Met. Blood Services, 1975-83, Atlantic Rural Exposition, 1976, Pvt. Industry Council Richmond, 1983-85, Federated Arts Council Richmond, 1979-85, Richmond Meml. Hosp. Found., 1980—, Richmond Renaissance, Inc., 1982—, Va. Coun. Econ. Edn., 1993; mem. Premier Edn. Coun. U.S.; bd. dirs. Maymont Found., 1973, pres., 1983-84, mem. exec. and fin. coms.; bd. dirs. Project AID-SIR, 1979-80, Cities in Schs. Found. of Va., 1989, Va. Housing Found., vice chmn. apptd. by gov., 1989; mem. adv. bd. Black Mus., 1984, The Arts Council of Richmond, Inc., 1986; mem. Gov's Econ. Adv. Council, 1982-85; adv. council Salvation Army Boys Club, 1970—; Va. Council on Econ. Edn., 1985, trustee Richmond Meml. Hosp., 1970—, Va. Mus. Fine Arts, 1983, mem. exec., exhibition and fin. coms.; trustee Va.

Union U., 1984, mem. exec. com., chmn. fin. com., past chmn. audit com.; trustee St. Paul's Coll., Lawrenceville, Va., 1976-84, bd. assocs., 1984; trustee J. Sargeant Reynolds Coll. Found., 1984; mem. nat. corp. com. United Negro Coll. Fund, 1975—; vice chmn. audit com. City of Richmond, 1983-85, chmn. 1986-88; mem. Richmond Police Meml. Found., 1985, debt policy com. City of Richmond; trustee univ. fund Va. Commonwealth U., 1986, Historic Richmond Found., 1986 ; mem. adv. bd. Sch. Social Work Va. Commonwealth U., 1985-88. Served to 1st lt. AUS, 1952-54. Decorated Bronze Star; recipient Order of Merit Boy Scouts Am., 1967; Man and Boy award Boys Club, 1969; Citizenship award NAACP, 1974; Citizenship award Astoria Beneficial Club, 1976; Brotherhood award Richmond chpt. NCCJ, 1979; Quest for Success award for Black Entrepreneurs Am., Miller Brewing Co. and Philip Morris Co., 1986. Mem. Am. Inst. Banking, Bank Adminstrn. Inst., Am. Banking Assn. (minority lending com. comml. lending divsn. 1976-79, exec. com. 1992-94, legis. com. 1988, 93—, fed. govt. rels. com. 1995—, bd. dirs. 1994—), Va. Bankers Assn. (bd. dirs. 1986-88, pres.-elect 1992, pres. 1993-94), Ctrl. Richmond Assn. (dir. 1971-72), Old Dominion Bar Assn. (lay mem., bd. dirs.), Ind. Order St. Luke (trustee 1970-88), Kiwanis, Owens & Minor, Inc. (bd. dirs. 1993), Alpha Phi Alpha, Alpha Beta Boule, Sigma Phi. Home: 1728 Hungary Rd Richmond VA 23228-2335 Office: Consol Bank & Trust Co PO Box 26823 Richmond VA 23261-6823*

HENN, FRITZ ALBERT, psychiatrist; b. Alden, Pa., Mar. 26, 1941; s. Fredrich and Luise (Kimm) H.; m. Suella Weiland, Aug. 1, 1964; children: Sarah, Stephen. BA, Wesleyan U., Middleton, Conn., 1963; PhD, Johns Hospkins U., 1967; MD, U. Va., 1971. Dir. rsch. tng. U. Iowa Hosps. and Clinics, Iowa City, 1975; asst. prof. U. Iowa, Coll. of Medicine, Iowa City, 1974-78, assoc. prof., 1978-81, prof. dept. psychiat., 1981; prof., chmn. SUNY, Stony Brook, 1982-94; dir. L.I. Rsch. Inst., Stony Brook, 1982-83, Inst. of Mental Health Rsch., Stony Brook, 1983—; prof. psychiatry U. Heidelberg, Germany, 1994; dir. Ctrl. Inst. for Mental Health, Germany, 1994; pres. Winter Conf. on Brain Rsch., 1990-92. Mem. editorial bd. Jour. Neurochemistry, 1980-90, Archives Gen. Psychiatry, 1983—. Cons. Project Dawn Justice Dept., 1973-74. Fellow Life Ins. Medicine Rsch. Fund, 1968-71, Falk fellow Am. Psychiat. Assn., 1972-74. Mem. AMA, Am. Coll. Psychiatrists, Am. Coll. Neuropsychopharmacology, Soc. for Neurol. Sci., Psychiat. Rsch. Soc. (pres. 1992), Am. Soc. Neurochemistry, Sigma Xi, Alpha Omega Alpha. Office: Mental Health Inst, PO 12 21 20, 68072 Mannheim Germany

HENNE, ANDREA RUDNITSKY, business educator; b. Phila., Sept. 11, 1952; d. Isadore and Florence (Sanders) Rudnitsky; m. Lawrence Michael Henne, May 27, 1984; children: Laura Joy, Michael Andrew. BS, Temple U., 1974; MA in Edn., UCLA, 1975, EdD, 1983. Prof. L.A. City Coll., 1975-90; dir. curriculum devel. Bridges Learning Ctr., Solana Beach, Calif., 1992-94; instr. San Diego Mesa Coll., 1995-98; web mgr./on-line edn. coord. Calif. Sch. Profl. Psychology, 1999—; bus. cons., San Diego, 1994—. Author: Intensive Records Management, 4th edit., 1998. Vol. Solana Beach Elem. Sch., San Diego, 1990—, Girl Scouts U.S.A., San Diego, 1995—. Edn. Professions Devel. Act fellow UCLA, 1975; named Outstanding Young Careerist, Bus. and Profl. Women, L.A., 1979. Mem. ASCD, Assn. Records Mgmt. and Adminstrn., Inc., Nat. Bus. Edn. Assn., Calif. Bus. Edn. Assn. (sec., v.p. and pres. 1976-79), Delta Pi Epsilon. Avocations: studying piano, computers, aerobics.

HENNEBERGER, LAWRENCE FRANCIS, lawyer; b. Princeton, Ind., Apr. 13, 1938; s. Francis James and Vera Juanita (Rogers) H.; m. Nancy E. Hanagan; children: Lawrence Francis, James John. B.B.A., Loyola U., New Orleans, 1960; LL.B., Loyola U., 1960-62; LL.M., George Washington U., 1969. With Loyola U.-Am. Inst. Banking, New Orleans, 1956-62; assoc. atty. Arent, Fox et al, Washington, 1965-70; ptnr. Arent, Fox, Kintner, Plotkin, Kahn, Washington, 1971—; mem. bd. visitors Sch. Law, Loyola U., New Orleans, 1983—; bd. advisors Dental Hygiene Dept., Loyola U., 1975—. Served to capt. U.S. Army, 1962-65. Decorated Army Commendation medal; Loyola U. scholar, 1956-60; recipient Leader of Yr. award Loyola U., 1960, Outstanding Student Athlete award, 1958-60, highest scholastic average award, 1960; Triangle award, Motor and Equipment Mfrs. Assn., 1975. Mem. D.C. Bar Assn., Ind. Bar Assn., La. Bar Assn., Bar of U.S. Supreme Ct. Republican. Roman Catholic. Avocations: reading; classical and jazz music; representational art; long distance running. Home: 2419 Mare Ln Oakton VA 22124-1514 Office: Arent Fox Kintner Plotkin & Kahn 1050 Connecticut Ave NW Ste 500 Washington DC 20036-5339

HENNECY, BOBBIE BOBO, English language educator; b. Tignall, Ga., Aug. 11, 1922; d. John Ebb and Lois Helen (Gulledge) Bobo; student, Wesleyan Conservatory, 1943-44; AB summa cum laude, Mercer U., Macon, Ga., 1950; postgrad. Oxford (Eng.) U. English-Speaking Union Scholar, 1961; MA, Emory U., 1962; postgrad. Cambridge U., Eng., 1987; m. James Howell Hennecy, Dec. 28, 1963; 1 child, Erin. Sec. Tattnall Sq. Bapt. Ch., 1943-48; sec., adminstrv. asst. to pres., instr. Mercer U., 1950-61, instr. English, 1961-76, asst. prof., 1976-89, emeritus assoc. prof. and adj. prof., 1989—; founder Tattnall Sq. Acad., Macon, 1968, sec. acad. corp., 1968-73, dir., 1968-78. Author numerous poems printed in anthologies Nat. Lib. Poetry. Bobbie Bobo Hennecy scholarship named in her hon. Tattnall Sq. Acad., Mercer U.; NDEA fellow Emory U., 1962; recipient plaque for thirty yrs. svc. as advisor to Psi Gamma Chi Omega, 1983, named outstanding Psi Gamma Chi Omega, 1995; recipient award for Poetry by U.D.C., 1995, Editors Choice awards for Outstanding Achievement in Poetry, Nat. Libr. Poetry, 1995, 96, 97, 98; named to Internat. Poetry Hall of Fame, 1997. Mem. AAUW (chpt. v.p. 1959, pres. 1964), AAUP, MLA, Nat. Libr. Poetry, S. Atlantic MLA, LWV, UDC (pres. 1994-96, award for poetry 1995), DAR (registrar 1980-82), YWCA (life), So. Comparative Lit. Assn., Am. Comparative Lit. Assn., Internt. Soc. Poetry (disting. mem. 1997), Internat. Comparative Lit. Assn., Nat. Assn. Tchrs. English, Ga. Assn. Tchrs. English, English Speaking Union, Collegiate Press (adv. bd.), Am. Acad. Poets, Soc. Am. Poets, Pres. Club of Mercer U., Mid. Ga. Art Assn., Hereditary Register, Soc. Genealogists London, Nat. Soc. So. Dames, Nat. Soc. Magna Charta, Daus. of 1812, Descendants, Colonial Clergy, Daus. of Am. Colonists, Jamestowne Soc., Colonial Dames XVII Century (chpt. 1st v.p. 1988-91), Colonial Order of the Crown (descendants of Charlemagne), Ams. of Royal Descent, Mid. Ga. Hist. Soc., Coosa County Ala. Hist. Soc., Marion County S.C. Mus., Friends of the Cannonball House, Cardinal Key, Sigma Tau Delta, Sigma Mu (pres., v.p., sec.-treas.), Phi Delta (advisor), Phi Kappa Phi, Alpha Psi Omega, Chi Omega (alumnae pres. 1953, advisor 1953-83). Baptist. Home: 1810 Winship St Apt 4 Macon GA 31204-5542

HENNEKE, EDWARD GEORGE, lawyer; b. Flint, Mich., Jan. 28, 1940; s. Edward G. and Anna I. (Kielhorn) H.; m. Donna M. Wardosky, Jan. 24, 1970; children: Dawn, Shelley, Charlene; stepchildren: Scott, Tracy, Kurt Fraim. AA, Flint Jr. Coll., 1960; BS, U. Mich., Flint, 1962; JD, U. Mich., Ann Arbor, 1965. Bar: Mich. 1965, U.S. Dist. Ct. (ea. dist.) Mich. 1967, U.S. Ct. Appeals (6th cir.) 1974, U.S. Supreme Ct. 1971. Asst. pros. atty. Genesee County Pros. Atty., Flint, 1965-67; assoc. Ransom, Fazenbaker & Ransom, Flint, 1967-74; prin. ptnr. Keil, Ransom & Henneke, Flint, 1975-88, Henneke, McKone & Fraim, Flint, 1988—. Mem. planning com. Flushing Twp., 1986-92; bd. appeals, 1993—. Named Outstanding Alumnus, Flint U. Mich., 1971. Mem. Genesee County Bar Assn. (dir. 1978-81, pres. 1981-83), ABA. Avocations: hunting, golf, skiing. Office: Henneke McKone & Fraim 2222 S Linden Rd Ste G Flint MI 48532-5460

HENNELLY, EDMUND PAUL, lawyer, oil company executive; b. N.Y.C., Apr. 2, 1923; s. Edmund Patrick and Alice (Laccorn) H.; m. Josephine Kline; children: Patricia A. Anglin, Pamela J. Farley. BCE, Manhattan Coll., 1944; JD, Fordham U., 1950. Bar: N.Y. 1950. Instr. Manhattan Coll., 1947-50; litigation assoc. Cravath, Swaine & Moore, 1950-51, sr. litigation assoc., 1953-54; asst. gen. counsel CIA, Washington, 1951-52; assoc. counsel Time, Inc., N.Y.C., 1954-56; asst. legis. cons. Mobil Oil Corp., N.Y.C., 1956-60, legis. cons., 1960-61, mgr. domestic govt. rels. dept., 1961-67, mgr. govt. rels. dept., 1967-73, gen. mgr. govt. rels. dept., 1974-78, gen. mgr. pub. affairs dept., 1978-86; pres., chief exec. officer Citroil Enterprises, N.Y.C., 1986—; bd. dirs. South Cay Trust, Republic Nat. Bank N.Y., N.Y.C. Contbr. articles on engring. and law to profl. jours. Trustee, vice chmn. Daytop Village Found.; mem. adv. com. N.Y. State Legis. Com. on Higher Edn., Nassau County (N.Y.) Energy Commn., L.I. Citizens' Com. for Mass Transit, N.Y. State Def. Coun.; mem. White House Conf. on Natural Beauty, 1963; bd. dirs. Nat. Coun. on Aging; exec. com. Pub. Affairs Rsch. Coun. of Conf. Bd.; mem. Nassau County Econ. Devel. Planning Coun.; commr. nat. com. Commn. for UNESCO, 1982-85, head U.S. del. with personal rank of amb. 22d Gen. Conf., 1983, mem. internat. adv. panel, 1989—; mem. Pres.' Intelligence Transition Team, 1980-81; cons. Pres.'s Intelligence Oversight Bd.; trustee Austen Riggs Ctr., Pub. Affairs Found. Lt., USNR, 1943-46, PTO, ETO. Decorated Knight of Malta, Knight of Holy Sepulchre. Mem. ABA, Fed. Bar Assn., Assn. Bar City of N.Y., Acad. Polit. and Social Scis., Am. Good Govt. Soc. (trustee), Tax Coun. (bd. dirs.), Pub. Affairs Coun. (bd. dirs.), Freedom House (trustee), Am. Mgmt. Assn., Pi Sigma Epsilon, Delta Theta Phi, Army-Navy Club, Meadows Country Club, Sarasota Yacht Club, Island Hills Country Club, Explorers Club, Knights of Malta, Knights Holy Sepulchre. Clubs: Army-Navy, Explorers. Lodges: K.M., Knights Holy Sepulcher. Home: 84 Sequams Ln E West Islip NY 11795-4508 also: 3941 Hamilton Club Cir Sarasota FL 34242-1109 Office: Citroil Enterprises 21 Argyle Sq Babylon NY 11702-2712

HENNEMAN, STEPHEN CHARLES, counselor; b. Chgo., June 17, 1949; s. Charles Philip Jr. and Marion Louise (Eichberger) H.; m. Patrica Ann York, Feb. 14, 1975 (div. Sept. 1980); 1 child Charles Philip III; m. Marion Jean McDermand, Oct. 4, 1980; stepchildren: Ervin F. Schrock Jr., Lisa Ann Schrock, Thomas M. Schrock. BA in Journalism, Colo. State U., 1971; MA in Counseling, U. N.D., 1987. Commd. 2d lt. USAF, 1971, advanced through grades to maj., 1984; missile launch officer 570th Strategic Missile Squadron, Davis Monthan AFB, Ariz., 1972-76; info. officer 321st Strategic Missile Wing, Grand Forks AFB, N.D., 1976-79; missile combat crew flight comdr. 446th Strategic Missile Squadron, Grand Forks AFB, 1980-82; missile combat crew comdr. evaluator 321st Strategic Missile Wing, Grand Forks AFB, 1982, wing nuclear surety officer, 1982-83, chief weapon safety branch, 1983-85; asst. ops. officer 320th Strategic Missile Squadron, F E Warren AFB, Wyo., 1985-86; dep. wing inspector 90th Strategic Missile Wing, F E Warren AFB, 1986-88; ops. officer 319th Strategic Missile Squadron, F E Warren AFB, 1988-89; dep. chief war res. materiel div. Hdqrs. U.S. Air Forces in Europe, Ramstein Air Base, Fed. Republic Germany, 1989-92; vol. and outreach coord. Safe House/Sexual Assault Svcs., Inc., Cheyenne, Wyo., 1992-93; quality control investigator Dept. Employment State of Wyoming, Cheyenne, 1993-95; counselor Wyo. State Penitentiary, Rawlins, 1995-96, counseling team leader, 1996-97; residential counselor Aurora (Colo.) Cmty. Mental Health Ctr., 1997—. Advocate, counselor Safehouse/Sexual Assault Svcs., Inc., Cheyenne, 1985-89; sec., bd. dirs. Carbon County Citizens Organized to See Violence Ended, 1996-97. Mem. ACA, Am. Mental Health Counselors Assn., Colo. Counselors Assn. Avocations: photography, popular music recordings collecting, reading.

HENNEMEYER, ROBERT THOMAS, diplomat; b. Chgo., Dec. 1, 1925; s. Rudolph Johannes and Mary Matilda (Petersen) H.; m. Joan Therese Renaud, Dec. 28, 1954; children—Christian, Paul, Robin. Ph.B., U. Chgo., 1947, M.A., 1950; student, Chgo. Tchrs. Coll., African area studies Oxford U., Eng., 1960-61, U. Md., 1965-67. Tchr. high schs. Chgo., 1948-50; instr. Woodrow Wilson Jr. Coll., Chgo., 1951; commd. fgn. service officer U.S. Dept. State, 1952; cultural officer Bremen, Fed. Republic Germany, 1952-53; officer-in-charge Bremerhaven, Fed. Republic Germany, 1953-54; asst. U.S. sec. Allied Gen. Secretariat, Bonn, Fed. Republic Germany, 1954-56, spl. asst. to ambassador, 1954-56; econ. officer Consulate Gen., Munich, 1956-58; internat. relations officer Dept. State, 1958-60; consul, dep. chief mission Dar es Salaam Tanganyika, 1961-64; faculty adviser U.S. Naval Acad., Annapolis, 1964-66; personnel officer Dept. State, Washington, 1966-68; chief polit. sec. Am. embassy Oslo, Norway, 1968-71; consul gen. Dusseldorf, Fed. Republic Germany, 1971-75; dep. asst. sec. Bur. of Security and Consular Affairs Dept. State, 1976-78; consul gen. Munich, 1978-80; sr. insp. and exec. dir. Dept. State, 1980-83, exec. asst. to Under Sec., 1983-84; U.S. ambassador Banjul, The Gambia, 1984-86; fgn. affairs advisor U.S. Cath. Conf., Washington, 1986-88, dir. office internat. justice and peace, 1988-90; pvt. cons., 1990—. Served with AUS, 1943-46. Mem. DACOR, Fgn. Service Assn., Alpha Delta Phi. Address: 1701 Clower Creek Dr Sarasota FL 34231-8928

HENNER, MARILU, actress; b. Chgo., Apr. 6, 1952; m. Frederic Forest, 1980 (div.); m. Rob Lieberman, 1990. Attended, U. Chgo. ppearances include (TV series) Taxi, ABC, 1978-82, NBC, 1982-83, Evening Shade, CBS, 1990-94, Marilu, 1994-95, (TV movies) Dream House, 1981, Stark, 1985, Love With A Perfect Stranger, 1986, Ladykillers, 1988, Chains of Gold, Fight for Justice: The Nancy Conn Story, 1995, My Son is Innocent, 1996, Titanic, 1996, Batman & Mr. Freeze: SubZero, 1998 (voice), 1998; TV mini-series) Titanic, 1996, (films) Between the Lines, 1977, Blood Brothers, 1978, Hammett, 1983, The Man Who Loved Women, 1983, Johnny Dangerously, 1984, Cannonball Run II, 1984, Perfect, 1985, Rustler's Rhapsody, 1985, L.A. Story, 1991, Noises Off, 1992, Chasers, 1994, The Titanic Chronicles, 1999, Man on the Moon, 1999; Broadway debut in Over Here; other Broadway prodns. include Pal Joey, Social Security; stage performances include Grease (nat. co.), Carnal Knowledge, Grown-Ups, Super Sunday. *

HENNER, MARTIN E., arbitrator, mediator; b. N.Y.C., Aug. 6, 1940; s. Isidore and Rose (Zabar) Henner; m. Karen Elaine Hemmingsen, Mar. 24, 1978 (div. Sept. 1984). BA, U. Chgo., 1960; JD, U. Wis., 1969; ADB, Columbia U., 1978. Bar: Wis. 1969, Calif. 1970, Oreg. 1974. Adminstrv. asst. to commr. U.S. Equal Employment Opportunity Commn., Washington, 1965; exec. dir. U.S. Equal Employment Opportunity Commn., 1969; compliance officer, affirmative action specialist, dir. Mich. Civil Rights Divsn., Detroit, 1965-67; atty. Henner, Wolpman, Constantinides & Cohen, 1970-71; pvt. practice, 1971-75, 95—; rschr. U.S. Vets. Adminstrn. Hosp., Palo Alto, Calif., 1976; adminstr., trainer U. Conn., 1977-79; dep. pub. defender Orange County (Calif.), 1980; atty./staff rep. Am. Fedn. State County and Mcpl. Employees, 1981-86; legis. aide to Senator William Dwyer Oreg. State Senate, 1995; vis. asst. prof. San Jose (Calif.) State U., 1976, 77; asst. prof. U. Conn., 1977-79, Calif. State U., Long Beach, 1979-82; Fulbright lectr. U. Paris, 1980-81; instr. Oreg. State U., Corvallis, 1986-88. Contbr. articles to profl. jours. Mem. Am. Arbitration Assn., Oreg. Mediation Assn., Oreg. Assn. Adminstrv. Law Judges, Oreg. State Bar Assn. (state bar counsel region 2), Indsl. Rels. Rsch. Assn. (trustee Oreg. chpt. 1995-96), Soc. Profls. in Dispute Resolution (treas. Pacific NW chpt. 1988-89). E-mail: henner@impartial.com. Home: 2675 Baker Blvd Eugene OR 97403-1680 Office: PO Box 1558 Eugene OR 97440-1558

HENNES, ROBERT TAFT, former management consultant, investment executive; b. Jamestown, N.Y., Mar. 8, 1930; s. Theodore Preston and Lucille (Kane) H.; m. Frances Walker Pratt, May 9, 1953 (div. 1962); children: Robert Taft, Duncan Pratt, Margaret Nickerson, Theodore Preston II; m. Grace Margaret Bruton, Oct. 9, 1971. A.B., Harvard U., 1951; M.B.A., U. Pa., 1952. With Lummus Co., N.Y.C., 1952-62; exec. v.p., dir. Conahay & Lyon, Inc. (advt.), N.Y.C., 1962-70; sr. v.p. Cole & Assos., Boston, 1970-72; chmn., dir. Hennes & Cox Inc., N.Y.C., 1972-77; sr. dir. Spencer Stuart & Assos., N.Y.C., 1977-88; dir. Oldwyck Industries, Inc., N.Y.C. Mem. Kennett Square Golf and Country Club, Harvard Club of N.Y. Home: PO Box 728 Kennett Square PA 19348-0728

HENNESSEY, AUDREY KATHLEEN, computer researcher, educator; b. Fairbanks, Apr. 4, 1936; d. Lawrence Christopher and Olga Virginia (Strandberg) Doheny; m. Gerard Hennessey, Mar. 10, 1963; children: Brian, Kate. BA, Stanford U., 1957; HSA, U. Toronto, Ont., Can., 1968; PhD, U. Lancaster, Eng., 1982. Asst. dir. European sales Univ. Soc., Heidelberg, Fed. Republic Germany, 1959-61; landman's asst. Union Oil Co. Calif., Anchorage, 1962; sys. analyst No. Telephones, New Liskeard, Can., 1962-63; adminstr. group pension Mfgs. Life Ins., Toronto, 1963-65; instr. office systems Adult Edn. Ctr., Toronto, 1965-68; lectr. office sys. Salford Coll. Tech., Lancashire, Eng., 1968-70; sr. lectr. data processing Manchester (Eng.) Met. U., 1970-79; lectr. computation U. Manchester, Eng., 1979-82; assoc. prof. computer sci. Tex. Tech. U., Lubbock, 1982-86, assoc. prof. info. sys., 1987-94, prof. info. sys., 1994—; dir. Inst. for Studies of Organized Automation, Lubbock, 1987-95; pres., CEO ISOA Inc., 1994—; dir. Internat. Ctr. Informatics Rsch., 1996—; vis. instr. Fed. Law Enforcement Tng. Ctr., Glynco, Ga., 1984-88; adj. prof. West Tex. A&M U., Canyon, 1994-95, U. Alaska, Anchorage, 1995, U. Tex., Dallas, 1995-98; mem. NATO panel of experts on visualization of massive data sets, 1996-98. Author: Computer Applications Project, 1982; contbg. author: Semiconductor International, 1996; editor (procs.) Office Document Architecture Internat. Symposium, English version, 1991; contbr. articles to profl. jours.; patentee in field. Organizer Explorer Scouts Computer Applications, Lubbock, 1983-85. Recipient various awards Tex. Instruments, 1982-86, 94, Xerox Corp., 1985, Halliburton, 1986, Sys. Exploration, 1987, State of Tex., 1988-93, 96—, Knowledge-based Image Analysis award USN Space Sys., 1991-96, Immunization Tracking Sys. award Robert Wood Johnson Found., 1993, Leica, 1994, Sematech ADC awards, 1994, Leica GmbH ADC, 1995—. Mem. IEEE (contbg. author Systems Man Cybernetics 1984, Soc. Mfg. Engrs., Assn. Computing Machinery, Assn. of Info. Tech. Profls. (pres. chpt. 1989, Disting. Info. Sci. award 1992), Sigma Xi Rsch. Soc. (chpt. pres. 1996-97), Spl. Interest Group for Artificial Intelligence (pres. 1996-98, chair JEDEC working group ISO semiconductor defect data stds. 1999—). Office: Tex Tech U MS #2101 Tex Tech U Lubbock TX 79409 also: ICIR 1221 W Campbell Rd Ste 231 Richardson TX 75080-2968

HENNESSEY, DAVID PATRICK, banker; b. Coos Bay, Oreg., Aug. 2, 1950; s. William Patrick and Beverly Ann (Curtis) H.; m. Kathryn Ann McCloskey, Aug. 2, 1975; 1 child, Kristin R. AA, Am. River Coll., 1970; BS, Calif. State U., Sacramento, 1974; MBA, Chico State U., 1978. V.p. Bank of Am. N.T. and S.A., Sacramento, 1974-85; exec. v.p. Sunrise Bank Calif., Curtis Heights, 1985-90; pres., chief exec. officer Sunrise Bancorp Sunrise Bank Calif., 1986-90; exec. v.p. Sacramento lst Nat. Bank. subs. West Coast Bancorp, 1990-92, Sacramento First Nat Bank, 1990-92; exec. v.p., CFO, bd. dirs. Step Ahead Investments Inc., North Highlands, Calif., 1992-95; pres., CEO, bd. dirs. Sentinel Savs. & Loan, A Fed. Assn., 1995-96; investment broker AG Edward & Sons Inc., Roseville, Calif., 1996—; chmn. bd. dirs. Data Corp., Roseville, Western Sunrise Mortgage Corp., Rancho Cordovia, Calif. Advisor Sch. Bus. Calif. State U., Sacramento, 1987. Named Outstanding Alumni Calif. State U., 1987. Republican. Home: 7800 Shelborne Dr Granite Bay CA 95746-8624 Office: AG Edwards & Sons Inc 3005 Douglas Blvd Ste 110 Roseville CA 95661-3854

HENNESSEY, JOHN WILLIAM, JR., academic administrator; b. Danville, Pa., Mar. 25, 1925; s. John William and Martha Scott (Braun) H.; m. Jean Marie Lande, June 26, 1948; children: John William III, Martha Scott. AB, Princeton U., 1948; MBA, Harvard U., 1950; PhD, U. Wash., 1956; MA (hon.), Dartmouth Coll., 1959; LHD (hon.), York Coll. of Pa., 1978, U. N.H., 1981. From instr. to assoc. prof. orgn. and adminstrn. Coll. Bus. Adminstrn., U. Wash., 1950-57; prof. Amos Tuck Sch. Bus. Adminstrn., Dartmouth Coll., 1957-87, assoc. dean, 1962-68, dean, 1968-76, Charles H. Jones 3d Century prof. mgmt., 1976-87, now emeritus; provost U. Vt., Burlington, 1987-89, interim pres., 1990; prof. Inst. pour l'Etude des Methodes de Direction de l'Enterprise, Lausanne, Switzerland, 1959; bd. dirs. Kendal at Hanover, chmn. bd. dirs., 1998—. Author: (with Austin Grimshaw) Organizational Behavior, 1960, (with others) Hospital Policy Decisions, 1966. Trustee Mary Hitchcock Meml. Hosp., Hanover, 1963-86, chmn. bd. 1977-83; trustee Ednl. Testing Svc. 1975-80, 81-85, chmn. bd. 1978-80, 84-85; chmn. governing coun. Dartmouth Hitchcock Med. Ctr., 1977-83, trustee, 1983-86, 91—, chmn. bd. trustees, 1992-95; bd. visitors Grad. Sch. Bus., U. Pitts., 1970-76, 79-88; mem. Pres.'s Coun. on Bus. Sch., U. Vt., 1982-87; dir. Milbank Meml. Fund, 1982-87; trustee U. Vt., 1985-87, Med. Ctr. Hosp. Vt., 1988-90. 1st lt. U.S. Army, 1943-46. Mem. Am. Assembly Collegiate Schs. Bus. (dir. 1970-77, pres. 1975-76), Phi Beta Kappa. Home: 4 Webster Ter Hanover NH 03755-1708

HENNESSEY, N. PATRICK, physician, clinical researcher; b. Detroit, Dec. 14, 1947; s. Norman Patrick and Rita Marie (Coffin) H. BA, BS, Aquinas Coll., 1971; MD, Mich. State U., 1975. Diplomate Am. Bd. Dermatology. Resident in internal medicine William Beaumont Hosp., Royal Oak, Mich., 1975-76, New Eng. Deaconess Hosp., Boston, 1976-77; resident in dermatology, malignant melonoma fellowship NYU Med. Ctr., N.Y.C., 1977-80; pvt. practice N. Patrick Hennessey, MD, N.Y.C., 1980—; assoc. prof. clin. dermatology NYU Sch. Medicine, N.Y.C., 1980—; cons. Bur. of Venereal Disease Control, N.Y.C., 1980-85, U.S. Dept. Def., Mil. Entrants Processing Sta., Ft. Hamilton, N.Y., 1984-92; chmn. med. adv. com. Body Positive, Inc., N.Y.C., 1992—; clin. investigator NIH-AIDS Clin. Trials Group-NYU, 1987—. Author: (chpt.) Color Atlas of Cutaneous Manifestations of AIDS, 1989; contbr. articles to profl. jours. Bd. dirs. N.Y. in '94-Gay Games IV, N.Y.C., 1991-94. Fellow Am. Acad. Dermatology; mem. AMA, Soc. for Investigative Dermatology, Am. Soc. Dermatol. Surgery, Internat. Soc. Dermatol. Surgery, N.Y. State Med. Soc., Internat. AIDS Soc., Dermatol. Soc. Greater N.Y. Home: 330 E 38th St Apt 27E New York NY 10016-2788 Office: 650 1st Ave New York NY 10016-3240

HENNESSEY, WILLIAM JOSEPH, physician; b. Troy, N.Y., Mar. 8, 1947; s. Joseph William and Loretta (Brooks) H.; m. Patricia McMahon, Jan. 23, 1983; children: Bridget Marie, Jason William, Matthew Brian, Mark Andrew. BS, Rensselaer Poly. Inst., 1969; MD, Albany Med. Coll., 1973. Cert. Am. Bd. of Ob/Gyn. Resident in ob-gyn Albany (N.Y.) Med. Ctr. Hosp., 1973-76; pvt. practice specializing in ob-gyn, Troy, N.Y., 1976—; mng. ptnr. Ob-Gyn Health Ctr. Assocs., 1985; attending physician Albany Med. Ctr. Hosp., Samaritan Hosp.; treas. med. staff Samaritan Hosp., 1988, sec. med. staff, 1989, v.p. med. staff, 1990, pres., 1991; clin. asst. dept. ob-gyn Albany Med. Ctr. and Albany Med. Coll., 1976—, clin. instr.; chmn. dept. ob-gyn Samaritan Hosp., 1991-95; bd. dirs. PSRO, 1981-85, PRO, 1985-86. Fellow Am. Coll. Ob-Gyn, Am. Fertility Assn.; mem. Am. Chem. Honor Soc., AMA, N.Y. State Med. Soc., Rensselaer County Med. Soc., Northeast Ob-Gyn Soc., Northeastern N.Y. Health Care Consortium, Am. Assn. Gynecol. Laporoscopists, Sampson Soc. (pres.). Republican. Roman Catholic.

HENNESSY, DANIEL KRAFT, lawyer; b. Summit, N.J., Jan. 4, 1941; s. Robert Emmett and Agnes Lyons (Lindle) H.; m. Susan Elizabeth (Bettina) Ware, June 17, 1972; children—Mary Elise, Daniel Joseph, Michael Ware, Catherine Anne. B.S. with highest honors, U.S. Naval Acad., 1963; J.D. cum laude, Harvard U., 1970. Bar: Tex. 1970. Commd. ensign U.S. Navy, 1963, advanced through grades to lt., 1966; service in Vietnam; resigned, 1967; since practiced law in Dallas; ptnr. Hughes & Luce (formerly Hughes & Hill), 1973—. Editor: Harvard Law Rev, 1969-70. Mem. bd. advisers Jesuit Coll. Prep. Sch., Dallas, 1975-88; bd. dirs. Dallas-North Tex. region NCCJ, 1976-83, Catholics United for Faith, Inc., 1982—, Greater Dallas Right to Life Ednl. Found., 1974-86, The Highlands Sch., 1986—. Decorated knight comdr. Equestrian Order of Holy Sepulchre of Jerusalem, Knight of Malta. Mem. Dallas Bar Assn., State Bar of Tex. Roman Catholic. Home: 4405 Beverly Dr Dallas TX 75205-3001

HENNESSY, DEAN MCDONALD, lawyer, multinational corporation executive; b. McPherson, Kans., June 13, 1923; s. Ernest Weston and Beulah A. (Dunn) H.; m. Marguerite Sundheim, Sept. 6, 1946 (div. Sept. 1979); children: Joan Hennessy Wright, John D., Robert D. (dec.), Scott D. (dec.); m. Darlene MacLean, Apr. 4, 1981. A.B. cum laude, Harvard U., 1947, LL.B., 1950; M.B.A., U. Chgo., 1959. Bar: Ill. 1951. Assoc. Carney, Crowell & Leibman, Chgo., 1950-53; atty. Borg-Warner Corp., Chgo., 1953-62; with Emhart Corp., Farmington, Conn., 1962-88, asst. sec., 1964-67, sec., gen. counsel, 1967-74, v.p., sec., gen. counsel, 1974-76, v.p., gen. counsel, 1976-86, sr. v.p., gen. counsel, 1986-88; ret. 1988. Incorporator Ill. Citizens for Eisenhower, 1952; chmn. Citizens Activities, Ill. Citizens for Eisenhower, 1952, 56; Justice of the peace, mem. bd. suprs. Proviso Twp., Ill., 1952-56; vice chmn. Jr. Achievement Chgo., 1959; program chmn. trade and industries divsn. United Rep. Fund Ill., 1961; trustee West Hartford Bicentennial Trust, Inc., 1976-77, Friends and Trustees of Bushnell Meml., Hartford, 1978-84; bd. dirs. Royal Homestead Condominium Assn., Juno Beach, Fla., 1990-93. Served to lt. (j.g.) USNR, 1943-46. Sheldon fellow Harvard U. Mem. ABA, Mfrs. Alliance for Productivity and Innovation. (vice chmn. law coun. 1984-87, chmn. 1987, 88), John Harvard Soc. Republican. Presbyterian. Home: 119 SW Hatteras Ct Palm City FL 34990-4325

HENNESSY, ELLEN ANNE, lawyer, benefits compensation analyst, educator; b. Auburn, N.Y., Mar. 3, 1949; d. Charles Francis and Mary Anne (Roan) H.; m. Frank Daspit, Aug. 27, 1974. BA, Mich. State U., 1971; JD, Cath. U., 1978; LLM in Taxation, Georgetown U., 1984. Bar: D.C. 1978, U.S. Ct. Appeals (D.C. cir.) 1978, U.S. Supreme Ct. 1984. Various positions NEH, Washington, 1971-74; atty. office chief counsel IRS, Washington, 1978-80; atty.-advisor Pension Benefit Guaranty Corp., Washington, 1980-82; assoc. Stroock & Stroock & Lavan, Washington, 1982-85; assoc. Willkie Farr & Gallager, Washington, 1985-86, ptnr., 1987-93; dep. exec. dir. and chief negotiator Pension Benefit Guaranty Corp., Washington, 1993-98; sr.

v.p. Actuarial Sci. Assocs., Inc., Washington, 1998—; adj. prof. law Georgetown U., Washington, 1985—; mem. com. on continuing profl. edn. Am. Law Inst./ABA, 1994-97. Mem. ABA (supervising editor taxation sect. newsletter 1984-87, mem. standing com. on continuing edn. 1990-94, chairperson joint com. on employee benefits 1991-92), Women in Employee Benefits (pres. 1987-88), D.C. Bar Assn. (mem. steering com. tax sect. 1988-93, chairperson continuing legal edn. com. 1993-95). Democrat. Avocation: whitewater canoeing. Home: 1926 Lawrence St NE Washington DC 20018-2734 Office: Ste 900 601 Pennsylvania Ave NW Washington DC 20004

HENNESSY, JAMES ERNEST, academic administrator, telecommunications executive, retired; b. Syracuse, N.Y., Dec. 24, 1933; s. Thomas Emmett and Mary Ann (Couvrette) H.; m. Barbara Ann Hahn, Sept. 1, 1956; children—Lawrence H., Paul J. B.M.E., Syracuse U., 1955, M.B.A., 1968. Vice pres.-bus. mktg. N.Y. Telephone Co., N.Y.C., 1978-81; v.p. regional sales N.Y. Telephone Co., 1981-82; v.p.-market research and services Bellcore, Basking Ridge, N.J., 1982-83; exec. v.p. mktg. and tech. Nynex Corp., White Plains, N.Y., 1984-90, ret.; exec. dir. Palisades Inst., Dominican Coll., Orangeburg, N.Y.; also chmn. bd. trustees Dominican Coll., Orangeburg, N.Y.; p. Chmn. bd. trustees Nyack (N.Y.) Hosp., 1981-89, 93—, Dominican Coll., Blauvelt, N.Y., 1982—; dep. county exec. County of Rockland, N.Y., 1994-95. Lt. USNR, 1956-58. Mem. Am. Soc. Quality Control, MENSA, Tau Beta Pi, Beta Gamma Sigma. Roman Catholic. Club: Rockland Country (Sparkill, N.Y.). Avocations: reading, golfing, walking, poetry. Home: 20 Rockford Dr West Nyack NY 10994-1125 Office: Dominican Coll Palisades Inst Off of Exec Dir Orangeburg NY 10962*

HENNESSY, JOHN FRANCIS, III, engineering executive, mechanical engineer; b. N.Y.C, Nov. 27, 1955; s. John Francis Jr. and Barbara (McDonnell) H. AB, Kenyon Coll., 1977; BSME, Rensselaer Poly Inst., 1978; MS, MIT, 1988. Registered profl. engr., N.Y., N.J., Mass., Va., Del., Calif. Project engr. Syska & Hennessy, N.Y.C., 1978-83; project mgr. Syska & Hennessy, San Francisco, 1983-86; v.p. Syska & Hennessy, L.A., 1986-87; v.p. Syska & Hennessy, Cambridge, Mass., 1987-88, sr. v.p., 1988-89; CEO Syska & Hennessy, N.Y.C., 1989—, chmn., 1992-96; chmn., bd. dirs. N.Y. Bldg. Congress, N.Y.C., 1988—; chmn. Times Square Subway Sta. Improvement Corp., N.Y.C., 1989—. Mem. USO of Met. N.Y.; vice-chmn. Salvation Army of N.Y., 1997—; mem. Bldg. Futures Coun. Sloan fellowship, 1987. Mem. ASHRAE, NSPE, ASME, Coun. on Tall Bldgs. and Urban Habitat, Univ. Club, Olympic Club, Union League Club, Met. Club (Washington), Lyford Cay Club (Nassau), Winged Foot Golf Club (Mamaroneck, N.Y.), Nat. Golf Links of Am., Princeton Club, The Links. Roman Catholic. Avocations: golf, tennis, skiing, squash. Office: Syska & Hennessy 11 W 42nd St New York NY 10036-8002

HENNESSY, JOHN M., brokerage house executive; b. 1936. Vice chmn. CS First Boston Inc., until 1989; group CEO Financiere Credit Suisse-First Boston, 1990-97; ret.; chmn. Credit Suisse First Boston Pvt. Equity, N.Y.C., 1997—. Office: Credit Suisse Pvt Equity 11 Madison Ave New York NY 10010-3698

HENNESSY, MARGARET BARRETT, health care executive; b. Oak Park, Ill., Apr. 16, 1952; d. Bernard Leo and Frances (Madigan) H. BA in Sociology and Psychology, St. Norbert Coll., DePere, Wis., 1974; MS, Rush U., Chgo. Communications specialist Ill. Cancer Coun., Chgo., 1983-84; adminstrv. asst. Rush-Presbyn./St. Luke's Med. Ctr., Chgo., 1984-85; adminstrv. intern Cook County Hosp., Chgo., 1985-86; fin. analyst Loyola U. Med. Ctr., Maywood, Ill., 1986-89; operating officer Howard Brown Meml. Clinic, Chgo., 1989-93; hematology-oncology adminstr. Loyola U. Med. Ctr., Maywood, Ill., 1993-96; assoc. dir. primary care svcs. Lake County Health Dept., Waukegan, Ill., 1996-98; ind. contractor Hennessy Cons., Evanston, Ill., 1998—; guest lectr. Loyola U. Law Sch., 1989-90. Contbr. articles to profl. jours. Tchr. English as a second lang. World Relief Orgn., Chgo., 1989; cons. United Charities Camps, Chgo., 1989. Recipient Foster G. McGaw scholar, Am. Coll. health Care Execs., 1985. Mem. Rush U. Alumni Assn. (pres.), Chgo. Health Execs. Forum, Am. Coll. Healthcare Execs., Assn. Ambulatory Care Adminstrs. Avocations: sports, reading. Office: Lake County Pub Health Dept 1217 Hull Ter Evanston IL 60202-3258

HENNESSY, THOMAS CHRISTOPHER, clergyman, educator, retired university dean; b. N.Y.C., Nov. 3, 1916; s. Thomas C. and Anna E. (Regan) H. A.B., Georgetown Coll., 1940; M.A. in Latin and Greek Classics, Fordham U., 1947, M.S. in Edn., 1957, Ph.D., 1962. Joined S.J., 1934, ordained priest Roman Cath. Ch., 1947. Tchr. Fordham Prep. Sch., N.Y.C., 1941-44, 49-52, high sch. counselor, 1952-61; counselor educator Fordham U. at Lincoln Ctr., N.Y.C., 1961-81; dean, prof. counselor edn. Sch. Edn. Marquette U., Milw., 1981-85. Editor: The Inner Crusade: The Closed Retreat in the U.S., 1965, The High School Counselor Today, 1966, The Interdisciplinary Roots of Guidance, 1966, Values and Moral Development, 1976, Value-Moral Education: The Schools and the Teachers, 1979, Fordham: The Early Years, 1998; cons. editor: Personnel and Guidance Jour., 1978-81; contbr. numerous articles to profl. jours. Mem. APA. Office: Fordham U Loyola Hall Bronx NY 10458

HENNESY, GERALD CRAFT, artist; b. Washington, June 11, 1921; s. Gerald Craft and Frances Lee (Moore) H.; m. Elizabeth Ann Lovering, Mar. 4, 1950; children: Kathleen, Paul Brian, Shawn, High, Craig. Student, Corcoran Sch. Art, 1939, George Washington U., 1940; BS, U. Md., 1948. Enlisted U.S. Navy, 1942, advanced through grades to comdr., 1956; mgmt. analyst U.S. Air Force Hdqrs., Pentagon, Washington, 1948-52, 53-56; asst dir. for orgn. and mgmt. AEC, 1956-72; artist, dir. Studio of Hennesy, Clifton, Va., 1972—. One man shows include PLA Gallery, McLean, Va., 1967, Tolley Galleries, Washington, 1983, Venable Neslage Galleries, Washington, 1993, Marin-Price Galleries, Chevy Chase Md., 1995, 96, 98; exhibited works at Corcoran Gallery Art, Washington, 1957, 59, 67, Smithsonian Inst., Washington, 1962, 64, Allied Artists of Am., N.Y.C., 1974, 75; represented in permanent collections at U.S. Ho. of Reps., Washington, Md. State Exec. Mansion, Annapolis, Nat. Hdqrs. Am. Legion, Washington, Nat. Hdqrs. DAR, Washington, Hdqrs. FDIC, Washington, others. Decorated Air medal with one star. Mem. Washington Soc. Landscape Painters. Republican. Home and Office: 6811 White Rock Rd Clifton VA 20124-1434

HENNIES, CLYDE ALBERT (LOU), military officer, state official, military academy administrator; b. Manly, Iowa, Oct. 31, 1935; s. William Albert and Dorothy Lucille (Harrington) H.; m. Connie Lee Baker, June 12, 1974; children: David Lowthian, Geoffrey Lowthian. BGS in Polit. Sci., U. Nebr., Omaha, 1972; MS in Journalism, U. Nebr., Lincoln, 1983; MS in Pub. Adminstrn., Shippensburg (Pa.) U., 1983. Commd. 2d lt. U.S. Army, 1963—, advanced through grades to major gen., 1988; comdr. 3 Units and S-3, 7th Squadron, 17th Cavalry, 17th Aviation Group, Vietnam, 1969-70; chief pub. affairs hdqrs. U.S. Army Europe and Seventh Army, 1983-84; dep. chief pub. affairs Office Chief of Pub. Affairs, Washington, 1986-89; commanding gen. U.S. Army Safety Ctr./Dir. Army Safety, Ft. Rucker, Ala., 1989-91; adj. gen. hdqrs. State Area Command, Ala. Army N.G., Montgomery, 1995-99; pres. Lyman Ward Mil. Acad., Camp Hill, Ala., 1999—; cons. Hennies Group, Inc., Ozark, Ala., 1991-95; advisor film industry on Firebird, 1989, 90. Pres. Broad St. Assn., Ozark, 1990—; bd. dirs. Flowers Performing Arts Ctr., 1992; exec. bd. Boys and Girls Club of Am., 1994—. Decorated D.S.M., Silver Star, Legion of Merit with oak leaf cluster, D.F.C., Bronze Star with 7 oak leaf clusters, with V device, Air medals with 2 V devices, Air medals (27), Purple Heart, Army Commendation medal with oak leaf cluster, Vietnam Svc. Medal, Vietnam Medal of Honor, Vietnam Gallantry Cross, D.S.M. with oak leaf cluster, Ala.; Order of Mil. Merit, Rep. of Korea. Mem. AAAA (exec. v.p.), Assn. U.S. Army, Nat. Wild Turkey Fedn., Army Aviation Assn. Am., Rotary. Methodist. Avocations: training gun dogs, hunting, music/performing arts, golf, handball. Home: Pres Qtrs Lyman Ward Mil Acad Camp Hill AL 36850 Office: PO Box 178 Camp Hill AL 36850

HENNIG, ALFRED W., lawyer; b. Istanbul, Turkey, July 15, 1952; came to the U.S., 1958; s. Rolf Alfred Hennig and Clara Del Favero. Student, Albert Ludwigs U., Freiburg, Germany, 1973; BA, U. Redlands, 1974; postgrad., Sorbonne, Paris, 1977; JD, Santa Barbara Coll. Law, 1979; postgrad., UCLA, 1993. Bar: Calif. Lab. asst. Dr. Paul Lohmann GmbH, Emmerthal, Germany, 1973; exec. ast. Sadolin & Stimman Co., Lima, Peru, 1974; legal asst. Santa Barbara (Calif.) County Pub. Defender, 1977; enumerator U.S. Dept. Commerce, Bur. of the Census, San Diego, 1980; atty. intern internat. law Barrera, Siqueiros & Torres Landa, Mexico City, 1981; atty. Cardenas & Fifield, El Centro, Calif., 1983-85, Read, Miguelez & Dib, L.A., 1985-90, Oliver Law Offices, L.A., 1990-92; pvt. practice L.A., 1993—; pres. Internat. Club, Redlands, Calif., 1973-74. Mem. Internat. Law Soc., Country Club Woods (bd. mem. 1997—), Turner Club, Alpha Mu Gamma, Pi Gamma Mu. Avocations: photography, equitation, cycling, travel, foreign languages. E-mail: derfla@jps.net. Office: Ste 104 3440 Torrance Blvd Torrance CA 90503

HENNIG, CHARLES WILLIAM, psychology educator; b. Queens, N.Y., May 7, 1949; s. Charles Joseph and Evelyn Mary (Gerstel) H.; m. Mary Christina Shamrock, Jan. 9, 1982; 1 child, Brian Steve. BA, SUNY, Buffalo, 1971; MS, Tulane U., 1976, PhD, 1978. Grad. teaching asst. Tulane U., New Orleans, 1974-78; vis. asst. prof. psychology U. Okla., Norman, 1978-79, Centre Coll. Ky., Danville, 1979-80; asst. prof. Salem (W.Va.) Coll., 1980-83, assoc. prof., 1983-88, prof., 1988-89, chair psychology, 1983-89; prof., chair psychology McMurry U., Abilene, Tex., 1989—. Contbr. articles to profl. jours. Bd. dirs. client advocacy coun. Abilene MH/MR, 1996—, chair, 1998—, mem. human rights com., 1998—; bd. dirs. Family Outreach of Abilene, 1999—. Mem. APA, Am. Psychol. Soc., Animal Behavior Soc., Psychonomic Soc., Midwestern Psychol. Assn., Southeastern Psychol. Assn., Abilene Psychol. Assn. (sec.-treas. 1990-91, 94-95, pres. 1992-93, 96-97), Psi Chi. Republican. Roman Catholic. Avocations: travel, reading. Home: 4701 Stonehedge Rd Abilene TX 79606-3429 Office: McMurry U Psychology Dept PO Box 86 Abilene TX 79697-0086

HENNIGAN, PAUL, municipal official. MPA, U. Pitts. Dir. fin., CFO City of Pitts., 1994—; exec. dir. City of Pitts. pension fund. Office: Finance Dept 200 City County Bldg 414 Grant St Pittsburgh PA 15219-2409*

HENNIGAR, DAVID JOHN, investment broker; b. Windsor, N.S., Can., July 5, 1939; s. Dean S. and Jean B. (Jodrey) H.; m. Carolyn Hiltz, June 8, 1964; children: Brian, Jan. B of Commerce, Mt. Allison U., 1960; MBA, Queen's U., 1962. Investment analyst Burns Fry Ltd. and predecessor co., Toronto, Ont., Can., 1963-66; br. mgr. Burns Fry Ltd. and predecessor co., Halifax, N.S., Can., 1966-71, Atlantic regional dir., 1971-93; chmn. bd. dirs. Annapolis Basin Group Inc.; chmn. Extendicare Inc., Acadian Securities Inc., Aquarius Coatings Inc., Cougar Aviation Inc., High Liner Foods, Inc., Tomanet Inc.; bd. dirs. Crown Life Ins. Co., Minas Basin Pulp & Power Co. Ltd., Ben's Holdings Ltd., Scotia Investment Ltd., Cobi Foods Inc., Atlantic Shopping Ctrs. Ltd., Landmark Corp., Maritime Paper Products Ltd., Sentex Systems Ltd., Alternative Fin. Corp. Bd. dirs., treas. Izaak Walton Killam Hosp. for Children, Halifax, 1976-82; bd. dirs. Inst. for Rsch. on Pub. Policy, Ottawa, Ont., 1983-89; chmn. Oceans Inst. Can.; mem. Trilateral Commn., 1988-94; bd. govs. Dalhousie U., 1983-90. Mem. Investment Dealers Assn. Can. (nat. bd. dirs. 1985-87), Internat. Oceans Inst., Halifax Club. Home: 51 Forest Ln, Bedford, NS Canada B4A 1H8 Office: 3 Bedford Hills Rd, Bedford, NS Canada B4A 1J5 also: Extendicare, 3000 Steeles Ave E, Ontario, ON Canada L3R 9W2

HENNIGAR, WILLIAM GRANT, JR., dentist; b. Buffalo, Dec. 25, 1947; s. William Grant and Donnette (Glaeser) H.; m. Jennie Carcaud, Mar. 22, 1975 (div.); children: William Grant III, Charlotte Carcaud, Travis Wellshofer, Brittany Lines. AB, Colgate U., 1970; DMD, U. Pa., 1973; cert., U. Rochester, 1975; JD, Cleve. State U., 1992. Bar: Mass., N.Y. 1993. With Harvard U. Health Inc., Cambridge, Mass., 1974; ptnr. Am. Family Dental Group, P.C., Cheektowaga, N.Y., 1982-97; pres. Grand Island, Cheektowaga, N.Y., 1988—; Bd. dirs. West River Homeowners Assn., Grand Island, 1985-88, Alumni Bd. Nichols Sch., Buffalo, 1988-89. Lic. capt. U.S. Coast Guard, 1989—. Fellow Acad. of Gen. Dentistry, ADA, Town of Grand Isl. Long Range Planning Com., 1998; mem. ABA, N.Y.State Bar Assn., Internat. Assn. for Orthodontics, Am. Acad. Dental Group Practice, U.S. Dental Inst. (cert. 1985), Erie County Bar Assn.,Buffalo Launch Club (Grand Island), Phi Kappa Psi, Psi Omega, U.S. Power Squadron. Libertarian. Episcopalian. Avocations: volleyball, boating, softball, genealogy. Home: 1275 W River Rd Grand Island NY 14072-2421 Office: Am Family Dental Group 2025 Whitehaven Rd Grand Island NY 14072-2024

HENNING, GEORGE THOMAS, JR., steel company executive; b. West Reading, Pa., Sept. 26, 1941; s. George Thomas and Helen Virginia (Spangler) H.; m. Susan Young, July 21, 1962; children: George Thomas III, Michael Kevin. B.A., Pa. State U., 1963; M.B.A., Harvard, 1965. Mgr. econ. analysis Eastern Gas & Fuel, Boston, 1967; mgr. gen. acctg. Ohio River Co., Cin., 1968; asst. to contr. Eastern Gas & Fuel Assos., Boston, 1969; dir. corp. planning Boston Gas Co., 1970; contr. Eastern Assoc. Coal Corp., Pitts., 1971-74; v.p., contr. Lykes Resources, Inc., 1974-78; asst. contr. Jones & Laughlin Steel Corp., 1979-85; gen. mgr. coal mine ops. and raw materials sales LTV Steel Co., Cleve., 1986, gen. mgr. asset mgmt., 1986-89; v.p., chief fin. officer Pioneer Chlor Alkali Co., Inc., Houston, 1988-95; v.p., CFO Pioneer Cos., Inc., 1995; v.p., contr. The LTV Corp., Cleve., 1995—. Mem. Pa. State Alumni Council. Mem. Omicron Delta Kappa, Pi Gamma Mu. Presbyterian. Office: The LTV Corp 200 Public Sq Cleveland OH 44114-2301

HENNING, JOEL FRANK, lawyer, author, publisher, consultant; b. Chgo., Sept. 15, 1939; s. Alexander M. and Henrietta (Frank) H.; m. Grace Weiner, May 24, 1964 (div. July 1987); children: Justine, Sarah-Anne, Dara; m. Rosemary Nadolsky, June 21, 1992; 1 child, Alexandra. AB, Harvard U., 1961, JD, 1964. Bar: Ill. 1965. Assoc. Sonnenschein, Levinson, Carlin, Nath & Rosenthal, Chgo., 1965-70; fellow, dir. program Adlai Stevenson Inst. Internat. Affairs, Chgo., 1970-73; nat. dir. Youth Edn. for Citizenship, 1972-75; dir. profl. edn. Am. Bar Assn., Chgo., 1975-78; asst. exec. dir. comm. and edn. ABA, 1978-80; ptnr. Joel Henning & Assocs., 1980-87; sr. v.p., gen. counsel, mem. exec. com. Hildebrandt, Inc., 1987—; pres., pub. LawLetters, Inc., 1980-89; pub. Lawyer Hiring and Tng. Report, 1980-89; Chgo. theater critic Wall St. Jour., 1989—; pub. Almanac of Fed. Judiciary, 1984-89; editor Bus. Lawyer Update, 1980-87; mem. faculty Inst. on Law and Ethics, Council Philos. Studies; chmn. Fund for Justice, Chgo., 1979-85. Author: Law-Related Education in America: Guidelines for the Future, 1975, Holistic Running: Beyond the Threshhold of Fitness, 1978, Mandate for Change: The Impact of Law on Educational Innovaiton, 1979, Improving Lawyer Productivity: How to Train, Manage and Supervise Your Lawyers, 1985, Law Practice and Management Desk Book, 1987, Lawyers Guide to Managing and Training Lawyers, 1988, Maximizing Law Firm Profitability: Hiring, Training and Developing Productive Lawyers, 1991-98, also articles. Chmn. Gov.'s Commn. on Financing Arts in Ill., 1970-71; bd. dirs. Ill. Arts Council, 1971-81, Columbia Coll., Chgo.; bd. dirs., v.p., pub. edn. exec. com. ACLU of Ill.; trustee S.E. Chgo. Commn.; mem. Joseph Jefferson Theatrical Awards Com. Fellow Am. Bar Found. (life); mem. Am. Law Inst., ABA (ho. of dels.), Chgo. Bar Assn., Chgo. Council Lawyers (co-founder), Social Sci. Edn. Consortium. Office: 150 N Michigan Ave Ste 3600 Chicago IL 60601-7572 *The hardest question for me to answer is, "What do you do?" I do a lot. Some of it returns money and satisfaction. Some returns more of one than the other. And, I do some things that make me feel fit. The best of what I do helps integrate my various selves and improves my relations with the world. But I have no facile way to say all of this at cocktail parties when, invariably, that question is popped.*

HENNING, JOHN EDWARD, secondary school educator in English, researcher; b. Canton, Ohio, Apr. 1, 1954; s. Edward Ira and Betty Lee (Vaughn) Gloekler; m. Maria Carmen Coluizzi, June 14, 1980; children: Carl John, Alex Christopher. BS in Agr., Pa. State U., 1977; MEd in Vocational Edn., Kent State U., 1982; AS in Computers, Stark Tech. Coll., 1985. Tchr. agr. West Br. H.S., Beloit, Ohio, 1978, Marlington H.S., Alliance, Ohio, 1978-87; tchr. of English Marlington H.S., Alliance, 1987—; presenter nat. conf. and rsch. confs. on Edn. and English Lang. Named Martha Holden Jennings scholar Martha Holden Jennings Found., Kent State U., 1993; finalist for Stark County Tchr. of Yr., 1993-94; Marlington H.S. Tchr. of Yr., Student Coun. Mem. NEA, APA, Ohio Edn. Assn., Nat. Coun. Tchrs. of English, Am. Edni. Rsch. Assn., Semiotic Soc. Am., Elks, Phi Delta Kappa (pres., v.p. 1995-97). Home: 1051 Briarcliff Ave Alliance OH 44601 Office: Marlington HS 10450 Moulin Ave Alliance OH 44601

HENNING, LORNE EDWARD, professional hockey coach; b. Melfort, Sask., Can., Feb. 23, 1952; s. Robert Henning; m. Cathye Henning, 7/25/74; children: Brett. Profl. hockey player N.Y. Islanders, NHL, 1972-81; player/asst. coach N.Y. Islanders, 1980-81, asst. coach, 1984; coach Springfield Indians (AHL), 1984-85, Minn. North Stars, NHL, 1985-87; asst. coach N.Y. Islanders, 1989, coach, 1994-95; asst. coach Chicago Blackhawks, 1995-98, N.Y. Islanders, 1998—. Office: NY Islanders Nassau Coliseum Uniondale NY 11553*

HENNING, MICHAEL ANTHONY, diversified financial company executive; b. N.Y.C., May 1, 1940. Grad., St. Francis Coll., BBA, 1961; grad., Harvard U. Intern Ernst & Young, N.Y.C., 1960, mem. audit staff, 1961-65, mem. internat. tax dept., 1965-73, ptnr., 1973-78, ptnr. in charge internat. tax, 1978-85, mng. ptnr. N.Y. office, 1985-91, vice chmn. tax svcs., 1991-93, co-chair U.S. firm, 1993-94; CEO Ernst & Young Internat., N.Y.C., 1994-98, chmn., 1995-98; dept. chmn. LLT, 1998—. Bd. dirs. BBB. Met. N.Y., Inc., Saint Francis Prep. Sch., Saint Francis Coll. Mem. Am. Inst. CPAs (chmn. internat. tax com.), N.Y. State Soc. CPAs (chmn. internat. tax com.). Office: Ernst & Young 787 7th Ave Fl 23 New York NY 10019-6018*

HENNING, NEIL SCOTT, financial consultant; b. S.I., N.Y., Nov. 30, 1961; s. Hugo L. and Janette (Tasker) H.; m. Robyn R. Cooper, Mar. 21, 1987; children: Samantha, Kirsten, Pamela. Retirement specialist Copeland Cos., Clark, N.J., 1983-92; account exec. Cigna, Hackensack, N.J., 1992-93, Lincoln Investment Planning, Florham Park, N.J., 1993—. Named to Summit Club, Am. Inst. Mgmt., 1992. Mem. Freemasons (sr. deacon Nutley, N.J. 1995—, chmn. scholarship com. 1997, mem. budget com. 1997, jr. warden 1999). Republican. Avocations: golf, model trains, philately. Home: 31 Terrace Ave Nutley NJ 07110-1139 Office: Lincoln Investment Planning 100 Campus Dr Florham Park NJ 07932-1006

HENNING, RUDOLF ERNST, electrical engineer, educator, consultant; b. Hamburg, Germany, Aug. 3, 1923; came to U.S., 1939; s. Ernest P. and Emmy (Rosenfeld) H.; m. Patricia Ann Miklas, Sept. 30, 1961; 1 child, Patricia Emerson Irwin. BSEE, Columbia U., 1943, MSEE, 1947, D Engring. Sci. in EE, 1954. Registered profl. engr., Fla. Jr. engr. Radio Receptor Co., N.Y.C., 1946; project engr., sect. head Sperry Gyroscope Co., Great Neck, N.Y., 1947-58; chief engr. Sperry Microwave Electronics Co., Clearwater, Fla., 1958-70; acting asst. dean U. South Fla. Coll. Engring., Tampa, 1970-71; assoc. dean U. South Fla., Tampa, 1971-82, prof. elec. engring., 1982-95, Disting. prof., 1995—; chmn. elect. engring. dept. U. South Fla., Tampa, 1986-87; dept. head Naval Electronics Lab. Ctr., San Diego, 1971; program evaluator Accreditation Bd. Engring. and Tech., N.Y.C., 1988-95; mem. rev. panel NSF, 1989; cons. in field. Mem. devel. coun. Morton F. Plant Hosp., Clearwater, Fla., 1970; bd. dirs. Clearwater Community Concert Assn., 1963-65, S.E. Consortium for Minorities in Engring., Atlanta, 1979-82; founder, dir., adviser Yes We Care! Minority Engring. Program, Pinellas County, Fla., 1983—, Hillsborough County, Fla., 1991—. With U.S. Army, 1944-46, ETO. Recipient Pres.'s Affirmative Action award U. South Fla., 1986, Disting. Svc. award, 1990; named Engr. of Yr. by Tampa Bay Engring. Socs., 1987. Fellow IEEE (Centennial medal 1984, U.S. Activities Bd. Citation of Honor 1992), Microwave Theory and Tech. Soc. IEEE (pres. 1968, chmn. Internat. Microwave Symposia 1965, 79, co-chmn. 1995, Automated Measurement Career award 1986, Disting. Svc. award 1996); mem. Electromagnetics Acad., Fla. Engring. Soc., Am. Soc. Engring. Edn., Sigma Xi (pres. U. South Fla. chpt. 1977-78). Presbyterian. Avocations: hiking, travel, gardening, orchids. Office: U South Fla Dept Elec Engring Tampa FL 33620

HENNING, SYLVIE DEBEVEC, French language educator; b. Cleve., Apr. 11, 1948; d. Ladislav Ignatius and Denise Celine (Hannais) Debevec; m. Eric Maxim Henning, May 31, 1975. BA in French, Case Western Res. U., 1970, MA in French, 1974, PhD, 1975. Asst. prof. U. Wis.-Parkside, Kenosha, 1975-77; assoc. prof. U. Rochester, N.Y., 1977-85; prof. French SUNY, Plattsburgh, 1985—; chmn. dept. lang. and lit. SUNY, Plattsburgh, 1989—; exec. coun. Assn. Dept. of Fgn. Lang., N.Y.C., 1993—. Author: Genet's Ritual Play, 1981, Beckett's Critical Complicity 1988 (Midwest MLA award 1987); contbr. articles to profl. jours. Recipient Disting. Faculty award Phi Eta Sigma, 1987, Cross Border Studies award U.S. Dept. Edn. Title VI, 1993, Faculty fellowship Mellon Found., 1981. Mem. MLA, Am. Coun. Teaching Fgn. Lang., Am. Assn. Tchrs. French, Beckett Soc. Office: SUNY Dept French Plattsburgh NY 12901

HENNING, TERESA BETH, English educator; b. Princeton, Ill., Dec. 16, 1967; d. John Francis and Diana K. (Parsons) H.; m. Gary Bruce Garcia, May 25, 1996. BA, Ill. State U., 1989; MA, Purdue U., 1991, PhD, 1998. Undergrad. tchg. asst. Ill. State U., Normal, 1988-89; grad. instr. Purdue U., West Lafayette, Ind., 1989-96; lectr. Ind. U./Purdue U., Indpls., 1996—; spkr. in field. Ill. State scholar, State of Ill., 1986-87; Purdue Rsch. Found. Summer grantee Purdue U., West Lafayette, 1994. Mem. MLA, Nat. Coun. Tchrs. English, Conf. on Coll. Composition and Comm., Ind. Tchrs. Writing, Golden Key. Office: IUPUI Dept English 502L Cavanaugh Hall 425 University Blvd Indianapolis IN 46202-5148

HENNING, WILLIAM THOMAS, museum director; b. Denver, Mar. 5, 1937; s. William Thomas Sr. and Rosalee (Bennett) H.; m. Eleanor Ann Whiteley, May 29, 1958; children: Cynthia Diane, Thomas Reed, David Randal. BFA, Phillips U., Enid, Okla., 1959; MA, U. Denver, 1963; postgrad., U. Iowa, 1966-69. Instr. Ariz. Western Coll., Yuma, 1963-66; asst. prof. Phillips U., 1969-75; curator Colorado Springs Fine Art Ctr., 1976-79, Hunter Mus. Art, Chattanooga, 1980-87, Ark. Arts Ctr., Little Rock, 1987-91, U. Ky. Art Mus., Lexington, 1991-96; dir. Rosemount Mus., Pueblo, Colo., 1996—; adj. faculty U. Ark., Little Rock, 1990-91, U. Ky., Lexington, 1995, U. So. Colo., Pueblo, 1997. Author: A Catalogue of the American Collection. Hunter Museum of Art, 1985; co-author: A Spectacular Vision: The George and Susan Proskauer Collection, 1994. Mem. Am. Assn. Museums, Mountain-Plains Mus. Assn., Nat. Trust for Historic Preservation, Rotary Club, Blue Key. Episcopalian. Avocations: reading, research writing. Home: 6B Windbridge Ln Pueblo CO 81001-1400 Office: Rosemount Mus 419 W 14th St Pueblo CO 81003-2707

HENNINGER, BRIAN, professional golfer; b. Sacramento, Oct. 19, 1962; m. Catherine Henninger; children: Carlin, Hunter. Degree in psychology, U. So. Calif., 1987. Profl. golfer, 1987—; winner Deposit Guaranty Golf Classic, 1994. Won Queen Mary Open, 1989, Pacific Coast Amateur, 1989, Macon Open, 1992, Tex. Open, 1992, Knoxville Open, 1992, Deposit Guaranty Golf Classic, 1994. Office: PGA Am Box 109601 100 Avenue Of Champions Palm Beach Gardens FL 33410*

HENNINGER, POLLY, neuropsychologist, researcher and clinician; b. Pasadena, Calif., Apr. 1, 1946; d. Paul Bennett and Mary (MacNair) Johnson; m. Richard Henninger Jr., 1966 (div. 1983); children: Marguerite, Nathan; m. Clyde Pechstedt, 1985 (div. 1992). BA, Ind. U., 1967, Pomona Coll., 1977; MA, U. Toronto, 1969, PhD, 1982; PhD (respecialization), Fuller Theol. Sem., 1995; LLD (hon.), Johnson and Wales U., 1993, Williams Coll., 1993, U. R.I., 1998. Registered psychologist, Ont., Can., Mass. Postdoctoral fellow Calif. Inst. Tech., Pasadena, 1982-84; doctoral respecialization in clin. psychology Fuller Theol. Sem., Pasadena, 1991-95; asst. prof. Pitzer Coll., Claremont, Calif., 1984-87, Brock U., St. Catharines, Ont., 1987-91; vis. assoc. divsn. biology Calif. Inst. Tech., Pasadena, 1984-94; asst. dir. neuropsychol. svcs. Ctr. for Aging Resources, Fuller Theol. Sem., Pasadena, 1991-92; psychology intern Boston VA Med. Ctr. and New Eng. Med. Ctr., 1994-95; neuropsychology fellow Tufts Med. Sch., Boston, 1995-96; staff neuropsychologist Fall River Outpatient Clinic Braintree Rehab. Hosp., 1996, Cambridge (Mass.) Hosp., Harvard Med. Sch., 1996-97; rsch. affil. McLean Hosp., Harvard Med. Sch., Belmont, Mass., 1997—. Contbr. chpts. to books, articles to profl. jours.; host cable tv program, 1996—. Recipient fellowships and grants. Mem. APA (div. 40 chair rsch. selection 1986-89), Nat. Acad. Neuropsychology, Cognitive Neurosci. Soc., Internat. Neuropsychol. Soc. Democrat. Episcopalian. Home: 16 Fainwood Cir # 2 Cambridge MA 02139-1110 Office: Cambridge Hosp Dept Psychiatry 1493 Cambridge St Dept Cambridge MA 02139-1099

HENNINGS, DOROTHY ANN, financial adviser; b. Spokane, Wash., Mar. 23, 1937; d. Theodore Baza LaRue and Florence Irene (Jaeger) Innes; m. Peter L. Sbarbaro Sr., May 16, 1959 (div. 1973); children: Peter L. Jr., David

A., John E. AS in Acctg., Napa Valley Coll., 1974; BS, Calif. State U., Sacramento, 1977. Cert. fin. planner. Acctg. asst. Napa (Calif.) County Counsel for Econ. Opportunity, 1972-73; owner, cons. Dash Enterprises, American Canyon, Calif., 1973-78; owner, bookkeeper Reliable Meats, American Canyon, 1973-74; fin. planner IDS Fin. Svcs., Napa, 1983-94, Am. Express Fin. Advisors, Napa, 1995—. Vol. Boy Scouts Am., Am. Canyon PTA, Little League, Pop Warner Football; sponsor T-ball and Babe Ruth Bambino and Babe Ruth League Teams; tax preparer Vita, Napa, 1973-74. Mem. Soroptimist Club, Order Ea. Star, Women of Moose, Greater Napa Valley Lions. Republican. Office: Am Express Fin Advisors 3033 California Blvd Napa CA 94558-3304

HENNINGS, DOROTHY GRANT (MRS. GEORGE HENNINGS), educational educator; b. Paterson, N.J., Mar. 15, 1935; d. William Albert and Ethel Barbara (Moll) Grant; m. George Hennings, June 15, 1968. AB, Barnard Coll., 1956; MEd (NSF Acad. Yr. Inst. grantee), U. Va., 1959; EdD (Field Enterprise grantee), Columbia, 1965. Tchr., Pierrepont Elem. Sch., Rutherford, N.J., 1956-58, Thomas Jefferson Jr. High Sch., Fair Lawn, N.J., 1959-64; prof. edn. Kean U. of N.J., Union, 1965-99, disting. prof. edn. 1999—. Recipient Edn. Press. award, 1974, Outstanding Article award, 1999. Author citation N.J. Inst. Tech., Div. Continuing Edn., 1982. Mem. Nat. Coun. Tchrs. English, N.J. Reading Assn. (Disting Svc. to Reading award 1993), Internat. Reading Assn. (Outstanding Tchr. Educator in Reading award 1992), Suburban Reading Coun., Phi Beta Kappa, Phi Delta Kappa, Phi Kappa Phi, Kappa Delta Pi. Author: (with B. Grant) Teacher Moves, 1971; Content and Craft: Written Expression in the Elementary Sch., 1973; Smiles, Nods and Pauses: Activities to Enrich Children's Communication Skills, 1974; Mastering Classroom Communication: What Interaction Analysis Tells the Teacher, 1975; (with G. Hennings) Keep Earth Clean, Blue and Green: Environmental Activities for Young People, 1976; Words, Sounds, and Thoughts: More Activities to Enrich Children's Communication Skills, 1977; Communication in Action: Teaching the Language Arts, 1978, 6th edit., 1997; (with D. Russell) Listening Aids Through the Grades, 1979; (with G. Hennings) Today's Elementary Social Studies, 1980, 2d edit., 1989; Written Expression in the Language Arts, 1981; Teaching Communication and Reading Skills in the Content Areas, 1982; (with L. Fay) Star Show, 1989, Grand Tour, 1989, Previews, 1989, Reading with Meaning: Strategies for College Reading, 1990, 4th rev. edit., 1999, Poets Journal, 1991, Beyond the Read Aloud: Learning to Read Through Listening to and Reflecting on Literature, 1992; contbr. articles to Edn., The Record, Lang. Arts, Sci. Tchr., The Reading Tchr., Jour. of Reading, Tchr. to Tchrs., Sci. and Children, Early Years, Reading Research and Instruction, New Eng. Jour. of History, Jour. Reading Edn., others. Home: 21 Flintlock Dr Warren NJ 07059-5014 Office: Kean U Morris Ave Union NJ 07083

HENNINGSEN, PETER, JR., diversified industry executive; b. Mpls., Oct. 6, 1926; s. Peter and Anna O. (Kjelstrup) H.; m. Donna J. Buresh, June 19, 1948; children—Deborah, Pamela, James. BBA, U. Minn., 1950. Packaging engr. govt. and aero. products div. Honeywell, Inc., Mpls., 1950-72; mgr. packaging Internat. Tel. & Tel., N.Y.C., 1972-80; v.p. Raymond Eisenhardt & Son, Inc., 1980-90; ind. packaging and material handling cons., 1990—; mem. Inst. Packaging Profls. (formerly Soc. Packaging and Handling Engrs.), 1951—, fellow, 1970, pres., 1970-71, chmn. bd., 1972-73, named Man of Yr., 1968. Editl. cons. mags. in field. With USNR, 1944-46. Elected to Packaging Hall of Fame, Packaging Edn. Forum, 1995. Mem. ASTM, Aerospace Industries Assn. (chmn. packaging com. 1967), Masons, Shriners. Methodist. Home and Office: 15717 Woodgate Rd N Minnetonka MN 55345-4533

HENNION, CAROLYN LAIRD (LYN HENNION), investment executive; b. Orange, Calif., July 27, 1943; d. George James and Jane (Porter) Laird; m. Reeve L. Hennion, Sept. 12, 1964; children: Jeffrey Reeve, Douglas Laird. BA, Stanford U., 1965; grad. Securities Industry Inst., U. Pa., 1992. CFP, fund specialist; lic. ins. agt.; registered gen. securities prin. Portfolio analyst Schwabacher & Co., San Francisco, 1965-66; adminstrv. coord. Bicentennial Commn., San Mateo County, Calif., 1972-73; dir. devel. Crystal Springs Uplands Sch., Hillsborough, Calif., 1973-84; tax preparer Household Fin. Corp., Foster City, Calif., 1982; freelance, 1983-87; sales promotion mgr. Franklin Distbrs., Inc., San Mateo, 1984-86, v.p. and regional sales mgr. of N.W., 1986-91; v.p. Viatech, Inc., 1986-92; proprietor Buncom Ranch, 1990—; v.p. Mid-Atlantic, 1991-94, Keypoint Svcs. Internat., 1992—; pres. Brock Rd. Corp., 1993—; v.p. Strand, Atkinson, Williams & York, Medford, Oreg., 1994—. Editor: Lest We Forget, 1975. Pres. South Hillsborough Sch. Parents' Group, 1974-75; sec. Vol. Bur. of San Mateo County, Burlingame, Calif., 1975; chmn. Cmty. Info. Com., Town of Hillsborough, 1984-86, mem., subcom. chmn. fin. adv. com., 1984-86; mem. adv. com. Jackson County Airport, 1996—, vice chair, 1999—; mem. coun. Town of Buncom, Oreg., 1990—; bd. dirs. Pacific N.W. Mus. Natural History, 1995-96; chmn. Jackson County Applegate Trail Sesquicentennial Celebration, 1995-97; treas. Sesquicentennial Wagon Train, 1995-97; founding dir. So. Oreg. Hist. Soc. Found., v.p., sec., 1995-98, pres., 1998—; trustee Oreg. Shakespeare Festival Endowment Fund, 1996—, sec., treas., 1997-98, pres., 1998—; bd. dirs. Providence Cmty. Health Found., 1996—, chmn. planned giving com., 1997—, sec., 1998—; dir. Rogue Valley Manor Cmty. Svcs., 1996—, vice-chair, 1997—; dir. Cratrian Performances Co., 1997—, chmn. mem. com., 1998—; dir. So. Oreg. Estate Planning Coun., 1997—, pres., 1998-99. Recipient awards Coun. for Advancement and Support of Edn., 1981, Exemplary Direct Mail Appeals Fund Raising Inst., 1982, Wholesaler of Yr., Golden Mic award Frederic Gilbert Assocs., 1993; named Wholesaler of Yr., Shearson Lehman Hutton N.W. Region, 1989, among Top 300 Fin. Advisors, Worth Mag., 1998. Home: 3232 Little Applegate Rd Jacksonville OR 97530-9303 Office: Strand Atkinson Williams & York 1 N Holly St Medford OR 97501-2720

HENNION, REEVE LAWRENCE, communications executive; b. Ventura, Calif., Dec. 7, 1941; s. Tom Reeve and Evelyn Edna (Henry) H.; m. Carolyn Laird, Sept. 12, 1964; children: Jeffrey Reeve, Douglas Laird. B.A., Stanford U., 1963, M.A., 1965. Reporter Tulare (Calif.) Advance-Register, 1960-62; reporter UPI, San Francisco, 1963-66; mgr. UPI, Fresno, Calif., 1966-68; regional exec. UPI, Los Angeles, 1968-69; mgr. UPI, Honolulu, 1969-72, San Francisco, 1972-75; Calif. editor UPI, 1975-77, gen. news editor, 1977-81, bus. mgr., 1981-83, v.p., gen. mgr. Pacific div., 1983-85; v.p., gen. mgr. Calif.-Oreg. Broadcasting, Inc., 1985-86; pres. Viatech Inc., 1986-92; propr. Buncom Ranch; pres. Keypoint Svcs. Internat., Inc., Medford, Oreg., 1992—; interim exec. dir. Rogue Valley Coun. of Govts., 1998. Editor: The Modoc Country, 1971, Buncom: Crossroads Station, 1995. Chmn. Calif. Freedom of Info. Com., 1983-84; mem. Jackson County Planning Commn., Jackson County Roads Com.; mayor of Buncom, Oreg.; pres. Buncom Hist. Soc.; trustee So. Oreg. Hist. Soc. Mem. Am. Planning Assn. (exec. bd. Oreg. chpt.), Delta Kappa Epsilon. Home: 3232 Little Applegate Rd Jacksonville OR 97530-9303 Office: PO Box 4518 Medford OR 97501-0178

HENRETTY, DONALD BRUCE, history educator; b. Washington, June 12, 1937; s. Malcolm Senseney and Ethel Louise (Kidwell) H.; m. Elizabeth Kathleen Talbot, June 21, 1986. BA, Randolph-Macon Coll., Ashland, Va., 1959; MEd, U. Va., 1967. Cert. secondary tchr., Va. Tchr. history Annandale (Va.) H.S., 1959-90, dir. athletics, 1978-80; tchr. history Centreville (Va.) H.S., 1990-92; coach varsity soccer St. Stephen's and St. Agnes Sch., Alexandria, 1991-96, interim chair dept. history, 1996-97, tchr. history, 1993—. Dir. Camp Pleasant, Dunfries, Va., 1964, Glayden Sch. and Camp, Lucketts, Va., 1967-68; legis. asst. Va. State Senate, Richmond, 1973; chmn. bd. trustees Fairfax (Va.) Retirement Sys., 1976-77; v.p. Va. Edn. Assn., 1972-73; bd. dirs. Fairfax Edn. Assn., 1969-73, Soc. Alumni Randolph-Macon Coll., 1980-83; pres. No. Va. Soccer Coaches, Fairfax, 1982-84; lay leader Calvary United Meth. Ch., Arlington, Va., 1968-69, 72-73, 90-92. Study grantee NEH, 1983. Mem. Va. Hist. Soc. Democrat. United Methodist. Home: 8325 Toll House Rd Annandale VA 22003-4630

HENRICH, JEAN MACKAY, painter, sculptor, educator; b. Halifax, N.S., Can., Sept. 19, 1909; m. John William Henrich, 1943 (dec. 1944); 1 child, Margaret Person. Student, Art Inst. Chgo., 1929-31; BA, Antioch Coll., 1932; cert., U. Vienna, 1933; MA, U. Buffalo, 1954. Instr. sculpture Art Inst. Buffalo, 1938-43, 45-46; chmn. art dept. Buffalo Sem., 1946-79, artist-in-residence, 1979-89. One-woman shows at AAO Galleries, Buffalo, 1979, Larkin House, Buffalo Sem., 1986, 88, 89, 90, Adams Gallery, Dunkirk, N.Y., 1989, Century Club, Rochester, N.Y., 1993, Genesee Falls, N.Y., 1996, Buffalo Grammar, 1998; works include Geneva (N.Y.) Vet.'s Meml., 1939. Mem. Buffalo Soc. Artists, 20th Century Club. Unitarian. Avocation: gardening. Home and Studio: 155 Saint James Pl Buffalo NY 14222-1457

HENRICH, WILLIAM JOSEPH, JR., lawyer; b. Phila., Jan. 13, 1929; s. William J. and Helen (Moylan) H.; m. Dorothy Kolsun; children: William III, Michael, David, Richard. BA in Econs., LaSalle U., 1950; JD, Temple U., 1956. Bar: Pa. 1957, Ct. Common Pleas 1957, U.S. Dist. Ct. (ea. dist.) Pa. 1957. Assoc. Dilworth, Paxson, Kalish & Kauffman, Phila., 1957-65, ptnr., 1965-84, sr. ptnr., 1988—; pres., gen. counsel Triangle Pub. Inc., Radnor, Pa., 1985-88; bd. mgrs. Beneficial Bank, Phila; corp. sec. The Annenberg Found., St. Davids, Pa., 1985—; bd. dirs. Phila. Consolidated Holding Corp. Bd. dirs. LaSalle U., Phila., Pa., 1985—; trustee The Annenberg Sch. Comm., U. Pa., 1985—, The Annenberg Sch. Comm., U. So. Calif., L.A., 1985—; active Union League of Phila. Mem. ABA. Office: Dilworth Paxson LLP 1735 Market St Fl 32 Philadelphia PA 19103-7503

HENRICHS, ALBERT MAXIMINUS, classicist, educator; b. Cologne, Germany, Dec. 29, 1942; came to U.S., 1971; s. Johannes and Berti H.; m. Ingrid Ursula Schaadt, June 4, 1965 (div. Mar. 1990); children: Markus, Helen Felicitas; m. Maura Giles, June 19, 1997. Student, U. Cologne, 1962-66, U. Bonn, 1962-63; Dr.phil., U. Cologne, 1966, habilitation, 1969; A.M. (hon.), Harvard U., 1972. Vis. lectr. U. Mich., Ann Arbor, 1967-69; prof. U. Cologne, 1970-71; asso. prof. classics U. Calif., Berkeley, 1971-73; prof. Greek and Latin. Harvard U., Cambridge, Mass., 1973-84; Eliot prof. Greek lit. Harvard U., 1984—, chmn. dept. classics, 1982-88, mem. affiliated faculty Div. Sch., 1982—; Sather prof. classical lit. U. Calif., Berkeley, 1990; sr. fellow Ctr. for Hellenic Studies, Washington, 1992-97. Author: Didymos der Blinde Kommentar zu Hiob (Tura-Papyrus), 2 vols., 1968, Die Phoinikika des Lollianos, 1972, Die Götter Griechenlands, 1987, Warum soll ich denn tanzen? Dionysisches im Chor der griechischen Tragödie, 1996; editor: Harvard Studies in Classical Philology, 1975-79; adv. bd. Harvard Libr. Bull., 1981-95, Greek, Roman and Byzantine Studies, 1984—; contbr. articles on ancient Greek lit., papyrology, mythology and religion to scholarly jours. Fellow Am. Acad. Arts and Scis.; mem. Am. Philos. Soc., Am. Philol. Assn., Assn. Internationale de Papyrologues., Egypt Exploration Soc. Home: 272 Concord Ave Cambridge MA 02138-1338 Office: Harvard U Dept Classics 319 Boylston Hall Cambridge MA 02138

HENRICHS, W(ALTER) DEAN, dermatologist; b. Smith Center, Kans., Oct. 26, 1936; s. Walter George and Mildred (Kubias) H.; m. Barbara Ann Bremer, Apr. 7, 1967; children: Matthew, Mark, Jonathan. BA, U. Kans., 1961, MD, 1965. Diplomate Am. Bd. Dermatology, Am. Bd. Dermatopathology. Commd. ensign USN, 1964, advanced through grades to capt.; chmn. dept. dermatology Winston-Salem (N.C.) Health Care Plan, 1984—. Methodist. Avocations: golf, reading. Fax: (336) 718-1050. Office: Winston Salem Health Care 250 Charlois Blvd Winston Salem NC 27103-1579

HENRICK, MICHAEL FRANCIS, lawyer; b. Chgo., Feb. 29, 1948; s. John L. and A. Madeline (Hafner) H.; m. Cissi F. Henrick, Aug. 9, 1980; children: Michael Francis Jr., Derry Patricia. BA, Loyola U., 1971; JD with honors, John Marshall Law Sch., 1974. Bar: Ill. 1974, U.S. Dist. Ct. (no. dist.) Ill. 1974, U.S. Supreme Ct. 1979, Wis. 1985, U.S. Dist. Ct. (ea. dist.) Wis. 1985. Ptnr. Hinshaw & Culbertson, Chgo., Waukegan, Ill., 1974—. Recipient Corpus Juris Secundum award West Publ. Co., 1974. Mem. ABA, Def. Rsch. Inst., Ill. Bar Assn., Lake County Bar Assn., Ill. Hosp. Attys. Assn., Internat. Assn. of Defense Counsel, Ill. Defense Attys. Assn., Soc. Trial Lawyers Def. Rsch. Inst., Am. Inns of Ct. Office: Hinshaw & Culbertson 110 N West St Waukegan IL 60085-4330

HENRICKS, ROGER LEE, retired social services administrator; b. Wauseon, Ohio, May 16, 1943; s. Clifford Seldon and Annabelle Mae (Perkins) H.; m. Judith Ann Shimp, Aug. 28, 1966 (div. Mar. 1981); children: Wendy, Craig, Joel; m. Helen Elizabeth Dennis, June 6, 1986. BA, Adrian (Mich.) Coll., 1966. Welfare caseworker Dept. Social Svcs., Adrian, Mich., 1966-68, protective svcs. caseworker, 1968-78, supr. protective svcs., 1978-94; exec. dir. Family Awareness Ctr., Adrian, 1994-97; youth specialist Adrian Tng. Sch., 1997-98; ret.; instr. Ea. Mich. U., Ypsilanti, 1977-82, Siena Heights Coll., Adrian, 1987—, Parent Nurturing Program, Adrian, 1985—; co-founder Family Awareness Ctr., Adrian, 1982-84; presenter in field. Founder, pres. Child Abuse and Neglect Coun., Adrian, 1977—, Sexual Abuse Task Force, Adrian, 1988-97; pres., bd. dirs. Call Someone Concerned, Adrian, 1972-86, hon. bd. dirs., 1986—. Recipient Nancy Nichols award Office Substance Abuse, 1983, Mich. Pub. Servant of Yr. award Govt. Adminstrs. Assn. Found, 1988, Ray Helfer award Mich. Commn. for Prevention Child Abuse, 1989. Avocations: woodworking, softball, basketball.

HENRICKSON, BONNIE, college basketball coach. BS in Phys. Edn., St. Cloud (Minn.) U., 1986; MS in Phys. Edn., Western Ill. U., 1988. Asst. coach U. Ia., 1995-97, Big 10 regular season conf. champions, 1995-96, Big 10 tournament conf. champions, 1996-97; asst. coach Va. Poly. U. Hokies, Blacksburg, Va., 1988-95, head coach, 1997—; Atlantic 10 tournament champions Va. Poly. U. Hokies, Blacksburg, 1997-98; ranked 14th in NCAA, 1998-99. Office: c/o Athletic Dept Womens Basketball Va Poly Inst State U Blacksburg VA 24061*

HENRICKSON, EILER LEONARD, retired geologist, educator; b. Crosby, Minn., Apr. 23, 1920; s. Eiler Clarence and Mabel (Bacon) H.; children: Eiler Warren, Kristin, Kurt Eric, Ann Elizabeth. BA, Carleton Coll., 1943; PhD, U. Minn., 1956. Geologist U.S. Geol. Survey, Calif., 1943-44; instr. Carleton Coll., 1946-47, 48-51, asst. prof., 1951-53, 54-56, assoc. prof., 1956-62, prof., 1962-70, Charles L. Denison prof. geology, 1970-87, chmn. dept., 1970-78, wrestling coach, 1946-58, 83-87, Emeritus prof. geology, 1987—; prof. geology, chmn. dept. Colo. Coll., 1987-96, Emeritus prof. geology, 1997—; pres. Concentrating Systems of Am., 1996—, U.S. Vermiculite Products, 1997—, C.S.A. Corp., 1985—; instr. U. Minn., 1947-48, 53-54; vis. lectr. numerous univs., Europe, 1962; cons. Jones & Laughlin Steel Corp., 1946-58, Fremont Mining Co., Alaska, 1958-61, G.T. Schieldahl Co., Minn., 1961-62, Bear Creek Mining Co., Mich., 1965-66, U. Minn. Messenia Expdn., 1966-75, Exxon Co., 1977-78, Cargill Corp., Mpls., 1983-84, Leslie Salt Co., San Francisco, 1985-86, various other cos.; research scientist, cons. Oak Ridge (Tenn.) Nat. Lab., 1985-86; cons. Argonne Nat. Lab., 1966-78, research scientist, summers, 1966-67; field studies metamorphic areas, Norway and Scotland; dir. young scholars program NSF, 1988-90. Author: Zones of Regional Metamorphism, 1957. Dir. Northfield Bd. Edn., 1960-63; steering com. Northfield Community Devel. Program, 1966-67. Served as 1st lt. USMCR, 1943, AUS, 1944-46. Fulbright research scholar archeol. geology, Greece, 1966-87. Mem. AAAS, Mineral Soc. Am., Nat. Assn. Geology Tchrs., Minn. Acad. Sci (vis. lectr.), Am. Geol. Inst., Geol. Soc. Am., Soc. Econ. Geologists, Rocky Mountain Assn. Geologists, Nat. Wrestling Coaches and Ofcls. Assn., Archaeol. Inst. Am. (vis. lectr.), Sigma Xi. Rsch. in archael. geology, Greece and North Africa, 1977-78, in mineral potential of Greece and Egypt, 1978-79, on ore deposits and archael. geology, province of copper and tin in artifacts in N.Am. and world. Fax: 507-645-4354. Home: 2107 Park Point Dr Northfield MN 55057 Address: PO Box 674 Northfield MN 55057

HENRICKSON, MARK, social worker, priest; b. Wilmington, Del., Nov. 28, 1955; s. Bruce and Elaine Mary (Fowler) H. BA, Trinity Coll., 1977; MDiv, Episcopal Div. Sch., 1980; MSW, U. Conn., 1990; PhD, UCLA, 1996. Ordained priest, Episc. Ch., 1981. Curate Trinity Episcopal Ch., Torrington, Conn., 1980-82; chaplain resident Hartford (Conn.) Hosp., 1982-83; priest-in-charge St. Monica's Episcopal Ch., Hartford, 1983-85; pvt. practice Hartford, 1985-91; dir. AIDS/HIV program Hartford Health Dept., 1988-91; NIMH, AIDS rsch. tng. fellow UCLA, 1992-94; field unit supervisor immunization program L.A. County Dept. Health Svcs., 1995-96; HIV divsn. dir. Northeast Valley Health Corp., 1996—; mem. Permanent Task Force on AIDS, Conn., 1989-91; cons. AIDS Ministries Regional Care Team, Hartford, 1990-91; mem. part-time faculty St. Joseph's Coll., Hartford, 1991; part-time faculty Calif. State U., Northridge, 1997—; interim and supply priest Diocese of L.A. Contbr. articles to profl. jours. Recipient various civic and profl. awards. Mem. NASW. Office: 8215 Van Nuys Blvd Ste 306 Panorama City CA 91402-4839

HENRICKSON, RICHARD RALPH, composer, lyricist, musician, record producer; b. Portland, Oreg., Nov. 27, 1948; s. Jack and Lorraine Mabel (Mahar) H.; m. Sahra-Jean Bricker, May 9, 1982 (div. 1989). BS, Juilliard Sch., 1972, MusM, 1973. Violinist, asst. prin. Orch. Festival Two Worlds, Spoleto, Italy, 1970, N.J. Symphony Orch., Newark, 1970-72; prin. violin N.Y. Pro Arte Chamber Orch., N.Y.C., 1974-86; pres. Beautiful Music Unlimited., Ltd., N.Y.C., 1975—; violinist, assoc. prof. music Hofstra String Quartet Hofstra U., Hempstead, N.Y., 1985-86; violinist Hampton String Quartet, 1986—. Performed as violinist/ soloist in Broadway shows including Gottu Go Disco, 1979, Barnum, 1980-82, understudy violin, actor Sherlock Holmes, 1974-76; assoc. concertmaster 1600 Pennsylvania Ave, 1976, Peg, 1983, Singin' in the Rain, 1985-86, Sweet Charity, 1986-87, Me and My Girl, 1987-89, Fiddler on the Roof, 1990-91, Les Misérables, 1991—, also 22 others; concertmaster violin Billy Ocean, Stephanie Mills, George Benson, Jennifer Holliday, Tom Jones, Freddie Jackson, Jeffrey Osborne Kenny Lattimore albums; freelance violinist with Gregg Allman, Rick Wakeman, Paul Anka, Dixie Carter, Frank Sinatra tours and hundreds of concerts with others; solo violinist, recording artist 8 Music Minus One violin duet albums, The Tango Project album, 4 Hampton String Quartet albums; composer, orchestrator, lyricist: (ballet) Ozone Hour, 1978, (songs) Lovely Dancer, 1976 (prix d'interprétation, Grand Prix Paris Internat. Chanson, 1976), How Do You Want to Love Me? (Médaille d'Or Acad. Internat. Lutèce, Grand Prix Paris Internat. Chanson 1978), The Ballerina, 1979 (Grand prize Sound & Light Internat. Song Festival Pyramids, Giza, Egypt 1985), (musical plays) The Joy and the Passion, 1991, Sonnets from a Wand'ring Bark, 1997; studio musician (violinist) for numerous major record labels, and nationaly broadcast commls.; violinist film soundtracks include The Wiz, The Verdict, Silkwood, The Cotton Club, When Harry Met Sally, Do the Right Thing, The Age of Innocence, The Chamber, Everyone Says I Love You, Marvin's Room, Michael Collins, Mo' Better Blues, My Blue Heaven, Scent of a Woman, Striptease, numerous others; violinist, records include Village People, Sheena Easton, Paul Simon, John Sebastian, Diana Ross, Billy Cobham, many others; artist (video) Get a Job Hampton String Quartet (Grammy nomination Artist for Best Concept Music Video), 1988. Mem. ASCAP, Am. Fedn. Musicians, Inst. Audio Rsch. (resident producer 1979), Nat. Acad. Rec. Arts Scis. (video screening com. 1989-90), Rec. Musicians U.S. and Can. (bd. dirs., N.Y. chpt. 1991-92). Democrat. Congregationalist. Office: Hampton String Quartet Inc 344 W 72nd St # 1 New York NY 10023-2625

HENRICSON, BETH ELLEN, microbiologist; b. Johnson City, N.Y., Apr. 22, 1947; d. Clifford Lyle and Margaret Addison (Moore) Hevenor; m. Lawrence Karl Henricson, Aug. 9, 1969; children: Erik Karl, Karen Jeanette. BS in Microbiology, Pa. State U., 1969; postgrad., U. Rochester, 1969-70; MEd Overseas Grad. program, Boston U., Sechenheim, Germany, 1987; PhD in Biomed. Sci., Uniformed Svcs. U. Hlth. Scis., 1992. Registered clin. pub. health microbiologist Am. Acad. Microbiologists. Med. technologist Dept. of Army, Ft. Hood, Tex., 1981-84; microbiologist, med. technician Dept. of Army 5th Gen. Hosp., Stuttgart, Germany, 1986-87; predoctoral rsch. fellow USUHS, Bethesda, Md., 1987-92; NRC fellow FDA Ctr. Biol. Evaluation & Rsch., NIH, Bethesda, Md., 1992-93; postdoctoral rsch. fellow Henry M. Jackson Found., Bethesda, Md., 1993-95; microbiologist supr., quality assurance coord. Va. Dept. Agrl. and Consumer Svcs., Warrenton, Va., 1995—. Contbg. author Endotoxin Research, 1990, Bacterial Endotoxins, 1995; author, editor VDACS Office of Animal Industry Lab. Svcs. Quality Assurance Guidance Manual; contbr. articles to profl. jours. including Infection & Immunity, Molecular Medicine, Jour. Endotoxin Rsch., Jour. Vet. Diagnostic Investigation. Leader Boy Scouts Am., Hawaii, Tex., Germany, 1978-85, Girl Scouts Am., Tex., Germany, 1982-87; vol. Washington AIDS Ride, 1996—. N.Y. State Regents scholar, 1965. Mem. Assn. Vet. Microbiologists (v.p. Colonial States chpt. 1996-98, pres. 1999), Am. Assn. Vet. Lab. Diagnosticians (Bacteriology, Mycoplasmology, Mycology steering com.), Am. Soc. Microbiology, Internat. Endotoxin Soc., Nat. Environ. Health Assn., Iota Sigma Pi, Phi Sigma, Phi Beta Kappa, Phi Kappa Phi. Achievements include research in endotoxin analogs, LPS (lipopolysaccharide)-inducible gene expression, acyloxyacyl hydrolase contbn. to LPS detoxification, LPS and Taxol activation of Lyn Kinase autophosphorylation and LPS-induced cytokine production; contribution of C. diphtheriae to wound infection in an equine. Office: Va Dept Agrl Warrenton Regional Lab 272 Academy Hill Rd Warrenton VA 20186-4305

HENRIKSEN, MELVIN, mathematician, educator; b. N.Y.C., N.Y., Feb. 23, 1927; s. Kaj and Helen (Kahn) H.; m. Lillian Viola Hill, July 23, 1946 (div. 1964); children—Susan, Richard, Thomas; m. Louise Levitas, June 12, 1964 (dec. Oct. 1997). B.S., Coll. City N.Y., 1948; M.S., U. Wis., 1949, Ph.D. in Math, 1951. Asst. math., then instr. extension div. U. Wis., 1948-51; asst. prof. U. Ala., 1951-52; from instr. to prof. math. Purdue U., 1952-65; prof. math., head dept. Case Inst. Tech., 1965-68; research assoc. U. Calif. at Berkeley, 1968-69; prof., chmn. math. dept. Harvey Mudd Coll., 1969-72, prof., 1972-97, prof. emeritus, 1997—; mem. Inst. Advanced Study, Princeton, 1956-57, 63-64; vis. prof. Wayne State U., 1960-61; rsch. assoc. U. Man., Winnipeg, Can., 1975-76; vis. prof. Wesleyan U., Middletown, Conn., 1978-79, 82-83, 86-87, 93-94. Author: (with Milton Lees) Single Variable Calculus, 1970; assoc. editor: Algebra Universalis, 1993—, Topology Atlas, 1996—, Topological Commentary, 1996—; author articles on algebra, rings of functions, gen. topology. Sloan fellow, 1956-58. Mem. Am. Math. Soc., Math. Assn. Am. (assoc. editor Am. Math. monthly 1988-91, assoc. editor Algebra Universalis 1993—). Office: Harvey Mudd Coll Math Dept Claremont CA 91711*

HENRIKSEN, THOMAS HOLLINGER, university official; b. Detroit, Nov. 16, 1939; s. Paul and Irene (Hollinger) H.; m. Margaret Mary Mueller, Sept. 9, 1968; children—Heather Anne, Damien Paul Hollinger. B.A., Va. Mil. Inst., 1962; M.A., Mich. State U., 1966, Ph.D., 1969. Asst. prof. SUNY, Plattsburgh, 1969-73, assoc. prof., 1973-79, prof., 1979-80; Peace fellow Hoover Instn. on War, Revolution and Peace Stanford (Calif.) U., 1979-80, research fellow, 1980-82, sr. research fellow, 1982-86, sr. fellow, 1986—, assoc. dir., 1983—, exec. sec. nat. fellows program, 1984—, mem. Pres.'s Commn. on White House fellows, 1987-93; mem. U.S. Army Sci. Bd., 1984-90. Author: Mozambique: A History, 1978, Revolutiona and Counterrevolution: Mozambique's War of Independence, 1964-74, 1983, The New World Order: War, Peace and Military Preparedness, 1992, Clinton's Foreign Policy in Somalia, Bosnia, Haiti, and North Korea, 1996, Using Power and Diplomacy to Deal With Rogue States, 1999; co-author: The Struggle for Zimbabwe: Battle in the Bush, 1981; contbg. author, editor: Soviet and Chinese Aid to African Nations, 1980; Communist Powers in Sub-Saharan Africa, 1981; assoc. editor Yearbook on Internat. Communist Affairs, 1982-91; contbg. author, editor: One Korea? Challenges and Prospects for Reunification, 1994. Trustee George C. Marshall Found., 1993—. Served to lt. U.S. Army, 1963-65. Home: 177 Lundy Ln Palo Alto CA 94306-4563 Office: Stanford U Hoover Instn Stanford CA 94305

HENRIKSEN MACLEAN, EVA HANSINE, former anesthesiology educator; b. Petaluma, Calif., Jan. 1, 1929; d. Peder Henrik Boas and Karen (Nielsen) Henriksen; m. Daniel Edward MacLean, Aug. 25, 1957 (dec. Dec. 1981); children: Elizabeth, Mary Ann. AA, U. Calif., Berkeley, 1948, BA, 1950; MD, Yale U., 1954. Diplomate Am. Bd. Anesthesiology. Intern, resident Los Angeles County Hosp., L.A., 1954-57; from instr. to asst. prof. anesthesia Loma Linda U. (formerly Coll. Med. Evangelists), L.A., 1957-68; from instr. to assoc. prof. surgery anesthesiology Sch. Medicine U. So. Calif., L.A., 1957-94, assoc. prof. anesthesiology emeritus, 1994—; anesthesia cons. L.A. Coroner's Office, 1992-99. Mem. governing coun. Angelica Luth. Ch., 1992-99. Democrat. Avocation: patchwork quilt making. Home: 957 Arapahoe St Los Angeles CA 90006-5703

HENRIKSON, ARTHUR ALLEN, political cartoonist, educator; b. Oak Park, Ill., June 1, 1921; s. Allen Bernhardt and Florence Ella (Dixon) H.; m. Lois Elizabeth Wessling, July 3, 1943; children: Diane Elizabeth, Janet Christine, Michele Charlene Smetana. Student, Austin Acad. Fine Arts, Chgo., Chgo. Acad. Fine Arts, 1936-37; BS, Northwestern U., 1946, postgrad., 1946-51. With advt. dept. Snips Mag., Chgo., 1947-56; advt. and layout Des Plaines (Ill.) Jour., 1956; with Wessling Svcs., Des Moines. Illustrator: Living the Good Live Microwave Recipebook, 1990, PMS-Solving the Puzzle, 1995; editl. polit. cartoonist for Des Plaines Jour., 1956-69, Rockford Newspapers, Inc., 1959-73, Reporter/Progress, Downers Grove, Ill., 1959—, The Doings, Hinsdale, Ill., 1960-73, Ill. Cartoon Svc., 1961-81, Ind. Register, Libertyville, Ill., 1961-75, Suburban Life, Berwyn, Ill., Harvey

(Ill.) Tribune, 1962-73, others; contbr. cartoons to Modern Medicine, Esquire, Nat. Enquirer, AMA, Christian Sci. Monitor, others; cartoons reprinted in Today's Cartoon, 1962, Best Gag Cartoons of the Year, 1964, Best Editorial Cartoons of the Year, 1972—, also in Chgo. Sun Times, Chgo. Daily News, Chgo. Tribune, L.A. Times, Sacramento Bee, San Diego Union, U.S. News and World Report, numerous others; cartoons exhibited at Columbia U., 1960, Art Inst. Chgo., 1962, White House, Washington, 1963, LWV, Washington, 1963, others; cartoons in permanent collections at Libr. of Congress, Lyndon Baines Johnson Libr., Mus. of Cartoon Art, State Hist. Soc. Mo., others. Mem. bd. deacons First Congl. Ch., United Ch. of Christ, Des Plaines, 1970-74, chmn., 1972, 74, moderator, 1976, also mem. mission bd. and music bd.; bd. dirs. Northwest Cmty. coun. Girls Scouts U.S., 1972-79; pres. Sch. Bd. Caucus, Des Plaines, 1968-72, pres., 1970. Capt., USAF, 1942-46. Recipient numerous awards for cartoons. Mem. Assn. Editl. Cartoonists. Avocations: music, theatre, art. Home: 27 N Meyer Ct Des Plaines IL 60016-2243

HENRIKSON, DIANE ELIZABETH, career counselor; b. Chgo., July 18, 1952; d. Arthur Allen and Lois Elizabeth (Wessling) H.; m. Darrell Lee Slider, May 31, 1975 (div. Dec. 1992). BA in Spanish, U. Ill., 1974; MA in Counselor Edn., U. South Fla., 1996. Employment counselor Crown Personnel Inc., Mt. Prospect, Ill., 1974-75; bilingual tchr.'s aide Sch. Dist. #21, Wheeling, Ill., 1975; sec., asst. registrar Yale U., New Haven, 1975-77; asst. to personnel dir., personnel coord. Housing Authority New Haven, 1977-79; benefits specialist Profl. Pensions Inc., New Haven, 1980-81, Chloride Inc., Tampa, Fla., 1981-83; personnel technician II human resources dept. U. South Fla., Tampa, 1984-86, personnel technician III, personnel svcs. specialist, 1986-90, coord. human resources dept., 1990-96, career specialist career ctr., 1996—. Mem. choir St. Mark United Ch., Valrico, Fla., 1987—; mem. chorus U. South Fla., 1986-88, women's chorale, 1993-95. Mem. AAUW (treas. 1976-78, 80-81), ACA, Am. Assn. Employment in Edn., Fla. Coop. Edn. and Placement Assn., Fla. Counseling Assn., Phi Kappa Phi, Phi Beta Kappa, Alpha Lambda Delta. Avocations: singing, theater, going to theme parks, traveling. Home: 723 Herlong Ct Brandon FL 33511-5903 Office: Career Ctr U South Fla 4202 E Fowler Ave # Svc2088 Tampa FL 33620-9951

HENRION, MARILYN J., artist, fiber graphics designer; b. N.Y.C., June 16, 1932; d. Samuel and Helen Greenfield; m. Edward J. Henrion, Dec. 6, 1952; children: Jacqueline, Michele, Claudia, Dan. Cert. graphic design, Cooper Union, 1952; BA, Fordham U., 1972. Assoc. prof. Fashion Inst. Tech. SUNY, 1969-89; quilt artist, lectr. N.Y.C., 1989—. One man shows include Decouvrir Gallery, Seattle, 1997, Atlantic C.C. Art Gallery, Mays Landing, N.J., 1997, Leman Publs. Gallery, Golden, Colo., 1997, AAAS, Washington, 1996, Merrill Lynch Corp. Hdqs., Plainsboro, N.J., 1994, Chauncey Gallery, Princeton, N.J., 1992, Conant Gallery, Princeton, 1992; exhibited in group shows at Gross McCleaf Gallery, Phila., 1997, 95, Nabisco Corp. Gallery, East Hanover, N.J., 1996, Janice Charach Epstein Mus. Gallery, West Bloomfield, Mich., 1996, 97, 98, All-Russia Mus. Decorative and Applied Art, 1993, 96, Sullivan County Art Mus., Hurleyville, N.Y., 1996, Nat. Patchwork Assn. Eng., 1995, Internat. Quilt Festival, Houston, 1995, Mus. Am. Quilters Assn., Paducah, Ky., 1995, N.Y. Quilt Festival, 1995, Rye (N.Y.) Arts Ctr., 1995, La Conner (Wash.) Quilt Mus., 1998, N.Y. State Mus., Albany, 1999, Tokyo Internat. Forum, 1998, San Diego Hist. Soc. Mus., 1999, Am. Craft Mus., N.Y.C., 1998; represented in permanent collection Kaiser Permanente, Denver, Comanche County Meml. Hosp., Lawton, Okla., Rodale Press, Emmaus, Pa., Dana Farber Cancer Inst., Boston. Mem. Studio Art Quilt Assocs. (bd. dirs.), Manhattan Quilters' Guild, Art Quilt Network, Am. Quilt Study Group, Friends of Fiber Art Internat., Textile Study Group N.Y., Am. Craft Coun., Am. Quilting Soc. Home: 505 Laguardia Pl Apt 23D New York NY 10012-2005

HENRIQUES, DIANA BLACKMON, journalist; b. Bryan, Tex., Dec. 17, 1948; d. Lawrence Ernest and Pauline (Webb) Blackmon; m. Laurence Barlow Henriques, Jr., June 7, 1969. BA with distinction, George Washington U., 1969. Editor Lawrence Ledger, Lawrenceville, N.J., 1969-71; reporter Asbury Park (N.J.) Press, 1971-74; copy editor Palo Alto (Calif.) Times, 1974-76; investigative reporter Trenton (N.J.) Times, 1976-82; bus. writer The Phila. Inquirer, 1982-86; writer Barron's Fin. Weekly, N.Y.C., 1986-89, The New York Times, 1989—; vis. fellow, cons. Woodrow Wilson Sch., Princeton U., N.J., 1981-82, Guggenheim Found., N.Y., N.J., 1981-82. Author: (books) The Machinery of Greed, 1986, Fidelity's World, 1995; contbr. articles to profl. jours. Recipient Bell Prize N.J. Press Assn., 1977, Investigative Reporting prize Deadline Club, 1997. Mem. N.Y. Fin. Writers Assn., Phi Beta Kappa, Lectr. Am. Press Inst. Avocations: race walking, reading. Office: The New York Times 229 W 43rd St New York NY 10036-3959*

HENRIQUEZ-FREEMAN, HILDA JOSEFINA, fashion design executive; b. Palmarito de Cauto, Oriente, Cuba, June 18, 1938; came to U.S., 1960; d. Matias and Isabel Beatrice (Freeman) Henriquez. BA, Bethune-Cookman Coll., 1963; postgrad., Tchrs. Coll., 1965-66, Roosevelt U., 1966, Northwestern U., 1969-70; cert., No. Ill. U., 1975; postgrad., Loop Coll., 1972-84. Modiste/couturier Fina Modas, Habana, Cuba, 1952-59; instr. English Habana Pub. Sch., Cuba, 1956-58; ct. reporter Govt. La Cabana, Habana, Cuba, 1959-60; language instr. Ft. Lauderdale Sch. Dist., Fla., 1963-64; custom design Freeman's Fashion Atelier, Chgo., 1965-68; pres. dir. Acad. for Fashion Art Design, Chgo., 1968—; head designer Eur-Am. Creations, Chgo., 1978-81; cons. Freeman's Enterprise, Chgo., 1982—. Mentor Spanish coalition, Youth Career Awareness Program, Chgo., 1987. Mem. Cuban C. of C., Cuban Liceo, Ill. Assn. Trade and Tech. Schs., NAFE. Avocations: dancing, writing, hiking, swimming, traveling. Office: Acad for Fashion Art Design 410 S Michigan Ave Chicago IL 60605-1302

HENRY, BARBARA A., publishing executive; b. Oshkosh, Wis., July 23, 1952; d. Robert Edward and Barbara Frances (Aylesworth) H. BJ, U. Nev. Reporter Reno Newspapers, 1974-78, city editor, 1978-80, mng. editor, 1980-82; asst. nat. editor USA Today, Washington, 1982-83; exec. editor Reno Gazette-Jour., 1981-86; former editor, dir. Gannett Rochester Newspapers, Rochester, N.Y.; pub. Great Falls (Mont.) Tribune(part of the Gannett group), 1992-96; pres., pub. Des Moines Register, 1996—. Mem. Soc. Profl. Journalists, Associated Press Mng. Editors, Am. Soc. Newspaper Editors, Calif.-Nev. Soc. Newspaper Editors (bd. dirs.). Avocation: skiing. Office: The Des Moines Register 715 Locust St Des Moines IA 50309-3767*

HENRY, BRIAN C., telephone company executive. Exec. v.p., CFO, Cin. Bell Inc., 1998; CEO Convergus, 1998—. Office: Cin Bell Inc 201 E 4th St Cincinnati OH 45202-4122*

HENRY, BRIAN THOMAS, lawyer; b. Chgo., Dec. 25, 1954; s. Thomas Joseph and Shirley Grace (Pfaff) H.; m. Mary Elizabeth Collins, Sept. 17, 1983; children: Kyle J., Erin Maureen, Colin Thomas. BA Honors in History magna cum laude, Loyola U., Chgo., 1977; JD, U. Ill., 1980. Bar: Ill. 1980, U.S. Dist. Ct. (no. dist.) Ill. 1980. Assoc. Pretzel & Stouffe Chtd., Chgo., 1980—; faculty instr. Ill. Assn. of Def. Trial Counsel Trial Acads., 1990-99; seminar speaker Chgo. Bar Assn. Comparative Negligence Seminar, 1990, '91; cons. health care com. Inst. of Medicine of Chgo.; frequent lectr. med. groups. Editor-in-chief Recent Decisions Sect. of Ill. Bar Jour., 1979-80. Mem. ASTL, ABA, Ill. Assn. Hosp. Attys., Ill. Assn. Defense Trial Counsel, Internat. Assn. Defense Counsel, Chgo. Bar Assn., Ill. Bar Assn., Phi Alpha Theta, Phi Alpha Delta. Office: Pretzel & Stouffer Chtd 1 S Wacker Dr Ste 2500 Chicago IL 60606-4617

HENRY, BUCK, actor, writer; b. N.Y.C., 1930; s. Paul and Ruth (Taylor) Zuckerman. B.A. in English, Dartmouth Coll., 1952. stage actor: Life With Father, 1948, Fortress of Glass, 1952, Bernardine, 1952, No Time for Sergeants, 1956, The Premise, 1961-62, House of Blue Leaves, 1987, King Fish, 1988, Three Viewings, 1995; TV actor, writer: The Gary Moore Show, The Steve Allen Show, 1961, That Was The Week That Was, 1964-65, Alfred Hitchcock Presents, 1985, The New Show, 1984 (also rotating host); TV dir., actor: Hunger Chic, 1989; rotating host: The Late Show, 1986; narrator: The Secret Life of 118 Green St., 1990; actor: The Edge, 1990-91, Beauty Rest, 1992, Keep the Change, 1992, Mastergate, 1992, Laughing Matters, 1993; co-creator: Get Smart!, 1965-69 (Emmy award outstanding writing in comedy series 1966), When Things Were Rotten, 1975; creator, prodr., writer: Captain Nice, 1967, creator: Quark, 1978; film actor: The Secret War of Harry Frigg, 1968, Taking Off, 1971, Is There Sex After Death, 1971, The Man Who Fell To Earth, 1976, Old Boyfriends, 1978, The Absent-Minded Waiter, 1979, Gloria, 1980, Eating Raoul, 1982, Aria, 1987, Dark Before Dawn, 1988, Rude Awakening, 1989, Tune in Tomorrow..., 1990, Defending Your Life, 1991, The Player, 1992, The Linguini Incident, 1992, Short Cuts, 1993, Grumpy Old Men, 1993, Even Cowgirls Get the Blues, 1994, To Die For, 1995, The Real Blonde, 1997, I'm Losin You, 1998; screenwriter: The Troublemaker, 1964, The Graduate, 1967 (Acad. award nomination best screenplay-adaptation 1967, Brit. Acad. award Best Script 1968, N.Y. Film Critics award 1968, Writers Guild Am. award 1968), Candy, 1968, What's Up Doc, 1972 (Screen Writers Guild award 1972), The Day of the Dolphin, 1973, Protocol, 1984, I Love N.Y., 1987; actor, screenwriter: Catch-22, 1970, The Owl and the Pussycat, 1970; actor, dir., screenwriter: First Family, 1980; actor, writer, co-prodr., dir.: Heaven Can Wait, 1978 (Acad. award nomination 1978). Served with U.S. Army, 1952-54. Recipient (with Calder Willingham) N.Y. Film Critics award and Writers Guild of Am. award for the Graduate. Mem. Writers Guild Am., Dirs. Guild. Office: William Morris Agy 151 S El Camino Dr Beverly Hills CA 90212-2775*

HENRY, CARL FERDINAND HOWARD, theologian; b. N.Y.C., Jan. 22, 1913; s. Karl F. and Johanna (Vaethroeder) H.; m. Helga Bender, Aug. 17, 1940; children: Paul Brentwood (dec. 1993), Carol Jennifer. B.A., Wheaton (Ill.) Coll., 1938, M.A., 1940; B.D., No. Baptist Theol. Sem., Chgo., 1941, Th.D., 1942; Ph.D., Boston U., 1949; Litt.D. (hon.), Seattle-Pacific Coll., 1963, Wheaton Coll., 1968; L.H.D. (hon.), Houghton Coll., 1973; D.D. (hon.), Northwestern Coll., 1979, Gordon-Conwell Theol. Sem., 1984; LL.D (hon.), Hillsdale Coll., 1989. Ordained to ministry Bapt. Ch., 1941; asst. prof., then prof. theology No. Bapt. Theol. Sem., 1942-47; acting dean Fuller Theol. Sem., Pasadena, Calif., 1947, prof., 1947-56, Peyton lectr., 1963, vis. prof., 1980; vis. prof. theology Wheaton Coll., Gordon Div. Sch., Columbia Bible Coll., 1977, 80, Japan Sch. Theology, 1974, systematic theology and Biblical studies Trinity Evang. Div. Sch., 1974, 87-91, 92-96, Bethel Theol. Sem., W. San Diego, 1988, Denver Conservative Bapt. Sem., 1981, 83, So. Bapt. Theol. Sem., 1988; vis. prof. Eastern Bapt. Theol. Sem., 1969-70, prof.-at-large, 1970-74; lectr.-at-large World Vision, 1974-87; Disting. vis. prof. Christian studies Hillsdale Coll., 1983-84; Disting. vis. prof. systematic theology Calvin Theol. Sem., 1986; faculty mem. flying seminar to Europe and Nr. East, Winona Lake (Ind.) Sch. Theology, 1952; daily radio commentator Sta. KPOL Let the Chips Fall, L.A., 1952-53; chmn. World Congress Evangelism, Berlin, 1966, Consultation Scholars, Washington, 1967; program chmn. Jerusalem Conf. Bibl. Prophecy, Israel, 1971; Latin Am. Theol. Frat. lectr., 1973; lectr. Evangelism Internat., Singapore, 1976, 78, 86, All-India Evang. Conf. on Social Action, Madras, 1979, Liberia Bapt. Theol. Sem., Monrovia, 1982, Cameroun Bapt. Theol. Coll., Ndu, 1982, Japan Christian Inst., Tokyo, 1989; vis. lectr. Asian Ctr. Theol. Studies and Mission, Seoul, Korea, 1974, 74, 76, 78, 80, Teoloski Facultet, Matija Vlacic Illrik, Zagreb, Yugoslavia, 1977, Asian Theol. Sem., Manila, 1980, Soong Sil Univ. Inst. Christian Culture Research, Seoul, 1987, C.S. Lewis Summer Inst., Oxford, 1988, Second Bapt. Ch., Oradea, Romania, 1988, 90, Rutherford Lectures, Edinburgh, Scotland, 1989, Chavanne Scholars' Colloquium on Bibl. Principles and Pub. Policy, Baylor U., 1989, Tyndale Sem., Amsterdam, The Netherlands, 1990, Washington Bapt. Coll. and Sem., 1990-95, Beeson Div. Sch. Samford U., 1994, Acton Soc., 1995, Korea Bapt. Coll. & Sem., Seoul, 1995, So. Baptist Theol. Sem., 1998—; bd. dirs. Inst. Advanced Christian Studies, 1976-79, 81-85, dir. emeritus, 1988—, pres., 1971-74; bd. dirs. Ethics and Pub. Policy Ctr., 1979-96, Inst. Religion and Democracy, 1981-95, v.p., 1985—, Prison Fellowship, 1981—, lectr.-at-large, 1990-94; M.E. Found., 1989—; trustee Gordon Conwell Theol. Sem., 1965-68, Christian Life Commn. Southern Baptist Conv., 1991-93, Elmer Bisbee Found., 1986-91; bd. dirs. Ministers Life and Casualty Union, 1968-77, Riverside Found., 1997, Carl F. H.Henry Inst. for Evangel. Engagement, Sothern Baptist Theological Seminary; co-chmn. Rose Bowl Easter Sunrise Service, 1950-56; main street com. Rockford Inst., 1990—; mem. Christian Life Commn., So. Bapt. Conv., 1991-93; addressed symposium Ctr. Human Values, Moscow, 1993. Author: A Doorway to Heaven, 1941, Successful Church Publicity, 1942, Remaking the Modern Mind, 1948, The Uneasy Conscience of Modern Fundamentalism, 1947, Giving a Reason for Our Hope, 1949, The Protestant Dilemma, 1949, Notes on the Doctrine of God, 1949, Fifty Years of Protestant Theology, 1950, The Drift of Western Thought, 1951, Personal Idealism and Strong's Theology, 1951, Glimpses of a Sacred Land, 1953, Christian Personal Ethics, 1957, Evangelical Responsibility in Contemporary Theology, 1957, Aspects of Christian Social Ethics, 1964, Frontiers in Modern Theology, 1966, The God Who Shows Himself, 1966, Evangelicals at the Brink of Crisis, 1967, Faith at the Frontiers, 1969, A Plea for Evangelical Demonstration, 1971, New Strides of Faith, 1972, Evangelicals in Search of Identity, 1976, God, Revelation and Authority, vols. 1 and 2, 1976, vols. 3 and 4, 1979, vol. 5, 1982, vol. 6, 1983, The Christian Mindset in a Secular Society, 1984, Christian Countermoves in a Decadent Culture, 1986, Confessions of a Theologian, 1986, Conversations with Carl Henry: Christianity for Today, 1986; Twilight of a Great Civilization, 1988, A Lifetime of Quotable Thoughts: Carl Henry at His Best, 1990, Toward a Recovery of Christian Belief, 1990, The Identity of Jesus of Nazareth, 1992, gods of this age or God of The Ages?, 1994, Has Democracy Had Its Day?, 1996; editor: Contemporary Evangelical Thought, 1957, Revelation and the Bible, 1959, The Biblical Expositor, 1960, Basic Christian Doctrines, 1962, Christian Faith and Modern Theology, 1964, Jesus of Nazareth: Saviour and Lord, 1966, Fundamentals of the Faith, 1969, Horizons of Science, 1978; editor in chief: Baker's Dictionary of Christian Ethics, 1973; co-editor: (with Kenneth Kantzer) Evangelical Affirmations, 1990; cons. editor: Baker's Dictionary of Theology, 1964; editor: Christianity Today, 1956-68, editor-at-large, 1968-77; contbg. editor: World Vision Mag., 1976-87; religion corr. World mag., 1995—. Mem. Capitol Hill Met. Bapt. Ch., Washington, 1956—. Recipient Freedoms Found. award, 1954, 66, Sem. Alumnus of Yr., No. Bapt. Theol. Sem., 1971, Religious Heritage Am. award, 1975, Disting. Social Svc. award Wheaton Coll. Alumni Assn., 1961, J. Elwin Wright award Nat. Assn. of Evangelicals, 1990, Disting. Svc. award Christian Life Commn., So. Bapt. Conv., 1992, 50 Yr. Svc. award Religious Heritage of Am., 1993; honored with Carl F.H. Henry manuscript collection Syracuse U., 1975—, The Carl F.H. Henry Study and Resource Ctr., Trinity Evang. Divinity Sch., Deerfield, Ill., 1987; fellow Christianity Today Inst., 1987-94; Soc. Sci. Study of Religion fellow, 1992—. Mem. AAAS, Am. Soc. Christian Ethics, Am. Acad. Religion, Am. Theol. Soc. (v.p. 1974-75, pres. 1979-80), Nat. Assn. Envangelicals (bd. adminstrn. 1956-70), Am. Philos. Assn., Am. Soc. Ch. History,Soc. Oreintal Rsch. Evang. Theol. Soc. (pres. 1969-70), Conf. Faith and History, Soc. Christian Philosophers, Nat. Assn. Bapt. Profs. of Religion, Evang. Press Assn. (hon. life), Soc. Bible Lit. Subject of festschift God and Culture, 1993. Address: 1141 Hus Dr Apt 206 Watertown WI 53098-3258 *To know God as the ultimate Who's Who nurtures gratitude for all the days of one's years, including creation life, regenerate life, and resurrection life to come.*

HENRY, CATHERINE THERESA, insurance company executive; b. N.Y.C., June 25, 1934; d. John Patrick and Bridie (Hartnett) H. Student, Queens Coll., 1960-63. With Equitable Life Assurance Soc., N.Y.C., 1952—, systems analyst, 1965-74, adminstrv. mgr., 1974-76, personnel mgr., 1976-80, asst. v.p., personnel officer, 1980-83, v.p., human resources officer, 1983-90, v.p. ins. svcs., 1990-94, v.p. tech. mgmt., 1994—. Exec. com. W. 89th St. Park Block Assn., N.Y.C., 1986—. Named to Acad. Women Achievers, YWCA, 1985. Mem. Am. Soc. Quality and Participation, Orgnl. Devel. Network, Orgnl. Devel. Network of Greater N.Y., N.Y. Human Resource Planners, Human Resource Planning Soc. (bd. dirs. 1990—, sec. 1993-95, pres. 1995-98). Avocations: theatre, travel, walking, reading. Office: The Equitable 1290 Ave of Ams New York NY 10104

HENRY, CECIL JAMES, JR., insurance sales broker; b. DeSoto, Mo., Nov. 20, 1937; s. Cecil J. and Gertrude M. (Waldron) H.; m. Jane A. Henry, May 2, 1959; children: Eric J., Jason C. AB, William Jewell Coll., 1959; postgrad., U. Kans., 1959-60; MS in Fin. Svcs., Am. Coll., 1982, MS in Mgmt., 1988. CLU. Asst. food dir. William Jewell Coll., Liberty, Mo., 1955-59; ops. mgr. Graybar Electric, Kansas City, Mo., 1961-65; with Alexander Proudfoot, Chgo., 1966; spl. agt. Prudential Ins. Co., Wichita, Kans., 1966-67; prin. Henry Ins. Ltd., Wichita, 1967—; bd. dirs. Kirkpatrick Sprazker & Co. CPAs; mem. adv. bd. Sta. KNSS Radio, 1991—. Contbr. articles to mag. Bur. mem. United Way Wichita, 1974—; bd. dirs. Presbyn. Family Support Svcs., 1988—, chair, 1992—. Mem. Kans. Assn. Life Underwriters (pres. 1982-83, cert. 1983), Wichita Assn. Life Underwriters (pres. 1974-75), Better Bus. Bur. (bd. dirs. 1974-75), Nat. Assn. Life Underwriters, Nat. Assn. Life Underwriters (pres. Wichita chpt. 1974-75), Am. Soc. of CLUs and Chartered Fin. Cons., Am. Risk and Ins., Knife and Fork Club, Downtown Lions. Republican. Baptist. Avocations: gardening, reading, traveling. Home: 1903 E Lockwood St Wichita KS 67216-3368 Office: Henry Ins Ltd 1224 E Harry PO Box 3728 Wichita KS 67201-3728

HENRY, CHARLES JAY, library director; b. Washington, June 17, 1950; s. Charles J. and June (Statz) H.; m. Nancy C. Todd, Oct. 4, 1986. BA, Northwest Mo., 1972; MA, Columbia U., 1977, MPhil, 1980, PhD, 1987. Instr. Columbia U., N.Y.C., 1981-82; asst. to dean Columbia Coll., N.Y.C., 1982-85; asst. dir., divsn. humanities, hist. Columbia Libr., N.Y.C., 1985-91; dir. libr. Vassar Coll., Poughkeepsie, N.Y., 1991-96; dir. Am. Arts and Letters Network, 1995-96; vice-provost Rice U., Houston, 1996—; exec. dir. Two Ravens Inst., 1998—; internat. rsch. fellow London Guildhall U., 1995—; chair nat. steering com. for computer scis. and humanities, 1998—. Co-author: Computing and Humanities: New Dir., 1990; contbr. articles to profl. jours; panel mem., speaker in field. Lectrs., symposia peace edn. UN, Peace Edn. Columbia U.; exec. com. Nat. Initiative for a Networked Cultural Heritage. Fulbright scholar Vienna, 1980-81; Lilian Becker scholar Middlebury Coll., 1977; MacArthur Found. grantee, 1984-87; Presidents fellow Columbia U. 1978-79, 79-80; recipient Best Paper award humanities architecture divsn. Conf. Cybernetics and Systems Rsch., Vienna, 1992, All Conf. award, 1996. Mem. AAAS, ALA, Assn. Computers and Humanities (exec. coun. 1994-96), Am. Soc. for Info. Sci., N.Y. Acad. Sci., Coalition for Networked Info. (project leader 1991—), Bd. of Governors, TX Digital Libr. Alliance. Democrat. Achievements include rsch. in cybernetics and systems rsch.

HENRY, CHRISTOPHER JOEL, software consultant; b. Santa Maria, Calif., Dec. 18, 1958; s. Stacey Chumard Henry and Elvera Pauline (Ruggerio) Talley. Student, City Coll. San Francisco, 1977-80, Dale Carnegie Sch., 1980; AS in Computer Sci., Andover Coll., Portland, Maine, 1994. Ops. mgr. MACCO, 1985-90; sr. lab technician IDEXX Labs., Portland, Maine, 1991-92; cons., subcontractor Douglass/400, Boston, 1993-94, EMC Corp., Hopkinton, Mass., 1994; programmer G.H. Bass Inc., Portland, 1994; cons. QCC, Inc., Westwood, Mass., 1995-96, Douglas Cons. Inc., info. mgmt., contract cons. svcs., Boston, 1997—. Mem. New Eng. Sys. Group. Republican. Roman Catholic. Avocations: road racing, camping, reading. Office: Douglas Cons Inc 8 Park Plz Ste 130 Boston MA 02116-3952

HENRY, DAVID ALLEN, advertising executive; b. Cedar Rapids, Iowa, Apr. 16, 1950; s. Don Albert and Anna Mae (Manwiller) H.; m. Elise Marie Cohen, June 7, 1981 (div. Apr. 1988); children: Lauren, Erica, Sylvia. BBA, U. Iowa, 1972. V.p. mktg. Movie Systems, Inc., Denver, 1975-77; chmn., chief exec. officer Henry Gill Advt., Denver, 1977—; mem. bd. advisors Entrepreneurial Inst. Denver, 1989. Bd. dirs. Direction 2,000 Found., Littleton, Colo., 1990-93, Littleton Pub. Schs. Found., 1993—; nat. advisor White House Conf. for Drug-Free Am., Washington, 1988. Recipient Award of Merit, United Way Mile High Child Care, Denver, 1988, Cert. of Appreciation, Communities for Drug-Free Colo., 1989, Sch. Restructuring Program, Gov. of Colo., 1990, Cert. of Merit, Keep Denver Beautiful, 1990. Mem. Am. Mktg. Assn., Am. Assn. Advt. Agys. (mem. western bd. govs. 1988-92, chmn. bd. dirs. Rocky Mountain Coun. 1988), Denver Advt. Fedn. (bd. dirs. 1987-91), Denver Press Club, Greater Denver C. of C. (mem. bd. advisors 1990, Cert. of Appreciation 1989). Avocations: reading, skiing, scuba diving, golf, travel. Office: Henry Gill Advt 1225 17th St Ste 2500 Denver CO 80202-5525

HENRY, DAVID HOWE, II, retired diplomat; b. Geneva, N.Y., May 19, 1918; s. David Max and Dorothy (Buley) H.; m. Margaret Beard, Nov. 16, 1946; children: David Beard, Peter York, Michael Max, Susan. Student, Hobart Coll., 1935-37, Sorbonne, 1937-38; A.B., Columbia U., 1939; student, Russian Inst., 1948-49, Harvard U., 1944-45, Nat. War Coll., 1957-58. Ins. agt., 1939-41; mem. fgn. service Dept. State, 1941-71; assigned Dept. State, Montreal, 1941-42, Beirut, 1942-44, Washington, 1944-45, 48-52, 57-66, 70, Moscow, 1945-48, 52-54, Vladivostok, 1945-46, Berlin, 1955-57; acting dir. Office Research and Intelligence Sino-Soviet bloc, 1958-59; dir. dept. polit. affairs Nat. War Coll., 1959-61; dep. dir. Office Soviet Affairs, 1961-64, dir., 1964-65; mem. Policy Planning Council, 1965-66; dep. chief of mission Am. embassy, Reykjavik, Iceland, 1966-69; information systems specialist, 1970; polit. and security council affairs UN, N.Y.C., 1971-78. Mem. Kappa Alpha. Presbyterian. Club: Rotarian. Home: 2551 SW Brookwood Ln Palm City FL 34990-4752

HENRY, DEWITT PAWLING, II, creative writing educator, writer, arts administrator; b. Wayne, Pa., June 30, 1941; s. John and Kathryn (Thralls) Henry; m. Constance Joy Sherbill, Aug. 25, 1973; children—Ruth Kathryn, David Jung Min. A.B., Amherst Coll., 1963; A.M., Harvard U., 1965, Ph.D., 1971; postgrad., U. Iowa-Iowa City, 1964-66. Editor Ploughshares, dir. Ploughshares, Inc., Watertown, Mass., 1971-89, exec. dir., 1989-95; dir. Book Affairs, Inc., Watertown, 1975-85; adj. prof. Emerson Coll., Boston, 1982-83, asst. prof. creative writing and lit., 1983-89, assoc. prof., 1989—, acting chair div. writing, pub. and lit., 1987-88, chair, 1989-93; mem. adv. panel Mass. Coun. on the Arts, Boston, 1981-83; literature panelist Nat. Endowment for the Arts, Washington, 1982-85, 92-93; mem. adv. bd. New England Found. for Arts, 1983-85; mem. Watertown Arts Lottery coun., 1987-92; bd. dirs., treas. Associated Writing Programs, 1988-90, pres., 1990-91. Author: The Ploughshares Reader, New Fiction for the 80s, 1985, Other Sides of Silence, New Fiction from Ploughshares, 1993, Fathering Daughters, 1998; columnist Wilson Libr. Bull., 1979-81; staff editor: The Pushcart Prize, 1978—. Fellow Woodrow Wilson found., 1963; fellow Coordinating Council of Literary Mags., 1979, Nat. Endowment for Arts, 1979. Mem. Associated Writing Programs, Phi Beta Kappa. Presbyterian. Home: 33 Buick St Watertown MA 02472-2176 Office: Emerson Coll Writing Lit Pub Divsn 100 Beacon St Boston MA 02116-1501

HENRY, EDGAR ROBERT, associate editor; b. N.Y.C., Oct. 30, 1937; s. Edgar Leopold and Jane Ann (James) H.; m. Leota Esma Burrows, June 9, 1963; children: Craig McNeal, Lyle Anthony. BA, CCNY, 1968; MA in Journalism, Columbia U., 1969. Reporter Wall St. Jour., N.Y.C., 1969-72; writer, reporter Money Mag., N.Y.C., 1972-79; Washington correspondent Money Mag., Washington, 1979-81; assoc. editor Kiplinger's Personal Fin. Mag. (formerly Changing Times), Washington, 1982—. Columnist: Changing Times Mag., 1985—; editor: (annual) Changing Times Car Book, 1985—; corr. Kiplinger Report syndicated TV show, 1994—; contbr. articles to How to books and mags. Recipient Rosebud award More Mag., N.Y.C., 1970. Mem. Washington Automotive Press Assoc. (founding mem., sec. 1986—, pres. 1993-95, found. pres. 1995-96), Nat. Press Club (Cert. of Merit 1983, Best Consumer Journalism awards 1990), U.S. Senate, Ho. of Reps. News Galleries. Avocations: photography, golf, desktop publishing, computers. Office: Kiplinger's Personal Finance 1729 H St NW Washington DC 20006-3904

HENRY, EDWARD FRANK, computer accounting service executive; b. East Cleveland, Ohio, Mar. 18, 1923; s. Edward Emerson and Mildred Adelia (Kulow) H.; m. Nicole Annette Peth, June 18, 1977. BBA, Dyke Coll., 1948; postgrad., Case Western Reserve U., 1949, Cleve. Inst. Music, 1972. Cert. Notary Public Ohio. Internal auditor E.F. Hauserman Co., 1948-51; sales and radio announcer Sta. WSRS, 1951; office mgr. Frank C. Grismer Co., 1951-52, Broadway Buick Co., 1952-55; sec., treas. Commerce Ford Sales Co., 1955-65; nat. mgr. Auto Acctg. div. United Data Processing Co., Cin., 1966-68; v.p. Auto Data Systems Co., Cleve., 1968-70; pres. Profl. Mgmt. Computer Sys., Inc., Cleve., ž, 1970—, ComputerEASE, Small Bus. Computer Ctrs. divsn. Profl. Mgmt. Computer Sys., Inc., 1985—, VideoEASE CompuAIDE Computerized Video Rental Sys. divsn. Profl. Mgmt. Computer Systems, Inc., 1987-89, CompuPRINT divsn. Profl. Mgmt. Computer Sys., Inc., 1995—, TravelEASE divsn. Profl. Mgmt. Computer Sys., Inc., 1996—. Photography published in Travel Agents Internat. mag., 1990 (hon. mention 1990). Exec. artistic dir. NorthCoast Cultural Centre, 1989—. Drum major, musician Wurlitzer Marching Band, Cleve., 1939-42, The Ed Henry Dance Band, 1939-42; with USAF Marching Band, Kearns, Utah, 1943; charter pres. No. Ohio Coun. Little Theatre, 1954-56; founder, artistic and mng. dir. Exptl. Theatre, Cleve., 1959-63; dramatic dir., actor Euclid Little Theatres, and various cmty. theatres including Jewish Cmty. Ctr.; actor Cleve. Playhouse, 1961-63. Bd. dirs. Cleve. Philharmonic Orch.,

1972-74, Cleve. Jazz Orch., 1991—; Cleve. Opera League. 1st lt. USAAF, 1943-46, PTO, capt. USAAF Res., 1946-57. Decorated Bronze Star (3); semi-finalist nature category Internat. Open Amateur Photography Contest, 1999. Mem. APA, Am. Mgmt. Assn., Inst. Mgmt. Accts., Mil. Order World Wars, Air Force Assn. (life), Ky. Cols., Data Processing Mgmt. Assn., Nat. Assn. Profl. Cons., Am. Soc. Profl. Cons., Res. Officers Assn., Mil. Order World Wars (Cleve. chpt., bugler, commdr., 1994-95), Mayfield Area C. of C., Associated Photographers Internat., Internat. Platform Assn., Internat. Soc. Photographers (disting. mem.), Nat. Assn. Met. Mus. Art of N.Y., Cleve. Mus. Art, Art Inst Chgo., Phi Kappa Gamma (charter pres. Gamma chpt., past nat. pres.), Am. Legion, VFW, Acacia Country, Hermit, Univ., Cleve. Grays, Deep Springs Trout, Nat. Sojourners (Nat. Pres.'s cert. 1977-78, pres. Cleve. chpt. #23 1978), Heroes of '76 (comdr. Cleve. 1977), DeMolay (master Cleve. chpt., 1942, Legion of Honor 1970), Masons (hon. 33d degree St. Bernard lodge, Doge City, 50 year hon., 1994), Cuyahoga County Meml. Lodge (worshipful master 1993-94) KT, Scottish Rite (dramatic dir. 1967—, thrice potent master 1982-84, class named in his hon. 1994), Grotto, Shriners (dramatic dir. 1968-88), Cleve. Ct. #14, Jesters (dir. 1981, impresario 1984—, dramatic dir. 1971—, producer, dir. Nat. Book of the Play Acapulco, Mexico, 1985; nat. prodr., dir. Nat. Book of the Play Reno, 1988—, Bally's Celebrity Rm., Las Vegas, 1989-96, Hyatt Regency O'Hare 1998, Royal Dramatist, 1989—, Chgo. Hyatt, 1998, nat. chmn. emeritus ritual com. 1990-96, nat. rep emeritus to nat. ct., 1996), Kachina, SOBIB, Rotary. Republican. Presbyterian. Fax: 216-663-9822. Home: 666 Echo Dr Gates Mills OH 44040-9606 Office: Profl Mgmt Computer Systems Inc 19701 S Miles Rd Cleveland OH 44128-4257

HENRY, EDWIN MAURICE, JR., lawyer, electrical engineer, consultant; b. Cambridge, Md., June 26, 1930; s. Edwin Maurice Henry Sr. and Emma Lee (Wilson) Clayton; m. Barbara Ann Brittingham, Feb. 2, 1952; children: Barbara Jo, Kim M. Student, U.S. Naval Acad., 1949-51; BSEE, John Hopkins U., 1957; JD, U. Balt., 1972. Bar: Md. 1974, U.S. Dist. Ct. Md. 1974; registered profl. engr., Md. Assoc. Pairo & Pairo, Balt., 1973-76; ptnr. Pairo & Henry, Ellicott City, Md., 1976-86; sole practice Ellicott City, 1986-95; pvt. practice LLC, 1996—; mem. Md. Atty. Grievance Rev. Bd., 1980-83. Author: Defense of Speeding Vascar, 1974. Served with USN, 1947-51. Mem. Md. Bar Assn., Howard County Bar Assn., Am. Legion, Masons, Shriners, Jesters, Eastern Shore Soc., St. Andrew's Soc., Cambridge Yacht Club. Methodist. Avocations: travel. Home: 9035 Overhill Dr Ellicott City MD 21042-5246 Office: PO Box 309 8433 Main St Ellicott City MD 21043-4665

HENRY, FRANCES ANN, journalist, educator; b. Denver, July 23, 1939; d. Lewis Byford and Betsy Mae (Lancaster) Patten; m. Charles Larry, June 28, 1963 (div. May 1981); children: Charles Kevin, Tracy Diane. BA in English, Carleton Coll., 1960; MA in Social Sci., U. Colo., Denver, 1988; MA in Journalism, Memphis State U., 1989. Cert. tchr. Lang. arts tchr. Rolla (Mo.) Pub. Schs., 1963-66; journalism tchr. Douglas County Pub. Schs., Castle Rock, Colo., 1976-99; retired Memphis State U., 1999; chmn. English dept. Douglas County Pub. Schs., Castle Rock, Colo., 1992-98; mng. editor Douglas County News-Press, Castle Rock, 1986-87; editor Fourth World Bulletin, 1988; exec. editor Daily Helmsman Memphis State U., 1988-89, gen. mgr. Daily Helmsman, 1991-92. Contbr. articles to profl. jours. Recipient Gov.'s award for excellence in edn. Colo. Endowment for Humanities, 1997. Mem. ACLU, Colo. Lang. Arts Soc., Colo. H.S. Press Assn. (sec. 1981-83, pres. 1983-91, bd. dirs., named Colo. Journalism Tchr. of Yr. 1985), Mensa, Kappa Tau Alpha. Democrat. Episcopalian.

HENRY, FREDERICK EDWARD, lawyer; b. St. Louis, Aug. 28, 1947; s. Frederick E. and Dorothy Jean (McCulley) H.; m. Vallie Catherine Jones, June 7, 1969; children: Christine Roberta, Charles Frederick. AB, Duke U., 1969, JD with honors, 1972. Bar: Ill. 1972, U.S. Dist. Ct. (no. dist.) Ill. 1972, Calif. 1982. Assoc. Baker & McKenzie, Chgo., 1972-79, ptnr., 1979—. Bd. dirs. Lincoln Park Conservation Assn., Chgo., 1983-85, Old Town Triangle Assn., Chgo., 1980-83, pres., 1984. Recipient Willis Smith award Duke U. Law Sch., 1972. Mem. ABA, Chgo. Bar Assn., Calif. State Bar, Order of Coif. Home: 164 W Eugenie St Chicago IL 60614-5809 Office: Baker & McKenzie 1 Prudential Pla 130 E Randolph St Ste 3700 Chicago IL 60601-6342*

HENRY, GARY NORMAN, air force officer, astronautical engineer; b. Fort Wayne, Ind., Nov. 3, 1961; s. Norman Thomas and Elaine Cathrine (Schabb) H. BS in Astro. Engring. with distinction, USAF Acad., 1984; MS in Aero./Astronautical Engring., Stanford U., 1988; grad., USAF Test Pilot Sch., 1994, USAF Air Command & Staff Coll., 1997. CFP. Commd. 2d lt. USAF, 1984, advanced through grades to maj., 1996; project engr. USAF Weapons Lab., Kirtland AFB, N.Mex., 1984-87; asst. prof. astronautics USAF Acad., Colorado Springs, 1989-93; flight test engr. 418 Flight Test Squadron, Edwards AFB, Calif., 1993-94, chief flight dynamics br., 1994-95; exec. officer USAF Flight Test Ctr., Edwards, 1995-96; dep. dir. test and evaluation Airborne Laser Sys. Program Office, Kirtland AFB, N.Mex., 1997—; sole proprietor Polaris Fin. Svcs., 1987—. Editor: (textbook) Space Propulsion Analysis and Design, 1995; contbr. articles to profl. jours. Recipient sci. and engring. award USAF, 1993. Mem. AIAA (sr. mem., hybrid rocket tech. com. 1993-94, Young Engr. of Yr. Rocky Mountain region 1993), Soc. Flight Test Engrs., Nat. Endowment for Fin. Edn. Achievements include research director of 1st successful Department of Defense land-based hybrid sounding rocket flight. Office: Airborne Laser Sys Program Office 3300 Target Rd SE Kirtland AFB NM 87117-6612

HENRY, HOLLY ANN, journalist; b. May 3, 1976. B in Journalism, Ohio U., 1998. Intern Parkersburg (W.Va.) News, 1997; staff writer San Angelo (Tex.) Standard-Times, 1998—; with The Post, Athens, Ohio, 1994-98. Pulliam fellow Indpls. Star/News, 1998. Mem. Soc. Profl. Journalists (pres. West Tex. chpt. 1999—, pres. Ohio U. chpt. 1997-98). E-mail: hollyhen@gte.net. Home: 34 Cielo Vista Plaza 11-C San Angelo TX 76904 Office: 34 W Harris Ave San Angelo TX 76903

HENRY, JAMES M., physician, neuropathologist; b. Harvey, Ill., July 9, 1935; m. Johanna M. Ludwig, 1967; children: Christian F., Mark M., Christoph J., James V. AB with high honors, U. Ill., 1956; MD magna cum laude, U. Wuerzburg, Germany, 1964. Diplomate in neuropathology and anat. pathology Am. Bd. Pathology. Intern New Britain (Conn.) Gen. Hosp., 1965-66; resident in neurology Letterman Army Med. Ctr., San Francisco, 1966-67, resident in anat. pathology, 1967-69; fellow in neuropathology Armed Forces Inst. Pathology, Washington, 1969-71, assoc. pathologist, 1971-75, chief divsn. diagnostic neuropathology, 1975-80; various command and staff positions U.S. Army, 1980-92; med. liaison officer U.S. Embassy, Tel Aviv, 1986-89, London, 1991-92; staff pathologist, chief divsn. diagnostic neuropathology Armed Forces Inst. Pathology, 1992—; neuropathology cons. Nat. Naval Med. Ctr., Bethesda, Md., 1969-72, 94—; assoc. prof. pathology Uniformed Svcs. U. Health Scis., 1976-80, adj. prof. pathology, 1988-92; lectr. U. Wuerzburg, 1984-86; vis. prof. Hebrew U., Jerusalem, 1986-89; clin. prof. pathology and neurol. surgery U. Louisville, 1991—. Contbr. articles to profl. jours. Decorated Legion of Merit with 2 oak leaf clusters, Meritorious Svc. medal with 3 oak leaf clusters, others. Mem. Am. Assn. Neuropathologists, Can. Assn. Neuropathologists, German Soc. Neuropathology and Neuroanatomy, German Soc. for Mil. Medicine and Pharamcy. Office: Armed Forces Inst Pathology Washington DC 20306-6000

HENRY, JOANNE LANDERS, writer; b. Indpls., Feb. 24, 1927; d. Delver Harold and Octavia (Greene) Landers; m. Earl W. Henry, Oct. 11, 1958 (div. 1989); children: David, Katherine. BA, U. Rochester, 1948. With promotion/publicity Oxford U. Press, N.Y.C., 1954-57; editor Bobbs-Merrill, Indpls., 1949-54, 57-58. Author: Elizabeth Blackwell, 1961, 96, Marie Curie, 1966, A Clearing in the Forest, 1992, Log Cabin in the Woods, 1988, others. Avocations: amateur musician (cello), sailing.

HENRY, JOHN MARTIN, urologist; b. Doylestown, Pa., Apr. 3, 1962; s. William and Marian (Abrams) H.; m. Regina Wheelan; children: Madison, John Griffin. BA, Franklin & Marshall U., 1984; MD, Johns Hopkins U., 1988. Diplomate Am. Bd. Urology. Resident U. Pa., Phila., 1994; urologist Berks Urol. Assoc., Wyomissing, Pa., 1994—. Fellow ACS; mem. Am. Urol. Assn., Reading Physician's Orgn., Phila. Urol. Soc. Office: Berks Urol Assocs 1075 Berkshire Blvd Ste 900 Wyomissing PA 19610-1264

HENRY, J(OHN) PORTER, JR., sales consultant; b. Webster Groves, Mo., Oct. 25, 1911; s. J(ohn) Porter and Imogen Edith (Adams) H.; m. Mary Lee Harney, Mar. 5, 1941 (dec. Dec. 1977); children: Barbara Henry Drews, Richard Adams; m. Martha Rush Philley, Mar. 10, 1978 (div. 1991). AB, Washington U., St. Louis, 1932. With St. Louis Star-Times, 1933-35, Cin. Post, 1937; asst. sec. Optimist Internat., 1936-39; mem. staff St. Louis Post-Dispatch, 1939-41, N.Y. Daily News, 1941-43; founder, pres. Porter Henry & Co., N.Y.C., 1946-75. Author: Handbook of Outboard Motors, 1948, Secrets of the Master Sellers, 1987, Secrets of the Master Sales Managers, 1993; co-author: Effective Sales Incentive Compensation, 1980, Greater Efficiency in the Small Office, 1983; contbr. articles to mags. and profl. jours. Served with USAAF, 1943-45, ETO. Decorated Medal of Freedom. Mem. Phi Beta Kappa, Sigma Chi. Office: 2401 Ingleside Ave Cincinnati OH 45206-2118

HENRY, JOHN RAYMOND, sculptor; b. Lexington, Ky., Aug. 11, 1943; s. Arthur Raymond and Catherine (Campbell) H.; m. Pamela Kathryn, May 12, 1984; 1 child from previous marriage, Katherine Leigh Henry-Barrett. Student, U. Ky., 1961-65, U. Wash., 1962, Ill. Inst. Tech., 1967, U. Chgo., 1968-69; BFA, Sch. of Art Inst., 1969; PhD of Art (hon.), U. Ky., 1996. Pres., CEO ConStruct Corp., 1979-81; vis. prof. sculpture U. Iowa, 1969, U. Wis. Green Bay, 1970, U. Chgo., 1971, Sch. of Art Inst. Chgo., 1979-80; coord., advisor Art Inst. Chgo., City of Chgo., 1974; advisor Art Coun., New Orleans, 1976; mem. adv bd. Lawyers for Creative Arts, Chgo.; spkr. in field. Solo exhbns. include retrospective Art Mus. South Tex., Corpus Christi, Mus. Art, Ft. Lauderdale, Fla., Mus. Fine Arts, St. Petersburg, Fla., Hunter Mus. Art, Chattanooga, 1988-89, Richard Gray Gallery, Chgo., 1969, 71, Ill. State Mus., 1973, Gallery 10, Aspen, Colo., 1980, Nina Owen Ltd., Chgo., 1990, Jaffee, Baker Gallery, Boca Raton, Fla., 1991, Ann Norton Sculpture Garden, Palm Beach, Fla., 1991, Ctr. for Arts, Vero Beach, Fla., 1991, Seo Hwa Gallery, Seoul, Korea, 1993, Springfield (Mo.) Art Mus., 1995, many others; exhbns. include U. South Fla. Art Mus., Tampa, 1988, traveling Marseille, France, Geneva, Hasselet, Belgium, Barcelona, Spain, 1988, Thomas Ctr. Gallery, Gainesville, Fla., 1989, North Miami (Fla.) Ctr. Contemporary Art, 1989-90, Internat. Art Expo, Tokyo, 1991, European Fine Art Fair, Maastricht, The Netherlands, 1992, Polk Mus. Art, Lakeland, Fla., 1992, Internat. Art Expo, Chgo., 1992, 93, Art Chgo., 1992, New Pier Show, Chgo., 1993, FIAC, Paris, 1993, Lineart, Ghent, Belgium, 1993, Manif 95, Manif 96, Seoul, Art Chgo. 96, Pier Walk 96, Chgo., Art in Chgo., Mus. Contemporary Art, 1996, numerous others; represented in permanent collections Mint Mus. Art, Charlotte, N.C., Springfield (Mo.) Art Mus., Ft. Worth Art Mus., Bradley Sculpture Garden, Milw. Art Mus., Oklahoma City Art Ctr., Brit. Mus., Miami Dade C.C., others, numerous pvt. collections. NEA Individual Artist fellow/grantee, 1975, State of Fla. Individual Artist fellow, 1989, Edward L. Reyerson fellow Art Inst. Chgo., 1969, Ford Found. grantee Sch. Art Inst. Chgo. Mem. Nat. Found. Advancement in Arts (trustee 1991—, chair programs 1993—), Internat. Sculpture Ctr. (bd. dirs., vice chmn. bd. dirs.), SE Sculptors Assn. (hon., life).

HENRY, JOHN W., professional sports team executive; b. Quincy, Ill.; m. Peggy Henry; 1 child. Founder, chmn. John W. Henry & Co., Inc., Boca Raton, Fla., 1981—, Westport, Conn., 1981—; chmn., majority owner Class AAA Tucson Toros, Pacific Coast League, 1989-97; co-owner W. Palm Beach Tropics, Sr. Baseball League, 1989—; limited ptnr. N.Y. Yankees, 1992—; chmn. Fla. Marlins Baseball Club, Miami, 1999—. Mem. Nat. Assn. Futures Trading Advisors (bd. dirs.), Managed Futures Trade Assn. (bd. dirs.), Nat. Futures Assn. (mem. nominating com.), Futures Industry Assn. (bd. dirs.). Office: Fla Marlins 2267 W 199th St Miami FL 33056

HENRY, JOSEPH LOUIS, university dean; b. New Orleans, May 2, 1924; s. Varice S. and Mabel (Mansion) H.; m. Dorothy L. Whittle, July 28, 1954 (dec. 1991); children: Joseph Louis, Ronald Maurice, Joan Alison, Leilani Cecile (Mrs. P. Smith), Peter Donald; m. Gracia Bautista Cua, Jan. 1995. D.D.S., Howard U., 1946; B.S., Xavier U., 1948, Sc.D., 1975; M.S., Ill. U., 1949, Ph.D., 1951; D.H.L., Ill. Coll. Optometry, 1973; M.A. (hon.), Harvard U., 1975. Diplomate Am. Bd. Oral Medicine. Instr. oral medicine Coll. Dentistry, Howard U., Washington, 1946-48, assoc. prof. oral medicine, 1951-53, supt. clinics, 1953-65, prof. oral medicine, 1958-66, dir. clinics, 1965-66, dean, 1966-75, dean emeritus, 1981—; chmn., prof. oral diagnosis and radiology Sch. Dental Medicine, Harvard U., 1975—, prof. emeritus, 1995, assoc. dean, 1978-93, interim dean, 1990-91; nat. adv. coun. dental rsch., HHS, 1991—; Joseph N. Pew Charitable Trust health prof. com. adv. panel for dent., 1991—; nat. adv. coun. on health professions edn. HHS, 1990-92, IOM Commn. on Educating Dentists for Future 1993-95, Nat. Affairs Commn., 1993—; minority audit panel mem. Clinton Health Care Program, 1993; rsch. fellow U. Ill.; extern U. Ill. Rsch. and Ednl. Hosp., Chgo., 1948-51; cons. Freedmen's Hosp., 1951—, Tuskegee VA Hosp., 1951—, Crownsville (Md.) State Hosp., 1960—; trustee Ill. Coll. Optometry, 1972—, chmn. bd. trustees, 1982-86; cons. Essex Community Coll., 1972, Roxbury Med.-Tech. Inst., 1969—, Bakers Dozen Youth Center, Project Headstart, Peace Corps, Mt. Altoe Vets. Hosp.; bd. govs. D.C. Gen. Hosp., 1971-72; mem. dental editorial award com. William J. Gies Found. Advancement Dentistry; mem. adv. panel for dentistry Pew Health Professions Commn., 1991—; mem. nat. adv. coun. for dental rsch. HHS, 1991—. Contbr. to: Optometry: Education for the Profession, 1973, Optometric Education, A Summary Report, 1973, also articles in profl. jours. Mem. White House Conf. Internat. Relations, 1965; cons. White House Conf. Employment Handicapped, 1967, Nat. Urban Coalition, 1971, Nat. Commn. on Optometry, 1971-72; sponsor Boys Town, 1955—; life mem. NAACP; sponsor Urban League, 1953—; program dir. YMCA, 1950-51; mem. St. Gabriel's PTA, 1960—; trustee D.C. div. Am. Cancer Soc., Ill. Coll. Optometry; bd. dirs. Inst. Myofunctional Therapy, 1973, Symposia and Seminars, Inc., 1974; mem. Commn. Ednl. Credit Am. Council Edn., 1974; trustee Roxbury Latin Sch.; bd. dirs. W.E.B. DuBois Inst. Harvard U. Afro-Am. Research, 1976, Urban Health Project, 1997. Served to 2d lt. ASTP, 1942-43. Recipient Student Body and Student Council Faculty award, 1964, Achievement award Howard U. Dental Coll., 1967, Wisdom award Honor, 1970, Dental Alumni award, 1971, Inter-Alumni award United Negro Coll. Fund, 1970, Pub. Service award Urban League, 1970, awards Nat. Dental Assts., 1970, awards Nat. Naval Dental Sch., 1971, awards Roxbury Med.-Tech. Inst., 1972, Founders award Nat. Optometric Assn., 1973, Triennial award Nat. Dental Assn., 1973, award services D.C. govt., 1975, Disting. Svc. award Am. Assn. Dental Schs., 1995, Disting. Friend award Ill. Coll. Optometry, 1995, Carel C. Koch Meml. Medal award Am. Acad. Optometry, 1996, Orgn. of Tchrs. of Oral Diagnosis award; named Dentist of Year D.C. Dental Soc., 1973. Fellow AAAS (v.p., chmn. sect. on dentistry, mem.-at-large sect. dentistry), Internat., Am. Coll. Dentists, Royal Soc. Health; mem. Nat. Dental Assn. (Achievement award 1967, dentist of year award 1972, Presdl. award 1976), ADA (Quiz bowl champion trophy 1970, chmn. sect. periodontics ann. meeting 1976), Am. Acad. Oral Medicine (Robert T. Freeman award 1972, numerous others), Inst. Medicine, D.C. Dental Soc., Maimonides Dental Soc., Internat. Assn. Dental Research, Nat. Acad. Scis., Washington Acad. Sci., N.Y. Acad. Scis., Am. Acad. Polit. and Social Scis., Am. Assn. Tchrs. Practice Adminstrn. (pres., v.p., mem. exec. com.), Greater Washington Periodontal Soc. (pres. 197O), Am. Acad. Periodontology, AAUP, Am. Assn. Dental Schs., Acad. Dental Practice Adminstrn. (chmn. profl. liaison com. 1972), Acad. History of Dentistry, Am. Coll. Health Orgn., Howard U., U. Ill., Xavier U. alumni clubs, Sigma Xi, Alpha Eta Epsilon, Alpha Kappa Mu, Chi Delta Mu, Chi Lambda Kappa, Omicron Kappa Upsilon. Roman Catholic. Home: Chestnut Hill 309 Winchester St Apt A Newton Hlds MA 02461-2049 Office: Harvard U Sch Dental Med 188 Longwood Ave Boston MA 02115-5819 *My success is primarily attributable to "the way the twig was bent" by my parents. They provided a home in which love for God, each other and our fellow man prevailed.*

HENRY, JOSEPH PATRICK, chemical company executive; b. Mansfield, Ohio, Mar. 3, 1925; s. Harold H. and Louise A. (Droxler) H.; student Bowling Green State U., 1943-44; B.S., Ohio State U., 1949; m. Jeanette E. Russell, Oct. 26, 1957; 1 dau., Jeanette Louise. Ohio sales mgr. NaChurs Plant Food Co., Marion, Ohio, 1949-55; organizer, pres. Growers Chem. Corp., Milan, 1955—, Sandusky Imported Motors, Inc. (Ohio), 1958-78; pres. Homestead Motors, Inc., 1978-83; co-owner Homestead Inn Restaurant, Homestead Farms; v.p. Homestead Inn, Inc. Motels, 1963—, South Avery Corp. Motels, 1961—; dir. Erie County Bank, Vermilion, Ohio., Soc. Bank of Firelands. Served with USMCR, 1943-46; PTO. Named to Lakewood (Ohio) H.S. Atheletic Hall Fame, 1997—; recipient Businessman of the Year award Republican Congressional Com., 1999. Mem. Nat. Fedn. Ind. Bus. (nat. adv. council), AAAS, Ohio Farm Bur. Fedn., Milan C. of C., Aircraft Owners and Pilots Assn., Internat. Flying Farmers, Ohio Restaurant Assn., Ohio Motel-Hotel Assn., Ohio Licensed Beverage Assn., Am. Horse Show Assn., Nat. Trust for Historic Preservation, N.A.M., Internat. Platform Assn., Huron County Hist. Soc., Ohio Farm Bur., (pres.), Ohio, Internat. (dir. 1978-84) Arabian horse assns. Clubs: Antique Automobile Am., Sports Car Am., N. Am. Yacht Racing Union, Sandusky Yacht, Sandusky Sailing, Catawba Island. Developer (with V.A. Tiedjens) foliage fertilization and direct to seed fertilization of comml. field crops. Home: 128 Center St Milan OH 44846-9757 Office: Growers Chem Corp PO Box 1750 Milan OH 44846-1750 also: Homestead Farms RR 1 Milan OH 44846-1700

HENRY, JULIETTA, commissioner, state and local; b. Chgo., Oct. 9, 1965. Assoc. in Acctg., Madison (Wis.) Bus. Coll., 1986; BBA, Cardinal Stritch U., 1997. Legis. asst. State Sen. John O. Norquist, Madison, 1983-86; adminstrv. asst. Opportunities Industrialization Ctr. Greater Madison, 1986-88; staff asst. Mayor John O. Norquist City of Milw., 1988-92, mgr. election svcs. Office Election Commrs., 1992-95, exec. dir. Office Elections Commrs., 1995—. Bd. dirs. YMCA (Black Achiever award), YWCA, Friends of the Milw. Pub. Libr. Recipient Top Ladies of Distinction award, 1995. Mem. Links Inc. Home: 6993 W Glenbrook Rd Milwaukee WI 53223-1111 Office: City of Milw Bd Election Commrs 200 E Wells St City Hall Milwaukee WI 53202

HENRY, KENNETH JAMES, JR., medicinal chemist, anti-infectives researcher; b. Akron, Ohio, July 6, 1965; s. Kenneth James and Patricia Ann (Young) H.; m. Cynthia Louise Long, July 30, 1988; children: Rachael Aliana, Calvin James. BS, U. Mich., 1987; PhD in chemistry, Ind. U., 1993. Postdoctoral rsch. assoc. Duke U., Durham, N.C., 1993-95; rsch. chemist Abbott Labs., Abbott Park, Ill., 1995-98; medicinal chemist Eli Lilly & Co., Indpls., 1998—. Contbr. articles to profl. jours.; patentee in pharms. Leader, organizer Monroe County Caulk, Bloomington, Ind., 1992. Mem. Am. Chem. Soc. Presbyterian. Avocations: fishing, canoeing, swimming, music. Office: Eli Lilly & Co Lilly Rsch Labs Lilly Corp Ctr Indianapolis IN 46285

HENRY, LAURIE JAYNE, writer, educator; b. Sioux City, Iowa, Dec. 3, 1956; d. Gordon Charles H. and Audrey Fae Roorda; m. John Drury, June 13, 1987; children: Eric, Rebecca. BA, Oberlin Coll., 1980; MA, Johns Hopkins U., 1981; MFA, U. Iowa, 1985. Editor F&W Pubs., Cin., 1986—; tchr. Raymond Walters Coll., Cin., 1989—; panelist Ohio Arts Coun., Columbus, 1997—. Author: Restoring the Chateau at the Marquis de Sade, 1986, Fiction Writer's Market, 1986, Fiction Dictionary, 1993, Novelist's Notebook, 1999. Provincetown Fine Arts Work Ctr. fellow, 1985-86. Mem. Author's League. Home: 2824 Werk Rd Cincinnati OH 45211

HENRY, LAURIN LUTHER, public affairs educator; b. Kankakee, Ill., May 23, 1921; s. Laurimer Luther and Jeanette Belle (Wagner) H.; m. Kathleen Jane Stephan, May 18, 1946; children—Stephanie Jane, Robin Leigh. B.A., DePauw U., 1942; M.A., U. Chgo., 1948, Ph.D., 1960. Staff asst. Public Adminstrn. Clearing House, Chgo. and Washington, 1950-55; research asso., sr. staff mem. Brookings Instn., Washington, 1955-64; prof. govt. and fgn. affairs U. Va., 1964-78; dean Sch. Community and Public Affairs, Va. Commonwealth U., Richmond, 1978-86, prof., 1986-87, prof. emeritus, 1987—; guest scholar U. Va., 1988-95; vis. prof. Johns Hopkins U.; cons. to govt. Author: Presidential Transitions, 1960, The NASA-University Memorandum of Understanding, 1967; co-author: Presidential Election and Transition of 1960-61, 1961; contbr. articles profl. publns. Served with USNR, 1942-46. Recipient L.D. White prize Am. Polit. Sci. Assn., 1961. Fellow Nat. Acad. Pub. Adminstrn. (sr.); mem. Nat. Assn. Schs. Public Affairs and Adminstrn. (pres. 1971-72), Am. Soc. Pub. Adminstrn., Phi Beta Kappa, Phi Kappa Phi. Home: 2401 Old Ivy Rd #1204 Charlottesville VA 22903

HENRY, LLOYD, councilman; m. Leonie Henry; children: Sean, Heather, Tracy. Student, United Theol. Coll., West Indies; MDiv, N.Y. Seminary, 1988, D in Ministry, 1991. City councilman N.Y.C. Coun., 1994—; chmn. immigration subcom. N.Y.C. Coun.; mem. gen. welfare, civil svc., labor and environ. protection coms. Rector St. Augustine's Episcopal Ch., 1981—. Recipient Spiritual Leadership award Mid-Bklyn. Polit. Club; named Priest of Yr., Nat. Chaplains Assn. Mem. NAACP, Jaycees Intenrat., Kiwanis, United Order Mechanics. Office: 1498 Flatbush Ave Brooklyn NY 11210-2441*

HENRY, LOIS HOLLENDER, psychologist; b. Phila., Jan. 19, 1941; d. Edward Hubert and Frances Lois (Nesler) Hollender; m. Charles L. Henry, Oct. 24, 1964 (div. 1971); children: Deborah Lee, Randell Huitt, Andrew Edward. BA, Thomas A. Edison Coll., 1979; MSW, Fordham U., 1981; PhD in Indsl. Psychology, City U. L.A., 1992. Diplomate cert. neurofeedback provider; cert. social worker, Ariz., N.Y., N.J., EEG Biofeedback Practitioners; lic. svc. profl., career counselor, Ariz. Pers. asst., sec. IBM, Paterson, N.J. and St. Louis, 1964-66; min.'s asst. Grace Luth. Ch., St. Cloud, Fla., 1966-68; adminstr./tchr. Fla. Finishing Acad., St. Cloud, 1968-70; adminstrv. asst. Newark Book Ctr., 1972-77; intern, med. social worker Jersey City Med. Ctr., 1979-80; intern, psychiatric/med. social worker VA Med. Ctr., Lyons, N.J., 1980-81; sch. social worker Lakeview Learning Ctr., Budd Lake, N.J., 1981-82; mgr. human resources Terak Corp., Scottsdale, Ariz., 1982-85; v.p. counseling and bus. devel. Murro & Assocs., Phoenix, 1985-88, exec. v.p. cons., 1988-91; prin. career cons. Henry & Assocs., Scottsdale, 1982—; staff psychologist Nelson O'Connor & Assocs., Phoenix, 1993-97; v.p. dir. profl. svcs. Lee Hecht Harrison, Phoenix, 1998—; cert. neurotherapist Forensic Psychol. Svcs., Phoenix, 1995-96; career cons., individual/family counselor/psychotherapist/neurotherapist, spkr., Henry & Assocs., Scottsdale, 1982—; adj. prof. Ottawa U.; mem. employers com. Ariz. Dept. Econ. Security; cons. in field. Coordinator-vol. Job-A-Thon, Phoenix, 1983. Fellow Am. Orthopsychiat. Assn., Internat. Assn. Outplacement Profls. (treas. Ariz. region 1992-95, assoc. editor Internation Jour. Neuronal Regulation), Nat. Registry of Soc. Neuronal Regulation (diplomate, charter mem.); mem. NASW, Soc. Human Resource Mgmt., Am. Assn. Psychophysiology. Office: 8628 E Granada Rd Scottsdale AZ 85257-2943

HENRY, MARGARET ROSE, state legislator; b. Rayne, La., June 20, 1944. BA, Tex. So. U.; MA, Springfield Coll. Mem. Del. Senate, Dover, 1994—, mem. bond bill, children, youth and their families, mem. health and social svcs., labor and pub. safety coms.; chmn. Combat Drug Abuse Coms. Mem. Gov.'s Commn. on Families, State Human Rels. Commn. and Del. Agy. to Reduce Crime; bd. dirs. Child Inc.; mem. Del. Adolescent Program; bd. dirs., trustee Med. Ctr. Del. & Wesley Coll.; chair Del. State Arts Coun.; past pres. Wilmington chpt. Links, Inc.; mem. Jr. League Wilmington. Mem. Brandywine Profl. Assn. Office: Del Senate State Capitol Dover DE 19901*

HENRY, MARIE ELAINE, poet; b. San Francisco, Oct. 4, 1948; d. Norbert Francis and Katharyne Elizabeth (Hedman) H. BA in English with honors, San Jose State U., 1970; MA in Creative Writing, San Francisco State U., 1972. Contbg. poet/short fiction writer: The Reed, Panjandrum, Gallimaufry, Beautitude, Alcatraz, Center, Boulevards, Rapscallions Dream, Yellow Silk, Another Small Magazine, California Oranges, Peace or Perish: A Crisis Anthology, Co-Evolution Quar., Apalachee Quar., Squaw Valley Community of Writers Poetry Anthology, Canvass, Noe Valley Voice, Only Morning in Her Shoes, Pudding Mag., Sacred River, Out of Season, Disability Rag, Range of Motion, Watch Out! We're Talking, Through the Mill, Bite to Eat Place, Poetry at the 33 Review, Dream Machinery, Buffalo Bones, Convolvulus, Exquisite Corpse, Full Court: A Literary Anthology of Basketball, Barnabe Mountain Rev., Beside the Sleeping Maiden. Recipient James D. Phelan writing awards San Jose State U., 1970, Bukowski Poetry Contest award, 1999. Mem. Marin Poetry Ctr., Bay Area Folk Harp Soc. Avocations: playing harp, guitar and blues harmonica, swimming. Home: 855 C St Apt 408 San Rafael CA 94901-2853

HENRY, MARY LOU SMELSER, elementary education educator; b. Russellville, Ala., Mar. 2, 1953; d. Jessie Clifton and Margie Lou (Willingham) Smelser; m. Don M. Henry, Aug. 26, 1972; children: Aaron,

Nathan. Student, N.W. Ala. State Jr. Coll., 1971-72; BS, Middle Tenn. State U., 1975; MA, Tenn. Tech. U., 1986, postgrad., 1998. Cert. elem. tchr., secondary tchr. history and sociology, Tenn., Ala. Substitute tchr. Warren County Bd. Edn., McMinnville, Tenn., 1979-82; tchr. LaPetite Acad., McMinnville, 1982-83; tchr. 2d grade Grundy County Bd. Edn., Altamont, Tenn., 1983—. Coord. Drug Awareness Task Force, 1990-92; mem. Grundy County Edn. Assn. Recipient Tchr. of Yr. award 1987-88, Trophy award 4H, 1988-91. Mem. NEA, Grundy County Edn. Assn. (sec. 1989-90, chmn. pub. rels. 1990-91, rep. North Elem. 1990-91, editor Tchr. Times 1989-91, pres. 1993-94, chair grievance com. 1994-95, negotiations com. 1993-99), Tenn. Edn. Assn. (Cert. of Appreciation 1991, women status com. 1994-96). Home: 212 Forest Dr Mc Minnville TN 37110-2333

HENRY, NANCY SINCLAIR, middle school educator; b. Alexandria, Va., Aug. 4, 1940; d. John Wilson and Margaret Lucille (Bryant) Sinclair; m. James Russell Henry, June 21, 1969; 1 child, Ryan Sinclair. BA in Elem. Edn., Coll. William and Mary, 1962; MA in Edn., Instrn. & Curriculum, Lynchburg Coll., 1997. Cert. tchr., Va. Primary tchr. Alexandria Pub. Schs., 1962-69, 70-73, Louisa County Pub. Schs., Louisa, Va., 1969-70; presch. tchr. St. Paul's Nursery and Day Sch., Alexandria, 1973-81; elem. and mid. tchr. Bedford County Pub. Schs., Bedford, Va., 1981—, math.-coop. learning cons., 1988—; cons. learning ctrs. Alexandria Pub. Schs., 1970-73; cons. math. and coop. learning Appomattox County Schs., Appomattox, Va., 1989, 90, 91, Bedford County Schs., 1990-96, mentor, 1996—. Vol. James Earl Carter U.S. Presdl. campaign, Alexandria, 1976; pres. Bookmark Club, Bedford, 1987-88, Bedford Hist. Soc., 1989-90 (pres. 1998—); trustee Bedford Regional Libr., 1988-96. Named Tchr. of Yr. Bedford County Mid. Sch., 1990-91, Otter chpt. DAR, 1996-97, 97-98; grantee Va. Commn. on Fine Arts, 1989-90. Mem. NEA, Nat. Coun. Tchrs. Math., Nat. Mic. Sch. Assn., Va. Edn. Assn., Piedmont Area Reading Coun., Va. Reading Assn., Bedford County Edn. Assn. (Tchr. of Month 1991), Phi Kappa Delta, Alpha Delta Kappa, Phi Delta Phi. Episcopalian. Avocations: quilting, camping. Home: 1096 Meadowbrook Dr Bedford VA 24523-3020 Office: Bedford Mid Sch Longwood Ave Bedford VA 24523-3402

HENRY, NICHOLAS LLEWELLYN, college president, political science educator; b. Seattle, May 22, 1943; s. Samuel Houston and Ann (Connor) H.; m. Muriel Bunney; children: Adrienne Richardson, Miles Houston. B.A., Centre Coll. Ky., 1965; M.A., Pa. State U., 1967; M.P.A., Ind. U., 1970, Ph.D., 1971. Asst. to dean Coll. Arts and Scis.; instr. Ind. State U., 1967-69; vis. asst. prof. U. N.Mex., 1971-72; asst. prof. polit. sci. U. Ga., 1972-75, assoc. prof., 1975-78, prof., 1978-87, dir. Ctr. Pub. Affairs, 1975-80, dean Coll. Pub. Programs, 1980-87; prof., pres. Ga. So. U., Statesboro, 1987-98; prof. polit. sci. Ga. So. U., 1998—. Author or editor 12 books; contbr. numerous articles to profl. jours. Recipient Author of Yr. award Assn. Sci. Jours.; named One of 100 Most Influential People in Ga., Ga. Trend, 1994. Fellow Nat. Acad. Pub. Adminstrn.; mem. Cosmos Club (Washington). Office: Ga So U PO Box 80331 Statesboro GA 30460-8033

HENRY, OLGA ELAINE, nursing educator, health care trainer; b. London, Ont., Can., Aug. 29, 1943; came to U.S., 1979; d. Andrej and Agafia (Schur) Olejar; m. Ronald John Chapchuk, June 4, 1965 (div. July 1980); children: Timothy Jon, Robin Anne Marie; m. Gilbert Armstrong Henry, Dec. 18, 1984; children: Douglas Richard, Valerie Jean, Pauline Michelle. RN, Atkinson Sch. Nursing, Toronto, Ont., 1965; BSN, U. Western Ont., London, 1966; MBA, cert. health svcs. adminstrn., Nova Southeastern U., Ft. Lauderdale, Fla., 1988. Cert. home health nurse, cert. corp. trainer, cert. continuing edn. provider. Dir. edn. Mississauga (Ont.) Hosp., 1974-79, North Ridge Hosp., Ft. Lauderdale, Fla., 1980-84; adminstr. Barna Inst., Inc., Ft. Lauderdale, 1984-85; coord. health care City of Ft. Lauderdale, 1985; supr. nursing Maxicare Home Health, Ft. Lauderdale, 1985-88; dir. nursing All-Care Health Svcs., Lauderhill, Fla., 1988-90, Enteral & Parenteral Support Svc., Sunrise, Fla., 1990; supr. nursing Mederi of Broward County, Inc., Coral Springs, Fla., 1991-93; coord. staff edn. Mederi of Broward County, Inc., 1993-98; adj. prof. Broward C.C., Ft. Lauderdale, 1993—; cons., corp. trainer Profl. Edn. Enterprises, Inc., Coral Springs, 1984—. Mem. South Fla. Dem. Club, Hollywood, 1996. Mem. ANA, NAFE, The Profl. Woman Spkrs. Bur., Fla. Nurses Assn., Women Healthcare Execs. Network, Nova Southeastern U. Sch. Bus. Alumni Assn. (bd. dirs. Broward County chpt. 1995—). Avocations: gardening, photography, needlework.

HENRY, PAUL EUGENE, JR., minister; b. Summit, N.J., Jan. 10, 1941; s. Paul Eugene and Arline Anita (Ferns) H; m. Carolyn Sandra Haas, July 16, 1966; children: Susan Beth, Thomas Paul, Carol Lee. BA, Gettysburg (Pa.) Coll., 1963; MDiv, Luth. Theol. Sem., Gettysburg, 1966. Ordained to ministry Luth. Ch. Am., 1966. Asst. pastor 1st Luth. Ch., Albany, N.Y., 1966-67; pastor St. John's Luth. Ch., Canajoharie, N.Y., 1967-70, Mamaroneck, N.Y., 1970-77; pastor Faith Luth. Ch., East Hartford, Conn., 1977—; chmn. Lay Workers Conf. Met. N.Y. Synod, 1974; sec. Capitol Dist., Upper N.Y. Synod, 1966-67; mem. worship com. Met. N.Y. Synod, 1975-76; mem. exec. bd. New Eng. Synod, 1979-85; mem. Common. on Budget and Fin., 1979-85, chmn., 1980-82; coord. Area V, No. Conn., 1979-85; chmn. New Eng. Synod Conv., 1991. Chaplain Mamaroneck Vol. Fire Dept, 1970-77, East Hartford Police Dept., 1982—. Mem. East Hartford Clergy Assn. (pres. 1986—), Greater Hartford Luth. Chs. (dean 1985—, sem. intern supr. 1994-95). Home: 22 Dartmouth Dr East Hartford CT 06108-1426 Office: 1120 Silver Ln East Hartford CT 06118-1329

HENRY, PETER YORK, lawyer, mediator; b. Washington, Apr. 28, 1951; s. David Howe II and Margaret (Beard) H.; children: Ryan York, Zachary Price, Chance Hagdorn; m. Deidra B. Hagdorn, May 1995; 1 child, Chance Hagdorn Henry; stepchildren: Nathan Hebert, Christopher Hebert. B.B.A., Ohio U., 1973; J.D. St. Mary's U., San Antonio, 1976. Bar: Tex. 1976. Sole practice, San Antonio, 1976—. Mem. ATLA, Tex. Bar Assn., Tex Trial Lawyers Assn., San Antonio Trial Lawyers Assn. (bd. dirs. 1989-90), San Antonio Bar Assn., Phi Delta Phi. Home: 7642 Bluesage Cv San Antonio TX 78249-2541 Office: 224 Casa Blanca St San Antonio TX 78215-1232

HENRY, PHILIP LAWRENCE, marketing professional; b. Los Angeles, Dec. 1, 1940; s. Lawrence Langworthy and Ella Hanna (Martens) H.; m. Claudia Antonia Huff, Aug. 9, 1965 (div. 1980); children: Carolyn Marie, Susan Michelle; m. Carrie Katherine Hoover, Aug. 23, 1985. BS in Marine Engring., Calif. Maritime Acad., 1961. Design engr. Pacific Telephone Co., San Diego, 1963-73; service engr. Worthington Service Corp., San Diego, 1973-78; pres. Realmart Corp., San Diego, 1978-81; dir. mktg. Orbit Inn Hotel and Casino, Las Vegas, 1981-84; pres. Comml. Consultants, Las Vegas, 1984—, Gray Electronics Co., Las Vegas, 1986—; chmn. bd. dirs. Las Vegas Accomodations Unltd., 1997—; mng. mem. G/Tracker Techs., LLC, 1998, Strobe Detector Techs., LLC, 1998; bd. dirs. Silver State Classic Challenge, Inc. Inventor electronic detection devices, 1986—. Served to lt. (j.g.) USNR, 1961-67. Republican. Avocation: amateur radio, open road auto racing, storm chasing. Home: 1843 Somersby Way Henderson NV 89014-3876

HENRY, PHYLLISS JEANETTE, United States Marshal. AA in Law Enforcement, Des Moines Area C.C., 1972; BGS, U. Iowa, 1984, MA in Comm. Studies, 1986, PhD in Comm. Rsch., 1988. Police officer Des Moines (Iowa) Police Dept., 1972-82; state adminstrv. dir. Roxanne Conlin for Gov. campaign, Iowa, 1982; intern Police Found., Washington, 1984; comm. rsch. analyst Starr and Assocs., 1985; mgr. support svcs. Dept. Pub. Safety Iowa State U., 1990-94; U.S. marshal so. dist. Iowa, apptd. by Pres. Clinton U.S. Dept. Justice, 1994—; adv. com. Dirs. Marshals, 1995-97. Named Woman of Yr., Metro. Woman's Network, 1991, Officer of Yr. Internat. Assn. of Women, 1991. Mem. Iowa Assn. Women Police (co-founder, Officer of Yr. 1991), Fed. Exec. Coun. Policy Com. (co-founder), Nat. ctr. for Women and Policing (adv. bd.). Office: Office US Marshal US Courthouse 123 E Walnut St Rm 208 Des Moines IA 50309-2035

HENRY, RANDOLPH MARSHALL, company executive, real estate broker; b. Houston, Jan. 23, 1946; s. Marshall Gambrell and Merriem Rue (Evans) H.; m. Janis Kay Frank, Apr. 5, 1979; children: Vernon Clark, Clark Marshall. BA, So. Meth. U., 1968; Diploma in Hist. Studies, Cambridge (Eng.) U., 1969; MBA, U. Pa., 1971. Lic. real estate broker. Asst. to pres. Surfcoat Inc., Houston and Fairbanks, Alaska, 1971-72; mgr. Gerald D. Hines Interests, Houston, 1972-75; pres. The Randolph Henry Co., Houston, 1975—, EcoPoly, Inc., 1993-98, AllPoly Corp., 1999—; pres. MGP Mgmt. Inc., Houston, 1976-87; adv. dir. Tex. Commerce Bank, Houston, 1982-96; v.p., bd. dirs. Brazos Mgmt. Co., 1976-90, Skyline Condominium Corp., 1983-90; co-chmn. bd. dirs. Pvt. Sector Initiatives, Houston; mem. adv. com. New Founds. for Neighborhoods. Mktg. network Houston Econ. Devel. Coun., 1987—; chmn. Post Oak Sch., Houston, 1987-89; founding pres. City of Post Oak Assn., 1974-75; Rep. precinct chmn., Houston, 1979; adminstrv. bd. Chapelwood Meth. Ch., 1987—, chmn. bldg. com., treas. Mem. Reusable Indsl. Container Assn. (chair plastic drum products group), Wharton Alumni Assn., Houston C. of C. (aviation com.), Reusable Indsl. Packaging Assn. (bd. dirs.). Methodist. Club: Univ. Avocations: astronomy, skiing, cattle ranching, basketball. Home: 640 Pifer Rd Houston TX 77024-5434 Office: 5858 Westheimer Rd Ste 703 Houston TX 77057-5647

HENRY, RENE ARTHUR, JR., environmental agency administrator; b. Charleston, W.Va., June 13, 1933; s. Rene A. and Lillian E. (Reveal) H.; children: Deborah Marie, Bruce Rexford. A.B., Coll. William and Mary, 1954; postgrad., W.Va. U., 1954-56. Account exec. Flournoy & Gibbs, Toledo, 1956-59; publicity dir. Lennen & Newell, Inc., San Francisco, 1959-67; sr. v.p., dir. Daniel J. Edelman, Inc., Los Angeles, 1967-70; pres. Rene A. Henry, Jr., Inc., L.A., 1970-74; ptnr. Allen, Ingersoll, Segal & Henry, Inc., L.A., 1974-75; prin. ICPR, L.A., 1975-81; pvt. practice mgmt. and sports mktg. cons., 1981-86, 90-91; pres., chief exec. officer Nat. Inst. Bldg. Scis., Washington, 1986-88; confidential asst. to adminstr. Farmers Home Adminstrn. USDA, 1989; cons., designate asst. adminstr. AID, Dept. State, 1989-90; spl. asst. to dir. Office of Fed. Contract Compliance Programs, U.S. Dept. Labor, Washington, 1991; exec. dir. univ. rels. Tex. A&M U., College Station, 1991-96; dir. Office of Comm. and Govt. Rels. U.S. EPA, Phila., 1996—; exec. sec. to bd. dirs. Coun. Housing Producers, 1968-78; spl. advisor The Pres.'s Coun. on Phys. Fitness and Sports, 1981-89; spl. cons. Nat. Fitness Found., 1981-89. Author: How to Profitably Buy and Sell Land, 1977, Marketing Public Relations, 1995; co-author: MIUS and You—The Developer Takes a Look at a New Utility Concept, 1980, Bears Handbook, 1996. Mem. U.S. Olympic Com., 1985-89, asst. to pres., mem. coms. internat. rels., pub. rels., long range strategic planning task force; campaign dir. for athletes and entertainers Bush for Pres. and Bush/Quayle '88 presdl. election campaigns. With U.S. Army, 1956-58. Named San Francisco Bay Area Pub. Relations Man of Year, 1963; recipient Clarion award for human rights Women in Communication, 1980. Mem. Acad. TV Arts and Scis. (past chair bldg. com.), Nat. Assn. Home Builders, Inst. Residential Mktg., Pub. Rels. Soc. Am. (Coll. Fellows, Disting. Citizen award L.A. chpt. 1979, 3 Silver Anvils, mem. bd. dirs. Phila. chpt., sec., treas. Coll. of Fellows, exec. com. environment section), Acad. Motion Picture Arts and Scis., Sigma Nu. Episcopalian. Office: US EPA 1650 Arch St Philadelphia PA 19103-2029

HENRY, RICHARD CONN, astrophysicist, educator; b. Toronto, Mar. 7, 1940; came to U.S., 1962, naturalized, 1973; s. Edwin Mackie and Jean Bonar (Conn) H.; m. Rita Mahon, May 10, 1975; children: George William, Mark Winston. B.Sc., U. Toronto, 1961, M.A., 1962; Ph.D., Princeton U., 1967. Rsch. assoc. Inst. Advanced Study, 1967; rsch. appointee E.O. Hulburt Ctr. Space Rsch., Naval Rsch. Lab., Washington, 1967-69; research physicist E.O. Hulburt Center Space Research, Naval Research Lab., 1969-76; asst. prof. Johns Hopkins U., Balt., 1968-74, assoc. prof., 1974-77, prof., 1977—, mem. prin. profl. staff Applied Physics Lab., 1991—; vis. staff Los Alamos Nat. Lab.; dep. dir. astrophysics divsn. NASA, 1976-78; dir. Md. Space Grant Consortium, 1989—. Recipient Gold medal Royal Astron. Soc. Can., 1961; Alfred P. Sloan fellow, 1971-75. Fellow AAAS; mem. Am. Phys. Soc., Am. Astron. Soc., Internat. Astron. Union. Home: 12515 Meadowood Dr Silver Spring MD 20904-2922 Office: Johns Hopkins U Dept Physics And Astro Baltimore MD 21218*

HENRY, RICHARD MICHAEL, educator; b. Urbana, Ill., May 22, 1957; s. Richard Warfield Henry and Marilyn Jean O'Connor. BA, St. Lawrence U., 1979; MPA, Bowling Green State U., 1983; PhD, U. Minn., 1996. Lectr. U. Minn., Mpls., 1996-97; cmty. faculty Met. State U., St. Paul, 1997; asst. prof. SUNY, Potsdam, 1997—. Author: Pretending and Meaning, 1996; editor Blueline, 1998—. Office: Dept English & Comm SUNY Potsdam Potsdam NY 13676

HENRY, RICK, broadcast executive. Degree in engring., Ripon (Wis.) Coll. Pres., gen. mgr. Sta. WISN-TV, Milw., 1997—. Office: Sta WISN-TV 759 N 19th St Milwaukee WI 53233-2126*

HENRY, ROBERT HARLAN, federal judge, former attorney general; b. Shawnee, Okla., Apr. 3, 1953. BA, U. Okla., 1974, JD, 1976. Bar: Okla. 1976. Atty. Henry, West, Still & Combs, Shawnee, Okla., 1977-83, Henry, Henry & Henry, Shawnee, 1983-87; mem. Okla. Ho. of Reps., 1976-86; atty. gen. State of Okla., Oklahoma City, 1987-91; dean, prof. law. Law Sch. Okla. City U., 1991-94; judge U.S. Ct. Appeals (10th cir.), Oklahoma City, 1994—; mem. Nat. Conf. Commrs. on Uniform State Law. Fellow Am. Bar Found.; mem. Okla. Bar Assn., Am. Coun. Young Polit. Leaders, Nat. Assn. Attys. Gen. (chmn. state constl. law adv. com., vice-chmn. civil rights com.). Office: US Ct Appeals 10th Cir 200 NW 4th St Oklahoma City OK 73102-3026*

HENRY, RONALD JAMES WHYTE, university official; b. Belfast, No. Ireland, Feb. 5, 1940; came to U.S., 1965; s. William James Louis and Mary Ann (Whyte) H.; children: Norah Lynn, Andrea Marie. BSc, Queen's U., Belfast, 1961, PhD, 1964. Asst. lectr. Queen's U., 1964-65; rsch. assoc. Goddard Space Flight Ctr., Greenbelt, Md., 1965-66; asst. physicist Kitt Peak Nat. Obs., Tucson, 1966-69; assoc. prof. La. State U., Baton Rouge, 1969-73, prof., 1973-89, chmn. dept. physics and astronomy, 1976-82, dean basic scis., 1982-89; v.p. acad. affairs Auburn (Ala.) U., 1989-91; provost, exec. v.p. for acad. affairs Miami U., Oxford, Ohio, 1991-94; provost, v.p. acad. affairs Ga. State U., Atlanta, 1994—; com. on undergrad. sci. edn. Nat. Rsch. Coun., 1998—. Fellow Am. Physics Soc. Republican. Avocation: golf. Office: Ga State U Atlanta GA 30303

HENRY, ROY MONROE, financial planner; b. Oct. 27, 1939; s. Roy Monroe and Nancy Lowe (Morse) H.; m. Meredith Elaine Hjelmstad, Aug. 20, 1961; children: Robin E., Roy M. III. BBA, Kennedy-Western, 1990. Registered prin., rep.-NASD; LUTCF. Airman 1st class USAF, Turkey, 1957-61; estimator Con P. Curran Printing Co., St. Louis, 1961-64; sales mgr. Prudential Ins. Co., St. Louis, 1964-72; pres. Roy M. Henry & Assocs., Chesterfield, Mo., 1972-76, St. Louis Fin. Planners, Chesterfield, Mo., 1976-83, First Fin. Planners, Chesterfield, Mo., 1983—; guest spkr. Purdue U., Yale U., Stanford U. Appeared on (TV show) 20/20, 1991; contbr. articles to profl. jours. Named Fin. Planner of Yr., 1987; commd. admiral by Commonwealth of Ky. Fellow Life Underwriting Tng. Counsel; mem. Internat. Assn. Fin. Planners (bd. dirs. 1984-86), Mo. Athletic Club, Internat. Assn. of Registered Fin. Cons. (pres.), Order of Ky. Cols. Republican. Lutheran. Avocations: travel, model trains, cars, video and career. E-mail: linamd@mail.ffp1.com. Home: 2031 Kehrsboro Dr Chesterfield MO 63005-6512 Office: First Fin Planners Inc c/o Debbie Linman 15455 Conway Rd Chesterfield MO 63017-2067

HENRY, SALLY MCDONALD, lawyer; b. Durham, N.C., Aug. 1, 1948; d. John Frederick and Mary Frances (McDonald) Henry; m. Bradley Lewis Rudin. BA, Duke U., 1970; MA in Anthropology, SUNY, Binghamton, 1973; JD, NYU, 1982. Tchr. Endicott (N.Y.) Pub. Schs., 1971-75, Monticello (N.Y.) Pub. Schs., 1975-79; clk. U.S. Bankruptcy Ct., Bklyn., 1982-83; assoc. Skadden, Arps, Slate, Meagher & Flom, N.Y.C., 1983-91, ptnr., 1991—. Editor articles Rev. Law and Social Change, 1981-83; contbr. numerous articles to profl. jours. Mem. rules com. E.D.N.Y., Bklyn, 1984. Home: 395 Riverside Dr Apt 6A New York NY 10025-1843 Office: Skadden Arps Slate Meagher & Flom 919 3rd Ave New York NY 10022-3902*

HENRY, SAMUEL DUDLEY, educator; b. Washington, Oct. 9, 1947; s. Dudley and Shendrine Eugene (Boyce) H.; m. Ana Maria Meneses, Dec. 23, 1988; children: Antonia, Adsilla. BS, D.C. Tchrs. Coll., 1969; MA in Edn., Columbia U., 1974, EdD, 1978. Tchr. engring. D.C. Pub. Schs., 1969-71, Binghamton Pub. Schs., Bing, N.Y., 1971-73; asst. prof. U. Mass., Amherst, 1977-79; dir. RDAC Tchrs. Coll., N.Y.C., 1979-81, San Jose (Calif.) State U., 1981-88, 89-92; assoc.dean Calif. State U., Northridge, 1988-89; exec. dir., assoc. prof. Portland State U., 1992—; Exec. dir., 1992-94, urban fellow, assoc. prof. of ed. Mem. Multi-County Com. Child & Family Svcs., Portland, 1993—, Evelyn Robinson Scholar Com., San Jose, 1985-92; mem., pres. exec. bd. United Campus Christian Ctr., San Jose, 1984-87; assoc. campaign mgr. Learned for City Coun., San Jose, 1986. With U.S. Army. Recipient Shiny Apple award L.A. Tchrs. Ctr., 1989, Disting. Svc. award Evelyn Robinson Sch. Com., San Jose, 1992. Mem. ASCD, Smithsonian Inst. Avocations: photography, reading, exercise, basketball, travel. Home: 1186 SW 12th Ct Troutdale OR 97060-1495 Office: Portland State U PO Box 751 Portland OR 97207-0751

HENRY, SHERRYE, federal agency administrator. Grad. magna cum laude, Vanderbilt U.; MBA, Fordham U. Asst. adminstr. Office Women's Bus. Ownership SBA; vice-chair interagy. com. on women's bus. enterprise. Author of 2 books including The Deep Divide: Why American Women Resist Equality; contbr. numerous articles to nat. mags.; creator, host Woman! program on Sta. WCBS-TV, N.Y.C.; ind. prodr., broadcaster Sherrye Henry Program WOR Radio, N.Y.C. Active Group for the South Fork, eastern end of L.I., N.Y., Fedn. Protestant Welfare Agys. N.Y., The Retreat, East Hampton, N.Y. Mem. Women's Forum N.Y. (founding mem.). Office: Office of Women's Bus Ownership 409 3rd St SW Washington DC 20024-3212

HENRY, STEPHEN LEWIS, state official, orthopedic surgeon, educator; b. Owensboro, Ky., Oct. 8, 1953; s. Virgil Lewis and Wanda (Harper) Henry. BS, We. Ky. U., 1976; MD, U. Louisville, 1981. Diplomate Am. Bd. Orthopaedic Surgery. Intern gen. surgery U. Louisville Med. Ctr., 1981-82, resident, 1982-86, instr. orthopedic surgery, 1986—; lt. gov. Commonwealth of Ky., 1995—; clin. investigator Richards Med. Co., Memphis, 1986—; athletic physician football teams U. Louisville, 1987—, Seneca High Sch., 1987—, Ky. State Football Championships, 1986—; commr. "A" dist. Jefferson County, 1992-95. Editor: Sports Medicine; contbr. abstracts and articles to profl. jours., chpts. to books. Treas. Louisville Tyler Park Neighborhood Assn., 1983-88, pres., 1988-89. Recipient best paper award So. Med. Assn., 1985, best clin. rsch. award U. Cin., 1986, outstanding resident rsch. award U. Louisville, 1988, Edwin G. Bovill rsch. award Orthopaedic Trauma Assn., 1989, Bell award for outstanding vol., Louisville, 1989, Presdl. recognition Nat. Vol. Week, The White House, 1989; named Outstanding Young Leader in Ky., 1988, One of 10 Outstanding Young Ams., U.S. Jaycees, 1989, Bell award, 1989, Jefferson award, 1989, Owensboro award for excellence, 1990, Lawrence-Grever award, 1990; grantee Richards Med. Co., 1986, Dept. Navy, 1989. Mem. Jefferson County Med. Soc., So. Orthopedic Assn., Ky. Med. Assn., U. Louisville House Staff Assn. (com. on health, phys. edn. and med. aspects of sports 1987—). Democrat. Home: 1361 Tyler Park Dr Louisville KY 40204-1539 Office: 700 Capitol Ave Frankfort KY 40601-3410*

HENRY, SUSAN ARMSTRONG, biology educator, university dean; b. Alexandria, Va., June 27, 1946; d. Frederic Sylvester and Frederica Ann (Thompson) A.; m. Peter Edward Henry, July 20, 1968; children: Rebecca Alice, Joshua Armstrong. BS in Zoology, U. Md., 1968; PhD in Genetics, U. Calif., Berkeley, 1971. Postdoctoral fellow Brandeis U., Waltham, Mass., 1971-72; asst. prof. genetics Albert Einstein Coll. Medicine, Bronx, N.Y., 1972-77, assoc. prof. genetics and molecular biology, 1972-82, prof., 1972-87, dir. Sue Golding grad. div., 1983-87; prof. biol. scis. Carnegie Mellon U., Pitts., 1987—, head dept. biol. scis., 1987-91, program dir. undergrad. biol. scis. edn. initiative, Howard Hughes Med. Inst., 1989—, dean Mellon Coll. Sci., 1991-98; mem. nat. adv. gen. med. scis. coun. NIH, 1995-98, adv. com. rsch. on minority health, 1998—, chmn., 1999—; co-dir. W.M. Keck Ctr. Advanced Tng. Computational Biology, 1992—. Contbr. over 70 articles to profl. jours. Recipient Merit award NIH, 1991, Career Devel. award, 1975-80, Irma T. Hirschl Faculty award Hirschl Found., 1980-85; rsch. grantee NIH, 1972—. Fellow AAAS, Am. Acad. Microbiology; mem. Genetics Soc. Am., Am. Soc. Biol. Chemists, Am. Soc. Microbiologists. Office: Carnegie Mellon U Mellon Coll Scis 4400 5th Ave Pittsburgh PA 15213

HENRY, THOMAS JOSEPH, research entomologist; b. Logansport, Ind., Jan. 8, 1948; s. Joseph Fouts Henry and Betty Jean (Vitello) Walker; m. M. L. Mee, Jan. 28, 1968 (div. 1974); children: Thomas Alan, Angela Marie; m. C. M. Kathryn Henderson, July 3, 1986. BS, Purdue U., 1971; MS, Pa. State U., 1980; PhD, U. Md., 1995. Entomologist Pa. Dept. Agr., Harrisburg, 1972-80; rsch. entomologist Systematic Entomol. Lab., Agrl. Rsch. Svc., U.S. Dept. Agr., Washington, 1980—. Co-editor, author: Catalog of the Heteroptera, or true bugs, of Canada and Continental United States, 1988; co-author: Synthesis of Holarctic Miridae, 1992, Monograph of the Stilt Bugs, or Berytidae, of the Western Hemisphere, 1997; contbr. over 130 articles to profl. jours. Recipient Vice Pres. Gore's Hammer award, 1998. Mem. Entomol. Soc. Am. (disting. achievement award in regulatory entomology), Entomol. Soc. Washington (editor 1992-95), Willi Hennig Soc., Internat. Heteropterists Soc. (founding mem. and editor 1997—), N.Y. Entomol. Soc. Avocations: gardening, native and tropical fish, woodworking. Office: Systematic Entomology Lab ARS USDA MRC 168 10th & Constitution Ave Washington DC 20560

HENRY, WILLIAM LOCKWOOD, sales and marketing executive; b. Pasadena, Calif., July 2, 1948; s. Edward Lockwood and Jane (Post) H.; m. Pamela Ann Henry; children: Thomas Edward, Michael Lockwood. BS, UCLA, 1971, MS, 1973. Fin. exec. Ford Motor Co., Dearborn, Mich., 1973-81; dir. fin. Stroh Brewery Co., Detroit, 1981-82, v.p., fin. planner, 1982-84, v.p., sales, mktg. adminstr., 1985-1986, v.p. mktg. and plannig, 1987-89; exec. v.p. Stroh Brewery Co, Detroit, 1989-91; pres., CEO Stroh Brewery Co., Detroit, 1991—; bd. dirs. Met. Affairs Corp., Century Coun. Mem. Detroit Athletic Club. Office: The Stroh Brewery Co 100 River Place Detroit MI 48207-4291*

HENRY, WILLIAM OSCAR EUGENE, lawyer; b. Ocala, Fla., Mar. 30, 1927; s. Jesse Dawson and Alice M. (Johnson) H.; m. Bobbie Moorhead, May 9, 1952; children: Carol Ann, Robert Dawson, Jean Elizabeth. BS in Journalism, U. Fla., 1950, JD, 1952. Bar: Fla. 1952; cert. cir. mediator Supreme Ct. Fla., tax lawyer Fla. Bd. Legal Specialization. Newspaperman The Marion Sun, Ocala, 1952-53; assoc. Holland, Bevis, McRae & Smith, Bartow, Fla., 1953-55; ptnr. Holland and Knight (and predecessor firms), Bartow, Lakeland and Orlando, Fla., 1955—; bd. dirs. Consol.-Tomoka Land Co., Daytona Beach, Fla.; arbitrator, mem. panel Am. Arbitration Assn. Contbr. articles to profl. jour. Legis counsel Office of Gov. of Fla., Tallahassee, 1963; bd. dirs. U. Fla. Found., Inc., 1977-87, Holland and Knight Found., Lakeland, 1982-97; v.p. Ctrl. Fla. coun. Boy Scouts Am., 1990-95; trustee Fla. Bar Found. Endowment Trust, 1991—. Recipient Disting. Eagle Scout award, 1990, Silver Beaver award, 1992; named Outstanding Past Pres. Vol. Bar Assn. award Fla. Coun. Bar Assn. Pres., 1991-92. Fellow Am. Bar Found., Am. Coll. Trusts and Estates Coun., Am. Coll. Tax Coun., Am. Judicature Soc., Nat. Health Lawyers Assn., Fla. Bar Found. (bd. dirs. 1983-89, pres. 1988-89, Medal of Honor 1996); mem. ABA (ho. of dels. 1984-89, 93—, exec. com. sect. officers conf. 1997—), Fla. Bar (pres. 1983-84, Fla. Outstanding Tax Atty. award 1986), U. Fla. Nat. Alumni Assn. (bd. dirs., pres. 1968, Disting Alumnus award 1972), Univ. Club, Citrus Club, Lakeland Yacht and Country Club, Elks, Sigma Alpha Epsilon (pres. Fla. Upsilon alumni 1993—). Methodist. Home: 985 S Helen Cir Bartow FL 33830-7444 Office: Holland & Knight LLP 200 S Orange Ave Ste 2600 Orlando FL 32801-3449

HENRY, WILLIAM RAY, business administration educator; b. Russellville, Ark., Dec. 30, 1925; s. Mace Leon and Violet May (Shinn) H.: m. Norma Talmadge Wright, Nov. 27, 1954; children—William Ray, Lisa Carolyn, Linda Carol, Lara Carline. B.S., U. Ark., 1948, M.S., 1953; Ph.D., N.C. State U., 1957. Asst. prof., then assoc. prof., prof. N.C. State U., Raleigh, 1956-70; prof. bus. adminstrn. Ga. State U., Atlanta, 1970—, prof. emeritus fin., 1993—. Author: (with others) Managerial Economics, 1978; contbr. (with others) articles to profl. jours. Served with USAAF, 1944-45. Recipient award of merit Am. Agrl. Econs. Assn., 1957, 61. Mem. Am. Econs. Assn., AAUP. Office: University Plaza Atlanta GA 30303

HENSCHEL, MILTON G., church administrator. Pres. Jehova's Witnesses. Office: Jehova's Witnesses 25 Columbia Heights Brooklyn NY 11201-2483*

HENSCHEL, SHIRLEY MYRA, licensing agent; b. N.Y.C., Dec. 18, 1932; d. Joseph and Leah Rose (Cooper) H. BA, Barnard Coll., 1954. Pub. rels., sales promotion exec. Louis Marx & Co., Inc., N.Y.C., 1954-59; acct. exec. Harold J. Siesel Co., N.Y.C., 1959-62; pres. U.S. Motor Sport Promotions, Inc., N.Y.C., 1962-66; v.p. Flora Mir Candy Corp., N.Y.C., 1966-71, Marden-Kane, Inc., N.Y.C., 1971-79; pres. Alaska Momma, Inc., N.Y.C., 1979—. Mem. Sch. and Home Products Assn. (assoc.), Licensing Industry and Merchandisers Assn. (charter mem. Achievement award 1988, nominated for Hall of Fame 1994), Women Inc., Women in Toys (charter mem.). Democrat. Jewish. Avocations: cooking, travel, reading, theatre, investing. E-mail: licensing@alaskamomma.com. Fax: 212 696 1340. Office: Alaska Momma Inc 303 5th Ave Rm 2009 New York NY 10016-6652

HENSEL, KATHERINE RUTH, investment strategist, securities analyst; b. Summit, N.J., Nov. 24, 1959; d. John Charles and Carolyn (Bahle) H.; m. Jean-Paul Fouillade, Sept. 24, 1994. AB, Harvard U., 1981, MBA, 1985. Securities analyst Donaldson Lufkin & Jenrette, N.Y.C., 1981-83; investment banker Paine Webber, N.Y.C., 1985; investment banker Shearson Lehman Bros., N.Y.C., 1986, sr. v.p., securities analyst, 1987-91; mng. dir. Lehman Bros., N.Y.C., 1992, chief investment strategist, 1993-95; sr. equity rsch. analyst Chancellor Capital Mgmt., N.Y.C., 1996; mng. dir. Chancellor LQT, N.Y.C., 1997-98, dir. rsch., sr. equity portfolio mgr., 1998—. Contbr. articles to profl. jours. Named Instl. Investor All Am. Rsch. Team, 1989-93. Office: 1166 Avenue Of The Americas New York NY 10036-2708

HENSELER, SUZANNE MARIE, state legislator, social studies educator, majority whip; b. Brookline, Mass., Dec. 7, 1942; d. Paul R. and Evelyn (Warren) McGoldrick; m. John L. Henseler, June 26, 1965; children: Sean Patrick, Warren Paul, Timothy Brian. BS in History Edn., Boston Coll., 1964. Tchr. Pilgrim High Sch., Warwick, 1964-66; clk. house labor com. R.I. Ho. Reps., Providence, 1977-82; tchr. St. Rocco Sch., Johnston, R.I., 1984—; mem. R.I. Ho. of Reps., Providence, 1982, majority whip, 1992—. Former mem., bd. mem. North Kingstown (R.I.) Soccer Assn., 1974-89; mem. North Kingstown Dem. Town Com., 1974—; mem. sch. com., Kingstown, 1974-76; co-chair pay equity commn., 1995—; co-chair Legis. Women's Health Commn., 1995—; chmn. R.I. Mobile Home Commn., 1988-93; chmn. Legis. Commn. to Study the Solid Waste Mgmt. Corp.; mem. leg. com. study Dept. of Environmental Mgmt. Named Outstanding Young Women of Yr., North Kingstown Jaycettes, 1977, Nat. Environ. award 1993. Mem. Nat. Orgn. Women Legislators, Women in Govt. Home: 210 Edmond Dr North Kingstown RI 02852-2416 Office: Majority Whip State House # 303 Providence RI 02903

HENSELL, LINDA MARIE, environmental scientist; b. Seoul, Korea, July 19, 1969; came to U.S., 1970; d. Thomas Edward and Yong Nang (Kim) H. BS in Biology, U. Tex., San Antonio, 1992; MS in Environ. Sci., U. Tex., 1994. Reg. environ. profl., Nat. Registry Environ. Profls. Environ. specialist Dynamic Corp., San Antonio, 1995-96; environ. planner Quadrant Cons. Inc., Houston, 1997; environ. specialist Turner Collie & Braden Inc., Dallas, 1997—. Co-author: Bexar County Environmental Resource Guide, 1993. Vol. ARC, San Antonio, 1992. Mem. Am. Planning Assn., N. Tex. Assn. Environ. Profls. Avocations: cooking, hiking, quilting, crafts, dancing. Office: Turner Collie & Braden Inc 5710 Lbj Fwy Ste 370 Dallas TX 75240-6399

HENSELMANN, CASPAR GUSTAV FIDELIS, sculptor; b. Mannheim, Germany, Mar. 13, 1933; came to U.S., 1950; s. Albert Edward and Lore Elfriede (Feist) Henselmann; m. Evangeline Carran, Dec. 30, 1981; children: Xavier, Samuel. Student, Northwestern U., 1950-52; diploma in med. art, U. Ill. Coll. Medicine, 1955; BFA, Art Inst., Chgo., 1956; postgrad. studies, Wayne State U., Columbia U., 1958-61. Fellow W. B. Saunders Pub. Co., Phila., 1956; med. illustrator pvt. practice, N.Y.C., 1968—; art dir. Aron & Falcone Advtg., Chatham, N.J., 1972-73; assoc. prof. sculpture CW Post Ctr. Long Island (N.Y.) Univ., 1976-77, Hofstra Univ., Hempstead, N.Y., 1987-88; assoc. prof. Long Island U., Brooklyn, 1996—; vis. artist St. Cloud (Minn.) State Coll., 1975, Ox-Bow Sch. of Painting, Sugatuck, Mich., 1976, Memphis Acad. Fine Arts, 1982, Md. Art Inst., 1982, Univ. N.C., Chapel Hill, 1983; lectr. and critic Grad. Sch. of Architecture, U. Pa., Phila., 1993, Grad. Sch. Architecture, Columbia U., N.Y.C., 1994; mem. Berlin-Spandau Internat. City Planning Project Team, Columbia U., 1993. Artist: one man shows include Rice Gallery, N.Y.C., 1961, 63, Kern County Mus., Bakersfield, Calif., 1965, Stable Gallery, 1968, 55 Mercer Gallery, 1972, 74, 75, 76, 77, Sculpture Now, NYC, 1979, Fredericksburg (Va.) Ctr. for Creative Arts, 1979, Walter Bischoff Gallery, Chgo., 1986, Drothea Van Der Koelen, Mainz, Germany, 1989, Walter Bischoff, Stuttgart, Berlin, Germany, 1990, 94, 97, Kunstverein Bielefeld Mus. in Waldhof, Germany, 1991, Bill Bace Gallery, N.Y.C., 1992, 95, Stadt Gallery, Lahr, Germany, 1993, Offenberg Mus., Germany, 1994, View Pardo Gallery, N.Y.C., 1996, Kingsborough Community Coll., Brooklyn, 1997, Lindenau Mus., Altenburg, Germany, 1991, Rosenberg & Kaufman Gall., NYC, 1995, Villa Heiss Mus., Altenburg, Germany; included in group shows Am. Painting and Sculpture Annual, Phila., 1964, Nat. Design Ctr., Chgo., 1964, New Eng. Artists Annual, Silvermine, Conn., 1964, Arts Coun. of Great Britain, Whitechapel Gallery, London, 1970, Marika Malacorda Gallery, Geneva, Switzerland, 1976, Memphis (Tenn.) Acad. Fine Arts, 1982, Nina Owen Gallery, Chgo., 1987, U. Mass., Amherst, 1989; represented in collections in Marshall-Isley Bank Lobby, Milw., 1971, Mannesmann Internat. Hdqtrs., Dusseldorf, Germany, 1985, Deutsche Bank, N.Y.C., 1990, Julius Baer Bank, N.Y.C., 1992, Kunsthalle, Bremen Germany, 1993, Collection Hurrtle, Durbach, Germany, 1994, Lindendau Mus., Altenburg, Germany, Villa Heiss Mus., Germany, Newburger Mus., Purchase, NY. Home and Studio: 21 Bond St New York NY 10012-2451

HENSELMEIER, SANDRA NADINE, retired training and development consulting firm executive; b. Indpls., Nov. 20, 1937; d. Frederick Rost Henselmeier and Beatrice Nadine (Barnes) Henselmeier Enright; m. David Albert Funk, Oct. 2, 1976; children: William H. Stolz, Jr., Harry Phillip Stolz II, Sandra Ann Stolz. AB, Purdue U., 1971; MAT, Ind. U., 1975. Exec. sec. to dean Ind. U. Sch. Law, Indpls., 1977-78; adminstrv. asst. Ind. U.-Purdue U., Indpls., 1978-80, assoc. archivist, 1980-81; program and comm. coord. Midwest Alliance in Nursing, Indpls., 1981-82; tng. coord. Coll./Univ. Cos., Indpls., 1982-83; pres. Better Bus. Comms., Indpls., 1983—; adj. lectr. lectr. U. Indpls. Center Continuing. Mgmt. Devel. and Edn., Indpls., 1984—. Author: Successful Customer Service Writing, Winning with Effective Business Grammar, Successful Telephone Communication and Etiquette, Management Writing; contbr. articles to profl. jours. Mem. Am. Soc. Indexers Soc., Soc. Tech. Comms., Econ. Club Indpls. Republican. Presbyterian. Avocations: traveling, walking, reading, learning new ideas.

HENSEN, STEPHEN JEROME, lawyer; b. Durango, Colo., Nov. 8, 1961; s. Ronald Jerome and Sandra Lucille (Monroe) H.; m. Janice Lynn Lamunyon; children: Amanda, Stephanie, Cory. BS in Econs., Colo. State U., 1984; JD, Gonzaga U., 1987. Bar: Colo. 1987, U.S. Dist. Ct. Colo. 1987, U.S. Ct. Appeals (10th cir.) 1988, U.S. Supreme Ct. 1994. Atty. Cortez Friedman, P.C., Denver, 1987-93; atty. McKenna & Cuneo, Denver, 1993-95; ptnr. Richman & Hensen, P.C., Denver, 1995—. Mem. Colo. Bar Assn., Denver Bar Assn., Colo. Supreme Ct. Bar Com. Republican. Office: Richman & Hensen PC 1775 Sherman St Ste 1717 Denver CO 80203-4318

HENSEY, CHARLES MCKINNON, retired lawyer; b. Ft. Bragg, N.C., Aug. 20, 1934; s. Charles Walter and Sarah McQueen (McKinnon) H.; m. Edna May Railey, July 9, 1966; children: Charles Gordon, Walter Thomas. BA in Bus. Adminstrn., Duke U., 1957; JD, U. N.C., 1962. Bar: N.C. 1962, U.S. Ct. Appeals (4th cir.) 1984, U.S. Supreme Ct. 1972. Assoc. Johnson, Biggs & Britt, Lumberton, N.C., 1962-65; asst. atty. gen. N.C. Dept. Justice, Raleigh, 1965-85, spl. dep. atty. gen., 1985-86, mem. spl. litig. counsel, 1985-91, counsel N.C. State Bd. Elections, 1991-97. Bd. dirs. Montessori Sch., Raleigh, 1978. Lt. (j.g.) USNR, 1957-59; capt. USNR ret. Mem. N.C. Bar Assn., N.C. State Bar. Democrat. Avocations: genealogy, historical research. Home: 2051 White Oak Rd Raleigh NC 27608-1449

HENSGEN, HERBERT THOMAS, medical technologist; b. Cin., May 28, 1947; s. Herbert and Carolyn Elizabeth (Stites) H. BS, U. Cin., 1973, MS, 1978; AAS, Cin. Tech. Coll., 1981. Reg. med. technologist. Grad. tchg. asst. U. Cin., 1976-77; lectr. Edgecliff Coll., Cin., 1977-78; tech. Our Lady of Mercy Hosp., Cin., 1979-81, med. lab. tech., 1981-84, med. technologist, 1984-86; rsch. asst. Children's Hosp. Med. Ctr., Cin., 1986—; instr. Cin. Tech. Coll, 1984-85. Contbr. article to Gen. and Comparative Endocrinology; co-author abstracts for Soc. for Pediat. Rsch., Endocrine Soc. Deacon Madisonville Bapt. Ch., 1977. Mem. Am. Soc. Clin. Pathologists, Triple Nine Soc., Am. Mensa, Ltd., N.Y. Acad. Scis. Achievements include production of data suggesting lack of insulin-like growth factor-I (IGF-I) may mediate growth retardation in the neonatal rat; discovery of evidence that IGF-I may be one of several growth factors regulating differentiation of the fetal brain; demonstration that the antigonadal effect of prolactin in the lizard Anolis carolinensis is directed toward the smaller ovarian follicles; research on effects of IGF-I and its binding proteins on fetal and neonatal development. Home: 7420 Drake Rd Cincinnati OH 45243-1422 Office: Children's Hosp Med Ctr Dept Endocrinology 3333 Burnet Ave Cincinnati OH 45229-3026

HENSHAW, BARBARA LOUISE HANBY, retired psychology tester, counselor; b. Washington, Apr. 5, 1926; d. Chauncey Bayard and Margarethe Elizabeth (Frederick) Hanby; m. Edmund Lee Jr., Aug. 5, 1950; children: Lynne Pope, Richard, Scott. AB, George Washington U., 1948, AM, 1952. Asst. registrar George Washington U., Washington, 1950-52; psychometrist Langly Sch., McLean, Va., 1965-73, Burgundy Farms Sch., Alexandria, Va., 1965-73; clerk U.S. Ho. Reps., 1976-83. Vol., precinct chmn. Dem. Party, Fairfax, Va., 1956-87. Mem. Phi Beta Kappa. Episcopalian. Avocations: travel, hiking, fishing, swimming. Home: 20522 Falcons Landing Cir Sterling VA 20165-7595 also: Apt 5109 20550 Falcons Landing Cir Sterling VA 20165-3586

HENSHAW, BEVERLY ANN HARSH, women's health nurse, consultant; b. Jasper, Mich., Aug. 26, 1937; d. Arthur Estol and Doris Ione (Lindsay) Harsh; m. Kenneth P. Wilkinson, Apr. 8, 1978; children: Kit, Jeff, Kim, Brad, Brian, David. BSN, U. Mich., 1960; cert. ob-gyn. nurse practitioner, Johns Hopkin's U., 1973; MSN, Pa. State U., 1983. RN, Pa.; cert. nurse practitioner. Instr. Sch. Nursing Pa. State U., University Park, NP women's health; NP, clinic mgr. Family Health Svcs., Inc., State College, Pa.; pvt. practice cons. 5; care coord. Health Beginnings Plus Project; cons. in field. Mem. Am. Acad. Nurse Practitioners, Assn. Women's Health, Ob. and Neonatal Nurses, ANA, NANPRH, Jacobs Inst. of Women's Health, Assn. Reproductive Health Profls., Lamaze Internat. Home: RD 1 Box 340 Port Matilda PA 16870-9426

HENSHAW, GUY RUNALS, management consultant; b. Moscow, Idaho, Sept. 27, 1946; s. Paul C. and Helen E. Henshaw; m. Susan S. Seigel, Dec. 29, 1968; children: Christine, Victoria. BA, Ripon Coll., 1968; MBA, U. Pa., 1970. V.p. Security Nat. Bank, Walnut Creek, Calif., 1970-80, Bank Am., San Francisco, 1980-84; pres., dir. CivicBan Corp., Oakland, Calif., 1984-93; chmn. Payday, Payroll Co., San Francisco, 1993-96; mng. dir. Henshaw/Vierra, LLC, San Francisco, 1996—; dir. Calif. Banker's Ins. Svcs., Inc., San Francisco, 1989-92, Fair Isaac & Co., San Rafael, Calif., 1994—. Chmn. bd. trustees Head Royce Sch., Oakland, 1982-90; trustee Ripon (Wis.) Coll., 1994—; dir. John Muir Health Sys., Walnut Creek, 1999—. Lt. col. U.S. Army, 1968-96. Mem. Royal Automobile Club (London), Pacific Union Club, Diablo Country Club. Episcopalian. Avocations: tennis, travel. E-mail: henvie@aol.com. Office: Henshaw/Vierra LLC 400 Montgomery St Ste 820 San Francisco CA 94104

HENSHAW, JONATHAN COOK, manufacturing company executive; b. Dobbs Ferry, N.Y., Jan. 29, 1922; s. Elmer Ellsworth and Leonora Agnes (Scott) H.; m. Martha Emily Stock, July 14, 1948; children: William, Jane, Mary, Thomas, Daniel, Anne. BS, Fordham U., 1950; MBA, NYU, 1952; AA in Real Estate, Bucks County Community Coll., 1988. C.P.A., N.Y. Staff accountant Coopers & Lybrand, N.Y.C., 1951-55, 68-69; v.p., treas. J.A. Ewing & McDonald, Inc., N.Y.C., 1955-62; asst. treas. Block Drug Co., Jersey City, 1962-64; controller, asst. treas. Turner Jones Co., Inc., N.Y.C., 1964-68; treas. Visual Electronics, N.Y.C., 1969—, Crane Co., N.Y.C., 1970-80; assoc. broker Fox & Lazo Realtors, Phila., 1980-83, John T. Henderson, Inc., 1983-87; broker, appraiser Richard A. Weidel Corp., Newtown, Pa., 1987—. Served as sgt. AUS, 1943-46. Decorated Purple Heart. Roman Catholic. Home: 48 Falcon Rd Levittown PA 19056-1906 Office: Richard A Weidel Corp PO Box 735 Newtown PA 18940-0735

HENSHAW, WILLIAM RALEIGH, middle school educator; b. Richmond, Va., Apr. 28, 1932; s. Edmund James Jr. and Dorothy Varnes (Carrier) H.; m. Joyce Winston Kuhn, Mar. 24, 1956; children: Mark Hutson, Marcia Lynne, Matthew Harrison. BA, Randolph-Macon Coll., 1957; postgrad., Va. Commonwealth U., 1964-89, Coll. William and Mary. Cert. collegiate profl. tchr. with endorsements, Va. Securities clk. Fed. Res. Bank, Richmond, 1960-62; mid. sch. tchr. Hanover County Pub. Schs., Ashland, Va., 1963—, adviser, yearbook specialist, 1988—. Author instrnl. manuals. Vice pres., pres. Pearson's Corner Elem. Sch. PTA, Mechanicsville, Va., 1980-84. With U.S. Army, 1952-60, Korea. Mem. NEA, Va. Edn. Assn., Hanover Edn. Assn., Va. Assn. Sci. Tchrs. (exec. bd.), Greater Richmond Assn. Sci. Educators, U.S. Boomerang Assn. Avocations: boomerangs, making custom knives. Home: 6450 Birch Tree Trce Mechanicsville VA 23111-5306 Office: Hanover County Pub Schs Ashland VA 23005 also: Chickahominy Mid Sch 9450 Atlee Station Rd Mechanicsville VA 23116-2600

HENSHEL, HARRY BULOVA, watch manufacturer; b. N.Y.C., Feb. 5, 1919; s. Harry D. and Emily (Bulova) H.; m. Joy Altman, Nov. 4, 1948; children—Dale, Patti, Diane, Judith. A.B., Brown U., 1940; grad., U.S. Army Command and Gen. Staff Sch., 1945; M.B.A., Harvard U., 1951. With Bulova Watch Co., Inc., Flushing, N.Y., 1938—; asst. sec. Bulova Watch Co., Inc., 1950, sec., 1951, v.p. finance, 1957, exec. v.p., 1958, pres., 1959-74, chmn., 1973-96, vice-chmn., 1996—; bd. dirs. Ampal Corp., mem. audit com., Universal Holdings Corp., mem. audit com.; chmn. bd. dirs. Bulova Internat., Ltd., 11961-81; chmn. Atlantic Time Products Corp., 1991—; chmn. chief execs. coun. The Omega Group, 1991; chmn. Bulova Watch Co., 1973-96, vice chmn., 1991—. vice chmn., trustee Adelphi U., 1955-88, emeritus trustee, 1989—; bd. overseers parsons Sch. Design; bd. dirs. U.S. Com. for UNICEF, 1979-87, Fedn. Employment and Guidance Svcs., Westchester Philharm. Orch., 1990; mem. bus. coun. UN Bus. Adv. Com., policy study com. Heller Inst., 1979-85; mem. adv. bd. N.Y.C. chpt. Am. Cancer Soc., N.Y. State Bus. Venture Partnership. Mem. Amateur Athletic Union U.S. (timing com.), N.Y. C. of C. (dir.), Am. Ordnance Assn (life), Newcomen Soc. N.Am., UN Assn. U.S. (dir.), Thoroughbred Owners and Breeders Assn., Sigma Chi (Significant Sig medal). Republican. Clubs: Harvard Business School, Sales Executives, New York (dir.), Brown Univ, Harmonie, Economic; Army and Navy (Washington); Old Oaks Country (Purchase, N.Y.); Turf and Field; Town (Scarsdale). Home: 24 Murray Hill Rd Scarsdale NY 10583-2828 Office: Bulova Corp 1 Bulova Ave Flushing NY 11377-7826

HENSINGER, MARGARET ELIZABETH, horticultural and agricultural advertising and marketing executive; b. Jackson, Mich., Aug. 31, 1950; d. John Kenneth and Inez Estelle (McVay) H.; m. William C. Pixley, Apr. 26, 1985; children: William Christopher, Patrick Edward. BS, Eastern Mich. U., 1973. Salesperson Hunter Pub. Co., Winston-Salem, N.C., 1974-76, Josten's-Am., Topeka, 1976-77; editorial asst. Mich. Dept. Agriculture, Lansing, 1977-80, U. Fla., Apopka, 1981-82; pres. Country Carousel, Inc., Mt. Dora, Fla., 1983—; editor, pres. Green Pages Ltd., Mt. Dora, 1984-88; owner, pres. Sunbelt Mktg. Services, Inc., Mt. Dora, 1982—; pub. Fax-It-Green The Hort Fax Directory, 1987-98; pres., treas. Duragreen Mktg. USA, Inc., Mt. Dora, 1990—. Mem. Leadership Am., Fairfax, Va., 1990. Mem. Tex. Assn. Nurserymen, Nat. Assn. Women in Horticulture (v.p., past pres., organizer), Am. Soc. of Advt. Promotion, Fla. Nurserymen and Growers Assn., Mt. Dora C. of C. (exec. bd. dirs., sec. 1988-89, v.p. 1989—, pres. 1996), Golden Triangle Reps. Women's Club (past pres.). Republican. Episcopalian. Avocations: reading, travel, golf, gardening, sewing. Home: PO Box 1483 Mount Dora FL 32756-1483 Office: Duragreen Mktg USA Inc PO Box 1486 Mount Dora FL 32756-1486

HENSLEIGH, HOWARD EDGAR, lawyer; b. Blanchard, Iowa, Oct. 29, 1920; s. Albert Dales and Eula Fern (Bair) H.; m. Janice Lee Pedersen, Aug. 15, 1948; children: Susan Lee Hensleigh Harvey, Nancy Ann Hensleigh-Quinn, Jonathan Blair. BA, Iowa U., 1943, JD, 1947; postgrad., Columbia U., 1954-55. Bar: Iowa 1947, N.Y. 1955, Mass. 1968. Commd. U.S. Army, 1943, advanced through grades to col., 1965, ret., 1973; legal adviser U.S. Mission to NATO, Paris, 1958-60; dep. asst. gen. counsel office of Sec. Def. U.S. Govt., Washington, 1960-67, dep. asst. to sec. treas., 1967-68; asst. gen. counsel Raytheon Co., Bedford, Mass., 1968-91, ret., 1991; pvt. practice Carlisle, Mass., 1991—; participated in U.S. Italy Internat. Ct. Justice, The Hague, 1989. Chmn. town com. Carlisle Reps., 1972-80, sch. com. Carlisle, 1973-75, bd. selectmen, 1977-80. Mem. ABA (chmn. region I), Fed. Bar Assn., Am. Soc. Internat. Law. Home and Office: 50 School St Carlisle MA 01741-1709

HENSLEY, ELIZABETH CATHERINE, nutritionist, educator; b. Mpls., Feb. 27, 1921; d. Erich Christian and Lulu Mabel (Elliott) Selke; m. Eugene B. Hensley, June 10, 1954 (dec. 1992). B.S. in Edn., U. N.D., 1942; M.S., Cornell U., 1944, postgrad., 1950-51. Instr. food and nutrition U. Del., 1944-47; asst. prof. Okla. A&M U., 1947-50; mem. faculty U. Mo., Columbia, 1951—, prof. food and nutrition, 1954-84, prof. emeritus, 1984—, chmn. dept. home econs., 1954-55, head dept. food and nutrition, 1955-65, co-chmn. dept. human nutrition, 1973-76. Author: Basic Concepts of World Nutrition, 1981. Mem. Am. Home Econs. Assn., Nutrition Today Soc., Mo. Home Econs. Assn., PEO, Pi Lambda Theta, Omicron Nu, Phi Upsilon Omicron, Gamma Sigma Delta, Kappa Alpha Theta. Mem. Christian Ch. (Disciples of Christ). Home: 802 Greenwood Ct Columbia MO 65203-2841

HENSLEY, MARY SUSAN MASK, emergency room nurse; b. Memphis, Jan. 10, 1958; d. John Carlin and Peggy Ann (Hodgson) M. AD, Belmont Coll., 1980; BSN, Union U., 1990. RN, Tenn. Charge nurse med./surg. fl. Bapt. Hosp., Nashville; staff nurse, relief charge nurse St. Francis Spl. Care, Memphis; staff nurse emergency rm. Eastwood Hosp., Memphis; staff nurse Unicoi Meml. Hosp., Erwin, Tenn.

HENSLEY, ROBERT BRUCE, psychology educator; b. Chicago Heights, Ill., Aug. 14, 1965; s. William Ralph and Frances Marie (Pahl) H. AA, Kirkwood C.C., Cedar Rapids, Iowa, 1986; BA, U. No. Iowa, 1990, MA, 1992. Cert. tchr., Iowa. Adj. instr. psychol. Kirkwood C.C., Cedar Rapids, 1992—, Mt. Mercy Coll., Cedar Rapids, 1995—. Area Ten scholar Coop Oil Co., 1985. Mem. Midwestern Psychol. Assn., Phi Alpha Theta, Delta Chi, Psi Chi, Kappa Delta Pi. Home: 2260 C St SW Cedar Rapids IA 52404-3022 Office: Mt Mercy Coll 1330 Elmhurst Dr NE Cedar Rapids IA 52402-4763

HENSLEY, ROSS CHARLES, dermatologist; b. Oklahoma City, Dec. 23, 1946; s. Ralph and Winona Marie (Clark) H.; m. Melba Carol Holliman, Apr. 11, 1968; children: Jason Scott, Jeffrey Alan. BS, Southwestern State U., 1968; MD, U. Okla., 1972. Intern U. Okla., 1972-73, resident in dermatology, 1973-76; pvt. practice dermatology, Lawton, Okla., 1978—. Maj. U.S. Army, 1976-78. Baptist. Avocation: ecology. Office: 4417 W Gore Blvd Ste 7 Lawton OK 73505-5978

HENSLEY, STEPHEN ALLAN, insurance executive; b. Portsmouth, Va., July 29, 1950; s. Theodore Allen and Lillie Mae (Costner) H. BA, U. W. Fla., 1976. Mgr. Carlyle & Co. Jewelers, Killeen, Tex., 1977-83; owner L.T., Ltd. Property, Killeen, 1983—; claims specialist State Farm Ins., Austin, 1985—; disaster rep. State Farm Fire & Casualty Ins. Co., Austin, 1989—; investigator State Farm Life Ins. Co., 1986—; chmn. Computers for Freedom project Amnesty Internat., 1998; mem. Pitsco Ask an Expert Group. Univac focus group Brasenose Coll., Oxford, England, 1993; contbr. articles to profl. jours. Active Friends of KNCT-TV, Belton, 1985—, Viva Les Arts Societe, Killeen, 1988—. Decorated Knight Grand Comdr., Order of the Commonwealth, Can., 1990, Knight Grand Cross, Order of St Joseph, B.C., 1994, Count, Order of the Sursum Corda, Belgium, 1991, Baron, Sovereign Order von Liechtenstein, 1991, Keeper of the Tomes Principality of St. Michel de Clermont, 1991, Adm., Tex. Navy, 1991, Knight Comdr., Mil. and Chivalric Order of Sword of Eng., 1996, Chevalier Comdr. Order St. Raphael, Eng., 1997, Comdrs. Cross Order of St. Stanislas, Poland, 1997. Mem. U.S. Golf Assn., Lake Belton Yacht Club, Am. Legion. Avocations: golf, sailing, fencing, tennis, riding.

HENSLEY, SUE L., communications director. BS, U. Ill., 1995. Office: Office of Sen Tim Hutchinson 245 Dirksen Senate Office Washington DC 20510

HENSON, (BETTY) ANN, media specialist, educator; b. Tampa, Fla., Dec. 20, 1944; d. James (Jim) and Beth (Tabb) H. BA, U. South Fla., 1966; MEd, U. Fla., 1980, EdS, 1985. Cert. tchr., Fla. English tchr. Hillsborough County Schs., Tampa, 1967-68; drama tchr. Cultural Enrichment Ctr., Gainesville, Fla., 1969-70, Title II Grant, Gainesville, 1970-72; lang. arts tchr. Alachua County Schs., Gainesville, 1972-74; team leader humanities ESAA Grant Alachua County, Gainesville, 1975-82; media specialist Alachua County Schs., Gainesville, 1982—, tech. coord., 1993—; adj. faculty Nova U., Gainesville, 1988-96, Ctr. for Distance Learning, Ocala Ctr., St. Leo's Coll., 1994—; part-time libr. Alachua County Libr. Dist., asst., 1996—. Presenter in field; slide show prodr. (Fla. ctr. for children and youth award 1984). Mem. Gainesville City Beautification Bd., 1995—; mem. com. Kanapaha Bot. Garden Festival. Recipient First Liberty Inst. award Ams. United Rsch. Found., Washington, 1991; grantee Fla. Ctr. Tchrs. Resident Scholar, 1993; grantee in field. Mem. Profl. Assn. Libr. and Media Specialists (sec. 1991-92, 94-96), Fla. Assn. Media in Edn., Alpha Delta Pi, Phi Delta Kappa. Avocations: reading, travel, floral arrangement. Home: 203 SW 41st St Gainesville FL 32607-2178 Office: Westwood Middle Sch 3215 NW 15th Ave Gainesville FL 32605-5097

HENSON, ANNA MIRIAM, otolaryngology researcher, medical educator; b. Springfield, Mo., Nov. 7, 1935; d. Bert Emerson and Esther Miriam (Crank) Morgan; m. O'Dell Williams Henson, Aug. 1, 1964; children: Phillip, William. BA, Park Coll., Parkville, Mo., 1957; MA, Smith Coll., 1959; PhD, Yale U., 1967. Instr. Smith Coll., Northampton, Mass., 1960-61; rsch. assoc. Yale U., New Haven, 1967-74; instr. U. N.C., Chapel Hill, 1975-78, rsch. asst. prof., 1978-83, rsch. assoc. prof., 1983-86, rsch. prof. dept. surgery Sch. Medicine, 1986—; mem. study sect. on hearing rsch. NIH, Bethesda, Md., 1990-93. Contbr. articles to profl. jours. Fulbright scholar, Australia, 1959-60; NIH grantee, 1975—. Mem. Assn. for Rsch. in Otolaryngology, Sigma Xi. Office: U NC Cb 7090 Taylor Hall Chapel Hill NC 27599

HENSON, C. WARD, mathematician, educator; b. Worcester, Mass., Sept. 25, 1940; s. Charles W. and Daryl May (Hoyt) H.; m. Faith deMena Travis, August 31, 1963; children: Julia Rebecca, Suzanne Amy, Claire Victoria. AB, Harvard U., 1962; PhD, MIT, 1967. Asst. prof. Duke U., Durham, N.C., 1967-74, N.Mex. State U., Las Cruces, 1974-75; asst. prof. U. Ill., Urbana, 1975-77, assoc. prof., 1977-81, prof., 1981—, chmn. dept. math., 1988-92; vis. assoc. prof. U. Wis., Madison, 1979-80; vis. prof. RWTH Aachen, Fed. Republic Germany, 1985-86, Univ. Tübingen, Fed. Republic Germany, 1992-93. Mem. Assn. for Symbolic Logic (sec.-treas. 1982—), Am. Math. Soc., Math. Assn. Am., London Math. Soc., European Assn. Theoretical Computer Sci. Office: U Ill Dept Math 1409 W Green St Urbana IL 61801-2943

HENSON, DANIEL P., III, housing and community development commissioner; b. Balt.; m. Del Carter; children: Darryn, Dana. AB in History and Polit. Sci., Morgan State U., 1966; postgrad. in bus. and ins., Johns Hopkins U., 1967-70. Jr. h.s. and spl. edn. tchr. Balt. City Pub. Schs., 1966-67; agt., sales mgr. Met. Life Ins. Co., Balt., 1967-74; gen. agt. Guardian Life Ins. Co. Am., Inc., Balt., 1974-77; regional adminstr. U.S. SBA, Phila., 1977-79; dir. Minority Bus. Devel. Agy., U.S. Dept. Commerce, Washington, 1979-81; dir., minority bus. devel. Greater Balt. Com., Inc., 1981-82; v.p., mktg. G & M Oil Co., Inc., Balt., 1982-84; v.p., ptnr., sr. devel. mgr. Struever Bros. Eccles & Rouse, Inc., Balt., 1984-93; commr., exec. dir., CEO Balt. City Dept. Housing and Cmty. Devel., 1993—. Past co-host (weekly TV show) City Line, Balt. Past bd. mem. Balt. Urban League, Balt. chpt. Home Builders Assn. Md.; past bd. mem. and chmn., Fed. Res. Bank Richmond, Balt. chpt.; mdm. bd. Balt. Mental Health Systems, Balt. Delta Alumnae Found., and Ctr. Ethics and Corp. Policy, Balt.; chmn. bd. Balt. Sch. Arts, and Investing in Balt. Com. Office: City of Baltimore Dept Housing & Cmty Devel 417 E Fayette St # Baltimore MD 21202-3431*

HENSON, DIANA JEAN, county official; b. Evanston, Ill., Feb. 11, 1949; d. Paul J. and Mary (Norris) Roberts; m. Jim Henson; 1 child, Richard Leslie Pruyn Jr. BS in Elem. Edn., Ball State U., 1971; MS in Elem. Edn., Ind. State U., 1979; EdS in Adminstrn./Supervision, West Ga. Coll., 1985; doctoral study, U. Ga., 1986—. Cert. in adminstrn. and supervision, middle grades edn., data collection, early childhood edn., elem. tchr., Ga., Ind. Tchr. 3rd grade Blue River Valley Sch. System, Mt. Summit, Ind., 1971-73; fin. analyst Dun & Bradstreet, Indpls., 1973-74; sec. to vice chmn. mktg. dept. Glenview (Ill.) State Bank, 1974-75; tchr. 6th grade St. John's Cath. Sch., Panama City, Fla., 1976-77; tchr. 3rd to 8th grades St. Ann's Cath. Sch., Terre Haute, Ind., 1978-79; pvt. preschool and elem. prin. Learning Tree Sch., Terre Haute, 1979-81; tchr., asst. prin. Haralson County Sch. System, Buchanan, Ga., 1981-83, tchr., reading dept. chair, 1983-88; tchr. 6th grade Carroll County Sch. System, Carrollton, Ga., 1988-89, asst. prin., 1989-94; dir. compensatory edn./testing, 1994—. Active Bowdon Hist. Commn.; pres. Ga. Compensatory Edn. Leaders. Mem. Bowdon Area Hist. Soc., Phi Delta Kappa, Phi Kappa Phi, Kappa Delta Pi. Home: PO Box 277 130 W College St Bowdon GA 30108-1306

HENSON, GENE ETHRIDGE, retired legal administrator; b. Lawrenceville, Ga., Sept. 26, 1924; d. Fred Golden and Cora Jewell (Smith) E.; m. James Arthur Henson, May 2, 1948 (dec.); 1 child, Gena Arlene. Grad. Interior Design, Gwinnett Tech. Inst., 1991. With Smith, Currie & Hancock, Atlanta, 1959-90; adminstr. Smith, Currie & Hancock, 1965-90; chair fashion & design adv. com. Gwinnett Tech. Inst., 1992-93; owner Gene Henson Interiors; Ofcl. hostess for State of Ga., So. Gov's Conf., Atlanta, 1971; past adult tchr. First Baptist Ch., Lawrenceville; mem. adv. coun. Ctr. for Profl. Edn. Ga. State U., 1980-84. Bd. dirs., v.p. County Seat Players Theatre Group; actress Steel Magnolias, The Foreigner, Harvey, Our Town; bd. dirs., sec. Gwinnett Coun. for Arts, 1997-98. Mem. Internat. Interior Design Assn., Atlanta Assn. Legal Execs. (1st pres. 1975), Assn. Legal Adminstrs. (life, nat. v.p. 1979—, bd. dirs. 1979-83, v.p. Atlanta chpt., pres.-elect, 1986-87, pres. 1987-88). Home and Office: 74 Scenic Hwy Lawrenceville GA 30045-5729

HENSON, HOWARD KIRK, lawyer; b. Chgo., Apr. 28, 1956; s. Howard I. and Constance M. (Evanhoff) H.; m. Annette Whorton, May 3, 1991. BA, Ga. State U., 1979; JD, U. Ga., 1982; postgrad., Harvard U., 1996. Bar: Ga. 1982, U.S. Dist. Ct. (no. dist.) Ga. 1983, U.S. Dist. Ct. (mid. dist.) Ga. 1986. Pvt. practice Atlanta, 1982-86; of counsel Corlew, Smith & Wright, Atlanta, 1984-86; house counsel Am. States Ins. Co., Atlanta, 1986-88; atty. Amoco Corp., Atlanta, 1988-95; pvt. practice Atlanta, 1995—. Mem. ABA, State Bar Ga., Atlanta Bar Assn., Ga. Trial Lawyers Assn., Am. Trial Lawyers Assn. State & Fed. Litigation. Home: 4615 Lake Forrest Dr NE Atlanta GA 30342-2537 Office: 3690 N Peachtree Rd Ste 250 Atlanta GA 30341-2389

HENSON, JAMES BOND, veterinary pathologist; b. Colorado City, Tex., Nov. 13, 1933; s. John Lee Henson and Beatrice (Porter) Walls; m. Janet Christine Neol; children: Sarah, Ben, James. B.S. in Animal Sci., Tex. A&M U., 1956, DVM, 1958, MS, 1959; PhD, Wash. State U., Pullman, 1962. Diplomate Am. Coll. Vet. Pathologists. Assoc. prof. Wash. State U., Pullman, 1962-68, prof., chair vet. pathology, 1968-73; dir. rsch. grad. edn. Coll. Vet. Medicine, Pullman, 1973-74, dir. internat. program devel., prof. vet. pathology, 1978—; prof. exptl. animal medicine U. Wash., Seattle, 1968-74; dir. Internat. Lab. Research in Animal Diseases, Nairobi, Kenya, 1974-78; project dir. Western Sudan Agrl. Research Project, 1979-83; cons. U.S. AID, WHO, FAO, others, also various developing countries; mem. sci. and tech. adv. com. Spl. Program on Tropical Diseases, WHO, 1978-82; trustee Consortium Internat. Devel., 1982-84, 90-93; mem. exec. com. Small Ruminant Collaborative Research Support Project, 1981-84, 90-93, chair, 1993. Contbr. articles to profl. jours., chpts. to books. Recipient Outstanding Tchg. award Tex. A&M U., 1964, Mary K. Dunkle award Mich. State U., 1966; NIH fellow, 1965. Mem. Assn. Internat. Agrl. Rsch. and Devel. (pres.). Home: PO Box 2684 Pullman WA 99165-2684 Office: Wash State U Pullman WA 99164*

HENSON, JANE ELIZABETH, information management professional, adult educati; b. Ft. Wayne, Ind., Dec. 1, 1946; d. Robert Eugene and Lucile Catherine (Feeney) Tucker; m. Phillip Likins Henson, Aug. 23, 1971; 1 child, Robert Likins. BS in Edn., Ind. U., 1970, MS in Edn., 1973, MLS, 1976. Tchr. pub. schs., Ft. Wayne, 1970-71, Nevada, Mo., 1971-72; libr., cataloger Ctrl. Conn. State U., New Britain, 1976-77; libr. numeric data U. Wis., Madison, 1978-80; adj. prof. libr. Navy Safety Sch. Ind. U., Bloomington, 1981-83, reference libr. Vocat. Edn. Project, 1984-86; asst. dir. ERIC Clearinghouse, Bloomington, 1988-95, assoc. dir., 1995-98, co-dir., 1999—. Co-author: Rising Expectations: A Framework for ERIC's Future in the National Library of Education, 1997; editor: Libraries Link to Learning: Final Report on the Indiana Governor's Conference on Libraries and Information Services, 1990. Chair ERIC tech. com. U.S. Dept. Edn. ERIC Program, Washington, 1990—, mem. ERIC exec. com., 1990—. Mem. Am. Soc. Info. Sci. (dept. dir. SIG cabinet 1993, chair behavioral and social sci. SIG 1994, cert. of appreciation 1993). Roman Catholic. Avocations: officiating track and field events (cert.), reading, travel. Office: ERIC Clearinghouse for Social Studies Social Sci Edn 2805 E 10th St Ste 120 Bloomington IN 47408-2601

HENSON, MICHELE, state legislator; b. Boston, Aug. 29, 1946. AA, LaSalle U., 1966; BA, U. Miami. Adminstr. Metro Dental Svcs., 1985—; mem. Ga. Ho. of Reps., Atlanta, 1990-92, 93—; mem. health and ecology com., appropriations com. Ga. Ho. of Reps. from dist. 65, vice chair ins. com., chmn. subcom. mental health-retardation and substance abuse; co-chmn. women's caucus Ga. Gen. Assembly, 1995-96. Democrat. Jewish. Office: Ga House of Reps State Capitol Atlanta GA 30334*

HENSON, O'DELL WILLIAMS, JR., anatomy educator; b. Kansas City, Mo., Jan. 11, 1934; s. O'Dell Williams and Natalie (Smith) H.; m. Miriam Morgan, Aug. 1, 1964; 1 child, Phillip William. BA, U. Kans., 1957, MA, 1960; PhD, Yale U., 1964. From instr. to assoc. prof. Dept. Anatomy, Yale U., New Haven, 1964-74; prof. Dept. Cell Biology and Anatomy U. N.C., Chapel Hill, 1974—. Chmn. Commn. Anatomy, N.C., 1982—. Recipient Phi Sigma award 1960, Alexander Von Humbolt award 1982, Cen. Carolina Bank Excellence in Teaching award 1982, NIH-Nat. Inst. Deafness and Other Communicative Disorders Claude Pepper award, 1989. Fellow AAAS. Home: 317 Reade Rd Chapel Hill NC 27516-1509 Office: U NC Dept Cell Biology and Anatomy Taylor Hall CB 7090 Chapel Hill NC 27599

HENSON, PAMELA TAYLOR, secondary education educator, biology; b. Mobile, Ala., Aug. 31, 1958; d. Richard Dowdy and Martha Jo (Hanson) Taylor; m. Thomas Baird Henson III, Mar. 7, 1987; 1 child, Joshua Taylor. BS in Secondary Edn./Biology, U. South Ala., 1983; MS in Secondary Edn./Biology, U. Mobile, 1989, Adminstrv. Cert., 1990; Edn. Specialist Adminstrn., Ala. State U., 1995. Cert. secondary edn. educator. Sci. tchr. Fairhope (Ala.) Middle Sch., 1984-91, Foley (Ala.) H.S., 1991—. Christa McAuliffe fellow State Dept. of Edn., 1994, Outstanding Biology tchr. Nat. Assn. Biology Tchrs., 1994, Outstanding Instr. in Environ. Edn., Legacy Found., 1995; recipient Presdl. award NSTA, 1994. Mem. NSTA, Nat. Assn. Biology Tchrs., Ala. Sci. Tchrs. Assn., Nat. Marine Educators Assn., Baldwin County Assn. Profl. Educators (pres. 1994—), Alpha Delta Kappa (treas. 1994-96). Republican. Baptist. Avocations: travel, walking, outdoor summer sports. Home: PO Box 1676 812 Trione St Daphne AL 36526

HENSON, RALPH EUGENE, sheriff, retired; b. Champaign, Ill., July 30, 1935; s. Archie David and Flossie Jane (Fox) H.; m. Betty Joan Reed, Dec. 18, 1955; 1 child, Cheryl Joanne. Grad. h.s., Paxton, Ill. Lic. law enforcement officer, Ill. Base film exch. supr. USAF, Chanute AFB, Ill., 1954-57; state police trooper Ill. State Police, Ashkum, 1957-82, state police lt., 1982-89; sheriff Ford County, Paxton, 1990—; bd. dirs. Ford County E9-1-1, Paxton. With USAR, Ill. N.G., 1955-92. Recipient Pres.' Nat. medal of patriotism Am. Police Hall of Fame, 1993. Mem. Am. Legion (comdr., past comdr.), Masons, Knights Templar, Order of Ea. Star (patron 1985, 88). Republican. Mem. Church of Christ. Avocations: autos, firearms.

HENSON, RAY DAVID, legal educator, consultant; b. Johnston City, Ill., July 24, 1924; s. Ray David and Lucile (Bell) Henson. B.S., U. Ill., 1947, J.D., 1949. Bar: Ill. 1950, U.S. Supreme Ct. 1960. Assoc. CNA Fin. Corp., Chgo., 1952-70; prof. law Wayne State U., 1970-75, Hastings Sch. Law, U. Calif., San Francisco, 1975—. Author: Landmarks of Law, 1960, Secured Transactions, 1973, 2d edit., 1979, Documents of Title, 1983, 2d edit., 1990, The Law of Sales, 1985; also various other books and numerous articles; editor: The Business Lawyer, 1967-68. Mem. legal adv. com. N.Y. Stock Exch., 1971-75. Served with USAAF, 1943-46. Mem. Am. Law Inst. (life), ABA (chmn. bus. law sect. 1969-70, adv. bd. jour. 1974-80), Ill. Bar Assn. (chmn. comml. banking and bankruptcy law sect. 1963-65), Chgo. Bar Assn. Club: Univ. (San Francisco). Home: 1400 Geary Blvd San Francisco CA 94109-6561 Office: U Calif Hastings Sch Law 200 Mcallister St San Francisco CA 94102-4707

HENSON, ROBERT FRANK, lawyer; b. Jenny Lind, Ark., Apr. 10, 1925; s. Newton and Nell Edith (Kessinger) H.; m. Jean Peterson Henson, Sept. 14, 1946; children: Robert F., Sandra Henson Curfman, Laura, Thomas, David, Steven. BS, U. Minn., 1948, JD, 1950. Bar: Minn. 1950, U.S. Supreme Ct. 1972. Atty. Soo Line R.R., 1950-52; ptnr. Cant, Haverstock, Beardsley, Gray & Plant, Mpls., 1952-66; sr. ptnr. Henson & Efron, Mpls., 1966-94, of counsel, 1995—; chmn. Minn. Lawyers Profl. Responsibility Bd., 1981-86; co-chmn. Supreme Ct. Study Com. on Lawyer Discipline, 1992-94. Trustee Mpls. Found., 1974-85, Emma Howe Found, 1986-90; chmn. Hennepin County Mental Health and Mental Retardation Bd., 1968-70. Served with USN, 1943-46. Fellow Am. Bar Found.; mem. ABA, Hennepin County Bar Assn. (pres. 1968-69), Minn. Bar Assn., Order of Coif. Unitarian. Office: 1200 Title Ins Bldg Minneapolis MN 55401

HENSON SCALES, MEG D(IANE), artist, writer, publisher; b. Portland, Oreg., Oct. 16, 1953; d. Kenneth Jack and Jessie Louise (Mott) Henson; m. Jeffrey Charles Henson Scales, Dec. 16, 1985; 1 child, Coco Tigre Roja. Student, San Francisco State U., 1972-73, 74-75, Friends' World Coll., Guatemala, 1974. Founding mem. Black Edn. Ctr., Portland, Oreg., 1970-71; mng. editor Woman's Bldg., L.A., 1979-81; pvt. investigator Kleinbauer Investigations, L.A., 1981-83; tchr. CUNY, N.Y.C., 1987-89, Mindbuilders, Bronx, N.Y., 1987-89; painter, writer, strategist Henson Scales Prodns., N.Y.C., 1989—; founder Com. for Rational African Americans Against the Parade, N.Y.C., 1995; pub., editor The Harlem Howl, N.Y.C., 1995—; Commn. Sacred banners for Grace Methodist Ch., Wilmington, Del., 1997; spkr. in field. Author: The Book of Love, 1988, Melisma, 1989 (Deming award 1989); co-creator, performer Tragedy in Black and White/A Race Record in One Act, 1981; dir., prodr. video documentary Class, 1989, Action/Reaction, 1998; author essays Tenderheaded; Man, God and the Okey-Doke; Be/Held; one-woman show U. Fla. at Gainesville Univ. Gallery, 1998, Smithsonian Anacostia Mus. and Ctr. for Afrianc Am. History and Culture, 1999. Founding mem. African Am. Against Violence, N.Y.C., 1995. Recipient N.Y. Found. Arts fellowship, N.Y.C., 1989. Avocations: comparative religion, peace studies, jyotish. Home: 1945 7th Ave Apt 4N New York NY 10026-2242

HENTGEN, PATRICK GEORGE, baseball player; b. Detroit, Nov. 13, 1968. Pitcher Toronto Blue Jays, 1986—; mem. Am. League All-Star Team, 1993-94; player World Series Games, 1993. Named Am. League Pitcher of Yr., The Sporting News, 1996; recipient Cy Young award Baseball Writers' Assn. Am., 1996. Office: Toronto Blue Jays, 1 Blue Jay Way Ste 3200, Toronto, ON Canada M5V 1J1*

HENTGES, DAVID JOHN, microbiology educator; b. LeMars, Iowa, Sept. 18, 1928; s. Romaine Francis and Geneva Mae (Kruger) H.; m. Kathleen Edwina Mullan, Dec. 28, 1957; children: Stephen Edward, Kathleen Marie, Margaret Ann. BS, U. Notre Dame, 1953; MS, Loyola U., Chgo., 1958, PhD, 1961. Asst. prof. Creighton U. Sch. Medicine, Omaha, 1964-67, assoc. prof., 1967-68; assoc. prof. U. of Mo. Sch. of Medicine, Columbia, 1968-72, prof., 1972-81, interim chmn., 1976-79; prof., chmn. Tex. Tech. U. Sch. Medicine, Lubbock, 1981-96, vice provost for rsch., dean grad. sch. biomed. scis., 1996-98, assoc. dean basic scis., 1996-98, dean emeritus, 1998—. Editor: Human Intestinal Microflora, 1983, Medical Microbiology, 1986, Microbiology and Immunology, 2d edit., 1995; regional editor Microbial Ecology in Health and Disease, 1987-96; mem. editl. bd. Infection and Immunity, 1983-92, Anaerobe, 1998—; contbr. chpts. to books and articles to profl. jours. Lay gen. chmn. Diocesan Cath. Appeal, Lubbock, 1989, 97, steering com., 1985—. Named Knight Comdr., Order of the Holy Sepulchre, 1995, Knight of Merit, Constantinian Order of St. George, 1997. Fellow Am. Acad. of Microbiology (emeritus); mem. Am. Soc. Microbiology, Assn. for Gnotobiotics, Cath. Acad. of Scis., Soc. for Microbial Ecology and Disease (pres. 1987-89), Serra Internat. (dist. gov. 1987-88, Serran of Yr. 1988), Sigma Xi. Republican. Roman Catholic. Avocations: gardening, fly fishing. Home: 4601 88th St Lubbock TX 79424-4107

HENTIC, YVES FRANK MAO, investment banker, industrial engineer; b. Paris, Dec. 7, 1946; came to U.S., 1947; s. Pierre Yves and Alberta Dorothy (Smith) H.; m. Donna May Woods, Aug. 3, 1981 (div. Dec. 1990); 1 child, Frank Hilton Wadsworth Hentic; m. Pandora Duke Biddle, Jan. 19, 1991; 1 child, Katherine Yvette Biddle Hentic. AB in Econs., Georgetown U., 1970; AS in Engring., Fashion Inst. Tech., N.Y.C., 1972; MBA, Harvard U., 1975. Plant engr. Lynn Lee Fabrics, N.Y.C., 1972-73; cons. Emanuel Weintraub Assocs., N.Y.C., 1974; securities analyst Wertheim & Co., N.Y.C., 1975-77; arbitrage analyst Colin Hochstin & Co., N.Y.C., 1977-78; rsch. ptnr. Bodkin, DePaolis, Hentic, Satloff & Co., N.Y.C., 1978-80; mng. ptnr. Y.H. Assocs., N.Y.C., 1980-95; pres. Yves Hentic & Co., Jersey City, 1983-86, Merger, Inc., Reno, 1987-95, Send It In, Mex., 1993-95, Archimedes Mgmt. Inc., 1995-97, OX Pasture Devel., Inc., Southampton, 1997—; pres. 18 pub. cos. for Merger Inc., Reno, 1987-92; mem. N.Y. Stock Exch., 1983-86. Mem. Southampton (N.Y.) Assn., 1992—. Mem. St. Nicholas Soc. (treas. 1990-95), Soc. Colonial Wars N.Y. (3d v.p. 1992-94), U.S. Croquet Assn., Kane Lodge, Met. Grotto, Shinnecock Marlin and Tuna Club, Colonial Order of the Acorn, Sons of the Revolution N.Y. Avocations: croquet (3rd 1st flight doubles Nat. Championship 1998), mineralogy, game fishing (holder world record for big eye trevally, Costa Rica 1983), technical scuba diving, cave exploring.

HENTOFF, NATHAN IRVING, writer; b. Boston, June 10, 1925; s. Simon and Lena (Katzenberg) H.; m. Miriam Sargent, 1950 (div. 1950); children: Jessica, Miranda; m. Margot Goodman, Aug. 15, 1959; children: Nicholas, Thomas. B.A. with highest honors, Northeastern U., 1945; postgrad., Harvard U., 1946; Fulbright fellow, Sorbonne, Paris, 1950. Writer, producer, announcer radio sta. WMEX, Boston, 1944-53; asso. editor Down Beat mag., 1953-57; co-founder, co-editor The Jazz Review, 1958-60; staff writer The New Yorker, N.Y.C., 1960-97; columnist and staff writer Village Voice, 1957—; columnist Washington Post, 1984—; faculty New Sch. Social Research; adj. asso. prof. N.Y. U. Mus. adviser: The Sound of Jazz, The Sound of Miles Davis, CBS-TV; editor: (with Nat Shapiro) Hear Me Talkin' to Ya, 1955, (with Nat Shapiro) The Jazz Makers, 1957, (with Albert McCarthy) Jazz, 1959, The Collected Essays of A.J. Muste, 1966, Black Anti-Semitism and Jewish Racism, 1970; author: The Jazz Life, 1961, Peace Agitator: The Story of A.J. Muste, 1963, The New Equality, 1964, Jazz Country, 1965, (Children's Spring Book Festival award N.Y. Herald Tribune 1965), Call the Keeper, 1966, Our Children Are Dying, 1966, Onwards, 1967, A Doctor Among the Addicts, 1967, I'm Really Dragged but Nothing Gets Me Down, 1967, Journey into Jazz, 1968, A Political Life: The Education of John V. Lindsay, 1969, In The Country of Ourselves, 1971, State Secrets: Police Surveillance in America, 1973, This School Is Driving Me Crazy, 1975, (Golden Archer award 1980), Jazz Is, 1976, Does Anybody Give a Damn? Nat Hentoff on Education, 1977, The First Freedom: The Tumultuous History of Free Speech in America, 1980, (Hugh M. Hefner First Amendment award Deadline Club, 1981), Does This School Have Capital Punishment?, 1981, Blues for Charles Darwin, 1982, The Day They Came to Arrest the Book, 1982, (Cranberry Award list Acton Pub. Libr. 1983), The Man From Internal Affairs, 1985, Boston Boy: A Memoir, 1986, American Heroes: In and Out of School, 1987, John Cardinal O'Conner at the Storm of a Changing American Church, 1988, Free Speech for Me--But Not for Thee, 1992, Listen To the Stories: Nat Henthoff on Jazz and Country Music, 1995; author numerous articles. Mem. steering com. Reporters Com. for Freedom of Press. Mem. AFTRA. Office: The Village Voice 36 Cooper Sq New York NY 10003-7149

HENTON, MELISSA KAYE, strategic technology and arms control analyst; b. Bossier City, La., Apr. 6, 1968; d. Harold Hayes and Nancy Lee (Bullers) H. BA, Creighton U., 1990; MA, George Washington U., 1995. Asst. dir. civil-mil. rels. Atlantic Coun. of U.S., Washington, 1991-93, dep. dir. civil-mil. rels., 1993-95, dep. dir. ops., 1995, dir. of planning, 1996-98; analyst strategic technol. and arms control analysis divn. Dyn Meridian, 1998—; mem. Gov.'s Edn. Coun., Lincoln, 1990, Gov.'s Youth Adv. Coun., Lincoln, 1989-90. Mem. Arms Control Assn., Atlantic Coun. of U.S., Columbian Women, Washington Tennis Found., Theta Phi Alpha. Home: 4601 31st Rd S Apt A1 Arlington VA 22206-1620 Office: Dyn Meridian 6101 Stevenson Ave Alexandria VA 22304

HENTON, WILLIS RYAN, bishop; b. McCook, Nebr., July 5, 1925; s. Burr Milton and Clara Vaire (Godown) H.; m. Martha Somerville Bishop, June 7, 1952; 1 son, David Vasser. B.A., U. Nebr., 1949; S.T.B., Gen. Theol. Sem., N.Y.C., 1952, D.S.T., 1972; D.D., U. of South, Sewanee, Tenn., 1972. Ordained priest Episcopal Ch., 1953; missionary St. Benedicts Mission, Besao, Mountain Province, Philippines, 1952-57; mem. staff St. Lukes Chapel, N.Y.C., 1957-58; rector Christ Ch., Mansfield, La., 1958-61, St. Augustine's Ch., Baton Rouge, 1961-64; archdeacon Diocese of La., 1964-71; bishop coadjutor Diocese N.W. Tex., 1971-72; bishop N.W. Tex., Lubbock, 1972-80, Western La., 1980-90; ret., 1990. Pres. Tex. Conf. Chs., 1978-80; pres. La. Inter-Ch. Conf., 1985-86. Served with inf. AUS, 1944-46. Decorated Bronze Star. Office: PO Box 10108 New Iberia LA 70562-0108

HENTZ, VINCENT R., surgeon; b. Jacksonville, Fla., Aug. 29, 1942. MD, U. Fla., 1968. Intern Stanford (Calif.) Hosp., 1968-69, resident in plastic surgery, 1969-74, now hand surgeon; fellow in hand surgery Roosevelt Hosp., N.Y.C., 1974-75; prof. functional restoration Stanford (Calif.) U. Office: Stanford Univ 900 Welsh Rd # 15 Stanford CA 94305-5343*

HENWOOD, WILLIAM SCOTT, lawyer; b. Toronto, Ont., Can., May 24, 1949; s. William John and Muriel Mae (Scott) H.; m. Carol Elizabeth Nichols, Nov. 17, 1973; children: William Scott Jr., Cameron Nichols. BBA, Ga. State U., 1976; JD, Woodrow Wilson Coll. Law, 1978. Bar: Ga. 1979. Law clk. to reporter of decisions Supreme Ct. Ga., Atlanta, 1974-80, asst. reporter of decisions, 1980-84, reporter of decisions, 1984—. Co-author: Georgia's Appellate Judiciary: Profiles and History, 1987. Pres. Leafmore-Creek Park Civic Assn., Decatur, Ga., 1982-83, Briarcliff Cmty. Sports, Decatur, 1986-87; mem. Sesquicentennial Com., Supreme Ct. of Ga. With Army N.G., 1968-74. Fellow Ga. Bar Found.; mem. Assn. of Reporters of Jud. Decisions (pres. 1988-89), Ga. Legal History Found. (treas. 1984-96), Gridiron Secret Soc., Lawyers Club Atlanta (mem. exec. com. 1998—), Advocates Club (exec. bd. 1996-98), Burns Club (sec. 1992-93), Old War Horse Lawyers Club. Democrat. Presbyterian. Avocations: travel, hunting, sports car racing. Home: 2247 Springwood Dr Decatur GA 30033-2722 Office: Supreme Ct Ga Judicial Bldg Atlanta GA 30334

HENZINGER, THOMAS ANTON, computer science educator; b. Linz, Austria, Dec. 8, 1962; came to U.S., 1985; s. Sigmund A. and Elisabeth H. Diplomas in computer sci. with distinction, Kepler U., Linz, 1984, 87; MS in Computer and Info. Sci., U. Del., 1986; PhD in Computer Sci. with distinction, Stanford U., 1991. Asst. prof. computer sci. Cornell U., Ithaca, N.Y., 1992-95; asst. prof. elec. engring./computer sci. U. Calif., Berkeley, 1996-97, assoc. prof. elec. engring./computer sci., 1997-98, prof. elec. engring./computer sci., 1998—; visitor AT&T Bell Labs., Murray Hill, N.J., 1991, 92, 93, 94, 95; vis. scientist dept. applied math. Weizmann Inst. Sci., Rehovot, Israel, 1989, 90; postdoctoral visitor Inst. Computer Sci. and Applied Math. Fourier U., Grenoble, France, 1991; jour. referee Distributed Computing, Formal Aspects of Computing, Formal Methods in System Design, Info. and Computation, Jour. Automated Resaoning, Jour. Symbolic Computation; lectr. in field. Contbr. articles to profl. jours. Recipient George E. Forsythe Meml. award Stanford U., 1989, Career Devel. award NSF, 1995, Young Investigator award Office Naval Rsch., 1995; Fulbright fellow, 1985-86, Grad. fellow IBM, 1988-91. Mem. AAAS, Math. Assn. Am., Assn. Computing Machinery (jour. referee conf. referee), IEEE (jour. referee, conf. referee), Assn. Symbolic Logic (jour. referee), Soc. Indsl. and Applied Math. (jour. referee, conf. referee), European Assn. Theoretical Computer Sci. (jour. referee), N.Y. Acad. Scis., Sigma Xi. Office: U Calif EECS Dept 519 Cory Hall Berkeley CA 94720-1770

HENZLIK, RAYMOND EUGENE, zoophysiologist, educator; b. Casper, Wyo., Dec. 26, 1926; s. William H. Henzlik and Adeline Adele (Brown) Wolff; m. Wilma Louise Bartels, Oct. 1, 1950; children: Randall Eugene, Nancy Jo. BS, U. Nebr., 1948, MS, 1952, PhD, 1960; postgrad., Cornell U., 1961-62. Tchr. biology and chemistry York (Nebr.) High Sch., 1948-50; sci. edn. supr. Tchrs. Coll., U. Nebr., Lincoln, 1951-53; tchr. biology Omaha North High Sch., 1953-56; instr. biology Nebr. Wesleyan U., Lincoln, 1957-59; asst. prof. zoology and biology U. Nebr., Lincoln, 1959-61; asst. prof. biology Ball State U., Muncie, Ind., 1962-67, assoc. prof. physiology, 1967-69, prof. physiology, 1970—; adj. vis. prof. vet. physiology Tex. A&M U., College Station, 1984-85; anatomy cons. Nat. Prescription Footwear Applicators Assn., Muncie, 1962—; lectr. Pedorthics Tech. Program, Muncie, 1977—; cons. ednl. affairs Argonne (Ill.) Nat. Lab., 1970-76; dir. ednl. program Am. Diabetes Assn., Muncie, 1979-83; vis. prof. health sci. USAF European Ctr., Ramstein and Rhein Main, Germany, 1977-78; lectr. Ind. Health Care Assn., 1985-91. Author: Human Physiology Lab Manual, 1976-92; contbr. articles to profl. jours. Pres. Muncie Tech. Soc., 1975-80; mem. bd. Am. Diabetes Assn. Delaware County, Muncie, 1979-85. Radiation biology fellow NSF/AEC, U. Mich., 1960, Radiobiology fellow AEC/NSF, Cornell U., 1961-62, Radiation Biology Rsch. fellow U.S. Radiobiology Lab N.C. State U., 1965, P.R. Nuclear Ctr., 1967. Mem. AAAS, Nutrition Today Soc., Ind. Acad. Sci., Muncie Tech. Soc., Mensa, Sigma Xi, Phi Delta Kappa. Avocations: renting houses, reading, book collecting. Home: 5009 N Somerset Dr Muncie IN 47304-6501 Office: Ball State U Physiology and Health Sci Dept 2000 W University Ave Muncie IN 47306-0002

HEPBURN, KATHARINE HOUGHTON, actress; b. Hartford, Conn., May 12, 1907; d. Thomas N. and Katharine (Houghton) H.; m. Ludlow Ogden Smith (div.). AB, Bryn Mawr Coll., 1928; LHD (hon.), Columbia U., 1992. Actress: (films) A Bill of Divorcement, 1932, Christopher Strong, 1933, Morning Glory, 1933 (Acad. award for best performance by actress 1934), Little Women, 1933, Spitfire, 1934, The Little Minister, 1934, Alice Adams, 1935, Break of Hearts, 1935, Sylvia Scarlett, 1936, Mary of Scotland, 1936, A Woman Rebels, 1936, Quality Street, 1937, Stage Door, 1937, Bringing up Baby, 1938, Holiday, 1938, The Philadelphia Story, 1940 (N.Y. Critic's award 1940), Woman of the Year, 1941, Keeper of the Flame, 1942, Stage Door Canteen, 1943, Dragon Seed, 1944, Without Love, 1945, Undercurrent, 1946, Sea of Grass, 1946, Song of Love, 1947, State of the Union, 1948, Adam's Rib, 1949, The African Queen, 1951, Pat and Mike, 1952, Summertime, 1955, The Rainmaker, 1956, The Iron Petticoat, 1956, The Desk Set, 1957, Suddenly Last Summer, 1959, Long Day's Journey into Night, 1962 (Best Actress, Cannes Internat. Film Festival), Guess Who's Coming to Dinner, 1967, (Acad. award for best actress 1968),The Lion in Winter, 1968 (Acad. award for best actress 1969), Madwoman of Chaillot, 1969, Trojan Women, 1971, A Delicate Balance, 1973, Rooster Cogburn, 1975, Olly, Olly, Oxen Free, 1978, On Golden Pond, 1981 (Acad. award for best actress 1981), George Stevens: A Filmmaker's Journey, 1984, The Ultimate Solution of Grace Quigley, 1985, Love Affair, 1994; (plays) The Czarina, 1928, The Big Pond, 1928, Night Hostess, 1928, These Days, 1928, Death Takes a Holiday, 1929, A Month in the Country, 1930, Art and Mrs. Bottle, 1930, The Warrior's Husband, 1932, Lysistrata, 1932, The Lake, 1933, Jane Eyre, 1937, The Philadelphia Story, 1939, Without Love, 1942, As You Like It, 1950, The Millionairess, Eng. and U.S.A., 1952, The Taming of the Shrew, The Merchant of Venice, Measure for Measure,, Eng. and Australia, 1955, Merchant of Venice, Much Ado about Nothing, Am. Shakespeare Festival, 1957, toured later, 1958, Twelfth Night, Antony and Cleopatra, Am. Shakespeare Festival, 1960, Coco, 1969-70, toured, 1971, The Taming of the Shrew, 1970, A Matter of Gravity, 1976-78, West Side Waltz, 1981, (TV movies) The Glass Menagerie, 1973, Love among the Ruins, 1975, The Corn Is Green, 1979, Mrs. Delafield Wants to Marry, 1986; Laura Lansing Slept Here, 1988, The Man Upstairs, 1992, This Can't Be Love, 1994, One Christmas, 1994; narrator, co-writer documentary Katharine Hepburn: All About Me, 1993; author: The Making of the African Queen, 1987, (autobiography) Me, 1991. Recipient gold medal as world's best motion picture actress Internat. Motion Picture Expn., Venice,

Italy, 1934, ann. award Shakespeare Club, N.Y.C., 1950, award Whistler Soc., 1957, Woman of Yr. award Hasty Pudding Club, 1958, outstanding achievement award for fostering finest ideals of acting profession, 1980, lifetime achievement award Coun. Fashion Designers Am., 1986, award Kennedy Ctr. Awards, 1990. Office: William Morris Agy 1325 Avenue Of The Americas New York NY 10019-6026*

HEPBURN, VALERIE ANN, state agency administrator; b. Iowa City, Iowa, Oct. 5, 1961; d. Lawrence Ronald and Mary Elizabeth (Zoghby) H. BA in Polit. Sci., Agnes Scott Coll., 1983; M in Pub. Adminstrn., Ga. State U., 1987. Legis. aide Ga. Gen. Assembly, Atlanta, 1980-82; asst. to coord. Ginn for Gov. Campaign, Atlanta, 1982; dir. gov. relations Sec. of State, Atlanta, 1983-84, dir. adminstrn., 1985—; mem. exec. bd. dirs. Ga. Fiscal Mgmt. Council, Atlanta; mem. legis. subcom. Council for Licensure, Enforcement and Regulation, Washington, council of state govts., 1986—. Vice-chmn. legis. com. Dem. Party of Ga., Atlanta, 1982-86; mem. Westover Plantation Homeowner's Assn., Atlanta, 1985—. Named one of Outstanding Young Women of Am., 1985, 86. Mem. Am. Mgmt. Assn., Am. Soc. Pub. Adminstrn., Bus. and Profl. Women (Young Careerist award 1984), Nat. Assn. Female Execs., Am. Polit. Sci. Assn. Democrat. Roman Catholic. Avocations: baseball, basketball, needlework, reading, tennis.

HEPGULER, GREGORY GOKHAN, petroleum engineer; b. Eskisehir, Turkey, Oct. 3, 1961; came to U.S., 1980; s. Memduh and Gülsen (Ertoglu) H.; m. Wendy Margaret Nicholson, Mar. 19, 1985. BS in Petroleum Engring., U. Tulsa, 1984, MS in Engring., 1988. Software engr. and cons. Fluid Flow Engring. Co. (now CEALC), Tulsa, 1984-88; tech. sales rep. Baker Oil Tools, Houston, 1988-89; engr./tech. sys. analyst Union Pacific Resources, Ft. Worth, Tex., 1989-95; engring. cons. Sci. Software-Intercomp, Houston, 1995-96; lead engr. Simulation Scis., Inc., Brea, Calif., 1996-97; advising reservoir engr. UNOCAL Spirit Energy 76, Lafayette, L.A., 1997—; mem. gas lift task group subcom. 11 Am. Petroleum Inst., Houston, 1991-93. Contbr. papers to profl. jours. including Jour. Petroleum Tech., (Soc. Petroleum Engrs.), Computer Applications Jour. Mem. Soc. Petroleum Engrs., Tau Beta Pi, Pi Epsilon Tau, Sigma Xi. Achievements include development of unique, comprehensive theoretical model for gas-lift valve performance; design and creation of production optimization program for oil and gas wells; establishment of the first Unix workstation network for Union Pacific Resources; development of reservoir simulation interface to surface and production networks. Avocations: reading computer journals, bicycling, classical music, watching documentaries. Home: 122 Cane Ridge Cir Lafayette LA 70508-4374 Office: 4021 Ambassador Caffery Pkwy Lafayette LA 70503-5262

HEPLER, KENNETH RUSSEL, manufacturing executive; b. Canton, Ohio, Mar. 31, 1926; s. Clifton R. and Mary A. (Sample) H.; m. Beverly Best, June 9, 1945; 1 child, Bradford R. Student, Cleve. Art Inst., 1946-47, Case Western Res. U., 1948-50. V.p., adminstr. A. Carlisle and Co., San Francisco, 1954-67; pres. K.R. Hepler and Co., Menlo Park, Calif., 1968-73, Paramount Press., Jacksonville, Fla., 1974-75; pvt. practice printing broker, 1976-80; chmn. Hickey and Hepler Graphics Inc., San Francisco, 1981—; instr. printing prodn., San Francisco City Coll. With USAAC, 1943-45. Mem. San Francisco Litho Club (pres. 1972), Phila. Litho Club (sec. 1975-76), Newtown Exchange Club (pres. 1976), Elks. Republican. Presbyterian. Office: Hickey & Hepler Graphics Inc 1633 Bayshore Hwy Ste 222 Burlingame CA 94010-1515

HEPLER, MERLIN JUDSON, JR., real estate broker; b. Hot Springs, Va., May 13, 1929; s. Merlin Judson and Margaret Belle (Vines) H.; m. Lanova Helen Roberts, July 25, 1952; children: Nancy Andora, Douglas Stanley. BS in Bus., U. Idaho, 1977; grad., Realtors Inst., 1979. Cert. residential specialist. Enlisted USAF, 1947, advanced through grades to sgt., 1960, ret., 1967; service mgr. Lanier Bus. Products, Gulfport, Miss., 1967-74; sales assoc. Century 21 Singler and Assn., Troy, Idaho, 1977-79; broker B&M Realty, Troy, 1979—. Mem. Nat. Assn. Realtors, Am. Legion, U. Idaho Alumni Assn., Air Force Sgts. Assn. Republican. Lodge: Lions. Avocations: hunting, fishing. E-mail: mhepler@idaho.tds.net. Home: 1081 Driscoll Ridge Rd Troy ID 83871-9605 Office: B&M Realty W 102 A St PO Box 187 Troy ID 83871-0187

HEPPE, KAROL VIRGINIA, lawyer, educator; b. Vinton, Iowa, Mar. 14, 1958; d. Robert Henry and Audry Virginia (Harper) H. BA in Law and Society, U. Calif., Santa Barbara, 1982; JD, People's Coll. of Law, 1989. Cmty. organizer Oreg. Fair Share, Eugene, 1983; law clk. Legal Aid Found. L.A., summer 1986; devel. dir. Ctrl. Am. Refugee Ctr., L.A., 1987-89; exec. dir. Police Watch-The Police Misconduct Lawyer Referral Svc., L.A., 1989-94; instr. People's Coll. of Law, L.A., 1992-94; dir. alternative sentencing project Ctr. Juvenile and Criminal Justice, 1994-95; cons. Bay Area Police Watch, 1996; investigator Office of Citizen Complaints City and County of San Francisco, 1998—; vol. law clk. Legal Aid Found. L.A., 1984-86, Lane County Legal Aid Svc., Eugene, 1983. Editor (newsletters) NLG Law Students in Action, 1986, Ctrl. Am. Refugee Ctr., 1986-89, Prison Break, 1994. Bd. dirs. People's Coll. of Law, 1985-90, Law Student Civil Rights Rsch. Coun., N.Y.C., 1986; bd. dirs., law student organizer Nat. Lawyers' Guild, L.A., 1984-87; mem. Coalition for Human Immigrants Rights, 1991-92, So. Calif. Civil Rights Coalition, 1991-92; bd. dirs. Bay Area Nat. Lawyers Guild, 1997—. Scholar, Kramer Found., 1984-88, Law Students' Civil Rights Rsch. Coun., 1986, Davis-Putter Found., 1988, Assn. for Cmty.-Based Edn. Prudential, 1988. Avocations: reading, travel. E-mail: karolúheppe@ci.sf.ca.us.

HEPPER, IONA LYDIA, gallery owner; b. Eureka, S.D., Mar. 10, 1918; d. Emanuel E. and Lydia (Koerner) Voll; m. Kenneth Melvin Hepper, May 1, 1938 (dec. Feb. 1998); children: Judy, Rod. Student, Calif. Sch. Arts & Crafts, 1936-37. Owner Flair Gifts & Interiors, Stockton, Calif., 1951-81, tchr. art, 1965—, designer, 1971—; owner GAlerie Iona, Stockton, Calif., 1993—. Cover designer (book) The Concepts of Bodily Objects, 1997. Mem. Nat. Watercolor Soc., Pastel Soc. Am., Pastel Soc. West Coast, Stockton Art League. Republican. Presbyterian. Avocations: painting, travel, reading. Home: 5469 Covey Creek Cir Stockton CA 95207-5210 Office: Galerie Iona 354 Lincoln Ctr Stockton CA 95207-2627

HEPPNER, GLORIA HILL, medical science administrator, educator; b. Gt. Falls, Mont., May 30, 1940; d. Eugene Merrill and Georgia M. (Swanson) Hill; m. Frank Henry Heppner, June 6, 1964 (div. 1975); 1 child, Michael Berkeley. BA, U. Calif., Berkeley, 1962, MA, 1964, PhD, 1967. Damon Runyon postdoctoral fellow U. Wash., Seattle, 1967-69; asst. and assoc. prof. Brown U., Providence, 1969-79, Herbert Fanger meml. lectr., 1988; chmn. dept. immunology, dir. labs., sr. v.p. Mich. Cancer Found., Detroit, 1979-91; dir. breast cancer program Karmanos Cancer Inst., 1991—, dep. dir., 1994—; assoc. chairperson for rsch. dept. internal medicine Wayne State U. Sch. Medicine, Detroit, 1991—; mem. external adv. com. basic sci. program M.D. Anderson Hosp. and Tumor Clinic, Houston, 1984-94; mem. external adv. com. Case Western Res. U. Cancer Ctr., Cleve., 1988—, Roswell Park Meml. Inst., Buffalo, 1991—; Sarah Stewart meml. lectr. Georgetown U., Washington, 1988; bd. sci. counselors Nat. Inst. Dental Rsch., 1993-97. Editor: Macrophages and Cancer, 1988; mem. editorial bd. Cancer Rsch., 1989-93, Jour. Nat. Cancer Inst., 1988, Sci., 1988-92; contbr. over 200 articles to sci. jours. Bd. dirs. Lyric Chamber Ensemble, 1996—. Recipient Mich. Sci. Trail-Blazer award State of Mich., 1987; fellow Damon Runyon-Walter Winchell Found., 1967-69. Mem. AAAS, Am. Assn. for Cancer Rsch. (bd. dirs. 1983-86, chmn. long-range planning com. 1989-91), Am. Assn. Immunologists, Metastasis Rsch. Soc. (bd. dirs. 1985-89), Women in Cancer Rsch. (nat. pres.), Internat. Differentiation Soc. (v.p. 1990-92, pres. 1992-94), LWV (bd. dirs. Grosse Pointe, Mich. 1989-95). Democrat. Avocations: music, theater. Office: Karmanos Cancer Inst 2nd Fl A100 John R Exec Office Detroit MI 48201

HEPTINSTALL, ROBERT HODGSON, physician; b. Keswick, Eng., July 22, 1920; s. James A. and Mabel (Sanders) H.; m. Ann Enraght Porter, Jan. 25, 1950; children: Bridget, Gillian, Jonathan, James, Caroline, Christopher. MB, BS, London U., 1944, MD, 1948. Intern, house surgeon Charing Cross Hosp., London, 1944; jr. lectr. pathology St. Mary's Hosp., London, 1947-50, sr. lectr. pathology, 1950-60; vis. prof. pathology Washington U., St. Louis, 1960-62; assoc. prof. pathology Johns Hopkins Med. Sch., Balt., 1962-67, prof. pathology, 1967-69, 88—, Baxley prof. pathology, dir. dept., 1969-88; pathologist in chief Johns Hopkins Hosp., 1969-88; disting. svc. prof. pathology, 1992—; pathology study sect. NIH, 1963-67, pathology tng. com., 1967-71; sci. adv. bd. Nat. Kidney Found., 1969-73. Author: Pathology of the Kidney, 1966, 5th edit., 1998; editor Lab. Invest, 1976-81; mem. editl. bd. Kidney Internat., Lab Investigation. With M.C., Royal Army, 1944-47. Recipient gold medal Danish Surg. Soc., 1984, David M. Hume Meml. award Nat. Kidney Found., 1986. Mem. Am. Assn. Pathologists, Internat. Acad. Pathology (Maude Abbott lectr. 1983), Renal Assn., Am. Soc. Nephrology (pres. 1972-73, Joh P. Peters award 1993), Internat. Soc. Nephrology (v.p. 1981-84, Jean Hamburger award 1999), Danish Soc. Nephrology (hon.), Renal Pathology Soc. (pres. 1980-83), Alpha Omega Alpha.

HEPWORTH, RICHARD GORDON, surgeon, writer; b. Leeds, Eng., Mar. 12, 1926; came to U.S., 1974; s. William and May Isobel (Richardson) H.; m. Rilla Scarlet Black, May 1974; children: Heather Gail, Eileen Maya. MD, U. Leeds, Eng., 1951. Intern Gen. Infirmary, Leeds, 1951; resident Toronto Western Hosp., 1955, Vancouver Hosp., 1960-62; chief urology St. Vincent's Hosp., Vancouver, B.C., Can., 1963-74; assoc. prof. Memphis-Bapt. Hosp., 1974-80; prof. surgery Western U. Pacific, Pomona, Claif., 1981-90; mem. faculty Med. Mgmt. Devel. Assn., San Diego, 1990-92. Author: The Making of a Chief, 1974. Lt. RCAF, 1959-62. Fellow Royal Coll. Surgeons, Am. Coll. Surgeons. Avocation: instrument rated pilot. E-mail: hepworth@whidbey.com. Home: 660 Highland Dr Point Robert WA 98281 Office: Hepworth Assocs 660 Highland Dr Point Roberts WA 98281

HERAKOVICH, CARL THOMAS, civil engineering, applied mechanics educator; b. East Chicago, Ind., Aug. 6, 1937; m. Marlene Vukowich, Apr. 23, 1960; children: Bradley, Douglas, Kristine, Russell. BSCE, Rose-Hulman Inst. Tech., 1959; MS in Mechanics, U. Kans., 1962; PhD in Mechanics, Ill. Inst. Tech., 1968. Registered profl. engr., Va. Prof. Va. Poly. Inst. and State U., Blacksburg, 1967-87; prof. civil engring. and applied mechanics U. Va., Charlottesville, 1987-98, Henry L. Kinnier prof. civil engring., 1990-98, prof. emeritus, 1998—, dir. applied mechanics, 1987-98; co-dir. NASA composites program Va. Poly. Inst. and State U., Blacksburg, 1974-87; dir. Ctr. for Innovative Tech., Inst. for Materials Sci. and Engring., 1984-86, Ctr. for High Temp. Composites, 1993-98. Editor: Handbook of Composites No. 2, 1989; author: Mechanics of Fibrous Composites, 1998. Fellow ASME (chmn. com. composite materials 1989-92, exec. com. 1992-97, divsn. chair 1996-97), ASCE, Am. Acad. Mechanics; mem. Internat. Union Theoretical and Applied Mechanics (gen. assembly), U.S. Nat. Com. on Theoretical and Applied Mechanics, Soc. Engring. Sci. (sec. 1983-90, bd. dirs. 1989-92, v.p. 1991, pres. 1992), Soc. Exptl. Mechanics, Soc. Advancement Materials Processing and Engring. Office: U Va Applied Mechs Thornton Hall Rm B-122 Charlottesville VA 22903-2442

HERALD, CHERRY LOU, research educator, research director; b. Beeville, Tex., Dec. 23, 1940; d. Edwin Sherley and Margaret Lucille (Caron) Bell; m. Delbert Leon Herald, Jr., July 31, 1964; children: Heather Amanda, Delbert Leon, III. BS, Ariz. State U., 1962, MS, 1965, PhD, 1968. Faculty rsch. assoc. Cancer Rsch. Inst. Ariz. State U., Tempe, 1973-74, sr. rsch. chemist Cancer Rsch. Inst., 1974-77, asst. to dir. and sr. rsch. chemist Cancer Rsch. Inst., 1977-83, asst. dir., assoc. rsch. prof. Cancer Rsch. Inst., 1984-88, assoc. dir., rsch. prof. Cancer Rsch. Inst., 1988—. Co-author: Biosynthetic Products for Cancer Chemotherapy, vols. 4, 5, & 6, 1984, 85, 87, Anticancer Drugs from Animals, Plants & Microorganisms, 1994, sci. jours. Mem. Am. Soc. Pharmacognosy, Am. Chem. Soc. E-mail: cherald@asu.edu. Office: Ariz State U Cancer Rsch Inst Tempe AZ 85287-2404

HERALD, GEORGE WILLIAM, foreign correspondent; b. Berlin, Jan. 3, 1911; came to U.S., 1941; s. Bruno H. and Paula J. (Levy) H.; m. Martha A. Dubois, Mar. 24, 1948; children—Steve Andrew, Patricia Claudia. LL.D. cum laude, Basle U. (Switzerland), 1934; postgrad. Columbia U., 1950-52. Staff corr. INS, N.Y., London and Paris, 1945-46, bur. chief, Berlin and Vienna, 1946-49; spl. writer United Features, N.Y.C., 1949-52; assoc. editor UN World mag., N.Y.C. and Europe, 1952-55; head bur. Vision, Inc., Paris, 1955—. Author: My Favorite Assassin, 1943; (with others) Off the Record, 1952, Tatiana, 1955 (adapted for TV movie); (with Soraya Esfandiary) My Life as an Empress, 1962; The Big Wheel, 1963, Art and Money, 1977; contbr. numerous articles to mags. including Reader's Digest, Harper's, McCall's; contbg. editor Am. Peoples Ency., 1952-62. Served to capt. U.S. Army, 1942-45. Recipient Best Spl. Reporting from Abroad award Mex. Press, 1989. Mem. Authors League Am., Internat. Press Inst., Overseas Press Club Am., Anglo-Am. Press Club, Internat. Arts Council. Unitarian. Office: Vision Inc Vision Bldg 310 Madison Ave Rm 1412 New York NY 10017-6009

HERALD, SANDRA JEAN, elementary education educator; b. Indpls., Aug. 3, 1950; d. Chester Lee and Mary Mae (Jeffras) H. BA, Marian Coll., Indpls., 1973; MA, Ind. U., Indpls., 1980. Dental asst. Dr. Jones, Indpls., 1969-73; instr. dance Garrison Sch. Dance, Indpls., 1968-73; elem. tchr. St. Gabriel Sch., Connersville, Ind., 1973—. Active in community theater, 1974-83. Sunday sch. tchr. Fairfax Ch., Indpls., 1966-72, East Side Meth. Ch., Connersville, 1984-86; camp counselor Meth. Ch. Summer Camp, Connersville, 1986; presiding pres. John Conner Players Bd., Connersville, 1983-84; participating staff instr. Ind. Dance Conv., Indpls., 1970-73; vol. local nursing home care ctrs.; active local gose; trio/quarter "Praise"; bd. dirs. Connersville United Way. Recipient Lavinnia Smith award John Conner Players, Connersville, 1980. Mem. Area Reading and Arts Assn. Avocations: choreography, reading, Bible study, choir directing, pet care. Home: 824 Western Ave Connersville IN 47331-1601 Office: St Gabriel Sch 224 W 9th St Connersville IN 47331-2074

HERB, EDMUND MICHAEL, optometrist, educator; b. Zanesville, Ohio, Oct. 9, 1942; s. Edmund G. and Barbara R. (Michael) H.; divorced; children—Sara, Andrew; m. Jeri Herb. O.D., Ohio State U., 1966. Pvt. practice optometry, Buena Vista, Colo., 1966—; past prof. Timberline campus Colo. Mountain Coll.; past clin. instr. Ohio State U. Sch. Optometry. Mem. Am. Optometric Assn., Colo. Optometric Assn. Home: 16395 Mt Princeton Rd Buena Vista CO 81211-9505 Office: 115 N Tabor St Buena Vista CO 81211 also: Leadville Colorado Med Ctr Leadville CO 80461

HERB, F(RANK) STEVEN, lawyer; b. Cin., Nov. 9, 1949; s. Frank X. and Jean M. (Zurcher) H.; m. Jean L. Jeffers, June 21, 1971; children: Tracy Lynn, Jacquelyn Anne. BS, Bowling Green U., 1971; JD, U. Cin., 1974. Bar: Ohio 1974, Fla. 1978, U.S. Dist. Ct. (no., mid., and so. dists.) Fla., U.S. Ct. Appeals (11th cir.). Assoc. Connaughton Law Offices, Hamilton, Ohio, 1974; jud. advocate gen., chief of civil law USAF, Tyndall AFB, Fla., 1975-78; mng. ptnr. Nelson Hesse, Sarasota, Fla., 1979—. Author: (with others) Bennedicts on Admiralty, 1996, 97, 98; contbr. chpts. to books. Bd. dirs. Brock Wilson Found., Sarasota, 1983-92; pres. Riegels Landing Assn., Sarasota, 1986-90, 98-2000; dir., vice chmn. Siesta Key Utilities Assn., 1994—; mem. govt. rels. com. Nat. Marine Mfrs. Assn. Capt. JAGC USAF, 1975-78. Decorated USAF Meritorious Svc. medal. Mem. Ohio Bar Assn., Fla. Bar Assn. (chmn. 12th Jud. cir. unauthorized practice of law com. 1986-93, fee arbitration com. 12th jud. cir. 1996—), Sarasota Bar Assn., Def. Rsch. Inst., Maritime Law Assn., Am. Boat and Yacht Counsel, Nat. Marine Mfrs. Assn. (govt. rels. com.), The Field Club (dir. exec. com.). Republican. Roman Catholic. Avocations: boating, woodworking, skiing, tennis. Office: Nelson Hesse 2070 Ringling Blvd Sarasota FL 34237-7002

HERB, JANE ELIZABETH, banker; b. Pottsville, Pa., Nov. 26, 1959; d. Wallace Lamar and Arlene Grace (Miller) Kimmel; m. David Glenn Herb, Dec. 22, 1978; 1 child, Jennifer Marie. Student, ICS, 1995—. Adminstrv. asst., customer svc. rep. Pa. Nat. Bank and Trust Co., Valley View, 1977-85; cosmetic salesperson Mary Kay Cosmetics, Dallas, 1980-84; fin. svc. salesperson for various firms, 1985-88; acct. supr., customer svc. rep. Jetson Direct Mail Svcs. Inc./Time Warner Inc.-N.Y.C., St. Clair, Pa., 1988-94; compliance mgr., br. mgr., asst. to pres. Gratz (Pa.) Nat. Bank, 1994—. Republican. United Methodist. Avocations: reading, running. Home: PO Box 565 Valley View PA 17983-0565 Office: Internat Correspondence Schs The Gratz Nat Bank PO Box 159 Gratz PA 17030-0159

HERB, MARVIN J., food products executive; b. 1937. BS, U. Buffalo, 1959; MBA, U. Toledo, 1964. Mgmt. trainee Kroger Co., Toledo, 1960-65; with Pepsi-Cola Co., Inc., 1965-72; various positions including pres. Pepsi-Cola Bottling Co. Indpls, Inc.; with Borden, Inc., N.Y.C., 1972-76, v.p. dairy and svc. divsn., 1976-77, pres. dairy and svc. divsn., 1977-78, corp. v.p., pres. dairy and svc. divsn., 1978-81; chmn. bd. Hondo, Inc., Niles, Ill., 1981—. Office: Hondo Inc 7400 N Oak Park Ave Niles IL 60714-3818*

HERB, SAMUEL MARTIN, manufacturing company executive; b. Yeadon, Pa., Nov. 29, 1938; s. Samuel F. and Mildred V. (Reitz) H.; m. Judith Ann Oesch, July 2, 1966 (dec.); children: Samuel S., Corinne M., David M. (dec.), Elizabeth A. BEE, Drexel U., 1969. Registered profl. engr., Calif. Tech. writer Honeywell Corp., Ft. Washington, Pa., 1964-73, applications engr., 1973-76, project engr., 1976-79; product application specialist Leeds & Northrup, North Wales, Pa., 1979-83, product line mgr., 1983-85, mgr. bus. devel., 1985-88, systems advt. mgr., 1988-91, market mgr. distributed systems, 1991-93, market mgr. control applications, 1993-94; dir. mktg. Procon Sys., Inc., Lansdale, Pa., 1994-95; corp. analyst Moore Process Automatic Solutions, Spring House, PA, 1996—; mem. faculty Spring Garden Coll., Chestnut Hill, Pa., 1976-82. Author: Understanding Distributed Process Control, 1983, Control System Architectures, 1994, Implementing Control Systems, 1995, Understanding Distributed Processor Systems for Control, 1999; contbr. articles to profl. jours. Commr. Boy Scouts Am., 1961—. Named to Legion of Honor Chapel of Four Chaplains, 1985; recipient Woodbadge, 1989, Disting. Commissioner Awd., Silver Beaver award, 1990, Boy Scouts Am. Mem. Instrument Soc. Am. (sr.), Indsl. Computing Soc., Engrs. Club (Phila.). Republican. Roman Catholic. Avocations: travel, swimming, outdoors, model railroading, house projects. Home: 117 Pawnee Rd Doylestown PA 18901-5142 Office: Moore Process Automation Solutions Spring House PA 19477

HERBAUGH, ROGER DUANE, computer and software company executive; b. Mt. Vernon, Wash., May 20, 1957; s. Donald Lloyd and Kathleen Joyce (Anderson) H.; m. Anne Louise Finlayson, May 8, 1993; children: Andrew David Miller, Celeste Jane Miller, Trevor Allan Miller, Vanessa Anne Herbaugh, Deirdre Rose Herbaugh. AA, Skagit Valley Coll., 1984; BA, Western Wash. U., 1986. Cert. Microsoft profl. Computer programmer Stockmar Northwestern, Mt. Vernon, 1986-87; CEO, computer cons. Herbaugh & Assocs., Inc. Computer Support Group, Mt. Vernon, 1987—; also pres. bd. dirs. Herbaugh & Assocs., Inc., Mt. Vernon; cons. Mobil, Ferndale, Wash., 1985-86, Shell Oil Co., Anacortes, Wash., 1986-98, BP Oil Co., Ferndale, Wash., 1986-93, ARCO, Blaine, Wash., 1989—, Tosco, Ferndale, Wash., 1993-97, Tosco, Seattle, 1993-97, Tesoro, Anacortes, Wash., 1998—; Microsoft Solutions provider; bd. dirs., pres. Software Plus, Inc., Mt. Vernon, 1991—; mem. tech. adv. coun. Mt. Vernon H.S.; trainer Kiwanis. Sgt. U.S. Army, 1975-81. Mem. Burlington C. of C., Mt. Vernon C. of C., Kiwanis (dist. chmn., immediate past lt. gov., past pres. Mt. Vernon chpt.). Republican. Mem. LDS Ch. Avocations: boating, fishing, travel. Office: Herbaugh & Assocs Inc Computer Support Group 1754 S Burlington Blvd Burlington WA 98233-3224

HERBECK, DALE ALAN, educator; b. Chgo., June 14, 1958; s. Delbert George and Virginia (Gerke) H.; m. Edith Haffenreffer, Aug. 15, 1997. BA, Augustana Coll., 1980; MA, U. Iowa, 1982, PhD, 1988. Instr., dir. forensics Boston Coll., Chestnut Hill, Mass., 1985-88, asst. prof., dir. forensics, 1988-91, assoc. prof., dir. forensics, 1991-94, assoc. prof., 1994-98, assoc. prof., chmn., 1998—. Author numerous debate handbooks; editor Free Speech Yearbook, 1992-94; contbr. articles to profl. jours. Recipient Midwest Forensic Assn. Rsch. award, 1987, Trzaszka Student Advising award, 1989, Robert M. O'Neil award for rsch. on freedom of expression, 1993, Svc. award Am. Debate Assn., 1994, Eastern Comm. Assn. Past Pres. award, 1995. Mem. Am. Forensic Assn. (pres. 1992-94, v.p. 1990-92), Am. Communication Assn. (exec. bd. 1994—), Ctrl. States Communication Assn., Ea. Communication Assn., Internat. Communication Assn., Nat. Communication Assn., Mortarboard, Phi Beta Kappa, Delta Sigma Rho, Omicron Delta Kappa. Democrat. Lutheran. Home: 15 Dover Farm Rd Medfield MA 02052-1130 Office: Boston Coll Lyon 215 Chestnut Hill MA 02167

HERBEL, LEROY ALEC, JR., telecommunications engineer; b. Ft. Carson, Colo., July 24, 1954; s. LeRoy Alec and Mabel Bertha (Huffman) H. BS, S.W. Mo. State U., 1976; MEd, Ga. So. U., 1978; MS in Telecommunications, Golden Gate U., 1987, MBA, 1990. Asst. mgr. toy dept. Dillard's Dept. Store, Springfield, Mo., 1971-76; material controller GTE of the South, Durham, N.C., 1979-80; asst. prof. mil. sci. Army ROTC, U. N.H., Durham, 1982-85; tech. instr. Northern Telecom Inc., Raleigh, N.C., 1988-91; sr. engr. No. Telecom Inc., Raleigh, N.C., 1991-93; field engr. mgr. Western Wireless Corp., Bellevue, Wash., 1994-95; switch supr. Palmer Wireless (CellularOne), Ft. Myers, Fla., 1995-96; sr. network analyst Sprint PCS, Lenexa, Kans., 1996-97; instrl. sys. specialist Dept. Def., Fort Gordon, Ga., 1997—; adj. prof. DeKalb (Ga.) C.C., 1978-79, N.C. Wesleyan Coll., Rocky Mount, 1991. Scoutmaster Troop 213 Boy Scouts Am., Cary, N.C., 1990-93, asst. dist. commr. Dan Beard dist., 1992-96, mem. merit badge staff Nat. Jamboree, 1993. Capt. U.S. Army, 1980-88; maj., USAR, 1988—. Recipient Scoutmaster award of merit Boy Scouts Am., 1991, Disting. Leadership citation Boy Scouts Am., 1991, Scoutmaster Key award Boy Scouts Am., 1992, Dist. Order of Merit Boy Scouts Am., 1994, Boy Scout Commr. Key award, 1995. Mem. Telephone Pioneers of Am., Phi Delta Kappa. Avocations: golf, running, trains, camping, music.

HERBENER, MARK BASIL, bishop; b. Chgo., Jan. 2, 1932; s. Otto Berthold and Elsbeth Marie (Mueller) H.; m. Donna Fay Gergens, Apr. 25, 1958; children: Matthew, Jenny Pickett. Student, Concordia Coll., Milw., 1949-51; BA, Concordia Sem., St. Louis, 1953, theol. diploma, 1956. Ordained to ministry Luth. Ch.-Mo. Synod, 1956, Evang. Luth. Ch. in Am., 1978. Intern St. John Luth. Ch., Durand, Wis., 1954-55; pastor Messiah Luth. Ch., Richardson, Tex., 1956-61, Mt. Olive Luth. Ch., Dallas, 1961-87; bishop No. Tex.—No. La. synod Evang. Luth. Ch. in Am., Dallas, 1987—; co-chair Dallas Interfaith Task Force, 1981-86; v.p. Greater Dallas Cmty. of Chs., 1983-85; dir. Dallas region NCCJ, 1983-86; pres. Tex. Conf. Chs., 1995-97; fellow Thanks-giving Sq. Pres. Dallas Opportunities Industrialization Ctr., 1983-85; co-convenor Martin Luther King Jr. Inst., Dallas, 1986-87; v.p. Greater Dallas Cmty. Rels. Commn., 1987; convenor Jewish-Christian-Muslim Dialogue, Dallas, 1990; co-chair Tex. Jewish-Christian Forum, 1992-95, 98—; chair chapel com. Thanks-Giving Square, 1992-95. Recipient Disting. Ch. Svc. award Tex. Luth. Coll., 1987, A. Maceo Smith award Dallas African-Am. Mus., 1987, Religious Liberty award Am. Jewish Congress, 1997; named Peacemaker of Yr., Dallas Peace Ctr., 1987. Mem. Tex. Conf. Chs. (pres. 1995-97), Dallas Pastors Assn. (chmn. 1978-80), Dallas Bach Soc. (pres. 1998—). Democrat. Office: Evang Luth Ch in Am No Tex—No La Synod PO Box 560587 Dallas TX 75356-0587 also: 1530 River Bend Ste 105 1230 River Bend Ste 105 Dallas TX 75247

HERBER, STEVEN CARLTON, physician; b. L.A., Aug. 25, 1960; s. Raymond and Marilyn Joyce (Dart) H.; m. Katherine Carol Jones, Apr. 23, 1989. BS, Pacific Union Coll., 1982; Dr.med., Loma Linda U., 1986. Diplomate Nat. Bd. Med. Examiners, Am. Bd. Plastic Surgery. Resident surgeon Med. Ctr. Loma Linda (Calif.) U., 1986-90; resident plastic surgery Yale U., New Haven, Conn., 1990-92; asst. prof. surgery Loma Linda (Calif.) U., 1993-98; med. dir. Ctr. for Plastic Surgery at St. Helena Hosp., 1998—. Contbr. articles to profl. jours. NIH grantee, 1988, MacPherson Soc. Clin. Sci. fellow, 1992; recipient Leadership award, AMA, 1991, 98. Fellow ACS; mem. Am. Soc. Plastic and Reconstructive Surgeons, Am. Cleft Palate, Craniofacial Assn., Calif. Med. Assn., San Bernardino County Med. Soc., Yale Plastic Surgery Soc. Republican. Adventist. Avocations: travel, collections of watches, books. Office: 1030 Main St Ste 206 St Helena CA 95574

HERBERG, PAUL THOMAS, state agency administrator; b. Hannibal, Mo., Nov. 26, 1964; s. Randall Owen and Marilyn Barrett Herberg; m. Mary Beth DeGeeter, Sept. 26, 1987; children: Amy, Kelly, Michael. BS in Recreation and Park Adminstrn., U. Mo., 1987; M of Pub. Adminstrn., U. Louisville, 1997. Recreation leader Ky. Dept. of Corrections, Pewee Valley, 1987-89; recreation leader Ky. Dept. of Parks, Louisville, 1989-91, recreation supr., 1991-93; pers. program analyst Ky. Pers. Cabinet, Frankfort, 1998—. City coun. mem. City of Orchard Hills, Crestwood, Ky., 1994-96; bd. dirs. Oldham County Parks, LaGrange, 1994-98. Mem. Am. Soc. for Pub. Adminstrn., Pi Alpha Alpha. Roman Catholic. Avocations: hunting, fishing, camping, canoeing, tennis. E-mail: pherberg@aol.com. Home: 7425

W Orchard Grass Blvd Crestwood KY 40014 Office: Ky Pers Cabinet 200 Fair Oaks Ln Ste 517 Frankfort KY 40601

HERBERS, JOAN MARIE, biology educator; b. St. Louis, Sept. 8, 1952; d. Vincent Theodore and Mary Janette (Buescher) H.; m. Thomas G. Gilson, Mar. 26, 1983; children: Emily, David. BS, U. Dayton, 1973; MS, Northwestern U., 1974, PhD, 1978; postgrad., Stanford U., 1978-79. Asst. prof. U. Vt., Burlington, 1979-85, assoc. prof., 1985-90, prof., assoc. dean, 1991-93; prof. biology, chmn. dept. Colo. State U., Ft. Collins, 1993—. Contbr. over 50 articles to sci. jours. Grantee NSF, 1988-89. Mem. Internat. Union for Study Social Insects (pres.-elect N.Am. sect. 1999). Avocations: piano and violin. E-mail: herbers@lamar.colostate.edu.

HERBERS, TOD ARTHUR, publisher; b. Cin., Sept. 11, 1948; s. Walter Fred and Jeanette Ruth (Dalton) H.; m. Suzanne Jeannine Daly, Sept. 7, 1974. B.A., Catholic U. Am., 1970. With Nation's Bus. mag., Washington, 1972-75; promotion dir. Nation's Bus. mag., 1974-75, Washingtonian mag., Washington, 1975-76; circulation and promotion dir., assoc. pub. Washingtonian mag., 1976-77; pub. Am. Film mag., Washington, 1977-82; mng. pub. Science 86 Mag., Washington, 1982-86; pub. Sci. Illustrated Mag., Washington, 1987-89; pres. Jour. NIH Rsch., Washington, 1989-94; pub. On Target Media, Inc., Washington, 1994—. Home: 8428 Holly Leaf Dr Mc Lean VA 22102-2224 Office: On Target Media Inc 1828 L St NW Ste 720 Washington DC 20036-5104

HERBERT, ADAM WILLIAM, JR., chancellor; b. Muskogee, Okla., Dec. 1, 1943; s. Addie (Hibler) H.; m. Karen Y. Lofty, Apr. 1980. BA, U. So. Calif., 1966, MPA, 1967; PhD, U. Pitts., 1971. Instr., asst. prof., coord. acad. programs Ctr. Urban Affairs Sch. Pub. Adminstrn., U. So. Calif., L.A., 1969-72; assoc. prof., chmn. urban affairs program div. environ. and urban systems Va. Poly. Inst. State U., Blacksburg, 1972-75, prof., dir. North Va. programs, Ctr. for Pub. Adminstrn. and Policy, 1978-79; White House fellow, spl. asst. sec. HEW, Washington, 1974-75; spl. asst. to under sec. HUD, Washington, 1975-77; prof., dean Fla. Internat. U., Miami, 1979-87, assoc. v.p. for acad. affairs, chief acad. officer North Miami campus, 1985-88, v.p., chief adminstrv. officer, 1987-88; pres. U. North Fla., Jacksonville, 1988-98; chancellor State Univ. Sys. of Fla., 1998—. Office: State Univ Sys of Fla 325 W Gaines St Ste 1514 Tallahassee FL 32399-1950*

HERBERT, ALBERT EDWARD, JR., interior and industrial designer; b. Detroit, June 12, 1928; s. Albert Edward and Gladys Mae (Speechley) H. Student, Pratt Inst., 1947-50. Owner, operator Albert Herbert Designs, 1957—; designer for V'Soske, Inc. Baker Furniture. Author: (with Roger P. Myers) The Last Survivor, 1976, Killer Pack, 1976; Contbr. articles on design to mags. Served with USAF, 1952-56. Fellow Am. Soc. Interior Designers (life). Home: Fords Colony 142 Blackheath Williamsburg VA 23188

HERBERT, AMANDA KATHRYN, special education educator; b. Cleve., Apr. 10, 1948; d. Ralph Earle and Nina Kathryn (Burkey) Herbert; m. John Davis Reeves, June 26, 1971 (div. 1978). Student, Coll. of Wooster, Ohio, 1966-68; BA, Defiance Coll., 1971; MEd, Lynchburg Coll., 1982. Cert. tchr., Va. Elem. tchr. Napoleon (Ohio) City Schs., 1970-72; substitute tchr. Juvenile Boys Correction Ctr., Maumee, Ohio, 1972-73; Title I reading tchr. Defiance City Schs., 1973-76, tchr. 4th grade, 1976-78; tchr. 4th to 6th grades Platte Valley Schs. RE3, Ovid, Colo., 1978-81; tchr. elem. and secondary spl. edn. Amherst County (Va.) Schs., 1982—; tchr. Camp Little Indian, Defiance, 1967-77. Contbr. to book. Deacon, elder First Presbyn. Ch., Defiance, 1973-78; singer Defiance Community Choir, 1972-77; actor, singer Fine Arts Ctr., Lynchburg, Va., 1983—; mem. choir Parkland United Meth. Ch., Lynchburg, 1982—. Mem. NEA, Coun. for Exceptional Children (div. learning disabilities), Va. Edn. Assn., People to People Citizen Ambassador Program to Peoples' Rep. China, Amherst Edn. Assn., Alpha Chi. Methodist. Avocations: travel, reading, swimming, acting, instrumental and vocal performance. Office: Amherst County High Sch Old Rt 29 Amherst VA 24521

HERBERT, CAROL SELLERS, farming executive, lawyer; b. Durham, N.C., Mar. 2, 1943; d. George Grover and Mae (Savage) Sellers; m. James Keller Herbert, Nov. 13, 1980; children: John, Katherine, Paul, Barry. BA, Duke U., 1964; JD cum laude, Whittier Coll., 1976. Bar: Calif. 1976, U.S. Dist. Ct. (cen. dist.) Calif. 1976. Tchr. h.s. Wasatch Sch. Dist., Heber, Utah, 1964-67; dir., tchr. Pinedale (Mont.) Sch. Dist., 1967-71; adminstr. Whittier Law Sch., L.A., 1971-76; lawyer Katz Granof Palarz, Beverly Hills, Calif., 1976-79; exec. dir. MBJ Legal and Profl. Pub., Inc., L.A., 1979-83; dean San Joaquin Coll. Law, Fresno, Calif., 1981-85; pres., co-founder Barrister Project, L.A., 1985-90, Herbert Found., Fresno and Lindsay, Calif., 1990—; dir., CFO HerCal Corp., Lindsay, Calif.; trustee Domus Mitus Found., Fresno, 1994-96; founder Beverly Hills Bar Assn. Com. on Women and Law, 1977; dir. CLI DreamWeavers Divsn., Lindsay, Calif., 1995; Reiki Master Usui Shiki Ryoho, 1996. Prodr. Lang. of Dreams (video series), 1994-97. Mem. ABA, Calif. Bar Assn.

HERBERT, CHESLEY C., psychiatrist, educator; b. Charlotte, N.C., June 7, 1943; m. Marie Genevieve Groszko, Aug. 10, 1975; Rachel G., Andrew G. AB in History, Duke U., 1961-65; MD, Columbia U., 1965-69. Diplomate Am. Bd. Psychiatry and Neurology; lic. physician and surgeon, Calif., Nat. Bd. Med. Examiners, DEA. Intern Harlem Hosp. Ctr., N.Y.C., 1969-70; resident in psychiatry U. Calif., San Francisco, 1970-73, fellow in social psychiatry, 1973-75; pvt. practice San Francisco, 1973—; asst. clin. prof. psychiatry U. Calif., San Francisco, 1975-83, assoc. clin. prof., 1983—; staff psychiatrist On Lok Sr. Health Svcs., San Francisco, 1980—; cons. Psychopathic divsn. Superior Ct., San Francisco, 1974-78, North of Market Sr. Alcohol Program, San Francisco, 1979-80; psychiatrist srs. unit N.E. Mental Health Ctr., San Francisco, 1975-79; chief divsn. psychiatry and psychology dept. medicine Davies Med. Ctr., San Francisco, 1996-98; mem., active staff, Calif. Pacific Med. Ctr., courtesy staff mem. St. Francis Meml. Hosp., Chinese Hosp. Contbr. articles to profl. jours. Mem. Am. Psychiat. Assn., No. Calif. Psychiat. Soc., Calif. Med. Assn., San Francisco Med. Soc. Office: 45 Castro St Ste 302 San Francisco CA 94114-1010

HERBERT, EDWARD FRANKLIN, public relations executive; b. N.Y.C., Jan. 30, 1946; s. H. Robert and Florence (Bender) H.; m. Rhonda J. Scharf, Aug. 20, 1967; children: Jason Dean and Heather Ann (twins). B.S. in Comm., Syracuse U., 1967, M.S., 1969. Assoc. dir. pub. relations Am. Optometric Assn., Washington, 1971; community relations specialist Gen. Electric Co., Columbia, Md., 1971-73, pub. relations account supr., 1973-75; dir. pub. affairs Nat. Consumer Fin. Assn., Washington, 1975-78; regional dir. pub. relations Montgomery Ward Co., Balt., 1978-80, fin. info. services dir., Chgo., 1980-81, internal comm. dir., 1981-82, corp. comm. dir., 1982-83; regional dir. pub. relations MCI Comm. Corp., Chgo., 1983-84; dir. comm. MCI Midwest, MCI Telecom. Corp., 1985-93; prin. Edward F. Herbert & Assoc., 1993—; Bd. dirs. United Cerebral Palsy of Chgo., Better Bus. Bur. Served with U.S. Army, 1969-71. Mem. Pub. Relations Soc. Am., Execs. Club of Chgo., Info. Industry Council. Home and Office: 830 Timberhill Ln Highland Park IL 60035-5121

HERBERT, GAVIN SHEARER, health care products company executive; b. L.A., Mar. 26, 1932; s. Gavin and Josephine (D'Vitha) H.; children by previous marriage Cynthia, Lauri, Gavin, Pam; 2d. m. Ninetta Flanagan, Sept. 6, 1986. B.S., U. So. Calif., 1954. With Allergan, Inc., Irvine, Calif., 1950—, v.p., 1956-61, exec. v.p., pres., 1961-77, chmn. bd., CEO, 1977-91, chmn. bd., 1992-95, chmn. emeritus; pres. Eye and Skin Care Products Group Smith Kline Beckman Corp., 1981-89; exec. v.p. Smith Kline Beckman Corp., 1986-89; bd. dirs. Beckman Instruments, Inc., Calif. Healthcare Inst. Mem. Rsch. to Prevent Blindness (bd. dirs.), Big Canyon Country Club, Newport Harbor Yacht Club, Pacific Club, Beta Theta Pi. Republican. Office: Allergan Inc PO Box 19534 2525 Dupont Dr Irvine CA 92612-1599*

HERBERT, JAMES ALAN, writer; b. Burlington, Vt., July 29, 1945; s. Alan Wells and Rose Marion H.; m. Martha Lebedzinski, June 20, 1976 (div. 1983); children: Denise M., Jeni Ayn; m. Margaret Harris, Oct. 20, 1992; 1 child: Alicia Ayn. Student, Wittenberg U., Springfield, Ohio, 1963-65, SUNY, Buffalo, 1986, Niagara U., 1991. McLean Trucking Co., 1969-86; Author, 1986—. Author: The Third Testament, 1988, Rock and Roll Politics, 1992. Committeeman Conservative Party, N.Y., 1971; pub. rels. Vietnam Vets. of Am., 1989-91. Served to cpl. USMC, 1966-69, Vietnam. Recipient conspicuous svc. award State of N.Y., 1991. Mem. Toastmasters Internat. (treas. Buffalo chpt. 1988-90), Niagara Falls Transp. Club, Buffalo Transp. Club. Avocations: boating, golf, swimming. Office: PO Box 83 North Boston NY 14110-0083

HERBERT, JAMES ARTHUR, artist, filmmaker; b. Boston, Feb. 13, 1938; s. James Arthur and Bernice Frances (Burns) H. A.B. magna cum laude, Dartmouth Coll., 1960; M.F.A., U. Colo., 1962. Instr. U. Colo., 1962; artist-in-residence Yale Summer Sch. Art and Music, 1965; mem. faculty dept. art U. Ga., Athens, 1962—; prof. U. Ga., 1973—, rsch. prof., 1992—. One-man shows, Babcock Galleries, N.Y.C., 1967, U. Colo., Boulder, 1972, Poindexter Gallery, N.Y.C., 1972, 73, 74, 76, Mus. Modern Art, N.Y.C., 1970, 72, 74, 77, 81, 88, Mus. Modern Art, 1994, 98, Walker Art Ctr., Mpls., 1973, 82, Harvard U., 1973, High Mus. Art, Atlanta, 1979, Kennedy Ctr., Washington, 1981, Libr. of Congress, Washington, 1983—, Museu Tropical, Lisbon, Portugal, 1993, Art Gallery Toronto Can., 1994, Oberhausen Internat. Film Festival, Germany, 1999, Brit. Coun., Cologne, Germany, 1999, Film Mus. Munich, 1999; group shows include Krannert Art Mus., Urbana, Ill., 1974, New Orleans Mus. Art, 1975, 80, 89, Whitney Mus. Am. Art, 1969, 73, 74, 83, Westdeutsche Kurzfilmtage, Oberhausen, W. Ger., 1970, 72, 89, 92, La Cinémathèque Royale de Belgique, Knokke-Heist, Belgium, 1974-75, Mus. Modern Art, 1979, P.S. 1, N.Y.C., 1979, Stedelijk Mus., Amsterdam, 1982, Kennedy Ctr., Washington, 1983, Monique Knowlton Gallery, N.Y.C., 1983, IRCAM, Pompidou Ctr., Beaubourg, France, 1984, Cinémateque Française, Beaubourg, 1985, Bibliotheque Nat., Avignon, France, 1985, Mus. Modern Art, N.Y.C., 1986, 91, Los Angeles County Mus. Art, 1988, Carnegie-Mellon U. Art Gallery, Pitts., 1988, Va. Mus. Fine Art, Richmond, Va., 1988, Southeastern Ctr. for Contemporary Art, Winston-Salem, N.C., 1988, Corcoran Gallery of Art, Washington, 1989, Kuznetsky Most Exhbn. Hall, Moscow, 1989, Art Gallery of Ont., 1989, Long Beach Mus. Art, Calif., 1989, 91, Norton Galley Art, Palm Beach, 1989, Sheridan Opera House, Telluride, Colo., 1989, 91, 93, Mus. Fine Arts, Boston, 1990, Art Inst., Chgo., 1990, Pacific Film Archive, Berkeley, Calif., 1991, Walker Art Ctr., Mpls., 1991, Sundance theatre, Park City, Utah, 1992, Melbourne Internat. Film Theatre, Australia, 1992, European Media Art Theatre, Osnabrück, Germany, 1992, Toronto (Can.) Film Festival Theatre, 1992, N.Y. Film Festival at Lincoln Ctr., 1992, Inst. de Estadios Norteamericanos, Barcelona, Spain, 1992, Eldorado Theatre, Royal Palace, Antwerp, Belgium, 1993, Odense (Denmark) Internat. Film Theater, 1993, Fifth Media Festival Theatre, Hertogenbosch, Netherlands, 1993, Vienna Shortfilm Mus., Antwerp (Belgium) Sinema festival Theatre, 1993, Rio Internat. Festival Hall, Rio de Janiero, Brazil, 1993, Melbourne (Australia) Internat. Film Mus., 1992, Sydney (Australia) Internat. Film Mus., 1994, Vherskě Hradiště, Czech Republic, 1994, Kunstencentrum, Leuveen, Netherlands, Gaumont Marignan Theater, Paris, 1995, Toronto Internat. Film Festival Theater, 1997, Toronto Internat. Film Festival, 1997, 99, Sundance Film Festival Theater, Park City, Utah, 1998, 99, Rotterdam Internat. Film Festival, The Netherlands, 1998, 99, Mus. Nat. Ctr. de Arte Reina Sofia, Madrid, Spain; represented in permanent collections, N.Y. U., Am. Fedn. Arts, Royal Film Archives Belgium, Centre Beaubourg, Paris, Mus. Modern Art, Whitney Mus. Am. Art, Cornell U., Am. Film Inst., Chase Manhattan Bank, Coca Cola USA, Herbert F. Johnson Mus. Art at Cornell U., Walker Art Ctr., Mlps.; author:Stills: Photographs by James Herbert, 1992. Recipient Awards in the Visual Arts, Rockefeller Found., 1987; Woodrow Wilson fellow, 1960-62, Guggenheim Found. fellow, 1971-72, 89-90; grantee Am. Film Inst., 1969, Nat. Endowment Arts, 1975, 78, 81, 82, Louis Comfort Tiffany Found., 1980, Rockefeller Found., 1993; commn. Libr. of Congress, 1983, Adolph and Esther Gottlieb Found., 1991. Office: Univ Ga Art Dept Athens GA 30602

HERBERT, JAMES CHARLES, education executive; b. Dayton, Ohio, Nov. 22, 1941; s. Charles August and Helen Louise (Korte) H.; m. Sandra Lynn Swanson, June 4, 1966; children: Kristen, Sonja. BA, U. Dayton, 1963; MA, Brandeis U., 1965, PhD in History of Ideas, 1970. Instr. history Cath. U. Am., Washington, 1967-69; asst. prof. history and philosophy U. D.C., Washington, 1971-73; asst. prof. gen. honors program U. Md., College Park, 1973-79; Am. Coun. on Edn. fellow U.S. Dept. Edn., Washington, 1979-80; dir. governance study Carnegie Found. for Advancement Teaching, Washington, 1980-82; dir. acad. rels. Coll. Bd., N.Y.C., 1982-84, exec. dir. acad. affairs, 1984-89; dir. edn. programs NEH, Washington, 1989-95; dir. rsch. and edn. programs NEH, 1995-99; mem. Nat. Performance Review, Office of V.P. of U.S., 1993; vis. rsch. scholar Inst. for Philosophy and Pub. Policy, U. Md., 1998-99. Gen. editor Academic Preparation Series, 6 vols., 1985-86; editor, writer: Academic Preparation for College, 1983; writer: Control of the Campus, 1982. GM scholar, 1959-63, NDEA fellow, 1963-66, Folger Shakespeare Libr. fellow, 1971, Am. Coun. on Edn. fellow, 1979-80. Mem. Am. Assn. for Higher Edn., AAUP, Nat. Collegiate Honors Coun. (exec. com. 1978-80, 81-84, pres. N.E. region 1978-79). Avocations: writing, swimming, travel, gardening. Office: NEH 1100 Pennsylvania Ave NW Washington DC 20004-2501

HERBERT, LEROY JAMES, retired accounting firm executive; b. Long Branch, N.J., Aug. 3, 1923; s. LeRoy J. and Edna Hazel (Keller) H. BS, U. Md., 1950. CPA, N.J., N.Y., Ohio, Tenn., La., N.C., Va.; chartered acct. South Africa. Profl. staff mem. Ernst & Ernst, Balt., 1950-58, asst. mgr., 1958-60; mgr. internat. ops. Ernst & Ernst, N.Y.C., 1960-63, ptnr., 1963-67; sr. U.S. ptnr. Whinney Murray Ernst & Ernst, London and Paris, 1967-70; ptnr. in charge internat. ops. N.Y.C., 1970-78; internat. exec. ptnr. Ernst & Whinney Internat., N.Y.C., 1979-83. Bd. dirs. U. Md. Found., St. Barnabas Health Care Sys.; past chmn. Monmouth Med. Ctr., Long Branch, N.J. With U.S. Army, 1942-46. Recipient Disting. Alumnus award U. Md. Coll. Bus. and Mgmt., 1980, Disting. Acctg. Alumnus award, 1991; named to Long Branch H.S. Disting. Alumni Acad. Hall of Fame, 1996. Mem. AICPA, N.Y. Assn. CPAs, Ohio Assn. CPAs, Md. Assn. CPAs, Transvaal Soc. Accts. (South Africa), Union League, Deal Country Club, Pres.'s Club (U. Md.), Beta Alpha Psi. Episcopalian. Home: Channel Club Tower Monmouth Beach NJ 07750

HERBERT, MARILYNNE, public relations executive, freelance photographer; b. Columbus, Ga., Aug. 12, 1944; d. Herbert Paul and Victoria (Raskin) Gruber; m. Victor Daniel Herbert, June 23, 1968 (div. 1990); children: Alissa, Laura. BA, Colo. Woman's Coll., 1966. Adminstrv. asst. pub. rels. dept. Mt. Sinai Med. Ctr., N.Y.C., 1966-68; freelance photographer N.Y.C., 1977—; sr. account exec. Ruder-Finn, Inc., N.Y.C., 1986-93; dir. pub. rels. Iona Coll., New Rochelle, N.Y., 1993-94; sr. account exec. Coll. Connections Inc., N.Y.C., 1994-96; sr. mgr. media rels. Halstead Comm., N.Y.C., 1997—; cmty. rels. coord. Osborn Retirement Cmty., 1995—. Bd. dirs. Women of Westchester, White Plains, N.Y., 1977—, Byrdcliffe Performing Arts Orgn., New Rochelle, 1987-91, Nat. Women's Polit. Caucus, Westchester County, 1988—, Sr. Pers. Placement Bur., Inc., 1989-92; bd. dirs., sec. New Rochelle Cmty. Fund, 1986-91. Recipient Spl. Recognition award Nat. Women's Polit. Caucus, 1989. Mem. Am. Soc. Mag. Photographers, Assn. for Women in Comm., Lake Katonah Club (bd. govs. 1995-98). Jewish. Home: 77 Upper Lake Shore Dr Katonah NY 10536-2646

HERBERT, MARY KATHERINE ATWELL, freelance writer; b. Grove City, Pa., Dec. 9, 1945; d. Stewart and Luella Irene (Brown) Atwell; m. Roland Marcus Herbert; children: Stephen Todd, Amy Elizabeth, Jill Anne. BA, Ariz. State U., 1968, MA, 1973; film cert., U. So. Calif., 1978. Film writer Scottsdale Daily Progress, 1976-79; dir. pub. relations Phoenix Theatre, 1980-85; script analyst, 1985-86; exec. asst. to v.p. prodn. De Laurentiis Entertainment Group, 1986; producer's assoc. film TRAXX, 1986-87; dir. of devel. Devin/DeVore Prodns., 1988-89; free-lance script analyst and writer Glendale, Calif., 1989-97. Script writer: (TV shows) Trial By Jury, Dick Clark Prodn., (feature films) Dry Heat, Blind Desire, others; author: Writing Scripts Hollywood Will Love, 1994, Selling Scripts to Hollywood, 1998. bd. mgrs. Hollywood-Wilshire YMCA, 1992-96. Mem. Ariz. Forum, Kappa Delta Pi, Pi Lambda Theta.

HERBERT, PETER NOEL, physician, medical educator; b. Troy, N.Y., Dec. 8, 1941; s. Martin James and Delia (Mangan) H.; m. Maureen Anne Darretta, Aug. 5, 1969; children—Tara, Kiki, Garth, Luke. B.S., Rensselaer Poly. Inst., Troy, N.Y., 1963; M.D., Yale U., 1967. Intern Yale-New Haven Hosp., 1967-68, resident, 1968-69; chief sect. on lipoprotein structure Nat. Heart, Lung and Blood Inst. NIH, Bethesda, Md., 1973-77; assoc. prof. Brown U., Providence, 1977-83, prof., 1983-91; chief div. nutrition and metabolism Miriam Hosp., Providence, 1977-90; chmn. dept. medicine Hosp. St. Raphael, New Haven, 1990—; clin. prof. medicine Sch. Medicine, Yale U., 1991—; program dir., nutrition ctr. Brown U. Gen. Clin. Rsch. Ctr., 1983-85, assoc. program dir., 1985-90; adj. prof. medicine Brown U., 1991—. Contbr. articles to profl. jours. Fellow ACP, Am. Heart Assn. (dir. R.I. chpt. 1978—, chmn. research com.), Soc. Behavioral Medicine, Am. Coll. of Nutrition, Am. Fedn. Clin. Research, Am. Soc. Clin. Investigation, Council on Epidemiology of Am. Heart Assn. Roman Catholic. Home: 57 Island View Ave Branford CT 06405-5629 Office: Office of St Raphael 1450 Chapel St New Haven CT 06511-4405

HERBERT, ROBERT LOUIS, art history educator; b. Worcester, Mass., Apr. 21, 1929; married; 3 children. BA, Wesleyan U., 1951; MA, Yale U., 1954, PhD, 1957. Instr. Yale U., New Haven, 1956-60, asst. prof., 1960-63, assoc. prof., 1963-66, prof., 1966-74, Robert Lehman prof. history of art, 1974—, chmn. dept., 1965-68; now Andrew W. Mellon prof. of humanities, emeritus Mount Holyoke Coll., South Hadley, Mass. Author: Barbizon Revisited, 1962, The Art Criticism of John Ruskin, 1964, Modern Artists on Art, 1964, Neo-impressionists and Nabis in the Collection of Arthur G. Altschul, 1965, Neo-impressionism, 1968, David, Voltaire, Brutus and the French Revolution, 1972, J.F. Millet, 1975, Impressionism: Art, Leisure and Parisian Society, 1989, Seurat, 1991, Monet on the Normandy Coast, 1994, Peasants and "Primitism:" French Prints from Millet to Gauguin, 1995; contbr. articles to profl. jours., chpts. to books. Decorated Officier de l'Ordre des Arts et des Lettres (France); recipient Frank Jewett Mather award Coll. Art Assn., 1963, Disting. Teaching of Art History award, 1982; Am. Coun. Learned Soc. grantee-in-aid, Paris, 1960; Morse fellow from Yale, London and Paris, 1960-61, Guggenheim fellow, 1971-72, Rockefeller Found. Humanities fellow, 1986. Mem. Am. Acad. Arts and Scis., Am. Philos. Soc. Office: Mt Holyoke Coll Dept Art South Hadley MA 01075

HERBERT, STEPHEN W., hospital executive; b. Montreal, Aug. 18, 1941; s. Theodore Herbert and Mary (Rothstein) Spector; m. Marcia Maislin, Feb. 7, 1982; children: Michele, Robbie. B.S., McGill U., 1963; M.H.A., U. Ottawa, 1968. With adminstrn. and paramed. depts. Hôpital de l'Est, Montreal, 1960-62; bus. mgr. Bayview Enterprises Inc., Montreal, 1963-64; personnel dir. Lakeshore Gen. Hosp., Pointe Claire, Que., Can., 1964-66; adminstrv. resident Hamilton Civic Hosps., Ont., Can., 1967-68; assoc. exec. dir. diagnostic and support services McMaster U. Med. Ctr., Hamilton, 1968-77; dir. patient, diagnostic, therapeutic and support services Royal Victoria Hosp., Montreal, 1977-78, pres., 1978-88; pres. Meditron Corp., Montreal, 1988-90; pres., chief exec. officer Baycrest Centre for Geriatic Care, North York, Ont., 1990—; assoc. prof. dept. health adminstrn. U. Toronto, Ont., 1991—; faculty Sch. Health Adminstrn., U. Ottawa, Ont., Can., part-time 1969-77, adj. prof. adminstrn., 1984-88; asst. prof. epidemiology and biostats. McGill U., 1981-86, assoc. prof., 1986-88, adj. prof. 1988, assoc. dean health care planning med. faculty, 1986-88; pres., bd. dirs. Royal Victoria Hosp. Found., Montreal, 1978-88; bd. dirs. Baycrest Centre, Baycrest Centre Foun., Met. Toronto Hosp. Coun., Canabec Health Svcs. Consulting, No. Am. Assn. Jewish Homes and Housing for the Aged; chmn. Region 3 Ont. Hosp. Assn., bd. dirs. Regional Geriatric Program, Nat. Chronic Care Consortium, Ont. Coun. Tchng. Hosps., Toronto Acad. Health Scis. Ctr.; former bd. dirs. A.M.I. Advancement Fund, Royal Victoria Hosp. Ctr., Sogec-Sante (Can.) Inc., Sogec-Lavalin Inc., Physiotherapie Hochelaga Inc, Syscor, Montreal Joint Hosp. Inst., RVH Kidney Fund, Cedars Cancer Fund; internat. fellow King's Fund Coll., London, 1988-94, med. sci. Dept. Medicine Royal Victoria Hosp., 1986, assoc. prof. Dept. Health Adminstrn. U. Toronto; chmn. Healthnet North; lectr. in field. Active Metro Toronto dist. Health Coun. Long Term Care Com.; dir. Hosp. Coun. Met. Toronto. Recipient Gov. Spl. medal 125th Ann. Confedn. Can., 1993. Mem. Assn. Can. Teaching Hosps. (past pres.), Assn. des Directeurs generaux des services de santé et des services sociaux du Quebec, Am. Hosp. Assn., Am. Pub. Health Assn., Am. Acad. Med. Adminstrn., Can. Coll. Health Service Execs. (Robert Wood Johnson award, Extendicare award), Can. Pub. Health Assn., Internat. Hosp. Fedn., Young Pres.'s Orgn. Northeast Can./Am. Health Council, Can. Health Econs. Assn., Centre Medicine, Ethics, Law, McGill U., Can. Hosp. Assn. (expert working group-econ., costs, funding), Ont. Hosp. Assn. (regional coun. exec. com.), Hosp. Coun. Met. Toronto (strategic issues com.), Toronto Acad. Health Sci. Coun., Internat. Health Econs. Mgmt. Assn., Internat. Health Policy and Mgmt. Inst., Inst. Health Svcs. Mgmt., Met. Toronto Dist. Health Coun. (priority and planning com., rsch., edn. and health industry sub-com, long term care steering com, resource allocation work group, hosp. mgmt. rsch. unit external adv. counc.), Regional Geriatric Prog. Mgmt. Coun., Royal Soc. Health, Toronto Jewish Fedn., World President's Orgn. Home: 1166 Bay St #504, Toronto, ON Canada M5S 2X8

HERBERT, VICTOR DANIEL, medical educator; b. N.Y.C., Feb. 22, 1927; s. Allan Charles and Rosaline (Margolis) H.; children from previous marriages: Robert, Steven, Kathy, Alissa, Laura. BS in Chemistry, Columbia U., 1948, MD, 1952, JD, 1974. Intern Walter Reed Army Med. Ctr., Washington, 1952-53; resident Montefiore Hosp., Bronx, N.Y., 1954-55; asst. instr., rsch. fellow Albert Einstein Coll. of Medicine, Bronx, 1955-57; rsch. asst. in hematology Mt. Sinai Hosp., N.Y.C., 1958-59; from instr. to asst. prof. Harvard U. Thorndike Lab., Boston, 1959-64; assoc. prof., prof. pathology and medicine Columbia U., N.Y.C., 1964-72; prof. medicine Mt. Sinai Sch. Medicine, N.Y.C., 1964—; prof., asst. chair of medicine SUNY Downstate Med. Ctr., Bklyn., 1976-84; chief hematology & nutrition rsch. lab. Bronx Vets. Affairs Med. Ctr., 1970—; chmn. medicine Hahnemann U. Sch. Medicine and Med. Ctr., Phila., 1984-85; prof. medicine, chair com. to strenghthen nutrition Mt. Sinai Sch. Medicine, N.Y.C., 1985—. Author: Nutrition Cultism: Facts & Fictions, 1981; co-author: Vitamins & Health Food: The Great American Hustle, 1981, Genetic Nutrition: Designing a Diet Based on Your Family Medical History, 1993 (republished, retitled The Healing Diet 1995), The Vitamin Pushers: How the Health Food Industry is Selling America A Bill of Goods, 1994; editor, author: The Mount Sinai School of Medicine Complete Book of Nutrition, 1990, Total Nutrition: The Only Guide You'll Ever Need: From the Mount Sinai Sch. Medicine, 1995; contbr. more than 800 articles to profl. jours. Lt. col. U.S. Army, ETO, 1944-46, Korea, 1952-54, Vietnam, 1965, 66, 73, Mid. East. 1990-91. Recipient Middleton award U.S. Dept. Vets. Affairs, 1978, Commr.'s Citation, FDA, 1984. Fellow ACP (master); mem. Am. Soc. Hematology (Parliamentarian 1975—), Am. Fedn. Clin. Research, Am. Soc. Clin. Investigation, Assn. Am. Physicians, Am. Inst. Nutrition (Fellow award 1993), Am. Soc. Clin. Nutrition (pres. 1980-81, Herman award 1986, McCollum award 1972, Van Slyke award 1990). Avocations: theatre, Judo. Office: Mt Sinai Sch of Medicine 130 W Kingsbridge Rd Bronx NY 10468-3992

HERBERT, VICTOR JAMES, foundation administrator; b. Follansbee, W.Va., Aug. 6, 1917; s. Oliver James and Gertrude Mae (Lazear) H.; m. Dorothy Clara Johnson, Sept. 2, 1942; children—Victor J., Dorothy Constance. A.B., Bethany (W.Va.) Coll., 1940. Adminstr., negotiator, airline employee orgns.; a founder Air Line Stewards and Stewardesses Assn., Internat., 1946, acting pres., 1946-51, asst. to pres., 1951-59; in charge edn. and orgn. dept. Air Line Pilots Assn. A.F.L., 1946-62; pres. Airline Employees Assn. Editor: Air Line Employee. Pres. bd. dirs. Bus. Indsl. Ministry. Mem. Beta Theta Pi. Presbyn. Club: Mason. Home: 14730 Greenview Rd Orland Park IL 60462 Office: Air Line Employees Assn Internat 6500 W 65th St Ste 201 Chicago IL 60638

HERBERT, WILLIAM CARLISLE, lawyer; b. Gainesville, Fla., Aug. 25, 1947; s. Thomas Walter and Jean Elizabeth (Linton) H.; m. Mary Lee Dedinsky. *In 1692, John Tilton, Jr., of Gravesend, Long Island, sold his house to Coert Stephense (Voorhees) of nearby New Amersfoort and moved to New Jersey. John and Coert became in-laws 244 years later, when Carlisle's parents were married. A descendant of Methodist ministers in South Carolina, Carlisle's father became a Distinguished Service Professor (English) at the University of Florida. A native of Philadelphia, Pa., Carlisle's mother formed the first racially integrated organization in Gainesville, Fla. Their children are T. Walter Herbert, Jr., a professor of English, Dr. M. Linton Herbert, a radiologist, and Carlisle.* AB, Princeton U., 1969; MSJ, Northwestern U., 1970, JD cum laude, 1976. Bar: Ill. 1976, U.S. Ct. Appeals (7th cir.) 1977, Fla. 1978, U.S. Dist. Ct. (no. dist.) Ill. 1978, U.S.

Supreme Ct. 1980, U.S. Tax Ct. 1982. Law clk. to Hon. Latham Castle U.S. Ct. Appeals (7th cir.), 1976-77; ptnr. Hopkins & Sutter, Chgo. *Carlisle developed and successfully defended a method, based on common law principles, of achieving nationwide settlement of claims against state life insurance guaranty associations.* Exec. editor Northwestern U. Law Rev., 1976. Mem. ABA, Ill. State Bar Assn., Fla. Bar, Chgo. Bar Assn., Legal Club Chgo., U. Club Chgo. Presbyterian. Office: Hopkins & Sutter 3 1st Nat Plz Chicago IL 60602

HERBERT ROSE, KATHY LYNNE, lawyer; b. Great Neck, N.Y., Mar. 18, 1959; d. Victor Daniel Herbert and Jacqueline Lois (Lubin) Edelstein. BA in Psychology, Brandeis U., 1980; JD, Columbia U., 1983. Bar: N.Y. 1984, Conn. 1995. Assoc. Simpson Thacher & Bartlett, N.Y.C., 1983-88; sr. v.p./gen. counsel Creditanstalt-Bankverein, N.Y.C., 1988-98, Bank Austria, 1998—; mem. Internat. Bank Regulatory Compliance Com., 1994. Mem. ABA, Inst. Internat. Bankers (lawyers divsn., mem. legis. and regulatory com.), N.Y. State Bar Assn. (vol. elderly project lifetime planning 1992—), Bar City N.Y. (mem. com. Ea. Europe 1992-94, mem. com. banking 1996—, Robert McKay cmty. outreach program 1993, 94). Office: Bank Austria 245 Park Ave Fl 32 New York NY 10167-0002

HERBIG, GEORGE HOWARD, astronomer, educator; b. Wheeling, W.Va., Jan. 2, 1920; s. George Albert and Glenna (Howard) H.; m. Delia Faye McMullin, Oct., 1943 (div. 1968); children: Marilyn, Lawrence, John, Robert; m. Hannelore Helene Tillmann, Sept. 3, 1968. AB, UCLA, 1943; PhD, U. Calif., Berkeley, 1948. From jr. astronomer to assoc. astronomer Lick Obs., U. Calif., Mt. Hamilton, 1948-60, astronomer, 1960-67; prof. astronomy U. Calif., Santa Cruz, 1967-87; astronomer Inst. for Astronomy, U. Hawaii, 1987—; asst. dir. Lick Obs., 1960-63, acting dir., 1970-71. Editor: Non-Stable Stars, 1955, Spectroscopic Astrophysics, 1970; author over 230 sci. papers, articles, revs. Martin Kellogg fellow U. Calif., Berkeley, 1946-48, NRC fellow Pasadena and U. Chgo., 1948-49, Washington, 1948-49; recipient Medaille U. de Liège, Belgium, 1970, Catherine Wolfe Bruce Gold medal Astron. Soc. Pacific, 1980, Petrie prize and lecture Can. Astron. Soc., 1995. Fellow Am. Acad. Arts and Scis; mem. Nat. Acad. Scis., Internat. Astron. Union, Am. Astron. Soc. (Warner prize 1955, Henry Norris Russell lectr. 1975), Max Planck Inst. für Astronomie (fgn. sci. mem.), Soc. Royale des Scis. de Liège (corr.). Democrat. Office: U Hawaii Inst for Astronomy 2680 Woodlawn Dr Honolulu HI 96822-1839

HERBIG, GÜNTHER, conductor; b. Aussig, Germany, Nov. 30, 1931; s. Emil and Gisela (Hieke) H.; diploma Franz-Liszt-Hochschule, Weimar, Germany, 1956; m. Jutta Czapski, Oct. 30, 1958; children: Beate, Thomas. Mus. asst. Erfurt Theatre, 1956-57; condr. Deutsches Nat. Theatre, Weimar, 1957-62; prin. condr. Potsdam (Ger.) Theatre, 1962-66; condr. Berliner Sinfonie-Orchester, Berlin, 1966-72, chief condr., artistic dir., 1977-83; chief condr., artistic dir. Dresden (Ger.) Philharmonic Orchester, 1972-77; prin. guest condr. Dallas Symphony Orch., 1979-81; prin. guest condr. BBC Philharm., 1982-85; music dir. Detroit Symphony Orch., 1984-90; artistic advisor Toronto Symphony Orch., 1988, music dir., 1988-94. Recipient Theodor Fontane Arts prize, 1964; German Dem. Republic Arts prize, 1970; Nat. prize German Dem. Republic, 1977. Roman Catholic.

HERBLOCK See BLOCK, HERBERT LAWRENCE

HERBOLD, ROBERT J., communications company executive. Exec. v.p., COO, Microsoft Corp, Redmond, Wa. Office: Microsoft Corp One Microsoft Way Redmond WA 98052-6399*

HERBRUCKS, STEPHEN, food products executive; b. 1950; s. Harry Herbrucks. Pres. Herbruck Poultry Ranch Inc., Saranac, Mich., Poultry Mgmt. Systems, Saranac, Mich., 1980—. Office: Herbruck Poultry Ranch Inc 6425 Grand River W Ave Saranac MI 48881-9669*

HERBST, ARTHUR LEE, obstetrician, gynecologist; b. N.Y.C., Sept. 14, 1931; s. Jerome Richard and Blanche (Vatz) H.; m. Lee Ginsburg, Aug. 10, 1958. A.B. magna cum laude, Harvard Coll., 1953, M.D. cum laude, 1959. Diplomate Am. Bd. Ob-gyn. (bd. dirs. 1985-93, dir. div. gynecol. oncology 1989-91). Intern Mass. Gen. Hosp., Boston, 1959-60; resident Mass. Gen. Hosp., 1960-62; resident in obstetrics and gynecology Boston Hosp. for Women, 1962-65; instr., assoc. prof. obstetrics-gynecology Mass. Gen. Hosp. and Harvard U. Med. Sch., Boston, 1965-76; Joseph B. DeLee prof. obstetrics and gynecology U. Chgo., 1976-84; chmn. dept. obstetrics-gynecology Chgo. Lying In Hosp., 1976—; Joseph B. DeLee Disting. Service prof. U. Chgo., 1984—; chmn. exec. com. U. Chgo. Hosps. and Clinics, 1980-84. Mem. editorial bd. Jour. Gynecol. Oncology; contbr. articles to profl. jours. Fellow Royal Coll. Obstetricians and Gynecologists (hon.), Inst. Med., Nat. Acad. Scis.; mem. AMA, ACS, ACOG, Am. Gynecol. and Obstet. Soc. (pres. 1997-98), Am. Assn. Profs. Ob-Gyn., Ctrl. Assn. Obstetricians and Gynecologists, Chgo. Gynecologic Soc., Soc. Pelvic Surgeons, Endocrine Soc., Infertility Soc., Soc. Gynecologic Oncologists. Home: 1234 N State Pky Chicago IL 60610-2219 Office: U Chgo Med Ctr 5841 S Maryland Ave Chicago IL 60637-1463

HERBST, EDWARD IAN, brokerage firm executive; b. N.Y.C., Aug. 22, 1945; s. Samuel B. and Grace Ann (Ballin) H.; m. Lois Gabbe (div. 1983); children: Sandra, Brian. AB, George Washington U., 1967; MBA, NYU, 1970. Corp. 1st v.p. Drexel Burnham Lambert, N.Y.C., 1970-83; mng. dir. Cowen & Co., N.Y.C., 1983—; now mng. dir. SG Cowen Securities Corp., N.Y.C.; mem. Chgo. Bd. Trade; mem. nominating com. for bd. govs. Am. Stock Exch., N.Y.C., 1991—; mem. nominating com. for bd. dirs. Options Clearing Corp., N.Y.C., 1991—; mem. permanent faculty com. on continuing edn. Am. Law Inst., N.Y.C., 1986—, AICPA, N.Y.C., 1986—. Chmn. Young Dem. Party, Harrison, N.Y., 1961-63; bd. dirs. Westchester Shore Humane Soc., White Plains, N.Y., 1970-74, George Washington U. Nat. Coun. for Arts and Scis., 1995—; Am. Italian Found. for Cancer Rsch., 1993—; bd. trustees Second Stage, 1991—. Mem. Securities Industry Assn. (com. on options and derivative products 1982-84), Metropolis Country Club (White Plains). Avocations: photography, antique cars. Office: SG Cowen Securities Corp Financial Sq # 27 New York NY 10005*

HERBST, ERIC, physicist, astronomer; b. N.Y.C., Jan. 15, 1946; s. Stuart Karl and Dorothy (Polakoff) H.; m. Judith Strassman, Oct. 15, 1972; children: Elisabeth, Andrea, Seth. AB, U. Rochester, 1966; MA, Harvard U., 1969, PhD, 1972. Asst. prof. chemistry Coll. of William and Mary, Williamsburg, Va., 1974-79, assoc. prof.chemistry, 1979-80; assoc. prof. physics Duke U., Durham, N.C., 1980-86, prof. physics, 1986-91; prof. physics Univ. zu Köln, Cologne, Germany, 1988-89; prof. physics Ohio State U., Columbus, 1991—, prof. astronomy, 1992—; cons. NASA, Washington, 1985-90, NSF, Washington, 1989-92. Contbr. over 190 articles and 25 revs. to profl. jours. Recipient Humboldt award Humboldt Found., 1988, Max Planck prize Max Planck Soc., 1993. Mem. Am. Astron. Soc., Am. Chem. Soc., Am. Phys. Soc., Sigma Xi. Achievements include theory of how organic molecules are formed in space; theory of floppy molecules. Office: Ohio State U Dept Physics 174 W 18th Ave Columbus OH 43210-1106

HERBST, JAN FRANCIS, physicist, researcher; b. Tucson, May 1, 1947; s. Alva and Frances Theresa (Feler) H.; m. Margaret Mae Priest, July 24, 1982; children: Helen, John, Mary. BA in Physics, U. Pa., 1968, MS, 1968; PhD, Cornell U., 1974. Postdoctoral rsch. assoc. Nat. Bur. Standards, Gaithersburg, Md., 1974-76; asst. physicist Brookhaven Nat. Lab., Upton, N.Y., 1976-77; assoc. sr. rsch. physicist GM Rsch. Labs., Warren, Mich., 1977-81, staff rsch. scientist, 1981-85, mgr. magnetic materials sect., 1984—, sr. staff rsch. scientist, 1985-93, prin. rsch. scientist, 1993—; mem. basic energy sis. adv. com. Dept. Energy, 1995—. Contbr. more than 85 articles to profl. jours.; patentee in field. Recipient Campbell award GM Rsch. Labs., 1983, McCuen award GM Rsch. Labs., 1987, Kettering award GM Corp., 1987. Fellow Am. Phys. Soc. (sec.-treas. div. condensed matter physics 1985-90, Internat. prize for new materials 1986). Avocations: reading, numismatics. Office: GM R & D Ctr MC 480-106-224 30500 Mound Rd Warren MI 48090-9055

HERBST, JURGEN, history and education educator; b. Braunschweig, Germany, Feb. 22, 1928; came to U.S., 1954, naturalized, 1957; s. Hermann and Annemarie (Otto) H.; m. Susan Lou Allen, Sept. 16, 1951; children—Christian, Annemarie, Stephanie. Student, U. Gottingen, 1947-48; B.A., U. Nebr., 1950; M.A., U. Minn., 1952; Ph.D., Harvard U., 1958. Instr. edn. and history Wesleyan U., Middletown, Conn., 1958-59; asst. prof. Wesleyan U., 1959-65, asso. prof., 1965-66; assoc. prof. ednl. policy studies and history U. Wis., 1966-69, prof., 1969-94, prof. emeritus, 1994—. Author: The German Historical School in American Scholarship, 1965, The History of American Education, 1973, From Crisis to Crisis: American College Government, 1636-1819, 1982, And Sadly Teach: Teacher Education and Professionalization in American Culture, 1989, The Once and Future School: 350 Years of American Secondary Education, 1996, Requiem for a German Past: A Boyhood among the Nazis, 1999; editor: Our Country, 1963, History of Elementary School Teaching Curriculum, 1990, Aspects of Antiquity in the History of Education, 1992, German Influences on Education in the United States to 1917, 1995, Mutual Influences on Education: Germany and the United States in the Twentieth Century, 1997. Am. Coun. Learned Socs. grantee, 1960; Fulbright Commn. grantee, 1963, 81; Nat. Endowment for Humanities grantee, 1972-73; Nat. Inst. Edn. grantee, 1973-76; Internat. Research and Exchanges Bd. grantee, 1977; Guggenheim Found. grantee, 1978-79; Wis. Inst. Research in Humanities grantee, 1978-79; Spencer Found. grantee, 1986, 99. Mem. Nat. Acad. Edn., Am. Hist. Assn., Orgn. Am. Historians, History of Edn. Soc. Historische Kommission der Deutschen Gesellschaft für Erziehungswissenschaft, Internat. Standing Conf. for the History of Edn. (mem. exec. com., pres. 1988-91). Democrat.

HERBST, MARIE ANTOINETTE, former state senator; m. Paul Herbst. BA, Albany State Tchr.'s Coll.; Masters, Columbia U.; postgrad. secondary sch. adminstrn., U. Conn. Pub. sch. tchr. East Windsor, Conn.; mem., asst. majority leader Conn. State Senate from 35th Dist.; 7th-9th grade tchr. E.W. H.S.; town councilor, 1994—; chmn. pub. safety com.; asst. minority leader, 1989-92; mem. fin., revenue, bonding com., 1989; mem. edn. com. Lector Sacred Heart Ch.; past chmn. H.S. DDC; past mem. Ladies of Sacred Heart; past mem. Tri-Town Disabled Com., Vernon Town Coun., 1975-79; past mem. Vernon Bd. Edn.; mem. Adult Edn. Adv. Commn., 1985; active New Rockville Youth Studies, 1995—; activities corporator Rockville Cen. Hosp., 1994—; bd. dirs. Tolland Health Inc., Hockarum Valley Cmty. Coun., 1995; apptd. to Vernon Town Coun., 1995; elected dep. mayor to Vernon Town Coun., 1995. Mem. Internat. Edn. Assn., Nat. Edn. Assn., Conn. Edn. Assn., Phi Delta Kappa, Gamma Kappa Rho. Democrat. Roman Catholic. Home: 245 Brandy Hill Rd Vernon Rockville CT 06066-5609*

HERBST, ROBERT LEROY, organization executive; b. Mpls., Oct. 5, 1935; s. Walter Peter and Bernice Mickey (Mikkelson) H.; m. Evelyn Clarice Elford, Sept. 22, 1956; children—Eric Elford, Peter Robert, Amy Jo. B.S. in Forest Mgmt, U. Minn., St. Paul, 1957. Dep. commnr. Minn. Conservation Dept., 1966-69; nat. exec. dir. Izaak Walton League Am., 1969-70; commr. natural resources State of Minn., 1971-77; asst. sec. fish, wildlife and parks Dept. Interior, Washington, 1977-81; sec. Dept. Interior, Jan. 20-26, 1981; exec. dir. Trout Unltd., 1981-90; pres. Lake Superior Ctr., Washington, 1990-92, A-S5 Energy Co., Reno, Nev., 1997-98; Washington rep. TVA, Washington, 1992-96; CEO, chmn. bd. dirs. Global Environment & Tech. Found., Annandale, Va., 1996—; instr. U. Minn., 1954; mem. adv. faculty N. Am. Sch. Conservation, 1969-77; chmn. Gt. Lakes Fisheries Commn., 1978-80, steering com. Nat. Fishing Week, 1991; mem. U.S. Commn. UNESCO, 1978-79, Pres. Carter's Interagency Coun., 1978-80; co-chmn. Nat. Adv. Coun. Environ. Edn., 1989, chmn., 1990-92; mem. U.S. bd. Environ. Ctr. for Ctrl. and Ea. Europe, 1997—; chmn. bd. dirs. Nat. Wildlife Refuge Assocs., 1998—. Author: Careers in Environment, 1973, also articles. Mem. nat. bd. Boy Scouts Am., 1969-77; exec. bd. Viking Coun., 1975-76; mem. bd. House of Prayer Luth. Ch., Richfield, Minn., 1969-77; bd. govs. African Inst. Econs. Edn. and Devel., 1980; pres. Nat. Watershed Protection Ctr., 1994. Recipient Nat. Service award Izaak Walton League Am., 1971; Silver Beaver award Boy Scouts Am., 1977; Distinguished Service award U. Minn., 1969; named Pub. Adminstr. of Year in Minn. Am. Soc. Pub. Adminstrn., 1976. Mem. Natural Resource Coun. Am. (chmn. 1989-91, Honor award 1994), Land Between Lakes Assn.(chmn. 1982-91, trustee 1981-91). Democrat. Office: Global Environment & Tech Found 7010 Little River Tpke Ste 300 Annandale VA 22003-3241

HERBSTER, WILLIAM GIBSON, university administrator, consultant; b. Poughkeepsie, N.Y., Jan. 15, 1933; s. John Zachary and Esther (Pedolski) H.; m. Mary Lee Talley, Sept. 21, 1957; children—David Easton, Michael Eugene, Susan Talley Fulghum. B.A., Hamilton Coll., 1955. Trainee C & P Bell Telephone Co., Charleston, W.Va., 1955; trainee Citibank N.A., N.Y.C., 1958-60, asst. cashier, 1961-63, asst. v.p., 1963-65, v.p., 1966-69, sr. v.p., 1969-76; sr. v.p. Cornell U., Ithaca, N.Y., 1976-87, sr. v.p. emeritus, 1987—; dir. Lin Broadcasting Corp., Kirkland, Wash., 1976-95, LIN Television Corp., Providence, R.I., 1994-98, Citizens Savs. Bank, Ithaca, N.Y., 1976-94, MRSI Inc., N.Y., 1981-93; dir. Cornell Rsch. Found., W-2 Publs., Inc., Ithaca, N.Y., 1989-97, Found. for Devel. Polish Agr., 1995—, Am. U. in Bulgaria, Blagowgrad, 1994—, Small Enterprise Equity Funds, St. Petersburg and Nishny Novograd, Russia, Sofia, Bulgaria, 1995—; mem. adv. com. M&T Trust Co. Ctrl. N.Y., 1995-98; chmn. bd. Am. Trust for Agr. in Poland, 1991—; sr. adv. Investment Fund for Founds., 1991—. Trustee Family and Children's Svc., Ithaca, N.Y., 1977-87, Ithaca Neighborhood Housing Svc., 1976-86, Bank St. Coll. of Edn., N.Y.C., 1970-76, Hamilton and Kirkland Colls., Clinton, N.Y., 1969-77, Tompkins Found., Ithaca, 1984-89; co-founder, chmn. exec. com. Cmty. Preservation Corp., N.Y.C., 1973-76; treas. Rsch. Librs. Group, Inc., 1986-92, exec. com.; mem. fin. com. The Coll. Bd., 1986-95; chmn. Ithaca Steering Com. Empire State Games, 1989. Capt. USMC, 1955-58. Named Man of Yr., Harlem Commonwealth Council, 1973. Mem. Univ. Club (N.Y.C.). Avocations: tennis; sailing; bridge; travel. Home and Office: 2700 Calvert St NW Washington DC 20008-2621

HERBSTMAN, LORETTA, sculptor; b. Bklyn., June 14; d. Berardino and Sabina (Senelli) Guicciardini; m. Martin Herbstman, Aug. 28; children: Jason, Dana. Instr. stone sculpture J. Reid Sch. Art, Buford, Ga. Sculptor in stone, cast bronze, cast resins and wire mesh; group exhibits in galleries throughout Manhattan, L.I., Staten Island, Ga., Fla. and shown on Joe Franklin TV Show, as well as Smithtown Art Coun. Mill Pond House, C.W. Post U. Hutchins Gallery, Gallery North, Suffolk County Bald Hill Cultural Ctr., Falconaire's Gallery, N.Y. Design Ctr.; jewelry designer/maker. Founder, pres. Farmingville (N.Y.) Improvement Coun.; mem. East End Arts Coun., Huntington Town Art League, Smithtown Art League, Westhampton Cultural Consortium. Recipient 1st prize for sculpture in a mixed-media juried show East Islip Arts Coun., numerous others. Mem. Nat. Sculpture Soc., Ga. Artists Registry. Home: 1490 S Orlando Ave Cocoa Beach FL 32931-2334

HERCULES, DAVID MICHAEL, chemistry educator, consultant; b. Somerset, Pa., Aug. 10, 1932; s. Michael George and Kathryn (Saylor) H.; m. Nancy Catherine Miller, Sept. 23, 1957 (div. 1968); 1 dau., Kimberly Ann; m. Shirley Ann Hoover, Dec. 14, 1970; children: Sherri Kathryn, Kevin Michael. B.S., Juniata Coll., 1954; Ph.D., MIT, 1957. Asst. prof. Lehigh U., 1957-60; assoc. prof. Juniata Coll., Huntington, Pa., 1960-63; asst. prof. MIT, 1963-68, assoc. prof., 1968-69; assoc. prof. U. Ga., Athens, 1969-74, prof., 1974-76; prof. dept. chemistry U. Pitts., 1976-94, chmn., 1980-89, Miles prof., 1990-94; Centennial prof. and chmn. Vanderbilt U., Nashville, Tenn., 1995—; mem. vis. com. for chemistry Lehigh U., 1980-84; vis. prof. Mich. State U., 1972; chmn. Gordon Research Conf. on Electron Spectroscopy, 1974, Gordon Research Conf. on Analytical Chemistry, 1966; co-chmn. Internat. Conf. Chemiluminescence, 1972; univ. rep. Council on Chem. Research, 1980-88; mem. program com. Pitts. Conf. on Analytical Chemistry and Applied Spectroscopy, 1977-94; mem. vis. scientist program NSF, 1964-76. Mem. editorial bds.: Applied Spectroscopy, 1963-65, Analytical Chemistry, 1964-67, Jour. Electron Spectroscopy, 1971-77, Environ. Analytical Chemistry, 1973—, Spectrochimica Acta, 1973-83, Talanta, 1974-80, Spectroscopy Letters, 1975—, The Scis., 1979-84, Trends in Analytical Chemistry, 1980-88, Jour. Trace and Microprobe Techniques, 1980-93; patentee (in field). Recipient Benedetti-Pichler award Am. Microchem. Soc., 1987, Achievement in Analytical Chemistry award Ea. Analytical Symposium, 1988, prize Alexander von Humboldt Found., 1984, Disting. Alumnus award Juniata Coll., 1989, Pres.'s Disting. Rsch. award U. Pitts., 1990; John Simon Guggenheim Meml. fellow, 1973. Mem. Am. Chem. Soc. (Petroleum Research Fund adv. bd. 1978-80, chmn. div. analytical chemistry 1977-78, analytical chemistry award 1986, Arthur W. Adamson award disting. svc. in advancement of surface chemistry 1993, Pitts. sect. award 1997), Soc. Applied Spectroscopy (Lester W. Strock medal New Eng. sect. 1981, Pitts. Spectroscopy award 1996), Am. Vacuum Soc., Photoelectric Spectrometry Group, Pa. Acad. Scis., Spectroscopy Soc. Pitts. (award 1996), Soc. Analytical Chemists Pitts., Sigma Xi. Home: 200 Olive Branch Rd Nashville TN 37205-3220 Office: Vanderbilt U Dept Chemistry Box 1822, Sta B Nashville TN 37235

HERD, HAROLD SHIELDS, state supreme court justice; b. Coldwater, Kans., June 3, 1918. B.A., Washburn U., 1941, J.D., 1942. Bar: Kans. 1943. Partner firm Rich and Herd, Coldwater, 1946-53; individual practice law Coldwater, 1953-79; justice Kans. Supreme Ct., 1979-93; ret., 1993; disting. jurist in residence Washburn Law Sch., Topeka, 1993—; mayor, Coldwater, 1949-53, county atty., Comanche County, Kans., 1954-58; mem. Kans. Senate, 1965-73, minority floor leader, 1969-73. Bd. govs. Washburn Law Sch., 1974-78, disting. jurist in residence, 1993-94; mem. Kans. Com. for Humanities, 1975-80, chmn. 1980, Hall Ctr. for Humanities, adv. coun. Kans. U. Mem. S.W. Bar Assn. (pres. 1977), Kans. Bar Assn. (exec. council 1973-80). Office: Washburn Law Sch Kans Jud Ctr 1700 SW College Ave Topeka KS 66621-0001*

HERD, JOANNE MAY BEERS, intravenous therapy nurse, educator; b. Nazareth, Pa., Nov. 28, 1934; d. Robert Albert and Marguerite (Small) Beers; m. Robert Von Steuben Herd, Oct. 25, 1958; 1 child, Scott Robert. Diploma, Allentown (Pa.) Hosp., 1955. Cert. intravenous nurse. Asst. instr. sci. Allentown Hosp., 1956-57, recruitment dir., 1957-58; staff nurse Tidewater Blood Bank Svcs., ARC, Norfolk, Va., 1959-60, Sentara Virginia Beach (Va.) Gen. Hosp., 1979-86; staff educator Virginia Beach (Va.) Gen. Hosp., 1986—; intravenous nurse educator, cons., 1997—. Designer intravenous nurse emblem lapel pin, mobile teaching unit. Mem. League Intravenous Therapy Edn., Intravenous Nurses Soc. (chmn. Ea. Va. chpt. 1983-85, pres. elect 1993-94, pres. 1994-95, presdl. advisor 1995-96, bd. mem. at large 1996—), Allentown Hosp. Alumni Assn. (life).

HERDECK, DONALD ELMER, publishing executive, retired humanities educator; b. Chgo., Nov. 19, 1924; s. Elmer and Violet (Cotter) H.; m. Margaret L. Laniak. BA, MA, U. Chgo., 1948; PhD, U. Pa., 1968. Tchr. French and English Girard Coll., Phila., 1952-54; fgn. svc. officer U.S. Dept. State, Washington, 1955-64; assoc. prof. humanities Georgetown U., Washington, 1965-87; pub., chmn., pres. Three Continents Press, Colorado Springs, 1973-96; pres., editor, publ. Passeggiata Press, Pueblo, Colo., 1996—. Author: African Authors: A Bio-Critical Bibliographical Ency., 1971, Caribbean Writers: A Bio-Critical Bibliographical Ency., 1974; editor, contbr. Three Dynamite Authors: Derek Walcott, Naguib Mahfouz, Wole Soyinka, 1994, Appreciating the Difference: The Biography of Three Continents Press, 1996. Pres. Cabin John Citizens Assn., Bethesda, Md., 1969-70. With U.S. Army, 1943-46, ETO. Mem. African Lit. Assn., 103d Infantry Assoc.

HERDEG, HOWARD BRIAN, physician; b. Buffalo, Oct. 14, 1929; s. Howard Bryan and Martha Jean (Williams) H.; m. Beryl Ann Fredricks, July 21, 1955; children: Howard Brian III, Erin Ann Kociela. Student Paul Smith's Coll., 1947-48, U. Buffalo, 1948-50, Canisius Coll., 1949; DO, Phila. Coll. Osteopathic Medicine, 1954; MD, U. Calif.-Irvine Coll. Medicine, 1962. Diplomate Am. Acad. Pain Mgmt. Intern, Burbank (Calif.) Hosp., 1954-55; practice medicine specializing in gen. medicine, surgery and pain mgmt., Woodland Hills, Calif., 1956—; chief med. staff West Park Hosp., Canoga Park, Calif., 1971-72, trustee, 1971-73; chief family practice dept. West Hills Regional Med. Center (formerly Humaua Hosp. West Hills, 1982-83, 84-85, 88-89), mem. exec. com., 1984-85, 88-89, Mem. Hidden Hills (Calif.) Pub. Safety Commn., 1978-82; bd. dirs. Hidden Hills Community Assn., 1971-73, pres., 1972; bd. dirs. Hidden Hills Homeowners Assn., 1973-75, pres., 1976-77; bd. dirs. Woodland Hills Freedom Season, 1961-67, pres., 1962; mem. Hidden Hills City Council, 1984—, mayor pro tem, 1987-90, mayor, 1990-92. Recipient disting. service award Woodland Hills Jr C. of C., 1966. Mem. Woodland Hills C. of C. (dir. 1959-68, pres. 1967), Theta Chi, Gamma Pi. Republican. Home: 24530 Deep Well Rd Hidden Hills CA 91302-1210 Office: 22600 Ventura Blvd Woodland Hills CA 91364-1414

HERDEG, JOHN ANDREW, lawyer; b. Buffalo, Sept. 15, 1937; s. Franklin Leland and Susannah Estelle (Clark) H.; m. Judith Coolidge Carpenter, June 24, 1961; children: Judith Leland Herdeg Wilson, Andrew Carpenter Herdeg, Fell Coolidge Herdeg. BA, Princeton U., 1959; LLB, U. Pa., 1962. Bar: Conn. 1963, Del. 1964. Atty. Wilmington (Del.) Trust Co., 1963-75, sr. v.p. in charge of trust dept., 1975-85, bd. dirs., chmn. trust com., corp. sec., 1977-85; ptnr. Herdeg & Assocs., Wilmington, 1986-98; pvt. practice Herdeg & duPont, P.A., Wilmington, 1998-99; with Herdeg, duPont & Dalle Pazze, LLP, Wilmington, 1999—; co-founder, chmn. bd. dirs. Christiana Bank & Trust Co., Greenville, Del., 1992—. Bd. trustees Henry Francis duPont Winterthur (Del.) Mus., 1970—, chmn., 1977-86; trustee Med. Ctr. of Del., Stanton, 1965—; supr. Pennsbury Twp., Chester County, Pa., 1968-74; mem. Westminster Presbyn. Ch. Mem. Wilmington Club (bd. govs. 1997—, treas. 1999—), Vicmead Hunt Club (bd. govs. 1977-84), Walpole Soc., Confrerie des Chevalier du Tastevin, West Chop Club. Avocations: tennis, photography, decorative arts. Home: PO Box 216 Mendenhall PA 19357-0216 Office: Herdeg & DuPont 12th & Orange St Ste 500 Wilmington DE 19801-1140

HERDENDORF, CHARLES EDWARD, III, retired oceanographer, limnologist, consultant; b. Lorain, Ohio, Oct. 2, 1939; s. Charles Edward, Jr. and Esther Kathryne Herdendorf; m. Ricki Sue Crowl, May 22, 1993. BS, Ohio U., 1961, MS, 1963; PhD, Ohio State U., 1970. Cert. profl. geologist, Am. Inst. Profl. Geologists. Geologist, section head Ohio Dept. Natural Resources, Sandusky, Ohio, 1960-71; assoc. prof. geol. scis. and zoology Ohio State U., 1971-76, prof., 1976-88, prof. emeritus, 1988--; dir. Franz Theodore Stone Lab. and Ctr. for Lake Erie Area Rsch., Put-in-Bay, Ohio, 1971-88; dir. Ohio sea grant coll. program Ohio State U., Columbus, 1978-88; sci. dir. Columbus-Am. Discovery Group, Columbus, 1988-95; apptd. by Ohio Gov. to Acid Rain Forest Task Force, 1984, Ohio Maritime Adv. Coun., 1999. Author: Ohio's Natural Heritage, 1979 (Ohioana Book Award 1980), Journal of Great Lakes Research, 1997; Author/Editor: Large Lakes of the World, 1990, Lake Erie Handbook, 1993, Science on a Deep-Ocean Shipwreck, 1995. Vol. naturalist Ohio Divsn. Nat. Areas and Preserves, Huron, Ohio, 1988--; pres. Beachwood Villas Assn., Huron, 1989-90; advisor Nat. Maritime Hist. Soc., Peekskill, N.Y., 1989--; trustee Ohio Hist. Soc., Columbus, 1995-96, Great Lakes Hist. Soc., Vermilion, Ohio, 1999--. With ROTC, USAF, 1957-58. Recipient Citizenship medal SAR, 1990; named to Hall of Fame F. T. Stone Lab., Ohio State U., 1996, Diver of Year Bay Area Divers, 1998. Fellow Geol. Soc. Am., Explorers Club; mem. Ohio Acad. Sci. (pres. 1995-96, Centennial Honoree 1991), Internat. Assoc. for Great Lakes Rsch. (bd. dirs. 1977-80, v.p. 1979-80, Best Paper of Yr. 1998), Am. Fisheries Soc. (cert. fisheries scientist, cert. underwater archaeologist), NSPE, Ohio Office Hist. Preservation, U.s. Nat. Park Svc. Republican. Methodist. Avocations: photography, scuba diving, boating, aircraft piloting, hiking. E-Mail: herdendorf.1@osu.edu. Home: 585 West Shore Blvd Put-in-Bay OH 43456 Office: Ohio State U Ste 410 1507 Clevelant Rd East Huron OH 44839

HERDER, GWENDOLIN ELISABETH MARIA, publishing executive; b. Freiburg, Germany, Aug. 23, 1961; d. Hermann Josef Romano and Mechtild Edith (Horten) H. Diploma, Complutense, Madrid, 1982; PhD, U. Bonn, Germany, 1989, MA in Spanish Lit., 1993. Asst. mktg. dir. Herder Publ., Freiburg, Germany, 1990-91, religious editor, 1992-93, dir. publ., 1993; CEO/pres. Crossroad Publ., N.Y.C., 1993—; adv. bd. Libreria Herder, Rome, 1994—. Mem. Religious Pubs. Group (bd. dirs.), Cath. Book Publisher Assn., German Cath. Book Publ. Assn. Office: Crossroad Publishing 370 Lexington Ave # 2600 New York NY 10017-6503*

HERDLEIN, RICHARD JOSEPH, III, college official and dean, educator; b. Valdosta, Ga., Dec. 8, 1944; s. Margaret D. Herdlein; 1 child, Richard J. IV. BA, St. John Fisher Coll., 1966; MA, Niagara U., 1970, MS, 1976; PhD, U. Pitts., 1985. Gen. mgr. Schmitt Sales, Inc., Amherst, N.Y., 1964-68; dir. residence Kent (Ohio) State U., 1969-72; dir. student ctr. D'Youville Coll., Buffalo, N.Y., 1974-76; dir. student activities Eckerd Coll., St. Petersburgh, Fla., 1976-77; asst. dir. univ. ctr. Adelphi U., Garden City, N.Y., 1978-80; dean student affairs U. Pitts., 1980-87; v.p. Thomas More Coll.,

Crestview Hills, Ky., 1987-90; v.p. student affairs, dean, assoc. prof. history Medaille Coll., Buffalo, 1990—; lectr. SUNY Coll. at Buffalo Grad. Sch. Higher Edn. Adminstrn., 1997—. Councilman Amherst Rep. Com., 1993-96; chmn. jingle bell run Arthritis Found., Tonawanda, N.Y., 1991—; bd. dirs., chmn. fundraising com. Leadership Buffalo, 1997—; bd. dirs. Buffalo Coun. on World Affairs; alumnus Ctr. for Entrepreneurial Leadership, SUNY, Buffalo, 1995—. Sgt. USAR, 1967-73. Named Person of Yr. Adelphia U., 1980, Most Respected Dr., Ctr. for Entrepreneurial Leadership SUNY Buffalo, 1996. Mem. Amvets. Republican. Roman Catholic. Avocations: golf, racquetball, running, reading, arts. Home: 47 Fairchild Dr Amherst NY 14226-3328 Office: Medaille Coll 18 Agassiz Cir Buffalo NY 14214-2601

HERDMAN, SUSAN, art educator, artist; b. Yonkers, N.Y., May 29, 1941; d. Raymond Charles and Ellen (Saunders) Herdman; m. John C. Barker, June 12, 1965 (div. July 1984); children: Jennifer, Carrie, John. BFA, Alfred U., 1963; MA, U. Iowa, 1965. Art educator Muscatine (Iowa) Pub. Schs., 1965-66, Iowa City Pub. Schs., 1966-67, Regina High Sch., Iowa City, 1967-68; artist, owner Herdman Photographic Archive (formerly Native Images), Bettendorf, Iowa, 1992—; art educator Davenport (Iowa) Cmty. Schs., 1985—. Group shows include Drake U., Des Moines, 1984, U. Iowa, Iowa City, 1987, 91, Davenport Mus. Art, 1987, Quad City Arts Coun., Rock Island, Ill., 1987, Whispering Winds Gallery, Iowa City, 1991, Quincy (Ill.) Art Ctr., 1992, Walton Art Ctr., Fayetteville, Ark., 1992, 93, Alias Gallery, Atlanta, 1992, Ga. Tech., Atlanta, 1992, Lincoln (Colo.) Art Ctr., 1992, 93, Davenport Mus. Art, 1992, Mus. Anthropology U. Calif., Chico, 1992, Red Mesa Art Gallery, Gallup, N.Mex., 1992, Putnam County Arts Coun., Mahopac, N.Y., 1992, Near Northwest Arts Coun., Chgo., 1993, North Platte Valley Art Guild, Scottsbluff, Nebr., 1993, U. Iowa, 1993, Chautaugua Art Assn. Galleries, 1993, Greater Harrisburg (Pa.) Arts Coun., 1993, 94, Fla. Soc. Fine Arts, Miami, Fla., 1993, Columbia Arts Ctr., Vancouver, Wash., 1993, Eiteljorg Mus. Am. Indian and Western Art, Indpls., 1994, Maude Kerns Art Center, Eugene, Oreg., 1994, Soc. Contemporary Photography, Kansas City, 1994, Mus. Northwest Colo., Craig, 1994, Fuller Mus. Art, Brockton, Mass., 1994, Perry House Galleries (Silver medal), Alexandria, Va., 1995, No. Colo. Artists Assn., Fort Collins, Colo., 1996, Photo Nat. 96 (2nd place award), Mo., 1996, Oscar Howe Art Ctr., S. Dakota, 1996; one-person show Cornell Coll., Mt. Vernon, Iowa, 1997; permanent collections include Am. Indian Art Ctr., Chgo., Mus. Anthropology U. Calif., Chico., Deere and Co., Moline, Ill, Eiteljorg Mus. Native Am. and Western Art, EverColor Corp., Wooster, Mass., Heard Mus. Libr. and Archives, Phoenix. Mem. Nat. Mus. Am. Indian, Nat. Mus. Women in Arts, Davenport Indian Parent Adv. Com., 1991-95. Recipient Best of Show award Quad City Arts Coun., 1987, Best of Photography Ann. Photographers Forum Mag., 1993, others; grantee Iowa Arts Coun., 1995. Mem. Iowa Alliance for Arts Edn., Quad City League of Native Ams. Home: 3303 Oxford Dr Bettendorf IA 52722-2667

HEREFORD, FRANK LOUCKS, JR., physicist, educator; b. Lake Charles, La., July 18, 1923; s. Frank L. and Marguerite (Roussel) H.; m. Ann Lane, Jan. 3, 1948; children—Frank, Sarah, Robert. BA, U. Va., 1943, PhD in Physics, 1947; DSc, Fla. Inst. Tech., 1974; LLD, Hampden-Sydney Coll., 1974. Physicist Bartol Research Found., Swarthmore, Pa., 1947-49; mem. faculty U. Va., 1949-92, prof. physics, 1952-92; dean U. Va. (Grad. Sch. Arts and Scis.), 1962-66, Robert C. Taylor prof. physics, 1966-92, provost, v.p., 1966-71, pres., 1974-85; vis. prof. U. St. Andrews, Scotland, 1971-72; dir. Gould, Inc., Rolling Meadows, Ill., 1980-88. Contbr. profl. jours. Bd. govs. Belfield Sch., Charlottesville, 1959-62, 63-65, chmn. bd., 1962; bd. dirs. St. Anne's Sch., Charlottesville, 1966-70; trustee Woodberry Forest Sch., 1968-74, Mariner's Mus., Newport News, Va., 1975-85. Fulbright scholar U. Birmingham, Eng., 1957-58; recipient Devel. award USN Ordnance Dept., 1945, Horsley Rsch. prize Va. Acad. Sci., 1953. Fellow Am. Phys. Soc. (chmn. Southeastern sect. 1961-62), Phi Beta Kappa, Sigma Xi, Omicron Delta Kappa, Alpha Tau Omega. Home: RR 5 Charlottesville VA 22901-9805

HEREK, STEPHEN, film director, producer. Motion picture dir., prodr. Dir. films Bill & Ted's Excellent Adventure, 1989, Don't Tell Mom the Babysitter's Dead, 1991, The Mighty Ducks, 1992, The 3 Musketeers, 1993, Mr. Holland's Opus, 1995, 101 Dalmations, 1996; dir., prodr. Holy Man, 1998; dir., writer Critters, 1986. Office: c/o DGA 7920 Sunset Blvd Los Angeles CA 90046*

HEREMANS, JOSEPH PIERRE, physicist; b. Leuven, Belgium, Jan. 8, 1953; came to U.S., 1984; s. Joseph Felix and Marie Therese (Bracke) H.; m. Claire Pierre Mali, July 1, 1978; children: Hilde Anne, Joseph Paul. Elec. Engr., U. Louvain, Belgium, 1975, PhD in Applied Physics, 1978. Aspirant Belgium Nat. Sci. Found., Louvain, 1978-80, charge de recherche, 1980-83; prin. scientist GM Rsch. and Devel. Ctr., Warren, Mich., 1984-85; group leader GM Rsch., Warren, Mich., 1985-87, sect. mgr., 1987-99; prin. scientist Delphi Automotive Systems R&D, Warren, 1999—; invited prof. U. Louvain, 1989; vis. scientist U. Tokyo, 1982, MIT, Cambridge, 1980-81. Editor: Growth, Characterization and Properties of Ultrathin Magnetic Films and Multilayers, 1989; contbr. articles to profl. jours. Fellow Am. Phys. Soc.; mem. AAAS, Materials Rsch. Soc., Sigma Xi. Achievements include patents in field. Office: GM R&D Ctr Physics and Phys Chem Dept 30500 Mound Rd Warren MI 48092-2031

HERENDEEN, CAROL DENISE, dietitian; b. Cleve., Dec. 10, 1955; m. Norman James Herendeen, June 30, 1979; children: Seth Ryan, Eric Kyle. AA, Lakeland Community Coll., 1976; BS, Kent State U., 1978. Lic. dietitian, Fla. Dietary supr. U. Hosps., Cleve., 1978-79, St. Luke's Hosp., Cleve., 1979; trainee Lake County Hosps., Willoughby, Ohio, 1980, Case Western Res. U., Cleve., 1980; clin. dietitian Lakeland (Fla.) Regional Med. Ctr., 1980-87; renal dietitian Watson Clinic, Lakeland, 1987—; cons. Pasco County Nursing and Rehab. Ctr., Dade City, 1981-84, City of Lakeland Employee Fairs, 1985, 87, 91, 92, Sta. WLKF-AM, Lakeland, 1989-91, Polk County Schs., Winter Haven, Fla., 1990; speaker diabetes and cardiac programs Watson Clinic, Lakeland, 1989-91, others. Mem. Am. Dietetic Assn. (registered, renal dietitians practice group), Am. Diabetes Educators Assn. (cert.), Am. Heart Assn. (CPR cert.), Cypress Dietetic Assn. (sec. 1987-88, pres. elect 1988-89, pres. 1989-90, chair nominating com. 1990-91, 91-92, membership 1991, 92), Nat. Kidney Found. (coun. renal nutrition 1981—), Fla. Coun. Renal Nutrition (sec. 1983-84, treas. 1987-89, pres. elect 1989-90, pres. 1990-91, chair nominating com. 1991-92). Methodist. Avocation: travel. Office: Watson Clinic 1550 Lakeland Hills Blvd Lakeland FL 33805-3261

HERENDEEN, ROBERT ALBERT, environmental scientist; b. Freeport, N.Y., Oct. 18, 1940; s. Lemuel Albert and Marjorie Bessie (Hatfield) H.; m. Gail Elizabeth Anderson, Nov. 22, 1971 (div. 1990); children: Laurel, Paul; m. Ann Elizabeth Burke, Aug. 12, 1995. BS in Physics, Rensselaer Polytech Inst., 1962; PhD, Cornell U., 1970. Assoc. prof. U. Ill., Champaign, 1985—; profl. scientist Ill. Natural History Survey, Champaign, 1985—. Contbr. articles to profl. jours. Postdoctoral fellow Norwegian Inst. Tech., Trondheim, 1975-77. Mem. Internat. Soc. Ecological Modelling, Internat. Soc. Ecological Econs. Avocations: wilderness canoeing, bee keeping, drumming. Home: 1618 W Church St Champaign IL 61821-2433 Office: Ill Natural History Survey 607 E Peabody Dr Champaign IL 61820-6917

HERENTON, WILLIE W., mayor; b. Memphis, Apr. 23, 1943; divorced; children: Errol, Rodney, Andrea. BS, LeMoyne-Owen Coll., 1963; MA, Memphis State U., 1966; PhD, So. Ill. U., 1971. Elem. sch. tchr. Memphis City Sch. System, 1963-67, elem. sch. prin., 1967-73; dept. supt. Memphis City Schs., 1974-78, supt. of schs., 1979-91; mayor Memphis, 1991—. Bd. dirs. Nat. Urban League Edn. Adv. Coun., 1978, Nat. Jr. Achievement, Jr. Achievement of Memphis 1979—, United Way Greater Memphis, 1979—; mem. Nat. Alliance of Black Educators, 1974—. Named one of Top 100 Sch. Adminstrs. in U.S. and Can., Exec. Educator Jour., 1980, 84. Fellow Rockefeller Found., 1973. Office: Office of the Mayor 125 N Main St Ste 200 Memphis TN 38103-2017*

HERETH, LYLE GEORGE, electrical engineering technologist; b. Everett, Wash., Oct. 14, 1947; s. L. Walter and Alvina Katharina (Weber) H.; m. Margaret Sue Brewer, Dec. 19, 1978; children: Christopher, Walter, Emilie, Jennifer, Jacob. BS in Elec. Engring. Tech., Weber State Coll., 1975; M of Engring. Adminstrn., U. Utah, 1981. Quality engr. Nat. Semiconductor, Salt Lake City, 1975-78, Beehive Internat., Salt Lake City, 1978-80; quality mgr. Sperry Univac, Salt Lake City, 1980-82; sys. devel. mgr. LDS Ch., Salt Lake City, 1982-85, dir. tech., arch., 1985-90, asst. coord., 1990-93, cons. emerging tech., 1993-99; dir. info. tech. FHD, 1999—; chmn. info. sys. VIM, CDC Corp., Minn., 1984-89; project mgr. geneal. sys. FamilySearch, 1987 (Smith award 1992, 95). Chmn. planning and zoning South Salt Lake City Govt., 1986-94. Recipient Pub. Svc. awards South Salt Lake Govt., 1983, 94. Mem. Am. Soc. Quality Control, Assn. for Info. and Image Mgmt. Mem. LDS Ch. Avocations: reading, camping, cooking, acting. Office: LDS Ch FHD 50E N Temple Salt Lake City UT 84150

HERGE, HENRY CURTIS, SR., education educator, dean emeritus; b. Bklyn., June 29, 1905; s. Henry John and Theresa (Maaz) H.; m. Josephine E. Breen, July 2, 1931 (dec. Oct. 8, 1975); children: Joel Curtis, Henry Curtis; m. Alice V. Wolfram, Apr. 21, 1976. BS, NYU, 1929, MA, 1931, EdD, 1942; MA (hon.), Wesleyan U., 1946; PhD, Yale U., 1956. Instr. English Sr. High Sch., Port Washington, N.Y., 1928-38; dist. prin. Bayville, N.Y., 1938-41, Bellmore, N.Y., 1941-45; asst. dir. study on implication of armed svcs. edn. programs Am. Council Edn., Washington., 1945-46; dir. higher edn., tchr. edn. cert. Conn. State Dept. Edn., 1946-53; adjunct prof. Hartford U., 1950-52, Fairfield U., 1950-53; dean, prof. edn. Rutgers U., 1953-64; adjunct prof. U. So. Calif., summer 1964, NYU, 1964-65; prof. edn., assoc. dir. Rutgers Ctr. for Internat. Programs, 1964-75; del. White House Conf. Edn., 1957; edn. cons. USOM Asuncion and ICA dir. ednl. priorities study for Ministry of Edn., Paraguay, 1961; team leader Rutgers-U.S. AID field survey, Zambia and Malawi, 1961-62; chief edn. devel. officer U.S. AID, Jamaica, 1966-68; Fulbright rapporteur Seminar in Univ. Adminstrn., U.S. and Italy, 1970; OAS sr. rsch. fellow, Paraguay and Jamaica, 1972-73. Author: Wartime College Training Programs of Armed Services, 1948; The College Teacher, 1966, Navy V-12, 1996; editor: Disarmament in the Western World, 1968; Common Concerns in Higher Education: An Italian-American Universities Project, Phase I, 1970; contbr. numerous articles to profl. publs. Pres. Shadow Lake Assn., Vt., 1976-78; sec. Fed. Lake Assns., No. Vt., 1980-84; project dir. Hilton Head Plantation Public Forum for Humanities, 1980-81; chmn. bd. trustees Coll. Hilton Head (S.C.), 1984-86, Town Council Com. for Higher Edn., 1986-88. Served as comdg. officer Wesleyan U.S. Navy V-12 unit 1943-45; lt. comdr. USNR (Ret.). Recipient cert. of recognition NCCJ, 1958, Honor citation, Rutgers Grad. Sch. Edn., 1993. Mem. N.J. Congress Parents and Tchrs. (hon. life), N.J. Secondary Sch. Tchrs. Assn. (trustee 1954-66, merit award 1966), N.J. Coun. on Edn., N.J. Schoolmasters Club, Fulbright Alumni Assn. (v.p. S.C. chpt. 1983-91), Naval Res. Assn. (life), Retired Officers Assn. (life), Phi Delta Kappa (emeritus), Epsilon Pi Tau (laureate trustee), Kappa Delta Pi (award 1976). Home: 104 Fleet Landing Blvd Atlantic Beach FL 32233-4585

HERGE, HENRY CURTIS, JR., consulting firm executive; b. Hartford, Conn., Sept. 13, 1950; s. Henry Curtis and Josephine (Breen) H.; m. Donna Gay Takeda, Dec. 20, 1974 (div. Dec. 1982); m. Madge Lynn Henley, Feb. 19, 1983; children: Whitney Meghan, H. Curtis III, Erika Ainsley, Alyssa Taylor. BS in Mech. Engring., Rutgers U., 1972, BA, 1972. Prodn. specialist GE, Columbia, Md., 1972-73, engring. foreman med. sys. divsn., Milw., 1973-74, buyer internat. sales div., N.Y.C., 1974-76; sr. sys. analyst Arthur Andersen & Co. (now Andersen Cons.), N.Y.C., 1976-78, cons. mgr., Stamford, Conn., 1978-85, ptnr., 1985—, practice dir. consulting divsn. Rochester, N.Y. office, 1987-92; v.p. Am. Prodn. and Inventory Control Soc., Rochester, 1985; sr. v.p. Tech. Solutions Co., 1992-94; ptnr. Diamond Tech. Ptnrs., Pittsford, N.Y., 1994-97; prin. A.T. Kearney divsn. of Electronic Data Sys, Plano, Tex., 1995—, global contracts mgr., 1997—, svc. delivery quality, 1998—. Presbyterian. Avocations: skiing, travel, canoeing, kites. Home: 16 Lancashire Way Pittsford NY 14534-9786

HERGE, J. CURTIS, lawyer; b. Flushing, N.Y., June 14, 1938; s. Henry Curtis and Josephine E. (Breen) H.; m. Joyce Dorean Humbert, Aug. 20, 1960 (div. 1988); children: Cynthia Lynda, Christopher Curtis; m. Shirley Brooks Labonte, Dec. 22, 1989. Student, Cornell U., 1956-58; BA, Rutgers U., 1961, JD (Sebastian Gaeta scholar), 1963. Bar: N.Y. 1964, U.S. Supreme Ct. 1970, U.S. Ct. Claims 1974, D.C. 1974, Va. 1976. Assoc. firm Mudge Rose Guthrie & Alexander, N.Y.C., 1963-71; spl. asst. to atty. gen. U.S. Dept. Justice, Washington, 1973; assoc. solicitor conservation and wildlife U.S. Dept. Interior, Washington, 1973-74; asst. to sec. and chief staff U.S. Dept. Interior, 1974-76; ptnr. Sedam & Herge, McLean, Va., 1976-85, Herge, Sparks & Christopher LLP, McLean, Va., 1985—; bd. dirs. Diversified Labs., Inc., Ann E.W. Stone & Assocs., Inc., Palmer Tech. Svcs., Inc., Eaton Design Group, Inc., George Washington Banking Corp., Eaton Purchase Mgmt., Inc., George Washington Nat. Bank, Congl. Inst. Inc., Citizens United for Am., Am. Def. Lobby, Coun. Nat. Def., Renascence Found., The Am. Lobby Econ. Recovery Taskforce, Nat. Bank No. Va., Am. Freedom Found., Creative Response Concepts Inc. With Congl. Inst. Inc.; mem. adv. bds. Washington Legal Found., Nat. Taxpayers Legal Fund; Va. Commonwealth escheator Loudoun County and City of Fairfax, 1979-83; co-dir. spokesmen resources Com. for Re-election of Pres., 1971-72; mem. No. Va. Estate Planning Council; mem. natural resources coun. Rep. Nat. Com.; mem. Fairfax County Rep. Com., Conservative Rep. Com.; mem. Office Pres.-Elect Fed. Election Commn. Transition Team, 1980; co-chmn. N.Y. Honor Am. Day, 1970; speaker state planning and fed. election laws; expert witness, charitable fund-raising, U.S. Tax Ct. Mem. Am., N.Y. State, Va., D.C. bar assns., Phi Kappa Sigma. Club: Capitol Hill. Home: 35 Rutherford Cir Potomac Falls VA 20165-6221 Office: Herge Sparks & Christopher LLP 6862 Elm St Ste 360 Mc Lean VA 22101

HERGENHAN, KENNETH WILLIAM, lawyer; b. N.Y.C., Apr. 21, 1931; s. William Otto and Neva H.; m. Jane Steinruck Stahl, Aug. 24, 1959; children: Lisa Fevery, Susan Mitchell, William, John. BS, Lehigh U., 1953; LLB, Harvard U., 1958. Bar: Oreg. 1958, U.S. Dist. Ct. Oreg. 1958. Assoc., then ptnr. Miller, Nash, Wiener, Hager & Carlsen and predecessors, Portland, Oreg., 1958-96; dir. Willamette Industries, Inc., Portland. Contbr. articles to legal publs. 1st lt. U.S. Army, 1953-55. Mem. ABA, Oreg. Bar Assn., Multnomah Athletic Club. Democrat. Episcopalian. Avocations: aviation, gardening. Home: 4237 SW Arthur Way Portland OR 97221-3203

HERGER, WALLY W., congressman; b. Yuba City, Calif., May 20, 1945. Formerly mem. Calif. State Assembly; mem. 100th-106th Congresses from 2d Calif. dist., 1987—; mem. agr., mcht. marine and fisheries coms. 100th-103rd Congresses from 2d Calif. dist.; mem. budget com., mem. ways and means com.; owner Herger Gas, Inc. Office: US Ho of Reps 2433 Rayburn Bldg Washington DC 20515-0502*

HERGERT, HERBERT LAWRENCE, consultant; b. Portland, Oreg., Feb. 20, 1927; s. John Edward and Elizabeth (Blahm) H.; m. Lois Marion Lilly, Dec. 20, 1949; children: Lawrence A., Gregory K., David E., Daniel W. BA, Reed Coll., 1948; MS, Oreg. State U., 1951, PhD, 1954. Asst. prof. Oreg. State U., Corvallis, 1952-54; rsch. chemist Rayonier Inc., Shelton, Wash., 1954-70; asst. dir. R&D ITT Rayonier Inc., N.Y.C., 1970-72, v.p., dir. R&D, 1972-80, dir. quality, 1971-79, v.p., dir. tech. mktg., 1980-87; sr. scientist Repap Techs. Inc., Valley Forge, Pa., 1987-97; trustee Textile Rsch. Inst., Princeton, N.J., 1976-82, Tech. Assn. Pulp & Paper Industries, Atlanta, 1980-83; forest products con., Pottstown, Pa., 1987-97; adj. prof. N.C. State U. Contbr. over 90 papers to profl. jours. and 7 chpts. to books. Chmn. bd. dirs. Shelton (Wash.) Gen. Hosp., 1962-66, Shelton Sch. Dirs., 1966-70; adv. bd. Cons. Bapt. Theol. Seminary, Denver, 1968-79. Corp. USAAF, 1945-46. Fellow Internat. Acad. Wood Sci.; mem. Am. Botanical Soc., Internat. Paleobotanical Soc., Soc. Wood Sci. and Tech., Am. Chem. Soc., TAPPI. Republican. Baptist. Achievements include 6 U.S. patents and 36 foreign patents. Home: 901 Burdan Dr Pottstown PA 19464-4475

HERGOTT, ALAN, laywer. Ptnr. Bloom Hergott Cook Diemer & Klein, Beverly Hills, Calif. Office: Bloom Hergott Cook Diemer & Klein 150 S Rodeo Dr Flr 3 Beverly Hills CA 90212-2410*

HERGUTH, ROBERT JOHN, columnist; b. Chgo., Apr. 4, 1926; s. Harry Conrad Herguth and Loretta (Oberreither) Herguth-Slimmer; m. Margaret Ann Silsbee, Apr. 16, 1966; children: Amy Rene, Robert Charles, Mary Jennifer. BA in Journalism, U. Mo., 1948. Copy editor, reporter Peoria Star, Ill., 1948-54; reporter, feature writer, columnist Chgo. Daily News, 1954-78; columnist Chgo. Sun Times, 1978-97, freelance weekly columnist, 1997—. Mem. editl. bd. Chgo. Sun Times., 1985-86. With U.S. Army, 1950-52. Inducted into Chgo. Journalism Hall of Fame, 1996. Mem. Chgo. Newspaper Guild (Page One award 1973), Chgo. Press Club (v.p. 1984-87, pres. 1987). Democrat. Roman Catholic.

HERING, DORIS MINNIE, dance critic; b. N.Y.C., Apr. 11, 1920; d. Harry and Anna Elizabeth (Schwenk) H. B.A. cum laude, Hunter Coll., 1941; M.A., Fordham U., 1985. Freelance dance writer, 1946-52; assoc. editor, prin. critic Dance mag., N.Y.C., 1952-72; exec. dir. Nat. Assn. for Regional Ballet, N.Y.C., 1972-87; adj. assoc. prof. dance history NYU, 1968-78; freelance dance writer, lectr., cons., 1987—; mem. dance panel NEA, 1972-75, cons., 1991—; mem. dance panel N.Y. State Coun. Arts, 1992-96, program auditor, 1997—; bd. dirs. Walnut Hill Sch., 1975—, Internat. Ballet Competition, 1981—; hon. bd. dirs. Phila. Dance Alliance, 1980—; cons. Regional Dance Am.; adj. assoc. prof. dance history NYU Grad. Sch. Edn. Author: 25 Years of American Dance, 1950, Dance in America, 1951, Wild Grass, 1965, Giselle and Albrecht, 1981; sr. editor Dance mag., 1989—. Howard D. Rothschild Rsch. fellow Harvard U., 1991-93; recipient 33d ann. Capezio Dance Found. award for lifetime svc., 1985, Award of Distinction Dance mag., 1987, Sage Cowles Land Grant chair in dance U. Minn., 1993; named to Hunter Coll. Alumni Hall of Fame, 1986. Mem. Dance Critics Assn., Assn. Dance History Scholars, Phi Beta Kappa, Chi Tau Epsilon (hon.).

HERING, WILLIAM MARSHALL, medical organization executive; b. Indpls., Dec. 26, 1940; s. William Marshall and Mary Agnes (Clark) H.; m. Suzanne Wolfe, Aug. 10, 1963. BS, Ind. U., 1961, MS, 1962; PhD, U. Ill., Urbana, 1973. Tchr. Indpls. pub. schs., 1962-66; asst. dir. sociol. resources project Am. Sociol. Assn., 1966-70; dir. social sci. curriculum Biomed. Interdisciplinary Project, Berkeley, Calif., 1973-76; staff assoc. Tchrs. Ctrs. Exchange, San Francisco, 1976-82; dir. research Far West Lab. Ednl. Research and Devel., San Francisco, 1979-82, sr. research assoc., 1982-85; mgr. human resource devel. Bank Am., San Francisco, 1985-94; dir. programs Am. Acad. Ophthalmology, San Francisco, 1994—; mem. Nat. Adv. Bd. Educ. Resource Info. Ctr.; cons. U.S. Dept. Edn.; pres. Social Sci. Educ. Consortium, 1981-82, bd. dirs., 1979-81; bd. dirs. San Francisco Chamber Orch., 1986-94. Nat. Inst. Educ. grantee, 1979-82. Mem. Am. Soc. Tng. and Devel. (v.p. 1986), Alliance Continuing Med. Edn., Alpha Tau Omega, Phi Delta Kappa. Republican. Episcopalian. Contbr. over 100 articles, book chpts. Home: 731 Duboce Ave San Francisco CA 94117-3214 Office: 655 Beach St San Francisco CA 94109-1342

HERINK, RICHIE, education company executive; b. Jersey City, Nov. 15, 1932; s. Reinhard and Anna (Golumb) H.; m. Nancy Gay Reck; children: Jennifer, Paul. ME, Stevens Inst. Tech., 1954; MS, Rensselaer Poly. Inst., 1957; EdD, Fairleigh Dickinson U., 1974; BA, Edison State U., 1976; BS, SUNY, 1976; PhD, Union Grad. Sch., 1979. Registered profl. engr., Vt., Mass. Staff engr. Western Electric Co., Kearney, N.J., 1957-67; systems analyst IBM Corp., White Plains, N.Y., 1967-76; mgr. IBM Corp., 1981-84, program mgr., 1976-81, 84—; workshop chmn. Nat. Rsch. Coun., Washington, 1986-87; mem. editorial bd., Internat. Jour. Tech. Mgmt., Milton Keynes, U.K., 1987-89, Jour. Engring. Tech. and Mgmt., Falls Church, Va., 1988-89. Patentee, transformer clamping device; author: College Level Statistics, 1965; editor: Psychotherapy Handbook. With U.S. Army, 1954-56. Recipient medallion for meritorious pub. svc., Econ. Devel. Coun. N.Y., 1977, medal for profl. accomplishment, U. Sofia, Bulgaria, 1988. Mem. Fairleigh Dickinson U. Doctoral Alumni Assn. (pres. 1981-85). Home: 786 Bingham Rd Ridgewood NJ 07450-2106 Office: Skillbuilders Inc Ridgewood NJ 07450

HERITAGE, LEE MORGAN, music educator, composer; b. Dover, Del., Nov. 15, 1958; s. Charles McKee and Virginia Catherine (Bateman) H.; m. Amy Heritage, Aug. 26, 1983. BMusic magna cum laude, Shenandoah Coll./Conservatory, Winchester, Va., 1984; MMusic, U. Wis., 1986; DMusical Arts, U. Ill., 1990. Prof. music U. Toledo, Ohio, 1989—; dir. composition studies Brevard (N.C.) Music Ctr., summers 1996—; adj. instr. Ind. State U., Terre Haute; propr. Heritage Music Engraving, Toledo, 1988-94. Composer: Two Poems, 1992, A Suffusion of Blue, 1996, Fling, 1996, Lullabye for Bear, 1997. Trustee Toledo Jazz Soc., 1993-96. Recipient 2d prize Carmichael Competition, Ind. U., 1989, 2d prize Composers Guild, 1998, others. Mem. Coll. Music Soc., Am. Music Ctr., Broadcast Music Inc., Phi Kappa Phi. Avocations: woodworking, golf. Office: U Toledo Dept Music Toledo OH 43606

HERKNER, BERNADETTE KAY, occupational health nurse; b. East Liverpool, Ohio, Apr. 29, 1947; d. Charles R. and Anna G. (Parr) Geon. Diploma in nursing, East Liverpool City Hosp., 1973; BS in Applied Sci., Youngstown (Ohio) State U., 1976. RN, Ohio, Mich., Fla; cert. in audiometrics, sipromety, ICD-9-CM; cert. case mgr.; cert. occupl. health nurse specialist. Charge nurse emergency rm. East Liverpool City Hosp., 1976-78; sr. occupl. health nurse specialist Dow Chem. N.Am., Midland, Mich., 1978—. Active Vol. Action Ctr. Midland County. Recipient Best Bedside Nurse, Centennial award for svc. to humanity, 1973, Ctrl. Mich. Outstanding Occupl. Health Nurse of Yr. award, 1993; named Miss Hope Columbiana County unit Am. Cancer Soc., 1977. Mem. Am. Assn. Occupl. Health Nurses (cert.), Mich. Assn. Occupl. Health Nurses (bd. dirs.), Emergency Nurses Assn., Mich. Nurses Assn., Ctrl. Mich. Assn. Occupl. Health Nurses (bd. dirs., corr. sec. 1986-90, rec. sec. 1990-91, pres. 1991-95, legis. chmn. 1995-96), East Ctrl. Mich. Emergency Nurses, Ohio Emergency Nurses Assn. (membership sec.), Case Mgmt. Soc. Am.

HERKNESS, LINDSAY COATES, III, securities broker; b. N.Y.C., Feb. 8, 1943; s. Lindsay C. and Harriett (Richard) H. B.A., Trinity Coll., Hartford, Conn., 1965. Sr. v.p. Morgan Stanley Dean Witter, N.Y.C., 1965—. Pres., bd. dirs. Manhattan Eye, Ear and Throat Hosp. Mem. Union Club, Downtown Assn., Piping Rock Club (Locust Valley, N.Y.), Bath and Tennis Club (Palm Beach, Fla.). Home: 160 E 65th St Ste 31C New York NY 10021-6654

HERKSTRÖTER, CORNELIUS, retired oil industry executive. Pres. Royal Dutch Petroleum Co., The Hague, The Netherlands, to 1998; also chmn. com. mng. dirs. Royal Dutch/Shell Group Cos., to 1998, ret., 1998. Office: Royal Dutch/Shell Group Cos. 30 Carel van Bylandtlaan, 2596 HR The Hague The Netherlands

HERLANDS, E. WARD, poet, printmaker; b. N.Y.C., Mar. 31, 1925; s. Max and Rose (Polaner) Schenker; m. Robert E. Herlands; children: Wendy, Nancy. BS, Pratt Inst., N.Y.C., 1946. Instr. U. Conn., Sterling Barn Theatre. Contbg. author: In A Word: A Harpers Magazine Dictionary of Words That Don't Exist But Ought To, McGraw Hill's Literature: Reading Fiction, Poetry, Drama and the Essay; contbr. works to Red Cedar Rev., Phoebus, Gryphon, N.Y. Times, Prairie Schooner, Midstream, Connecticut River Rev., No. New Eng. Rev., Ubiquitous, Fairfield County, The Prose Poem: An Internat. Jour., Ladies Home Jour., others; graphic arts/designs appeared in Mademoiselle, Vogue, Harpers Bazaar, Glamour, Good Housekeeping; author book revs. Mem. Poets and Writers, Poetry Soc. Am., Acad. Am. Poets, Conn. Poetry Soc., Stanford Art Assn., Pratt Inst. Alumni Assn. Home: 179 Fox Ridge Rd Stamford CT 06903-2216

HERLEMAN, LAURA ANN, nursing administrator; b. Allegheny County, Pa., Mar. 27, 1949; d. Frank K. and Ellen Louise (Hogg) Sweeny; m. William H. Herleman, Aug. 22, 1970 (dec.); children: William H. Jr., Amy S. Diploma in nursing, Allegheny Valley Hosp., Natrona Heights, Pa., 1970; student, Pa. State U., New Kensington, 1985-88; BSN, La Roche Coll., Pitts., 1995; postgrad., Duquesne U., 1998—. RN, Pa. Staff nurse med.-surg. units Allegheny Valley Hosp., Natrona Heights, Pa., 1970-76, 79-86; supr. nursing Allegheny Valley Hosp., 1986-91; staff nurse med.-surg. unit St. Clair Meml. Hosp., Pitts., 1977-79; asst. DON Allegheny Gen. Hosp., Pitts., 1990-93; staff nurse Allegheny Homecare, 1993-95, coord., 1995-96, mgr., 1996—; nursing supr. Forbes Nursing Ctr., Pitts., 1995-96; substitute sch. nurse Freeport (Pa.) Area Sch. Dist., Highlands Sch. Dist., Natrona Heights, 1988-94. Office: Allegheny Home Care 4 Allegheny Ctr Pittsburgh PA 15212-5255

HERLIHY, JAMES EDWARD, retail executive; b. Englewood, N.J., Dec. 29, 1942; s. James Edward and Agnes Cecilia (McNeil) H.; m. Marilyn Minor,Dec. 31, 1986; children: Courtney, Kimberly Ann, Laurel, Michael. BS in Acctg., Fairleigh Dickinson U., 1965. Sr. mgr. Price Waterhouse, 1964-79; fin. dir. Allied Suppliers Ltd., London, 1979-80; v.p., contr. Grand Union Co., Paramus, N.J., 1980-83, sr. v.p., CFO, 1983-86; exec. v.p., CFO Odd Lot Trading Inc., Elizabeth, N.J., 1987-88; sr. v.p. fin., CFO, bd. dirs. S.E. Nichols Inc., N.Y.C., 1988-91; exec. v.p., CFO The Bombay Co. Inc., Ft. Worth, 1991-97, Illuminations.com, Inc., Petaluma, Calif., 1998—. Treas., mem. bd. dirs. Van Cliburn Found., Inc., 1995—. Mem. AICPAs, N.J. State Soc. CPAs, Fin. Execs. Inst., Nat. Retail Fedn. (fin. divsn. bd. dirs.). Home: 1401 Hillcrest St Fort Worth TX 76107-1522 Office: Illuminations.com Inc 1995 S McDowell Blvd Petaluma CA 94954

HERLIHY, THOMAS MORTIMER, lawyer; b. N.Y.C., Apr. 8, 1953; s. John Wilfred and Mary Frances (O'Sullivan) H.; m. Janice Anne Lazzaro, Aug. 26, 1978; children: Carolyn Jane, John Wilfred II. BA in History, Columbia U., 1975; JD, Fordham U., 1978. Bar: Calif. 1978, U.S. Dist. Ct. (no. dist.) Calif. 1978, U.S. Dist. Ct. (ea. and so. dists.) Calif. 1979, U.S. Dist. Ct. (cen. dist.) Calif. 1984, U.S. Ct. Appeals (9th cir.) 1979. Assoc. Pettit & Martin, San Francisco, 1978-82; ptnr. Kornblum, Kelly & Herlihy, San Francisco, 1982-88, Kelly, Herlihy, Advani & Klein, San Francisco, 1988—; lectr. Rutter Group, trial skills program Calif. Continuing Edn. of Bar, 1983-86, 87, 88; adj. faculty Nat. Inst. Trial Advocacy, 1997-98. Mem. ABA (litigation sect., torts and ins. practice sect.), Calif. Bar Assn., San Francisco Bar Assn., Calif. Def. Counsel, Def. Research Inst. Republican. Roman Catholic. Clubs: Olympic, Columbia U. Alumlni Club. Home: 1424 Cortez Ave Burlingame CA 94010-4711 Office: Kelly Herlihy Advani & Klein 44 Montgomery St Ste 2500 San Francisco CA 94104-4712

HERLIHY-CHEVALIER, BARBARA DOYLE, mental health nurse; b. Cambridge, Mass., June 28, 1935; d. William A. and Aloyse V. (Mahoney) Doyle; m. Timothy J. Herlihy, Aug. 20, 1955 (dec. Oct. 1983); children: Michael, Ann-Marie, Sharon, Ellen, Stephen, Kathleen, James; m. Robert J. Chevalier, May 28, 1994 (dec. Oct. 1995); 1 stepchild, Ron. RN, Mass. Gen. Hosp., 1956; BS in Human Svcs., N.H. Coll., 1983; MS in Nursing, Anna Maria Coll., 1987. Nat. cert. instr. and coord. remotivation therapy. Pvt. duty nurse N.E. Bapt. Hosp., MGH, Boston, 1956-58, St. John's Hosp., Lowell, Mass., 1966-70; charge nurse Tewksbury (Mass.) Hosp. Mass. Dept. Pub. Health, 1970-76; coord. remotivation therapy Danvers (Mass.) State Hosp., 1976-79; registered community mental health nurse Mass. Dept. Mental Health, Lawrence, 1979-91; mental health nurse Lowell (Mass.) Adult Day Treatment, 1991-94. Mem. Nat. Remotivation Therapy Orgn. (nat. instr., coord.), Internat. Adv. Coun. Remotivation Therapy, Bay State Remotivation Coun. Home: 142 Trull Rd Tewksbury MA 01876-1705

HERLING, MICHAEL, steel company executive; b. Cernauti, Romania; arrived in Canada, 1950; m. Marta Klein; children: Dorothy Herling Chaikelson, Joyce Herling Saifer. B in Econs., U. Vienna, Austria, 1933; D in Econs., U. Florence, 1935. Sr. v.p. Ivaco, Inc., Montreal, Que., Can., 1969—. Office: Ivaco Inc 770 Rue Sherbrooke Ouest, Montreal, PQ Canada H3A 1G1

HERLINGER, DANIEL ROBERT, hospital administrator; b. Boskovice, Czechoslovakia, Oct. 27, 1946; came to U.S., 1950, naturalized, 1956; s. Rudolf and Ingeborg (Gessler) H.; m. Susanne Reiter, June 1, 1969; children: Lisa, Rebecca, Joanna. BS, Loyola U., Chgo., 1968; MBA, George Washington U., 1971. Asst. adminstr. Michael Reese Hosp., Chgo., 1971-73; v.p. Mercy Hosp., Chgo., 1973-84; pres. St. John's Regional Med. Ctr., Oxnard, Calif., 1984-94, Mercy Healthcare Ventura County, 1994-96, CHW Ctrl. Coast, Santa Barbara, Calif., 1996—. Fellow Am. Coll. Hosp. Adminstrs.; mem. World Pres. Orgn., Rotary. Jewish. Home: 15 Camino Verde Santa Barbara CA 93103-2144 Office: CHW Ctrl Coast 511 Bath St Santa Barbara CA 93101-3403

HERLONG, HENRY MICHAEL, JR., federal judge; b. Washington, June 1, 1944; s. Henry Michael Sr. and Josie Payne (Blocker) H.; m. Frances Elizabeth Thompson, Dec. 30, 1983; children: Faris Elizabeth, Henry Michael III. BA, Clemson U., 1967; JD, U. S.C., 1970. Bar: S.C. 1970, U.S. Ct. Appeals (4th cir.) 1972, U.S. Dist. Ct. S.C. 1972. Legis. asst. U.S. Senator Strom Thurmond, Washington, 1970-72; asst. U.S. atty. Dept. Justice, Greenville, S.C., 1972-76, Columbia, S.C., 1983-86; U.S. Magistrate judge U.S. Dist. Ct., Columbia, S.C., 1986-91; U.S. Dist. judge U.S. Dist. Ct., Greenville, S.C., 1991—; prin. Coleman & Herlong, Edgefield, S.C., 1976-83. Dir. Edgefield (S.C.) Devel. Bd., 1978-83, S.C. Assn. of Counties, 1980-83; active S.C. Rural Devel. Bd., 1980-83, Edgefield County Coun., 1979-83. Capt. USAR , 1970-75. Mem. S.C. Bar, Edgefield County Bar, Lions Club, Sertoma Club. Republican. United Methodist. Avocations: hunting, fishing, gardening. Office: US Dist Courts PO Box 10469 300 E Washington St Greenville SC 29603-1000*

HERMACH, FRANCIS LEWIS, consulting engineer; b. Bridgeport, Conn., Jan. 8, 1917; s. Frank and Barbara (Dauenheimer) H.; m. Frances M. Roberts, June 22, 1940 (dec. Feb. 1996); children: George, William (dec.); m. Elfriede Groen, Oct. 11, 1998. B.E.E., George Washington U., 1943. Sci. aid Nat. Bur. Standards, Washington, 1939-42; elec. engr., 1942-63, chief elec. instruments sect., 1963-72, dep. chief electricity div., 1970-72, cons., 1972-76; cons. engr. Elec. Measurements, Silver Spring, Md., 1976—. Contbr. articles on elec. measurements to profl. jours. Served with USNR, 1945-46. Recipient Disting. service award Dept. Commerce, 1954; Morris E. Leeds award IEEE, 1976, Centennial medal, 1984; Engr. Alumni Achievement award George Washington U., 1985. Fellow IEEE, Instrument Soc. Am., Washington Acad. Scis.; mem. Precision Measurements Soc., Philos. Soc. Washington. Methodist. Patentee in field. Home: 2850 Aquarius Ave Silver Spring MD 20906-1811

HERMAN, ALEXIS M., federal official; b. Mobile, Ala., July 16, 1947. Grad., Xavier U., 1969. Founder, CEO A.M. Herman & Assocs., Washington; nat. dir. Minority Women's Employment Program, Washington, until 1977; dir. Women's Bur. Dept. Labor, Washington, 1977-81; chief staff, then dep. chair Dem. Nat. Conv. Com., Washington, until 1991, CEO, 1991-92; dep. dir. Clinton-Gore Presdl. Transition Office, Washington, 1992-93; asst. to President U.S., Pub. Liason dir. White House, Washington, 1993-96; sec. labor U.S. Dept. Labor, Washington, 1997—. Mem. Nat. Coun. Negro Women, Delta Sigma Theta. Office: US Dept Labor Office Sec Washington DC 20210-0001

HERMAN, ALLEN IAN, foundation administrator; b. Pitts., June 16, 1950; s. Harry W. and Ann (Burke) H.; m. Jacqueline Wadler, July 5, 1981; children: Zvi, Ari, Michal. BA, U. Pitts., 1972; MBA, U. Pa., 1974. Cancer coordinator Jamaica (N.Y.) Hosp., 1975-76; asst. adminstr. Health Sci. Ctr., SUNY, Bklyn., 1976-79, assoc. adminstr., 1979-83; chief exec. officer Nephrology Found. Bklyn., 1983—; lectr. SUNY Health Sci. Ctr. Health Related Professions, Bklyn., 1983—; mem. council ESRD Network #25, N.Y.C., 1980-88. Mem. editorial bd.: Jour. Greater N.Y. Med. Records Assn., 1984; contbr. articles to profl. jours. bd. dirs. Hebrew Acad. West Queens, Jackson Heights, N.Y., 1987—; chmn. Youth Dept. Young Israel of Kew Gardens Hills, 1998—, coach little league baseball, 1990-98. Fellow Am. Coll. Healthcare Execs.; mem. Am. Hosp. Assn., Nat. Dialysis Assn. (bd. dirs. 1985-87, v.p. 1988, pres. 1989-90), Nat. Renal Adminstrs. Assn., Wharton Health Care Alumni Assn. Democrat. Jewish. Avocations: sports, music, photography. Office: Nephrology Found Bklyn 342 Flatbush Ave Brooklyn NY 11238-4902

HERMAN, ANDREA MAXINE, newspaper editor; b. Chgo., Oct. 22, 1938; d. Maurice H. and Mae (Baron) H.; m. Joseph Schmidt, Oct. 28, 1962. BJ, U. Mo., 1960. Feature writer Chgo.'s Am., 1960-63; daily columnist News Am., Balt., 1963-67; feature writer Mainichi Daily News, Tokyo, 1967-69; columnist Iowa City Press-Citizen, 1969-76; music and dance critic San Diego Tribune, 1976-84; asst. mng. editor features UPI, Washington, 1984-86, asst. mng. editor news devel., 1986-87; mng. editor features L.A. Herald Examiner, 1987-91; editor/culture We/Mbl Newspaper, Washington, 1991—. Recipient 1st and 2d prizes for features in arts James S. Copley Ring of Truth Awards, 1982, 1st prize for journalism Press Club San Diego, 1983. Mem. Soc. Profl. Journalists, Am. Soc. Newspaper Editors, AP Mng. Editors, Women in Communications. Avocations: music, art. Office: We/ Mbl Newspaper 1350 Connecticut Ave NW Washington DC 20036-1722

HERMAN, BARRY MARTIN, international economist; b. Bklyn., June 27, 1943; s. Aaron and Fannie Herman; m. Martha Feldman, Mar. 19, 1967; children: Alicia, Mark. AB, Columbia U., 1965; MBA, U. Chgo., 1967; PhD, U. Mich., 1974. Mgmt. analyst U.S. Bur. of the Budget, Washington, 1967; lectr. in econs. U. Mich., Dearborn, 1972-73; asst. prof. Dickinson Coll., Carlisle, Pa., 1973-75; instr. Lehman Coll., CUNY, Bronx, 1975-76; econs. affairs officer UN, N.Y.C., 1976-89, chief developed economies sect., 1989-95, chief internat. econ. rels. br., 1995—. Editor, author: International Finance and Developing Countries in a Year of Crisis, 1998, Financial Turmoil and Reform, 1999; contbr. articles to profl. jours. Mem., rev. panel, children in a globalizing world UNICEF, N.Y.C., 1997—; resource person, expert group on capital market volatility Commonwealth Secretariat, London, 1998; mem. conf. planning com. Global Interdependence Ctr., Phila., 1995—. Mem. Am. Econs. Assn. E-mail: herman@un.org. Office: Dept Econs and Social Affairs UN New York NY 10017

HERMAN, CHESTER JOSEPH, physician; b. Cin., Nov. 24, 1941; s. Chester and Aline (Reilley) H. Student, Xavier U., Cin., 1959-62, Fordham U., 1962-64; PhD, MD, U. Rochester, 1970. Diplomate Am. Bd. Pathology. Research assoc. NIH, Bethesda, Md., 1970-72, resident in anatomic and clin. pathology, 1972-76; pathologist Nat. Cancer Inst., Bethesda, 1972-79, Cath. U., Nijmegen, Holland, 1979-83, City Hosps., Delft, Holland, 1983-86; prof. pathology Loyola U., Chgo., 1986-91, Emory U. Sch. Medicine, 1991—; dir. pathology Grady Meml. Hosp., Atlanta, 1991—. Contbr. numerous articles to profl. jours. Served with USPHS, 1970-79. Recipient Commendation medal USPHS, 1978; named Fgn. Specialist, Japanese Govt., 1978. Mem. Internat. Acad. Pathology, Coll. Am. Pathologists, Soc. Analytic Cytology.

HERMAN, DAVID HENRY, artist, violin restorer and dealer; b. N.Y.C., Apr. 28, 1940; s. Morris and Elsie (Lass) H.; m. Sandra Lois Pinker, June 27, 1972; children: Lori, Tammy, Deanne. BS, NYU, 1961; MA, Bklyn. Coll., 1970. Tchr. orchestral music J.H.S. 210, N.Y.C., 1961-64, Elmont (N.Y.) Meml. H.S., 1964-94; violin restorer, dealer East Meadow, N.Y., 1975—; painter L.I. and N.Y.C., 1991—; mem., organizer Rudolf Baranik Art Seminar, N.Y.C., 1996—; panelist Fitting into 21st Century Heckscher Mus., Huntington, N.Y., 1996. One-man shows include Hewlett-Woodmere Libr., N.Y., 1994, Gallery Swan, Soho, N.Y., 1995, Gallery Emanuel, Kings Point, N.Y., 1996, Nexus Gallery, N.Y.C., 1998, Caelum Gallery, 1998, 99; group exhbns. include Nassau County Mus. Annex, 1993, Heckscher Mus., Huntington, N.Y., 1997, Mills Pond House, St. James, N.Y., 1998, Amos Eno Gallery, N.Y. With USAR, 1961. Mem. Appraisers Assn. Am. Jewish. Avocations: walking, reading, playing the piano.

HERMAN, DAVID JAY, orthodontist; b. Rome, N.Y., Oct. 4, 1954; s. Maurice Joseph and Bettina S. (Stiener) H.; m. Mary Beth Appleberry, Apr. 11, 1976; children: Jeremiah D., Kellin A. BA in Biology, San Jose State U., 1976; DDS, Emory U., 1981; MS in Orthodontics, U. N.C., 1992, MPH, 1992. Comdr. USPHS, 1981-97; advanced gen. practice resident Gallup (N. Mex.) Indian Med. Ctr., 1983-84; Navajo area dental br. chief Window Rock, Ariz., 1986-89; mem. grad. residency com. U. N.C., Chapel Hill, 1990-91; Navajo area orthodontic specialist Shiprock, N. Mex., 1992-97; clin. dir. Nizhoni Smiles Inc., 1997-99; pvt. practice Farmington, N.Mex., 1998—; pres. Four Corners Orthodontics, Inc., 1998—; mem. health adv. bd. Navajo Reservation Headstart, 1986-89; health promotion/disease prevention cons. USPHS-Indian Health Svc. Navajo Area, Window Rock, 1986-89; cons. Ariz. IHS Periodontal Health Task Force, 1986-90. Asst. wrestling coach Winslow (Ariz.) H.S., 1984-86, Gallup High Sch., 1987-89, Chapel Hill H.S., 1991-92, Farmington H.S., 1992-97, Aztec H.S., 1998—; mem. Farmington Youth Wrestling Program, 1992—. Recipient Healthy Mothers/Healthy Babies Disease Prevention award, 1988, USPHS Achievement medal, 1985, Headstart Achievement award, 1989, Ariz. Pub. Health Assn. Hon. award, 1989; Nat. Health Svc. Corp. scholar Emory U., 1977-81. Mem. ADA (v.p. N.Mex. soc. 1998—), Am. Assn. Orthodontists, Rocky Mountain Soc. Orthodontists, N.Mex. Soc. Orthodontists (v.p. 1996-97, pres. 1998—), Northwestern N.Mex. Sco. Orthodontists (v.p.), Navajo Area Dental Soc. (pres. 1985), Am. Assn. Mil. Orthodontists (sec.reas. 1992, v.p. 1993-94, pres. 1995-97). Avocations: wrestling, weight lifting, jogging, skiing, backpacking.

HERMAN, DEBORAH ANN, secondary education educator; b. Chester, Pa., Sept. 6, 1972; d. Glen Jean Jr. and Deborah Lee (Lay) Keiser; m. Gregg Alan Herman, July 13, 1996. BS in Edn. in English, West Chester (Pa.) U., 1995. Cert. instrnl. I tchr., Pa. Tchr. English, Coatesville (Pa.) Area Sch. Dist., 1996—; cons. Lincoln U., Pa., 1997. Recipient Gift of Time award Am. Family Inst., 1996. Mem. Nat. Coun. English Tchrs., Lions. Republican. Methodist. Avocations: weightlifting, reading, gardening.

HERMAN, DONALD ALOYS, radio station personality and official; b. Detroit, Aug. 3, 1927; s. Aloys Frank and Rose Catherine (Daugherty) H.; m. Mary Frances Morley, July 19, 1949; children: Frank, Rebecca Herman Hartglass, Barbara Herman Middleton, Carolyn Herman Murray, Monica Herman André, Patricia (dec.), Stephanie (dec.). BA, U. Mich., 1950, MA, 1954. Announcer, disc jockey Sta. WPAG, Ann Arbor, Mich., 1947-50, Sta. WHRV, Ann Arbor, 1950-61; news anchor, host talk show Community Forum, commentator Sta. WCKY, Cin., 1961-67, 70-94; adminstrv. asst. to supt. Cin. Pub. Schs., 1967-70; morning show personality, features and news dir. Sta. WSAI, Cin., 1994—; part-time mem. faculty U. Mich., Ann Arbor, 1952-61; mem. adj. faculty No. Ky. U., Highland Heights, 1985-94. Narrator 1937 flood TV documentary, Cin., 1987; comml. tapes include Cincinnati Christmas Past, Don Herman's Poets Corner. Past pres. Ann Arbor chpt. Mich. Assn. for Emotionally Disturbed Children. With USN, 1945-46. Named to Hall of Fame, Queen City chpt. Soc. Profl. Journalists, Cin., 1996. Avocations: historic radio, classic cars, photography, vintage radio sets. Office: Sta WSAI 1111 St Gregory St Cincinnati OH 45202-1770

HERMAN, EDITH CAROL, journalist; b. Edgewood, Md., July 1, 1944; d. Herbert R. and Thirza E. (Simmons) H.; m. Leonard Wiener. B.A., Purdue U., 1966. Reporter Hollister Newspaper Chain, Wilmette, Ill., 1966-68; reporter Chgo. Tribune Newspaper, 1968-79, edn. editor, 1971-74, feature writer, 1976-79; sr. editor TV Digest Inc., 1980-83; pub. rels. mgr. AT&T, 1983-90; pub. rels. cons. Bethesda, 1990-94; sr. editor Warren Publishing, 1994—. Bd. dirs. Sigma Delta Chi Found. of Washington. Recipient Journalism award Ill. Edn. Assn., 1969-70; Editorial award Ill. Automatic Merchandising Council, 1977. Mem. Soc. Profl. Journalists. Home: 5501 Burling Ct Bethesda MD 20817-6309

HERMAN, ELVIN E., retired consulting electronic engineer; b. Mar. 17, 1921; s. John Lawrence and Martha Elizabeth (Conner) H.; m. Grace Winifred Eklund, Sept. 29, 1945; 1 child, Jane Ann Herman Fischer. BSEE, State U. Iowa, 1942. Engr., sect. head Naval Rsch. Lab., Washington, 1942-51; sect. head Corona (Calif.) Labs., Nat. Bur. Stds., 1951-53; sect. head, lab. mgr., tech. dir. radar sys. group Hughes Aircraft Co., El Segundo, Calif., 1953-83; cons. electronic engr., Pacific Palisades, Calif., 1983-88; ret., 1988. Recipient Meritorious Civilian Svc. award Naval Rsch. Lab., 1946. Fellow IEEE. Achievements include 24 patents in field. Home: 1200 Lachman Ln Pacific Palisades CA 90272-2228

HERMAN, GEORGE ADAM, writer; b. Norfolk, Va., Apr. 12, 1928; s. George Adam and Minerva Nevada (Thompson) H.; m. Patricia Lee Glazer, May 26, 1955 (div. 1989); children: Kurt, Erik, Karl, Lisa, Katherine, Christopher, Jena, Amanda; m. Patricia Jane Piper Dubay, Aug. 25, 1989; children: Lizette, Paul, Kirk, Victoria. PhB, Loyola Coll., 1950; MFA, Cath. U., 1954; cert. fine arts, Boston Coll., 1951,52,53. Asst. prof. Clarke Coll., Dubuque, Iowa, 1955-60, Villanova (Pa.) U., 1960-63; asst. prof., playwright in residence Coll. St. Benedict, St. Joseph, Minn., 1963-65; chmn. theatre dept. Coll. Great Falls, Mont., 1965-67; media specialist Hawaii State Dept. Edn., Honolulu, 1967-75, staff specialist, 1975-83; sr. drama critic Honolulu Advertiser, 1975-80; artistic dir. Commedia Repertory Theatre, Honolulu, 1978-80; freelance writer, lectr., composer Portland, Oreg., 1983—. Author: (plays) Company of Wayward Saints, 1963 (McKnight Humanities award 1964), Mr. Highpockets, 1968, A Stone for Either Hand, 1969, Tenebrae, 1984, (novels) Carnival of Saints, 1994 (finalist Oreg. Book Awards 1994), A Comedy of Murders, 1994, Tears of the Madonna, 1995; composer (ballets) The Dancing Princesses, Fraidy Cat. Pres. local chpt. Nat. Sch. Pub. Rels. Assn., Honolulu, 1981-83; bd. dirs. Honolulu Community Theatre, 1981-82, Hawaii State Theatre Coun., Honolulu, 1981. With U.S. Army, 1950-52. Recipient Hartke Playwrighting award Cath. U., 1954, Excellence award Am. Security Coun., 1967. Avocations: directing theatre, lecturing.

HERMAN, GEORGE EDWARD, radio and television correspondent; b. N.Y.C., Jan. 14, 1920; s. Sydney H. and Tessie Samuels (Dryfoos) H.; m. Patricia Kerwin, Feb. 19, 1955; children—Charles, Scott, R. Douglas. A.B. cum laude, Dartmouth Coll., 1941; M.S., Columbia U., 1942. Night news editor radio sta. WQXR, N.Y.C., 1942-44; joined CBS, 1944; bur. mgr. CBS, Tokyo, Japan, 1950-53; Washington corr. CBS, 1954-87; moderator Face the Nation, 1969-84; also lectr.; free-lance corr., contbr. Nat. Pub. Radio and World Monitor TV, 1987—. Contbr. articles to mags. Mem. AFTRA (v.p. 1970-78), Am. Automobile Assn., Press Club (Tokyo), Cosmos Club. Home: 4500 Q Ln NW Washington DC 20007-2569

HERMAN, HANK, writer; b. N.Y.C., Nov. 13, 1949; s. Philip and Stella (Rubenfeld) H.; m. Carol K. Korngut, Dec. 30, 1972; children: Matt, Greg, Robby. BA, U. Pa., 1971. Advt. copywriter Prentice-Hall, Englewood Cliffs, N.J., 1972-73; assoc. editor Travel Mgmt. Daily, N.Y.C., 1973-74; mng. editor TravelScene, N.Y.C., 1975-77; mng. editor Health Mag., N.Y.C., 1978-79, editor in chief, 1980-88; freelance writer, 1989—; health reporter Sta. WINS-Radio, N.Y.C., 1987-90. award-winning columnist Westport News, 1993—; author numerous mag. articles and youth sports fiction books, 1973—. Avocations: running, tennis, skiing, coaching youth sports.

HERMAN, HERBERT, materials science educator; b. N.Y.C., June 15, 1934; s. Samuel and Frances (Friedman) H.; m. Barbara R. Budin, July 1, 1963; 1 child, Daniel. B.S., DePaul U., 1956; M.S., Northwestern U., 1958, Ph.D., 1961. Fulbright scholar U. Paris, 1961-62, Argonne Nat. Lab., 1962-63; asst. prof. U. Pa., 1963-68, Ford Found. prof. in industry, 1967-68; prof. dept. materials sci. SUNY, Stony Brook, 1968—, chmn., 1974-80; leading prof., 1993—; dir. NSF Materials Rsch. Sci. & Engring. Ctr./Ctr. Thermal Spray, 1996—; liaison scientist U.S. Office Naval Research, London, 1975-76; mem. and chmn. NRC panels, 1978-81; indsl. cons. Editor-in-chief Treatise on Materials Science and Technology, 1972—, Materials Sci. and Engring., internat. jour.; contbr. articles to profl. jours. NSF grantee, 1964—, Office Naval Rsch. grantee, 1974—, U.S. Army Corps of Engrs. grantee, 1992—. Fellow Am. Ceramic Soc., Am. Soc. Metals; mem. AIME, ASM (chmn. thermal spray divsn. 1986-89), Acad. Ceramics, Am. Soc. Engring. Edn., Sigma Xi. Office: SUNY Dept Materials Sci Old Engring 314 Stony Brook NY 11794-2275*

HERMAN, IRVING LEONARD, business administration educator; b. Seattle, June 6, 1920; s. Joseph and Elizabeth Mitzie (Silverstone) H.; m. Jeanne Shirley Hasson, Aug. 31, 1946; children: Michelle (Mrs. Richard Dennis Ferkel), Deborah (Mrs. Tad Steven Shapiro). BA magna cum laude, U. Wash., 1942; MA, Stanford U., 1949, PhD, 1952. Research psychologist Air Force Personnel and Tng. Research Ctr., Lackland AFB and Mather AFB, Calif., 1950-58; engring. psychologist Lockheed Aircraft Corp., Sunnyvale, Calif., 1958; mgr. personnel devel. Aerojet-Gen. Corp., Sacramento, Calif., 1958-68; mgr. mgmt. devel. So. Calif. Gas Co., Los Angeles, 1968-69; assoc. prof. bus. and pub. adminstrn. Calif. State U., Sacramento, 1969-72, prof., 1972-90, prof. emeritus, 1990—, chmn. dept., 1978-80; mgmt. cons. to local bus. and industry. Bd. dirs. Community Svcs. Planning Coun., 1990—. 1st lt. AUS, 1942-45. Recipient Presdl. award Sacramento City-County C. of C., 1965; Irving L. Herman Day proclaimed by Mayor of Sacramento, May 12, 1990. Mem. AARP (mem. Calif. Capital City task force 1991-95), Soc. Human Resource Mgmt. (cert. life, sr. prof. human resource), Sacramento Human Resource Mgmt. Assn. (life), Sacramento City-County C. of C. (chmn. edn. com. 1964-65), Sacramento Pres. Assn. (pres. 1979-81), Phi Beta Kappa, Sigma Xi, Beta Gamma Sigma, Delta Sigma Pi. Home: 889 Commons Dr Sacramento CA 95825-6652 Office: Calif State U 6000 J St Sacramento CA 95819-2605

HERMAN, JOAN ELIZABETH, healthcare company executive; b. N.Y.C., June 2, 1953; d. Roland Barry and Grace Gales (Goldstein) H.; m. Richard M. Rasiej, July 16, 1977. AB, Barnard Coll., 1975; MS, Yale U., 1977. Actuarial student Met. Life Ins. Co., N.Y.C., 1978-82; asst. actuary Phoenix Mut. Life Ins. Co. (now Phoenix Home Life Mut. Ins.), Hartford, Conn., 1982-83; assoc. actuary, dir. underwriting research Phoenix Mut. Life Ins. Co., Hartford, Conn., 1983-84, 2d v.p., 1984-85, v.p., 1985-89, sr. v.p., 1989-98; pres. specialty businesses Wellpoint Health Networks, Woodland Hills, Calif., 1998; group pres. Well Point Health Networks, 1999—; bd. dirs. PM Holdings, Inc., Phoenix Group Holdings, Inc., Phoenix Am. Life Ins. Co., Emprendimiento Compartido, S.A., v.p.; bd. dirs. ProFuturo S.A., ProRenta S.A., La Construccion Seguros de Vida, S.A., BC Life & Health Co., Profl. Claims Svcs Inc., Proserv. Contbr. articles to profl jours. Capt. fundraising team Greater Hartford Arts Coun., 1986; bd. dirs. Hadassah, Glastonbury, Conn., Temple Beth Hillel, South Windsor, Conn., 1983-84, Children's Fund Conn., 1992-98, My Sister's Place, Shelter, Hartford, 1989-94, Western Mass. Regional Nat. Conf. Conn., 1995-98, Greater Hartford Arts Coun., 1997-98; bd. dirs. Hartford Ballet, 1989-95, corporator, 1995-98; bd. dirs. Leadership Greater Hartford, 1989-94, chmn. bd. dirs., 1993-94; mem. bd. founders Am. Leadership Forum of Hartford, 1991-98; corporator Hartford Sem., 1994-98. Fellow Soc. Actuaries (chairperson health sect. coun. 1994-95); mem. Am. Acad. Actuaries (bd. dirs. 1994-97), Am. Leadership Forum, Home Office Life Underwriters Am. Jewish. Avocations: reading, swimming, bicycling, jogging, aerobic dancing, hiking. Office: Wellpoint Health Networks 1 Well Point Way Thousand Oaks CA 91367

HERMAN, JOSH SETH, actor, clown, magician; b. Passaic, N.J., Aug. 13, 1957; s. George and H. Lillian (Lissak) H. BS, U. Houston, 1980; student, HB Studio, 1984. Corp., radio, TV spokesman, symbol Rockaway's Playland, Rockaway Beach, N.Y., 1984; actor Royal Ct. Repertory Co., N.Y.C., 1984-85; clown Herriott Circus at Kid's World, Longbranch, N.J., 1985; illusionist, magician's asst. John Bundy Prodns., Woodbridge, N.J., 1985; magic demonstrator Mecca Magic, Bloomfield, N.J., 1985—; corp. symbol Little Jake Welsh Farms, Long Valley, N.J., 1985—; creator of clown team (with Dawn Spaven) Smilin Josh and Miss Silly Bubbles, 1985; local advance publicity clown Great Am. Circus, Allan C. Hill Entertainment Corp., Sarasota, Fla., 1986; clown in TV comml., performer Powerplant Entertainment Ctr., Six Flags Corp., Balt., 1986; prin. nat. TV comml. Dial Soap, 1987; performer Macy's TV comml., 1989; co-producer TV show (with Dawn Spaven) The Neighborhood Playground, 1990. Appeared in TV commls. Great Adventure Amusement Park, 1991, Wendy's Internat., 1992, Delta Airlines, 1997, 98; performer Good Living Exposition Home Shows, 1992-97. Mem. Nutley (N.J.) Little Theatre, 1984—, Studio Players Essex County, Montclair, N.J., 1985-86; bd. dirs. New Theatre North Jersey, Pompton Plains, N.J., 1984-86. Mem. Screen Actors Guild, World Clown Assn., Clowns Am. Internat., Merri Makers Clown Alley, Internat. Brotherhood Magicians. Office: PO Box 553 Clifton NJ 07012-0553

HERMAN, KENNETH BEAUMONT, lawyer; b. Medford, Mass., Jan. 23, 1944; s. Beaumont Alexander and Winifred (Small) H.; m. Agnes Anne Burch, Sept. 18, 1976; children: Alexander Beaumont, Juliana Burch. AB, Harvard U., 1966, JD, 1969. Bar: N.Y. 1971. Tchr. St. Dominic Savio High Sch., East Boston, Mass., 1969-70; assoc., then ptnr. Fish & Neave, N.Y.C., 1970—. Mem. Larchmont (N.Y.) Recreation Com., 1983—, trustee Larchmont Hist. Soc., 1987-88. Mem. ABA, N.Y. State Bar Assn., N.Y. Intellectual Property Law Assn. (chmn. com. on incentives for innovation 1987-88), Licensing Execs. Soc., Internat. Trade Commn. Trial Lawyers Assn., Fed. Cir. Bar Assn., Am. Intellectual Property Law Assn., Assn. Bar of City of N.Y., Am. Arbitration Assn. (panel arbitrators). Avocations: sailing, skiing, kayaking, reading. Home: 810 Pirates Cv Mamaroneck NY 10543-4717 Office: Fish & Neave 1251 Avenue Of The Americas New York NY 10020-1104

HERMAN, LLOYD ELDRED, curator, consultant, writer; b. Corvallis, Oreg., Mar. 19, 1936; s. Raymond R. and Luella Jane (McNabb) H. BS, Am. U., 1960. Pub. rels. mgr. Nat. Housing Ctr., Nat. Assn. Home Builders, Washington, 1965-66; adminstrv. officer Office Dir. Gen. Mus. Smithsonian Instn., Washington, 1966-71; dir. Renwick Gallery, Smithsonian Instn., 1971-86; dir. emeritus Renwick Gallery, Smithsonian Instn., Washington, 1993; dir. Can. Craft Mus., Vancouver, B.C., 1988-91; mem. adv. bd. Internat. Tapestry Network, 1991—, Friends Fiber Art Internat., 1991—. Author: Art that Works: The Decorative Art of the 80's, Crafted in America, 1990, Clearly Art: Pilchuck's Glass Legacy, 1992, Trashformations: Recycled Materials in Contemporary American Art and Design, 1998; co-author: Tales and Traditions: Storytelling in 20th Century American Craft, 1993. Chair Mcpl. Arts Commn., Bellingham, Wash., 1995. With USN, Pacific Fleet, 1956-58. Mem. Am. Craft Coun. (hon. fellow, 1991), Am. Assn. Mus., Glass Art Soc., Internat. Coun. Mus., Order Daneborg (Chevalier, 1981), Order Leopold II. Democrat. Avocations: swimming, theatre. Home: 8500 32nd Ave NW Seattle WA 98117-3901

HERMAN, LYNN BRIGGS, state legislator; b. Philipsburg, Pa., Oct. 30, 1956; s. Frederick Jr. and Barbara Ann (Briggs) H.; m. Barbara A. Gette, May 14, 1987. BA, U. Pitts., Johnstown, 1978; MPA, U. Pitts., 1980. Adminstrv. asst. Pa. Dept. Edn., Harrisburg, 1980-81; adminstrv. analyst Pa. Dept. Transp., Harrisburg, 1981-82; mem. Pa. Ho. of Reps., Harrisburg, 1982—. Named Outstanding Legislator, Pa. Rifle and Pistol Assn., 1987. Mem. Frat. Order Police, Grange, Pa. State Club, Elks, Kiwanis, Masons. Republican. Office: Pa Ho of Reps State Capitol Harrisburg PA 17120

HERMAN, MARK NORMAN, translator; b. Bklyn., Dec. 9, 1942; s. Joseph and Sylvia (Shapiro) H.; m. Ronnie Susan Apter, June 18, 1967; children: Daniel Arthur, Jeffry Michael. BS, Columbia U., 1963; MS, U. Calif., Berkeley, 1965. Pvt. practice Shepherd, Mich. Translator (with Ronnie Apter) of eighteen operas and operettas performed in the U.S., Can., and Eng.; author or translator numerous poems; contbr. articles to profl. jours.; pub. 1st Performing Edition of Alessandro Scarlatti's Eraclea. Mem. Am. Translators Assn. E-mail: herman.apter@sensible-net.com. Home and Office: 5748 W Brooks Rd Shepherd MI 48883-9202

HERMAN, MARTIN NEAL, neurologist, educator; b. Washington, July 19, 1939; s. Karl and Zina (Bratt) H.; m. Sydney Beryl Epstein, July 1, 1962; children: Kenneth Dayan, Heidi Felice. AA, George Washington U., 1960; BS, Northwestern U., 1961, MD, 1964. Diplomate Am. Bd. Electroencephalography, Am. Bd. Psychiatry and Neurology, Nat. Bd. Med. Examiners; lic. N.J. Intern Georgetown U./D.C. Gen. Hosp., Washington, 1964; resident psychiatry U. Rochester (N.Y.)/Strong Meml. Hosp., 1964; resident neurology U. Va., Charlottesville, 1967-70; rsch. fellow clin. neurophysiology NIH, Bethesda, Md., 1970-71; asst. prof., dir. electroencephalography N.J. Coll. Medicine and Dentistry, Newark, 1971-74; dir. neurology Monmouth Med. Ctr.; Long Branch, N.J., 1974—; asst. clin. prof. Hahnemann Med. Coll. and Hosp., 1974-91; clin. assoc. prof. Pa. U., Hahnemann U., 1991—; attending physician Martland Hosp., Newark, 1971-74, East Orange (N.J.) VA Hosp., 1971-74, Riverview Med. Ctr., Red Bank, N.J., 1983—. Contbr. chpts. in books and articles to profl. jours. Mem. AMA, Am. Acad. Neurology, Am. Med. Electroencephalographic Soc., Am. Clin. Neurophysiology Soc., N.J. Med. Soc., N.J. Acad. Medicine, Ea. Assn. Electroencephalographers, Phi Eta Sigma.

HERMAN, MARY MARGARET, neuropathologist; b. Plymouth, Wis., July 26, 1935; d. Elmer Fredolein and Esther Lydia (Bross) H.; m. Lucien Jules Rubinstein, Jan. 31, 1969. BS in Med. Sci., U. Wis., 1957, MD, 1960. Diplomate Nat. Bd. Med. Examiners, Am. Bd. Anatomic Pathology, Am. Bd. Neuropathology. Intern Mary Hitchcock Meml. Hosp., Hanover, N.H., 1960-61; resident in neurology U. Wis. Hosps., 1961-62; intern in pathology Yale U., New Haven, 1962-63, asst. resident in pathology, 1963-64, fellow neuropathology, 1964-65, rsch. assoc. pathology, 1967-68; fellow neuropathology Stanford U., Palo Alto, Calif., 1965-66, fellow, acting instr. neuropathology, 1966-67, asst. prof. pathology, 1967-74, assoc. prof., 1974-81; prof., co-dir. divsn. neuropathology U. Va. Sch. Medicine, Charlottesville, 1981-91, prof. clin. pathology, 1991-92; spl. expert neuropathology in clin. brain disorders br. NIMH, Washington, 1991-96, sr. staff scientist, 1996—; neuropathologist NIMH Brain Collection, 1992—, Stanley Fund Brain Collection, 1992—; vis. asst. prof. Albert Einstein Coll. Medicine, Bronx, N.Y., 1971-72; mem. program project rev. com. Nat. Inst. Neurol. and Communicative Diseases, NIH, 1973-77; cons. lab. svc. VA Hosp., Salem, Va., Ctrl. Va. Tng. Ctr., Lynchburg, 1982-92, ad hoc mem. pathology A study sect., 1986-91; cons. neuropathologist D.C. Med. Examiner's Office, Washington, 1992—, D.C. Gen. Hosp., 1992—; mentor scientist NIH Intramural Rsch. Tng. award, Fogarty Fellows, Howard Hughes Med. Inst./MCPS/NIH student and tchr. internships program, Stanley Found. scholar's program. Mem. edit. bd. Jour. Neuropathology and Exptl. Neurology, 1989-93; contbr. numerous articles to profl. jours. Recipient Rsch. Career Devel. award NIH, 1967-72, Faculty Devel. award Merck Found., 1969. Mem. AAAS, AMA, Am. Soc. Biol. Psychiatry, Am. Assn. Neuropathologists (Weil award 1974), Am. Soc. for Investigative Pathology, Soc. for Devel. Biology, Internat. Soc. Neuropathology, Am. Soc. Cell Biology (rsch. fellowship program, mentor scientist summer tchr. 1994), Internat. Acad. Pathology, Soc. In Vitro Biology, Soc. Neurosci. Achievements include work on neuropathology of serious mental disorders, embryonal tumors of CNS and aluminum neurotoxicity. Avocations: gardening, music, tennis. Home: 19022 Canadian Ct Gaithersburg MD 20886-3937 Office: Clin Brain Disorders Br NIMH/NIH MSC 4091 Bethesda MD 20892

HERMAN, RICHARD CHARLES, educator; b. Rochester, N.Y., Jan. 16, 1950; s. Donald Isaac and Opal Mae (Page) H.; children: Jileen, Matthew, Katrina, Stephanie. BS in Math., Roberts Wesleyan, 1972. Tchr. H.S. sci., math. Webster (N.Y.) Ctrl. Sch., 1972—, coach boys track, 1973-83, 89—, coach boys soccer, 1973-98; coach boys track Wayne Ctrl. H.S., Ontario, N.Y., 1984-89; pvt. practice roofer pvt. practice, Ontario, N.Y., 1990—. Republican. Free Methodist. Avocations: racquetball, tennis, soccer, auto mechanics, auto restoration. Home: 284 Boston Rd Ontario NY 14519-9367 Office: Webster HS 275 Ridge Rd Webster NY 14580

HERMAN, ROBERT JOHN, artist manager, author, music industry advisor; b. Aug. 30, 1955. Stage hand, asst. house mgr., talent booker Ungano's/Ritz Theatre, S.I., N.Y.; talent booker, from mid-1970s; cofounder the factory a music club, mid 1970s; exec. v.p. Moviola/J&R Film Co., N.Y.C., 1980-92; founder, pres. Consol. Video Svcs., from 1992; campaigned to save Fillmore East Theatre, N.Y.C.; Am. music corr. BBC Radio, London; pres. Pinnacle Artists. Author articles and music revs. for various publs. Home: 15 Egbert Ave Staten Island NY 10310

HERMAN, ROBERT LEWIS, cork company executive; b. N.Y.C., July 16, 1927; s. Nat W. and Ruth (Stockton) H.; m. Susan Marie Volper, Dec. 10, 1966; children: Candia Ruth, William Neal. AB, Columbia U., 1948, BS, 1949. V.p. Joseph Samuels & Sons, Inc., Whippany, N.J, 1953-62; pres. Dependable Cork Co., Inc., Morristown, N.J, 1962—; sr. chmn. Amorim Indsl. Solutions, Inc., Trevor, Wis., 1999—; bd. dirs. Concorco LDA, Lisbon, Portugal, Oporto, Portugal, Amorim Indsl. Solutions, LDA, Oporto, Portugal. Inventor Corticiera natural cork wallcovering. Comdr. C.E. Corps, USNR, 1949-53. Mem. N.J. Mfrs. Assn., Naval Res. Assn., U.S. C. of C., Navy League Club, Columbia U. Club, Princeton Club (N.Y.C.). Home: PO Box 1023 Morristown NJ 07962-1023 Office: PO Box 1102 Morristown NJ 07962-1102

HERMAN, ROBERT SAMUEL, former state official, economist, educator; b. Newburgh, N.Y., Dec. 18, 1919; s. Bernard O. and Leona (Gottlieb) H.; m. Beatrice Hirsch, June 20, 1942; children: Gerald W., Arthur P. AB, Union Coll., 1941; MA, U. Cin., 1942; PhD, NYU, 1950. Lectr. Syracuse U., 1947-60; vis. prof. Russell Sage Coll., 1948-57, State U. N.Y., 1960-62; vis. lectr. Econ. Devel. Inst., Washington, 1958-69; dir. research and fiscal policy div. budget N.Y. State Exec. Dept., Albany, 1950-63, dir. budget planning and devel., 1963, asst. budget dir., 1963-66; exec. dir. Commn. on Constl. Conv., 1966-67; exec. asst. to pres. N.Y. State Constl. Conv., 1967; dir. N.Y. Senate Com. on Higher Edn., 1968-72; prof. CUNY, 1968; prof. SUNY-Albany, 1968-69, vis. prof., 1970—; prof. econs. and pub. adminstrn., chmn. dept. Union Coll., Schenectady, 1969-74; spl. adviser N.Y. State Assembly, 1974-80; chmn. Kennerman Assos., 1979-89, Ednl. Planning and Mgmt. Assocs., 1982-86; cons. UN; former U.S. adviser to, Venezuela, Peru, India, Greece, Ecuador, Nigeria, Turkey, Iran, Guatemala, Iran, U.S. State Dept. lectr., India, Nepal, Iran, 1972. Author: poems; contbr. articles to profl. jours. Mem. adv. com. Nat. Planning Assn., Ctr. for Econ. Projections, Rand Corp., Ford Found.; adviser Assoc. Arts Councils, Inst. Man and Sci.; staff v.p. Nat. Conf. State Legislatures, 1974—; dir. Traffic Safety Inst. Recipient Charles Evans Hughes award for Excellence in Pub. Svc., 1991, award for Excellence in Hwy. Safety Rsch., U.S. Dept. Transp., 1992. Mem. Phi Beta Kappa. Home: 2 Creekside Ct Slingerlands NY 12159-9335 Office: SUNY 80 Wolf Rd Albany NY 12205-2608

HERMAN, R(OBERT) THOMAS, journalist. BA, Yale U., 1968. Intern Washington bur. Wall St. Jour., 1967, reporter N.Y. bur., 1968-69, 74-76, reporter Atlanta bur., 1969-74, reporter Asian edit., 1976-77; econ. reporter Wall St. Jour., N.Y.C., 1978—. Co-author: The Flat-Tax Primer, others; columnist: The Wall Street Jour.'s "Tax Report", 1994—. Office: Wall St Jour 200 Liberty St New York NY 10281-1003

HERMAN, ROGER ELIOT, professional speaker, consultant, futurist, writer; b. San Francisco, Cal., Dec. 11, 1943; s. Carlton Martin and Estelle (Nadler) H.; m. Janet I. Meyer, June 22, 1969 (div. Feb. 1974); 1 child, Scott Philip; m. Sandra Jean Steckel, May 2, 1974 (div. Sept. 1997); children: Bruce, Jeffrey, Jennifer; m. Joyce L. Gioia, Dec. 27, 1997. BA in Sociology, Hiram Coll., 1969; MA in Pub. Adminstrn., Ohio State U., 1977. Cert. mgmt. cons.; cert. speaking profl. Mgr. Rayco, Inc., Kent, Ohio, 1970-72; pvt. practice sales Stow, Ohio, 1972-76; pub. service dir. City Hilliard, Ohio, 1976-78; city mgr. City Rittman, Ohio, 1978-80; pres. Herman Assocs., Inc., Greensboro, N.C., 1980—. Author: Disaster Planning for Local Government, 1982, Emergency Operations Plan, 1983, The Process of Excelling, 1988, Keeping Good People, 1990, 99, Turbulence!, 1995, Lean & Meaningful, 1998, Signs of the Times, 1999; contbg. editor: Workforce and Workplace Trends, The Futurist mag.; contbr. mag. columns, articles to profl. jours. Commr. Ohio Boy Scouts Am., 1970, scoutmaster Texas (Ohio) Boy Scouts Am., 1966-70. Served with U.S. Army, 1965-68. Named Most Interesting Person In Northeast Ohio, Cleve. mag., 1981, named one of Outstanding Young Men Am., 1976, 77, 78, 79; recipient Arrowhead award Boy Scouts Am., Ohio, 1969. Mem. ASTD (chmn. profl. devel. 1987-88, program chmn. 1985-86, newsletter editor N.E. Ohio chpt. 1985-86), Nat. Spkrs. Assn. (cert. speaking profl.), Inst. Mgmt. Cons. (cert. mgmt. cons., pres. Ohio chpt. 1991-95, nat. bd. dirs. 1996—, vice chair 1999—), World Future Soc., Ohio Jaycees (Hilliard pres. 1976-77, Blue Chip Disting. Svc. award 1977), Toastmasters (dist. lt. gov. Texas, Ohio 1965-80, Able Toast master award 1969). Republican. Jewish. Avocations: writing, classic car restoration. Office: The Herman Group 3400 Willow Grove Ct Greensboro NC 27410-8600

HERMAN, SCOTT HUNT, radio station executive; b. Bklyn., Dec. 9, 1958; s. Morton and Sheila Marcia (Weiss) H.; m. Beth Amey, Dec. 20, 1981; children: Sean Michael, Jamie Lynn, Gregory Daniel. BA in TV and Radio, Bklyn. Coll., 1980. Unit mgr. WINS Radio, N.Y.C., 1981-82, asst. news dir., 1982-83, news dir., 1983-85, v.p., gen. mgr., 1994—; program dir. KYW Radio, Phila., 1985-88; program dir., exec. dir. WMAQ Radio, Chgo., 1988-90; news dir. KYW TV, Phila., 1990-92; dir. news programming KYW TV, KYW Radio and WMMR Radio, Phila., 1992-93; v.p. news CBS Radio Networks, 1997-98; v.p., gen. mgr. WINS-AM, WNEW-FM, N.Y.C., 1998—. Recipient Best Radio Newscast award UP Internat., 1983, 84, 40 Under 40 award Phila. Bus. Jour., 1993, Tree of Life award Jewish Nat. Fund, 1998. Mem. AP Broadcasters (v.p. radio 1993-95, pres.-elect 1995-97, pres. 1998—), N.Y. Market Radio Broadcasters Assn. (vice chmn. 1997, treas. 1994—), N.Y. State Broadcasters Assn. (bd. dirs. 1995—, state coord. 1985-87), Internat. Radio and TV Soc. (bd. dirs. found. 1994—), N.Y. Press Club. Jewish. Avocations: sports, softball, baseball, movies. Office: 1010 WINS Radio 888 7th Ave New York NY 10106-0001*

HERMAN, SIDNEY N., lawyer; b. Chgo., May 14, 1953; s. Leonard M. and Suzanne (Nierman) H.; m. Meg Dobies. BA, Haverford Coll., 1975; JD, Northwestern U., 1978. Bar: Ill. 1978, U.S. Dist. Ct. (no. dist.) Ill. 1978, U.S. Ct. Appeals (7th cir.) 1982, U.S. Supreme Ct. 1983. Assoc. Kirkland & Ellis, Chgo., 1978-84, equity ptnr., 1984-93; founding ptnr. Bartlit Beck Herman Palenchar & Scott, Chgo., 1993—; bd. dirs. Todd Shipyards Corp., Sigmatron, Inc., Chgo., Am. Steel Wool Mfg., Inc., Chgo. Articles editor Northwestern U. Law Rev. Trustee Francis W. Parker Sch. Mem. ABA, Ill. Bar Assn. Jewish. Office: Bartlit Beck Et Al Courthouse Pl 54 W Hubbard St Chicago IL 60610-4645

HERMAN, STEPHEN ALLEN, lawyer; b. Suffolk, Va., Nov. 27, 1943; m. Sally Jean Mansbach, Sept. 7, 1968; children: Braden, Andrew. BS, U. Pa., 1965; LLB, U. Va., 1968. Bar: Va. 1968, D.C. 1970, U.S. Ct. Appeals (D.C. cir.) 1970. Instr. law U. Chgo., 1968-70; assoc. Kirkland & Ellis, Washington, 1970-75, ptnr., 1975-90; sr. v.p., gen. counsel U.S. Generating Co., Bethesda, Md., 1990—. Author: FERC Practice and Procedure, 1984. Mem. Energy Bar Assn. (past pres.). Office: US Generating Co 7500 Old Georgetown Rd Ste 1300 Bethesda MD 20814-6161

HERMAN, STEPHEN CHARLES, lawyer; b. Johnson City, N.Y., Apr. 28, 1951; s. William Herman and Myrtle Stella (Clark) Keithline; m. Jeanne Ellen Nelson, Sept. 9, 1972; children: Neelie Kristine, Stefanie Anne, Christopher William. Student, Cedarville Coll., 1969-72; BA, Wright State U., 1973; JD, Ohio No. U., 1976. Bar: Mo. 1977, Ill. 1977, U.S. Dist. Ct. (no. dist.) Ill. 1979, U.S. Dist. Ct. (ea. dist.) Mo. 1978, U.S. Dist. Ct. (ea. dist) Mich. 1988, U.S. Dist. Ct. (so. dist.) Tex. 1997, U.S. Ct. Appeals (7th cir.) 1979, U.S. Ct. Appeals (10th cir.) 1992, U.S. Supreme Ct. 1986, U.S. Ct. Internat. Trade, 1998. Atty. Mo. Pacific Railroad Co., St. Louis, 1977-78; assoc. Belnap, McCarthy, Spencer, Sweeney & Harkaway, Chgo., 1978-82; ptnr. Belnap, Spencer & McFarland, Chgo., 1982-83, Belnap, Spencer, McFarland & Emrich, Chgo., 1983-84, Belnap, Spencer, McFarland, Emrich & Herman, Chgo., 1984-89, Belnap, Spencer, McFarland, Herman, 1990-96, McFarland & Herman, 1996—. Mem. ABA, Mo. Bar Assn., Met. Bar Assn. St. Louis, Ill. State Bar Assn., Chgo. bar Assn., Met. Bar Assn. St. Louis, Assn. Transp. Law, Logistics and Policy, Tower Club, Univ. Club (Chgo.). Home: 440 E Wisconsin Ave Lake Forest IL 60045 Office: McFarland & Herman 20 N Wacker Dr Ste 1330 Chicago IL 60606-2902

HERMAN, STEVEN DOUGLAS, cardiothoracic surgeon, educator; b. Budapest, Hungary, Apr. 7, 1945; came to U.S., 1949; s. Frank Elroy and Marta (Fischer) H.; m. Jacqueline Lee Forman, Aug. 14, 1983; children: Andrew Scott, Rebecca Sue. Student, Cornell U., 1962-64; BA, Johns Hopkins U., 1966, MD, 1969. Diplomate Am. Bd. Surgery, Am. Bd. Thoracic Surgery. Intern, resident, chief resident in surgery N.Y. Hosp.-Cornell Med. Ctr., N.Y.C., 1969-75, resident, chief resident in cardiovasc. and thoracic surgery, 1975-77; asst. prof., attending surgeon adult and pediatric cardiothoracic surgery Hahnemann Med. Sch. and Hosp., Phila., 1977-79; chief cardiovasc. and thoracic surgery St. Vincent's Med. Ctr., Bridgeport, Conn., 1979-88; attending cardiothoracic surgeon St. Michael Med. Ctr., Univ. Hosp., Newark, 1990—; attending thoracic surgery Mt. Sinai Med. Ctr., N.Y.C.; clin. asst. prof. surgery Univ. Medicine and Dentistry N.J., Newark, 1991-94, clin. assoc. prof., 1994—; instr. surgery med. coll. Cornell U., N.Y.C., 1974-77; cons. cardiothoracic surgery Milford (Conn.) Hosp., 1979-90; attending surgeon cardiothoracic surgery Bridgeport Hosp., 1979-84, Park City Hosp., Bridgeport, 1989-90, Clara Maass Med. Ctr., Belleville, N.J., 1991—, Mountainside Hosp., Montclair, N.J., 1992—, St. Barnabas Med. Ctr., Livingston, N.J., 1992—; mem. courtesy staff cardiothoracic surgery Park City Hosp., 1978-89, Bridgeport Hosp., 1984-90, Univ. Medicine and Dentistry N.J.-Univ. Hosp., 1990-97; adj. prof. cardiothoracic surgery Mt. Sinai Med. Sch., N.Y.C., 1997—; mem. cardiovasc. task force Health Sys. Agy., Fairfield County, Conn., 1980-81; mem. exec. com. St. Michael's Med. Ctr., 1993-96; presenter in field. Contbr. articles to profl. jours. Trustee Congregation Ahavath Achim, Fairfield, Conn., 1983-90, Hillel Acad. Sch., 1984-87, Aleh Found., Bnai Brak, Israel. Thoracic Surgery fellow Meml. Hosp., Sloan-Kettering Cancer Ctr., 1975. Fellow ACS, Am. Coll. Cardiology, Coll. Physicians Phila.; mem. Am. Heart Assn. (mem. cardiovasc. coun., bd. dirs. Fairfield County br. 1980-83, program chmn. Ea. Fairfield County region 1985), N.Am. Soc. Pacing and Electrophysiology, N.J. Soc. Thoracic Surgeons, N.Y. Acad. Scis., N.J. Med. Soc., Essex County Med. Soc. (mem. spkrs. bur. com. 1992—), Soc. Thoracic Surgeons, Internat. Soc. Cardiothoracic Surgeons, Internat. Soc. Heart Transplantation, Internat. Assn. Cardiac Biol. Implants, Assn. Acad. Surgery, C. Walton and Richard C. Lillehei Surg. Soc., Johns Hopkins Med. & Surg. Soc., Gen. Thoracic Surg. Club. Republican. Jewish. Avocations: skiing, tennis, computers. Home: 160 E Linden Ave Englewood NJ 07631-3622 Office: 268 Dr Martin Luther King Newark NJ 07102

HERMAN, THERESA JOAN (TERRI), quality assurance professional; b. Omaha; d. Maurice Brice and Rita Claire Breen; m. David Allan Herman, Aug. 24, 1985; children: James David, Michael Thomas. BS in Criminal Justice, U. Nebr., 1984, MPA, 1996. Security officer Omaha Pub. Power Dist., Ft. Calhoun, Nebr., 1985-87, emergency planning planner, 1987-90, plant rev. com. tech. coord., 1994-95, sr. quality assurance lead auditor, 1990—. Bd. edn. St. Philip Neri Sch., Omaha, 1999. Mem. Am. Soc. Quality, Pi Alpha Alpha. Republican. Roman Catholic. Avocation: singing. Office: Omaha Pub Power Dist PO Box 399 Fort Calhoun NE 68023

HERMAN, WILLIAM ARTHUR, physics and engineering laboratory administrator; b. Washington, Mar. 9, 1947; s. William Jackson and Alma Rebecca (Wattwood) H. BSEE, George Washington U., 1968. Chief microwave sect. Southeastern Radiol. Health Lab., Montgomery, Ala., 1968-70; chief microwave measurements unit FDA, Rockville, Md., 1970-73, dep. chief, electromagnetics br., 1973-74, sr. engr. electromagnetics br., 1974-79, assoc. dir. divsn. electronic products, 1979-83, dir. divsn. phys. scis., 1983—; mem. Interagy. Group on Sci. Performance Measures, Rockville, 1994—; staff mem. Blue Ribbon Panel on FDA, Washington, 1990; expert panelist NAS Symposium on Video Display Terminals and Vision; 1981, NIH Bioengring. Symposium: Bldg. the Future of Biology and Medicine, Instruments and Devices Panel, 1998. Contbr. articles to profl. jours.; patentee in field. With USPHS, 1968-74. Mem. IEEE (sr.), World Future soc., Inst. Noetic Scis., Mensa, Tau Beta Pi (sec. 1968), Washington Ethical Soc., Amnesty Internat., Sigma Tau, Omicron Delta Kappa, Phi Eta Sigma, Alpha Theta Nu. Buddhist. Avocations: musician, writing.

HERMAN, WILLIAM GEORGE, municipal government executive; b. West Chester, Pa., Sept. 2, 1956; s. Albert William Jr. and Beverly Lou (Marshall) H.; m. Mary Jo Batchelder, July 7, 1983; children: Brian William, Andrew Albert. Grad. H.S., Weare, N.H., 1974. Cert. pub. mgr. Reporter, photographer Union Leader Corp., Manchester, N.H., 1973-80; prin., owner Herman Assocs. P.R., Manchester, 1980-82; press sec. Gov. John H. Sununu, Concord, N.H., 1982-83; programs info. officer N.H. Divsn. Human Svcs., Concord, 1984-86, Divsn. Econ. Devel., Concord, 1986-92; pub. info. officer Fed. Emergency Mgmt., Boston, 1992—; town adminstr. Town of Milton, N.H., 1993-95, Town of New Durham, N.H., 1995—; affiliate, cons. Mcpl. Resources, Inc., Concord, 1995—; dir. N.H. Pub. Works Mut. Aid Program, 1999—; mem. U.S. Selective Svc. #4, Merrimack County, 1999—. Mem., vice chmn. U.S. Selective Svc. #10, Hillsborough County, 1982-98; mem., chmn. Bd. Selectmen, Weare, N.H., 1984-96; commr., officer So. N.H. Planning Commn., Manchester, 1984-96; chmn. Concord Regional SW/RRC, Corcord, 1987—; dir. Greater Manchester ARC, 1988-94; trustee YMCAA Camp Coniston, Grantham, N.H., 1989-93; dir. ARC Blood Svc., Dedham, Mass., 1989-98. Recipient George Washington honor medal Freedom Found., Valley Forge, Pa., 1973, Svc. award Town of Weare, 1996, Grassroots govt. leadership award Nat. Assn. Towns & Twps., Washington, 1991. Mem. Internat. City/County Mgmt. Assn., N.H. Assn. Cert. Pub. Mgrs., N.H. Mcpl. Mgmt. Assn., N.H. Govt. Fin. Officers. Republican. Avocations: reading, travel, computers, tennis. Home: 203 Loudon Rd Unit 721 Concord NH 03301-6088 Office: Town of New Durham PO Box 207 New Durham NH 03855-0207

HERMANCE, JOHN FRANCIS, geophysics educator, environmental geophysics and hydrology consultant; b. Kingston, N.Y., Jan. 9, 1939; s. H. Louis and Mary R. Hermance; children: Scott, Travis. BSc, SUNY, New Paltz, 1961; MSc, Syracuse U., 1964; PhD, U. Toronto, 1967. OSHA cert. health and safety ops. at hazardous materials sites. Rsch. assoc. MIT, 1967-68; asst. prof., assoc. prof., prof. dept. geol. scis. Brown U., Providence, 1968—; dir. numerous geophys. field projects in Iceland, the Azores, the Yukon, Can., N.E. U.S. and major volcanic ctrs. in western U.S.; vis. faculty fellow Petroleum Rsch. Ctr., Bartlesville, Okla., 1974; vis. sr. rsch. assoc. Lamont-Doherty Geol. Obs., 1975-76; chmn. thermal regimes panel Nat. Acad. Scis. Continental Sci. Drilling Com., 1982-85; chmn. workshop Nat. Geomagnetic Initiative, NRC, NAS, 1992; mem. NASA/MAGSAT Investigator's Tem; mem. Inter-Union Commn. on the Lithosphere/CC-5; exec. com., bd. mem. Deep Observation and Sampling of the Earth's Continental Crust through Sci. Drilling, 1984-87; sci. adv. com. Long Valley Deep Exploration Well, DOE/GTD and Sandia Nat. Labs., 1985-94. Assoc. editor Environ. Geology, 1980-82, Tectonophysics, 1987-92. Mem. AAAS, Am. Geophys. Union, Soc. Exploration Geophysicists (best presentation award ann. meeting 1974), Nat. Ground Water Assn./Assn. Ground Water Scientists and Engrs., Soc. Environ. and Engring. Geophysicists. Office: Brown U Dept Geol Scis Providence RI 02912-1846

HERMANCE, LYLE HERBERT, college official; b. Lincoln, Nebr., Dec. 10, 1939; s. Milo Lee Sr. and Amelia Henrietta (Schoneman) H.; m. Dorothy Kay Stanislav, June 12, 1960 (div.); children: Lane Alan, Lori Ann, Russell Joel; m. Janette Kay Sims, Oct. 11, 1986. BS, U. Nebr., 1964, MS, 1970. Cert. agr. edn. tchr., Nebr. Tchr. vocat. agr. and indsl. arts Emerson (Nebr.)-Hubbard Pub. Schs., 1964; tchr. vocat. agr. Waverly (Nebr.) Pub. Schs., 1964-79, chmn. dept. vocat. edn., 1973-79; coord. adult agr. program area cmty. svcs. div. S.E. C.C., Lincoln, 1979—, dir. Adult Edn. Ctrs. area cmty. svcs. div., 1991—, interim dir. div., 1992-94, dir. div., 1994-96, dir. continuing edn., 1996—; rep. Nebr. Turkey Coun., 1968-72, Nebr. Grassland and Forage Coun., 1969—; nat. coord. computers in agr. demonstration contest Future Farmers Am. 1990-93; mem. adult edn. task force Nat. Coun. for Agrl. Edn., 1991—; mem. adv. coun. agrl. edn. dept. U. Nebr., 1987—; mem. S.E. Rsch. and Ext. Ctr. adv. team Inst. Agr. and Natural Resources, 1992—; asst. supt. Future Farmers Am. div. sheep show Nebr. State Fair, 1988-90, supt., 1990—; pres. Nebr. Vocat. Agrl. Found., 1970-71, bd. dirs., 1991-92. Bd. dirs. Lancaster County Pub. Nursing Adv. Com., 1972-76; mem. Lancaster County Extension Bd., 1990-95, pres., 1992-95; mem. Nebr. affiliate task force Am. Heart Assn., 1992—; mem. spl. com. on agrl. edn. Nebr. Coun. Vocat. Edn., 1986-88; charter bd. dirs., advisor Nebr. Agrl. Leadership Coun., Inc., 1980-82; charter mem. Nebr. Coalition for Agrl. Fin. Mgmt. Edn., 1990—, state co-chmn., 1991—; bd. dirs. Nebr. Assn. Vocat. Indsl. Clubs Am., 1995—, state coord. leadership and skills contest, 1996—. Recipient hon. degree Future Farmers Am., 1970, 71, 94, Nebr. Disting. Svc. award, 1994, Nebr. Lifetime Svc. award, 1996. Mem. NEA, Nebr. Edn. Assn., Waverly Edn. Assn. (pres. 1970-71, Lancaster County Agrl. Soc. (bd. dirs. 1991), Nebr. Vocat. Agrl. Assn. (dist. v.p. 1967-68, state pres. 1968-69, dist. chmn. 1966-67, 87-89, 97—, state sec./treas. 1971-73, 77-81, dist. vice chmn. 1996-97, Outstanding Young Mem. award 1969, Outstanding Post Secondary Instr. award 1988, 30 Yrs. of Dedicated Svc. to Agrl. Edn. award 1994), Nebr. Vocat. Assn. (bd. dirs. 1976-80, state pres. 1980-81), Nat. Farm Ranch Bus. Mgmt. Edn. Assn. (nat. sec. 1989-90, nat. pres. 1991-92), Nebr. Assn. for Adult Agrl. Educators (charter, pres. 1988-89), Am. Vocat. Assn., Nat. Assn. Agrl. Educators, U. Nebr. Alumni Assn.,Waverly Kiwanis. Home: 13305 N 112th St Lincoln NE 68517

HERMANIES, JOHN HANS, lawyer, retired; b. Aug. 19, 1922; s. John and Lucia (Eckstein) H.; m. Dorothy Jean Steinbrecher, Jan. 3, 1953. A.B., Pa. State U., 1944; JD, U. Cin., 1948, D of Law (hon.), 1992. Bar: Ohio 1948. Atty. Indsl. Commn. Ohio, 1948-50; asst. atty. gen. State of Ohio, 1951-57, asst. to gov., 1957-59; ptnr. Hermanies & Major (formerly Beall, Hermanies, Bortz & Major), Cin., 1958-99; mem. bd. grievances and discipline Supreme Ct. Ohio, 1976-82; ret., 1999; mem. Ohio Bd. Bar Examiners, 1963-68. Mem. Southwest Ohio Regional Transit Authority, 1973-76; trustee U. Cin, 1977-92, Found. Bd., 1992—; mem. bd. elections Hamilton County, Ohio, 1984-88; chmn. exec. com. Hamilton County Rep. Party, 1974-88. With USMC, WWII. Mem. ABA, Ohio Acad. Trial Lawyers Assn., Am. Judicature Soc., Bankers Club, Queen City Club, Highland Country Club, Hyde Park Golf and Country Club. Home: 1201 Edgecliff Pl Cincinnati OH 45206-2847

HERMANN, ALLEN MAX, physics educator; b. New Orleans, July 17, 1938; s. Edward Frederick and Miriam (Davidson) H.; m. Leonora Christopher, May 19, 1979 ; children: Miriam, Mary, Neil, Scott. BS with honors in Physics, Loyola U., New Orleans, 1960; MS in Physics, U. Notre Dame, 1962; PhD in Physics, Tex. A&M U., 1965. Sr. research scientist Jet Propulsion Lab, Pasadena, Calif., 1965-67, tech. mgr., 1985-86; asst. prof. physics Tulane U., New Orleans, 1967-70, assoc. prof. physics, 1970-75, prof. physics, 1975-81; task mgr. Solar Energy Research Inst., Golden, Colo., 1980-85; prof., chmn. dept. physics U. Ark., Fayetteville, 1986-89, Disting. prof., 1989; prof. dept. physics U. Colo., Boulder, 1990—; cons. Jet Propulsion Lab., 1978-81, 86-87, NASA-Lewis Rsch. Ctr., Cleve., 1978-80, Cardiac Pacemakers Inc., Mpls., 1976-79, Radiation Monitoring Devices, Newton, Mass., 1990-93, Superconducting Core Techs., Denver, 1989-95. Founding co-editor Applied Physics Communication; editor: Applied Physics Book Series; contbr. numerous articles to profl. jours. Bd. dirs. Colo. Assn. Retarded Citizens, Denver, 1983-85. Recipient NASA Outstanding Achievement award 1970, 72, Disting. Scientist award Am. Assn. Physics Tchrs., 1987; named Hero, State of Ark., Ark. Times mag.; named Person of the Yr., Superconductivity Week, 1989; elected to Acad. Disting. Grads., Coll. Sci., Tex. A&M U., 1999. Fellow Am. Phys. Soc.; mem. IEEE (sr.), Electrochem. Soc., Materials Research Soc. Home: 2704 Lookout View Dr Golden CO 80401-2520 Office: U Colo PO Box 390 Boulder CO 80309-0390

HERMANN, DONALD HAROLD JAMES, lawyer, educator; b. Southgate, Ky., Apr. 6, 1943; s. Albert Joseph and Helen Marie (Snow) H. AB (George E. Gamble Honors scholar), Stanford U., 1965; JD, Columbia U., 1968; LLM, Harvard U., 1974; MA, Northwestern U., 1979, Ph.D., 1981; MA in Art History, Sch. Art Inst. Chgo., 1993; postgrad., U. Chgo. Bar: Ariz. 1968, Wash. 1969, Ky. 1971, Ill. 1972, U.S. Supreme Ct. 1974. Mem. staff, directorate devel. plans U.S. Dept. Def., 1964-65; With Legis. Drafting Research Fund, Columbia U., 1966-68; asst. dean Columbia Coll., 1967-68; mem. faculty U. Wash., Seattle, 1968-71, U. Ky., Lexington, 1971-72; mem. faculty DePaul U., 1972—, prof. law and philosophy, 1978—, dir. acad. programs and interdisciplinary study, 1975-76, assoc. dean, 1975-78, dir. Health Law Inst., 1985—; lectr. dept. philosophy Northwestern U., 1979-81; counsel DeWolfe, Poynton & Stevens, 1984-89; vis. prof. Washington U., St. Louis, 1974, U. Brazilia, 1976, U. P.R. Sch. Law, 1993; lectr. law Am. Soc. Found., 1975-78, Sch. Edn. Northwestern U., 1974-76, Christ Coll. Cambridge (Eng.) U., 1977, U. Athens, 1980; vis. scholar U. N.D., 1983; mem. NEH seminar on property and rights Stanford U., 1981; participant law and econs. program U. Rochester, 1974; mem. faculty summer seminar in law and humanities UCLA, 1978; Bicentennial Fellow of U.S. Constitution Claremont Coll., 1986; Law and Medicine fellow Cleve. Clinic., 1990; bd. dirs. Coun. Legal Edn. Opportunity, Ohio Valley Consortium, 1972, Ill. Bar Automated Rsch. Corp., 1975-81, Criminal Law Consortium Cook County, Ill., 1977-80; cons. Adminstrv. Office Ill. Cts., 1975-90; reporter cons. Ill. Jud. Conf., 1972-90; mem. Ctr. for Law Focused Edn., Chgo., 1977-81; faculty Instituto Superiore Internazionale Di Science Criminali, Siracusa, Italy, 1978-82; cons. Commerce Fedn., State of São Paulo, Brazil, 1975. Editor: Jour. of Health and Hosp. Law, 1986-96, DePaul Jour. Healthcare Law, 1996—, AIDS Monograph Series, 1987—. Bd. dirs. Ctr. for Ch.-State Studies, 1982—, Horizons Cmty. Svcs., 1985-88, Chgo. Area AIDS Task Force, 1987-90, Howard Brown Health Ctr., 1994—; dir., v.p. Inst. for Genetics, Law and Ethics, Ill. Masonic Hosp., 1993—; trustee 860 N. Lakeshore Trust, Chgo., Ill., 1993-95; bd. visitors Oriental Inst., U. Chgo., 1995—, bd. dirs. Renaissance Soc., 1995—; mem. Cook County States Atty. Task Force on Drugs, 1985-90, Cook County States Atty. Task Force on Gay and Lesbian Issues, 1990—; mem. Ill. HIV Prevention Cmty. Planning Group, Ill. Dept. Pub. Health. John Noble fellow Columbia U., 1968, Internat. fellow, NEH fellow, Law and Humanities fellow U. Chgo, 1975-76, Law and Humanities fellow Harvard U., 1973-74, Northwestern U., 1978-82, Criticism and Theory fellow Stanford U. 1981, NEH fellow Cornell U., 1982, Judicial fellow U.S. Supreme Ct., 1983-84; Univ. scholar Northwestern U., 1979. Mem. ABA, Ill. Bar Assn., Chgo. Bar Assn., Am. Acad. Polit. and Social Sci., Am. Law Inst., Am. Soc. Law and Medicine, Am. Soc. Polit. and Legal Philosophy, Nat. Health Lawyers Assn., Am. Judicature Soc., Am. Philos. Assn., Soc. for Bus. Ethics, Soc. for Phenomenology and Existential Philosophy, Internat. Assn. Philosophy of Law and Soc., Soc. Writers on Legal Subjects, Internat. Penal Law Soc., Soc. Am. Law Tchrs., Am. Assn. Law Schs. (del., sect. chmn., chmn. sect. on jurisprudence), Am. Acad. Healthcare Attys., Ill. Assn. Hosp. Attys., Evanston Hist. Soc., Northwestern U. Alumni Assn., Signet Soc. of Harvard, Hasty Pudding Club, University Club, Quadrangle Club, Tavern Club, Cliff Dwellers Club, Arts Club Chgo., Legal Club Chgo., Law Club Chgo. Episcopalian. Home: 1243 Forest Ave Evanston IL 60202-1451 Office: DePaul U Coll Law 25 E Jackson Blvd Chicago IL 60604-2287 also: 880 N Lake Shore Dr Chicago IL 60611-1761

HERMANN, GEORGE ARTHUR, pathologist, educator; b. Dayton, Ky., Dec. 30, 1932; s. George Joseph and Ruth Flossie (Sauer) H.; m. Myrl Duncan, Aug. 14, 1954; children: Heather, George. AB, Harvard U., 1954; MD, Boston U., 1958. Diplomate Am. Bd. Pathology, Am. Bd. Nuclear Medicine. Tchg. asst. Harvard Med. Sch., Boston, 1961-62; instr. in pathology U. Pa., Phila., 1963-69, assoc. in pathology, 1969-73, clin. asst. prof. pathology, 1973-79, clin. assoc. prof. pathology, 1979-85, clin. prof. pathology, 1985—; chmn. imaging resource com. Coll. Am. Pathologists, Skokie, Mich., 1983-87; chmn. Am. Bd. Nuclear Medicine, L.A., 1991. Contbr. over 75 articles to profl. jours. Fellow Coll. Am. Pathologists, Coll. Physicians; mem. Soc. Nuclear Medicine, Am. Coll. Nuclear Physicans (imaging com. 1994). Avocation: tennis. Home: 705 Gt Springs Rd Bryn Mawr PA 19010

HERMANN, PAUL DAVID, retired association executive; b. Chgo., Feb. 1, 1925; s. Edgar Paul and Marjory (Alexander) H.; m. Joan Louise Mullin, Nov. 10, 1948; children: Bruce Phillip, Susan Marie. Student, Lawrence U., 1942-45; B.S. in Bus. Adminstrn, Northwestern U., 1948. Cert. assn. exec. Asst. dir. news bur. Ill. Inst. Tech., Chgo., 1945-48; editor Constrn. Equipment News, Chgo., 1948-49; exec. v.p. Assn. Equipment Distbrs., Oak Brook, Ill., 1950-90; pres. AED Research & Services Corp., 1974-90. Contbr. articles on assn. mgmt. to various jours. Mem. Am. Soc. Assn. Execs. (hon., pres. 1974, Key award 1985), Chgo. Soc. Assn. Execs. (life, pres. 1969), U.S. C. of C. (dir. 1980-82, chmn. assn. com. 1981-86, small bus. council 1976-82), Nat. Chamber Alliance for Politics (adv. council 1978-82), Inst. Orgn. Mgmt. (mem. bd. regents 1969-72), Delta Tau Delta (Alumni Achievement award 1982). Home: 411 S Prospect St Galena IL 61036-2159

HERMANN, PHILIP J., lawyer; b. Cleve., Sept. 17, 1916; s. Isadore and Gazella (Gross) H.; m. Cecilia Alexander, Dec. 28, 1945; children: Gary, Ann. Student, Hiram Coll., 1935-37; B.A., Ohio State U., 1939; J.D., Western Res. U., 1942. Bar: Ohio 1942. With Hermann Cahn & Schneider and predecessors, Cleve., 1946-86; founder, former chmn. bd. Jury Verdict Rsch., Cleve.; pres. Legal Info. Pubs. Author: 1956, Better Settlements Through Leverage, 1965, Do You Need a Lawyer?, 1980, Better, Earlier Settlements through Economic Leverage, 1989, Injured? How to Get All the Money You Deserve, 1990, The 96 Billion Dollar Game: You are Losing, 1993, How to Select Competent Cost-effective Legal Counsel, 1993, Profit With the Right Lawyer; contbr. articles to profl. jours. Served to lt. comdr. USNR, 1942-46, PTO. Mem. ABA (past vice chmn. casualty law com., past chmn. use of modern tech. com.), Ohio Bar Assn. (past chmn. ins. com., past chmn. fed. ct. com., past mem. ho. of dels.), Cleve. Bar Assn. (past chmn. membership com.), Am. Law Firm Assn. (past chmn. bd.), Fedn. Ins. Counsel. Club: Walden Golf and Tennis. Home: 615 Acadia St Aurora OH 44202 *Being what some people label "a perfectionist" is not easy and certainly not popular. It takes time and effort to collect information, to analyze it, to apply these to decisions and to insist upon careful work, but in the long run it is rewarding.*

HERMANN, ROBERT BELL, physical chemist, consultant; b. Bellevue, Pa., Dec. 12, 1930; s. Gustave Adolph and Alida Mae (Bell) H.; m. Phyllis Ann Halley, Aug. 7, 1958 (div. Feb. 1982); children: Deborah, David, Stephen; m. Carol Sue Lester, June 12, 1985. BS in Chemistry, U. Mich., 1953; MS, Wayne State U., 1960, PhD, 1962. Organic chemist Parke-Davis & Co., Detroit, 1953-58; NSF postdoctoral fellow U. Wis., Madison, 1962-63; postdoctoral fellow Ill. Inst. Tech., Chgo., 1963-64; computational chemist Eli Lilly & Co., Indpls., 1964-93; vis. prof. Ind. U.-Purdue U. Ind., Indpls., 1994—; cons. Eli Lilly & Co., 1994—. Contbr. articles to profl. jours. Presbyterian. Achievements include research of relationship between molecular surface area and solubility especially with regard to hyrdophobic interactions; patent for inhibitors of phospholipase A2. Office: Ind U Purdue U Indpls Dept Chemistry 402 N Blackford St Indianapolis IN 46202-3217

HERMANN, ROBERT EWALD, surgeon; b. Highland, Ill., Jan. 28, 1929; s. Ewald E. and Erna (Pabst) H.; m. Barbara Bower, Aug. 23, 1952 (dec. Aug. 1980); m. Polly Dreher, Mar. 8, 1986; childrn: Robert Jr., Barry, Monty. AB cum laude, Harvard U., 1950; MD, Washington U., St. Louis, 1954. Diplomate Am. Bd. Surgery. Intern, resident Univ. Hosps., Cleve., 1954-61; chmn. gen. surgery Cleve. Clinic, 1969-94, emeritus cons. dept. gen. surgery, 1994—; clin. prof. surgery Case Western Res. Sch. Medicine, Cleve., 1970—; dir. Am. Bd. Surgery, Phila., 1975-81; mem. Residency Rev. Com., Chgo., 1975-81. Author: Surgery of Gallbladder, Bile Ducts, Pancreas, 1979, Surgical Practice of Cleveland Clinic, 1985; contbr. over 180 articles to med. jours., 53 chpts. to books. Trustee Cleve. Clinic Found., 1976-77. Capt. M.C. U.S. Army, 1956-57. Recipient Roswell Park Gold medal Buffalo Surg. Soc., 1993. Mem. ACS (gov. 1981-87, v.p. 1996-97, Disting. Svc. award 1994), Am. Surg. Soc., German Surg. Soc. (hon.), Internat. Surg. Soc., Internat. Coll. Surgeons (hon.), Soc. Surg. Oncology, Soc. Surgery Alimentary Tract (pres. 1988-89), Assn. Program Dirs. Surgery (pres. 1979-81), Ea. Surg. Soc. (pres. 1985-86), Pan-Pacific Surg. Assn. (v.p. 1991-93), Joint Commn. on Accreditation of Healthcare Orgns. (bd. commrs. 1997—). Republican. Avocations: tennis, golf, sailing, music. Home: 1 Bratenahl Pl Apt 1403 Bratenahl OH 44108-1156 Office: Cleve Clinic A-80 9500 Euclid Ave Cleveland OH 44195-0001

HERMANN, ROBERT JAY, manufacturing company engineering executive, consultant; b. Sheldahl, Iowa, Apr. 6, 1933; s. John and Ellen Melinda (Ericson) H.; m. Darlene Velda Lowman, Mar. 20, 1954; children: Scott Alan, Sherie Lynn. BSEE, Iowa State U., 1954, MSEE, 1959, PhD, 1963. Dep. dir. research and engrng. Nat. Security Agy., Ft. Meade, Md., 1973-75; spl. asst. to supreme allied comr. Europe SHAPE, Casteau, Belgium, 1975-77; dep. under sec. of def. for research and engring. Dept. Def., Washington, 1977-79, asst. sec. of Air Force for research, devel. and logistics, 1979-81, spl. asst. for intelligence to under sec. of def. for research engring., 1981-82; v.p. systems tech. and analysis United Techs., Hartford, Conn., 1982-84, v.p. advanced systems def. and space group, 1984-87, v.p. sci. and tech., 1987-92, sr. v.p. sci. and tech., 1992-98; cons. Dept. Def., 1982—, Def. Sci. Bd.; mem. vis. com. advanced tech. Nat. Inst. Stds. and Tech., 1992-97; mem. Pres. Fgn. Intelligence Adv. Bd., 1993—; mem. commn. on phys. scis., math. and applications NRC, 1993-98; bd. dirs. Draper Labs., 1992—, Am. Nat. Stds. Inst., 1994—. 1st lt. USAF, 1955-57. Recipient Arthur Fleming Washington Jaycees, 1972; recipient Nat. Capital Nat. Capital Area Architects and Engrs., Washington, 1967, Air Force Disting. Service medal USAF, Washington, 1980. Mem. NAE, AIAA, Armed Forces Comms. and Electronics Assn. (bd. dirs. 1979-83), Security Affairs Support Assn. (pres. 1983-86, award 1994), Navy League (chmn. indsl. exec. bd. 1989). Home: 5 Stonepost Simsbury CT 06070-2511 Office: Conn Tech Assoc 160 Farmington Ave Farmington CT 06032-1728

HERMANN, ROBERT JOHN, lawyer, corporate executive; b. Chgo., Apr. 17, 1944; s. Jacob L. and Rose E. (McCrudden) H.; m. Lyn D. Johnson; children by a previous marriage: Kelly, Brenna, Richard, Edana. Student, U. Ill., 1962-65; BS, No. Ill. U., 1967; JD, DePaul U., 1970. Bar: Ill. 1970, U.S. Supreme Ct. 1988; CPA, Ill., Tex. Tax staff Deloitte Haskins & Sells, Chgo., 1968-81; dir. corp. tax Houston Natural Gas, 1981-82, v.p. corp. tax, 1982-85; v.p. corp. tax Enron Corp., Houston, 1985—. Mem. ABA, Nat. Assn. Mfrs. (taxation com.), Tax. Execs. Inst., Sweetwater Country Club. Home: 4002 S Oak Cir Sugar Land TX 77479-2426 Office: Enron Corp PO Box 1188 1400 Smith St Houston TX 77002-7369

HERMANSEN, JOHN CHRISTIAN, computational linguist; b. Athens, Greece, Oct. 21, 1949; s. John Theodore and Lois Ann (Shope) H.; m. Sharyl Lynn Miner (div. 1994); children: John Theodore, Janet Lois. BA in Speech, BA in Linguistics, Pa. State U., 1975; PhD in Computational Linguistics, Georgetown U., 1985. Cert. knowledge engr., 1992. Propr. CompAssociates, Inc., Washington, 1974-78; lectr., univ. fellow computational linguistics Georgetown U., Washington, 1980-83, dir. Lang. Processing Ctr., Sch. Langs. and Linguistics, 1982-85; artificial intelligence rsch. scientist Planning Rsch. Corp., McLean, Va., 1985-88, computational linguistics cons., 1988-90; cons. knowledge engring. Sterling Software, Inc., McLean, Va., 1991-95; lead scientist linguistics analysis team State Dept. CLASS Project, Lang. Analysis Systems, Inc., Herndon, Va., 1986—; computational linguistics cons. Ctr. for Applied Linguistics, Washington, 1985-94; CEO Lang Analysis Systems, Inc., Herndon, Va., 1991—. Co-author: Southeast Asia Refugee Testing Report, Vols. I and II, 1985, Report on the Evaluation of Kenya Radio Language Arts Project, 1985, PAKTUS Version 1 User's Guide, 1986, Building NLU Systems in the PAKTUS Environment: Developer's Introduction, 1987, Message Processing Systems: Evaluation Factors, 1987, Meronomy, Word Experts and Prepositional Phrase Attachment in PAKTUS, 1989, Techniques in Multilingual Name Searching, 1989, The Automated Templating System for Database Update from Unformatted Message Traffic, 1995, The On-line Name Reference Library Project, 1999, Automated Name Reference Library, 1999; contbr. articles to profl. jours.; patentee in field. Mem. IEEE, Assn. for Computational Linguistics, Internat. Assn. Knowledge Engrs., Soc. for Psychology and Philosophy, Data Adminstrn. Mgmt. Assn. Home: 12012 Robin Dr Catharpin VA 20143-1307 Office: Lang Analysis Systems Ctr for Innovative Tech 2214 Rock Hill Rd Herndon VA 20170-4214

HERMANSON OGILVIE, JUDITH, foundation executive; b. London, Oct. 16, 1945; d. John Herbert and Estella Barbara (Osborne) Hermanson; m. Keith William Ogilvie, Nov. 19, 1976. AB magna cum laude, Smith Coll., Northampton, Mass., 1967; student, Am. U., Paris, 1965; MA, George Washington U., 1968, PhD, 1983. Ops. tng. officer Peace Corps, Washington, 1968-70; assoc. dir. Peace Corps, Uganda, 1970-71, Philippines, 1971-72; policy analyst VISTA, Washington, 1972-73; spl. asst. to commr., vice chair Consumer Product Safety Commn., Washington, 1973-76; dir. program devel. evaluation Dept. HUD, Washington, 1976-77; co-founder, exec. v.p. Newman & Hermanson Co., Washington, 1977-83; dep. regional dir. African region Coop. Housing Found., Washington, 1984; program and tng. chief Peace Corps, Washington, 1984-86, regional dir. for Europe, Africa, Middle East, 1986-92; exec. v.p. internat. programs Coop. Housing Found., Washington, 1992-96, v.p., 1996—; cons. World Bank, U.S. AID; bd. dirs. Overseas Coop. Devel. Coun.; bd. trustees Am. U. Paris, 1999—. Contbr. articles to profl. jours. Mem. Montgomery County Housing and Community Devel. Adv. Com. Recipient John D Lange Internat. award Nat. Assn. Housing and Redevel. Ofcls., 1995, Disting. Alumni Profl. Achievement award Am. U. Paris, 1999. Mem. Phi Beta Kappa, Smith Club. Episcopalian. Office: Coop Housing Found 8300 Colesville Rd Silver Spring MD 20910-6225

HERMEL, SIDNEY H., artist; b. Mar. 26, 1922. BS, NYU, 1942. Artist, illustrator, jewelry designer N.Y.C.; art instr. various orgns., N.Y.C. With USAF. Office: 41 Union Sq W New York NY 10003-3208

HERMES, FRANK, marketing executive. BA, Dartmouth Coll.; MBA, U. Pa. Mktg. rep. IBM; v.p. Citibank N.A., 1973-84; sr. v.p. Standard & Poor's Corp., 1985-95; v.p. instnl. markets group OneSource Info. Svcs., Inc., Cambridge, Mass., 1995—. Office: OneSource Info Svcs Co 150 Cambridge Park Dr Cambridge MA 02140-2322*

HERMES, MARJORY RUTH, machine embroidery and arts educator; b. Caldwell, Kans., June 28, 1931; d. Truman Homer and Olive Ruth (Ridings) Brown; m. Ogden S. Jones, Jr., Dec. 17, 1949 (div. Aug. 1956); m. Richard Lawrence Hermes, July 18, 1963; children: Penelope, Peter, Deborah, Patricia, Pamela, Kristin. Student, U. Kans., 1949-50, Arkansas City Jr. Coll., 1953-54. Sec. Maurer-Neuer Corp., Arkansas City, Kans., 1954-56, Lesh, Bradley & Barrand, Lawrence, Kans., 1959-60; exec. sec. Houston Corp., Wichita, Kans., 1956-57; mgr. Ind. Ins. Co., Landstuhl, Fed. Republic Germany, 1960-62; sec. U. Kans., Lawrence, 1962-63; photograph restorer Herb's Studio, Lawrence, 1977-78; ptnr., agt. Hayes-Richardson-Santee Inc., Lawrence, 1978-83; instr. sewing and machine embroidery Self & Bob's Bernina, Lawrence, 1985—; mem. Lawrence Ins. Bd., 1980-83. Bd. dirs. United Way, Lawrence, 1981-83; host Am. Indian Athletic Hall of Fame, 1980-82; treas. local polit. campaigns, 1984, 88; leader Therapeutic Horse Riding Instrn., Lawrence, 1992-95. Mem. Nat. Machine Embroidery Instrs. Assn. (bd. dirs. for N.D., S.D., Nebr., Iowa, Mo., Minn. and Kans. 1987-90), Am. Sewing Guild, Am. Bus. Women's Assn. (v.p. Lawrence 1980-81, pres. 1981-82, Inner Circle award 1982, Woman of Yr. award 1984), Lawrence C. of C. (envoy 1978-83). Republican. Avocations: horsemanship, travel, sailing. Home: 2513 W 24th Ter Lawrence KS 66047-2818

HERMES, MOTHER THERESA MARGARET, prioress; b. Hallettsville, Tex., Sept. 30, 1906; d. Anthony Thomas and Teresa (Drysee) H. BA, U. Tex., 1930. Novice Discalced Carmelite Nuns, New Orleans, 1934-36; foundress Discalced Carmelite Nuns, Lafayette, La., 1936, directress of novices, 1936-48, prioress, 1948-82, 85-94; organizer, coord. St. Teresa Assn., Lafayette, 1978; organizer, counselor Carmelite Guild, 1950—. Collaborator Satutes/St. Teresa's Assn., 1979. Recipient Papal medal Pope John Paul II, Lafayette, 1990, Jerusalem Cross, Patriarch Maximos V Hakim, Lafayette, 1991, Mission Cross Rev. Giovanni Salerno, Lafayette, 1990, Mother-Counselor-Emerita, 1994—. Office: Discalced Carmelite Nuns 1250 Carmel Ave Lafayette LA 70501-5211 *Jesus prayed: "Father...that they may be one even as we are one...that they may be perfected in unity." John 17:22-23. As I observe the chaotic conditions prevailing in humanity today, it seems that Division (among nations, families, within Man himself) is the chief menace to its unity and consequent peace. May Jesus' prayer be realized through the action of the Spirit of Love in men's hearts.*

HERMINGHOUSE, PATRICIA ANNE, foreign language educator; b. Melrose Park, Ill., Mar. 13, 1940; m. 1964, 2 children. BA, Knox Coll., 1962; MA, Washington U., 1965, PhD in German, 1968. Asst. prof. German, U. Mo.-St. Louis, 1966-67, vis. lectr., 1968-69; asst. prof. Washington U., St. Louis, 1967-78, assoc. prof. German, 1978-83; Fuchs prof. German studies, U. Rochester, N.Y., 1983—, also chmn. dept. fgn. langs., lits. and linguistics, 1983-89; lectr. German, Fontbonne Coll., 1965-66. Internat. Research & Exchanges Bd. ad hoc grantee, 1976. Sr. fellow Nat. Endowment for the Humanities, 1991. Mem. MLA, Am. Assn. Tchrs. German (exec. council 1979-81), German Studies Assn. (exec. com.), Coalition Women German (coord. 1974-75, nat. steering com. 1976-79, 94—), Assn. Depts. Fgn. Langs. (exec. com.). Contbr. articles to profl. jours.; editor or co-editor: Literatur der DDR in den siebziger Jahren, 1983; Literatur und Literaturtheorie in der DDR, 1976; Frauen in Mittelpunkt, 1987, Gender and Germaness, 1997; editor GDR Bull.: Newsletter Lit. and Culture in German Dem. Republic, 1975-83; co-editor Women in German Yearbook. Address: U Rochester Dept Modern Langs Cult Rochester NY 14627

HERMUS, LANCE JAY, art appraiser; b. Bklyn., Mar. 2, 1954; s. William Hermus and Ethel (Tychman) Kornberg; m. Hoa Thi Ngueyn, July 1, 1980 (div. mar. 1993); children: Jennifer Barbara, Christopher; m. Tzipora Ingrid Corber, June 5, 1994; 1 child, Benjamin. BA in Art with highest honors, Coll. S.I., 1992; Cert. in Art Appraising, NYU, 1996. Registered art appraiser Appraiser Assn. of Am. Freelance photographer, artist S.I., 1972-92; video prodn. art dir. Master Prodns., S.I., 1988-90; conservator, curator, appraiser Santo Bruno Fine Art, S.I., 1992-96; conservator, curator William Myers Collection, N.Y.C., 1993-94; appraiser, art cons. Hermus Fine Arts, S.I., 1996—; asst. lectr., edn. dept. Met. Mus. of Art, N.Y.C., 1990-93; artist, photo restoration Snug Harbor Cultural Ctr., S.I., 1990-93. Mem. Dem. County Com., S.I., 1974, poll watcher, 1975. Mem. Appraiser Assn. of Am. (assoc.), Am. Inst. for Conservation of Hist. and Artistic Works. Jewish. Avocations: mus. and collection rsch., writing, coaching basketball, art collecting, reading. Home and Office: 312 Travis Ave Staten Island NY 10314-6251

HERNANDEZ, AMIE SUSAN, academic director; b. Manhattan, N.Y., Feb. 26, 1973; d. Alexander Peter Hernandez and Karen Gail Levitan. BA, SUNY, Oswego, 1995; MA, NYU, 1997. Bldg. mgr. student union SUNY, Oswego, 1993-95; asst. mgr. Third North Residence Hall NYU, N.Y.C., 1995-97; area coord. Manhattan Coll., Riverdale, N.Y., 1997-98; asst. dir. campus life Fairleigh Dickinson U., Teaneck, N.J., 1998—; program coord. Multicultural Camp, Teaneck, 1998—. Mem. AAUW, Am. Coll. Pers. Assn., Nat. Assn. Student Pers. Adminstrn., Coll. Student Pers. Assn., Hispanic Assn. for Higher Edn. N.J., Inc. Avocations: reading, advising, mentoring, movies, relaxing. Office: Fairleigh Dickinson U. 1000 River Rd T010C-FDU Teaneck NJ 07666

HERNANDEZ, ANGEL, umpire; b. Havana, Cuba, Aug. 26, 1961; m. Mireya Lopez, Nov. 10, 1984; children: Jennifer, Melissa. Former umpire Fla. State League, Carolina League, So. League, Venezuelan League, Fla. Instrnl. League, Triple Alliance, Am. Assn.; umpire maj. league baseball Nat. League, N.Y.C., 1993—; with Umpires Union, Phila. Active youth baseball Khoury League, Pony League. Avocations: hunting, motorcycles. Office: Nat League 350 Park Ave New York NY 10022 also: Umpires Union 1735 Market St Philadelphia PA 19103

HERNANDEZ, CHRISTINE, educational consultant; b. San Antonio, July 23, 1951; d. Joe and Aurora (Zapata) H. BA, Our Lady of the Lake Coll., 1973; MA, U. Tex., 1981. Cert. elem. tchr. Tchr. San Antonio Ind. Sch. Dist., 1973-83; pres. San Antonio Fedn. of Tchrs., 1983-86; ednl. cons. Bexar County Fedn. Tchrs., San Antonio, 1986-90; dir. Southwest Policy Leaders Forum, Ctr. Policy Alternatives, 1999—. Mem. Dist. 124 Tex. Ho. of Reps., 1991-99, mem. legis. budget bd., 1994-99, select. com. on revenue & pub. edn. funding, 1997-99, calendars com., 1997-99, mem. appropriations com., 1993-99, mem. pub. edn. com., 1993-99; bd. edn. San Antonio Ind. Sch. Dist., 1986-91; pub. mem. bd. dirs. State Bar Tex., 1989-92; bd. dirs. So. Regional Coun., 1990-98, mem. exec. com., 1993-95, v.p., 1995-98; bd. dirs. Target '90 Goals for San Antonio, 1987-91, Providence High Sch., 1987-90; bd. dirs. Tex. Lyceum, 1990-97, sec., 1991-93, v.p. 1993-94; exec. com. San Antonio River Corridor com. 1987-89, Govs. Commn. for Women, 1985-87, Tex. Task Force on Indigent Health Care, 1983-84; bd. mgrs. Bexar County Hosp. Dist., 1982-84; bd. review Hist. Dists. and Landmarks, 1981-82; task force Southland Corps. Coll. Program, 1985; mem. San Antonio Commn. on Literacy, 1987-89; trustee United Way, 1988—; founder, pres. La'Tina Found., 1997—, San Antonio-Mex. Found. for Edn., 1997-99; mem. nat. adv. bd. Found. for Women's Resources, 1993-95. Named Hispanic Woman of Yr., 1984, Young Woman of Promise, Good Housekeeping Mag., 1985, Sunday's Woman, S.A. Light, 1985, Alumnus of Yr., U. Tex., San Antonio, 1993, Friend of Bus., Tex. C. of C., 1994, San Antonio Women's Hall of Fame, 1992; recipient Outstanding Leadership award YWCA, 1989, Spirit of the Am. Woman award J.C. Penney Co., 1992, Pacesetter award Stennis Ctr. for Pub. Svc., 1998. Mem. Tex. Assn. Sch. Bds. (bd. trustees 1989-90), Leadership Am. Alumnae Assn., Hispanic Women's Network of Tex. (bd. dirs.), Leadership San Antonio Alumni Assn., Tex. Women's Forum, Any Baby Can Alliance, Leadership Tex. Alumnae Assn., San Antonio 100 (charter), Am. Fedn. Tchrs. (v.p. 1978-81, treas. 1981-83, pres. 1983-86). Democrat. Roman Catholic. Avocations: traveling, reading novels and biographies. Office: 1875 Connecticut Ave NW Ste 710 Washington DC 20009-5740

HERNANDEZ, DANIEL ARTHUR, elementary school educator; b. Galveston, Tex., Dec. 8, 1945; s. Reyes and Irene (Unzueta) H.; m. Bettye Ann Sing, Aug. 4, 1972; children: Angelica Dana, Michael Stephen. BA in Music Edn., Howard Payne U., 1969; M of Ch. Music, Southwestern Sem., 1973; postgrad., Sam Houston State U., 1977-78, 1981-84, Tex. Woman's U., 1981, U. Tex., Arlington, 1979. Cert. music tchr., Tex. Minister music, youth Rocky Creek Bapt. Ch., Brownwood, Tex., 1967-69; tchr. elem. music Galveston (Tex.) ISD, 1969; minister music, youth First Bapt. Kennedale, Tex., 1971-72, Pleasant Glade Bapt. Ch., Grapevine, Tex., 1972-74; tchr. elem. music Birdville ISD, Ft. Worth, Tex., 1974—; clinician Chorister's Guild, Ft. Worth 1981, Edn. Service Ctr., Region XI, Ft. Worth 1981, 84. Deacon Birdville Bapt. Ch., Ft. Worth, 1975, dir. young musicians choir, 1977-91; founder Snow Heights Soundbusters Boys' Choir; founder, dir. John D. Spicer Elem. Colt Chorale; exec. bd. Tex. Boys' Choir, Ft. Worth, 1985; pres. Walton Band Friends, 1992-93. With U.S. Army, 1969-71, Vietnam. Decorated with Bronze Star, Air medal. Named Outstanding Young Men Am., U.S. Jaycees, 1982. Mem. NEA (chmn. Region XI elem. music 1978), Tex. Tchrs. Assn. (chmn. elem. music 1978), Tex. Music Educators Assn. (regional chmn. 1979-80, nominating com. 1980-82, mem. agenda com. 1986, clinician region X, 1982), Kodaly Educators Tex. (clinician 1980), Orgn. Am. Kokaly Educators, Ft. Worth Arts Coun., S.W. Vietnam Vets. (charter), Phi Mu Alpha (charter mem. Nu Omega chpt.). Avocations: military history, music, racquetball, coaching men's flag football and children's soccer. Home: 6909 McCoy Dr Fort Worth TX 76148-2318 Office: John D Spicer Elem Sch 4300 Estes Park Rd Fort Worth TX 76137

HERNÁNDEZ, FERNANDO VARGAS, lawyer; b. Irapuato, México Sept. 8, 1939; came to U.S., 1942, naturalized, 1957; s. José Espinosa and Ana Maria (Vargas) H.; m. Bonnie Corrie, Jan. 8, 1966 (div. Feb. 1991); children: Michael David, Alexandra Rae, Marcel Paul. BS, U. Santa Clara, 1961, MBA, 1962; JD, U. Calif.-Berkeley, 1966. Bar: Calif. 1967, U.S. Dist. Ct.

(no. dist.) Calif. 1967. Sole practice law, San Jose, Calif., 1967—; lectr. law Lincoln U.; lectr. bus. U. Santa Clara. Mem. San Jose Housing Bd., 1970-73; arbitrator, judge protem Santa Clara County Superior Cts., 1979-98. Chmn. bd. trustees Calif. Rural Legal Assistance, 1973-75; bd. dirs. San Jose Civic Light Opera, 1981-83. Served with AUS, 1962-63. Mem. Calif. State Bar Assn., Santa Clara County Bar Assn. (chmn. torts sect. 1977-78, features editor In Brief mag. 1990-93), Calif. Trial Lawyers Assn., (bd. govs. 1979-82), Santa Clara County Trial Lawyers Assn. (pres. elect 1981), U. Santa Clara Alumni Assn. (pres. San Jose chpt. 1977-78), La Raza Lawyers Assn. Democrat. Roman Catholic. Club: Democratic Century. Contbg. editor to legal pleadings books. Office: 64 W Santa Clara St Fl 2D San Jose CA 95113-1806

HERNANDEZ, GILBERTO JUAN, accountant, auditor, management consultant; b. Havana, Cuba, July 12, 1943; came to U.S., 1960; s. Gilberto E. and Zoila M. (Mendez) H.; m. Maria-Elena Diaz Lugo, Jan. 19, 1968 (div. 1971); 1 child, A. Patrick; m. Maria-Carmen Marcet, Dec. 23, 1972; children: Martin J., David J., Thomas J. BBA, Pace U., 1968. CPA, N.Y., Fla. Auditor sr. Arthur Andersen LLP, N.Y.C., Tampa, Fla., 1968-73; v.p., treas. Coaxial Comms., Inc., Sarasota, Fla., 1973-81; tax mgr. Laventhol & Horwath, Tampa, Fla., 1981-83; ptnr. ValienteHernandez, CPAss member Firm IA Internats, Tampa and Tallahassee, Fla., 1983—; dir. Ind. Accts. Internat. Commr. City of Tampa Housing Authority, 1981-95; treas., bd. dirs. Ybor City Devel. Corp., Tampa, 1988—; chmn. Tampa Bay Econ. Devel. Corp., 1990—; active City of Tampa Mayor's Hispanic Adv. Coun., 1984-96. Mem. AICPA, N.Y. State Soc. CPAs, Fla. Inst. CPAs (bd. dirs., sec. West Coast chpt., past chmn. com. on unauthorized practice of pub. accountancy 1993-94, Outstanding Chmn. of Yr. 1994), Nat. Assn. Housing and Redevel. Ofcls. (bd. govs. 1988-94), Govt. Fin. Officers Assn., Fla. Assn. Govt. Fin. Officers, Ybor City C. of C. (pres. 1997-98, chmn. 1998-99), Ybor City Rotary Club (pres. 1990-91). Avocations: geography, travel, hiking. Office: ValienteHernandez 918 E Busch Blvd Tampa FL 33612-8542

HERNANDEZ, JACQUELINE CHARMAINE, lawyer; b. Trinidad, W.I., Nov. 1, 1960; came to U.S., 1975; d. Desmond and Jocelyn Virginia (Felix) H. BA, L.I. U., 1982; JD, NYU, 1985. Bar: N.Y. 1986, N.J. 1987, U.S. Dist. Ct. (so. and ea. dists.) N.Y. 1988, U.S. Dist. Ct. N.J. 1996. Assoc. Cooper and Kenny, N.Y.C., 1985-87, Semel, Boeckmann, Diamond, Schepp & Yuhas, N.Y.C., 1987-88, Wood, Williams, Rafalsky & Harris, N.Y.C., 1988-90; from assoc. to ptnr. Cooper, Liebowitz, Royster & Wright, Elmsford, N.Y., 1990-96; assoc. Gordon & Silber, P.C., N.Y.C., 1996—. Mem. ABA, Nat. Bar Assn., Black Bar Assn. Bronx County, Assn. Black Lawyers of Westchester County Inc., Internat. Platform Assn. Roman Catholic. Avocations: theatre, travel. Home: Paladins Keep 24 Carhart Ave White Plains NY 10605-1448 Office: Gordon & Silber PC 355 Lexington Ave New York NY 10017-6603

HERNANDEZ, JO FARB, museum curator, consultant; b. Chgo., Nov. 20, 1952. BA in Polit. Sci. & French with honors, U. Wis., 1974; MA in Folklore and mythology, UCLA, 1975; postgrad., U. Calif., Davis, 1978, U. Calif., Berkeley, 1978-79, 81. Registration Mus. Cultural History UCLA, 1974-75; Rockefeller fellow Dallas Mus. Fine Arts, 1976-77; asst. to dir. Triton Mus. Art, Santa Clara, Calif., 1977-78, dir., 1978-85; adj. prof. mus. studies John F. Kennedy U., San Francisco, 1978; grad. advisor arts adminstrn. San Jose (Calif.) State U., 1979-80; dir. Monterey (Calif.) Peninsula Mus. Art, 1985-93, cons. curator, 1994—; prin. Curatorial and Mus. Mgmt. Svcs., Watsonville, Calif., 1993—; adj. prof. gallery mgmt. art dept. U. Calif., Santa Cruz, 1999; cons. Archives Am. Art, 1998-99, Arts Coun. Silicon Valley, 1998-99; lectr., panelist, juror, panelist in field USIA, Calif. Arts Coun., Calif. Confedn. for Arts, Am. Assn. Mus., Western Mus. Assn., Am. Folklore Soc., Calif. Folklore Soc., others; vis. lectr. U. Wis., 1980, Northwestern U., 1981, San Jose State U., 1985, UCLA, 1986, Am. Cultural Ctr., Jerusalem, 1989, Tel Aviv, 1989, Binat. Ctr., Lima, Peru, 1988, Daytona Beach Mus. Art, 1983, UCLA, 1986, Israel Mus., 1989, U. Chgo., 1981, Mont. State U., 1991, Oakland Mus., 1996, High Mus. Art, Atlanta, 1997, Mus. Am. Folk Art, N.Y., 1998, San Francisco Mus. Modern Art, 1998, U. Calif., 1998, Calif. Arts Coun., 1997, 99, Grinnell (Iowa) Coll., 1999; guest curator San Diego Mus. Art, 1995-98; guest on various TV and radio programs. Contbr. articles to profl. publs.; author: (mus. catalogs) The Day of the Dead: Tradition and Change in Contemporary Mexico, 1979, Three from the Northern Island: Contemporary Sculpture from Hokkaido, 1984, Crime and Punishment: Reflections of Violence in Contemporary Art, 1984, The Quiet Eye: Pottery of Shoji Hamada and Bernard Leach, 1990, Alan Shepp: The Language of Stone, 1991, Wonderful Colors: The Paintings of August Francois Gay, 1993, Jeannette Maxfield Lewis: A Centennial Celebration, 1994, Armin Hansen, 1994, Jeremy Anderson: The Critical Link/A Quiet Revolution, 1995, A.G. Rizzoli: Architect of Magnificent Visions, 1997 (one of 10 Best Books in field Amazon.com), Misch Kohn: Beyond the Tradition, 1998, Fire and Flux: An Undaunted Vision/The Art of Charles Strong, 1998. Bd. dirs. Bobbie Wynn and Co. of San Jose, 1981-85, Santa Clara Arts and Hist. Consortium, 1985, Non-Profit Gallery Assn., 1979-83, v.p., 1979-80; mem. nat. adv. bd. The Fund for Folk Culture, Santa Fe, 1995-98. Recipient Golden Eagle award Coun. Internat. Non-theatrical Events, 1992, Leader of Decade award Arts Leadership Monterey Peninsula, 1992, merit award N.Y. Book Show, 1997. Mem. Am. Assn. Mus. (mus. assessment program surveyor 1990, 94, lectr. 1986, nat. program com. 1992-93), Calif. Assn. Mus. (chair ann. meeting 1990, chair nominating com. 1988, 90, 93, bd. dirs. 1985-94, v.p. 1987-91, pres. 1991-92), Art Table, Am. Folklore Soc., Western Mus. Conf. (bd. dirs., exec. com. 1989-91, program chair 1990), Nat. Coun. for Edn. in Ceramic Arts, Alliance for Calif. Traditional Arts, Phi Beta Kappa. Office: Curatorial and Mus Mgmt Svcs 345 White Rd Watsonville CA 95076-0429

HERNANDEZ, MARK ALAN, educator in Spanish; b. San Antonio, May 29, 1964; s. John c. and Mary Antonieta (Gonzalez) H. BA, Yale U., 1986; postgrad. studies, Duke U., 1987-88; MA, U. Kans., 1990, PhD, 1996. Mng. editor Intercultural Devel. Rsch. Assn., San Antonio, 1986-87; instr. in Spanish Duke U., Durham, N.C., 1987-88; grad. tchg. asst. U. Kans., Lawrence, 1988-94; dissertation fellow Grinnell (Iowa) Coll., 1994-96, asst. prof. Spanish, 1996-98; asst. prof. Spanish Bowling Green State U., 1998—. Recipient Duke Endowment fellowship, Duke Univ., 1987-88, scholarship Nat. Hispanic Scholarship Fund, 1987-94, Postbaccalaureate fellowship U. Kans., 1989-91, Grad. Tchg. Asst. award, 1993, Dissertation fellowship Grinnell Coll., 1994-96. Mem. MLA, Am. Assn. Tchrs. of Spanish and Portugese, Latin Am. Studies Assn. Avocations: travel, Latin Am. music, tennis, basketball. Office: Dept Romance Langs Bowling Green State U 203 Shatzel Hall Bowling Green OH 43403

HERNANDEZ, MIKE, city official; m. Sylvia Hernandez; children: Michelle, Emiliano. Past hon. mayor City of Highland Park; city councilman 1st dist. City of L.A., 1991—, chmn. adminstrv. svcs. com., mem. govt. efficiency & arts com., health & humanities com., chmn. cmty. & econ. devel. com.; vice chair info. tech. gen. svcs. com.; mem. Northeast Bus. Devel. Coun., Northeast L.A. Cmty. Planning Adv. Com. Mem. L.A. Jaycees, Highland Park Optimists, Kiwanis of Highland Park. *

HERNANDEZ, PROSPERO MEDALLA, book publisher, consultant; b. Manila, Jan. 10, 1944; came to U.S., 1984; s. Perfecto Meer Hernandez and Mena Medalla; m. Marita Gamboa, Dec. 18, 1982; 1 child, Alyssa. BSBA, De La Salle Coll., Manila, 1966; MA, Universidad de Navarra, Pamplona, Spain, 1968. Communication dir. Ctr. for Rsch. and Communication, Manila, 1970-71; rsch. dir. Philippines Herald/A. Soriano Group of Cos., Manila, 1971-73; mng. dir. Sinag-tala Pubs. Inc., Manila, 1973-80; asst. to pres. Lyceum of the Philippines, Manila, 1980-82; v.p. Island Pub. House, Inc., Manila, 1982-84; asst. dir., bus. mgr. Rutgers U. Press, New Brunswick, N.J., 1986-91; assoc. dir., chief operating officer Rutgers U. Press, 1991—; cons. U.S. Nat. Acad. Scis. Bd. on Sci. and Tech., Washington, 1985-86, Swiss Ctr. for Appropriate Tech., St. Gallen, Switzerland, 1985-86, Appropriate Tech. Internat., Washington, 1985. Author newspaper column, 1966. Mem. Philippine Hist. Conservation Soc., 1983—. Mem. Internat. Assn. of Scholary Pubs., Am. Assn. Univ. Presses (assoc. mem.), De La Salle Alumni Assn. (bd. dirs. Eastern U.S., N.Y.C. 1986). Roman Catholic. Avocations: squash, oil painting. Home: 123 Prentice Ave South River NJ 08882-2210 Office: Rutgers Univ Press 100 Joyce Kilmer Ave Piscataway NJ 08854

HERNANDEZ, RAMON ROBERT, retired clergyman and librarian; b. Chgo., Feb. 23, 1936; s. Eleazar Dario and Marie Helen (Stange) H.; m. Fern Ellen Muschinske, Aug. 11, 1962; children: Robert Frank, Maria Marta. BA, Elmhurst (Ill.) Coll., 1957; BD, Eden Theol. Sem., St. Louis, 1962; MA, U. Wis., 1970. Co-pastor St. Stephen United Ch. Christ, Merrill, Wis., 1960-64; dir. youth work Wis. Conf. United Ch. Christ, Madison, 1964-70; dir. T.B. Scott Free Library, Merrill, 1970-75, McMillan Meml. Library, Wisconsin Rapids, Wis., 1975-83, Ann Arbor (Mich.) Pub. Library, 1983-94; pastor Comty. Congl. Ch., Pinckney, Mich., 1994-98; seminar leader on pub. libr. long-range planning, budgeting and handling problem patrons. Editl. com. mem. Songs of Many Nations Songbook, 1970; contbr. articles to profl. jours. Treas. Ann Arbor Homeless Coalition, 1985-88; bd. dirs., sec., v.p. Riverview Hosp. Assn., Wisconsin Rapids, 1977-83; bd. dirs. Hist. Soc. Mich., 1988-90. Mem. ALA, Wis. Libr. Assn. (Leadership award 1980, pres. 1980), Rotary (pres. Merrill chpt. 1974-75, Community Svc. award 1975, pres. Ann Arbor chpt. 1990-91, Paul Harris fellow 1994).

HERNANDEZ, ROBERTO REYES, secondary school educator; b. Juarez, Chihuahua, Mex., Apr. 30, 1950; came to U.S., 1953; s. Felipe de Jesus and Juanita (Reyes) H.; m. Joanne Dora Richard; adopted children: Rosellor, Ledores, Joetta, Harriett, Barbara, Richard, Ray. AA in Edn., El Paso C.C., 1976; BS in Psychology, U. Tex., El Paso, 1978, BE in Secondary Edn., 1981, BS in Biology, 1982, MS in Biology, 1986; grad. sci. fellow, Baylor Coll. Medicine, 1984-85. Cert. secondary edn. teacher, Tex. Pharmacy technician Southwestern Gen. Hosp., El Paso, 1974-79, William Beaumont Army Med. Ctr. U.S. Civil Svc., Ft. Bliss, Tex., 1979-81; tchr. life and earth sci. Houston Ind. Sch. Dist., 1984-85; tchr. phys. sci., anatomy, physiology, biology Socorro Ind. Sch. Dist., El Paso, 1981-84; tchr. phys. sci., biology, astronomy, chemistry, computer sci. and GED Ysleta Ind. Sch. Dist., El Paso, 1985—; instr. English El Paso C. C., spring, 1986; grad. asst. interdisciplinary edn. Tex. A & M U., summer, 1989, 90; mem. evaluation team So. Assn. of Accreditation, El Paso, 1984; mem. textbook adoption team Tex. Biology Textbook Adoption Com., El Paso, 1983-84. Pres. Tex. Student Edn. Assn., El Paso, 1980-81; vol. instr. ESL The Westin Paso Del Norte Hotel, El Paso, 1990; den leader Wolf and Bear Cub Scout Pack 201, 1994-95. Recipient Hidalgo award Heitel Broadcasting Corp., 1997. Mem. NEA, Tex. State Tchrs. Assn., sYsleta Tchrs. Assn. (area rep. 1994-97), Vista Hills Lions Club (lion tamer 1992-94, Leo advisor 1992—, editor newsletter 1993-95, 2d v.p. 1994-95, dir. 1995-96, Lion of Yr. 1992-93, 96-97, dist. 2T3 Leo Clubs chair 1997-99, exec. v.p. 1998-99). Home: 10310 Kellogg St El Paso TX 79924-2902 Office: Eastwood HS 2430 Mc Rae Blvd El Paso TX 79925-6097

HERNÁNDEZ, ROGER EMILIO, newspaper columnist; b. Havana, Cuba, Jan. 9, 1955; s. Roger Rómulo and Mabel Lydia (Vazquez) H.; m. Dianne Beth Doctor, Nov. 27, 1988; children: Elena Rose, Benjamin Mark. BA in Mass Media and Journalism, Rutgers U., 1977. Rschr. MacNeil-Lehrer Report, 1977; assoc. prodr. N.J. Network, 1977-78, news assignment editor, 1978-83; news assignment editor WWOR-TV, N.Y.C., 1983-84; freelance writer, 1984—; syndicated columnist King Features Syndicate, 1990—; prof. English composition and journalism Fairleigh Dickinson U., N.J., 1991-97, Bloomfield Coll., N.J., 1991—; writer-in-residence N.J. Inst. Tech., 1997—. Contbr. syndicated column to approximately 40 newspapers, including Miami Herald, Washington Post, Dallas Morning News, also articles to mags.; prodr. TV documentaries, 1992. Roman Catholic. Avocations: birding, food and wine, Napoleonic miliatary miniatures, world soccer. Office: King Features Syndicate 235 E 45th St Fl 2 New York NY 10017-3367*

HERNANDEZ, ROLAND, broadcast executive. Pres., CEO Telemundo Group, Inc., Hialeah, Fla. Office: Telemundo Group Inc 2290 W 8th Ave Hialeah FL 33010-2017 Address: 2425 Olympic Blvd Santa Monica CA 90404*

HERNANDEZ-DENTON, FEDERICO, supreme court justice; b. Santurce, P.R., Apr. 12, 1944; s. Federico and Teresa (Denton) Hernandez-Morales; m. Isabel Pico, 1966. BA, Harvard U., 1966, JD, 1969. Bar: P.R. 1971. Dir. Consumer Rsch. Ctr. and Bus. Adminstrn. Rsch. Ctr. U. P.R., 1970-72; dir. P.R. Consumer Svc. Adminstrn., 1973; sec. P.R. Dept. Consumer Affairs, 1973-76; asst. prof. Law Sch. Interam. U., P.R., 1977-84, dean, 1984-85; now justice Supreme Ct. P.R, San Juan; chair Bd. Bar Examiners. Mem. ABA, Am. Law Inst., P.R. Bar Assn. Office: Supreme Ct of PR PO Box 9022392 San Juan PR 00902-2392

HERNANDEZ-LEDEZMA, JOSE JUAN, laboratory administrator; b. Jalpan, Mex., Mar. 7, 1951; came to U.S., 1991; s. Alfredo and Amada (Ledezma) H.; m. Valantin Solyman; children: Alfredo, Daniel, David, Mariam. DVM, U. Veracruzana, Mex., 1975; MS, U. Mo., 1980; PhD, Wash. State U., 1988. Diplomate Am. Bd. Bionalysts. Regional dir. INIP, Veracruz, 1974-79; sr. rschr. INIFAP, Queretaro, Mex., 1988-90; rsch. asst. U. Mo., 1991-93; dir. labs. Infertility and IVF Ctr., St. Louis, 1992—. Author: Handbook of Immunology/Radioisotopes in Animal Research, 1986, Hot Bioclimates in Selected Livestock Species: Sheep, 1987, Trophoblast Cells: Pathways for Maternal-Embryonic Communications, 1993, Biotechnology and Policy, A Latin-American Perspective, 1995. Founding mem. Sierra Gorda ecological group, Jalpan, 1990. Conacyt scholar, Mex., 1978, 85; travel grantee IETS, Arrowhead, Colo., 1988. Mem. Soc. Study Reproduction, Am. Soc. Reproductive Medicine, Soc. Male Reproduction and Urology, Reproductive Biology Profl. Group, European Soc. Human Reproduction and Embryology, Internat. Embryo Transfer Soc. Roman Catholic. Avocation: coaching soccer. Office: Infertility & IVF Ctr 3009 N Ballas Rd Ste 359C Saint Louis MO 63131-2322

HERNDON, ANNE HARKNESS, sales executive; b. Knoxville, Tenn., July 21, 1951; d. Alexander Jones and Mary Belle (Lothrop) Harkness; m. David S. Egerton, Apr. 21, 1972 (div. 1979); children: David, Mary; m. Morris Herndon, Nov. 26, 1993. Student, Agnes Scott Coll., Decatur, Ga., 1969-71, U. Tenn., 1971-73. Mktg., advt. mgr. Volunteer Realty, Knoxville, 1975-77; adminstrv. asst. nat. sales Creative Displays, Knoxville, 1977-81; salesperson Sta. WJXB Radio, Knoxville, 1981-86, sales mgr., 1988—; sales and mktg. mgr. Cellular One, Knoxville, 1986-87; cons. nat. ourdoor advt. Berkline Corp., Morristown, Tenn., 1978-81, Knoxville C. of C.; speaker nat. convs. Contbr. articles to profl. jours. Bd. dirs. Knoxville Polit. Action Com., Knoxville Arts Coun., Knoxville Beautification Bd., Boy Scouts Fin. Com.; com. mem. Dogwood Arts Festival, United Way. Recipient Pres.'s award South Ctrl. Comm. Corp., 1991, 92, 93. Mem. Ad Club. Republican. Presbyterian. Avocations: water skiing, hiking, boating. Home: 346 Okema Way Loudon TN 37774-3148 Office: WJXB 1100 Sharps Ridge Knoxville TN 37917-7122

HERNDON, CATHY CAMPBELL, artist, art educator; b. Richmond, Va., Sept. 25, 1951; d. Kenneth Holcomb and Grace (Brooks) Campbell. BS in Art and Drama, Radford (Va.) U., 1973; MS in Art Edn., Va. Commonwealth U., 1980. Art tchr. Hanover County Schs., Ashland, Va., 1973-76, Stafford County Schs., Va., 1976-86; neon mixed media constrn. artist, signmaker Fredericksburg (Va.) City Schs., 1985—; artist, tchr. Rappahannock Security Ctr., Fredericksburg, 1989-91, Fredericksburg Ctr. for Creative Arts, 1984—, Fredericksburg City Schs., 1991—; curator, 1991-94, bd. dirs., 1984—; exchange tchr. Kingston U., Eng., 1995. One-person shows include Fredericksburg Ctr. for Creative Arts, 1986, Southside Va. C.C., Alberta, 1992, Art First Gallery, Fredericksburg, 1992, 94, 96, 98, Shenandoah Valley Art Ctr., Waynesboro, Va., 1993, Geico Corp. Hdqs., Fredericksburg, 1994, 96, Riverby's Gallery 97, Fredericksburg, Frejus, France, 1997, others; exhibited in group shows in Karpathos, Greece, London, England, Montross Galleries, Fredericksburg, 1992, Va. Ctr. Creative Arts, Sweetbriar, Va., Rocquebrune, France, 1995, Recycled Show, London; founding mem. Exposure Unltd. Art Group; executed various murals. Fredericksburg Sister City Assn., 1992—. Recipient numerous awards for works; named Best in Show, Hanover Arts Festival, 1995, Geico Educator of Yr., 1996, Fredericksburg Jaycees Educator of The Year, 1998. Mem. Nat. Art Edn. Assn., Lioness. Avocations: car racing, beach, travel, dancing. Home and Studio: PO Box 7955 408 Frederick St Fredericksburg VA 22401-6028

HERNDON, DAVID N., surgeon. Chief staff Shriners Burn Inst., Galveston, Tex., 1981—; prof. surgery, Jesse H. Jones disting. chair burn surgery U. Tex., Galveston. Office: U Tex Med Br 815 Market St Galveston TX 77550-2725*

HERNDON, JAMES HENRY, orthopedic surgeon, educator; b. L.A., Oct. 31, 1938; s. James Greene and Kathleen Theresa (Murphy) H.; m. Geraldine Grace Armiger, Feb. 26, 1971; children: Jennifer, Jonathan. BS, Loyola U., L.A., 1961; MD, UCLA, 1965; MA, Brown U., 1979; MBA, Boston U., 1990. Diplomate Am. Bd. Orthopaedic Surgery (bd. dirs., pres. 1991-92). Intern Hosp. of U. Pa., Phila., 1965-66, resident in surgery, 1966-67; resident in orthopaedics Mass. Gen. Hosp., Boston, 1970, chief resident in orthopaecids, 1967-70; asst. clin. prof. orthopaecid surgery Mich. State U., Grand Rapids, 1974-77, assoc. clin. prof., 1977-78; prof., chmn. dept. orthopaedics Brown U., Providence, 1979-88; surgeon-in-chief dept. orthopaedic surgery R.I. Hosp., Providence, 1979-88; Silver prof., chmn. dept. orthopaedic surgery U. Pitts., Pitts.; chief dept. orthopaedics and rehab. Presbyn. U. Hosp., Pitts., 1988-98, Montifiore U. Hosp., Boston, 1998—; assoc. sr. vice chancellor Health Svcs. U. Pitts. Med. Ctr., 1995—, v.p. Med. Svcs., 1995—, chmn. ptnrs. dept. orthopaedic surgeons; examiner Am. Bd. Orthopaedic Surgery, Chgo., 1977—, pres., 1990-91. Reviewer Jour. Bone and Joint Surgery, 1975—; contbr. articles to profl. jours., chpts. to books; author books in field. Trustee Meeting St. Sch., Providence, 1984-88, Harmarville Rehab. Hosp., Pitts., 1989-95; mem. bd. govs. Arthritis Found., Providence, 1984-88, Pitts., 1989—; bd. dirs. Make A Wish Found. Maj. U.S. Army, 1971-73. Recipient Edith and Carl Lasky Meml. award UCLA Med. Sch., 1965, Bronze award Am. Congress Rehab. Medicine, 1972, Clin. Rsch. award N.Y. Med. Soc., 1974. Fellow ACS, Am. Acad. Orthopaedic Surgeons (treas. 1994—); mem. Am. Orthopaedic Assn., Orthopaedic Rsch. Soc., Residence Rev. Com. Orthopaedic Surgery (past chmn.), Am. Soc. Surgery of Hand, Agawam Hunt Club, Hope Club, Longue Vue Club. Office: Massachusetts Gen Hosp Gray 624 55 Fruit St Boston MA 02114-2617

HERNDON, JOHN LAIRD, consulting firm executive; b. Shreveport, La., 1958; s. Jack and Irene Herndon. BS Econs., Millsaps Coll., Jackson, Miss., 1981; MBA, U. Miss., Oxford, 1997. Cons. Jackson, Miss., 1981-84; fin. analyst Coldwell Banker, L.A., 1984-86; sr. fin. analyst Kenneth Leventhal & Co., L.A., 1986-87; asst. contr. E&Y Real Estate Group, L.A., 1987-89, contr., 1989-95; dir. Ernst & Young LLP, N.Y., 1996—. Developer Computational Bus. web site, e-business authority, GalleryNetwork.com., 1999; author numerous articles; speaker in field. John Palmer scholar U. Miss., Oxford, 1996-97. Mensa Internat. Episcopalian. Avocation: tennis. Office: Ernst & Young LLP 125 Chubb Ave Lyndhurst NJ 07071-3504

HERNDON, ROY CLIFFORD, physicist; b. Washington, Sept. 25, 1934. BS, Washington and Lee U., 1955; PhD, Fla. State U., 1962. Staff physicist Lawrence Livermore (Calif.) Lab., 1962-67; prof. Nova U., Ft. Lauderdale, 1967-75; dir. CBTR Ctr. for Biomed. & Toxicological Rsch., Fla. State U., Tallahassee, 1983—; dir. Inst. for Ctrl. and Eastern European Coop. Environ. Rsch.; exec. dir. Fla. Hazardous Waste Adv. Coun., Tallahassee, 1980-82; mem. adv. bd. Fla. State U. System, Tallahassee, 1988—; hon. prof. Tech. U. Budapest, 1992. Author: (with others) Methods of Computational Physics, 1966, Land Use: A Spatial Approach, 1980, Theories of Electrons in Disordered Systems, 1982; contbr. over 100 articles to profl. jours. Mem. AAAS, Am. Inst. Biol. Scis., N.Y. Acad. Sci., Fla. Acad. Sci., Phi Beta Kappa. Office: CBTR Fla State U 226 Morgan Bldg 2035 E Paul Dirac Dr Tallahassee FL 32310-3760

HERNON, JOSEPH MARTIN, JR., history educator; b. Washington, June 30, 1936; s. Joseph Martin and Lucille (Mearns) H. A.B. magna cum laude, Cath. U. Am., 1959; Ph.D., Trinity Coll., Dublin U., 1963. Instr., Ohio State U., 1963-65; asst. prof. Cath. U. Am., 1965-67; vis. asst. prof. history U. Md., 1967-68; asst. prof. U. Mass., Amherst, 1968-69; assoc. prof. U. Mass., 1969-77, prof., 1978—; vis. prof. Dublin U., 1970, U. Stirling, 1976; lectr. Amherst Coll., Bentley Coll., Georgetown U.; The O'Donnell lectr. Trinity Coll., Dublin, 1976, Nat. Archives, 1999; cons. NEH, World Book Ency., U.S. Capitol Hist. Soc., ACLS; Theodore Sorensen fellow John F. Kennedy Libr. Found., 1991-92. Author: Celts, Catholics and Copperheads: Ireland Views the American Civil War, 1968, (with T.E. Hachey and L.J. McCaffrey) The Irish Experience, 200 B.C.-A.D, 1996, A Concise History, 1996, Profiles in Character: Hubris and Heroism in the U.S. Senate, 1789-1990, 1997; contbr. numerous articles and poems to profl. jours. Mem. exec. com. Coll. Young Dems., 1959; U.S. del. NATO Conf. Young Polit. Leaders, 1960; del. Mass. Dem. Conv., 1987, 88; mem. Amherst Dem. Town Com., 1988-89. Am. Philos. Soc. grantee, 1970, U. Mass. Faculty grantee, 1970; Theodore Sorensen fellow John F. Kennedy Libr. Found., 1991-92. Fellow Royal Hist. Soc.; mem. Am. Hist. Assn., Am. Cath. Hist. Assn., Am. Conf. Irish Studies (treas. 1966-71), Phi Beta Kappa, Delta Epsilon Sigma, Pi Gamma Mu, Blue Key. Home: 2909 N 19th St Tacoma WA 98406-7038 Office: U Mass Dept History Amherst MA 01003

HERNREICH, NANCY, federal official; b. State College, Miss., July 27, 1946; d. Bernard Francis and Nancy Davis (Martin) McAvoy; m. Robert Eastman Hernreich, Sept. 21, 1968 (div. 1979); 1 child, Ashley Proulx. BA, Webster Coll., 1968; postgrad., Ark. State U. Social worker Jonesboro (Ark.) Sch. Dist., 1970-76; scheduling sec. Gov. of Ark., Little Rock, 1985-92; dep. asst. to pres., dir. Oval Office White House, Washington, 1993—. Mem. Ft. Smith Jr. League, Little Rock Jr. League; chmn. bd. Ft. Smith Pride; social worker, Jonesboro; bd. dirs. Big Bros./Big Sisters Ft. Smith, Spl. Olympics; mem. state steering com. Mondale for Pres.; mem. state Dem. Exec. Com.; del. Dem. Nat. Conv., 1980; election commr. Sebastion County; coord. Sebastion County Clinton Campaign, 1980, 82, 84; dir. March of Dimes Telethon, 1985; head state pub. affairs com. Jr. League. Democrat. Avocations: running, cooking. Office: White House 1600 Pennsylvania Ave NW Washington DC 20500-0003*

HERNSTADT, JUDITH FILENBAUM, city planner, real estate executive, broadcasting executive; b. N.Y.C., Nov. 18, 1942; d. Alex and Ruth Selena (Silberman) Filenbaum. BA, NYU, 1964, M Urban and Regional Planning, 1966; cert. smaller co. mgmt. program, Harvard Bus. Sch., 1977. With Office Planning Coordination, State of N.Y., 1966-68; ptnr. Devel. Planning Assocs., N.Y.C., 1967-68; with engrng. scis. dept. Svc. Bur. Corp., N.Y.C., 1968-69; planning cons. Llewelyn-Davies Assocs., N.Y.C., 1969-71, Arlen Realty & Devel. Corp., N.Y.C., 1971-73; ptnr. Planning & Devel. Team, N.Y.C. and Las Vegas, 1974—; v.p. Sta. KVVU-TV Nev. Ind. Broadcasting Corp., Las Vegas, 1974-75; pres. Sta. KVVU-TV Nev. Ind. Broadcasting Corp., 1976-77, Hernstadt Broadcasting Corp., 1978-81; bd. dirs. Internat. Film and TV Exch., Inc.; bd. adv. program Transitions to Democracy Elliot Sch. Internat. Affairs George Washington U., mem. coun. Rockefeller U., 1998. Condr. TV interview programs. Del. Fine Arts Fedn. N.Y., 1970-90; mem. Hudson Inst., 1980-92; mem. fine arts com. U.S. Dept. State, 1976—; bd. dirs. Hebrew Immigrant Aid Soc., Nat. Com on Am. Fgn. Policy, Decorative Arts Trust, Eastside Internat. Cmty. Ctr., 1988-96. Mem. Internat. Film and TV Exch. (bd. dirs.), Harvard Club (N.Y.C.), Hadji Baba Soc., Lotos Club, Explorers Club. Home: 927 5th Ave New York NY 10021-2650

HERNTON, CALVIN COOLIDGE, African American studies educator, artist, writer; b. Chattanooga, Apr. 28, 1932; s. Magnolia Jackson; m. Mildred Webster, June 5, 1958 (dec. July 1982); 1 child, Antone; m. Mary O'Callaghan Garvey, Nov. 24, 1998. BA in Sociology, Talladega Coll., 1954; MA in Sociology, Fisk U., 1956; postgrad., Columbia U., 1961-62. Instr. social sci. Benedict Coll., Columbus, S.C., 1957-58, Edward Waters Coll., Jacksonville, Fla., 1958-59, Ala. A&M Coll., Montgomery, 1959-60, So. U., Baton Rouge, 1960-61; writer-in-residence Cen. State U., Wilberforce, Ohio, fall 1970; writer-in-residence Oberlin (Ohio) Coll., 1970-72, prof. African Am. studies and creative writing, 1972—; lit. cons. Nat. Black Arts Festival, Atlanta, Ga., 1994-98; tech. cons. TV series Man Called Hawk, Sta. WBTV, Burbank, Calif., 1987-88; mem. adv. bd. Tenn. Writers Alliance, Nashville, 1991—, Sisters in Support of So. Africa, St. Croix, V.I., 1997—. Author: (books) Sex and Racism in America, 1965, Coming Together, 1974, Sexual Mountain and Black Women Writers, 1987. Fellow Phila. Assn., London, 1965-69; sabbatical Lilly Found., 1974-75. Mem. Writers Guild of Am. East, Authors League of Am. Avocations: swimming, basketball, reading, movies. Home: 35 N Prospect St Oberlin OH 44074

HERO, BARBARA FERRELL, visual and sound artist, writer; b. L.A., Jan. 3, 1925; d. Paul C. and Lucile (Evans) Ferrell; children: Alfred O. III, Barbara Ann, Michelle Claire, David Evans. BA in Art, George Washington U., 1950; EdM in Math., Boston U., 1980; cert. in techniques of computer sound Synthesis, MIT, 1981. Art tchr. Marjory Webster Jr. Coll., Washington, 1953-54; printmaker, painter, 1948—; vis. artist, lectr. U. Mass., Amherst, 1970s, Rochester (N.Y.) Inst. Tech., 1970s, U.S. Psychotronics Assn., Chgo., 1981-89; mus. sound creator Acoustic Brain Rsch., N.C., 1989; founder, dir. Internat. Lambdoma Rsch., Wells, Maine, 1994. Inventor Lambdoma Harmonic Keybd.; exhibited in Contemporary Am. Artist series Corcoran Gallery of Art, 1950; paintings represented in collections at Chase Manhattan Bank, N.Y.C., 1960s, Miami (Fla.)-Dade U., 1960s; author: Lambdoma Unveiled (The Theory of Relationships), The Glass Bead and Knot Theory of Relationships, The Lambdoma Resonant Harmonic Scale (P, Q, R, S, T, U, V and W); contbr. articles to profl. jours. Recipient Davina Winslow Meml. prize Nat. Soc. Painters in Casein, 1964, Cert. of Achievement, Interant. Assn. Colour Healers, London, 1982, J.A. Gallimore cert. for tech. R&D in psychotronics U.S. Psychotronics Assn., Chgo., 1994. Mem. Math. Assn. Am., N.Y. Acad. Scis. Office: Internat Lambdoma Rsch Inst 496 Loop Rd Wells ME 04090-7622

HEROLD, JEFFREY ROY MARTIN, library director; b. Chgo., Aug. 9, 1941; s. Roy George and Anne (Polacek) H.; m. Carol Ann Courtial, June 20, 1964; children: Kristin Ann, Timothy Scott. MEd, SUNY, Buffalo, 1966; PhD, Ohio State U., 1969; MLS, Kent State U., 1986. Teaching assoc. Ohio State U., Columbus, 1965-69; asst. prof. edn. SUNY, Cortland, 1969-74, Ind. U. Pa., 1974-75; lectr. in edn. Kelvin Grove Coll., Brisbane, Australia, 1976-78; assoc. dir. office continuing edn. Ohio State U., Columbus, 1979-84; extension libr. Columbus Pub. Libr., 1985-87; dir. Bucyrus (Ohio) Pub. Libr., 1987—, Bucyrus Libr. Consortium, 1989—; bd. dirs. North Ctrl. Libr. Cooperative, Mansfield, Ohio, 1991-93; adv. coun. Classical WOSB-FM, The Ohio State U., Marion, 1998—. Book reviewer: Libr. Jour., 1988-97. Chair McGovern for Pres. Com., Cortland County, N.Y., 1972; founder and pres. SUNY Founds. of Edn. Assn., 1971-72. Grantee Timken Found., 1989, 96, Ohio Humanities Coun., 1994, 95, 97, Libr. Svcs. and Tech. Act, 1998. Mem. ACLU, ALA, Pub. Libr. Assn. (Univ. Press books for pub. librs. com. 1990-93), Ohio Libr. Coun. Avocations: reading, walking. Office: Bucyrus Pub Libr 200 E Mansfield St Bucyrus OH 44820-2381

HEROLD, KARL GUENTER, lawyer; b. Munich, Feb. 3, 1947; came to U.S., 1963; s. Guenter K.B. and Eleonore E.E. H.; children: Deanna, Donna, Nicole, Jessica, Christine, Karl-Matthäus. BS, Bowling Green State U., 1969; JD, Case Western Res. U., 1972. Bar: Ohio 1972, N.Y. 1985, Conseil Juridique, France, 1990, Rechtskundiger, Germany, 1991, Avocat, France, 1992. Ptnr.-in-charge, European bus. practice coord. Jones, Day, Reavis & Pogue, Frankfurt, Germany, 1972—; coord. bus. practice Europe and Ctrl. and Ea. Europe Jones, Day, Reavis & Pogue; trustee Internat. and Comparative Law Ctr. Southwest Legal Found., Dallas, 1983; bd. dirs. Didier Taylor Refractories Corp., Cin., Redland Corp., San Antonio, v.p., Redland Credit Corp., San Antonio, v.p., Redland Fin. Inc., San Antonio, v.p., 1979-86, Zircoa Inc., Solon, Ohio, 1988-92. Contbr. numerous articles to legal jours. Trustee Cleve. Internat. Program, 1982-88; chmn. bd. dirs. Frankfurt Internat. Sch., 1991-93. Mem. ABA, Internat. Bar Assn., Order of Coif, Omicron Delta Kappa. Office: Jones Day Reavis & Pogue 599 Lexington Ave Fl C1A New York NY 10022-6030 also: Jones Day Reavis & Pogue, Hochhaus am Park Grueneburg Weg, 60323 Frankfurt Germany

HERON, DAVID WINSTON, librarian; b. Los Angeles, Mar. 29, 1920; s. Charles Morton and Elizabeth (Atsatt) H.; m. Winifred Ann Wright, Aug. 24, 1946; children—Holly Winston, James, Charles. A.B., Pomona Coll., 1942; B.L.S., U. Calif. at Berkeley, 1948; M.A., U. Calif. at Los Angeles, 1951. Reference asst. U. Calif. at Los Angeles Library, 1948-52; librarian Am. embassy, Tokyo, Japan, 1952-53; staff asst. to librarian Grad. Reading Room U. Calif. at Los Angeles, 1953-55; asst. to dir. Stanford Libraries, 1955-57, asst. dir., 1959-61; asst. librarian Hoover Instn., Stanford, 1957-59; dir. libraries U. Nev., Reno, 1961-68, U. Kans., Lawrence, 1968-74; univ. librarian U. Calif. at Santa Cruz, 1974-78, emeritus librarian, 1979—; sr. lectr. Sch. Library and Info. Studies, 1978-79; head reader services Hoover Instn., 1980-86; library adviser U. Ryukyus, Naha, Okinawa, 1960-61; mem. Kans. Library Adv. Commn., 1973-74. Author: Forever Facing South, 1991, Night Landing, 1999; editor: A Unifying Influence, 1981; mem. editorial bd. Coll. and Rsch. Librs.; contbr. articles to gen. and profl. jours. Served as 1st lt. AUS, 1942-46, ETO. Mem. ALA (exec. bd.), Kans. Library Assn., Nev. Library Assn. (pres. 1963-65), Assn. Research Libraries (bd. dirs. 1974), ACLU, Assn. Coll. and Research Libraries (editor monographs; chmn. U. libraries sect. 1970-71). Democrat. Home: 120 Las Lomas Dr Aptos CA 95003-3221

HERON, FRANCES DUNLAP, author, educator; b. Fulton, Mo., Dec. 26, 1906; d. Elijah Scott and Emma Susan (Owen) Dunlap; m. Laurence Tunstall, June 17, 1931 (dec.); children: Susan Heron Wollam, Alfred, Frances E. (dec.), Donald (dec.). AA, William Woods Coll., Fulton, 1925; BJ, U. Mo., 1927. Mem. editl. staff Christian Bd. Publ., St. Louis, 1927-31, Christian Advocate, Chgo., 1944-56; book reviewer Chgo. sunday Tribune, 1943-56; dir. edn. Grace United Protestant Ch., Park Forest, Ill., 1959-60; pub. sch. tchr. Dist. 147, Harvey, Ill., 1966-85; vol. preserving history Flossmoor (Ill.) Cmty. Ch., 1940—; lectr., writer Spiritual Frontiers Fellowship, Evanston, Ill., 1962-68. Author: Betty Ann, Beginner, 1930, With My Whole Heart, 1950, The Busy Berrys, 1950, Kathy Ann, Kindergartner, 1955, Here Comes Elijah, 1959, Jay Bain, Junior Boy, 1963; writer articles for Nat. Coun. Chs. Elections judge, 1950-68; neighborhood solicitor Am. Cancer Soc., 1997. Recipient Spl. Distinction prize Sch. Journalism, Columbia, Mo., 1927. Mem. PEO Sisterhood (historian 1949-67, 71—), Callaway County Hist. Soc., Perry County Historians. Democrat. Avocations: travel, genealogy, antiques, parapsychology. Home: 18520 Stewart Ave Homewood IL 60430-3036

HERON, JULIAN BRISCOE, JR., lawyer; b. Washington, Dec. 17, 1939; s. Julian B. Sr. and Doris S. (Strange) H.; m. Kathleen Ann Sweeney, Aug. 13, 1983; children: Kimberle, Melissa, Julian III, Kevin, Kathleen. BS, U. Ky., 1962, LLB, 1965. Bar: Ky. 1965, D.C. 1966, U.S. Dist. Ct. D.C. 1966, Md. 1968, U.S. Ct. Appeals (D.C. cir.) 1968, U.S. Supreme Ct. 1968. Ptnr. Pope, Ballard & Loos, Washington, 1968-81, Heron, Burchette, Ruckert & Rothwell, Washington, 1981-90, Tuttle, Taylor & Heron, Washington, 1990—; chmn. U.S. Agrl. Export Devel. Coun., 1983-85. Pres. Washington Internat. Horse Show, 1984, 85, Nat. Horse Show, 1994-96. Capt. USAF, 1965-68. Fellow ABA (chmn. agr. com. of adminstrv. law sect.); mem. D.C. Bar Assn. (chmn. ethics com.), Ky. Bar Assn., Md. Bar Assn., Bar Assn. D.C., Barristers, Faquier Springs Country Club. Republican. Roman Catholic. Office: Tuttle Taylor & Heron Ste 407 1025 Thomas Jefferson St NW Washington DC 20007-5201

HERON, VIRGINIA GRACE, secondary education educator; b. Burlington, Vt., Sept. 16, 1932; d. Frank Aloysius Heron and Grace Irene Couture Sharon. BA, Rivier Coll., Nashua, N.H., 1964, MA, 1973. Tchr. Presentation of Mary Acad., Biddeford, Maine, 1953-54, Island Pond, Vt., 1954-57, Bellingham, Mass., 1957-63, Lewiston, Maine, 1963-67, Methuen, Mass., 1967-71; tchr. Rice H.S., Burlington, 1971-73; Presentation of Mary Acad., Methuen, 1979—. Trustee Rivier Coll., 1979-81. Democrat. Roman Catholic. Avocations: quiltmaking, creative cooking, reading, arts and crafts. Home and Office: Presentation of Mary Acad 209 Lawrence St Methuen MA 01844-3884

HERONEN, MARIE F., nursing administrator, medical/surgical nurse; b. Flint, Mich., June 14, 1946; d. Jack Charles and Marie Anna (Lucke) Smith; m. Daniel J. Heronen, Dec. 6, 1969; children: Donna, Elizabeth. Diploma, St. Joseph Sch. Nursing, Flint, 1967; BS, Calif. Poly. State U., San Luis Obispo, 1981. RN, Mich., Calif.; cert. ACLS, CPR instr., cert. nursing adminstr. Team leader McClaren Hosp., Flint; staff nurse Sierra Vista Hosp., San Luis Obispo; dir. nursing Calif. Mens Colony, San Luis Obispo. Lt. (j.g.) USN, 1967-69. Mem. Am. Correctional Health Svcs. Assn., Nursing Adv. Coun., Calif. State Employees Assn., Cen. Coast Nursing Coop. Coun., Calif. Assn. Mgmt.

HERPEL, GEORGE LLOYD, marketing educator; b. St. Louis, Aug. 31, 1921; s. George Martin and Irene (Lloyd) H.; m. June L. Stamm, Nov. 22, 1949; children: John, Mark. BA, Vanderbilt U., 1943, MBA, 1955; PhD, St. Louis U., 1958. Gen. sales mgr., dir. pub. relations C.V. Mosby Pub. Co., St. Louis, 1947-54; dir. mgmt. devel. Internat. Shoe Co., St. Louis, 1954-62; sr. prof. mktg. Temple U., Phila., 1962-83, prof. emeritus, 1988—; prof. bus. adminstrn. Villanova U., 1983-88; pres. Hedgerow Theatre Corp., 1971-76; chmn. bd. trustees Sales Mktg. Execs. Grad. Sch. Sales and Mktg. Mgmt., Syracuse U., 1962-64, dean faculty, 1964-83; nat. ednl. cons. Splty. Advt. Assn., Dallas, 1972-89; trustee Accreditation Inst., Sales Mktg. Execs., 1986-90. Author: Specialty Advertising in Marketing, 1972, New Dimensions in Creative Marketing, 1983. Mem. Regional Export Expansion Com., 1966-74, U.S. Dept. of Commerce; chmn. Export Planning Com., Phila. With USNR, 1943-46. Recipient Educator of Yr. award Internat. Sales Mktg. Execs., 1985; named to Hall of Fame, Splty. Advt. Assn. Internat., 1991. Mem. Am. Mktg. Assn. (pres. St. Louis 1957-58, nat. v.p. 1963-65, chpt. bd. dirs. 1999—), Am. Soc. Internat. Execs. (bd. dirs., sec. 1975-94), Sales Mktg. Execs. Internat. (bd. dirs., v.p., exec. com. 1954-64), Nat. Spkrs. Assn. (charter), Sales Execs. Assn. St. Louis (pres. 1954-56), Vanderbilt U. Alumni Assn. (pres. St. Louis 1950), Pi Sigma Epsilon (bd. dirs. 1960-69), Beta Theta Pi (pres. St. Louis 1949). Home: 5323 Bermuda Vlg Advance NC 27006-9455

HERPST, ROBERT DIX, lawyer, optics and materials technology executive; b. Teaneck, N.J., Jan. 23, 1947; s. Harold Dix and Anita Augusta (Adams) H.; children: Katherine Elizabeth, Lauren Gabriel; m. Theresa M. Jacobini, Oct. 24, 1987. BS, NYU, 1969; JD, Rutgers U., 1972. Bar: N.J., U.S. Supreme Ct. Assoc. Pitney, Hardin & Kipp, Morristown, N.J., 1972-77, BOC Group, Inc., Montvale, N.J., 1977-89; div. counsel BOC Group, Inc., Montvale, 1978-82, corp. counsel, asst. sec., 1982-88; pres. Internat. Crystal Labs., Garfield, N.J., 1982-88, mng. dir., chmn. bd. dirs., 1988—. Patentee in field. Avocations: golf, politics, stock market, graphic arts. Office: Internat Crystal Labs 11 Erie St Garfield NJ 07026-2307

HERR, EDWIN LEON, educator, academic administrator; b. Carlisle, Pa., Nov. 23, 1933; s. Samuel Leon and Ruth Estelle (McGonigal) H.; m. Patricia Ann Green, July 27, 1963; children: Amber Leigh, Christopher Alan, Alicia Estelle. BS in Bus. Edn., Shippensburg State Tchrs. Coll, 1955; MA in Psychol., Columbia U., 1959, Profl. Diploma, 1961, EdD, 1963. Lic. counseling psychologist, Pa. Instr. Columbia U. Tchrs. Coll., N.Y.C., 1959-63; from asst. to assoc. prof. dept. counselor edn. SUNY, Buffalo, 1963-66; dir. bur. guidance svcs., dir. bur. pupil pers. Pa. Dept. Pub. Instrn., Harrisburg, 1966-68; prof. edn. Pa. State U. Coll. Edn., State College, 1968-89; disting. prof. edn. Pa. State U. Coll. Edn., University Park, 1989—; dept. head counselor edn., counseling psychology & rehab. svcs. Pa. State U. Coll. Edn., State College, 1968-92, acting asst. dean for grad. studies, 1972-74, dir. vocat. edn., 1972-77, 85-90, acting dir. divsn. edn. policy studies, 1973-76, interim dean Coll. Edn., 1974, 98-99, dir. addictions prevention lab., 1978-79, assoc. dean grad. programs, rsch. and tech., 1992—; dir. Coll. Edn. Counseling Ctr., 1974-92; vis. prof. Inst. for the Devel. Nations/U. Reading, Eng., 1967, U. British Columbia, Vancouver, Can., 1989; ext. prof. Temple U., 1967-68; aux. prof. psychology adolescence Lebanon Valley Coll., 1967-68; faculty Nat. Ctr. for Rsch. in Vocat. Edn./Ohio State U., 1978-85. Co-author: (with Evans) Foundations of Vocational Education, 1978, Guidance and Counseling in the Schools: Perspectives on the Past, Present, and Future, 1979; (with Pinson), Foundations of Policy for Guidance and Counseling, 1982; (with Long) Counseling for Youth Employability, 1983; (with Cramer) Career Guidance and Counseling Through the Life Span: Systematic Approaches, 1988, fifth edit., 1996, Controversies in the Mental Health Professions, 1989, Multicultural Diversity in Britain and the U.S.: Implications for Counseling, 1990, (with Rayman and Garcia) Handbook for the College and University Career Center, 1993, Counseling Employment-Bound Youth, 1995; (with K. Gray) Other Ways to Win. Creating Alternatives for High School Graduates, 1995 (with K. Gray) Workforce Education: The Basics, 1998, Counseling in a Dynamic Society, Contexts and Practices for the 21st Century, 1998; editor Jour. Counseling and Devel., 1992-96; mem. various editl. bds.; contbr. articles to profl. jours. Co-chmn. Centre County Cancer Crusade, State College, 1978-79; lay leader St. Pauls United Meth. Ch., State College, 1978-81, chmn. adminstrv. bd., 1978-81, chmn. edn. commn., 1975-78, pastor-parish com., 1981-83; active State College Mcpl. Band, 1989—; asst. baseball coach Teener League, 1982-83. Capt USAF Res. Ditchley Found. fellow Eng., 1972, Rsch. fellow Japan Soc. for Promotion Sci., Sophia U., Tokyo, 1979, Vis. fellow Nat. Inst. for Careers Edn. and Counseling, Cambridge, Eng., 1976; Disting. scholar Chi Sigma Iota, 1993; recipient Jesse S. Heiges Disting. Alumni award Shippensburg U., 1984, Govt. Rels. award Am. Counseling Assn., 1993, Career Achievement award Pa. State U. Coll. Edn., 1996. Fellow Am. Assn. Applied and Preventive Psychology (com. mem.), Am. Psychol. Assn. (com. mem.), Am. Psychol. Soc. (com. mem.), Pa. Psychol. Assn. (com. mem.); mem. AACD (pres. 1983-84, Profl. Devel. award 1990), Nat. Vocat. Guidance Assn. (Merit award 1976, Outstanding Svc. award 1990), Internat. Round Table for the Advancement Counseling (bd. dirs. 1976-84, pres. 1979-80), Internat. Assn. for Ednl. and Vocat. Guidance (bd. dirs. 1991—), Assn. for Counselor Edn. and Supervision (pres. 1974-75, pres. North Atlantic region 1969-70, Outstanding Svc. award 1975, Profl. Leadership award 1990), Am. Pers. and Guidance Assn. (bd. dirs. 1975-78, 82-85, Arthur A. Hitchcock Disting. Profl. Svc. award 1980), Am. Sch. Counselor Assn., Am. Vocat. Assn., Assn. for Multi-Cultural Counseling and Devel., Nat. Career Devel. Assn. (pres. 1978-81, Eminent Career award 1986), Assn. for Measurement and Evaluation in Guidance, Am. Mental Health Counselors Assn., Internat. Assn. for Applied Psychology, World Future Soc., Am. Counseling Assn. (life, pres. 1982-85, Profl. Devel. Leadership award 1990), Pa. Counseling Assn. (life, Presdl. award 1993), Nat. Coun. for Cert. Career Counselor (cert.), Phi Delta Kappa. Republican. United Methodist. Avocations: fishing, flying, travel, music. Home: 860 Saxton Dr State College PA 16801-4236 Office: The Pa State Univ College Edn 241 Chambers Bldg University Park PA 16802-3206

HERR, PETER HELMUT FRIEDERICH, sales executive; b. Hamburg, Germany, Apr. 23, 1951; came to U.S., 1978; s. Helmut and Ellen (Schmidt) H.; m. Kim Lovett, Sept. 29, 1984 (div. Nov. 1991); 1 child, Andrew; m. Monika Berns, Nov. 19, 1991; children, Jan, Maximilian. BS in Mech. Engring., U. Braunschweig, 1974, MS in Aero. Engring., 1978. Aero. engr. R&D Beech Aircraft Corp., Wichita, Kans., 1978-81; regional mgr. Beech Aircraft Corp., Wichita, 1981-86, sr. regional mgr., 1987-92, dir. internat. market devel., 1992-93, regional dir. western Europe and Africa, 1993-94; v.p. internat sales Raytheon Aircraft, Wichita, 1994—; sec., treas. Euroflight, Inc., Wichita, 1985—. Cpl. German Air Force, 1970-72. Lutheran. Avocations: flying, comml. and instrument rated multi engine pilot, golf, boating. Home: 15229 E Zimmerly Ct Wichita KS 67230-9244 Office: Raytheon Aircraft Co 10511 E Central Ave Wichita KS 67206-2557

HERR, PHILLIP RAY, federal agency administrator; b. Mt. Pleasant, Pa., Aug. 12, 1956; s. Herbert Eugene and Mary Elizabeth Herr; m. Maria Magdalena Enamorado; 1 child, Alejandra. AB, Ind. U., 1979; PhD, Columbia U., 1988. Edn. assoc. N.Y.C. Bd. of Edn., Bklyn., 1983-88; rsch. assoc. Metis Assocs., N.Y.C., 1988-89; sr. evaluator U.S. Gen. Acctg. Office, Washington, 1989—; adj. lectr. York Coll., CUNY, Jamaica, Queens, 1985-88. Fulbright-Hays fellow U.S. Dept. Edn., 1984, fellowship NSF, 1984, Inter-Am. Fedn., 1981, PRA fellowship Orgn. of Am. States, 1984. Fellow Am. Anthropol. Assn. (workshop leader 1997-98). Avocations: photography, travel. E-mail: herrp.NSIAD@gao.gov. Office: US GAO Internat Rels and Trade 441 G St NW Washington DC 20548

HERR, RICHARD, history educator; b. Guanajuato, Mexico, Apr. 7, 1922; s. Irving and Luella (Winship) H.; m. Elena Fernandez Mel, Mar. 2, 1946 (div. 1967); children: Charles Fernandez, Winship Richard; m. Valerie J. Jackson, Aug. 29, 1968; children: Sarah, Jane. A.B., Harvard U., 1943; Ph.D., U. Chgo., 1954. Instr. Yale U., 1952-57, asst. prof., 1957-59; assoc. prof. U. Calif., Berkeley, 1960-63, prof. history, 1963-91, prof. emeritus, 1991—, chancellor's fellow, 1987-90; directeur d'études associé, sixième sect. Ecole Pratique des Hautes Etudes, Paris, 1973; dir. Madrid Study Ctr., U. Calif., 1975-77; chair Portuguese Studies Program, U. Calif., Berkeley, 1994-98; vis. life mem. Clare Hall, Cambridge, Eng., 1985—; vis. prof. U. Alcalá. Henares, Spain, 1991; bd. dirs. Internat. Inst. Found. in Spain, Boston; fellow Ctr. for History of Freedom, Washington U., St. Louis, 1994. Author: The Eighteenth Century Revolution in Spain, 1958, Tocqueville and the Old Regime, 1962, Spain, 1971, Rural Change and Royal Finances in Spain at the End of the Old Regime, 1989 (Leo Gershoy award Am. Hist. Assn. 1990); co-author: An American Family in the Mexican Revolution, 1999; editor: Memorias del cura liberal don Juan Antono Posse, 1984; co-editor, contbr.: Ideas in History, 1965, Iberian Identity, 1989; editor, contbr.: The New Portugal Democracy and Europe, 1993, Themes in Rural History of the Western World, 1993; asst. editor: Jour. Modern History, 1949-50; mem. editl. bd. French Historical Studies, 1966-69, Revista de Historia Economica, 1983—. With AUS, 1943-45. Decorated Comendador of the Orden de Isabel la Católica (Spain); recipient Bronze medal Collège de France, Paris, The Berkeley citation U. Calif., 1991; Social Sci. Rsch. Coun. grantee, 1963-64; Guggenheim fellow, 1959-60, 84-85; NEH sr. fellow, 1968-69. Fellow Am. Acad. Arts and Scis.; mem. Am. Philos. Soc., Real Academia de la Historia Madrid (corr.), Soc. for Spanish and Portuguese Hist. Studies. Office: U Calif Dept History Berkeley CA 94720-2550

HERR, RICHARD JOSEPH, sculptor, educator; b. Sheboygan, Wis., Jan. 17, 1937; s. George E. and Mollie (Rammer) H.; m. Anya Van Dulm, Dec. 21, 1995; children: Gretchen, Kurt, Eric. Pvt. instrn., Oscar Binder, Stuttgart, Germany, 1955-58; student, Layton Sch. Art, Milw., 1959-61, Marquette U., 1960-61, U. Wis., Milw., 1961-62. Prin./dir. Art Independent Gallery, Lake Geneva, Wis., 1968-84; artist-in-residence The Prairie Sch., Racine, Wis., 1970-71; art instr. The Prairie Sch., 1971-76, U. Wis. Parkside, Kenosha, 1972-73, Santa Barbara (Calif.) City Coll., 1983-88; prin./dir. The New Gallery, Santa Barbara, 1985-87; pres. Richard J. Herr Corp. Fine Art Acquisition, Milw., 1995—; mem. Visual Art in Pub. Places com. appointed by Santa Barbara city coun., 1983-85; bd. dirs. Wis. Art Edn. Assn., 1974-75, Artists Equity Santa Barbara (v.p. 1984-86); exec. bd. Art Affiliates U. Calif. Santa Barbara, 1986-87. Exhbns. include Painters and Sculptures Show, Milw. Art Ctr., 1965, Old Orchard Invitational Show, Skokie, Ill., 1972, group show Artists Equity, Santa Barbara, 1984, Art Milw., Pfister Hotel, 1995; sculpture reproduced in Milw. Sentinel, Chgo. Sun-Times, Playboy others; lectr., workshop presenter in field. Bd. dirs. Repertory West Dance Co., Santa Barbara, 1986-87. Recipient numerous awards including Marquette U. Fine Arts Festival award for sculpture, 1967, 1st award for sculpture Racine Invitational, Wustum Mus., 1970, 1972, Duo Critic's award Chgo. Tribune, Chgo. Art Inst., 1972. Mem. Am. Internat. Sculptors. Home: 1020 E Lyon St Apt 104 Milwaukee WI 53202-2155

HERR, SHARON MARIE, librarian; b. St. Cloud, Minn., June 23, 1950; d. Lawrence James and Avis Christina (Klein) Blenkush; m. Dennis Wilfred Herr, June 8, 1985. BA cum laude, Coll. St. Benedict, 1972; MA in LS, U. Mich., 1974. Scheduling asst. South Jr. H.S., St. Cloud, 1968; asst. to libr. Coll. of St. Benedict, St. Joseph, Minn., 1972-73; sci. libr. Ohio No. U., Ada, 1974-78, cataloging libr., 1978—; mem. univ. coun. Ohio No. U., Ada, 1989-91, 97—, mem. pers. com., 1979-80. Judge elections Hardin County Bd. Elections, Kenton, Ohio, 1995—. Recipient Betty Crocker Homemaker award Gen. Mills, 1968. Mem. ALA, Assn. Coll. and Rsch. Librs., Assn. Libr. Collections and Tech. Svcs., Acad. Libr. Assn. of Ohio, Libr. of Congress Assocs., Smithsonian Instn. Democrat. Avocations: antiques, gardening, Christmas tree ornament collecting, investing. Home: 822 S Johnson St Ada OH 45810-1521 Office: Ohio No U Ada OH 45810

HERR, STANLEY SHOLOM, law educator; b. Newark, Aug. 7, 1945; s. Louis J. and Ruth G. (Greenberg) H.; m. Raquel Schuster, June 17, 1979; children: David Louis, Deborah Ann, Ilana Ruth. BA cum laude, Yale U., 1967, JD, 1970; DPhil, Oxford U., 1979. Bar: D.C. 1971, U.S. Dist Ct. D.C. 1971, U.S. Ct. Appeals (5th cir.) 1972, Md. 1984, U.S. Supreme Ct. 1984. Staff atty. Stern Community Law Office, Washington, 1970-71; sr. staff atty. Nat. Law Office of Nat. Legal Aid Defender Assn., Washington, 1971-73; Joseph P. Kennedy Jr. fellow Balliol Coll. Oxford (Eng.) U., 1973-76; vis. scholar, instr. Law Sch. Harvard U., Cambridge, Mass., 1976-80; Rockefeller Found. fellow, vis. scholar Law Sch. Columbia U., N.Y.C., 1980-82; project dir. mental patients' rights guidebook NIMH, Northampton, Mass. and Bethesda, Md., 1982-83; vis. assoc. prof. law U. Md., Balt., 1983-84, assoc. prof. law, 1984-95, prof. law, 1995—; sr. rsch. fellow Schell Ctr. for Internat. Human Rights, Yale Law Sch., 1995—; cons. U.S. Dist. Ct. Mass., Boston, 1979-81; co-founder, v.p. Homeless Persons Representation Project, Balt., 1987—; vis. prof. Tel Aviv U., 1990-91; vis. scholar Law Sch., Hebrew U., Jerusalem, 1990-91; Kennedy Pub. Policy fellow, The White House, 1993-95; cons. NAS. Author: The New Clients: Legal Services for Mentally Retarded Persons, 1979, Rights and Advocacy for Retarded People, 1983, Legal Rights and Mental Health Care, 1983, A Guide to Consent, 1999; contbr. articles to legal jours., chpts. to books. Bd. dirs. Am. Jewish Soc. for Svc., N.Y.C., 1972—, Am. Assn. Mental Retardation, Internat. Acad. Law & Mental Health; cons. U.S. Pres.'s Com. on Mental Retardation, 1978-80; mem. Md. Gov.'s Commn. to Revise Mental Retardation and Devel. Disability Laws, 1985-86; pres. Greater Balt. Shelter Network, 1987. Recipient Rosemary F. Dybwad Internat. award Nat. Assn. Retarded Citizens, 1973, Leadership award Region IX Am. Assn. Mental Deficiency, 1984, Thomas Ferciot Disting. Profl. Svc. award Balt. Assn. Retarded Citizens, 1987, Swartz medallion for Humanitarian Svc., Swartz found., 1990, Burton Blatt award Young Adult Inst., Rights of the Disadvantage award Md. Bar Found., 1999, Regent's faculty award for excellence in pub. svc., 1999; named Fulbright scholar 1990-91, fellow World Inst. on Disability, 1993; Switzer Disting. Rsch. fellow, 1999—. Fellow Am. Assn. Mental Retardation (pres. legal process divsn. 1978-80, 82-84, bd. dirs. 1993-95, v.p. 1996, pres.-elect 1997, pres. 1998, Humanitarian award 1996, Sandra Jensen Humanitarian award Region II 1997); mem. ABA (commn. on mental and phys. disability law 1997, chair editl. adv. bd., mental and phys. disability law reporter), Assn. Retarded Citizens U.S. (chmn. legal advocacy com. 1984-90). Avocations: long-distance running, foreign travel. Office: U Md Law Sch 500 W Baltimore St Baltimore MD 21201-1701

HERRANEN, KATHY, artist, graphic designer; b. Zelienople, Pa., Dec. 22, 1943; d. John and Helen Elizabeth (Sayti) D'Biagio; m. John Warma Herranen, Dec. 31, 1974 (div. Feb. 1994); 1 child, Michael John. Student, Scottsdale (Ariz.) C.C., 1990—. Cert. tchr. art, State Bd. Dirs. for Cmty. Coll. of Ariz. Horseback riding instr. Black Saddle Riding Acad., Lancaster, Calif., early 1960's; tel. company supr. Bell Tel., Bishop, Calif., 1965; reporter, part-time photographer Ellwood City (Pa.) Ledger, 1967-70; backcountry guide and cook Mammoth Lakes (Calif.) Pack Outfit, 1970; motel mgr. Mountain Property Mgmt., Mammoth Lakes, 1970-72; reporter, bookkeeper Hungry Horse (Mont.) News, 1973-74; pig farmer Columbia Falls, Mont., 1973-75; fine artist, illustrator, graphic designer Mont., Calif., and Ariz., 1980—; fine arts cons. Collector's Gallery, Galleri II, Yuma, Ariz., 1983-84; wind chime designer, creator Phoenix, 1995—; represented by Marcella's Ariz. Collection, Phoenix, 1995—, Backstreet Furniture and Art, Phoenix, 1995—, Hohn Gallery Fine Arts, Ltd., Scottsdale, 1997—; guest lectr. Paradise Valley Tchrs Acad., Phoenix, 1993, Sr. Adult Edn. Program, Scottsdale (Ariz.) Cmty. Coll., 1994, pastel painting instr., 1996; guest demonstrator Binder's Art Ctr., Scottsdale, 1995, Backstreet Furniture and Art, Phoenix, 1995-96; guest lectr., demonstrator Summer Edn. Program Paradise Valley Sch. Dist. Solo shows include Pinnacle, Phoenix, 1993, Villas of Sedona, Ariz., 1995. Sec. Young Dems., Ellwood City, late 1960's, Vistas Home Owners Assn., Phoenix, 1995—; troubleshooter Maricopa County Elections Dept., Phoenix, 1994-96. Recipient 1st place award Potpourri Artists, Yuma, Ariz., 1981, Subscriber award Butte (Mont.) Arts Coun., 1981, 2nd place award Desert Artists, Yuma, 1982, honorable mention Yuma County Fair, Yuma, 1983, Wildlife Painting Exhibit, Scottsdale, 1993, honorable mention Scottsdale Studio 13, 1991, 92, Special award, 1993, Merit award, 1993, 94 (2). Mem. Nat. Assn. Sr. Friends Fine Artists (chair 1995—, honorable mention 1993, People's Choice award 1996), Nat. and Ariz. chpts. of Women's Caucus for Art, Phoenix Artists Guild, Ariz. Pastel Artists Assn. (charter mem., membership chair 1995-96, 2d v.p., show chair 1996, guest demonstrator 1995, guest lectr. 1998, Merit award 1995), Artists and Craftsmen of Flathead Valley (founder, charter mem., pres. 1981-82), Phi Theta Kappa. Republican. Lutheran. Avocations: public speaking and acting, dancing, stamp collecting, photography, interior decorating. Office: 4114 E Union Hills Dr Unit 1011 Phoenix AZ 85050-3355

HERRANS-PEREZ, LAURA LETICIA, psychologist, educator, research consultant; b. Vega Baja, P.R., June 16, 1935; d. Juan B. and María T. (Pérez)) Herrans. BA, U. P.R., 1955; MA, Cath. U. Am., 1957, PhD, 1969. Lic. psychologist, P.R. Psychologist I, Dept. Health, San Juan, P.R., 1957-60, rsch. cons. mental health secretariat, 1983—; prin. investigator WISC-R rsch. project U. P.R., Rio Piedras, 1960-63, instr. psychology, 1963-69, assoc. prof., 1969-77, prof., 1977—; prin. investigator, WISC-R rsch. project U. P.R., San Juan, P.R., 1987-92. Author: Psicologia y Medición, 1985, Manual of Instructions for the Puerto Rican WISC-R, 1992; co-author: Dos Modelos Psicometricos para el Diagnostico Diferencial, 1989, Manual WISC-R, 1992; translator Wechsler Intelligence Scale for Children-Revised, 1992. Pres. ICPE de P.R., Inc., 1989-98. Mem. APA, Assn. Psychologists P.R. (pres. 1970-71), Assn. Univ. Profs. Roman Catholic. Avocations: sailing, swimming. Office: ICPE de PR Inc Ste 107 Med Ophthalmic Pla Hnas Davila Bayamon PR 00959

HERRELKO, DAVID A., career officer. BS in Elec. Engring., MIT, 1969; disting. grad., Res. Officer Tng. Corps, MIT, 1969; MS in Sys. and Info. Sci., Syracuse U., 1970; student pilot tng., Webb AFB, Tex., 1970-71; MS in Bus. Adminstrn., U. Dayton, 1975; student, Squadron Officer Sch., 1975; disting. grad. Air Force Inst. Tech., UCLA, 1976, PhD in Engring., 1976; student, Air Command and Staff Coll., 1978, Def. Sys. Mgmt. Coll., 1981. Commd. 2d lt. USAF, 1970, advanced through grades to brig. gen., 1995; computer sys. design engr. aero. sys. div. Wright-Patterson AFB, Ohio, 1971-73; chief Data Processing br. Joint Tactical Info. Distbn. Sys. Program Office, Hanscom AFB, Mass., 1976-77; lead sys. engr. Tactical Air Control Ctr. Automation Program, Hanscom AFB, Mass., 1977-79; stationed at Hdqs. Air Force Sys. Command, Andrews AFB, Md., 1979-81; various positions Hdqs. USAF, Pentagon, Washington, 1981-85; sr. rsch. fellow Nat. Def. U., Ft. Lesley J. McNair, Washington, 1985-86; stationed at Hanscom AFB, 1986-91; insp. gen. Air Force Sys. Command, Andrews AFB, 1991-92, Air Force Logistics Command, Wright-Patterson AFB, 1991-92, Air Force Materiel Command, Wright-Patterson AFB, 1992; comdr. Wright Lab., Wright-Patterson AFB, 1992-95, Joint Logistics Sys. Ctr., Wright-Patterson AFB, 1995-98; vice comdr. Aero. Sys. Ctr., Wright-Patterson AFB, 1998—. Decorated Legion of Merit with oak leaf cluster. Recipient Golden Knight award Nat. Mgmt. Assn., 1993. Office: ASC/CV 1865 Fourth St Rm 208 Wright Patterson AFB OH 45433

HERRELL, VIRGIL LEE, secondary education educator, English educator; b. Jefferson City, Tenn., Apr. 25, 1962; s. Virgil and Mattie Lee (Stansberry) H.; m. Pamela Kay Lowe, Oct. 22, 1994. BA, Lincoln Meml. U., 1983. Profl. cert. Tenn. State Bd. Edn. Tchr. Claiborne County H.S., Tazewell, Tenn., 1983—; instr. Walter's State C.C., Morristown, Tenn., 1997—. Bd. mem. Spl. Olympics, Tazewell, 1985-93. Mem. NEA, Tenn. Edn. Assn., Claiborne County Edn. Assn., Tenn. Col., Ky. Col. Democrat. Baptist. Avocations: music, reading, theater. Office: Claiborne County HS 1325 Claiborne St Tazewell TN 37879-4134

HERREN, CLINE CHAMPION, real estate agent; b. Marshfield, Mo., Mar. 29, 1935; s. Cline Champion and Audrey Lorene (Rader) H.; m. Barbara Sue Dugan, Mar. 24, 1974; 1 child, Cline Champion Herren III. Farmer Marshfield, 1953-54, 56-60; laborer GM, Berkley, Mo., 1961-63; engring. technician Wright & Assocs., Springfield, Mo., 1965-68, Sho-Me Power Corp., Marshfield, 1968-76; real estate broker Century Realty, Marshfield, 1976—; pres. Webster County Land Title Co., Marshfield, 1976—. With U.S. Army, 1954-56, 63-65. Mem. Greater Springfield Bd. Realtors (pres. 1987; Realtor of Yr. 1986). Republican. United Methodist. Office: Century Realty PO Box I-44 & Spu Marshfield MO 65706-0001

HERRENKOHL, ROY CECIL, psychology educator; b. Huntington, W.Va., Aug. 26, 1932; s. Roy Cecil and Anna Marie (Ashworth) H.; m. Ellen Madeline Cohen, Nov. 26, 1964; children: Eric Brian, Todd Ian, Joshua David. BA, Washington and Lee U., 1954; student, Reading (Eng.) U., 1954-55; postgrad., Union Theol. Sem., N.Y.C., 1955-57; PhD in Psychology, NYU, 1966. Cert. psychologist, Pa. Assoc. sec. W.T. Grant Found., N.Y.C., 1957-62; lectr. in psychology Long Island U., N.Y.C., 1964-66; asst. prof. social rels. Lehigh U., Bethlehem, Pa., 1966-69, assoc. prof., 1969-75, prof. psychology, 1975-96, dir. Ctr. for Social Rsch., 1974-90, vice provost for R&D, 1990-96, Disting. Univ. Svc. prof., 1996—; cons. Computing Devices Internat., Mpls., 1995-97. Contbr. articles to profl. jours. Recipient Outstanding Rsch. Article award Am. Profl. Soc. on the Abuse of Children, 1998. Mem. APA, Am. Psychol. Soc. Avocation: carpentry. Office: Lehigh U Ctr for Social Rsch 520 Brodhead Ave Bethlehem PA 18015-3008

HERRERA, ARTURO, artist; b. Caracas, Venezuela, 1959. BFA, U. Tulsa, 1982; MFA, U. Ill., Chgo., 1992. resident ArtPace, San Antonio, 1999—. One-person shows include MWMWM Gallery, Chgo., 1993, 94, The Ctr. for Contemporary Arts, Santa Fe, 1993, Randolph St. Gallery, Chgo., 1995, Hermetic Gallery, Milw., 1995, Mus. Contemporary Arts, Chgo., 1995, Revolution Gallery, Ferndale, Mich., 1996, Univ. Club, Chgo., 1996, Gahlberg Gallery, Coll. DuPage, Glen Ellyn, 1996, Brent Sikkema/Wooster Gardens, N.Y.C., 1998, The Renaissance Soc. U. Chgo., 1998, Worcester (Mass.) Art Mus., 1998, The Art Inst. Chgo., 1998, Dia Ctr. for the Arts, 1998; group exhbns. include Gallery 400, Chgo., 1992, Nomadic Site, L.A., 1992, MWMWM Gallery, Chgo., 1993, Klein Art Works, Chgo., 1993, Sch. Art and Design, U. Chgo., 1994, Sotheby's Inc., Chgo., 1994, The Drawing Ctr., N.Y.C., 1994, Layton Gallery, Milw. Inst. Art and Design, 1994, Feature, N.Y.C., 1994, 95, PS 122, N.Y.C., 1994, Ten in One Gallery, Chgo., 1994, LACE, L.A., 1995, 213 Inst. Pl., Chgo., 1995, TBA Exhbn. Space, Chgo., 1995, Chgo. Cultural Ctr., 1996, NIU Gallery, Chgo., 1996, Randolph St. Gallery, Chgo., 1996, Thread Waxing Space, N.Y., 1996, Gallery 312, Chgo., 1996, Gallery 16, San Francisco, 1997, Real Art Ways, Hartford, Conn., 1997, Stephen Friedman Gallery, London, 1998, Brent Sikkema, N.Y., 1999. Recipient award Art Matters, Inc., N.Y.C., 1995, The Marie Walsh Sharpe Art Found., N.Y.C., 1997, Louis Comfort Tiffany Found., N.Y.C., 1997, Pollock-Krasner Found., N.Y.C., 1998; SA grantee Ill. Arts Coun., Chgo., 1995, CAAP grantee Dept. Cultural Affairs, Chgo., 1995; visual arts fellow Ill. Arts Coun., Chgo., 1996. Office: c/o Brent Sikkema 530 W 22nd St New York NY 10011*

HERRERA, HENRY FRANCIS, career officer; b. Miami Springs, Fla.; m. Ruth Underwood; children: Cynthia Driscoll, Suzanne, Sara Elliot, Steven. BS in Naval Sci., U.S. Naval Acad., 19966. Commd. ensign USN, 1966, advanced through grades to rear adm.; stationed on USS James K. Polk, USS Sand Lance, USS Von Steuben, USS Sculpin; asst. force nuclear power officer Staff Commdr. Submarine Force U.S. Atlantic Fleet; exec. officer Nuclear Propulsion Examining Bd. Commdr. Chief U.S. Atlantic Fleet; commdr. USS Lafayette, 1984-87, USS Mich., 1987-90; br. head Ballistic Missile Submarine Security Program Office Asst. Chief Naval Ops., 1990-91; chief Asia-Pacific Divsn. Strategic Plans & Policy Joint Staff, 1991-92; dir. Command Control, Comm., Computers & Intelligence Sys. U.S. Strategic Command, 1992-94; commdr. Submarine Group 9/Submarine Force Rep., 1994-96; pres. Bd. Insp. & Survey, 1996—. Decorated Def. Superior Svc. Medal, 2 Legion of Merit Medals, 2 Meritorious Svc. Medals, 2 Navy Commendation Medals, Navy Achievement Medal, Nat. Def. Svc. Medal with bronze star, others. Office: USN 2600 Tarawa Ct Ste 250 Norfolk VA 23521-3235*

HERRERA, JOHN, professional football team executive; married; 8 children. BA in History, U. Calif., Davis. Tng. camp asst. Oakland Raiders, 1963-68, pub. rels. asst., 1968, dir. pub. rels., 1978-80, sr. exec., 1985—; dir. player pers. B.C. Lions, 1981-82; gen. mgr. Sask. Roughriders, 1983-84; with scouting depts. Tampa Bay Buccaneers, 1975-76, Washington Redskins, 1977. Office: Oakland Raiders 1220 Harbor Bay Pkwy Alameda CA 94502-6570

HERRERA, MARY CARDENAS, education educator, music minister; b. Sugar Land, Tex., Feb. 21, 1938; d. Jose Chavez and Juanita (Lira) Cardenas; m. Saragosa Martin Herrera, Sept. 20, 1960 (dec.); children: Michael (dec.), Patricia Ann Zagrzecki, Aaron Martin Herrera, Katherine Ann Nava. Grad., Sugar Land (Tex.) High Sch., 1957, Patricia Stevens Bus. Sch., 1960; student, Houston C.C., 1991, 92. Sec. William Penn Hotel, Houston, 1959-66; payroll clk. Peakload, Inc., Houston, 1967-69; acctg. clk. Am. Gen., Inc., Houston, 1970-73; nurse asst. Ft. Bend Ind. Sch. Dist., Stafford, Tex., 1973-88; tchr.'s asst. Ft. Bend Ind. Sch. Dist., Sugarland, Tex., 1988—; numerous offices Holy Family Cath. Ch., Missouri City, Tex., 1981-90, Hispanic choir dir., 1981-89; Hispanic choir dir. Notre Dame Cath. Ch., 1990-91; Hispanic del. Galveston-Houston Diocese, 1987-89; regional del. Encuetro Dioceseno Conf., San Antonio, 1983, 84, 85; dir., coord. Diocesan Hispanic Choir, 1982-86, music workshops, 1982-88. Songwriter in field. Mem., tchr. PTO, 1973—; mem. Holy Family Hispanic Com.; mem. choir Iglesia del Pueblo, Pasadena, Tex., 1991, 92, asst. Sunday sch. tchr., 1992-93, coord. monthly Women's Praise Gathering, 1994-97; music min. local prayer groups Houstong area, 1990—. Mem. Women's Aglow (praise and worship music min. Pasadena chpt. 1988-90). Democrat. Avocations: jogging, playing guitar. Home and Office: 4506 Ludwig Ln Stafford TX 77477-5219

HERRERA, PALOMA, dancer; b. Buenos Aires, Dec. 21, 1975; d. Alberto Oscar and Diana Lia (Rube) H. Attended, Olga Ferri Studio, 1982, Ballet Sch. of Minsk, 1987, English Nat. Ballet, London, 1990, Sch. Am. Ballet, N.Y.C., 1991; diploma, Inst. Superior Art at The Colon Theatre, Buenos Aires, 1991. Soloist Am. Ballet Theatre, N.Y.C., 1992-95, prin. dancer, 1995—. Dancer (ballets) Don Quixote, 1987, 88, soloist La Bayadere, The Sleeping Beauty, Don Quixote, Met. Opera, N.Y.C., 1992, Etudes, The Sleeping Beauty, Swan Lake, Symphonie Concertante, Voluntaries, 1993, prin. Symphonie Concertatne, Symphonic Variations, 1993; prin. Peasant Pas de Deux in Giselle, Colon Theatre, Buenos Aires, 1992, La Bayadere, 1993; prin. Don Quixote, soloist Etudes, Voluntaries, Theme and Variations, Kennedy Ctr., Washington, 1993; prin. The Nutcracker, Dorothy Chandler Pavilion, L.A., 1993, Palace Theatre, Stamford, Conn., 1993; repertoire Met. Opera House Symphonic Variations, Theme and Variations, The Nutcracker, Cruel World, Symphonie Concertante, Gala Performance, 1994, La Bayadera, Don Quixote, Paquite, How Near Heaven, Les Sylphides, Cruel World , Tchaikovsky Pas de Deux, Romeo and Juliet, 1995; guest artist Ballet Gala, Toronto, 1993, Colon Theatre, Buenos Aires, 1993, Gala Ballet of Aix-En-Provence, France, 1993, New Generation Ballet, Moscow, Gala Tribute to Nureyev, Toronto, Le Gala des Etoiles, Montreal, Internat. Evenings of Dance, Vail, Colo., Don Quixote, Kremlin Palace, Moscow, 1995. Recipient First prize Latino Am. Ballet Contest, Lima, Peru, 1985, Coca-Cola Contest of Arts and Scis., 1986, Finalist diploma XIV Varna (Bulgaria) Internat. Competition of Ballet, 1990; scholar Colon Theatre Found., 1989; Dance scholar Antorchas Found., 1991. Home: One Lincoln Plz 20 W 64th St Apt F New York NY 10023-7129 also: Billinghurst 2553 10 Piso Dto, CP 1425 Buenos Aires Argentina Office: American Ballet Theatre 890 Broadway Fl 3 New York NY 10003-1278

HERRERA, SANDRA JOHNSON, school system administrator; b. Riverside, Calif., June 21, 1944; d. William Emory Johnson and Mildred Alice (Alford) Wimer; m. Wynn Neal Huffman, Feb. 19, 1962 (div. May 1967); 1 child, Kristen Lee; m. Steven Jack Herrera, June 21, 1985 (div. Dec. 1997). AA in Purchasing Mgmt., Fullerton Coll., 1983; BSBA, U. Redlands, 1985, MA in Mgmt., 1988. Sr. purchasing clk Fullerton (Calif.) Union High Sch. Dist., 1969-77, buyer, 1977-79, coord. budgets and fiscal affairs, 1979-83; asst. dir. fin. svcs. Downey (Calif.) Unified Sch. Dist., 1983-85; dir. acctg. Whittier (Calif.) Union High Sch. Dist., 1985-89; asst. supt. bus. Whittier City Sch. Dist., 1989-91, Oxnard Elem. Sch. Dist., 1991—; cons. Heritage Dental Lab., El Toro, Calif, 1981-97. Spl. dep. sheriff Santa Barbara (Calif.) County Sheriff's Mounted Posse, 1986-90; spl. dep. marshal U.S. Marshals Posse, Los Angeles, 1987-95. Mem. Calif. Assn. Sch. Bus. Ofcls. (treas. S.E. sect. 1985, mem. acct. R & D com. 1983-89, mem. chief bus. officials com. 1989—), So. Calif. Paraders Assn. (exec. sec. 1976-97), Calif. State Horsemens Assn. (regional v.p. 1986-87, sec. 1988), Alpha Gamma Sigma. Avocations: horseback riding, golf, reading, micro-computers, model trains. Home: 1720 Ironbark Ct Oxnard CA 93030-3410 Office: Oxnard Elem Sch Dist 1051 S A St Oxnard CA 93030-7442

HERRERA, SHIRLEY MAE, personnel and security executive; b. Lynn, Mass., Apr. 5, 1942; d. John Baptiste and Edith Mae Lagasse; m. Christian Yanez Herrera, Apr. 30, 1975; children: Karen, Gary, Ivan, Iwonne. AS in Bus., Burdett Bus. Coll., Lynn, 1960; student, Wright State U., 1975-78. Cert. facility security officer, med. asst. in pediatrics. Med. asst. Christian Y. Herrera, M.D., Stoneham, Mass., 1972-74; human resource adminstr. MTL Systems, Inc., Dayton, Ohio, 1976-79; dir. pers. and security Tracor GIE, Inc., Provo, Utah, 1979-95; cons. on family dynamics family enrichment program Hill AFB, Utah, 1980-82; cons. on health care memt. Guam 7th Day Adventist Clinic, 1983; cons. on basic life support and CPR, Projecto Corazon, Monterrey, Mex., 1987—; faculty mem. Inst. for Reality Therapy, 1991—. Contbg. editor Inside Tractor, 1991—. Chmn. women's aux. YMCA Counselling Svcs., Woburn, Mass., 1970; chmn. youth vols. ARC, Wright-Patterson AFB, Dayton, 1974-76; trustee Quail Valley Homeowner's Assn., Provo, 1988-89; rep. A Spl. Wish Found., Provo, 1989. Recipient James S. Cogswell award Def. Investigative Svc., Dept. Def., 1987. Mem. Inst. for Realty Therapy (cert.), Pers. Assn. Ctrl. Utah, Women in Mgmt. (coun. mem. 1991-95), Nat. Classification Mgmt. Soc. (chairperson Intermountain chpt. 1992-94). Republican. Avocations: writing, skiing, reading. Home: 3824 Little Rock Dr Provo UT 84604-5234

HERRES, PHILLIP BENJAMIN, computer software executive; b. Spokane, Wash., Nov. 5, 1941; s. Benjamin Jacob and Ollie Lee (Bell) H.; m. Lorelei Norma Munroe, June 15, 1963; children: Michele Marie, Anthony Phillip, Jason Randall. BSEE, Gonzaga U., 1963; MBA, U. Oreg., 1965. Registered profl. engr., Calif. Engr. Pacific N.W. Bell, Portland, Oreg., 1965-66; chief engr. Electronic Splty., Portland, Oreg., 1966-71; dir. engring. Arcata Communications, Mountain View, Calif., 1971-73; engring. mgr. Clare-Pendar, Post Falls, Idaho, 1973-76; v.p. network systems Northern Telecom, Dallas, 1976-87; sr. v.p. engring. Avanti Communications, Newport, R.I., 1987-89; chief oper. officer Aldus Corp., Seattle, 1989-92; mgmt. cons. Mercer Island, Wash., 1993-94; pres. Evergreen Software Tools, Redmond, Wash., 1994-95; mgmt. cons. Herres Co., Mercer Island, Wash., 1995—; pres. ST Labs., Bellevue, Wash., 1997-98. 1st lt. U.S. Army, 1967-71. Mem. IEEE, Columbia Tower Club. Republican. Roman Catholic. Avocations: golf, scuba diving, target shooting, collections. Office: The Herres Co 8460 W Mercer Way Ste 244 Mercer Island WA 98040-5633 also: ST Labs 3535 128th Ave SE Bellevue WA 98006-1261

HERRES, ROBERT TRALLES, financial services executive; b. Denver, Dec. 1, 1932; s. F. Willard and Edna Margaret (Tralles) H.; m. Shirley Jean Sneckner, Apr. 16, 1957; children: Julie Latenser, Michael, Jennifer Babeon. BS, U.S. Naval Acad., 1954; MS in Elec. Engring., Air Force Inst. Tech., 1960; MPA, George Washington U., 1965. Commd. 2d lt. U.S. Air Force, 1954, commdr. comms. command, 8th air force, dir. command, control and comms. sys., joint chiefs of staff; commdr. in chief NORAD; 1st commdr. in chief U.S. Space Command; advanced to 4 star gen. U.S. Air Force, 1984; v.p. Joint Chiefs of Staff, 1987; ret., 1990; pres. property and caualty divsn. United Svcs. Automobile Assn., 1990, pres., COO, 1992, chmn., CEO, 1993—, pres. property and casualty divsn., chmn., CEO, 1993—. Chmn. Nat. Bd. Junior Achievement; bd. mem Nat. Mentoring Ptnrshp., Neighborhood Housing Svcs. Am., Atlantic Coun.; nat. exec. bd. Boy Scouts Am.; bd. trustees Trinity U., San Antonio; chmn. Ins. Inst. Hgwy Safety, 1998, Ins. Info. Inst.; mem. Naval Acad. Endowment Trust, USNA Found., Air Force Acad. Found.; nat. adv. coun. Fannie Mae, 1999—. Mem. Nat. Assn. Independent Insurers (vice chmn., chmn.-elect), Am. Inst. Chartered Property Casualty Underwriters (bd. mem.). Office: United Svcs Automobile Assn 9800 Fredericksburg Rd San Antonio TX 78288-0325

HERRETT, RICHARD ALLISON, agricultural research institute administrator; b. Buffalo, Aug. 4, 1932; s. Wilbert Atherton and Loys (Richards) H.; m. Virginia Walker, July 28, 1958 (div. July 1978); children: Steven Jay, Jeffrey James, William Allan; m. Joan Hanhauser Maurer, Aug. 26, 1978; 1 child, Maxwell. BS in Agrl. Rsch., Rutgers U., 1954; MS in Agronomy/Organic Chemistry, U. Minn., 1956, PhD in Plant Biochemistry/Organic Chemistry, 1959; postgrad., George Washington U., U. Calif., Berkeley. Leader rsch. team Boyce Thompson Inst., Yonkers, N.Y., 1959-61, Union Carbide Corp., Clayton, N.C., 1961-70; tech. mgr. ICI Ams. Inc., Wilmington, Del., 1970-75, dir. rsch. and devel., 1975-87, mem. govt. rels., sci. liaison, 1987-92; pres., cons. EnvirAg Assocs., Bethesda, Md., 1992-94; exec. dir. Agrl. Rsch. Inst., Bethesda, 1995—; bd. dirs., treas., trustee N.C. Biotech Ctr., Research Triangle Park; bd. dirs. Agrl. Rsch. Inst./Bio, Washington; treas. C.V. Riley Found., Washington, 1988-92; vice chmn. exec. bd. Bus. Coun. on Indoor Air; appointee N.C. Bd. Sci. and Tech.; presenter in field. Contbr. chpts. to books, articles to profl. jours.; patentee in field. Upton Meml. scholar Rutgers U. Mem. AAAS, Internat. Union of Pure and Applied Chemists (fin. chmn.), Nat. Agrl. Chems. Assn. (chmn., mem. rsch. dirs. com.), Am. Chem. Soc., Weed Sci. Soc. Am., Sigma Xi, Inst. Food Technologists. Avocations: racquetball, skiing. E-mail: ariherrett@aol.com. Home: 23 Sonneborn Ln Severna Park MD 21146-4803 Office: Agrl Rsch. Inst 236 Massachusetts Ave NE Washington DC 20002-4980

HERRICK, GREGORY EVANS, technology corporation executive; b. Ottumwa, Iowa, Nov. 23, 1951; s. Walter Edward and Doris Ann (Evans) H. BS, U. Iowa, 1974. Gen. mgr. retail stores Amana (Iowa) Soc., 1975-77; mktg. mgr. Meredith Corp., Des Moines, 1977-80; mktg. devel. mgr. Fingerhut Corp., Minnetonka, Minn., 1980-82; founder, pres., chief exec. officer, chmn. Zeos Internat., Mpls., 1982-95; CEO Yellowstone Aviation, Inc., Jackson, Wyo., 1996—, Old Faithful Land & Cattle Co., Jackson; founder, mgr. Golden Wings Flying Mus., Mpls., 1998—; pres. Historic Aviation and Flying Books, 1999—. Editor: Complete Desk Reference, 1973; patentee and inventor electronics equipment. Mem. Inst. Am. Entrepreneurs (Minn. Entrepreneur of Yr., 1991). Republican. Roman Catholic. Avocations: flying, skiing, sailing. Address: PO Box 6291 Jackson WY 83002-6291

HERRICK, JOHN DENNIS, financial consultant, former law firm executive, retired food products executive; b. St. Paul, Oct. 8, 1932; s. Willard R. and Gertrude (O'Connor) H. BA, U. St. Thomas, 1954; MBA (hon.), U. Laval. Field auditor Gen. Mills, Inc., Mpls., 1954-59; acctg. supr. Gen. Mills, Inc., Kankakee, Ill., 1959-61; adminstrv. mgr. Gen. Mills, Inc., Chgo., 1961-62; mgr. auditing Gen. Mills, Inc., Mpls., 1962-65; mgr. new bus. devel. Gen. Mills, Inc., 1965-66; dir. adminstrn. and controller Smiths Food Group (subs.) Gen. Mills, Inc., London, 1966-68; pres. Gen. Mills Cereals Ltd., Toronto, Ont., Can., 1969-71; chmn. bd., pres., chief exec. officer Gen. Mills Canada, Inc., Toronto, Ont., Can., 1971-86; chief operating officer Borden & Elliot, Toronto, 1986-89; cons. Palm Beach Gardens, Fla., 1989—; pres. J.D. Herrick Found.; past chmn. Grocery Products Mfrs. of Can., Toronto; dir. CP Express & Transport, Toronto. Past pres. Jr. Achievement Can., Toronto, 1970-71; past chmn. Toronto Area Indsl. Devel. Bd.; past pres., mem. coun. Bd. Trade Met. Toronto; past chmn. Emmanuel Convalescent Found., Toronto; past pres. Am. Club; past vice-chmn. Nat. Theater Sch. Can., Montreal; past chmn. Toronto Harbour Commn.; bd. dirs., pres. Cath. Charities Palm Beach; bd. dirs. Pub. Voice for Food and Health Policy, Washington; mem. pres.'s coun. U. St. Thomas; chmn.'s adv. bd. Rep. Nat. Com., pres. Roundtable NRSC. Capt. USAF, 1954-57. Recipient Queen's Silver Jubilee medal, 1978; decorated Knight Comdr., Knights of Holy Sepulchre, Order of St. John, Order of Polonia Restituta. Mem. Can. C. of C. (past chmn., gov.), Beefeater Club, Empire Club, Royal Can. Yacht Club, Lambton Golf and Country Club, N.Y. Athletic Club, Old Port Yacht Club, Hot Stone Club, Palm Beach Roundtable, Accademia Italiana Della Cucina Club, K.C., Capital Hill Club (Washington), Poinciana Club (Palm Beach, Fla.), Ibis Golf & Country Club. Roman Catholic. Home: 15100 Palmwood Rd Palm Bch Gdns FL 33410-1026 Office: PO Box 31828 Palm Bch Gdns FL 33420-1828

HERRICK, KATHLEEN MAGARA, social worker; b. Mpls., Oct. 18, 1943; d. William Frank and Mary Genevieve (Gill) Magara; m. John M. Herrick, Feb. 5, 1966; children: Elizabeth Jane, Kathryn Mary. BA in Social Work and French, Coll. St. Benedict, St. Joseph, Minn., 1965; MSW (Mildred B. Erickson fellow), Mich. State U., 1976. Cert. diplomate Am. Psychotherapy Assn., 1998. Social worker II Carer County Social Svcs., Chaska, Minn., 1965-70; therapist St. Lawrence Cmty. Mental Health Ctr., Lansing, Mich., 1974-75; sch. social worker Ingham Intermediate Sch. Dist., Mason, Mich., 1975-76; home/sch. coord. Eaton Intermediate Sch. Dist., Charlotte, Mich., 1976-81; sch. social worker, 1994—; caseworker St. Vincent Home for Children, Lansing, 1979-80; tchr. cons. for severely emotionally impaired, 1981-83; behavior disorder cons., 1983-85; sch. social work cons., 1985-87, preention splst. profl. and program svcs., 1987-94. Chmn. bd. dirs. Eaton CountyChild Abuse and Neglect Prevention Coun., 1986—; Dem. precinct del.; bd. dirs. Cath. Socia Svcs., Lansing; splst. substance abuse prevention region XIII SAPE, 1987-94. Recipient Eaton County Svc. to children award Eaton County Child ABuse and Neglect Prevention Coun., 1997. Mem. NASW, NEA, NOW, Nat. Women's Health Network, Nat. Platform Assn., Mich. Edn. Assn., Nat. Assn. Retarded Citizens, Am. Orthopsychiat. Assn., Mich. Assn. Sch. Social Workers, Mich. Assn. Emotionally Disturbed Children, Eaton County Assn. Retarded Citizens, Amnesty Internat., Mich. Assn. Suicidology, Glasser Inst. Reality Therapy and Choice Theory, Phi Kappa Phi, Phi Alpha. Democrat. Home: 2113 Long Leaf Trl Okemos MI 48864-3210 Office: 1790 Packard Hwy Charlotte MI 48813-9717

HERRICK, KENNETH GILBERT, manufacturing company executive; b. Jackson, Mich., Apr. 2, 1921; s. Ray Wesley and Hazel Marie (Forney) H.; m. Shirley J. Todd, Mar. 2, 1942; children: Todd Wesley, Toni Lynn. Student public and pvt. schs., Howe, Ind.; LHD (hon.), Siena Heights Coll., 1974; HHD (hon.), Adrian Coll., 1975, Detroit Inst. Tech., 1980; LLD, Judson Coll., 1975; D Engring. (hon.), Albion Coll., 1981. With Tecumseh Products Co., Mich., 1940-42, 45—; v.p. Tecumseh Products Co., 1961-66, vice chmn. bd., 1964-70, pres., 1966-70, chmn. bd., chief exec. officer, 1970-86, chmn. bd., 1986—. Bd. dirs. Howe Mil. Sch., 1970-81, from Herrick Found., 1970; mem. exec. adv. bd. St. Jude Children's Hosp., from 1978. Served with USAAC, 1942-45. Recipient Hon. Alumni award Mich. State U., 1975; Disting. Svc. award Albion Coll., 1975. Mem. Lenawee Country Club, Elks, Tecumseh Country Club, Masons. Presbyterian. Office: Tecumseh Products Co 100 E Patterson St Tecumseh MI 49286-2087*

HERRICK, KRISTINE FORD, graphic design educator; b. Bryn Mawr, Pa., Feb. 7, 1947; d. Charles Burton and Leah (Bosler) Ford; m. Stephen Wickes Herrick, Oct. 11, 1969 (div. Apr. 1982); 1 child, Katharine Wickes; m. Lee M. Smith, June 6, 1987; 1 stepchild, Suzannah Stuart Smith. BS, Skidmore Coll., 1969; MFA, Temple U., 1983. Cert. art tchr., N.Y. Layout artist Capital Newspapers, Albany, N.Y., 1969-70; designer Slocum House Pub., Albany, N.Y., 1970; asst. art dir. Gen. Electric Co., Schenectady, N.Y., 1970-72; art dir. Kirkman 3 Advt., Albany, 1972-75; from instr. to asst. prof. Tyler Sch. Art Temple U., 1980-85; design cons. Springhouse (Pa.) Corp., 1983-85; asst. prof., program coordinator graphic design Coll. St. Rose, Albany, 1985-92, assoc. prof., 1992—. Author: Trademarks, A History, 1982, Trademarks, An Evolution, 1983. V.p. Ctr. Sq. Assn., Albany, 1972—; founding mem. Historic Albany Assn., 1974—; bd. dirs. Berkshire Ballet Co., Albany, 1988—. Grantee for excellence in teaching Sears Roebuck Found., 1990. Mem. Am. Inst. of The Graphic Arts, Univ. and Coll. Designers Assn., Graphic Design Edn. Assn., The Creative Club (bd. dirs. 1997—). Office: Coll St Rose 432 Western Ave Albany NY 12203-1419

HERRICK, SYLVIA ANNE, health service administrator; b. Minot, N.D., Oct. 5, 1945; d. Sylvester P. and Ethelina (Harren) Theis; m. Michael M. Herrick, Nov. 8, 1989; children: Leo J., Mark A. BSN, U. N.D., 1967; MS in Pub. Health Nursing, U. Colo., Denver, 1970; sch. nurse credential, San Jose State U., 1991; postgrad., Golden Gate U. RN, Calif.; cert. pub. health nursing, health svc. Pub. health nurse Dept. Pub. Health City of Mpls.; instr. nursing San Francisco State U., 1967-69; cons. exec. search Med-Power Resources, Alameda, 1974-88; coord. health svcs. Alameda Unified Sch. Dist., 1977-91; team mgr. home care nursing and program devel. coord. Vis. Nurse Assn. and Hospice of No. Calif., 1991-99, quality mgmt. and edn. specialist; mgr. disease mgmt. and health awareness East Bay Med. Network, 1999—; project mgr. disease mgmt. programs East Bay Med. Network, 1997-99; spkr. in field. Mem. Nat. Nurses Bus. Assn., Calif. Sch. Nurses Orgn. (bd. dirs., chair edn Bay Coast sect.), Delta Kappa Gamma. Home: 1711 Encinal Ave Alameda CA 94501-4020

HERRICK, TODD W., manufacturing company executive; b. Tecumseh, Mich., 1942. Grad., U. Notre Dame, 1967. Pres., chief exec. officer Tecumseh (Mich.) Products Co. Office: Tecumseh Products Co 100 E Patterson St Tecumseh MI 49286-2087

HERRICK, TRACY GRANT, fiduciary; b. Cleve., Dec. 30, 1933; s. Stanford Avery and Elizabeth Grant (Smith) H.; B.A., Columbia U., 1956, M.A., 1958; postgrad. Yale U., 1956-57; M.A., Oxford U. (Eng.), 1960; m. Maie Kaarsoo, Oct. 12, 1963; children: Sylvi Anne, Alan Kalev. economist, Fed. Res. Bank, Cleve., 1960-70; sr. economist Stanford Research Inst., Menlo Park, Calif., 1970-73; v.p., sr. analyst Shuman, Agnew & Co., Inc., San Francisco, 1973-75; v.p. Bank of Am., San Francisco, 1975-81; pres. Tracy G. Herrick, Inc., 1981—; lectr. Stonier Grad. Sch. Banking, Am. Bankers Assn., 1967-76; commencement speaker Memphis Banking Sch., 1974; bd. dirs. Jefferies Group, Inc., chmn. bd. audit com. 1989-96, chmn. bd. compensation com. 1991-96, dir. 1983-99; bd. dirs. Jefferies & Co., Inc., Anderson Capital Mgmt., Inc. Mem. adv. bd. San Xavier Found. Monterey, Calif. Fellow Fin. Analysts Fedn.; mem. Assn. Investment Mgmt. Rsch., San Francisco Soc. Security Analysts, dir. Com. for Monetary Rsch. and Edn., Inc. Republican. Congregationalist. Author: Bank Analyst's Handbook,

1978; Timing, 1981; Power and Wealth, 1988; contbr. articles to profl. jours. Home: 1150 University Ave Palo Alto CA 94301-2238

HERRIFORD, ROBERT LEVI, SR., army officer; b. Lewistown, Ill., May 4, 1931; s. John and Lola (Braden) H.; m. Muriel Jean Davis, July 10, 1949; children: Robert Levi, Thomas Merle, David William, Deborah S., Traci Ann. B.S., U. Ariz., 1966, M.B.A., 1968. Enlisted in U.S. Army, 1948, commd. 2d lt., 1952, advanced through grades to maj. gen., 1979; service in Vietnam, 1966-67; comdr. 269th Ordnance Group Ft. Bragg, N.C., 1969-71; chief spl. items mgmt. Tank Automotive Command Detroit, 1971-72; comdr. Korean Procurement Agy. Seoul, 1973-74; dir. procurement Armaments Command Rock Island, Ill., 1974-76; comdr. Def. Contracts Region N.Y., 1976-78; asst. dep. chief of staff logistics Pentagon, 1978-80; dir. procurement and prodn. Devel. and Readiness Command Alexandria, Va., 1980-83; assoc. chief ops. officer, dir. support services Argonne Nat. Lab., 1983-95. Chmn. Minority Bus. Opportunity Council, N.Y.C., 1976-78. Decorated Legion of Merit, D.S.M., Def. Superior Service medal, Bronze Star, Airmedal, numerous others. Mem. Am. Def. Preparedness Assn., Assn. U.S. Army, Am. Legion, Nat. Contracts Mgmt. Assn. (chpt. pres. 1975-76). Office: 104 N Pittsburg Lndg Springfield IL 62707-7959 *There is no substitute in any career, but particularly in an Army officer's career, for hard work, dedication and absolute integrity. Subordinates, peers, and superiors can sense it in training, in garrison, and in battle. Many people, in all pursuits and professions, are created equal in talent. Only a very few are willing to give to that talent all the care and dedication that is required to bring it to the top of their chosen field. It is often easier to explain why you didn't make it than to devote all that is required to develop this talent.*

HERRIMAN, JEAN ANN, elementary education educator; b. Charleston, W.Va., Aug. 14, 1953; d. John Charles and Dorothy Gwinn (Dearman) McIntosh; 1 child, John Phillip Raiford. BEd, Ga. So. Coll., 1981; early childhood endorsement, Tenn. Tech. U., 1984; M in Early Childhood, Piedmont Coll., 1997. Tchr. elem. Chickamauga (Ga.) City Sch. Sys., 1984-85, Whitfield County Sch. Sys., Dalton, Ga., 1985-86; tchr. Jackson County Schs., Jefferson, Ga., 1986—. Mem. Internat. Reading Assn. Republican. Avocations: kayaking, horseback riding, guitar, piano, arts and crafts. Office: Maysville Elem Sch 9270 Highway 82 Spur Maysville GA 30558-2101

HERRIN, FRANCES E., critical care nurse; b. Blairsville, Ga., Mar. 27, 1930; d. George W. and Iris C. (Tramell) Anderson; widowed; children: Naguyalti, Warren. AA, L.A. Trade Tech. Coll., 1973; postgrad., Calif. State U., 1973, Chapman Coll., 1987. RN, Calif.; ACLS, Calif. Nurse emergency rm. Oak Ridge (Tenn.) Hosp., 1950-57; staff nurse Cen. Rec. Hosp., L.A., 1958-68; charge nurse Hollywood Pres. Hosp., L.A., 1970-74; coronary care nurse Kaiser Permanent Med. Ctr., Fontana, Calif., 1974-90; nurse in med. unit De Kalb Med. Ctr., Decatur, Ga., 1992—; pediat. care nurse PSA Home Health, 1995-96. Mem. Hosp. Christian Fellowship (pres.), Black Nurses Assn. (quality assurance com.).

HERRIN, MORELAND, civil engineering educator, consultant; b. Morris, Okla., Nov. 14, 1922; s. Birney D. and Lucille (Moreland) H.; m. Nancy M. Jameson, Dec. 24, 1946; children—Jeannie N., Stanley M., Gwen M. BSCE, Okla. State U., 1947, MS, 1949; PhD, Purdue U., 1954. Instr. Okla. State U., 1947-49, assoc. prof., 1954-58; prof. civil engring. U. Ill., Urbana, 1958—; dir. Ill. Coop. Transp. Program; design engr. Hudgins, Thompson & Ball (engrs.), Oklahoma City, 1949-50; materials engr. Garnett, Fleming, Cordray and Carpenter, Belvidere, Ill., 1957; asst. materials engr., road test Am. Assn. State Hwy. Ofcls., Ottawa, Ill., 1958; cons. hwy. materials, pavement design, 1955—. Contbr. articles to profl. jours. Served to capt. USAAF, 1943-46. Recipient Epstein award U. Ill., 1962. Mem. Transp. Research Bd., Assn. Asphalt Paving Technology (pres. 1978), ASCE, Am. Soc. Engring. Edn., ASTM, Chi Epsilon, Tau Beta Pi. Mem. Disciples of Christ Ch. Home: 1414 W William St Champaign IL 61821-4407 Office: 1208 NCEL 205 N Mathews Ave Urbana IL 61801-2350

HERRIN, STEPHANIE ANN, retired aerospace engineer; b. Oakland, Calif., May 13, 1950; d. Thomas Edgar Herrin and Mary Teresa Silva; m. Este Stovall, May 20, 1989. BSc, U. Pacific, 1976; MSc, Columbia Pacific U., 1978; PhD in Engring. & Applied Scis., U. Bradford, West Yorkshire, U.K., 1994. Reliability engr. Applied Tech. Litton Industries, Sunnyvale, Calif., 1979-80; sr. reliability engr., reliability project mgr. ESL, Inc., Sunnyvale, 1980-84; sr. reliability & quality assurance engr. Martin Marietta, Balt., 1984-85; lead, sr. reliability engr. Los Alamos Tech. Assn., Albuquerque, 1985-86; sr. reliability engr. Boeing, Houston, 1987-89; sr. sys. engr., knowledge capture engr. Astrobiology Inst. NASA-Ames Rsch. Ctr., Moffett Field, Calif., 1988-99; cons. Lawrence Livermore Labs., Livermore, Calif., 1985-87; failure analysis engring. radiographer, analyst Ford Aerospace & Comm. Corp., Palo Alto, Calif., 1973-79; owner, analyst Fail Safe Radiography, Palo Alto, 1975-81. Contbr. articles to profl. jours. Recipient U.S. govt. Manned Flight Awareness award, 1994, Woman of Yr. award Am. Biographical Inst., 1999; NASA grantee, 1987-89, 90-93, 94-95; named to Outstanding Scientists of 20th Century, Internat. Biog. Ctr., Cambridge, Eng., 1999. Mem. IEEE (reliability & maintainability soc., engring. in medicine & biology computer soc., info. theory, sys., man & cybernetics, oceanic engring. soc.), AAUW. Achievements include patent for real-time automated diagnosis and intelligent utility for maintainability. Home: 343 Center St Redwood City CA 94061-3883

HERRING, GROVER CLEVELAND, lawyer; b. Nocatee, Fla., Dec. 9, 1925; s. Joseph I. and Martha (Selph) H.; m. Dorothy L. Blinn, Apr. 17, 1947; children: Stanley T., Kenneth Lee. JD, U. Fla., 1950. Bar: Fla. 1950. Assoc. Haskins & Bryant, 1950-52; sole practice West Palm Beach, Fla., 1952-60, 64—; ptnr. Blakeslee, Herring & Bie and predecessor firm, 1953-60, Warwick, Paul & Herring, 1964-70, Herring & Evans now Arnstein & Lehr, 1970-95, Baldwin & Herring, West Palm Beach, Fla., 1995—; atty. City of Atlantis, Fla., City of West Palm Beach, 1960-63, Town of Ocean Ridge, Fla., 1953-61, 64-66, Village of Royal Palm Beach, Fla., 1964-72, Town of South Palm Beach, Fla., 1966-72; spl. master-in-chancery 15th Jud. Cir. Palm Beach County, 1953-54; judge ad litem Mcpl. Ct., West Palm Beach, 1954-55; bd. dirs. Lawyers Title Services Inc., West Palm Beach. Contbr. legal articles to profl. revs. Active PTA, Family Service Agy., Palm Beach County Mental Health Assn.; chmn. profl. sect. ARC, 1960; mem. Charter Revision Com. West Palm Beach, 1960-65, Palm Beach County Resources Devel. Bd., 1959—, Dem. Exec. Com., 1965-70; apptd. mem. Govtl. Study Commn. by Fla. Legis.; bd. dirs. Community Chest. Served with USNR, 1944-46. Mem. ABA, Palm Beach County Bar Assn. (treas. 1960), John Marshall Bar Assn., Fla. Bar Assn., Am. Judicature Soc., Lawyers Title Guaranty Fund (field rep. 1955-60, 64—), East Coast Estate Planning Council, Nat. Inst. Mcpl. Law Officers, Law-Sci. Acad., Assn. Trial Lawyers Am. (assoc. editor 1960—), Lawyers Lit. Club, Nat. Mcpl. League, U. Fla. Law Ctr. Assn., World Peace Through Law Ctr., Fla. Sheriff's Assn. (hon.), U. Fla. Alumni Assn., VFW, Am. Legion, West Palm Beach C. of C., Civic Music Assn., Palm Beach County Hist. Soc. (pres. 1969-72), New Eng. Hist. Geneal. Soc. Boston. Clubs: West Palm Beach Country (hon.); Airways (N.Y.C.). Lodges: Eight Oaks River, Masons (32 deg.), Elks, Moose. Home: 3507 N Australian Ave West Palm Bch FL 33407-4511 Office: Baldwin & Herring Ste G 1675 P B Lakes Blvd West Palm Beach FL 33401

HERRING, JACK WILLIAM, retired English language educator; b. Waco, Tex., Aug. 28, 1925; s. Benjamin Oscar and Bertha (Shiplet) H.; m. Daphne L. Norred, June 10, 1944; children—Penny Elizabeth, Paul William. B.A., Baylor U., 1947, M.A., 1948; Ph.D., U. Pa., 1958. English instr. Howard Coll., Birmingham, Ala., 1948-50; assoc. prof., acting chmn. dept. English Grand Canyon Coll., Phoenix, 1951-55; asst. prof. English Ariz. State U., Tempe, 1955-59; dir. Armstrong Browning Library, Baylor U., 1959-85, asso. prof. English, 1959-62, prof. English, 1962-73, Margaret Root Brown prof. Robert Browning studies, 1973-97; ret.; English prof. Beijing Second Fgn. Lang. Inst., 1984-85, Shaghai Inst. Mech. Engring., 1989-90, People's Republic China. Author: Browning's Old School Fellow, 1972; editor: Complete Poetry of Robert Browning. Club: Kiwanis (pres. Waco club 1976-77, lt. gov. div. 23 1983-84). Avocations: travel to United Kingdom, Europe, China and Soviet Union. Home: PO Box 6169 Waco TX 76706-0169 *There is no substitute for tested truth.*

HERRING, JERONE CARSON, lawyer, bank executive; b. Kinston, N.C., Sept. 27, 1938; s. James and Isabel (Knight) H.; m. Patricia Ann Hardy, Aug. 6, 1961; children—Bradley Jerone, Ansley Carole. A.B., Davidson Coll., 1960; LL.B., Duke U., 1963. Bar: N.C. 1963. Assoc. McElwee & Hall, North Wilkesboro, N.C., 1965-69; ptnr. McElwee, Hall & Herring, North Wilkesboro, 1969-71; exec. v.p., sec., gen. counsel Br. Banking & Trust Co., Winston-Salem, N.C., 1971—, BB&T Corp., Winston-Salem, 1995—. Served to capt. U.S. Army, 1963-65. Mem. ABA, N.C. Bar Assn., Am. Soc. Corp. Secs., Am. Corp. Counsel Assn. Presbyterian. Office: 200 W 2d St Winston Salem NC 27101

HERRING, OLIVER, artist. BFA, U. Oxford, Eng., 1988; MFA, Hunter Coll., 1991. One-man shows include Work Space Gallery, New Mus. Contemporary Art, N.Y.C., 1993, Mannheimer Kunstverein, Mannheim, 1993, Max Protetch Gallery, N.Y.C., 1994, 96, 97, 98, Space Untitled, N.Y., 1994, Bernard Toale Gallery, Boston, 1994, Solomon R. Guggenheim Mus., N.Y., 1996, Mus. Modern Art, N.Y.C., 1996, Manfred Baumgartner Gallery, Washington, 1996, Newlyn Art Gallery, Penzance, Eng., 1997, Camden Art Ctr., London, 1997, Ace Galleries, L.A., 1999; exhibited in group shows at List Art Ctr., Brown U., Providence, 1995, Queens (N.Y.) Lib. Gallery, 1996, New Mus. Contemporary Art, N.Y., 1996, Randolph Street Gallery, Chgo., 1996, The Contemporary Mus., Honolulu, 1996, Max Protetch Gallery, N.Y.C., 1997, Galerie Thaddaeus Ropac, Paris, 1997, numerous others. Mass. Arts Lottery grantee, 1989; N.Y. Found. Arts grantee, 1995. Office: care Max Protetch Gallery 511 West 22d St New York NY 10011

HERRING, RALPH MCNEELY, nurse; b. Charlotte, N.C., June 12, 1962; s. Ralph Alderman Jr. and Alice Lenora (McNeely) H.; m. Jill Paxton Stubbs, Oct. 24, 1992; children: Nell, Van. BA, Guilford Coll., 1984; ADN, Charlotte Meckenburg Hosp., 1995. CRRN. Asst. nurse mgr. for brain injury and spinal cord units Charlotte Inst. Rehab., 1995—; dir. nursing Med. Staff Contract Nursing, Charlotte, 1995-96; CPR instr. Am. Heart Assn., Charlotte, 1995-98. Mem. juvenile prison outreach program 1st Presbyn. Ch., Mooresville, N.C., 1990-96. Mem. Internat. Dyslexia Assn. Democrat. Avocations: gardening, beer and wine making, scuba diving, family. E-mail: rmherring@mindspring.com. Home: 735 N Main St Mooresville NC 28115-2313

HERRING, SUSAN WELLER, dental educator, oral anatomist; b. Pitts., Mar. 25, 1947; d. Sol W. and Miriam (Damick) Weller; m. Stephen E. Herring, Nov. 18, 1967 (div. Oct. 1983); m. Norman S. Wolf, May 27, 1995. BS in Zoology, U. Chgo., 1967, PhD in Anatomy, 1971. NIH postdoctoral fellow U. Ill., Chgo., 1971-72, from asst. prof. to prof. oral anatomy and anatomy, 1972-90; prof. orthodontics U. Wash., Seattle, 1990—; vis. assoc. prof. biol. sci. U. Mich., Ann Arbor, 1981; cons. NIH study sect., Washington, D.C., 1987-89; sci. gov. Chgo. Acad. Sci., 1982-90; mem. pub. bd. Growth Pub. Inc., Bar Harbor, Maine, 1982—. Mem. editl. db. Acta Anatomica, 1989—, Jour. Dental Rsch., 1995-98, Jour. Morphology, 1997—; contbr. articles to profl. jours. Predoctoral fellow NSF, 1967-71; rsch. grantee NIH, 1975-78, 81—, NSF, 1990-92, 94-95. Fellow AAAS; mem. Internat. Assn. Dental Rsch. (dir. craniofacial biology group 1994-95, v.p. 1995-96, pres.-elect 1996-97, pres. 1997-98, Craniofacial Biology Rsch. award 1999), Am. Soc. Zoologists (chmn. vertebrate zoology 1983-84, exec. com. 1986-88), Am. Soc. Biomechanics, Am. Assn. Anatomists (chmn. Basmajian com. 1988-90), Soc. Vertebrate Paleontology, Am. Soc. Mammalogists, Internat. Soc. Vertebrate morphology (convenor 4th congress 1994, pres. 1994-97), Sigma Xi. Avocation: semi-profl. violin. Office: U Wash Box 357446 Seattle WA 98195-7446

HERRING, WILLIAM CONYERS, physicist, emeritus educator; b. Scotia, N.Y., Nov. 15, 1914; s. William Conyers and Mary (Joy) H.; m. Louise C. Preusch, Nov. 30, 1946; children—Lois Mary, Alan John, Brian Charles, Gordon Robert. A.B., U. Kans., 1933; Ph.D., Princeton, 1937. NRC fellow Mass. Inst. Tech., 1937-39; instr. Princeton, 1939-40, U. Mo., 1940-41; mem. sci. staff Div. War Research, Columbia, 1941-45; prof. applied math. U. Tex., 1946; research physicist Bell Telephone Labs., Murray Hill, N.J., 1946-78; prof. applied physics Stanford (Calif.) U., 1978-81, prof. emeritus, 1981—; mem. Inst. Advanced Study, 1952-53. Recipient Army-Navy Cert. of Appreciation, 1947; Distinguished Service citation U. Kans., 1973; J. Murray Luck award for excellence in sci. reviewing Nat. Acad. Scis., 1980; von Hippel award Materials Rsch. Soc., 1980, Wolf prize in Physics, 1985. Fellow Am. Phys. Soc. (Oliver E. Buckley solid state physics prize 1959), Am. Acad. Arts and Scis.; mem. AAAS, NAS, Am. Soc. Info. Scis. Home: 3945 Nelson Dr Palo Alto CA 94306-4524 Office: Stanford U Dept Applied Physics Stanford CA 94305

HERRINGER, FRANK CASPER, diversified financial services company executive; b. N.Y.C., Nov. 12, 1942; s. Casper Frank and Alice Virginia (McMullen) H.; m. Maryellen B. Cattani; children: William, Sarah, Julia. AB magna cum laude, Dartmouth, 1964, MBA with highest distinction, 1965. Prin. Cresap, McCormick & Paget, Inc. (mgmt. cons.), N.Y.C., 1965-71; staff asst. to Pres., Washington, 1971-73; adminstr. U.S. Urban Mass Transp. Adminstrn., Washington, 1973-75; gen. mgr. San Francisco Bay Area Rapid Transit Dist., 1975-78; exec. v.p. Transam. Corp., San Francisco, 1979-86, pres., dir., 1986—, CEO, 1991—, chmn., 1996—; bd. dirs. Unocal Corp., Charles Schwab & Co. Trustee Calif. Pacific Med. Ctr. Mem. Cypress Point Club, San Francisco Golf Club, Olympic Club, Pacific Union Club, Stock Farm Club, Phi Beta Kappa. Office: Transam Corp 600 Montgomery St San Francisco CA 94111-2702

HERRINGTON, JAMES BENJAMIN, JR., job recruiting executive; b. New Orleans, Jan. 17, 1953; s. James Benjamin Sr. and Ruby Mae (Collins) H. BS in Edn., La. Tech U., 1975; MEd, Tarleton State U., 1982. Tchr., coach Briarfield Acad., Lake Providence, La., 1975-76; material expeditor Brown & Root Constrn. Corp., Luling, La., 1976-77, Mid-Tex Constrn., Ft. Worth, 1977; tchr., coach Glen Rose (Tex.) High Sch., 1977-78; tchr., head coach Smith Middle Sch., Killeen, Tex., 1978-82, Manor Middle Sch., Killeen, 1982-84; tchr., coach Channelview (Tex.) High Sch., 1984-85; sci. tchr. Miller Intermediate Sch., Pasadena, Tex., 1985-88; counselor San Jacinto Intermediate Sch., Pasadena, 1988-93; orgnl. specialist Tex. Faculty Assn., 1993-97; owner DataTrain Inc., Houston, 1996—. Mem. NEA (rec. sec. Rep. Educators Caucus 1991-93), Tex. Tchrs. Assn. (pub. rels. chmn. Dist. IV 1989-92, polit. activist team 1986-93, instrnl. and profl. devel. com. 1986-91, media rels. chmn. Dist. IV 1990-92, bd. dirs. 1990-92), Pasadena Educators Assn. (bd. dirs. 1986-87, pres. 1988-90, v.p. 1990-91, sec.-treas. 1991-92, editor 1986-87), Optimists. Presbyterian. Avocations: sports, baseball card collector. Home: PO Box 631806 Houston TX 77263-1806 Office: DataTrain Inc 6363 Richmond Ave Ste 260 Houston TX 77057-5914

HERRINGTON, JAMES PATRICK, secondary education educator; b. East St. Louis, Apr. 10, 1950; s. James Lindsey and Anna (Kotras) H.; m. Therisa Marie Hawk, July 31, 1981. BS in Math. Edn., Northwestern U., 1972; MS in Math. Edn., So. Ill. U., 1974, EdD in Instructional Process, 1980. Cert. secondary tchr., gen. adminstr., supt., Ill. Grad. rsch. asst. So. Ill. U., Edwardsville, 1972-74, 78-79; math. and sci. tchr. Pontiac Sch. Dist. #105, Fairview Heights, Ill., 1974-78; math. tchr. O'Fallon (Ill.) Twp. High Sch., 1979—, chmn. math. dept., 1986—, chmn. sci. dept., 1993-99. Contbr. articles to profl. publs. Mem. S.W. Math. Conf. (bd. dirs. 1985—), Nat. Coun. Tchrs. Math., Ill. Coun. Tchrs. Math. (bd. dirs. 1989-92), Math. Assn. Am., Belleville Weightlifting Club (bd. dirs. 1975—), Kappa Delta Pi. Avocations: weight training, basketball. Office: O'Fallon Twp High Sch 600 S Smiley St O'Fallon IL 62269-2399

HERRINGTON, JOHN DAVID, III, lawyer; b. Warren, Ohio, Nov. 19, 1934; s. John David, Jr. and Gertrude Francis (Herlinger) H.; m. Phoebe Jane Henderson, Mar. 16, 1957; children: Gay Annette, Joy Ann, Jennifer John. BSBA, Ohio State U., 1956. C.P.A., Pa. With Price Waterhouse & Co., Pitts., 1956-63; asst. to sec.-treas. Fisher Sci. Co., Pitts., 1963-65, controller, 1965-71, v.p. fin., treas., 1971-78, sr. v.p. fin., treas., 1979-82; exec. dir. Reed Smith Shaw & McClay, Pitts., 1982-86; ret., 1986; dir. Hi Pure, Inc., Rochester Sci., Pfeiffer Glass, E & A Bldg. Corp., F.S.C. de Mexico, Conco Inc. Bd. dirs. Family and Childrens Service Pitts. Served with AUS, 1957-58. Mem. Fin. Execs. Inst., Tax Execs. Inst., Planning Execs. Inst., Am. Inst. C.P.A.s, Pa. Soc. C.P.A.s, Assn. Legal Adminstrs. Home: 9402 Babcock Blvd Allison Park PA 15101-2011 also: 9721 S Old Oregon Inlet Rd Nags Head NC 27959-9376

HERRIOTT, DONALD RICHARD, optical physicist; b. Rochester, N.Y., Feb. 4, 1928; s. William T. and Lois Emily (Denton) H.; m. Karis Kernow Smith, Feb. 3, 1951; children—Jean Elizabeth, Ann Barbara, Nancy Jane, Donald Richard, Jr. Student, U. Richmond, 1945; student, Duke U., 1945-49, U. Rochester, 1950-51, Poly. Inst. Bklyn., 1961-63. Optical engr. Bausch & Lomb Co., Rochester, N.Y., 1949-56; mem. tech. staff Bell Telephone Lab., Murray Hill, N.J., 1956-68, head dept., 1968-81; sr. sci. advisor Perkin-Elmer, Norwalk, Conn., 1981-91. Patentee in field. Served with USN, 1945-46. Recipient Patent of Yr. award N.J. Research Council, 1978, Thomas Alva Edison Patent award N.J. Research Council, 1986. Fellow Optical Soc. Am. (Fraunhofer award 1983); mem. Nat. Acad. Engring., IEEE (sr.; Cledo Brunetti award 1980), Beta Theta Pi. Republican. Presbyterian. Avocations: bird photography, sailing, skiing. Home: 1237 Isabel Dr Sanibel FL 33957-3509

HERRLINGER, STEPHEN PAUL, air force officer, flight test engineer, educator; b. Louisville, Ky., Nov. 23, 1959; s. John Howard and Josephine Doris (Martin) H.; m. Julie Louise Nelson, Feb. 4, 1989; children: Kyle H., Heidi K. BS in Chemistry, U. Akron, 1981; BS in Aero. Engring., USAF Inst. Tech., 1985; MS in Engring. Mgmt., Golden Gate U., 1989; M in Aero. Sci., Embry Riddle Aero. U., 1992. Registered Engr. in Tng., Ohio. Commd. 2d lt. USAF, 1981, advanced through grades to lt. col., 1998; rsch. chemist USAF Rocket Propulsion Lab., Edwards AFB, Calif., 1981-83; aerodynamic engr. advanced cruise missile 4200 Test and Evaluation Squadron USAF, Edwards AFB, 1985-86; chief advanced cruise missile aerodynamics sect. 31st Test and Evaluation Squadron USAF, Edwards AFB, 1986-87, chief advanced cruise missile performance, environ. sect., 1987-89; projct mgr E-9A surveillance aircraft program 4484th Test Squadron, Tyndall AFB, Fla., 1989-91; missile scoring flight test dir. 4484th Test Squadron, Tyndall AFB, 1991-92; dir. C-27A operational flight test 84th Test Squadron USAF, Tyndall AFB, 1992-94; chief of advanced testing ESC/ZJ USAF, Hanscom AFB, 1994-95, advanced sensor TBM program mgr., 1995-98; sys. program office dir. range threat sys. SM-ALC/LHR USAF, McClellan AFB, Calif., 1998—; adj. instr. Gulf Coast C.C. U. West Fla., Embry Riddle Aero. U., 1991-99. Contbr. articles to Jour. Organic Chemistry, Soc. Flight Test Engrs. Jour., Jour. Aircraft. Leader youth group Calif. Luth. U. Chapel, Thousand Oaks, 1986-89; guitarist Luth. Ch. of the Savior, Bedford, Mass., 1995-97. Decorated USAF Meritorious Svc. medal with one oak leaf cluster, USAF Commendation medal, USAF Achievement medal with 1 oak leaf cluster, USAF Aerial Achievement medal, Spl. Achievement award Internat. Test and Evaluation Assn., 1994, Electronic Systems Ctr.'s Lt. Gen. O'Neill award for Acquisition Excellence, 1995. Achievements include U.S. patent for aerodynamic fairing /nose cone for M-130 chaff/flare dispenser design. Home: 8246 Prior Way Antelope CA 95843-4477 Office: SM-ALC/LHR Mcclellan AFB CA 95652

HERRMAN, MARCIA KUTZ, child development specialist; b. Boston, June 16, 1927; d. Cecil and Sonia (Schneider) Kutz; m. Bayard F. Berman, July 23, 1949 (div. 1960); m. William H. Herrman, June 23, 1961; 1 child, Fred. BA, Smith Coll., 1949; MA, Pacific Oaks Coll., 1974. Credentialed tchr., Calif. NIMH intern Cedars-Sinai Med. Ctr., L.A., 1966-67; ednl. therpist L.A. Child Guidance Clinic, 1967-69, Child and Family Study Ctr., Cedars-Sinai Med. Ctr., 1969-71; dir. tng., asst. project dir. handicapped early edn. program Dubnoff Ctr., North Hollywood, Calif., 1972-76; child devel. cons. schs., agys. and families Studio City, Calif., 1969—; cons. L.A. Child Guidance Clinic, Head Start, Child Care and Devel. Svcs., 1969-73; cons. child and parenting program St. Joseph's Ctr., Venice, Calif., 1992-98; profl. expert L.A. Unified Sch. Dist., 1976-80; vis. faculty Pacific Oaks Coll., Pasadena, Calif., 1970-76. Vol. Alliance for Children's Rights, 1992-94, Child Advocate's Office, Superior Ct., L.A., 1983—; mem. Dependency Ct. Com., 1988-92, Task Force on Rep. of Children in Dependency Ct., Superior Ct., L.A. County, 1994; mem. oversight and resource coms. Placement Project, joint com. of program policy adv. com. Dept. Children and Family Svcs., 1995-98; steering com. Cmty. Based Placement Project, Joint Effort of Youth Law Ctr., L.A. Dept. Children & Family Svcs. and Calif. Dept. Social Svcs., 1995; mem. L.A. Foster Care Network, 1987-94, L.A. County MacLaren Children's Ctr. Task Force, 1990-95, cmty. mem., 1996—; cmty. adv. com. St. Joseph's Ctr., 1992-96; policy and implementation coms. Cmty. of Care Integration Project, 1998—, L.A. County bd. suprs., policy and implementation coms.; bd. chair Keeping Families Together, L.A., 1987-88; trustee Ruth Pearce Fund for Therapeutic Companions, 1994—. Recipient Vol. of Yr. award L.A. County Bd. Supr., 1986, Commendation for Dedicated Svc. to Cmty., 1991, Recognition award for Outstanding Svc. to Children L.A. County Inter-Agy. Coun. on Child Abuse, 1991; Sophia Smith scholar, 1949. Fellow Am. Orthopsychiat. Assn. (life); mem. N.Y. Acad. Scis., Assn. Child Devel. Specialists, Nat. Ct. Appointed Spl. Advocate Assn. Democrat. Jewish. Avocations: music, theater, hiking, travel. Home and Office: 3919 Ethel Ave Studio City CA 91604-2204

HERRMANN, BENJAMIN EDWARD, former insurance executive; b. Bensonhurst, N.Y., May 9, 1919; s. Benjamin Edward and Ethel (Cuff) H.; m. Jean Clare Yancey, Oct. 19, 1946 (dec. Mar. 1, 1994); children: Benjamin E., Elizabeth M.; m. Mary Anne O'Connor, Oct. 20, 1995. B.S., Columbia, 1941. C.L.U. With Home Life Ins. Co. N.Y., N.Y.C., 1941-68; regional v.p. Northeastern U.S., P.R., 1960-68; agy. v.p. Acacia Mut. Life Ins. Co., Washington, 1968-75; exec. com., dir. Acacia Nat. Life Ins. Co.; Acacia Equity Sales Corp. regional v.p. Met. N.Y., Home Life Ins. Co., N.Y.C., 1975-78; v.p. sales adminstrn. Met. N.Y., Home Life Ins. Co., 1978-80, v.p. mktg., 1980-84; pres. Nat. Benefit Plans Inc., Norfolk, Va., 1986-93. Mem. Planning Bd., Madison, N.J., 1963-68, chmn., 1967-68; mem. Zoning Bd. Adjustment, 1964-68, chmn., 1966. Served to 1st lt. USAAF, 1943-46, PTO. Fellow Life Mgmt. Inst.; mem. Life Ins. Mgmt. and Rsch. Assn. (exec. devel. com., chmn. agy. officers roundtable com. 1968-76, chmn. 1976, chmn. tng. dirs. subcom. 1974-76, grad. sch. agy. mgmt., agy. officer sch., sr. mktg. officers' seminar), Soc. CLUs, Golden Key Soc., U.S. Squash Racquets Assn. (bd. dirs. 1986-95), Va. Squash Racquets Assn. Inc. (pres. 1986-91, chmn. 1991-95), Intertel, Mensa, Kingsmill Golf Club, The Jesters Club. Republican. Presbyterian. Home: 105 Elizabeth Page Williamsburg VA 23185-5108

HERRMANN, DEBRA MCGUIRE, chemist, educator; b. Ft. Benning, Ga., Dec. 28, 1955; d. Delbert Wayne and Twyla Pauline (Moran) McGuire; m. David Read Herrmann, Aug. 2, 1980; children: Adam James, Jesse Read, Aaron Matthew. BS in chemistry, U. Tex., 1979, U. Ark., 1989. Rsch. chemist Dow Chem., Oyster Creek, Freeport, Tex., 1980-84; chemist Aluminum Co. Am., Bauxite, Ark., 1984-87; tchr. Little Rock (Ark.) Sch. Dist., 1987-90. Pres., bd. dirs. Little Peoples Acad. Sch. Montessori, Ottumwa, Iowa, 1990-93; den leader Cub Scouts. Mem. PEO, Phi Beta Kappa. Democrat. Presbyterian. Avocations: walking, watercolor, dogs, school vol., sailing, gardening. Home: 1349 Lakeview Dr Southlake TX 76092-4853

HERRMANN, GEORGE, mechanical engineering educator; b. USSR, Apr. 19, 1921. Diploma in Civil Engring., Swiss Fed. Inst. Tech., 1945, PhD in Mechanics, 1949. Asst., then asso. prof. civil engring. Columbia, 1950-62; prof. civil engring. Northwestern U., 1962-69; prof. applied mechanics Stanford, 1969-, prof. emeritus; cons. SRI Internat., 1970-80. Contbr. 260 articles to profl. jours.; editl. bd. numerous jours. Fellow ASME (hon. mem. 1990, Centennial medal 1980); mem. ASCE (Th. v. Karman medal 1981), Nat. Acad. Engring., AIAA (emeritus). Office: Stanford U Div Mechanics/Computation Durand Bldg 281 Stanford CA 94305-4040

HERRMANN, JANE MARIE, physical therapist; b. St. Louis, Aug. 13, 1961; d. Harold Jack and Elizabeth Joan (Hogan) H. BS in Phys. Therapy, St. Louis U., 1984; M. Health Sci., Washington U., St. Louis, 1991. Registered phys. therapist, Ill., Mo.; registered/cert. athletic trainer, Ill. Staff phys. therapist St. Anthony's Med. Ctr., St. Louis, 1985-87; profl. staff coord. Divsn. of Med. Rehab. Profl. Phys. Therapy, Inc., St. Louis, 1987-91; dir. of phys. therapy Hillsboro (Ill.) Area Hosp. Med. Rehab., Hillsboro, 1991-94; phys. therapy cons. Continental Med. Svcs., Hillsboro, 1992-95, Sundance Corp., Litchfield, Ill., 1994—; clin. dir. MedRehab, Inc., Hillsboro, 1994-96; dir. rehab. Hillsboro Area Hosp., 1996—. Mem. Am. Phys. Therapy Assn., Nat. Athletic Trainers Assn., Ill. Phys. Therapy Assn. Roman Catholic. Avocations: tennis, golf, drawing. Office: Hillsboro Area Hosp 1200 E Tremont St Hillsboro IL 62049-1912

HERRMANN, KENNETH JOHN, JR., social work educator; b. Lackawanna, N.Y., Apr. 13, 1943; s. Kenneth John and Alice Jane (Gray) H.; m.

Kathleen Wolf, Oct. 1969 (div. 1986); m. Kathleen T. Morris-Costanza, 1994; children: Aaron Kim-Eui, Gabe Sang-Koo, Mark Hoi-Duk, Rachele Hoi-Im, Ruth Myung-Hee, James Thomas, Joseph Costanza. BA, Canisius Coll., 1972; MSW, SUNY, Buffalo, 1975. Tchr. St. Monica's Sch., Buffalo, 1963-67; sr. caseworker Erie County Child Welfare, Buffalo, 1969-73; family therapist Wyndham Lawn Home for Children, Lockport, N.Y., 1975-77; dir. children's svcs. Dept. Social Svc. County of Genesee (N.Y.), 1977-78; assoc. prof. social work SUNY, Brockport, 1978—; pvt. practice psychotherapy East Pembroke, N.Y., 1975—; adoption social worker Dillon Children's Svcs. Intercountry Adoption Program, 1982-84; internat. adoption social worker New Beginnings Child and Family Svcs., 1989—; exec. dir. Vets. Svcs. Ctr. of West N.Y., Batavia, 1991-94; domestic violence group therapist YWCA, 1995-97; cons. E.J. Noble Hosp., 1997—; mem. state bd. for social work N.Y. State Edn. Dept., 1984—; cons. UN Children's Fund, U.S. Senate, U.S. Congress; radio and TV appearances, lectr., cons. on children's rights, child abuse and neglect, fmaily violence. Author: I Hope My Daddy Dies, Mister, 1975, I'm Nobody's Child, 1982; author studies on internat. children's issues; contbr. articles to profl. jours. With U.S. Army, 1967-69. N.Y. State Soc. for Social Work clin. fellow. Fellow N.Y. State Soc. Clin. Social Work; mem. NASW, VFW, Def. for Children Internat., OURS, Bertha Capen Reynolds Soc., Americal Assn. Home: 2614 E Main Rd East Pembroke NY 14056-0067 Office: SUNY Faculty Office Bldg Brockport NY 14420

HERRMANN, LACY BUNNELL, investment company executive, financial entrepreneur, venture capitalist; b. New Haven, May 12, 1929; s. James Joseph and Helen Georgia (Bunnell) H.; m. Elizabeth Ocumpaugh Beadle, May 23, 1953; children: Diana Parsons, Conrad Beadle. AB, Brown U., 1950; postgrad., London Sch. Econs., 1953-54; MBA, Harvard U., 1956. Asst. to purchasing mgr. and buyer Westinghouse Elec. Corp., Metuchen, N.J., 1956-60; asst. v.p. Douglas T. Johnston & Co., Inc., N.Y.C., 1960-66; v.p. Johnston Mut. Fund, Inc., N.Y.C., 1964-66; gen. ptnr. Tamarack Assocs., N.Y.C., 1966-84; chmn. bd., pres. Family Home Products, Inc., N.Y.C., 1972-84, Buxton's Country Shops, Jamesburg, N.J., 1973-86; chmn., CEO Aquila Mamgt. Corp., 1983—; founder, pres. STCM Corp., moneymarket fund, N.Y.C., 1974-76; vice chmn. bd. trustees, v.p. Centennial Capital Cash Mgmt. Trust, N.Y.C. successor to STCM Corp., 1976-81; chmn. bd. trustees, pres. successor fund Capital Cash Mgmt. Trust, 1981—; founder, chmn. bd. trustees, pres. Trinity Liquid Assets Trust, 1982-85, Oxford Cash Mgmt. Fund, 1982-88, Prime Cash Fund, 1982—; chmn., CEO, Aquila Mgmt. Corp., 1983—; founder, sponsor, mgr. Pacific Capital Cash Assets Trusts, 1984—, Hawaiian Tax-Free Trust, 1985—, Churchill Cash Reserves Trust, 1985—, Tax-Free Trust Ariz., 1986—, Tax-Free Trust Oreg., 1986—, Tax-Free Fund Colo., 1987—, Churchill Tax-Free Fund of Ky., 1987—, Pacific Capital Tax-Free Cash Assets Trusts, 1988—, Pacific Capital U.S. Govt. Securities Cash Assets Trust, 1988—, Narragansett Insured Tax-Free Income Fund, 1992—, Tax-Free Fund for Utah, 1992—, Aquila Rocky Mountain Equity Fund, 1994—, Aquila Cascadia Equity Fund, 1996—, VP Aquila Distributors, Inc.; bd. dirs. Quest for Value Fund Investment Trust, Quest for Value Accumulation Trust, Quest Cash Res., Inc.; trustee Oppenheimer/Quest group funds global Value Fund, 1994—, Oppenneimer Rochester Funds; organizer, bd. dirs. and/or cons. to numerous sml. to medium sized-corps. and orgns.; founding dir. mgmt. cons. firm merged with Towers, Perrin, Forster & Crosby; instr. Rutgers U., 1958-59; chmn., pres. bd. dirs. In-Cap Mgmt. Corp, 1984—; speaker various profl. investment orgns. Contbr. articles to profl. jours. Organizer, trustee endowed award Internat. div. Grad. Sch. Journalism, Columbia U., 1962—; trustee Meml. and Endowment Trust of St. Paul's Ch., Westfield, N.J., 1968-96; mem. capital devel. com. St. Luke's Ch., Darien, Conn., 1978-85, mem. coll. scholarship fund com., 1976-85; trustee Brown U., 1990-96, trustee emeritus, 1996—, Hopkins Sch., New Haven, 1993—. Lt. (j.g.) USN, 1951-54, Korea; lt. USNR ret. Mem. N.Y. Soc. Security Analysts, Harvard Bus. Sch. Club N.Y. (bd. dirs., officer, 1958-71), Assoc. Alumni Brown U. (bd. dirs. 1978-87, exec. com. 1980-85, pres. 1983-85), Harvard Club, N.Y. Athletic Club, Brown U. Club, N.Y.C. Club (bd. dirs. 1981-88), Brown U. of Fairfield Country Club (pres. 1977-82, bd. dirs. 1977—), Univ. Club (R.I.), Faculty Club Brown U., Stratton Mountain Country Club, Orleans Yacht Club, Ariz. club, Outrigger Canoe Club (Honolulu), Lahaina Yacht Club (Maui). Republican. Episcopalian. Home: 6 Whaling Rd Darien CT 06820-5930 Office: 380 Madison Ave New York NY 10017-2513

HERRMANN, ROBERT LAWRENCE, biochemistry, science and religion educator and administrator; b. N.Y.C., July 17, 1928; s. Philip Charles and Florence Gertrude (Benn) H.; m. Elizabeth Ann Cook, Aug. 12, 1950; children—Stephen, Karen, Holly, Anders. B.S. in Chemistry, Purdue U., 1951; Ph.D. in Biochemistry, Mich. State U., 1956. Postdoctoral fellow MIT, 1956-59; from asst. prof. to assoc. prof. biochemistry Boston U. Sch. Medicine, 1959-76; prof., chmn. dept. biochemistry Oral Roberts U. Sch. Medicine and Dentistry, Tulsa, 1976-81, assoc. dean biomed. sci., 1978-79; lectr. chemistry Gordon Coll., Wenham, Mass., 1981, adj. prof., 1982-97; exec. dir. Am. Sci. Affiliation, 1981-93; program dir. John Templeton Found. 1992—; judge Templeton Prize for Progress in Religion, 1999—. Editor: Prog. in Theology newsletter of John Templeton Found; contbr. chpts. to books, articles to profl. jours. Trustee Christian Med. Soc., 1976-79, Barrington Coll., 1975-78, Templeton Found., 1987-95, 96—, Southeastern Mass. U., 1988-91; mem. Bd. Health, Bedford, Mass., 1975-76. Served with USN, 1946-48, 51-52. Fellow AAAS, Gerontol. Soc.; mem. Am. Soc. Biochem. and Molecular Biology, Victoria Inst., Sci. and Religion Forum, European Soc. for Study Sci. and Theology, Am. Sci. Affiliation. Evangelical Christian. Home: 12 Spillers Ln Ipswich MA 01938-2430 Office: Gordon Coll 255 Grapevine Rd Wenham MA 01984-1899

HERRMANN, WALTER, retired laboratory administrator; b. Johannesburg, Republic of South Africa, May 2, 1930; came to U.S., 1953; s. Gottlob Friedrich and Gertrud Louise (Retzlaff) H.; m. Betty Allard (div.); children: Peter Friedrich, Inga Louise; m. Ednarae B. Gross. BSc in Engring. cum laude, U. Witwatersrand, Republic South Africa, 1950; PhD in Mech. Engring., U. Witwatersrand, 1955. Rsch. engr. MIT, Boston, 1953-55, sr. rsch. engr., 1957-64; lectr. U. Cape Town, Rep. South Africa, 1955-57; div. supr. Sandia Nat. Labs., Albuquerque, 1964-67, dept. mgr., 1967-82, dir. engring. scis., 1982-90, sr. fellow, 1990-93; ret. Sandia Nat. Labs., 1993; W.W. Clyde prof. U. Utah, Salt Lake City, 1971-72. Contbr. articles to profl. jours. Mem. ASME, Am. Phys. Soc., Nat. Acad. Engring.

HERRNSTADT, RICHARD LAWRENCE, American literature educator; b. N.Y.C., Nov. 4, 1926; s. Oscar Edward and Helen (Lidz) H.; m. Helen Lea Appel, June 18, 1950; children—Steven, Ellen Sara, Owen. B.S., U. Wis., 1948, M.S., 1950; Ph.D., U. Md., 1960. Instr. English Iowa State U., Ames, 1954-58; asst. prof. Iowa State U., 1958-61, assoc. prof., 1961-65, prof., 1965-92, prof. emeritus, 1992—. Editor: The Letters of A. Bronson Alcott, 1969; contbr. articles to profl. jours. Bd. dirs. Ames Cmty. Sch. Dist., 1967-74, Iowa Humanities Programs, 1973-79, v.p., 1978-79; bd. dirs. Area Edn. Agy. 11, Johnston, Iowa, 1977-91, v.p., 1980-84, pres., 1984-87; bd. dirs. Youth and Shelter Svcs., Ames, 1980-91, v.p., 1984-85, pres., 1985-87; bd. dirs. Joint Action in Cmty. Svc., 1994—. Served with USN, 1945-46. Recipient faculty citation Iowa State U. Alumni Assn., 1983. Mem. MLA, Am. Studies Assn. (exec. council 1969-76), Thoreau Soc., Mid-Am. Am. Studies Assn. (v.p. 1961-62, pres. 1962-63), AAUP, Phi Beta Delta. Democrat. Jewish. Home: 5320 N Via Sempreverde Tucson AZ 85750-5970

HERRO, JOHN JOSEPH, software specialist; b. Watertown, Wis., Oct. 3, 1945; s. Alexander Chris and Lyla Victoria H.; m. Beverly Lynn Franz, June 26, 1976; children: Carla Lynn, Brian Peter, Emily Anne. BS, Ill. Inst. Technology, Chgo., 1967; MS, Ill. Inst. Technology, 1968, PhD, 1973. Electronic engr. Motorola, Inc., Schaumburg, Ill., 1968-71; assoc. engr. Ill. Inst. Technology Rsch. Inst., Chgo. and Dayton, Ohio, 1972-75; tech. staff Logicon, Inc., Dayton, 1975-77; systems analyst Cin. Electronics Corp., 1977-78; sr. software engr. GE Co., Cin., 1978-86; staff software engr. Grumman Aerospace, Melbourne, Fla., 1986-88, Harris Corp., Palm Bay, Fla., 1988-89; software specialist Golden Enterprises, Inc., Melbourne, 1989—; pres. Software Innovations Technology, Palm Bay, 1988—; tchr. SUNY at Binghamton, 1985-86, Fla. Inst. Technology, Melbourne, 1988-89. Author: ADA Tutor, 1988. Recipient Spl. Fellowship Ill. Inst. Technology, 1969, Traineeship NSF, 1971. Mem. Tau Beta Pi, Sigma Xi, Sig-ADA, Four Sigma Soc. Roman Catholic. Avocations: amateur radio, home computing, classical music. Home: 1083 Mandarin Dr NE Palm Bay FL 32905-4706

HERROD, HENRY GRADY, III, allergist, immunologist; b. Oakland, Calif., Apr. 30, 1945. MD, U. Ala., 1972. Cert. allergy and immunology; cert. pediats. Intern U. Wash., Seattle, 1972-73, resident in pediats., 1973-74; resident rsch. assoc. in allergy and immunology NIH, Bethesda, Md., 1974-76; fellow in allergy and immunology Duke U., Durham, 1976-78; physician Le Bonheur Childrens Med. Ctr., Memphis; prof. U. Tenn., Memphis, dean, 1998—. Mem. AAAI, AAI, AAP, APS. E-mail: Hherrod@utmem.edu. Office: Dean Coll Medicine U Tenn 62 S Dunlap St Ste 400 Memphis TN 38163-4903*

HERRON, EDWIN HUNTER, JR., energy consultant; b. Shreveport, La., June 7, 1938; s. Edwin Hunter and Helen Virginia (Russell) H.; B.S. in Chem. Engring., Tulane U., 1959, M.S., 1963, Ph.D. (NSF fellow, 1963-64), 1964; m. Frances Irvine Hunter, June 27, 1959; children—Edwin, David, Ashley. Rsch. engr. Exxon Rsch. & Engring. Co., Linden, N.J., 1959-61; sr. rsch. engr. Exxon Prodn. Rsch. Co., Houston, 1964-66; corp. planning advisor Esso Europe, London, Eng., 1966-74; fin. analyst Exxon Corp., N.Y.C., 1974-78; v.p. Gruy Petroleum Tech., Inc., McLean, Va., 1978-84; pres. Petro-Analysis Inc. (name changed to Hunter Trading Co. Inc.), 1984—; pres. Petroleum Equities, Inc., 1987—; dir. petroleum projects CORE Internat., Inc., 1989—; pres. Petroleum Holdings, Inc., 1993—. Recipient Levey award, Tulane U., 1970. Mem. Soc. Petroleum Engrs., Am. Inst. Chem. Engrs., Sci. Rsch. Soc., Soc. Tulane Engrs., Tau Beta Pi. Contbr. articles to profl. publs.

HERRON, HOLLY LYNN, flight nurse, educator; b. Kirksville, Mo., Sept. 20, 1959; d. Rolland Edward Herron and Sonia Ann (Meisner) Bray; m. Robert Meader, June 20, 1992; 1 child, Lauren Meader. Diploma, Grant Hosp. Sch.Nursing, 1980; AAS, Otterbein Coll., 1980; BSN, Ohio U., 1984; MSN, Ohio State U., 1990. Charge nurse surg. ICU, preceptor, contingent staff Grant Med. Ctr., Columbus, Ohio, 1980-83, nurse open heart ICU, 1983-84, flight nurse, clin. coord., other positions for LifeFlight, 1984—; instr. critical care & med.-surg. nursing Otterbein Coll., Westerville, Ohio, 1990—. Contbr. articles to profl. jours.and textbooks. Mem. AACN, ANA (Excellence in Nursing award 1990), Nat. Flight Nurses Assn. (pres. Ohio chpt. 1989-93, past v.p.), Assn. Air Med. Svcs. (edn. com.), Emergency Nurses Assn., ASTM, Sigma Theta Tau. Republican. Lutheran. Avocations: reading, rock collecting. Office: Grant Med Ctr Life Flight 111 S Grant Ave Columbus OH 43215-4701

HERRON, JANET IRENE, industrial manufacturing engineer; b. Zanesville, Ohio, Oct. 14, 1949; d. Lincoln and Freda Louise (Nolan) Estep; m. Wade Harold Herron, June 10, 1967; children: Toni Renee, Dawnise Renee. AAS, Muskingum Area Tech. Coll., 1978; BS, Ohio U., 1990. Elec., mech. designer Nat. Cash Register, Cambridge, Ohio, 1978-83; restructuring engr. Cooper Ind., Zanesville, 1983-87; sr. product engr., quality mgr. Tomkins Ind., Malta, Ohio, 1990-93; pres., owner Herron Engring. & Design, Chandlersville, Ohio, 1993—; engring. instr. Mid-East Ohio Joint Vocat. Sch., 1987-88, Ctrl. Ohio Tech. Coll., 1987-88, Muskingum Area Tech. Coll., 1990—; mfg. outreach engr. Edison Welding Inst. Columbus, Ohio, 1996-98. Mem. NAFE, AAUW, Am. Soc. Quality, Inst. Indsl. Engrs., Soc. Mfg. Engrs., Soc. Engrs. in Mfg., Soc. Women Engrs., Mid-East Ohio Women's Entrepreneurs. Democrat. Presbyn. Avocations: hosting foreign exchange students, attending concerts, travel, home restoration. Home: 9945 Claysville Rd Chandlersville OH 43727-9765

HERRON, ORLEY R., college president; b. Olive Hill, Ky., Nov. 16, 1933; s. Orley R. and Hyllie W. (Weaver) H.; m. Donna Jean Morgan, Aug. 24, 1956; children: Jill Donette, Morgan Niles, Mark Weaver. BA, Wheaton Coll., 1955; MA, Mich. State U., 1959, PhD, 1965; LittD (hon.), Houghton Coll., 1972; LHD (hon.), Lesley Coll., 1983. Dean of students Westmont Coll., Santa Barbara, Calif., 1961-67; dir. doctoral program/student pers. U. Miss., 1967-68; asst. to pres. Ind. State U., 1968-70; pres. Greenville (Ill.) Coll., 1970-77, Nat Louis U. (formerly Nat. Coll. Edn.), Evanston, Ill., 1977-97; chmn. Herron Techs., Inc., 1998—; mem. Ill. Commn. for Improvement Elem. and Secondary Edn., 1983-1985; chmn. bd. Harris Bank, Wilmette, Ill., 1991—, also bd. dirs.; bd. dirs. Corp. Cmty. Schs. Am., 1989—. Author: Role of the Trustee, 1969, Input-Output, 1970, New Dimensions in Stude Personnel Administration, 1970, A Christian Executive in a Secular World, 1979, Who Controls Your Child?, 1980, Words to Live By, 1997, (cassette tape) Governing Higher Education in the 70's, 1970. Rep. of Pres. U.S. 25th Anniversary UNESCO, 1971; mem. adv. bd. Expt. on Internat. Living, Santa Barbara, 1961-67; mem. Gov.'s Task Force on Encouraging Citizen Involvement in Edn., 1986-87; bd. dirs. Ch. Centered Evangelism; mem. Chgo. Sun. Evening Club, 1987-97. Lt. comdr. U.S. Naval Res., 1973-77. Recipient Crusader Christian Contbn. award Wheaton Coll., 1955, 74, Outstanding Citizen award Greenville Jaycees, 1971, Outstanding Educator award Religious Heritage of Am., 1987, Disting. Alumnus award Wheaton Coll., Outstanding Alumnus award New Philadelphia H.S., Amicus Polonae award, 1996. Mem. Am. Assn. Higher Edn., AAUP, Coun. on Inter-Instnl. Cooperation (pres.), Council Advancement Small Colls. (sec.), Christian Coll. Consortium (exec. com.), Fedn. Ind. Ill. Colls. (exec. bd. 1971-97), Assn. Free Meth. Ednl. Instns. (pres. 1973-75), Rotary, Kiwanis. Office: 727 Roslyn Ter Evanston IL 60201-1721

HERRON, SIDNEY EARL, sales executive; b. Aberdeen, Wash., May 25, 1952; s. Marshall Elbie and Martha Elizabeth (Nicholson) H.; m. Gloria Annette Hanson, Mar. 17, 1973 (div. Mar 1983); children: Jason, Angela; m. Alison Marie Young, Oct. 12, 1985; children: Jeff, Amanda, Shane. Student, U. Washington, Seattle, Grays Harbor Coll., 1970-71, Northwest Coll., 1971-72. Field service engr. Teltone Corp., Kirkland, Wash., 1973-77, sales engr., 1977-80, area sales mgr. component products, 1980-81, area sales mgr. data products, 1981-83, nat. accounts mgr. pvt. label div., 1983-84, western regional sales mgr., 1985-86; product mgr. data products Teltone Corp., Kirkland, 1986-89; western regional sales mgr. Teltrend, Inc., Kirkland, Wash., 1989-90; with mktg. and sales Rapcom Corp., Bellevue, Wash., 1990-91; pres., founding ptnr. Avicom, Inc., Bothell, Wash., 1991-97; sales mgr. Moose Logic, Inc., Woodinville, Wash., 1997—; mgmt. cons. TRC Systems Corp., Federal Way, Wash., 1986-87. Author, editor and actor videotaped tech. tng., 1976; author sales tng. manual for Teltone Corp., 1983. Mem. Internat. Airline Passangers' Assn. Republican. Club: Columbia Athletic (Kirkland, Wash.). Avocations: music, basketball, skiing, boating, raquetball. Home: Avicom Inc 2506 171st Pl SE Bothell WA 98012-6512 Office: Moose Logic Inc Ste 202B 14522 NE No Woodinville Way Woodinville WA 98072

HERRSTROM, DAVID STEN, banking executive; b. Oakland, Calif., Oct. 18, 1946; s. Sten Gunnar and Norma Hazel (Stratford) H.; m. Constance Joy Harmon, Nov. 6, 1945; 1 child, Tristen. BA, Nyack Coll., 1968; MA, NYU, 1969, PhD, 1975. Mgr. sys. devel. Citicorp. Author: Jonah's Disappearance, 1990, Appearing by Daylight, 1992. v.p. Roosevelt (N.J.) Sch. Bd., 1981; pres. Roosevelt Arts Project, 1989-99. N.J. State Coun. Arts fellow, 1983. Mem. Am. Acad. Poets, Poetry Soc. Am. Home: 15 Farm Ln Roosevelt NJ 08555

HERSCH, RUSSELL LEROY, secondary education educator; b. Waterloo, Iowa, May 17, 1916; s. John David and Ethel Grace (Owen) H.; m. Irma Lucille Selg, Nov. 30, 1940; children: Jon Craig, Geri Kay, Janene Joy, James Jay Russell. BA, U. No. Iowa, 1939; MA, U. Minn., 1949; postgrad., St. Cloud U., 1960-64, Columbia U., summer, 1962, U. Alaska. Cert. tchr., Minn. Tchr. Geneseo Consol. Schs., Buckingham, Iowa, 1939-42, Lindstrom-Center City (Minn.) Sch., 1942-43; math. tchr., asst. prin. Cambridge (Minn.) High Sch., 1946-57; secondary sch. prin. Osseo (Minn.) Sch. Dist., 1957-82, substitute tchr., 1983—. Bd. dirs. Metro Bd. for Aged, 1992-95; treas., bd. dirs. Christian Reaching Out in Social Svc., 1979-85. With USAF, 1943-46, ETO. Republican. Baptist. Avocations: Boy Scouting. Home: 9459 Prairieview Trl N Champlin MN 55316-2692

HERSCHBACH, DUDLEY ROBERT, chemistry educator; b. San Jose, Calif., June 18, 1932; s. Robert Dudley and Dorothy Edith (Beer) H.; m. Georgene Lee Botyos, Dec. 26, 1964; children: Lisa Marie, Brenda Michele. BS in Math., Stanford U., 1954, MS in Chemistry, 1955; AM in Physics, Harvard U., 1956, PhD in Chem. Physics, 1958; DSc (hon.), U. Toronto, 1977, Cornell Coll., 1988, Framingham State Coll., 1989, Adelphi U., 1990, Dartmouth Coll., 1992, Charles U., Prague, 1993, U. Ill., Chgo., 1994, Wheaton Coll., 1995. Jr. fellow Harvard U., Cambridge, Mass., 1957-59, prof. chemistry, 1963-76, Frank B. Baird prof. sci., 1976—, mem. faculty council, 1980-83, master Currier House, 1981-86; asst. prof. U. Calif., Berkeley, 1959-61, assoc. prof., 1961-63; cons. editor W.H. Freeman lectr. Haverford Coll., 1962; Falk-Plaut lectr. Columbia U., 1963; vis. prof. Gottingen (Germany) U., summer 1963, U. Calif., Santa Curz, 1972; Harvard lectr. Yale U., 1964; Debye lectr. Cornell U., 1966; Rollefson lectr. U. Calif., Berkeley, 1969; Reilly lectr. U. Notre Dame, 1979; Phillips lectr. U. Pitts., 1971; disting. vis. prof. U. Ariz., 1971, U. Tex., 1977, U. Utah, 1978; Gordon lectr. U. Toronto, 1971; Clark lectr. San Jose State U., 1979; Hill lectr. Duke U., 1988; Priestly lectr. Pa. State U., 1990; Kaufman lectr. U. Pa., 1990; Polanyi lectr. U. N.C., 1991; Dreyfus lectr. Dartmouth Coll., 1992; Paulins lectr. Calif. Inst. Tech., 1993; Bernstein lectr. UCLA, 1994; Brown lectr. Rutgers U., 1995. Assoc. editor: Jour Phys. Chemistry, 1980-88.. Guggenheim fellow U. Freiburg, Germany, 1968; vis. fellow Joint Inst. for Lab. Astrophysics U. Colo., 1969; Fairchild Disting. scholar Calif. Inst. Tech., 1976; Sloan fellow, 1959-63, Exxon Faculty fellow, 1980—; recipient pure chemistry award Am. Chem. Soc., 1965, Centenary medal, 1977, Pauling medal, 1978; Spiers medal Faraday Soc., 1976, Polanyi medal, 1981, Langmuir prize, 1983, Nobel Prize in Chemistry, 1986, Nat. Medal of Sci. NSF, 1991, Heyrovsky medal 1992, Sierra Nevada Disting. Chemist award, 1993, Kosolapoff medal, 1994, William Walker prize, 1994; named to Calif. Pub. Edn. Hall of Fame, 1987. Fellow Am. Phys. Soc. (chmn. chem. physics div. 1971-72), Am. Acad. Arts and Scis.; mem. AAAS, Am. Chem. Soc., Nat. Acad. Scis., Royal Soc. Chemistry (fgn. hon. mem.), Am. Philos. Soc., Phi Beta Kappa (orator Harvard U. 1992), Sigma Xi. Office: Harvard U Dept Chemistry 12 Oxford St Cambridge MA 02138-2902*

HERSCHENSOHN, BRUCE, film director, writer; b. Milw., Sept. 10, 1932. Ed., Los Angeles. With art dept. RKO Pictures, 1953-55; dir., editor Gen. Dynamics Corp., 1955-56; dir., writer, editor Karma for Internat. Communications Found.; editor, co-dir. Friendship Seven for NASA; dir., editor Tall Man Five-Five for Gen. Dynamics Corp. and SAC; dir. motion picture and TV Service USIA, 1968-72, spl. cons. to dir., 1972—; staff asst. to Pres. U.S., 1972; dep. spl. asst. to Pres., 1973-74, mem. transition team, 1981; sr. fellow Claremont (Calif.) Inst., 1993; Rep. nominee U.S. Senate (Calif.), 1992; tchr. U. Md., 1972; spl. cons. to Rep. Nat. Conv., 1972; polit. analyst KABC-TV and KABC radio, 1978-91. Directed and wrote films for USIA, including Bridges of the Barrios, The Five Cities of June, The President, John F. Kennedy: Years of Lightning, Day of Drums, Eulogy to 5:02; recipient Acad. award for Czechoslovakia 1968 as best documentary short 1969; author: The Gods of Antenna, 1976; contbg. editor: Conservative Digest. Bd. govs. Charles Edison Meml. Youth Fund; Rep. nom. U.S. Senate, Calif., 1992. Served with USAF, 1951-52. Recipient Arthur S. Flemming award as 1 of 10 outstanding young mem in fed. govt., 1969; Distinguished Service medal USIA, 1972; Ann. award Council Against Communist Aggression, 1972. Office: Claremont Inst 250 W 1st St Claremont CA 91711-4736

HERSCHMAN, JEFFREY D., lawyer; b. Chgo., Sept. 30, 1948. BS, Drake U., 1970; JD with honors, U. Ill., 1973. Bar: Md. 1973. Mem. Piper & Marbury, Balt. Address: Piper & Marbury 36 S Charles St Baltimore MD 21201-3020

HERSETH, ADOLPH SYLVESTER (BUD HERSETH), classical musician; b. Lake Park, Minn., July 25, 1921. Student, New England Conservatory, Boston. Prin. trumpet player Chgo. Symphony Orch., 1948—. With U.S. Army, World War II. Named Instrumentalist of Yr., Musical Am., 1996. Office: care Chgo Symphony Orch Orchestra Hall 2590 220 S Michigan Ave Chicago IL 60604-2501*

HERSEY, DAVID FLOYD, information resources management consultant, retired government official; b. Balboa, C.Z., Jan. 7, 1928; s. Ralph George and Marie M. (Ortiz) H.; m. Phyllis May Peterson, Aug. 26, 1961; children: David Floyd, Ruth Ellen, Thomas Owen. B.S., Trinity U., 1948; M.S., U. Ill., 1949; Ph.D., Washington U., St. Louis, 1952. Diplomate: Am. Acad. Microbiology. Assoc. dir. Sci. Info. Exch., Smithsonian Instn., Washington, 1961-63; dep. dir. Sci. Info. Exch., Smithsonian Instn., 1964-71, pres., 1972-82; health sci. adminstr. FDA, 1984-90; mem. virus and rickettsial study sect. USPHS, 1957-61; cons. Microbiol. Assos., Inc., 1960-70, Cooke Engring. Co., Arlington, Va., 1969-72. Contbr. articles on microbiology and info. sci. to profl. jours. Commd. 1st lt. U.S. Air Force, 1952; advanced through grades to col. Res. 1973; chief clin. lab. 3700th USAF Hosp., 1952-54, Lackland AFB, Tex.; established 1st USAF Epidemiol. Lab., 1957-58; asst. chief virology br. Armed Forces Inst. Pathology, 1960-61, Washington; resigned 1961. Decorated Air Force Commendation medal. Mem. Acad. Medicine. Home: 11602 Gilsan St Silver Spring MD 20902-3123

HERSEY, GEORGE LEONARD, art history educator, retired; b. Cambridge, Mass., Aug. 30, 1927; s. Milton Leonard and Katharine (Page) H.; m. Jane Maddox Lancefield, Sept. 2, 1953; children: Donald, James. B.A., Harvard U., 1951; M.F.A., Yale U., 1954, M.A., 1961, Ph.D., 1964. Instr. art Bucknell U., Lewisburg, Pa., 1954-55; asst. prof. Bucknell U., 1955-59, acting chmn., 1958-59; instr. Yale U., New Haven, Conn., 1963-65; asst. prof. Yale, 1965-68; assoc. prof. Yale U., 1968-74, prof., 1974-98, ret., 1998; mem. adv. bd. Conn. Preservation Trust, 1977-79; mem. Conn. State Commn. Capitol Restoration, 1977-79; lectr. Princeton U., Columbia U., other univs., orgns. Author: Alfonso II and the Artistic Renewal of Naples, 1969, The Aragonese Arch at Naples, 1443-1475, 1973; High Victorian Gothic: A Study in Associationism, 1972, Pythagorean Palaces: Magic and Architecture in the Italian Renaissance, 1975, Architecture, Poetry and Number in the Royal Palace at Caserta, 1983, The Lost Meaning of Classical Architecture, 1988, (with R. Freedman) Possible Palladian Villas, 1992, High Renaissance Art in St. Peter's and the Vatican, 1993, The Evolution of Allure, Sexual Selection from the Medici Venus to the Incredible Hulk, 1996, The Monumental Impulse: Architecture's Biological Roots, 1999; also numerous articles and revs.; co-editor: Architectura, 1971—; editor: Yale Publs. in History of Art, 1974-90; art exhbn. co-organizer The Taste of Angels: Neapolitan Paintings in North America, 1650-1750, Yale Univ. Art Gallery and other museums, 1987-88. With U.S. Merchant Marine, 1945-46, U.S. Army, 1946-47. Recipient Monticello prize, 1961; Fulbright scholar, Italy, 1962; Morse fellow, 1966, Schepp fellow, Florence, Italy, 1972; resident Am. Acad. Rome, 1994. Mem. Soc. Archtl. Historians (bd. dirs. 1971-73), Renaissance Soc. Am., Dunky Club hon.). Democrat. Home: 167 Linden St New Haven CT 06511-2407

HERSH, BURTON DAVID, author; b. Chgo., Sept. 18, 1933; s. Maurice Henry and Florence Nita Hersh; m. Ellen Eiseman, Aug. 3, 1957; children: Leo Joseph, Margery Clara. BA, Harvard Coll., 1955. Cons. Sundance Inst., Park City, Utah, 1991; elected to Acad. Sr. Profls. at Eckerd Coll., St. Petersburg, Fla., 1993. Author: (novel) The Ski People, 1968, (nonfiction books) The Education of Edward Kennedy 1972 (Book Find Club award 1972), The Mellon Family (Fortune Club award 1978, Book of the Month Club award), The Old Boys, 1992, The Shadow President: Ted Kennedy in Opposition, 1997. Dir. N.H. Civil Liberties Union, Concord, 1983-86; founding chmn. Bradford Conservation Com., N.H., 1970s; fin. com. N.H. Dem. Party, 1970s. With U.S. Army, 1957-59, Germany. Fulbright scholar U.S. Govt., 1955-56; Bread Loaf fellow Bread Loaf Writer's Workshop, Middlebury, Vt., 1964, others. Mem. Authors Guild Am., Am. Soc. Journalists and Authors, Assn. Former Intelligence Officers (bd. dirs. New Eng. br. 1992—), Internat. Soc. for Comparative Lit. and Theatre, PEN, Phi Beta Kappa. Democrat. Jewish. Avocations: print collecting, skiing, tennis, investing. Home and Office: PO Box 433 Bradford NH 03221-0433

HERSH, IRA PAUL, tax and financial planning consultant; b. Bklyn., July 14, 1948; s. Saul and Mildred (Leibowitz) Hershkowitz; m. Jan Bennett; children: Marcy Fay, Gregory Alexander, Carrie Elizabeth. BA, Queens Coll., 1969. Tax mgr. Wiss and Co., N.Y.C., 1970-77; contr. Assets Adminstrn. and Mgmt., Stamford, Conn., 1978-79; tax mgr. Exec. Monetary Mgmt., Inc., N.Y.C., 1980-84; pvt. practice tax and fin. planning, 1985—; pres. MacArthur Equities Ltd., 1985—. Mem. Rolling Hills Country Club. Home and Office: 20 Branch Brook Rd Wilton CT 06897-1520

HERSH, RICHARD H., academic administrator; b. N.Y.C.; m. Judith C. Meyers. BA in Polit. Sci. and History, Syracuse U., 1964, MA in Social Sci. Edn., 1965; EdD, Boston U., 1969. Prof., chmn. secondary edn. Coll. Edn. U. Toledo, Ohio, 1968-75; assoc. dean tchr. edn., prof. edn. Coll. Edn. U.

Oreg., 1976-80, dean grad. sch., assoc. provost rsch., 1980-83; v.p. rsch. U. Oreg., Eugene, 1983-85; v.p. acad. affairs U. N.H., Durham, 1985-89; v.p. acad. affairs, provost Drake U., Des Moines, 1989-91; pres. Hobart and William Smith Coll., Geneva, N.Y., 1991—; vis. prof., dir. moral edn. project Ont. Inst. Studies Edn. U. Toronto, 1975-76, Ctr. Moral Devel., Harvard U., Cambridge, Mass., 1975-76; vis. prof. Western Australia Inst. Tech., Perth, 1978; speaker in field. Co-author: No G.O.D.'s in the Classroom: Inquiry into Inquiry, 1972, Inquiry and Elementary Social Studies, 1972, Inquiry and Secondary Social Studies, 1972, Perspectives in Moral and Values Education, 1976, Promoting Moral Growth: From Piaget to Kohlberg, 1979, 83, Models of Values and Moral Education, 1980, The Structure of School Improvement, 1983. Stanford U. fellow, 1979, Congl. fellow, 1982-83, Ger. Acad. Exch. Svc. fellow, 1983. Avocations: skiing, tennis, rowing (mem. U.S. rowing team competed World Championships, Bled, Yugoslavia, 1966). Office: Hobart and William Smith Coll Pres Office Geneva NY 14456-3397 Home: Presidents House 690 S Main St Geneva NY 14456-3109

HERSH, ROBERT MICHAEL, lawyer, insurance company executive; b. N.Y.C., Feb. 12, 1940; s. Esaac and Esther (Cohen) H.; m. Louise Jersh, ept. 23, 1984; 1 child, Lauren. BA, Columbia U., 1960; JD, Harvard U. Bar: N.Y. 1964. Assoc. Malcolm & Hoffmann, N.Y.C., 1964-66, Valicenti, Leighton, Reid & Pine, N.Y.C., 1966-68; atty. Lraftco Corp., N.Y.C., 1968-74; assoc. counsel Equitable Life Assurance Soc. U.S., N.Y.C., 1974-76, asst. gen. counse., 1976-78, v.p., counsel, 1978-83, v.p., assoc. gen. counsel, 1983-88; v.p., gen. counsel Integrity Life Ins. Co., N.Y.C., 1988-93; assoc. gen. counsel Met. Life ins. Co., N.Y.C., 1994—; dir. Ideal Mut. Ins. Co., 1972-74; chief announcer Madison Sq. Garden Track Meets, 1974—; chief Eng. lang. athletics announcer Olympic Games, 1984, 88, 92, 96 World Championships, 1991, 93, 95, 97, 99 World Indoor Championships, 1987, 99, World Jr. Championships, 1994-98. Columnidst: Track & Field News, 1973-84, sr. editor, 1974—; contbg. editor Runner Mag., 1980-87; contbr. articles to profl. jours. With USAR, 1963-69. Mem. Assn. of Bar of City of N.Y. (com. profl. and jud. ethics 1978-81, consumer affairs com. 1984-85, ins. com. 1985-88), USA Track & Field (dir. 1979—, chmn. records com. 1979-88, chmn. rules com. 1989-98, gen. counsel 1989-98, chmn. grand prix 1982-96, Robert Giegengack award for outstanding svc. 1997), Internat. Amateur Athletic Fedn. (tech. com. 1984—), Assn. Track & Field Statisticians, Fedn. Am. Statisticians of Track. Home: 92 Club Dr Roslyn Heights NY 11577-2732 Office: MetLife 1 Madison Ave New York NY 10010-3603

HERSH, SID, real estate developer; b. Bayonne, N.J., Aug. 28, 1920; s. Adolph and Esther Hersh; m. Selma Roy; children: Carol Ann, Michael, Danny, Bonnie. Grad., Bayonne Sr. H.S. Pres. State Lumber & Millwork Co., Hillside/South Plainfield, N.J., 1945-60, Sid Hersh Assoc. Inc., Miami, 1962-99; ptnr. Canam Assoc., Miami, 1962—, S.K.A. Assoc., Miami, 1973—. Home: 19372 Cherry Hills Ter Boca Raton FL 33498-4653

HERSHAFT, ALEX, organization executive; b. Warsaw, Poland, July 1, 1934; came to the U.S., 1951; s. Jozef and Sabina (Kalina) H.; m. Eugenie Crystal, Oct. 1, 1962; 1 child, Monica. BA in Chemistry, U. Conn., 1955; PhD in Chemistry, Iowa State U., 1961. Lectr. Israel Inst. Tech., Haifa, 1961-63; ops. analyst Ctr. for Naval Analyses, Arlington, Va., 1963-65; staff analyst Avco Corp., Wilmington, Mass., 1965-68; rsch. scientist Grumman Corp., Bethpage, N.Y., 1968-72; prin. scientist Booz Allen & Hamilton, Bethesda, Md., 1972-74; dir. environ. studies Enviro Control, Rockville, Md., 1974-76; sr. scientist MITRE Corp., McLean, Va., 1977-81; founder League for Abolition of Religious Coercion in Israel, 1961, Environ. Tech. Seminar, 1969, Vegetarian Info. Svc., 1976, Farm Animal Reform Movement, 1981; co-founder U.S. animal rights movement, 1981; launched the Great Am. Meatout, 1985, World Farm Animals Day, 1983. Contbr. articles to profl. jours. Pres. Farm Animal Reform Movement, 1981—. Named to Vegetarian Hall of Fame, 1998. Home: PO Box 5888 Bethesda MD 20824-5888

HERSHAFT, ELINOR, space planner, interior designer; b. N.Y.C., Aug. 12, 1940; d. Solomon and Rose (Cohen) Klausner; m. Arthur Hershaft, June 21, 1959 (div. 1983); children: Karin, Peter; m. Alan J. Hoffman, Sept. 2, 1990. Student, Skidmore Coll., 1956-58; BA, N.Y.U., 1960; postgrad., N.Y. Sch. Interior Design, 1977-78. Lic. home improvement contractor, Conn. Interior designer Elinor Hershaft Interiors, Greewich, Conn., 1979—. Major projects house constrn. with interior design, 1985-87, additions, 1982—; projects pub. in House Beautiful, 1988, Tile News, 1988, Kitchen and Bath Concepts, 1989; numerous comml. and residential interior design projects in Fairfield, Conn. and Westchester, N.Y. Counties, Mass., So. Fla., Wilmington, N.C.; also custom furniture design and fabrication. Creative dir. Greenwich Jewish Fedn., 1983-86; developer design format, logo and calligraphy spl. fund raising campaign Temple Sholom, Greenwich, 1994-95; pro bono office design and space planning Jewish Cmty. Svcs. Recipient Svc. award Jewish Community Svcs. of Greewich, 1985, Greewich Jewish Fedn., 1983, 84, 85. Mem. ASID (allied mem.), Allied Bd. Trade, AIA (allied individual), AAF (allied individual). Jewish. Avocations: calligraphy, reading, swimming, piano, writing verse. Studio: 115 Old Mill Rd Greenwich CT 06831-3015

HERSHATTER, RICHARD LAWRENCE, lawyer, author; b. New Haven, Sept. 20, 1923; s. Alexander Charles and Belle (Blenner) H.; m. Mary Jane McNulty, Aug. 16, 1980; children by previous marriage: Gail Brook, Nancy Jill, Bruce Warren; 1 stepdau., Kimberly Ann Matlock Kleiman. BA, Yale U., 1948; JD, U. Mich., 1951. Bar: Conn. 1951, Mich. 1951, U.S. Supreme Ct. 1959. Pvt. practice New Haven, 1951-85, Clinton, Conn., 1985—; state trial referee, 1984—; mem. Clinton Rep. Town Com., Conn., 1982—, chmn., 1984-88. Author: The Spy Who Hated Licorice, 1966, Fallout For a Spy, 1968; The Spy Who Hated Fudge, 1970, Hung Jury, 1999. Mem. Clinton Rep. Town Com., Conn., 1982—, chmn., 1984-88; mem. Branford (Conn.) Bd. Edn., 1963-71. With Air Corps, U.S. Army, 1942-44, AUS, 1944-46. Mem. Conn. Sch. Attys. Coun. (pres. 1977), Middlesex County Bar Assn., Mystery Writers Am., West Haven C. of C. (pres. 1956), Masons. Office: 41 West Rd Clinton CT 06413-2316 also: 166 Route 81 Killingworth CT 06419-1469

HERSHBERGER, ROBERT GLEN, architect, educator; b. Pocatello, Idaho, Apr. 4, 1936; s. Vernon Elver and Edna Syvilla (Kinsley) H.; m. Deanna Marlene Van Dyke, Mar. 25, 1961; children: Vernon, Andrew. AB, Stanford U., 1958; BArch, U. Utah, 1959; MArch, U. Pa., 1961, PhD, 1969. Registered architect, Idaho, Ariz. Project architect Spencer & Lee, Architects, San Francisco, 1961-63; project designer GBQC Architects, Phila., 1967-69; asst. prof. Idaho State U., Pocatello, 1963-65; adj. asst. prof. Drexel U., Phila., 1967-69; practicing architect Archtl. & Planning Cons., Tempe, Ariz., 1969-87; prof. Sch. of Architecture Ariz. State U., Tempe, 1969-87, acting dir. Sch. Architecture, 1986-87, assoc. dean. Coll. of Architecture and Environ. Design, 1987; prof. U. Ariz. Coll. Arch., Tucson, 1988—, dean, 1988-96; chmn. Environ. Design Rsch. Assoc., Washington, 1976-79, chair Archs. in Edn. Com. AIA, Washington, 1983-85; v.p. Arch. Rsch. Ctrs. Consortium, 1994-96; prin. Hershberger, Arch. and Planner, Tucson, 1997—. Prin. works include Covenant Bapt. Ch. (AIA Excellence award), Urban Renewal Plan Downtown Tempe (AIA Citation), Hershberger residence (AIA honor 1990). Bd. dirs. Rio Salado Found.; mem. Tempe Design Rev. Com., 1985-87, Tempe Elec. Adv. Com., 1982-85, Pocatello Planning Commn., 1962-65; mem. pub. arts com. U. Ariz., 1988-96, chmn., 1994-96, mem. campus design rev. adv. com., 1990-96, chmn., 1990-93; chair staff parish com. Catalina United Meth. Ch., 1995; bd. dirs. Catalina Day Care Ctr., 1990-93, So. Ariz. chpt. Make-A-Wish Found., 1995-96. Recipient Crescordia Environ. Excellence award Valley Forward Assn., 1986, Hon. Mention award Ariz. Hist. Mus. competition, 1985. Fellow AIA (pres. Rio Salado chpt. 1981, 74-88, bd. dirs. So. Ariz. chpt. 1988—, pres., 1993, Gold medal adv. bd. 1992-95). Democrat. Methodist. Avocations: fly fishing, skiing, hunting, tennis, golf, photography. Office: U Ariz Capla Sch Arch PO 21-0075 Tucson AZ 85721*

HERSHBERGER, STEVEN KAYE, controller; b. Dover, Ohio, Jan. 10, 1953; s. Paul Abraham and Marilyn Jean (Gerber) H. BA, Eastern Mennonite Coll., 1975; MBA, Kent State U., 1987. Office mgr. Goodville (Pa.) Ins. Mgmt., 1977-78; underwriter Great Am. Ins. Co., Lancaster, Pa., 1978-80; vol. svc. Way Internat., Inc., Grand Forks, N.D., 1980-82; co-owner, mgr. Total Fitness Ctr., New Philadelphia, Ohio, 1982-85; budget analyst Sch. Speech Pathology and Audiology, Kent, Ohio, 1986-87; sales assoc. J.C. Penney, New Philadelphia, 1987-89; acct. Africa Inter-Mennonite Mission, Elkhart, Ind., 1989-91, contr., 1991-96; contract auditor Roche Diagnostics, Indpls., 1996-97, svc. contract specialist, 1997—, sales analyst, 1998—. Avocations: photography, swimming, horseback riding, walking my dog.

HERSHCOPF, BERTA RUTH, psychotherapist, writer; b. N.Y.C., Oct. 1, 1924; d. Samuel and Marian (Gzinterman) Feinman; m. Jack Hershcopf, June 11, 1947; children: Shelley, Amy, David. AA, Morris Jr. Coll., Morristown, N.J., 1942; BA, Douglass Coll., 1944; cert., Postgrad. Ctr. for Mental Health, N.Y.C., 1973, N.Y. Med. Coll., N.Y.C., 1977. Dir. U.S.O., Nebr., Wyo., N.Y., 1944-46; psychiatric clin. counselor Long Island Jewish Hillside Med. Ctr., New Hyde Park, N.Y., 1974-75; counseling therapist Mt. Sinai Hosp., N.Y.C., 1977-78; asst. dir. Psychoanalytic Ctr., N.Y.C., 1980-82; pvt. practice N.Y.C., 1973—; dir. Am. Counseling and Psychotherapy Svcs., N.Y.C., 1981—; cons., workshop leader Women's Rsch. Project CUNY, N.Y.C., 1975-76; cons. Nat. Urban League, 1979; workshop leader Ctr. for Interpersonal Growth at Fordham U., N.Y.C., 1979-80. Articles in jour. and nat. newpapers. Environ. activist, N.Y.C., 1993—. Mem. N.Y. State Assn. Practicing Psychotherapists (cert.), Am. Asn. for Counseling and Devel., Am. Mental Health Counselors Assn. Avocations: classical music, ballroom dancing, table tennis, nature, theatre. Home and Office: 875 Park Ave New York NY 10021-0341

HERSHENOV, BERNARD ZION, electronics research and development company executive; b. N.Y.C., Sept. 22, 1927; s. Joseph and Rebecca (Landes) H.; m. Miriam Leah Gold, Oct. 27, 1950; 1 dau., Ruth Lois. B.S., U. Mich., 1950, M.S., 1952, Ph.D., 1959. Asso. research engr. U. Mich., Ann Arbor, 1951-59; devel. engr. Gen. Electric Co., Schenectady, 1959-60; mem. tech. staff, head microwave integrated circuits RCA Research Labs., Princeton, N.J., 1960-72; dir. Research Labs., Tokyo, 1972-75; head energy systems Research Labs., Princeton, 1976-79, dir. Solid State Devices Lab., 1979-83, dir. Optical Systems and Display Materials Lab., 1983-84, dir. Optoelectronics Research Lab., 1984-87; dir. mktg. coordination David Sarnoff Research Ctr. (subs. of SRI Internat.), Princeton, 1987-88; dir. internat. bus. devel., 1989-93; sr. advisor Sarnoff Research Ctr. (subs. of SRI Internat.), Princeton, 1994-95; cons., 1993-95. Contbr. articles in field. V.p. Jewish Community Center, Princeton, 1970-71, pres., 1971-72, trustee, 1977-79; mem. physics adv. com. U. Mich., 1988—. Served with USN, 1946-47. Recipient RCA Outstanding Achievement awards, 1963, 66, Microwave Application award Microwave Theory and Techniques Soc. of IEEE, 1992. Fellow IEEE; mem. Sigma Xi, Phi Kappa Phi. Jewish. Home: 22 Raleigh Rd Kendall Park NJ 08824-1007

HERSHENSON, MIRIAM HANNAH, librarian; b. Springfield, Mass., July 23, 1944; d. David and Thelma (Wasserman) Ratner; m. Frank J. Hershenson, July 7, 1968; children: Trent M., Scott D. AB, Syracuse U., 1966; MS, Simmons Coll., 1967; postgrad., Nova U., 1987-89. Cert. tchr., librarian, Mass. Media specialist Quincy (Mass.) Pub. Schs., 1967-71, Virginia Beach (Va.) Pub. Schs., 1982-84, Portsmouth (Va.) Pub. Schs., 1984; regional children's coord. Broward County Libr., Ft. Lauderdale, Fla., 1985-88, br. liaison, 1988-89, br. librarian, 1989-93, regional br. supr., 1993—. Mem. ALA, Pub. Libr. Assn., Fla. Libr. Assn. (caucus chair 1990-91), Broward County Libr. Assn. (pres. 1994-95), Hadassah (life, chpt. pres. 1983-84), Nat. Coun. Jewish Women (life), Jewish Women Internat. (life), Brandeis Univ. Women (life). Office: 100 S Andrews Ave Fort Lauderdale FL 33301-1830

HERSHENSON, ROBERTA MANTELL, writer, photographer; b. Newark, Nov. 24, 1940; d. Milton A. and Florence Braun) Mantell; m. Paul Hershenson; children: Nina, Michael. BS in Edn., Simmons Coll., Boston, 1962. Writer, prodr. Warren Schloat Prodns., Pleasantville, N.Y., 1969-72; freelance photographer Westchester County, N.Y., 1972-83; freelance writer and photographer N.Y., 1983—; contbr. N.Y. Times, N.Y.C., 1983—; cons. Scarsdale (N.Y.) Adult Sch., 1997; lectr. Westchester Photog. Soc., Valhalla, N.Y., Scarsdale Adult Sch., 1997; pres. Ground Glass, Irvington, N.Y., 1980s, Film Workshop of Westchester, Tarrytown, N.Y., 1970s. Author news and feature articles N.Y. Times, Opera News, Wildlife Conservation Mag, Opera News, Wildlife Conservation mag. 1999. Mem. Am. Soc. Journalists and Authors, Oratorio Soc. N.Y., Ontario Soc. of N.Y. Avocations: music, writing fiction, choral singing. Home: 45 Popham Rd Scarsdale NY 10583

HERSHEY, COLIN HARRY, management consultant; b. Everett, Pa., Aug. 31, 1935; s. Harry and Marjorie (Nycum) H.; m. Jacqueline Anderson, June 14, 1974; children: Barclay Harry, Marjorie Anderson. BSCE, Lehigh U., 1957; MBA, U. Pitts., 1967, postgrad., 1968. Registered profl. engr., Pa. Civil engr. contracting divsn. Dravo Corp., Pitts., 1957-59, cost engr., 1961-63; field engr. Army Corps Engrs., Pitts., 1958-61; mgr. mgmt. info. systems, atomic power divsn. Westinghouse Electric Co., Pitts., 1964-67; counselor Planning Dynamics, Inc., Pitts., 1968-70, v.p., 1970-72, pres., 1972-77, pres., chmn., 1977—. Author, editor: Strategic Planning Concepts, 1985; contbr. articles to profl. jours. Mem. Am. Mgmt. Assn. (adv. com. Strategic Mgmt. Program), Strategic Leadership Forum, Duquesne Club, Alpha Tau Omega, Chi Epsilon. Office: Planning Dynamics Inc 135 Industry Dr Pittsburgh PA 15275-1035

HERSHEY, DALE, lawyer; b. Pitts., Mar. 24, 1941; s. Henry E. and Elizabeth (Loeffler) H.; m. Susanne Jarrett Wilson, July 8, 1967; children: Lauren Olivia, Justin Alexander. BA, Yale U., 1963; LLB, Harvard U., 1966. Bar: Pa. 1966, U.S. Dist. Ct. (we. dist.) Pa. 1966, U.S. Ct. Appeals (3d cir.) 1971, U.S. Tax Ct. 1978, U.S. Supreme Ct. 1979. Assoc. Eckert Seamans Cherin & Mellott, LLC, Pitts., 1966-75, ptnr., 1975—; adj. prof. indsl. adminstrn. and law, Carnegie Mellon U., 1986—; pres. Charleston Trust/U.S.A. Bd. dirs. Legal Aid Soc. Pitts., pres., 1983-89; pres. Gateway to the Arts, Inc.; bd. dirs. Friends of Carnegie Libr., Pitts. Chamber Music Soc., pres., 1992-94; fellow Carnegie Inst. Mus. Art. Mem. ABA, Pa. Bar Assn. (Pro Bono award 1988), Allegheny County Bar Assn. (bd. dirs. Bar Found., mem. judiciary com.), Am. Law Inst., Harvard Law Sch. Assn. Western Pa. (pres. 1985-86), Hist. Soc. Western Pa. (bd. dirs., exec. com.), Harvard-Yale-Princeton Club, Yale Club (N.Y.C.), Yale Club (Pitts.) (pres. 1987-89). Unitarian. Home: 311 Dorseyville Rd Pittsburgh PA 15215-1022 Office: Eckert Seamans Cherin & Mellott 600 Grant St Ste 4400 Pittsburgh PA 15219-2703

HERSHEY, GERALD LEE, psychologist; b. Detroit, Mar. 7, 1931; s Von Waltz and Clementine H.; m. Shirley Gauld, Oct. 2, 1954; children: Bruce, Dale, James. Student, UCLA, 1949-54; B.A. with honors, Mich. State U., 1957, M.A., 1958, Ph.D., 1961. Asst. instr., research assoc. Mich. State U., East Lansing, 1958-61; mem. faculty dept. psychology Fullerton Coll., Calif., 1961—, prof., 1965—, chmn. dept., 1980—; vis. prof. Chapman Coll., Calif., 1962-69. Co-author: Human Development (2d edit.), 1978, Living Psychology (3d edit.), 1981. Served to 1st lt. AUS, 1954-56. Mem. Am. Psychol. Assn., Assn. Humanistic Psychology, NEA. Lodge: Lions. Office: Fullerton College 321 E Chapman Ave Fullerton CA 92832-2011

HERSHEY, H(OWARD) GARLAND, JR., university administrator, orthodontist; b. Iowa City, Nov. 6, 1940; m. Barbara Thompson; children—Brooke Janssen, Dru Ann, Paige Marie, Alexandra Elizabeth, Howard Garland III. B.S., U. Iowa, 1962, D.D.S., 1965, M.S., 1971. Diplomate Am. Bd. Orthodontics; fellow Am. Coll. Dentists. Inst. dept. oral diagnosis U. Iowa, Iowa City, 1968-69; staff research asst. dept. otolaryngology U. Iowa, 1969-71, asst. instr. dept. orthodontics, 1970-71; asst. prof. dept. orthodontics U. N.C., Chapel Hill, 1971-74; assoc. prof. U. N.C., 1974-78, prof., 1978—; asst. dean acad. affairs Sch. Dentistry, U. N.C., 1975-80, assoc. dean, 1980-83, dir. grad. edn., 1975-83, vice chancellor for health affairs, 1983—, vice provost, 1988—, interim provost, 1992-93; practice dentistry specializing in orthodontics, 1971—; mem. staff N.C. Meml. Hosp., 1973—; mem. N.C. Orthodontic Health Care Com., 1974—; mem. bd. govs. Research Triangle Inst., 1991—, mem. exec. com., 1992—; cons. on dental health to U. Alexandria, Arab Republic of Egypt, 1980—. Mem. editorial cons. Am. Jour. Phys. Anthropology, 1974-80, Jour. ADA, 1975—; mem. editorial rev. bd. Jour. Dental Edn., 1979-82, Clin. Preventive Dentistry, 1980—, Am. Jour. Orthodontics, 1986—; cons. editor Dental Student Jour., 1978—; So. Soc. Orthodontists, 1976—, Am. Jour. Orthodontics, 1980—; contbr. articles to profl. Jours. Bd. dirs. Chapel Hill-Carrboro United Way, 1979-82, pres., 1980-81, N.C. Meml. Hosp., 1983—; mem. Parks and Recreation Commn., Chapel Hill-Carrboro, 1980-85, vice chmn., 1983-85; bd. dirs. Triangle Univs. Ctr. for Advanced Studies, 1991—, mem. exec. com., 1994—, vice chair 1995. Capt. U.S. Army, 1965-68. Recipient Disting. Svc. award Assoc. Schs. Allied Health Professions, 1996. Fellow Internat. Coll. Dentists, Am. Coll. Dentists; mem. AAAS, APHA, ADA (cons. coun. on dental edn. 1978—, vice chmn. sect. on orthodontics and oral devel. 1978-79, chmn. 1979-80), Assn. Acad. Health Ctrs. (bd. dirs. 1992—, chair elect 1995, chair 1996), Internat. Assn. Dental Rsch., N.C. State Dental Soc., Am. Assn. Dental Schs., So. Soc. Orthodontists (edn. com.), N.C. Orthodontic Soc. (chmn. manpower evaluation 1974—), Durham-Orange Dental Soc., Am. Soc. Dentistry for Children, Internat. Assn. Dentofacial Abnormalities, Edward H. Angle Soc. Orthodontics, Charles H. Tweed Found., Assn. Am. Med. Colls., N.C. Parks and Recreation Soc., Rsch. Triangle Inst. (bd. dirs.), Order of the Golden Fleece, Delta Sigma Delta, Omicron Kappa Upsilon, Sigma Xi. Home: 722 E Franklin St Chapel Hill NC 27514-3823 Office: U NC 214 S Bldg Chapel Hill NC 27599*

HERSHEY, JODY HENRY, public health physician; b. Roanoke, Va., Nov. 1, 1956; s. Jay Henry Hershey and Maryann (Thomas) Shane. BS, Roanoke Coll., 1978; MD, Ea. Va. Med. Sch., 1982; MPH, Johns Hopkins U., 1987. Diplomate Am. Bd. Family Practice; bd. cert. pub. health and gen. preventive medicine. Pub. health officer Piedmont Health Dist. Va. Dept. Health, Farmville, 1987-89; genetics program dir. Va. Dept. Health, Richmond, 1989-90; med. dir. Va. Dept. Corrections, Dillwyn, 1990-92; adminstrv. dir., family/ambulatory care physician Carilion Healthcare Corp., Roanoke, 1992-95; pub. health dir. New River Health Dist. Va. Dept. Health, Christiansburg, 1995—; vis. cons., prof. The Second Clin. Coll., People's Hosp. Beijing Med. U., 1995—; mem. steering com. Inst. for Cmty. Health, Blacksburg, Va., 1995—, Ctrl. Highlands Appalachia Leadership Initiative on Cancer, Abingdon, Va., 1996—; bd. dirs. Western Va. Cmty. Health Svcs. Bd., Wytheville, 1995—. Contbr. articles to profl. jours. Bd. dirs. Mill Mountain Theatre, Roanoke, 1994—, New River Valley Hospice, Christiansburg, 1995—, Big Bros., Roanoke, 1995—, The New Century Coun., Roanoke, 1995—. Recipient Leadership award Luth. Brotherhood, 1993, Leadership and Scholarship award Lions Club, 1994, Outstanding Cmty. Svc. and Leadership award Kiwanis Club, 1995, Pub. Health Leadership Inst. award The Ctrs. for Disease Control and Prevention, Atlanta, 1996-97. Fellow Am. Coll. Preventive Medicine; mem. APHA (com. chmn./adv. bd. 1988—, adv. bd./steering com. 1996—), Am. Acad. Family Physicians, Va. Acad. Family Physicians, Med. Soc. Va. (com. chmn. 1995—), Va. Acad. Preventive Medicine and Pub. Health (adv. bd.). Avocations: triathlete, gentleman farmer. Office: New River Health Dist 210 Pepper St S Ste A Christiansburg VA 24073-3522

HERSHEY, LINDA ANN, neurology and pharmacology educator; b. Marion, Ind., Jan. 15, 1947; d. Matthew John and Janice Elaine Kwolek; m. Charles Owen Hershey, May 1, 1976; children: Edward, William, Erin. BS, Purdue U., 1968; PhD, Washington U., St. Louis, 1973, MD, 1975. Diplomate Am. Bd. Psychiatry and Neurology. Resident in neurology Barnes Hosp., St. Louis, 1976-78; fellow in clin. pharmacology Strong Meml. Hosp., Rochester, N.Y., 1978-80; asst. prof. neurology Case Western Res. U., Cleve., 1980-86; assoc. prof.neurology and pharmacology SUNY, Buffalo, 1986-94, prof. neurology and pharmacology, 1994—; chief neurology svc. Buffalo VA Med. Ctr., 1986—; mem. neurology adv. group VA, Washington, 1994—; sr. examiner ABPN, 1997—. Co-author: Handbook of Dementing Illnesses, 1994, Essentials of Pharmacology, 1995, Practice of Geriatrics, 1998, Hypertension Primer, 1999; mem. editl. bd. Clin. Pharmacology and Therapeutics, 1993—, Stroke, 1995—. Co-dir. Alzheimers Disease Assistance Ctr., Buffalo, 1994-98; elder Univ. Presbyn. Ch., Buffalo, 1995-99. Grantee Sterling-Winthrop Co., 1992-96, Lorex Pharms., 1995-96, Parke-Davis, 1990-92, 96-98, Nat. Inst. Neurol. and Communicative Disorders and Stroke, 1994-98, Bayer Pharms., 1998-99, Ortho-McNeil Pharms., 1999—, VISN-2, 1999—. Fellow Am. Acad. Neurology, Am. Neurol. Assn.; mem. Am. Soc. Clin. Pharmacology and Therapeutics, Am. Heart Assn. (mem. exec. com. stroke coun. 1993-97, chmn. program com. stroke coun. 1993-97). Achievements include evaluating use of MRI in patients with vascular dementia, describing natural history of vascular and mixed dementia, validating cognitive and functional screening instruments in patients with vascular dementia, reviewing stroke types and prevention strategies in women, comparing various presenile dementias and assessing the role of hypertension in the development of dementia and developing practice guidelines for treatment of Alzheimer's disease. E-mail: hershey.linda@buffalo.va.gov. Office: VA WNH Healthcare Sys 3495 Bailey Ave Buffalo NY 14215-1129

HERSHEY, NATHAN, lawyer, educator; b. N.Y.C., Apr. 28, 1930; s. Harry and Hannah (Horwitz) H.; m. Carol Fine, July 13, 1958; children—Suzanne, Madeleine. A.B., N.Y. U., 1950; LL.B., Harvard U., 1953. Bar: D.C. 1953, Pa. 1977. Individual practice law N.Y.C., 1955-56; research assoc. in health law U. Pitts., 1956-58, asst. prof., 1958-63, assoc. prof., 1963-68, prof., 1968—; mem. Pa. Bd. Med. Edn., 1974-80; of counsel Markel, Schafer, and Goldman P.C., Pitts., 1977—, Post & Schell, Phila., 1984-94; cons. Pa. State Com. on Public Health and Welfare, 1973-80. Author: (with others) Hospital Law Manual, 1959, (with Robert D. Miller) Human Experimentation and the Law, 1976, Hospital-Physician Relations, 1982; editor: Hosp. Law Newsletter; contbr. articles to profl. jours. Bd. dirs. Women's Health Services, 1976-91, bd. v.p., 1982-91; Bd. dirs. Hill House Assn., Pitts., 1964-71. Served with U.S. Army, 1953-55. Mem. Inst. Medicine-NAS, Am. Soc. Hosp. Attys. (past pres.), Soc. Hosp. Attys. Western Pa. (dir. 1974-85, past pres.), Am. Pub. Health Assn. Democrat. Jewish. Home: 5423 Northumberland St Pittsburgh PA 15217-1128 Office: 1120 Grant Bldg Pittsburgh PA 15219

HERSHEY, ROBERT LEWIS, mechanical engineer, management consultant; b. Chgo., Dec. 18, 1941; s. Maurice and Rose Beverly (Barrish) H. BSME summa cum laude, Tufts U., 1963; MSME, MIT, 1964; PhD in Engring., Cath. U. Am., 1973. Registered profl. engr., D.C., N.Y.; cert. mfg. engr. Engr. Bell Telephone Labs., Whippany, N.J., 1963-67; acoustics mgr. Weston Instruments, Inc., Poughkeepsie, N.Y., 1967-68; sr. scientist Bolt Beranek & Newman, Washington, 1968-71; acoustics program mgr. Booz Allen & Hamilton, Bethesda, Md., 1971-79; program v.p. Sci. Mgmt. Corp., Washington, 1979-80, divsn. v.p., 1980-88; exec. engr. O'Donnell Cons. Engrs., Inc., Washington, 1988—; sec. Engring. Registration Bd., D.C., 1987—, D.C. Profl. Coun., Washington, 1974; mem. coordinating com. on productivity Am. Assn. Engring. Socs., Washington, 1984-88. Author: How to Think With Numbers, 1982. Sci. policy analyst George Bush Presdl. Campaign, Washington, 1988, 92, Bob Dole Presdl. Campaign, Washington, 1996; pres. Hamilton House Assn. Resident Tenants, Washington, 1987-88, 90—; mem. Joint Bd. on Sci. Engring. Edn., Washington, 1972-78. Recipient Design award Machinery Mag., 1963. Fellow ASME (chmn. Washington chpt. 1978-79); mem. AAAS, D.C. Sci. Writers Assn., Nat. Energy Resources Orgn., Mensa, Capital PC User Group, Acoustical Soc. Am. (chmn. Washington chpt. 1982-83), D.C. Soc. Profl. Engrs. (pres. 1975-76, nat. dir. 1980-86, Young Engr. of Yr. 1974), D.C. Coun. Engring. and Archtl. Socs. (del. 1969—, pres. 1978-79, Pres.'s award 1989, Nat. Capital award 1974), Soc. Mfg. Engrs. (chmn. Washington Robotics Internat. chpt. 1986-87), Washington Coal Club, MIT Club of Washington (pres. 1979-80), Washington Tufts U. Alumni Club (v.p. 1970-71), Tau Beta Pi (pres. Tufts student chpt. 1962-63, v.p. Washington alumni chpt. 1988-89), Sigma Xi. Republican. Avocations: chess, tennis, sports cars, golf. Home: Apt 1033 1255 New Hampshire Ave NW Washington DC 20036-2328

HERSHISER, OREL LEONARD, IV, professional baseball player; b. Buffalo, Sept. 16, 1958; s. Orel Leonard H. III and Millie H.; m. Jaimie (Byars) Hershiser, Feb. 7, 1981; 2 sons, Orel Leonard V, Jordan Douglass. Student, Bowling Green State U. Pitcher minor league teams Clinton, Ia., 1979, San Antonio, 1980-81, Albuquerque, 1982-83; with Los Angeles Dodgers, 1983-94, Cleve. Indians, 1995-97; pitcher San Francisco Giants, 1997-98, New York Mets, 98-; mem. Nat. League All-Star Team, 1987, 88. Named Nat. League Cy Young award winner, 1988, Most Valuable Player 1988 World Series. NL Gold Glove, 1988, Major League Player of Yr. Sporting News, 1988, Nat. League Pitcher of Yr. Sporting News, 1988, Sporting News Nat. League All-Star Team, 1988, Sporting News Silver Slugger Team, 1993, All-Star Games, 1987-89. Player World Series, 1988. Office: New York Mets 123-10 Roosevelt Ave Flushing NY 11368

HERSHMAN, JACK IRA, urologist; b. Bklyn., Oct. 7, 1955; s. Seymour and Sonia Elaine (Kamins) H.; m. Ingrid Gail Bernstein, Aug. 25, 1986; children: Melissa Paige, Jennifer Whitney, Neil Ross. BA in Biology magna cum laude, U. Rochester, 1977; MD, Mt. Sinai Sch. Medicine, 1981. Diplomate Am. Bd. Urology. Resident in surgery Lenox Hill Hosp., N.Y.C., 1981-82; resident in urology Montefiore Med. Ctr., Bronx, N.Y., 1983-86; chief urology Phelps Meml. Hosp., North Tarrytown, N.Y., 1986—; attending urologist Dobbs Ferry (N.Y.) Hosp., 1986—, Westchester County Med. Ctr., Valhalle, N.Y., 1986—, No. Westchester Hosp., Mt. Kisco, N.Y., 1998—; clin. instr. urology N.Y. Hosp., N.Y.C., 1987—; chief section urology Phelps Meml. Hosp., North Tarrytown, 1990—. Fellow Am. Coll. Surgeons; mem. Am. Urologic Soc., N.Y.S. Urologic Soc., N.Y. State Med. Soc., Westchester County Med. Soc., Phi Beta Kappa. Office: 777 N Broadway Ste 309 Sleepy Hollow NY 10591-1040

HERSHMAN, JEROME MARSHALL, endocrinologist; b. Chgo., July 20, 1932; s. Maurice and Gertrude (Zemel) H.; m. Fleurette Kram, Dec. 22, 1957; children: Daniel, Michael, Jeffrey. BS, Northwestern U., 1952; MS, Calif. Inst. Technology, 1953; MD, U. Ill., 1957. Diplomate Am. Bd. Internal Medicine, Endocrinology & Metabolism. Fellow in endocrinology New England Ctr. Hosp., Boston, 1961-63; clin. investigator Northwestern U. Med. Sch., Chgo., 1964-67; chief clin. nuclear medicine Birmingham (Ala.) VA Hosp., 1967-71, chief endocrine sect., 1971-72; prof. Sch. Medicine U. Ala., Birmingham, 1967-72, UCLA, 1972—; chief endocrinology and metabolism West L.A. VA Med. Ctr., 1972—. Editor: Thyroid, 1991—; mem. editorial bd. Am. Jour. of Medicine 1989-95; editor: Practical Endocrinology, 1981, Endocrine Pathophysiology, 2d edit., 1982, 3d edit., 1988, Syllabus of 38th Annual Postgraduate Assembly of the Endocrine Soc., 1986. Capt. USAF, 1959-61. col. USAR, 1985-91. Mem. Am. Thyroid Assn. (dir. 1989-92, pres. 1992-93). Jewish. Achievements include demonstration of thyrotropin-releasing hormone for diagnosis of pituitary and thyroid disease in 1969; discovered thyroid-stimulating activity of human chorionic gonadotropin. Home: 15970 Meadowcrest Rd Sherman Oaks CA 91403-4714 Office: West LA VA Med Ctr 11301 Wilshire Blvd Los Angeles CA 90073-1003

HERSHMAN, JUDITH, advertising executive; b. Boston, Sept. 16, 1949; d. Max and Mollie (Cohen) H. BFA, Boston U., 1971. Pres., owner Hershman Advt. & Design, Foxboro, Mass., 1979—. Executed mural Kenmore Subway Sta., Boston, 1970. Adv. com. Tri-County Vocational Tech. High Sch. Avocations: sewing, volleyball, softball, crewel embroidery, refinishing furniture. Home and Office: 41 Mechanic St Foxboro MA 02035-2027

HERSHMAN, LYNN LESTER, artist; b. Cleve.; 1 dau., Dawn. B.S., Case-Western Res. U., 1963; M.A., San Francisco State U., 1972. Prof. U. Calif., Davis, 1984—; Vis. prof. art U. Calif., Berkeley, Calif. Coll. Arts and Crafts, San Jose State U., 1974-78; assoc. project dir. Christo's Running Fence, 1973-76; founder, dir. Floating Mus., 1975-79; ind. film/video producer and cons., 1979—. Author works in field; one-man shows include Santa Barbara Mus. Art, 1970, Univ. Art Mus., Berkeley, Calif., 1972, Mills Coll., Oakland, Calif., 1973, William Sawyer Gallery, 1974, Nat. Galleries, Melbourne, Australia, 1976, Mandeville Art Gallery, U. Calif., San Diego, 1976, M.H. de Young Art Mus., 1978, Pallazo dei Diamonte, Ferrara, Italy, 1978, San Francisco Art Acad., 1980, Portland Center Visual Arts, 1980, New Mus., New Sch., N.Y.C., 1981, Inst. Contemporary Art, Phila., 1981, Anina Nosai Gallery, N.Y.C., 1981, Contemporary Art Center, Cin., 1982, Toronto, Los Angeles Contemporary Exhibits, 1986, Univ. Art Mus. Berkeley, 1987, Madison (Wis.) Art Ctr., 1987, Intersesction for the Arts, San Francisco, Pacific Film Archive, A. Space, "Guerilla Tactics" Toronto, Can., Venice Bienalle Global Village; group exhbns. include Cleve. Art Mus., 1968, St. Paul Art Ctr., 1969, Richmond (Calif.) Art Ctr., 1970, 73, Galeria del Sol, Santa Barbara, Calif., 1971, San Francisco Art Inst., 1972, Richard Demarco Art Gallery, Edinburgh, Scotland, 1973, Laguna Beach (Calif.) Art Mus., 1973, Univ. Art Mus., Univ. Calif., Berkeley, 1974, Bronx (N.Y.) Mus., 1975, Linda Ferris Gallery, Seattle, 1975, Madenville Art Gallery, San Diego, Contemporary Arts Mus., Houston, 1977, New Orleans, 1977, Ga. Mus. Art, Athens, 1977, New Mus., N.Y., 1981, Calif. Coll. Arts and Crafts, 1981, San Francisco Mus. Modern Art, 1979, 80, 90, Art-Beaubourg, Paris, 1980, Ars Electronica, 1989, Am. Film Inst., 1989, Mus. Moving Image Internat. Ctr. for Photography, 1989, Kitchen Ctr. for Video-Music, N.Y., 1990, Robert Koch Gallery, San Francsico, 1990, Inst. Contemporary Art, London, 1990, Frankfurt (Germany) Art Fair, 1990, Inst. Conteporary Art, Boston, 1991, Oakland (Calif.) Mus., 1991, La Cite des Arts et des Nouvelles Technologies, Montreal, 1991, Richard F. Brush Art Gallery, Canton, N.Y., 1992, Jack Tilton Gallery, N.Y., 1992, Southeastern Ctr. for Contemporary Art, Winston-Salem, N.C., 1992, Bonner Kunstverein, Bonn, Germany, 1992, Chgo. Ave. Armory, 1992, Retrospective, Tribute, 1994, Nelson Gallery, Paris, 1994, Hess Collection, 1994. Bd. dirs. San Francisco Art Acad., Spectrum Found., Motion a Performance Collective. Western States Regional fellow (film/video), 1990; grantee Nat. Endowment for the Arts, (2) Art Matters Inc., San Francisco Found., N.Y. State Coun. for the Arts, Zellerbach Family Fund, Inter Arts of Marin, Gerbode Found., The Women's Project; recipient Dirs. Choice award San Francisco Internat. Film Festival, 1987, tribute 1987 Mill Valley Video Festial, Exptl. Video award 1988, 1st prize Montbelliard, France, 1990, 2d prize, Vigo, Spain, 1992, 1993 Ars Electronica, Austria, WRO Poland, Nat. Film Theatre, London, Gerber award Seattle Art Mus., 1994, ZKM/Siemans award, 1995. Mem. Assn. Art Pubs. (dir., Annie Gerber award 1995). Office: 1201 California N San Francisco CA 94123-3503*

HERSHMAN, SCOTT EDWARD, lawyer; b. N.Y.C., Mar. 31, 1958; s. Harold Martin and Barbara (Goldberg) H. BA, Am. U., 1980; JD, Yeshiva U., 1983. Bar: N.Y. 1984, U.S. Dist. Ct. (so. and ea. dists.) N.Y. 1986, U.S. Supreme Ct. 1994. Asst. dist. atty. N.Y. County Dist. Atty.'s Office, N.Y.C., 1983-86; ptnr. Graubard, Mollen & Miller, N.Y.C., 1986—. Mem. ABA, N.Y. State Bar Assn., Assn. Bar City of N.Y. Office: Graubard Mollen & Miller 600 3rd Ave New York NY 10016-1901

HERSHNER, ROBERT FRANKLIN, JR., judge; b. Sumter, S.C., Jan. 21, 1944; s. Robert Franklin and Druie (Goodman) H.; m Sally Sinclair, May 19, 1990; children: Bryan, Andrew. AB, Mercer U., 1966, JD, 1969. Bar: Ga. 1971, U.S. Dist. Ct. (mid. dist.) Ga. 1971, U.S. Dist. Ct. (so. dist.) Ga. 1979, U.S. Ct. Appeals (11th cir.) 1981, U.S. Supreme Ct. 1978. Atty. Ga. Legal Services Corp., Macon, 1972; assoc. Adams, O'Neal, Hemingway & Kaplan, Macon, Ga., 1972-76; ptnr. Kaplan & Hershner, P.A., Macon, 1976-80; judge U.S. Bankruptcy Ct. for Middle Dist. Ga., Macon, 1980—, chief bankruptcy judge, 1986—; chair Fed. Jud. Ctr. Com. on Bankruptcy Edn., 1994—, active, 1990—. V.p. Macon Heritage Found., 1977-78; pres. student body Mercer U., 1965-66, interfraternity coun., 1964-65. Capt. U.S. Army, 1970-75. Mem. Ga. Bar Assn., Macon Bar Assn., Nat. Conf. Bankruptcy Judges (gov., v.p. 1996-97, pres. 1997-98), Blue Key Honor Soc., Phi Eta Sigma. Methodist. Contbr. Georgia Lawyers Basic Practice Handbook, 2d edit., Post-Judgment Procedures, 1979; cons. Norton Bankruptcy Law and Practice. Office: US Bankruptcy Ct PO Box 86 Macon GA 31202-0086

HERSI, DOROTHY TALBERT, education educator; b. Pine Bluff, Ark., Nov. 13, 1953; d. Ernest and Dorothy Georgie (Burkett) Talbert; m. Hersi M. Hersi, May 29, 1977; 1 child, Sidin. BA cum laude, Howard U., 1975, MEd, 1976, postgrad., 1983-84, PhD, 1991. Counselor Alexandria (Va.) City Schs.; tchr. English, Charles County Pub. Schs., La Plata, Md.; instr. Upward Bound, Howard U., Washington, instr. devel. skills; adj. asst. prof., coord./dept. chair Ctr. for Academic Reinforcement Howard U., 1991-94; assoc. prof., asst. v.p. Student and Acadademic Support Svcs. Del. State U., Dover, Del., 1997—; presenter Coll. Bd. Forum, 1984. Author: How To Develop a Better Memory: The ICARE System of Memorization. Mem. APGA, ACPA, Internat. Reading Assn. (past mem. U.S. legis. com.), D.C. Reading Coun. (past bd. dirs.), Phi Delta Kappa, Kappa Delta Pi (past sec.). Home: 35 Deer Cir Bear DE 19701-2718

HERSKOVITZ, S(AM) MARC, lawyer; b. Munich, Jan. 1, 1949; came to U.S., 1949; s. Max and Bella Herskovitz; 1 child from previous marriage, David Michael; m. Barbara Hobbs, Nov. 28, 1990; 1 child, Daniel Max. BA, Pa. State U., 1970; MS in Edn. with high honors, So. Ill. U., 1974; JD with honors, Fla. State U., 1987. Bar: Fla. 1987, U.S. Dist. Ct. (mid. dist.) Fla. 1988, U.S. Ct. Appeals (11th cir) 1988. Agy. mgr. Sun Personnel Svcs., Inc., Sarasota, Fla., 1978-80; claims adjuster Allstate Inc. Co., Lake Worth, Fla., 1980-84; sr. litigation atty. Fla. Dept. Ins., Tallahassee, 1987—. Mem. ABA, Assn. Trial Lawyers Am., Phi Kappa Phi. Democrat. Jewish. Avocations: volleyball, softball, reading, photography. Home: 707 Lothian Dr Tallahassee FL 32312-2858 Office: Fla Dept Ins 612 Larson Bldg Tallahassee FL 32399-0333

HERSKOWITZ, IRA, educator, molecular geneticist; b. Bklyn., July 14, 1946. BS in Biology, Calif. Inst. Tech., 1967; PhD in Microbiology, MIT, 1971; PhD (hon.), St. Louis U., 1997. From asst. to full prof. biology U. Oreg., Eugene, 1972-81; assoc. Inst. Molecular Biology, U. Oreg., Eugene, 1972-81; prof. dept. biochemistry and biophysics U. San Francisco, 1981—, chmn. dept., 1990-95, head divsn. genetics, 1981—, co-dir. program in human genetics, 1997—; mem. genetics study sect. NIH, Bethesda, Md., 1986-90; mem. sci. rev. bd. in genetics Howard Hughes Med. Inst., Bethesda, 1986-94, mem. med. adv. bd., 1995-97; vis. prof. Coll. de France, Paris, 1992; sci. adv. bd. Tularik, Inc., 1992-96; mem. awards jury Albert Lasker Med. Rsch., 1994—; mem. sci. adv. com. Inst. Cancer Rsch., Fox Chase Cancer Ctr., 1995—; bd. sci. counsellors Nat. Cancer Inst., 1996—; advisor Merck Genome Rsch. Inst., 1996—. Assoc. editor Virology, 1976-81, Genetics, 1982-87, Ann. Rev. Genetics, 1984-89; editor Jour. Molecular Biology, 1982-86, assoc. editor 1986-87; mem. editl. bd. Molecular and Cellular Biology of the Cell, 1989—, Trends in Genetics, 1990—; mem. bd. reviewing editors Sci., 1991-96. Mem. vis. com. for dept. biology MIT, 1982—. Recipient Eli Lilly award Am. Soc. Microbiology, 1983, Disting. Tchg. award U. Calif., San Francisco, 1984, medal Genetics Soc. Am., 1988, Howard Taylor Ricketts award, U. Chgo., 1992, Disting. Alumni award Calif. Inst. Tech., 1994; named Streisinger lectr. U. Oreg., 1984, Harvey Soc. lectr., 1986, Mendel lectr. Genetical Soc. Gt. Britain, 1991, Bateson lectr. John Innes Inst., Norwich, UK. Fellow AAAS, MacArthur Found., Am. Acad. Arts and Scis., Am. Soc. Microbiology; mem. Nat. Acad. Scis. (sci. reviewing award 1985), Genetics Soc. Am. (pres. 1985). Rsch. in control of gene expression in yeast, pathogen-host interactions, cell signalling and growth control, cell morphogenesis. Office: U Calif San Francisco Dept of Biochem & Biophys 513 Parnassus Ave San Francisco CA 94143-0448*

HERSLEY, DENNIS CHARLES, environmentalist, software systems consultant; b. Idaho Falls, Idaho, July 11, 1947; s. Cyril R. and Bardella (Webb) H.; m. Jane Anne Lilly, Jan. 16, 1993; children: Cary Connolly, Laura Lilly, Claire Lilly. Student, U. So. Calif., 1964-65; electronics tech. cert., Idaho State U., 1970; postgrad., U. Santa Clara, 1979. Cert. FCC 1st class radio engr. with TV and radar endorsements.;. Ptnr. Intensive Care Tech. Svcs., Pocatello, Idaho, 1972-74; test engring. mgr. Nat. Semiconductor, Sunnyvale, Calif., 1975-76; test ops. mgr. Amdahl Ireland, Ltd., Dublin, 1978; engr., planner, analyst Amdahl Corp., Sunnyvale, 1979-85; CFO, chmn. Provista Software Internat., San Jose, Calif., 1985-86; pres. Almaden Consulting, Santa Cruz, Calif., 1985—; co-founder, pres., dir. non profit sci. rsch. Citizens United for Responsible Environmentalism, Inc., Santa Cruz, Calif., 1994—; CFO Rsch. Consultation, Inc., Santa Cruz, Calif., 1998—; planner, sponsor Fusewest Regional Tech. Conf., Scottsdale, Ariz., 1988-89; tech. curriculum advisor Idaho State U., 1970-75; participant 3d Internat. Conf. on bioaerosols, Fungi and Mycotoxins, 1998. Inventor calculator design, 1975; featured on BBC documentary, 1998. Recipient Outstanding Alumnus award Idaho State U., 1975, Honored Donor award Monterey Bay Aquarium, 1996. Mem. Calif. Assn. Non-Profits, No. Calif. Focus Users Group (asst. editor 1988-90), Santa Cruz Tech. Alliance. Office: CURE 2375 Benson Ave Santa Cruz CA 95065-1674

HERSON, ARLENE RITA, producer, journalist, television program host; b. N.Y.C.; d. Sam and Mollie (Friedman) Hornreich; m. Milton Herson, June 16, 1963; children: Michael, Karen. Student, Queens Coll., 1957, New Sch. for Social Rsch., N.Y.C., 1960. Exec. sec. Tex McCrary, Inc., N.Y.C., 1958-60; asst. to William L. Safire Safire Pub. Rels., N.Y.C., 1960-62; columnist The Advisor, Inc., Middletown, N.J., 1974-78; prodr., host The Arlene Herson Show, N.Y.C., 1978—; syndicated nationally on Tempo TV, 1988, Channel Am., 1989-93; spokesperson Storer Cable TV, Monmouth County, 1989-91, Nutri/Systems, Monmouth and Ocean Counties, 1989-90; news anchor Nostalgia Cable TV Network at Rep. Nat. Conv., 1993; cons., talent coord. Super Annuities, 1993-94; moderator debate on capital punishment, 1998; guest lectr. Polo Plus Lecutre Series, 1997; moderator panel on assisted suicide, 1999. Contbg. writer The Washington/Hampton Connection Dan's Papers, 1993—, The Hill Newspaper, 1994-98; columnist, Boomer Times and Senior Life, 1999—; exec. producer The Magic Flute, conductor Victor Borge, DAR Constitution Hall, Washington, 1995, 1776, 1997; exec. producer, casting dir. (musical) 1776, DAR Constitution Hall, Washington, 1996, encore prodn., 1998; prodr. 1776 (featuring current mems. of Congress), 1998; interviewer Steven Spielberg's Shoah Found., 1997—; celebrity interviewer, panelist Am. Sr. Side, Nat. Pub. Radio, 1999; co-host radio program Changing Times, 1999. Bd. dirs. women's activities campaign for Sen. Jacob J. Javits, N.Y.C., 1968, Monmouth (N.J.) Mus., 1982-86, Will Rogers Inst., 1992—, Washington Symphony Orch., 1994-98, v.p., 1994; mem. 92d St. Y Benefit com., Variety-The Children's Charity; mem. Women's Project and Prodns., 1992; com. mem. Children's Psychiat. Ctr., 1971-90, Monmouth Park Charity Fund, 1980-90; mem. corp. exec. bd. Family and Childrens' Svcs., 1985-90, Ctrl. Park Conservancy, Women of Washington, also mentor program Women's Econ. Devel. Coun.; life mem. N.Y. chpt. Brandeis U. Libr. Fund; mem. dir.'s resource coun. Nat. Women's Econ. Alliance; mem. social com. Westbridge Condominium; fin. chmn. Mike Herson for Congress, 1994, fin. com. March of Dimes, 1995; mem. profl. women's coun. Nat. Mus. of Women in the Arts, 1994; com. mem. Vincent T. Lombardi Cancer Rsch. Ctr., 1994-98, Parkinson's Action Network, 1996; publicity chmn. exhbn. for Israel Tennis Ctrs. Excalibur Soc. of Lyn U., 1996—; mem. adv. coun. to co-chmn. Rep. Nat. Com., 1997—; mem. Power of Women Effecting Renewal, 1997; mem. 2d decade coun. Am. Film Inst., 1998; bd. dirs. A Healing Among Nations, 1999; mem. Soc. of 100, Fla. Philharm. Orch., 1999. Recipient CAPE award for best talk show on Cable TV Network, 1984-93, Woman of Achievement in Comm. award Adv. Commn. on Status of Women, 1986, Pub. and Leased Access (PAL) award for best talk show Paragon Cable TV, N.Y.C., 1988, spl. resolution N.J. Assembly, 1988, Willie award for outstanding svc. Will Rogers Inst., 1992; named Disting. Alumni mem. Waldorf Astoria, 1998; nominee Cable ACE award for best talk show series nationwide. Mem. NAFE, NATAS, Nat. Acad. Cable Programming, Nat. Assn. Profl. Women, Women in Commn., Women in Cable, Women in Film and Video, Am. Women in Radio and TV, Power Women Effecting Renewal, Internat. Radio and TV Soc., Internat. Newswoman's Assn., Nat. Press Club, Friends for Life, Friars Club, Bethesda Country Club, Lotos Club, East River Tennis Club, Excalibur Soc. of Lynn U., Seagate Beach Club. Avocations: tennis, swimming, reading. E-mail: aherson123@aol.com. Fax #: (561) 998-4776.

HERSPRING, DALE R., political science educator, consultant; b. Oakland, Calif., Sept. 28, 1940; s. Frank E. and Ruby F. Herspring; m. Maureen C. Phillip, June 11, 1965; children: Larissa, Kurt, Kyle. AB, Stanford U., 1965; MA, Georgetown U., 1967; PhD, U. So. Calif., 1972. Fgn. svc. officr Dept. State, Washington, 1971-91; ret., 1991; prof. Nat. War Coll., Washington, 1991-93; prof. polit. sci., head dept. Kans. State U., Manhattan, 1993—; weekly contbr. Manhattan Mercury, 1993-97. Author 7 books; mem. editl. bd. Communist and Post Communist Studies, 1995—; contbr. over 50 articles to profl. jours. Capt. USNR, 1967-69. Fulbright fellow. Republican. Roman Catholic. Home: 3912 Barbara Ln Manhattan KS 66503 Office: Kans State U Dept Polit Sci Waters Hall Manhattan KS 66506

HERSTAND, THEODORE, theatre artist, educator; b. N.Y.C., May 14, 1930; s. Max Arthur and Rose (Shyatt) H.; m. Jo Ellen Gillette, Aug. 23, 1957; children: Sarah Ellen, Michael Simpson. Cert. Advanced Studies, U. Birmingham (Eng.), 1951; BA, U. Iowa, 1953, MA, 1957; PhD, U. Ill., 1963. Instr. theatre Parsons Coll., Fairfield, Iowa, 1953-54, Eastern Ill. U., Charleston, 1957-59; asst. prof. SUNY, Plattsburgh, 1960-64, asso. prof., 1963-64; asst. prof. U. Ill., 1964-66; asso. prof. U. Minn., Mpls., 1966-70; prof., chmn. dept. theatre, drama and dance Case Western Res. U., Cleve., 1970-77; chmn. faculty senate Case Western Res. U., 1975-76; dir. Sch. Drama, U. Okla., Norman, 1977-79, prof., 1979-92; prof. emeritus U. Okla., Norman, 1992—; artistic dir., actor Okla. Profl. Theatre, 1978; vis. prof. Mpls. Coll. Art and Design, 1969; vis. dir. Colo. Shakespeare Festival, Boulder, 1968, 82; theatre bldg. cons. Eastern Ill. U., Charleston, Ill. State U., Bloomington, Jewish Community Center Theater, Mpls.; ednl. cons. in arts; spl. contbr. Silver Burdett Music Series. Profl. actor, dir. over 70 plays; author: (plays) Sugar and Lemon, 1968; new version Oedipus, 1978, Dov, 1982, The Emigration of Adam Kurtzik, 1985, 89, It Should Be So, 1989, The Minor Matter of Cynthia Smith, 1990, Bittersweet, 1996, others; assoc. editor: Drama Survey, 1967-70; contbr. revs., articles to profl. jours.; founder Klein Nat. Playwriting award, 1974, Bliss Nat. Playwriting award, 1980. Bd. dirs. Theater-in-the=Round, Mpls., 1968, v.p., 1969; bd. dirs. Gt. Lakes Shakespeare Festival, 1970-71, Okla. Arts Inst., mem. theatre panel, 1991—, chair 1994—; chmn. bd. dirs. Okla. Hillel Found., 1981-82; trustee Karamu House, 1975-77, Temple B'nai Israel, Oklahoma City, 1989-92, 1999—; chmn. new plays program S.W. Theatre Assn., 1985-89; mem. Coun. of Jewish Theatres, 1993—. Mem. Nat. Theatre Conf., Dramatists Guild, Omicron Delta Kappa. Home: 4418 Manchester Ct Norman OK 73072-3915 Office: Flora Roberts Inc 157 W 57th St New York NY 10019-2210

HERSTEIN, CARL WILLIAM, lawyer; b. Plainfield, N.J., Jan. 8, 1953; s. Robert L. and Marie (Burke) H.; m. Charlene Ruth Mosher, Aug. 16, 1975; children: Janette, Matthew, Diana, Jennifer. BA in Polit. Sci. with high distinction, highest honors, U. Mich., 1973; JD, Yale U., 1976. Bar: Mich. 1976. Congl. intern to Congressman Clarence Long Washington, 1972; acting divsnl. paymaster Parts Divsn. GM, Flint, Mich., 1973; law clk. Benton Hicks Beltz Behm & Nikola, Flint, 1974; ptnr. Honigman Miller Schwartz and Cohn, Detroit, 1976—; mem. fin. instns. adv. bd. U. Detroit-Mercy, 1985-95. Editor Yale Law Jour., 1975-76. Chair Cath. Social Svcs. of Washtenaw County, 1992-93, treas., 1990-92, trustee, 1985-90; trustee John and Marnee Devine Found., 1992-97; active Detroit Zool. Soc., Ann Arbor Hands-on Mus., Nat. Trust for Hist. Preservation, Detroit Art Inst., Mich. Hist. Soc.; bd. dirs. St. Francis Parish, Ann Arbor, 1985-91, mem. edn. commn., edn. commn. rep, 1990-91. Recipient William Jennings Bryan prize, 1973; James B. Angell scholar, 1973. Mem. ABA (real property and trust law sect.), State Bar Mich., Cath. Lawyers Guild, U. Mich. Pres. Club, U. Mich. Victors Club, U. Mich. Alumni Assn., Yale U. Alumni Assn., KC, Otsego Ski Club, Ann Arbor Golf & Outing Country Club, Huron Valley Swim Club, Phi Beta Kappa. Republican. Roman Catholic. Avocations: reading, snow skiing, golf, travel, drawing. Office: Honigman Miller Schwartz & Cohn 2290 1st National Bldg Detroit MI 48226

HERSTEIN, HOWARD JOSEPH, author; b. Regent, N.D., Sept. 20, 1927; s. Oliver Daniel and Mantie Esther (Bratcher) H. Student, Mankato (Minn.) Comml. Sch., 1946-47, MacPhail Sch. Drama, Mpls., 1947-49. Supply supr. U.S. Army, Mpls., 1959-63, Grand forks, N.D., 1963-71; supply mail supr. Traveler's Ins., Des Moines, 1971-87. Author: (radio plays) Rejection Slip Theatre "WHO", 1995-96, Iowa Radio Project WOI, 1993-94, (quizes) Sky-Delta Airlines Mag., 1987-89. With USN, 1945-46. Mem. Des Moines Area Writers Network (newsletter staff 1986—), Iowa Scriptwriters Alliance, Rosicrucian Order.

HERTA, BRYAN, race car driver; b. Warren, Mich., May 23, 1970; s. Toma and Nina Herta; m. Janette Herta; 1 child, Calysta. Student, U. Calif., Irvine, Ohio State U. Driver Chip Ganassi Racing, 1995-98; pilot Shell Ford-Cosworth/Reynard Championship car Team Rahal, Indpls, 1998—; with A.J. Foyt Ent., Indpls. Captured Indy Lights title, 1993; winner Barber-Saab Pro Series championship, 1991, 1989 Skip Barber Formula Ford Series title, 1987 World Karting Assn. championship; recipient Am.'s Choice award as one of N.Am.'s top young drivers, 1992, scored first career pole position, 1995, awarded Most Important Driver, by fellow drivers, 1996. Achievements include earning CART victory from the pole Grand Prix of Monterey at Laguna Seca Raceway, 1998; pole positions and podium finishes Long Beach, Portland; finished 8th in championship standings with career-best 97 PPG Cup points. Office: c/o Team Rahal 4601 Lyman Dr Hillard OH 43026*

HERTENSTEIN, MYRNA LYNN, publishing executive; b. Detroit, July 19, 1937; d. Bernard Franklin and Alice Agnes (Stewart) Aller; m. George Ronald Hertenstein, June 21, 1958 (div. July 1979); children: Dale Ronald, Robert Mark. AS in Bus., Wayne State U., 1957; student, Huntingdon Coll., 1980-84. Departmental sec. Sch. of Bus. Wayne State U., Detroit, 1957-59; county and vol. coord. Montgomery (Ala.) Area Coun. on Aging, 1977-80; admissions counselor Coastal Tng. Inst., Montgomery, 1981-83; rural volunteerism coord. State of Ala., Montgomery, 1983-84; account exec. Ala. Bus. Rev., Montgomery, 1984-85, Sta. WRJM-FM, Montgomery, 1985-86; asst. local sales mgr. Sta. WCOV-TV Fox Affiliate, Montgomery, 1986-90; owner, assoc. pub. TRAVELHOST of Cen. Ala., Montgomery, 1990—; mem. Dirs. of Vols. in Agys., Montgomery, 1978-82, Montgomery County Health Coun., 1979-81, Area Agy. on Aging Adv. Coun., Montgomery, 1981-83, Pres.' Coun. Montgomery, 1983, 84; asst. to instr. Dale Carnegie & Assocs., Montgomery, 1978-83. Editor (newsletter) Montgomery Area Coun. on Aging, 1978-80; dir., writer (commls.) Sta. WCOV-TV, 1986-90; writer (commls.) Sta.WRJM-FM, 1985-86. Mem. adminstrv. coun. Whitfield United Meth. Ch., Montgomery, 1977, coord. Meals-on-Wheels, 1978-86; mem. pub. rels. coun. First United Meth. Ch., Montgomery, 1992-94, mem. comms. com. 1995—, vice chmn., 1997, chmn., 1998, mem. coun. of ministries, 1998, mem. adminstrv. bd., 1998; den leader coach Boy Scouts Am., Bellevue, Nebr., 1969-71; editor Capitol Jr. Woman's Club, Montgomery, 1975-82; pres. Parents Without Ptnrs., 1983-85; bd. dirs. Arthritis Found., 1992—, vice chair, 1995, chair, 1996, mem. Ala. chpt. exec. com., 1996; dance com. Ala. Dance Theatre, 1996—; bd. dirs. Montgomery chpt. Am. Cancer Soc., 1998—. Recipient Emerging 30 award Montgomery Area C. of C., 1992, small business of yr. award, 1994, corp. vol. of yr. award Voluntary Action Ctr., Montgomery, 1992, award Montgomery Com. for Arts, 1993, Spl. Achievement award U.S. Small Bus. Administrn., 1995, Silver Medal award Montgomery Advt. Fedn. and Am. Advt. Fedn., 1996. Mem. Pub. Rels. Coun. Ala., Ala. Travel Coun., Montgomery Restaurant Assn., Montgomery Hotel/Motel Assn. (bd. dirs. 1992-94, 99—), Sales and Mktg. Execs. (editor newsletter 1995—, bd. dirs. 1998—), Montgomery Assn. Bus. Communicators, Montgomery Advt. Fedn. (bd. dirs. 1985-92, 96—, newsletter editor 1996-97), Montgomery C. of C. (vice chmn. ambs. 1992, chmn. ambs. 1993, chmn. advt. promotions and publs. 1994, hospitality devel. and mktg. task force 1995—, chmn. spl. projects com. 1996), Montgomery Civitans. Avocations: ballroom dancing, photography, ceramics. Home: 3005 Baldwin Brook Dr Montgomery AL 36116-3803 Office: Travelhost of Cen Ala PO Box 20666 Montgomery AL 36120-0666

HERTING, ROBERT LESLIE, pharmaceutical executive; b. Aurora, Ill., Jan. 26, 1929; s. Herold Edward and Marie Christine (Parr) H.; m. Claireen LaVern Molzan, June 5, 1954; 1 son, Robert Leslie. BS, U. Ill., 1950, MD, 1954; MS in Biochemistry, Ill. Inst. Tech., 1961, PhD in Biology, 1970. Diplomate Am. Bd. Internal Medicine. Intern Ill. Central Hosp., Chgo., 1954-55; from assoc. dir. clin. rsch. to divsnl. v.p. Abbott Labs., North Chicago, Ill., 1957-76; v.p. med. rsch. Schering-Plough Corp., Bloomfield, N.J., 1977-80; v.p. internat. clin. rsch. and med. affairs G.D. Searle & Co., Skokie, Ill., 1980-84, v.p. clin. rsch., 1984-94, sr. dir. R & D clin. safety, 1994-98; ret., 1998, v.p. specialized med. cons., 1998—; clin. assoc. prof. medicine U. Ill., 1957-77; mem. research adv. com. Agy. for Internat. Devel. U.S. Dept. State, 1986-92; cons. Specialized Med. Consulting, Ltd., 1998—. Mem. editorial bd.: Antimicrobial Agents and Chemotherapy, 1963-65. Served with U.S. Army, 1955-57. Fellow ACP; mem. AMA, Chgo. Soc. Internal Medicine, Am. Soc. Microbiology, Am. Soc. Clin. Pharmacology and Therapeutics, Sigma Xi. Home: 1281 N Northwest Hwy Park Ridge IL 60068-1662

HERTOG, ROGER, investment company executive. Pres., COO Sanford C. Bernstein & Co., Inc. Office: Sanford C Bernstein & Co Inc 767 5th Ave New York NY 10153-0023*

HERTWECK, ALMA LOUISE, sociology and child development educator; b. Moline, Ill., Feb. 6, 1937; d. Jacob Ray and Sylvia Ethel (Whitt) Street; m. E. Romayne Hertweck, Dec. 16, 1955; 1 child, William Scott. A.A., Mira Costa Coll., 1969; B.A. in Sociology summa cum laude, U. Calif.-San Diego, 1975, M.A., 1977, Ph.D., 1982. Cert. sociology instr., multiple subjects teaching credential grades kindergarten-12, Calif. Staff research assoc. U. Calif.-San Diego, 1978-81; instr. sociology Chapman Coll., Orange, Calif., 1982-87; instr. child devel. MiraCosta Coll., Oceanside, Calif., 1983-87, 88-89; instr. sociology U.S. Internat. U., San Diego, 1985-88 ; exec. dir., v.p. El Camino Preschools, Inc., Oceanside, 1985—. Author: Constructing the Truth and Consequences: Educators' Attributions of Perceived Failure in School, 1982; co-author: Handicapping the Handicapped, 1985. Mem. Am. Sociol.

Assn., Am. Ednl. Research Assn., Nat. Council Family Relations, Nat. Assn. Edn. Young Children, Alpha Gamma Sigma (life). Avocations: foreign travel; sailing; bicycling. Home: 2024 Oceanview Rd Oceanside CA 92056-3104 Office: El Camino Preschs Inc 2002 California St Oceanside CA 92054-5693

HERTWECK, E. ROMAYNE, psychology educator; b. Springfield, Mo., July 24, 1928; s. Garnett Perry and Nova Gladys (Chowning) H.; m. Alma Louise Street, Dec. 16, 1955; 1 child, William Scott. BA, Augustana Coll., 1962; MA, Pepperdine U., 1963; EdD, Ariz. State U., 1966; PhD, U.S. Internat. U., 1978. Cert. sch. psychologist, Calif. Night editor Rock Island (Ill.) Argus Newspaper, 1961; grad. asst. psychology dept. Pepperdine Coll., L.A., 1962; counselor VA, Ariz. State U., Tempe, 1963; assoc. dir. Conciliation Ct., Phoenix, 1964; instr. Phoenix Coll., Phoenix, 1965; prof. Mira Costa Coll., Oceanside, Calif., 1966—, mem. senate coun., 1968-70, 85-87, 89-91, chmn. psychology-counseling dept., 1973-75, chmn. dept. behavioral sci., 1976-82, 87-88, 90-91; part-time lectr. dept. bus. adminstrn. San Diego State U., 1980-84, Sch. Human Behavior U.S. Internat. U., 1984-89; prof. psychology Chapman Coll. Mem. World Campus Afloat, 1970; pres. El Camino Preschs., Inc., Oceanside, Calif., 1985—; CEO Nutri-Cal, Inc., Oceanside, Calif., 1996—. Bd. dirs. Lifeline, 1969, Christian Counseling Center, Oceanside, 1970-82; mem. City of Oceanside Childcare Task Force, 1991—; mem. City of Oceanside Community Rels. Commn., 1991-96, vice chair, 1994; mem. steering com. Healthy Cities Project City of Oceanside, Calif., 1993-95. Mem. Am., Western, North San Diego County (v.p. 1974-75) psychol. assns., Am. Assn. for Counseling and Devel., Nat. Educators Fellowship (v.p. El Camino chpt. 1976-77), Am. Coll. Personnel Assn., Phi Delta Kappa, Kappa Delta Pi, Psi Chi, Kiwanis (charter mem. Carlsbad club, dir. 1975-77). Home: 2024 Oceanview Rd Oceanside CA 92056-3104 Office: Mira Costa Coll PO Box 586312 Oceanside CA 92058-6312 also: El Camino Preschs Inc 2002 California St Oceanside CA 92054-5673

HERTWECK, GALEN FREDRIC, minister; b. St. Louis, May 31, 1946; s. Vernon L. and Erma G. (Giger) H.; m. Bronte L. McGuire, July 8, 1967; children: John L., Jill R. AA, Mesa (Ariz.) Community Coll., 1967; BA, So. Calif. Coll., 1968; MDiv, Fuller Theol. Sem., Pasadena, Calif., 1972; D of Ministry, Fuller Theol. Sem., 1977. Ordained to ministry Assemblies of God Ch., 1973. Assoc. pastor Harbor Assembly of God, Costa Mesa, Calif., 1972-75, Faith Assembly Ch., Monterey Park, Calif., 1975-76; asst. min. Christian Life Ch., LaCrescenta, Calif., 1976-77; dir. adult ministries Evang. Temple Christian Ctr., Springfield, Mo., 1977-79; pastor King's Chapel Christian Ctr., Springfield, 1979-93; adj. faculty So. Calif. Coll., 1972-75, 97—; pastor Orange Coast Cmty. Ch., Lake Forest, Calif., 1994—; vis. lectr. Continental Theol. Sem., Brussels, 1983, Asia Pacific Theol. Sem. Baguio City, The Philippines, 1988, Asia Theol. Ctr. for Evangelism and Missions, 1984; pres. Springfield Ministerial Alliance, 1984-85; adj. faculty Assemblies of God Theol. Sem., Springfield, 1986-90. Contbr. articles to publs. Pres. Child Advocacy Coun., Springfield, 1989-91. Mem. Lake Forest C. of C. (v.p. 1997—). Republican. Office: Orange Coast Cmty Ch 24331 Muirlands Blvd D4-132 Lake Forest CA 92630

HERTZ, ARTHUR HERMAN, business executive; b. Bklyn., Sept. 10, 1933; s. Edwin Carl and Blanche H.; Stephen R., Andrew P. B.B.A., U. Miami, Fla., 1955, postgrad., 1955-56. Acct. Aetna Mortgage Co., Miami, Fla., 1955; acct. Wometco Enterprises, Inc., Miami, 1955-60, controller, v.p., 1960-64, sr. v.p., 1964-71, exec. v.p., treas., chief fin. officer, 1971-81, chief ops. officer, 1981-84, chmn., chief exec. officer, 1985—; exec. v.p., chief ops. officer WEI Enterprises Corp., Miami, 1984-85; exec. v.p. Wometco Broadcasting Co., Inc., Miami, 1984-85. Past pres. Orange Bowl Com.; mem. City of Miami Off St. Parking Authority; vice chair Fla. Comn. on Tourism; chair Visit Fla., Pub. Health Trust, Miami-Dade County; chair Pub. Health Trust, Miami Dade County; chair fin. and audit com. bd. trustees U. Miami. Mem. AICPA, Fla. Inst. CPAs, Greater Miami C. of C. (gov. 1975-78), Iron Arrow, Phi Kappa Phi, Omicron Delta Kappa, Phi Eta Sigma. Home: 610 Fluvia Ave Coral Gables FL 33134-7016 Office: Wometco Enterprises Inc PO Box 141609 Coral Gables FL 33114-1609

HERTZ, DANIEL LEROY, JR., entrepreneur; b. Montclair, N.J., Feb. 27, 1930; s. Daniel Leroy and Elizabeth Nielsen (Beet) H.; m. Valerie A. Smith, Mar. 15, 1956 (div. 1962); m. Isabel Waud Hurd, Apr. 18, 1970; children: Valerie H. Boyle, Suzanne E., Daniel L. III, Seana L. Burdge. Degree in mech. engring., Stevens Inst. Tech., 1952, MS in Mech. Engring. (hon.), 1982. Sales engr. C.E. Conover & Co., Fairfield, N.J., 1953-58; founder, pres. Seals Eastern, Red Bank, N.J., 1958—; mem. adv. bd. polymer tech. cons. Tex. A&M U., College Station, 1990-94, CHEMTECH, Washington, 1983-91, Elastomerics, Atlanta, 1984-92. Contbr. chpts. to Intermediate Rubber Technology, 1983, Handbook of Elastomers, 1988, Vanderbilt Handbook, 1990, Engineering with Rubber, 1992, Rubber Products Manufacturing Technology, 1993, also numerous tech. papers in field. Mem. vis. com. mech. engring. dept. Stevens Inst. Tech., 1992-96; sec. Riverside Dr. Assn., Red Bank, 1980-85. Cpl. U.S. Army, 1950-51, Korea. Mem. Am. Chem. Soc. (treas. rubber divsn. 1988-90, chmn. 1996), N.Y. Rubber Group (chmn. 1983), Rumson Country Club, Nassau Club, Seabright Tennis Club. Republican. Episcopalian. Achievements include 5 U.S. patents. Home: 734 Navesink River Rd Red Bank NJ 07701-6354 Office: 134 Pearl St Red Bank NJ 07701-1525

HERTZ, HARRY STEVEN, government official; b. N.Y.C., Feb. 25, 1947; s. Marcus and Alice (Oppenheimer) H.; m. Francine Turkowitz, June 21, 1969; children: Matthew Adam, Joshua Lee. BS in Chemistry, Poly. Inst. Bklyn., 1967; PhD in Organic Chemistry, MIT, 1971. Alexander von Humboldt fellow U. Munich, Fed. Republic Germany, 1971-73; research chemist Nat. Bur. Standards (now Nat. Inst. Standards and Tech.), Gaithersburg, Md., 1973-78, chief organic analytical rsch. div., 1978-83; dir. Ctr. for Analytical Chemistry Nat. Bur. Standards, Gaithersburg, Md., 1983-91, acting dir. Nat. Measurement Lab., 1989, dir Chem. Sci. and Tech. Lab., 1991-92, dep. dir. Office Quality Programs and Malcolm Baldrige Nat. Quality Award, 1992-96; dir. Baldrige Nat. Quality Program and Malcolm Baldrige Nat. Quality award, 1996—; mem. health environ. research adv. com. Dept. Energy, Washington, 1984-89, good mfg. practices adv. com. FDA, 1988-90; mem. steering com. conf. bd. Global Ctr. Performance Excellence, 1996—; mem. nat. quality com. United Way Am., 1997—. Co-editor: Trace Organic Analysis, 1979; mem. editorial adv. bd. Analytical Chemistry, 1984-86, Chem. and Engring. News, 1990-92; contbr. numerous articles to profl. jours. Recipient Bronze medal Dept. Commerce, 1981, Arthur S. Flemming award for Outstanding Fed. Service, 1985, Silver medal Dept. Commerce, 1986, Gold medal Dept. Commerce, 1998. Fellow AAAS, mem. Am. Soc. for Mass Spectroscopy (sec. 1983-85), Am. Chem. Soc., Nat. Com. for Clin. Lab. Standards (pres. 1986-88), Sigma Xi. Avocations: racquetball, hiking. Office: Nat Inst Standard & Tech A635 Adminstrn Bldg Gaithersburg MD 20899

HERTZ, KENNETH THEODORE, health care executive; b. Jackson Heights, N.Y., Aug. 19, 1951; s. Irwin R. and Dorothy S. H.; m. Debra Pitre, July 12, 1997. BA in Spl. Studies, SUNY, Fredonia, 1974; cert. med. and dental practice mgmt., Loyola U., 1992. Gen. mgr. Cape Cod Symphony, West Barnstable, Mass., 1974-75; mng. dir. Tulsa Philharm., 1975-78; pres., gen. mgr. Atlanta Ballet, 1979-89; instr. continuing edn. Oglethorpe U.; dir. Atlanta Great Artists Series, 1989-90, Atlanta Arts Devel. Svcs., 1989-90; exec. dir. New Orleans Symphony, 1990-91; adminstr. M.D. Care, Inc., New Orleans, 1991-95; dir. acquisitions and network devel. Tenet Healthcare, New Orleans, 1995-96, area mgr. practice ops., 1996-97; adminstr. MacArthur Surg. Clinic, Alexandria, La., 1997—; mem. dance panel City of Atlanta, 1983-89, Ga. Coun. for Arts, 1984-88, NEA, 1985-87; dir. Dance/USA, 1985-89; mem. adv. bd. cert. program in med./dental practice mgmt. Loyola U., 1993—; mem. Pres.'s Adv. Coun., De La Salle H.S., 1993—. Chmn. Atlanta C. of C. Cultural Programming Task Force, 1987-89, Atlanta C. of C. "Arts Alive," art celebration, 1986; former chmn. Ga. Profl. Arts Caucus, 1983-85; former bd. dirs. Am. Jewish Com., Atlanta, 1987, Big Bros./Big Sisters, Atlanta, 1988-89, Arts Festival Atlanta, BVA, Atlanta, 1986-90, Bus. Vols. for the Arts, Atlanta; bd. dirs. New Orleans Ballet Assn., 1996—, Rapides Symphony Orch., 1998—. Mem. Midtown Bus. Assn. (dir. 1984-89), Ga. Citizens for Arts, Am. Symphony Orch. League, Alpha Phi Omega.

HERTZ, LEON, publishing executive; b. Perth, Australia, Aug. 1, 1938; came to U.S., 1975; s. A. and Rose (Traub) H.; m. Linda Paula Cooper, June 1, 1980; 1 child, Monique. Student, U. Western Australia, Perth. Dir. Mirror Newspapers News Ltd., Sydney, Australia, 1967-75; gen. mgr., dir. Australian Nationwide News, Sydney, Australia, 1969-75; v.p., gen. mgr. Express News Corp. Am., San Antonio, 1975-80; v.p., assoc. pub., gen. mgr. N.Y. Post Am., N.Y.C., 1980-86; gen. mgr., dir. News Internat., London, 1986-87; exec. v.p. in charge global mktg. News Corp. Ltd., N.Y.C., 1987; exec. v.p. News Am., N.Y.C., 1987—; bd. dirs. Media Council of Australia, Sydney, 1970-75; chmn. Australian Newspaper Council, Sydney, 1973-75. Mem. Internat. Advt. Assn. (bd. dirs. 1987—, treas. 1987—), Am.-Scandinavian Found., Am. Australian Assn. (dir.), Spanish-Am. C. of C. Clubs: Cruising Yacht (Sydney); Friars (N.Y.C.), Metro. Club (N.Y.C.). Avocation: sailing. Home: 4 E 88th St New York NY 10128-0509 Office: News America Inc Ste 303 1211 Avenue Of The Americas New York NY 10036-8795

HERTZ, RICHARD CORNELL, rabbi; b. St. Paul, Oct. 7, 1916; s. Abram J. and Nadine (Rosenberg) H.; m. Mary Louise Mann, Nov. 25, 1943 (div. July 1971); children: Nadine Hertz Urben, Ruth Mann Joyaux; m. Renda Gottfürcht Ebner, Dec. 3, 1972. A.B., U. Cin., 1938; M.H.L., Hebrew Union Coll., 1942, D.D. (hon.), 1967; Ph.D., Northwestern U., 1948. Ordained rabbi, 1942; asst. rabbi N. Shore Congregation Israel, Glencoe, Ill., 1942-47; asso. rabbi Chgo. Sinai Congregation, 1947-53; sr. rabbi Temple Beth El, Detroit, 1953-82, rabbi emeritus, 1982—; adj. prof. Jewish Thought U. Detroit, 1970-80, disting. prof. Jewish studies, 1980—; spl. asst. to pres. Cranbrook Edn. Community, 1983-84; del. to internat. conf. World Union for Progressive Judaism, London, 1959, 61, Amsterdam, 1978, bd. dirs. union, 1973—; Lectr. Jewish Chautauqua Soc., 1942-80; former mem. plan bd. Synagogue Council Am.; past mem. chaplaincy commn., former bd. dirs. Nat. Jewish Welfare Bd.; former mem. exec. com., vice chmn. Citizen's Com. for Equal Opportunity, Am. Jewish Com.; mem. Mich. Gov.'s Com. on Ethics and Morals, 1963-69; mem. Mich. adv. council U.S. Commn. on Civil Rights, 1979-85; past mem. nat. bd. dirs. Religious Edn. Assn.; past adv. bd. Joint Distbn. Com.; former mem. nat. rabbinical council United Jewish Appeal; mem. rabbinic cabinet Israel Bonds, 1972—; pres. Hyde Park and Kenwood Council Chs. and Synagogues, Chgo., 1952. Author: Rabbi Yesterday and Today, 1943, This I Believe, 1952, Education of the Jewish Child, 1953, Our Religion Above All, 1953, Inner Peace for You, 1954, Positive Judaism, 1955, Wings of the Morning, 1956, Impressions of Israel, 1956, Prescription for Heartache, 1958, Faith in Jewish Survival, 1961, The American Jew in Search of Himself, 1962, What Counts Most in Life, 1963, What Can A Man Believe, 1967, Reflections for the Modern Jew, 1974, Israel and the Palestinians, 1974, Roots of My Faith, 1980, also articles in sci., popular publs. Dir. Am. Jewish Com., mem. nat. exec. bd., former hon. vice-chmn. Detroit chpt.; past dir. Mich. Soc. Mental Health, Jewish Family and Children's Services, United Community Services, Jewish Welfare Fedn. Detroit; v.p. Jewish Community Council Detroit; dir. United Found., Boys Clubs, Mich. region Anti-Defamation League; chmn. bd. overseers Hebrew Union Coll.-Jewish Inst. Religion, 1968-72; bd. govs. Detroit Inst. Tech., 1955-70; trustee Marygrove Coll., Detroit, 1986—. Served as chaplain AUS, 1943-46. Recipient Key of the City, Detroit, 1966, Histadrut award, 1984, Dove award Ecumenical Inst., 1995. Fellow Am. Sociol. Soc.; mem. Assn. Jewish Studies, Detroit Hist. Soc., Central Conf. Am. Rabbis (former nat. chmn. com. on Jews in Soviet orbit), Am. Jewish Hist. Soc., Am. Legion (dept. chaplain 1956-57), Jewish War Vets. (dept. chaplain 1958-59, 72-74), Alumni Assn. Hebrew Union Coll.-Jewish Inst. Religion (past dir.), Nat. Assn. Ret. Reform Rabbis (pres. 1989). Attended spl. mission for White House to investigate status Jews and Judaism in USSR 1959, mission for chief chaplains Def. Dept. to conduct retreats for Jewish chaplains and laymen, Berchtesgaden, Germany, 1973; mem. mission to Arab countries and Israel, Nat. Council Chs.-Am. Jewish Com., 1974; 1st Am. rabbi received in pvt. audience at Papal Palace by Pope Paul VI, 1963; Eisenhower amb. People to People Program to Moscow, Warsaw, Krakow, Budapest to study Jewish studies in univs. in Eastern Bloc, 1994. Home: 4324 Knightsbridge Ln West Bloomfield MI 48323-1621 Office: Temple Beth El 7400 Telegraph Rd # 14 Mile Bloomfield Hills MI 48301-3876 *My life has fallen in pleasant places. I have been fortunate enough and lived long enough to enjoy my life as a Rabbi and teacher. To be able to help people become better Jews and appreciate their Jewish heritage has been a source of great satisfaction.*

HERTZ, ROY, physician, educator, researcher; b. Cleve., June 19, 1909; s. Aaron Daniel and Bertha (Lichtman) H.; m. Pearl Fennell, June 24, 1934 (dec. 1962); children: Margaret, Jeremy; m. Dorothy Anne Wright Oberdorfer, Nov. 9, 1965. AB, U. Wis., 1930, PhD, 1934, MD, 1939, DSc (hon.), 1986; MPH, Johns Hopkins U., 1940. Rsch. assoc. U. Wis., Madison, 1930-34; instr. pharmacology Howard U., Washington, 1934-35; rsch. fellow Brown U., Providence, 1935-36, U. Wis., 1936-39; chief endocrinology br. Nat. Cancer Inst., Bethesda, Md., 1941-66; sci. dir. Nat. Inst. Child Health, Bethesda, 1966-67; prof. ob-gyn George Washington U., Washington, 1967-68, chief reprodn. rsch., 1968-69; assoc. dir. The Population Council, N.Y.C., 1969-73; rsch. prof. pharmacology, ob-gyn. George Washington U., Washington, 1973-83, prof. emeritus, 1983—; scientist emeritus NIH, Bethesda, Md., 1987—. Recipient Lasker Med. Research award, N.Y.C., 1972, Cancer Research award Internat. Coll. Surgeons, 1969. Fellow ACP, Am. Coll. Ob-gyn, Am. Assn. Ob-gyn (hon.); mem. AAAS, Nat. Acad. Scis., The Endocrine Soc. (v.p. 1960, Fred Conrad Koch award 1996), Chilean Med. Soc. (hon.), Argentine Med. Soc. (hon.). Avocations: gardening, travel. Home: 25006 Half Pone Point Rd Hollywood MD 20636-2948

HERTZBERG, ABRAHAM, aeronautical engineering educator, university research scientist; b. N.Y.C., July 8, 1922; s. Rubin and Paulien (Kalif) H.; m. Ruth Cohen, Sept. 3, 1950; children: Eleanor Ruth, Paul Elliot, Jean R. BS in Aero. Engring., Va. Poly. Inst., 1943; MS in Aero. Engring., Cornell U., 1949; postgrad., U. Buffalo, 1949-53. Engr. Cornell Aero. Lab., 1949-57, asst. head aerodynamics research, 1957-59, head aerodynamics research, 1959-65; dir. aerospace & energetic rsch. program U. Wash., 1966-93, prof. astronautics, 1966-93; prof. emeritus astronautics, 1993—; prin. investigator numerous federal rsch. grants; cons. Aerospace Corp., past mem. sci. adv. bd. USAF, Olin-Rocket Rsch., STI Optronics; past mem. electro-optics panel SAB, mem. various ad hoc coms.; mem. space sys. and tech. adv. com., rsch. and tech. subcom., past mem. rsch. and tech. adv. coun. NASA; mem. plasma dynamics rev. panel NSF, U.S. Army; honored spkr. Laser Inst. Am., 1975, Citizens of Sendai, 1991; past mem. theory adv. com. Los Alamos Nat. Lab.; vis. lectr. Chinese Acad. Scis., Beijing, 1983, 88, 97; Paul Vieille lectr. 7th Internat. Shock Tube Symposium, 1969, 89, 17th Internat. Symposium on Shock Waves and Shock Tubes, 1989; Irvine I. Glass Meml. lectr. U. Toronto, 1996. Editor Physics of Fluids, 1968-70; contbr. numerous articles on modern gas dynamics, high powered lasers, controlled thermonuclear fusions processes, space laser solar energy concepts, space energy concepts and new ultra velocity propulsion concepts to profl. jours. Served with AUS, 1944-46. Honored speaker Laser Inst. Am. Fellow AIAA (Dryden lectr. 1977, Agard lectr. 1978, Plasmadynamics and Lasers award 1992), Internat. Acad. Astronautics; mem. AAAS, NAE, Am. Phys. Soc., Sigma Xi. Achievements include patents in field. Office: U Wash Aerospace & Energetics PO Box 352250 Seattle WA 98195-2250

HERTZBERG, ARTHUR, rabbi, educator; b. Lubaczow, Poland, June 9, 1921; s. Zvi Elimelech and Nehamah (Alstadt) H.; m. Phyllis Cannon, Mar. 19, 1950; children: Linda, Susan. A.B., Johns Hopkins U., 1940; M.H.L., Jewish Theol. Sem., 1943; Ph.D., Columbia U., 1966; D.D., Lafayette Coll., 1970; D.H.L., Balt. Hebrew Coll., 1974, Jewish Theol. Sem., 1987, Balt. Hebrew U., 1997, Boston Hebrew Coll., 1999. Rabbi, 1943; Hillel dir. Mass. State and Smith Coll., 1943-44; rabbi Congregation Ahavath Israel of Oak Lane, Phila., 1944-47, West End Synagogue, Nashville, 1947-56, Temple Emanu El, Englewood, N.J., 1956-85; rabbi emeritus Temple Emanu El, 1985—; prof. religion Dartmouth Coll., 1985-91, prof. emeritus, 1991—; lectr. Columbia U., 1961-68, adj. prof. history, 1968-90; vis. scholar Mideast Inst., 1991—; vis. assoc. prof. Jewish studies Rutgers U., 1966-68; lectr. religion Princeton U., 1968-69; vis. prof. history Hebrew U., Jerusalem, 1970-71; vis. prof. Ecole des Hautes Etudes, Paris, 1989; vis. scholar St. Antony's Coll., Oxford, 1989; pres. Conf. Jewish Social Studies, 1967-72; mem. exec. com. World Zionist Orgn., 1969-78, Jewish Agy. for Israel, 1969-71, bd. govs., 1971-78; pres. Am. Jewish Congress, 1972-78, Am. Jewish Policy Found., 1978—; v.p. World Jewish Congress, 1975-91, co-chmn. adv. coun., 1991—; vis. prof. humanities NYU, 1991—. Author: The Zionist Idea, 1959, (with Martin Marty and Joseph Moody) The Outbursts that Await Us, 1963, The French Enlightenment and the Jews, 1968, Being Jewish in America, 1979, The Jews in America: Four Centuries of an Uneasy Encounter, 1989, Jewish Polemics, 1992, (with Aron Hirt-Manheimer) Jews: The Essence and Character of a People, 1998; editor: Judaism, 1961, 2d rev. edit., 1991; introduction author At Home Only With God, 1992; sr. editor: Ency. Judaica, 1972; contbr.: Ency. Britannica, 1975. Vice pres. bd. dirs. Meml. Found. for Jewish Culture, 1965-98. Served 1st lt., chaplain USAF, 1951-53. Recipient Amram award, 1967; award for Lifetime Achievement Present Tense, 1989; Inst. Advanced Studies fellow, Jerusalem, 1982. Home: 83 Glenwood Rd Englewood NJ 07631-1909 Office: 147 Tenafly Rd Englewood NJ 07631-2231 also: NYU 19 University Pl Rm 505 New York NY 10003-4556 *I cannot even imagine improving on Hillel's dictum, nearly 20 centuries ago: what is hateful to you, don't do to your fellow man.*

HERTZBERG, HENRY, radiologist, educator; b. Bklyn., Oct. 21, 1933; s. Louis and Bessie (Eisman) H.; m. Dori Balter, June 10, 1962; children: Richard, Lisa. BS, CCNY, 1955; MD, SUNY, Bklyn., 1959. Diplomate Am. Bd. Radiology. Intern Kings County Med. Ctr., Bklyn., 1959-60; resident Roosevelt Hosp., N.Y.C., 1960-63; dir. radiology Fort Gordon (Ga.) Army Hosp., 1963-65; pvt. practice Green Brook, N.J.; assoc. dir. dept. radiology Somerset Med. Ctr., Somerville, N.J., 1975-85; dir. dept. radiology Muhlenberg Med. Ctr., Plainfield, N.J., 1985-92; attending radiologist Muhlenberg Med. Ctr., 1992—; clin. asst. prof. radiology Rutgers U. Med. Ctr., 1985—. Capt. M.C., U.S. Army, 1963-65. Mem. AMA. Avocation: travel. Home: 182 Deer Run Watchung NJ 07060-6222 Office: Assoc Radiologists PA 239 Us Highway 22 Green Brook NJ 08812-1916

HERTZBERG, RICHARD WARREN, materials science and engineering educator, researcher; b. N.Y.C., Aug. 17, 1937; s. Nelson Bert and Alice (Sobin) H.; m. Linda Judith Wishnow, June 18, 1961; children: Michelle, Ilyce, Jason Lyle. B.S.M.E., CCNY, 1960; M.S. in Metallurgy, MIT, 1961; Ph.D. in Metallurgy, Lehigh U., 1965. Research asst. MIT, 1960-61; research scientist United Aircraft Corp., East Hartford, Conn., 1961-64; dir. mech. behavior Lehigh U., Bethlehem, Pa., 1964—, N.J. Zinc prof. metallurgy, 1978—, short course organizer, 1977—, chmn., 1987-92; vis. prof. Ecole Polytechnique Fédérale de Lausanne (Switzerland), 1976; v.p. Del Rsch. Corp., Hellertown, Pa., 1969-74. Author: Deformation and Fracture Mechanics of Engineering Materials, 1976, 89, 96, (with John A. Manson) Fatigue of Engineering Plastics, 1980; co-editor: Conference on In Situ Composites II, 1980. Bd. dirs. Temple Beth El, Allentown, Pa., 1973-76; sec. Temple Beth El Endowment Found., 1979-84; bd. dirs. Congregation Am Haskalah, Allentown, 1982-88. Recipient award for outstanding rsch. Alcoa Found., Bethlehem, 1972, 73, Bradley Stoughton award Lehigh Valley chpt., 1992, R.R. and E.C. Hillman award for advancing the interests of Lehigh U., 1994; co-recipient Eleanor and Joseph Libsch award for outstanding achievement and distinction in rsch. Lehigh U., 1983, award for teaching excellence Lehigh U., 1991. Fellow Am. Soc. Metals (chmn. nat. young mems. com. 1969-72, Phila. chpt. Notable Achievement award, Lehigh Valley chpt. Bradley Stoughton award 1992); mem. ASTM, AIME. Office: Lehigh U Dept Material Sci 5 E Packer Ave Bethlehem PA 18015-3102

HERZ, ANDREW LEE, lawyer; b. N.Y.C., Nov. 12, 1946; s. John W. and Elise J. H.; m. Jill K. Herz; children: Adam, Matthew, Daniel, Michael. BA, Columbia U., 1968, JD, 1971. Bar: N.Y. 1972. Assoc. Milbank, Tweed, Hadley & McCloy, N.Y.C., 1971-75, Nickerson, Kramer, Lowenstein, Nessen, Kamin & Soll, N.Y.C., 1975-76, Marshall, Bratter, Greene, Allison & Tucker, N.Y.C., 1977-80; gen. counsel N.Y. State Mortgage Loan Enforcement and Adminstrn. Corp., N.Y.C., 1980-81; ptnr. Richards & O'Neil, LLP, N.Y.C., 1981—; lectr. Real Estate Inst., NYU, 1988-93; cons. N.Y. Real Property Svcs., 1987; pres., dir. Hotel Carlyle Owners Corp. Author: Office Lease Operating Expense Clauses-Definitional Problems, 1986, Renegotiating Commercial Leases, 1993, Liability Risks for Ducting Loan Commitments, 1995; co-author: Japanese Yen Financing of U.S. Real Estate, 1989, Real Estate Management Agreements, 1990. Chmn. zoning bd. appeals Village of Ossining, N.Y., 1980-88; bd. dirs. Planned Parenthood N.Y.C., 1987-94, AIDS Resource Ctr., 1991-94. Harlan Fiske Stone Scholar, 1971. Mem. ABA (real property divsn., comml. office leasing com. 1999—, chair real estate mgmt. com. 1990-91, vice chmn. 1988-90, co-chair real estate asset mgmt. com. 1992-94, chair real estate asset mgmt. com. 1994-95, lending and financing subcom. 1997-99, co-chair comml. leasing com. 1999—), Am. Coll. Real Estate Lawyers (vice chair office leasing com. 1997-98, chair office leasing com. 1999—), N.Y. State Bar Assn. (co-chmn. comml. leasing com. 1991-96, exec. com. 1991-96, real property sect., editor N.Y. Real Property Jour. 1996-97), Assn. of Bar of City of N.Y., Real Estate Bd. N.Y., Urban Land Inst. Democrat. Home: 31 Flint Ave Larchmont NY 10538-3807 Office: Richards & O'Neil LLP 885 3rd Ave New York NY 10022-4834

HERZ, LEONARD, financial consultant; b. Bronx, N.Y., June 25, 1931; s. Emanuel and Henrietta (Morris) H.; m. Sally Jampolsky, May 2, 1954 (dec. Apr. 1994); children: Michael, Hildee, Larry; m. Debra Brody, July 28, 1995. B.B.A., CCNY, 1952. C.P.A., N.Y. Auditor Lybrand Ross Bros., C.P.A.s, N.Y.C., 1954-60; asst. controller Merritt Chapman Scott, N.Y.C., 1960-66; treas. Baker Industries Inc., Parsippany, N.J., 1966-73; v.p. finance Del Labs. Inc., Farmingdale, N.Y., 1973-74; exec. v.p. Holmes Protection, Inc., N.Y.C., 1974-82; fin. cons. L. Herz, Denver, 1982—; dir. Oliver Exterminating Corp., Am. Med. Alert Corp.; bd. dirs. Ctrl. Sta. Electric Protective Assn. With AUS, 1952-54. Mem. N.Y. State Soc. C.P.A.s, Am. Inst. C.P.A.s, Exec. Assn. Greater N.Y. (bd. dirs.). Home and Office: 254 Garfield St Denver CO 80206-5519

HERZ, MARVIN IRA, psychiatrist, educator; b. N.Y.C., Dec. 24, 1927; s. Jules Edward and Vivian M. (Becker) H.; m. Beatrice Leslie Mittelman, Sept. 13, 1952; 3 children. BA, U. Mich., 1949; MS in Psychology, Yale U., 1950; MD, Chgo. Med. Sch., 1955; cert. in psychoanalysis, Columbia U., 1968. Diplomate Am. Bd. Psychiatry and Neurology (sr. examiner). Intern U. Ill. Research and Ednl. Hosps., 1955-56; resident in psychiatry Michael Reese Hosp., Chgo., 1956-59; dir. inpatient service div. psychiatry Montefiore Hosp., N.Y.C., 1961-63; dir. Westchester Sq. Day Hosps., N.Y.C., 1963-65; asst. prof. psychiatry Albert Einstein Coll. Medicine, N.Y.C., 1963-65; asso. in psychiatry Columbia U., 1965-68, asst. prof. clin. psychiatry, 1968-72, asso. prof., 1972-77; ward adminstr. Washington Heights Community Service, N.Y. State Psychiat. Inst., 1965-68; asst. attending psychiatrist Vanderbilt Clinic, Presbyn. Hosp., N.Y.C., 1965-68; dir. Washington Hts. Community Service, 1968-72; dir. community services N.Y. State Psychiat. Inst., 1972-77, acting clin. dir., 1975-76; med. dir. Ga. Mental Health Inst., Atlanta, 1977-78; dir. ops. research, 1977-78; prof. psychiatry Emory U., 1977-78; prof., chmn. dept. psychiatry SUNY Sch. Medicine, Buffalo, 1978-91; dir. psychiatry Erie County Med. Center, Buffalo, 1978-91; head dept. psychiatry Buffalo Gen. Hosp., 1978-91; prof. U. Rochester, N.Y., 1991—; cons. in psychiatry VA Hosp., Buffalo, 1978-91; sr. sci. advisor to dir. NIMH, 1989-91, cons. psychiatry edn. br., 1978; cons. Robert Wood Johnson Found., 1992; cons. Nat. Heart and Lung Inst., Task Panel of Pres.'s Commn. on Rsch. in Mental Illness, 1977; chmn. psychiat. adv. com. N.Y. State Office Mental Health, 1980-87. Contbr. articles to med. jours. Served to lt. comdr. USNR, 1959-61. Recipient award for outcomes rsch. World Assn. for Psychosocial Rehab., U.S. Br., 1994, Heinz Lehmann rsch. award N.Y. State Office Mental Health, 1994. Fellow Am. Psychiat. Assn. (chmn. com. to develop practice guidelines for schizophrenia 1992-97, prize in hosp. psychiatry rsch. 1988, chair rsch. prize com. 1996—), Am. Coll. Psychiatrists (bd. regents 1990-93, 2d v.p. 1994-95, v.p. 1995-96, pres. elect 1996-97, pres. 1997-98, Dean award for rsch. in schizophrenia 1993), Am. Coll. Psychoanalysts (treas. 1991-95, v.p. 1996-97, pres. elect 1997-98, pres. 1998-99); mem. Assn. for Clin. Psychosocial Rsch. (pres. 1993-95), Assn. Psychoanalytic Medicine (chmn. com. on comm. psychiatry 1975-76), Am. Psychopathol. Assn., Alpha Omega Alpha. Home: 5 Vineyard Hl Fairport NY 14450-4601 Other Address: Strong Ties 1650 Elmwood Ave Rochester NY 14620-3427

HERZ, SYLVIA BEATRICE, clinical and community psychologist; b. N.Y.C., May 1, 1930; d. Jacob and Minnie (Glucksman) Schnipper; m. Jean A. Herz, Apr. 29, 1955; 1 child, Howard Todd Jaffe. BS, Hunter Coll., 1940; MS, NYU and Oreg. State U., Corvallis, 1945; PhD, NYU, 1964. Lic. psychologist; diplomate Am. Bd. Family Psychology, Am. Bd. Sexology. Clin. psychologist cmty. and pvt. practice, N.J., 1964—; pres. Essex County

Coun. on Drug Addiction, N.J., 1975-85; chmn. Essex County Mental Health Bd., 1970-76; cons. N.J. Dept. Health, 1972-93; mem. adv. bd. Gov.'s Commn. on Children and Families, 1970-80; mem. N.J. Bd. Psychology Examiners, 1980-90; cons., advisor Gov.'s Task Force on Children and Families, 1980-94. Editor Jour. Family Psychology, 1970-80; contbr. articles to profl. jours. Recipient Nat. Rohrer award APA, 1990, award N.J. Pub. Health Assn., 1985, others. Mem. N.J. Pub. Health Assn. (pres. 1989-94). Avocations: writing, walking, reading, piano, art. Home: 220 Tillou Rd South Orange NJ 07079-1522 also: 1201 S Ocean Dr Apt 9055 Hollywood FL 33019-2121 Office: Doctors Offices 1130 Raritan Rd Cranford NJ 07016-3328

HERZBERG, PETER JAY, lawyer; b. Newark, Feb. 3, 1950; s. Arno and Annelie (Baruch) H.; m. Lisa F. Chrystal, Mar. 13, 1982. B.A., Haverford Coll., 1972; J.D., U. Pa., 1975. Dep. atty. gen. N.J. Dept. Law and Pub. Safety, Trenton, 1975-78, 80, 82-83; staff atty. Sierra Club Legal Def. Fund, Washington, 1978-80; acting asst. counsel to gov. of N.J., Trenton, 1981. John F. Baker scholar, 1971. Mem. Phi Beta Kappa. Office: Pitney Hardin Kipp & Szuch PO Box 1945 Morristown NJ 07962-1945

HERZBERG, SYDELLE SHULMAN, lawyer, accountant; b. N.Y.C., July 24, 1933; d. Hyman and Rose (Green) S.; m. Norman Joseph Herzberg, June 23, 1962; 1 child, Gilbert. BS, NYU, 1955; JD, Bklyn. Law Sch., 1957. Bar: N.Y. 1958; CPA, N.Y. Pub. acct. M. Sharlach & Co, N.Y.C., 1955-62; pvt. practice acctg. and law New Rochelle, N.Y., 1962—. Mem. bd. edn. Solomon Schechter Sch. of Westchester, White Plains, N.Y., 1975-78, bd. dirs. PTA, 1975-78; pres. PTA bd. Westchester Hebrew High Sch., Mamaroneck, N.Y., 1980-82; mem. budget adv. bd. City of New Rochelle, N.Y., 1975. Mem. ABA, AICPA, N.Y. State Soc. CPA, N.Y. State Bar Assn., Huguenot-Thomas Paine Hist. Assn. (treas. 1987—, trustee 1987—), LWV (pres. New Rochelle chpt. 1983-85, treas. Westchester chpt. 1989—, budget chair N.Y. 1989-91, treas. N.Y. state 1991—). Jewish. Home: 46 Longvue Ave New Rochelle NY 10804-4119 Office: 519 Main St New Rochelle NY 10801-6365

HERZBERG, THOMAS, artist, illustrator; b. Chgo., Feb. 3, 1954; s. Carroll Alexander and Victoria Herzberg; m. Rosemary Ann Morrissey, Aug. 11, 1979; 1 child, Kyli Rose. BA, Northeastern U., 1975; MFA, Northern Ill. U., 1979. illustrations appeared in Chgo. mag., Advertising Age, Playboy mag., World Book, Chgo. Tribune, Washington Post, Art Inst. Chgo., Goodman Theatre, Chgo. Exhibited Art Inst. Chgo., 1978, 84, De Cordova Mus., Lincoln., Mass., 1978, 79, 83, Silvermine Guild Artists, New Canaan, Conn., 1980, Met. Mus. and Art Ctr., Coral Gables, Fla., 1980, 82, Hunterdon Art Ctr., Clinton, N.J., 1982, U. Dallas, 1983, 10th, 12th and 13th Ann. Soc. Newspaper Design, Am. Soc. Illustrators 28th, 39th and 41st Ann. Exhbns.; represented in permanent collections De Cordova Mus., Terrance Gallery, Palenville, N.Y., Met. Mus. and Art Ctr., Silvermine Guild Artists, Carnegie Inst., Art Inst. Chgo., Lincoln Park Zoo, Chgo. Symphony Orch.; over 1500 illustrations in newspapers, mags., books, mus. graphics, 1981—. Named Best of Show 3 Ann. Ill. Regional Print Show, 1980; recipient Award of Excellence New Horizons in Art North Shore Art League, 1980-82, Weston Press and Gallery award 8th Internat. Miniature Print Exhbn. Pratt Graphic Ctr., 1981, Cert. of Design Excellence Print's Regional Design Ann., 1994-96, 97, also numerous awards Art Direction mag. creativity show, 1992-93, Soc. Newspaper Design, Cert. of Merit Soc. Illustrators Print Regional Design Annual.

HERZBERGER, EUGENE E., retired neurosurgeon; b. Sotchi, USSR, June 7, 1920; came to U.S., 1957, naturalized, 1964; s. Eugene S. and Mary P. H.; married; children—Henry, Monica. M.D., U. King Ferdinand I, Cluj, Rumania, 1947. Diplomate Am. Bd. Neurol. Surgery. Intern Univ. Hosp., Cluj, Rumania, 1946-47, resident in surgery, 1947-48; resident in neurosurgery Beilinson Hosp., Tel Aviv, 1949-53; chief neurosurgeon Tel Hashomer Govt. Hosp., Tel Aviv, 1953-57; research asst. Yale U., 1958-59; instr. neurosurgery Med. Coll. Ga., 1959-60; attending neurosurgeon St. Clare Hosp., Monroe, Wis., 1960-76, Mercy Hosp. and Finley Hosp., Dubuque, Iowa, 1976-94. Contbr. articles to med. jours. Mem. Am. Assn. Neurol. Surgeons, Iowa Midwest Neurosurg. Soc., Congress Neurol. Surgeons, Am. Acad. Neurology, Iowa State Med. Soc. Office: 15649 E El Lago Blvd Fountain Hills AZ 85268

HERZECA, LOIS FRIEDMAN, lawyer; b. N.Y.C., July 7, 1954; d. Martin and Elaine Shirley (Rapoport) Friedman; m. Christian S. Herzeca, Aug. 15, 1980; children: Jane Leslie, Nicholas Cameron. BA, SUNY-Binghamton, 1976; JD, Boston U., 1979. Bar: N.Y. 1980, U.S. Dist. Ct. (so. and ea. dist.) N.Y. 1980. Atty. antitrust div. U.S. Dept. Justice, Washington, 1979-80; assoc. Fried, Frank, Harris, Shriver & Jacobson, N.Y.C., 1980-86, ptnr., 1986—. Editor Am. Jour. Law and Medicine, 1978-79. Mem. ABA, N.Y.C. Bar Assn. Office: Fried Frank Harris Shriver Jacobson 1 New York Plz Fl 22 New York NY 10004-1980

HERZENBERG, ARVID, physicist, educator; b. Vienna, Austria, Apr. 16, 1925; s. Harry and Wilhelmine (Pfeiffer) H.; m. Marjorie Swift, Nov. 30, 1949; children: Catherine, Anne, Stephen. B.S., U. Manchester, Eng., 1949, D.Sc., 1964. Mem. faculty U. Manchester, 1952-69; prof. applied physics Yale, 1969—. Contbr. articles to profl. jours. Fellow Brit., Am. phys. socs. Home: 6 Legrand Rd North Haven CT 06473-1013 Office: 313 Becton Ctr Yale University New Haven CT 06520

HERZENBERG, CAROLINE STUART LITTLEJOHN, physicist; b. East Orange, N.J., Mar. 25, 1932; d. Charles Frederick and Caroline Dorothea (Schulze) L.; m. Leonardo Herzenberg, July 29, 1961; children: Karen Ann, Catherine Stuart. SB, MIT, 1953; SM, U. Chgo., 1955, PhD, 1958; DSc (hon.), SUNY, Plattsburgh, 1991. Asst. prof. Ill. Inst. Tech., Chgo., 1961-66, research physicist ITT Research Inst., 1967-70, sr. physicist, 1970-71; lectr. Calif. State U., Fresno, 1975-76; physicist Argonne (Ill.) Nat. Lab., Ill., 1977—; prin. investigator NASA Apollo Returned Lunar Sample Analysis Program, 1967-71; producer and host TV sci. series Camera on Sci.; disting. vis. prof. SUNY, Plattsburgh, 1991; mem. final selection com. 1993 Bower award and Prize for Achievement in Sci., 1993-94; bd. adv. the Bower award and Prize for Achievements in Sci.; mem. nat. panel of advisors PBS TV sci. series Bill Nye the Sci. Guy, 1991-95; steering com. mem. Midwest Consortium for Internat. Security Studies, 1994-95. Author: Women Scientists from Antiquity to the Present: An Index, 1986. Contbr. articles to profl. jours. Candidate for alderman, Freeport, Ill., 1975; past chmn. NOW chpt., Freeport. Am. Phys. Soc. Congl. Scientist fellow finalist, 1976-77; recipient award in sci. Chgo. Women's Hall of Fame, 1989. Fellow AAAS, Am. Phys. Soc. (past chmn. com., past sec.-treas. forum on Physics and Soc., past exec. bd. Forum on the History of Physics, panel pub. affairs), Assn. Women in Sci. (nat. sec. 1982-84, pres. 1988-90); mem. Sigma Xi. Home: 1700 E 56th St Ste 2707 Chicago IL 60637-1935 Office: Argonne Nat Lab DIS Divsn Bldg 900 Argonne IL 60439

HERZENBERG, LEONARD ARTHUR, medical educator; b. Bklyn., Nov. 5, 1931; m. 1953; 4 children. BA, Bklyn. Coll., 1952; PhD in Biochemistry, Calif. Inst. Tech., 1956. From asst. to assoc. prof. genetics Stanford (Calif.) U., 1959-69, prof., 1969—; mem. genetics study sect. NIH. Co-contbr. articles to sci. publs. Fellow Am. Cancer Soc., Pasteur Inst., Paris, 1955-57. Fellow AAAS, Internat. Soc. Analytical Cytology (hon. award for sci. and technol. achievements 1998); mem. Am. Acad. Microbiology, Genetics Soc. Am., Am. Assn. Immunologists (Lifetime Svc. award 1998), Soc. Devel. Biology. Achievements include invention of fluorescence-activated cell sorter; research in redox regulation of gene expression and diseases, regulation of lymphocyte development, in apoptosis in the immune system and in disease processes, in cell biology of AIDS in model systems and patients; development of multi-parameter flow cytometry and scanning cytometry. Office: Stanford U Dept Genetics Beckman Center B009 Stanford U Med Ctr Stanford CA 94305-5138*

HERZER, RICHARD KIMBALL, franchising company executive; b. Ogden, Utah, June 2, 1931; s. Arthur Vernon and Dorothy (Cortez) H.; m. Phyllis Ann McCullough, Mar. 29, 1958; children: Diane E., Mark V., Craig K. BS, UCLA, 1958. Vice-pres., contr. United Rent All, Inc., L.A., 1967-71; dir. fin. planning Internat. Industries Inc., North Hollywood, Calif., 1971-73, v.p., controller, 1973-75, v.p. fin., 1975-79, pres., 1979—, chmn. bd., CEO, 1983—; bd. dirs. IHOP Corp., 1979—. Trustee So. Calif. chpt. Multiple Sclerosis, 1984—. 1st lt. U.S. Army, 1953-56. Mem. Calif. Restaurant Assn. (dir. 1985-94), Phi Delta Theta. Republican. Home: 4411 Woodleigh Ln La Canada Flintridge CA 91011-3542 Office: IHOP Corp 525 N Brand Blvd Glendale CA 91203-1903

HERZFELD, CHARLES MARIA, physicist; b. Vienna, Austria, June 29, 1925; came to U.S., 1942, naturalized, 1949; s. August Alfred and Frieda Auguste (Poehlman) H.; children: Charles Christopher, Thomas Augustine, Paul Vincent; m. Shannon Stock Shuman, June 9, 1990. BS in Chem. Engring. cum laude, Cath. U. Am., 1945; PhD (Carnegie Found. fellow), U. Chgo., 1951. Lectr. chemistry Cath. U. Am., 1946; lectr. gen. sci. Coll. U. Chgo., 1946-47; lectr. physics DePaul U., Chgo., 1948-50; physicist Ballistic Research Lab., Aberdeen, Md., 1951-53, Naval Research Lab., Washington, 1953-55; lectr. physics U. Md., 1953-57, prof. physics, 1957-61; cons. chief heat and power div. Nat. Bur. Standards, 1955-56, acting asst. chief, 1956-57, chief heat div., 1957-61, asso. dir. bur., 1961; asst. dir. Advanced Research Project Agy., Dept. Def., 1961-63, dir. ballistic missile def., 1963; dep. dir. Advanced Research Projects Agy., 1963-65, dir., 1965-67; tech. dir. def. space group ITT, Nutley, N.J., 1967-74; tech. dir. aerospace-electronics-components-energy group ITT, 1974-76, tech. dir. telecommunications and electronics group N.Am., 1978-79; v.p., dir. research ITT Corp., 1979-83, v.p., dir. research and tech., 1983-85; vice chmn. Aetna, Jacobs and Ramo, N.Y.C., 1985-90; dir. def. rsch. and engring. Dept. Def., Washington, 1990-91; cons. to Office Sci. and Tech. Policy, Exec. Office Pres. of U.S., Washington, 1991; chmn. bd. Westronix Co., Midvale, Utah, 1985-88; mem. Def. Sci. bd., 1968-83, Def. Policy Bd., 1985-90, Nat. Commn. on Space, 1985-86; cons. in field; fellow Hudson Inst., 1970-90; mem. Brookings Inst. 5th Conf. for Career Execs. in Fed. Govt., 1958, mem. chief of Naval Ops. exec. panel, 1970—; mem. Tech. Review Bd. Hong Kong, 1993-94, Nat. Security Advisory Bd., Los Alamos Nat. Lab.; adj. fellow Ctr. Strategic and Internat. Studies, Washington, 1995—. Editor: Temperature, Its Control in Science and Industry, vol. III, 1962; contbr. articles to profl. jours. Recipient Flemming award, 1963; Meritorious Civilian Service medal Dept. Def., 1967. Fellow AAAS, Am. Phys. Soc., Conf. on Sci., Philosophy and Religion, Coun. Fgn. Rels., Ctr. for Strategic and Internat. Studies (Washington); mem. Explorers Club, Inst. for Strategic Studies (London), Cath. Assn. Internat. Peace (pres. 1959-61), Cosmos Club (Washington).

HERZFELD-KIMBROUGH, CIBY, mental health educator; b. Mobile, Ala., Oct. 10, 1941; d. Julius Sr. and Nettie (Fraizer) Herzfeld; m. Charles C. Kimbrough, Nov. 28, 1964; children: Carolos R., Choron F. BS, U. Mo., 1970; MA, Wash. U., 1980; MAT, AGC, Webster U., 1982. Cert. tchr., Mo. Coord. children-adolescent svcs. Metro Comprehensive Mental Health Ctr., St. Louis; cons. C. Kimbrough and Assocs.; instr. minority mental health Wash. U., St. Louis; founder, exec. dir. Creative Inovative and Behavioral Experences, CIBE; mng. dir. CKAN Ltd., Nigeria; project coord. Children's Devel. Ctr., Lagos, Nigeria; intervention specialist, counselor Ferguson Florissant Schs.; adj. instr. St. Louis U.; developer Children's Treatment Program; established Metroties Day Treatment Sch., 1987. Creator (line of African greeting cards) KenteKards. Trustee Children's Devel. Ctr., Lagos, Nigeria. Knoxville Coll. acad. scholarship, 1961; NIMH fellow, 1979; recipient Outstanding Leadership award Woman's Collaboration Conf., 1985, Exceptional Tchr. award INROADS Pre-Coll. Inst., 1986, Devel. award MTS, Lagos, Nigeria. Mem. Nat. Black Child Devel. Inst. (pres. St. Louis affiliate, Outstanding Svc. award), St. Louis Assn. of Black Psychologists (membership chair), St. Louis Mental Health Assn. (children's svcs. coun., membership chair), Mo. Psychol. Assn. (St. Louis network for women psychologists sec.), Nigerian Field Soc. (membership chair), Internat. Platform Soc., 100 Black Women, Nigerian Federated Women, Am. Woman's Club. Home: 11752 Russet Meadow Dr Saint Louis MO 63146-4231

HERZIG, DAVID JACOB, pharmaceutical company executive, immunopharmacologist; b. Cleve., Dec. 13, 1936; s. Marvin Laurence and Lillian Gertrude (Blaine) H.; m. Phyllis Glicksberg, Sept. 2, 1962; children—Michael, Pamela, Roberta, Karen. BA, Oberlin Coll., 1958; PhD in Chemistry, U. Cin., 1963. Vis. scientist NIH, Bethesda, Md., 1963-65, staff fellow, 1965-67; sr. rsch. assoc. NYU Sch. Medicine, N.Y.C., 1967-68, Warner Lambert, Parke-Davis Co., Ann Arbor, Mich., 1968-77, dir. immunopharmacology, 1977-81, dir. sci. devel., 1981-99, v.p. drug devel. and sci. devel. Mich. Biotechnology Inst., also bd. dirs. Contbr. articles to profl. jours. Bd. dirs. Mich. Ctr. High Tech., 1992-95. Fellow Damon Runyon Meml. Fund. Mem. AAAS, Am. Soc. Pharmacology and Exptl. Therapeutics, Am. Acad. Allergy Immunology, Mich. Biotech. Assn. (bd. dirs. 1993-96, pres. 1994-96), N.Y. Acad. Scis., N.Y. Fencers Club (bd. dirs. 1970-77), Sigma Xi. Avocations: squash, fencing, furniture building. Home and Office: 3540 Windemere Dr Ann Arbor MI 48105-2842 Office: Warner Lambert Parke-Davis 2800 Plymouth Rd Ann Arbor MI 48105-2430

HERZIG, JULIE ESTHER, designer; b. N.Y.C., Jan. 23, 1951; d. Philip R. and Helene J. (Phillips) H.; m. Robert J. Desnick, Oct. 23, 1988; 1 child, Jonathan Phillips. BA, Mt. Holyoke Coll., 1973; BArch with honors, Pratt Inst., 1983. With Red Roof Design, N.Y.C., 1977-80, Phillips Janson Group, N.Y.C., 1983-84, Herzig, Knechtel Assocs., N.Y.C., 1984-85, Herzig Design, N.Y.C., 1985—. Mt. Holyoke Coll. grantee, 1972. Mem. AIA (assoc.), Mt. Holyoke Club.

HERZING, ALFRED ROY, computer executive; b. Kitchener, Ont., Can., June 23, 1958; naturalized, 1982; s. Alfred Georg and Kaethe (Binder) H.; m. Marjorie, Aug. 20, 1983; 1 child, Adam. BSEE, Calif. Poly. Inst., 1981. Telecom. engr. Union Oil Co., L.A., 1982-84; computer planning analyst Union Oil-UNOCAL, 1984-86; supr. facilities mgmt. UNOCAL Corp. Info. Svcs., Anaheim, Calif., 1986-89, bus analyst, 1989, mgr. planning and analysis, 1989-91, mgr. tech. & bus. assessment, 1991-96, exec. dir. Year 2000 Project Office, 1997—; speaker ENTELEC, Dallas, San Antonio, 1983, 85. Host athletic tournament Alfred Roy Herzing Invitational Frisbee Golf Tournament, 1980—. Mem. Toastmasters (L.A. chpt. pres. 1986-87, gov. area 12 1987-88, arminstrv. lt. gov. dist. 52 1988-89, ednl. lt. gov. dist. 52 1989-90, dist. gov. 1990-91, Toastmaster of Yr. 1990, region II conf. edn. presenter 1992, 93, chmn. dist. 52 1992-93, 93-94, pres. speakers forum club 1993-94, CTM/ATY.DTM chmn. founder's dist. 1993-94, 94-95, internat. dir. 1995-97, 3rd v.p. 1998-99, 2nd v.p. 1999—), Yorba Linda Achievers Club (charter mem., pres. 1993-94). Republican. Avocations: frisbees, computer simulations. Home: 20365 Via La Vieja Yorba Linda CA 92887-3211 Office: UNOCAL 376 S Valencia Brea CA 92823

HERZLICH, HAROLD J., chemical engineer; b. Bklyn.; m. Carol Ast; children: Amy, Adam. BSChemE, NYU, 1956; student, So. Conn. Coll., Quinnipiac Coll. Mem. prodn. squadron Goodyear Tire & Rubber Co., Akron, Ohio, 1956-57, mem. process devel., 1957-58; prodn. compounder Armstrong Rubber Co., New Haven, 1958-61, sr. compounder, 1961-62, divsn. compounder, 1962-65, mgr. pass tire comp. devel., 1965-66, mgr. auto tire comp. devel., 1966-68, mgr. pass car tire comp. devel., 1968-70, sr. rsch. chemist, 1970-73, mgr. compound rsch., 1973-75, mgr. compound devel., 1975-85, dir. tire engring., legal matters and product reliability, 1985-88; dir. tire engring., legal matters and product reliability Pirelli Armstrong Tire Co., New Haven, 1988-90; consulting tire engr. Tire Engring., Chemistry and Safety, Las Vegas, 1990—; pres. Elasphalt Corp.; chmn. Internat. Tire Conf.; speaker in field. Tech. editor Rubber and Plastics News. With USCG. Mem. ASTM (mem. E-40), Am. Chem. Soc. (chmn. rubber divsn. 1982—, chmn.-elect 1981, mem. membership com., mem. edn. com., mem. budget and fin. com., treas. rubber divsn. 1978-81, bus. mgr. rubber chemistry and tech., mem. divsn. chemistry and law, hon. life), Soc. Automotive Engrs., Acad. Forensics Sci. (engring. divsn.), Tire Soc., Conn. Rubber Group (edn. chmn., vice chmn., chmn. 1966, hon. life). Avocations: sports, community svc., travel. Home and Office: Tire Engring Chemistry & Safety 8908 Desert Mound Dr Las Vegas NV 89134-8801

HERZOG, ARTHUR, III, author; b. N.Y.C., Apr. 6, 1927; s. Arthur Jr. and Elizabeth Lindsay (Dayton) H.; 1 son by previous marriage, Matthew Lennox. Student, U. Ariz., 1945-46; BA, Stanford U., 1950; MA, Columbia U., 1956. Editor Fawcett Publs., 1957-59; cons. Peace Corps, 1967-68; polit. cons., 1969-71; bd. dirs. Leslie Mandel Enterprises, Mandel Airplane Funding and Leasing Co. Author: (with others) Smoking and the Public Interest, 1963, The War-Peace Establishment, 1965, The Church Trap, 1968, McCarthy for President, 1969, The B.S. Factor,m 1973, The Swarm, 1974, Earthsound, 1975, Orca, 1977, Heat, 1977, rev. edit., 1989, IQ 83, 1978, Make Us Happy, 1978, Glad to be Here, 1979, Aries Rising, 1989, The Craving, 1982, L.S.I.T.T., 1983, Vesco-From Wall Street to Castro's Cuba, The Rise, Fall and Exile of the King of White Collar-Crime, 1987, Takeover, 1987 (formerly L.S.I.T.T.), The Woodchipper Murder, 1989, Seventeen Days: The Katie Beers Story, 1993, How to Write Almost Anything Better and Faster, 1995, (almost all works transl. and published in Hungary); contbr. articles to leading Am. pubs. Campaign mgr. Oreg., nat. pub. rels. dir. Eugene McCarthy Presdl. Campaign, 1968; founder New Democratic Coalition, N.Y. and nationally, 1968-69, Lexington Dem. Club, 1974. With USNR, 1944-45. Mem. PEN, Authors Guild, Authors League. Address: PO Box 294 Wainscott NY 11975-0294 *I do not believe that money and success should figure as strongly as it does in our estimate of what is a good life. Since it often does, though, I would point to perseverance as a major element of success. Another, mostly overlooked, is a lack of dogmatism and a belief in skepticism and personal happiness as ends in themselves.*

HERZOG, BARBARA JEAN, secondary school educator, administrator; b. Fond du Lac, Wis.; d. Charles Victor and Helen Jean (Gutsch) H. BS in Social Studies, U. Wis., Oshkosh, 1970, MS in Teaching in History-Social Sci., 1975; PhD in Ednl. Adminstrn., U. Wis., Madison, 1984. Cert. tchr., Wis.; cert. prin., Wis. Tchr. Woodworth Jr. H.S., Fond du Lac, 1970-75, 76-81; adminstrv. intern Fond du Lac Pub. Schs., 1983, mem. insvc. edn. coun., 1978-84; grad. asst. U. Wis., Madison, 1982-83; tchr. Sabish Jr. H.S., Fond du Lac, 1981-82, 83-84, Shattuck Jr. H.S., Neenah, 1984-87; asst. prin. Neenah Jr. H.S. Dist., 1984-87; tchr., curriculum dir. Oshkosh Area Sch. Dist., 1987-97, asst. supt. instrn., 1997—; ad hoc prof. U. Wis. Oshkosh Coll. Edn., 1977—; presenter U. Wis. Oshkosh NSF Conf., 1976, Wis. Ednl. Rsch. Assn., Milw., 1976, Nat. Coun. for the Social Studies Conf., Mpls., 1978, Tex., 1978, Wis. Coun. for the Social Studies, Oconomowoc, 1978, 83, , 84, 86, Milw. Tchrs. Edn. Assn., 1978, Great Lakes Regional Social Studies Conf., Chgo., 1979, Nat. U. Extension Assn. Region IV Conf., Kalamazoo, 1979, Wis. Edn. Assn. Coun., Milw., 1979, Assn. Tchr. Educators, Washington, 1980, San Diego, 1988, Nat. Coun. on States on Insvc. Edn., San Diego, 1980, 14th Annual Mid. and Jr. H.S. Conf., U. Wis., Oshkosh, 1986, 15th Annual Conf., 1987, Assn. Tchr. Educators Regional Spring Miniclinic, Oak Brook, Ill., 1986, Globescope Wis. 88, Oshkosh, 1988, Assn. Wis. Sch. Adminstrs., Madison, 1988, U. Wis. Oshkosh and Green Bay, 1990, 91, among others. Co-author: (with others) Programming for Staff Development: Fanning the Flame, 1990; contbr. articles to profl. jours. Mem. exec. com. Oshkosh Human Rels. Coun., 1993-96; chairperson, mem. faith formation com. St. Peter Cath. Ch., Oshkosh, 1993-95, communion min., 1982—; mem. South Winnebago pub. edn. com. Am. Cancer Soc., Oshkosh, 1992-96; bd. dirs. Silvercrest Girls' Group Home, Neenah, 1986-87, So. Fox Valley Child Svcs. Soc., Oshkosh 1990-96; mem. ednl. outreach subcom. Oshkosh Cmty. U. Human Rels. Coun., 1989—; alt. Oshkosh Addictions Coord. Bd., 1990-92; mem. bd. visitors Sch. Edn. U. Wis., Madison, 1997—. Recipient Advocacy award Wis. Sch. Counselors Assn., 1992, Best Overall Paper award Wis. Ednl. Rsch. Assn., 1986, Rsch. award Wis. Improvement Program, 1986, U. Wis. Sch. Edn. Alumni Achievement award, 1995, Citation award Wis. AHPERD, 1997. Mem. ASCD, Assn. Am. Sch. Adminstrs., Wis. Coun. for the Social Studies (exec. com. 1980-87), Oshkosh Area Sch. Dist. Adminstrs. Assn., TESOL, Wis. ASCD, Wis. Staff Devel. Coun., Oshkosh Area United Way, Oshkosh Southwest Rotary, Oshkosh C. of C. (edn. com. 1987-96), Phi Delta Kappa (chpt. pres. 1989-90), Delta Kappa Gamma (Helen Duling scholarship 1982). Recipient Adminstr. of Yr. award Oshkosh Area Sch. Dist., 1995. Home: 1632 Menominee Dr Oshkosh WI 54901-2523 Office: Oshkosh Area Sch Dist 215 S Eagle St Oshkosh WI 54901-5624

HERZOG, BEVERLY LEAH, hydrogeologist; b. Fond du Lac, Wis., Aug. 27, 1954; d. Charles Victor and Helen Jean (Gutsch) H.; m. Craig Warren Cutbirth, June 2, 1979. BS in Geology, U. Wis., Oshkosh, Wis., 1976; MS in Hydrology, Stanford U., 1978. Cert. groundwater profl., cert. profl. geologist. Asst. hydrogeologist Donohue & Assocs., Sheboygan, Wis., 1977; cons. Hydrocomp Internat., Palo Alto, Calif., 1977-78; asst. hydrogeologist Camp, Dresser & McKee, Champaign, Ill., 1978-79; asst. geologist Ill. State Geol. Survey, Champaign, 1980-84, assoc. hydrogeologist, 1985-90, sr. hydrogeologist, head groundwater resources & protection, 1991-98, head environ. geology group, 1997—. Mem. editorial bd. Ground Water, 1985-90, Ground Water Monitoring Rev., 1987-97; contbr. numerous articles on ground water in profl. jours. and symposium procs. Bd. dirs. DeWitt County chpt. ARC, Clinton, Ill., 1984-90, CPR and first aid instr. Champaign County ARC, 1978-93; bd. dirs. Green Meadows coun. Girl Scouts U.S., 1994-99, 2d v.p., 1997-99, camp counselor Fox River Area coun., Appleton, Wis., 1972, 73, 76; bd. dirs. Ctr. for Women in Transition, 1999—. Named outstanding vol. Champaign County ARC, 1987; recipient best paper award Ground Water Monitoring Rev., 1988, disting. achievement award Ill. State Geol. Survey, 1989; named woman of distinction Green Meadows Girl Scout Coun., 1994. Mem. ASTM, Assn. Ground Water Scientists and Engrs., Am. Inst. Profl. Geologists (sec. Ill.-Ind. sect. 1992-93), Am. Geophys. Union, Ill. Groundwater Assn. (bd. dirs. 1991, vice chmn. 1992, chmn. 1993), Altrusa (bd. dirs. Champaign-Urbana chpt. 1996-98, pres.-elect 1998—), Sigma Xi. Avocations: racquetball, travel, companion animals. Home: RR 1 Box 45 Bellflower IL 61724-9721 Office: Ill State Geol Survey 615 E Peabody Dr Champaign IL 61820-6918 *When we are striving for success, however we define it, we must take care not to lose our humanity or integrity. Without these, success means nothing. We must still be able to look in the mirror and like the person looking back.*

HERZOG, FRED F., law educator; b. Prague, Czech Republic, Sept. 21, 1907; s. David and Anna (Reich) H.; m. Betty Ruth Cohen, Mar. 27, 1947 (dec. Sept. 1984); children: Stephen E., David R. Dr. Juris, U. Graz (Austria), 1931; JD with high distinction U. Iowa, 1942; LL.D. (hon.), John Marshall Law Sch., 1983. Bar: Iowa 1942, Ill. 1946, U.S. Supreme Ct. 1965. Judge, Vienna, Austria, 1937-38; prof. and dean Chgo.-Kent Coll. Law, 1947-73; spl. atty. Met. San. Dist. Greater Chgo., 1962-70; 1st asst. atty. gen. Ill., 1973-76; dean John Marshall Law Sch., Chgo., 1976-83, prof., 1976—. Recipient Americanism award DAR, 1978; Golden Doctor diploma U. Graz, 1981; award of Excellence, John Marshall Law Sch. Alumni Assn., 1981; cert. of Appreciation, Ill. Dept. Registration and Edn., 1978; Ill. Atty. Gen.'s award for Outstanding Pub. Service, 1976; Torch of Learning award Am. Friends of the Hebrew U., 1986; named to Sr. Citizens Hall of Fame, City of Chgo., 1983. Mem. ABA, Ill. Bar Assn., Chgo. Bar Assn., Ill. Appellate Lawyers Assn., Decalogue Soc. Lawyers, Mid-Am. Club, Internat. Club (Chgo.), Union League Club (Chgo.). Contbr. articles to legal jours. Office: John Marshall Law Sch 315 S Plymouth Ct Chicago IL 60604-3969

HERZOG, JOHN E., securities dealer; b. N.Y.C., Mar. 18, 1936; s. Robert I. and Norma (Englander) H.; m. Diana E. Rigby; children: Mary, Sarah. BA, Cornell U., 1957; postgrad. N.Y. Inst. Fin., 1958; MBA, NYU, 1970. With Eastman Dillon (Paine Weber), Phila., 1957-59; chmn. Herzog, Heine, Geduld, N.Y.C., 1959—, R.M. Smythe & Co., Inc.; charter mem. regulatory policy adv. com. N.Y. Stock Exchange, 1981—, mem. regional firms adv. com.; trustee Securities Industry Inst. Bd. dirs. Resources for Children with Spl. Needs, N.Y.C.; trustee The Knox Sch., 1986-91, Randolph Macon Woman's Coll., Securities Industry Inst.; bd. regents L.I. Coll. Hosp., Bklyn.; founder Mus. Am. Fin. History. Mem. Securities Industry Assn. (chmn. N.Y. area firms com., econ. edn. com. N.Y. dist.). Office: Herzog Heine Geduld Inc 26 Broadway Ste 232 New York NY 10004-1788

HERZOG, LAWRENCE ARTHUR, city planning educator; b. N.Y.C., July 7, 1951; s. Arthur Lawrence and Bernice Herzog; m. Vivienne Lee Bennett, Aug. 19, 1990; 1 child, Adin Jacob. BA, SUNY, Albany, 1973; MA, Syracuse U., 1975, PhD, 1980. Sr. planner Middlesex County Planning Bd., New Brunswick, N.J., 1975-77; sr. Fulbright lectr. Nat. U. Engring., Lima, Peru, 1980; prof. urban studies U. Calif., San Diego, La Jolla, 1981-89; sr. advisor Junin Dept., U.S. Agy. Internat. Devel., Lima, Peru, 1982-83; prof. city planning San Diego State U., 1989—; cons. U.S. Agy. Internat. Devel., Bolivia, 1985, Am. Inst. Archs., Tex., 1988, Calif. Dept. Transport, San Diego, 1991-93; editor, writer Pacific News Svcs., San Francisco, 1988-95; vis. scholar London Sch. Econs., 1990, Autonomous U. Madrid, 1993, Columbia U. Sch. Arch. and Planning, 1994. Author: Where North Meets South, 1990, From Aztec to High Tech, 1999; editor: Planning the International Border Metropolis, 1986, Changing Boundaries in the Americas, 1992. Advisor Citizen Coordinating for Century III, San Diego, 1992-95, New

Sch. Architecture, 1992—; mem. adv. bd. San Diego Dialogue, 1997—. Recipient Donald Robertson Memorial prize, Scotland, 1990; fellow Graham Found. Advanced Studies in Fine Arts, 1998, Ctr. U.S.-Mexican Studies, U. Calif., 1999. Mem. Latin Am. Studies Assn., Urban Affairs Assn., Assn. Collegiate Schs. Planning. Avocations: road bicycling, sea kayaking, hiking, travelling, photography. E-mail: laherzog@mail.sdsu.edu. Office: San Diego State U Sch Pub Adminstrn and Urban Studies MC 4505 San Diego CA 92122-4505

HERZOG, LESTER BARRY, lawyer, educator; b. Presov, Czechoslovakia, July 3, 1953; came to U.S., 1965; s. Alexander and Flora (Braun) H.; m. Terry Lynn Hochhauser, Feb. 6, 1979; children: Simcha, Sarah, Chaim, Judah, Leah. BA, Rabbinical Sem. Belz, Bklyn., 1974; MBA with distinction, L.I. U., 1977; JD cum laude, Bklyn. Law Sch., 1983. Bar: N.Y. 1984, U.S. Dist. Ct. (ea. and so. dists.) N.Y. 1984; CPA, N.Y. Sr. auditor Seidman & Seidman, N.Y.C., 1977-83; sr. trial atty. Office Corp. Counsel N.Y.C. Law Dept., Bklyn., 1983-89; pvt. practice N.Y.C., 1989—; adj. assoc. prof. law and acctg. L.I. U., Bklyn., 1985—. Contbr. articles to profl. jours. Mem. ABA, AICPA (exam grader 1981-83), N.Y. State Bar Assn. Democrat. Jewish. Avocations: chess, fishing, gardening. Home and Office: 1729 E 15th St Brooklyn NY 11229-2084

HERZOG, PETER EMILIUS, legal educator; b. Vienna, Austria, Dec. 25, 1925; came to U.S., 1950, naturalized, 1955; s. Paul and Leopodine (Manhart) H.; m. Brigitte Ecolivet, June 29, 1970; children: Paul, Elizabeth Ann. Student, U. Vienna, 1949-50; BA, Hobart Coll., 1952; LLB summa cum laude, Syracuse U., 1955; LLM, Columbia U., 1956. Bar: N.Y. 1957. Dep. asst. atty. gen. N.Y. State Dept. Law, Albany, 1955-57; asst. atty. gen. N.Y. State Dept. Law, 1957-58; asst. prof. law Syracuse U. Coll. Law, 1958-62, assoc. prof., 1962-66, prof., 1966-83, Crandall Melvin prof., 1983-94, Crandall Melvin prof. emeritus, 1995—, law librarian, 1960-68; staff mem. Columbia U. Project on Inter Procedure, 1960-63; assoc. dir. Project on European Legal Instns., 1968-73; staff mem. UN Commn. on Internat. Trade Law, 1968-69; rsch. fellow Procedural Aspects Internat. Law Inst., 1968-71; lectr. Hague (Netherlands) Acad. Internat. Law, 1992; cons. N.Y. State Eminent Domain Commn., 1971; vis. prof. U. Paris, 1976-77, U. Dijon, France, 1987, U. Fribourg, Switzerland, 1987. Author: (with Martha Weser) Civil Procedure in France, 1967, (with Ivan Head and Frank Dawson) International Law, National Tribunals and the Rights of Aliens, 1971, (with Hans Smit) The Law of the European Economic Community, A Commentary, 1976, (with Schlesinger, Baade and Wise) Comparative Law, 6th edit., 1998; contbr. articles to legal publs.; mem. bd. editors: Am. Jour. Comparative Law, 1977—. Jervey fellow Columbia U., 1956. Mem. Am. Soc. Internat. Law, Soc. de Législation Comparée, Internat. Law Assn., Internat. Acad. Comparative Law (assoc.), Wissenschaftliche Gesellschaft für Verfahrensrecht, Order of Coif, Phi Beta Kappa. Roman Catholic. Home: 112 Erregger Rd Syracuse NY 13224-2220 Office: Syracuse U Coll Law Syracuse NY 13244-1030

HERZOG, RICHARD F., retired science educator; b. Vienna, Austria, Mar. 13, 1911. PhD, U. Vienna, 1933, hon. degree, 1983. Prof. physics U. Vienna, 1950-53, Air Force Cambridge Rsch. Ctr., Bedford, Mass., 1953-58; dir. space sci. lab. GCA Corp., Bedford, 1958-73; prof. physics and astronomy U. So. Miss., Hattiesburg. Hon. chmn. Sims-V Conf., 1985. Issue of Jour. Mass Spectrometry and Ion Physics in his honor, 1971. Mem. Am. Soc. for Mass Spectrometry, Am. Inst. Physics, Sigma Pi Sigma. Home: 601 SW 141st Ave Apt 209 Pembroke Pines FL 33027-1517

HERZSTEIN, ROBERT ERWIN, lawyer; b. Denver, Feb. 26, 1931; s. Sigmund Edwards and Estelle Ruth (Borwick) H.; m. Priscilla Holmes, July 11, 1956; children: Jessica Anne, Emily Holmes, Robert Holmes. AB, Harvard U., 1952, LLB, 1955. Bar: Colo. 1956, D.C. 1959, U.S. Supreme Ct. 1962. Sr. ptnr., other positions Arnold & Porter, Washington, 1958-80, sr. ptnr., 1981-89; undersec. for Internat. Trade U.S. Dept. Commerce, Washington, 1980-81; ptnr. Shearman & Sterling, Washington, 1989-95, counsel, 1995-99; ptnr. Miller & Chevalier, Washington, 1999—. Contbr. articles to profl. jours. Trustee Internat. Law Inst., Washington, 1974—; bd. dirs. Ptnrs. for Dem. Change, Appleseed Found., Coun. of Ams., N.Y., Internat. Human Rights Law Group, Washington, chmn., 1989-93; bd. dirs., faculty Salzburg Seminar in Am. Studies, 1986-93. Mem. ABA, Am. Soc. Internat. Law (exec. coun. 1981-84), Coun. on Fgn. Rels. Home: 4710 Woodway Ln NW Washington DC 20016-3241 Office: 801 Pennsylvania Ave NW Ste 900 Washington DC 20004-2667

HESBURGH, THEODORE MARTIN, clergyman, former university president; b. Syracuse, N.Y., May 25, 1917; s. Theodore Bernard and Anne Marie (Murphy) H. Student, U. Notre Dame, 1934-37; PhB, Gregorian U., 1939; postgrad., Holy Cross Coll., Washington, 1940-43; STD, Cath. U. Am., 1945; 124 hon. degrees awarded between 1954-92. Joined Order of Congregation of Holy Cross, 1934, ordained priest Roman Cath. Ch., 1943. Chaplain Nat. Tng. Sch. for Boys, Washington, 1943-44; vets. chaplain U. Notre Dame, 1945-47, 138 hon. degrees awarded between 1954-98, 1948-49, exec. v.p., 1949-52, pres., 1952-87, pres. emeritus, 1987—, instr., asst. prof. religion, 1945-48, chmn. dept. religion, 1948-49; Fellow Am. Acad. Arts and Scis.; mem. Internat. Fedn. Cath. Univs., Commn. on Humanities, Inst. Internat. Edn. (pres., dir.), Cath. Theol. Soc., Chief Execs. Forum, Am. Philos. Soc., Nat. Acad. Edn., Coun. on Fgn. Rels. (trustee), Nat. Acad. Scis. (hon.), U.S. Inst. Peace (bd. dirs.). Author: Theology of Catholic Action, 1945, God and the World of Man, 1950, Patterns for Educational Growth, 1958, Thoughts for Our Times, 1962, More Thoughts for Our Times, 1965, Still More Thoughts for Our Times, 1966, Thoughts IV, 1968, Thoughts V, 1969, The Humane Imperative: A Challenge for the Year 2000, 1974, The Hesburgh Papers: Higher Values in Higher Education, 1979, God, Country, Notre Dame, 1990, Travels with Ted and Ned, 1992. Former dir. Woodrow Wilson Nat. Fellowship Corp.; mem. Civil Rights Commn., 1957-72; mem. of Carnegie Commn. on Future of Higher Edn.; chmn. U.S. Commn. on Civil Rights, 1969-72; mem. Commn. on an All-Volunteer Armed Force, 1970; chmn. with rank of ambassador U.S. delegation UN Conf. Sci. and Tech. for Devel., 1977-79 ; Bd. dirs. Am. Council Edn., Freedoms Found. Valley Forge, Adlai Stevenson Inst. Internat. Affairs; past trustee, chmn. Rockefeller Found.; trustee Carnegie Found. for Advancement Teaching, Woodrow Wilson Nat. Fellowship Found., Inst. Internat. Edn., Nutrition Found., United Negro Coll. Fund, others; chmn. Overseas Devel. Council; chmn. acad. council Ecumenical Inst. for Advanced Theol. Studies, Jerusalem. Decorated comdr. L'ordre des Arts et des Lettres. Recipient U.S. Navy's Disting. Pub. Service award, 1959; Presdl. Medal of Freedom, 1964, Gold medal Nat. Inst. Social Scis., 1969, Cardinal Gibbons medal Cath. U. Am., 1969, Bellarmine medal Bellarmine-Ursuline Coll., 1970; Meiklejohn award AAUP, 1970, Charles Evans Hughes award Nat. Conf. Christians and Jews, 1970; Merit award Nat. Cath. Ednl. Assn., 1971, Pres.' Cabinet award U. Detroit, 1971; Am. Liberties medallion Am. Jewish Com., 1971; Liberty Bell award Ind. State Bar Assn., 1971; Laetare medal Univ. Notre Dame, 1987, Pub. Welfare medal NAS, 1984; Pub. Svc. award Common Cause, 1984, Disting. Svc. award Assn. Cath. Colls. and Univs., 1982, Jefferson award Coun. Advancement and Support of Edn., 1982. Fellow Am. Acad. Arts and Scis.; mem. NAS (hon.), Internat. Fedn. Cath. Univs., Commn. on Humanities, Inst. Internat. Edn. (pres., bd. dirs.), Cath. Theol. Soc., Chief Execs. Forum, Am. Philos. Soc., Nat. Acad. Edn., Coun. on Fgn. Rels. (trustee). Office: U Notre Dame 1315 Hesburgh Libr Notre Dame IN 46556*

HESKETH, THOMAS R., chemical engineer; b. Balt., May 4, 1954; s. Herbert T. and Arline H. Hesketh; m. Susan P. Hesketh, July 29, 1978; children: Lisa M., Eric T. BSChemE, Princeton U., 1975; MSChemE, U. Wis., 1977; MBA, U. Chgo., 1978. Process engr. Corning Glassworks, Wilmington, N.C., 1979-80, process engrng. mgr., 1980-86; applications engrng. mgr. Corning Glassworks, Corning, N.Y., 1986-88; plant mgr. Heraeus Amersil, Buford, Ga., 1988-89; fiber optics bus. mgr. Heraeus Amersil, Duluth, Ga., 1989-99; ptnr. Proactive Corp. Consolidators, Buford, 1997—. Avocation: sailing. E-mail: tomhesketh@bigplanet.com. Home: 6421 Cannon Dr Flowery Branch GA 30542 Office: Proactive Corp Consolidators 4445 Commerce Dr Buford GA 30518

HESKETT, ROBERT EARL, psychologist. BA, Eastern Coll.; BDiv, Ea. Bapt. Theol. Seminary; MA in Philosophy, U. Pa.; M of Sacred Theology, Boston U.; D of Ministry, Andover Newton Theol. Sch. Ordained to min., Am. Bapt. Chs.; lic. psychologist, Mass. Min. First Bapt Ch. and Eden Bapt. Ch., Bar Harbor, Nebr., 1956-75, Roslindale Bapt. Ch., Boston, 1956-75, First Bapt. Ch., New Bedford, Mass., 1956-75; staff mem. Inter-Ch. Coun. of Greater New Bedford, 1975-83; psychologist Ctr. for Human Svcs., Inc., New Bedford, 1983-92, New Bedford Child and Family Svc., 1993-96; cons. psychologist Mass. Rehab. Commn., 1996—; exec. dir. Cmty. Ctr. for Non-Violence, New Bedford, 1992—; presenter in field. Mem. Southeastern Mass. Psychol. Assn., Internat. Soc. for Traumatic Stress Studies, Internat. Inst. of Bioenergetic Analysis, Delta Kappa Gamma. Home: 8 Cooke St Fairhaven MA 02719

HESLIN, CATHLEEN JANE, artist, designer, entrepreneur; b. Bklyn., Feb. 24, 1929; d. Charles Jenkins and Katherine (Bauer) Hunter; m. John Thomas Heslin, June 24, 1950. AA, Packer Collegiate Inst., Bklyn., 1950; postgrad., Duke U., Pratt Inst. Sr. artist, designer Klopman Mills, Rockleigh, N.J., 1966-72; free-lance designer, 1972-90; propr. Quilters Corner, Tappan, N.Y., 1978-90. Author: History of Rockleigh, N.J., 1648-1973, 1973, Old Order Amish-The People and Their Quilts, 1988; inventor Quilters Quarter measuring device. Councilwoman Borough of Rockleigh, 1973-85, 90-92, pres. coun., 1983-85, historian, 1973-90, chmn. anniversary dedication com., 1973, environ. com., 1974, action com., 1974-75, borough hall com., 1975, acquisition com., 1975, chmn. bicentennial com., 1974-76, chmn. fin. com., 1977-78, chmn. hist. adv. com., 1977-86, liaison to Bergen County hist. programs, 1978, pub. safety com., 1979-84, chmn. bldg. com., 1983-85, housing commn., 1984, Hist. Preservation Commn., 1987-90, ins. com., 1990, liaison to planning bd., 1990, designs for Rockleigh Commons; mem. Rockleigh Planning Bd., 1973, 87-89; Rep. mayoral nominee Borough of Rockleigh, 1988; founder Cathleen Heslin Found., 1990p; trustee Abram Demaree Homestead, 1982-84; established Rockleigh Wildlife Sanctuary and Land Preserve. Recipient various certs. of appreciation. Mem. Tappantown Hist. Soc. (dir.), Soc. Archtl. Historians, Am. Soc. Planning Ofcls., Bergen County Hist. Soc. (trustee 1984-90), Historic Homes Assn. N.J. Obtained State and Nat. Historic Dist. status for Borough of Rockleigh. Home & Office: Haring Farm 5 Piermont Rd Rockleigh NJ 07647-2715

HESLIN, JOHN THOMAS, entrepreneur, historic preservationist; b. Bklyn., Jan. 24, 1927; s. John Joseph and Edna (Young) H.; m. Cathleen Jane Hunter Heslin, June 24, 1950. AB, Duke U., 1952; MSc in Edn., Hofstra U., 1955; MDiv, Union Theol. Sem., 1990; postgrad., Art Students League, 1991. Ordained to Anglican Ch. Holy Order of Deacons, 1993, Sacred Order of Priests, 1995. Supr. E.I. duPont de Nemours & Co., Inc., 1953; owner John T. Heslin Design Studio, 1955-60; freelance editor, 1960-66; pres. John T. Heslin & Co., Inc., 1966-86; bd. dirs. Quilter's Corner, Inc.; career advisor Career Devel. Ctr., Duke U., 1992-98. Author: A Consideration of the Condition of Creation, the Creator and Evil, 1990; author poetry. Fire chief Rockleigh (N.J.) Vol. Fire Dept., 1974-75; chmn. shade tree com. Borough of Rockleigh, 1975-80, marshall, 1975, historic adv. com., 1978-79; vice chmn. Rockleigh Bd. of Adjustment, 1977; chmn. Rockleigh Planning Bd., 1980; establishor Rockleigh Wildlife Preserve, 1977; co-founder, pres. N.J. Historic Homes Assn., 1977-79; founder, dir. Hopewell Found., 1981-84; chmn., bd. trustees Abram Demarest Homestead Restoration, 1981-84; trustee Cathleen Heslin Found., 1991-98. With USN, 1944-46. Mem. N.J. State Vol. Fire Chiefs Assn., Duke U. Alumni Assn., Masons (Free and Accepted, Ancient Accepted Scottish Rite), Shriners, Phi Alpha Kappa, Mu Sigma. Home: Haring Farm 5 Piermont Rd Rockleigh NJ 07647

HESS, BARTLETT LEONARD, clergyman; b. Spokane, Wash., Dec. 27, 1910; s. John Leonard and Jessie (Bartlett) H.; BA, Park Coll., 1931, MA (fellow in history 1931-34), U. Kan., 1932, PhD, 1934; B.D., McCormick Theol. Sem., 1936; m. Margaret Young Johnston, July 31, 1937; children: Daniel Bartlett, Deborah Margaret, John Howard and Janet Elizabeth (twins). Ordained to ministry Presbyn. Ch., 1936; pastor Effingham, Kan., 1932-34, Chgo., 1935-42, Cicero, Ill., 1942-56, Ward Meml. Presbyn. Ch., Detroit, 1956-68, Ward Presbyn. Ch., Livonia, Mich., 1956-92; pastor emeritus, Ward Presbyn. Ch., 1992—; organizing pastor, Knox Presbyn. Ch., Ann Arbor, 1992-96; pastor in residence Cornerstone Evang. Presbyn. Ch., Brighton, Mich., 1997—; interim pastor First Presbyn. Ch., Trenton, Mich., 1998-99. Tchr. ch. history, bible Detroit Bible Coll., 1956-60, bd. dirs., 1956—; minister radio sta. WHFC, Chgo., 1942-50, WMUZ-FM, Detroit, 1958-68, 78—, WOMC-FM, 1971-72, WBFG-FM, 1972-92, WWCN-AM, 1992—; missioner to Philippines, United Presbyn. Ch. U.S.A., 1961; mem. Joint Com. on Presbyn. Union, 1980; adviser Mich. Synod coun. United Presbyn. Ch.; mem. com. Billy Graham Crusade for S.E. Mich., 1976; mem. adminstrv. com. Evang. Presbyn. Ch., 1980-85; mem. joint com. missions Evang. Presbyn. Ch. and the Presbyn. Ch. of Brazil. Mem., organizer Friendship and Svc. Com. for Refugees, Chgo., 1940. Bd. dirs. Beacon Neighborhood House, Chgo., 1945-52, Presbyns. United for Bibl. Concerns, 1975-80; pres. bd. dirs. Peniel Community Center, Chicago, 1945-52. Named Pastor of Year, Mid-Am. Sunday Sch. Assn., 1974; recipient Svc. to Youth award Detroit Met. Youth for Christ, 1979, Father of Evangelical Presbyn. Ch. award, 1991. Mem. Cicero Mins. Coun. (pres. 1951), Phi Beta Kappa, Phi Delta Kappa. Author: (with Margaret Johnston Hess) How To Have a Giving Church, 1974; (with M.J. Hess) The Power of a Loving Church, 1977, How Does Your Marriage Grow, 1982, Never Say Old, 1984; contbr. articles in field to profl. jours. Traveled in Europe, 1939, 52, 55, 68; also in Greece, Turkey, Lebanon, Syria, Egypt, Israel, Iraq; condr. tour of Middle East and Mediterranean countries, 1965, 67, 73, 74, 76, 78, 80, 84, 90, China and Far East, 1982; missioner, India, 1981, 89, Brazil, 85, 86, 87, 89, 95, Argentina, 87, 89, 91, 95. Home: 15191 Ford Rd Dearborn MI 48126-4699 Office: 40000 Six Mile Rd Northville MI 48167-3956 *In the increased velocity and pace of current history, the hunger for God's revelation in the Bible and in Christ is greater than at any time in my ministry of sixty-five years.*

HESS, CHARLES EDWARD, environmental horticulture educator; b. Paterson, N.J., Dec. 20, 1931; s. Cornelius W. M. and Alice (Debruyn) H.; children: Mary, Carol, Nancy, John, Peter; m. Eva G. Carroad, Feb. 14, 1981. BS, Rutgers U., 1953; MS, Cornell U., 1954, PhD, 1957; DAgr (hon.), Purdue U., 1983; DSc (hon.), Delaware Valley Coll., Doylestown, Pa., 1992. From asst. prof. to prof. Purdue U., West Lafayette, Ind., 1958-65; rsch. prof., dept. chmn. Rutgers U., New Brunswick, N.J., 1966, assoc. dean, dir. N.J. Agrl. Exptl. Sta., 1970, acting dean Coll. Agrl. and Environ. Sci., 1971, dean Cook Coll., 1972-75; assoc. dir. Calif. Agrl. Exptl. Sta., 1975-89; asst. sec. sci. and edn. USDA, Washington, 1989-91; dean Coll. Agrl. and Environ. Scis. U. Calif., Davis, 1975-89, prof. dept. environ. horticulture, 1975-94; prof. emeritus, 1994—; dir. internat. programs Coll. Agrl. and Environ. Scis. U. Calif., Davis, 1992-98, spl. asst. to provost, 1994—; cons. U.S. AID, 1965, Office Tech. Assessment, U.S. Congress, 1976-77; chmn. study team world food and nutrition study NAS, 1976; mem. Calif. State Bd. Food and Agr., 1984-89; mem. Nat. Sci. Bd., 1982-88, 92-98, vice-chmn., 1984-88; co-chmn. Joint Coun. USDA, 1987-91. Mem. West Lafayette Sch. Bd., Ind., 1963-65, sec., 1963, pres., 1964; mem. Gov.'s Commn. Blueprint for Agr., 1971-73; bd. dirs. Davis Sci. Ctr., 1992-94; trustee Internat. Svc. for Nat. Agrl. Rsch., The Hague, The Netherlands, 1992-98, bd. chmn., 1995-96. Mem. U.S. EPA (mem. biotech. sci. adv. com. 1992-96), AAAS (chmn. agriculture sect. 1989-90), Am. Soc. Hort. Sci. (pres. 1973), Internat. Plant Propagators Soc. (pres. 1973), Agrl. Rsch. Inst., Phi Beta Kappa, Sigma Xi, Alpha Zeta, Phi Kappa Phi. Office: U Calif Coll Agrl and Environ Scis Dept Environ Horticulture Davis CA 95616

HESS, DARLA BAKERSMITH, cardiologist, educator; b. Valparaiso, Fla., June 4, 1953; d. James Barry and Irma Marie (Baker) Bakersmith; m. Leonard Wayne Hess, July 20, 1988; 1 child, Ever Marie. BS, Birmingham So. Coll., 1975; MD, Tulane U., 1979. Diplomate Am. Bd. Internal Medicine, Am. Bd. Cardiovascular Disease. Commd. ensign USN, 1979, advanced through grades to lt. comdr., 1988; resident in internal medicine Portsmouth (Va.) Naval Hosp., 1979-82, cardiologist, head non-invasive cardiology, 1986-88; fellow in cardiology San Diego Naval Hosp., 1982-84; cardiologist, head med. officer in charge ICU Camp Lejeune (N.C.) Naval Hosp., 1984-85; asst. prof. medicine U. Miss. Med. Ctr., Jackson, 1988-91, asst. prof. ob/gyn., 1990-91; dir. noninvasive sect. cardiology, dir. fetal echocardiograp U. Mo., Columbia, 1991—; co-dir. Adult Cogenital Heart Disease Clinic, 1991—, assoc. prof. medicine, assoc. prof. ob/gyn., 1998—. Author: (with others) Obstetrics and Gynecology Clinics, 1992, Clinical Problems in Obstetrics & Gynecology, 1993, General Medical Disorders During, 1991; editor: Fetal Echocardiography, 1999; contbr. articles to So. Med. Jour., Ob/Gyn. Clinics N.Am., So. Med. Assn. Annual Meeting, Soc. Perinatal Obs., Jour. Reproductive Medicine; co-editor Fetal Echocardiography, 1998. Fellow Am. Coll. Cardiology; mem. Am. Heart Assn. (fellow stroke coun.), Am. Soc. Echocardiography, Am. Assn. Nuclear Cardiology, Phi Beta Kappa, Alpha Omega Alpha. Republican. Episcopalian. Home: PO Box 10200 Columbia MO 65205-4003 Office: U Mo Health Sci Ctr 1 Hospital Dr Columbia MO 65201-5276

HESS, DAVID WILLARD, journalist; b. Moundsville, W.Va., Sept. 19, 1933; s. Willard Cary and Flora Ruth (Marling) H.; m. Dorthea Lee West, Sept. 29, 1956; children—Daniel Robert, Laura Cary (dec.). BA, Ohio State U., 1958, MA, 1964. Washington corr. Beacon Jour., Akron, Ohio, 1971-80; asst. news editor Knight-Ridder Newspapers, Washington, 1980-81, congl. corr., 1981-83, 88—, nat. polit. corr., 1983-84, White House corr., 1984-88; chmn. bd. Nat. Press Bldg. Corp., 1985-87, corp. exec. com., 1987-88, also bd. dirs. Bd. dirs. Washington Press Found., 1985-92, treas., 1989-91, v.p., 1991-92; mem. standing com. Corrs. for Ho. and Sen. Press Galleries, 1992-94. Recipient Worth Bingham prize for investigative journalism Bingham Found., 1978, grand prize for consumer journalism Nat. Press Club, 1978, Media award for best gen. reporting Akron Press Club, 1979; Profl. Journalism fellow Stanford U.,1970. Mem. Soc. Profl. Journalists (Washington chpt. Hall of Fame 1997). Presbyterian. Club: Nat. Press (pres. 1985).

HESS, DENNIS JOHN, investment banker; b. Manila, July 7, 1940; s. Carl and Anna (Harris) H.; m. Marilyn Golchert, July 7, 1977; children: Whitney, Christine, Craig. B.S., U. Calif., Berkeley, 1962. With Merrill Lynch & Co., 1969—, v.p., 1977-80; chmn. bd., chief exec. officer Merrill Lynch, Hubbard, Inc., N.Y.C., 1980—; dir. diversified fin. svcs. Merrill Lynch, Pierce, Fenner & Smith, 1985—; pres., chief oper. officer ML Realty, 1983—; chmn., CEO, ML Equity Mgmt. Corp., 1984—, Paine Webber Life Ins. Co.; chmn. bd. Tandem Fin. Corp.; CEO, Merrill Lynch Ins. Group, 1986—; pres. DJH, Inc., Greenwich, Conn.; bd. dirs. United First Mortgage Corp., M.L. Huntoon Paige, Inc., MLH Puerto, SA, Family Life Ins. Co., DJH, Inc.; exec. v.p. Payne Webber Inc.; chmn., CEO Paine Webber Life Ins. Co. Served to 1st lt. USAF, 1962-66. Mem. Greenwich Country Club. Republican. Roman Catholic. Office: 1200 Harbor Blvd Weehawken NJ 07087-6728

HESS, DONALD F., retired manufacturing executive, accountant; b. Manheim, Pa., Feb. 13, 1919; s. Elam Gross and Marcelia Edna (Farmer) H.; m. Christina Leed Lamparter, Oct. 1, 1937; children: Donald L., David A. Controller Bearings Co. of Am., Lancaster, Pa., 1948-52, prodn. planning mgr., 1952-61; materials mgr. Jamesbury Corp., Worcester, Mass., 1961-64; dir. materials mgmt. Keuffel & Esser Co., Hoboken, N.J., 1964-66; seminar instr. Donald F. Hess Assocs., Lancaster, 1966-72; materials mgr. Rutt Custom Kitchens, Goodville, Pa., 1972-92; leader in-plant and pub. seminars throughout U.S. Developer various prodn. and mgmt. publs.; contbr. articles and book chpts. to profl. pubs. Donald F. Hess award York (Pa.) Coll. created in his honor by the Am. Prodn. and Inventory Control Soc., 1983. With U.S. Army, 1944-46. Decorated Bronze Star medal. Mem. Am. Prodn. and Inventory Control Soc. (founding mem., 1st v.p. edn. and research 1959, exec. v.p. 1960, nat. pres. 1961, hon. life mem. 1962; founder, 1st pres. Lancaster chpt. 1958-59, hon. life mem. 1960). Home: 401 L6 Eden Rd Lancaster PA 17601

HESS, EMERSON GARFIELD, lawyer; b. Pitts., Nov. 13, 1914. A.B., Bethany Coll., 1936; J.D., U. Pitts., 1939. Bar: Pa. 1940. Sr. ptnr. Hess, Reich, Georgiades, Wile & Homyak and predecessor firm Emerson G. Hess & Assocs., Pitts., 1940-92; of counsel DeMarco & Assocs., Pitts., 1992—; solicitor Scott Twp. Sch. Bd., 1958-65; legal counsel Judiciary com. Pa. Ho. of Reps., 1967-69; solicitor Scott Twp., 1968-69, Crafton Borough, 1974-78, Authority for Improvements in Municipalities of Allegheny County, 1977-80. Bd. dirs. Golden Triangle YMCA, Pitts., 1945—, WQED Ednl. TV, Pitts., 1952-68; pres., dir. Civic Light Opera Assn., Pitts., 1967-68; mem. internat. com. YMCA World Svc., N.Y.C., 1968-78; trustee, chmn. Cen. Christian Ch., Pitts., 1962-63; pres. Anesthesia and Resuscitation Found., Pitts., 1964-88, Pa. Med. Rsch. Found., 1960-88. Mem. ABA, Pa. Bar Assn., Allegheny County Bar Assn. Home: 43 Robin Hill Dr Mc Kees Rocks PA 15136-1238 Office: DeMarco & Assocs 946 Gulf Tower 707 Grant St Pittsburgh PA 15219-1908

HESS, EVELYN VICTORINE (MRS. MICHAEL HOWETT), medical educator; b. Dublin, Ireland, Nov. 8, 1926; came to U.S., 1960, naturalized, 1965; d. Ernest Joseph and Mary (Hawkins) H.; m. Michael Howett, Apr. 27, 1954. MB, B.Ch, BAO, U. Coll., Dublin, 1949; MD, Univ. Coll., Dublin, 1980. Intern West Middlesex Hosp., London, Eng., 1950; resident Clare Hall Hosp., London, 1951-53, Royal Free Hosp. and Med. Sch., London, 1954-57; rsch. fellow in epidemiology of Tb Royal Free Med. Sch., London, 1955; asst. prof. internal medicine U. Tex. Southwestern Med. Sch., 1960-64; assoc. prof. dept. medicine U. Cin. Coll. Medicine, 1964-69, McDonald prof. medicine, 1969—, dir. div. immunology, 1964-95; sr. investigator Arthritis and Rheumatism Found., 1963-68; attending physician Univ. Hosp., VA Hosp.; cons. Children's Hosp., Cin., 1967—, Jewish Hosp., Cin., 1968—; mem. various coms., mem. nat. adv. coun. NIH; mem. various coms. FDA, Cin. Bd. Health. Contbr. articles on immunology, rheumatic diseases to jours., chpts. to books. Active Nat. Pks. Assn., Smithsonian Instn., others. Recipient Arthritis Found., 1973, 78, 83, Am. Lupus Soc., 1979, Am. Acad. Family Practice, 1980, award for AIDS work State of Ohio, 1989, Spirit of Am. Women award, 1989; travel fellow Royal Free Med. Sch., Scandinavia, 1956, Empire Rheumatism Coun., 1958-59. Master ACP (Master Tchr. award 1995), ACR (Disting. Rheumatologist award 1996); fellow AAAS, Am. Acad. Allergy, Royal Soc. Medicine; mem. Heberden Soc., Am. Coll. Rheumatology, Pan-Am. League Assns. for Rheumatology, Ctrl. Soc. Clin. Rsch., Am. Fedn. Clin. Rsch., Am. Assn. Immunologists, Am. Soc. Nephrology, Am. Soc. Clin. Pharmacology and Therapeutics, Transplantation Soc., N.Y. Acad. Scis., Soc. Exptl. Biology and Medicine, Rheumatological Soc. Colombia (hon.), Rheumatological Soc. Peru (hon.), Rheumatological Soc. Italy (hon.), Clin. Immunol. Soc. Japan (hon.), Alpha Omega Alpha. Home: 2916 Grandin Rd Cincinnati OH 45208-3418 Office: U Cin Med Ctr Cincinnati OH 45267

HESS, FREDERICK J., lawyer; b. Highland, Ill., Sept. 22, 1941; s. Fred and Matilda (Maiden) H.; m. Mary V. Menkhus, Nov. 13, 1976; children—Frederick, M. Elizabeth. B.S. in Polit. Sci. and History, St. Louis U., 1963; J.D., Washburn Sch. Law, Topeka, 1971. Bar: Kans. 1971, Ill. 1975, U.S. Supreme Ct. 1975, D.C. 1977, U.S. Tax Ct. 1977. Asst. U.S. atty. Dept. Justice, East St. Louis, Ill., 1971-73, 1st asst. U.S. atty., 1973-76; ct. appt. U.S. Atty. E. Dist. of Ill., 1977; ptnr. Stiehl & Hess, Belleville, Ill., 1977-82; U.S. atty. U.S. Dist. Ct. (so. dist.) Ill., East St. Louis, 1982-93; pvt. practice Lewis Rice & Fingersh, Belleville, 1993—; past pres. Nat. Assn. Former U.S. Attys., 1996; part-time judge Ill. Ct. of Claims, 1997—. Served to capt. USAF, 1964-68. Fellow ABA, ABA Found., Ill. Bar Assn., Ill. Bar Found.; mem. Kans. Bar Assn., D.C. Bar Assn. Republican. Clubs: Tamarac Golf (Shilo, Ill.). Office: Lewis Rice & Fingersh 325 S High St Belleville IL 62220-2116

HESS, FREDERICK SCOTT, artist; b. Balt., July 12, 1955; s. Charles Stevens and Katherine Ruth Hess; m. Gita Tabatabai, Dec. 28, 1989; children: Ava Katarina, Atiyeh Mehri. BS, U. Wis., 1977; postgrad., Vienna Acad. Fine Art, 1979-84. artist in residence Bahman Cultural House, Tehran, Iran, 1992, Cité Internat. des Arts, Paris, 1993. Solo exhibitions include Gallery Herzog, Vienna, Austria, 1979, Galerie im Tabak Museum, Vienna, Austria, 1982, Ousey Gallery, L.A., Calif., 1985, 86, 88, 89, 90, 92, 94, U. So. Calif. Fisher Art Gallery, 1987-88, Santa Clara U. de Saisset Mus., Santa Clara, Calif., 1987-88, Mt. San Jacinto Coll., San Jacinto, Calif., 1989, Fresno (Calif.) Art Mus., Calif., 1991, Underground Exhibition, Tehran, Iran, 1993, Art Inst. So. Calif., Laguna Beach, 1996, Mt. S. Antonio Coll. Walnut, Calif., 1997; exhibited in group shows at Taipei (Taiwan) Fine Arts Mus., 1987, U. So. Calif., L.A., 1987-88, Laguna Art Mus., Laguna Beach, Calif., 1988, Henry Art Gallery, U. Washington, Seattle, 1988, Fresno (Calif.) Art Mus., 1988-89, Flint (Mich.) Inst. Art, 1991, San Diego Mus. Art, 1991, Triton Mus., Santa Clara, Calif., 1992, Oakland (Calif.) Mus., 1992, Flint (Mich.) Inst. Art, 1992, Nev. Inst. Contemporary Art, Las Vegas, 1995, L.A. County Mus. Art, 1997, Armory Ctr. for Arts, Pasadena, 1997, Laband Art Gallery, L.A., 1998. Recipient Theodor Koerner award Austrian Min. Culture, Vienna, 1981, WESTAF award Nat. Endowment for the Arts, 1990; fellow J. Paul Getty Trust, 1991, Nat. Endowment for the

Arts, 1991. Mem. The Drawing Group. Avocations: writing, polo, sailing. Address: 1830 Lake Shore Ave Los Angeles CA 90026-1716

HESS, GARY RAY, historian; b. Pitts., Mar. 23, 1937; s. John C. and Dorothy (Brombach) H.; m. Rose Cycler, Aug. 20, 1966; 1 child, Ryan Charles. BA, U. Pitts., 1959; MA, U. Va., 1962, PhD, 1965. From asst. prof. to assoc. prof. history Bowling Green (Ohio) State U., 1964-71, prof., 1971-88, disting. rsch. prof., 1988—, chair history dept., 1973-81, 85-92, acting dean arts & scis., 1981-82, interim dir. Ctr. Rsch. & Pub. Svc., 1998-99. Author: America Encounters India, 1971, U.S. at War 1941-45, 1985, U.S. Emerges as Southeast Asian Power, 1987, Vietnam & United States, 1987, rev. edit., 1998; mem. editl. bd. Diplomatic History, 1998—. Mem. city coun. City of Bowling Green, 1990-92. Mem. Soc. Historians Am. Fgn. Rels. (mem. coun. 1986-93, pres. 1991). E-mail: ghess@bgnet.bgsu.edu. Office: Bowling Green State U History Dept Bowling Green OH 43403

HESS, GEORGE FRANKLIN, II, lawyer; b. Oak Park, Ill., May 13, 1939; s. Franklin Edward and Carol (Hackman) H.; m. Diane Ricci, Aug. 9, 1974; 1 child, Franklin Edward. BS in Bus., Colo. State U., 1962; JD, Suffolk U., 1970; LLM, Boston U., 1973. Bar: Pa. 1971, Fla. 1973, U.S. Tax Ct. 1974, U.S. Dist. Ct. (so. dist.) Fla. 1975. Assoc. Hart, Childs, Hepburn, Ross & Putnam, Phila., 1970-72; instr. Suffolk U. Law Sch., Boston, 1973-74; ptnr. Henry, Hess & Hoines, Ft. Lauderdale, Fla., 1974-79; with Mousaw, Vigdor, Reeves & Hess, Ft. Lauderdale, Fla., 1979-94; pvt. practice Ft. Lauderdale, Fla., 1995—. Bd. dirs. Childrens Home Soc., Ft. Lauderdale, 1985-89, Nadeau Charitable Found., 198—. Lt. USNR, 1963-66. Mem. ABA, SAR, Fla. Bar Assn., Broward County Bar Assn., Lauderdale Yacht Club, USN League, Phi Alpha Delta. Episcopalian. Home: 2524 Castilla Is Fort Lauderdale FL 33301-1505 Office: 333 N New River Dr E Fort Lauderdale FL 33301-2241

HESS, GEORGE PAUL, biochemist, educator; b. Vienna; came to U.S., 1938; s. Henry Steven Hess and Edith Muller; m. Betsey S. Williams, Oct. 1953 (div. Dec. 1979); children: Peter, Richard, Paul, David; m. Susan Elizabeth Coombs, 1980. AB, U. Calif., Berkeley, 1951, PhD, 1953. Postdoctoral fellow MIT, 1951-53, Nat. Infantile Paralysis, 1953-55; instr. Cornell Med. Sch., 1955; asst. prof. biochemistry Cornell U., Ithaca, N.Y., 1956-60; assoc. prof. Cornell U., Ithaca, 1960-64, prof., 1964—; vis. fellow chemistry Yale U., 1960, U.S. State Dept. Cultural Exchange prof. to Europe, 1963; vis. prof. biophysics U. Pa., Phila., 1964-65, biochemistry U. Hawaii, Honolulu, Jan. 1966, chemistry U. Ariz., Tucson, Feb. 1968, biology MIT, 1990; U.S. State Dept. Cultural Exch. prof. to Europe, 1970; lectr. Naito Found., Japan, 1988. Mem. Biochemistry Editl. Adv. Bd.; adv. bd. Ctr. Molecular and Behavioral Neuroscis., Universidad del Caribe, P.R. With U.S. Army, 1945-47. Recipient Alexander von Humboldt Sr. Scientist award U. Konstanz, 1982, Outstanding Educator Recognition award Cornell Merrill Presdl. scholar, 1994, 97, Wellcome vis. professorship, 1998; Guggenheim fellow, sr. Fulbright grantee Max-Planck-Inst. fur physikalische Chemie, 1962-63; spl. NIH fellow Med. Rsch. Coun. Lab Molecular Biology, 1969-70; Churchill Coll. U. Cambridge vis. fellow 1969-70; NIH Nat. Inst. of Neurol. Diseases and Storke Fogarty scholar-in-residence, 1999—. Fellow AAAs, Am. Acad. Microbiology; mem. NAS, Am. Chem. Soc., Biophys. Soc., Fedn. Am. Soc. of Exptl. Biologists, N.Y. Acad. Scis., Soc. Neurosci., Protein Soc. Home: 123 Heights Ct Ithaca NY 14850-2450 Office: Cornell Univ 216 Biotechnology Bldg Ithaca NY 14853-2703

HESS, HANS OBER, lawyer; b. Royersford, Pa., Nov. 8, 1912; s. Samuel Harley and Annamae (Wenger) H.; m. Dolores Groke, May 18, 1940; children: Antonine (Mrs. Joseph J. Gal), Roberta (Mrs. Edward S. Trippe), Liese (Mrs. Arleigh P. Helfer, Jr.), Kristina (Mrs. Charles H. Bonner). A.B., Ursinus Coll., 1933, LL.D. (hon.), 1979; LL.B., Harvard U., 1936; LL.D. (hon.), Muhlenberg Coll., 1964; D.F.A. (hon.), Phila. Coll. Art, 1981. Of counsel to Ballard, Spahr, Andrews & Ingersoll, Phila. Editor: Fiduciary Rev, monthly, The Nature of a Humane Society, 1976. Former mem. exec. coun. Luth. Ch. in Am.; trustee Lankenau Hosp., Phila. U. of the Arts; former chmn. Mary J. Drexel Home, Lankenau Med. Rsch. Ctr.; former bd. dirs., sec. Phila. Orch. Assn., Acad. Music Phila.; former mem. Harvard Overseers Com. to Visit Law Sch.; former nat. chmn. Harvard Law Sch. Fund. Mem. ABA, Pa., Phila., Montgomery County bar assns., Harvard Law Sch. Assn. Clubs: Philadelphia, Union League, Philadelphia Country (Phila.). Home: 1400 Waverly Rd #41 Gladwyne PA 19035-1274 Office: 1735 Market St Fl 51 Philadelphia PA 19103-7502

HESS, JANICE BURDETTE, nursing administrator; b. LaGrange, Ga., July 4, 1946; d. Carl Alton and Bennetta Felton (Hipp) Burdette; m. John Randall Hess, Aug. 19, 1966; children: Heather Bennetta, Laurie Ellen. Diploma, Orange Meml. Sch. Nursing, Orlando, Fla., 1967; certificate nurse practitioner, Brigham Young U., 1976; BSN cum laude, So. Missionary Coll., Collegedale, Tenn., 1980; MS in Nursing, U. Fla., 1984. Cert. nurse practitioner in adult health; cert. in nursing adminstr. ICU staff nurse West Volusia Meml. Hosp., Deland, Fla., 1967-69; dir. health svcs., nurse practitioner coll. health Stetson U., Deland, 1969-85; coord. nursing, nurse practitioner adult health & amb. care VA Outpatient Clinic, Daytona Beach, Fla., 1985-95; clin. dir., nurse practitioner family health svcs. Munroe Regional Health Systems, Ocala, Fla., 1995-98; nurse practitioner, primary care and employee health svcs. VA Outpatient Clinic, Daytona Beach, Fla., 1998—; nurse practitioner, adj. faculty U. Fla., Orlando, 1991—. Mem. adv. com. grad. nursing program U. Ctrl. Fla., Head Start Marion County. Mem. Fla. Nurses Assn., VA Ambulatory Care Nurse Network, Ctrl. Fla. Advanced Coun. Nursing (pres., editor newsletter), Sigma Theta Tau. Home: 865 N Summit Ave Lake Helen FL 32744-2002

HESS, JEANETTE RUTH, county official; b. Columbus, Wis., July 5, 1938; d. Lester M. and Laura A. (Adams) Schmidt; m. John E. Hess, Dec. 30, 1961. BA, Milw.-Downer Coll., 1960. Tchr. Aurora East (Ill.) H.S., 1960-67; sec. No. Ill. U., DeKalb, 1967-69; continuity writer Sta. KDTH Radio, Dubuque, Iowa, 1970-72; asst. advt. mgr. Flexsteel Industries, Dubuque, 1972-74; adminstr. County of Dubuque, 1974—; mgmt. chair Dubuque Area Labor-Mgmt. Coun., 1995—; chair Dubuque County Sesquicentennial Commn., 1994-97. Bd. dirs. Iowa Assn. Hosps. and Health Systems, 1997—, Substance Abuse Svcs. Ctr., Dubuque, 1988-93; vice-chair bd. dirs. Mercy Health System, Dubuque, 1991—; pres. Dubuque Area Congregations United, 1986; sec. bd. Dubuque Cmty. Food Pantry, 1987—; pres. Project Concern Bd., Dubuque, 1989-90. Named 1st Citizen Dubuque Telegraph Herald, 1996, hon. chairperson WalkAmerica, 1997; recipient Labor-Mgmt. Partnership award Dubuque Area Labor-Mgmt. Coun., 1994-95. Mem. Iowa Pub. Employment Rels. Assn., Iowa State Assn. Counties. Democrat. Lutheran. Avocations: gardening, embroidery, quilting.

HESS, JOHN B., oil industry executive. Chmn., CEO Amerada Hess Corp., N.Y.C., 1995—. Office: Amerada Hess Corp 1185 Avenue Of The Americas New York NY 10036-2601*

HESS, JOHN WARREN, scientific institute administrator, educator; b. Lancaster, Pa., May 6, 1947; s. John Warren and Barbara Kathryn (Spencer) H.; m. Letitia Jean Schrantz, Mar. 20, 1971; children: Nathan James, Joshua Kyle. BS in Geol. Scis., Pa. State U., 1969, PhD in Geology, 1974. Asst. rsch. prof. water resources ctr. Desert Rsch. Inst., Las Vegas, Nev., 1974-78, assoc. rsch. prof., 1978-86, rsch. prof., 1986—, dir. environ. isotope lab., 1981-87, dep. dir., 1987-89, exec. dir., 1989—, interim v.p. rsch., 1994-95, v.p. acad. affairs, 1995—; chmn. bd. dirs. Karst Waters Inst., Charlestown, W.Va. Contbr. over 75 articles to profl. jours. Adult leader Boy Scouts Am., Las Vegas, 1978—. Hon. Rsch. fellow U. Glasgow, Scotland, 1980-81. Fellow Geol. Soc. Am. (2nd vice chmn. 1993-94, 1st vice chmn. 1994-95, chair 1995-96), Nat. Speleological Soc.; mem. AAAS, Am. Geophys. Union, Internat. Assn. Hydrogeologists, Geochem. Soc. Home: 7205 Fury Ln Las Vegas NV 89128-4219 Office: Desert Rsch Inst 755 E Flamingo Rd Las Vegas NV 89119-7363

HESS, KARL, electrical and computer engineering educator; b. Trumau, Austria, June 20, 1945; came to U.S. 1977; naturalized 1988; s. Karl Joseph and Gertrude (Resch) H.; m. Sylvia Horvath, Sept. 1967; children—Ursula, Karl. Ph.D., U. Vienna, Austria, 1970. Rsch. asst. U. Vienna, 1969-71, asst. prof., 1971-77, univ. lectr., 1977; vis. assoc. prof. U. Ill., Urbana, 1977-80, prof. elec. and computer engring., 1988—, adj. prof. supercomputing applications, 1990—, Swanlund Endowed chair, 1996—, prof. physics. Contbr. articles to profl. jours.; patentee in field. Univ. scholar U. Ill., 1982-83; Fulbright scholar, 1973-74. Fellow AAAS, IEEE (J.J. Ebers award 1994, David Sarnoff field award 1995), Am. Phys. Soc., Am. Acad. Arts and Scis. Avocations: classical music; chess. Home: 1805 Bentbrook Dr Champaign IL 61822-9220 Office: U Ill Beckman Inst 405 N Mathews Ave Urbana IL 61801-2325

HESS, LEONARD WAYNE, obstetrician gynecologist, perinatologist; b. Richlands, Va., Nov. 23, 1949; s. Ralph Eugene and Lucille Cindy (Kennedy) H.; m. Sarah Mahala Leedy, Nov. 27, 1969 (div. July 1988); children: Gregory Scott, Lauren Ashley; m. Darla Irma Bakersmith, July 20, 1988; 1 child, Ever Marie. BSChemE, Va. Poly. Inst., 1973; MD, Va. Commonwealth U., 1977. Diplomate Nat. Bd. Med. Examiners, Am. Bd. Ob-Gyn., also sub.-bd. Maternal-Fetal Medicine. Intern U.S. Naval Hosp., Portsmouth, Va., 1977-78; resident in ob-gyn. U.S. Naval Hosp., Portsmouth, 1978-81; fellow in maternal-fetal medicine Naval Med. Command, Walter Reed Army Med. Ctr., Washington and Bethesda, 1981-83; staff dept. ob-gyn. U. Health Scis., Bethesda, 1981-85; dept. ob-gyn. U.S. Naval Hosp., Portsmouth, 1985-87; comdr. USNR, 1987-88; asst. prof. dept. ob-gyn. U. Miss. Med. Ctr., Jackson, 1987-91; assoc. prof. ob-gyn. U. Mo. Med. Ctr., Columbia, 1991-96, head obstetrics and maternal-fetal medicine, 1991-96, prof., chmn. ob-gyn., 1996—, chmn.ob-gyn., 1996—; mem. Med. Ethics Com., U.S. Naval Hosp., Portsmouth, 1985-87; mem. Patient Care Com., U. Miss. Med. Ctr., Jackson, 1988-91, Infection Control Com., 1988-91; bd. examiner Am. Bd. Ob-Gyn., 1997—. Author: Fetal Echocardiography, 1999; cons. editor Obstetrics and Gynecology, 1988—, Am. Jour. Obstetrics and Gynecology, 1988—, Am. Jour. Med. Genetics, 1989—; contbr. numerous articles to profl. jours. Mem. AMA, USP (ob-gyn. adv. panel 1995—), Am. Coll. Obstetricians and Gynecologists, Soc. Perinatal Obstetricians, Am. Inst. Ultrasound in Medicine, Assn. Profs. Gynecology and Obstetrics, Cen. Assn. Obstetricians and Gynecologists, Am. Soc. Human Genetics, So. Med. Assn., Winifred L. Wiser Soc., Miss. State Obstet. and Gynecol. Soc., Cen. Med. Soc., Gynecic Soc., Med. Soc. Va., Portsmouth Acad. Medicine, Med. and Surgical Soc. of Md., Miss. State Med. Assn., Assn. Mil. Surgeons, Miss. Perinatal Assn., So. Perinatal Assn. Republican. Episcopalian. Office: U Mo Med Ctr HSC N625 Columbia MO 65212 Address: PO Box 10200 Columbia MO 65205-4003

HESS, MARCIA WANDA, retired educator; b. Cin., Mar. 15, 1934; d. Edward Frederick Lipka and Rose (Wirtle) Lipka Stanley; m. Edward Emanuel Grenier, Aug. 9, 1952 (div.); m. Thomas Benton Hess, Mar. 25, 1960; children: Kathleen Ann, Cynthia Jean, Thomas Allen. Grad. high sch., Cin. Instr. asst. Cin. Pub. Schs., 1970-95, also mem. staff desegregation workshop and unified K-12 reading communication arts program staff tng. com.; ret., 1995. Contbr. tchr.-instr. asst. handbook, instr. asst. tng. film. Mem. Winton Place Vets of World War II Women's Aux. (pres. 1982-84, bd. dirs. 1982-86, 89-91, v.p. 1997-99). Republican. Roman Catholic. Avocations: travel, reading. collecting first editions, needlepoint, photography. Home: 157 Palisades Pt Apt 4 Cincinnati OH 45238-5660

HESS, MARGARET JOHNSTON, religious writer, educator; b. Ames, Iowa, Feb. 22, 1915; d. Howard Wright and Jane Edith (Stevenson) Johnston; m. Bartlett Leonard Hess, July 31, 1937; children: Daniel, Deborah, John, Janet. BA, Coe Coll., 1937. Bible tchr. Cmty. Bible Classes, Ward Presbyn. Ch., Livonia, Mich., 1959-96, Christ Ch. Cranbrook (Episcopalian), Bloomfield Hills, Mich., 1980-93, Luth. Ch. of the Redeemer, Birmingham, Mich., 1993—. Co-author: (with B.L. Hess) How to Have a Giving Church, 1974, The Power of a Loving Church, 1977, How Does Your Marriage Grow?, 1983, Never Say Old, 1984; author: Love Knows No Barriers, 1979, Esther: Courage in Crisis, 1980, Unconventional Women, 1981, The Triumph of Love, 1987; contbr. articles to religiouos jours. Home: 15191 Ford Rd Apt 302 Dearborn MI 48126-4696 *A lifetime of teaching the Bible, mainly to women, has shown me how it meets people's needs, in the home, in the work place, in the world.*

HESS, MARILYN ANN, state legislator; m. Dennis J. Hess; children: Christine, Craig. AA, NYU, 1977; BBA in Mgmt. cum laude, Pace U., 1980. Assoc. Merrill Lynch, N.Y.C., 1972-77; home improvement contractor Conn., 1982-90; mem. Conn. Ho. of Reps., 1993—; state rep. 150th Assembly Dist., Conn., 1993—; chmn. Conn. Internat. Trade Coun., 1995—; mem. Rep. Roundtable of Greenwich, 1993—, Amb. Roundtable, 1994—, Conn. Reps. for Choice, 1992—; dir. Rep. Town Com., 1989—. Organizer pack 516 Boy Scouts Am., N.Y.C., 1976; fund raiser, chmn. Lewisboro Neighbor's Club, South Salem, 1979; sec. Ridgefield HIst. Dist. Commn., 1984-85, Greenwich Hist. Dist. Commn., 1988-90, Friends of the Byram Shubert Libr. Bd., 1989-93; del. Parents Together, 1980; underwriting com. Bruce Mus. Ball, 1990-91; alternate Greenwich Planning and Zoning Commn., 1990-93; founding trustee Byram Scholarship fund, 1991—; co-founder Byram River Watershed Alliance, 1995—; bd. dirs. YMCA, Greenwich, 1997—. Named Mother of Yr., Town and Village Newspaper, 1974. Home: 29 Field Point Dr Greenwich CT 06830-7013 Office: Ho of Reps State Capitol Hartford CT 06106

HESS, MILTON SIEGMUND, computer company executive; b. Balt., Apr. 22, 1941; s. Fred and Bernice (Goldstick) H.; m. Sheila Lee Rosenzwog, Aug. 31, 1963 (div. Mar. 1985); children: Frederick Michael, Sanford Fairfax; m. Cecia Ohringer, June 16, 1985. B of Engring. Sci. with highest honors, Johns Hopkins U., 1962; MS, Columbia U., 1963, D in Engring. Sci., 1966. Mem. tech. staff Bell Telephone Labs., Inc., Allentown, Pa., 1966-69, supr., 1969-72; supr. Piscataway, N.J., 1972-77; prin. cons. Am. Mgmt. Systems, Inc., Arlington, Va., 1977-86, v.p., 1986-96; sr. cons. Am. Mgmt. Systems, Inc., Arlington, 1996-97, v.p., 1998—. Contbr. articles to profl. jours. NSF fellow, 1962, 63-65; David and Florence Guggenheim fellow, 1962; Md. State Engring. scholar, 1958-62, Engring. Profs. Emeriti scholar Johns Hopkins U., 1961. Mem. IEEE (computer soc.). Jewish. Achievements include research in design and quality improvement strategies for information systems. Avocations: motorcycle touring, indoor gardening, running, weight training. Office: Amer Mgmt Systems Inc 4050 Legato Rd Fairfax VA 22033-4087

HESS, P. GREGORY, lawyer; b. Wheeling, W.Va., Sept. 15, 1946; s. Philip Tilman and Virginia Lamberton (Jackson) H.; m. Susan Marion Kyff, Aug. 16, 1969; children: Philip Andrew, Peter Gregory, Michael Trevor, Aimee Suzanne. AB, Princeton U., 1968; JD, Yale U., 1971; LLM in Taxation, NYU, 1976. Bar: N.Y. 1972, Fla. 1976. Assoc. Breed, Abbott and Morgan, N.Y.C., 1971-73; ptnr. Williamson and Green, N.Y.C., 1973-76, Williamson and Hess, N.Y.C., 1976-80; of counsel Christy & Viener, N.Y.C., 1980, ptnr., 1980-98; ptnr. Salans, Hertzfeld, Heilbronn, Christy & Viener, N.Y.C., 1999—; bd. dirs. Barr and Barr, Inc., N.Y.C. Trustee N.Y. Sch. for Deaf, White Plains, 1982—, pres., 1990-93, chmn., 1993—; trustee Princeton (N.J.) Campus Club, 1972-97; bd. dirs. Greater Westchester Youth Orchs. Assn., Inc., Millwood, N.Y., 1986-91, chmn., 1988-91; bd. dirs., v.p. Westchester Found. for the Deaf, Inc., Hawthorne, N.Y., 1997—. Mem. Princeton Club N.Y. Home: 47 Quaker Bridge Rd Ossining NY 10562-1624 Office: Salans Hertzfeld Heilbronn Christy & Viener 620 5th Ave New York NY 10020-2402

HESS, PATRICK HENRY, chemist; b. Albia, Iowa, Aug. 6, 1931; s. John Henry and Mary Ellen (Judge) H.; m. Ann Marie Malone, June 6, 1959; children: Michelle, Maria, Margaret, Catherine, John. B.S. in Chemistry, U. Iowa, 1953; M.S. in Organic Chemistry, U. Nebr., 1958, Ph.D. in Organic Chemistry, 1960. Chemist Iowa State Hygienic Labs., 1953-54; teaching asst. U. Nebr., 1956-57, rsch. asst., 1957-58, rsch. fellow, 1958-60; rsch. chemist Chevron Research Co., Richmond, Calif., 1960-64, Chevron Oil Field Rsch. Co., La Habra, Calif., 1964-65; sr. rsch. chemist Chevron Oil Field Research Co., La Habra, Calif., 1965-69, sr. rsch. assoc., 1969-92; ret., 1992; rsch. group supr. Chevron Corp. Contbr. articles to profl. jours.; patentee crude oil recovery. Active youth sports PTA. Served with USAF, 1954-55. Rsch. fellow 3-M, 1958-59, Monsanto, 1959-60. Mem. Am. Chem. Soc., Soc. Petroleum Engrs., Sigma Xi, Alpha Chi Sigma, Alpha Tau Omega. Republican. Roman Catholic. Home: 12463 Jeremiah Dr Auburn CA 95603-9051 *Retirement is great - so long as one doesn't become too retired.*

HESS, PETER ANDREAS, German language educator; b. Sept. 20, 1955. BA, U. Zurich, 1977; MA, U. Mich., 1980, PhD, 1984. Assoc. prof. German, U. Tex., Austin, 1987—, grad. advisor, 1994—; vis. asst. prof. U. Ky., 1984-85, U. Ariz., 1985-86; dir. Austria-Ill. Exch. program, Vienna, 1986-87. Pres. Barton Hills Neighborhood Assn., Austin, 1998—. E-mail: phess@mail.utexas.edu. Home: 2502 Rock Terr Dr Austin TX 78704-3840 Office: U Tex Dept German 3 102 Ep Schoch Bldg Austin TX 78712-1190

HESS, RICHARD LOWELL, broadcast executive; b. Forest Hills, N.Y., Oct. 19, 1951; s. Richard Farmer and Barbara Evelyn (McCann) H.; m. Mary Elizabeth McIntyre, Sept. 17, 1983; children: Robert Ogilvie, Michael McIntyre. BS, St. Johns U., 1973. Audio/video sys. engr. ABC-TV, N.Y.C., 1973-81; dir. engring. McCurdy Radio Ind., Toronto, Ont., 1981-83; v.p Nat. Tele Cons., Glendale, Calif., 1983—. Patentee in field. Mem. Audio Engring. Soc., Soc. Motion Picture and TV Engrs., Sons of the Revolution. Episcopalian. Avocations: wildlife/nature photography, music, computers. E-mail:rlhess@mindspring.com. Office: Nat Tele Cons 700 N Brand Blvd Fl 10 Glendale CA 91203-1202

HESS, SIDNEY J., JR., lawyer; b. Chgo., June 26, 1910; s. Sidney J. and Alma (Katz) H.; m. Jacqueline Engelhardt, Aug. 28, 1948; children—Karen E. Hess Freeman, Lori Ann. PhB, U. Chgo., 1930, JD, 1932. Bar: Ill. 1932. Practiced in Chgo., 1932—; mem. firm Aaron, Schimberg & Hess, 1933-84, D'Ancona & Pflaum, 1985—; bd. dirs., legal counsel Jewish Fedn. of Met. Chgo., 1968-77, v.p., 1972-74, pres., 1974-76; dir., legal counsel Jewish United Fund Met. Chgo., 1971-77, pres., 1974-76; legal counsel Jewish Welfare Fund Met. Chgo., 1969-73; bd. dirs. S. Silberman & Sons, Chgo. Metallic Products, Inc., Vienna Sausage Mfg. Co. Mem. exec. com. Anti-Defamation League, 1954-57, HIAS, 1974-90; mem. nat. devel. coun., aims com., citizens bd. U. Chgo.; bd. dirs. Schwab Rehab. Hosp., 1954-65, pres., 1959-64; trustee Michael Reese Founds., 1991—. Recipient Judge Learned Hand Human Rels. award Am. Jewish Com., Julius Rosenwald Meml. award Jewish Fedn. Met. Chgo., 1994, Army Commendation Medal (USAF); elected to Jewish Cmty. Ctrs. Hall of Fame, City of Chgo. Sr. Citizens Hall of Fame. Mem. ABA, Ill. State Bar Assn., Chgo. Bar Assn., Am. Judicature Soc., U. Chgo. Law Sch. Assn. (dir.), Std. Club (past pres., dir.), Mid-Day Club (Chgo.), Northmoor Country Club (Highland Park, Ill.), Tamarisk Country Club (Rancho Mirage, Calif.), Phi Beta Kappa, Pi Lambda Phi. Home: 1040 N Lake Shore Dr Chicago IL 60611-1165 Office: 111 E Wacker Dr Chicago IL 60601-4205 *In my judgment the principles and standard of conduct which one must observe in daily life include a clear recognition of the rights and privileges of others, coupled with a desire to provide assistance to those who are less fortunate and unable to provide for themselves. No conduct of one's affairs can be adequate and fulfilling without recognition and observance of relationships with family. In all dealings, one must act with the highest degree of integrity and conscientious application.*

HESS, SIDNEY WAYNE, management consultant; b. Ames, Iowa, Oct. 21, 1932; s. Edwin M. and Mina Larson H.; m. Grayce Ann Medici, Oct. 9, 1954; children: Debra, Peter, Diana. B.S., M.I.T., 1953; postgrad., Delft Technische Hogeschool, 1953-54; Ph.D., Case Inst. Tech., 1960; M.A. (hon.), U. Pa., 1971. Mgr. ops. research Atlas Chem. Industries, Inc., Wilmington, Del., 1959-66; assoc. prof., dir. Mgmt. and Behavioral Sci. Center, U. Pa., 1966-75; dir. pharm. program devel. ICI Americas, 1974-76; v.p. planning and research ICI Americas, Wilmington, Del., 1976-80; v.p., gen. mgr. aerospace div. ICI Americas, 1980-86; v.p. mfg. Synthes Ltd. (USA), 1986; sr. v.p. Chase Enterprises, 1987-89; prof. mgmt. Drexel U., Phila., 1989-94; pres. Hess Assoc., 1986—; bd. dirs. Ketron, Inc.; prin. Becknell, Frank, Gross & Hess, Inc., 1968-71. Contbr. articles to profl. jours. Bd. dirs. Girls Inc. of Del., 1980-96, 98—, also sec.; trustee Concord Presbyn. Ch., 1978-80; mem. Adv. Com. on Indsl. Innovation, Dept. Commerce, 1978-79. Served to 1st lt. U.S. Army, 1954-56. Fulbright fellow, 1953. Mem. Inst. Mgmt. Sci. (past internat. sec. and pres., Disting. Svc. medal 1992), Ops. Rsch. Soc. Am. (past pres. Delaware Valley sect.), Am. Def. Preparedness Assn. (bd. dirs. Phila. sect.), Chem. Mktg. Rsch. Assn. (Meml. award), Inst. for Ops. Rsch. and Mgmt. Sci. (pub. info. com.), Coun. of Ringfield Pvt. Resdl. Devel. (pres.), Greenville Country Club, MIT Club of Delaware Valley (bd. dirs., pres.), Tau Beta Pi, Theta Chi.

HESS, STEPHEN, political scientist, author; b. N.Y.C., Apr. 20, 1933; s. Charles and Florence (Morse) H.; m. Elena Shayne, Aug. 23, 1959 (div. 1979); children: Charles P., James R.; m. Beth Amster, Aug. 22, 1982. Student, U. Chgo., 1950-52; BA, Johns Hopkins U., 1953. Jr. instr. polit. sci. Johns Hopkins U., 1953-55; staff asst. to U.S. Pres., 1959-61; asst. to minority whip U.S. Senate, 1961; assoc. fellow Inst. for Policy Studies, 1964-65; fellow Inst. Politics J.F. Kennedy Sch. Govt., Harvard, 1967-68; dep. asst. to U.S. Pres. for urban affairs, 1969; nat. chmn. White House Conf. on Children and Youth, 1969-71; sr. fellow Brookings Instn. Washington, 1972—; mem. Washington regional selection panel Pres.'s Commn. on White House Fellows, 1973; cons. Ford Found., 1974-76; mem. D.C. Bd. Higher Edn., 1973-76; chmn. D.C. Coun. Home Rule Transition Commn., 1974; U.S. alt. rep. UNESCO Gen. Conf., 1974; mem. alumni fellows adv. com. Inst. Politics, J.F. Kennedy Sch. Govt., Harvard U., 1974—; mem. 20th Century Fund task forces, 1975, 78; mem. U.S. Nat. Commn. for UNESCO, 1975-77; editor in chief Nat. Rep. Platform, 1976; mem. adv. coun. on gen. govt. Rep. Nat. Com., 1978-81; U.S. alt. rep., UN Gen. Assembly, 1976; cons. USIA, 1976, U.S. Office Mgmt. and Budget, 1977, German Marshall Fund of U.S., 1978—; bd. dirs. Internat. Writers Svc., 1978—; mem. vis. com. Gerald R. Ford Inst. for Pub. Svcs., Albion Coll., 1979-82; fellow faculty govt. Harvard U., 1979-82; cons. Russell Sage Found., 1980; mem. adv. com. Fund for Investigative Journalism, 1981—; mem. steering com. project on media and sci. Georgetown U. Med. Ctr., 1985; mem. sr. adv. bd. ctr. for press, politics and pub. policy John F. Kennedy Sch. Govt., Harvard U., 1987—; vis. prof. Johns Hopkins U., 1990, UCLA, Washington program, 1990. Author: (with Malcolm Moos) Hats in the Ring: The Making of Presidential Candidates, 1960, America's Political Dynasties, 1966, rev. edit., 1996; (with David S. Broder) The Republican Establishment, 1967; (with Milton Kaplan) The Ungentlemanly Art: A History of American Political Cartoons, 1968, rev. edit., 1975; (with Earl Mazo) Nixon: A Political Portrait, 1968, rev. edit., 1969, The Presidential Campaign, 1974, rev. edit., 1987, Organizing the Presidency, 1976, rev. edit., 1988, The Washington Reporters, 1981; The Government/Press Connection: Press Officers and Their Offices, 1984; The Ultimate Insiders: U.S. Senators in the National Media, 1986, Live from Capitol Hill! Studies of Congress and the Media, 1991, International News & Foreign Correspondents, 1995, rev. edit., 1997, Presidents & The Presidency, 1995, News & Newsmaking, 1995, (with Sandy Northrop) Drawn & Quartered, 1996, The Little Book of Campaign Etiquette, 1998. With AUS, 1956-58. Fellow Nat. Acad. Pub. Adminstrn. Home: 3705 Porter St NW Washington DC 20016-3103 Office: Brookings Instn 1775 Massachusetts Ave NW Washington DC 20036-2188

HESS, SUZANNE HARRIET, newspaper administrator, photographer; b. Steubenville, Ohio, Nov. 8, 1941; d. Roswell J. and Ruth R. (Feuer) Caulk; m. Richard Robert Hess, Aug. 28, 1960 (div. Oct. 1989); children: Richard, Rebecca. Student, Lane C.C., 1961. Cert. radiologist, Oreg.; cert. ofcl. USA Track and Field, 1992-97. Med. asst. Dr. John Burket, Medford, Oreg., 1970-72; sec. receptionist Dr. Paul Saarinen, Eugene, Oreg., 1982-84; office mgr. Europcar Internat., Sicily, Italy, 1989-91; visitor svcs. mgr. Conv. and Visitors Assn. Lane County, Eugene, Oreg., 1991-94; office mgr. Nat. Masters News, Eugene, Oreg., 1994-97; adminstrv. editor Nat. Masters News, Eugene, 1998—; bd. dirs. U.S. Amateur Track and Field, Oreg., Photographer Nat. Masters News; nat. sec. USA Track and Field-Masters Com., 1997-98. Sec. Oreg. Track Club, Eugene, 1993-96, com. person for preservation of Prefontaine Rock, 1995; protester Preservation of Old Growth Timber, Eugene, 1994; elected nat. sec. USA Track and Field Masters Com., 1996. Recipient Appreciation award Oreg. Track Club, 1995, 2 Nat. Championship awards U.S. Amateur Track and Field, 1995, Silver medal 16# and 25# weight throw U.S. Amateur Track and Field Nat. Masters Indoor Championship, 1995, Bronze medal discus and hammer U.S. Amateur Track and Field Nat. Masters Outdoor Championships, 1995, Gold medal 16# weight throw and 25# superweight throw U.S. Amateur Track and Field Nat. Masters Weight and Superweight Championships, 1995, Gold medal U.S. Amateur Track and Field Nat. Masters Weight Pentathlon, 1995, Bronze medal 16# weight throw, Silver medal 25# super weight throw U.S. Amateur Track & Field Indoor Nat. Championships, Boston, 1997, Gold medals 16# and 25# superweight U.S. Amateur Track and Field Indoor Nat. Championships, Boston, 1998; named All Am. U.S. Amateur Track and Field, 1995, 97, 98. Democrat. Avocations: track and field, bicycling, travel. Office: Nat Masters News 1675 Willamette St Eugene OR 97401-4013

HESSE, CHRISTIAN AUGUST, mining and underground construction consultant; b. Chemnitz, Germany, June 20, 1925; s. William Albert and Anna Gunhilda (Baumann) H.; B. Applied Sci. with honors, U. Toronto (Ont., Can.), 1948; m. Brenda Nora Rigby, Nov. 4, 1964; children: Rob Christian, Bruce William. Registered profl. engr., Can.; chartered engr., U.K. In various mining and constrn. positions, Can., 1944-61; jr. shift boss N.J. Zinc Co., Gilman, Colo., 1949; asst. layout engr. Internat. Nickel Co., Sudbury, Ont., 1949-52; shaft and tunnel engr. Perini-Walsh Joint Venture, Niagara Falls, Ont., 1952-54; constrn. project engr. B. Perini & Sons (Can.) Ltd., Toronto, Ottawa, and New Brunswick, 1954-55; field engr. Aries Copper Mines Ltd., No. Ont., 1955-56; instr. in mining engring. U. Toronto, 1956-57; planning engr. Stanleigh Uranium Mining Corp. Ltd., Elliot Lake, Ont., 1957-58, chief engr., 1959-60; subway field engr. Johnson-Perini-Kiewit Joint Venture, Toronto, 1960-61; del. Commonwealth Mining Congress, Africa, 1961; with U.S. Borax & Chem. Corp., 1961-90; mng. dir. Yorkshire Potash, Ltd., London, 1970-71, gen. mgr., pres. Allan Potash Mines Ltd., Allan, Sask., Can., 1974, chief engr. U.S. Borax & Chem. Corp., L.A., 1974-77, v.p. engring., 1978-81, 87-90, v.p. and project mgr. Quartz Hill molybdenum project, 1981-90; v.p. Pacific Coast Molybdenum Co., 1981-90, v.p. mining devel., 1984-90. Co-author publs. on submarine tailings disposal. Sault Daily Star scholar, Sault Sainte Marie, Ont., Can., 1944. Fellow Inst. Mining and Metallurgy; mem. SME/AIME (chmn. So. Calif. mining sect. 1994-95), Can. Inst. Mining and Metallurgy (life), Assn. Profl. Engrs. Ont., Prospectors and Developers Assn., N.W. Mining Assn., Alaska Miners Assn., L.A. Tennis Club. Lutheran.

HESSE, DOUGLAS DEAN, English educator; b. DeWitt, Iowa, July 25, 1956; s. Donald Glen and Coral Ardis (Krukow) H.; m. Dawn Dannenbring, June 7, 1981 (div. 1996); children: Monica, Andrew; m. Becky Bradway, Mar. 7, 1998. BA, U. Iowa, 1978, MA, 1980, PhD, 1986. Editor ACT, Iowa City, 1978-80; instr. English Findlay (Ohio) Coll., 1980-83; prof., dir. grad. studies Ill. State U., Normal, 1986—; editor WPA, 1994-98. Actor, stage mgr. cmty. theatre, Bloomington, Ill., 1991—; coord. Earth Day Observance, Bloomington, 1991; vol. Metcalf Sch., Bloomington, 1988—. Mem. MLA, Assn. Tchrs. Advanced Composition, Coun. Writing Program Adminstrs. (pres.), Conf. Coll. Composition (exec. com.), Nat. Coun. Tchrs. English, Rhetoric Rev. Soc. Democrat. Lutheran. Avocations: acting, singing, swimming, tennis. Home: 204 William Dr Normal IL 61761-1851 Office: Ill State U 4240 Dept English Normal IL 61790-4240

HESSE, KAREN (SUE), writer, educator; b. Balt., Aug. 29, 1952; d. Alvin Donald and Frances Broth Levin; m. Randy Hesse; children: Kate, Rachel. BA, U. Md., 1975. Reference libr. U. Md., 1973-75, leave benefit coord., 1975-76; advt. sec. Country Journal mag., 1976-77, typesetter, proofreader, 1978-88; mental health care provider, 1989-91, children's lit. reviewer, 1993-94. Author: (children's books) Wish on a Unicorn, 1991 (Hungry Mind Rev. Children's Book of Distinction 1992), Letters From Rifka, 1992 (Nat. Jewish Book award 1993, IRA Children's Book award 1993, Christopher award 1992, Sydney Taylor Book award 1992, ALA Notable Book 1992, ALA Best Book for Young Adults 1992, Sch. Libr. Jour. Best Book of Yr. 1992, Horn Book Outstanding Book of Yr. 1992, Booklist Editors' Choice 1992, N.Y. Pub. Libr. 100 Titles for Reading and Sharing 1992), Poppy's Chair, 1993 (Am. Booksellers Assn. Pick of List 1993), Lester's Dog, 1993 (Best Book of Yr. Sch. Libr. Jour. 1993, Notable Children's Trade Book in Field of Social Studies 1993), Lavender, 1993, Sable, 1994 (Sch. Libr. Jour. Best Book of Yr. 1994, N.Y. Pub. Libr. 100 Titles for Reading and Sharing 1994, Boston Globe 10 Best Trade Books 1994, Parenting Mag. 40 Outstanding Children's Books 1994), Phoenix Rising, 1994 (Sch. Libr. Jour. Best Book of Yr. 1994, IRA Tchr.'s Choice 1995, N.Y. Pub. Libr. Books for the Teenage 1995, Best Book for Young Adults ALA 1995, Notable Book, 1995, Wilson Libr. Bull. 33 Favorite Reads 1994 (S.C. Jr. Book award, 1996, 97, others), A Time of Angels, 1995 (IRA Tchr's Choice 1996, IRA Young Adults' Choice, 1997, N.Y. Pub. Libr. Books for the Teenager 1995), The Music of Dolphins, 1996 (Pub.'s Weekly Best Book of Yr. 1996, Best Book of Yr. Sch. Libr. Jour. 1996, Book Links, 100 Titles for Reading and Sharing N.Y. Pub. Libr. Children's Book 1996, Best Books for Young Adults ALA, 1997, Golden Kite Honor Book, 1997), Out of the Dust, 1997 (Newbery medal 1998, Scott O'Dell award 1998), Just Juice, 1998 (100 Titles for Reading and Sharing N.Y. Pub. Libr. 1998, Notable Children's Trade Book in the Field of Social Studies 1998), Come On, Rain!, 1999 ; contbr. When I Was Your Age, Vol. II, 1999, articles to profl. jours. Chmn. Sch. Bd., 1989; sec. bd. dirs. Moore Free Libr., 1989-91; active Hospice, 1988—. Mem. Soc. Children's Book Writers and Illustrators, So. Vt. Soc. Children's Book Writers (leader 1985-92), Ctr. for Children's Environ. Lit., Author's Guild. Avocations: reading, hiking, cultivating friendships, music, dowsing. Office: Scholastic 555 Broadway New York NY 10012-3919

HESSE, MARTHA O., natural gas company executive; b. Hattiesburg, Miss., Aug. 14, 1942; d. John William and Geraldine Elaine (Ossian) H. B.S., U. Iowa, 1964; postgrad., Northwestern U., 1972-76; M.B.A., U. Chgo., 1979. Research analyst Blue Shield, 1964-66; dir. div. data mgmt. Am. Hosp. Assn., 1966-69; dir., chief operating officer SEI Info. Tech., Chgo., 1969-80; assoc. dep. sec. Dept. of Commerce, Washington, 1981-82; exec. dir. Pres.' Task Force on Mgmt. Reform, 1982; asst. sec. mgmt. and adminstrn. Dept. of Energy, Washington, 1982-86; chmn. FERC, Washington, 1986-89; sr. v.p. 1st Chgo. Corp., 1990; now pres. Hesse Gas, Houston; bd. dirs. Pinnacle West Capital Corp., Ariz. Pub. Svc. Co., , Mut. Trust Life, Laidlaw, Aqua Alliance Inc., The Beacon Coun., CIGNA Utilities Adv. Bd. Office: Box 2160 Winnemucca NV 89446-2160

HESSE, THURMAN DALE, welding and metallurgy educator, consultant; b. Plymouth, Wis., Nov. 28, 1938; s. Leonard Ferdinand and Eileen H.; m. Virginia Raynoha, Sept. 5, 1959; children: Daniel Jacob, David Tyler, Laura Alice. BS, Wis. State Coll. & Inst. Tech., 1962; MS, Stout State U., 1965; postgrad., U. Wis., 1974-75. Tchr. welding State Vocat. Tech. & Adult Edn., Madison, 1965-96, tchr. machine shop, 1966-96, tchr. welding tech., 1968-96; welding instr. indsl. div. Madison (Wis.) Area Tech. Coll., 1966-96; weld test condr. Wis. Dept. Industry Labor & Human Rels., Madison, 1976—; owner Tech. Welding Svcs., Cottage Grove, Wis., 1978—; lectr. U. Wis. Engring. Extension, Madison, 1978-85. Producer videotape on welding career options; contbr. articles to Welding Jour. Mem. coun. St. Stephens Luth. Ch., Monona, Wis., 1982-85. Mem. ASTM, Am. Welding Soc. (cert. welding inspector, chmn. bd. dirs. Madison-Beloit chpt., membership com. 1989-92, Howard Adkins award 1975, Dist. 12 dir. 1992-99), Am. Soc. Metals. Home and Office: Tech Welding Svc 2302 Whiting Rd Cottage Grove WI 53527-9724

HESSELBEIN, FRANCES RICHARDS, foundation executive, consultant, editor; b. South Fork, Pa.; d. Burgess Harmon and Anne Luke (Wicks) Richards; widowed, 1978; 1 child, John Richards. DHL (hon.), Buena Vista Coll., 1987, Juniata Coll., 1990, Hood Coll., 1991; D Mgmt. (hon.), GM Inst., 1990; LLD (hon.), Wilson Coll., 1991; LHD (hon.), Marymount-Tarrytown Coll., 1993; DHL (hon.), Boston Coll., 1994, U. Nebr., Kearney, 1994, Lafayette Coll., 1995, Carroll Coll., 1996, Fairleigh Dickinson U., 1996, Muhlenburg Coll., 1996. CEO Talus Rock Girl Scout Coun., Johnstown, 1970-74, Penn Laurel Girl Scout Coun., York, Pa., 1974-76, Girl Scouts U.S., N.Y.C., 1976-90; pres., CEO Peter F. Drucker Found. Nonprofit Mgmt., N.Y.C., 1990-99, chmn., 1999—; bd. dirs. Mut. of Am. Ins. Co., N.Y.C.; mem. nat. bd. visitors Peter F. Drucker Grad. Mgmt. Sch. Claremont (Calif.) Grad. Sch., 1987—; chmn. bd. govs. Josephson Ethics Inst.; mem. adv. com. to bd. dirs. N.Y. Stock Exch., 1988-91; bd. govs. Ctr. for Creative Leadership, Greensboro, N.C., 1992—; mem. adv. bd. Harvard Bus. Sch.'s Initiative on Social Enterprise, Harvard's Kennedy Sch. Govt. Nonprofit Policy and Leadership Program. Editor-in-chief Leader to Leader; co-editor The Leader of the Future, The Organization of the Future, The Community of the Future, Drucker Found. Future Series. Trustee Juniata Coll., Huntingdon, Pa., 1988—, Allentown (Pa.) Coll., 1988-97; mem. Pres.'s Adv. Com. on Points of Light Initiative Found., 1989; bd. dirs. Nat. Exec. Svc. Corps., N.Y., Commn. on Nat. and Cmty. Svc., 1991-94, Village Found., also vice-chmn.; mem. adv. bd. The Leadership Inst., U. So. Calif., 1991, Harvard Bus. Sch.'s Initiative on Social Enterprise, Harvard U.'s John F. Kennedy Sch. Govt. Nonprofit Policy and Leadership Program. Recipient Outstanding Achievement award Inter-Svc. Club Coun., Johnstown, 1976, Entrepreneurial Woman award Women Bus. Owners of N.Y., 1984, Nat. Leadership award United Way of Am., Washington, 1985, Disting. Cmty. Svc. award Mut. of Am. Ins. Co., 1985, Dir.'s Choice-award Nat. Women's Econ. Alliance, 1989, Pa. Soc. Disting. Citizen award, 1991, Wilbur M. McFeeley award Internat. Mgmt. Coun. YMCA, 1993; inducted into the Bus. Hall of Fame, Johnstown, 1995; named Outstanding Exec., Savvy Mag., 1985; on cover BusinessWeek, 1990, Presdl. Medal of Freedom, 1998; featured in Chief Exec. mag., 1995, Fortune, 1995, 96, Chapel of Four Chaplains Gold Legion of Hon. medal, 1999; named Disting. Alumni Fellow U. Pitts., 1999. Mem. Sky Club, Pa. Soc. Club. Office: Peter F Drucker Found Nonprofit Mgmt 320 Park Ave 3d Fl New York NY 10022-6815

HESSELINK, ANN PATRICE, financial executive, lawyer; b. Tokyo, July 20, 1954; d. Ira John Jr. and Etta Marie (Ter Louw) H.; 1 child, Katherine Marie Hesselink Hicks. AB in Psychology, Hope Coll., 1975; JD, St. Johns U., 1980; advanced profl. cert. in fin., NYU, 1983. Bar: N.Y. 1981; CPA, N.Y. Tax mgr. Coopers & Lybrand, N.Y.C., 1980-82; asst. v.p. Bankers Trust Co., N.Y.C., 1982-83; dir. internat. taxes PepsiCo, Inc., Purchase, N.Y., 1983-85; sr. v.p., dir. taxes Young & Rubicam Inc., N.Y.C., 1986-94; v.p. taxes, tax counsel AT&T Capital Corp., Morristown, N.J., 1994-97. Trustee, v.p. Blue Rock Sch., Palisades, N.Y., 1987-89; treas., bd. dirs. Plays for Living, 1991-98; trustee New Brunswick Sem., 1993-98; bd. trustees Ctrl. Coll., 1999—. Mem. ABA, N.Y. State Bar Assn., AICPA, Am. Sch. in Japan Alumni Assn. (chmn. N.Y. region). Democrat. Presbyterian. Home: 27 Ballantine Rd Mendham NJ 07945-3004

HESSELINK, LAMBERTUS, electrical engineering and physics educator; b. Enschede, The Netherlands, Dec. 4, 1948; came to U.S., 1971; s. Lambertus and Wilhelmina (ten Tye) H. BSME, Twente Inst. Tech., Enschede, 1970, BS in Applied Physics, 1971, postgrad., 1974; MSME, Calif. Inst. Tech., 1972, PhD in Applied Mechs., Physics, 1977. Research fellow Calif. Inst. Tech., Pasadena, 1977-78, instr. applied physics, 1978-80, sr. research fellow fluid mechs., 1979-80; asst. prof. aeros. and astronautics Stanford (Calif.) U., 1980-85, asst. prof., 1985—, assoc. prof. elec. engring., 1980-85, asst. prof., 1985-90, prof. electrical engring. and aeronautics/astonautics, 1990—; cons. Hughes Aircraft Corp., Culver City, Calif., 1978-79, MCC Corp., 1986-92; invited scientist image processing work group for Hubble Space Telescope, 1990; assoc. editor Jour. Applied Sci. and Applied Optics, 1990; founder Optitek, Inc.; cons. to industry and govt.; mem. scientific adv. bd. USAF, 1995—. Patentee in field. Recipient Stheeman prize Twente Inst. Tech., 1970; Fulbright fellow 1971-74; Josephine de Karman fellow, 1974-75. Fellow Optical Soc. Am.; mem. AIAA (Engr. of Yr. 1982), Soc. Photo-Optical Instrumentation Engrs. Optical Soc. Am., Am. Phys. Soc., Royal Dutch Acad. Arts and Scis. (corr.), Sigma Xi. Office: Stanford U Dept Electrical Engring Durand 353 Stanford CA 94305-4035

HESSELLUND-JENSEN, PETER LYKKE, lawyer; b. Stockholm, Sweden, Mar. 22, 1945; s. Aage and Juliette (Mathiassen) H.-J.; m. Julia Deane O'Connor, Sept. 24, 1973. Student, U. Copenhagen, Denmark, 1971; LLM, Columbia U., 1972. Bar: N.Y. 1976, U.S. Dist. ct. (so. dist.) N.Y. 1976, D.C. 1989, U.S. Dist. Ct. D.C. 1989, U.S. Ct. Appeals (D.C.cir.) 1989. Sec. in legal dept. Danish Ministry of Fgn. Affairs, Copenhagen, 1973-74; internat. law cons. Baker & McKenzie, N.Y.C., 1975; assoc. Burlingham Underwood & Lord, N.Y.C., 1975-81, Cardillo & Corbett, N.Y.C., 1981-83; pvt. practice N.Y.C., 1983-87; ptnr. Foyen & Peri, N.Y.C., 1987-90, Orlando Conseils, N.Y.C., 1990-91, O'Connor, Reddy & Jensen, P.C., N.Y.C., 1992-95; of counsel Schürmann & Partners, N.Y.C., 1997—; pvt. practice, N.Y.C. Woods Hole fellow, 1972; Fulbright grantee Danish-Am. Found., 1971, Columbia U. grantee, 1971. Mem. ABA, N.Y. State Bar Assn., Am. Soc. Internat. Law, Maritime Law Assn., Danish Am. C. of C. (bd. dirs. 1990—, pres. 1997—), European Am. C. of C. (bd. dirs. 1990-98), Am. Scandinavian Soc. (pres. 1994-97). Fax: 212-370-1614. Office: Law Offices 230 Park Ave Ste 2240 New York NY 10169-2299

HESSERT, WILFRED O., military officer. BS in Acctg. magna cum laude, Husson Coll., 1969; M in Bus. Adminstrn., Auburn U., 1974; grad., Air Command and Staff Coll., 1974, Air War Coll., 1982, CAPSTONE, 1997. Commd. 2d lt. USAF, 1968, advanced through grades to maj. gen., 1997; pilot 132d Fighter Inceptor Squadron, Maine Air N.G., Dow AFB, Maine, 1967-72; aircraft maintenance and flight test officer Maine Air N.G., Bangor Internat. Airport, 1972-76, chief of maintenance, 1976-79; comdr. 101st Consol. Aircraft Maintenance Squadron Maine Air N.G., Bangor Air N.G. Base, 1979-84, dep. comdr. for maintenance 101st Consol. Aircraft Main. Sq., 1984-87, dep. comdr. for ops. Hdqs., 1987-91, vice wing comdr. 101st Air Refueling Wing, 1991, wing comdr. 101st Air Refueling Wing, 1991-96; Air N.G. asst. to comdr. U.S. Air Forces in Europe, Ramstein Air Base, Germany, 1996-97; dep. inspector gen. Hdqs. USAF, Washington, 1997—. Decorated Legion of Merit, Meritorious Svc. medal with oak leaf cluster. Office: SAF/IG 1140 Air Force Pentagon Washington DC 20330-1140

HESSION, ALICE IRENE, principal; b. Lafayette, Ind., July 17, 1949; d. George E. and Francis M. (Jarka) H. BA, Purdue U., 1971; M in Religious Edn., St. Meinrad Sch. Theology, Ind., 1977; EdS, Spalding U., 1997. Tchr. Ctrl. Cath. H.S., Lafayette, 1971-79; asst. prin. St. Xavier H.S., Louisville, 1979-90, Mount St. Joseph H.S., Balt., 1990-96; prin. Cath. H.S., Huntsville, Ala., 1996—; mem. bd. overseers St. Meinrad (Ind.) Sem., 1986-92, bd. dirs. Mount St. Joseph H.S., 1984-90. Mem. Nat. Cath. Edn. Assn., Nat. Assn. Secondary Sch. Prins., Women in Sch. Adminstrn. Office: Catholic High Sch 4810 Bradford Dr NW Huntsville AL 35805-1949

HESSLER, DAVID WILLIAM, information and multimedia systems educator; b. Oak Park, Ill., May 9, 1932; s. William Wigney and Gwendolyn Eileen (Butler) H.; m. Helen Montgomery, Aug. 27, 1955; children: Leslie Susan, Laura Lynne. BA, U. Mich., 1955, MA, 1961; PhD, Mich. State U., 1972. Comml. photographer Oscar & Assocs., Chgo., 1950; equipment engr. Western Electric Co., Chgo., 1958-59; dir. librs. and media Ann Arbor (Mich.) Pub. Schs., 1966-67; asst. prof. edn. Western Mich. U., 1967-72, assoc. prof., 1974-77; dir. instrnl. svcs., prof. edn. U. S.C., 1973-74; cons., asst. dir. Audio-Visual Edn. Ctr. U. Mich., Ann Arbor, 1960-66, prof. Sch. Info., 1977-98, prof. emeritus, 1998—, dir. instrnl. strategy svcs. for schs. of edn., libr. sci., 1979-81, pres. Ann Arbor sys. and tech., 1987—, exec. dir. for info. svcs. Info-Span, 1991-92; exec. v.p. Infotronix, Ann Arbor, 1993-97; cons. Presdl. Commn. on World Hunger; cons. media and tech.; instrnl. designer and evaluator; bd. dirs. Kirsch Techs.; vis. prof., cons. dept. biblioteconomia U. Brazil, 1981. Author: (with J. Smith) Student Production Guide, 1975, Technology for Communication and Instruction, 1983; producer/dir. numerous films, filmstrips, TV programs and sound/slide programs for various ednl. levels. Lt. USAF, 1955-58; capt. Res. ret. Decorated Air Force Commendation medal; named Most Valuable Tchr. Chrysler Corp., 1965; Ednl. Profl. Devel. Act fellow, 1968-69. Mem. ALA, ASTD, Assn. Image and Info. Mgmt., M Club, Phi Kappa Phi. Home: 3677 Frederick Dr Ann Arbor MI 48105-2887 Office: Univ Mich Sch Info W Hall 550 E University Ave Ann Arbor MI 48109-1092

HESSLER, DOUGLAS SCOTT, screenwriter; b. Hagerstown, Md., July 22, 1948; s. Chester Scott (dec.) and Betty Jane (Martin) H.; m. Fumiko Hamada, June 11, 1993. BFA, Va. Commonwealth U., 1971; MFA, Md. Inst. Coll. of Art, 1974; Postgrad. Degree, Am. Film Inst., L.A., 1985. Painter, filmmaker, N.Y.C., 1974-82; creative dir. J. Walter Thompson Advt., N.Y.C., 1977-83; prodn. exec. Cannon Films, L.A., 1985-88, Walt Disney Co., L.A., 1988-90; artistic dir. Landmark Entertainment, L.A., 1990-92; with German TV and feature film prodn. cos., TV networks; condr. screenwriting workshops, L.A., Germany, 1995-96. Screenwriter: Out of Nowhere, Bend in the River, Over the Line, 1993, Eye of the Storm, 1993, Judgement Day, 1994, Adrenaline, 1995, Code Red, 1996, Side Swipe, 1996; prodr. Intruder, Paramount Pictures, 1990, Because the Night, Penthouse German film sub., 1998; (German TV movies) GUN, 1998, Extreme, 1998, The Bitch, 1998. Staff sgt. USAFR, 1967-72. Recipient Adolf-Grime award, Germany, 1995, award Houston Film Internat. Festival, 1996, N.Y. Film Festival, 1996; N.Y. State Arts grantee N.Y. State Coun. on Arts, 1979, 80, 81; Am. Film Inst. Writer/Dir. fellow, 1984-85. Avocations: fly fishing, traveling, writing. Address: 32 W Potomac St Williamsport MD 21795-1036

HESSLER, GENE JOSEPH, retired musician, retired museum curator; b. Cin., July 13, 1928; s. Joseph August and Clara (Schmidt) H. BS in Music Edn., U. Cin., 1955; MM in Musicology, Manhattan Sch. Music, 1957. Trombonist Band of Elliot Lawrence, 1949-51, Band of Billy May, 1954, Band of Woody Herman, 1955, Band of Sauter-Finnegan, 1956, Band of Buddy Rich, 1959; prin. trombonist San Antonio Symphony, 1957-59, Cin. Symphony World Tour, 1966; trombonist various Broadway musicals, N.Y.C., 1959-67; curator Chase Manhattan Bank Money Mus., N.Y.C., 1967-77, St. Louis Mercantile Bank Money Mus., 1986-88. Author: The Comprehensive Catalog of U.S. Paper Money, 1997, U.S. Essay, Proof and Specimen Notes, 1979, An Illustrated History of U.S. Loans, 1988, The Engraver's Line, 1993; editor: Paper Money, 1985-98; contbg. editor: The Numismatist, 1986—; columist Numismatist, 1992—, Coin World, 1993—. Mem. sch. bd. St. Louis Cathedral Sch., 1994-96, vol. tchr., 1990-96; vol. tchr. St. Boniface Sch., 1997—. Recipient Medal of Merit, Soc. Internat. Numismatics; named Numismatic Amb., Numismatic News. Fellow Am. Numismatic Soc.; mem. Am. Numismatic Assn., Internat. Bank Note Soc. Avocations: photography, cooking, wine. Office: PO Box 31144 Cincinnati OH 45231-0144

HESSLER, WILLIAM GERHARD, tax consultant; b. Chgo., May 20, 1926; s. William Gerhard and Rosemary (Kalb) H.; m. Kazuko Yonetsu, June 2, 1956 (dec. Mar. 1, 1995); children: Martha, George, Kay, Emmy. BSEE, Purdue U., 1946; MBA, Northwestern U., 1956. Cert. data processor; cert. individual tax profl. Tech. intelligence investigator U.S. Army, Tokyo, 1947-50; electronics engr. signal corps. U.S. Army, Yokohama, Japan, 1952-54; mfg., devel. engr. Western Electric, Chgo., 1955-61; engring. specialist Goodyear Aerospace Corp., Akron, Ohio, 1961-65; computer applications programmer analyst Goodyear Tire & Rubber Co., Akron, 1965-83, computer operating systems programmer, 1983-87; cons. Cutler-Williams, Independence, Ohio, 1987; systems engineer Profl. Support, Inc., Brecksville, Ohio, 1989; tax cons. and return preparer H & R Block, Greater Akron, 1969-80, Akron Nat. Tax & Notary, 1981, Hammer Tax Svc., Akron, 1982—; cons. in field, 1982—; agt. enrolled to practice before the U.S. Dept. Treasury IRS, 1984—. Scoutmaster Boy Scouts Am., Silver Lake, Ohio, 1972-77. With U.S. Army, 1950-52, Japan. Mem. Nat. Assn. Tax Practitioners. Roman Catholic. Avocation: amateur radio (W8DXT). Home: 3046 Lake Rd Cuyahoga Falls OH 44224-3814

HESSLUND, BRADLEY HARRY, product manager; b. Mpls., June 27, 1958; s. Harry A. and Dorothy (Tishi) H.; m. Diane M. Mahoney, June 13, 1992. AA, Normandale C.C., 1978; BS, U. Wis., Menomonie, 1981; MBA, U. Pitts., 1984. Cert. sr. indsl. technologist. Indsl. engr. Thermo King Corp. subs. Westinghouse Electric Corp., Bloomington, Minn., 1981-82; project engr. Westinghouse Electric Corp., Beaver, Pa., 1983; cost engr. IBM Corp., East Fishkill, N.Y., 1984-85; mfg. engring. supr. Hoffman Engring. Co. subs. Pentair Inc., Anoka, Minn., 1985-88; sr. cost analyst Naval Sys. divsn. FMC Corp., Fridley, Minn., 1988-90; project mgr. Deltak Corp., Plymouth, Minn., 1990-94; mgr. project engring., sr. program mgr. Despatch Industries, Mpls., 1994—. Avocations: auto-mechanics, hockey, weight-lifting, softball, reading. Home: 3220 Pineview Ln N Plymouth MN 55441-2864 Office: Despatch Industries PO Box 1320 Minneapolis MN 55440-1320

HESTAD, BJORN MARK, metal distributing company executive; b. Evanston, Ill., May 31, 1926; s. Hilmar and Anna (Aagaard) H.; m. Florence Anne Ragusi, May 1, 1948; children: Marsha Anne, Patricia Lynn Krueger, Peter Mark. Student Ill. Inst. Tech., 1947. Sales corr., Shakeproof, Inc., Chgo., 1947-50; indsl. buyer Crescent Industries, Inc., Chgo., 1950-51; purchasing agt. Switchcraft, Inc., Chgo., 1951-73, materials mgr., 1973-74, dir. purchasing, 1974-77; pres. Tool King, Inc., Wheeling, Ill., 1977-95, CEO, chmn. bd. dirs., 1995—; pres. Hestad Inc.; gen. ptnr. Hestad Ltd. Partnership; gen. ptnr. H & H Enterprises of Northfield. Mgr. youth orgns. Northfield Jr. Hockey Club, 1968-71, Winnfield Hockey Club, 1972-73; bus. mgr. West Hockey Club, 1973-74. Served as cpl. U.S. Army Air Corp, 1944-46. Mem. Tooling and Mfg. Assn., Steel Svc. Ctr. Inst., Sons of Norway, Waukegan Yacht Club, Lions. Republican. Mem. United Ch. Christ. Home: 850 Happ Rd Northfield IL 60093-1005 Office: Tool King Inc 275 Larkin Dr Wheeling IL 60090-6457

HESTAD, MARSHA ANNE, educational administrator; b. Evanston, Ill., Apr. 25, 1950; d. Bjorn Mark and Florence Anne (Ragusi) H. BS, U. Ill., 1972; MEd, Nat. Coll. Edn., Evanston, Ill., 1978; postgrad., Purdue U., 1985; PhD, Loyola U., Chgo., 1991. Cert. in elem. edn., spl. reading, gifted edn., gen. adminstrn., Ill., Ind. Tchr. 5th grade Deerfield (Ill.) Sch. Dist. 109, 1972-78; head tchr. North Aegean Acad., Kavala, Greece, 1978-81; gifted resource tchr. Alief Ind. Sch. Dist., Houston, 1983-84, TeKoppel, Evansville, Ind., 1984-85; field supr. Purdue U., West Lafayette, Ind., 1987; gifted coord. MSD Mt. Vernon, Ind., 1985-88; gifted resource Libertyville (Ill.) Sch. Dist. 70, 1988-91; instr. Coll. Lake County, Grayslake, Ill., 1991; clin. prof. Loyola U., Chgo., 1991; prof. Ind. State U., Terre Haute, 1992-93; tchr. lang. arts/lit. 7th grade, co-dir./prin. summer sch. Libertyville (Ill.) Sch. Dist. 70, 1993-94; prin. Chippewa Sch., Bensenville (Ill.) Dist. 2, 1994-96, Rockland Sch., Libertyville Ill., 1996—; adj. prof. Loyola U., Chgo., 1998—; bd. dirs. Odyssey of the Mind, Ind. and Ill.; cons. in field. Exec. co-producer Countdown interactive cable program, 1995-96; exec. producer Blast Off cable program, 1997—; contbr. articles to profl. jours. Mem. ASCD, Am. Ednl. Rsch. Assn., Nat. Coun. Staff Devel., Midwest Ednl. Rsch. Assn., Ill. Assn. for Gifted Children (v.p. 1998, pres.-elect 1999), Phi Delta Kappa. Home: 2016 Walters Ave Northbrook IL 60062-4526

HESTAND, JOEL DWIGHT, minister, evangelist; b. Henrietta, Tex., May 23, 1939; s. Dee Lathell and Jack Fern (Gamble) H.; m. Carolyn Somers, June 12, 1959; children: Paul Daniel, Joe Randall. Student, Odessa (Tex.) Coll., 1963-66; diploma, Brown Trail Sch. Preaching, Ft. Worth, Tex., 1968-70, Sunset Sch. Missions, Lubbock, 1973; BTh, Trinity Theol. Sem., 1988. Evangelist Ch. of Christ, various locations, 1968—; missionary Tanzania, E. Africa, 1973-75, Chimala Mission and Hosp., Mbeya, Tanzania, 1994-95; police chaplain Naperville (Ill.) Police Dept., 1977-83; ednl. dir. Rockford (Ill.) Christian Camp, 1977-82, bd. dirs., 1977-82; instr. Fishers of Men Evangelism, Frankfort, Ky., 1984—. With USAF, 1957-66. Republican. Office: Myrtle Ave Ch of Christ 134 Myrtle Ave Frankfort KY 40601-3114 *"Now all has been heard: here is the conclusion of the matter: Fear God and keep His Commandments, for this is the whole of man." Ecclesiastes 12:13.*

HESTENES, DAVID, physics educator; b. May 21, 1933. PhD, UCLA, 1963. Rsch. physicist UCLA, 1963-64; NSF fellow Princeton (N.J.) U., 1964-66; prof. physics Ariz. State U., Tempe, 1966—. Fulbright scholar Cambridge (Eng.) U., 1994-95. E-mail: hestenes@asu.edu. Home: 2416 Palm Dr Tempe AZ 85282 Office: Ariz State U Dept Physics PO Box 871504 Tempe AZ 85287-1504

HESTER, ALBERT LEE, retired journalism educator; b. Sweetwater, Tex., May 31, 1932; s. Albert Harderick and Katharine Louise (Wood) H.; m. Mary Conoly Cullum, Aug. 18, 1963; children: Albert Cullum, Katherine Leigh. BJ, So. Meth. U., 1958; MA, U. Wis., 1970, PhD, 1972. Reporter Dallas Times Herald, 1957-65, asst. city editor, 1965-67, city editor, 1967-68; from asst. prof. to prof. Coll. Journalism U. Ga., Athens, 1972—, head dept. Coll. Journalism, 1983-91; dir. Cox Ctr. Internat. Tng. and Rsch. Author: Handbook for 3rd World Journalists, 1987, Creating a Free Press in Eastern Europe, 1993. Sgt. AUS, 1952-54, Korea. Mem. Assn. Edn. in Journalism (div. sec. 1976-78). Democrat. Episcopalian. Avocations: hiking, photography, computer music composition. Home: 184 Milledge Ter Athens GA 30606-4936 Office: Univ Ga Coll Journalism 191 E Broad St Athens GA 30601-2847

HESTER, BRUCE EDWARD, library media specialist, lay worker; b. Clarksville, Tenn., June 26, 1956; s. Edward Vaughan and Mabel Sarah (Chandley) H. BS, Middle Tenn State U., 1978; MEd, Trevecca Nazarene Coll., 1987. Cert. elem. tchr., cert. secondary tchr. and libr., Tenn. Tchr. Met.-Davidson County Schs., Nashville, 1993-98; libr. Clarksville/Montgomery County Schs., Clarksville, Tenn., 1998—; adj. faculty-vol. State C.C., Gallatin, Tenn., 1993—; choir dir. First Christian Ch., Dover, Tenn., 1983—, Sunday sch. tchr., deacon, 1988-93, chmn. bd. dirs., 1989-93; dir. Stewart County Cmty. Choir, 1987-89. Co-chmn. Stewart County Rep. Party, 1986-89. Recipient Vol. Svc. award Cystic Fibrosis Found., 1984, Mayor's Acts of Excellence award, 1994; named E. Middle Sch. Tchr. of Yr., 1996. Mem. NEA, Tenn. Edn. Assn., Tenn. Assn. Sch. Librs., Tenn. Assn. Mid. Schs., Clks. Montgomery County Edn. Assn. (East Mid. Sch. Tchr. of Yr. 1995). Mem. Disciples of Christ Ch. Home: 1724 Valley Rd Clarksville TN 37043-4537 Office: Northeast Middle Sch 3703 Trenton Rd Clarksville TN 37040 *Our heritage is the foundation of our future. As children, our parents help to build us to be able to meet the challenge of life and embrace* *the future. The option is ours; to add to that foundation or remain unfinished.*

HESTER, DONALD DENISON, economics educator; b. Cleve., Nov. 6, 1935; s. Donald Miller and Catherine (Denison) H.; m. Karen Ann Helm, Oct. 24, 1959; children: Douglas Christopher, Karl Jonathan. BA, Yale U., 1957, MA, 1958, PhD, 1961. Asst. prof., assoc. prof. Yale U., New Haven, Conn., 1961-68; jr. vis. prof. Bombay Univ., India, 1962-63; econs. prof. U. Wis., Madison, 1968—, dept. chmn., 1990-93; cons. Fed. Res., 1969-84; vis. prof. People's U. China, Beijing, 1987. Author: Indian Banks: Their Portfolios, Profits and Policy, 1964; co-author: Bank Management and Portfolio Behavior, 1975; co-editor: Risk Aversion and Portfolio Choice, 1967; contbr. numerous articles to profl. jours. Mem. Wis. Coun. Econ. Affairs, 1983-87. Guggenheim fellow 1972, Econometric Soc. fellow, 1977; recipient faculty fellowship Ford Found., 1967, other rsch. awards. Avocations: classical music, art, hiking, traveling. Home: 2111 Kendall Ave Madison WI 53705-3915 Office: U Wis Dept Econs 1180 Observatory Dr Madison WI 53706-1320

HESTER, DOUGLAS BENJAMIN, lawyer, federal official; b. McKenzie, Ala., Sept. 18, 1927; s. Mack Ellis and Carrie Lottie (Taylor) H.; m. Melissa Hood Fuller, Apr. 16, 1960; children: Carlotta Marie, Benjamin Alexander. B.S., U. Ala., 1950, LL.B., 1952. Bar: Ala. 1952, D.C. 1960, U.S. Supreme Ct. Law asst. Office Legis. Counsel-U.S. Senate, Washington, 1952-54, asst. counsel, 1954-69, sr. counsel, 1969-80; legis. counsel U.S. Senate, 1980-91; mem., liaison between Ala. and U.S. Congress Svc. Corps. of Retired Execs., 1992-93. Trustee Centro Anglo-Espanol, Washington, 1990. Served with AUS, 1945-47. Mem. ABA, D.C. Bar Assn., Ala. Bar Assn., Farah Order of Jurisprudence, Pi Alpha Delta, Omicron Delta Kappa, Sigma Delta Pi, Pi Kappa Phi. Home: 2171 Vaughn Ln Montgomery AL 36106-3252

HESTER, GERALD LEROY, retired school system administrator; b. Seattle, Aug. 6, 1928; s. Ernest Orien and Louise (Drange) H.; m. Carol Joyce Johnston, Aug. 2, 1953; children—Mark Wyn, Sue Ann. B.S., Wash. State U., 1950, B.Ed., 1953; M.Ed., Western Wash. State Coll., 1957; Ed.D., Columbia U., 1964. Prin. jr. high sch. Bellevue Sch. Dist., Wash., 1959-64, dir. guidance, 1964-65; supt. Vashon Sch. Dist., Wash., 1965-69, Auburn Sch. Dist., Wash., 1969-73, Vancouver Sch. Dist., Wash., 1973-80, Spokane Sch. Dist., Wash., 1980-93; exec. com. People to People, 1985—; Gov.'s High Tech Com., 1988—; mem. Provost Commn. on Tchr. Edn., Wash. State U., Pullman, 1983-84; mem. adv. bd. U. Wash. Sch. Edn., Seattle, 1974; mem. Citizens Adv. Com. Higher Edn. Consortium, Spokane, Wash., 1984; bd. mem. Wash. Council for Econ. Edn., Seattle, 1984. Bd. dirs. Inland Empire coun. Boy Scouts Am., 1981-89 , YMCA, 1982—; chmn. edn. div. United Way, Spokane, 1981-82. Served to 1st lt. U.S. Army, 1951-52. Recipient Civic Fame award Rotary Club 21, Spokane, 1982; listed among Top 100 Educators, Exec. Educator Mag., 1984, 87, 89, 90; recipient Alumni Achievement award Wash. State U., 1984; named Ednl. Adminstr. of Yr. Nat. Assn. Edn. Office Pers., 1989. Mem. Am. Assn. Sch. Adminstrs. (adv. com., finalist nat. supt. of yr. 1990, leadership for learning award 1992, disting. svc. award 1995), Suburban Sch. Supts. (pres. 1982-83), Wash. Assn. Sch. Adminstrs. (exec. bd. 1971-74), 1st Class Sch. Dist. Supts. (pres. 1984), Spokane C. of C. (bd. trustees 1983-87, exec. com. 1985-88), Phi Delta Kappa. Clubs: Royal Oaks Country (Vancouver, Wash.) (pres. 1979-80); Spokane Country, Spokane, Prosperity (Spokane, Wash., pres. 1993). Lodge: Rotary. Home: 41340 Woodhaven Dr W Palm Desert CA 92211-8106 also: 5203 S St Andrews Ln Spokane WA 99223*

HESTER, JAMES MCNAUGHTON, foundation administrator; b. Chester, Pa., Apr. 19, 1924; s. James Montgomery and Margaret (McNaughton) H.; m. Janet Rodes, May 23, 1953; children: Janet McN., Margaret, Martha. B.A., Princeton U., 1945, LL.D. (honoris causa), 1962; B.A. (Rhodes scholar 1947-50), Oxford (Eng.) U., 1950, D.Phil., 1955; LL.D., Lafayette Coll., 1964, Morehouse Coll., 1967; L.H.D., Hartwick Coll., 1964; LHD (hon.), Pace U., 1971, U. Pitts., 1971, Colgate U., 1974; L.H.D., N.Y. U., 1977; DCL, Alfred U., 1965; LLD (hon.), Hofstra U., 1967, Hahnemann Med. Coll., 1967, Fordham U., 1971, Amherst Coll., 1975, New Sch. for Social Rsch., 1975, Union Coll., 1983. Civil information officer Fukuoka Mil. Govt. Team, Japan, 1946-47; asst. to Am. sec. to Rhodes Trustees, 1950; asst. to pres. Handy Assocs., Inc. (mgmt. cons.), N.Y.C., 1953-54; account supr. Gallup and Robinson, Inc., Princeton, N.J., 1954-57; provost Bklyn. center L.I. U., 1957-60, v.p., 1958-60; prof. history, exec. dean arts and sci., dean Grad. Sch. Arts and Sci. N.Y.U., 1960-61, pres., 1962-75; rector UN U., Tokyo, 1975-80; pres. N.Y. Bot. Garden, 1980-89; pres. The Harry Frank Guggenheim Found., N.Y.C., 1989—, also bd. dirs.; bd. dirs. Alliance Fund and related funds. Trustee Lehman Found. Served with USMCR, 1943-46, 51-52. Mem. Assn. Am. Rhodes Scholars. Clubs: Century Assn., University, Pretty Brook Tennis. Office: H Frank Guggenheim Found 527 Madison Ave New York NY 10022-4304

HESTER, JULIA A., lawyer; b. L.A., Nov. 14, 1953; d. Robert William and Bertie Ella (Gilbert) H.; m. Fred M. Haddad, Aug. 2, 1980; children: Allison Hester-Haddad, Nancy Hester-Haddad. BA, Fla. Atlantic U., 1984; JD, Nova U., 1990. Bar: Fla. 1990, U.S. Dist. Ct. (mid. dist.) Fla. 1993. Asst. pub. defender Broward Pub. Defender, Ft. Lauderdale, Fla., 1990-93; atty., ptnr. Haddad & Hester, Ft. Lauderdale, 1993-95, 97—. Bd. dirs. St. Anthony Found., Ft. Lauderdale, 1995—, Ft. Lauderdale Billfish Tournament, 1992-96, BACDL, St. Thomas Aquinas Found., 1999—; mem. Sunrise Intracoastal Bd., Ft. Lauderdale, 1995; bd. dirs., officer Kids Inn Distress Aux., Ft. Lauderdale, 1984-87; bd. dirs. St. Thomas Found., 1999—, mem. exec. bd., 1999. Avocations: skiing, fishing, swimming. Office: 1 Financial Plz Ste 2612 Fort Lauderdale FL 33394-0061

HESTER, KARA-LYN ANNETTE, software engineer; b. Phila., Feb. 27, 1963; d. Javis Leon and O. Elizabeth (Seals) W. BS in Computer Sci., Drexel U., 1986, MS in Computer Sci., 1992. Intake worker Wheel's Inc., Phila., 1983; staff cons. computer ctr. Drexel U., Phila., 1984, sr. cons., 1984-85; programmer E. I. duPont, Phila., 1985; sr. programmer, computer scientist RMS Techs., Inc., Marlton, N.J., 1986-94, tech. mgr. Geophys. Scis. Lab.; project mgr. EDS, Lawrenceville, N.J., 1994—. Author manual: AFCAD Revisited, 1984; co-designer, implementor software. Recipient Letter of Commendation, U.S. Naval Acad., 1990. Mem. IEEE, Assn. for Computing Machinery. Avocations: woodworking, reading, gardening. Home: 9 Timothy Ln Burlington NJ 08016-4115 Office: EDS Princeton Pike Corp Ctr 989 Lenox Dr Lawrenceville NJ 08648-2315

HESTER, KARLTON EDWARD, composer, performer, music educator; b. El Paso, Tex., Feb. 11, 1949; s. Webb and Clara (Briggs) H.; m. Bette Jean Hered; 1 child, Karlton William. MusB, U. Tex., El Paso, 1971; MusM, San Francisco State U., 1978; PhD in Composition, CUNY, 1990. Music dir. Eisenhower High Sch., Rialto, Calif., 1971-74, San Francisco and Oakland (Calif.) Pub. Schs., 1977-82, Contempory Jazz Art Movement, San Francisco and N.Y.C., 1977-82; pres. Hesteria Records & Pub. Co., San Francisco and N.Y.C., 1981—; adj. prof. Bronx (N.Y.) Community Coll., 1985-88; adj. prof. Coll. of S.I., N.Y., 1988-91, asst. prof., 1990-91; artist in residence N.Y. Found. for Arts, N.Y.C., 1984-88, N.Y. Found. for the Arts, N.Y.C., 1984-91; composer in residence Western Edition Cultural Ctr., San Francisco, 1980-81; asst. prof. Coll. S.I., N.Y., 1990-91; Herbert Gussman dir. jazz studies Cornell U., Ithaca, N.Y., 1991—; pres. Interdisciplinary Artists Aggregation, Inc., Ithaca, N.Y.; composer in residence, music dir. Cazadero Music Camp, Berkeley, Calif., 1982. Producer, composer record albums. Mem. Rosicrucian Order, San Jose, Calif., 1980—. Recipient S.I. Cmty. TV NOVA video award for A Children's Jazz Video; grantee NEA, 1985, 89, New Engl. Coun. for Arts, 1986, S.I. Coun. for Arts, 1987, 90, 91, Fund for U.S. Artists at Internat. Festival & Exhbns., 1994-95, Howard Found. merit award in composition, 1996; fellow Mellon Found., 1991-92. Mem. ASCAP (popular and standard awards), Nat. Flute Assn., Am. Fedn. Musicians. Avocation: sports. Home: 139 Burleigh Dr Ithaca NY 14850-1709 Office: Cornell U Music Dept Lincoln Hal Ithaca NY 14853

HESTER, MELVYN FRANCIS, labor union executive; b. Kingston, Jamaica, Dec. 9, 1938; came to U.S., 1957; s. Glen Owen and Ditta Ann (White) H.; m. Sarita Stair, 1963 (div. 1970); m. Laura Pires, Feb. 17, 1990. BA in History with hons., Anderson U., 1961; MA in Govt. and History, Ind. U., 1962; MSW with distinction, Columbia U., 1969. Cert. social worker. Grad. asst. Ind. U., Bloomington, 1961-62; asst. to the pastor Lafayette Ch. of God, Bklyn., 1962-69; caseworker Bur. of Child Welfare, N.Y.C., 1963-66, supr./case supr., 1966-72, asst. to dir., 1973-76; asst. to asst. commr. Spl. Svcs. for Children, N.Y.C., 1972-73; dir. Office of Adminstrv. Svcs., N.Y.C., 1976-79; exec. dep. commr. Human Resources Adminstrn., N.Y.C., 1979-90; gen. mgr. United Fedn. Tchrs., N.Y.C., 1990—; field instr. Columbia Univ. Sch. Social Work, N.Y.C., 1972-78; adj. prof. Fordham Univ. Sch. Social Work, N.Y.C., 1979-80, Columbia Univ. Sch. Social Work, 1978-82; mentor Nat. Urban/Rural Fellows, N.Y.C., 1988-90. Contbr. articles to profl. jours. Bd. dirs. N.Y. Urban Coalition, 1992—, Nat. Forum for Black Pub. Adminstrs., Washington, 1986-92, Caribbean Action Lobby, Washington, 1985-87; trustee Riverside Ch., 1992-94; minister Bronx-Westchester Cmty. Ch., 1993—. Recipient Fgn. Student scholarship Anderson, Ind., 1957-62; grad. fellowship Univ. Wis., Madison, 1961. Mem. One Hundred Black Men (chmn. internat. affairs 1989-92), New Life on the Lower East side (bd. dirs. 1988-90), Columbia U. Sch. of Social Work Alumni Assn. (bd. dirs. 1992-94). Democrat. Church of God. Avocations: travel, history, Biblical scholarship, Afro-Brazilian music, Caribbean Art and Lit. Home: 555 Kappock St Apt 18E Bronx NY 10463-6453 Office: United Fedn Tchrs 260 Park Ave S New York NY 10010-7214

HESTER, NANCY ELIZABETH, county government official; b. Miami, Fla., Jan. 20, 1950; d. George Temple and Lorraine Patricia (Cluney) Hester; BA, Bucknell U., 1972; MIA, Columbia U., 1974; MBA, Fla. Internat. U., 1979. Treasury rep. Westinghouse Elec. Co., N.Y.C., 1974-76; adminstrv. officer serving in bldg. and zoning, gen. services, and corrections and rehab. depts. Metro Dade County, Fla., 1979—, bur. comdr. corrections and rehab. dept., 1990—; adj. prof. Fla. Internat. U., Miami, 1980-83. Bd. dirs. YWCA Greater Miami, 1988-92, LWV Dade County, 1993—, pres. bd. dirs., pres. bd. trustees edn. fund, 1994-96; mem. adv. bd. SafeSpace, 1995—. Mem. Zool. Soc. Fla., Miami City Ballet Guild.

HESTER, NORMAN ERIC, chemical company technical executive, chemist; b. Niangua, Mo., Dec. 16, 1946; s Eric Ira and Norma Josephine (Wright) H.; m. Sylvie Jean Hunt, June 16, 1973; children: Jenay Aimee, Yvette Joy, Trinity Marie. AA, El Camino Coll., 1966; BS, Calif. State U., Long Beach, 1968; MS, U. Calif., Riverside, 1971, PhD, 1972. Postdoctoral rsch. chemist U. Calif. Air Pollution Ctr., Riverside, 1972-74; air quality chemist EPA, Las Vegas, Nev., 1974-77; program mgr. Rockwell Internat., Newbury Park, Calif., 1977-80; group head Occidental Petroleum Rsch. Ctr., Irvine, Calif., 1980-83; tech. dir. Truesdail Labs. Inc., Tustin, Calif., 1983—; pvt. environ. cons., Mission Viejo, Calif., 1983. Contbr. articles to profl. jours. Mem. ASTM, Am. Chem. Soc., Assn. Hazardous Materials Profls. Republican. Avocations: growing hybrid roses, hiking, travel. E-Mail: norman@truesdail.com. Office: Truesdail Labs Inc 14201 Franklin Ave Tustin CA 92780-7008

HESTER, PATRICK JOSEPH, lawyer; b. Worcester, Mass., Aug. 14, 1951; s. Joseph P. and Anne T. (O'Brien) H.; m. Ann E. Riley, July 11, 1987; children: Maureen M., Colleen A., Margaret R., Molly E. BS in Civil Engr., W.P.I., Worcester, Mass., 1973; MS in Civil Engr., Northeastern U., Boston, 1979; JD, Suffolk Law Sch., Boston, 1983. Bar: Mass. 1983, U.S. Dist. Ct. Mass. 1984, 1st Cir. Ct. Appeals, 1999. Civil engr. Stone & Webster, Boston, 1973; dist. engr. Algonquin Gas Transmission Co., Boston, 1973-75, engr., 1975-78, sr. engr., 1978-79, supr.-engr., 1979-82, project mgr., 1982-83, asst. mgr. gas supply, 1983-84, corp. atty., 1984-92, v.p., gen. counsel, 1992-97; asst. gen. counsel Duke Energy Corp., Boston, 1998—; gen. counsel M & N Mgmt. Co., 1998—; profl. engr., Mass. Mem. Am. Bar Assn., Mass. Bar Assn., Fed. Energy Bar Assn., Boston Bar Assn., New England Corp. Counsel Assn., Guild Gas Mgrs., Chi Epsilon, Phi Delta Phi. Democrat. Roman Catholic. Avocation: sports. Office: Duke Energy Corp 1284 Soldiers Field Rd Boston MA 02135-1064

HESTER, PAUL V., career officer. BSBA in Accountancy, U. Miss., 1969, MBA in Accountancy, 1970; student pilot tng., Columbus AFB, Miss., 1971; student, Squadron Officer Sch., 1974, Air Command and Staff Coll., 1979; M in Mil. Arts and Scis., U.S. Army Command and Gen. Staff Coll., 1980; student, Nat. War Coll., 1990, Harvard U., 1992; sr. def. fellow, Harvard U., 1993. Commd. 2d lt. USAF, 1970, advanced through grades to maj. gen., 1998; stationed at Davis-Monthan AFB, Ariz., 1972, 73-74; aircraft comdr. 354th Tactical Fighter Squadron, Korat Royal Thai AFB, Thailand, 1973; various positions Luke AFB, Ariz., 1974-76; F-15 instr., flight examiner 525th Tactical Fighter Squadron, Bitburg Air Base, W. Germany, 1977-79; stationed at Langley AFB, Va., 1980-86; chief Ho. of Reps. liaison, sec. Air Force legis. liaison Hdqs. USAF, Washington, 1986-89; stationed at Kadena Air Base, Japan, 1990-92; div. chief weapons tech. control div. Joint Chiefs of Staff, Washington, 1993-94; Joint Chiefs of Staff rep. Com. Security and Cooperation Europe, Vienna, Austria, 1994-95; comdr. 35th Fighter Wing, Misawa Air Base, Japan, 1995-97, 53rd Wing, Eglin AFB, Fla., 1997; dir., legis. liaison Office Sec. Air Force, Washington, 1997—. Decorated Legion of Merit with oak leaf cluster, Air medal with four oak leaf clusters, Rep. Vietnam Gallantry Cross with Palm, Rep. Vietnam Campaign medal. Office: SAF/LL 1160 Air Force Pentagon Washington DC 20330-1160

HESTER, RANDOLPH THOMPSON, JR., landscape architect, educator; b. Danville, Va., Dec. 12, 1944; s. Randolph Thompson and Virginia (Green) H.; m. Marcia Jeanne McNally, Mar. 17, 1983; 1 child, Nathaniel Christopher. BA, N.C. State U., 1969, BS in Landscape Architecture, 1968; M in Landscape Architecture, Harvard U., 1969. Registered landscape architect, N.C. Prof. Pa. State U., State Coll., 1969-70; prof. N.C. State U., Raleigh, 1970-80, city univ. coord., 1972-75; prof. U. Calif., Berkeley, 1981—, chmn. dept. landscape architecture, 1987-92; assoc. dir. Ctr. Environ. Design Rsch., Berkeley, 1982-85; designer community devel. sect., Cambridge, Mass., 1969-72. Author: Rural Housing Site Planning, 1974 (award 1975), Neighborhood Space, 1975, (Am. Soc. Landscape Archs. Merit award 1986), Community Goal Setting, 1982, Planning Neighborhood Space with People, 1984, The Meaning of Gardens, 1990, Community Design Primer, 1990; founder planning process Goals for Raleigh, 1972-76 (All Am. City award 1976); designer urban wilderness Runyon Canyon, 1986 (Am. Soc. Landscape Arch. Honor award 1987), Big Wild Park, Big Sky Gateway, 1990-95; mem. editl. bd. Places mag., 1985—. Chmn. Five Points Citizens Adv., Coun., Raleigh, 1973, Georgetown-Roanoke Neighborhood Assn., Raleigh, 1979; councilman City of Raleigh, 1975-77; commr. Parks and Recreation Bd., Berkeley, 1982-86; bd. dirs. Ctr. for Environ. Change, 1985—; trustee Small Town Inst., 1988—. Recipient Outstanding Extension Svc. award N.C. State U., 1974, Virginia Dare award City of Manteo, N.C., 1981. Mem. Am. Soc. Landscape Archs. (Nat. Merit award 1976, Nat. Honor award 1984, Honor award 1991, Coun. of Educators in Landscape Architecture, Nat. Outstanding Educator award 1995, numerous other awards). Democrat. Methodist. Avocations: water color painting, leaded glass, drawing, gardening. Office: U Calif Dept Landscape Architecture 202 Wurster Hall Berkeley CA 94720-2000

HESTER, ROSS WYATT, retired business forms manufacturing executive; b. Amarillo, Tex., Aug. 23, 1924; s. Wyatt Langford and Nettie Estelle (Horne) H.; m. Elizabeth Ruth Hobbs, May 28, 1948 (div. Aug. 1984); children: Sherry Gail, Randal Ross, Debra Renee, Stephen Keith, Jeffry Wyatt. BA, Austin Coll., Sherman, Tex., 1947. Vice pres. Hester's Office Supply, Inc., Lubbock, Tex., 1947-60; pres. Caprock Bus. Forms, Inc., Lubbock, 1960-90, chmn. bd., 1990-96; ret., 1996. Trustee Austin Coll., 1987-99. With USAAF, 1943-46, CBI. Recipient Disting. Alumnus award Austin Coll., 1984. Mem. Printing Industry Assn. Tex. (pres. 1988-89). Republican. Presbyterian. Avocations: tennis, skiing, reading, travel. Office: Hester Books 3504 34th St Lubbock TX 79410-2832

HESTER, THOMAS PATRICK, lawyer, business executive; b. Tulsa, Okla., Nov. 20, 1937; s. E.P. and Mary J. (Layton) H; m. Nancy B. Scofield, Aug. 20, 1960; children: Thomas P. Jr., Ann S., John L. BA, Okla. U., 1961, LLB, 1963. Bar: Okla. 1963, Mo. 1967, N.Y. 1970, D.C. 1973, Ill. 1975. Atty. McAfee & Taft, Okla. City, 1963-66, Southwestern Bell Telephone Co., Okla. City, St. Louis, 1966-72, AT&T, N.Y.C., Washington, 1972-75; gen. atty. Ill. Bell Telephone Co., Springfield, 1975-77; gen. solicitor Ill. Bell Telephone Co., Chgo., 1977-83, v.p., gen. counsel, 1983-87; sr. v.p., gen. counsel Ameritech, Chgo., 1987-91, exec. v.p., gen. counsel, 1991-97; ptnr. Mayer, Brown & Platt, Chgo., 1997—; sr. v.p., gen. counsel, sec. Sears, Roebuck and Co., 1998-99; corp. counsel ctr. adv. bd. Northwestern U., 1987-97. Mem. Taxpayers' Fed. of Ill., Springfield, 1987-97, chmn. bd. trustees 1987-88; mem. adv. bd. Ill. Dept. Natural Resources, 1991—, chmn., 1993-98; mem. Am. arts com. Art Inst. Chgo., 1994—, trustee, 1995—. Fellow Am. Bar Found.; mem. Am. Law Inst. Office: Mayer Brown & Platt 190 S LaSalle St Chicago IL 60603-3441

HESTER, THOMAS ROY, anthropologist; b. Crystal City, Tex., Apr. 28, 1946; s. Jim Tom and Mattie Laura (Umphres) H.; m. Lynda Sue Broadway, July 2, 1966; children: Lesley Elise, Amy Lynne. BA with honors, U. Tex., Austin, 1969; PhD, U. Calif., Berkeley, 1972. Acting asst. prof. anthropology U. Calif., Berkeley, 1972-73; asst. prof. anthropology U. Tex., San Antonio, 1973-75, asso. prof., 1975-77, prof., 1977-87; prof. anthropology U. Tex., Austin, 1987—; dir. Ctr. for Archaeol. Research, 1974-87, Tex. Archeol. Research Lab., 1987—; vis. assoc. prof. U. Calif., Berkeley, 1976. Author: (with R. Heizer and J. Graham) Field Methods in Archaeology, 1975, Digging into South Texas Prehistory, 1980, (with R. Heizer and C. Graves) Archaeology: A Bibliographical Guide to the Basic Literature, 1980, (with G. Ligabue, S. Salvatori, M. Sartor) Colha e I Maya Dei Bassipiani, 1983, (with E.S. Turner) A Field Guide to the Stone Artifacts of Texas Indians, 1985, 2d edit., 1993, (with G. Ligabue) Robert F. Heizer's Age of Giants, 1990, (with H.J. Shafer) Maya Stone Tools, 1991; Ethnology of Texas Indians, 1991, (with H.J. Shafer and K.F. Feder) Field Methods in Archaeology, 7th edit., 1997; editorial bd. numerous jours.; contbr. articles to profl. jours. Woodrow Wilson fellow, 1969-70. Fellow Tex. Archeol. Soc. (pres. 1993); mem. Soc. Am. Archaeology (exec. com. 1984-86), Assn. Field Archaeology (exec. com. 1979-82), Soc. Archaeol. Sci., Accademia Nazionale die Lincei (fgn.), Sigma Xi (pres. Alamo chpt. 1979). Democrat. Methodist. Home: 1205 Falcon Ledge Dr Austin TX 78746-5117 Office: U Tex Archeol Rsch Lab Austin TX 78712-1100 also: U Tex Dept Anthropology Austin TX 78712-1086

HESTON, CHARLTON (JOHN CHARLTON CARTER), actor; b. Evanston, Ill., Oct. 4, 1924; s. Russell Whitford and Lilla (Charlton) Carter; m. Lydia Marie Clarke, Mar. 17, 1944; children—Fraser Clarke, Holly Ann. Student, Northwestern U., 1941-43. Mem. Nat. Council on the Arts, 1967-72. Author: The Actor's Life, 1979, In the Arena, 1995; performances include: (stage) Antony and Cleopatra, 1947, Leaf and Bough, 1948, Design for a Stained Glass Window, 1949, The Tumbler, 1960; (TV appearances) Wuthering Heights, Macbeth, Taming of the Shrew, Of Human Bondage, Jane Eyre, The Nairobi Affair, 1984, The Proud Men, 1987, TNT, 1988, 90, 91, A Man For All Seasons (also dir.), 1988, Original Sin, 1989, Treasure Island, 1990, The Little Kidnappers, 1990, The Crucifer of Blood, Crash Landing: The Rescue of Flight 232, 1992, The Avenging Angel, 1995; (TV series) The Colbys, 1985-87, Chiefs (miniseries), 1983, (also writer) Charleton Heston Presents the Bible, 1993; (films) Dark City, Greatest Show on Earth, 1952, The Savage, 1952, Ruby Gentry, 1952, The President's Lady, 1952, Pony Express, 1983, Arrowhead, 1953, Bad for Each Other, 1954, Naked Jungle, 1954, The Secret of the Incas, 1954, The Far Horizons, 1955, Lucy Gallant, 1955, Private War of Major Benson, 1955, The Ten Commandments, 1956, Three Violent People, 1956, Touch of Evil, 1958, The Big Country, 1958, Ben Hur, 1959 (Acad. award for best actor), The Wreck of Mary Deare, 1959, El Cid, 1961, The Pigeon That Took Rome, 1962, 55 Days of Peking, 1963, Diamond Head, 1963, The Agony and The Ecstasy, 1963, The War Lord, 1965, The Greatest Story Ever Told, 1965, Khartoum, 1966, Planet of the Apes, 1967, Will Penny, 1968, Number One, 1969, Beneath The Planet of the Apes, 1969, Julius Caesar, 1970, The Hawaiians, 1970, The Omega Man, 1971, Antony and Cleopatra (also dir.), 1971, Skyjacked, 1972, Call of the Wild, 1972, Soylent Green, 1973, The Three Musketeers, 1973, Airport, 1974, The Four Musketeers, 1974, Earthquake, 1974, Midway, 1976, Two-Minute Warning, 1976, The Last Hard Men, 1976, The Prince and the Pauper, 1977, Gray Lady Down, 1977, Mountain Men, 1980, The Awakening, 1980, Mother Lode (also dir.), 1982, Solar Crisis, 1989, Almost An Angel, 1990 (cameo), Wayne's World 2 (cameo), Tombstone, 1993, True Lies, 1994, In the Mouth of Madness, 1995, Hamlet, 1996, Alaska, 1996, Ben Johnson: Third Cowboy On The Right, 1996, Hercules (voice), 1997, Illusion Infinity, 1998, Gideon's Webb, 1998, Armageddon (voice), 1998, Toscano, 1999, Any Given Sunday, 1999, Town & Country, 1999; TV movie Avenging Angel, 1995, I Am Your Child, 1997; dir. The Caine Mutiny Court-Martial (Beijing), 1988. Trustee Los Angeles Center Theatre Group, Am. Film Inst., 1971—, chmn., 1973; head President's Task Force on Arts and Humanities, 1981—; led the Pledge of Allegiance at the Republican Conv., New Orleans, 1988. Served in USAAF, World War II. Recipient Jean Hersholt award as Humanitarian of Yr. Am. Acad. Motion Picture Arts and Scis., 1978, Citizenship medal VFW, 1982, Golden medal City of Vianna, 1995. Mem. Screen Actors Guild (pres. 1966-71), NRA (pres.). Office: care Jack Gilardi ICM 8942 Wilshire Blvd Beverly Hills CA 90211-1934 Office: care NRA 11250 Waples Mill Rd Fairfax VA 22030-7400*

HESTON, RENATE, nursing administrator; b. Gross-Strehlitz, Germany; came to U.S., 1960; d. Guenter and Elisabeth (Englich) Paetzold; m. Leonard Lancaster Heston; children: Barbara and Ardis (twins). BSN; BS in Human Svcs., U. Minn., 1987. RN, Minn., Iowa, Oreg.; cert. nursing supr.-adminstr.; bd. cert. gerontolog. nurse. Staff nurse, asst. head nurse; head nurse psychiat. unit Oreg. State Hosp., U. Oreg., U. Iowa Med. Sch.; nurse supr. The Wilder Found., New Brighton, Minn.; cons. in field. Co-author: The Medical Casebook of Adolf Hitler. Bd. dirs., dir. vol. svcs. U. N.A. Minn., 1973-88. Mem. AAUW, U. Minn. Alumni Assn. Avocations: classical music, reading, gardening, visual arts, gourmet cooking. E-mail: rheston1@fiarview.org. Home: 128 Windsor Ct New Brighton MN 55112-3372 Office: Ebenezer Social Ministry 2545 Portland Ave Minneapolis MN 55404-4406

HETH, DIANA SUE, therapist; b. Robinson, Ill., Sept. 25, 1948; d. Quentin Wilson and Marguerite (Byrd) Abraham; m. Kenneth Lewis Greider, Aug. 16, 1970 (div. Mar. 1985); children: Kathryn Elizabeth, Susan Nicole, Jonathan Abraham; m. Harold Eugene Heth; children: Joseph Brockwell, Kiley Joy, Mark Quentin. BSE, Eastern Ill. U., 1970; MSW, U. Ill., 1992. Lic. clin. social worker; cert. criminal justice specialist. Exec. dir. Nat. Assn. Downs Syndrome, Chgo., 1977-78, Heartland Hospice, Effingham, Ill., 1983-88; office adminstr. Am. Family Life Assurance, Effingham, Ill., 1988-90; sec. design engring. dept. Fedders N.Am., Effingham, Ill., 1990; co-owner H&S Vending, 1990-98; therapist sexual abuse Heartland Human Svcs., Effingham, Ill., 1992-94; child welfare specialist II Ill. Dept. of Children and Family Svcs., Effingham, 1994—; profl. adv. com. Hospice Lincolnland. Author: One Gift to the Next, 1983, Sundance Lady, 1990. Vol. Belleville (Ill.) Hospice, 1981-83; co-chmn. svc. and rehab. com. Am. Cancer Soc.; mem. parent adv. bd. Ill. State U., 1996—; social work cons. Effingham County Health Dept., 1995; steering com. Coun. on Domestic Violence, 1998. Mem. NASW, Assn. for Christian Counselors, Ill. State Hospice Orgn. (bd. dirs. 1985-86), Ill. Pub. Health Assn., County Orgn. Svc. Providers, Newcomers Club (pres. 1984-85), Compassionate Friends Club (bd. dirs. 1985-86), Topnotcher's 4-H Club (leader), Ill. State U. Parents Assn. (adv. bd. 1996—), Nat. Assn. for Forensic Counselors. Republican. Methodist. Avocations: bridge, bowling, needlework, gardening, cooking. Home: RR 1 Box 63 Shumway IL 62461-9722 Office: Effingham Field Office Ill Dept Child/Family Svcs 401 Industrial Ave Ste 2 Effingham IL 62401-2835

HETHERINGTON, BONITA ELIZABETH, elementary education educator; b. Sully, Iowa, May 27, 1946; d. Marion Peter and Florence Lucille Swank; m. Thomas Olson Hetherington, Aug. 17, 1968; children: Eric Hunter, Cori Joanne. BA, Cen. Coll., Pella, Iowa, 1968; postgrad., Tex. A&M U., 1979, Tex. Tech. U., 1983-87, Clarion (Pa.) U., 1990, Carlisle U., Millersville U.; Pa. Master's equivalency, Ind. U. of Pa., 1992. Cert. tchr., Pa., Tex. Elem. tchr. Schley County Schs., Ellaville, Ga., 1968-71; 3d grade tchr Montezuma Ind. Sch., Buena Vista, Ga., 1971; 2d grade tchr. Bryan (Tex.) Ind. Schs., 1979-82; tchr. Lubbock (Tex.) Ind. Sch., 1982-88; 3d grade tchr. Lewisburg (Pa.) Area Schs., 1989—, K-12 lang. arts instnl. specialist, 1991—, 4th grade tchr., 1991—; supr. student tchrs. Ga. S.W. Coll., 1971, Tex. A&M U., 1978-82, Tex. tech., 1987, Susquehanna U., 1992, Bloomsburg U., 1993-94, 96-99, Bucknell U., 1999; cons. Lubbock Schs., 1983-88, Muleshoe (Tex.) Ind. Schs., 1986-88, Region XI Ext. Day Insvc., Mason, Tex., 1987; instr. Inst. for Tchrs. of Disadvantaged Gifted, Lubbock, 1987-88; bd dirs. Regional Insvc. Bd., Montandon, Pa., 1989—, chmn., 1996—; strategic planning steering com., sec. Lewisburg Area Sch. Dist., 1993—, policies and procedures com., 1992-97, act 178 profl. devel. com., 1991-93,

94—, insvc. presenter, 1994—, sch. improvement team, 1995—, Blue Ribbon sch. prep. com., 1996—, Goals 2000 Consortium, 1996-98, Educate Am. Consortium, 1998—; Foreign Lang. Dist. com., 1999. Leader Brownies, Girl Scouts U.S., Lubbock, 1983-86, Cub Scouts, Bryan, 1979-81; pres. PTA, Canton, Tex., 1975-76, PTO, Lubbock, 1985-86; edn. com. Union County Hist. Soc.; mem. Packwood House Mus. Vols., vol. Am. Heart Assn., Am. Cancer Soc.; lector, usher, mem. social concern com., substitute tchr. for Sunday sch. nursery to adult Luth. Ch. Named one of 17 showcased tchrs. Pa. Assn. Childhood Edn. Internat., 1993; named one of Outstanding People of 20th Century Internat. Biog. Ctr., Cambridge, Eng., 1998. Fellow Internat. Biog. Assn.; mem. NEA, NCTE, AAUW, Nat. Coun. Tchrs. of English, Pa. State Edn. Assn., Lewisburg Edn. Assn., Internat. Reading Assn., Susquehanna Valley Reading Coun., Keystone State Reading Assn., Alpha Delta Gamma, Epsilon Sigma Alpha. Republican. Avocations: reading, travel, cooking, crafts, personal computing. E-mail: boto2@yahoo.com. Fax #: 570-524-4120. Home: 1615 Market St Lewisburg PA 17837-1231

HETHERINGTON, EILEEN MAVIS, psychologist, educator; b. Nov. 27, 1926. BA, U. B.C., 1947, MA, 1948; PhD in Psychology, U. Calif.-Berkeley, 1958. Clin. psychologist B.C. Child Guidance Clinic, 1948-51, sr. psychologist, 1951-52; clin. internship Langley Porter Clinic, 1956-57; instr. psychology San Jose State Coll., 1957-58; asst. prof. Rutgers U., 1958-60; from asst. prof. to prof. U. Wis., 1960-70; prof. psychology U. Va., Charlottesville, 1970—, James Page prof. psychology, 1976—, dept. chmn., 1980-84. Editor Child Devel., 1971-77; rschr. in personality devel. and childhood psychopathology, the role of family process and parent characteristics on normal and deviant behavior in children, the effects of divorce and remarriage on families, parents and children. Bd. dirs. Found. for Child Devel. Recipient Disting. Scientist award Am. Assn. for Marriage and Family Therapy, 1988, Am. Family Therapy Assn., 1992. Mem. APA (pres. divsn. 7, 1978-79, Stanley Hall Disting. Scientist award 1987, Disting. Scientist award 1993), Soc. Rsch. in Child Devel. (pres. 1985-87, Disting. Scientist award 1995), Soc. Rsch. in Adolescents (pres. 1986-88, Disting. Scientist award 1988, William James Disting. Scientist award 1994), Am. Psychol. Soc. Office: U Va Dept Psychology Gilmer Hall Charlottesville VA 22903*

HETHERINGTON, JOHN SCOTT, principal; b. Burlington, Iowa, June 3, 1945; s. Willard and Mara Lea (Scott) H.; m. Patricia Dyane Ladd, Aug. 19, 1967; children: Joseph Scott, Dyane, Kara Lynn., Tara Lea. BA in Social Studies, Graceland Coll., 1967; MS in Phys. Edn., Ctrl. Mo. State U., 1973. Tchr., coach Washington Jr. High Sch., Clinton, Iowa, 1969-72, South Harrison High Sch., Bethany, Mo., 1972-77, Clear Creek High Sch., Tiffin, Iowa, 1977-78; owner restaurant, Lamoni, Iowa, 1978-82; tchr., coach King City (Mo.) High Sch., 1982-84; prin., tchr., coach Miami-Amoret (Mo.) High Sch., 1984-87; asst. prin., coach Logan-Rogersville (Mo.) High Sch., 1987-93, prin., 1993—. Mem. Nat. Assn. Secondary Sch. Prins., Mo. Assn. Secondary Sch. Prins., Southwest Mo. Assn. Secondary Prins., Ctrl. Ozark Conf. Schs. (pres. 1997-98), Phi Delta Kappa. Democrat. Home: 4120 Tipparary St Rogersville MO 65742-9431

HETHERINGTON, JOHN WARNER, lawyer; b. N.Y.C., Aug. 15, 1938; s. John Kells and Susanna Louisa (Warner) H.; m. Hope Luke, Nov. 6, 1976; children: Kells, Jane. BA, Yale U., 1960, JD, 1963. Bar: N.Y. 1964, U.S. Dist. Ct. (ea. and so. dists.) N.Y. 1965, U.S. Ct. Mil. Appeals 1974, Conn. 1987. Atty. Fed. Res. Bank, N.Y.C., 1964-65; assoc. Dickerson & Reilly (formerly Brown, Hyde & Dickerson), N.Y.C., 1965-67; atty. Westvaco Corp., N.Y.C., 1967-77, asst. sec., asst. gen. counsel, 1977-78, sec., asst. gen. counsel, 1978—, v.p., 1987—; apptd. to adv. com. on shareholder comm. SEC, 1981-82. Mem. planning and zoning commn. Town of New Canaan, Conn., 1986-89, mem. town coun., 1989-97. Capt. JAGC, USNR ret. Mem. SR, Am. Soc. Corp. Secs., Inc. (chmn. tender offers com. 1986-89, dir. 1990-93), Assn. of Bar of City of N.Y., Country Club of New Canaan. Republican. Congregationalist. Avocation: sailing. Office: Westvaco Corp 299 Park Ave New York NY 10171

HETHERWICK, GILBERT LEWIS, lawyer; b. Winnsboro, La., Oct. 30, 1920; s. Septimus and Addie Louise (Gilbert) H.; m. Joan Friend Gibbons, May 31, 1946 (dec. Aug. 1964); children: Janet Hetherick Pumphrey, Ann Hetherwick Lyons Winegeart, Gilbert, Carol Hetherwick Sutton, Katherine Hetherwick Hummel; remarried Mertis Elizabeth Cook, June 7, 1967. BA summa cum laude, Centenary Coll., 1942; JD, Tulane U., 1949. Bar: La. 1949. With legal dept. NorAm Energy Corp., Shreveport, La., 1949-53; dir. Blanchard, Walker, O'Quin & Roberts, PLC, Shreveport, 1953—. Mem. Shreveport City Charter Revision Com., 1955; Shreveport Mcpl. Fire and Police Civil Svc. Bd., 1956-92, vice chmn., 1957-78, chmn., 1978-88. Served with AUS, 1942-46. Recipient Tulane U. Law Faculty medal, 1949. Mem. ABA, La. Bar Assn., Shreveport Bar Assn. (pres. 1987), Fed. Energy Bar Assn., Order of Coif, Phi Delta Phi, Omicron Delta Kappa. Episcopalian. Home: 4604 Fairfield Ave Shreveport LA 71106-1432 Office: Bank One Tower Shreveport LA 71101

HETLAGE, ROBERT OWEN, lawyer; b. St. Louis, Jan. 9, 1931; s. George C. and Doris M. (Talbot) H.; m. Anne R. Willis, Sept. 24, 1960; children: Mary T., James C., Thomas K. AB, Washington U., St. Louis, 1952, LLB, 1954; LLM, George Washington U., 1957. Bar: Mo. 1954, U.S. Dist. Ct. (ea. dist.) Mo. 1954, U.S. Supreme Ct. 1957. Ptnr., Hetlage & Hetlage, 1958-65, Peper, Martin, Jensen, Maichel & Hetlage, St. Louis, 1966-97, chmn., 1994-97; of counsel Blackwell Sanders Peper Martin LLP, 1998—. Served to 1st lt. U.S. Army, 1954-58. Fellow Am. Bar Found. (life); mem. Bar Assn. Met. St. Louis (pres. 1967-68), Mo. Bar (pres. 1976-77), ABA (chmn. real property, probate and trust law sect. 1981-82), Am. Coll. Real Estate Lawyers (pres. 1985-86), Am. Bar Found. (bd. trustees 1996—), Am. Judicature Soc., Anglo-Am. Real Property Inst. (chmn. 1991). Office: Blackwell Sanders Peper Martin LLP 720 Olive St Saint Louis MO 63101

HETLAND, JAMES LYMAN, JR., banker, lawyer, educator; b. Mpls., June 9, 1925; s. James L. and Evelyn E. (Lundgren) H.; m. Barbara Anne Taylor, Sept. 10, 1949; children: Janice E., James E., Nancy L., Steven T. B.S.L., U. Minn., 1948, J.D., 1950. Bar: Minn. 1950. Law clk. Minn. Supreme Ct., 1949-50; asso. firm Mackall, Crounse, Moore, Helmey & Palmer, Mpls., 1950-56; prof. U. Minn. Coll. Law, 1956-71; v.p. urban devel. First Nat. Bank Mpls., 1971-75, sr. v.p. law and urban devel., 1975-82, sr. v.p., gen. counsel, sec., 1982-88; sr. v.p. First Bank System, 1987-88; counsel to bd. and sec. First Bank, N.A., 1988-90; of counsel Rasmussen & Assocs., Ltd., 1990—; adj. prof. Hubert Humphrey Inst., U. Minn., 1976-90, Bus. Coll. extension, 1975-81, Coll. Law, 1980-90; labor arbitrator, 1967—; chmn. Minn. Citizens Coun. Crime and Delinquency, 1978-83; chmn. adv. coms. Minn. Supreme Ct., 1958-90; regents adv. com. Hubert Humphrey Inst., U. Minn., 1982-90; chmn. Telecommuters, Inc., 1992-96. Co-author: Minnesota Jury Instruction Guides, 1963, 2d edit., 1974, Minnesota Practice, 3 vols., 1970. Chmn. Met. Coun. Twin Cities, St. Paul, 1967-71, Mpls. Charter Commn., 1963-70; chmn. Mpls. Citizens League, 1963-64, bd. dirs., 1953-67; bd. dirs. Mpls. Downtown Coun., 1971—, vice chmn., 1978-82, chmn., 1982-83; chmn. bd. Minn. Zool. Garden, 1978-83; nat. v.p., mem. exec. com. Nat. Mcpl. League, 1979-82, pres., 1982-85, chmn. bd., 1985-87; vice chmn. Minn. Press Coun., 1973-81; vice chmn. bd. Minn. Health Care Cost Coalition, 1980; bd. dirs. Interstudy, 1972-79, chmn., 1974; mem. Bus. Urban Issues Coun., Conf. Bd., 1980-89; bd. dirs. Freshwater Biol. Rsch. Found., 1971-85, adv. bd., 1985—; bd. dirs. Mpls. Community Coll. Found., 1978-83, Minn. Exptl. City, 1972-75, Minn. Campfire Girls, 1974-79, Mpls. YMCA, 1957-76; bd. dirs. Health Central, Inc., 1973-87, exec. com., 1977-87; bd. dirs. Citizen Coun. on Crime and Justice, 1977—, chmn., 1979-82; bd. dirs. Ctr. for Policy Studies, 1983—, Twin Cities Habitat for Humanity, 1988-95; mem. exec. com. Partnership Dataline U.S.A., 1983; bd. dirs., exec. com. Health One, 1987-93; trustee Metro State U., 1989-98, Mpls. United Way, 1988—; chmn. Mpls. Urban Tennis, 1987-94. With AUS, 1943-46. Mem. ABA, Am. Bankers Assn., Minn. Bar Assn., Hennepin County Bar Assn. Republican. Lutheran. Clubs: Mpls. Athletic, N.W. Tennis Assn. Lodge: Rotary. Office: 2116 2nd Ave S Minneapolis MN 55404-2606 *Seeking to improve services for urban citizens through new public and private service delivery systems has been a keystone for setting involvement priorities. Effective service delivery systems are essential if an urban society is to preserve a free public-private economic democracy. Involvement and change in the private sector is as important as in the public sector.*

HETRICK, THEODORE LEWIS, JR., emergency medicine physician; b. Danville, Pa., Nov. 5, 1949; s. Theodore Lewis and Betty Jane (Saylor) H.; m. Cynthia Ellen Smith, June 14, 1986; children: Keturah Ellen, Kimberly Lauren. BS summa cum laude, Dickinson Coll., 1971; MD, Temple U., 1975. Family practice resident Geisinger Med. Ctr., Danville, Pa., 1975-78; emergency room physician Sunbury (Pa.) Cmty. Hosp., 1979—, med. dir. paramed. svcs., 1989—; staff physician Yellowstone Nat. Park (Wyo.) Med. Svcs., 1984—; emergency room physician Shamokin Area Cmty. Hosp., Coal Twp., Pa., 1994—; med. dir. Rescue Hose Co., Beavertown, Pa., 1991—. Contbr. wildlife photographs to numerous mags. Mem. Phi Beta Kappa, Alpha Omega Alpha. Home: RR 1 Box 1029 Beavertown PA 17813-9707 Office: Sunbury Cmty Hospital Emergency Room 350 N 11th St Sunbury PA 17801-1600

HETT, JOAN MARGARET, civic administrator; b. Trail, B.C., Can., Sept. 8, 1936; s. Gordon Stanley and Violet Thora (Thors) Hett; B.Sc., U. Victoria (B.C., Can.), 1964; M.S., U. Wis., Madison, 1967, Ph.D., 1969. Ecologist, Eastern Deciduous Forest Biome, Oak Ridge Nat. Lab., 1969-72; coor. sites dir. Coniferous Forest Biome, Oreg. State U., Corvallis and U. Wash., Seattle, 1972-77; ecol. cons., Seattle, 1978-84; plant ecologist Seattle City Light, 1984-86; supr. Rights-of-Way, Seattle City Light, 1986-91, vegetation mgmt. mgr., Seattle City Light, 1991—. Mem. Ecol. Soc. Am., Brit. Ecol. Soc., Am. Inst. Biol. Scis., Am. Forestry Assn., Sigma Xi. Contbr. articles to profl. jours.; research in plant population dynamics, land use planning, forest sucession.

HETTCHE, L. RAYMOND, research director; b. Balt., Mar. 24, 1938; s. Leroy and Dorothy (Curtain) H.; m. Patricia Durkan, July 1965; children: Lisa, Kathleen, Matthew, Craig. BSCE, AB in Math., Bucknell U., 1961; MSCE, Carnegie-Mellon U., 1961, PhD in CE, 1965. Asst. prof. Rutgers U., New Brunswick, N.J., 1964-66; resident rsch. assoc. Nat. Bur. Standards, Washington, 1966-68; structural engr. metallurgy div. Naval Rsch. Lab., Washington, 1968-71, head thermomech. effect sect., 1971-73, head mech. br. metallurgy div., 1973-75, supt. materials sci. div., 1975-81; now, dir. Applied Rsch. Lab. Pa. State U., State College, 1981—; navy rep. Tech. Working Group Export Control, Washington, 1979-81; navy rep. subgroup P materials panel for metals Tech. Cooperation Program, Washington, 1977-81; session chmn. Submarine Tech. Symposium, Columbia, Md., 1990. Contbr. numerous articles to profl. jours. Tau Beta Pi Nat. fellow, 1961-63; NSF fellow, 1963; recipient Outstanding Achievement award Am. Def. Preparedness Assn., 1986. Mem. ASME (com. on mgmt. 1976-80), Acoustical Soc. Am., Am. Soc. Engring. Edn., Sigma Xi. Office: Pa State U Applied Rsch Lab PO Box 30 State College PA 16804-0030

HETTICH, PAUL JOSEPH, theatre designer, technician, military officer; b. Fort Jackson, S.C., June 16, 1965; s. Paul Ignatious and Mary Ann (Kloida) H. BA, Barat Coll., 1987; MA, No. Ill. U., 1992; cert. mktg., Coll. Lake County, Grayslake, Ill., 1990. Grad. asst. No. Ill. U., Dekalb, 1989-92; tech. dir. Ctr. State Prodns., Zion, Ill., 1988-92; asst. tech. dir. Coll. of Lake County, Grayslake, Ill., 1989-89; tech. dir. Absolute Theatre Co., Chgo., 1988-90, Lake Forest (Ill.) Symphony, 1985-93, The Genessee Theatre, Waukegan, Ill., 1987-90; cons. Chgo. Theatre's, 1987-92; tech. dir. Barat Coll., Lake Forest, Ill., 1994-95; tech. dir., theatre facilities mgr. Barrington (Ill.) H.S., 1997—; owner Frisco Boarding Kennels. Ranger, police officer Lake County Forest Preserve, Libertyville, Ill., 1988—; mem. 1982 —, Boy Scouts Am., 1980. Maj. USAR, 1987—. Mem. USNG Assn. (life), USROA Assn. (life), Res. Officers Assn. (life), U.S. Spl. Forces Assn. (life), Psychol. Ops. Assn. (life). Republican. Roman Catholic. Home and Office: Ctr Stage Prodns 4000 Il Route 173 Zion IL 60099-5107

HETTRICK, GEORGE HARRISON, lawyer; b. Piney River, Va., Aug. 15, 1940; s. Ames Bartlett and Frances Caryl (O'Brian) H.; children: Heather White Hettrick Brugh, Edward Lord. BA, Cornell U., 1962; JD, Harvard U., 1965. Bar: Va. 1965. Assoc. Hunton & Williams, Richmond, Va., 1965-73, ptnr., 1973—; ptnr. in charge Church Hill Neighborhood Law Office Hunton & Williams, 1990—, chmn. Community Svc. com.; dir. Richmond Community Hosp., 1992—. Contbr. articles to profl. jours. Spl. counsel Gov. of Va., Richmond, 1971-72; vice chmn. bd. dirs. Va. Port Authority, Norfolk, 1970-75, former commr., vice chmn.; pres. bd. trustees Va. Episcopal Sch., Lynchburg, 1978-81; mem. Va. State adv. com. Neighborhood Assistance Program; past dir., chmn. Peter Paul Devel. Ctr., Inc.; bd. dirs. Richmond Better Housing Coalition, St. Mary's Hosp., Stuart Circle Hosp., Richmond Cmty. Hosp., 1995—, Regional Meml. Med. Ctr.; mem. Henrico County (Va.) Cmty. Svcs. Bd., 1997—. Capt. U.S. Army, 1966-68. Fellow Va. Law Found.; mem. ABA, Va. Bar Assn. (chmn. substance abuse com. 1995-96, Lawyers Helping Lawyers), Va. State Bar, Richmond Bar Assn. (chmn. pro bono om. 1998—). Republican. Episcopalian. Home: 6350 Memorial Dr Sandston VA 23150-6307 Office: Hunton & Williams PO Box 1535 Richmond VA 23218-1535

HETZEL, ALICE M., statistician, researcher; b. Guthrie, Okla., Feb. 9, 1922; d. Eugene Tilden and Ina (Pence) H. BS, Okla. State U., 1942; postgrad., Georgetown U., 1945. Economist Navy Dept., Washington, 1943-46; statistician USPHS, Washington, 1946-50, U.S. Navy Dept., Washington, 1950-61; spl. asst. to chief Nat. Office Vital Stats., Washington, 1961-68, chief marriage and divorce stats., 1968-74; dep. dir. divsn. vital stats. NCHS, Washington, 1974-83; rschr. self employed, Silver Spring, Md., 1983—. Author: U.S. Vital Statistics System 1950-1995, 1997, Marriage and Divorce Statistics and the Health Department, 1971, Health Survey of the Trust Territory of the Pacific Islands, 1959; co-author: Vital Statistics Rates in the U.S. 1940-1960, 1968. Mem. Argule Country Club. Home: 1300 Ednor Rd Silver Spring MD 20905-5110

HETZEL, FREDRICK WILLIAM, biophysicist, educator; b. Toronto, June 28, 1946; came to U.S., 1974; BS, U. Waterloo, Ont., Can., 1970, MS, 1971, PhD, 1974; JD, Wayne State U., 1994. Sr. CA rsch. scientist Radiation Med. Dept. Div. Radiology, Buffalo, N.Y., 1976-78; asst. prof. Biophysics Dept. SUNY, Buffalo, N.Y., 1977-78; rsch. prof. Grad. Div. Niagra (N.Y.) U., 1978; sr. radiation biologist Therapeutic Radiology, Henry Ford Hosp., Detroit, 1978-82; adjunct asst. prof. Biology Dept. Wayne State U., Detroit, 1979-85; clin. assoc. prof. Physics Dept. Oakland U., Rochester, Mich., 1982-85; assoc. prof. Physics Dept. Oakland U., Rochester, 1985-87; dir. radiobiology Neurology Dept. Henry Ford Hosp., Detroit, 1982-90; prof. Physics Oakland U., Rochester, Mich., 1987-93, dir. radiation oncology rsch., 1991-93; dir. R & D Presbyn./St. Luke's Med. Ctr., Denver, 1993-94; dir. R&D HealthOne, Denver, 1994-96, v.p., dir. rsch., 1996—; co-organizer, guest faculty Hyperthermia and Cancer Therapy, Seattle, 1984, Madison, Wis., 1985, Durham, N.C., 1987; profl. cons. hyperthermia FDA Regulations, Protocol Design, 1986; mem. med. staff bylaws com. Henry Ford Hosp., 1989; mem. radiation study sect. DHHS/NIH/DRG, 1989-93. Assoc. editor: Radiation Rsch., 1987-91. Grantee NIH, 1979-88, 86-90 (2), 87-90, 92—. Mem. N.Am. Hyperthermia Group (memberhsip com. 1987-88, sec.-treas. 1989-91), Am. Assn. Physicians in Medicine (chmn. task group), Am. Soc. Clin. Oncology, Am. Coll. Med. Physics. Home: 201 Locust Ln Denver CO 80220-5973 Office: HealthOne Rsch 1850 High St Denver CO 80218-1308

HETZEL, WILLIAM GELAL, executive search consultant; b. New Rochelle, N.Y., May 19, 1933; s. William Gelal and Nan (Sanes) H.; m. Karen Marie Ross; children: William Gelal III, Tara L., John F., Janda B. Student, Washington Coll., 1949-51; B.B.A., U. Miami, 1953; postgrad., Xavier U., 1957-58; M.B.A., Northwestern U., 1962. Cons. McKinsey & Co., Inc., Chgo., 1961-64; various sales mgmt. positions Xerox Corp., Chgo., Rochester, N.Y., Louisville, 1964-69; dir. mktg. Maremont Corp., Chgo., 1969-70; pres. Medelco, Inc., Schiller Park, Ill., 1970-72; div. gen. mgr., v.p. ITT Service Industries Corp., Cleve., 1972-74; v.p. Lamalie Assos., Inc., Chgo., 1974-78; sr. v.p. Eastman & Beaudine, Chgo., 1978-81; pres. The Hetzel Group, Inverness, Ill., 1981—; speaker in field. Contbr. numerous articles on exec. recruitment to profl. jours. Mem. adv. bd. Coll. of Bus. and Mgmt. Northeastern Ill. U., 1986—, mem. found. bd., 1993—. Served to lt. (j.g.) USN, 1953-56. Mem. Internat. Assn. Corp. and Profl. Recruitment, Am. Assn. Exec. Search Cons. Republican. Lutheran. Office: 1601 Colonial Pky Inverness IL 60067-4732

HETZLER, SUSAN ELIZABETH SAVAGE, educational administrator; b. Monticello, Iowa, Mar. 18, 1947; d. Robert Engelbert and Josephine May (Ricklefs) Savage; children: Stephanine, Michael. BS in Edn., Rockford (Ill.) Coll., 1971; 2MS in Edn., No. Ill. U., 1978, cert. advanced study, 1984; PhD, Walden U., Mpls., 1989. Cert. elem. tchr., adminstr., Ill., Iowa; supr., sociology tchr., Ill. Elem. tchr. Freeport (Ill.) Sch. Dist., 1971-86; prof. elem. edn. Iowa State U., Ames, 1986-90; dir. tchr. edn. and devel. Iowa Dept. Edn., Des Moines, 1990-96; prof. edn., dean sch. edn. Buena Vista U., Storm Lake, Iowa, 1996-99; program adminstr. for educator preparation State of Tex., Austin, 1999—; curriculum cons. Ames Sch. Dist., 1985-90, Des Moines Sch. Dist., 1985-90; mem. ISU adv. bd., Ames, 1991—. Author: Elementary Education Practicum Teaching, 1988, Learning Centers, 1989. Comsnr. Drug and Alcohol Prevention Project, Freeport, 1976-85; chairperson Stephenson County (Ill.) Cancer Soc., 1976-78, small bus. dvsn. United Way, Freeport, 1980-85; vol. BSA and GSA, Freeport, 1974-85. Recipient Excellence in Teaching award Iowa State U., 1989-90, Outstanding Elem. Tchrs. Am. Ill., 1974, 81. Mem. AAUP, ASCD, NEA, Iowa ASCD, Am. Assn. Colls. of Tchr. Edn., Iowa Assn. Colls. of Tchr. Edn., Iowa Ednl. Rsch. and Eval. Assn., Assn. Tchr. Educators, Delta Kappa Gamma, Phi Delta Kappa, Rotary, Kiwanis. Presbyterian. Avocations: reading, skiing, tennis, piano, antiques, golf. Home: 3712 Bratton Heights Dr Austin TX 78728 Office: State Bd Edn Cert Buena Vista Univ 1001 Trinity St Austin TX 78701

HETZMARK, ABBY M., secondary education educator; b. Waterbury, Conn., May 10, 1974; d. Alan H. and Janet C. (Cross) H. BA magna cum laude, Duke U., 1996; MA, U. Va., 1997. Cert. tchr., N.C. Tchr. h.s. Friends Acad., Locust Valley, N.Y., 1997—. Mem. Phi Beta Kappa. Avocations: reading, running, hiking.

HETZNER, DONALD RAYMUND, social studies educator, forensic social scientist; b. Ottawa, Ill., Jan. 1, 1938; s. James Hyatt and Thelma Margaret (Sheedy) H.; m. Coralia Josefina Lora, July 9, 1966; children: Sean, Matthew. AA, LPO Jr. Coll., 1957; BA in Social Sci., Shimer Coll., 1961; MA in Polit. Sci., No. Ill. U., 1965; EdD in Social Studies, SUNY, Buffalo, 1972. Cert. tchr. social studies, N.Y. Tchr. English, social studies Medina (N.Y.) Pub. Sch. System, 1966-68; tchr. Kenmore-Tonawanda (N.Y.) Union Free Sch. Dist. 1, 1968-69; prof. SUC, Buffalo, 1970—; scholar in residence Am. Assn. Cmty. and Jr. Colls., Washington, 1986-87; cons. restructuring post-secondary edn. in The Acad. Namibia, Southwest Africa, 1989; founder Applecore Consulting. Co-author: Practical Methods for the Social Studies, 1977, Working in America, 1976, Historian: Building a New Nation in 1789; editor: The Social Science Record, 1975-78; contbr. articles to ednl. jours. Mem. World Assn. for Case Rsch. and Application, Nat. Coun. for Social Studies, N.Y. State Coun. for Social Studies (exec. bd. dirs. 1975-78, jour. editor), Rsch. and Planning for the Future (founder). Democrat. Avocations: travel, historical research. Home: 67 Lancaster Ave Buffalo NY 14222-1403 Office: SUC Dept History & Social Studies 1300 Elmwood Ave Buffalo NY 14222-1004

HETZNER, MARC ANDREW, lawyer; b. Logansort, Ind., Apr. 24, 1953; s. John R. and Nelma L. (Byrt) H.; m. Rosalie M.; children: Collette N., Christopher R., Kimberly A. BA, Ind. U., 1975, MBA, 1983, JD, 1983. Bar: Ind. 1983, U.S. Dist. Ct. (so. dist.) Ind. 1983, U.S. Tax Ct. 1983, U.S. Ct. Appeals (7th cir.) 1988. Ptnr. Krieg Devault Alexander & Capehart, Indpls., 1989—. Contbr. articles to profl. jours. Mem. Indpls. Zoo Planned Giving Com., 1995—, St. Vincent Hosp. Found., Planned Giving Com., 1995—. 1st lt. U.S. Army, 1975-79. Fellow Am. Coll. Trust & Estate Counsel; mem. Ind. Estate Bar Found., Indpls. Estate Planning Coun. Office: Krieg DeVault Alexander & Capehart 1 Indiana Sq Ste 2800 Indianapolis IN 46204-2079

HEUER, ARTHUR HAROLD, ceramics engineer, educator; b. N.Y.C., Apr. 29, 1936; s. William Jacob and Hannah (Kaye) H.; m. Roberta Feinstein, Dec. 22, 1956 (div. 1974); children: Howard, Michael, James; m. Joan McKnee Hulburt, May 8, 1976. BS, CCNY, 1956; PhD, U. Leeds, Eng., 1965, DSc, 1977. Rsch. chemist Ind. Gen. Corp., Keasbey, N.J., 1956-60; rsch. engr. Electron Tube Div. Bendix Co., Eatontown, N.J., 1960-61; staff scientist AVCO Space Systems Div., Lowell, Mass., 1965-67; asst. prof. ceramics div. metall. and materials Case Western Res. U., Cleve., 1967-70, assoc. prof., 1970-74, prof., 1974—, dir. materials rsch. lab. Case Inst. Tech., 1974-80, Kyocera Prof. Ceramics, 1985—; external sci. mem. Max-Planck Inst. fur Metalforschung, Germany, 1990—. Editor: Zirconia I, Zirconia II; contbr. over 340 articles to profl. jours. Recipient Alexander von Humboldt award Max-Planck Inst., 1983, Gold Medal award ASM. Fellow Am. Ceramic Soc. (chmn. basic sci. com., Sosman Meml. lectr. 1986, editor jour. 1988-90, John Jeppson award 1990, Orton lectr. 1991, Disting. Life mem. 1996), U.K. Inst. Physics; mem. AAAS, NAE, ASM (Gold medal). Achievements include research in transformation toughening in Zirconia, electron microscopy in ceramics, dislocations in ceramics, phase transformations in ceramics, biomimetic processing of materials, materials science aspects of MEM, rapid prototyping technology/solid freeform fabrication of engineering materials, mechanical properties of hand and soft tissue; cofounder CAM-LEM Inc. Home: 2043 Random Rd Apt 303 Cleveland OH 44106-5916 Office: Case Western Res U Materials Sci and Engring 10900 Euclid Ave Cleveland OH 44106-1712

HEUER, GERALD ARTHUR, mathematician, educator; b. Bertha, Minn., Aug. 31, 1930; s. William C.F. and Selma C. (Rosenberg) H.; m. Jeanette Mary Knedel, Sept. 5, 1954; children—Paul, Karl, Ruth, Otto. BA, Concordia Coll., 1951; MA, U. Nebr., 1953; PhD, U. Minn., 1958. Math. instr. Hamline U., 1955-56; math. instr. Concordia Coll., 1956-57, asst. prof., 1957-58, assoc. prof., 1958-62, prof., 1962-95, Sigurd and Pauline Prestegaard Mundhjeld prof., 1988-95, chmn. dept., 1963-70, research prof., 1970-71, prof. emeritus and mathematician-in-residence, 1995—; mathematician Remington Rand Univac, summer 1958; vis. prof. U. Nebr., 1960-61; mathematician Control Data Corp., summers 1960-62, cons., 1960-63; vis. lectr. Math. Assn. Am., 1964-66; cons. NSF-AID, India, 1968-69; guest speaker Minn. sect. Math. Assn. Am., 1956, Neb. sect., 1961, No. Central sect., 1974; vis. prof. dept. pure and applied math. Wash. State U., Pullman, 1980-81; vis. prof./scholar Math. Inst., Cologne (Germany) U., 1973-74, Inst. Stats., Econs. and Ops. Research, Graz U., Austria, 1987-88, rsch. prof. fall semester 1990; dir. U.S. Math. Olympiad Tng. Session, leader U.S. team Internat. Math. Olympiad, 1988-90; vis. prof. Graz U., Austria, 1994, 97; invited plenary spkr. Internat. Symposium Ops. Rsch., Passau, Germany, 1995. Co-author: (With Ulrike Leopold-Wildburger) Balanced Silverman Games on General Discrete Sets, 1991, Silverman's Game, 1995; reviewer Zentralblatt für Mathematik, Berlin, 1967—, Math. Revs., Ann Arbor, Mich., 1978—; contbr. articles to profl. jours. NSF Faculty fellow, 1966-67; NSF rsch. grantee, 1963, 64, 66; Bush Rsch. scholar Concordia Coll., 1983-84, Centennial Rsch. scholar, 1992, 93, 94, 95. Mem. Math. Assn. Am. (com. on Am. math. competitions 1988—, nat. bd. govs. 1971-73, com. on Putnam prize 1987-90, local and regional competitions com. 1998—, pres. Minn. sect. 1959-60, cert. meritorious svc. 1994), Am. Math. Soc., Nat. Geographic Soc., Deutsche Math.-Vereinigung E.V. (Berlin), Österreichische Math. Gesellschaft (Vienna), Sigma Xi. Lutheran. Home: 1216 Elm St S Moorhead MN 56560-4049 Office: Concordia Coll Dept Math Moorhead MN 56562

HEUER, MARGARET B., retired microcomputer laboratory coordinator; b. Juneau, Alaska, Sept. 12, 1935; d. William George and Flora (Rusk) Allen; m. Joseph Louis Heuer; children: Leilani, Joseph (dec.), Daniel, Suzanne, Karen, Mark, Jerina. AA, San Bernardino Valley Coll., 1980. Cert. data processing, computer repair and maintenance, microcomputer support specialist. Coord. microcomputers lab. Oakton Community Coll., Skokie, Ill., 1981-93; ret., 1993.

HEUER, MARTIN, temporary services company executive; b. Algoma, Wis., Oct. 16, 1934; s. Orland Fred and Gertrude Mayme (Zimmerman) H.; m. Rita Mae Prokash, Oct. 27; children: Martin Joseph, Ronald James. AA, SUNY, 1973, AS, 1975. Commd. 2d lt. C.E., U.S. Army, 1954, advanced through grades to lt. col., 1968; flight comdr., adminstrv. and maintenance officer 1st Aviation Co., Fort Riley, 1958-61; with 937th Engr. Aviation Co., Panama, Lima, Peru, 1961-65; maintenance officer 174th Aviation Co., Vietnam, 1966; adj. 14th Combat Aviation Bn., 1966-67; dir. systems, curriculum and spl. projects div. Army Primary Helicopter Sch., Fort Wolters, Tex., 1967-69; aviation advisor Wis. Army N.G., West Bend, 1969-70; airfield comdr. Cu Chi Army Airfield, Vietnam, 1970; adj. 165th Combat

Aviation Group, Vietnam, 1970-71; engr. advisor Wis. N.G., Eau Claire, 1971-73; mgr., area mgr. Manpower Temp. Services, 1973-76; exec. v.p. Aide Services, Inc. and KARI Services, Inc., Tampa, Fla., 1976-80, pres., chmn., 1980—; pres., chmn. Capitol Services, Inc., Tallahassee, 1982-86; pres., chmn. AIDE 2000, Inc. 1998—, pres. bd. dirs. Fort Wolters Fed. Credit Union, 1967-69; chmn. bd. Digital Control Corp., Seminole, Fla., 1981-98 . Pres., Seminole High Sch. Band Boosters, 1974-79, v.p. Pinellas County Band Boosters, 1977-78; bd. dirs. Seminole High Sch. Booster Assn., 1975-79, pres., 1978-79. Decorated Legion of merit with 1 oak leaf cluster, Bronze star medal with 3 oak leaf clusters, Air medal with 3 oak leaf clusters; recipient First Band Booster Pres. award Seminole High Sch., 1979, Service to Mankind award Sertoma, 1980. Mem. Assn. Manpower Franchise Owners (dir. 1980-82, 83-86, treas. 1981-82, chmn. 1984-86), Assn. U.S. Army (chmn. bd. govs. 1981-82, asst. state v.p. Suncoast chpt. and Fla., 1981-82, state v.p. 1982-84, chmn. chpt. communications com. nat. adv. bd. 1982-86, mem. corp. adv. council 1985-90, Fla. exec. council 1985-90, bd. dirs. Sun Coast chpt. 1994—), Army Aviation Assn. Am., Air Force Assn., Soc. Am. Mil. Engrs., Res. Officers Assn., Retired Officers Assn., Future Farmers Am. Alumni Assn., Nat. Assn. Temp. Svcs. (treas./sec. Fla. chpt. 1991-94), Vietnam Helicopter Pilots Assn. (bd. dirs. Fla. chpt. 1993—, v.p. 1996-98, pres. 1998—). Republican. Office: Ste 102 5402 Beaumont Center Blvd Tampa FL 33634-5202

HEUER, MICHAEL ALEXANDER, dean, endodontist educator; b. Grand Rapids, Mich., Apr. 27, 1932; s. Harold Maynard and Gwendolyn Ruth (Kremer) H.; m. Barbara Margaret Naines, Nov. 23, 1955; children—Kristan M., Karin E., Katrina A. DDS, Northwestern U., 1956; MS, U. Mich., 1959. Pvt. practice Chgo., 1959-86; asst. prof. Northwestern U., 1960-66; assoc. prof. Loyola U., Chgo., 1968-73; prof., chmn. dept. endodontics Northwestern U., 1974-83, assoc. dean acad affairs, 1983-88, sr. assoc. dean, 1988-93, dean, 1993-98; dir. Am. Bd. Endodontics, 1971-77, sec.-treas., 1973-76, pres., 1976-77; chmn. subcom. Am. Nat. Standards Inst.; mem. com. on advanced edn. Commn. on Accreditation of Dental Edn., 1974-77, endodontic cons., 1986-91, curriculum cons., 1986-92. Contbr. articles in field to profl. jours. Served with USNR, 1956-58. Fellow Am. Coll. Dentistry (sec.-treas. Ill. sect. 1986-92, vice chair 1992-94, chair 1994-96), Internat. Coll. Dentistry, Am. Assn. Endodontists (life; exec. coun. 1967-71, sec. 1979-84, v.p. 1984-85, pres.-elect 1985-86, pres. 1986-87); mem. AAAS, ADA (life; coun. dental materials and devices 1972-78, chmn. 1977-78, sci. coun. 1980-97), Internat. Assn. Dental Rsch., Am. Assn. Dental Schs., Chgo. Odontographic Soc. (pres. 1982-84), Edgar D. Coolidge Endodontic Soc. (charter sec. 1961, pres. 1964, trustee), Phi Eta Sigma, Omicron Kappa Upsilon, Chi Psi, Delta Sigma Delta. Home: 1552 Treeline Ct Naperville IL 60565-2015 Office: Northwestern U Dental Sch Chicago IL 60611

HEUER, ROBERT MAYNARD, II, opera company executive; b. Detroit, Nov. 27, 1944; s. Robert Maynard and May Elizabeth (Quinn) H. Student, Capital U., 1963-64; B.A., Wayne State U., 1976. Youth dir. Grace Luth. Ch., Detroit, 1964-66; costume designer, prodn. mgr. U. Windsor, Ont., Can., 1967-69; program coord. Detroit Youtheatre, Detroit Inst. Arts, 1970-71; mng. dir. Mich. Opera Theatre, Detroit, 1971-79; prodn. dir. Fla. Grand Opera (formerly Greater Miami Opera), 1979-83; asst. gen. mgr. Greater Miami Opera, 1984-85, gen. mgr., CEO, 1986-97, gen. dir., CEO,, 1997—. Mem. Performing Arts Ctr. Found. Greater Miami. Recipient Grand Decoration of Honor Republic of Austria, 1990. Mem. Opera Am. (bd. dirs.), Greater Miami C. of C. Home: 547 Navarre Ave Coral Gables FL 33134-4231 Office: Fla Grand Opera 1200 Coral Way Miami FL 33145-2927

HEUER, SAM TATE, lawyer; b. Batesville, Ark., July 11, 1952; s. Albert A. and Mary (Baker) H.; children: Noal Tate, Polly Anna, Charles Albert; m. Max Parker. BBA in Banking and Fin., U. Miss., 1974; JD, U. Ark., 1978. Bar: Ark. Dep. pros. atty. 4th Jud. Dist., Fayetteville, Ark., 1979-80; assoc. Davis Bracey & Heuer, Springdale, Ark., 1980-81; pvt. practice, Batesville, 1981-86; pros. atty. 16th Jud. Dist., Batesville, 1983-86; assoc,, salesman Crews & Assocs., Little Rock, 1987-88; assoc. John Wesley Hall P.C., Little Rock, 1988-93; ptnr. Thurman, Lawrence & Heuer, PLC, Little Rock, 1994—. Mem. ATLA, Ark. Prosecutor's Assn. (bd. dirs. 1984-86, v.p. 1985-86), Ark. Trial Lawyers Assn., Am. Trial Lawyers Assn., Pulaski County Attys. Assn. Democrat. Episcopalian. Office: Thurman Lawrence & Heuer 124 W Capitol Ave Ste 1650 Little Rock AR 72201-3758

HEUMAN, DONNA RENA, lawyer; b. Seattle, May 27, 1949; d. Russell George and Edna Inez (Armstrong) H. BA in Psychology, UCLA, 1972; JD, U. Calif., San Francisco, 1985. Cert. shorthand reporter, Calif. Owner Heuman & Assocs., San Francisco, 1978-86; real estate broker Calif., 1990—; co-founder, chair, CFO Atherton Park Foods, Inc., 1996—; Mem. Hastings Internat. and Comparative Law Rev., 1984-85; bd. dirs. Saddleback, 1987-89. Jessup Internat. Moot Ct. Competition, 1985, bBd. dirs. N. Fair Oaks Adv. Coun., vice chair, sec. 1993-95. Mem. ABA, NAFE, ATLA, AOPA, Nat. Shorthand Reporters Assn., Women Entrepreneurs, Mensa, Calif. State Bar Assn., Nat. Mus. of Women in the Arts, Calif. Lawyers for the Arts, San Francisco Bar Assn., Commonwealth Club, World Affairs Coun., Zonta (bd. dirs.). Home: 750 18th Ave Menlo Park CA 94025-2018 Office: Superior Ct Calif Hall Of Justice Redwood City CA 94063

HEUMANN, JUDITH, federal agency administrator; m. Jorge Pineda. BA Speech and Theatre, Long Island U., 1969; MPH, U. Calif., Berkeley, 1975. Spl. edn. and 2d grade tchr. N.Y.C. Pub. Schs., 1970-73; legis. asst. to chair Senate Com. Labor and Pub. Welfare, Washington, 1974; sr. dep. dir. Ctr. Independent Living, Berkeley, 1975-82; spl. asst. to exec. dir. State Dept. Rehab., Sacramento, Calif., 1982-83; v.p., co-founder, dir. Rsch. Tng. Ctr. Pub. Policy in Independent Living, Berkeley, Calif., 1983-93; co-founder World Inst. Disability, Berkeley, Calif.; U.S. asst. sec. U.S. Dept. Edn., Washington, 1993—; also chair, vice chair, bd. mem. Archtl. & Transp. Barriers Compliance Bd., Washington, 1998—. Office: Dept of Edn Spl Edn & Rehabilitative Svcs 330 C St SW Ste 3006 Washington DC 20201-0001 also: Archtl & Transp Barriers Compliance Bd 1331 F St NW Ste 100 Washington DC 20004-1107*

HEURING, WAYNE ROBERT, newspaper journalist; b. East St. Louis, Ill., Sept. 8, 1947; s. Allen B. and Esther E. (Baldus) H.; m. Ellen Zucker, June 29, 1970 (div. Jan. 1974); m. Laura Appelbaum, Apr. 21, 1974 (div. Jan. 1975). BA in Psychology, U. Ill., 1969, MS in Journalism, 1971. Sports dir. WPGU Radio, Urbana, Ill., 1966-68; sportswriter Champaign-Urbana (Ill.) News-Gazette, 1969-71; reporter, copy editor Champaign-Urbana Courier, 1971-75; copy editor Milw. Sentinel, 1975-79; night bus. desk chief Chgo. Tribune, 1979-86; night copy desk chief San Francisco Examiner, 1986—; writing coach San Francisco State U., 1989-97, 1999; journalism instr. Marquette U., Milw., 1976-78. Co-chmn. judging com. Nat. Ednl. Media Network, Oakland, Calif., 1994-96, mem. judging com. 1993—, trustee 1995-96. Avocations: reading, computing, foreign languages, bridge, squash, photography. Home: 60 Parkridge Dr Apt 6 San Francisco CA 94131-1428 Office: San Francisco Examiner 110 5th St San Francisco CA 94103-2918

HEUSCH, CLEMENS AUGUST, physicist, educator; b. Aachen, Germany, Apr. 19, 1932; s. Hermann and Elisabeth (Pauli) H.; m. Karin von Gilgenheimb, July 6, 1968; children: Marina, Bettina. Student, Bowdoin Coll., 1951-52; Dipl. Phys., U. Aachen, 1955; postgrad., U. Paris, 1956; Dr. rer. nat., Tech. U. Munich, 1959. Rsch. asst. Tech. U., Munich, 1956-59; project leader rsch. div. AEG, Frankfurt, Germany, 1960-61; rsch. scientist DESY Accelerator Lab., Hamburg, Germany, 1961-63; from rsch. fellow to assoc. prof. Calif. Inst. Tech., Pasadena, 1963-69; prof., co-prin. investigator U. Calif., Santa Cruz, 1969—; cons., referee Am. Inst. Physics, N.Y.C., European Orgn. for Nuclear Rsch., Geneva; cons. Nat. Acad. Scis.; mem. various internat. adv. coms., 1965—; founding dir. Santa Cruz Inst. for Particle Physics; lectr. musical criticism Porter Coll., U. Calif., vis. prof., RWTH Aachen, Germany, 1995—. Free-lance music critic. Recipient Humboldt prize, 1990; Fulbright scholar, 1951; grantee Dept. Energy, NSF, 1963—. Roman Catholic. Office: U Calif Inst for Particle Physics Dept Physics 1156 High St Santa Cruz CA 95064*

HEUSEL, BARBARA STEVENS, English scholar and educator; b. Louisville, Jan. 12, 1935; d. Jay T. and Ruth L. Stevens; children: Heidi Heusel Freeman, Lisa Gillig, Gretchen Heusel. BA, Heidelberg Coll., 1957; MA, U. Louisville, 1967; PhD, U. S.C., 1983. Instr. dept. of English U. Louisville, 1965-68, Furman U., Greenville, S.C., 1968-84; vis. asst. prof. English Wake Forest U., Winston-Salem, N.C., 1985-88; lectr. in English U. N.C., Chapel Hill, 1984-85, 88-89; assoc. prof. English N.W. Mo. State U., Maryville, 1990-98, prof. English, 1998—; dir. of curriculum The ArtSchool, Carrboro, N.C., 1988-90; cons. PENULTIMA, Chapel Hill, N.C., 1988—; lectr. in field. Author: Patterned Aimlessness: Iris Murdoch's Novels of the 1970s and 1980s, 1995; contbr. articles to profl. jours. Mellon grant Furman U., 1979-80, grant Nat. Endowment for the Humanities, 1989. Mem. AAUW, Iris Murdoch Soc. (founder, sec.-treas. 1986-93, pres. 1993—), MLA, James Joyce Soc., South Atlantic MLA. Avocations: traveling, aerobics, birding, canoeing, films. Office: NW Mo State U Dept English Maryville MO 64468

HEUSER, GEORGE KELLY, physician; b. Honolulu, Oct. 21, 1957; s. Gustave Fredrick and Bernice (Johnson) H. BSChemE, U. Va., 1979; MD, Ea. Va. Med. Sch., 1984. Assoc. chief staff for ambulatory care Va. Med. Ctr., Hampton, 1987-98; med. dir. Sentora Health Care, Virginia Beach, Va., 1998—. Mem. ACP. Home: 1744 Jack Frost Rd Virginia Bch VA 23455-3221 Office: Sentarch Health Mgmt. 4417 Corporation Ln Virginia Beach VA 23462-3162

HEUSSER, CALVIN JOHN, biology educator, researcher; b. North Bergen, N.J., Sept. 10, 1924. BS, Rutgers U., 1947, MS, 1949; PhD, Oreg. State U., 1952. Am. Geog. Soc., N.Y.C., 1952-67; MS NYU, 1967-91, prof. emeritus, 1991—; mem. Heusser & Heusser, cons., Tuxedo, N.Y., 1991—. Author: Late Pleistocene Environments, 1960, Pollen and Spores of Chile, 1971. Pfc. U.S. Army, 1944-45, ETO. Recipient David Livingstone medal Am. Geog. Soc., 1987; Guggenheim Found. fellow, 1963, Fulbright Commn. fellow, 1963, Clare Hall U. Cambridge (Eng.) fellow, 1985. Mem. Am. Quaternary Assn., Am. Assn. Stratigraphic Palynologists, Torrey Bot. Club (pres. 1975-76). Avocations: classical music, art. Home: Clinton Woods Tuxedo NY 10987 Office: Heusser & Heusser Clinton Rd Tuxedo Park NY 10987

HEVESI, ALAN G., muncipal or county official; b. Queens, N.Y., Jan. 31, 1940; m. Carol Hevesi; children: Laura, Dan, Andrew. BA, Queens Coll.; PhD in Pub. Law and Govt., Columbia U. Faculty mem. Queens Coll., 1967-93; comptr. City of N.Y., 1994—; adj. prof. Fordham Law Sch., Columbia U. Sch. Internat. and Pub. Affairs. Author: Legislative Politics in New York State: A Comparative Analysis, 1975; co-editor: The Politics of Urban Education, 1969; contbr. articles to profl. jours. Office: Comptrollers Office 1 Centre St Rm 530 City of New York New York NY 10007*

HEWES, LAURENCE ILSLEY, III, lawyer, management, development, legal consultant; b. Palo Alto, Calif., Sept. 18, 1933; s. Laurence Ilsley, Jr. and Patricia Esther (Jackson) H.; m. Mary Clarke Darling, Oct. 1, 1960; children: Laurence Ilsley IV, Henry Patrick Darling, Mary Clarke Danforth. AB, Yale U., 1956, LLB, 1959. Bar: D.C. 1961, U.S. Dist. Ct. D.C., 1961, U.S. Ct. Appeals (D.C. cir.) 1961, U.S. Supreme Ct. 1966. Assoc. counsel U.S. Senate Comm. Labor and Human Resources, Washington, 1961; assoc. counsel Econ. Devel. Adminstrn. U.S. Dept. Commerce, Washington, 1961-62; staff dir., counsel Pres.'s Com. on Equal Opportunity in Armed Forces, Washington, 1962-63; assoc. then ptnr. Hydeman & Mason and successor firms, Washington, 1963-72; ptnr. Boasberg & Hewes (and successor firms), Washington, 1972-80, Wald Harkader & Ross, Washington, 1980-85; exec. dir., gen. counsel The Support Ctr., 1985-88; pres., chief exec. officer, gen. counsel Corp. Against Drug Abuse, 1989-93; legal, devel. and mgmt. cons. Washington, 1994—; bd. dirs., Officer Taft Corp., Washington and N.Y.C., 1967-72; bd. dirs., mgr. Grants Mgmt. Adv. Svc., Inc., 1975-80; lectr. non-profit orgn. field. Contbr. articles to profl. jours., chpts. to books. Bd. trustees, Wooster Sch., Danbury Conn., 1981-89, Friends of Superior Ct. of D.C., 1973-87. Served with USAFR, 1959-66. Mem. ABA, D.C. Bar Assn., Cosmos Club, Yale Club (N.Y.C.), Mountain View Country Club. Democrat. Avocations: music, reading, bicycling, fly fishing, tennis.

HEWES, ROBERT CHARLES, radiologist; b. Balt., Feb. 14, 1953; s. Gordon Cecil and Gladys Dorothy (Barringham) H.; m. Judith Renee Lacy, Mar. 23, 1975; children: Christy, Amy, Jeremy. Student, Columbia Union Coll., 1973, Kettering Coll. of Med. Arts, 1971; BS, Loma Linda U., 1976, MD. Diplomate Am. Bd. Med. Examiners, Am. Bd. Radiology with subspecialty in vascular and internat. radiology. Resident in radiology Loma Linda (Calif.) U., 1978-81, asst. prof. radiology, 1983-84; fellow in orthopedic radiology Hosp. for Spl. Surgery Cornell U. Med. Ctr., N.Y.C., 1981-82; fellow in interventional radiology Johns Hopkins U. Hosp., Balt., 1982-83; assoc. prof. Wright State U.; mem. staff Kettering (Ohio) Med. Ctr., vice chmn. dept. radiology, 1985-87, chmn., 1988-95; pres. Patient First Imaging Network, 1994-95, med. dir., 1996-98; pres. Kettering Radiologists, Inc., 1987-95, 97-99; bd. dirs. Spring Valley Acad., chmn. fin. mgmt. com., 1998-99; pres. Alumni Assn. Spring Valley Acad., 1987-89. Contbr. articles on radiology to profl. jours. Bd. mem. Seventh Day Adventist Ch., Kettering, Ohio. Recipient Cert. of merit Am. Roentgen Ray Soc., 1983, Disting. Alumnus award Kettering Coll. of Med. Arts, 1990. Mem. AMA, Radiol. Soc. N.Am., Soc. Cardiovascular and Interventional Radiology, Miami Valley Radiol. Soc. (pres. 1994), Alpha Omega Alpha (award). Republican. Adventist. Avocations: radio-controlled airplanes, ham radio, woodworking, sports. Office: Kettering Med Ctr Dept Radiology 3535 Southern Blvd Dayton OH 45429-1221

HEWES, THOMAS FRANCIS, physician; b. Boston, Mar. 5, 1929; s. Walter Raymond and Margaret Frances (Fallon) H.; m. Catherine Rene Lemaitre; June 29, 1958; children: Christine, Philip, Gerald, Nancy. AB, Coll. of the Holy Cross, 1950; MD, Tufts U., 1954. Diplomate Am. Bd. Internal Medicine. Intern U. Rochester (N.Y.) Strong Meml. Hosp., 1954-55, resident, 1955-56; sr. med. resident VA Hosp., Boston, 1958-59; clin. and rsch. fellow in gastroenterology Mass. Gen. Hosp., Boston, 1959-60; physician Am. Hosp. Paris, Neuilly-sur-Seine, France, 1961-98, dir. ICU, 1968-87, v.p. med. staff, 1978-80, 82-85, pres. med. staff, 1980-82, 85-87, chmn. dept. medicine, 1978-92; adj. clin. prof. medicine Tufts U. Sch. Medicine, Boston, 1993—; bd. govs. Am. Hosp. Paris, 1976-87. Trustee Am. Sch. Paris, Garches, France, 1971-80, Am. Aid Soc., Paris; pres. bd. regents Marymount Internat. Sch., Nevilly. Capt. U.S. Army, 1956-58. Recipient Profl. Svc. citation FAA, 1994. Mem. AMA, Mass. Med. Soc., Polo de Paris. Democrat. Roman Catholic. Avocations: sailing, gardening, travel. Home: 46 Blvd Inkermann, 92200 Neuilly Sur Seine France Office: Am Hosp Paris, 63 Blvd Victor Hugo, 92200 Neuilly Sur Seine France

HEWES, WILLIAM GARDNER, III, insurance executive, real estate agent, legislator; b. New Iberia, La., Oct. 27, 1961; s. William Gardner and Sarah Lee (Smith) H.; m. Paula Christine Morton, Aug. 31, 1985; children: Katherine C., Sarah M., William G. BSBA, U. So. Miss., 1984. Agt., owner Billy Hewes III Ins. Agy., Gulfport, Miss., 1985—, broker, assoc., 1989—; senator Dist. 49 Harrison County State of Miss., Jackson, 1992—, chmn. ports and marine resources com., 1993—. Named Conservation Legislator of Yr. Miss. Wildlife Fedn., 1993, Top 40 Under 40 Bus. Leaders, 1996; Henry Toll fellow Coun. of State Govts., 1994. Fellow Life Underwriter Tng. Coun.; mem. Gulf Coast Assn. Underwriters (pres., v.p., com. chmn. 1985—, Achievement award 1992), West Gulf Coast Bd. Realtors, Gulfport Jaycees (pres., v.p., com. chmn. 1985—), U. So. Miss. Alumni Assn. (pres. Harrison County chpt. 1987-88), Gulf Coast C. of C. (amb. 1990, Grad. Leadership award 1991-92), Am. Legis. Exch. Coun. (Outstanding Legislator award 1994, 96, bd. dirs.). Republican. Roman Catholic. Avocations: fishing, racquetball, music, golf. Home: 200 Locust St Gulfport MS 39507-4341 Office: B Hewes Ins and Real Estate PO Box 2387 Gulfport MS 39505-2387*

HEWETT, DAVID EDGAR, journalist; b. Windsor, Vt., Mar. 31, 1938; s. Stanton Hewett and Susan (Sargent) Jones; m. Judith Cram Hewett, 1963 (div. 1970); children: Deborah, James, Mary; m. Janna Teuscher, June 5, 1976. Student, Goddard Coll., 1971-73. Antiques dealer Putney, Vt., 1971-77; freelance writer Brattleboro, Vt., 1977-83; contbg. editor Maine Antiques Digest, Waldoboro, Maine, 1983—. Author: The Antiques Game, 1980; author series of investigative reports Maine Antique Digest (Spl. Citation for accuracy and fairness Mormon History Assn., Brigham Young U., Salt Lake City, 1989); contbr. articles to Washington Post, Christian Sci. Monitor, other publs.; designer, creator computer software: Hewett's Database of American Cabinetmakers, 1997. Head UE-218 (union) Polit. Action Com., Springfield, Vt., 1968-70. Mem. Philatelic Assn., Bur. Issues Assn., Machine Cancel Soc. Democrat. Avocations: stamp collecting, building model airplanes. Office: Maine Antique Digest Main St Waldoboro ME 04572

HEWETT, THOMAS AVERY, petroleum engineer, educator; b. Lansing, Mich., Apr. 23, 1944; s. Richard Eugene and Frances Marion (Perry) H.; m. Marilyn Roberta Lawley, July 11, 1970 (div. Mar. 1979); m. Evro Lynn Stylianides, Nov. 3, 1984 (div. Nov. 1992); m. Janet M. Bostrom, Mar. 17, 1994. BS, Mich. State U., 1966; MS, MIT, 1968, ME, 1969, PhD, 1970. Asst. prof. CUNY, 1970-75; rsch. scientist Union Carbide Corp., Tarrytown, N.Y., 1975-79; sr. engring. assoc. Chevron Oil Field Rsch. Co., Lahabra, Calif., 1979-91; prof. petroleum engring. dept. Stanford (Calif.) U., 1991—. Contbr. over 40 articles to profl. jours. Recipient Engring. Merit award Orange County Engring. Coun., 1991. Fellow Inst. for Advancement of Engring.; mem. AAAS, Soc. Petroleum Engrs. Achievements include two patents on solar heating; pioneering use of fractals in petroleum reservoir modeling. Office: Stanford U Dept Petroleum Engring Rm 096 Green Earth Scis Bldg Stanford CA 94305-2220

HEWITSON, WILLIAM CRAIG, physician, career officer; b. Park City, Utah, July 4, 1961; s. William Glenn and Darlene Marie Hewitson; m. Deanne Gomm, July 15, 1983; children: William Brent, Staci Anne. BA with honors, U. Utah, 1986; MD, USUHS, 1991; MPH, Johns Hopkins U., 1995. Diplomate Am. Bd. Preventive Medicine. Officer U.S. Army, advanced through grades to maj., 1986; transitional intern Fitzsimons Army Med. Ctr., Aurora, Colo., 1991-92; 2d brigade surgeon 7th Inf. Divsn. Fitzsimons Army Med. Ctr., Ft. Ord, Calif., 1992-93; divsn. surgeon Fitzsimons Army Med. Ctr., Ft. Lewis, Wash., 1993-94; resident in general preventive medicine Walter Reed Army Inst. Rsch., Washington, 1994-96; chief injuries and occupation illnesses U.S. Army Ctr. for Health Promotion and Preventive Medicine, Aberdeen Proving Grounds, Md., 1996-98; chief preventive medicine divsn. Gen. Leonard Wood Army Cmty. Hosp., Ft. Leonard Wood, Mo., 1998—; dir. The Preventive Health Care Mgmt. Group, Salt Lake City, 1996-97; cons. Med. Adv. Sys., Owings, Md., 1995-98. Contbr. articles to profl. jours. Advancement chmn. Big Piney dist., Boy Scouts Am., Waynesville, Mo., 1999, Four Rivers dist. health and safety com., 1998, Pack # 1036 com. chmn., Ft. George G. Meade, 1995-97; missionary LDS Ch. Sch., Argentina, 1980-82. Mem. AMA (Physician Recognition award 1997), Assn. Mil. Surgeons U.S., Masons. Avocations: running, fitness, flying, golf, tennis. Office: Gen Leonard Wood Army Cmty Hosp 126 Missouri Ave Fort Leonard Wood MO 65473-8952

HEWITT, CHARLES C., broadcast executive; b. Pratt, Kans., Dec. 24, 1939; s. Harold E. and Leola (Bratty) H.; m. Barbara J.; children: Elizabeth, Rebecca; m. Pamela Villiars Hewitt (Sept. 29, 1990); step children: Jesse Garcia, Sara Lyn Garcia. BA, U. Kans., 1963, JD, 1966. Exec. dir. Nat. Space Inst., 1974-80; corporate dir. Comms. Fairchild Industries, 1986; exec. dir. Soc. for Pvt. and Comml. Earth Stations, 1980-86; pres. Satellite Broadcasting and Comms. Assn. Am., 1986—. Mem. Satellite Broadcasting and Comms. Assn. Am. (officer). Office: Satellite Broadcasting & Communications Assn of Am 225 Reinekers Ln Ste 600 Alexandria VA 22314-2875

HEWITT, CONRAD W., state superintendant of banks. Supt. of banks State of Calif.; commr. Calif. State Dept. Financial Inst. Office: 111 Pine St Ste 1100 San Francisco CA 94111-5613

HEWITT, DENNIS EDWIN, financial executive; b. Los Angeles, Apr. 9, 1944; s. Robert Sherwood and Anna Marie (Linge) H.; m. Kathryn Dale Lefler, June 11, 1966; children—Denise, Dawn. B.S., UCLA, 1966; M.B.A., U. So. Calif., 1968. Fin. analyst Rockwell Internat., L.A., 1967-72; div. contr. Arcata Co., N.Y.C., 1972-76; v.p., contr. Weeden Co., N.Y.C., 1976-78; sr. v.p., treas. Young & Rubicam Inc., N.Y.C., 1979-88; treas. Omnicom Group Inc., N.Y.C., 1988—. Republican. Avocations: golf, tennis. Home: 1 Richmond Dr Old Greenwich CT 06870-1413 Office: Omnicom Group Inc 437 Madison Ave New York NY 10022-7001

HEWITT, DON S., television news producer; b. N.Y.C., Dec. 14, 1922; s. Ely S. and Frieda (Pike) H.; children: Jeffrey, Steven, Jill, Lisa; m. Marilyn Berger, Apr. 14, 1979. Student, NYU, 1941; hon. degree, Brandeis U., 1990; DFA (hon.), Am. Film Inst., 1993. War corr., World War II; prodr. 1st Kennedy-Nixon TV debate, 1960; exec. prodr. CBS Evening News with Walter Cronkite, 1960-65, 60 Minutes, 1968—. Delivered 1st ann. William S. Paley lectr. Mus. of TV and Radio, 1993. Recipient Paul White award Radio and TV News Dirs. Assn., 1987; Gold medal Internat. Radio and TV Soc., 1987, Broadcaster of Yr. award, 1980; Gold Baton award Columbia DuPont, 1988, Peabody award, 1989, Lowell Thomas Centennial award, 1992, 1st ann. Goldsmith award for Investigative Reporting, John F. Kennedy Sch. Govt. Harvard U., 1992, Lifetime award Prodrs. Guild Am., 1993, Founders award Internat. Coun. of TV Acad. Arts and Scis., 1995; named to Hall of Fame, NATAS, 1990. Office: CBS News/60 Minutes 524 W 57th St New York NY 10019-2924 *Sometimes I think I am not sure of what I absolutely know is so.*

HEWITT, EMILY CLARK, lawyer, minister; b. Balt., May 26, 1944; d. John Frank and Margaret Genevieve (Gray) H. AB, Cornell U., 1966; MPhil, Union Theol. Sem., 1975; JD, Harvard U., 1978. Bar: Mass. 1978, U.S. Dist. Ct. Mass. 1979, U.S. Ct. Appeals (1st cir.) 1984; ordained priest Protestant Episcopal Ch. 1974. Adminstr. Upward Bounds Programs Cornell and Hofstra U., N.Y.C., 1967-69; asst. min. St. Mary's Epsicopal Ch., Manhattanville, N.Y., 1972-73; lectr. Union Theol. Sem., N.Y.C., 1972-73, 74-75; asst. prof. Andover Newton Theol. Sch., Newton Centre, Mass., 1973-75; assoc. Hill & Barlow, Boston, 1978-85, ptnr., 1985-93; gen. counsel GSA, 1993-99; judge U.S. Ct. of Fed. Claims, Washington, 1999—. Co-author: Women Priests: Yes or No?, 1973; contbr. works in field. Bd. dirs. Mass. Found. for Humanities and Pub. Policy, South Hadley, 1983-89. Mem. ABA, Mass. Bar Assn. (council mem. real property sect. 1983-86), Women's Bar Assn., Mass., New Eng. Women in Real Estate (bd. dirs. 1985-89), Mass. Conveyancers Assn., ACLU (ch.-state com. 1971-75). Office: Gen Srvs Admin Gen Counsel 1800 F St NW Ste 4140 Washington DC 20405-0002*

HEWITT, FRANKIE LEA, theater producer; b. Roger Mills Cty, Okla., June 17, 1931; d. Frank David and Mary Lou (Wood) Teague; m. Alonzo Robert Childers, Dec. 10, 1951 (div. 1955); m. Don S. Hewitt, June 8, 1963 (div. 1974); children: Jilian, Lisa. Grad., Napa (Calif.) High Sch., 1949. Women's editor Napa Daily Register, 1949-51; asst. advt. dir. Rose Marie Reid Swim Suits, L.A., 1951-52; writer Calif. Inst. Social Welfare, L.A., 1954-55; writer, legis. aide Nat. Inst. Social Welfare, Washington, 1956-58; staff dir. U.S. Senate Subcom. to Investigate Juvenile Deliquency, Washington, 1959-61; pub. affairs advisor U.S. Mission to UN, N.Y.C., 1961-63; founder, producing dir. Ford's Theatre Soc., Washington, 1967—. Recipient Congl. Arts Caucus award, 1993; named Washingtonian of Yr., Washingtonian Mag., 1978, Woman of Yr., Women's Equity Action League, 1981, YWCA, 1986. Avocations: needlepoint, hiking. Office: Ford's Theatre 511 10th St NW Washington DC 20004-1402

HEWITT, JAMES WATT, lawyer; b. Hastings, Nebr., Dec. 25, 1932; s. Roscoe Stanley and Willa Manners (Watt) H.; m. Marjorie Ruth Barrett, Aug. 8, 1954; children: Mary Janet, William Edward, John Charles, Martha Ann. Student, Hastings Coll., 1950-52; BS, U. Nebr., 1954, JD, 1956. Bar: Nebr. 1956. Practice Hastings, 1956-57, Lincoln, Nebr., 1960—; v.p., gen. counsel Nebco, Inc., Lincoln, 1961—; vis. lectr. U. Nebr. Coll. Law, 1970-71. Mem. state exec. com. Rep. Party, 1967-70, mem. state ctrl. com., 1967-70, legis chmn., 1968-70; bd. dirs. Lincoln Child Guidance Ctr., 1969-72, pres., 1972; bd. dirs. Lincoln Cmty. Playhouse, 1967-73, pres., 1972-73; trustee Bryan Meml. Hosp., Lincoln, 1968-74, 76-82, chmn., 1972-74; bd. dirs. Lincoln Libr., 1990-97; trustee U. Nebr. Found., 1979—; dir. Bryan Meml. Hosp. Found., Lincoln, 1994—; exec. v.p., dir. Nebr. State Hist. Soc. Found., Lincoln, 1994—; dir. Nebr. state chpt. The Nature Conservancy, 1993-99. Capt. USAF, 1957-60. Fellow Am. Bar Found. (Nebr. state chmn. 1988-92, 99—, chmn. 1994-95); mem. ABA (Nebr. state del. 1972-80, bd. govs. 1981-83), Nebr. State Bar (chmn. ins. com. 1972-76, chmn. pub. rels. com. 1982-84, pres. 1985-86), Fed. Bar Assn., Lincoln Bar Assn., Newcomen Soc. (Nebr. chair 1995—), Am. Rose Soc., Nebr. Rose Soc., Lincoln Rose Soc., Nebr. Club, Country of Lincoln Club, Round Table, Beta Theta Pi, Phi Delta Phi. Congregationalist. Home: 2990 Sheridan Blvd Lincoln NE 68502-4241 Office: PO Box 80268 1815 Y St Lincoln NE 68508-1233

HEWITT, JENNIFER LOVE, actress, singer; b. Waco, Tex., Feb. 21, 1979; d. Danny and Pat. Appeared in (film) I Still Know What You Did Last Summer, 1998, Can't Hardly Wait, 1998, I Know What You Did Last Summer, 1997, Trojan War, 1997, House Arrest, 1996, Sister Act 2: Back in the Habit, 1993, Little Miss Millions, 1993, Munchie, 1992, (TV) Party of Five, 1995—, The Byrds of Paradies, 1994, McKenna, 1994, Shaky Ground, 1992, Kids Incorporated, 1989; host The Senior Prom, 1997; appearance on Boy Meets World, 1996. Albums include Jenniver Love Hewitt, 1996, Let's Go Bang, 1995, Love Songs, 1992. Office: William Morris Agy 151 El Camino Dr Beverly Hills CA 90212*

HEWITT, JOHN HAMILTON, JR., editor, writer; b. N.Y.C., Aug. 20, 1924; s. John Hamilton and Agatha (Benjamin) H.; m. Vivian Ann Davidson, Dec. 26, 1949; 1 child, John Hamilton III. Student, Harvard U., 1941-43; BS, NYU, 1948, MA, 1949. Instr. English Morehouse Coll., Atlanta, 1948-50, co-chmn. dept. humanities, 1950-52; reporter N.Y. Amsterdam News, N.Y.C., 1952-56; adminstrv. sec. St. Philip's Ch., N.Y.C., 1956-61; staff writer Med. Tribune, N.Y.C., 1961-72; sr. editor, mng. editor Hosp. Practice, N.Y.C., 1972-75; assoc. editor Med. Tribune, N.Y.C., 1975-83, Emergency Med., 1983-86. Author articles on African-Am. art and 19th century N.Y.C. history. Home: 862 W End Ave Apt 1 New York NY 10025-4959

HEWITT, LESTER L., lawyer; b. Houston, Mar. 11, 1942. BSME, U. Houston, 1965, LLB cum laude, 1968. Bar: Tex. 1968. Examiner U.S. Patent Office, 1968-69; atty. Pravel, Hewitt, Kimball & Krieger, Houston; Assoc. prof. engring. law U. Houston, 1973-80. Mem. Am. Intellectual Property Law Assn. (treas. 1985-88), Houston Intellectual Property Law Assn. (pres. 1991-92), Order of the Barons, Phi Delta Phi, Pi Tau Sigma, Tau Beta Pi, Omicron Delta Kappa. Office: Pravel Hewitt Kimball & Krieger 1177 West Loop S Fl 10 Houston TX 77027-9006*

HEWITT, PAUL BUCK, lawyer; b. St. Louis, July 27, 1949; s. John York and Kathryn Louise (Buck) H.; m. Marla Ivy Zimmers, Feb. 17, 1985; children: Anna Ruth, Rachel Elizabeth. BA in Econs., Northwestern U., 1971; JD cum laude, U. Wis., 1974. Bar: D.C. 1979, Wis. 1974. Law clk. to chief justice Wis. Supreme Ct., Madison, 1974-75; atty. Bureau of Competition FTC, Washington, 1975-78; assoc. Akin Gump Strauss Hauer and Feld, Washington, 1978-82, ptnr., 1983—; articles editor Wis. Law Rev., Madison, 1973-74. Mem. ABA, D.C. Bar, Wis. Bar Assn. Office: Akin Gump Strauss Hauer and Feld Ste 400 1333 New Hampshire Ave NW Washington DC 20036-1564

HEWITT, THOMAS F., hotel executive. Grad., Bryant Coll., 1967; hon. doctorate, Johnson and Wales U. With Sheraton Corp., pres. N.Am. divsn., 1983-85; pres., COO Carnival Resorts and Casinos, Miami, Fla., 1997—. Chmn. Am. Hotel Found., Greater Miami Conv. and Visitors Bur.; dean Pres. Acad.; bd. dirs. Fla. Internat. Univs. Sch. of Hospitality; bd. trustees Bryant Coll., Smithfield. Mem. Am. Hotel and Motel Assn. Ednl. Inst. (bd. dirs.), Am. Hotel and Motel Assn. (officer's adv. coun.), Dade County's Beacon Coun., Coconut Grove C. of C. Office: Carnival Hotels and Resorts 3250 Mary St Miami FL 33133

HEWITT, TIMOTHY MARTIN, museum curator; b. Lakewood, Ohio, Nov. 16, 1963; s. Martin Alexander Hewitt and Janet Natalie Steinke. BA in History/Anthropology, Pacific Luth. U., 1986. Mus. curator The Presdl. Mus., Odessa, Tex., 1992—. Author exhibit texts; composer chamber music, 1982—; arranger sml. ensemble music, 1992—. Youth counselor Redeemer Luth. Ch., Odessa, 1992—, dir. handbell choir, 1993—, leader brass ensemble, 1995—, dir. youth bd., 1998—; mem. French Horn sect. Odessa Coll. Concert Band, 1992—. Recipient Don Jerke Leadership award Pacific Luth. U., Tacoma, Wash., 1985, John Philip Sousa Band award Mead H.S. Band, Spokane, 1982; mem. All-State H.S. Band, Wash. State Music Educators Assn., Richland, 1982. Mem. Aid Assn. Luths. (treas. local br. 1996—, v.p. 1995). Avocations: playing piano and French Horn, composing music, genealogy, bicycle touring. Office: The Presdl Mus 622 N Lee Ave Odessa TX 79761-4426

HEWITT, VIVIAN ANN DAVIDSON (MRS. JOHN HAMILTON HEWITT, JR.), librarian; b. New Castle, Pa.; d. Arthur Robert and Lela Luvada (Mauney) Davidson; m. John Hamilton Hewitt, Jr., Dec. 26, 1949; 1 son, John Hamilton III. AB with honors, Geneva Coll., 1943, LHD, 1978; BSLS, Carnegie Mellon U., 1944; postgrad., U. Pitts., 1947-48. Sr. asst. libr. Carnegie Libr., Pitts., 1944-49; instr., libr. Sch. Libr. Sci. Atlanta U., Atlanta U., 1949-52; with Readers Reference Svc., Crowell-Collier Pub. Co., N.Y.C., 1953-55; libr. Rockefeller Found., N.Y.C., 1955-63; librarian Carnegie Endowment Internat. Peace, N.Y.C., 1963-83; librarian Mexican Agrl. Program, Rockefeller Found., summer 1958; dir. libr. and info. svcs. Katherine Gibbs Sch., N.Y.C., 1984-86; reference asst. Coun. on Fgn. Rels., 1986-89; lectr. spl. librarianship at grad. schs. of L.S. and info. throughout U.S. and Can., 1968-88; condr. profl. seminars Am. Mgmt. Assn., 1968-69, UN Inst. Tng. and Rsch., 1973, 74, Grad. Sci. Libr. and Info. Sci., Rutgers U., 1986; SLA rep. to Internat. Fedn. Libr. Assns., 1970-73, 73-75, 75-77; mem. nat. adv. com. Ctr. for the Book, Libr. of Congress, 1979-84; mem. adv. bd. Who's Who Among African Ams., 1975—. Contbr. chpt. to: The Black Librarian in America, 1970, What Black Librarians Are Saying, 1972, New Dimensions for Academic Library Service, 1975, A Century of Service, 1976, Handbook of Black Librarianship, 1977, The Black Librarian in America Revisited, 1994, Notable Black American Men, 1999. Bd. dirs. Graham-Windham, 1967, sec., 1980-87; bd. dirs. Laymen's Club, Cathedral Ch. of St.John the Divine, 1975—, sec., 1986-93. Recipient Outstanding Cmty. Svc. awards United Fund N.Y., 1965-77, Disting. Alumna award U. Pitts.-Carnegie Libr. Schs. Alumni Assn., 1978, Merit award Carnegie Mellon U. Alumni Assn., 1979. Mem. ALA (Disting. Svc. to Librarianship award Black Caucus 1978, Leadership in Profession award Black Caucus 1992), Spl. Librs. Assn. (pres. N.Y. chpt. 1970-71, nat. pres. 1978-79, named to Hall of Fame, condr. seminar 1969, rep. to Pacem In Terris Convocation 1965, rep. to White House Conf. Internat. Cooperation Yr. 1965), Jack and Jill Am., Inc. (ea. regional dir. 1967-69), Alpha Kappa Alpha. Democrat. Episcopalian. Home: 862 W End Ave New York NY 10025-4959

HEWITT, WILLIAM HARLEY, investment and marketing executive; b. Ithaca, N.Y., June 29, 1954; s. William Leonard and Myrtie Mae (Van Etten) H.; m. Marilyn J. Butler, Feb. 12, 1994. Student, Cornell U., 1972-74, Syracuse U., 1974-77. Broker First Jersey Securities, Peabody, Mass., 1979-80; rep. Garrett Arthur Assoc., Cambridge, Mass., 1980-82; pres. Wealth Adv. Group, Boston, 1982-85; cons. The New Eng., Boston, 1985-89; mng. prin. Century Cos. of Am., Waverly, Iowa, 1989-93; regional dir. Nationwide Life/Variable Products, 1993—; cons. Ednl. Tng. Systems, Boston, 1990-91. Author: (reference) Investment Product Selling System, 1989, Market Secrets, 1991. Mem. Nat. Trust for Hist. Preservation, Washington, 1989-92. Mem. Investment Tng. Assn. (mng. ptnr.), Aircraft Owners and Pilot Assn., Internat. Platform Assn., Ducks Unltd. Avocations: skiing, sailing, flying, golf, cooking, jazz. Home: 99 Golf Pky Madison WI 53704-7080 Office: Nationwide Life Ins Columbus OH 50677-9202

HEWLETT, GLORIA LOUISE, rancher, retired educator, civic volunteer; b. Clifton, Tex., Nov. 28, 1930; d. Dock Simpson and Leona Martha (Fricke) Martin; m. Robert Eckhart Hewlett, Jr., Sept. 3, 1950; children: Robert Eckhart, III, Jeffrey Martin Hewlett. BA, U. Corpus Christi, 1962; MEd, Northwestern State U., Natchitoches, La., 1974; DEd, East Tex. State U., 1988. Tchr. Terrebonne Parish Sch. Dist., Houma, La., 1962-69, Natchitoches (La.) Parish Sch. Dist., 1970-76, Mesquite (Tex.) Sch. Dist., 1977-91; ret., 1991. Author: A Descriptive Study of Textbook Preparation Programs and State Level Textbook Adoption in Texas, 1988. Mem. sr. affairs commn. Dallas City Coun., 1995-97; pres. Eta Zeta chpt. of Delta Kappa Gamma, Dallas, 1992-94. Named Gift to the Ednl. Found. of AAUW, 1992-93, 94-95. Mem. AAUW (pres. Dallas br. 1991-93, v.p. Tex. 1994-96), Dallas Ret. Tchrs. Assn. (pres. 1997-99), The Women's Coun., Dallas Hist. Soc., Am. Legion Aux. Presbyterian. Avocations: reading, genealogy, gardening. Home and Office: 9402 Mill Hollow Dr Dallas TX 75243-6338

HEWLETT, RICHARD GREENING, historian; b. Toledo, Feb. 12, 1923; s. Timothy Younglove and Gertrude Josephine (Greening) H.; m. Marilyn Eloise Nesper, Sept. 6, 1946. Student, Dartmouth, 1941-43, Bowdoin Coll., 1943-44; MA, U. Chgo., 1948, PhD, 1952. Intelligence specialist USAF Hdqrs., Washington, 1951-52; reports analyst AEC, Washington, 1952-57; chief historian AEC, 1957-75, ERDA, Washington, 1975-77; chief historian U.S. Dept. Energy, 1977-80; sr. assoc., sr. v.p., chmn. bd. History Assoc., Inc., Rockville, Md., 1980—; Regents' lectr. U. Calif., 1982; historiographer Episcopal Diocese of Washington, also Washington Cathedral, 1978—; chmn. fed. govt. resource group Nat. Coordinating Com. for Promotion of History, 1977-81; mem. U.S. Del. 2d UN Internat. Conf. on Peaceful Uses Atomic Energy, 1958. Author: Jessie Ball du Pont, 1992; co-author: The New World, 1939-46, 1962, Atomic Shield, 1947-52, 1969, Nuclear Navy, 1946-52, 1974, Atoms for Peace and War, 1953-61, 1989. Served with USAAF, 1943-46. Recipient David D. Lloyd prize Harry S. Truman Libr. Found., 1970; Distinguished Service award AEC, 1973. Mem. Am. Hist. Assn., Orgn. Am. Historians (Richard W. Leopold prize 1970), Soc. History Tech., Hist. Soc. Episc. Ch., Nat. Coun. Pub. History, Soc. for History in Fed. Govt. (v.p. 1983-85, Henry Adams prize 1990, Franklin D. Roosevelt award 1994), Cosmos Club. Episcopalian. Home: 7909 Deepwell Dr Bethesda MD 20817-1927 Office: History Assocs Inc 5 Choke Cherry Rd Ste 280 Rockville MD 20850-4004

HEWLETT, WILLIAM (REDINGTON), manufacturing company executive, electrical engineer; b. Ann Arbor, Mich., May 20, 1913; s. Albion Walter and Louise (Redington) H.; m. Flora Lamson, Aug. 10, 1939 (dec. 1977); children: Eleanor Hewlett Gimon, Walter B., James S., William A., Mary Hewlett Jaffe; m. Rosemary Bradford, May 24, 1978. BA, Stanford U., 1934, EE, 1939; MS, MIT, 1936; LLD (hon.), U. Calif., Berkeley, 1966, Yale U., 1976, Mills Coll., 1983, Marquette U., 1994; DSc (hon.), Kenyon Coll., 1978, Poly. Inst. N.Y., 1978; LHD (hon.), Johns Hopkins U., 1985; EngD (hon.), U. Notre Dame, 1980, Utah State U., 1980, Dartmouth Coll., 1983; PhD, Rand Grad. Inst.; D Electronic Sci. (hon.), U. Bologna, Italy, 1989; HHD (hon.), Santa Clara U., 1991. Electromedical researcher, 1936-39; co-founder Hewlett-Packard Co., Palo Alto, Calif., 1939, ptnr., 1939-46, exec. v.p., dir., 1947-64, pres., 1964-77, chief exec. officer, 1969-78, chmn. exec. com., 1977-83, vice chmn. bd. dirs., 1983-87, emeritus dir., 1987—; mem. internat. adv. council Wells Fargo Bank, 1986-92; trustee Rand Corp., 1962-72; trustee Carnegie Inst., Washington, 1971-90, trustee emeritus, 1990—, chmn. bd. 1980-86; dir. Overseas Devel. Council, 1969-77; bd. dirs. Inst. Radio Engrs. (now IEEE), 1950-57, pres. 1954; coord. chpt. on rsch. in industry for 5-Yr. Outlook Report, NAS, 1980-81; mem. adv. coun. on edn. and new techs. The Tech. Ctr. of Silicon Valley, 1987-88; past bd. dirs. Chrysler Corp., FMC Corp., Chase Manhattan Bank, Utah Internat. Inc. Contbr. articles to profl. jours.; patentee in field. Trustee Stanford U., 1963-74, Mills Coll., Oakland, Calif., 1958-68; mem. Pres.'s Gen. Adv. Com. on Fgn. Assistance Programs, Washington, 1965-68, Pres.'s Sci. Adv. Com., 1966-69; mem. San Francisco regional panel Commn. on White House Fellows, 1969-70, chmn., 1970; pres. bd. dirs. Palo Alto Stanford Hosp. Ctr., 1956-58, bd. dirs., 1958-62; dir. Drug Abuse Council, Washington, 1972-74, Kaiser Found. Hosp. & Health Plan Bd., 1972-78; chmn. The William and Flora Hewlett Found., 1966-94, chmn. emeritus, 1994—; dir. emeritus Monterey Bay Aquarium Rsch. Inst., 1998—; bd. dirs. San Francisco Bay Area Council, 1969-81, Inst. Medicine, Washington, 1971-72, The Nat. Acads. Corp., 1986-98, Monterey Bay Aquarium Rsch. Inst. , 1987-98, emeritus dir., Univ. Corp. for Atmospheric Rsch. Found., 1986-88. Lt. col. AUS, 1942-45. Recipient Calif. Mfr. of Yr. Calif. Mfrs. Assn., 1969, Bus. Statesman of Yr. Harvard Bus. Sch. No. Calif., 1970, Medal of Achievement Western Electronic Mfrs. Assn., 1971, Industrialist of Yr. (with David Packard) Calif. Mus. Sci. and Industry and Calif. Mus. Found., 1973, Award with David Packard presented by Scientific Apparatus Makers Assn., 1975, Corp. Leadership award MIT, 1976, Medal of Honor City of Boeblingen, Germany, 1977, Herbert Hoover medal for disting. service Stanford U. Alumni Assn., 1977, Henry Heald award Ill. Inst. Tech., 1984, Nat. Medal of Sci. U.S. Nat. Sci. Com., 1985, Laureate award Santa Clara County BUs. Hall of Fame Jr. Achievement, 1987, World Affairs Coun. No. Calif. award, 1987, Degree of Uncommon Man award Stanford U., 1987, Laureate award Nat. Bus. Hall of Fame Jr. Acievement, 1988; Decorated Comdr.'s Cross Order of Merit Fed. Republic Germany, 1987, John M. Fluke Sen. Meml. Pioneer award, Electronics Test Mag., 1990, Silicon Valley Engring. Hall of Fame award Silicon Valley Engring. Coun., 1991, Exemplary Leader award Am. Leadership Forum, 1992, Alexis de Tocqueville Soc. award United Way, Santa Clara County, 1991, Nat. Inventors Hall of Fame award Nat. Inventors Hall of Fame Found. Akron, 1992, Howard Vollum Leadership award Oreg. Grad. Inst. Sci. and Tech., 1993, Internat. Citizens award World Forum of Silicon Valley, 1994, Lifetime Achievement award Lemelson-MIT prize, 1995; named to Lowell H.S. Alumni Assn. Wall of Fame, 1995; named hon. fellow Harris-Manchester Coll. Oxford U., 1996, Benjamin Franklin medal Royal Soc. Encouragement of Arts, Manufactures & Commerce, London, 1997. Fellow NAE (Founders award 1993), IEEE (life fellow, Founders medal with David Packard 1973), Franklin Inst. (life, Vermilye medal with David Packard 1976), Am. Acad. Arts and Scis.; mem. NAS (panel on advanced tech. competition 1982-83, president's circle 1989—), Instrument Soc. Am. (hon. life), Am. Philos. Soc., Calif. Acad. Sci. (trustee 1963-68), Assn. Quadrato della Radio, Century Assn. N.Y.C. Office: Hewlett-Packard Co 3000 Hanover St Palo Alto CA 94304-1181

HEWLETT-KIERSTEAD, NANCY CARRICK, psychologist; b. Schenectady, Feb. 19, 1927; d. Clarence Wilson and Mary Stephens (Carrick) Hewlett; BFA, Cornell U., 1949; MA (Univ. fellow), U. Mich., 1952; PhD (Univ. fellow), U. Conn., 1972; registered clin. psychologist; m. Andrzej T. Romer, June 19, 1952 (div. 1969); children: Jan Edward, Anna Louise, Mary Helena; m. Henry A. Kierstead, July 26, 1981 (dec. Feb. 1990). Tchr. art Thomaston (Conn.) High Sch., 1960-63; freelance artist, potter, 1962-67; assoc. prof. psychology Eastern Conn. State U., Willimantic, 1969-84; ret. 1984; clin. psychologist Effective Coping Strategies, Ill., Conn., 1982-91; writer 1987—. Author: The Green Ribbon, 1997. Asst. clk. Storrs (Conn.) monthly meeting Soc. of Friends, 1978-80, clk., 1980. Mem. ACLU, ADL, Hemlock Soc., Choice in Dying, Brunswick (Maine) Friends Mtg.

HEXT, KATHLEEN FLORENCE, internal audit college adminstrator; b. Bellingham, Wash., Oct. 7, 1941; d. Benjamin Byron and Sarah Debell (Youngquist) Gross.; m. George Ronald Hext, June 13, 1964 (div. 1972); m. William H. Lewis, Nov. 14, 1992. BA magna cum laude, Lewis & Clark Coll., Portland, Oreg., 1963; MA, Stanford U., 1964; MBA, UCLA, 1979. CPA; chartered bank auditor; cert. info. systems auditor. Chief exec. officer Internat. Lang. Ctr., Rome, 1970-77; sr. auditor Peat, Marwick, Mitchell & Co., L.A., 1979-81; mgr. fin. audit Lloyds Bank, L.A., 1981-83, mgr. EDP audit, 1983-85; dir. corp. auditor First Interstate Bancorp, L.A., 1985-89, sr. v.p., gen. auditor, 1989-91, sr. v.p., chief compliance officer, 1991-94; compliance cons. Proactive, Inc., 1993—; dir. internal audit Calif. State U., Long Beach, 1996—; treas., Arcadia H.O. Assoc., El Monte, Calif., 1982-84, 86-88, pres., 1985. Recipient Edward W. Carter award UCLA, 1979. Mem. AICPA, Calif. Soc. CPA. Republican. Avocations: photography, microcomputers, reading. Home: 2703 N Studebaker Rd Long Beach CA 90815-1628 *I sincerely believe that the key to a happy, successful life is to do all that you do in truth and love.*

HEXTALL, RON, professional hockey player; b. Winnipeg, Man., May 3, 1964; m. Diane H.; children: Kristen, Bretton. With Phila. Flyers, 1982-92, 96—, Quebec Nordiques, 1992-93, N. Y. Islanders, 1993-96; mem. AHL All-Star team, 1985-86, NHL All-Star first team, 1986-87, NHL All-Rookie team, 1986-87; player NHL All-Star game, 1988. Recipient Vezina Trophy (NHL top goaltender), 1986-87, Conn Smythe Trophy (Stanley Cup Playoff Most Valuable Player), 1986, 87., Dudley (Red) Garrett Meml. trophy, 1985-86; named Rookie of the Year Sporting News, 1986-87. Office: Phila Flyers First Union Ctr 3601 S Broad St Philadelphia PA 19148*

HEY, ROBERT PIERPONT, editor association bulletin; b. E. Providence, R.I., Jan. 24, 1935; s. Daniel Chase and Grace (Pierpont) H.; m. Nancy Henson, July 4, 1959; 1 dau., Julie. A.B., Harvard U., 1955. Gen. assignment reporter, local edn. reporter Christian Sci. Monitor, Boston, 1960-64; asst. to Am. news editor, then asst. Am. news editor Christian Sci. Monitor, 1964-67, S.E. U.S. corr., then Washington corr., 1967-76, asst. mng. editor, 1976-79; mng. editor features Christian Sci. Monitor, Boston, 1979-83, editorial writer, 1983-86; Washington Corr. Christian Sci. Monitor, 1986-91; mng. editor AARP Bull., 1991—; purchasing agt. Arkell Safety Bag Co., N.Y.C., 1956-58; with public relations dept. U. Pitts., 1964. Served with AUS, 1958-60. Office: 601 E St NW Washington DC 20049-0001

HEYBURN, JOHN GILPIN, II, federal judge; b. 1948; m. Martha Keeney, 1976. BA, Harvard U., 1970; JD, U. Ky., 1976. Ptnr. Brown, Todd & Heyburn, Louisville, 1976-92; fed. judge U.S. Dist. Ct. (we. dist.), Louisville, 1992—. Bd. dirs. Kentuckians for Jud. Improvement, 1975-76; mem. Budget Com. Jud. Conf.of U.S., 1994—, chmn. 1997—; chair Jefferson County Crime Commn.; mem. vis. com. U. Ky., 1980; active Leadership Louisville Found. With USAR, 1970-76. Mem. ABA, Ky. Bar Assn., Louisville Bar Assn., U. Ky. Coll. Law Alumni Assn., Louisville Com. Fgn. Rels. Office: US Dist Ct 601 W Broadway Ste 450 Louisville KY 40202-2249

HEYCK, THEODORE DALY, lawyer; b. Houston, Apr. 17, 1941; s. Theodore Richard and Gertrude Paine (Daly) H. *Theodore Daly Heyck, son of Gertrude Paine Daly and Theodore Richard Heyck. Gertrude Daly, daughter of David Daly and Gertrude Paine and granddaughter of Robert Paine, all instrumental in the formation of early Houston social and business life. The Paine lineage includes Thomas Paine, colonial revolutionary and David Daly, Harvard graduate, descended from a line of Boston Irish. Theodore Richard Heyck, son of Theodore Frantz Valentin Heyck and Frances Catherine Girand, whose ancestries trace back respectively through Friedrich Heinrich Theodore Heyck who emmigrated to Galveston, Texas from Holstein in 1852 and through Sophia Caroline Hanauer whose ancestors emmigrated from Wiltenheim, Alsace in 1843.* BA, Brown U., 1963; postgrad. Georgetown. U., 1963-65, 71-72; JD, N.Y. Law Sch., 1979. Bar: N.Y. 1980, Calif. 1984, U.S. Ct. Appeals (2nd cir.) 1984, U.S. Supreme Ct. 1984, U.S. Dist. Ct. (so. and ea. dists.) N.Y. 1980, U.S. Dist. Ct. (we. and no. dists.) N.Y. 1984, U.S. Dist. Ct. (cen. and so. dists.) Calif. 1984, U.S. Ct. Appeals (9th cir.) 1986. Paralegal dist. atty. Bklyn., 1975-79; asst. dist. atty. Bklyn. dist., Kings County, N.Y., 1979-85; dep. city atty., L.A., 1985—; bd. dirs. Screen Actors Guild, N.Y.C., 1977-78. Mem. ABA, AFTRA, NATAS, SAG, Bklyn. Bar Assn., Assn. Trial Lawyers Am., N.Y. Trial Lawyers Assn., N.Y. State Bar Assn., Calif. Bar Assn., Fed. Bar Council, L.A. County Bar Assn., Actors Equity Assn. Home: 2106 E Live Oak Dr Los Angeles CA 90068-3639 Office: Office City Atty City Hall E 200 N Main St Los Angeles CA 90012-4110

HEYD, EVA, photographer; b. Prague, Czech Republic, Aug. 26, 1953; came to U.S., 1985; naturalized, 1989; d. Otto Anthony Heyd and Miluska (Sindelarova) H.; m. Jan Mach, June 3, 1975 (div. June 1979); 1 child, Kristyna; m. Vaclav Victor Krakora, Aug. 13, 1985; 1 child, Thomas. M in Journalism, Charles U., Prague, 1977. Freelance journalist Prague, 1974-77, freelance photographer, 1977-79; editor Horizon Pub. Ho., Prague, 1979, Architekt mag., Prague, 1979-85; freelance photographer N.Y.C., 1985—; lectr. Faculta Zurnalistiky Fotoklub, Strahovsky Fotoklub, Prague, 1975; juror photog. competitions, Prague, 1976-78. Illustrator: A Sort of Life (Graham Green), 1974, Photographer (Pierre Boulle), 1982; artist multimedia project (with dancer, painter Lisa Pilot), Jean Gibson Gallery, N.Y., 1991, Paula Cooper Gallery, N.Y., 1992; exhibited in group shows at Silver Image Gallery, Seattle, 1990, Nakama Gallery, Tokyo, 1991, Gallery Manes, Prague, 1993, Eisler, N.Y., 1993, Heller Gallery, N.Y., 1995, Smithtown Arts Coun., 1996, Barret Ho. Galleries, Poughkeepsie, N.Y., 1997, Bohemian Gallery, N.Y., 1997, City Hall, N.Y.C., 1997, Cast Iron Gallery, N.Y.C., 1998; one-woman shows include Gallery USM Rubin, Prague, 1979, Gallery Sztuky Wspolcesnej, Warsaw, 1982, Gallery Fotochema, Prague, 1982, Thermal, Karlovy Vary, Czech Republic, 1985, Gallery Junge Kunstler, Berlin, 1985, Ekazent Gallery, Vienna, 1987, UMPRUM Mus. Expresso, Prague, 1994, New Horizon Gallery, Prague, 1994, Bohemian Gallery, N.Y., 1998; represented in permanent collections at UMPRUM Mus., pvt. collection; contbr. articles and revs. to mags. and jours., Czech Republic and U.S. Mem. Bohemian Gallery Group. Home and Studio: 84-28 63rd Rd Middle Village NY 11379

HEYDE, MARTHA BENNETT (MRS. ERNEST R. HEYDE), psychologist; b. New Bern, N.C., Jan. 31, 1920; d. George Spotswood and Katherine (McIntosh) Bennett; AB, Barnard Coll., 1941; MA, Columbia, 1949, PhD, 1959; m. Ernest R. Heyde, Aug. 17, 1946. Instr. psychol. founds. and services Tchrs. Coll., Columbia U., N.Y.C., 1953-60, research asst., career pattern study Horace Mann-Lincoln Inst., Tchrs. Coll. Columbia U., 1957-59, research assoc., 1960-70, cons., 1970-73. Mem. Barnard Coll. Alumnae Council, 1956-61, 69—, pres. class, 1956-61. Trustee, Barnard Coll., 1974-78, hon. vice-chmn. Barnard Coll. Centennial, 1987-89. Mem. Am. Psychol. Assn., Sigma Xi, Kappa Delta Pi, Pi Lambda Theta. Contbr. to research monograph The Vocational Maturity of Ninth Grade Boys, 1960, Floundering and Trial After High Sch, 1967; co-author: Vocational Maturity During the High School Years, 1979. Home: 530 E 23rd St Apt 8E New York NY 10010-5030

HEYDEBRAND, WOLF VON, sociology educator; b. Kl. Tschunkawe, Germany, June 15, 1930; came to U.S., 1954; s. Georg Von and Sigrid Von (Waldersee) H.; m. Ruth Keiling, Sept. 1954 (div. 1973); 1 child, Gitry V.; m. Sarah Rosenfield, June 1974 (div. 1979); m. Elizabeth Robinson, Mar. 1987; children: Daniel Adam V., Sophia Ingrid V. MA, U. Chgo., 1961, PhD, 1965. Asst. prof. sociology U. Chgo., 1964-67; assoc. prof. Washington U., St. Louis, 1967-71; prof. NYU, N.Y.C., 1973—; vis. assoc. prof. Columbia U., 1972-73, 85; co-dir. Comparative Orgn. Rsch. Program, U. Chgo., 1964-67; rsch. assoc. Med. Care Rsch. Ctr., St. Louis, 1967-71; co-prin. investigator Explorat's Health Svc., N.Y.C., 1972-74; prin. investigator Adjudication vs. Adminstrn., Russell Sage Found., 1974-75; Max Weber prof. U. Heidelberg, 1996. Author: Hospital Bureaucracy, 1973; (with others) Rationalizing Justice: The Political Economy of Federal District Courts, 1990; editor: Comparative Organizations, 1973, Max Weber, 1994; assoc. editor Am. Jour. Sociology, 1964-67, Contemporary Sociology, 1972-74, Social Problems, 1981-84, Law and Soc. Rev., 1985-87. Grantee NSF, 1964; grantee USPHS, 1967, Nat. Ctr. Health Service, 1972, Russell Sage Found., 1974-75. Mem. Am. Sociol. Assn. (pres. sect. orgns. and occupations 1987-88), Ea. Sociol. Assn. (exec. coun. 1979-82), Law and Soc. Assn. (trustee), Internat. Sociol. Assn. Jewish. Office: NYU Dept Sociology 269 Mercer St Rm 411 New York NY 10003-6633

HEYDERMAN, ARTHUR JEROME, engineer, civilian military employee; b. Bklyn., Jan. 1, 1946; s. Herbert Robert and Sally (Baron) H.; m. Renee Linda Pearlman, July 4, 1967; children: Brian Douglas, Deborah Ann, Cathy Ruth. BS in Applied Math., Poly. Inst. Bklyn., 1966, MS in Applied Math., 1973; postgrad., Stevens Inst. Tech., 1982, Brookings Inst., 1992, Wharton Sch. Bus., U. Pa., 1993. Nuclear weapons engr. U.S. Army Armaments R&D Ctr., Picatinny Arsenal, N.J., 1971-83; asst. tech. dir. U.S. Army Armaments R&D Ctr., Picatinny Arsenal, 1983-84, chief prodn. program planning, 1984, assoc. tech. dir., 1984-86; armaments rsch. and devel. prog. mgr. U.S. Army Armaments Munitions and Chem. Command, Rock Island, Ill., 1986-93, chief of rsch. devel., test and evaluation integration, 1993-94; chief improved armor engring. U.S. Army Armaments Rsch., Devel. and Engring. Ctr., Rock Island, Ill., 1994-96; chief armor engring. U.S. Armaments Rsch. Devel. & Engring. Ctr., Rock Island, Ill., 1996-98, chief artillery sys. & armor divsn., 1998—; bd. dirs., sec./treas., pres. Iowa-Ill. chpt. Am. Def. Preparedness Assn., Rock Island; lt. col. nuclear weapons officer USAR, Ft. Sheridan, Ill., 1989-93; pres. OPICON, Bettendorf, Iowa, 1989—; nat. coun. Am. Def. Preparedness Assn.; coun. mem. Quad-Cities Engring. and Sci. Coun.; adj. faculty U.S. Army Command and Gen. Staff Coll., Ft. Leavenworth, Kans., 1981-89, Scott C.C., 1997. Contbr. column to Rock Island Argus/Moline Dispatch; guest editor Quad Cities Times; contbr. tech. papers on weapons and weaponry assessment to profl. meetings. Pres., bd. dirs. Sussex County Jewish Ctr., Newton, N.J., 1979-86; fundraiser United Jewish Fedn., Davenport, Iowa, 1986—; mem. Rock Island Arsenal Com. for Disabled, 1987-93, Quad Cities Coalition for Choice; dir. intake Quad City chpt. ACLU; mem. platform com. Scott County Dem. Ctrl. Com., 1994—; mem. 1st dist. Iowa Dem. Ctrl. Com., 1994—; mem. platform com. Iowa State Dem. Party; chmn. Quad Cities WWII Commemoration Com., 1995, Quad Cities Vietnam Wall Com., 1997; mem. Iowa Sesquecentennial Commemoration Com., 1995, Rock Island County, Ill. C. of C. Spkrs. Bur., 1996; bd. dirs. Jewish Fedn. of Quad Cities, 1996-99; bd. dirs. Iowa Civil Liberties Union, 1997—, Iowa Civil Liberties Found., 1997—. Capt. U.S. Army, 1968-71, Vietnam; maj./lt. col. USAR, 1971-93. Decorated Bronze Star; Cross of Gallantry (Vietnam); named to Hon. Order St. Barbara, U.S. Army Field Arty. Assn.; recipient Civilian of Yr. award Fifth Region Assn. of the U.S. Army, 1998. Mem. VFW, ACLU (nat. bd. dirs. 1998—), NAACP (bd. dirs. Quad Cities chpt. 1996—), U.S. Army Acquisitions Corps, U.S. Army Engr. Assn., Assn. U.S. Army (v.p. Ft. Armstrong chpt. 1993—, acting pres. chpt. 1996-97), Soc. Am. Mil. Engrs. (scholar 1966),

Soc. Am. Mil. Comptrs., Federally Employed Women, Planned Parenthood (mem. cmty. coun.), Nat. Soc. Scabbard and Blade (chpt. v.p. 1965-66), Nat. Def. Indsl. Assn. (pres. Iowa Ill. chpt.), Res. Officers Assn., Poly. Alumni Assn. (pres. Quad City chpt. 1989—), Mensa, Intertel, Vietnam Vets. Jewish. Avocations: horticulture, art, bonsai, cooking, photography. Home: 1430 Grappler Ct Bettendorf IA 52722-1847

HEYDERMAN, MARK BARON, sales and marketing company executive; b. Bklyn., July 14, 1942; s. Herbert Robert and Sally (Baron) H.; m. Carol Ann Woulfin, May 26, 1963; children: Janice, Richard, Alysia, Tracey. AAS, N.Y. Community Coll., 1962. Dir. ops. Sloves Orgn., N.Y.C., 1962-86; v.p. Sloves Presentations Inc., Floral Park, N.Y., 1986-93; pres. MBH Presentations Inc., Floral Park, 1993—; cons. Graphic Image, Hempstead, N.Y., 1992—, E&M Bindery, L.I., 1992—. Co-inventor, record album for The Franklin Mint, 1976; book style video case, 1990. Mem. Binders and Finishers Assn. (recruiter 1986—, bd. dirs. 1995-97), Pied Picas (pres. 1961-62), Gamma Epsilon Tau. Avocations: model airplanes and railroads, horseback riding, home and auto mechs., printing and binding, instructional work. Office: MBH Presentations Inc 10 Terrace Ave Floral Park NY 11001-2915

HEYDET, NATHALIE DURBIN, gifted and talented education educator; b. Terre Haute, Ind., Nov. 20, 1948; d. Howard Border and Hersilia (Warren) Durbin; m. Raymond Thomas Heydet, Sept. 20, 1974; 1 child, Lisa. AA in Elem. Edn., Broward C.C., Davie, Fla., 1971; BEd, Fla. Atlantic U., 1973, MEd, 1978. Cert. tchr., Fla. Tchr. Broadview Elem. Sch., Pompano, Fla., 1973-74; tchr. Tamarac (Fla.) Elem. Sch., 1974-85, tchr. gifted, 1986-88; tchr. gifted Country Hills Elem., Coral Springs, Fla., 1988-94, Horizon Elem., Sunrise, Fla., 1994-98, Eagle Ridge Elem., 1996-98; tchr. spl. assignment in program devel. Broward County Schs., Coral Springs, Fla., 1998—; adj. English instr. Broward C.C., Coconut Creek, Fla., 1979-81; speaker in field. Mem. Coral Springs Bicentennial Com., 1991. Recipient Fla. award of Excellence, 1986, Little Red Sch. House award Fla. Prins. Assn., 1987, 90, 91; named Broward County Math. Tchr. of Yr., 1998; finalist Broward County Tchr. of Yr. Mem. Fla. Assn. of the Gifted, North Area Gifted Assn., Broward County Guild of Tchrs., Delta Kappa Gamma. Republican. Methodist. Avocations: crafts, traveling, reading. Home: 3091 NW 112th Ave Coral Springs FL 33065-3547

HEYDMAN, ABBY MARIA, dean; b. Des Moines, June 1, 1943; d. Frederick Edward and Zeta Margaret (Harrington) Hitchcock; m. Frank J. Heydman, Dec. 20, 1967; 1 child, Amy Lee. BS, Duchesne Coll., 1967; MN, U. Wash., 1969; PhD, U. Calif., Berkeley, 1987. Registered nurse, Calif. Staff nurse Bergan Mercy Hosp., Omaha, 1964-65; student health nurse St. Joseph's Hosp., Omaha, 1965-66, instr. sch. nursing, 1966-68; staff nurse Ballard Community Hosp., Seattle, 1968-69; instr. Creighton U., Omaha, 1969-70, asst. prof., 1970-74, acting dean, 1971-72; chairperson nursing dept. St. Mary's Coll., Moraga, Calif., 1978-85; dean nursing program Samuel Merritt-Saint Mary's Coll., Oakland and Moraga, Calif., 1985-93; acad. dean Samuel Merritt Coll., Oakland, 1989—; lectr. U. Calif., San Francisco, 1974-75. Contbr. articles to profl. jours. Chmn. Newman Hall Community Council, Berkeley, 1985-87; bd. dirs. Oakland YMCA, 1981-83. Mem. AAHE, ANA, Am. Assn. Higher Edn., Oakland Higher Edn. Consortium, Calif. Nurses Found. (bd. dirs. 1986-88, vice chair 1997-98), Sigma Theta Tau (chair fundraising com. Nu Xi chpt. 1998), Phi Kappa Delta. Roman Catholic. Avocations: swimming, writing, travel, reading. E-mail: aheydman@samuelmerritt.edu. Home: 51 Vicente Rd Berkeley CA 94705-1603 Office: Samuel Merritt Coll 370 Hawthorne Ave Oakland CA 94609-3108

HEYDON, PETER NORTHRUP, farmer, educator, philanthropist; b. Hackensack, N.J., Nov. 25, 1940; s. Clark A. and Elizabeth VanFleet (Northrup) H.; m. Henrietta M. Heydon, Aug. 24, 1968. BA, Princeton U., N.J., 1962; MA, U. Mich., Ann Arbor, 1963, PhD, 1970. Instr. in humanities & English U. Mich., Ann Arbor, 1963-80, adj. prof., 1980-86; dir., chmn. The Clements Library Assocs., Ann Arbor, 1970—; trustee Folger Shakespeare Libr., Washington D.C., 1986—, Nat. Pub. Radio Found., 1994—; dir. Farrar, Straus & Giroux, N.Y.C., 1970-94; dir. Richard Cohen Books, London, 1994-98; founder, dir. The Mosiac Found. Mem. The Lotos Club, The Grolier Club, The Century Assn. Avocations: restoration of classic special interest automobiles, historic preservation of national register buildings. Office: Heydon Washington St Prop 324 E Washington St PO Box 7801 Ann Arbor MI 48107-7801

HEYDRICK, LINDA CAROL, consulting company executive, editor; b. Pomona, Calif., July 25, 1947; d. Robert Bruce and Wanda Georgine (Wellman) Middough; m. Stephen R. Bova, Jan. 20, 1968 (div. May 1981); children: Karen E., Lori L.; m. Allen L. Heydrick, Mar. 15, 1995. Student, El Camino Coll., Gardena, Calif., 1965-66. Sec. TRW, Inc., Manhattan Beach, Calif., 1967-68, USAF NCO Clubs, Mildenhall, Eng., 1968-70; adminstrv. asst. Prudential-Bache Securities, N.Y.C., 1970-73, Tex. Instruments, Inc., Dallas, 1980-83; asst. to pres. Acclivus Corp., Dallas, 1983-85, mgr. design and prodn., 1985-88, mgr. ops., 1988-89, v.p. ops., 1989—; cons. Digital Equipment Corp., Boston, 1984-89, internat. translations of books, audiotapes and videotapes. Editor: (books and videotapes) BASE for Sales Performance, 1984, Acclivus Sales Negotiation, 1985, The New BASE for Sales Excellence, 1989, Major Account Planning and Strategy, 1993, rev., 1996, Building on the BASE (award for best new tng. products Human Resource Exec.), 1993, R3 Service, (award for best new tng. product Human Resource Exec. 1998) 1997. Organizer Meals on Wheels, Denton, Tex., 1977; editor, pub Denton Bible Ch., 1993—. Mem. ASTD, Instructional Systems Assn., Nat. Soc. for Performance and Instrn., Soc. for Aplied Learning Tech., Soc. for Accelerative Learning and Tchg., Internat. Listening Assn. Republican. Avocations: Christian studies, fine arts, design, performing arts. Office: Acclivus Corp 14500 Midway Rd Dallas TX 75244-3109

HEYEN, BEATRICE J., psychotherapist; b. Chgo., June 23, 1925; d. Carl Edwin and Anna W. (Carlson) Lund; m. Robert D. Heyen, June 16, 1950 (dec. Feb. 1981); children: Robin, Jefferson, Neil; m. Robert Christiansen, Nov. 24, 1984. BS, U. Chgo., 1949. Instr. Boone (Iowa) Jr. Coll., 1959-64, Rochester (Minn.) Jr. Coll., 1967-68, Winona (Minn.) State Coll., 1965-68; dir. social svc. State Clinic, Kirksville, Mo., 1968-71; supr., dir. Family Counseling Agy., Joliet, Ill., 1971-85; pvt. practice Muskegon, Mich., 1985—; cons. Homes for Aged, Programs for Aged, Winona, 1965-68, Spl. Programs and Individuals in Psychotherapy, Muskegon, 1984—; dir. Christiansen Fine Art Gallery, North Muskegon. Mem. Gov.'s Com. on Status of Women, Iowa, 1957-62, Gov.'s Com. on Aging, Minn., 1966-68; bd. mem. Mission for Area People, Muskegon, 1998. Grantee for Pilot Projects in Svc. to Women 1971-84. Mem. AAUW, NASW, Acad. Cert. Social Workers, C.G. Jung Inst. (Chgo.). Methodist. Avocations: ecological interests, day lily gardening, contemporary art. Home: 1610 N Weber Rd Muskegon MI 49445-8615

HEYER, CAROL ANN, illustrator; b. Cuero, Tex., Feb. 2, 1950; d. William Jerome and Merlyn Mary (Hutson) H. *Ms. Heyer's grandparents are Joseph and Verna Heyer, and Mary and Harold Hutson. William Jerome Heyer was world traveler, veteran of WWII, and member of 82nd Aiborne. He carried out, through enemy lines, an injured RAF pilot from jungles of India where he had crashed. Merlyn Hutson Heyer, world traveler, professional singer, was a member of the Hutson Sisters singing troop (Ailsa and Sybil Hutson). She performed with ENSA during WWII and at the front lines to entertain the troops. Merlyn met and married William J. Heyer and traveled to the States as a war bride. They were married for 48 years.* BA, Calif. Lutheran U., 1974. Freelance artist various cos., Thousand Oaks, Calif., 1974-79; computer artist Image Resource, Westlake Village, Calif., 1979-81; staff writer, artist Lynn-Davis Prodns., Westlake Village, Calif., 1981-87; art dir. Northwind Studios Internat., Camarillo, Calif., 1988-89; illustrator Touchmark, Thousand Oaks, 1989—; cons. art dir., writer Lynn-Wenger Prodns., 1987-89; guest spkr. Thousand Oaks Libr., Author's Faire, Calif. Luth. U., Soc. Children's Book Writers and Illustrators, Illustrators Day, Ventura County Reading Assn.'s Author's Faire; guest artist/spkr. Oxnard Libr.; booksignings/appearances Anaheim Conv. Ctr., L.A. Conv. Ctr., Am. Booksellers Assn.; guest 1996 Readout, grand opening Barnes and Noble, Thousand Oaks; represented by Art Works, N.Y.C.; invited artist Ann. Art Show, Chemers Gallery. Illustrator (children's books) A Star in the Pasture, 1988, The Dream Stealer, 1989, The Golden Easter Egg, 1989, All Things Bright and Beautiful, 1992, Rapunzel, 1992, The Christmas Carol, 1995, Prancer, Gift of the Magi, Dinosaurs Strange and Wonderful, Down the Great Unknown, 1999, Flame and Clay (teachers' big book) 1998, 3 Repeat Jobs for Hampton/Brown (teacher's big book), (illustrator) Night Journey, 1999, (illustrator)Black Beauty, 999, Here Come the Brides, (adult book) The Artist's Market, also L.A. Times, Daily News, The Artist's Mag., News Chronicle; also cover art for Troll Assoc., Top Secret, The Loveless Cafe (cookbook), Ellery Queen's Mystery Mag., Frontispiece Collectors Leather Bound Edition, Crippen and Landru Mystery Covers, Dragon mag., Dungeon mag., Aboriginal Sci. Fiction mag., Wizards of the Coast, (game covers) F.X. Schmid - Puzzle Wizards of the Coast (fantasy collector cards, Dune and Hobbit) and various novels, books and games; illustrator Bugs Bunny Coloring Book, Candyland Work Book, The Dragon Sleeps Step Ahead Workbook, City of Sorcers, CD-ROM cover for Memorex/Roaring Mouse Prodns.; interior art for various publs. including (mags.) Amazing Stories two covers, Interzone, Aboriginal Sci. Fiction Mag., Alfred Hitchcocks Myster Mag., Ideals mag., Realms of Fantasy mag., Sci. Fiction Age mag., Tomorrow mag., (book) Tome of Magic, (book) Top Secret, (book) Loveless Cafe, (book, interiors) Star Trek Next Generation, (also art for game cards), (repeat covers) Crippen and Landru, (game book cover) Wizards of the Coast; writer (screenplay) Thunder Run, 1986; illustrator, writer (children's books) Beauty and the Beast, 1989, The Easter Story, 1989, Excalibur, Robin Hood, 1993, Sleeping Beauty in the Wood, 1996, The Christmas Story, 1996, Down the Great Unknown, 1999, Flame and Clay, 1998; paintings for line of Fantasy Art Prints, Scafa/Tornabene, religious art prints; rep. by Every Picture Tells a Story Gallery, Worlds of Wonder; 2 covers for young adults Hyperion/Disney Press; one-woman show Adventures for Kids Gallery; illustrator poster for motion picture and TV fund; writer Disney ednl. prodns., others; freelance artist Disney Interactive. Recipient Lit. award City of Oxnard Cultural Arts Commn. and Carnegie Art Inst., 1992, Best Cover Art Boomerang award, 1989, Cert. of Merit, Career Achievement award Calif. Luth. U., 1993, Cert. of Excellence Alumni Career Achievement award, 1993, Print's Regional Design Ann. award, 1992, Best Paper Backs award Internat. Reading Assn./Children s Book Coun. Joint Com., 1994, Spectrum Internat. Competition for Best in Contemporary Fantastic Art. Mem. Soc. Children's Book Writers (judge 1990, Mag. Merit award 1988, Keynote spkr.), Assn. Sci. Fiction and Fantasy Artists, Soc. Illustrators (Cert. of Merit 1990-92, winner Ann. Illustration West show, award L.A. chpt. 1998). Featured in articles. Home and Office: Touchmark 925 Ave Arboles Thousand Oaks CA 91360

HEYER, JOHN HENRY, II, lawyer; b. Rochester, N.Y., May 4, 1946; s. Joseph Lester and Margaret Mary (Darcy) H.; m. Charla Ann Prewitt (dec.); children: Thomas, William, John III, Richard, Mary. BA, U. Colo., 1969; JD, U. Denver, 1972. Bar: Colo. 1973, U.S. Dist. Ct. Colo. 1973, N.Y. 1976, Pa. 1979, U.S. Dist. Ct. (we. dist.) N.Y. 1980, U.S. Supreme Ct. 1982. Atty. Texaco, Inc., Denver, 1973-75; sole practice Olean, N.Y., 1975—; pres. Northeastern Land Svcs., Inc., Olean, N.Y., 1982—; v.p. Vector Capital Corp., Rochester, N.Y., 1985-87; chpt. 7 trustee U.S. Bankruptcy Ct., we. dist. N.Y., 1986—. Editor: New York Oil and Gas Statutes, 1985. Asst. dist. atty. Cattaraugus County, Olean, 1978-81; bd. dirs. Olean YMCA, 1989—, v.p. 1993-94, pres., 1994-99; bd. dirs. Buffalo Philharm. Symphony Cir., v.p., 1993, pres., 1994-95; bd. dirs. Friends of Good Music, pres. 1994-95. Mem. N.Y. State Bar Assn. (real property sect., real property devel. com.), Erie County Bar Assn., Cattaraugus County Bar Assn. (sec.-treas. 1997, v.p. 1998, pres. 1999), Eastern Mineral Law Found. (trustee 1984—, exec. com. 1994-95), Ind. Oil and Gas Assn. N.Y. (bd. dirs. 1986—, sec. 1986-87, v.p. 1988—), SAR, Selden Soc. Roman Catholic. Office: PO Box 588 201 N Union St Olean NY 14760-2738

HEYL, ALLEN VAN, JR., geologist; b. Allentown, Pa., Apr. 10, 1918; s. Allen Van and Emma (Kleppinger) H.; student Muhlenberg Coll., 1936-37; BS in Geology, Pa. State U., 1941; PhD in Geology, Princeton U., 1950; m. Maxine LaVon Hawke, July 12, 1945; children: Nancy Caroline, Allen David Van. Field asst. major regional exploration, govt. geologist Nfld. Geol. Survey, summers 1937-40, 42; jr. geologist U.S. Geol. Survey, Wis., 1943-45, asst. geologist, 1945-47, assoc. geologist, 1947-50, geologist, Washington and Beltsville, Md., 1950-67; staff geologist, Denver, 1968-90; cons. geologist 1990—; disting. lectr. grad. coll. Beijing, China and Nat. Acad. Sci., 1988; disting. invited lectr. Internat. Assn. Genesis Ore Deposits 9th Symposium, Beijing, 1994; chmn. Internat. Commn. Tectonics of Ore Deposits. Fellow Instn. Mining and Metallurgy (Gt. Brit.), Geol. Soc. Am., Am. Mineral. Soc., Soc. Econ. Geologists; mem. Inst. Genesis of Ore Deposits, Geol. Soc. Wash., Colo. Sci. Soc., Rocky Mountain Geol. Soc., Friends of Mineralogy (hon. life), Evergreen Naturalist Audubon Soc., Sigma Xi, Alpha Chi Sigma. Lutheran. Contbr. numerous articles to profl. jours., chpts. to books. Home: PO Box 1052 Evergreen CO 80437-1052

HEYLER, GROVER ROSS, retired lawyer; b. Manila, The Philippines, June 24, 1926; s. Grover Edwin and Esther Viola (Ross) H.; m. Caroline Yarbrough, Aug. 10, 1949; children: Richard Ross, Sue Louise, Randall Arthur. BA, UCLA, 1949; LLB, U. Calif., Berkeley, 1952. Bar: Calif. 1953. Assoc. Latham & Watkins, L.A., 1952-60, ptnr., 1960-93, chmn., corp. securities dept., 1967-89. Bd. dirs. Nat. Alliance for Rsch. into Schizophrenia and Depression, N.Y.C.; bd. dirs. Mental Health Assn., L.A. Mem. Calif. Bar Assn. (com. on drafting Calif. corps. code 1971-75), Order of Coif, UCLA ALumni Assn. (bd. dirs. 1966-70, 1988-90), L.A. Country Club, Riviera Tennis Club. Home: 491 Homewood Rd Los Angeles CA 90049-2713

HEYMAN, IRA MICHAEL, federal agency administrator, museum executive, law educator; b. N.Y.C., May 30, 1930; s. Harold Albert and Judith (Sobel) H.; m. Therese Helene Thau, Dec. 17, 1950; children: Stephen Thomas (dec.), James Nathaniel. AB in Govt., Dartmouth Coll., 1951; JD, Yale U., 1956; LLD (hon.), U. Pacific, 1981, Hebrew Union Coll., 1984, U. Md., 1986, SUNY, Buffalo, 1990. Bar: N.Y. 1956, Calif. 1961. Legis. asst. to U.S. Senator Ives, 1950-51; assoc. Carter, Ledyard & Milburn, N.Y.C., 1956-57; law clk. to presiding justice U.S. Ct. Appeals (2d cir.), New Haven, 1957-58; chief law clk. to Supreme Ct. Justice Earl Warren, 1958-59; acting assoc. prof. law U. Calif., Berkeley, 1959-61, prof. law, 1961-66, prof. city and regional planning, 1966-93, prof. emeritus, 1993—, vice chancellor, 1974-80, chancellor, 1980-90; counselor to Sec. of Interior Dept. Interior, Washington, 1993-94; sec. Smithsonian Inst., Washington, 1994—; vis. prof. Yale Law Sch., 1963-64, Stanford Law Sch., 1971-72. Editor Yale Law Jour.; contbr. articles to profl. jours. Sec. Calif. adv. com. U.S. Commn. Civil Rights, 1962-67; trustee Dartmouth Coll., 1982-93, chmn., 1991-93; mem. Lawyers' Com. for Civil Rights under Law, 1977-95; chmn. exec. com. Nat. Assn. State Univs. and Land Grant Colls., 1986; bd. regents Smithsonian Instn., 1990-94. 1st lt. USMC, 1951-53, capt. Res. ret. Decorated chevalier Legion of Honor (France).

HEYMAN, LAWRENCE MURRAY, printmaker, painter; b. Washington, June 30, 1932; s. Philip I. and Gertrude B. H.;. BFA, Tyler Sch. Fine Arts, Temple U., 1954; BS in Edn., Temple U., 1955; MFA, Am. U., 1972. Instr. fine arts in printmaking R.I. Sch. Design, 1967-69, asst. prof. fine arts and printmaking, 1972-79, dir. printmaking program, 1976-79; lectr. Am. U., 1971-72. Exhibited in one-man shows, Mickelson Gallery, Washington, 1966, 77, R.I. Sch. Design, 1969, 79, St. John's U., St. Paul, 1980, Mus. City of N.Y., 1984, Starr Gallery, Newton, Mass., 1985, Plum Gallery, Kensington, Md., 1986, 88, NIH, Bethesda, Md., 1990, Vets.' Meml. Auditorium, Providence, 1991; group shows including, Providence Art Club, (prize 1974, 76), Bibliotheque Nationale, Paris, 1977 (purchase honor 79), San Francisco Art Museum, 1977, Plum Gallery, Kensington, Md., 1985, 86, 89, Starr Gallery, Newton, Mass., 1990; represented in permanent collections Bibliotheque Nationale, Paris, Bklyn. Mus., Brooks Meml. Mus., Tenn., Mus. City of N.Y., Portland (Oreg.) Art Mus.; U.S. rep. Art in Embassies program exhbn., Istanbul, Turkey, 1976; Commd.: print edits. for Associated Am. Artists, N.Y.C., 1964, 68, 69, Antares Editions d'Art, Paris, 1970, 71, 72, Judith Selkowitz Fine Arts, N.Y.C., 1978. Served with U.S. Army, 1955-57. Nominee and finalist for Nat. Arts medal Nat. Endowment for Arts, 1987; finalist 1989 Portrait Painting Competition Artist's Mag. Mem. Whitegate Features Syndicate Fine Arts. Office: 71 Faunce Dr Providence RI 02906-4805

HEYMAN, MELVIN BERNARD, pediatric gastroenterologist; b. San Francisco, Mar. 24, 1950; s. Vernon Otto and Eve Elsie Heyman; m. Jody Ellen Switky, May 8, 1988. BA in Econs., U. Calif., Berkeley, 1972; MD, UCLA, 1976, MPH in Nutrition, 1981. Diplomate Am. Bd. Pediatrics (assoc. 1997—), Am. Bd. Pediatric Gastroenterology (assoc. 1997—). Intern, resident Los Angeles County-U. So. Calif. Med. Ctr., 1976-79; fellow UCLA, 1979-81; asst. prof. U. Calif., San Francisco, 1981-88, assoc. prof., 1988-94, prof., 1994—, chief pediatric gastroenterology, hepatology and nutrition, 1990—; dir. UCSF/Stanford Combined Tng. Program Pediatric Gastroenterology/Nutrition; assoc. dir. Pediatric Gastroenterology/Nutrition, San Francisco, 1986-89; mem. cons. staff San Francisco Gen. Hosp., Natividad Med. Ctr., Salinas, Calif., Scenic Gen. Hosp., Modesto, Calif. Contbr. articles to profl. jours. Chmn. scientific adv. com. San Francisco chpt. Crohn's and Colitis Found. Am., 1987-94, bd. dirs., 1986—. Rsch. grantee Children's Liver Found., 1984-85, John Tung grantee Am. Cancer Soc., 1985-89. Mem. N.Am. Soc. Pediat. Gastro Nutrition (chair patient care com. 1997—), Am. Acad. Pediat., Am. Inst. Nutrition, Am. Gastroenterol. Assn., Soc. Clin. Nutrition, Am. Soc. Parental Enteral Nutrition, Am. Bd. Pediatric Gastroenterology (subbd. mem.). Avocations: skiing, swimming, hiking, tennis, biking. Office: U Calif Dept Pediatrics Box 0136 San Francisco CA 94143-0136*

HEYMAN, RALPH EDMOND, lawyer; b. Cin., Mar. 14, 1931; s. Ralph and Florence (Kahn) H.; m. Sylvia Lee Schottenstein, Jan. 2, 1984; children: Michael Cary, Cynthia Ann Heyman Eeg, Ginger Florence. A.B. magna cum laude (Rufus Choat scholar), Dartmouth Coll., 1953; LLB cum laude, Harvard U., 1956; LLM, U. Cin., 1957. Bar: Ohio 1956, Ill. 1957. Pvt. practice Cin., 1956-58, Dayton, 1958—; assoc. Freiden & Wolf, 1956-58; from assoc. to ptnr. Smith & Schnacke, 1958-88; ptnr. Chernesky, Heyman & Kress, Dayton, Ohio, 1988—; lectr. estate planning U. Cin., 1958-61; lectr. participant Southwestern Ohio Tax Inst., 1957-65; lectr., moderator Dayton Bar Assn. Tax Insts., 1975-79, 94; lectr. continuing edn. program U. Dayton, 1989; lectr. estate planning Dayton Area Tax Profls., 1993; lectr. on venture capital Miami Valley Venture Assn., 1998; dir., gen. counsel Towne Properties, Ltd., Sachs Mgmt. Corp., Inc., Outdoor Consulting, Inc., Precision Photo Labs., Inc., Aristocrat Products, Inc., K.k. Motorcycle Supply, Inc., The Sportsman's Guide. Recipient Robert A. Shapiro Vol. award 1998. Commr. Bd. Rural Zoning Commn. Montgomery County, 1969-71; bd. dirs., pres. Jewish Fedn. Dayton, 1993-97; nat. trustee NCCJ; past pres. Temple Israel, Temple Israel Found.; dir. United Way Greater Dayton Area, 1999. Recipient Humanitarian award NCCJ, 1997. Mem. ABA, Ohio Bar Assn., Dayton Bar Assn. (chmn. tax com.), Cin. Bar Assn., Lawyers Club, Meadowbrook Club, Dayton City Club (past pres.), B'nai Brith, Phi Beta Kappa. Jewish. Office: Chernesky Heyman & Kress PLL PO Box 3808 1100 Courthouse Plz SW Dayton OH 45401-3808

HEYMAN, SAMUEL J., chemicals and building materials manufacturing company executive; b. N.Y.C., Mar. 1, 1939; s. Lazarus S. and Annette (Silverman) H.; m. Ronnie Feuerstein, Nov. 1970; children: Lazarus, Eleanor, Jennifer, Elizabeth. BS magna cum laude, Yale Coll., 1960; LLB, Harvard U., 1963. Bar: Conn. 1963. Atty. U.S. Dept. Justice, Washington, 1963-64; asst. U.S. atty. Dist. of Conn., New Haven, 1964-67; chief asst. U.S. atty. New Haven div., 1967-68; pres. Heyman Properties, Westport, Conn., 1968-83; chmn., chief exec. officer GAF Corp., Wayne, N.J., 1983—; chmn., CEO Internat. specialty Products Inc., Wayne, N.J., 1991—. Office: International Specialty Products Inc 1361 Alps Rd Wayne NJ 07470-3700*

HEYMAN, WILLIAM HERBERT, financial services executive; b. N.Y.C., Apr. 20, 1948; s. George Harrison and Edythe Jane (Forman) H., Jr.; AB magna cum laude, Princeton U., 1970; JD cum laude, Harvard U., 1973. Bar: N.Y. 1974, D.C. 1991. Assoc. White & Case, N.Y.C., 1973-75, Cravath, Swaine & Moore, N.Y.C., 1975-78, Stroock & Stroock & Lavan, N.Y.C., 1978-79; gen. ptnr., COO Mercury Securities, N.Y.C., 1979-88; mng. dir. Smith Barney, Harris Upham & Co., Inc., 1989-91; dir. divsn. market regulation, SEC, Washington, 1991-93; mng. dir. Salomon Bros. Inc., 1993-95; exec. v.p. Travelers Investment Group, Citigroup, N.Y.C., 1995—; CEO Tribecca Investments LLC, N.Y.C., 1996—. Trustee Mt. Sinai-NYU Med. Ctr., 1994—, Hosp. for Joint Diseases, 1994—; mem. N.Y. area firms adv. com. N.Y. Stock Exch., 1996—; mem. adv. bd. fin. math. Courant Inst. Math. Scis. NYU; bd. dirs. Student/Sponsor Partnership of N.Y., 1989-91, 93—, 92d St. YM&YWHA, N.Y.C., 1979-90; council overseers United Jewish Appeal-Fedn. N.Y., 1986-88; mem. fin. com. N.Y. State Reps., 1986-90, v.p. N.Y. County Reps. Com., 1987-90; mem. nat. fin. com. George Bush for Pres., 1987-88; hon. chmn. Bicentennial Presdl. Inaugural, 1989; pub. mem. Adminstrv. Conf. of the U.S., 1989-90; mem. N.Y. regional panel for selection of White House Fellows, 1989; mem. fin. products adv. com. Commodity Futures Trading Commn., 1992-93. Mem. Harvard Law Sch. Assn. (nat. council 1986-90), Econ. Club N.Y., Phi Beta Kappa. Jewish. Clubs: Century Country (Purchase, N.Y.); Army and Navy (Washington). Office: Citigroup 388 Greenwich St Fl 36 New York NY 10013-2362

HEYMANN, C(LEMENS) DAVID, author; b. N.Y.C., Jan. 14, 1945; s. Ernest Frederick and Renee K. (Vago) H.; m. Jeanne Ann Lunin, Nov. 10, 1974 (div. 1995); children: Chloe Colette, Paris Kent Fineberg-Heymann; m. Rebecca Ellen Coughlan, 1995 (div. 1996). BS, Cornell U., 1966; MFA, U. Mass., 1969. Lectr. English lit. SUNY-Stony Brook, 1969-74, Antioch Coll., N.Y.C. campus, 1975; mem. judges panel Am. Book Awards, 1979-80, Nat. Book Critics Circle, 1978-79. Author: (poetry) The Quiet Hours, 1969; Ezra Pound: The Last Rower, 1976, American Aristocracy: The Lives and Time of James Russell, Amy and Robert Lowell, 1980, Poor Little Rich Girl: The Life and Legend of Barbara Hutton, 1983, A Woman Named Jackie: An Intimate Biography of Jacqueline Bouvier Kennedy Onassis, 1989, Liz: An Intimate Biography of Elizabeth Taylor, 1995, RFK: A Candid Biography of Robert F. Kennedy, 1998; also book revs. and articles for nat. mags. and newspapers. Israeli govt. writer's grantee, 1984-85.

HEYMANN, PHILIP BENJAMIN, law educator, academic director; b. Pitts., Oct. 30, 1932. B.A., Yale U., 1954; LL.B., Harvard U., 1960. Bar: D.C. 1960, Mass. 1969. Trial atty. gen. Dept. Justice, Washington, 1961-65, asst. atty. gen. criminal div., 1978-81, dep. atty. gen., 1993-94; dep. adminstr. Bur. Security and Consular Affairs, Dept. State, Washington, 1965; acting adminstr. Bur. Security and Consular Affairs, Dept. State, to 1967; dep. asst. sec. of state for Bur. Internat. Orgns., 1967, exec. asst. to under sec. of state, 1967-69; with Legal Aid Agy. of D.C., 1969; faculty law Harvard U., 1969—, James Barr Ames prof. law, dir. Harvard Law Sch. Ctr. for Criminal Justice; assoc. prosecutor and cons. to Watergate Spl. Prosecution Force, summers 1973-75. Served with USAF, 1955-57.

HEYMANN, S. RICHARD, lawyer; b. Chgo., Sept. 18, 1944; s. Samuel R. and Ann (Menning) H.; m. Jane Ann Gebhart, June 14, 1980; children: Elizabeth Jane, Catherine Claire. BS, U. Wis., 1966; JD, U. Mich., 1969. Bar: Mo. 1969, Wis. 1988. Law clk. Minn. Supreme Ct., St. Paul, 1970-72; assoc. Bryan, Cave, McPheeters & McRoberts, St. Louis, 1972-79, ptnr., 1980-87; ptnr. Foley & Lardner, Madison, Wis., 1987—; adj. prof. U. Wis. Law Sch. Mem. U. Wis. Found., Wis. Alumni Assn. (bd. dirs. 1985-87). Clubs: Madison, Maple Bluff Country. Office: Foley & Lardner PO Box 1497 150 East Gilman St Madison WI 53701-1497

HEYMANN, STEPHEN, marketing management consultant; b. N.Y.C., Dec. 7, 1940; s. Harold Joseph and Estelle Olga H.; m. Elaine Puciat, June 24, 1962; children: Elizabeth Jill, Michael Carroll, Andrew Harold. BS, Wharton Sch., U. Pa., 1962. Div. mgr., mdse. mgr. Sears, Roebuck & Co., Phila., 1962-65; brand mgr. Household Products div. Procter & Gamble Co., Cin., 1965-69; pres., dir., mgmt. cons. Glendinning Assos., Westport, Conn., 1969-81; founder, pres. New Eng. Cons. Group, 1981-90, Tech. Transfer Assocs., Wilton, Conn., 1990-96; pres., COO Netalk, Internet Svcs., Los Gatos, Calif., 1996-97; with Paladin Cons. Group, Los Altos, Calif., 1997—; founder, pres. Paladin Consulting Group, 1992-98; dir. Penniman Chems. Inc., Glenco Enterprises Ltd., Glendinning Cos. Inc., Aficionado. Author: More People on Skis, 1972, Like, series of children's books, 1972-74. Mem. ASTM, Am. Mgmt. Assn., Am. Mktg. Assn., Young Pres. Orgn., Assn. Nat. Advertisers. Clubs: Stratton Mountain, Wharton, Lotos. Office: Paladin Cons Group 262 Pasa Robles Ave Los Altos CA 94022-1157

HEYMOSS, JENNIFER MARIE, librarian; b. Detroit, Apr. 14, 1958; d. John Joseph and Virginia Marie (Kern) H. BA in English and German,

Wayne State U., 1980, MS in Libr. Sci., 1981. Libr. asst. Wayne State U. Librs., Detroit, 1982-83; asst. libr. Plunkett & Cooney, Detroit, 1983-86, Henry Ford Mus. & Greenfield Village Rsch. Ctr., Dearborn, Mich., 1986-90; libr. Henry Ford Mus. & Greenfield Village Rsch. Ctr., Dearborn, 1990-92; asst. head tech. svcs. Flint (Mich.) Pub. Libr., 1992—. Literacy vol., 1987—. Mem. ALA. Spl. Librs. Assn. (various coms. 1988-92), Mich. Libr. Assn., Pub. Librs. Assn., Phi Beta Kappa, Beta Phi Mu. Democrat. Methodist. Avocations: reading, music. Office: Flint Pub Libr 1026 E Kearsley St Flint MI 48503-1994

HEYN, ARNO HARRY ALBERT, retired chemistry educator; b. Breslau, Germany, Oct. 6, 1918; s. Myron and Margarete M.E.C. (Cierpinski) H.; m. Helen A. Pielemeier, Mar. 14, 1942; children: Evan A., Margaret L., Robert E. BS, U. Mich., 1940, MS, 1941, PhD in Analytical Chemistry, 1944. Exptl. chemist Sun Oil Co., Norwood, Pa., 1944-47; from instr. to prof. chemistry Boston U., 1947-84, prof. emeritus, 1984; vis. scientist Brookhaven Nat. Lab., summers 1954-56; acad. guest Eidg. Techn. Hochschule, Zurich, 1965, Gesellschaft F. Kernforschung, Karlsruhe, 1973, 80, 81, 82, Landesanst. F. Wasserbiologie, Vienna, 1973; sci. adviser Boston Dist. U.S. FDA, 1967-72. Contbr. articles to profl. jours. Fellow AAAS; mem. Am. Chem. Soc. (councilor 1967-97, alt. councilor 1998—, chmn. coun. com. on constn. and bylaws 1983-85, coun. policy com. 1986-91, vice-chmn. 1987-88, com. on coms. 1992-94, Henry Hill award N.E. sect. 1986, editor Nucleus 1989—), AAUP (treas. Boston U. chpt. 1979-83), Sigma Xi, Phi Lambda Upsilon, Sub Sig Outing Club (Boston). Avocation: locksmithing. Home: 21 Alexander Rd Newton MA 02461-1830

HEYNEMAN, DONALD, parasitology and tropical medicine educator; b. San Francisco, Feb. 18, 1925; s. Paul and Amy Josephine (KLauber) H.; m. Louise Davidson Ross, June 18, 1971; children: Amy J., Lucy A., Andrew P., Jennifer K., Claudia G. AB magna cum laude, Harvard U., 1950; MA, Rice U., 1952, PhD, 1954. Instr. zoology UCLA, 1954-56, asst. prof., 1956-60; head dept. parasitology U.S. Navy Med. Research unit, Cairo; also co-dir. U.S. Navy Med. Research unit, Malakal, Sudan, 1960-62; assoc. research parasitologist Hooper Found. U. Calif., San Francisco, 1962-64, assoc. prof., 1966-68, prof., 1968-91, prof. emeritus, 1991—, asst. dir. Hooper found., 1970-74, acting chmn. dept. internat. health, 1976-78; assoc. dean Sch. Pub. Health U. Calif., Berkeley and San Francisco, 1987-91, assoc. dean emeritus, 1991—, chmn. joint med. program, 1987-91, chmn. emeritus, 1991—; research coordinator U. Calif. Internat. Ctr. Med. Research and Tng., Kuala Lumpur, Malaysia, 1964-66; cons. physiol. processes sect. NSF, 1966-91; environ. biology div. NIH, 1968-91; mem. tropical medicine and parasitology study sect. NIAID-NIH, 1973-76; mem. adv. sci. bd. Gorgas Meml. Inst., 1967-90; cons. WHO, 1967, mem. sci. tech. rev. com. on Leishmaniases, 1984; cons. UN Devel. Program, 1978-91, US-AID, others; panel reviewer Internat. Nomenclature of Diseases, 1984—; Am. cons. and U.S. prin. investigator U. Linkage Project, Egypt-U.S., 1984—; mem. Calif. Health Adv. Com., 1983—. Author: (with R. Boolootian) An Illustrated Laboratory Text in Zoology, 1962, An Illustrated Laboratory Text in Zoology, A Brief Version, 1977, International Dictionary Medicine and Biology, (with R. Goldsmith) Textbook of Tropical Medicine and Parasitology, 1989;co-author, contbg. editor Phytolacca dodecandra: Endod, 1984, Endod II, 1987; contbr. articles to jours., chpts. to books.; editorial cons. Am. Jour. Tropical Medicine and Hygiene, Jour. Parasitology, Jour. Exptl. Parasitology, Sci., 1968—, other jours. Served with AUS, 1943-46. NIH grantee, 1966-85. Mem. Am. Soc. Parasitologists (council 1970-74, pres. 1982-83), Am. Micros. Soc. (exec. com. 1971-75), Am. Soc. Tropical Medicine and Hygiene (councilor 1981-84), So. Calif. Parasitol. Soc. (pres. 1957-58), No. Calif. Parasitologists (sec.- treas. 1969-72, pres. 1977-78), Phi Beta Kappa. Home: 1400 Lake St San Francisco CA 94118-1036 Office: U Calif Dept Epidemiology and Biostatistics Box 0560 San Francisco CA 94143

HEYSER, WILLIAM H., landscape contractor; b. Norristown, Pa., Mar. 26, 1928; s. Ellsworth and Ruth (Woodland) H.; m. Janice Marie Knerr, June 27, 1953; children: Susan Marie, Holly Ruth. BS in Horticulture, Pa. State U., 1950. Registered landscape architect, Pa. Mgr. Heyser Landscaping and Tree Svc., Norristown, Pa., 1952-62; pres. Heyser Landscaping, Inc., Norristown, 1962-86, CEO, 1986-98; landscape contracting competition judge The Landscape Contractors Assn. Met. Washington, Inc., 1985; judge Phila. Flower Show, 1985-93. Columnist Tri-State Real Estate Jour., 1986-87. Mem. Worcester Twp. Planning Commn., Pa., 1968-70, Montgomery County Pvt. Industry Coun., Norristown, 1982-83; founder Mid-Atlantic Student Landscape Field Day, 1985; bd. trustees Lower Providence Presbyn. Ch., 1962-64; pres. Worcester Home and Sch. Assn., 1968-69; chmn. com. disting. citizens award Boy Scouts Am., 1990. Recipient Disting. Citizen of Yr. award Boy Scouts Am., 1992; named to Norristown Area H.S. Hall of Fame, 1994. Mem. Pa. Nurserymens assn. (com. chmn. 1983-84, 89-90), Assoc. Landscape Contrs. Am. (com. mem. 1983-86), Del. Valley Landscape Contrs. Assn. (pres. 1966-67), Pa. Hort. Soc. (Gold Plant award com. 1984—), Norristown Jaycees (pres. 1960-61). Republican. Clubs: Montgomery Count Pa. State, Penn State (past pres. 1961-62). Lodge: Rotary (pres. 1969-70). Avocations: reading, horseback riding, tennis, skiing. Office: Heyser Landscaping Inc 400 N Park Ave Norristown PA 19403-1399

HEYSSEL, ROBERT MORRIS, physician, retired hospital executive; b. Jamestown, Mo., June 19, 1928; s. Clarence D. and Meta and (Reusser) H.; m. Maria McDaniel, Aug. 7, 1955; children: James Olin, Maria Lisa, Robert Morris, Kurt Frederick, Helen Perrier. B.S., U. Mo., 1951; M.D., St. Louis U., 1953, D.Sc. (hon.), 1985; LHD, John Hopkins U., 1992. Postgrad. tng. St. Louis U. Hosp., 1953-56, Barnes Hosp., St. Louis, 1953-56; hematologist, acting dir. dept. medicine Atomic Bomb Casualty Commn., Nagasaki and Hiroshima, Japan, 1956-58; mem. faculty Sch. Medicine, Vanderbilt U., Nashville, 1959-68; dir. div. nuclear medicine Sch. Medicine, Vanderbilt U., 1962-68, assoc. prof. medicine, 1964-68; assoc. dean Sch. Medicine, Johns Hopkins U., Balt., 1968-72; dir. health care programs and outpatient services Sch. Medicine, Johns Hopkins U., 1968-72, prof. medicine, 1971—, prof. health care orgn., 1972-83; exec. v.p., dir. Johns Hopkins Hosp., 1972-83, pres., CEO, 1983-92; pres., chief exec. officer Johns Hopkins Health System, Balt., 1986-92; trustee Johns Hopkins U.; bd. dirs. Signet Bank Corp., Signet Bank of Md., Monsanto Co.; chmn. Commonwealth Fund on Acad. Health Ctrs., 1983. Contbr. articles to profl. jours. Mem. gen. assembly Assn. Am. Med. Colls., 1974-80, mem. exec. council, 1978, chmn. council teaching hosps., 1978-80, chmn. 1983-84; chmn. com. on emergency med. services Nat. Acad. Scis., 1973-76; mem. Joint Commn. on Prescription Drugs, 1976, Gov's Commn. on High Tech., 1983-86; numerous other local, state and nat. coms. on health, medicine and med. edn.; bd. dirs., trustee St. Louis U., 1989. Recipient USPHS Career Devel. award, 1962; Distinguished Alumnus award U. Mo., 1972. Fellow ACP, Am. Coll. Physician Execs., Internat. Soc. Hermatology; mem. Inst. Med. of NAS, Assn. Am. Physicians, Soc. Med. Adminstrs., numerous other sci. assns. Club: Elk Ridge (Balt.).

HEYWARD, ANDREW JOHN, television producer; b. Roslyn, N.Y., Oct. 29, 1950; s. E.J.R. and Elisabeth Heyward; m. Jody Gaylin Heyward, May 23, 1976; children: David, Emily, Sarah. BA, Harvard U., 1972. Producer Sta. WNEW-TV News, N.Y.C., 1974-76; producer Sta. WCBS-TV News, N.Y.C., 1976-78, exec. producer, 1978-81; producer CBS Evening News CBS News, N.Y.C., 1981-84, sr. producer, 1984-87; exec. producer 48 Hours, N.Y.C., 1987-93, Eye to Eye, 1993-94; v.p. CBS News, 1994-96; exec. producer CBS Evening News, 1994-96; pres. CBS News, 1996—. Mem. NATAS (Emmy award 1977-78, 84, 88-93, 95). Office: CBS News 524 W 57th St New York NY 10019-2924

HEYWARD, HAROLD, financial consultant; b. Chgo., July 2, 1942; s. Frank J. and Annette (Siegel) H.; m. Frida E. Isaacs, Feb. 7, 1937; 1 child, Leslie A. Davis. Student, Ill. Inst. Tech., 1932-33. Lic. pvt. pilot. Dist. mdse. mgr. Sears Roebeck & Co., Chgo., 1931-44; owner, mgr. Nat. Wholesale Mdse. Co., Chgo., 1945-50; Chgo. rep. Swingline Inc., Long Island City, N.Y., 1950-80; fin. cons., stock broker, real estate salesman, bus. owner, Highland Park, Ill., 1980—. Patentee in fields photography, vending machines and staple guns.

HEYWOOD, ANNE, artist, educator; b. Newport, R.I., Sept. 15, 1951; d. Albert Paul and Eileen Frances (Laforest) Boretti; m. Ciro DiGiovanni, May 24, 1969 (div. 1980); 1 child, Carlo; m. Henry Robert Heywood, Nov. 9, 1985. BA in Art summa cum laude, Bridgewater (Mass.) State Coll. Tchr. drawing and pastels Silver Lake Reg. H.S. Adult Edn., Kingston, Mass., 1991-95; art educator pastels, drawing South Shore Art Ctr., Cohasset, Mass., 1996—; art educator pastels Fuller Mus. Art, Brockton, Mass., 1996—, Pastel Painters Soc. Cape Cod, Barnstable, Mass., 1997—; art educator drawing Swinburne Sch., Newport, R.I., 1995, Round Top Ctr. for Arts, Damariscotta, Maine, 1996; pastel demonstrator spkr. numerous art orgns., Weymouth, Milton, Mass., 1995—; sec. Artists Cir. at Fuller Mus., Brockton, Mass., 1995-97. Contbg. artist: (included in books) Best of Pastel, 1996, Landscape Inspirations, 1997, Best of Sketching and Drawing 1999; one-woman shows include East Bridgewater (Mass.) Pub. Libr., 1992, 95, Mass. Audubon Soc., Marshfield, 1992, South Shore Natural Sci. Ctr., Norwell, Mass., 1993, Marion (Mass.) Art Ctr., 1994, Fuller Art Mus., Brockton, Mass., 1995, Passage Gallery, South Shore Art Ctr., Cohasset, Mass., 1996, 98, Sparrow House, Plymouth, Mass., 1997; exhibited in group shows at Pembroke (Mass.) Art Festival, 1991, Earth Kingdom Gallery, Hanover, Mass., 1992, Duxbury Art Assn., Mass., 1993, Trenton (N.J.) State Coll., 1994, Bridgewater State Coll., 1994, Audubon Soc., Marshfield, Mass., 1994-97, Zullo Gallery, Medfield, Mass., 1995-99, Maine Art Gallery, Wiscasset, 1995, Pastel Soc. Am., N.Y.C., 1995, 97, Internat. Assn. Pastel Socs., 1997, East Bridgewater Pub. Libr., 1996, 97, Joseph A. Driscoll Gallery, Brockton, 1996, Left Bank Gallery, Wellfleet, Mass., 1997, Gallery at C3TV, South Yarmouth, Mass., 1997, Salmagundi Club, N.Y., 7th Nat. Biennial Exhbn. Degas Soc., La. (La. Watercolor Soc. award of merit), 48th Nat. Exhbn. Contemporary Realism in Art, Mass., Soc. Western Artists, 1999; also corp. collections; included in book: The Best of Sketching and Drawing, 1999; contbr. articles to profl. jours.; editor Pastel Painter's Soc. of Cape Cod newsletter, 1998-99. Sec. East Bridgewater Arts Coun., 1992-97. Recipient 1st pl. drawing East Bridgewater Art Festival, 1991, 1st pl. awards Wickford (R.I.) Art Assn., 1992, Taunton (Mass.) Art Assn., 1993, South Shore Art Ctr. Blue Ribbon Members Show, Cohasset, 1994, Fuller Art Mus., Brockton, 1994, 1st pl. pastels Plymouth Guild May Members Show, 1994, award Providence Art Club, 1996, award of distinction All New Eng. Color Show, Cohasset, 1996, convention image award Internat. Assn. Pastel Socs., 1997; Vt. Studio Ctr. Residency fellow, 1999. Mem. Am. Artists Profl. League, Associated Pastelists on Web (signature mem.), Pastel Painters Soc. Cape Cod (signature mem., bd. dirs. 1999—, Canson-Talens award 1997), Conn. Pastel Soc., Pastel Soc. Am. (Holbein award 1995, award 1997), Oil Pastel Assn./United Pastellists Am., Nat. Assn. Women Artists. Roman Catholic. Avocations: reading, walking, biking, choir. Home and Studio: 85 Ashley Dr East Bridgewater MA 02333-1703

HEYWOOD, JOHN BENJAMIN, mechanical engineering educator; b. Sidcup, Kent, Eng., Jan. 11, 1938; s. Harold and Frances Dora (Weaver) H.; m. Marguerite Gilkerson, Dec. 28, 1961; children: James, Stephen, Benjamin. BA, Cambridge U., 1960, DSc, 1984; MS, MIT, 1962, PhD, 1965; DTech (hon.), Chalmers U. Tech., 1999. Lectr. Northeastern U., Boston, 1963-65; rsch. assoc. mech. engring. dept. MIT, Cambridge, 1964-65, asst. prof. mech. enginrg., 1968-70, assoc. prof., 1970-76, prof., 1976-92, dir. Sloan Automotive Lab., coord. transp. programs in Energy Lab., 1972—; co-dir. leaders for mfg. program MIT, 1991-93; Sun Jae prof. mech. engring., 1992—; rsch. officer Cen. Electricity Generating Bd., Leatherhead, Eng., 1965-67, group leader, 1967-68; cons. in field. Author, editor: (with others) Open-Cycle MHD Power Generation, 1969; author: (with others) The Automobile and the Regulation of its Impact on the Environment, 1975, Internal Engine Combustion Fundamentals, 1988; contbr. Ency. Britannica, chpts. to books, numerous articles, papers to profl. jours., confs., symposia U.S.A, Eng., Europe. Recipient Ayerton Premium Inst. Elec. Engrs., U.K., 1969; Fulbright travel scholar, 1960; Richard C. Mellon Overseas fellow Churchill Coll., Cambridge, Eng., 1976-77; recipient Nat. award for Advancement of Motor Vehicle Rsch. and Devel., US DOT, 1996. Fellow U.K. Instn. Mech. Engrs. (George Stephenson Internat. Lectr. 1997), Soc. Automotive Engrs. (Ralph R. Teeter Outstanding Young Engr. award 1971, Arch T. Colwell Merit award 1973, 81, 89, Outstanding Oral Presentation award 1980, Horning Meml. Best Paper award 1984); mem. ASME (Freeman scholar 1986, Honda lectr. 1990), Nat. Acad. Engring. Rsch. interests in thermodynamics, combustion, energy, power and propulsion, performance, efficiency and emissions of spark-ignition and diesel engines, control of air pollution, engine design and manufacture. Office: MIT Dept Mech Engring 77 Mass Ave # 3-340 Cambridge MA 02139-4307

HEYWOOD, ROBERT GILMOUR, lawyer; b. Berkeley, Calif., May 18, 1949; m. Carolyn Cox, June 10, 1972. AB with distinction, Stanford U., 1971; MA, U. Calif., Berkeley, 1972; JD cum laude, Santa Clara U., 1975. Bar: Calif. 1975, U.S. Dist. Ct. (no. and ea. dists.) Calif. 1975, U.S. Ct. Appeals (9th cir.) 1976, U.S. Supreme Ct. 1979; cert. specialist workers' compensation law Calif. Bd. Legal Specialization, State Bar Calif. Ptnr. Hanna, Brophy, MacLean, McAleer & Jensen, Oakland, Calif., 1976—; instr. Santa Clara U., 1975-77, advocacy skills workshop Stanford U. Law Sch., 1994—; faculty ctr. for trial and appellate adv. Hasting Coll. of Law, San Francisco; mem. faculty Calif. Ctr. for Jud. Edn. and Rsch., 1998; mem. intensive advocacy program faculty U. San Francisco Sch. Law, 1995—; adj. prof. law U. Calif., Hastings, 1982-86; arbitrator Alameda County Superior Ct. Mem. bd. editl. cons. Calif. Compensation Cases. Bd. dirs. Alameda County Legal Aid Soc., Oakland, 1978-87, Cazadero Performing Arts Camp, 1994—; bd. govs. Oakland East Bay Symphony, pres., 1991-93. Mem. ABA, Calif. Bar Assn., Calif. Continuing Edn. of Bar (editor, lect., author), Alameda County Bar Assn., Calif. Compensaton Def. Attys. Assn. Office: Hanna Brophy MacLean Et Al 155 Grand Ave Ste 600 Oakland CA 94612-3747

HEZIR, JOSEPH S., energy and environmental company executive; b. Pitts., Aug. 27, 1950; s. Joseph F. and Elizabeth G. H.; m. Joyce Ann Martincic, May 12, 1979; children: Alexandra M., Damjan S. BS, Carnegie-Mellon U., 1972, MS, 1974. Rsch. engr. St. Joe Minerals Corp., Monaca, Pa., 1971, Carnegie-Mellon U., Pitts., 1972; planning analyst City of N.Y., 1973; budget examiner U.S. Office Mgmt. and Budget, Washington, 1974-82, dep. assoc. dir., 1982-92; sr. corp. analyst Exxon Rsch. and Engring. Corp., Florham Park, N.J., 1982; mng. ptnr. The EOP Group, Inc., Florham Park, 1992—; mem. adv. bd. Competitiveness Policy Coun., Washington, 1992-94, NASA Adv. Coun., Washington, 1992-93. Dir. nat. capital chpt. ARC, Washington, 1987-90. Fellow Coun. Excellence in Govt.; mem. NAS (mem. study bds.), Croatian Fraternal Union Am. Roman Catholic. E-mail: EOPGROUP@PRIMENET.COM. Home: 1509 Pennycress Ln Vienna VA 22182 Office: EOP Group Inc 819 7th St NW Washington DC 20001

HIAPO, PATRICIA KAMAKA, lay worker; b. Honolulu, May 18, 1943; d. Ward Charles and Violet Kaopua (Nicholas) McKeown; m. Bernard Joseph Hiapo, July 9, 1960; children: Bernard Jr., Beatrice, Jacqueline, Mary-Louise. Grad. high sch., Honolulu. Cert. catechist, 1988. Area del. St. John Apostle and Evangelist, Mililani, Hawaii, 1981-84; eucharistic min. St. John Apostle and Evangelist, Mililani, 1981-88; hospice and bereavement ministry St. Francis Hosp., Honolulu, 1983, eucharistic min., 1983-88; religious edn. coord. Resurrection of The Lord, Waipahu, Hawaii, 1984-88; dir. religious edn. St. Jude, Ewa Beach, Hawaii, 1988-91; home visitor Hana Like, Honolulu, 1990-98; parent educator Alu Lke Pulama I Na Keiki/Lee Town Ctr., Waipahu, Hawaii, 1998—; mem. marriage encounter team Cath. Ch., Honolulu, 1981-83. Recipient award Our Lady of Peace, 1991. Office: 87-117 Pulapa Pl Waianae HI 96792 also: Parents and Children Together-Hana Like 45-955 Kamehameha Hwy Ste 404 Kaneohe HI 96744-3222

HIATT, ARNOLD, shoe manufacturer, importer, retailer; b. May 26, 1927; s. Alexander and Dorothy H.; m. Anne Wechsler. B.A., Harvard U., 1948. Pres., founder Blue Star Shoe Co., Lawrence, Mass., 1952-69; pres., chief exec. officer Stride Rite Corp., Boston, 1969-89, chmn. bd., 1982-92; chmn. Stride Rite Found., Boston, 1982—; bd. dirs. Dreyfus Fund., Cabot Corp. Former mem. bd. regents of higher edn. Commonwealth of Mass.; mem. bd. trustees Isabela Stewart Gardner Mus., The John Merck Found.; former mem. vis. com. Boston U. Sch. Medicine; bd. overseers Harvard U., 1984-90; chair Bus. for Social Responsibility. Mem. Am. Footwear Industries Assn. (dir., chmn. 1980).

HIATT, CHARLES F., II, secondary education educator; b. Daytona Beach, Fla., Oct. 20, 1955; s. Charles F. and Marilyn June (Meyers) H.; m. Lori Ann Nadenik, Feb. 26, 1994. BS, Stetson U., 1978. Cert. tchr., Fla. Tchr. Bishop Moore H.S., Orlando, Fla., 1979-81, Warner Christian Acad., South Daytona, Fla., 1982-84, 86-90, Seabreeze Sr. H.S., Daytona Beach, 1984-85, Silver Sands Middle Sch., Port Orange, Fla., 1990—. Mem. ASCD, NEA, Volusia Coun. Social Studies (dist. rep. 1995-97), Volusia Educators Assn., Nat. Geographic Soc., Smithsonian Inst., Masons. Avocations: traveling, motorcycling. Home: 132 Highland Ave Ormond Beach FL 32174-5616 Office: Silver Sands Middle Sch 1300 Herbert St Port Orange FL 32119-4134

HIATT, FRED, editorial writer; b. Washington, 1955. BA in History, Harvard U., 1977. City Hall reporter Atlanta Journal-Constitution, 1979-80; reporter The Washington Star, 1981; Va. reporter The Washington Post, 1981-83, Pentagon reporter, 1983-86, Northeast Asia co-bur. chief, 1987-90, Moscow co-bur. chief, 1991-95, editl. writer, 1996—. Author: (novel) The Secret Sun, 1992, (children's book) If I Were Queen of the World, 1997. Office: The Washington Post 1150 15th St NW Washington DC 20071-0001

HIATT, HOLLY MARLANE, history educator; b. Mesa, Ariz., Sept. 28, 1972; d. Phillip Rudger and Roma Lee (Willis) H. BA in Edn., Ariz. State U., 1994. Cert. secondary edn., Ariz. Tchr. history Snowflake (Ariz.) Unified Sch. Dist., 1995-97; asst. to sen. State of Ariz., 1998—. Bd. dirs. local chpt. Gov.'s Alliance Against Drugs, Snowflake, 1988-90. Mem. Ariz. Coun. Social Studies, Nat. Coun. Social Studies, Lambda Delta Sigma (pres. 1993-94), Phi Alpha Theta. Republican. Mem. Latter-Day Saints Ch. Avocations: music, reading, team sports, racquetball, genealogy. Home: 930 N Mesa Dr Mesa AZ 85201-4323

HIATT, HOWARD H., physician, educator; b. Patchogue, N.Y., July 22, 1925; s. Alexander and Dorothy (Askinas) H.; m. Doris Bieringer, Nov. 29, 1947; children—Jonathan, Deborah, Frederick. M.D., Harvard U., 1948. Intern, then resident medicine Beth Israel Hosp., Boston, 1948-50; research fellow Cornell U. Med. Coll., 1950-53; clin. investigator USPHS, 1953-55; mem. faculty Med. Sch., Harvard U., 1955—, H.L. Blumgart prof. medicine, 1963-72, prof. medicine, 1972—, prof. medicine Sch. Pub. Health, 1984-92, dean Sch. Pub. Health, 1972-84; physician-in-chief Beth Israel Hosp., 1963-72; sr. physician Brigham Women's Hosp., boston, 1984—. Mem. NAS Inst. Medicine, Am. Soc. Clin. Investigation, Assn. Am. Physicians, Am. Acad. Arts and Scis. (sec. 1992-97, dir. Initiatives for Childrens 1992—), Alpha Omega Alpha. Home: 130 Mt Auburn St Cambridge MA 02138-5757 Office: Brigham and Women's Hosp Boston MA 02115

HIATT, JANE CRATER, arts agency administrator; b. Winston-Salem, N.C., May 26, 1944; d. Howard Rondthaler Jr. and Irene (Sides) Crater; m. K.W. Everhart Jr. (div. June 1973); m. Wood Coleman Hiatt, May, 1978; 1 child, Jonathan David. BA, U. N.C., 1966; MA, Wake Forest U., 1972. Eng. tchr. Winston-Salem (N.C.)/Forsyth County Schs., 1966-70; exec. dir. Tenn. Com. for the Humanities, Nashville, 1973-77; cons. various ednl. and cultural agys. Ocean Springs, Miss., 1978-80; asst. dir. Miss. Humanities Coun., Jackson, Miss., 1981-85; exec. dir. Arts Alliance of Jackson and Hinds County, Miss., 1985-89, Miss. Arts Commn., Jackson, 1989-95; participant Arts Leadership Inst. of Humphrey Inst. for Pub. Affairs, Mpls., 1986, Leadership, Jackson, 1987. Co-editor Peoples of the South, 1976; exec. producer (TV series) The South with John Siegenthaler, 1976; host, reporter Miss. Ednl. TV, Jackson, 1981-87. Mem. Miss. Econ. Coun., 1986-87, Miss. R & D Coun., 1984-88; pres. Mental Health Assn. of Hinds County, Jackson, 1986; treas. Miss. for Ednl. Broadcasting, 1987, 88, 89, Premier Class Leadership, Jackson, 1987, 88; mem. comty. adv. coun. Jr. League of Jackson, 1995-98; mem. cmty. adv. bd. Jr. League of Jackson, 1995—; mem. Friends of Art and Preservation in Embassies Millenium Com. representing Miss. Recipient Heritage award City of Biloxi, 1984. Mem. Nat. Assembly of Local Arts Agys., Nat. Coun. on Arts, Nat. Assembly State Arts Agys. (bd. dirs. 1992-95, 2d v.p. 1995), So. Arts Fedn. (bd. dirs. 1989-95), Miss. Ctr. for Nonprofits (vice chmn., bd. dirs. 1993-96, adv. bd. 1997—), Pub. Edn. Forum (bd. dirs. 1993—), Greater Jackson Found. (bd. dirs. 1996—), Phi Beta Kappa. Home: 507 Roses Bluff Dr Madison MS 39110-7545

HIATT, MARJORIE MCCULLOUGH, service organization executive; b. Cin., July 12, 1923; d. Robert Stedman and Mildred (Rogers) McCullough; m. Homer E. Lunken, Apr. 15, 1944 (dec. 1970); children: Karen (dec. 1948), Kathryn Lunken Summers, Margo Lunken Yesner; m. William McLeod Ittmann, Mar. 17, 1972 (dec. 1982); m. Harold Hiatt, Apr. 14, 1984 (dec. 1999). Student, U. Cin., 1941-43. Active Girl Scouts U.S., 1962—, chmn. conv. com., 1972, del. world convs., 1969, 72, 75, 78, 81, 84, 87, 93, chmn. pub. relations com., 1963-66, mem. nat. exec. com., 1963-75, mem. nat. bd., 1962—, 4th v.p., 1966-69, 1st v.p., 1969-72, nat. pres., 1972-75, chmn. nat. adv. council, 1975-82, mem. birthplace adv. com., 1980-97; vice chmn. world conf., Orleans, France, 1981; mem. world com. World Assn. Girl Guides and Girl Scouts, 1978-87, vice chmn., 1984-87. Regional dir. Assn. Jr. Leagues Am., 1958-60, nat. pres., 1960-62; mem. br. Jr. League Cin., 1944-58, Nat. Tng. Labs., 1963-66, Nat. Assembly for Social Policy and Devel., 1968-71; mem. exec. com. Council Nat. Orgns. for Children and Youth, 1960-62, 68-72; bd. dirs. United Way Am., 1962-67, sec., 1965-66, v.p., 1966-67, 1989—; mem. policy com. Center Vol. Soc., 1971-72; bd. dirs. Coll. Prep. Sch., Cin., 1962-69, pres., 1964-69; bd. dirs. Cin. Speech and Hearing Center, 1955-66, v.p., 1958-62, pres., 1963-66, trustee emeritus, 1966—; mem. bd. Children's Theatre, Cin., 1948-58, pres., 1948-50; bd. dirs. Community Health and Welfare Council Cin., 1957-63, Hamilton County (Ohio) Research Found., 1963-65, Cancer Family Care, Cin., 1971-72, Boys Clubs Greater Cin., Marjorie P. Lee Home for Aged, Music Hall Assn., Cin. Symphony Orch.; bd. dirs. Beechwood Home for Incurables, 1975-87; bd. dirs. St. Margaret Hall, 1991—, Cin. Civic Garden Ctr., 1992-95; mem. Ohio Citizens Coun., 1956-58; mem. bd. 7th Presbyterian Ch., 1967-74, 85—, ruling elder, 1976-78, 95—, chmn. bd. trustees, 1992-94; sr. warden St. Martin's in the Field, Biddeford Pool, Maine; bd. dirs. Greater Cin. Found., 1979-87; bd. dirs. U. Cin. Found., 1979—, pres. 1986-88, vice chmn. 1988—, trustee emeritus, 1993—; pres. Garden Club Cin., 1984-86, co-chmn. zone X meeting, 1989, zone X chmn. pub.; bd. dirs. Friends Cin. Parks, 1987-98, corr. sec., 1989-92; trustee Cin . Arts Assn.; founding bd. dirs. Emery Soc. Children's Hosp; pres. protem Cin. Parks Found., 1995, bd. dirs., 1997—. Mem. Olave Baden-Powell Soc. (v.p. 1991-93, pres. 1993-97), World Found. for Girl Guides and Girl Scouts (v.p. 1989—), Garden Club Am. (vice chmn. founder's fund 1991-92), Am. Psychiat. Assn. Aux. (bd. dirs., rec. sec. 1991-92). Home: 2353 Bedford Ave Cincinnati OH 45208-2656

HIATT, PETER, retired librarian studies educator; b. N.Y.C., Oct. 19, 1930; s. Amos and Elizabeth Hope (Derry) H.; m. Linda Rae Smith, Aug. 16, 1968; 1 child, Holly Virginia. B.A., Colgate U., 1952; M.L.S., Rutgers U., 1957, Ph.D., 1963. Head Elmora Br. Library, Elizabeth, N.J., 1957-59; instr. Grad. Sch. Library Service Sci. Rutgers U., 1960-62; library cons. Ind. State Library, Indpls., 1963-70; asst. prof. Grad. Library Sch., Ind. U., 1963-66, assoc. prof., 1966-70; dir. Ind. Library Studies, Bloomington, 1967-70; dir. continuing edn. program for library personnel Western Interstate Commn. for Higher Edn., Boulder, Colo., 1970-74; dir. Grad. Sch. Library and Info. Sci., U. Wash., Seattle, 1974-81, prof., 1974-98; prin. investigator Career Devel. and Assessment Center for Librarians, 1979-83, 90-93; dir. library insts. at various colls. and univs.; adv. project U.S. Office Edn.-ALA, 1977-80; prof. emeritus U. Wash., 1998—; bd. dirs. King County Libr. Sys., 1989-97, pres., 1991, 95, sec., 1993, 94; prin. investigator Career Devel. and Assessment Ctrs. for Librs.: Phase II, 1990-93. Author: (with Donald Thompson) Monroe County Public Library: Planning for the Future, 1966, The Public Library Needs of Delaware County, 1967, (with Henry Drennan) Public Library Services for the functionally Illiterate, 1967 (with Robert E. Lee and Lawrence A. Allen) A Plan for Developing a Regional Program of Continuing Education for Library Personnel, 1969, Public Library Branch Services for Adults of Low Education, 1964; dir., gen. editor: The Indiana Library Studies, 1970; author: Assessment Centers for Professional Library Leadership, 1993; mem. editorial bd. Coll. and Rsch. Librs., 1969-73; co-editor Leads: A Continuing Education Newsletter for Library Trustees, 1973-75, Octavio Noda; author chpts., articles on library continuing edn., staff devel. and libr. adult svcs. Mem. ALA (officer), Pacific N.W. Libr. Assn., Assn. Libr. and Info. Sci. Educators (officer, Outstanding Svc. award 1979), ACLU. E-mail: phiatt@waypt.com. Home: 111 E Rhododendron Dr Port Townsend WA 98368-9414 *I know of no other profession which helps so many people and organizations change and grow--from pre-school years through retirement, as does librarianship. It is a joy to be part of that.*

HIBBARD, CARL ROGER, social services administrator; b. Charlotte, N.C., Aug. 21, 1944; s. Carl Hiram and Doris May (Foster) H.; m. Nancy

Rosalyn Cude, June 18, 1967; children: Alison Elizabeth Hibbard Hager, Christopher Roger. BA in Bus. Adminstrn., Furman U., 1966; MEd in Cmty. Leadership and Devel., Springfield Coll., 1967. Cert. camp dir. Am. Camping Assn.; cert. YMCA sr. dir. Phys. dir. Johnston Meml. YMCA, Charlotte, 1967-68; exec. dir. YMCA Camp Cheerio, High Point, N.C., 1970-74; asst. gen. dir. Durham (N.C.) YMCA, 1974-76; adminstrv. dir. YMCA Blue Ridge Assembly, Black Mountain, N.C., 1976-85; exec. dir. YMCA Blue Ridge Assembly, Black Mountain, 1985—. Contbr. articles to profl. jours. Chmn. Black Mountain Recreation Commn., 1985-87; mem. Buncombe County Recreation Adv. Com., Asheville, N.C., 1991—, chmn., 1993-96, 97—; mem. Black Mountain Correctional Ctr. for Women Cmty. Resource Coun., 1996—; exec. bd. Daniel Boone Coun. Boy Scouts Am., 1997—; bd. dirs. Asheville-Mountain Area chpt. ARC, 1998—. 1st lt. U.S. Army, 1968-70. Mem. Internat. Assn. Conf. Ctr. Adminstrs. (first v.p. 1984-86), Assn. Profl. YMCA Dirs. (cert., pres. Carolinas' chpt. 1981-84, dist. v.p. S.E. dist. 1984-87, dist. v.p. S.E. dist. adminstrn. sect. 1991-93), Black Mountain-Swannanoa C. of C. (bd. dirs. 1980-81, 85-88, 93-98, pres. 1987), Rotary Club (pres. 1980-81, Paul Harris fellow). Methodist. Home and Office: YMCA Blue Ridge Assembly Inc 84 Blue Ridge Cir Black Mountain NC 28711-9750

HIBBARD, RICHARD PAUL, industrial ventilation consultant, lecturer; b. Defiance, Ohio, Nov. 1, 1923; s. Richard T. and Doris E. (Walkup) H.; BS in Mech. Indsl. Engring., U. Toledo, 1949; m. Phyllis Ann Kirchoffer, Sept. 7, 1948; children: Barbara Rae, Marcia Kae, Rebecca Ann, Patricia Jan, John Ross. Mech. engr. Oldsmobile div. Gen. Motors Corp., Lansing, Mich., 1950-56; design and sales engr. McConnell Sheet Metal, Inc., Lansing, 1956-60; chief heat and ventilation engr. Fansteel Metall. Corp., North Chicago, Ill., 1960-62; sr. facilities and ventilation engr. The Boeing Co., Seattle, 1962-63; ventilation engr. environ. health div. dept. preventive medicine U. Wash., 1964-70, lectr. dept. environ. health, 1970-82, lectr. emeritus, 1983—; prin. Indsl. Ventilation Cons. Svcs., 1983—; chmn. Western Indsl. Ventilation Conf., 1962; mem. com. indsl. ventilation Am. Conf. Govtl. Indsl. Hygienists, 1966—; mem. staff Indsl. Ventilation Conf., Mich. State U., 1955—. With USAAF, 1943-45, USAR, 1946-72. Recipient Disting. Svc. award Indsl. Ventilation Conf., Mich. State U., 1975, 93. Mem. Am. Soc. Safety Engrs. (R.M. Gillmore Meml. award Puget Sound chpt.), ASHRAE, Am. Inst. Plant Engrs., Am. Indsl. Hygiene Assn. (J.M. Dallevalle award 1977), Am. Foundryman's Soc. Lodges: Elks, Masons. Contbr. articles on indsl. hygiene and ventilation to profl. jours. Home: 41 165th Ave SE Bellevue WA 98008-4721

HIBBARD, WALTER ROLLO, JR., retired engineering educator; b. Bridgeport, Ct., Jan. 20, 1918; s. Walter R. and Helen S. (Kenworthy) H.; m. Charlotte H. Tracy, Mar. 21, 1942 (dec. 1970); children: Douglas, Lawrence, Diana; m. Louise A. Brembeck, Jan. 29, 1972. AB, Wesleyan U., 1939; DEng, Yale U., 1942; LLD (hon.), Mich. Tech. U., 1968; DEng,of Engring. (hon.), Montana Coll. Mineral Scis. and Tech., 1970. Asst., then assoc. prof. Yale U., New Haven, 1946-51; rsch. assoc., then mgr. metallurgy and ceramics Gen. Electric Research Lab., Schenectady, N.Y., 1951-65; dir. U.S. Bur. Mines, Washington, 1965-68; v.p. Owens Corning Fiberglas Corp., 1968-74; prof. engring. Va. Poly. Inst. and State U., Blacksburg, 1974-87, prof. emeritus, 1987—; dir. Va. Ctr. for Coal and Energy Research, Blacksburg, 1977-87. Contbr. numerous articles to profl. publs. Served to lt. comdr. USNR, 1942-46. Recipient Yale U. Engring. Alumni award, 1955, Wesleyan U. Disting. Alumnus award, 1979. Mem. Nat. Acad. Engring., AIME (R.W. Raymond award 1950, J. Douglas medal 1969, Mineral Econs. award 1983), Am. Soc. Metals, Am. Ceramic Soc. Home: 1403 Highland Cir Blacksburg VA 24060-5624

HIBBEN, CELIA LYNN, psychiatric mental health nurse practitioner; b. Birmingham, Ala., July 16, 1953; d. Kenneth Gordon and Bobbie Rae (Barnum) H. BSN, U. Tex., Tyler, 1990; postgrad., U. Tex., Arlington, 1993-97. Relief house supr. Glenoaks Hosp. (Psychiatric Hosp.), Greenville, Tex., 1990-92; coord. psychiat. nursing Tex. Longevity Healthcare Inst., Ft. Worth, 1992-93; case mgr., home health psychiat. cons. All Saints Hosp., Ft. Worth, 1993-97; collaborative practice with Dr. Robert Guzman, 1996, health care cons., 1996—; system analyst Care Centric Solutions, Duluth, Ga., 1996—. Vol. AIDS Outreach Ctr., Ft. Worth, 1991-96. Recipient Outstanding Clin. Achievement award U. Tex., Arlington, 1996; ANA scholar, 1990. Mem. Dallas Songwriters Assn., Sigma Theta Tau, Alpha Chi. Republican. Baptist. Avocations: guitar, writing and performing music. Home: 2705 Tree Summit Pkwy Duluth GA 30096-7931

HIBBERT, ROBERT GEORGE, lawyer, food company executive; b. Marlboro, Mass., July 3, 1950; s. Charles Harris and Mary Barbara (Sauage) H.; m. Cynthia Joan Miller, June 12, 1971; children: Lauren, Meg, Robert J. BA, Columbia U., 1972; JD, Am. U., 1975. Bar: Mass. 1975, Md. 1975, D.C. 1985. Trial atty. office of gen. counsel USDA, Washington, 1975-79, dir. standards and labeling divsn. food safety inspection service, 1980-85; v.p., gen. counsel Am. Meat Inst., Arlington, Va., 1985-88; with McDermott, Will & Emery, Washington. Mem. ABA, Mass. Bar Assn., Md. Bar Assn., D.C. Bar Assn., Am. Agrl. Law Assn. Home: 621 Whittingham Dr Silver Spring MD 20904-6332 Office: McDermott Will & Emery 600 13th St NW Fl 12-8 Washington DC 20005-3005*

HIBBS, JOHN DAVID, software executive, engineer, business owner; b. Del Norte, Colo., Jan. 26, 1948; s. Alva Bernard and Frances Ava (Cathcart) H.; m. Ruthanne Johnson, Feb. 28, 1976. BSEE, Denver U., 1970. Elec. engr. Merrick and Co., Denver, 1972-73; lighting engr. Holophane div. Johns Manville, Denver, 1973-79; lighting products mgr. Computer Sharing Svcs., Inc., Denver, 1979-83; pres., owner Computer Aided Lighting Analysis, Boulder, Colo., 1983-86, Hibbs Sci. Software, Boulder, Colo., 1986—; chmn. bd. Sport Sail Inc., 1996-97; co-founder Sport Sail, Inc. Author CALA, CALA/Pro and PreCALA lighting programs; patentee in field. With USNR, 1970-72. Recipient 1st prize San Luise Valley Sci. Fair, 1963. Mem. IEEE, Illuminating Engring. Soc. North Am. (chmn. computer com. 1988-91), Computer Soc. IEEE (chmn. computer problem set com. 1991-95). Avocations: woodworking, bicycling, sailing. Home and Office: PO Box 400 Fraser CO 80442-0400

HIBBS, JOHN STANLEY, lawyer; b. Des Moines, Sept. 19, 1934; s. Ray E. Hibbs and Jean Waller (Lackey) Gravender; m. John S. II, Kari S. Hibbs Carroll, Jennifer R. Hibbs-Kraus. BBA, U. Minn., 1956, JD cum laude, 1960. Bar: Minn. 1960, U.S. Dist. Ct. Minn. 1960, U.S. Ct. Appeals (8th cir.) 1963, U.S. Tax Ct. 1965, U.S. Supreme Ct. 1970. Ptnr. Dorsey and Whitney, Mpls., 1960—, Health Practice Group; chmn. Adv. Task Force on Minn. Corp. Law, Mpls., 1979-82, tax policy study group of Minn. Bus. Climate Task Force, Mpls., 1978-80; coun. Med. Group Practice Attys. Author: Minnesota Nonprofit Corporations-A Corporate and Tax Guide, 1979; contbr. over 150 profl. papers to publs. Served to capt. USAR, 1956-66. Fellow Am. Coll. Tax Counsel; mem. ABA (cons. com. on corp. laws 1981-82), Nat. Health Lawyers Assn., Am. Acad. Healthcare Attys., Coun. Med. Group Practice Attys., Minn. Bar Assn., Hennepin County Bar Assn. Republican. Lutheran. Avocations: sports, reading, travel, gardening. Home: 25 Cooper Cir Minneapolis MN 55436-1316 Office: Dorsey & Whitney 220 S 6th St Ste 2200 Minneapolis MN 55402-1498*

HIBBS, LOYAL ROBERT, lawyer; b. Des Moines, Dec. 24, 1925; s. Loyal B. and Catharine (McClymond) H.; children: Timothy, Theodore, Howard, Dean. BA, U. Iowa, 1950, LLB, JD, 1952. Bar: Iowa 1952, Nev. 1958, U.S. Supreme Ct. 1971. Ptnr. Hibbs Law Offices, Reno, 1972—. Moderator radio, TV Town Hall Coffee Breaks, 1970-72; mem. Nev. State Bicycle Adv. Bd., 1996—, Reno Bicycle Coun., 1995—, Reno Park Recreation Commn., 1999—. Fellow Am. Bar Found. (Nev. chmn. 1989-94); mem. ABA (standing com. Lawyer Referral Svc. 1978-79, steering com. state dels. 1979-82, consortium on legal svcs. and the pub. 1979-82, Nev. State Bar del. to Ho. of Dels. 1978-82, 89-90, bd. govs. 1982-85, mem. legal tech. adv. coun. 1985-86, standing com. on nat. conf. groups 1985-91, chmn. sr. lawyers divsn. Nev. 1988—), Nat. Conf. Bar Pres.'s Iowa Bar Assn., Nev. Bar Assn. (bd. govs. 1968-78, pres. 1977-78), Washoe County Bar Assn. (pres. 1966-67), Nat. Jud. Coll. (bd. dirs. 1986-92, sec. 1988-92), Assn. Def. Counsel No. Calif., Assn. Def. Counsel Nev., Assn. Ski Def. Attys., Aircraft Owners and Pilots Assn. (legal svcs. plan 1991—), Washoe County Legal Aid Soc. (co-founder), Lawyer-Pilots Bar Assn. (chmn. Nev.), Greater Reno C. of C. (bd. dirs. 1968-72), Phi Alpha Delta. Home: 1489 Foster Dr Reno NV 89509-1209 Office: Ste 250 290 S Arlington Ave Reno NV 89501-1713

HIBEL, BERNARD, financial consultant, former apparel company executive; b. N.Y.C., Dec. 22, 1916; s. Jacob and Leah (Singer) H.; m. Annette; children: Laurel, Karen, Miriam; adopted children: Michael Weiser, Scott Weiser, John Weiser. B.B.A. magna cum laude, St. John's U., 1937. C.P.A. Mng. exec. charge contract termination Cleve. Ordnance Dist., 1945-46; mng. acct. Bernard M. Joffe & Co., N.Y.C., 1946-48, Aronson & Oresman (C.P.A.s.), N.Y.C., 1948-55; exec. v.p. Kayser-Roth Corp., N.Y.C., 1975-81, also dir.; cons., 1982—; tchr. acctg. Bklyn. Coll., U.S. Army. Bd. dirs. Miss Universe Beauty Pageant. With AUS, 1943-45. Decorated Bronze Star. Mem. Am. Inst. C.P.A.s, N.Y. State Soc. C.P.A.s. Office: 300 E 56th St New York NY 10022-4136

HIBNER, RAE A., insurance company official, nurse; b. Libertyville, Ill., Jan. 31, 1956; d. Richard Douglas and Raelene Ann (Warren) Lyons; m. John Paul Hibner, June 21, 1986; children: Kevin John, Thomas Ivan. Diploma, Luth. Gen. Hosp. Sch. Nursing, Park Ridge, Ill., 1979; BS in Nursing, U. Ill., Chgo., 1984; MS, No. Ill., 1987. RN. Staff nurse Cardiac Telemetry Luth. Gen. Hosp., 1979-81, staff nurse CCU, 1981-82; staff nurse coronary ICU U. Ill. Hosp., Chgo., 1982-83, asst. head nurse coronary ICU, 1983-86, head nurse coronary ICU, 1986-88, staff nurse coronary-med. ICU, 1988-90; coord. utilization rev. Parkside Health Mgmt. Corp., Chgo., 1989-91; asst. dir. utilization mgmt. U. Ill., Chgo., 1991-93; risk mgr. Rush-Presbyn.-St. Lukes Med. Ctr., Chgo., 1993-96; claims cons. CNA Ins. Cos., Chgo., 1996; dir. claims corp. accts. CNA Health Pro, Chgo., 1996—. Republican. Roman Catholic. Avocations: needlepoint, crochet, swimming, camping.

HICE, MICHAEL, editor, marketing professional; b. Carlsbad, N.Mex., June 8, 1946; s. William Elmer and Jewell Irene (Holcomb) H. BA, Tulane U., 1968. Asst. dir. ESL Lang. Ctrs., Houston, 1970-77; program dir. St. Marys Coll., Moraga, Calif., 1977-78; with Savin Corp., San Francisco, 1978-82; gen. sales mgr. Radio Sta. KLSK, Santa Fe, N.Mex., 1983-90; ptnr., v.p. Mountain Time Tours, Santa Fe, N.Mex., 1987-88; ptnr., v.p. sales mktg. cons. Nightingale Hice Inc., Santa Fe, N.Mex., 1990-96; ptnr., editor Indian Artist, Inc., Santa Fe, N.Mex., 1994—; co-founder, arts dir., promoter Homogenesis, San Francisco, 1981-82; freelance writer. Founder, editor Indian Artist, 1994-99; founder, editor-in-chief Native Artists mag., 1999—; co-author: (play) Song of Myself, 1984; founder, assoc. pub. Native Artists mag., 1999. Co-founder AID and Comfort, Santa Fe, 1989, Bus. for Social Responsibility, 1993. Recipient Best of Show award N.Mex. Advt. Fedn., 1990, Best Multi-Media Pub. Svc. Campaign award, 1993, Cowles Media award, 1998, Folio Editorial Excellence award, 1998. Mem. Nat. Mktg. Assn. Avocations: hiking, snow skiing, gardening, swimming, yoga. Home: 48A Ojo De La Vaca Rd Santa Fe NM 87505-1457 Office: Native Artists Ste 303 320 Galisteo Santa Fe NM 87501

HICK, KENNETH WILLIAM, business executive; b. New Westminster, B.C., Can., Oct. 17, 1946; s. Les Walter and Mary Isabelle (Warner) H. BA in Bus., Eastern Wash. State Coll., 1971; MBA (fellow), U. Wash., 1973, PhD, 1975. Regional sales mgr. Hilti, Inc., San Leandro, Calif., 1976-79; gen. sales mgr. Moore Internat., Inc., Portland, 1979-80; v.p. sales and mktg. Phillips Corp., Anaheim, Calif., 1980-81; owner, pres., chief exec. officer K.C. Metals, San Jose, Calif., 1981-87; owner, pres., chief exec. officer Losli Internat. Inc., Portland, Oreg., 1987-89; pres. Resources N.W. Inc., 1989—; communications cons. Asso. Pub. Safety Communication Officers, Inc., State of Oreg., 1975-93; numerous cons. assignments, also seminars, 1976-98. Contbr. articles to numerous publs. Mem. Oreg. Gov.'s Tax Bd., 1975-76; pres. Portland chpt. Oreg. Jaycees, 1976; bd. fellows U. Santa Clara, 1983-90. Served with USAF, 1966-69. Decorated Commendation medal. Mem. Am. Mgmt. Assn., Am. Mktg. Assn., Assn. M.B.A. Execs., Assn. Gen. Contractors, Soc. Advancement Mgmt., Home Builders Assn. Roman Catholic. Home: 25659 Cheryl Dr West Linn OR 97068-4589 Office: Resources N/W Inc 19727 Highway 99E Hubbard OR 97032-9716

HICKCOX, LESLIE KAY, health educator, consultant, counselor; b. Berkeley, Calif., May 12, 1951; d. Ralph Thomas and Marilyn Irene (Stump) H. BA, U. Redlands, 1973; MA in Exercise Physiology, U. of the Pacific, 1975; MEd, Columbia U., 1979; MEd in Health Edn., Oreg. State U., 1987, MEd in Guidance & Counseling, 1988, EdD in Edn., 1991. Cert. state C.C. instr. (life), Calif. Phys. edn. instr., dir. intramurals SUNY, Stony Brook, 1981-83; instr. health edn. Linn-Benton C.C., Oreg., 1985-94; health and phys. edn. instr. Portland C.C., 1994-95; edn. supr., instr. Oreg. State U., Corvallis, 1988-90; instr. human studies and comm. Marylhurst Coll., Portland, Oreg., 1987-96; instr. health edn. U. (New Zealand) Auckland, 1991; instr. health curriculum and supervision Concordia Coll., Portland, Oreg., 1992; instr., coord. dept. health, phys. edn. and recreation Rogue C.C., Grants Pass, Oreg., 1995-97; assoc. prof., coord. health and phys. edn. Western Mont. Coll., Dillon, 1997-99; asst. prof. health edn. Northwestern Ill. U., Chgo., IL, 1999—; founder Experiential Learning Inst., 1992—, found., Lilly N.W. High Edn. Tchg. Conf., 1996; founding v.p. Home Health Diagnostics, Portland, Oreg., 1996. Contbr. articles to profl. jours. Mem. ASCD, Nat. Ctr. for Health Edn., Assn. for Advancement of Health Edn., Higher Edn. R & D Soc. Australasia, Coun. for Adult and Exptl. Learning, Kappa Delta Phi, Phi Delta Kappa. Home: 2635 N Baldwin St Portland OR 97217 Office: Dept Health Phys Edn Recreation and Athletics Northeastern Ill Univ 5500 N Saint Louis Ave Chicago IL 60607

HICKEL, WALTER JOSEPH, investment firm executive, forum administrator; b. nr. Claflin, Kans., Aug. 18, 1919; s. Robert A. and Emma (Zecha) H.; m. Janice Cannon, Sept. 22, 1941 (dec. Aug. 1943); 1 child, Theodore; m. Ermalee Strutz, Nov. 22, 1945; children: Robert, Walter Jr., Jack, Joseph, Karl. Student pub. schs., Claflin; D.Eng. (hon.), Stevens Inst. Tech., 1970, Mich. Tech. U., 1973; LL.D. (hon.), St. Mary of Plains Coll., St. Martin's Coll., U. Md., Adelphi U., U. San Diego, Rensselaer Poly. Inst., 1973, U. Alaska, 1976, Alaska Pacific U., 1991; D.Pub. Adminstrn. (hon.), Willamette U. Founder Hickel Investment Co., Anchorage, 1947—; gov. State of Alaska, 1966-69, 90-94; sec. U.S. Dept. Interior, 1969-70; sec. gen. The Northern Forum, 1994—; former mem. world adv. council Internat. Design Sci. Inst.; former mem. com. on sci. freedom and responsibility AAAS; nominated for pres. at 1968 Republican Nat. Convention; co-founder Yukon Pacific Corp.; founder Inst. of the North, 1996—. Author: Who Owns America?, 1971; contbr. articles to newspapers. Mem. Republican Nat. Com., 1954-64; bd. regents Gonzaga U.; bd. dirs. Salk Inst., 1972-79, NASA Adv. Coun. Exploration Task Force, 1989-91; mem. Governor's Econ. Com. on North Slope Natural Gas, Alaska, 1982. Named Alaskan of Year, 1969, Man of Yr. Ripon Soc., 1970; recipient DeSmet medal Gonzaga U., 1969, Horatio Alger award, 1972, Grand Cordon of the Order of Sacred Treasure award His Imperial Majesty the Emperor of Japan, 1988. Mem. Pioneers of Alaska, Alaska C. of C. (former chmn. econ. devel. com.), Equestrian Order Holy Sepulchre, Knights Malta, KC. Leader of the first Alaska Chamber economic trade mission to Japan. Home: 1905 Loussac Dr Anchorage AK 99517-1225 Office: PO Box 101700 Anchorage AK 99510-1700 *We shall never understand peace, justice and the living of life until we recognize that all people are human and that humans are the most precious things on earth.*

HICKEN, JEFFREY PRICE, lawyer; b. Macomb, Ill., Oct. 25, 1947; s. Victor and Mary Patricia (O'Connell) H.; m. Mary Sarah Schmidt, Aug. 23, 1969; children: Andrew, Molly, Elizabeth. BA, Cornell Coll., 1969; JD, U. Ill., 1972. Bar: Minn. 1972, U.S. Dist. Ct. Minn. 1980, U.S. Ct. Appeals (8th cir.). Assoc. Weaver, Talle & Herrick, Anoka, Minn., 1972-77; sr. ptnr. Hicken, Scott & Howard, P.A., Anoka, 1977-97, 1998—. Bd. dirs. Anoka Lyric Arts; precinct chair Dem. Farmer-Labor Party, Anoka, 1976—. Capt. U.S. Army, 1969-77. Recipient J. Franklin Littel scholarship Cornell Coll., Mt. Vernon, Iowa, 1969. Fellow Am. Acad. Matrimonial Lawyers (cert. arbitrator, bd. mgrs.); mem. Minn. State Bar Assn., Anoka County Bar Assn. (pres. 1990-91), City of Anoka Charter Commn. (chmn. 1978-84). Democrat. Avocations: running, violin. Home: 1700 West Ln Anoka MN 55303-1923 Office: Hicken Scott & Howard PA 2150 3rd Ave Ste 300 Anoka MN 55303-2200

HICKEN, RUSSELL BRADFORD, art dealer, appraiser; b. Jacksonville, Fla., Dec. 24, 1926; s. Leslie Adames and Nettie Bradford (Frazee) H.; m. Margot Louise Ward, Apr. 14, 1978. BS, Fla. State U., 1951. Tchr. Fletcher H.S., Jacksonville, 1951-57; dir. Jacksonville Art Mus., 1957-64, 69-75, Tampa (Fla.) Art Inst., 1964-67, Mint Mus. Art, Charlotte, 1967-69, Hollywood (Fla.) Art & Culture Ctr., 1975-77; art dealer Russel B. Hicken, Fine Arts Ltd., Tampa, Miami, 1977—. Mem. Bakehouse Art Ctr., Miami, 1996—, Sesquicentennial Commn., Jacksonville, 1972. With U.S. Army, 1944-46; ETO. Mem. Am. Assn. Mus., S.E. Mus. Conf. (pres. 1969-70, AAM rep. 1970-76). Democrat. Avocations: chess, backgammon, travel. Fax: 850-907-0066. Home and Office: 5403 Widefield Rd Tallahassee FL 32308-6454

HICKERSON, GLENN LINDSEY, leasing company executive; b. Burbank, Calif., Aug. 22, 1937; s. Ralph M. and Sarah Lawson (Lindsey) H.; m. Jane Fortune Arthur, Feb. 24, 1973. BA in Bus. Adminstrn., Claremont Men's Coll., 1959; MBA, NYU, 1960. Exec. asst. Douglas Aircraft Co., Santa Monica, Calif., 1963; sec., treas. Douglas Fin. Corp., Long Beach, Calif., 1964-67, regional mgr. customer financing, 1967; exec. asst. to pres. Universal Airlines, Inc., Detroit, 1967-68, v.p., treas., asst. sec., 1968-69, pres., 1969-72; v.p., treas., asst. sec. Universal Aircraft Service, Inc., Detroit, 1968-69, chmn. bd., 1969-72; v.p., treas. Universal Airlines Co., Detroit, 1968-69, pres., 1969-72; group v.p. Marriott Hotels, Inc., Washington, 1972-76; dir. sales Far East and Australia Lockheed Calif. Co., 1976-78, dir. mktg. Americas, 1978-79, dir. mktg. Internat., 1979-81, v.p., internat. sales, 1981-83; v.p. comml. mktg. internat. Douglas Aircraft Co., McDonnell Douglas Corp., 1983-89; mng. dir. GPA Asia Pacific, El Segundo, Calif., 1989-90; exec. v.p. GATX Air Group, San Francisco, 1990-95, pres., 1995-98, chmn., dir. adv. bd., 1998—; chmn., dir. adv. bd. GATX Capital Corp., San Francisco, 1998—; pres. Hickerson Assocs., 1998—. Bd. govs. Keck Ctr. for Internat. Strategic Studies; mem. Calif. Export Adv. Council. Served to lt. (j.g.) USCGR, 1960-62. H.B. Earhart Found. fellow, 1962. Mem. Internat. Assn. Charter Airlines (exec. com. 1971), Pacific Union Club, San Francisco Yacht Club, San Francisco Founders Club, Am. One, St. Francis Yacht Club.

HICKEY, BERNARD J., bank executive; b. Jan. 6, 1942. BA, St. Ambrose Coll., 1963. Sr. v.p., dir. Camp Grove (Ill.) State Bank, 1968—; dir. Camp Grove Bancorp, 1980—. Address: 608 E Swords Dr Edelstein IL 61526

HICKEY, DAMON DOUGLAS, library director; b. Houston, Tex., Oct. 30, 1942; s. Thomas Earl and Ethel Elizabeth (Place) H.; m. Mary Lyons Temple, May 27, 1967; 1 child, Doralyn Temple Hickey Edwards. BA, Rice U., 1965; MDiv, Princeton (N.J.) Theol. Sem., 1968; cert. in clin. pastoral care, Inst. of Religion, Houston, 1969; MSLS, U. N.C., 1975; MA, U. N.C., Greensboro, 1982; PhD, U. S.C., 1989. Assoc. pastor First Presbyn. Ch., Irving, Tex., 1969-71, Southminster Presbyn. Ch., Oklahoma City, Okla., 1971-72; pastor First Presbyn. Ch., Moore, Okla., 1971-72; catalog librarian U. N.C., Chapel Hill, 1972-73; acting curator rare books Duke U., Durham, N.C., 1973-74; assoc. libr. dir. Guilford Coll., Greensboro, N.C., 1975-91, curator Friends Hist. Collection, 1980-91; dir. libr. Coll. Wooster, Ohio, 1991—; mem. Libr. Adv. Coun., OhioLINK; adj. asst. prof. history Guilford Coll., 1990-91. Author: Sojourners No More: The Quakers in the New South, 1895-1920, 1997; editor jour. The Southern Friend, 1983-91; contbr. chpts. to books, articles, book reviews to profl. jours. Chair fund distbn. com. United Way Wooster, 1998-99. Mem. ALA, Ohio Acad. History, Assn. Coll. and Rsch. Librs. (mem. exec. com. coll. librs. sect.), Orgn. Am. Historians, So. Hist. Assn., N.C. Friends Hist. Soc. (bd. dirs. 1977-91), Friends Hist. Assn., Hist. Soc. N.C. (elect), Phi Alpha Theta, Beta Phi Mu. Democrat. Religious Soc. Friends. Avocations: reading, baseball, choral music. Office: Coll of Wooster Libraries Wooster OH 44691-2364

HICKEY, DELINA ROSE, education educator; b. N.Y.C., Mar. 25, 1941; d. Robert Joseph and Marie (Ripa) H.; m. David Andrews; 1 child by previous marriage, Jon Robert. BS in Edn., SUNY, Oneonta, 1963; MA, Manhattan Coll., 1967; EdD in Counselor Edn. and Psychology, U. Idaho, 1971; postgrad., Harvard U., 1995. sch. tchr., counselor pub. schs., Westchester, N.Y., 1963-68; part-time instr. psychologist St. Thomas Aquinas Coll., Sparkhill, N.Y., 1971-72; asst. prof. edn. Nathaniel Hawthorne Coll., Antrim, N.H., 1972-75; mem. faculty Keene (N.H.) State Coll., 1975—, assoc. prof. edn., 1978-87, prof., coord. faculty, 1987—, interim dean profl. studies, 1887, v.p. student affairs, 1990—; mem. adv. council Title IV, 1979-82; fellow Nat. Ctr. Rsch. chin Vocat. Edn., 1984-85; assoc. in edn. Harvard U., 1984-85, Inst. Ednl. Mgmt., 1995. Contbr. articles to ednl. jours. Mem. N.H. Ho. of Reps., 1981-85; trustee Big Bros.-Big Sisters, Keene, 1978-80, Family Planning Svcs. S.W. N.H., 1976-85, Monadnock Family Svcs., 1995—; trustee Monadnock Hospice, 1994-96, also chmn. pers. com.; mem. N.H. Juvenile Conf. Com., 1976-81; bd. dirs. Cheshire Med. Ctr., 1996—; pres. bd. dirs. CHESCO. Grantee Marion Jasper Whitney Found. Mem. Nat. Assn. Student Pers. Adminstrs. (adv. com. region I, editor, chief Net Results electronic mag. 1997-99), Am. Vocat. Assn., New Eng. Assn. Tchrs. and Educators, New Eng. Rsch. Orgn., N.H. Order Women Legislators, N.H. Pers. and Guidance Assn., N.H. Assn. Student Pers. Adminstrs. (adv. bd.). Office: Keen State Coll Student Ctr Keene NH 03431

HICKEY, DENNIS WALTER, retired bishop; b. Dansville, N.Y., Oct. 28, 1914; s. Walter Morris and Aloysia (Sullivan) H. B.A., Colgate Univ., 1935; postgrad. St. Bernard's, 1941. Ordained priest Roman Catholic Ch., 1941; asst. pastor St. Mary's Ch., Auburn, N.Y., 1941-46; notary Diocesan Tribunal, Rochester, N.Y., 1946-61; pastor St. Theodore Ch., Rochester, 1961-68; consecrated bishop, 1968; aux. bishop Diocese of Rochester, 1968-89; pastor St. Thomas More Ch., Rochester, 1982-85; gen. mgr. Courier-Jour., 1985. Address: 415 Ames St Rochester NY 14611-1225

HICKEY, DIXIE MARIE, school system administrator; b. Little Rock, Mar. 23, 1940; d. Richard Glenville and Vera Marie Gill; m. Robert Franklin Hickey, Aug. 1, 1959; children: Evelyn Diane, Steven Marcus. AA, Motlow State C.C., 1974; BS, Middle Tenn. State U., 1977, postgrad., 1979-80; postgrad., U. Tenn., 1980-86, UCLA, 1990; MA in Spl. Edn., Calif. State U., Dominguez Hills, 1993. Tchr. King George County Sch. Dist., King George, Va., 1959; math data aide U.S. Navy, Dahlgren, Va., 1960-61; reading paraprofl. Tullahoma (Tenn.) City Schs., 1974-75; substitute tchr. Tullahoma City Schs., 1977; tchr. St. Paul the Apostle Sch., Tullahoma, Tenn., 1977-80; instrnl. aide Oak Ridge (Tenn.) City Schs., 1980-82; dir. spl. edn. Ridgeview Psych. Hosp., Oak Ridge, Tenn., 1982-86; learning handicapped specialist, dir. edn. Del Amo Hosp. Schs., Torrance, Calif., 1986-90; ednl. therapist Switzer Ctr. for Spl. Edn., Torrance, Calif., 1987-92; dir. edn., learning and severely handicapped specialist South Bay Children's Health Ctr., Redondo Beach, Calif., 1990-94; pvt. practice ednl. therapist, 1992-94; asst. dir. spl. edn., coord. spl. edn. programs Smith-Green West Allen Spl. Edn. Coop., Ft. Wayne, Ind., 1994—; condr. prosocial skills groups Acad. for Acad. and Individual Excellence, Torrance, 1992-94. Author: (with others) Intercultural Education in the Classroom, 1986. Tchr. Vietnamese resettlement, Oak Ridge, 1988; CPR instr. Am. Red Cross, Oak Ridge, Torrance, 1981-87. Mem. DAR, Coun. for Exceptional Children, Ind. Coun. Adminstrs. Spl. Edn., Colonial Dames XVII Century. Mem. Christian Ch. Avocations: nature, reading, crafts, sewing, genealogy. Home: 8207 Rockbrook Ct Fort Wayne IN 46825-7105 Office: MSD SW Allen County Schs Adminstrn Office 4824 Homestead Rd Fort Wayne IN 46804-5461

HICKEY, GREGORY JOSEPH, priest, educational administrator; b. Darby, Pa., Aug. 10, 1947; s. Joseph Thomas and Helen Gertrude (Lockard) H. BA, Temple U., 1973; MDiv, St. Charles Sem., 1979; MA, Villanova U., 1989. Ordained priest Roman Cath. Ch., 1979. Tchr. St. Patrick Grade Sch., Norristown, Pa., 1969-74; mem. ednl. testing staff Montgomery County I.U., Norristown, 1972-73, Phila. I.U., 1974-75; asst. pastor Ss. Simon & Jude Ch., Westtown, Pa., 1979-81, St. Augustine Ch., Bridgeport, Pa., 1981-82, St. Leo Ch., Phila., 1982-87; tchr. Cardinal Dougherty High Sch., Phila., 1987-88; campus minister Bishop Conwell High Sch., Levittown, Pa., 1988-90; dir. studies St. Hubert High Sch., Phila., 1990-91; tchr. Cardinal Dougherty High Sch., 1991-92; dir. guidance and psychology Roman Cath. High Sch., 1992-96; prin. Kennedy-Kenrick Cath. H.S., Norristown, Pa., 1996—. Mem. Nat. Assn. Secondary Sch. Prins., ASCD, Nat. Cath. Edn. Assn., Ancient Order Hibernians, Kappa Delta Pi. Republican. Avocations: music, theater, reading. Home: 3160 Gaul St Philadelphia PA 19134-4447

HICKEY, JAMES ALOYSIUS CARDINAL, archbishop; b. Midland, Mich., Oct. 11, 1920; s. James P. and Agnes (Ryan) H. J.C.D., Lateran U., Italy, 1950; S.T.D., Angelicum U., Italy, 1951; M.A., Mich. State U., 1962.

Ordained priest Roman Catholic Ch., 1946; sec. to Bishop of Saginaw, 1951-60; rector St. Paul Sem., Saginaw, Mich., 1960-68; aux. bishop Saginaw, 1967-69; chmn. bishops' com. on Priestly Formation, 1968-69; rector N.Am. Coll., Rome, 1969-74; bishop of Cleve., 1974-80, archbishop of Washington, 1980—; chancellor Cath. U. Am., 1980—; elevated to cardinal, 1988; mem. Ctrl. Com. for 1975 Holy Year, 1973-75; chmn. Bishop's Com. Pastoral Rsch. and Practices, 1974-77, Bishop's Com. for Doctrine, 1979-82; chmn. bd. trustees Basilica of the Nat. Shrine of Immaculate Conception, 1980—; chmn. Bishops' Com. Human Values, 1984-87; chmn. Bishop's Com. on N.Am. Coll., 1988-92, 94-97. Episc. advisor to Serra Internat., 1981-88; Episc. moderator Holy Childhood Assn., 1984-93; elected mem. Secretariat Synod of Bishops, 1991-94. Address: Archdiocese Washington Archdiocesan Pastoral Ctr PO Box 29260 Washington DC 20017-0260

HICKEY, JEROME EDWARD, investment company executive; b. Chgo., June 25, 1937; s. Matthew Joseph and Naomi (Pope) H.; m. Denise Coakley, May 20, 1967; children: J. Graham, Matthew, Elizabeth, George, Peter. BS in Econs., Coll. of the Holy Cross, 1959; MA in Philosophy, Boston Coll., 1964. Instr. Cranwell Sch., Lenox, Mass., 1964-66; acct. exec. Paine Webber, N.Y.C., 1966-68; v.p. Hickey & Co., Chgo., 1968-72, Ralph W. Davis, Chgo., 1972-75, Weeden & Co., Chgo., 1975-78; founder, pres. Jerome Hickey Assocs., Chgo., 1979-84; pres. No. Trust Brokerage, Chgo., 1984-87; sr. v.p. Stein Roe & Farnham, Chgo., 1988-93; sr. v.p., mng. dir. SEI Corp., Chgo., 1993-96; founder, mng. dir. Dearborn Ptnrs., Chgo., 1997—. Dir. Western Golf Assn., Golf, Ill., 1979—, chmn. exec. com., 1991-96; trustee St. Ignatius Coll. Prep., Chgo., 1988-93, chmn., 1990-93. Named Outstanding Young Man in Am., 1971. Mem. Knollwood Club (Lake Forest, Ill., dir. 1976-79), Bond Club Chgo. (dir. 1974-75), Econ. Club Chgo., Desert Forest Golf Club, The Boulders. Roman Catholic. Home: 1923 N Fremont St Chicago IL 60614-5016 Office: Dearborn Ptnrs 200 W Madison St Chicago IL 60606-3414

HICKEY, JOHN HEYWARD, lawyer; b. Miami, Fla., Dec. 18, 1954; s. Weyman Park Hickey and Alice Joan (Heyward) Brown. BA magna cum laude, Fla. State U., 1976; JD, Duke U., 1980. Bars: Fla. 1980, U.S. Dist. Ct. (so. dist) Fla. 1980, U.S. Dist. Ct. (mid. dist.) Fla. 1982, U.S. Ct. Appeals (5th cir.) 1982, U.S. Ct. Appeals (11th cir.) 1983, U.S. Supreme Ct. 1985. Trial lawyer Smathers & Thompson, Miami, 1980-85; trial lawyer Hornsby & Whisenand P.A., Miami, 1985—, ptnr., 1988; ptnr. Hickey & Jones, Miami, 1988—; lectr. securities litigation Internat. Assn. Fin. Planners, 1989, 90, Fla. Inst. CPAs, 1990, Flood Ins. Conf., Columbus, Ohio, 1991, Scottsdale, Ariz., 1992, Orlando, Fla., 1993; lectr. admiralty law, Fla. Bar, 1994. Contbg. author: Fla. Bar Jour., 1990. Interviewer of prospective undergrads. Duke U. Alumni Adv. Com., 1984—; arbitrator Miami Marine Arbitration Coun. Mem. ABA (litigation mgmt./econs. com. 1986—, comml. transactions and banking com. 1986—), Fla. Bar (chmn. grievance com. 1986-89, vice chmn. 1999—, lectr. Bridge the Gap seminars 1984-85, jud. evaluation com. 1985, chmn. 11th cir. fee arbitration com. 1991—, cert. civil trial lawyer 1990, lectr. admiralty law 1994, vice chair admiralty law com. 1997—), Dade County Bar Assn. (bd. dirs. 1998—, media rels. com. 1982-83, membership com. 1982-83, legal edn. com. 1983-84, cir. ct. com. 1983-84, dir. 1984-86, chmn. young lawyers sect. meetings and programs com. 1985-86, chmn. young lawyers sect. sports com. 1984-85, exec. com. 1985—, chmn. profl. arbitration subcom. 1986—, cert. of merit 1985, 88, 89, 91, 921, 93, bd. dirs. 1990-93, 97—, chmn. banking and corp. litigation com. 1990, 91, 92, chmn. civil litigation com. 1992-93, exec. com. 1992-93, treas. 1999—), Greater Miami C. of C., Coral Gables C. of C., Propellor Club of U.S. (Miami divsn.), Marine Coun. So. Fla. (bd. dirs.), Southeastern Admiralty Law Inst. (proctor), Maritime Law Assn., Miami Marine Arbitration Coun., Phi Beta Kappa. Office: Hickey & Jones PA 1401 Brickell Ave Ste 510 Miami FL 33131-3501

HICKEY, JOHN MILLER, lawyer; b. Cleve., June 4, 1955; s. Lawrence Thomas and Margaret (Miller) H.; m. Sharon Salazar, Aug. 4, 1984; children: Theodore James, John Salazar, Margaret Maureen. Student, U. Wales, U.K., 1975-76; BA, Tulane U., 1977; JD cum laude, Calif. We. Sch. Law, 1981; LLM in tax, NYU, 1982. Bar: Calif. 1981, N.Mex. 1983, U.S. Dist. Ct. N.Mex. 1983, U.S. Tax Ct. 1983, U.S. Ct. Appeals (10th cir.) 1983. Prodn. control mgr. Randall-Textron, Inc., Wilmington, Ohio, 1977-78; assoc. Montgomery & Andrews, Santa Fe, 1983-88; shareholder, dir. Compton, Coryell, Hickey & Ives, Santa Fe, 1988-93, Hickey & Ives, Santa Fe, 1993-97, Hickey & Johnson PA, Santa Fe, 1998—. Bd. dirs. Los Alamos (N.Mex.) Econ. Devel., Hospice Ctr., Inc., Santa Fe; sec. Inst. Water Policy Studies, Santa Fe. Republican. Roman Catholic. Avocations: bicycling, squash, reading. Home: 806 Camino Zozobra Santa Fe NM 87505-6101 Office: Hickey & Johnson 1660 Old Pecos Trl Ste H Santa Fe NM 87505-4768

HICKEY, JOHN THOMAS, retired electronics company executive; b. Chgo., Oct. 28, 1925; s. Matthew J., Jr. and Naomi (Pope) H.; m. Joanne R. Keating, Sept. 17, 1949; children: Kathleen Hickey Coakley, John, Michael, James, Roger. B.S. in Commerce, Loyola U., Chgo., 1948; M.B.A., U. Chgo., 1952. With Motorola Inc. (and subs.), 1943-96, gen. mgr. semicondr. div., 1955-58, asst. to pres., 1958-62, dir. long range planning, 1962-65, v.p. planning, 1965-70, v.p. finance, sec., 1970-74, sr. v.p., chief fin. officer, dir., 1974-84, exec. v.p., chief fin. officer, dir., 1984-86, chmn. fin. com., dir., 1986-96. Served with AUS, 1944-46. Mem. Skokie Country Club (Glencoe, Ill.), Ocean Forest Golf Club (Sea Island, Ga.), Sea Island Club. Home: 614 South Ave Glencoe IL 60022-1674 also: PO Box 31065 Sea Island GA 31561-1065

HICKEY, JOHN THOMAS, JR., lawyer; b. Evanston, Ill., July 9, 1952; s. John Thomas and Joanne (Keating) H.; m. Candis Bailey, July 7, 1979; children: Alison, Jack, Patrick, Claire, Matthew. AB, Georgetown U., 1974; JD, U. Chgo., 1977. Bar: Ill. 1977, U.S. Dist. Ct. (no. dist.) Ill. 1977, U.S. Ct. Appeals (7th cir.) 1977, U.S. Ct. Appeals (10th cir.) 1987. Assoc. Kirkland & Ellis, Chgo., 1977-83, ptnr., 1983—. Fellow Am. Coll. Trial Lawyers. Listed in Leading Ill. Attys. Office: Kirkland & Ellis 200 E Randolph St Fl 59 Chicago IL 60601-6609

HICKEY, JOSEPH MICHAEL, investment banker; b. Greensburgh Pa., June 6, 1940; s. Joseph Michael and Margaret (Nelson) H.; m. Suzanne Klempay, July 2, 1970. BS, Ind. U. Pa., 1963. Sales rep. 3M Co., St. Paul, Minn., 1967-69; account exec. Hornblower & Weeks, Hemphill, Noyes, Cleve., 1970-75; pres. Prescott, Ball & Turben, 1976-88; dist. chmn. Nat. Assn. Security Dealers, 1979-81; mem. mktg. com. SIA, N.Y.C., 1982-86, mem. regional firms com., 1989; chmn. bd. Carnegie Capital Mgmt. Co., Cleve., 1983-86; pres. J.W. Charles Group, 1988-90; chmn. Pierman Golf Co., North Palm Beach, Fla., 1991-92; pres. Greyfriar Capital Corp., North Palm Beach, Fla., bd. vis. U. Dallas Grad. Sch. of Mgmt., 1995—; bd. dirs. No. Trust Corp. Fla. Capt. U.S. Army, 1963-67. Mem. Kirtland Country Club (Willoughby, Ohio), Loxahatchee Club (Fla.), Castle Pines Golf Club (Castle Rock, Colo.), Lost Tree Club (Fla.).

HICKEY, KEVIN FRANCIS, healthcare executive; b. Bridgeport, Conn., June 20, 1951; s. Herbert Augustine and Anne Therese (Pisani) H.; m. Christine Marie Hackett, June 10, 1973 (div. 1978); m. Eileen Michael O'Gara, July 4, 1981; children: Frances, Augustine. AB, Harvard U., 1973; MHSA, U. Mich., 1976; JD, Loyola U., Chgo., 1984. Bar: Ill. 1984. Dir., office human resources Am. Hosp. Assn., Chgo., 1978-83; exec. v.p. First Health Assocs., Chgo., 1983-85; v.p., gen. counsel Metlife Healthcare Mgmt. Corp., St. Louis, 1985-88; sr. v.p. Lincoln Nat. Life Ins. Co., Ft. Wayne, Ind., 1988-92; regional v.p. Aetna Health Plans, Chgo., 1992-94; sr. v.p. ops. Aetna Health Plans, Hartford, Conn., 1994-96; pres. Health Plans of Am., Farmington, Conn., 1996-97; exec. v.p. Oxford Health Plans, Norwalk, Conn., 1997-98; prin. First Health Assocs., Avon, Conn., 1998—. Contbr. articles to profl. publs. Office: First Health Assocs 302 W Main St Avon CT 06001-3681

HICKEY, LEO J(OSEPH), museum curator, educator; b. Phila., Apr. 26, 1940; s. James J(oseph) and Helen Marie (Schwartz) H.; m. Judith McKendry, June 29, 1968; children: Geoffrey Alan, Damian Michael, Jason Alexander. B.S., Villanova U., 1962; M.A., Princeton U., 1964; postgrad., Rutgers U., 1963-65; Ph.D., Princeton U., 1967; M.A. (privatim), Yale U., 1983. Postdoctoral fellow NRC-Smithsonian Inst., Washington, 1966-69, assoc. curator, 1969-80; chmn. exhibits com. Natural History Mus., Smithsonian, 1973-75, curator, 1980-82; prof. geology Yale U., New Haven, Conn., 1982—; dir. Peabody Mus., Yale U., 1982-87; prof. biology Yale U., 1982-97; curator of paleobotany Peabody Mus. Nat. History; adj. prof. botany U. Md., College Park, 1981-85; adj. prof. geology U. Pa., Phila., 1982-86; past pres., pres., v.p. Yellowstone-Bighorn Rsch. Assn., Red Lodge, Mont., 1979-86; dir. Mus. of Am. Theatre, New Haven, 1983-87. Author: Stratigraphy and Paleobotany of Golden Valley Formation, 1977; co-author: The Great Dinosaur Mural, 1990; editor: (with D.W. Taylor) Origin, Early Evolution, and Phylogeny of the Flowering Plants, 1996. Recipient H.A. Gleason award N.Y. Bot. Gardens, 1977, Best Paper award Geol. Soc. Washington, 1981, Disting. Alumnus award Villanova U., 1982, Ann. Book award Dinosaur Soc., 1992; grantee Smithsonian Rsch. Found., 1972-76, Nat. Geog. Soc., 1979, 84, 85, NSF, 1984, 90, 92. Mem. Geol. Soc. Am., Bot. Soc. Am., AAAS, Paleontol. Soc. Democrat. Roman Catholic. Club: Morys (New Haven). Office: Peabody Mus Natural History PO Box 208118 170 Whitney Ave New Haven CT 06511-8902

HICKEY, PAUL ROBERT, anesthesiologist , educator; b. Corinth, N.Y.; s. William Joseph Hickey; m. Ann Marie Murphy, Oct. 9, 1956; children: Julia, Brendan, Claire, Connor, Meghan. BA cum laude, Yale U., 1966; MD, Columbia U., 1970. Diplomate Am. Bd. Anesthesiology, Nat. Bd. Med. Examiners; lic. physician, N.Y., Mass., Ohio. Surg. intern Columbia Presbyn. Med. Ctr., N.Y.C., 1970-71, asst. resident, 1971-72; resident anesthesia Mass. Gen. Hosp., Boston, 1978-80, fellow cardiac anesthesia svc., 1980-81; clin. and rsch. assoc. in surgery Nat. Heart and Lung Inst., NIH, Bethesda, Md., 1972-74; clin. fellow anesthesia Harvard Med. Sch., 1978-80, rsch. fellow anesthesia, 1980-81, instr. anesthesia, 1981-83, asst. prof., 1983-86, assoc. prof., 1986-96, prof. anaesthesia, 1996—, chair exec. com. dept. anesthesia, 1997—; staff physician emergency rm. St. Anne's Hosp., Fall River, Mass., 1974-78, Falmouth (Mass.) Hosp., 1974-78; asst. in anesthesia Children's Hosp. Med. Ctr., Boston, 1981-83; clin. assoc. in anesthesia, Mass. Gen. Hosp., 1981—; cons. in anesthesia Brigham and Women's Hosp., Boston, 1982—; assoc. in anesthesia The Children's Hosp., 1984-86, sr. associ. in anesthesia, 1986-92, anesthesiologist-in-chief, 1992—, chmn. physican orgn., 1998—; cons. cardiac anesthesia Project Hosp., Washington, 1984—; vis. prof. various univs., 1983—; chmn. anesthesia/intensive care subcom. Project Hope steering com. for Sino-Am. Children's Med. Ctr., 1990-93; assoc. examiner Am. Bd. Anesthesiology, 1988—, assoc. oral examiner, 1991—; lectr. various orgns., univs., hosps. Cons., editl. bd. Anesthesiology, 1981-91, Jour. Thoracic and Cardiovascular Surgery, 1984—, New Eng. Jour. Medicine, 1992—, Pediatric Rsch., 1994—; editl. bd. Jour. Cardiothoracic Anesthesia, 1986-92, Anesthesia and Analgesia, 1987-97; contbr. articles to profl. jours., chpts. to books. Grantee Janssen Pharmecutica, Inc., 1982-83, 85-88, NIH, 1985—, Mass. Humane Soc., 1982-83, Medasonics, 1990-91. Fellow Am. Acad. Pediatrics; mem. AAAS, Andrew G. Morrow Surg. Soc., Am. Soc. Anesthesiologists (com. on circulation 1983-85, com. on pediatric anesthesia 1992-94), Internat. Anesthesia Rsch. Soc., Soc. Cardiovascular Anesthesiologists (internat. affairs com. 1987—), Assn. Univ. Anesthetists, Soc. Pediatric Anesthesia, Soc. Acad. Anesthesia Chmn., Mass. Med. Soc. Office: Children's Hosp Anesthesia Dept 300 Longwood Ave Boston MA 02115-5724*

HICKEY, SHARON MARIE, middle school educator; b. Chgo., Dec. 23, 1970; d. Daniel J.and Mary A. (Jablonski) T.; m. Gregory M. Hickey; June 12, 1993; children: Megan Elizabeth, Sean Myers. BS in Elem. Edn. magna cum laude, Ball State U., 1992; MEd Reading Specialist, George Mason U., 1997. Reading, study skills coord. No. Va. C.C., Annandale, Va., 1992-94; reading, lang. arts educator Loudoun County Pub. Schs., Sterling, Va., 1994—; faculty advisor Helping Hands Club, Seneca Ridge Mid. Sch., Sterling, Va., 1992-94. Mem. Nat. Coun. Tchrs. of English, Kappa Delta Pi, Phi Mu.

HICKEY, SHIRLEY LOUISE COWIN, elementary education educator; b. Moscow, Idaho, Nov. 20, 1950; d. George Theodore and Shirley Phyllis (Stokes) Cowin; m. Leonard Arnold Hickey, Aug. 19, 1973 (div. Sept. 1994); 1 child, Alisa Hadley; m. Stephen S. Tellari, Aug. 1, 1998. BA, Mt. Holyoke Coll., 1973; MA, Gonzaga U., Spokane, Wash., 1977. Cert. tchr., Wash. Substitute tchr. Cen. Valley Sch. Dist. and West Valley Sch. Dist., Spokane, Wash., 1973-77; svc. rep. Pacific NW Bell Telephone, Seattle, 1978-83; substitute tchr. Tahoma Sch. Dist., Maple Valley, Wash., 1983-87, St. Anthony Sch., Renton, Wash., 1983-87, St. James Sch., Kent, Wash., 1983-87; elem. tchr. Cedar Valley Sch., Kent, 1987-93, tchr., 1996—; pvt. tchr. piano, 1983-93. Cellist Women in Music Internat., 1990-91; class agt. Mt. Holyoke Coll., South Hadley, Mass., 1972-89, class libr. chmn., 1989-92; bd. dirs. Cedar Valley PTA, Kent, 1989-90. Mem. Kent Edn. Assn. (bldg. rep. 1988-92, polit. action com. 1990-93, crisis team 1990-91, sec. 1992-93, pres. 1993-96), Music Tchrs. Nat. Assn., Wash. State Music Tchrs. Assn., Mt. Holyoke Alumnae Assn. (bd. dirs. 1990-93), Mt. Holyoke Coll. Club (western rep. 1987-90, com. chmn. 1990-93). Episcopalian. Avocation: music. Home: 12313 SE 280th St Kent WA 98031

HICKEY, WINIFRED E(SPY), former state senator, social worker; b. Rawlins, Wyo.; d. David P. and Eugenia (Blake) Espy; children: John David, Paul Joseph. BA, Loretto Heights Coll., 1933; postgrad. U. Utah, 1934, Sch. Social Service, U. Chgo., 1936; LLD (hon.) U. Wyo., 1991. Dir. Carbon County Welfare Dept., 1935-36; field rep. Wyo. Dept. Welfare, 1937-38; dir. Red Cross Club, Europe, 1942-45; commr. Laramie County, Wyo., 1973-80; mem. Wyo. Senate, 1980-90; dir. United Savs. & Loan, Cheyenne; active Joint Powers Bd. Laramie County and City of Cheyenne. Pub. Where the Deer and the Antelope Play, 1967. Pres., bd. dirs. U. Wyo. Found., 1986-87; pres. Meml. Hosp. of Laramie County, 1986-88, Wyo. Transp. Mus., 1990-92; chmn. adv. council div. community programs Wyo. Dept. Health and Social Services; pres. county and state mental health assn., 1959-63; trustee, U. Wyo., 1967-71, St. Mary's Cathedral, 1986—; active Nat. Council Cath. Women, Gov. Residence Found., 1991-93, Wyo. Transp. Mus., 1993—; chair Am. Heritage Assocs. of U. Wyo., 1992-96; com. chair Citizen of the Century State of Wyo., Am. Heritage Ctr., 1966—. Named Outstanding Alumna, Loretto Heights Coll., 1959, Woman of Yr. Commn. for Women, 1988, United Med. Ctr., Cheyenne, 1998, Legislator of Yr. Wyo. Psychologists Assn., 1988, Family of the Yr. U. Wyo., 1995, Person of Yr., United Med. Ctr., Cheyenne, Wyo., 1998. Mem. Altrusa Club (Cheyenne).

HICKINGBOTHAM, FRANK D., food product executive; b. 1936. With Nat. Investors Life Ins., 1959; prin. McGehee High School, 1958-61; pres., CEO FDH Entprs. Inc., 1970; founder TCBY Entprs. Inc., 1981-87, chmn., CEO, 1981-97. Office: TCBY Enterprises Inc 425 W Capitol Ave Ste 1200 Little Rock AR 72201-3409*

HICKINGBOTHAM, NANCY BENNETT, nursing case manager; b. Binghamton, N.Y., Aug. 10, 1957; d. William E. and Iris Lucille (Neild) Bennett; m. J. Mark Hickingbotham, Aug. 29, 1981. BS in Nursing, So. Conn. State U., New Haven, 1979. Staff nurse med.-surg. Hartford (Conn.) Hosp., 1979-81; vis. nurse Meriden (Conn.) Pub. Health Vis. Nurse Assn., 1981-85; med. rsch. nurse Hartford (Conn.) Hosp., 1985-93; case mgr. Conn. Cmty. Care Inc., Wethersfield, 1993—. Home: 35 Oakdale St Wethersfield CT 06109-1535 Office: Conn Cmty Care Inc 43 Enterprise Dr Bristol CT 06010

HICKMAN, BERT GEORGE, JR., economist, educator; b. Los Angeles, Oct. 6, 1924; s. Bert George and Caroline E. (Douglass) H.; m. Edythe Anne Warshauer, Feb. 9, 1947; children: Wendy Elizabeth, Paul Lawrence, Alison Diane. B.S., U. Calif.-Berkeley, 1947, Ph.D., 1951. Instr. Stanford U., 1949-51; research asso. Nat. Bur. Econ. Research, 1951-52; asst. prof. Northwestern, 1952-54; mem. sr. staff Council Econ. Advisers, 1954-56; research assoc. Brookings Instn., 1956-58, mem. sr. staff, 1958-66; prof. Stanford U., 1966-95, prof. emeritus, 1996—; vis. prof. U. Calif. at Berkeley, 1960, London Grad. Sch. Bus Studies, 1972-73, , Inst. Advanced Studies, Vienna, Austria, 1974, 1975, Kyoto U., 1977; NSF fellow Netherlands Economic Inst., Rotterdam, 1964-65; Ford Found. Faculty research fellow, 1968-69; mem. com. econ. stability Social Sci. Research Council, 1959-61, chmn., 1962-95; chmn. exec. com. Project Link, 1969—; hon. prof. U. Vienna, 1985—; chmn. Energy Modeling Forum working group on macroecon. impacts of energy shocks Stanford U., 1982-83; Am. coord. US-USSR program on econ.-math. macromodeling Am. Coun. Learned Socs., 1988-90. Author: Growth and Stability of the Postwar Economy, 1960, Investment Demand and U.S. Economic Growth, 1965, (with Robert M. Coen) An Annual Growth Model of the U.S. Economy, 1976; Editor: Quantitative Planning of Economic Policy, 1965, Econometric Models of Cyclical Behavior, 1972, Global International Economic Models, 1983, International Monetary Stabilization and the Foreign Debt Problem, 1984, International Productivity and Competitiveness, 1992; co-editor: Global Econometrics, 1983, Macroeconomic Impacts of Energy Shocks, 1987, Link Proceedings, 1991, 92, Studies in Applied Economics, Vol. 1, 1997; contbr. articles to profl. jours. Served with USNR, 1943-46. Vis. fellow Internat. Inst. Applied Systems Analysis, 1979, 80; resident fellow Rockefeller Found., 1989; named Hon. Prof. U. Vienna, Austria. Fellow Econometric Soc.; mem. Am. Econ. Assn. (chmn. census adv. com. 1968-71, tech. subcom. to rev. bus. cycle devels. 1962-68, nominating com. 1978-79, chmn. seminar on global modeling, conf. on econometrics and math. econs. 1975-83), Phi Beta Kappa, Phi Eta Sigma. Home: 904 Lathrop Dr Stanford CA 94305-1060 Office: Stanford U Dept Econs Stanford CA 94305

HICKMAN, CHARLES WALLACE, educational association administrator; b. Des Moines, Sept. 19, 1952; s. James Charles and Margaret Wallace (McKee) H.; m. Rebecca Ann Nyman, July 31, 1993; children: Matthew, Heidi. BBA, U. Iowa, 1974, MA, 1975. Economist U.S. Dept. Labor, Washington, 1976; project coord. Ind. U., Bloomington, 1977; dir. projects and svcs. Am. Assembly Collegiate Schs. Bus., St. Louis, 1978—. Office: AACSB 600 Emerson Rd Ste 300 Saint Louis MO 63141-6762

HICKMAN, CLEVELAND PENDLETON, JR., biology educator; b. Greencastle, Ind., Oct. 29, 1928; m. Ethel Rae Rickenbacher, Aug. 19, 1950; children: Andrew Richard, Diane Elaine. A.B., DePauw U., 1950; M.S., U. N.H., 1953; Ph.D. in Zoology (B.C. Elec. scholar), U. B.C., 1958. Fishery researcher U. Wash., Seattle, 1954-55; asst. prof. U. Alta., 1958-63, asso. prof., 1963-67; assoc. prof. biology Washington and Lee U., Lexington, Va., 1967-70, prof., 1970-93, prof. emeritus, 1993—. Author: (with L.S. Roberts) Animal Diversity, 1995, (with L.S. Roberts) Biology of Animals, 7th edit., 1998, (with L.S. Roberts and A. Larson) Integrated Principles of Zoology, 10th edit., 1997, A Field Guide to Sea Stars and Other Echinoderms of Galápagos, 1998, A Field Guide to Marine Molluscs of Galápagos, 1999, (with William S. Hoar) A Laboratory Companion for General and Comparative Physiology, 3d edit., 1983; contbr. numerous articles to profl. jours. Nat. Research Council Can. grantee, 1959-67; sr. research fellow, 1965-66; NIH grantee, 1962-65; NSF grantee, 1970-74. Office: Washington and Lee U Dept Biology Lexington VA 24450

HICKMAN, ELIZABETH PODESTA, retired counselor, educator; b. Livingston, Ill., Sept. 30, 1922; d. Louis and Della (Martin) Podesta; BE summa cum laude, Eastern Ill. State U.; MA, George Washington U., 1966; postgrad. U. Chgo., 1945, U. Va., 1964-66, (fellow) Northeastern U., 1967-68; EdD (Exxon Found. grantee, Raskob Found. grantee), George Washington U., 1979; m. Franklin Jay Hickman, Mar. 17, 1944 (dec.); children: Virginia Hickman Hellstern, Franklin. Tchr. public schs., Ill., Ohio, Va., Naples, Italy, 1944-64; dir. coll. transfer guidance Marymount Coll. of Va., Arlington, 1964-67, dir. Counseling Center, 1974-81, assoc. dean counseling and residence life, 1981-84; community counselor div. Mass. Employment Security, Newton, 1968-69; tchr. English conversation, Fuchu, Japan, 1969-73; placement dir., career counselor Coll. Great Falls (Mont.), 1973-74; assoc. researcher George Washington U., 1986; lectr. Far East divsn. U. Md., Fuchu, 1971-73; spl. adv. Internat. Ranger Camps, Denmark and Switzerland, 1974-81; spl. cons. Internat. Quaker Sch., Werkhoven, The Netherlands, 1959-63; mem. steering com. Pres.'s Com. on Employment of Handicapped, 1974-95. Vol., ARC, 1967-78, Family Services, 1954-75, White House Agy. Liaison, 1986—, Kennedy Ctr. Adminstrn., Washington, 1984—. Served with WAVES, 1943-44. Recipient Disting. Alumnus award Eastern Ill. U., 1984. Lic. counselor, Va. Mem. Brent Soc., Rose Soc. Potomac, Ill. Soc., Italian Am. Soc., Marymount Univ. Angels Soc., Women's Com. Nat. Symphony Orch., Washington Opera Guild, Delta Epsilon Sigma, Pi Lambda Theta. Roman Catholic. Home: 4708 38th Pl N Arlington VA 22207-2915

HICKMAN, FREDERIC W., lawyer; b. Sioux City, Iowa, June 30, 1927; s. Simeon M. and Esther (Nixon) H.; m. Katherine Heald, July 15, 1964; children: Mary Sanders, Sara Ridder. AB, Harvard U., 1948, LLB magna cum laude, 1951. Bar: Ill. 1951. Asso. firm Sidley & Austin, Chgo., 1951-55; partner firm Hopkins & Sutter, Chgo., 1956-71, 75-92, sr. counsel, 1993—; asst. sec. for tax policy Dept. Treasury, Washington, 1972-75; draftsman Ill. Income Tax, 1969; author and lectr. on taxation. Mem. Ill. Humanities Council, 1977-82; mem. Citizens Commn. on Public Sch. Fin., 1977-78; chmn. bd. trustees Am. Conservatory Music, 1980-90; pres. Nat. Tax Assn., 1989-90. Served with USN, 1945-46. Mem. ABA (chmn. com. on depreciation 1966-68, com. on capital formation 1976-78, coun. 1980-83, chmn. com. on tax structure and simplification 1991-92, Internat. Fiscal Assn. (dr. 1973-77), Am. Coll. Tax Counsel (regent 1989-92), Comm. Club (Chgo.), Union League (Chgo.), Mid-Day (Chgo.), Cliff Dwellers (Chgo.), Legal (Chgo., pres. 1980-81), Chikaming Country (Lakeside, Mich.) Club. Republican. Methodist. Home: 360 Green Bay Rd # 4E Winnetka IL 60093-4032 Office: Hopkins & Sutter 3 First National Plz Chicago IL 60602

HICKMAN, HUGH V., science educator, researcher; b. Washington, June 3, 1947; s. Jack Wallis Hickman and Mary Cecelia (Regar) McCoy; m. Kayoko K. Hickman, Dec. 30, 1997; 1 child, Hugh Yamato. BSEE, U. South Fla., 1984, PhD, 1989. Entrepreneur, 1969-80; vis. prof. elec. engring. U. South Fla., Tampa, 1989-90; vis. prof. computer sci. Eckerd Coll., St. Petersburg, Fla., 1990-91; prof. physics Hillsborough Community Coll., Tampa, 1991—. Contbr. articles to profl. jours. Mem. AAAS, IEEE, Am. Assn. Physics Tchrs., Am. Phys. Soc., Ye Mystic Krewe of Gasparilla, Phi Kappa Phi. Republican. Roman Catholic. Achievements include research into temporal dynamics. Home: 5010 W Dante Ave Tampa FL 33629-7513 Office: Hillsborough Community Coll PO Box 30030 Tampa FL 33630-3030

HICKMAN, J. KENNETH, accounting company executive; b. Bklyn., July 8, 1928; s. Walter E. and Mildred C. (Ehrhardt) H.; m Irene A. Davis, May 12, 1956; children: Patricia, Carolyn, Beth. B.S. cum laude, Fordham U., 1951. With Arthur Andersen & Co. CPAs, 1953-91, mng. ptnr. N.J. office, 1963-72, ptnr. N.Y. office, 1972-91; bd. dirs. Gunther Internat., Ltd. Trustee Fordham U., 1983—, Am. Irish Legal Rsch. and Edn. Found., Inc., 1995—. 1st lt. AUS, 1951-53. Mem. AICPA, U.S. Coun. for Internat. Bus., Nat. Com. Am. Fgn. Policy, Inc., Carnegie Coun. Ethics and Internat. Affairs, Bus. Coun. Internat. Understanding (dir. 1981-98), Fgn. Policy Assn. (gov. 1982-94, dir. 1984-94), Bus. Coun. for UN, Am. Coun. on Germany, Nat. Com. for U.S.-China Rels., Inst. Mgmt. Accts., Fordham U. Alumni Fedn. (nat. chmn. 1973-75), N.J. Soc. CPAs (trustee 1971-73), Ireland-U.S. Coun. for Commerce and Industry (trustee 1978-93, v.p. 1979-93), Am.-Irish Hist. Soc. (exec. coun. 1981—), Econ. Club N.Y., Beacon Hill Club, Alpha Kappa Psi, Beta Gamma Sigma. Home: 45 Templar Way Summit NJ 07901-3730 Office: Grubb & Ellis Inc 55 E 59th St New York NY 10022 *Never fold. Play every hand as it is dealt to you.*

HICKMAN, JAMES CHARLES, business and statistics educator, business school dean; b. Indianola, Iowa, Aug. 27, 1927; s. James C. and Mabel L. (Fisher) H.; m. Margaret W. McKee, June 12, 1950; children—Charles Wallace, Donald Robert, Barbara Jean. B.A., Simpson Coll., 1950; M.S., U. Iowa, 1952, Ph.D., 1961. Actuarial asst. Bankers Life Co., Des Moines, 1952-57; asst. prof. dept. statistics U. Iowa, 1961-64, asso. prof., 1964-67, prof., 1967-72; prof. bus. and statistics U. Wis., Madison, 1972-93; dean Sch. Bus. U. Wis., 1985-90; emeritus prof. and dean U. Wis., Madison, 1993—; Warren prof. U. Manitoba, 1990; Bowles prof. George State U., 1996; mem. panel of cons. on social security fin. Senate Fin. and House Ways and Means Com., 1975-76; mem. adv. com. to Joint Bd. for Enrollment of Actuaries, 1976-78; mem. Actuarial Standards Bd., 1985-92; dir. Century Investment Mgmt. Co. Mem. bd. dirs. Blue Cross and Blue Shield United of Wis.; bd. pensions Presbyn. Ch. in U.S.A., 1989-95. With USAAF, 1945-47. Recipient Alumni Achievement award Simpson Coll., 1979, David Halmstad award for actuarial rsch. Actuarial Edn. Rsch. Fund, 1979, 81, Disting. Alumni Achievement award U. Iowa, 1993. Fellow Soc. Actuaries (v.p. 1975-77, bd. govs. 1971-74, 91-94); mem. Soc. Actuaries Found. (bd. dirs. 1994—), Casualty Actuarial Soc., Am. Acad. Actuaries (Jarvis Farley award for svc.), Am. Statis. Assn., Swiss Assn. Actuaries (corr. mem.), Beta Gamma Sigma (bd. govs. 1988-92). Presbyterian. Home: 4917 Woodburn

Dr Madison WI 53711-1347 Office: U Wis Sch Bus 975 University Ave Madison WI 53706-1324

HICKMAN, JANET SUSAN, college administrator, educator; b. Bklyn., Aug. 28, 1948; d. Richard and Frances J. (Falconer) Liberth; m. C. Kennedy Hickman, June 21, 1970; 1 child, Kennedy R. BSN cum laude, U. Bridgeport, 1970; MS, No. Ill. U., 1976; EdD, Temple U., 1987. RN, Ill., Ohio, Pa., Del., N.Y. Instr. St. Joseph Hosp., Joliet, Ill., 1974-77, Wright State U., Dayton, Ohio, 1977-78; asst. prof. Neumann Coll., Aston, Pa., 1979-81; assoc. dean health professions Ea. Coll., St. Davids, Pa., 1982-92; coord. grad. program, prof. West Chester (Pa.) U., 1992—. Author: (with others) Nursing Theories, 4th edit., 1995, Mental Health and Psychiatric Nursing, 1992, Health Assessment in Nursing, 1995; contbr. articles to profl. jours. Mem. APHA, Temple U. Alumni Assoc., Sigma Theta Tau. Home: 1435 Clover Ln West Chester PA 19380-5906 Office: West Chester Univ Dept Nursing West Chester PA 19383

HICKMAN, JOHN NORWOOD, marketing executive; b. Sept. 1, 1964. BS in Agrl. Econs., N.C. State U., 1986; MBA, Coll. William & Mary, 1992. Dealer credit mgr. Wachovia, Burlington, N.C., 1986-90; regional mktg. dir. AMF, Atlanta, 1992-93; COO/mgr. E.S. Mktg. Co-op, Melfa, Va., 1993-96; mgr. specialty food products VESCorp, Belle Haven, Pa., 1996—. E-mail: bontemp@shore.intercom.net. Home: Box 8 Melfa VA 23410

HICKMAN, MAXINE VIOLA, social services administrator; b. Louisville, Miss., Dec. 24, 1943; d. Everett and Ozella (Eichelberger) H.; m. William L. Malone, Sept. 5, 1965 (div. 1969); 1 child, Gwendolyn. BA, San Francisco State U., 1966; MS, Nova U., 1991; postgrad., Calif. Coast U., 1991—. Lic. State of Calif. Dept. Social Svcs. IBM profl. mechanic operator Wells Fargo Bank, San Francisco, 1961-65; dept. mgr. Sears Roebuck & Co., San Bruno, Calif., 1966-77; adminstr. Pine St. Guest House, San Francisco, 1969-88; fin. planner John Hancock Fin. Svcs., San Mateo, Calif., 1977-81; chief exec. officer Hickman Homes, Inc., San Francisco, 1981—; cons. BeeBe Meml. Endowment Found., Oakland, Calif., 1990—, Calif. Assn. Children's Home-Mems., Sacramento, 1989—. Mem. NAACP, San Francisco. Named Foster Mother of Yr., Children's Home Soc. Calif., 1985, Woman of Yr., Gamma Nu chpt. Iota Phi Lambda, 1991. Mem. Foster Parents United, Calif. Assn. Children's Homes, Nat. Bus. League, Order of Ea. Star, Masons (worthy matron), Alpha Kappa Alpha. Democrat. Baptist. Avocations: singing, walking, interior design, real estate. Office: Hickman Homes Inc 67 Harold Ave San Francisco CA 94112-2331

HICKMAN, PATRICIA, artist, craftswoman. BA, U. Colo., 1962; MA in Design and Textiles, U. Calif., Berkeley, 1977. Prof., head fiber program art dept. U. Hawaii at Manoa, Honolulu. One-woman shows U. Hawaii, 1991, Contemporary Mus., Honolulu, 1995-96, Banker Gallery, San Francisco, 1996, San Francisco Craft and Folk Art Mus., 1998-99; exhibited in Kanezawa, Japan, 1982, Kassel, Germany, 1982, Savaria Mus., Szombathely, Hungary, 1984, Lausanne, Switzerland, 1985, Maya Behn Gallery, Zurich, Switzerland, 1985, Gelerie de Sluis, Leidschendam, The Netherlands, 1984, Copenhagen, 1986, Kyoto, Japan, 1987, N.D. Mus. Art tour in Far East, 1988-90,Bradford, Eng., 1990, Philharm. Gallery, Liege Belgium, 1991-93, Am. Embassy, Warsaw, Poland, 1991-93, Africa tour, 1992-94; represented in permanent collections Contemporary Mus., Honolulu, State Found. Culture and Arts, Honolulu, Honolulu Acad. Art, Ark. Arts Ctr., Little Rock, Am. Craft Mus., N.Y.C., Erie (Pa.) Art Mus., Oakland (Calif.) Mus., Wadsworth Atheneum, Hartford, Conn., Savaria Mus., Smithsonian Instn., Washington, also corp. collections; commd. by Maui Arts and Cultura Ctr., Kahului, Hawaii, 1991-94; contbr. essays to exhbn. catalogs; work represented in various publs. Individual artist grantee Nat. Endowment for Arts, 1986-87, 94-95; individual artist visual arts fellow Hawaii State Found. on Culture and Arts, 1998. *

HICKMAN, RICHARD LONNIE, advertising executive; b. Atlanta, Oct. 18, 1950; s. Lonnie C. and Dean (Wilder) H.; m. Margaret Mary Capellini, Nov. 6, 1982; children: Wilder Anthony, Langdon Bond. BA, U. S.C., 1973, MA, 1973. V.p. mktg. Mowbray Pub., Providence, 1977-80; pres. Indianhead Advt., Gloucester, Mass., 1980-87; v.p., dir. prodn. Barry Blau & Ptnrs., Fairfield, Conn., 1987-89; pres. Oxford Direct, Boston, Va., 1990-92; v.p. new bus. NAIM, Fredericksburg, Va., 1993-94, exec. v.p., 1994; v.p. DiMark Va., 1994-95; dir. market devel. Harte-Hanks Direct Mktg., Fredericksburg, 1995-97, sr. cons., 1997-98; mgr. Kinko's, Fredericksburg, 1998—; Vietnam War Vet. Author: The Four Color Primer, 1983, The Direct Mail Package from Hell, 1989, Credit Card Retention in a Shark's Feeding Frenzy, 1994; inventor in field. Active Rep. Nat. Com. Sgt. U.S. Army, 1969-71. Named Eagle Scout. Mem. Direct Mktg. Assn., Direct Mktg. Assn. Washington, Internat. Platform Soc., Ednl. Funding Group (chair 1992—), Am. Legion, VFW. Republican. Episcopalian. Avocations: gardening, cooking, hunting, fishing. Home and Office: 10717 Wellington St Fredericksburg VA 22407-1272

HICKMAN, R(OBERT) HARRISON, political pollster, strategist; b. Whiteville, N.C., Feb. 10, 1953; s. Robert Raymond and Marietta (Harrison) H.; m. Caroline Isabelle Mesrobian, Aug. 15, 1981; 1 child, Ralfe Harrison. AB, Guilford Coll., 1975; MA, U. Nebr., 1977; postgrad., Tulane U., 1978, U. Mich., 1979. V.p. Hamilton & Staff, Inc., Chevy Chase, Md., 1980-84; ptnr. Hickman-Brown Rsch., Inc., Washington, 1984—; adj. prof. George Washington U., Washington, 1993—; election cons. CBS News, N.Y.C., 1982—. Disting. Alumni lectr. Guildford Coll., Greensboro, N.C., 1987; named most valuable pollster 1986 elections, U.S. News & Report, 1986; recipient Good Guy award Nat. Women's Polit. Caucus, 1987, Alumni Excellence award Guilford Coll., 1991; named Best in the Bus., Cable News Network Inside Politics, 1988. Mem. Am. Assn. Polit. Cons., Am. Assn. Pub. Opinion Rsch., Am. Polit. Sci. Assn., Kenwood Country Club (Bethesda, Md.). Democrat. Methodist. Avocations: golf, reading. Home: 3828 Gramercy St NW Washington DC 20016-4226 Office: Hickman-Brown Rsch Inc 1350 Connecticut Ave NW Ste 206 Washington DC 20036-1739

HICKMAN, RUTH VIRGINIA, Bible educator; b. Sac City, Iowa, Oct. 15, 1931; d. Ronald Minor and Ida E. (Willcutt) Wilson; m. Charles Ray Hickman, Aug. 25, 1962; children: Ronald Everett, Lisa Michelle. BS in Home Econs., Morningside Coll., 1953. Ordained to ministry Christian Ch., 1985. Instr. Nat. Ednl. TV, 1964-76; staff coord., tchr. Life for Layman, Denver, 1974-77; founder, tchr. Abundant Word Ministries, Lakewood, Colo., 1980—; tchr. Bible Calvary Temple, Denver, 1980—; sales/trainer Hillestad Internat., Woodruff, Wis., 1978—; Women's com. Billy Graham Assn., Denver, 1986-87. Author: (book) Hope for Hurting People, 1987; speaker, instr. audio and video tape series, 1980—. Leader pilgrimages to Israel, 1984, 87, 94, 96, 98. Mem. Rocky Mountain Fellowship Christian Leaders. Republican. Home: 3043 S Holly Pl Denver CO 80222-7010 Office: Abundant Word Ministries 6900 W Alameda Ave Ste 106 Lakewood CO 80226-3312

HICKMAN, TERRIE TAYLOR, administrator; b. Rapid City, S.D., Dec. 2, 1962; d. William Adrian and Carolyn Gene (Habben) T.; children: Matthew, Kalie. BS, Okla. State U., 1985; MEd, Cen. State U., 1988. Cert. elem tchr., presch. tchr., Okla. Mktg. dir. Tealridge Manor, Edmond, Okla., 1989-90; owner Oxford Pointe Jazzercize, Edmond, Okla., 1989-90; adminstr. Retirement Inn at Quail Ridge, Oklahoma City, Okla., 1991-92, Country Club Square, Edmond, 1992-93; planner Areawide Aging Agency, Oklahoma City, 1992-97; mem. adv. coun., co-chmn. Okla. Bus. and Aging Leadership Coalition, newsletter Networker editor; presenter in field; adv. coun. sr. companion planning com. State of Okla. Conf. on Aging; mem. Oklahoma City Reading Coun. Co-editor Sage Age; contbr. articles to various pubs. Co-chmn. media hosting party Olympic Festival, Norman, Okla., 1989; co-coord. jazzercize for hope Benefit for Hope Ctr., Edmond, The McGruff Safe House Program, Stillwater, Okla.; com. chmn. Coalition for Elderly Concerns, Oklahoma City; vol. Stillwater Domestic Violence Shelter, Payne County Employment Svcs., Stillwater; mem. renter's adv. bd. Okla. State U. Student Senate. Mem. ASCD, Women in Bus., Edmond Area C. of C., Okla. Bus. and Aging Leadership Coalition, Phi Kappa Delta, Alpha Gamma Delta, Sigma Phi Omega, Kappa Delta Pi. Republican. Lutheran. Avocation: biking.

HICKMAN, TRAPHENE PARRAMORE, library director, storyteller, library and library building consultant; b. Dallas, Jan. 31, 1933; d. Redden Travis and Stella (Moore) P.; m. John Robert Hickman, June 9, 1950; children—Lynn Kleifgen, Laurie Ward. A.A., Mountain View Community Coll.; B.A., U. Tex-Arlington; M.L.S., U. North Tex. Cert. librarian, Tex. Librarian Cedar Hill Pub. Library, Tex., 1959-77; dir. Dallas County Library System, Dallas, 1977-93; libr. cons. Dallas County, 1993-95; chair leadership coun. and family ministries IUMC of Cedar Hill. Editor: History and Directory of Cedar Hill, 1976; editor News and Views newsletter Dallas county Employees, 1986-92. Chmn. Bicentennial Com., Cedar Hill, 1976; del. Dem. Nat. Conv. 9th Senate Dist., Tex., 1976; chmn. Sesquicentennial Com., Cedar Hill, 1984-86; Dallas County Dem. Forum; mem. Electoral Coll., 1988; chairperson Women's Bd. Northwood Inst., Cedar Hill; active Dallas County Sesquicentennial Com., 1996—. Recipient Newsmaker of Yr. award Cedar Hill Chronicle, 1976; named Ambassador of Goodwill, State of Tex., 1976. Mem. ALA, Tex. Libr. Assn. (legis. com. 1984-95, councillor 1982-83, trustee com. 1987-95, pub. info. com. 1987-95), Pub. Libr. Adminstrs. of North Tex. (sec., v.p., pres. 1980, 87), Dallas County Libr. Assn., N.E. Tex. Libr. Sys. (legis. commn. 1978-95, Libr. of Yr. 1987), U. North Tex. Sch. Libr. and Info. Scis. Alumni Assn. (pres. 1987-88), Cedar Hill C. of C., Cedar Summit Book Club (officer), Dallas Area Storytelling Guild (pres. 1995—). Democrat. Methodist. Avocations: writing, reading, storytelling, gardening, bridge, travel, square dancing. Home and Office: 421 Lee St Cedar Hill TX 75104-2697

HICKOK, EUGENE W., state agency administrator; m. Katharine Pauley; 2 children. Tchr. polit. sci. Dickinson Coll., 1980—, adj. prof. Dickinson Sch. Law; spl. asst. Office of Legal Counsel U.S. Dept. Justice, 1986, 87; sec. Edn. Commonwealth of Pa. Dept. Edn., Harrisburg, 1995—; dir. Clarke Ctr. Interdisciplinary Study of Contemporary Issues. Mem. Carlisle Area Sch. Bd. Adj. scholar Heritage Found. Office: Commonwealth of Pa State Dept Edn 333 Market St Harrisburg PA 17101-2210*

HICKOK, GLORIA VANDO, publisher, editor, poet; b. N.Y.C., May 21, 1936; d. Erasmo Vando and Anita Velez-Mitchell; m. Maurice Peress, July 2, 1955 (div. Sept. 1980); children: Lorca, Paul, Anika; m. William H. Hickok, Oct. 4, 1980. Student, NYU, 1951-56, U. Amsterdam, The Netherlands, 1953-54; BA, Tex. A&I U., 1975; postgrad., L.I. U., 1982-83. Ednl. ombudsman Mayor's Spl. Sch. Task Force, N.Y.C., 1969-70; ednl. cons. Youth Diversion project City of Kansas City (Mo.) Mayor's Office, 1977-79; pub., editor Helicon Nine Editions, Kansas City, 1977—; exec. dir. Ctrl. Exch., Kansas City, 1980; contbg. editor N.Am. Rev., Cedar Falls, Iowa, 1996—; mem. adv. bd. Mo. Ctr. for the Book, Jefferson City, Mo., 1993-95; mem. lit. panels Nat. Endowment for Arts, Washington, 1991, 94; bd. BkMk Press, U. Mo., Kansas City, 1998—. Author: (poems) Promesas: Geography of the Impossible, 1993 (Thorpe Menn Book award 1994), Shadows and Supposes, 1998 (Alice Fay DiCastagnola award); editor, pub.: Spud Songs: Anthology of Potato Poems, 1999. Pres., founder Midwest Ctr. for Lit. Arts, Inc., Kansas City, 1991-96; bd. dirs., co-founder Writers Pl., Kansas City, 1991; trustee, arts chair Clearinghouse for Midcontinent Found., Kansas City, 1988-90; pres. N.W. Dible Found., Shawnee Mission, Kans., 1998—. Editors grantee Coord. Coun. Lit. Mags., 1986; poetry fellow Kans. Arts Commn., 1989; recipient Billee Murray Denny prize for poetry, 1991, Gov.'s Arts award State of Kans., 1991. Mem. PEN Internat., poetry Soc. Am., Acad. Am. Poets, Coun. Lit. Mags. and Presses, Mo. Citizens for Arts. Avocation: photography. E-mail: helicon9@aol.com. Office: Helicon Nine Editions 3607 Pennsylvania Kansas City MO 64111

HICKOK, RICHARD SANFORD, retired accountant; b. Elizabeth, N.J., Nov. 3, 1925; s. Ernest Sherlock and Amy (McFadden) H.; m. Janet E. Allsopp, Sept. 24, 1948; children: Sanford, Steven, Jonathan, Wendy. B.S. in Econs, U. Pa., 1948. C.P.A., N.Y., other states. With firm KMG Main Hurdman, N.Y.C., 1948—, ptnr., 1958—, mem. policy bd., 1971—, mng. ptnr., 1975—, chmn., 1980-83; pres. Klynveld Main Goerdeler (internat. firm), 1981-83, ret., 1983; chmn. Hickok Assocs., Inc., 1989—; bd. dirs. Marsh & McLennan Cos., Comstock Resources, Inc., Projectavison, Inc. Contbr. articles to profl. jours. Trustee Fin. Accounting Found., 1978-80. Served to lt. (j.g.) USNR, 1943-47. Mem. AICPA (coun.), N.Y. State socs. CPAs, Nat. Assn. Corp. Dirs., Am. Arbitration Assn. Clubs: Univ. (N.Y.C.), Eastward Ho. Home: 36 Cockle Way Brewster MA 02631-1149*

HICKS, ALLEN MORLEY, hospital administrator; b. Toronto, Iowa, May 11, 1928; s. Perle and Grace (Mowry) H.; m. Sue Hicks; children by previous ma rriage: David, Dennis, Wendy, Patricia. Student, Long Beach City Coll., 1949-50; B.S., U. Iowa, 1952, M.S., 1954. Adminstrv. resident St. Lukes Hosp., Davenport, Ia., 1953-54; adminstr. Schmitt Meml. Hosp., Beardstown, Ill., 1954-57, Pekin (Ill.) Meml. Hosp., 1957-63, Ill. Masonic Hosp. and Med. Center, Chgo., 1963-72; pres. Community Hosp., Indpls., 1972-84, Meth. Health Care Systems, Memphis, 1984-85, VHA Enterprises, 1985-90; adminstr. Midwest Med. Ctr., Indpls., 1991-93; sr. advisor St. Vincent's Hosp. and Health Care Corp.; chmn. bd. Vol. Hosps. Am., 1980-84, Multi-Mut. Ins. Cos. of Bermuda and Cayman Islands; bd. dirs. Am. Coll. Testing, Ind. Blue Cross, Am. Health Capital, Indpls. Conv. Ctr.; preceptor masters degree program in health and hosp. adminstrn. U. Iowa; chmn. com. extended care Coun. on Assn. Svc., 1963; pres. Chgo. Hosp. Coun., 1970-71. Campaign chmn., bd. dirs., chmn. indsl. div. United Fund, Pekin, Ill., 1959-64; pres. Tazwell County United Cerebral Palsy, 1960-61; chmn. Cancer Crusade, Pekin, 1960-61; service chmn. Tazewell County, 1958-60; chmn. bd. Tomahawk dist. Creve Coeur council Boy Scouts Am., 1963-64, bd. dirs. Crossroads council; bd. dirs. Cancer Soc., Hosp. Research and Devel. Inst., Inc.; pres. Meth. Health Systems Memphis, 1984-85. H. Served with USNR, 1945- 49, 51-52. Recipient Outstanding Young Man of Year award State Ill., 1960; Distinguished Service award Pekin Jr. C. of C., 1960; Boss of Year award Marquette chpt. Nat. Secs. Assn., 1962. Fellow Am. Coll. Health Adminstrn.; mem. Am. Hosp. Assn. (del. 1971—, chmn. com. community relations), Ill. Hosp.Assn. (trustee, chmn. com. personnel relations), Am. Coll. Hosp. Adminstrs., Am. Assn. Maternal and Infant Health, Ill. Welfare Assn., Ill. C. of C., Am. Legion, Am. Vets., 500 Assn., Beta Gamma Sigma. Presbyterian (elder, trustee). Clubs: Mason, Elks, Kiwanis (bd. dirs. Internat. Found. 1981-85, pres. local chpt. 1983). Office: St Vincents Hosp PO Box 40970 2001 W 86th St Indianapolis IN 46260-1902

HICKS, BETHANY GRIBBEN, judge, lawyer, commissioner; b. N.Y., Sept. 8, 1951; d. Robert and DeSales Gribben; m. William A. Hicks III, May 21, 1982; children: Alexandra Elizabeth, Samantha Katherine. AB, Vassar Coll., 1973; MEd, Boston U., 1975; JD, Ariz. State U., 1984. Bar: Ariz. 1984. Pvt. practice Scottsdale and Paradise Valley, Ariz., 1984-91; law clk. to Hon. Kenneth L. Fields Maricopa County Superior Ct. S.E. dist., Mesa, 1991-93; commr., judge pro tem Maricopa County Superior Ct. Ctrl. and S.E. Dists., Phoenix and Mesa, 1993-99, judge domestic rels. and juvenile divsns., 1993-99; magistrate Town of Paradise Valley, Ariz., 1993-94; judge Maricopa County Superior Ct., 1999—. Mem. Jr. League of Phoenix, 1984-91; bd. dirs. Phoenix Children's Theatre, 1988-90; parliamentarian Girls Club of Scottsdale, Ariz., 1985-87, 89-90, bd. dirs., 1988-91; exec. bd., sec. All Saints' Episcopal Day Sch. Parents Assn., 1991-92, pres., 1993-94; active Nat. Charity League, 1995—, Valley Leadership Class XIX, 1997-98; vol., Teach for Am., 1997—. Mem. ABA, State Bar Ariz., Maricopa County Bar Assn., Ariz. Women Lawyers' Assn. (steering com. 1998—). Republican. Episcopalian. Club: Paradise Valley Country. Office: 1810 S Lewis St Mesa AZ 85210-6234

HICKS, C. FLIPPO, lawyer; b. Fredericksburg, Va., Feb. 24, 1929; s. Robert A. and Nell (Jones) H.; m. Patricia DeHardit (dec. 1983); children: Robert, Patricia Shull, J. Flippo (dec. 1995), Paula Mooradian. BS in Commerce, U. Va., 1950, LLB, 1952. Bar: Va. 1952, U.S. Supreme Ct. 1955. Asst. atty. gen. Commonwealth of Va., Richmond, 1953-59; ptnr. Martin, Hicks, Ingles, Ltd., Gloucester, Va., 1959-91; gen. counsel Va. Assn. Counties, Richmond, 1991—; bd. dirs., v.p. Williamsburg (Va.) Nat. Bank, 1965-75; bd. dirs. 1st Va. Bank, Commonwealth Williamsburg. Presdl. elector 1968, 76, 80; pres. exec. coun. Episcopal Diocese of Va., 1970-71, mem. standing com., 1971-74. Fellow Am. Bar Found.; mem. ABA (Leader of Yr. award Gen. Practice Sect., Constbar Leader of Yr. 1992), Va. State Bar (pres. 1990-91). Democrat. Episcopalian. Avocations: gardening, college sports. Office: Va Assn Counties Old City Hall 10th and Broad Sts Richmond VA 23234

HICKS, C. THOMAS, III, lawyer; b. N.Y.C., Sept. 14, 1945; s. Charles Thomas and Jeane (Merritt) H.; m. Susan Massie, Dec. 30, 1967 (div. Dec. 1997); children: Melissa, Merritt. BSCE, Va. Tech. U., 1967; JD, U. Ga., 1970; LLM in Tax, Georgetown U., 1975. Bar: Ga. 1970, Va. 1972, D.C. 1981. Assoc. Boothe, Prichard & Dudley, Fairfax, Va., 1975-78; ptnr. Wickwire, Gavin & Gibbs, P.C., Vienna, Va., 1978-83, Shaw, Pittman, Potts & Trowbridge, McLean, Va., 1983-98, Greenberg Traurig, McLean, 1998—; gen. counsel Wolf Trap Found. Performing Arts, 1998—. Judge advocate USMC, Washington, 1971-75; co-founder, dir. No. Va. Transp. Alliance, McLean, Va., 1987, gen. counsel, 1987—. Mem. Va. Bar Assn. (mem. bus. law coun.), Va. State Bar (bus. law sec. bd. governors, chmn.), Fairfax Bar Assn., Nat. Assn. Bond Lawyers, Va. Assn. Comml. Real Estate (pres., co-founder, dir.), NAIOP (pres., dir. Va. chpt. 1990), No. Va. Tech. Coun. (dir., gen. counsel 1996—), Greater Washington Bd. Trade, Fairfax County C. of C. (dir. 1998—). Avocations: sailing, tennis, golf. Home: 6443 Madison McLean Dr McLean VA 22101 Office: Greenberg Traurig 1750 Tysons Blvd Fl 12 Tysons Corner VA 22102-3823

HICKS, CADMUS METCALF, JR., financial analyst; b. Hagerstown, Md., Dec. 21, 1952; s. Cadmus Metcalf Sr. and Marie Elizabeth (Keefauver) H.; m. Elizabeth Ann Dressel, May 31, 1980; children: Liza, Alethea, Cadmus III. BA, Wheaton (Ill.) Coll., 1974; MA, U. Chgo., 1976; PhD, Northwestern U., Evanston, Ill., 1980. Chartered fin. analyst. Rsch. analyst John Nuveen & Co. Inc., Chgo., 1980-85, asst. v.p., 1985-90, v.p., 1990—, asst. mgr. rsch. dept., 1993-96, mgr. rsch. dept., 1996—. Author: (with others) The Municipal Bond Handbook, 1983; contbr. articles to profl. jours. Mem. Nat. Fedn. of Mcpl. Analysts (bd. govs. 1991-93), Chgo. Mcpl. Analysts Soc. (pres. 1991-92), Investment Analysts Soc. of Chgo., Assn. for Investment Mgmt. and Rsch. Republican. Office: 333 W Wacker Dr Chicago IL 60606-1220

HICKS, CECILIA PERKINS, editor; b. Lincolnton, N.C., Apr. 2, 1974. BS, Appalachian State U., 1996. Income maintenance caseworker Dept. Social Svcs., Lenoir, 1998; reporter Lenoir (N.C.) News-Topic, 1996-98, lifestyles editor, 1998—. Email: Ntnews@btwave.net. Office: 123 Pennton Ave Lenoir NC 28645

HICKS, CLAUDE W., JR., federal judge; b. 1945. BA, Furman U., 1967; JD, Mercer U., 1970. Pvt. law practice Macon, Ga., 1970-86; magistrate judge U.S. Dist. Ct. (mid. dist.) Ga., 1983—. Served with U.S. Army, 1974-75. Office: US Courthouse 475 Mulberry St Macon GA 31201-3385

HICKS, DOLORES KATHLEEN (DE DE HICKS), association executive; b. Mount Vernon, Iowa, Sept. 22, 1932; d. Edward M. and Olga Marie (Hekl) Staskal; m. Roswell Allen Hicks, Sept. 5, 1952; children: Thomas, Gregory, Bryan, Kevin. Student, Colo. Coll., 1950-52. Exec. women's wardrobe cons. Bullock's, Torrance, Calif., 1985-86; exec. dir. The Vol. Ctr., Torrance, 1986—; pres. Vol. Ctrs. So. Calif., 1988; coord. First Lady of Calif. Outstanding Vol. Awards, Sacramento, 1993; nat. bd. dirs. Vol. Ctrs.-Points of Light Found., Washington, 1993-96. Pres. LWV, Palos Verdes Peninsula, Calif., 1981-83; chair Year of the Coast, Calif. LWV, Sacramento, 1984; active in state and local polit. campaigns. Named YWCA Woman of the Yr., YWCA, Torrance, 1986, Woman of Distinction, Soroptimist, Torrance, 1988. Mem. Pvt. Industry Coun. (bd. mem. 1994-97), Cmty. Assn. of the Peninsula (life, pres. 1984-87, Palos Verdes Peninsula Citizen of Yr. 1987, Outstanding Vol. award 1988), So. Bay Prodrs. Guild (Outstanding Interviewer 1995), Vol. Ctrs. of Calif. (bd. mem. 1988—, Founders award 1991), Gamma Phi Beta (alumni mem., Internat. Carnation award 1992, Achievement award 1993). Democrat. Roman Catholic. Avocations: gourmet cooking, home decorating, entertaining, reading, traveling.

HICKS, DONALD W., SR., councilman; b. Mar. 15, 1951. BBA, U. Houston, 1976; JD cum laude, Tex. So. U., 1979; postgrad., So. Meth. U.. Broker Tex. Real Estate, 1981-94; assoc. tax atty. Office Chief Counsel-IRS, Office of Regional/Dist. Counsel, San Francisco & Dallas; city councilman Dist. 5 Dallas City Coun., 1992—; pvt. practice law, mediator. Author (lecture series 2000) Vision of Dallas' Future, 1994. Commr. Dallas County Sheriff's Civil Svc. Commn.; exec. dir. North Ctrl. Tex. Coun. Govts.; vice chmn. Dallas/Ft. Worth Regional Film Commn.; chmn. Minority/Women-Owned Bus. Enterprises Com. Recipient Dallas Black Chamber Quest for Success award, 1991, Cmty. and Econ. Devel. award Oak Cliff Bible Fellwship, Juanita Craft Legal award NAACP-Dallas, A. Maceo Smith Legal award NAACP-Regional. Mem. Tex. Assn. Black City Coun. Mems. (bd. dirs.), Nat. League Cities (mem. cmty. and econ. devel. steering com.), Dallas Bar Assn., JL Turner Legal Soc. (Pres. award 1986), Greater Dallas C. of C. Office: 1500 Marilla St Rm 5fn Dallas TX 75201-6300*

HICKS, DOROTHY JANE, obstetrician and gynecologist, educator; b. Cleve., Apr. 18, 1919; d. Arnell R. and Marvel M. (Hale) H. AB, Case Western Reserve U., 1941; MD, Temple U., 1944. Diplomate Am. Bd. Obstetrics and Gynecology. Asst. prof. dept. ob-gyn. U. Miami, 1967-85, prof., 1985—; bd. dirs. rape treatment ctr. Jackson Meml. Hosp., Miami, med. dir., 1974-93, cons., 1993—; dir. pedigyn clinic Jackson Meml. Hosp. Contbr. articles to profl. jours. Fellow Am. Coll. Ob-Gyn., N.Am. Soc. Pediatric and Adolescent Gynecology, South Atlantic Ob-Gyn. Soc., Fla. Soc. Ob/Gyn, Miami Ob/Gyn Soc. Avocations: dog training, golf. Office: U Miami Sch Medicine Dept Ob-Gyn PO Box 16960 Miami FL 33101-6960

HICKS, GEORGE WILLIAM, automotive and mechanical engineer; b. Ypsilanti, Mich., Jan. 15, 1948; s. Troy Diamond Sr. and Clara (Sehl) H.; m. Carol Ann Kohorst, Aug. 5, 1967; children: Lorelei Lynn, Dawn Marie, Heather Nicole. BSME, U. Mich., 1977. Registered profl. engr., Mich; ACTAR cert. traffic accident reconstructionist; cert. OSHA safety instr.; diplomate Am. Bd. of Forensic Engring. and Tech. Test and devel. engr. Chrysler Corp., Chelsea, Mich., 1976-81; sr. engr. Alexander Proudfoot Co., Chgo., 1981; mech. engr. Polytechnic, Lincolnwood, Ill., 1981-82; mgr. tech. svcs. Shackson Assocs., Ann Arbor, Mich., 1982-84; forensic engr. Joscelyn & Treat, Ann Arbor, 1984-86; staff cons. Packer Engring., Troy, Mich., 1986-90; owner, prin. cons. Ingenium Engring. Svcs., Rochester Hills, Mich., 1990—; cons. Backplane Tech., Clinton, 1984-86, Shackson Assocs., Ann Arbor, 1984-86; spkr. ADED Midwest Conf., Cleve., 1992. Author: Anatomy of an Instrumented Generic Quadriplegic Evaluation Van, 1993, Safety Standards and the Rehabilitation Vehicle, 1991; editor: Roll Over Protective Structures Manual, 1989, Safety Belt Components manual (Internal Distribution), 1992-94. Mem. ASME, NSPE, Nat. Mobility Equipment Dealers Assn., Engring. Soc. Detroit, Assn. Driver Educators for the Disabled, Mich. Assn. Traffic Accident Investigators, Soc. Automotive Engrs., Nat. Fire Prevention Assn., Am. Welding Soc., Internat. Assn. Arson Investigators. Office: Ingenium Engring Svcs 3889 Mildred Ave Rochester Hills MI 48309

HICKS, GREGORY STEVEN, marketing professional; b. Ft. Wayne, Ind., Dec. 24, 1959; s. Earl Hoyt and Sarah Helen (Bobo) H.; m. Nita Dawn Noblitt, Nov. 9, 1985. BS in Fin., Ind. U., 1983; MBA, U. Indpls., 1995. Asst. v.p. Fidelity Fed. Savs. and Loan, Seymour, Ind., 1983; fin. dir. Devel. Svcs., Columbus, Ind., 1983-85; account coord. Devel. Services, Columbus, Ind., 1985-86; exec. dir. Jennings County Econ. Devel., North Vernon, Ind., 1986-88; dir. Columbus (Ind.) Econ. Devel. Bd., 1989-91; mgr. nat. devel. PSI Energy, Plainfield, Ind., 1992-95; acct. mgr. comml. and indsl. sales PSI Energy, Plainfield, 1995-97; strategic mktg. rep. Cinergy Power Mktg. and Trading, Cin., 1997-98, mgr. retail aggregation, 1998; v.p. mktg. and bus. devel. Gaylor, 1998—. Active Assn. for Retarded Citizens, North Vernon, 1983-86, Jennings County Econ. Devel., 1985-88; head coach Hayden Elem. Girls and Boys Basketball, North Vernon, 1984-86; sec. bd. dirs. Jennings Community Hosp. Found., 1987-88. Mem. South Cen. Savs. and Loan League (v.p. 1983), Kiwanis (treas. local chpt. 1985-86, pres. 1987-88, lt. gov. 1991-92), Kappa Delta Rho (bd. dirs. 1984-92). Home and Office: 565 Persimmon Dr North Vernon IN 47265-6730

HICKS, HAROLD EUGENE, chemical engineer; b. Mpls., Jan. 20, 1919; s. Julius and Della (Beebe) H.; m. Ruth Esther Nelson, Oct. 4, 1941 (dec. Mar. 1989); children: Barbara H. Young, Charlotte H. Silvia, David H., Douglas E.; m. Virginia C. Hobson, Mar. 31, 1990. B Chem. Engring., U. Minn., 1941; postgrad., U. Del., 1946-47. Chemist Hercules Powder Co., Wilmington, Del., 1941, rsch. chemist, 1941, 46-50; prodn. supr. Hercules Powder Co., Hattiesburg, Miss., 1950-64; plant mgr. Hercules Powder Co., Chicopee,

Mass., 1964-66; plant mgr. Hercules Inc., Franklin, Va., 1966-68, Brunswick, Ga., 1968-76, Louisiana, Mo., 1978-80; tech. advisor Dawood-Hercules, Lahore, Pakistan, 1976-78; vol. exec. Internat. Exec. Svc. Corp., 1986-94; pres. The Book Shop, Inc., Brunswick, 1991—; bd. dirs. Downtown Devel. Authority, Brunswick. Mem. county cos. Glynn County; dir. St. Mark's Towers, Glynn-Brunswick Navy League of the U.S., Pine Belt Savings & Loan Assn, Hattiesburg, Miss., 1958-64, dir., 1st Nat. Bank of Brunswick, Ga., 1969-76. Maj. U.S. Army, 1941-46, ETO. Mem. AIChE (emeritus), Am. Chem. Soc. (emeritus), Rotary. Methodist. Avocations: computers, photography, travel, reading, gardening. Home: 133 Shore Rush Dr Saint Simons GA 31522

HICKS, IRLE RAYMOND, retail food chain executive; b. Welch, W.Va., Dec. 21, 1928; s. Irle Raymond and Mary Louise (Day) H. B.A., U. Va., 1950. Bus. mgr. Hicks Ford, Covington, Ky., 1952-58; acct. Firestone Plantations Co., Harbel, Liberia, 1958-60; auditor Kroger Co., Cin., 1960-66; gen. auditor Kroger Co., 1966-68, asst. treas., 1968-72, treas., 1972—. Bd. dirs. Old Masons' Home Ky. Served with AUS, 1950-52. Mem. Fin. Execs. Inst., Bankers Club, Alpha Kappa Psi, Phi Kappa Psi. Episcopalian. Clubs: Mason, Cincinnati. Home: 454 Oliver Rd Cincinnati OH 45215-2507 Office: 1014 Vine St Cincinnati OH 45202-1141

HICKS, JACK ALAN, library director; b. Ft. Dodge, Iowa, Sept. 14, 1939; s. Thomas D. and Calma J. (Voss) H.; m. Donna Marie Westervelt; children: Maren Lydia, Sarah Marie. BA, Hamline U., 1967; MLS, Rosary Coll., 1972. Librarian Deerfield (Ill.) Pub. Libr., 1972—; vice chair Joint Computer Program for Librs., Skokie, Ill., 1988—; spkr. in field. Contbr. articles to profl. publs. Mem. adv. bd. Coll. of Lake County, Highland Park, Ill., 1988-95; fundraiser Girl Scouts U.S., Moraine Coun., 1975—. Sgt. U.S. Army, 1961-65. Mem. ALA, Ill. Libr. Assn., Ch. and Synagogue Libr. Assn., Deerfield C. of C., Pi Gamma Mu. Episcopalian. Avocations: motorcycles, kayaking.

HICKS, JIM, secondary education educator. Tchr. Physics Barrington (Ill.) H.S. Recipient Innovative Teaching and Secondary Sch. Physics award, 1992. Office: Barrington HS 616 W Main St Barrington IL 60010-3099*

HICKS, JOHN BERNARD, internist; b. Deer Lake, Nfld., Can., Aug. 22, 1933; came to U.S., 1960; s. William Francis and Mary Esther (Dalton) H.; m. Bernice Elizabeth Algee; children: Ann Elizabeth, Joan Marie, Cathie, John Bernard, Carolyn Andrea. BS, St. Francis Xavier U., Antigonish, N.S., 1953; MD, Dalhousie U., 1958. Intern Dalhousie Affiliated Hosps., 1957-58; gen. practice, 1958-59; resident in pathology Regina (Sask.) Hosp., 1959-60; resident in internal medicine Baylor Coll. Medicine Affiliated Hosps., Houston, 1960-62, fellow in renal and hypertensive diseases, 1962-63; pvt. practice Houston, 1964—; assoc. clin. prof. Baylor Coll. Medicine, U. Tex. Med. Sch., Houston; attending physician Meth. Hosp., St. Luke's Episcopal Hosp., St. Anthony's Ctr. Mem. Am. Soc. Internal Medicine, Tex. Med. Soc., Houston Soc. Internal Medicine (pres. 1988), Harris County Med. Soc. (chmn. splty. coun. 1990, exec. com. 1990, med. grievance com. 1993, ethics com. 1994-96). Roman Catholic. Home: 2111 Mcclendon St Houston TX 77030-2109 Office: Med Clinic Houston 1707 Sunset Blvd Houston TX 77005-1713

HICKS, JUDITH EILEEN, nursing administrator; b. Chgo., Jan. 1, 1947; d. John Patrick and Mary Ann (Clifford) Rohan; m. Laurence Joseph Hicks, Nov. 22, 1969; children: Colleen Driscoll, Patrick Kevin. BSN, St. Xavier Coll., Chgo., 1969, U. Ill., Chgo., 1975. Staff nurse Mercy Hosp., Chgo., 1969-70, nursing supr., 1970-73; cons. continuing edn. Ill. Nurses Assn., Chgo., 1974-75; dir. ob-gyn. nursing Northwestern Meml. Hosp., Chgo., 1975-81; v.p. nursing Children's Meml. Hosp., Chgo., 1981-86; pres. Children's Meml. Home Health, Inc., 1986—, Children's Meml. Nursing Svcs., 1986—; pres. Allied & Children's Home Health and Nursing Services, 1988, CM Healthcare Resources, Inc., 1988—, The Pediatric Place, Inc., 1994—; dir. Near North Health Corp., Chgo., 1982-85; pres. Pediatric Excellence Program Svc.; bd. dirs. Infant Welfare Soc. Chgo., Nat. Breast Cancer Assn. Recipient Jonas Salk Leadership award March of Dimes, 1998. Mem. Am. Soc. Nursing Adminstrs., Women's Health Exec. Network (1984-85), Ill. Hosp. Assn. (chmn. coun. on nursing 1982-83), Inst. Medicine. Home: 2206 Beechwood Ave Wilmette IL 60091-1508 Office: CM Health Care Resources Ste 200 1000 Sunset Ridge Rd Northbrook IL 60062-4010

HICKS, LESLIE ELIZABETH, museum curator; b. Brunswick, Ga., Jan. 27, 1965; d. Edward Arthur and Elizabeth Jean (Sullivan) Snow; m. Charles Andrew Hicks, Sept. 17, 1988; children: Shelby Andrew, Frances Elizabeth. BS, Presbyn. Coll., Clinton, S.C., 1987. Interpretive ranger Hofwyl-Broadfield Plantation Ga. Dept. Natural Resources, Brunswick, 1987-90; curator of edn. mus. divsn. Jekyll Island (Ga.) Authority, 1990—. Mem. Ga. Assn. Museums and Galleries, Southeastern Museums Conf. (local arrangements com., transp. chair 1996). Democrat. Presbyterian. Office: Jekyll Island Authority Mus Divsn 381 Riverview Dr Jekyll Island GA 31527-0874

HICKS, M. ELIZABETH (LIZ HICKS), pharmacist; b. Shawnee, Okla., Aug. 16, 1944; d. Joseph Robert and Betty Ruth (Thomas) Coughlin; m. Frank Jack Hicks, July 16, 1965 (dec. 1978); 1 child, Felicia Jeanette. BS, Okla. U., 1967. Lic. pharmacist. Pharmacy intern Liberty Drug, Chickasha, Okla., 1967-68; pharmacist St. Francis Hosp., Wichita, Kans., 1968, Hart Drug, Wichita, 1968-70; pharmacist, dir. Home Drug/PrePrep Med. Div., Wichita, 1970-82; pharmacist, mgr. Revco Drug, Wichita, 1982-87; pharmacist Gessler's Drug, Wichita, 1987—, pharmacist in charge, 1994-95; author, presentor continuing edn. programs for nursing home adminstrs., dental technicians, nurses, nurses aides, and pharmacists. Author, presentor: Women You'll Wish You Had Known, Parts 1 and 2. Mem. Commn. on the Status of Women, Wichita Housing Authority, 1989-91; precinct committeewoman Dem. Ctr. Com., Sedgwick County, Kans., 1984—; co-chair Woman Fair, Wichita, 1985; chair Sedgwick County Coun. on Aging, Wichita, 1982-83; mem. Wichita-Sedgwick County Bd. Health, 1992-96, chmn. 1996; pres.-elect Kans. Employee Pharmacists Coun., 1997, pres. 1998. Recipient Wichita NOW Trophy, 1991. Mem. Wichita Acad. Pharmacists (pres. 1983-84), Kans. Pharmacists Assn. (chair PAC 1986-89), Am. Pharm. Assn., NOW (pres. Wichita Chpt. 1981-82, state coord. 1988-90). Avocations: travel, reading mysteries, performing as Women from History. Home: 5233 W 1st N Wichita KS 67212-2402

HICKS, MARILYN SUE, lay worker; b. Clarksville, Tenn., Mar. 21, 1949; d. Roy Davis and Ada La Una (Powers) Wright; m. James Ray Hicks, July 5, 1970; children: Jason, Susan, Stephen. Student, Trevecca Nazarene Coll., Nashville, Ind. U., 1991—. Dir. children's ministries Grace Ch. of Nazarene, Nashville, 1971-72, Bloomington 1st Ch. of the Nazarene, 1995—; youth dir. 1st Ch. of Nazarene, Bloomington, Ind., 1988—, sec., del., 1989—. Author: (songs) I Want to Be More Like You, 1990; The Land That I Love, 1992; I Just Want To Be, 1992; contbr. articles to profl. jours. Mem. Nazarene World Mission Soc. (treas. S.W. Ind. Dist. 1990-95, S.W. Ind. dist. mission pres. 1998—). Home: 1105 E Allendale Dr Bloomington IN 47401-8708 Office: 1st Ch of Nazarene 700 W Howe St Bloomington IN 47403-2233 *I always look at the positives in life and smile at whatever comes my way. God has given us each day, and if we dwell on the negatives, we will miss what He wants to give us.*

HICKS, MARION LAWRENCE, JR. (LARRY HICKS), lawyer; b. Bethlehem, Pa., Sept. 5, 1945; s. Marion Lawrence and Martha (McCracken) H.; m. Beverly Brickman, Nov. 28, 1970; children: Yale McCracken, Hadley Brook, Kelley Hayden. BA History, Duke U., 1967; JD with honors, U. Tex., 1970. Bar: Tex. 1970. Law clerk 9th cir. U.S. Ct. Appeals, L.A., 1970-71; assoc. Thompson, Knight, Simmons & Bullion, Dallas, 1971-77; ptnr., shareholder Thompson & Knight, Dallas, 1977—; speaker in field. Editor Tex. Law Review; contbr. articles to profl. jours. Mem. ABA (real property, trust and probate sect.), Am. Coll. Mortgage Attys., State Bar Tex., Dallas Bar Assn. (past chmn. real property sect., legal aid and legal svcs. com.), Tex. Acad. Real Estate, Probate and Trust Lawyers (founding mem.), Coll. State Bar Tex., Order of Coif, Tower Club (bd. govs.), Phi Delta Phi. E-mail: Hicks, L.@TKLaw.com. Avocations: sports, hunting, fishing. E-mail: hicksl@tkla.com. Home: 3915 Prescott Ave Dallas TX 75219-2240 Office: Thompson & Knight 1700 Pacific Ave Ste 3300 Dallas TX 75201-4693

HICKS, NORM, airport operations executive; b. 1941. BBA, Golden Gate U., 1964; postgrad., U.S. Naval Postgrad. Sch., 1971. Exec. dir., COO Mohave County Airport Authority, Bullhead City, Ariz. Office: Mohave County Airport Auth 600 Highway 95 Bullhead City AZ 86429-5007*

HICKS, NORMAN WILLIAM, physical science educator; b. Middletown, Conn., Apr. 1, 1949; s. Irving and Marjorie (Gastler) H.; m. Charlene Ann Serra, June 19, 1971; 1 child, Meredith. BS, Ea. Conn. State Coll., 1971; MS, Ctrl. Conn. State Coll., 1978; 6 year diploma, So Conn. St. U., 1988. Lab. asst., lab. instr. Middlesex Cmty. Coll., Middletown, Conn., 1968-71; tchr. Center Sch., East Hampton, Conn., 1971-72; sci. tchr. Baldwin Mid.Sch., Guilford, Conn., 1972—; cons. Xerox Edn. Publs., Middletown, 1973-75. Vice chmn. Regional Sch. Dist. 13 Bd. Edn., Durham, Conn., 1996—, chmn. policy dist. 13, 1996—; chmn. curriculum devel. com. Guilford Bd. Edn., 1993—; bd. dirs. Durham Fair Found., 1994—; vice chmn. Zoning Bd. Appeals, Durham, 1983-89; bd. dirs. Guilford Cmty. TV, 1974-80; treas. Dem. Town Com., Durham, 1982—. Fellow Inst. Sci. Instrn. & Study; mem. Nat. Sci. Tchrs. Assn., Guilford Edn. Assn., Nat. Sci. Tchrs. Assn., Assn. Conn. Fairs. Democrat. Episcopalian. Avocations: skiing, woodworking, technology. Home: PO Box 554 Durham CT 06422-0554

HICKS, PHYLLIS ANN, medical, surgical nurse; b. Croghan, N.Y., July 4, 1935; d. Leonard B. and Doris A. (Schack) Bush; m. Patrick Clare, Aug. 1, 1953 (dec. Jan. 1976); m. Charles L. Hicks, May 26, 1979; children: Michael Clare, Maureen (dec.), Martin (dec.); stepchildren: Lynn, Melinda, Kevin. ADN, St. Elizabeth's Hosp., Utica, N.Y., 1988; cert. pharmacology, Bd. Coop. Ednl. Svcs., Verona, N.Y., 1989, phlebotomy cert., 1994; student, Mercy Hosp. Sch. Nursing, Watertown, N.Y., 1952-53. RN, N.Y. Nurse med.-surg. unit Rome (N.Y.) Murphy Meml. Hosp., 1988-90; head nurse geriatrics Stonehedge Nursing Home, Rome, N.Y., 1990; nurse I Mohawk Valley Psychiatric Ctr., Utica, N.Y., 1990-91; charge nurse ventilator unit Oneida (N.Y.) City Hosp., 1993—. Home: 10276 State Route 26 Ava NY 13303-2213 Office: Oneida Health Care Assn 321 Genesee St Oneida NY 13421-2699

HICKS, ROBERT RUIZ, JR., army officer; b. Tampa, Fla., Oct. 12, 1943; s. Robert Ruiz Sr. and India Elizabeth (Gormley) H.; m. Judy Ann Smith, June 18, 1966; children: Robert Ruiz III, Richard Ryan. BS, U.S. Mil. Acad., 1966; M of Ops. Rsch., Tulane U., 1973. Commd. 2d lt. U.S. Army, 1966, advanced through grades to maj. gen., 1995; asst. dir. compensation Office of Sec. of Def., Washington, 1987-89; comdr. div. arty., 8th inf. div. U.S. Army Europe and 7th Army, 1989-91, chief staff 8th inf. div., 1991-92, chief reduction br., dep. chief of staff for ops., 1992, asst. div. comdr. 1st armored div., 1992-93; chief staff I Corps, Ft. Lewis, Wash., 1993-94; dep. dir. for assessment J8 The Joint Staff, Washington, 1994-95; comdr. JTF-Olympics, Atlanta, 1995-96; comdg. gen. U.S. Army, Japan and 9th Taacom, 1996-98; dir. programs, analysis and evaluation U.S. Army Office of Chief of Staff, Washington, 1998—. Decorated DDSM, Legion of Merit, DFC, Bronze Star medal with V device, Purple Heart, Air medal with 3 V devices, Army Commendation medal with V device. Office: Chief of Staff 200 Army Pentagon Washington DC 20310-0200*

HICKS, SHERMAN GREGORY, pastor; b. Bklyn., June 22, 1946; s. Charles Sr. and Sarah Mae (Rollins) H.; m. Anna Marie Peck, Sept. 12, 1970 (div.); children: Andrea, Geoffrey, Christopher. BA, Wittenberg U., 1968; MDiv, Hamma Sch. Theology, 1973; DD (hon.), Carthage Coll., 1988, Elmhurst Coll., 1989, Wittenberg U., 1990. Ordained to ministry Luth. Ch., 1973. Pastor Concordia Luth. Ch., Buffalo, 1973-77; co-pastor Holy Trinity Luth. Ch., East Orange, N.J., 1977-79; asst. to bishop Ill. Synod, Luth. Ch. Am., Chgo., 1979-87; bishop Met. Chgo. Synod, Evang. Luth. Ch. in Am., Chgo., 1988-95; sr. pastor First Trinity Luth. Ch., Washington, 1996—. Pres. Interfaith Coun. for Homeless, Chgo., 1988, AIDS Nat. Interfaith Network, 1991; trustee Carthage Coll., Kenosha, Wis., 1988, Nat. AIDS Fund, 1997; bd. dirs. Luth. Social Svcs. Ill., 1988-95, Bethphage, Omaha; mem. Coun. Religious Leaders, Chgo., 1988-95; bd. dirs. Leadership Coun. for Met. Open Cmty. Named One of Outstanding Young Men in Am., Jaycees, 1974; recipient Alumni Citation, Wittenberg U., 1993. Office: First Trinity Luth Ch 309 E St NW Washington DC 20001-2711 *In my experiences with life I have discovered that there are three very basic questions that we humans have the need to know answers for: (1) Who am I? (2) For what purpose am I here? (3) What am I going to do? Within the context of our faith we can find the answers.*

HICKS, STEVE L., artist, art educator; b. Fayetteville, Ark.; s. Shelby and Lucie H.; m. Cynthia B., March, 1970; children: Jessica, Spencer. BA, U. Ky., 1969; MA, Murray State U., 1972; MFA, U. Ark., 1975. Instr. art La. State U., Eunice, 1978-80; assoc. prof. art, chair art divsn. Okla. Bapt. U., Shawnee, 1980—; adv. conservationist Mabee-Gerver Mus., Shawnee, 1985—. Mem. Coll. Art Assn. Office: Okla Bapt U Art Divsn #61197 500 University Shawnee OK 74804

HICKS, SUSAN LYNN BOWMAN, small business owner; b. Flint, Mich., Mar. 24, 1952; d. Richard and Carol Joanne (Haney) Bowman; m. Duane James Hicks, Aug. 6, 1977. BA, U. Mich., Flint, 1975; MA, Cen. Mich. U., 1981. Med. social worker Flint Osteo. Hosp., 1974-77; dir. med. social work and patient rels. Crittenton Hosp., Rochester, Mich., 1978-89; coord. geriatric social work Genesys Regional Med. Ctr., 1990—; owner, Susan Hicks Enterprises, 1988—; mgmt. tng. and devel. cons. Buick, Oldsmobile, Cadillac div. GM, Grand Blanc, Mich., 1985. Bd. dirs., chmn. com. Rochester Area Youth Guidance, Mich., 1986, chmn., 1988; bd. dirs. E. ctrl. Mich. chpt. Alzheimer's Assn., 1994. Mem. Soc. for Hosp. Social Work Dirs. (Recognition award 1984, 85, pres.-elect 1985-86, pres. 1986-87, chmn. polit. and social action com. 1988—), Nat. Assn. Social Workers, NAFE, Soc. Patient Representatives. Methodist. Avocations: tap dancing, writing. Home and Office: 8201 Sawgrass Trl Grand Blanc MI 48439-1874

HICKS, TERRELL COHLMAN, surgeon, educator, health facility administrator, academic administrator; b. Seminole, Okla., 1949. MD, U. Tex., 1977. Diplomate Am. Bd. Surgery, Am. Bd. Colon and Rectal Surgery. Intern U. Louisville, 1977-78, resident in surgery, 1979-82; fellow in colon and rectal surgery Ochsner Clinic, New Orleans, 1982-83, now surgeon, assoc. chmn. dept. colon and rectal surgery, program dir. CRS tng. fellowship program; assoc. clin. prof. surgery Sch. Medicine La. State U. Mem. AMA, Am. Soc. Colon and Rectal Surgery (treas.), So. Med. Assn. Office: Ochsner Clinic 1514 Jefferson Hwy New Orleans LA 70121-2483

HICKS, THOMAS O., buyout firm executive, professional baseball team executive; b. N.Y.C., 1946. BBA, Univ. of Tex., 1968; MBA, Univ. So. Cali., 1970. Invest. officer Morgan Guaranty Trust Co., New York, 1968-74; pres. First Dallas Capital Corp., Dallas, 1974-77; co-managing partner Summit Partners, Dallas, 1977-83; co-chair., co-ceo Hicks & Haas Inc., Dallas, 1983-89; chair., ceo Hicks, Muse, Tate & Furst Inc., Dallas, 1989-; chair., owner Texas Rangers, Arlington, 1995-, Dallas Stars, Dallas, 1996-. Contributor: United Way, Goodwill, The Dallas Art Museum, The Dallas Symphony Orchestra, The Science Place at Fair Park. chairman, Chancellor Media Corp., Capstar Broadcasting Corp.; director, Sybron Intl. Corp., CorpGroup Ltd., Intl. Home Foods., MVS Corp., Olympus Real Estate Corp., Regal Cinemas Inc., Triton Energy Ltd., Viasystems Grp., Home Interiors & Gifts Inc.; board of dirs. Crow Family Holdings., advisory bd. Chase Manhattan Corp.; chair., Univ. of Texas Investment Management Co. Office: Hicks Muse Tate & Furst 200 Crescent Ct Ste 1600 Dallas TX 75201-1844*

HICKS, TYLER GREGORY, publishing company executive, writer; b. N.Y.C., June 21, 1921; s. Ernest Tyler and Mary B. (O'Brien) H.; m. Saretta M. Gratke, Feb. 23, 1946 (dec. Mar. 1974); children: Gregory T., Barbara L., Steven D.; m. Mary T. Shanley, Aug. 29, 1975. Engr. Merport Realty Co., 1943-46; design engr. Lockwood-Greene Engrs. Inc., 1946-49; editor in chief Profl. and Reference Books div. McGraw-Hill Co., N.Y.C., 1962-85, pres., chmn. bd. dirs. employees fed. credit union, 1970-95, bd. dirs., 1995—; instr. Cooper Union, N.Y.C.; owner Internat. Engring. Assocs.; pres. Internat. Wealth Success Inc., Rockville Centre, N.Y.; lectr. in field. *Tyler Hicks is a publishing executive who has combined several careers into a highly successful business. Starting as a mechanical engineer, he moved into magazine and book publishing for a major U.S. publisher. He writes engineering books, a number of which have become classics in their field. After buying a small business, he quickly learned the many problems faced by small business owners. He then created two business-opportunity newsletters which have been published for more than 30 years. A number of business books also grew out of this small-business experience, one of which has sold more than one million copies.* Author: How To Borrow Your Way to a Great Fortune, 1970, Magic Mind Secrets for Building Riches Fast, 1971, How To Make One Million Dollars in Real Estate in Three Years Starting with No Cash, 1988, Tyler Hicks' Encyclopedia of Wealth-Building Secrets, 1980, How to Borrow Your Way to Real Estate Riches, 1987, Business Capital Sources, 1984, Financial Broker, Finder, Business Broker Complete Success Kit, 1988, Real Estate Riches Success Kit, 1988, Complete Business Borrowers Success Kit, 1988, 101 Ways to 100% Financing of Business and Real Estate, 1997, How to Get Rich on Other People's Money, 1988, Standard Handbook of Engineering Calculations, 1995, Handbook of Mechanical Engineering Calculations, 1998; co-author: Handbook of Electric Power Calculations, 1984, Handbook of Chemical Engineering Calculations, 1984; co-editor: Standard Handbook of Consulting Engineering, 1986, How to Get Rich on Other People's Money, 1988, How to Build A Million Dollar Fortune, 1989, Mail Order Success Secrets, 1990, How to Make Big Money in Real Estate in the Tighter, Tougher 90s Market, 1992, 199 Greate Home Businesses You Can Start (and Prosper In), for Under $1,000, 1993, How to Start Your Own Business on a Shoestring and Make Up to $500,000 a Year, 1995, Handbook of Civil Engineering Calculations, 1999, 203 Home-Based Businesses, 1999. With U.S. Mcht. Marines, 1936-43. Mem. IEEE, ASME, U.S. Naval Inst., Internat. Oceanographic Found. Clubs: Rockville Links Golf, Huntington Yacht. Home: 24 Canterbury Rd Rockville Centre NY 11570-1310 Office: McGraw-Hill 2 Penn Plaza Ste 1500 New York NY 10121 *The clearest and strongest thought permeating my life is based on my own experience and observation of lives of thousands of people throughout the world. This thought is: Men and women can achieve in life whatever goals they set for themselves if a person combines careful planning and analysis of each objective with mental images of successful achievement. This approach seems to work everywhere—for everyone. Choosing to do what one enjoys also contributes to success because better performance occurs when people like what they're doing. Helping others achieve their goals in life brings great rewards to both the helper and the person assisted.*

HICKS, VIRGINIA HOBSON, bookstore owner, educator; b. Birmingham, Ala., June 15, 1923; d. Earle Pegram and Virginia (Robinson) Calvin; m. John Lewis Hobson, Sept. 9, 1950 (div. 1974); children: John Lewis, Ginger Hobson Watson; m. Harold Eugene Hicks, Mar. 31, 1990. AB, Vanderbilt U., 1948, MS, 1979, PhD; postgrad., Sullins Coll., Memphis State U., Jacksonville U., U. North Fla., George Peabody Coll. Cert. tchr., N.Y. Head gen. cargo Brit. Ministry, N.Y. Ctrl. R.R., N.Y.C., 1944; with United Air Lines, N.Y.C., 1945; tchr. Caldwell Sch., Nashville, 1948-50, Venetia Sch., Jacksonville, Fla., 1950-51, Hutchison Sch., Memphis, 1959-65; owner, operator Lee St. Book and Art Shops, Brunswick, Ga., 1970-74, Golden Isles Book Distbn., Brunswick, 1970-74; antiquarian bookseller, 1970—; owner The Book Shop Inc., Brunswick. Bd. dirs. St. Mark's Towers Home for Elderly, Brunswick, 1981—. Recipient Charles S. Haslam award for excellence in bookselling, book appraisal and mktg. Mem. Am. Booksellers Assn., Southeastern Booksellers Assn., Ga. Antiquarian Booksellers Assn., Jr. League Savannah. Home: 133 Shore Rush Dr Saint Simons Is GA 31522-1437 Office: The Book Shop Inc 1519 Newcastle St Brunswick GA 31520-6806

HICKS, WALTER JOSEPH, electrical engineer; b. Lawrence, Mass., Mar. 10, 1935; s. Walter Francis and Ethel Mary (Royds) H.; m. Faith Winifred McCrum, Apr. 4, 1959; children: Janet Lee, Walter David, Pamela Jean. BSEE, MIT, 1957, MSEE, 1957; PhD in Plasma Physics, N.Mex. State U., 1969. Elec. engr. Raytheon Co., Bedford, Mass., 1957-67; radar system engr., dept. mgr. Raytheon Co., 1970-74; tech. advisor Raytheon Co., Lowell, Mass., 1974-84; cons. engr. Raytheon Co., Bedford, 1984-98; owner Paradox Scientific of Acton, Mass., 1998—; mem. sci. adv. bd. USAF, Washington, 1983. Patentee in field. Elder United Presbyn. Ch., Newton, Mass., 1978-82. Home: 7 Pinewood Rd Acton MA 01790

HICKS, WENDELL LEON, history educator, publisher, political scientist; b. Pitts., July 2, 1946; s. John Verris and Juanita H.; m. Patricia Ann Du Hart, Jan. 15, 1977 (div. Jan. 1980); children: Wendell Leon Jr., Gregory Moore. BA, Fayetteville State U., 1971; MA, N.C. Ctrl. U., 1973. Grad. asst. N.C. Ctrl. U., Durham, 1972; asst. prof. Saint Augustine's Coll., Raleigh, N.C., 1973; grad. asst. U. Toledo, 1974-79; prof. history Bowling Green (Ohio) State U., 1979; pub. Azaka Publs., Pitts., 1983—. Author: The Bloody Flux: The World's No. 1 Killing Disease for the Past Six Centures, 1982, The Ku Klux Klan: A Psychoanalytical and Medical Perspective, 1992. Co-chmn. Operation PUSH, Pitts., 1983; active NAACP, Pitts., Vet. Club, Fayetteville, N.C. With USN, 1965-71. Mem. AAUP, Internat. Platform Assn., Pi Gamma Mu, Phi Alpha Theta (v.p. 1976-77, pres. 1977-78). Democrat. Methodist. Avocations: football, track and field, swimming, weightlifting, boxing. Home and Office: Azaka Publs 2154 Centre Ave Pittsburgh PA 15219-6315

HICKS, WILLIAM ALBERT, III, lawyer; b. Welland, Ont., Can., Apr. 6, 1942; s. William Albert and June Gwendolyn (Birrell) H.; m. Bethany G. Galvin, May 21, 1982; children: James Christopher, Scott Kelly, Alexandra Elizabeth, Samantha Katherine. AB, Princeton U., 1964; LLB, Cornell U., 1967. Bar: N.Y. 1967, Ariz. 1972, U.S. Dist. Ct. Ariz. 1972. Assoc. Seward & Kissel, N.Y.C., 1967-68; assoc. Snell & Wilmer LLP, Phoenix, 1972-75, ptnr., 1976—; instr. Ariz. State U., 1974-75. Mem. U.S. Olympic fencing squad, 1964; mem. bd. advisors Casino USA, Inc. 1981-84; bd. dirs. Scottsdale Arts Ctr. Assn., 1984-88, v.p. devel., 1985-87; bd. dirs. Valley Leadership, Inc., 1987-91, sec. 1988-89, sec.-treas., 1989-90; bd. dirs. Scottsdale Cultural Coun., 1988-97, vice chmn., 1992-95, chmn. 1995-96; active mem. The Luke's Men, 1992—, bd. dirs., 1993-97, sec., 1993-94, v.p., 1995-96, pres. 1996-97; mem. adv. bd. Scottsdale Arts Ctr., 1988-91, chmn. 1988-90; bd. dirs. Ariz. Coun. on Econ. Edn., 1998—. Capt. JAG Corps, USAF 1968-72. Recipient DSM. Mem. ABA, N.Y. State Bar Assn., Ariz. Bar Assn., Maricopa County Bar Assn., Nat. Assn. Bond Lawyers (vice chmn. com. on financing health care facilities 1982-83, chmn. com. on financing health care facilities 1983-86, mem. securities law and disclosure com. 1994—), Princeton U. Alumni Assn. Ariz. (pres. 1978-81, sec. 1981—), Paradise Valley (Ariz.) Country Club. Office: Snell & Wilmer LLP One Arizona Ctr Phoenix AZ 85004-0001

HICKSON, MARCUS LAFAYETTE, III, communication educator, consultant; b. Macon, Ga., Aug. 10, 1945; s. Marcus Lafayette Jr. and Edna Lucille (Cribb) H.; m. Joyce Horton, Sept. 1, 1968 (div.); m. Nancy Dorman, Dec. 13, 1986. BS, Auburn U., 1966, MA, 1968; MA, Miss. State U., 1981; PhD, So. Ill. U., 1971; JD, Birmingham Sch. Law, 1993. Asst. prof. Miss. State U., Starkville, 1970-71, prof., chmn., 1974-87; prof. comm., chmn. dept. U. Ala., Birmingham, 1987—. Co-author: The Southern Redneck, 1982, NVC: Nonverbal Communication, 1989, Introduction to Communication Theory, 1991, Effective Communication for Academic Chairs, 1993. With U.S. Army, 1971-74. Home: 1004 Oak Tree Rd Birmingham AL 35244 Office: U Alabama 1612 10th Ave S Birmingham AL 35205-3514

HICKSON, ROBIN JULIAN, mining company executive; b. Irby, Eng., Feb. 27, 1944; s. William Kellett and Doris Matilda (Martin) H.; m. P. Anne Winn, Mar. 28, 1964; children: Richard, Sharon, Nicholas, Steven. BS in Mining Engring. with honors, U. London, 1965; MBA, Tulane U., 1990. Mining engr. N.J. Zinc Co., Austinville, 1965-70; divisional mgr. N.J. Zinc Co., Jefferson City, Tenn., 1970-71; spl. project engr. Kerr McGee Corp., Grants, N.Mex., 1971-72; gen. mgr. Asarco, Inc., Vanadium, N.Mex., 1972-78; gen. mgr. Gold Fields Mining Corp., Ortiz, N.Mex., 1978-83, Mesquite, Calif., 1982-86; v.p. Freeport Mining Co., New Orleans, 1986-91, Freeport Indonesia Inc., Irian Jaya, 1991-92; pres. Freeport Rsch. and Engring. Co., New Orleans, 1992-93; sr. v.p. Cyprus Climas Metals Co., Tempe, Ariz., 1993-94; pres. Cyprus Amax Engring. and Project Devel. Co., Tempe, 1994—; v.p. engring. and devel. exec. officer Cyprus Amax Minerals Co., 1994—. Author: (with others) Interfacing Technologies in Solution Mining, 1981. Recipient Robert Earll McConnell award AIME, 1998. Mem. Instn. Mining and Metallurgy, Am. Inst. Mining and Metallurgy, Mining and Metall. Soc., N.Mex. Mining Assn. (bd. dirs. Santa Fe, N.Mex. chpt. 1975-83), Calif. Mining Assn. (bd. dirs. Sacramento chpt. 1982-86), Beta Gamma Sigma. Episcopalian. Avocations: ornithology, travel. Home: 12246 S

Honah Lee Ct Phoenix AZ 85044-3455 Office: PO Box 22015 1501 W Fountainhead Pkwy Tempe AZ 85282-1868

HICOK, BETHANY FAITH, English educator; b. Troy, N.Y., May 18, 1958; d. Kenneth and Bethany (Tyler) H.; m. Jonathan Miller, Sept. 13, 1986; 1 child, Samuel. BA cum laude, Russell Sage Coll., 1980; MAT, U. Rochester, 1990, MA, 1992, PhD, 1996. Asst. mgr. Albany (N.Y.) Symphony Orch., 1980-81; arts writer, editor The Saratogian, Saratoga Springs, N.Y., 1981-84; county govt. recorder The Recorder, Amsterdam, N.Y., 1984-85; ESL instr. Centro Electronico de Idiomas, Maracaibo, Venezuela, 1985-86; sales asst. Perstorp Warerite, London, 1986-88; asst. prof. English Mt. St. Clare Coll., Clinton, Iowa, 1996—. Contbr. article to profl. jour. Mem. MLA, AAUW, Elizabeth Bishop Soc., Marianne Moore Soc. Democrat. Avocations: hiking, cycling, music, travel. Home: 500 Oakhurst Dr Apt 4 Clinton IA 52732-3665

HIDA, GEORGE T., chemical and ceramic engineer; b. Cluj, Romania, June 9, 1946; came to U.S. 1987; s. Tiberiu and Ilana (Lazarovics) H.; m. Veronica-Irma Torok, Feb. 17, 1967 (div. 1975); m. Rodica Silvia Jeleapov, Sept. 19, 1975; children: Sven, Sever. MS, Poly. Inst., Bucharest, Romania, 1970; PhD, Technion, Haifa, Israel, 1987. Glass engr. TV Screen Factory, Bucharest, 1970-73; ceramic engr. Ceramic Engring. divsn. Rsch. Inst. Electrotechnic Ind., Bucharest, 1973-75, rsch. engr., 1975-77, rsch. scientist, 1977-80, sr. rsch. scientist, 1980-82; rsch. assoc. prof. Technion/U. Buffalo, Haifa/Buffalo, 1983-88; v.p. engring. Benchmark Structural Ceramics, Buffalo, 1988—; lectr. Coll. for Bldg. Materials, Bucharest, 1975-79, Rsch. Inst. Electrotechnic Ctr., 1978-81. Contbr. more than 80 articles to profl. jours.; holder 14 U.S. patents. Served with Israeli Army, 1984-87. Mem. ASTM, Am. Ceramic Soc., Am. Chem. Soc., N.Y. Acad. Scis., Nat. Inst. Ceramic Engring., Am. Assn. Combustion Synthesis. Achievements include patents for Mechanochemical Alloying of Reactants for Reaction-Sintering Technology, Sialons, Bonded Carbides, Silicon Carbides, Nitrides, Silicides and Refractory Oxides within Low-to-Zero Shrinkage Technology; introduction of mechanochemical activation to combustion-synthesis reactants prior to ignition, to achieve full control of combustion occurence and predetermined composition and structure of the product; esatblished and defined the principles of controlled combustion-synthesis CCS; applied CCS to produce needle like single crystals (wiskers) of silicon carbide titanium carbide and sialon; developed CCS based chemical furnaces. Home: 63 Eastwick Dr Amherst NY 14221-2627 Office: Benchmark Structural Ceramics 235 Aero Dr Buffalo NY 14225-1429

HIDALGO, MIGUEL, transportation company executive; b. Detroit, Nov. 10, 1958; s. Manuel and Ann (Molina) H.; m. Rausdha Nelly Cachoa, Nov. 14, 1992; children: Jesahel, Monica Natasha, Samuel. BA in Communications, Pepperdine U., 1981; MS in Aero. Mgmt., Nat. U., 1992, MBA in Internat. Bus. Mktg., 1999. Owner Pacific Trans Service, L.A., 1981-83, Disneyland, Anaheim, Calif., 1984; legal adminstr. Hidalgo & Assocs., L.A., 1985-90; ops. and customs Aero Calif. Airlines, San Diego, 1990-91; pres. AeroCargo, San Diego, 1992-96; owner AeroCargo, Inc., Baja AirWest Express, Nelly's Pilot/Aircraft Supply, Brown Field Rental Car Svc., Nelly's Airport Sta.; mgr. U.S. Airways, 1997—. Author: Baja Nelly's Flightguide to Mexico, 1994; contbr. articles to profl. jours. Active S.W. Rep. Project; advisor Polit. Edn. Project. With USN, mem. Res., ret., 1985-91. Mem. Pepperdine Assocs., San Marino Alumni Assn., Huntington Libr. Republican. Roman Catholic.

HIDAY, VIRGINIA ALDIGÉ, sociologist educator; b. New Orleans, Jan. 28, 1939; d. Robert Joseph and Mary Boagni (Anding) A.; m. L.L. Hiday, Sept. 5, 1970 (div. June 2, 1997). AB, U. N.C., 1960, MEd, 1961, PhD, 1973. Asst. prof. U. Colo., Boulder, 1972-75; postdoctoral fellow Duke U. Med. Ctr., Durham, N.C., 1975-76; asst. prof., prof. N.C. State U., Raleigh, 1976—; vis. prof. U. N.C., Chapel Hill, 1974-75; referee for various sci. jours. in sociology, law, psychiatry; cons. N.C. Divsn. Mental Health, Raleigh, 1986, 89, Nat. Health Svc., London, 1999. Mem. editl. bd. Contemporary Sociology, 1986-91, 98—, Rose Monograph Series, 1982-88; contbr. numerous articles to profl. jours. Mem., com. AAUP, Boulder, Colo., 1972-75; worker Campaigns for local, state, nat. offices, Chapel Hill, 1966—, Habitat for Humanity, Chapel Hill, 1996-97; bd. dirs. Orange County Mental Health Assn., Chapel Hill, 1995—. Named NIMH Postdoctoral fellow, Population Predoctoral fellow NICHD. Mem. APA, Am. Sociol. Assn. (coun. mem. med sect., sec., treas. mental health), So. Sociol. Soc. (coun. mem.), Internat. Acad. Law & Mental Health (coun. mem. 1993—), Soc. for Study of Social Problems, Phi Kappa Phi, Sigma Xi. Democrat. Episcopalian. Avocations: tennis, skiing, dancing. Office: NC State U Dept Sociology/Anthropology Box 8107 Raleigh NC 27695-8107

HIDDING, GEZINUS JACOB, information technology and strategy educator; b. Vlagtwedde, The Netherlands, Apr. 11, 1958; came to U.S., 1982; s. Pieter J. H. and Martje (Veldhuis) H.; m. Antje Kuiper, June 5, 1987. BS in Econometrics, U. Groningen, The Netherlands, 1979, MS in Econometrics/DSS, 1982; MS in Info. Systems, GSIA/Carnegie Mellon U., 1985, PhD in Info. Systems, 1992. Staff Andersen Consulting, Chgo., 1986-87; cons. Andersen Informatique, Paris, 1987-88; various positions Andersen Consulting, Chgo., 1988-94, sr. methodologist, 1994-96; vis. asst. prof. Loyola U., Chgo., 1996-97, asst. prof., 1997—; mem. adv. bd. Eolas Devel. Corp., 1998—; lectr. in U.S., Europe and Japan. Contbr. articles to profl. jours. and chpt. to book. Mem. Assn. Computing Machinery, Dutch Assn. Informatics, Inst. Ops. Rsch. and Mgmt. Scis. Avocations: playing and listening to music, languages: Dutch, French, German. E-mail: ghidding@aol.com. Home: 1237 W Victoria St Chicago IL 60660-3448 Office: Loyola Univ Chgo 25 E Pearson St Chicago IL 60611-2001

HIDDLESTON, RONAL EUGENE, drilling and pump company executive; b. Bristow, Okla., Mar. 21, 1939; s. C.L. and Iona D. (Martin) H.; m. Marvelene L. Hammond, Apr. 26, 1959; children: Michael Scott, Mark Shawn, Matthew Shane. Student, Idaho State U., 1957-58. With Roper's Clothing and Bishop Redi-Mix, Rupert, Idaho, 1960-61; pres., chmn. bd., gen. mgr. Hiddleston Drilling, Rupert, 1961-66, Mountain Home, Idaho, 1966—; bd. dirs. Baker Mfg. Mem. Mountain Home Airport Adv. Bd., 1968—; hon. mem. Idaho Search and Rescue. Mem. Nat. Ground Water Assn. (past pres.); Idaho Ground Water Assn. (hon. life, past pres.), Pacific N.W. Water Well Assn., N.W. Mining Assn., Nat. Fedn. Ind. Businessmen, Ground Water Inst. (bd. dirs.), Aircraft Owners and Pilots Assn., Ducks Unltd., Nat. 210 Owners Club, Nat. Sporting Clays Assn., Masons, Royal Arch, Scottish Rites, El Korzh Shrine. Home: 105 Goodall St Mountain Home ID 83647-1629 Office: RR 3 Box 610D Mountain Home ID 83647-9206

HIDEN, ROBERT BATTAILE, JR., lawyer; b. Boston, May 8, 1933; s. Robert Battaile Sr. and Clotilda (Waddell) H.; m. Ann Eliza McCracken, Mar. 27, 1956; children: Robert B. III, Elizabeth Patterson, John Hughes. BA, Princeton U., 1955; LLB, U. Va., 1960. Bar: N.Y. 1961, U.S. Ct. Appeals (2d cir.) 1974, U.S. Dist. Ct. (so. dist.) N.Y. 1975. Assoc. Sullivan & Cromwell, N.Y.C., 1960-67, ptnr., 1968-98, of counsel, 1999—. Articles editor and contbr. U. Va. Law Rev., 1959-60; contbr., mem. bd. editors Futures Internat. Law Letter, 1987-92. Trustee Hampton (Va.) U. and Hampton Inst., 1984—; commr. Larchmont Little League, N.Y., 1964-68; chmn. Larchmont Jr. Sailing Program, 1977-78; vestry, jr. warden St. John's Episc. Ch., Larchmont, 1982-86, 99—. Served to lt. (j.g.) USNR, 1955-57. Mem. ABA, N.Y. State Bar Assn., Assn. of Bar of City of N.Y., N.Y. County Bar Assn., Am. Judicature Soc., Raven Soc., Order of Coif, Omicron Delta Kappa. Democrat. Clubs: Larchmont U. (pres. 1976-77), Larchmont Yacht (trustee 1979-85, sec. 1990—); N.Y. Yacht (N.Y.C.); Scarsdale Golf (N.Y.). Avocations: skiing, golf, sailing, tennis. Home: 2 Walnut Ave Larchmont NY 10538-4232 Office: Sullivan & Cromwell 125 Broad St Fl 28 New York NY 10004-2489

HIDORE, JOHN JUNIOR, geographer, educator; b. Cedar Falls, Iowa, July 6, 1932; s. John Henry and Vearle Lluela (Thomas) H.; m. Suzanne C. Freeman, Feb. 25, 1995; children: Jill Helen, John Warren. B.A. in Math. and Earth Sci, State Coll. Iowa, Cedar Falls, 1954; M.A. in Phys. Geography, U. Iowa, 1958, Ph.D., 1960. Instr. geography U. Wis., Madison, 1960-62; asst. prof. Okla. State U., Stillwater, 1962-64; asso. prof. Okla. State U., 1964-66; dir. NDEA Inst. Geography, 1966; asso. prof. U. Ind., Bloomington, 1966-68; acting chmn. U. Ind., 1968-71, prof., 1972-80; prof. and head dept. geography U. N.C., Greensboro, 1980-87; vis. prof. U. Ife, Nigeria, 1971-72, U. Khartoum, Sudan, 1974-75, Ben Gurion U. of Negev, Beer Sheva, Israel, 1978. Author: Introduction to Physical Geography, 1967, A Geography of the Atmosphere, 1972, Physical Geography: Earth Systems, 1974, A Workbook of Weather Maps, 1976, Physical Geography: A Laboratory Manual, 1978, 85, 89, Weather and Climate, 1985, Climatology, 1984, Climatology: An Atmospheric Science, 1993, Global Environmental Change, 1996; contbr. articles, abstracts and book revs. to profl. jours. Home: 3505 Terrault Dr Greensboro NC 27410-8240 Office: U NC Dept Geography Greensboro NC 27412

HIDY, GEORGE MARTEL, chemical engineer, executive; b. Kingman, Ariz., Jan. 5, 1935; s. John William and Margaret (Coqueron) H.; m. Dana Sexton Thomas, Oct. 15, 1958; children—Anne, Adrienne, John; m. 2d, Doris A. Wilson, Sept. 28, 1990. A.B., Columbia U., N.Y.C., 1956, B.S., 1957; M.S.E., Princeton U., N.J., 1958; D.Eng., Johns Hopkins U., Balt., 1962. Asst. dir. chemistry and microphysics Nat. Ctr. Atmospheric Research, Boulder, Colo., 1967-69; group leader chem. physics Rockwell Internat. Sci. Ctr., Thousand Oaks, Calif., 1969-73, assoc. dir., 1973-74; gen. mgr. Environ. Research & Tech., West Lake, Calif., 1974-76, v.p., 1976-84; pres. Desert Research Inst., Reno, Nev., 1984-87; v.p. Electric Power Research Inst., Palo Alto, Calif., 1987-94; assoc. dir. coll. engring. Ctr. Environ. Rsch. and Technol. U. Calif., Riverside, 1994-96; prin. Aerochem Assocs., Riverside, 1995—; Ala. Indsl. prof. environ. engring. U. Ala., Birmingham, 1996—. Commr., Calif. Youth Soccer Assn., Los Angeles, 1982-84. Fellow AAAS, Air and Waste Mgmt. Assn.; mem. AIChE, Am. Meteorol. Soc., Am. Chem. Soc., Am. Geophys. Union. Home: 2504 Woodfern Cir Birmingham AL 35244-6406

HIEATT, ALLEN KENT, language professional, educator; b. Indpls., Jan. 21, 1921; emigrated to Can., 1968, returned to U.S., 1986; s. Allen Andrew and Violet Rose (Kent) H.; m. Constance Bartlett, Oct. 25, 1958; children by previous marriage: Alice Allen, Katherine Marsh. A.B., U. Louisville, 1943; Ph.D., Columbia U., 1954. Lectr. Columbia U., N.Y.C., 1944-45, instr., 1945-55, asst. prof., 1956-59, assoc. prof., 1960-69; prof. English U. Western Ont., London, 1969-86, emeritus, 1987—; sr. founding editor Spenser Newsletter, London, Ont., 1970-75. Mem. editorial bd. Duquesne Studies, Pitts., 1976—, Spenser Studies, 1979—; editorial cons. Spenser Ency., 1990; co-editor: College Anthology of British and American Verse, 1964, Poetry in English: An Anthology, 1987; author: Short Time's Endless Monument, 1960, (with C. Hieatt) The Canterbury Tales of Geoffrey Chaucer, 1964, rev. edit., 1981, Spenser: Selected Poetry, 1970, Chaucer, Spenser, Milton, 1975; translator: (with M. Lorch) Lorenzo Valla, On Pleasure, 1977; co-author: (with C. Hieatt) (children's book) The Canterbury Tales of Geoffrey Chaucer, 1961. Cutting fellow, 1946-47; leave grantee Can. Council, Oxford, Eng., 1977-78; research fellow Social Sci. and Humanities Research Council of Can., 1981-82. Fellow Royal Soc. Can.; mem. MLA (chmn. div. English lit. Renaissance 1978-79, William Riley Parker Prize, 1984), Spenser Soc. (pres.), Renaissance Soc. Am. (chmn. north central div. 1973-79). Home: 304 River Rd Deep River CT 06417-2120

HIEATT, CONSTANCE BARTLETT, English language educator; b. Boston, Feb. 11, 1928; d. Arthur Charles and Eleonora (Very) Bartlett; m. Allen Kent Hieatt, Oct. 25, 1958. Student, Smith Coll., 1945-47; AB, Hunter Coll., 1953, AM, 1957; PhD, Yale U., 1959. Lectr. City Coll., CUNY, 1959-60; from asst. prof. to assoc. prof. English Queensborough C.C., CUNY, 1960-65; from assoc. prof. to prof. St. John's U., Jamaica, N.Y., 1965-69; prof. English U. Western Ont., London, Can., 1969-93, prof. emeritus, 1993—. Author: (with A.K. Hieatt) The Canterbury Tales of Geoffrey Chaucer, 1964, rev. edit., 1981, Spenser: Selected Poetry, 1970; The Realism of Dream Visions, 1967, Beowulf and Other Old English Poems, 1967, rev. edit., 1983, Essentials of Old English, 1968, The Miller's Tale By Geoffrey Chaucer, 1970; (with Sharon Butler) Pleyn Delit: Medieval Cookery for Modern Cooks, 1976, rev. edit., 1979, (with Brenda Hosington) rev. 2d edit., 1996, Karlamagnus Saga, Vols. I and II, 1975, Vol. III, 1980; (with Sharon Butler) Curye on Inglysch, 1985; An Ordinance of Pottage, 1988, (with Robin F. Jones) La Novele Cirurgerie, 1990; (with Minnette Gaudet) Guillaume de Machaut's Tale of the Alerion, 1994; (with Brian Shaw and Duncan Macrae-Gibson) Beginning Old English, 1994; also children books (with Hieatt) The Canterbury Tales of Geoffrey Chaucer, 1961, Sir Gawain and the Green Knight, 1967, The Knight of the Lion, 1968, The Knight of the Cart, 1969, The Joy of the Court, 1971, The Sword and the Grail, 1972, The Castle of Ladies, 1973, The Minstrel Knight, 1974. Yale U. fellow, and Lewis-Farmington fellow, 1957-59; Can. Council and Social Sci. and Humanities Rsch. Coun. grantee; Yale U. vis. fellow, 1985-86, 89-93. Fellow Royal Soc. Can.; mem. MLA, Medieval Acad. Am., Internat. Soc. Anglo-Saxonists, Assn. Can. Univ. Tchrs. English, New Chaucer Soc. Episcopalian. Home: 304 River Rd Deep River CT 06417-2120

HIEB, MARIO KIRK, broadcast engineer, inventor, writer, consultant; b. Rapid City, S.D., Oct. 22, 1958; s. Harry Melvin and Carolyn (Opp) H. BSEE, S.D. Tech., 1982. Chief engr. Sta. KIMM/KGGG-FM, Rapid City, 1977-84, Sta. KLTQ-FM, Salt Lake City, 1985-87; engr. Centro Corp., Salt Lake City, 1987-88; chief engineer KXRK-FM, Salt Lake City, 1992-98; producer Sta. X-96 Radio, Salt Lake City; audio engr. ESPN TV, 1991, 93; pres., founder Microcast Communications, 1997—; v.p., dir. engring. Acme Broadcasting, Inc., 1998—; project engr. Post Perfect, N.Y.C., 1987, Gramercy Broadcast Ctr., N.Y.C., 1988; producer, editor, engr. Wasatch Imagination Ctr., Salt Lake City, 1990; chief engr. Sta. KJQ-FM, Salt Lake City, 1991. Contbr. Radio World mag. Com. mem. capital campaign KRCL Radio, 1993—. Mem. Soc. of Broadcast Engrs. (cert. profl. broadcast engineer, chmn. Utah chpt. 1997, 98), Mensa. Avocation: skiing.

HIEBEL, WILLIAM RAYMOND, writer, artist, composer, retired English educator; b. Chgo.; s. Joseph James and Catherine Theresa (Walsh) H. AB, Loyola U., Chgo.; MA, Northwestern U., Evanston, Ill., PhD. Tchg. asst. English Northwestern U.; instr. Ill. Inst. Tech., Chgo., Georgetown U., Washington; asst. prof. Ill. Inst. Tech., Chgo.; asst. prof. Loyola U., Chgo., prof. emeritus. Avocations: bicycle riding, tennis.

HIEBER, WILLIAM GEORGE, JR., stockbroker; b. Astoria, N.Y., Feb. 16, 1937; s. William George and Marie (Siegel) H.; m. Jean Helen Frankenheimer, Apr. 23, 1967; children: Jennifer Maria, Christina Jean. AB, Colgate U., 1958; JD, Harvard U., 1961. Bar: N.Y. 1962; chartered fin. analyst. Trust investor First Nat. City Bank, N.Y.C., 1962-63; security analyst C.J. Lawrence, N.Y.C., 1963-67; stock broker Bacon Stevenson, N.Y.C., 1967-69; dir. research Muller & Co., N.Y.C., 1969-70; pres. Shoenberg, Hieber, Inc., N.Y.C., 1970—. Mem. Chartered Fin. Analysts, N.Y. Soc. Security Analysts, N.Y. State Bar Assn., N.Y. Stock Exchange (assoc.), Am. Stock Exchange (allied), Phi Beta Kappa. Republican. Lutheran. Home: 314 Cambridge Ave Garden City NY 11530-5419 Office: Shoenberg Hieber Inc 66 Reade St New York NY 10007-1834

HIEBERT, CLEMENT ARTHUR, surgeon, consultant, educator; b. Boston; s. Joelle Cornelius and Susie (Pauls) H.; m. Mary Anne Tremaine, June 10, 1956; children: Timothy, Sarah, Katherine, Amy, John; m. May Cameron, Dec. 9, 1978. AB magna cum laude, Bowdoin Coll., 1947; MD, Harvard U., 1951. Diplomate Am. Bd. Gen. Surgery, Am. Bd. Thoracic Surgery, Am. Bd. Vascular Surgery; lic. MD, Maine. Intern, resident Mass. Gen. Hosp., Boston, 1951-56; rsch. fellow Harvard U., Strangeways Rsch., Cambridge, Eng., 1956-57; chief resident West Surgical Svcs, Mass. Gen. Hosp., Boston, 1957-58; senior registrar in thoracic surgery Frenchay Hosp., Cambridge, Eng., 1958-59; dir. surg. clinics Mass. Gen. Hosp., Boston, 1959-60; attending surgeon Maine Med. Ctr., Mercy Hosp., Portland, Maine, 1960—; chmn. dept. surgery Maine Med. Ctr., Portland, 1086-89, chmn. emeritus dept. surgery, 1990—; dep. med. dir. voyage IV rotation to W. Africa, Project Hope, 1964; instr. in Thoracic Surgery, Harvard Med. Sch., Gen. Hosp. Post-Grad course: guest lectr. U. Toronto, ann. refresher course in Gen. Thoracic Surgery; staff surgeon divsn. thoracic surgery, Toronto Gen. Hosp., 1984-85, U. Paris (OSEO), 1984, Curzo Internat. de Actualizacion en Circugia, Madrid, 1984, Medizinische Hochschule, Hannover, Germany, 1985, U. Rio Grande de Norte, Natal, Brazil, 1985; lectr. Royal Coll. Surgeons Can., Meml. U. St Johns, Newfoundland, U. Leuven, Belgium, 1985, 96, U. Conn., 1989, Ctr. Med. de Forcilles, Attilly, Paris, 1991, Kantonspital, Basel, Switzerland, 1993, Dartmouth Med. Sch., Bay State Med. Ctr. U. Mass.; rep. Am. Bd. of Surgery to the inaugural Arab Bd. of Surgery Examinations, Baghdad, Iraq, 1986. Co-editor (with others) 2 vol. textbook in Thoracic Surgery, 1995; contbr. over 60 articles to profl. jours including Annals of Thoracic Surgery, Surgery, JAMA, Am. Jour. of Surgery, World Jour. of Surgery and chpts. in a variety of textbooks. Past mem., bd. dirs. Portland Symphony Orch., Opportunity Farm for Boys, New Gloucester, Maine; bd. dirs. World Affairs Coun., Portland, Maine, 1995-98; instr. Maine Handicapped Skiing, 1995. With U.S. Navy, Atlantic Fleet, 1944-48. Recipient Santos Dumont medal of merit, Govt. of Brazil., Brazilian Embassy, Washington, 1086; named Scholar-in-Residence, Rockefeller Found., Lake Como, Italy, 1990. Fellow ACS, Am. Coll. Cardiology; mem. Am. Bd. Surgery (sr. mem., bd. dirs.), Soc. of Thoracic Surgeons, Boston Surgical Soc., Internat. Soc., Soc. for Cardiovascular Surgery. Avocations: landscape gardening, photography, skiing. E-mail: hiebert@ime.net. Home: 268 Rte 115 Windham ME 04062

HIEBERT, RAY ELDON, educator, author, consultant; b. Freeman, S.D., May 21, 1932; s. Peter Nicholas and Helen (Kunkel) H.; m. Roselyn Lucille Peyser, Jan. 30, 1955 (div. Apr. 1985); children: David, Steven, Emily, Douglas; m. Sheila Jean Gibbons, Dec. 21, 1985. B.A., Stanford U., 1954; M.S., Columbia U., 1957; M.A., U. Md., 1961, Ph.D., 1962. Faculty Am. U., 1958- 67, prof. journalism, chmn. dept. journalism, 1962-67; dir. Washington Journalism Center, 1965-68; head dept. journalism U. Md., College Park, 1968-72; dean Coll. Journalism, 1973-79, prof., 1980-98, prof., dean emeritus, 1998—; dir. Am. Journalism Ctr., Budapest, Hungary, 1991-95; pres. Comm. Rsch. Assocs., 1979—; dir. Am. Journalism Ctr., Budapest, Hungary, 1991-95; acad. adv. U.S. Voice of Am., 1983-91. Author or editor more than 20 books on history and comm. Fulbright fellow to Africa, 1982. Mem. Soc. Profl. Journalists (pres. Md. chpt. 1977-78), Cosmos Club (Washington), Kappa Tau Alpha, Phi Kappa Phi, Omicron Delta Kappa. Home: 10606 Mantz Rd Silver Spring MD 20903-1247 Office: U Md College Park MD 20742-7111

HIEKEN, CHARLES, lawyer; b. Granite City, Ill., Aug. 15, 1928; s. Samuel and Margaret (Isaacs) H.; m. Donna Jane Clanin, Jan. 6, 1961; children: Tina Jane, Seth Paul. SBEE, MIT, 1952, SMEE, 1952; LLB, Harvard U., 1957. Bar: Ill., 1957, Mass., 1958, U.S. Supreme Ct., 1960, U.S. Ct. Customs and Patent Appeals, 1961, U.S. Ct. Claims, 1963, U.S. Ct. Appeals (fed. cir.), 1982. Patent asst. Lab. Electronics, Boston, 1954-56, Fish, Richardson & Neave, Boston, 1956-57; assoc. Hill, Sherman, Meroni & Simpson, Chgo., 1957, Joseph Weingarten, Boston, 1957-58; assoc. Wolf, Greenfield & Hieken, Boston, 1958-61, ptnr., 1961-70; prin. Charles Hieken Law Offices, Waltham, Mass., 1970-87; ptnr. Fish & Richardson, Boston, 1987-94, prin., 1995—. Mem. pres.'s adv. coun. Bentley Coll., 1993—; mem. coun. Harvard Law Sch. Assn., 1998—. Mem. Boston Bar Assn. (mem. civil procedure com. 1959—), Mass. Bar Assn. (chmn. intellectual property com. 1977-80), Ill. State Bar Assn. Served with U.S. Merchant Marine, 1944-47, U.S. Army, 1952-54. Mem. Boston Patent Law Assn. (chmn. pub. relations com. 1965-66, chmn. antitrust law com. 1966-70, 78-80, treas. 1970-71, v.p. 1971-72, pres.-elect, 1972-73, pres. 1973-74), IEEE (life), Harvard Law Sch. Assn. (coun. 1998—), Down Town Club (bd. govs.), Tau Beta Pi, Eta Kappa Nu. Home: 193 Wilshire Dr Sharon MA 02067-1561 Office: Fish & Richardson PC 225 Franklin St 31st Fl Boston MA 02110-2809

HIEMIER, PAIGE DANA, nurse; b. N.Y.C., May 11, 1954; d. Stanley Richard and Faith Mae (Dow) H. AS, Bergen C.C., 1985; student, William Paterson Coll., 1989, New Sch., N.Y.C., 1990, William Paterson Coll., 1996—. RN, N.Y. Nurse neonatal ICU St. Luke's Hosp., N.Y.C., 1986-90, nurse emergency and pediat. emergency rm., 1990—, nurse pediat. AIDS Clinic, 1991-93; chair collective bargaining unit St. Luke's Hosp., N.Y.C., 1989-91; nurse emergency rm. Kennedy Meml. Hosp., Saddlebrook, N.J., 1991-93; pres. Computer Tut*her, Ridgefield Park, N.J., 1997—; owner online vitamin and health product co. AHOOO! Health, Ridgefield Park, 1997—; chair St. Luke's Collective Bargaining Unit, N.Y.C., 1989-91. Author: Another Side of Innocence, 1989; author numerous poems. Citizen's adv. com. Bergen C.C., 1985-86. Avocations: rock climbing, fishing, roller blading, movies, snowboarding. Home: PO Box 375 Ridgefield Park NJ 07660-0375

HIEMSTRA, MARVIN ROY, poet, humorist, literary consultant; b. Pella, Iowa, July 27, 1939; s. Martin Jess and Henrietta Catherine Hiemstra. BA with honors, State U. Iowa, 1962; MA, Ind. U., 1966. Poet, humorist, 1967—; lit. cons., San Francisco, 1967—; book arts cons. Juniper Von Phitzer Press, San Francisco, 1975—. Author: Cats in Charge, 1989, Dream Tees, 1991; author, performer: (CD) In Deepest USA, 1996, (performance video) A Turquoise Coyote Under Your Pillow, 1998. Recipient Narrative Poetry award Browning Soc., 1975, Three Poem prize Montalvo Ctr. for the Arts, 1985, Poet in Performance award Carmel Festival for the Performing Arts, 1998. Mem. Poetry Soc. Am., Acad. Am. Poets, The Dramatists Guild, Inc., MBS Internat. (Disting. Book award 1990). Avocations: piano, folk humor, architecture, horticulture. E-mail: drollmarv@aol.com. Office: Zippy Digital 166 Bonview St San Francisco CA 94110-5147

HIEMSTRA, ROGER, adult education educator, writer, networker; b. Plainwell, Mich., Sept. 15, 1938; s. Claude and Frances (Anson) H.; m. Janet Louise Werner, June 23, 1968; children: Nancy, David. A.A., Pasadena City Coll., Calif., 1958; B.S., Mich. State U., 1964; M.S., Iowa State U., 1967; Ph.D., U. Mich., 1970. Mott Intern Flint (Mich.) Community Schs., 1968-69; program coordinator Wayne State U., Detroit, 1969-70; dept. asst. U. Mich., Ann Arbor, 1969-70; prof. adult edn. U. Nebr., Lincoln, 1970-76; prof., chmn. adult edn. Iowa State U., Ames, 1976-80; prof. adult edn., instrnl. design Syracuse (N.Y.) U., 1980-97, chmn. dept. adult edn., 1980-96, prof. emeritus, 1996—; prof., program dir. of adult edn. Elmira Coll., 1997—; chmn. Commn. Profs. Adult Edn., Washington, 1981-83; co-dir. adult edn. resource worldwide Kellogg Project, 1986-90, dir., 1991-93. Co-author, editor: Changing Approaches to Studying Adult Education, 1980; co-author: Individualizing Instruction, 1990, Self-Direction in Adult Learning, 1991, Professional Writing, 1994; editor: Environments for Effective Adult Learning, 1991; co-editor, author Overcoming Resistence to Self-Direction in Adult Learning, 1994; author: The Educative Community, 1972, Lifelong Learning, 1976; sr. editor Lifelong Learning: The Adult Years, 1980-83; editor Adult Edn. Quar., 1985-88. Mem. Commn. of Profs. of Adult Edn. With USNR, 1960-62. Named Tchr. of Yr. for Grad. Studies, Elmira Coll., 1999. Mem. Adult Edn. Assn. U.S.A. (exec. bd. 1977-82, svc. award), Am. Assn. Adult and Continuing Edn., Assn. for Continuing Higher Edn. (Nat. Leadership award 1991). Democrat. Unitarian. Home: 318 Southfield Dr Fayetteville NY 13066-2253

HIENTON, JAMES ROBERT, lawyer; b. Phoenix, July 25, 1951; s. Clarence J. Jr. and Lola Jean (Paxton) H.; m. Diane Marie DeBrosse, July 22, 1977. BA, U. Ariz., 1972; MBA, Ariz. State U., 1975, JD, 1975; LLM, Washington U., St. Louis, 1977. Bar: Ariz. 1975, U.S. Dist. Ct. (Ariz.) 1975. Corp. atty. Ariz. Pub. Service, Phoenix, 1975-76; asst. prof. Ariz. State U., Tempe, 1977; assoc. then ptnr. Gust, Rosenfeld, Divelbess et al, Phoenix, 1978-85; sr. tax ptnr. Evans, Kitchel and Jenckes, Phoenix, 1985-89; ptnr. Jennings, Strouss and Salmon, Phoenix, 1989-93; sr. shareholder Bonnett, Fairbourne, Friedman, Hienton, Miner & Fry, P.C., Phoenix, 1993-95, Ridenour, Swenson, Cleere & Evans, P.C., Phoenix, 1995—. Officer, bd. dirs. Charter Govt., Phoenix, 1978-82; mem. Phoenix Citizens Charter Rev. Com., 1982; participant Phoenix Together; participant 1st Phoenix Town Hall, 1981, 2d, 1982, 3d, 1983, recorder, 1983, 85; mem. Balanced Govt. Com., 1983; mem Phoenix Police and Fire Pension Bds., 1982-89; bd. dirs. Ariz. Theater Co., 1979-89; mem. class V, Valley Leadership, 1983-84; founding life mem. Ariz. Mus. Sci. and Industry. Mem. ABA, Ariz. Bar Assn., Maricopa County Bar Assn., Phi Kappa Phi. Republican. Club: Phoenix City. Home: 441 W Mclellan Blvd Phoenix AZ 85013-1141 Office: Ridenour Swenson Cleere & Evans PC 40 N Central Ave Ste 1400 Phoenix AZ 85004-4457

HIER, DANIEL BARNET, neurologist; b. Chgo., Mar. 23, 1947; s. Stanley W. and Jean (Schrager) H.; m. Myra Goldberg, Aug. 30, 1981 (dec. Jul. 1995); m. Linda Lesky (sep. 1998); children: Benjamin Philip, David Samuel. BA, Harvard U., 1969, MD, 1973. Medical intern Bronx Mcpl. Hosp., N.Y.C., 1973-74; neurology resident Mass. Gen. Hosp., Boston, 1974-77, neurology fellow, 1977-79; neurologist Michael Reese Hosp., Chgo., 1979-89, chmn. neurology, 1987-89; head neurology U. Ill., Chgo., 1989—, assoc. prof. neurology, 1989-91; prof. Ul. Ill., 1991—. Fellow Am. Acad.

Neurology, Am. Heart Assn. (stroke council). Home: 553 W Fullerton Pkwy Chicago IL 60614-6431

HIER, MARSHALL DAVID, lawyer; b. Bay City, Mich., Aug. 24, 1945; s. Marshall George and Helen May (Copeland) H.; m. Nancy Speed Brown, June 26, 1970; children: John, Susan, Ann. BA, Mich. State U., 1966; JD, U. Mich., 1969. Bar: Mo. 1969. Assoc. Peper, Martin, Jensen, Maichel and Hetlage, St. Louis, 1969-76, ptnr., 1976-95; prin. Bertram, Peper and Hier, P.C., St. Louis, 1996—; bd. dirs. Gateway Ctr. Met. St. Louis, Mercantile Libr. Assn., St. Louis Soc. Blind and Visually Impaired. Contbr. articles to profl. jours. Mem. St. Louis Bar Assn. (editor jour. 1988—), St. Louis Civil Round Table (former pres.). Baptist. Home: 17141 Chaise Ridge Rd Chesterfield MO 63005-4457

HIERONYMUS, EDWARD WHITTLESEY, lawyer; b. Davenport, Iowa, June 13, 1943. B.A. cum laude, Knox Coll., 1965; J.D. with distinction, Duke U., 1968. Bar: Calif. 1969, Iowa 1968. Ptnr. O'Melveny & Myers, Los Angeles, 1974-96, of counsel, 1996—. Contbr. articles on law to profl. jours. Exec. sec. Los Angeles Com. Fgn. Relations, 1975-86. Served with Judge Adv. Gen. U.S. Army, 1965-74. Mem. ABA (award for profl. merit 1968), Calif. Bar Assn. (founding co-chair natural resources subsect., real property sect. 1986-88), Los Angeles County Bar Assn., Iowa Bar Assn. Office: O'Melveny & Myers 400 S Hope St Los Angeles CA 90071-2899

HIERS, MARY A., museum director. Dir. Fernbank Science Ctr., Atlanta, Ga. Office: Fernbank Science Center 156 Heaton Park Dr NE Atlanta GA 30307-1398*

HIETT, EDWARD EMERSON, retired lawyer, glass company executive; b. Toledo, Nov. 24, 1922; s. Stanley J. and Clara I. (Jones) H.; m. Margaret J. Winter, July 1, 1944; 1 dau., Katherine L. B.B.A., U. Mich., 1946, M.B.A., LL.B., 1949. Bar: Ohio bar 1949. Practice in Toledo, 1949-52; mem. legal dept. Libbey-Owens-Ford Co., Toledo, 1952-63; sec. Libbey-Owens-Ford Co., 1963-78, asst. gen. counsel, 1963-73, v.p. gen. counsel, 1973-78; sr. counsel Owens-Corning Fiberglas, 1978-86; sole practice, 1986-91, ret., 1991; lectr. econs., bus. law U. Toledo, 1949-69. Served as officer USNR, 1942-46. Mem. Toledo Club. Home and Office: 3723 Brookside Rd Toledo OH 43606-2615

HIGASHIDA, RANDALL TAKEO, radiologist, neurosurgeon, medical educator; b. L.A., Oct. 26, 1955; s. Henry and Alice Higashida; m. Jean Kim, May 17, 1986. BS, U. So. Calif., 1976; MD, Tulane U. Diplomate Am. Bd. Radiology. Intern Harbor UCLA Med. Ctr., 1980-81, resident in radiology, 1981-84, fellow in diagnostic/interventional neuroradiology, 1984-85; asst. prof. radiology UCLA Med. Ctr., 1985-86; assoc. prof. radiology U. Calif. San Francisco Med. Ctr., 1986-94, prof. radiology and neurosurgery, 1994—; cons. Target Therapeutics Corp., Fremont, Calif., 1989-93, Interventional Therapeutics Corp., Fremont, 1986-93, Cordis Corp., Miami Lakes, Fla., 1993-96; mem. exec. com. stroke rsch. grants Abbott Labs., Chgo., 1994-96. Mem. editl. bd. Jour. Endovasc. Surgery, 1994-96, Jour. Minimally Invasive Neurosurgery, 1994-96; manuscript reviewer Am. Jour. Neuroradiology, 1992—. Recipient rsch. award Am. Heart Assn., Dallas, 1978-79. Mem. AMA, Am. Soc. Neuroradiology (sr. mem., exec. coun. joint section of cerebrovascular neurosurgery), Soc. Cardiovascular and Interventional Radiology, Am. Soc. Interventional and Therapeutic Neuroradiology (exec. com. 1994-96), Internat. Soc. Endovascular Surgery. Republican. Protestant. Avocations: hiking, tennis, biking, photography, travel. Office: UCSF Medical Ctr 505 Parnassus Ave # L352 San Francisco CA 94143-0628

HIGBEE, ANN G., public relations executive, consultant; b. Newark, May 6, 1942; d. Roger Herald German and Charlotte May (Ryan) Wentzell; m. James Lyman Higbee, June 25, 1965; 1 child, Travis James. BS, U. Md., 1964. Field rep. Am. Field Svc., N.Y.C., 1964-65; from acct. exec. to v.p. Rath Orgn., Syracuse, N.Y., 1965-71, T.A. Best Co., Skaneateles, N.Y., 1971-75; dir. devel. Manlius Pebble Hill Sch., Jamesville, N.Y., 1975-79; dir. pub. rels., mng. ptnr. Eric Mower and Assocs., Syracuse, 1980—. Chair Pub. Broadcasting Coun./CNY, Syracuse, 1977-84; dir. Crouse Health, Syracuse, 1983—; trustee Coll. Environ. Sci. and Forestry Found., Syracuse, 1991—. Named Women of Achievement by Post-Standard, Syracuse, 1973, Outstanding Young Woman by Jaycees, Syracuse. Mem. Pub. Rels. Soc. Am. (accredited, counselors sect.), Am. Assn. Advt. Agys. (pub. rels. com.). Avocations: golf, travel. Office: Eric Mower and Assocs 500 Plum St Ste 300 Syracuse NY 13204-1481*

HIGBEE, DONALD WILLIAM, electronics company executive; b. Stonewall, Okla., Jan. 7, 1931; s. James W. and Nannie M. (Driver) H.; m. Joan M. Diamond; children: Bradley, Carter, Phillip, Lisa. AB cum laude, U. So. Calif., 1956, JD, 1962. Bar: Calif. 1963; U.S. Supreme Ct. Quet. Pacific Press, Inc., Los Angeles, 1956-60; sec., treas. Utah Research and Devel. Co., Salt Lake City, 1964; controller Interstate Electronics, Anaheim, Calif., 1960-63; dir. contracts Interstate Electronics, Anaheim, 1965-74, v.p., sec., 1974-86, also bd. dirs.; pres. Higbee Investments, 1989—. Bd. dirs. Silverado (Calif.) Water Dist., 1965-70, Silverado-Modjeska Recreation and Park Dist., 1965-70. Served with USMC, 1950-51, Korea. Decorated Purple Heart, 1951. Mem. State Bar of Calif., Orange County Bar Assn., Nat. Contract Mgmt. Assn., Nat. Assn. Accts., Machinery and Allied Products Inst., Nat. Security Indsl. Assn., VFW, Masons, Elks, Moose. Republican. Lodges: Elks, Masons, Moose. Avocations: gardening, computers, tennis, golf. Home: 3502 Cazador Ln Fallbrook CA 92028-9426

HIGBEE, JOAN FLORENCE, librarian; b. Washington, Jan. 1, 1945; d. Florence Salick H. Student, U. Sorbonne, 1962-63, U. Nancy, 1967-68; BA in French, George Washington U., 1967; MA and PhD in Romance Langs., Johns Hopkins U., 1975; MLS, Cath. U. Am., 1976. Libr. Collection Svcs. Dept., Libr. of Congress, Washington, 1976-98; specialist French Caribbean culture Area Studies Dept., Libr. of Congress, Washington, 1998—; collections specialist Woodrow Wilson Internat. Ctr. Scholars, Smithsonian Inst., 1981—; instr. Johns Hopkins U., 1968-72; asst. d'anglais, Lycée Frédéric Chopin, Nancy, France, 1967-68; guest lectr. George Washington U., 1997—. Author: Southwest European Studies, 1989, Western Europe Since 1945, 1996; creator, editor Libr. of Congress Houdini home page, 1996—; contbr. articles to profl. jours. Mem. ALA (councilor at large 1980-88, founding coordinator Library Union Task Force, past mem. policy monitoring com., resolutions com., com. profl. standards), Assn. Coll. and Research Libraries (past chair Western European specialists sect.), Internat. Brotherhood Magicians (award of outstanding merit 1996), Soc. Am. Magicians, Houdini Hist. Assn. (hon. bd. 1995—). Office: Libr of Congress 1st and Independence Ave SE Washington DC 20540

HIGBY, EDWARD JULIAN, safety engineer; b. Milw., June 9, 1939; s. Richard L. Higby and Julie Ann (Bruins) O'Kelly; m. Frances Ann Knoodle, 1959 (div. 1962); 1 child, Melinda Ann Mozader. BS in Criminal Justice, Southwestern U., Tucson, 1984. Tactical officer Miami Police Dept., Fla., 1967-68; intelligence officer Fla. Divsn. Beverages, 1968-72; licensing coord. Lums Restaurant Corp., Miami, 1972-73; legal asst. Walt Disney World, Lake Buena Vista, Fla., 1973-78; loss control cons. R.P. Hewitt & Assocs., Orlando, Fla., 1978-79; safety coord. City of Lakeland, Fla., 1979-94. Author: Safety Guide for Health Care, 1979. Councilman City of Bay Lake, 1974-76, mayorr, 1975-76; active Fla. League of Cities, 1974-76, Tri-County League of Cities, 1974-76, Orange County Criminal Justice Coun., 1974-78, Ctrl. Fla. Safety Coun., 1978-79; bd. dirs. Greater Lakeland chpt. ARC, 1980-86, chmn. bd. dirs., 1983-84, 85-86, chmn. health svcs., 1980-86; mem. budget com. United Way Ctrl. Fla., 1983-85; bd. dirs. Tampa Area Safety Coun., 1983-92, pres., 1990-91; bd. dirs. Imperial Traffic Safety Coun., 1983-89; mem. Polk County Disaster Coordination Com., bd. dirs., 1984-92; bd. dirs. Employers Health Care Group Polk County, 1987-89, Parent Resources and Info. on Drug Edn., 1989-92; bd. dirs. ARC Polk County chpt., 1990-92, 94-96, coord. Mass Care, 1994-95, chmn. Health and Safety, 1994-95, chmn. Risk Mgmt., 1995-96; active ARC Disaster Svcs. Human Resources Sys., 1994-99; mem. Fla. Adv. Com. Arson Prevention, Local Emergency Planing Com., State of Fla., 1987-92, 94—, Fla. Disaster Mortuary Team, 1995—; mem. adv. panel Polk County Industry Cmty., 1997—; mem. adv com. Charlotte Harbor Nat. Estuary, 1997. With U.S. Army, 1963-64. Named Vol. of Yr., Greater Lakeland chpt. ARC, 1983-84. Mem. NRA (life), World Safety Orgn., Fla. Sheriffs Assn. (hon. life), Internat. Assn. Identification (life, Fla. divsn., Russian divsn.), Nat. Found. Mortuary Care, Automatic Fire Alarm Assn., Disaster Emergency Response Assn. (life), Environ. Assessment Assn., U. Fla. Nat. Alumni Assn. (life), Fla. Pub. Health Assn., Fla. Fedn. Safety, Am. Soc. Safety Engrs. (mem. regional oper. com. 1983-85, 88-90, profl. devel. conf. com. 1983, 85, chpt. bd. dirs. 1983-87, chpt. pres. 1984-85, v.p. profl. devel. region VIII 1988-90, Safety Profl. of Yr. 1984-85, Albert G. Mowson award 1995-96), Heartland Safety Soc. (life, pres. 1982-83, 94-95), Fla. Citrus Safety Assn. (pres. 1981-83), Nat. Fire Protection Assn., Am. Indsl. Hygiene Assn. (Fla. chpt.), Fire Marshals Assn. N.Am., Soc. Fire Protection Engrs. (bd. dirs. Fla. chpt. 1994-99), So. Health Assn., Fla. Affiliation of Ins. Safety Reps., Internat. Critical Incident Stress Found., Critical Incident Stress Debriefers Fla., Nat. Assn. Search and Rescue, Fla. Funeral Dirs. Assn., Fla. Emergency Preparedness Assn., Fla. Assn. Code Enforcement, Internat. Assn. Arson Investigators, Fla. Cracker Cattle Assn. (life), Harley Owners Group (life), Am. Motorcycle Assn. (life), Lakeland Rifle and Pistol Club. Republican. Avocations: hunting, fishing.

HIGBY, GREGORY JAMES, historical association administrator, historian; b. Dearborn, Mich., Dec. 24, 1953; s. Warren James and Gertrude (Mosebach) H.; m. Marian Fredal, June 2, 1979. BS in Pharmacy, U. Mich., 1977; MS in Pharmacy, U. Wis., 1980, PhD in Pharmacy, 1984. Staff pharmacist Higby's Pharmacy, Bad Axe, Mich., 1977-78; asst. to dir. Am. Inst. of the History of Pharmacy, Madison, Wis., 1981-84, asst. dir., 1984-86, assoc. dir., 1986, acting dir., 1986-88, dir., 1988—; rsch. assoc. U. Wis., Madison, 1984-86; adj. asst. prof. U. Wis., Madison, 1984-94, adj. assoc. prof., 1994—; cons. Smithsonian Instn., Washington, 1987, Am. Soc. Hosp. Pharmacists, Bethesda, Md., 1990, U.S. Pharmacopeial Conv., 1992-95, Am. Assn. Colls. Pharmacy, 1993—; mem. adv. com. Fed. Drug Law Inst., Washington, 1989-90. Author: In Service to American Pharmacy: The Professional Life of William Procter, Jr., U. Ala. Press, 1992; co-author: The Spirit of Voluntarism...The United States Pharmacopeia 1820-1995, 1995; editor: One Hundred Years of the National Formulary, 1989, Pill Peddlers: Essays on the History of the Pharmaceutical Industry, 1990, Historical Hobbies for the Pharmacist, 1994, The History of Pharmacy, A Selected Annotated Bibliography, 1995, The Inside Story of Medicines, 1997; author poetry; editor Pharmacy in History Jour., 1986—; contbr. articles to profl. jours. Recipient Edward Kremers award 1995. Mem. Am. Pharm. Assn., Am. Chem. Soc. (assoc.), Am. Assn. for History of Medicine, Hist. Sci. Soc., Orgn. Am. Historians, Soc. for History of Tech., Internat. Acad. History of Pharmacy. Avocations: bird watching, racquetball, jazz musician. Office: Am Inst of the History of Pharmacy 425 N Charter St Madison WI 53706-1508

HIGBY, (DONALD) WAYNE, artist, educator; b. Colorado Springs, Colo., May 12, 1943; s. Donald W. and Betty (Bates) H.; m. Donna Claire Bennett, Mar. 12, 1966; children: Austin Myles, Sarah Lark. BFA, U. Colo., 1966; MFA, U. Mich., 1968. Prof. art N.Y. State Coll. Ceramics, Alfred U., 1973—; chair divsn. ceramic art, 1983-91; panelist Task Force for Individual Artists N.Y. State Coun. Arts, 1980-82, chair, 1978, mem. visual arts panel, 1976, 77; mem. NEA Visual Artists Fellowship/Crafts, 1986, NEA Visual Arts Overview Panel, 1989-90; hon. prof. art Hubei Acad. Fine Arts, Wuhan, People's Republic of China, 1992, ceramic art Jingdezhen Ceramic Inst, People's Republic of China, 1994. One-man exhbns. include Helen Drutt Gallery, 1988, 90, Mus. of Art and Design, Helsinki, Finland, 1999; invitational exhbns. include 8th and 13th Chunichi Internat. Exhbn. Ceramic Art, Nagoya, Japan, 1980, 85, respectively, Everson Mus. Art, Syracuse, N.Y., 1981, 87, 89, Am. Craft Mus., N.Y.C., 1982, 89, Jacksonville (Fla.) Mus. Art, 1982, Nelson-Atkins Mus. Art, Kansas City, 1983, Boston Mus. Fine Arts, 1984, Victoria and Albert Mus., London, 1986, Seoul Olympics Arts Festival, 1988, Nat. Mus. Ceramic Art, Balt., 1989, Kanazawa, Ishibkawa Pref, Japan, 1991, Nat. Mus. Modern Art, Tokyo, 1992-93, Met. Mus. Art, N.Y.C., 1999; public collections include Met. Mus. Art, N.Y.C., Mpls. Mus. Art, Phila. Mus. Art, Everson Mus. Art, Joslyn Mus. Art, Omaha, Am. Craft Mus., Victoria and Albert Mus., Boston Mus. Fine Arts, Bklyn. Mus. Art, L.A. County Mus. Art. Bd. dirs. Haystack Mountain Sch. Crafts, Deer Isle, Maine, 1983—, pres., 1989-92. Howard Found. fellow, 1985-86, 89-90; recipient Master Tchr. award U. Hartford, 1990, Chancellor's award SUNY, 1993; named visionary of Am. craft Am. Craft Mus., 1995. Mem. Coll. of Fellows Am. Craft Coun. Office: N Y State Coll Ceramics Alfred U Alfred NY 14802

HIGDON, LEO I., JR., dean, finance educator. Dean Grad. Sch. Bus. Adminstrn. U. Va., Charlottesville; pres. Babson Coll., Babson Park, Mass. Office: Babson Coll Babson Park MA 02157-0901

HIGDON, POLLY SUSANNE, federal judge; b. Goodland, Kans., May 1, 1942; d. William and Pauline Higdon; m. John P. Wilhardt (div. May 1988); 1 child, Liesl. BA, Vassar Coll., 1964; postgrad., Cornell U., 1967; JD, Washburn U., 1975; LLM, NYU, 1980. Bar: Kans. 1975, Oreg. 1980. Assoc. Corley & Assocs., Garden City, Kans., 1975-79, Kendrick M. Mercer Law Offices, Eugene, Oreg., 1980-82; pvt. practice law Eugene, 1983; judge U.S. Bankruptcy Ct., Eugene, 1983-95; judge U.S. Bankruptcy Ct., Portland, Oreg., 1995-97, chief judge, 1997—. Active U.S. Peace Corps, Tanzania, East Africa, 1965-66. Mem. Am. Bankruptcy Inst., Nat. Conf. Bankruptcy Judges, Oreg. Women Lawyers. Office: US Bankruptcy Ct 1001 SW 5th Ave Fl 7 Portland OR 97204-1147

HIGDON, SHIRLEY A., medical/surgical nurse; b. El Paso, Tex., Feb. 28, 1953; d. Raymond J. and Beatrice H. Tarang; 1 child, Adam D. Higdon. Diploma, Tex. Ea. Sch. Nursing, Tyler, 1982; AS in Nursing, Tyler Jr. Coll., 1981; BS, U. Tex., Tyler, 1990. Sch. nurse Tyler Ind. Sch. Dist.; staff nurse Tyler Square Ambulatory Ctr.; health edn. Zales Lipshy U. Hosp., Dallas; utilization rev./admissions nurse Med. City Hosp., Dallas. Mem. ANA, Tex. Nurses Assn. (program chair), Sigma Theta Tau.

HIGGENS, WILLIAM JOHN, III (TREY HIGGENS), sales executive; b. Evanston, Ill., May 26, 1951; s. William John Jr. and Delores May (Fuller) H.; m. Melanie Ann Mayer (div.); children: Melissa Lee, Tracy Ann; m. Barbara Carrie Simcoe, July 8, 1989. BS in Mktg. Mgmt., Miami U., Oxford, Ohio, 1973. Sales rep. A.B. Dick Co., Chgo., 1973-76; dist. sales mgr. McGraw-Hill Pub. Co., Chgo., 1976-85, CMP Publ., Inc., Chgo., 1985-91, McGraw-Hill Pub. Co., Chgo., 1991-96; Ea. regional sales mgr., dir. Europe and Middle East Lightwave mag. PennWell Pub. Co., Oak Brook, Ill., 1996—. Mem. Bus. Mktg. Assn. (bd. dirs. 1984—, cert. bus. communicator 1989). Republican. Episcopalian. Avocations: flying, golf, reading, travel, computers. Home: 230 Weidner Rd Buffalo Grove IL 60089-1949 Office: PennWell Pub Co 2625 Butterfield Rd Ste 138S Oak Brook IL 60523-1244

HIGGINBOTHAM, EDITH ARLEANE, radiologist, researcher; b. New Orleans, Sept. 14, 1946; d. Luther Aldrich and Ruby (Clark) H.; m. Terry Lawrence Andrews (div. 1979); m. Donald Temple Ford (div. 1989). *Sister, Eve J. Higginbotham MD, is chairman of ophthalmology at University of Maryland Hospital in Baltimore. She is an internationally known ophthalmologist with many publications. She has a BS and an MS in Chemical Engineering from MIT and an MD from Harvard. Sister, Cecelia B. Higginbotham is a medical librarian at Bayne Jones Army Community Hospital. She has a BSN from Catholic University, an MLS from Atlanta University, and has been responsible for the medical library since 1984.* BS, Howard U., 1967, MS, 1970, MD, 1974. Diplomate Am. Bd. Radiology, Am. Bd. Nuclear Medicine. Intern St. Vincent's Hosp., N.Y.C., 1974-75, resident in diagnostic radiology, 1975-78, resident in nuclear radiology, 1978-79; asst. prof. radiology, chief nuclear medicine Howard U., Howard U. Hosp., Washington, 1979-82; assoc. prof. clin. radiology, dir. nuclear medicine U. Medicine and Dentistry N.J., Newark, 1982-90; locum tenens radiologist Sterling Med., Cin., 1991—, Med. Nat., San Antonio, 1990-91; diagnostic radiologist Diagnostic Health Imaging Systems, Lanham, Md., 1994-97; radiologist, dir. radiology N.E. Wash. Med. Group, Colville, Wash., 1997—; radiologist Mount Carmel Hosp., Colville, 1997—; cons. Biotech. Rsch. Inst., Rockville, Md., 1989-94; profl. assoc. Ctr. for Molecular Medicine and Immunology, Newark, 1984-90; asst. prof. radiology George Washington U., Washington, 1990; presenter in field. Contbr. articles to profl. jours. Named Outstanding Working Woman, Glamour mag., 1981, Hon. Dep. Atty. Gen., State of La., 1982. Mem. Am. Coll. Radiology, Radiol. Soc. N.Am., Soc. Nuclear Medicine, Sigma Xi, Phi Delta Epsilon. Roman Catholic. Avocations: aerobics, reading, self-improvement, music. travel. Home: 1139 SE Park Dr Colville WA 99114-9336 also: 3926 Chestnut St New Orleans LA 70115-2662 also: Mt Carmel Hosp 982 E Columbia Ave Colville WA 99114-3316

HIGGINBOTHAM, JOHN TAYLOR, lawyer; b. St. Louis, Feb. 10, 1947; s. Richard Cann and Jocelyn (Taylor) H.; m. Lauren Flint Totty, Aug. 9, 1975 (div. 1979). BA, UCLA, 1969; JD, Columbia U., 1972. Bar: N.Y. 1975, Calif. 1976. Assoc., Kirlin, Campbell & Keating, N.Y.C., 1972-74; atty. Nat. Bank of N.Am., N.Y.C., 1974-76, Bank of Am., 1977; assoc. Barger & Wolen, L.A., 1977-78, Halperin, Shivitz, Scholer, Schneider & Eisenberg, 1978-79; atty., dir. real estate Korvettes Inc., N.Y.C., 1979-82; assoc. Leon Katz, Bklyn., 1983-84; assoc. Finley, Kumble, Wagner, Heine, Underberg, Manley & Casey, N.Y.C., 1984-86; assoc. regional counsel HUD, N.Y.C., 1986-88, Sterling Securities, Inc., Manhasset, N.Y., 1989-93, Willkie, Farr & Gallagher, N.Y.C., 1993. Editor: Safe Deposit Decisions and Practice, 1977—. Mem. NARAS, NATAS, Acad. Motion Picture Arts and Scis., League Am. Theatres and Producers, Inc.

HIGGINBOTHAM, KENNETH JAMES, financial services executive; b. Phila., Aug. 3, 1942; s. James V. and Elizabeth R. (Roebas) H.; m. Ruth M. Schaffer, Apr. 12, 1969; children: Jennifer K., Scott G. BA, Rutgers U., 1971; MBA, Drexel U., 1973. Fin. analyst, discount window Fed. Res. Bank of Phila., 1972-77; corp. cash mgmt. cons. First Pa. Bank NA, Phila., 1977-79; EFT cons. Control Data Corp., Mpls., 1979-84; dist. rep. Aid Assn. for Lutherans, Appleton, Wis., 1984-94; reg. rep. Lincoln Fin. Advisors, Richboro, Pa., 1994—; adj. faculty LaSalle U., Phila., 1977—. With USN, 1963-67. Mem. Am. Assn. U. Profs., Soc. Fin. Svc. Profls., Nat. Assn. Life Underwriters, Internat. Assn. Fin. Planners, Bucks County Estate Planning Coun. Home: 21 Holly Hill Rd Richboro PA 18954-1917 Office: Lincoln Financial Advisors 21 Holly Hill Rd Richboro PA 18954-1917

HIGGINBOTHAM, PATRICK ERROL, federal judge; b. Ala., Dec. 16, 1938. Student, U. Ala., 1956, Arlington State Coll., 1957, North Tex. State U., 1958, U. Tex., 1958; B.A., U. Ala., 1960, LL.B., 1961; LLD (hon.), So. Meth. U., 1989. Bar: Ala. 1961, Tex. 1962, U.S. Supreme Ct. 1962. Assoc. to ptnr. Coke & Coke, Dallas, 1964-75; judge U.S. Dist. Ct. (no. dist.) Tex., Dallas, 1976-82, U.S. Ct. Appeals (5th cir.), Dallas, 1982—; adj. prof. So. Meth. U. Law Sch., 1971—, adj. prof. constl. law, 1981—; conferee Am. Assembly, 1975, Pound Conf., 1976; bd. suprs. Inst. Civil Justice Rand. Contbr. articles, revs. to profl. publs.; note editor: Ala. Law Rev., 1960-61. With USAF, 1961-64, JAG. Recipient Dan Meador award U. Ala., Samuel E. Gates Litigation award Am. Coll. Trial Lawyers, 1997; named Outstanding Alumnus U. Tex., Arlington, 1978, One of Nation's 100 Most Powerful Persons for the 80's Next Mag. Fellow Am. Bar Found.; mem. ABA (chmn. com. to compile fed. jury charges antitrust sect., mem. coun. antitrust sect., bd. editors Jour. chair appellate judges conf. 1989—), Dallas Bar Assn. (dir., chmn. cons. legal aid civic affairs), Dallas Bar Found. (bd. dirs.), Am. Law Inst., S.W. Legal Found. (chmn. bd. of trustees), Am. Judicature Soc. (bd. dirs., trustee), Nat. Jud. Coun. State and Fed. Cts., Dallas Inn of Ct. (pres. 1996—, chair adv. com. on civil rules jud. conf. U.S. 1993-96), Farrah Law Soc., Order of Coif (hon.), Bench and Bar, Am. Inns. of Ct. Found. (pres. 1996—), Omicron Delta Kappa. Office: US Ct Appeals 13E1 US Courthouse 1100 Commerce St Dallas TX 75242-1027

HIGGINBOTHAM, WENDY JACOBSON, political adviser, writer; b. Salt Lake City, Oct. 23, 1947; d. Alfred Thurl and Virginia Lorraine (LaCom) Jacobson; m. Keith Higginbotham, July 12, 1969; children: Ann Elizabeth Morley, Ryan Keith, Laura Carol. Student, Occidental Coll., 1965-66, U. Grenoble, France, 1967; BA cum laude with highest honors, Brigham Young U., 1969. Teaching instr. Brigham Young U., Provo, Utah, 1969-70, editor univ. press, 1970-71; freelance editor Camarillo, Calif., 1971-78; freelance newspaper writer Vienna, Va., 1983-85; mem. profl. staff U.S. Senate Labor Com., Washington, 1985-86; exec. asst. U.S. Senator Orrin G. Hatch, Washington, 1986-88, legis. dir., 1988-91, chief of staff/adminstrv. asst., 1991-94, chief policy adviser, 1994-95; polit. adviser, freelance writer Washington, 1996—. Mem. Profl. Rep. Women, Phi Kappa Phi. Mormon. Avocations: traveling, hiking. Home: 2022 Willow Branch Ct Vienna VA 22181-2972

HIGGINBOTTOM, SAMUEL LOGAN, retired aerospace company executive; b. North Lawrence, Ohio, Oct. 5, 1921; s. Samuel Bradlaugh and Vera Abbie (Gutchess) H.; m. Fair Steinschneider, Aug. 30, 1947 (dec. May 1997); children: Samuel Logan, Marie Fair, Michele Rowan Maclaren; m. Janaina Dornelles, Aug. 4, 1998. BS in Civil Engring, Columbia, 1943; grad. Advanced Mgmt. Program, Harvard U. Design engr. Parsons, Brinckerhoff, Hogan & McDonald, N.Y.C., 1945-46; v.p. engring., flight, test and inspection Trans World Airlines, Inc., 1946-64; v.p. engring. and maintenance Eastern Air Lines, Inc., 1964-67, v.p. operations group, 1967-69, sr. v.p., 1969, exec. v.p., 1969-70, pres., chief operating officer, 1970-73; chmn., pres., chief exec. officer Rolls-Royce Inc., N.Y.C., 1974-86. Emeritus chmn. bd. trustees Columbia U.; vice-chmn. St. Thomas U. Capt. USAAF, WWII, ETO. Decorated hon. comdr. Order Brit. Empire; recipient Egleston medal Columbia U. Engring. Sch., 1977. Fellow AIAA; mem. Soc. Automotive Engrs., Conquistadores del Cielo, Wings Club (pres.1980-81), Deering Bay Yacht and Country Club, Tau Beta Pi, Psi Upsilon, Theta Tau. Roman Catholic. Home: 6741 SW 140th St Miami FL 33158 Office: 1 Alhambra Plz Ste 1115 Coral Gables FL 33134-5217

HIGGINS, BRIAN ALTON, art gallery executive; b. Brookline, Mass., Oct. 26, 1930; s. Gerald and Catherin (Walsh) H.; m. Jane Edgington, July 1, 1975; children: Brenda, Belinda, Devon. With film dept. Sta. WNAC-TV, Boston, 1951-53; mgr. Ctrl. European Film Exch., Karlsruhe, Germany, 1953-54; ops. mgr. Sta. WMTW-TV, Portland, Maine, 1954-68; gen. mgr., dir. devel. Leghorn Cable TV Sys., 1969; v.p., gen. mgr. Sta. WSMW-TV, Worcester, Mass., 1974-84; pres. Brian Edgington Collection Am. Art, 1974—. Contbr. articles to publs. Chmn. bd. Ctrl. Mass. Symphony Orch., 1979—, Ctrl. Mass. chpt. Am. Heart Assn.; bd. dirs. Ctrl. Mass. chpt. ARC; mem. coun. YMCA, Worcester Art Mus.; past vice-chmn. Maine Project Hope. With Signal Corps, U.S. Army, 1952-54. Recipient numerous civic awards. Mem. Danforth Mus. Art (life), Worcester Art Mus., Atlantic City Hist. Mus. (life). Republican. Home: Ridge Rd West Brookfield MA 01585 Office: PO Box 1011 West Brookfield MA 01585-1011

HIGGINS, DICK (RICHARD CARTER HIGGINS), writer, publisher, composer, artist; b. Cambridge, Eng., Mar. 15, 1938; came to U.S., 1939; s. Carter Chapin and Katharine (Bigelow) H.; m. Alison Knowles, May 31, 1960 (div. 1970); children: Hannah and Jessica (twins); m. Alison Knowles, 1984. Student, Yale U., 1957; BS in English, Columbia U., 1960; postgrad., Manhattan Sch. Printing, 1960-61; MA in English, NYU, 1977; studied with John Cage and Henry Cowell, 1958-59. Co-founder Happenings (Theater) movement, N.Y.C., 1958, Fluxus movement, N.Y.C., 1961; founder Something Else Press, N.Y.C., 1963-73; originator concept, developer (visual, mus. and lit. publs.) Intermedia, 1965; founder, operator Unpublished Edits., West Glover, Vt., 1972-85 (renamed Printed Editions, 1978, in operation until 1986); operator Something Else Gallery, 1966-69; tchr. Calif. Inst. Arts, 1970-71; mem. lit. panel N.Y. State Coun. on Arts, 1979-81; rsch. assoc. in visual arts, SUNY-Purchase, 1983-89; vis. Clark prof. in art Williams Coll., fall 1987, rsch. assoc. in history of art, 1989—; tchr. Salzburg (Austria) Sommerakademic, 1973, Lund (Sweden) U., 1997. Author: What are legends, 1960, Jefferson's birthday/Postface, 1964, foew & ombwhnw, 1968, Die fabelhafte Geträume von Taifun-Willi, 1969, Computers for the arts, 1970, amigo, 1972, A book about love and war and death, 1972, The Ladder to the moon, 1973, For Eugene in Germany, 1973, Spring Game, 1973, City with all the angles, 1974, Modular Poems, 1975, classic plays, 1976, Legends and Fishnets, 1986, Cat alley, 1977, The Epitaphs/Gli epitaphi, 1977, George Herbert's pattern poems: in their tradition, 1977, Everyone has sher Favorite (his or hers), 1977, The epickall quest of the brothers Dichtung and other outrages, 1977, A dialectic of centuries: notes towards a theory of the new arts, 1978, some recent snowflakes (and other things), 1979, of celebration of morning, 1980, Ten ways of looking at a bird, 1981, Selected early works, 1982, 1959/60, 1982, Art contemporain 10-20, 1983, Horizons: the poetics and theory of the intermedia, 1982 (Japanese edit. 1985), Intermedia, 1985, 2d edit., 1991, Poems, Plain and Fancy, 1986, Visible Language, 1986, Pattern Poetry: A Guide to an Unknown Literature, 1987, The Journey, 1991, The Autobiography of the Moon, 1992, Happytime the Medicine Man, 1992, Buster Keaton Enters Into Paradise, 1994, Octette, 1994, Life Flowers, 1997, Modernism Since Postmodernism, 1997; translator Novalis' Hymne an die

Nacht, 1978, 2d edit., 1984, 3d edit., 1988, Czternascie tlumaczen telefonicznych dla Steve'a McCaffery, Poland, 1987, The Journey, 1991, The Autobiography of the Moon, 1992, Happytime the Medicine Man, 1992, Octette, 1994, Buster Keaton Enters Into Paradise, 1994, (with others) The Book, Spiritual Instrument, 1996; editor, annotator On the composition of images, sign and ideas by Giordano Bruno, 1991; musical works include first electronic opera Stacked Deck (with Richard Maxfield), 1958-59, Piano Album: short pieces, 1962-84, 1980, Sonata for prepared piano, 1981, 26 Mountains for Viewing the Sunset From, 1981, Variation on a natural theme, for orch., 1981, 1959/60, 1982, Song for any voice(s) and instrument(s), 1983, Sonata No. 2 for piano, 1983; author numerous plays, movies; editor: (with Wolf Vostell) Pop Architektur, 1969, Fantastic Architecture, 1971; 150 book inclusions; contbr. to numerous periodicals, 1962-95; author mimeo books, acting scripts, small multiples, buttons, postcards, pamphlets, booklets; films include A tiny movie, 1959, The flight of the Florence bird, 1960, The flaming city, 1961-62, The End, 1962, Invocation of canyons and boulders for Stan Brakhage, 1962, Plunk, 1962, For the dead, 1965, Scenario, 1968, Hank and Mary without apologies, 1969, Mysteries, 1969, Men & women and bells, 1970; videotapes include Gentle talk, 1977, A lecture on The Something Else Press and since, 1981, The flaming city, 1961-62, 81, Fluxus at Williams, 1987; radio performance pieces include Die fabelhafte Geträume von Taifun-Willi, 1970, City with all the angles, 1973, Scenes forgotten and otherwise remembered, 1985, Girlande für John, 1987, Five professionals whom you can trust, 1989, Three double helixes that aren't for sale, 1989; mus. publs. include Graphis 144, Wipeout for orchestra, Graphis 143, Softly for orchestra, 1967, Suggested by small swallows, 1973, Emmett Wiliams' ear/L'orecchio di Emmett Williams, 1978; recordings include Telephone music, 1979, Eine zweite heutliche deutliche Sprache, 1972, Danger music 17, 1977, Plug: an acid novel, 1977, "glaslass" in Baobab, 1978, Poems and metapoems, 1983, Session with Bern Porter, 1983, Telephone translation #9, 1983, Bodies electric: arches and requiem for Wagner the criminal mayor, 1985, Glasslass, 1985, Constellations, 1986, Music by Dick Higgins, 1989; one or two-artist shows include Galerie Rene Block, Berlin, 1973, Centro de Arte y Communicacion, Buenos Aires, 1974, Galerie St. Petri, Lund, Sweden, 1974, Galerie Vehicule, Montreal, 1974, Museu de ArtContemporanea, Sao Paulo., Brazil, 1976, Galerie Ecart, Geneva, 1977, La Mamelle, San Francisco, 1977, Studio Morra, Naples, 1977, Galerie Inge Baecker, Bochum, 1978,82, C Space, N.Y.C., 1978, Galleri Sudurgata, Reykjavik, Iceland, Galerie Ars Viva, Berlin, 1982, Galerie A, Amsterdam, 1982, Emily Harvey Artworks, N.Y.C., 1986, 89, Art Gallery, San Diego State U., Calexico, Calif., 1987, Mid-Hudson Arts and Sci. Ctr., Poughkeepsie, N.Y., 1988, Emily Harvey artworks, N.Y, 1989, Galeria Potocka, Krakow, Poland, 1989, Emily Harvey Gallery, N.Y.C., 1990, 93, Gallery Office Art Berry Coll., Rome, Ga., 1991, Schüppenhauer Gallery, Cologne, Germany, 1991, Galérie J.-et-J. Paris, 1993, Emily Harvey Gallery, N.Y.C., 1993, Henie Onstad Art Ctr., Oslo, 1995, Mpls. Mus., 1995, Mcpl. Gallery, Pori, Finland, 1995, Archivio di Nuova Scrittura, Milan, Italy, 1995, Ctr. for Contemporary Art, Warsaw, 1996, Gallery 479, N.Y.C., 1996, Caterina Gualco, Genova, 1997; group exhbns. include Judson Gallery, N.Y.C., 1960, Fine Arts Gallery, U. B.C., 1969, Copenhagen Mus. Modern Art, 1972, Los Angeles Inst. of Contemporary Arts, 1978, Detroit Art Inst., 1979, Neuberger Mus., SUNY, Purchase, N.Y., 1981, Galerie Ars Viva, Berlin, 1982, Hayward Gallery, London, 1983, Staatsgalerie Stuttgart, 1984, Nexus Gallery, Phila., 1985, Mappin Art Gallery, Sheffield, Eng., 1986, Harlekin Art, Wiesbaden, 1987, Galleria Vivita 1, Florence, 1988, Stux Gallery, N.Y.C., 1990, others; represented in permanent collections and archives including Berlinische Galerie, Berlin, Gallery of Modern Art, Vienna, Austria, Sonja Henie-Niels Onstad Found., Oslo, Norway, Museu de Arte Contemporanea, Sao Paulo, Brazil, Museum of Modern Art, Copenhagen, Neue Staatsgalerie Stuttgart, Museo Vostell, Caceres, Spain, Jean Brown Archive, John Paul Getty Art Ctr., Los Angeles, Ruth and Marvin Sackner Archive of Visual Poetry, Miami Beach, Fla., Archiv Hanns Sohm, Neue Staatsgalerie Stuttgart; included in pvt. collections of Marcel Fleiss, Paris, Dr. Kenneth Friedman, N.Y.C., Emily Harvey, N.Y.C., Gil Williams, Binghamton, N.Y., Rene Block, Berlin, others; fluxus performances numerous locations U.S.A. and Europe including Moderna Galerija Ljubljana, Solvenia, 1997; numerous creative works including music, art and ephemeral publications since 1958. Ctr. for 20th Century Studies fellow U. Wis., Milw., 1977, DAAD fellow, Berlin, 1981-82, Banff (Alta., Can.) Centre fellow, 1990; N.Y. State Coun. on Arts grantee, 1968—, Collaborations grantee visual arts program N.Y. State Coun. on Arts, 1989—, Purchase Coll. grantee for pattern poetry projects, 1984-86, 88—, Pollock-Krasner Found. grantee, 1993; recipient Bill C. Davis Drama award for The Journey (1986-87), 1988—; residency Banff (Alberta) Centre, 1990. Home: PO Box 27 Station Hill Rd Barrytown NY 12507 *I find I never feel quite complete unless I'm doing all the arts--visual, musical and literary. I guess that's why I developed the term 'intermedia,' to cover my works that fall conceptually between these.**

HIGGINS, DOROTHY MARIE, academic dean; b. Lawrence, Mass., May 1, 1930; d. John Daniel and Mary Jane (Herbertson) H. AB, Emmanuel Coll., 1951; MS, Cath. U., 1961; PhD, Boston Coll., 1966. Assoc. prof. chemistry Emmanuel Coll., Boston, 1966-88, chair chemistry dept., 1974-85; div. chair math., sci., tech. Roxbury Community Coll., Roxbury Crossing, Mass., 1988-90; dean arts and scis. Teikyo-Post U., Waterbury, Conn., 1990-97; part-time instr. organic chemistry Naugatuck Valley Cmty.-Tech. Coll., 1998; grant cons. N.E. coll. Optometry, Boston, 1986; faculty cons. Zymark Corp., Hopkinton, Mass., 1982; rsch. assoc. U. Mass., Boston, 1975-84. Editor: (workbook) Geometry: Development Students, 1989; editor sci. newsletter, 1989; editorial adv. bd. Jour. Coll. Sci. Teaching, 1984-88. Instrumentation grantee NSF, 1985, Chautauqua grantee NSF, 1981-82, Instrumentation grantee George Alden Trust, 1985, Boston Globe Found., 1985, Extramural Assoc. grantee NIH, 1984. Mem. Am. Chem. Soc., Nat. Sci. Tchrs. Assn., New Eng. Chem. Tchrs., Soc. Coll. Sci. Teaching, Am. Assn. Higer Edn., Sigma Xi. Democrat. Roman Catholic. Avocations: needlework, crocheting, cross-country skiing.

HIGGINS, EDWARD ALOYSIUS, retired newspaper editor; b. St. Louis, Aug. 22, 1931; s. Edward Aloysius and Elsie (Gummersbach) H.; m. Mary Suzanne Vallar, May 15, 1954; children—Nancy Elizabeth, David Francis, Carol Marie. A.B., St. Louis U., 1953; Stanford Journalism fellow, Stanford U., 1968-69. Gen. assignment reporter St. Louis Post-Dispatch, 1953-67, editorial writer, 1967-84, editor Commentary Page, 1984-87, asst. editor editorial page, 1986-87, editor editorial page, 1987-97; ret., 1997. Home: 15340 Braefield Dr Chesterfield MO 63017-1832

HIGGINS, GEORGE EDWARD, sculptor; b. Gaffney, S.C., Nov. 13, 1930. B.A., U. N.C. Instr. sculpture Parsons Sch. Design, N.Y.C., 1961-62. vis. prof. Cornell U., 1968, U. Wis., 1968-69, U. Ky., 1969-70, Sch. Visual Arts, N.Y.C., 1964-72. One man shows, Leo Castelli Gallery, N.Y.C., 1960, 63, 66, Richard Feigen Gallery, Chgo., 1964, Mpls. Inst. Art, 1964, exhibited group shows Art, USA, 1959, Detroit Inst. Art, 1959-60, Carnegie Inst., 1961, Mus. Modern Art, N.Y.C., 1961, 63, Martha Jackson Gallery, N.Y.C., 1960, Andrew Dickson White Gallery, 1960, Bernard Gallery, Paris, France, 1960, Whitney Mus., N.Y.C., 1964, 66, Documenta, Kassel, Germany, 1968, Art Inst. Chgo., Brandeis U., Tate Gallery, London, Phila. Mus. Arts, New Sch. Art Center, N.Y.C., Smithsonian Instn., numerous others; represented in permanent collections, Whitney Mus., N.Y.C., Guggenheim Mus., N.Y.C., Albright-Knox Gallery, Buffalo, Houston Mus. Fine Arts, Mus. Modern Art, N.Y.C., Albright Art Gallery, Chase Manhattan Bank, N.Y.C., others. Address: 2655 Henley Rd Sanford NC 27330-7549

HIGGINS, JACK, editorial cartoonist; b. Chgo., Aug. 19, 1954; s. Maurice James and Helen Marie (Egan) H.; m. Mary Elizabeth Irving, Apr. 26, 1997. BA in Econs., Coll. Holy Cross, 1976. Editorial cartoonist The Daily Northwestern, Evanston, Ill., 1978-81; freelance editorial cartoonist Chgo. Sun-Times, 1980-84, editorial cartoonist, 1984—. Vol. worker Jesuit Vol. Corps, Washington, 1977. Recipient Peter Lisagor award Chgo. Soc. Profl. Journalists, 1984, 87, 91, 94, 96, 97, 98, 1st prize Internat. Salon Cartoons, Montreal, Que., Can., 1988, Pulitzer prize for editl. cartooning, 1989, Disting. Svc. award Sigma Delta Chi, 1988, 98, John Fischetti editl. cartooning award, 1998, media svc. award Chgo. Lung Assn., 1993, Herman Kogan media awards Chgo. Bar Assn., 1993, 95; named Alumnus of Yr., St. Ignatius Coll. Prep. Sch., Chgo., 1992, Ill. Journalist of Yr., 1996; finalist for Pulitzer prize, 1986, for Robert F. Kennedy journalism award, 1993, 94, others. Mem. Nat. Soc. of Profl. Journalists (Disting. Svc. award). Roman Catholic. Avocations: oil painting, bicycling. Office: Chgo Sun-Times 401 N Wabash Ave Chicago IL 60611-5642

HIGGINS, JAMES HENRY, III, marketing executive; b. Providence, May 8, 1940; s. James Henry Jr. and Betty (Hall) H. AB, Brown U., 1962. Mem. faculty Gov. Dummer Acad., Byfield, Mass., 1964-66; rsch. assoc. Entelek Inc., 1966-69; mgr. sch. svcs. group Sterling Inst., 1969-72; vice pres. Vickerman and Schultz, Inc., Washington, 1985-87; sr. v.p. Complete Communications, Inc., Washington, 1987-90; dir. devel. The Brit. Consortium, Washington, 1990—; mktg. cons. Time Life Video, N.Y.C., 1972-73, Longman Group Ltd., Eng., 1973-74, McGraw-Hill Publs. Co., N.Y.C., 1975-85. lectr., contbr. articles to boating publs. Mem. mgmt. com. A.S.K. Brown Mil. Collection, Brown U., 1990—. With USAR, 1964-70. Mem. Am Soc. Assn. Execs., Found. for Internat. Meetings (bd. dirs. 1987—), Naval War Coll. Found. (assoc.), Mystic Seaport Mus. (yachting com. 1986—), Antique and Classic Boat Soc. (pres., v.p., bd. dirs. 1978-94), Lake Placid Inst. (bd. dirs. 1996—, sec. 1999—), City Tavern Club (bd. govs. 1998—, sec. 1999—), Agawam Hunt Club, Hope Club, St. Regis Yacht Club. Home: 2807 O St NW Washington DC 20007-3130 Office: 1101 30th St NW Ste 500 Washington DC 20007-3708

HIGGINS, JAMES JACOB, statistics educator; b. Canton, Ill., Oct. 31, 1943; married, 1967; 2 children. BS, U. Ill., 1965; MS, Ill. State U., 1967; PhD in Stats., U. Mo., 1970. Asst. prof. math. U. Mo., Rolla, 1970-74; from asst. prof. to assoc. prof. math. U. South Fla., 1974-80; prof. stats. Kans. State U., Manhattan, 1980—; dept. head, 1990-95. Mem. Am. Statis. Assn., Inst. Math. Stats. Achievements include research in reliability theory; classical and Bayesian estimation theory; statistical modelling; experimental design; textbook author. E-mail: jhiggins@ksu.edu. Office: Kans State U Stats Lab Dickens Hall Manhattan KS 66506

HIGGINS, JAY FRANCIS, financial executive; b. Gary, Ind., June 25, 1945; s. J. Francis and Veronica (Conroy) H.; AB, Princeton U., 1967; MBA, U. Chgo., 1970; m. Gail Marie Joy, Nov. 23, 1979; children: Maura Ellis, Kerry Elizabeth, Erin Leigh, Conor Francis. With Salomon Bros., N.Y.C., 1970-92, v.p., 1976, gen. ptnr. in charge merger and acquisition dept., 1978, head corp. fin. dept., 1986, vice chmn., 1987-92; mng. ptnr. Cloverleaf Ptnrs., Inc., Greenwich, Conn., 1992—. With USAR, 1967. Mem. Knights of Malta. Roman Catholic. Home: 2 Hope Farms Bedford NY 10506-2102 Office: Cloverleaf Ptnrs Inc 411 W Putnam Ave Greenwich CT 06830-6261

HIGGINS, JOHN EDWARD, JR., lawyer; b. Medford, Mass., Dec. 27, 1939; s. John E. and Catherine (Grant) H.; m. Frances Litton, Oct. 18, 1968; children: David, Elizabeth, John. BA, Boston Coll., 1961; JD, Boston U., 1964; MS, Cornell U., 1970. Bar: Mass. 1964. Atty. NLRB, Memphis and Washington, 1964-76; dep. gen. counsel NLRB, Washington, 1976-88, mem. bd., 1988-89, 96-97, solicitor, 1989-95, 97—, acting insp. gen., 1994-96; adj. prof. Cath. U. Law Sch., Washington, 1982—. Mem. village coun. Sect. 5, Village Chevy Chase, Md., 1976-92; scoutmaster Boy Scouts Am., Washington, 1986-91. With USMCR, 1960-66. Mem. ABA (pub. co-chmn. on developing law under nat. labor rels. act), Am. Law Inst. Office: NLRB 1099 14th St NW Washington DC 20570

HIGGINS, KATHRYN O'LEARY, government official; b. Sioux City, Iowa, Oct. 11, 1947; d. Paul C. and Mary Kathryn (Callaghan) O'Leary; widowed; children: Liam James, Kevan Paul. BS, U. Nebr., 1969. Manpower specialist U.S. Dept. Labor, Washington, 1969-78; asst. dir. employment policy White House Domestic Policy, Washington, 1978-81; staff dir. minority U.S. Senate Labor & Human Resources Com., Washington, 1981-86; chief of staff U.S. Representative Sander Levin, Washington, 1986-93, Sec. of Labor Robert Reich, Washington, 1993-95; cabinet sec. White Ho. Cabinet Affairs, Washington, 1995-97, dep. sec. of labor, 1997-99. Vol. Gonzaga Mother's Club, Washington, 1988—; vol., host parent Project Children, Washington, 1987—. Democrat. Roman Catholic. Avocations: cooking, antiques, book club. Home: 6915 Ridgewood Ave Chevy Chase MD 20815-5149 Office: Nat Trust for Historic Preservation 1785 Massachusettes Ave NW Washington DC 20036*

HIGGINS, KENNETH MICHAEL, electrician; b. Erwin, Tenn., Aug. 5, 1951; s. Charles William and Dolores Lucretia (Fanning) H.; m. Bella Ekonomides, Nov. 23, 1985; children: Michael Keith, Karvis. Student, Poly. Inst., Balt., 1969; Elec. Engr. Assoc., Essex (Md.) Coll., 1977. Lic. master electrician. Nuclear technician Calvert Cliffs Nuclear Power, Lusby, Md., 1976-84; electric technician, mechanic Md. Port Adminstrn., Balt., 1986—; owner So. Bella Elec., Balt., 1990—. Pres. Md. Classified Employee Assn., chpt. 140, Cundalk, Md., 1996; mem. exec. bd. Am. Fed., State, County, Mcpl. Employees Union, #2801, Balt., 1997. Office: So Bella Elec PO Box 12052 Baltimore MD 21281-2052

HIGGINS, MARGARET CHRISTIE, photographer; b. San Francisco, Apr. 10, 1951; d. James Sloane and Rachel Hall H.; 1 foster child, Lastone Mundo. BA, Calif. Western U., 1974. Jr. counselor, lifeguard Camp Beaverbrook, Clear Lake, Calif., 1969; resident asst. Calif. Western U., San Diego, 1973-74; asst. tchr. Challenge to Learning, San Francisco, 1985-90; water safety instr. San Francisco, 1985. Author of poems. With U.S. Army, 1975-78. Episcopalian. Avocations: singer, gardening, crafts, poetry, pets.

HIGGINS, MARIKA O'BAIRE, registered nurse, philosophy educator, novelist, entrepreneur; b. Manila, The Philippines, Oct. 3, 1947; d. Gerald John and Giovanna (BelForti) Barry; m. Dean. J. P. Higgins, July 1, 1978; children: Matthew, Alexei, Rita, Dean Patrick. Student, U. Conn., 1964-65; diploma, Ellis Hosp. Sch. Nursing, 1977; BSN, Russell Sage Coll., 1980, postgrad., 1983, 94; grad. ontological design, Logonet Inc. ODC-J, 1993; postgrad. in humanities, Calif. State U., Dominguez Hills, 1995—. RN, N.Y. English tchr. Lang. Inst., Taipei, Taiwan, 1971-73; team leader, staff nurse in acute psychiatry Samaritan Hosp., Troy, N.Y., 1978-80; staff nurse, pediatric ICU Albany (N.Y.) Med. Ctr., 1980-84, 97—; rsch. nurse Commn. on Quality Care for Mentally Disabled, Albany, 1984; staff nurse Columbia-Greene Med. Ctr., Catskill, N.Y., 1984-89; night charge nurse Conifer Park, Scotia, N.Y., 1991-92; nursing educator St. Clare's Hosp., Schenectady, N.Y., 1992-96; founder, designer Future Design & Co., 1995—; nurse Pediat. High Tech Home Care, 1996—; adjunct clin. educator Albany Med. Ctr. So. Vt. Coll., Bennington, 1997—; philosophy coaching Cmty. Hospice Saratoga, N.Y., 1998—; founder Future Design. Publ. poet, lit. writer; comml. artist Echo Mag. Vol. curriculum designer in gifted and talented programs; mem. Red Cross Disaster Team. Mem. Amnesty Internat. Childreach Plan Internat., Thorobred Toastmasters (pres.). Home and Office: PO Box 5102 166 Lincoln Ave Saratoga Springs NY 12866

HIGGINS, MARK C., development banker; b. Sac City, Iowa, Aug. 13, 1951; s. Charles Frank and Helen Yvonne (Lamoureux) H. BA, St. John's U., Collegeville, Minn., 1975; MA, Cath. U. Am., 1982, postgrad., 1985-90. Writer, editor Liturgical Conf., Washington, 1979-80; prodn. mgr. Cambridge Theol. Publs., Bethesda, Md., 1980-82; assoc. dir. Evang. Refugee Svcs., Tübingen, Fed. Republic Germany, 1982-83; rsch. asst. Nat. Conf. Cath. Bishops, Washington, 1986-89; budget officer World Bank, Washington, 1990—; teaching asst. religion Cath. U. Am., Washington, 1985-87, dir. liturgy and worship Campus Ministry, 1987-88; peer counselor Whitman-Walker Clinic, Washington. Contbr. articles to profl. publs. Gay educator police tng. program Lesbian and Gay Task Force, Washington; founder New Cath. Community Project, Washington, Gertrude Stein Soc.; active Gay and Lesbian Alliance Against Defamation, Women's Ordination Conf., Call-To-Action, Cath. reform. Mem. Am. Acad. Religion, Cath. U. Gay and Lesbian Alumni Assn. (bd. dirs. 1989—), Mensa. Avocations: partraiture, historic reconstruction of St. Mary's City, Md. Home: 1419 R St NW Apt 14 Washington DC 20009-3832 Office: World Bank 1818 H St NW Washington DC 20433-0002

HIGGINS, MARY ELLEN See HAWKINS, MARY ELLEN HIGGINS

HIGGINS, MICHAEL EDWARD, finance executive; b. Easton, Md., Nov. 15, 1955; s. George Herman and Margaret Jane (Jones) H. AA, Goldey Beacon Coll., 1975; BS, Salisbury State U., 1981, MBA, 1989. Cost acct. Cambridge (Md.) Wire Cloth Co., 1975-82; adminstrv. asst. Air Plaza West, Church Creek, Md., 1983-84; mktg. svcs. mgr. Nationwide Fulfillment, Cambridge, 1984-86; fin. dir. Dorchester County Commn. Aging, Inc., Ridgely, Md., 1987—; instr. bookkeeping Chesapeake Coll., Cambridge, 1992-95. Bd. dirs. United Fund Dorchester, 1996-99; tchr. Sunday sch. Ch. of Jesus Christ LDS, Cambridge, 1983-97, fin. clk., 1992-97. Democrat. Avocations: gardening, cooking, reading, geneology. Home: 113 Somerset Ave Cambridge MD 21613-1251 Office: Dorchester County Commn on the Aging 2474 Cambridge Beltway Cambridge MD 21613-0219

HIGGINS, NANCY BRANSCOME, management and counseling educator; b. New Castle, Pa.; d. Otis and Ola May (Vaughn) Branscome; m. Bernard F. Higgins, Nov. 15, 1969; 1 child, Bernard F. II. BBA, Westminster Coll., 1967, MEd, 1970; MA, Pepperdine U., 1979; EdD, Vanderbilt U., 1990. Cert. counselor; full life cmty. coll. cert. in bus. mgmt. and indsl. human resources mgmt., psychology, office svcs. and related technologies. Counselor U. Md., College Park, 1976-77, now adj. prof. bus. mgmt.; prof. part-time Hartnell Coll., Salinas, Calif., 1977-80; prof. mgmt. Monterey (Calif.) Peninsula Coll., 1977-80; coord., adminstr. Pepperdine U., Ft. Ord, Calif., 1977-80; prof. part-time Park Coll., Ft. Myer, Va., 1980-82, No. Va. C.C., Annandale, 1980-82, Prince George's Coll., Largo, Md., 1980-82; prof. mgmt. and mktg., coord. Montgomery Coll., Rockville, Md., 1982—, chmn. mgmt. dept., 1993—, mem. faculty congress, 1985-87; mem. task force Nat. Coun. for Occupl. Edn., 1994; adj. prof. U. Md., 1998. Vol. ARC, Washington, Lakeside Hosp., Cleve., 1990; mem. WETA-Edn. TV, Fairfax, Va.; mem. bus./mgmt. adv. bd. U. Md., 1997—. Recipient Student Devel. award Montgomery Coll., 1982, Svc. award, 1982, Faculty and Counseling Excellence award, 1997, Faculty/Counseling Excellence award. Mem. AAUW, ASTD (membership com. and career devel. 1994—), Soc. Human Resources Mgmt., Nat. Soc. Exptl. Edn., Am. Assn. Women in C.C.'s, Pepperdine U. Alumni Assn., Vanderbilt U. Alumni Assn., Westminster Coll. Assn., Montgomery Coll. Alumni Assn. (50th Anniversary com. 1996, Continuing Edn. Leadership Inst. com. 1996-97, Alumni Tchr.-Counselor Excellence award 1997), Chi Omega (rush chairperson 1994—). Avocation: travel. Home: 7764 Heatherton Ln Potomac MD 20854-3212

HIGGINS, PETER THOMAS, technology consultant; b. Hackensack, N.J., Aug. 17, 1943; s. Joseph Alexander and Rita Barth (Buckley) H.; m. Kathleen Mary Melehan, June 6, 1970; 1 child, Kelton Charles. BS in Math., Marist Coll., 1967; MS in Math., Computer Sci., Stevens Inst. Tech., 1968. Front desk clk. Carlyle Hotel, N.Y.C., 1964-67; sci. programmer CIA, Washington, 1968-74, project engr., 1974-80, ops. engr. mgr., 1981-86; congl. fellow U.S. House of Reps., Washington, 1986-87, U.S. Senate, Washington, 1987; mgr. rsch. and devel. CIA, Washington, 1987-89, chief info. officer, 1989-92; dep. asst. dir. engring. FBI, Washington, 1992-95; founder & prin. cons. Higgins & Assocs., Washington and London, 1995—; speaker in field; bd. dirs. CTX Corp., Cabin John, Md., Printrak Internat., Inc., Anaheim, Calif. Local leader Jaycees, McLean, Va., 1970; vol. Dem. Nat. Conv., Atlantic City, 1964; Sun. sch. tchr. Holy Trinity Ch., Washington, 1983-91; vol. instr. Presdl. Classroom for Young Ams., 1994-97, 99. Recipient Intelligence medal of merit CIA, 1994. Mem. Am. Polit. Sci. Assn. (Fgn. Affairs Congl. fellow 1986), Congl. Fellows Alumni Steering Com., Internat. Assn. Identification (chmn. automated fingerprint identification com. 1996—), Assn. Pub. Safety Comm. Ofcls., Assn. Work Process Improvement (industry leadership coun. 1997—). Roman Catholic. Avocations: reading, walking, automobiles. Office: Higgins & Assocs Internat 3116 Woodley Rd NW Washington DC 20008-3448

HIGGINS, RICHARD J., educational administrator. BS in Metallurgy, MIT, 1960; PhD in Materials Sci., Northwestern U., 1965. Prof. physics U. Oreg., Eugene, founding dir. materials sci. inst.; prof. elec. engring. Ga. Tech., Atlanta, 1987-99, prof. emeritus, 1999—, dir. microelectronics rsch. ctr., 1988-95; founder, dir. Global Innovation for Engrs. Ga. Inst. Tech., 1995—; vis. rschr. Bell Labs, 1972-73, U. Paris, 1981, Thomson-CSF, Paris, 1982, MIT, 1983-85; cons. Analog Devices, 1983-85, Tektronix, 1985-87, NSF, UNESCO, Ford Found. Author: Electronics with Digital and Analog ICs, 1983, Digital Signal Processing in VLSI, 1989, 2 others; contbr. 80 tech. articles to profl. jours. Fellow Am. Phys. Soc. Achievements include research in GaAs heterostructure devices for next-generation ultra-high speed integrated circuits and optoelectronics; roadmap studies for future semiconductor devices, electronic packaging, optoelectronic packaging. E-mail: higginsrj@aol.com. Office: 845 Penn Ave NE Atlanta GA 30308

HIGGINS, ROBERT ARTHUR, electrical engineer, educator, consultant; b. Watertown, S.D., Sept. 5, 1924; s. Arthur C. and Nicoline (Huseth) H.; m. Barbara Jeanne Fagerlie, 1958; children—Patricia Suzanne, Daniel Alfred, Steven Robert. BEE with honors, U. Minn., 1948; MSEE, U. Wis., 1964; PhDEE, U. Mo., 1969. Registered profl. engr. Engr. Schlumberger Well Survey Corp., Tex., 1948-57; rsch. technologist Mobil Rsch. and Devel. Corp., Tex., 1958-61; rsch. engr. United Aircraft Rsch. Labs., Conn., 1965; staff specialist Remote Sensing Inst., S.D., 1969-71; asst. prof. elec. engring. S.D. State U., 1969-74, assoc. dir. Engring. Expt. Sta., 1973-77, prof. elec. engring., 1974-79; cons. Mankato State U., 1980; prin. engr. Sperry Univac, 1981-85; prof. elec. engring. St. Cloud (Minn.) State U., 1985-95, prof. emeritus, 1995—; cons. Control Data Corp., 1977-80, Lawrence Livermore Lab., 1971-73, USAF Office Sci. Rsch., Fla., 1976, NCR-Comten, 1988-90, FMC Corp., 1991-92, Ontrack Computer Sys., 1993-98; project dir., cons. NSF, 1973-80, 87-89. Contbr. articles to profl. jours. Bd. dirs. Eden Prairie Bd. Edn., Minn., 1982-85, Nat. Storage Industry Consortium, 1995-98. With CE, AUS, 1943-46. NASA fellow, 1966-68; grantee NSF, 1966, 72, 74, 86, AEC, 1971-73, Office Water Resources Research, 1971-74. Mem. IEEE (sr., life), Am. Soc. Engring. Educators, Sigma Xi, Eta Kappa Nu. Lutheran. Home: 11260 Windrow Dr Eden Prairie MN 55344-4055

HIGGINS, ROBERT FREDERICK, lawyer; b. Olney, Ill., July 8, 1944; s. Robert Kenneth and Betty (Travers) H.; m. Barbara Bowman, Aug. 27, 1966 (dec.); children: Jennifer M., Matthew B., Kathryn C. BA, Marietta Coll., 1966; JD, Wash. U., St. Louis, 1969. Bar: Fla. 1972, Mo. 1969, Ohio 1969. Asst. county counselor legal dept. St. Louis County, St. Louis, 1969; judge advocate USAF, Keesler AFB, Biloxi, Miss., 1969-71; trial counsel USAF, Southeast U.S., 1971-72; mil. judge USAF, Calif. and Nev., 1972-73; assoc. Van Den Berg, Gay & Burke, PA, Orlando, Fla., 1974-76, Lowndes, Piersol, Drosdick & Doster, Orlando, 1977-79; ptnr. Lowndes, Drosdick, Doster, Kantor & Reed, PA, Orlando, 1979—. Pres. Christian Svc. Ctr., Orlando, 1983-85; chmn. Ctrl. Fla. chpt. ARC, Orlando, 1992-94; bd. dirs. ARC in Ctrl. Fla., 1990—; mem. cmty. redevelopment adv. bd. City Winter Park, 1995-97. Mem. Fla. Bar Assn. (UCC/bankruptcy com. 1990—), Orange County Bar Assn. (exec. coun. 1983-89), Comml. Law League, Orlando Area Dolfins (pres. 1983-84), Interlachen Country Club. Lutheran. Office: Lowndes Drosdick Doster Kantor & Reed PO Box 2809 215 N Eola Dr Orlando FL 32802*

HIGGINS, ROBERT (WALTER), military officer, physician; b. Uniontown, Wash., Nov. 9, 1934; s. Nelson Leigh and Abbie Elizabeth (Rowe) H.; m. Barbara Jean Wright, Aug. 19, 1956; children: Fred, Colleen, Jay. BS in Pharmacy, Wash. State U., 1957; MD, U. Wash., 1965. Pharmacist Wenatchee (Wash.) Thrifty Drugs, 1957-59; owner Higgins Drug Store, Pullman, Wash., 1959-61; intern L.A. County Harbor Gen. Hosp., Torrance, 1965-66; commd. lt. USN, 1966; ships surgeon USS Tutuila, Vietnam, 1966-68; ptnr. Ludwick, Zook & Higgins Family Medicine, Wenatchee, 1968-72; commd. lt. comdr. USN, 1972, advanced through grades to rear adm., 1988; chmn. dept. family medicine Naval Hosp., Charleston, S.C., 1972-78, Camp Pendleton, Calif., 1978-80, Bremerton, Wash., 1980-86; comdg. officer Naval Hosp., Camp Pendleton, 1986-87; med. officer USMC Washington, 1987-89; dep. surgeon gen. USN, 1989-93; specialty advisor surgeon gen. USN, Washington, 1973-86. Contbg. author: Behavioral Disorders, 1984, 90; contbr. articles to profl. jours. Scoutmaster Boy Scouts Am., Charleston, 1974-78, Camp Pendleton, 1978-80; trustee Family Health Found. Am., Wash. State U. Found., 1992-98; bd. visitors Wash. State U. Coll. Pharmacy, 1998—. Decorated Disting. Svc. medal, Legion of Merit, Meritorious Svc. medal, Navy Commendation medal; recipient Alumni Achievement award Wash. State. U., 1988, Disting. Alumnus award U. Wash. Sch. Medicine, 1996. Fellow Am. Acad. Family Physicians (pres. 1984-85, arl. del. to AMA 1985-91, del. 1992—), Philippine Acad. Family Physicians (hon. 1999); mem. Uniformed Svcs. Acad. Family Physicians (pres. 1974-76), World Orgn. Family Medicine (v.p. 1986, pres. elect 1995-98, pres. 1998—), Elks, Masons. Avocations: bird watching, fly fishing, model airplanes, stamp collection, jogging. Home and Office: 2303 Highland Dr Anacortes WA 98221-3143

HIGGINS, SHAUN O'LEARY, media executive; b. Princeton, Ind., Mar. 22, 1948; s. John Frank and Laura Dorothea (Thompson) H.; m. Ann

Glendening, Nov. 23, 1975; children: Flannery Maeve, Ian Dashiell. BA in Comm., DePauw U., 1971. Reporter, city editor Lu-Mar Newspapers, Inc., Bloomington, Ind., 1967-69; mng. editor The Times, Brazil, Ind., 1969-72; congl. cand. 7th Dist. Ind. Dem., Brazil, 1972; cons. Keep's Creek Assocs., Indpls., 1972-73; wire editor Times & Times World, Roanoke, Va., 1973-74; freelance writer, editor self-employed, N.Y.C., 1974-75; news editor, state bur. chief Lee Newspapers, Inc., Billings, Helena, Mont., 1975-79; asst. mng. editor Cowles Pub. Co., Spokane, Wash., 1973-83; mktg. dir. Cowles Pub. Co., Spokane, 1983-88, dir. mktg. and sales, 1988—; pres., COO New Media Ventures, Inc., Cowles Pub. Co., Spokane, 1993—; chmn., CEO Print Mktg. Concepts, Inc., Houston, 1996—; cons. in field; instr. in field; owner The Oxalis Group, Spokane, 1979—. Co-prodr. "Good Paper" TV comml., 1986 (Telly award 1988; 2 Emmy awards 1987); dir. "The Arts Can Change Your Life," 1988 (MAX award 1988); author: Review Tower, 1985 (MAX award 1985), Toward Greater Understanding, 1989, Database Marketing Applications for Newspapers, 1995, Effective Direct Mail Letters for Newspapers, 1995, The Newspaper in Art, 1997, Measuring Spokane, 1998, Vachel Lindsay: Troubadour in the Wild Flower City, 1999; editor: Ice Storm '96, 1996, Team of Destiny, 1997, Zagmania, 1999; contbr. more than 60 articles to profl. publs. Bd. dirs., trustee Wash. Commn. for Humanities, Seattle, 1988-93, United Way of Spokane County, 1988-91; mem. pub. rels. adv. bd. DePauw U., 1996—; bd. dirs. Spokane Regional Conv. and Visitors Bur., 1991-94, Spokane Symphony Orch., 1991-96, Cmty. Devel. Bd., Spokane, 1986-88; trustee, chmn. Spokane Area Econ. Devel. Coun., 1983-91, chair, 1990; chmn. Festival of Four Cultures, 1989. Recipient Emmy(s) N.A.T.A.S., 1987, Telly award Cin. Broadcasters, 1988, MAX Best of Show award Spokane Advt. Fedn., 1988, Best of Show award Internat. Newspaper Mktg. Assn., 1987, Silver Strand award INMA-West, 1993; named Spokane Advt. Profl. of Yr., 1988, Media, Inc. Northwest Print Media Person of the Year, 1992. Mem. Spokane Advt. Fedn. (pres. 1988-89), Direct Mktg. Assn., Pub. Rels. Soc. Am., Soc. Profl. Journalists, Am. Statis. Assn., Internat. Newspaper Mktg. Assn. (trustee, internat. pres. 1993—, Silver Shovel award 1996), Newspaper Assn. Am. (retail coun., bus. devel. com., chair nat. polit. task force), Fedn. Internationale des editeurs des Journaux (exec., dir.), Chautauqua Soc. of Eastern Wash. U., Voltaire Soc. Am. (founding mem.). Avocations: book collecting, reading, travel. Home: 428 W 27th Ave Spokane WA 99203-1854 Office: Cowles Pub Co 999 W Riverside Ave Spokane WA 99201-1006

HIGGINS, SISTER THERESE, English educator, former college president; b. Winthrop, Mass., Sept. 29, 1925; d. James C. and Margaret M. (Lennon) H. AB cum laude, Regis Coll., 1947; MA, Boston Coll., 1959, DHL, 1993; PhD, U. Wis., 1963; DHL, Emmanuel Coll., 1977, Lesley Coll., 1991; postgrad. in lit. and theology, Harvard U., 1965-66; LLD (hon.), Northeastern U., 1982, Bentley Coll., 1992, Regis Coll., 1994. Joined Congregation of Sisters of St. Joseph, Roman Cath. Ch., 1947; asst. prof. English, Regis Coll., Weston, Mass., 1963-65, asst. prof., 1965-67, assoc. prof. English lit., 1968—, pres., 1974-92, also trustee; book reviewer Boston Globe, 1965—. Trustee Waltham (Mass.) Hosp., 1978-85, Cardinal Spellman Philatelic Mus., 1976-92; mem. Mass. Gov.'s Commn. on Status Women, 1977-79, Nat. Com. Ecclesial Role Women, Archdiocesan Fin. Coun., 1991—. U. Wis. research grantee Eng. Mem. Nat. Cath. Ednl. Assn., AAUW, MLA, AAUP, Assn. Ind. Colls. and Univs. Mass. (exec. com.), New Eng. Colls. Fund, NEASC (commn.). Office: Regis Coll 235 Wellesley St Weston MA 02493-1505

HIGGINS, THOMAS A., federal judge; b. 1932. AA, Christian Bros. Coll., 1952; BA, U. Tenn., 1954; LLB, Vanderbilt U., 1957. Bar: U.S. Dist. Ct. (mid. dist.) Tenn., U.S. Ct. Mil. Appeals, U.S. Ct. Appeals (6th cir.), U.S. Supreme Ct. Ptnr. Willis & Higgins, 1960-61; assoc., then. ptnr. Cornelius, Collins, Higgins & White, 1961-84; judge U.S. Dist. Ct. (mid. dist.) Tenn., Nashville, 1984—. Served with AUS, 1957-60. Fellow Am. Coll. Trial Lawyers; mem. ABA, Tenn. Bar Assn., Nashville Bar Assn. Office: US District Court A-845 US Courthouse Nashville TN 37203-3816*

HIGGINSON, JERRY ALDEN, JR., bank executive; b. Mt. Vernon, Ill., July 21, 1957; s. Jerry Alden Sr. and Beverly Joyce (York) H.; m. Leah Jane Murray, June 11, 1983; children: Sara Elisabeth, Jon Patrick Alden. BA, Graceland Coll., Lamoni, Iowa, 1979; postgrad., So. Ill. U., 1979; M in Fin. and Banking, So. Meth. U., 1988. Trust officer, asst. cashier Salem (Ill.) Nat. Bank, 1979-80; trust officer MidAm. Bank and Trust, Carbondale, Ill., 1980-82; v.p., city mgr. NationsBank Tex., San Antonio, 1982-97; v.p. Norwest Bank, San Antonio, 1997-98; dir. devel. and planned giving Jewish Family Svc., 1998—; instr. Am. Inst. Banking, San Antonio, 1984—; mem. Estate Planners Coun., San Antonio, 1982—; mem. faculty Palo Alto Community Coll., 1989-90. Pres. San Antonio Symphony Soc., 1985-86; treas., pres. San Antonio Clean and Beautiful Com., 1986-87, pres. bd. dirs., 1987-89; pres. bd. trustees San Antonio Area Found., 1986-90; bd. dirs. Beautify San Antonio, 1987—, pres., 1988-89; bd. dirs. Keep Tex. Beautiful, Inc.; bd. dirs. Mental Health Assn. Tex., 1989-90, chmn., 1991—, treas., 1992—, v.p., bd. dirs. , treas. 1992—, past pres.; pres. Keep San Antonio Beautiful Inc., 1986-89; mem. bd. vol. Alamo Area Coun. Boy Scouts Am., 1990, pack chmn., 1998—; bd. dirs. San Antonio Jr. Achievement, 1990, San Antonio Botanical Soc., 1992—, Planned Giving Coun. San Antonio, 1993—, treas., 1993—, Mission Rd. Devel. Ctr.; chmn. Koehler Found., 1991—; mem. adv. bd. Salvation Army, San Antonio, bd. dirs.; mem. devel. bd. Our Lady of Pillar, 1992—; mem. Nat. Jewish Ctr. for Immunology-Regional Coun., 1995—; mem. bd. Friends of San Antonio Pub. Libr., 1997—, Musical Offerings, 1997—; mem. adv. bd. Salvation Army, 1994—. Mem. Nat. Soc. Fund Raising Execs., Symphony Soc. San Antonio, San Antonio Baroque Music Soc., San Antonio Conservation Soc., San Antonio Bot. Soc. (bd. dirs. 1992—), Knife and Fork Club San Antonio (bd. dirs. 1990-91, v.p. 1991-92, pres. 1992—), The Witte Mus. (bd. 1994—), San Antonio Geneal. Soc., Alden Kindred of Am., Mayflower Soc. Am. Republican. Mem. Reorganized Ch. Jesus Christ of Latter-day Saints.

HIGGINSON, JOHN, retired military officer; b. St. Louis, Oct. 24, 1932; s. John and Clara Elizabeth (Lindemann) H.; married; children: Robert, Mark, Patrick, Paul. BA, St. Mary's U., 1954; BS, Naval Postgrad. Sch., 1966; MS, George Washington U., 1968. Ensign USN, advanced through grades to Rear Adm., ret.; comdr. Helicopter Anti-submarine Squadron 2, 1973-74, Helicopter Anti-submarine Squadron 10, 1976-78, Amphibious Squadron 7, 1981-83, Amphibious Group 3, 1985; comdr. Naval Surface Group, Long Beach, 1986, ret., 1990-92; pres. Long Beach C. of C.; prof. mgmt. Naval War Coll., Newport, R.I. Co-author: Sea and Air, The Marine Environment, 1962, 2nd. edit., 1973. Bd. dirs. United Way, L.A., Long Beach Symphony, Long Beach Youth Activities, DARE, Inc., USO, Leadership Long Beach, St. Mary's Med. Ctr., Meml. Med. Ctr. of Long Beach; trustee Long Beach City Coll. Found., Long Beach Civic Light Opera; mem. exec. bd. of Long Beach Boy Scouts of Am.; mem. exec. coun. Industry-Edn. Coun. of Calif.; former chmn. L.A. Combined Fed. Campaign; pres., CEO Am. Gold Star Manor Charitable Trust, 1993—. Mem. Navy Helicopter Assn. (former pres.), Fed. Exec. Bd. (former chmn.), Rotary (commr. Calif. Vets. Meml. Commn.). Home: 5341 Las Lomas Park Estates Long Beach CA 90815

HIGGINSON, KAREN ANN DOROTHY, librarian; b. June 1, 1953. AA, Mt. Ida Coll., 1974; BLS, So. Conn. State U., 1979, MLS, 1990. Asst. libr. music divsn. Sterling Libr. Yale U., New Haven, 1979-86; asst. libr. Harcourt Wood Meml. Libr., Derby, Conn., 1986-89, dir., 1989—; coord., facilitator writer's roundtable Harcourt Wood Meml. Libr. Violinist with contemporary choir St. Stanislaus Ch., Meriden, Conn. E-mail: khigginson@juno.com.

HIGGS, JOHN H., lawyer; b. Balt., Mar. 10, 1934; s. E. Homer and Josephine (Doughty) H.; m. Helen Platt, Aug. 25, 1956; children: Sarah, Anne, Julia, Susan. AB, Dartmouth Coll., 1956; LLB, U. Pa., 1960. Bar: N.Y. 1961. Founder Higgs Pavements Co., Milford, Conn., 1953-56; assoc. Sullivan & Cromwell, N.Y.C., 1960-61, 62-68; assoc. Wickes, Riddell, Bloomer, Jacobi & McGuire, N.Y.C., 1968, ptnr., 1969-79; ptnr. Morgan, Lewis & Bockius, LLP, N.Y.C., 1979-97, counsel, 1997—; ptnr. Skyport Indsl. Park, Newark, N.J.; sec. Ea. States Bankcard Assn., Lake Success, N.Y., 1970-88; bd. dirs. Indsl. Bank Japan Trust Co., N.Y., 1974—, IBJ Found. Inc., N.Y., 1989—; mem. staff adv. com. on comml. bank supervision State N.Y., 1965-66. Contbr. articles to profl. jours. Mayor Village of Pelham Manor, N.Y., 1979-81. Home: 20 Beechtree Ln Pelham NY 10803-3502 Office: Morgan Lewis & Bockius 101 Park Ave Fl 44 New York NY 10178-0060

HIGGS, JON SCOTT, computer company executive, researcher; b. Manhasset, N.Y., Dec. 18, 1956; s. Donald Robert and Jean Marie Higgs. BA, Haverford Coll., 1978. Area mgr. U.S. Treasury USSBD, Phila., 1978-84; tech. cons. NSTL, Plymouth Meeting, Pa., 1984-89; project mgr. NSTL, Plymouth Meeting, 1989-93; pres. PC Wizards, Wayne, Pa., 1993—; internat. computer lab. cons. NSTL/Groupe Tests, Paris, 1992. Author: Early One Morning, 1985; author, rschr. Software Digest, 1989-98; contbr. articles to profl. jours. Recipient Choreography award County Dance and Song Soc., 1993. Avocation: choral singing. Home: 588 Forest Rd Wayne PA 19087 Office: PC Wizards 588 Forest Rd Wayne PA 19087

HIGH, LINDA OATMAN, author; b. Ephrata, Pa., Apr. 28, 1958; d. Robert and Mary (Millard) Haas; m. John David High; four children. Author: Maizie, 1995, Hound Heaven, 1995, A Christmas Star, 1997, A Stone's Throw from Paradise, 1997, Hogwash, History & Horse Sense, 1997, Beekeepers, 1998. Mem. Soc. Children's Book Writers & Illustrators, Pennwriters. Home: 1209 Reading Rd Narvon PA 17555-9352

HIGH, MELVIN C., protective services official. Police chief Norfolk, Va. Office: 100 Brooke Ave Norfolk VA 23510-1826*

HIGH, S. DALE, diversified company executive; b. Lancaster, Pa., May 2, 1942; s. Sanford H. and Erma (Denlinger) H.; m. Sadie S. Horst; children from previous marriage: Steven D., Gregory A., Suzanne M. BSBA, Elizabethtown Coll., 1963, LDH (hon.), 1993. Exec. v.p. High Steel Structures, Inc., Lancaster, 1963-77; ptnr. High Properties, Lancaster, 1963—; chmn., pres. High Industries, Inc., Lancaster, 1977—; gen. ptnr. High Employee Svcs., Ltd., Lancaster; bd. dirs. High Investors, Ltd., Lancaster, High Food Svcs., Ltd., Lancaster, High Hotels Ltd., Lancaster, Lancaster Alliance, Educators Mut. Life Ins. Co., Lancaster, EXCEL Pa. Chamber, Inc., Penn Sq. Gen. Corp.; mem. panel of judges Ctrl. Pa. Entrepreneur of the Yr. Award Program, 1994-95, chmn., 1996. Mem. Pa. State Rep. com., Harrisburg, 1985; co-chmn. fin. Lancaster County Rep. Com., 1985-88; trustee High Found., Lancaster, Lancaster County Found., Elizabethtown Coll., Pa., 1979—, Lancaster Gen. Hosp., 1976-84; bd. dirs. United Way Lancaster County, 1975-78, Lancaster County Rev. Commn., 1984-86, Pa. Chamber of Bus. and Industry, Harrisburg, 1991—, Modern Transit Partnership, 1998—; chmn. Pa. Chamber PAC, 1997. Named Outstanding Young Man, Lancaster Jaycees, 1977, Disting. Pennsylvanian, Phila. C. of C., 1981; recipient Exemplar award Lancaster C. of C. and Industry, 1995, Disting. Bus. Alumni award Elizabethtown Coll., 1995, Jr. Achievement Spirit Achievement award, 1997, Pa. Dutch Coun./BSA Disting. Citizen award, 1999; named Ctrl. Pa. Master Entrepreneur of Yr. Ernst & Young, 1999. Mem. World Pres.'s Orgn., Lancaster C. of C. (bd. dirs. 1976-82, chmn. 1981), Hamilton Club, Lancaster Country Club, Tuesday Club, Delta Mu Delta (hon.). Republican. Presbyterian. Avocations: reading, bicycling, hiking, travel. Office: High Industries Inc PO Box 10008 1853 William Penn Way Lancaster PA 17601-6713

HIGH, THOMAS W., energy services executive; b. Oakland, Calif., Dec. 7, 1947; s. William A. and Vera D. (Blumann) H.; m. Nancy J. Hughes, June 8, 1969. BA, U. Calif., Berkeley, 1968; grad. advanced mgmt. program, Harvard U., 1992. Rep. govt. and pub. affairs Pacific Gas and Electric Co., San Francisco, 1973-82, dir. legis. svcs., 1982-84, asst. sec., 1984-85, corp. sec., 1985-86, v.p., corp. sec., 1986-91, v.p., asst. to chmn., 1991-94, v.p., asst. to CEO, 1994-95, sr. v.p. corp. svcs., 1995-97; sr. v.p. adminstrn. and external rels. PG&E Corp., San Francisco, 1997—. Trustee Am. Conservatory Theatre, 1991—; mem. coun. Friends of the Bancroft Libr., 1993-95. Office: PG & E Corp Ste 2400 One Market Spear Tower San Francisco CA 94105

HIGH, TIMOTHY GRIFFIN, artist, educator, writer; b. Memphis, Tenn., Mar. 10, 1949; s. Warren Barrett and Jo Ellen (Wise) H.; m. Cynthia Spikes, Aug. 10, 1973. BFA, Tex. Tech U., 1973, MA, 1975; MFA, U. Wis., 1976. Assoc. prof. U. Tex., Austin, 1976—; visual artist drawings, serigraphs, papermaking, monoprints, monotypes, water-media painting, installation and papier maché sculpture; free-lance writer. Over 150 solo, invitational and gallery group shows since 1976, including Amarillo (Tex.) Art Mus., 1993, Martin-Rathburn Gallery, San Antonio, 1997; group exhbns. include Adair Margo Gallery, El Paso, Tex., 1996; represented in permanent collections including Art Inst. Chgo., Bklyn. Mus., Mus. Fine Art, Boston, Met. Mus. Art, N.Y.C., Fogg Mus., Cambridge, Mass., Mus. Fine Art, Houston. Travel fellow Ford Found., Peruvian Andes, 1978; individual artist fellow Nat. Endowment Arts, 1989. Mem. So. Graphics Coun. (conf. coord. 1988-89), Mid-Am. Coll. Art Assn. (1998 conf. spkr.), Nat. Assn. Scholars (panelist conv. 1993), Tex. Fine Arts Assn., Austin Visual Artists Assn. Avocations: travel, photography, backpacking, fly fishing, reading. Address: care/ Terra Rosa Studio 2308 Lawnmont Ave Austin TX 78756-1915 Office: Univ of Tex Austin Dept Art & Art History Austin TX 78712

HIGHAM, JOHN, history educator; b. N.Y.C., Oct. 26, 1920; s. LLoyd Stuart and Margaret (Windred) H.; m. Eileen Moss, Aug. 26, 1948; children: Margaret, Jay, Daniel, Constance Vidor. BA, Johns Hopkins U., 1941; PhD, U. Wis., 1949. Instr. history UCLA, 1948-50; asst. prof. UCLA, 1950-54; asso. prof. Rutgers U., 1954-58, prof., 1958-60; prof. history U. Mich., Ann Arbor, 1961-67; Moses Coit Tyler Univ. prof. U. Mich., 1968-71, 72-73; vis. assoc. prof. Columbia U., 1958-59; John Martin Vincent prof. Johns Hopkins U., 1971-89, prof. emeritus, 1989—; directeur d'études associé Ecole des Hautes Etudes en Sciences Sociales, Paris, 1981-82; Newman vis. prof. Am. civilization Cornell U., Ithaca, N.Y., 1991-92. Author: Strangers in the Land, 1955, 2nd edit., 1988, History: Humanistic Scholarship in America, 1965, rev. edit., 1989, Writing American History, 1970, Send These to Me, 1975, rev. edit., 1984; editor: The Reconstruction of American History, 1962, Ethnic Leadership in America, 1978, New Directions in American Intellectual History, 1979, Civil Rights and Social Wrongs: Black-White Relations Since World War II, 1997; co-author: (Peter Kivisto, Dag Blanck, editors) American Immigrants and Their Generations, 1990, Conceptions of National History, 1994. Served with USAAF, 1943-45. Princeton U. Coun. Humanities fellow, 1960-61; Commonwealth Fund lectr. Univ. Coll., London, 1968; Ctr. Advanced Study Behavioral Scis. fellow, 1965-66; Phi Beta Kappa vis. scholar, 1972-73; mem. Inst. Advanced Study, 1973-74; Fulbright-Hays lectr. Kyoto Am. Studies Seminar, 1974; fellow Woodrow Wilson Internat. Ctr. for Scholars, 1976-77, Guggenheim Found. fellow, 1984-85, Fulbright 40th Anniversary Disting. fellow, Argentina, 1986, Mellon Sr. fellow Nat. Humanities Ctr., 1988-89. Mem. Am. Acad. Arts and Scis., Am. Hist. Assn. (council and exec. com. 1971-74, rep. to Am. Council Learned Socs. 1977-80, gen. editor: Guide to Historical Literature, 3d edit. 1987-90), Orgn. Am. Historians (pres. 1973-74), Mich. Soc. Fellows (sr. fellow 1971-73), New Soc. Letters Lund (Sweden), Am. Antiquarian Soc., Am. Studies Assn., Soc. Am. Historians, Immigration History Soc. (pres. 1979-82), Century Club (N.Y.C.). Office: Johns Hopkins U Dept History Baltimore MD 21218

HIGHAM, PAUL H., marketing professional. Sr. v.p. mktg. and sales promotions Wal-Mart Stores, Inc., Bentonville, Ark. Office: Wal-Mart Stores Inc 702 SW 8th St Bentonville AR 72716*

HIGHBERGER, WILLIAM FOSTER, lawyer; b. Suffern, N.Y., May 15, 1950; s. John Kistler and Helen Stewart (Foster) H.; m. Carolyn Barbara Kuhl, July 12, 1980; children: Helen Barbara, Anna Mary. AB, Princeton U.; JD, Columbia U. Bar: Calif. 1976, U.S. Dist. Ct. (cen. dist.) Calif. 1976, U.S. Ct. Appeals (2d cir.) 1976, U.S. Ct. Appeals (9th cir.) 1977, U.S. Dist. Ct. (so. and ea. dists.) Calif. 1979, U.S. Supreme Ct. 1980, D.C. 1981, U.S. Dist. Ct. (no. dist.) Calif. 1981, U.S. Dist. Ct. D.C. 1982, U.S. Ct. Appeals (D.C. cir.) 1982, U.S. Ct. Appeals (3d cir.) 1983, N.Y. 1984, U.S. Dist. Ct. (so. dist.) N.Y. 1984, U.S. Dist. Ct. (ea. dist.) N.Y. 1985. Law clk. to judge U.S. Ct. Appeals (2d cir.), Bridgeport, Conn., 1975-76; assoc. Gibson, Dunn & Crutcher, Washington and L.A., 1976-82, ptnr., 1983—. Notes and comments editor Columbia U. Law Rev., 1974. Mem. Nature Conservatory, Calif., 1981—; active Pacific Palisades (Calif.) Presbhn. Ch., 1987—. James Kent scholar Columbia U., 1973. Mem. ABA (com. on individual rights and responsibilities in workplace, labor sect.), L.A. County Bar Assn., Indsl. Rels. Rsch. Assn., Am. Employment Law Coun., Univ. Cottage Club. Republican. Office: Gibson Dunn & Crutcher 333 S Grand Ave Ste 4400 Los Angeles CA 90071-3197*

HIGHFILL, PHILIP HENRY, JR., retired language educator; b. Petersburg, Va., Aug. 12, 1918; s. Philip Henry and Grace (Jones) H.; m. Annabelle Hollowell (Molly), 1943; children: Mary Hollowell, Philip Henry III. BA, Wake Forest Coll., 1942; postgrad., Middlebury Coll., 1946; MA, U. N.C., 1948, PhD, 1950. Reporter Daily Advance, Elizabeth City, N.C., 1942, 46, Shreveport (La.) Times, 1942; instr. U. Rochester, N.Y., 1950-53, asst. prof., 1953-55; assoc. prof. George Washington U., Washington, 1955-61, prof., 1961-89, prof. emeritus, 1989; cons. lit. Folger Shakespeare Library, Washington, 1964-68. Co-author: (with Kalman A. Burnim and Edward A. Langhans) A Biographical Dictionary of Actors, Actresses, Musicians, Dancers, Managers and Other Stage Personnel in London, 1660-1800, 16 vols., 1973-93; (with George Winchester Stone) In Search of Restoration and 18th-Century Theatrical Biography, 1976, (with Kalman A. Burnim) John Bell, Patron of Theatrical Portraiture, 1998; editor: Shakespeare's Craft, 1982; contbr. numerous articles and revs. to scholarly jours. With U.S. Army, 1942-46. Grantee Huntington Library, 1959, NEH, 1967-68, 70-71, 74-76, 84-87; fellow John Simon Guggenheim Found., 1959-60, Folger Shakespeare Library, 1968, Theodore Stewart fellow Nat. Library Scotland, 1975; fellow Washington Evening Star, 1963; recipient George Freedley award Theatre Library Assn., 1980. Mem. MLA, South Atlantic MLA, Soc. for Theatre Rsch. (Eng.), Am. Soc. Theatre Rsch. (spl. award 1994), Am. Soc. for 18th Century Studies, Shakespeare Soc. Am., Am. Handel Soc. (bd. dirs. 1986-93), Lit. Soc. Washington (v.p. 1991, pres. 1992-93), Wafflers Club, George Washington Univ. Club, Cosmos Club (v.p. 1979, pres. 1980, bd. dirs. 1976-81). Avocations: traveling, music, cooking. Home: 5105 Westpath Ct Bethesda MD 20816-2319

HIGHLAND, CECIL BLAINE, JR., newspaper publisher, lawyer, banker; b. New Martinsville, W.Va., Nov. 23, 1918; s. Cecil Blaine and Ella C. (Clark) H.; m. Barbara Brennan, June 4, 1955; 1 child, Ellen Highland Fernandez. AB, W.Va. U., 1939; JD, Harvard U., 1949. Bar: W.Va. 1949. Practiced in Clarksburg, W.Va., 1949—; now of counsel McNeer, Highland, McMunn and Varner; chmn. One Valley Bank of Clarksburg, 1957-98; dir. Clarksburg Pub. Co., 1949—, pres., gen. mgr., treas., 1957—. Served with AUS, 1940-46; lt. col. Res. ret. Mem. Am., W.Va., Harrison County bar assns., Am. Legion, Harvard, W.Va. law sch. assns., Phi Beta Kappa, Phi Kappa Psi. Republican. Episcopalian. Clubs: Mason (32 deg., Shriner), Elk. Office: Clarksburg Pub Co Clarksburg WV 26301

HIGHLAND, MARILYN M., principal. Prin. Bay Haven Sch. Basics Plus, 1986—. Recipient Elem. Sch. Recognition award U.S. Dept. Edn., 1989-90. Office: Bay Haven Sch Basics Plus 2901 W Tamiami Cir Sarasota FL 34234-5709*

HIGHLAND, MARTHA (MARTIE), retired education educator, consultant; b. Lexington, Ky., June 3, 1934; d. William Thomas and Lyda Bruce (Wilson) H.; foster children: Barbara O. Noe, Teresa O. McKenzie, Debby O. Hodges, Joseph Owens, Kathy S. Coddington. AA, Cumberland Jr. Coll., 1955; BA in Edn., U. Ky., 1958; MA in Edn., U. Louisville, 1981. Cert. tchr., Ky. Tchr. Jefferson County Bd. Edn., Louisville, 1958-59, Ft. Knox (Ky.) Dependent Schs., 1959-65; tchr. Louisville City Schs., 1965-66, reading specialist, 1966-75; reading specialist Jefferson County Sch. System, Louisville, 1975-89, remedial specialist in reading and math., 1989-91; ret., 1991; substitute tchr., vol. Jefferson County Bd. Edn., Louisville, 1991—; faculty rep. Jefferson County Tchrs. Assn., 1981-91. Nominated Disney Tchr. of Yr., 1989. Mem. ASCD, Am. Bus. Women's Assn. (sec. 1989-92, v.p. 1988-89, 92-93, Woman of Yr. 1990). Avocations: academic coaching, reading, gardening. Home: 126 Stevenson Ave Louisville KY 40206-3125

HIGHLEN, LARRY WADE, music educator, piano rebuilder, tuner; b. Warren, Ind., Oct. 31, 1936; s. Lawrence Wade and Anna Belle (Dungan) H.; m. Camille Pence (div. 1975); children: Laurel, Wade, Jennifer, Tanna. Student, Niles Bryant Coll., 1967, Ivy Tech. Coll., Kokomo, Ind., 1975-76, Ivy Tech. Coll., Ft. Wayne, Ind., 1983-84. Pvt. piano tchr. Kokomo, 1967-85; piano tchr. Barbara Martin Piano Svc., Indpls., 1985-88, 1990—, Van Wezel Performing Arts Hall, Sarasota, Fla., 1988-90. Author: Piano Abstract, 1981. Fellow Ancient and Mystical Order Rosae Crucis. Avocation: building experimental musical instruments. Home and Office: 1912 W Deffenbaugh St Kokomo IN 46902-6032

HIGHMAN, BARBARA, dermatologist; b. Washington; d. Benjamin and Helen (Wienshienk) H. Student, Northwestern U., 1960-63; MD, U. Mich., 1967. Diplomate Am. Bd. Dermatology. Intern Baylor U. Affiliated Hops., Houston, 1967-68; dermatology residency Henry Ford Hosp., Detroit, 1968-71; fellow in dermatology Johns Hopkins U., Balt., 1971-72; pvt. practice Laurel, Md., 1972—; staff North Charles Hosp., Balt., 1972-77, Laurel Regional Hosp.; cons. in dermatology U.S. Army, Ft. Myer, Va., 1972-77. Fellow Am. Acad. Dermatology (continuing med. edn. award 1978-80, 80-83, 83-86, 86-89, 89-92, 92-95, 95-98, 98-2001); mem. AMA (physicians recognition award 1971-74, 74-77, 77-80, 80-83, 83-86, 85-89, 88-90, 90-92, 92-95, 95-98, 98-2001), Soc. for Investigative Dermatology, Nat. Found. for Dermatology, Anne Arundel County Med. Soc., Med. and Chirugical Soc. State of Md., Laurel Med. Soc., Prince George's Women's Med. Soc. Office: 3335 Old Line Ave Laurel MD 20724-2234

HIGHSMITH, JASPER HABERSHAM, sales executive; b. Waycross, Ga., Dec. 3, 1940; s. Jasper H. and Linda (Weatherly) H.; m. Constance Orr Fitzgibbons, Aug. 26, 1963 (div. 1969); m. Linda Inez Diaz, Aug. 25, 1979; children: Richard, Eric, Jason. BBA, U. Ga., 1963. Engring. assoc. Western Electric Co., Atlanta, 1964-66; engr. No. Electric Co., Montreal, Que., Can., 1966-68, Gen. Telephone Co., Tampa, Fla., 1969-74; staff engr. No. Telecom, Inc., Tampa, 1974-76, regional mgr., 1977-85, dir. sales, 1986-94; v.p. ea. ops. Goldfield Telecom Inc., Tampa, 1994-97; pres. Marine Tech. Resources Inc., Tampa, 1997—. Mem. IEEE, U.S. Telephone Assn., Ind. Telephone Pioneers Assn. (mem. adv. coun. mfrs. chpt. 1987-88), Nat. Telephone Coop. Assn., Telephone Assns. of Ga., Fla., N.C., S.C., Tenn., and Ala., Treasure City Jaycees (v.p. 1969, pres. 1971), Orgn. for the Protection and Advancement of Small Telephone Cos., Phi Delta Theta. Methodist. Avocations: flying, boating, water sports. Home: 13714 Halliford Dr Tampa FL 33624-6903 Office: 5364 Ehrlich Rd Ste 114 Tampa FL 33624

HIGHSMITH, SHELBY, federal judge; b. Jacksonville, Fla., Jan. 31, 1929; s. Isaac Shelby and Edna Mae (Phillips) H.; m. Mary Jane Zimmerman, Nov. 25, 1972; children—Holly Law, Shelby. A.A., Ga. Mil. Coll., 1948; B.A., J.D., U. Kansas City, 1958. Bar: Fla. 1958. Trial atty. Kansas City, Mo., 1958-59, Miami, Fla., 1959-70; circuit judge Dade County, Fla., 1970-75; sr. ptnr. Highsmith, Strauss, Glatzer & Deutsch, P.A., Miami, 1975-91; judge U.S. Dist. Ct. (so. dist.) Fla., Miami, 1991—. Chief legal adviser Gov.'s War on Crime Program, 1967-68; spl. counsel Fla. Racing Commn., 1969-70; mem. Inter-Agy. Law Enforcement Planning Counsel of Fla., 1969-70. Served to capt. AUS, 1949-55. Decorated Bronze Star; recipient Outstanding Alumni Achievement Law award, U. Mo., 1998. Fellow Internat. Soc. Barristers; mem. ABA, Dade County Bar Assn., Bench and Robe, Torch and Scroll, Miami Nat. Golf Club, Wildcat Cliffs Country Club, (Highlands, N.C.), Omicron Delta, Phi Alpha Delta. Republican. Roman Catholic. Office: Fed Justice Bldg 99 NE 4th St Rm 1027 Miami FL 33132-2138

HIGHSMITH, WANDA LAW, retired association executive; b. Cleveland, Mo., Oct. 25, 1928; d. Lloyd B. and Nan (Sisk) Law; student U. Mo., 1954-56; 1 child, Holly. Legal sec., firms in Mo. and D.C., until 1960; various staff positions Am. Coll. Osteopathic Surgeons, 1960-72, asst. exec. dir., conv. mgr., Alexandria, Va., 1974-94; ret., 1994. Mem. NAFE, Profl. Conv. Mgmt. Assn., Washington Soc. Assn. Execs., Am. Soc. Assn. Execs. Republican. Methodist. Home: 1600 S Joyce St Apt 1523 Arlington VA 22202-5130

HIGHSTEIN, JENE ABEL, sculptor; b. Balt., June 16, 1942; s. Gustav and Ada Abel Highstein; m. Alanna Heiss (div.); 1 child, Lokke Abel; m. Katharine Duane; children: Alex, Jesse. BA, U. Md., 1963; postgrad., U. Chgo., 1963-65, N.Y. Studio Sch., 1966, Royal Acad. Schs., London, 1967-70. vis. artist Yale U., New Haven, 1975, Sarah Lawrence Coll., Bronxville, N.Y., 1976, C.W. Post Coll, Old Westbury, N.Y., 1979, Emily Carr Coll. Art, Vancouver, B.C., Can., 1980, Rutgers U., Camden, N.J., 1982, Tyler Sch. Art, Phila., 1990, R.I. Sch. Design, Providence, 1991, SUNY Albany, 1991, Vt. Studio Ctr., Johnsonville, Vt., 1993, Brandeis U., Waltham, 1995;

instr. Sch. Visual Arts, N.Y., 1974, NYU, N.Y.C., 1984-86, Parsons Sch. Design, N.Y., 1983; artist in residence C.W. Post Coll., Old Westbury, N.Y., 1975; vis. prof. UCLA, 1987, Boston Mus.Sch., 1988, Cranbrook Acad. Art, Bloomfield Hills, Mich., 1990; vis. lectr. Harvard U., Cambridge, Mass., 1995-96. One-man shows include Galeria Comicos, Lisbon, 1992, Baumgartner Galleries, Washington, 1993, Ace Contemporary Exhbns., L.A., 1993, Portland (Oreg.) Art Mus., 1993, Laura Carpenter Fine Art, Santa Fe, N.Mex., 1993, St. Gauden's Meml., Cornish, N.H., 1993, Secea, Winston-Salem, N.C., Ace Gallery N.Y., Art Space, Seoul, 1996, Stark Gallery, N.Y., 1997, Hill Gallery, Birmingham, Mich., 1998, 5501 Columbia Arts Ctr., Dallas, 1998; group shows include Kunstmuseum, Passau, Germany, 1992, Rhona Hoffman Gallery, Chgo., 1992, Anders Tornberg Gallery, Lund, Sweden, 1993, Bklyn. Mus., 1993, Portland Art Mus., 1993, Andre Emmerich Gallery, N.Y.C., 1993, Galerie Art 4, Galerie de l'Explanade, Paris, 1993, Werkstaat Kollerschlag, Austria, 1993, Kunst Halle Krems, Austria, 1993, Caldas Da Rainha, Portugal, 1993, Drawing Ctr., N.Y.C., 1993, Baumgartner Galleries, Washington, 1994, Neuberger Mus. Art, Purchase, N.Y., 1994, Michael Klein Gallery, N.Y.C., 1995, Galerij S 65, Aalst, Belgium, 1995, others; represented in permanent collections at Balt. Mus. Art, Bklyn. Mus., Collection Panza di Biumo, Varese, Italy, Dallas Art Mus., Detroit Inst. Arts, Musee Pleine Aire, Paris, Met. Mus. Art, N.Y.C., Mus. Contemporary Art, N.Y.C., Mus. Modern Art, N.Y.C., New Mus. Contemporary Art, N.Y.C., N.Y. Pub. Libr., Portland Art Mus., Rose Art Mus., Brandeis U., Waltham, Mass., San Diego Mus. Contemporary Art, La Jolla, Calif., David & Alfred Smart Art Mus., Chgo., Solomon R. Guggenheim Mus., N.Y.C., Victoria and Albert Mus., London, L.A. County Mus., others. Grantee Change Inc., 1974, Creative Artists Pub. Svc., 1975, Theo Doran award Ninth Paris Beinnale, 1975, Nat. Endowment for Arts, 1976, 77, 78, 84, 94, Creative Artists Pub. Svc., 1979; recipient John Simon Guggenheim award, 980, St. Gauden's Meml. prize, 1992. Office: 515 W 36th St New York NY 10018-1100

HIGHT, B. BOYD, lawyer; b. Lumberton, N.C., Feb. 15, 1939; s. Boyd B. and Mary Lou (Lennon) H.; m. Mary Kay Sweeney, Mar. 31, 1962; children: Kathryn, Kevin. BA, Duke U., 1960; LLB, Yale U., 1966; diploma in comparative law, U. Stockholm, 1967. Assoc. O'Melveny & Myers, Los Angeles, 1967-74, ptnr., 1974-79, 81-84, 89—; dep. asst. sec. trans. and telecommunications U.S. Dept. State, Washington, 1979-81; exec. v.p., gen. counsel Sante Fe Internat. Corp., Alhambra, Calif., also bd. dirs. Bd. dirs. Planned Parenthood L.A., 1986-95, pres., 1992-94; mem. bd. overseers Rand Ctr. Russian and Eurasian Studies, 1987—, chair, 1994—; trustee Am. U. Cairo, 1987—; bd. dirs. Calif. Supreme Ct. Hist. Soc., 1993—; bd. overseers The Huntington, 1996—. Mem. Coun. Fgn. Rels., Calif. Club, Los Angeles Country Club. Democrat. Office: O'Melveny & Myers 400 S Hope St Los Angeles CA 90071-2899

HIGHT, HAROLD PHILIP, retired security company executive; b. Crescent City, Calif., Apr. 17, 1924; s. Vernon Austin and Mary Jane (Gontau) H.; m. Margaret Rose Edelman, Nov. 19, 1945 (div. 1949); children: Linda Marie, Beverly Sue; m. Doris Louise Dunn, June 20, 1982 (dec. 1998). Student police sci., Coll. of Redwoods, 1969. With Pan Am. World Airways, South San Francisco, Calif., 1945-51, 52; officer Richmond (Calif.) Police Dept., 1952-54; aircraft electrician Internat. Atlas Svc., Oakland, Calif., 1954-56; security officer radiation lab. AEC, Livermore, Calif., 1956-58; chief police Port Orford (Oreg.) Police Dept., 1958-61; dep. sheriff, sgt., evidence technician Del Notre County Sheriff's Dept., Crescent City, 1961-85; ret., 1985; security officer, sgt. Del Notre Security Svc., Crescent City, 1985. With USN, 1941-45, 51-52. Mem. Internat. Footprint Assn. (sec., treas. bd. dirs. Crescent City 1985—), Navy League U.S. (2d v.p. Crescent City 1984—), Tin Can Sailors, Masons, Scottish Rite (32d degree), Elks, Grange. Republican. Roman Catholic. Avocations: model railroads, walking. Home: 110 Lafayette Way Crescent City CA 95531-8351

HIGHT, JOE IRVIN, editor; b. Guthrie, Okla., July 14, 1958; s. Wilber Eugene and Pauline Ruth (Kingston) H.; m. Nannette Louise Bloch, Sept. 20, 1986; children: Elena Nicole, Elyse Christine. BA, U. Cen. Okla., 1980. From sports editor to mng. editor Guthrie Daily Leader, 1980-81; reporter, wire editor Shawnee (Okla.) News-Star, 1981-82, city editor, 1983-84; reporter Lawton (Okla.) Constn., 1982-83; from reporter to mng. editor The Oklahoman, Oklahoma City, 1985—; freelance writer USA Today, 1987; bd. mem. People in the Media Program, U. Ctrl. Okla., adv. bd. nat. Dart award; instr. Mich. State U.; site dir. Nat. Writer's Workshop Okla. Adv. Bd.; bd. dirs. Mid-Am. Press Inst. Bd. dirs., spokesman Red Andrews Christmas Dinner for Poor, Oklahoma City, 1985-98; bd. dirs. Okla. Archdiocese Young Adults, Oklahoma City, 1985-86; bd. dirs. Chelsea Sta. Neighborhood Assn., Edmond, Okla., pres., 1992-93, 95-96, v.p., 1993-94; mem. pastoral coun. St. John's Cath. Ch., Edmond, 1987-91, chmn. planning commn.; mem. Okla. Youth Arts Hon. Adv. Coun., 1992-93; mem. outreach com. Ctrl. Okla. 2020, 1993-94; parade marshal Celebrating Our Future Parade, 1994; mem. comm. com. Ctrl. Okla. Citizens League, 1995—; grad. Leadership Oklahoma City, 1995, alumni mem., 1995—, alumni bd., 1998—; fourth-grade girls basketball coach St. Elizabeth Ann Seton Sch., Edmond, Okla., 1998-99. Recipient E.K. Gaylord award Okla. Gridiron Club, 1979, Sweepstakes trophy Okla. Press Assn., 1984, Carl Rogan award AP, 1986, 95, gov.'s commendation, 1991, 1st Excel award Internat. Assn. Bus. Communicators, 1994, Nat. Dart award for coverage of victims of Okla. bombing, also other nat., regional and state awards; named Outstanding Vol., Okla. Archdiocese Young Adults, 1985, Red Andrews Christmas Dinner, 1987. Mem. Soc. Profl. Journalists (nat. team deadline reporting and photography awards for coverage of Okla. bombing), Am. Soc. of Newspaper Editors. Democrat. Avocations: reading, swimming, tennis, collecting, family. Office: The Oklahoman PO Box 25125 Oklahoma City OK 73125-0125

HIGHTOWER, CAROLINE WARNER, arts management consultant; b. Cambridge, Mass., Feb. 22, 1935; d. William Lloyd and Mildred (Hall) Warner; children—Amanda Brantley, Matthew Lloyd. Student, Northwestern U., 1953-54, Cambridge U., 1954-55; B.A., Pomona Coll., 1958. Advt. mgr. U. Calif. Press, Berkeley, 1959-61; editor McGraw Hill, N.Y.C., 1961-64, Saturday Rev., N.Y.C., 1967-69; found. officer Carnegie Corp., N.Y.C., 1969-71; cons. Internat. Ctr. Photography, Children's TV Workshop, Rockefeller Found., Ford Found., N.Y.C., 1971-77; dir. Am. Inst. Graphic Arts, N.Y.C., 1977-94; cons. N.Y.C., 1994—; faculty Arts Adminstrn. NYU, 1998; vice chmn. creative artists pub. svc. program N.Y. State Coun. on Arts, N.Y.C., 1974-84; panelist Nat. Endowment Arts, Washington, 1979, 81, 83; scholarship juror Art Dept. Yale U., 1982, Nat. Inst. for the Deaf, RIT, 1988; commencement speaker, Art Ctr. Coll. of Design, Pasadena, 1987; moderator opening session Graphic Design in Am., Walker Art Ctr., Minn., 1989; bd. dirs. Pub. Ctr. for Cultural Resources, N.Y.C., 1984-89; mem. adv. bd. Documents of Am. Design, N.Y.C., Lubalin Ctr. Cooper Union, Ctr. for Book Libr. Congress, Innovative Design Fund, Coll. Applied and Fine Arts, Rochester Inst. Tech. Office: 333 Central Park W New York NY 10025-7145

HIGHTOWER, JACK ENGLISH, former state supreme court justice, congressman; b. Memphis, Tex., Sept. 6, 1926; s. Walter Thomas and Floy Edna (English) H.; m. Colleen Ward, Aug. 26, 1950; children—Ann, Amy, Alison. B.A., Baylor U., 1949; JD, 1951; LLM, Univ. Va., 1992. Bar: Tex. 1951. Since practiced in Vernon; mem. Tex. Ho. of Reps., 1953-54; dist. atty. 46th Jud. Dist. Tex., 1955-61; mem. Tex. Senate, 1965-75, pro tempore, 1971; mem. 94th-98th Congresses from 13th Tex. Dist., 1975-85; 1st asst. atty. gen. State of Tex., 1985-87; justice Texas Supreme Ct., Austin, 1988-95; ret., 1996. Mem. Tex. Law Enforcement Study Commn., 1957; del. White House Conf. Children and Youth, 1970; alt. del. Democratic Nat. Conv., 1968; bd. regents Midwestern U., Wichita Falls, Tex., 1962-65; trustee Baylor U., 1972-81, acting gov., 1971; trustee Wayland Bapt. Univ., Plainview, Tex., 1991—, Tex. Bapt. Children's Home, 1959-62, Tex. Scottish Rite Hosp. Children, 1991—, Human Welfare Commn.; bd. dirs. Bapt. Standard, 1959-68. With USNR, 1944-46. Named Outstanding Dist. Atty. Tex., Tex. Law Enforcement Found., 1959, Disting. Alumnus, Baylor U., 1978; recipient Knapp-Porter award Tex. A&M Univ., 1980. Mem. Tex. Dist. and County Attys. Assn. (pres. 1958-59), Scottish Rite Ednl. Assn. Tex. (exec. com. 1990—), Tex. Supreme Ct. Historical Soc. (pres. 1991-98), Tex. Bar. Found. (fellow 1992), SAR, U.S. Supreme Ct. Historical Soc., Tex. State Historical Assn. (exec. coun. 1998—), Masons (grand master Tex. 1972), Lions (pres. Vernon 1961).

HIGHTOWER, JOE WALTER, chemical engineering educator, consultant; b. Morrilton, Ark., Sept. 14, 1936; s. Walter Eugene and Verda Mae (Poindexter) H.; m. Ann Grekel, May 11, 1980. B.S., Harding Coll., Searcy, Ark., 1959; M.S., Johns Hopkins U., 1961, Ph.D., 1963. Postdoctoral fellow Queens U., Belfast, No. Ireland, 1963-64; research assoc. Mellon Inst., Pitts., 1964-67; assoc. prof. chem. engring. Rice U., Houston, 1967-70; prof. Rice U., 1970—, dir. Office Sponsored Rsch., 1988-90; chair chem. engring. dept., 1995-98; cons. Exxon Rsch. & Engring. Co., Linden, N.J., 1970-80; sci. adv. bd. Haldor Topsoe A-S, Copenhagan, 1976-89; adv. bd. Catalytica Assocs., Stanford, Calif., 1975-80; chmn. bd. trustees Gordon Rsch. Conf., 1980-81; chmn. adv. bd. Petroleum Rsch. Fund, 1980-90; chmn. 5 coms. NRC, 1972-78; tchr., organizer courses in catalysis. Editor Procs. 4th Internat. Congress on Catalysis, 1972, Procs. 5th Internat. Congress on Catalysis, 1976, Procs. 11th Internat. Congress on Catalysis, 1996; mem. editl. bd. Energy Sources, 1978-93, Indsl. and Engring. Chemistry, Process Design and Devel., 1981-84, Jour. Catalysis, 1984-94; contbr. articles to sci. jours. Co-founder, pres. Human Resources Devel. Found., Houston, 1968—. Recipient Jefferson award for pub. service Houston, 1982, Honor Scroll, Tex. Inst. Chemists, 1987, Leadership in Action award, Houston, 1992, Disting. Alumni award Alpha Chi, 1997. Mem. Am. Chem. Soc. (chmn. petroleum chemistry divsn. 1974-75, Nat. award in petroleum chemistry 1973, award Southeastern Tex. sect. 1976, gen. chair S.W. Regional meeting 1996), Am Inst. Chem. Engring. Republican. Mem. Ch. of Christ. Home: 2346 Quenby St Houston TX 77005-1504 Office: Rice U Dept Chem Engring Houston TX 77251*

HIGHTOWER, JOHN BRANTLEY, arts administrator; b. Atlanta, May 23, 1933; s. Edward A. and Margaret (Kimzey) H.; m. Martha Ruhl, Feb. 25, 1984; children: Amanda, Matthew. BA in English, Yale U., 1955; DFA, Calif. Coll. Arts and Crafts. Asst. to pub. Am. Heritage Pub. Co., Inc., N.Y.C., 1961-63; exec. asst. N.Y. State Coun. Arts, N.Y.C., 1963-64, exec. dir., 1964-70; dir. Mus. Modern Art, N.Y.C., 1970-72; pres. Am. Coun. Arts, N.Y.C., 1972-74; pres. South St. Seaport, 1977-83, dir., vice chmn., 1983-84; exec. dir. Richard Tucker Music Found., 1977-89, Maritime Ctr. at Norwalk, 1984-89; dir. planning and devel. for the arts U. Va., 1989-93; pres., CEO The Mariners' Mus., Newport News, Va., 1993—; exec. com. WHRO, Norfolk; founder, chmn. Advs. for Arts, 1974-77; instr. arts mgmt. Wharton Sch., U. Pa., 1976-77, New Sch., 1976-77; cultural advisor Rockefeller Mission to Latin Am., 1969; vis. critic in arts adminstrn. Grad. Sch. Drama, Yale U., 1972-77; chmn. Planning Corp. for Arts, Urban Arts Corps. Bd. dirs. N.Y. State Coun. on Arts, Poets and Writers. Capt. USMCR, 1955-63. Fulbright fellow; recipient N.Y. State award, 1970. Mem. Century Assn. (N.Y.C.), 1805 Club (London). Home: 101 Museum Pkwy Newport News VA 23606-3635

HIGHTOWER, PAULINE PATRICIA, elementary education educator; b. Lewisburg, Tenn., May 13, 1941; d. Floyd L. Tidwell and Celestine (Hill) Tidwell-Walker; m. Bennie Fisher, Oct. 1961 (div. Mar. 1966); 1 child, Patricia Denise Fisher Wilcox; m. Charles Hightower, Jan. 1968 (div. Apr. 1998). BS Elementary Edn., Tenn. State U., 1963; MS in Spl. Edn./Learning Disabilities, Calif. Luth. Coll., 1980. Cert. elem. educator, Tenn., N.D., Nebr., Calif. Tchr. 3rd and 4th grades Jones Sch., Lewisburg, Tenn., 1964-65; tchr. 5th and 6th grades Cornersville (Tenn.) Sch., 1965-66; tchr. 5th grade Buena Vista Elem. Sch., Nashville, 1966-70; tchr. 6th grade Westmeade Elem. Sch., Nashville, 1970-71; tchr. 5th and 6th grades Twining Elem. Sch., Grand Forks, N.D., 1971-76; tchr. learning disabilities Fillmore Elem. Sch., Lompoc, Calif., 1979-80; tchr. remedial reading, and 6th gr. Ft. Crook Elem. Sch., Omaha, 1980-83; tchr. learning disabled Vogelweh Elem. Sch., Kaiserslautern, Fed. Republic of Germany, 1984-86; tchr. pre-sch. and severely handicapped Bowie Spl. Edn. Ctr., Wichita Falls, Tex., 1987; tchr. 2d and 6th grades Ft. Crook Elem. Sch., Omaha, 1987—; tchr. assistance team Ft. Crook Elem. Sch., 1989-94, mentor tchr., 1990—, team leader, 1994-96. Mem. Bellevue Edn. Assn. Republican. Mem. A.M.E. Ch. Avocations: reading, sewing, museums, hiking, collecting stuffed animals, crystal miniatures and coffee mugs. Home: 2536 Mose Ave Bellevue NE 68147 Office: Ft Crook Elem Sch 12501 S 25th St Bellevue NE 68123-5525

HIGHWATER, JAMAKE, author, lecturer; s. Jamie and Amana (Bonneville) H.; adopted by Alexander and Marcia Marks. Lectr. primal and 20th century culture various univs. in U.S. and Can., 1970—; grad. lectr. NYU Continuing Edn., 1979-83; asst. adj. prof. Grad. Sch. Architecture, Columbia U., 1983-84; cons. N.Y. State Council on the Arts, 1975-85; founding mem. Indian Art Found., Santa Fe, 1980-87, Cultural Council, Am. Indian Community House, N.Y.C., 1976, pres., 1976-78; mem. task force on individual artist N.Y. State Council on Arts, 1981, mem. lit. panel, 1982-83; mem. lit. panel N.Y. Found. of the Arts, 1989-90, Mass. Artists Fellowship, 1990-91; adj. faculty Inst. Am. Indian Art, Santa Fe, 1979—; lectr. UCLA Entertainment and Performing Arts Dept., 1999—. Host, narrator and writer of: TV series Native Land, 1986, The Primal Mind, Public Broadcasting Svc. Network, 1986 (best film yr. Nat. Ednl. Film Festival, 1986, Ace award Discovery Channel 1991); Author: Indian America: A Cultural and Travel Guide, 1975, Song From the Earth: American Indian Painting, 1976 (Anisfield-Wolf award in race relations 1980), Ritual of the Wind: No. American Indian Ceremonies, Music and Dances, 1977, Many Smokes, Many Moons, 1978 (Jane Addams Peace Book award), Dance: Rituals of Experience, 1978, The Sweet Grass Lives On: 50 Contemporary North American Indian Artists, 1980, Masterpieces of American Indian Painting, 2 vols., 1978-80, The Primal Mind: Vision and Reality in Indian America, 1981 (Virginia McCormick Scully Lit. award 1982), Native Land (based on PBS program), 1986, Shadow Show: An Autobiographical Insinuation, 1987, Myth and Sexuality, 1990, The World of 1492, 1992, The Language of Vision, 1994, The Mythology of Transgression, 1997,; novels Anpao: An American Indian Odyssey (Newbery Honor award 1978), 1977 (Named Best Book for Young Adults, ALA 1978), Journey to the Sky: Stephens and Catherwood's Rediscovery of the Maya World, 1978, The Sun, He Dies: The End of the Aztec World, 1980 (named Best Book for Young Adults, Sch. Library Jour. 1980), Legend Days (Notable Book, ALA 1985), The Ceremony of Innocence, (Best book for Young Adults, ALA) 1986, I Wear the Morning Star, 1986, Eyes of Darkness, (Notable Book, ALA) 1985, I Took the Fire: A Memoir, 1988, Kill Hole, 1992, Dark Legend, 1994, Rama, 1994 (Best Books for Young Adults N.Y. Pub. Libr.), (poetry) Moonsong Lullaby, 1981, Songs for the Seasons, 1995; (as J. Marks) Rock and Other Four Letter Words, 1968, Mick Jagger: The Singer Not the Song, 1973; contbr. critiques to various lit. jours.; classical music editor: Soho Weekly News, 1975-79; sr. editor: Fodor Travel Guides, 1970-75; contbg. editor: N.Y. Arts Jours, 1978-84, Indian Trader, 1977-80, Stereo Rev., 1972-79, Native Arts/West, 1980-81; nat. adv. bd. PEW Fellowships in the arts, 1991-92; mem. bd. Am. Poetry Ctr., 1991—; contbg. arts critic Christian Sci. Monitor, 1988-92; mem. adv. bd. Visions Mag., 1992—, The Highwater papers, N.Y. Pub. Libr. Mem. art task panel Pres.'s Commn. on Mental Health, 1977-78; gen. dir. S.W. Native Arts Festival, U.Tex., Houston, 1985-86; gen. dir. Festival Mythos, Phila., 1991; mem. adv. bd. Wheelwright Mus. Indian Art, 1980-82, Lame Deer Coll., 1981—; mem. nat. adv. bd. Native Am. Rights Fund, 1980-83; nat. adv. Joseph Campbell Libr./Archives, 1989—; creative adv. Griot: N.Y., Great Performances, PBS, Star Trek Voyager, Paramount Pictures, Brian Wilson Documentary, Don Was, BBC. Named Hon. Citizen of Okla., 1977, New Mex., 1978. Mem. AFTRA, PEN (children's lit. com. Am. Ctr., 1990—, exec. bd. PEN Am. Ctr. 1983-86), Authors Guild, Dramatists Guild, Authors League. Office: Native Land Found 8491 W Sunset Blvd Los Angeles CA 90069-1911 *I attempt in my writing and lecturing to use tribal peoples as a metaphor for a separate, primal reality which is alternative to Western mentality and possesses significance and vitality in its own distinctive values and traditions.*

HIGI, WILLIAM L., bishop; b. Anderson, Ind., Aug. 29, 1933. Student, Mt. St. Mary of the West Sem., Xavier U. Ordained priest Roman Cath. Ch., 1959. Bishop Roman Cath. Diocese of Lafayette, Lafayette, Ind., 1984—. Home: 610 Lingle Ave Lafayette IN 47901-1740 Office: Bishops Officee PO Box 260 Lafayette IN 47902-0260*

HIGLEY, BRUCE WADSWORTH, orthodontist; b. Iowa City, Dec. 1, 1928; s. Lester Bodine and Harriet (Wadsworth) H.; m. Marta Beatriz Velasco, Sept. 23, 1966. D.D.S., State U. Iowa, 1952, M.S., 1953; student, Grinnell Coll., 1946-48, orthodontic certificate, 1953. Diplomate Am. Acad. Pain Mgmt. Research, instr. Iowa Dental U., 1952-53; practice dentistry, specializing in orthodontics South Miami, Fla., 1955—; Owner, chmn. bd. M.B.H. Enterprises, Inc., Miami, Fla., 1960—. Vice chmn. dist. council Boy Scouts Am., 1959-62; Mem. Personnel Bd., South Miami, 1959. Served as 1st lt. Dental Corps AUS, 1953-55. Fellow Internat. Coll. Cranio-Mandibnlar ORthopaedics, World Fedn. Orthodontists; mem. Am. Assn. Orthodontics, Fla. Orthodontic Soc., So., Miami socs. orthodontists, Fla., Am. socs. dentistry for children, Fla., Fla. East Coast, Miami dental socs., Am., S. Dade dental assns., Fedn. Dentaire Internat., English Royal Acad., C. of C. (past dir., sec., treas.), Psi Omega, Omicron Kappa Upsilon. Presbyn. (deacon). Clubs: Rotarian (pres. 1961-62), Elk, Coral Reef Yacht, Coral Gables Country, Royal Palm Tennis; Bankers, Executive (Miami); Army-Navy. Home: 2000 Brickell Ave Miami FL 33129-1721 Office: 7210 S Red Rd Miami FL 33143-5321

HIGMAN, SALLY LEE, company executive; b. Hinsdale, Ill., Sept. 12, 1945; d. Lee Fulton and Freda Margaret (Doehle) H. AB in Social Scis., Shimer Coll., Mt. Carroll, Ill., 1967; MA in Govt., Claremont (Calif.) Grad. Sch., 1969; M of Planning, U. So. Calif., 1973; Cert. in Higher Studies in Ekistics, Athens Tech. Orgn., Athens Ctr. of Ekistics, 1970. Cons. Doxiadis Assocs., Athens, Greece, 1971; rsch. asst. U. So. Calif., 1971-72; cons. Republic of Ecuador, Quito, 1973-75, UN Devel. Prog., Quito, 1975-76; environ. analyst Tetra Tech Inc., Pasadena, Calif., 1976-78; sr. environ. planner Nus Corp., Sherman Oaks, Calif., 1978-81; project mgr. ACT, Inc., Westminster, Calif., 1981-87; owner Higman Doehle Environ. Cons., L.A., 1987-88; pres. Higman Doehle Inc., L.A., 1988—. Contbr. articles to profl. jours. Ford Found. scholar U. So. Calif., 1971-73, jr. rsch. fellow Athens Ctr. of Ekistics, 1969-71; intern Social Sci. Rsch. Coun., Ford Found., 1973-75. Mem. Shimer Coll. Scholastic Soc. Democrat. Episcopalian. Avocations: stamp collecting, travel.

HIGNITE, MICHAEL ANTHONY, computer information systems educator, researcher, writer, consultant; b. Baxter Springs, Kans., Jan. 23, 1954; s. Denver and Goldie Beatrice (Farris) H.; m. Lisa Jo Barger, May 15, 1976; 1 child, Anna. BS in Bus. Adminstrn., Okla. State U., 1976, MS in Bus., 1979; PhD in Bus. Edn., U. Mo., 1990. Computer programmer Atlantic Richfield Co., Dallas, 1979-80, 85-86; programmer, analyst Atlantic Richfield Co., Tulsa, 1980-82; systems analyst Atlantic Richfield Co., Anchorage, 1982-85, cons., 1987-88; asst. prof. S.W. Mo. State U., Springfield, 1990-95, assoc. prof., 1995—; adj. prof. computer sci. Anchorage C.C., 1982-85. Mem. Internat. Assn. Computer Info. Systems, Sierra Club, Delta Sigma Pi, Beta Gamma Sigma. Republican. Methodist. Avocations: reading, running, collecting antiques, kayaking. Home: 4760 S Connor Ave Springfield MO 65804-7518 Office: Southwest Mo State U 901 S National Ave Springfield MO 65804-0088

HIJUELOS, OSCAR, novelist; b. N.Y.C., Aug. 24, 1951; s. Pascual and Magdalena (Torrens) H. BA, CCNY, 1975, MA, 1976. Prof. English Hofstra U., Hempstead, N.Y., 1988-89. Author: Our House in the Last World, 1983, The Mambo Kings Play Songs of Love, 1989 (Pulitzer Prize for fiction 1990), The Fourteen Sisters of Emilio Montez O'Brien, 1993, Mr. Ive's Christmas, 1995 (Pulitzer prize nominee 1996). Recipient "Outstanding Writer" citation from Pushcart Press for "Columbus Discovering America", 1978; Oscar Cintas fiction writing grantee, 1978-79; Breadloaf Writers conference scholarship, 1980; Creative Artists Programs Service fiction writing grantee, 1982; Ingram Merrill Found. fiction writing grantee, 1983; Creative Writers fellow Nat. Endowment for the Arts, 1985; Am. Acad. in Rome fellow Am. Acad. and Inst. of Arts and Letters, 1985. *

HILBERT, ELROY E. "BUCK", retired airline pilot; b. Chgo., Nov. 16, 1924; s. Elroy Lawrence Hilbert and Florence Rose (Nuber) Martin; m. Elizabeth A. Briegel, Oct. 27, 1951 (dec. Aug. 1960); children: Christine Yvonne; m. Dorothy E. Bortkivitch, Dec. 2, 1961; children: Robert, Christine, Alice, Elroy II, Lee, Leslie. Student, Tex. Tech U., 1942-43, United Airlines Tng. Ctr., 1953-84. Commd. 2d lt. USAAF, 1944, advanced through grades to 1st lt., 1948, multi-engine pilot, 1944-46; aviator U.S. Army Arty., U.S., Japan and Korea, 1952-53; pilot United Airlines, Chgo., 1953-84; ret.; lectr. in field. Contbr. articles to profl. publs.; recreated 1st flight of Varney Airlines, 1976 (Medal 1977). Mem. exec. res. group CAP, Chgo., 1964-84. Named to Ill. Aviation Hall of Fame, 1987, Sport Aviation Hall of Fame, 1993; recipient Paul Tissandier diploma Fed. Aeronautique Internat., Paris, 1996. Mem. Nat. Aero. Assn. (chmn. contest records 1989—), Exptl. Aircraft Assn. (pres. antique and classic divsn. 1971-76), United Airlines Hist. Found., EAA Aviation Found. (bd. dirs. 1975—), Antique Airplane Assn. Avocation: aviation heritage. Home: 8102 Leech Rd PO Box 424 Union IL 60180-0424

HILBERT, OTTO KARL, II, lawyer; b. Colorado Springs, Colo., Feb. 9, 1962; s. Otto Karl and Mary Rachel (Shine) H.; m. Lucille Megan O'Shaughnessy, Apr. 21, 1995. BA, U. Notre Dame, 1984, postgrad., 1985; JD, U. Colo., 1988. Bar: Colo. 1989, Ariz. 1989, Wis. 1998, U.S. Dist. Ct. (no. dist.) Calif, U.S. Ct. Appeals (9th cir.) 1991, U.S. Tax Ct. 1992, U.S. Ct. Appeals (10th cir.) 1993, U.S. Supreme Ct. 1995. Assoc. Kelly, Stansfield & O'Donnell, Denver, 1988-89, 92-93, Russell Piccoli, Ltd., Phoenix, 1989-92, LeBoeuf, Lamb, Greene & MacRae LLP, Denver, 1993-96; shareholder Reinhart, Boerner, Van Deuren, Norris & Rieselbach PC, Denver, 1996—; arbitrator Nat. Assn. Securities Dealers, Inc., 1993—, Nat. Futures Assn., 1993—. Mem. law sch. adv. coun. U. Notre Dame, 1989-92; cons. Ariz. Spl. Olympics, Phoenix, 1989-92; mem. Edward Frederick Sorin Soc., Notre Dame, Ind., 1989—. Mem. ABA, Colo. Bar Assn., Denver Bar Assn., Ariz. Bar Assn., Wis. Bar Assn., Notre Dame Club of Phoenix (1st v.p. 1991-92, bd. dirs. 1989-92, Award of the Yr. 1992), Notre Dame Club of Denver (bd. dirs. 1995-97), Lakewood Country Club (bd. dirs. 1998—). Republican. Roman Catholic. Avocations: piano, guitar, golf. Office: Reinhart Boerner Van Deuren Norris Rieselbach PC 1 Norwest Ctr 1700 Lincoln St Ste 3725 Denver CO 80203-4537

HILBERT, RITA L., librarian; b. Orange, N.J., Nov. 1, 1942; d. Ralph P. LaSalle and Arlene (Julian) Strobel; children: Toby Gayle Buchanan, Stacey Giordano, Joseph, Matthew. AA, NYU, 1988, BA, 1990; MLS, Rutgers U., 1992. Merchandising rsch. analyst Burrelle's, Livingston, N.J., 1975-82; teaching asst. Montessori Sch., Millburn, N.J., 1982-84; outreach specialist Rockwood Meml. Libr., Livingston, 1984-90, head spl. svcs., 1990-92; libr. dir. Lincoln Park (N.J.) Pub. Libr., 1992-94, Mount Olive Township Pub. Libr., 1994—; mem. Adult Sch. Bd., Livingston, 1990—, Lincoln Pk. Bd. of Edn., 1995-98, chair policy com., 1997-98, negotiations com., 1997-98. Member Livingston Adv. Com. for the Handicapped, 1985—, Livingston Coun. for Sr. Citizens, 1985—, Region III Com. for Svcs. to Spl. Populations, sec., 1987-88; elected mem. Lincoln Park Bd. Edn., 1995-98, chair policy and negotiations coms., 1995-98; trustee Lincoln Park Libr., 1997-98. Recipient Founder's Day award NYU, 1990. Mem. ALA, AAUW (scholarship 1987), N.J. Libr. Assn. (scholarship 1990), N.J. Assn. Libr. Assts. (pres. 1989-90, scholarship in her name 1994), Morris Automated Info. Network (sec. 1993-94, v.p. 1995, pres. 1996), Mt. Olive Township Historical Soc., Kiwanis (Mt. Olive chpt.), Mt. Olive C. of C., Kiwanis, Alpha Sigma Lambda. Avocations: walking, painting, traveling. Office: Wolfe Rd Budd Lake NJ 07828

HILBERT, ROBERT BACKUS, county water utility administrator; b. Pleasant Grove, Utah, Jan. 4, 1929; s. Rudy and Sarah M. (Whitecar) H.; m. Dora Jean Davis, Aug. 26, 1949; children—Susan Jean (Mrs. Brian Oakden), Robert Jeffrey, Richard Wayne, Robert Layne. Student, U. Utah at Salt Lake City, 1946-47. Engring. aide U.S. Bur. Reclamation, Salt Lake City, 1947-52; field engr. Templeton, Linke & Alsup (cons. engrs.), Salt Lake City, 1952-54; gen. mgr., sec.-treas. Salt Lake County Water Conservancy Dist., Salt Lake City, 1954-89, ret., 1989; pres., chmn. bd. dirs. Central Utah Water Conservancy Dist., Orem, 1964-91; chmn. State of Utah Drinking Water Bd., 1979-95; sr. cons. Montgomery-Watson Cons. Engrs., Salt Lake City, 1990-95; water cons. Summit County, Utah, 1997—. Mem. water policy task force of nat. resource com. Utah State Legislature, 1974—. Served with AUS, 1950-52. Named Water Utility Man of the Year Intermountain sect. Am. Water Works Assn., 1969; named Am. Water Works Assn. leader to Goodwill People to People Tour of Iron Curtain Countries, 1972, Led Water Industry Tour of Soviet Union, 1989. Mem. Am. Water Works Assn. (dir. 1969-72, pres. 1974-75), Utah Water Users Assn. (pres. 1970-73), Salt Lake County Water and Wastewater Assn. (pres. 1971-72). Democrat. Mem. Ch. of Jesus Christ of Latter-day Saints. Home: PO Box 71721 Salt Lake City UT 84171-0721

HILBERT, ROBERT S(AUL), optical engineer; b. Washington, Apr. 29, 1941; s. Philip G. and Bessie (Friend) H.; m. Angela Cinel Ferreira, June 19, 1966; children: David M., Daniel S. BS in Optics, U. Rochester, 1962, MS in Optics, 1964. Optical design engr. Itek Corp., Lexington, Mass., 1963-65, supr. lens design sect., 1965-67, asst. mgr. optical engr. dept., 1967-69, mgr. optical engring. dept., 1969-74, dir. optics, 1974-75; v.p. engring. Optical Rsch. Assocs., Pasadena, Calif., 1975-84, sr. v.p., 1985-91, pres., COO, 1991—, also bd. dirs.; lectr. Northeastern U., Burlington, Mass., 1967-69; mem. trustees vis. com. Sch. Engring. and Applied Sci., U. Rochester, 1995-97. Patentee in lens systems. Recipient Future Scientist of Am. award, 1957; Am. Optical Co. fellow U. Rochester, 1962. Fellow Soc. Photo-Optical Instrumentation Engrs.; mem. Optical Soc. Am. (engring. coun. 1990-92), Lens Design Tech. Group (chmn. 1975-77). Jewish. Avocations: reading, the cinema. Home: 5055 Indianola Way La Canada Flintridge CA 91011-2657 Office: Optical Rsch Assocs 3280 E Foothill Blvd Pasadena CA 91107-3103

HILBERT, STEPHEN C., insurance company executive; b. 1946. Student, Ind. State U. Agent Aetna Life Ins. Co., Indpls., 1967-70, United Home Life Ins. Agy., Indpls., 1970-75, Aetna Life Ins., Indpls., 1975-79; chmn., CEO Conseco Inc. (now Conseco Cos.), Carmel, Ind., 1979—. Bd. dirs. Ind. State U. Found., Indpls. Conv. and Visitors Assn., Indpls. Zoo, St. Vincent Hosp. Found.; trustee Ctrl. Ind. Coun. on Aging Found., U.S. Ski Team; vol. Jr. Achievement, Multiple Sclerosis Soc., Park Tudor Sch., Indpls. Symphony Orch., Am. Heart Assn., Mental Health Assn. Marion County, Ind., Indpls. 500 Festival Com. Office: Conseco Cos 11815 N Pennsylvania St Carmel IN 46032-4555*

HILBERT, VIRGINIA LOIS, computer consultant and training executive; b. Detroit, June 4, 1935; d. Howard G. and Lois (Garner) Swaggerty; m. James R. Hilbert, Nov. 24, 1958; children: James Jr., Jennifer, Douglas, Alexandra. BA with honors, U. Mich., 1957. Govt. analyst dept. of health City of Detroit, 1957-60; owner, dir. Profl./Tech. Devel., Inc. dba Lansing Computer Inst., 1978—; bd. dirs. Physicians Health Plan. Contbr. articles to profl. jours. Tech. bd. Capital Region Cmty. Found.; sec. Tennis Patrons Bd., Lansing, 1984-89, Pro Symphony, 1984—; active Lansing Art Gallery, 1978-84; adv. com. for sml. bus. Mich. Jobs. Commn., 1997; small bus. chmn. Capital City United Way, 1998, bd. dirs., 1999. Listed in Entrepreneurial mag., Dun & Bradstreet chpt. on woman-owned firms, 1998; named one of Top Ten Women to own firms in the nation. Mem. ASTD, ASCD, Nat. Fedn. Ind. Bus. (guardian), CEO Network, Women Bus. Owners Assn., Mich. Tech. Coun., Nat. Bus. Edn. Assn., Gov.'s Small Bus. Conf. (del. gov.'s work group), Mich. Opportunity Card, Accrediting Commn. of Career Schs. and Colls. of Tech., Bus. Edn. Alliance for Progress, U.S. C. of C., Lansing C. of C. (small bus. coun., co-chair info. and seminar Small Bus. Edn.), Capital Area Health Alliance (Cmty. Health Info. Network-Tech. Adv. Group com., Mich. del. White House Conf. on Small Bus. 1995), Human Capital (state chmn. 1995, chair region V for implementation 1996-97, Entrepreneurial award for edn. Greater Lansing 1997, Diana award 1999), Rotary, Zonta, Alpha Phi (pres. heart equip. fund bd. 1975-96, alumnae pres.). Episcopalian. Home: 938 Wildwood Dr East Lansing MI 48823-3050 Office: Lansing Computer Inst Profl Tech Devel Inc 3001 Coolidge Rd Ste 403 East Lansing MI 48823-6337

HILBOLDT, JAMES SONNEMANN, lawyer, investment advisor; b. Dallas, July 21, 1929; s. Grover C. and Grace E. (Sonnemann) H.; m. Martha M. Christian, Sept. 5, 1953; children: James, Katherine Hilboldt Farrell, Susanna Jean, Thomas. AB in Econs., Harvard U., 1952; postgrad., U. Chgo., 1952-53; JD, U. Mich., 1956. With comml. and trust dept. No. Trust Co., Chgo., 1952-53; sole practice Kalamazoo, 1956—, pvt. practice as registered investment advisor, 1971—; bd. dirs. Lafourche Realty Co., Inc., Kalamazoo, pres., 1971—, Meijer, Inc., Grand Rapids, Mich., Old Kent Bank S.W. (formerly Am. Nat. Bank and Trust Co.), Mich., 1966-94. Bd. dirs. Kalamazoo Tennis Patrons, Inc., 1974-95, Downtown Devel. Authority, Kalamazoo, 1982-88, Downtown Tomorrow, Inc., Kalamazoo, 1985—, sec., treas., 1995, Downtown Kalamazoo Inc., 1988-91; treas., trustee The Power Found., 1967—, sec., 1967-94. Sgt. USMC, 1946-48. Mem. ABA, Mich. Bar Assn., Kalamazoo County Bar Assn., Harvard Club Western Mich. (pres. 1972-74), Kalamazoo Country Club, Park Club, Harvard Club N.Y.C. Avocations: tennis, swimming. Home: 4126 Lakeside Dr Kalamazoo MI 49008-2814 Office: 136 E Michigan Ave Kalamazoo MI 49007-3936

HILBORN, MICHAEL G., lawyer, real estate development executive; b. Chgo., May 10, 1943; s. Harold and Isabelle H.; m. Helene Wiczer, June 26, 1966; children: Harold, Jamie, Jeremy. B.S. in Accountancy, U. Ill., 1965; J.D., DePaul U., 1968. Bar: Ill. 1968. Atty. firm Tenney & Bentley, Chgo., 1968-72; atty. Urban Investment & Devel. Co., Chgo., 1972-76; asst. gen. counsel Urban Investment & Devel. Co., 1976-79, v.p., gen. counsel, sec., 1979-82, sr. v.p., gen. counsel, sec., 1983-93; sr. v.p., gen. counsel, sec. Urban Shopping Ctr., Inc., Chgo., 1993—. Mem. Ill. Soc. C.P.A.s, Ill. Bar Assn., Chgo. Bar Assn., ABA, Am. Corporate Counsel Assn., Internat. Council Shopping Ctrs.

HILBRECHT, NORMAN TY, lawyer; b. San Diego, Feb. 11, 1933; s. Norman Titus and Elizabeth (Lair) H.; m. Mercedes L. Sharratt, Oct. 24, 1980. B.A., Northwestern U., 1956; J.D., Yale U., 1959. Bar: Nev. 1959, U.S. Supreme Ct. 1963. Assoc. counsel Union Pacific R.R., Las Vegas, 1962; ptnr. Hilbrecht & Jones, Las Vegas, 1962-69; pres. Hilbrecht, Jones, Schreck & Bernhard, 1969-83, Hilbrecht & Assocs, 1983—, Mobil Transport Corp., 1970-72; gen. counsel Bell United Ins. Co., 1986-94; mem. Nev. Assembly, 1966-72, minority leader, 1971-72; mem. Nev. Senate, 1974-78; legis. commn., 1977-78; asst. lectr. bus. law U. Nev., Las Vegas.; oper. mem. Corp. Svcs. Group, 1998—; pres. Corp. Svcs. Co., 1998—, Nev. Incorporating Co., 1998—. Author: Nevada Motor Carrier Compendium, 1990. Mem. labor mgmt. com. NCCJ, 1963; mem. Clark County (Nev.) Dem. Ctrl. Com., 1959-80, 1st vice chmn., 1965-66; del. Western Regional Assembly on Ombudsman; chmn. Clark County Dem. Conv., 1966, Nev. Dem. Conv., 1966; pres. Clark County Legal Aid Soc., 1964, Nev. Legal Aid and Defender Assn., 1965-83; assoc. for justice Nat. Jud. Coll., 1993, 94, 95, 96. Capt. AUS, 1952-67. Named Outstanding State Legislator Eagleton Inst. Politics, Rutgers U., 1969, Best Lawyers in Am., Bar of Nev., 1993. Mem. ABA, ATLA, Am. Judicature Soc., Am. Acad. Polit. and Social Sci., State Bar Nev. (chmn. adminstrv. law 1991-94, chmn. sect. on adminstrv. law 1996), Nev. Trial Lawyers (state v.p. 1966), Am. Assn. Ret. Persons (state legis. com. 1991-94), Rotary, Elks, Phi Beta Kappa, Delta Phi Epsilon, Theta Chi, Phi Delta Phi. Lutheran. Office: 723 S Casino Center Blvd Las Vegas NV 89101-6716

HILBRINK, WILLIAM JOHN, violinist; b. Cleve., June 16, 1928; s. William and Caroline (Theil) H.; m. Patricia Anne Schultz, Aug. 6, 1955; children: Mark David, Holly Lee. B of Music Edn., Baldwin-Wallace Coll., 1955; MusM, U. Rochester, 1960. Cert. tchr. Tchr. strings, orch. Cleve. Pub. Schs., 1955-57; tchr. strings, dir. orch. MacMurray Coll., Jacksonville, Ill., 1958-62; tchr. violin, viola, string pedagogy, theory U. N.C., Greensboro, 1962-67; tchr. strings, grades 1-12, dir. orch. Fairfax (Va.) County Schs., 1967-83; asst. condr., assoc. concertmaster Fairfax Symphony Orch., 1977-84; ops. mgr. Fairfax (Va.) Symphony Orch., 1983-84; founder, 1st violinist Fairfax String Quartet, 1983—; orch. condr. MacMurray Coll. Community Orch., Jacksonville, 1958-62; founding mem. Collegium Musicum, Jacksonville, 1960-62; concertmaster Springfield (Ill.) Symphony Orch., 1962; 1st violinist Piano Trio, String Quartet, U. N.C., Greensboro, 1962-67; freelance violinist Washington area, 1977—. Reviewer of concerts, Civic Music Assn., 1960-62; violinist in several hundred concerts and recitals, 1958—. Organizer, condr. Fairfax All-County Orch., 1977-78; organizer Washington Met. area Spl. Olympics Orch., 1979; mem. music com. and admin. bd. Fairfax United Meth. Ch., 1990—; music contractor for several choral groups, Washington; adjudicator for numerous festivals, Va., N.C., and Md. Recipient scholarship Eastman Sch. Music, 1957-58, Suzuki Inst., 1966. mem. Am. Fedn. Musicians. Avocations: woodworking, model trains, house remodeling, astronomy, boat-building. Home: 5112 Forsgate Pl Fairfax VA 22030-4507

HILBURN, HEDWIG ALISON, electrician; b. Lubbock, Tex., Mar. 10, 1947; d. Marvin Benson and Naomi Hilburn. B of Music Edn., Tex. Tech. U., 1969, MEd, 1972; postgrad., Ind. U., 1994—. Spl. edn. tchr. Shelbyville (Ky.) Sch. System, 1972-74, Louisville Sch. System, 1974-75; musical dir. Blue Apple Players, Louisville, 1977-78; electrician' apprentice Louisville, 1979-84; electrician Internat. Brotherhood of Elec. Workers, 1984-85, Ford Motor Co./United Auto Workers, Louisville, 1985—; intern pub. rels. and publs. dept. Internat. Union United Auto Workers, Detroit, 1998-99. Mem. Newspaper Guild/Comms. Worker of Am., Nat. Writers, United Auto Workers (Svc. Recognition 1996). Democrat. Avocations: haphazard flower gardening, song writing, reading, playing instruments. E-mail: hhilburn@ix.netcom.com.

HILBURN, JOHN CHARLES, geologist, geophysicist; b. Dallas, Sept. 16, 1946; s. William Grant and Catherine (Thorwald) H.; 1 child, John C. Jr. BS in Geol. Scis., U. Tex., Austin, 1978. Mfg. mgr. Scorpio, Inc., Austin, 1972-74; rsch. engr., scientist U. Tex., Austin, 1974-78; corp. v.p. Reeves, Inc., Houston, 1978-79; mgr. acqusitions S.A.M. Western Geophys. Corp., Houston, 1979-80; sr. mktg. geophysicist GECO Geophys. Co., Inc., Houston, 1980-85; pres. John Hilburn & Assocs., Inc., Austin, 1985—. Mem. Soc. Exploration Geophysicists, European Assn. Exploration Geophysicists, Can. Soc. Exploration Geophysicists, Am. Assn. Petroleum Geologists, Geol. Soc. Am. Avocations: gem cutting, stamp collecting, skiing, scuba diving, cooking. Home and Office: 6302 Mountainclimb Dr Austin TX 78731-3908

HILDEBRAND, CAROL ILENE, librarian; b. Presho, S.D., Feb. 15, 1943; d. Arnum Vance and Ethel Grace (Cole) Stoops; m. Duane D. Hildebrand, Mar. 21, 1970. BA, Dakota Wesleyan U., Mitchell, S.D., 1965; M in Librarianship, U. Wash., 1968. Tchr. Watertown (S.D.) H.S., 1965-67; libr. dir. Chippewa County Libr., Montevideo, Minn., 1968-70, The Dalles (Oreg.)-Wasco County Libr., 1970-72; libr. Salem (Oreg.) Pub. Libr., 1972-73; libr. dir. Lake Oswego (Oreg.) Pub. Libr., 1973-82; asst. city libr. Eugene (Oreg.) Pub. Libr., 1982-91, acting city libr., 1991-92, libr. dir., 1993—; cons., condr. workshops in field. Vice-chair LWV, Lane County, 1987; bd. dirs. People for Oreg. Librs. Polit. Action Com., 1986—; sec. Citizens for Lane County Libr., 1985-88. Named Woman of Yr., Lane County Coun. of Orgns., 1995, Oreg. Libr. of Yr., 1993. Mem. ALA (chpt. councilor 1990-94), AAUW (bd. dirs. 1986, sec. 1995-96), Pacific N.W. Libr. Assn. (pres. 1989-90), Oreg. Libr. Assn. (pres. 1976-77), Rotary, Phi Kappa Phi. Methodist. Avocations: reading murder mysteries, baking. Office: Eugene Public Libr 100 W 13th Ave Eugene OR 97401-3433

HILDEBRAND, DANIEL WALTER, lawyer; b. Oshkosh, Wis., May 1, 1940; s. Dan M. and Rose Marie (Baranowski) H.; m. Dawn E. Erickson; children: Daniel G., Douglas P., Elizabeth A., Rachel E., Jacob E. BS, U. Wis., 1962, LLB, 1964. Bar: Wis. 1964, U.S. Dist. Ct. (we. dist.) Wis. 1964, N.Y. 1965, U.S. Dist. Ct. (so. and ea. dists.) N.Y. 1967, U.S. Ct. Appeals (2d cir.) 1968, U.S. Dist. Ct. (ea. dist.) Wis. 1970, U.S. Ct. Appeals (7th cir.) 1970, U.S. Supreme Ct. 1970, U.S. Tax Ct. 1986, U.S. Ct. Appeals (8th cir.) 1988, U.S. Ct. Appeals (D.C. cir.) 1991. Assoc. Willkie, Farr & Gallagher, N.Y.C., 1964-68; from assoc. to ptnr. DeWitt Ross & Stevens S.C., Madison, Wis., 1968—; lectr. U. Wis. Law Sch., Madison, 1972—; mem. Joint Survey Com. on Tax Ememptions Wis. Editor: U. Wis. Law Rev., 1963-64. Pres. Wis. Law Foun., 1993-95, Wis. Jud. Commn., 1992-98, chairperson, 1997-98. Fellow Am. Bar Found.; mem. ABA (mem. fed. cts. com. litigation sect., ho. of dels. 1992—, standing com. on ethics 1997—, Wis. state delegate 1995—), Wis. Bar Assn. (bd. govs. 1981-85, 86-93, mem. exec. com. 1987-93, chmn. 1988-89, pres. 1991-92), N.Y. State Bar Assn., Dane County Bar Assn. (pres. 1980-81), 7th Cir. Bar Assn., Am. Law Inst., Am. Acad. Appellate Lawyers, James E. Doyle Inn of Ct. Roman Catholic. Office: 2 E Mifflin St Ste 600 Madison WI 53703-2890

HILDEBRAND, DAVID KENT, statistics educator; b. Mpls., June 24, 1940; s. Frank Childs and Joyce (Wadmond) H.; m. Patricia Jane Gach, Mar. 30, 1964; children: Martin Victor, Jeffrey David. BA, Carleton Coll., 1962; MS, Carnegie Inst. Tech., 1965, PhD, 1967; MA (hon.), U. Pa., 1972. Asst. prof. stats. U. Pa., Phila., 1965-71, assoc. prof., 1971-76, prof., 1976—, chair dept. stats., 1985-90; vis. asst. prof. Carnegie-Mellon U., 1970-71; chair Faculty Senate, U. Pa., 1992-93. Author: Statistical Thinking for Behavioral Scientists, 1986; co-author: Prediction Analysis of Cross-Classification, 1977, Statistical Thinking for Managers, 4th edit., 1998, Basic Statistical Ideas for Managers, 1995. Mem. Am. Statis. Assn. Office: Univ of Pa Dept of Stats Philadelphia PA 19104-6302

HILDEBRAND, DON, science foundation executive. Pres. Rhone Merieux, Inc., 1985-97; v.p. biol. divsn. Merial Limited, Athens, 1997—. Address: 115 Trans Tech Dr Athens GA 30601-1649*

HILDEBRAND, FRANCIS BEGNAUD, mathematics educator; b. Washington, Pa., Sept. 1, 1915; s. Frank Alonzo and Inez (Patin) H.; m. Eleanor Maclaren Jenkins, Sept. 18, 1943; children—Susan Lee, Robert Craig, Jean Ellen. B.S., Washington and Jefferson Coll., 1936, M.A., 1938, Sc.D. (hon.), 1969; Ph.D., MIT, 1940. Mem. faculty MIT, Cambridge, 1938—, assoc. prof. math., 1950-67, prof., 1967-84, prof. emeritus, 1984—. Author: Advanced Calculus for Applications, 1949, 62, 76; Methods of Applied Mathematics, 1952, 65; Introduction to Numerical Analysis, 1956, 74; Finite-Difference Equations and Simulations, 1968. Mem. Am. Math. Soc., Math. Assn. Am., Sigma Xi, Phi Beta Kappa, Phi Delta Theta. Home: 7 Bucknell Rd Wellesley MA 02481-1201

HILDEBRAND, JOHN FREDERICK, newspaper columnist; b. Chgo., Dec. 23, 1940; s. Paul Hedden and Harriet L. (Cummins) H.; m. Vasana Lohitkoopt, June 24, 1972; children: Marisa Cummins, Shana Victoria, Brent Daniel. B Journalism, U. Mo., 1965; MS in Journalism, Columbia U., 1966. Reporter Poplar Bluff (Mo.) Daily Am. Republic, 1963, Joplin (Mo.) Globe, 1964, AP, Jefferson City and Kansas City, Mo., 1965; fgn. svc. officer U.S. Info. Svc., Washington and Bangkok, 1966-70; reporter Newsday, Melville, N.Y., 1970-74, asst. city editor, 1974-76, edn. writer, 1976—; adj. prof. journalism Chulalongkorn U., Bangkok, 1967; pres. Lloyd Neck (N.Y.) Holding Corp., 1988-91, bd. dirs., 1986-95. Vestryman St. John's Episcopal Ch., Cold Spring Harbor, N.Y., 1992-98. Recipient citation Adelphi U., Garden City, N.Y., 1987, citation Kappa Delta Pi, Oakdale, N.Y., 1988. Mem. Edn. Writers Assn. (1st prize opinion article 1978, 1st prize article series 1982, 97, 1st prize article package 1992), Phi Gamma Delta (sec. Chi Mu chpt. 1964). Home: 23 Target Rock Dr Huntington NY 11743-1464 Office: Newsday Inc 235 Pinelawn Rd Melville NY 11747-4250

HILDEBRAND, JOHN G(RANT), neurobiologist, educator; b. Boston, Mar. 26, 1942; s. John G. and Helen S. Hildebrand; m. Gail Deerin Burd, July 24, 1982. AB, Harvard U., 1964; PhD, Rockefeller U., 1969. Instr. neurobiology Harvard U. Med. Sch., Boston, 1970-72, asst. prof., 1972-77, assoc. prof., 1977-80, vis. prof., 1980-81; prof. biol. scis. Columbia U., N.Y.C., 1980-85; prof. neurobiol., biochemistry, molecular and cell biology, entomology U. Ariz., Tucson, 1985—, Regents prof., 1989—, dir. div. neurobiology, 1985—; assoc. behavioral biology Harvard U. Mus. Comparative Zoology, Cambridge, Mass., 1980-97; trustee Marine Biol. Lab., Woods Hole, Mass., 1981-89, mem. exec. com., 1981-88; Jan de Wilde lectr. U. Wageningen, The Netherlands, 1992; King Solomon lectr., Hebrew U., Jerusalem, 1995; K.D. Roeder lectr. Tufts U., 1995; Felix Santschi lectr. U. Zurich, Switzerland, 1995. Co-editor: Chemistry of Synaptic Transmission, 1974, Receptors for Neurotransmitters, Hormones, and Pheromones in Insects, 1980, Molecular Insect Science, 1990; devel. neurosci. sect. editor Jour. Neurosci., 1983-88; co-editor Jour. Comparative Physiology A, 1990—; mem. editorial bd. various other jours. Trustee Rockefeller U., N.Y.C., 1970-73. Recipient Javits Neurosci. award Nat. Isnt. Neurol. and Communicative Disorders and Stroke, NIH, 1986-94, Merit award Nat. Inst. Allergy and Infectious Diseases, NIH, 1986-97, R.H. Wright award Simon Fraser U., B.C., Can., 1990, Max Planck Rsch. award Max Planck Gesellschaft and Alexander von Humboldt-Stiftung of Germany, 1990, Founder's Meml. award Entomol. Soc. Am., 1997, Humboldt rsch. award, 1997; Helen Hay Whitney Found. fellow, 1969-72, A.P. Sloan Found. fellow, 1973-77. Fellow AAAS, Royal Entomol. Soc. U.K.; mem. Am. Soc. Biochemistry and Molecular Biology, Assn. for Chemoreception Scis. (IFF Innovative Rsch. award 1997), Soc. for Neurosci. (treas. 1993-94), Internat. Soc. Neuroethology (pres. 1995-98), Soc. Integrative and Comparative Biology, Internat. Soc. Chem. Ecology (pres. 1998-99), Deutsche Akademie der Naturforscher Leopoldina, Norwegian Acad. Sci. and Letters. Avocations: music, lower brass instruments. Home: 629 N Olsen Ave Tucson AZ 85719-5136 Office: U Ariz ARL Div Neurobiology PO Box 210077 Tucson AZ 85721-0077

HILDEBRAND, ROGER HENRY, astrophysicist, physicist; b. Berkeley, Calif., May 1, 1922; s. Joel Henry and Emily (Alexander) H.; m. Jane Roby Beedle, May 28, 1944; children: Peter Henry, Alice Louise, Kathryn Jane, Daniel Milton. AB in Chemistry, U. Calif., Berkeley, 1947, PhD in Physics, 1951. Physicist, U. Calif., 1942-51; physicist Tenn. Eastman Corp., Oak Ridge Nat. Lab., 1945; asst. prof. dept. physics Enrico Fermi Inst., U. Chgo., 1952-55, asso. prof., 1955-60, prof., 1960—, prof. dept. astronomy and astrophysics, 1978—, Samuel K. Allison Disting. Service prof., 1985—, chmn. dept. astronomy and astrophysics, 1984-88; dir. Enrico Fermi Inst., 1965-68, dean coll., 1969-73; assoc. lab. dir. for high energy physics Argonne (Ill.) Nat. Lab., 1958-64; chmn. sci. policy com. Stanford (Calif.) Linear Accelerator Ctr., 1962-66; mem. physics adv. com. Nat. Accelerator Lab., 1967-69; mem. sci. and ednl. adv. com. Lawrence Berkeley Lab., 1972-80; chmn. com. to rev. U.S. medium energy sci. AEC and NSF, 1974; chmn. airborne obs. users group NASA, 1983-84; chmn. sci. cons. group Stratopheric Obs. for Infrared Astronomy (SOFIA), NASA, 1985-89, mem. sci. working group, 1995—; mem. space astronomy and astrophysics Space Sci. Bd., 1987-90; mem. coun. Columbus Project, 1987-88; mem. sci. and tech. adv. panel for the submillimeter array Harvard/Smithsonian Ctr. for Astrophysics, 1989-95; mem. astronomy and astrophysics survey com. NAS Panel for Infrared Astronomy, 1989-90; chmn. Dannie Helneman prize com. Am. Inst. Physics, 1990; mem. sci. and tech. adv. group Large Millimeter Telescope, 1995—; mem. obs. vis. com. Assn. Univs. for Rsch. in Astronomy, 1993-96, chmn. Stratospheric Obs. Infrared Astronomy sci. coun., 1997—. Guggenheim fellow, 1968-69, Alfred P. Sloan Found. fellow, 1975. Fellow Am. Phys. Soc., Am. Acad. Arts and Scis.; mem. Am. Astron. Soc., Internat. Astron. Union, Midwestern Univs. Rsch. Assn. (dir. 19956-58, 62-68), Phi beta Kappa, Sigma Xi. Office: U Chgo Enrico Fermi Inst 5640 S Ellis Ave Chicago IL 60637-1433

HILDEBRAND, VERNA LEE, human ecology educator; b. Dodge City, Kans., Aug. 17, 1924; d. Carrell E. and Florence (Smyth) Butcher; m. John R. Hildebrand, June 23, 1946; children: Carol Ann, Steve Allen. BS, Kans. State U., 1945, MS, 1957; PhD, Tex. Women's U., 1970. Tchr. home econs. Dickinson County H.S., Chapman, Kans., 1945-46; tchr. early childhood Albany (Calif.) Pub. Schs., 1946-47; grad. asst. Inst. Child Welfare U. Calif., Berkeley, 1947-48; tchr. kindergarten Albany Pub. Schs., 1948-49; dietitian commons and hosp. U. Chgo., 1952-53; instr. Kans. State U., Manhattan, 1953-54, 59, Okla. State U., Stillwater, 1955-56; asst. prof. Tex. Tech U., Lubbock, 1962-67; from asst. prof. to prof. Mich. State U., East Lansing, 1967-97, prof. emeritus, 1997—; legis. clk. Kans. Ho. of Reps., Topeka, 1955. Author: Introduction to Early Childhood Education, 1971, 6th edit., 1997, Guiding Young Children, 1975, 6th edit., 1998, Parenting and Teaching Young Children, 1981, 90, Management of Child Development Centers, 1984, 4th edit., 1997, Parenting: Rewards and Responsibilities, 1994, 2d edit., 1997; co-author: China's Families: Experiment in Societal Change, 1985, Knowing and Serving Diverse Families, 1996. Mem. Nat. Assn. for the Edn. Young Children (task force 1975-77), Am. Home Econs. Assn. (bd. dirs., Leader award 1990), Women in Internat. Devel., Nat. Assn. Early Childhood Tchr. Edn. (award for meritorious and profl. leadership 1995). Home and Office: #904 4570 E Yale Ave Denver CO 80222

HILDEBRANDT, DARLENE MYERS, information scientist; b. Somerset, Pa., Dec. 18, 1944; d. Kenneth Geary and Julia (Klim) Myers; m. Peter Anton Hildebrandt, May 26, 1983; 1 child, Robin Adaire. BA, U. Calif., Riverside, 1969; MA, U. Wash., 1970. Info. specialist U. Wash. Acad. Computer Ctr., Seattle, 1970-73, library assoc., 1974-75, mgr. computing info. services adminstr., 1976-85, adminstr. computing info. services, 1986-91; head sci. librs. Wash. State U., Pullman, 1991—; spl. librs. rep. Wash. State Adv. Coun. Librs., 1992-98; mem. Wash. State Librs. Database Selection Com., 1997—. Editor: (newsletter) Points Northwest (Elaine D. Kaskela award 1973, 75, Best ASIS 1974), Wash. State Tribal Librs. Info. Newsletter, 1998—; compiler and editor Computing Info. Directory, 1985-96. Recipient Civitan award, 1963. Mem. Am. Soc. for Info. Sci. (founding mem. Pacific Northwest chpt. 1971, chairperson 1975, 76, bd. dirs. 1980-83, chpt. award 1978). Office: Wash State U Owen Sci & Engring Libr Pullman WA 99164-3200

HILDEBRANDT, GEORGE FREDERICK, lawyer; b. Claverack, N.Y., Mar. 28, 1959; s. Harry K. and Sophie Evelyn (Reutenauer) H. BA, Syracuse U., 1981, JD, 1984. Bar: N.Y. 1985, U.S. Dist. Ct. (no. dist.) N.Y. 1986, U.S. Supreme Ct. 1997, U.S. Ct. Appeals (2d cir.) 1998. Atty. Frank H. Hiscock Legal Aid Soc., Syracuse, N.Y., 1985-88; pvt. practice Syracuse, 1988—. Mem. Nat. Assn. Criminal Def. Lawyers, N.Y. State Trial Lawyers Assn., Onondaga County Bar Assn. Office: 300 Crown Bldg 304 S Franklin St Syracuse NY 13202-1233

HILDEBRANDT, H(ENRY) M(ARK), pediatrician; b. Ann Arbor, Mich., Oct. 23, 1926; s. Theophil Henry and Dora (Ware) H.; m. Jennie Parker (div. 1974); children: Marian, Carl, Janet, Jonathan, Lisabeth; m. Linda Figen (div. 1984); 1 child, Ursula; m. Deborah Bush-Black, 1986 (div. 1996). BA, U. Mich., 1948, MD, 1952. Diplomate Am. Bd. Pediatrics. Intern, resident in pediatrics City Hosps. Cleve. and Babies and Children's Hosp., 1952-55; from clin. assoc. prof. to clin. asst. prof. U. Mich., Ann Arbor, Mich., 1958-71, clin. assoc. prof., 1971—; pvt. practice Ann Arbor, 1955-87, Ypsilanti, Mich., 1987—; established U. Mich. Hosp. SCAN (Suspected Child Abuse and Neglect) team, 1971; clin. assoc. prof. U. Mich., Ann Arbor, 1969-78, mem. affiliate faculty, 1978—. Mem. Am. Acad. Pediatrics, Ambulatory Pediatric Assn. Episcopalian. Avocations: playing cello in string quartets, rail and trolley history. Home: 1930 Cambridge Rd Ann Arbor MI 48104-3651 Office: 5333 McAuley Dr Ste R 6011 Ypsilanti MI 48197-1014

HILDEBRANDT-WILLARD, CLAUDIA JOAN, banker; b. Inglewood, Calif., Feb. 12, 1942; d. Charles Samuel and Clara Claudia (Palumbo) H.; m. I. LeRoy Willard, Nov. 5, 1993. BBA, U. Colo. Head teller First Colo. Bank & Trust, Denver, 1969-70; asst. cashier First Nat. Bank, Englewood, Colo., 1975-79, asst. v.p., 1979-83, v.p., 1983-92; owner CJH Enterprises, Inc., Breckenridge, Colo., 1980—, Garden Tea Shop, Georgetown, Colo., Laudiac, Inc., Breckenridge, 1993—. Mem. Nat. Assn. Bank Women, Fin. Women Internat. (pres. elect. 1989-92), Am. Soc. for Pers. Adminstrn., Am. Inst. Banking, Mile High Group. Roman Catholic. Home: PO Box 665 Georgetown CO 80444-0665 Office: 612 A 6th St Georgetown CO 80444

HILDENBRAND, DONALD GERALD, editor; b. Klamath Falls, Oreg., Dec. 18, 1941; s. Gerald Edward and Mary Elizabeth (Lasater) H. BS in Gen. Studies, Southwestern Oreg. Coll., 1972; MFA in Creative Writing, U. Oreg., 1975. Cert. black belt Chinese Gung Fu; cert. instr. Hsing-i Kung Fu, Taiwan Martial Arts Inst., 1978. Instr. phys. activities Lane C.C., Eugene, Oreg., 1978—; editor Poetic Space Mag., Eugene, 1989—. Avocations: writing, poetry, film, martial arts. Home: PO Box 11157 Eugene OR 97440-3357

HILDERBRANDT, DONALD FRANKLIN, II, urban designer, landscape architect, artist; b. Bloomsburg, Pa., Aug. 30, 1939; s. Donald Franklin and Beatrice May (Kirchman) H.; m. M. Caroline Housenick, Aug. 27, 1960; children: Mark Berwind, John Thomas, Johanna Lynn. BS in Landscape Architecture, Pa. State U., 1961; MS in Landscape Architecture, U. Mich., 1963. Registered landscape architect, Md. Sr. designer, assoc. Johnson, Johnson & Roy, Inc., Ann Arbor, Mich., 1963-68; chief landscape architect The Rouse Co., Columbia, Md., 1968-71; co-founder, pres. Land Design/Rsch., Inc. (now LDR Internat., Inc.), Columbia, 1971—; chmn. bd. dirs. LDR Internat., Ltd., London; vis. lectr. Pa. State U., University Park, 1968—; vis. critic Harvard U., mem. design arts program panel; cons. NEA, Washington, 1983—; bd. dirs. Landscape Architecture Found., 1986-93. Author: Cost Effective Site Planning, 1976 (award 1978), New Life for Maryland's Old Towns, 1979 (award 1980), Cuyahoga Valley, 1975 (award 1976), Centennial Park (award 1989). Pa. State U. Alumni fellow, 1983; recipient Design award, spl. mention HUD, 1974, Grand award Associated Landscape Contractors Am., 1978. Fellow Am. Soc. Landscape Architects (nat. awards jury mem. 1975, 81). Democrat. Episcopalian. Home: 11101 Youngtree Ct Columbia MD 21044-2715

HILDING, JEREL LEE, music and dance educator, former dancer; b. New Orleans, Sept. 24, 1949; s. Oscar William and Loeta Dana (Boldra) H.; m. Krystyna Zofia Jurkowski, July 1, 1978; children: Dennis Jozef, Kristopher Jay. BA, La. State U., New Orleans, 1971. Prin. dancer Joffrey Ballet, N.Y.C., 1975-89; dir. arts in edn. N.J. Ballet, 1989-90; assoc. prof. music and dance U. Kans., 1990—. Avocations: piano, sports, carpentry. Office: U of Kansas Dept of Music & Dance 452 Murphy Hall Lawrence KS 66044-7523

HILDNER, ERNEST GOTTHOLD, III, solar physicist, science administrator; b. Jacksonville, Ill., Jan. 23, 1940; s. Ernest Gotthold Hildner Jr. and Jean (Johnston) Duffield; m. Sandra Whitney Shellworth, June 29, 1968; children: Cynthia Whitney, Andrew Duffield. BA in Physics and Astronomy, Wesleyan U., 1961; MA in Physics and Astronomy, U. Colo., 1964, PhD in Physics and Astronomy, 1971. Experiment scientist High Altitude Obs., Nat. Ctr. Atmospheric Rsch., Boulder, Colo., 1972-80, vis. scientist, 1985-86; chief solar physics br. NASA Marshall Space Flight Ctr., Huntsville, Ala., 1980-85; dir. Space Environment Ctr. NOAA Environ. Rsch. Labs. and Nat. Ctrs. Environ. Prediction, Boulder, 1986—; mem. com. on solar and space physics NRC, Washington, 1986-90; chmn. Com. on Space Environment Forecasting, fed. coord. for meteorology, Washington, 1988-97; co-chmn. com. space weather Office of Fed. Coord. for Meteorology, 1998—. Contbr. rsch. papers in solar and interplanetary physics, 1971—; co-inventor spectral slicing X-ray telescope with variable magnification. Mem. AAAS, Am. Geophys. Union (assoc. editor Geophys. Rsch. Letters 1983-85), Am. Astron. Soc. (councillor solar physics div. 1979-80), Internat. Astron. Union, Sigma Xi. Achievements include patent for Spectral Slicing X-Ray Telescope with Variable Magnification. Office: NOAA Space Environment Ctr 325 Broadway St Boulder CO 80303-3337

HILDRETH, EUGENE A., physician, educator; b. St. Paul, Mar. 11, 1924; s. Eugene A. V and Lila K. (Clator) H.; m. Dorothy Anne Myers, Mar. 23, 1946; children: Jeffrey Reed, William Myers, Anne Sarver, Katherine Clator. BS, Washington Jefferson Coll., 1943; MD, U. Va., 1947. Diplomate: Am. Bd. Internal Medicine (mem. 1969-72, 75-82, cons., com. mem. 1972-75), Am. Bd. Allergy and Immunology (founding com. 1970, mem. 1970-72, 1st co-chmn.). Intern Johns Hopkins, 1947-48; resident in medicine Hosp. U. Pa., 1948-49, USPHS Postdoctoral Research fellow in cardiovascular disease, 1949-51, chief resident in medicine, 1953-54, fellow in allergy and immunology, 1954-58, faculty, 1954-69, 71—; instr. medicine U. Pa., Phila., 1953-54; asso. medicine U. Pa., 1954-55, asst. prof. medicine, 1955-60, assoc. prof., 1960-69; assoc. dean U. Pa. (Sch. Medicine), 1964-69, prof. clin. medicine, 1971-90, prof. emeritus, 1990—, acting chmn. dept. research medicine, 1960-64; chmn. dept. medicine Reading (Pa.) Hosp. and Med. Center.; Cons. project site visits USPHS, 1965-70 ; cons. VA Hosp. Phila., 1955—; nat. adv. com. Medic Alert Found. Internat., 1964-83; cons. Citizens' Com. to Study Grad. Med. Edn., 1966; Am. Bd. Med. Spltys. rep. of subsplty. Bd. Allergy and Immunology of Am. Bd. Internal Medicine, 1969-72; chmn. certifying exam. com. Am. Bd. Internal Medicine, 1978-81, mem. core exam. com., 1986-87, mem. exec. com., 1978-82, chmn., 1981-82; mem. rep. Am. Bd. Med. Spltys., 1976-83, chmn. nominating com., 1979-80, mem. med. adv. bd. Lupus Found. Del. Valley, 1979—; chmn. Federated Council Internal Medicine; appeals bd. liaison Council of Grad. Med. Edn., 1980—. Co-author: Low Fat Diet, 1953, also research articles, 150 chpts. in textbooks.; Editorial bd.: Annals Internal Medicine, 1960-68, Postgrad. Medicine, 1969-75, Jour. Berks County Med. Soc, 1969-73, Internal Medicine Digest, 1971-75. Served with USNR, 1943-45, 51-53. John and Mary R. Markle scholar in acad. medicine, 1958-63; USPHS Research grantee. Master ACP (mem. bd. regents 1985-92, chmn. bd. regents 1989-91, pres. 1991-92, immediate past pres. 1992—, mem. ethics com. 1986-90, chmn. com. to delineate privileges of med. procedures, mem. nominating com. 1997—); fellow Am. Clin. and Climatologic Assn., Acad. Medicine of Singapore (hon.); mem. AAAS, Peripatetic Soc., Fedn. Am. Socs. for Exptl. Biology, N.Y. Acad. Scis., Inst. Medicine of NAS (mem. nominating com. 1982-84, mem. coun. 1986-90, chmn. nominating com. for coun. memberships 1989-90, mem. fin. com. 1988-90), Phila. Art Mus., Am. Acad. Allergy, Federated Coun. Internal Medicine, Royal Soc. Medicine, ACGME (mem. residency rev. com. internal medicine), Working Group on Disability of U.S. Presidents. Home: RR 3 Box 3960 Mohnton PA 19540-9265

HILDRETH, JAMES ROBERT, retired air force officer; b. Pine Bluff, Ark., May 4, 1927; s. William Wilson and Martha Leah (Chidester) H.; m. Beth Dixon Baker, July 12, 1955; children: John Baker, William Reid, Margaret Leah, Mark Dixon, Amy Beth. B.A. cum laude, La. Poly. Inst., 1952. Commd. 2d lt. USAF, 1952, advanced through grades to maj. gen., 1976; ret., 1981; comdr. 1st Air Commando Sqdn., 1967; comdr. 4th Tactical Fighter Wing, 1970-72; dep. dir. ops. Office of Joint Chiefs of Staff, 1972-73; dep. comdr. 13th Air Force, 1973-75, sr. Air Force rep. Weapons Systems Evaluation Group, Office of Sec. Def., 1975-76, comdr. Tactical Fighter Weapons Center, 1976-79, comdr. 13th Air Force, 1979-81. Pres. So. Nev. Fed. Exec. Agy., 1975-76; mem. adv. bd. United Way, Las Vegas, Nev., 1975-79; bd. dirs. Las Vegas C. of C., 1976-79; dist. chmn. Boy Scouts Am., 1979-81. Decorated D.S.M. (2), Silver Star, Legion of Merit (3), D.F.C. (3), Bronze Star, Air medal (14), Def. Superior Svc. medal, Meritorious Svc. Medal, Air Force Commendation medal (3), Purple Heart, Cross of Gallantry (Vietnam), Rep. Phillipines Legion of Honor. Mem. Kappa Sigma, Phi Kappa Phi, Omicron Delta Kappa, Sigma Tau Delta. Methodist. Club: Masons. Home: 315 Branch St PO Box 897 Spring Hope NC 27882-0897 Office: 9070 Edgerton Rd Spring Hope NC 27882-8916

HILDRETH, PATRICIA YVONNE, accounting executive; b. Clinton, Ind., Mar. 15, 1934; d. Leonard Adam and Wilma Vivian (Scifres) Prulhiere; m. James A. Hildreth, Jan. 20, 1954; children: John Alan, Patti Virginia, David Michael, Brian Spencer. Student, Jackson (Mich.) C.C., 1974-80, Ea. Mich. U., 1980-81. Sales clk. Yeager Co., Akron, Ohio, 1951-52; acctg. clk. B.F. Goodrich Co., Akron, 1952-54; owner P.Y. Hildreth, bookkeeping firm, Akron, 1965-72; owner, mgr. Jackson Small Bus. Svc., 1972—; cons. in field. Village campaign chmn. Jackson Pub. Schs., 1977, mem. various coms., 1972-81; acctive Girl Scouts U.S.A., Akron and Jackson; pres. PTA, Akron, 1968-70; treas. Jackson Med. Ctr. Inc., 1980-82; treas. Jackson Interfaith Shelter, 1985-97, pres. 1998-99. Mem. Ind. Accts. Assn. Mich. (various offices). Office: Jackson Small Bus Svc 1602 W Washington Ave Jackson MI 49203-1476

HILDRETH, R(OLAND) JAMES, foundation executive, economist; b. Des Moines, Nov. 26, 1926; s. Roland James and Emma (Lehman) H.; m. May Helen Carlson, June 8, 1947; children: Christine, Jeffrey, Paul. BS, Iowa State U., 1949; MS in Indsl. Econs., 1950; PhD in Econs., 1954; postgrad. in econs., U. Minn., 1950-52. Instr. Augsburg Coll., Mpls., 1950-52; asst. prof. agrl. econs. and sociology Tex. A&M U., 1954-58; with Tex. Agr. Experiment Sta., 1954-62, research coordinator W. Tex., 1958-59, asst. dir., 1959-62; asso. mgr., dir. Farm Found., Chgo., 1962-70; mgr., dir. Farm Found., 1970-91; mem. joint coun. Food and Agrl. Scis., USDA, 1978-85; cons. coun. edn. AVMA, 1977-87. Contbg. author: Changing Patterns in Fertilizer Use, 1968; Editor: Readings in Agricultural Policy, 1967; Co-editor, contbg. author: Methods for Land Economics Research, 1966. Mem. nat. coun. Boy Scouts Am., 1973-75; mem. adv. com. Coun. Rural Health, AMA, 1970-77; mem. adv. coun. on consumer affairs Am. Bankers Assn., 1971-73; mem. citizens adv. com. Coll. Phys. Edn., U. Ill., 1966-69; bd. dirs. Luth. Gen. Hosp., Park Ridge, Ill., 1968-82; Nat. Ctr. for Vol. Action, 1970-72. With U.S. Army, 1945-47. Recipient Henry A. Wallace award Iowa State U., 1981. Fellow AAAS, Soil and Water Conservation Soc., Am. Agrl. Econs. Assn. (pres. 1977-78); mem. Internat. Assn. Agrl. Economists (sec.-treas. 1973-91), Am. Country Life Assn. (past pres.). Home: 381 Poplar Ave Elmhurst IL 60126-4011

HILER, EDWARD ALLAN, agricultural and engineering educator; b. Hamilton, Ohio, May 14, 1939; s. Earl and Thelma (Kolb) H.; m. Patricia Burke; children: Karen, Richard, Scott. BS in Agrl. Engring., Ohio State U., 1963, MS in Agrl. Engring., 1963, PhD in Agrl. Engring., 1966. Registered profl. engr., Tex. Asst. prof. Tex. A&M U., College Station, 1966-69, assoc. prof., 1969-73, prof., 1973—, head dept. agrl. engring., 1974-88, dep. chancellor for acad. program planning and rsch., 1989-91, interim chancellor, 1991, exec. dep. chancellor, 1991, dep. chancellor for acad. and rsch. programs, 1991-92; vice chancellor, dean agrl. and life scis., dir. Tex. Agrl. Expt. Sta., 1992—; cons. on water conservation, environ. quality, energy and biol. processes and future agrl. engring. Office Tech. Assessment, U.S. Congress, Office of Water Rsch. and Tech., Dept. Interior, various univs. Contbr. over 100 articles to profl. publs. Recipient numerous ednl. and rsch. awards. Fellow AAAS, Instn. Agrl. Engrs. Eng., Am. Soc. Engring. Edn., Am. Soc. Agrl. Engrs. (bd. dirs., pres. 1991-92, trustee Found.); mem. NAE. Presbyterian. Avocations: golf, photography, reading novels. Office: Tex A&M Univ Sys Vice Chancellor and Dean Agr and Life Scis College Station TX 77843-2142

HILER, JOHN PATRICK, former government official, former congressman, business executive; b. Chgo., Apr. 24, 1953; s. Robert J. and Margaret F. Hiler; m. Catherine Sands. B.A., Williams Coll., 1975; M.B.A., U. Chgo., 1977. Mktg. dir. Charles O. Hiler and Son, Inc., Walkerton, Ind., 1977-80, Accurate Castings Co., La Porte, 1977-80; mem. 97th-101st congresses from 3d Ind. Dist., 1981-90; dep. adminstr. GSA, Washington, 1991-93; exec. Accurate Castings, Inc., La Porte, Ind., 1993—. Del. Ind. Rep. Conv., 1978, 90, 94, Rep. Nat. Conv., 1984, 88, White House Conf. on Small Bus., 1980; trustee Meml. Hosp. Mem. Ind. Mfrs. Assn., North Ctrl. Ind. Med. Edn. Found. Roman Catholic. Office: Accurate Castings Inc PO Box 639 La Porte IN 46352-0639

HILES, BRADLEY STEPHEN, lawyer; b. Granite City, Ill., Nov. 11, 1955; s. Joseph J. and Betty Lou (Goodman) H.; m. Toni Jonine Failoni, Aug. 12, 1977; children: Eric Stephen, Nina Catherine, Emily Christine. BA cum laude, Furman U., 1977; JD cum laude, St. Louis U., 1980. Bar: Mo. 1980, U.S. Dist. Ct. (ea. dist.) Mo., 1980, Ill. 1981. From assoc. to ptnr. Blackwekk Sanders Peper Martin, St. Louis, 1980—; v.p., sec., gen. counsel Miss. Lime Co., 1992. Editor-in-chief St. Louis Univ. Law Jour., 1979-80; contbr. articles to profl. jours. Pres. Second Baptist Ch. of St. Louis, 1988. Mem. Bar Assn. of Met. St. Louis (chmn. environ. and conservation law com. 1993-94). Republican. Baptist. Avocations: gospel singing, cycling. Home: 34 Meditation Way Ct Florissant MO 63031-6535 Office: Blackwell Sanders Peper Martin 720 Olive St Fl 24 Saint Louis MO 63101-2338

HILF, RUSSELL, biochemist; b. Bklyn., Aug. 13, 1931; s. Jerome Joseph and Sydel Ruth (Kaufman) H.; m. Beverly Sydelle Polak, May 29, 1955; children: Elise Rachel, Merrill Jean, Lawrence Michael. B.S., CCNY, 1952; M.S., Rutgers U., 1953, Ph.D., 1955. Head biochemistry sect., nutrition div. QM Food and Container Inst., Chgo., 1958-59; head, cancer endocrinology sect. Squibb Inst. for Med. Research, New Brunswick, N.J., 1959-69; prof. biochemistry dept. U. Rochester Sch. Medicine and Dentistry, N.Y., 1969—; chmn. diagnosis working group Breast Cancer Task Force, Nat. Cancer Inst., NIH, 1978-80; mem. merit rev. bd. in oncology VA, 1979-83; mem. cancer edn. rev. com. Nat. Cancer Inst., NIH, 1985-86, mem. reproductive endocrinology study sect., 1986-89, 97—; mem. sci. rev. panel Am. Inst. Cancer Rsch., 1990—; mem. N.Y. State Hlth. Sci. Rsch. Bd., 1997—. Editor: (with J.A. Kellen) Influences of Hormones in Tumor Development, 1979; assoc. editor Cancer Rsch., 1967-78, 83-94; mem. editl. adv. bd. Biochem. Pharmacology, 1973-83; mem. internat. adv. bd. Cancer Biochemistry BioPhysics, 1974—; mem. editl. bd. Oncology Rsch., 1989—; contbr. articles to profl. jours. Wellcome vis. prof., 1994. With Med. Svc. Corps U.S. Army, 1955-58. Grantee Nat. Cancer Inst., 1969—, Am. Cancer Soc., 1970-75, 83-88. Fellow AAAS, N.Y. Acad. Sci.; mem. Am. Soc. Biol. Chemists, Am. Assn. for Cancer Research, Endocrine Soc., Am. Soc. Photobiol., Soc. Exptl. Biology and Medicine, Am. Cancer Soc. (adv. com. biochemistry and chem. carcinogenesis 1986-89, vice chmn., chmn. adv. com. biochemistry and endocrinology 1990-91). Home: 85 Willowcrest Dr Rochester NY 14618-4337 Office: 601 Elmwood Ave Rochester NY 14642-0001

HILFERTY, BRYAN CAREY, English language educator; b. Arlington, Mass., Aug. 10, 1960; s. Walter Gerard and Ruthe (Hughes) H.; m. Shawna LaNaye Patton, Aug. 16, 1991. BA, U. Mass., 1987; MA, Colo. State U., 1996. Commd. 2d lt. U.S. Army, 1987, advanced through grades to maj., 1997; asst. prof. English U.S. Mil. Acad., West Point, N.Y., 1996—. Contbr. articles to profl. jours. Recipient Bronze Star U.S. Army, 1991. Mem. MLA, Assn. U.S. Army, VFW, Am. Acad. Poetry, Nat. Coun. Tchrs. English. Roman Catholic. Avocations: chess, boating. Home: 561A Connor Rd West Point NY 10996-1208 Office: Dept English Lincoln Hall West Point NY 10996

HILFSTEIN, ERNA, science historian, educator; b. Krakow, Poland; came to U.S., 1949, naturalized, 1954; d. Leon and Anna (Schornstein) Kluger; BA, CCNY, 1967, MA, 1971, PhD, City U. N.Y., 1978; m. Max Hilfstein; children: Leon, Simone Juliana. Tchr. secondary schs., N.Y.C., 1968-84, 86-92; collaborator Polish Acad. Scis., 1968-85; vis. prof. Queens Coll., 1973; affiliate Grad. Sch./Univ. Ctr., City U. N.Y. NEH grantee, 1984-85; recipient Rector's medal Univ. M. Kopernik, Torun, 1989, Order of Merit Silver medal Republic of Poland, 1991. Mem. History Sci. Soc., Polish Inst. Arts and Scis. in Am., CUNY Acad. for the Humanities and Scis., N.Y. Acad. Scis., Kościuszko Found., United Fedn. of Tchrs. (chpt. chmn. 1978-84, 86-92, del. 1980-92), Am. Mus. Nat. History, Libr. of Congress; mem. Nat. Commn. Am. Fgn. Policy. Democrat. Jewish. Author: Starowolski's Biographies of Copernicus, 1980; collaborator English version of Nicholas Copernicus Complete Works, vol. 1, 1972, vol. 2, 1978, vol. 3, 1985, vols. 2 & 3, 2d edit., 1992; co-translator: The Leviathan in the State Theory of Thomas Hobbes: Meaning and Failure of a Political Symbol, 1996; contbr. articles and revs. to profl. jours. Editor: Science and History, 1978, Copernicus and His Successors, 1995, Sebastian Petrycy, A Polish Renaissance Scholar, 1997. Home: 1523 Dwight Pl Bronx NY 10465-1121

HILGARD, ERNEST ROPIEQUET, psychologist; b. Belleville, Ill., July 25, 1904; s. George Engelmann and Laura (Ropiequet) H.; m. Josephine Rohrs, Sept. 19, 1931; children: Henry Rohrs, Elizabeth Ann Jecker. B.S., U. Ill., 1924; Ph.D., Yale, 1930; D.Sc., Kenyon Coll., 1964; LL.D., Centre Coll., 1974; D.Sc., Northwestern U., 1987, Colgate U., 1987; PhD (hon.), U. Oslo (Norway), 1994. Asst. instr. in psychology Yale U., 1928-29, instr., 1929-33; successively asst. prof., asso. prof., prof. psychology Stanford, 1933-69, emeritus prof., 1969—, exec. head dept., 1942-50, dean grad. div., 1951-55; Bd. dirs., pres. Ann. Reviews, Inc., 1948-73; With USDA, Washington, 1942, OWI, 1942-43, Office Civilian Requirements, WPB, 1943-44; Collaborator, div. child devel. and tchr. personnel Am. Council Edn., 1940-41; nat. adv. mental health council USPHS, 1952-56; fellow (Center Advanced Study Behavioral Scis.), 1956-57; Mem. U.S. Edn. Mission to Japan, 1946. Author: Theories of Learning, 1948, rev. edit., 1981, Introduction to Psychology, 1953, rev. edit., 1987, Hypnotic Susceptibility, 1965, Hypnosis in the Relief of Pain, 1975, rev. edit., 1983, Divided Consciousness, 1977, rev. edit., 1986, American Psychology in Historical Perspective, 1978, Psychology in America: A Historical Survey, 1987; editor: Fifty Years of Psychology, 1988. Bd. curators Stephens Coll., Mo., 1953-68. Recipient Warren medal in exptl. psychology, 1940; Wilbur Cross medal Yale U., 1971; Gold medal Am. Psychol. Found., 1978. Hon. fellow British Psychol. Assn.; mem. Am. Psychol. Assn. (pres. 1948-49, Outstanding Lifetime Achievement award 1994), Am. Acad. Arts and Scis., Nat. Acad. Edn., Soc. Psychol. Study Social Issues (chmn. 1944-45), AAAS, Nat. Acad. Scis. (sci. rev. award 1984), Am. Philos. Soc., Internat. Soc. Hypnosis (pres. 1973-76, Benjamin Franklin gold medal 1979), Sigma Xi. Home: # 226 850 Webster St Apt 226 Palo Alto CA 94301-2857 Office: Stanford U Psychology Dept Bldg 420 Rm 206 Stanford CA 94305-2130

HILGARTNER, MARGARET WEHR, pediatric hematologist, educator; b. Balt., Nov. 6, 1924; d. Andrew Henry and Margaret Elizabeth (Wehr) H.;m. Albert Milton Arky; children: George, Elizabeth, John. AB, Bryn Mawr Coll., 1946; MA, Duke U., 1951, MD, 1955. Diplomate Am. Bd. Pediatrics, Am. Bd. Pediatric Hematology/Oncology. Intern Bellevue Hosp., N.Y., 1955-56; resident in pediatrics N.Y. Hosp.-Cornell Med. Ctr., 1956-58, fellow in hematology/oncology, 1958-61, instr. in pediatrics, 1961-67, physician-in-charge pediatric coagulation, 1965-95, asst. prof., 1967-73, dir. hemophilia comprehensive treatment, 1970-95, assoc. prof., assoc. attending pediatrician outpatient dept., 1973-78, prof., dir. pediatric hematology/oncology div., attending pediatrician, 1978-94, Harold Weill prof. pediatric hematology, 1988—; assoc. attending pediatrician N.Y. Hosp., 1974—; adj. attending physician Sloan-Kettering Cancer Ctr., N.Y., 1979-97; bd. dirs., mem. exec. com. N.Y. Blood Ctr., 1989; cons. Bur. Handicapped Children, N.Y., 1971, Factor VIII Inhibitor Study Group, 1974, Ho. Reps. Ways and Means Com., 1977, Senate and Ho. Reps. Health Subcom. on Health, 1978-80, Fgn. and Interstate Commerce Com.-Ho. Reps. Subcom. on Pub. Health and Environment, 1979, N.Y. State Com. on Transfusion, 1979-84, Ad Hoc Com. Rev. Rsch. in Edn., 1981-82; cons. in medicine Englewood (N.J.) Hosp., 1974-86, in pediatric hematology, 1982-; lectr.-in-medicine Mt. Sinai Hosp., N.Y., 1979—; vis. prof. Rochester (Minn.) Hemophilia Ctr. 1979, 1980, Marshfield (Wis.) Clinic, 1979, Oakland Children's Hosp., 1981, Hangchow, Beijing, Kian, Peoples Republic of China, 1981, Johns Hopkins U. 1982, Rochester Strong Meml., 1985, Duke U. 1985; chmn. Gov.'s adv. coun. to N.J. Dept. Health Hemophilia Program, 1973-80; mem. task force Factor VIII-Inhibitors Nat. Heart Lung Inst., 1975-80; mem. adv. com. publ. health #94-63 Health Svcs. Adminstrn., 19761blood disease and resources Nat. Hear Lung Inst. NIH, 1985-89; chmn. Feiba Study Com., U.S. chpt., 1981-86, pediatric working group World Fedn. Hemophilia, 1982; mem. ad hoc AIDS adv. com. Nat. Heart Lung Blood Inst. NIH, 1985-87. Mem. profl. adv. bd. mag. Baby Talk, 1987—; contbr. numerous articles to profl. jours. Mem. Am. Acad. Pediat. (chmn. sect. program oncology/hematology), Am. Heart Assn., Am. Med. Women's Assn., Am. Pediatric Soc., Am. Soc. Hematology, Assn. Women in Sci. (treas. 1974-76), Harvey Soc., Internat. Soc. Blood Transfusion, Internat. Soc. Thrombosis and Hemostasis, Nat. Hemophilia Found. (bd. dirs. met. chpt. 1965-69, trustee 1968-88, med. dir. met. chpt. 1970-90, mem. med. and sci. bd. 1973-87, v.p. 1979-84, mem. edn. resources project 1979-84), N.Y. Acad. Sci., N.Y. Soc. Study Blood, World Fedn. Hemophilia (chmn. child care com. 1990), Am. Soc. Pediatric Hematology/Oncology, Children's Blood Found. (med. dir 1978—, bd. dirs. 1987—, pres. 1995-96), Cooley's Anemia Found. (bd. dirs. 1987—). Office: Cornell U Med Coll Dept of Pediatrics 525 E 68th St New York NY 10021-4873

HILGEMANN, DONALD WILLIAM, medical educator; b. Postville, Iowa, Aug. 20, 1952; married. Student, U. Iowa, 1972; MS in Biology, Univ. Tübingen, Germany, 1977, PhD in Pharmacology & Physiology, 1980. Rsch. and tchg. asst. Dept. Pharmacology U. Tübingen, 1977-80; rsch. assoc. Merrell Internat., Strasbourg, France, 1980-81; asst. rsch. physiologist UCLA Sch. Medicine, 1981-87; asst. clin. prof. nursing UCLA Sch. Nursing, 1982-87; asst. prof. Dept. Physiology U. Tex. Southwestern Med. Ctr., Dallas, 1988-91, assoc. prof., 1991-96, prof. physiology, 1996—; tchr., lectr. UNISEF, 1992, Univ. Kaiserlautern, 1994; vis. rsch. fellow Oxford U., Eng., 1985-88; invited spkr. Kyoto u., Japan, 1993-94, Northwestern U., Chgo., 1994, U. Konstanz, Germany, 1994, Johns Hopkins U., Balt., 1994, Tokyo Med. Coll., 194, Univ. Laussane, Switzerland, 1994, Pa. U., Phila., 1994, Oreg. Health Sci. Ctr., Portland, 1995, N.Y. Acad. Scis., Woods Hole, Mass., 1995, Rush Med. Ctr., Chgo., 1995, Swiss Fed. Inst. Tech., Zurich, 1994, Tel Aviv U., Israel, 1995. Fellow Binational Israeli-USa Found., Japan Soc. for Promotion Sci.; mem. Biophys. Soc. (young investigator award 1997), Soc. Neurosci., Soc. Gen. Physiologists, Physiol. Soc. Office: U Tex Southwestern Med Ctr 5323 Harry Hines Blvd Dallas TX 75235-7208*

HILGENBERG, JOHN CHRISTIAN, financial executive, corporate director, consultant; b. Balt., Sept. 6, 1941; s. Carl R. and Elizabeth (Rianhard) H.; m. Evelyn Brantley Handy, Apr. 1, 1971; children—Rodney, Crady. B.A., Yale U., 1963; M.B.A., U. Va., 1965. With internat. lending divsn. Md. Nat. Bank, Balt., 1970-75; v.p., dir. fin. svcs. S.M. Hyman Co., Balt., 1975-78; v.p. fin. Eastmet Corp., Balt., 1978-85 . Trustee Harbor Hosp. Ctr., 1975—; v.p., treas., dir. Sky Alland Rsch. Corp., 1986, 89-90; pres., bd. dirs. Ski Tech. Holdings, Inc. and CADS USA, Inc., 1987-89; pres. The Eager St. Group, Inc., Balt., 1991—; cons., investor in early-stage cos., 1986—; bd. dirs. Synthecell Corp., pres. 1992-95; bd. dirs. Genetic MediSyn Corp., The Tech. Group, 1991-95, U. Pharmaceuticals Md., 1996-99, L. Gordon Packaging Corp., 1996—. Lt. USNR 1965-70. Mem. Elkridge Club, Maryland Club. Republican. Episcopalian. Home: 2705 Greenspring Valley Rd Owings Mills MD 21117 Other: 6 E Eager St Baltimore MD 21202-2514

HILGERS, JOHN JACK WILLIAM, management and transportation consultant; b. Carmel-by-the-Sea, Calif., Nov. 17, 1934; s. Rudolph Joseph and Eleanor Maude (King) H.; m. Sharon Ann Hilgers, Dec. 15, 1968; children: Jon Marc, John Jack William Jr. BA in Psychology, San Jose State U., 1956; BA in Criminology, U. Calif., Berkeley, 1963; MS in Sys. Mgmt., U. So. Calif., 1984; MS in Urban Studies, Old Dominion U., 1995, PhD in Urban Svcs., 1998. Enlisted USMC, 1957, advanced in grades to col.; sr. dir. plans and ops. NATO USMC, Norfolk, Va., 1981-83; exec. dir. spl. tng. Fleet Marine Force Atlantic USMC, Jacksonville, N.C., 1983-84; v.p. resources prepositioning USMC, Norfolk, 1984-88, ret., 1988; rsch. asst. Bur. Rsch. Old Dominion U., Norfolk, 1988-90, program mgr. Coll. Bus. and Pub. Adminstrn., 1991-98, assoc. dir. Internat. Maritime Ports and Logistics Inst., 1993-98; exec. asst. Va. Legislature, 1999—; dir., mem. exec. com. Atlantic Rim Network, Boston, 1995—; exec. sec. Maritime Adv. Coun., Norfolk, 1991—; mem. tech. com. Met. Planning Orgn., Hampton Roads, Va., 1996-98; internat. maritime com. chmn. Conf. of World Regions, 1997—. Editor (newsletter) Bulletts and Cannonballs, 1993-98, Bus. and Econ. Quar., 1992-96. Divsn. dir. United Way, Norfolk, 1996, 97, Va. Beach Sister City Group, Virginia Beach, 1995—. Mem. ASPA (exec. com. transp. policy and adminstrn. com. 1997—), Rotary (pres. Sunrise Norfolk chpt. 1997-98, Paul Harris fellow 1996), Econs. Club (Hampton Rds), Internat. Bus. Coun., Pepper Lovers Club Va. Internat. (dir. 1994-96), Propeller Club U.S. (dir. Port of Norfolk 1996—), Hampton Rds. Fgn. Commerce Club (pres. 1996), Phi Kappa Phi, Phi Alpha Alpha. Avocation: antique and classic automobiles. Home and Office: 2505 Forehand Ln Virginia Beach VA 23454-2744

HILGERT, ARNIE, management and marketing educator; b. Detroit, Feb. 24, 1944; d. Norris Bersford and Romayne Catherine (Kent) Clarke; m. Jeffrey L. Hilgert, Dec. 21, 1964 (div. Dec. 1981); children: Michele LEanne, Tracy Lee. BA, U. Redlands, 1982; MBA, Peter F. Drucker Sch. Mgmt., 1984; MA Ctr. Ednl. Studies, The Claremont Grad. U., The Claremont Grad. Sch., 1991, PhD Ctr. Ednl. Studies, 1992. Ptnr. Durawood Shasta Pacific Industries, Chico, Calif., 1971-78; mgr., owner Homefront Home Improvement Stores, Chico, Calif., 1975-78; rsch. assoc. exec. mgmt. program The Claremont (Calif.) Grad. Sch., 1984-85, adminstr. exec. mgmt. program, 1985-89; sponsored rsch. analyst Calif. State U., L.A., 1989-90; assoc. prof. mngmt. and mktg. No. Ariz. U., Yuma, 1992—; participant in nat. and internat. profl. confs.; rschr. in multimedia and distance learning, implementation of ADA Act. Contbr. articles to profl. jours. Participant Rio Colorado Commn., Yuma, 1993—. State of Calif. Grad. fellow, Claremont, 1982-84; Econs. scholar John Randolph Haynes and Dora Haynes Found., 1981, Elizabeth Malpass scholar Zonta Club Redlands, 1980. Mem. Acad. Bus. Adminstrn., Acad. Mgmt., Acad. Internat. Bus., Ctr. for Study of Intellectual Devel., Claremont U. Sch. Womans Scholars. Home: 11843 E Calle Del Cid Yuma AZ 85367-7216 Office: No Ariz U PO Box 6236 Yuma AZ 85366-6236

HILGERT, RAYMOND LEWIS, management and industrial relations educator, consultant, arbitrator; b. St. Louis, July 28, 1930; s. Lewis Francis and Frieda Christine (Keune) H.; m. Bernice Alice Nerl, Apr. 28, 1951; children—Brenda, Diane, Jeffrey. BA, Westminster Coll., Fulton, Mo., 1952; MBA, Washington U., St. Louis, 1961; DBA, Washington U., 1963. Mgmt. positions with Southwestern Bell Telephone Co., 1956-60; mem. faculty Olin Sch. Bus. Washington U., St. Louis, 1963—, dir. summer workshop Olin Sch. Bus., 1964-68; dir. mgmt. devel. programs Olin Sch. Bus. Washington U., St. Louis, 1967-84; asst. dean, dir. undergrad. program Olin Sch. Bus. Washington U., St. Louis, 1968-69; cons.; lectr.; labor arbitrator. Author: (with C. Ling and Ed Leonard Jr.) Cases and Experiential Exercises in Human Resource Management, 1990, 3d edit., 2000, Cases in Collective Bargaining and Industrial Relations: A Decisional Approach, 1969, 9th edit., 1999, Labor Agreement Negotiations, 1983, 5th edit., 1998; (with Ed Leonard Jr.) Supervision: Concepts and Practices of Management, 1972, 7th edit., 1998; contbr. articles to profl. jours. Mem. adv. coun. St. Louis region SBA, 1983-91. Served to 1st lt. USAF, 1952-56. Named Tchr. of Yr., Washington U. Sch. Bus., 1968, 81, 85, 89. Mem. Acad. Mgmt., Indsl. Rels. Rsch. Assn., Soc. for Human Resource Mgmt. (sr. profl. in human resource mgmt.), Am. Mgmt. Assn. Lutheran. Avocations: sports, movies. Home: 1744 Lynkirk Ln Kirkwood MO 63122-2251 Office: Washington U Olin Sch Bus PO Box 1133 Saint Louis MO 63188-1133

HILKER, HELEN-ANNE, journalist; b. Springfield, Ohio, July 5, 1920; d. Albert John and Mary-Anne (Shanahan) Hilker. BA, Allegheny Coll., 1941; MA in Journalism, U. Iowa, 1942. Part-time reporter Meadville (Pa.) Tribune, 1938-41; reporter Dayton (Ohio) Journal-Herald, 1942-45; disaster reporter Eastern Area ARC, Alexandria, Va., 1945-46; asst. press officer Libr. of Congress, Washington, 1946-51; reporter Washington Bur. Scripps-Howard Newspapers, 1951-54; press officer Libr. of Congress, 1954-69, interpretive projects officer, 1969-77; ind. writer, editor Washington, 1977—; curator restoration needs exhbn., Libr. of Congress, 1980. Author: Ten First Street Southeast: Congress Builds a Library, 1980; news columnist Allegheny Coll. weekly newspaper, 1938-41; editor Allegheny Lit. Mag., 1940-41. Pres. Dayton Newspaper Guild, 1944-45; active Women's Nat. Press Club, Nat. Press Club, 1954—. Recipient 1st prize Allegheny Lit. Mag., 1937, Ohio Newspaper Women's Assn., 1945, Ednl. Press Assn. Am., 1965, Fed. Editors Assn. Blue Pencil awards, 1973; recipient citation, Soc. Tech. Communicators, 1973; recipient several other awards for writing and editing. Mem. Nat. Mus. Women in the Arts, Washington Print Club, Writers Ctr., Phi Beta Kappa, Kappa Tau Alpha. Avocations: family history, drawing, painting.

HILL, ALFRED, lawyer, educator; b. N.Y.C., Nov. 7, 1917; m. Dorothy Turck, Aug. 12, 1960; 1 dau., Amelia. B.S., Coll. City N.Y., 1937; LL.B., Bklyn. Law Sch., 1941, LL.D., 1986; S.J. D., Harvard U., 1957. Bar: N.Y. State bar 1943, Ill 1958. With SEC, 1943-52; prof. law So. Meth. U., 1953-56, Northwestern U., 1956-62; prof. law Columbia U., 1962-75, Simon H. Rifkind prof. law, 1975-87, Simon H. Rifkind prof. law emeritus, 1988—. Contbr. articles on torts, conflict of laws, fed. cts. constl. law to legal jours. Mem. Am. Law Inst. Home: 79 Sherwood Rd Tenafly NJ 07670-2734 Office: Columbia Law Sch New York NY 10027

HILL, ALICE LORRAINE, history, genealogy and social researcher, educator; b. Moore, Okla., Jan. 15, 1935; d. Robert Edward and Alma Alice (Fraysher) H.; children: Debra Hrboka, Pamela Spangler, Eric Shiver, Lorraine Smith. Grad., Patricia Stevens Modeling Sch., Orlando, Fla., 1963; student, Draughton Sch. Bus., Oklahoma City, 1968-69, Troy State U., 1970-71, Ventura Coll., 1974; AA in Gen. Edn., Rose Coll., Midwest City, Okla.; BS in Bus. and Acctg., Ctrl. State U., 1977; student, U. Okla., 1977-78; postgrad., Calif. Luth. U., 1988; ed. Sch. Edn., UCLA, 1990. Cert. cmty. coll. life instr. acctg., bus. and indsl. mgmt., computer and related techs., and real estate, Calif.; ordained min., Gospel Ministry, 1982; lic. in real estate sales. Former model, 1990-95; with L.A. Unified Sch. Dist., 1990-95; founder A. Hill & Assocs. (formerly America, We Love You), Oxnard, Calif., 1993—; co-founder Law of Moses Common Law Legal Assn., Kingfisher, Okla., with Internat. Hdqs. at Brussett, Mont., 1994; founder The Los Artistas for creative activities for young people, 1996; rschr. Americana 2000. Author: America, We Love You (Congl. Record Poem, made into World's 1st Internat. Patriotic song), 1975, Land of Lands (now world's first internat. patriotic song); ghost writer book for Shafenberg Rsch. Found., 1981; author: (lyrics) Come Listen to the Music, 1996, Someday John, 1996; contbr. various articles and poems to profl. publs. Mem. bd. dirs. Family Health Rsch., Seattle; mem. Wash. Home-schooling Orgn. Named hon. grad. Patricia Stevens Modeling Sch. (Fla.); recipient scholarship Leadership Enrichment Program, Okla., 1977, Hon. recognition Okla. State Bd. of Regents for Higher Edn., 1977, Presdl. citations for Pres. Ford, 1975, 76, Admired Woman of the Decade award, 1994, Life Time Achievement award, 1995, Most Gold Record award, 1995, Key award for Rsch., Internat. Cultural Diploma of Honor, 1995, Woman of Yr. award, 1995, Internat. Woman of Yr. award Order Internat. Fellowship, 1994/95, Disting. Mem. Internat. Poetry Soc.; named to Internat. Hall of Fame Internat. Poetry Soc., 1996. Mem. NAFE, NEA, AAUW, Internat. Platform Assn., Ventura County Profl. Women's Networking, Wash. Homeschooling Assn. Home: 11327 148th Ave SE Renton WA 98059 also: 1646 Lime Ave Oxnard CA 93033

HILL, ANITA CARRAWAY, retired state legislator; b. Chatfield, Tex., Aug. 13, 1928; d. Archie Clark and Martha (Butler) Carraway; BA in Journalism, Tex. Woman's U., 1950; m. Harris Hill, Sept. 20, 1952; children: Stephen Victor, Virginia Evelyn. Reporter Garland (Tex.) Daily News, 1950-51; ednl. dir. First Meth. Ch., Garland, 1951-53; chemist Kraft Foods Co., Garland, 1953-56; legis. aide, Tex. Legislature, 1975-77; mem. Tex. Ho. of Reps., 1977-92, mem. mcpl. bond and revenue sharing coms., 1971-74; ret., 1992. Awards chmn. City of Garland Environ. Council; mem. City of Garland Park and Recreation Bd., 1971-77, chmn., 1976-77; life mem. PTA; mem. Dallas County Mental Health Mental Retardation bd. trustees. Named Disting. Alumna, Tex. Woman's U., 1981. Mem. Garland C. of C., Rowlett C. of C., Bus. and Profl. Women's Club (Garland Woman of Year, 1980), AAUW, Tex. Assn. Elected Women. Republican. Methodist.

HILL, ANITA GRIFFITH, retired principal; b. Gadsden, Ala., Feb. 14, 1939; d. Charles Henry and Sue (McMeekin) Griffith; m. Lillon S. Hill, Aug. 15, 1973; children: Judy, Patty, Susan, Jimmy, Mark. BS, Auburn U., 1961; MA, U. Ala., Birmingham, 1971; AA, U. Ala., Tuscaloosa, 1973. Tchr. Marine Corps Air Sta. Sch., Beaufort, S.C., 1961-62, John Jones Elem. Sch., Gadsden, Ala., 1970-79, Southside Elem. Sch., Gadsden, Ala., 1979-83; prin. Ivalee Elem. Sch., Gadsden, Ala., 1983-85, Southside Elem. Sch., Gadsden, Ala., 1985-98. Recipient Nat. Sch. of Excellence Tchr. of Yr. award U.S. Dept. Edn., 1989-90. Mem. Ala. Coun. Sch. Adminstrs. and Suprs., State Prins. Exec. Com. (pres. dist. V prins. 1992—), DAR (sec. 1989-92), Altrusa Club, Delta Kappa Gamma (pres. 1978-80). Baptist. Avocations: water sports, reading. Home: 303 River Ridge Rd Gadsden AL 35901-9212 Office: Southside Elem Sch 2551 Highway 77 Southside AL 35907-7909*

HILL, ANNA MARIE, manufacturing executive; b. Great Falls, Mont., Nov. 6, 1938; d. Paul Joseph and Alexina Rose (Doyon) Ghekiere. AA, Oakland Jr. Coll., 1959; student, U. Calif., Berkeley, 1960-62. Mgr. ops. OSM, Soquel, Calif., 1963-81; purchasing agt. Arrow Huss, Scotts Valley, Calif., 1981-82; sr. buyer Fairchild Test Systems, San Jose, Calif., 1982-83; materials mgr. Basic Test Systems, San Jose, 1983-86; purchasing mgr. Beta Tech., Santa Cruz, Calif., 1986-87; mgr. purchasing ICON Rev., Carmel, Calif., 1987-88; materials mgr. Integrated Components Test System, Sunnyvale, Calif., 1988-89; mfg. mgr. Forte Comm., Sunnyvale, 1989-94; new products mgr. Cisco Sys., San Jose, 1994—; cons., No. Calif., 1976—. Counselor Teens Against Drugs, San Jose, 1970, 1/2 Orgn., Santa Cruz, 1975-76. Mem. Am. Prodn. Invention Control, Nat. Assn. Female Execs., Nat. Assn. Purchasing Mgmt., Am. Radio Relay League. Democrat. Avocations: amateur radio operator, music, gardening. Home: 733 Rosedale Ave # 4 Capitola CA 95010-2248 Office: Cisco Systems 110 W Tasman Dr San Jose CA 95134-1700

HILL, BARON P., congressman; b. Seymour, Ind., 1954; m. Betty Schepman; children: Jennifer, Cara, Elizabeth. BS in History, Furman U., 1975. Fin. analyst Merrill Lynch; mem. U.S. Congress from 9th Ind. dist., 1999—; mem. Agr., Armed Forces coms., Blue Dog Dems., New Dem. Coalition. Elected to Ind. Ho. Reps., 1982; served to 1990. Appointed by Speaker of the House to serve as chmn. House Rules Com. Served as asst. whip for Dem. Caucus, as chmn. Ind. House Campaign Com. from 1985-89. In 1992 Gov. Evan Bayh named Hill exec. dir. State Student Assistance Commn. Office: 1208 Longworth HOB Washington DC 20515*

HILL, BEN, broadcast executive. Gen. mgr. Sta. WCAO, Balt.; v.p. Sta. WXYV, Balt., Sta. WPGC-AM and WPGC-FM, Washington; v.p. and gen. mgr. CBS Radio. Office: 6301 Ivy Ln Ste 800 Greenbelt MD 20770-6329*

HILL, BETTY JEAN, nursing educator, academic administator; b. Ishpeming, Mich., Nov. 27, 1937; d. Azarius William and Evelyn (Herring) Parsons; m. Edwin E. Hill, Nov. 27, 1959 (dec. 1979); children: Cheryl, Kenneth; m. Harold Ralph Pawley, June 27, 1981. B in Nursing, No. Mich. U., Marquette, 1972, MEd, 1974; M in Nursing, Wayne State U., 1977, PhD, 1979. RN, Mich. Staff nurse St. Luke's Hosp., Marquette, 1958-60; supr. Meadowbrook Hosp., Bellaire, Mich., 1959-60; head nurse St. Luke's Hosp., Marquette, 1960-62, clin. instr., 1868-70; asst. prof. No. Mich. U., Marquette, 1972-75, assoc. prof., 1978-80, asst. dean, 1980-82, dean, prof., 1982—. Contbr. articles to jours.; author: (with others) Theory Construction, 1981. Fund Chairperson Hospice, Marquette, 1988. Fellow AASCU Acad. Leadership, 1991-93, Harvard Inst. for Ednl. Mgmt., 1992, No. Econ. Initiatives Corp., 1992—. Mem. Mich. and Nat. League for Nursing, Mich. Assn. Colls. of Nursing (treas. 1986-90), Midwest Alliance in Nursing, Am. Assn. State Coll. and Univs., Am. Assn. Colls. and Nursing, Marquette Econ. Club (pres. 1989-90), Rotary Club, Planned Parenthood, Sigma Theta Tau. Methodist. Avocations: boating, dancing, reading, golf. Home: 643 Lakewood Ln Marquette MI 49855-9517 Office: Allied Health Scis 202 Magers Hall Marquette MI 49855-5342*

HILL, BONNIE GUITON, company executive; b. Springfield, Ill., Oct. 30, 1941; d. Henry Frank and Zola Elizabeth (Newman) Brazelton; m. Walter Hill Jr.; 1 child, Nichele Monique. BA, Mills Coll., 1974; MS, Calif. State U., Hayward, 1975; EdD, U. Calif., Berkeley, 1985. Adminstr. asst. to pres.'s spl. asst. Mills Coll., Oakland, Calif., 1970-71; adminstrv. asst. to asst. v.p. Mills Coll., Oakland, 1972-73, student svcs. counselor, adv. to resuming students, 1973-74, asst. dean of students, interim dir. ethnic studies, lectr., 1975-76; exec. dir. Marcus A. Foster Ednl. Inst., Oakland, 1976-79; adminstrv. mgr. Kaiser Aluminum & Chem. Corp., Oakland, 1979-80; v.p., gen. mgr. Kaiser CTR Inc., Oakland, 1980-84; vice chair Postal Rate Commn., Washington, 1985-87; asst. sec. for vocat. and adult edn. Dept. Edn., Washington, 1987-89; sec. State and Consumer Svcs. Agy. State of Calif.; spl. adv. to Pres. for Consumer Affairs, dir. U.S. Office Consumer Affairs, 1989-90; pres., CEO Earth Conservation Corps, Washington, 1990-91; sec. State and Consumer Svcs. Industry, State of Calif., 1991-92; dean McIntire Sch. Commerce U. Va., Charlottesville, 1992-97; v.p. The Times Mirror Co., 1997—; sr. v.p. comm. and pub. affairs L.A. Times, 1998—; pres., CEO The Times Mirror Found., 1997—; bd. dirs. La.-Pacific Corp., Niagara Mohawk Power Corp., Hershey Foods Corp., AK Steele Corp. Office: The Times Mirror Co Times Mirror Sq Los Angeles CA 90053

HILL, BOYD H., JR., medieval history educator; b. Dunedin Isles, Fla., Feb. 21, 1931; s. Boyd Howard and Minnie Cauthen (Buchanan) H.; m. Alette Louise Olin, Jan. 26, 1956; children: Boyd Buchanan, Michael Howard. A.B., Duke U., 1953; M.A., U. N.C., 1957, Ph.D., 1963; postgrad., UCLA, 1957-58. Instr. La. State U., Baton Rouge, 1962-64; asst. prof. medieval history U. Colo., Boulder, 1964-66, assoc. prof., 1967-71, prof., 1971—, chmn. dept. history, 1981-85, chmn. dept. classics., 1986-87; scholarship dir. Coll. Arts and Sci., U. Colo., Boulder, 1992-96; vis. asst. prof. UCLA, 1966-67. Author: Medieval Monarchy in Action, 1972; editor: The Rise of the First Reich, 1969, The Western World, 1974; contbr. articles to profl. jours. Town trustee Jamestown, Colo., 1990-92. With U.S. Army, 1953-55. Wellcome Hist. Med. Library fellow, 1962; Am. Philos. Soc. grantee, 1968; Council Research and Creative Work U. Colo. grantee, 1980. Mem. Am. Hist. Assn. (councillor Pacific Coast br. 1971-74), Medieval Acad. Am. (councillor 1973-76), Rocky Mountain Medieval and Renaissance Assn. (pres. 1983), Phi Kappa Psi. Democrat. Presbyterian. Home: 1433 Tulip St Longmont CO 80501 Office: U Colo Campus Dept History PO Box 234 Boulder CO 80309-0234

HILL, BRIAN, professional basketball team coach; b. East Orange, N.J., Sept. 19, 1947; m. Kay Hill; children: Kimberly, Christopher. BS in Phys. Edn., Kennedy Coll., 1969. Basketball coach Clifford Scott High Sch., 1970-72; asst. coach Montclair State U., 1972-74, Pa. State U., 1983-86; asst. coach Lehigh U., 1974, head coach, 1975-83; asst. coach Atlanta Hawks, 1986-90; asst. coach Orlando (Fla.) Magic, 1990-93, head coach, 1993-97; head coach Vancouver Grizzlies, 1997—; head coach NBA Ea. Conf. All-Stars, 1995. Office: Vancouver Grizzlies, 800 Griffiths Way, Vancouver, BC Canada V6B 6G1*

HILL, BRUCE MARVIN, statistician, scientist, educator; b. Chgo., Mar. 13, 1935; s. Samuel and Leah (Berman) H.; m. Linda Ladd, June 18, 1958; children—Alec Michael, Russell Andrew, Gregory Bruce; m. Anne Edith Gardiner Bruce, Aug. 5, 1972. B.S. in Math., U. Chgo., 1956; M.S. in Stats., Stanford U., 1958, Ph.D. in Stats., 1961. Mem. faculty U. Mich., Ann Arbor, 1960—, assoc. prof. stats. and probability theory, 1964-70, prof., 1970—; vis. prof. bus. Harvard U., 1964-65; vis. prof. systems engring. U. Lancaster, U.K., 1968-69; vis. prof. stats. U. London, 1976; vis. prof. econs. U. Utah, 1979; vis. prof. math. U. Milan, U. Rome, 1989. Editor Jour. Am. Statis. Assn., 1977-83, Jour. Bus. and Econ. Stats, 1982—; contbr. articles to profl. jours., chpts. to books on stats, encys. Grantee NSF, 1962-69, 81-86, 89—, USAF, 1971-73, 87-89. Fellow Am. Statis. Assn. (pres. Ann Arbor chpt. 1986-91), Inst. Math. Stats.; mem. AAUP, Am. Math Assn., Rsch. Club U. Mich., Psi Upsilon, Sigma Chi. Home: 1657 Glenwood Rd Ann Arbor MI 48104-4133 Office: U Mich Dept Stats Ann Arbor MI 48109-1027

HILL, BRYCE DALE, school administrator; b. Seminole, Okla., Mar. 5, 1930; s. Charles Daniel and Ollie (Nichols) H.; B.S., East Central State Coll., 1952, M.Teaching, 1957; postgrad. U. Okla., 1959-70; profl. adminstrs. certificate, 1969; m. Wilma Dean Carter, Aug. 16, 1956; children: Bryce Anthony, Brent Dale. Tchr. pub. schs., New Lima, Okla., 1952-56, supt. pub. schs., 1956-95; owner New Lima Gas Co., 1958-82. Chmn. bd. dirs. Seminole County chpt. ARC, 1969-90; v.p. bd. dirs. Redland Community Action Program, 1968-71; mem. Seminole County Bd. Health, 1985-95, v.p., 1986-88, chmn., 1988-95; mem. Seminole County Rural Devel. Council, edn. leader com. Okla. Farmers Union, 1990-93, exec. com. Okla. Commn. for Ednl. Leadership, 1993-95; v.p., bd. dirs. Okla. Assn. Acad. Competition, 1991-95; chmn. Seminole County Dem. Ctrl. Com., 1962-64, 70-95. Named to Seminole Jr. Coll. Hall of Fame, 1995. Mem. NEA, Okla. Edn. Assn. (Friend of Edn. award 1996), Am. Assn. Sch. Adminstrs., Okla. Assn. Sch. Adminstrs. (exec. com. 1976-78, 79-81, bd. dirs. 1979-81, 93-95, Dist. 8 Adminstr. of Yr. 1983, 94, Lifetime Achievement award 1996), Orgn. Rural Okla. Schs. (bd. dirs. 1986-92, pres. 1993-94, Pioneer award 1998), Seminole County Tchrs. Assn. (pres. 1964-65, 71-72, 79-80, 90-91), Seminole County Sch. Adminstrs. Assn. (chmn. 1969-70, 93-95), Seminole County Schoolmasters Club (pres. 1963-64, 69-70, 77-78), Seminole County Ret. Tchrs. Assn. (pres. 1996—), Seminole Hist. Soc. (v.p. 1971-73, 74-76), Okla. Assn. Svc. Impact Schs. (bd. dirs. 1987-95). Baptist. Home: 32 Sequoyah Blvd Shawnee OK 74801-5570

HILL, CAROL DECHELLIS, writer, novelist; b. Jan. 20, 1942. BA, Chatam Coll., 1962; MA, NYU. Freelance journalist, creative writing tchr.; v.p., editor-in-chief, pub. Harcourt Brace Jovanovich, N.Y.C., 1980-87. Author: Henry James' Midnight Song.

HILL, CAROL JEAN, library director. BS, Mo. Western State, 1974; MLS, Emporia State U., 1980. Libr. dir. City of Fort Walton Beach, Fla., 1995—. E-mail: fwblibr@fwb.org. Office: 105 Miracle Strip Pksy SW Fort Walton Beach FL 32548-6614

HILL, CHARLES GRAHAM, JR., chemical engineering educator; b. Elmira, N.Y., July 28, 1937; s. Charles Graham and Ethel Mayburn (Pfleegor) H.; m. Katherine Mertice Koon, July 11, 1964; children: Elizabeth, Deborah, Cynthia. BS, MIT, 1959, MS, 1960, ScD, 1964. Asst. prof. MIT, Cambridge, 1964-65; asst. prof. U. Wis., Madison, 1967-71, assoc. prof., 1971-76, prof. chem. engring., 1976—, John T. and Magdalen L. Sobota prov. chem. engring., 1995—, prof. food sci., 1989—, chair dept. chem. engring., 1989-92; cons. A.D. Little, Cambridge, 1964-65, Joseph Schlitz Brewing Co., Milw., 1973-76, Nat. Bur. Stds., 1979-95. Author: Introduction to Chemical Engineering Kinetics and Reactor Design, 1977; contbr. articles to profl. jours. Capt. U.S. Army, 1965-67. Gen. Motors Nat. scholar, 1955-59; NSF fellow, 1959-62, Ford Found. fellow, 1964-65. Fellow AIChE; mem. Am. Chem. Soc., Inst. Food Technologists, Sigma Xi, Tau Beta Pi, Phi Lambda Upsilon. Republican. Presbyterian. Avocation: sailing. Home: 2241 Fox Ave Madison WI 53711-1922 Office: U Wis Dept Chem Engring 1415 Engineering Dr Madison WI 53706-1607

HILL, CHRISTOPHER THOMAS, administrator, educator; b. Clarksburg, W.Va., Aug. 29, 1942; s. Ransel Lewis and Roberta Gweneth (Hill) H.; m. Sheila Poleselli, Aug. 21, 1965. BS, Ill. Inst. Tech., Chgo., 1964; MS, U. Wis., 1966, PhD, 1969. Registered profl. engr., Mo. Rsch. engr Uniroyal Inc., Wayne, N.J., 1968-70; from asst. to assoc. prof. Washington U., St. Louis, 1970-78; sr. profl. staff Office of Tech. Assessment, Washington, 1977-78; sr. rsch. assoc. MIT, 1978-83; sr. specialist in sci. and tech. policy Congl. Rsch. Svc., Libr. of Congress, Washington, 1983-90; dir. Mfg. Forum Nat. Acads. Engring. and Scis., Washington, 1990-93; sr. analyst RAND, Washington, 1993-94; prof. pub. policy and tech. George Mason U., Fairfax, Va., 1994—, vice provost for rsch., 1997—; Contbr. articles to profl. jours. Fellow AAAS; mem. ACS, Am. Econs. Assn. E-mail: chill2@gmu.edu. Home: 2853 Ontario Rd NW Apt 105 Washington DC 20009-2237 Office: George Mason U Office of the Provost 4400 University Dr Fairfax VA 22030

HILL, CLAUDIA ADAMS, tax consultant; b. Long Beach, Calif., Oct. 14, 1949; d. Claude T. Adams and Geraldine (Jones) Crosby; m. W. Eugene Hill, Sept. 14, 1968 (div. Oct. 1983); children: Stacia Heather, Jonathan Eugene; m. Larry C. Enoksen, June 4, 1988. BA, Calif. State U., Fullerton, 1972; MBA, San Jose State U., 1978. Systems analyst quality assurance group United Technology Ctr., 1972-73; with Commrs. Adv. Group IRS, 1987; prin., owner Tax Mam, Inc., 1974—; noted lectr. in field of taxation; tax advisor, liaison to profl. assns. IRS. Editor-in-chief CCH Jour. of Tax Practice and Procedure; contbg. editor PPC Guide to Dealing with IRS, 7061709 Deskbook. Mem. Nat. Assn. Enrolled Agts., Calif. Soc. Enrolled Agts. Republican. Office: TAX MAM Inc 10680 S De Anza Blvd Cupertino CA 95014-4446

HILL, CLINTON, artist; b. Payette, Idaho, Mar. 8, 1922; s. Samuel Edgar and Iva Marie (Horn) H. B.S. U. Oreg., 1947; postgrad., Bklyn. Mus. Sch., 1949-51, Academie de la Grande Chaumiere, Paris, France, 1951, Instituto d'Arte Statale, Florence, Italy, 1951-52. Prof. Queens Coll., N.Y.C., 1968-87, now prof. emeritus. One-man shows include Marilyn Pearl Gallery, N.Y.C., 10 shows 1979-92, Monclair Mus., N.J., 1981, Galleria Blu, Milan, Italy, 1984, Worcester Mus., Mass., 1992, Andre Zarre Gallery, N.Y.C., 1993-95; represented in permanent collections Mus. Modern Art, N.Y.C., Met. Mus., N.Y.C., Phila. Mus., Albright Knox Gallery, Buffalo, Nat. Gallery Australia, Canberra, Bklyn. Mus., Phoenix Art Mus., Whitney Mus., N.Y.c., Brit. Mus., London, Fogg Mus., Harvard U., Princeton (N.J.) U. Libr. Rare Books Divsn., others. Served to lt. (j.g.) USN, 1943-47. Fulbright grantee India, 1956; Creative Artists Pub. Service grantee, 1975; Nat. Endowment for Arts grantee, 1976, 80. Home: 178 Prince St New York NY 10012-2905

HILL, COURTNEY KING, marketing professional; b. N.Y.C., Feb. 17, 1957; d. Henry King and Delores Paula (Daggett) H. Pres. Hill Comms. Inc., Hilton Head, S.C.; real estate broker Homes of Distinction, Hilton Head, 1981—; bd. dirs. Mid Tenn. Third Mobile, Cookeville. Mem. Rotary (Paul Harris fellow). Republican. Avocations: photography, travel, investments. Office: Hill Comm Inc 42 New Orleans Rd Hilton Head Island SC 29928

HILL, DAVID, broadcast executive. V.p. of Sports Nine Network, Australia, 1977-88; head Eurosport, Great Britain, 1988-91, Sky Sports, Great Britain, 1991-93; pres. Fox Sports, Los Angeles, CA, 1993—; CEO Fox Sports Network, 1996—; chmn., CEO Fox TV, 1996—. Office: Fox Sports PO Box 900 Beverly Hills CA 90213-0900*

HILL, DAVID, city human resources director; m. Linda Hill; 1 child, Jon. BA in Polit. Sci., UCLA, 1966; MPA, U. So. Calif., 1972. Staff City of L.A. Civil Svc. and Police Depts., 1965-66; human resources staff, various positions City of Anaheim, Calif., 1966-83, asst. dir. human resources dept., 1983-88; asst. dir. labor rels. dept. City of Anaheim, 1988-94, human resources dir., 1994—; past bd. dirs. So. Calif. Pub. Labor Rels. Coun.; City of Anaheim rep., bd. dirs. Coop. Pers. Svcs.; participant Sr. Human Resources Mgrs. Roundtable, Orange County, Calif. Mem. gov. bd., 1st Congl. Ch. Anaheim; vol. bd. mem. Anaheim Area Credit Union. Mem. Internat. Pers. Mgmt. Assn. (past mem. resolutions com., author Comparable Worth resolution, western region pres. 1983-84, active participant numerous region confs., Excellence award 1990), So. Calif. Pers. Mgmt. Assn. (past bd. dirs., pres. 1978-79, chair ann. tng. conf. 1978, Emery E. Olson Achievement award 1996). Office: Dept Human Resources City Hall 200 S Anaheim Blvd Anaheim CA 92805-3820*

HILL, DAVID ALLAN, electrical engineer; b. Cleve., Apr. 21, 1942; s. Martin D. and Geraldine S. (Yoder) H.; m. Elaine C. Dempsey, July 9, 1971. BSEE, Ohio U., 1964, MSEE, 1966; PhD in Elect. Engring., Ohio State U., 1970. Vis. fellow Coop. Inst. for Rsch. Environ. Sci., Boulder, Colo., 1970-71; rsch engr. Inst. for Telecommunication Scis., Boulder, 1971-82; sr. scientist Nat. Inst. Standards and Tech., Boulder, 1982—; adj. prof. U. Colo., Boulder, 1980—. Editor Geosci. and Remote Sensing Jour., 1980-84, Antennas and Propagation Jour., 1986-89; contbr. over 100 articles to profl. jours., chpts. to books. Recipient award for best paper Electromagnetic Compatability Jour., 1987. Fellow IEEE (chpt. chmn. 1975-76, editor 1986-89); mem. Electromagnetic Soc. (bd. dirs. 1980-86), Internat. Union Radio Sci. (nat. com. 1986-89), Colo. Mountain Club (Boulder), Sierra Club. Office: Nat Inst Standards & Tech 813-07 325 Broadway St Boulder CO 80303-3337

HILL, DAVID GEOFFREY, college administrator; b. Montgomery, Ala., May 29, 1954; s. William David and Norma Zell Dorsey Hill. BA in Journalism, Auburn U., 1976; MA in Pub. and Pvt. Mgmt., Birmingham-So. Coll., 1994. Comm. tng. specialist SouthTrust Bank, Birmingham, Ala., 1976-77; writer Blue Cross/Blue Shield, Birmingham, 1977-80; comms. dir. Fed. Res. Bank, Atlanta, 1980-81; asst. dir. comms. United Way of Ctrl. ala., Birmingham, 1984-85; asst. dir. pub. info. Birmingham-So. Coll., 1985-90, dir. publs., 1990-98, dir. comms., 1998—. Vol. ARC, 1978-80, Am. Cancer Soc., 1988, Birmingham C. of C., 1990; pub. rels. vol. Drum Corps Internat., Chgo., 1978-89, south dir., 1986-89; pub. rels. dir. Winter Guard Internat., Denver, 1988-91. Recipient Outstanding Chpt. Pres. award Internat. Assn. Bus. Communicators, 1980, Outstanding Comms. Program award Coun. for Advancement and Support of Higher Edn., 1991. Mem. Pub. Rels. Soc. Am., Pub. Rels. Coun. Am., Ala. Press Assn. Methodist. Avocations: music, reading, cooking, writing, studying current culture. E-mail: idlewilders@mindspring.com. Home: 678 Idlewild Cir Birmingham AL 35205

HILL, DAVID LAMAR, lawyer; b. Gadsden, Ala., Oct. 31, 1941; s. Jasper O. and Ulma I. (Jones) H.; m. Nita J. Neal, Nov. 7, 1970; 1 child, Heather A. BS, U. Ala., 1963; JD, George Washington U., 1968. Bar: D.C. 1969, U.S. Dist. Ct. D.C., U.S. Ct. Appeals (D.C. cir.), U.S. Supreme Ct. Ptnr. Keller & Heckman, Washington, 1973-82; pvt. practice, 1982-88; ptnr. O'Connor & Hannan, Washington, 1988—. Mem. ABA (adminstrv. law sect.), Fed. Comm. Bar Assn., D.C. Bar Assn., Nat. Lawyers Club. Home: 5119 Wessling Ln Bethesda MD 20814-1232 Office: O'Connor & Hannan 1919 Pennsylvania Ave NW Washington DC 20006-3483

HILL, DAVID LAWRENCE, research corporation executive; b. Boonville, Miss., Nov. 11, 1919; s. David Alexander and Mabel Clair (Brown) H.; BS, Calif. Inst. Tech., 1942; PhD (Socony Vacuum Co. fellow), Princeton U., 1951; m. Mary M. Shadow, Dec. 31, 1950 (dec. Jan. 1992); children: David A., Mary C., Robert L., John F., Cynthia A., Sandra E., James A. With U. Chgo. Metall. Lab. and Argonne Nat. Lab., 1942-46, assoc. physicist, group leader, 1944-46; asst. prof. physics Vanderbilt U., Nashville, 1949-52, assoc. prof., 1952-54; guest scholar Inst. Theoretical Physics, Copenhagen, summer 1950; cons. theoretical physics U. Calif., Los Alamos (N.Mex.) Sci. Lab., 1952-54, staff mem., 1954-58, group leader theoretical nuclear physics, 1955-58; mgmt. cons., 1958-60; pres. Phys. Sci. Corp., Fairfield, Conn., 1960-62, Nanosecond Systems, Inc., Fairfield, 1963-72, Particle Measurements, Inc., Southport, Conn., 1965-81, Harbor Rsch. Corp., 1978—; chmn. bd. Integrated Total Systems, Inc., Hingham, Mass., 1968-81; pres. Southport Computers, Inc., Conn., 1973-81, Valutron N.V., Netherlands Antilles, 1980—; pres. Patent Enforcement Fund, Inc., Southport, Conn., 1990—, Inventors' Def. Fund, Inc., 1996—; chmn. bd. dirs. Cassar Hill L.L.C., mgr., 1996—; lectr. in field; sci. advisor to Vice Presdl. nominee, Senator Estes Kefauver, 1956; incorporator, exec. v.p. dir. Los Alamos Investment Corp., 1956-58; cons. physicist in field. Adv. com. on sci. and tech. of Adv. Coun. of Dem. Nat. Com., 1959-61. Fellow Am. Phys. Soc., AAAS; mem. IEEE, Fedn. Am. Scientists (nat. chmn. 1953-54), Sigma Xi. Contbr. articles to profl. jours. Office: Patent Enforcement Fund PO Box 569 Southport CT 06490-0569

HILL, DAVID MARK, city planning director; b. Binghamton, N.Y., May 24, 1955; s. Robert Steven Hill and Miriam Joyce (Constable) Emmett; m. Kathleen Ann Gavin, Aug. 8, 1981; children: Katherine Leigh, Rachel Elizabeth, Sarah Danielle. AAS in Forest Tech., SUNY-CESF, Wanakena, N.Y., 1975; BS in Environ. Studies, SUNY-CESF, Syracuse, N.Y., 1981, M in Landscape Arch., 1984. Planner City of Buffalo Planning Dept., 1983-85; project planner City of Winston Salem/Forsyth County Planning Bd., Winston-Salem, N.C., 1985-88; prin. planner City of Binghamton (N.Y.) Planning Divsn., 1988-91; planning dir. City of Victoria (Tex.) Planning Dept.,

1991-97; planning dir. City of Denton (Tex.) Planning and Devel. Dept., 1997-99, asst. city mgr. devel. svcs., 1999—. Mem. Am. Planning Assn. (cert. planner, Hon. Mention Comprehensive Plan 1989), Am. Soc. Landscape Architects, Urban and Regional Info. Systems Assn., Urban Land Inst. Home: 3220 Nottingham Dr Denton TX 76201-1349 Office: Planning & Devel Dept 221 N Elm St Denton TX 76201-4107

HILL, DEBORA ELIZABETH, author, journalist, screenwriter; b. San Francisco, July 10, 1961; d. Henry Peter and Madge Lillian (Ridgeway-Aarons) H. BA, Sonoma State U., 1983. Talk show host Rock Jour. Viacom, San Francisco, 1980-81; interviewer, biographer Harrap Ltd., London, 1986-87; editor North Bay Mag., Cotati, Calif., 1988; guest feature writer Argus Courier, Petaluma, Calif., 1993-95; concept developer BiblioBytes, Hoboken, N.J., 1994-95, White Tiger Films, San Francisco, 1995—; feature writer The Econs. Press, 1996-97; literary agt. The Thornton Agy., Portland, Oreg., 1997—; assoc. prodr. White Tiger Films, 1995—; concept developer Star Trek: Voyager and Star Trek: Deep Space Nine, 1997-98; mem. Writers Net The Online Wordbiz Directory, Writers for Hire, The Hollywood Direct Access Directory. Author: The San Francisco Rock Experience, 1979, CUTS from a San Francisco Rock Journal, 1982, Punk Retro, 1988, Gale Research-Resourceful Woman, 1994, St. James Guide to Fantasy Writers, 1996, A Ghost Among Us, 1996, St. James Guide to Famous Gays and Lesbians, 1997, Jerome's Quest, 1997, SuperGirls: The Co-Ed Murders, 1999; co-author: Rumour Has a Memory, 1999, The Land of the Wanal, The Lost Myths Saga, vol. 1; co-writer, cons. producer The Danger Club, Danger Club II; contbr. stories and articles to profl. jours. Democrat. Avocations: clothing design, cooking, internet, reading, interior design. E-mail: debora.h111@mailcity.com. Home: 110 Grant Ave Petaluma CA 94952-4809 Address: Thronton Lit Agy 1431 SE Knight St Portland OR 97202

HILL, DEBORAH ANN, special education educator; b. Dover, N.J., May 7, 1957; d. George Fred and Mary Ann (Marks) Lutz; m. Robert Charles Hill, Sept. 6, 1980. BS in Spl. Edn., Coll. Misericordia, Dallas, Pa., 1979. Cert. tchr., N.C. Tchr. Murdoch Ctr., Butner, N.C., 1979-87, Chapel Hill (N.C.) Carrboro City Schs., 1987—. Asst. leader Girl Scouts U.S., Wilkes Barre, Pa. 1978, Raleigh, N.C., 1985. Named Tchr. of Orange County Assn. Retarded Citizens, 1989-90; recipient Zora Rashkis Personal & Profl. Committment to Students & Staff award, 1995; Edn. grantee, 1989-90. Mem. ASCD, Am. Fedn. Tchrs. (N.C. chpt.), Coun. Exceptional Children, N.C. Mental Health Assn., Assn. Retarded Citizens. Democrat. Roman Catholic. Avocations: sewing, fishing, bicycling. Home: PO Box 25333 Durham NC 27702-5333 Office: Ephesus Elem Sch Ephesus Church Rd Chapel Hill NC 27514

HILL, DELINDA JEAN, medical/surgical nurse, enterostomal therapy nurse; b. Okmulgee, Okla., Jan. 11, 1957; d. Robert Winfield and Phillis Lucille (Locker) Davis; m. Stanton Robert Hill, Nov. 26, 1976. AAS in Nursing with honors, Tulsa Jr. Coll., 1979; BSN with high honors, Langston U., 1990; MS, U. Okla., 1996. Cert. med.-surg. nurse, ANCC, cert. enterostomal therapy nurse. Enterostomal therapy nurse clin. specialist Hillcrest Med. Ctr., Tulsa, 1979—; mem. skin integrity task force Hillcrest Med. Ctr. Mem. Sigma Theta Tau (Beta Delta chpt. at large). Office: Hillcrest Med Ctr 1120 S Utica Ave Tulsa OK 74104-4012

HILL, DIANE SELDON, corporate psychologist; b. Mpls., Sept. 17, 1943; d. Earl William and Geraldine (Le Veille) Seldon; m. David Reuben Hill, May 14, 1986 (div. Feb. 1988); children: Anna Marion, Jason David. BA, Mt. Holyoke Coll., 1965; MA in Psychology, U. Minn., 1968, PhD in Psychology, 1974; Advanced Mgmt. Program, U. Pa. Wharton Sch., 1992. Lic. psychologist, Colo; diplomate in clin. psychology Am. Bd. Profl. Psychologists. Instr., counselor Student Counseling Bur. U. Minn., Mpls., 1968-70, advisor women's programs, Student Activities Bur., 1970-71; instr. psychology Augsburg Coll., Mpls., 1970-71; counselor, tchr. humanities Emma Willard Sch., Troy, N.Y., 1972-75; dir. counseling and re-engagement Colo. Women's Coll., Denver, 1976-77; clin. field supr., Sch. Profl. Psychology U. Denver, 1977—; asst. clin. prof. psychology U. Colo. Health Scis., Denver, 1981-89, Ctr. for Creative Leadership, Colorado Springs, 1981—; pvt. practice Denver, 1977-89; mgmt. and organizational cons. Somerville and Co., Inc., Denver, 1989—; dir. Profl. Exams. Svc., N.Y.C., 1991-97; presenter at profl. meetings; expert witness on psychology ethics; presenter testimony before Colo. legis. hearing coms. and Colo. Ins. Commn.; lobbyist for psychology licensure Parliament of Finland, 1989. Mem. vestry St. Thomas Episcopal Ch., Denver, 1997—; bd. dirs. Rocky Mountain Women's Inst., Denver, 1997—. Named NDEA IV fellow U. Minn., 1967-68. Fellow Am. Psychol. Assn.; mem. Colo. Psychol. Assn. (bd. dirs. 1979-82, dir. polit. action com.), Am. Assn. State Psychology Bds. (del. 1982-83, mem.-at-large exec. com. 1983, pres. 1988-91), Colo. Bd. Psychologist Examiners (bd. dirs. 198-187, chmn. 1983-88), Women's Forum Colo. (mem. com. 1979—). Episcopalian. Avocations: alpine and nordic skiing, scuba diving, snorkeling, cycling, hiking. Home: 2052 Bellaire St Denver CO 80207-3722 Office: Somerville End Co Inc Cairn Bldg 1625 Broadway 727 E 16th Ave Denver CO 80203

HILL, DONALD DEE, management consultant, lecturer, writer; b. Moultrie, Ga.; s. Thomas Dee and Vivan Mae (Monk) H. BCE, Ga. Inst. Tech. Registered profl. engr., Ala. Structural engr. Patchen & Zimmerman Cons. Engrs., Augusta, Ga.; asst. dir. F.S.D. Am. Plywood Assn., Tacoma; mng. dir., CEO ASME Internat. Gas Turbine Inst., Atlanta; lectr. and spkr. in field; spl. cons., lectr. to Czech Republic, 1996; lectr. pilot program, Vietnam, 1997. Monthly columnist Convene mag. Vice pres. Letterman's Club; ruling elder Presbyn. Ch. 1st lt. U.S. Army. Named Eagle of the Acropolis, Palais de Congres, Nice, France; named to Coll. of 17 Gentlemen, Netherlands Congress Bur.; named Ark. Traveler, Gov. of Ark.; recipient R. Tom Sawyer Gas Turbine award ASME, 1996. Mem. Am. Soc. Assn. Execs. (coun. internat. sect.), Meeting Planners Internat., Ga. Tech. Alumni Assn., Chi Epsilon, Kappa Sigma. Avocation: weight lifting. Home and Office: 6870 Lisa Ln Atlanta GA 30338-3952

HILL, DONALD S., commissioner, state; married; 2 children. BS cum laude, U. N.H., 1971; MBA, Plymouth State Coll., 1983. Acct. I, II, III N.H. Dept. Edn., Concord, 1971-76; bus. adminstr. III N.H. Dept. Edn., 1976-82, chief of bus. mgmt., 1982-83; sr. bus. supr. N.H. Dept. of Adminstrv. Svcs., 1983-88, asst. commr., budget officer, 1988-96, commr., 1996—. Budget com. Town of Pembroke, N.H., 1981-87, town treas., 1981-84, bd. of selectman, 1972-81. Office: NH Adminstrv Svcs Dept State House Annex 25 Capitol St Rm 120 Concord NH 03301-6312

HILL, DONALD WAIN, education accreditation commission executive; b. Montfort, Wis., June 14, 1924; s. Victor Charles and Emma Grace (Carr) H.; m. Phyllis Kay Hogan, July 2, 1949; children: Leslie Scott Hill Barnett, Lance Howlett Hill, Lawson Wain Hill. BBA, U. Wis., 1949, MBA, 1953. Budget analyst City of Milw., 1950-53; adminstrv. analyst State of Wis., Madison, 1953-54; bus. mgr. U. Wis., Milw., 1954-56; mem. joint staff Coord. Comm. for Higher Edn., Madison, 1956-59; asst. supt. schs. Chgo. Pub. Schs., 1959-66; exec. vice chancellor City Colls. of Chgo., 1966-84; ednl. cons. Hill Assocs., Carlsbad, Calif., 1984-86; asst. dir., sr. accreditation specialist Accreditation Commn. of Career Sch. and Colls. of Tech., Arlington, Va., 1986—; chmn. fin. com. Ill. Task Force on Edn., Springfield, 1965-66; mem. Ill. Higher Edn. Master Plan Com., Urbana, 1963-64; chmn. facilities com. Task Force to Form U. of Wis.-Milw., 1956; mem. fin. study com. U.S. Office Edn., Washington, 1963. Contbr. articles to profl. jours. Mem. ednl. credentials and credit rev. team Am. Coun. on Edn., Abu Dhabi, 1987; mem. task force on collective bargaining Carnegie Found., N.Y.C., 1975-76. With U.S. Infantry, 1942-46, ETO. Mem. Wis. Acad. Scis., Arts and Letters (higher edn. rep. for Wis. Acad. Rev. 1957-59), Econ. Club Chgo. Methodist. Avocations: golf, tennis, genealogy, travel. Home: 8435 W Tonto Ln Peoria AZ 85382-8802 Office: Accreditation Commn Career Schs and Colls Tech 2101 Wilson Blvd Ste 302 Arlington VA 22201-3062

HILL, DONNA MARIE, communications executive; b. Amesbury, Mass., July 25, 1957; d. Robert and Marie Doris (Lucier) Menzigian. BS in Math., U. Lowell, 1979, MBA in Ops., 1983. Material control analyst AVCO Corp., Wilmington, Mass., 1979-81; ops. analyst Blue Cross & Blue Shield, Boston, 1981-83, risk analyst, 1983-84; systems analyst Bell Atlantic Corp., Bethesda, Md., 1984-86; cons. internal Bell Atlantic Corp., Bethesda, 1986-89, project mgr., 1989-91, new tech. strategic planning mgr., 1992-97, sr mgr. sales channel devel., 1997—; speaker FUSE Nat. and Regional Confs., 1988, 91. inventor (software) User-assisted Adhoc Reporting, 1988, Natural English Report Access, 1988. Vol. Montgomery County Vol. Assn., Montgomery, Md., 1983—, PALS Montgomery County, 1984—; chair spl. events New Mem. Svcs. John F. Kennedy Ctr. Performing Arts, Washington, 1985—, mem. vol. adv. com., 1991, 92; chair vol. adv. com. Kennedy Ctr., 1992—; bd. dirs. Sister City Corp., Rockville, 1992—, v.p., 1993-95, pres.-elect, 1994-95, pres., 1995—. Mem. NAFE, Ops. Rsch. Soc., Intelligent Computer Rsch. Inst., Focus User Group (co-chmn. artificial intelligence group 1989, leader, coord. spl. interest groups for Nat. Com., 1989, nat., regional spkr. 1988, 91), Rockville Jr. C. of C. (sec. 1992-93), Md. Jr. C. of C. (program mgr. internat. involvement 1992-93, dist. dir. 1993-94, cmty. devel. v.p. 1994-95, U.S. Jr. C. of C. internat. affairs commn. 1995-98, JCI individual devel. commn. 1996, spl. asst. to world pres. 1997—), Internat. Spkrs. Platform, Jr. C. of C. Republican. Roman Catholic. Avocations: photography, travel. Office: Bell Atlantic 1320 Courthouse Rd 9th Fl Arlington VA 22201

HILL, DOROTHY BENNETT, community activist; b. Union Springs, Ala., Nov. 6, 1955; d. William Davis and Carrie Lou Bell Davis-Cody; m. Simon James Hill I, Dec. 15, 1976; children: Angela Elizabeth, Carrie LaVonna Denise, Simon James II. BA in Human Resource Adminstrn., St. Leo Coll., 1992. Asst. tchr., bus driver Econ. Opportunity Authority, Savannah, Ga., 1978-84; paraprofl. Chatham County Bd. Edn., Savannah, 1984-86; owner, dir. Hill's Daycare and Preschool, Savannah, 1986-89; suspense tech. Aetna Medicare, Savannah, 1989-93; family support coord. Youth Futures Authority, Savannah, 1993-94, finance specialist family resource ctr., 1994-95; cmty. campaigner Ga. Campaign for Adolescent Pregnancy Prevention, Savannah, 1996-98; owner, dir. Lesye-Anye Scholastic Inst. of Achievement, Savannah, 1998—; cons. Daycare Home Providers The La Nourriture Co., Decatur, Ga., 1989—. V.p. Windsor Forest High Sch. PTA/PTO; mem. parent adv. team to supt. Savannah-Chatham Bd. Edn.; bd. dirs. Neighborhood Improvement Assn.; citizen rev. panelist Juvenile Ct. Chatham-Savannah Youth in Foster Care; mem. family to family steering com. Alternative Placement to Foster Care; bd. dirs. Healthy Start Initiative Male Involvement; exec. com. Youth Crime Watch of Savannah; mem. neighborhood coun. Cmty. Change for Youth Devel., youth advisor; sec. Eastside Concerned Citizens; mem. adv. com. Summer Youth Roundtable; vol. Meml. Med. Ctr.; founder, advisor Chatham-Savannah Youth Action Team; pres. stewardess bd. #2 St. Philip A.M.E. Ch., mem. pulpit aid bd., usher bd. # 1, communication com.; troop leader Girl Scouts U.S.A.; den mother Cub Scouts. Mem Savannah State U. Alumni Assn., St. Leo Coll. Alumni Assn. Avocations: sewing, horticulture, reading, travel. Home: PO Box 15132 Savannah GA 31416-1832

HILL, DRAPER, editorial cartoonist; b. Boston, July 1, 1935; s. L. Draper and Jean Hutchins (Thompson) H.; m. Sarah Randolph Adams, Apr. 22, 1967; children: Jennifer Randolph, Jonathan Draper. B.A. magna cum laude, Harvard C., 1957; postgrad, Slade Sch. Fine Arts, Univ. Coll., London, Eng., 1960-63. Reporter and cartoonist Quincy (Mass.) Patriot Ledger, 1957-60; editorial cartoonist Worcester (Mass.) Telegram, 1964-71, Comml. Appeal, Memphis, 1971-76, The Detroit News, 1976-99; dir. Play of Month Guild, N.Y.C., 1958-82; instr. drawing Worcester Art Sch., 1967-71; lectr. Thomas Nast, Garibaldi, Beerbohm, Gillray, and others. Author: Mr. Gillray, The Caricaturist, 1965, Fashionable Contrasts, 1966, (with James Roper) The Decline and Fall of the Gibbon, 1974, The Satirical Etchings of James Gillray, 1976, (essay) Cartoons & Caricatures in Ency. of Collectibles, 1978, Political Asylum: Editorial Cartoons by Draper hill, 1985; also catalogs; one-person shows include Detroit Hist. Mus., 1996. Mem. adv. bd. Swann Found. for Caricature and Cartoon, N.Y.C., 1980-93, 98—. Winner Thomas Nast prize for editorial cartooning Landau-in-der-Pfalz, Fed. Republic Germany, 1990. Mem. Assn. Am. Editorial Cartoonists (2d v.p. 1972-74, 1st v.p. 1974-75, pres. 1975-76, author quar. column History Corner assn. Notebook, 1974—), Club of Odd Vols. Home: 368 Washington Rd Grosse Pointe MI 48230-1616

HILL, EARLENE HOOPER, state legislator; b. Balt., Oct. 22; d. Otis Barnett Hooper and Thelma E. (Richardson) Young; 1 child, Charisse E. BA, Norfolk State U.; MSW, Adelphi U.; DHL, Five Towns Coll., 1997. Mgr. N.Y. State Dept. Social Svcs., N.Y.C.; mem. N.Y. State Assembly, 1988—; mem. women's program, shop steward Pub. Employees Fedn., 1980-88, exec. bd. Exec. bd. Jack & Jill of Am., Inc., Nassau County, N.Y., 1985—; mem. Nat. Women's Polit. Caucus, N.Y.C., 1987—. Mem. Negro Bus. and Profl. Women (Cen. Nassau chpt.), Delta Sigma Theta. Democrat. Office: NY State Legislature State Capitol Albany NY 12224

HILL, EDITH MARIE, medical/surgical nurse; b. Wailuku, Maui, Hawaii, June 10, 1947; d. John Arthur and Sally Ayako (Oda) Pratt; m. Michael Eliott Hill, Mar. 29, 1969; children: Laura Marcienne, Adam Jeffrey. Diploma in nursing, Rochester (N.Y.) State Hosp., 1968; BSN, Nazareth Coll. Rochester, 1981; postgrad., SUNY Brockport. RN, N.Y. Staff nurse Strong Meml. Hosp., Rochester, 1968-69, various facilities, Tex., Calif., Ala., Ohio, 1969-73; staff nurse Genesee Hosp., 1973-93, perioperative nurse clinician, 1993-98; educator oper. rm. Strong Meml. Hosp., Rochester, 1998—. Contbg. author of chpt. in book Core Curriculum in Perioperative Nursing, 1995; contbr. articles to profl. publs. Mem. ANA, Assn. Oper. Rm. Nurses (cert., sec. Upstate N.Y. chpt. 1994-96, treas. 1997—). Avocations: reading, travel. Office: Univ Rochester Med Ctr Strong Meml Hosp 601 Elmwood Ave Rochester NY 14642-0001

HILL, ELEANOR JEAN, lawyer; b. Miami Beach, Fla., Dec. 19, 1950; d. Elbert Cray and Florence Louise (Strzycki) Hill; m. Thomas Paul Gross, April 7, 1990; 1 child, Bryan Michael Gross. BS, Fla. State U., 1972, JD, 1974. Bar: Fla. Asst. atty. U.S. Atty's Office, Tampa, Fla., 1975-78; spl. atty. Organized Crime Strike Force, U.S. Dept. Justice, Tampa, Fla., 1978-80; asst. counsel U.S. Senate Permanent Subcommittee on Investigations, Washington, 1980-82, chief counsel to minority, 1982-87, staff dir., chief counsel, 1987-95; inspector gen. U.S. Dept. Defense, Arlington, Va., 1995-99; ptnr. King & Spalding, Washington, 1999—. Mem. Fla. Bar Assn., Phi Beta Kappa, Phi Kappa Phi. Office: King & Spalding 1730 Pennsylvania NW Washington DC 20006

HILL, ELIZABETH ANNE, academic administrator, lawyer; b. N.Y.C., Dec. 29, 1942; d. Harry Gerald and Grace Marie (Byrne) H. BA, St. Joseph's Coll., Bklyn., 1964; MA, Columbia U., 1965; JD, St. John's Law Sch., Jamaica, N.Y., 1978. Bar: N.Y. 1979, U.S. Dist. Ct. (ea. dist.) N.Y. 1979; cert. tchr. English and social studies K-12, N.Y. H.s. tchr. Acad. St. Joseph, Brentwood, N.Y., 1967-70, Bishop Kearney H.S., Bklyn., 1970-71; co-dir. formation program Sisters of St. Joseph, Brentwood, 1971-76; atty. Cath. Migration Office, Bklyn., 1978-80; exec. asst. to pres. St. Joseph's Coll., Bklyn., 1980-97, pres., 1997—; bd. dirs. Brookhaven (N.Y.) Hosp., L.I. Assn.; mem. bd. trustees L.I. Reg. Adv. coun. Higher Edn. Mem. Bishop's Commn. on Pub. Policy, Bklyn., 1978-81; mediator Diocesan Mediation and Arbitration Panel, Bklyn., 1981—. Mem. Nat. Assn. Coll. and Univ. Attys., Bklyn. C. of C. (bd. dirs.). Office: St Joseph's Coll 245 Clinton Ave Brooklyn NY 11205-3602

HILL, ELIZABETH STARR, writer; b. Lynn Haven, Fla., Nov. 4, 1925; d. Raymond King and Gabrielle (Wilson) Cummings; m. Russell Gibson Hill, May 28, 1949; children: Andrea van Waldron, Bradford Wray. Student, Finch Jr. Coll., 1941-42, Columbia U., 1970-73. Freelance writer; past dir. Princeton Creative Ctr.; tchr. writing Princeton Adult Sch. Author: (juvenile books) The Wonderful Visit to Miss Liberty, 1961, The Window Tulip, 1964, Evan's Corner, 1967, 91 (ALA Notable Book for Children), Master Mike and the Miracle Maid, 1967, Pardon My Fangs, 1969, Bells: A Book to Begin On, 1970, Ever-After Island, 1977, Fangs Aren't Everything, 1985, When Christmas Comes, 1989, The Street Dancers, 1991, Broadway Chances, 1992 (ABA Pick of the Lists), The Banjo Player, 1993, Curtain Going Up!, 1995, Bird Boy, 1999; contbr. articles to mags. including Reader's Digest, many others. Mem. Authors Guild Am., Authors League Am., Univ. Club Winter Park. Office: Langford Apts PO Box 940 Winter Park FL 32790-0940

HILL, ELLEN BROWN, emergency medicine/gerontology professional, nurse; b. Pitts., Dec. 21, 1944; d. F. Gordon and Muriel Edith (Dunkerley) Brown. Diploma in nursing, St. Francis Gen. Hosp., Pitts., 1969; AA magna cum laude, Butler County Community Coll., Butler, Pa., 1982; BSN, La Roche Coll., Pitts., 1986; postgrad., Slippery Rock (Pa.) U., 1987. Cert. sch. nurse, EMT, pre hosp. trauma technician. Gerontology staff nurse St. Barnabas Free Home, Gibsonia, Pa., 1970-76; head athletic trainer BCCC, Butler, 1981-84; spl. dep. Butler county Sheriff's Dept., 1982—; trauma technician Richland Emergency Med. Svcs., Gibsonia, Pa., 1983—; head athletic trainer Mars (Pa.) Area Sch. Dist., 1984-86, sch. nurse substitute, 1984-98; spl. dep. Butler county Sheriff's Dept., Greentree, Pa., 1982—; trauma technician Richland Emergency Med. Svcs., Gibsonia, Pa., 1983—; head athletic trainer LaRoche Coll., 1983-84; head athletic trainer Mars (Pa.) Area Sch. Dist., 1984-86, sch. nurse substitute, 1984-98; staff and emergency rehab. nurse Olsten Health Svcs., Greentree, Pa., 1986—; gerontology staff nurse Vincentian Home, Pitts., 1992-93; test adminstr. for nursing assts. in long-term care facilities Pa. state cert., 1990-92; mem. rehab. staff D.T. Watson Rehab. Hosp. for Children and Adults, 1987-93; profl. tractor-trailer driver for Storming Eagle Transport, Gibsonia, Pa., 1992—; staff agy. nurse Polk (Pa.) Ctr., 1997. Disaster health svcs. specialist, shelter mgr. ARC, 1976—, instr. CPR, first aid; Sunday sch. tchr. Presbyn. Ch., 1959-70; cub scout leader Boy Scouts Am., 1977-79; leader Girl Scouts U.S., 1971-74; cmty. resource person PTO, 1969-82; women's day program chmn. Gulf Oil Corp. (Mellon Inst.), Pitts., 1967-69; athletic trainer, statistician Am. Legion Baseball, 1985-86; statistician Baseball BCE, 1981-84. Recipient Thanks for Helping at fires, blood drives, disasters award ARC, 1984. Mem. Emergency Nurses Assn., Pa. Assn. EMTs, St. Francis Gen. Hosp. Alumni Assn., Internat. Arabian Horse Assn., Cmty. Vol. Fire Dept. Valencia Aux., Pa. Arabian Horse Assn. (sec. 1976-77), Mars Area Bowling Assn., Butler Horsemen's Assn. (horse show sec. 1972-79, treas. 1972-79), Butler County Saddle Club (sec., horse show treas.), Traildusters of Western Pa. Snowmobile Club, Friends of the Nat. Parks of Gettysburg, Pa. Sheriff's Assn. (charter), Jacques Cousteau Soc., BCCC Alumni Assn., Valencia Area Hist. Soc., Am. Motorcycle Assn, Phi Theta Kappa (scholar 1982). Avocations: community resource person, neighborhood veterinarian, acupressure and relaxation through massage therapist. Home: 122 Butler Street Ext Valencia PA 16059-1606

HILL, EMITA BRADY, academic administrator; b. Balt., Jan. 31, 1936; d. Leo and Lucy McCormick (Jewett) Brady; children: Julie Beck, Christopher, Madeleine, Vedel. BA, Cornell U., 1957; MA, Middlebury Coll., 1958; PhD, Harvard U., 1967. Instr. Harvard U., 1961-63; asst. prof. Western Reserve U., 1967-69; from asst. prof. to v.p. Lehman Coll. CUNY, Bronx, N.Y., 1970-91; chancellor, grad. faculty Ind. U., Kokomo, Ind., 1991-99, chancellor emerita, 1999—. Mem. Am. Assn. Higher Edn., Assn. Am. Coll., Am. Soc. for 18th Century Studies, Am. Assn. State Colls. and Univs., Internat. Assn. Univ. Pres., Internat. Soc. for 18th Century Studies, Phi Beta Kappa. Avocations: music, scuba diving, tennis. Office: Ind U PO Box 9003 2300 S Washington St Kokomo IN 46902-3557

HILL, ERIK BRYAN, newspaper photographer; b. Eugene, Oreg., Feb. 17, 1957; s. Robert Donald and Dagmara (Grislis) H.; m. Robin Mackey, Aug. 30, 1986; children: Mara, Emma. BA in Internat. Rels., Stanford U., 1979; MS in Journalism, Ohio U., 1987. Photographer, photo editor The Kansas City (Mo.) Star, 1981-84; photographer The Anchorage Daily News, 1984—; adj. instr. U. Alaska, Anchorage, 1990—. Recipient Pulitzer prize gold medal for pub. svc. Columbia U., 1989, finalist Pulitzer prize for feature photography, 1990. Mem. Nat. Press Photographers Assn. Avocations: political pin collecting, family hikes, travel. Office: Anchorage Daily News 1001 Northway Dr Anchorage AK 99508-2098

HILL, ESTHER DIANNE, business education educator; b. Maysville, Ky., Apr. 14, 1943; d. Frank Hinson and Jean Pepper (Yelton) H. BS, Ea. Ky. State Coll., 1966. Cert. bus. edn., typing and English tchr., Ohio. Tchr. Milton-Union Schs., West Milton, Ohio, 1966-68, Forest Hills Sch. Dist., Cin., 1968-96; tchr. evenings Cin. Tech. Coll., 1977-80; software verifyer South Western Pub. Co., Cin., 1982-83, ret., 1996; writer Dist. Curriculum, Cin., 1975-96; dist. mem. County Textbook Com., Cin., 1982-96. Mem. NEA, Ohio Edn. Assn., Nat. Bus. Edn. Assn., Ohio Bus. Tchrs. Assn., Forest Hills Tchrs. Assn., Eastern Ky. U. Alumni assn. Republican. Mem. Ch. of Christ. Avocations: embroidery, counted cross stitching, golf, reading. Home: 40 Bonnie Ln Fort Thomas KY 41075-2532

HILL, FAY GISH, librarian; b. Rensselaer, Ind., Sept. 19, 1944; d. Roy Charles and Vergie (Powell) Gish; m. John Christian Hill, May 20, 1967; 1 child, Christina Gish. BA, Purdue U., 1967; MLS, U. Tex., 1971. Asst. librarian basic reference dept. Tex. A&M U., College Station, 1972, assoc. librarian sci. ref. dept., 1972-74, acting head librarian sci. reference dept., 1975; reference librarian Cen. Iowa Regional Library, Des Moines, 1984—. Troop leader Girl Scouts U.S., Ames, Iowa, 1983-88; bd. dirs. Friends of Fgn. Wives, Ames, 1982-86. Mem. ALA, Iowa Libr. Assn., Iowa Libr. Assn. Found. (bd. dirs. 1990-95). Presbyterian. Avocation: collecting antiques. Home: 5604 Thunder Rd Ames IA 50014-9448 Office: Cen Iowa Regional Libr Reference 515 Douglas Ave Ames IA 50010-6215

HILL, G. RICHARD, lawyer; b. Chapel Hill, N.C., Oct. 22, 1951. BA magna cum laude, U. Minn., 1973, MA, 1975; JD, Yale U., 1978. Bar: Wash. 1978. Atty. Phillips McCullough, Seattle; adj. prof. law U. Wash., 1987-88; co-founder Pacific Real Estate Inst. Mem. ABA (mem. urban, state and local govt. law sect., chair 1995-96, mem. exec. com. 1992-95, chmn. land use planning and zoning com. 1990-92, co-chmn. subcom. hazardous waste and mcpl. liability 1984-86, chmn. subcom. on land use litigation and damages 1986-88). Office: Phillips McCullough 2025 1st Ave # 1130 Seattle WA 98121-2100

HILL, GARY, video artist; b. Santa Monica, Calif., Apr. 4, 1951. Student, Art Students League, Woodstock, 1969. founder, dir. Open Studio Video, Tarrytown, N.Y., 1977-78; artist-in-residence Exptl. TV Ctr., Binghamton, N.Y., 1975-77, Portable Channel, Rochester, N.Y., 1978, Sony Corp., Hon. Atsugi, Japan, 1985, Chgo. Art Inst., 1986, Calif. Inst. Arts, Valencia, 1987, Hopital Ephémère, Paris, 1991; vis. assoc. prof. Ctr. Media, SUNY, Buffalo, 1979-80; vis. prof. art Bard Coll., Annandale-on-Hudson, N.Y., 1983; art faculty Cornish Coll. Arts, Seattle, 1985-92. One person shows include Mus. Modern Art, N.Y.C., 1980, 90, Whitney Mus. Am. Art, N.Y.C., 1983, Galerie des Archives, Paris, 1990, 91, Galerie Huset-Glyptotek Mus. Mus., Copenhagen & YYZ Artist's Outlet, Toronto, 1990, OCO Espace d'art contemporain, Paris, 1991, Watari Mus. Contemporary Art, Tokyo, 1992, Mus. Modern Art, Oxford, Eng., 1993, Mus. Contemporary Art, L.A., 1994, Mus. Contemporary Art, Chgo., 1994, Fundaicó La Caixa, Barcelona, Spain, Busch-Reisinger Mus., Harvard U. Art Mus, Cambridge, Mass., 1995, Moderna Museet, Stockholm, 1995, Inst. Contemporary Art, Phila., 1996, Kunst-und Ausstellungshalle der Bundesrepublik Deutschland (Forum), Bonn, Germany, 1996, Centro Cultural Banco do Brazil, Rio de Janeiro, 1997, Musée d'Art Contemporain de Montréal, Can., 1998, Donald Young Gallery, Seattle, 1998, Museu d'Art Contemporani, Barcelona, Spain, 1998, others; exhibited in group shows Am. Ctr., Paris, 1983, Whitney Mus. Am. Art, N.Y., 1986, St. Gervais, Geneva, 2d Seminar on Internat. Video, 1987, ELAC Art Contemporain, Lyon, France, 1988, Biennial Exhbn., Whitney Mus. Am. Art, 1991, 93, Performing Objects, Inst. Contemporary Art, Boston, 1992, Cocido y Crudo, Centro Reina Sofia, Madrid, 1994, Light Into Art, Contemporary Arts Ctr., Cin., 1994, Facts and Figures, Lannan Found., L.A., 1994, Multiplas Dimensoes, Centro Cultural de Belem, Lisbon, Portugal, 1994, Beeld, Mus van Hedendaagse Kunst, Ghent, Belgium, 1994, Crossings, Kunsthalle Wien, Austria, 1998, Voices, Witte de with Rotterdam, The Netherlands, 1998; author: Primarily Speaking, 1981-83, Whitney Mus. Am. Art, 1983, Primarily Speaking Communications, 1988, And if the Right Hand did not Know What the Left Hand is Doing, Illuminating Video, 1990, Unspeakable Images, Camera Obscura, 1991, Finnish Nat. Gallery, Helsinki, Finland, 1995, Mus. Modern Art, N.Y.C., 1995, Albert Knox Gallery, Buffalo, 1996, World Wide Video Festival, Amsterdam, The Netherlands, 1997. Recipient prize ARTEC 91 Internat. Biennale, Nagoya, Japan, 1991; Rockefeller Intercult Media Arts fellow, 1989-90, Guggenheim fellow, 1990; recipient JOhn D. and Catherine T. MacArthur grant. Office: Donald Young Gallery 933 W Washington Blvd Chicago IL 60607-2218*

HILL, GARY D., lawyer; b. Eugene, Oreg., Apr. 7, 1952; s. Virgil R. and Doris H.; m. Patricia L. Hill, July 10, 1976. BA, Linfield Coll.,

McMinnville, Oreg., 1974; JD, Northwestern Sch. of Law, Portland, 1981. Bar: Oreg. 1982. News anchor KPTV, Portland, Oreg., 1976-92; pvt. practice Portland, Oreg., 1981-84, 88-92; atty. Hergert & Assocs., Oregon City, Oreg., 1992—. Vol. Oreg. Rep. Party, Portland, 1996, Oregon Dole-Kemp presdl. campaign, 1996. Recipient Am. Juris Prudence award, Lawyers Coop. Pub. Co., 1981; recognized for participation in CLE Oreg. State Bar, 1985, 91. Mem. Oreg. State Bar Assn. (law related edn. com. 1996—, chair-elect small firm and sole practitioner sect. 1997-98, Juvenile and Family Law Sect. 1992—, chair 1998-99), Oreg. Assn. of Family Law Practitioners. Avocations: golf, sailing, fishing. Office: Hergert & Assocs 1001 Molalla Ave Ste 201 Oregon City OR 97045-3768

HILL, GEORGE JAMES, physician, educator; b. Cedar Rapids, Iowa, Oct. 7, 1932; s. Gerald Leslie and Essie Mae (Thompson) H.; m. Helene Zimmermann, July 16, 1960; children: James Warren, David Hedgcock, Sarah, Helena Rundall. A.B., Yale U., 1953; M.D., Harvard U., 1957; MA, Rutgers U., 1999. Intern N.Y. Hosp., 1957-58; fellow and resident in surgery Peter Bent Brigham hosp. and Harvard Med. Sch., 1958-61, 63-66; clin. assoc. NIH, Bethesda, Md., 1961-63; instr. surgery U. Colo., 1966-67, asst. prof., 1967-72, asso. prof., 1972-73; prof. Washington U., 1973-76; prof., chmn. Marshall U., 1976-81; prof., dir. surg. oncology U. of Medicine and Dentistry of N.J.-N.J. Med. Sch., Newark, 1981-96; prof. emeritus U. of Medicine and Dentistry of N.J. - N.J. Med. Sch., Newark, 1997—; Am. Cancer Soc. prof. clin. oncology U. Medicine and Dentistry N.J.-N.J. Med. Sch., Newark, 1989-92; pres. faculty N.J. Med. Sch., Newark, 1991-92; clin. prof. surgery Uniformed Svcs. U. of the Health Scis., Bethesda, Md., 1989—; acting pres. Sterling Coll., Craftsbury Common, Vt., 1996; rsch. coord. St. Barnabas Med. Ctr., Livingston, N.J., 1997—; chmn. clin. cancer edn. com. Nat. Cancer Inst., 1978-80; vis. fellow in molecular biology Princton U., 1988. Author: Leprosy in Five Young Men, 1970, paperback edit., 1979, Outpatient Surgery, 1973, 3d edit., 1988, Clinical Oncology, 1977; contbr. articles to med. jours. Pres. Tri-State Area coun. Boy Scouts Am., Huntington, W.Va., 1980-82, v.p. Essex coun., 1983-89, commr., 1998, 1998, commr. No. N.J. Coun., 1998-99, chmn. nat. health careers exploring com., 1987-92; pres. W.Va. divsn. Am. Cancer Soc., 1980-81, pres. N.J. divsn., 1987-89; pres. Am. Assn. Cancer Edn., 1985-86; mem. N. J. State Commn. on Cancer Rsch., 1983-84; trustee Frost Valley YMCA, 1986—, Sterling Coll., Craftsbury Common, Vt., 1990—; nat. dir.-at-large Am. Cancer Soc., 1989-96, mem. nat. exec. com., 1990-91, hon. life mem., 1996—; vestry Ch. of the Holy Innocents, 1994-96. Capt. M.C., USNR; active duty USN, 1990-91, ret., 1992. Recipient Civic Actions medal Republic South Vietnam, 1972, Lederle Med. Faculty award, 1970, Silver Beaver award Boy Scouts Am., 1981, Silver Antelope award, 1998, Am. Cancer Soc. Nat. Divisional award, St. George medal, 1992, Gorgas medal Assn. Mil. Surgeons U.S., 1991, Outstanding Svc. medal Uniformed Svcs. U. Health Scis., 1992, Meritorious Svc. medal USN, 1993, Nat. William Spurgeon III award Boy Scouts Am., 1994; named Jerseyan of Week, Newark Star Ledger, 1987, 93; Damon Runyon fellow, 1973-76. Mem. ACS (mem. com. on cancer 1987-93), Acad. Medicine N.J. (pres. 1992-93), Soc. Univ. Surgeons, Soc. Surg. Oncology (exec. coun. 1985-88), Ctrl. Surg. Assn., Am. Assn. Cancer Edn. (pres. 1985-86, Edwards medal 1994), Am. Assn. Cancer Rsch., Essex County Med. Soc. (pres. 1995-96), Med. Soc. N.J. (chmn. com. cancer control 1985-94, sec. 1995-96), AAUP (pres. chpt. 1988-89), SAR (chpt. sec. 1999—), Harvard Club (N.Y.C. and Boston), Univ. Club (Denver), Army and Navy Club, Explorers Club, Soc. Mayflower Descs., Order of Founders and Patriots of Am., Soc. of Colonial Wars, Yale Club of Ctrl. N.J. (pres. 1991-93), Sigma Xi (chpt. pres. 1986-87), Alpha Omega Alpha. Republican. Episcopalian. Office: St Barnabas Med Ctr 94 Old Short Hills Rd Livingston NJ 07039-5672

HILL, GEORGE RICHARD, chemistry educator; b. Ogden, Utah, Nov. 24, 1921; s. George Richard and Elizabeth (McKay) H.; m. Melba Parker, Aug. 25, 1941; children: George Richard IV, Margaret Hill Nielson, Robert Parker, Carolyn Hill Allen, Susan Hill Mann, Nancy Hill Bauman, David Parker. AB in Chemistry, Brigham Young U., 1942, DSc (hon.), 1980; PhD in Phys. and Inorganic Chemistry, Cornell U., 1946. Chemist Am. Smelting & Refining Co., 1937-42; asst. part-time instr. Cornell U., Ithaca, N.Y., 1942-46; mem. faculty U. Utah, Salt Lake City, 1946-72, prof. chemistry, 1950-72, chmn. fuels engring., 1951-65, dean Coll. Mines and Mineral Industries, 1966-72, Envirotech. endowed prof., 1977-82, Eimco endowed prof., 1982—; project dir. Air Force Combustion Rs.h, 1952-57; dir. Office Coal Rsch., Dept. Interior, Washington, 1972-73; dept. dir. fossil fuels Electric Power Research Inst., Palo Alto, Calif., 1973-77; dir. fossil fuel power plants dept. Electric Power Rsch. Inst., Palo Alto, Calif., 1976-77; project dir. Air Force Office Sci. Rsch., 1956-61, Equity Oil Shale Rsch.h, 1961; mem. NRC com. Mineral and Energy Resources, 1976-81; mem. fossil energy adv. com. Dept. Energy, 1977—; vice chmn. Utah Coun. Energy Conservation and Devel., 1978-83; chmn. Utah Task Force on Power Plant Siting, 1978; chmn. editorial com. NRC, 1977-81; com. chmn. Chemistry of Coal Utilization, 1981; mem. Nat. Coal Coun., 1985—. Contbr. papers on kinetics of coal conversion, oil shale, corrosion, catalysis. Mem. exec. bd. region XII Boy Scouts Am., 1961; chmn. Explorer activities sect. 6, 1959-61; mem. Explorer com. nat. exec. bd. 1965-72; mem. quorum of the 70 area presidency Mormon Ch., 1987-92; bd. dirs. Deseret Gymnasium, 1967. Recipient Silver Beaver, Silver Antelope and Silver Buffalo awards, Boy Scouts Am.; Disting. Svc. award Utah Petroleum Coun., 1968, Outstanding Profl. Engr. award Utah Engring. Coun., 1970. Fellow Nat. Acad. Engring., Am. Inst. Chemists; mem. AAAS, AIME, Am. Chem. Soc. (Utah award Salt Lake sect. 1969, Henry H. Storch award 1971), Am. Inst. Chem. Engrs., Nat. Coal Council, Nat. Acad. Eng., Sigma Xi, Phi Kappa Phi, Sigma Pi Sigma, Alpha Phi Omega. Home: 241 N Vine St Apt 1203W Salt Lake City UT 84103-1938 *There's no limit to the amount of good you can do if you don't care who gets the credit.*

HILL, GEORGE ROY, film director; b. Mpls., Dec. 20; s. George Roy and Helen Frances (Owens) H.; m. Louisa Horton, Apr. 7, 1951. B.A., Yale U.; B of Lit., Trinity Coll., Dublin, Ireland. Acting debut: (play) The Devil's Disciple, Dublin, 1948; other stage appearances include The Creditors, 1950; toured with Margaret Webster's Shakespeare Repertory Co.; writer, actor: (teleplay) My Brother's Keeper, 1953; writer, producer, dir.: (teleplay) Judgement at Nuremberg, 1957; dir.: (Broadway plays) Look Homeward, Angel, 1957, The Gang's All Here, Period of Adjustment, Greenwillow, 1960, Henry, Sweet Henry, 1967, (off-Broadway show) Moon on a Rainbow Shawl, 1962, (films) Period of Adjustment, 1962, Toys in the Attic, 1963, The World of Henry Orient, 1964, Hawaii, 1966, Thoroughly Modern Millie, 1967, Butch Cassidy and the Sundance Kid, 1969, Slaughterhouse-Five, 1972, The Sting, 1973, The Great Waldo Pepper, 1975, Slap Shot, 1977, A Little Romance, 1979, The World According to Garp, 1982, The Little Drummer Girl, 1984, Funny Farm, 1988. Served as pilot USMC, World War II and Korean War. Recipient Acad. award for best dir. of The Sting, 1973; Emmy award nominations for A Night to Remember, The Helen Morgan Story, Child of Our Time; Acad. award nomination for Butch Cassidy and the Sundance Kid, 1969; Cannes Internat. Film Festival Jury Prize for Slaughterhouse Five, 1972. Office: Pan Arts Prodns 59 E 54th St Rm 73 New York NY 10022-4211

HILL, GRACE LUCILE GARRISON, education educator, consultant; b. Gastonia, N.C., Sept. 26, 1930; d. William Moffatt and Lillian Tallulah (Tatum) Garrison; m. Leo Howard Hill, July 24, 1954; children: Lillian Lucile, Leo Howard Jr., David Garrison. BA, Erskine Coll., 1952; MA, Furman U., 1966; PhD, U. S.C., 1980. Lic. sch. psychologist, S.C. Tchr. Bible, Clinton (S.C.) Pub. Schs., 1952-53; tchr. English Parker High Sch., Greenville, S.C., 1953-55; elem. tchr. Augusta Circle Sch., Greenville, 1955-57; tchr. homebound children Greenville County Sch. Dist., Greenville, 1961-64, psychologist, 1966-77; adj. prof. grad. studies in edn. Furman U., Greenville, 1977—, U. S.C., Columbia, 1982—; ednl. cons. Ednl. Diagnostic Svcs., Greenville, 1980—; exec. dir. Camperdown Acad., Greenville, 1986-87; cons. learning disability program Erskine Coll., Due West, S.C., 1978—. Contbr. articles to profl. jours. Pres. Lake Forest PTA, Greenville, 1970-71; pres. of Women A.R. Presbyn. Ch., Greenville, 1973-75, adult Bible tchr., 1978—; sec. bd. trustees Erskine Coll., 1982-88; bd. dirs. Children's Bur. S.C., Columbia, 1981-87, YWCA, Greenville, 1984-88; bd. advisors for adoption S.C. Dept. Social Svcs., Columbia, 1987-92. Recipient Order of the Jessamine, Greenville News award, 1994-95; Disting. Lectr Erskine Coll., 1999. Mem. Am. Edn. Rsch. Assn. (southeastern rep. 1982-84, editor newspaper for SIG group 1982-83), Jean Piaget Soc., Assn. for Supervision and Curriculum Devel., Orton Dyslexia Soc. (pres. Carolinas br. 1984-88), Ea. Ednl. Rsch. Assn., S.C. Psychol. Assn., Order of the Jessamine, 21st Century Living Initiative, Delta Kappa Gamma. Democrat. Avocations: travel, writing. Home and Office: 28 Montrose Dr Greenville SC 29607-3034 *Where did we get the idea that for children to succeed we must set them up to fail? Poverty, crime and abuse beget poverty, crime and abuse—not success and achievement . When will America wake up?.*

HILL, GRAHAM RODERICK, librarian; b. Richmond, Surrey, Eng., Apr. 4, 1946; s. Herbert Edgar and Elsie (Davies) H.; m. Penelope Mary Potts, Aug. 31, 1968; 1 child, Lindsay. B.A., U. Newcastle-on-Tyne, 1968; M.A., U. Lancaster, 1969; M.L.S., U. Western Ont., 1970. With Univ. Libraries, McMaster U., Hamilton, Ont., Can., 1971—; assoc. univ. librarian Univ. Libraries, McMaster U., 1977-79, univ. librarian, 1979—. Chmn. bd. govs. Hillfield-Strathallan Coll., 1989-91. Recipient Can. Assn. Rsch. Librs. award for disting. svc. to rsch. librarianship, 1998 and various grants. Mem. Assn. Research Libraries (bd. dirs. 1983-86), Can. Assn. Research Libraries (pres. 1984-86), Ont. Council Univ. Libraries (chmn. 1984-86). Home: 15 Forestview Dr, Dundas, ON Canada L9H 6M9 Office: McMaster U, 1280 Main St W, Hamilton, ON Canada L8S 4L6

HILL, GRANT, professional basketball player; b. Dallas, Oct. 5, 1972; s. Calvin and Janet Hill. BA in History, Duke U., 1994. Forward Detroit Pistons, 1994—. Named to Dream Team II U.S. Olympic Team, 1996, Corookie of Yr., 1994. Office: Detroit Pistons Two Championship Dr Auburn Hills MI 48326*

HILL, GREG, newspaper bureau chief. San Francisco bur. chief Wall St. Jour. Office: Wall St Jour 201 California St Ste 1350 San Francisco CA 94111-5015*

HILL, HAROLD NELSON, JR., lawyer; b. Houston, Apr. 26, 1930; s. Harold Nelson and Emolyn Eloise (Geeslin) H.; m. Betty Jane Fell, Aug. 16, 1952; children: Douglas, Nancy. B.S. in Commerce, Washington and Lee U., Lexington, Va., 1952; JD, Washington & Lee U., 1981; LL.B., Emory U., 1957, JD, 1986. Bar: Ga. 1957. Assoc., then partner firm Gambrell, Harlan, Russell, Moye & Richardson, 1957-66; asst. atty. gen. Ga., 1966-68; exec. asst. atty. gen., 1968-72; partner firm Jones, Bird & Howell, 1972-74; assoc. justice Supreme Ct. Ga., 1975-82, chief justice, 1982-86; ptnr. Hurt, Richardson, Garner, Todd & Cadenhead, Atlanta, 1986-92, Judicial Resolutions Inc., Atlanta, 1993-94; of counsel Long, Aldridge & Norman, Atlanta, 1994-95. Served with AUS, 1952-54. Fellow Am. Bar Found.; Mem. Am. Law Inst., State Bar Ga., Lawyers Club Atlanta, Old War Horse Lawyers Club. Methodist.

HILL, HELEN MARGUERITE THACKER, academic administrator; b. Pike County, Ky., Feb. 16, 1923; d. Arvle and Ellen (Turner) Thacker; m. Wallace Charles Hill, Nov. 25, 1959 (dec. Oct. 18, 1968). BA, U. Ky., 1944, MA, 1953; student, U. Fla., 1956; EdD, Okla. State U., 1970; post doctoral, U. Ky., 1973, 76. Cert. secondary tchr., Ky. Instr. Pike County Schs., Pikeville, Ky., 1944-53; counselor U. Houston, 1956-59; dir. counseling, women's residence halls Purdue U., Lafayette, Ind., 1959-61; asst. dean of women Okla. State U., Stillwater, 1962-66; dean of women W.V. Inst. Tech., Montgomery, W.V., 1970-72, assoc. dean students, 1972-73; dir. commuter student affairs U. Mass., Amherst, 1973-75; prof., counselor Ea. Ky. U., Richmond, 1976; clin. psychologist Logan-Mingo Area Mental Health, Inc., Williamson, W.V., 1976-78; assoc. dean student Ga. Coll., Milledgeville, 1978-82, dir. student support svcs., 1982—; bd. Ga. Rehab. Svcs., Atlanta, 1996—. Named to U. Ky. Coll. Edn. Hall of Fame, 1998. Mem. Nat. Rehab. Assn., Ga. Rehab. Assn., Ga. Assn. Women Deans, Counselors and Adminstrns. (treas. 1994-96), Order of Omega, Kappa Delta Phi, Phi Delta Kappa. Avocations: sewing, antique collecing. Home: 601 W Charlton St Milledgeville GA 31061-2302

HILL, HENRY ALLEN, physicist, educator; b. Port Arthur, Tex., Nov. 25, 1933; s. Douglas and Florence Hill. B.S., U. Houston, 1953; M.S., U. Minn., 1956, Ph.D., 1957; M.A. (hon.), Wesleyan U., 1966. Research asst. U. Houston, 1952-53; teaching asst. U. Minn., 1953-54, research asst., 1954-57; research assoc. Princeton U., 1957-58, instr., then asst. prof., 1958-64; assoc. prof. Wesleyan U., Middletown, Conn., 1964-66; prof. physics Wesleyan U., 1966-74, chmn. dept., 1969-71; prof. physics U. Ariz., Tucson, 1966-95, prof. emeritus, 1995—; chmn. bd. Zetetic Inst., 1992—; researcher on nuclear physics, relativity, astrophysics, and optics. Contbr. articles to profl. jours. Sloan fellow, 1966-68. Fellow Am. Phys. Soc.; mem. AAAS, Am. Astron. Soc., Optical Soc. Am., Am. Geophys. Union. Office: Zetetic Inst 1665 E 18th St Ste 206 Tucson AZ 85719-6809

HILL, HENRY CARL, college administrator; b. Buckholts, Tex., Sept. 15, 1934; s. Henry C. and Athie (Kirk) H.; m. Jimmye Rae Colburn, Oct. 10, 1959; children: Stephen, Cathryn, Henry C. II. BS, Tex. A&M U., 1956; MBA, Baylor U., 1971; PhD, Tex. A&M U., 1993. Commd. 2d lt. USAF, 1956, advanced through grades to col., 1977, served as pilot, 1956-84; comdr. 2nd Comm. Squadron USAF, Denver, 1978-81; comdr., prof. aerospace studies Det 805 Tex. A&M U., College Station, 1981-84; ret. USAF, 1984; CEO pvt. business, College Station, Tex., 1984-86; instr. Blinn Coll., College Station, 1986-87, dir., 1987-93, assoc. v.p., 1993-95; assoc. v.p. Blinn Coll., Brazos County, 1995—. Mem. Tex. Jr. Coll. Tchrs. Assn., Air Force Assn. (pres., sec. Chpt. 292 1985-86), Air Force Assn. Tex. (parliamentarian 1989-95, exec. v.p. 1995-97, pres. 1997-99, past pres. 1999—). Office: Blinn Coll PO Box 6030 2520 E Villa Maria Rd Bryan TX 77805-6030

HILL, HUGH FRANCIS, III, lawyer, physician; b. Roanoke, Va., Mar. 15, 1949; s. Hugh Francis Jr. and Beatrice (Wray) H.; m. Sandra I. Read, Aug. 31, 1974; children: Hugh F. IV, Andrea Read. BS, Washington and Lee U., 1971; MD, Med. Coll. Va., 1975; JD, U. Va., 1979. Bar: Va. 1980, D.C. 1981. Intern PG Y-1 St. Louis U. Med. Ctr.; pvt. practice Washington, 1980—; pres. Legal Medicine Ctr., Bethesda, Md., 1992—; med. dir. Montgomery Hospice, Md., 1996-98, consulting med. dir., 1998—; instr. dept. emergency medicine Johns Hopkins U., Washington, 1996—; internat. cons. Health Care Fin. Adminstrn., 1999—. Author: Pennsylvania Medical Malpractice, 1988; editor Emergency Dept. Law, 1989-91; contbr. chpts. to books. Recipient President's award Am. Coll. Legal Medicine, 1988. Fellow Am. Coll. Emergency Physicians, Am. Bd. Legal Medicine, Am. Bd. Emergency Medicine (examiner), Nat. Health Lawyers Assn. Democrat. Office: 6915 Radnor Rd Bethesda MD 20817-6328

HILL, HULENE DIAN, accountant; b. Salisbury, N.C., Mar. 17, 1948; d. Hulon Clive and Marie Cordelia (Plyler) H.; m. Ed Adkins; 1 child, Daren Steven Starnes. BS in Acctg., U. N.C., Charlotte, 1971. CPA, N.C. Staff acct. Peat, Marwick Mitchell & Co., Charlotte, 1971-74; sr. tax acct. Arthur Andersen & Co., Charlotte, 1974-76; tax mgr. Ernst & Young (formerly Clarkson, Harden & Gantt), Columbia, 1976-79; ptnr. Deloitte & Touche, Charlotte, 1979-92; v.p. tax Hodge, Steward & Co., P.A., Raleigh, N.C., 1992—. Recipient Hon. Mention as Bus. Woman of Yr. Shearson Lehman and Queens Coll., 1986, 89, 90, 91; named Acct. of Yr. Acad. Women Achievers YWCA, 1985. Mem. AICPA, Women Execs. (pres. 1987-88), Univ. N.C. Charlotte Athletic Found. (v.p. 1986-87), U. N.C. Charlotte Alumni Assn. (pres. 1985-86), Beta Alpha Psi (Acct. of Yr. U. N.C. chpt. 1985). Republican. Roman Catholic. Avocations: bridge, travel, reading. Home: 204 Rosehaven Dr Raleigh NC 27609-3880 Office: PO Box 41168 Raleigh NC 27629-1168

HILL, I. KATHRYN, medical certification agency executive; b. Phila., Apr. 6, 1950; d. Joseph Anthony and Irma Lorraine (Walther) Piehs; m. John Patrick McElwain, May 17, 1969 (div. Aug. 1979); children: John Charles, Brian Patrick; m. David Terence Hill, Sept. 27, 1980. BA, Widener Coll., 1979; MEd, Temple U., 1982. Cert. secondary tchr., Pa. Translator, transcriber Sci-Tech, Inc., Phila., 1970-77; tchr. West Chester (Pa.) East High Sch., 1978, Garnet Valley Jr.-Sr. High Sch., Concordville, Pa., 1979; asst. to dir. Nat. Bd. Med. Examiners, Phila., 1980-81, evaluation program asst., 1981-82, evaluation program assoc., 1982-84, sr. program assoc., 1984-85; asst. exec. v.p. Fedn. State Med. Bds., Ft. Worth, 1985-86, asst. exec. v.p., exec. dir. of the examination bd., 1986-94, sr. v.p., exec. dir. examination bd., 1995-96; exec. dir. Nat. Commn. on Cert. of Physician Assts., Atlanta, 1996—. Editor: FLEX/SPEX Guidelines, 1985, 87, 90, FLEX/SPEX Info. Bull., 1987-94; co-editor Fedn. Exchange, 1986-95; contbr. articles to profl. jours. Mem. Am. Ednl. Rsch. Assn., Nat. Coun. on Measurement in Edn., Assn. of Am. Med. Colls. Republican. Lutheran. Office: NCCPA 157 Technology Pkwy Ste 800 Norcross GA 30092

HILL, ISABEL THIGPEN, urban planner; b. Montgomery, Ala., Sept. 9, 1951; d. Wiley Croom and Sarah Isabel (Dunn) H.; m. James David Sweeny, Jan. 11, 1992; 1 child, Anna Reese. BA, Hollins Coll., 1973; MA, George Washington U., 1982. Survey worker Va. Historic Landmarks Commn., Richmond, 1973; staff asst. U.S. Ho. Reps., Washington, 1974-76; rsch. specialist NEH, Washington, 1976; historian Historic Am. Engring. Record, Washington, 1977-83; program analyst N.Y. State Coun. Arts, N.Y.C., 1984-85; cmty. planner N.Y.C. Dept. Housing Preservation & Devel., 1985-87; assoc. city planner N.Y.C. Dept. City Planning, 1987-93; exec. dir. Southwest Bklyn. Indsl. Devel. Corp., 1994-95; econ. devel. urban planning cons. PDS Assocs., Bklyn., 1993—; bd. dirs. Nat. Affordable Housing Network, Econ. Devel. Assistance Consortium; project advisor Bklyn. Hist. Soc., 1995—; mem. New Day Films. Producer, dir. (film) Made In Brooklyn, 1993. Mcpl. Art Soc. fellow, 1989. Mem. Am. Planning Assn., Nat. Trust Historic Preservation, Women Make Movies, Assn. Independent Video and Filmmakers, Architects, Designers, Planners for Social Responsibility. Office: PDS Assocs 562 4th St Brooklyn NY 11215-3009

HILL, JACK, motion picture director, writer, educator; b. Oxnard, Calif., Jan. 28, 1933; s. Roland E. and Mildred (Pannill) H.; m. Estelle Chamberlin; children: Mark, Dorian, Amanda; m. Elke Baumgarten, Nov. 26, 1973. BA, UCLA, 1963. Freelance motion picture writer and dir. L.A., 1965—; instr. Columbia Coll., L.A., 1980—. Writer, dir. (film) Spider Baby, 1964, Pit Stop, 1967, The Big Bird Cage, 1971, Coffy, 1972, Foxy Brown, 1973, The Swinging Cheerleaders, 1974, dir. (film) The Big Doll House, 1970, Switchblade Sisters, 1975; writer, dir., producer (film) Sorceress, 1981; writer (film) City on Fire, 1978, The Bees, 1978, Death Ship, 1979. Home: 1445 N Fairfax Ave # 105 West Hollywood CA 90046-3924

HILL, JAMES CLINKSCALES, federal judge; b. Darlington, S.C., Jan. 8, 1924; s. Albert Michael and Alberta (Clinkscales) H.; m. Mary Cornelia Black, June 7, 1946; children: James Clinkscales, Albert Michael. BS in Commerce, U. S.C., 1948; JD, Emory U., 1948. Bar: Ga. 1948, U.S. Supreme Ct. 1969. Assoc. Gambrell, Russell, Killorin & Forbes, Atlanta, 1948-55, ptnr., 1955-63; ptnr. Hurt, Hill & Richardson, Atlanta, 1963-74; judge U.S. Dist. Ct. (no. dist.) Ga., 1974-76, U.S. Cir. Ct. (5th cir.), Atlanta, 1976-81, U.S. Cir. Ct. (11th cir.), Atlanta, 1981-89; sr. U.S. cir. judge U.S. Ct. Appeals, Atlanta, 1989—; past chmn. com. on appellate ednl. programs Fed. Jud. Ctr.; former mem. com. on intercir. assignments Jud. Conf. U.S. With USAAF, 1943-45. Fellow ACTL, Am. Bar Found. (life); m. ABA, Am. Law Inst., World Assn. Judges, State Bar Ga., Atlanta Bar Assn., Am. Judicature Soc., Lawyers Club Atlanta (life), Old War Horse Lawyers. Republican. Baptist. Office: US Ct Appeals PO Box 52598 Jacksonville FL 32201-2598

HILL, JAMES EDWARD, insurance company executive; b. Chgo., Mar. 3, 1926; s. George and Mary Luella (Hutchens) H.; m. Jessie Mae Birmingham, Jan. 29, 1949; children: James R. (dec.), Ellen M. Student Denver U., 1947, MS in Fin. Svcs., Am. Coll., Bryn Mawr, Pa., 1980. CLU; chartered fin. cons.; cert. fin. planner. Office mgr., purchasing agt., acct. Steve Tojek Co., Milw., 1948-54; office mgr., acct. Oreg. Athletic Equipment Co., Portland, 1954-56; spl. agt. Prudential Ins. Co., Portland, 1956-58, div. mgr., 1958-70; gen. agt. Gt. Am. Res. Ins. Co., Portland, 1970—; v.p. Robert A. Amey Co. Inc., mfrs. reps., 1971-75; pres. Diversified Plans, Inc., 1979-89, v.p., 1989-96, pres., 1996—. V.p. Multnomah County Young Republicans, 1957-58; vice chmn. Washington County Parks Adv. Bd., 1978, chmn., 1979-83; local sch. committeeman Beaverton, Or. Sch. Dist., 1993 (elected), instr. Life Underwriter Tng. Coun.; mem. task force for curriculum and instrn. Oreg. Sch. Dist., Beaverton; dir. Citizens for Pub. Edn. Inc., 1991—; bd. dirs. Christian Heritage Month Assn., 1997—; treas. Evergreen Presbyn. Ch., 1993—, elder, 1997—. With U.S. Army, 1944-47. Recipient Edgar M. Kelly award Prudential, 1967. Mem. Oreg. Life Underwriters Assn. (edn. chmn. 1981-82, pres.-elect 1982-83, pres. 1983-84), Portland Life Underwriters Assn. (dir. 1978-80, chmn. edn. com. 1978-80, pres. 1980-81, Am. Soc. C.L.U.s (C.L.U. of Yr. award Portland chpt.; instr.), Am. Family Assn. (Oreg. state dir. 1993—). Home and Office: 12980 NW Saltzman Ct Portland OR 97229-4668

HILL, JAMES SCOTT, lawyer; b. Boston, Mar. 21, 1924; s. Benjamin B. and Dorothy (Scott) H.; m. Sally C. Foss, June 28, 1945; children: Richard B., Chessye F., Cynthia C., Michael O. B.A. magna cum laude, Williams Coll., 1947; JD, Columbia U., 1949. Bar: N.Y. 1949, N.J. 1958. Assoc. Baldwin, Todd & Lefferts, N.Y.C., 1949-50; corp. sec., atty. Johnson & Johnson, N.J., 1950-66; v.p., sec., gen. counsel Celanese Corp., N.Y.C., 1966-74; v.p., gen. counsel, dir. Liggett & Myers, Durham, N.C., 1974-76; v.p. law and govt. affairs CBS Inc., N.Y.C., 1976-78; group pres. law and regulatory affairs Am. Hosp. Supply Corp., Evanston, Ill., 1978-81; of counsel Shanley & Fisher, 1981-88, Smith, Stratton, Wise, Heher & Brennan, Princeton, N.J., 1988—; judge Princeton (N.J.) Twp., 1959-65. Treas. N.J. Republican Fin. com., 1965-70; trustee John Seward Johnson Sr. Charitable Trusts, Princeton Med. Ctr., N.J. State Aquarium, Trinity Counselling Svc., Princeton, N.J.; chmn. Williams Coll. Devel. Coun.; chmn. Boyden Soc.-Deerfield Acad.; bd. dirs. Friends of Channel 13; mem. exec. com. Friends of the Inst. for Advanced Study, Princeton. Served to 1st lt. USAAF, 1943-46. Fellow Am. Coll. Trust and Estate Counsel (mem. charitable planning and exempt orgn. com.); mem. Assn. Gen. Counsel, Nassau Club (trustee 1983—), Met. Club (Washington), Princeton Club (N.Y.C.), Mid-Ocean Club (Bermuda), Bedens Brook Club (bd. govs. 1995—), Springdale Club, Nassau Club (trustee 1993-96), Jasna Polana Golf Club (Princeton), Gasparilla Club (Boca Grande, Fla.), Chi Psi. Republican. Episcopalian (warden). Home: 155 Lambert Dr Princeton NJ 08540-2306 Winter Home: PO Box 1767 Boca Grande FL 33921-1767 Office: 600 College Rd E Princeton NJ 08540-6636

HILL, JAMES STANLEY, computer consulting company executive; b. Merrickville, Ont., Can., July 24, 1914; m. Doris C. Huelster, 1938; children: George, Janice, Mary, Beverly, Richard. With Minn. Mut. Life Ins. Co., 1930-69, sr. v.p., 1966-69; pres. Digiplan, Inc., White Bear Lake, Minn., 1969—, Red Oak Press, 1994-98; bd. dirs., chmn. audit com. Hadco Inc., 1981-98; pub. spkr., 1994—. Author: Confessions of an 80 Year Old Boy, 1994, Almost Immortal, 1996. Treas. Minn. State H.S. Math. League, St. Paul Area Coun. of Chs. Found.; bd. dirs. United Hosp. Fellow Soc. Actuaries (bd. govs., v.p.). Home and Office: Digiplan Inc 5011 Lake Ave Apt 205 Saint Paul MN 55110-2655 *To live each day free from guilt, worry and fear, with opportunities to serve and love others and to exercise both mind and body vigorously—with these goals (and it's taken me over 60 years to come even close), the other things (money, recognition, love from others, and appreciation) come automatically. Christ and others have said it better, but the important thing is: It Works.*

HILL, J(AMES) TOMILSON, investment banker; b. Westbury, N.Y., May 24, 1948; s. James Tomilson Jr. and Dorothy H. (Kutcher) H.; m. Janine A. Wolf, Feb. 2, 1980; children: Margot Langdon, Astrid Tomilson. BA, Harvard U., 1970, MBA, 1973. Vice pres. mergers and acquisitions 1st Boston Corp., N.Y.C., 1973-79; sr. v.p. Smith Barney, Harris Upham & Co. Inc., N.Y.C., 1979-82; mng. dir., dir. mergers and acquisitions, co-head investment banking div. Shearson Lehman Bros. Inc., N.Y.C., 1982-90; vice-chmn., co-chief exec. officer Lehman Bros., N.Y.C., 1990-93; also bd. dirs. Shearson Lehman Bros. Holdings, Inc., co-pres., co-chief operating officer, 1993; co-chief exec. officer Lehman Bros., 1993, Shearson Lehman Bros., 1993, SLB Asset Mgmt., 1993; gen. ptnr. and mem. investment and mgmt. com. Blackstone Group, N.Y.C., 1993—; pres., CEO Blackstone Alternative Asset Mgmt., 1995—. Contbr. articles to profl. pubs. Bd. dirs. N.Y.C. Econ. Devel. Corp., Hirshhorn Mus. and Sculpture Garden, Whitney Mus. Am. Art, Lincoln Ctr. Theater, Milton Acad., Nightingale-Bamford Sch. Mem. Coun. Fgn. Rels., Piping Rock Club, Meadow Brook Club, Links Club, River Club. Home: 4 E 72nd St New York NY 10021-4144 Office: Blackstone Group 345 Park Ave Ste 3101 New York NY 10154-0004

HILL, JAMES WARREN, college dean; b. Nashville, Nov. 1, 1951; s. James Warren Hill Sr. and Vernelle B. Hickerson; m. Caffie Hill; children: Phlilip, Jamie. BS, Ctrl. Mo. State U., 1975; M Counseling Edn., U. Mo., Kansas City, 1980, EdS, 1982. Coord. fin. aid U. Mo., Kansas City, 1976-

87; assoc. dir. fin. aid U. Wis., Milw., 1987-92, asst. dean students, 1992-94, assoc. dean of students, 1994-96, dean of students, 1996—. Sec. bd. dirs. Future Milw. Inc., 1997—, Wis. Cmty. Fund., Madison, 1996-98; bd. dirs. AChoice, Milw., 1996—; mem. Milw. Forum, 1994—. Mem. NAACP, NASPA, WCPA. Avocations: jogging, music. E-mail: jimhill@csd.uwm.edu. Office: U Wis-Milw PO Box 413 Milwaukee WI 53201

HILL, JAY, member of parliament; b. Ft. St. John, B.C., Can., 1952; m. Carol Phillips, 1973; three children. Elected to House of Commons, Prince George-Peace River, B.C., 1993—; apptd. Reform Deputy Critic for Immigration, 1995, Critic for Regional Devel. Program, 1995; Offcl. Opposition Dep. Whip, Chief Critic for Agr. and Agri-Foods. Mem. B.C. Grain Producers Assn. (past pres.), B.C. Fedn. of Agr. (bd. dirs.), Soil Conservation Can. 9bd. dirs.), B.C. Provincial Seed Fair (chmn.). Office: House of Commons, Ottawa, ON Canada K1A OA6*

HILL, JEFFERSON BORDEN, regulatory oversight officer, lawyer; b. Wilmington, Del., Nov. 5, 1941; s. Julian Werner and Mary Louisa (Butcher) H.; m. Gabrielle Marie Tourville, Mar. 19, 1976; children: Corinna Borden Hill, Lydia Richards Hill. BA, Harvard U., 1963, LLB, 1967. Bar: Del. 1967, D.C. 1972. Legis. asst. Congressman William V. Roth, Jr., Washington, 1967-70; attorney Antitrust div. U.S. Dept. Justice, Washington, 1970-76; asst. dir. Office of Policy Planning and Legis., Antitrust Div., U.S. Dept. Justice, Washington, 1976-77; br. chief Office Info. and Regulatory Affairs, Office Mgmt. Budget, Washington, 1977—; adj. prof. Georgetown U., Washington, 1987-96. Mem. Met. Club. Republican. Home: 639 E Capitol St SE Washington DC 20003-1234 Office: Office Mgmt and Budget 17th and Pennsylvania Ave NW Washington DC 20503

HILL, JESSE HOYT, training specialist, economics & business educator; b. Memphis, Mar. 3, 1950; s. James Richard and Mary Althea (Ruby) H.; m Sheri Loree Robinson, July 17, 1970; children: Christ Corrine, Jesse Jaron. BS, U North Tex., 1975; MS, Amber U., 1986; EdD, Nova Southeastern U., 1996. Provisional tchr. cert., Tex., 1975. Tng. specialist City of Dallas, 1972—; tchr. econs. and bus. mgmt. Grad. SCh. Amber U., 1999—; adj. faculty No. Lake Coll., Irving, Tex., 1987-94, No. Ctrl. Tex. Coll., Gainesville, 1995-96, U. Dallas, Irving, 1996—. Deacon First Presbyn. Ch., Grapevine, Tex., 1984-87; pres., bd. dirs. First Presbyn. Pre-Sch., Grapevine, 1985-88; referee U.S. Soccer Fedn. Recipient award Jaycee of the Yr., 1985. Mem: Tex. Jr. Coll. Tchrs. Assn., Tex. Assn Coll. Tech. Educators. Avocations: Little League coach, painter. Home: 3719 High Dr Grapevine TX 76051-4553 Office: City of Dallas 1500 Marilla St # 6an Dallas TX 75201-6390

HILL, JIM, state official; 1 child, Jennifer. BA in Econs., Mich. State U., 1969; MBA, Indiana U., 1971, JD, 1974. Asst. atty. gen. Oreg. Dept. of Justice, 1974-77; hearing referee Oreg. Dept. of Revenue, 1977-81; personnel specialist and cons. State Farm Ins., 1984-86; elected mem. Oreg. House of Reps., 1983-87, Oreg. State Sen., 1987-93; dir. mktg. PEN-NOR, Inc., Portland Gen. Contractors, 1986-88; corp. accts. mgr. for Latin Am. Mentor Graphics, 1988-93; state treas. State of Oreg., Salem, 1994—. Office: Oreg State Treasury 159 State Capitol Salem OR 97310-0840

HILL, JIM TOM, chemical company executive; b. Cushing, Okla., Apr. 27, 1939; s. Wilburn C. and Susie (Ruckman) H.; m. Linda J. Archer, Aug. 30, 1963; children: Sheri, David, Susan. BS in Chemistry, Abilene Christian U., 1961; MS in Biochemistry, U. Tenn., 1964, PhD, 1968. Sr. rsch. scientist E.R. Squibb & Sons, New Brunswick, N.J., 1968-69, Lakeside Labs., Milw., 1969-75; sr. rsch. specialist Monsanto, St. Louis, 1975-78; dir. chemistry Hazelton Labs. Am., Vienna, Va., 1978-80; mgr. toxicology Phelps Dodge, Washington, 1980-81; dir. sci. affairs Chem. Specialties Mfrs. Assn., Washington, 1981-86, dir. product ingredient rev. program, 1987-97; v.p. Specialty Product Group, SRS Internat., Washington, 1997—. Contbr. articles to profl. jours. Mem. Am. Coll. Toxicology, Am. Soc. Pharmacology and Exptl. Therapeutics, Environ. Mutagen Soc., Am. Chem. Soc., Soc. Toxicology, Sigma Xi. Home: 2477 Freetown Dr Reston VA 20191-2527 Office: 1625 K St NW Ste 1000 Washington DC 20006-1619*

HILL, JIMMIE DALE, retired government official; b. Fort Worth, Tex., Dec. 28, 1933; s. William Haden and Myrtle Maude H.; m. Martha Lea Hoad, May 26, 1956; children: William, Loretta, Carol, Patricia. Student, DelMar Coll., 1955-57, U. Okla., 1957-58, U. Wichita, 1963-64. Enlisted in U.S. Air Force, 1951, advanced through grades to maj., 1974; comptroller for space systems acquisition Los Angeles, 1963-70; adv. CIA, 1970-73; ret., 1974; spl. asst. to undersec. Air Force, Washington, 1974-78; dir. Office of Space Systems, Dept. Air Force, 1978-82; dep. undersec. Air Force Space Systems, 1982-96; dep. dir. Nat. Reconnaissance Office, 1982-96. Scoutmaster Boy Scouts Am., 1971-76. Decorated Legion of Merit; recipient Disting. Civilian Svc. medal Dept. Def., 1974, 76, 87, 96, Presdl. Rank award of Meritorious Exec., 1980, 88, Presdl. Rank of Disting. Exec., 1981, 91, Air Force sr. exec. award, 1982-87, 89, 90, 92, 93, 94, 95, Air Force Exceptional Civilian Svc. award, 1987, 96, Nat. Intelligence Disting. Svc. medal, Ctrl. Intelligence Agy. Disting. Intelligence medal, Disting. Svc. medal NASA, Goddard Meml. Trophy, Nat. Space Club, 1996, Goddard Astronautics award AIAA, 1998. Mem. Air Force Assn. Methodist. Home: 7920 Lewinsville Rd Mc Lean VA 22102-2407 Office: Space OSAF SAF/USS The Pentagon Washington DC 20330 *Choose an occupation or profession because you like it, not for recognition and reward. For if you're happy in your work, with loyalty, dedication and hard work, ample recognition and reward will follow.*

HILL, JOANNE FRANCIS, retired elementary education educator; b. Holland, Mich., Jan. 12, 1937. BA in Elem. Edn., Western Mich. U., 1961; postgrad., Mich. State U., 1961-65, Oxford U., 1965. Cert. elem. tchr. Sec. Am. Bus. Woman, Holland, 1972-74; tchr. West Ottawa Pub. Sch., Holland, 1957-97. Former leader Camp Fire Girls, Inc., Holland; mem. Holland Cmty. Theatre, 1972-89; Sunday sch. tchr. Ref. Ch., 1970-81, mem. choir, 1972—, elder, 1981-94. Mem. ASCD, Nat. Coun. Tchrs., Nat. Coun. Tchrs. English, Mich. Edn. Assn. (pres. 1993-94, past pres. 1994-95), Area Bargaining Coun. (sec. 1992-95), Sch. Employees Coun. (sec. 1992-93), West Ottawa Edn. Assn. (sec. 1984-85, v.p. 1985-86, pres. 1986-97). Republican. Home: 1008 Bluebell Dr Holland MI 49423-6861

HILL, JOE H., legislative staff member; b. Paris, Oct. 28, 1946; s. James W. and Erin Lucile Hill; m. Wanda Susan Cranford, Dec. 19, 1971; children: Adam, Judith, Travis. BS, Bethel Coll., 1968. Project dir. N.W. Tenn. Devel. Dist., Union City, 1968-70; asst. dir. N.W. Tenn. Devel. Dist., Martin, 1970-73; dist. dir. U.S. Rep. Ed Jones, Yorkville, Tenn., 1973-89, U.S. Rep. John Tannes, Union City, Tenn., 1989—. Officer Henry County Dem. Party, Davis, Tenn., 1968-73, Gibson County Dem. Party, Trenton, Tenn., 1982-90. Mem. Masons, Moose, Elks. Democrat. Methodist. Avocations: fishing, hunting, jogging. Home: 1513 Julie St Union City TN 38261

HILL, JOHN EARL, mechanical engineer; b. Ely, Nev., July 18, 1953; s. Earl M. and Florence (Lagos) H.; m. Terry Lynn Biederman, Oct. 3, 1981; 1 child, Felicia Biederman. BA in Social Psychology, U. Nev., 1974, BSME, 1981. Cert. engr. in tng. Machinist B&J Machine and Tool, Sparks, Nev., 1977-78; designer, machinist Screen Printing Systems, Sparks, Nev., 1978, Machine Svcs., Sparks, 1978-81; computer programmer U. Nev., Reno, 1980-81; design engr. Ford Aerospace and Communications Corp., Palo Alto, Calif., 1981-82, 86-88; contract design engr. Westinghouse Electric Corp., Sunnyvale, Calif., 1982-83; contract project engr. Adcotech Corp., Milpitas, Calif., 1983-84; sr. engr. Domain Tech., Milpitas, 1984-85; project engr. Exclusive Design Co., San Mateo, Calif., 1985-86; automation mgr. Akashic Memories Corp., San Jose, Calif., 1988-94; ptnr. Automated Bus. Svcs., San Jose; dir. automation engring. Seagate Rec. Media, Fremont, Calif., 1994-97; mgr., equipment engr. FormFactor, Inc., Livermore, Calif., 1997—. Mem. Robotics Internat. of Soc. Mfg. Engrs., Tau Beta Pi, Pi Mu Epsilon, Phi Kappa Phi. Avocations: music, art, hang gliding. Home: 147 Wildwood Ave San Carlos CA 94070-4516 Office: Form Factor Inc 5666 La Ribera St Livermore CA 94550-9275

HILL, JOHN HOWARD, lawyer; b. Pitts., Aug. 12, 1940; s. David Garrett and Eleanor Campbell (Musser) H. B.A., Yale U., 1962, J.D., 1965. Bar: Pa. 1965, U.S. Dist. Ct. (we dist.) Pa. 1965, U.S. Ct. Appeals (3d cir.) 1965, U.S. Supreme Ct. 1982. Assoc. Reed, Smith, Shaw & McClay, Pitts., 1965-75, ptnr., 1975-90; of counsel Jackson, Lewis, Schnitzler & Krupman, Pitts., 1991—. Bd. dirs. Travelers Aid Soc., Pitts., 1972—, treas., 1982-87, pres., 1987-90; bd. dirs. Pitts. Opera. Mem. ABA, Pa. Bar Assn., Allegheny County Bar Assn., Hosp. Assn. Pa., Pa. Soc., Pitts. Symphony Soc., Duquesne Club, Fox Chapel Golf Club, Rolling Rock Club, Phi Gemma Delta. Republican. Presbyterian. E-mail: hillj@jacksonlewis.com. Home: 4722 Bayard St Pittsburgh PA 15213-1708 Office: Jackson Lewis Schnitzler & Krupman One PPG Pl 28th Fl Pittsburgh PA 15222-5414

HILL, JOHN WALLACE, special education educator. BA in Elem. Edn. cum laude, Am. U., 1970, MEd in Spl. Edn., 1971, PhD in Edn., 1974. Dir. Learning Disabilities Clinic Meyer Children's Rehab. Inst., U. Nebr. Med. Ctr., Omaha, 1974-87; prof. spl. edn. Coll. of Edn., U. Nebr., Omaha, 1974—, Regents prof., 1989-95; adj. prof. Coll. of Pharmacy, U. Nebr. Med. Ctr.; lectr. various univs., assns. and confs.; former mem., bd. dirs. Omaha Head Start Program, Child and Family Devel. Corp. Contbr. articles to profl. jours. Fellow Am. Acad. for Cerebral Palsy and Devel. Medicine; mem. Phi Delta Kappa, Sigma Xi. Office: Univ Nebr at Omaha Dept Spl Edn Omaha NE 68182

HILL, JOHN-EDWARD, theater executive; b. Buffalo, June 19, 1947; s. John Vernon and Charlotte Adele (Brandel) H.; m. Barbara Ann Harris, Aug. 19, 1982; 1 child, David Harrison. BS, Northwestern U., 1970; MFA, Yale U., 1974. Lic. 1st class FCC. Theater mgr. Yale Cabaret Theater, New Haven, 1971-73; asst. mng. dir. Yale Repertory Theatre, New Haven, 1973-74; gen. mgr. Spingold Theater Ctr. Brandeis U., Waltham, Mass., 1974—; mng. dir., co-producer Brandeis Repertory Co., Waltham, 1988-89; producer, gen. ptnr. The Personals Co. Ltd. Partnership., N.Y.C., 1985-86. Mgr. USO Show Tour, Fed. Republic of Germany, Italy, 1980. Mem. Assn. Performing Arts Presenters, New Eng. Theatre Conf. Jewish. Avocations: collector of antique phonographs, records, magic lanterns, slides and ephemera. Office: Brandeis U Spingold Theater Arts Ctr PO Box 9110 Waltham MA 02454-9110

HILL, JOSEPHINE CARMELA, realtor; b. Tulsa, Feb. 27, 1932; d. Raphael and Jennie (Ferro) C.; m. Billy Gene Hill, Aug. 10, 1957; children: Patricia Ann, Barbara Jo. BEd, Chgo. State U., 1954; postgrad., Southwestern State U., 1957-58, Tulsa U., 1962. Cert. tchr.; lic. real estate broker; cert. residential specialist; cert. in referral and relocation. Clk. typist part-time Glidden Paint Co., Chgo., 1954-57; tchr. Chgo. Pub. Schs., 1954-57, Clinton (Okla.) Pub. Schs., 1958-59; sales rep. and bookkeeper Hill's Drug Shop, Tulsa, 1962-74; realtor assoc. Carriage Co. Realtors, Tulsa, 1974-77; broker assoc. John Hausam Realtors, Tulsa, 1977-87, 95—, J. Menger Elite Realtors, Tulsa, 1987-95, John Hausam Realtors, Tulsa, 1995—; mem. adv. bd. Tulsa Jr. Coll., 1991-93; divsn. v.p. Womens coun. Realtors Referral and Relocation,1993. Contbr. articles to profl. jours. Mem. St. Francis Hosp. Aux., Tulsa, 1986—; mem. exec. bd. March of Dimes, 1991—. Mem. Nat. Assn. of Realtors (realtors active in politics 1990-91, polit. calling network 1988—, meetings com. 1996-97, Outstanding award 1990, Svc. award), Women's Coun. of Realtors (regional v.p. 1991, state chpt. pres. 1988, gov. 1989), Okla. Assn. of Realtors (mem. legis. com. 1988—, Okla. State Mem. of Yr. 1990, Mem. of Yr. local chpt. 1990, bd. dirs. 1993-94, mem. edn. com. 1994), Greater Tulsa Assn. of Realtors (vice chair realtors polit. action com. 1991, mem. profl. stds. com. 1992—, mem. profl. bylaws com. 1992, bd. dirs. 1992-94, treas. 1994, sales assoc. of yr. 1991, chmn. fin. and budget 1994, mem. exec. com. 1993, 94), Women's Coun. of Realtors, Real Estate Sales Assocs., Omega Tau Rho. Roman Catholic. Avocations: aerobic dancing, scuba diving, ballroom dancing, walking, reading. Office: John Hausam Realtors 6550 E 71st St Tulsa OK 74133-2754

HILL, JUDITH DEEGAN, lawyer; b. Chgo., Dec. 13, 1939; d. William James and Ida May (Scott) Deegan; children: Colette M., Cristina M. BA, Western Mich. U., 1960; cert., U. Paris, Sorbonne, 1962; JD, Marquette U., 1971; postgrad., Harvard U., 1984. Bar: Wis. 1971, Ill. 1973, Nev. 1976, D.C. 1979. Tchr. Kalamazoo (Mich.) Bd. Edn., 1960-62, Maple Heights (Ohio) Bd. Edn., 1963-64, Shorewood (Wis.) Bd. Edn., 1964-68; corp. atty. Fort Howard Paper Co., Green Bay, Wis., 1971-72; sr. trust adminstr. Continental Ill. Nat. Bank & Trust, Chgo., 1972-76; atty. Morse, Foley & Wadsworth Law Firm, Las Vegas, 1976-77; dep. dist. atty., criminal prosecutor Clark County Atty., Las Vegas, 1977-83; atty. civil and criminal law Edward S. Coleman Profl. Law Corp., Las Vegas, 1983-84; pvt. practice law, 1989-99, ret., 1999. Bd. dirs. YMCA, Highland Park, 1973-75, Planned Parenthood of So. Nev., 1977-78, Nev. Legal Svcs., Carson City, 1980-87, state chmn., 1984-87; bd. dirs. Clark County Legal Svcs., Las Vegas, 1980-87, bd. dirs. St. Jude's Ranch for Children, 1999—; mem. Star Aux. for Handicapped Children, Las Vegas, 1986-96, Greater Las Vegas Women's League, 1987-88; jud. candidate Las Vegas Mcpl. Ct., 1987, New Symphony Guild, Variety Club Internat., 1992-93, Las Vegas Preservation Group; mem. Nat. Conf. for Cmty. and Justice, So. Nev., 1998—, St. Jude's Aux. for Abused Children, 1999—. Scholar Auto Specialities, St. Joseph, Mich., 1957-60, St. Thomas More scholar Marquette U. Law Sch., Milw., 1968-69; juvenile law internship grantee Marquette U. Law Sch., 1970. Mem. Nev. Bar Assn., So. Nev. Assn. Women Attys., Ill. Bar Assn., Children's Village Club (pres. 1980). Home: 521 Sweeney Ave Las Vegas NV 89104-1436

HILL, JUDITH SWIGOST, business analyst, information systems engineer; b. Harvey, Ill., Dec. 31, 1942; d. J.W. and M.J. (Kuczaik) Swigost; m. Wallace H. Hill, May 16, 1982; stepchildren: Scott, Amy, Molly, Elizabeth. BA in English/Theater, U. Ill., 1964; postgrad., Am. U., 1967-69, New Sch. for Social Research, N.Y.C., 1977-82, 83-85. Vol. U.S. Peace Corps, Philippines, 1964-66; recruiter U.S. Peace Corps, Washington, 1966-67; program mgr. U.S. Peace Corps, Micronesia, 1968; dir. corr. U.S. Peace Corps, Washington, 1969; editor, prin. Congl. Monitor, Inc., Washington, 1970-76; legis. analyst Philip Morris, Inc., N.Y.C., 1976-77; tech. analyst, writer Jesco, Inc., N.Y.C., 1978-79; assoc. pub. Thomas Pub. Co., N.Y.C., 1980-84; bus. analyst AGS, Inc. Ind. Cons., N.Y.C., 1984-93; dir. MIS N.Y.C. Sch. Constrn. Authority, 1993-94; ind. cons. in project mgmt. N.Y.C., 1994—; ind. cons. info. engring. and tech. orgn., N.Y.C., 1987—. Contbr. articles to profl. jours. Active Murray Hill Com., N.Y.C., 1986—. Mem. IEEE, ACM, Assn. Systems Mgmt., Am. Assn. for Artificial Intelligence, Spl. Interest Group on Artificial Intelligence, Internat. Assn. Knowledge Engrs., Nat. Assn. Returned Peace Corps Vols., Returned Peace Corps Vols. Greater N.Y. (by-laws com. 1985-86, spkrs. bur. 1987). Jewish. Avocations: cross-country skiing, golf, writing, banjo, jazz piano. Home and Office: 155 E 34th St Apt 12C New York NY 10016-4751

HILL, KATHLEEN LOIS, performing art school executive; b. Denver, Sept. 11, 1955; d. James Jenkins and Elaine (Marcella) Hill; 1 child Terrence Drake. BA, Colo. Women's Coll., 1977. Choreographer Fashion Bar TV Comml., Denver, 1981, Pure Gold Cheerleaders USFL, Denver, 1985, Kenny Rodgers Western Wear, Denver, 1990; exec., art dir. Hill Acad. of Dance and Dramatics, Denver, 1976—; bd. dirs. Colo. Dance Alliance, Denver, 1986-89; guest judge I Love Dance, Portland, Oreg., 1991—. Performer Met. Troupers Charity Entertainers, Colo., 1970-76. Named Young Careerist, Bus. and Profl. Women of Am., 1978; recipient Scholastic scholarships Colo. Women's Coll., 1973-77. Mem. Colo. Dance Alliance (bd. dirs. 1986-89), Colo. Dance Festival, Internat. Tap Assn. Democrat. Roman Catholic. Avocations: avid reader, performing arts advocate, travel. Office: Hill Dance Acad/Dramatics 6265 E Evans Ave Ste 14 Denver CO 80222-5822

HILL, KENNETH O., performing company executive. Pres. Ballet West, Salt Lake City, 1990—. Chmn. bd. dirs. United Way, 1990; past chmn. fed. rels. com. Salt Lake C. of C. Named Hon. Pub. Utah Press Assn.; recipient Friend of Utah award Gov. Utah. Office: Ballet West Capitol Theatre 50 W 200 S Ste 100 Salt Lake City UT 84101-1663*

HILL, KENT RICHMOND, college president; b. Nampa, Idaho, May 24, 1949; s. Double E. and Helen Louise (Robertson) H.; m. Janice Elaine Hurn, June 12, 1972; children: Jennifer Lynn, Jonathan Kent. BA in History, N.W. Nazarene Coll., 1971; diploma for basic Russian lang., Def. Lang. inst., 1972; postgrad., Georgetown U., 1973-74; MA in Russian and East European Studies, U. Wash., 1976, PhD in History, 1980. Teaching asst. in history N.W. Nazarene Coll., Nampa, Idaho, 1969-71; Russian translator, 1972-74; teaching asst. in history of Christianity U. Wash., Seattle, 1980, asst. prof. history, 1980-85, assoc. prof. history, 1985-86; pres. Inst. on Religion and Democracy, Washington, 1986-92, Ea. Nazarene Coll., Quincy, Mass., 1992—; interviews, speaker, presenter in field. Author: The Puzzle of the Soviet Church: An Inside Look at Christianity and Glasnost, 1989, Turbulent Times for the Soviet Church, 1991, The Soviet Union on the Brink, 1991; contbr. articles to profl. publs. Bd. dirs. Peter Deyneka Russian Ministries, 1991—, Keston Coll., 1985—; mem. nat. exec. bd. World Without War Coun., Berkeley, Calif., 1986—; bd. advisors Inst. on Religion and Democracy, 1984-86, bd. dirs., 1993—; mem. ch. bd. 1st Ch. of Nazarene, Seattle, 1980-85; bd. trustees Russian-Am. Christian U., Moscow, 1998—; bd. dirs. Quincy Hist. Soc., 1997—. Named Alumnus of Yr., N.W. Nazarene Coll., 1988; presented with Key to City, Mayor of City of Nampa, 1983; named Prof. of Yr. Seattle Pacific U., 1986; grantee Seattle Pacific U., 1981-82, 82-83, 84, 85, U. Wash., 1979-80; Nat. Def. Fgn. Lang. fellowship, 1976-77, Earhart fellow Internat. Rsch. and Exchs. fellow, 1978; recipient Pushkin award for Outstanding Scholarship, Def. Lang. Inst., 1972. Mem. Conf. on Faith and History, Rotary. Home: 148 Monroe Rd Quincy MA 02169-1936 Office: Eastern Nazarene Coll 23 E Elm Ave Quincy MA 02170-2905

HILL, LARKIN PAYNE, real estate company data processing executive; b. El Paso, Tex., Oct. 30, 1954; d. Max Lloyd and Jane Olivia (Evatt) H. Student Coll. Charleston, 1972-73, U. N.C., 1973. Lic. real estate broker, N.C. Sec., property mgr. Max L. Hill Co., Inc., Charleston, S.C., 1973-75, sec., data processor, 1979-82, v.p. adminstrn., 1982—; resident mgr. Carolina Apts., Carrboro, N.C., 1975-77; sales assoc., Realtor, Southland Assocs., Chapel Hill, N.C., 1977-78; cons. specifications com. Charleston Trident Multiple Listing Service, 1985. Bd. dirs. Charleston Area Arts Coun., 1992-93. Mem. Royal Oak Found., Scottish Soc. Charleston (bd. dirs. 1989-91), Preservation Soc., Charleston Computer Users Group, N.C. Assn. Realtors, Spoleto Festival USA (chmn. auction catalog com. 1990-92); co-chair Beaux Arts Ball, Sch. Arts. Republican. Methodist. Avocations: reading, crossword puzzles, Am. Staffordshire Terriers, T'ai Chi. Home: 7 Riverside Dr Charleston SC 29403-3217 Office: Max L Hill Co Inc/Relmax Realty Svcs 824 Johnnie Dodds Blvd Mount Pleasant SC 29464-3103

HILL, LAURYN, vocalist; b. South Orange, N.J., 1975. Student, Columbia U. appeared on TV in serial "As the World Turns"; featured in "Sister Act II; Back in the Habit." Teamed with Prakazrel "Pras" Michel and Wyclef Jean as the Fugees while still in H.S.; trio produced 2 albums: Blunted on Reality, 1994, and The Score, 1996 (17 million copies sold). Solo debut The Miseducation of Lauryn Hill earned 10 Grammy award nominations including Album of the Yr. and Best New Artist. Wrote and produced On That Day for gospel artist CeCe Winans; wrote A Rose is Still a Rose for Aretha Franklin album; also directed song's accompanying video. Founder non-profit The Refugee Youth Camp Youth Project. With Fugees received 2 1996 Grammy awards--Best Rap Album for The Score and Best R&B Performance by a Duo or Group With Vocal (Killing Me Softly). Recipient 1999 Grammy awards for Album of Yr., Best New Artist, Best R&B Song, Best R&B Album, Best Female R&B Vocal Performance. Nominated for several awards at 13th Annual Soul Train Music Awards in L.A. Recipient 4 awards (Outstanding New Artist, Outstanding Female Artist, Outstanding Album and NAACP President's award) 30th Annual NAACP Image Awards, Pasadena, Calif., 1999. Other awards include Favorite New Soul/R&B Artist (26th Annual Am. Music Awards), Best New Artist (Danish Grammy Awards), Entertainer of Yr. (Entertainment Weekly), #1 Album of Yr. (Time mag., N.Y. Times), Best R&B Album of 1998 (USA Today), Artist of Yr. (Spin mag.), Artist of Yr. (Details mag.), 3 Rolling Stone Music Awards. Office: Sony Music 550 Madison Ave New York NY 10022-3211*

HILL, LAWRENCE SIDNEY, management educator; b. Gary, Ind., Nov. 10, 1923; m. Evelyn Honig, Mar. 22, 1964; 1 child, Robert J. BSE, Purdue U., 1947; MBA, U. So. Calif., L.A., 1960; MSIE, U. So. Calif., 1962, Engr. I.E., 1965, PhD, 1968. Registered profl. engr., Calif. Asst. indsl. engr. USX Corp., Gary, Ind., 1947; indsl. hygiene engr. Ill. Dept. Pub. Health, Chgo., 1948-51; indsl. engr. USX Corp., Gary, 1951-52; sr. engr. Nat. Safety Coun., Chgo., 1953; sr. indsl. engr. Martin Marietta Co., Balt., 1953-55; group head McDonnell Douglas Co., Santa Monica, Calif., 1955-57; sr. mem. staff The Rand Corp., Santa Monica, 1957-71; prof. mgmt. Calif. State U., L.A., 1969—; cons., prin. engr. Ralph M. Parsons Co., Pasadena, 1973-82; cons., sr. mem. tech. staff TRW Inc., Redondo Beach, Calif., 1982-90; cons., environ. mgr. USN, Long Beach, Calif., 1991-94; vis. lectr. Ops. Rsch. Soc. Am./ Inst. Mgmt. Scis., 1973-95, expert witness in safety, mgmt., 1986—. Contbr. articles to profl. jours., books. Mem. Alpha Pi Mu, Alpha Iota Delta. Avocations: profl. and coll. sports. Home: 3653 Oceanhill Way Malibu CA 90265-5637

HILL, LEDA KATHERINE, librarian; b. Bklyn., Feb. 16, 1952; d. David and Leda Louise (Jones) H. BA, Bklyn. Coll., 1974, MS in Edn., 1989; MLS, Queens (N.Y.) Coll., 1995. New bus. coord. INAC Corp., Cranford, N.J., 1974-80; paralegal Orgn. Women for Legal Awareness, Inc., East Orange, N.J., 1980-83; tchr. Roselle (N.J.) Bd. Edn., 1983-84; libr., tchr. N.Y.C. Bd. Edn., Bklyn., 1985—. Mem. Bklyn. Reading Coun., N.Y.C. Sch. Librs. Assn., Am. Libr. Assn., Am. Assn. Sch. Librs. Office: Middle School 2 655 Parkside Ave Brooklyn NY 11226-1505

HILL, LORIE ELIZABETH, psychotherapist; b. Buffalo, Oct. 21, 1946; d. Graham and Elizabeth Helen (Salm) H. Student, U. Manchester, Eng., 1966-67; BA, Grinnell Coll., 1968; MA, U. Wis., 1970, Calif. State U., Sonoma, 1974; PhD, Wright Inst., 1980. Instr. English U. Mo., 1970-71; adminstr., supr. Antioch-West and Ctr. for Ind. Living, San Francisco, Berkeley, 1975-77; dir. tng. Ctr. for Edn. and Mental Health, San Francisco, 1977-80, exec. dir., 1980-81; pvt. practice Berkeley and Oakland, Calif., 1976—; instr. master's program in psychology John F. Kennedy U., Orinda, Calif., 1985, 94—; founder group of psychotherapists against racism; spkr. on cross-cultural psychology; creater Jump Start, a violence prevention and unlearning racism program for youth; trainer for trainers 3rd Internat. Conf. Conflict Resolution, St. Petersburg, Russia; sr. facilitator Color of Fear. Organizer against nuclear war; founding mem. Psychotherapists for Social Responsibility; psychologist Big Bros. and Big Sisters of the East Bay, 1986-88; vol. instr. City of Oakland Youth Skills Devel. Program; active Rainbow Coalition for Jesse Jackson's Presdl. Campaign, Ron Dellums Re-election Com.; campaigner for Clinton-Gore; founder, dir. Providing Alternatives to Violence; creator JumpStart program. Mem. Calif. Psychol. Assn. (chairperson pub. interest divsn. 1997, Helen MAargulies Mehr Pub. Svc. award 1996, chair social issues 1996—, Silver Psi award 1999). Democrat-Socialist. Avocations: sports, travel, music, reading. Office: 2955 Shattuck Ave Berkeley CA 94705-1808

HILL, LOUIS ALLEN, JR., former university dean, consultant; b. Okemah, Okla., May 18, 1927; s. Louis Allen and Gladys Adelia (Dietrich) Hill Wise; m. Jeanne Rose Murray, June 14, 1951; children: Dawn, David, Dixon. B.A., Okla. State U., 1949, B.S.C.E., 1954, M.S.C.E., 1955; Ph.D., Case Inst. Tech., 1965. Registered profl. engr., Okla., Ariz. Engr. Lee Hendricks Engring., Tulsa, 1955-57, Hudgins, Thompson, Ball & Assocs., Oklahoma City, 1957-58; asst. prof. civil engring. Ariz. State U., 1958-66, assoc. prof., 1966-70, prof., 1970-74, chmn. dept. civil engring., 1974-81; dean Coll. Engring. U. Akron, 1981-88, assoc. v.p. rsch. and grad. studies, 1988; chmn. Ohio Engring. Dean's Council, 1983-85; trustee Engring. Found. of Ohio, 1985-88; staff engr. Salt River Project, Ariz., 1962; cons. in field. Author: Fundamentals of Structures, 1975, Compendium of Structural Aids, 1975, Structured Programming in Fortran, 1981; contbr. numerous articles to profl. jours.; designer numerous bridges, hwys. Ch. leader-tchr. 1st Bapt. Ch., 1971-88, Scottsdale Presbyn. Ch., 1990—. Served to capt. C.E., U.S. Army, 1945-47, 51-53, The Philippines, Japan. Recipient Disting. award Akron Coun. Engring. and Sci. Socs., 1987, commendation Minorities in Mainstream Tech. Com., 1990, Disting. Svc. award U. Akron Coll. Engring., 1994; named Educator of Yr., Inroads N.E. Ohio, Inc., 1986; Louis A. Hill Jr. award established in his honor Qua Tech., 1987, Mayor Plusquellic proclaimed April 23, 1997 as Dr. Louis A. Hill Day in City of Akron; fellow Continental Oil Co., 1955, faculty fellow NSF, 1963. Fellow ASCE (life); mem. NSPE (sec., profl. engr. in edn. 1986-88), Am. Soc. Enging. Edn. (life, Western Electric Fund award 1967), Sigma Xi, Tau Beta Pi, Omicron Delta

Kappa. Republican. Home and Office: 3208 N 81st Pl Scottsdale AZ 85251-5800

HILL, LOWELL DEAN, agricultural marketing educator; b. Delta, Iowa, Apr. 27, 1930; s. Frederick Carl and Harriet Jane (Atwood) H.; m. Betty Elaine Carpenter, Dec. 9, 1951; children: Rebecca Elaine, Brent Howard. BS in Agrl. Edn., Iowa State U., 1951; MS in Agrl. Econs., Mich. State U., 1961, PhD in Agrl. Econs., 1963. Asst. prof., then assoc. prof. dept. agrl. econs. U. Ill., Urbana, 1963-72, prof., 1972-77, L.J. Norton prof. agrl. mktg., 1977-98, L.J. Morton prof. emeritus, 1998—; cons. Office Tech. Assessment, Washington, 1986-88, South Am. and Europe, 1995, FAO, Rome, 1978-80, U.S. AID, 1983, World Bank, Washington, 1989-90, 92-93, Argentina, Colombia, Chile, 1989-94, U.S. Feed Grains Coun., Venezuela, Japan, Korea, 1990-93, USDA, Russia, 1993-96. Author: Grain Grades and Standards: Historical Issues, 1990; editor: Role of Government in a Market Economy, 1982, Corn Quality in World Markets, 1985. Cpl. U.S. Army, 1952-54. Fellow East West Ctr.; recipient Quality of Comm. award, 1980, 88, Disting. Policy Contbr. award 1988, Extension Programs award, 1989, Disting. Svc. award USDA, 1989, Internat. Mktg. Support award Am. Soybean Assn., 1989, Faculty award for rsch. excellence, 1991; Univ. scholar, 1992. Fellow Am. Agrl. Econ. Assn. (Andersons' award for outstanding rsch. accomplishments 1999); mem. Coun. Agrl. Sci. and Tech. (chmn. 1989-90), Rotary. Office: Univ Ill Mumford Hall 1301 W Gregory Dr Urbana IL 61801-3608

HILL, LUTHER LYONS, JR., lawyer; b. Des Moines, Aug. 21, 1922; s. Luther Lyons and Mary (Hippee) H.; m. Sara S. Carpenter, Aug. 12, 1950; children—Luther Lyons III, Mark Lyons. BA, Williams Coll., 1947; LLB, Harvard U., 1950; LLD (hon.), Simpson Coll., 1979. Bar: Iowa 1951. Law clk. to Justice Hugo L. Black U.S. Supreme Ct., 1950-51; assoc., ptnr. Henry & Henry, Des Moines, 1951-69; mem. legal staff Equitable Life Ins. Co. of Iowa, 1952-87, exec. v.p., 1969-87, gen. counsel, 1970-87; of counsel Nyemaster, Goode, McLaughlin, Voigts, Wiest, Hansell O'Brien, Des Moines, 1992—; counsel, adminstr. Iowa Life and Health Ins. Guaranty Assn. Bd. dirs., past pres. United Comty. Svcs. Greater Des Moines; past trustee, past chmn. Simpson Coll., Indianola, Iowa; bd. chmn. Iowa State Hist. Found., 1997—; trustee The Hoyt Sherman Pl. Found. Capt. M.I., AUS, WWII, ETO. Mem. ABA, Iowa Bar Assn., Polk County Bar Assn., Assn. Life Ins. Counsel, Des Moines Club, Wakonda Club. Republican. Avocation: walking in the Swiss mountains. Home: 2801 Park Ave Des Moines IA 50321-1515 Office: 1900 Hub Tower 699 Walnut St Des Moines IA 50309-3929

HILL, MACK, career officer; b. Tampa, Fla.. Commd. officer U.S. Army, advanced through grades to brig. gen.; brig. gen., comdg. gen. Madigan Army Med. Ctr./Western Regional Med. Command, Tacoma, 1998—. Office: Madigan Army Med Ctr Western Reg Med Command Tacoma WA 98431

HILL, MARK C., lawyer; b. Marshall, Tex., Aug. 25, 1951; s. James E. and Gussie L. (Chastain) H.; m. Kathryn Jane Kilgore, June 14, 1975; children: James K., Elizabeth W., John T. BBA, Tex. Christian U., 1973; JD, U. Tex., 1976. Bar: Tex. 1976, U.S. Dist. Ct. (no., ea. and we. dists.) Tex., U.S. Dist. Ct. (ea. dist.) Okla., U.S. Dist. Ct. Nebr., U.S. Ct. Appeals (5th, 10th and 14th cirs.), Temporary Emergency Ct. Appeals, U.S. Tax Ct., U.S. Supreme Ct. Atty., ptnr. Cantey & Hanger, Ft. Worth, 1976-84; ptnr. in charge Haynes & Boone, Ft. Worth, 1984-97, mem. mgmt. com., 1984-92; sr. v.p., corp. sec., gen. counsel Tandy Corp., Ft. Worth, 1997—. Chmn. Tarrant County CSC, Ft. Worth, 1988-90. Named Outstanding Young Leader Ft. Worth C. of C., 1986; recipient Honarary State FFA Degree Tex. Future Farmers Am., 1987. Fellow Tex. Bar Found.; mem. ABA, Tarrant County Bar Assn. (dir. 1986-88), Internat. Assn. Def. Counsel, Am. Soc. Corp. Secs., Am. Corp. Counsel Assn., Sigma Alpha Epsilon. Presbyterian. Home: 5336 Collinwood Ave Fort Worth TX 76107-3634 Office: Tandy Corp 100 Throckmorton Ste 1900 Fort Worth TX 76102

HILL, MARS ANDREW, writer, retired civil engineer; b. Pine Bluff, Ark., Nov. 18, 1922.; BS in Archtl. Engring., U. Ill., 1954; M in African Am. Studies, SUNY, Albany, 1974, D in Humanistic Studies, 1997. Civil engr. N.Y. State Dept. Transp., Albany, 1958-83; tchr. writing Marist Coll., Glenmount, N.Y., 1993-94; tchr. Black Playwrights SUNY, Albany, 1987, tchr. Black theatre, 1970; tchr. Black history Albany Acad., 1977; tchr. writing seminar Coxsackie (N.Y.) Prison, 1979. Author: (play) Cavorting with the Wartons, 1979 (N.Y. State CAPS prize 1979), (fiction) Moaners' Bench, 1989 (Pulitzer prize nominee). Founder Black Experience Ensemble, Albany, 1969; founder, mem. Black Arts Festival. Recipient Kuumba award Black Arts Festival, 1984. Mem. Black Theatre Network. Avocations: skiing, tennis, swimming, running, fishing. Home: 5 Homestead Ave Albany NY 12203-1905

HILL, MARY LOU, accountant, business consultant; b. Phila., July 8, 1936; d. Norman Findlay and Gladys Louise (Weigand) Tompkins; m. Ernest Clarke Hill Jr., Mar. 15, 1958; children: Sally, Holly, Randy, Chuck, Jim. Student, U. Miami, 1954-55, U. Okla., 1955-57; BBA, Portland State U., 1979, M in Taxation, 1982. CPA, Oreg. Staff acct. Fordham & Fordham, Hillsboro, Oreg., 1982-84; instr. Portland (Oreg.) State U., 1984-85; owner The Bookshelf, Sunriver, Oreg., 1985-88; instr. Cen. Oreg. Community Coll., Bend, 1986, 88-89; small bus. cons., 1988—; staff acct. Richard Rocci CPA, Portland, Oreg., 1990-91, Scribner & Scribner, PC, Portland, 1992-94, Alten & Sakai & Co., Portland, 1994-95, Napier & Co., Tigard, Oreg., 1996—. Mem. AAUW, Oreg. Soc. CPAs, Kappa Kappa Gamma. Democrat. Christian Scientist. Avocations: travel, reading, swimming, computers. Home and Office: 9172 SW Wilshire St Portland OR 97225-4059

HILL, MELODIE ANNE, special education educator; b. Cortez, Colo., May 24, 1959; d. DaleWentworth and Lette Belle (Green) Higman; m. Jeffrey A. Hill, Feb. 16, 1985; children: Kevin Patrick, Virginia Laurel. BA in Edn. & Psychology, U. Denver, 1983; MA in Curriculum, Adams State Coll., 1987; postgrad., N.Mex. State U., 1995—. Reading specialist Kemper Elem. Sch., Cortez, Colo., 1983-85, sci. specialist, 1985-89; sci. curriculum team, sci. tchr. trainer Ctrl. Consol. Sch. Dist., Shiprock, N.Mex., 1989—; tchr. spl. edn. Shiprock H.S.; presenter in field, 1995—. Mem. Good-Samaritan Ctr., Cortez, 1990—, Colo. Rep. Women, Cortez, 1996—. NSF grantee, 1990, Los Alamos Nat. Lab. grantee, 1998; Hornbeck scholar, 1983. Mem. ASCD, AAUW, NEA, N.Mex. CEC, Nat. Assn. Sci. Tchrs. Episcopalian. Avocations: hiking, photography, mountain biking, swimming, writing. Office: Ctrl Consol Sch Dist PO Box 280 Shiprock NM 87420-0280

HILL, MELVIN JAMES, oil company executive; b. Santa Ana, Calif., May 19, 1919; s. Albert Frederick and Alice Lucile (Moody) H.; m. Daphne G. Langston, Mar. 1, 1947; children: Patricia (Mrs. Michael Michalek), Candace A. A.B., U. Cal. at Berkeley, 1941. With Western Gulf Oil Co., Cal., 1941-56, Gulf Research & Devel. Co., Harmarville, Pa., 1956-63; with Gulf Oil Corp., Pitts., 1963-75; v.p. Gulf Oil Corp., 1971-74, sr. v.p., 1974-75, exec. v.p., 1981-84; ret., 1984; pres. Gulf Energy and Minerals Co.-Internat., Houston, 1975-78, Gulf Exploration & Prodn. Co., 1978-81. Mem. Am. Petroleum Inst., Am. Assn. Petroleum Geologists, Am. Inst. Profl. Geologists, Geol. Soc. Am., Soc. Exploration Geophysicists, Am. Geophys. Union. Office: 2711 Ebbtide Rd Corona Del Mar CA 92625-1403

HILL, MICHAEL J., film editor. Works include TV movies Berlin Tunnel 21, 1981, Cagney & Lacey, 1981, The First Time, 1982, Baby Sister, 1983, Obsessive Love, 1984, Combat High, 1986, (films with Daniel P. Hanley): (also with Robert J. Kern) Night Shift, 1982, Splash, 1984, Cocoon, 1985, Gung Ho, 1986, (also with Gregory Prange) Armed and Dangerous, 1986, Willow, 1988, Parenthood, 1989, Pet Sematary, 1989, Problem Child, 1990, Backdraft, 1991, Far and Away, 1992, The Paper, 1994, Apollo 13, 1995 (Acad. award for best film editing 1996), Ransom, 1996, EdTV, 1999. Office: Broder Kurland Webb Uffner Agency 9242 Beverly Blvd Ste 200 Beverly Hills CA 90210-3731

HILL, MICHAEL JOHN, newspaper editor; b. Joliet, Ill., Dec. 28, 1954; s. Elton John and Dolores Congetta (Romano) H.; m. Mary Louise Bergin, June 6, 1981 (div. 1993). BS in Journalism, No. Ill. U., 1977. Reporter gen. Muncie (Ind.) Star newspaper, 1977-78; reporter police-courts Oshkosh (Wis.) Northwestern newspaper, 1978-80; reporter govt. Messenger-Inquirer newspaper, Owensboro, Ky., 1980-82, Jour. Times newspaper, Racine, Wis., 1982-87; reporter capitol Capital Times, Madison, Wis., 1987-89, city editor, 1989-93; asst. city editor Las Vegas Rev. Jour., Las Vegas, 1993-96; weekend editor Augusta (Ga.) Chronicle, 1996-98; free-lance writer/editor, 1999—. Contbr. articles to publs. Recipient 1st place investigative reporting Wis. Newspaper Assn., 1990, Wis. Am. Legion Auxiliary Assn. best stories on youth issues award, 1986, Wis. Press Assn. honorable mention investigative reporting, 1985, Inland Daily Press Assn. honorable mention, investigative, interpretive and background reporting, 1984, Wis. Press Assn., 3rd place, investigative reporting, 1983, 2d pl. freedom of info. Ky. Press Assn., 1982, 3rd place, best news story, 1982. Mem. ACLU, Investigative Reporters and Editors. Avocations: gardening, coin collecting, stamp collecting, tennis. Home: 2330 Chalet Gardens Rd #4 Fitchburg WI 53711

HILL, MILTON KING, JR., lawyer; b. Balt., Nov. 29, 1926; s. Milton King and Mary Fusselbaugh (Hall) H.; m. Agnes Ciotti, June 11, 1949; children: Thomas Michael, Milton King, III, Susan Hill. BS in Bus. and Pub. Adminstrn., U. Md., 1950, JD, 1952. Bar: Md. 1952, U.S. Dist. Ct. Md. 1952, U.S. Ct. Appeals (4th cir.) 1952. Assoc. Smith, Somerville & Case, Balt., 1952-55, ptnr., 1955-90; ret.; mem. faculty Md. Hosp. Ednl. Inst. Served with USAF, 1944-46. Fellow Am. Coll. Trial Lawyers, Internat. Soc. Barristers; mem. Md. State Bar Assn., Md. Bar Assn., Nat. Conf. Commrs. Uniform State Laws (pres. 1981-83, chmn. model punitive damages act drafting com.), Assn. Def. Trial Counsel (pres. 1964-65), Internat. Assn. Ins. Counsel, ABA (ho. of dels. 1981-83), Md. Bar Found., Am. Acad. Hosp. Attys. Clubs: Potapskut Sailing Assn., Wednesday Law. Home: 8810 Walther Blvd Apt 2329 Parkville MD 21234-0025

HILL, NORMA LOUISE, librarian; b. Somerville, Mass., Oct. 27; d. Southern G. and Marguerite M. (Smith) Smallwood; m. George Forris Hill, Dec. 30, 1954; children: Gregory Harrison, Jonathan Smallwood. AB, Wheaton Coll., 1952; MS in Libr. Sci., Our Lady of the Lake Coll., 1975; postgrad., Harvard U., 1994. Grad. asst. Our Lady of the Lake Coll., San Antonio, 1974-75; libr. Cmty. Guidance Ctr., San Antonio, 1975; 86th tactical fighter wing 86th Tactical Fighter Wing, Ramstein, Fed. Republic Germany, 1976-79; info. mgmt. specialist Exec. Office of the Pres., Washington, 1980; dept. head Howard County (Md.) Libr., 1980-81, asst. dir., 1981-86, dir., 1996—; del. Gov.'s Conf. on Libr. and Info. Sci., 1991. Mem. Friends of the Howard County Libr., Howard County Literacy Coalition, 1984, Md. Adv. Coun. on Librs., 1987-88; adv. bd. State Libr. Resource Ctr., 1986-88, network planning and resource sharing task force, 1988-89; bd. dirs. Columbia Found., 1992-98, sec. 1994-98, Howard County Housing Alliance, 1992-93; mem. adv. bd. Johns Hopkins U. Columbia Ctr., 1994—; mem. cmty. rels. coun. Howard County Gen. Hosp., 1995—; mem. bd. Equal Bus. Opportunity Commn., 1996—; mem. leadership team Bd. Health Improvement, 1996—. Recipient Insp. Gen. Spl. Achievement award USAF, 1977, 78. Mem. Md. Assn. Pub. Libr. Adminstrs., Md. Libr. Assn. (chair nominations com. 1984-85, co-chmn. fed. rels. subcom. 1985-86, 1st v.p., pres.-elect 1986-87, pres. 1987-88, exec. bd. 1988-89, chair awards com. 1991, legis. com. 1997—, award 1993), ALA (pub. libr. divsn., nominations com. 1989-90), Pub. Libr. Assn., NAFE, Leadership Howard County, Nat. Coun. of Negro Women, Alpha Kappa Alpha. Democrat. Office: Howard County Libr 6600 Cradlerock Way Columbia MD 21045-4912

HILL, PAT, coach; married; children: Michael, Matthew, Zachary. B, Univ. Calif., 1973. Offensive coach L.A. Valley Coll., 1974-76; offensive line coach Utah Univ., 1977-80; offensive coord. UNLV, 1981-82, Calgary Stampeders, 1983; offensive coach Univ. Ariz., 1990-91; offensive line coach Cleveland Browns, 1992; head football coach Calif. State U., Fresno, 1996—. Office: Calif State U 6020 E Bulldog Ln Fresno CA 93740-8020*

HILL, PATRICIA JO, special education educator; b. Muncie, Ind., Oct. 28, 1944; d. Frederic Burnside and Elizabeth Becom (Zaring) Harbottle; widowed; 1 son, Thomas Frederic. BS, Ball State U., 1964, MA, 1978, EdS, 1981. Cert. EMT, 1997. Instr., head immunology dept. Ball Meml. Hosp., Muncie, Ind., 1963-74; tchr. emotionally disturbed Indpls. Pub. Schs., 1974-75, lead tchr. severe/profound mentally retarded, 1979-84, tchr. moderately mentally handicapped, 1986-87; media specialist in spl. edn., 1984-86; cons. Prescription Learning Corp., 1975-76; tchr. mildly mentally handicapped, 1987-93, cross categorical spl. edn. tchr., 1993—; seminar presenter Ind. State Prevent Child Abuse Conf., 1998. Participant 21st Leadership Series between C. of C. and Inpls. Pub. Schs., Area 15 Spl. Olympics Coach; Black History Liaison, Ind. Chpt. Prevention of Child Abuse; chair Indy PAC, instnl. and profl. devel. com.; vol. first aid team, disaster team ARC; vol. Protect the Promise Coalition; del. Ind. State Rep. Convention, Rep. Leadership Conf. for Midwestern States, 1997; mem. staff to elect 10th Dist. Rep. Congresswoman Virginia Blankenbaker, 1998. NSF grantee, 1961; Shroyer scholar Mchts. Nat. Bank Muncie, 1972; Indpls. Pub. Schs. scholar, 1981. Mem. Assn. Behavioral Analysts, Coun. Exceptional Children (med. and health problems), Ind. State Tchrs. Assn. (spl. edn. com.), Indpls. Edn. Assn. (exec. bd., sec. 1998—), Greater Indpls. Rep. Women. Methodist. Home: 7330 Scarborough Blvd East Dr Indianapolis IN 46256-2053 Office: 3445 Central Ave Indianapolis IN 46205-3705

HILL, PAUL CHRISTIAN, dean; b. Berea, Ohio, Dec. 24, 1958; s. Russell J. and Barbara Jean Hill; m. P.J. Ursey, GFeb. 19, 1994 (dec. July 1998). MusB, Kent State U., 1982; MusM in Choral Conducting, New Eng. Cons., 1987. Music master Roxbury Latin Sch., West Roxbury, Mass., 1986-89; asst. prof. music Delta Coll., University Center, Mich., 1989-96, chair humanities, 1996-99, assoc. dean acad. adminstrn., 1999—. Bd. dirs. ACDA-Mich., 1991-96. Mem. Nat. Coun. for Staff, orgn. and Program Devel. Home: 304 Hart St Bay City MI 48706 Office: Delta Coll 1961 Delta Rd University Center MI 48710

HILL, PAUL DRENNEN, lawyer, banker; b. Bklyn., Jan. 8, 1941; s. John Drennen and Margaret Henrietta (Gens) H.; m. Ann Kilbourne Patch, June 6, 1964; children: Hal Chase, John Andrew. BA, Williams Coll., 1962; LLB cum laude, Columbia U., 1966. Bar: Ga. 1966. Mgmt. asso. Time Inc., 1962-63; partner firm Gambrell, Russell & Forbes, Atlanta, 1970-75; sr. v.p., gen. counsel First Atlanta Corp., 1975-78, exec. v.p., chief fin. officer, 1978-85; exec. v.p. First Wachovia Corp., Atlanta, 1985-87; mng. ptnr. Hansell & Post, Atlanta, 1987-88; exec. v.p., chief oper. officer Fed. Home Loan Bank of Atlanta, 1988-96, pres., CEO, 1997—; bd. dirs. Builders' Transport, Inc., Camden, S.C., Std. Fed. Savs. & Loan, Columbia, S.C., First Atlanta Corp., Ga. Affordable Housing Corp., Enterprise Social Investment Corp.; adj. prof. Emory U. Law Sch., Atlanta, 1975; bd. dirs. Atlanta Midtown Alliance, 1994—, mem. exec. com., 1995—. Mem. Met. Atlanta Crime Commn., 1984-87; mem. bd. visitors Grady Meml. Hosp., Atlanta, 1983-96; trustee Ga. Inst. CLE, Atlanta, 1985-87, St. Andrew's Sch., Middletown, Del., 1986-88, Paideia Sch., Atlanta, 1980-84; v.p., treas., trustee Atlanta Bot. Garden, 1979-92; trustee, treas. Southeastern Flower Show; trustee Atlanta Preservation Ctr., 1992-98; mem. fin. com., trustee Westminster Schs., Atlanta, 1985-87; chmn. devel. opportunities task force Ctrl. Atlanta Progress, 1983-84; rep. Williams Coll. Devel. Coun., Williamstown, Mass., 1983-85; bd. dirs. Shepherd Spinal Clinic, Atlanta, 1983-84. With USAR, 1963-66. Mem. ABA, Am. Inst. Banking, Conf. Board (exec. conf.), Ga. Bar Assn. (chmn. corp. and banking law sect. 1974, mem. corp. counsel sect.), Atlanta Bar Assn. (chmn. continuing legal edn. com. 1981-82), Am. Bankers Assn., Commerce Club, Piedmont Driving Club, Atlanta Rotary Club. Congregationalist. Office: Fed Home Loan Bank PO Box 105565 1475 Peachtree St NE Atlanta GA 30348

HILL, PEGGY SUE, principal; b. Roswell, N.Mex., Aug. 4, 1953; d. Cecil Vecoe and Edith Augustine (Raney) H. BS, U. Ark., 1978, MEd, 1982; EdS, 1994. Cert. elem. prin., tchr. music and libr. Music tchr., K-6 Springdale (Ark.) Schs., 1978-83, elem. prin., 1983-98, tech. coord., 1998—. Named Outstanding Young Educator Springdale Jaycees, 1983, Prin. of Ark. Exemplary Sch., Ark. Dept. Edn., 1989-90, 91-92, 93-94; recipient nat. award for teaching of econs. Joint Coun. Econ. Edn., 1990, 91, 92, 94. Mem. ASCD, Internat. Reading Assn., Ark. Assn. Edn. Administrs., Ark. Assn. Elem. Sch. Prins., (presenter conf. 1990), Phi Delta kappa (Outstanding Administr. award 1991), Kiwanis (bd. dirs. Springdale Breakfast chpt. 1991). Office: Lee Elem Sch PO Box 8 Springdale AR 72765*

HILL, PETER WAVERLY, lawyer; b. White River Junction, Vt., June 24, 1953; s. Richard Bert and Elaine Etta (Kimball) H.; m. Eileen Winderman, Aug. 27, 1994; 1 stepchild, Marshall Jackson Miller. BA in Philosophy and Govt., U. Ariz., 1975, JD, 1978. Bar: Ariz. 1978, U.S. Dist. Ct. (no. dist.) N.Y. 1979, N.Y. 1980, U.S. Ct. Appeals (2d cir.) 1982. Staff atty. Legal Aid Soc. Mid N.Y., Utica, 1978-79, Oneonta, 1979-83; assoc. Law Offices of Paternoster & O'Leary, Walton, N.Y., 1983-84; pvt. practice, Oneonta, 1985—. Contbr. articles to profl. jours. Mem. N.Y. State com. Socialist Party, Syracuse. Mem. Nat. Lawyers Guild, Nat. Orgn. Social Security Claimants Reps., N.Y. State Bar Assn., Otsego County Bar Assn., Delaware County Bar Assn., Injured Workers' Bar Assn., Inc. Unitarian Universalist. Office: 384 Main St Oneonta NY 13820-1930

HILL, PHILIP, retired lawyer; b. East Saint Louis, Ill., Mar. 13, 1917; s. Nehemiah William and Lulu Myrtle (Johnson) H.; m. Betty Jean Stone, July 4, 1942; children: William Stone, Thomas Chapman, Nancy Layton, Mary Anne. AB in Chemistry, U. Ill., 1937; PhD in Chemistry, Ohio State U., 1941; JD, John Marshall Law Sch., Chgo., 1968. Bar: Ill. 1968, U.S. Patent Office 1969, U.S. Ct. Appeals (fed. cir.) 1982. With Standard Oil Co. Ind., 1941-78, patent atty., 1969-73, dir. petroleum and corp. patents and licensing, 1973-78; ptnr. Hill & Hill, Lansing, Ill., 1978-86, pvt. practice law Philip Hill, P.C., 1987-96; ret., 1996; cons. Univ. Patents, Inc., Norwalk, Conn., 1980-89; treas. Am. Waste Reduction Corp., 1992-96. Mem. ABA, AAAS, Ill. State Bar Assn., Am. Intellectual Property Law Assn., Chgo. Patent Law Assn., Am. Chem. Soc., Phi Beta Kappa, Sigma Xi, Phi Kappa Phi. Methodist. Clubs: Kiwanis (Lansing, pres. 1959, 84). Contbr. articles to profl. jours.; patentee in field. Home: 3241 N Schultz Dr Lansing IL 60438-3205 Office: PO Box 187 Lansing IL 60438-0187

HILL, RAY ALLEN, educator. BS, Howard U., 1964, MS, 1965; PhD, U. Calif., Berkeley, 1977. Instr. So. U., Baton Rouge, 1965-66, Howard U., Washington, 1966-75; asst. prof. Fisk U., Nashville, 1977-80; assoc. prof. C.C. Balt., 1980-82, Morgan State U., Balt., 1982-85; instr. biology Lowell Coll. Prep., San Francisco, 1986—; vis. assoc. prof. U. Calif., San Francisco, 1985; staff scientist EPA Hqrs., Washington, 1978, NASA hqrs., Washington, 1979, Lawrence Berkeley Lab., 1980, 93; vis. scientist Genetech, Inc., San Francisco, 1992; vis. minority prof. Purdue U., West Lafayette, Ind., 1989, 90, 91. E.E. Worthing scholar, 1960-64, vis. scholar Stanford U., Palo Alto, Calif., 1984, 85, Siemens scholar, 1995; Ford Found. fellow 1975-76, 76-77, IISME fellow, 1992. Home: 8751 Fehler Ln Cotati CA 94931-5374

HILL, RAYMOND HEIT, management consultant; b. Long Branch, N.J., Oct. 29, 1962; s. Lawrence G. and Marcia L. (Hinz) H.; m. Debra A. Dumont, Aug. 31, 1986; children: Cameron, Connor. BS in Natural Resources, Cornell U., 1985; M of Environ. Mgmt., Resources, Econ. Policy, Duke U., 1989. Environ. scientist Alliance Tech. Corp., Bedford, Mass., 1985-87, Durham, N.C., 1987-88; sr. cons. Booz Allen & Hamilton, N.Y.C., 1988-90, assoc., 1990-92, sr. assoc., 1992-94; prin. A.T. Kearney, N.Y.C., 1994-97, v.p., 1997—; speaker in environ./chem. field; cons. environ., chem. and pharm. issues. Contbr. articles to profl. publs. Mem. Cornell U. Club, Saugatuck Rowing Assn., U.S. Rowing Assn. (master's nat. champion 1996, 97). Avocations: sailing, bicycling, rowing.

HILL, RAYMOND JOSEPH, packaging company executive; b. Chanute, Kans., May 4, 1935; s. Raymond Joseph and Emma Leona (Arthurs) H.; Asso. in Engring., Coffeyville (Kans.) Coll., 1955; m. Bettie Anne Handshumaker, Mar. 2, 1957; children: David, Dianne, Todd, Scott, Jennifer. MBA, U. Denver, 1977. Field engr. Phillips Petroleum Co., Bartlesville, Okla., 1957-59; design engr. Thiokol Chem. Corp., Brigham City, Utah, 1959-60; tech. supr. Hercules Chem. Corp., Salt Lake City, 1960-68; project mgr. aerospace div. Ball Corp., Boulder, Colo., 1968-70, plant mgr. and v.p. mfg. metal container div., Findlay, Ohio and Denver, Colo., 1970-78, pres. agrl. systems div., Westminster, Colo., 1978-85; v.p. plastic ops., sr. v.p. mfg. tech., ex. v.p. food metal, exec. v.p. food plastics Am. Nat. Can Corp., Chgo., 1985-90, sr. v.p. mfg. tech., 1990-93, exec. v.p. food plastics N.Am.; pres. Chesnee Assocs., Inc., Internat. Cons., 1993-97; exec. v.p. The Pop-Straw Co., also bd. dirs.; bd. dirs. Navaho Agrl. Products Industries, United Energy Devel., Packaging Adv. Coun., Flex Packing Assn., The Hallmark Group, Packaging Ptnrs., Classic Signatures, Inc., PopStraw Co.; mem. policy adv. com. to Office of U.S. Trade Rep., 1980—. Mem. Am. Ordnance Assn., Nat. Food Processors Assn., Soc. Tool Engrs., Irrigation Assn., Rotary. Republican. Episcopalian. Home: 509 Aurora Ave Apt 611 Naperville IL 60540-6262 Office: Chesnee Assocs Inc 2010 E Algonquin Rd Ste 210 Schaumburg IL 60173-4168

HILL, REBECCA SUE HELM, educator; b. Winchester, Ind., Sept. 8, 1955; d. Edward Arthur and Jacqueline Sue (Cassel) Helm; m. Paul Mark Hill, Dec. 29, 1977; children: Aaron Israel, Revkah Lauren, Hadassah Sue. BS, Asbury Coll., 1973; MEd, Purdue U., 1993. Cert. tchr., Ind. Tchr. N.W. Christian Acad., St. Louis, 1977-78, Monroe Ctrl. H.S., Parker, Ind., 1979-80, Dayspring Acad., Parker, 1983-85; tchr. literacy and lang. McCutcheon H.S., Lafayette, Ind., 1997-98, East Tipp Mid. Sch., Lafayette, Ind., 1998—; instr. Greenwood Cmty. Sch. Fine Arts, Indpls., 1990-93, Purdue U., West Lafayette, Ind., 1991—; instr. literacy and lang. Ind. Vocat. Coll., Lafayette, 1994—; bd. tchr. edn. coun. Sch. Edn. Purdue U., 1994-97; edn. supt. Stockwell (Ind.) United Meth. Ch., 1997—; presenter in field. Contbr. articles to profl. publs.. Performer Arts Ind. Mag., 1994, 95, 96; tchr. vol. New Cmty. Sch., Lafayette, 1995-96; mentor Curriculum and Instrn. Grad. Student Orgn., Purdue U., 1993-95. Andrews fellow, 1994-96; recipient Disting. Hoosier award Gov. of Ind., 1995. Mem. Alpha Upsilon Alpha (pres. 1994-96), Kappa Delta Pi. Avocations: family, music, outdoor activities, reading, gardening. Home: 6931 Church St PO Box 176 Stockwell IN 47983-0176 Office: Purdue U Dept Curr and Instruction Liberal Arts & Edn Bldg West Lafayette IN 47907

HILL, RICHARD A., advertising executive; b. Detroit. Student, Mich. State U.; MS in Mktg., Wayne State U. With J. Walter Thompson, Young & Rubicam; media supr. Buick/GMC Truck divsn., assoc. media dir. McCann-Erickson, Troy, Mich., 1970-75; sr. account exec. Buick account McCann-Erickson, Troy, 1975-77; v.p. media, mktg. dir. McCann-Erickson, Detroit, 1977-79, account supr. multi-products group, 1979-81, account supr. Buick, 1981-86, sr. v.p., mgmt. rep., 1986-91, dep. mgr., chmn. mgmt. bd., 1991-93, exec. v.p., gen. mgr., 1993-97, dir. profl. devel., 1997—, also exec. v.p., 1993—. Avocation: golf. Office: McCann-Erickson 755 W Big Beaver Rd Ste 2500 Troy MI 48084-0230*

HILL, RICHARD DEVEREUX, retired banker; b. Salem, Mass., Nov. 6, 1919; s. Robert W. and Grace (Dennis) H.; m. Polly Bergstedt, Sept. 13, 1947; children: Steven D., Johanna Hill Simpson, Richard Devereux. AB, Dartmouth Coll., 1941; MCS, Amos Tuck Sch. Adminstrn. and Finance, 1942; postgrad. in banking, Rutgers U., 1951; LLD (hon.), Babson Coll.; LLD, Northeastern U., Salem State Coll.; D in Bus. Adminstrn. (hon.), Boston Coll., Tufts U. With The First Nat. Bank of Boston, 1946-84, loan officer, 1948-51, asst. v.p., 1951-55, v.p., 1955-65, exec. v.p., 1965-66, pres., 1966-71, chmn. bd., chief exec., 1971-83, chmn. exec. com., 1983-84, chmn. bd., chief exec. officer, 1971-83; chmn. bd., chief exec. officer Bank of Boston Corp., 1971-83, chmn. exec. com., 1983-84; bd. dirs. Raytheon Co.; pres. fed. adv. coun. Fed. Res. System, 1977; chmn. Inst. Internat. Fin. Inc., 1983-86. Former chmn. transp. com. New Eng. Coun.; mem. vis. com. Sloan Sch. Mgmt., MIT, 1967-70; mem. Greater Boston adv. bd. Salvation Army; mem. bd. visitors Fletcher Sch. Internat. Law and Diplomacy, 1980—; chmn. bd. trustees Dartmouth Coll., 1981-83, trustee emeritus, former mem. investment com.; pres. emeritus, hon. trustee Mus. Fine Arts, Boston; former trustee Boston Urban Found.; hon. mem. Corp. Woods Hole Oceanographic Instn.; former overseer Crotched Mountain Found.; former chmn. Bus. Coun. for Internat. Understanding. Recipient Acad. Disting. Bostonians award Greater Boston C. of C., Christian A. Herter award World Affairs Coun. Mem. Internat. Monetary Conf. (hon.; past pres.), Transp. Assn. Am. (bd. dirs., past chmn. investor panel), Assn. Res. City Bankers (hon.; past pres.), Am. Inst. Banking (adv. com. Boston chpt. 1967-82), Dartmouth Alumni Assn. Boston (past v.p.), New Eng. Exeter Alumni Assn. (past pres.), Mass. Hist. Soc., Sigma Nu, Federal Club. Republican. Congregationalist. Clubs: Algonquin, Comml. (Boston); Eastern Yacht (Marblehead); Royal Bermuda Yacht, Riddell's Bay Golf and Country (Bermuda), Coral Beach and Tennis (Bermuda). Lodge: Masons. Home: Sargent Rd Marblehead MA 01945 Office: 100 Federal St Boston MA 02110-1802

HILL, RICHARD EARL, academic administrator; b. Clintonville, Wis., Mar. 30, 1929; s. Lyle Earl and Gladness Josephine (Love) H.; m. Marilyn Jean Thompson, June 5, 1951; children: Mark R., Kenneth L., Richard Earl, Joy A., Sarah J. B.A., Carroll Coll., Waukesha, Wis., 1951, L.H.D., 1974; M.Div., McCormick Theol. Sem., 1956. Ordained to ministry Presbyterian Ch., 1956; pastor chs. in Wis., 1955-62; pastor Frame Meml. Presbyn. Ch., Stevens Point, Wis.; also univ. pastor U. Wis., Stevens Point, 1962-69; asst. to pres. Carroll Coll., 1969-74; pres. Huron (S.D.) Coll., 1974-77; pres. Lakeland Coll., Sheboygan, Wis., 1977-89, pres. emeritus, 1991—, chancellor, 1989-91; pres. S.D. Fedn. Pvt. Colls., 1977; exec. com. Colls. Mid-Am., 1975-77; mem. 6th Congl. Dist. Acad. Selection Com., 1978-89; v.p. Wis. Found. Ind. Colls., 1983-85, pres., 1985-86. Mem. Am. Assn. Colls., Council Advancement and Support Small Colls., Council Advancement and Support Edn., Wis. Assn. Ind. Colls. and Univs. (pres. 1980-83), Am. Mgmt. Assn., Sheboygan Econ. Club (pres. 1985), Pi Kappa Delta, Pi Gamma Mu. Club: Rotary. Address: 1557 Navigator Rd Punta Gorda FL 33983-6221

HILL, RICHARD LEE, lawyer; b. Spanish Fork, Utah, May 17, 1951; s. Von and Maxine (Chambers) H.; m. Kathryn Smith, July 10, 1980; children: Natalie Kathryn, Nicole Charlene, Kristina Michelle, Kara Alexandra, Alexis Marie. BS cum laude, Brigham Young U., Hawaii, 1976; JD, Brigham Young U., 1979. Bar: Utah 1979, U.S. Dist. Ct. (cen. dist.) Utah 1979, U.S. Supreme Ct. 1979. Ptnr. Parker, McKeown, McConkie, Salt Lake City, 1979-82, Hill, Johnson, Schmutz, & P.C., Provo, Utah, 1982—; gen. counsel Marie Osmond Inc., Provo, 1984—, Covey Leadership Ctr., Inc. Mem. Utah Arts Coun., 1994—; bd. dirs. Provo Theatre Co., 1987—. Mem. ABA, ATLA, Utah Bar Assn., Riverside Country Club. Mormon. Avocation: acting. Office: Hill Johnson & Schmutz Ste 200 3319 N University Ave Provo UT 84604-4484

HILL, RICK ALLAN, congressman; b. Grand Rapids, Minn., Dec. 30, 1946; m. Betti Christie, June 10, 1983; children: Todd, Corey, Mike. BA in Econs. and Polit. Sci., St. Cloud State U., 1968. Surety bonding businessman, owner InsureWest, 1968-90; real estate and investment ptnr., 1983—; committeeman State Rep. Party, 1990-94; legis. liaison to Gov. Marc Racicot, Mont., 1993; mem. 105th-106th Congress from Mont dist., 1997—; mem. banking and fin. svcs. com. 105th Congress from Mont dist., mem. resources com., mem. small bus. com.; fin. chair State Rep. Party, 1989-91, state chair, 1991-92. Bd. dirs. Mont. Sci. and Tech. Alliance, 1992. Office: 1037 Longworth Bldg Washington DC 20515-2601*

HILL, ROBERT FOLWELL, JR., information systems specialist; b. High Point, N.C., July 24, 1946; s. Robert Folwell Sr. and Antilee (Dinkins) H.; Cynthia Hightower, Mar. 5, 1971 (div. Dec. 1977); 1 child, Robert Folwell III; m. Linda Kay Frier Balfour, June 7, 1978. BS in Computer Sci., N.C. State U., 1971. Supr. quality control Mac Panel Computer Tape Co., High Point, N.C., 1965-68; computer programmer U. N.C., Wilmington, 1972-74; programmer, analyst Gen. Adminstrn. U. N.C., Chapel Hill, 1974-79, dir. info. systems Gen. Adminstrn., 1979—. Pres. Triangle chpt. Nat. Found. for Ileitis and Colitis Rsch., Triangle Park, N.C., 1983, treas., 1984, v.p., 1985-88; pres. Crohn's and Colitis Found. Am., 1989-91, v.p. membership, 1991-99; spl. registrar Orange County Bd. Elections, Hillsborough, N.C., 1984; mem. exec. com., mem.-at-large N.C. Vol. Health Agys., 1990, sec., 1991; bd. mem. Combined Health Appeal of N.C., 1991-95, treas. 1993-95. Recipient Mary Ann Mobley Vol. Leadership award, 1996. Mem. Data Processing Mgmt. Assn., N.C. Assn. Instnl. Rsch., State Employees Assn. N.C., Coll. and Univ. Sys. Exch., Nat. Assn. Stock Car Auto Racing, Toastmasters Internat. Democrat. Avocation: auto racing. Home: 203 Northwood Dr Chapel Hill NC 27516-1122 Office: U NC Gen Adminstrn PO Box 2688 Chapel Hill NC 27515-2688

HILL, ROBERT FRED, medical educator; b. Oklahoma City, Nov. 4, 1936; s. Harold Meredith Hill and Hazel Marie (Zipse) Hilbert; m. Judith Anne Walker, May 31, 1964; children: Vanessa, Jonathan. BS in Social Sci., Okla. State U., 1964; MA in Anthropology, Am. U., 1968; PhD in Anthropology, U. Pitts., 1975. Fellow cmty. psychiatry U. Pitts., 1969-72; asst. prof. pub. health U. Okla., Oklahoma City, 1972-74, asst. prof., assoc. prof. cmty. medicine, 1974-84, assoc. prof. pediatrics, 1984-94, prof. pediatrics, 1994—; adv. bd. mem. Ctr. Cultural Dynamics, Denver, 1987—. Author: The Ethnic Imperative, 1977, The Culture of Oklahoma, 1993; contbr. articles to profl. jours. Adolescent health subcom. mem. Okla. Commn. on Children and Youth, 1990—. Recipient Certificate Achievement Okla. Sec. Commerce, 1988, Gov.'s Commendation State of Okla., 1993. Fellow Am. Anthropol. Assn., Soc. Applied Anthropology; mem. AAAS, Soc. Adolescent Medicine, Am. Profl. Soc. on Abuse of Children, High Plains Soc. Applied Anthropology (adv. bd.). Avocations: vocal music, golf. Home: 1113 Hemstead Pl Oklahoma City OK 73116-6210 Office: Univ Okla Childrens Hosp PO Box 26901 Oklahoma City OK 73126-0901

HILL, ROBERT JOHN, aviation executive; b. Unity, Ohio, June 29, 1932; s. Harry H. and Alice Jo (Blair) H.; m. Eve Marie Duke, Feb. 16, 1957; children: Kathleen, Randall, Scott. BBA, Youngstown State U., 1960; postgrad. in aviation tech., U. Miami, 1963; postgrad. in aviation, Flight Safety Inst., 1973-86. Cert. various instr. and transp. ratings, FAA. Pilot Beckett Aviation, Youngstown and Cleve., Ohio, 1967-77; ops. inspector FAA, Indpls., 1977-78; pilot Republic Steel, Cleve., 1979-82; pres. R.J. Hill, Inc., Strongsville, Ohio, 1983—; chief pilot Flight Ops., Inc., Cleve., 1984-89; capt. Corp. Wings, 1989—; cons. Savors Aviation, Negley, Ohio, 1968-71, Brunswick (Ohio) Aviation, 1985-86, Grafton-Ea. Aviation Group, 1988-90. Asst. leader Boy Scouts Am., North Lima, Ohio, 1968-71; advisor Youth Riding Club, Strongsville, 1974-76; co-leader Teen Aviation Group, Columbiana, Ohio, 1984. Served with USN, 1950-54, Korea. Mem. Nat. Bus. Aircraft Assn. (assoc.), Exptl. Aircraft Assn. (v.p. 1983—), Quiet Birdmen, DAV. Methodist. Avocations: aircraft restoration, golf. Home: 16554 Whitney Rd Cleveland OH 44136-2411 Office: Corporate Wings 355 Richmond Rd Cleveland OH 44143-1420

HILL, ROBERT MARTIN, police detective, forensic document examiner, consultant, lecturer; b. Hammond, Ind., Dec. 10, 1949; s. Donald Edwin and Norma Jeanne (Beal) H.; m. Connie Carolina Nordquist, Dec. 19, 1970. BA, U. Minn., 1974; postgrad., U. Phoenix; cert. in fin. fraud, IRS, Glynco, Ga., 1984; cert. in questioned documents, U.S. Secret Service, Glynco, Ga., 1986. Cert. police officer, Ill., Minn., Ariz.; cert. fraud examiner. Police officer Rolling Meadows (Ill.) Police Dept., 1970-72, St. Paul Police Dept., 1972-79; police officer Scottsdale (Ariz.) Police Dept., 1980-81, police fraud detective, 1981—; com. mem. Fraud Ariz. Banker's Assn., 1985-86; lectr. various colls. and orgns.; pres. Assoc. Document Labs., Inc.; forensic document examiner. Recipient Dirs. Commendation U.S. Secret Svc., Washington, 1986, Commendation, Dept. Defense, 1993; named Investigator of Yr. Econ. Crime Investigators, 1991. em. Internat. Assn. Credit Card Investigators (v.p. 1985-86, pres., bd. dirs. 1 986-88, 1986-88), Internat. Law Enforcement Officer of the Yr. award 1986, Ariz. chpt. Police Officer of the Yr. 1984, 86, 93), Internat. Assn. Auto Theft Investigators, Am. Acad. Forensic Scis., Internat. Police Assn., Assn. Cert. Fraud Examiners, Southwest Assn. Forensic Document Examiners, Internat. Assn. for Identification. Republican. Baptist. Avocations: travel, photography, weightlifting. Office: 9065 E Via Linda Scottsdale AZ 85258-5400

HILL, ROGER L., principal; b. July 24, 1964. BSE in Math., John Brown U., 1986; MEd in Ednl. Adminstrn., U. Ark., 1991. Tchr. math. Gentry (Ark.) Mid. Sch., 1987-90, Westwood Jr. H.S., Richardson, Tex., 1993-94; asst. prin. Ramay Jr. H.S., Fayetteville, Ark., 1990-93, 94-96; prin. Kirksey Mid. Sch., Rogers, Ark., 1996—. E-mail: rhill@kirksey.nwsc.k12.ar.us. Office: 316 Bluff Dr Lowell AR 72745

HILL, RONALD CHARLES, surgeon, educator; b. Parkersburg, W.Va., Sept. 4, 1948; s. Lloyd E. and Margaret (Pepper) H.; m. Lenora Jane Rexrode, June 12, 1971; children: Jeffrey, Mandy. BA, W.Va. U., 1970, MD, 1974. Diplomate Am. Bd. Surgery, Am. Bd. Thoracic Surgery. Intern dept. of surgery Duke U. Med. Ctr., Durham, N.C., 1974-75; resident in surgery Duke U., Durham, N.C., 1974-85, rsch. assoc., 1976-79, tchg. scholar, 1984-85; asst. prof. surgery W.Va. U., Morgantown, 1985-90, assoc. prof., 1990-96, prof. surgery, 1996—; cons. VA Med. Ctr., Clarksburg, W.Va., 1985—; dir. surg. rsch. dept. surgery W.Va. U., 1986-88, student coord. dept. surgery, 1986-97; mem. ad hoc com. merit rev. bd. for cardiovasc. studies VA, Washington, 1988-90; mem. Surg. Edn. and Self-Assessment Program '99 Com.; chmn. instnl. rev. bd. Protection Human Subjects, 1994—, program chmn. dept. surgery, 1998—. Contbr., co-contbr. numerous book chpts. and articles to profl. publs. Mem.-at-large adminstrv. bd. Drummond Chapel United Meth. Ch., Morgantown, 1987-89, 93-95, fin. com. 1994-96, lay del. to ann. conf., 1995-97, chmn. coun. on evangelism, 1999—. Recipient Lange Med. Book award, 1971, 73, 74, Merck Med. Book award, 1974, Roche Med. award, 1972, Sowers award Duke U., 1992. Fellow ACS (coun. W. Va. chpt. 1999—), Southeastern Surg. Congress, Assn. Acad. Surgery, Sabiston Soc., Am. Coll. Cardiology, Am. Coll. Chest Physicians, Am. Coll. Angiology, So. Thoracic Surg. Assn. (coun. mem.), Soc. Thoracic Surgeons; mem. Am. Heart Assn., (v.p., pres. elect, pres. W. Va. affiliate 1994-96), Soc. Univ. Surgeons, Am. Assn. Thoracic Surgery, Internat. Surg. Soc., So. Surg. Assn., W. Va. Med. Assn., Southern Thoracic Surgical Assn. (coun. 1999—), Mended Hearts, Lakeview Country Club, Pines Country Club, Phi Beta Kappa, Alpha Omega Alpha, Alpha Epsilon Delta, Profl. Assn. Diving Instrs. Soc. (cert. master scuba diver). Republican. Avocations: fishing, photography, scuba diving, shell collecting. Home: 10 Flegal St Morgantown WV 26505-2240 Office: WVa U Med Ctr Dept of Surgery Medical Center Dr Morgantown WV 26506

HILL, RONALD GUY, non-profit organization consultant; b. Andrews, N.C., Aug. 18, 1934; s. H. Guy and Martha Floriede (Henson) H.; m. Shirley Hendrix, Nov. 15, 1955; children: Ronald Guy Jr., Rebecca, William Felix. BS, U. Nebr., Omaha, 1969; postgrad., Indsl. Coll. Armed Forces, Washington, 1970. Enlisted U.S. Army, 1952, advanced through grades to capt.; comdg. officer 198th Pers. Svc. Co. and 61st Army Band, Fed. Republic Germany, 1967-69; dir. entertainment divsn. U.S. and free world forces, Vietnam, 1969-70; procurement officer Joint Mil. Svcs., Gunter AFB, Ala., 1970-71; exec. Chief Staff Mil. Ops., Washington, 1971-73; ret., 1973; active duty Operation Desert Storm, 1991; county mgr. Cherokee County, Murphy, N.C., 1974-81; mgr. Saudi Corp., Taif, Saudi Arabia, 1981-85; dir. John C. Campbell Folk Sch., Brasstown, N.C., 1985-91; founding dir. Allison's Wells Sch. Arts & Crafts and Small Bus. Incubator for Artists, 1991-96. Founder The Jeff Hailen Enloe, Jr. Meml. Fund, 1998—; founder orphanage, Fed. Republic Germany, 1968, Cherokee County Hist. Mus., 1977; founder, builder 12 community ctrs., Cherokee County, 1976, former mem. bd. dirs. Nat. Assn. Counties; bd. dirs. Western N.C. Assoc. Communities, Smoky Mountain Host N.C., Cherokee County Arts Coun., Western N.C. Tomorrow, Appalachian Consortium, So. Appalachian Highlands Conservancy, Mountain Outdoor Recreation Alliance, SE Tourism Soc.; past mem. Southwestern N.C. Planning and Econ. Devel. Commn.; bd. dirs. John C. Campbell Folk sch.; also numerous other orgns. Decorated Legion of Merit, Bronze Star; Bravery Gold medal (Greece), Presdl. citation (Republic of Korea), Gallantry Cross (Republic of Vietnam); recipient numerous other medals, badges, letters of appreciation and commendation. Mem. Cerkokee County C. of C., Am. Craft Coun., N.C. Arts Advs., Artists and Blacksmiths Assn. N.Am., Tenn. Artist-Craftsmen's Assn., N.Am. Folk Music and Dance Alliance, Cherokee County Hist. Soc. (past bd. dirs.), Am. Legion, VFW, Ret. Officers Assn., Soc. 3d Inf. Div. U.S.A., Masons (32 degree), Shriners. Democrat. Methodist. Avocations: blacksmithing, collecting pottery and antiques, weaving, woodworking, genealogy. E-mail: rhill@stc.net. Address: 2127 Duncan Bridge Rd Sautee Nacoochee GA 30571-3614

HILL, RUSSELL J., federal judge; b. 1931. BA, St. Olaf Coll., 1952; JD, U. Iowa, 1959. Pvt. law practice San Diego, Webster City, Iowa, 1966-72; judge Iowa Dist. Ct., Webster City, 1972-87; chief bankruptcy judge U.S. Dist. Ct. (so. dist.) Iowa, Des Moines, 1987—. Served with USNR, 1952-56. Office: US Courthouse Annex 110 E Court Ave Ste 447 Des Moines IA 50309-2044

HILL, RUTH FOELL, language consultant; b. Houston, Sept. 13, 1931; d. Ernest William and Florence Margaret (Kane) Foell; children: Linden Ruth, Andrea Grace. Student, Principia Coll., 1950; BA, U. Calif., Berkeley, 1952; postgrad., San Diego State, 1955, Cen. Piedmont, 1981. Cert. tchr., Calif. Owner, dir. Art Gallery of Chapel Hill (N.C.), 1966-75; ecumenical bd. Campus Ministry, Charlotte; with referral svc. Charlotte (N.C.) Bed and Breakfast Registry, 1980-90; lang. cons. Berlitz Internat., Raleigh, N.C., 1988-91; cert. cons. Performax Internat.; rep. UN Decade for Women Conf., NGO Forum, Nairobi, Kenya, 1985, Women and Global Security Conf., 1986; rep. emerging issues forum N.C. State U., 1987-93; presenter Southeastern Women's Studies Conf. Contbr. poetry to Nat. Libr. of Poetry. Bd. dirs., chmn. natural resources com. LWV; coord. USIA grant region 6, Internat. Exch. Network; mem. N.C. Leadership Forum, N.C. Citizens Assembly, 1989; chmn. Week of Edn. Pub. Forum on Energy, Union Concerned Scientists, 1990-93; bd. dirs. Nat. Women's Conf. Commn., 1994—; mem. edn. subcom. Mayor's Internat. Cabinet, 1995; mem. Congress House Spkr.'s Citizen Task Force, 1995—; mem. Rep. Platform Com. and Nat. Presdl. Task Force, 1995, Rep. Inner Cir., 1995. Named Outstanding Athlete Women's Athletic Assn., Woman of the Yr., Am. Biog. Inst., 1994, Internat. Poetry Hall of Fame, 1998; Hewlett Found. scholar. Mem. AAUW (v.p. membership com., bd. dirs.), Ams. for Legal Reform (adv. bd.), Am. Farm Land Trust, UN Assn. U.S.A. (chpt. pres. 1991-93, co-chair UN Day Queens Coll. 1992, N.C. divsn. sec. 1993-94, UN50 chair 1995), Am. Biog. Inst. Rsch. Assn. (nominated to bd. govs.), Am. Biog. Inst. (apptd. adv. bd.), Carolina Coun. on World Affairs, Chapel Hill-Carrboro Sch. Art Guild (pres.), Midwest Acad., World Wide Women in Environment, N.Y. Acad. Sci. Republican. Christian Scientist. Avocations: travel, environmental issues, international exchange networking. Office: PO Box 220802 Charlotte NC 28222-0802

HILL, SAMUEL RICHARDSON, JR., retired medical educator; b. Greensboro, N.C., May 19, 1923; s. Samuel Richardson and Nona (Sink) H.; m. Janet Redman, Oct. 28, 1950; children: Susan Hill Lindley, Samuel Richardson III, Elizabeth Hill Humphreys, Margaret Hill Cohn. BA, Duke U., 1943; MD, Bowman Gray Sch. Medicine, 1946; DSc (hon.), U. Ala., 1975, Wake Forest U., 1979. Intern medicine Peter Bent Brigham Hosp., Boston, 1947-48; asst. resident medicine Peter Bent Brigham Hosp., 1948-49, asst. medicine, 1949-50; teaching fellow medicine Harvard Sch. Medicine, 1948-49, research fellow medicine, Dazian Med. Found. research fellow, 1949-50; chief resident medicine N.C. Bapt. Hosp., instr. medicine Bowman Gray Sch. Medicine, 1950-51; asst. medicine Harvard Sch. Medicine, also Peter Bent Brigham Hosp., 1953-54; asst. prof. medicine, dir. metabolic and endocrine div. Med. Coll. Ala., also chief metabolic div. VA Hosp., Birmingham, 1954-57; assoc. prof. medicine, dir. metabolic and endocrine div. U. Ala. Med. Ctr. and VA Hosp., Birmingham, 1957-62; prof. medicine, dean U. Ala. Sch. Medicine, Birmingham, 1962-68; prof. medicine U. Ala. Med. Coll., Birmingham, 1968-94; v.p. for health affairs, dir. Med. Ctr., 1968-77; pres. U. Ala., Birmingham, 1977-87, Disting. prof., 1987-93, Disting. prof. emeritus and cons., 1994-98; dir. med. edn. program U. Ala. System, 1972-79; bd. dirs. Birmingham br. Fed. Res. Bank Atlanta, 1981-83, chmn. Birmingham br., 1983. Contbr. articles to med. jours. Bd. regents Nat. Library Medicine, 1978-80, chmn. bd. regents, 1979-80. Served to maj. M.C., USAF, 1951-53. Fellow ACP (Willard O. Thompson Meml. traveling scholar 1960), AAAS, Royal Soc. Medicine; mem. Soc. Exptl. Biology and Medicine, Am. Fedn. Clin. Research (pres. 1961-62), Endocrine Soc., Am., Ala. diabetes socs., Mass., Jefferson County med. socs., Am. Thyroid Soc., AMA, Inst. Medicine of Nat. Acad. Scis., So. Soc. Clin. Investigation, Med. Assn. State Ala. (councillor), Assn. Am. Med. Colls., Assn. for Acad. Health Centers (pres. 1972), Sigma Xi, Alpha Omega Alpha. Episcopalian. Home: 109 Mountain Brook Park Dr Birmingham AL 35213-3639

HILL, SHIRLEY ANN, mathematics educator; b. Kansas City, Mo., Aug. 26, 1927; d. George Haddon and Lena (Oberdiek) H. BA, U. Mo., 1948; MA, U. Kansas City, 1956; PhD, Stanford U., 1961; LHD (hon.), U. Nebr., Omaha, 1984. Tchr. Kansas City Sch. Dist., 1956-58, Jefferson Union Dist., Santa Clara, Calif., 1958-60; research assoc. Stanford (Calif.) U., 1960-63; prof. U. Mo., Kansas City, 1963—, Curator's prof., 1987—. Author: (with others) Introduction to Logic, 1964, Elementary Geometry, 1976; editor: Education in the 80s: Mathematics, 1982.. recipient Howard J. McGraw, Jr. Prize in Education, McGraw-Hill, 1992. Mem. Nat. Coun. Tchrs. Math. (pres. 1978-80), Math. Scis. Edn. Bd. (chmn. 1985-90), U.S. Commn. on Math. Instrn. (chmn. 1976-80), Nat. Bd. Profl. Teaching Standards (bd. dirs. 1988-92), Phi Beta Kappa.

HILL, STAN WAYNE, video producer; b. Marion, Ill., Dec. 30, 1945; s. Clayal Clint and Okie Magdalene (Rodgers) H.; m. Judith Elaine Hobbs, Aug. 18, 1967; children: Amanda C., Kirstan C. BS in Communications, So. Ill. U., 1967; M in Religious Edn., So. Bapt. Thol. Sem., 1969. Producer talk show Sta. WJCL-TV, Savannah, Ga., 1971-72, producer news, 1977-78; pres. Video Media Prodns., Statesboro, Ga., 1975-78; freelance producer Birmingham, Ala., 1978-83; video producer Woman's Missionary Union So. Bapt. Conv., Birmingham, 1983—. Exec. prodr. (documentary video) "One Common Need", 1996 (Bronze Telly award 1996, Silver Angel award 1996, Silver medal Houston Internat Film Festival 1996); prodr., dir., writer (video program) Christian Women's Job Corps, 1998 (Silver Angel award 1998, Communicator award 1998); prodr., dir. over 750 shows, sports events; writer, prodr. over 100 ednl. videos. Mem. Internat. TV Assn. (regional v.p. 1986-88, chpt. pres. 1989-90), Religion Communicators Coun., Bapt. Communicators Assn. Baptist. Avocations: Victorian architecture, science fiction. Office: Woman's Missionary Union 100 Missionary Ridge Birmingham AL 35242

HILL, STEPHEN L., JR., lawyer; m. Marianne Matteson; 2 children. BS in Polit. Sci., Southwest Mo. State U., 1981; JD, U. Mo., 1986; postgrad., London U. Trial atty. Smith, Gill, Fisher & Butts, Kansas City, 1986-94; U.S. atty. Western Dist. Mo., Kansas City, 1994—. Office: Office US Atty We Dist Mo 400 E 9th St Ste 5510 Kansas City MO 64106-2117*

HILL, STEVEN, actor; b. Seattle, Feb. 24, 1922; m. Selma Stern, 1951; 4 children. Actor appearings in films: Lady Without Passport, 1950, Storm Fear, 1956, Goddess, 1958, Kiss Her Goodbye, 1959, A Child is Waiting, 1963, Slender Thread, 1965, It's My Turn, 1980, Rich and Famous, 1981, Eyewitness, 1981, Yentl, 1983, Garbo Talks, 1984, On Valentine's Day, 1986, Brighton Beach Memoirs, 1986, Raw Deal, 1986, Legal Eagles, 1986, Heartburn, 1986, Courtship, 1987, Running on Empty, 1988, Billy Bathgate, 1991, White Palace, 1991, The Firm, 1993, (tv series): Sacco-Vanzetti Story, 1960, Mission: Impossible, 1966, King, 1978, One Life to Live, 1968, Between Two Women, 1986, Columbo: Murder, Smoke & Shadows, 1989, Law & Order, 1990—, Where's the Money, Noreen?, 1995; TV guest appearances include: Actor's Studio, 1948, Goodyear TV Playhouse, 1951, Philco TV Playhouse, 1948, Alfred Hitchcock Presents, 1955, The Untouchables, 1959, Route 66, 1960, Naked City, 1958, The Fugitive, 1963, thirtysomething, 1987. Nominated Emmy, 1998, SAG award, 1998, 99. Office: Wolf Films Inc c/o Universal TV 100 Universal City Plz #69 Universal City CA 91608-1085*

HILL, STEVEN JOHN, journalist, political reformer; b. New London, Conn., June 6, 1958; s. William John and Patricia (Rogers) H. BA in Geology and Geophysics, Yale U., 1982. Freelance journalist San Francisco, 1991—; program dir. Labor Net @ IGC, San Francisco, 1995-96; west coast dir. Ctr. for Voting and Democracy, San Francisco, 1993—. Co-author: Reflecting All of Us, 1998; contbr. articles to newspapers, profl. publs., and mags., including Wall St. Jour., Ms., Seattle Times, Cleve. Plain Dealer, Christian Sci. Monitor, L.A. Times, Miami Herald, San Francisco Chronicle, The Nation, others, also poetry and short fiction to small publs. Mem. adv. com. Citizens for Proportioned Representation, San Francisco, 1993-96; mem. steering com. LaborNet @ IGC, 1996; campaign mgr., chmn. San Franciscans for Preference Voting, 1996. Avocations: hiking, bicycling, oil painting, music composition, writing novels.

HILL, SUSAN SLOAN, safety engineer; b. Quincy, Mass., June 1, 1952; d. Ralph Arnold and Grace Elenore (Sloan) Crosby; m. William Loyd Hill, Dec. 16, 1973 (div. July 1982); m. William Joseph Graham, Sept. 10, 1983 (div. Feb. 1985). Assoc. Sci. in Gen. Engring., Motlow State C.C., Tullahoma, Tenn., 1976; BS in Indsl. Engring., Tenn. Technol. U., 1978. Intern, safety engr. Intern Tng. Ctr., U.S. Army, Red River Army Depot, Tex., 1978-79, Field Safety Activity, Charlestown, Ind., 1979, system safety engr. Comm.-Electronics Command, Ft. Monmouth, N.J., 1979-84, gen. engr., 1984-85; chief system safety Arnold Air Force Sta., USAF, Tullahoma, 1984; system safety engr. U.S. Army Safety Ctr., Ft. Rucker, Ala., 1985-91; medically retired; ind. cons. system safety, 1991—; founder Fibromyalgia Support Group; leader Arthritis Found. Support Group; active Arthritis Found. Recipient 5 letters of appreciation U.S. Army. Mem. NAFE, Assn. Fed. Safety and Health Profls. (regional v.p. 1980-84), Assn. Women Engrs., Nat. Safety Mgmt. Soc., Am. Soc. Safety Engrs., System Safety Soc., Order Engr. Republican. Episcopalian. Avocations: bowling, needlework, sewing, cooking, golf. Home and Office: PO Box 1075 Tullahoma TN 37388-1075

HILL, TERRELL LESLIE, chemist, biophysicist; b. Oakland, Calif., Dec. 19, 1917; s. George Leslie and Ollie (Moreland) H.; m. Laura Etta Gano, Sept. 23, 1942; children: Julie Lisbeth Eden, Carolyn Jo (Mrs. Gary Lineburg), Ernest Evan. A.B., U. Calif. at Berkeley, 1939, Ph.D., 1942; postgrad., Harvard U., 1940. Instr. chemistry Western Res. U., 1942-44; rsch. assoc. radiation lab. U. Calif. at Berkeley, 1944-45; rsch. assoc. chemistry, then asst. prof. chemistry U. Rochester, 1945-49; chemist U.S. Naval Med. Rsch. Inst., 1949-57; prof. chemistry U. Oreg., 1957-67; prof. chemistry U. Calif. at Santa Cruz, 1967-71, adj. prof., 1977-89, prof. emeritus, 1989—, vice chancellor for scis., div. natural scis., 1968-69; research chemist NIH, Bethesda, Md., 1971-88, scientist emeritus, 1988—; Mem. biophysics study sect. USPHS, 1954-57; chemistry panel NSF, 1961-64. Author: Statistical Mechanics, 1956, 87, Statistical Thermodynamics, 1960, 86, Thermodynamics of Small Systems, vol. I, 1963, 94, vol. II, 1964, 94, Matter and Equilibrium, 1965, Thermodynamics for Chemists and Biologists, 1968, Free Energy Transduction in Biology, 1977, Cooperativity Theory in Biochemistry, 1985, Linear Aggregation Theory in Cell Biology, 1987, Free Energy Transduction and Biochemical Cycle Kinetics, 1989, also rsch. papers. Guggenheim fellow Yale, 1952-53; recipient Arthur S. Flemming award U.S. Govt., 1954; Distinguished Civilian Service award U.S. Navy, 1955; award Washington Acad. Scis., 1956; Disting. Service award USPHS, 1981; Disting. Service award U. Oreg., 1983; Sloan Found. fellow, 1958-62. Mem Nat. Acad. Scis., Am. Chem. Soc. (Kendall award 1969), Biophys. Soc., NAACP, ACLU, Phi Beta Kappa. Home: 433 Logan St Santa Cruz CA 95062-3607

HILL, THOMAS ALLEN, lawyer; b. Salem, Ohio, Mar. 29, 1958; s. Charles Spencer and Dorothy Jane (Allen) H. *During WWII father Charles served in the 586th B-26 Bomb Squadron of the 397th Bomb Group, U.S. Army Air Force, and was in France in 1945 with the 1259th Combat Engineer Batallion. Mother Dorothy worked for Lockheed Aircraft Corp., 1943-1945. Father descends from Sir Moyses Hill, who accompanied the Earl of Essex to Ireland in 1573 and was dubbed a Knight Bachelor in 1616. Mother descends from the immigrant Ralph Allen of Sandwich, Mass. and his son, Jedediah Allen, the latter having been a minister among the Quakers as early as 1685 and a member of the first New Jersey Colonial Assembly in 1703.* BA magna cum laude, Hiram Coll., 1980; JD, George Washington U., 1984. Bar: Ohio 1984, Pa. 1987, D.C. 1988, U.S. Supreme Ct. 1989, Tex. 1990, Okla. 1991; registered rep. series 6 and 63 Nat. Assn. Securities Dealers. Legis. intern Office of Hon. John Conyers, Jr., Washington, 1979; asst. to dean campus Life for Housing, conf. dir. Hiram (Ohio) Coll., 1980-81; corp. counsel Capital Oil & Gas Inc., Austintown, Ohio, 1984-93; gen. counsel, sec. North Coast Energy, Inc., Bedford Heights, Ohio, 1987—, Trinity Oil & Gas, Inc. subs. North Coast Energy Inc., Warren, Ohio, 1990-93; mem. mini-task force on notices of violation Ohio Div. Oil and Gas, Columbus, 1988-90; part-time fin. analyst Primerica Fin. Svcs., Inc., 1997—. *Tom Hill has been the General Counsel of North Coast Energy, Inc. (NCE) since its acquisition of Capital Oil & Gas, Inc. in 1987. NCE is publicly traded on NASDAQ under the symbol NCEB and is a major Appalachian Basin exploration and production company which in 1998 acquired the assets of BTI Energy, Inc. and Kelt-Ohio, Inc. Since 1997 NCE has been an affiliate of NUON International, whose parent is the second largest public utility company in the Netherlands and a leader in the development of cogeneration facilities. NCE's second largest shareholder is Fort Worth-based Range Resources Corporation.* Mem. ABA, Ohio Bar Assn., Mahoning County Bar Assn., Pa. Bar Assn., Okla. Bar Assn., D.C. Bar Assn., State Bar Tex., Trumbull County Bar Assn., Ohio Oil and Gas Assn., Christian Legal Soc., Ea. Mineral Law Found., Fed. Energy Bar Assn., Ohio Land Title Assn., Ohio Geneal. Soc., Mahoning Valley Hist. Soc., Austintown Hist. Soc., Gen. Soc., War of 1812, SAR, Order of Arrow, Kappa Delta Pi, Pi Gamma Mu. Republican. Avocations: local history, study of Amaranth. Home: 4841 Westchester Dr Apt 102 Youngstown OH 44515-2548 Office:

North Coast Energy Inc 1993 Case Pkwy Twinsburg OH 44087-2343 *Motto: I Peter 1: 23-25.*

HILL, THOMAS BOWEN, III, lawyer; b. Montgomery, Ala., Oct. 21, 1929; s. Thomas Bowen, Jr. and Mildred (Abrams) H.; m. Maria Paschall, Dec. 29, 1955; children: Thomas Bowen IV, Mason P., William I. III, Chappell H. BS, U. Ala., 1951, LLB, 1953. Bar: Ala. 1953. Assoc. atty., pres. Hill, Hill, Carter, Franco, Cole & Black, 1953-57, ptnr., 1957—; bd. dirs. Regions Bank Montgomery; mem. Gov.'s staff, 1963—. Former trustee YWCO; past chmn., bd. of deacons Presbyn. Ch. Recipient Algernon Sydney Sullivan medallion as outstanding male grad. U. Ala., 1953; recipient Unsung Hero award Trinity Presbyn. Ch. Mem. ABA, Ala. Bar Assn. (com. chmn., award of merit), Montgomery County Bar Assn. (past pres.), Am. Coll. Mortgage Attys., Ala. Bar Found. (founder), U. Ala. Nat. Alumni Assn. (past v.p.), Montgomery C. of C. (past bd. dirs.), Ala. Motorists Assn. AAA Alabama (bd. dirs.), Com. of 100, Pioneers of Montgomery, Ala. Assn. Canterbury Clubs, Half Snapper Club, Druids, Jasons, Quadrangle, Kiwanis (past pres.), Tau Kappa Alpha, Phi Delta Phi, Alpha Tau Omega, Omicron Delta Kappa. Avocations: hunting, fishing, boating. Home: 3721 Vaughn Rd Montgomery AL 36106-2726

HILL, THOMAS CLARK, lawyer; b. Prestonsburg, Ky., July 17, 1946; s. Lon Clay and Corinne (Allen) H.; m. J. Barbarie Friedly, June 13, 1968; children: Jason L., Duncan L. BA, Case Western Reserve U., 1968; JD, U. Chgo., 1973. Bar: Ohio 1973, U.S. Supreme Ct. 1976. Assoc. atty. Taft, Stettinius & Hollister LLP, Cin., 1973-81, ptnr., 1981—. Author: Monthly Meetings in North America: A Quaker Index, 4th edit., 1998. Trustee, treas. Wilmington (Ohio) Coll., 1982-94, 99—; treas. Friends World Commn. for Consultation, Sect. of the Ams., 1990-95, presiding clk., 1995-99; trustee Wilmington Yearly Meeting of Friends (Quakers), 1986-98. Mem. ABA, Ohio State Bar Assn., Cin. Bar Assn., Friends Hist. Assn. (bd. dirs. 1994-95). Republican. Mem. Soc. of Friends. Avocation: Quaker history. Office: 1800 Firstar Tower 425 Walnut St Cincinnati OH 45202-3923

HILL, THOMAS CLARKE, IX, accountant, systems specialist, entrepreneur; b. Chgo., July 5, 1969; s. Thomas Clarke VIII and Arlene Mae (Wertz) H. BA in Polit. Economy and Politics, Lake Forest Coll., 1992; postgrad., DePaul U., 1998—. Legis. asst. State Rep. William E. Peterson, Prairie View, Ill., 1989-92, State Sen. William E. Peterson, Prairie View, 1992-94; project mgr. Vernon Twp., Prairie View, 1992-94; cons. Resource Tech. Assocs., Des Plaines, Ill., 1994-95; acct., systems specialist Green Acres Country Club, Northbrook, Ill., 1995—; owner IX Designs, 1997—. Precinct com. Lake County (Ill.) Rep. Ctrl. Com., 1990—; chmn. Lake County Young Reps., 1993; del. state conv. Rep. Ctrl. Com., Peoria, Ill., 1992; election judge Office of County Clk., Lake County, 1988-90; treas. Medinah Investment Club. Frances Beidler scholar Lake Forest Coll., 1990-91, 91-92. Mem. Nat. Eagle Scout Assn., Club Accts. Assn. Am. (assoc.), Shriners, Scottish Rite, Masons, Mensa, York Rite, Phi Beta Kappa, Pi Sigma Alpha. Avocations: camping, trapshooting, woodworking. Home: 64 Berkshire Ln Lincolnshire IL 60069-3203 Office: Green Acres Country Club 916 Dundee Rd Northbrook IL 60062-2798

HILL, THOMAS GLENN, III, dermatologist; b. Atlanta, Dec. 15, 1942; s. Thomas Glenn, Jr. and Wilella (Burns) H.; BA in History, Emory U., 1964; MD, Med. Coll. Ga., Augusta, 1968; m. Barbara Brown; children: Elizabeth Burns, Jennifer Michelle, Thomas Glenn IV. Diplomate Am. Bd. Dermatology Intern, USAF Med. Center, Keesler AFB, 1968-69; resident in dermatology Med. Coll. Va., 1972-75; practice medicine specializing in dermatology, cutaneous and cosmetic surgery, Decatur, Ga., 1975—; mem. staff DeKalb Gen., Grady Meml., Rockdale County, Newton County hosps.; pres. Physician's Skin Care Services, Inc. clin. asst. prof. dermatology Emory U. Med. Sch., 1975—. Mem. Ga. Gov.'s Medicaid Adv. Panel, 1978-79. Mem. editorial bd. Jour. Dermatologic Surgery and Oncology, 1988—; guest editor Jour. Dermatol. Surgery and Oncology. Served as officer M.C., USAF, 1967-72. Decorated Disting. Service award, Presdl. Unit citation. Fellow Am. Acad. Cosmetic Surgeons, Internat. Assn. Cosmetic Surgeons; mem. AMA (Physician Recognition awards 1975, 90), Am. Acad. Dermatology, Am. Soc. Dermatologic Surgery, Internat. Soc. Dermatologic Surgery, Am. Dermatologic Soc. Allergy and Immunology, So. Med. Assn., Ga. Soc. Dermatologists, Ga. Soc. Dermatologic Surgeons (sec.-treas. 1986, bd. dirs. 1985-88, pres. 1986-87), Atlanta Dermatologic Assn., Chattahoochee Country Club. Office: 5071 Snapfinger Woods Dr Decatur GA 30035-4019

HILL, THOMAS WILLIAM, JR., lawyer, educator; b. N.Y.C., Dec. 25, 1924; s. Thomas William Sr. and Marion (Bond) H.; m. Elizabeth Rowe, June 18, 1949; children: Gretchen P., Catharine B., Thomas William III. BS, U. Pa., 1948; MBA, NYU, 1950; JD, Columbia U., 1953. Bar: N.Y. 1953, D.C. 1954, U.S. Supreme Ct. 1958, Fla. 1989; CPA, N.Y. Sr. tax acct. Hurdman & Cranstoun, 1949-50; asst. U.S. atty. So. Dist. N.Y., 1953-54; assoc. Cahill, Gordon, Reindel & Ohl, 1954-58; sr. ptnr. Spear & Hill, 1958-75; ptnr. Sidley & Austin, 1981-86; pres. Belco Petroleum Co., N.Y.C., 1962-63; legal adviser Sultanate of Oman, 1972-76; adj. prof. law U. Miami, 1986-97. Contbr. articles to profl. jours. Vice chmn., pres., trustee Internat. Coll., Beirut, Lebanon, 1978-91. 1st lt. AUS, 1943-46. Decorated Bronze Star, Purple Heart, Medal of Oman (Sultanate of Oman), Order of Homayun (Iran). Mem. ABA, Assn. of Bar of City of N.Y., IBA, Racquet and Tennis Club (N.Y.C.), Mayacoo Golf Club, Taconic Golf Club, Phi Delta Phi, Kappa Sigma. Home: 2627 Muirfield Ct West Palm Beach FL 33414-7019

HILL, TYRONE, professional basketball player; b. Cin., Mar. 19, 1968. BA in Comm. Arts, Xavier U., 1986-90. Forward Golden State Warriors, San Francisco, 1990-93, Cleve. Cavaliers, 1993-97, Milw. Bucks, 1997-99, Philadelphia 76ers, 1999—. Active NBA Stay In Sch. Program. All-time leading rebounder, scorer Xavier U.; leader Cleve. Cavaliers field-goal percentage, 1993-94; named to NBA All-Star Game Eastern Conf., 1995. Avocation: music. Office: Philadelphia 76ers First Union Ctr 3601 S Broad St Philadelphia PA 19148*

HILL, VALERIE CHARLOTTE, nurse; b. Shaftsbury, Vt., Dec. 2, 1932; d. William Henry Harrison and Angeline Margaret Stella (Fuller) Hill; m. Edward Joseph Klanit (dec. July 1984); 1 child, Joyce Ellen Klanit Artadi. Grad., Mt. Sinai Hosp. Sch. Nursing, 1955. RN, N.Y. Nurse The Jack Martin Respiratory Ctr. of The Mt. Sinai Hosp., N.Y.C., 1955-57; v.p. Chauffeurs Unlimited, Inc., N.Y.C., 1957-77; nurse Rusk Inst., N.Y.C., 1957-58, Beth Israel Med. Ctr., N.Y.C., 1978-79; owner, mgr. Powers Fish Market, Inc., N.Y.C., 1977-84; tchr. Techs. for Creating, Albany, N.Y., 1983-97, Snohomish, Wash., 1997—; nurse Doctors Hosp., N.Y.C., 1984-86; pvt. duty nurse Personal Health Care Svcs., Albany, N.Y., 1987-88; nurse Albany Med. Ctr. Hosp., 1987-95; real estate sales assoc. Century 21-Stanley Major Ltd., West Sand Lake, N.Y., 1988, Century-21 Home Towne Properties, Albany, 1989-92. Author numerous poems. Recipient Outstanding Service to Community award Mayor Koch City of N.Y., 1983. Mem. Alumnae Assn. Mt. Sinai Hosp. Sch. Nursing (bd. dirs. 1968). Democrat. Avocations: reading, writing poetry, home videos, piano, walking, painting. Home: 7618 129 Dr SE Snohomish WA 98290-6248

HILL, VIRGIL, professional boxer; b. Bismarck, N.D., Jan. 18, 1964. Recipient Silver medal 1984 Olympics; named WBA Light Heavyweight Champion, 1987-91, 92. Achievements include record of 42 wins and 1 loss with 20 knock-outs.

HILL, W. CLAYTON, management consultant; b. New Hampton, Mo., Sept. 24, 1916; s. Charles A. and Elva E. (Riggins) H.; m. Dorothy L. Crosby, Aug. 24, 1938; children: Charles W., Douglas L. BS Bus. Adminstrn., U. Mo., 1937. Acct. GE, Bridgeport, Conn., 1937-41; sales mgr. IBM, Phila., 1941-49; asst. to pres. GE X-Ray Corp., Milw., 1949-53; v.p. Hotpoint Co. divsn. GE, Chgo., 1953-57; mgr. planning GE, N.Y.C., 1957-62; dir. planning Am. Can Co., N.Y.C., 1962-64; mgmt. cons. Clay Hill & Assocs., Greenwich, Conn., 1964-80, Prarie Village, Kans., 1980—; instr. Marquette U., 1950-53; cons. RCA Corp., Sperry Co., Ford Motor Co., Pet, Inc., GE, Monsanto Co., H&R Block, Inc., Farmland Industries, Inc., Sprint Corp., others. Pres. King Merit Estates; mem. town bd. Greenwich, Conn., 1976-80, adv. bd. Bus. Sch. U. Mo., City of Prarie Village; bd. dirs. Internat. Fedn. Bus. Edn., 1992; cons. to pres. N.W. Mo. State U., 1994. With Signal Corps AUS, 1943-46. Recipient Pres. citation merit award, Outstanding Achievement and Meritorious Svc. award, 1988, Faculty-Alumni award, Disting Achievement, 1988, W. Clayton Hill Innovator award GE Med. Systems, 1989, Alumnus of Yr. award U. Mo., 1992, Disting. Svc. award 1993. Mem. Am. Mktg. Assn., U. Mo. Bus. Sch. Alumni Assn. (pres. Kansas City chpt. 1985-94. Office: 8713 Catalina St Shawnee Mission KS 66297-2351

HILL, WALLACE HARRY, sports television consultant; b. Chgo., Oct. 14, 1935; s. Wallace George and Evelyn Teresa (O'Connor) H.; m. Mary Helen Du Beau, Oct. 21, 1956 (div. Jan. 1970); children: Scott, Amy, Molly, Betsi; m. Judith Ellen Swigost, May 16, 1982;. BA in Comm., Am. U., 1960. TV prodn. mgr. NBC Sports, N.Y.C., 1973-92; pvt. practice sports TV cons. N.Y.C., 1992—; mem. broadcast adv. bd. NBA, N.Y.C., 1992-98. Prodr. (film) Skills That Last A Lifetime, 1972 (Silver award), In Search of Spring, 1973 (Silver award), Internat. Film & TV Festival N.Y. With U.S. Army, 1954-56. Mem. Internat. TV Assn., Nat. Assn. Broadcasters (assoc.). Avocation: golfer. Home and Office: 155 E 34th St Apt 12C New York NY 10016-4751

HILL, WALTER, film director, writer, producer; b. Long Beach, Calif., Jan. 10, 1942. Student, Mexico City Coll., Mich. State U. Screenplays include Hickey and Boggs, 1972, The Getaway, 1972, 1994, The Thief Who Came to Dinner, 1973, The Mackintosh Man, 1973, The Drowning Pool, 1975, The Warriors, 1979; writer, dir.: Hard Times, 1975, The Driver, 1978, The Warriors, 1979, Southern Comfort, 1981, 48 Hrs., 1982, Streets of Fire, 1984, Wild Bill, 1995; producer: Alien, 1979, Blue City, 1986; writer, prodr. (with Gordon Carroll and David Giler) Aliens, 1986, Alien 3, 1992; dir.: The Warriors, The Long Riders, 1980, Brewster's Millions, 1985, Crossroads, 1986, Extreme Prejudice, 1987, Johnny Handsome, 1989, Another 48 Hrs., 1990, Tresspass, 1992, Geronimo, 1993 (also prodr.); dir., writer, producer: Red Heat, 1988, Tales from the Crypt, 1989-92. Office: William Morris Agy c/o J Burnham 151 S El Camino Dr Beverly Hills CA 90212-2775*

HILL, WALTER A., agricultural sciences educator, researcher; b. New Brunswick, N.J., Aug. 9, 1946; s. Henry Solomon and Tessie Paisley H.; m. Jill Karen Harris; children: Shaka W.T., Askia A.H., Osei J.E. BA in Chemistry, Lake Forest Coll., 1968; MAT in Chemistry, U. Chgo., 1970; MS in Soil Chemistry, U. Ariz., 1973; PhD in Agronomy, U. Ill., 1978. From asst. prof. to assoc. prof. dept. agrl. scis. Tuskegee (Ala.) U., 1978-84, adminstr. USDA Cooperative Extension Program, 1987-91, prof. dept. agrl. scis., 1984—, rsch. dir. USDA Cooperative State Rsch. Program, 1986—, dir. G.W. Carver Agrl. Experiment Sta., 1986—, dean Sch. Agriculture and Home Economics, 1987—; bd. dirs. Agrl. Satellite Corp., 1990-93; chair 1890 Coun. Deans and Dirs., 1992—, Profl. Agrl. Workers Conf., 1988—, Internat. Symposium Sweetpotato Tech. for 21st Century, 1991; co-dir. Nat. Sweetpotato Info. Ctr., 1991—; dir. NASA Ctr. Food Prodn., Processing and Waste Mgmt. for CELSS, 1991—, So. Food Systems Edn. Consortium; mem. various coms. Nat. Rsch. Coun.; mem. adv. bd. NSF, 1992—; USAID sci. liaison Asian Vegetable Rsch. and Devel. Ctr., Taiwan, 1989—; mem. agrl. biotech. rsch. adv. com. USDA, 1992—; vis. sci. NASA Kennedy Space Ctr., 1987, Internat. Inst. Tropical Agriculture, Nigeria, 1985, Dept Agronomy Purdue U., summer 1981. Founder Tuskegee Horizons Mag./Jour., 1990—; editor Sweetpotato Technology for the 21st Century, 1993; contbr. numerous articles, books, book chpts., procs., abstracts; patentee in field. Trustee Lake Forest Coll., Ill., 1989—; vol. Cub Scouts Am., Tuskegee, 1990—; mem. PTA, Washington Chapel A.M.E. Recipient Outstanding Rsch. and Teaching award Ala. Soil & Water Conservation Soc., 1992, Futurist in Sci. and Tech. award Black Enterprise Mag., 1990, Faculty award excecllence in sci. & tech. White House Initiative on HBCU, 1988, Disting. Alumni Svc. citation Lake Forest Coll., 1986; named Exec. of Yr. by Profl. Secs. Internat., 1991, Danforth assoc. for excellence in undergrad. teaching Danforth Found., 1980; Kellogg fellow, 1988; USDA grantee, NASA grantee, U.S. Dept. Edn. grantee, USAID grantee, others. Fellow Am. Soc. Agronomy (Outstanding Minority Educator award 1990); mem. Am. Soc. Gravitational & Space Biology, Am. Soc. Horticultural Sci., Crop Sci. Soc. Am. (strategic planning com. 1993), Internat. Soil Sci. Soc., Internat. Soc. Tropical Root Crops (Plucknett Outstanding Rsch. Paper award 1983), Internat. Soc. Horticultural Sci., Soil Sci. Soc. Am., Assn. Rsch. Dirs. (chair elect 1992—), Phi Beta Kappa, Sigma Xi, Gamma Sigma Delta. Office: Tuskegee Univ Carver Agrl Expt Sta Campbell Hall Rm 100 Tuskegee Institute AL 36088*

HILL, WALTER WATSON, JR., political science educator; b. Chgo., Nov. 1, 1951; s. Walter and Phyllis Hill. BS, MIT, Cambridge, 1973; MS, MIT, 1977, PhD, 1984. Lectr., asst. prof. Howard U., Washington, 1980-90; assoc. prof. St. Mary's Coll. Md., St. Mary's City, 1990—; vis. prof. U. N.C., Chapel Hill, 1993-94, vis. scholar U. Mich., Ann Arbor, 1997-98. Contbr. articles to profl. jours. Gallatin fellow, Geneva, 1978-79; travel grantee NSF, Paris, 1985. Avocations: running, chess. Office: St Marys Coll Md Dept Polit Sci Saint Marys City MD 20686

HILL, WAYNE THOMAS, school administrator, minister; b. Miss., Mar. 30, 1942; s. Bill Gully and Nona Zona (Smith) H.; m. Sandra Smith, Oct. 4, 1963 (dec. Apr. 1992); children: Shelye, Renee, William; m. Joyce R. Rogers, Dec. 18, 1994. BS in Edn., Miss. State U., 1975, M in Sch. Adminstrn., 1984; M in Bible Studies, So. Bapt. Coll., 1989, DD, 1990; DM, Trinity Bible Coll., 1991. Spl. project engr. Taylor Machine Works, Louisville, Miss., 1963-75; instr. Webster County Vocat. Ctr., Europa, Miss., 1975-78, East Ctrl. C.C., Decatur, Miss., 1978-85; adminstr. Millsaps Vocat. Ctr., Starkville, Miss., 1985-96, Kosciusko (Miss.) Attala Vocat. Ctr., 1996—; adv. bd. So. Bapt. Ctr., Jacksonville, Fla., 1995-96. Exec. bd. Winston Bapt. Assn., Louisville, 1992-96, trustee, 1993-96, tchr., 1990—. With USAR, 1959-62. Recipient Small Ch. Pastor Yr. award So. Bapt. Assn., Jackson, Miss., 1990. Mem. VICA, MAVE, AVA, Miss. State U. Alumni Assn. Avocations: fishing, reading, restoring old cars. Home: 432 Boon Rd Louisville MS 39339-7242

HILL, WILLIAM A(LEXANDER), judge; b. Carmel, Calif., Aug. 21, 1946; s. R. William and Ruth M. (McDonald) H.; m. Diane K. Hartman, Apr. 25, 1981; children: Erin, Georgia. B.S., U. N.D., 1968, J.D., 1971; cert. Hastings Coll. Law Coll. Advocacy, 1977; grad. in fed. evidence U. Mich. Law Sch., 1981. Bar: N.D. 1971, Minn. 1974, U.S. Dist. Ct. N.D. 1971, U.S. Tax Ct. 1973, U.S. Ct. Appeals (8th cir.) 1973. Dep. sec. of state State of N.D., 1971-72; law clk. to judge U.S. Dist. Ct. N.D., 1972-74; ptnr. Pancratz Law Firm, Fargo, N.D., 1974-83; magistrate U.S. Dist. Ct., N.D. 1975-83; judge, U.S. Bankruptcy Ct, 1983—; mem. 8th cir. bankruptcy appellate panel, 1996—; part-time magistrate U.S. Dist. Ct. N.D., 1975-83; active N.D. Supreme Ct. Joint Procedures Com. Commr., 1978-83; mem. exec. bd. No. Lights coun. Boy Scouts Am., 1993-98; bd. dirs. Fargo Moorhead Symphony; chmn. Gethemane Episcopal Found., Fargo, 1981-83; pres. Plains Art Mus., Moorhead, Minn., 1982. Office: US Bankruptcy Ct Quentin N Burdick US Courthouse 655 1st Ave N Ste 350 Fargo ND 58102-4952

HILL, WILLIAM E., director technology services city government; b. 1955. BA, Southwest U., 1995, MBA, 1998. Dir. info. tech. svcs. City of Dayton, Ohio, 1997—. Office: Info Tech Svcs 1 First National Plz Dayton OH 45402-1705

HILL, WILLIAM FRANK, history educator; b. East Liverpool, Ohio, Dec. 23, 1947; s. John and Mary (McGrew) H. BS, Bowling Green State U., 1969. History tchr. McCord Jr. H.S., Sylvania, 1969-77, Southview H.S., Sylvania, 1977—. Mem. NEA, Northwest Ohio Edn. Assn., Ohio Edn. Assn., Ohio Hist. Assn., Sylvania Edn. Assn. (bd. dirs. 1970-76, v.p. 1973-74), Phi Alpha Theta.

HILL, WILLIAM U., state supreme court justice. Atty. gen. Cheyenne, Wyo., 1995-98; justice Wyo. Supreme Ct., Cheyenne, 1998—. Office: Wyoming Supreme Court 2301 Capitol Ave Cheyenne WY 82001-3644

HILL, WILLIAM VICTOR, II, retired army officer, secondary school educator; b. Carlisle, Pa., Dec. 14, 1936; s. William Victor and Frances Ellen (Swanson) H.; m. Doris Ann Cox, Nov. 11, 1961; children: William Victor III, David C., Stephanie C. Hill Trede. BBA, Tex. A&M U., 1959; MPA, U. Mo., Kansas City, 1972; diploma, Command and Gen. Staff Coll., 1969, Air War Coll., 1982. Lic. realtor. Commd. 2d lt. U.S. Army, 1959, advanced through grades to col.; tank bn. comdr. 2d Bn., 13th Armor, Ft. Knox, Ky., 1976-78; prof. mil. sci. Sam Houston State U., Huntsville, Tex., 1979-81; insp. gen. 5th U.S. Army, Ft. Sam Houston, Tex., 1982-85; ret. U.S. Army, 1987; dir. army Jr. Res. Officers Tng. Corps South San Antonio (Tex.) Ind. Sch. Dist., 1988-95; sr. army instr. South San Antonio H.S., 1988-97, ret., 1997. Author army materials. City Coun. apptd. mem. San Antonio Conv. Ctr. Contract Rev. Com., 1998-99. Decorated Legion of Merit, Bronze Star medal, Combat Inf. badge, Airborne-Ranger, Silver medal Order of St. George, others. Mem. U.S. Armor Assn. Avocations: fishing, conservation activities. Home: 3208 Bent Bow Dr San Antonio TX 78209-3518

HILL, WILMER BAILEY, administrative law judge; b. Washington, May 18, 1928; s. Wilmer A. and Matilda F. (Nabor) H.; m. Joan C. Brunelle, June 24, 1967; children: Stuart Michael, Stephen Mark. A.B., Dartmouth Coll., 1950; LL.B., J.D., Georgetown U., 1953. Bar: D.C. 1956. Sec.-treas., dir. Ames, Hill & Ames, Washington, 1955-81; sole practice Washington, 1981-86; sr. adminstrv. law judge Social Security Adminstrn., Portland, Oreg., 1986—. Vice-pres. Brookdale Citizens Assn., 1975-76. Served with AUS, 1953-55. Mem. Fed. Adminstrn. Law Judges Conf., Assn. Adminstrn. Law Judges, Transp. Lawyers Assn. (pres. 1984-85), Sigma Phi Epsilon, Delta Theta Phi. Republican. Methodist. Clubs: Portland Golf. Home: 8492 SW Chevy Pl Beaverton OR 97008-6894

HILLARD, CAROLE, state official; b. Deadwood, S.D., Aug. 14, 1936; m. John M. Hillard (dec.); children: David, Sue Ellen, Todd, Eddie, Lornell. BA in Edn., Univ. of Ariz., 1957; MA in Edn., S.D. State Univ., 1982; MA in Polit. Sci., Univ. of S.D., 1984. State rep. State of S.D., 34th dist., 1991-95; lt. gov. State of S.D., 1995—; dir. Mich. Nat. Bank., Black Hills Regional Eye Inst., YMCA; mem. exec. bd. Nat. Crime Prevention Coun. Active Rapid City Common Coun., Rapid City C. of C., S.D. Bd. of Charities and Corrections, McGruff Crime Prevention Coun. (exec. bd.), S.D. Corrections Commn., Cmty. Care Ctr., S.D. Children's Home Soc., S.D. Assurance Alliance, Nat. Child Protection Partnership, First United Methodist Ch. (exec. bd.), Rapid City Econ. Devel. Partnership, F.L.A.G.S. Found.; mem. exec. bd. Bog Bros./Big Sisters. Recipient Pub. Svc. award, 1987, Gov.'s Outstanding Citizen award, 1988, George award Rapid City C. of C., 1994; named Outstanding Chirperson, United Way, 1986, S.D. Guardian Small Bus., 1994. Mem. LWV, Women's Network, Mt. Rushmore Soc., Indian-White Coun., Toastmasters, Ninety-niners, Rapid City Fine Arts Coun. Republican. Methodist. Avocations: flying (lic. pvt. pilot), snow skiing, scuba diving, reading. Office: Office of Lt Governor State Capitol 500 E Capitol Ave Ste 215 Pierre SD 57501-5070*

HILLARD, ROBERT ELLSWORTH, public relations consultant; b. St. Paul, Nov. 17, 1917; s. Homer Ellsworth and Barbara Mary (Smith) H.; m. Nancy Jane Oxenhandler, Dec. 30, 1973. B.A. summa cum laude, U. Minn., 1940. Reporter Des Moines Tribune, 1939-40; rotogravure editor Des Moines Register, 1940-41; feature editor St. Louis Star-Times, 1941, 45-46; ptnr. Fleishman-Hillard, Inc., St. Louis, 1946-74, sr. ptnr., 1974-82, cons., 1982—. Editor-in-chief: The Minn. Daily, 1938-39. Pres. Urban League St. Louis, 1950-52, Health and Welfare Council Met. St. Louis, 1957-59, Family and Children's Service Greater St. Louis, 1960-62. Served as lt. USNR, 1942-45, PTO. Inductee Minn. Daily Hall of Distinction, 1998. Mem. Pub. Rels. Soc. Am. (accredited), St. Louis Pub. Rels. Soc. (pres. 1953-56, Nat. Lifetime Achievement award 1996), Phi Beta Kappa, Beta Theta Pi, Sigma Delta Chi. Home: PO Box 104 Caledonia MO 63631-0104 Office: 200 N Broadway Saint Louis MO 63102-2730

HILL-DAVIS, DEBORAH ANN, school psychologist; b. St. Louis, Feb. 22, 1952; d. W.H. and Betty (Emmert) Muenster; m. Edward C. Hill, Mar. 21, 1975 (div. May 1991); children: Sarah Margaret, Bridget Kelley; m. Todd A. Davis, June 22, 1996. Attended, St. Andrews U., Scotland, 1972-73; BA with Honors, Drury Coll., Springfield, Mo., 1974; edn. specialist, U. Nebr., Kearney, 1978. Cert. Iowa. Sch. psychology intern Meyer's Children's Rehab. Inst., Omaha, Nebr., 1978; sch. psychologist Edni. Svc. Unit #10, Holdredge, Nebr., 1978-79; sch. psychology cons. Dept. Pub. Instrn., Des Moines, 1982-83; sch. psychologist Des Moines Pub. Schs., 1979—; pres. bd. dirs. Des Moines Adolescent-Child Guidance Ctr., 1983-89; mem. adv. panel Statewide Task Force-Families of Prisoners, Des Moines, 1990-92. Editor: (newsletter) Iowa Sch. Psychology Newsletter, 1981-83, (resource manual) Pvt. Practice of Sch. Psychology, 1983. Democrat. Avocations: biking, reading, gardening, traveling, camping. Home: 1139 Polk Blvd Des Moines IA 50311-3334 Office: Des Moines Ind.-Cmty. Sch. 1800 Grand Ave Des Moines IA 50309-3310

HILLE, BERTIL, physiology educator; b. New Haven, Oct. 10, 1940; s. C. Einar and Kirsti (Ore) H.; m. Merrill Burr, Nov. 21, 1964; children: Erik D., J. Trygve. BS, Yale U., 1962; PhD, Rockefeller U., 1967. H.H. Whitney fellow Cambridge U., 1967-68; asst. prof. U. Wash., Seattle, 1968-71, assoc. prof., 1971-74, prof. physiology, 1974—; vis. prof. U. Saarland, Hamburg, Germany, 1975-76. Author: Ionic Channels of Excitable Membranes, 1984, 92; mem. editl. bd. Jour. Gen. Physiology, 1971—, Am. Jour. Physiology, 1984-87, Jour. Neurosci., 1984-87, Neuron, 1987—, Curr. Opin. Neurobiol., 1990—, Procs. of NAS, 1996—; contbr. articles to profl. jours. Recipient Alexander von Humboldt Sr. Scientist award, 1975, Bristol-Myers Squibb award, 1990, (with Dr. Clay Armstrong) Louisa Gross Horowitz prize for biology or biochemistry Columbia U., 1996. Mem. NAS, Biophys. Soc. (K.S. Cole award 1975, 86). Home: 10630 Lakeview Ave NE Seattle WA 98125 Office: U Wash Box 357290 Seattle WA 98195-7290

HILLE, ROBERT ARTHUR, healthcare executive; b. Hartford, Conn., June 19, 1931; s. Henry Oscar and Mary (Zelanski) H.; m. Barbara White, Nov. 20, 1954; children: Richard, Marilyn, David, Thomas, Catherine. BS in Edn. and Biology with honors, U. Conn., 1954; MS in Healthcare Adminstrn., Baylor U., 1969. Commd. 2d lt. U.S. Army, 1954, advanced through grades to col., ret., 1978, various positions in healthcare, 1954-69; adminstr. U.S. Army Hosp., Ft. Benjamin Harrison, Ind., 1969-71, Seoul, Korea, 1971-72; dep. dir., asst. prof. grad. program Baylor U., Waco, Tex., 1972-74; chief patient adminstrn. Office Surgeon Gen., Washington, 1974-77; assoc. dir. med. staff Baylor U. Med. Ctr., Dallas, 1978-79; adminstr. Reynolds Army Hosp., Ft. Sill, Okla., 1977-78; assoc. exec. dir. Baylor U. Med. Ctr., Dallas, 1979-80, sr. v.p., 1980-84, exec. v.p., COO, 1984-95; internal cons. Baylor U. Med. Ctr., 1995-96; retired; adj. instr. health svcs. adminstrn. Washington U., St. Louis, 1981-96; adj. prof. U. Ala., Birmingham, 1981-95; mem. edn. com. Dallas-Ft. Worth Hosp. Coun., 1981-88, trustee, 1989-90; trustee Baylor Inst. Rehab., 1982-87, chmn., 1984-85; bd. dirs., assoc. dir. Tex. Cmty. Bank; trustee Baylor Ctr. Restorative Care, 1990, Helicopter Ambulance Svc. North Tex., 1987-96, chmn., 1994-95, sec. bd. dirs. Transplant Inst. S.W. Active Our Lady of the Lake Cath. Ch.; mem. long range planning com. Heath, Tex., 1995-96; mem. Planning and Zoning Commn., Heath, Tex., 1997—. Decorated Legion of Merit. Fellow ACHE; mem. Am. Hosp. Assn., Tex. Hosp. Assn. (mem. ho. of dels. 1984-85, chmn. dist. V 1984-85), Fed. Health Care Execs. Inst., KC (4th degree).

HILLEARY, VAN, congressman; b. Rhea County, Tenn., June 20, 1959. BS in Bus. Adminstrn., U. Tenn., 1981; JD, Samford U., 1990. With SSM Industries, Inc., 1984-86, dir. planning and bus. devel., 1992—; mem. 104th-106th Congress from 4th Tenn. dist., 1995—; mem. budget com. 104th Congress from 4th Tenn. dist., mem. edn. and the workforce com., mem. armed svcs. com. With USAF, 1982, Persian Gulf; with USAFR, 1982—. Decorated 2 U.S. Air medals, Nat. Svc. medal, Kuwaiti Liberation medal. Mem. Am. Legion, Sigma Chi. Republican. Presbyterian. Office: US Ho of Reps 114 Cannon Bldg Washington DC 20515-4204

HILLEMAN, MAURICE RALPH, virus research scientist; b. Miles City, Mont., Aug. 30, 1919; s. Robert A. and Edith (Matson) H.; m. Lorraine Witmer, Aug. 3, 1963; children—Jeryl Lynn, Kirsten Jeanne. BS, Mont. State U., 1941, DSc (hon.), 1966; DSc (hon.), U. Md., 1968, Washington and Jefferson Coll., 1992; D hon. causa (hon.), U. Leuven, 1984; PhD, U. Chgo., 1944. Asst. bacteriologist U. Chgo., 1942-44; research asso. virus labs. E.R. Squibb & Sons, 1944-47, chief virus dept., 1947-48; chief research and diagnostic sects. virus and rickettsial diseases Army Med. Service Grad. Sch., Walter Reed Army Med. Center, 1948-56, asst. chief lab. affairs, 1953-56; chief respiratory diseases Walter Reed Army Inst. Research, Washington, 1956-57; dir. virus and cell biol. research Merck Inst. Therapeutic Research,

Merck & Co. Inc., 1957-66, exec. dir., 1966-71, v.p., 1971-78, sr. v.p., 1978-84; dir. Merck Inst., 1984—; dir. virus and cell biology research, v.p. Merck, Sharp & Dohme Research Labs., 1970-78, sr. v.p., 1978-84; vis. investigator Hosp. of Rockefeller Inst. for Med. Rsch., 1951; vis. prof. bacteriology U. Md., 1953-57; adj. prof. virology pediatrics Sch. Medicine U. Pa., 1968—; cons. Children's Hosp. of Phila., 1968—; mem. coun. divsn. biol. scis. Pritzker Sch. Medicine, 1977-95; John Herr Musser lectr. Musser-Burch Soc., Tulane U. Sch. Medicine, 1969, 19th Graugnard lectr., 1978; mem., spl. cons. panel respiratory and related viruses USPHS, 1960-64; mem. Nat. Cancer Inst. primate study group, 1964-70; mem. coun. analysis and projection Am. Cancer Soc., 1971-76; mem. expert adv. panel on virus diseases WHO, 1952—; bd. dirs. W. Alton Jones Cell Sci. Ctr., Lake Placid, N.Y., 1980-82, Am. Liver Found. (hon.), 1986—, Am. Type Culture Collect, 1992-95, Nat. Found. Infectious Diseases, 1987—, Nat. Cancer Inst. Bd. Sci. Counselors, 1990-95, Bd. Sci. Counselors Paul Erlich Found. (Frankfurt, Germany), 1993—; bd. dirs. Jos. J. Stokes Rsch. Inst. U. Pa.; mem. overseas med. rsch. labs. com. Dept. Def., 1980; mem. virology dept. rev. com. Am. Type Culture Collection, 1980; mem. Ad Hoc Vaccine Subcom. AIDS Program NIH, 1991, AIDS Rsch. and Devel. Vaccine Working Group, 1992—, panel 1995—, Panel Internat. Task Force NIH Strategic Plan, 1992; mem. vaccine design and evaln. group, NIAID, NIH, 1995—; trustee Internat. Vaccine Inst., Korea; mem. program evaluation task force NIH Office AIDS Rsch., 1996-97. Mem. editl. bd. AIDS Rsch. and Human Retroviruses, 1995—, Internat. Jour. Cancer, 1964-71, Inst. Sci. Information, 1968-70, Am. Jour. Epidemiology, 1969-75, Infection and Immunity, 1970-76, Excerpta Medica, 1971—, Proc. Soc. Exptl. Biology and Medicine, 1976—, Jour. Antiviral Research, 1980—, Vaccine, 1983, Virus Genes, 1986, Vaccine Research, 1990; contbr. 480 articles to sci., profl., med. jours. Decorated by King Hassan II of Morocco, 1997; Phi Kappa Phi fellow, 1941-42, Koessler fellow, 1943-44; recipient Howard Taylor Ricketts prize, 1945, 83, Disting. Civilian Svc. award Sec. Def., 1957, Walter Reed Army Med. Incentive award, 1960, Dean M. McCann award, 1970, Procter award, 1971, Lasker Med. Rsch. award, 1983; Achievement award Indsl. Research Inst., 1975, Joseph E. Smadel award, 1984, Alumni medal, U. Chgo., 1987, Albert B. Sabin medal, 1988, Nat. Medal Sci., Pres. of U.S., 1988, San Marino award, 1989, Robert Koch Gold medal, 1989, Spl. Lifetime Achievement award Children's Vaccine Initiative of WHO, 1996, Albert B. Sabin Found. gold medal, Lifetime Achievement award 1997, Maxwell Finland award Nat. Fedn. Infectious Disease, 1998. Fellow Am. Acad. Microbiology; mem. Am. Acad. Arts and Scis., Nat. Acad. Sci., Inst. of Medicine of Nat. Acad. Sci., Am. Philos. Soc., Am. Soc. Microbiology, Soc. Exptl. Biology and Medicine (mem. editl. and publs. com. 1977—), Tissue Culture Assn. (mem. coun. 1977—), Am. Assn. Immunologists, Am. Assn. Cancer Rsch., Infectious Diseases Soc., Permanent sect. Microbiol. Standardization Internat. Assn. Microbiol. Socs., Internat. Vaccine Inst. (UN bd. trustees 1995—), Russian Acad. Biotechnology (hon. fgn. mem.), L'Acadèie Nationale de Pharmacie (fgn. corr.). Office: Merck Rsch Labs WP53C 350 West Point PA 19486 *Once the problem is defined and the facts are known, decision and action are little more than the implementation of the obvious.*

HILLENBRAND, MARTIN JOSEPH, diplomat, educator; b. Youngstown, Ohio, Aug. 1, 1915; s. Joseph John and Mary Magdalene (Walter) H.; m. Faith Stewart, June 27, 1941; children: Ruth Marie, David Martin, John Steven. A.B., U. Dayton, 1937, Litt.D. (honoris causa), 1963; M.A., Columbia U., 1938, Ph.D., 1948; postgrad., Harvard U., 1949-50; LL.D. (hon.), U. Md., 1973. Joined fgn. service, 1939; vice consul Zurich, Switzerland, 1939, Rangoon, Burma, 1940, Calcutta, India, 1942, Lourenco Marques, S.E. Africa, 1944; fgn. service officer Bremen, Ger., 1945; consul, 1946; officer in charge div. govt. and adminstrn. Bur. German Affairs, Dept. State, 1950-52, 1st sec., Paris, 1952-56, U.S. polit. adviser, Berlin, 1956-58; dir. Office of German Affairs Dept. State, 1958-62, dir. Berlin Task Force, 1962-63; minister, dep. chief of mission Bonn, Ger., 1963-67; ambassador to Hungary, 1967-69; asst. sec. for European affairs Dept. State, 1969-72; ambassador to Fed. Republic Germany, 1972-76; dir. gen. Atlantic Inst. Internat. Affairs, Paris, 1977-82; Dean Rusk prof. internat. relations U. Ga., Athens, 1982-97, Dean Rusk prof. emeritus, 1997—, dir. Global Policy Studies, 1983-91, co-dir. Ctr. for East-West Trade Policy (name changed to Ctr. Internat. Trade and Security 1995—), 1987-97, co-dir. emeritus Ctr. Internat. Trade and Security, 1997—; ret., 1997; chmn. Fulbright commn. for Germany, 1963-67; head U.S. del. Four Power Working Group on Germany and Berlin, 1959; mem. del. Fgn. Mins. Conf., Geneva, 1959; head, mem. U.S. del. numerous internat. mtgs. and confs.; chmn. fellowship selection com. Robert Bosch Found., 1983-92, hon. chmn., 1992-96; trustee So. Ctr. Internat. Studies, 1986—, chmn., 1987-90; bd. dirs. Mercedes Benz NA, 1990-94. Author: Power and Morals, 1949; Germany in an Era of Transition, 1983, Fragments of Our Time: Memoirs of a Diplomat, 1998; co-author: Zwischen Politik und Ethik, 1968; co-author, editor: The Future of Berlin, 1980; co-editor: Global Insecurity, 1982; contbr. numerous chpts. to books, also articles. Decorated Grand Cross of Merit, Germany, others. Mem. Internat. Studies Assn., Coun. Fgn. Rels., Am. Fgn. Svc. Assn., Am. Coun. on Germany (diplomatic adv. com.), Am. Acad. Diplomacy. Roman Catholic. Office: U Ga Ctr Internat Trade & Secur Athens GA 30602

HILLENMEYER, JOHN, medical center executive. MS in Healthcare Adminstrn., Duke U., 1974. Pres., CEO Orlando Regional Med. Ctr., 1997—. Mem. Am. Coll. Health Care. Office: 1414 Kuhl Ave Orlando FL 32806

HILLER, ARTHUR, motion picture director; b. Edmonton, Alta., Can., Nov. 22, 1923. Ed., U. Toronto and U. B.C., Alta., Toronto and B.C.; F.V.Ch.C., Victoria Coll., Glasgow, 1967; MA in Psychology; LHD, London Inst. Applied Research, 1973; DFA (hon.), U. Victoria, 1995; LLD, U. Toronto, 1995. Dir. TV prodns. Matinee Theatre, Playhouse 90, Alfred Hitchcock Presents, Route 66, Naked City; dir. films Americanization of Emily, 1965, Out of Towners, 1970, Love Story, 1970, Plaza Suite, 1971, Hospital, 1971, Man of La Mancha, 1972, The Man in the Glass Booth, 1975, Silver Streak, 1976, The In-Laws, 1979, Making Love, 1982, Teachers, 1984, Outrageous Fortune, 1987, The Babe, 1992. Decorated comdr. Internat. Order Sursam Corda; doctor laureate Imperial Order Constantine Brussels, 1972; recipient Can. radio awards, 1951, 52; awards for edn. by radio Ohio U., 1952, 53; best dir. nomination Nat. Acad. TV Arts and Scis., 1962; best dir. nomination Acad. Motion Picture Arts and Scis., 1970; Golden Globe award for best dir., 1970; Dir.'s award nomination Dirs. Guild Am., 1970; Best Dir. award N.Y. Fgn. Press, 1970. Mem. Directors' Guild of Am. (pres. 1988-92), Acad. Motion Picture Arts and Scis. (pres. 1993-97), Am. Film Inst. Ctr. Advanced Film and TV Studies. Office: Golden Quill 8899 Beverly Blvd Ste 702 Los Angeles CA 90048-2431

HILLER, GEORGE MEW, financial advisor, investment manager, lawyer; b. Washington, July 21, 1956; s. William Eugene and Vera Ellen (Mew) H.; m. Marie Naomi Aliceaacosta, Mar. 24, 1979; children: George Mew Jr., Danielle Celeste, Emory Durell. BBA in Bus. Mgmt., Tex. A&M U., 1977, MBA in Fin., 1978; JD, Emory U., 1982, LLM in Taxation, 1986. Bar: Ga., 1982; CFP. Prin. Hiller & Assocs., Attys. at Law, Atlanta, 1985—; owner George M. Hiller Cos., L.L.C., Atlanta, 1985—. Author: Christian Financial Concepts Will Kit, 1993; contbg. author (booklet): Estate Planning Addendum Christian Financial Concepts, Gainesville, Ga., 1992—; co-author (textbook chpt.) Developing a Personal Portfolio in Real Estate, 1988; contbr. articles profl. jours. Bd. dirs. Christian Fin. Planning Inst.; trustee Galilee Gospel Found. Mem. State Bar of Ga., Inst. CFPs. Republican. Avocations: reading, travel. Home: 1165 Clifton Rd NE Atlanta GA 30307-1229 Office: George M Hiller Cos 3414 Peachtree Rd NE Ste 1110 Atlanta GA 30326-1167

HILLER, SUSAN, artist. Lectr. Slade Sch. Art, Univ. Coll., London, 1980-91; prof. art and design U. Ulster, Belfast, No. Ireland, 1991-98; resident Karolyi Found., Vence, France, 1968, Ministry Fine Arts, Morocco, 1969; contract tchg. and lectures Royal Coll. Art, Ealing Poly., Godard Coll., Vt., 1972-78; artist-in-residence U. Sussex, Brighton, Eng., 1975; lectr. II, Maidstone (Kent, Eng.) Coll. Art, 1975-80; disting. vis. prof. dept. art Calif. State U., Long Beach, 1988; vis. art coun. chmn. dept. art UCLA, 1991; vis. prof. art UCLA, 1992; vis. lectr. numerous instns. and colls., including N.S. Coll. Art and Design, Kunst Akademi, Oslo, Sch. Visual Arts, N.Y.C., Sydney (Australia) Coll. Arts Power Inst., Leeds (Eng.) U., U. London, Calif. Inst. Arts, U. Plymouth, Brighton U., Ruskin Sch. Fine Art, Oxford U., Bath Acad. Fine Art, Ctrl. Sch. Art and Design, Glasgow Coll. Art, Royal Coll. Art, Rotterdam Art Acad., Byam Show Sch. Art; external examiner dept. art. U. London Goldsmith's Coll., 1984-88, 93-96, Stourbridge Coll. Art and Tech., St. Martin's Sch. Art, London Inst., 1993-96, U. Northumbria, Newcastle, Eng., 1993-96, dept. art and design Gwent Coll. Higher Edn., Newport, Eng., 1984-88, South Glamorgan Coll. Higher Edn., Cardiff, Wales, 1987-91, dept. painting Wimbledon Sch. Art, London, 1997-99, dept. printmaking and electronic imaging Royal Coll. Art, London, 1997-00; mem. visual arts panel Greater London Arts Assn., 1976-80, guest curator Brit. Coun.-Franklin Furnace Gallery, N.Y.C., 1981; mem. visual art panel Arts Coun. Eng., 1997-99, also others. Numerous one-woman shows, latest being Gimpel Fils, London, 1980, 82, 83, 94, 95, Roslyn Oxley Gallery, Sydney, 1982, Exptl. Art Found., Adelaide, Australia, 1982, 98, Andre Emmeich Gallery, Zurich, Switzerland, Vivienne Esders Galerie, Paris, 1984, Orchard Gallery, Londonderry, No. Ireland, 1984, Pat Hearn Gallery, N.Y.C., 1987, 89, 91, 92, Univ. Mus., Calif. State U., Long Beach, 1988, Pierre Birtschansky Galerie, Paris, 1989, Mappin Mus. and Art Gallery, Sheffield, Eng., 1990, 91, Nicole Klagsbrun Gallery, N.Y.C., 1991, Foksal Gallery, Warsaw, Poland, 1997, Oriel Gallery, Cardiff, 1997, Projektgalerie, Leipzig, Germany, 1998, Ctr. for Contemporary Photography, Melbourne, Australia, 1998, Inst. Contemporary Art, Phila., 1998, Berry House, London, 1998, Henie Onstad Kunstcenter, Oslo, 1999; 2-woman show Entwistle Gallery, London, 1994; retrospective show Inst. for Contemporary Art, London, 1986, Tate Gallery, Liverpool, Eng., 1996; exhibited in numerous group shows, latest being Tate Gallery, 1995, 97, Inst. Contemporary Art, Boston, Mus. Women, Washington, Mus. Modern Art, N.Y.C., 1999; represented in permanent collections, including Tate Gallery, Arts Coun. Gt. Britain, Victoria and Albert Mus., Tokyo Met. Mus. Photography, Nat. Gallery Art South Australia, Adelaide, Leeds City Mus. and Art Gallery, Imperial War Mus., London; author: (with David Coxhead) Dreams: Visions of the Night, 1981, revised 1989, 91, 94, 96; also articles. Recipient visual artist's award Gulbenkenian Found., 1976, 77; grantee Greater London Arts Assn., 1981, Nat. Endowment Arts, 1982; travel fellow Visual Arts Bd., Australia, 1982, Guggenheim fellow in visual art practice, 1988, hon. fellow Dartington Coll. Arts, 1998. E-mail: aceposible@aol.com. Studio: 83 Loudoun Rd, London NW8 OD6, England*

HILLERMAN, TONY, writer, former journalism educator; b. Sacred Heart, Okla., May 27, 1925; s. August Alfred and Lucy Mary (Grove) H.; m. Marie Elizabeth Unzner, Aug. 16, 1948; children: Anne, Janet Hillerman Grado, Anthony Jr., Monica Hillerman Atwell, Steven, Daniel. Student, Okla. State U., 1942-43; BA, U. Okla., 1948; MA in English, U. N.Mex., 1965, LittD (hon.), 1990; LittD (hon.), Ariz. State U., 1991. Police reporter Borger (Tex.) News-Herald, 1948; reporter, city editor constn. Morning Press, Lawton, Okla., 1949-50; polit. reporter UP, Oklahoma City, 1950-52; bur. mgr. UP, Santa Fe, 1952-54; reporter, then city editor and editor The New Mexican, Santa Fe, 1954-62; prof. journalism U. N.Mex., Albuquerque, 1965-87, asst. to pres., 1963-65, 81-84. Author: (novels) The Blessing Way, 1970, The Fly on the Wall, 1971, The Boy Who Made Dragonfly, 1972, Dance Hall of the Dead, 1973 (Edgar Allan Poe award 1973), Listening Woman, People of Darkness, The Dark Wind, The Ghostway, Skinwalkers, 1986 (Anthony award 1987), A Thief of Time, 1988 (Macavity award Mystery Readers Internat. 1988, Dept. Interior award 1990), Talking God, 1988 (Media award Am. Anthrop. Assn. 1990), The Joe Leaphorn Mysteries, Coyote Waits, 1990, Sacred Clowns, 1993, Finding Moon, 1995, The Fallen Man, 1996, The First Eagle, 1998; (non-fiction) The Great Taos Bank Robbery, New Mexico, Rio Grande, The Spell of New Mexico, Indian Country, The Best of the West, The Oxford Book of American Detective Stories, 1996; also articles, audio recs.; editor: The Mysterious West, 1994. With inf. U.S. Army, 1943-45; ETO. Decorated Bronze Star, Silver Star, Purple Heart; recipient Golden Spur award Western WRiters Am., 1987, Spl. Friend of Dineh award Navajo Tribal Coun., 1987, Grand Prix de Littérature Policière award, France, Ambassador award Ctr. for the Indian, 1992. Mem. Mystery Writers Am. (Edgar Allen Poe award 1974, pres. 1988, Grand Master award 1991), Internat. Crime Writers Assn. Democrat. Roman Catholic. Avocation: trout fishing.

HILLERS, DELBERT ROY, Near East language educator; b. Chester, S.D., Nov. 7, 1932; s. William Albert and Emma Rose (Gienapp) H.; m. Patricia Mays Turnbaugh, June 29, 1958; children: Eve Elizabeth, Samuel Thomas. Diploma, Concordia Coll., Milw., 1952; BA, Concordia Sem., St. Louis, 1954, BD, 1957; MA, Johns Hopkins U., 1958, PhD, 1963. Instr. Hebrew and ancient Near East studies Concordia Sr. Coll., Fort Wayne, Ind., 1958-60; asst. prof. Johns Hopkins U., Balt., 1963-66, assoc. prof., 1966-70, prof., 1970—, W.W. Spence prof. Semitic Langs., 1971-94; W.W. Spence prof. emeritus, 1994—; acting chmn. dept. Near Eastern Studies Johns Hopkins U., Balt., 1964-70, chmn. dept. Near Eastern Studies, 1976-79; ann. prof. Am. Sch. Oriental Rsch., Jerusalem, 1968-69; Annenberg vis. prof. Dropsie Coll., 1985-86; Albright lectr. Johns Hopkins U., 1992; apptd. vis. prof. Pontifical Bib. Inst., Rome, 1996. Author: Treaty Curses and the Old Testament Prophets, 1964, Covenant: The History of a Biblical Idea, 1969, Lamentations, The Anchor Bible, 1972, rev. edit., 1992, Micah, Hermeneia Series, 1983; editor: Comprehensive Aramaic Lexicon, 1985-92, (with E. Cussini) Palmyrene Aramaic Texts, 1996; mem. Revised Standard Version Old Testament Com., 1983-86. Fellow Johns Hopkins U., 1961-63, 1957-58; Schaff lectr. Pitts. Theol. Sem., 1970. Mem. Soc. Bibl. Lit., Am. Schs. Oriental Rsch., Cath. Bibl. Assn. Home: 3923 Canterbury Rd Baltimore MD 21218-1704

HILLERS, ELLEN MARSH, film-television production coordinator; b. Syracuse, N.Y., Feb. 19, 1961; d. Robert Stilphen and Eleanor Hunter (Marsh) H. BA, Wells Coll., 1983. Production coord.: (films) Scrooged, Paramount Pictures, N.Y.C., 1987, Reversal of Fortune, Pressman Film, N.Y.C., 1989, Lorenzo's Oil, Universal City Studios, Pitts., 1991, Quiz Show, Disney, N.Y.C., 1993, Little Big League, Castlerock Entertainment, L.A./Mpls., 1993, Twelve Monkeys, Universal City Studios, Phila./Balt., 1995, Men in Black, Columbia Pictures, N.Y., 1996, Fear and Loathing in Las Vegas, 1997, Hoofbeats, Columbia Tri-Star, 1998; (TV) Miami Vice, 911; (other) The Super, Funny About Love, A Kiss Before Dying, The Accidental Tourist, Beaches, True Love. Mem. Internat. Alliance Theatrical Stage Employees and Moving Picture Machine Operators of U.S. and Can. Republican. Episcopalian. Avocations: computer hacking, running, cooking. Home: 124 Rim Rock Dr Durango CO 81301-8603

HILLERT, MATS, materials scientist, educator; b. Goteborg, Sweden, Nov. 28, 1924; s. Hilding and Anna (Jonsson) H.; m. Gerd Hagberg; children: Jan, Lena, Sven, Nils. Chem. engr., C.T.H. Goteborg, 1947, Dr h.c., 1979; DSc, MIT, 1956; Dr h.c., U. Grenoble, 1987, U. Trondheim, 1994. Rschr. Swedish Inst. Metals Rsch., Stockholm, 1948-61; prof. phys. metallurgy K.T.H., Stockholm, 1961-90. Contbr. articles to profl. jours. Recipient Gold medal Acta Metall. Inc., 1978, Bakhuis Roozeboom Gold medal K. Vet. Akad. The Netherlands, 1977, Tawara Gold medal Iron Steel Inst. Japan, 1993. Fellow AIME (R.F. Mehl award 1974), Royal Acad. Scis.; mem. Inst. Metals Japan (hon.; Murakami gold medal 1982), Fgn. Assoc. Nat. Acad. Engring., 1997. Home: Vegabacken 9, 18163 Lidingo Sweden Office: KTH Dept Materials Sci, SE-10044 Stockholm Sweden

HILLERT, RICHARD WALTER, composer, educator, author; b. Granton, Wis., Mar. 14, 1923; s. Richard Henry and Amelia Matilde (Trimberger) H.; m. Gloria Rose Bonnin, Aug. 20, 1960; children: Kathryn, Virginia, Jonathan. BS in Edn., Concordia U., 1951; MusM, Northwestern U., Evanston, Ill., 1955, MusD, 1968. Tchr., dir. music Bethlehem Luth. Ch., St. Louis, 1951-53, Trinity Luth. Ch., Wausau, Wis., 1953-59; prof. music Concodia U., River Forest, Ill., 1959-91, distn. prof. music, 1987, prof. emeritus, 1991—. Music editor: Inter Lutheran Commission on Worship, 1966-78, Lutheran Church-Missouri Synod, 1968-69, Chrismas Annual, 1985-89; assoc. editor Ch. Music, 1966-81; contbr. articles to profl. jours.; composer: Sonata for Violin and Piano, 1953, Sonata for Flute and Piano, 1954, Symphony in Three Movements, 1955, Prelude and Toccata for Organ, 1956, Alternations Number One for 7 Instruments, 1966, Divertimento for 5 Instruments, 1967, Angus Dei for 3 Choirs and Percussion, 1974, Partita for Organ: Picardy, 1978, Divertimento Number Two for 11 Players, 1983, Evening Prayer for Cantor, Congregation, and Organ, 1984, The Pillars for Wind Symphony, 1989, Fantasia on The Nunc Dimittis for Chamber Orch., 1990, Sine Nomini for Symphonic Band, 1995, Suite for Strings, 1996, Sonata for Flute and Harpsichord, 1997, Seven Psalms of Grace for Baritone Solo, Choirs and Orch., 1998. Recipient 1st prize Internat. Soc. Contemporary Music, 1961-62. Mem. Assn. Luth. Ch. Musicians (life), Pi Kappa Lambda, Sigma Alpha Iota. Avocations: traveling, American popular music before 1950, political and music biography. Home: 1620 Clay Ct Melrose Park IL 60160-2419

HILLERY, THOMAS HUNGIVILLE, journalist, financial consultant; b. Boston, Dec. 15, 1962; s. Thomas Hungiville and Mary Jane (Larato) H.; s. Thomas Hungiville and Mary Jane (Larato) H. *Great great grandfather Thomas Hillery left County Clare, Ireland, and great great grandmother Mary O'Donnell arrived in Cambridge, Massachusetts in 1868, where the family lived for 101 years. Grandfather Paul Frederick Hillery, Cambridge City councillor 1932-33, Chairman Trustees Cambridge City Hospital 1938-39. Mother Mary Jane Larato Hillery, first female military aide-de-camp to Governor, Commonwealth of Massachusetts, appointed one of first five female liason officers, United States Military Academy at West Point 1976, host/producer cable television program "For the Record".* BA, Clark U., 1985; Magistri in Artibus Liberalibus, Harvard U., 1997. Accredited assessor # 666, Mass. Promotions dept. WCRB-FM, Waltham, Mass., 1990-92; journalist Dorchester News, Boston, 1992—. Author: "Make Advertising Work!" Use Demographics, Psychographics and Purchasing Data. Bd. assessors Town of Sudbury, 1987-96. Mem. Internat. Assn. Assessing Officers, Mass. Assn. Assessing Officers, U.S. Libr. Congress, Jonas Clark Fellows, Clark U. Alumni Coun., Clark Legacy Soc., Harvard Club Boston, Harvard Investment Assn., Nat. Press Club, Nat. Trust for Hist. Preservation, Internat. Platform Assn., New Eng. Hist. Geneaol. Soc., Sons Union Vets. Civil War, KC, Masons (past master Charles A. Welch Lodge, past high priest Houghton Royal Arch, Grand Royal Arch chpt. exemplification degree team 1992-93, dist. dep. grand treas. 1992-93), Scottish Rite, Order Eastern Star, Shriners, Mil. Order Loyal Legion U.S., Sons of Am. Legion Post 191 (chaplain), Ancient and Honorable Artillery Co. Home: 66 Willow Rd Sudbury MA 01776-2663 Office: 299 Savin Hill Ave Ste 1 Boston MA 02125-1055

HILLESTAD, CHARLES ANDREW, lawyer; b. McCurtain, Okla., Aug. 30, 1945; s. Carl Oliver and Aileen Hanna (Sweeney) H.; m. Ann Ramsey Robertson, Oct. 13, 1973. BS, U. Oreg., 1967; JD, U. Mich., 1972. Bar: Colo. 1972, U.S. Dist. Ct. Colo. 1972, U.S. Ct. Appeals (10th cir.) 1972, Oreg. 1993; lic. real estate broker, Colo. Law clk. to presiding justice Colo. Supreme Ct., Denver, 1972-73; ptnr. DeMuth & Kemp, Denver, 1973-83, Cornwell & Blakey, Denver, 1983-90, Scheid & Horlbeck, Denver, 1990-93, Gablehouse & Epel, Denver, 1993-94; pvt. practice Cannon Beach, Oreg., 1994—; co-developer award winning Queen Anne Inn, Capitol Hill Mansion and Cheyenne Canyon Inn Hotels (4-diamond award AAA); mem. ad hoc com. Denver Real Estate Atty. Specialists. Author: Preventive Law for Innkeepers, co-author: Annual Surveys of Real Estate Law for Colorado Bar Association; contbr. articles to profl. jours.; assoc. editor Inn Times. Past coun. mem. Denver Art Mus.; past chmn. Rocky Mountain chpt. Sierra Club; past v.p., bd. dirs. Seaside C. of C.; past bd. dirs. Hist. Denver, Inc. Staff sgt. U.S. Army, 1968-70. Recipient Colo. Co. of Yr. award Colo. Bus. Mag., Award of Honor Denver Ptnrship., Newsmaker of Yr. and Outstanding Achievement awards Am. Assn. Hist. Inns, Tourism Person of Yr. award Denver Conv. and Visitor's Bur., Rocky Mountain Spectacular Inn award B&B Rocky Mountains Assn., Best Inns of Yr. awards County Inns Mag. and Adventure Rd. Mag., Best of Denver award Westward newspaper. Mem. ABA, Colo. Bar Assn., Oreg. Bar Assn., Denver Bar Assn., Colo. Lawyers for the Arts, POETS, Astoria C. of C., Seaside C. of C., Cannon Beach C. of C. Avocations: photography, art collecting, historic and environmental preservation, history and architecture reading, rafting. Office: PO Box 1065 1347 S Hemlock Cannon Beach OR 97110

HILLEY, JOSEPH HENRY, lawyer; b. Birmingham, Ala., June 29, 1956; s. Howard Guy and Ruby Josephine (Mann) H.; m. Joy Elaine Fitzgerald, Aug. 11, 1984. BA, Asbury Coll., 1978; MDiv, Asbury Theol. Sem., 1984; JD, Cumberland Sch. Law, 1988. Bar: Ala. 1988, Ga. 1988, U.S. Dist. Ct. (no. dist.) Ala. 1988, U.S. Tax Ct. 1988, U.S. Ct. Appeals (11th cir.) 1993, U.S. Supreme Ct. 1995. Sports photographer World Wide News Svc., 1978-84; law clk. Gen. Counsel to Sec. of Def., Washington, 1987; assoc. Redden, Mills and Clark, Birmingham, Ala., 1988—; pvt. practice, 1996-98; assoc. Carr Allison Pugh Howard Oliver & Sisson, Birmingham, Ala., 1998—; coord. capital campaign Asbury Coll., Wilmore, Ky., 1989-91. Author: (screenplays) Wake Up, 1994, Union Town, 1995. Mem. Pinnelas County Dem. Exec. Com., St. Petersburg, Fla., 1984; trustee Woodlawn United Meth. Ch., Birmingham, 1988; chmn. bd. dirs. Children of the World, Inc. Named to Dean's List, Cumberland Sch. of Law, 1985-88, Nat. Dean's List, 1985-88. Mem. ABA, Ala. Bar Assn., Ga. Bar Assn., Birmingham Bar Assn., Bar of U.S. Tax Ct., Bar U.S. Supreme Ct., Phi Alpha Delta. Democrat. Episcopalian. Avocations: sports, theatre, writing. Office: 6251 Monroe St Ste 100 Daphne AL 36526

HILL-FESSENDEN, ANNE LYNN, multi-faceted food and beverage consultant; b. Uniontown, Pa., Sept. 3, 1944; d. Robert Benjamin and Katherine Rebecca (Reynolds) Rankin; m. Howard Harry Hill, Aug. 23, 1964 (div. Dec. 1979); children: Jennifer Leigh, Carolyn Jeanne; m. Thomas A. Fessenden, Apr. 29, 1990. BS, U. Md., 1966. Elem. tchr. Prince George's County Bd. Edn., Upper Marlboro, Md., 1966-68; food svc. mgr. Bloomingdales, White Flint, Md., 1976-78; dist. mgr. ice cream parlors/restaurants Drug Fair, Inc., Alexandria, Va., 1978-80; dir. quality assurance and product devel. Marriott Internat., Washington, 1980-88, sr. dir. corp. procurement, 1988-90, sr. v.p. food and beverage, 1990-97; pres. ALH & Assocs., Germantown, Md., 1997—; bd. dirs. Balt. Internat. Culinary Coll. Mem. NAFE, DAR, AAUW, Soc. for Advancment of Foodservice Rsch., Internat. Dairy/Deli/Baking Assn., Internat. Assn. Women Chefs and Restaurateurs, Nat. Assn. Convenience Stores, Inst. Food Techs., Roundtable for Women in Foodservice (Pacesetter award 1986), Restaurant Assn. Md., Rsch. Chefs Assn. (founding). Republican. Presbyterian. Avocations: gourmet cooking, needlework, wreathmaking, ceramics, furniture refinishing. Office: ALH & Assocs 21525 Davis Mill Rd Germantown MD 20876-4419

HILLGREN, SONJA DOROTHY, journalist; b. Sioux Falls, S.D., May 17, 1948; d. Ralph Oliver and Priscilla Adaline (Mannes) Hillgren; m. Ralph Lee Hill (dec.). BJ, U. Mo., 1970, MA, 1972; postgrad. (Nieman fellow), Harvard U., 1982-83. Washington corr. Ohio-Washington News Svc., 1972-73; reporter UPI, Annapolis, Md., 1974-76; reporter, editor UPI, Washington, 1976-78; farm editor UPI, 1978-88; Washington corr. Knight-Ridder, Washington, 1988-90; Washington editor Farm Jour., 1990-95, editor, 1995—, exec. v.p., 1997—; exec.-in-residence U. Mo., 1997. Chair bd. dirs. Nat. Press Bldg. Corp., 1997; bd. dirs. Winrock Internat. Inst. Agrl. Devel., 1996—. Recipient J.R. Russell award Newspaper Farm Editors Am., 1985, Reuben Brigham award Agrl. Communicators in Edn., 1988; named Old Master, Purdue U., 1992, Agrl. Communicator of Yr., Nat. Agri-Mktg. Assn., 1996; Woodrow Wilson vis. fellow, 1993—, Oscar in Agr. for Excellence in Agrl. Reporting U. Ill., 1998. Mem. AAUW, Nat. Assn. Agrl. Journalists (pres. 1987-88), Nat. Press Club (bd. govs. 1991-96, chair 1993-94, v.p. 1995, pres. 1996), Soc. Profl. Journalists, Investigative Reporters and Editors, Am. Soc. of Mag. Editors, Am. Agrl. Editors' Assn., Nat. Agri-Mktg. Assn., Farm Found., Coun. on Fgn. Rels., Congl. Country Club, Pi Beta Phi (Carolyn Helman Lichtenberg Crest award 1999), Alpha Zeta. Lutheran. Avocations: sports, reading. Home: 201 S 18th St Apt 1916 Philadelphia PA 19103-5937 Office: Farm Jour 1500 Market St Fl 28 Philadelphia PA 19102-2100

HILL-HULSLANDER, JACQUELYNE L., nursing educator and consultant; b. Melrose Park, Ill., Jan. 9, 1940; d. Richard C. and Marian L. (Hamlin) Hill; m. Gale Franklin Hulslander, June 5, 1993; children: Daryl, Gary. Diploma, Evanston (Ill.) Hosp. Assn., 1961; BS, Elmhurst (Ill.) Coll., 1977, BSN, 1981; MS, Nat.-Louis U., Evanston, 1986; PhD, U. Ill., 1990. Cons. in course devel. Ill. Bell Telephone Co., Chgo.; cons. for employee devel. Glen Oaks Med. Ctr., Glendale Hts., Ill.; prof. Triton Coll., River Grove, Ill.; staff nurse OB Evanston (Ill.) Hosp. Assn., 1961-62; staff and charge nurse OB Gottlieb Mem. Hosp., Melrose Park, Ill., 1962-65; faculty OB Proviso Sch. Practical Nursing, Maywood, Ill., 1965-67; charge nurse OB Gottlieb Meml. Hosp., Melrose Park, 1970-75; grad. rsch. asst. dept. vocat. edn. U. Ill., Champaign-Urbana, Ill., 1988-89; faculty prof. basic med. surg. nursing and obstetrics Triton Coll., River Grove, Ill., 1976—; cons. Dawson Tech. Inst., Chgo. City Coll.; cons. Engring. Systems Inc., Aurora, Ill.; presenter in field. Multicompetencies for Practical Nurses grantee, 1986, Patient Care Plans Visual Assessment Guide grantee, 1998-99. Mem. Chateau Lorraine Homeowners Assn. (sec., v.p., pres. 1992-96), U. Ill.

Alumn Assn., Phi Delta Kappa, Phi Kappa Phi. Home: 222 Lorraine Cir Bloomingdale IL 60108-2546 Office: Triton Coll 2000 N 5th Ave River Grove IL 60171-1907

HILLI, MARY ELIZABETH, rehabilitation nurse, administrator; b. Bklyn., Nov. 14, 1939; d. Joseph and Mary Elizabeth (Drew) Wagner; m. Karl A. Hilli, Mar. 1, 1969; chilren: Kathryn, Karl, Thomas. Diploma, Mary Immaculate Hosp., Jamaica, N.Y., 1960; BSN, Adelphi U., 1966; MA, Framingham State Coll., 1987. Cert. in nursing adminstrn.; lic. nursing home adminstr.; diplomate Am. Coll. Healthcare Execs. Head nurse Mary Immaculate Hosp., 1964-66; instr. Children's Hosp., Boston, 1966-69; dir. nursing Franciscan Children's Hosp., Brighton, Mass.; sr. v.p. patient care Franciscan Children's Hosp. and Rehab. Ctr., Brighton, 1976-94; nurse cons., dir. quality improvement and outpatient svcs. Clinton Hosp., Mass., 1994-95; asst. adminstr. subacute and rehab. ctr. Advantage Health Corp., Lowell, Mass., 1995-97; dir. clin. svcs., adminstr. TCU Symmes Hosp. Mec. Ctr., Arlington, Mass., 1997—. Mem. Am. Coll. Healthcare Execs., Mass. Orgn. Nurse Execs. (com. chair, newsletter editor), Sigma Theta Tau (bd. dirs. Pi Epsilon chpt.-at-large).

HILLIARD, BONNIE JEAN, writer, editor; b. Akron, Ohio, Aug. 10, 1953; d. James Norman and Doris Mae (Jagger) Lasher; m. Mark Daniel Hilliard, May 28, 1977; children: Jason, Leah. BA in English, Kent (Ohio) State U., 1975; postgrad., Wheaton (Ill.) Coll., 1976-77. Songwriter Kent, 1983-86; staff writer, reporter Record-Courier, Kent, 1986-91; writer I ALLTEL Pub., Hudson, Ohio, 1991-94; writer II ALLTEL Pub., Hudson, 1994—; owner Class Act Copywriting; comml. freelance writer, 1998—; profl. singer. Contbr. articles to profl. jours., popular mags.; assoc. editor Akron Bus. Mag., 1999—. Recipient award of excellence in print journalism Ohio Pub. Images, Inc., 1990. Mem. Soc. Profl. Journalists, Kent C. of C., Bd. Room Group, Women's Network. Avocations: songwriting, guitar, showing horses, reading. Home and Office: 7608 Seasons Rd Kent OH 44240-6031

HILLIARD, DAVID CRAIG, lawyer, educator; b. Framingham, Mass., May 22, 1937; s. Walter David and Dorothy (Shortiss) H.; m. Celia Schmid, Feb. 16, 1974. BS, Tufts U., 1959; JD, U. Chgo., 1962. Bar: Ill. 1962, U.S. Supreme Ct. 1966. Mng. ptnr. Pattishall, McAuliffe, Newbury, Hilliard & Geraldson, Chgo., 1984—; adj. prof. law Northwestern U., 1971—, chmn. Symposium Intellectual Property Law and the Corp. Client, 1987—. Author: Unfair Competition and Unfair Trade Practices, 1985, Trademarks, 1987, Trademarks and Unfair Competition, 1994, 3d edit., 1998, Trademarks and Unfair Competition Deskbook, 1996, 3d edit., 1998; editor-in-chief Chgo. Bar Record, 1978-81. Trustee Art Inst. Chgo., 1980—, chmn. sustaining fellows, 1981-85, chmn. adv. com. dept. architecture, 1981—, pres. aux. bd., 1977-79, chmn. exhbns. com., 1993—, exec. com., 1995—, chmn. bd. govs. of the sch., 1997—; trustee Newberry Libr., 1983—, exec. com., 1987—; pres. Lawyers Trust Fund Ill., 1985-88; mem. vis. com. DePaul U. Law Sch., U. Chgo. Sch. of Law, chmn., 1987-88, Northwestern U. Assocs., 1985—; mem. profl. adv. bd. Atty. Gen. Ill., 1982-84; mem. Ill. Commn. on Rights of Women, 1983-85; bd. dirs. Ill. Inst. Continuing Legal Edn., 1980-82; pres. Planned Parenthood Assn. Chgo., 1975-77. Lt. JAGC, USN, 1962-66. Recipient Maurice Weigle award, 1974, Chgo. Coun. Lawyers award for jud. reform, 1983. Fellow Am. Coll. Trial Lawyers (chmn. courageous adv. com. 1995-97); mem. ABA (chmn. trademark divsn. 1986-87, mem. coun. 1991-95, intellectual property law sect.), Ill. Bar Assn., Chgo. Bar Assn. (pres. 1982-83, founding chmn. young lawyers sect. 1971-72), Internat. Trademark Assn. (bd. dirs. 1989-91, ADR panel of neutrals 1994—), Arts Club, Chgo. Club, Econ. Club, Grolier Club, Law Club, Legal Club (pres. 1989-90), Univ. Club, Casino, Wayfarers Club (pres. 1994-95). Home: 1320 N State Pky Chicago IL 60610-2118 Office: Pattishall McAuliffe Newbury Hilliard & Geraldson 311 S Wacker Dr Ste 5000 Chicago IL 60606-6622

HILLIARD, EARL FREDERICK, congressman, lawyer; b. Apr. 9, 1942; s. Mary Franklin Hilliard; m. Iola H. Hilliard, June 9, 1967; children: Alesia, Earl F. BA, Morehouse Coll., 1964; JD, Howard U., 1967; MBA, Atlanta U., 1970. Rsch. asst. Howard U., 1965-67; instr. Miles Coll., 1967-68; asst. to pres. Ala. State U., 1968-70; ptnr. Hilliard, Jackson, Little & Stansel, Birmingham, 1974-78; pvt. practice Birmingham; pres. Am. Trust Life Ins. Co.; mem. Ala. Ho. of Reps., 1974-80, chmn. Black legis. caucus, 1975; mem. Ala. Senate, 1980-93, 103d-106th Congresses from 7th Ala. dist., 1993—; mem. agrl. com., mem. small bus. com., mem. internat. rels. com. Life mem. NAACP. Reginald Herber Smith Comty. Lawyer fellow, 1970-71. Mem. Nat. Bar Assn. (life), Ala. Black Lawyers Assn., Morehouse Coll. Alumni Assn. (life), Alpha Phi Alpha (life). Baptist. Home: 1625 Castleberry Way Birmingham AL 35214-4867 Office: US Ho of Reps 1314 Longworth HOB Washington DC 20515-0107

HILLIARD, JOHN MAUK, university official; b. Clovis, N.Mex., Sept. 19, 1945; s. John Kent and Jane Elizabeth (Mauk) H. BA, Ea. N.Mex. U., 1967, MA, 1970. Edn. and leadership cons. Sigma Alpha Epsilon Frat., Evanston, Ill., 1967-68; lectr. Lehman Coll. CUNY, Bronx, 1970-82, dir. special programs, 1983-92, dir. recruitment, 1992—. Author: Back to Basics, 1981; contbr. articles to mags. Mem. exec. com., edn. chair St. George's Soc. N.Y., 1990-94; bd. trustees Robert R. Livingston Libr., N.Y.C., 1991—. Recipient cert. of merit Philalethes Soc. Internat., Washington, 1981; Paul Harris fellow Rotary Club, Bronx, 1990-91. Mem. SAR (bd. mgrs.). Democrat. Episcopalian. Avocations: genealogy, history of fraternal societies, history of American frontier. Home: 100 Sullivan St Apt 2-g New York NY 10012-3630 Office: CUNY Lehman Coll Bedford Pk Blvd W Bronx NY 10468-1589

HILLIARD, KELLY MCCOLLUM, employment manager; b. May 13. BS in Finance, U. N.C., Greensboro, 1988, student. Benefits coord. U. N.C., Greensboro, N.C., 1990-94, recruitment coord., 1994-98, employment mgr., 1998—. Office: Univ North Carolina Greensboro PO Box 26170 Greensboro NC 27402-6170

HILLIARD, SAM BOWERS, geography educator; b. Hart County, Ga., Dec. 21, 1930; s. Asa Farris and Flora Elizabeth (Bowers) H.; m. Joyce Collier, June 4, 1955; children—Steven Glen, Anita Joy. A.B., U. Ga., 1960, M.A., 1962; M.S., U. Wis., 1963, Ph.D., 1966. Electrician Savannal River Valley plant Dupont Co., Aiken, S.C., 1954-59; teaching asst. U. Wis., 1961-65; instr. U. Wis., Milw., 1965-67; asst. prof. geography So. Ill. U., 1967-71; prof. La. State U., Baton Rouge, 1971-82, alumni prof., ret., 1983-93; chmn. dept. geography La. State U., 1976-79, 85-86, dir. Sch. Geosci., 1977-79; columnist The Hartwell Sun newspaper. Author: Hog Meat and Hoecake: Food Supply in the Old South, 1972, An Atlas of Antebellum Southern Agriculture, 1984; co-author: Louisiana: Its Land and People, rev. edit., 1987, The South Revisited: Forty Years of Change, 1992; contbr. articles to profl. jours. County historian, 1998. Served with U.S. Navy, 1950-54. Mem. Nat. Geog. Soc., Agrl. History Assn.

HILLIER, JAMES, technology management executive, researcher; b. Brantford, Ont., Can., Aug. 22, 1915; came to U.S., 1940; s. James Sr. and Ethel Anne (Cooke) H.; m. Florence Marjory Bell, Oct. 24, 1936 (dec. 1992); children: James Robert, William Wynship. BA, U. Toronto, 1937, MA, 1938, PhD, 1941, DSc (hon.), 1978; DSc (hon.), N.J. Inst. Tech., 1981. Rsch. asst. Banting Inst. U. Toronto Med. Sch., 1938-40; head electron microscope rsch. RCA Labs., Camden and Princeton, N.J., 1940-53; adminstrv. engr. corp. rsch. and engring. RCA Corp., Princeton, 1954-55; chief engr. comml. electronic products RCA Corp., Camden, 1955-57; gen. mgr. labs. RCA Corp., Princeton, 1957-58, v.p. labs., 1958-68; v.p. corp. rsch. and engring. RCA Corp., N.Y.C., 1968-69, exec. v.p. rsch. and engring., 1969-76, exec. v.p., sr. scientist, 1976-77, ret., 1977; dir. corp. rsch. Westinghouse Air Brake Co., Pitts. and Alexandria, Va., 1953-54; mem. higher edn. study com. Gov.'s Office, State of N.J., 1963-64; mem. commerce tech. adv. bd. U.S. Dept. Commerce, Washington, 1964-70; chmn. adv. coun. dept. elect. engring. Princeton U., 1963-65; mem. adv. coun. Coll. Engring., Cornell U., Ithaca, N.Y., 1966-99; mem. joint consultative com. U.S. AID/Egyptian Acad. Sci. Rsch. and Tech., Cairo, 1978-84. Co-author: Electron Optics and the Electron Microscope, 1945; co-contbr.: Medical Physics, 1944, vol. II, 1950, Colloidal Chemistry, vol. VI, 1946; contbr. Ency. Britannica, 1948. Pres., founder James Hillier Found., Inc., 1996—. Decorated officer Order of Can., 1997; inducted into Nat. Inventors Hall of Fame, 1980, N.J. Inventors Hall of Fame, 1992; recipient James Loudon Gold medal U. Toronto, 1937, Albert Lasker award APHA, 1960, Commonwealth award, 1980, Presdl. award Microbeam Analysis Soc., 1989. Fellow AAAS (chmn. nomination com. sect. M 1965), IEEE (David Sarnoff award 1967, Founders medal 1981), Am. Phys. Soc. (mem. at large, governing bd. 1964-65); mem. Microscope Soc. Am. (pres. 1944, Disting. Scientist award 1977), Indsl. Rsch. Inst. (bd. dirs. 1960-65, pres. 1964, Inst. medal 1975), Nat. Inventors Hall of Fame Found., Inc. (bd. dirs. 1992—), Nat. Acad. Engring. (coun. 1971), Rotary (bd. dirs. 1988-91), Nassau Club, Sigma Xi. Achievements include 41 patents in field; co-design of first successful electron microscope in North America, of first commercially available electron microscope in North America; discovery of principle of Stigmator for correcting astigmatism of electron microscope objective lenses; invention of electron microprobe microanalyser; first to picture tobacco mosaic virus, bacterial viruses and ultra-thin section of a single bacterium. Home: 22 Arreton Rd Princeton NJ 08540-1402

HILLIER, J(AMES) ROBERT, architect; b. Toronto, Ont., Can., July 24, 1937; came to U.S., 1941, naturalized, 1961; s. James and Florence (Bell) H.; m. Barbara Ann Weinstein, Apr. 7, 1986; 1 child, Jordan Rebecca Hillier; children by previous marriage-Kimberly (dec.), James Baldwin. BA, Princeton U., 1959, MFA, 1961; MBA (hon.), Bryant Coll., 1992. Project designer J. Labatut, Princeton, N.J., 1961-62; project mgr. Fulmer & Bowers, Princeton, 1961-66; prin. J. Robert Hillier, Princeton, 1966-72; pres. The Hillier Group, Princeton, 1972-87, chmn. bd., 1987—; adj. faculty mem. Sch. Arch. Princeton U.; bd. dirs. Hershey Trust Co. Prin. works include Bryant Coll. campus, Smithfield, R.I., 1969, Rutgers U. Athletic Center, Piscataway, N.J., 1977, Butler Hosp. Providence, 1978, N.J. State Justice Complex, Trenton, 1985, Harbor Island Design, Tampa, Fla., 1981, Beneficial Corp. Complex, 1982, Merritt Tower, 1985, Wharton Sch. Exec. Ctr., 1986, N.J. Aquarium, 1991, Am. Home Products Corp. Headquarters, 1992, Sprint World Hqrs., 1997, Smith-Kline Beecham Headquarters, 1998. Trustee Peddie Sch., Hightstown, N.J., 1981—, McCarter Theatre, Prinecton, 1983-89, Bryant Coll., Smithfield, R.I., 1993-96, Edison Coll. Found., Milton Hershey Sch. Recipient over 250 design awards from archtl. assns., 1966—; Architect of Yr. award N.J. Contractors Assn., 1976, 87, 92, 97, Disting. Svc. award Internat. Assn. Conf. Ctrs., 1988, Award of Excellence N.J. Bus. and Industry Assn., 1988, N.J. Entrepreneur of Yr., 1989, Community Svc. Human Rels. award, 1992. Fellow AIA (v.p. N.J. chpt. 1974); mem. Nat. Coun. Archtl. Registration Bds., Princeton Quadrangle Club, Nassau Club, Princeton Club, Union League. Avocations: running, swimming. Home: 2846 River Rd New Hope PA 18938-9527 Office: The Hillier Group 500 Alexander Rd Princeton NJ 08540-6002

HILLIKER, GRANT GILBERT, writer, former diplomat and educator; b. Tomah, Wis., June 26, 1921; s. Vernon Gilbert and Celeste C. (Reich) H.; m. Miriam L. Chrisler, Apr. 3, 1943 (div. Dec. 1979); children: Janet Lee, Laurie Ann; m. Adele Chafetz, Dec. 9, 1979. BA in Journalism, U. Wis., 1942; cert. radio engr., Northwestern Tech. Inst., Evanston, Ill., 1943; postgrad., George Washington U., 1950-55. From clk. to consul gen. U.S. Dept. State, Washington, and fgn. countries, 1946-71; mem. sr. faculty Ohio State U. Mershon Ctr., Columbus, 1971-95; program developer Urban Alternatives Group, Columbus, 1976-85; exec. dir. Internat. Visitors Coun., Columbus, 1989-92; freelance writer, book reviewer Columbus Dispatch, 1995-97. Author: Politics of Reform in Peru, 1971; contbr.: Communicating for Peace, 1990. Mem. Falls Church (Va.) City Coun., 1953-55; chmn. Task Force To Organize Area Commn., Columbus, 1974, Task Force on Cable TV, Columbus, 1975; pres. Cmty. Resources Ctr., Columbus, 1972-73, UN Assn., Columbus, 1983-85, Columbus Internat. Program, 1985-87. 1st lt. U.S. Army, 1942-46. Fed. exec. fellow Brookings Instn., Washington, 1965-66. Mem. Phi Beta Kappa. Avocations: gardening, carpentry, hiking, biking, swimming. Home and Office: 5268 Rush Ave Columbus OH 43214-1218

HILLINGER, CHARLES, journalist, writer; b. Evanston, Ill., Apr. 1, 1926; s. William Agidious H. and Caroline Bruning; m. Arliene Otis, June 22, 1948; children: Brad, Tori. BS in Polit. Sci., UCLA, 1951. Circulation mgr., columnist Park Ridge (Ill.) Advocate, 1938-41; copy boy, libr., feature writer Chgo. Tribune, 1941-43; reporter, feature writer, syndicated columnist L.A. Times, 1946-92, ret., 1992. Author: California Islands, 1957, Bel-Air Country Club, A Living Legend, 1993, Charles Hillinger's America, 1996, Charles Hillinger's Channel Islands, 1998, Hillinger's California, 1997. Mem. adv. bd. Sant Cruz Is. Found., Santa Barbara, Calif., 1992—; treas. 8-Ball Welfare Found. Greater L.A. Press Club, 1992—. With USN, 1943-46. Mem. Greater L.A. Press Club (sec. 1978-88, v.p. 1988-90, pres. 1990-92), Dutch Treat Club W. Avocations: tennis, golf, hearts. Home: 3131 Dianora Dr Rancho Palos Verdes CA 90275-6200

HILLIS, JOHN DAVID, television news executive, producer, writer; b. Washington, Dec. 28, 1952; s. Willard E. and Holly M. Hillis; m. Catherine H. McQuaig, Nov. 21, 1975; children: Faith Courteney, David Esten, Elizabeth Nicole. AB in Journalism, U. Ga., 1975. Film editor Sta. WSB-TV, Atlanta, 1973-74, asst. producer, 1974-76, news producer, 1976; exec. news producer Sta. KOTV-TV, Tulsa, 1976-79; news producer Sta. WRAL-TV, Raleigh, N.C., 1979-80; news producer Cable News Network, Inc., Atlanta, 1980-81, exec. producer, Newswatch, 1981-83, exec. producer, 1983-84, spl. events producer, 1984; news dir. Cablevision Systems Corp., Woodbury, N.Y., 1984-86; gen. mgr. Rainbow News 12 Co., Woodbury, 1986-89; pres., CEO Allnewsco, Inc., Washington, 1989—, Newschannel 8 Cable Svc., Springfield, Va., 1991—. Contbr. articles to profl. jours. Recipient Radio Newscast award Ga. AP Broadcasters, 1973, TV Newscast award Okla. AP Broadcasters, 1978, TV Series award News Acad. Cable Programming, 1985, Washington Region Emmy award, 1997. Mem. NATAS (Bd. of Govs. award Washington chpt.), Soc. Profl. Journalists, Radio TV News Dirs. Assn., Nat. Press Club, Assn. Regional News Channels (founder, chmn. 1993), Nat. Cable T.V. Assn. (satellite network com.). Methodist. Office: Newschannel 8 7600 Boston Blvd # D Springfield VA 22153-3136

HILLIS, STEPHEN KENDALL, secondary education educator; b. Hillsboro, Oreg., Jan. 5, 1942; s. Earnest Howard Hillis and Phyllis Noreen (Bagley) Gortner; m. Sharon Ione Arbogast, Aug. 5, 1967; children: Jeff Wise, Teryl Dorothy, Tonya Noreen. BA, Pacific U., 1965. Cert. Std. Oreg. Dept. Edn. H.s. tchr. Eagle Grove, Iowa, 1967-73, Madras, Oreg., 1973—. Precinct com. Jefferson County Dems., Madras, 1978-89, chair precinct com. 1988-91. With USAR, 1959-65. Mem. ASCD, NEA (human civil rights com. 1990-96, bd. dirs. 1993—), Oreg. Edn. Assn. (bd. dirs. 1983—, v.p. 1988-93). Democrat. Home: 375 NE Chestnut St Madras OR 97741-1910 Office: 509J Sch Dist 390 S Tenth St Madras OR 97741

HILLIS, WILLIAM DANIEL, biology educator; b. Paris, Ark., June 12, 1933; s. Charles Raymond Hillis and Carra Elizabeth (Daniel) Coffee; m. Argye Idell Briggs, Dec. 23, 1952; children: William Daniel Jr., David Mark, Argye Elizabeth Trupe. BS, Baylor U., 1953; MD, Johns Hopkins U., 1957. Lic. in medicine and surgery, Md., Tex. Asst. prof. pathobiology Johns Hopkins U. and Sch. Hygiene and Pub. Health, Balt., 1965-68, assoc. prof., 1968-72; asst. prof. Johns Hopkins U. Sch. Medicine, Balt., 1972-76, assoc. prof., 1976-82; prof., chmn. dept. biology Baylor U., Waco, Tex., 1982-85, Cornelia Marshall Smith prof. biology, 1985-98; disting. prof. biology Baylor U., Waco, 1995—; exec. v.p. Baylor U., Waco, Tex., 1985-89, v.p. student affairs, 1989-98; cons. Nat. Cancer Inst., Bethesda, Md., 1965-68, Nat. Heart and Lung Inst., Bethesda, 1977-82; dir. Health Professions Rsch. Tng. Program, Balt., 1979-82, Out-Patient Clin. Rsch. Ctr., Balt., 1975-82. Contbr. articles to profl. jours. Pres. Bapt. Home Md., Balt., 1972-81; Md. rep. exec. com. So. Bapt. Conv., NAshville, 1977-82; bd. dirs. Food for Hungry, Glendale, Calif., 1972-82, Caritas, Waco, Tex., chair, 1989-95. Col. USAF, 1960-65, USAFR, 1965-85. Recipient Louis Livingston Seaman award Assn. Mil. Surgeons U.S., 1978, Disting. Alumnus award Baylor U., 1998; named Outstanding Prof. Baylor U., 1985. Mem. Am. Assn. Immunologists, Soc. for Exptl. Biology and Medicine, Am. Soc. for Microbiology, N.Y. Acad. Sci., McLennan County Med. Soc., Waco C. of C. (bd. dirs. 1987), Johns Hopkins Soc. of Scholars, Mortar Bd., Phi Beta Kappa, Alpha Omega Alpha, Omicron Delta Kappa. Democrat. Clubs: Brazos (Waco); Johns Hopkins (Balt.). Avocations: vocal music, drama, gardening, carpentry, philately. Home: 3640 Alta Vista Dr Waco TX 76706-3741 Office: Baylor Univ PO Box 97388 Waco TX 76798-7388

HILLJE, BARBARA BROWN, lawyer; b. Carlisle, Pa., Dec. 18, 1942; d. R. Morrison and Gladys M. (Lauver) Brown; m. John W. Hillje, Mar. 23, 1968. AB, Vassar Coll., 1964; BS in Edn., Ind. U. Pa., 1965; MA, Temple U., 1971, ABD, 1977; JD, Villanova U., 1984. Bar: Pa. 1984, U.S. Dist. Ct. (ea. dist.) Pa. 1984, N.J. 1985, U.S. Dist. Ct. N.J. 1985, U.S. Supreme Ct. 1990. English tchr. Council Rock Sr. High Sch., Newtown, Pa., 1965-68; assoc. Harry J. Agzigian and Assocs., Levittown, Pa., 1985-87; pvt. practice Langhorne, Pa., 1987—. Contbr. articles to profl. journals. Bd. dirs., pres. bd. Children of Aging Parents, Levittown, 1985-93; mem. facility ethics com. Statesman Health & Rehab. Ctr., Levittown, Pa., 1996—. Recipient Women Helping Women award Soroptimists of Indian Rock, Inc., 1995; named Woman of Yr., Lower Bucks AAUW, 1985, Neshaminy BPW, 1987, Legal Humanitarian of Yr., Bucks County United Way, 1994, Consumer Connection award, 1996. Mem. ABA, AAUW (bd. dirs. 1978—, legis. cons. Pa. division 1990-92), Middletown-Newtown LWV (bd. dirs. 1983-89, citizen campaign watch adv. panel 1992, 94, 96), Pa. Bar Assn., Bucks County Bar Assn. (bd. dirs. 1991-93), Nat. Acad. Elder Law Attys., Older Women's League (legis. chair 1984-94, Women of Worth award 1993). Office: 506 Corporate Dr W Langhorne PA 19047-8011

HILLMAN, ALAN L., internist, educator, researcher; b. N.Y.C., July 12, 1956; s. Herman David and Edith (Geilich) H.; m. Janice Kubo, July 9, 1983; children: Jennifer, Abigail. BA cum laude, Cornell U., 1978, MD, 1981; MBA, U. Pa., 1986. Intern in internal medicine N.Y. Hosp., 1981-82, asst. resident in internal medicine, 1982-84; dir. clin. programs Hosps. of U. of Pa., Phila., 1986-90, med. dir. Health Pass, 1987-90; assoc. dir. med. group U. Pa., Phila., 1987-90, sr. scholar clin. epidemiology, 1990—, dir. Ctr. for Health Policy, 1990-98, mem. comprehensive cancer ctr., 1992; assoc. prof. health care Wharton Sch., U. Pa., Phila., 1993—; assoc. prof. medicine Sch. of Medicine, U. Pa., Phila., 1993—; assoc. dean health svcs. rsch. U. Pa., Phila., 1995-98; asst. instr. dept. of medicine N.Y. Hosp.-Cornell Med. Ctr., N.Y., 1981-84; asst. prof. of medicine and health care mgmt. Sch. of Medicine and The Wharton Sch., U. Pa., Phila., 1986-93, assoc. prof., 1993-99, prof., 1999—; mem. Inst. for Human Gene Therapy, U. Pa. Med. Ctr., Phila., 1995—; discharge planning com. Hosp. of Univ. of Pa., 1986-88, drug use effects com., 1990-91; admissions and awards com. Health Care Mgmt. Dept., The Wharton Sch., 1990-92; exec. com. The Leonard Davis Inst. of Health Econs., 1990—, sr. fellow, 1984—; co-dir. Health of the Pub. Program, Sch. of Medicine, 1991-92; com. on jud. ethics U. Pa., 1993—; ctr. for bioethics adv. com. Sch. of Medicine, 1994—, faculty senate, 1994—, master's program in med. ethics adv. com. Coll. of Arts and Scis., 1995—, com. on health svcs. rsch. Sch. Medicine, 1995—, com. on multiculturalism in rsch. Inst. on Aging, 1995—, info. sys. strategic planning steering com. Sch. Medicine, 1996; cons. Solvay Pharms., Marietta, Ga., U. Mo. Sch. of Medicine, Columbia, 1994, UNISYS Corp., Blue Bell, Pa., 1993, Prudential Ins. Co., Atlanta, 1993—, PACC Bd. of Dirs., Clackamas, Oreg., 1993, Gate Pharms., Kulpsville, Pa., 1994-95, Exogen Co., Princeton, N.J., 1994—, Forest Labs., N.Y.C., 1994—, VidaMed Corp., Palo Alto, Calif., 1993-95, Health Industry Mfrs. Assn., Washington, 1993—, Proctor & Gamble, Morris Plains, N.J., 1993, Syntex, 1993—, Eli Lilly Corp., Indpls., 1993-95, Amgen, Thousand Oaks, 1993—, Rhone-Poulenc Rorer, Antony Cedex, France, 1992—, Abbott Labs., Abbott Park, Ill., 1991—, and all others. Contbr. numerous articles to profl. jours. and newspapers. Recipient Article of the Year award Assn. for Health Svcs. Rsch., 1990, Young Investigator's award, 1993. Fellow ACP, Am. Bd. Internal Medicine; mem. Group Health Assn. of Am., Internat. Soc. of Tech. Assessment in Health Care, Soc. of Gen. Internal Medicine, Phila. Coll. of Physicians, Internat. Soc. for Econ. Evaluation of Medicines, Am. Fedn. for Clin. Rsch., Assn. for Health Svcs. Rsch., Physicians for Social Responsibility, Soc. of Gen. Internal Medicine, Am. Soc. for Clin. Investigation, Alpha Omega Alpha. Office: U Pa Blockley Hall Rm 1123 423 Guardian Dr Philadelphia PA 19104-6021

HILLMAN, CAROL BARBARA, communications executive; b. Sept. 6, 1940; d. Joseph Hoppenfeld and Elsa (Spiegel) Hoppenfeld Resika; m. Howard D. Hillman, May 25, 1969. BA with honors, U. Wis., 1961; postgrad., U. Lyon, France, 1961-62; MA, Cornell U., 1966. Asst. editor Holt Rinehart & Winston Pubs., 1965-66; staff assoc. pub. rels. Ea. Airlines, N.Y.C., 1966-74; pub. affairs mgr. Squibb Corp., N.Y.C., 1974-75; asst. dir. corp. pub. rels. Burlington Industries, N.Y.C., 1975-77, dir. corp. pub. rels., 1977-80, v.p. pub. rels., 1980-82; v.p. corp. comms. Norton Co., Worcester, Mass., 1982-89, sr. cons., 1989-90; nat. dir. pub. rels. and comms. Deloitte & Touche, Wilton, Conn., 1990-91; v.p. univ. rels. Boston U., 1991-95; prin. Hillman & Kersey Strategic Comms., 1995—; mem. pub. affairs coun. Machinery & Allied Products Inst., 1982-89; mem. dep. policy com., agenda com. Mass. Bus. Roundtable, 1982-89; bd. dirs. Mass. Econ. Stabilization Trust, Corp. Bus., Work & Learning. Mem. Cornell Coun., Ithaca, 1981-85, pub. rels. com., 1981-88; mem. adv. coun. Coll. Human Ecology, Cornell U., Ithaca, 1982-84; mem. adv. bd. Ct. Apptd. Spl. Advocates, Worcester, 1983-87; voting mem. Wis. Union Trustees, U. Wis., Madison, 1982-90, trustee, 1990—; mem. bd. visitors coll. letter sci., U. Wis., 1996—, Clark U. Assocs., Worcester, 1983-89; bd. dirs. Planned Parenthood League Mass., 1986-90, pub. affairs com., 1991—; trustee Quinsigamond C.C., Worcester, 1987-98. Fulbright scholar U. Lyon, 1961-62; Cornell grad. fellow, 1962. Mem. Internat. Women's Forum, Mass. Women's Forum, Arthur Page Soc., The Wisemen, Phi Beta Kappa, Mortar Bd., Phi Kappa Phi. Home: 299 Belknap Rd Framingham MA 01701-4716 Office: Hillman & Kersey 299 Belknap Rd Framingham MA 01701-4716

HILLMAN, CHARLENE HAMILTON, public relations executive; b. Akron, Ohio; d. Charles Edward and Maeton (Anderson) Hamilton; m. Robert Edward Hillman; 1 child, Robert Edward (dec.). Student, Youngstown Coll., Ind. U. Extension. Mem. Bob Long Assocs., Indpls., 1959-62; pub. relations dir. Paul Lennon Advt. Agy., Indpls., 1962-63, Clowes Meml. Hall, Indpls., 1963-64; owner, pres. Charlene Hillman Pub. Rels. Assocs., Indpls., 1964-75; sr. v.p., dir. pub. rels. Caldwell-van Riper, Inc., Indpls., 1975-90, also dir.; pvt. practice. Editor: Hoosier Ind. quar. mag., 1966-95. (Frances Wright award 1984), Pub. Rels. Soc. Am. (pres. Hoosier chpt. 1967, nat. bd. dirs. 1974-75, inducted to coll. fellows, 1992). Fax: (317) 879-9584. Home and Office: 2216 Oak Run Pl Indianapolis IN 46260-5123

HILLMAN, DOUGLAS WOODRUFF, federal judge; b. Grand Rapids, Mich., Feb. 15, 1922; s. Lemuel Serrell and Dorothy (Woodruff) H.; m. Sally Jones, Sept. 13, 1944; children: Drusilla W., Clayton D. Student, Phillips Exeter Acad., 1941; A.B., U. Mich., 1946, LL.B., 1948. Bar: Mich. 1948, U.S. Supreme Ct. 1967. Assoc. Lilly, Luyendyk & Snyder, Grand Rapids, 1948-53; partner Luyendyk, Hainer, Hillman, Karr & Dutcher, Grand Rapids, 1953-65, Hillman, Baxter & Hammond, 1965-79; U.S. dist. judge Western Dist. Mich., Grand Rapids, 1979—; chief judge Western Dist. Mich., 1986-91, sr. judge, 1991—; instr. Nat. Inst. Trial Adv., Boulder, Colo; dir. Fed. Judges Assn.; mem. jud. conf. com. on Adminstrn. of Magistrate Judges Sys., 1993—; chair 6th Circuit Standing Com. on Jud. Conf. Planning; mem. exec. com. ABA jud. adminstrn. divsn. Nat. Conf. Fed. Trial Judges, 1995-98. Co-author articles in legal publs. Chmn. Grand Rapids Human Relations Commn., 1963-66; chmn. bd. trustees Fountain St. Ch., 1970-72; pres. Family Service Assn., 1967. Served as pilot USAAF, 1943-45. Decorated DFC, Air medal; recipient Annual Civil Liberties award ACLU, 1970, Disting. Alumni award Ctrl. High Sch., 1986, Raymond Fox Advocacy award, 1989, Champion of Justice award State Bar Mich., 1990, Profl. & Cmty. Svc. award Young Lawyers Sect., 1996, Svc. to Profession award Fed. Bar Assn., 1991; named one of 25 Most Respected Judges Mich. Lawyers Weekly. Fellow Am. Bar Found.; mem. ABA, Mich. Bar Assn. (chmn. client security fund), Grand Rapids Bar Assn. (pres. 1963), Am. Coll. Trial Lawyers (Mich. chmn. 1979, com. on teaching trial and appellate adv.), 6th Circuit Jud. Conf. (life), Internat. Acad. Trial Lawyers, Fedn. Ins. Counsel, Internat. Assn. Ins. Counsel, Internat. Soc. Barristers (pres 1977-78, chair annual Hillman Trial Adv. Seminar 1982—), M Club of U. Mich. (com. visitors U. Mich. Law Sch.), Univ. Club (Grand Rapids), Torch Club. Office: US Dist Ct 682 Fed Bldg 110 Michigan St NW Grand Rapids MI 49503-2363

HILLMAN, GILBERT ROTHSCHILD, medical educator; b. New Haven, Conn., May 1, 1943; s. Jacob D. and Clara (Rothschild) H.; m. Rachel Read, Aug. 27, 1965; child: Laura. BA, Harvard, 1965; PhD, Yale, 1969. Asst. prof. Brown U., 1970-76; assoc. prof. U. Tex. Med. Br., Galveston, 1976-82, prof., 1982—. Contbr. articles to profl. jours. Grantee NIH, NSF, 1976—. Office: U Tex Med Br Dept of Pharmacology Galveston TX 77555-1031

HILLMAN, HENRY L., investment company executive; b. Pitts., Dec. 25, 1918; s. J.H. (Jr.) and Juliet Cummins (Lea) H.; m. Elsie Mead Hilliard, May 12, 1945; children: Lea, Audrey, Henry, William. A.B., Princeton U., 1941. Chmn. exec. com. Hillman Co. Emeritus mem. exec. com. Allegheny Conf. on Community Devel.; chmn. Hillman Found., Inc.; trustee Carnegie Inst.; mem. Bus. Coun. Lt. USNR, 1942-45. Clubs: Duquesne (Pitts.), Pitts. Golf, Fox Chapel Golf, Rolling Rock (Ligonier, Pa.) (hon. gov.), Laurel Valley Golf (Ligonier, Pa.) (dir.), Links (N.Y.C.), Princeton (N.Y.C.), Augusta (Ga.) Nat. Golf, Lyford Cay (Nassau), Seminole Golf (Fla.). Home: Morewood Heights Pittsburgh PA 15213 Office: Hillman Co 330 Grant St Pittsburgh PA 15219-2202

HILLMAN, HOWARD BUDROW, author, editor, publisher, consultant; b. Hollywood, Calif, Dec. 8, 1934; s. Donald Edward and Rebecca (Budrow) H. B.A., Calif. State U.-Long Beach, 1959; M.B.A., Harvard U., 1961. Pres. Nat. Acad. Sports, N.Y.C., 1961, Howard Hillman Co., N.Y.C., 1966—; editor, pub. Howard Hillman Publs., N.Y.C., 1982—; pres. Customer Satisfaction Inst., N.Y.C., 1986—; editor, pub. Quality Digest, N.Y.C., 1987—; v.p. Am. Film Theatre, N.Y.C., 1972-74; internat. lectr. and cons. in field. Author: Hillman's Insiders Guide to New York Restaurants, 1969, The Ins and Outs of Living in New York, 1970, New York at a Glance, 1971, San Francisco at a Glance, 1971, Chicago at a Glance, 1971, Hawaii at a Glance, 1972, Washington at a Glance, 1972, Boston at a Glance, 1972, Florida at a Glance, 1972, The Complete New Yorker, 1972, The Art of Winning Foundation Grants, 1975, The Art of Winning Government Grants, 1977, The Diner's Guide to Wine, 1978, The Book of World Cuisines, 1979, The Art of Winning Corporate Grants, 1980, The Art of Writing Business Reports and Proposals, 1980, The Cook's Book, 1981, Kitchen Science, 1981, Great Peasant Dishes of the World, 1983, The Gourmet Guide to Beer, 1983, The Art of Dining Out, 1984, The Macmillan Complete Computer Buyer's Checklist, 1984, The Computer Log, 1985, Avoiding Computer Nightmares, 1985, Public Domain Software on File for the Apple, 1985, Hillman's Restaurant Ratings, 1986, Public Domain Software on File for the IBM, 1986, New Kitchen Science, 1989, The Educated Palate, 1991, Quality Digest, 1992, The Art of Satisfying Customers, 1993, Quality Consensus, 1994, The CSI Critique Book, 1995, The Art and Psychology of Pleasing Diners, 1996, Hillman Travel Wonders of the World, 1998; contbr. articles to various mags., newspapers and jours.; guest radio, TV talk shows. Served with U.S. Army, 1954-56. Episcopalian. Club: Harvard (N.Y.). Home and Office: 220 E 63rd St New York NY 10021-7660

HILLMAN, JAMES V., pediatrician; b. Youngstown, Ohio, Jan. 8, 1943; m. Rita Cerveny, Aug. 2, 1969; children: Joanna, Kathleen, Michael, Victoria, Daniel. BS, Notre Dame U., 1965; MD, St. Louis U., 1971. Diplomate Am. Bd. Pediatrics, Am. Bd. Pediatric Emergency Medicine, Am. Bd. Emergency Medicine, Am. Bd. Med. Toxicology, Am. Bd. Med. Examiners; cert med. rev. officer Cert. Coun. Am. Coll. Occupational and Environ. Medicine. Intern in pediatrics The Children's Hosp. Med. Ctr., Akron, Ohio, 1971-72; resident in pediatrics The Children's Hosp. Med. Ctr., Akron, 1972-73, chief resident in pediatrics, 1973-74; from staff pediatrician to asst. dir. emergency dept. Children's Hosp. Med. Ctr., Akron, 1976-78; clin. instr. Chgo. Med. Sch., 1974-76; asst. prof. pediatrics Northeastern Ohio U. Coll. Medicine, 1978; asst. dir. emergency dept. Tampa (Fla.) Gen. Hosp., 1978-80, co-dir. emergency dept., 1980-90, chief emergency med. svcs., 1990—; clin. asst. prof. pediatrics U. S. Fla. Coll. Medicine, Tampa, 1978-93, clin. assoc. prof. pediatrics, 1993—; co-med. dir. Fla. Poison Info. Ctr., Tampa Gen. Hosp., 1978—, dir. pediatric emergency care ctr., 1981-90, dir. occupational health svcs., 1992-95; dir. Med. Toxicology Cons., Tampa; pres. The Emergency Assocs. for Medicine.; med. dir., cons. Fla. Steel Corp., Tampa Elec. Co., Lykes Bros., Inc. Author: (with others) Clin. Practice of Emergency Medicine, 1989, 2d rev. edit., 1994; contbr. articles to profl. jours and sci. papers and case histories to med. confs. Bd. dirs. Judeo-Christian Coalition Clinic, Tampa, at present, Family Hostel Found., 1980-90; med. advisor Hillsborough County Emergency Med. Svc., Tampa, Tampa Fire Rescue, Rape Crisis Ctr., Tampa and other civic orgns; chmn. of bd. Tampa Bay Regional Poison Control Found.; past med. dir. Basic Trauma Life Support State of Fla.; mem. State Appointed Task Force on Trauma, 1989-90, State Pesticide Rev. Coun., 1990—; chair Health Effects Team, 1992—, Pesticide Rev. Coun., 1994-95. Lt. commdr. USN, 1974-76. Recipient James Kramer award Children's Hosp. Med. Ctr., Akron, Ohio, 1974. Fellow Am. Coll. Emergency Physicians (bd. dirs., past treas., sec., pres. Fla. chpt., mem. nat. toxicology standards com. 1990-94); mem. Am. Acad. Pediatrics, Soc.Emergency Pediatric Medicine (bd. dirs.). Avocation: sailing. Office: Emergency Assocs Medicine Ste 400 6200 W Courtney Campbell Cswy Tampa FL 33607-1496*

HILLMAN, JORDAN JAY, law educator; b. 1924. M.A. in Polit Sci., U. Chgo., 1947, JD, 1950; SJD, Northwestern U., 1965. Bar: Ill. 1950. Mem. legal staff Ill. Commerce Commn., 1950-53; with Chgo. and Northwestern Ry., 1954-67, gen. counsel, 1963-67, v.p. law, 1966-67; prof. emeritus law Northwestern U., 1967-89, prof., rsch. counsel, prof. transp. ctr., 1989-91; sr. legal cons., gen. counsel U.S. Ry. Assn., 1974-76, spl. counsel, 1976-79; legal cons. Amtrak, 1978. Mem. Constn. Study Commn., State of Ill., 1963-67; mem. Zoning Amendment Com., Evanston, Ill., 1963-68; mem. Bd. Edn., Dist. 202, Evanston Twp. H.S., 1968-71; mem. Chgo. Transit Authority Bd., 1981-87. Mem. Phi Beta Kappa. Author: Competition and Railroad Price Discrimination, 1968; The Parliamentary Structuring of British Road-Rail Freight Coordination, 1973; The Export-Import Bank at Work; Promotional Financing in the Public Sector, 1982; Price Level Regulation for Diversified Public Utilities, 1989. Office: Northwestern U Sch Law 317 E Chicago Ave Chicago IL 60611-3008

HILLMAN, REED V., protective services official. BSBA, Babson Coll.; JD, Suffolk U. Trooper Mass. State Police, 1974-85, corporal, 1985-87, sgt., 1987-89, staff sgt., 1989-92, lt., 1992-94, capt., 1994-96, col., supt., 1996—. Office: Commonwealth of Mass Dept State Police 470 Worcester Rd Framingham MA 01702

HILLMAN, RICHARD EPHRAIM, pediatrician, educator; b. Pawtucket, R.I., Oct. 6, 1940; s. Harold S. and Anne (Chernick) H.; m. Laura S. Smith, June 14, 1970; children: Helena, Stuart, Noah, Paul, Andrew, Anne. AB, Brown U., 1962; MD, Yale U., 1965. Diplomate: Am. Bd. Med. Examiners, Am. Bd. Pediatrics, Am. Bd. Human Genetics. Intern Grace-New Haven Hosp., 1965-66, resident, 1966-67; asst. prof. pediatrics Washington U., St. Louis, 1971-75, assoc. prof., 1975-78, prof. pediatrics, 1981-87, assoc. prof. genetics, 1977-81, prof. genetics, 1981-87; prof. biochemistry and child health U. Mo., Columbia, 1987—; chmn. mental retardation research com. Nat. Inst. Child Health and Human Devel., Bethesda, Md., 1983-87, assoc. chmn., 1995—. Lt. comdr. USN, 1969-71. Fellow Am. Acad. Pediatrics; mem. Soc. Pediatric Research (council), Am. Pediatric Soc., Am. Soc. Clin. Investigation, Soc. for Inherited Metabolic Disorders (pres.). Office: U Mo Dept Child Health 1 Hospital Dr Columbia MO 65201-5276*

HILLMAN, RITA, investor; b. N.Y.C., May 16, 1912; d. Rudolf and Bertha (Goodman) Kanarek; m. Alex L. Hillman, Aug. 23, 1932 (dec. 1968); children: Richard Alan (dec.), Alex L. Student NYU, 1929-32. Mem. Met. Mus. Art (mem. vis. com. 20th century art dept.), Am. Friends Israel Mus. (exec. com.), Bklyn. Acad. Music (mem. exec. com.), Internat. Ctr. Photography (hon. chmn.), Alex Hillman Family Found. (pres.). Home: 895 Park Ave New York NY 10021-0327 Office: 630 5th Ave New York NY 10111-0100

HILLMAN, ROBERT ANDREW, law educator, former university dean; b. N.Y.C., Dec. 23, 1946; s. Herman D. and Edith N. (Geilich) H.; m. Elizabeth Hall Kafka, Aug. 24, 1969; children: Jessica H., Heather D. BA, U. Rochester, 1969; JD, Cornell U., 1972. Bar: N.Y. 1973, Iowa 1976. Law clk. to judge U.S. Dist. Ct., N.Y.C., 1972-73; assoc. Debevoise & Plimpton, N.Y.C., 1973-74; prof. law U. Iowa, Iowa City, 1975-82; prof. law Cornell U., Ithaca, N.Y., 1982—, acad. dean, 1990-97, Edwin Woodruff prof. law. Author: (with others) Common Law and Equity Under the UCC, 1985, Law: Its Nature, Functions, and Limits, 1986, Contract and Related Obligation: Theory, Doctrine, and Practice, 1987, 2d edit., 1992, 3d edit., 1997, The Richness of Contract Law, 1997; contbr. articles to profl. jours. Mem. Am. Arbitration Assn. (arbitrator 1980—), Am. Law Inst. Avocations: tennis, bicycling. Office: Cornell U Law Sch Myron Taylor Hall Ithaca NY 14853*

HILLMAN, SANDRA SCHWARTZ, public relations executive, marketing professional; b. Chester, Pa., 1941; m. Robert S. Hillman, Apr. 1964; children: Pamela Hillman Loeb, Allison Hope. BA, Pa. State U., 1962. Assoc. editor McFadden-Bartell Pub., N.Y.C., 1963-64; pub. rels. account exec. Edward M. Meyers & Assocs., N.Y.C., 1964-66; info. officer Nat. Tchr. Corps, U.S. Office Edn., Washington, 1966-68, Balt. Dept. Housing and Cmty. Devel., 1968-71; exec. dir. Balt. Office Promotion and Tourism, 1971-84; pub. info. mgr. The Nat. Tchr. Corps, 1963-68; pub. rels. acct. exec. Edward M. Meyers & Assocs.; pub. rels. officer Balt. Dept. Housing and Cmty. Devel., 1968-70; exec. dir. Balt. Office Promotion and Tourism, 1970-84; prin., exec. v.p. Trahan, Burden & Charles Inc., 1984—; mktg., pub. rels. cons. to cities of Pitts., San Diego, Buffalo, Niagara Falls, N.Y., N.Y.C., Miami, Milw., Curacao, Netherlands Antilles, Charleston, Chattahooga, Edinburg; mem. bd. Gov.'s Tourism Task Force; presenter, lectr. in field. Bd. dirs. Balt. Symphony Orch., World Trade Ctr. Inst., Balt. City Found., Boy Scouts Am., Md. Film Commn., The Nat. Aquarium, Jr. League Cmty. Coun., Urban League; pres. Balt. Ctr. for Performing Arts, 1976-92. Recipient Lifetime Achievement award Balt. Pub. Rels. Soc., 1996. Fellow Pa. State U. (Disting. 1991); mem. Gov.'s World Trade Ctr. Inst. (mem. bd., coms.), Md. C. of C. (strategic planning com.), Children's Theater Assn. Office: Trahan Burden & Charles 1030 N Charles St Baltimore MD 21201-5442*

HILLMAN, STEPHEN J., federal judge; b. 1950. BA, U. Calif., Berkeley, 1972; JD, U. Wash., 1975. Bar: Calif. Dep. chief dep. fed. pub. defender for ctrl. dist. Calif., 1979-86; ptnr. Berman & Clark, Santa Monica, Calif., 1986-92; magistrate judge for ctrl. dist. Calif., U.S. Magistrate Ct., L.A., 1992—. Office: US Magistrate Ct 339 US Courthouse 312 N Spring St Los Angeles CA 90012-4701

HILLMAN, WILLIAM CHERNICK, federal bankruptcy judge, educator; b. Providence, R.I., Oct. 15, 1935; s. Harold S. and Anne (Chernick) H.; m. Edith Boren, June 22, 1958 (div. 1982) ; children: Harold S. II, Daniel C.A. JD cum laude, Boston U., 1957, LLM, 1968. Bar: R.I. 1957, U.S. Supreme Ct. 1965, Mass. 1990. Ptnr. Strauss, Factor, Hillman & Lopes (and predecessors), Providence, R.I., 1957-91; U.S. bankruptcy judge U.S. Bankruptcy Ct., Boston, 1991—; judge of probate Town of Barrington and West Greenwich, R.I., 1975-91; program chmn. Practicing Law Inst., N.Y.C., 1978—, chmn. Banking Law Inst., N.Y.C., 1983-88, R.I. Law Inst., Providence, 1982-86; adj. prof. law Suffolk U., 1996-98, Northeastern U., 1998—. Author: Commercial Loan Documentation, 1986, 3d edit., 1990, Secured Transactions Law and Documentation, 1986, Documenting Secured Transactions: Problem Avoidance and Effective Drafting, 1987, 10th edit., 1997, Personal Bankruptcy, 1993, 2d edit., 1995; editor Letters of Credit: Current Thinking in America, 1987; contbr. articles to profl. jours. Capt. U.S. Army, 1958. Mem. ABA, Boston Bar Assn., R.I. Bar Assn., Nat. Conf. Commrs. on Uniform State Laws (life, commr. 1969—), Scribes. Office: US Bankruptcy Ct 10 Causeway St Rm 1101 Boston MA 02222-1009*

HILL-MCDONALD, LINDA, professional basketball coach; b. Morton, Pa.. B.Health, Phys. Edn. and Recreation, West Chester U., 1970, MEd, 1984. Coach basketball and lacrosse Ridley Sr. H.S., Phila.; head coach Temple U., Phila., 10 yrs., U. Minn., Mpls., 7 yrs., Cleve. Rockers, WNBA, 1997—; head coach Olympic Sports Festival Team, 1989; coach Big Ten All-Star Team, summer 1993. Recipient Carol Echman award Women's Basketball Coaches' Assn.; named Coach of the Yr., Atlantic 10, 1987, 89, Big 5, 1989; Recipient Outstanding Female Athlete award West Chester U., 1970; Inductee West Chester U. Women's Athletic Hall of Fame, 1989. Mem. Women's Basketball Coaches Assn. Office: Cleveland Rockers 1 Center Ct Cleveland OH 44115-4001

HILLMER, MARGARET PATRICIA, library director; b. Cirencester, Gloucestershire, Eng., Mar. 17, 1936; came to U.S., 1960; naturalized, 1973; d. John Albert and Margaret Evelyn (Richardson) Hall; m. Max Lorraine Hillmer, Mar. 24, 1962; children: Felicity Margaret, Jennifer Anne. ALAM, London Acad. Music Dram. Art, London, 1955; AB magna cum laude, Heidelberg Coll., 1976; AM in Libr. Sci., U. Mich., 1977. Cert. libr. Ohio. Speech and ballet tchr. Cirencester, 1955-58; governess NSW, Australia, 1959-60; ballet instr., choreographer Heidelberg Coll., Tiffin, Ohio, 1969-73, adminstrv. asst. pub. rels. Water Quality Lab., 1978-79; head reference dept. Tiffin-Seneca Pub. Libr., 1979-80, libr. dir., 1980—. Contbr. articles to profl. publs. Chair Take Our Daughters to Work Day, 1993—; bd. dirs. Tiffin-Seneca Teen Ctr., 1992—; mem. Tiffin City Schs. Bd. Edn., 1991—, pres., 1995-96; mem. Seneca County Dept. Human Svcs. Bd., 1984-91, pres., 1987-89. Recipient Liberty Bell award Seneca County Bar Assn., 1990, People's Law Sch. award Ohio Acad. Trial Lawyers, 1993, Athena award Tiffin Area C. of C., 1999. Mem. ALA, AAUW, LWV (pres. Tiffin chpt. 1980-82, chair internat. rels. Ohio 1975-76), Ohio Libr. Assn. (legislation com. 1985-89, chair legis. network 1989-93, chair awards and honors com. 1995-96, seminar spkr. 1985—), Pub. Libr. Assn., Freedom to Read Assn., Tiffin Rotary Club, Beta Phi Mu. Democrat. Episcopalian. Avocations: reading, theater, classical music. Home: 25 Southview Pl Tiffin OH 44883-3312 Office: Tiffin-Seneca Pub Libr 77 Jefferson St Tiffin OH 44883-2339

HILLS, ALAN R., artistic director; b. Cleve.. Past student, Wright State U. Past live entertainment dir. Funtime, Inc.; past sales mgr., spl. events coord. Visitor's Bur. Greater Cleve.; with Cleve. San Jose Ballet, 1989, past interium gen. mgr., ops. dir. Office: San Jose Ballet PO Box 1666 San Jose CA 95109-1666*

HILLS, ARTHUR W., architectural firm executive. BS in Horticulture, Mich. State U., 1953; student, U. Toledo, 1957-58; B of Landscape Architecture, U. Mich., 1961. Registered architect, Mich., Ohio, Fla. Prin. Arthur Hills, Landscape Architect, 1960-66, Arthur Hills and Assocs., Toledo, 1966—. Prin. works include (golf courses) Golf Club Ga. (Best New Pvt. Course Golf Digest 1992), Harbour Pointe (Best New Pub. Course Golf Digest 1991), The Champions, Lexington, Ky., Bighorn Golf Club, Palm Desert, Calif., Dunes West, Charleston, S.C., Arthur Hills Course at Palmetto Dunes and Palmetto Hall Plantation, Hilton Head Island, Bonita Bay's Marsh Course, Bonita Springs, Fla. (one of Top 100 Courses in U.S. Golf Digest 1988—), TPC at Eagle Trace, Coral Springs, Fla. (one of Top 100 Courses in U.S. Golf Digest), Egypt Valley Country Club, Grand Rapids, Mich., Wingpointe, Salt Lake City, River Islands Golf Club, Knoxville, Tenn., Walking Stick, Pueblo, Colo., Windsor Parke, Jacksonville, Fla., The Legacy at Green Valley, Las Vegas, Nev., others. With U.S. Armed Svcs., 1952-54. Mem. Am. Soc. Golf Course Architects (officer, trustee), Am. Soc. Landscape Architects, Golf Course Supt.'s Assn. Am., Nat. Golf Found., Nat. Reacreation and Pks. Assn., Ohio Pks. and Recreation Assn., Ohio Turfgrass Found., Urban Land Inst. Office: Arthur Hills & Assoc 7351 W Bancroft St Toledo OH 43615-3014*

HILLS, AUSTIN EDWARD, vineyard executive; b. San Francisco, Oct. 13, 1934; s. Leslie William and Ethel (Lee) H.; m. Erika Michaela Brunar, May 20, 1978; children—Austin, Justin. A.B., Stanford U., 1957; M.B.A., Columbia U., 1959. Chmn. bd. dirs. Hills Bros. Coffee, Inc., San Francisco, 1976, Grgich Hills Cellar, Rutherford, Calif., 1977—; bd. dirs. North Fulton Bancshares, Inc.; pres. Hills Vineyards, Inc., Rutherford, 1975-97; pres. Pacific Coast Coffee Assn., San Francisco, 1975-76. Pres., San Francisco Soc. for Prevention of Cruelty to Animals, 1972-78, No. Calif. Soc. for Prevention of Cruelty to Animals, 1972-78. Served with Air N.G. Mem. Am. Soc. Enologists. Republican. Office: 490 Post St Ste 1049 San Francisco CA 94102-1301

HILLS, CARLA ANDERSON, lawyer, former federal official; b. Los Angeles, Jan. 3, 1934; d. Carl H. and Edith (Hume) Anderson; m. Roderick Maltman Hills, Sept. 27, 1958; children: Laura Hume, Roderick Maltman, Megan Elizabeth, Alison Macbeth. AB cum laude, Stanford U., 1955; student, St. Hilda's Coll., Oxford (Eng.) U., 1954; LLB, Yale U., 1958; hon. degrees, Pepperdine U., 1975, Washington U., 1977, Mills Coll., 1977, Lake Forest Coll., 1978, Williams Coll., 1981, Notre Dame U., 1993, Wabash Coll., 1997. Bar: Calif. 1959, DC 1974, U.S. Supreme Ct. 1965. Asst. U.S. atty. civil divsn. L.A., 1958-61; ptnr. Munger, Tolles, Hills & Rickershauser, L.A., 1962-74; asst. atty. gen. civil divsn. Justice Dept., Washington, 1974-75; sec. HUD, 1975-77; ptnr. Latham, Watkins & Hills, Washington, 1978-86, Weil, Gotshal & Manges, Washington, 1986-88; U.S. trade rep. Exec. Office of the Pres., 1989-93; chmn., CEO Hills & Co., 1993—; bd. dirs. Inter-Am. Dialogue, Am. Internat. Group, Time-Warner, Lucent Techs., Inc., Bechtel Enterprises Holdings, Chevron Corp., TCW Group, Inc.; adj. prof. Sch. Law, UCLA, 1972; mem. Trilateral Commn., 1977-82, 93—, Am. Com. on East-West Accord, 1977-79, Internat. Found. for Cultural Cooperation and Devel., 1977-89, Fed. Acctg. Standards Adv. Council, 1978-80; mem. corrections task force L.A. County Sub-Regional; adv. bd. Calif. Council on Criminal Justice, 1969-71; standing com. discipline U.S. Dist. Ct. for Central Calif., 1970-73; mem. Adminstrv. Conf. U.S., 1972-74; exec. com. law and free soc. State Bar Calif., 1973; bd. councillors U. So. Calif. Law Center, 1972-74; trustee Pomona Coll., 1974-79; trustee Brookings Instn., 1985; mem. at large exec. com. Yale Law Sch., 1973-78; mem. com. on Law Sch. Yale U. Council; Gordon Grand fellow Yale U., 1978; mem. Sloan Commn. on Govt. and Higher Edn., 1977-79; advisory com. Princeton U., Woodrow Wilson Sch. of Pub. and Internat. Affairs, 1977-80; trustee Am. Productivity and Quality Ctr., 1988; council mem. Calif. Gov. Coun. Econ. Policy Adv., 1993—, Coun. on Fgn. Rels., 1993—; vice-chair Nat. Com. on U.S.-China Rels., 1993—; bd. dirs., U.S.-China Bus. Coun., vice-chair, 1995—. Co-author: Federal Civil Practice, 1961; co-author, editor: Antitrust Adviser, 1971, 3d edit., 1985; contbg. editor: Legal Times, 1978-88; mem. editorial bd. Nat. Law Jour., 1978-88. Trustee U. So. Calif., 1977-79, Norton Simon Mus. Art, Pasadena, Calif., 1976-80; trustee Urban Inst., 1978-89, chmn., 1983-89; co-chmn. Alliance to Save Energy, 1977-89; vice chmn. adv. coun. on legal policy Am. Enterprise Inst., 1977-84; bd. visitors, exec. com. Stanford U. Law Sch., 1978-81; bd. dirs. Am. Coun. for Capital Formation, 1978-82, Interam. Dialogue, 1997—; mem. exec. com. Inst. for Internat. Econs., 1993—; mem. adv. com. MIT-Harvard U. Joint Ctr. for Urban Studies, 1978-82. Fellow Am. Bar Found.; mem. L.A. Women Lawyers Assn. (pres. 1964), ABA (chair publs. com. antitrust sect. 1972-74, council 1974, 77-84, chair 1982-83), Fed. Bar Assn. (pres. L.A. chpt. 1963), L.A. County Bar Assn. (fed. rules and practice com. 1963-72, chair issues and survey 1963-72, chair sub-com. revision local rules for fed. cts. 1966-72, jud. qualifications com. 1971-72), Am. Law Inst., Am. China Soc. (bd. dirs. 1995—), Yale of So. Calif. Club (bd. dirs. 1972-74), Yale Club. Clubs: Yale of So. Calif. (dir. 1972-74); Yale (Washington). Office: Hills & Co 1200 19th St NW Ste 201 Washington DC 20036-2429

HILLS, FREDERIC WHEELER, editor, publishing company executive; b. East Orange, N.J., Nov. 26, 1934; s. Frederic Wheeler and Mildred Chambers (Hood) H.; m. Patricia Schulze, Jan. 17, 1958 (div. Dec. 1973); children: Christina, Bradford; m. Kathleen Matthews, Apr. 21, 1980; children: Gregory, Frederic. BA, Columbia U., 1956; MA, Stanford U., 1959. Editor F.W. Dodge Corp., San Francisco, 1959-60, N.Y.C., 1960-61; editor McGraw-Hill Book Co., N.Y.C., 1961-68, editor-in-chief Coll. divsn., 1968-72, editor-in-chief Gen. Books divsn., 1972-78; mem. editorial bd. Simon & Schuster Book Co., N.Y.C., 1979—, v.p., 1981—. With AUS, 1958. Mem. PEN, Assn. Am. Pubs. Home: 218 Monterey Ave Pelham NY 10803-2310 also: PO Box 1061 Shelter Island Heights NY 11965-1063 Office: Simon & Schuster Book Co 1230 Ave of the Americas New York NY 10020-1586

HILLS, JOHN MERRILL, educational administrator, consultant, former public policy research center executive; b. Wethersfield, Conn., May 6, 1944; s. Merrill Clarke and Elizabeth (Tarrant) H.; m. Irene Jeanne Lavallee, Oct. 7, 1974 (div.); children: John M. Jr., Sara Clarke. Student, U. Hartford, 1963; BBA, Nichols Coll., 1969; postgrad., U. Md., 1976. Salesman Peter A Frasse and Co., Inc., Hartford, Conn., 1963-64; dir. alumni relations, asst. dir. admissions Nichols Coll., Dudley, Mass., 1969-72; regional dir. Georgetown U., Washington, 1972-74; dir. devel. cen. adminstrn. U. Md., College Park, 1974-77; v.p. Roanoke Coll., Salem, Va., 1977-86, The Brookings Instn., Washington, 1986-98; pres. JMH Assocs., 1998—; pres. J.M.H. Assocs., Alexandria, Va., 1979—; cons. Am. Assn. Univ. Cons., Inc., Washington, 1975-77; mgmt., pub. relations and fund raising cons. Trustee, mem. exec. com. Nichols Coll., Dudley, Mass., 1993—, Higher Edn. Roundtable, Lamplighters; judge U.S. Steel Alumni Award, Pitts., 1979-86; bd. dirs. Mill Mountain Theater, Roanoke, 1983-86, Roanoke ARC, 1984-86, Roanoke Valley C. of C., 1983-86; mem. adv. bd. Phoenix Soc. Georgetown U. Sch. Law.; mem. Little Theater of Alexandria. With U.S. Army, 1965-67, N.G. Recipient Alumni Achievement award Nichols Coll., 1991; named one of Outstanding Young Men Am., U.S. Jaycees, 1980, Outstanding Nat. Advisor, Pi Lambda Phi, Conn., 1983, 86. Mem. Nat. Soc. Fund Raiser Execs., Coun. for Advancement and Support of Edn. (faculty chmn.), Alexandria Sportsman's Club (mem. exec. com.), Hunting Hills Club, Jefferson Club (Roanoke), Met. Club Washington, Paul Hill Choral Soc. (mem. corp. bd.). Roman Catholic. Avocations: sailing, jogging. Home: 1272 New Hampshire Dr NW Washington DC 20036-2188 also (summer): 17 Josephine St Rehoboth Beach DE 19971-2017 Office: Annenberg Rural Challenge 808 17th St NW Washington DC 20006

HILLS, LEE, foundation administrator, newspaper executive, consultant; b. Granville, N.D., May 28, 1906; s. Lewis Amos and Lulu Mae (Loomis) H.; m. Leona Hass, Dec. 25, 1933 (div. 1944); 1 child, Ronald L.; m. Eileen Whitman, June 7, 1948 (dec. 1961); m. Argentina Schifano, Oct. 31, 1963. Attended, Brigham Young U., 1924-25, U. Mo., 1927-29; LLB, Okla. City Univ., 1934; hon. degree in Bus. Adminstrn., Cleary Coll., 1958; LLD (hon.), Eastern Mich. U., 1969; LHD (hon.), U. Utah, 1969, U. Mo., 1988; D. in Journalism (hon.), U. Miami, Fla., 1986. News/edit. exec. Scripps-Howard Newspapers, Cleve., Indpls., Okla. City, 1933-41; mng. editor Miami (Fla.) Herald, 1942-51; exec. editor, pub. Miami Herald and Detroit Free Press, 1951-79; pres. Knight Newspapers, 1967-73; chmn., chief exec. officer Knight-Ridder, Inc., Miami, 1974-81; trustee, vice chmn., chmn. John S. & James L. Knight Found., Miami, chmn. emeritus, 1999—. Co-author: Facsimile, 1949. Trustee Am. Fedn. Arts, N.Y.C., Ctr. Fine Arts, Miami, Fla.; life trustee Detroit Inst. Arts.; pres. Detroit Arts Commn., 1966-80. Recipient Maria Moors Cabot Gold Medal for disting. contbn. to inter-Am. rels. Columbia U., N.Y.C., 1946, Disting. Svc. Journalism, U. Mo., Columbia, 1950, 63, Pulitzer Prize in Journalism, 1950, 56, William Allen White Found. award journalistic merit U. Kans., 1983; named to Hall of Honor U. Mo. Sch. Journalism, 1959, Okla. Journalism Hall of Fame, 1973; first inductee Comm. Hall of Fame, Brigham Young U., 1992; named in his honor Lee Hills Hall U. Mo. Sch. Journalism, 1992, Lee Hlls Journalism fellowship Stanford U. within Knight Fellowship Program, 1992, Lee Hills Award Disting. Career Svc. to Detroit Theater, 1986, Lee Hills chair in Free-Press Studies, U. Mo., 1997. Home: Bay Point 4450 Banyan Ln Miami FL 33137-3302 Office: John & James Knight Found One Herald Plz 6th Fl Miami FL 33132-1693*

HILLS, LINDA LAUNEY, advisory systems engineer; b. New Orleans, June 21, 1947; d. Edgar Sebastien and Isabel (James) Launey; m. Marvin Allen Hills Sr. Jan. 29, 1977 (div. July 1982); 8 stepchildren. Student, Navy Avionics Schs., Memphis and San Diego, 1979-89; certs. in tech. tng., IBM, Chgo. and Kingston, N.Y., Sys. Mgmt. Schs., Chgo. and Dallas. Cert. disaster recovery planner. Sec. Calhoun and Barnes Inc. Co., New Orleans, 1965; clk.-typist, stenographer, med. transcriptionist, teletypist Social Security Adminstrn., New Orleans, 1965-67; dep. U.S. marshal U.S. Marshal's Office, New Orleans, 1967-69; supr. U.S. Atty.'s Office, New Orleans, 1969; with clk.'s office, dep. U.S. clk., courtrom dep. U.S. clk. U.S. Dist. Ct. (ea. dist.) La., New Orleans, 1969-73; steno, sr. sec. Kelly Girl and Norrell Temp Services, New Orleans, 1974; customer engr. trainee IBM, Dallas, 1979; customer engr., sys. mgmt. specialist IBM, San Diego, 1979-84; sys. ctr. rep. NSD Washington System Ctr. IBM, Gaithersburg, Md., 1984-87; ops. specialist mktg. dept. IBM, San Diego, 1987—, adv. sys. engr., 1988-91; lectr., cons. in field. Author 3 workbooks on recovery mgmt., also presentation guide for execs. with cost evaluation, presentation guide for company coms. Vol. Touro Infirmary, Dialysis Unit, New Orleans, 1965-67, New Orleans Recreation Dept. 1964-68, PALS-Montgomery County Mental Health Orgn., Bethesda, Md., 1984-87, various polit. candidates, 1965-3; mem. Calif. Gov.'s Subcom. on Disaster Preparedness. Petty officer USN, 1974-78. Mem. NAFE, ACP, DAV, Info. System Security Assn., Women Computer Profls. San Diego, Data Processing Mgmt. Assn., San Diego Zoolog. Soc., Assn. System Mgmt., Smithsonian Instn. (resident assoc.), Nat. Trust Hist. Preservation. Avocations: travel, piano, crocheting, carpentry, woodworking. Office: PO Box 261806 San Diego CA 92196-1806

HILLS, PATRICIA GORTON SCHULZE, curator; b. Baraboo, Wis., Jan. 31, 1936; d. Hartwin A. Schulze and Glennie Gorton Baker; m. Frederic W. Hills, Jan. 17, 1958 (div. Feb. 1974); children: Christina, Bradford; m. Guy Kevin Whitfield, Jan. 3, 1976; 1 child, Andrew. BA, Stanford U., 1957; MA, Hunter Coll., 1968; PhD, NYU, 1973. Curatorial asst. Mus. Modern

Art, N.Y.C., 1960-62; guest curator Whitney Mus. Am. Art, 1971-72, assoc. curator 18th and 19th Century art, 1972-74; vis. asst. prof. art dept. Hunter Coll., 1973; adj. assoc. prof. fine arts Inst. Fine Arts NYU, 1973-74; assoc. prof. fine arts and performing arts York Coll. CUNY, 1974-78; assoc. prof. dept. art history Boston U., 1978-88, prof., 1988—, chmn. dept., 1995-97; adj. assoc. prof. Grad. Sch. Arts and Scis., Columbia U., 1974-75; adj. curator Whitney Mus. Am. Art, 1974-87. Author: Eastman Johnson, 1972, The American Frontier: Images and Myths, 1973, The Painters' America: Rural and Urban Life, 1810-1910, 1974, Turn-of-Century America: Paintings, Graphics, Photographs, 1890-1910, 1977, Social Concern and Urban Realism: American Painting of the 1930s, 1983, Alice Neel, 1983, John Singer Sargent, 1986, Stuart Davis, 1996; co-author: The Figurative Tradition and the Whitney Mus. Am. Art, 1980, Jacob Lawrence: Thirty Years of Prints: 1963-93, Eastman Johnson: Painting America, 1999. Danforth Found. grad. fellow for women, 1968-72, John Simon Guggenheim Meml. Found. fellow, 1982-83, Charles Warren Ctr. for Studies in Am. History fellow, 1982-83, W.E.B. DuBois Inst. for Afro-Am. Rsch. fellow, Harvard U., 1991-92, NEH fellow, 1995. Mem. Coll. Art Assn., Women's Caucus for Arts, Am. Studies Assn., Am. Assn. Mus. Home: 238 Putnam Ave Cambridge MA 02139-3767 Office: Boston U Dept Art History Boston MA 02215

HILLS, REGINA J., journalist; b. Sault Sainte Marie, Mich., Dec. 24, 1953; d. Marvin Dan and Ardithanne (Tilly) H.; m. Vincent C. Stricherz, Feb. 25, 1984. B.A., U. Nebr., 1976. Reporter UPI, Lincoln, Nebr., 1976-80, state editor, bur. mgr., 1981-82; state editor, bur. mgr. UPI, New Orleans, 1982-84, Indpls., 1985-87; asst. city editor Seattle Post-Intelligencer, 1987-99, online prodr., 1999—; panelist TV interview show Face Nebr., 1978-81; vis. lectr. U. Nebr., Lincoln, 1978, 79, 80; columnist weekly feature Capitol News, Nebr. Press Assn., 1981-82. Recipient Outstanding Coverage awards UPI, 1980, 82. Mem. U. Nebr. Alumni Assn., Zeta Tau Alpha. Office: Seattle Post-Intelligencer 101 Elliott Ave W Ste 200 Seattle WA 98119-4295

HILLS, RODERICK M., lawyer, business executive, former government official; b. Seattle, Mar. 9, 1931; s. Kenneth Maltman and Sarah B. (Love) H.; m. Carla Helen Anderson, Sept. 27, 1958; children: Laura, Roderick Jr., Megan, Allison. BA in History, Stanford U., 1952, LLB, 1955. Bar: Calif. 1957, U.S. Supreme Ct. 1960, D.C. 1977. Law clk. to Justice Stanley F. Reed U.S. Supreme Ct., 1955-57; assoc. Musick, Peeler & Garrett, L.A., 1957-62; ptnr. Munger, Tolles & Hills, L.A., 1962-75; chmn. Republic Corp., L.A., 1971-75; counsel to Pres. U.S., 1975; chmn. SEC, 1975-77; chmn., CEO Peabody Coal Co., St. Louis and Washington, 1977-79; ptnr. Latham, Watkins & Hills, Washington, 1978-82; chmn. Sears World Trade, Inc., Washington, 1982-84; chmn., mng. dir. The Manchester Group, Ltd. (renamed Hills Enterprises, Ltd.), Washington, 1986—; mng. ptnr. Donovan, Leisure, Rogovin, Huge & Schiller, Washington, 1989-92; chmn. internat. practice group Shea & Gould, Washington, 1992-94; ptnr. Mudge Rose Guthrie Alexander & Ferdon, Washington, 1994-95; vis. prof. law Harvard U., 1969-70; lectr. law Stanford U., 1960-69; disting. faculty fellow internat. fin. Yale U. Sch. Mgmt., 1986-89; bd. dirs., vice-chmn. Oak Industries, Fed. Mogul Corp., chmn. 1996, Wasto Mgmt., Medaphis. Bd. editors, comment editor: Stanford Law Rev, 1953-55. Trustee Com. Econ. Devel., 1978—; dir. U.S.-ASEAN Coun. for Bus. and Tech., Inc., 1982—, chmn., 1986-90, vice chmn., 1990—; mem. Bretton Woods Com. Fellow Am. Bar Found.; mem. ABA, U.S. Supreme Ct. Bar Assn., L.A. County Bar Assn., State Bar Calif., Order of Coif, Chancery Club, Lowes Island Club, Chevy Chase Club, Phi Delta Phi. Republican. Episcopalian. Avocations: tennis, golf, history. Home: 3125 Chain Bridge Rd NW Washington DC 20016-3411 Office: Hills Enterprises Ltd 1200 19th St NW Washington DC 20036-2412

HILLSTROM, THOMAS PETER, engineering executive; b. Lakewood, Ohio, Apr. 20, 1943; s. Harry Edward and Mary Pauline (Mauss) H.; m. Jean Elizabeth Greenfield; children: Edward, Mary. BS in Mech. Engring., Northwestern U., Evanston, 1966; MBA, Northwestern U., Chgo., 1977. Design engr. Internat. Harvester, Hinsdale, Ill., 1966-74, project engr., 1974-78, product safety engr., 1978-82; mgr. engring. Fire Apparatus Div., FMC, Tipton, Ind., 1982-85; mgr. contract engring. FMC Naval Systems Div., Mpls., 1985-87, program mgr., 1987-90, mgr. splty. engring., 1990-91; program mgr. United Def., L.P., Mpls., 1985—. Patentee in field. Mem. Soc. Automotive Engrs., Am. Soc. Agrl. Engrs., System Safety Soc., Boy Scouts Am. Order of the Arrow. Republican. Home: 4340 Hackley Point Ln Muskegon MI 49441-4818 Office: United Def LP 4800 E River Rd Minneapolis MN 55421-1402

HILLYARD, IRA WILLIAM, pharmacologist, educator; b. Richmond, Utah, Mar. 23, 1924; s. Neal Jacobsen and Lucille (Duce) H.; m. Venice Lenore Williams, July 10, 1945 (dec.); children: Christine, Kevin, Eric; m. Norma Larsen, May 1, 1970. B.S., Idaho State U., 1949; M.S., U. Nebr., 1951; Ph.D., St. Louis U., 1957. Pharmacologist Mead Johnson Co., Evansville, Ind., 1957-59; sr. pharmacologist, sect. leader Warner-Lambert Research Inst., Morris Plains, N.J., 1959-69; assoc. prof. pharmacology Idaho State U. Coll. Pharmacy, Pocatello, 1969-73, 77-79, dean, 1979-87, prof. pharmacology, 1979-91, prof. emeritus, 1991—; dir. pharmacology and toxicology ICN Pharms., Irvine, Calif., 1973-77, cons., 1977-80; cons. Pennwalt Pharm. Co., Rochester, N.Y., 1978-83. Contbr. articles to profl. jours. Served with USN, 1943-45, 51-53. Decorated Purple Heart. Fellow Am. Found. Pharm. Edn.; mem. Western Pharmacology Soc., Am. Assn. Colls. Pharmacy, Am. Soc. Pharmacology and Exptl. Therapeutics, N.Y. Acad. Scis., Sigma Xi, Rho Chi, Phi Delta Chi. Lodge: Rotary. Home: 2750 Mt Borah Pl Pocatello ID 83201-2637 Office: Idaho State U Dept Pharmacology Pocatello ID 83209 *I firmly believe that we make individual contributions to the welfare and progress of mankind only if every action is based on truth. If we remain honest and open-minded in our approach, truth will always be recognized and those challenging decisions which must precede every action, will be correctly made even though each decision may not always be agreeable to us or to others. In the end, however, if truth prevails, progress will be made because we will all recognize the correctness of what is said or done.*

HILLYARD, LYLE WILLIAM, lawyer; b. Logan, Utah, Sept. 25, 1940; s. Alma Lowell and Lucille (Rosenbaum) H.; m. Alice Thorpe, June 24, 1964; children: Carrie, Lisa, Holly, Todd, Matthew. BS, Utah State U., 1965; JD, U. Utah, 1967. Bar: Utah 1967, U.S. Supreme Ct. 1977. Pres. Hillyard, Anderson & Olsen, Logan, 1967—; senator State of Utah, Salt Lake City, 1985—. Rep. chmn. Cache County, Logan, 1970-76; Utah State Rep., 1981-84; pres. Cache County C. of C., 1977. Named one of Outstanding Young Men of Am., Utah Jaycees, 1972; recipient Disting. Svc. award, Logan Jaycees, 1972, Merit award Cache Valley coun. Boy Scouts Am., 1981. Mem. ABA, Utah State Bar Assn., Cache County Bar Assn., Assn. Trial Lawyers Am., Am. Bd. Trial Advocates. Mormon. Club: Big Blue (Logan). Lodge: Kiwanis. Office: Hillyard Anderson & Olsen 175 E 1st N Logan UT 84321-4601

HILPERT, EDWARD THEODORE, JR., lawyer; b. Frazee, Minn., Apr. 29, 1928; s. Edward Theodore Sr. and Hulda Gertrude (Wilder) H.; m. Susan Hazelton, May 5, 1973. AB, U. Wash., 1954, JD, 1956. Bar: Wash. 1956, U.S. Dist. Ct. (we. dist.) Wash. 1956, U.S. Tax Ct. 1959, U.S. Ct. Appeals (9th cir.) 1959, U.S. Supreme Ct. 1970. Law clk. to Hon. George H. Boldt U.S. Dist. Ct. (we. dist.) Wash., Tacoma, 1956-58; assoc. Ferguson & Burdell, Seattle, 1958-63, ptnr., 1963-91; sr. ptnr. Schwabe, Williamson, Ferguson & Burdell, Seattle, 1992—; mem. exec. com. 9th cir. Jud. Conf., San Francisco, 1987-90. Judge pro tem Seattle Mcpl. Ct., 1971-80. Capt. USAR, 1946-49, 50-52, Korea. Mem. ABA, Mensa, Rainer Club, Seattle Tennis Club, Broadmoor Golf Club. Republican. Lutheran. Home: 1434 Broadmoor Dr E Seattle WA 98112-3744 Office: Schwabe Williamson Ferguson & Burdell US Bank Ctr 1420 5th Ave Ste 3400 Seattle WA 98101-2339

HILSENRATH, BARUCH M., principal. Prin. Bess and Paul Sigel Hebrew Acad. Greater Hartford, Bloomfield, Conn., 1987—. Recipient Elem. Sch. Recognition award U.S. Dept. Edn., 1989-90. Office: Bess and Paul Sigel Hebrew Acad Greater Hartford 53 Gabb Rd Bloomfield CT 06002-2306*

HILSMAN, ROGER, government educator; b. Waco, Tex., Nov. 23, 1919; s. Roger and Emma (Prendergast) H.; m. Eleanor Willis Hoyt, June 22, 1946; children—Hoyt R., Amy, Ashby, Sarah. BS, U.S. Mil. Acad., 1943; MA, Yale U., 1950, PhD, 1951. Commd. 2d lt. U.S. Army, 1943, advanced through grades to maj., 1951; with (Merrill's Marauders), Burma, 1944; comdg. officer (OSS guerrilla group in), Burma, 1944-45; asst. chief Far East intelligence operations, Hdqrs. OSS, Washington, 1945-46; spl. asst. to exec. officer CIA, 1946-47; planning officer NATO affairs, Joint Am. Mil. Adv. Group, London, Eng., 1950-52; internat. politics br. Hdqrs. U.S. European Command, 1952-53; resigned, 1953; research fellow Center Internat. Studies, Princeton, 1953-54; research asst. Center Internat. Studies, 1954-55; research assoc., lectr. Woodrow Wilson Sch.; lectr. internat. relations Columbia, 1958; research asso. Washington Center Fgn. Policy Research, lectr. internat. affairs Sch. Advanced Internat. Studies, Johns Hopkins, 1957-61; chief fgn. affairs div., legislative reference service Library Congress, 1956-58, dep. dir. for research, 1958-61; dir. bur. intelligence and research State Dept., 1961-63; asst. sec. state Far Eastern affairs, 1963-64; prof. govt. Columbia U., 1964-89, prof. emeritus, 1990—; lectr. Nat. War Coll., Air U., Army War Coll., Indsl. Coll. Armed Forces.; Fulbright Disting. lectr., India, 1985; USMC Found. chair mil. affairs, 1991. Author: Strategic Intelligence and National Decisions, 1956, To Move a Nation, 1967, The Politics of Policy Making in Defense and Foreign Affairs, 1971, The Crouching Future: International Politics and U.S. Foreign Policy—A Forecast, 1975, To Govern America, 1979, The Politics of Governing America, 1985, The Politics of Policy Making: Conceptual Models and Bureaucratic Politics, 1987, 90, 92, American Guerrilla: My War Behind Japanese Lines, 1990, George Bush vs Saddam Hussein: Military Success! Political Failure?, 1992, The Cuban Missle Crisis, The Struggle Over Policy, 1996, From Nuclear Military Strategy to a World Without War, A History and Proposal, 1999; co-author: Military Policy and National Security, 1956, Alliance Policy in the Cold War, 1959, NATO and American Security, 1959, Foreign Policy in the Sixties, 1965, The Superpowers and Revolution, 1986, Nuclear Strategy and Arms Control, 1986. Rockefeller fellow, 1958.

HILSON, DIANE NIEDLING, nursing administrator; b. Balt., May 28, 1956; d. John William and Marlyn Elaine (Weber) Niedling; m. James Earl Hilson, Sept. 18, 1982 (div.); children: James Ross, Katherine Michelle. BSN, Med. Coll. of Ga. Sch. Nursing, 1977, MSN, 1990. RN, Ga. Staff nurse, RN CCU St. Joseph Hosp., Augusta, Ga.; charge and staff nurse ICU Med. Coll. of Ga. Hosp., Augusta, nurse mgr. med./surg. unit. Recipient Nurses Make a Difference award Am. Hosp. Assn., 1985, Excellence in Nursing award, 1994. Mem. Ga. Nurses Assn., Sigma Theta Tau. Home: 3632 Bermuda Cir E Augusta GA 30909-2604 Office: Med Coll of Ga 1120 15th St Augusta GA 30912-0006

HILT, MARY LOUISE, artist; b. Muskegon, Mich., May 17, 1947; d. Jack Lyle and Martha Campbell (Van Epps) H. Student, Layton Sch. Art (now Milw., Inst. Design and Art), 1966-68. art tchr. for spl. needs adults Kelliher Ctr., Arlington, Mass., 1994-96. One-woman show Harvard Law Sch., Cambridge, 1987, Armenian Genocide Collection, Mass. State House, Boston, 1995, Armenian Libr. and Mus. of America, Watertown, Mass., 1995-96; two-person show Fruenthal Ctr. for Performing Arts, Muskegon, 1989; exhibited in group shows at Bravos Gallery, Georgetown, Mass., 1987, 90-92, 94, 96, Nat. Arts Club, N.Y.C., 1997, Fed. Res. Bank, Boston, 1998, others. Mem. Cambridge C. of C. Episcopalian. Office: Hilt Studio 33 Richdale Ave Cambridge MA 02140-2627

HILTNER, DAWN MARIE, elementary education educator; b. Phila., Feb. 19, 1966; d. Cloyd Edward Jr. and Elizabeth Ann Weidenmoyer; m. William James Hiltner III, Aug. 12, 1995. BA in Journalism cum laude, Temple U., 1988, postgrad., 1996—; MA in Elem. Edn., Trenton State Coll., Hillwood Lakes, N.J., 1993; postgrad., Temple U., 1996—. Cert. elem. tchr., N.J., Pa. Asst. mgr. Eyelab, Inc., Langhorne, Pa., 1985-89; tchr. Epiphany of Our Lord Sch., Phila., 1989, St. Frances Cabrini Sch., Fairless Hills, Pa., 1989-91; tchr. Galloway Twp. Pub. Schs., Absecon, N.J., 1991—, dist. coord. for pub. info., 1994-95; unit leader Roland Rogers Sch., Absecon. Mem. AAUW, APA, Internat. Reading Assn., Galloway Twp. Edn. Assn. (negotiations com. 1998-99, com. of 21), Golden Key, Kappa Tau Alpha. Avocations: reading, sewing, scholarly pursuits. Home: 1000 Station Ave Langhorne Manor PA 19047 Office: Galloway Twp Pub Schs 101 S Reeds Rd Box 968 Absecon NJ 08201

HILTON, ANDREW CARSON, investor, management consultant, former manufacturing company executive; b. D'Lo, Miss., Nov. 20, 1928; s. A.C. and Pearl (Walters) H. BA, U. Md., 1952; MA, George Washington U., 1953; PhD, Western Res. U., 1956. Former research asso. Personnel Research Inst., Western Res. U.; cons. Psychol. Corp., N.Y.C.; dir. personnel relations Raytheon Co.; then dir. personnel Internat. Tel.& Tel. Corp.; sr. v.p. adminstrn. Coltec Industries Inc., N.Y.C., 1963-83, exec. v.p., 1983-91, vice chmn., 1991—, also bd. dirs.; vice chmn. Coltec Industries Inc, 1991-94; proprietor Hilton Mgmt. Enterprises, 1994—. Contbr. articles to profl. jours. Mem. APA, N.Y. Acad. Scis. Club: University (N.Y.C.). Office: Hilton Mgmt Enterprises Inc 147 E 48th St New York NY 10017-1223

HILTON, BARRON, hotel executive; b. Dallas, 1927; s. Conrad Hilton. Founder, pres. San Diego Chargers, Am. Football League, until 1966; v.p. Hilton Hotels Corp., Beverly Hills, Calif., 1954; pres., chief exec. officer Hilton Hotels Corp., Beverly Hills, 1966—, chmn., 1979—, also dir.; chmn. Hilton Equipment Corp, Beverly Hills, Calif; mem. gen. adminstrv. bd. Mfrs. Hanover Trust Co., N.Y.C. Office: Hilton Hotels Corp 9336 Civic Center Dr Beverly Hills CA 90210-3604*

HILTON, CLAUDE MEREDITH, federal judge; b. Scott County, Va., Dec. 8, 1940; s. Claude Swanson and Edna (Fletcher) H.; m. Joretta Cabaniss, June 16, 1963; children: John, Rachel. BS, Ohio State U., 1963; JD, Am. Univ., 1966. Bar: Va. 1966, U.S. Ct. Appeals (4th cir.) 1967, U.S. Supreme Ct. 1981. Dep. clk. of cts. Arlington County, Va., 1964-66, asst. commonwealth atty., 1967-68, commonwealth atty., 1974; sole practice Arlington, 1967-85; judge U.S. Dist. Ct. (ea. dist.) Va., Alexandria, 1985—, now chief judge; asst. commonwealth atty., Arlington, 1967-68, commonwealth atty., 1974; dep. clk. ct., Arlington, 1964-66; commr. in chancery U.S. Ct. Appeals (4th cir.), 1976-85; bd. govs. criminal law sect. Va. State Bar, 1979-84, chmn., 1982-83, mem. ins. com., 1981-85. Mem. ABA, Va. Bar Assn., Arlington County Bar Assn. Republican. Methodist. Lodges: Masons, Alexandria Lodge of Perfection, Kena Temple. Home: 3912 N Upland St Arlington VA 22207-4642 Office: US Courthouse 401 Courthouse Sq Alexandria VA 22314-5704*

HILTON, DEANIE HERMAN, human resources executive, telecommunications manager; b. Hickory, N.C., Mar. 23, 1947; d. Ruel Franklin and Daisy (Loftin) Herman; m. Kenneth James Massagee, Aug. 19, 1967 (div. 1976); 1 child, Amy Celeste; m. William Glenn Hilton, May 18, 1996. Diploma, Catawba Valley Community Coll., 1966, student, 1979, 89; student, Clemson U., 1988. Accounts receivable clk. Hickory Springs Mfg. Co., Hickory, N.C., 1966-68, cashier, 1968-72, sec., v.p. mfg., 1972-79, pers. adminstr., 1979-81, sr. pers. rep., 1981-83, human resources adminstr., 1983—. Bd. dirs. Flynn Christian Fellowship Houses, Hickory, 1989-92; vol. ARC, Hickory, 1989—. Named Outstanding Young Woman Hickory Jaycettes, 1981. Mem. NAFE, Piedmont Personnel Assn., Am. Bus. Women's Assn. (sec., 1981-82, pres. 1982-83, Woman of Yr. 1982, 89), Foothills Exchange of Am. Bus. Women's Assn. (chmn. 1983), Outstanding Bus. Woman of Catawaba County (chmn. 1988). Lutheran. Avocations: calligraphy, walking. Home: 4391 Fox Trl Hickory NC 28601-6704 Office: Hickory Springs Mfg Co 235 2nd Ave NW Hickory NC 28601-4950

HILTON, JAMES GORTON, pharmacologist; b. Balt., Sept. 21, 1923; s. George Edward and Ethel Alberta (Schaefer) H.; m. Elizabeth Earline Lindsay, Sept. 21, 1946; children: James Lindsay, William Edward. B.S. in Chemistry, Va. Poly. Inst., Blacksburg, 1947; M.S. in Pharmacology, U. Tenn., 1952, Ph.D., 1954. Teaching fellow dept. pharmacology U. Tenn., Memphis, 1950-53; asst. prof. to assoc. prof. pharmacology U. Miss., Oxford and Jackson, 1953-58; assoc. prof. pharmacology Marquette U., Milw., 1959-61; assoc. prof. U. Tex., Galveston, 1961-63, prof. dept. pharmacology, 1963-92, acting chmn. dept. pharmacology and toxicology, 1979-82; chief div. pharmacology Shriners Burn Inst., Galveston, 1976-90; prof., chmn. pharmacology St. Georges U., Grenada, W.I., 1990. Contbr. in field. Served with USNR, 1941-46. Fellow Am. Heart Assn.; mem. Am. Physiol. Soc., Am. Soc. Pharmacology and Exptl. Therapeutics, Internat. Soc. Burn Injuries, Peruvian Pharmacology Soc., Am. Burn Assn. Episcopalian. Club: Masons. Home: 2626 Gerol Dr Galveston TX 77551-1530

HILTON, PETER JOHN, mathematician, educator; b. London, Apr. 7, 1923; s. Mortimer and Elizabeth (Freedman) H.; m. Margaret Mostyn, Sept. 14, 1949; children: Nicholas, Timothy. MA, Oxford (Eng.) U., Eng., 1948; PhD, Oxford (Eng.) U., 1950, Cambridge (Eng.) U., Eng., 1952; HHD (hon.), No. Mich. U., 1977; DSc (hon.), Meml. U. Nfld., Can., 1983, U. Autonoma Barcelona, Spain, 1989. Lectr. Manchester U., Eng., 1948-52; sr. lectr. Manchester U., 1956-58; lectr. Cambridge U., 1952-55; Mason prof. pure math. Birmingham U., Eng., 1958-62; prof. math. Cornell U., 1962-71, U. Wash., 1971-73; Beaumont prof. Case Western Res. U., 1973-82; disting. prof. SUNY, Binghamton, 1982-93, emeritus, 1993—; disting. prof. U. Ctrl. Fla., Orlando, 1993—; guest prof. Swiss Fed. Inst. Tech., Zurich, 1966-67, 81-82, 88-89, Courant Inst. Math. Scis., NYU, 1967-68, Ohio State U., 1977, U. Autonoma, Barcelona, 1989, Univ. de Lausanne, 1996; Mahler lectr. Australian Math. Soc., 1997; vis. fellow Battelle Seattle Rsch. Ctr., 1970-71, fellow, 1971—; co-chmn. Cambridge Conf. on Sch. Math., 1965; chmn. com. applied math. tng. NRC, 1977—; sec. Internat. Commn. Math. Instrn., 1979-82. Author: Homotopy Theory, 1953, (with S. Wylie) Homology Theory, 1960, Homotopy Theory and Duality, 1966, (with H.B. Griffiths) Classical Mathematics, 1970, General Cohomology Theory and K-Theory, 1971, (with U. Stammbach) Course in Homological Algebra, 1971, 2d edit., 1997, Le Langage des Categories, 1973, (with Y.C. Wu) Course in Modern Algebra, 1974, (with G. Mislin and J. Roitberg) Localization of Nilpotent Groups and Spaces, 1975 (with J. Pedersen) Fear No More, 1982, Nilpotente Gruppen und Nilpotente Räume, 1984, (with J. Pedersen) Build Your Own Polyhedra, 1987, (with J. Pedersen) College Preparatory Mathematics, 1992, (with D. Holton and J. Pedersen) Mathematical Reflections, 1997; editor: Ergebnisse der Mathematik, 1964—, Ill. Jour. Math., 1962-68, Jour. Pure and Applied Algebra, 1970-75, Topics in Modern Topology, 1968, Miscellanea Mathematica, 1991; contbr. articles to profl. jours. Recipient Silver medal U. Helsinki, Finland, 1975, Centenary medal John Carroll U., 1985. Mem. Am. Math. Soc., Math. Assn. Am. (1st v.p. 1978-80), Can. Math. Soc., Math Soc. Belgium (hon.), London Math. Soc., Cambridge Philos. Soc., Brazilian Acad. Scis. (hon.). Home: 29 Murray St Binghamton NY 13905-4504 Office: SUNY Dept Math Scis Binghamton NY 13902-6000

HILTON, ROBERT PARKER, SR., national security affairs consultant, retired naval officer; b. Atlanta, Mar. 17, 1927; s. William Linwood and Elizabeth Shumate (Parker) H.; m. Joan Maxine Mader, Sept. 3, 1955; children: Robert Parker, Wendy Hilton-Jones. B.A., U. Miss., 1948; postgrad., Naval War Coll., 1961, Nat. War Coll., 1968; M.A. in Russian Affairs, Georgetown U., 1964; postgrad., Sino-Soviet Inst. George Washington U., 1964-68. Commd. ensign U.S. Navy, 1948, advanced through grades to rear adm., 1972; svc. all operational fleets cruisers/destroyers Korea, Japan, Vietnam, Italy, Belgium; asst. chief staff logistics CINCSOUTH, Naples, Italy, 1972-74; dep. dir. force devel. and strategic plans Office Joint Chiefs Staff, 1974-76; dir. East Asia and Pacific region Office Sec. Def., Washington, 1976-77; dir. strategy plans and policy div. OPNAV (OP60), 1977-78; asst. dep. CNO, Plans and Policy, 1979; dep. asst. chief staff Plans and Policy SHAPE, 1979-81; vice dir. ops. Office Joint Chiefs Staff, 1981-83; retired USN, 1983; sole proprietor Hilton Assocs., Alexandria, Va., 1984-98; cons. nat. security affairs, also nat. security and def. matters Inst. Def. Analyses, Alexandria, Va., 1984-94, mem. rsch. staff, 1994—. Decorated Def. D.S.M., Navy D.S.M., Def. Superior Svc. medal, Legion of Merit, Bronze Star, Joint Service Commendation medal. Mem. Coun. Fgn. Rels., Councillor Atlantic Coun. (sr.), U.S. Naval Inst., Nat. Trust Historic Preservation, Pi Sigma Alpha, Pi Kappa Phi, Phi Delta Theta. Episcopalian. Clubs: Masons, Army Navy Country. Home: 3628 Orlando Pl Alexandria VA 22305-1147 Office: Inst Def Analyses 1801 N Beauregard St Alexandria VA 22311-1733

HILTON, STANLEY GOUMAS, lawyer, educator, writer; b. San Francisco, June 16, 1949; s. Loucas Stylianos and Effie (Glafkides) Goumas; m. Raquel Estrella Villalba, Feb. 25, 1996. BA with honors, U. Chgo., 1971; JD, Duke U., 1975; MBA, Harvard U., 1979. Bar: Calif. 1975, U.S. Dist. Ct. Calif., U.S. Ct. Appeals (9th cir.), U.S. Supreme Ct. Libr. asst. Duke U. Libr., Durham, N.C., 1972-75, Harvard U. Libr., Cambridge, Mass., 1977-79; minority counsel U.S. Senator Bob Dole, Washington, 1979-80; adminstrv. asst. Calif. State Senate, Sacramento, 1980-81; pvt. practice San Francisco, 1981—; adj. assoc. prof. Golden Gate U., San Francisco, 1991—. Author: Bob Dole: American Political Phoenix, 1988, Senator for Sale, 1995, Glass Houses, 1998 (best writer 1998). Pres. Com. to Stick With Candlestick Park, San Francisco, 1992-96, Value Added Tax Now, San Francisco, 1994—, Save the 4th Amendment, San Francisco, 1995—. Mem. Calif. State Bar, Hellenic Law Soc., Bechtel Toastmasters Club (pres.). Democrat. Avocations: philately, photography, classical music, ancient Greek and Roman history. Office: 580 California St Ste 500 San Francisco CA 94104-1000

HILTON, THEODORE CRAIG, computer scientist, computer executive; b. Oakland, Calif., June 14, 1949; s. Theodore Caldwell and Maxine (Donnelly) H.; m. Peggy Estes, May 21, 1990; children: Christopher, Kelly, Clark. BS in Internat. Rels., Occidental Coll., 1972; BS, Calif. Inst. Tech., 1972; MS in Computer Sci., N.Y. Inst. Tech., 1980. Ptnr., founder Cen. Data Corp., L.A., 1971—, CEO, 1988—; engr. RSK, L.A., 1972-73; prof. Lake (Fla.) Coll., 1981-85, dept. chmn., 1983-85; prin. rsch. invest. U.S. Dept. Def., L.A., 1985-88; chmn. Access LLC, 1996—; chmn., CEO E-City Corp., 1996—; chmn. WEB Holdings Corp., 1998; bd. dirs. TBS S.A., Versailles, France, Carolina Access LLC, S.E. Data Comms.; U.S. presenter SOLE Internat. Conv., 1991, CALS presenter, 1995; chmn. Web Holdings Corp., 1996—; chmn., CEO E-City LLC, 1996—. Creator: (computer systems) E-City, 1956 Broadcast Management System, 1972, ICSS, 1974, EBook, 1993, Quality Assurance System, 1994; patentee Autonomous Network Smart Labels, filterable ditigal advertising, Internet database mgmt. sys.; contbr. over 59 articles to profl. jours. Mem. IEEE, IEEE Computer Soc., Am. Mgmt. Assn., Logistics Engrs. Soc., Data Processing Mgmt. Assn., N.Y. Acad. Scis., Rotary (Paul Harris fellow). Achievements include patents on image system and public network exchange systems. Office: Cen Data Corp 145 N Church St Spartanburg SC 29306-5163

HILTS, EARL T., lawyer, government official; educator; b. Ilion, N.Y., Mar. 31, 1946; stepson Leon Thomas and Gertrude Annette (Daly) Butler; m. Mae Hwa Kim, Apr. 13, 1973; children: Troy Alan, Kimberly Michelle. BS, St. Lawrence U., 1967; JD, Albany Law Sch., 1970. Bar: N.Y. 1972. Gen. atty.-advisor Dept. Army, Watervliet Arsenal, N.Y., 1978-80, supervisory atty.-advisor, Watervliet 1980—; adj. prof. Schnectady C.C., 1985—. Catechism instr. St. Mary's Ch., 1990-92; pee wee football coach, wrestling coach Shenendehowa Sch., 1983-87; little league coach West Crescent Halfmoon Baseball League, 1980-90. Capt. JAGC, U.S. Army, 1972-76. Scholar St. Lawrence U., 1963-67, Albany Law Sch., 1967-70. Mem. N.Y. State Bar Assn., Am. Legion, Pi Mu Epsilon. Republican. Roman Catholic. Home: 28 Oakwood Blvd Clifton Park NY 12065-7413 Office: Legal Office Watervliet Arsenal Watervliet NY 12189

HILTS, PHILIP JAMES, correspondent; b. Chgo., May 10, 1947; s. Edward Leonard and Katherine (Bonn) H.; m. Mary Donna McKeown, Apr. 26, 1974 (dec. Apr. 1987); children: Benjamin, Alexis, Sean; m. Carisa Cunningham, Apr. 3, 1993; 1 child, Katherine Cassidy. Student, Georgetown U., 1965-67, 69. Writer Suburban Life Newspapers, LaGrange, Ill., 1968, Va. Sentinel, Fairfax, 1969, Washington Daily News, Washington, 1970-72; freelance writer Washington, 1972-80; nat. staff writer Washington Post, Washington, 1980-89; Washington Corr. N.Y. Times, Washington, 1989—; writer N.Y. Times, Boston, 1996—. Author: Behavior Mod, 1974, Scientific Temperaments, 1982, Memory's Ghost, 1995, Smokescreen, 1996. Bd. dirs. Howard Simons Found. for Native Am. Journalists. Nieman fellow Harvard U., 1984-85, Sci. Writing fellow Marine Biol. Lab., 1986, Harvard Sch. Pub. Health fellow, 1995—; recipient 1st prize nat. reporting Washington-Balt. Newspaper Guild, 1982, Pub. award N.Y. Times, 1990, 92, 94, 1st Place Journalism award for coverage of lung disease Am. Lung Assn., 1996. Mem. NAS Inst. Medicine (com. on clin. rsch. 1996-97). Home: 12 Monmouth Ct Brookline MA 02446-5634 Office: NY Times Boston Bur Boston MA 02205*

HILTS, RUTH, artist; b. Sparks, Nev., Dec. 4, 1923; d. William and Nellie Elisa (DeGoosh) Gonzales; m. Robert Norton Hilts, Sept. 28, 1942; children:

Robert Norton, Jr., Deirdre Lynne. BA, U. Nev., 1962. Grad. teaching asst. dept. English U. Nev., Reno, 1962-63, editor-interviewer dept. oral history, 1967-74; profl. artist Reno, 1975—. One-woman shows include Sierra Nev. Mus. Art, 1987-88, Nev. Gallery, Reno, 1990, River Gallery, Reno, 1995, 98, Red Mountain Gallery at Truckee Meadows C.C., Reno, 1995, Nevada Leg. Bldg., Carson City, Nev., 1997; exhibited in group shows at Watercolor West XIV, Riverside, Calif., 1982, Nev. Mus. Art Biennial, Reno, Las Vegas, 1990, 96, Sierra Nev. Coll., Tahoe, 1992-93, Stremmel Gallery, Reno, 1992-94, River Gallery, 1993-94, Sierra Arts Found. Gallery, Reno, 1994-95; represented in permanent collections including Nev. Mus. Art, Kafoury, Armstrong & Co., Reno, Helms Constrn. Co., Reno, Dean Witter, Reynolds, Inc., Reno, Tournament Players Club Summerlin, Las Vegas, Comstock Bank, Reno; contbr. art to publs. Nev. Mag., 1988, Encore, 1995, 98, Neon, 1995, 97. Mem. Comstock Arts Coun., Reno-Sparks Theater Coalition. Mem. Nat. Mus. Women in the Arts, Nev. Mus. Art, Sierra Arts Found. (grantee for excellence 1995), Phi Kappa Phi. Avocations: reading, hiking, mountain and desert camping. Home and Office: 1895 Wren St Reno NV 89509-2334

HILTY, PETER DANIEL, retired English educator, poet; b. Fortuna, Mo., July 16, 1921; s. Peter P. and Barbara (Koller) H.; m. Nancy Wismer, Aug. 16, 1969; 1 child, Daniel. BA, U. Mo., 1950, MA, 1951, PhD, 1958. Instr. English, U. Mo., Columbia, 1952-58; prof. English, Park Coll., Kansas City, Mo., 1959-62; prof. English, S.E. Mo. State U., Cape Girardeau, 1962-92, founding editor Cape Rock Jour., 1962—. Author: (poetry) How Far Is Far?, 1985, Exotic Birds, 1992; editor: Letters of Thomas Crooks, 1992. Mem. Cape Girardeau City Coun., 1985-91; bd. dirs. Cape Girardeau Hist. Soc. Mem. Rotary (bd. dirs. Cape Girardeau 1996—). Methodist. Avocations: woodworking, genealogy, German linguistics, onomastics. Home: 632 Bellevue St Cape Girardeau MO 63701

HILTZ, STARR ROXANNE, sociologist, educator, computer scientist, writer, lecturer, consultant; b. Little Rock, Sept. 7, 1942; d. John Donald and Mildred V. (Koons) Smyers; A.B., Vassar Coll., 1963; M.A., Columbia U., 1964, Ph.D., 1969; m. Murray Turoff, 1985; children—Jonathan David, Katherine Amanda. Prof. sociology, Upsala Coll., 1969-85, CIS N.J. Inst. Tech., 1985-93, disting. prof. computer and info. sci., 1993—; assoc. dir. Computerized Conferencing and Communications Center, N.J. Inst. Tech., 1978—; pres. Computerized Conferencing, Inc., 1978—; cons. social impacts of computer systems. Recipient Computer Pioneer award Electronic Frontier Found., 1994. Mem. Am. Sociol. Assn., Assn. Computing Machinery. Unitarian. Author: Creating Community Services for Widows, 1976; (with M. Turoff) The Network Nation, 1978, 2d edit. 1993; (with E. Kerr) Computer-Mediated Communication, 1982, Online Communities, 1984, The Virtual Classroom, 1994, (with L. Harasim, L. Teles and M. Turoff) Learning Networks, 1995. Home: 19 Meadowbrook Rd Randolph NJ 07869-3808 Office: CIS NJ Inst Tech Newark NJ 07102

HILTZIK, MICHAEL, journalist. Journalist L.A. Times. Recipient Pulitzer prize for Beat Reporting, 1999. E-mail: Michael.Hiltzik@latimes.com. Office: c/o LA Times Bus Sect Times Mirror Sq Los Angeles CA 90053*

HIMBURG, SUSAN PHILLIPS, dietitian, educator; b. Norfolk, Va., May 17, 1946; d. Claude Ralph Jr. and Sarah Ann (Gilbert) Phillips; m. James Donald Himburg, Feb. 9, 1968; 1 child, Karlene Susan. BS, Fla. State U., 1968; M in Med. Sci., Emory U., 1972; PhD, U. Miami, Fla., 1979. Dietetic intern Emory U., Atlanta, 1971; clin. dietitian Emory U. Hosp., Atlanta, 1971, 72-73; from instr. to prof. Fla. Internat. U., Miami, 1973—, dir. coordinated program in dietetics, 1979-99, dir. health scis. recruitment and retention program, 1985—, chmn. dietetics and nutrition, 1992-97, self-study dir., 1997—; grant reviewer disadvantaged assistance program HHS, Rockville, Md., 1989—; site visitor So. Assn. Colls. and Schs., Atlanta, 1987—. Author: (tng. manual) ADA Self-Study, 1988, 91, 95; contbr. articles to profl. jours. Fellow Am. Dietetic Assn. (site visitor 1985—, chairperson commn. on accreditation 1992-93, medallion 1996); mem. Soc. Nutrition Edn., Fla. Dietetic Assn. (del. 1990—, Disting. Dietitian 1995), Miami Dietetic Assn. (mem. nominating com. 1989, Disting. Dietitian 1994), Phi Kappa Phi, Kappa Omicron Nu. Office: Fla Internat Univ CH 201 Coll Health Scis Miami FL 33199

HIMELEIN, LARRY M., judge; b. Buffalo, June 27, 1949; s. Levant Maurice and Barbara McKenzie (Neilson) H.; m. Julie Ann Peglowski, Mar. 20, 1982; children: Ryan Charles, Brendan Levant, Meghan Lee. BA, Ithaca Coll., 1971; JD, Suffolk U., 1975. Bar: N.Y. 1976. Pvt. practice, Gowanda, N.Y., 1977-79; assoc. Levant Himelein, Jr., Gowanda, 1979-82; dist. atty. Cattaraugus County, Little Valley, N.Y., 1982-92; judge Cattaraugus County, Little Valley, 1993—; mem. Arson Task Force, Little Valley, 1982-92, Traffic Safety Bd., 1982-92, Cattaraugus County Police Chiefs, Little Valley, 1982-92. Bd. dirs. Tri-County Meml. Hosp., Gowanda, N.Y., 1987-96. Mem. N.Y. State Bar Assn., N.Y. State County Judges Assn., N.Y. State Family Judges Assn., N.Y. State Surrogate Ct. Assn., Cattaraugus County Bar Assn., Erie County Bar Assn., Am. Legion, Slovenian Club, Gowanda Country Club (bd. dirs. 1997—). Democrat. Episcopalian. Home: 40 W Hill St Gowanda NY 14070-1428 Office: 303 Court St Little Valley NY 14755-1028

HIMELFARB, RICHARD JAY, securities firm executive; b. Balt., Feb. 3, 1942; s. Jacob and Jennie (Willen) H.; m. Margaret Conn, Sept. 7, 1969; children: Elizabeth Jayne, Michael Ross. BA, Johns Hopkins U., 1962; LLB, Yale U., 1965. Bar: Md., 1965. Employed, then ptnr. Weinberg & Green (now Saul, Ewing, Remick & Saul), Balt., 1967-83; sr. exec. v.p. Legg Mason, Inc., Balt., 1983—, also bd. dirs. Trustee Center Stage, Inc., Balt., 1984—, Balt. Goodwill Industries, 1984-93, Kennedy Krieger Inst., 1993—; Bryn Mawr Sch., 1991-94; mem. bd. visitors U. Md., Balt., 1990-96, chmn., 1996—; bd. visitors Inst. of Human Virology, 1997—; bd. dirs. Balt. Devel. Corp. Mem. Phi Beta Kappa. Home: 116 Taplow Rd Baltimore MD 21212-3312 Office: Legg Mason Inc 100 Light St Baltimore MD 21202-1099

HIMELFARB, STEPHEN ROY, lawyer; b. Washington, Feb. 19, 1954; s. Jordan Sheldon and Marion (Soloman) H.; m. Anne Patricia Spille, June 26, 1983; children: Kara Michelle, Bradley Richard. BSBA, Am. U., 1976; JD, George Mason U., 1980. Bar: D.C. 1982, Md. 1982, Va. 1988, U.S. Dist. Ct. D.C. 1982, U.S. Dist. Ct. Md. 1982, U.S. Ct. Appeals (D.C. and 4th cirs.) 1982, U.S. Dist. Ct. (ea. dist.) Va. 1988, U.S. Tax Ct. 1990, U.S. Bankruptcy Ct. (ea. div.) Va. 1988, U.S. Supreme Ct. 1985. From v.p. to pres. ECA Bus. Comm. Network, Washington, 1982-85; ptnr. Himelfarb & Podryhula, Washington, 1984-93, Speights & Micheel, Washington, 1986-88, Sheeskin, Hillman & Lazar, PC, Rockville, Md., 1989-90, Ahmad & Himelfarb, PC, Rockville, Md., 1993-95; pvt. practice Bethesda, Md., 1995—; v.p. Video Shack Inc., Woodbridge, Va., 1984-95. Mem. ABA, Md. State Bar Assn., Va. Bar Assn., Assn. Trial Lawyers Am., Phi Delta Phi. Democrat. Jewish. Avocations: electronics, coin-op/americana collecting, model trains, radio control models. Home: 1214 Winter Hunt Rd Mc Lean VA 22102-2434 Office: 4701 Sangamore Rd Ste S-225 Bethesda MD 20816-2508

HIMELSTEIN, SUSAN, psychologist; b. Norwalk, Ohio, Feb. 27, 1951; d. Warren and Frances (Jenkins) Holzhauser. BS, Miami U., Oxford, Ohi, 1973; MA, UCLA, 1981, PhD with honors, 1987. Lic. psychologist, sch. psychologist, counselor, tchr., Calif. Staff psychologist Verdugo Psychotherapy Inst., Glendale, Calif., 1987-88; counselor, psychologist Beverly Hills (Calif.) Unified Schs., 1988-98; pvt. practice Beverly Hills, 1989—; psychologist, cons., sr. faculty mem. Reiss-Davis Child Study Ctr., 1987-96; adj. prof. Pepperdine U., Culver City, 1989—, vis. prof., 1996—; supr. interns for various univs.; spkr. UCLA Ext. Confs., 1994—. Acad. scholar Calif. State Fellowship, 1981-83. Mem. APA, L.A. County Psychol. Assn., Calif. Psychol. Assn. Office: 9107 Wilshire Blvd Ste 215 Beverly Hills CA 90210-5522

HIMES, JAMES ALBERT, veterinary medicine educator emeritus; b. Lucas, Ohio, Aug. 12, 1919; s. Albert Merle and Nina Grace (Galleher) H.; m. Ruth Naomi Banks, Apr. 26, 1958 (div. 1973); children: Leslie Jo, Jillyn Alicia; m. Genia Lee, May 10, 1973. BS, Muskingum Coll., 1941; postgrad., U. Nebr., 1941-42, 46; VMD, U. Penn., 1950; PhD, Cornell U., 1965. Veterinarian Tenn., Va., Fla., 1950-62; rsch. asst. Cornell U., Ithaca, N.Y., 1962-65; from asst. prof. to assoc. prof. U. Fla., Gainesville, 1965-76, dir. vet. medicine edn., 1975-77, prof., 1976-90; from asst. dean to assoc. dean U. Fla. Coll. Vet. Medicine, Gainesville, 1977-90; prof. emeritus U. Fla., Gainesville, 1990—. Editor: Part X, Spontaneous Animal Models of Human Disease, 1979. Sgt. U.S. Army, 1942-45. Mem. AVMA, Fla. Vet. Med. Assn. (Vet. of Yr. 1987, Exec. Disting. Svc. award 1992), Alachua Vet. Med. Assn. (sec.-treas. 1973-74, pres. 1995), Marion County Vet. Assn. Avocations: reading, music, walking, jogging, cooking. Home: 2841 SW 37th Pl Apt 59F Gainesville FL 32608-3122

HIMES, JOHN HARTER, medical researcher, educator; b. Salt Lake City, July 25, 1947; s. Ellvert Hiram and Mildred Anna (Harter) H.; m. Kathleen Cox (div.); children: Rachel Anne, Matthew Hiram, Sarah Elizabeth; m. LaVell Gold. BS, Ariz. State U., 1971; PhD, U. Tex., 1975; MPH, Harvard U., 1982. Rsch., sr. scientist Fels Rsch. Inst., Yellow Springs, Ohio, 1976-79; Fels asst. prof. Wright State U. Sch. Medicine, Dayton, Ohio, 1977-79; sr. analyst, project dir. Abt Assocs., Cambridge, Mass., 1979-82; assoc. prof. CUNY, Bklyn., 1982-87; from assoc. prof. to prof. U. Minn. Sch. Pub. Health, Mpls., 1987—, dir. nutrition coord. ctr., 1995—; expert com physical status WHO, Geneva, Switzerland, 1991-94, expert adv. panel nutrition, 1994—; mem. tech. working groups Ctrs. for Disease Control, Washington and Atlanta, 1988-97. Author: Parent-specific Adjustment for Assessment of Recumbent Length & Stature, 1981, Anthropometric Assessment of Nutritional Status, 1991; contbr. articles to profl. jours. Recipient Nathalie Masse Meml. prize Internat. Children's Ctr., Paris, 1979. Fellow Human Biology Coun.; mem. Am. Inst. Nutrition, Am. Pub. Health Assn., N.Am. Assn. Study of Obesity, Internat. Assn. Human Auxology, Pan Am. Health Orgn. (tech. adv. nutrition 1994—), Nat. Ctr. Health Stats. (tech. working group 1994-97), Am. Soc. Nutritional Scis., Soc. for Study of Human Biology, Phi Kappa Phi, Sigma Xi, Delta Omega.

HIMES, KENNETH ALAN, retired marketing executive; b. Phila., Nov. 2, 1937; s. Kenneth Elwood and Thelma Frances (Diffenbacher) H.; m. Diane Margaret Zurinsky, Sept. 14, 1959; children: Christine Ann Himes Daly, Susan Leigh. BS in Bus., Lycoming Coll., 1959. With Woolrich (Pa.) Inc., 1959-90, sales rep., 1960-85, sr. v.p. mktg., 1985-90. Founder, sec. Woolrich Vol. Fire Co., 1960; trustee Lycoming Coll., 1987-95, Williamsport Hosp. and med. Ctr., 1988-95; fire commr. Bluffton Twp., 1995—; co-chmn. Fire Commn., 1997-98. Named Outstanding Alumnus Lycoming Coll., 1987. Mem. Nat. Assn. Men's and Boys' Apparel, Somerset Hills Jaycees, Masons, Rotary. Republican. Methodist. Avocations: golf, travel, fishing. Office: Woolrich Inc Mill St Woolrich PA 17779

HIMM, EMILIE GINA, records and information manager, consultant; b. Huntington, N.Y., July 12, 1946; d. Joseph Pratte and Constance Delores (Carioli) Walker; m. Thomas Robert Himm, Apr. 23, 1966; 1 child, Thomas Francis II. Student, Thomas Edison State Coll., 1990-93, 96—. Cert. Pub. Mgr., Rutgers State U. Acct. corr. McGraw Hill, Inc., Hightstown, N.J., 1966-68; various supervisory and adminstrv. positions various state agencies, Trenton, N.J., 1973-85; mcpl. court adminstr. Pemberton (N.J.) Twp., 1985-86; records and info. mgr. N.J. Dept. Transp., Trenton, 1986-97, supr. records and info., 1997—; co-chair State Govt. Industry Action Com., Prairie Village, Kans., 1989, chair, 1990-92, 95-96, chmn. industry specific group-transp., 1996-98; mem. impact study group N.J. Dept. State, Trenton, 1991; co-chair programs Princeton ARMA, 1997-98; mem. govt. rels. com. GRECO, 1998—; mem. N.J. State Task Force on Imaging Tech. Best Practices Methodology, 1998—; spkr. at nat. and internat. seminars and confs. Contbg. writer various local govt. publs. including N.J. Dept. Transp. Records Control and Preservation Tng. Workbook. Bd. dirs. Soroptimists Internat., 1986-88; publicity chair Little League Aux., Pemberton Twp., 1982-84; post-prom com. Bordentown (N.J.) Residents Against Drugs, 1991-93; mem. Prin.'s Adv. Coun., Bordentown, 1992; co-leader Girl Scouts Am., 1971-73; mem. N.J. Image Enabled Document Processing Storage, Retrieval and Workflow Taskforce. Named Employee of Yr., N.J. Dept. Transp., 1993. Mem. ASPA, Nat. Assn. State Info. Resource Execs., Assn. Records Mgrs. and Adminstrs. (co-founder so. N.J. chpt., sec. 1981, 82, bd. dirs. ctrl. N.J. chpt. 1990-92, pres. 1993-95, program chair 1997—, spkr. internat. seminars). Democrat. Roman Catholic. Avocations: Native American studies, gardening, travel, reading. Office: NJ Dept of Transportation PO Box 600 Trenton NJ 08625-0600

HIMMELBERG, CHARLES JOHN, III, mathematics educator, researcher; b. North Kansas City, Mo., Nov. 12, 1931; s. Charles John and Magdalene Caroline (Batliner) H.; m. Mary Patricia Hennessy, Jan. 27, 1962; children: Charles, Ann, Mary, Joseph, Patrick. BS, Rockhurst Coll., 1952; MS, U. Notre Dame, 1954, PhD, 1957. Assoc. analyst Midwest Rsch. Inst., Kansas City, Mo., 1957-59; asst. prof. math. U. Kans., Lawrence, 1959-65, assoc. prof., 1965-68, prof., 1968—, chmn. dept. math., 1978-99. Mem. editorial bd. Rocky Mountain Jour. Math, 1972-88; contbr. articles to profl. jours. Mem. Am. Math. Soc., Math. Assn. Am. Roman Catholic. Office: U Kans Dept Math Lawrence KS 66045

HIMMELBERG, ROBERT FRANKLIN, historian, educator; b. Kansas City, Mo., July 16, 1934; s. Alexander Franklin and Genevieve Fay (Leonard) H.; B.A., Rockhurst Coll., 1956; M.A., Creighton U., 1958; Ph.D., Pa. State U., 1963; m. Josephine Ann Boone, Dec. 27, 1958; children: Thomas A., Robert A., Juliana Ruth. Instr. Am. history Fordham U., Bronx, N.Y., 1961-63, asst. prof., 1963-68, asso. prof., 1968-77, prof., 1977—, dept. chmn., 1969-72, pres. faculty senate, 1989-92, dean Grad. Sch. Arts and Scis., 1993—; Hoover Presdl. Library fellow, 1984-85, grantee, 1993. Am. Philos. Soc. grantee, 1978. Mem. Am. Hist. Assn., Orgn. Am. Historians. Republican. Roman Catholic. Author: The Origins of the National Recovery Administration: Business, Government and the Trade Association Issue, 1921-1933, 1976, rev. edit., 1994; editor: Business and Government in America Since 1870, 1994; co-editor: Historians and Race: Autobiography and the Writing of History, 1996; contbr. articles to profl. jours. Office: Fordham Univ Dept History Bronx NY 10458

HIMMELBLAU, DAVID MAUTNER, chemical engineer; b. Chgo., Aug. 29, 1923; s. David and Roda (Mautner) H.; m. Betty H. Hartman, Sept. 1, 1948; children—Andrew, Margaret Ann. B.S., MIT, 1947; M.B.A., Northwestern U., 1950; Ph.D., U. Wash., 1957. Cost engr. Internat. Harvester Co., Chgo., 1946-47; cost analyst Simpson Logging Co., Seattle, 1952-53; mgr. Excel Battery Co., Seattle, 1953-54; teaching asst., instr. U. Wash., Seattle, 1955-57; successively asst. prof., asso. prof., prof. chem. engrng. U. Tex., Austin, 1957—; chmn. dept. U. Tex., 1973-77; pres. RAMAD Corp.; Univ. Fed. Credit Union, 1964-68; exec officer CACHE Corp. of Mass., 1984—. Author: Basic Principles and Calculations in Chemical Engineering, 1962, 67, 74, 82, 89, 96, Process Analysis and Simulation, 1968, Process Analysis by Statistical Methods, 1970, Applied Nonlinear Programming, 1974, Optimization of Chemical Processes, 1989; contbr. numerous articles in field to profl. jours. With U.S. Army, 1943-46, 51-52. Served with U.S. Army, 1943-46, 51-52. NSF grantee, 1953-94; NATO Sci. Com. grantee, 1969. Mem. Am. Inst. Chem. Engrs. (dir. 1973-76), Am. Chem. Soc., Am. Math. Soc., Ops. Research Soc. Am., Soc. Indsl. and Applied Mathematics, Sigma Xi, Delta Mu Delta. Club: Headliners (Austin). Home: 4609 Ridge Oak Dr Austin TX 78731-5211 Office: Univ Texas Coll Engring Austin TX 78712

HIMMELFARB, JOHN DAVID, artist; b. Chgo., June 3, 1946; s. Samuel and Eleanor (Gorecki) H.; m. Mary Louise Day. AB, Harvard U., 1968; MA, Grad. Sch. Edn., 1970. One-man shows: Ill. Arts Council, Chgo., 1974, Graphics I&II, Boston, 1974, Ill. Center, Chgo., 1975, U. Nebr., Omaha, 1976, Dorothy Rosenthal Gallery, Chgo., 1976, Ill. State Mus., Springfield, 1978, Albrecht Mus. Art, St. Joseph, Mo., 1978, Ball State U., 1978, 89, Sheldon Meml. Art Gallery, 1978, Ill. Wesleyan U., 1979, Terry Dintenfass Inc., N.Y.C., 1979, 83, 86, 89, 91, Gallery 72, Omaha, 1979, 83, 85, 87, 90, 92, 94, 96, Fountain Gallery, Portland, Oreg., 1980, Hull Gallery, Washington, 1980, Barbara Balkin Gallery, Chgo., 1982, Area X Gallery, N.Y.C., 1985, Brody's Gallery, Washington, 1985, 90, Sioux City Art Ctr., 1985, Davenport Mus., 1986, John Nichols, N.Y.C., 1986, Blanden Art Mus., 1987, Evanston Art Ctr., 1987, 96, Fundacio Josep Artigas, Barcelona, Spain, 1989, Kalamazoo Inst. Arts, 1989, Miami U. Art Mus., 1990, Ark. Art Ctr., 1990, Madison Art Ctr., 1990, Huntington Mus. Art, 1990, Cissie Peltz Gallery, 1991, Anchor Graphics, 1992, U. No. Iowa, 1993, Gallery 1756, Chgo., 1995, Chgo. Cultural Ctr., 1995, Spaightwood Gallery, Madison, Wis., 1996, 99, Jean Albano Gallery, Chgo. 1996, 98; group shows include: Minn. Mus. Art, Total Mus. Contemporary Art, Seoul, Korea, Bklyn. Mus., Indpls. Mus. Art, Art Inst. Chgo., Walker Art Ctr., Nat. Mus. Am. Art; represented in permanent collections: Art Inst. Chgo., Indpls. Mus. Art, Nat. Mus. Am. Art, Fogg Mus. Art, Cleve. Mus. Art, Mpls. Inst. Art, Portland Mus. Art, Ill. State Mus., Bklyn. Mus., Balt. Mus. Art, Des Moines Art Center, High Mus. Art, Atlanta, Toledo Mus. Art, Univs. Wis., Minn., Oreg., Iowa, Total Mus. of Contemporary Art, Seoul, Korea, others. NEA fellow in painting, 1982, in drawing, 1985; Ill. Arts Council fellow, 1986. Studio: 2400 S Oakley Ave Chicago IL 60608-4902

HIMMELFARB, MILTON, editor, educator; b. Bklyn., Oct. 21, 1918; s. Max and Bertha (Lerner) H.; m. Judith Siskind, Nov. 26, 1950; children: Martha, Edward, Miriam, Anne, Sarah, Naomi, Dan. B.A., CCNY, 1938, M.S., 1939; B.Hebrew Lit., Jewish Theol. Sem. Coll., 1939; diplôme, U. Paris, 1939; postgrad., Columbia U., 1942-47. Dir. information and research Am. Jewish Com., N.Y.C., 1955-86; editor Am. Jewish Year Book, N.Y.C., 1959-86; contbg. editor Commentary mag., N.Y.C., 1960-86; vis. prof. Jewish Theol. Sem., N.Y.C., 1967-68, 71-72; vis. lectr. Yale, 1971; vis. prof. Reconstructionist Rabbinical Coll., Phila., 1972-73. Author: The Jews of Modernity, 1973. Mem. U.S. Holocaust Meml. Council, 1986-89.

HIMMELRIGHT, ROBERT JOHN, JR., rubber company executive; b. Canton, Ohio, Mar. 29, 1926; s. Robert John and Katherine Dewees (Nusly) H.; m. Suzanne Hadley, Mar. 11, 1950; children: Robert John III, Christina S., George H., Anne D. BA, U. N.Mex., 1951; LLD (hon.), Kenyon Coll., 1987. With Teledyne Monarch Rubber Co., Hartville, Ohio, 1950-84, asst. to pres., then v.p., 1955-62, pres., 1963-84; chmn. Monarch South Seas Ltd., Delray Beach, Fla., 1984—. Alt. del. Republican Nat. Conv., 1972, 76; trustee Kenyon Coll., Gambier, Ohio. With USNR, 1944-46, 50-51. Mem. Pine Valley Golf Club. Lutheran. Home and Office: 200 N Ocean Blvd Delray Beach FL 33483-7126

HIMMS-HAGEN, JEAN MARGARET, biochemist; b. Oxford, Eng., Dec. 18, 1933; d. Frederick Hubert and Margaret Mary (Deadman) Himms; m. Paul Hagen, Sept. 29, 1956; children: Anna, Nina. BSc, U. London, 1955; PhD, Oxford U., 1958. Postdoctoral fellow Harvard U., 1958-59; asst. prof. physiology U. Man., 1959-64; assoc. prof. biochemistry Queen's U., 1964-67; assoc. prof. biochemistry U. Ottawa, 1967-71, prof., 1971-99, acting chmn. dept., 1975-77, 87, chmn. dept., 1977-82, prof. emeritus, 1999—; mem. coun. Med. Rsch. Coun., 1970-75; mem. Exec. Med. Rsch. Coun., 1970-73, mem. grants coms., 1969-75, chmn. metabolism grants com., 1972-75. Assoc. editor Can. Jour. Biochemistry, 1967-71, Can. Jour. Physiology and Pharmacology, 1971-75, Am. Jour. Physiology, 1979-89, 92—; mem. editl. bd. proc. Soc. Exptl. Biology and Medicine, 1984-90, Obesity Rsch., 1993—; contbr. over 150 articles and revs. to sci. jours., chpts. to books. Recipient research grants Med. Research Council, 1960—, career award, 1968-77, Bond award Am. Oil Chemists Soc., 1972. Fellow Royal Soc. Can.; mem. Can. Biochem. Soc. (Ayerst award 1973), Am. Soc. Nutritional Scis., Biochem. Soc. U.K., Soc. for Exptl. Biology and Medicine (coun. 1991-94), N.Am. Assn. Study of Obesity (coun. 1995-98), Am. Physiol. Soc., Am. Soc. Pharmacology and Exptl. Therapeutics. Home: 233 Tudor Pl, Ottawa, ON Canada K1L 7Y1 Office: U Ottawa Dept Biochemistry, 451 Smyth Rd, Ottawa, ON Canada K1H 8M5

HINCH, STEPHEN WALTER, telecommunications industry executive; b. Seattle, July 13, 1951; s. Harlan Delmer and Ivy Roslyn (Thrush) h.; m. Nicolette Constance Obritsch, Sept. 11, 1976; children: Gregory P., Juliana G. BS, MS in Engring., Harvey Mudd Coll., 1974. Mfg. engr. Hewlett-Packard Co., Santa Rosa, Calif., 1974-78; mfg. engring. mgr. Hewlett-Packard Co., Rohnert Park, Calif., 1978-84; corp. SMT program mgr. Hewlett-Packard Co., Palo Alto, Calif., 1984-88, Santa Rosa, Calif., 1988—; rsch. and devel. mgr. Hewlett-Packard Co., Santa Rosa, 1988—; instr. Inst. Interconnection and Packaging of Electronic Circuits, Lincolnwood, Ill., 1985-93. Author: Handbook of Surface Mount Technology, 1988, Guide to State Parks of Sonoma Coast and Russian River, 1998; contbr. chpts. to books, tech. articles to profl. jours.; patentee in field. Mem. Bennett Valley Sch. Bd. Trustees, 1994-98, pres. 1996-97. Mem. IEEE, Telecomms. Industries Assn. Avocations: freelance writing, photography. Office: Hewlett-Packard Co 1400 Fountain Grove Pkwy Santa Rosa CA 95403-1799

HINCHEY, BRUCE ALAN, environmental engineering company executive; b. Kansas City, Mo., Jan. 24, 1949; s. Charles Emmet and Eddie Lee (Scott) H.; m. Karen Adele McLaughlin, Nov. 27, 1969 (div. Nov. 1983); children: Scott Alan, Traci Denise, Amanda Lee, Richard Austin; m. Karen Robitaille, Apr. 10, 1993. Student, U. Mo., Rolla, 1967-71. Source testing crew chief Ecology Audits, Inc., Dallas, 1971-76; lab. mgr. Ecology Audits, Inc., Casper, Wyo., 1976-78; mgr. ops. Ecology Audits, Inc., Dallas, 1978-79; v.p. Kumpe & Assoc. Engrs., Casper, 1979-81; pres. Western Environ. Svcs. and Testing, Inc., Casper, 1981—, Hawk Industries, Inc., 1993—; pres. Mining Assocs. Wyo., Cheyenne, 1986-87. Mem. Wyo. State Ho. of Reps., Cheyenne, 1989—, spkr. of house, mgmt. coun., rules com., energy coun., select water com., sel. edn. com., active Natrona County Rep. precinct, Casper, 1986—, Am. Legis. Exch. Coun., 1989; chair Natrona County Rep. Party, 1988-89. Mem. Am. Inst. Mining Engrs., Nat. Fedn. Ind. Bus. (Guardian award), Air Pollution Control Assn., Casper C. of C., Rotary, Shriners, Masons. Methodist. Office: Western Environ Svcs and Testing Inc 913 N Foster Rd Casper WY 82601-1640

HINCHEY, MAURICE D., JR., congressman; b. N.Y.C., Oct. 27, 1938; s. Maurice D. and Rose (Bonack) H.; m. Ilene Marder, 1985; children: Maurice Scott, Josef L., Michelle R. BA, SUNY, New Paltz, 1968; MA, NYU, New Paltz, 1970. Mem. N.Y. State Assembly, 1974-93; mem. 103rd-106th Congress from 26th N.Y. dist., 1993—, mem. banking and fin. svcs. com.; chmn. N.E. Task Force Food & Farm Policy & Assembly Environ. Conserv. Comm., Higher Edn!. Rules & Racing & Wagering Comm., Joint Legis. Comm. Solid Waste Mgmt., Interstate Coun. on Migrant Edu., N.Y. Urban Cultural Parks Adv. Coun. Author: (with others) Organized Crime and the Solid Waste Industry, 1986; N.Y. City Water Supply, A History, 1988. Hudson River Greenway Coun.; bd. dirs. Children's Rehab. Ctr., WAMC Nat. Pub. Radio. Recipient of Legislator of the Yr. award, Environ Planning Lobby, 1975, 1979, N.Y. State Bar Assn. Environ award, 1989. Founding mem. Saugerties Dem. Club, vice chmn. N.Y. State Dem. Commn. Roman Catholic. Office: US Ho of Reps 2431 Rayburn HOB Washington DC 20515-3226*

HINCKLEY, DAVID MALCOLM, journalist, editor, critic; b. Hartford, Conn., Nov. 23, 1948; s. Malcolm Slate and Evelyn Gladys (Nason) H.; m. Francis McCarthy, May 24, 1986; children: Marcia, Kip, Ric, Nell. BA, Drew U., 1970. Writer, editor Morristown (N.J.) Record, 1972-80; writer, editor, critic-at-large N.Y. Daily News, N.Y.C., 1980—; judge Ralph J. Gleason Book Awards, N.Y.C., 1990—. Author: The Rolling Stones: Black & White Blues, 1995. Office: NY Daily News 450 W 33rd St Fl 3 New York NY 10001-2681

HINCKLEY, DEBORAH CLARK, language services professional; b. Cin., Sept. 16, 1947; d. Timothy Dwight and Helen Marilyn (Clark) H.; m. Richard Austin Beaumont, Feb. 26, 1993. BA cum laude, Brown U., 1969; postgrad., Sorbonne U., Paris, 1970-71. Instr. English Lang. Studies, Ltd., Paris, 1969-71; self-employed instr. English Paris, 1971-73; instr. French and English Cincilingua, Cin., 1973-76; tchr., trainer, dir. Nat. Inst. of Langs., N.Y.C., 1976-84; pres. inlingua Lang. Ctrs., Ridgewood and Summit, N.J., 1984—; pres. inlingua Americas' Nat. Commn., 1987-93, 96—, inlingua Internat. Commn., 1992-93; bd. dirs. inlingua Internat., 1993-96. Mem. ASTD, Sietar Internat. Office: inlingua Lang Ctr 171 E Ridgewood Ave Ridgewood NJ 07450-3824

HINCKLEY, GORDON B., church official; s. Bryant S. and Ada (Bitner) H.; m. Marjorie Pay, Apr. 29, 1937; children: Kathleen Hinckley Barnes, Richard G., Virginia Hinckley Pearce, Clark B., Jane Hinckley Dudley. Asst. to Council of Twelve Apostles, Church of Jesus Christ Latter Day Saints, 1958-61, mem. council, 1961-81, Counselor in the First Presidency, 1981-82, Second Counselor in the First Presidency, 1982-85, First Counselor in the First Presidency, 1985-95; pres. of ch., 1995—. Office: First Presidency LDS Ch 47 E South Temple Salt Lake City UT 84150-1005

HINCKLEY, GREGORY KEITH, financial executive; b. San Francisco, Oct. 3, 1946; s. Homer Clair and Josephine F. (Gerrick) H. BS in Math. and Physics, Claremont Men's Coll., 1968; MS in Applied Physics, U. Calif.-San Diego, 1970; MBA, Harvard U., 1972. CPA, Ill. Second v.p. Continental Bank, Chgo., 1972-78; dir. fin. ITEL Corp., San Francisco, 1978-79; group contr. Raychem Corp., Menlo Park, Calif., 1979-83; v.p. fin., CFO Bio-Rad Labs., Richmond, Calif., 1983-89; sr. v.p. fin., CFO Crowley Maritime Corp., San Francisco, 1989-91; sr. v.p., CFO VLSI Tech. Inc., San Jose, 1992-97; exec. v.p., COO Mentor Graphics Corp., Wilsonville, Oreg., 1997—; bd. dirs. OEC Med. Systems, Inc., Salt Lake City, Amkor Tech., West Chester, Pa., Oreg. Mus. Sci. and Industry, Portland. Fulbright fellow, Eng., 1968. Mem. AICPAs. Home: 2417 SW 16th Ave Portland OR 97201-2308

HINCKLEY, TED C., historian, educator, writer; b. N.Y.C., Oct. 4, 1925; s. Theodore Charles and Eunice Marguerite (Platt) H.; m. Caryl Fay Chesmore, June 17, 1948; children: Susan Platt Hinckley Koester, Deborah Christine Hinckley Riche. BA in Bus. Adminstrn., Claremont McKenna Coll., Claremont, Calif., 1950; BS in History, N.W. Mo. State U., Maryville, 1951; MA in Edn., U. Mo., Kansas City, 1953; PhD in History, Ind. U., 1961. Jr. exec. Chesmore Seed Co., St. Joseph, Mo., 1950; tchr. history Barstow Sch., Kansas City, Mo., 1951-53; asst. to pres. Claremont McKenna Coll., 1953-55; headmaster St. Katharine's Sch., Davenport, Iowa, 1955-57; tchg. asst. Ind. U., Bloomington, 1957-59; prof. history San Jose (Calif.) State U., 1959-90; adj. prof. Western Wash. U., Bellingham, 1991—; lectr. Fulbright Assocs., Yogyakarta, Indonesia, 1994-95; PACE lectr. USS Boxer, 1997, USS A. Lincoln, 1998, USS Leyte Gulf, 1999. Author: John G. Brady, 1982, The Canoe Rocks, 1995; War, Wings. . .1945, 1996, The Americanization of Alaska, 1972; mem. editl. bd. Pacific N.W. Quar., 1974-93, Alaska History, 1984—, Jour. of the West, 1977—. Mem. Calif. Hist. Preservation Commn., Sacramento, 1980-85; elder Saratoga (Calif.) Presbyn. Ch., 1968-70; assoc. Danforth Found., St. Louis, 1962—. With USN, 1943-46, 2d lt. U.S. Army Res., 1950-53, ensign USNR, 1953-56. Huntington Libr. summer fellow, 1971; Alaska Hist. Commn. fellow 1983-84; grantee Am. Philos. Soc., 1962, 66. Mem. Am. Hist. Assn., Western Hist. Assn. (coun. 1987-90), Alaska Hist. Soc., Wash. State Hist. Assn., Fulbright Assn., Phi Beta Kappa. Christian. Avocations: play writing, gardening, carpentry. Home: 950 Chesley Park Dr Sedro Woolley WA 98284-9565

HIND, HARRY WILLIAM, pharmaceutical company executive; b. Berkeley, Calif., June 2, 1915; s. Harry Wyndham and B.J. (O'Connor) H.; m. Diana Vernon Miesse, Dec. 12, 1940; children—Leslie Vernon Hind Daniels, Gregory William. BS, U. Calif., Berkeley, 1939; LLD, U. Calif.-Berkeley, 1968; DSc (hon.), U. Scis. Phila., 1982. Founder Barnes-Hind Pharms., Inc., Sunnyvale, Calif., 1939—; pres. Hind Health Care, Inc. Contbr. articles to profl. jours.; designer ph meter and developer of ophthamic solutions. Mem. chancellor's assocs. U. Calif.; trustee emeritus U. Calif.-San Francisco Found. Recipient Ebert award for pharm. research, 1948, Eye Research Found. award, 1958, Helmholtz Ophthalmology award for research, 1968, Carbert award for sight conservation, 1973, Alumnus of Yr. award U. Calif. Sch. Pharmacy, 1965, Disting. Service award U. Calif. Proctor Found., 1985, Commendation by Resolution State of Calif., 1987, Pharmaceutical Achievements commendation State of Calif. Assembly, Hon. Recognition award Contact Lens Mfrs. Assn., 1990. Fellow AAAS; mem. Am. Pharm. Assn. (Man of Yr. Pharmacist's Planning Svc. 1987), Am. Optometric Assn. (Man of Yr. award, 1987), Contact Lens Soc. Am. (Hall of Fame 1989), Am. Assn. Pharm. Scientists, Am. Chem. Soc., Calif. Pharm. Assn., N.Y. Acad. Scis., Los Altos Country Club, Sigma Xi, Rho Chi, Phi Delta Chi. Office: 3707 Williams Rd San Jose CA 95117-2700

HINDEN, STANLEY JAY, newspaper editor; b. N.Y.C., Jan. 27, 1927; s. Edward I. and Rose (Kroshinsky) H.; m. Sara Leopold, May 24, 1953; children: Alan, Lawrence, Pamela. B.A., Syracuse U., 1950. Successively reporter, polit. editor, editor editorial pages, nat. corr. Washington Newsday, Garden City, N.Y., 1952-71; successively exec. editor, editor Nat. Jour., Washington, 1971-73; editl. page features editor, editor Dist., Md. and Va. weekly sects., fin. reporter, columnist Washington Post, 1973-96, fin. writer column Washington Investing. Contbr. polit. column. Inside Politics, Newsday, 1955-65, Retirement Jour. column Washington Post, 1996—. Served with AUS, 1945-46. Home: apt 630 3310 N Leisure World Blvd Silver Spring MD 20906-5664 Office: 1150 15th St NW Washington DC 20071-0001

HINDERAKER, IVAN, political science educator; b. Hendricks, Minn., Apr. 29, 1916; s. Theodore and Clara (Hanson) H.; m. Evelyn Birkholz, June 7, 1941; 1 child, Mark. B.A., St. Olaf Coll., 1938; M.A., U. Minn., 1942, Ph.D., 1949. Mem. faculty UCLA, 1948—, prof. polit. sci., 1956—, chmn. dept., 1960-62; vice chancellor acad. affairs U. Calif.-Irvine, 1962-64; chancellor U. Calif.-Riverside, 1964-79, chancellor emeritus, 1979—. Mem. Minn. Ho. of Reps., 1941-43; mem. Calif. Transp. Commn., 1978-84, chmn., 1982. Served to 1st lt. USAAF, 1943-46. Home: 943 Goldenrod Ave Corona Del Mar CA 92625-1504

HINDERY, LEO JOSEPH, JR., media company executive; b. Springfield, Ill., Oct. 31, 1947; s. Leo Joseph and E. Marie (Whitener) H.; m. Deborah Diane Sale, Feb. 20, 1980; 1 child, Robin Cook. BA, Seattle U., 1969; MBA, Stanford U., 1971. Asst. treas. Utah Internat., San Francisco, 1971-80; treas. Natomas Co., San Francisco, 1980-82; exec. v.p. fin. Jefferies & Co., L.A., 1982-83; chief fin. officer A.G. Becker Paribas, N.Y.C., 1983-85; chief officer planning and fin. Chronicle Pub. Co., San Francisco, 1985-88; mng. gen. ptnr. InterMedia Ptnrs. (merged with ATT Broadband/Internet Svcs.), San Francisco, 1988-97; pres. Tele-Communications, Inc., 1997—; bd. dirs. DMX, Inc., NETCOM On-Line Comm. Svcs., Inc., Nat. Cable TV Assn., Cable Telecomms. Assn., C-Span. With U.S. Army, 1968-70. Mem. Calif. Golf Club. Avocation: golf. Office: ATT Broadband & Internet Svc 9197 South Peoria St Englewood CO 80112*

HINDIN, SEYMOUR, lawyer; b. N.Y.C.; s. Joseph S. and Sara L. (Altman) H.; m. Vera (dec. Mar. 1987); children: Steven D., Joel S. BA, NYU, 1939, JD, 1941. Bar: U.S. Dist. Ct. (so. dist.) N.Y. 1947, U.S. Dist. Ct. (ea. dist.) N.Y. 1959, U.S. Supreme Ct. 1961, U.S. Ct. Appeals (2d dist.) 1980. Atty. pvt. practice, N.Y.C., 1943—; mem. Environ. Conservation Adv. Bd., Port Jefferson, N.Y., 1975-90; arbitrator U.S. Dist. Ct., Ea. Dist. N.Y., 1988—, Dist. Ct. Suffolk County, 1985—, Nassau County, 1985-90; adult edn. instr. Earl L. Vandermeulen H.S., Port Jefferson, 1975-86, Miller Place, 1983-85. Mem. Score-Counselor to Am. Small Bus., 1988—. Recipient Ten Yr. award for Svc. Small Bus. Cmty., 1988. Mem. Suffolk County Bar Assn. (Golden Anniversary Award of Practice of Law 1993), Knights of Pythias (Cosmopolitan Lodge chancellor comdr. 1946). Home: 105 E Gate Rd Port Jefferson NY 11777

HINDLE, PAULA ALICE, nursing administrator; b. Cambridge, Mass., Feb. 26, 1952; d. Edward Adam and Geraldine Ann (Donahue) H. BSN, Fitchburg State Coll., 1974; MSN, Duke U., 1980; MBA, Simmons Coll., 1988. Staff nurse Mt. Auburn Hosp., Cambridge, Mass., 1974-75; staff nurse U. Hosp., Boston, 1975-77, head nurse, 1977-79; staff nurse Duke U. Med. Ctr., Durham, N.C., 1979-80, clin. instr., 1980-81, area mgr., 1981; nurse leader, clin. dir. New Eng. Med. Ctr., Boston, 1981-87; cons. Ctr. for Nursing Case Mgmt., Boston, 1984-87; v.p. nursing Faulkner Hosp., Boston, 1987-94; v.p. nursing and support svcs. Alexandria (Va.) Hosp., 1994-97; v.p. for patient care, chief nurse exec. Loyola U. Med. Ctr., Maywood, Ill., 1997—; mem. adv. com. Regis Coll. Nursing, 1993; mem. planning and resource com. Simmons Coll., 1993-94; mem. affiliate faculty George Mason U., 1994-95. Active Am. Heart Assn. Mem. Am. Orgn. Nurse Execs., Va. Orgn. Nurse Execs., Mass. Orgn. Nurse Execs. (treas. 1991-93), Humane Soc., Simmons Coll. Grad. Sch. Mgmt. Alumni Assn. (bd. dirs. 1991-93, pres. 1992-93), Sigma Theta Tau. Democrat. Roman Catholic. Avocations: ballroom dancing, bicycling, reading, theatre, music. Home: 1322 Tall Oaks Ln Wheaton IL 60187-3039 Office: Loyola U Med Ctr 2160 S 1st Ave Maywood IL 60153-3304

HINDMAN, MARGARET HORTON, college administrator; b. Salisbury, Md., Feb. 15, 1947; d. Herbert Elwood and Imogene (Caruthers) Horton; m. Don C. Hindman, Aug. 9, 1969; 1 child, Annemarie H. BA, Hood Coll., 1969; postgrad., Antioch Coll., 1974-77. Reporter Frederick (Md.) News-Post, 1969-72; counselor, project coord. Community Mental Health Svcs., Frederick, 1972-73; editor weekly newspaper Sentinel Newspapers, Gaithersburg, Md., 1973-74; writer, editor Nat. Clearinghouse for Alcohol Info., Gaithersburg, 1974-76; dir. pub. info. Hood Coll., Frederick, Md., 1976-79; publs. mgr. Nat. Clearinghouse for Alcohol Info., Rockville, Md., 1979-84; dir. communications Hood Coll., Frederick, 1984-89, assoc. v.p. communications, 1989—; freelance writer Balt. Sun, 1973-76, Nat. Inst. on Alcohol Abuse, Rockville, 1976-77. Contbr. articles to mags. and profl. jours. Mem. Md. Judicial Nominating Commn., 6th Dist., State of Md., Annapolis, 1986-88; alternate mem. Md. Water Quality Adv. Commn., Annapolis, 1991—. Recipient awards for mag. editing and direct mail Md. Press Women, 1984. Mem. Coun. for Advancement and Support of Edn., Ednl. Writers Assn. Office: Hood Coll Rosemont Ave Frederick MD 21701

HINDS, EDWARD DEE, insurance and investment professional, financial planner; b. Madera, Calif., May 13, 1949; s. Edward Dee Jr. and Donna (Parker) H.; m. Olga P. Hinds; children: Sarah, Stephen, Rebekah. Grad., Life Underwriting Tng. Coun. CLU. Sr. acct. agt. Allstate, Lemoore, Calif., 1983-90; gen. agt. Ohio Nat. Life Ins. Cos., Midland Nat. Life Ins. Co., Paso Robles, Calif, 1990—; gen. ptnr. Edward D. Hinds, Ins. and Fortress Fin. Strategies, Paso Robles, 1990—, Edward D. Hinds, Ins., 1995—; founder, gen. ptnr. Fortress Fin. Strategies, A Registered Investment Adviser, 1995-97; founder, gen. mgr. Hinds Fin. Group, LLC, 1998—; benefits cons. U-Haul Dealers, Cen. Calif., 1992—, KOA, Calif., 1997. Mem. Soc. of Fin. Svc. Profls., Nat. Assn. of Life Underwriters, Nat. Assn. of Health Underwriters, Million Dollar Roundtable.

HINDS, GLESTER SAMUEL, financier, program specialist, tax consultant; b. N.Y.C., July 4, 1951; s. Glester Samuel and Kathryne Elizabeth (Ellison) H. *Mother Kathryne Elizabeth (Ellison) received B.S. in Nursing from C.W. Post College and M.A. from Columbia University's Teacher's College in New York City. Born in Philadelphia, lived in New York until retirement to Georgia. Her entire career in medicine, retired as Director of Nursing. A former "Who's Who" in Nursing and having travelled around the world, currently chairperson of local newspaper and director of Nannie L. Jenkins Learning Center. A secretary and member of Randolph County Retired Teacher's Association, also involved in local community, educational and political organizations.* BBA, Bernard M. Baruch Coll., 1973; MBA in Fin., Columbia U., 1975. Stock broker, ins. broker, notary pub. Staff acct. Peat Marwick Mitchell, N.Y.C., 1975-77; fin. analyst Citicorp, N.Y.C., 1977-79; sr. fin. analyst Am. Express, N.Y.C., 1979-80; owner, cons. Hinds Fin. Svcs., Long Island, N.Y., 1980-87; owner, founder, pres. Emerald Advt. Co., 1985—; program specialist Calif. FTB, Manhasset, N.Y., 1987—; cons. Am. Entrepreneur's Assn., L.A., 1980-89, Mildred Burke Prodns., 1982-84, Worldwide Diamonds Assn., 1983-85, Acad. Fin. Aid Matching Svcs., 1983-87; licensee Creative Capital Pubs., Inc., 1983; with Mail Order Assocs., Inc., 1984—; holder minority interest Carlton Blues Football Team, Australia. Editor: Financial Newsletter the H-Club, 1978-82; actor: On Camera TV Acting, 1986; contbr. articles to profl. jours., to Passport For Travel newsletter. Mem. Presdl. Nat. Steering Com., Rep. Presdl. Task Force; founder Heritage Found., Washington, 1981, Ronald Reagan Rep. Ctr., 1989; founding mem. FDR Meml. Constrn. Project, 1996; mem. chmn.'s com. U.S. Senatorial Bus. Adv. Bd., 1981, 82; mem. Nassau-Suffolk Neighborhood Network; mem. Jim Valvano Found. for Cancer Rsch., Am. Heart Assn., The Children's Charity Fund, N.Y. Sportscene Children's Found. Recipient Edward M. Paster Meml. award, Sigma Alpha award, Beta Gamma Sigma award, Beta Alpha Psi award, Bernard M. Baruch Coll., 1973, Distinction award Am. Express, 1993, Humanitarian Gold Record of Achievement ABI, 1994, Leader in sci. award, 1995, Internat. Man of the Yr. award in Sci., 1993; named Toronto Sports Club Athlete of Yr., 1987. Mem. USA Amateur Athletes, Interval Internat., Am. Mus. Natural History (assoc.), Am. Soc. Notaries, U.S. Olympic Soc., N.Y. Pub. Interest Rsch. Group, 24K Club, USA Wrestling, Franklin Mint Collectors Soc., Pro-Wrestling Hall of Fame (chmn. until 1994), U.S. Tennis Assn., Nat. Amateur Wrestling Hall of Fame (ptnr., fundraiser), Insiders Money Club, Internat. Platform Assn., Am. Cancer Soc., Am. Inst. Cancer Rsch., Troy Aikman Found., Carter Ctr., Environ. Def. Fund, Internat. Soc. Financiers, Coram Civic Assn. (acting pres.), Oxford Fin. Club, Carlton Blues Football Team (Australia), World Trade Ctr. Club. Methodist. Home: PO Box 971 Coram NY 11727-0971 Office: California Franchise Tax Bd 1325 Franklin Ave Fl 5 Garden City NY 11530-1666

HINE, ROBERT VAN NORDEN, JR., historian, educator; b. Los Angeles, Apr. 26, 1921; s. Robert Van Norden and Elizabeth (Bates) H.; m. Shirley M. McChord, June 24, 1949; 1 child, Allison. BA, Pomona Coll., 1948; MA, Yale U., 1949, PhD, 1952. Instr. history U. Calif., Riverside, 1954-55; asst. prof. U. Calif., 1955-61, asso. prof., 1961-66, prof., 1966-90, prof. emeritus, 1990—; prof. recalled U. Calif., Irvine, 1990—. Author: California's Utopian Colonies, 1953, rev. edit., 1983, Edward Kern and American Expansion, 1962, rev. edit., In the Shadow of Fremont, 1982, Bartlett's West: Drawing the Mexican Boundary, 1968, The American Frontier: Readings and Documents, 1972, The American West: An Interpretive History, 1973, (with John Mack Faragher) 3rd edit., 1999, Community on the American Frontier: Separate But Not Alone, 1980, California Utopianism: Contemplations of Eden, 1981; editor: William Andrew Spalding, Los Angeles Newspaperman, 1961, Soldier in the West: Letters of Theodore Talbot, 1972, Josiah Royce: West As Community in Writing Western History, 1991, Josiah Royce: From Grass Valley to Harvard, 1992 (Commonwealth Club award 1992), Second Sight, 1993 (N.Y. Times Notable Book of 1993); contbr. articles to profl. jours. Recipient Harbison award for disting. teaching Danforth Found., 1968, Wagner Meml. award Calif. Hist. Soc., 1986; Huntington Libr. fellow, 1953, 60, Guggenheim fellow, 1958, 68, Nat. Endowment for Humanities sr. fellow, 1977, Calif. Coun. for Promotion of History award, 1994. Mem. Western History Assn. (life, hon. 1990, Award of Merit 1996), Orgn. Am. Historians, Phi Beta Kappa. Home: 19191 Harvard Ave # 317 Irvine CA 92612-4670

HINER, ELIZABETH ELLEN, pharmacist; b. Balt., Aug. 11, 1943; d. Samuel Joseph and Zola Mae (Hedrick) Bracken; m. William O. Hiner (div.); children: Christine Ellen, Oliver Joseph; m. Ray Danforth Crossley, Aug. 3, 1985. BS in Pharmacy, W.Va. U., 1966; postgrad., Johns Hopkins U., 1984-87; cert. in pub. health pharmacy, Royal Soc. Health, London, 1996. Registered pharmacist, W.Va., Md., Va. Staff pharmacist U. Va. Hosp., Charlottesville, 1965-66; pharmacy supr. Andrew Rader Army Health Clinic, Ft. Meyer, Va., 1977; pharmacist NIH, Bethesda, Md., 1977-78; consumer safety officer Bur. Biologics FDA, Bethesda, 1978-80, freedom of info. officer, 1980-81, biologics adverse reaction coord., 1981-84, sr. regulatory officer divsn. bacterial products, 1984-92; dir. health promotion fed.-state rels. FDA, Rockville, Md., 1992—; mem., chair pharmacy adv. com. USPHS, Rockville, 1991—; ad hoc mem. Bur. Voluntary Compliance, Nat. Assn. Bds. of Pharmacy, Chgo., 1993-98; mem. faculty Food and Drug Law Inst., 1996-97. Contbr. articles to sci. jours. Mem. parent adv. bd. Beaver Coll., Glenside, Pa., 1993-97; mem. Olney (Md.) Women's League, 1986—. Capt. USPHS, 1978—. Recipient Cert. of Recognition, Nat. Assn. Bds. of Pharmacy, 1993, 94, 95, 96, 97, 98. Mem. Am. Pharm. Assn., Am. Soc. Health Sys. Pharmacists, Commd. Officers Assn., Lambda Kappa Sigma Alumni. Avocation: sailing.

HINER, GLADYS WEBBER, psychologist; b. Mt. Park, Okla., Mar. 10, 1907; d. Santford and Erie Emma (Rose) Webber; m. Wayman Hiner, Aug. 11, 1927 (dec. Mar. 1967); children: Waynel Cook, Sandra Homer. BS, U. Okla., 1934, MS, 1955, PhD, 1962; HHD (hon.), Wagon Wheel Found., McCloud, Okla., 1973. Bd. cert. devel. psychologist. Tchr. Okla. City Pub. Schs., 1953-61; dir. Dale Rogers Tng. Ctr., Okla. City, 1962-63; prof. Okla. City U., 1963-72, Rose State Coll., Okla. City, 1972-86; cons. Wagon Wheel Sch. McLoud, Okla., 1962-82, pvt. practice, Okla. City, 1986—. Supr. Sunday Sch. Trinity Baptist Ch., Okla. City, 1940-72; bd. dirs. Okla. State Assn. for Mentally Retarded Children, 1963-67, Youth and Child Coun. Okla. U. Med. Sch., 1966-69, Bridge Builders, Okla. City; Dem. state del., 1986. Fellow Okla. Psychol. Assn., Am. Assn. on Mental Deficiency; mem. The Acad. Ret. Profls., Okla. Hist. Soc., DAR, Colonial Dames, Psi Chi, Phi Theta Kappa. Avocations: reading, swimming, bridge. Home: 800 S Canadian Trails Dr Norman OK 73072-7627

HINER, GLEN HAROLD, JR., materials company executive; b. Morgantown, W.Va., July 22, 1934; s. Glen Harold and Dorothy M. (Brown) H.; m. Ann Hiner; children: Stephanie, Greg. BS, W.Va. U., 1957, DSc (hon.), 1989. Registered elec. engr. Sales mgr. GE, 1965-67, mgr. mktg., 1967-70, plant mgr., 1970-72, gen. mgr., 1972-77; mng. dir. GE Plastics, The Netherlands, 1977-78; v.p., gen. mgr. GE Plastics, Pittsfield, Mass., 1978-81, sr. v.p., gen. mgr., 1981-83, sr. v.p., group exec., 1983-92; chmn., CEO Owens-Corning, Toledo, 1992—; bd. dirs. Dana Corp., Huntsman Corp. Bd. dirs. Toledo Symphony. Capt. USAF, 1957-60. Mem. Bus. Coun., Bus. Roundtable, The Toledo Club, Toledo Country Club, Links Club, Inverness Club. Republican. Methodist. Office: Owens Corning One Owens Corning Pkwy Toledo OH 43659-0002*

HINER, JOHN PATRICK, newspaper editor; b. Dearborn, Mich., July 18, 1960; s. John Henry and Rose Mary (Nagy) H.; m. Cheryl Ann Zarosley, Aug. 24, 1985 (div. May 1997); 1 child, Alexander Cassidy. BA, Adrian (Mich.) Coll. Reporter Daily Telegram, Adrian, 1982-84, news editor, 1984-86; reporter Citizen-Patriot, Jackson, Mich., 1986-89, asst. metro editor, 1989-94; metro editor Bay City (Mich.) Times, 1994—; chmn. bus. wire story com. AP Mich., Detroit, 1996. Author: The Pocket Pro, 1994. Chmn. devel. com. Leadership Bay County, Bay City, 1994—; bd. dirs. Bay Area Family Y, Bay City, 1997—. Newswriting award AP, 1983, 87, 88, 90, 91, 90, 88, UPI, 1990; Sch. Bell award Mich. Edn. Assn., 1988. Mem. Rotary (bd trustee 1995—). Avocations: writing, reading, tennis, golf, travel. Home: 1577 Dawn Marie Ct Auburn MI 48611-9209 Office: Bay City Times 311 5th St Bay City MI 48708-5853

HINERFELD, LEE ANN, veterinarian; b. San Francisco, Apr. 24, 1955; d. Norman Martin and Ruth Jean (Gordon) H. BA, Vassar Coll., 1977; DVM, Tufts U., 1986; MS, U. Wyo., 1987. Lic. Conn., Mass. Sr. rsch. technician U. Mass. Med. Ctr., Worcester, 1977-80; small animal clinician, assoc. vet. Mt. Pleasant Hosp. for Animals, Newtown, Conn., 1987, Shakespeare Vet. Hosp., Stratford, Conn., 1988-90, New London (Conn.) Vet. Hosp., 1990—. Fellow Conn. Acad. Vet. Practice, Am. Vet. Med. Assn., Conn. Vet. Med. Assn., Assn. Women Vets; mem. Defenders of Wildlife, Population Comm. Internat., Common Cause, New Forests Project, Phi Kappa Phi. Avocations: jogging, skiing, hiking, cooking, photography. Office: New London Vet Hosp 122 Cross Rd Waterford CT 06385-1204

HINERFELD, NORMAN MARTIN, manufacturing company executive; b. N.Y.C., May 17, 1929; s. Benjamin B. and Anne (Blitz) H.; m. Ruth Jean Gordon, Dec. 25, 1952; children—Lee Ann, Thomas Benjamin, Joshua Gordon. A.B., Harvard U., 1951, M.B.A., 1953. Security underwriter, underwriting dept. Goldman Sachs & Co., 1953; asst. to pres. Julius Kayser & Co., 1955-56; asst. to pres. Catalina, Inc., 1956-57, v.p. mfg., 1957-64, sr. v.p., 1964-67; v.p. Kayser-Roth Corp., 1964-67, exec. v.p., 1967-74, mem. exec. com., 1972—, pres., COO, 1974-76, dir., 1958-85, chmn. exec. com., 1976-85; chmn., CEO Wingspread Corp., 1985-88, Pandora Industries, Inc., N.Y.C., 1988—, Tica Industries, Inc., N.Y.C., 1990—, Delta Pharm. Group Ltd., 1993—; sec.-treas. Thermacon Industries Inc., 1989—; bd. dirs. Supermarkets Gen. Corp.; chmn. council Ctr. for Study Democratic Instns.; mem. U.S.A.-BIAC to OECD, 1978—; mem. exec. com. Dist. Export-Council U.S. Dept. Commerce, 1978—; mem. adv. council on Japan-U.S. Econ. Relations, 1980—. Author: (with D. Moross) Automation-Challenge to Management, 1953; patentee self-programmed automatic machinery. Bd. overseers NYU Sch. Bus., 1984-88; chmn. Metro N.Y.-Bus. Execs. for Nat. Security, 1990—, mem. exec. com., 1992—. 1st lt. U.S. Army, 1953-55. Mem. Am. Arbitration Assn. (chmn. bd. 1984-90, exec. com., bd. dirs. 1969—), Am. Apparel Mfrs. Assn. (bd. dirs., past pres., mem. exec. com.), Internat. Apparel Fedn. (past pres.), Nat. Knitted Sportswear Assn. (exec. com., bd. dirs.), U.S. C. of C. (chmn. export policy com. 1979-89). Home: 11 Oak Ln Larchmont NY 10538-3917 Office: Thermacon Industries Inc 1983 Marcus Ave New Hyde Park NY 11042-1016

HINERFELD, ROBERT ELLIOT, lawyer; b. N.Y.C., May 29, 1934; s. Benjamin B. and Anne (Blitz) H.; m. Susan Hope Slocum, June 27, 1957; children: Daniel Slocum, Matthew Ben. AB, Harvard U., 1956, JD, 1959. Bar: Calif. 1960. Asst. U.S. atty So. Dist. Calif., 1960-62; assoc. Leonard Horwin, Beverly Hills, Calif., 1962-66; mem. Simon, Sheridan, Murphy, Thornton & Hinerfeld, Los Angeles, 1967-74, Murphy, Thornton, Hinerfeld & Cahill, 1975-83, Murphy, Thornton, Hinerfeld & Elson, 1983-85, Manatt, Phelps & Phillips LLP, 1985—; arbitrator bus. panel Los Angeles Superior Ct., 1979-82; assoc. ind. counsel (diGenova), 1993-95; judge pro tempore Beverly Hills Municipal Court, 1967-74; clin. lectr. U. So. Calif. Law Center, 1980-81, guest lectr., 1993-96; expert witness, 1987—, legal affairs on-air guest spkr. sta. KCRW-FM, Santa Monica, Calif., 1998-99. Contbr. articles to profl. jours. Trustee Westland Sch., Los Angeles, 1970-75, Pacific Hills Sch., 1971-72. Fellow Am. Bar Found.; mem. ABA, Fed. Bar Assn., Los Angeles County Bar Assn. (spl. com. jud. evaluation 1978-82, arbitration com. 1981-83, settlement officer 2d appellate dist. appellate case settlement project 1996—, spl. com. on appellate evaluation 1996—), Beverly Hills Bar Assn., State Bar Calif. (mem. com. on criminal law and procedure, chmn. spl. com. revision fed. criminal code, mem. disciplinary investigation panel dist. 7 1977-80, hearing referee State Bar Ct. 1981-83, referee rev. dept. 1984-87, exec. com. litigation sect. 1983-85, civil litigation adv. group 1985-88), Am. Arbitration Assn. (arbitrator comml. panel 1966—), Calif. Acad. Appellate Lawyers (membership com. 1983-88, 2d v.p. 1985-87, 1st v.p. 1987-88, pres. 1988-89), Harvard Club So. Calif. (dir. 1974-73, sec. 1978-80, mem. prize book com. 1992-94), Harvard Club N.Y.C. Home: 371 24th St Santa Monica CA 90402-2517 Office: Manatt Phelps & Phillips LLP 11355 W Olympic Blvd Los Angeles CA 90064-1614

HINERFELD, RUTH G., civic organization executive; b. Boston, Sept. 18, 1930; m. Norman Hinerfeld, children: Lee, Thomas, Joshua. A.B., Vassar Coll., 1951; grad., Program in Bus. Adminstrn., Harvard-Radcliffe Coll., 1952. With LWV, 1954—, UN observer, 1969-72, chairperson internat. relations com., 1972-76, 1st v.p. in charge legis. activities, 1976-78, pres., 1978-82; dir. LWV Overseas Edn. Fund, 1975-76, trustee, 1975-86; chairperson LWV Edn. Fund, 1978-82; mem. White House Adv. Com. for Trade Negotiations, 1975-82; sec. UN Assn. of U.S., 1975-78, vice chmn., 1983—, bd. govs., 1975—, mem. econ. policy coun., 1976-93; bd. dirs. Overseas Devel. Coun.; trustee Inst. of Internat. Edn., 1997—; mem. U.S. del. auspices of Nat. Com. on U.S.-China Rels. and Chinese People's Inst. Fgn. Affairs, 1978. Mem. coun. Nat. Mcpl. League, 1977-80, 83-86; del.-at-large Internat. Women's Yr. Conf., Houston, 1977; mem. exec. com. Leadership Conf. on Civil Rights, 1978-82; trustee Citizens Rsch. Found., 1978—; mem. Nat. Petroleum Coun., 1979-82; mem. U.S. del. to World Conf. on UN Decade for Women, 1980; mem. adv. com. Nat. Inst. for Citizen Edn. in the Law, 1981-91; mem. North South Roundtable, 1978-88; mem. nat. gov. bd. Common Cause, 1984-90; vice chmn. U.S. com. UNICEF, 1986-90, treas., 1990-91; mem. vis. com. Harvard U. Bus. Sch., 1984-90; mem. Bretton Woods Com.; bd. dirs. Com. for Modern Cts., 1993-96. Recipient Disting. Citizen award Nat. Mcpl. League, 1978; Outstanding Mother award Nat. Mother's Day Com., 1981; Aspen Inst. Presdl. fellow, 1981. Mem. Council on Fgn. Relations, Phi Beta Kappa. Office: 11 Oak Ln Larchmont NY 10538-3917

HINES, ANDREW HAMPTON, JR., utilities executive; b. Lake City, Fla., Jan. 28, 1923; s. Andrew Hampton and Louise Dixie (Howland) H.; m. Ann Groover, June 28, 1947' children: Andrew Hampton III, Elizabeth Renee, John Bradford, Daniel Howland. BME with high honors, U. Fla., 1947; degree (hon.), Stetson U., 1987, U. South Fla., 1989, Rollins Coll., 1989, Fla. So. Coll., 1994. Registered profl. engr., Fla. With R&D depts. GE, 1947-51; pres. Fla. Power Corp., 1972-82; chmn. bd. Fla. Progress Corp., St. Petersburg, 1982-91, chmn. emeritus, 1991—; chmn. bd. Precise Power Corp., Bradenton, Fla., 1990-97; cons. Triangle Cons. Group; bd. dirs. Templeton Mut. Funds, Franklin Mutual Series Funds; past chmn. N.Am. Electric Reliability Coun.; exec.-in-residence Eckerd Coll. Trustee Asbury Theol. Sem.; bd. dirs. Fla. Coun. Econ. Edn., U. Fla. Found., Tampa Bay Rsch. Inst.; Sunday sch. tchr. Meth. Ch.; chmn. Pinellas County Cmty. Reuse Orgn., 1994-97; chmn. No Casinos in Fla., Inc. 2d lt. USAAF, 1943-45. Decorated Air medal, Prisoner of War medal. Fellow ASME; mem. U.S. Energy Assn., Acad. Sr. Profls. Eckerd Coll., Blue Key, St. Petersburg Yacht Club, Sigma Tau, Phi Kappa Phi, Tau Beta Pi, Beta Gamma Sigma. Methodist. Office: Triangle Cons Group 150 2nd Ave N Ste 1170 Saint Petersburg FL 33701-3342 *You cannot out give God. If you cast your bread upon the waters it will come back buttered.*

HINES, ANGUS IRVING, JR., petroleum marketing executive; b. Suffolk, Va., Aug. 7, 1923; s. Angus Irving and Lois E. (Howell) H.; m. Genevieve Hopkins McCollum, Nov. 24, 1949 (div. 1977); children: Ann Russell Hines Mauer, Marilyn N. Hines Stulb, A. McCollum, Angus Irving III. Pres. Sentry Petroleum Inc. (now Angus I. Hines, Inc.), Suffolk, 1945—; Angus Hines, Inc., Svc. Gas Co., Inc. Served with U.S. Maritime Service, 1943-45; ETO. Mem. Va. Petroleum Jobbers Assn. (past pres.), Rotary (past pres.), Quiet Birdmen. Methodist. Office: Angus I Hines Inc PO Box 1080 1426 Holland Rd Suffolk VA 23439-1080

HINES, ANNA GROSSNICKLE, author, illustrator; b. Cin., July 13, 1946; d. Earl Stanton and Ruth Marie (Putman) Grossnickle; m. Gary Roger Hines, June 19, 1976; children: Bethany, Sarah, Lassen. Art major, San Fernando Valley St, 1964-67, 72; BA in Human Devel., Pacific Oaks Coll., 1974, MA in Human Devel., 1978. Tchr. L.A. City Day Care Ctrs., 1967-70, Columbia Elem. Sch., Calif., 1975-78. Author: Taste The Raindrops, 1983, Come To The Meadow, 1984, Maybe A Band-Aid Will Help, 1984, Bethany For Real, 1985, All By Myself, 1985, Cassie Bowen Takes Witch Lessons, 1985, Don't Worry I'll Find You, 1986, Daddy Makes The Best Spaghetti, 1986, I'll Tell You What They Say, 1987, Keep Your Old Hat, 1987, It's Just Me, Emily, 1987, Grandma Gets Grumpy, 1988, Boys Are Yucko!, 1989, They Really Like Me, 1989, Sky All Around, 1989, Big Like Me, 1989, Mean Old Uncle Jack, 1990, The Secret Keeper, 1990, Remember The Butterflies, 1991, The Greatest Picnic In The World, 1991, Jackie's Lunch box, 1991, Tell Me Your Best Thing, 1991, Moon's Wish, 1992, Rumble Thumble Boom!, 1992, Moompa, Toby and Bomp, 1993, Gramma's Walk, 1993, Even If I Spill My Milk?, 1994, What Joe Saw, 1994, BIG HELP!, 1995, When the Goblins Came Knocking, 1995, When We Married Gary, 1996, Miss Emma's Wild Garden, 1997, My Own Big Bed, 1998, What Can You Do in the Rain?, 1999, What Can You Do in the Snow, 1999, What Can You Do in the Sun?, 1999, What Can You Do in the Wind", 1999; illustrator: A Ride in the Crummy, 1991, Flying Firefighters, 1993, Day of the High Climber, 1994, Bean, Gean's Games, Bean's Night, 1998, Bouncing on the Bed, 1999. Children's Book Coun., 1988. Mem. Soc. Children's Book Writers and Illustrators, Internat. Reading Assn., Nat. Assn. Edn. of Young Children. Office: care Greenwillow Books 1350 Ave of the Americas New York NY 10016-7418 also: Clarion Books 215 Park Ave S New York NY 10003-1603

HINES, ANSON H., museum director; b. Honolulu, Jan. 4, 1947. BA, Pomona Coll., 1969; PhD, U. Calif., Berkeley, 1976. Postdoctoral rsch. geologist U. Calif., Santa Cruz, 1975-79; sr. marine biologist TEARA Corp., 1978-79; marine ecologist SERC, Washington, 1979-88; asst. dir. Smithsonian Environ. Rsch. Ctr., Edgewater, Md., 1988—; adj. prof. Dept. Zoology U. Md., College Park, 1989—, Dept. Marine, Earth & Atmosphere Scis. N.C. State U., 1992—. Disting. rsch. fellow New Zealand Nat. Inst. Water & Atmospheric Rsch., 1993, rsch. fellow Japan Soc. Promotion Scis., 1995; recipient Vailie prize Pomona Coll., Claremont, Calif., 1969. Mem. Ecol. Soc. Am., Soc. Integrative & Comparative Biology, Crustacean Soc., Estuarine Rsch. Found. Office: Smithsonian Environ Rsch Ctr PO Box 28 Edgewater MD 21037-0028*

HINES, ANTHONY LORING, automotive executive; b. Altus, Okla., Sept. 19, 1941; s. William A. and Edna Lee (Allen) H.; m. Nancy Campbell, Sept. 19, 1959 (div. 1962); children: William, Todd; m. Jo Ann Willoughby, June 22, 1963; children: Donna, Larry, Teresa, Toni, Michael. BSChemE, U. Okla., 1967; MSChemE, Okla. State U., 1969; PhDME, U. Tex., 1973. Registered profl. engr., Tex. Asst. prof. chem. engring. Ga. Inst. Tech., Atlanta, 1973-75; asst. to assoc. prof. chem. engring. Colo. Sch. Mines, Golden, 1975-80; prof. chem. engring., head dept. U. Wyo., Laramie, 1980-83; assoc. dean engring. rsch. Okla. State U., Stillwater, 1983-87; prof. chem. engring., dean engring. U. Mo.-Columbia, 1987-93; v.p. Honda of Am., Mfg., Inc., Marysville, Ohio, 1993-97; now sr. v.p. Honda of Am., Mfg. Inc., Marysville, Ohio, 1997; v.p. mfg. Navistar Internat. Corp., Springfield, Ohio, 1998—; site visitor NSF, 1988-90; mem. Mo. Corp. for Sci. & Tech., 1991—; mem. rev. panel on air quality Internat. Energy Agy., 1991; mem. rev. panel Laser, 1990; mem., lead reviewer Lumcon, 1990. Co-author: Mass Transfer Fundamentals and Applications, 1984, Mass Transfer Solutions Manual, 1985, Indoor Air, Quality and Control, 1993; contbr. articles to profl. jours. Mem. Okla. Coun. Sci. and Tech. Rsch. Task Force, 1984, Regional Commerce and Growth Assn., St. Louis, 1988—; assoc. mem. Columbia Regional Econ. Devel., Inc., 1989—; mem. Columbia Area Regional Econ. Devel., Inc., 1989—. Mem. NSPE, ASHRAE (com. on sorption 1988—), Nat. Inst. for Engring. Mgmt. and Systems (bd. govs. 1990—), Am. Inst. Chem. Engrs. (sec. separations div. 1991), Mo. Soc. Profl. Engrs., Am. Soc. Engring. Edn.. Avocations: hunting, fishing, handball, basketball. *

HINES, BETTY TAYLOR, women's center administrator; b El Paso, Aug. 23, 1927; d. Harold Baldwin and Mary Agnes (Baldwin) Taylor; m. H. Andrew Hines, Jan. 29, 1950; children: Andrew T., Bettina L., Daniel A., D.E.G. AS in Liberal Arts, Grossmont Coll., El Cajon, Calif., 1968; B of Applied Arts and Sci. in Sociology, East Tex. State U., Texarkana, 1990, MS in Counseling Psychology, 1995. Classified advt. clk. L.A. Times, 1961-63; with Realty World Brokers, Calif., 1976-82; sexual assault counselor, adv./vol. Domestic Violence Prevention, Inc., Texarkana, Tex., 1983-89; exec. dir. Bi-State Women's Ctr., Texarkana, 1989—; mem. steering com. Women's Involvement, Texarkana, 1988—; Goodwill amb. Ladies Aux. Fleet Res. Assn., 1993-94. Recipient Christine Nelson award YWCA, 1992, Leadership Texarkana Wilbur award in human rels., 1994; named Woman of Yr., Am. Bus. Women's Assn., 1994. Mem. SCORE. Avocations: needlepoint, sewing, travel. Office: BSWC Now Mabel Bryan Morriss Ctr 124 W Broad St Texarkana TX 75501-5609

HINES, DEAN HOWARD, military officer; b. Barnesville, Ohio, May 22, 1935; s. Stewart Shannon and Gertrude (Bishop) H.; m. Betsy Shannon Graham, May 30, 1962; children: Nathan, Todd, Amy, Cynthia. BS, U.S. Naval Acad., 1957; MS in Naval Architecture, MIT, 1965. Commd. ensign USN, 1957, advanced through grades to rear adm., 1989; current ship's maintenance officer Comdr.-in-chief Pacific Fleet USN, Pearl Harbor, Hawaii, 1977-79; prodn. officer USN, 1979-82; asst. maintenance engr. USN, San Diego, 1982-84; shipyard commdr. USN, Charleston, S.C., 1984-88; dep. comdr. indsl. and facilities mgmt. Naval Sea Systems Command USN, Washington, 1988-90. Mem. U.S. Naval Inst. (life). Office: Fleet Maintenance Officer Norfolk VA 23511

HINES, EARL S., federal judge; b. 1943. BA, U. Tex., 1965, JD, 1967. Law clk. to Hon. Joe Fisher, 1967-68, asst. atty. gen. Tex., 1969-71; with Brown and Hines, Beaumont, Tex., 1971-84; apptd. magistrate judge ea. dist. U.S. Dist. Ct. Tex., 1984. Mem. ABA, State Bar Tex., Jefferson County Bar Assn. Office: 234 Fed Bldg/US Courthouse 300 Willow St Beaumont TX 77701-2222

HINES, EDWARD FRANCIS, JR., lawyer; b. Norfolk, Va., Sept. 5, 1945; s. Edward Francis and Jeanne Miriam (Caulfield) H.; m. Elaine Geneva Carroll, Aug. 21, 1971; children: Jonathan Edward, Carolyn Adele. AB, Boston Coll., 1966; JD, Harvard U., 1969. Bar: Mass. 1969. Assoc. Choate Hall & Stewart, Boston, 1969-77, ptnr., 1977—; bd. dirs. Univ. Hosp., Boston, 1990-96, vice-chmn., 1994-96. With USAR, 1969-75. Mem. Boston Bar Assn. (pres. 1988-89), Boston Bar Found. (pres. 1995-97), Mass. CLE (pres. 1985-87), Carroll Ctr. for Blind (bd. dirs. 1983-89, 90-96, chmn. 1994-96), Mass. Taxpayers Found. (bd. dirs. 1987—), Am. Heart Assn. (bd. dirs. Dallas 1984-86, 91—, chmn. 1998—, award of merit 1983), Assoc. Industries Mass. (bd. dirs. 1990—, chmn. 1996-98), Am. Coll. Greece (Athens, bd. dirs., vice chmn. (trustee 1988-97), Fed. Tax Inst. New Eng. (treas. 1994—), Social Law Libr. (trustee 1993-98), Supreme Jud. Ct. Hist. Soc. (trustee 1989-96), North Andover Country Club, Boston Coll. Club, Bay Club. Office: Choate Hall & Stewart Exchange Pl 53 State St Boston MA 02109-2804

HINES, GEORGE LAWRENCE, surgeon; b. Bklyn., June 10, 1946; s. Frank and Ruth (Katzman) H.; m. Helene Anne Reitman, Aug. 23, 1969; children: Brian, Jennifer. BA, Boston U., 1969, MD, 1969. Diplomate Am. Bd. Gen. Surgery, Am. Bd. Thoracic Surgery, Am. Bd. Gen. Vascular Surgery. Intern Maimonides Med. Ctr., Bklyn., 1969-70; resident Sinai Hosp., Detroit, 1970-71; to chief resident L.I. Jewish Med. Ctr., N.Y.C., 1971-74; cardiothoracic resident NYU Med. Ctr., N.Y.C., 1974-76; attending physician Winthrop U. Hosp., Mineola, N.Y., 1976—; pvt. practice Mineola; chief div. vascular surgery Winthrop U. Hosp., Mineola, N.Y., 1995—. Maj. U.S. Army Res., 1970-79. Fellow Am. Coll. Surgeons; mem. Am. Assn. for Thoracic Surgery, Soc. of Thoracic Surgeons, Internat. Soc. for Cardiovascular Surgery. Democrat. Jewish. Avocations: jogging, piano. Office: Winthrop Cardiothoracic Vascular Surgery Group 120 Mineola Blvd Mineola NY 11501-4073

HINES, GREGORY OLIVER, actor, dancer; b. N.Y.C., Feb. 14, 1946; s. Maurice Robert and Alma Iola (Lawless) H.; m. Pamela Koslow, Apr. 12, 1981; children: Daria Hines, Jessica Koslow, Zachary Evan. Appeared with Hines Kids, 1949-55, Hines Bros., 1955-63, Hines, Hines and Dad, 1963-73, An Evening of Tap at Carnegie Hall, 1989; appeared in plays: The Girl in Pink Tights (Broadway debut) 1954, Severance, 1974-77, Eubie!, 1978 (Theater World awazrd), Comin' Uptown, 1980 (Tony award nomination), Sophisticated Ladies, 1981, (Tony award nomination), Parade of Stars Playing the Palace, 1983, I Love Liberty, 1981-82, Twelfth Night, 1989, Jelly's Last Jam, 1992-93 (Tony award, best actor in a musical, 1992); appeared in films: Wolfen, 1981, History of the World Part I, 1981, The Deal of the Century, 1983, The Muppets Take Manhattan, 1984, The Cotton Club, (also choreographer) 1984, White Nights, 1985, Running Scared, 1986, Off Limits, 1988, Tap (also choreographer) 1989, Eve Of Destruction, 1991, A Rage in Harlem, 1991, Renaissance Man, 1994, Waiting to Exhale, 1995; TV appearances: Tap Dance in America (PBS) 1989, Motown Returns to the Apollo, Saturday Night Live (host), (movies) White Lie, 1991, T-Bone and Weasel, 1992, Dead Air, 1994, A Stranger in Town, 1995. Recipient 3 Tony nominations, 1979, 80, 81, Theater World award, Tor award, Dance Educators Am. award. Mem. Actors Equity, Screen Actors Guild, AFTRA.

HINES, JEFF G., environmental protection administrator; b. L.A., Jan. 17, 1954; s. Elden A. and Lucille R. (Bare) H.; m. Thereé M. Adams, Oct. 11, 1975; children: Todd A., Ryan M., Renée L. Student, Ind. U., 1972-73; BS in Environ. Health Scis., Wright State U., 1977. Registered sanitarian, Ohio. Pub. health sanitarian Auglaize County Health Dept., Wapakoneta, Ohio, 1977-78; staff and mgmt. positions in hazardous waste & water program Ohio EPA, Dayton, 1978-86, environ. supr. hazardous waste programs, 1986-89, environtl. mgr. emergency and remedial response, 1989-94, asst. dist. chief, 1994—, acting chief divsn. of remedial response, 1998-99; instr. N.E. Hazardous Waste Project, Boston, 1987-88, Environ. Law Inst. & U.S. EPA, Washington, 1988; ops. improvement task force implementation steering com. Ohio EPA, Columbus, 1992-93; watershed enhancement program steering com. Lower Great Miami River Basin County, Miami (Ohio) Valley Regional Planning Commn., Dayton, 1996—; curriculum adv. bd. Inst. for Environ. Quality, Wright State U., Dayton, 1993—. Named Employee of Yr. Ohio EPA, 1987, Chief Negotiator of grant, 1991-92, Prin. Negotiator of grant, 1991-92. Mem. Glen Helen Nature Preserve Assn., Beavercreek Wetlands Assn. Avocations: stained glass craftsmanship. Office: 401 E 5th St Dayton OH 45402-2911

HINES, JOANN R., professional association executive and consultant; b. Balt., Dec. 16, 1948; d. Donald Reed Russell and Marjorie Louise Heller Scott; m. Rex Michael Hines, Apr. 5, 1980. Student, Temple U., 1971-75. Sales rep. Union Camp Corp., Atlanta, 1976-79; market devel. Crown Zellerbach, Atlanta, 1979-83; bus. devel. mgr. Advanced Design and Packaging, Atlanta, 1983-86; market devel. mgr. Chesapeake Display and Packaging, Winston-Salem, N.C., 1986-88; ind. packaging cons., pres. Globalpak (formerly Hines & Assocs), Acworth, Ga., 1988—; pres. Global Assn. Mgmt. (formerly Hines & Accos.), 1988—; founder, exec. dir. Women in Packaging, Inc., Acworth, 1993—; judge for CorrPak '92, '93, AmeriStar Packaging Competition, Package Printing and Converting's Excellence Awards, 1992, 93, Drummer Merchandising and Promotion Award; chmn. First Internat. Packaging Symposium; lectr. in field; chmn. Large Events Planning Packaging Coun.; cons. to Ga. So. U. to develop packaging curriculum; sr. cons. to Pub. Affairs Group. Contbg. author: Board Converting News; contbr. articles to profl. jours.; editl. adv. bd. The Profl. Jour. of Packaging; exec. editor: Packaging Horizons Mag., 1996-99. Mem. TAPPI (mktg. chmn. mktg. adv. com. internat. corrugated container dir.), Western Packaging Assn. (bd. dirs. 1999—), Soc. Competitive Intelligence, Internat. Assn. Design and Package Printing Industry (founding bd. dirs. 1994—), AICC, Nat. Inst. Packaging, Handling, and Logistics Engrs., Inst. Packaging Profls. (packaging cons. coun.), Internat. Packaging Cons. Avocations: sewing, fishing, reading, travel, knitting, gourmet cooking.

HINES, MARION ERNEST, electronic engineering consultant; b. Bellingham, Wash., Nov. 30, 1918; s. William Robert and Zella (Mudge) H.; m. Julie Warren Viele, May 3, 1947; children: Sheldon Knickerbocker, Julian Bigelow, Hadley Warren. B.S. in Applied Physics, Calif. Inst. Tech., 1940, B.S. in Meteorology, 1941, M.S.E.E., 1946. Mem. tech. staff, head dept. Bell Telphone Labs., Inc., Murray Hill, N.J., 1946-60; sr. scientist, v.p. Microwave Assoc. Inc., Burlington, Mass., 1960-78; v.p., M/A-COM Inc., Burlington, 1978-88; ind. cons., 1988—. Contbr. numerous articles to profl. jours.; holder 41 U.S. and fgn. patents. Maj. AC, U.S. Army, 1940-45. Fellow IEEE (life, mem. editorial bds., Lamme medal 1983, Centennial medal 1984), IEEE Electron Devices Soc. (J.J. Ebers award 1975), IEEE Microwave Theory and Techniques Soc. (Microwave prize 1971, 78, Microwave Career award 1983), Tau Beta Pi. Home: 44 W Cedar St Boston MA 02114-3302

HINES, MARSHALL, construction engineering company executive; b. Chgo., Dec. 29, 1923; s. Herbert Waldo and Helen (Gartside) H.; m. Janet Young, July 28, 1945; children: Karen Lynn, Keith Douglas, Dori Hines Alton. BCE, Mich. State U., 1947, MCE, 1948. Registered profl. engr., Mich. Project engr. The Christman Co., Lansing, Mich., 1948-55, supt., 1955-70, gen. supt., 1971-83, exec. v.p., 1983—. With U.S. Army, 1943-45. Mem. NSPE, Mich. Soc. Profl. Engrs. (bd. dirs. 1986, Constrn. Engr. Yr. 1990, Engr. of Yr. award 1994), Builders Exch. of Lansing (pres. 1988), Rotary (bd. dirs. Lansing club 1986-87). Republican. Methodist. Home: 1137 Rebecca Rd East Lansing MI 48823-5210 Office: The Christman Co 408 Kalamazoo Plz Lansing MI 48933-1990*

HINES, N. WILLIAM, dean, law educator, administrator; b. 1936. AB, Baker U., 1958; LLD, U. Kans., 1999, LLB, 1961; LLD, Baker U., 1999. Bar: Kans. 1961, Iowa 1965. Law clk. U.S. Ct. Appeals 10th cir., 1961-62; tchg. fellow Harvard U., 1961-62; asst. prof. law U. Iowa, 1962-65, assoc. prof., 1965-67, prof., 1967-73, disting. prof., 1973—, dean, 1976—; vis. prof. Stanford U., 1974-75. Notes and comments editor Kans. Law Rev. Grad. fellow Harvard U., 1961-62. Fellow ABA Found., Iowa State Bar Found.; mem. Environ. Law Inst. (assoc.), Jo. Co. Her. Trust (founder, pres.), Order of Coif. Office: U Iowa Coll Law Iowa City IA 52242-0001

HINES, PATRICIA, social worker, educator; b. Watertown, N.Y., Nov. 4, 1947; d. Arthur and Bella (O'Neil) H. BS, SUNY, Oswego, 1969; MSW, SUNY, Buffalo, 1975; MPA, Fairleigh Dickinson U., 1982. Cert. Dr. Thomas Gordon Parent Effectiveness Trainer. Supr. social work Ocean County Bd. Social Svcs., Toms River, N.J., 1973-77; adminstrv. supr. social work Ocean County Bd. Social Svcs., Toms River, 1977-83, dep. dir., 1983-96; exec. dir. Ocean Fedn. Found., Toms River, 1996—; social work cons. Ocean County Vis. Homemaker Svc., Inc., Toms River, 1975-80, Cmty. Meml. Hosp., Toms River, 1978-79, Manchester Manor, Bartley Manor Convalescent Ctr., Ocean Convalescent Ctr., Barnegat Nursing Facility, Burnt Tavern Convalescent Ctr., Logan Manor, Medicenter, Freehold Care Ctr., Keswick Lifecare, So. Ocean, Madison Ctr., Royal Health, Regal Manor, Green Acres Manor; prin. in Sr. Care Planning Assocs.; instr. social work Gorgian Court Coll., Lakewood, 1975—. Chmn. Ocean County Title XX Coalition, 1977-82; bd. dirs. Ocean County Family Planning Program, Toms River, 1969-73, Mental Health Bd., 1983-84; mem. exec. bd. United Way, 1983-96; mem. Aging Network Svc., 1992—. Mem. NASW (nat. register clin. social workers), Acad. Cert. Social Workers (diplomate clin. social work). Home: 13 Bay Harbor Blvd Brick NJ 08723-7303 Office: 975 Hooper Ave Toms River NJ 08754-2009

HINES, PRESTON HARRIS, state supreme court justice; b. Atlanta, Sept. 6, 1943. AB in Polit. Sci., Emory U., 1965, JD, 1968. Bar: Ga. 1968, U.S. Dist. Ct. Ga. 1973. Law clk. Civil Ct. Fulton County, 1968-69; pvt. practice Marietta, Ga., 1969-74; judge State Ct. of Cobb County, 1974-82, Superior Ct. of Ga., 1982—. Chmn. attys. divsn. Cobb County United Appeal, 1972; participant Leadership Ga., 1975, Leadership Atlanta, 1978-79; pres. YMCA Cobb County, 1976; co-treas. Cobb Landmarks Soc., 1976-77; former bd. dirs. Cobb County Emergency Aid Assn., Cobb-Marietta Girls Club, Ga. chpt. Leukemia Soc. Am., Cobb County Children's Ctr., Met. Atlanta Red Cross, First Presbyn. Day Kindergarten; mem. cmty. adv. com. Marietta-Cobb County LWV; bd. dirs. Kennesaw Coll. Found.; trustee Cobb Cmty. Symphony. Named Outstanding Young Man of Yr., Ga. Jaycees, 1975, Boss of Yr., Cobb County Legal Secs. Assn., 1975-76, 83-84. Mem. ABA, State Bar Ga. (chmn. Law Day com. 1975, mem. exec. com. younger lawyers sec. 1974-76), Cobb Jud. Cir. (sec. 1972-73, chmn. Law Day com. 1972), Joseph Henry Lumpkin Inn of Ct. Ga., Atlanta Lawyers Club, Kiwanis (bd. dirs. Marietta chpt., chmn. Key Club com., past chmn. spiritual aims com., past pres.), Cobb County C. of C., Sigma Alpha Epsilon (Atlanta and Marietta chpts.). Office: Supreme Court 504 State Judicial Bldg Atlanta GA 30334*

HINES, ROBERTA LEIGH, medical educator; b. Manchester, N.H., Sept. 18, 1952. BA, U. N.H., 1974; MD magna cum laude, Dartmouth U, 1978. Diplomate Am. Bd. Anesthesiology, critical care cert.; lic. physician, Conn. Intern surgery Yale-New Haven Med. Ctr., 1978-79, asst. resident surgery, 1979-81, asst. resident anesthesiology, 1981-83, chief resident, 1982-83, cardiovascular fellow, 1983-84, assoc. physician, 1983-84, attending physician, 1984—, dir. recovery rm., 1984-87, dir. cardiothoracic ICU, 1984—, chief dept. anesthesiology, 1995; instr. anesthesiology Yale U. Sch. Medicine, 1982-83, asst. prof., 1984-90, assoc. prof., 1990-94, acting chair, 1994, prof., chmn. dept. anesthesiology, 1994—; assoc. examiner Am. Bd. Anesthesiologists, 1991—; lectr., vis. profs. various univs. and hosps. Mem. editl. bd. Soc. Cardiovascular Anesthesia, 1985-89, Jour. Clin. Anesthesia, 1992, 93, 94, 95, Seminars in Anesthesia, 1995; editor Heart Failure, 1988-92; editl. cons. Anesthesia and Analgesia, 1992, 93, 94, 95, Anesthesiology, 1992, 93, 94, 95, Am. Soc. Obstetrics and Gynecology, 1993, 94, 95; reviewer, editl. cons. Clin. Anesthesia, 1993, 94, 95; reviewer Critical Care Medicine, 1992, 93, 94, 95, Jour. Clin. Monitoring, 1992, 93, 94, 95; editor: (with C. Blitt) Monitoring in Anesthesia and Critical Care, 1994; contbr. articles to profl. jours., chpts. to books. Mem. Soc. Edn. in Anesthesia, Internat. Anesthesia Rsch. Soc., Am. Soc. Anesthesiologists (clin. circulation subcom. 1990, 91, critical care medicine subcom. 1991), Soc. Critical Care Medicine (program chair 1994, 95), Soc. Cardiovascular Anesthesiologists (program com. 1990, 91, 92, editl. bd. 1983-88), Assn. Univ. Anesthesiologists, Am. Soc. Critical Anesthesiologists, Conn. State Soc. Anesthesiologists. Office: Yale U Sch of Medicine PO Box 208051 333 Cedar St New Haven CT 06520-8051*

HINES, SUSAN CAROL, English language educator; b. Atlanta, Aug. 6, 1965; d. William Walter and Gretchen Ann (Heers) H. BA, U. Alaska, 1987; MA, U. B.C., Vancouver, Can., 1989; PhD, Ga. State U., 1998. Instr. English George Soros Found., Pragu, Czech Republic, 1991-92; prof. English Mid. Ga. Coll., Cochran, 1993-98, La Salle U., Phila., 1998—; founder Texts2000. Contbr. articles to profl. jours. Grantee Ga. Humanities Coun., 1995, NSF, 1996. Mem. MLA, AACE. Office: La Salle U Dept English Philadelphia PA 19141

HINES, VONCILE, special education educator; b. Detroit, Dec. 1, 1945; d. Raymond and Cleo (Smith) H. AA, Highland Park Community Coll., 1967; BEd, Wayne State U., 1971, MEd, 1975; MA, U. Detroit, 1978. Tchr. primary unit Detroit Bd. Edn., 1971-79, spl. educator, 1979-94; tchr. trainee Feuerstein's Instrumental Enrichment, 1988—; cons. Queen's Community Workers, Detroit, 1977—; evaluator Teen Profl. Parenting Project, New Detroit Inc., 1986-87; guest educator, critic "Express Yourself", Sta. WQBH 1400 AM, 1989. Author: I Chose Planet Earth, 1988; inventor in field. Recipient cert. of merit State of Mich., 1978, 88, cert. of appreciation Queen's Cmty. Workers, 1980, Wayne County Bd. Commrs., 1988, award of recognition Detroit City Coun., 1984, 88. Mem. Assn. for Children and Adults with Learning Disabilities, Assn. Supervision and Curriculum Devel., Nat. Thinking Skills Network, NAFE, Nat. Council Negro Women (presenter 1987), Met. Detroit Alliance of Black Sch. Educators. Democrat. Avocation: travel.

HINES, WILLIAM EUGENE, banker; b. N.Y.C., July 5, 1914; s. William J. and Alice M. (Callahan) H.; m. Dorothy H. Moore, June 4, 1949; children—Alice M., Dorothy H., Margaret M., William J., Elizabeth A., Robert J. Student, Columbia; grad., Rutgers U. Grad. Sch. Banking, 1948. With Bankers Trust Co., N.Y.C., 1950—; asst. v.p. Bankers Trust Co., 1958-63, v.p., 1963—; instr. Am. Inst. Banking, 1948-64, Am. Youth Hostels, 1954-65, former chmn., now dir. Chmn. planning bd. Village of Quogue, N.Y., 1991—; trustee Quogue Libr., 1995—. Mem. N.Y. Soc. Security Analysts, Accts. Club N.Y.C., Nat. Assn. Mental Health (nat. treas., dir. 1966, nat. trustee), Quogue (N.Y.) Assn. (pres. 1994-96, trustee 1992—), Shinnecock Yacht Club (commodore 1974-76, treas. 1980-94). Office: 119 E Parkway Rd Scarsdale NY 10583

HINES, WILLIAM EVERETT, publisher, producer, cinematographer, writer; b. San Bernardino, Calif., Apr. 2, 1923; s. Everett Ellsworth and Etta Elvira (Gillard) H. Student, UCLA, 1941-43, 46; BA, U. So. Calif., L.A., 1950, MA, 1951. Cameraman, film editor N.Am. Aviation, Inc., L.A. and Downey, Calif., 1951-53; founder, pres. Ed-Venture Films, L.A., 1954—; sec., treas. Sampson Prodns., S.A., Panama, 1956-60; v.p. Intro-Media Prodns., Inc., L.A., 1971-75; pres., pub. Ed-Venture Films/Books, L.A., 1985—; cons., expert witness, L.A., 1965—; lectr., instr., L.A., 1958—. Author: Job Descriptions For Film, Video & CGI, 5 edits., 1961-98, Operating Cinematography for Film and Video, 1997; writer Operating Tips column for Internat. Photographer mag., 1987—; contbr. numerous features to profl. jours.; producer: (ednl. film) Running For Sheriff, 1954 (Merit award 1955, 56); producer films., commls. Mem. profl. adv. bd. Calif. State U., Long Beach, 1973—, Northridge, 1974—; chmn. bd. trustees Producers and Film Craftsmen Pension and Health Plans, L.A., 1965-79. Sgt. USAAF, 1943-46. Recipient Spl. citation City of L.A., 1966. Mem. Nat. Assn. Broadcast Employees and Technicians, Internat. Cinematographers Guild, Internat. Alliance Theatrical Stage Employees (nat. exec. bd. dirs. 1989—, dir. tng. 1992—), Soc. Oper. Cameramen (charter, sec. 1978—, corp. liaison 1991—), recipient President's award for Lifetime Achievement Soc. Operating Cameramen, 1995, Am. Film Inst., Publishers Mktg. Assn., Nat. Geog. Soc., Assn. Film Craftsmen (pres., mem. exec. bd. 1957-79), Masons, Shriners, Ephebian Soc., Sigma Nu (Epsilon Pi chpt.). Avocations: tennis, fishing, travel, reading. Office: Ed-Venture Films/Books 1122 Calada St Los Angeles CA 90023-3115

HINESLEY, J. HOWARD, superintendent. Supt. Pinellas County Schs., Largo, Fla., 1990—. Recipient State Finalist for Nat. Supt. of Yr. award, 1993. Office: Pinellas County Schs Adminstrn PO Box 2942 Largo FL 33779-2942*

HINGLE, PAT, actor; b. Miami, Fla., July 19, 1924; s. Clarence M. and Marvin (Patterson) H.; m. Julia Wright, Oct. 25, 1979; children—Jody, Billy, Molly. BFA, U. Tex., 1949; PhD (hon.), Otterbein Coll., 1974. Numerous acting roles on stage, screen and TV, including End as a Man, 1953, On the Waterfront, 1953, The Long Grey Line, 1954, Festival, 1954, Cat on a Hot Tin Roof, 1955, 83, 93, Girls of Summer, 1956, The Strange One, 1956, Dakr at the Top of the Stairs, 1957, No Down Pavement, 1957, J.B., 1958, The Deadly Game, 1960, Macbeth, 1961, Troilus and Cressida, 1961, Strange Interlude, 1963, Blues for Mr. Charlie, 1964, A Girl Could Get Lucky, 1964, Invitation to a Gunfighter, 1964, The Glass Menagerie, 1965, The Odd Couple, 1966, Nevada Smith, 1966, Johnny No-Trump, 1967, Hang 'Em High, 1968, The Price, 1968, Bloody Mama, 1969, Child's Play, 1970, Norwood, 1970, Wusa, 1970, The Selling of the President, 1972, That Championship Season, 1973, Super Cops, 1973, Hazel's People, 1973, Running Wild, 1973, The Lady from the Sea, 1976, Independence, 1976, The Gauntlet, 1977, Norma Rae, 1979, When You Comin'Back, Red Ryder, 1979, Thomas A. Edison, Reflections of a Genius, 1978, A Life, 1980, Running Brave, 1982, Sudden Impact, 1983, Falcon and the Snowman, 1984, Brewster's Millions, 1985, Blue Skies, 1988, Rescue of Jessica McClure, 1989, Batman, 1989, The Kennedys of Massachusetts, 1989, The Drifters, 1990, Moon for the Misbegotten, 1990, The Habitation of Dragons, 1991, Gunsmoke III, 1991, Batman Returns, 1992, Citizen Cohn, 1992, Simple Justice, 1992, Will and Bart Show, 1992, Cheers, 1993, In the Heat of the Night, 1993, Lightnin' Jack, 1994, The Quick and the Dead, 1994, Friendly Suit, 1994, One Christmas, 1994, Batman Forever, 1995, Truman, 1995, Wings, 1996, Larger Than Life, 1996, Bastard Out of Carolina, 1996, A Thousand

Acres, 1996, Batman and Robin, 1997, The Shining, 1997, 1776, 1997-98, Touched By an Angel, 1999. Served with USNR, 1942-46, 51-52.

HINGSON, RALPH W., medical educator; b. July 21, 1948. BA in Internat. Relations, Johns Hopkins U., 1969, ScD, 1974; MPH, U. Pitts., 1970. Prof. dept. Socio-Med. Scis. and Community Medicine and Dept. of Pediatrics Boston U. Sch. of Medicine, 1986—; now dept. chair social behavioral scis. dept. Boston U. Sch. Pub. Health; cons. Nat. Inst. on Alcoholism and Alcohol Abuse, Nat. Ctr. for Substance Abuse Prevention, Nat. Trans. Rsch. Bd., Am. Cancer Soc., others; nat. bd. dirs. MADD; v.p. Pub. Policy. Contbr. numerous articles to profl. jours. Named one of America's 10 Outstanding Young Men U.S. Jaycees, 1984; recipient Hero award MADD. Home: 4 Louisburg Sq Boston MA 02108-1203 Office: Boston U Sch Medicine Sch Pub Health 715 Albany St Boston MA 02118-2526

HINGTGEN, JOSEPH NICHOLAS, psychologist, neuroscientist, educator; b. Dubuque, Iowa, Nov. 18, 1936; s. Joseph Theodore and Clara Adelaide (Jungers) H.; m. Eleanor Anita Quinn, June 26, 1965; children—Cynthia, Christina, Charles. B.S., Loras Coll., 1958; Ph.D., Loyola U., Chgo., 1963. Cert. psychologist, Ind. Instr. Ind. U. Sch. Medicine, Indpls., 1963-66; asst. prof. Ind. U. Sch. Medicine, 1966-70, assoc. prof., 1970-77, prof. psychology and neurobiology, 1977—, research assoc. Inst. Psychiat. Research, 1962-74, chief sect. research service, 1974-79, mem. exec. bd., 1974—, dir. grad. and postdoctoral program in med. neurobiology, 1984—, chair instnl. animal care and use com., 1989-97, chair grad. sch. admissions com., 1996—; lectr. psychology Marian Coll., 1963-88, adj. prof., 1988—. Mem. editorial bd.: Annual vols. Internat. Symposium on Neuronal Control of Bodily Function; author over 200 books, chpts. and articles on neurochem. correlates behavior, methods of psychobiology, animal models depression, stress and psychiatric disorders, infantile autism in profl. jours. Mem. Soc. for Neurosci. Roman Catholic. Office: Inst Psychiat Rsch Ind U Med Ctr Indianapolis IN 46202

HINKELMAN, RUTH AMIDON, insurance company executive; b. Streator, Ill., June 4, 1949; d. Olin Arthur and Marjorie Annabeth (Wright) Amidon; m. Allen Joseph Hinkelman, Jr., Oct. 28, 1972; children: Anne Elizabeth, Allen Joseph III. AB in Econs., U. Ill., 1971. Underwriter Kemper Ins. Group, Chgo., 1971-75; acct. exec. Near North Ins. Agy., Chgo., 1975-76; underwriter Gen. Reinsurance Corp., Chgo., 1976-78, asst. sec., 1978-79, asst. v.p., 1979-83, 2nd v.p., 1983-87, v.p., 1987—. Home: 133 Linden Ave Wilmette IL 60091-2838 Office: Gen Reinsurance Corp 233 S Wacker Dr Ste 4100 Chicago IL 60606-6379

HINKLE, BARTON LESLIE, retired electronics company executive; b. Miami Beach, Fla., Nov. 2, 1925; s. Frank Leslie and Kathryn Barton (Paddock) H.; m. Christine Smith, Aug. 22, 1949 (dec. Aug. 1955); m. Sabrena Sanford, Apr. 4, 1959; children—Karen, Douglas, Jean, Maria, Elizabeth. B.S. in Chem. Engring, Purdue U., 1949; M.S., Inst. Textile Tech., 1951; Ph.D., Ga. Inst. Tech., 1953. Research asst. Ga. Inst. Tech. Exptl. Sta., Atlanta, 1951-53; research engr. E.I. duPont de Nemours & Co., Inc., Richmond, Va., 1953-55; research supr. E.I. duPont de Nemours & Co., Inc., 1955-57, tech. supt., 1957-61, mfg. supt., 1961-62, asst. plant mgr., 1962-64; plant supt. E.I. duPont de Nemours & Co., Inc., Clinton, Iowa, 1964-69; product mgr. E.I. duPont de Nemours & Co., Inc., Wilmington, Del., 1969-71; lab. mgr. E.I. duPont de Nemours & Co., Inc., 1971-75, adminstrv. and planning asst., 1976-77, personnel mgr., 1977-84; v.p. human resources Electromagnetic Scis., Inc., Norcross, Ga., 1984-87, cons. human resources, 1987—. Sr. warden, vestryman St. Davids Episcopal Ch., 1975-78. Served with AUS, 1944-46, ETO. Republican. Patentee in field aerosol electrification, viscous polymers, cellophane. Home: 5773 Hunton Wood Dr Broad Run VA 20137-2019

HINKLE, BETTY RUTH, educational administator; b. Atchison, Kans., Mar. 18, 1930; d. Arch W. and Ruth (Baker) Hunt; m. Charles L. Hinkle, Dec. 25, 1950 (div.); children: Karl, Eric. BA, U. Corpus Christi, 1950; MS, Baylor U., 1956; MA, U. North Colo., 1972, EdD, 1979. Cert. tchr., Tex., Mass., Colo.; cert. adminstr., Colo. Tchr. Alice (Tex.) Ind. Sch. Dist., 1950, Waco (Tex.) Ind. Sch. Dist., 1951-52, 53-58, Hawaii Pub. Schs., Oahu, 1952-53, Newton Pub. Schs., Newtonville, Mass., 1962-63, Colorado Springs (Colo.) Pub. Schs., 1966-78; cons., exec. dir. spl. project unit Colo. State Dept. Edn., Denver, 1978-92, asst. commr., 1995, ret., 1995, rep. fed. rels. Office Commr. Edn., 1995-96, ret., 1996; pvt. cons., 1997—; pres. BH Cons., Colorado Springs, 1997—; mem. cabinet Colo. Dept. Edn., mem. Quality Coun., fed. liaison rep. to chief state sch. officers, Washington, chmn. 1996; alt. foreman Denver Grand Jury, 1983. Recipient Dept. Edn. Specialists award Colo. Assn. Sch. Execs., 1979, Employee Yr. award Colo. Dept. Edn., 1986, Fed. Ednl. Program Adminstrv. Coun. ann. award for Distinctive Svc. to Colo. Children, 1988. Mem. ASCD, Am. Assn. Sch. Adminstrs., Colo. Assn. Sch. Execs. (coord. coun. 1976-79, v.p. dept. edn. specialists 1974-75, pres. 1975-76), Colo. Assn. Sch. Execs., Phi Delta Kappa. E-mail: betty.hinkle@worldnet.att.net. Home: 1011 N 18th St Colorado Springs CO 80904-2852

HINKLE, BUCKNER, JR., lawyer; b. Lexington, Ky., May 14, 1948. BA, U. of South, 1970; JD, U. Ky., 1974. Bar: Ky. 1974. Ptnr. Stites & Harbison, Lexington, Ky. Bd. regents Morehead State U. Mem. ABA (governing com. Forum on Constrn. Law, sects. on litigation, pub. contract and surety law), Am. Coll. Constrn. Lawyers, Ky. Bar Assn., Fayette County Bar Assn. Office: Stites & Harbison 250 W Main St Ste 2300 Lexington KY 40507-1758

HINKLE, CHARLES FREDERICK, lawyer, clergyman, educator; b. Oregon City, Oreg., July 6, 1942; s. William Ralph and Ruth Barbara (Holcomb) H. BA, Stanford U., 1964; MDiv, Union Theol. Sem., N.Y.C., 1968; JD, Yale U., 1971. Bar: Oreg. 1971; ordained to ministry United Ch. of Christ, 1974. Instr. English, Morehouse Coll., Atlanta, 1966-67; assoc. Stoel Rives LLP (formerly Stoel, Rives, Boley, Jones & Grey), Portland, Oreg., 1971-77, ptnr., 1977—; adj. prof. Lewis and Clark Law Sch., Portland, 1978—; bd. govs. Oreg. State Bar, 1992-95. Oreg. pres. ACLU, Portland, 1976-80, nat. bd. dirs., 1979-85; bd. dirs. Kendall Cmty. Ctr., 1987-93, Youth Progress Assn., 1994-98, Portland Baroque Orch., 1999—; mem. pub. affairs com. Am. Cancer Soc., 1994-99; mem. Oreg. Gov.'s Task Force on Youth Suicide, 1996. Recipient Elliott Human Rights award Oreg. Edn. Assn., 1984, E.B. MacNaughton award ACLU Oreg., 1987, Wayne Morse award Dem. Com. Oreg., 1994, Tom McCall Freedom of Info. award Women in Comm., 1996, Civil Rights award Met. Human Rights Commn., 1996, Pub. Svc. award Oreg. State Bar, 1997. Fellow Am. Bar Found.; mem. ABA (ho. of dels. 1998—), FBA, Multnomah County Bar Assn., City Club Portland (pres. 1987-88). Democrat. Home: 14079 SE Fair Oak Way Milwaukie OR 97267 Office: Stoel Rives 900 SW 5th Ave Ste 2600 Portland OR 97204-1268

HINKLE, CHARLES NELSON, retired agricultural engineering educator; b. Lafayette, Ind., Sept. 12, 1930; s. Clifford Nelson and Ura L. (Frickey) H.; m. Delores J. Riemer, Aug. 18, 1951; children: Chris Nelson, Andrew John, Karen Sue, Laura Kay. Registered profl. engr., Ind. Agrl. market specialist Armco Steel Corp., Middletown, Ohio, 1953; assoc. prof. agrl. engring. S.D. State U., Brookings, 1957-65; prof. Purdue U., West Lafayette, Ind., 1965-70, 72-90, prof. agrl. engring dept., freshman engring dept., 1970-72, prof. emeritus, 1990—. Contbg. author: Ventilation of Animal Structures, 1983; contbr. articles to tech. jours. Preconstrn. coord. group. Laborers for Christ, mission bd. Lutheran Ch., Mo. Synod. With U.S. Army, 1953-55. Fellow Am. Soc. Agrl. Engrs. (dir. 1976-78); mem. Optimist Club (Optimist of Yr. Lafayette club 1990). Home: 400 N Sharon Chapel Rd West Lafayette IN 47906-4838 Office: Purdue U Dept Agrl Engring West Lafayette IN 47907

HINKLE, DOUGLAS PADDOCK, retired languages educator; b. Stamford, Conn., June 9, 1923; s. Frank Leslie and Kathryn B. Paddock Hinkle; m. Rose-Marie Hecker, Apr. 14, 1966; children: Anthony Barton, Monica Kathryn. BA, U. Va., 1952, MA, 1954. Lic. law enforcement officer, Ohio. Tchr. English Va. Pub. Schs., Nelson County, 1948-49; dir. binat. ctr. U.S. Info. Svc., La Paz, Bolivia, 1955-57, Caracas, Venezuela, 1958; asst. prof. Spanish and French Sweet Briar Coll., Amherst, Va., 1958-62, Southwestern U., Memphis, 1962-63; coll. editor modern langs. D.C. Heath & Co., Boston, 1963-65; assoc. prof. modern langs. Ea. Ky. U., Richmond, 1965-67; sr. lectr. modern langs. Ohio U., Athens, 1967-93, prof. emeritus modern langs., 1994—; program evaluator NEH, Washington, 1975-78. Author: (books) Faces of Crime, 1989, Mug Shots, 1990, (book of poetry) Poetry Is You, 1977, (slideshow/video program) Remembering Faces, 1990; mem. editl. bd. NAMES, 1968-74. Chmn. drug abuse com. Kiwanis Club, Athens, Ohio, 1983-87; cert. aux. Athens Police Dept., 1982-87, forensic artist, 1981-87; bd. dirs. Cen. Va. Crime Clinic, Richmond, 1994-97. Cpl. U.S. Army, 1943-46. Recipient Caballero, Order of Condor award Republic of Bolivia, 1957. Mem. Athens Bar Assn. (Citizenship award 1983), Fraternal Order of Police (hon. permanent mem.), Raven Soc., Phi Beta Kappa. Republican. Roman Catholic. Avocations: painting, historical linguistics, marksmanship. Home: 9305 Cason Rd Glen Allen VA 23060

HINKLE, JO ANN, English language educator; b. Alton, Ill., Feb. 7, 1961; d. Joe and Dorothy Louise (Stoneburner) Christen; m. Robert Eugene Hinkle, Aug. 19, 1989. BA, So. Ill. U., Edwardsville, 1984; MA, So. Ill. U., 1992. Instr. English, Lewis and Clark Coll., Godfrey, Ill., 1988—. Democrat. Unitarian. Avocations: fiction writing, violin. Home: 11 Maple Dr Dorsey IL 62021-1733

HINKLE, MURIEL RUTH NELSON, naval warfare analysis company executive; b. Bayonne, N.J., Mar. 17, 1929; d. Andrew and Florence Martha Ida (Nuber) Nelson; m. David Randall Hinkle, June 5, 1954; children: Valerie Nelson, Janet Lee, Sally Ann. Student, Md. Coll. for Women, 1947-49; BA, U. Md., 1951. Mgr. Wildacres Thoroughbred Horse Farm, Waterford, Conn., 1960-70; illustrator naval warfare predictions/computer simulated naval engagements Analysis & Tech., Inc., North Stonington, Conn., 1970-73; pres. Sonalysts, Inc., Waterford, Conn., 1973-88, 94-98, chmn., CEO, 1973—; also founder, past dir. Command Engring. & Tech. Svcs. Co.; pres., CEO, chmn. Stonington Farms Inc. (now Mystic Valley Hunt Club), 1983; adv. bd. Conn. Nat. Bank, 1988-92; chmn., CEO Anglers Assocs., 1989-96, S.I. Devel. Corp., 1989—; bd. dirs. Sonalysts Studios, Inc.; cons. anti-submarine warfare cruise missile weapon sys. GE Co., 1974-76; cons. Def. Nuclear Agy. for Tactical Nuclear Effects in anti-submarine warfare, 1974-75; spl. edn. substitute tchr. Waterford Pub. Schs., 1968-74. Co-author: Scope of Acoustic Communications Systems in Naval Tactical Warfare, 1974, Non-Acoustic Anti Submarine Warfare, 1974, Nuclear Weapons Effects in Anti Submarine Warfare, 1974, Measures of Effectiveness, Naval Tactical Communications, 1975, Destroyer ASW Barrier, 1977. Bd. trustees Thames Sci. Ctr., 1979-82. Recipient commendation for svcs. to submarine force Comdr. Submarine Squadron Ten, 1973, SBA New Eng. Contractor of Yr. award, 1986, SBA Adminstr.'s award for excellence, 1985, 86, bus. assoc. of yr. award Naval Inst., 1999. Mem. Am. Horse Shows Assn., Nat. Audubon Soc., Submarine Devel. Group Two Wives Club (pres. 1968), Sigma Kappa (pres. Senesk chpt. 1987-89), Navy Wives Club. Republican. Baptist. Home: 9 Cove Rd Stonington CT 06378-2304 Office: Sonalysts Inc PO Box 280 215 Parkway N Waterford CT 06385-1209

HINKLEY, EVERETT DAVID, JR., physicist, business executive; b. Augusta, Maine, Nov. 19, 1936; s. Everett David and Julina Margaret (Nolan) H.; m. Christine Marie Caso, June 18, 1960; children: Anne, Mark, Kristin, David. Student, Rensselaer Poly. Inst., 1954-56; BS in Engring. Physics, Washington U., St. Louis, 1958; MS in Physics, Northwestern U., 1961, PhD in Physics, 1963. Mem. rsch. staff Gen. Telephone Labs., Northlake, Ill., 1958-59; rsch.-teaching assoc. Northwestern U., Evanston, Ill., 1960-63; mem. tech. staff MIT Lincoln Lab., Lexington, Mass., 1963-76; v.p. Laser Analytics, Inc., Lexington, 1976-77; sect. mgr., program mgr., sr. rsch. scientist Calif. Inst. Tech. Jet Propulsion Lab., Pasadena, 1976-86; chief electronics scientist Lockheed Aero. Rsch. Lab., Valencia, Calif., 1986-87; chief scientist Hughes Aircraft Co., El Segundo, Calif., 1987-89; chief scientist, global change initiative TRW Space & Tech. Group, Redondo Beach, Calif., 1989-92; v.p., chief scientist Bainbridge Tech. Group, Ltd., L.A., 1992-93; sr. scientist, mgr. Sci. and Tech. Corp., 1993—; sr. rsch. fellow Ctr. for Internat. Rels., UCLA, 1991-94, mem. physics dept. adv. coun., 1993-95, chmn. atmospheric scis. adv. coun., 1991-98; mem. space systems and tech. adv. com. NASA, 1991-94. Author, editor: Laser Monitoring of the Atmosphere, 1976; contbr. articles to tech. jours., chpts. to books. Mem. Pasadena Lung Assn., 1980-86. Fellow Optical Soc. Am. (co-chmn. Conf. on Lasers and Electro-Optics 1986); mem. IEEE (sr., chmn. aerospace policy com. 1993-96, co-chmn. spaceborne photonics conf. 1991, co-chmn. combined optical-microwave earth and atmospheric sensing conf. 1993), IEEE Lasers and Electro-Optics Soc. (sec.-treas. 1987-89, bd. govs. 1987—), Wash. U. Alumni Coun., Sigma Xi, Tau Beta Pi. Avocations: racquetball, tennis, hiking.

HINKLEY, GERRY, newspaper editor. Now dep. mng. editor Milw. Jour. Sentinel, 1995—. Office: Milw Sentinel PO Box 661 333 W State St Milwaukee WI 53203-1305*

HINKLEY THOMPSON, CAROL JOYCE, philanthropy consultant, motivational speaker, writer; b. Detroit, Oct. 28, 1939; d. Carl O. and Vivial Louise (Hoover) Hinkley; m. Keith Francis MacKechnie Thompson, Oct. 6, 1962 (div. Aug. 1979); children: Kathryn M. Thompson Timms, Gregory R., Rebecca E. Thompson Cecin, Gwendolynne Thompson, Monica Clare. Student, Mercy Coll. Sch. Nursing, Detroit, 1960-62; BS magna cum laude, Tex. Woman's U., Denton, Tex., 1988. Office nurse Miller & Shore, Boston, 1962; pvt. perinatal educator Cambridge, Dallas, Tulsa, Mass., 1965-90; S.W. regional dir. Am. Soc. Psychoprophylaxis in Obs., Inc., Dallas, 1967-71; exec. dir. Family Life Info. Ctr., Dallas, 1973-81; mgr., co-founder Dallas Chamber Orch., 1979-82; major gifts officer U. North Tex., Denton, 1989-92; pvt. cons. nationwide, 1992—; chmn., exec. producer LORAC, Inc., Dallas, 1994—. Author: Childbirth Today: Prepared and Positive, 1978; columnist Grapevine Sun, 1980-81; contbr. articles to profl. jours.; established website on new breast cancer cells and diagnosis, micrometastatis, via cytokeratin staining. Originator, lobbyist for passage Child Safety Act U.S. Congress, Washington, 1965-66, The Breast and Ovarian Cancer Treatment Act, 1999; co-founder Stop the Hwy., Tulsa, 1966, Family Life Info. Ctr., Dallas, 1973; trustee Family Counseling and Children's Svcs., Big Bros., Big Sisters, Lenawee County, Mich., Estate and Fin. Planning Coun.; founder Project-Abandoned Mother and Child, Dallas, 1978, Leadership Dallas; bd. dirs. YWCA, Richardson, Tex., 1996-97; trustee, sec., dir. Tex. Meml. Mus., Austin; opened clinics in Dallas for perinatal care, parenting, and teenage pregnancy. Mem. AAUW, Internat. Platform Assn., Nat. Soc. Fund Raising Execs., Internat. Trade Assn., Dallas, Ind. Colls. Advancement Assn., The Dallas 40, Dallas Coun. World Affairs, Univ. Ind., Ctr. on Philanthropy. Avocations: the arts, econ. devel., flying, traveling, history, geneology. E-mail: lorac1@airmail.net. Office: LORAC Inc 11915 Stonehollow Dr Apt 1112 Austin TX 78758-3104

HINMAN, ALAN RICHARD, public health administrator, epidemiologist; b. New Orleans, Mar. 23, 1937; s. E. Harold and Katharine Ellen (Fradenburgh) H.; m. Donna Virgene Graham, Dec. 21, 1959 (div. 1962); m. Lucy Winkler Householder, May 30, 1965; children: Johanna Mary, Katharine Emily. BA, Cornell U., 1957; MD, Western Res. U., 1961; MPH, Harvard U., 1969. Intern in internal medicine Cleve. Met. Hosp., 1961-62, resident, 1962-64, chief resident, 1964-65; with USPHS, 1965-70, 77-96; advanced through grades to asst. surgeon gen., 1988; epidemic intelligence svc. officer Ctr. for Disease Control, Calif. State Dept. Health, 1965-66; regional evaluation officer malaria eradication program Ctrs. for Disease Control, Atlanta, 1966-67, San Salvador, El Salvador, El Salvador, 1967-68; asst. chief viral diseases br. epidemiology program Ctrs. for Disease Control, Atlanta, 1969-70; dir. Bur. Epidemiology, N.Y. State Dept. Health, Albany, 1970-71, asst. commr. epidemiology and preventive health svcs., 1971-75; asst. commr., dir. Bur. Preventive and Med. Svcs., Tenn. Dept. Pub. Health, Nashville, 1975-77; dir. divsn. immunization Ctr. for Prevention Svcs., Ctrs. for Disease Control, Atlanta, 1977-88; coord. nat. vaccine program Office of Asst. Sec. for Health, 1987-90; asst. surgeon gen. USPHS, 1988-96; dir. Nat. Ctr. for Prevention Svcs. Ctrs. for Disease Control, 1988-95; sr. advisor to dir. Ctrs. for Disease Control and Prevention, 1995-96; sr. cons. pub. health programs, coord. CDC World Bank collaboration on immunizations Task Force Child Survival and Devel., Atlanta, 1996—; adj. asst. prof. preventive and cmty. medicine Albany Med. Coll., Union U., 1970-75; adj. asst. prof. pub. health Rensselaer Poly Inst., 1971-75; assoc. clin. prof. dept. preventive medicine Vanderbilt U., 1975-77; clin. asst. prof. dept. cmty. medicine Divsn. Healthcare Svcs., U. Tenn., 1975-77; clin. asst. prof. dept. family and cmty. health Meharry Med. Coll., 1975-77; clin. assoc. prof. dept. preventive medicine-cmty. health Emory U. Sch. Medicine, Atlanta, 1978-90; vis. prof. Case Western Res. U. Sch. Medicine, 1984; adj. prof. Emory U. Sch. Pub. Health, 1990—; vis. lectr. Shanghai 1st Med. Coll., 1981; sr. cons. for pub. health programs, The Task Force for Child Survival and Devel., 1996—. Contbr. over 250 articles to profl. jours. Decorated D.S.M.; recipient Indian Health Svc. Dir. Spl. Excellence award, 1992. Fellow ACP, APHA (mem. gov. coun. 1975-77, mem. program devel. bd. 1984-86, mem. nominating com. 1984-86, chair 1985-86, chair-elect epidemiology sect. 1985-87, chair sect. 1987-89, past chair 1989-91, mem. exec. bd. 1991-95, spkr. governing coun. 1995—), Am. Acad. Pediat., Am. Coll. Epidemiology (mem. exec. bd. 1990-94, v.p. 1991-92, pres. 1992-93), Am. Coll. Preventive Medicine (regent 1974-75, 77-81, v.p. for pub. health 1975-76); mem. AMA, Am. Epidemiol. Soc., Am. Soc. Tropical Medicine and Hygiene, Am. Venereal Disease Assn. (bd. dirs. 1972-75, sec.-treas. 1975-77), Assn. Tchrs. Preventive Medicine, Infectious Diseases Soc. Am., Internat. Epidemiol. Assn., Physicians for Social Responsibility, Soc. Epidemiol. Rsch., Soc. Med. Decision Making. Home: 2194 Creek Park Rd Decatur GA 30033-2714

HINMAN, EVE CAISON, academic administrator; b. Charleston, S.C., May 17, 1951; d. Robert Lee Jr. and Ella Louise (Cross) Caison; m. William DeLeon Thrasher, June 9, 1972 (div. 1997); 1 child, Beverly Ann Thrasher Varner; m. Charles Steven Hinman, Feb. 27, 1998. Student, Francis Marion Coll., 1974-78, Trident Tech. Coll., 1990-91. Adminstrv. asst. to dean, acad. v.p. Francis Marion Coll., Florence, S.C., 1973-78; bus. mgr. dept. neurology Med. U. S.C., Charleston, 1978—. Pianist, asst. choir dir. Friendship United Meth. Ch., Cross, S.C., 1988-96, chairperson worship com., 1993. Mem. Assn. Am. Med. Colls. (group on bus. affairs), Southeastern Bluegrass Assn. Avocations: bluegrass rhythm guitar, singing and performing, classical guitar, piano, reading. Office: Med U SC Dept Neurology PO Box 250606 96 J Lucas St Charleston SC 29425

HINMAN, FRANK, JR., urologist, educator; b. San Francisco, Oct. 2, 1915; s. Frank and Mittie (Fitzpatrick) H.; m. Marion Modesta Eaves, Dec. 3, 1948. AB with great distinction, Stanford U., 1937; MD, Johns Hopkins U., 1941. Diplomate Am. Bd. Urology (trustee 1979-85). Intern Johns Hopkins Hosp., 1941-42; resident Cin. Gen. Hosp., 1942-44, U. Calif. Hosp., 1945-47; pvt. practice San Francisco, 1947-85; assoc. clin. prof. urology U. Calif., San Francisco, 1954-62, clin. prof., 1962—; urologist-in-chief Children's Hosp., 1957-85; adv. council Nat. Inst. Arthritis, Diabetes, Digestive and Kidney Diseases, 1983-86. Lt. USNR, 1944-46. Named Disting. Alumnus, Johns Hopkins U., 1995. Fellow ACS (regent 1972-80, vice-chmn. 1978-79, v.p. 1982-83), Royal Coll. Surgeons (hon., Eng.); mem. Am. Urol. Assn. (hon.), Am. Assn. Genito-Urinary Surgeons (hon., pres. 1981, Keyes medalist 1998), Clin. Soc. Genito-Urinary Surgeons (pres. 1979), Internat. Soc. Urol. (pres. Am. sect. 1980-84), Am. Assn. Clin. Urologists, Am. Fedn. Clin. Research, Soc. Pediatric Urology (founding mem., pres. 1971), Soc. Univ. Urologists (founding mem., pres. 1973), Am. Acad. Pediatrics (pres. urology sect. 1986), Urodynamics Soc. (founding mem., pres. 1980-82), Genito Urinary Reconstructive Soc. (founding mem.), Pan Pacific Surg. Assn. (v.p. 1980-83), Internat. Continence Soc., Brit. Assn. Urologic Surgeons (hon.) (St. Paul Medalist 1991), Soc. Française d'Urologie, Australasian Soc. Urologic Surgeons (hon.), Phi Beta Kappa, Alpha Omega Alpha. Clubs: Bohemian, St. Francis Yacht, San Francisco Yacht. Home: 1000 Francisco St San Francisco CA 94109-1127 Office: U Calif Med Ctr San Francisco CA 94143-0738 *Devoting two afternooons each week to research, teaching and other academic pursuits, uninterrupted by surgery and clinical practice, can result in satisfying advances.*

HINMAN, HARVEY DEFOREST, lawyer; b. Binghamton, N.Y., May 7, 1940; s. George Lyon and Barbara (Davidge) H.; m. Margaret Snyder, June 23, 1962; children: George, Sarah, Marguerite. BA, Brown U., 1962; JD, Cornell U., 1965. Bar: Calif. 1966. Assoc. Pillsbury, Madison & Sutro, San Francisco, 1965-72, ptnr., 1973-93, v.p., gen. counsel Chevron Corp., 1993—; bd. dirs. Legal Aid Soc., San Francisco. Bd. dirs., sec. Holbrook Palmer Park Found., 1977-86; bd. dirs. Phillips Brooks Sch., 1978-84, pres. 1983-84; trustee Castillija Sch., 1988-89; bd. govs. Filoli Ctr., 1988—, pres. 1994-95. Fellow Am. Bar Found.; mem. ABA, San Francisco Bar Assn. Office: Chevron Corporation 575 Market St San Francisco CA 94105-2856

HINMAN, ROSALIND VIRGINIA, storyteller, drama educator; b. London, May 5, 1938; d. Frederick and Gladys Molly (Seabrook) Ellam; m. Richard Leslie Hinman, Sept. 23, 1967; children: Katherine, Jeremy, Adrian, Isabel. Diploma in Dramatic Art, U. London, 1958; cert. in Edn., Cen. Sch. Speech and Drama, London, 1959; MALS, Wesleyan U., Middletown, Conn., 1998. Lectr. Ministere d'Edn. Nat. U. France, Tourcoing, Albi, 1960-63, U. de Caen, France, 1960-63; domestic & overseas exhibit adminstr. The Design Coun., London, 1963-66; artist Boces, Westchester, N.Y., 1968-70, Eugene O'Neill Theater Ctr., Waterford, Conn., 1980—; freelance performer Old Lyme, Conn., 1982—; performing artist Conntours Conn. Commn. on the Arts, Hartford, 1988—; artistic dir. Conn. Student Performing Arts Festival, Middletown, 1988-95. Author: Three Hairs From The Devil's Beard and Other Tales, 1990 (Parents' Choice Gold award 1992, ALA Notable 1992). Trustee Old Lyme (Conn.) Phoebe Griffin Noyes Libr., pres., 1992-95; mem. adv. bd. Conn. Storytelling Ctr., pres., 1994-97. Avocations: sailing, skiing, flyfishing, flytying. Home and Office: 1 Smith Neck Rd Old Lyme CT 06371-2617

HINNANT, CLARENCE HENRY, III, health care executive; b. Richmond, Va., June 7, 1938; s. Clarence Henry Jr. and Billie Louise (Chewning) H.; m. Barbara Ann Livingston, June 10, 1966 (div. Feb. 1971); children: C.H. IV, W.W. Tuck. BS, Va. Poly. Inst. and State U., 1961; BS magna cum laude, Med. Coll. Va., 1981. Math. tchr. Hopewell (Va.) High Sch., 1961-64; staff mem. Harper & Row Pub., N.Y.C., 1964-67; stockbroker Merrill Lynch & Co., Richmond, Va., 1967-71; pres. Lancaster Corp., White Stone, Va., 1971-81; v.p., treas. Westminster Canterbury, Lynchburg, Va., 1981-89; pres. Westminster Canterbury of Blue Ridge, Charlottesville, Va., 1989—; faculty Am. Coll. Healthcare Adminstrn., Washington, 1982-84. Contbr. articles to profl. jours. Rep. del. to State Conv., Richmond, 1973; pres., bd. dirs. Westminster Canterbury Blue Ridge Found. Fellow Am. Coll. Healthcare Adminstrs.; mem. Va. Assn. Non-Profit Homes for Aging (bd. dirs. 1983-84), S.R., Country Club of Va. (Richmond), Keswick Club, Rotary. Republican. Episcopalian. Avocations: golf, sailing. Home: 407 Key West Dr Charlottesville VA 22911-8423 Office: Westminster Canterbury Blue Ridge 250 Pantops Mountain Rd Charlottesville VA 22911-8694

HINNANT, HILARI ANNE, educator, educational consultant; b. Coral Gables, Fla., Mar. 23, 1953; d. William Walker and Margaret Elizabeth (Ennis) H.; m. M. Greg Miller. BS in Edn., U. Ga., 1974; MS in Edn., Fla. Internat. U., 1976. Art tchr. Banyan Elem. Sch. Dade County, Miami, 1974-79; tchr. Hilliard (Fla.) Sr. H.S., 1979-80, Callahan (Fla.) Jr. H.S., 1980-81, Duval County Pub. Schs., Jacksonville, Fla., 1981-83, The Am. Sch., Hamburg, West Germany, 1983-84, Brevard County Pub. Schs., Rockledge, Fla., 1984-86; clin. experience facilitator U. Wis., LaCrosse, 1987-88; tchr. Sarasota (Fla.) County Pub. Sch., Sarasota, Fla., 1988-90; asst. dir., exploratorium specialist Ednl. Rsch. Ctr. for Child Devel. U. South Fla., Tampa, 1990-91; dir. cen. and VA brs. YMCA Child Care, Milw., 1991-92; ednl. coord. Portage (Wis.) Project transition grant Coop. Edn. Svc. Agy. # 5, 1992-93; project transition grantee Coop. Svc. Agy. # 5, 1992-93; instr. child care & devel. Madison (Wis.) Area Tech. Coll., 1993-94; ednl. cons., 1994—; tchr. Bedford County Pub. Schs., 1994-96, Prince William Public Schs., 1996—; illustrator, writer Brevard County Maths. Curriculum Guide Rockledge; presenter Va. Assn. Early Childhood Edn. Conf., 1998; presenter and cons. in field. Author poems; contbr. articles to profl. jours. Selby grantee, 1989, tchg. tolerance grantee So. Poverty Law Ctr., 1997-98, Nat. Tree Trust grantee, 1998—. Mem. Nat. Assn. for Edn. Young Children, So. Early Childhood Assn., Midwest Assn. for Edn. Young Children (conf. presenter 1992, 93), Kappa Delta Pi (presenter internat. convocation 1988), Phi Delta Kappa (past pres. Sarasota-Bradenton chpt. 1989, rsch. grantee 1996), Delta Gamma. Democrat. Roman Catholic. Avocations: running, writing poetry, painting. Home: 3953 Conquest Ct Lake Ridge VA 22192-5185

HINNRICHS-DAHMS, HOLLY BETH, middle school educator; b. Milw., Oct. 31, 1945; d. Helmut Ferdinand and Rae W. (Beebe) H.; m. Raymond H. Dahms, June 11, 1983 (dec. Oct. 2, 1983). Student U. Wis., Milw., 1963-64, 66, 79—, Chapman Coll., 1965, 67, Internat. Coll. Copenhagen, summer 1968, Temple U., summer 1970, BA, Alverno Coll., 1971; postgrad.

Marylhurst Coll., 1972, Chapman Coll. World Campus Afloat, summers 1973, 74, Inst. Shipboard Edn., 1978, 79, 94. V.p. Hinnrichs Inc., Germantown, Wis., 1964-72; tchr. Germantown Recreation Dept., 1965; coach Milw. Recreation Dept., 1966-67; rep. for Wis., Chapman Coll., Orange, Calif., 1967; clk. Stein Drug Co., Menomonee Falls, Wis., 1967-72; tchr. Milw. area Cath. Schs., 1967-72, 83, 90-91, 1996—, maths 96-8), German Town Schs., St. Lawrence Sch., 1991-92; asst. mgr. Original Cookie Co. (Mother Hubbard's) Cookie Store, Northridge Mall, Milw., 1977-84, SAU-U Warehouse Deli, 1984-85, mgr. office, 1985-90; with Pilgrim Message Ctr., 1987—; substitute tchr. cath. schs. Milw. area, 1975-80, 83-89, 90, 92—, St. Rose Sch., 1989-90; tchr. Indian Community Sch., Milw., 1971-72, 88, 94—, Martin Luther King Sch., 1973-74, Crossroads Acad., Milw., 1974-75, Harambee Community Sch., 1980-83; tutor Brookfield (Wis.) Learning Ctr., 1986-87; Midwest rep. World Explorer Cruises, 1978-82; mem. replacement crew Hallmark Cards, 1997—. Mem. Wis. Math. Coun., Nat. Coun. Tchrs. Math., Internat. Inst. Milw. Friends of Mus., U.S. Lighthouse Soc., Great Lakes Lighthouse Soc., Miniss Kitigan Drum (Milw. chpt.), Golden Rule, Order Ea. Star, Alpha Theta Epsilon. Christian Scientist. Home: N88w15041 Cleveland Ave # 3 Menomonee Falls WI 53051-2239

HINOJOSA, DAVID, fraud examiner; b. Monterrey, Mex., Apr. 27, 1968; came to U.S., 1971; s. Antonio Florencio and Maria Del rosario (Jimenez) H.; m. Kimberly Evans, Dec. 22, 1996. BBA in Acctg. cum laude, Tex. A&I U., 1991. Cert. assoc. in ins. acctg. and fin. designation, cert. fraud examiner. Acctg. supr. State Farm Ins., Austin, Tex., 1992-95; fin. auditor State Farm Ins., Bloomington, Ill., 1995-96, fraud examiner, 1996—. Vol. income tax assistance V.I.T.A., Kingsville, Tex., 1991; State Farm liaison Hispanic Bus. Student Assn., Austin, 1993-95. Mem. Inst. Internal Auditors, Assn. cert. Fraud Examiners, Inst. Mgmt. Accts. (v.p. edn. and profl. devel. 1995, dir. acad. rels. 1994). Avocations: photography, computer graphics, genealogy. Office: State Farm Ins 112 E Washington St Bloomington IL 61701-1002

HINOJOSA, FEDERICO GUSTAVO, JR., judge; b. Edinburg, Tex., Apr. 16, 1947; s. Federico Gustavo and Zulema (Trevino) H.; m. Yolanda Silva, 1970 (div. 1977); 1 child, Cynthia; m. Magdalena Garza, Oct. 30, 1992. BA, Pan Am. U., 1969; JD, U. Houston, 1977. Bar: Tex. 1977, U.S. Dist. Ct. (so. dist.) Tex. 1977, U.S. Ct. Appeals (5th cir.) 1980, U.S. Supreme Ct. 1980. Assoc. Clark, Lowes & Carrithers, Houston, 1977-79; ptnr. Clark & Hinojosa, Houston, 1979-81; child support atty. Tex. Dept. Human Resources, McAllen, 1981-83; asst. dist. atty. Hidalgo County, Edinburg, 1983-84; assoc. Atlas & Hall, McAllen, 1984-87; ptnr. Lewis, Pettitt & Hinojosa, McAllen, 1987-91; justice Tex. Ct. Appeals for 13th Dist., Corpus Christi, 1991—. Sgt. USAF, 1970-74. Mem. State Bar Tex., Mexican-Am. Bar Tex., Mexican-Am. Bar Assn. Coastal Bend (dir. 1993-94), Hidalgo County Bar Assn. (dir. 1986-90). Democrat. Office: 13th Ct Appeals 100 E Cano St Edinburg TX 78539-4548

HINOJOSA, MARIA L., news correspondent; b. Mexico City, July 2, 1961; d. Raul and Berta (Ojeda) H.; m. German E. Perez, July 20, 1991. BA magna cum laude, Barnard Coll., 1984. Reporter Enfoque Nacional, San Diego, 1985, prodr., 1987; asst. prodr. weekend edit. NPR, Washington, 1986; freelance reporter, prodr. NPR, N.Y.C., 1989, correspondent, 1990—; prodr. CBS News Radio, N.Y.C., 1988; asst. prodr. CBS This Morning, N.Y.C., 1988; reporter Sta. WNYC Radio, N.Y.C., 1990; host radio Latino USA, N.Y.C., 1993—; host TV show Visiones Sta. WNBC, N.Y.C., 1993-95; urban affairs corr. CNN, N.Y.C., 1995—; lectr. in field. Author: CREWS--Gang Members Talk to Maria Hinojosa, 1995; mem. editl. bd. NACLA, N.Y. Bd. dirs. Columbia U. Coun. on Urban Affairs, N.Y.C., 1994. Recipient Unity award for radio feature Lincoln U., 1992, Cindy award Assn. Visual Communicatoes, 1993, Best Radio Feature award Soc. Profl. Journalists, 1993, Robert F. Kennedy Journalism award, 1995. Mem. Nat. Assn. Hispanic Journalists (Best Radio Report 1992), Nat. Alliance Third World Journalists, Newswoman's Club of N.Y. Avocations: reading, writing, dancing, hiking, yoga. Office: CNN 5 Penn Plz Fl 20 New York NY 10001-1878*

HINOJOSA, RAUL, physician, ear pathology researcher, educator; b. Tampico, Tamulipas, Mexico, June 18, 1928; came to U.S., 1962, naturalized, 1968; s. Raul Hinojosa-Flores and Melida (Prieto) Hinojosa; m. Berta Ojeda, Sept. 25, 1953; children—Berta Elena, Raul Andres, Jorge Alberto, Maria de Lourdes. B.S. in Biology, Inst. Sci. and Tech., Tampico, 1946; M.D., Nat. Autonomous U. Mexico, Mexico City, 1954. Asst. prof. U. Chgo, 1962-68, assoc. prof., 1968-97, assoc. prof. emeritus, 1998—, dir. temporal bone program for ear rsch., 1962—, rsch. assoc., 1968-88; rsch. fellow biophysics Harvard U., Boston, 1963; rsch. assoc. in neuropathology, Harvard U., 1964, rsch. fellow in anatomy, 1965. Editor temporal bone histopathology update Am. Jour. of Otolaryngology, 1989-94. Recipient Rsch. Career Devel. award NIH, 1962-65, rsch. grantee, 1962—, hearing rsch. study sect. grantee, 1988-92. Mem. AAAS, Internat. Otopathology Soc., Microscopy Soc. Am., Midwest Soc. Electron Microscopists, Assn. Rsch. in Otolaryngology, Am. Otological Soc., N.Y. Acad. Scis., Internat. Otopathology Soc. Home: 5316 S Hyde Park Blvd Chicago IL 60615-5706 Office: U Chgo 5841 S Maryland Ave Chicago IL 60637-1463

HINOJOSA, RICARDO H., federal judge; b. 1950. BA, U. Tex., 1972; JD, Harvard U., 1975. Judge U.S. Dist. Ct. (so. dist.) Tex.; law clk. Tex. Supreme Ct., 1975-76; assoc. Ewers & Toothaker, McAllen, Tex., 1976-79, ptnr., 1979-83; judge U.S. Dist. Ct. (so. dist.) Tex., McAllen, 1983—. Office: US Dist Ct So Dist Tex 1701 W Bus Hwy 83 Ste 1028 Mcallen TX 78501

HINOJOSA, RUBEN, congressman; m. Marty Hinojosa; 5 children. BBA, U. Tex., Austin; MBA, U. Tex.-Pan Am. Pres., CFO H & H Foods; mem. 105th-106th Congress from 15th Tex. dist., 1996—. Mem. Tex. State Bd. Edn.; mem. coordinating bd. Tex. Higher Edn. Named Hispanic Man of the Yr. Rio Grande Valley, 1994; recipient Lifetime Achivement award Hispanic Bus. Mag. Office: 1032 Longworth Washington DC 20515-4315*

HINOJOSA-SMITH, ROLAND, English language educator, writer; b. Mercedes, Tex., Jan. 21, 1929; s. Manuel Guzman and Carrie Effie (Smith) H.; divorced; children: Clarissa Elizabeth, Karen Louise, Robert Huddleston. BS, U. Tex., 1953; AM, N.Mex. Highlands U., 1963; PhD, U. Ill., 1969. Chmn. dept. modern langs. Tex. A&I U., Kingsville, 1970-74, dean Coll. Arts and Scis., 1974-76, v.p. acad. affairs, 1976-77; prof. English U. Minn., Mpls., 1977-81; Ellen Clayton Garwood prof. English U. Tex., Austin, 1981—, Mari Sabusawa Michener chair English, 1989-93, dir. Tex. Ctr. for Writers, 1989-93; USIA cons., Panama, Mex., Iraq, Germany, Austria, Poland, Spain, France, Wales. Author: Estampas del Valle, 1973 (Quinto Sol 1973), Klail City, 1976 (Casa de las Americas 1976), Korean Love Songs, 1978, The Valley, 1983, Dear Rafe, 1985, Partners in Crime, 1985, Fair Gentlemen of Belken County, 1986, Klail City, 1987, Becky and Her Friends, 1990, Los Amigos de Becky, 1991, Korea Liebes Lieder, 1992, The Useless Servants, 1993, Ask a Policeman, 1998; guest editor Am. Short Fiction, 1993-94. Illini (U. Ill.) Comback Guest, 1996; grand marshal for commencement U. Tex., 1994—. Recipient Outstanding Latino faculty mem. Hispanic Caucus Am. Assn. Higher Edn.; named Disting. Alumnus U. Ill. Coll. Liberal Arts, 1988, 98, Disting. Vis. Prof. U. Kans., summer 1994; Ford Found. fellow, 1979, Marshal of the Univ. U. Tex., 1995—. Fellow Soc. Spanish and Spanish Am. Studies; mem. MLA, Am. PEN, Academia Real de la Lengua, Hispanic Soc. Democrat. Roman Catholic. Home: 1800 E Stassney Ln Apt 802 Austin TX 78744-2749 Office: U Tex Dept English Austin TX 78712

HINSCH, GERTRUDE WILMA, biology educator; b. Chgo., Oct. 20, 1932; d. Hans Rudolph and Gertrude (Kalb) H. BSEd, No. Ill. U., 1953; MS, Iowa State U., 1955, PhD, 1957. Instr. Mt. Holyoke Coll., South Hadley, Mass., 1957-60; asst. prof., then assoc. prof. Mt. Union Coll., Alliance, Ohio, 1960-67; assoc. prof. U. Miami (Fla.), 1966-74; assoc. prof. U. South Fla., Tampa, 1974-80, prof., 1980—. Office: U S Fla Dept Biology Tampa FL 33620

HINSDILL, RONALD DWIGHT, bacteriology educator, immunotoxicologist; b. Chgo., Dec. 6, 1933; s. Kenneth Arthur and Mary Frances (Woodruff) H.; m. Jeanette Wilma, Aug. 27, 1960; children—Kevin, Tyson, Dawn. B.S. in Pharmacy, U. Ill.-Chgo., 1956, M.S. in Med. Microbiology, 1958; Ph.D. in Bacteriology, U. Wis., 1963. Research assoc. Rockefeller U., N.Y.C., 1962-66; asst. prof. bacteriology U. Wis., Madison, 1966-70, assoc. prof. bacteriology, 1970-76, prof. bacteriology, 1976-96; prof. preventive medicine U. Wis., 1976-96, chmn. dept. bacteriology, 1982-96, dir. Environ. Toxicology Ctr., 1974-83, prof. Emeritus, 1996—. Author: (with others) Fundamentals of Microbiology, 1974. Mem. Madison Area Commodore Users Group (co-founder 1982, pres. 1983-84). Home: 3006 Park St Middleton WI 53562-1604

HINSHAW, CHESTER JOHN, lawyer; b. Sacramento, Mar. 10, 1941; s. Chester Edward and Gertrude Lorraine (Miller) H.; m. Karen Forbes Breakey, Feb. 19, 1977. AB, Stanford U., 1963; JD, U. Calif., Berkeley, 1966. Bar: Calif. 1966, U.S. Dist. Ct. (no. dist.) Calif. 1967, U.S. Ct. Appeals (9th cir.) 1967, N.Y. 1968, U.S. Dist. Ct. (so. dist.) N.Y. 1972, U.S. Dist. Ct. (ea. dist.) N.Y. 1974, U.S. Ct. Appeals (2d cir.) 1974, U.S. Dist. Ct. (no. dist.) N.Y. 1980, U.S. Dist. Ct. (ea. dist.) Mich. 1982, U.S. Dist. Ct. (no. dist.) Tex. 1983, Tex. 1984, U.S. Ct. Appeals (5th cir.) 1984, U.S Supreme Ct. 1991. Assoc. Chadbourne & Parke, N.Y.C., 1967-74, ptnr., 1974-83; ptnr. Jones, Day, Reavis & Pogue, Dallas, 1983—; lectr. U. Calif. Berkeley, 1966. Mem. ABA, Tex. Bar Assn., Calif. Bar Assn. Office: Jones Day Reavis & Pogue PO Box 660623 2001 Ross Ave Ste 2000 Dallas TX 75201-2958

HINSHAW, DAVID B., SR., retired hospital administrator; b. 1923. Grad., Loma Linda U., 1947, post grad., 1947-48. Intern White Meml. Hosp., L.A., 1946-47; resident gen. and vascular surgery VA Hosp., U. Oreg., 1950-54; pvt. practice, 1954—; instr. Sch. Medicine, Loma Linda U., Calif., 1954-83; pres. Loma Linda Faculty Med. Group, 1973—, Adventist Health System Loma Linda Inc., Loma Linda, Calif., 1982—, Loma Linda U. Med. Ctr., Calif., 1983-94; pres. Loma Linda (Calif.) Mecantile Inc., 1988-94, ret., 1994; bd. dirs. Loma Linda U. Med. Ctr. With U.S. Army, 1948-50. Office: Loma Linda U Med Ctr PO Box 2000 Loma Linda CA 92354-0200*

HINSHAW, DAVID B., JR., radiologist; b. L.A., Dec. 28, 1945; s. David B. Sr. and Mildred H. (Benjamin) H.; m. Marcia M. Johns, Aug. 7, 1966; children: Amy, John. BA in German and Pre Medicine, Loma Linda U., Riverside, Calif., 1967; MD, Loma Linda U., 1971. Diplomate Am. Bd. Radiology in diagnostic radiology and neuroradiology. Intern Loma Linda U. Med. Ctr., 1971-72, resident diagnostic radiology, 1972-74; neuroradiologist 2d Gen. Army Hosp., Landstuhl, Fed. Republic Germany, 1975-77; asst. prof. Loma Linda U. Sch. Medicine, 1975-80, assoc. prof., 1981-85, prof., 1986—, vice chmn. dept. radiation scis., 1988-90, chmn. dept. radiology, 1990—; pres. med. staff Loma Linda U. Med. Ctr., 1994-95; vice chair faculty practice plan Loma Linda U., 1995—; dir. sect. magnetic resonance imaging, Loma Linda, 1983—; cons. U.S. Army Med. command, Europe, 1976-77, Jerry L . Pettis Meml. VA Hosp., 1980—. Contbr. numerous articles to profl. jours., book chpts. in field of radiology. Maj. U.S. Army, 1975-77. Recipient Pres's. award Loma Linda U., 1971, Donald E. Grggs award Internal Med. Fellow Am. Coll. Radiology, Walter E. McPherson Soc. (Outstanding Faculty Research award 1987); mem. AMA (Physicians Recognition award 1980-83, 84—), Am. Soc. Neuroradiology (sr., program com. 1989, chmn. pub. rels. com. 1989-90), Western Neuroradiol. Soc., Radiol. Soc. N.Am., Calif. Med. Assn., San Bernadino County Med. Assn., Inland Radiol. Soc. (pres. 1989-90), Calif. Radiol. Soc., Assn. Univ. Radiologists, Soc. Magnetic Resonance Imaging, Soc. Magnetic Resonance in Medicine, Fedn. Western Socs. Neurol. Scis., Am. Roentgen Ray Soc., Am. Soc. Head and Neck Radiology, L.A. Radiol. Soc., Soc. Chmn. Acad. Radiology Depts., Alpha Omega Alpha (pres. Epsilon chpt. 1987). Republican. Seventh-day Adventist. Avocations: traveling, electronics. Office: Loma Linda U Med Ctr Dept Radiology 11234 Anderson St MRI B 624 Loma Linda CA 92354-2804*

HINSHAW, EDWARD BANKS, broadcasting company executive; b. Aurora, Ill., Feb. 27, 1940; s. Lorenzo M. and Emily (Roach) H.; m. Victoria Leone Biggers, Jan. 16, 1965; children: Eric, Brian. Student, Harvard Coll., 1958-59, U. Minn., 1959-62. Announcer Sta. KSTP-Radio-TV, Mpls., 1959-64; announcer Voice of America, Washington, 1964-65; reporter, anchorman Jour. Broadcast Group, Inc. (formerly Sta. WTMJ, Inc.), Milw., 1965-70, editorialist, 1970-74, editorial dir., 1974—, mgr. public affairs, 1979-90, mgr. pers. and editorial affairs, 1990-94, v.p. human resources, 1994—; instr. broadcast journalism U. Wis., Whitewater, 1976, 79, 86. Trustee Nat. First Amendment congress, 1980-83; chair Wis First Amendment Congress, 1985; bd. chair Milw. Urban League, 1987; bd. dirs. Children's Outing Assn., 1987-90, Ko-Thi Dance Co., 1992—, pres., 1994-96; bd. dirs. Richard and Ethel Herzfeld Found., 1997—. Recipient DuPont-Columbia Citation in Broadcast Journalism, 1978; Abe Lincoln Merit award So. Baptist Radio-TV Commn., 1978; NCCJ Gold Media Medallion, 1977. Mem. Nat. Broadcast Editorial Assn. (pres. 1980-81), Wis. Broadcasters Assn. Found. (bd.), Milw. Press Club (bd. dirs. 1990—, pres.-elect 1992, pres. 1993, past pres. 1994), Knight of the Golden Quill, Sigma Delta Chi (Disting. Svc. award 1977, Excellence in Journalism award 1988, Freedom of Info. award 1994). Office: Jour Broadcast Group Inc 720 E Capitol Dr Milwaukee WI 53212-1308

HINSHAW, ERNEST THEODORE, JR., private investor, former Olympics executive, former financial executive; b. San Rafael, Calif., Aug. 26, 1928; s. Ernest Theodore and Ina (Johnson) H.; m. Nell Marie Schildmeyer, June 24, 1952; children: Marc Christopher, Lisa Anne, Jennifer, Amy Lynn. AB, Stanford U., 1951, MBA, 1957. Staff asst. to pres. Capital Research and Mgmt. Co., Los Angeles, 1957-58; dir. planning Capital Research and Mgmt. Co., 1967-68; fin. analyst Capital Research Co., Los Angeles, N.Y.C., 1958-68; v.p. Capital Research Co., 1962-71, mgr. N.Y.C. office, 1962-66; dir., exec. v.p. Am. Funds Service Co., Los Angeles, 1968-69; pres. Am. Funds Service Co., 1969-72, chmn. bd., 1972-82; dir. pres. Capital Data Systems, Inc., Los Angeles, 1971-73; chmn. Capital Data Systems, Inc., 1973-79; v.p. Capital Group, Inc., Los Angeles, 1973-83; sr. v.p. Growth Fund Am., 1973-74, pres., 1974-76, chmn. bd., 1976-82, dir., 1974-96; sr. v.p. Income Fund Am., 1973-74, pres., dir., 1974-76, chmn. bd., 1976-82, dir., 1974-96; commr. yachting 1984 Olympic games Los Angeles Olympic Organizing Com., 1980-84; dir. Capital Research & Mgmt. Co., 1972-83; mem. guest faculty Northwestern U. Transp. Center, 1965-66; mem. ops. com. Investment Co. Inst., 1970-74. Bd. dirs. Newport Harbor Nautical Mus., 1989-92, Girl Scout Coun. Orange County, 1993—, chair fin. com., 1996-97, treas., 1998—; trustee Friends of Girl Scouts Trust; mem. investment com. Hoag Hosp. Found., 1992-97. Served to 1st lt. USMC, 1951-53. Mem. Soc. Airline Analysts (sec. 1965-66), Los Angeles Soc. Fin. Analysts, N.Y. Soc. Security Analysts, Am. Statis. Assn., Town Hall Calif., Nat. Kite Class (pres. 1968-69), Lido 14 Internat. Class Assn. (pres. 1978-79), Assn. Orange Coast Yacht Clubs (commodore 1976), So. Calif. Yachting Assn. (commodore 1979), B.O.A.T., Inc. (dir. 1977-81), Pacific Coast Yachting Assn. (dir. 1979-80), U.S. Yacht Racing Union (dir. 1980-81), U.S. Sailing Ctr. Long Beach, Calif. (adv. coun. mem.). Democrat. Clubs: Wall Street (N.Y.C.); University (Los Angeles); Lido Isle Yacht (Newport Beach, Calif.) (commodore 1973); Stanford U. Sailing (trustee 1984-96); St. Francis Yacht (San Francisco); Ft. Worth Boat. Home: 729 Via Lido Soud Newport Beach CA 92663-5530

HINSHAW, KEITH C., veterinarian. DVM, U. Calif., Davis, 1980, MPVM, 1981. V.p. animal health Phila. Zool. Garden, 1982—. Office: Phila Zool Garden 3400 W Girard Ave Philadelphia PA 19104-1139

HINSHAW, MARK LARSON, architect, urban planner; b. Glendale, Calif., Aug. 17, 1947; s. Lerner Brady and Alice Elaine (Larson) H.; m. Caryl Ann Kunsemuller, Dec. 21, 1968 (div. 1982); 1 child, Erica; m. Marilyn Kay Smith, June 18, 1983 (div. 1997); children: Lindsay, Christopher. BArch magna cum laude, U. Okla., 1970; M Urban Planning, CUNY, 1972. Registered architect, Wash. Sr. planner Planning Dept., Anchorage, 1976-77; project planner TRA, Seattle, 1977-82; urban designer City of Bellevue, Wash., 1982-90; ind. cons., 1991-97; dir. urban design Loschky Marquardt Nesholm Architects, Seattle, 1997—; architect-in-the-sch. Seattle Sch. Dist., 1979. Columnist on architecture, urban design Seattle Times, 1993—; author: Citistate Seattle: Shaping a Modern Metropolis, 1999; contbr articles to profl. publs. and books. Mem. Urban Beautification Commn., Anchorage, 1975, Design Jury, Hemet (Calif.) Civic Ctr. Competition, Seattle Design Commn., 1990-91; mem. Downtown Seattle Design Rev. Bd. 1st lt. USAF, 1972-76. NEA grantee, 1975; recipient merit award for Hist. Preservation, City Seattle, 1983. Fellow AIA (pres. Seattle chpt. 1992-93); mem. Am. Planning Assn. (sec. Wash. chpt. 1982, v.p. 1983-85, pres. 1987-89), Am. Inst. Cert. Planners (mem. nat. bd. 1994-98). Office: 801 2nd Ave Fl 5 Seattle WA 98104-1509

HINSON, CLAUDIA BURNS, elementary school educator; b. Dallas, July 2, 1921; d. Claude L. and Madge I. Burns; children: Kathleen D. Hinson Baillargeon, C. Daniel Hinson. BA, Baylor U., 1943; MA, Pepperdine U., 1977. Cert. elem. and spl. edn. tchr., Calif. Copywriter Moody Bible Inst., Chgo.; dir. youth program Cen. Tex. Conf., Meth. Ch., Waco, Tex.; tchr. Corona (Calif.)-Norco Unified Sch. Dist.; dir. seminars on religious edn.; freelance writer; artistic dir. musical theater; mem. Colleagues Pepperdine U. Contbr. articles and poetry to profl. publs. Recipient hon. svc. award Calif. PTA. Mem. Nat. Coun. Tchrs. English, Corona-Norco Tchrs. Assn. (rep.), Instrnl. Improvement Coun., Tchrs. and Writers Collaborative, Poetry Soc. Am.

HINSON, DAVID RUSSELL, airline company executive, federal agency administrator; m. Ursula; 3 children. Student, U. Wash. Fighter pilot USN, 1956-60; airline and engring. pilot, 1960-72; pilot Northwest Airlines; flight instr. United Airlines; chief pilot for flight tng. West Coast Airlines; dir. flight stds. and engring. Hughes Air West; founder Hinson-Mennella Inc.; founder, dir. Midway Airlines Inc., Chicago, Ill., 1979—, chmn., chief exec. officer, 1985—; exec. v.p. mktg. bus. devel. McDonnell Douglas Corp.; adminstr. FAA, Washington, 1993-96; bd. dirs. The Continental Bank, Chgo., Northwestern Railroad, Penwest Inc. Trustee Lewis & Clark Coll., U. Chgo. Grad. Sch. Bus., U. Wash. Grad. Sch. Bus. Recipient Ops. award Aviation Week and Space Tech., 1997. Avocations: aviation history, collecting aviation art. Office: Fed Aviation Adminstrn 800 Independence Ave SW Washington DC 20591-0001

HINSON, GALE MITCHELL, social worker; b. Bklyn., June 29, 1951; d. Albert Lee and Doris (Purdie) Mitchell; m. Lawrence Hinson, Aug. 31, 1975; 1 child, Terrence. Assocs degree in Community Svcs., SUNY, Farmingdale, 1972; BSW, Adelphi U., 1984, MSW, 1986. Cert. social worker II, N.Y.; cert. criminal justice specialist. Mem. staff Nassau County Dept. Mental Health, Mental Retardation, Mineola, N.Y.; forensic mental health specialist Nassau County Correctional Ctr., East Meadow, 1987; psychiat. social worker I Nassau County Correctional Ctr., East Meadow, N.Y., 1987—; forensic mental health specialist. Commr.'s rep. multicultural adv. com.; mem. Ryan White Title I HIV Health Svcs. Planning, Nassau and Suffolk Counties; mem. Christian Edn., trustee bd. Naomi Temple AME Zion Ch., Roosevelt, N.Y. Mem. NASW, Nat. Assn. Forensic Social Workers. Home: 6 Brown Ave Hempstead NY 11550-6907 Office: Nassau County Dept Mental Health Mental Retardation 240 Old Country Rd Mineola NY 11501-4245

HINSON, HOWARD HOUSTON, petroleum company executive; b. Fletcher, Okla., Mar. 3, 1913; s. Jasper Lafayette and Dana (Wunsch) H.; m. Louise Lawson, May 31, 1934 (dec.); children: Barbara Ann Hinson Brightwell, Larry Howard; m. Doris Lloyd Findley, 1976. B.S., Tex. Tech Coll., Lubbock, 1934, M.S., 1945; postgrad., Advanced Mgmt. Program, Harvard U. Registered profl. engr., Tex. Jr. petroleum engr. helium plants U.S. Bur. Mines, Tex., 1936-40; asst. petroleum engr. U.S. Bur. Mines, 1940-42, asso. petroleum engr., 1942-43, petroleum engr., 1943-44, sr. petroleum engr., 1944-47, asst. supervising engr., 1947-48; chief prodn. research engr. Continental Oil Co., 1948-50, asst. mgr. prodn., 1950-52, southwestern regional gen. mgr., 1952, v.p. fgn. dept., 1953-57, dir., 1958-66, v.p. fgn. exploration and prodn., 1957-61, v.p., gen. mgr. internat. exploration, prodn., 1961-66, cons., 1966-68; pres., dir. Imperial-Am. Mgmt. Co., Houston, 1968-69; partner Hinson & Hall, 1969-72, Hinson, Hall & Smith, 1971-72; pres., chmn. and CEO Tex. Pacific Oil Co., Inc., Dallas, 1972-82. *Howard Houston Hinson as Vice President-exploration-worldwide for Conoco, had the major responsibility for finding oil and gas in Libya, Dubai and the North Sea. He assisted in establishing Conoco's oil and gas production offshore the Gulf of Mexico. He was a member of Conoco's Executive Management Committee and Board of Directors. The production of over one million barrels per day of oil from Libya made Conoco, Marathon and Amerada into large international oil companies. The combined production from the properties in Libya and Dubai provided over two percent of the world's oil production for many years.* Contbr. articles to profl. jours. Recipient Distinguished Engr. award Tex. Tech U., 1975, Distinguished Alumnus award, 1976. Mem. Soc. Petroleum Engrs., Am. Assn. Petroleum Geologists, Willowbrook Club, Holytree Club, Tau Beta Pi.

HINSON, JACK ALLSBROOK, research toxicologist, educator; b. Mullins, S.C., Aug. 18, 1944; s. Layton Liston and Will (Allsbrook) H.; m. Joanne Edwards Kidd; children: Edward Thomas, Richard William. BS, Coll. of Charleston, 1966; MS, U. S.C., 1968; PhD, Vanderbilt U., 1972. Postdoctoral fellow Nat. Inst. of Health, Bethesda, Md., 1972-75, sr. staff fellow, 1975-80; rsch. toxicologist Nat. Ctr. Toxicological Rsch., Jefferson, Ark., 1980-90, chief biochem. mechanisms br., 1989-90; adj. prof. U. Ark. Med. Sci., Little Rock, 1980-90; prof., dir. div. toxicology U. Ark. Med. Sci., Little Rock, 1990—; dir. interdisciplinary toxicology program, occupl. and environ. health program U. Ark. Med. Sci., 1990-95; chmn. Ark. Toxicology Symposium, 1992—; adj. assoc. prof. U. Tenn. Ctr. for Health Scis., Memphis, 1982-90; vis. fellow Middlesex Hops. Med. Sch., London, 1982; vis. prof. U. Leiden, The Netherlands, 1986. Editor Drug Metabolism Revs., 1997—, mem. editl. bd., 1995-97; mem. editl. bd. Toxicology and Applied Pharmacology, 1980-89, 96—, Jour. Toxicology and Environ. Health, 1991—; contbr. chpts. to books and articles to profl. jours. Mem. Soc. Toxicology (pres. South Ctrl. chpt. 1990-92), Am. Soc. Pharmacology and Exptl. Therapeutics, Internat. Soc. for Study of Xenobiotics, Am. Indsl. Hygiene Assn. Episcopalian. Home: 8 Piedmont Ln Little Rock AR 72223-2232 Office: U Ark Med Sci Divsn Toxicology 4301 W Markham St # 638 Little Rock AR 72205-7101

HINSON, KAREN ELIZABETH, secondary education educator; b. Balt., Sept. 16, 1966; d. William Dean and Gertrude Elizabeth (Gramlich) H. Student, Randolph Macon Woman's Coll., 1984-86; BA, Washington Coll., Chestertown, Md., 1988; MS, Johns Hopkins U., 1999. Cert. social studies tchr. grades 5-12, earth scis. tchr. 7-12, Md. Sports info. dir. Washington Coll., 1988-89; educator Echo Hill Outdoor Sch., Worton, Md., 1989; edn. asst. mgr. Chesapeake Bay Found., Annapolis, Md., 1990-93; instr. Hurricane Island Outward Bound Sch., Balt., 1994; tchr. Western Sch. Tech. and Environ. Sci., Balt., 1993-95, social studies dept. chair, 1995—, sci. and tech. dept. chair, 1999—; mem. Md. State Dept. Edn. Coun. Ednl. Equity, Balt., 1995-98; multicultural liaison Balt. County Pub. Schs., 1995-98, svc. learning coord., 1996-99, testing coord., 1996-99; presenter in field. Author (curricula) Living Lessons, 1994, Gender Equity in Education, 1995; editor (curricula) Communications in the Workplace, 1997; adv. com. (video prodn.) Gender/Equity Video, 1996. Earthwatch-Bell Atlantic/Lotus Tchr. fellow, Bell Atlantic Found., Oxford, Eng., 1997; recipient Health Svcs. award ARC, Balt., 1987, Nat. Women's Collegiate Athletic award, 1988; C-SPAN Nat. Equipment for Edn. grantee, 1998. Mem. ASCD, Nat. Coun. Social Studies, Nat. Coalition for Sex Equity in Edn. Avocations: kayaking, opera, reading, flute, hiking. Office: Western Sch Tech & Environ Sci 100 Kenwood Ave Baltimore MD 21228-3610

HINSON, ROBERT C., career officer. BS in Edn., U. Tenn., 1970; student, Squadron Officer Sch., 1977; MA in Humanities and Edn., Ark. State U., 1977; student, Air Command and Staff Coll., 1982, Nat. War Coll., 1989, Harvard U. Commd. 2d lt. USAF, 1971, advanced through grades to maj. gen., 1998; adminstrv. specialist 379th Aeromed. Airlift Wing, Scott AFB, Ill., 1970-71; officer trainee Officer Tng. Sch., Lackland AFB, Tex., 1971; B-52 co-pilot, aircraft comdr. and instr. pilot 97th Bombardment Wing, Blytheville AFB, Ark., 1973-77; air staff tng. officer Sec. Air Force Personnel Coun., Pentagon, Washington, 1977-78; pilot, instr. pilot and flight evaluator 529th Bomb Squadron, Plattsburgh AFB, N.Y., 1979-82; various assignments Plattsburgh AFB, N.Y., 1986-88, 1982-86; chief strategic nuc. policy br., joint staff and J-5 Pentagon, Washington, 1989-91, exec. officer strategic plans and policy directorate, 1989-91; comdr. 99th Ops. and Maintenance Group, Ellsworth AFB, S.D., 1991-93; wing comdr. 99th Tactics and Tng. Wing, Ellsworth AFB, S.D., 1991-93; various assignments USAF, 1993-97; dir. ops. Hdqs. Air Force Space Command, Peterson AFB, Colo., 1997—. Decorated Legion of Merit. Office: HQ AFSPCI DO 150 Vandenberg St Ste 1105 Peterson AFB CO 80914-4170

HINSON, ROBERT WILLIAM, advertising executive, consultant; b. Neptune, N.J., Nov. 30, 1944; s. Herbert William and Bernice (Stadelhofer) H. AB in Econs. and Sociology, Boston Coll., 1966. Media planner Benton & Bowles, Inc., N.Y.C., 1968-70; v.p., assoc. media dir. SSC&B: Lintas Worldwide, N.Y.C., 1970-74, sr. v.p., dir. media ops., 1976-80; v.p., assoc. media dir. Foote Cone & Belding, Inc., L.A., 1974-76; exec. v.p., chmn. mgmt. com., chmn. ops. com., dir. media svcs. Rosenfeld, Sirowitz & Lawson, Inc., N.Y.C., 1980-85, exec. v.p., dir. mktg. and media svcs., chief adminstrv. officer, 1986-87; pres., chief exec. officer Hinson and Assocs., Inc., N.Y.C., N.J., 1987-91; cons. in field, 1991—. Author: Media Leverage, 1985. Media dir. Tuesday Team, Reagan-Bush '84 campaign, 1984; sustaining mem. Rep. Nat. Com.; mem. Ronald Reagan Presdl. Libr. Found., Monmouth County (N.J.) Rep. Orgn.; bd. dirs. Monmouth (N.J.) Symphony Orch. Mem. NATAS, Internat. Assn. TV, Arts and Scis., Internat. Radio and TV Soc., Media Dirs. Industry Coun., Am. Assn. Advt. Agys. (media policy com. 1980-87), Am. Rsch. Found. (media com. coun. 1983-86), Boston Coll. Alumni Assn., Wagner Soc. N.Y., Monmouth County Hist. Soc., Alliance Francaise of Monmouth County (N.J.), Alliance Francaise of Ft. Lauderdale, Nature Conservancy, Nat. Trust for Hist. Preservation, N.Y. Athletic Club, Deal (N.J.) Golf and Country Club, Allenhurst (N.J.) Beach Club, Coral Ridge (Fla.) Country Club. Roman Catholic. Home: PO Box 33 Allenhurst NJ 07711-0033 also: 133 N Pompano Beach Blvd Pompano Beach FL 33062-5725

HINSON, SUE ANN, legal assistant, orthopedic nurse; b. Springfield, Ohio, Oct. 27, 1952; d. William H. and Joanna M. (Waits) H. Diploma, Cmty. Hosp. Sch. Nursing, Springfield, 1973; AS in Legal Assisting, Fla. Met. U., 1998, student. RN, Fla.; cert. legal nurse cons. Fla. Risk Mgmt. Inst. Staff nurse Cmty. Hosp., Springfield, 1973-78, 79-86, Mt. Carmel Med. Ctr., Columbus, Ohio, 1978-79; staff nurse orthopedics dept. North Ridge Med. Ctr., Ft. Lauderdale, Fla., 1986-90; nurse Prison Health Svcs., Ft. Lauderdale, Fla., 1990-93; orthopedic nurse Nurse Care, Ft. Lauderdale, Fla., 1993-94, Fla. Med. Ctr., Ft. Lauderdale, Fla., 1995-96, Colonial Palms West, 1994-95; legal asst. Michael B. Morsillo, Ft. Lauderdale, 1996—. Mem. Nat. Assn. Orthopedic Nurses (cert.), Nat. League Nursing, Nat. Assn. Legal Assts.

HINTHORN, MICKY TERZAGIAN, volunteer, retired; b. Jersey City, N.J., July 5, 1924; d. Bedros H. and Aznive (Hynelian) Terzagian; m. Wayne L. Hinthorn, Aug. 11, 1957. BS in Occupational Therapy, U. So. Calif., 1953; MBA, Coll. Notre Dame, Belmont, Calif., 1984. Registered occupational therapist. Gen. office worker Drake Secretarial Coll., Jersey City, 1941-42; sec., expediter Western Electric Co., Kearny, N.J., 1943-45; sec. div. edn. CBS, NYC, 1945-46; sec. to v.p. sales Simon and Schuster, Inc., NYC, 1947-51; gen. office worker in Sch. of Edn. U. So. Calif., L.A., 1951-52; occupational therapist Palo Alto (Calif.) Clinic, 1954-55; chief occupational therapist Children's Health Coun., Palo Alto, 1954-56; sec. to chief mil. engr. Lenkurt Electric Co., San Carlos, Calif., 1956-58; sr. sec. re-entry program Bank of Am., Redwood City, Calif., 1979-80; ret., 1980; organizer occupational therapy dept. Children's Health Coun., Palo Alto, Calif., 1954, chief 1954-56. Author, editor numerous newsletters and orgns.' papers. Charter mem., membership chair U. So. Calif. Pres. Cir., San Francisco, 1978-80; treas. North Peninsula chpt. San Francisco Opera Guild, San Mateo, Calif., 1979; vol. pub. info. chair re-election San Mateo County Supr., Redwood City, Calif., 1978; founder, charter pres. Friends of Belmont (Calif.) Libr., 1974-75; mem. Coastside Fireworks Com., 1989-94, chair corp. sponsorship, 1992-93. Recipient Hon. Mem., Friends of San Francisco Pub. Libr., 1974. Mem. AAUW (pres. San Mateo br. 1976-77; Half Moon Bay br. chair local scholarships 1992, 99, historian 1992-94, corr. sec. 1995-97, name grant honoree Edn. Found. Jodi Gordon Endowment 1991-92), Half Moon Bay Coastside C. of C. (chair bus. edn. scholarships 1992, 93, Recognition award 1993), Seton Med. Ctr. Coastside Aux. (scholarship com. 1996—), U. So. Calif. Alumni Assn. (life), Coll. of Notre Dame Alumni Assn., Friends of Filoli, Friends of Half Moon Bay Libr., Coastside Women's Club (scholarship com. 1999). Avocations: photography, walking, reading, writing, attending performing arts events. Home: PO Box 176 Half Moon Bay CA 94019-0176

HINTIKKA, JAAKKO, philosopher, educator; b. Helsingin pitäjä, Finland, Jan. 12, 1929; s. Toivo Juho and Lempi J. (Salmi) H.; m. Merrill Bristow Provence, Feb. 11, 1978 (dec.); m. Ghita Holmström, Dec. 19, 1987. Cand. Phil. Lic. Phil., U. Helsinki, Finland, 1952, Dr.Phil., 1956; exchange student, Williams Coll., 1948-49; post-doctoral scholar, Harvard U., 1954; hon. doctorate, U. Liège, 1984, Jagiellonian U., 1995. Jr. fellow Soc. Fellows, Harvard U., 1956-59; prof. philosophy U. Helsinki, 1959-70; research prof. Acad. Finland, 1970-81; prof. philosophy Fla. State U., Tallahassee, 1978-90, McKenzie prof., 1986-90, also prof. computer sci., 1986-90; prof. Boston U., 1990—; vis. prof. Brown U., 1962, U. Calif., Berkeley, 1963, Hebrew U. Jerusalem, 1974; part-time prof. philosophy Stanford U., 1964-82, Immanuel Kant lectr., 1985; John Locke lectr. Oxford (Eng.) U., 1964; fellow Center for Advanced Study in Behavioral Scis., 1970-71; Hägerström lectr. U. Uppsala, 1983; co-chair Am. organizing com. Twentieth World Congress Philos., 1998. Author: Knowledge and Belief, 1962, Models for Modalities, 1969, Tieto on valtaa, 1969, Logic, Language-Games and Information, 1973, Time and Necessity, 1973, Knowledge and the Known, 1974, (with U. Remes) The Method of Analysis, 1974, The Intentions of Intentionality, 1975, The Semantics of Questions and the Questions of Semantics, 1976, Aristotle on Modality and Determinism, 1977, The Game of Language, 1983, (with J. Kulas) Anaphora and Definite Descriptions, 1985, (with Merrill B. Hintikka) Investigating Wittgenstein, 1986, (with Martin Kusch) Kieli ja maailma, 1988, (with Merrill B. Hintikka) The Logic of Epistemology, 1989, Intentionnalite et mondes possibles, 1989, (with James Bachman) What If? Toward Excellence in Reasoning, 1990, (with Gabriel Sandu) On the Methodology of Linguistics, 1991, Eseje Logiczno-Filozoficzne, 1992, Fondements d'une theorie du langage, 1994, The Principles of Mathematics Revisited, 1996, Ludwig Wittgenstein: Half-truths and One-and-a-Half Truths, 1996, Lingua Universalis vs. Calculus Ratiocinator, 1996, Language, Truth and Logic in Mathematics, 1997, Paradigms for Language Theory, 1997, El Viaje Filosófico más Largo, 1998, Inquiry as Inquiry, 1999; contbr. over 300 articles to profl. jours.; editor-in-chief: Internat. Jour. Synthese, 1965-76, 82—; editor: Synthese Libr., 1965—, Acta Philosophica Fennica, 1973-79, Synthese Lang. Libr., 1976-84, (with Patrick Suppes) Aspects of Inductive Logic, 1966, Philosophy of Mathematics, 1969, (with Donald Davidson) Words and Objections, 1969, (with Patrick Suppes) Information and Inference, 1970, (with others) Approaches to Natural Language, 1973, Rudolf Carnap, Logical Empiricist, 1976, (with others) Essays on Wittgenstein in Honor of G.H. von Wright, 1976, (with Robert Butts) Procs. 5th Internat. Congress Logic, Methodology and Philosophy of Science (4 vols.), 1977, (with Lucia Vaina) Cognitive Constraints on Communication, 1984, (with S. Knuuttila) The Logic of Being, 1986, (with Leila Haaparanta) Frege Synthesized, 1987, Aspects of Metaphor, 1994, From Dedekind to Gödel, 1995. Decorated comdr. Order of the Lion of Finland, 1st class, 1987; recipient Wihuri Internat. prize, 1976, E.J. Nyström prize Soc. Scientiarum Fennica, 1988, Suomen Kulttuurirahasto grand prize, 1989; Guggenheim fellow, 1979-80. Mem. Assn. Symbolic Logic (v.p. 1968-70), Internat. Inst. Philosophy (v.p. 1993-96), Internat. Union History and Philosophy Sci. (v.p. 1971-75, pres. 1975), Finnish Acad. Sci. and Letters (coun. 1972-79), Philosophy of Sci. Assn. (governing bd. 1970-72), Societas Scientiarum Fennica, Internat. Fedn. Philos. Socs. (governing bd. 1978-88, 93-98, v.p. 1993-98), Am. Philos. Assn. (v.p. Pacific divsn. 1974-75, pres. 1975-76), Am. Acad. Arts and Scis., Norwegian Acad. Sci., C.S. Peirce Soc. (pres. 1997), Russian Acad. of Scis. (fgn. mem.), Phi Beta Kappa (hon.). Home: 38 Flint Dr Marlborough MA 01752-6701 Office: Boston U Dept Philosophy Boston MA 02215 also: U Helsinki Inst Philosophy, PO Box 24 FIN, 00014 Helsinki Finland

HINTON, CHARLES, lawyer; b. Wilmington, Del., Mar. 22, 1948; s. Eleanor Mary (McBride) H.; m. Debra Ann Dawson, May 22, 1976; 1 child, Jennie Leslie. BS, Wilmington Coll., 1974; JD, South Tex. Coll., 1978. Bar: Tex. 1978, U.S. Dist. Ct. (so. dist.) Tex. 1984, U.S. Supreme Ct. 1987, U.S. Ct. Appeals (5th cir.) 1987. Asst. dist. atty. Harris County, Houston, 1978-82; pvt. practice Houston, 1982—; city atty. Tex., 1990—. Avocations: carpentry, fishing, roller skating. Home: 6407 Castle Lane Dr Houston TX 77066-3921 Office: Office of the City Attorney PO Box 469002 Garland TX 75046-9002*

HINTON, DAVID OWEN, retired electrical engineer; b. Guilford County, N.C., May 12, 1938; s. George Owen Hinton and Barbara Elizabeth (Greeson) Wilder; m. Thelma Marie Arrington, Jan. 26, 1963; 1 child, David Scott. BSEE, N.C. State U., 1965. Electronics officer USN Destroyer, Norfolk, Va., 1965-67; naval flight officer Patrol Squadron 23, Brunswick, Maine, 1967-70; aircraft maintenance officer USN Rsch. Lab., Patuxent River, Md., 1970-72; project officer Health Effects Rsch. Lab. U.S. EPA, Research Triangle Park, N.C., 1972-79, dep. dir. Human Exposure & Field Rsch. Divsn., 1992; dir. Quality Assurance and Tech. Support Divsn., Research Triangle Park, N.C., 1993-95; ret., 1995; mem. Air Sampling Instruments Com., Cin., 1976-84; chmn. Electronics Tech. Adv. Com., Durham, N.C., 1981-85. Author: (with others) Air Sampling Instruments for Evaluation of Atmospheric Contaminants, 1983; contbr. papers, articles to profl. jours. Capt. USPHS, 1977-95, ret. Recipient Nat. Def. medal USN, 1972, Commendation medal USPHS, 1986, Bronze medal U.S. EPA, 1988. Mem. Internat. Soc. Exposure Analysis, Am. Conf. Govt. Indsl. Hygienists, Soc. Am. Inventors, Commd. Officers Assn. (sec., treas. 1988), Navy Res. Assn. (life), Res. Officers Assn. (life). Achievements include patents in field. Home: 8616 Bluff Point Ct Raleigh NC 27615

HINTON, JAMES FORREST, JR., lawyer; b. Gadsden, Ala., Nov. 19, 1951; s. James Forrest Sr. and Juanita Grey (Weems) H.; m. Rosalind Flynn, Nov. 10, 1979. BA, Vanderbilt U., 1974; JD, U. Ala., 1977. Bar: Ala. 1977, D.C. 1979, U.S. Dist. Ct. (so. dist.) Ala. 1979, U.S. Ct. Appeals (5th cir.) 1980, U.S. Ct. Appeals (11th cir.) 1981, La. 1982, U.S. Dist. Ct. (ea. and mid. dists.) La. 1982, U.S. Dist. Ct. (no. dist.) Ala 1982, U.S. Supreme Ct. 1982, U.S. Dist. Ct. (we. dist.) La. 1983, U.S. Dist. Ct. (no. dist.) Ohio 1983, U.S. Ct. Appeals (D.C. cir.) 1984, U.S. Ct. Appeals (fed. cir.) 1985, U.S. Dist. Ct. (so. dist.) Tex. 1987, U.S. Dist. Ct. (no. dist.) Tex. 1991, Tex. 1992, Tenn. 1992, U.S. Dist. Ct. (ea. and we. dists.) Ark. 1992, U.S. Ct. Appeals (6th and 8th cirs.) 1992, U.S. Dist. Ct. (ea. and we. dists.) Tex. 1993, U.S. Dist. Ct. (mid. dist.) Ala. 1993, U.S. Dist. Ct. (ea. and mid. dist.) Tenn. 1994. Law clk. to chief judge U.S. Dist. Ct. (so. dist.) Ala., Mobile, 1977-79; ptnr. Darby, Myrick & Hinton, Mobile, 1979-82; dir. McGlinchey Stafford Lang, New Orleans, 1982-93; ptnr. Adams & Reese, New Orleans, 1993-97; shareholder Berkowitz, Lefkovits, Isom & Kushner, Birmingham, 1997—. Contbr. articles to profl. jours. Mem. ABA (antitrust, intellectual property, litigation sects.), FBA, La. Assn. Def. Counsel, Order of Coif, Phi Beta Kappa. Office: Berkowitz Lefkovits Isom & Kushner 1600 South Trust Twr 420 20th St N Birmingham AL 35203-5200

HINTON, PAULA WEEMS, lawyer; b. Gadsden, Ala., Dec. 5, 1954; d. James Forrest and Juanita (Weems) H.; m. Steven D. Lawrence, Mar. 31, 1984; 1 child, David Hinton Lawrence. BA, U. Ala., 1976, MPA, 1979, JD, 1979. Bar: Ala. 1979, Tex. 1982, U.S. Dist. Ct. (so. dist.) Ala. 1980, U.S. Dist. Ct. (so. dist.) Tex. 1981, U.S. Dist. Ct. (no. dist.) Tex. 1988, U.S. Dist. Ct. (ea. and we. dists.) Tex. 1989, U.S. Dist. Ct. (no. and mid. dists.) Ala. 1993, U.S. Ct. Appeals (5th and 11th cirs.) 1981. Law clk. to magistrate U.S. Dist. Ct. Ala., Mobile, 1979-80; assoc. Vinson & Elkins, Houston, 1981-88; ptnr. Akin Gump Strauss Hauer & Feld, L.L.P., Houston, 1989—; mem. gender bias task force implementation com. Tex. Supreme Ct., 1998—. Rotary fellow U. Sevilla, Spain, 1980-81. Mem. State Bar Tex. (chair women in the profession com. 1996-97, 97-98), Houston Bar Found. (bd. dirs. 1994-96, chmn. 1996), U. Houston Law Found. (adv. bd.). Office: Akin Gump Strauss Hauer & Feld LLP 711 Louisiana St Houston TX 77002-2716*

HINTON, S(USAN) E(LOISE), author; b. Tulsa, 1948; m. David Inhofe, 1970; 1 child, Nicholas David. BS, U. Tulsa, 1970. Author (teen-age fiction) The Outsiders, 1967 (N.Y. Herald Tribune Best Teenage Book list 1967, Chgo. Tribune Book World Spring Festival Honor Book 1967, Media and Methods Maxi award 1975, Mass. Children's Book award 1979), That Was Then, This Is Now, 1971 (ALA Best Books for Young Adults list 1971, Chgo. Tribune Book World Spring Festival Honor Book 1971, Mass. Children's Book award 1978), Rumble Fish, 1975 (ALA Best Book for Young Adults list 1975, Sch. Libr. Jour. Best Books of Yr. list 1975, Land of Enchantment award N.Mex. Libr. Assn. 1982), Tex, 1979 (ALA Best Books for Young Adults list 1979, Sch. Libr. Jour. Best Books of Yr. list 1979, Am. Book award nominee 1981, Calif. Young Reader medal nominee 1982, Sue Hefly award 1983), Taming the Star Runner, 1988, Big David, Little David, 1994; (screenplay, with Francis Ford Coppola) Rumble Fish, 1983; film appearances Tex, 1982, The Outsiders, 1983, The Puppy Sister, 1995. Recipient Golden Archer Award, 1983; Author award ALA Young Adult Svcs. Divsn./Sch. Libr. Jour., 1988. Office: care Dell Publ Press Rels 1540 Broadway New York NY 10036-4039*

HINTZ, CHARLES BRADLEY, diversified financial executive; b. Chgo., Dec. 6, 1949; s. Charles Frank and Helen (Bernadette) H.; m. Kristine Ingrid Falsetta, July 23, 1980. BS, Purdue U., 1971; MS, U. So. Calif., 1976; MBA, U. Pa., 1978. Various treasury positions Standard Oil Co. of Calif., San Francisco, 1978-82; v.p., dir. treasury ops. The Northern Trust Co., Chgo., 1982-83, group v.p. corp. devel., 1983-84; v.p., treas. Anderson, Clayton & Co., Houston, 1984-86; prin. Morgan Stanley & Co., N.Y.C., 1986-91; treas., mng. dir. Morgan Stanley Group, N.Y.C., 1992-96; chief fin. officer, managing dir. Lehman Bros. Holdings, N.Y.C., 1996-98. Alumni bd. dirs. Krannert Sch. Purdue U.; bd. visitors Marshal Sch. U. So. Calif. Lt. comdr. USNR, 1971-76. Mem. Fin. Execs. Inst., Treasury Mgrs. Assn. (v.p.). Club: Houston, Plainfield Country, Penn.

HINTZ, NORMA A., cardiac care nurse; b. Earling, Iowa., Feb. 1, 1940; d. John D. and Maurine R. (Klein) Lehan; m. Donald F. Hintz, Apr. 30, 1960; children: Susan, Donald Jr. (dec.), Daniel, Mark, Michelle. BSN, Bishop Clarkson Coll. Nursing, Omaha, 1988. Primary care nurse Bishop Clarkson Hosp., Omaha, 1988—. Named Bishop Clarkson Hosp. Nurse of Yr., 1991. Mem. AACN, Clarkson Alumni Soc., Sigma Theta Tau. Home and Office: 229 W Plains St Gretna NE 68028-4409

HINTZ, ROBERT LOUIS, transportation company executive; b. Chgo., May 25, 1930; s. Louis A. and Gertrude V. (Herman) H.; m. Gloria Mae Safbom, Nov. 12, 1955; children—Cary, Leslie, David, Erin. BS in Bus. Adminstrn. magna cum laude, Northwestern U., 1960, MBA, 1965. With Chessie System Inc., from 1963; internal audit officer C.&O. Ry., Cleve., 1963-65; staff asst. to v.p. C.&O. Ry.-B.&O. R.R., Cleve., 1965-68, asst. to v.p., 1968-70; compt. C.&O. Ry.-B.&O. R.R., Balt., 1970-72; asst. to pres. parent co. C.&O. Ry.-B.&O. R.R., Cleve., 1972-74, v.p. corp. svcs., 1974-76, v.p. fin., 1976-78, sr. v.p.-fin., 1978-80; sr. v.p. fin. CSX Corp., Richmond, Va., 1980-83, exec. v.p., 1983-88, ret.; chmn., CEO, CSX Energy Corp., Richmond, 1985-88, ret., Sea-Land Corp., Edison, N.J., 1986-88; pres., CEO, CSX Properties Group, 1985-88; chmn., CEO R.L. Hintz & Assocs., 1989; bd. dirs. Scott & Stingfellow Fin., Inc., Chesapeake Corp., Reynolds Metals Co., Arch Coal, Inc. Chmn. St. Joseph's Villa; chmn. Hosp. Hospitality House; bd. dirs. Christian Children's Fund. With USAF, 1950-54. Mem. Fin. Execs. Inst., Commonwealth Club, Country Club Va. Roman Catholic. Home and Office: 10002 Walsham Ct Richmond VA 23233-5401

HINZ, CARL FREDERICK, JR., physician, educator; b. Cleve., Apr. 9, 1927; s. Carl Frederick and Marie (Jones) H.; m. Joan Herndon, June 5, 1953; children—Elizabeth, Richard, Catherine, Gretchen. B.S., Western Res. U., 1948, M.D., 1951. Faculty dept. medicine Western Res. U. Sch. Medicine, Cleve., 1953-67; asst. prof. Western Res. U. Sch. Medicine, 1961-67, research asso. div. research in med. edn., 1964-67; prof., asso. dean U. Conn. Sch. Medicine, 1967-92, acting head dept. medicine, 1979-80, emeritus, 1992—; mem. Conn. Med. Exam. Bd., 1976-80. Chmn. bd. dirs. blood svcs. Conn. region ARC, 1993-95, chair coun. of chairs North Atlantic area, 1995—. Markle scholar, 1959-64; scholar-in-residence Inst. Medicine, Nat. Acad. Sci., 1987-88. Fellow ACP; mem. Am. Soc. Clin. Investigation, Am. Assn. Immunologists, Am. Soc. Hematology, Central Soc. Clin. Research, Am. Fedn. Clin. Research, Conn. Med. Soc., Hartford County Med. Assn. (dir. 1976-92, pres. 1986-87), Conn. Lung Assn. (pres. 1979-81). Home: 11 Highwood Dr Avon CT 06001-2411 Office: U Conn Sch Medicine Farmington CT 06032

HINZ, DOROTHY ELIZABETH, writer, editor, international corporate communications and public affairs specialist; b. N.Y.C.. AB, Hunter Coll.; student, Columbia U. Asst. to dir. devel. Columbia U., N.Y.C., 1953-55; mng. editor, econs. rschr.-analyst, writer speeches, position papers, mgr. pubs. W.R. Grace & Co., N.Y.C., 1955-64; staff writer Oil Progress, fgn. news media, speeches, films, internat. petroleum ops., pub. rels. dept. Caltex Petroleum Corp., N.Y.C., 1964-69; fin. editor Merrill Lynch, Pierce, Fenner & Smith, 1969-74; mgr. publs., mgr. speakers' bur., assoc. speech writer mktg. and corp. comm. dept. Mfrs. Hanover Corp., N.Y.C., 1974-88; mem. Internat. Seminars, Columbia U., N.Y.C., 1988—. Contbr. articles on multinat. corps., developing nations, trade and fin. to various publs.; researcher of policy proposals for J.P. Grace's book, It's Not Too Late in Latin America. Mem. The Ams. Found. Mem. N.Y. Press Club, Americas Soc., Bolivarian Soc. (sec., bd. dirs.), Fgn. Press Assn., Coun. of Ams. Home and Office: 600 W 115th St Apt 104 New York NY 10025-7720*

HINZ, SHIRLEY SORENSEN, administrative secretary; b. Denver, Sept. 28, 1942; m. Dale Edward Hinz, Sept. 3, 1966; children: Andrew Christian, Tammy Lynn Dahl. Student, Ft. Lewis Coll., 1961, Barnes Bus. Coll., 1982; diploma in spl. pub., Inst. Children's Lit., 1994. Adminstrv. asst. USDA, Ft. Collins, Colo., 1989; divsn. sec. U.S. Dept. Energy, Golden, Colo., 1991; sect. sec. U.S. Dept. Interior, Ft. Collins, 1992—; mem. labor mgmt. partnership coun. U.S. Dept. Interior, 1994-95. Author numerous poems; writer/songwriter. Active Ault (Colo.) Sr. Ctr., 1989—. Recipient Editor's Choice award Nat. Libr. Congress, Nat. Libr. Poetry, 1995-96, Accomplishment of Merit award Creative Arts & Sci. Enterprises, 1996, Nat. Merit Award cert. Larimer County Fed. Exec. Assn., 1996, awards Poetry Guild, 1996-97; named to Internat. Poetry Hall of Fame, Nat. Libr. Congress, 1997. Mem. Internat. Soc. Poets (disting.), Famous Poets Soc. (Diamond Homer award 1996), Acad. of Am. Poets. Lutheran. Avocations: gardening, studying and working in bonsai, song writing. Home: PO Box 1063 304 Cherry Ln Ault CO 80610 Office: US Dept of Interior 4512 Mcmurry Ave Fort Collins CO 80525-3400

HINZ, THEODORE VINCENT, architect; b. Bklyn., June 6, 1933; s. Theodore V. and Lillian (Adolph) H.; m. Louise R. Symmons; 1 child, Linda. BArch, Pratt Inst., 1956. Registered arch., N.Y., N.J., Va., Md., Conn., Ill. Draftsman, designer Muller & Ash Archs., N.Y.C., 1956-59; designer Urban, Brayton & Burrows, N.Y.C., 1959; designer, project arch. Goldstone & Dearborn, N.Y.C., 1959-66, assoc., 1966-70; ptnr. Goldstone, Dearborn & Hinz, N.Y.C., 1970-73, Goldstone & Hinz, N.Y.C., 1973—. Capt. C.E., U.S. Army, 1956-57. Recipient cert. Merit for Excellence in Design NYSA, award of honor for Excellence in Design for Greenacre Park, 1972, Good Neighbor award Volvo Hdqs. N.J. Mfg. Assn., 1973, Bus. Friend of Arts award, 1988, Lumen citation Illumination Engring. Soc., 1990, Spl. Recognition award Concrete Industry Bd., 1993, Build N.Y. award Gen. Bldg. Contractors of N.Y., 1993. Mem. AIA, N.Y. Soc. Archs., N.Y. State Assn. Archs., Constrn. Specifications Inst., Bayside Hist. Soc. (trustee 1975-77, 81-83, v.p. 1977-79, pres. 1979-81), Queens Hist. Soc. (trustee 1980-87). Office: Goldstone & Hinz Architects PC 104 E 40th St Rm 803 New York NY 10016-1838

HIPP, KENNETH BYRON, lawyer; b. Charlotte, N.C., Aug. 4, 1945; s. Junius B. and Jeanne Carol (Gwaltney) H.; m. Ann Winfield Birmingham, Sept. 23, 1966; children: Kenneth Byron Jr., Andrew Clay. AB, Duke U., 1967; JD with high honors, U. N.C., Chapel Hill, 1971. Bar: N.C. 1971, Hawaii 1987, U.S. Dist. Ct. (no. dist.) Tex. 1978, U.S. Dist. Ct. Hawaii 1987, U.S. Ct. Appeals (2d, 4th and 5th cirs.) 1972, U.S. Ct. Appeals (9th cir.) 1976, U.S. Ct. Appeals (10th cir.) 1977, U.S. Supreme Ct. 1993. Assoc. Micronesian Claims Com., Saipan, Northern Mariana Islands, 1973-74; regional dir. Micronesian Claims Co., Palau, Western Caroline Islands, 1974-76; atty. enforcement litigation NLRB, Washington, 1971-73, 76-77, supr. atty. enforcement litigation, 1977, dep. asst. gen. counsel spl. litigation, 1977-78, dep. asst. gen. counsel appellate litigation, 1978-86, dep. asst. gen. counsel contempt litigation, 1986-87; ptnr. Goodsill Anderson Quinn & Stifel, Honolulu, 1987-95; mem. Nat. Mediation Bd., Washington, 1995-98, chmn., 1996-98; ptnr. Marr Hipp Jones & Pepper, Honolulu, 1998—; bar examiner State of Hawaii, 1988-92; vis. assoc. prof. Law Sch., Boston Coll., 1983-84; adj. prof. Law Sch., Cath. U. Am., 1978-79, Law Ctr., Georgetown U., Washington, 1984-87; adj. prof. Grad. Sch. Bus. U. Hawaii, 1989-94. Mem. Hawaii State Bar Assn. (chair labor and employment law sect. 1990-91), Order of Coif. Presbyterian. Home: 314 Poipu Dr Honolulu HI 96825-2125 Office: Marr Hipp Jones and Pepper Ste 1550 1001 Bishop St Pauahi Tower Honolulu HI 96813

HIPP, WILLIAM HAYNE, insurance and broadcasting executive; b. Greenville, S.C., Mar. 11, 1940; s. Francis Moffett and Mary Matilda (Looper) H.; m. Anna Kate Reid, June 14, 1963; children: Mary Henigan, Francis Reid, Anna Hayne. BA, Washington and Lee U., 1962; MBA, U. Pa., 1965. With Met. Life Ins. Co., 1965-69; v.p. Liberty Life Ins. Co., Greenville, S.C., 1969-74, exec. v.p., 1977-79, chmn. bd. dirs., 1979—; chief exec. officer Liberty Corp., Greenville, 1979—, also bd. dirs.; bd. dirs. Wachovia Corp., SCANA Corp., S.C. Rsch. Authority,. Trustee, vice-chmn. Nat. Urban League, 1979-89; trustee Com. Econ. Devel., N.Y., 1988—, Episcopal H.S., Alexandria, Va., 1982-88; chmn. Greenville Urban League, 1978, Greenville YMCA, 1979; trustee Greenville County Sch. Sys., 1975-76, Washington and Lee U., Lexington, Va., 1985-95, Greenville C. of C., 1985; trustee, chmn. Alliance for Quality Edn., 1986—, Greenville Hosp. Sys., 1989-95; bd. dirs. Am. Coun. Life Ins., 1995—, S.C. State Devel. Bd., 1980-85, and others. Mem. Greenville C. of C. (chmn. 1985). Office: Liberty Corp PO Box 789 2000 Wade Hampton Blvd Greenville SC 29615-1037*

HIPPAUF, GEORGETTE LAURIN, company executive; b. Lowell, Mass., June 13, 1936; d. Mathias R. and Helene Marie (Rousseau) Laurin; m. Frank V. Mann, Sept. 21, 1957 (div. Oct. 1973); children: Frank V. Jr., Richard, Helene, Jacqueline; m. Walter M. Hippauf, Oct. 3, 1974. BA in English Lit., Boston U., 1957; MA in Edn., SUNY, Albany, 1971. Lang. arts tchr. St. Thomas Sch., Delmar, N.Y., 1972-73; v.p. Rosetta Stone Assocs., Nashua, N.H., 1977-78, Resources of N.H., Inc., Nashua, 1979—. Co-author: Birth of the Republican Party, 1995; editor: The Candidates: See How They Run, 1990, A Tall State Revisited, 1993; editor commemorative booklet: 140th Birthday of the Republican Party, 1993. Del. Rep. Nat. Conv., Houston, 1992, Rep. State Conv., Concord, N.H., 1992; mem. N.H. Commn. on Status of Women, Concord, 1990-92, chmn., 1992; asst. chmn. Rep. State Com., Concord, 1993-95, 95—; mem. Bush Presdl. Primary Campaign Adv. Bd., N.H., 1979-80, Reagan Presdl. Primary Campaign Adv. Bd., 1975-76. Mem. N.H. Fedn. Rep. Women (sec. 1988-89, 3d v.p. 1990-91, pres. 1992-93), Nashua Fedn. Rep. Women (pres. 1988-89), Amos Tuck Soc. (founder, v.p. 1994, 95, 96—). Roman Catholic. Avocations: travel, reading, photography. Home: 15 Browning Ave Nashua NH 03062-2478 Office: Resources of NH Inc 20 Gregg Rd Nashua NH 03062-1003

HIPPE, ANNE ELAINE, nursing educator; b. Lincoln, Nebr., Mar. 23, 1951; d. Thomas Dean and Arlene (Foreman-Elliott) Buffington; children: Kim, Debbie, Rob, Jenney, Eric, Bryce; m. Robert Hippe, July 4, 1986. Diploma, Nebr. Meth. Hosp., 1974; postgrad., Chadron State Coll.; BSN with distinction, Bishop Clarkson Coll., Omaha, 1991; MSN, U. Nebr. Med. Ctr., 1997. RN, Nebr. RN ICU, CCU St. Elizabeth Community Health Ctr., Lincoln, 1974-75, RN labor and delivery, 1975-77; RN pediatrics Bryan Meml. Hosp., Lincoln, 1979, RN PAR/OR, 1979-82; RN ICU Regional West Med. Ctr., Scottsbluff, Nebr., 1982; instr. Western Nebr. C.C., Scottsbluff, 1982—, divsn. chair for health occupations, 1994—. Active Christ the King Parish, Gering, Nebr., 1987. Democrat. Roman Catholic. Avocations: music, needlework, computers. Home: 1018 E 35th St Scottsbluff NE 69361-4535 Office: Western Nebr Community Coll 1601 E 27th St Scottsbluff NE 69361-1815

HIPPEAU, ERIC, book publishing executive; b. Paris, Aug. 16, 1951; came to U.S., 1986; Attended, Sorbonne Univ., Paris. V.p. computer publs. IDG, N.Y.C.; publisher IDG Info World; publisher Computer World Ziff-Davis, N.Y.C., 1989-90, exec. v.p., 1990-91, pres., COO, 1991, chmn., CEO, 1991-93; chmn., CEO Ziff Comms. Co., N.Y.C., 1993—. Office: Ziff-Davis Inc 28 E 28th St New York NY 10016-5802*

HIPPEE, WILLIAM H., JR., lawyer; b. Des Moines, 1946. BS, U. Pa., 1968; JD, Stanford U., 1972. Bar: Minn. 1972. Ptnr. Dorsey & Whitney LLP, Mpls. Office: Dorsey & Whitney LLP 220 S 6th St Ste 2200 Minneapolis MN 55402-1498*

HIPPLE, WALTER JOHN, English language educator; b. Chgo., Mar. 14, 1921; s. Walter John and Emilie (Scheu) H.; m. Anne Ruth Poier, Nov. 27,

1962; children: Heidi Kristina, Ethan John; m. Kay F. Moomaw. BA, U. Chgo., 1947, MA, 1948, PhD, 1954; postdoctoral, U. London, 1957, Cambridge (Eng.) U., 1961-62; LittD, Shimer Coll., 1977. Lectr. Roosevelt U., Chgo., 1948; instr. U. Chgo., 1948-50, U. Ark., 1951-52; asst. prof. U. Fla., Gainesville, 1952-56; assoc. prof. Cornell Coll., Mt. Vernon, Iowa, 1957-61; prof. U. Pacific, Calif., 1962, Idaho State U., 1963, U. So. Calif., 1963; prof., chmn. dept. humanities Ind. State U., Terre Haute, 1963-72; dean Shimer Coll., Mt. Carroll, Ill., 1972-76; acad. v.p. West Chester (Pa.) State Coll., 1976-77; prof. philosophy West Chester (Pa.) U., 1977-91, assoc. to pres., 1977-79, dir. honors, 1979-91, prof. emeritus, 1991; prof. English Heilongjiang (People's Republic of China) U., Harbin, 1991-92; chmn. Com. on Humanities in Secondary Schs. Ind., 1965-69; prof. univs. and insts. in Peoples Republic of China, 1986-92; guest prof. U. Autonomous Region Caribbean Coast Nicaragua, 1997, U. Zambia, 1999. Author: The Beautiful, the Sublime and the Picturesque in Eighteenth Century British Aesthetic Theory, 1957; editor, author introduction: Alexander Gerard, An Essay on Taste, 1963; contbr. articles to profl. jours. With U.S. Army, 1943-45. Guggenheim fellow, 1961-62. Home: 328 S Darlington St West Chester PA 19382-3341 Office: U Zambia Dept Lit & Langs, PO Box 32379, Lusaka Zambia

HIPPS, ALBERTA, city councilwoman. BSN, U. N. Fla., 1981; MBA, Jacksonville U., 1986. City councilwoman Jacksonville (Fla.) City Coun. Republican. Office: 117 W Duval St Ste 425 Jacksonville FL 32202-3700

HIPPS, LARRY CLAY, clergyman, evangelistic association executive; b. Huntsville, Ala., Aug. 11, 1953; s. William B. and Clara M. (Yance) H.; m. Cathy Ann Dees, Mar. 22, 1975; children: Betsy Ann, Allison Renee, Jonathan Clay. BS, Ala. A&M U., 1975; MinM, Internat. Bible Inst. and Sem., 1983, MinD, 1984. Ordained minister Bapt. Ch., 1975. Dir. ministry Flint River Bapt. Ch., Huntsville, 1973-76; assoc. pastor West Rome Bapt. Ch., Rome, Ga., 1976-80, Broadway Bapt. Ch., Memphis, 1980-87; pres. Bring Them In Evangelist Assn., Inc., Memphis, 1976-88, Houston, 1988—; bus. and children's ch. min. Sagemont Ch., Houston, 1989—; pres. BTI Home Bus. Dirs. Inst., Memphis and Houston, 1984-89. Author: Bring Them in Sunday School Lesons, 1980, BTI Bus Director Manual, 1981, BTI Bus Captain's Handbook, 1987; pub., editor Bring Them In Mag., 1975—; pub. Puppet UpDate mag., Tulsa, 1978. Mem. Nation Wide Bus Ministry Assn. (pres. 1978-79), Internat. Bus. Dirs. Assn. Republican. Avocation: Disneyana collecting, golf. Office: Bring Them In 11323 Hughes Rd Houston TX 77089-4637

HIPSCHMAN, DAVID, editor; b. Long Branch, N.J., Oct. 13, 1952; s. Leonard and Olga (Weiss) H.; m. Dorrie Dale, Dec. 2, 1987; children: Robert William, Katie. BA in English, Anthropology, Trenton State Coll., 1976. Reporter Delaware Valley News, Frenchtown, N.J., 1977-98; reporter, bur. chief Easton (Pa.) Express, 1978-80; internat. editor San Francisco Chronical, 1980-90; editor, publisher Kinesis, Whitefish, Mont., 1991-95; editor-in-chief Casper (Wyo.) Star-Tribune, 1995—. Author: Flying Sounds, 1978. Mem. Wyo. Press Assn. (bd. dirs. 1997-98). Avocations: aviation, fly-fishing. Office: Fargo Forum 101 5th St N Fargo ND 58102

HIRAHARA, PATTI, public relations executive; b. Lynwood, Calif., May 10, 1955; d. Frank C. and Mary K. Hirahara; m. Terry K. Takeda, Sept. 1995. AA, Cypress Coll., 1975; BA, Calif. State U., Fullerton, 1977. Pub. affairs dir. United TV, L.A., 1977-80; v.p. Asian Internat. Broadcasting Co., L.A., 1980-81; mktg. cons. Disneyland, Anaheim, Calif., 1982; pub. rels. agt. Japan External Trade Orgn., L.A., 1982-86, 87-92; owner, pres. Prodns. By Hirahara, Anaheim, 1982—; comml. photographer Hirahara Photography, Anaheim, 1977-83; publicist Tokyo Met. Govt., 1981, World Trade Week So. Calif., 1997, 98, 99; advisor State Colo. Trade Mission to Japan, 1986, State Ariz. Trade/Investment Mission to Japan, 1987, County Riverside, Calif. for Japanese trade, investment, tourism, 1986-88; coord. JETRO's bus. Study Series, L.A., 1988; advisor Japan External Trade Orgn., 1987-88, TV Prodr./Host: Images, 1980, 1980, Expressions, 1994. Mem. reader panel Golf for Women Mag. Bd. dirs. Nisei Week Japanese Festival, L.A., 1980-81; mem. anaheim H.S. 20 Yr. Reunion Com., 1993. Nat. scholar Seventeen Mag. Youth Adv. Coun., 1973; named Orange County Niesi Queen, Suburban Optimist Club, Buena Park, Calif., 1974, nat. semi-finalist Outstanding Working Women Competition Glamour Mag., 1975; recipient svc. award Suburban Optimist Club of Buena Park, 1975. Mem. NAFE, Soc. Profl. Journalists (bd. dirs. 1980-81), World Trade Ctr. Assn. Orange County, Japanese Am. Citizens League, Am. Women in Radio and TV (bd. dirs. So. Calif. chpt. 1980-82, vice-chair western conf. 1981), So. Calif. Golf Assn., No. Calif. Golf Assn., Pub. Rels. Soc. Am. (Orange County chpt. 1990), Adelaide Price Elem. Sch. (30 yr. reunion chair 1997), Suburban Optimist Club of Buena Park (bd. dirs. 1993-96, chairperson 30th Anniversary Celebration 1996, Optimist of Yr. 1995-96), L.A. Dept. Water and Power Golf Club, Hunter Ranch Golf Club, Alpha Gamma Sigma.

HIRAI, DENITSU, surgeon; b. Yokkaichi, Mie, Japan, July 27, 1943; came to U.S. 1969; s. Denyomu and Shizuo (Tanaka) H.; m. Fumiko Hada, June 14, 1969; 1 child, R. Lisa. MD, U. Tokyo, 1968. Diplomate Am. Bd. Surgery, Am. Bd. Quality Assurance and Utilization Rev. Physicians, Am. Bd. Surg. Critical Care; cert. nutrition support physician. Intern and residency Waterbury (Conn.) Hosp., 1969-74; fellow Mt. Sinai Hosp., 1974-75; asst. chief surgery VA Med. Ctr., Lincoln, Nebr., 1975-80; chief surgery VA Med. Ctr., Lincoln, 1981—; asst. clin. prof. surgery Creighton U., Omaha, 1982-84, asst. prof. surgery, 1984—; clin. instr. U. Nebr., Omaha, 1986-88, clin. asst. prof. surgery, 1988—. Author: Brain Ticklers (Japanese), 1983. Fellow ACS, Am. Coll. Critical Care Medicine; mem. AAAS, AMA, ACS, Am. Soc. Parenteral and Enteral Nutrition, Soc. Am. Gastrointestinal Endoscopic Surgeons, Southwestern Surg. Congress, Soc. Critical Care Medicine, Assn. VA Surgeons. Avocations: photography, Braille transcription, karate (Okinawa Black Belt). Office: VA Med Ctr 600 S 70th St Lincoln NE 68510-2451

HIRANO, ASAO, neuropathologist; b. Tomioka, Gunma, Japan, Nov. 26, 1926; s. Yoshiro and Miyoe Hirano; m. Keiko Okubo, May 23, 1959; children—Michio, Ikuo, Yoko, Shigeo. B.D., Kyoto U., 1952. Chief resident neurology Montefiore Hosp., Bronx, 1957-58; head div. neuropathology Montefiore Med. Ctr., Bronx, 1965—, Harry M. Zimmerman prof. neuropathology, 1995; vis. scientist NIH, 1959-65; head div. neuropathology Montefiore Med. Ctr., Bronx, 1965—, Harry M. Zimmerman prof. neuropathology, 1995—; prof. pathology Albert Einstein Coll. Medicine, 1971—, prof. neurosci., 1974—; vis. prof. Kansai Med. U., Osaka, Japan, 1985, Nippon Med. Sch., Tokyo, 1993; neuropathology cons. surg. neurology, 1996—; mem. internat. adv. bd. med. electron microscopy, 1997—. Author: A Guide to Neuropathology, 1981, Metastatic Tumors of the Nervous Systems, 1982, Color Atlas of Neuropathology, 1988; editor: Neuropsychiatric Disorders in the Elderly, 1983, Patholoy of the Myelinated Axon, 1985, Amyotrophic Lateral Sclerosis, Progress and Perspectives in Basic Research and Clinical Application, 1995; mem. internat. editorial bd. Sec. 5 Excerpta Medica, 1976—; mem. editorial com. Neurol. Medicine, 1978—; mem. adv. bd. Jour. Neuropathology and Exptl. Neurology, 1971-81, mem. editorial bd., 1981-84; mem. editorial bd. Progress in Computerized Tomography, 1978—, Annals of Neurology, 1983-89, Acta Neuropathologica (mem. editorial bd.), 1991—; mem. adv. bd. Clinical Neuropathology, 1982—, Neuropathology and Applied Neurobiology, 1983—; hon. editor Brain Tumor Pathology, 1993—, Neuropathology, 1994—; mem., neuropathology cons. Surg. Neurology, 1996—; mem. internat. adv. bd. Med. Electron Microscopy, 1997—. Recipient Billings Silver medal AMA, 1959, Key to Osaka City, Japan, 1977, Royal Coll. Lectr. award Can. Assn. Neuropathologists, Royal Coll. Physicians and Surgeons Can., 1980, 1st Jack Prichard Meml. Lectr. award Queen's U., Belfast, 1981, 1st Endowment Lectr. of Neuropathology in memory of Mrs. Rajan Bharati and 150th Yr. Celebration of Madras Med. Coll., 1984, Commendation award Hon. Ben Blaz, 1992, Plaque, U.S. Ho. Reps., 1992. Mem. Am. Assn. Neuropathologists (pres. 1977-78, Weil award 1968, award for meritorious contbn. to neuropathology 1995), Am. Neurol. Assn., Assn. for Rsch. in Nervous and Mental Diseases, Am. Soc. Cell Biology, Internat. Soc. Neuropatholgy, Am. Acad. Neurology (assoc.), Japanese Soc. Neuropathology (councilor 1984, hon.), Western Pacific Neurol. Soc. (hon.), Australian and New Zealand Soc. for Neuropathology (hon.), Brit. Neuropathologists, World Fedn. Neurology (rsch. com. 1978), Japanese Soc. Neurosurgery, (sr. mem.), Japanese Soc. Neurology (hon.). Office: Montefiore Med Ctr 111 E 210th St Bronx NY 10467-2401

HIRASAKI, GEORGE JIRO, chemical engineer, educator; b. Beaumont, Tex., Sept. 26, 1939; s. Tokuzo and Toki (Kishi) H. BSChemE with honors, Lamar U., 1963; PhDChemE, Rice U., 1967. With Shell Devel. Co., Houston, 1967-93; A.J. Hartsook prof. in chem. engrg. Rice U., Houston, 1993—; prof. Rice U., Houston, 1993—. Contbr. articles to profl. jours.; patentee in field. Mem. NAE, Am. Chem. Soc., AIChE, Soc. Petroleum Engrs. (Lester C. Uren award 1989), Soc. Core Analysts, SIAM. Avocations: windsurfing, skiing, mountaineering. Office: Rice U Dept Chem Engring 6100 Main St Houston TX 77005-1892

HIRD, MARY, nursing administrator; b. Jamaica, May 24, 1940; d. Robert and Miriam (Fullerton) Johnson; m. Sylvester Hird, Feb. 11, 1967; children: York, Claudia. RN degree, U. W.I. Sch. Nursing, Kingston, Jamaica, 1965; diploma, Victoria Jubilee Midwifery, Kingston, 1966; student, CUNY, Brooklyn, 1979-80; BS magna cum laude, St. Joseph's Coll., Brooklyn, 1984. Cert. low risk neonatal nursing, 1995, RCLS. Dep. matron St. Joseph's Hosp., Kingston, 1971-74; organizer Glen Vincent Clinic Ministry of Health, Kingston, 1975-77; administrv. nursing care coord. Brookdale U. Hosp. Med. Ctr., Bklyn., 1989—; adj. prof. nursing CUNY, 1990—. Mem. NAACOG. Home: 1218 E 49th St Brooklyn NY 11234-1513

HIRES, WILLIAM LELAND, psychologist, consultant; b. South Orange, N.J., July 5, 1918; s. Harrison Streeter and Christine B. (Leland) H.; m. Karen Reynolds Perrott, July 12, 1975; 1 child, Jennifer Leland. BS, Haverford Coll., 1949; PhD, U. Pa., 1972. Asst. to dean of admissions, asst. dir of scholarships U. Pa., 1952-55; supr. psychol. svcs., spl. classes, asst. supt. Office Supt. Chester County (Pa.) Schs., 1956-59; assoc. prof. West Chester Coll., 1960-61; adminstrv. asst. Office of Pres., asst. to sec. U. Pa., 1961-64; assoc. Edward N. Hay & Assocs., 1964-65; asst. supt. pub. schs. Chester County, 1966-68, pvt. cons., 1968-75; dir. diagnostic and consultative svc. Chester County Intermediate Unit, 1975-76, pvt. practice psychology, 1976-78; dir. pupil svcs. Upper Darby (Pa.) Sch. Dist., 1978-81; dean acad. studies Curtis Inst. Music, Phila., 1981-86; ptnr. Hires Assocs., Phila., 1987—. With USMC, 1942-46; with AUS, 1941-42, 50-52; lt. col. AUS ret.; col. Pa. Army N.G. ret. Mem. AAAS, APA, Soc. of Cin. (bd. dirs.), Welcome Soc., Hist. Soc. Pa. (bd. dirs.), 1st Troop Phila. City Cavalry (hon.), Soc. Colonial Wars Pa. (gov.), Phila. Club, Franklin Inn Club, Merion Cricket Club, The Rabbit.

HIRN, DORIS DREYER, health service administrator; b. N.Y.C., Dec. 3, 1933; d. James Howard and Dorothy Van Nostrand (Young) Dreyer; m. John D. Hirn, Oct. 27, 1956; children: Deborah Lynn, Robert William. Student, Colby Jr. Coll., 1950-51, Hofstra U., 1953-56. Owner Dutchlands Farm, Albany, N.Y., 1957-62, Hickory Hill Farm, Galena, Ill., 1965-75; adminstr. Home Health Svc., Chgo., 1972-74; exec. dir. Suburban Home Health Svc., 1974-87, Home Health Svc. Chgo. North, 1987-95, Columbia Home Care, 1995-96; v.p., pub. Caregivers Resource Co., Hampshire, Ill., 1995—; ptnr. Candor Assocs.; pres. Hirn Assocs. Ltd.; dir. Nat. Health Delivery Systems, Serengeti Prodns., Inc.; bd. dirs. Lifeline Pilots, Inc., NAHC, Fin. Mgrs. Forum, Ill. Long Term Task Force, Ill. Homecare Coun., BBH Assocs., Inc.; pub. Caregivers Resource Director; presenter in field. Author: Survey Process in Home Health Manual; contbr. articles to profl. jours. With WAVES, 1951-52. Recipient Ill. Govs. award for Excellence Home Care Agy. Office: Caregivers Resource Co 48W685 Immelman Ln Hampshire IL 60140-8334

HIRNING, FREDRIC CARL, pharmacist; b. Lodi, Calif., Aug. 20, 1947; s. Clarence Christian Reuben and Gertrude (Hoff) H.; m. Marilyn Kay Truitt, Aug. 31, 1968; children: Lindsay Ann, Katherine Erin, John Michael. BS in Pharmacy cum laude, U. of the Pacific, 1970, PharmD cum laude, 1972; cert. pharmacy mgmt., U. N.C., 1989; cert. health care mgmt., U. So. Calif., 1991. Registered pharmacist, Calif. From pharmacist to dir. pharmacy Mercy Hosp., Sacramento, 1970-76; dir. pharmacy St. Josephs Med. Ctr., Stockton, 1976-80, pharmacist, 1980-82; dir. pharmacy svcs. Sutter Davis (Calif.) Hosp., 1983-85; pharmacist Relief Pharmacy Svc., Stockton, 1985-87; dir. pharmacy svcs. Drs. Hosp. Manteca, Calif., 1987—; adj. prof. U. of the Pacific Sch. Pharmacy, Stockton, 1987-89, new dean search com., 1994-95; instr. chemical dependency studies Calif. State U., Sacramento, 1991-95; instr. drug & alcohol counselor cert. program U. of the Pacific, Stockton, 1993-95, bd. dirs. pharmacy assoc., 1990—; field monitor Occupl. Healthcare Svcs., Larkspur, Calif., 1988-93; chmn. Calif. Vet. Diversion Com., 1993-95; vice-chmn. Calif. Nursing Diversion Com., 1992-94; cons. and presenter in field. Co-author: Purchasing and Inventory Control, 1992, Points of Light, A Guide for Helping..., 1996; contbr. articles to profl. jours. Active Bishops Adv. Com. on Drug and Alcohol, Fresno, 1987—, Partners in Prevention/Parents Who Care, Stockton, 1987-95, Pharmacists Against Drug Abuse, 1986—, Calaveras County Drug Abuse Task Force, San Andreas, Calif., 1986-87, Leadership, Manteca, 1989-90; asst. scoutmaster Boy Scouts Am., Stockton, 1991—; bd. dirs. PALS-Drug Treatment Program, Stockton, 1993-95; coun. mem. Lincoln H.S., Stockton, 1991-93. Recipient Geigy Leadership award Sacramento Valley Soc. Hosp. Pharmacists, 1976, Commendation award San Joaquin County Sheriff, 1982, Appreciation award Boy Scouts Am., 1990, Nat. Cmty. Svc. award U.S. Pharmacist jour., 1993; named Disting. Pharmacist, Roerig Pharmaceuticals, 1989, Disting. Alumni, U. of the Pacific Alumni Assn., 1997; named to Lodi Union H.S. Sports Hall of Fame, 1994. Mem. Internat. Pharmacy Fedn., Am. Pharm. Assn. (del. 1990-95), Acad. Pharmacy and Practice & Mgmt. (edn. standing com. 1993-94, vice-chmn. awards standing com., sect. chmn. 1994-95), Am. Soc. Health-Sys. Pharmacists, Calif. Pharmacists Assn. (editl. rev. com. 1993—, ednl. found. adv. com. 1997—, Bowl of Hygeia award 1991), Am. Inst. for the History of Pharmacy, Christian Pharmacists Fellowship Internat., Internat. Pharmacists Anonymous, Am. Pharm. Assn. Found., Am. Soc. Health-Sys. Pharmacists Found., Internat. Coalition Addiction Studies Educators, Acad. Hosp. Pharmacists (bd. dirs. 1994-96, Quality Commitment award 1995), San Joaquin Pharmacists Assn. (bd. dirs. 1989-94, pres. 1993), Cen. Valley Soc. Hosp. Pharmacists (bd. dirs. 1988-93, pres. 1992, Pharmacist of Yr. 1992), San Francisco Zool. Soc., U.S. Holocaust Meml. Mus. Assn., Nat. Eagle Scout Assn., Rho Chi. Republican. Episcopalian. Avocation: travel. Home: 1707 Lakeshore Dr Lodi CA 95242-4223 Office: Drs Hosp Manteca 1205 E North St Manteca CA 95336-4932

HIRNING, KATIE, information officer. Grad., Calif. State U.; MBA, Golden Gate U. V.p. NewGeneration Software, Inc., 1989-94; ind. cons. for electronic data interchange translation, 1996-97; chief info. officer Fed. Energy Regulatory Commn., Washington; dir. Office of Chief Info. Officer, Fed. Energy Regulatory Commn.; rep. Commn. on Pres.'s Coun. on Yr. 2000 Conversion; mem. Small Agy. Coun. Dem. nominee for Congress, Calif.'s 4th Dist., 1994, 96. FAX: 202-208-1259. Office: Fed Energy Regulatory Commn Office Chief Info Officer 888 1st St NE Ste 11J Washington DC 20426-0002

HIROHATA, DEREK KAZUYOSHI, career officer; b. Dos Palos, Calif., June 26, 1963; s. Vincent Yoshinobu and Gertrude Sumiko (Kimura) H. BA in Polit. Sci., Calif. State U., Fresno, 1987; grad., Italian Mil. Jump Sch., 1989, USAFE Command & Control Sch., 1990, Brit. Army Jump Sch., 1990; MA in Aerospace Sci., Embry riddle U., Carbondale, 1992; JD, So. Ill. U., Carbondale, 1996. Bar: Calif. 1997, U.S. Ct. Appeals (armed forces) 1997, U.S. Ct. Criminal Appeals (air force) 1997. Commd. 2d lt. U.S. Air Force, advanced through grades to capt., 1991; ground launched cruise missile launch control officer Italy and U.K., 1988-90; emergency actions officer 501 Tactical Missile Wing, RAF Greenham Common, U.K., 1989-90; chief force mgmt. 513 Svcs. Squadron, RAF Mildenhall, U.K., 1990-92; billeting & food svc. coord., laison officer Air Fete, Eng.; treaty inspector escort Conventional Forces Europe; USAFR, 1993—, 932 SVS ops. officer, 1993-97; dept. judge advocate gen. USAF, 1997—. Contbr. to poetry anthologies Am. Poetry Soc., 1993, Poets Pen Quarterly, 1993, Memories Anthology, 1994, Delta. Coord. peer support network Sch. Law So. Ill. U., Carbondale, founder, capt. trial advocacy competition team, 1994-95; mem. Jessup Internat. Moot Ct. team. Mem. ABA, ATLA (founder So. Ill. U.-Carbondale chpt.), Calif. State Bar Assn. Am. Psychology and Law Soc., Christian Legal Soc., Internat. Law Soc., So. Ill. U.-Carbondale Student Bar Assn., So. Ill. U.-Carbondale Law & Medicine Soc., Air and Space Smithsonian, Officers' Christian Fellowship, Airforce Assn., Air Force Edn. Soc., U.S. Capitol Hist. Soc., Calif. State U.-Fresno Alumni Orgn., West Coast Karate Assn., Assn. Air Force Missileers (assoc.), Sigma Nu (alumni advisor So. Ill. U.-Carbondale chpt., dist. comdr., div. comdr. Far West), Fed. Bar Assn., State Bar Calif., Lawyer-Pilots Bar Assn., Ground Launched Cruise Missile Hist. Found. Republican. Methodist. Avocations: karate, flying, scuba diving, sky diving, photography. Home: PO Box 243 South Dos Palos CA 93665-0243

HIRONDELLE, ANNE ELIZABETH, ceramic artist; b. Vancouver, Wash., July 8, 1944; d. John Wayne and Alice G. (Tokola) Harvey; m. Robert Lee Schwiesow, Aug. 26, 1967. BA in English, U. Puget Sound, 1966; MA in Counseling Psychology, Stanford U., 1967; postgrad. Sch. Law, U. Wash., 1972-73; student ceramics program, Factory of Visual Art, Seattle, 1973-74; postgrad., U. Wash., 1974-76. Assoc. dir. U. Wash. YMCA, Seattle, 1967-69, dir., 1969-72; lectr., artist-in-residence, workshop leader Pacific Luth. U., Tacoma, 1980, Multnomah Art Ctr., Portland, 1982, Brookhaven Coll., Farmers Branch, Tex., 1988, Internat. Clay Seminar, Calgary, Alta., Can., 1989, Sonoma State Coll., Santa Rosa, Calif., 1990, Emily Carr Sch. Art and Design, Vancouver, B.C., Can., 1990, Tulane U., New Orleans, 1991, Santa Rosa Jr. Coll., 1991, Newport H. S., Bellevue, 1992, Arrowmont Sch. Arts and Crafts, Gatlinburg, Tenn., 1993, Boise State U., 1993, Craft Students League, N.Y.C., 1994. One person shows include Pacific Luth. U., Tacoma, Wash., 1980, Seattle Ctr., 1985, Lawrence Gallery, Portland, Oreg., 1986, 88, Foster/White Gallery at Frederick & Nelson, Seattle, 1986, Martha Schneider Gallery, Highland Park, Ill., 1987, Franklin House Gallery, Port Townsend, Wash., 1985, 87, 90, Garth Clark Gallery, Kansas City, Mo., 1990, Maveety Gallery, Salishan, Oreg., 1991, Schneider-Bluhm-Loeb Gallery, Chgo., 1992, Joanne Rapp Gallery, Scottsdale, Ariz., 1991, 93, The Works Gallery, Phila., 1991, 94, Garth Clark Gallery, N.Y.C., 1992, 94, Garth Clark Gallery, L.A., 1987, 89, 90, 93, 95; exhibited in group shows Oreg. Sch. Arts and Crafts, Portland, 1979, Sussler Gallery, U. Mich., Ann Arbor, 1980, Henry Gallery, U. Wash., Seattle, 1981, Lawrence Salishan Gallery, Gleneden Beach, Oreg., 1982, Hockaday Ctr. for Arts, Kalispel, Mo., 1983, Bellevue (Wash.) Art Mus., 1984, Tacoma Art Mus., 1984, Foster/White Gallery, Seattle, 1985, 87, 93, Gallery Eight, La Jolla, Calif., 1986, 87, 93, Martha Schneider Gallery, Chgo., 1986, 90, Safeco Plaza, Seattle, 1986, Garth Clark Gallery, N.Y.C., 1986, 87, 88, 89, 91, 92, Susan Cummings Gallery, Walnut Creek, Calif., 1987, Pewabic Pottery, Detroit, 1987, Athenaem Mus., Alexandria, Va., 1988, Lawrence Gallery, Portland, 1988, Faith Nightingale Gallery, San Diego, 1988, 91, Nora Eccles Harrison Mus. Art, Utah State U., Logan, 1989, Cedar Creek Gallery, Creedmore, N.C., 1989, Sonoma State U. Art Gallery, Rohnert, Calif., 1990, Moira-James Gallery, Green Valley, Nev., 1990, 91, Swidler Gallery, Royal Oak, Mich., 1989, 90, 91, The Works Gallery, Phila., Pa., 1990, Am. Craft Mus., N.Y.C., 1991, Conterprary Crafts gallery, Portland, 1991, Pro Art Gallery, St. Louis, 1992, 93, Kirkland (Wash.) Arts Ctr., 1992, MacKenzie Fine Arts Ctr, Dearborn, Mich., 1993, The 1004 Gallery, Port Townsend, Wash., 1993, Craft Alliance, St. Louis, 1993, 94, Ferrin Gallery, Northampton, Mass., 1993, Art Ctr. Gallery Seattle Pacific U., 1993, Schmidt-Bingham Gallery, N.Y.C., 1994, Galleries of Dept. Art Tex. Tech. U., 1994, Artworks Gallery, Seattle, 1994; represented in numerous pub. and pvt. permanent collections including Am. Craft Mus., Ariz. State U. Art Mus., Boise State U., Gateway Tower, Newark Mus., Nora Eccles Harrison Mus. Art, Pacific Lut. U., Oreg. Arts Commn., U. Iowa Mus. Art, The White House, Charles A. Wustum Mus. Fine Arts, others; featured in numerous profl. jours., art. mags., mags. and newspapers. Recipient 1st pl. awards, 1989; Nat. Endowment for Arts visual artist fellow, 1988. Avocation: gardening. Office: Foster/White Gallery 123 S Jackson St Seattle WA 98104*

HIRONO, MAZIE KEIKO, state official; b. Fukushima, Japan, Nov. 3, 1947; came to U.S., 1955, naturalized, 1957; d. Laura Chie (Sato) H. B.A., U. Hawaii, 1970; J.D., Georgetown U., 1978. Dep. atty. gen., Honolulu, 1978-80; Shim, Tam, Kirimitsu & Naito, 1984-88; mem. Hawaii Ho. of Reps., Honolulu, 1980-94; elected lt. gov., 1994. Bd. dirs. Nuuanu YMCA, Honolulu, 1982-84, Moiliili Cmty. Ctr., Honolulu, 1984; dep. chair Dem. Nat. Com., 1997. Mem. U.S. Supreme Ct. Bar, Hawaii Bar Assn., Phi Beta Kappa. Democrat. Office: State Capitol Lt Governor's Office PO Box 3226 Honolulu HI 96801-3226

HIROSE, AKIRA, physics educator, researcher; b. Kijimadaira, Nagano, Japan, Aug. 16, 1941; came to Can., 1971; s. Genji and Katsuyo (Yamada) H.; m. Kimiko Yamamoto, Feb. 4, 1969; children: Tadashi, Kyoko. B Engring., Yokohama (Japan) Nat. U., 1965, M Engring., 1967; PhD, U. Tenn., 1969; DSc, U. Sask., 1994. Mem. rsch. sect. Oak Ridge (Tenn.) Nat. Lab., 1969-71; rsch. scientist U. Sask., Saskatoon, Can., 1971-77, assoc. prof., 1977-79, prof. physics, 1979—; corr. Plasma Phys. Controlled Fusion, 1984—; chmn. Internat. Conf. on Plasma Sci., Saskatoon, 1986; vis. prof. FOM Inst. Plasmafysica, The Netherlands, 1989, Tokyo Met. Inst. Tech., 1996; disting. fgn. rschr. Japan Atomic Energy Rsch. Inst., 1995. Author: Introduction to Wave Phenomena, 1985; contbr. over 180 articles to profl. jours. Recipient IEEE Merit award Nuclear and Plasma Scis. Soc., 1993, Disting. Rschr.'s award U. Sask., 1995, Plasma Sci. and Applications award IEEE Nuclear Plasma Sci. Soc., 1998; Fulbright scholar, 1967; Nat. Sci. Engring. Rsch. Coun. grantee, 1977; Japan Soc. Promotion Sci. rsch. fellow, 1984. Fellow IEEE (assoc. editor Trans. Plasma Sci. 1983—), Am. Phys. Soc.; mem. Can. Assn. Physicists (chmn. divsn. plasma physics 1981-82, 94-95). Home: 2914 East View, Saskatoon, SK Canada S7J 3H9 Office: U Sask, Dept Physics & Engring Phys, Saskatoon, SK Canada S7N 5E2

HIROSE, TERUO TERRY, surgeon, educator; b. Tokyo, Jan. 20, 1926; s. Yohei and Seiko (Ogushi) H.; m. Tomiko Kodama, June 1, 1976; 1 son, George Philamore. BS, Tokyo Coll., 1944; MD, Chiba U., Japan, 1948, PhD, 1958. Diplomate Am. Bd. Surgery, Am. Bd. Thoracic Surgery. Intern Chiba U. Hosp., 1948-49, resident in surgery, 1949-52; resident in surgery Am. Hosp., Chgo., 1954; resident in thoracic surgery Hahnemann Med. Coll., Phila., 1955-56, N.Y. Med. Coll., N.Y.C., 1961-62; practice medicine specializing in surgery Chiba, Japan, 1952-53; chief of surgery Tsushimi Hosp., Hagi, Japan, 1958-59; asst. prof. surgery Chiba U., 1959; research fellow advanced cardiovascular surgery Hahnemann Hosp., Phila., 1959; teaching fellow surgery N.Y. Med. Coll., 1959-60, instr., 1961-62; pvt. practice N.Y.C., 1965-89, N.J., 1965-89; dir. cardiovascular lab. St. Barnabas Hosp., N.Y.C., 1975-84; sr. attending surgeon St. Barnabas Hosp., 1965-81; chief vascular surgery Union Hosp., Bronx, N.Y., 1966-67; attending surgeon Flower and Fifth Ave Hosp., N.Y.C., 1973-80, Jewish Hosp. Med. Center, Bklyn., 1976-80, St. Vincent Hosp., N.Y.C., 1976-88, Mamonides Hosp., Bklyn., 1976-78, Passaic Gen. Hosp., 1977-88, Westchester (N.Y.) County Hosp., 1977-78, Yonkers (N.Y.) Profl. Hosp., 1978-79, Westchester Sq. Hosp., 1978-84, Yonkers Gen. Hosp., 1980-89, St. Joseph Hosp., Yonkers, 1980-89; clin. prof. surgery N.Y. Med. Coll., 1974-89; dir. KPMG Health Care, Japan, 1997—. Author: (in Japanese) A Chaos of American Medicine, 1987, Japanese Doctor, 1987, Where American Medicine Is Going, 1988, Major Surgery Without Blood Transfusion, 1990, Problems and Solutions of American Medicine, 1991, Warning for Modern Medical Science (New Medical Ethics), 1992, Comparative Studies of Medical System in the World, 1992, The Changing Face of Geriatrics, 1994, Monologue of Japanese American Physician, 1995, Environmental Medicine, 1998, Japan! Do Not Follow American Health Care System, 1998, Quality of Life in Modern Medicine, 1998, Medicine About Life and Death, 1998, 99, Why AIDS Can Not Be Conquered, 1999; author 10 med. monograms, 1968-80; editor Japanese Med. Planner Ltd.; contbr. over 700 articles to profl. jours. Recipient Hektoen Bronze medal AMA, 1965, Gold medal, 1971. Fellow Am. Coll. Angiology, Am. Coll. Chest Physicians, Am. Coll. Cardiology, Internat. Coll. Surgeons, N.Y. Acad. Medicine; mem. Am. Assn. Thoracic Surgery, N.Y. Soc. Thoracic Surgery, Pan-Pacific Surg. Assn., Internat. Cardiovascular Soc., Am. Geriatric Soc., Am. Fedn. Clin. Rsch., Am. Writers Assn. Achievements include invention of single pass low prime oxygenator; pioneer aortocoronary direct bypass surgery, open heart surgery without blood transfusion. *One should respect another's religion or creed and offer assistance regardless of whether or not one is in agreement with the other's belief, provided that belief harms no other.*

HIRSA, AMIR H., aerospace engineer, educator; b. Tehran, Nov. 23, 1962; came to U.S., 1975; s. Hossein and Forough (Khonsari) H.; m. Azita Hosseini-Ara, Oct. 5, 1991. BS in Aeronautics, San Jose State U., 1983; MS in Aerospace Engring., U. Mich., 1986, PhD in Aerospace Engring., 1990. From asst. prof. to assoc. prof. Rensselaer Poly. Inst., Troy, N.Y., 1990—; Navy faculty fellow David Taylor Model Basin, Carderock, Md., 1992; cons.

Arthur D. Little, Inc., Cambridge, Mass., 1990-91. Grantee NSF, 1992, 98, Office of Naval Rsch., 1993, 96, 97. Mem. Am. Phys. Soc. Achievements include discovery of novel methods to generate and study vortex flows, novel methods to quantify the intrinsic viscoelastic properties of gas-liquid interfaces in the presence of surfactants; fundamental contributions to understanding the role of surfactants on interfacial hydrodynamics. Office: Rensselaer Poly Inst Dept Mech Engring Aero Engring & Mechs 110 8th St Dept Mech Troy NY 12180-3590

HIRSCH, BARRY, lawyer; b. N.Y.C., Mar. 19, 1933; s. Emanuel M. and Minnie (Levenson) H.; m. Myra Seiden, June 13, 1963; children—Victor Terry II, Neil Charles Seiden, Nancy Elizabeth. BSBA, U. Mo., 1954; J.D., U. Mich., 1959; LL.M., N.Y. U., 1964. Bar: N.Y. bar 1960. Assoc., then partner firm Seligson & Morris, N.Y.C., 1960-69; v.p., sec., gen. counsel dir. B.T.B. Corp., 1969-71; v.p., sec., gen. counsel Loews Corp. (and subsidiaries), 1971-86, sr. v.p., sec., gen. counsel, 1986—; bds. dirs. Neuberger and Berman Fixed Income Funds. Served to 1st lt. AUS, 1954-56. Mem. ABA, Assn. of Bar of City of N.Y., N.Y. State Bar Assn., Zeta Beta Tau, Phi Delta Phi. Home: 1010 5th Ave New York NY 10028-0130 Office: Loews Corp 667 Madison Ave Fl 7 New York NY 10021-8087

HIRSCH, BARRY L., lawyer; b. Chgo., Nov. 11, 1933. Student, UCLA; LLB, U. So. Calif., 1957. Bar: Calif. 1957, N.Y. 1985. Ptnr. Armstrong, Hirsch, Jackoway, Tyerman & Wertheimer, L.A. Mem. State Bar Calif., L.A. County Bar Assn., Beverly Hills Bar Assn., L.A. Copyright Soc. Office: Armstrong Hirsch Jackoway Tyerman & Wertheimer 1888 Century Park E Los Angeles CA 90067-1702*

HIRSCH, BRUCE ELLIOT, anatomy educator; b. Chgo., Apr. 22, 1944; s. Sidney Harold and Esther (Gershon) H.; m. Charlene Zaslawsky, Aug. 15, 1976; 1 child, Joel. BS, U. Chgo., 1966; PhD, U. Pa., 1974. Lectr. U. Ibadan, Nigeria, 1975, Immaculata (Pa.) Coll., 1976-78; vis. investigator Hadassah Med. Sch./Hebrew U., Jerusalem, 1979-80; assoc. prof. biomed. scis. Pa. Coll. Podiatric Medicine, Phila., 1976-98; assoc. prof. anatomy and cell biology Temple U., Phila., 1998—; adj. asst. prof. U. Pa., Phila., 1993—. Author: Foot and Ankle, 1993; contbr. articles to profl. jours. Mem. AAUP, Am. Assn. Anatomists, Am. Assn. Clin. Anatomists, Internat. Orgn. Optical Engring. Jewish. Avocations: photography, woodworking.

HIRSCH, CARL HERBERT, retired manufacturing company executive; b. Pontiac, Mich., Aug. 24, 1934; s. Robert Reynolds and Charlotte (Zeiss) H.; BS in Mech. Engring., U. Mich., 1957; M in Indsl. Engring., U. Toledo, 1962, MBA, 1967; grad. Advanced Mgmt. Program, Harvard U., 1974; m. Anne Louise Dearing, June 27, 1959; children: Jeffrey Todd, Gregory Scott. Product engr. Babcock & Wilcox Co., Barberton, Ohio, 1959-60; product engr. Dana Corp., Toledo, 1960-67, mfg. mgr. Perfect Circle div., 1967-69, pres. C.A. Danaven subs. Dana Corp., Valencia, Venezuela, 1969-72, v.p. Latin Am. Dana Internat. div., Toledo, 1972-73, v.p., gen. mgr. Spicer Clutch div., Ft. Wayne, Ind., 1973-75, Spicer Universal Joint div., Toledo, 1975-76, group v.p. Dana Corp., 1977-78, exec. v.p. vehicular, 1979-80, v.p. corp. planning, 1980-85, sr. v.p., 1985-91, exec. v.p., 1991-95, pres. Dana Internat., 1996-98, ret., 1998; instr. Earlham Coll., 1967-69, U. Toledo, 1962-65; mem. Mfg. Alliance for Productivity and Innovation, Global Bus. Coun.; industry adv. com. Coll. Engring., U. Mich.; adv. com. Ctr. Internat. Bus. Edn. U. Mich. Bd. dirs. ATA Found., World Trade Ctr. Toldeo, Toledo Area council Boy Scouts Am., NW Ohio Jr. Achievement, Child Abuse Prevention Center, Toledo Zool. Soc., Maumee Valley Country Day Sch., Sta. WGTE-PBS. Served to lt. USN, 1957-59. Registered profl. engr., Mich. Mem. Nat. Mgmt. Assn., Sigma Alpha Epsilon. Presbyterian. Home: 110 Treetop Pl Holland OH 43528-8450*

HIRSCH, CHARLES FLYNN, writer, editor; b. St. Paul, Oct. 6, 1947; s. Bernard Aloysius and Margaret Ruth (Horn) H. BA, U. Minn., 1969; MS, Syracuse U., 1982. Instr. Newhouse Sch. Comms. Syracuse (N.Y.) U., 1981-83; dir. editl. svcs. PI Advt., N.Y.C., 1983-85; project editor, writer, prodr., dir. Zaner Bloser, Honesdale, Pa., 1987-88; editor Globe/Prentice Hall, Teaneck, N.J., 1988; cons. editor Weekly Reader Field Publs., Middletown, Conn., 1988-90; developmental editor Highlights for Children, Honesdale; 1991; curriculum cons. Calif. Dept. Edn., San Diego, San Francisco, 1991-94; project editor Oxford U. Press., N.Y.C., 1996-98; spkr. in field; artistic dir. La Rue Geneva Film Festival, Ithaca, N.Y., 1981. Author: (curriculum materials) World of Reading, 1987, Sports Pages, 1987, Muppet Bedtime Stories, 1989; Learning to Be a Healthy Kid, 1991-94, (book/tape series) The Joinables: Meet the Joinables, Ms. Grace Gives a Party, Baby Di Changes Color, 1991, Primary Place, 1994, (non-fiction) Taxation, 1993, (ednl. games) Geo Safari Sports Pages, 1996; co-author: (with Debbie Beres Supple) 61 Cooperative Learning Activities in ESL, 1996; writer, developer for internet: Cyberseniors, 1998; editor: Spelling Connections: Words Into Language, 1988, World of Language, 1988, The Oxford Picture Dictionary for the Content Areas, 1999; writer, prodr., dir. (videotapes) Spelling Connections, 1989; host, prodr. TV newsmag. Are We On, 1980-81. Cons. artistic dir. Franco-Am. Arts Assn., Bozouls, France, 1991-98; policy advisor Alameda (Calif.) County Office Edn., 1994-96; shelter coord. St. Francis Xavier Homeless Shelter, N.Y.C., 1996-98; mem., cons. for curriculum devel. Gay, Lesbian, Straight Ednl. Network. Recipient Achievement award for cable programming Am. TV Corp., 1979, 80; grantee Lila H. Wallace Found., 1981, Far West Labs., 1995, Daedulus Ednl. Found., 1995. Mem. ASCD, Nat. Coun. Tchrs. English, Tchrs. English to Students of Other Langs. Home: 183 Prospect Pl Brooklyn NY 11238-3801

HIRSCH, DANIEL, lawyer; b. Bklyn., Feb. 26, 1940; s. Burton and Lee (Roller) H.; m. Trina Lutter, July 15, 1965 (div.); children: Jessica Elyse, Jeremy Bram. BS, U. Pa., 1960; JD, Columbia U., 1963. Bar: N.Y. 1964. Assoc. Carter Ledyard & Milburn, N.Y.C., 1964-68; pvt. practice N.Y.C., 1968-74; prin. Jones, Hirsch, Connors & Bull, P.C., N.Y.C., 1974—; dir. Loral Orion. Lt. USNR, 1965-75. Mem. N.Y. State Bar Assn., Assn. of Bar of City of N.Y., Fedn. Ins. and Corp. Counsel, Univ. Club. Office: Jones Hirsch Connors & Bull 101 E 52nd St Fl 22 New York NY 10022-6061

HIRSCH, DAVID L., lawyer, corporate executive. BA, Pomona Coll., 1959; JD, U. Calif., Berkeley, 1962. Bar: Calif. 1963. V.p. Masco Tech./NI Industries, Inc., Taylor, Mich., 1966—; v.p. mem. commn. on Govt. Procurement for U.S. Congress, 1971. Mem. editorial bd. Bur. Nat. Affairs' Fed. Contracts Report. Fellow Am. Bar Found.; mem. ABA (life fellow of fellows, chair emerging issues com. sect. pub. contract law, sec. pub. contract law sect. 1977-78, mem. council 1978-80, chmn. 1981-82), Calif. Bar (bd. advisors pub. law sect.), Los Angeles County Bar Assn., Fed. Bar Assn., Nat. Contract Mgmt. Assn. (nat. bd. advisors), Fin. Exec. Inst. (legal advisor com. on govt. bus.). Office: Masco Tech Corp/NI Industries Inc 21001 Van Born Rd Taylor MI 48180-1300

HIRSCH, EDWARD MARK, poet, English language educator; b. Chgo., Jan. 20, 1950; s. Kurt and Irma (Ginsburg) H.; m. Janet Landay, May 29, 1977. BA, Grinnell Coll., 1972; PhD, U. Pa., 1978. Asst. prof. Wayne State U., Detroit, 1978-82, assoc. prof., 1982-85; assoc. prof. U. Houston, 1985-87, prof. English, 1987—. Author: (poems) For the Sleepwalkers, 1981 (Lavan Younger Poets award 1985), Wild Gratitude, 1986 (Nat. Book Critics Cir. award), The Night Parade, 1989, Earthly Measures, 1994, On Love, 1998, (prose) How to Read a Poem and Fall in Love with Poetry, 1999, Responsive Reading, 1999; editor: Transforming Vision: Writers on Art, 1994. Nat. Endowments for Arts Creative Writing fellow, 1982, Guggenheim fellow, 1985; recipient Tex. Inst. of Arts and Letters award, 1987, Lit. award Am. Acad. Arts Letters, 1998; recipient Prix de Rome, 1988, Lyndhurst prize, 1994-96; MacArthur fellow, 1998. Home: 1528 Sul Ross St Houston TX 77006-4730 Office: U Houston Dept English Houston TX 77204

HIRSCH, ELOISE, city administrator. BA in Polit. Sci., Sarah Lawrence Coll., 1967. Dir. City Planning Dept. City Pitts., 1992—. Bd. dirs. Bethlehem Haven Women's Shelter, Architrace-Pitts. Found. Architecture. Mem. Internat. Women's Forum, Am. Planning Assn. Office: John P Robin Civic Bldg 200 Ross St Ste 4 Pittsburgh PA 15219-2014*

HIRSCH, ERIC DONALD, JR., English language educator, educational reformer; b. Memphis, Mar. 22, 1928; s. Eric Donald and Leah (Aschaffenburg) H.; m. Mary Monteith Pope, June 15, 1958; children: Eric, John, Frederick, Elizabeth. BA, Cornell U., 1950; MA, Yale U., 1955, PhD (Fulbright fellow), 1957; LittD (hon.), Williams Coll., 1989, Rhodes Coll., 1993, Rollins Coll., 1994, Marietta Coll., 1997. Instr. Yale, 1956-61, asst. prof. English, 1961-64, assoc. prof., 1964-66; prof. U. Va., Charlottesville, 1966—, chmn. dept. English, 1968-71, 81-83; dir. composition U. Va., 1971—, Kenan prof. English, 1973—; Linden Kent prof. English U. Va., Charlottesville, 1989-94, Univ. prof. edn. and humanities, 1994; founder, pres. Core Knowledge Found., Charlottesville, 1986—; bd. dirs. U. Press; lectr. in field; supervising com. English Inst., 1972-74; mem. nat. adv. coun. N.Y. Regent's Competency Tests in Writing, 1979; advisor Nat. Coun. Ednl. Rsch., 1983; bd. dirs. Founds. Literacy Project, 1985—; pres. Cultural Literacy Found., 1987, Core Knowledge Found., 1990; dir. Albert Shanker Inst., 1997—. Author: Wordsworth and Schelling: A Typological Study of Romanticism, 1960, Innocence and Experience: An Introduction to Blake, 1964 (Explicator award), Validity in Interpretation, 1967, The Aims of Interpretation, 1976, The Philosophy of Composition, 1977, Cultural Literacy: What Every American Needs to Know, 1987; co-author: A Dictionary of Cultural Literacy, 1988; editor: A First Dictionary of Cultural Literacy, 1989, The Core Knowledge Series, Book I: What First Graders Need to Know, 1991, Book II: What Second Graders Need to Know, 1991, Book III: What Third Graders Need to Know, 1992, Book IV: What Fourth Graders Need to Know, 1992, Book V: What Fifth Graders Need to Know, 1993, Book VI: What Sixth Graders Need to Know, 1993, The Schools We Need and Why We Don't Have Them, 1996; mem. adv. bd. Jour. Basic Writing, Blake Studies, Critical Inquiry, Genre New Lit. History, Lit. in Performance; contbr. articles to profl. jours. Pres. Coalition for Core Curriculum, 1989—. Served with USNR, 1950-52. Morse fellow, 1961-62; Guggenheim fellow, 1964-65; sr. fellow NEH, 1971, 80-81; fellow Center for Humanities Wesleyan U., 1973; fellow Council Humanities Princeton U., 1976; fellow Center for Advanced Study in Behavioral Scis., 1980-81; fellow Humanities Research Ctr., Australian Nat. U., 1982; Bateson lectr. Oxford U., 1983. Fellow Internat. Acad. Edn. in Royal Acad. Sci. Lit. and Arts (Brussels); mem. Am. Acad. Arts and Scis. (supervisory com. 1981-86), MLA, Byron Soc., Am. Fedn. Tchrs. (Biennial Quest award 1997). Home: 2006 Pine Top Rd Charlottesville VA 22903-1233

HIRSCH, GEORGE AARON, publisher; b. N.Y.C., June 21, 1934; s. George J. and Sylvia (Epstein) H.; m. Shay Yandell Scrivner; children: David Aaron, William George; stepchildren: Ian Gregory Scrivner, Sean Gabriel Scrivner. A.B. magna cum laude, Princeton U., 1956; M.B.A., Harvard U., 1962. With Time-Life Internat., 1962-67; founding pub., pres. New York Mag., N.Y.C., 1967-71; chmn., pres., CEO New Times Comm. Corp., N.Y.C., 1973-79; founding pub. New Times mag., N.Y.C., 1973-79; founder, pub. The Runner Mag., N.Y.C., 1978-87; v.p., pub. Runner's World mag. Mag. divsn. Rodale Press, Inc., 1987—; group pub. Rodale Active Network, 1987—; pub. dir. Men's Health mag., 1987—; dir. internat. mags. Rodale Press, 1995—; TV sports commentator, 1979—. A founder N.Y.C. Marathon, 1976; hon. mem. exec. com. alumni coun. Princeton U.; Dem. candidate for 15th Congl. Dist., N.Y., 1986; del. Dem. Nat. Conv., 1988. With USNR, 1957-60. Mem. Century Assn. Club. Office: Runner's World 733 3rd Ave Fl 15 New York NY 10017-3204*

HIRSCH, GILAH YELIN, artist, writer; b. Montreal, Quebec, Can., Aug. 24, 1944; came to U.S., 1963; d. Ezra and Shulamis (Borodensky) Y. BA, U. Calif., Berkeley, 1967; MFA, UCLA, 1970. Prof. of art Calif. State U., Dominguez Hills, L.A., 1973—; adj. prof. Internat. Coll., Guild of Tutors, L.A., 1980-87, Union Grad. Sch., Cin., 1990. Founding mem. Santa Monica (Calif.) Art Bank, 1983-85; bd. dirs. Dorland Mountain Colony, Temecula, Calif., 1984-88. Recipient Disting. Artist award Calif. State U., 1985, Found. Rsch. award, 1988, 89, 97, 98; grantee Nat. Endowment for the Arts, 1985; Dorland Mountain Colony fellow, 1981-84, MacDowell Colony fellow, N.H., 1987, Banff Ctr. for the Arts fellow, Can., 1985; named artist-in-residence RIM Inst., Payson, Ariz., 1989-90, Tamarind Inst. of Lithography, Albuquerque, 1973, Rockefeller Bellagio Ctr., Italy, 1992, Tyrone Guthrie Ctr. for Arts, Annamahkerrig, Ireland, 1993, creative rsch. award Sally Canova Rsch. Scholarship and Creative Activities awards program, 1997, 98, 99. Office: Calif State Univ Dominguez Hills 1000 E Victoria St Carson CA 90747-0001

HIRSCH, HORST EBERHARD, business consultant in metals and semiconductors; b. Woelsendorf, Fed. Republic Germany, July 26, 1933; came to U.S., 1984; s. Albert and Emilie (Eberhardt) H.; m. Helga G. Gruber, May 2, 1961; children: Manon K., Fabiane M., Erin A. Diploma in chemistry, Tech. U. Karlsruhe, Fed. Republic Germany, 1959, D in Chem. Tech., 1961. Postdoctoral fellow NRC of Can., 1961-62; research and devel. engr., mgr. Cominco Ltd., Trail, B.C., Can., 1962-84; pres., chief exec. officer Cominco Electronic Materials Inc., Spokane, Wash., 1984-88; pres. Johnson Matthey Electronics N.Am., Spokane, 1989-91, MSM, 1991—; vis. exec. IESC, 1992, field assoc., 1993—; mem. bd. mgmt. B.C. Rsch. Coun., Vancouver, 1980-84; senate U. B.C., Vancouver, 1981-85; mem. adv. com. Wash. Tech. Ctr., 1992-94. Contbr. articles on chemistry and metallurgy to profl. publs., chpts. to books; patentee in field. Recipient Excellence in Innovation award Fed. Govt. Can., 1985. Mem. Soc. German Mining and Metall. Engrs. Lutheran. Avocations: reading, skiing, swimming, golfing.

HIRSCH, JAMES ALAN, executive director; b. Evanston, Ill., Feb. 24, 1953; s. Walter James and Marjorie (Abrahms) H.; m. Michelle Wilder, May 23, 1988. Student, So. Ill. U., 1973-74. Dir. Evanston br. Old Town Sch. Folk Music, 1978-82; instr. Old Town Sch. Folk Music, Chgo., 1975-78, exec. dir., 1982—; dir., cons. Chgo. Area Bluegrass Assn., Chgo., 1983-85; dir. Urban Traditions, Chgo., 1987—. Performer, writer: (albums) Working on Steel, 1978, Tricky Fingers, 1983. Recipient Excellence award Beatrice Found., 1987; named Entrepreneur of Yr. Columbia Coll. Arts, 1996, Chicagoan of Yr., Chgo. Mag., 1998. Avocations: bowling, golfing, music, books. Office: Old Town Sch Folk Music 4544 N Loncoln Ave Chicago IL 60625

HIRSCH, JEFFREY ALLAN, lawyer; b. Chgo., June 14, 1950; s. Leo Paul And Dorthy (Seidman) H.; m. Lennie Sue Henderson, June 16, 1979; children: Lea, Ashley. BSBA, U. Fla., 1972, JD with honors, 1975. Bar: Fla. 1975, U.S. Dist. Ct. (so. and mid. dists.) Fla. 1975. Assoc. Swann & Glass, Coral Gables, Fla., 1975-76, Glass, Schultz, Weinstein & Moss, Coral Gables, 1976-80; ptnr. Holland & Knight, Ft. Lauderdale, Fla., 1980-93; prin. shareholder Greenberg, Traurig, Hoffman, Lipoff, Rosen & Quentel, P.A., Ft. Lauderdale, Fla., 1993-98, Greenberg, Traurig, P.A., Ft. Lauderdale, Fla., 1998—; exec. dir. Govtl. Research Ctr., Gainesville, Fla., 1975. Active Leadership Broward, Ft. Lauderdale, 1986—, Leadership Fla., 1994—. Mem. ABA, Fla. Bar Assn., Broward County Bar Assn. Avocations: reading, travel. Office: Greenberg Traurig PA Ste 1500 515 E Las Olas Blvd Fort Lauderdale FL 33301-2296*

HIRSCH, JEROME S., lawyer; b. N.Y.C., 1948. BA in Econs., SUNY, Binghamton, 1970; JD, Fordham U., 1974. Bar: N.Y. Assoc. Skadden, Arps, Slate, Meagher & Flom, N.Y.C., 1974-81, ptnr., 1982—. Mem. ABA (class action and derivative lawsuits subcom. 1982-85, corp. counsel com., co-chmn. subcom. on settlement techniques), N.Y. State Bar Assn., Assn. of Bar of City of N.Y. Office: Skadden Arps Slate Meagher & Flom 919 3rd Ave New York NY 10022-3902

HIRSCH, JUDD, actor; b. N.Y.C., Mar. 15, 1935; s. Joseph Sidney and Sally (Kitzis) H.; m. Bonni Chalkin, Dec. 24, 1992. BS in Physics, CCNY, 1960. Broadway appearances in Barefoot in the Park, 1966, Knock Knock, 1976 (Drama Desk award for best featured actor), Chapter Two, 1977-78, Talley's Folly, 1980, I'm Not Rappaport, 1985-86 (Tony award for best actor in play 1986, Outer Critics Circle award, 1986), Conversations with My Father, 1992 (Tony award for best actor in play 1992, Outer Critics Circle award, 1992), A Thousand Clowns, 1996; off-Broadway appearances in On the Necessity of Being Polygamous, 1963, Scuba Duba, 1967-69, King of the United States, 1972, Mystery Play, 1972, Hot L Baltimore, 1973, Prodigal, 1973, Knock Knock, 1975, Talley's Folly, 1979 (Obie award), The Seagull, 1983, I'm Not Rappaport, 1985, Below the Belt, 1996; regional appearences include Theater for Living Arts, Phila., 1969-70, Line of Least Existence, Harry Noon and Night, The Recruiting Officer, Annenberg Ctr., Phila., 1971, Hough in Blazes, Conversations with My Father, Seattle Repertory, 1991, L.A., 1993, Scarborough, Eng., 1994, London, 1995, Death of a Salesman, Chapel Hill, N.C., 1994, Robbers, Long Wharf Theater, 1995, Death of a Salesman Manitoba Theatre Ctr., Winnipeg and Royal Alexandra Theatre, Toronto, 1997; stock and tour appearances in A Thousand Clowns, Threepenny Opera, Fantastiks, Woodstock, N.Y., 1964, Peterpat, Houston and Ft. Worth, 1970, Harvey, Chgo., 1971, And Miss Reardon Drinks a Little, Palm Beach, Fla., 1972, I'm Not Rappaport, nat. tour, 1987; TV appearances include The Keegans, 1975, Medical Story, 1975, Delvecchio series, 1976-77, Rhoda, 1977, Taxi series, 1978-83 (Emmy award for best actor in a comedy series, 1981, 1983), Noel Edmunds Saturday Road Show, 1990 (Eng.), Dear John series (Golden Globe award 1988), 1988-92, George and Leo, 1997; TV movies include The Law, 1974, Fear on Trial, 1975, The Legend of Valentino, 1975, The Halloween That Almost Wasn't, 1979, Sooner or Later, 1979, Marriage Is Alive and Well, 1980, First Steps, 1985, Brotherly Love, 1985, The Great Escape-Untold Story, 1988, She Said No, 1990, Betrayal of Trust, 1993, Color of Justice, 1997, Rocky Marciano and Man on the Moon, 1999; films include King of the Gypsies, 1978, Ordinary People (nominated Acad. Award), 1980, Without a Trace, 1983, Teachers, 1984, The Goodbye People, 1984, Running on Empty, 1988, Independence Day, 1996. Mem. Acad. Motion Picture Arts and Scis., Acad. TV Arts and Scis., Screen Actors Guild, Actors Equity Assn., AFTRA. Office: care J Wolfe Provident Fin Mgmt 10345 W Olympic Blvd Los Angeles CA 90064-2548

HIRSCH, JULES, physician, scientist; b. N.Y.C., Apr. 6, 1927. Student, Rutgers U., 1943-45; MD, U. Tex., 1948; DSc (hon.), SUNY, 1988. Intern pathology and medicine Duke Hosp., N.C., 1948-50; from asst. resident to resident coll. medicine SUNY, Syracuse, 1950-52; asst. prof., assoc. physician Rockefeller U., N.Y.C., 1954-60, assoc. prof., physician, 1960-67, prof., sr. physician, 1967—; Sherman Fairchild prof. Rockefeller U., 1988-98, emeritus, 1998—; sr. physician, 1967—; physician-in-chief Rockefeller U. Hosp., 1992-96, emeritus, 1996—. Recipient Robert H. Herman award, 1994, McCollum award, 1984. Fellow Am. Coll. of Physicians, fellow Royal Coll. Physicians Edinburgh; founding mem. Assn. for Patient Oriented Rsch. (APOR)' mem. AAAS, NAS (Inst. Medicine), Am. Soc. Clin. Investigation, Am. Soc. Clin. Nutrition, Assn. Am. Physicians, Am. Fedn. Clin. Rsch., Harvey Soc. Achievements include research in obesity, human behavior, internal medicine, biochemistry and physiology of lipids, lipid metabolism and nutrition. Office: Rockefeller U 1230 York Ave New York NY 10021-6399

HIRSCH, JUNE SCHAUT, chaplain; b. Green Bay, Wis., Sept. 30, 1925; d. Clifford Charles and Eleanor Josephine (Arts) Schaut; m. Marshall E. Gilette, Jan. 23, 1946 (div. 1974); children: Ronald Leigh, Patrick Allen, Vicki Jeanne Baumann; m. Hubert L. Hirsch, Nov. 7, 1975. Student, St. Mary's Sch. Nursing, Rochester, Minn., 1943-45, U. Wis., Sheboygan, 1974-75. Cert. med. asst., 1966. Med. asst. James W. Faulkner, M.D., Phoenix, 1953-56; med. office mgr. Edward E. Houfek, M.D., Sheboygan, Wis., 1956-75; med. office cons. Profl. Mgmt. Inc., Milw., 1975-77; office mgr., adminstrv. asst. Schroeder & Holt Architects Ltd., Milw., 1977-90; vol. chaplain St. Camillus Health Ctr., Milw., 1991—, Children's Hosp. and Froedent Meml. Hosp., Milw., 1991-95; staff chaplain Froedert Meml. Hosp., 1995—; instr. med. asst. program Lake Shore Tech., 1975-76. Mem. Am. Assn. Med. Assts. (nat. trustee 1963-66), Wis. Soc. Med. Assts. (life, exec. bd. 1975-89), Lake ShoreMed. Assts. (exec. bd. 1959-75), Nat. Assn. Cath. Chaplains (cert.). Republican. Roman Catholic. Home: 10200 W Bluemound Rd Apt 918 Milwaukee WI 53226-4372 Office: Froedtert Meml Luth Hosp 9200 W Wisconsin Ave Milwaukee WI 53226-3522

HIRSCH, LARRY JOSEPH, retail executive, lawyer; b. Boston, July 1, 1938; s. Samuel and Anne (Rossman) H.; m. Kay Pollock, Mar. 16, 1974. BA, Syracuse U., 1962; JD, Suffolk U., Boston, 1968; grad. gemologist, Gem Inst. Am., Los Angeles, 1981. Bar: Mass. 1968, R.I. 1968, Fla. 1970.; cert. gemologist, Los Angeles, 1986. Mgr. Vality Dept. Store, Groton, Conn., 1962-63; asst. area dir. Am. Jewish Com., Miami, Fla., 1968-69; asst. city atty. City of Miami, Fla., 1969-71; atty Feuer & Feuer, Miami, Fla., 1971-74, Turano & Turano, Westerly, R.I., 1974—; asst. town solicitor Town of Westerly, R.I., 1975-76; pres. Westerly Jewelry Co. Inc., Westerly, R.I., 1978—; Mem. adv. bd. Fleet Bank, Westerly, 1984-90; bd. dirs. Washington Trust Bancorp, Inc. Pres. Chariho-Westerly Animal Rescue League, 1976—; incorporator bd. govs. Cmty. Hosp. of Westerly, 1985—, bd. trustees, 1984-94, fin. com., 1984—, human resources com., 1998—; mem. Ctr. for the Arts, Westerly, 1984; v.p. Westerly Heart Assn., 1986; bd. dirs. Am. Heart Assn., Westerly, 1986-93; mem. Charter Revision Com., Westerly, 1985-89; bd. dirs., v.p. Joint Devel. Task Force, Westerly, 1988—, v.p., 1994-99, pres., 1999—; bd. dirs. Animal Rescue League of So. R.I., 1988-94, North End Cmty. Watch, 1996-97; mem. adv. coun. Westerly Integrated Social Svcs. Program, 1996, chmn., 1997—, Westerly Fire Dist. Salary Rev. & Benefits Coms., 1996—; incorporator Westerly Pub. Libr., 1997—; mem. site planning group West High Sch., 1998—. With U.S. Army, 1958-60. Larry Hirsch Day named in his honor, Town of Westerly, 1980; recipient Someone Spl. award, Channel 26 WTWS TV, New London, Conn., 1987; named Columbus Citizen of Yr., Golden Key Club, Westerly, 1989. Mem. Nat. Assn. Jewelry Appraisers, New Eng. Appraisers Assn., Am. Gem Soc., Gemological Inst. Am., Westerly Track Club (pres. 1976, bd. dirs. 1976—), Elks (Larry Hirsch Run 1980—), Fraternal Order Police (assoc., scholar com.). Avocations: long distance running, humane treatment of animals. Office: Westerly Jewelry Co PO Box 324 Westerly RI 02891-0324

HIRSCH, LAURENCE ELIOT, construction executive, mortgage banker; b. N.Y.C., Dec. 19, 1945; s. S. Richard and Lillian (Avenet) H.; m. Susan Judith Creskoff, Dec. 23, 1967; children: Daria Lee, Bradford Richard. BS in Econs., U. Pa., 1968; JD cum laude, Villanova U., 1971. Bar: Pa. 1972, Tex. 1973. Assoc. Wolf, Block, Schorr & Solis Cohen, Phila., 1971-73; assoc. Bracewell & Patterson, Houston, 1973-76, ptnr., 1976-78; pres. Southdown, Inc., Houston, 1977-85, CEO, 1984-85; pres. Centex Corp., Dallas, 1985-88, CEO, 1988—, also chmn. bd. dirs., 1991—; chmn. Centex Constrn. Products, Inc., Dallas, 1994—; Trustee The Blackrock Group; adv. dir. Heidelberger Zement, A.G. Mem. bd. cons. Villanova U. Law Sch.; mem. undergrad. exec. bd. U. Pa. Wharton Sch. With USAR, 1968-75. Office: Centex Corp PO Box 199000 Dallas TX 75219-9000 also: 2728 N Harwood St Dallas TX 75201-1516

HIRSCH, LAWRENCE LEONARD, physician, retired educator; b. Chgo., Aug. 20, 1922; m. Donna Lee Sturm; children: Robert, Edward, Sharon. BS, U. Ill., 1943; MD, U. Ill., Chgo., 1950. Diplomate: Am. Bd. Family Practice. Intern. Ill. Masonic Med. Ctr., Chgo., 1950-51; practice medicine specializing in family medicine Chgo., 1951-70; dir. ambulatory care Ill. Masonic Med. Ctr., Chgo., 1970-71; dir. family practice residency program Ill. Masonic Med. Ctr., 1971-75; prof., chmn. dept. family medicine Chgo. Med. Sch., 1975-89, prof. emeritus, 1989—; mem. med. licensing bd. State of Ill., 1982-94, chmn., 1988-94, hosp. licensing bd., 1994—; bd. dirs. Ill. Coun. for continuing Med. Edn., 1981-85, pres., 1986-87; cons. recombinant DNA Abbott Labs., 1980-87; lectr. in field; staff pres. Ill. Masonic Med. Ctr., 1970. Book rev. editor: Soc. of Tchrs. Family Medicine, 1979-89; book reviewer: Jour. AMA, 1969—; contbr. articles to profl. jours. Bd. dirs. Mid-Am. chpt. ARC, Chgo., 1978-88; nat. pres. Alpha Phi Omega, Kansas City, Mo., 1974-78; exec. com. Chgo. Found. Med. Care and PSRO, 1977-84, Ill. State Inter-Ins. Exchange, 1975—; bd. dirs. Crescent Counties Found. for Med. Care, 1985-91; commr. Northbrook (Ill.) Park Dist., 1987-91, pres., 1990—; mem. Village of Northbrook Planning Commn., 1987-89. Served with U.S. Army, 1943-46. Recipient Silver Beaver award Boy Scouts Am., 1963; recipient Silver Antelope award Boy Scouts Am., 1967, Disting. Eagle award Boy Scouts Am., 1969, Brotherhood award Lakeview Interfaith Council, 1968, Physician Speaker award AMA, 1981; inducted into City of Chgo. Sr. Citizens Hall of Fame, 1991. Fellow AAAS, Am. Acad. Family Physicians (mem. congress of dels.); mem. Chgo. Med. Soc. (pres. 1979, Pub. Svc. award 1990), Ill. Acad. Family Physicians (pres. 1977), Assn. Depts. Family Medicine (exec. com.), Masons, Shriners, Kiwanis (dir. local club). Democrat. Unitarian. Office: 1324 Coventry Ln Northbrook IL 60062-4339

HIRSCH, MARTIN ALAN, dentist; b. N.Y.C., Mar. 26, 1947; s. Arthur Morris and Lillian (Brachfeld) H.; m. Noreen Ellen Hirsch, July 20, 1980; children: Jennifer, Kimberly. BS, CUNY, 1968; DMD, U. Pa., 1972; splty. in prosthodontics, U. Iowa, 1975; splty. in maxillofacial prosthetics, U. Chgo., 1976. Dental extern The Coatsville (Pa.) Hosp., 1971-72; dental intern Mt. Sinai Hosp., N.Y.C., 1972-73; resident VA Hosp., Iowa City, 1973-75, U. Chgo. Hosp. and Clinics, 1975-76; asst. prof. dept. otolaryngology Abraham Lincoln Sch. of Medicine U. Ill. Med. Ctr., Chgo., 1976-77; dir. maxillofacial prosthetics clinic Ctr. for Craniofacial Anamolies U. Ill. Med. Ctr., Chgo., 1976-77; asst. prof. U. Ill. Coll. Dentistry, Chgo., 1977-93; staff dept. dentistry U. Ill. Hosp. Med. Ctr., Chgo, 1979-83; staff dept. surgery dental section Cuneo Hosp., Chgo., 1979-87, Cabrini Hosp., Chgo., 1979-92; staff dept. dentistry Ill. Masonic Med. Ctr., Chgo., 1979—, mem. head and neck treatment ctr., 1981—; sr. staff Columbus Hosp. dept. surgery dental sect., Chgo., 1979-98; pvt. practice gen., cosmetic and prosthetic dentistry Chgo., 1979—; attending Cath. Health Ptnrs., Chgo., 1998—; adj. instr. U. Chgo. Hosps. and Clinics, 1975-76; spkr. dental confs., symposiums, seminars; made presentations to lay audiences on radio and TV. Spkr. Am. Cancer Soc., Chgo. divsn., 1981-87, chmn. profl. edn. com., 1981-85, mem. oral cancer com., 1982-86. Mem. ADA, Ill. Dental Soc., Chgo. Dental Soc. Avocations: swimming, reading. Home: 1578 Hazel Ln Winnetka IL 60093-1313 Office: 2800 N Sheridan Rd Chicago IL 60657-6156

HIRSCH, MICHAEL, lawyer; b. Hamilton, Ohio, Aug. 27, 1949. BA, Duke U., 1971; JD, George Washington U., 1974. Atty. advisor U.S. Gen. Acctg. Office, Washington, 1974-76, Dept. Housing and Urban Devel., Washington, 1976-79; atty. advisor Fed. Emergency Mgmt. Agy., Washington, 1979-90, assoc. gen. counsel, 1991-96, dep. gen. counsel, 1997—. Office: Fed Emergency Mgmt Agy 500 C St SW Ste 840 Washington DC 20472-0001

HIRSCH, MILTON CHARLES, lawyer; b. Chgo., Sept. 10, 1952; s. Charles Ira and Beverly Ruth (Kelner) H.; m. Ilene Lonnie Schreer, Feb. 16, 1986. BA, U. Calif., San Diego, 1974; MS, DePaul U., 1979; JD, Georgetown U., 1982. Bar: Fla. 1982, U.S. Dist. Ct. (so., mid. dists.) Fla. 1983, U.S. Dist. Ct. (no. dist.) Fla. 1985, U.S. Ct. Appeals (5th and 11th cirs.) 1983, U.S. Tax Ct. 1983, U.S. Ct. Claims 1983, U.S. Supreme Ct. 1988. Acct. Arthur Young & Co., CPAs, Chgo., 1977-79; asst. state atty. Office State Atty., Miami, Fla., 1982-84; assoc. Finley, Kumble, Wagner, Heine, Underberg, Manley et al, Miami, 1985-87; pvt. practice Miami, 1987—; adj. prof. Nova U. Law Sch., Ft. Lauderdale, Fla., 1988, 94, 95. Author: Florida Criminal Trial Procedure; contbg. editor Jour. Nat. Assn. Criminal Def. Attys., 1987—; contbr. articles to profl. jours. Mem. ABA (litigation sect.), Nat. Assn. Criminal Def. Lawyers, Fla. Bar Assn.), Fla. Criminal Def. Attys. Assn. (former pres., Presdl. award for Disting. Svc. 1987-88). Office: 9130 S Dadeland Blvd Ste 1504 Miami FL 33156-7850

HIRSCH, PAUL J., orthopedic surgeon, medical executive, educator; b. Bklyn., Oct. 12, 1937; s. Morris M. and Dorothy (Wolitzer) H.; 1 child, Jeremy S. BA in English, Roanoke Coll., 1957; MD, U. Va., 1961. Diplomate Am. Bd. Orthopedic Surgery. Intern NYU-Bellevue Med. Ctr., N.Y.C., 1961-62, resident, 1964-68; chief orthopedic surgery Raritan Valley Hosp., Green Brook, N.J., 1969-71; pvt. practice orthopedic surgery Bridgewater, N.J., 1971—; clin. prof. orthopaedic surgery Seton Hall Sch. Grad. Med. Edn.; pres., med. dir. InterMedix, Lawrenceville, N.J.; active staff, orthopaedic svc. Somerset (N.J.) Med. Ctr.; courtesy staff Robert Wood Johnson U. Hosp., New Brunswick, N.J.; clin. asst. prof. orthopedic surgery Rutgers Med. Sch., 1971-79; clin. instr. orthopedic surgery NYU-Bellevue Med. Ctr., 1969-79; clin. assoc. prof. orthopedic surgery N.J. Med. Sch., 1980—; clin. prof. orthopedic surgery Seton Hall Sch. Postgrad. Medicine; chmn., bd. trustees Jour. Bone and Joint Surgery, 1999; mem. practicing physicians adv. group Nat. Com. Quality Assurance, 1996-98; vice chmn., bd. dirs. MIIX Group, Inc. Chmn. publs. com. Jour. Med. Soc. N.J., 1980-85; contbr. articles, editor profl. jours.,; mem. editorial bd. N.J. Medicine; editor-in-chief N.J. Medicine. Trustee Rutgers Prep. Sch., pres. bd. trustees, 1983-86; trustee Raritan Valley C.C.; bd. dirs. N.J. Med. Polit. Action Com., 1983—, chmn. N.J. Com. for Quality Orthopedic Care; bd. trustees Orthopaedic Rsch. and Edn. Found., 1989-94. Mem. ACS, AMA, Am. Orthopaedic Assn., Am. Acad. Orthopaedic Surgeons (bd. councilors 1982-88), Am. Coll. Physician Execs., Eastern Orthopaedic Assn. (trustee 1981-84), N.J. Orthopaedic Soc. (pres. 1979-80), Med. Soc. N.J. (chmn. orthopaedic sect. 1977-78, ho. of dels. 1976—, treas. 1982-86, 2d v.p. 1986-87, 1st v.p. 1987-88, pres. elect 1988-89, pres. 1989-90, trustee 1982-91), Somerset County Med. Soc., Acad. Medicine of N.J. (chmn. orthopaedic sect. 1975-78, trustee 1978-91, 95—, pres. elect 1982-83, pres. 1983-84), Am. Trauma Soc. (pres. ctrl. Jersey unit 1977-81), Internat. Soc. Orthopaedic Surgery and Traumatology, N.J. Health Scis. Group (treas. 1982-83), N.J. Hosp. Assn. (trustee 1986-89), N.J. Assn. Med. Splty. Socs. (pres. 1979-80, dir. 1981-85), Ind. Sch. Chmn. Assn., Med. Inter-Ins. Exch. N.J. (bd. govs. 1987-90), N.J. State Med. Underwriters, Inc. (bd. dirs. 1990-99, vice chmn. bd. dirs. 1991-99). Office: Green Knoll Profl Park US Hwy 202-206 Bridgewater NJ 08807-1746

HIRSCH, PHILIP FRANCIS, pharmacologist, educator; b. Stockton, Calif., June 24, 1925; s. Harold and Elsa (Frohman) H.; m. Eugenia Isaeff, Sept. 21, 1956; children—Steven, Lisa, Kenny, Nancy. B.S. in Chemistry, U. Calif., Berkeley, 1950, Ph.D. in Physiology, 1954. Lectr. physiology U. Calif., Berkeley, 1954-55; instr. pharmacology Sch. Dental Medicine, Harvard U., Boston, 1955-57; asso. in pharmacology Sch. Dental Medicine, Harvard U., 1957-63, asst. prof. pharmacology, 1964; physiologist Lawrence Livermore Lab., 1964-66; asso. prof. pharmacology Sch. Medicine, U. N.C., Chapel Hill, 1966-70; prof. Sch. Medicine, U. N.C., 1970-92; dir. dental research ctr. U. N.C., 1975-83, prof. dental ecology Sch. of Dentistry, 1988-92, prof. emeritus, 1992—; mem. gen. medicine B study sect. NIH, 1974-78, clin. scis. study section, 1981-85. Contbr. articles to profl. jours. Bd. dirs. YMCA, Chapel Hill, 1981-83. Served with AUS, 1943-46. Mem. AAAS, Am. Soc. for Bone and Mineral Rsch., Endocrine Soc., Am. Soc. Pharmacology and Exptl. Therapeutics, Internat. Bone and Mineral Soc., Sigma Xi. Home: 2008 S Lakeshore Dr Chapel Hill NC 27514-2031 Office: U NC Dental Research Ctr Cb # 7455 Chapel Hill NC 27599

HIRSCH, RAYMOND ROBERT, chemical company executive, lawyer; b. St. Louis, Mar. 20, 1936; s. Raymond Winton and Olive Frances (Gordon) H.; m. Joanne Therese Dennis, Jan. 30, 1960; children: Amy Elizabeth, Thomas Christopher, Timothy Joseph, Mary Patricia. LL.B., St. Louis U., 1959. Bar: Mo. 1959. With Treasury Dept., 1960-62, Petrolite Corp., St. Louis, 1962—; sec. Petrolite Corp., 1971—, v.p., gen. counsel, 1973-82, sr. v.p., gen. counsel, 1982-92; of counsel Guilfoil, Petzall & Shoemake, St. Louis, 1992—; mem. Pub. Defender Commn., Mo. Mcpl. judge City of Bridgeton, Mo., 1970-73; mem. City of Des Peres Planning and Zoning Commn., 1974-78; mem. bd. edn. Spl. Sch. Dist. St. Louis County, 1981-83. Mem. Mo. Air N.G., 1959-60; trustee Childhaven. Mem. ABA, Am. Soc. Corp. Secs., Mo. Bar Assn., Bar Assn. St. Louis. Roman Catholic. Clubs: Missouri Athletic. Home: 3 W Walinca Walk Saint Louis MO 63105-2007 Office: Guilfoil Petzall & Shoemake 100 S 4th St Saint Louis MO 63102-1800

HIRSCH, RICHARD GARY, lawyer; b. L.A., June 15, 1940; s. Charles and Sylvia (Leopold) H.; m. Claire Renee Recsei, Mar. 25, 1967; 1 child, Nicole Denise. BA, UCLA, 1961; JD, U. Calif., Berkeley, 1965. Bar: Calif. 1967, U.S. Dist. Ct. (ctrl. dist.) Calif. 1967, U.S. Supreme Ct. 1972, U.S. Ct. Appeals (9th cir.) 1989, U.S. Dist. Ct. (ea. dist.) Calif. 1991. Dep. dist. atty. L.A. Dist. Atty.'s Office, 1967-71; ptnr. Nasatir, Hirsch & Podberesky, Santa Monica, Calif., 1971—; commr. Calif. Coun. Criminal Justice, 1977-81; mem. Spl. Com. on Cts. in the Media/Judicial Coun. Calif., 1979. Co-author: California Criminal Law Proceedings/Practice, 1986, 2d edit. 1994. Pres. bd. trustees Santa Monica Mus. Art, 1984-91; chmn. Greek Theatre Adv. Com., L.A., 1976-79; mem. L.A. Olympic Organizing Com., 1981-84; bd. dirs. Ocean Park Cmty. Ctr., 1995—, bd. chair, 1997—. Recipient Spl. Merit Resolution, L.A. City Coun., 1984, Criminal Def. Atty. of Yr. award Century City Bar Assn., 1996. Fellow Am. Bd. Criminal Lawyers (bd. dirs., v.p. 1998—); mem. Calif. Attys. Criminal Justice (pres. 1987, bd. trustees), Criminal Cts. Bar Assn. (pres. 1981, Spl. Merit award 1988), L.A. County Bar Assn. (Criminal Def. Atty. of Yr. 1999), Santa Monica C. of C. (bd. dirs. 1995-97). Avocations: cooking, reading, community service. Office: Nasatir Hirsch Podberesky 2115 Main St Santa Monica CA 90405-2215

HIRSCH, ROBERT LOUIS, energy research-development-management consultant; b. Evanston, Ill., Mar. 6, 1935; s. Louis Aaron and Dorothy Jean (Block) H.; m. Evelyn Podhouser, Feb. 1, 1959 (div. 1999); children—Allen, Lauri, Scott. B.S., U. Ill., 1958, Ph.D., 1964; M.S., U. Mich., 1959. Research engr. Atomics Internat., 1959-60; physicist, later dir. ITT Indsl. Labs., Fort Wayne, Ind., 1964-68; sr. physicist controlled thermonuclear research AEC (now Dept. Energy), Washington, 1968-72; div. dir. 1972-76; asst. adminstr. solar, geothermal and advanced energy sys. ERDA (presdl. appointment), 1976-77; dep. mgr. sci. and tech. dept. Exxon Corp., 1977; gen. mgr. exploratory petroleum research Exxon Research and Engring. Co., 1977-80; mgr. Synthetic Fuels Research Lab. Exxon Research and Engring. Co., Baytown, Tex., 1980-83; v.p., mgr. rsch. and tech. svcs. dept. Arco Oil and Gas Co., Dallas, 1983-91; chief exec. officer ARCO Power Techs., Inc., 1986-91; v.p. Washington office Electric Power Rsch. Ins., 1991-94; cons. in tech. and mgmt., 1994—; exec. advisor Advanced Power Technologies, 1997—; pres. The Energy Tech. Collaborative, Inc., 1995-97; chmn. bd. on energy and environ. sys. NRC, 1996—; mem. bds. Annappolis Ctr. and Fusion Power Assocs.; participant in Atlantic Coun. Studies; mem. LDRD Bd. Lawrence Livermore Nat. Lab., 1993-95; mem. U.S.-USSR Joint Commn. on Peaceful Uses of Atomic Energy, 1970s; chmn. U.S. del. U.S.-USSR Joint Fusion Power Coord. Com., 1970s; mem. Internat. Fusion Rsch. Coun., 1970s, Dept. Energy Rsch. adv. bd., 1980s; vice chmn. com. on sci., engring. and tech. Fed. Coord. Coun. for Sci. Engring. and Tech., 1976; adv. bd. Princeton Plasma Physics Lab., 1980s, Oak Ridge Nat. Lab., 1993-97; rsch. coord. coun. Gas Rsch. Inst., 1980s. Contbr. articles to profl. jours. Recipient Meritorious award William Jump Found., 1971, Disting. Service award AEC, 1974, spl. achievement award Fusion Power Assocs., 1982, spl. Achievement award ERDA, 1976, 77, commendation NASA, 1982, merit award U. Mich. Engring. Alumni Soc., 1997; AEC Spl. fellow, 1960-63. Fellow AAAS; mem. Am. Nuclear Soc. (chmn. fusion tech. group, dir. 1975-76, 78-79, outstanding tech. achievement award 1983), Am. Phys. Soc., Tau Beta Pi (U. Ill. Alumni Honor award), Phi Epsilon Pi. Patentee in field. Home: 201 Commonwealth Ave Alexandria VA 22301-2317

HIRSCH, ROSEANN CONTE, publisher; b. N.Y.C., Feb. 5, 1941; d. Frank and Anna (Burzycki) Conte; m. Barry Jay Hirsch, Oct. 1, 1967; children: Brian Christopher, Nicholas Benjamin, Jonathan Alexander. Student, Boston U., 1958-61. Editorial asst. Grolier, Inc., 1962-64; editor Ideal Pub. Corp., N.Y.C., 1968-74; editorial dir. Sterling's Mags., Inc., N.Y.C., 1975-78, Hearst Spl. Publs., Hearst Corp., N.Y.C., 1978-84; v.p. Ultra Communications, Inc., N.Y.C., 1984-89; pub., pres. Dream Guys, Inc., N.Y.C., 1986-93; pres. Lamppost Press, Inc., N.Y.C., 1989-. Author: Super Working Mom's Handbook, 1986; editor: Young & Married Mag., 1976-77, 100 Greatest American Women, Good Housekeeping's Moms Who Work; contbr. articles to various mags. Home and Office: Lamppost Press Inc 1172 Park Ave # 8 B New York NY 10128-1213

HIRSCH, STUART, orthopaedic surgeon; b. N.Y.C., June 7, 1941; m. Lisa; children: Todd, Scott. MD, U. Va., 1966. Diplomate Am. Bd. Orthopaedic Surgeons. chmn. dept. orthopaedics Somerset Med. Ctr., Somerville, N.J.; cons. in field. Capt. USAF, 1968-70. Fellow Am. Coll. Surgeons; mem. Am. Orthopaedic Assn. 9exec. com.).

HIRSCH, SYROLA RUTH, gerontology rehabilitation nurse; b. Tripp, S.D., Dec. 17, 1921; d. Theodore and Pauline (Heinrich) Schaefer. Diploma, Luth. Sch. Nursing, Sioux City, Iowa, 1942; B. of Philosophy, Northwestern U., 1961; BSN, DePaul U., 1978; MA in Gerontology, Roosevelt U., 1987. RNC, CRRN; recert. gerontol. nurse, RNC; cert. registered rehab. nurse. Courier nurse Santa Fe RR, Chgo. and L.A., 1946-47; pvt. duty nurse First Dist. Nursing, Chgo., 1948-69; gen. duty cardiac nursing U. Chgo. Clinics, 1969-74; staff nurse surg. Michael Reese Hosp., Chgo., 1974-79; sr. staff nurse med.-surg. Johnston Bowman Rehab. Ctr., Rush Presbyn. St. Lukes Med. Ctr., Chgo., 1979-96; ret. Rush Presbyn. St. Lukes Med. Ctr., Chgo., 1996; rep. unit adv. com. Johnston Bowman Rehab. Ctr., Rush Presbyn. St. Lukes Med. Ctr., Chgo., 1984-87; mem. Citizen Ambassador Program Chinese Nursing Assn., Beijing, lectr. Hon. citizen Boys Town. Mem. ANA, Assn. for Rehab. Nursing, Ill. State Nurses Assn., Nat. Gerontol. Nursing Assn., Am. Assn. Neurosci. Nurses, Internat. Clown Assn., Am. Assn. for Therapeutic Humor, Nat. Assn. Orthopedic Nursing, Profl. Nursing Assn., Am. Diabetes Assn., Holistic Nursing Assn., Med.-Surg. Nurse Assn., Sigma Theta Tau. Avocations: reading, music, traveling, photography. Home: 4800 S Chicago Beach Dr Chicago IL 60615-7001

HIRSCH, WALTER, economist, researcher; b. Phila., Apr. 21, 1917; s. Arnold Harry and Ann Belle (Feldstein) H.; m. Leanore Brod, Feb. 12, 1939 (dec. 1985); stepchild, Stephen M. Gold; children: Jeffrey A., Robert A.; m. June Freedman Gold Clark, Dec. 16, 1986. BS in Econs., U. Pa., 1938; LLD (hons.), Chapman Coll., 1968. Economist U.S. Bur. Stats., Washington and N.Y.C, 1946-50, Dept. USAF, Washington, 1950-51, Nat. Prodn. Auth., Washington, 1952-53; dir. indsl. mobilization Bur. Ordnance Dept. USN, Mechanicsburg, Pa., 1954-56; ops. rsch. analyst Bur. Supplies and Accts. Dept. USN, Arlington, Va., 1956-58; economist, ops. rsch. analyst Internat. Security Affairs Office Sec. of Def., Arlington, 1958-61; chief ops., rsch. analyst Gen. Svcs. Adminstrn., Washington, 1961-63; ops. rsch. analyst Spl. Projects Office Sec. of Def., Arlington, 1963-67; dir. ednl. rsch. U.S. Office Edn., San Francisco, 1967-72; cons. on loan to Office of Dean Acad. Planning San Jose (Calif.) State U., 1972-74. Author: Unit Man-Hour Dynamics for Peace or War, 1957, Internal Study for Office Secretary of Defense: Sharing the Cost of International Security, 1961. Vol. De Young Mus., San Francisco, 1981-84, Calif. Palce of Legion of Honor, Phila. Mus. Art, 1984-86; pres. Met. Area Reform Temples, Washington, Nat. Fedn. Temple Brotherhoods; supporter Phila. Orch., San Francisco Symphony, San Francisco Conservatory Music, Curtis Inst. With USAAF, 1942-46. Recipient Meritorious Civilian Svc. award Navy Dept., 1956. Mem. Pa. Athletic Club, Commonwealth Club of Calif., World Affairs Council, Press Club of San Francisco, Phi Delta Kappa. Avocations: collecting art, music, chess, poetry.

HIRSCHBECK, JOHN F., umpire; b. Bridgeport, Conn., Sept. 17, 1954; married; 4 children. BS in Phys. Edn., Ctrl. Conn. State. Former umpire Fla. State League, Ea. League, Instrnl. League, Puerto Rican League, Internat. League; umpire maj. league baseball Am. League, N.Y.C., 1984—; with Umpires Union, Phila. Avocations: hunting, fishing, golfing. Office: Am League 350 Park Ave New York NY 10022 also: Umpires Union 1735 Market St Philadelphia PA 19103

HIRSCHBECK, MARK, umpire; b. Bridgeport, Conn., Sept. 22, 1960; m. Mary Frances Mallon, Nov. 20, 1982; children: Jaclyn, Nikki, Monica, Mark Jr. Umpire maj. league baseball Nat. League, N.Y.C., 1987—; with Umpires Union, Phila.; former umpire Gulf Coast League, Fla. State League, Midwest League, Ea. League, Dominican Republic League, Fla. Instrnl. League, Am. Assn. Avocations: hunting, fishing, golfing. Office: Nat League 350 Park Ave New York NY 10022 also: Umpires Union 1735 Market St Philadelphia PA 19103

HIRSCHBERG, VERA HILDA, writer; b. N.Y.C., Sept. 19, 1929; d. Bernard and Minnie (Margolis) Lieberman; m. Peter Hirschberg, Aug. 21, 1949; children: Karen Hirschberg Reses, Paul. BJ, Hunter Coll., 1950. Staff writer Pacific Stars and Stripes, Tokyo, 1956-64; corr. Newsweek, Guatemala, 1964-65; transp. staff writer N.Y. Jour. Commerce, Washington, 1969-70; transp. editor Nat. Jour. Mag., Washington, 1970-72; dir. women's programs, presdl. speechwriter The White House, Washington, 1972-74; dir. tech. transfer HUD, Washington, 1974-75; dep. spl. asst. to Sec. Pub. Affairs Dept. Treasury, Washington, 1975-77; press. sec. U.S. Sen. William Roth, Jr., Washington, Jan. to Dec. 1977; editorial cons. various govt. and non-govt. clients, 1977-78; pub. affairs dir. White House Conf. on Libr. and Info. Svcs., Washington, 1978-80; sr. writer, adminstr.'s speechwriter NASA, Washington, 1980-92; cons. in field. Editor: Israel at the Polls, 1977; author numerous newspaper and mag. articles. Recipient Outstanding Svc. citation The White House, 1973, Meritorious Svc. award Dept. Treasury, 1977, Exceptional Performance award NASA, 1982, Exceptional Svc. medal, 1988. Mem. Exec. Women in Govt. (founding mem. 1973), Zionist Orgn. Am. Republican. Jewish. Avocations: gourmet cooking, foreign travel, reading, museums, art collecting.

HIRSCHFELD, ALBERT, artist; b. St. Louis, June 21, 1903; s. Isaac and Rebecca (Rothberg) H.; m. Florence Ruth Hobby, July 13, 1927 (div. Mar. 1941); m. Dorothy Dolly Haas, May 8, 1943 (dec. Sept. 1994); 1 child, Nina; m. Louise Kerz, Oct. 23, 1996. Student, Nat. Acad., Art Students Leaque, County Council, London, Julienne's, Paris; DFA (hon.), U. Hartford, 1982; LHD (hon.), Acad. of Art, 1984; DFA (hon.), NYU, 1985; LHD (hon.), CUNY, 1985, Brandeis U., 1989; DFA (hon.), Pratt Inst., 1994. Caricaturist N.Y. Times, 1926—; theatre corr. in Moscow for N.Y. Herald Tribune, 1927. Sculptor one-man exhbns. include Newhouse Gallery, 1928, Waldorf Astoria, 1932, Morgan Gallery, 1936, Guy Mayer Gallery, 1942, John Heller Gallery, 1959, Hammer Gallery, 1967, Mus. City N.Y., 1973, Margo Feiden Gallery, 1973, Wako Galleries, Tokyo, 1975, Katonah Art Mus., 1998, Harvard Theater Collection, 1998; theater caricaturist, N.Y. Times, 1925—; represented in permanent collections St. Louis Art Mus., Butler Inst. Am. Art, Whitney Mus. Am. Art, N.Y.C., Cleve. Art Mus., N.Y.C. Mus., N.Y. Pub. Library, Fogg Mus., Bklyn. Mus., Met. Mus. Art, Mus. Modern Art, Davenport Municipal Art Gallery, Mus. U. Wis., Lincoln Center Mus. Performing Arts, N.Y.C., murals in Fifth Ave. Playhouse, Am. Pavilion, World's Fair, Brussels, 1958; author: Manhattan Oases, 1932, Harlem, 1942; musical comedy Sweet Bye and Bye, 1946; The American Theatre, 1961, (with S.J. Perelman) Westward Ha, 1949, Show Business is No Business, 1951, Hirschfeld Folio, 1964, The World of Hirschfeld, 1970, (with Brooks Atkinson) The Lively Years, 1973, Rhythm folio 10 lithographs, Hirschfeld by Hirschfeld, 1979; The Entertainers, 1977, Art and Recollections from 8 Decades, 1991, Hirschfeld on Line, Applause, 1998; U.S. postage stamps of comedians, 1991, of Silent Screen, 1994; (documentary film) The Line King, 1997. Recipient Am. Specialist grant U.S. State Dept., 1960, Spl. Tony award for theatre caricature, 1974, Creative award Art Inst. Boston, 1976, City of N.Y. Arts and Culture award, 1979, Brooks Atkinson Tony award, 1984, Weissberger award Theatre Hall of Fame, 1985, New Eng. Theatre award, 1984, award of honor City of N.Y., 1979, League of N.Y. Theatres and Producers Theatre award, 1975, Life Achievement award Houston Film Festival, 1989, Edwin Booth award CUNY Grad. Sch., ASCAP, 1991, Lotus Club award, 1990, National Arts Club, 1992, Stage Dirs. and Choreographers award, 1992. Mem. Illustrators Club (Hall of Fame 1986, Theater Hall of Fame 1990, N.Y. Living Landmark 1996). Home: 122 E 95th St New York NY 10128-1705

HIRSCHFELD, ARLENE F., civic worker, homemaker; b. Denver, Apr. 6, 1944; d. Hyman and Gertrude (Schwartz) Friedman; m. A. Barry Hirschfeld, Dec. 17, 1966; 2 children. Student, U. Mich., 1962-64; BA, U. Denver, 1966. English tchr. Abraham Lincoln High Sch., Denver, 1966-70. Pres. Jr. League of Denver, 1986-87, v.p. ways and means, 1985-86, v.p. mktg., 1982-83, chmn. Colo. Cache cookbook mktg. com., 1978-79, chair holiday mart, 1981, 85-87, participant in Nat. Jr. League Mktg. Conf.; trustee Graland Country Day Sch., 1988-97, bd. sec., 1990-95, chmn. edn. com., 1989-95, pres. parent coun., 1982-83, auction chmn., 1980, 81; bd. dirs. Allied Jewish Fedn., 1988-96, 98—; chair bd. dirs. Allied Women's Camp, 1999—, Allied Jewish Fedn. of Colo., 1999—; co-chmn. collector's choice event Denver Art Mus., 1989, 94, bd. trustees, 1995—, co-chair mktg. com.; co-chair Inst. Internat. Edn. Annual Dinner, 1997; co-chmn. benefit luncheon Pub. Edn. Coalition, 1990, mini grants selection com., 1985-87; mem. bd. Minoru Yasui Comty. Vol. award, 1986-87; mem. Greater Denver C. of C. Leadership Denver, class of 1987-88; bd. dirs. Women's Found. Colo., 1992-97, hon. trustees coun., 1997—; bd. dirs. Anti-Defamation League, 1994-96, Colo. Spl. Olympics Coun. Advisors, Mizel Mus. Judaica and LMG Found., Rose Cmty Found., Jewish Life com., Mile High Coun. Girl Scouts U.S; trustee Women's Found., 1991-97; mem. dean's coun. Harvard Div. Sch., 1992—; mem. nat. leadership com. Harvard Women's Studies in Religion Program; exec. com. Children's Diabetes Found., Denver, 1993—; bd. trustees mem. Girls Scouts Mile Hi Coun. Named Humanitarian of Yr. Nat. Jewish Ctr., 1988, named to Colo. Women's Econ. Devel. Coun. by Gov. of Colo., 1989—, Sustainer of Yr. Jr. League, 1992; recipient Nat. Women's Mus. of the Arts. Colo. Chpt. award, 1991, U. Denver Founder's Day Alumni Community Svc. award; recipient Woman of Distinction award Rocky Mtn. News and Hyatt Beaver Creek, 1993, Colo. I Have A Dream Found. award, 1992, Volunteer Award, Am. Assn. of U. Women (Denver Br.), 1998, Allied Jewish Fedn. of Colo. Golda Meir award, 1999. Mem. Colo. Women's Forum. Avocations: aerobics, snow and water skiing, golf. Office: 5200 Smith Rd Denver CO 80216-4525

HIRSCHFELD, MICHAEL, lawyer; b. Bronx, N.Y., July 4, 1950; s. Lawrence John and Ida (Miller) H.; m. Heidi P. Greenspan, June 17, 1973; children: Adam Lawrence, Philip Richard. BEE summa cum laude, CCNY, 1972; JD cum laude, U. Pa., 1975; LLM in Taxation, NYU, 1980. Bar: N.Y. 1976, U.S. Dist. Ct. (so. and ea. dists.) N.Y. 1976, U.S. Tax Ct. 1978. Assoc. Shearman and Sterling, N.Y.C., 1975-80, Roberts and Holland, N.Y.C., 1980-83; assoc. Carro, Spanbock, Kaster and Cuiffo, N.Y.C., 1983-85, ptnr., 1985-88; ptnr. Winstown & Strawn, N.Y.C., 1988-98, Dechert, Price & Rhoads, N.Y.C., 1998—; lectr. NYU, Assn. of Bar of City of New York, ABA, ALI-ABA, PLI, Syracuse U., U. Tex., Tulane U., Georgetown U.; chmn. NYU Inst. Real Estate Taxation; co-chmn. 49th, 50th, 52d, 53d and 54th ann. Fed. Income Taxation Confs.; 11th-21st ann. NYU Confs. on Fed. Taxation of Real Estate Taxations: mem. nat. edn. bd., Business Entities (RIA publ.) Real Estate Tax Digest, Jour. of Internat. Tax, Tax. Mgmt. Real Estate Jour.; mem. adv. bd. Tax Mgmt. Real Estate, Inst. Fed. Tax. Co-author: Real Estate Limited Partnerships, 3rd edit., 1991; bd. editors Real Estate Tax Digest, BNA Tax Mgmt.; editl. adv. bd. NYU Real Estate Adv. Bd. Mem. ABA (lectr. taxation sect., mem. coun. 1997—, co-chmn. govt. subcom. 1992-94, chmn. govt. subcom. 1994-97, chmn. real estate tax problems com. 1989-91, chmn. syndications subcom. 1985-87, vice chmn. ACRS depreciation recapture subcom. 1983-85, task force pres.'s tax reform proposals minimum tax subcom. 1985-86, vice chmn. gov. submission com. 1992-95), Am. Law Inst. (lectr.), N.Y. State Bar Assn. (lectr., co-chmn. coms. on income from real property tax sect. 1988-91, co-chmn. com. on preferences and minimum tax 1991-92, co-chmn. com. in individuals 1992-93, co-chmn. com. U.S. activities of fgn. taxpayers 1993-96, co-chmn. com. on real property, 1996-98, co-chmn. tax accts. 1998—, exec. com. 1987—, com. on internat. members), Assn. of Bar of City of N.Y. (mem. com. on internat. transactions), Internat. Tax Assn., Am. Coll. Tax Counsel. Avocation: music (drum). Fax: (212) 698-3599. E-mail: Mhirschf@Dechert.com. Office: Dechert Price & Rhoads 30 Rockefeller Plz Fl 22 New York NY 10112-2200*

HIRSCHFELD, RONALD COLMAN, retired consulting engineering executive; b. Amsterdam, N.Y., Nov. 23, 1930; s. John Anton and Catherine (Schuyler) H.; m. Erma Lou Jones, Aug. 8, 1964; children: Amy Karen, Carl Schuyler. B.S. in Civil Engring, Union Coll., 1950; S.M., Harvard U., 1951, Ph.D., 1958. Teaching fellow Harvard U., 1951-54, instr. soil mechanics, 1958-60, asst. prof., 1960-64; assoc. prof. civil engring. M.I.T., 1964-72; prin. Geotech. Engrs. Inc., Winchester, Mass., 1970-92, pres., 1974-78, 82-86; mem. dean's adv. coun. Sch. Engring., U. Mass., 1978-95. Co-editor: Embankment-Dam Engineering, 1963. Bd. dirs. Winchester A Better Chance Inc., 1979-84; chmn. governing bd. Winchester Unitarian Soc., 1981-82; trustee Engring. Ctr. Edn. Trust, Boston, 1990-96, chmn., 1992-93. Mem. ASCE (hon., pres. Mass. sect. 1973-74, nat. dir. 1981-84), Am. Cons. Engrs. Council (pres. New Eng. 1982-83, nat. dir. 1983-84), Assn. Engring. Geologists (chmn. New Eng. sect. 1971-73, nat. dir. 1972-73), Geol. Soc. Am. Unitarian. Home: 47 Emerson Rd Winchester MA 01890-3407

HIRSCHFIELD, JIM, artist, educator; b. Pitts., Mar. 7, 1951. BFA, Kansas City Art Inst., 1976; MFA, U. Oreg., 1978. Vis. lectr. U. Oreg., Eugene, 1978; vis. artist U. Wash., Seattle, 1984; cons. Seattle Arts Commn., 1982-84, King County Arts Commn., Seattle, 1988-98; full prof. U. N.C., Chapel Hill, 1988—; vis. asst. prof. U. Nev., Reno, 1986; vis. lectr. Ohio State U., Columbus, 1987. Solo exhbns. include Factory of Visual Art, Seattle, 1980, and/or, Seattle, 1980, 80 Langton St., San Francisco, 1982, U. Wash., Seattle, 1983, Mattress Factory, Pitts., 1985, A.R.C. Raw Space, Chgo., 1986, Nev. Art Mus., Reno, 1986, Sierra Nevada Coll., 1986, Ohio State U., 1987, U. Hawaii, 1987, U. Nev.-Reno, 1987, U. Calif.-Santa Cruz, 1988, Henry Art Gallery, Seattle, 1989, Seattle Art Mus., 1989, N.C. Art Mus., Raleigh, 1989, Wake Forest U., Winston-Salem, 1990, Nexus Contemporary Arts Ctr., Atlanta, 1991, Sarratt Gallery, Nashville, 1991, Kala Inst., Berkeley, Calif., 1992, ACME Arts, Columbus, 1994, SPACES, Cleve., 1994, Asheville (N.C.) Art Mus., 1994, Southeastern Ctr. for Contemporary Art, Winston-Salem, 1994; groiup shows include and/or, Seattle, 1976, 80, U. Oreg. Art Mus., 1978, Museo Carillo Gil, Mexico City, 1980, Whitcom Mus. History and Art, Bellingham, 1982, Artquke, Portland, 1984, San Francisco Mus. Modern Art, 1985, Brockton (Mass.) Art Mus., 1986, King County Arts Commn., Mercer Island, Wash., 1988, Atlanta Coll. Art, 1990, Weatherspoon Gallery, Greensboro, N.C., 1990, Ackland Art Mus., Chapel Hill, 1992, Fayerweather Gallery, 1992, Painted Bride Gallery, Phila., 1996; commns. include Seattle ARts Commn. Rainier Sq., 1981, Passage Point Parks, 1978, Pub. Art Study, 1984, Wash. Arts Commn., 1984, Connemara

Found., 1986, Mass. Coun. on the Arts, 1986, duke Med. Ctr., 1989, 90, 93, City of Atlanta Detention Ctr., 1994, South Reg. Libr., Charlotte, 1996, N.C. Zoo, 1996, others; co-author: (public art studies) Artwork/Network, 1984, Public Art Master Plan for the Kingdome, 1988; contbr. articles to profl. jours. Bd. dirs. Ctr. on Contemporary Art, Seattle, 1984-88; pub. art commr. Chapel Hill Arts Commn., 1994-97. Nat. Endowment for Arts/Rockefeller Found. grantee, 1986, Pollock Krasner Found., 1987, King County Art Commn., 1988, Art Matters Inc., 1988, Artist Trust, 1989, Seattle Arts Commn. via Allied Arts Found., 1989, N.C. Art Coun., 1995; fellow Nat. Endowment for the Arts, 1989, 90, Inst. Art and Humanities, 1990, 93, Phillip and Ruth Hettleman Prize for Artistic Excellence, 1993, N.C. Art Coun., 1991, 96; recipient award in visual arts Graham Found., 1990. Office: Univ of North Carolina Dept Art Hanes Art Ctr CB 3405 Chapel Hill NC 27599

HIRSCHHORN, AUSTIN, lawyer; b. Detroit, Feb. 20, 1936; s. Herman and Dena Grace (Ufberg) H.; m. Susan Carol Goldstein, June 30, 1963; children: Laura Elsie, Carol Helen, Paula Gail. B.A. with honors, Mich. State U., 1957; LL.B., Wayne State U., 1960. Bar: Mich. 1961. Assoc. Arnold M. Gold Law Offices, Detroit, 1960-63; ptnr. Gold & Hirschhorn, Detroit, 1963-65; pvt. practice Detroit, 1965-68; ptnr. Boigon, Hirschhorn & Winston, Detroit, 1968-69, Boigon & Hirschhorn, Detroit and Southfield, 1969-78; pvt. practice Southfield, 1979-80; ptnr. Zemke & Hirschhorn (P.C.), Southfield, Mich., 1980-83, Austin Hirschhorn, P.C., Southfield, 1983-91; of counsel Rubenstein, Isaacs, Haroutunian & Sobel, P.C., Southfield, 1991-92; pvt. practice Austin Hirschhorn, P.C., Birmingham, Mich., 1992-96, Troy, Mich., 1996—; lectr. Inst. Continuing Legal Edn., Mich. Trustee The Internat. Sch., Farmington Hills, Mich. With AUS, 1960-62. Mem. ABA, Mich. Bar Assn., Oakland County Bar Assn., Am. Bankruptcy Inst., Comml. Law League Am. Jewish. Home: 26903 York Rd Huntington Woods MI 48070-1361 Office: 201 W Big Beaver Rd Ste 710 Troy MI 48084-4162*

HIRSCHHORN, ERIC LEONARD, lawyer; b. N.Y.C., Apr. 28, 1946; m. Leah Wortham, Oct. 31, 1981; children: Alexander, Elizabeth, Anne. BA, U. Chgo., 1965; JD, Columbia U., 1968. Bar: N.Y. 1968, U.S. Supreme Ct. 1972, D.C. 1973. Reginald Heber Smith Community Lawyer fellow MFY Legal Svcs., N.Y.C., 1968-71; counsel Dem. Study Group N.Y. State Assembly, Albany, 1971; legis asst. to Rep. Bella Abzug, U.S. Ho. of Reps., Washington, 1971-73; assoc. Cadwalader, Wickersham & Taft, N.Y.C., 1973-75; chief counsel subcom. on govt. info. and individual rights U.S. Ho. of Reps., Washington, 1975-77; dep. assoc. dir. internat. affairs & trade U.S. Office Mgmt. & Budget, Washington, 1977-80; dep. asst. sec. for export adminstrn. U.S. Dept. Commerce, Washington, 1980-81; ptnr. Winston & Strawn (formerly Bishop, Cook, Purcell & Reynolds), Washington, 1981—; exec. sec. Industry Coalition on Tech. Transfer, Washington, 1986—. Contbr. articles to profl. jours. Mem. Assn. Bar City N.Y., Computer Law Assn., Thurgood Marshall Am. Inn of Ct., ABA Ctr. on Profl. Responsibility, D.C. Bar (legal ethics com. 1997-98). Office: Winston & Strawn 1400 L St NW Ste 800 Washington DC 20005-3508

HIRSCHHORN, KURT, pediatrics educator; b. Vienna, Austria, May 18, 1926; came to U.S., 1940, naturalized, 1945; s. Emanuel and Helen (Mayberger) H.; m. Rochelle Reibman, Dec. 20, 1952; children—Melanie D., Lisa R., Joel N. Student, U. Pitts., 1944; BA, NYU, 1950, MD, 1954, MS (Bergquist fellow), 1958. Intern Bellevue Hosp., N.Y.C., 1954-55; resident Bellevue Hosp., 1955-56; fellow N.Y. U., 1956-57, U. Upsala, Sweden, 1957-58; instr. N.Y. U. Sch. Medicine, 1956-58, asst. prof., 1958-63, asso. prof., 1963-66; Arthur J. and Nellie Z. Cohen prof. genetics and pediatrics Mt. Sinai Sch. Medicine, City U. N.Y., 1966-76, Herbert H. Lehman prof., chmn. pediatrics, 1977-95, prof. pediat., human genetics and medicine, 1995—; adj. prof. biology N.Y. U., 1966-74; Established investigator Am. Heart Assn., 1960-65; career scientist N.Y.C. Health Research Council, 1965-75. Author numerous sci. publs.; editor: (with Harry Harris) Advances in Human Genetics, 1969-95; mem. editl. bd. 16 sci. jours. Mem. council Village Community Sch., 1968-73, chmn., 1972-73. Served with AUS, 1944-47. Recipient Rudolph Virchow medal, 1974, Alumni Achievement award NYU Sch. Medicine, 1982, Jacobi medallion Mt. Sina Med. Ctr., 1993, Wm. Allan award Am. Soc. Human Genetics, 1995. Fellow AAAS, Am. Acad. Pediatrics, N.Y. Acad. Medicine; mem. Inst. of Medicine of NAS, Am. Coll. Med. Genetics, Am. Soc. Clin. Investigation, Am. Assn. Physicians, Am. Pediatric Soc., Am. Soc. Human Genetics (pres. 1969, dir. 1964-65, 68-71), Pediatric Travel Club, Am. Assn. Immunologists, Harvey Soc. (v.p. 1979-80, pres. 1980-81, coun. 1981-84), Genetics Soc. Am., Environ. Mutagen Soc. (coun. 1969-76), Am. Soc. Pediatric Chairmen (coun. 1983-86), Am. Cancer Soc. (coun. 1989-92), Phi Beta Kappa, Sigma Xi, Alpha Omega Alpha. Home: 29 Washington Sq W New York NY 10011-9180 Office: Mt Sinai Sch Medicine 1 Gustave L Levy Pl New York NY 10029-6500

HIRSCHHORN, ROCHELLE, genetics educator; b. Bklyn., Mar. 19, 1932; d. Hyman and Anna Reibman; m. Kurt Hirschhorn; children: Melanie D., Lisa R., Joel N. BA, Barnard Coll., 1953; MD, NYU, 1957. Intern NYU-Bellevue Med. Divsn., N.Y.C., 1958-59; rsch. fellow, teaching asst. NYU Sch. Medicine, N.Y.C., 1963-65, assoc. rsch. scientist, 1965-66, instr. in medicine, 1966-69, asst. prof. medicine, 1969-74, assoc. prof. medicine, 1974-79, prof. medicine, 1979-95, head divsn. med. genetics, 1984—, prof. medicine and cell biology, 1996—; hon. fellow Galton Lab. Human Genetics & Biometry Univ. Coll., London, 1971-72; assoc. attending physician in medicine Bellevue Hosp., N.Y.C., 1969-80, Univ. Hosp., NYU Sch. Medicine, 1974-81; attending physician Bellevue Hosp., 1980—, Univ. Hosp., 1981—; mem. numerous NIH coms. & study sects., 1973—; vis. prof. Harvard U., 1995, U. Calif. San Francisco, 1995. Senator NYU Senate, mem. pediatrics search com., 1987-89, human subjects instl. rev. bd., 1989-94, co-dir. second year med. genetics course, 1989-93, NYU appointments and promotions com. 1995—; trustee AIDS Med. Found./AMFAR; judge Westinghouse Nat. Sci. Talent Search; founding mem. Village Cmty. Sch. Fellow AAAS, Am. Coll. Rheumatology, Am. Coll. Med. Genetics (founder); mem. NAS, Inst. Medicine, Am. Soc. for Clin. Investigation, Assn. Am. Physicians, Am. Assn. Immunologists, Am. Soc. Human Genetics (cert. 1987), Interurban Clin. Club (pres. 1987-88), Peripatetic Soc., Soc. for Inherited Metabolic Diseases, Harvey Soc. (coun. 1989-92), Alpha Omega Alpha (councillor Delta of N.Y. 1982—). Achievements include elucidation of pathophysiologic mechanisms, delineation of molecular and biochemical defects of genetic disorders including adenosine deaminase and glycogen storage disease type II. Office: NYU Med Ctr 550 1st Ave New York NY 10016-6481

HIRSCHKLAU, MORTON, lawyer; b. N.Y.C., Mar. 9, 1932; s. Joseph I. and Sylvia (Kleiner) H.; m. Martha R. Silverstein, June 21, 1953; children: Mitchell L., Deborah E. Hirschklau Loeber, Susan I. AB, Syracuse U., 1953, JD, 1959. Bar: N.Y. 1959, N.J. 1960, U.S. Supreme Ct. 1963, U.S. Ct. Appeals (3d cir.) 1982. Law sec. Superior Ct. N.J., Paterson, 1959-60; assoc. Theodore D. Rosenberg, Esquire, Paterson, 1960-63; ptnr. Hirschklau, Wasserman & Welch, Oakland, N.J., 1963-73; pvt. practice Fair Lawn, N.J., 1973-76; ptnr. Hirschklau, Feitlin & Trawinski, Fair Lawn, 1976-84, Muscarella, Hirschklau, Bochet, Feitlin, Trawinski & Edwards, Fair Lawn, 1984-90, Karas, Kilstein, Hirschklau, Feitlin & Youngman, Fair Lawn, 1990-99, Morton Hirschklau, Esq. and Assocs., 1999—; planning bd. atty. Borough of Fair Lawn, 1961-65, Borough atty., 1965, 81-83; planning bd. atty., Borough of Emerson, 1967-71, zoning bd. atty., 1971-83; zoning bd. atty. Village of Ridgewood, 1977—, Borough of Saddle River, 1996—; spl. counsel Bergen County Park Commn., Paramus, N.J., 1987-88; chmn. N.J. Supreme Ct. Com. on Ethics, 1987-88. Bd. dirs., atty. Fair Lawn Mental Health Ctr., 1965—; bd. dirs., past pres. Opportunity Ctr., Inc., Fair Lawn; pres. Fair Lawn Clean Govt. Assn., 1968-70. Lt. USNR, 1953-56. Mem. N.J. Bar Assn., Bergen County Bar Assn. (chmn. real estate com.), Fair Lawn Rotary Club (past pres.). Avocations: golf, tennis, collecting porcelains. Office: Karas Kilstein Hirschklau Feitlin & Youngman 9-10 Saddle River Rd Fair Lawn NJ 07410-5721

HIRSCHMAN, ALBERT OTTO, political economist, educator; b. Berlin, Apr. 7, 1915; s. Carl and Hedwig (Marcuse) H.; m. Sarah Chapiro, June 22, 1941; children: Catherine Jane, Elisabeth Nicole. Student, U. Sorbonne, Paris, Hautes Etudes Commerciales, Paris, London Sch. Econs., 1933-36; D in Econs. Sci., U. Trieste, 1938; hon. degree, Rutgers U., 1978, U. So. Calif., 1986, U. Turin, Italy, 1987, New Sch. for Social Rsch., 1988, Free U. of Berlin, 1988, U. Paris, 1989, U. Buenos Aires, 1989, U. Campinas, Brazil, 1990, Georgetown U., 1990, Yale U., 1990, U. Trier, Germany, 1990, Santander, Spain, 1992, U. Coimbra, Portugal, 1993, U. Paris, Nanterre, France, 1993, Williams Coll., 1993. Rockefeller fellow U. Calif., Berkeley, 1941-433; Economist Fed. Res. Bd., Washington, 1946-52; fin. adviser Nat. Planning Bd., Bogotá, Colombia, 1952-54; pvt. econ. cons. Bogotá, 1954-56; research prof. econs. Yale U., 1956-58; prof. internat. econ. relations Columbia U., 1958-64; prof. polit. economy Harvard U., 1964-74, Littauer prof. polit. economy, 1967-74; prof. Inst. for Advanced Study, Princeton, 1974-85, prof. emeritus, 1985—; fellow Ctr. Advanced Study Behavioral Scis., 1968-69; mem. Inst. for Advanced Study, 1972-73; fellow Wissenschaftskolleg zu Berlin, 1990-91. Author: National Power and the Structure of Foreign Trade, 1945, The Strategy of Economic Development, 1958, Journeys Toward Progress: Studies of Economic Policy-Making in Latin America, 1963, Devlopment Projects Observed, 1967, 2d edit., 1995, Exit, Voice, and Loyalty: Responses to Decline in Firms, Organizations and States, 1970, A Bias for Hope: Essays on Development and Latin America, 1971, The Passions and the Interests: Political Arguments for Capitalism Before Its Triumph, 1977, Essays in Trespassing: Economics to Politics and Beyond, 1981, Shifting Involvements: Private Interest and Public Action, 1982, Getting Ahead Collectively: Grassroots Experiences in Latin America, 1984, Rival Views of Market Society and Other Recent Essays, 1986, 2nd edit., 1992, The Rhetoric of Reaction: Perversity, Futility, Jeopardy, 1991, A Propensity to Self-Subversion, 1995, Crossing Boundaries: Selected Writings, 1998; editor Latin Am. Issues-Essays and Comments, 1961; contbr. articles to profl. jours. Served with AUS, 1943-45. Decorated Orden de San Carlos (Colombia); recipient Frank E. Seidman Disting. award in polit. economy, 1980, Talcott Parsons prize for social sci., 1983, Kalman Silvert prize L.Am. Studies Assn., 1986, 1st prize for social sci. articles Fritz Thyssen Found., 1992, Toynbee prize, 1998. Fellow Am. Econ. Assn.; mem. NAS, Council Fgn. Relations, Am. Acad. Arts and Scis., Am. Philos. Soc. (Thomas Jefferson medal 1998); fgn. mem. Brit. Acad., Accademia Nazionale dei Lincei (Rome), Acad. Scis. Berlin-Brandenburg. Address: Inst for Advanced Study Princeton NJ 08540

HIRSCHMAN, CHARLES, JR., sociologist, educator; b. Atlanta, Nov. 29, 1943; s. Charles Sr. and Mary Gertrude (Mullee) H.; m. Josephine Knight, Jan. 29, 1968; children: Andrew Charles, Sarah Lynn. BA, Miami U., Oxford, Ohio, 1965; MS, U. Wis., 1969, PhD, 1972. Vol. Peace Corps, Malaysia, 1965-67; prof. Duke U., Durham, N.C., 1972-81, Cornell U., Ithaca, N.Y., 1981-87; prof. U. Wash., Seattle, 1987—, chair dept. sociology, 1995-98; Cons. Ford Found., Malaysia, 1974-75; chair social scis. and population study sect. NIH, Washington, 1987-91; vis. scholar Russell Sage Found., 1998-99. Author: Ethnic and Social Stratification in Peninsula Malaysia, 1975; contbr. articles to profl. jours. Fellow Ctr. Advanced Study in the Bahavioral Scis., Stanford, Calif., 1993-94. Fellow AAAS; mem. Assn. for Asian Studies (bd. dirs. 1987-90), Population Assn Am. (bd. dirs. 1992-94, v.p. 1997). Office: U Wash Dept Sociology PO Box 353340 Seattle WA 98195-3340

HIRSCHMAN, SHALOM ZARACH, physician; b. Troy, N.Y., Aug. 5, 1936; s. Meyer and Anne Hirschman; divorced; children: Orin, Raquel; m. Frances E. Neumann Ron, 1995. B.A., Yeshiva U., 1957; M.D., Albert Einstein Coll. Medicine, 1961; Ph.D. equivalent, NIH Grad. Sch., 1966. Intern medicine Mass. Gen. Hosp., Harvard Med. Sch., 1961-62, resident, 1962-63; research assoc. NIH, Nat. Insts. Arthritis, Metabolic and Digestive Diseases, 1963-65, sr. investigator, 1965-66; NIH fellow in medicine Columbia-Presbyn. Med. Center, N.Y.C., 1966-67; sr. investigator Nat. Cancer Inst., NIH, 1967-69; instr. medicine George Washington U. Sch. Medicine, 1963-65; assoc. prof. medicine, dir. div. infectious diseases Mt. Sinai Sch. Medicine, CUNY, 1969-71, prof. medicine, dir. div. infectious diseases, 1971—, vice chmn. dept. medicine, 1972-75; attending physician Mt. Sinai Hosp., N.Y.C., 1971—; dir. emeritus divsn. infectious diseases Mt. Sinai Med. Ctr., 1996—; mem. merit rev. bd. VA, 1976-79; mem. virology and microbiology exec. bd. Am. Cancer Soc., 1981-86; pres., CEO Advanced Viral Rsch. Corp., 1996—. Founder, trustee Touro Coll., Touro Law Sch., N.Y.C., 1970. Served with USPHS, 1963-69. NIH fellow, 1964; research grantee, 1970—. Fellow ACP, Am. Soc. Infectious Diseases (councillor N.Y. chpt. 1995-96), Am. Coll. Clin. Pharmacology, Royal Coll. Hygiene and Tropical Medicine; mem. AAAS, Am. Biophys. Soc., Am. Soc. Microbiology, Soc. Gen. Virology, Am. Soc. Liver Diseases, Soc. Exptl. Biology and Medicine, Am. Soc. Clin. Investigation, Assn. Am. Physicians, Am. Fedn. Clin. Rsch., Am. Fedn. Med. Rsch., N.Y. Acad. Scis. (chmn. microbiology sect. 1975), Harvey Soc. Office: 200 Corporate Blvd S Ste 145 Yonkers NY 10701-6805

HIRSCHOWITZ, BASIL ISAAC, physician; b. Bethal, South Africa, May 29, 1925; came to U.S., 1953, naturalized, 1961; s. Morris and Dorothy (Drieband) H.; m. Barbara L. Burns, July 6, 1958; children: David E., Karen, Edward A., Vanessa. BSc, Witwatersrand U., Johannesburg, 1943, MB.BCh, 1947, MD, 1954. Intern, resident Johannesburg Gen. Hosp., 1948-50; house physician Postgrad. Med. Sch., London, Eng., 1950; registrar Central Middlesex Hosp., London, 1951-53; instr., asst. prof. U. Mich., 1953-56; asst. prof. Temple U., 1957-59; assoc. prof. medicine U. Ala. Med. Center, Birmingham, 1959-64; prof. medicine U. Ala. Med. Ctr., 1964-95, emeritus prof., 1995; prof. physiology U. Ala. Med. Center, 1970—; Disting. faculty lectr. U. Ala., 1988; chmn. faculty coun. U. Ala. Sch. Medicine, 1989-90; dir. div. gastroenterology medicine U. Ala. Hosp. and Clinics, 1959-87; chmn. exec. com. U. Ala. Hosp., 1986-88. Recipient Charles F. Kettering Prize, Gen. Motors Cancer Found., 1987, Seale Harris award So. Med. Assn., 1992; named to Ala. Acad. Honor, 1991. Master ACP (Laureate award 1989); fellow AAAS, Assn. Am. Physicians, Royal Coll. Physicians (Edinburgh), Royal Coll. Physicians (London), Royal Soc. Medicine (hon.), Royal Philatelic Soc., (London); mem. AMA, South African, Brit., Ala. Med. Assns., Med. Rsch. Soc. Gt. Britain, Am. Fedn. Clin. Rsch., So. Soc. Clin. Investigation, Am. Physiol. Soc., Biophys. Soc., Am. Gastroent. Assn. (Friedenwald medal 1992), Am. Soc. Gastro-Intestinal Endoscopy (Schindler medal 1974, Disting. lectr. 1994), Am. Coll. Gastroenterology (Disting. Sci. Achievement award 1982), Brit. Soc. Gastro-Intestinal Endoscopy (hon.), Brit. Soc. Gastroenterology (Founders lectr. 1988, Astra internat. lectr. 1997), Italian Soc. Gastroenterology corr.), William Beaumont Soc. (Eddy Palmer award for contbns. to endoscopy 1976), Soc. Exptl. Biology and Medicine, Sigma Xi, Alpha Omega Alpha. Office: U Ala at Birmingham Med Ctr Birmingham AL 35294

HIRSCHY, GORDON HAROLD, real estate agent, auctioneer; b. Sturgis, Mich., Jan. 28, 1942; s. Harold L. and Clara L. (Roy) H.; m. Alice Ann Grossman, Aug. 8, 1964 (dec. 1983); m. Sarah Lee Gerber, Nov. 20, 1994; children: Daniel, Benjamin, Matthew, Kurtt, Lori, Hannah. BS in Gen. Agriculture, Purdue U., 1964; degree in auctioneering sci. and mgmt., Am. Acad. Auctioneers, 1990. FIC, LUTCF. State nitrogen engr., constrn. supr. Smith-Douglass Fertilizer Co., Indpls., 1965-67; asst. mgr. LaGrange County (Ind.) Farm Bur. Corp., 1967-72; county office mgr., agt. LaGrange County Farm Bur. Ins., 1972-80; owner, operator Community Ins. Svcs., Inc., LaGrange, 1980-88; ins. agt. Ins. Market Place, Inc., LaGrange, 1988-89; dist. rep. Modern Woodmen of Am., Inc., Rock Island, Ill., 1989-91; auctioneer Century 21 Fairfield Real Estate, Fort Wayne, Ind., 1971—. Named one of Outstanding Young Men Am., 1972, Rookie of Yr. Mich. Football Ofcls. Assn., 1988. Mem. N.E. Ind. Assn. Life Underwriters (pres. 1983, Mem. of Yr. 1982), Ind. Life and Health Ins. Leaders Club (exec. dir., sec. 1978-91), Ind. Auctioneers Assn., Am. Soc. Farm Equipment Appraisers, Gideons Internat. (meml. Bible sec.), Ind./Mich. Football Ofcls. Athletic Assns. Republican. United Methodist. Avocation: football officiating, auctioneering. Office: 3501 Fairfield Ave Fort Wayne IN 46807-1805

HIRSH, ALLAN THURMAN, JR., publishing executive; b. Cumberland, Md., Aug. 19, 1920; s. Allan Thurman and Ellinor Goldsmith (Ottenheimer) H.; m. Eleanor B. Rosenthal, June 17, 1944; children: Helene, Allan III, Eleanor. BS in Econs., Johns Hopkins U., 1941. CPA, Md. Acct. Burke Landsberg Gerber, Balt., 1941-42; pres. Ottenheimer Pubs., Inc, Balt., 1946-89, chmn. bd., 1989—; v.p. Allan Pubs., Inc., Balt., 1980—, Creative Horizons (formerly Ottenheimer Creations Inc.), Balt., 1994—, Thurman House, Hong Kong, 1994—. Bd. dirs. Balt. Hebrew Congregation, 1960-63, 83-86; assoc. Jewish Charities, Balt., 1972-79; pres. Forest Park H.S. PTA, 1968, Balt. City Coll. PTA, 1971; bd. dirs. Hebrew Burial and Social Service Soc., 1946—, pres. 1972-79; bd. dirs. 11 Slade Apt. Corp., 1985-88, 98—, pres., 1987-88, treas., 1998—, bd. dirs. With USN, 1942-46. Democrat. Jewish. Club: Suburban (Balt.) (dir. 1974-79, v.p. 1976-79); Presidents (West Palm Beach, Fla.). Home: 11 Slade Ave Baltimore MD 21208 Office: Ottenheimer Publishers Inc 5 Park Center Ct Ste 300 Owings Mills MD 21117-4200

HIRSH, BERNARD, supply company executive, consultant; b. Seguin, Tex., July 18, 1916; s. Samuel and Sarah (Marks) H.; m. Johanna Charlotte Cristol, Feb. 14, 1941 (dec. Jan. 1977); children: Richard, Robert, Terry, Cristy; m. Beatrice Castelle, Feb. 11, 1978. BA, U. Tex., 1939, LLB, JD, 1939. Bar: Tex. 1939. Claims rep. Handley Claim Svc., Dallas, 1939-41; spl. agt. War Food Adminstrn., U.S. Govt., Dallas, 1941-44; pres. Milliners Supply Co., Dallas, 1945-82, chmn. bd., 1982-85, chmn., owner, 1985—. Pres. Temple Emanu-El Brotherhood, Dallas, 1960-62, Temple Emanu-El, Dallas, 1970-72, Nat. Fedn. Temple Brotherhoods, N.Y.C., 1974-76; chancellor Jewish Chautauqua Soc., N.Y., 1970-72. Mem. Dallas Bar Assn., State Bar Tex., Columbian Country Club. Avocations: travel, reading. Office: Milliners Supply Co 911 Elm St Dallas TX 75202-3101

HIRSH, CRISTY J., school counselor; b. Dallas, Oct. 3, 1952; d. Bernard and Johanna (Cristol) H. BS in Early Childhood and Elem. Edn., Boston U., 1974; MS in Spl. Edn., U. Tex., Dallas, 1978; MEd in Counseling and Student Svcs., U. North Tex., 1991. Nat. cert. counselor; lic. profl. counselor, Tex.; cert. tchr., Tex., Mass.; cert. sch. counselor, Tex. Dir., learning specialist Specialized Learning, Dallas, 1981-93; counselor, mem. adj. faculty Eastfield Coll., Mesquite, Tex., 1992-95; counselor Grapevine (Tex.)-Colleyville Ind. Sch. Dist., 1995—; mem. adj. faculty Richland Coll., Dallas, 1991-92. Mem. ACA, Am. Sch. Counselor Assn., Coun. for Exceptional Children, Pi Lambda Theta, Phi Delta Kappa. Avocations: travel, theater, film, cooking, reading. Office: VISTA Alternative Campus 3051 Ira E Woods Ave Grapevine TX 76051-3817

HIRSH, IRA JEAN, psychology educator, researcher; b. N.Y.C., Feb. 22, 1922; s. Ellis Victor and Ida (Bernstein) H.; m. Shirley Helene Kyle, Mar. 21, 1943; children—Eloise, Richard, Elizabeth, Donald. A.B., N.Y. Coll. for Tchrs., 1942; A.M., Northwestern U., 1943; M.A., Harvard, 1947, Ph.D., 1948. Research asst. psycho-acoustic lab. Harvard, Cambridge, Mass., 1946-47; research fellow Harvard, 1947-51; with Central Inst. for Deaf, St. Louis, 1951—; asst dir. research Central Inst. for Deaf, 1958-65, dir., 1965-83; dir. Central Inst. Deaf, 1992-94; mem. faculty or adminstrn. Washington U., St. Louis, 1951-92, prof. psychology, 1961-92, dean faculty arts and scis., 1969-73, Mallinckrodt Disting. Univ. prof., 1984-92, prof. emeritus, 1992—, chmn. psychology dept., 1983-87; vis. prof. U. Paris, 1962-63, U. Tsukuba, Japan, 1982; U.S. del Internat. Standards Orgn., 1962-76; mem. Internat. Acoustics Commn., 1969-75; chmn. behavioral scis. and edn. NRC, 1982-87. Author: The Measurement of Hearing, 1952; Contbr. articles to profl. jours. Served with USAAF, 1943-45; Served with AUS, 1945-46. Recipient Biennial award, 1956, Gold medal, 1992 Acoustical Soc. Am., Assn. Honors Am. Speech and Hearing Assn., 1968. Fellow Acoustical Soc. Am. (pres. 1967-68, gold medal 1992), Am. Psychol. Assn., Am. Speech and Hearing Assn. (exec. council 1958-61, 65-68); mem. NAS. Home: 6629 Waterman Ave Saint Louis MO 63130-4660*

HIRSH, NORMAN BARRY, management consultant; b. N.Y.C., Apr. 20, 1935; s. Samuel Albert and Lillian Rose (Minkow) H.; m. Christina M. Poole, Sept. 21, 1957 (div. 1967); children: Richard Scott, Lisa Robin; m. Sharon Kay Girot, Dec. 29, 1973; 1 child, Sharon Margaret. BSME, Purdue U., 1956; cert. in mgmt., UCLA, 1980. Mech. engr. Ford Motor Co., Dearborn, Mich., 1956-58; design engr. Gen. Dynamics, San Diego, 1958-62; mech. engr. aircraft divsn. Hughes Tool Co., Culver City, Calif., 1962-65, project engr. aircraft divsn., 1965-69, engr. mgr. aircraft divsn., 1969-72; dep. program dir. Hughes Helicopters, Culver City, 1972-79, v.p., 1979-84; v.p., gen. mgr. Hughes Helicopters, Mesa, Ariz., 1984-85; exec. v.p. McDonnell Douglas Helicopter Co., Mesa, 1986-90; pres. Rogerson Hiller Corp., Port Angeles, Wash., 1990-93, Rogerson Aircraft Corp. Flight Structures Group, Port Angeles, 1990-93; cons. in field. Served with U.S. Army. Recipient Disting. Engrng. Alumnus award Purdue U., 1990, Outstanding Mech. Engrng. Alumnus award, 1991. Hon. fellow Am. Helicopter Soc. (chmn. 1986-87); mem. Assn. U.S. Army, Army Aviation Assn. Am., Am. Def. Preparedness Assn., Nat. Aeronautic Assn., Helicopter Assn. Internat. Achievements include devel. and prodn. of the AH-64 Apache helicopter, devel. and FAA cert. of the NOTAR (No Tail Rotor) concept for the MD520N helicopter; initiated design, devel. and FAA cert. of the MD Explorer light twin engine helicopter.

HIRSH, THEODORE WILLIAM, lawyer; b. Gary, Ind., Nov. 16, 1934; s. Phillip and Libby (Krieger) H.; m. Beatrice Elaine Given, Aug. 28, 1955; children: Robert, Margo, Elizabeth, Irwin. AB, Ind. U., 1954, JD, 1957. Bar: Ind. 1957, Ill. 1958, Md. 1965. Atty. Montgomery Ward & Co., Chgo., 1958; pvt. practice Gary, 1958-60; trial lawyer, chief counsel IRS, Chgo., 1960-65; ptnr. Venable, Baetjer & Howard, Balt., 1965-76, Miles & Stockbridge, Balt., 1978-86; prin. Sussman & Hirsh, P.A., Balt., 1976-78; ptnr. Melnicove, Kaufman, Weiner, Smouse & Garbis, P.A., Balt., 1986-89, Miles & Stockbridge, Balt., 1989-96; with Law Offices of Peter G. Angelos, P.C., Balt., 1996-99, Ballard, Spahr, Andrews & Ingersoll, LLP, Balt., 1999—. Office: Ballard Spahr Andrews & Ingersoll LLP Ste 1900 300 E Lombard St Baltimore MD 21202

HIRSHFIELD, STUART, lawyer; b. N.Y.C., Dec. 31, 1941; s. William Louis and Anne (Frank) H.; m. Susanne Drucker, Jan. 22, 1967; children: Matthew S., Edward R. BA, Syracuse U., 1963, JD, 1966. Bar: N.Y. 1966, U.S. Dist. Ct. (so. and ea. dists.) N.Y. 1968, U.S. Ct. Appeals (2nd cir.) 1968. Assoc. Krauss & Krauss, N.Y.C., 1966-67; atty. N.Y. Cen. RR, N.Y.C., 1967-69; assoc. Blum, Haimoff, Gersen, Lipson & Szabad, N.Y.C., 1969; atty. CIT Fin., N.Y.C., 1970-72; assoc. Shea & Gould, N.Y.C., 1972-77, ptnr., 1977-88; ptnr., chmn. bankruptcy practice group Dewey Ballantine, N.Y.C., 1988—; Bd. dirs. 565 Tenants Corp. Contbr. Asset Based Financing--A Transactional Guide, 1985. Assn. atty. Allenwood Civic Assn., Great Neck, N.Y., 1984; bd. visitors Syracuse U. Coll. Law, 1990—, exec. com., 1991-96. With USAR, 1966-72. Fellow Am. Coll. Bankruptcy (2d cir. admissions coun. 1994—, chair 1998—, bd. regents 1998—), Am. Bar Found.; mem. ABA (com. on bankruptcy 1983—), N.Y. Bar Assn., Assn. Bar City N.Y. (corp. reogn. com. 1975-78, 82-85), Assn. Comml. Fin. Attys. (dir. 1980-93), Rockefeller Ctr. Club. Office: Dewey Ballantine 1301 Avenue Of The Americas New York NY 10019-6022

HIRSHMAN, HAROLD CARL, lawyer; b. Durham, N.C., Apr. 22, 1945; s. Morry and Florence Miriam (Goldman) H.; m. Linda Redlick, Dec. 21, 1966 (div. May 1984); 1 child, Sarah Anne; m. Lorie Chaiten, Feb. 19, 1989; children: Samuel David, Emma Lillian, Jacob Edwin. BS, Cornell U., 1966; JD, U. Chgo., 1969. Bar: Ill. 1969, U.S. Supreme Ct. 1976. Ptnr. Sonnenschein, Nath & Rosenthal, Chgo., 1969—. Author: (with others) Commercial Damages, 1986—. Bd. dirs. Lawyers Com. for Civil Rights, Chgo., Am. Jewish Congress Midwest Region; bd. dirs. Chgo. Opera Theatre, 1983-90. Mem. ABA, ACLU (past mem. bd. dirs. Chgo. chpt.), Chgo. Bar Assn., Chgo. Coun. Lawyers. Democrat. Office: Sonnenschein Nath Et Al 233 S Wacker Dr Ste 8000 Chicago IL 60606-6342

HIRSHON, ROBERT EDWARD, lawyer; b. Portland, Maine, Apr. 2, 1948; s. Selvin and Gladys (Wein) H.; m. Roberta Lynn Miller, Aug. 16, 1969; children: Todd, Sara, Jason, Miriam. BA, U. Mich., 1970, JD, 1973. Bar: Maine 1973, U.S. Dist. Ct. Maine 1973, U.S. Ct. Appeals (1st cir.) 1977. Shareholder Drummond, Woodsum & MacMahon P.A., Portland, 1973—; adj. prof. law U. Maine Law Sch. Contbr. articles to profl. jours. Chairperson Breakwater Sch Bd., Portland, 1978-85; mem. Zoning Bd. Appeals, Cape Elizabeth, Maine, 1983-90. Mem. ABA (mem. Ho. of Dels. 1992—, chair standing com. lawyers pub. svc. responsibility 1990-93, chair steering com. pro bono ctr. 1991-96, chair torts and ins. practice sect. 1996-97, chair standing com. on membership 1997—), Maine Bar Assn. (pres. 1986, chair continuing legal edn. com. 1975-83), Cumberland County Bar Assn., Maine Bar Found. (pres. 1990). Avocations: reading, tennis, skiing. Home: 2 Oakhurst Rd Cape Elizabeth ME 04107-1406 Office: Drummond Woodsum & MacMahon PO Box 9781 Portland ME 04104-5081

HIRSHSON, STANLEY PHILIP, history educator; b. Bklyn., June 8, 1928; s. Morris M. and Rose (Gallant) H.; m. Claire Shibin, Nov. 21, 1965; 1 son, Mark Robert; m. Janet N. Feldman, Mar. 4, 1974; 1 son, Scott

Garad. A.B., Rutgers U., 1950; M.A., Columbia U., 1951, Ph.D., 1959. Lectr. history Seton Hall U., South Orange, N.J., 1957-59; asst. prof. Paterson (N.J.) State Coll. (now William Paterson Coll.), 1959-62; asso. prof. Queens Coll., City U. N.Y., Flushing, 1963-66; prof. Queens Coll., City U. N.Y., 1966—. Author: The White Tecumseh: A Biography of General William T. Sherman, 1997, The Lion of the Lord, A Biography of Brigham Young, 1969, Grenville M. Dodge, Soldier, Politician, Railroad Pioneer, 1967, Farewell to the Bloody Shirt, Northern Republicans and the Southern Negro, 1962, My History Is Holy, A Biography of Mary Baker Eddy. Served with AUS, 1946-47, 53-55. Am. Coun. Learned Socs. fellow, 1962-63, Guggenheim fellow, 1966-67, Rockefeller Found. fellow, 1981-82, Andrew W. Mellon fellow Huntington Libr., 1993. Home: 59 Wilson Pl Closter NJ 07624-2321 Office: Queens Coll Dept History Flushing NY 11367

HIRSHTAL, EDITH, concert pianist, educator, chamber musician; b. Bregenz, Austria, May 31, 1950; d. Izak and Sabina (Silbershein) H. B of Music, Temple U., 1973, M of Music, 1975; artist diploma, Peabody Conservatory, 1983. Adj. faculty mem. Temple U., Phila., 1973-83, Bryn Mawr (Pa.) Conservatory, 1980-83; pianist, mem. faculty Downeast Summer Chamber Inst., 1983, Dobbs Ferry Chamber Inst., 1984; prof. piano Calif. State U., Long Beach, 1984—; founder, artistic dir. Oasis Chamber Ensemble, Long Beach, 1996—; collaborations with Phila. Opera Co., Sequoia Quartet, Joanne Faletta Mostovoy Concerto Soloists, Stephanie Chase Jonathan Mack, Antoinette Perry, Peter Marsh, Michael Carson. Artist compact disc Impromptu, Despite the Odds; debut recital at Weill Recital Hall, N.Y.C., Carnegie Hall, Lincoln Ctr., Alice Tully Hall. Recipient Galica prize Paderewski Found., Phila., 1970. Democrat. Jewish. Office: Calif State U Dept Music 1250 N Bellflower Blvd Long Beach CA 90840-0006

HIRST, HESTON STILLINGS, former insurance company executive; b. Concord, N.H., Nov. 8, 1915; s. Edgar Clarkson and Mary Walker (Stillings) H.; m. Ruth Elizabeth Galway, Sept. 9, 1939; children—Ann, Edgar, George. A.B., Dartmouth Coll., 1936, postgrad., 1937. Chem. engr. Factory Mut. Engring. Corp., 1937-44; chief engr. Blackstone Mut. Ins. Co., 1945-49, sec., asst. treas., 1949-52, v.p., sec., 1952-65, exec. v.p., 1965-68; sr. v.p. engring.-underwriting MFB Mut. Ins. Co., Providence, 1968-72; sr. v.p., sec. corp. affairs Allendale Mut. Ins. Co., Johnston, R.I., 1972-81; ret., 1981; sr. v.p., sec. corp. affairs Affiliated FM Ins. Co., Appalachian Ins. Co., New Providence Corp. Mem. Republican Town Com., Barrington, R.I., 1952-76, Com. on Appropriations, Barrington, 1961-70, town moderator, Barrington, 1970-76. Mem. Am. Chem. Soc., Soc. Fire Protection Engrs., Providence Engring. Soc., Dartmouth Soc. Engrs., Univ. Club (Providence). Republican. Unitarian.

HIRST, JOANNE FLIP, community health nurse; b. N.Y.C., Nov. 15, 1951; d. Martin Irvin and Marianne (Ghetler) Goldstein; m. Charles Stanley Hirst, Mar. 26, 1978; children: Roland C., Brian J. Schleifer. AAS, Jr. Coll. of Albany, N.Y., 1984; BS, SUNY, Utica, 1990, MSN, 1997. Staff nurse primary care unit St. Peter's Hosp., Albany, 1984-85; charge nurse, team leader Community Hosp. of Schoharie County, Cobleskill, N.Y., 1985-86; pub. health nurse Schoharie (N.Y.) County Health Dept., 1986—; part-time adult nurse practitioner Dr. Lorraine E. Davis Family Practice, 1998—. Capt. USAR, 1975—. E-mail: flip51@midtel.net.

HIRST, PETER CHRISTOPHER, consulting actuary; b. Nairobi, Kenya, Aug. 22, 1943; s. Harold Rupert and Maureen (Doherty) H.; B.A., Balliol Coll., Oxford U., 1965, M.A., 1969; m. Audrey Kennett, July 27, 1968; children—Philippa Anne, Sara Elizabeth. Supr. group pension dept. Imperial Life of Can., Toronto, Ont., 1967-70; cons. actuary Peat, Marwick & Partners, Toronto, 1970-74; asst. v.p., sr. cons. actuary Johnson & Higgins, Willis, Faber, Toronto, 1974-76; founder, actuary Hirst Cons. Ltd., Toronto, 1976-80; pres., actuary Tillinghast, Nelson & Warren, Inc., Toronto, 1980-86; co-founder, pres. Actrex Ptnrs. Ltd., 1986-93; exec. v.p. Buck Consultants Ltd., 1993—; hon. faculty Centre for Continuing Studies in Employee Benefits, Humber Coll., bd. dirs. Fellow Can. Inst. Actuaries (past pres.), Inst. Actuaries; mem. Soc. Actuaries (assoc.), Conf. Consulting Actuaries (bd. dirs.), Internat. Assn. Actuaries, Internat. Assn. Cons. Actuaries, Can. Pension & Benefits Inst. (past pres.), Assn. Can. Pension Mgmt., Human Resources Profl. Assn. Ont. Toronto (bd. dirs.). Clubs: Bd. Trade of Met. Toronto, Canadian, Mississauga Golf and Country. Contbr. articles on pensions and actuarial topics to profl. jours. Home: 19 Chisholm St, Oakville, ON Canada L6K 3W2 Office: Buck Consultants Ltd, Box 15 Ste 1500 95 Wellington St W, Toronto, ON Canada M5J 2N7

HIRT, JOAN B., education educator; b. Huntington, N.Y., Feb. 20, 1951; d. Warren G. and Ruth T. Hirt. BA in Russian Studies, Bucknell U., 1972; MAEd, U. Md., 1979; PhD, U. Ariz., 1992. Asst. dir. housing and dining svcs. Humboldt State U., Arcata, Calif., 1979-88; assoc. dean students U. Ariz., Tucson, 1988-92; assoc. prof. higher edn. and student affairs Va. Tech. U., Blacksburg, 1992—; cons. in edn.; corp. cons. Contbr. chpts. to books, articles to profl. jours. Mem. Am. Coll. Pers. Assn. (bd. dirs. 1996-99), Assn. for Study of Higher Edn., Nat. Assn. Student Pers., Am. Coll. Pers. Assn. Office: ELPS-Va Tech U 307 E Eggleston Hall Blacksburg VA 24061

HIRTH, JOHN PRICE, metallurgical engineering educator; b. Cin., Dec. 16, 1930; s. John Willard and Betty Ann (Price) H.; m. Martha Joan Davis, Nov. 28, 1953; children: John Marcus, Laura Ellen, James Gregory, Christina Louise. B. Metall. Engring., Ohio State U., 1953; M.S., Carnegie-Mellon U., 1953, Ph.D., 1957; DSc (hon.), Ohio State U., 1995. Asst. prof. metall. engring. Carnegie-Mellon U., Pitts., 1958-61; Mershon prof. Ohio State U., 1961-67; vis. prof. Stanford, 1967-68; prof. Ohio State U., Columbus, 1967-88, Wash. State U., Pullman, 1988—; Aizen vis. prof. Nat. U. Mex., Mexico City, 1976; cons. in field; bd. overseers Acad. for Contemporary Problems, 1971-76. Author: Condensation and Evaporation, 1964, Theory of Dislocations, 1968, 82; editor: Scripta Metallurgica, 1974-94. Served with USAF, 1953-55. Fulbright fellow Bristol U., Eng., 1957-58. Fellow AIME (Hardy medal 1960, Mehl medal 1980, Mathewson medal 1982), Am. Soc. Engring. Edn. (McGraw award 1967), Am. Soc. Medals (Stoughton award 1964, Campbell lectr. 1972, White award 1989, Gold medal 1994, Sauveur Achievement award 1998); mem. NAS, NAE, Norwegian Acad. Scis. and Letters, Sigma Xi. Home: 114 Ramsey Canyon Rd Hereford AZ 85615

HIRUKI, CHUJI, plant virologist, science educator; b. Fukue, Nagasaki, Japan, June 16, 1931; arrived in Can., 1966; s. Chuichi and Mitsu (Kawamuko) H.; m. Yasuko Hijikata, Dec. 26, 1961; children: Tadaaki, Lisa. BSc, Kyushu U., Fukuoka, 1954, PhD, 1963. Plant pathologist Hatano Tobacco Expt. Sta., Hatano, Japan, 1954-65; asst. prof. U. Alberta, Edmonton, Can., 1966-70, assoc. prof., 1970-76, prof., 1976-91, univ. prof., 1991-96; univ. prof. emeritus U. Alberta, Edmonton, 1996—; vis. plant pathologist, U. Calif., Berkeley, 1963-64; vis. scientist INRA, Versailles, France, 1972; vis. prof. Agrl. U., Wageningen, The Netherlands, 1973; CSFP vis. prof. U. Queensland, Brisbane, Australia, 1984, vis. prof., 1984-85; hon. disting. scientist China Paulownia Rsch. Ctr., 1993-95; internat. cons. forest pathology FAO UN, 1993-95; chmn. Internat. Working Group Plant Viruses with Fungal Vectors, 1988-93, IUFRO Working Party on Virus and Mycoplasma Diseases, 1982—. Editor: Tree Mycoplasmas and Mycoplasma Diseases, 1988; over 150 scientific rsch. papers, 300 rsch. paper presentations. Fellow U. Wis., 1964-66, The Netherlands Internat. Ctr., 1973; recipient rsch. award Disting. Fgn. Specialist Govt. Japan, 1991, J. Gordin Kaplan award U. Alberta, 1993; named Nat. Sci. Coun. lectr. Govt. Republic China, 1989. Fellow Royal Soc. Can., Am. Phytopathological Soc. (Pacific divsn., Lifetime Achievement award 1993), Can. Phytopathological Soc. (pres. 1990-91, award for outstanding rsch. 1996); mem. Internat. Soc. Plant Pathologists (treas. 1998—), N.Y. Acad. Scis., Phytopathological Soc. Japan (award excellence in rsch. 1990). Avocations: reading, classical music, swimming. Home: 152 Windermere Cres, Edmonton, AB Canada T6R 2H6 Office: U Alta, U Alta, Dept Agr Food and Nutrition, Edmonton, AB Canada T6G 2P5

HISCHAK, THOMAS STEPHEN, theater educator, writer; b. Rochester, N.Y., Nov. 17, 1951; s. Thomas M. and Helen (Lomaglio) H.; m. Catherine M. Nieland, May 22, 1976; children: Mark, Karen. BA in English and Theater, St. Louis U., 1973; MFA in Theater, So. Ill. U., 1978. Instr. theater Point Park Coll., Pitts., 1978-82; audience devel. dir. Del. Theater Co., Wilmington, 1982-83; prof. theater SUNY, Cortland, 1983—; cons. N.Y. Coun. on the Arts, N.Y.C., 1985—. Author: Word Crazy: Broadway Lyricists from Cohan to Sondheim, 1991, Stage It With Music: An Encyclopedic Guide to the American Musical Theatre, 1993, American Musical Theatre Song Encyclopedia, 1995, Theatregoer's Almanac, 1997, Am. Musical Film Song Encyclopedia, 1999. Recipient Stanley Drama award, Wagner Coll., Staten Island, N.Y., 1996, Outstanding Acad. Book award ALA, 1996. Mem. Dramatist's Guild (assoc.). Office: SUNY Performing Arts Dept Cortland NY 13045

HISCOCK, RICHARD CARSON, marine safety investigator; b. Washington, Dec. 18, 1944; s. Earle Francis and Alice Morgan (Carson) H.; m. Nancy Lynn Schafer, Oct. 12, 1968 (div. Jan. 1986); m. Virginia Murray Brierley, July 6, 1996. Student, Am. U., 1964-66. Coast Guard license master near coastal. Fisherman F/V Benjo, Chatham, Mass., 1977-78; asst. harbormaster Town of Chatham (Mass.), 1977-87; exec. dir. U.S. Lifesaving Mfrs. Assn., North Chatham, Mass., 1984-86; investigator Marine Safety Cons., Fairhaven, Mass., 1987-91; pres. ERE Assocs. Ltd., North Chatham, 1991—; instr. hypothermia, cold water survival, emergency rescue equipment and fishing vessel safety, 1979-87; mem. Comm. Fishing Industry Vessel Adv. Com., 1991-98; mem. Cape Cod Coastal Zone Mgmt. Adv. Com., 1977-92, chmn., 1986-91; mem. Barnstable County Coastal Resources Com., 1992-93; mem., chmn. Chatham Waterways Adv. Com., 1983-87; founder, bd. dirs. Marine Safety Found., Inc., Mass., 1993; mem. Chatham Fin. Com., 1993-95; mem. Chatham Bylaw Rev. Com., 1995-97; industry advisor USCG Fishing Vessel Casualty Task Force, 1999. Contbr. articles to profl. jours. Recipient Pub. Svc. Commendation, USCG, 1984, Cert. of Merit, USCG, 1998. Mem. Soc. Naval Architects and Marine Engrs., U.S. Marines Safety Assn. Achievements include drafting a bill to establish crew licensing, inspection and additional safety requirements of certain fishing industry vessels; rsch. on comml. fishing, uninspected vessel safety, fishing vessel safety and hypothermia. Home and Office: ERE Assocs Ltd 24 Briar Spring Rd Orleans MA 02653-3702

HISE, MARK ALLEN, dentist; b. Chgo., Jan. 17, 1950; s. Clyde and Rose T. (Partipilo) H. AA, Mt. San Antonio Coll., Walnut, Calif., 1972; BA with highest honors, U. Calif., Riverside, 1974; MS, U. Utah, 1978; DDS, UCLA, 1983. Instr. sci. NW Acad., Houston, 1978-79; chmn. curriculum med. coll. prep program UCLA, 1980-85; instr. dentistry Coll. of Redwoods, Eureka, Calif., 1983; practice dentistry Arcata, Calif., 1983—; participant numerous radio and TV appearances. Editor: Preparing for the MCAT, 1983-85; contbr. articles to profl. jours.; speaker in field. Recipient awards for underwater photography; Henry Carter scholar U. Calif., 1973, Calif. State scholar 1973, 74, Regents scholar U. Calif., 1973; Calif. State fellow, 1975, NIH fellow, 1975-79. Mem. AAAS, ADA, Calif. Dental Assn., Acad. Gen. Dentistry, Nat. Soc. for Med. Rsch., North Coast Scuba Club. Roman Catholic. Avocation: underwater photography. Home and Office: 1225 B St Arcata CA 95521-5936

HISEY, LYDIA VEE, educational administrator; b. Memphis, Tex., July 10, 1951; d. Murray Wayne Latimer and Jane Kathryn (Grimsley) Webster; m. Gregory Lynn Hisey, Oct. 4, 1975; children: Kathryn Elizabeth, Jennifer Kay, Anna Elaine. BS in Edn., Tex. Tech U., 1974, MEd, 1990. Cert. tchr., mid-mgmt., Tex.x. Tchr. phys. edn. Lubbock (Tex.) Ind. Sch. Dist., 1975-79, tchr., 1982-91, asst. prin., 1991-95, prin., 1995—. Recipient Way-To-Go award Lubbock Ind. Sch. Dist., 1989, Impact II grantee, 1991. Mem. Tex. Elem. Prins. and Suprs. Assn., Lubbock Elem. Prins. and Suprs. Assn. (v.p. 1997-98, pres. 1998—), Delta Kappa Gamma, Phi Delta Kappa. Baptist. Avocation: cross-stitching. Home: 4417 87th St Lubbock TX 79424-4231

HISKES, DOLORES G., educator; b. Chgo.; d. Leslie R. and Dagmar (Brown) Grant; m. John R. Hiskes; children: Robin Caproni, Grant. Student, U. Ill., Chgo. Presenter workshops in devel. and implementation of tutoring programs and ednl. materials. *Dolores has tutored reading for over 30 years, collected classic old reading and spelling texts from all over the world, and developed a special teaching technique ("eyerobics") that helps prevent or correct reversals. She has simplified and incorporated the best of all this information into one comprehensive reading and spelling text. Phonics Pathways is the result of that effort. She continues to write new educational material and publish articles in professional journals such as The California Reader, Winter 1997; Reading Matters, Association of American Educators, October/November 1997; and the National Right To Read Report, February 1998.* Author/illustrator: Phonics Pathways, Pyramid, The Short-Vowel Dictionary; developer ednl. games: The Train Game, Blendit!, Wordwatch, The Long and the Short of It. Mem. Assn. Am. Educators, Assn. Ednl. Therapists, Calif. Assn. of Res. Specialists, Orton Dyslexia Soc., Learning Disabilities Assn., Nat. Right to Read Found., The Calif. Reading Assn., Pubs. Mktg. Assn., Pacific Ednl. Mktg. Assn., Calif. Watercolor Soc., Commonwealth Club of Calif., Bay Area Ind. Pubs. Assn. Avocations: watercolors, travel, reading, exercise. E-mail: dolores@dorbooks.com. Office: Dorbooks PO Box 2588 Livermore CA 94551-2588

HISKEY, J. BRENT, metallurgical engineer, educator; b. Salina, Utah, Aug. 18, 1944; m. 1967; 2 children. BS, U. Utah, 1967, MS, 1971, PhD in Metallurgy, 1973. Rschr. Alcoa Labs, 1973-74; asst. prof. N. Mex. Inst. Mining & Tech., 1974-77; rsch. scientist US Steel Rsch. Labs, 1977-80; mgr. metallurgy rsch. Kennecott Copper Corp., 1980-84; dir. Ariz. Mining & Mineral Resources Rsch. Inst., 1985-96; prof. U. Ariz., 1984—, assoc. dean Coll. Engring. and Mines, 1999—; dir. Copper Rsch. Ctr., 1989-97; lectr. Carnegie Mellon U., 1977-79; cons. E.I. du Pont de Nemours & Co., Inc., 1984—, Phelps Dodge, 1985—, Newcrest Gold Co., 1985-95, Kennecott Corp., 1985-96; chmn. Nat. Assn. Mineral Inst. Dirs., 1990-91, Cyrus AMAX Metals Corp., 1994—; bd. dirs. Am. Chemet Corp., 1993—. Recipient James Douglas Gold medal Am. Inst. Mech. Engrs., 1993. Mem. Nat. Acad. Engrs., Soc. Metallurgy Engrs. (Taggart award 1974), Soc. Mining Metallurgy & Exploration Inc. (chmn. mineral & metallurgy processing div. 1991-92), Sigma Xi. E-mail: jbh@bigdog.engr.arizona.edu. Fax: 520-621-8159. Home: 7078 E Chipmunk Ct Tucson AZ 85750-0807 Office: Dept Math Science & Engineering Univ Arizona Tucson AZ 85721

HISLOP, MERVYN WARREN, health advocate administrator, psychologist; b. Vancouver, B.C., Apr. 26, 1937; s. George and Freda (Wickenden) H.; m. Marilyn Gail Johnson, July 24, 1965; children: Lawren Nyall, Mylene Lorelle. B.A. with honors, U. B.C., 1965; M.A., McMaster U., 1967, Ph.D., 1970. Cert. health adminstr. Dir. behaviour mgmt. services Surrey Place Centre, Ministry of Health, Toronto, Ont., 1970-73; dir. psychol. services Woodlands Ministry of Human Resources, New Westminster, B.C., 1973-78; coordinator life edn. program New Westminster, 1975-77; exec. dir. Riverview Hosp., Port Coquitlam, B.C., 1978-85, Valleyview Hosp., Port Coquitlam, B.C., 1985-86; dir. legis. and regulatory affairs Mental Health Services Div., B.C. Ministry of Health, 1986-89; psychiat. adv. Govt. Alberta, Can., 1989—; research proposal submission cons. Can. Council, 1973; mem. edn. adv. com. Douglas Coll., 1983-86. Demonstration model grantee Province Ont., 1971; province Ont. grad. fellow McMaster U., 1969; recipient David and Jean Bolocan Meml. prize U. B.C., 1965; Nat. Rsch. Coun. Can. scholar, 1965, 66, 67, 68. Mem. Can. Coll. Health Service Execs. (cert.), Can. Inst. Law and Medicine. Home: 17203-57 Ave, Edmonton, AB Canada T6M 1B8

HISS, ROLAND GRAHAM, physician, medical educator; b. Newark, Oct. 9, 1932; s. George Crosby and Adrianne (Graham) H.; m. Margaret Barringer McGrath, Aug. 23, 1957; children: John Barringer, Meredith Graham Brown. BS, U. Mich., 1955, MD, 1957. Diplomate Am. Bd. Internal Medicine. Intern in medicine Phila. Gen. Hosp., 1957-58; resident in medicine U. Mich. Hosp., Ann Arbor, 1961-64; fellow hematology Simpson Meml. Inst., Ann Arbor, 1964-66; faculty medicine U. Mich. Med. Sch., Ann Arbor, 1966—, chmn. dept. med. edn., 1982—; coordinator edn. Mich. Diabetes Research and Tng. Ctr., Ann Arbor, 1977—. Contbr. 50 articles to profl. jours. Served to capt. USAF, 1958-61. Recipient Teaching award Kaiser Permanente Found. and U. Mich., 1976. Fellow ACP; mem. Am. Diabetes Assn., AMA, Mich. State Med. Soc. Home: 3551 Chatham Way Ann Arbor MI 48105-2827 Office: U Mich Med Sch Towsley Ctr Box 0201 G-1103 Ann Arbor MI 48109-0201

HISS, TONY, writer; b. Washington, Aug. 5, 1941; s. Alger and Priscilla Harriet (Fansler) H.; m. Lois Cynthia Metzger, Feb. 22, 1986; 1 child, Jacob. AB, Harvard Coll., 1963. Staff writer The New Yorker, N.Y.C., 1963—; vis. scholar Taub Urban Rsch. Ctr. NYU, N.Y.C., 1994—; Regents' lectr. landscape architecture dept. U. Calif., Berkeley, Davis, 1992. Author: Laughing Last, 1977, The Experience of Place, 1990, The View from Alger's Window, 1999; co-author: All Aboard With E.M. Frimbo, 1974, 97, A Region at Risk, 1996, Disarming the Prairie, 1998, Prairie Passage: The I&M Canal Corridor, 1998; illustrator: The Bird Who Steals Everything Shining, 1987. Cons. Hudson River Greenway Coun., Albany, N.Y., 1990; juror Rudy Bruner Found., N.Y.C., 1991; trustee Conservancy Hist. Battery Pk, 1995; bd. dirs. Village Alliance, 1998; adv. bd. Scenic Am., Inc., 1999. Recipient best content article in non-geog. periodical award Nat. Coun. for Geog. Edn., 1990, Nat. Lit. award Nat. Recreation and Park Assn., 1995, George S. Lewis award Am. Inst. Archs. (local chpt.); Guggenheim fellow, 1994. Mem. Pen Am. Ctr., N.Y. Inst. Humanities. Avocation: train travel. Home: 22 E 8th St New York NY 10003-5920 Office: NYU Taub Urban Rsch Ctr 269 Mercer St Fl 2 New York NY 10003-6633

HITCHBORN, JAMES BRIAN, telecommunications executive; b. Grand Junction, Colo., Aug. 26, 1938; s. Louis Bryan and Sarah Alice (McCarty) H.; children: Kimberley, James Bryan, Jennifer Leigh, David Everett; m. Jan Pamela Schuster, Jan. 8, 1983. BS in Gen. Engring., U.S. Naval Acad., 1962; BS in Meteorology, USN Postgrad. Sch., 1967; cert. in mgmt., USN Sr. War Coll., 1977. Ensign USN, 1962, advanced through grades to capt., 1982, ret., 1988; nat. support dir. Teknekron Infoswitch, DFW Airport, Tex., 1988-91; mgr. internat. sales support Intervoice, Inc., Dallas, 1991, internat. sales exec., 1991-93, dir. internat. support, 1993-95, dir. project mgmt., 1994-95, dir. field ops., 1995-96, dir. office adminstrn., 1996-98, dir. CPE line bus. opr., 1998—. Mem. Olympic Rowing Team (U.S.), Rome, 1960; leader Boy Scouts Am., Newport, R.I., 1976-77. Mem. Nat. Model R.R. Assn., North Tex. Garden R.R.S., U.S. Golf Assn., Thorntree Country Club, Pebble Beach Automobile Club, Corvette Club of North Tex. Republican. Methodist. Avocations: model railroading, cross-country skiing, golf, power walking, biking.

HITCHCOCK, ETHAN ALLEN, lawyer; b. Milton, Mass., July 12, 1909; s. George Collier and Elizabeth (Fiske) H.; m. Elizabeth French, 1937 (dec.); children: Constance, Mary Elizabeth Bigham; m. Jane Chace Nicholas, 1976 (dec. 1987); m. Mari B. Watts, 1987. Grad., St. Louis Country Day Sch., 1927; A.B., Yale U., 1931; LL.B., Harvard U., 1934. Bar: N.Y. 1935. Practiced in N.Y.C., 1934-41, 46—; ptnr. Webster & Sheffield, 1961-83, of counsel, 1984-91; chmn. bd. dirs. Olivetti Corp. Am., 1959-78. Pres. bd. Lenox Hill Neighborhood Assn., 1938-40, chmn. Brearley Sch., 1954-60; mem. Yale U. Council; chmn. Com. on Med. Affairs, 1970-75; trustee Lenox Hill Hosp., 1950-70; trustee WNET/Thirteen Ednl. Broadcasting Corp., 1967-82, chmn., 1968-81; vice chmn. bd. dirs. N.Y. Philharm., 1965-74; bd. govs. Pub. Broadcasting Service, 1973-75; bd. dirs. Moblzn. for Youth, 1965-68; chmn. bd. dirs. MFY Legal Services, 1968-70; v.p., bd. dirs. Alzheimer's Disease and Related Disorders Assn. Inc., 1980-90; mem. U.S. Congress Office of Tech. Assessment Adv. Panel on Alzheimer's Disease, 1987-90. Served from lt. to lt. comdr. USNR, 1941-46. Mem. Chi Psi. Home: PO Box 143 28 King St Oldwick NJ 08858-0143

HITCHCOCK, FRITZ, automotive company executive. CEO, owner Hitchcock Automotive Resources, City of Industry, CA, 1980—. Office: Hitchcock Automotive Resour 17340 Gale Ave La Puente CA 91748-1512*

HITCHCOCK, JOANNA, publisher; b. London. BA, Oxford (Eng.) U., 1960, MA in Modern History, 1965. Asst. publicity dept. Oxford U. Press, London, 1962-66; asst. promotion mgr. Princeton (N.J.) Univ. Press, 1966-68, advt. and exhibits mgr., 1968-69, staff editor, 1970-72, mng. editor, 1972-80, exec. editor, 1980-84, asst. dir., 1985-87, exec. editor for humanities, 1988-92; dir. U. of Tex. Press, Austin, 1992—. Mem. Princeton U. Libr. Coun., 1986-95. Mem. Am. Assn. Univ. Presses (bd. dirs. 1984-87, chair equal opportunities com. 1985-86, ann. program planning com. 1986-87, pres. 1997-98, past pres. 1998-99). Home: 1507 Preston Ave Austin TX 78703-1903 Office: Univ of Texas Press PO Box 7819 Austin TX 78713-7819

HITCHCOCK, KAREN RUTH, biology educator, university dean, academic administrator; b. Feb. 10, 1943; d. Roy Clinton and Ruth (Wardell) H. BS in Biology, St. Lawrence U., 1964; PhD in Anatomy, U. Rochester, 1969. Postdoctoral fellow in pulmonary cell biology Webb-Waring Inst. Med. Rsch., 1968-70; asst. prof. dept. anatomy Tufts U. Sch. Medicine, Boston, 1970-75, assoc. prof. dept. anatomy, 1975-80, assoc. prof., acting chmn. dept. anatomy, 1978-80, prof., chmn. dept. anatomy and cellular biology, 1980-82, George A. Bates prof. histology, 1982-85, chmn. dept. anatomy and cellular biology, 1982-85; prof. dept. cell biology and anatomy Tex. Tech. U. Health Scis. Ctr.; assoc. dean Tex. Tech. U. Sch. Medicine, Lubbock, 1985-87; vice chancellor rsch., dean grad. coll. U. Ill., Chgo., 1987-91, prof. cell biology, anatomy and biol. scis., 1987-91; v.p. acad. affairs, prof. biol. scis. U. at Albany, SUNY, 1991-95, interim pres., 1995-96, pers., 1996—; mem. nat. adv. rsch. resources coun. NIH, 1992-96, Nat. Bd. Med. Examiners, 1987-95; bd. dirs. N.Y. Capital Region Ctr. Econ. Growth, 1996—; mem. steering com. Assn. Colls. & Univs. State N.Y., 1995—; mem. N.Y. State Senate Higher Edn. com. adv. com., 1995—; pres., bd. dirs. Capital Region Info. Svc., N.Y., 1995—; bd. dirs. Charter One Bank F.S.B., 1999. Mem. exec. com. Gov.'s Sci. Adv. Com., Ill., 1991; pres. Albany-Colonie C. of C., 1999. Mem. Am. Assn. Anatomists (exec. com. 1981-85, v.p. 1986-88, pres. 1990-91), Nat. Assn. for Biomed. Rsch. (bd. dirs. 1990-92), Nat. Assn. State Univs. and Land-Grant Colls. (chair coun. acad. affairs com. 1994-95), Ill. Soc. Med. Rsch. (pres. 1988-91). Home: 286 Riverview Rd Rexford NY 12148-1649 Office: U at Albany Office of Pres 1400 Washington Ave Albany NY 12222-0100

HITCHCOCK, KEN, professional hockey coach; b. Edmonton, Alta., Can., Dec. 17, 1951; m. Nancy; children: Emily, Alex, Noah. Student, U. Alta., Edmonton, Can. Head coach Kamloops Blazers, 1984-90; asst. coach Phila. Flyers, 1990-93; head coach Kalamazoo Wings, 1993-94; coach All-Star Games IHL, 1993-94, 94-95; coach Dallas Stars, 1996—. Named Coach of Yr. Minor Hockey, 1982-83, Alta. Minor Hockey Assn., 1983-84, WHL, 1986-87, 89-90, top coach Canadian Major Jr. Hockey, 1989-90. Office: Dallas Stars 211 Cowboys Pkwy Irving TX 75063-5931*

HITCHCOCK, WALTER ANSON, educational consultant, retired educational administrator; b. Shelton, Wash., Dec. 9, 1918; s. Paul H. and Hazel (Boyington) H.; m. Helen Nadine Rainbolt, Mar. 13, 1944; children: Paul H., Walter Anson, Larry W. BABA, Wash. State U., 1940, BEd, 1941, MA in Edn., 1948; postgrad., U. Okla., 1943-44, summer 1946; EdD, Wash. State U., 1966. Tchr. bus. subjects Omak (Wash.) Sr. High Sch., 1941-42; counselor Weatherwax Sr. High Sch., Aberdeen, Wash., 1946-47; prin. Wilbur (Wash.) High Sch., 1947-49; supt. schs. Nespelem, Wash., 1949-50, Wilbur, 1950-55, Moxee, Wash., 1955-59; supt. schs. West Valley schs., Spokane, 1959-66, Kennewick schs., 1966-69; dep. supt. Spokane city schs., 1969-72, supt., 1972-80; assoc. Interpacific Investors Services, 1980-85; mem. adv. com. on tchr. edn. Ea. Wash. State U., 1959-63, ednl. imperatives com., 1984-86; adminstrv. adv. com. State Sch. Supt., mem. spl. edn. com., 1976-79; mem. Wash. State Ednl. TV Adv. Com., 1972-74; mem. spl. edn. adv. com. Cen. Wash. State U., 1975-79. Mem. Tri-Cities United Cmty. Svcs., 1967-69, v.p., 1968; active Benton-Franklin Govtl. Conf., 1968-69; bd. dirs. Expo 74, 1972-75, United Way, Spokane County, 1972-79, Inland Empire Red Cross, Inland Empire Coun. Boy Scouts Am., Spokane Area Youth Com., OK Boys Ranch sponsored by Olympia Kiwanis, 1993-94; panel mem. Eastern Wash. Area Agy. on Aging, 1984-85. Served with AUS, 1942-45. Mem. Am. Assn. Sch. Adminstrs. (mem. SASA-AASA rels. com. 1971-74), NEA, Wash. Edn. Assn. (bd. dirs. dept. adminstrn. and supervision 1968-69), Inland Empire Edn. Assn. (pres. 1972-73), Northwest Regional Sch. Adminstrs. (chmn.), Yakima Valley Sch. Adminstrs. (chmn.), Spokane Area Supts. Assn. (pres.), Lincoln-Adams Bi-County Activities Assn. (pres.), Wash. Assn. Sch. Adminstrs. (pres. 1969-70, mem. exec. com.), Wash. State Ret. Tchrs. Assn. (del. 1986-98, mem. fin. com. 1994—, chmn. 1996-97, actuarial study com. 1998-99, faculty need com. 1999), Thurston County Ret. Tchrs. Assn. (bd. dirs. 1986-95, found. com. 1996—), Phi Kappa Phi, Alpha Kappa Psi, Phi Delta Kappa, Sigma Phi Epsilon. Presbyterian. (trustee 1957-59, ruling elder). Clubs: Lion, Wilbur Commercial (pres. 1952-54), Kiwanis (trustee 1961-63, 67-69, 72-76).

HITCHING, HARRY JAMES, retired lawyer; b. N.Y.C., Nov. 20, 1909; s. Harry and Sara (James) H.; m. Virginia Wyber, June 1933 (dec. Feb. 12, 1972); children: Virginia B. (Mrs. Daniel Andrews), James F.; m. Jeanne Austin Buckner, Aug. 25, 1972. A.B., Columbia, 1929, LL.B. (Kent scholar), 1931, J.D., 1969. Bar: N.Y. 1932, Tenn. 1938, Ga. 1969. Pvt. practice N.Y.C., 1931-37; prin. atty. TVA, 1937-40, asst., gen. counsel, 1940-44; mem. firm Miller and Martin, Chattanooga, 1944-46; partner Miller & Martin and predecessor firm Miller, Martin and Hitching, 1946-92; Gen. counsel Skyland Internat. Corp., Benwood Found., Chattanooga Area Regional Transp. Authority; div. counsel Vulcan Materials Co.; dir. Krystal Co. Mem. Miller Park Bd.; Chmn. bd. Tonya Meml. Found., Estate Planning Council Chattanooga; chmn. advisory bd. Chattanooga Salvation Army; bd. dirs. Chattanooga Opthalmol. Found., Community Found. Greater Chattanooga. Served to ensign USCGR, 1943-45. Mem. ABA, Tenn. Bar Assn., Ga. Bar Assn., Chattanooga Bar Assn. (v.p.), Chattanooga Bar Found., Chattanooga C. of C. (treas., dir., Newcomen Soc. N.Am. Episcopalian. Clubs: Lookout Mountain Fairyland, Mountain City (Chattanooga), Lookout Mountain Golf (Chattanooga), Geology (Chattanooga), Torch (Chattanooga) (pres.). Home: 1701 Wood Nymph Trail Lookout Mountain GA 30750-2640

HITCHMAN, CAL MCDONALD, SR., secondary education educator; b. Houston, July 9, 1948; s. Robert McDonald and Isabel Mary (Shugert) H.; 1 child, Cal McDonald Jr. BA, Houston Bapt. U., 1972. Cert. vocat./tech. edn. mktg. Tex. Auditor, pers. adminstr., tng. coord. Rice Food Markets, Inc., Houston, 1968-76; tchr., coord. Houston (Tex.) Ind. Sch. Dist., Sterling High Sch., 1976-80; dir. edn. Airco Tech. Inst., Houston, 1980-81; tchr., coord. Houston (Tex.) Ind. Sch. Dist., Sterling High Sch., 1981-91, Houston (Tex.) Ind. Sch. Dist., Sam Houston High Sch., 1991—; adj. prof. U. Houston, 1997-98. Named Outstanding Young Men of Am., 1975, 77. Mem. Am. Vocat. Assn., Mktg. Educators Tex., Mktg. Edn. Assn., DECA (profl. div.), DECA Tex. Assn. (dist. dir. mktg. edn. 1990—), sec., v.p. 1987-90), Metrodet, Tex. Adv. Coun. for Mktg. Edn./DECA, 1990— (chair 1995-96), Kappa Alpha Order. Methodist. Avocations: tennis, swimming, music, theatre. Home: 923 Gober St Houston TX 77017-4116 Office: Houston Ind Sch Dist Sam Houston H S 9400 Irvington Blvd Houston TX 77076-5224

HITE, CATHARINE LEAVEY, orchestra manager; b. Boston, Oct. 1, 1924; d. Edmond Harrison and Ruth Farrington Leavey; m. Robert Atkinson Hite, Aug. 28, 1948; children: Charles Harrison, Patricia Hite Barton, Catharine Hite Dunn. BA, Coll. William and Mary, 1945. Restoration guide Williamsburg Restoration, 1944-45; asst. edn. dept. Honolulu Acad. Arts, 1945-46; sec., tour guide edn. dept. office chief curator Nat. Gallery Art, 1946-48; opera liason/coord. Honolulu Symphony, 1972-73, asst. to gen. mgr., 1973-75, community devel. dir./opera coord., 1975-77, dir. ops./opera prodn. coord., 1977-79, orch. mgr., 1979-84, mem. exec. com., 1965-69, pres. women's assn., 1965-66; com. chmn., opera assn. chmn. Hawaii Opera Theatre, 1966-69. Mem. W. R. Farrington Scholarship Com., 1977—, chmn., 1982-94; mem. community arts panel State Found. Culture and the Arts, 1982, State Found. Music and Opera, 1984; docent Iolani Palace, 1990—; docent Honolulu Acad. Arts, 1996—. Mem. Jr. League, Alliance Française, Hawaii Watercolor Soc. Mem. Phi Beta Kappa. Episcopalian.

HITE, JUDSON CARY, retired pharmaceutical company executive; b. Canton, Ohio, Oct. 12, 1939; s. Everett Corbett and Dorothy Elizabeth (Caley) H.; m. Mary Kay Woodman, July 14, 1962 (div. Mar. 1970); children: Judson Cary III, Kenneth Woodman; m. Elsie Adeline Lilly, Oct. 1, 1977; 1 child, Julie Christina. BS, Ohio State U., 1962. Mgmt. trainee The Upjohn Co., Kalamazoo, Mich., 1962-64, programming analyst, 1964-67, profl. acct., 1967-70, adminstrv. mgr., 1970-74, gen. audit mgr., 1974-81, dir gen. audit, 1981-85, dir. med. affairs, 1985-89, dir. info. systems, 1989-91, dir. rsch. contracts, 1991-93, dir. office mgmt. svcs., 1993-95; ret., 1995. Mem. Nat. Assn. Accts. (dir., v.p., 1964-74), Inst. Internal Auditors (dir. 1974-85), Lic. Execs. Soc., Sigma Chi (v.p. 1960-61). Republican. Avocations: golf, boating. Home: 5961 Scenic Way Dr Kalamazoo MI 49009-9112

HITES, RONALD ATLEE, environmental science educator, chemist; b. Jackson, Mich., Sept. 19, 1942; s. Wilbert T. and Evelyn J.H.; m. Bonnie Rae Carlson, Dec. 26, 1964; children: Veronica, Karin, David. BA in Chemistry, Oakland U., 1964; PhD in Analytical Chemistry, MIT, 1968. NAS fellow Agrl. Rsch., Peoria, Ill., 1968-69; mem. rsch. staff, dept. chemistry MIT, Cambridge, 1969-72, asst. prof. chem. engring., 1972-76, assoc. prof., 1976-79; prof. Ind. U., Bloomington, 1979-89, Disting. prof. pub. and environ. affairs and chemistry, 1989—; cons. EPA, 1974—. Assoc. editor Environ. Sci. Tech., 1990—; mem. editorial bd. Chemosphere, 1979-99; contbr. articles to prof. jours. Grantee NSF, 1974—, EPA, 1974—, Dept. Energy, 1977-95. Fellow AAAS; mem. Am. Chem. Soc. (award in environ. sci. 1991), Am. Soc. for Mass Spectrometry (pres. 1988-90, mem. editl. bd. 1990-96), Soc. Environ. Toxicol. Chemistry (bd. dirs. 1997—, Founders award 1993), Sigma Xi. Office: Ind U Sch Pub and Environ Affairs 410H Bloomington IN 47405

HITLIN, DAVID GEORGE, physicist, educator; b. Bklyn., Apr. 15, 1942; s. Maxwell and Martha (Lipetz) H.; m. Joan R. Abramowitz, 1966 (div. 1981); m. Abigail R. Gumbiner, 1982 (div. 1998). BA, Columbia U., 1963, MA, 1965, PhD, 1968. Instr. Columbia U., N.Y.C., 1967-69; research assoc. Stanford (Calif.) Linear Accelerator Ctr., 1969-72, asst. prof., 1975-79, mem. program com., 1980-82; asst. prof. Stanford U., 1972-75; assoc. prof. physics Calif. Inst. Tech., Pasadena, 1979-85, prof., 1985—; mem. adv. panel U.S. Dept. Energy Univ. Programs, 1983; mem. program com. Fermi Nat. Accelerator Lab., Batavia, Ill., 1983-87, Newman Lab., Cornell U., Ithaca, N.Y., 1986-88; mem. rev. com. U. Chgo., Argonne Nat. Lab., 1985-87; chmn. Stanford Linear Accelerator Ctr. Users Orgn., 1990-93; mem. program com. Brookhaven Nat. Lab., Upton, N.Y., 1992-95; spokesman BaBar Collaboration, 1994—. Contbr. numerous articles to profl. jours. Fellow Am. Phys. Soc. Rsch. in elementary particle physics. Home: 1704 Skyview Dr Altadena CA 91001-2143 Office: Calif Inst of Tech Dept Physics 356-48 Lauritsen Pasadena CA 91125

HITT, DAVID HAMILTON, retired hospital executive; b. Tuscaloosa, Ala., May 14, 1925; m. Frances Ford, Aug. 12, 1949; children: David Hamilton, Kathryn Ann. BS, MS in Commerce and Bus. Adminstrn, U. Ala.; MHA, U. Minn., 1952. Hosp. adminstr. U. Ala. Hosp., 1947-50; various positions, including chief exec. officer Baylor U. Med. Center, 1952-79; sr. v.p. James A. Hamilton Assocs. (hosp. consultants), Dallas, 1979-84; pres., chief exec. officer Meth. Hosps. of Dallas, 1984-96, also bd. dirs., pres. emeritus; bd. dirs. Swiss Ave. Bank, Bapt. Med. Ctr., Jacksonville, Fla.; pres. Dallas Hosp. Coun., 1959; mem. adminstrv. bd. Coun. Tchg. Hosps. of Assn. Am. Med. Colls., 1972-79; assoc. clin. prof. Washington U., St. Louis, 1961-96; adj. assoc. prof. Trinity U., San Antonio, 1964-96. Contbr. numerous articles to profl. jours. Mem. exec. bd. council Boy Scouts Am.; v.p. Community Council Greater Dallas. Recipient Earl M. Collier award Distinguished Hosp. Adminstrn. Tex., 1973, Dean Conley award, Silver Beaver award Boy Scouts Am. Fellow Am. Coll. Healthcare Execs. (Gold medal award for excellence in healthcare mgmt. 1990, past regent, editl. bd. Frontiers Health Svcs. Mgmt. 1991-93); mem. Am. Hosp. Assn. (Citation for Meritorious Svc. 1987, Disting. Svc. award 1992, trustee, past chmn. coun. financing), Tex. Hosp. Assn. (trustee, treas., v.p., pres., chmn. ho. of dels. 1967), Am. Protestant Hosp. Assn. (past trustee), Alumni Assn. U. Minn. Program Hosp. Adminstrn. (past pres.), Marine Corps Assn., Exch. Club (East Dallas, pres. 1957), Dallas Wood and Waters, Masons, Shriners, Grotto, Rotary (Dallas) (bd. dirs., dist. Ethics Bus. award 1993). Home: 7231 Twin Tree Ln Dallas TX 75214-1941

HITT, JOHN CHARLES, academic administrator; b. Houston, Dec. 7, 1940; s. John Charles and Mary W. (Green) H.; m. Martha Ann Halsted, Dec. 23, 1961; children: John Charles, Sharon Aileen. AB cum laude, Austin Coll., 1962; MS (Danforth fellow, NSF fellow), Tulane U., 1964, PhD (Danforth fellow, NSF fellow), 1966. Cert. psychologist, Tex. Asst. prof. psychology Tulane U., 1966-69; assoc. prof. psychology Tex. Christian U., Ft. Worth, 1969-77; assoc. dean of univ. Tex. Christian U., 1972-77; v.p. Tex. Christian U. Research Found., 1974-77; dean Grad Sch. Tex. Christian U., 1975-77; v.p. acad. affairs Bradley U., Peoria, Ill., 1977-87; provost Bradley U., 1981-87; v.p. acad. affairs, prof. psychology U. Maine, Orono, 1987-92, interim pres., 1991-92; pres. U. Cen. Fla., Orlando, 1992—; bd. dirs. Space Coast Devel. Commn., Orlando Regional Health Care Sys.; bd. trustees EDUCOM, 1993—; adv. bd. World Trade Ctr., 1993-94, Orlando Sci. Ctr., 1992—; bd. dirs. Seminar on Acad. Computing, 1984-88, chmn. bd. dirs., 1986-87; chair task force distance learning State U. Sys. of Fla., 1993; pres.'s commn. NCAA, 1993—; nat. adv. bd. Ctr. for the Study of Sports in Soc., 1994—. Mem. bd. co-editors Psychological Research, 1973-77; editl. bd. TQM in Edn., 1993—; editl. adv. bd. Met. Univs., 1993—; contbr. articles in psychology and neurosci. to profl. jours. Chmn. com. on social scis. Austin Coll. 125th Anniversary Commn., 1973-77; charter mem. Austin Coll. Bd. Edn. Visitors, 1976-80; Tex. Christian U. rep. Leadership Ft. Worth, 1973-74; program chmn. Forum Ft. Worth, 1976-77; mem. Tarrant County United Way Budget Com., 1975-77, Forward Ft. Worth, 1976-77, Econ. Devel. Commn. Mid-Fla., Found. Orange County Pub. Schs., Fla Info. Resource Network; chmn. loaned exec. program Heart of Ill. United Way, 1979, chmn. edn. unit, 1980, bd. dirs. 1983-87; bd. dirs. Greater Peoria YMCA, 1980-84, SunBank, 1992—, mem. community adv. council St. Francis Med. Ctr., Peoria, 1984-87; bd. dirs. Inst. Phys. Medicine and Rehab., Peoria, 1981-87, pres. bd. dirs., 1986-87, Heart of Fla. United Way, 1993—; v.p. Penobscot Valley United Way, Bangor, Maine, 1989-92; trustee Bangor YWCA, 1991-92; vestry St. John's Episcopal Ch., Bangor, 1990-91. Mem. APA, AAAS, Psychonomic Soc., Soc. for Neurosci., Am. Assn. Higher Edn., Peoria Area C. of C. (bd. dirs. 1986-87), Greater Orlando C. of C., Winter Park C. of C., Fla. Assn. of Colls. and Univs. (bd. dirs.), Sigma Xi, Alpha Chi, Psi Chi, Phi Kappa Phi, Beta Gamma Sigma, Omicron Delta Kappa. Home: 1000 Central Florida Blvd Orlando FL 32826-2404 Office: U Ctrl Fla PO Box 160002 Orlando FL 32816-0002*

HITTINGER, WILLIAM CHARLES, electronics company executive; b. Bethlehem, Pa., Nov. 10, 1922; s. John Tilghman and Pearl (Heimbach) H.; m. Elizabeth Herman, July 9, 1944; children—Patricia, William, David, Nancy. B.S. with honors in Metall. Engring, Lehigh U., 1944, D.Engring. (hon.), 1973. Engr. Western Electric Co., 1946-52; prodn. mgr. Semiconductor div. Nat. Union Radio Corp., 1952-54; exec. dir. Bell Telephone Labs., 1954-66; pres. Bellcomm Inc., Washington, 1966-68, Gen. Instrument Corp., N.Y.C., 1968-70; v.p., gen. mgr. RCA Corp., Somerville, NJ., 1970-72; exec. v.p. RCA Corp., N.Y.C., 1972-86; bd. dirs. UNC Inc., Annapolis, Md., Stabler Cos., Inc., Harrisburg, Pa., Biotechnica Internat. Inc., RCA Corp., Thomas & Betts, Recognition Equipment, Allen Bradley, Am. Fletcher Corp., Bethlehem Steel. Bd. dirs. Bethlehem Fgn. Policy Assn., 1960-62, Nat. Action Council for Minorities in Engring., Inc.; trustee, interim pres. Lehigh U., 1997. Served to capt. AUS, 1943-46. Named hon. citizen Bethlehem, 1966. Fellow IEEE, Royal Acad. Arts; mem. Nat. Acad. Engring., Omicron Delta Kappa, Phi Gamma Delta, Sigma Xi, Tau Beta Pi. Home and Office: 52 Pippins Way Morristown NJ 07960-6984

HITTLE, JAMES DONALD, writer, business consultant; b. Bear Lake, Mich., June 10, 1915; s. Harry F. and Margaret Jane (McArthur) H.; m. Edna Jane Smith, Dec. 9, 1939 (dec. 1969); children: Harry McArthur, James Richard; m. Patricia Ann Herring, Sept. 5, 1970. B.A., Mich. State U., 1937; M.S. in Oriental History and Geography, U. Utah, 1952. Commd. 2nd lt. USAR cav., 1937; resigned USAR, 1937; directly commd. 2nd lt. USMC, 1937, advanced through grades to brig. gen., 1958, legis. asst. to comdt., 1952-58; asst. to sec. def. legis. affairs, 1958-60, ret., 1960; dir. nat. security and fgn. affairs VFW, 1960-67; syndicated columnist Copley News Service, 1964-69; mil. commentator MBS, 1964-69; dir. DISC, Inc., 1960-67; spl. counsel Senate Armed Services Com., 1968-69; cons. House Armed Services Com., 1968-69; founder, dir. D.C. Nat. Bank, 1965-69; asst. sec. navy for manpower and res. affairs, 1969-71; sr. v.p. govt. affairs Pan Am. World Airways, Washington, 1971-73; cons. to adminstr. VA, 1973-77; cons. to pres. Overseas Pvt. Investment Corp., 1974-75; participant comml. air mgmt. survey S.E. Asian Transp. and Communications Commn., 1975; cons. Gleason Assocs. Inc., 1974-90, LTV Aerospace and Def. Corp., 1975-88, Marriott Corp., 1975—, KMS Industries, Inc., 1985-90; comdt. U.S. Marine Corps, 1979-81; sec. U.S. Navy, 1981-82; counselor to Sec. of Navy, 1982-87; mem. adv. com. USN Postgrad. Sch. 1983-87, 89-94. Author: History of the Military Staff, 1949; also articles; editor: Jomini's Art of War, 1945; columnist: Navy Times, 1974-95, N.Y. Times Regional Newspapers, 1993—. Bd. dirs. Stafford County (Va.) Indsl. Devel. Authority, 1974-88, 90-96, vice chmn., 1993-96; vice chmn. Belleau Woods U.S. Mil. Cemetery Meml. Day Svcs., 1978—. Decorated Legion of Merit with combat V, Purple Heart, Medal of Combat Merit France, Cross of Chevalier, Mil. Order European Vets.; recipient Alfred Thayer Mahan award Navy League U.S., 1960, Scroll of Honor, 1967, silver medal City of Paris, 1961, gold medal, 1972, George Washington award Freedom Found., 1967, 69, Selective Svc. Sys. Disting. Svc. award, 1971, U.S. Navy Civilian Disting. Svc. award, 1971, 87, Meritorious Pub. Svc. citation U.S. Marine Corps, 1981, Outstanding Alumnus award Mich. State U., 1987, Disting. Alumni award Coll. Arts and Letters, 1994, Commemorative medal China duty, Republic of China, Commemorative medal Murmansk convoy svcs., Russian Fedn. Mem. VFW, Am. Legion, Brit. Legion (hon.), La. State Hist. Soc. (hon. life), Mil. Order World Wars, Clan MacArthur Soc. Am., Navy League, U.S. Marine Corps League (legis. com. 1980-82), Battleship Assn. U.S., 1st Marine Div. Assn. (life), 3d Marine Div. Assn. (life), Co. Mil. Historians, Mil. Order of Carabao, China-Burma-India Vets. Assn., China Marine Assn., Sons of Union Vets. of Civil War, Sons of the Revolution, Naval and Maritime Correspondents Circle, USS Washington Reunion Group, Army-Navy Club of Washington (pres. 1983-87, pres. emeritus 1988—), Phi Kappa Phi, Phi Kappa Delta. Address: 3137 14th St S Arlington VA 22204-4330

HITTLE, RICHARD HOWARD, corporate executive, international affairs consultant; b. Columbus, Nebr., Apr. 30, 1923; s. Arthur Howard and Frieda Margaret (Poppe) H.; m. Catherine Louise Dethlefsen, May 11, 1951; children: Ann-Louise, Thomas Woodford, Bradley Arthur. Student, Cambridge (Eng.) U., 1945; BS, U. Denver, 1950, LLB, 1951; MBA, Harvard U., 1955. With Conoco Inc., 1955-87, mgr. internat. acquisitions, 1964-75; pres. Continental Overseas Oil Co., N.Y.C. also Stamford, Conn., 1969-75; gen. mgr., v.p. internat. govt. affairs Conoco, Inc., Stamford, 1975-83, Wilmington, Del., 1983-87. Bd. govs. Dorset Field Club; bd. dirs. Dorset Hist. Soc.; bd. trustees Merck Forest and Farmland Ctr., Rupert, Vt. Mem. Harvard Club (N.Y.C.), Stanwich Club, Dorset Field Club (Vt.), Met. Club (Washington), Dorset Field Club (bd. dirs.), Dorset Hist. Soc., Merck Forest and Farmland Ctr. (bd. trustees). Republican. Lutheran. Clubs: Harvard (N.Y.C.); Stanwich, Greenwich Horseneck Club (Greenwich, Conn.); Dorset Field. (Vt.); Metropolitan (Washington). Home: PO Box 325 Dorset VT 05251-0325 Office: PO Box 469 Old Greenwich CT 06870-0469

HITTNER, DAVID, federal judge; b. Schenectady, N.Y., July 10, 1939; s. George and Sophie (Moskowitz) H.; children: Miriam, Susan, George. BS, NYU, 1961, JD, 1964. Bar: N.Y. 1964, Tex. 1967. Pvt. practice, Houston, 1967-78; judge Tex. 133d Dist. Ct., Houston, 1978-86, U.S. Dist. Ct. (so. dist.) Tex., Houston, 1986—. Author 2 books; contbr. articles to profl. jours. Mem. Nat. coun. Boy Scouts Am. Capt. inf., paratrooper U.S. Army, 1965-66. Recipient Silver Beaver award Boy Scouts Am., 1974, Silver Antelope award Boy Scouts Am., 1988, Samuel E. Gates award Am. Coll. Trial Lawyers. Mem. ABA (merit award), State Bar Tex. (Outstanding Lawyer in Tex. award), Houston Bar Assn. (president's and Dirs.' award), Am. Law Inst., Masons (33d degree). Office: US Courthouse 515 Rusk St Ste 8509 Houston TX 77002-2603

HITZ, FREDERICK PORTER, educator, lawyer; b. Washington, Oct. 14, 1939; s. Frederick Porter and Elizabeth (Hume) H.; m. Mary Buford Bocock, Sept. 7, 1963; 1 child, Eliza. AB, Princeton U., 1961; JD, Harvard U., 1964. Bar: Mass. 1965, Va. 1966, D.C. 1976, U.S. Supreme Ct. 1988. Asst. lectr., law dept. U. IFE, Ibadan, Nigeria, 1964-65; fgn. svc. officer U.S. Dept. State, Abidjan, Ivory Coast, 1967-73; congl. rels. officer U.S. Dept. State, Washington, 1974-75; dep. asst. sec. legis. affairs U.S. Dept. Def., Washington, 1975-77; mem. energy policy and planning staff Exec. Office of Pres., Washington, 1977; dir. congl. affairs U.S. Dept. Energy, Washington, 1977-78; legis. counsel CIA, Washington, 1978-81; ptnr. Schwabe, Williamson & Wyatt, Washington, 1982-90; inspector gen. CIA, Washington, 1990-98; lectr. in pub. and internat. affairs Woodrow Wilson Sch., Princeton U., 1998—, Weinberg prof. of pub. policy, 1999—; councillor Atlantic Coun. of U.S., 1988-90. Co-author: Report to ABA Standing Com. on Law and Nat. Security: Oversight and Accountability of U.S. Intelligence Agencies: An Evaluation, 1985. Trustee Potomac Sch., McLean, Va., 1989-95, chmn. bd. trustees, 1992-94; vestry St. Paul's Ch., Alexandria. Mem. ABA, Deer Isle Yacht Club (Maine), Met. Club (Washington, bd. govs. 1994—, sec. 1995-96, pres. 1998-99), Ivy Club (Princeton, N.J.). Democrat. Episcopalian. Avocations: sailing, skiing, squash. Office: Princeton U Woodrow Wilson Sch Ctr Internat Studies Princeton NJ 08540

HITZMAN, DONALD OLIVER, microbiologist; b. Milw., Dec. 2, 1926; s. Walter John and Irene (Smith) H.; m. Mary Elizabeth Neumann, Aug. 20, 1952; children: Murray W., Daniel C. AB, Carleton Coll., Northfield, Minn., 1948; MS, U. Ill., 1950, PhD, 1954. Resident microbiologist Texaco Co., Long Beach, Calif., 1951; sr. rsch. assoc. Phillips Petroleum Co., Bartlesville, Okla., 1954-85; v.p. rsch. Geo-Microbial Tech., Inc., Ochelata, Okla., 1985—. Contbr. articles to sci. publs. With USAAF, 1944-45. Fulbright scholar, Australia, 1951. Mem. Soc. Microbiology, Soc. Indsl. Microbiology, Am. Chem. Soc. Republican. Episcopalian. Achievements include over 60 patents; numerous fgn. patents. Office: Geo-Microbial Tech East Main St Ochelata OK 74051

HIXON, ALLEN WENTWORTH, landscape architect, land planner; b. Worcester, Mass., Aug. 12, 1929; s. Allen Wentworth and Olive Fletcher (Gates) H.; m. Dorothy Beals, June 28, 1952; children: Donna Jeannette, Allen Loring, David Newell. BS with honors, U. Mass., 1952, M cum laude in Landscape Architecture, 1956. Registered landscape architect, Conn., Fla., Mass., N.Y., N.J. Designer Yarwood & Block, 1955-58; pvt. practice Simsbury, Conn., 1958-90; prin. Allen Hixon Assocs., Simsbury, 1958—; Pioneer in "open space planning" concepts and environ. conservation easements; over 1,600 projects including Simsbury (Conn.) Farms Recreation Complex, Sugar Mills Woods, Homassasa, Fla., Prudential Computer Complex, N.J., Nabisco Global Headquarters, N.J., Stanadyne Headquarters, Windsor, Conn., 17 Simsbury Subdivsns.; instr. landscape architecture, student fellow U. Mass., 1954-56. Prin. works exhibited in group and one-man shows in Ft. Walton Beach, Fla., Amherst, Mass. and Simsbury; designer town seal and town flag for Simsbury; jazz drummer; bandleader That Jazz Band, Swingtime. Active Simsbury Planning Commn.; bd. dirs. Farmington Valley Art Ctr., Avon, Conn., Simsbury Art and Crafts Assn.; judge major gardens New England Flower Show, Boston; mem. Blue Ribbon Gulf of Mexico Dr. Improvement Com., Longboat Key, Fla., 1990, 91; mem. site plan rev. com. City of Middletown, Conn. Lt. USAF, 1952-54. Recipient 1st Prize award Springfield Mus. Fine Arts, 1954, Merit award South Ch. Parking Garden, Am. Assn. Nursery, 1961, Merit award Longmeadow Mall, Am. Assn. Nursery, 1969, Outstanding Svc. award Nat. Soc. Interior Decorators, 1971, 1st Prize award Am. Land Developers Assn., 1984, Pub. Places award Conn. AIA, Conn. Am. Soc. Landscape Archs., 1985; named Hometown Hero, Simsbury, Conn., 1991. Fellow Am. Soc. Landscape Architects (Merit award; chmn. ethics com., vice chmn. open com. on housing, exec. com. Conn. chpt., pres. 1968-70, v.p. and program chmn. 1966, 67, nominating com.); mem. Am. Planning Assn., Am. Hort. Soc., Worcester Hort. Soc., Hartford County Soil Conservation Dist., Nat. Park and Recreation Assn., Nat. Assn. Home Builders, Phi Kappa Phi. Contbr. articles to profl. jours. *

HIXON, ANDREA KAYE, healthcare quality specialist; b. Clifton Forge, Va., Jan. 15, 1955; d. Leon Malcolm and Mary Ruth (Bowyer) Whitmer; m. Charles L. Hixon Jr., Sept. 11, 1976. ADN, Frederick (Md.) Community Coll, 1974; BSN, George Mason U., Fairfax, Va., 1981; MS, U. Md., Balt., 1986. Cert. profl. for healthcare quality, 1993. Staff ambulatory care VA Med. Ctr., Martinsburg, W.Va., 1974-82; nursing home adminstr. VA Med. Ctr., 1982-86; quality assurance coord. nursing James A. Haley VA Hosp., Tampa, Fla., 1987-93; coord. med. ctr. CQI Program, Tampa, 1993—. Mem. Am. Assn. Spinal Cord Injury Nurses, Nat. Assn. for Healthcare Quality. Home: 2610 Bridle Dr Plant City FL 33567-6742

HIXON, JAMES EDWARD, physiology educator; b. Ames, Iowa, July 5, 1938; s. Ralph Malcom and Stella Viola (Sadler) H.; m. Anna Elsbeth Ripken, Nov. 25, 1967; children: Jill Elizabeth, Ernest Rudolf. BS, U. Calif., Davis, 1961, PhD, 1968. Rsch. fellow Harvard U. Med. Sch., Boston, 1968-69; postdoctoral fellow U. Western Ont., London, Can., 1969-71; rsch. assoc. Cornell U., Ithaca, N.Y., 1971-77; asst. prof. physiology U. Ill., Urbana, 1977-81, assoc. prof., 1981-86, prof., 1986—, interim asst. dean of students Coll. Vet. Medicine, 1995-96, 97—. Contbr. numerous articles to profl. jours. Fogarty Sr. Internat. fellow NIH, 1985; recognized as an Excellent Tchr. by students, 1982, 87-92. Mem. Am. Soc. Animal Sci., Endocrine Soc., Soc. for Study Reproduction. Achievements include research into the role of estradiol in regulating corpus luteum function in food-producing animals. Office: U Ill 2001 S Lincoln Ave Urbana IL 61802-6178

HIXON, JANET KAY ERICKSON, education specialist; b. Holdrege, Nebr., Dec. 28, 1940; d. Vernon Eugene and Lucile (Petersen) Erickson; children: Cheryl, Christie. Diploma in nursing, Mary Lanning Meml. Hosp. Sch. of Nursing, 1961; BSN, Marycrest Coll., 1978; MA in Edn., Loras Coll., 1981. RN, Colo. Asst. head nurse med. Mary Lanning Meml. Hosp., Hastings, Nebr., 1961-62; head nurse med-surg. Good Samaritan Hosp., Kearney, Nebr., 1962-68; staff nurse med. Xavier Hosp., Dubuque, Iowa, 1968-69; staff nurse Med. Assocs. Clinic, Dubuque, Iowa, 1970-72; instr. Sch. Nursing Finley Hosp., Dubuque, Iowa, 1972-81; mgr. employee edn. Mercy Health Ctr., Dubuque, Iowa, 1981-82; dir. edn. and nursing practice Assn. Oper. Rm. Nurses, Inc., Denver, 1982-92, coord. congress and world conf. programs, 1992-94, prof. edn. specialist, 1994—. Contbr. articles to profl. jours. Mem. ANA (continuing edn. coun.), Assn. Oper. Rm. Nurses, Am. Soc. Assn. Execs., Sigma Theta Tau. Home: 11925 E Harvard Ave # 6108 Aurora CO 80014-1805 Office: Assn Oper Rm Nurses Inc 2170 S Parker Rd Ste 300 Denver CO 80231-5711

HIXON, ROBIN RAY, food service executive, writer; b. Vancouver, Wash., May 4, 1954; s. Charles Donovan and Leona Margaret (Teske) Hixson. Exec. chef, Am. Culinary Fedn., 1972-77; BA in Bus., Purdue U., 1992. Cert. Am. Restaurant Assn., 1992. Apprentice Redlion Inns, Vancouver, 1972-77, exec. chef, 1977-80; exec. chef Hilton Hotel, Baton Rouge, 1981; chief steward Delta Queen Steamboat Co., New Orleans, 1981-86, gen. mgr., 1986-88; exec. chef Icicle Seafoods Inc., Seattle, 1989-92, Sea Spirit Cruise Lines, Inc., 1992-93, Petersburg Fisheries, Inc., Alaska, 1993-96; dir. ops. The Calzone-Co. Inc., Duncan & Ptnrs., Pete's Pizza Inc., Spokane, Wash., 1996-97; writer, layout coord. Dream Works, Seattle, 1997—; cons. RSVP Travel Prodns., Inc., Mlps., 1992—, Arctic Storm, Inc., Seattle, 1998—. Author: American Regional Cuisines, 1987; contbr. articles to profl. jours. Mem. Nat. Trust for Hist. Preservation, 1982-92, Wash. Hist. Preservation, 1990-92, Oreg. Pub. Broadcating, 1990-92, N.Y. Met. Opera, 1973-80; performer Peruvian Singers, 1972-74, A Chorus-Line, 1975-76, Spokane's Mens Chorus, 1996-97. Mem. Am. Culinary Fedn. (writer 1985-91), Chefs De Cuisine Soc. Oreg. (sgt. at arms 1974-80), N.Y.C. Acad. Theatre and Dance, Am. Film Inst. Democrat. Home: 1701 Broadway St # 262 Vancouver WA 98663-3436

HIXSON, ELMER L., engineering educator. Prof. emeritus dept. elec. engring. U. Tex., Austin. Recipient Fellow Mems. award Am. Soc. Engring. Educators, 1992. Fellow Acoustical Soc. Am.; mem. IEEE (life), Inst. for Noise Control Engring. (founding mem.). Office: U Tex Dept Elec & Computer Engring Austin TX 78712

HIXSON, SHEILA ELLIS, state legislator; b. L'Anse, Mich., Feb. 9, 1933; divorced; children: Denise, Lynn, Andy, Todd. AB, No. Mich. U., 1953. Tchr. Head Start; campaign mgr., aide Congressman William Ford, Mich., 1963-64; adminstrv. aide to state senator, 1965-66, legal aide to sec. of Dem. Nat. Conv., 1966-76; mem. Md. Ho. of Dels., Annapolis, 1976—, mem. ways and means com., environ. matters com., budget and audit com., house rules and exec. nominations com., procurement com., lottery com., others, chair joint com. fed.-state rels., chair task force on child abuse and neglect; chmn. Ways and Means com.; mem. Gov. Work Force Investment Bd. Mem. Montgomery County Dem. State Cen. Com. Mem. Nat. Assn. Sunday Sch. Instrs., Nat. Profl. and Bus. Women's Orgn., Women's Polit. Caucus, Plowmen and Fishermen, NOW. Home: 1008 Broadmore Cir Silver Spring MD 20904-3108 Office: Md Gen Assembly Ways and Means Com Rm 100 Lowe House Office Bl Annapolis MD 21401-1991

HIXSON, STANLEY G., speech, language and computer technology educator; b. Chgo., Nov. 25, 1947; s. George Samuel and Alice Elizabeth (Domino) H.; m. Alice Jean Ray, May 25, 1975; children: Polly Alice, Jay Stanley, Christa Renee, Michael Wayne. BA, William Jewell Coll., Liberty, Mo., 1969; MS, Cen. Mich. U., 1986; postgrad., U. Kans. Dir. comm. and retail mktg. Successful Living, Inc., Mpls., 1975-78; pres. LightShine Comm., Shawnee Mission, Kans., 1979-91; editor-in-chief Successful Living, Inc., Mpls.; pub. affairs specialist U.S. Army C.E., Kansas City, Mo., 1983-84; instr. leadership, speech and lang. U.S. Army Command and Gen. Staff Coll., Ft. Leavenworth, Kans., 1984-91; sr. tng. instr. total quality leadership Naval Supply Sys. Command, Washington, 1991-92; dir. quality and process improvement Bur. of Naval Pers., Washington, 1992-94; pres. Great Ideas! in Edn., Alexandria, Va., 1994—; adj. prof. William Jewell Coll., 1989-90; presenter computer tech., leadership, mktg. and mgmt. seminars, 1973—. Author: Research and Study Skills, 1989, Implementing Total Quality Leadership in the U.S. Navy, 1992, Professional Graphics Presentations, 1995, Intermediate and Advanced Relational Database Management Using MS Access, 1996; co-author: Effective Staff Communications, 1985, 89, Visions and Revisions, 1981, Total Quality Leadership: Customers, Teams and Tools, 1992; editor: An Application of Multiple Intelligences Theory in an Elementary Music Classroom, 1998. With USAF, 1969-73. Recipient Achievement cert. Dept. Army, 1988, Outstanding Svc. award Successful Living, Inc., 1979, 81-82, 84. Mem. Fed. Info. Coun., Washington Deming Study Group, Navy Total Quality Leadership Advocates Network, Genealogy Club (Loudon County, Va.), Assn. Philippe Du Trieux, Alpha Phi Omega (life). Home: 5211 Leeward Ln Kingstowne VA 22315-3944

HJELMSTAD, WILLIAM DAVID, lawyer; b. Apr. 4, 1954; s. Alvin Gordon and a. thecla (Walz) H.; m. Jenny M. Dube, Nov. 27, 1993; children: Jennifer Ashley, Allison Caitlin. AA in Social Sci., Casper Coll., 1974; BS in Psychology, U. Wyo., 1976, JD, 1979. Bar: Wyo. 1979, U.S. Dist. Ct. Wyo. 1979. Dept. county pros. atty. Hot Springs County, Thermopolis, Wyo., 1979-80; asst. pub. defender Natrona County, Casper, Wyo., 1980-82; sole practice Casper, Wyo., 1981—. Mem. ATLA, ABA (mem. family law com. 1983-84, adoption com. 1983-84), Wyo. State Bar Assn. (mem. alcohol and substance abuse com., lawyers assistance com. 1988-95, computer and technical com. 1997-99), Natrona County Bar Assn., Wyo. Trial Lawyers Assn., Am. Judicature Soc., Acad. Family Mediators, U. Wyo. Alumni Assn., Casper Coll. Alumni Assn., Wyo. Cowboy Shootout Com., Elks, Kiwanis. Home: PO Box 90001 Casper WY 82609-1001

HJERPE, EDWARD ALFRED, III, finance and banking executive; b. Worcester, Mass., Jan. 25, 1959; s. Edward Alfred Jr. and Nancy Ann (O'Connor) H.; m. Macrina Groody, Aug. 17, 1985; children: Christine G., Edward A. IV, Catherine Ann. BA in Econs. and Bus., St. Anselm Coll., 1981; MA in Econs., U. Notre Dame, 1984, PhD in Econs., 1985. Industry economist Commodity Futures Trading Commn., Washington, 1985-86; fin. economist Fed. Home Loan Bank Bd., Washington, 1986-88; v.p., chief economist Fed. Home Loan Bank, Boston, 1988-89, sr. v.p., 1989-92, exec. v.p., CFO, 1992-97; sr. v.p., treas., CFO First Fed. Am. Bancorp, Inc., Fall River, Mass., 1997—; now exec. v.p., COO, CFO First Fed. Am. Bancorp, Inc., Swansey, Mass. Contbr. articles to profl. jours. Bd. trustees St. Anselm Coll., 1992—; chmn. fin. com. Medway Town, 1995-98. Recipient A. Schmitt Dissertation fellowship. Mem. Am. Econ. Assn., Boston Econ. Club, Bus. Assocs. Club, Omicron Delta Epsilon, Delta Epsilon Sigma, Pi Gamma Mu. Roman Catholic. Home: One Great Rd Barrington RI 02806-1579 Office: First Fed Savs Bank Am One First Park Swansey MA 02777*

HJORT, HOWARD WARREN, consultant, economist; b. Plentywood, Mont., Dec. 20, 1931. BS, Mont. State U., 1958, MS, 1959; postgrad., N.C. State U. Staff economist Office of Sec. Agr., Washington, 1963-65; spl. asst. to under sec. Office of Sec. Agr., 1965; dir. staff for program planning and analysis Office of Sec., 1965-69; planning and mgmt. adviser with Ford Found., India, 1969-72; dir. Office of Econs., Policy Analysis and Budget, 1977-81; co-founder Schnittker Assocs. (agrl. cons.), Washington, 1972-77; ptnr. EPI (McLean), Va., 1981-84; dir. policy analysis div. FAO, Rome, 1984-90; dir. liaison office for N.Am. FAO, Washington, 1990-91; dep. dir. gen. FAO, Rome, 1992-97; cons., 1998—. Office: 1910 Franklin Ave Mc Lean VA 22101-5307

HJORTSBERG, WILLIAM REINHOLD, author; b. N.Y.C., Feb. 23, 1941; s. Helge Reinhold and Anna Ida (Welti) H.; m. Marian Souidee Renken, June 2, 1962 (div. 1982); children—Lorca Isabel, Max William.; m. Sharon Leroy, July 21, 1982 (div. 1985). BA, Dartmouth Coll., 1962; postgrad., Yale U., 1962-63, Stanford U., 1967-68. Ind. author, screenwriter, 1969—; adj. prof. media and theatre arts Mont. State U., 1991—. Author: Alp, 1969, Gray Matters, 1971, Symbiography, 1973, Toro! Toro! Toro!, 1974, Falling Angel, 1978, Tales & Fables, 1985, Nevermore, 1994, films: Thunder and Lightning, 1977, Legend, 1986; co-author TV film: Georgia Peaches, 1980; contbg. editor Rocky Mountain Mag., 1979; contbr. fiction to Realist, Playboy, Cornell Rev., Penthouse, Oui, Sports Illustrated; contbr. criticism to N.Y. Times Book Rev. Recipient Playboy Editorial award, 1971, 78; Wallace Stegner fellow, 1967-68; Nat. Endowment Arts grantee, 1976. Mem. Authors Guild, Writers Guild Am. Avocations: fly fishing, skiing, collecting modern first editions, art, antique toys. Home and Office: Main Boulder RT Mc Leod MT 59052

HLAD, GREGORY MICHAEL, psychometrist, assessment services coordinator; b. McKeesport, Pa., Feb. 14, 1947; s. Michael Gregory Jr. and Helen Delores (Harman) H.; m. Carol Ann Huzinec, July 15, 1972; 1 child, Kristen. BEd, U. Miami, Coral Gables, 1969; MEd, Calif. (Pa.) State U., 1974. Cert. tchr., Fla., Pa.; cert. work evaluator; cert. occupational specialist. Tchr. Wilkinsburg (Pa.) Sch. Dist., 1969-79; asst. prof. Pasco-Hernando Community Coll., New Port Richey, Fla., 1979-83; occupl. specialist Pasco-Pvt. Industry Coun., Fla., 1983-93; assessment coord. Workforce Devel. Authority, Ocala, Fla., 1993-96, Pasco-Hernando C.C., New Port Richey, Fla., 1996—; cons. Xerox Ednl. div. New Haven, 1977-79, Pasco-Hernando Community Coll., 1983—, mem. learning lab. adv. com., 1985-86; v.p. Ednl./Psychol. Assessments Inc. Mem. budget adv. com. Safety Harbor (Fla.), 1986-87. Recipient Cert. of Appreciation Dept. of Corrections, 1982, Appreciation of Service award Boy Scouts Am., 1986. Mem. Nat. Assn. Psychometrists, Nat. Assn. Workforce Profls. Avocations: jogging, sports car racing, home computers. Home: 39 Friendship Ct Safety Harbor FL 34695-2644 Office: Pasco-Hernando CC 10230 Ridge Rd New Port Richey FL 34654-5199

HLADKY, WILLIAM GEORGE, protective service official; b. Bangor, Maine, Dec. 13, 1951; s. George W. and Catherine (Lewis) H.; m. Mary Wallbaum, Aug. 23, 1976. B in Gen. Studies, U. Iowa, 1974; MPA, Fla. Atlantic U., 1982. News editor Indianola (Iowa) Reminder, 1974-76; reporter Savannah (Ga.) Morning News/Evening Press, 1976-78, Ft. Lauderdale (Fla.) Sun Sentinel, 1978-79; adminstrv. asst. to chief Opa-locka (Fla.) Police Dept., 1979-81; instr., dir. law enforcement program Ctrl. Tex. Coll., Frankfurt, Germany, 1984-85; officer Metro-Dade Police Dept., Miami, Fla., 1981-84, 85-87, detective, 1987—. Contbr. articles to newspapers (1st and 3rd pl. W. Herschel Lovell local govt. awards Ga. Press Assn.). Active Dade County Police Benevolent Assn., 1982—. NEH journalism fellow Ga. Tech. U., 1978. Mem. Profl. Law Enforcement Assn., Fla. Tae Kwon Do Inst. (tchr., 1st Dan award 1989, 2nd Dan award 1996), Phi Kappa Phi. Avocations: Tae Kwon Do, poetry, travel, reading, bicycling.

HLATKY, MARK ANDREW, cardiologist, health services researcher; b. Windber, Pa., June 4, 1950; s. George Andrew and Rose Annette (Gonnella) H.; m. Donna Marie Alvarado, May 12, 1984; 1 child, Nicholas Michael. BS, MIT, 1972; MD, U. Pa., 1976. Diplomate Am. Bd. Internal Medicine, Am. Bd. Cardiovasc. Disease; lic. physician, Calif. Intern, resident U. Ariz., Tucson, 1976-79; Robert Wood Johnson clin. scholar U. Calif., San Francisco, 1979-81; fellow in cardiology Duke U., Durham, N.C., 1981-83, asst. prof. medicine, 1983-89; assoc. prof. health rsch. and policy, assoc. prof. medicine Stanford (Calif.) U., 1989-96, prof. health rsch. and policy, prof. medicine, 1996—; attending physician, cardiovasc. medicine svc. Stanford U. Med. Ctr., 1989—; mem. Health Care Tech. Study sect. NIH, Rockville, Md., 1992-96. Contbr. more than 100 articles to profl. jours. Sloan scholar, 1972. Fellow Am. Coll. Cardiology; mem. Am. Heart Assn. (fellow coun. on clin. cardiology), Am. Fedn. Clin. Rsch., Internat. Soc. for Tech. Assessment in Health Care, Phi Beta Kappa. Achievements include research in outcomes after coronary surgery, coronary angioplasty, acute myocardial infarction, and cardiac arrhythmias. Home: 168 Rinconada Ave Palo Alto CA 94301-3725 Office: Stanford U Sch Medicine HRP Redwood Bldg Rm 150 Stanford CA 94305

HLAVACEK, ROY GEORGE, publishing executive, magazine editor; b. Chgo., Sept. 17, 1937; s. George Louis and Lillian Barbara (Vasovic) H.; m. Nancy Elaine Wroblaski, Aug. 3, 1963; children: Carrie Lee Felix, Alexander Michael. BS, U. Ill., 1960; MBA, U. Chgo., 1969. Project engr. Research and Devel. Center, Swift & Co., Chgo., 1960-65; v.p., editor, pub. Food Processing mag., Foods of Tomorrow mag. Food Publs. div. Putman Pub. Co., Chgo., 1965-92; v.p., group pub. Food Group, Delta Communications Inc., Chgo., 1992—; adv. com. dept. food sci. U. Ill., Urbana-Champaign, 1988—. Commr. Oak Park (Ill.) Landmarks Commn., 1972-79, chmn., 1976-79; treas. Oak Park Bicentennial Commn., 1973-76, Ernest Hemingway Found. of Oak Park, 1983—. Mem. ASME, Food Processing Machinery and Supplies Assn. (dir. 1987-91), Inst. Food Technologists (councilor 1975-81, chmn. Chgo. sect.), Pi Tau Sigma, Sigma Tau. Patentee in field. Home: 904 Forest Ave Oak Park IL 60302-1310 Office: Food Group Reed Elsevier Bus Info 1350 E Touhy Ave Des Plaines IL 60018-3303

HLAVATY, PATRICK DENNIS, educator, musician; b. Chgo., Mar. 17, 1941; s. Frank James and Irene Hlavaty; m. Kathleen Ann Lore, Aug. 4, 1961 (div. Nov. 1974); children: Nina, Patrice, Patrick; m. Deborah Ann Oldham, May 17, 1981; 1 child, Timothy. BM, DePaul U., Chgo., 1963, MMusic, 1964. Musician Chgo., 1964-73, N.Y.C., 1973-90; computer lab mgr. Brumby Elem. Sch., Marietta, Ga., 1993—; mem. program com. Ga. Ednl. Tech. Conf., Macon, 1995-98. Contbr. articles to profl. jours.; newspaper columnist Technology in Edn., North Ga. Star. Named Vol. of Yr., Rocky Mount Elem. Sch., 1991. Republican. Avocations: collecting music stamps, building web pages. E-mail: patrickh@mindspring.com. Home: 3571 Clementine Ct Marietta GA 30066-4591 Office: Brumby Elem Sch 1306 Powers Ferry Rd SE Marietta GA 30067-5410

HLEDE, KORIE, professional basketball player; b. Mar. 29, 1975. BS in Psychology and Comm., Duquesne U. Guard Montig, Croatia, Detroit Shock. Named 1995 Atlantic 10 Rookie of the Yr., 1997-98 Atlantic 10 Player of the Yr. Achievements include becoming first athlete in Duquesne history to have jersey number retired; ranks second in Atlantic 10 history in career points; Duquesne's all-time leading scorer, male or female, with 2,631 points. Avocations: tennis, travel, reading. Office: Detroit Shock 2 Championship Dr Auburn Hills MI 48326*

HLOUSEK, JOYCE B(ERNADETTE), school system administrator; b. Chgo., Sept. 7, 1949; d. Theodore P. and Helen J. (Pietrzak) Brewer. BSEE, DePaul U., Chgo., 1971, MA, 1976; EdD, Vanderbilt U., 1993. Cert. in elem. edn., learning disabilities, gen. adminstrn., Ill. Tchr., asst. prin. Chgo. Pub. Schs., 1970-71; tchr. Community Consol. Sch. Dist. 54, Schaumburg Twp., Ill., 1971-73, learning disabilities specialist, 1973-80, 1980-85, dir. program assessment, 1985-96, adminstr., 1996—; instr. Ill. Adminstrv. Acd., North Cook Region, Ill., 1989-92; due process hearing officer Ill. State Bd. Edn., 1976-84. Author: The Missing Piece of Change, 1993, Understanding Your Child's Test Scores, 1982, (series) Action Mathematics , 1976; feature writer Chgo. Daily Herald and Chgo. Tribune, 1996—. Sec. Community Communicators, Schaumburg Twp., 1978-81; bd. dirs., edn. Strays Halfway House; electee Parish Religious Edn. Bd., 1997. Named Outstanding Educator, Schaumburg Jaycees, 1974. Mem. ASCD, Am. Assn. Sch. Adminstrs., Ill. Assn. for Supervision and Curriculum Devel., Inst. for Ednl. Rsch. (bd. editorial advisors), Phi Delta Kappa. Office: Schaumburg Twp Cmty Consol Sch Dist 54 Lakeview Sch 524 E Schaumburg Rd Schaumburg IL 60194-3510

HLOZEK, CAROLE DIANE QUAST, financial services company officer; b. Dallas, Apr. 17, 1959; d. Robert E. and Bonnie (Wootton) Quast. BS, BBA, Tex. A&M U., 1982. CPA, Tex. Internal auditor Brown & Root Inc., Houston, 1982-84; asst. contr. Wilson Supply Co., Houston, 1984-86; sr. acctg. supr. Hydro Conduit Corp., Houston, 1986-87; fin. analyst Am. Capital, Houston, 1989-94; dir. adminstrn., CFO, Am. Gen. Securities, Inc., Houston, 1994-98; contr. 1st Fin. Group Am., Houston, 1998—. Chmn. bd. dirs. On Our Own Inc., 1987-91. Mem. Tex. Soc. CPA's, Mensa, Houston Zool Soc., Houston Livestock Show and Rodeo, CPA's Helping Schs., Houston Mus. Natural History. Home: 15405 Mauna Loa Ln Houston TX 77040-1344 Office: 1st Fin Group Am 3801 Kirby 7th Fl Houston TX 77098

HLYWA, JENNIFER LYN, secondary educator; b. N.Y.C., Aug. 26, 1970; d. Peter Jr. and Dorothy Ellen (Siolek) H. BS in Biology, SUNY, Albany, 1992; MEd, Dowling Coll., 1995. Tchr. L.I. Sch. for the Gifted, Huntington Station, N.Y., 1994-96; h.s. chemistry tchr. N. Babylon (N.Y.) H.S., 1996-98; 7th/8th grade math. and sci. tchr. New Haven Sch., Manteca, Calif., 1998—; tchr. rsch. assocs. program Dept. of Energy, Brookhaven Labs., 1995. Mem. Sci. Tchrs. Assn. N.Y. State, Inc.

HMURCIK, LAWRENCE VINCENT, electrical engineering educator; b. Bridgeport, Conn., Aug. 9, 1952; s. Joseph Peter and Helen Barbara (Klosiewicz) H.; m. Catherine Mary Marczak, Aug. 17, 1990. BS, Fairfield U., 1974; MS, Clarkson U., 1976, PhD, 1980. Registered profl. engr., Conn. Rsch. physicist Diamond Shamrock Corp., Painesville, Ohio, 1980-83; prof. physics and engring. U. Bridgeport, 1983—; cons. in field, 1983—. Co-author: Physics for Scientists and Engineers, 1982, Instructor's Manual for Engineers, 1986; contbr. 45 articles to profl. publs.; book reviewer for jours. in field. Grantee Cottrell Corp., 1985, State of Conn., 1986, United Illuminating Energy, 1998; recipient Teaching Excellence award Sears Roebuck Co., 1990. Mem. IEEE, Am. Phys. Soc., Am. Soc. Engring. Edn. Roman Catholic. Office: U Bridgeport Dept Physics & Elec Engring Bridgeport CT 06601

HO, CHIH-MING, physicist, educator; b. Chung King, China, Aug. 16, 1945; came to U.S., 1968; s. Shao-Nan and I-Chu Ho; m. Shirley T.S. Ho, Mar. 4, 1972; 1 child, Dean. BSME, Nat. Taiwan U., 1967; PhD, Johns Hopkins U., 1974. Assoc. rsch. scientist Johns Hopkins U., Balt., 1974-75; asst. prof. U. So. Calif., L.A., 1976-81, assoc. prof., 1981-85, prof., 1985-91; prof. UCLA, 1991—, Ben Rich-Lockheed Martin prof., 1996—; dir. Ctr. for Micro Systems, 1993—; cons. Flow Industries, Kent, 1982, Dynamics Tech., Torrance, Calif., 1977, Rockwell Internat., Canoga Park, Calif., 1980-83. Contbr. articles to profl. jours.; patentee in field. Fellow AIAA, Am. Phys. Soc.; mem. Nat. Acad. Engring., Academia Sinica, Phi Beta Kappa. Achievements include research in micro-electro-mechanical systems, biomedical engineering, turbulence, aerodynamics, nois.

HO, CHI-TANG, food chemistry educator; b. Fuzhou, Fujian, China, Dec. 26, 1944; came to U.S., 1969; s. Chia-jue and Siu (Lin) H.; m. Mary Shieh, June 29, 1974; children: Gregory, Joseph. MS, Washington U., 1971, PhD, 1974. Postdoctoral assoc. sch. chemistry Rutgers U., New Brunswick, N.J., 1975-76, postdoctoral assoc. dept. food sci., 1976-78, asst. prof. dept. food sci., 1978-83, assoc. prof., 1983-87, prof., 1987—. Co-editor: Thermal Generation of Aromas, 1989, Food Extrusion Science and Technology, 1991, Phenolic Compounds and Their Effects on Health, I and II, 1992, Food Phytochemicals for Cancer Prevention, I and II, 1994; contbr. over 200 articles to profl. jours. Fellow Am. Chem. Soc. (chmn. agrl. and food chemistry divsn. 1995-96); mem. Inst. Food Technologists. Achievements include patents for rosemary antioxidant and butter flavor. Home: 32 Jernee Dr East Brunswick NJ 08816-5308 Office: Rutgers U Dept Food Sci New Brunswick NJ 08903

HO, DAVID D., research physician, virologist; b. Taichung, Taiwan, Nov. 3, 1952; came to U.S. 1964.; s. Paul and Sonia H.; m. Susan Kuo; children: Kathryn, Jonathan, Jaclyn. Attended, MIT; BS summa cum laude, Calif. Inst. Tech., 1974; MD, Harvard, 1978. Res. internal medicine UCLA Sch. Medicine, 1981, chief res., 1982; clinical and rsch. fellow Infectios Disease Unit Mass. Gen. Hosp., 1982-85; rsch. fellow medicine Harvard U., 1982-85; physician, rsh. scientist divsn. infectious diseases, dept. med. Cedars-Sinai Med. Ctr., 1986-90; dir. Diamond AIDS Rsch. Ctr., N.Y., 1990—; prof. med. and microbiol., co-dir. Ctr for AIDS Rsch. NYU, 1990-96, dir., 1994-96; asst. prof. med. in res. UCLA, 1986-89, assoc. prof. 1989. Contbr. over 110 articles to profl. jours. Recipient Mayor's award (N.Y.C.) for Excellence in Sci. and Tech., Scientific award Chinese Amer. Med. Soc.; named 1996 Man of Yr., Time mag. Mem. AmFAR (bd. dirs. sci. bd.), Com. of 100 (Chinese Am. leadership org.), NIH vaccine working group; fellow AAAS (Ernst Jung prize in medicine). Office: Aaron Diamond AIDS Rsch Ctr 455 1st Ave Fl 7 New York NY 10016-9102*

HO, DAVID KIM HONG, educator; b. Honolulu, Mar. 5, 1948; s. Raymond T.Y. and Ellen T.Y. (Fong) H.; m. Joan Yee, July 6, 1968 (div. Apr. 1982); 1 child, Michael J.; m. Patricia Ann McAndrews, June 25, 1983. BS in Indsl. Engring., U. So. Calif., 1970; MBA, Butler U., 1976; MS in Acctg., U. Wis., Whitewater, 1981. Cert. fellow in prodn. and inventory mgmt. Indsl. engr. FMC Corp., L.A., 1970-73; mgr. prodn. planning and inventory control FMC Corp., Indpls., 1973-77; materials mgr. Butler Mfg. Co., Ft. Atkinson, Wis., 1977-81; systems mgr. Butler Mfg. Co., Kansas City, Mo., 1981-82; dir. materials and systems Behlen Mfg. Co., Columbus, Nebr., 1982-84, v.p. operations, bd. dirs., 1984-86; mgr. corp. materials Lozier Corp., Omaha, 1986-90, plant mgr., 1990-91; v.p. mfg. Heatilator Inc., Mt. Pleasant, Iowa, 1991-93; prof. profl. studies Bellevue (Nebr.) U., 1993—; instr. Met. C.C., Omaha, 1989—, Iowa Wesleyan Coll, Mt. Pleasant, 1991-92. Mem. Nat. Assn. Purchasing Mgmt. (acad.), Am. Prodn. and Inventory Control Soc. Home: 11729 Fisher House Rd Bellevue NE 68123-1112 Office: Met CC PO 3777-Soc 121 Omaha NE 68103-0777

HO, HIEN VAN, pediatrician; b. Hue, Thuathien, Vietnam, Aug. 1, 1947; came to U.S., 1982.; s. Vinh Van Ho and Te (Thi) Truong; m. Huong Xuan Diep, Aug. 2, 1972; children: Hoa, Hieu, Hiep, Stephen Huy. MD, Saigon U., 1972. Diplomate Am. Bd. Pediatrics. Resident in pediatrics Georgetown U. Hosp., Washington, 1983-86; chief resident Arlington Hosp., Va., 1985-86; pediatrician Seven Corners Pediatrics, Falls Church, Va., 1986—; instr. Georgetown U. Hosp., 1986. First lt. Republic of Vietnam Army, 1972-75. Fellow Am. Acad. Pediatrics; mem. AMA, N.Y. Acad. Scis., Vietnamese Med. Assn. Home: 10001 Robindale Ct Great Falls VA 22066-1848 Office: Seven Corners Pediatrics 6079 Arlington Blvd Falls Church VA 22044-2707

HO, HWA-SHAN, engineering executive, civil engineer, consultant, drilling engineer; b. Hualien, Taiwan, Sept. 10, 1941; came to U.S., 1964; s. Tung-Mu and Mien (Lin) H.; m. Rita Ying-Huei Chau, Aug. 24, 1969 (dec. Dec. 1993); m. Jenny Shijin Wang, Oct. 24, 1994; children: Yvonne Y.F., Isaac Y.J., Yvette Y.F. BSCE, Nat. Taiwan U., 1963; MS in Engring., Brown U., 1966, PhD in Engring., 1969. Assoc. in rsch. Brown U., Providence, R.I., 1968-69; asst. prof. civil engring. Univ. So. Calif., L.A., 1969-74; sr. engring. technologist Ralph M. Parsons Co., Pasadena, Calif., 1974-76; assoc. prof. civil engring. U. Utah, Salt Lake City, 1976-81; sr. rsch. specialist Exxon Production Rsch. Co., Houston, 1981-84; cons. scientist Sperry-Sun Drilling Svcs., Houston, 1984-92; pres. Tapong RTI, Inc., Spring-Klein, Tex., 1992—; cons. Diamant Boart Stratabit, Brussels, 1991-95, Geothermal Energy Rsch. & Devel. Co., Tokyo, 1994-96. Mem. Orgn. of Chinese Americans, Houston, 1990—, Chinese Profl. Club (officer 1993), Houston, 1992-94. 2nd lt. USAF, 1963-64, Taiwan. Mem. ASCE, Soc. Petroleum Engrs. Achievements include 10 U.S. patents on directional drilling tech.; first to use software program to correct error in MWD Survey due to drillstring deformations enabling elimination of gyro wireline re-survey; first to devel. comprehensive rock-bit interaction model in drilling trajectory prediction; first to propose designed PDC Bits with specific walk tendencies and anti-walk bits; first to study the effect of drillstring stiffness in torque-drag monitoring calculations; first to propose "compliance-based" torque-drag monitoring; improved self-consistent forward stepping algorithm in trajectory prediction; first to infer formation dip and strike from directional drilling data; rsch. on a new gen. variational method to solve boundary value problems in linear sys. with interfaces, multiple connectivities. E-mail: HwashanHo@aol.com. Home: 5411 Mineral Creek Ct Spring TX 77379-8869 Office: TAPONG RTI INC PO Box 11170 Spring TX 77391-1170

HO, IWAN, research plant pathologist; b. Souzhou, Jiangsu, China, Apr. 15, 1925; came to U.S., 1956; m. Mei-Chun Chang, Nov. 29, 1975; 1 child, Tomur M. BS, Nat. Shanghai U., 1946; MS, La. State U., 1958; PhD, Oreg. State U., 1984. Microbiologist Seattle Pub. Health Dept., 1962-66; research plant physiologist Forestry Scis. Lab., Corvallis, Oreg., 1970—; courtesy asst. prof. Coll. Forestry, Oreg. State U. Mem. Mycol. Soc. Am., Am. Soc. Plant Physiologists, Internat. Soc. Plant Molecular Biology, Sigma Xi. Democrat. Episcopalian. Avocations: painting, violin, stamp collecting. Home: 1686 SW Bullevard St Philomath OR 97370-9538 Office: Forestry Sci Lab Pacific NW Rsch Sta 3200 SW Jefferson Way Corvallis OR 97331-8550

HO, JOHN WING-SHING, biochemistry educator, researcher; b. Hong Kong, Sept. 10, 1954; came to U.S., 1979; s. Tak-Kam and Sam-Mui (Tong) H. BS in Biochemistry, U. Alberta, Can., 1979; MA in Chemistry, SUNY, Buffalo, 1982, PhD in Chemistry, 1985. Teaching asst. dept. chemistry SUNY, Buffalo, 1979-82, rsch. asst. dept. chemistry, 1982-85; chemistry lectr. Millard Fillmore Coll., SUNY, Buffalo, 1985; postdoctoral fellow SUNY, Buffalo, 1985-87; rsch. assoc. dept. chemistry U. Utah, Salt Lake City, 1987-88, rsch. faculty Ctr. for Human Toxicology, 1988—; vis. prof. dept. applied biology and chem. tech. Hong Kong Poly., 1992; lectr. dept. biochemistry Chinese U. of Hong Kong, 1994—; spkr. seminars and confs., 1983—. Reviewer Jour. Chromatography (Biomedical Applications), 1990—; contbr. articles to profl. jours. IBR fellow Inst. Basic Rsch., 1986-88; recipient traineeship Health and Human Svcs., 1985-86. Fellow Am. Inst. Chemists; mem. AAAS, Am. Chem. Soc., N.Y. Acad. Scis., U.S. Tennis Assn.

HO, LOW-TONE, physician, researcher, educator; b. Chousan, Chekiang, China, May 1, 1947; s. Tzen and Jo-Hsiu (Yen) H.; m. Shu-Hsia Tu, Nov. 12, 1973; children: Pei-Ling, Pei-SHuan, Ming-Han. MD, Nat. Def. Med. Ctr., Taipei, Taiwan, 1971. Med. diplomate; lic. physician, China, U.S. Resident Vets. Gen. Hosp., Taipei, 1971-75, attending physician, 1975—, chief endocrine function unit, 1982-85, chief divsn. endocrinology and metabolism, 1985-94, chmn. dept. med. rsch. and edn., 1994—; prof. medicine Nat. Def. Med. Ctr., Taipei, 1986—, prof. nuclear medicine, 1991—; prof. medicine Nat. Yang-Ming U., Taipei, 1986—, prof. physiology, 1988—, dean Sch. Medicine, 1999—; prof. biomed. sci. Nat. Tsing-Hua U., Taipei, 1991—; prof. Grad. Inst. Clin. Medicine, NYMU, 1995—, prof. and dean, NYMU Sch. of Med., 1999—. Contbr. articles to profl. jours. Col. Taiwan Nt. Def. Med. Ctr., 1971-89. Recipient Outstanding Rsch. Accomplishment award Nt. Sci. Coun., 1989-91; faculty fellow U. Mich., Ann Arbor, 1977-79; Nat. Health grantee, 1983-86. Mem. Diabetes Assn. China (exec. bd. 1988—), Endocrine Soc. China (exec. bd. 1988—), Soc. Lipid and Atherosclerosis China (exec. bd. 1994—). Avocations: chess, bridge, philosophy, computer, golf. Office: Vets Gen Hosp, Shipai Rd Sect 2 # 201, Taipei 112, Taiwan

HO, PAUL SIU-CHUNG, physics educator; b. Canton, China, Oct. 6, 1936; came to U.S., 1959; s. Chi and Sue S. (Wong) H.; m. Mary H. J. Sung, Oct. 21, 1967; children: Susan, Alexander. BS, Nat. Chengkung U., Taiwan, 1957; MS, Nat. Tsinghua U., Taiwan, 1959; PhD, Rensselaer Poly. Inst., Troy, N.Y., 1965. Asst. prof. Cornell U., Ithaca, N.Y., 1967-72; assoc. prof. Cornell U., 1972; mem. research staffT.J. Watson Rsch. Ctr. IBM, Yorktown Heights, N.Y., 1972-75; mgr. IBM, 1975-85, sr. mgr., 1985-91; prof. materials sci. U. Tex., Austin, 1991—. Mem. editorial bd. Jour. Thin Solid Films, 1981-86, Nonstructured Materials, 1991—, Materials Physics and Chemistry, 1991—; editor 6 books; patentee in field. Recipient Outstanding Contbn. award, IBM Research Div., 1977, Outstanding Tech. Achievement award, 1986. Fellow Am. Phys. Soc., Am. Vacuum Soc. (exec. com. 1985-87); mem. Materials Rsch. Soc. Office: Univ Tex Austin Ctr for Mats Sci & Engring Austin TX 78712*

HO, REGINALD CHI SHING, medical educator; b. Hong Kong, Mar. 30, 1932; came to U.S., 1940; s. Chow and Elizabeth (Wong) Ho; m. Sharilyn Dang , Nov. 14, 1964; children: Mark, Reginald, Gianna Masca, Timothy. Student, St. Louis U., 1954, MD, 1959. Diplomate Nat. Bd. Med. Examiners, Am. Bd. Internal Medicine. Rotating intern U. Cin. Hosps., 1959-60, resident in internal medicine, 1960-62; fellow in hematology and oncology Barnes Hosp./Washington U., St. Louis, 1962-63; attending physician in oncology, hematology and internal medicine Queen's Med. Ctr., 1962—; instr. in medicine Sch. Medicine U. Hawaii, Honolulu, 1967-69, asst. clin. prof. medicine, 1969-72, assoc. clin. prof., 1972-77, clin. prof., 1977—; attending physician dept. hematology and oncology Straub Clinic and Hosp., Honolulu, 1973—; mem. tech. rev. com. Regional Med. Program Hawaii, 1970-71, long range planning com. 1971; prin. investigator Hawaii Community Clin. Oncology Program, Honolulu, 1983-86; adj. prof. clin. sci. Cancer Rsch. Ctr. Hawaii, 1989—, mem. various coms. Contbr. articles to med. jours. Bd. dirs. Cath. Svcs. for Families, 1987-91. Mem. AMA, ACP, Am. Cancer Soc. (divsn. del. 1982-93, del. dir. 1983-92, exec. com. 1989—, chair med. and sci. exec. com. 1991-92, past officer dir. 1994—, v.p. 1991-92, pres. 1992-93, immediate past pres. 1993-94, Clin fellow 1962, bd. dirs. Hawaii divsn. 1968—, v.p. 1970-71, chmn. exec. com. 1971-73, v.p. 1973-75, pres. 1976-77, chmn. bd. dirs. 1977-78, hon. life mem. 1989—, bd. dirs. Honolulu chpt. 1980-86, bd. dirs. Oahu unit 1966-71, chair svc. and rehab. com. 1967-71), Hawaii Med. Assn. (Hawaii cancer commn. 1980-85, chair cancer com. 1981-90), Honolulu County Med. Assn. (del. to Hawaii Med. Assn. 1969-72, alt. del. 1972-74, bd. govs. 1972), Exptl. Med. Care Rev. Orgn. (exec. com., chair ambulatory care edn. audit com. 1972), Alpha Omega Alpha. Roman Catholic. Avocation: tennis. Office: Straub Clinic and Hosp 888 S King St Honolulu HI 96813-3083

HO, STUART TSE KONG, investment company executive; b. Manila, Nov. 18, 1935; came to U.S., 1936; s. Chinn and Betty (Ching) H.; m. Mary Lois Lee, June 17, 1961; children: Peter, Cecily, Heather. BA, Claremont (Calif.) McKenna, 1957; JD, U. Mich., 1963. Bar: Hawaii. Asst. sec. to chmn. bd. Capital Investment of Hawaii, Honolulu, 1965—; chmn. bd. Gannett Pacific Corp., 1987—; trustee Coll. Retirement Equities Fund, N.Y.C.; bd. dirs. Pacific Century Fin. Corp., Honolulu, Gannett Co., Inc., Rosslyn, Va., Aloha Airgroup, Inc., Honolulu. Representative Hawaii Ho. of Reps., Honolulu, 1966-70, majority fl. leader, 1968-70; del. Constnl. Conv. of 1968, Honolulu, 1968; regent U. Hawaii, Honolulu, 1971-74. 1st lt. U.S. Army, 1958-60, ETO. Democrat. Office: Capital Investment Hawaii 733 Bishop St Ste 1700 Honolulu HI 96813-4017

HO, THOMAS INN MIN, computer scientist, educator; b. Honolulu, Oct. 17, 1948; s. Herbert Low Seu and Rose (Lee) H.; m. Laura Loh; children: Brian Koon Leong, Tabitha En Hui. BS, Purdue U., 1970, MS, 1971, Ph.D., 1974. Asst. prof. computer sci., mgmt. Purdue U., West Lafayette, Ind., 1975-78, assoc. prof., 1978-84, prof., 1984-90, head computer tech., 1978-88; exec. dir. Intelenet Commn., Indpls., 1986-88; dir. Info. Networking Inst. Carnegie Mellon U., Pitts., 1990-92; sr. fellow info. systems and computer sci. Nat. U. Singapore, 1993-94; chairperson, prof. computer tech. Ind. U. Purdue U., Indpls., 1995—; cons. in field. Author: (with J.L. Whitten and L.D. Bentley) Systems Analysis and Design Methods, 1986; contbr. articles to profl. jours. NSF fellow, 1970-72. Mem. Am. Soc. Engring. Edn., Assn. Info. Sys., Internet Soc. Office: Ind U Purdue U Indpls Dept Computer Tech 723 W Michigan St Indianapolis IN 46202-5191

HO, WEIFAN LEE, merchandise executive; b. N.Y.C., Mar. 11, 1951; d. Ho chee and Kwan Fong Lui. Student, Middlebury Coll.; BA, CCNY, 1972. Furniture buyer Gimbels East, N.Y.C., 1972-86; buyer Carson Pirie Scott, Chgo., 1986-89, Bloomingdales, N.Y.C., 1989-92; divsnl. mdse. mgr. Conran's-Habitat, N.Y.C., 1992-93; buyer Abraham and Straus/Jordan Marsh, N.Y.C., 1994, Macy's East, N.Y.C., 1995—. Mem. NAFE. Office: Macy's East 151 W 34th St New York NY 10001-2180

HO, YHI-MIN, university dean, economics educator; b. Nanking, China, Nov. 18, 1934; came to U.S., 1958, naturalized, 1972; s. Yung-Tung and Hsing-In H.; m. Shu-Fen Ma, Nov. 23, 1962; Andrew M., Katherine. B.A. in Econs., Nat. Taiwan U., 1955; M.S. in Econs., Utah State U., 1961; Ph.D. in Econs., Vanderbilt U., 1965. Mem. managerial staff mktg. div. Chinese Petroleum Corp., 1955-58; asst. prof. U. So. Miss., 1963-65, U. Houston, 1965-66, Tulane U., New Orleans, 1966-70; chmn. dept. econs. and bus. adminstrn. U. St. Thomas, Houston, 1970—, acting dean Cameron Sch. Bus., 1978-80, dean, 1980—, Cullen Found. chair in econs., 1989—. Author: Agricultural Development of Taiwan, 1903-1960, 1966; contbr. articles to profl. jours. Mem. adb. bd. Vols. for Arts; mem. adminstrv. bd. Houston-Taipei Soc., Inc., 1978—; trustee Meml. Hosp. Sys., Houston, 1987-97, Meml. Found. Bd., 1997—. Ford scholar, 1960-61; Rockefeller fellow, 1961-63; NSF grantee, 1973-75. Mem. Am. Econ. Assn., So. Econ. Assn. Office: U St Thomas 3800 Montrose Blvd Houston TX 77006-4626

HO, YIK HONG, colon and rectal surgeon; b. Singapore, Apr. 21, 1956; s. Peng Yoke Ho and Mei Yiu (Lucy) Fung; m. Chui Wah Ludmilla Tung, Sept. 13, 1984; 1 child, Elaine Jo-Lan. MBBS with honors, U. Queensland, 1980. Intern Princess Alexandra Hosp., Brisbane, Australia, 1980-81, resident, 1981-82; med. officer Sai Ying Pun Hosp./Tang Shiu Kin Hosp., Hong Kong, 1982-83; registrar U. Surg. Unit Queen Mary Hosp., Tung Wah Hosp., Hong Kong, 1983-89; sr. registrar Singapore Gen. Hosp., 1989-93, cons., 1993-98, dir. Pelvic Floor Lab., 1996—, sr. cons., 1998—; rsch. fellow U. Hosp., U. Nottingham, U.K., 1989; part-time clin. lectr. Nat. U. Singapore, 1990—; dep. chmn. Electronics Med. Records Workgroup, Singapore Gen. Hosp., 1994—. Mem. editl. rev. com. Annals of Acad. of Medicine, 1994—; mem. editl. com. Singapore Gen. Hosp. Procs., 1995-99, assoc. editor, 1995-98, editor, 1999—; contbr. articles to profl. jours. Scholarship Australian Kidney Found., 1977. Fellow Royal Australasian Coll. Surgeons, Royal Coll. Surgeons (Edinburgh), Royal Coll Physicians and Surgeons (Glasgow), Internat. Coll. Surgeons (Singapore sect. com. mem. 1994-96, 98-99, treas. 97-99, sec. 1999, gov. internat. bd. 1999); mem. Singapore Soc. Continence (v.p. 1993—), Biomed. Rsch. and Exptl. Therapeutics Soc. Singapore (hon. sec. 1993-95, pres. 1995-97). Avocations: fitness, computer, photography, swimming, tai-chi. Office: Dept Colorectal Surgery, Singapore Gen Hosp Outram Rd, Singapore 16908, Singapore

HOADLEY, WALTER EVANS, economist, financial executive, lay worker; b. San Francisco, Aug. 16, 1916; s. Walter Evans Sr. and Marie Howland (Preece) H.; m. Virginia Alm, May 20, 1939; children: Richard Alm, Jean Elizabeth (Mrs. Donald A. Peterson). AB, U. Calif., 1938, MA, 1940, PhD, 1946; D in Comml. Sci., Franklin and Marshall Coll., 1963; LLD (hon.), Golden Gate U., 1968, U. Pacific, 1979; hon. degree, El Instituto Technologico Autonomo de Mexico, 1974. Collaborator U.S. Bur. Agrl. Econs., 1938-39; rsch. economist Calif. Gov.'s Reemployment Commn., 1939, Calif. Gov.'s State Planning Bd., 1941; rsch. economist, teaching fellow U. Calif., 1938-41, supr. indsl. mgmt. war tng. office, 1941-42; econ. adviser U. Chgo. Civil Affairs Tng. Sch., 1945; sr. economist Fed. Res. Bank Chgo., 1942-49; economist Armstrong World Industries, Lancaster, Pa., 1949-54, treas., 1954-60, v.p., treas., 1960-66, dir., 1962-87; sr. v.p., chief economist, mem. mng. com. Bank of Am. NT & SA, San Francisco, 1966-68, exec. v.p., chief economist, mem. mng. com., mem. mgmt. adv. council, chmn. subs., 1968-81; ret., 1981; sr. research fellow Hoover Inst., Stanford U., 1981—; dep. chmn. Fed. Res. Bank, Phila., 1960-61, chmn., 1962-66; chmn. Conf. Fed. Res. Chmn., 1966; faculty Sch. Banking U. Wis., 1945-49, 55, 58-66; adviser various U.S. Govt. Agys.; Wright Internat. Bd. Econ. and Investment Advisors, 1987—; spl. adviser U.S. Congl. Budget Office, 1975-87; mem. pub. adv. bd. U.S. Dept. Commerce, 1970-74; mem. White House Rev. Com. for Balance Payment Stats., 1963-65, Presdl. Task Force on Growth, 1969-70, Presdl. Task Force on Land Utilization, Presdl. Conf. on Inflation, 1974; gov. Com. on Developing Am. Capitalism, 1977—, chmn., 1987-88; dir. PLM Internat., 1989-97, Transisco Industries, Inc., 1981-95, Davis/Selected/Venture Advisors, 1981-96. Mem. Meth. Ch. Commn. on World Svc. and Fin. Phila. conf., 1957-64, chmn. investment com., 1964-66; bd. dirs., exec. com. Internat. Mgmt. and Devel. Inst., 1976-97; trustee Pacific Sch. Religion, 1968-89; adviser Nat. Commn. to Study Nursing and Nursing Edn., 1968-73; trustee Duke U., 1968-73, pres.'s assoc., 1973-80; trustee Golden Gate U., 1974-94, chmn. investment com., 1977-93; trustee World Wildlife U.S. Fund The Conservation Found., 1987-90; mem. periodic chmn. adminstrv. bd. Trinity United Meth. Ch., Berkeley, Calif., 1966-84; mem. adminstrv. bd., advisor Lafayette (Calif.) United Meth. Ch., 1984—; mem. bd. overseers vis. com. Harvard Coll. Econs., 1969-74; chmn. investment com. Calif.-Nev. Meth. Found., 1968-75, mem., 1976-91; mem. Calif. Gov.'s Coun. Econ. and Bus. Devel., 1978-82, chmn., 1980-82; trustee Hudson Inst., 1979-84; co-chmn. San Francisco Mayor's Fiscal Adv. Com., 1978-81, mem. 1981-96; chmn. Bay Area Econ. Advisers, 1982—; spl . adviser Presdl. Cabinet Com. Innovation, 1978-79; mem. Calif. State Internat. Adv. Com., 1986-94; regent U. Calif., 1990-91; mem. adv. coun. Calif. Environ. Tech. Ptnrship., 1993-94; mem. econ. adv. coun. Calif. Inst. Fed. Policy Rsch., 1994—; trustee Internat. Ho. U. Calif., 1991—, Devel. Com., 1994—, chmn., 1995-97. Fellow Am. Statis. Assn. (v.p., bd. dirs. 1952-54, pres. 1958), Nat. Assn. Bus. Economists (San Francisco chpt. exec. com. 1989—); mem. Am. Fin. Assn. (bd. dirs. 1955-56, pres. 1969), Conf. Bus. Economists (chmn. 1962), Atlantic Coun. of U.S. (bd. dirs. 1985—), Internat. Acad. Mgmt., 1980—; U.S. Coun. for Internat. Bus. (sr. trustee 1992—), Commonwealth Club of Calif. (pres. 1987, chmn. pub. affairs-comm. com. 1995—), Am. Econ. Assn., Am. Mktg. Assn., Am. Bankers Assn. (chmn. urban and cmty. affairs com. 1972-73, mem. econ. adv. coun. 1976-78), Nat. Bur. Econ. Rsch. (bd. dirs. 1965-81), Western Econ. Assn. (bd. dirs., mem. steering com. 1966-94), U. Calif. Alumni Assn. (pres. 1989-91, chmn. investment com. 1983-89, 94-96, 97—, Alumnus of Yr. 1993), U.S. Nat. Com. on Pacific Econ. Coop. (vice chmn. 1984-89, mem. exec. com. 1989-94), Caux Internat. Roundtable (chmn. steering com. 1993-97), St. Francis Yacht Club, Pacific Union Club, Bankers Club, Silverado Country Club, Phi Beta Kappa Assocs. (bd. dirs. 1986-95), Kappa Alpha. Office: Bank of AmRet Execs Dept 3001-B 11th Fl 555 California St San Francisco CA 94104-1502 *From long observation and living, I've concluded that faith in a Supreme Being is the most powerful force enabling an individual to deal with the ongoing challenges of human existence.*

HOAG, DAVID GARRATT, aerospace engineer; b. Boston, Oct. 11, 1925; s. Alden Bomer and Helen Lucy (Garratt) H.; m. Grace Edward Griffith, May 10, 1952; children—Rebecca Wilder, Peter Griffith, Jeffrey Taber, Nicholas Alden, Lucy Seymour. BS, MIT, 1946, MS, 1950. Staff engr. instrumentation lab. MIT, Cambridge, 1946-57; tech. dir. Polaris Missile Guidance, 1957-61; tech. dir., program mgr. Apollo Spacecraft Guidance, 1961-72; advanced system dept. head C.S. Draper Lab., Inc., Cambridge, 1972-86. Recipient Pub. Svc. award NASA, 1969, Spl. award Royal Inst. Navigation, Britain, 1970, Laurels, Aviation Week, 1970. Fellow AIAA (Louis W. Hill Space Transp. award 1972, chmn. New Eng. sect. 1979-80); mem. Nat. Acad. Engring., Inst. Navigation (Thurlow award 1969, pres. 1978-79), Internat. Acad. Astronautics (assoc. editor ACTA Astronautica 1973-79). Home: 116 Winthrop St Medway MA 02053-2310

HOAG, JOHN ARTHUR, retired bank executive; b. Freeport, N.Y., Sept. 29, 1932; s. John Hoag and Viola (Babcock) Hobson; m. Jeanette Makaio, Dec. 5, 1959; children: Steve, Vanessa, Kanani. BS, U. Mo., 1955; grad., Pacific Coast Banking Sch., Wash., 1970; MBA, U. Hawaii, 1977. Account exec. Walston & Co., N.Y.C., 1960; mgmt. trainee 1st Hawaiian Bank, Honolulu, 1960, br. mgr., Hilo, 1968, Island v.p., 1970-76, sr. v.p., mgr., 1976, exec. v.p. loan group, 1979, pres., 1989-94, also bd. dirs.; vice chmn. bd. dirs., 1994; retired 1st Hawaiian Bank, 1995; pres. 1st Hawaiian Inc., Honolulu, 1991-95, also bd. dirs.; vice chm. 1st Interstate Bank Hawaii, Honolulu, 1991—; vice chmn. of bd., 1994—, ret., 1995; chmn. bd. Hawaii Reserves, Inc.; vice chmn. Pioneer Fed. Savs. Bank; bd. dirs. Castle Med. Ctr., BancWest Corp. Bd. regents Tokai Internat. Coll., 1992-95, U. Hawaii, 1995—; bd. dirs. Hawaii Med. Svc. Assn., 1981-93, Honolulu Polynesian Cultural Ctr, 1990-93, Kapiolani Med. Ctr. for Women and Children, Honolulu, 1989-95. Capt. USMC, 1955-60. Mem. Pres.' Club U. Hawaii, C. of C. of Hawaii (chmn. bd. 1992-93). Mem. LDS Ch. Office: PO Box 3200 999 Bishop St Honolulu HI 96847 also: 1st Hawaiian Bank PO Box 3200 Honolulu HI 96847-0001

HOAG, PAUL STERLING, architect; b. Spokane, Aug. 7, 1913; s. Percival Doane and Emma Imogen (Rusk) H.; m. Nancy Jean Lawrence, Oct. 21, 1967. Student, Washington State Coll., Pullman, 1930-31, Stanford U., 1932-33. Lic. architect, Calif., Colo., Tex., Wash. Gen. mgr. Hoag X-Ray Co., Spokane, 1933-42; designer various war industry cos., 1942-45; architect apprentice Richard Neutra, L.A., 1945-46, Paul Robinson Hunter and others, L.A., 1946-48; prin. Paul Sterling Hoag, L.A., 1948-87, Crane Island, Wash., 1987—; intr. advanced design So. Calif. Inst. Architecture; entire body of archtl. design drawings placed in archives U. Calif. Art History Dept. Prin. works include Falcon Plastics Factory, Oxnard, Calif. (top plant of 1970 award Modern Mfg.), Old Ranch Country Club, Seal Beach, Calif., Huntington Harbor (Calif.) Beach Club, Happy Valley Sch., Ojai, Calif., Adobe Hotel, Yachats, Oreg., Sterling Holloway residence, Laguna Beach, Calif., Beatrice Wood studio and residence, Ojai; author: (novel) Life of Antonio Vivaldi, 1994-98; monthly columnist The Listener, L.A. Architect; contbr. articles to profl. jours. and newspapers. Architect mem. Bel-Air Archtl. Com., L.A., 1982-88, San Vicente Design Rev. Bd., 1980-86; design cons. San Juan County (Wash.) for Eastsound town redesign, 1990-94. Fellow AIA. Home and Office: 403 W Lake Sammamish Pkwy NE Bellevue WA 98008-4224 *The most exciting discovery of my professional life was Carl Jung's revelatory concept of "archaic memories" because it enabled me to understand how intuitive design makes it possible to create building forms and interior spaces which are free of fashion and therefore timelessly meaningful, my constant goal.*

HOAGLAND, ALBERT JOSEPH, JR., psychotherapist, hypnotherapist, minister; b. Clayton, N.J., July 2, 1939. Cert. psychiat. tech., Ancora State Hosp., 1958; RN, Monmouth Med. Ctr., 1961; BS, Monmouth Coll., 1964; MSW, Rutgers U., 1966; M.Div., Fuller Theol. Sem., 1978; D in Ministry, Boston U., 1981; PhD, Am. Inst. Hypnotherapy, 1989, D.C.H., 1991; MS in Oriental Medicine, Samra U. of Oriental Medicine, 1995; PhD in Nutritional Medicine/Homeopathy, Curentur U., 1997. Ordained to ministry Disciples of Christ, 1978; lic. clin. social worker, Calif., marriage, family and child counselor, Calif.; cert. sch. counselor, anger therapist, eating disorders therapist. Pvt. practice counseling, 1966-96; psychiat. technician, RN N.J. State Hosp., Marlboro, 1958-66; instr., cons. Los Angeles County Dept. Probation, 1972-75; instr. psychology Calif. Grad. Inst., 1973; instr. Chapman Coll., 1972-74; instr. psychology Calif. State U., Dominguez Hills, 1974; instr. Torrance (Calif.) Adult Sch., 1977-79, 81-85; pastor Ariz., 1984-85, Calif., 1978-79, 81-84, Mass., 1979-81; subs. tchr. Marana (Ariz.) Sch. Dist., 1985; instr. Beverly Hills Adult Sch., 1984—; exec. dir. Personal Counseling Svcs. and Hypnotherapy Ctr. (name changed to Hoagland Healing Arts Complex), San Pedro, 1986-96; instr. Samra U. of Orienta Medicine, 1994-95; dean Curentur U., 1995-98; religious educator various retreats, programs, summer camps, etc., 1975—; bd. dirs. Inst. Psychostructural Balancing, 1998; pres. Oriental Medicine Inst., 1995—. Author: Anger to Intimacy, 1988; editor Jonestown Collection, 1978, Professional Papers from the Desert, 1970, What's Your Problem?, 1989; producer (film) Gestalt Art Therapy, 1974. Mem. Congress of Disciples Clergy, Disciples of Christ Hist. Soc., Disciples Peace Fellowship; trainer, cons. L.A. Coun. Exploring divsn. Boy Scouts Am., 1971-73, 88—, explorer post advisor, 1988—; coach Palos Verdes (Calif.) Soccer Program, basketball and soccer Torrance City Sports Program; dir. YWCA Delinquency Prevention Program, San Pedro, 1986-89; chair cmty. adv. coun. San Pedro High Sch.; campaigned for mayor of San Pedro, 1988. Recipient Adult God and Svc award, 1989. Mem. Nat. Tchrs. Assn., Nat. Assn. Social Workers, Am. Assn. Marriage and Family Therapists, Am. Osteo. Assn., Nat. Assn. Christians in Social Work, Harbor Area Police Clergy Coun. (pres.), Am. Bd. Hypnotherpaists, Nat. Assn. Clergy Hypnotherapists, World Fedn. Mental Health, Clowns of Am., San Pedro Rotary (sec.), Phi Delta Kappa. Democrat. Home: 3318 Torrance Blvd Torrance CA 90503-5011 Office: Oriental Medicine Inst PO Box 2825 Torrance CA 90509

HOAGLAND, ALBERT SMILEY, electrical engineer; b. Berkeley, Calif., Sept. 13, 1926; s. Dennis Robert and Jessie Agnes (Smiley) H.; m. Janine Maryse Simart, May 23, 1950; children: Catherine, Nicole, Richard. B.S., U. Calif.-Berkeley, 1947, M.S., 1948, Ph.D., 1954. Registered profl. engr., Calif. Asst. prof. elec. engring. U. Calif.-Berkeley, 1954-56; sr. engr. IBM, San Jose, Calif., 1956-59; mgr. engring sci. San Jose Research Lab., 1959-62; sr. tech. cons. IBM World Trade, The Hague, Holland, 1962-64; mgr. engring. sci. IBM Research Ctr., N.Y.C., 1964-68, dir. tech. planning Research Div., 1968-71; corporate program coordinator IBM, Boulder, Colo., 1971-76; mgr. exploratory magnetic rec. San Jose Research Lab., 1976-82; tech. adv. Gen. Products Div., 1982-84; acting dir. Ctr. for Magnetic Recording Research, U. Calif. San Diego, 1983-84; prof. elec. engring., dir. Inst. Info. Storage Tech. Santa Clara U., Calif., 1984—; lectr. computer design U. Calif. Berkeley, 1948-54, 56-62; adj. prof. U. Calif. San Diego, 1986; cons. State Calif., 1955-56, IBM, 1954-56, also numerous cons. in data storage industry, 1984—; chmn. Nat. Computer Conf. Bd., 1976-78; adj. prof. Harvey Mudd Coll. Author: Digital Magnetic Recording, 1963, 2d edit., 1991, reprinted, 1998; contbr. articles on magnetic rec. and info. storage tech. to profl. publs. Trustee Charles Babbage Inst.; regent Inst. Info. Mgmt.; chmn. adv. com. TMRC, 1991-95, chair adv. com., 1993—. Served with USNR, 1943-46. Recipient outstanding paper award IEEE, 1957. Fellow IEEE (dir. 1974-77), Am. Fedn. Info. Processing Socs. (dir. 1969-78, pres. 1978-80); mem. IEEE Computer Soc. (pres. 1971-73), Research Soc. Am. (pres. Sequoia chpt. 1962-63), Sigma Xi, Phi Beta Kappa, Eta Kappa Nu, Tau Beta Pi. Club: Golden Bear. Patentee in field. Home: 13834 Upper Hill Dr Saratoga CA 95070-5334 Office: Santa Clara U Inst Info Storage Tech Santa Clara CA 95053

HOAGLAND, DONALD WRIGHT, lawyer; b. N.Y.C., Aug. 16, 1921; s. Webster Comley and Irene (Wright) H.; m. Mary Tiedeman, May 14, 1949; children—Peter M., Mary C., Sara H., Ann W. BA, Yale U., 1942; LLB, Columbia U., 1948. Bar: N.Y. 1948, Colo. 1951. Assoc. firm Winthrop, Stimson, Putnam & Roberts, N.Y.C., 1948-51; ptnr. Davis, Graham & Stubbs, Denver, 1951-63, 66-87, of counsel, 1987—; with AID, 1964-66, asst. adminstr. devel. finance and pvt. enterprise, 1965-66; cons. AID, Indonesia, 1967-75; lectr. U. Denver Sch. Law, 1971-75; chmn. bd. Bi-Nat. Devel. Corp., 1968-70; dir. Centennial Fund, Inc., 2d Centennial Fund, Inc., Gryphon Fund, Inc., 1959-63; mem. Colo. Supreme Ct. Grievance Com., 1992-98. Mem. Denver Planning Bd., 1955-61, 67-70, chmn., 1959-61; bd. dirs., vice chmn. Denver Art Mus., 1959-63, 72-76, 79-82; bd. dirs. Colo. Urban League, 1960-63, 66-72, chmn. bd., 1968-72; adv. bd. Vols. Tech. Assistance vice chmn. bd. Denver chpt. ARC, 1959-61; bd. dirs. Legal Aid Soc. Colo., 1972-84, pres., 1975-79; trustee Phillips Exeter Acad., 1960-67, Colo. Rocky Mountain Sch., 1981-84, Am. U., Washington, 1982-85; chmn. bd. dirs. Legal Aid Found., Colo., 1983-87; chmn. Social Sci. Found. Denver U., 1995—; chmn. Colo. Health Data Commn., 1986-88; bd. dirs. Colo. Bus. Coalition for Health, 1988-89, Covington-Colo. Found. for Ednl. Excellence, 1998—; exec. dir. Ctr. for Health Ethics and Policy U. Colo., Denver, 1987-91; chmn. Gov. Romer's panel health advisors, 1992-94; pres. Colo. Found. Pub. Health and Environ., 1995-98; chmn. Caring for Colo. Found., 1999—. Served as dive bomber pilot USNR, 1943-45. Decorated Air medal with oak leaf cluster. Mem. ABA, Colo. Bar Assn., Denver Bar Assn. E-mail: Donald.Hoagland@DGSlaw.com. Home: 355 Garfield St Denver CO 80206-4509 Office: Davis Graham & Stubbs PO Box 185 Denver CO 80201-0185

HOAGLAND, EVERETT H., poet, English educator; b. Dec. 18, 1942. BA in English, Lincoln U., 1964; MA in Creative Writing, Brown U., 1973. Univ. fellow Brown U., 1971-73; from instr. to assoc. prof. English U. Mass., Dartmouth, 1973—. Author: (poetry) Black Velvet, 1970, Scrimshaw, 1976, This City and Other Poems; contbg. editor The Am. Poetry Review, 1984—. Recipient Gwendolyn Brooks Fiction award; Arts fellow in poetry Mass. Artists Found., 1974, 85; named Poet Laureate, City of New Bedford, Mass.; honoree 4th Ann. Celebration of Black Scholarship, 1994. Office: Dept English 285 Old Westport Rd North Dartmouth MA 02747-2356

HOAGLAND, JENNIFER HOPE, accountant; b. N.Y.C., Nov. 29, 1955; d. John Joseph and Winifred Adele (Strohmann) Vetter; m. John Grinnell Hoagland, Jr., Jan. 24, 1983; 1 child, John Grinnell III. BS in Acctg., Case We. Res. U., 1977; postgrad., U. Tex., El Paso, 1989—. CPA, Tex.; cert. internal auditor; cert. in mgmt. acctg. Rsch. analyst Predicasts, Inc., Cleve., 1977-79; internal auditor El Paso Electric Co., 1979-80; acct. Exxon Corp., Houston, 1980-81; sr. acct. Colton, Starr, Pena & Co., El Paso, 1981-83, Paul J. Ellenburg Corp., El Paso, 1983-85; dir. of acctg. Life Mgmt. Ctr., El Paso, 1985—. Mem. AICPA, Inst. Mgmt. Accts. Office: Life Mgmt Ctr 8929 Viscount Blvd El Paso TX 79925-5823

HOAGLAND, JIMMIE LEE, newspaper editor; b. Rock Hill, S.C., Jan. 22, 1940; s. Lee Roy and Edith Irene (Sullivan) H.; m. Jane Stanton Hitchcock, July 14, 1995; children: Laura Lee, Lily Hue, Lee Clayton. A.B. in Journalism, U. S.C., 1961; student, U. Aix-en-Provence, France, 1961-62, Columbia U., 1968-69. Reporter Evening Herald, Rock Hill, 1960; copy editor N.Y. Times Internat. Edit., Paris, France, 1964-66; reporter Washington Post, 1966-69, Africa corr., 1969-72, Middle East corr., 1972-75, Paris corr., 1975-77, fgn. editor, 1979-81, asst. mng. editor, 1981-86, assoc. editor, chief fgn. corr., 1986—. Author: South Africa: Civilizations in Conflict, 1972. Bd. trustees Inst. for Study of Diplomacy, Georgetown U., Washington. Ford Found. fellow Columbia U., 1968-69; recipient Pulitzer prize internat. report, 1970; Overseas Press Club award internat. reporting, 1977; Pulitzer prize for commentary, 1991; Eugene Meyer Career Achievement award, 1994. Mem. Council on Fgn. Relations, Phi Beta Kappa, Pi Kappa Alpha. Office: Washington Post 1150 15th St NW Washington DC 20071-0002*

HOAGLAND, KARL KING, JR., lawyer; b. St. Louis, Aug. 21, 1933; s. Karl King and Mary Edna (Parsons) H.; m. Sylvia Anne Naranick, July 13, 1957; children: Elizabeth Parsons, Sarah Stewart, Karl King III, Alison T. BS in Econs., U. Pa., 1955; LLB, U. Ill., 1958. Bar: Ill. 1958, U.S. Dist. Ct. (so. dist.) Ill. 1958. V.p., gen. counsel, sec. Jefferson Smurfit Corp., St. Louis, 1960-92, Container Corp. Am., St. Louis, 1986-92; of counsel Hoagland, Fitzgerald, Smith & Pranaitis, Alton, Ill., 1987—; chmn. bd. dirs. Millers' Mut. Ins. Assn. Ill., 1989-92. Asst. editor: U. Ill. Law Forum, 1957-58. Trustee, treas. Monticello Coll. Found., 1965—. 1st lt. USAF, 1958-60. Mem. Ill. Bar Assn., Madison County Bar Assn., Alton-Wood River Bar Assn., Lockhaven Country Club, Mo. Athletic Club, Crystal Lake Club, Order of the Coif, Beta Gamma Sigma. Episcopalian. Avocations: tennis, skiing, hunting, fishing, golf. Home: Fairmount Addition 91 Hawthorne Dr Alton IL 62002-3209

HOAGLAND, LAURANCE REDINGTON, JR., investment executive; b. Palo Alto, Calif., Dec. 18, 1936; s. Laurance Redington and Naomi Ann (Carpenter) H.; m. Grace Updegraff Mohns, Sept. 5, 1959; children: Laurance Redington, III, Craig C., David B., Edward L. AB, Stanford U., 1958; BA, Oxford (Eng.) U., 1960, MA, 1963; MBA, Harvard U., 1962. Chartered financial analyst. With Irwin Mgmt. Co., Columbus, Ind., 1962-74; v.p., portfolio mgr. Irwin Mgmt. Co., 1965-74; exec. dir. fin. services Cummins Engine Co., Columbus, 1975; v.p., treas. Cummins Engine Co., 1975-80; founder, prin. Anderson, Hoagland and Co., investment mgmt. co., St. Louis, 1980-91; pres., chief exec. officer Stanford Mgmt. Co., Menlo Park, Calif., 1991—; bd. dirs. ProCard, Inc., Rio Grande Med. Techs. Dir. bd. pensions Presbyn. Ch. USA, 1981-92, chmn. investment com., 1987-91; trustee Louisville Sem., 1994—, Lucile Packard Found. for Children, 1998—; fin. com. Rockefeller Found., 1995—; investment com. Hewlett Found., 1996—. Mem. Soc. Chartered Financial Analysts. Home: 115 Fox Hollow Rd Woodside CA 94062-3607 Office: Stamford Mgmt Co 2770 Sand Hill Rd Menlo Park CA 94025-7020*

HOAGLAND, MAHLON BUSH, biochemist, educator; b. Boston, Oct. 5, 1921; s. Hudson and Anna (Plummer) H.; m. Olley Virginia Jones, Jan. 10, 1961; children from previous marriage: Judith, Mahlon Bush, Robin. Student, Williams Coll., 1940-41, Harvard U., 1941-43; M.D., Harvard U., 1948; Sc.D. (hon.), Worcester Poly. Inst., 1973, U. Mass., 1984. From rsch. fellow to asst. prof. medicine Med. Sch. Harvard U. at Mass. Gen. Hosp., 1948-60; assoc. prof. bacteriology and immunology Med. Sch. Harvard U., 1960-67; prof. biochemistry, chmn. dept. Med. Sch. Dartmouth, 1967-70; pres., sci. dir. Worcester Found. for Biomed. Rsch., Shrewsbury, Mass., 1970-85, pres. emeritus, 1985—; rsch. assoc. Carlsberg Labs., Copenhagen, 1951-52, Cavendish Labs., Cambridge, Eng., 1957-58; cancer rsch. scholar Am. Cancer Soc., 1953-58; founder, spokesman Del. for Basic Biomed. Rsch., 1978-85. Author 5 books and 65 articles to profl. publs. Recipient Franklin medal, 1976; 2 book awards Am. Med. Writers Assn., 1982, 96. Fellow Am. Acad. Arts and Scis.; mem. NAS. Achievements include discovery of mechanism of amino acid activation and (with P.C. Zamecnik) of transfer ribonucleic acid. Home: Academy Rd Thetford VT 05074

HOAGLAND, SAMUEL ALBERT, lawyer, pharmacist; b. Mt. Home, Idaho, Aug. 19, 1953; s. Charles Leroy and Glenna Lorraine (Gridley) H.; m. Karen Ann Mengel, Nov. 20, 1976; children: Hiliary Anne, Heidi Lynne, Holly Kaye. BS in Pharmacy, Idaho State U., 1976; JD, U. Idaho, 1982. Bar: Idaho 1982, U.S. Dist. Ct. Idaho 1982, U.S. CT. Appeals (9th cir.) 1984. Lectr. clin. pharmacy Idaho State U., Pocatello, 1976-78, lectr. pharmacy law, 1985-86, dean's adv. council Coll. Pharmacy, 1987-92; hosp. pharmacist Mercy Med. Ctr., Nampa, Idaho, 1978-79; retail pharmacist Thrifty Corp., Moscow, Idaho, 1980-82; assoc. Dial, Looze & May, Pocatello, 1982-89, Prescott & Foster, Boise, Idaho, 1989-90; pvt. practice, 1990—; gen. counsel Design Innovations and Rsch. Corp., 1991-95; chmn. malpractice panel Idaho Bd. Medicine, Boise, 1983-92, adminstrv. hearing officer, 1989-92. Contbr. to law publs. Bd. dirs. Cathedral Pines Camp, Ketchum, Idaho. Mem. Idaho State Bar Assn., Idaho Pharm. Assn., Idaho Trial Lawyers Assn., Boise Bar Assn., Capital Pharm. Assn., Am. Pharm. Assn., Idaho Soc. Hosp. Pharmacists (bd. dirs.), Am. Soc. Pharmacy Law, Flying Doctors Am. (Atlanta) (bd. dirs.). Home: 11901 W Mesquite Dr Boise ID 83713-0813 Office: 1471 Shoreline Dr Ste 100 Boise ID 83702

HOAGLUND, LEORA MAE, emergency nurse, radiology nurse; b. Cadillac, Mich., June 13, 1950; d. Merle and Betty Mae (Hall) Fewless; m. Elmo V. Hoaglund, May 17, 1969; children: Shawanee, Cherokee, Cheyenna, Joshua. ADN, Ferris State U., 1986; cert. EMT-S, Muskegon Community Coll., 1983; BSN, Ferris State U., 1991. RN, Mich.; CEN; cert. EMT specialist, ACLS, APLS, CPR instr. Nurses aide Lakeview Manor Nursing Home, Cadillac, 1977-78; respiratory therapist Reed City (Mich.) Hosp., 1983-86, float nurse, 1986-87; staff nurse ICU-SCU Mercy Hosp., 1987-88, staff nurse emergency room, 1988—, profl. practice com. mem., 1991-96, radiology nurse, 1997—; home health nurse In Home Help, Big Rapids, Mich., 1988—, Amicare, 1994; instr. CPR, 1990—. Vol. EMT-S, Osceola County Emergency Med. Svc., Reed City, 1982—; leader 4-H, Osceola County, 1980-88; vol. fire and rescue person Tustin (Mich.) Area Fire Dept., 1980—, sec., 1986-92; 1st lt. vol. fire and rescue svc., 1992-94, 2d capt., 1994—.

HOANG, DUC VAN, theoretical pathologist, educator; b. Hanoi, Vietnam, Feb. 17, 1926; came to U.S. 1975, naturalized 1981; s. Duoc Van and Nguyen Thi (Tham) H.; m. Mau-Ngo Thi Vu, 7 children. M.D., Hanoi U. Sch. Medicine, Vietnam, 1952; DSc, Open Internat. U., Sri Lanka, 1989. Dean Sch. Medicine Army of the Republic of Vietnam, Saigon, 1959-63; dean Minh-Duc U. Sch. Medicine, Saigon, 1970-71; clin. prof. theoretical pathology U. So. Calif. Sch. Medicine, L.A., 1978—; adj. prof. Emperor's Coll. Traditional Oriental Medicine, Santa Monica, Calif., 1988-91; initiator of attitudinal immunology. Author: Towards an Integrated Humanization of Medicine, 1957; The Man Who Weights the Soul, 1959; Eastern Medicine, A New Direction?, 1970; also short stories; author introdn. to work of Marie Noël, Vietnamese transl. of La Rose Rouge; translator: Pestis, introduction to the work of Albert Camus, Vietnamese translation of La Peste; editor: The East (co-founder); jour. Les Cahiers de l'Asie du Sud-Est. Founder, past pres. Movement for Fedn. Countries S.E. Asia; co-founder, past v.p. Movement for Restoration Cultures and Religions of Orient; active Vo-Vi Meditation Assn. Am.; mem. The Noetic Inst., 1988—, Internat. Found. for Homeopathy, 1987; founder, pres. Intercontinental Found. for Electro-Magnetic Resonance Rsch., 1989—; coord. Unity and Diversity World Health Coun., 1992—. Named hon. dean The Open Internat. U. of Complementary Medicines, Sri Lanka, 1989; Unity-and-Diversity World Coun. fellow, 1990—. Mem. AAUP, Assn. Clin. Scientists, Am. Com. for Integration Eastern and Western Medicine (founder), Assn. Unitive Medicine (founder, pres.), U. So. Calif. Faculty Member Club (L.A.). Republican. Roman Catholic. Home: 3630 Barry Ave Los Angeles CA 90066-3202

HOANG, HUNG MANH, information systems analyst, consultant; b. Hanoi, Vietnam, July 6, 1954; came to U.S., 1975; s. Frank Dinhue and Dianne (Nguyen) H.; m. Candice Kim Truong, Apr. 6, 1986; 1 child, Judy Anh. BSME, Tex. A&M U., 1982; postgrad., Sch. Engring. and Logistics, 1987; MS in Software Engring., Monmouth Coll., 1988. Mech./electronics engr. Dept. Army, Texarkana, Tex., 1984-88, Ft. Monmouth, N.J., 1984-88; programmer/analyst Computer Scis. Corp., Houston, 1988-89; engr. specialist McDonnell Douglas Space Systems Co., Houston, 1989-91; info. sys. analyst Texaco Inc., Houston, 1991-95; consulting database adminstr. Brown and Root Inc., Houston, 1995-96; software engr. Landmark Graphics Corp., Houston, 1996—. Sec. gen. Phat Quang Temple, South Houston, 1984; com. mem. Vietnamese-Am. Space Tech. Assn., Houston, 1991; pres. Vietnamese-Am. Student Assn., Tex. A&M U., College Station, 1981-83, spring 1983. Mem. IEEE, Assn. Computing Machinery, Phi Theta Kappa. Home: 8210 Creek Glen Dr Sugar Land TX 77478-4747 Office: Landmark Graphics Corp 15150 Memorial Dr Houston TX 77079-4304

HOANG, LOC BAO, electrical engineer; b. Saigon, Vietnam, Feb. 26, 1964; came to U.S., 1980; s. Chau Van Hoang and Quy Thi Bui; m. Tracy Phuong-Nga Doan, Dec. 7, 1990; children: Kimberly Bao, Christopher Dang-Khoa. BSEE, U. Calif., Berkeley, 1988; MSEE, San Jose State U., 1993. Design engr. Xicor, Inc., Milpitas, Calif., 1989-90; sr. design engr. Nat. Semiconductor Corp., Santa Clara, Calif., 1991-93, Silicon Storage Tech., Inc., Sunnyvale, Calif., 1993-94; design mgr. Winbond Memory Lab., San Jose, Calif., 1994-97; dir. design Winbond Electronics Corp. Amer., San Jose, Calif., 1997—; presenter Internat. Symposium on VLSI Tech., 1993. Mem. IEEE. Achievements include patent for Row Decoder and Driver with Switched-Bias Bulk Regions; semiconductor mem. device with dataline undershoot detection and reduced read access time, electrically byte selectable and byte alterable mem. arrays, flash cell having self-timed progamming and other patents; patent pending for notable findings of methods and design techniques to improve performance and/or reliability of non-volatile semiconductor memories. Avocations: music, movies, swimming, table tennis. Office: Winbond Electronics Corp Am 2727 N 1st St San Jose CA 95134-2029

HOAR, FREDERICK M., public relations executive. With Miller/Shandwick, 1989—; pres. Miller/Shandwick West, L.A., 1992-98; chmn. Miller/Shandwick Technologies, Boston, 1998—. Office: Miller/Shandwick Technologies 4 Copley Pl Ste 605 Boston MA 02116*

HOAR, SUSAN REMILLARD, library media specialist; b. Woonsocket, R.I., Aug. 9, 1949; d. Lionel Jeremie and Germaine Dorothy (Benjamin) Remillard; m. Timothy J. Hoar, Nov. 17, 1973; children: Catherine Merena, Jessica L., T. Matthew. BS, Fitchburg State U., 1971; postgrad., Bridgewater (Mass.) State U., 1994—. Cert. tchr. English, Mass. Tchr. English Bellingham (Mass.) Meml. H.S., 1971-78; tchr. English Blackstone Valley Reg. Vocat. Tech. H.S., Upton, Mass., 1983-94, libr. media specialist, 1994—, gen. adv. bd., 1994—, sch. coun., 1995—. Named Tchr. of the Yr., Millbury Am. Legion, 1989. Mem. ALA, ASCD, Am. Assn. Sch. Librs., Nat. Tchrs. Assn., Blackstone Valley Tech. Tchrs. Assn. (scholarship com. 1983-97, v.p. 1993-97, pres. 1997—), Mass. Computer Using Educators, Mass. Sch. Libr. Media Assn., Mass. Tchrs. Assn. Avocations: acting, directing. Office: Blackstone Valley Reg Vocat Tech High Sch 65 Pleasant St Upton MA 01568-1431

HOAR, WILLIAM PATRICK, editor, author; b. Haverhill, Mass., Nov. 7, 1945; s. John Patrick and Helen Rose (Powers) H.; m. Louisa Miller, July 29, 1978; children: Meredith Miller Hoar, Emily Erin Hoar. AB, Bowdoin Coll., 1967. Contbg. editor Am. Opinion, Belmont, Mass., 1971-85; assoc. editor The Rev. of the News, Belmont, 1971-85; exec. editor, v.p. Conservative Digest, Washington, 1985-89, World Networks, 1989-91; Washington corr. Southern Africa Spl. Dispatch, 1990-91, Newslink Africa, 1990-91; exec. dir. Second Decade Found., 1991—; Washington editor, sr. v.p. World News Digest, Silver Spring, Md., 1991-94; consulting editor Conservative Review, 1993-97; Washington editor New American, 1992—; mng. editor CD Publs., Silver Spring, 1996—. Author: Architects of Conspiracy: An Intriguing History, 1984 (updated Japanese edit. 1991), Our Corrupt Congress, 1992, Handouts and Pickpockets, 1996: editor various jours. including Regions in Transition, 1990, Counter-Terrorism, 1997; contbr. articles to profl. jours. Mem. Bel Pre Civic Assn., Silver Spring, Md., 1985—. Staff sgt. U.S. Army, 1968-70. Decorated Army Commendation medal. Mem. White House Corres. Assn., Congl. Periodical Press Gallery, Soc. Profl. Journalists, Am. Legion, Nat. Press Club, Internat. Policy Forum (bd. govs.), Chi Psi. Home: 2916 Bluff Point Ln Silver Spring MD 20906-3043 Office: CD Pubs 8204 Fenton St Silver Spring MD 20910-4509

HOAR, WILLIAM STEWART, zoologist, educator; b. Moncton, N.B., Can., Aug. 31, 1913; s. George W. and Nina (Steeves) H.; m. Margaret MacKenzie, Aug. 13, 1941; children: Stewart George, David Innes, Kenzie Margaret, Melanie Frances. B.A. hon., U. N.B., 1934, D.Sc. (hon.), 1965; M.A., U. Western Ont., 1936, D.Sc. (hon.), 1978; Ph.D., Boston U., 1939; D.Sc. (hon.), Meml. U. Nfld., 1967, St. Francis Xavier U., 1976; LL.D. (hon.), Simon Fraser U., 1980, Toronto U., 1981, Mt. Allison U., 1998. Asst. prof. biology U. N.B., 1939-42, prof. zoology, 1943-45; research assoc. U. Toronto, 1942-43; prof. zoology and fisheries U. B.C., Vancouver, 1945-64; head dept. zoology U. B.C., 1964-71, prof., 1971-79, prof. emeritus, 1979—; research scientist Fisheries Research Bd. Can., 1935-57. Author: General and Conparative Physiology, 3d edit., 1983; sr. editor 14 vol. treatise on fish physiology; contbr. articles to profl. jours. Decorated Order of Can.; recipient Flavelle medal, 1965, Fry medal, 1974, Shinkishi Hatai medal Pacific Sci. Assn., 1991. Fellow Royal Soc. Can., Canadian, U.S. socs. zoology and physiology. Home: 3561 W 27th Ave, Vancouver, BC Canada V6S 1P9

HOARD, HEIDI MARIE, lawyer; b. Mt Clemons, Mich., Feb. 8, 1951; d. Duane Jay and Elizabeth Hoard; m. John B. Lunseth II, Jan. 11, 1980; children: John B. III, Steven J. BA, Macalester Coll., 1972; JD cum laude, U. Minn., 1976. Bar: Minn. 1976, U.S. Dist. Ct. Minn. 1976. Assoc. Faegre & Benson, Mpls., 1976-83, ptnr., 1984-93; sr. legal counsel Medtronic, Inc., 1993-95; v.p., gen. counsel, corp. sec. The Musicland Group, Minnetonka, 1995—; mem. State Bd. Women in the Legal Profession Task Force, State Bd. Legal Cert., 1986-88, pres. Tel-Law, Bar Assn. Com., Mpls., 1978-80; bd. dirs. Fund for Legal Aid Soc. Mem. Minn. Region G, Law Enforcement Assistance Assn. Com., 1971-72; vol. aide U.S. Senate Nursing Home Investigation and Hearing, Mpls., 1971-72; student dir. Legal Aid Clinic, U. Minn., Mpls., 1975-76. Mem. Am. Soc. Corp. Secs. (bd. dirs. Minn. sect.), Am. Corp. Counsel Assn., Minn. Bar Assn., Phi Beta Kappa. Democrat. Office: Musicland Group 10400 Yellow Circle Dr Minnetonka Mills MN 55343*

HOARD, LEROY, professional football player; b. New Orleans, May 15, 1968. Student, U. Mich. Running back Cleve. Browns, Minnesota Vikings, 1996—. Named to NFL Pro Bowl Team, 1994. Office: Minnesota Vikings 9520 Viking Dr Eden Prairie MN 55344*

HOART, GLADYS GALLAGHER, English language educator; b. N.Y.C., June 27, 1914; d. Martin and Edna (Parker) Gallagher; m. Francis Xavier Hoart, June 25, 1939; children: Robert, Helen, Andrew. AB cum laude, NYU, 1967, MA, 1970; MA in Liberal Studies, New Sch. for Social Rsch., 1975. Cert. mem. N.Y. Stock Exchange. Adj. prof. English Nassau C.C., Garden City, N.Y., 1970—; dir. Career Seminars for Teenage Girls, Flushing, N.Y., 1963-64; tutor Black Studies Program, Manhasset, N.Y., 1968-69. Pres., co-founder Broadway Homeowners' Assn., Flushing, N.Y., 1964-65; committeewoman Dem. Party, Manhasset, N.Y., 1970; organizer Parkchester (N.Y.) Golden Age Club, 1953; trustee Dalcroze Sch. of Music, 1998—. Mem. AAUW, Alliance Floor Brokers, Musicians Club (bd. dirs. 1993—). Roman Catholic. Avocations: architecture, equitation, gardening, music.

HOBAN, GEORGE SAVRE, lawyer; b. Faribault, Minn., Nov. 20, 1914; s. George W. and Margaret (Savre) H.; m. June Tullar, Feb. 4, 1939; children: William J., Robert G. B.A., Ripon Coll., 1936; J.D., Northwestern U., 1938. Bar: Ill. 1938. Practiced in Chgo., 1938-80; partner firm Hinshaw, Culbertson, Moelmann, Hoban & Fuller, 1949-80; ret., 1980. Trustee Ripon Coll., 1965-80, hon. trustee, 1981—; trustee N.W. Community Hosp., Arlington Heights, Ill., 1963-70; trustee Ravenswood Hosp. Med. Center, 1970-80, hon. trustee, 1981—. Served to capt. AUS, 1942-46. Mem. Am., Ill., Chgo. bar assns., Am. Acad. Orthopaedic Surgeons (hon.), Ill. C. of C. (chmn. legis. com. 1963-64), Phi Delta Phi. Club: Kingsway Country. Home: 1750 Jamaica Way Apt 215 Punta Gorda FL 33950-5162 Office: 222 N La Salle St Chicago IL 60601-1003

HOBAN, LILLIAN, author, illustrator; b. Phila., May 18; d. Jules and Fanny (Godwin) Aberman; children: Phoebe, Abrom, Esmé, Julia. Student, Phila. Mus. Sch., Hanya Holm Sch. Dance, N.Y.C., Martha Graham Sch. Dance. Author, illustrator: (children's books) I Can Read, Arthur Series, 1972—; illustrator: (children's books) Frances Series, 1964— (Notable Book award), First Grade Series, 1967—, Jim Books, Charlie the Tramp (Christopher award). Mem. PEN, Authors Guild, Soc. Children's Book Writers. Democrat. *

HOBART, BILLIE, education educator, consultant; b. Pitts., Apr. 19, 1935; d. Harold James Billingsley and Rose Stephanie (Sladack) Green; m. W.C.H. Hobart, July 20, 1957 (div. 1967); 1 child, Rawson W. BA in English, U. Calif., Berkeley, 1967, EdD, 1992; MA in Psychology, Sonoma State U., 1972. Cert. tchr., Calif. Asst. prof. Coll. Marin, Kentfield, Calif., 1969-78; freelance cons., writer, 1969—; asst. prof. Contra Costa Coll., San Pablo, Calif., 1986—. Author: (cookbook) Natural Sweet Tooth, 1974, (non-fiction) Expansion, 1972, Purposeful Self: Coherent Self, 1979, (non-fiction) Talking to Dead People, 1996, (biographee) Captain Granville Perry Swift, California Pioneer and Sonoma Bear, 1999; contbr. articles to profl. jours. Served with WAC, 1953-55. Mem. No. Calif. Coll. Reading Tchrs. Assn. (pres. 1996-98), Mensa, Commonwealth Club San Francisco, Phi Delta Kappa. E-mail: www.unseenworlds.com. Home and Office: PO Box 1542 Sonoma CA 95476-1542

HOBART, THOMAS YALE, JR., union president; b. Buffalo, Dec. 26, 1936; s. Thomas Yale and Anne Rita (Mulloy) H.; m. Dorothy A., Aug. 10, 1963; children: Elizabeth Anne Rottner, Catherine Marie, Thomas Yale III. BS in Edn., SUNY, Buffalo, 1960; MS in Edn., Canisius Coll., Buffalo, 1964. Cert. tchr., N.Y. Tchr. Buffalo Bd. Edn., guidance counselor; pres. N.Y. State United Tchrs., Albany; v.p. Am. Fedn. Tchrs., Washington, N.Y. State AFL-CIO, Albany; pres. Buffalo Tchrs. Fedn., 1969; mem. Tchr. Edn. and Cert. Bd; vice chmn. N.Y. State Employment Tng. Coun., 1979; mem. Job Tng. and Partnership Coun., 1983, vice chairperson coun., 1985; co-chair Task Force on Career Pathways, 1991; v.p. Tchr. Edn. Conf. Bd., Commrs. Task Force on Edn. and Cert., 1975; chair Pub. Employee Benefit Fund, 1975-91; mem. Gov.'s Task Force on Taylor Law, 1974, Gov.'s Task Force on Financing of Elem., Sec. and Continuing Edn., 1975; mem. N.Y. State Adv. Coun. on Vocat. Edn., 1977, v.p., 1982; mem. Regents and Gov.'s Task Force on Equity and Excellence in Edn., 1978; mem. State Plan Com. for Vocat. Edn., 1979; mem. adv. bd. Northeast Lab.; founder, co-chair N.Y. State Labor-Religion Conf.; co-chair Task Force on Tchg. Profession; commr. N.Y. State Gov.'s Conf. on Libr. and Info. Svcs., 1990, Child Labor Law Edn. Fund; del. World Confedn. Orgns. Tchg. Profession, Internat. Fedn. Free Tchr. Unions, state and nat. AFL-CIO, Jewish Labor Coun., Coun. Profl. Employees, AFL-CIO, Pub. Employment Dept. AFL-CIO, Edn. Internat.; mem. adv. coun. Cornell Sch. Labor/Mgmt. Rels., St. Joseph's Guild, Am. Labor Coun. Chair, bd. dirs. United Way N.Y., Albany; charter mem. Martin Luther King Commn.; bd. dirs. Welfare Rsch. Inst.; mem. adv. bd. N.Y. State Occupational Disease Diagnostic Ctr. Network Study; mem. N.Y. State Svc. Coun., ARC. Staff sgt. U.S. Army, 1960-68. Mem. NEA (bd. dirs.), Am. Fedn. Tchrs. (v.p. 1974—), Ft. Orange Club, Shaker Ridge Country Club, Transit Valley Country Club. Democrat. Roman Catholic. Home: 157 Bassett Rd Amherst NY 14221-2641 Office: NY State United Tchrs 159 Wolf Rd # Albany NY 12205-1106

HOBBIE, RUSSELL KLYVER, physics educator; b. Albany, N.Y., Nov. 3, 1934; s. John Remington and Eulin Pomeroy (Klyver) H.; m. Cynthia Ann Borcherding, Dec. 28, 1957; children: Lynn Katherine, Erik Klyver, Sarah Elizabeth, Ann Stacey. B.S. in Physics, Mass. Inst. Tech., 1956; A.M., Harvard U., Ph.D., 1960. Research asso. U. Minn., 1960-62, mem. faculty, 1962—, prof. physics, 1972-98, prof. physics emeritus, 1998—, assoc. dean, 1984-95, dir. Space Sci. Ctr., 1978-84. Author: Intermediate Physics for Medicine and Biology, 1978, 3d edit. 1997. Mem. Am. Assn. Physics Tchrs. (exec. bd. 1980-83), Am. Phys. Soc., Am. Assn. Physicists in Medicine, AAAS., IEEE. Home: 2151 Folwell Ave Saint Paul MN 55108-1306

HOBBINS, ROBERT LEO, lawyer; b. Des Moines, June 5, 1948; s. Leo Michael and Margaret Ellen Hobbins; m. Carmela Theresa Tursi, Dec. 27, 1974; children: Brian, Patrick, Edward. BA magna cum laude, Creighton U., 1970; JD, NYU, 1973. Bar: Minn. 1973. Assoc. Dorsey & Whitney, Mpls., 1973-78, ptnr., 1979—; clin. faculty Law Sch. Hamline U., 1971-72. Root-Tilden scholar. Mem. ABA (labor sect., EEO law com.), Minn. State Bar Assn., Hennepin County Bar Assn., Creighton U. Alumni Assn. (v.p. 1994). Office: Dorsey & Whitney 220 S 6th St Ste 2200 Minneapolis MN 55402-1498

HOBBINS, THOMAS EBEN, physician; b. N.Y.C., Dec. 7, 1939; s. Richard Redfield and Nancy (Minahan) H.; m. Jeannette Murkland, Aug. 31, 1968; children: Wendy Cromwell, Thomas Eben Jr. BA, U. Pa., Phila., 1961; MD, Hahnemann Med. Coll., Phila., 1965. Diplomate Am. Bd. Internal Medicine, Am. Bd. Sleep Medicine. Intern Hosp. U. Pa., Phila., 1965-66; staff assoc. Lab Viral Immunology, Divsn. Biologics Stds. NIH, Bethesda, Md., 1966-69; resident physician internal medicine U. Wash., Seattle, 1969-71; pulmonary med. fellow Hosp. U. Pa., Phila., 1971-72; asst. prof., assoc. prof. medicine Univs. Md. Hosp., Balt., 1972-85; med. dir. Md. Sleep Disorders Ctr., Balt., 1985—; chair environ. com. Med. and Chirurgical Faculty Md., 1997-98. Bd. mem. Friends Sch. Balt., 1981-88; activist Cardin for Congress, Md. 3rd Congl. Dist., 1988—; mem. Gov.'s Air Quality Task Force, Balt., 1989-90; mem. diesel exhaust adv. panel Md. Dept. Environ., Balt., 1991-95. Lt. col. USPHS, 1966-69. Recipient Disting. Svc. awards Am. Lung Assn. Md., Balt., 1995, Cmty. Svc. award Med. and Chirurgical Faculty Md., Balt., 1997. Fellow ACP; mem. Physicians for Social Responsibility (nat. pres. 1999), Am. Acad. Sleep Medicine (bd. dirs. 1999—), Balt. County Med. Assn. (bd. govs. 1995—, disting. svc. award 1996), Md. Thoracic Soc. (pres. 1981-83). Mem. Soc. of Friends. Avocations: in-line skating, backcountry skiing, sailing. Office: Md Sleep Disorders Ctr 6701 N Charles St GBMC Baltimore MD 21204

HOBBS, AVANEDA DORENZA, publishing company executive, minister, singer; b. Charlottesville, Va., July 23, 1955; d. Frederick Douglass and Viola Marie H. BS in Sociology, Va. Wesleyan, 1976; MA in Ednl. Adminstrn., Spirit of Truth Inst., Richmond, Va., 1994, EdD in Ednl. Adminstrn., 1994; PhD in Comm. and Counselling, Spirit of Truth Inst., 1995. Ordained minister, Charismatic Ch., 1990. Lead singer Gospel Equattes, Washington, 1971; vocalist Mighty Clouds of Joy, 1972, various orgns., 1975—; agt. Rev. Demond Wilson., Washington, 1996—; CEO, World Resource Outreach Co., Forestville, Md., 1991—; bd. dirs. Solid Rock Records, In The Beginning Ministries, Inc., CAPublishing; i nat. dir. pub. rels. Gospelrama conv., 1985-88; internat. comm. and ednl. cons. Idahosa World Outreach, Nigeria, 1990-93; mem. Worldwide Accreditation Commn. of Christian Ednl. Instns. vocalist: popular gospel singer since early 1970's, concert, TV and radio appearances; author: Guide to Black Religious and Supporting Orgns., 1990. Participant in Congl. and White House Briefings as influential religious leader in D.C., 1992. Recipient Outstanding Svc. award Christian Music Conf., 1980, D.C. Mayoral commendation, 1990. Mem. NAFE, Broadcast Music, Inc. (assoc.), Christian Mgmt. Assn., Black Nat. Religious Broadcasters, Christian Mgmt. Assn., Worldwide Accreditation Commn. of Restoration House of Am., Christian Ednl. Instns., Prince Georges County Educators Assn., Prince Georges County Pub. Rels. Assn. Democrat. Avocations: swimming, travel, tennis, writing, entertaining.

HOBBS, C. FREDRIC, artist, filmmaker, author; b. Phila., Dec. 30, 1931; s. Robert Frederic and Gertrude (Madison) H.; children: Leslie Newbold, Mary Alison. Grad., Menlo Sch.; BA, Cornell U., 1953; grad., Academia de San Fernando de Belles Artes, Madrid, 1955-56. Pres. Fredric Hobbs Films, Inc., 1975; chmn., chief exec. officer Virginia City (Nev.) Restoration Corp., 1978-85. Writer, dir., producer 4 feature films, (TV series) Taiwan, The Other China, 1988-90, (TV/multimedia series) Fastfuture, 1998—; author: The Richest Place on Earth, 1978, Eat Your House: Art Eco Guide to Self Sufficiency, 1980, The Spirit of the Monterey Coast, 1990, and others; also articles.; one-man shows include, Calif. Palace Legion of Honor, San Francisco, 1958, Mus. Sci. and Industry, Los Angeles, 1976, San Francisco Mus. Modern Art, 1980-81, Sierra Nevada Mus. Art, 1984; maj. mus. exhbns. include Concurso Internat. Palacio de la Virreina, Barcelona, Spain (17 countries), Art USA, Madison Sq. Garden, N.Y., Pa. Acad. Fine Arts., Phila, Internat. Drawing Competition II, Nat. Fine Arts Collection, Smithsonian Inst., Washington, Drawings USA 63" II Biennial, St. Paul Art Ctr., Minn., Ann. Sculpture-Painting Exhbns., SFAI, San Francisco Mus. Art, III and V Invitationals, Finch Coll. Mus. Art., N.Y.C., Gallery Modern Art., N.Y.C., Nat. Gallery Art, Washington, Reed Coll., Portland, Oreg., U. Pacific, Stockton, Calif., San Diego Mus. Art., Mills Coll., Oakland, Calif., Touring Am. Mus., Ebert Gallery, 1994, 95, 97, others; permanent collections include Mus. Modern Art, N.Y.C., Met. Mus. Art, N.Y.C., Spencer Meml. Ch., N.Y.C., Calif. Palace Legion of Honor, Finch Coll. Mus. Art, St. Paul Art Gallery, San Francisco Mus. Modern Art, Fine Arts Mus. San Francisco, Sierra Nevada Mus. Art, Reno, Stanford (Calif.) U. Mus. Art., San Francisco State Coll., U. Calif. Media Ctr., San Jose (Calif.) Mus. Art., Oakland (Calif.) Mus. Art., Johnson Mus., Cornell U., others; galleries include Twentieth Century West Galleries, N.Y.C., Braunstein Gallery, San Francisco, Heritage Gallery, L.A.; represented by Ebert Gallery, San Francisco. 1st lt. USAF, 1953-55. Mem. Film Arts Found. Democrat. Episcopalian. Address: The Madison Hobbs Studio 1000 Noriega St San Francisco CA 94122-4514 *To create a work of art is an act of faith in the human spirit and in God. Art must always transcend materialist values and monuments to success. It is often the work of fools and children yet it is the ultimate reality.*

HOBBS, CATHERINE LYNN, English language and literature educator; b. Guymon, Okla., Feb. 13, 1951; d. Dan Stewart and Betty Jean (Ray) H. m. Cecil L. Peaden, Mar. 23, 1975 (div. Feb. 15, 1994). BA in Journalism, U. Okla., 1973; MA in Modern Letters, U. Tulsa, 1983; PhD in English, Purdue U., 1989. Instr. Rogers State Coll., Tulsa, Okla., 1983-84; vis. lectr. comms. U. Tulsa, 1984-85; teaching asst. English dept. Purdue U., West Lafayette, Ind., 1985-89; asst. prof. English Ill. State U., Normal, 1989-92; asst. prof. English dept. U. Okla., Norman, 1992-95, assoc. prof., 1995—; mem. bd. H-Rhetor History of Rhetoric discussion group, 1993—. Editor: Nineteenth-Century Women Learn to Write, 1995; mem. editl. bd. Women in Science; contbr. articles to profl. jours. NEH fellow, 1990, 93. Mem. AAUW, MLA, Am. Soc. Eighteenth Century Studies, Internat. Soc. History of Rhetoric, Nat. Coun. Tchrs. of English, Rhetoric Soc. Am., Phi Kappa Phi. Democrat. Office: U Okla English Dept Norman OK 73019

HOBBS, DAVID ELLIS, mechanical engineer. BA in Engring. Sci., Dartmouth Coll., 1963; BSME, Case Inst. Tech., 1964; MSME, Rensselaer Poly. Inst., 1967, PhD in Mech. Engring., 1983. With turbine component design group Pratt & Whitney, East Hartford, Conn., 1964-67, with turbine analysis and tech. devel. group, 1967-77, with compressor analysis and tech. devel. group, 1977-94; gas turbine design sys. cons. FTS Cons., Inc., East Hartford, Conn., 1995—, TurboVision Cons. Group, Miami, Fla., 1995—. Contbr. articles to profl. jours. Recipient Horner citation United Technologies Corp., 1993. Fellow AIAA (assoc.); mem. ASME (gas turbine turbomachinery com., axial compressor panel, Gas Turbine award 1988). Home: 20 Bayberry Trl South Windsor CT 06074-3809

HOBBS, GREGORY JAMES, JR., state supreme court justice; b. Gainesville, Fla., Dec. 15, 1944; s. Gregory J. Hobbs and Mary Ann (Rhodes) Frakes; m. Barbara Louise Hay, June 17, 1967; children: Daniel Gregory, Emily Mary Hobbs Wright. BA, U. Notre Dame, 1966; JD, U. Calif., Berkeley, 1971. Bar: Colo. 1971, Calif. 1972. Law clk. to Judge William E. Doyle 10th U.S. Cir. Ct. Appeals, Denver, 1971-72; assoc. Cooper, White & Cooper, San Francisco, 1972-73; enforcement atty. U.S. EPA, Denver, 1973-75; asst. atty. gen. State of Colo. Atty. Gen.'s Office, Denver, 1975-79; ptnr. Davis, Graham & Stubbs, Denver, 1979-92; shareholder Hobbs, Trout & Raley, P.C., Denver, 1992-96; justice Colo. Supreme Ct., Denver, 1996—; counsel No. Colo. Water Conservancy, Loveland, Colo., 1979-96. Contbr. articles to profl. jours. vol. Peace Corps-S.Am., Colombia, 1967-68; vice chair Colo. Air Quality Control Com., Denver, 1982-87; mem. ranch com. Philmont Scout Ranch, Boy Scouts Am., Cimarron, N.Mex., 1988-98; co-chair Eating Disorder Family Support Group, Denver, 1992—. Recipient award of merit Denver Area Coun. Boy Scouts, 1993, Pres. award Nat. Water Resources Assn., Washington, 1995. Fellow Am. Bar Found.; mem. ABA, Colo. Bar Assn., Denver Bar Assn. Avocations: backpacking, fishing, writing poetry. Office: Colo Supreme Ct 2 E 14th Ave Denver CO 80203-2115

HOBBS, GUY STEPHEN, financial executive; b. Lynwood, Calif., Feb. 23, 1955; s. Franklin Dean and Bette Jane (Little) H.; m. Laura Elena Lopez, Jan. 6, 1984; 1 child, Mariah Amanda. BA, U. Calif., Santa Barbara, 1976; MBA, U. Nev., 1978. Sr. rsch. assoc. Ctr. for Bus. and Econ. Rsch., Las Vegas, Nev., 1978-80; pvt. practice mgmt. cons. Las Vegas, 1979-82; mgmt. analyst Clark County, Las Vegas, 1980-81, sr. mgmt. analyst, 1981-82, dir. budget and fin. planning, 1982-84, comptroller, dir. fin., chief fin. officer, 1984-96; pres. Hobbs, Ong & Assocs., Inc., 1996—; lectr. in mgmt. Coll. Bus. and Econs., U. Nev., Las Vegas, 1977-88; pres. Pacific Blue Ent., 1991—; mem. Interim Legis. Com. Infrastructure Fin., 1993-94; mem. Interim Legis. Com. Studying Laws Relating to the Distbn. of Taxes in Nev., 1995-96, 97—. Author publs. in field. Mem. exec. bd. Miss Nevada USA and Miss NEVADA Teen USA, 1996—; instr. Las Vegas Baseball Acad., 1998—. Mem. Am. Soc. Pub. Adminstrn. (Pub. Adminstr. of Yr. 1987), Govt. Fin. Officers Assn. (Fin. Reporting Achievement award 1984-95, Disting. Budget Presentation, award 1993-96), Nev. Taxpayers Assn. Republican. Avocations: sports, photography, travel. Office: Hobbs Ong & Assocs Inc 3900 Paradise Rd Ste 152 Las Vegas NV 89109-0928

HOBBS, HORTON HOLCOMBE, III, biology educator; b. Gainesville, Fla., Dec. 17, 1944; s. Horton Holcombe Jr. and Georgia Cates (Blount) H.; m. Susan Claire Krantz, Oct. 12, 1967; children: Heather H. Killion, Horton Holcombe IV. BA, U. Richmond, 1967; MS, Miss. State U., 1969; PhD, Ind. U., 1973. Instr. Christopher Newport Coll., Newport News, Va., 1973-75; asst. prof. George Mason U., Fairfax, Va., 1975-76; prof. biology Wittenberg U., Springfield, Ohio, 1976—; com. mem. Nongame Wildlife Tech. Adv. Com., Columbus, Ohio, 1989-95; trustee Island Cave Rsch. Ctr., 1987—. Author: The Crayfishes and Shrimp of Wisconsin, 1988; life scis. editor: Nat. Speleological Soc. Bull., Huntsville, Ala., 1985-96; contbr. 150 articles to profl. jours. Campaign co-chair County Park Dist., Springfield, 1980. Fellow Nat. Speleological Soc. (bd. govs. 1985-88), The Explorers Club, Ohio Acad. Sci.; mem. Crustacean Soc. (coun. mem. 1980-83), Biol. Soc. Wash. (exec. coun. 1976-77), Cave Conservancy of the Virginias (bd. dirs. 1988—). Achievements include development of Ohio's Cave Protection Law; participation in International Speleological Expeditions to Costa Rica. Office: Wittenberg U Dept Biol Springfield OH 45501

HOBBS, J. TIMOTHY, SR., lawyer; b. Yakima, Wash., Sept. 23, 1941; s. Leonard M. and Virginia (Snider) H.; m. Barbara J. Hatfield, June 14, 1964; children: Amy Elizabeth, J. Timothy Jr. BA in Polit. Sci., U. Wash., 1964; JD, Am. U., 1968. Bar: D.C. 1969, U.S. Ct. Supreme Ct. 1973, U.S. Ct. Appeals Fed. Crct. 1982, U.S. Ct. Appeals (11th cir.) 1986, U.S. Ct. Appeals (5th cir.) 1989, U.S. Ct. Appeals (6th cir.) 1996. Assoc. Mason Fenwick & Lawrence, Washington, 1969-76, ptnr., 1977-82, sr. ptnr., 1982-91; ptnr., head intellectual property dept. Dykema Gossett, 1991—. Author chpt. on copyright law, West's Federal Practice Manual, 1983. Pres. Arlington Outdoor Edn. Assn., 1990-92. Mem. D.C. Bar (chmn. trademark com. 1982-84), U.S. Trademark Assn. Forums (speaker 1988), Washington Golf and Country Club. Home: 6135 Lee Hwy Arlington VA 22205-2134 Office: Dykema Gossett Franklin Square Ste 300 West 1300 I St NW Washington DC 20005

HOBBS, JAMES BEVERLY, business administration educator, writer; b. Topeka, Sept. 9, 1930; s. Kenneth Beverly and Ida (Burkholder) H.; m. Peggy Genevieve Whitney, Nov. 2, 1957; children: David Beverly, Nancy Ruth. AB, Harvard U., 1952; MBA, U. Kans., 1957; DBA, Ind. U., 1962. Fin. analyst Hotpoint divsn. GE, Chgo., 1957-60; asst. prof. mgmt. and acctg. Kans. State U., 1962-66, assoc. dean, 1964-66; assoc. prof. mgmt. and acctg. Lehigh U., 1966-70, prof., 1970-79, Frank L. Magee Disting. prof. bus. adminstrn., 1979-91, Frank L. Magee Disting. prof. bus. adminstrn. emeritus, 1991—, chmn. dept. mgmt., fin., mktg. and law, 1970-75, chmn. dept. mgmt., fin. and mktg., 1982-83, dir. MBA program, 1986-89, co-chmn. mgmt. dept., 1989-90, assoc. dean Coll. Bus. and Econ., 1993, assoc. dean Coll. Arts and Scis., 1993-95, chmn. art and architecture dept., 1996, assoc. dean emeritus Coll. Arts & Scis., 1999—; vis. prof. acctg. U. Canterbury, New Zealand, 1976, Mich. Technol. U., 1975; vis. prof. mgmt. U. Edinburgh, Scotland, 1984, Ecole Superieure Commerce de Poitiers, France, 1990, Acad. Ednl. Devel., Bishkek, Kyrghystan, 1999; participant mission to Ulan Bator, Mongolia, UN Devel. Program, 1992; participant missions to Ternopil, Ukraine, Vladivostok, Russia, Bratislava, Slovak Republic and Kishnev, Moldova, Internat. Exec. Svc. Corps, 1993, 95, 97, 98, mission to Skopje, Macedonia, U.S. Energy Assn., 1997; acad. cons. Author: Financial Accounting, 1984, Corp. Staying Power, 1987, Homophones & Homographs, 1999. Served as naval aviation cadet USN, 1952, as regtl. sgt. maj. U.S. Army, 1953-54, Korea. Mem. Dictionary Soc. N.Am., Mensa, Phi Beta Kappa, Phi Kappa Phi, Beta Gamma Sigma, Beta Alpha Psi, Sigma Iota Epsilon, Omicron Delta Epsilon, Omicron Delta Kappa, Delta Mu Delta, Phi Beta Delta. Unitarian. Home: 1915 Black River Rd Bethlehem PA 18015-8920

HOBBS, KAREN FRENCH, development officer; b. Huntsville, Ala., Dec. 5, 1958; d. John Andrew and Maggie (Menes) French; m. Jeff Dale Hobbs, May 19, 1979. BA, Abilene Christian Univ., 1991, MA, 1993. Development officer Abilene Christian Univ., 1994—. Home: 817 Chanticleers Ln Abilene TX 79602-3150 Office: Abilene Christian Univ ACU Box 29130 Abilene TX 79699

HOBBS, LEWIS MANKIN, astronomer; b. Upper Darby, Pa., May 16, 1937; s. Lewis Samuel and Evangeline Elizabeth (Goss) H.; m. Jo Ann Faith Hagele, June 16, 1962; children: John, Michael, Dara. B of Engring. Physics, Cornell U., 1960; MS, U. Wis., 1962, PhD in Physics, 1966. Jr. astronomer Lick Obs., U. Calif., Santa Cruz, 1965-66; faculty U. Chgo., 1966—, prof. astronomy and astrophysics, 1976—; dir. Yerkes Obs. Williams Bay, Wis., 1974-82; mem. Space Telescope Inst. Coun., 1982-87; astronomy com. of bd. trustees Univs. Rsch. Assn., Inc., Washington, 1979-83, chmn., 1979-81; bd. govs. Astrophys. Rsch. Consortium, Inc., Seattle, 1984-91; mem. Users Com. for Hubble Space Telescope, NASA, 1990-94. Contbr. articles to profl. jours. Bd. dirs. Mil. Symphony Assn. of Walworth County, 1972-88. Alfred P. Sloan scholar, 1955-60. Mem. Am. Astron. Soc., Am. Phys. Soc., Internat. Astron. Union, Wis. Acad. Scis. Arts and Letters. Office: U Chgo Yerkes Observatory Williams Bay WI 53191

HOBBS, MARVIN, engineering executive; b. Jasper, Ind., Nov. 30, 1912; s. Charles and Madge (Ott) H.; B.S. in Elec. Engring., Tri-State Coll., Angola, Ind., 1930; postgrad. U. Chgo., 1932; PhD in Elec. Engring. Greenwich U., 1990; m. Bernadine E. Weeks, July 4, 1936 (dec.). Radio receiver engr. U.S. Radio & TV Corp., Zenith Radio Corp., Gen. Motors Corp., 1930-38; aircraft radio designer E.K. Cole Ltd., England, 1935-36; cons. radio & TV engr., Europe, 1938-39; chief engr. Scott Radio Labs., Chgo., 1939-46; cons. engr. RCA, Camden, N.J., 1946-49; v.p. Harvey-Wells Electronics, Southbridge, Mass., 1952-54; asst. to exec. v.p. Gen. Instrument Corp., Newark, N.J., 1958-62; mgr., cons. engr. Design Service Co., N.Y.C., 1963-68; v.p. Gladding Corp., Syracuse, N.Y., 1968-71, cons. corporate devel., 1971-79; mem. adminstrv. group Bell Telephone Labs., Naperville, Ill., 1979-82; chief electronics br. W.P.B., 1942-43, head radio cons. radio & radar divsn., 1943-44; chief electronics divsn. Munitions Bd., 1950-51, adviser for electronics, chmn., 1951-52. Mem. Electronics Prodn. Bd., ODM, Washington, 1951-52; operations analyst Far East Air Force, 1945. Recipient Certificate of Appreciation War Dept., 1945, Certificate of Commendation, Navy Dept., 1947. Registered profl. engr., Ill. Mem. IEEE (life). Author: Basics of Missile Guidance and Space Techniques, 1959, Fundamentals of Rockets, Missiles and Spacecraft, 1962; Modern Communications Switching Systems, 1974, 2d edit., 1981; Modern CB Radio Servicing, 1979; Servicing Home Video Cassette Recorders, 1982; Techniche Moderne Di Riparazione Delle Radio CB, 1982; E.H. Scott—The Dean of DX-A History of Classic Radios, 1985; Video Cameras and Camcorders, 1989; RISC/CISC Development and Test Support, 1992; Servicing Facsimile Machines, 1992, Manual De Raparacion y Servicio De Maquinas De Fax, 1993. Inventor low radiation radio receiver installed on all USN ships during WWII. Home and Office: 9051C Siempre Viva Rd San Diego CA 92173-3604

HOBBS, MICHAEL EDWIN, broadcasting company executive; b. Washington, Nov. 26, 1940; s. Robert Boyd and Barbara Alberta (Davis) H.; m. Ann Reed, Sept. 16, 1989. A.B. cum laude, Dartmouth Coll., 1962; J.D., Harvard U., 1965. Bar: Mass. 1966. Staff counsel, asst. to gen. mgr. Sta. WGBH Ednl. Found., Boston, 1966-67; exec. asst. ednl. TV stas. Nat. Assn. Ednl. Broadcasters, Washington, 1967-70; sec. PBS, Washington, 1970-87, gen. counsel, 1970-71, dir. adminstrn., 1970-73, v.p., 1973-76, sr. v.p., 1976-87, sr. v.p. for policy and planning, 1987-91; sr. fellow Hartford Gunn Inst., Alexandria, Va., 1991—. Alexandria Rep. city com., 1997—, chmn. 1998—. Mem. ABA (intellectual property law sect.), Mass. Bar Assn., Nat. Acad. TV Arts and Scis., George Town Club, Phi Beta Kappa. Home and Office: Hartford Gunn Inst 419 Cameron St Alexandria VA 22314-3221

HOBBS, RAY DAVID, editor; b. Pensacola, Fla., July 13, 1951; s. Richard Alton and Louise Adell (Williams) H.; m. Pamela A. Aiello, Dec. 17, 1977; children: Ray David Jr., Brian Joseph. BA in English Lit., Ill. State U., 1975. Reporter Pine Bluff (Ark.) Comml., 1977-79; bur. chief Ark. Dem., Pine Bluff, 1979-81; asst. city editor Ark. Dem., Little Rock, 1981-83, night city editor, 1983-85, city editor, 1985-93; exec. city editor Ark. Dem.-Gazette, Little Rock, 1993-96; asst. mng. editor/news Ark. Dem.-Gazette, 1996-98, dep. mng. editor, 1998—. Contbg. editor: World Book Ency., 1988-92. Recipient Disting. Svc. award Wehco Media Inc., 1994, Community Svc. award Ark. Children's Dreams Fedn., 1986. Avocations: fly fishing, men's amateur soccer league, travel. Office: Ark Democrat-Gazette Capitol Ave and Scott St Little Rock AR 72201

HOBBS, ROY JERRY, military career officer, health services administrator; b. Whiteville, N.C., July 24, 1950; s. Roy Jacob Hobbs and Tracy Jane (Register) Shupla; m. Diane Hobbs; children: Michael, Rebecca, Stephanie, Sarah. BA in History and Edn., U. N.C., 1974; MA in Personnel Mgmt., Ctrl. Mich. U., 1977, MA in Health Care Adminstrn., 1981; AAS, C.C. of Air Force, 1978. Cert. emergency mgr. Internat. Assn. Emergency Mgrs. Commd. 2d lt. USAF, advanced through grades to col., 1998; air traffic contr. Seymour Johnson AFB, N.C., 1975-79; squadron comdr. USAF Hosp., Whiteman AFB, Mo., 1979-80; resource mgr. USAF Hosp., Yokota AB, Japan, 1980-83; patient adminstrn. officer RAF, Bentwaters, U.K., 1983-86; chief tng. Jt. Med. Readiness Tng. Ctr., Ft. Sam Houston, Tex., 1986-89; med. plans fellow HQ Tactical Air Command, Langley AFB, Va., 1989-90; med. advisor HQ LANDSOUTHEAST (NATO), Izmir, Turkey, 1990-91; chief med. ops. HQ Air Combat Command, Langley AFB, 1991-94; comdr. 24th Med. Spl. Squadron, Howard AFB, Panama, 1994-95; command adminstr. Air Force Spl. Ops. Command, Hurlburt Field, Fla., 1995-97; comdr. 35th Med. Squadron, Misawa, Japan, 1997—. Decorated Armed Forces Expeditionary medal, Oman & Somalia, 1989, 93, Southwest Asia Svc. medal, 1991, Chief Med. Svc. Corps. Badge, 1992. Fellow Am. Coll. Healthcare Execs. Avocation: martial arts (9th Dan master instr. Okinawan Karate & Kobudo). Office: 35 MDSS Unit 5024 APO AP 96319-5024

HOBBS, TRUMAN MCGILL, federal judge, lawyer; b. Selma, Ala., Feb. 8, 1921; s. Sam F. and Sarah Ellen (Greene) H.; m. Joyce Cummings, July 9, 1949; children—Emilie C. Reid, Frances John Rose, Dexter Cummings, Truman McGill. A.B., U. N.C., 1942; LL.B., Yale U., 1948. Bar: Ala. 1948. Practiced in Montgomery, 1951-80; law clk. U.S. Supreme Ct., 1948-49; ptnr. Hobbs, Copeland, Franco & Screws, 1951-80; U.S. dist. judge Montgomery, 1980—; now sr. judge; Chmn. Ala. Unemployment Appeal Bd., 1952-58. Pres. United Appeal Montgomery; pres. Montgomery County Tb Assn.; v.p. Ala. Com. for Better Schs.; Chmn. Montgomery County Exec. Democratic Com., 1970. Served to lt. USNR, 1942-46, ETO, PTO. Decorated Bronze Star medal. Fellow Am. Coll. Trial Lawyers; mem. Internat. Acad. Trial Lawyers, Ala. Plaintiffs Lawyers Assn. (past pres.), Ala. Bar Assn. (pres. 1970-71), Montgomery County Bar Assn. (past pres.). Home: 2301 Fernway Dr Montgomery AL 36111-1603

HOBBS, WALTER CLARENCE, retired educator; b. Richmond Hill, N.Y., Dec. 15, 1932; s. Clarence Wellington and Ella Marie (Schmidt) H.; m. June Florence Anderson, Mar. 16, 1957; 1 child, Eric E. BA, U. Buffalo, 1961; MA, SUNY, Buffalo, 1963, PhD, 1968, JD, 1976; LLD (hon.), Houghton Coll., 1988. Dir. instnl. rsch. SUNY, Buffalo, 1963-70, mem. faculty, 1969-93, emeritus, 1993—; vis. prof. Trinity Evang. Div. Sch., Deerfield, Ill., 1987, 89; lectr., manuscript reviewer in field. Editor: Government Regulation of Higher Education, 1978, Understanding Academic Law, 1982, Jour. Higher Edn. Mgmt., 1992-94; contbr. articles to profl. publs., chpts. to books. Tchr., officer Randall Bapt. Ch., Williamsville, N.Y., 1960-77; sec. Patkai Ministries, Inc., U.S. and India, 1963—; pres. Coalition for Common Ground, Buffalo, 1993-95; bd. dirs. Coun. Chs., Buffalo and Erie County, N.Y., 1993-96. Mem. Am. Assn. for Higher Edn., Assn. for Study of Higher Edn. (legal counsel 1987—, Spl. Merit award 1993), Gospel and Our Culture Network. Democrat. Home: 623 Lake Bluff Rd Thiensville WI 53092-1286

HOBBY, WILLIAM PETTUS, broadcast executive, retired; b. Houston, Jan. 19, 1932; s. William Pettus and Oveta (Culp) H.; m. Diana Poteat Stallings, Sept. 11, 1954; children: Laura Poteat Beckworth, Paul William, Andrew Purefoy, Katherine Pettus Gibson. B.A., Rice U., 1953. Pres. H & C Communications, Inc., 1979-83, chmn. bd., chief exec. officer, 1983-96; lt. gov. Tex., 1973-91; chancellor Univ. of Houston Sys., 1995-97; Sid Richardson prof. Lyndon B. Johnson Sch. Pub. Affairs, U. Tex., Austin, 1990-97; Radoslav Tsanoff prof. Rice U., Houston, 1991—. Served to lt. (j.g.) USNR, 1953-57. Office: Hobby Comm LLC 2131 San Felipe Houston TX 77019-5620

HOBDAY, JOHN CHARLES, foundation administrator; b. Richmond, Surrey, Eng., July 7, 1935; emigrated to Can., 1952, naturalized, 1967; s. Stephen Henry and Kathleen Hawtrey (White) H.; m. Helga Stock, June 22, 1962; children: Heidi Andrea, Oliver John, Tina Karina. Ed., Rugby Sch., Eng. Producer, dir. radio drama and features CBC, 1957-64; theatre dir. Confedn. Centre for Arts, Charlottetown, P.E.I., Can., 1966-68; adminstrv. dir. Neptune Theatre, Halifax, N.S., Can., 1968-71; nat. dir. Can. Conf. Arts, Toronto and Ottawa, Ont., 1971-82; exec. dir. corp. donations Joseph E. Seagram and Sons, Ltd., Montreal, Que., Can., 1982—; exec. dir. Samuel and Saidye Bronfman Family Found., Montreal, 1983—; mem. adv. com. on culture and communications UNESCO. Freelance writer, actor, dir., lectr.

HOBELMAN, CARL DONALD, lawyer; b. Hackensack, N.J., Dec. 26, 1931; s. Alfred Charles and Marion (Gerrish) H.; m. Grace Palumbo, Apr. 25, 1964. BCE, Cornell U., 1954; JD, Harvard U., 1959. Bar: N.Y. 1960, U.S. Supreme Ct. 1975, D.C. 1980, Calif. 1993. Assoc. LeBoeuf, Lamb, Greene & MacRae, N.Y.C., 1959-64; ptnr. LeBoeuf, Lamb, Greene & MacRae, L.A., N.Y.C., Washington, 1965-94; of counsel LeBoeuf, Lamb, Greene & MacRae, Washington, 1995—. Contbr. articles on energy-related topics to profl. jours. Served to 1st lt. U.S. Army, 1954-56. Mem. ABA, Fed. Energy Bar Assn. (pres. 1980-81), D.C. Bar Assn., Met. Club (Washington), Univ. Club (N.Y.C.). Avocations: travel, philately. Office: LeBoeuf Lamb Greene & MacRae 1875 Connecticut Ave NW Washington DC 20009-5728

HOBERMAN, MARY ANN, author; b. Stamford, Conn., Aug. 12, 1930; d. Milton and Dorothy (Miller) Freedman; m. Norman Hoberman, Feb. 4, 1951; children: Diane, Perry, Charles, Meg. BA, Smith Coll., 1951; MA, Yale U., 1984. With advt. dept. Gimbel's Dept. Store, N.Y.C., 1951-52; newspaper reporter Harrisburg, Pa., 1952; editor N.Y. Graphic Soc., Greenwich, Conn., 1963-64; poetry cons.: lectr. in field; program coord. C.G. Jung Ctr., N.Y.C., 1981; adj. prof. Fairfield (Conn.) U., 1980-83; instr. Yale U., New Haven, 1989; founder, mem. The Pocket People, 1968-75; founder, performer Women's Voices, 1983-93. Author: All My Shoes Come in Two's, 1957, How Do I Go?, 1958, Hello and Good-by, 1959, What Jim Knew, 1963, Not Enough Beds for the Babies, 1965, A Little Book of Little Beasts, The Raucous Auk, 1973, The Looking Book, 1973, Nuts to You and Nuts to Me, 1974, I Like Old Clothes, 1976, Bugs, 1976, A House Is a House for Me, 1978, Yellow Butter, Purple Jelly, Red Jam, Black Bread, 1981, The Cozy Book, 1982, Mr. and Mrs. Muddle, 1988, A Fine Fat Pig and Other Animal Poems, 1991, Fathers, Mothers, Sisters, Brothers, 1991; editor: My Song is Beautiful, 1994, The Cozy Book, 1995, The Seven Silly Eaters, 1997, One of Each, 1997, Miss Mary Mack, 1998, The Llama Who Had No Pajama, 1998. Bd. dirs. Greenwich Libr., 1988-91, Literacy Vols., 1997—. Recipient Nat. Book award, 1984. Mem. Authors Guild. Avocations: dancing, gardening, hiking, tennis. Home: 98 Hunting Ridge Rd Greenwich CT 06831-3134*

HOBERMAN, STUART A., lawyer; b. N.Y.C., Nov. 21, 1946. BBA, Baruch Coll., N.Y.C., 1969; JD, Bklyn. Law Sch., 1972; LLM, NYU, 1973. Bar: N.Y. 1973, N.J. 1977, Pa. 1979, U.S. Supreme Ct. 1976. Assoc. Windels & Marx, N.Y.C., 1973-77, Wilentz, Goldman & Spitzer, Woodbridge, N.J., 1977-80; ptnr. Wilentz, Goldman & Spitzer, 1980—. Trustee, Emmanuel Cancer Found., Kenilworth, N.J., 1983-90. Mem. N.J. State Bar Assn. (trustee 1990-94, 97—, corp. and bus. law sect. chmn. 1988-90, bank law sect. chmn. 1986-87, chmn. exec. com. of gen. coun. 1990-92, trustee N.J. State Bar Found. 1992—, treas. 1995, 96, 1st v.p. 1997—). Office: Wilentz Goldman & Spitzer PO Box 10 90 Woodbridge Ctr Dr Ste 900 Woodbridge NJ 07095-1142

HOBEROCK, LAWRENCE LINDEN, mechanical engineer, educator; b. Wichita, Kans., Oct. 21, 1939; s. Lawrence H. and Teresa B. (Gornick) H.; m. Judith L. Anderson, June 6, 1964; children: Michael Jo, Barbara T., Timmothy M. BSME, U. Mo.-Rolla, 1961, MSME, 1963; PhD, Purdue U., 1966. Registered profl. engr., Tex., Okla. Asst. prof., then assoc. prof. U. Tex., Austin, 1968-78; rsch. assoc. Amoco Prodn. Co., Tulsa, 1978-81, rsch. supr., 1981-85; v.p. rsch. Derrick Mfg. Corp., Buffalo, 1985-86; pvt. practice engring. cons. Buffalo, 1986-87; prof., head mech. and aero. engring. Okla. State U., Stillwater, 1987—; cons. Amoco Prodn. Co., 1977-78, 88, Shell Devel. Co., Houston, 1989-91, Conoco, Ponca City, Okla., 1990, Cagle Oilfield Svcs., Tulsa, 1990. Contbr. articles to profl. publs. Capt. U.S. Army, 1966-68. Fellow ASME (dedicated svc. award, chair dynamic sys., v.p. sys. and design, assoc. editor); mem. AIAA, IEEE, IEEE Control Sys. Soc., Soc. Petroleum Engrs. (assoc. editor), Am. Soc. Engring. Edn. Avocations: carpentry, bird watching, wines, upland bird hunting. Office: Okla State U Sch Mech and Aero Engring 218 EN Stillwater OK 74078

HOBGOOD, BURNET MCLEAN, theater educator; b. Lotumbe, Zaire, June 23, 1922; s. Henry Clay and Tabitha (Alderson) H.; m. Mary Jane Bishop, June 1, 1957; children: Laurence Bishop, Cathleen Stuart, Brent McLean. AB, Transylvania U., 1947; MA, MFA, Western Res. U., 1950; PhD, Cornell U., 1964. Chair, prof. dept. speech and drama Catawba Coll., Salisbury, N.C., 1950-61; prof., chair dept. theater So. Meth. U., Dallas, 1964-75; prof., head dept. theater U. Ill., Urbana, 1975-95, prof. of theatre emeritus, 1995—; dir. various summer theater programs. Author, editor: Master Teachers of Theatre, 1988; co-author: Framework for Directing in the Theatre, 1999, Director's Work in Theatre, 1998; editor: Directory of American College Theatre; contbr. articles, papers to jours. acad. theater. Sgt. U.S. Army, 1943-46, PTO. Recipient Lifetime Achievement award Assn. for Theatre in Higher Edn., 1992. Fellow Am. Theatre Assn. (pres. 1970), S.W. Theatre Conf., Mid-Am. Theatre Conf.; mem. Am. Soc. Theatre Rsch., Assn. Theatre in Higher Edn. Democrat. Unitarian. Avocation: swimming. Home: 3 Illini Cir Urbana IL 61801-5813 Office: U Ill Dept Theatre Krannert Ctr Performing Arts Urbana IL 61801

HOBGOOD, E(ARL) WADE, college dean; b. Wilson, N.C., June 28, 1953; s. Max Earl and Mary (Carpenter) H.; m. Dianne Bland, Apr. 24, 1977; children: Courtney, Heather. BFA, E. Carolina U., 1975, MFA, 1977; postgrad., Am. Inst. for Philanthropic, Studies, 1995, Harvard U., 1997, Sashakawa Fellowship/AACSCU, 1998. Asst. prof. art Ark. State U., Jonesboro, 1977-78; design dir. and asst./assoc. prof. art Western Carolina U., Cullowhee, N.C., 1978-84; chmn., assoc. to full prof. art and design Winthrop U., Rock Hill, S.C., 1984-88, acting chmn. dept. music, 1991-92, assoc. dean and prof. Coll. Visual and Performing Arts, 1988-92; dean Coll. of Fine Arts Stephen F. Austin State U., Nacogdoches, Tex., 1992-93; dean Coll. of Arts Calif. State U., Long Beach, 1993—; panelist ann. conf. Coun. Coll. Arts & Scis., 1995; panelist Internat. Coun. Fine Arts Dean's Ann. Conf., 1995, 97; faculty cons. Ednl. Testing Svcs., 1993—; field reader/evaluator, field-initiated studies grants U.S. Dept. Edn., 1992—; sr. evaluator Nat. Assn. Schs. of Art and Design, 1987—; chair grants rev. panel Pub. Corp. for Arts, 1994, mem. allocations com., 1996—; bd. dirs. Rancho Los Cerritos Found., Am. Jazz Philharmonic, Internat. Coun. Fine Arts Deans; mem. cultural planning com. City of Long Beach; evaluator/cons. Arts Edn. Partnership Grants, Ky. Arts Coun., 1992; evaluator/panelist Challenge grants, NEA, 1991, correspondent/cons. Arts Edn. Rsch. Briefing, 1991. Mem. selection com. Pub. Corp. for the Arts, Long Beach, 1993; bd. dirs. Rock Hill Arts Coun., 1985-89; mem. planning com. Cultural/City of Rock Hill, 1988-92, County of York, S.C., 1989-92; mem. Long Beach Mus. of Art, 1993—, Univ. Art Mus., 1993—, KLON Jazz Radio, 1993—; mem. Mayor's Task Force on Smithsonian, City of Long Beach, 1996—. Recipient medallion in arts edn. Kennedy Ctr. for Performing Arts, Washington, 1988. Mem. Internat. Coun. Fine Arts (editor publs., mem. futures com., chair editl. bd. 1996-99), Long Beach C. of C., Long Beach Mus. Art, Phi Kappa Phi. Office: Calif State Univ Coll of the Arts 1250 N Bellflower Blvd Long Beach CA 90840-0001

HOBLIT, GREGORY, film director, television executive; b. Abilene, Tex.. Dir. (TV series): Hill Street Blues, 1981 (Emmy awards Outstanding Drama Series, 1981, 82, 83, 84, nominated 1985, 86), L.A. Law, 1986 (nominated Emmy award Outstanding Drama Series, 1986), NYPD Blue, 1993 (DGA awaaaard Outstanding Directorial Achievement in Dramatic Shows-Night, pilot episode, 1993, TV Prodr. of Yr. award 1994, Emmy award Outstanding Drama Series, 1995); dir.: (TV movie) Roe vs. Wade, 1989, Primal Fear, 1996, Fallen, 1998; assoc. prodr. (TV) Dr. Strange, 1978; supervising prodr. (TV series) Paris, 1979; prodr. (TV movies): Vampire, 1979, Roe vs. Wade. Office: c/o DGA 7920 Sunset Blvd Los Angeles CA 90046 and: Steven Bochco Prodns PO Box 900 Beverly Hills CA 90213*

HOBLITZELLE, GEORGE KNAPP, former state legislator; b. St. Louis, Sept. 28, 1921; s. Harrison and Mary D. (Jones) H.; m. Katharine L. Wells, Nov. 18, 1950; children—Katharine, Laura Trimble, Lucy. A.B. summa cum laude, Princeton, 1943. With Gen. Steel Industries, Inc., 1946-73, successively spl. apprentice, asst. to v.p., treas., 1946-53, sec., asst. to pres., 1953-60, v.p., 1960-65, v.p., sec., 1965-73; mem. Mo. Ho. of Reps., 1973-89. Bd. dirs. Arts and Edn. Coun., Capt. F.A., AUS, 1943-46, 51-53, ETO. Decorated Bronze Star. Episcopalian. Home: 7801 Pershing Saint Louis MO 63105-3864

HOBSON, ALESA, medical/surgical nurse; b. Brigham City, Utah, Feb. 29, 1960; d. Clifford James and Berniece (Tanner) H. BSN, U. Utah, 1983. RN, Utah. Staff nurse cardiovascular-thoracic unit, nurse care mgr. LDS Hosp., Salt Lake City, 1988—99; cardiovascular-thoracic clin. nurse eductor LDS Hosp., 1988—; instr. and dir. EKG course, preceptor LDS Hosp., Salt Lake City, 1986—; academic, scholarship advisor Xi Alpha chpt. Chi Omega Fraternity, U. Utah. Youth group leader/advisor Ch. of Jesus Christ of Latter-Day Saints, 1992-98, Sunday sch. tchr., 1998—; alumni amb. U. Utah. Mem. Utah Nurses Assn. Democrat. Avocations: reading, needlepoint, waterskiing, music, theatre.

HOBSON, DAVID LEE, congressman, lawyer; b. Cin., Oct. 17, 1936; m. Carolyn Alexander; children: Susan Marie, Lynn Martha, Douglas Lee. BA, Ohio Wesleyan U., 1958; JD, Ohio State Coll. Law, 1963; hon. degree Ctrl. State U., Wittenberg U. Former resident counsel Kissell Co., Springfield, Ohio; former atty. Union Central Life Ins. Co., Cin.; mem. Ohio Senate, 1982-90, majority whip, 1986-88, pres. pro tem, 1988-90; mem. 102nd-105th Congresses from 7th Ohio dist., Washington, D.C., 1991—; house coms. appropriations, budget, standards of ofcl. conduct. Former trustee Wilberforce U., Ohio, Urbana U.; trustee Ohio Wesleyan; bd. dirs. Ohio. Mem. ABA, AMVETS, Ky. Bar Assn., Ohio Bar Assn., Springfield Bd. Realtors, Springfield Area C. of C. (past bd. dirs.), Non-Commissioned Officers Assn., Masons (32 degrees), Am. Legion, VFW, Moose, Elks, Rotary, Shrine Club. Home: # 200 5 W North St Springfield OH 45501-2690 Office: US Ho of Reps 1514 Longworth Bldg Washington DC 20515-3507*

HOBSON, DOUGLAS PAUL, psychiatrist; b. Louisville, July 22, 1952; s. Charles Paul and Stella Mae (Billings) H.; m. Vicki Lyn Hoofnel, Dec. 18, 1976; children: Zachary, Lucas. BA, U. Louisville, 1974, MD, 1978; MA, Baylor U., 1983. Diplomate Am. Bd. Psychiatry and Neurology. Resident in psychiatry Yale U. Sch. Medicine, New Haven, 1978-82; fellow in psychosomatic medicine Mass. Gen. Hosp., Boston, 1982-83; dir. psychiatry residency Med. Coll. Ga., Augusta, 1983-87, St. Louis U., 1987-89; regional med. officer Dept. of State, Abidjan, Cote d'Ivoire, 1989-91, Vienna, Austria, 1991-95; asst. prof. psychiatry U. Louisville, 1995—. Contbr. articles to profl. publs. Named Ky. Col., Hon. Order of Ky. Cols., 1974. Mem. AMA, Acad. Psychosomatic Medicine. Mem. Ch. of God. Avocations: antiquarian books, classical music, genealogy. Office: Louisville VA Med Ctr Dept Psychiatry 800 Zorn Ave Louisville KY 40206-1433

HOBSON, GEORGE DONALD, retired geophysicist; b. Hamilton, Ont., Can., Jan. 8, 1923; s. Robert Charles and Agnes Hamilton (Mathieson) H.; m. Arletta Louise Russell, May 21, 1948; children: Robert, Linda, Douglas, Donna. BA, McMaster U., 1946, DSc (hon.), 1991; MA, Toronto U., 1948. Registered profl. geophysicist, Can. Party chief, ptnr. Heiland Exploration Can. Ltd., Calgary, Alta., 1948-55; geophysicist Can. Fina Oil Co., Calgary, 1955-56; chief geophysicist Merrill Petroleums Ltd., Calgary, 1956-57; geophysicist Pacific Petroleums Ltd., Calgary, 1957-58; chief seismic sect. Geol. Survey Can., Ottawa, Ont., 1958-69, chief geophysics div., 1969-71; dir. Polar Shelf Project, Ottawa, 1972-88, sr. advisor, 1988-90; rsch. assoc. Nunavut Rsch. Inst., Iqaluit, NWT, Can., 1997—. Author or co-author over 200 articles in field. Recipient No. Sci. award and Centennial medal Dept. Indian and No. Affairs, Can., 1991, Ind. Achievement award Am. Soc. Mech. Engrs., Massey Medal, 1991, Royal Can. Geog. Soc. Fellow Exploration Geophysicists India, Royal Can. Geog. Soc. (bd. govs. 1987-94, Massey medal 1991, Camsell award 1998), Arctic Inst. N.Am. (bd. govs. 1984-91); mem. Sci. Inst. N.W. Territory (bd. govs. 1990-93), Soc. Exploration Geophysicists (v.p. 1968), Assn. Profl. Engrs., Geologists, Geophysicists Alta., Can. Soc. Exploration Geophysicists. Mem. United Ch. Can. Avocations: genealogy, barbershop singing. Home: PO Box 161, 5428 Long Island Rd, Manotick, ON Canada K4M 1A3

HOBSON, HARRY LEE, JR., lawyer; b. Ada, Okla., May 14, 1929; s. Harry Lee and Sevilla Amanda V. (Saufferer) H.; m. Lois Hanna Helmick, Jan. 21, 1961; children: Harry Lee III, Winifred Louise. AB, U. Wichita, 1951; LLB, NYU, 1956. Bar: Kans. 1956, Colo. 1972. Law clk. U.S. Supreme Ct., Washington, 1956-57; successively assoc., ptnr., counsel Jochems, Sargent & Blaes, Wichita, Kans., 1957-72; ptnr. Holland and Hart, Denver, 1972—; instr. U. Wichita, 1957-59; moderator Sta. KARD-TV, Wichita, 1958-59; v.p., gen. counsel Safelite Industries, Wichita, 1968-69; advocate Am. Bd. Trial Advocates. Mng. editor NYU Law Rev., 1955-56. Chmn. Wichita Pub. Libr., 1962-66. 1st lt. USAF, 1951-53. Fellow Am. Coll. Trial Lawyers; mem. ABA, Colo. Bar Assn., Kans. Bar Assn., Fed. Bar Assn., Denver Bar Assn., Wichita State U. Alumni Assn. (pres. 1962), NYU Club, Petroleum Club, Phi Delta Phi, Pi Sigma Alpha, Delta Sigma Rho, Phi Alpha Theta, Phi Delta Theta. Democrat. Presbyterian. Avocations: ranching, real estate, hunting, fishing, spectator sports. Home: 4001 S Clermont St Englewood CO 80110-5084 Office: Holland & Hart 555 17th St Ste 2900 Denver CO 80202-3979

HOBSON, JAMES RICHMOND, lawyer; b. Atlanta, Sept. 13, 1937; s. Richmond Pearson and Alice Chambers (Carey) H.; m. Nancy Hulbert Saussy, Nov. 29, 1963; children: Kathleen Hunter, Caroline Richmond, Susan Saussy. BA in English, Cornell U., 1959; MA in Govt., Georgetown U., 1963; JD, U. San Francisco, 1971. Bar: Calif. 1972, U.S. Ct. Appeals (9th cir.) 1972, U.S. Dist. Ct. (no. dist.) Calif. 1972, D.C., 1973, U.S. Ct. Appeals (D.C. cir.) 1973, U.S. Dist. Ct. D.C. 1973. Staff writer Charlotte (N.C.) Observer, 1963; rschr., writer Rep. Nat. Com., Washington, 1964-65; Washington editor Med. Econs. Mag., 1965; info. officer Hoover Instn., Stanford, Calif., 1966-72; atty., mgr. FCC, Washington, 1972-78; asst. v.p. GTE Svc. Corp., Washington, 1978-81; Washington counsel GTE Corp., Washington, 1982-91; v.p. Donelan, Cleary, Wood & Maser, PC, Washington, 1991-95, prin., 1995—, pres., 1997—. Bd. dirs. Mid-Peninsula Citizens for Fair Housing, Palo Alto, Calif., 1971-72; sr. warden Immanuel Ch. on the Hill, Alexandria, Va., 1977, 90, jr. warden, 1976, 88; traffic and parking bd. City Alexandria, 1980-82; mem. Alexandria Libr. Co., 1991—, pres., 1995-96; mem. panel arbitrators Am. Arbitration Assn., 1994-97; adv. bd. Inst. for Conflict Analysis and Resolution, George Mason U., 1989—, chmn., 1995-98; bd. trustees Goodwin House, Inc., 1996—, exec. com., 1998—. Mem. ABA, Fed. Comm. Bar Assn. (exec. com. 1984-87, 94-96), Met. Club. Washington), Sigma Alpha Epsilon. Episcopalian. Home: 3613 Trinity Dr Alexandria VA 22304-1840 Office: Donelan Cleary Wood & Maser 1100 New York Ave NW Ste 750W Washington DC 20005-3934

HOBSON, JOHN ALLAN, psychiatrist, researcher, educator; b. Hartford, Conn., June 3, 1933; s. John Robert and Anne Barnard (Cotter) H.; m. Joan Merle Harlowe, June 18, 1956 (div. Jan. 1993); children: Ian, Christopher, Julia; m. Lia Cesarea Silvestri, May 19, 1995; children: Andrew, Matthew. BA, Conn. Wesleyan U., 1955; MD, Harvard U., 1959. Diplomate Am. Bd. Psychiatry and Neurology; lic. physician, Mass. Intern, Bellevue Hosp., N.Y.C., 1959-60; resident in psychiatry Mass. Mental Health Ctr., Boston, 1960-61, 64-66; NIMH spl. fellow dept. physiology U. Lyon, France, 1963-64; research assoc. dept. physiology Harvard Med. Sch., Boston, 1964-67, instr. psychiatry, 1966-67, assoc. in psychiatry, 1967-69, asst. prof., 1969-74, 74-78, prof. psychiatry, 1978—, prof. psychiatry (neurosci.), 1983—; sr. psychiatrist Mass. Mental Health Ctr., Boston, 1965-67, dir. lab. neurophysiology, 1967, prin. psychiatrist, 1967—, dir. group psychotherapy tng. program, 1972-80; lectr. psychiatry Brown U., Providence, 1972-74; clin. assoc. NIMH, Bethesda, Md., 1961-63; vis. sci., lectr. U. Bordeaux, France, 1973; Sandoz lectr. U. Edinburgh, Scotland, 1975; lectr. Italian Nat. Health Research Inst., Rome, 1978; vis. prof. Istituto di Psicologia, U. degli Studi, Rome, 1983; participant internat. confs.; mem. sci. adv. bd. NIMH Intramural program, NIH, Bethesda, 1981-84, Max Planck Inst. Psychiatry, Munich, 1985—; scholar in residence Rockefeller Study Ctr., Bellagio, Italy, 1987; Decade of the Brain lectr. Soc. Neurosci. 1991, Am. Acad. Neurology, 1993; Joseph P. Erlanger Disting. lectr. Am. Physiol. Soc., Sleep Research Soc. Disting. Scientist Award, 1998; Author: The Dreaming Brain, 1988, Sleep, 1989, The Chemistry of Conscious States, 1994, Consciousness, 1998; mem. editl. bd. Jour. Cellular and Molecular Neurobiology, 1980—, Archives Itallienes de Biologie, 1983—; contbg. editor Sleep Revs., 1970-72, assoc. editor, 1972-73, editor-in-chief, 1973-74, book rev. editor, 1975-76; sect. editor Neuroreport, 1990—, Psychophysiology, 1993—; assoc. editor Dreaming; contbr. articles to profl. jours. Olin scholar, 1951. Mem. AAAS, Assn. Psychophysiol. Study of Sleep, Soc. Neurosci. (program com. 1974-76, chmn. museum adv. group 1976), Boylston Med. Soc., Mind-Body Network, John D. and Catherine T. MacArthur Found., Sigma Xi. Club: Thursday. Office: Harvard Med Sch 74 Fenwood Rd Boston MA 02115-6113

HOBSON, KEITH LEE, civil engineer, consultant; b. Nevada, Iowa, Feb. 16, 1958; s. Bobby Lee and Marjorie Pearl (Breeden) H.; m. Brenda Hunter, June 6, 1981; children: Leah Christine, Rebecca Marie. BSCE, Iowa State U., 1980; MSCE, U. Mo., 1983. Registered profl. engr., Kans., Mo., Iowa, Ill. Design engr. Black & Veatch, Kansas City, Mo., 1980-85, project engr., 1985-93; city engr. City of Nevada, Iowa, 1993-94; project mgr. Fox Engring., Ames, Iowa, 1994—. Coun. mem. City of Nevada, Iowa, 1996-97; youth counselor, program adminstr. Red Bridge United Meth. Ch., Kansas City, 1980-93; choir mem., staff parish rels. First United Meth. Ch., Nevada, Iowa, 1993—; mem. Nev. Economic Devel. Commn.; mem. adv. com. Nev. Sch. Dist. Mem. ASCE (chpt. program chmn. 1985-86), Water Environ. Fedn., Kans. and Iowa Water Pollution Control Assn. (editor newsletter 1991-92, 97—), Engrs. Club Kansas City (chmn. attendance com. 1986-88, student assistance com.), Toastmasters (toastmaster of yr. club award 1986), Chi Epsilon, Tau Beta Pi, Rotary. Republican. Home: 21101 620th Ave Nevada IA 50201-7926 Office: Fox Engring 1531 Airport Rd Ames IA 50010-8230

HOBSON, ROBERT WAYNE, II, surgeon; b. DeKalb, Ill., Dec. 21, 1939; s. Robert Wayne and Jean Helen (Sampson) H.; m. Joan Patricia Souza, Dec. 5, 1985; children: Lisa, Wayne, Laura, Matthew. BS in Chemistry, George Washington U., 1959, MD, 1963. Diplomate Am. Bd. Surgery; cert. of spl. qualification in gen.-vascular surgery. Intern Tripler Gen. Hosp., Honolulu, 1963-64; resident gen. surgery Walter Reed Gen. Hosp., Washington, 1967-71, fellow peripheral vascular surgery, 1972-73; group surgeon 3rd Spl. Forces Group, Ft. Bragg, N.C., 1964-65; surgeon Detachment C-3, 5th Spl. Forces Group, Republic of Vietnam, 1965-66; chief exptl. surgery, dep. dir. Div. Surgery, Walter Reed Inst. Rsch., Washington, 1971-75; asst. chief peripheral vascular surgery svc. Walter Reed Army Med. Ctr., Washington, 1973-75; chief surg. svc. East Orange VA Med. Ctr., N.J., 1975-83; chief sect. vascular surgery Univ. Medicine and Dentistry of N.J., Newark, 1978-86, assoc. prof. surgery, 1975-79, prof. surgery, 1980-86, vice chmn. dept. surgery, 1980-86; James Utley prof. surgery, chmn. dept. surgery Boston U. Sch. Medicine. 1986-88; surgeon-in-chief Univ. Hosp., Boston U. Med. Ctr., 1986-88; prof. surgery, chief sect. vascular surgery U. Medicine and Dentistry of N.J., Newark, 1988—, prof. physiology, 1990; editorial cons. Jour. AMA, 1982—; mem. editorial bd. Jour. Surg. Rsch., 1983-88, Jour. Vascular Surgery, 1989-99, Stroke: Clinical Updates, 1990—, International J Angiol, 1992—, Vascular Surgery, 1995—; contbr. articles to profl. jours. Served to col. M.C., U.S. Army, 1963-75. Recipient Franklin Metcalfe award for surg. rsch. U.S. Army Med. Dept., 1969-70, Acad. award in Vascular Disease NHLBI, NIH, 1995—; decorated Bronze Star, Air Medal, Medal of Honor (RVN), Cross of Gallantry, Airborne (all Republic of Vietnam); NIH grantee, 1979-82, 95—, other rsch. project grants. Fellow ACS, Am. Surg. Assn., Stroke Coun. (exec. com. 1987-89, 95—), Am. Heart Assn.; mem. Internat. Cardiovascular Soc., Soc. Vascular Surgery (treas. 1989-93), Ea. Vascular Soc. (pres. 1996), Am. Venons Forum (pres. 1997), Assn. Program Direction in Vascular Surg. (pres. 1998—), Soc. Univ. Surgeons., Assn. VA Surgeons (v.p. 1983), Southeastern Surg. Congress, Am. Fedn. Clin. Rsch., Chesapeake Vascular Soc., Assn. Mil. Surgeons, Assn. Acad. Surgery (pres.-elect 1980, pres. 1981), Assn. Surg. Edn., Soc. Med. Cons. to Armed Forces, Assn. Internat. Vascular Surgeons, Soc. Surgeons of N.J., Boston Surg. Soc., Vascular Soc. N.J. (pres. 1981), Am. Coll. Surg. (sec. N.J. chpt. 1998). Republican. Office: U Medicine and Dentistry NJ Sect Vascular Surgery 185 S Orange Ave Newark NJ 07103-2757

HOBURG, JAMES FREDERICK, electrical engineering educator; b. Pitts., Dec. 30, 1946; s. William Lawrence and Virginia (Stewart) H.; m. Margaret Jean Ryan, Mar. 4, 1978. BS, Drexel U., 1969; SM, MIT, 1971, PhD in Elec. Engring., 1975. Instr. MIT, Cambridge, Mass., 1973-75; asst. prof. elec. engring. Carnegie-Mellon U., Pitts., 1975-80, assoc. prof. elec. engring., 1980-84, prof. elec. and computer engring., 1984—, assoc. head, dept. elec. and computer engring., 1985-91; cons. to rsch. and devel. orgns. Contbr. articles to profl. jours. Recipient teaching award MIT, 1972, Ryan award for Excellence in Undergrad. Edn., Carnegie-Mellon U., 1980; named Outstanding Prof. in Elec. Engring. Dept., Carnegie-Mellon U., 1977, 80, 84, 90, 95. Mem. IEEE, Electrostatics Soc. Am., Am. Soc. Engr. Edn., Sigma Xi, Tau Beta Pi, Eta Kappa Nu. Avocations: long distance running; walking; mountaineering. Home: 1000 Oak Creek Ln Baden PA 15005-2856 Office: Carnegie-Mellon U Dept Elec and Computer Engring Schenley Park Pittsburgh PA 15213-3830

HOBUS, ROBERT ALLEN, minister; b. Milw., Apr. 11, 1924; s. Herbert Walter and Clara (Hass) H.; m. Alice Olinda Jacobsmeyer, July 10, 1949; children: Paul Alan, David Andrew, Steven Robert, Michael Jon. MST, So. Meth. U., 1970; MDiv, Concordia Theol. Sem., St. Louis, 1971; DMin, Luth. Sch. Theology, Chgo., 1988. Ordained to ministry Luth. Ch.-Mo. Synod., 1949; cert. secondary tchr., Wis., Kans. Pastor 1st Luth. Ch., Rosebud, Tex., 1949-52; assoc. pastor Mt. Olive Luth. Ch., Milw., 1952-56; pastor Peace Luth. Ch., Antigo, Wis., 1956-58, Our Shepherd Luth. Ch., Greendale, Wis., 1958-65, Hope Luth. Ch., Friendswood, Tex., 1970-73; pastor Redeemer Luth. Ch., Wichita, Kans., 1973-78, Arkansas City, Kans., 1980-89; assoc. pastor Hope Luth. Ch., Des Moines, 1989-91; asst. pastor Redeemer Luth. Ch., Springfield, Mo., 1993—; dir. pilot '92 project Young Adult/Apt. Ministry, Dallas, 1965-70; chaplain VA Hosp., Temple, Tex., 1949-52; exec. dir. Inter-Faith Ministries, Wichita, 1978-80. Editor (South Wis. dist. supplement) Luth. Witness, 1959-65. Chaplain Wichita Police Dept., 1974-79. Home: 1705 W Primrose St Springfield MO 65807-4482 Office: Redeemer Luth Ch Springfield MO 65807

HOCH, DAVID ALLEN, physical education educator, athletic director; b. Northampton, Pa., July 26, 1946; s. Sterling Palmer and Evelyn Mae (McCallister) H.; m. Diane Duffy, June 18, 1977; children: Matthew David, Jennifer Lynn. AB in German, Grove City (Pa.) Coll., 1968; MEd in Phys. Edn., The Coll. N.J., 1972; EdD in Phys. Edn., Temple U., 1989. Tchr., coach Washington Twp. H.S., Sewell, N.J., 1968-71, Upper Dublin H.S., Ft. Washington, Pa., 1972-78, Ramsey (N.J.) H.S., 1978-79, Germantown Acad., Ft. Washington, 1981-89; instr., coach Pa. State U., Altoona, 1979-80; instr. phys. edn., basketball coach U. Pitts., Bradford, 1989-93; athletic dir. Eastern Tech. H.S., Baltimore County, 1994—; presenter in field. Contbr. articles to profl. jours., chpts. to books. Mem. AAHPERD, NEA, Pa. Assn. Health, Phys. Edn., Recreation and Dance, Nat. Interscholastic Athletic Adminstrs. Assn., Nat. Fedn. Interscholastic Coaches Assn., Nat. H.S. Athletic Coaches Assn., N.Am. Soc. for Sports Mgmt., Md. State Athletic Dirs. Assn. (mem. exec. coun.), Md. Assn. for Health, Phys. Edn., Recreation and Dance. Presbyterian. Avocations: running, marathons, gardening, photography. Home: 1207 Peachtree Rd Fallston MD 21047-1804 Office: Eastern Tech HS 1100 Mace Ave Baltimore MD 21221-3315

HOCH, EDWARD DENTINGER, author; b. Rochester, N.Y., Feb. 22, 1930; s. Earl George and Alice Mary (Dentinger) H.; m. Patricia Ann McMahon, June 5, 1957. Student, U. Rochester, 1947-49. Research asst. Rochester (N.Y.) Public Library, 1949-50; circulation asst. Pocket Books, N.Y.C., 1952-54; public relations writer Hutchins Advt. Co., Rochester, N.Y., 1954-68. Author: The Shattered Raven, 1969, The Judges of Hades, 1971, The Transvection Machine, 1971, The Spy and the Thief, 1972, City of Brass, 1972, The Fellowship of the Hand, 1973, The Frankenstein Factory, 1975, The Thefts of Nick Velvet, 1978, The Monkey's Clue and the Stolen Sapphire, 1978, The Quests of Simon Ark, 1984, Leopold's Way, 1985, The Night My Friend, 1991, Diagnosis: Impossible, 1996, The Ripper of Storyville, 1997; editor: Dear Dead Days, 1972, Best Detective Stories of the Year, 1976-81, All But Impossible, 1981, Year's Best Mystery and Suspense Stories, 1982-95, Murder Most Sacred, 1989, Twelve American Detective Stories, 1997. Trustee Rochester Public Libr., 1981-98. Served with U.S. Army, 1950-52. Mem. Mystery Writers Am., Inc. (dir., Edgar award 1967, Edgar scroll 1980, pres. 1982), Sci. Fiction Writers Am., Authors Guild, Crime Writers Assn. (Gt. Brit.). Roman Catholic. Home and Office: 2941 Lake Ave Rochester NY 14612-5529 *After publishing over 800 short stories and 30 books, I have to admit that I write primarily to entertain. But I've yet to decide whether it's more to entertain the reader or myself.*

HOCH, FREDERIC LOUIS, medical educator; b. Vienna, Austria, Apr. 14, 1920; came to U.S., 1922, naturalized, 1928; s. Samuel and Dore (Glinert) H.; m. Martha Louise Ludwig, Apr. 8, 1961. B.S., CCNY, 1939; M.D., N.Y. U., 1943; M.S., M.I.T., 1951. Intern Michael Reese Hosp., Chgo., 1943; resident in pathology Tufts Med. Sch., Boston, 1947; research asso. in biology MIT, 1948-51; research fellow in biochemistry Mass. Gen. Hosp., Boston, 1951-53; research asso., asst. prof. medicine Harvard Med. Sch., Boston, 1953-66; jr. asso., sr. asso. medicine Peter Brent Brigham Hosp., Boston, 1953-66; asso. prof. internal medicine and biol. chemistry U. Mich. Med. Sch., Ann Arbor, 1967-77; prof. internal medicine and biol. chemistry U. Mich. Med. Sch., 1977-86, prof. emeritus internal medicine, biol. chemistry, 1987—. Author: Energy Transformations in Mammals: Regulatory Mechanisms, 1971. Served to capt. M.C. U.S. Army, 1944-46. Fellow Baruch Found., 1948, NIH, 1949-51, Jane Coffin Childs Found., 1951-53, Howard Hughes Med. Inst., 1957-64. Mem. AAAS, Am. Chem. Soc., Biochem. Soc. (London), Am. Soc. Biol. Chem. Molecular Biology, Phi Beta Kappa, Sigma Xi.

HOCH, ORION LINDEL, corporate executive; b. Canonsburg, Pa., Dec. 21, 1928; s. Orion L.F. and Ann Marie (McNulty) H.; m. Jane Lee Ogan, June 12, 1952 (dec. 1978); children: Andrea, Brenda, John; m. Catherine Nan Richardson, Sept. 12, 1980. BS, Carnegie Mellon U., 1952; MS, UCLA, 1954; PhD, Stanford U., 1957. With Hughes Aircraft Co., Culver City, Calif., 1952-54; with Stanford Electronics Labs., 1954-57; sr. engr., dept. mgr., divsn. v.p., divsn. pres. Litton Electron Devices div., San Carlos, Calif., 1957-68; group exec. Litton Components divsn., 1968-70; v.p. Litton Industries, Inc., Beverly Hills, Calif., 1970, sr. v.p., 1971-74, pres., 1982-88, chief exec. officer, 1986-93, chmn., 1988-94, chmn. emeritus, 1994—, also dir.; pres. Intersil, Inc., Cupertino, Calif., 1974-82; chmn. exec. com. Western Atlas, Inc., Beverly Hills, Calif., 1994-98; bd. dirs. Litton Industries, Inc., Bessemer Trust Cos., Unova, Inc. Trustee Carnegie-Mellon U. Served with AUS, 1946-48. Mem. IEEE, Sigma Xi, Tau Beta Pi, Phi Kappa Phi. Office: Unova Inc 21,900 Burbank Blvd Woodland Hills CA 91367-7418

HOCH, PEGGY MARIE, computer scientist; b. Balt., Dec. 2, 1959; d. Stanley Elijah Hoch, Jr. and Nancy Irene (Bishop) Austin; 1 child, Kiana Mariah Shurkin. AA, Catonsville (Md.) Community, Coll., 1982; BS, Towson State U., 1987; MS, Johns Hopkins U., 1989. Lab. technician McCormick & Co., Hunt Valley, Md., 1980-84; computer scientist U.S. Army Concepts Analysis, Bethesda, Md., 1985-88; sr. assoc. programmer IBM Corp., Rockville, Md., 1989-91; computer programmer Nat. Oceanic and Atmospheric Adminstrn., Silver Spring, Md., 1991—. Author: (software) Design CDRLs for IBM/FAA, 1991, Design CDRLs for NOAA, 1994. Recipient Nat. Computer Sci. award U.S. Achievement Acad., 1987, Computer Sci. award Towson (Md.) State U., Chemistry award Catonsville Community Coll., 1980. Mem. AIAA, Am. Assn. Artificial Intelligence, Johns Hopkins U. Alumni Assn. Avocations: gourmet cooking, chess, reading, movies, walking. Home: 10551 Twin Rivers Rd Apt D2 Columbia MD 21044-2120 Office: Nat Weather Svc 1325 E West Hwy Silver Spring MD 20910-3280

HOCH, SCOTT MABON, professional golfer; b. Raleigh, N.C., Nov. 24, 1955; m. Sally Hoch; children: Cameron, Katie. B in Comm., Wake Forest U., 1978. Profl. golfer, 1978—. Named All-Am., 1977-78; mem. NCAA Championship Team, 1975; mem. (nat. teams) World Amateur Team Championships, 1978, Walker Cup, 1979, Pres.'s Cup, 1994, 96, Ryder Cup, 1997; mem. PGA Tour Charity Team, Deposit Guaranty Golf Classic, 1999; won Walker Cup, 1979, Quad Cities Open, 1980, Pacific Masters (Japan), 1982, Casio World Open (Japan), 1982, USF&G Classic, 1982, Lite Quad Cities Open, 1984, Vardon Trophy, 1986, Casio World Open (Japan), 1986, Las Vegas Invitational, 1989, Korea Open, 1990, Bob Hope Chrysler Classic, 1994, Pres.'s Cup, 1994, Heineken Dutch Open, 1995, Greater Milw. Open, 1995, 97, Michelob Championship, 1996. Avocations: sports. *

HOCHBAUM, GODFREY MARTIN, retired behavioral scientist; b. Vienna, Austria, Nov. 19, 1916; came to U.S., 1938, naturalized, 1942; m. Jean Fent, Nov. 14, 1942 (dec.); m. Lore Hochbaum, Dec. 2, 1994. B.A. in Psychology, Am. U., 1947; M.A. in Psychology, George Washington U., 1949; Ph.D. in Psychology and Sociology, U. Minn., 1953. Research psychologist, asst. chief behavioral sci. sect., chief sect. USPHS, 1952-67, dep. dir. social and econ. analysis div., 1967-68; dir. Office Internat. Health Research, Nat. Center Health Services Research and Devel., 1968-72; prof. dept. health edn. Sch. Public Health, U. N.C., Chapel Hill, 1972-88, prof. emeritus dept. health behavior and health edn., 1988—; cons. WHO, Pan Am. Health Orgn., Am. Lung Assn., Nat. Cancer Inst., Nat. Heart and Lung Inst.; Bur. Health Edn. (Center for Disease Control, USPHS), Nat. Center for Health Services Research (USPHS), Nat. Center Health Edn., VA. *In the 1950's, Hochbaum pioneered the application of social and psychological concepts and theories to the study of factors affecting people's health-related behaviors. His research in the psycho-social determinants of preventive health-behaviour, "Public Participation in Medical Screenings Programs" published in 1958, led to the formulation of the "Health Belief Model". This model is one of the most widely used theoretical formulations for the planning of health educational programs throughout the world.* Editorial reviewer Public Health Reports, Chronic Diseases, Am. Jour. Health Promotion; mem. editorial bd. Brit. Jour. Health Edn., Health Edn. Quar., Mature Health; author: Public Participation in Medical Screening Programs, 1958, 2d edit., 1970, Health Behavior, 1970; contbr. chpts. to books, articles to profl. jours. Served with Armed Forces, 1941-45. Recipient Nat. Honor award Eta Sigma Gamma; Ann. Hochbaum Disting. Lectr. award established by Sch. Pub. Health, U. N.C., 1990. Fellow APHA (Svc. award, Mayhew Derryberry award health edn. sect.); mem. Am. Psychol. Assn., Soc. Public Health Educators, AAAS, Internat. Union Health Edn., Am. Sch. Health Assn., Assn. for Advancement Health Edn. (Profl. Service award), Eta Sigma Gamma (Lifetime Achievement writing award). Home: 306 Azalea Dr Chapel Hill NC 27514-9206

HOCHBERG, AUDREY G., state legislator; b. Stamford, Conn., June 26, 1933; m. Herbert Hochberg; children: Carol, Brenda, Judith. BA in Econs. magna cum laude, Radcliffe Coll., 1955. Mem. Westchester County Bd. Legislators, 20 yrs.; mem. N.Y. State Assembly, Albany, 1992—, mem. edn., social svcs., energy, local govts., transp. coms.; minority leader Westchester County Bd. Legislators, 1976-79; chair Westchester County Criminal Justice Coord. Council, 1980-82; mem. Westchester County Task Force on Jail Overcrowding, 1980-92; co-chair Spl. Commns. Additional Revenues and Reducing Expenditures, 1990-92; bd. dirs. Hudson Valley Health Sys. Agy.; mem. task force on Corrections Overcrowding, Westchester Health Planning Coun., Westchester County Bd. of Health; mem. adv. bd. N.Y. State Cmty. Affairs. Bd. dirs. Boy's and Girls' Glub New Rochelle, WESCOP. Recipient Woman of Yr. award NOW, 1973. Mem. Phi Beta Kappa. Office: NY State Assembly Rm 557 LOBtol Albany NY 12224*

HOCHBERG, BAYARD ZABDIAL, lawyer; b. N.Y.C., May 16, 1932; s. Abraham and Sonia (Pincus) H.; m. Arlene Beethoven, Feb. 15, 1953; children: Ronny Mark, Randy Jean, Elizabeth Joyce. BA, CCNY, 1953; LLB, JD, U. Va., 1958. Bar: Md. 1958, Va. 1958. Law bailiff to Hon. Joseph Allen, Supreme Bench of Balt., 1958-59; asso. law office Paul Berman, Esq., Balt., 1959-68; ptnr. Levin, Hochberg & Chiarello, Balt., 1968-82; sr. ptnr. Hochberg, Chiarello & Costello, Balt., 1983—. Mem. editorial bd.: Va. Law Rev, 1956-58. Served to maj. U.S. Army Res., 1953-75. Fellow Am. Coll. Trial Lawyers, Md. Bar Found.; mem. ABA (Md. del. standing com. on state legis. 1970-73, tort and ins. practice sect. 1979—), Md. Bar Assn. (chmn. ins., negligence and workmens compensation sect. 1973, exec. bd., state-city medicolegal com. 1979-91, chmn. 1983-86, ct. of appeals rules com. 1993—), ATLA, Balt. Bar Assn. (chmn. legis. com. 1968-69, bd. govs. 1969-70, jud. adminstrn. com. 1980-86, family law com. 1985-88), Balt. County Bar Assn. (family law com.), Md. Trial Lawyers Assn. (bd. govs. 1970-76, co-chmn. com. on legis. 1970-72, v.p. Balt. 1975, Amicus brief com. 1979-81), Order of Coif (bd. dirs. 1993—), Cavalier King Charles Spaniel Club (v.p. 1998—). Home: 710 Cliveden Rd Baltimore MD 21208-4765 Office: 528 E Joppa Rd Baltimore MD 21286-5403

HOCHBERG, FAITH S., prosecutor. BA summa cum laude, Tufts U., 1972; JD magna cum laude, Harvard U., 1975. Law clk. to Hon. Spottswood W. Robinson III U.S. Ct. Appeals (D.C. cir.), 1975-76; pvt. practice Washington, Boston, Roseland, N.J., 1977-83; asst. U.S. atty. Dist. N.J., Newark, 1983-87, U.S. atty., 1994—; ptnr. Cole, Schotz, Bernstein, Meisel & Forman, Hackensack, N.J., 1987-90; past sr. dep. chief counsel Office Thrift Supervision, Jersey City; former dep. asst. sec. law enforcement U.S. Treasury Dept., Washington; U.S. Atty. Dist. of N.J., 1994—. Office: US Attorney for District of NJ Federal Bldg 970 Broad St Newark NJ 07102-2506*

HOCHBERG, MARK STEFAN, foundation president, cardiac surgeon; b. Providence, Nov. 26, 1947; s. Robert and Gertrude (Meth) H.; m. Faith Shapiro, June 6, 1976; children: Alyssa T., Asher R. BA, Brown U., 1969; MD, Harvard U., 1973; MD (Honoris Causa), Chongqing Sch. Med. Sci., China, 1987. Diplomate Am. Bd. Thoracic Surgery, Am. Bd. Surgery. Chief resident cardiothoracic surgery Mass. Gen. Hosp., Boston, 1980; clin. fellow in surgery Harvard Med. Sch., Boston, 1980; attending cardiac surgeon Newark Beth Israel Med. Ctr., 1981-93, dir. cardiac surgery, 1988-93; cons. cardiac surgeon Overlook Hosp., Summit, N.J., 1983-93; asst. prof. surgery U. Medicine and Dentistry of N.J., Newark, 1981-87, assoc. prof. surgery, 1987-93; spl. asst. to pres., vis. prof. surgery George Washington U., Washington, 1993-94, dean of univ. affairs, prof. surgery, 1994-95; sr. scholar Assn. Acad. Health Ctrs., 1995-96; pres. Healthcare Found. N.J., Roseland, 1996—; chmn. grant rev. com. N.J. affiliate Am. Heart Assn., New Brunswick, 1986-88, bd. dirs., 1986-93; bd. dirs., mem. com. on med. affairs Corp. of Brown U., Providence, 1987—. V.p. Temple B'nai Jeshurun, Short Hills, 1988-92; trustee Coun. N.J. Grantmakers, 1997—. Lt. comdr. USPHS, 1975-77. Fellow ACS, Am. Coun. Edn.; mem. Soc. Thoracic Surgery, Am. Assn. Thoracic Surgery, Alpha Omega Alpha. Office: Healthcare Found NJ 75 Livingston Ave Roseland NJ 07068

HOCHBERG, RONALD MARK, lawyer; b. Bklyn., Apr. 3, 1955; s. Fred S. and Adele (Gunsberg) H.; m. Sharon A. Berg, Aug. 11, 1985; children: Rachel, Sarah. BA, Rutgers U., 1977; JD, Bklyn. Law Sch., 1980; LLM, U. Miami, 1982. Assoc. Klatsky & Klatsky, Red Bank, N.J., 1980-81, Fuerst, Singer & Yusem, Somerville, N.J., 1982-83, Law Offices of Steven Schanker, Melville, N.Y., 1983-86; ptnr. Schanker & Hochberg, Attys., Huntington, N.Y., 1986—; frequent lectr. on estate planning; instr. Adelphi U., 1984-93. Columnist Financial World Mag., 1993-97; contbr. articles to profl. publs. Mem. ABA, N.Y. State Bar Assn., Estate and Tax Planning Coun. Avocations: skiing, sailing. Office: Schanker & Hochberg 27 W Neck Rd Huntington NY 11743-2618

HOCHE, PHILIP ANTHONY, life insurance company executive; b. Cape Girardeau, Mo., Jan. 29, 1906; s. Philip Aloysius and Mary Edith (Meyers) H.; m. Angela Genevieve Hayes, Jan. 2, 1941 (dec.); children: A. Henry, John Philip. B.A., Southeast Mo. State U., 1926. Sales rep. Sherwin-Williams Co., Chgo., 1926-31; agt., ednl. dir. New Eng. Mut. Life Ins. Co., Chgo., 1932-39; gen. agt. Kansas City Life Ins. Co., Bloomington, Ill., 1940-43, Orlando, Fla., 1946-91; mem. ins. bd. Winter Park, Fla., 1965-76; chmn., 1973-76; mem. ins. bd. Orlando, Fla., 1976-81; trustee Life Underwriters Tng. Council, 1956-59, Nat. Assn. Life Underwriters, 1961-63, sec., 1964, v.p., 1965, pres., 1966; also life mem. nat. council; chmn. Fla. Life Underwriters Polit. Action Com., 1970-81. Pres. Orange County (Fla.) Heart Assn., 1963-64; chmn. fund raising adv. com. So. region Am. Heart Assn., 1969, 71; gov.'s ambassador good will for Fla., 1965-66; pres. Central Fla. Estate Planning Council, 1957-58, 68-69; Life mem. bd. dirs. Fla. affiliate Am. Heart Assn., chmn., 1976-77. Served to lt. comdr. USNR, 1943-45. Recipient C.G. Snead Meml. award Fla. Assn. Life Underwriters, 1961. Mem. Am. Soc. C.L.U. (emeritus), Guild Former Pipe Organ Pumpers, Navy League, Am. Mensa Ltd. Clubs: University, Rotary (pres. 1958-59, Man of Yr. award 1959, sec. 1972-83); Rotary (Winter Park) (Paul Harris fellow). Home and Office: Inn at Freedom Sq 10801 Johnson Blvd Seminole FL 33772-4746

HOCHHALTER, GORDON RAY, advertising communications executive; b. Jerome, Idaho, Oct. 3, 1946; s. Ralph R. and Evelyn (McClellan) H. BA, Brigham Young U., 1972. Asst. promotion supr. Armstrong World Industries, Lancaster, Pa., 1972-74, promotion supr., 1974-76, sr. promotion supr., 1976; asst. advt. mgr. R.R. Donnelley & Sons Co., Chgo., 1976-79, asst. mgr. advt., sales promotion, 1979-81, advt. mgr., 1981-84, group mgr. mktg. com., creative devel., 1984-86, dir. mktg. com., creative dir., 1986-91; v.p., gen. mgr., creative dir. Mobium Corp. Design & Communications, Chgo., 1991-96, v.p., creative dir. design and conceptual devel., 1996-97; chief creative officer Mobium Creative Group, Chgo., 1998—; v.p., creative cons. Caviale Fashions, N.Y.C., 1987—. Author: Strategies for a New Age of Business Communications, New Media in a New Age of Business Communications, Creative Leverage in a New Age of Business Communications, Integrating Communications in a New Age of Business Marketing; monthly columnist Integrated Mktg. and Promotion Mag.; contbr. to profl. jours. and Libr. of Congress. Recipient London Internat. Advt. awards, 1987, One Show, Type Dirs. Club, Clio awrds, Art Dirs. Club awards, Andy awards, Addy awards, Internat. Advt. Festival AIGA awards, ProCom awards, Ace awards, Chgo. Tower awards, 1987-99, Am. Bus. Press Objective and Results award, 1992, Cresta Internat. Advt. award, 1993, Sawyer award Bus. Mktg. Mag., 1993, High-Tech. Advt. award MARCOM, 1994-96, Pinnacle award MARCOM, 1994, Icon award Bus. Week Mag., 1994-95, 98, 99. Mem. Am. Ctr. for Design, Am. Advt. Fedn., Am. Inst. Graphic Arts, Chgo. Advt. Fedn., Bus. Mktg. Assn., N.Y. Art Dirs. Club. Office: Mobium Corp The Merchandise Mart 200 World Trade Ctr Ste 2000 Chicago IL 60654

HOCHHAUSER, RICHARD MICHAEL, marketing professional; b. N.Y.C., Aug. 25, 1944; s. Stanley and Rita (Weingarten) H.; m. Carole Beth Wasserstein, Sept. 6, 1969; children: Jonathan, Jennifer. BS, Carnegie Mellon U., 1966; MBA, Columbia U., 1968. Systems engr. U.S. Dept. of Navy, Washington, 1968-70; v.p. market research Quayle Plesser & Co., N.Y.C., 1970-75; pres. research RMH Research, Inc. subs. Harte-Hanks Communications, Fort Lee, N.J., 1975-80; pres. mktg. services Harte Hanks Inc., Fairlawn, N.J., 1980-84; pres. direct mktg. Harte Hanks Inc., N.Y.C., 1984-95, exec. v.p., 1996—, COO, 1998—, pres., 1999—; faculty NYU. Mem. Direct Mktg. Assn. (exec. com., bd. dirs., chmn.). Avocations: horticulture, antique watches. Home: 1025 5th Ave # 9dn New York NY 10028-0134 Office: Harte Hanks Inc 260 Madison Ave New York NY 10016-2401

HOCHHEIMER, FRANK LEO, brokerage executive; b. N.Y.C., Sept. 27, 1943; s. Arthur A. and Alice (Schoenthal) H.; m. Beverly Widman, Dec. 24, 1967; 1 child, Martin. BA in Math., Queens Coll., 1965; MA in Econometrics, New Sch. Social Rsch., 1973; MA in Math., Hofstra U., 1966. Instr., chmn. math dept. N.Y. Inst. Tech., 1966-74; mgr. S. Bauer & Sons, N.Y.C., 1974-75; analyst Merrill Lynch, N.Y.C., 1974-75, computer specialist, commodity div., 1976-78, mgr., tech. analysis, 1978-79; v.p., dir. rsch. Merrill Lynch, N.Y.C., 1980-83; v.p., dir. Futures Info. Svcs., N.Y.C., 1983-85, v.p., mgr. global securities data and pricing svc., 1985-90; v.p., mgr. CMO dept. Merrill Lynch Mortgage Capital, N.Y.C., 1990-95; v.p., mgr. Merrill Lynch Ops. Sys. and Telecomm., N.Y.C., 1995—. Contrbr. articles to profl. jours. Mem. Am Econs. Assn., Nat. Assn. Bus. Economists, Market Technicians Assn., Futures Industry Assn. (former dir., teas. rsch. div.), Securities Industry Assn. (data mgmt. divsn.).

HOCHLERIN, DIANE, pediatrician, educator; b. N.Y.C., Feb. 4, 1942; d. William J. and Bertha Hochlerin. BS, U. City of N.Y., 1958; MD, Med. Coll. Pa., 1966. Diplomate Am. Bd. Pediats. Intern Albert Einstein Hosp., Phila., 1966-67; resident Phila. Gen. Hosp., 1967-69; attending pediatrician St. Luke's Roosevelt Hosp., N.Y.C., 1969—; clin. assoc. prof. pediats. Columbia U., N.Y.C., 1969—; asst. attending physician Cath. Med. Ctr., N.Y.C., 1993—; faculty advisor Adelphi U., N.Y.C., 1994. Fellow Am. Acad. Pediats.; mem. N.Y. State Med. Soc., County Med. Soc. Home and Office: 305 E 86th St Apt 20 New York NY 10028-4702

HOCHMAN, DAVID, economic development consultant; b. N.Y.C., Mar. 10, 1957; s. Stanley and Eleanor (Bell) H.; m. Eugenia Siegler, Jan. 15, 1983; children: Daniel B., Joel L. AB, Princeton U., 1978; MBA, NYU, 1984. Newsman The Associated Press, Buffalo, 1978-79; pubs. editor Wharton Analysis Ctr., Phila., 1979-81; pres., chief ops. officer Millennium Group, Inc., N.Y.C., 1982-85; assoc. dir. N.J. Commn. Sci. & Tech., Trenton, 1986-90, deputy dir., 1990-95; cons. pvt. practice, N.Y.C., 1995—; project mgr. Battelle Meml. Inst., N.Y.C., 1997—; adj. assoc. prof. pub. adminstrn., Wagner Sch., NYU, 1998—. Contbr. articles to profl. jours. Officer, dir. Spruce Hill Cmty. Assn., Phila., 1988-95; officer 27th Ward Dem. Com., Phila., 1988-95. Mem. Soc. Tech. Comm. Jewish. Home: 305 E 24th St Apt 2C New York NY 10010-4021

HOCHMAN, KENNETH GEORGE, lawyer; b. Mt. Vernon, N.Y., Nov. 12, 1947; s. Benjamin S. and Lillian (Gilbert) H.; m. Carol K. Hochman, Apr. 8, 1979; children: Brian Paul, Lisa Erin. BA, SUNY, Buffalo, 1969; JD, Columbia U., 1972. Bar: Ohio 1973, Fla. 1977, N.Y. 1979. Assoc. Jones, Day, Reavis & Pogue, Cleve., 1972-79, ptnr., 1980—; trustee Katharine Kenyon Lippitt Found., Cleve., 1988, Kenridge Fund, Cleve., 1989, Bolton Found., Cleve., 1990, Elisha-Bolton Found., Cleve., 1993. Harlan Fiske Stone scholar Columbia U., 1971, 72. Fellow Am. Coll. Trusts and Estate Counsel; mem. Phi Beta Kappa, Oakwood Club (Cleve.) (trustee 1997). Office: Jones Day Reavis & Pogue 901 Lakeside Ave E Cleveland OH 44114-1116

HOCHMAN, NAOMI LIPSON, special education educator, consultant; b. Bklyn.; d. William Lipson and Tillie Silverstein-Beech Lipson; m. Elihu Hochman (div. Mar. 1978); children: Richard, Lisa, Lauren. BA cum laude, Bklyn. Coll., 1956; MA, William Paterson U., 1973. Cert. spl. edn. tchr., N.Y., learning disability cons., N.J. Tchr. Bd. Edn., N.Y.C., 1956-58; spl. edn. tchr. Bd. Edn., Wayne, N.J., 1968-73; instr. edn. William Paterson U., Wayne, N.J., 1973—; learning disability cons. Wayne Bd. Edn., 1973—; mem. Thorough & Efficient Steering Com., N.J., 1975-80, Adv. Panel Spl. Edn., 1985-93; spkr. Literacy Vols. N.J. Passaic C.C., 1991—; bd. dirs. Wayne Counseling Youth, 1987-90. Mem. LWV, Wayne, 1965-73, Wayne Arts League, 1968-72. Recipient Honors Edn. award Bklyn. Coll., 1956. Mem. N.J. Edn. Assn., Profl. Svcs. Coun. N.J., N.J. Assn. Learning Cons. (pres. 1989-91). Avocations: tennis, bldg. doll houses. Home: 201 Zeppi Ln West Orange NJ 07052-4130 Office: Wayne Child Study Team 50 Nellis Dr Wayne NJ 07470-3555

HOCHMUTH, ROBERT MILO, mechanical and biomedical engineer, educator; b. Berkeley, Calif., May 29, 1939; s. Harold Robert and Marjorie Evelyn (Strawn) H.; m. Doris Ann Schwartz, June 6, 1964; 1 child, Carolyn Ann. B.S., U. Colo., 1961; M.S., Ohio State U., 1962; Ph.D., Brown U., 1967. Mem. faculty dept. chem. engring. Washington U., St. Louis, 1967-78; prof. Washington U., 1975-78; prof. dept. biomed. engring. Duke U., Durham, N.C., 1978—; prof. dept. mech. engring. and materials sci. Duke U., 1986—; chmn., 1986-94; acting dir. ctr. for biochem. engring. Duke U., 1986-90; cons. NIH, NSF, Whitaker Found. Mem. editl. bd. Biophys. Jour., 1980-84, Critical Revs. in Bioengring., 1977-84, Jour. Biomech. Engring., 1987-93, Cell Biophysics, 1989-94; contbr. articles to profl. jours. NSF fellow, 1961-62; Brown U. fellow, 1962-63; NIH research career devel. grantee, 1973-78. Fellow Am. Inst. Biol. Engr. (founder); mem. AAAS, ASME (chmn. bioprocess engring. program 1989-91), Biophys. Soc., Soc. Rheology, Biomed. Engring. Soc. (pres. 1993-94), N.Am. Soc. Biorheology (pres. 1996-98). Achievements include research on elastic, viscous, and adhesive properties of cells, cellular biomechanics. Office: Duke U Dept Mech Engring Durham NC 27708-0300

HOCHREITER, JOHN ALLEN, computer company owner, firefighter; b. Buffalo, Mar. 5, 1949; s. Robert Allen and Dorothy Eileen (Scully) H.; m. Shelley Cunningham, July 30, 1977; children: Sean Scully, Mark Andrew. BA, Niagara U., 1971; MEd, Boston Coll., Chestnut Hill, Mass., 1975. Mid. sch. tchr. sci. St. Rose of Lima Sch., Buffalo, 1971-73; mgr., dir. Snowflake Ventures, Ellicottsville, N.Y., 1973-74; itinerant tchr. for blind and visually impaired Buffalo Pub. Schs., 1975-77, itinerant tchr. coord., 1977-79; dept. mgr. Computac, Inc., West Lebanon, N.H., 1979-87, exec. v.p., 1987-92, pres., CEO, 1992—; bd. dirs. Mascoma Savs. Bank, Lebanon, N.H. Baseball coach Sr. Babe Ruth League; bd. dirs. Hanover (N.H.) Improvement Soc.; chmn. Dresden Sch. Bd., Hanover, 1988-89, Hanover Sch. Bd., 1987; lt. Hanover Fire Sta.-Etna Sta., 1983—. Mem. Conn. and Ompompanoosuc R.R., Hanover Country Club, Rotary (pres. 1996, presdl. citation 1996, Paul Harris fellow 1998). Republican. Roman Catholic. Avocation: golf. Fax: 603-298-6189. E-mail: john@computac.com.

HOCHREITER, JOSEPH CHRISTIAN, JR., engineering company executive; b. Bristol, Pa., Jan. 29, 1955; s. Joseph Christian and Mary Claire (Boyer) H.; m. Eileen Grace Wachtman, Aug. 31, 1984; children: Erich, Kristen. BA, Temple U., 1978; postgrad., Drexel U., 1983-85. Cert. ground water prof. Hydrologic tech. U.S. Geological Survey, Trenton, N.J., 1973-78, hydrologist, 1979-87; hydrologic mgr. Environ. Resources Mgt., Inc., Princeton, N.J., 1987-90, br. mgr., 1990-92, principal, 1991-92; v.p. Blasland, Bouck & Lee, Cranbury, N.J., 1992—; lectr. Pa. State U., Trevose, Pa., 1980-84. Author and co-author numerous reports, papers in related field; editl. bd Jour. Ground Water, Columbus, Ohio, 1989-93. Founder Bucks County Homeless Shelter, Levittown, Pa., 1985; bd. dirs. ARC, Langhorne, Pa., 1985-91, Human Growth Ctr., Holland, Pa., 1987-92, 96—. Recipient Adult Vol. award Bucks County Courier Times, 1987. Mem. Am. Geophysical Union, Nat. Ground Water Assn. (mem. fellowship com. 1995), Assn. Ground Water Scientists and Engrs., N.J. Acad. Sci., Geol. Assn. N.J. Home: 252 Hollow Branch Ln Yardley PA 19067-5791 Office: Blasland Bouck & Lee 8 S River Rd Cranbury NJ 08512-3698

HOCHSCHILD, ADAM, writer, commentator, journalist; b. N.Y.C., Oct. 5, 1942; s. Harold K. and Mary (Marquand) H.; m. Arlie Russell, June 26, 1965; children: David, Gabriel. A.B. cum laude (hon. nat. scholar 1960-61), Harvard U., 1963. Reporter San Francisco Chronicle, 1965-66; writer, editor Ramparts mag., 1967-68, 73-74; commentator Nat. Pub. Radio, 1982-83; bd. dirs. Nuclear Times mag., 1982-89; regents lectr. U. Calif.-Santa Cruz, 1987; lectr. Grad. Sch. Journalism U. Calif., Berkeley, 1992, 95, 97—; Fulbright lectr., India, 1997-98. Author: Half the Way Home: A Memoir of Father and Son, 1986 (Notable Book of Yr. ALA and N.Y. Times Book Rev.), The Mirror at Midnight: A South African Journey, 1990, The Unquiet Ghost: Russians Remember Stalin, 1994 (Notable Book of Yr. N.Y. Times Book Rev. and Libr. Jour., Madeline Dane Ross award Overseas Press Club Am., Gold medal Soc. Am. Travel Writers), Finding the Trapdoor: Essays, Portraits, Travels, 1997 (PEN/Spielvogel-Diamanstein award for the art of the Essay), King Leopold's Ghost: A Story of Greed, Terror and Heroism in Colonial Africa, 1998 (finalist Nat. Book Critics Circle award, Mark Lynton History prize); freelance writer nat. mags., 1966—; co-founder, editor, now writer Mother Jones mag., 1974—; commentator Pub. Interest Radio, 1987-88. Recipient Cert. of Excellence, Overseas Press Club, N.Y.C., 1981, Spann prize Eugene V. Debs Found., 1984, Thomas Storke Internat. Journalism award World Affairs Coun. No. Calif., 1987. Mem. PEN, Nat. Writers Union, Nat. Book Critics Circle. Home: 84 Seward St San Francisco CA 94114-2337

HOCHSCHILD, CARROLL SHEPHERD, medical equipment and computer company executive, educator; b. Whittier, Calif., Mar. 31, 1935; d. Vernon Vero and Effie Corinne (Hollingsworth) Shepherd; m. Richard Hochschild, July 25, 1959; children: Christopher Paul, Stephen Shepherd. BA in Internat. Rels., Pomona Coll., 1956; Teaching credential, U. Calif., Berkeley, 1957; MBA, Pepperdine U., 1985; cert. in fitness instrn., U. Calif., Irvine, 1988. Cert. elem. tchr., Calif. Elem. tchr. Oakland (Calif.) Pub. Schs., 1957-58, San Lorenzo (Calif.) Pub. Schs., 1958-59, Pasadena (Calif.) Pub. Schs., 1959-60, Huntington Beach (Calif.) Pub. Schs., 1961-63, 67-68; adminstrv. asst. Microwave Instruments, Corona del Mar, Calif., 1968-74; co-owner Hoch Co., Corona del Mar, 1978—; rep. Calif. Tchrs. Assn., Huntington Beach, 1962-63. Mem. AAUW, P.E.O. (projects chmn. 1990-92, corr. sec. 1992-94, 98-99, 99—, chpt. pres. 1994-95), Internat. Dance-Exercise Assn., NAFE, ASTD (Orange County chpt.), Assistance League Newport-Mesa, Toastmistress (corr. sec. 1983), Jr. Ebell Club (fine arts chmn. Newport Beach 1966-67). Republican.

HOCHSCHILD, JENNIFER L., political scientist, educator; b. Pitts., Sept. 17, 1950; d. Reinhard George and Barbara Elizabeth (Fox) H.; m. Charles Anthony Broh, Aug. 27, 1978; children: Eleanor Hochschild, Raphael Fox. BA, Oberlin Coll., 1971; PhD, Yale U., 1971. Asst. prof. polit. sci. Duke U., Durham, N.C., 1978-81, Columbia U., N.Y.C., 1981; from asst. prof. to prof. polit. sci. Princeton U., 1981-98, William Stewart Tod prof. pub. and internat. affairs, 1998—; cons. U.S. Dept. Def., 1996. Author: What's Fair? American Beliefs about Distributive Justice, 1981, The New American Dilemma: Liberal Democracy and School Desegregation, 1984, Facing Up to the American Dream: Race, Class, and the Soul of the Nation, 1995 (Gustavus Myers Ctr. for Study of Human Rights award 1996); editor: (with Sara McLanahan and Irwin Garfinkel) Social Policies for Children, 1996; trustee, mem. editl. bd. Princeton U. Press, 1988-95. Mem. adv. coun. Lyndon B. Johnson Sch. Pub. Affairs, U. Tex., 1998—; mem. bd. overseers Gen. Social Survey, 1999—; trustee Russell Sage Found., 1998—. Spencer Found. rsch. grantee, 1996-98; fellow Ctr. for Advanced Study in Behavioral Scis., 1987-88. Fellow Am. Acad. Arts and Scis.; mem. Am. Polit. Sci. Assn. (v.p. 1997-98), Assn. for Pub. Policy Analysis and Mgmt. (policy coun. 1997—), Jewish. Office: Princeton U Dept Politics Princeton NJ 08544

HOCHSCHWENDER, HERMAN KARL, international consultant; b. Heidelberg, Federal Republic Germany, Mar. 1, 1920; came to U.S., 1930, naturalized, 1935; s. Karl G. and Maria (Recken) H.; m. Janet Elliott (div. 1961); children: Lynn Anne Hochschwender McGowin, Herman Karl Jr., Irene Hochschwender Harris, James E.; m. Mary Koger, July 3, 1965; 1 child, J. Michael. BS, Yale U., 1941; postgrad., Harvard U. Asst. indsl. rels. mgr. Sargent and Co., New Haven, 1943-45; mgr. corp. planning Firestone Tire and Rubber Co., Akron, Ohio, 1945-56; pres. Mohawk Rubber Co., N.Y.C., 1959; founder, pres. Hochschwender and Assocs., Akron, 1959-72; founder, pres. Smithers Sci. Svcs., Inc., Akron, 1972-90, bd. dirs., 1972-96, chmn. bd., 1996—; lectr. in field. Contbr. articles to profl. jours. Vice chmn. bd. trustees Akron Gen. Med. Ctr. Inducted into Tire Ind. Hall of Fame, 1994. Mem. ASTM, Am. Coun. Ind. Labs., Union Internat. des Laboratoires Independents (pres. 1987-93, bd. govs.), Soc. Automotive Engrs., Am. Assn. Lab. Accreditation, Yale U. Alumni Assn. Clubs: Akron City (trustee), Portage Country (Akron), Yale (N.Y.C.), Naples Yacht, Royal Poinciana Golf. Lodge: Rotary. Address: Smithers Sci Svcs 425 W Market St Akron OH 44303-2045

HOCHSCHWENDER, KARL ALBERT, international trade and government relations consultant; b. Mannheim, Germany, Feb. 1, 1927; came to U.S., 1931, naturalized, 1938; s. Karl Georg and Maria Irma (Recken) H.; m. Lilli Gettinger, July 4, 1964. BA, Yale U., 1947, MA, 1949, PhD, 1962. Instr. polit. sci. Fla. State U., Tallahassee, 1949-51; assoc. Mott of Washington & Assocs., Washington, 1954-58; rsch. analyst U.S. Govt., Washington, 1959-60; asst. to mgmt. Am. Hoechst Corp., Bridgewater, N.J., 1961-63, mgr. govt. rels., 1963-68, dir. pub. rels., 1968-72, dir. pub. affairs, 1972-83; prin. Palatine Assocs., Princeton, N.J., 1983—; mem. roster of tech. specialists Office of Spl. Rep. for Trade Negotiations, Exec. Office Pres., 1964-67. Trustee United Fund Somerset Valley, N.J., 1969-75; mem. Princeton Site Plan Rev. Adv. Bd., 1992-99, vice chmn., 1994-99. Recipient Leonard D. White Meml. award Am. Polit. Sci. Assn., 1963; fellow Yale U., 1952-54. Mem. Am. Assn. Exporters and Importers (bd. dirs. 1963—, v.p. 1967-83, pres. 1983, chmn. 1983-85), Chem. Comm. Assn. (bd. dirs. 1976-80), Soc. Plastics Industry (chmn. food, drug and cosmetics packaging material com. 1972-76), Yale Club N.Y.C. Office: Palatine Assocs PO Box 1466 Princeton NJ 08542-1466

HOCHSTEIN, ANATOLY BORIS, maritime ports and waterways educator, researcher, consultant; b. Minsk, Belarus, Oct. 15, 1932; came to U.S., 1973; s. Boris A. and Esphir S. (Shapiro); m. Marina E Edidovich; 1 child Leonard. MS in water transp. and hydraulics with honors, Inst. Water Transp., Leningrad, USSR, 1955; PhD, Cen. Navigation Inst., Moscow, 1963. Dir. Waterways Lab. Cen. Navigation Inst., Moscow, 1963-73; sr. assoc. CACI, Inc., Washington, 1974-77; v.p., cons. Louis Berger Internat., Inc., East Orange, N.J., 1977—; dir., disting. prof. Nat. Ports and Waterways Inst., La. State U., Baton Rouge and Washington, 1982—; bd. dirs. Nat. Waterway Conf., Inc.; prin. U.S. rep. Internat. Navigation Congress, 1989—; chmn. Inland Waterways Com., Transp. Rsch. Bd., 1990-95. Author 5 books, over 50 articles in field. Bd. dirs. Hebrew Immigration Aid Soc., N.Y.C., 1987—. Mem. Am. Assn. Port Authorities. Home: 11905 Latigo Ln Oakton VA 22124-2314 Address: National Ports And Waterways Institu 2300 Clarendon Blvd Ste 300 Arlington VA 22201-3367

HOCHSTRASSER, DONALD LEE, cultural anthropologist, community health and public administration educator; b. Taylorsville, Ky., June 10, 1927; s. Emil John and Mary E. (Schad) H.; m. Marie Emlen, Apr. 9, 1960; 1 child, Letitia Cope; stepchildren—Eloise Q. Hatch, Laura A. Hatch. B.A., U. Ky., 1952, M.A., 1955; postgrad. (univ. fellow) Northwestern U., 1955-56; Ph.D. in Anthropology, U. Oreg., 1963; M.P.H., U. Calif.-Berkeley, 1969. Research asst. dept. rural sociology U. Ky., Lexington, 1954-55, instr. dept. anthropology, 1956-57, 1959-60, instr. dept. community medicine, 1961-63, asst. prof., 1963-66, assoc. prof., 1966-73, prof., 1973-80, assoc. dir. Ctr. Developmental Change, 1970-73, prof. community health Coll. Allied Health, prof. anthropology Coll. of Arts and Scis., prof. pub. adminstrn. Grad. Ctr. Pub. Adminstrn., 1980-93, prof. emeritus dept. health svcs., 1993—; teaching fellow dept. anthropology U. Oreg., Eugene, 1957-58, instr., 1958-59, NSF research fellow, 1960-61; USPHS spl. research fellow Sch. Pub. Health, U. Calif.-Berkeley, 1968-69; chmn. state family planning rev. com. Ky. State Comprehensive Health Planning Council, 1972-74; mem. state family planning task force Council Health Services, Ky. State Dept. Human Resources, 1974-78; cons., adv. numerous orgns.; vis. scholar dept. adminstrv. and social health scis. Sch. Pub. Health, U. Calif.-Berkeley, 1979; dir. Bluegrass Regional Birth Planning Council, Inc., Lexington, 1978-81, Lexington Planned Parenthood, Inc., 1982-89; mem. adv. coun. Ctr. of Creative Living/Adult Care Program of Lexington-Fayette County Health Dept., 1989. Mem. Union of Concerned Scientists, Am. Farmland Trust, Wilderness Soc. Served with USN, 1946-47. Grantee pub. health, family planning, sickle cell anemia, Tb control and occupational health-risk factors. Fellow Am. Anthrop. Assn., Soc. Applied Anthropology; mem. Soc. Med. Anthropology (founding), Am. Pub. Health Assn. (founding mem. population sect.), Assn. Tchrs. Preventive Medicine, AAAS, AAUP, Phi Beta Kappa, Sigma Xi, Alpha Kappa Delta, Delta Omega. Democrat. Clubs: Univ. Faculty, Alumni. Contbr. numerous articles to profl. pubs. Home: 953 Holly Springs Dr Lexington KY 40504-3119 Office: Univ Ky Med Ctr 208A Annex 2 Lexington KY 40536

HOCHSTRASSER, JOHN MICHAEL, environmental engineer, industrial hygienist; b. Cin., July 19, 1938; s. Alvin Louis and Helen Augusta (Furst) H.; m. Wilma Ruth Reckman, Feb. 27, 1960; children: Ronald, Jennifer, Caroline. BSME, U. Cin., 1963, MS in Environ. Engring., 1972, PhD in Environ. Health, 1976. Registered profl. engr., Ohio, Ill., N.J.; diplomate of environ. engring. Am. Acad. Environ. Engrs.; qualified environ. profl. Inst. Profl. Environ. Practice; cert. indsl. hygienist Am. Bd. Indsl. Hygiene; registered occupational hygienist, Can. Reliability and safety engr. GE Co., Evendale, Ohio, 1963-72; dir. environ. affairs G.D. Searle & Co., Skokie, Ill., 1975-78; dir. indsl. hygiene Tenneco Chems., Inc., Piscataway, N.J., 1978-83; project dir. Roy F. Weston, Inc., West Chester, Pa., 1983-85; dir. health and safety CH2M Hill, Inc., Parsippany, N.J., 1985-89; tech. dir. First Environ., Inc., Riverdale, N.J., 1989-92; dir. environ. health and safety Tastemaker, Cin., 1992-97, Am. Tool Cos., Inc., Wilmington, Ohio, 1998—. Mem. ASCE, NSPE, Am. Indsl. Hygiene Assn. (bd. dirs. 1987-90, chair ethics com. 1992-93), Am. Soc. Safety Engrs., Am. Acad. Indsl. Hygiene (councilor 1995-98), Am. Acad. Environ. Engrs. (chair indsl. hygiene com. 1995—), Air and Waste Mgmt. Assn., Water Pollution Control Fedn., System Safety Soc., Soc. for Risk Analysis. Achievements include research on the use of fault tree analysis to solve environmental problems; research of short circuit flow in cyclone dust collectors; established occupational exposure limits for estrogen dusts and availability requirements for incinerators. Home: 11317 Longden Way Union KY 41091-8004

HOCHSTRASSER, ROBIN M., chemist, educator; b. Edinburgh, Scotland, Jan. 4, 1931; U.S. citizen; married; 2 children. BSc, Heriot-Watt U., Scotland, 1952, DSc honoris causa, 1984; PhD in Pure Chemistry, U. Edinburgh, 1955. Mem. faculty dept. chemistry U. B.C., Can., 1957-63; mem. faculty dept. chemistry U. Pa., Phila., 1963—, Blanchard prof., 1971-83, Doonner prof. sci., 1983—, dir. Regional Laser Lab., 1978—; vis. prof. Cambridge (Eng.) U., 1972, Australian Nat. U., Canberra, 1973, U. Grenoble, France, 1974, Calif. Inst. Tech., 1975, others. Contbr. articles to profl. jours. Recipient Bourke medal Faraday Soc., 1981; Courtald scholar, 1952-55, Alfred P. Sloan Found. fellow, 1963-67, John Simon Guggenheim fellow, 1972, Alexander von Humboldt sr. fellow, 1978. Mem. AAAS, AAUP, Am. Chem. Soc. (Phila. Sect. award 1990, Peter Debye award 1997), Royal Inst. Chemistry, Am. Phys. Soc., Am. Inst. Physics, Biophys. Soc., Optical Soc. Am. (Spl. Pres.'s award 1986, Ellis R. Lippincott award 1997), Nat. Acad. Sci., Am. Acad. Arts and Scis. Office: U Pa Dept Chemistry 3301 Spruce St Philadelphia PA 19104-6323*

HOCK, FREDERICK WYETH, lawyer; b. Newark, July 10, 1924; s. Herbert Hummel and Carol (Wyeth) H.; m. Alfeld Catherine Larsen, Mar. 4, 1945; children: Carolyn, Sandra, Rhonda; m. 2d, Ellen Barbara Weidner, June 28, 1975. AA, Princeton U., 1944; BA, Rutgers U., 1948, LLB, 1950, JD, 1968. Bar: N.J. 1949. Assoc. Stevenson, Willette & McDermott, 1949-51; sole practice, 1951-65; ptnr. Hock & Sharkey, East Orange, N.J., 1965-79; sr. ptnr. Hock Silverlieb & Kramer, Livingston, N.J., 1979-93, Gulkin, Hock & Lehr, 1994—; acting judge East Orange Mcpl. Ct., 1954-57; mem. adv. bd. Maplewood Bank and Trust Co., Livingston, 1987-91, Summit Trust Co., 1991-98. Chmn. Juvenile Conf. Com. 1958-62; trustee Community Day Nursery of the Oranges & Maplewood, 1962-75, pres., 1973-75; trustee Founders Endowment Fund, 1954-87, House of Good Shepherd 1970-90, Nu Beta Found., 1970-91; bd. dirs. Essex County chpt. ARC, 1987-91; post adv. VFW post 5445, 1955-90. Served with USMC 1942-46. Mem. ABA, N.J. Bar Assn., Northwestern N.J. Estate Planning Council (dir. 1981-90), No. N.J. Estate Planning Coun. Office: 354 Eisenhower Pkwy Livingston NJ 07039-1023

HOCK, MORTON, entertainment advertising executive; b. N.Y.C., June 24, 1929; s. Louis and Grace Dora (Solomon) H.; m. Anita Zagerman, Nov. 8, 1959; children—Jennifer, Jonathan. With Blaine Thompson Co., N.Y.C.; acct. supr. David Merrick Productions, 1954-60; advt. mgr. Paramount Pictures, N.Y.C., 1960-63, v.p., 1967-71; dir. advt. United Artists Corp., N.Y.C., 1963-67; exec. v.p. Charles Schlaifer & Co., Inc., N.Y.C., 1972-83; exec. v.p. entertainment div. DDB Needham Worldwide, N.Y.C., 1983—; mgmt. supr. Universal Pictures Account, United Artists Theatres Account, Gramercy Pictures Account. Contbr. articles to Variety. Mem. adv. com., bd. dirs. Will Rogers Found., 1983—. Named Showman of Yr. Nat. Assn. Theatre Owners; recipient Nat. Screen Svc. award for best theatre trailer. Mem. Acad. Motion Picture Arts and Scis. (bd. dirs.), Motion Picture Pioneers. Clubs: Variety of N.Y. (pres. 1979-80); Friars (admission com.). Lodge: B'nai Brith (trustee cinema unit 1980—). Avocations: sports; music; reading; travel.

HOCKADAY, IRVINE O., JR., greeting card company executive; b. Ludington, Mich., Aug. 12, 1936; s. Irvine Oty and Helen (McCune) H.; m. Mary Ellen Jurden, July 8, 1961; children: Wendy Helen, Laura DuVal. A.B., Princeton U., 1958; LL.B., U. Mich., 1961, J.D., 1961. Bar: Mo. 1961. Atty. firm Lathrop, Koontz, Righter, Clagett and Norquist, Kansas City, 1961-67; atty., asst. gen. counsel, asst. to pres., v.p. Kansas City So. Industries, Inc., 1968-71, pres., chief ops. officer, 1971-80, pres., chief exec. officer, 1981-83; exec. v.p. Hallmark Cards, Inc., 1983-85, pres., chief exec. officer, 1986—, also bd. dirs., 1978—; Bd. dirs. Ford Motor Co., UtiliCorp United, Dow Jones and Co., Sprint; trustee Hall Family Found., Aspen Inst.; past chmn. bd. dirs. 10th dist. Fed. Res. Bank; past chmn. Civic Coun. Kansas City, 1987-89, Midwest Rsch. Inst. Club: Kansas City Country. Office: Hallmark Cards Inc PO Box 419580 2501 McGee Trafficway Kansas City MO 64141-6580

HOCKEIMER, HENRY ERIC, business executive; b. Winzig, Germany, Apr. 3, 1920; came to U.S., 1946, naturalized, 1951; s. Erich and Gertrude (Masur) H.; m. Margaret Feeny, May 26, 1956; children: Ellen Patricia, Henry Eric. Student, RCA Insts., 1946-47; electronics and bus. mgmt., N.Y.U., 1948-51. With Philco-Ford Corp., Phila., 1947—, gen. mgr. communications and tech. services div., 1962-63, corp. v.p., 1963-72; v.p., gen. mgr. refrigeration products div. Connorsville, Ind., 1972-75; pres. Ford Aerospace & Communications Corp., Dearborn, Mich., 1975-85; v.p. Ford Motor Co., 1981-85; cons. USIA, Washington, 1985, dep. dir. TV and film service, 1986-87, asst. dir., 1987-88, assoc. dir. for mgmt., 1988-91, cons.,

1991—; commr. RIAS, 1991—; exec. adv. bd. mem. Starmountain Inc., 1995—. Mem. Engring. Soc. Detroit, Smithsonian, University Club Washington, Washington Arts Soc.

HOCKENBERG, HARLAN DAVID, lawyer; b. Des Moines, July 1, 1927; s. Leonard C. and Estyre M. (Zalk) H.; m. Dorothy A. Arkin, June 3, 1953; children: Marni Lynn, Thomas Leonard, Edward Arkin. BA, U. Iowa, 1949, JD, 1952. Bar: Iowa 1952. Assoc. Abramson & Myers, Des Moines, 1952-58, Abramson, Myers & Hockenberg, Des Moines, 1958-64; sr. ptnr. Davis, Hockenberg, Wine, Brown, Koehn & Shors, Des Moines, 1964-95; shareholder, dir. Sullivan & Ward, P.C., Des Moines, 1995—; bd. dirs. West Des Moines State Bank, Partnership for a Drug-Free Iowa, Nat. Jewish Coalition, Smoother Sailing Found, Connections Program Des Moines Jewish Found.; mem. Iowa State Bar Assn. Prof. com.; co-chair Mentor Program. Mem. bd. editors U. Iowa Law Review. Pres. Des Moines Jewish Social Svc. Agy., 1958-60; mem. Internat. Rels. and Nat. Security Adv. Coun., Rep. Nat. Com., 1978; chmn. Coun. Jewish Fedns., Small Cities Com., 1970-71; mem. exec. com. Am. Israel Pub. Affairs Com.; pres. Wilkie House, Inc., Des Moines, 1965-66, Des Moines Jewish Welfare Fedn., 1973-74; mem. Presdl. Commn. on White House Fellowships, 1988-92; mem. Mayor's Select Com. on Drug Abuse, co-chair prevention subcom.; mem. steering com. Des Moines Vision Plan; mem. ins. devel. bd. Iowa Dept. Econ. Devel. With USNR, 1945-46. Mem. Des Moines C. of C. (pres. 1986, chmn. bur. econ. devel. 1979, 80, bd. dirs. 1986, chmn. Metro Forum), Des Moines Club, Pioneer Club, Delta Sigma Rho, Omicron Delta Kappa, Phi Epsilon Pi. Home: 2880 Grand Ave Des Moines IA 50312-4274 Office: Sullivan & Ward PC 801 Grand Ave Ste 3500 Des Moines IA 50309-8004

HOCKERSMITH, CHARLES EDWIN, information technology educator; b. Chambersburg, pa., Nov. 12, 1947; s. Charles Samuel and Marietta Maxine (Potter) H.; m. Nancy Nickles, Nov. 21, 1970; children: Michael Charles, Alexander Nickles. BSEd, Shippensburg U., 1973; MLS, Syracuse U., 1998. Humanities librarian Christiana H.S., Newark, Del., 1973-78; librarian Newark H.S., 1978-80; libr. dir. Cecil C.C., North East, Md., 1980-95; ops. officer Del. NG, Wilmington, 1995—. Dir. 1st State Symphonic Band, Chesapeake Brass Band, 287th Army Band; pres. Christiana Bd. Edn., 1994-97. With U.S. Army, 1980. Mem. ALA, Libr. Info. Tech. Assn. Methodist. Home: 1 Andries Rd Newark DE 19711-5616 Office: Del NG First Regiment Rd Wilmington DE 19808

HOCKETT, CHARLES FRANCIS, anthropology educator; b. Columbus, Ohio, Jan. 17, 1916; s. Homer Carey and Amy (Francisco) H.; m. Shirley Orlinoff, Apr. 25, 1942; children: Alpha, Asher Orlinoff, Amy Roberta, Rachel, Carey Beth. BA, MA in Ancient History, Ohio State U., 1936; PhD in Anthropology, Yale U., 1939. Mem. faculty Cornell U., Ithaca, N.Y., 1946—, prof. linguistics and anthropology, 1957—, Goldwin Smith prof. linguistics and anthropology, 1970-82; prof. emeritus, 1982—; adj. prof. linguistics Rice U., Houston, 1991—. Author: A Course in Modern Linguistics, 1958, Man's Place in Nature, 1973, Refurbishing our Foundations, 1987; composer (opera) Doña Rosita, 1962; also instrumental works, songs. Named to Hon. Order Ky. Cols.; Ctr. Advanced Study Behavioral Scis. fellow, 1955-56. Mem. NAS, Linguistic Soc. Am. (pres. 1964), Linguistic Soc. Can. and U.S. (pres. 1982), Am. Acad. Arts and Scis., Phi Beta Kappa, Sigma Xi. Home: 145 N Sunset Dr Ithaca NY 14850-1459

HOCKING, MARIAN RUTH, women's health nurse; b. Detroit, Aug. 31, 1934; d. John Frederick and Clara Elizabeth (Numbers) Johnson; m. Wilbert Joseph Hocking, June 19, 1954; children: David, James, Debra, Timothy, Thomas, John. ADN, Grand Rapids (Mich.) Jr. Coll., 1975; student, Wayne State U. Cert. inpatient obstet. care, cert. in fetal monitoring. Receptionist dental office, Royal Oak, Mich., 1955-56; nurse's aide Ctrl. Mich. Cmty. Hosp., Mt. Pleasant, 1959-66; nurse FDF Hosp., Grand Rapids, 1966-75; from staff nurse to asst. coord. Met. Hosp., Grand Rapids, 1975-94; nurse No. Mich. Hosp., 1988-99; ret., 1999; relief nurse Dr. Joseph Sypniewski, DO, Petoskey, Mo., 1999—. Home: 4512 Chessie Ln Central Lake MI 49622-9724

HOCKMUTH, JOSEPH FRANK, physicist, psychotherapist; b. Buffalo, N.Y., Mar. 6, 1942; s. Joseph Frank and Gertrude Marie (Merkley) H.; m. Sharon Louise Van Deusen Tiernan, June 30, 1965 (div.); children: Joseph Fess, Catherine Marie; m. Katherine Nancy Genco, June 1, 1991 (div.). BS in Physics, Calif. State U., 1965; MA in Psychology, Norwich U., 1992. Cert. substance abuse counselor, Ariz. Bd. Behavioral Health Examiners; cert. coll. instr., Ariz. State Bd.; cert. profl. counselor. Rsch. engr. Westinghouse Astroelectronics, Newbury Park, Calif., 1965-66; rsch. engr. Lockheed Missile & Space Co., Sunnyvale, Calif., 1966-69, sr. rsch. engr., 1972-78; radiation effects engr. IRT Corp., San Diego, 1969-72, staff scientist, 1984-87; addictions counselor Charter Hosp., Glendale, Ariz., 1992-93; prin. staff engr. Motorola Govt. Sys. & Tech. Group, Scottsdale, Ariz., 1978-84; tech. staff engr. Motorola GSTG, Scottsdale, Ariz., 1987—, divsn. cons. for radiation effects, 1987—; psychotherapist Fountain Hills, Ariz., 1992—. Contbr. Awakenings mag., 1992—. Funds coord. United Way, Scottsdale, 1988-90; class sponsor Wounded Knee (Wyo.) Tribal Elem. Sch., 1992—. Sgt. Calif. NG, 1960-68. Fellow Am. Counseling Assn., Ariz. Counselors Assn., Noetic Scis. Inst.; mem. ASTM (com. 1985—), IEEE (ofcl. tech. paper reviewer 1993). Roman Catholic. Avocations: guitar, piano, fishing, camping, American Indian culture studies. Home: 15024 E Windyhill Rd Fountain Hls AZ 85268-1323 Office: Motorola GSTG 8201 E Mcdowell Rd # H2550 Scottsdale AZ 85257-3893

HOCKNEY, DAVID, artist; b. Bradford, Yorkshire, Eng., July 9, 1937; s. Kenneth and Laura H. Attended, Bradford Coll. Art, 1953-57, Royal Coll. Art, London, 1959-62; D (hon.), U. Aberdeen, 1988; hon. degree, Royal Coll. Art, London, 1992. Lectr. U. Iowa, 1964, U. Colo., 1965, U. Calif. Berkeley, 1967; lectr. UCLA, 1966, hon. chair of drawing, 1980. One-man shows include Kasmin Gallery, 1963-89, Mus. Modern Art, N.Y.C., 1964, 68, Stedelijk Mus., Amsterdam, Netherlands, 1966, Whitechapel Gallery, London, 1970, Andre Emmerich Gallery, N.Y.C., 1972-96, Musee des Arts Decoratifs, Paris, 1974, Museo Tamayo, Mexico City, 1984, L.A. Louver, Calif., 1986, 89—, Nishimura Gallery, Tokyo, 1986, 89, 90, 94, Met. Mus. Art, 1988, L.A. County Mus. Art, 1988, 96, Tate Gallery, London, 1988, 92, Royal Acad. Arts, London, 1995, Hamburger Kunsthalle, 1995, Nat. Mus. Am. Art, Washington, 1997, 98, Mus. Ludwig, Cologne, 1997, MFA, Boston, 1998, Centre Georges Pompidou, Paris, 1999, Musee Picasso, Paris, 1999, others; designer: Rake's Progress, Glyndebourne, Eng., 1975; sets for Magic Flute, Glyndebourne, 1978, Parade Triple Bill, Stravinsky Triple Bill, Met. Opera House, 1980-81, Tristan und Isolde, Los Angeles Music Ctr. Opera, 1987; Turandot Lyric Opera, Chgo., 1992—, San Francisco Opera, 1993, Die Frau Ohne Schatten, Covent Garden, London, 1992, L.A. Music Ctr.Opera, 1993; author: David Hockney by David Hockney, 1976, David Hockney: Travels with Pen, Pencil and Ink, 1978, Paper Pools, 1980, David Hockney Photographs, 1982, Cameraworks, 1983, David Hockney: A Retrospective, 1988, Hockney Paints the Stage, 1983, That's the Way I See It, 1993, David Hockney's Dog Days, 1998; illustrator: Six Fairy Tales of the Brothers Grimm, 1969, The Blue Guitar, 1977, Hockney's Alphabet, 1991. Recipient Guinness award and 1st prize for etching, 1961, Gold medal Royal Coll. Art, 1962, Graphic prize Paris Biennale, 1963, 1st prize 8th Internat. Exhbn. Drawings Lugano, Italy, 1964, 1st prize John Moores Exhbn. Liverpool, Eng., 1967, German award of Excellence 1983, 1st prize Internat. Ctr. of Photography, N.Y., 1985, Kodak photography book award for Cameraworks, 1984, Praemium Imperiale Japan Art Assn., 1989, 5th Ann. Gov. Calif. Visual Arts award, 1994; named Companion of Honour, Her Majesty, the Queen of Eng., 1997. Office: 7508 Santa Monica Blvd Los Angeles CA 90046-6407

HOCOTT, JOE BILL, chemical engineer, educator; b. nr. Big Flat, Ark., Sept. 19, 1921; s. Jeiks Edmonds and Frances Clara (Berry) H.; BS, U. Ark., 1945; MS, Okla. State U., 1951. Insp. Maumelle Ordnance Works, U.S. Army Ordnance Dept., Little Rock, 1942-43; head sci. dept. Joe T. Robinson H.S., Little Rock, 1945-46; instr. chemistry U. Tulsa, 1946-47; teaching fellow Okla. A. and M. Coll., Stillwater, 1947-49; research chem. engr. Deep Rock Petroleum Corp., Cushing, Okla., 1950, Kerr-McGee Oil Corp., Stillwater, 1951; chem. engr. cons. Joe Bill Hocott, Little Rock, 1952-55, 63-—; med. technician U. Ark. Med. Center, Little Rock, 1955-56, research asso., 1956-57, instr. internal medicine, 1957-62; head chemistry dept. Little Rock Central High Sch., 1963-66; head sci. dept. Met. Vocat.-Tech. High Sch., Little Rock, 1967-73. Asst. scoutmaster Boy Scouts Am., 1945-46, troop committeeman, 1945-46, 57-58, neighborhood commr., 1969-70. Bd. dirs. Ark. Jr. Sci. and Humanities Symposium, 1965-75, asst. dir., 1972. Mem. Am. Inst. Chem. Engrs., Nat. Soc. Profl. Engrs., Ark., Ark. Jr. (dist. dir. 1966-70) acads. sci., Sigma Xi, Phi Lambda Upsilon, Unitarian. Home: 1010 Rice St Little Rock AR 72202-4536

HOCUTT, MAX OLIVER, philosophy educator; b. Berry, Ala., July 3, 1936; s. Harry Juell and Edith Pauline (Skelton) H.; m. Dorothy Lois Etheredge, Nov. 22, 1957; children—James Max, Cassandra Diane. B.A. with honors in philosophy (honors scholar), Tulane U., 1957, M.A., 1958; Ph.D. (So. Fellowships Career Teaching fellow), Yale, 1960. Instr. U. South Fla., Tampa, 1960-62; asst. prof., chmn. dept. philosophy U. South Fla., 1962-65; asso. prof. U. Ala., 1965-70, prof., 1970—, chmn. dept., 1978-91; vis. fellow Princeton U., 1979, St. Andrews U., 1987; bd. dirs. ACLU, University, 1969. Author: The Elements of Logical Analysis and Inference, 1979, First Philosophy, 1980; editor: Behavior and Philosophy, 1992-96; contbr. articles to profl. jours. Mem. Ala. Philos. Soc. (pres. 1967), So. Soc. Philosophy and Psychology, Am. Philos. Assn., Phi Beta Kappa. Home: 5510 Golden Pond Ave Northport AL 35473-1529 Office: U Ala Dept Philosophy Tuscaloosa AL 35487

HODAKIEVIC, JAMES JOSEPH, secondary education educator; b. Cleve., Aug. 21, 1947; s. Joseph Edward and Genevieve Sophie (Chodakowski) H.; m. Johanna Rita Dolphin, Feb. 15, 1969; children: Peter James, Bethany Nanette. BS in Edn., Bowling Green State U., 1969, MEd, 1972; postgrad., Kent State U., 1980-82. Cert. edn., Ohio. Driver edn. tchr. Lakota Local Schs., Kansas, Ohio, 1969; tchr., coach Western Res. H.S., Warren, Ohio, 1969-71; instr., football coach Bowling Green (Ohio) State U., 1971-72; tchr., head football coach West Holmes H.S., Millersburg, Ohio, 1972-75, Defiance (Ohio) H.S., 1975-79, Bedford (Ohio) H.S., 1979—; guest lectr. Bowling Green State U. Athletics, 1975-77; summer sch. tchr. Maple Heights (Ohio) H.S., 1981; staff dir. Ozzie Newsome Football Camp, Cleve., 1987; spkr. Youngstown (Ohio) State U. Athletics, 1994; staff Ohio State Summer Football Camp, 1997, Pa. State Summer Football Camp, 1997. Recipient Dr. Lee Tressel Meml. Coaching award Cleve. Touchdown Club, 1994; named Coach of Yr., Coshocton (Ohio) Tribune, 1974, Greater Cleve. Conf., 1993, Lake Erie League Erie Divsn., 1998. Mem. NEA, Nat. Fedn. Interscholastic Coach, Am. Football Coaches Assn. (assoc.), Ohio H.S. Football Coaches Assn., Greater Cleve. Football Coaches Assn. (pres., league dir., Golden Deeds award 1997). Avocation: golf. Home: 907 School Ave Cuyahoga Falls OH 44221-4113 Office: Bedford City Schs Bedford HS 481 Northfield Rd Bedford OH 44146-2201

HODAL, MELANIE, public relations executive. Pres. Dennis Davidson Assocs., Inc., L.A. Office: Dennis Davidson Assocs Inc US Divsn DDA Ltd London 5670 Wilshire Blvd Ste 700 Los Angeles CA 90036-5607*

HODAPP, DON JOSEPH, food company executive; b. Madelia, Minn., Dec. 24, 1937; s. Philip Henry and Katherine Lillian (Quinn) H.; m. Dorothy Ann Berg, Sept. 7, 1959; children: Don Jr., Jennifer, Paul, Patrick, Laurie. BA in Math., St. John's U., Collegeville, Minn., 1959. Adv. mktg. rep. IBM Corp., Mpls., 1959-66; dir. data processing Geo. A. Hormel & Co., Austin, Minn., 1966-69, asst. controller, 1969-81; gen. mgr. Geo. A. Hormel & Co., Fremont, Nebr., 1981-85; v.p. strategic planning Geo. A. Hormel & Co., Austin, 1985-86, group v.p., 1986-92, exec. v.p., CFO, 1992—, also bd. dirs., 1986—; bd. dirs., treasl. Hormel Found. Bd. regents St. John's U., Collegeville, Minn.; bd. dirs. Ctr. for Rural Policy and Devel. Republican. Roman Catholic. Lodge: Rotary. Office: Hormel Foods Corp 1 Hormel Pl Austin MN 55912-3680

HODAPP, LARRY FRANK, accountant; b. Dayton, Ohio, Feb. 13, 1956; s. Ruey Frank Jr. and Carol Rose (Coons) H.; m. Susan Ann Harris, July 1, 1978; children: Ryan Frank Harris, Lauren Elizabeth, Benjamin Andrew. BS in Acctg. with honors, Ind. U., 1978. CPA, Ohio. Staff acct. Deloitte Haskins & Sells, Dayton, Ohio, 1978-79, sr. asst. acct., 1979-81, sr. acct., 1981-84, mgr., 1984-89, sr. mgr., 1989-90; sr. mgr. Deloitte & Touche, Dayton, 1989-90; v.p. fin. Bush Leasing, Wilmington, Ohio, 1990-96, sr. v.p., CFO, 1996—, mem. challenge 95 environ. com., 1991-93. Chmn. Miami Valley Regional Bicycle Com., Dayton, 1985-90, 98—; dir. safety Thunder Rd. Bike-A-Thon, Dayton, 1982-90. Mem. AICPA, League Am. Wheelmen/Bicycle USA (nat. dir., treas. Balt. 1986-92), Ohio Soc. CPAs, Toastmasters (pres. 1985-86), Rotary (Kettering club pres. 1990-91, dist. treas. 1993-94, 99—), Ind. U. Alumni Assn. (pres. Dayton chpt. 1992-95, exec. coun. 1996—). Avocations: bicycling, golf. Home: 4724 Bokay Dr Dayton OH 45440-2025 Office: Bush Leasing 1600 W Main St Wilmington OH 45177-1085

HODAPP, SHIRLEY JEANIENE, curriculum administrator; b. Uniontown, Pa., July 10, 1934; d. James Sylvester and Nellie Mae (Kennedy) Amos; children: Holly Hodapp Vining, Curtis, David, Gordon. BS in Elem. Edn., Otterbein Coll., 1956; MEd, Wright State U., 1973; EdS, U. Toledo, 1990. Cert. elem. tchr., local supt., Ohio. Tchr. 3rd grade Elyria (Ohio) City Schs., 1955-56; tchr. 2nd grade Beavercreek Local Schs., Xenia, Ohio, 1956-57; tchr. elem. Xenia City Schs., 1965-73; ednl. facilitator Wright State U., Dayton, Ohio, 1973-74; adminstr. Marion S. Kinsey PreSch., Xenia, 1974-79; adminstr. elem. Northea. Local Schs., Defiance, Ohio, 1979-85; supr. elem. Defiance County Bd. Edn., 1985-92, dir. curriculum and related svcs., 1992-94; nat. cons. ITE Ednl. Cons., 1995—; adj. prof. Defiance Coll., 1985-93, U. Toledo, 1989, N.W. Tech. Coll., Archbold, Ohio, 1989-90, Bowling Green State U., 1994; dir. Little Gnat Kindergarten Readiness program, Babson Park Elem. Sch., 1996—; cons. in field. Author: Learning About Our World-Germany, 1993, Integrated Thematic Experiences, Implementation Guide, 1994; author and editor: Solving The Puzzles of Early Childhood, 1986, Integrated Thematic Experiences, Vol. I, 1993; contbr. articles to profl. jours. Chmn. Tng. Ohio's Parents for Success Program, Defiance County, 1989-92; mem. Early Childhood Intervention Collaborative, Defiance County, 1988-92, Four County Early Childhood Adv. Coun., Archbold, 1986-90; host Ohio Coop. Ext. Svc. Internat. Exch. Program, Defiance, 1990; chmn. Defiance 2000 Sch. Readiness Fair, 1994; coord. Lake Wales Pub. Libr. Time to Rhyme Presch. Summer Program, 1995; bd. dirs. Lake Wales Cmty. Theatre, 1995—; presch. planning com. Babson Park Elem. Sch., 1995—; corr. sec. Fla. Fedn. Music Clubs, 1995—; vol. dir. Little Gnat Program, Babson Park Elem. Sch.; mem. adv. bd. Renaissance Abbey Acad., Lakeland, Fla. Martha Holden Jennings grantee 1993; named Early Childhood Advocate of Yr., Defiance Assn. for Edn. Young Children, 1988, Leader of Lang. Arts Support Groups in Ohio, Ohio Dept. Edn., 1990, Outstanding Fla. Sch. Vol., Fla. Dept. Edn., 1997, Polk County Sch. Vol. of Yr., 1997, Nat. Points of Light award, 1998. Mem. ASCD, AAUW, Nat. Coun. Tchrs. Social Studies, Nat. Coun. Tchrs. Math., Nat. Assn. for Edn. of Young Children, Polk Coun. for Edn. of Young Children, Assn. Childhood Edn. Internat., Nat. Fedn. Music Clubs. Avocations: music, theatre, reading, travel. Home: 493 N Crooked Lake Dr Babson Park FL 33827

HODASH, BOB (ROBERT A. HODASH), principal; b. Bronx, N.Y., Aug. 25, 1957; s. Robert and Anne Marie (Buckley) H.; m. Wendy Kapstrom, Apr. 7, 1990; children: Liam Kapstrom, Jeniann. BA, Lehman Coll., 1980, MS, 1981. Profl. clear tchg. credential sci. and phys. edn.; preliminary adminstrv. svcs. credential. Health and phys. edn. chair athletic dir. Beth Am/Herzl Sch., Beverly Hills, Calif., 1982-84; assoc. athletic dir. Windward Sch., Mar Vista, Calif., 1984-86; tchr. phys. edn. and sci. L.A. Unified Sch. Dist., 1986-91, chair sci. dept., 1987-91; sci. tchr. Curran Jr. H.S. Bakersfield (Calif.) City S.D., 1991-95, sci. mentor tchr., 1994-95, program specialist, 1995-99; prin. Benjamin Franklin Sch., Bakersfield, 1999—; press rels. asst. dir. L.A. Olympics, 1984; pres. Ocean Valley Athletic League, L.A. County, 1984-86; advisor MESA (Math, Engring., Sci. Achievement), L.A. and Bakersfield, 1986—; mem. steering com. and chair sci. task force MS 3(cubed), 1992—; co-dir. Bakersfield Sch. Gardens Project, 1998—. Author: Historical Trail of the Bronx, 1976; prodr. (animated films) Anti Smoking Shorts, 1990. Water safety instr. trainer ARC, N.Y., 1976-81; com. mem. Anti Grafitti Program, Bakersfield, 1995—. Named Presdl. Vol. of the Yr., Pres. of the U.S., 1984; IBM Assist grantee IBM, L.A., 1990, Middle Sch. Restructing grantee State of Calif., 1990, 91. Mem. ASCD, Nat. Sci. Tchrs. Assn., Calif. Sci. Tchrs. Assn., Calif. State Tchrs. Assn., Phi Delta Kappa. Home: 9501 Benet Way Bakersfield CA 93311-1423 Office: Benjamin Franklin Sch 2400 Truxton Ave Bakersfield CA 93305

HODDER, JAMES EDWARD, industrial engineer; b. Bay City, Mich., June 27, 1937; s. Wilbert and Henrietta Mae (Howson) H.; m. Judy Jean Johnson, May 21, 1960; children: Tanya Kay Hodder Clark, Leann Marie, Stephen James. Degree in Indsl. Engring. Tech., Lake Superior State Coll., Sault Ste. Marie, Mich., 1985. Salesman Miles Homes, Mpls., 1976-77; plant mgr. Bldg. Components Inc., Kincheloe, Mich., 1977-80; clk. U.S. Postal Svc., Sault St. Marie, 1980-87; indsl. engr. U.S. Postal Svc., Sioux Falls, S.D., 1987-90, Columbus, Ohio, 1990-93; indsl. engr. ops. support specialist U.S. Postal Svc., Pitts., 1993-98; workforce planning specialist U.S. Postal Svc., Washington, 1998—. Exec. bd. Chippewa County United Way, Sault Ste. Marie, 1979. With USAF, 1958-76. Mem. Inst. Indsl. Engrs. (pres.-elect, v.p. 1988-89). Lutheran. Avocations: camping, travel, home remodeling. Home: 3565 Tuscarawas Rd Beaver PA 15009-9119 Office: US Postal Svc Hdqrs 475 L Enfant Pl SW Washington DC 20260-1604

HODDER, WILLIAM ALAN, fabricated metal products company executive; b. Lincoln, Nebr., May 6, 1931; s. Ernest Chesley and Velma Catherine (Warren) H.; m. Suzanne Holmes, Apr. 3, 1954; children: Kent, Laurie, Susan, Mark, Beth. BA, U. Nebr., 1954; postgrad., Harvard U., 1961. Mktg. positions IBM Corp., 1954-66; v.p. orgn. planning and devel. Dayton Co., Mpls., 1966-68; sr. v.p. Dayton Hudson Corp., 1970-73, dir., 1971-73; pres. Target Stores, 1968-73; pres., dir. Donaldson Co., Inc., Mpls., 1973-96, CEO, 1982-96, chmn. bd., 1984-96, ret., 1996; bd. dirs. Norwest Corp., Tennant Co., Cowles Media Co., ReliaStar Fin. Corp., Musicland Group Inc., Supervalu Inc. Mem. bd. overseers Carlson Sch. Mgmt. U. Minn. With AUS, 1954-56. Mem. Chief Execs. Orgn., Inc., Harvard U. Bus. Sch., Club Minn. (bd. dirs., past pres.), Mpls. Club, Minikahda Club. Address: 4900 IDS Ctr 80 S 8th St Minneapolis MN 55402-2100

HODDY, GEORGE WARREN, electric company executive, electrical engineer; b. Columbus, Ohio, Mar. 7, 1905; s. Arthur H. and Mary E. (Lutz) H.; m. Lois L. Mitchell, May 30, 1947; children: John, Peter, Matthew, Elizabeth Hoddy Howe, Rebekah Hoddy Smith, Melissa Hoddy. BEE, Ohio State U., 1926, MEE, 1932; LHD (hon.), Baker Coll., 1991. Elec. engr. Day-Fan Electric Co., Dayton, Ohio, 1926-29, Robbins & Myers, Inc., Springfield, Ohio, 1929-31; chief engr. Pioneer divsn. Master Electric Co., Dayton, 1932-34; v.p., gen. mgr. Redmond Co., Inc., Owosso, Mich., 1934-41; founder, pres., CEO Universal Electric Co., Owosso, 1942-71, chmn. bd. dirs., dir. internat. rels., 1971-79, vice chmn., 1979-85; chmn. Universal Electric Ltd., Gainsboroguh, Eng., 1974-82; chmn., bd. dirs. Am. Universal Electric Ltd., New Delhi, 1962-92; vice chmn., bd. dirs. Intertherm, Inc., 1972-74, chmn., 1974-84; owner, pres. Fiji Marina, L.A., 1968-76; pres., bd. dirs. Ventrola Mfg. Co., Owosso, 1968-76; chmn. Team 21, Inc., 1995—. Patentee in field. Bd. dirs. Mich. Accident Fund, 1945-61, Owosso Cmty. Concert Assn., 1946-53, Shiawassee United Way, 1956-59, Shiawassee County Mental Health Bd., 1963-67, United Cerebral Palsy Assn., 1963-65; trustee Meml. Hosp., Owosso, 1948-84, pres. 1954-58; chmn. Owosso Charter Rev. Commn., 1956-57, Owosso Citizens Savs. Bonds, 1971-80; mem. Owosso Pub. Sch. Bd., 1957-76, pres., 1975-76; trustee Flint Osteo. Hosp., 1985-90, A.M. Bentley Found., Owosso, 1986—; trustee Baker Coll., Flint, Mich., 1985—; regent Baker Coll. of Owosso, 1987—, chmn., 1993—; bd. dirs., pres. Shiawassee Found., 1973-77; trustee, chmn. Shiawassee County Bldg. Authority Comm., Corunna, Mich., 1986-95; mem. Tall Pine cou. Boy Scouts Am., 1942—, dist. chmn., 1954-58, mem. adv. bd., 1954—; trustee Oak Hill Cemetary Co., 1997—. 2nd lt. U.S. Army, 1931-36. Recipient Silver Beaver award Boy Scouts Am., 1958, Disting. Alumnus award Coll. Engring., Ohio State U., 1970, Alumni Citizenship award Ohio State U., 1975, Paul Harris fellow Rotary, 1997; others. Mem. NAM, Mich. Mfrs. Assn., U.S. C. of C., Owosso Corunna Area C. of C. (bd. dirs. 1948-61, adv. bd. 1961-78), Ohio State U. Alumni Assn., Newcomen Soc., Shriners, Masons, Sigma Xi, Tau Beta Pi, Pi Mu Epsilon, Eta Kappa Nu, Lambda Chi Alpha. Congregationalist. Home: 508 W Williams St Owosso MI 48867-2238 also: Lakeside Rd Cedarville MI 49719

HODEL, MARY ANNE, library director; b. St. Louis, Aug. 12; d. William George and Florence Marie (Betz) H.; children: Courtney Hodel Denham, Christian Hodel Denham. BA, U. Wis., 1972; MLS, Catholic U., 1973. Project libr. TRACOR-JITCO, Rockville, Md., 1973-74; from project mgr. to database mgr. Nat. Resources Libr. U.S. Dept. of Interior, Washington, 1974-77; cataloger USAF Base Libr., Ramstein, Germany, 1977-79; from project libr. to automation libr. Law Libr. Georgetown U., Washington, 1984-85, automation libr. Law Libr., 1985-91; chief state libr. resource ctr. Enoch Pratt Free Libr., Balt., 1991-95; dir. Ann Arbor (Mich.) Dist. Libr., 1995—; network coord. Coun. Md. Librs., 1991-95; mem. Sailor Implementation group, 1992-95, grants and devel. task force liaison, 1993-95; v.p. Mich. Libr. Consortium, 1998-99, pres. 1999—. Recipient Libr. of Yr. award Libr. Jour., 1997-98. Mem. ALA (Libr. of the Yr. award 1997/98), Mich. Libr. Assn., Am. Assn. Law Librs. (chair innovative interfaces users com. 1988-89, editor innovative interfacers survey 1989, program coord. ann. meeting 1987), Pub. Libr. Assn. (sys. sect. v.p./pres.-elect 1994-95, pres. 1995—), Md. Assn. Profl. Libr. Adminstrs., Md. Libr. Assn. (del. to ALA legis. day 1992, co-chair tech. interest group 1994, conf. planning com. 1993, 94, program coord. 1994), Law Librs. Soc. Washington (program coord. 1989, 90, chair innovative interfaces users workshop 1989, pres. acad. spl. interest sect. 1988-89, rec. sec. 1989-91). Avocations: travel, photography. Home: 1881 Snowberry Ridge Rd Ann Arbor MI 48103-9692 Office: 343 S 5th Ave Ann Arbor MI 48104-2217

HODES, BERNARD S., advertising agency executive; b. Newark, Dec. 27, 1931; s. Irving H. and Shirley (Baron) Ettenberg; 1 child, Jeffrey; m. Bonnie; stepchildren: Vicki, Wendy. Student, NYU, 1954-58. Advt. exec. various agys., N.Y.C., 1954-70; pres. Bernard Hodes Advt., N.Y.C., 1970—; chmn., bd. dirs. The Friars Nat. Found., Inc., N.Y.C.; pres., then ceo Bernard Hodes Advt Inc, N.Y.C., 1970—; dir. Community Guidance Service, N.Y.C., 1979—. Author: Principles and Practice of Recruitment Advertising: A Guide for Personnel Professionals, 1982; contbg. author Managing the Nursing Shortage: A Guide to Recruitment and Retention; bd. of advisors The Journal of Staffing and Recruitment, The Human Resource Professional. Club: Friars. Office: Bernard Hodes Advt Inc 555 Madison Ave Fl 15 New York NY 10022-3479*

HODES, MARION EDWARD, genetics educator, physician; b. N.Y.C., Aug. 6, 1925; s. Louis and Esterre (Berman) H.; m. Halina Zora Markowicz, Nov. 23, 1949; children: Marquis Z., Zachary I., Jonathan E., Abigail J. Student, Cornell U., 1941-43, U. Rochester, 1943-44; MD, U. Buffalo, 1947; PhD, Columbia U., 1955. Diplomate Am. Bd. Med. Genetics; cert. Am. Bd. Clin. Chemistry. Intern Jewish Hosp., Bklyn., 1947-48; officer-in-charge dept. physiol. chemistry U.S. Naval Med. Sch., 1951-52; resident Goldwater Meml. Hosp., N.Y.C., 1955-56; faculty mem. sch. medicine Ind. U., Indpls., 1956—; prof. medicine and biochemistry Ind. U., 1966-72, prof. med. and molecular genetics and medicine, 1972-91, prof. med. and molecular genetics, medicine and pathology, 1991—; sr. Fogarty Internat. fellow, Lady Davis vis. prof. Hebrew U., 1977-78; cons. Eli Lily & Co., 1958-62; med. cons. City of Hope Med. Ctr.; mem. adv. screening com. for sr. Fulbright awards in life scis. Coun. Internat. Exch. of Scholars, 1981-84. Chmn. internat. sci. coun., Israel Cancer Rsch. Fund, 1988-94, chmn. sci. rev. panel, 1988-95. Eleanor Roosevelt fellow, 1962-63; Guggenheim fellow, 1969-70; Leukemia Soc. scholar, 1961-66. Fellow Am. Coll. Med. Genetics (founder), Ind. Acad. Sci.; mem. AAAS, Am. Assn. Cancer Rsch., Am. Soc. Biochemistry and Molecular Biology, Am. Assn. Clin. Chemists, Am. Chem. Soc., Cen. Soc. for Clin. Rsch., Am. Soc. Human Genetics, Am. Fedn. Clin. Rsch., Soc. for Neurosci., N.Y. Acad. Scis., Sigma Xi. Home: 648 Edgemere Dr Indianapolis IN 46260-4107 Office: Ind U Med Ctr Dept Med & Molec Genetics 975 W Walnut St Indianapolis IN 46202-5251

HODES, PAUL WILLIAM, record company executive, lawyer; b. N.Y.C., Mar. 21, 1951; s. Robert Bernard and Florence (Rosenberg) H.; m. Margaret Ann Horstmann; children: Maxwell, Ariana. BA, Dartmouth Coll., 1972; JD, Boston Coll., 1978. Bar: N.H. 1978, Mass. 1980. Asst. atty. gen. Office of N.H. Atty. Gen., Concord, 1978-82; pres. Big Round Records, Inc., Concord, N.H., 1986—; co-owner Peggosus Music, 1986—. Bd. dirs. Capital Ctr. for Arts, 1990-97, chair 1990-96; bd. dirs. Children's Entertainment Assn., 1995-99, Concord Cmty. Music Sch., 1997—, N.H.

Children's Alliance, 1997—. Recipient hon. award Parents Choice Found., 1987, 96. Mem. Am. Bd. Trial Advocates, NARAS, ASCAP, ATLA, Nat. Assn. Criminal Def. Lawyers, N.H. Assn. Criminal Def. Lawyers, N.H. Trial Lawyers. Office: Shaheen & Gordon PA PO Box 2703 Concord NH 03302-2703 also: Big Round Records Inc PO Box 610 Concord NH 03302-0610

HODES, RICHARD J., think tank executive, immunologist, researcher. Grad., Yale U.; MD, Harvard U. Diplomate Am. Bd. Internal Medicine. Clin. investigator Nat. Cancer Inst. NIH, Bethesda, Md., dep. chief, acting chief immunology br. Nat. Cancer Inst., dir. Nat. Inst. Aging, 1993—; program coord. U.S.-Japan Coop. Cancer Rsch. Program, 1982—; mem. sci. adv. bd. Cancer Rsch. Inst., 1992—. Editor scholarly jours. including Jour. Exptl. Medicine and Therapeutic Immunology; contbr. numerous rsch. papers to profl. publs. Office: Nat Inst on Aging Bldg 31 Rm 5C35 MSC 2292 31 Center Dr Bethesda MD 20892-2292*

HODES, ROBERT BERNARD, lawyer; b. Bklyn., Aug. 25, 1925; s. James and Florence (Cohen) H.; m. Florence R. Rosenberg, Dec. 22, 1946 (div. Nov. 1984); 1 child, Paul; m. Cecilia Mendez, Dec. 18, 1984; children: James, Maria Paz. AB, Dartmouth Coll., 1946; LLB, Harvard U., 1949. Bar: N.Y. Supreme Ct. 1950, U.S. Dist. Ct. (so. dist.) N.Y. 1951, U.S. Tax Ct. 1955, U.S. Claims Ct. 1957, U.S. Ct. Appeals (2d cir.) 1959. Assoc. Willkie Farr & Gallagher, N.Y.C., 1949-56, ptnr., 1956-95, co-chmn., 1982-95, counsel, 1995—; bd. dirs. K&F Industries, Inc., W.R. Berkley Corp., LCH Investments N.V., Loral Space & Telecomm., Ltd., Globalstar Telecom. Ltd., Mueller Industries, Inc., Space Systems/Loral Inc., RV1 Guaranty Co., Ltd., Restructured Capital Holdings, Ltd. Active Cremer Found., Beaver Dam Sanctuary, Inc., Westchester Land Trust, The Riverkeeper, Inc. Home: 860 United Nations Plz New York NY 10017-1810 Office: Willkie Farr & Gallagher 1 CitiCorp Ctr 787 7th Ave New York NY 10019-6099

HODES, SCOTT, lawyer; b. Chgo., Aug. 14, 1937; s. Barnet and Eleanor (Cramer) H.; m. Maria Bechily, 1982; children—Brian Kenneth, Valery Jane, Anthony Scott. AB, U. Chgo., 1956; JD, U. Mich., 1959; LLM, Northwestern U., 1962. Bar: Ill. 1959, D.C. 1962, N.Y. 1981. Assoc. Arvey, Hodes, Costello & Burman, Chgo., 1959-61; ptnr. Arvey, Hodes, Costello & Burman, 1965-91, Ross & Hardies, Chgo., 1992—; bd. dirs. First Investors Life Ins. Co. N.Y., Richardson Electronics, Ltd., State Ill. Savs. and Loan Bd. Author: The Law of Art and Antiques, 1966, What Every Artist and Collector Should Know About the Law, 1974; Assoc. news editor: Fed. Bar News, 1963-70; co-editor: Conf. Mut. Funds, 1966, Legal Rights in the Art and Collectors' World, 1986; Contbr. articles to profl. jours. Chmn. Philippine Exch. Nurses award com., 1966; nat. chmn. Lawbooks U.S.A., 1962-73; co-chmn. Chgo. World Friendship Day, 1967; mem. Ill. Arts Coun., 1973-75; Committeeman Ill. 9th Dist. Dem. Com., 1970-82; bd. dirs. Michael Reese Hosp. Rsch. Inst., 1965-73, Found. of Fed. Bar Assn., 1970—, United Cerebral Palsy Chgo., 1976-84; governing bd. Chgo. Symphony Soc., 1978—; governing mem. Art Inst. Chgo., 1980—; mem. com. on internat. investment and tech. Dept. State, 1980-83; bd. dirs. Chgo. Neighborhood Theatre Found., 1980-92, The Harold Washington Found., 1988—; exec. com. Anti Defamation League, 1990—; chmn. Mayor's Task Force on Neighborhood Land Use, 1986-88; chmn. Navy Pier Devel. Authority, 1988-89; mem. Ill. Atty. Gen. adv. com., 1991-95; spl. counsel Art in Embassies Program, Dept. State, 1992-94; co-chmn. Private Enterprise Rev. and Adv. Bd., Ill., 1992-94. Capt. JAGC, AUS, 1962-64. Decorated Army Commendation medal; named one of Chicago's ten outstanding young men Jr. Assn. Commerce and Industry, 1968, Chgo. Artist's award for Support of Visual Arts, 1996, Disting. Svc. award Lawyer's for the Creative Arts, 1997. 02169408, Fed. Bar Assn. (chmn. council financing 1966-71, chmn. younger lawyers div. 1963-64, nat. council 1965—, Distinguished Service award 1971, 75, 86, Earl Kintner award for Outstanding Service, 1998), Ill. Bar Assn., Chgo. Bar Assn., Chgo. Art Inst. (life), Chgo. Hist. Soc. (life), Judge Adv. Gens. Assn. (life), Zeta Beta Tau, Tau Epsilon Rho. Jewish. Clubs: Standard, Econ. (Chgo.), Mid-Day. Lodge: Masons (32 degree). Home: 1540 N Lake Shore Dr Chicago IL 60610-1623 Office: Ross & Hardies 150 N Michigan Ave Ste 2500 Chicago IL 60601-7567

HODESS, ARTHUR BART, cardiologist; b. N.Y.C., Jan. 15, 1950; s. Samuel and Dora (Rosenkrantz) H.; m. Carol Yasuna, Aug. 31, 1969 (div. May 1985); children: Joshua David, Jeremy Scott; m. S. Christina Ellsworth, Dec. 23, 1987; children: Jonathan Ellsworth, Jason Dorian, Jordan Gottier. BA, Boston U., 1970; MD, Columbia U., 1974. Intern Hosp. of U. Pa., Phila., 1974-75, resident in medicine, 1975-77, fellow in cardiology, 1977-79; asst. instr. dept. medicine Hosp. U. of Pa., Phila., 1974-79; instr. physiology, dept. animal biology U. Pa., Sch. Veterinary Medicine, Phila., 1977-78; clin. assoc. dept. medicine U. Pa., Phila., 1979-81; attending cardiologist Brandywine Hosp., Coatesville, Pa., 1979—; dir. critical care Brandywine Hosp., Coatesville, 1989—, chief of cardiology, 1990—, chmn. dept. medicine, 1991-95; pres. Brandywine Valley Cardiovascular Assocs., Thorndale, Pa., 1991—. Contbr. articles to profl. jours. V.p. Chestnut Hollow Homeowners Assn., West Chester, Pa., 1990-94, bd. dirs. 1995; bd. dirs. Beth Israel Congregation, Chester County, 1991-96. Fellow Clin. Coun. Cardiology Am. Heart Assn. Fellow ACP, Am. Coll. Cardiology, Am. Coll. Chest Physicians; mem. Am. Soc. Echocardiography, Cardiac Electrophysiology Soc., Soc. Critical Care Medicine. Office: Brandywine Valley Cardio 3025 Zinn Rd Thorndale PA 19372-1131

HODGDON, HARRY EDWARD, association executive, wildlife biologist; b. Brattleboro, Vt., Sept. 4, 1946; s. Roscoe Burns and Ruth Noyes (Shattuck) H.; m. Sharyn Jane Post, Nov. 25, 1967 (div. Apr. 1992); children: Christopher Ross, Scott Gerald, Ryan David; m. Mary Susan Gordon, Aug. 7, 1993. B.S. in Wildlife Biology, U. Maine, 1968; M.S., U. Mass., 1971; Ph.D, U. Mass., 1978. Conservation mgr. NRA, Washington, 1975-76, dir. hunting and conservation, 1976-77; field dir. Wildlife Soc., Bethesda, Md., 1977-82; exec. dir. Wildlife Soc., Bethesda, 1982—; mem. nat. nongame bird steering com. Dept. Agr., Washington, 1976-80, mem. rangeland policy com. Office of Sec., 1978-80; mem. dept. agrl. forest svc. Nat. Threatened Endangered and Sensitive Species Task Force, 1988-89; mem. U.S. implementation bd. N.Am. Waterfowl Mgmt. Plan, 1988—; mem. steering com. Internat. Wildlife Mgmt. Congress, 1991-94, 98—; mem. info. and comm. study team Pres.'s Commn. on Am. Outdoors, 1985-86; mem. planning for environ. quality com. ASCE, N.Y.C., 1982—; mem. conservation adv. coun. U.S. Senate Subcom. on Soil Conservation, Forestry and Environment, 1983-84; mem. nat. adv. com. for evaluation of conservation title Food Security Act of 1985, Soil and Water Conservation Soc., 1988-92; mem. exec. com. Renewable Natural Resources Found., Bethesda, 1981-92, 96—, bd. dirs., 1981—; mem. Hunter Edn. Rev. Team, Wildlife Mgmt. Inst., 1994-96. Editor The Wildlifer Newsletter, 1982—; mem. editl. adv. bd. Human Dimensions of Wildlife Jour., 1994—; contbr. articles to profl. jours. Mem. nat. conservation com. Nat. Coun. Boy Scouts Am., Irving, Tex., 1981—. Recipient Disting. Alumnus award U. Mass., 1989. Mem. Wildlife Soc. (cert. wildlife biologist, chmn. com. 1977-84), Internat. Assn. Fish and Wildlife Agys. (legis. com. 1979-88, internat. affairs com. 1981—, profl. improvement com. 1981-87, Hunter edn. adv. coun. 1980—, proactive strategies for fish and wildlife mgmt. task force 1990-94), Am. Fisheries Soc., Soc. Am. Foresters, Soc. Range Mgmt., Sigma Xi, Phi Kappa Phi, Xi Sigma Pi, Alpha Zeta, Washington Biologist Field Club (bd. mgrs. 1981-83). Achievements include research in long-term field study of beaver (castor canadensis) behavior and population dynamics using individually marked animals of known sex and age documenting numerous sex and age differences in social and construction behaviors. Office: The Wildlife Soc 5410 Grosvenor Ln Bethesda MD 20814-2197

HODGE, ANN LINTON, artist; b. Long Beach, Calif., Aug. 24, 1934; d. Mills Schuyler and Irma Jean (Linn) Hodge; m. Quentin Conitz Becker, Dec. 19, 1968 (dec. May 1978); children: Susan Jean Becker Pedersen, Kathryn Ann Becker Michlitsch, Deborah Rena Becker Lippert, Naomi Ruth, David Mills, Sharon Elizabeth Becker Glutting. Student, U. So. Calif., Long Beach, Carroll N. Jones Jr.'s Sch. Fine Arts, Stowe, Vt., 1990-92. Fine arts portrait artist individual commns. Whittier and Long Beach, Calif., 1958-68; mural artist for local businesses Whittier and Long Beach, 1958-68; fine arts portrait artist individual commns. Mandan & Bismarck, N.D., 1968—; instr. basic drawing and advanced portraiture The Renaissance Palette Sch. Fine Arts, Mandan, 1970—; adj. prof. basic drawing Bismarck State Coll., Mandan, 1996; ofcl. state portrait artist Rough Rider Hall of Fame, N.D. State Capital, Bismarck, 1994—; judge art show Glen Ullin (N.D.) Art Assn., 1995; guest lectr. art Shiloh Christian Sch., Bismarck, 1988, Hughes Jr. H.S., Bismarck, 1996. Portraits on display on Internet, 1995—. Bible tchr., Bismarck, 1980's. Avocations: building furniture, Bible teaching, writing poetry, reading, making Christmas decorations. Address: The Renaissance Palette 1008 6th Ave NW Mandan ND 58554-2407

HODGE, BOBBY LYNN, mechanical engineer, manufacturing executive; b. Yadkinville, N.C., Oct. 14, 1956; s. Robert Henry and Betty Jean (Martin) H.; m. Robin Mayhue Renegar, June 8, 1979; children: Andrew, Adam. AAS with honors, Forsyth Tech. Inst., Winston-Salem, N.C., 1976; BS in Engring. Tech., U. N.C., Charlotte, 1978. Design engr. Clark/Gravely Corp., Clemmons, N.C., 1978-79; project engr. Clark/Gravely Corp., 1979-80; design engr. Ingersoll-Rand, Davidson, N.C., 1980-83, devel. engr., 1983-85; sr. applications engr. INA Bearing Co., Ft. Mill, S.C., 1985-87, mgr. automotive driveline engring. group, 1987-88, mgr. automotive applications engring., 1988-89, dir. automotive applications engring., 1989-96, dir. automotive engring., 1996-99; v.p. engring./product devel. The Setco Group, Cin., 1999—; internat. spkr. on design and application of anti-friction bearings. Contbr. articles to profl. jours.; inventor, 9 patents in field. Mem. adv. coun. U. N.C.-Charlotte Coll. Engring. Mem. ASME, SAE (mem. manual transmission com., mem. automatic transmission com., mem. clutch stds. com.), Soc. Tribologists and Lubrication Engrs., Am. Soc. Metals. Republican. Baptist. Avocations: golf, hunting, woodworking. Home: 1518 Jolee Dr Hebron KY 41048 Office: The Setco Group 5880 Hillside Ave Cincinnati OH 45233 *One of the most important tasks anyone can undertake is to establish a vision for their life. Without a vision there can not be direction. Without direction, any success or achievement comes merely by accident.*

HODGE, DANIEL RAY, auditor; b. Rochester, Pa., July 26, 1966; s. Earl Ray and June Opal (Laughner) H.; m. Lori Ann Ondick, Sept. 12, 1992; 1 child, Kayla Nicole. BS in Acctg., Mount Union Coll., 1988. Audit sr. Ernst & Young, Pitts., 1988-90, S.R. Snodgrass & Co., A.C., Wexford, Pa., 1990-94; audit sr. mgr. D.G. Sisterson & Co. LLP, Pitts., 1994-98; mgr. acctg. Montauk Inc., Pitts., 1998—; adv. com. D.G. Sisterson & Co., LLP, Pitts., 1996-98; mem. small bus. com. PICPA, 1998—, bar com., 1998—. Mem. Waldesnian Task Force, Beaver-Butler Presbytery, Zelienople, Pa., 1997—, mem. interpretation and stewardship com., 1997—; mem. Pitts. Regional Renaissance Tax Com., 1997. Mem. AICPA, Pa. Inst. CPAs, Inst. Cert. Mgmt. Accts. Republican. Avocatins: golf, tennis, baseball, listening to music, yardwork. E-mail: dhodge@worthshore.com. Home: 40 Bock Ln Baden PA 15005-2402

HODGE, DONALD RAY, systems architect; b. Springfield, Mo., Aug. 22, 1939; s. William Orin Jr. and Ruth Mildred (Jones) H. BS, Drury Coll., 1961; MS, U. Wis., 1963, PhD, 1968. Analyst Ctr. for Naval Analysis U. Rochester, Arlington, Va., 1968-71; staff mem. NAS, Washington, 1971; ops. rsch. analyst Dept. Army, Washington, 1971-73; sr. scientist The BDM Corp., Vienna, Va., 1973-77; sr. project engr. TRW, Fairfax, Va., 1977-88; sr. scientist Jaycor, Vienna, 1988-89; exec. staff Computer Scis. Corp., Falls Church, Va., 1989-96; pres. D.R. Hodge & Assocs., Alexandria, Va., 1996-97; system engr. Harris Corp., Melbourne, Fla., 1997—; panel moderator Internat. Command Ctr. Facilities Interoperability, Honolulu, 1987. Contbr. to Van Nostrand's Scientific Encyclopedia, 1976. Recipient Disting. Alumni award Drury Coll., Springfield, Mo., 1980. Mem. IEEE, Ops. Rsch. Soc. Am., Am. Phys. Soc., Mil. Ops. Rsch. Soc. (chmn. tactical command and control workshop). Achievements include development of measure 6B8 of NATO Long Term Defense Program, Defense Transportation System Information System Technical Reference Model. Home and Office: D R Hodge & Assocs 3865 Shady Run Rd Melbourne FL 32934-8548

HODGE, DOUGLAS, entertainment executive; b. Aug. 22, 1945. Acting student, Alliance Theatre; studied with, Cynthia Stillwell; student, Clayton SMTE Coll., 1995-96. Pres. Hodge Comms., Rex., 1995—. Model, actor (TV shows) Savannah, Mama Flora's Family, Arsenio Hall Show, Selma Lord Selma. Master sgt. U.S. Army, 1995; ret. Address: 4172 Peachtree Farms Rd Rex GA 30273

HODGE, ETTA LEE, director of surgical services, nurse; b. Houston, Mar. 6, 1955; d. Johnny and Lee Etta (Mason) Hawkins; m. Ralph Eugene Hodge, May 2, 1981; children: Jarvas Dionn, April LaTrice. BSN, Tex. Women's U., 1977; MBA in Health Adminstrn., Our Lady of the Lake U., 1997. RN, Tex.; cert operating room nurse Perioperative Nursing Inst. Operating room svc. coord. St. Joseph Hosp., Houston, 1988-90, assoc. dir. operating room, 1990-95, dir. surgical svcs., 1995—. 1st v.p. Mass Choir, Bella Vista Bapt. Ch., Houston, 1995-97; pres. Deacons and Ministers Wives, 1996-97, mem. Youth Adv. Bd., 1997. Mem. Assn. Operating Room Nurses, Mgmt. Specialty Assembly. Avocations singing, reading, cooking, mentoring. Office: St Joseph Hosp 1919 La Branch St Houston TX 77002-8321

HODGE, IDA LEE, physical therapist assistant; b. Ala., Aug. 5, 1940; d. John Louie and Rubye Lee (Williams) Hodge; m. Jimmie Arthur Beard, Mar. 12, 1959 (div. Aug. 1984); children: Tammie, Benita, Patti, Starr. AS, Wallace State C.C., Hanceville, Ala., 1982; AAS, U. Ala., Birmingham, 1984. Lic. phys. therapist asst., Tenn. Phys. therapist asst. Merihil Healthcare Ctr., Lewisburg, Tenn., 1984-86, Lincoln Skilled Care Ctr., Fayetteville, Tenn., 1986-89, Kennewick (Wash.) Gen. Hosp. Phys. Therapy Ctr., 1989-94, Lifecare Ctrs. of Am., 1996-98; pvt. practice Wallula, Wash., 1998—. Author poetry in anthologies. Tribal councilwoman Echota Cherokee tribe, Birmingham, 1981-83. Recipient Cert. of Exceptional Artistry and Creativity, Nat. Libr. Poetry, 1988, 1st prize sand sculpture Benton-Franklin County Fair, 1990, Stillwaters award Lifecare Ctrs. of Am., 1996. Mem. Am. Phys. Therapy Assn. (mem. affiliate assembly, oncology group), Lifecare Ctrs. Am. (Whatever It Takes award 1997). Democrat. Avocations: sculpting, painting, poetry writing, hiking, camping. Home and Office: 128 Ross Way Wallula WA 99363

HODGE, JAMES LEE, German language educator; b. Harrisburg, Pa., Sept. 18, 1935; s. Earl Henry and Catherine Margaret (Ferber) M.; m. Janice Ellen Dunn, June 21, 1958; children: Geoffrey Lee, Stephen Charles. A.B., Tufts U., 1957; A.M., Pa. State U., 1960, Ph.D., 1961. Grad. asst. Pa. State U., 1957-60; instr. German Bowdoin Coll., Brunswick, Maine, 1961-63; asst. prof. Bowdoin Coll., 1963-68, asso. prof., 1968-74, prof., 1974—, George Taylor Files prof. modern langs., 1977, chmn. dept. German, 1974-93; mem. IIE Fulbright Screening Com., 1973, 91. Author: Portable German Tutor, 1970; editor: (with Buehne and Pinto) Helen Adolf Festschrift, 1968; editor: (with T. Beebe and S. Cerf) The Speech of Richard von Weizsacker on May 8, 1985; editorial staff German Quar, 1976-83; contbr. articles to profl. jours. and reference works. Cubmaster Pine Tree council Boy Scouts Am., Brunswick, 1974. NDEA grantee, 1966-67; Bowdoin Mellon grantee, 1977, 84. Mem. AAUP, Am. Assn. Tchrs. German, MLA. Republican. Home: 37 Meadowbrook Rd Brunswick ME 04011-3421 Office: Bowdoin Coll Dept German Brunswick ME 04011

HODGE, MARY GRETCHEN FARNAM, manufacturing company distributor, manager and executive; b. DeFuniak Springs, Fla., Sept. 24, 1943; d. Thomas Dewey and Mary Catherine (Mixon) Farnam; m. Spessard L. Hodge, Apr. 28, 1962; children: Jennifer Robin, Monica Leigh Hodge Schulz, Stephanie Lea Hodge Glascock. Student, Orlando Coll.; grad., Citizens' Police Acad., Maitland, Fla., 1996. Adminstrv. asst. The Cameron and Barkley Co., Orlando, Fla., 1961-68, office mgr. machine tool divsn., 1975-76; mgr., corp. officer Frazer Machinery and Supply Co., Orlando, 1976-93, sec.-treas., 1988-93. Founder parent support groups for gifted edn., Seminole County, 1979; sec. Parent of Gifted Edn., Seminole County, 1980-87; mem. adv. bd. Exceptional Student Edn., Seminole City, Fla., 1980-87; chair Maitland (Fla.) Centennial Founders Bd. 1985; tour guide Orlando Opera Guild, Winter Park, Fla., 1985, bd. dirs., 1997—, v.p., 1999—; celebrity waitress Leukemia Soc. Am., Orlando, 1986; co-chair Project Graduation Lyman H.S., Seminole County, 1986-87; chair Alzheimers Resource Auction Dinner, Winter Park, 1987-88; bd. dirs. Maitland Civic Ctr., 1983-86, sec. 1983-84, v.p. 1987-88, 1993-94, pres. 1988-89, 1994-96, ex-officio bd. dirs., 1989-90; v.p. Maitland Woman's Club, 1994-98, pres. 1997-99; mem. Cultural Corridor Com., Maitland, 1994-98, fin. com., mem. grant com., 1998-99, mem. planning com., 1994-98; bd. dirs. non-profit Showcase Group, 1994-95, chair 1996; bd. dirs. Maitland Hist. Soc., 1996-99, So. Sem. C. of C., 1998—, Maitland/So. Sem. C. of C., chair Taste of Maitland, 1999; co-chair Am. Heart Assn. Lock-up Vol., 1995-96; vol. Golden Orch. and Chorus Aux., Over the Rainbow Auction, 1995-97; house mgr. Designer's Showhouse, 1998, 99, Orlando Opera; ch. coun. College Park United Meth. Ch., 1999, Orlando; co-chair Attic, 1999. Recipient Appreciation plaque Dividends, Seminole City, 1974-75, Cert. Appreciation Maitland Civic Ctr., 1986, 97, Alzheimer Resource Ctr., Winter Park, 1987, Pres.'s Gavel, 1989, 96, Northam award, 1995, Chamber Plaque, 1998, Designers' Showhouse Appreciation Cert, 1998-99. Mem. Am. Machine Tool Ditbrs., Soc. Mfg. Engrs., Maitland Woman's Club (several offices 1970—). Democrat. Methodist. Avocations: horticulture, bridge, reading.

HODGE, PATRICIA MARIE CASCIO, nurse practitioner in psychiatry; b. Bklyn., Nov. 1, 1955; d. Vincent J. and Mary (Farrell) Cascio; children: George E. IV, Kristen Lenore. AAS in Nursing with Distinction, Suffolk county Community Coll., 1981; BS in Community Health with distinction, St. Joseph's Coll., 1987; postgrad., Inst. Pastoral Formation, Rockville Centre N.Y.; MS Nurse Practitioner in Psychiatry, Stony Brook U., 1997. Cert. health counseling; cert. clin. specialist in adult psychiat. mental health nursing, chem. addictions registered nurse. Day nursing supr. Sisters of St. Joseph, Maria Regina Convent, Brentwood, N.Y., 1986-90; psychiat. nurse mental health div. Cath. Charities, Diocese Rockville Centre (N.Y.), 1990—, first psychiatric nurse, 1990—. Mem. Assn. Christian Therapists, Network of N.Y. Clin. Specialists in Psychiatric/Mental Health Nursing, The Nurse Practitioner Assn. of Long Island, Sigma Theta Tau Internat.

HODGE, PAUL WILLIAM, astronomer, educator; b. Seattle, Nov. 8, 1934; s. Paul Hartman and Frances H.; m. Ann Uran, June 14, 1962; children: Gordon, Erik, Sandra. BS, Yale U., 1956; PhD, Harvard U., 1960. Lectr. Harvard, 1960-61; asst. prof. astronomy U. Calif. at Berkeley, 1961-65; asso. prof. U. Wash., Seattle, 1965-69; prof. astronomy U. Wash., 1969—, chmn. Astronomy dept., 1987-91; fellow Mt. Wilson, Palomar Obs., Calif. Inst. Tech., Pasadena, 1960-61; physicist Smithsonian Astrophys. Obs., Cambridge, Mass., 1956-74. Author: Solar System Astrophysics, 1964, Galaxies and Cosmology, 1966, The Large Magellanic Cloud, 1967, Concepts of the Universe, 1969, Galaxies, 1972, Concepts of Contemporary Astronomy, 1974, The Small Magellanic Cloud, 1977, An Atlas of the Andromeda Galaxy, 1981, Interplanetary Dust, 1982, The Universe of Galaxies, 1985, Galaxies, 1986, The Andromeda Galaxy, 1992, Meteorite Craters and Impact Structures of the World, 1994, An Atlas of Local Group Galaxies, 1999; editor: The Astron. Jour., 1984—. Mem. Am. Astron. Soc. (v.p. 1990-93), Internat. Astron. Union, Meteoritical Soc., AAAS (pres. sect. D 1978-79, 83-84), Astron. Soc. Pacific (v.p. 1974-75), Korean Astron. Soc. Office: U Wash Dept Astronomy Box 351580 Seattle WA 98195-1580

HODGE, PHILIP GIBSON, JR., mechanical and aerospace engineering educator; b. New Haven, Nov. 9, 1920; s. Philip Gibson and Muriel (Miller) H.; m. Thea Drell, Jan. 3, 1943; children: Susan E., Philip T., Elizabeth M. AB, Antioch Coll., 1943; PhD, Brown U., 1949. Research asst. Brown U., 1947-49, asso., 1949; asst. prof. math. UCLA, 1949-53; assoc. prof. applied mechanics Poly. Inst. Bklyn., 1953-56, prof., 1956-57; prof. mechanics Ill. Inst. Tech., 1957-71; prof. mechanics U. Minn., Mpls., 1971-91, prof. emeritus, 1991—; Russell Severance Springer vis. prof. U. Calif., 1976; vis. prof. emeritus Stanford U., 1993—; sec. U.S. nat. com. Theoretical and Applied Mechanics, 1982—. Author: 5 books, the most recent being Limit Analysis of Rotationally Symmetric Plates and Shells, 1963, Continuum Mechanics, 1971; also numerous rsch. articles in profl. jours.; tech. editor Jour. Applied Mechanics, 1971-76. Recipient Disting. Service award Am. Acad. Mechanics, 1984; Karman medal ASCE, 1985. NSF sr. postdoctoral fellow, 1963. Mem. NAE, ASME (hon., Worcester Reed Warner medal 1975, ASME medal 1987), Internat. Union Theoretical and Applied Mechanics (asst. treas. 1984-92). E-mail: hodge@am-sun2.stanford.edu. Home: 580 Arastradero Rd Apt 701 Palo Alto CA 94306-3948 Office: Stanford U Applied Mech Div Durand Bldg Palo Alto CA 94305-4040

HODGE, RICHARD L., federal judge; b. 1946. JD, Mercer U., 1977. Magistrate judge U.S. Dist. Ct. (mid. dist.) Ga., Albany, 1993—. Office: Albany Towers Ste 316 235 Roosevelt St Albany GA 31701

HODGE, ROBERT JOSEPH, retail executive; b. St. Louis, July 5, 1937; s. Joseph Edward and Alberta Marie (Oehler) H.; m. Carmen Maria Villalobos, Sept. 1, 1960; children: Ralph, Robert, Carmen. BS in Indsl. Relations, St. Louis U., 1959. Meat dept. merchandiser Kroger Co., Cleve., 1972-74; corp. v.p. deli/bakery Kroger Co., Cin., 1981-83; v.p. Atlanta div. Kroger Co., 1983-85; meat merchandiser Kroger Co., St. Louis, 1977-80, v.p. gateway region, 1985-87; v.p. meat ops. Ralph's Grocery Co., Los Angeles, 1974-77; gen. mgr. Super X Drug, Melbourne, Fla., 1980-81; sr. v.p. Dillon Co., Hutchinson, Kans., 1987-89; sr. v.p. merchandising, manufacturing Kroger Co., Cin., 1989-92, pres. Cin./Dayton mktg. area, 1992—. Sgt. U.S. Army, res., 1959-66. Avocations: golf, skiing. Home: 614 Watchcove Ct Cincinnati OH 45230-3777 Office: Kroger Co 150 Tri County Pkwy Cincinnati OH 45246-3246

HODGE, VERNE ANTONIO, judge; b. St. Thomas, V.I., Nov. 16, 1933; s. John Wesley Hodge and Idalia Victoria Stout; children: Verne Jr., Bridget, Teresa. BS magna cum laude, Hampton U., 1956; JD cum laude, Howard U., 1969. Bar: V.I. 1969, D.C. 1969, U.S. Ct. Appeals (3d cir.) 1970, U.S. Supreme Ct. 1973. Internal auditor, internal revenue agt. V.I. Govt., 1958-61; pub. accountant, comptroller Mannassah Busline, Inc., St. Thomas, 1961-65; bus. mgr., personnel dir. V.I. Dept. Pub. Works, 1965-66; private practice law V.I., 1969-73, atty. gen., 1973-76; chief judge V.I. Territorial Ct., St. Thomas, 1976—; past chmn. Eastern region Nat. Assn. Attys. Gen.; Mem. V.I. Indsl. Incentive Bd., 1963-64, V.I. Bd. Elections, 1964-66. Author: The Need for Constitutional Courts in U.S. Territories, 1968, The Mirror Theory and Its Effects, 1969. Served to 1st lt., inf. U.S. Army, 1956-58. Recipient Am. Jurisprudence awards in state, local and fed. taxation, 1968-69, certificate in advanced income tax law Internal Revenue Service, 1960, award of merit 9th Inf. Div. U.S. Army, 1958. Mem. Am. Judges Assn., Am., Nat., V.I. bar assns. Democrat. Lutheran. Office: Territorial Ct PO Box 7603 Saint Thomas VI 00801-0603 *Nothing is so complicated that it cannot be simplified by hard work.*

HODGELL, MURLIN RAY, university dean; b. Mankato, Kans., Jan. 6, 1924; s. Ray Darius and Lora Henrietta (Overman) H.; m. Billie RoJean Seward, July 20, 1947; children—Janet, Kristen, Kevin. B.S., Kans. State U., 1949; M.S., U. Ill., 1952; M.R.P., Cornell U., 1956, Ph.D., 1959. Licensed architect, engr. and planner. Prof. U. Ill., 1950-54, Kans. State U., 1957-63; chmn. dept. city and regional planning Rutgers U., 1963-64; dir. Sch. Architecture, U. Nebr., 1964-69; dean Coll. Environ. Design, U. Okla., 1969—, dean emeritus; prin. Hodgell Assocs. in Architecture, Engring. and Planning; City planning dir., Manhattan, Kans., 1957-58, planning commr., 1959-63; dir. Kans. State U. Center Community Devel., 1959-63. Author: Contemporary Farmhouses, 1956, Forgotten Millions, 1959, Zoning, 1957. Trustee Weigal Found., Leonard Bailey Found. Served to lt. (j.g.) USNR, 1943-45. Named Kan. Outstanding Young Man of Yr. Kans. Jr. C. of C., 1959, Man of Yr. Manhattan, Kans., 1960; recipient citation distinguished community service Lane-Bryant Found., 1960. Fellow AIA, ASCE; mem. Am. Inst. Cert. Planners, Am. Soc. Planning Ofcls., Assn. Collegiate Schs. Architecture, Asso. Schs. Constrn. Home: 1301 Avondale Dr Norman OK 73069-4407

HODGEN, MAURICE DENZIL, foundation executive; b. Timaru, New Zealand, Aug. 7, 1929; s. William Arnold and Lindsey Frances (Neill) H.; m. Rhona Brandstater, June 20, 1951; children: Philip Denzil, Victoria Anne. Student, Avondale Coll., Cooranbong, Australia, 1948-50; B.S., Pacific Union Coll., 1953; M.A., Columbia U., 1956, Ed.D., 1958. Asst. prof. La Sierra Coll., Riverside, Calif., 1958-64; lectr. Solusi Coll., Bulawayo, Zimbabwe, 1964-66; dir. tchr. edn. Helderberg Coll., Somerset W., S. Africa, 1966-68; assoc. prof. Sch. Edn. Loma Linda (Calif.) U., 1968-72, prof., 1972—, dean grad. sch., 1978-87; adminstr. fin. devel. Claremont (Calif.) Grad. U., 1987-93. Exec. dir. Community Found. of Riverside County, 1993—. Served with U.S. Army, 1953-55. Office: 3800 N Orange St Ste 230 Riverside CA 92501-3622

HODGES, ANN, actress, singer, dancer; b. Elizabethtown, Ky., June 24; d. Henry Lavely and Margaret Rhodes (Lewis) H.; m. Richard Angleine; 1 child, Michael Christian Angleine; m. Barry C. Tuttle, Sept. 16, 1969 (div.

1972). Cert. yoga tchr.; ordained min. Congl. Ch. Practical Theology. Yoga instr., Tampa, St. Petersburg, Safety Harbor, Clearwater, Fla., 1994—; pvt. instr. Yoga, Fla. Appeared in (Broadway shows) No Strings, The Rothchilds, Heathen, (off-Broadway shows) The Boys From Syracuse, There Goes The Old Ballgame, Bella, (TV shows) The Jackie Gleason Show, The Steve Allen Show, The Ed Sullivan Show, Bell Telephone Hour, Ellery Queen, Omnibus, The Vic Damone Show, The Big Record, (TV spls.) Once Upon A Mattress, The G.M. Spectacular, The Esso Spectacular, (motion pictures) The Cardinal, The New Life Style, Oldsmobile, (plays) Hello Dolly!, Sugar Babies, Chicago, Can Can, Sweet Charity, Mame, Applause The Best Little Whorehouse in Texas, Gypsy, Damn Yankees, See How They Run, Catch Me If You Can., Legends!, I Ought to Be in Pictures, How the Other Half Loves, Pajama Tops, The Last of the Red Hot Lovers, Pal Joey, Cole Porter Reveiw, Gone with the Wind (role of Belle Watling in American Premiere Production), The Greenwich Village Scandals of 1923; also many commls., voice overs and indsls.; performer numerous charities including Am. Cancer Soc., Am. Heart Assn., Handicapped, Abused Wives and Children; star performer Gasparilla Coronation, 1991, guest performer Fla. Orch. at Clearwater Jazz Festival. Yoga instr. Safety Harbor Spa, Don CeSar, Harbour Island Athletic Club, Spa Emporium, Casa Bella Vista, Gold's Gym; min. Congl. Ch. of Practical Theology. Named the Queen of Mus. Theatre by the Press, one of Tampa Bay's top achievers, Leading Ladies of Ruth Eckerd Hall. Mem. Internat. Yoga Tchrs. Assn. (cert. in integral yoga therapy), Suncoast Yoga Tchrs. Assn. (past pres., bd. dirs.). Avocations: yoga, swimming, horse back riding, piano playing, embroidery.

HODGES, BENJAMIN, JR., management consultant; b. Amsterdam, Ga., Aug. 18, 1932; s. Fred Benjamin and Jessie Elizabeth (Pound) H.; m. Nell Davis, Feb. 10, 1957 (dec. June 1986). BS in bus. adminstrn., Fla. State Univ.; grad., Coll. Fin. Planners; D, LaSalle Univ. Founder Frederick B. Hodges Co. Contbr. articles to profl. jours. Developed Planned Gifts for Christian Ministries. Mem. Fla. Econ. Club, Quincy Exchange Club, Quincy C. of C., Masonic Blue Lodge, Scottish Rite, Shrine, Demolay, Alpha Kappa Psi, Arnold Air Soc., Kappa Sigma, Toast Masters, Am. Coll. Life Underwriters, Coll. Fin. Planners, Million Dollar Round Table, N. FL. Estate Planning Coun. Republican. Avocations: golf, history, fishing, genealogy. Office: Frederick B Hodges Cos 423 E Shotwell St Apt 1 Bainbridge GA 31717-4069

HODGES, DAVID ALBERT, electrical engineering educator; b. Hackensack, N.J., Aug. 25, 1937; s. Albert R. and Katherine (Rogers) H.; m. Susan Spongberg, June 5, 1965; children: Jennifer, Alan. B.E.E., Cornell U., 1960; M.S., U. Calif., Berkeley, 1961, Ph.D. in Elec. Engring, 1966. Mem. tech. staff Bell Telephone Labs., Murray Hill, N.J., 1966-69; head system elements research dept. Bell Telephone Labs., Holmdel, N.J., 1969-70; asso. prof. dept. elec. engring. and computer scis U. Calif., Berkeley, 1970-74, prof., 1974-98, chmn. dept., 1989-90, dean Coll. Engring., 1990-96, prof. Grad. Sch., 1998—. Contbr. articles to profl. jours. Fellow AAAS, IEEE.; mem. NAE. Patentee in field. Office: Univ Calif Coll Engring 516 Cory Hall Berkeley CA 94720-1770

HODGES, DEWEY HARPER, aerospace engineer, educator; b. Clarksville, Tenn., May 18, 1948; s. Plummer Maxwell Sr. and Etha Maude (Harper) H.; m. Margaret Elin Jones, Aug. 14, 1971; children: Timothy, Jonathan, David, Philip, Benjamin. BS in Aerospace Engring., U. Tenn., 1969; MS in Aero. and Astronautical Engring., Stanford U., 1970, PhD in Aero. & Astronautical Engring., 1973. Rsch. scientist U.S. Army Aeroflight Dynamics Directorate, Ames Rsch. Ctr., Moffett Field, Calif., 1970-80, sr. rsch. scientist, theoretical group leader, 1980-86; prof. aerospace engring. Ga. Inst. Tech., Atlanta, 1986—; instr. No. Calif. Bible Coll., San Jose, 1974-86; lectr. Stanford U., 1980-86; guest rsch. scientist DLR Inst. Structural Mechanics, Braunschweig, Fed. Republic of Germany, 1984. Contbr. more than 190 articles to profl. jours. and conf. procs.; co-patentee hingeless helicopter rotor with improved stability, 1976, real time missle guidance system, 1995. Elder Christian Comty. Ch., San Jose, 1980-86, Mt. Paran Ch., Atlanta, 1992-94. Fellow AIAA; mem. Am. Helicopter Soc., Am. Acad. Mechanics, Sigma Xi, Tau Beta Pi, Pi Tau Sigma. Republican. Presbyterian. Home: 1172 Branch Water Ct Atlanta GA 30338-4026 Office: Sch Aerospace Enging Ga Inst Tech Atlanta GA 30332-0150 *We know the story of how the wise men sought the Lord Jesus at his birth. I believe that wise men still seek him and that his promise of abundant life to those who follow him is still being fulfilled today.*

HODGES, GEORGE R., federal judge. Bankruptcy judge for western dist. N.C., U.S. Bankruptcy Ct., Charlotte. Office: US Bankruptcy Ct Charles R Jonas Fed Bldg 401 W Trade St Rm 104 Charlotte NC 28202-1619

HODGES, JAMES H., governor; married; 2 children: Luke, Sam. BBA, U. S.C., 1979, JD, 1982. Rep. Dist. 45 (Lancaster County) S.C. House of Reps., 1986-99, chmn. house judiciary com., 1992-94, chmn. joint com. judicial screening, 1993-94, minority leader of house, 1995-98; gov. State of S.C., 1999—; sec., gen. counsel The Springs Co. Named. Legislator of Yr., S.C. C. of C., 1993; recipient Compleat Lawyer Silver medallion U. S.C. Sch. of Law, 1994. Mem. Phi Beta Kappa. Office: Gov's Office PO Box 11829 Columbia SC 29211*

HODGES, JOHN HENDRICKS, physician, educator; b. Harpers Ferry, W.Va., Aug. 1, 1914; s. Joseph Howard and Edna (Hendricks) H.; m. Elizabeth May Wallace, Jan. 27, 1940; 1 child, John Hendricks Jr. BS, Cath. U. Am., 1935; MD, Jefferson Med. Coll., Phila., 1939. Diplomate Am. Bd. Internal Medicine. Intern Phila. Gen. Hosp., 1939-41; gen. practice Martinsburg, W.Va., 1941-42; resident medicine Jefferson Med. Coll. Hosp., 1942-46; faculty Jefferson Med Coll., 1944—, dir. course in clin. lab. medicine, 1944-72, Ludwig A. Kind prof. medicine, 1964-79, emeritus, 1979—, dir. div. gen. medicine, 1967-77; cons. hematology Lankenau Hosp., Phila., 1963-88, emeritus, 1988; pres. Henry K. Mohler Physicians Offices, Phila., 1955-75; S. Weir Mitchell assoc., treas. Coll. Physicians of Phila., 1978-84, coun. mem.; assoc. Cardeza Found., emeritus 1985—. Editor: Manual for Laboratory Medicine, 1946, 11 editions, 1966; Contbr. articles to profl. jours. Bd. dirs. Mercy Cath. Med. Ctr., 1972-82; trustee Thomas Jefferson U., 1978—, Children's Rehab. Hosp., 1979-89, Magee Rehab. Hosp., 1987-93; mem. Physicians Rev. Bd., United Fund, Pa. Hosp. Trustee Assn., 1979-88. Recipient Christian R. and Mary F. Lindback Found. award for excellence in teaching, 1966, Dean's medal Jefferson Med. Coll., 1989, Ann. award in medicine Cath. U. Am., 1969, Alumni Achievement award Jefferson Med. Coll., 1990, Gold Headed Cane award Jefferson Med. Coll.; 1992; Mary Markle Found. fellow in tropical medicine, 1944; portrait presented to Thomas Jefferson U., 1981. Fellow ACP; mem. AMA, Pa. Med. Soc., Phila. Med. Soc., Montgomery County Med. Soc., Internat. Soc. Hematology, Am. Soc. Hematology (emeritus), y, Internat. Soc. Internal Medicine, Alumni Assn. Jefferson Med. Coll. (past pres.), Meigs Med. Assn. (past pres. emeritus), Jefferson X-Soc., Sigma Xi, Alpha Omega Alpha, Phi Eta Sigma, Nu Sigma Nu. Home: 436 Sabine Ave Wynnewood PA 19096-1402

HODGES, JOT HOLIVER, JR., lawyer, business executive; b. Archer City, Tex., Nov. 16, 1932; s. Jot Holiver and Lola Mae (Hurd) H.; m. Virginia Cordray Pardue, June 11, 1955; children: Deborah, Jot, Darlene. BS, BBA, Sam Houston State U., 1954; JD, U. Tex., 1957. Bar: Tex., U.S. Dist. Ct. (so. dist.) Tex., U.S. Ct. Appeals (5th cir.). Asst. atty. gen. State of Tex., Austin, 1958-60; chmn. bd. Presidio Devel. Corp., Missouri City, Tex.; organizer, founder 3 banks, several corps. and ltd. partnerships; residential and comml. real estate developer. Contbr. articles to legal, med., pharm., and hosp. jours. Capt. U.S. Army. Mem. Houston Club. Home: 3527 Thunderbird St Missouri City TX 77459-2445 Office: 3660 Hampton Dr Ste 200 Missouri City TX 77459-3044

HODGES, JUDITH ANNE, artist, art educator; b. San Antonio, Sept. 22, 1951; d. Robert Marc and Betty A. H.; 1 child, Elan Young. BA in Liberal Arts, Prescott Coll., 1973; student, San Antonio Art Inst., 1985; Profl. Clear Multiple Subject Tchg. Credential, Nat. U., 1989; student, Monart Sch. of Arts, 1989, Otis Art Inst., 1990, Idylwild Sch. Music and the Arts, 1990, Art Ctr., Pasadena, 1997. Massage therapist pvt. practice, San Antonio, 1981-86, Murrieta Hot Springs, Calif., 1986-90; tchr. art Creative Arts Group, Temecula, Calif., 1988-90; tchr., artist Butterfield Visual and Performing Arts Magnet Sch., Moreno Valley, Calif., 1991—; tchr. Art Club Butterfield Elem. Sch. Arts, Moreno Valley, 1973, 94-97; juror Temecula Student Art Fair, 1990; art cons. Fallbrook (Calif.) Union Elem. Sch. Dist., 1990; site organizer Festival of Arts Moreno Valley Unified Sch. Dist., 1992-96, active gifted and talented and visual and performing arts student assessment, 1995-96; founder, owner White Moon Edits., artist prints, 1999—. Exhibited in group shows at Upstairs Gallery, Claremont, Calif., 1994, 95, Newport Beach Jazz Festival, Calif., 1996, Tubac Ctr. for Arts, Ariz., 1997, Art 2000 Group Exhbn., Moreno Valley, 1997 (hon. mention), Ariz. Aqueous XI Nat. Juried Exhibit, 1997, Riverside (Calif.) Art Mus., 1997, Fallbrook Wildlife Art Show, Calif., 1997, Art Works Gallery, Claremont, Calif., 1997 (first place award); artist: (published prints) The Bug Collection, 1997. Recipient San Antonio Art Inst. grant., 1985. Mem. Art 2000. Avocations: gardening, hiking, biking, gourmet cooking.

HODGES, KENNETH STUART, controlller; b. Bronx, N.Y., Nov. 2, 1955; s. Arthur Stuart and Arlene Marilyn (Hemme) H.; m. Diane Jean Lama, Aug. 20, 1977; children: Jonathan Stuart, Erika Jean. BBA, Iona Coll., 1977; MS in Adminstrn., Western Conn. State U., 1987. CPA, Conn. Staff acct. Coopers and Lybrand CPAs, Stamford, Conn., 1977-79; sr. acct. U.S. Surg. Corp., Norwalk, Conn., 1979-80; supr. accts. receivable Howmet Turbine Components, Greenwich, Conn., 1980-84; mgr. acctg. Guinness Import Co., Stamford, 1985-86; contr. Fujitsu Imaging Systems Am., Danbury, Conn., 1986-90; dir. fin. Ultimate Data Systems, Wilton, Conn., 1990-91; contr. Prentice Hall Legal & Fin. Svcs., N.Y.C., 1991-93, Mal Dunn Assoc. Inc., Croton Falls, N.Y., 1994-95, The Patterson Club, Inc., Fairfield, Conn., 1995-97; v.p., CFO Shared Techs. Comms., Hartford, Conn., 1997-99; CFO Discount Trophy & Co., South Windsor, Conn., 1999—. Mem. Am. Inst. CPAs, Conn. Soc. CPAs. Republican. Avocations: golf, tennis, boating, swimming, cycling.

HODGES, LAWRENCE H., agricultural engineer. Cons. agrl. and mech. engring. Racine, Wis. Home and Office: PO Box 307 Racine WI 53401-0307

HODGES, LOUIS WENDELL, religion educator; b. Eupora, Miss., Jan. 24, 1933; s. John Calvin and Lorene (Phillips) H.; m. Helen Elizabeth Davis, June 6, 1954; children: John David, George Kenneth. BA, Millsaps Coll., 1954; BD, Duke U., 1957, PhD, 1960. Ordained to ministry Meth. Ch., 1958. Asst. prof. religion Washington and Lee U., Lexington, Va., 1960-64, assoc. prof., 1964-67, prof., 1967-87, Fletcher Otey Thomas prof. Bible, 1987-97; Knight prof. journalism Washington and Lee U., Lexington, 1997—; vis. prof. U. Va., 1967-71; vis. disting. prof. applied and profl. ethics Ohio U., 1990. Co-author: The Christian and His Decisions, 1969; editor Social Responsibility: Bus., Journalism, Law, Medicine, 1974—; mem. editl. bd. Jour. Mass Media Ethics, 1988—; prodr., anchor TV program series, 1984. Chmn. Coun. on Human Rels., Lexington, 1965-68; mem. Va. adv. com. U.S. Commn. on Civil Rights, Richmond, 1968-74; founder, pres. Rockbridge Area Housing Corp., Lexington, 1968-74; 1st v.p. bd. dirs. Lexington-Rockbridge United Fund, 1972. Gurney Harris Kearns fellow Duke U., 1958-60, Univ. Ctr. in Va. fellow, 1965-66, The Hastings Ctr. fellow, 1985—, Fulbright Lectr. India Journalism, 1995-96. Mem. Assn. for Edn. in Journalism and Mass Comm., Soc. Profl. Journalists (mem. nat. ethics com.). Democrat. Home: 688 Still House Dr Lexington VA 24450-6319 Office: Washington and Lee U Dept Journalism Lexington VA 24450

HODGES, MARGARET MOORE, author, educator; b. Indpls., July 26, 1911; d. Arthur Carlisle and Anna Marie (Mason) Moore; m. Fletcher Hodges, Jr., Sept. 10, 1932; children: Fletcher III, Arthur Carlisle, John Andrews. AB with honors, Vassar Coll., 1932; MLS; Carnegie Libr. Staff scholar, Carnegie Inst. Tech., 1958. lectr. U. Pitts. Grad. Sch. Library and Info. Services, 1964-68, asst. prof., 1968-72, assoc. prof., 1972-75, prof., 1975-77, emeritus, 1977—. Children's librarian, radio and TV storyteller, Carnegie Library Pitts., 1953-64, story specialist, Pitts. Pub. Schs., 1964-68, also storyteller, WQED Schs. Services Dept. NIT network, 1965—; Author: (juvenile books) One Little Drum, 1958, What's for Lunch, Charley?, 1961, Club Against Keats, 1962, Tell It Again, 1963, Secret in the Woods, 1963, Wave, 1964 (runner-up Caldecott award), Hatching of Joshua Cobb, 1967, Constellation, a Shakespeare Anthology, 1968, Sing Out, Charley!, 1968, Lady Queen Anne, 1969 (named Best Book for Young Adults by Ind. Author, Ind. U. Writers Conf.), Making of Joshua Cobb, 1971, Gorgon's Head, 1972, Hopkins of the Mayflower, 1972, Fire Bringer, 1972, Persephone and the Springtime, 1973, Baldur and the Mistletoe, 1974, Freewheeling of Joshua Cobb, 1974, Knight Prisoner, The Tale of Sir Thomas Malory and His King Arthur, 1976, The High Riders, 1980, The Little Humpbacked Horse, 1980, The Avenger, 1982, If You Had a Horse, 1984, Saint George and the Dragon, 1984 (Caldecott medal 1985), Making a Difference, 1989, The Voice of the Great Bell, 1989, The Arrow and the Lamp, 1989, The Kitchen Knight, 1990, Buried Moon, 1990, Brother Francis and the Friendly Beasts, 1991, Saint Jerome and the Lion, 1991, Hauntings, 1991, Don Quixote and Sancho Panza, 1992, Of Swords and Sorcerers, 1993, St. Patrick and the Peddler, 1993, The Hero of Bremen, 1993, Hidden in Sand, 1994, Gulliver in Lilliput, 1995, Comus, 1996, Molly Limbo, 1996; co-editor: Elva S. Smith's The History of Children's Literature, 1980, The True Tale of Johnny Appleseed, 1997, Silent Night, the Song and Its Story, 1997, Up the Chimney, 1998. Mem. ALA (Newbery-Caldecott com. 1960), Pa. Library Assn., Am. Assn. Library Schs., Pitts. Bibliophiles, Zonta Internat., Distinguished Daus. Pa. Republican. Episcopalian. Home: G-48 Longwood at Oakmont 48 Garden Ct Verona PA 15147-3852 Office: U Pitts Bellefield Ave Pittsburgh PA 15260

HODGES, MITCHELL, computer executive; b. Fayetteville, N.C., Mar. 10, 1959; s. Eddie Jr. and Phyliss Marie (Dill) H.; Ilene Michelle Cohen; m. Aug. 16, 1986. BS in Philosophy, Randolph-Macon Coll., 1981; MS in Info. Systems, Nova U., 1992. Applications engr. Anderson Jacobson, Inc., Gaithersburg, Md., 1983-85; sr. product engr. Baxter Sys./Compucare, 1985-89; PC coord. Racal-Datacom, Sunrise, Fla., 1988-92; mgr. global electronic messaging W.R. Grace & Co., Boca Raton, Fla., 1992-95; mgr. workgroup opers. Delta Tech., Inc., Atlanta, 1995—. Mem. Alpha Psi Omega (chpt. pres. 1980-81), Theta Chi (chpt. chaplan 1979-80), Omnicron Delta Kappa. Republican. Home: 976 Oakleigh Manor Ct Powder Springs GA 30127-4941

HODGES, NORMAN, retired district judge; b. Silver City, N. Mex., Aug. 5, 1925; s. Joseph William and Eva Irene H.; m. Tressie Lee Murdock Weiland, Oct. 5, 1963; 1 stepchild, William V. Weiland. BA, U. N. Mex., 1947, BS, 1948, LLB, 1951, JD, 1968. Bar: N. Mex. 1951, U.S. Dist. Ct. N. Mex. 1952, U.S. Ct. Appeals 1960, U.S. Ct. Mil. Appeals 1960, U.S. Supreme Ct. 1960. Prin. Hodges, Hodges & Hodges, Attorneys, Silver City, 1951-52; assoc. H. Vearle Payne 6th Judicial Dist., Lordsburg, N. Mex., 1952-56; dist. attorney Grant, Luna, Hidalgo Counties, Silver City, 1957-63; dist. judge 6th Judicial Dist., Silver City, 1963-86, retired, 1986—. Mem. N. Mex. Supreme Ct. Children's Ct. Rules com., Albuquerque, 1970-73. Capt. USN, 1942-99. Recipient Judge of Yr. award N. Mex. State Bar Assn., Albuquerque, 1982. Mem. Retired Officers Assn., Copper Crest Country Club (bd. dirs. 1965-69), Elks Club, Sigma Chi (pres. 1944). Democrat. Protestant. Avocations: books, Southwestern America. Home: PO Box 390 Silver City NM 88062

HODGES, RALPH B., state supreme court justice; b. Anadarko, Okla., Aug. 4, 1930; s. Dewey E. and Pearl R. (Hodges) H.; m. Janelle H.; children: Shari, Mark, Randy. B.A., Okla. Baptist U.; LL.B., U. Okla. Atty. Bryan County, Okla., 1956-58; judge Okla. Dist. Ct., 1959-65; justice Okla. Supreme Ct., Oklahoma City, 1965—. Office: Okla Supreme Ct State Capital Bldg Oklahoma City OK 73105*

HODGES, ROBERT H., JR., federal judge; b. 1944. BS, U. S.C., 1966, JD, 1969. Legis. aide to Sen. Strom Thurmond, 1969-71, legis. aide to Congressman Floyd Spence, 1971-77; v.p., gen. counsel First Nat. Bank of S.C., Columbia, 1977-85; exec. v.p., gen. counsel S.C. Bankers Assn., Columbia, 1985-86; with Quinn, Arndt & Manning, Columbia, 1986-90; judge U.S. Claims Ct., Washington, 1990—. With Air Force Guard USAF Guard Res., 1963-69. Mem. ABA, S.C. Bar, So. Assn. Bank Counsel, Richland County Bar Assn. Office: US Court of Federal Claims 717 Madison Pl NW Rm 605 Washington DC 20005-0002*

HODGES, THOMPSON GENE, librarian, retired university dean; b. Clinton, Okla., Jan. 30, 1913; s. Kiah and Allie Lee (Thompson) H.; m. Claire Surbeck, June 19, 1935 (dec. 1979); 1 son, Thompson Gene (dec. 1995); m. Dorothea Arnold Ray, 1980. *Mr. Hodges only son was killed in the bombing of the federal building in Oklahoma City, April 19, 1995.* B.S., U. Okla., 1934, M.L.S., 1955; B.D., McCormick Theol. Sem., Chgo., 1939. Ordained to ministry Presbyn. Ch., 1939; minister supply Ch. of Scotland, 1939; pastor Pawhuska and Lawton, Okla., 1939-47; aquisitions librarian U. Okla., 1955-58; dean library services Central State U., Edmond, Okla., 1958-76; dean emeritus Central State U., 1976—; library cons. Univ. Microfilms, 1977; vis. prof. bibliography U. Okla., 1980-81; library cons. Moderator Tulsa Presbytery, 1943. Mem. ALA, Southwestern Library Assn., Okla. Library Assn. (pres. 1965-66), Okla. Ednl. Assn., Kappa Sigma, Beta Phi Mu, Kappa Kappa Psi. Home and Office: 415 Macy St Norman OK 73071-5024

HODGES, VERNON WRAY, mechanical engineer; b. Roanoke, Va., Dec. 26, 1929; s. Charlie Wayne and Kathleen Mae (Williams) H.; m. Lorraine Patricia Smart, Apr. 1, 1955 (div. 1966); children: Vernon Wray Jr., Gregory Elmer, MIchelle Lynn; m. Linda Lou Wall, Feb. 3, 1967; children: Kenneth Wray, Kelly Dianne. BS in Mech. Engring., Va. Poly. Inst. and State U., 1951; MS in Systems Mgmt., U. So. Calif., 1979. Registered profl. engr., Kans., Wash., Calif. Commd. 2d lt. USAF, 1951, advanced through grades to major, 1964, ret., 1965; flight test engr. Boeing Co., Wichita, Kans., 1966-71; sr. engr. Boeing Co., Seattle, 1971-76; systems test engr. Rockwell Internat., Edwards AFB, Calif., 1976-77; sr. engr. Rockwell Internat., Palmdale, Calif., 1981-90, Hughes Helicopters, Inc., Culver City, Calif., 1977-81, Computer Scis. Corp., Edwards AFB, 1990-93; pvt. comml. pilot, 1953—; asst. prof. air sci. Boston U., 1958-61. Elder, deacon Presbyn. Ch. USA, Lancaster, 1981—; active Calif. Rep. Cen. Com., Sacramento, 1977—, Rep. Cen. Com., Washington, 1977—. Recipient Letter of Commendation, USAF. Mem. ASME, NSPE (sec. 1972-75), Air Force Assn., Masons, Shriners. Home: 2731 W Avenue J8 Lancaster CA 93536-5832

HODGES, WILLIAM TERRELL, federal judge; b. Lake Wales, Fla., Apr. 28, 1934; s. Haywood and Clara Lucy (Murphy) H.; m. Peggy Jean Woods, June 8, 1958; children: Judson, Daniel, Clay. B.S.B.A., U. Fla., 1956, J.D., 1958. Bar: Fla. 1959. Mem. firm Macfarlane, Ferguson, Allison & Kelly, Tampa, 1958-71; instr. bus. law U. South Fla., Tampa, 1961-66; judge U.S. Dist. Ct. (mid. dist.) Fla., Tampa, 1971-82, 89—; mem. com. on ops. jury system Jud. Conf., 1982-87, cir. coun., 11th cir., 1981-86; adv. com. on rules criminal procedure and evidence Jud. Conf., 1987—, ad hoc com. on habeas corpus reform; mem. bench book com. Fed. Jud. Ctr., 1984—, chmn., 1987—. Exec. editor, U. Fla. Law Rev., 1957-58. Mem. Am., Tampa-Hillsborough County bar assns., Fla. Bar (chmn. grievance com. 1967-70, chmn. uniform comml. code com. 1970-71), Dist. Judges Assn. 5th Circuit (co-chmn. com. on pattern jury instrn. 1977-81), Dist. Judges Assn. 11th Circuit (chmn. jury instrns. com. 1982—, pres. 1981-82) Am. Judicature Soc. Office: US Dist Ct 512 US Courthouse 311 W Monroe St Jacksonville FL 32201-3558*

HODGE-SPENCER, CHERYL ANN, orthodontist; b. Dorchester, Mass., Apr. 1, 1952; d. Herbert Thomas and Edwina Catherine (Morey) Hodge; m. John Lawrence Spencer, June 10, 1978; children: Devin Thomas, Ian Nicholas. BS in Biology cum laude, Boston Coll., 1974; DMD, Tufts Sch. Dental Medicine, 1977; MPH, Harvard U. Sch. Pub. Health, 1981; Cert. in Orthodontics, Harvard Dental Sch., 1983. Orthodontist Brockton/Bridgewater, Mass., 1984—; orthodontic cons. Mass. Hosp. Sch., Canton, Mass., 1990-95; vice chmn. Bd. of Investment, Bridgewater Savs. Bank, 1989-92; asst. coach Duxbury Youth Hockey Bantam Team, 1993-94. Chmn. bd. dirs. Southeastern Mass. ARC. Lt. Dental Corps USN, 1977-80. Recipient Johnson & Johnson Dentistry award, 1977. Mem. Am. Assn. Orthodontists, Mass. Dental Soc., South Shore Dist. Dental Soc. (sec. 1990-92, peer rev. bd. 1990-92), Northeastern Soc. Orthodontists, Harvard Club Boston, Harvard Soc. Advancement Orthodontics, Metro South C. of C., Rotary (bd. dirs. charitable and ednl. fund 1989-92), Pierre Fouchard Acad., Ma. Amateur Hockey Assn. (intermediate patched hockey coach). Roman Catholic. Avocations: acoustic guitar, singing, cross stitch. Office: 124 South St Bridgewater MA 02324-2425

HODGETTS, RICHARD MICHAEL, business management educator; b. Bronx, N.Y., Mar. 10, 1942; s. Harold Thomas and Regina Gertrude (McDermott) H.; m. Sara Josefina Fontana, Aug. 1, 1970; children: Steven Michael, Jennifer Anne. BS, NYU, 1963; MBA, Ind. U., 1964; PhD, U. Okla., 1968. Mem. faculty U. Nebr., Lincoln, 1966-76, prof. mgmt., 1966-76; prof. mgmt. Fla. Internat. U., Miami, 1976—. Author: Effective Supervision, 1987, Real Managers, 1988, Business Communication, 1990, Social Issues in Business, 1990, Management, 1990, Organizational Behavior, 1991, Managerial communication, 1991, Personnel and Human Resource Management, 1992, Economics, 1993, Business, 1993, Blueprints for Continuous Improvement, 1993, International Business, 1995, TQM in Small and Medium-Sized Organizations, 1996, Internat. Mgmt., 1997, Effective Small Business Management, 1998, Entrepreneurship, 1998, Human Resource Management: A Customer-Oriented Approach, 1998, Measures of Quality and High Performance, 1998, Modern Human Relations at Work, 1999. Fellow Acad. Mgmt.; mem. Acad. Internat. Mgmt., So. Mgmt. Assn. Democrat. Roman Catholic. Avocations: jogging, racquetball. Home: 3930 Durango St Miami FL 33134-6438 Office: Coll Bus Adminstrn Fla Internat U Tamiami Trl Miami FL 33199

HODGIN, JEAN, English educator; b. Cin., June 2, 1936; d. Marston Dean Hodgin and Lucile Jeanette Loofbourrow. BS, Miami U., Oxford, Ohio, 1958; MA, Columbia U., 1960. Instr. Bloomfield (N.J.) Coll., 1963-65; asst. prof. Corning (N.Y.) C.C., 1965-69; prof., dept. chair North Shore C.C., Danvers, Mass., 1969—. Contbr. articles to lit. publs. Mem. Nat. Coun. Tchrs. English, Conf. on Coll. Composition and Comm., Two-Yr. Coll. Assn. (exec. officer). Avocations: photography, tennis, poetry. Office: North Shore CC 1 Ferncroft Rd Danvers MA 01923

HODGKIN, JOHN E., pulmonologist; b. Portland, Oreg., Aug. 22, 1939; s. Williard E. and Dorothy (Rigsby) H.; m. Jeanie Walker, Sept. 6, 1980; children: Steve, Kathryn, Carolyn, Jonathan, Jamie. BS, Walla Walla Coll., 1960; MD, Loma Linda U., 1964. Fellow in pulmonology Mayo Clinic, Rochester, Minn., 1970-72; chief pulmonary sect. Loma Linda (Calif.) U., 1974-80; clin. prof. medicine U. Calif., Davis, 1983—; med. dir. respiratory care St. Helena Hosp., Deer Park, Calif., 1983—, med. dir. pulmonary rehab., 1983—, med. dir. ctr. for health promotion, 1983-96, asst. to pres., 1994—; med. dir. Adventist Health No. Calif., Roseville, Calif., 1995-98, Calif. Med. Found., 1995-98. Editor: Chronic Obstructive Pulmonary Disease: Current Concepts in Diagnosis and Comprehensive Care, 1979, Respiratory Care: A Guide to Clinical Practice, 1977, 4th 1997, Pulmonary Rehabilitation: Guidelines to Success, 1984, 2d edit., 1993, Lung Sounds: A Practical Guide, 1988, 2d edit., 1996. Decorated bronze star U.S. Army, 1968. Fellow Am. Assn. Cardiovas. & Pulmonary Rehab. (pres. 1995-96), Am. Coll. Chest Physicians, Am. Coll. Physicians, Am. Thoracic Soc., Nat. Assn. Med. Direction of Respiratory Care, Am. Assn. Respiratory Care (bd. med. advisors). Avocations: tennis, softball, skiing. Home: 1330 Crestmont Dr Angwin CA 94508-9634 Office: Saint Helena Hosp Lloyd Bldg Ste 502 Deer Park CA 94576

HODGKINS, FRANCIS IRVING (BUTCH HODGKINS), county official. BS in civil engring., Calif. State U., Sacramento, 1972. Dep. dir. pub. works Sacramento County (Calif.), 1991-93; exec. dir. Flood Ctrl. Agy. Sacramento Area, 1993—. Mem. Calif. Flood Plain Mgrs. Assn. Office: Flood Ctrl Agy Sacramento Area 1007 7th St Fl 5 Sacramento CA 95814-3407

HODGKINS, WILLIAM F., career officer. BS in Secondary Edn., Auburn U., 1970, M in Edn. Adminstrn., 1973; grad., Squadron Officer Sch., 1974, USAF Fighter Weapons Sch., 1982, Air Command and Staff Coll., 1983, Can. Forces Command and Staff Coll., 1986; student, Air War Coll., 1995; student program for execs., Carnegie-Mellon U., 1997. Commd. 2d lt. USAF, 1974, advanced through grades to brig. gen., 1998; F-15 aircraft comdr., instr. pilot 33rd Tactical Fighter Wing, Eglin AFB, Fla., 1982, standardization and evaluation pilot, 1982, unit weapons and tactics officer, 1982; instr. pilot, wing weapons and tactics officer 18th Tactical Fighter Wing, Kadena AFB, Japan, 1983-85; air ops. joint staff officer various weapons programs Can. Forces Nat. Def. Hdqs., Ottawa, Ont., 1986-88; chief weapons and tactics div. 1st Tactical Wing Fighter, Langley AFB, Va.,

1988-89; chief spl. programs div., dep. chief staff ops. Hdqs. Tactical Air Command, Langley AFB, 1989-92; dep. chief staff ops. Hdqs. 17th Air Force, Sembach Air Base, Germany, 1992-93; comdr. 32d Fighter Group, Soesterberg Air Base, The Netherlands, 1993-94; chief war plans and mobilization div., various positions Hdqs. USAF, the Pentagon, Washington, 1995-97; dir. ops. J-3 US Forces Japan, Yokota Air Base, 1997-98; dep. comdr. Can. N.Am. Aerospace Def. Command Region, Winnipeg, 1998—. Decorated Legion of Merit. Office: CAN/DCR Aircom, Hq Box 17000 Station Forces, Winnipeg, Canada R35 3Y5

HODGKINSON, WILLIAM JAMES, marketing company executive; b. Bklyn., July 31, 1939; s. William James and Augusta Anne (Botka) H.; A.B., Bucknell U., 1961; M.B.A., Columbia U., 1963; m. Virginia Evelyn Humphreys, Sept. 7, 1963; 1 dau., Elizabeth Anne. Mktg. research analyst Singer Co., N.Y.C., 1963-66; asst. adminstrn. Writing Paper div. Am. Paper Inst., N.Y.C., 1966-67; market rsch. mgr. Diners Club, N.Y.C., 1967-68; with Dun & Bradstreet Cos., Inc., 1968-92, mgmt. cons. William E. Hill Co. div., N.Y.C., 1971-73, mgr. fin. svcs. group Donnelley Mktg. div., Stamford, Conn., 1973-86, v.p., 1987-92; COO Career Systems, Inc., Fairfield, Conn., 1993-97; pres. Marketview Pub. Corp., Fairfield, Conn., 1997—. Bd. dirs. Bklyn. Pub. Libr. br., 1974-79, Enlightenment Together, Inc., 1971-76; rsch. coord. Presdl. Task Force on Improving Small Bus., 1969-70; v.p., trustee Montessori Sch. Bklyn., 1975-79; trustee Greens Farms Congl. Ch., 1983-85; co-chmn. Save Fairfield Com., 1984—. Served with U.S. Army, 1963. Grantee Columbia U., 1962-63; recipient Brotherhood award Bucknell U., 1960. Mem. Bank Mktg. Assn., Am. Mktg. Assn., Direct Mail Mktg. Assn., Princeton Club (N.Y.C.), Phi Lambda Theta. Congregationalist. (bd. deacons 1971-78, pres. 1977-78). Contbr. articles to profl. jours. Home: 4454 Black Rock Tpke Fairfield CT 06430-1807

HODGSON, ARTHUR CLAY, lawyer; b. Little River, Kans., Aug. 22, 1907; s. Edward Howard and Flora Cleveland (Perry) H.; m. Annie Letitia Green, Jan. 5, 1939; children: Richard, David, Edward, Alice Anne, James. AB, U. Kans., 1929; JD, George Washington U., 1937. Bar: Kans. 1936, D.C. 1936, U.S. Supreme Ct. 1950. Sole practice law, Washington, 1936-38; practice, Lyons, Kans., 1938—, ptnr. Hodgson & Kahler, 1969—. Pres. Lyons Jaycees; bd. dirs. Lyons C. of C. With USN, 1943-45. Recipient Disting. Svc. award Lyons C. of C. Mem. ABA (ho. of dels. 1976-82), Kans. Trial Lawyers Assn. (bd. govs. 1957-89, pres. 1972-73), ATLA (bd. govs. 1973-76), Rice County Bar, S.W. Kans. Bar, Kans. Bar Assn. (del., disting. service award 1985), City Attys. Assn. Kans. (pres. 1960-61), Kans. State Hist. Soc. (pres. 1996-97), Rotary, Masons. Democrat. Congregationalist. Home: 1240 28th Rd Little River KS 67457-9004 Office: Hodgson & Kahler 119 1/2 W Main St Lyons KS 67554-1927

HODGSON, CHRIS, Canadian provincial official; b. Haliburton, Ont., Can., Dec. 7, 1961; m. Marie Hodgson; children: Clayton, Cody, Charlotte, Caroline. BA in Polit. Sci. with honors, Trent U., Peterborough, 1985. Min. of natural resources, min. no. devel. and mines Province Ont., Toronto, 1995-97, chair mgmt. bd. of cabinet, 1997, dep. house leader, 1997. Mem. Haliburton Men's Hockey League (past pres., mem.), Haliburton Highlands Outdoors Assn., Lion's Club. Office: 5th Fl, 99 Wellesley St West, Toronto, ON Canada M7A 1W3

HODGSON, ERNEST, toxicology educator; b. Durham, Eng., July 26, 1932; came to U.S., 1955; s. Ernest Victor and Emily (Moses) H.; m. Mary Kathleen Devlin, Dec. 21, 1957; children: Mary Elizabeth, Audrey Catherine, Patricia Emily Devlin, Ernest Victor Felix. B.Sc. with honors, Kings Coll. U. Durham, Eng., 1955; Ph.D., Oreg. State U., 1959. Rsch. fellow Oreg. State U., Corvallis, 1955-59, U. Wis., Madison, 1959-61; asst. prof. N.C. State U., Raleigh, 1961-63, assoc. prof., 1963-65, prof. toxicology, 1965—, William Neal Reynolds prof., 1977—, chmn. toxicology dept., 1982-97, Disting. Alumni Rsch. prof., 1987-90; mem. adv. panel U.S. EPA, Washington, 1982-85; mem. toxicology study sect. NIH, Washington, 1985-89, mem. NIEHS study sect., 1992-96, chmn. 1994-96; pres. Toxicology Comm., Raleigh, 1982—; vis. scientist U. Wash., Seattle, 1975. Author, editor: Introduction to Biochemical Toxicology, 1980, 2d edit., 1994, Modern Toxicology, 1987, 2d edit., 1997, Dictionary of Toxicology; editor: Reviews in Biochemical Toxicology, 1979—, Reviews in Environmental Toxicology, 1984—, Jour. Biochemical Toxicology; mem. editorial bd. Chemico-Biol. Interactions, Jour. Toxicology and Applied Pharmacology; contbr. articles to profl. jours. Chmn. policy rev. com. Gov.'s Waste Mgmt. Bd., Raleigh, 1984. NIH grantee, 1962—. qem. AAAS, Soc. Toxicology (edn. com. 1984—, Edn. award 1984, Merit award 1994, pres. mechanisms sect. 1991-92, pres. N.C. chpt. 1984-85), Am. Soc. Pharmacology (drug metabolism com. 1981-84), Am. Chem. Soc. (Burdick and Jackson Internat. award in pesticide chemistry, Sterling Hendricks award USDA, 1997), Internat. Soc. Study Xenobiotics (coun. 1986-89, sec.-elect 1990-92, sec. 1992-94, pres.-elect 1996-97, pres. 1998—), Sigma Xi (chpt. pres. 1974). Democrat. Avocations: history, writing, travel. E-mail address: ernestúhodgson@mcsu.edu. Office: NC State U Dept Toxicology Box 7633 Raleigh NC 27695

HODGSON, FREDERICK KIMMEL, radio station executive; b. May 17, 1942; s. Newton C. and Sarah (Ritnmel) H.; m. Judy Hodgson; children: David, Elizabeth Marberry, Jennifer Marberry, Steve. BA in Drama, Antioch Coll.; MA in Speech, U. Wis. Program dir. Sta. KTDB-FM Ramah (N.Mex.) Navajo Sch. Bd., Inc., 1971-73; devel. dir. Sta. WVWC-FM W.Va. Wesleyan Coll., Buckhannon, 1973-74; sta. mgr. Sta. KRSW-FM Minn. Pub. Radio, St. Paul, 1974-78; gen. mgr. Sta. KUOW-FM U. Wash., Seattle, 1978-83; v.p., gen. mgr. Sta. WETA-FM GWETA, Inc., Washington, 1983-86; cons. San Diego State U., 1987; gen. mgr. Sta. WAMU-FM The Am. U., Washington, 1987—; chmn. bd. dirs. Nat. Pub. Radio; bd. dirs. Nat. Pub. Radio, mem. audience doubling task force, mem. tng. adv. com.; mem. fin. mgmt. adv. com. CPB, mem. radio program fund rev. panel; vicechmn. Ea. Pub. Radio, 1991-93, chmn., 1993—; mem. Monitor Radio Adv. Com.; instr. English Instituto Cultural Argentino Norteamericano; radio prodr. local and nat. broadcasts, 1966-85. Mem. semi-profl., comty. and coll. theater groups, 1958-66; mem. ch. coun. Luther Pl. Meml. Ch., 1989-92, treas., 1990-93, vol. women's shelter, former chmn. parish edn. com.; active Leadership Wash. Recipient Best Spot News award Minn. AP Broadcasters, Best Edn. Program award Minn. Edn. Assn., Ohio State award for cultural documentary; NDEA fellow U. Wis. Office: Sta WAMU-FM Am U 4400 Massachusetts Ave NW Washington DC 20016-8082*

HODGSON, GREGORY BERNARD, software systems architect; b. Chgo., July 17, 1946; s. John George and Lucille (Nass) H.; m. Kathleen Patricia, Aug. 11, 1972 (div. July 1974); m. Kathryn Marie Maytum, Feb. 14, 1976. BS in Computer Engring., U. Ill., 1972. Computer programmer specialist Lockheed Missiles and Space Co., Sunnyvale, Calif., 1972-81, software systems engr., 1981-89; software sys. cons. Lockheed Missiles and Space Co., Sunnyvale, 1989-95; engr./scientist Hewlett-Packard Co., Sunnyvale, Calif., 1995; software system architect Lockheed Martin Missile and Space Ctr., Sunnyvale, Calif., 1995—; cons. in field. Served with U.S. Army, 1966-69. State of Ill. VA scholar, 1970-72. Mem. Ill. VA Assn. (coord. fed. and state affairs 1970-72). Roman Catholic. Avocations: boating, camping, bowling, softball, volleyball. Home: 469 1/2 Curie Dr San Jose CA 95123-4925

HODGSON, JAMES STANLEY, antiquarian bookseller; b. Detroit, Apr. 26, 1942; s. Norman Thomas and Marion Phyllis (Konat) H.; m. Nancy Irons Mercer, Aug. 10, 1968 (div. Feb. 1996); children: Emily Harcourt, William Mercer. AB, Brown U., 1964; MS, Simmons Coll., 1967. Acquisitions librarian Fogg Art Mus. Harvard U., Cambridge, Mass., 1968-83, librarian, 1983-84, chief librarian faculty Grad. Sch. of Design, 1984-90; pres. James Hodgson Books, Inc., Boston, 1990—; mem. adv. bd. Boston Archtl. Ctr., Boston, 1984—. Contbr. numerous articles to profl. jours. Trustee Rotch House and Garden Mus., New Bedford, 1984—; v.p. Coalition for Buzzard's Bay, 1994—. Mem. Art Libraries Soc. N.Am. Home and Office: 39 Chestnut St South Dartmouth MA 02748-3508

HODGSON, JANE ELIZABETH, obstetrician and gynecologist, consultant; b. Crookston, Minn., Jan. 23, 1915; d. Herbert and Adelaide (Marin) H.; m. Frank Walter Quattlebaum, Feb. 22, 1940; children: Gretchen, Nancy. BS, Carleton Coll., 1934, DSc (hon.), 1994; MD, U. Minn., 1939, MS in Ob-Gyn., 1947. Diplomate Am. Bd. Ob.-Gyn. Fellow Mayo Clinic, Rochester, Minn., 1941-44; pvt. practice in ob-gyn. St. Paul, 1947-72; med. dir. Preterm Clinic, Washington, 1972-74; med. dir. fertility control clinic St. Paul Ramsey Med. Ctr., 1974-79; med. dir. Planned Parenthood Minn., St. Paul, 1980-82, Midwest Health Ctr. Women, Mpls., 1981-83, Women's Health Ctr., Duluth, Minn., 1981-84; mem. staff Women's Health Ctr., Duluth, 1986—, also bd. dirs.; ostetrician/gynecologist Project Hope, Grenada, West Indies, 1984; vis. prof. ob-gyn. project hope Zheijiang Med. Sch., Hangzhou, People's Republic of China, 1985-86; clin. assoc. prof. ob-gyn. U. Minn., Mpls., 1986—; vis. med. educator Project Hope, Cairo, 1979-80; vis. prof. dept. ob-gyn. U. Calif., San Francisco, 1983. Editor: Abortion & Sterilization, 1981; contbr. numerous articles to profl. jours. Bd. dirs. Genesis II Women, Mpls., 1988—, Pro Choice Resources, Mpls., 1991—, Wellstone Alliance, Mpls., 1992—, Ctr. for Reproductive Law and Policy, N.Y.C., 1995—. Recipient Ann. Humanitarian award Nat. Abortion Fedn., 1981, Woman Physician of Yr. award Med. Women Minn. Med. Assn., 1983, Ann. Jane Hodgson Reproductive Freedom award Nat. Abortion Rights Action League, 1989, Hanah G. Solomon award Nat. Coun. Jewish Women, 1990, Margaret Sanger award Planned Parenthood Fedn. of Am., 1995, Harold Swanberg award Am. Med. Writer's Assn., 1996. Fellow Am. Coll. Ob-Gyn. (founding); mem. Am. Med. Women's Assn. (E. Blackwell award 1992, Reproductive Health award 1994), Minn. Ob-Gyn. Soc. (pres. 1967), Minn. Med. Assn. (So. Minn. Med. award 1952), Minn. Women's Polit. Caucus (16th Ann. Founding Feminist award 1988), Mayo Clinic Alumni Assn. Home and Office: 1537 N Fisk St Saint Paul MN 55117-3415

HODGSON, LYNN MORRISON, marine biologist; b. Atlanta, July 30, 1948; d. Fred Grady Jr. and Florence Kimball (Morrison) H. BS, Coll. of William and Mary, 1970; MS, U. Wash., 1972; PhD, Stanford U., 1979. Asst. rsch. scientist U. Fla., Gainesville, 1979-81; vis. asst. prof. U. Ark., Fayetteville, 1981-82; asst. rsch. scientist Harbor Br. Found., Ft. Pierce, Fla., 1982-85; asst. prof. biology Northern State U., Aberdeen, S.D., 1985-88, chair dept. math. and natural scis., 1988-92, prof. biology, 1989-92; assoc. prof. biology U. Hawaii at West Oahu, Pearl City, 1992-95, prof. biology, 1995—. Contbr. articles to Botanica Marina, Marine Biology, Jour. of Phycology and others. Grantee S.D. Dept. of Water and Natural Resources, 1987-88, Hawaii Natural Areas Reserves, 1990-91, Ednl. Improvement Fund, 1992-93, Hawaii Dept. of Health, 1993-94. Mem. Internat. Phycological Soc., Brit. Phycological Soc., Phycological Soc. Am. (nominations chmn. 1986-87), S.D. Acad. Scis. (pres. 1992), Hawaii Environ. Educators Assn., Sigma Xi (pres. U. Hawaii chpt. 1998-99, Kappa Mu Epsilon. Avocations: backpacking, scuba, canoeing, sailing, philately. Office: U Hawaii at West Oahu 96-129 Ala Ike St Pearl City HI 96782-3626

HODGSON, PAUL EDMUND, surgeon; b. Milw., Dec. 14, 1921; s. Howard Edmund and Ethel Marie (Niemi) H.; m. Barbara Jean Osborne, Apr. 22, 1945; children: Ann, Paul. BS summa cum laude, Beloit Coll., 1943; M.D. cum laude, U. Mich., 1945. Diplomate: Am. Bd. Surgery. Intern U. Mich. Hosp., 1945-46, resident in surgery, 1948-52; mem. faculty dept. surgery U. Mich., 1952-62, assoc. prof., 1956-62; prof. surgery U. Nebr. Coll. Medicine, Omaha, 1962-88; prof. emeritus U. Nebr. Coll. Medicine, 1988—, asst. dean for curriculum, 1966-72, chmn. dept. surgery, 1972-84; Trustee Beloit Coll., 1977-80. Served to capt. M.C. U.S. Army, 1946-48. Mem. A.C.S., Frederick A. Coller Surg. Soc., Soc. Univ. Surgeons, Central Surg. Assn., Soc. Surgery Alimentary Tract, Am. Assn. Surgery Trauma, Western Surg. Assn., Am. Surg. Assn. Presbyterian. Office: U Nebr Med Ctr 600 S 42nd St Omaha NE 68198-3280

HODGSON, PETER JOHN, music educator, composer; b. Birmingham, Eng., Apr. 6, 1929; came to U.S., 1965, naturalized, 1974; s. Eric Christopher and Dorothy (Price) H.; m. Mary Thatcher, 1958; 1 son, Michael. MusB, U. London, 1964; MusM, Royal Coll. Music, 1965; Ph.D. in Music (Univ. fellow), U. Colo., 1970. Resident music master Univ. Sch., Victoria, B.C., Can., 1952-55; mem. faculty, adminstr. Mt. Royal Coll., Calgary, Alta., Can., 1955-65; mem. faculty Banff (Alta.) Sch. Fine Arts, 1960-66; mem. faculty, adminstr. Sch. of Music, Ball State U., Muncie, Ind., 1968-78; dean New Eng. Conservatory of Music, 1978-83; prof. music, chmn. dept. music Tex. Christian U., Ft. Worth, 1983-87; dean faculty Principia Coll., Elsah, Ill., 1987-94, prof. music, 1987-96; freelance performer, teacher, cons., 1996—. Author: Music of Herbert Howells, 1971, Toward an Understanding of Renaissance Musical Structure, 1972, Benjamin Britten: A Composer Resource Manual, 1996; composer: 39 pieces for piano and/or organ, 1996, 10 vocal solos, 1996-98. Served with Brit. Army, 1947-49. Recipient award Brit. Council, 1964. Home: 7032 Via Valverde San Jose CA 95135-1339

HODGSON, REGINALD HUTCHINS, JR., corporate executive; b. Atlanta, Mar. 10, 1939; s. Reginald Hutchins and Dorothy (Roberts) H.; m. Sigrid Lund, June 6, 1961 (div. 1974); children: Dorothy Louise, Edward Lund; m. Janice Crook, Dec. 4, 1976; children: Daniel Clayton Patrick, Matthew Benjamin. BA in Econs., Kenyon Coll., 1961; MBA, Harvard Bus. SCh., 1968. Trainee Coca-Cola Co., Toronto, Canada, 1961-63; dist. mgr. Coca-Cola Export, Johannesburg, S. Africa, 1963-66; mktg. mgr. Coca-Cola Export, London, 1968-73; region mgr. Coca-Cola, U.S.A., Atlanta, 1973-74; area mgr. Coca-Cola, U.S.A., San Francisco, 1974-75, Chgo., 1975-79; v.p. Coca-Cola Far East, Hong Kong, 1980-84; pres. Paradise Foods Inc., Atlanta, 1984—. Mem. fin. com. Holy Innocents Episcopal Ch., Atlanta, 1991; mem. Blue Ribbon com. to assure quality growth for North Fulton County; team capt. YMCA Ptnrs. with Youth Campaign, 1996; bd. trustees Montreat Coll., 1997—. Inductee Kenyon Coll. Athletic Hall of Fame for football and lacrosse, 1998; named Small Bus. Person of Yr., Greater North Fulton C. of C., 1999. Mem. Rotary (dir. cmty. svc. Roswell East chpt. 1992—, pres.-elect 1993-94, pres. 1994-95). Republican. Episcopalian. Avocations: jogging, tennis, reading, movies. Home: 831 N Island Ter NW Atlanta GA 30327-4626

HODGSON, RICHARD, electronics company executive; b. Anyox, B.C., Can., Jan. 7, 1917; s. Arthur R. and Mabel (Malmstrom) H.; m. Geraldine Coursen Reed, Nov. 26, 1945; children: Philip, Morgan, Brooke, Peter. A.B. in Engring, Stanford U., 1937; M.B.A., Harvard U., 1939. With Radiation Lab., Mass. Inst. Tech., 1942-45; head engr. mgmt. div. Brookhaven Nat. Lab., AEC, 1946; dir. TV Paramount Pictures, 1947-50; pres., dir. Chromatic TV Labs., 1950-56; exec. v.p. Fairchild Camera & Instrument Corp., Syosset, L.I., 1955-62; pres., dir. Fairchild Camera & Instrument Corp., 1962-68; corp. sr. v.p., group mgr. ITT Corp., 1968-80; dir. McCowan Assocs. Inc., N.Y.C., 1980-98; expert cons. to U.S. sec. war, 1943-45; bd. dirs. Intel Corp., I-Stat Corp., Inc., IBIS Tech. Corp., Accent Color Sci. Inc. Mem. IEEE (sr.), Tau Beta Pi. Home: 881 Ponus Rdg New Canaan CT 06840-3417

HODGSON, W(ALTER) JOHN B(ARRY), surgeon; b. Middlesborough, England, Sept. 17, 1939; came to U.S., 1975; s. Walter Aggett and Constance Lillian (Nelson) H.; m. Jean C. Morgan, Apr. 20, 1967; children: Sean, Russell, Miranda. MB, BS, Charing Cross Med. Sch., London, 1964; M of Surgery, London U., 1976. Rotating intern, resident London U., 1964-75; surgeon Bronx (N.Y.) VA Med. Ctr., 1975-78, asst. chief surg. service, 1977-82; pvt. practice specializing in surgery Mt. Sinai Hosp., N.Y.C., 1978-81; chief gastro-intestinal surgery Westchester Med. Ctr., Valhalla, N.Y., 1981-94; dept. surg. Montefiore Med. Ctr. and Einstein Hosp., Bronx, NY, 1997—; prof. surgery N.Y. Med. Coll., Valhalla, 1987—, course organizer for laparoscopic surgery, 1990-92, prof. cell biol. and anatomy, 1993—; clin. prof. surgery NYU, 1995—; prof. surgery Albert Einstein Coll. Medicine, 1998—. Contbr. articles to profl. jours.; editor: Liver Tumors: Multidisciplinary Management, 1987; inventor cavitron surg. technique for livor tumor surgery. Organizer, coach Larchmont Jr. Soccer League, 1977; mem. Larchmont Rep. Com., 1985. Cavitron Co. grantee, 1978, Cavitron Lasersonics grantee, 1987. Fellow ACS, Am. Coll. Gastroneterology; mem. N.Y. Sur. Soc. for Acad. Surgery, Am. Assn. Clin. Anatomists, Am. Soc. Colon & Rectal Surgery, Soc. Am. Gastroendoscopic Surgery. Episcopalian. Club: Larchmont Yacht. Avocations: sailing, hill walking, skiing. Office: Montefiore Med Park Dept Surgery 1575 Blondell Ave Dept Surgery Bronx NY 10461-2660

HODJAT, YAHYA, metallurgist; b. Tehran, Iran, Aug. 8, 1950; came to U.S., 1977; s. Javad and Robabeh (Fayaz) H.; m. Patricia Anne Gray, Dec. 17, 1980. BS, Arya-Mehr U., Tehran, Iran, 1972; MS, Ohio State U., 1978, PhD, 1981. Engr. trainee August Thyssen Corp., Oberhausen, Fed. Republic Germany, 1974-75; project mgr. Pahlavi Steel Corp., Ahwaz, Iran, 1975-77; grad. rsch. assoc. Ohio State U., Columbus, 1977-81; dir. ops. Intercontinental Metals, Miami, Fla., 1981-82; rsch. scientist The Standard Oil Co., Cleve., 1982-83; mgr. ops. devel. Gates Corp., Farmington Hills, Mich., 1983—; cons. Intercontinental Metals Corp., Miami, 1978-80. Asst. inventor Pyro-Technique Silver Refining, 1980; inventor pulley Poly-V Belt, 1989. Served to lt. Iranian Imperial Army, 1972-74. Mem. AIME, Am. Soc. Metals, Am. Foundrymen's Soc., Alpha Sigma Mu. Home: 410 N Baldwin Rd Oxford MI 48371-3410 Office: Gates Corp 37684 Enterprise Ct Farmington Hills MI 48331

HODKINSON, SYDNEY PHILLIP, composer, educator; b. Winnipeg, Man., Can., Jan. 17, 1934; s. Ernest and Irene (Pilgrim) H.; m. Elizabeth Jane Deischer, July 22, 1955; children: Mark, Scott, Grant. MusB, U. Rochester, 1957, MusM, 1958; D of Mus. Arts, U. Mich., 1968. Mem. faculty U. Va., 1958-63, Ohio U., Athens, 1963-66, U. Mich., Ann Arbor, 1968-73; prof. composition, chair conducting and ensembles Eastman Sch. Music, Rochester, N.Y., 1973-98; artist-in-residence, Mpls.-St.Paul, 1970-72; Meadows chair composition So. Meth. U., Dallas, 1984-86; vis. prof. composition U. Western Ont., London, Can., 1990, Aspen Music Festival, 1998, 99. Composer numerous works for brass, woodwinds, strings and percussion, 1958—, also for orch., chorus, stage, opera, wind and chamber ensembles; artist various recs. Guggenheim fellow, 1978-79; grantee U. Va., 1961, Ohio U., 1964, Can. Coun., 1966, 69, 77-78, Danforth Found., 1966-68, U. Mich., 1969, 70-73, Ford Found., 1976, Nat. Endowment for Arts, 1975-76, 78, 83-84, 90-91, Martha Baird Rockefeller Found., 1976. Mem. Broadcast Music Inc., Am. Composers Alliance, Am. Music Ctr., Am. Fedn. Musicians, Phi Mu Alpha Sinfonia. Home: 2589 John Anderson Dr Ormond Beach FL 32176-2417

HODNICAK, VICTORIA CHRISTINE, pediatric nurse; b. Detroit, Dec. 29, 1960; d. Roderick Lewis and Beverly Caroline (Backus) Turner; m. Mark Michael Hodnicak, Sept. 20, 1986; children: Christopher Alan and Matthew Lewis (twins). ADN, Henry Ford C.C., Dearborn, Mich., 1982. RN, Mich., Tenn. Charge nurse, surg. nurse Harper Grace Hosp., Detroit, 1982-86; neonatal nurse St. John Hosp., Detroit, 1986; home care nurse, coord. med. mgmt. Bloomfield Nursing Svcs., Clawson, Mich., 1986-88; coord. pediatric endocrine growth study So. Health Sys., Memphis, 1988-92; nurse specialist, growth study coord. U. Tenn. Med. Group/St. Jude Children's Rsch. Hosp., Memphis, 1992-98; care coord., educator Pediatric Svcs. Am., Memphis, 1998—; home care pediatric nurse Personal Pediatric Nursing Profls., Pontiac, Mich., 1987-88; staff nurse Nancy Kissick's Profl. Nursing Svc., Mt. Clemens, Mich., 1988. Inventor Growth Hormone new dose form, 1991, Hydrocortisone dose and stress dosing card, 1990; contbr. articles to profl. jours.; inventor equipment care for vent. patients. Mem. Pediatric Endocrinology Nursing Soc. (membership com. 1992), Endocrine Nursing Soc., Human Growth Found., Neurofibromatosis Found., Turner Syndrome Soc., MAGIC Found., Alexander Graham Bell Assn. for Deaf. Lutheran. Avocations: crafts, doll collecting, travel.

HODNIK, DAVID F., retail company executive; b. 1947. Grad., Western Ill. U., 1970. Sr. auditor Paul Pettengill & Co., 1969-72; with Ace Hardware Corp., Hinsdale, Ill., 1972—, acct., 1972-74, mgr. acctg., 1974-76, controller, 1976-80, v.p., treas., 1980—; now pres., ceo ACE Hardware Corp., Oak Brook, IL. Office: ACE Hardware Corp 2200 Kensington Ct Oak Brook IL 60523-2100*

HODO, EDWARD DOUGLAS, university president. Dean Coll. Bus., U. Tex., San Antonio, until 1987; pres. Houston Bapt. U., 1987—. Office: Houston Baptist U Office of Pres 7502 Fondren Rd Houston TX 77074-3298*

HODOUS, ROBERT POWER, lawyer; b. Zanesville, Ohio, July 29, 1945; s. Robert Frank and Nancy Aurelia (Power) H.; m. Susan Cottrell Birkhead, Feb. 1, 1969; children: Robert Everett, Shannon Alycia. BA, Miami U., Oxford, Ohio, 1967; JD, U. Va., Charlottesville, 1970. Bar: Va. 1970. Assoc. firm McGuire, Woods & Battle, Charlottesville, 1970-71; asst. trust officer Nat. Bank & Trust Co., Charlottesville, 1971-72, trust officer, 1972-75, sec., 1975-79; sec. Jefferson Bankshares, Inc. (formerly NB Corp.), Charlottesville, 1979-91, v.p., sec., 1985-91, sr. v.p., sec., 1987-91; asst. to pres. Jefferson Nat. Bank, Charlottesville, 1987-91; pvt. practice law Charlottesville, 1991-92; mem. firm Payne & Hodous, Charlottesville, 1992—. Chmn. profl. div. Thomas Jefferson Area United Way, 1973, vice-chmn., 1978-79, campaign chmn., 1979-80, v.p. planning, 1981, pres., 1983; bd. dirs. Central Va. chpt. ARC, 1972-78, treas., 1972-75, chmn., 1975-77; commr. Charlottesville Redevel. and Housing Authority, 1974-78; mem. Region X Community Mental Health and Retardation Services Bd., 1973-79, chmn., 1974-76, mem. exec. com., 1976-78; v.p. Soccer Orgn. of Charlottesville-Albemarle, 1985-86, pres., 1986-88; co-pres. Greenbier Sch. PTA, 1985-86; chmn. recreation precinct Charlottesville City Dem. Com., 1971, Rep. com., 1992—; bd. dirs. Charlottesville-Albemarle Community Found., 1987—, chmn. devel. com., 1991-93, mem. exec. and fin. coms., 1991—, chmn. fin. com., 1997—. Mem. Va. Bar Assn., Charlottesville-Albemarle Bar Assn., Va. State Bar, Va. Bankers Assn. (com. drafted Va. Trust Subs. Act 1973, trust com. 1974-77, legal affairs com. 1986-91, large bank legis. coord. 1987-91), Computer Law Assn., Albemarle C. of C. (legis. action com. 1996—), Fairview Club (Charlottesville, pres. 1974-75). Roman Catholic. Home: 1309 Lester Dr Charlottesville VA 22901-3143 Office: 412 E Jefferson St Charlottesville VA 22902-5109 *To me success is indicated by feelings of personal peace and satisfaction, not by external possessions. My goals are to do my best in contributing to the success of endeavors in which I become involved and to remember that the people involved in activities are the most important part of the activities. I feel my family is my most important endeavor. I hope never to become so involved in activities that I cannot enjoy my family, my surroundings and people I meet, or that I cannot spend the time necessary to do well those activities in which I am involved.*

HODSOLL, FRANCIS SAMUEL MONAISE, government official; b. Los Angeles, May 1, 1938; s. Frank and Adelaide (Monaise) H.; m. Margaret Mimi McEwen, Aug. 18, 1963; children—Lisa-Monaise, Francis Hamill McEwen. B.A., Yale U., 1959; M.A., LL.b., Cambridge U., 1963; J.D., Stanford U., 1964; Fgn. Service econ. course, Washington, 1972; D.F.A. (hon.), Pratt Inst., 1983, U. Mass., 1986. Assoc. Sullivan & Cromwell, N.Y.C., 1965-66; fgn. service officer Adminstrv. Office Am. embassy, Belgium, 1966-68; asst. polit. advisor SHAPE, Belgium, 1968-69; controlling dir. Warner, Barnes & Co., Manila, 1964-71; oceans policy officer State Dept., Washington, 1969-71; spl. asst. chmn. Council on Environ. Quality, Washington, 1972-73; spl. asst. adminstr. EPA, Washington, 1973-74; dir. energy conservation div. Commerce Dept., Washington, 1974, staff dir. cabinet work edn. task force, 1974, exec. asst. to undersec., 1974-76, dept. asst. sec. commerce for energy and strategic resources, 1976-77; dir. Office of Law of Sea Negotiation State Dept., Washington, 1977, dep. U.S. spl. rep. for nonproliferation, 1978-80; mem. White House transition team Exec. Office Pres., Washington, 1980-81; dep. asst. to Pres. and dep. to chief of staff White House, Washington, 1981; chmn. Nat. Endowment for Arts, Washington, 1981-89; exec. assoc. dir., chief fin. officer U.S. Govt. Office Mgmt. and Budget, Exec. Office of Pres., Washington, 1989-91; dep. dir. for mgmt. Office Mgmt. and Budget, Exec. Office of Pres., Washington, 1991-93; bd. dirs. Unique Mobility; co-chmn. Sally Mae Edn. Svcs. Coun., 1995-96, Am. Assembly Arts and the Pub. Purpose, 1996-97; CEO Southwest Colo. Data Ctr., 1994-97; cons. in field. Chmn. Ouray County Rep. com., 1995-96; dir. Colo. River Water Conservation Dist., 1997—; v. chair Nat. Assn. Counties Geospatial Data com., 1998—; mem. Gen. Govt. Transition Team Colo. Gov. elect Bill Owens, 1998-99; mem. review com. New Century Colo., 1999—. Served as lt. U.S. Army, 1959-60. Mem. N.Y. State Bar Assn., Stanford U. Alumni Assn., Yale Club, Met. Club, Zeta Psi. Republican. Episcopalian.

HODSON, NANCY PERRY, real estate agent; b. Kansas City, Mo., Nov. 19, 1932; d. Ralph Edward Perry and Juanita (Youmans) Jackman; m. William K. Hodson, Oct. 4, 1974 (div. Jan. 1985); children: Frank Tyler, Lisa Thompson, Suzanne Desforges, Robert Hodson. Student, Pine Manor Jr. Coll., 1950-51, Finch Coll., 1951-53. Cert. real estate agt., Calif.; cert. interior designer. Owner Nancy Perry Hodson Interior Design, L.A. and Newport Beach, Calif., 1974-82; agt. Grubb and Ellis, Newport Beach, 1990, Turner Assocs., Laguna Beach, Calif., 1990-92. Founder U. of Calif. Arboretum, Irvine, 1987, Opera Pacific, Costa Mesa, Calif., 1987; mem. U. of

Calif. Rsch. Assocs., Irvine, 1986; pres. Big Canyon Philharm., Newport Beach, 1990; bd. dirs. Jr. Philharm., L.A., 1975-78. Mem. Big Canyon Country Club, L.A. Blue Ribbon 400 (1975-78), Jr. League Garden Club (pres. 1990-91), Big Canyon Garden Club (pres. 1989-91), Inst. of Logopedics (chmn. 30th Anniversary 1965), Guilds of Performing Arts Ctr. Presbyterian. Avocations: art, music, gardening.

HODSON, ROY GOODE, JR., retired logistician; b. Enon, Ala., July 22, 1927; s. Roy Goode and Ilda Fern (Jinks) H.; m. Mildred Bernice Parlier, Dec. 3, 1966 (dec. July 1992); children: Joan Hodson Bash, Scott Daniel, Jayne Clymer. Student, San Diego Jr. Coll., 1947-49, San Diego Vocational, 1947-49, San Diego State Coll., 1949-50. Security officer US Naval CB Ctr. (Civil Service), Port Hueneme, Calif., 1950-52; logistician Gen. Dynamics, San Diego, 1952-64, GTE Govt. Systems, Inc., Mt. View, Calif., 1964-89. Bd. dirs. San Jose Civic Light Opera Assn., 1988-95; advisor San Jose Children's Musical Theater, 1995—; active Yu-Ai Kai Japanese Am. Cmty. Sr. Svc., Sta. WNIT-TV PBS, Mishiana. With U.S. Army, 1945-47. Recipient Bravo award Silhoutte mag., 1988, Ginny award, 1989. Mem. AMVETS, Am. Assn. Ret. Persons, Am. Film Inst., Humane Soc. U.S., Am. Legion, Nat. Arbor Day Found., Easter Seals Found., Nat. Svc. Found., Nature Conservancy, Internat. Freelance Photographers Orgn., Internat. Platform Assn., Nat. Pks. and Conservation Assn., Calif. State Pks. Found., Milpitas C. of C., Spiceland Hist. and Tourism Soc., Am. Image Press Club, Nat. Humane Edn. Soc., Ind. Sheriffs Assn., Humane Soc. Noble County, Greenpeace. Democrat. Mem. Church of Christ. Avocations: photography, lapidary, geneaology, music. Home: 4611 W 300 S Albion IN 46701-9449

HOE, RICHARD MARCH, insurance and securities consultant, writer; b. Plainfield, N.J., June 16, 1939; s. Arthur James Hoe and Marjorie (Vandergrift) Beeson; m. Lynne Hovell, Sept. 26, 1964; children: Joshua Blake, Susan Brooke, Seth Jamieson. Student, Pace U., 1964-67, U. Tenn., 1976. CLU. Asst. to controller, fleet mgr., asst. purchasing agt. Hoe & Co. Inc., Bronx, N.Y., 1964-66; pres. OJS Mfg. Co., Bklyn., 1966-68, Fresh Impressions Inc., N.Y.C., 1968; agt. Fidelity Mut. Life, N.Y.C., 1968-72; asst. mgr. Fin. Life, N.Y.C., 1972-73; brokerage mgr. Am. Life N.Y., N.Y.C., 1973-75; exec. Provident Life & Accident Ins. Co., Chattanooga, 1975-78; mgr. Jefferson Standard, Tulsa, 1978-81; pres. Hoe & Co. Inc., Tulsa, 1981-93; fin. planner, designer, cons. Tulsa, 1978—; splst. Am. Citizens Fin. Svcs., Tulsa, 1998—; lectr. project bus. Tulsa Pub. Schs., 1983, 85, cons., 1984-86; lectr. in field; founder employee and exec. benefit plans, residual split-dollar, money purchase flexible spending plans, pvt. sector social security alternative portable plans, satellite split-dollar, satellite supplemental pensions, lifetime income nontaxable retirement plans, balanced funding plans. Author: Love in Pasadena, 1996; columnist (monthly) Broker World, 1985-86, 89—, Probe, Life Assn. News; contbr. articles to profl. jours., novelist. Chmn. fund raising Grimes Elem. Sch., Tulsa Pub. Schs., 1984-87; mem. gifted and talented com. Tulsa Pub. Schs., 1982; bd. dirs. Nat. ALS Found., N.Y.C., 1971-82. Fellow Life Underwriter Tng. Coun. (moderator 1979-86); mem. Reach Across Divs., Am. Soc. CLUs (student devel. chmn. 1990, mem. chmn. 1991, advt. and pub. rels. 1992-93), Tulsa Estate Planning Forum, Nat. Okla. Multiple Sclerosis Soc. (chmn. 150 tour com. 1992), Rotary Club of Will Rogers. Republican. Episcopalian. Avocations: writing, jazz, chess, bicycling. Home and Office: 5843 E 50th St Tulsa OK 74135-6885

HOECKER, DAVID, engineering executive; b. Cin., July 7, 1948; s. Vernon and Ruth (Schnake) H.; m. Susan Ameling, Aug. 15, 1970; children: Sarah, Paul. B.S., Rose Poly. Inst., Terre Haute, Ind., 1969; M.S.I.A., Purdue U., 1970; grad. program for execs., Carnegie-Mellon U., 1991. Cert. quality engr.; cert. quality mgr. Project mgr. Timken Co., Canton, Ohio, 1970-73, gen. supr., 1973-78; chief quality control engring. Timken Co., Lincolnton, N.C., 1978-82; chief engr. engring. services. Timken Co., Canton, Ohio, 1982-84; mgr. European Rsch. Timken Co., Northampton, Eng., 1984-89; gen. mgr. product engring. Timken Co., Canton, Ohio, 1989-93; gen. mgr. Timken Tooling Bus., Canton, 1993—, gen. mgr. quality & tech., 1996—; v.p. The Wilderness Ctr. Inc., 1995-97, pres., 1997—. V.p. Canton Jaycees, 1973-74, Trinity United Ch. of Christ, 1983-84, 91-92, pres., 1993, chmn. endowment com., 1996, Brit. Timken Sports Club, 1986-89; dir. Young Life, Canton, 1975-78. Named Spoke of Yr. Canton Jaycees, 1972; named Key Man Canton Jaycees, 1974. Mem. ASME, Am. Soc. Quality Control (sr. mem., sec. Charlotte sect. 1980-81, treas. 1981), Canton Club. Republican. Office: Timken Co Mail Drop BON-07 PO Box 6929 Canton OH 44706-0929

HOECKER, JAMES JOHN, lawyer; b. Rhinelander, Wis., July 12, 1945; s. Raymond Anton and Elizabeth Augusta (Kaiser) H. BA, Northland Coll., 1967; MA, U. Ky., 1970, PhD, 1975; JD, U. Wis., 1978. Bar: Wis. 1978, D.C. 1988, U.S. Dist. Ct. (we. dist.) Wis. 1978, U.S. Ct. Appeals (6th and D.C. cirs.) 1988, U.S. Supreme Ct. 1988. Asst. prof. Adrian Coll., 1973-74; atty. office commr. ins. State of Wis., Madison, 1978; assoc. Bell & Fox, Madison, 1979; atty., advisor Fed. Energy Regulatory Commn., Washington, 1979-84, asst. gen. counsel rulemaking and legis. analysis, 1984-86, asst. gen. counsel gas and oil litigation, 1986-88; ptnr. Keck, Mahin and Cate, Washington, 1988-90, Jones, Day, Reavis & Pogue, Washington, 1990—; chmn. Fed. Energy Regulatory Commn., Washington, 1992; advisor legal affairs to commrs. Holden and Sheldon, 1981-82. Author: Joseph Priestley and the Idea of Progress, 1987; contbr. articles to profl. jours. Mem. ABA, Fed. Energy Bar Assn., Wis. Bar Assn., D.C. Bar Assn., U.S. Supreme Ct. Bar Assn., Phi Delta Phi, Phi Alpha Theta. Democrat. Congregationalist. Avocations: etching, oil painting. Office: Fed Energy Regulatory Commn 888 1st St NE Washington DC 20426-0002*

HOECKER, THOMAS RALPH, lawyer; b. Chicago Heights, Ill., Dec. 14, 1950; s. William H. and Norma M. (Wynkoop) H.; m. V. Sue Thornton, Aug. 28, 1971; children: Elizabeth T., Ellen T. BS, No. Ill. U., 1972; JD, U. Ill., 1975. Bar: Ill. 1975, Ariz. 1985. Assoc. Davis and Morgan, Peoria, Ill., 1975-80, ptnr., 1980-84; assoc. Snell and Wilmer, Phoenix, 1984-86, ptnr., 1986-; mem. steering com. Western Pension Conf., Phoenix, 1986-92, pres., 1991-92. Fellow Ariz. Bar Found.; mem. ABA (vice chair tax sect. employee benefits com., co-chair legis. and adminstrv. subcom. of labor sect. employee benefits com. 1994-96), Ariz. Bar Assn., Ill. Bar Assn., Marciopa County Bar Assn., (mem. investment com. 1988-94). Avocation: fly fishing. Office: Snell and Wilmer 1 Arizona Ctr Phoenix AZ 85004

HOEFFEL, JOSEPH M., congressman, lawyer; b. Phila., Sept. 3, 1950; m. Francesca Montori; children: Mary, Jake. BS, Boston U., 1972; JD, Temple U., 1988. Lawyer Murphy, Oliver, Caiola & Gowen, Norristown, Pa.; mem. PA state senate, 1976-1984, 106th congress from PA 13th dist., 1999—; mem. budget com., 1999—, mem. internat. relations com., 1999—. Mem. Pa. Ho. of Reps., 1976-84; dem. candidate U.S. House 13th dist., 1984, 86, 96; Montgomery County commr., Pa., 1992—; chmn. Pa. Leadership Coun.; Montgomery County chmn. Clinton-Gore Campaign, 1992. Served with USAR. Office: Ho of Reps 1229 Longworth HOB Washington DC 20515*

HOEFFLIN, RICHARD MICHAEL, lawyer, judicial administrator, contractor; b. L.A., Oct. 20, 1949; s. David Greenfield and Gloria (Harrison) H.; m. Susan J. Amoroso, Mar. 29, 1969; children: Alyssa, Jennifer, Richard, II. BS in Acctg. cum laude, Calif. State U.-Northridge, 1971; JD, Loyola U., Los Angeles, 1974. Bar: Calif. 1974, U.S. Dist. Ct. (cen. dist.) Calif. 1974, U.S. Tax Ct. 1976, U.S. Dist. Ct. (no. and so. dists.) Calif. 1976, U.S. Supreme Ct. 1982. With Lewitt, Hackman, Hoefflin, Shapiro, Marshall & Harlan, 1974—, ptnr., 1977—; judge pro tem L.A. Superior Ct., 1982—, family law mediator, 1982-86; judge pro tem, Ventura County, Superior Ct., 1991—; arbitrator Am. Arbitration Assn., Fee Dispute Resolution Svcs. For L.A. County Bar. Co-founder Ventura County Homeowners For Equal Taxation, Westlake Village, Calif., 1978-79; pres. counsel Westlake Hills Homeowners Assn., 1975-77; chmn. celebrity Love Match Tennis Tour. for John McEnroe United Cerebral Palsy/Spastic Children Found., 1990—. Mem. ABA, L.A. Bar Assn., Ventura County Bar Assn., San Fernando Valley Bar Assn. (co-chair bus. and real estate sect. 1995-97), Westlake Hills Owners Assn. (pres. 1977-78), North Ranch Country Club (pres. tennis assn. 1984-85). Republican. Roman Catholic. Office: Lewitt Hackman Hoefflin Shapiro Marshall & Harlan 16633 Ventura Blvd Ste 1100 Encino CA 91436-1865

HOEFLICH, CHARLES HITSCHLER, banker; b. Phila., Apr. 4, 1914; s. Llewellyn Ashbridge and Mary Ann (Osterheldt) H. BS in Econs., U. Pa., 1936; cert. in banking, Rutgers U., 1949; cert. in bank mktg., Northwestern U., 1955; LLD, Okla. Christian U., 1972. V.p. Phila. Nat. Bank, 1951-62; pres. Union Nat. Bank & Trust Co., Souderton, Pa., 1962-76, chmn. bd. dirs., 1976-84, chmn. exec. com., 1984-86; chmn. Univest Corp. Pa., Souderton, 1973-86, chmn. emeritus, 1986—; mem. Rep. presdl. task force, 1981-97. Sec.-treas. Intercollegiate Studies Inst., Wilmington, Del., 1955—; trustee Okla. Christian U., Oklahoma City, 1974—. Recipient Presdl. citation USAAF, 1946, Citizen of Yr. award Fed. Bar Assn., 1960. Mem. Bank Mktg. Assn. (pres. 1964-65), Am. Bankers Assn., Union League Club (Phila.), Indian Valley Country Club (Telford, Pa.). Republican. Avocations: collecting Americana antiques and art; painting; horticulture. Office: Univest Corp Pa Main And Broad St Souderton PA 18964

HOEFLICH, MICHAEL HARLAN, law school dean; b. N.Y.C., Jan. 11, 1952; s. Sterling Martin and Barbara Su (Junger) H.; m. Karen Nordheden, Sept. 13, 1986. BA, MA in Canon Law, Haverford (Pa.) Coll., 1973; MA, Cambridge (Eng.) U., 1976; JD, Yale U., 1979. Bar: N.Y. 1980. Rsch. fellow Cambridge U., 1975-77; tax assoc. Cravath, Swaine & Moore, N.Y.C., 1978-79, 79-81; asst. prof. law U. Ill., Champaign, 1981-84, assoc. prof., 1984-86, prof., univ. scholar, dir. rsch. on legal history, 1986-88; prof. law and history Syracuse (N.Y.) U., 1988-94, dean coll. law, 1988-94; dean sch. law U. Kans., Lawrence, 1994—, John M. and John H. Kane Disting. prof., 1997—. Author: Roman and Civil Law, and the Development of Anglo-American Jurisprudence, 1997; co-author: Cases and Materials on Federal Taxation of Deferred Compensation, 1989; co-editor Property Law and Legal Education, 1988; editor The Gladsome Light of Jurisprudence, Learning the Law in England and the United States in the 18th and 19th Centuries, 1988; legal columnist Lawrence Jour.-World, 1994—; contbr. numerous articles to profl. publs. Housing commr. Champaign County Housing Authority, 1987-88; host weekly radio show on sta. WILL-AM, Champaign, 1986-88; bd. dirs. U. Ill. Libr. Friends, Champaign, 1988-90. Recipient Surrency Prize Am. Soc. Legal History, 1985. Fellow Am. Bar Found., Am. Philos. Soc. (Phillips); mem. Onondaga County Bar Assn. (bd. dirs. 1991-93), N.Y. State Bar Assn. (com. on professionalism 1988-94), Am. Law Inst. (advisor restatement, property, security and mortgages coms. 1989-93), Fund for Modern Cts. (bd. dirs. 1988-90), Kans. Bar Assn. Office: U Kansas Sch Law Green Hall Lawrence KS 66044-7577*

HOEFLIN, RONALD KENT, philosopher, test designer, newsletter publisher; b. Richmond Heights, Mo., Feb. 23, 1944; s. William Eugene and Mary Elizabeth (Dell) H. Student, Calif. Inst. Tech., 1962-63, U. Calif., Berkeley, 1966-67, U. N.C., 1970-71; BA, U. Minn., 1968, Shimer Coll., 1974; MLS, Ind. U., 1970; MA, New Sch. Social Rsch., 1979, PhD, 1987. With various librs., 1969-85; publisher, editor Triple Nine Soc., N.Y.C., 1985-89; publisher, editor, founder Top One Percent Soc., N.Y.C., 1989—, One-in-a-Thousand Soc., N.Y.C., 1992—. Designer (intelligence tests) Mega Test, 1985, Titan Test, 1990. Mem. Am. Philos. Assn. (Fifth Ann. Rockefeller prize 1988), Mensa, Mega Soc. (founder 1982), Prometheus Soc. (founder 1982). Office: PO Box 539 New York NY 10101-0539 *It's a godless universe. Only intelligent and resourceful people can guide it. But don't forget kindness. That was Communism's biggest failing.*

HOEFT, ROBERT GENE, agriculture educator; b. David City, Nebr., May 21, 1944; s. Otto O. Hoeft and Lula (Barlean) Pleskac; m. Nancy A. Bussen, Sept. 1, 1990; children: Jeffrey, Angela. BS, U. Nebr., 1965, MS, 1967; PhD, U. Wis., 1972. Asst. prof. S.D. State U., Rapid City, 1972-73; asst. prof. U. Ill., Urbana, 1973-77, assoc. prof., 1977-81, prof., 1981—. Author: Modern Corn Production, 1986; editor Jour. Prodn. Agr., 1986-92. Recipient Funk award U. Ill., 1990, Robert E. Wagner award Potash and Phosphate Inst., 1998. Fellow Soil Sci. Soc. Am., Am. Soc. Agronomy (CIBA-Geigy award 1978, Agronomic Extension award, grantee 1988, Agronomic Achievement award-soils 1995, Werner Nelson award for diagnosis of yield limiting factors 1996); mem. Coun. for Sci. and Tech. Office: U Ill 1102 S Goodwin Ave Urbana IL 61801-4730

HOEG, DONALD FRANCIS, chemist, consultant, former research and development executive; b. Bklyn., Aug. 2, 1931; s. Harry Herman and Charlotte (Bourke) H.; m. Patricia Catherine Fogarty, Aug. 30, 1952; children—Thomas Edward, Robert Francis, Donald John, Mary Beth, Susan Catherine. B.S. in Chemistry summa cum laude, St. John's U., N.Y., 1953; Ph.D. in Chemistry, Ill. Inst. Tech., 1957. Fellow in chemistry and chem. engring. Armour Research Found., 1953-54; grad. research asst. Ill. Inst. Tech., 1954-56; research chemist W.R. Grace & Co., 1956-58, sr. research chemist, 1958-61; group leader addition polymer chemistry Roy C. Ingersoll Research Center, Borg-Warner Corp., Des Plaines, Ill., 1961-64; mgr. polymer chemistry Roy C. Ingersoll Research Center, Borg-Warner Corp., 1964-66, assoc. dir., head chem. research dept., 1966-75, dir., 1975-88; pres. DFH Assocs., 1988—; former mem. solid state scis. adv. bd. NAS; bd. overseers Lewis Coll. Scis. and Letters of Ill. Inst. Tech., 1980-91; bd. dirs. Ill. Inst. Tech. Alumni, 1979-82, Mt. Prospect Combined Appeal, 1963-65. Bd. editors: Research Mgmt. Mag, 1979-82; contbr. numerous articles tech. publs., chpts. in books. TaPing Lin scholar, 1955-56; AEC asst., 1954; Armour Research Found. fellow, 1953-54; Ill. Inst. Tech. Achievement award, 1983. Mem. Am. Chem. Soc., AAAS, N.Y. Acad. Scis., Dirs. Indsl. Research, Am. Mgmt. Assn. (v.p. council 1984-88), Research Dirs. Assn. Chgo. (pres. 1977-78), Indsl. Research Inst. (bd. dirs. 1986-88), Sigma Xi. Patentee in field. *I've counseled myself that all ideas and concepts, no matter how seemingly difficult, are products of man's mind, and, therefore fundamentally understandable.*

HOEGERMAN, STANTON FRED, cytogeneticist; b. Bklyn., May 13, 1944; s. Fred and Edith (Rost) H.; m. Georgeanne Stengele, Mar. 5, 1966 (div. Dec. 1989); children: Elizabeth, David; m. Carol Park, May 16, 1992. BS, Cornell U., 1965; PhD, N.C. State U., 1972. Diplomate Am. Bd. Med. Genetics, Am. Bd. Clin. Cytogenetics. Instr. dept. biology Lincoln (Pa.) U., 1970-72; asst. biologist Argonne (Ill.) Nat. Lab., 1972-76; assoc. prof. dept. biology Coll. William and Mary, Williamsburg, Va., 1976—; adj. assoc. prof. dept. pediatrics Ea. Va. Med. Sch., Norfolk, Va., 1986—. contbr. articles to profl. jours. Mem. Am. Soc. Human Genetics, Genetics Soc. Am., Am. Genetics Assn., Botan. Soc. Am. Unitarian-Universalist. Achievements include research on chromosome breakage and the Fragile X syndrome and aneuploidy in sperm. Office: Coll William & Mary Dept Biology Williamsburg VA 23187

HOEHN, ELMER LOUIS, lawyer, state and federal agency administrator, educator, consultant; b. Memphis, Ind., Dec. 19, 1915; s. Louis and Agnes (Goss) H.; m. Frances Cory, June 10, 1943; children: Kathleen Gillmore, G. Patrick. B.S., Canterbury Coll., 1936, Northwestern U., 1937; J.D., U. Louisville, 1940. Bar: Ky. 1940, D.C. 1969, U.S. Supreme Ct. 1969, U.S. Ct. Appeals 1970, Ind. 1981. Prof. bus. and law Jeffersonville High Sch., Ind., 1937-41, Ind. U., 1940-41; with legal and personnel div. Am. Barge Lines, 1942-44; realtor Ind., 1949—; apptd. dir. by Gov. Ind. Oil and Gas, 1949-53; apptd. adminstr. by Pres. U.S. Oil Import Adminstrn., 1965-69; sec.-treas. Am. Assn. Oil Well Drilling Contractors, 1956-60; exec. sec. Ind. Oil Producers and Land Owners Assn., 1953-64; pvt. practice law Washington, 1969-91, Indiana, 1981—; ADR civil mediator, Ind., 1993; gov's. rep. Interstate Oil & Gas Compact Commn., 1949-53, 61-65; apptd. commr. by gov. Ohio River Greenway Devel. Commn., 1994; cons. petroleum, natural resources, energy and environment; chmn. Clark County Redevel. Commn., 1996—, Charlestown Ammo Reuse Authority, 1997—. Mem. Ind. Gen. Assembly, 1945- 49, minority floor leader, 1947, chief clk., 1949, Democratic chmn., Clark County, Ind., 1945-52; Ind. del. Dem. Nat. Conv., 1964, chmn. 8th Congl. Dist., 1952-58; mem. Ind. Dem. Exec. Com., 1952-58, Ind. and Midwest campaign mgr., LBJ campaign for president, 1960. Named hon. citizen Ind., Ky., citoyen honneur Soufflenheim, France, Ambassador Clark County, Ind. Mem. ABA, Fed. Bar Assn., Ky. Bar Assn. (Disting. sr. counselor 1990), D.C. Bar Assn., Ind. Bar Assn. (Disting. Sr. Counselor 1990), Coop. Oil and Gas Assn. (liason com. Washington 1969-91), Am. Inn of Ct., Sigma Delta Kappa. Roman Catholic. Clubs: Nat. Lawyers, Nat. Press (Washington); Ind. Legislators (Indpls.); Filson (Louisville), Elks Country (Jeffersonville). Home: 2105 Utica Pike Jeffersonville IN 47130-5005

HOEHN, NATASHA DIANE, elementary education educator; b. San Francisco, Dec. 18, 1974; d. Charles John Phillip and Janet Dale (Sedan) H. BA, Yale U., 1996. Cert. PPT, N.Y. Mid. sch. tchr. English, N.Y.C. Bd. Edn., Bronx, 1996—; mem., site-based coord. Teach for Am., N.Y.C., 1996—. Contbr. articles to profl. publ. Avocation: singing. Home: 344 E 76th St Apt 12A New York NY 10021-2569

HOEHN, RICHARD ALBERT, association executive, clergyman; b. Butler, Pa., Oct. 12, 1936; s. Clarence Albert and Mary Catherine (Rieger) H.; m. Patricia Joyce Brehm, Aug. 18, 1958 (div. Feb. 1980); m. Carole Lee Zimmerman, Oct. 28, 1990; children: Christine Joyce, Thomas Albert, Karen Elizabeth, Benjamin Douglass, Kristin Nicole Sizemore. BA, Capital U., 1958; BD, Trinity Luth. Sem., Columbus, Ohio, 1962; MA, U. Chgo., 1970, PhD, 1972. Ordained to ministry Evang. Luth. Ch. in Am. Pastor Good Shepherd Luth. Ch., Brunswick, Maine, 1962-65; prof. ch. in society Brite Div. Sch., Tex. Christian U., Ft. Worth, 1970-88; regional organizer Bread for the World, Washington, 1988-91; sr. rschr. Bread for the World Inst., Washington, 1991-92; dir. Bread for the World Inst., Silver Spring, Md., 1992—; dir. Internat. Devel. Conf., Washington, InterAction, Washington. Author: Up from Apathy, 1983; contbr. articles to profl. jours. Bd. dirs. Tex. Impact, Austin, numerous others. Recipient rsch. awards Tex. Christian U. Found.; Lily Found. postdoctoral fellow, 1976; Fulbright tchg. fellow, 1986; grantee Ford Found., W.K. Kellogg Found., Kraft Foods, others. Mem. Soc. Christian Ethics. Democrat. Home: 2007 Wooded Way Adelphi MD 20783-1348 Office: Bread for the World Inst 1100 Wayne Ave Ste 1000 Silver Spring MD 20910-5643

HOEKSTRA, PETER, congressman, manufacturing executive; b. Groningen, The Netherlands, Oct. 30, 1953; m. Diane M. Johnson; children: Erin, Allison, Bryan. BA, Hope Coll., 1975; MBA, U. Mich., 1977. Furniture exec. Herman Miller, Inc., 1977-92, project mgr., product mgr., dir. product mgmt., dir. dealer mktg., v.p. dealer mktg., 1988-92, v.p. product mgmt., 1992-93; mem. 103rd-106th Congresses from 2d Mich. dist., 1993—, mem. budget com., mem. edn. and the workforce com.; mem. Budget Com; chmn. edn. and the workforce ctr. subcom. on oversight and investigations. Contbr. to project devel. Equa Chair, recognized as outstanding product of 1980s by Time Mag. Republican. Office: US Ho of Reps Office Of Ho Mems 1122 Longworth Bldg Washington DC 20515-2202*

HOEKWATER, JAMES WARREN, treasurer; b. Grand Rapids, Mich., Nov. 4, 1946; s. William Harold and Sena (Hoeksema) H.; m. Roberta Joyce Paczala, July 12, 1975; children: William Paczala, Elizabeth Veronica. BA, Mich. State U., 1970. CPA, Mich. With Touche Ross & Co., Detroit, 1970-77; v.p., controller Great Lakes div. Nat. Steel Corp., Detroit, 1977-83; treas. Nat. Steel Corp., Pitts., 1983-89, v.p., 1987-89; corp. contr. ITT Rayonier Inc., Stamford, Conn., 1989-94; treas. Acme Metals Inc., Riverdale, Ill., 1994—. Mem. AICPA. Republican. Episcopalian. Home: 6420 Lane Ct Hinsdale IL 60521-5354 Office: Acme Metals Inc 13500 S Perry Ave Riverdale IL 60827-1148

HOEL, LESTER A., civil engineering educator; b. Bklyn., Feb. 26, 1935; s. Johannes and Julia (Michelsen) H.; m. Unni Sonja Blegen, Jan. 24, 1959; children: Julie Britt, Sonja Leslie, Lisa Maureen. B.C.E., City Coll., N.Y., 1957; M.S. in Civil Engring, Bklyn. Poly. Inst., 1960; D.Eng., U. Calif. at Berkeley, 1963. Registered profl. engr. Calif., Pa., Va. Asst. prof. engring. San Diego State Coll., 1962-64; Fulbright research scholar Inst. Transport Economy, Oslo, Norway, 1964-65; prin. engr. Wilbur Smith & Assoc., San Francisco, 1965-66; faculty Carnegie-Mellon U., Pitts., 1966-74; prof. civil engring. Carnegie-Mellon U., 1970-74; assoc. dir. Transp. Research Inst., 1966-74; Hamilton prof. dept. civil engring. U. Va., 1974—, chmn. dept., 1974-89. Author: Traffic and Highway Engineering, revised 2d edit., 1999; editor: Public Transportation, 1979, rev. 2d edit., 1992; mem. editl. bd. trnsp. jours.; author tech. papers, books and articles. Recipient Alumni award in Civil Engring. Coll. City N.Y., 1957, Stanley W. Gustafson Leadership award Hwy. Users Fedn., 1989, Pyke Johnson award Transp. Rsch. Bd., 1977, W.N. Carey Jr. award, 1991, S.S. Steinberg Edn. award Am. Rd. and Transp. Builders, 1991; Fulbright travel grantee, 1964-65. Fellow ASCE (Huber Rsch. prize 1976, Frank Masters award 1990, James Laurie prize 1999), Nat. Acad. Engring., Inst. Transp. Engrs.; mem. Transp. Rsch. Bd. (chmn. exec. com. 1986, chmn. com. on transp. profl. needs, truck weight study, chair SNO), Am. Soc. Engring. Edn., Sigma Xi, Chi Epsilon, Tau Beta Pi. Home: 1703 Old Forge Rd Charlottesville VA 22901-2111

HOEL, ROBERT FREDRICK, JR., construction executive, civil engineer; b. St. Louis, Apr. 14, 1949; s. Robert F. Sr. and LaVerne (Schaller) M. BSCE, U. Mo., 1971. Registered profl. engr., Mo., Fla. Project mgr. Hoel-Steffen Constrn. Co., St. Louis, 1971-79; project dir. Sverdrup Corp., St. Louis, 1979-82; regional mgr. Vector Constrn. Co., Orlando, Fla., 1982-84; sr. project mgr. Fed. Constrn. Co., St. Petersburg, Fla., 1984-87; v.p. dir. ops., regional mgr. Brown & Root Bldg. Co., Clearwater, Fla., 1987-99; v.p. Centex-Rooney Constrn. Co., 1999—. Mem. Mo. Soc. Profl. Engrs., Fla. Engring. Soc., Mo. Athletic Club. Roman Catholic. Home: 4909 SW 5th Pl Cape Coral FL 33914-6501 Office: Brown & Root Bldg Co 5830 142nd Ave N Clearwater FL 33760-2819

HOELSCHER, ROBERT JAMES, lawyer; b. Cleve., July 5, 1952; s. Max W. and Loraine A. (Bass) H.; m. Constance J. Fiske, Sept. 20, 1986; children: Ann, Carol. BA, Pa. State U., 1974; JD, Harvard U., 1977. Bar: Pa. 1977, N.J. 1992, U.S. Dist. Ct. (ea. dist.) Pa. 1978, U.S. Ct. Appeals (3d. cir.) 1983, U.S. Dist. Ct. N.J. 1992. Law clk. Supreme Ct. Pa., Pitts., 1977-78; assoc. Drinker Biddle & Reath, Phila., 1978-86; ptnr. Drinker, Biddle & Reath, Phila., 1986-97; counsel CoreStates Bank N.A. (now First Union Nat. Bank), Phila., 1997—. Articles editor Harvard Jour. on Legislation, 1977. Trustee Old Pine St. Ch., Phila., 1984-87, sec. bd. trustees, 1990-93; elder First Presbyn. Ch., Ardmore, Pa., 1995—. Mem. ABA, Pa. Bar Assn., Phila. Bar Assn., Phi Beta Kappa. Presbyterian. Office: First Union Nat Bank 15th Flr Widener Bldg 1339 Chestnut St Philadelphia PA 19107-3519

HOELZEL, SALLY ANN, lawyer; b. Knoxville, Iowa, Apr. 5, 1962; d. Clement C. and Helen J. (Falck) H.; m. Peter M. Eckblad, Oct. 11, 1986. BS, U. Wis., 1984, JD, 1987. Bar: Wis. 1987, U.S. Dist. Ct. (we. dist.) Wis. 1987. Assoc. McBurney, Perina, Wyngaard, Wilson & Raymond, Madison, Wis., 1987-88; staff atty. Office of State Pub. Defender, Racine, Wis., 1988-96; pvt. practice Racine, 1996—. Mem. ACLU, NOW, State Bar Wis., Racine County Bar Assn., People for the Ethical Treatment of Animals, ASPCA, Planned Parenthood, Ctr. for Reproductive Law and Policy. Office: 201 6th St Ste 300 Racine WI 53403-1264

HOENACK, AUGUST FREDERICK, architect; b. N.Y.C., Apr. 1, 1908; s. Hugo H. and Hulda (Kilian) H.; m. Mary Margery Course, June 14, 1939; children—Stephen A., Judith (Mrs. Paul Schultz), Francis A., August Jeremy. B.Arch., Pratt Inst., 1938; student, Columbia, 1930-31; postgrad., George Washington U., 1940-41. Architect PBA, Washington, 1938-41; asso. architect hospital facilities USPHS, Washington, 1942-46; asst. chief USPHS, 1946-55, chief architecture, engring. equipment br., 1955-68; v.p. firm Jensen & Halstead (Architects, Engrs. & Consultants), Chgo., 1968-73; asso. Dalton, Dalton, Litte, Newport, Bethesda, Md., 1973-80. Contbr. profl. jours. Recipient Superior Service award HEW, 1967, Outstanding Alumnus award Pratt Inst., 1968. Fellow AIA (mem. health environment com. 1960-67), Am. Assn. Hosp. Planning (Distinguished Service to Hosp. Design award 1967), Am. Hosp. Assn., Internat. Hosp. Fedn. Home: 8409 Seven Locks Rd Bethesda MD 20817-2006

HOENIGSWALD, HENRY MAX, linguist, educator; b. Breslau, Germany, Apr. 17, 1915; s. Richard and Gertrud (Grunwald) H.; m. Gabriele Schoepflich, Dec. 26, 1944; children: Frances Gertrude, Susan Ann. Student, U. Munich, 1932-33, U. Zurich, 1933-34, U. Padua, 1934-36; DLitt, U. Florence, 1936, Perfezionamento, 1937; LHD (hon.), Swarthmore Coll., 1981, U. Pa., 1988; MA (hon.), U. Pa., 1971. Staff mem. Istituto Studi Etruschi, Florence, 1936-38; lectr., rsch. asst., instr. Yale U., 1939-42, 44-45; lectr., instr. Hartford Sem. Found., 1942-43, 45-46; lectr. Hunter Coll., 1942-43, 46; lectr. charge Army specialized tng. U. Pa., Phila., 1943-44, assoc. prof., 1948-59, prof. linguistics, 1959-85, prof. emeritus, 1985—, chmn. dept. linguistics, 1963-70, co-chmn., 1978-79, cn. Caldwell Prize com., 1989-91; P-4 Fgn. Service Inst., Dept. State, 1946-47; asso. prof. U. Tex., 1947-48; sr. linguist Deccan Coll., India, 1955; Fulbright lectr., Kiel, summer 1968, Oxford U., 1976-77; corp. vis. com. fgn. lits. and linguistics MIT, 1968-74; chmn. overseers com. to visit dept. linguistics Harvard U., 1978-84; vis. assoc. prof. U. Mich., 1946, 52, Princeton U., 1959-60; vis. assoc. prof.

Georgetown U., 1952-53, 54, Collitz prof., 1955; vis. prof. Yale U., 1961-62, U. Mich., 1968; mem. Seminar, Columbia U., 1965—; vis. staff mem., Leuven, 1986; fellow St. John's Coll., Oxford U., 1976-77; del. Comparative Linguistics Internat. Rsch. and Exchs. Bd., 1986; cons. Etymological Dictionary of Old High German, 1980—; Poultney lectr. Johns Hopkins U., 1991; co-promotor, Leuven, 1992; mem. acad. com. Yarmouk U., 1997. Author: Spoken Hindustani, 1946-47, Language Change and Linguistic Reconstruction, 1960, Studies in Formal Historical Linguistics, 1973; editor: Am. Oriental Series, 1954-58, The European Background of American Linguistics, 1979, (with L. Wiener) Biological Metaphor and Cladistic Classification, 1987, (with M.R. Key) General and American Ethnolinguistics, 1989; assoc. editor Indian Jour. Linguistics, 1977—; cons. editor Jour. History of Ideas, 1978—; adv. bd. Lang. and Style, 1968—, Jour. Indo-European Studies, 1973—, Diachronica, 1984-94, Lynx, 1988—; mem. editl. bd. Internat. Ency. Linguistics, 1986-91; editl. cons. Biographical Dictionary of Western Linguistics, 1994—. Am. Council Learned Socs. fellow, 1942-43, 44, Guggenheim fellow, 1950-51, Newberry Library fellow, 1956, NSF and Center Advanced Study Behavioral Scis. fellow, 1962-63, Faculty fellow Modern Langs. Coll. House, 1990-91; Festschrift in his honor, 1987. Fellow British Acad. (corr.), Am. Acad. Arts and Scis.; mem. AAAS, NAS, Am. Philos. Soc. (rsch. com. 19784, libr. com. 1984-94, chmn. 1988-94, membership com. class IV 1984-90, chmn. 1987-90, exec. com. 1988-94, chmn. 1988-94, publs. com. 1994—, Henry Allen Moe prize 1991), N.Y. Acad. Scis., Linguistic Soc. Am. (pres. 1958), Am. Oriental Soc. (editor 1954-58, pres. 1966-67), Philol. Soc. (London), Linguistic Soc. India, Societas Linguistica Europaea, Linguistics Assn. Gt. Britain, Internat. Soc. Hist. Linguistics, Indogermanische Gesellschaft, Am. Philol. Assn., Classical Assn. Atlantic State, Soc. Linguistica Italiana, Henry Sweet Soc., Studienkreis Geschichte der Sprachwissenschaft, N.Am. Assn. History of Lang. Scis., Fulbright Assn., Internat. Soc. Friends of Wroclaw U. Home: 908 Westdale Ave Swarthmore PA 19081-1804 Office: U Pa 618 Williams Hall Philadelphia PA 19104-6305

HOEPFNER, KARLA JEAN, designer, artist; b. Bridgeton, N.J., Nov. 24, 1958; d. Victor Robert and Thelma J. Hoepfner. Student, U. Md., 1977-78; BFA cum laude, Va. Commonwealth U., 1983; postgrad., Sch. Visual Arts, N.Y.C., 1993, Empire State Coll., 1994-95. Designer Fortress, Phila., 1985-88, Total Concept Inc., N.Y.C., 1989-92; mgr. Archetype Gallery, N.Y.C., 1994-96; self employed painter N.Y.C., 1992—. Exhibited in group shows at Cabell Libr., Richmond, Va., 1980, Anderson Gallery, Richmond, 1983, Montauk Club, Brooklyn, 1993, Empire State Coll., N.Y.C., 1995. Mem. Phi Kappa Phi. Avocations: philosophy, metaphysics. Home: 121 8th Ave Brooklyn NY 11215-1709

HOEPRICH, PAUL DANIEL, physician educator; b. Alliance, Ohio, Jan. 3, 1924; s. Michael and Katharina (Wagner) H.; m. Muriel Lucy Blackwell, July 11, 1948; children: Martha Sue Kennedy, Paul Daniel Jr., Thomas Eric, Kurt Lincoln. Student, Harvard Coll.; MD, Harvard Med. Sch., 1947. Diplomate Am. Bd. Internal Medicine. Instr. medicine Johns Hopkins Sch. Medicine, Balt., 1956; instr. epidemiology Johns Hopkins Sch. Hygiene & Pub. Health, Balt., 1956; asst., assoc. prof. medicine U. Utah Coll Medicine, Salt Lake City, 1957-67, asst., assoc. prof. pathology, 1959-67; prof. medicine U. Calif. Sch. Medicine, Davis, 1967-91, emeritus, 1991—, prof. pathology, 1968-86, chief infectious and immunlogic diseases, 1967-80, chief med. mycology, 1986-91; cons. physician in field. Editor, author: The Fluids of Parenteral Body Cavities, 1959, Infectious Diseases, 1972-94; editor The Infectious Diseases Newsletter, 1985-90; contbr. chpts. to books and articles to med. and scientific jours. Capt. U.S. Army M.C., 1950-53. Recipient Soma Weiss award Harvard Med. Sch., 1947, Disting. Faculty award U. Calif. Davis Med. Ctr., 1986; Fogarty sr. fellow NIH, 1976. Fellow Am. Coll. Physicians, Infectious Disease Soc. Am.; mem. AAAS, Am. Soc. Clin. Investigation, Assn. Am. Physicians.

HOERIG, GERALD LEE, retired chemical company executive; b. Appleton, Wis., Aug. 18, 1943; s. Francis Sebastian and Joyce Isabelle (Jack) H.; m. Jacqueline Kaminski, Jan.22, 1966 (div. Oct. 1974); children: David, Andrea, Paul; m. Nicola Sue Postma, Jan. 11, 1975. BSChemE, U. Wis., 1966. Mgmt. trainee Parke-Davis Co., Detroit and Holland, Mich., 1966-67, process devel. chemist, 1967-68; chem. dept. sect. head Parke-Davis Co., Holland, Mich., 1968-73, pers. mgr., 1973-74, mgr. chem. dept., 1974-78; prodn. mgr. Arapahoe Chemicals (div. Syntex Co.), Boulder, Colo., 1978-79; plant mgr. Syntex Chems. Inc., Boulder, Colo., 1979-82, dir. ops., 1982-85; dir. ops. Syntex Ireland Ltd., Clarecastle, County Clare, Ireland, 1985-86; v.p., gen. mgr. Syntex Chems. Inc., Boulder, Colo., 1986-93, pres., 1993-94; v.p. USA Chem. Ops., 1993-94; v.p. chem. mfg. Syntex Chems. Inc., Boulder, Colo., 1994-97; pres. Syntex; bd. dirs. BankOne Boulder (formerly Affiliated Nat. Bank, Boulder). Pres. Golden West Found., Boulder; bd. dirs., advisor Vol. Boulder County, 1987-88, 89; exec. bd. Longs Peak coun. Boy Scouts Am., Boulder, 1988—, trustee, 1991—, chmn.-elect, 1993, pres.-elect, 1995, pres. 1996-98, exec. bd. Student Leadership Inst., Boulder, 1988—, Pvt. Industry Partnership, Boulder, 1984-85; mem. dean's adv. coun. U. Colo. Sch. Bus.; campaign chair Boulder County United Way, 1991, trustee, 1991-98; bd. dirs. Boulder Tech. Incubator, 1991—; chair Exec. Leadership Group/CMA, Responsible Care Coord. Group/CMA, 1991—; mem. Credibility Group/CMA, 1991—; bd. Colo. Alliance Bus., 1994—, Boulder Cmty. Hosp. Found., 1996—; mem. Engring. Sch. Adv. Coun. U. Colo., 1996—, Engring. Sch. Adv. Coun. U. Wis.; mem. Vision 2000 Colo. Cmty. Found. Mem. Chem. Mfrs. Assn. (bd. dirs. 1989-91, 96—), AIChE, Rotary Internat. (Boulder), Boulder C. of C. (fin. com., bd. dirs., chmn. 1992), U. Wis. Alumni Assn. Avocations: fishing, golfing, hunting, antique collecting, traveling.

HOERNEMAN, CALVIN A., JR., economics educator; b. Youngstown, Ohio, Sept. 30, 1940; s. Calvin A. and Lucille A. (Leiss) H.; m. Cheryl L. Morand, Aug. 10, 1973; children: David, Jennifer, Christina. BA, Bethany Coll., 1962; MA, Mich. State U., 1964, postgrad., Cambridge U. Mem. faculty, Delta Coll., University Center, Mich., 1966—, prof. econs., 1976—; cons. Prentice-Hall, Acad. Press, Goodyear Pub., Random House Pub.; econ. expert witness; Author: Poverty, Wealth and Income Distribution, 1969; co-author: "Caper" Principles of Economics Software Study Guide; contbr. articles to various publs. Recipient Recognition award AAUP, 1972, Bergstein award Delta Coll. Grad. Class, 1972, Competition for Excellence award IBM and the League for Innovation, 1988. Mem. AAUP, Am. Econ. Assn., Midwest Econ. Assn., Nat. Assn. Forensic Economist. Home: 5712 Lamplighter Ln Midland MI 48642-3137 Office: Delta Coll Dept Econs University Center MI 48710

HOERNER, ROBERT JACK, lawyer; b. Fairfield, Iowa, Oct. 12, 1931; s. John Andrew and Margaret Louise (Simmons) H.; m. Judith Chandler, Apr. 21, 1954 (div. Feb. 1975); children: John Andrew II, Timothy Chandler, Blayne Marie, Michelle Margaret Hoerner Smith; m. Mary Paolano, June 3, 1989. BA, Cornell Coll., 1953; JD, U. Mich., 1958. Bar: Ohio 1960, U.S. Supreme Ct. 1964, U.S. Ct. Appeals (6th cir.) 1972, U.S. Ct. Appeals (Fed. cir.) 1990. Law clk. to hon. Chief Justice Earl Warren U.S. Supreme Ct., Washington, 1958-59; assoc. Jones, Day, Reavis & Pogue, Cleve., 1959-63, 65-66; chief evaluation sect. antitrust divsn. Dept. Justice, Washington, 1963-65; ptnr. Jones, Day, Reavis & Pogue, Cleve., 1967-93. Contbr. articles to prof. jours. Trustee New Orgn. of the Visual Arts, Cleve., 1976-80, 87-90. With Counter Intelligence Corps, U.S. Army, 1953-55. Mem. ABA (antitrust sect., patent sect.), Ohio Bar Assn., Greater Cleve. Bar Assn., Cleve. Intellectual Property Law Assn., Leland (Mich.) Country Club, Order of Coif, Phi Beta Kappa. Democrat. Home: 360 Darbys Run Bay Village OH 44140-2968 Office: Jones Day Reavis & Pogue 901 Lakeside Ave E Cleveland OH 44114-1190

HOESSLE, CHARLES HERMAN, zoo director; b. St. Louis, Mar. 20, 1931; m. Marilyn Mueller, Jan. 5, 1952; children: Maureen, Kirk, Tracy, Bradley. AA, Harris Tchrs. Coll., 1951; student, Am. Assn. Zool. Parks and Aquariums Zoo Mgmt. Sch., 1976-77; LLD (hon.), Maryville Coll., 1986, St. Louis U., 1990, U. Mo., St. Louis, 1994. Reptile keeper St. Louis Zoo, 1963, asst. curator, 1964, curator reptiles and curator edn., 1968-69, gen. curator and dep. dir., 1969-82, dir., 1982—; adj. prof. dept. biology St. Louis U., 1973-74, 81-82, 83; owner, operator Exotic Pet Shop, St. Louis; host St. Louis Zoo Show, 1968-78. Chmn. Reptile Study Merit Badge counselors, St. Louis; mem. adv. bd. Mo. Coalition for Environment, 1997; state chmn. UN Day, 1982; mem. St. Louis County Counts; bd. dirs. Harris-Stowe State Coll. Found., City Mus. With U.S. Army, 1952-54. Recipient Disting. Alumnus award Harris-Stowe State Coll., 1987. Mem. Internat. Union Dirs. Zool. Gardens, Am. Zoo and Aquarium Assn. (bd. dirs. 1977-79, 85-87, v.p. 1988, pres. 1990-91, past pres. 1991-92, rep. to species survival commn. Internat. Union for Conservation Nature and Natural Resources), St. Louis Naturalists Club, St. Louis Ctr. for Internat. Rels. (bd. dirs. 1993—), St. Louis Mus. Collaborative (pres. 1993), Animal Protective Assn. (bd. dirs.), Internat. Friendship Alliance St. Louis County (chmn. cultural com.), Explorers, St. Louis Herpetological Society, Hawthorne Soc., St. Louis Rotary Club, St Louis Ambassadors Club (bd. dir.). Home: 10814 Forest Circle Dr Saint Louis MO 63128-2007 Office: St Louis Zoo Forest Park Saint Louis MO 63110-1380

HOEVELER, WILLIAM M., federal judge; b. Aug. 23, 1922; m. Mary Griffin Smith, 1950; 4 children. Student, Temple U., 1941-42; B.A., Bucknell U., 1947; LL.B., Harvard U., 1950. Bar: Fla. 1951. Practice law Miami, Fla., 1951-77; firm individual practice law; judge U.S. Dist. Ct. for Fla. So. Dist., 1977—; federal judge U.S. Dist., Miami, Fla., now sr. judge; lectr. in field. Incorporator, bd. dirs. Youth Industries, Inc.; mem. vestry St. Stephens Episcopal Ch., 1973-75, chancellor, 1973. Served to lt. USMC, 1942-46. Mem. Am. Judicature Soc., Fla. Bar (personal injury and wrongful death adv. com. 1976), Phila. Bar Assn., Dade County (Fla.) Bar Assn. (chmn. charity drives com. 1966), Am. Bar Assn. (chmn. com. on products, profl. and gen. liability law 1972-73, program chmn. sec. ins., negligence and compensation law 1975, mem. sect. governing council 1975-78, mem. governing com. of forum com. on constrn. industry), Omicron Delta Kappa. Office: US Dist Ct 301 N Miami Ave Fl 9 Miami FL 33128-7702*

HOEY, RITA MARIE, public relations executive; b. Chgo., Nov. 4, 1950; d. Louis D. and Edith M. (Finnemann) Hoey; m. Joseph John Dragonette, Sept. 4, 1982. BA in English and History, No. Ill. U., 1972. Asst. dir. Nat. Assn. Housing and Human Devel., Chgo., 1975; public relations account exec. Weber Cohn & Riley, Chgo., 1975-76; publicity coordinator U.S. Gypsum Co., Chgo., 1976-77; with Daniel J. Edelman, Inc., Chgo., 1977-84, sr. v.p., 1981-84; exec. v.p. Dragonette, Inc., Chgo., 1984-91, pres., 1991—. Mem. Pub. Rels. Soc. Am. Home: 3416 Cherry Valley Rd Woodstock IL 60098-8173 Office: Dragonette Inc 205 W Wacker Dr Ste 2200 Chicago IL 60606-1215

HOFELDT, JOHN W., lawyer; b. Elkhart Lake, Wis., Sept. 6, 1920; s. Johann Heinrich and Matilda A. (Kuester) H.; m. Marion Ruth Meyer, Nov. 27, 1943; children: Nancy R. Hofeldt Werley, William A., Mark R. Ph.B., U. Wis.-Madison, 1943, LL.B. (editor Law Rev. 1946-47), 1947. Bar: Wis. 1947, Ill. 1948. Since practiced in Chgo.; ptnr. Haight & Hofeldt (and predecessors), 1955-89, ret.; lectr. John Marshall Grad. Sch., Chgo., 1971-91. Mem. Ill. Sch. Dist. 194 Bd. Edn., 1964-72. Served with USN, 1943-46. Mem. Am., Wis., Ill. bar assns., Patent Law Assn. Chgo. Republican. Clubs: Masons (Chgo.), Shriners (Chgo.), Union League (Chgo.). Home: 5418 Old Middleton Rd Madison WI 53705-2606

HOFENER, STEVEN DAVID, civil engineer; b. Portsmouth, Va., Jan. 12, 1954; s. Harold Ralph and Becky Dean (Jeffries) H.; m. Sherryl Marie Roush, May 24, 1974; children: Michael Steven, Stephanie Marie. BSCE, Okla. State U., 1975; MCE, Tex. A&M U., 1977. Registered profl. engr., Okla., Tex., Mo., Ark., Kans. Rsch. assoc. Tex. Transp. Inst., College Station, 1976-79; chief traffic engr. City of Oklahoma City, 1979-84; pres. Traffic Engring. Cons., Oklahoma City, 1984—; adj. prof. civil engring. U. Okla., 1994. Contbr. technical articles to profl. jours. Recipient Fred Burgraf award Transp. Rsch. Bd. 1978. Fellow Internat. Inst. Transp. Engrs.; mem. Am. Pub. Works Assn., Mo. Valley Inst. Transp. Engrs. (pres. 1991), Okla. Traffic Engrs. Assn. (pres. 1984-85), Oklahoma City C. of C. Republican. Lutheran. Avocations: fishing, basketball, golf. Office: Traffic Engring Cons 6301 N Meridian Ave Ste 100 Oklahoma City OK 73112-1267

HOFER, CHARLES WARREN, strategic management, entrepreneurship educator, consultant; b. Phoenixville, Pa., Nov. 11, 1940; s. Charles Emil and Alice May (Howard) H.; m. Judith Racella Millner, Oct. 22, 1980. BS in Engring. Physics summa cum laude, Lehigh U., 1962; MBA in Mktg. with distinction, Harvard U., 1965, MS in Applied Math., 1966, D in Bus. Policy, 1969. Research asst. Harvard Bus. Sch., Boston, 1965-66; asst. prof. Northeastern U., Boston, 1968-69; vis. lectr. Singapore Inst. Mgmt., 1969-70; asst. prof. Northwestern U., Evanston, Ill., 1970-75; assoc. prof. Northwestern U., 1975-76; vis. assoc. prof. Stanford (Calif.) U., 1976-77, Columbia U., N.Y.C., 1978, NYU, 1978-80; vis. prof. U. Calif., Riverside, 1980; regents prof. strategy, entrepreneurship U. Ga., Athens, 1981—; vis. chair in entrepreneurship Rutgers U., 1988; lectr. Chgo. C. of C., 1976-78; Donald W. Riegle campaign cons., Flint, Mich., 1968-72; vis. lectr. Ga. Tech., 1993; lectr. Nova U., 1981-96, Ga. State U., 1995-99. Author: Toward a Contingency Theory of Business Strategy, 1975 (ranked 16th in world Acad. Mgmt. survey 1985), Strategy Formulation: Analytical Concepts, 1978 (ranked 30th in world Acad. Mgmt. survey 1985); co-author: Strategic Management: A Casebook in Policy and Planning, 1980, 84, Future Firms: How America's High Tech Companies Work, 1998, Creating Value with Entrepreneurial Leadership in Skill-Based Strategy, 1999; co-editor: Strategic Management: A New View of Business Policy and Planning, 1979 (ranked 6th in world Acad. Mgmnt. survey 1985); editor: Strategic Planning Management, 1987-90; and others. Baker scholar Harvard U., 1965; NSF fellow, 1962-63, Ford Found. fellow, 1966-67; recipient Rsch. award U. Ga., 1990, Leavey award Freedoms Found. Valley Forge, 1991, Coleman Entrepreneurship Mentor award Acad. Mgmt., 1992, Internat. Hall Fame Entrepreneur award Inventors Club Am., 1992, Williams A. Owens Rsch. award U. Ga., 1993, Sargent Americanism award Soc. Mfg. Engrs., 1994. Fellow U.S. Assn. Small Bus. and Entrepreneurship (chmn. corp. entrepreneurship divsn. 1989-90, v.p. devel. 1990-92, v.p. programs 1995-96, pres. 1998, Nat. Model Entrepreneurship MBA Program award 1991, Disting. Entrepreneurship Educator of Yr. award 1992, Nat. Model Entrepreneurship PhD Program award 1998); mem. Acad. Mgmt. (chmn. policy div. 1977-78, First Outstanding Contbns. entrepreneurship divsn. award 1989), Strategic Mgmt. Soc. (charter), Decision Scis. Inst. (chmn. policy track 1985-86), Inst. Mgmt. Scis., Am. Econ. Assn., Harvard Bus. Sch. Club Atlanta, Harvard Club Ga., Phi Beta Kappa, Phi Eta Sigma, Pi Mu Epsilon, Tau Beta Pi, Sigma Iota Epsilon, Beta Gamma Sigma. Lutheran. Avocations: chess, bridge, jogging, traveling, brandy tasting. Home: 4445 Stonington Cir Atlanta GA 30338-6621 Office: U Ga Mgmt Dept Terry Coll Bus Athens GA 30602

HOFER, MYRON A(RMS), psychiatrist, researcher; b. N.Y.C., Dec. 20, 1931; s. Philip and Frances Louise (Heckscher) H.; m. Lynne Hofer, June 12, 1954; children: Timothy Philip, Adeline Van Nostrand; Andrew Paul. AB, Harvard U., 1954, MD, 1958. Diplomate Am. Bd. Psychiatry and Neurology. Resident in medicine Mass. Gen. Hosp., Boston, 1958-60; rsch. assoc. N.Y. Hosp. - Cornell, N.Y.C., 1960-62, Nat. Inst. Mental Health, Bethesda, Md., 1962-64; resident in psychiatry N.Y. State Psychiat. Inst., N.Y.C., 1964-66; asst. prof. to prof. psychiatry & neurosci. Albert Einstein Coll. Medicine, Bronx, N.Y., 1966-84; prof. psychiatry Coll. Physicians and Surgeons Columbia U., N.Y.C., 1984—; dir., Dept. Devel. Psychobiology, N.Y. State Psychiatric Inst., 1984—; Thomas William Salmon lectr., 1996. Author: Roots of Human Behavior, 1981; editor jours. Psychosomatic Medicine, 1972—, Devel. Psychobiology, 1981—, Behavioral Neurosci., 1993—, Perinatal Devel., 1987. Mem. adv. bd. Soc. for the Right to Die, N.Y.C., 1979; trustee Dalton Sch., N.Y.C., 1970-71. Lt. comdr. USPHS, 1962-64, Washington. Recipient Rsch. Scientist award, NIMH, Bethesda, 1993, Merit award, 1986-96. Mem. Am. Psychosomatic Soc. (pres. 1982-83), Internat. Soc. Devel. Psychobiology (pres. 1980-81), Psychiatric Rsch. Soc., Acad. Behavior Medicine Rsch., Century Club. Avocations: sailing, gardening, squash, prints, drawings. Office: NY State Psychiat Inst 722 W 168th St Unit 40 New York NY 10032-2603

HOFER, ROY ELLIS, lawyer; b. Cin., Oct. 10, 1935; s. Eric Walter and Elsie Katherine (Ellis) H.; m. Suzanne Elizabeth Sturtz, June 6, 1956 (div. 1974); m. Cynthia Ann Corson, June 5, 1981; children: Kimberly, Tracy, Eric. BChemE, Purdue U., 1957; JD, Georgetown U., 1961. Patent examiner U.S. Patent & Trademark Office, Washington, 1957-59; patent agt. Exxon Corp., Washington, 1959-61; ptnr. Brinks Hofer Gilson & Lione, Chgo., 1961—, pres., 1995—; adv. com. No. Dist. Ill., 1991-95. Contbr. articles to profl. jours. Bd. dirs. Chgo. Lung Assn., 1982-83, Ctr. for Conflict Resolution, 1983-88, 90-91, pres., 1991-97; bd. dirs. Union League Boys and Girls Club, Chgo., 1985-94, Ill. Inst. Continuing Legal Edn., Chgo., 1986-88. Mem. ABA (dir. litigation sect. 1982-87), Fed. Cir. Bar Assn. (pres. 1993-94), Ill. State Bar Assn., Chgo. Bar Assn. (pres. 1988-89), Patent Law Assn. Chgo., Am. Intellectual Property Law Assn., Law Club Chgo., Phi Eta Sigma, Tau Beta Pi, Omega Chi Epsilon. Republican. Office: Brinks Hofer Gilson & Lione Ste 3600 455 N Cityfront Plaza Dr Chicago IL 60611-5599

HOFER, THOMAS W., landscape company executive. Pres. Spring Green Lawn Care Corp., Plainfield, Ill. Office: Spring Green Lawn Care Corp 11909 S Spaulding School Dr Plainfield IL 60544-9501*

HOFEREK, MARY JUDITH, database administrator; b. East Orange, N.J., Nov. 1, 1943; d. George William and Jessie (Rucki) H. BA, Trenton State Coll., 1965; MA, U. Mich., 1969; PhD, U. Wis., 1978. Sys. analyst Fed. Govt., Kansas City (Mo.), Washington, 1984-88; sr. sys. engr. CDSI, Rockville, Md., 1988-90; sr. database adminstr. IBM/Loral/Lockheed Martin, Reston, Va., 1990—; adj. prof. U. Md. Univ. Coll., College Park, 1988—. Author: Going Forth: Leadership Issues for Women in Sport, 1978; co-editor: Women and Leadership, 1978; contbr. articles to profl. jours. Mem. Women's Polit. Caucus, Washington, Polish Am. Arts Assn., Washington. Mem. IEEE. Avocation: tennis. Home: 218 Rabbitt Rd Gaithersburg MD 20878-1051

HOFERT, JACK, consulting company executive, lawyer; b. Phila., Apr. 6, 1930; s. David and Beatrice (Schatz) H.; m. Marilyn Tukeman, Sept. 4, 1960; children: Dina, Bruce. BS, UCLA, 1952, MBA, 1954, JD, 1957. Bar: Calif. 1957; CPA, Calif. Tax supr. Peat, Marwick Mitchell & Co., L.A., 1959-62, tax mgr., 1974-77; v.p. fin. Pacific Theaters Corp., L.A., 1962-68; freelance cons. L.A., 1969-74; tax mgr. Lewis Homes, Upland, Calif., 1977-80; pres. Di-Bru, Inc., L.A., 1981-87, Scolyn, Inc., L.A., 1988-95; bus. cons., 1995—; dir. Valley Fed. Savs. and Loan Assn., 1989-92. Mem. UCLA Law Rev., 1956-57; contbr. articles to tax, fin. mags. Served with USN, 1948-49. Avocation: tennis. Home and Office: 2479 Roscomare Rd Los Angeles CA 90077-1812

HOFF, CHARLES WORTHINGTON, III, banker; b. Balt., Mar. 1, 1934; s. Charles Worthington Jr. and Sarah Durant (Yearley) H.; m. Margaret Elizabeth Ober, Sept. 7, 1967; children: Zoe Carey, Alexandra Yearley, Juliana Macgill, Margaret Frazier, Charles Worthington IV. BS in Bus., Johns Hopkins U., 1961; postgrad., Stonier Sch. Banking, 1964-66. With First Nat. Bank Md., Balt., 1955-77, div. v.p., 1968-77; exec. v.p. Farmers & Mechanics Nat. Bank, Frederick, 1977-81, pres., 1981-93, chmn., 1993—, also bd. dirs.; bd. dirs. F & M Bancorp, pres., 1983-93, chmn., 1993—; bd. dirs. Frederick Brick Works. Bd. dirs. Children's Aid and Family Svc. Soc. Balt., 1972-77, exec. com., fin. com., 1974-76; pres. Oriole Advocates, Inc., 1963, treas., 1964-65; trustee Frederick Meml. Hosp.,1 983-89; mem. exec. com., mem. fin. com., trustee Hood Coll., 1985-97, chmn. fin. coms., trustee emeritus, 1997—; trustee Cmty. Found. Frederick County, Md., 1987-92. Mem. Am. Bankers Assn. (coun., v.p. for Md. 1983, edn., policy and devel. coun. 1990-93, bd. dirs. 1995-98), Am. Inst. Banking, Md. Bankers Assn. (bd. dirs. 1988-90, v.p. 1992-93, pres.-elect 1993-94, pres. 1994-95), Frederick County C. of C. (bd. dirs. 1980-82), Holly Hills Country Club, Cap and Gown Club (Princeton, N.J.), Rotary, Bryce Resort Country Club (Bayse, Va.), Frederick Cotillion Club, Club 18. Republican. Methodist. Home: 231 E Church St Frederick MD 21701-5405 Office: Farmers & Mechanics Nat Bank 110 Thomas Johnson Dr Frederick MD 21702-4377

HOFF, GERHARDT MICHAEL, lawyer, insurance company executive; b. Vienna, Austria, June 12, 1930; came to U.S., 1951, naturalized, 1955; s. Erich Theodor and Vilma (Frank) Klockenhoff; m. Lisa Decristoforo, June 1, 1970; children: Michael, Elisabeth, Anne-Christine. Student, U. Munich Law Sch., Germany, 1948-51, Columbia U., 1951-52; LL.B., NYU, 1958; LL.M. in Taxation, Emory U., 1982; C.L.U., 1961. Bar: Mass. 1959, D.C. 1968, Ga. 1984. With Mass. Mut. Life Ins. Co. and Variable Annuity Life Ins. Co., 1958-67; v.p. Variable Annuity Life Ins. Co. Am., Washington, 1967-68; mem. staff fin. services group ITT Corp., 1968-69; pres. ITT Hamilton Life Ins. Co., also ITT Variable Annuity Ins. Co., St. Louis, 1970-72, Sun Life Ins. Co. Am., Balt., 1972-78, 81-83; chief exec. officer Sun Life Ins. Co. Am., 1972-83; pres. Sun Life Group Am., Inc., Atlanta, 1978-83; chmn. law practice Bus. Planning Corp. Am., Atlanta, 1983—; founder (with Lisa Hoff) Cities in Color, Inc., 1985—. Served with AUS, 1955-57. Decorated Commendation ribbon with pendant. Mem. Am. Soc. C.L.U.'s, ABA. Presbyterian. Clubs: Capital City (Atlanta). Office: 12 Braemore Dr NW Atlanta GA 30328-4845 *We'll get along better with others if we recognize their right to be hard or easy on themselves, depending on their own choice of priorities.*

HOFF, JAMES EDWIN, university president; b. Milw., June 23, 1932; s. James E. and Lydia Elisabeth (Kuhn) H. BS in Biology, Spring Hill Coll., 1958, MA in Philosophy, 1959; MA in Theology, St. Louis U., 1966; PhD in Theology, Gregorian U., Rome, 1969. Joined J.S., Roman Cath. Ch., 1953, ordained priest, 1965. Lectr. Creighton Prep. Sch., Omaha, 1959-62; lectr. in theology St. Thomas Coll., St. Paul, 1970-75, dir. novices Jesuit Novitiate, 1970-75; assoc. prof. Creighton U., Omaha, 1976-91, acting dean Sch. Medicine, 1980-82, v.p. univ. rels., pres. Creighton Found., 1983-91; faculty Coll. Medicine, U. Nebr., Omaha, 1980-86; pres. Xavier U., Cin., 1991—; bd. dirs. 1st Franklin Savs., Cin.; lectr., presenter in field. Contbr. articles to profl. jours. Bd. dirs. Creighton U., St. Joseph's U., Phila., St. Xavier H.S., Cin., Loyola U., New Orleans, The Jewish Hosp., Cin., Cystic Fibrosis Found., Cin.; retreat dir. Jesuit Retreat House, Lake Elmo, Minn.; mem. Leadership Omaha. Mem. Nat. Assn. Cath. Chaplains, Cath. Theol. Soc. Am., Coun. for Advancement and Support Edn., Nat. Assn. Ind. Colls. and Univs., Am. Coun. on Edn. Office: Xavier U 3800 Victory Pkwy Cincinnati OH 45207-1092*

HOFF, JOHN SCOTT, lawyer; b. Des Moines, Jan. 2, 1946; s. John Richard and Valetta R. (Scott) H.; m. Susan Murial Felver, June 21, 1972 (div. 1975); m. Shirley Jo Ward, June 21, 1975; children: Jennifer Jo, John Baron. BSBA, Drake U., 1967; MBA, Calif. State U., Fullerton, 1971; postgrad., Oxford (Eng.) U., 1973; JD, Southwestern U., L.A., 1975; MA in Mil. History, Am. Mil. U., 1995. Bar: Iowa 1976, U.S. Ct. Claims 1976, U.S. Ct. Customs and Patent Appeals 1976, U.S. Ct. Mil. Appeals 1976, Ill. 1977, U.S. Dist. Ct. (no. dist.) Ill. 1977, U.S. Ct. Appeals (7th cir.) 1979, Calif. 1980, U.S. Supreme Ct. 1982, Nebr. 1983, D.C. 1983, Wis. 1984, U.S. Dist. Ct. (so. dist.) Iowa 1987, U.S. Ct. Appeals (9th and 10th cirs.) 1988, U.S. Dist. Ct. Ariz. 1990, U.S. Ct. Appeals (6th cir.) 1990, Mich. 1991, U.S. Ct. Appeals (8th cir.) 1991, N.Y. 1995, Minn. 1996, U.S. Dist. Ct. (cen. dist.) Ill. 1996; CPCU; chartered cost analyst. Staff atty. FAA Hdqrs., Washington, 1975-76; assoc. Lord, Bissell & Brook, Chgo., 1976-81; ptnr. Lapin, Hoff, Slaw & Laffey, Chgo., 1981-92, John Scott Hoff & Assocs., P.C., Chgo., 1992—; real estate broker Ill. Dept. Profl. Regulation, Springfield, 1980—;. Contbr. articles to profl. jours. Capt. USAF, 1967-75; col. USAFR, 1975—. Mem. Aviation Ins. Assn. (v.p. 1990-92, pres. 1992-94), Air Force Assn. (v.p., pres. 1980-93), Internat. Soc. Air Safety Investigation (v.p.), Aircraft Owners and Pilots Assn., Exptl. Aircraft Assn., Nat. Assn. Flight Instrs., Aero. Club Chgo. Republican. Presbyterian. Avocations: flying, military history. Office: 20 S Clark St Ste 2210 Chicago IL 60603-1805*

HOFF, JULIAN THEODORE, physician, educator; b. Boise, Idaho, Sept. 22, 1936; s. Harvey Orval and Helen Marie (Boraas) H.; m. Diane Shanks, June 3, 1962; children—Paul, Allison, Julia. BA, Stanford U., Calif., 1958; MD, Cornell U., N.Y.C., 1962. Diplomate Am. Bd. Neurol. Surgery (sec. 1987-91, chmn. 1991-92). Intern N.Y. Hosp., N.Y.C., 1962-63; resident in surgery N.Y. Hosp., 1963-64, resident in neurosurgery, 1966-70; Asst. prof. neurosurgery U. Calif., San Francisco, assoc. prof. neurosurgery, 1974-78, prof. neurosurgery, 1978-81; prof. neurosurgery U. Mich., Ann Arbor, 1981—; head sect. neurosurgery U. Mich., 1981—; mem. Am. Bd. Neurol-Surgery, 1986-92, chmn., 1991-92; mem. bd. sci. councillors Nat. Inst. Neurol. Diseases and Stroke-NIH, 1993-97; nat. adv. coun. NINDS, 1999—. Editor: Practice of Neurosurgery, 1979-85; Current Surgical Management of Neurological Diseases, 1980; Neurosurgery: Diagnostic and Management Principles, 1992, Mild to Moderate Head Injury, 1989; co-editor: Neurosurgery: Scientific Basis of Clinical Practice, 1985, 3rd edit., 1999;

contbr. articles to profl. jours. Served to capt. US Army, 1964-66. Recipient NIH Tchr.-Investigator award, 1972-77, Javits neurosci. investigator award NIH, 1985-99; Macy Faculty scholar, London, 1979. Fellow ACS (2d v.p.-elect 1998—); mem. Am. Assn. Neurol. Surgeons (v.p. 1991-93, pres. 1993-94), Am. Surg. Assn., Congress Neurol. Surgeons (v.p. 1982-83), Am. Acad. Neurosurgeons (treas. 1989-92, sec. 1992—, pres. 1996—), Cen. Neurosurg. Soc. (pres. 1985-86), Soc. Neurol. Surgeons (pres. elect 1998—). Republican. Presbyterian. Home: 2120 Wallingford Rd Ann Arbor MI 48104-4563 Office: U Mich Hosp TC 2128 Ann Arbor MI 48109

HOFF, MARCIAN EDWARD, JR., electronics engineer; b. Rochester, N.Y., Oct. 28, 1937; s. Marcian Edward and Mary Elizabeth (Fitzpatrick) H.; m. Judith Schless Rytand, May 19, 1977; children: Carolyn, Lisa, Jill. B.E.E., Rensselaer Poly. Inst., Troy, N.Y., 1958; M.S., Stanford U., 1959, Ph.D., 1962. Research asso. Stanford U., 1962-68; mgr. applications research Intel Corp., Santa Clara, Calif., 1968-83; v.p. research and devel. Atari Inc., Sunnyvale, Calif., 1983-84; Chief Technologist Teklicon Inc. Author articles on adaptive systems, microcomputers. NSF fellow, 1958-60; recipient Stuart Ballantine medal Franklin Inst., 1979. Mem. IEEE (Cledo Brunetti award 1980, Centennial Medal 1984), Sigma Xi, Eta Kappa Nu, Tau Beta Pi. Patentee track circuits, electrochem. memory, digital filters, integrated circuits, invented microprocessor. Home: 12226 Colina Dr Los Altos CA 94024-5299 Office: Teklicon Inc 3031 Tisch Way Ste 1010 San Jose CA 95128-2533*

HOFF, PHILIP HENDERSON, lawyer, former state senator, former governor; b. Turners Falls, Mass., June 29, 1924; s. Olaf and Agnes (Henderson) H.; m. Joan Brower, Aug. 28, 1948; children: Susan Brower, Dagny Elizabeth, Andrea Clark, Gretchen Henderson. A.B., Williams Coll., 1948; LL.B., Cornell Law Sch., 1951; hon. degrees, Am. Internat. Coll., U. Vt., Middlebury Coll., Windham Coll., Norwich U.; Williams Coll., Vt. Law Sch. Assoc. Black & Wilson, Burlington, Vt., 1951-54; ptnr. Black, Wilson, Coffrin & Hoff, Burlington, 1955-62; mem. Vt. Gen. Assembly, Montpelier, 1961; gov. State of Vt., 1963-69; ptnr. Hoff, Wilson, Powell & Lang, Burlington, 1969-89; mem. Vt. Senate, 1984-90; chmn. U.S. Civil Rights Com., Vt., New Eng. Natural Resources Com., Vt. Supreme Ct. Adv. Com.; mem. standing adv. com. Vt. Supreme Court; mem. Commn. on Civil Rights; mem. Friends of Health Care; of counsel Hoff, Curtis, Pacht, Cassidy & Frame, Burlington, 1989—. Co-chair, mem. New Eng. Gov.'s Conf., 1967-69; chmn. Vt. Dem. Com., 1974-75, adv. com. on Vt. bar admission requirements, Vt. Senate Com. on Edn.; trustee Vt. Law Sch., past pres. bd.; mem., past chair New Eng. Natural Resources Com.; bd. dirs. Law Conservation Found., New Eng. Environ. Policy Ctr. Mem. ABA, Vt. Bar Assn., Chittenden County Bar Assn. Episcopalian. Office: Hoff Curtis Pacht Cassidy & Frame 100 Main St Burlington VT 05401-8420*

HOFF, SAMUEL BOYER, political science educator; b. Williamsport, Pa., June 7, 1957; s. Samuel Romberger and J. Mattie (Schultz) H.; m. Phyllis Rose Oliveto, Aug. 16, 1986. BA in Polit. Sci., Susquehanna U., 1979; MA in Polit. Sci., Am. U., 1981, SUNY, Stony Brook, 1983; PhD in Polit. Sci., SUNY, Stony Brook, 1987. Instr. SUNY, Stony Brook, 1982-86; asst. prof. SUNY, Geneseo, 1987-88; asst. prof. dept. history and polit. sci. Del. State U., Dover, 1989-92, assoc. prof. dept. history and polit. sci., 1992-96, prof., 1996-99, ROTC dir., 1993-99, George Washington Disting. prof., 1999—; adj. instr. dept. social sci. N.Y. Inst. Tech., Old Westbury, N.Y., 1986; adj. asst. prof. Wittenberg U., Springfield, Ohio, 1987; vis. asst. prof. dept. govt. and politics Ohio Wesleyan U., Delaware, 1986-87; vis. asst. prof. Wichita (Kans.) State U., 1988-89; congl. intern U.S. Rep. Allen Ertel, Washington, 1978; mem. canvass staff Clean Water Action Project, Washington, 1980; rsch. asst. subcom. on human resources U.S. Ho. of Reps., Washington, 1980; asst. Senator Jacob Javits, Stony Brook, 1983-85. Contbr. articles to profl. jours. Committeeman Suffolk County Dems., L.I., 1984-86; presdl. candidate Dem. Party, 1988, Ind. Party, 1992, 96. Freedoms Found. scholar, 1990, 94; USMA-ROTC Mil. History fellow, 1994; Nat. Security Law fellow, 1995, Carnegie Coun. fellow, 1997. Fellow Carnegie Coun.; mem. Am. Polit. Sci. Assn., Acad. Polit. Sci., Nat. Social Sci. Assn., Northeastern Polit. Sci. Assn., Midwest Polit. Sci. Assn., Western Polit. Sci. Assn., So. Polit. Sci. Assn., Nat. Capital Area Polit. Sci. Assn., Pa. Polit. Sci. Assn., N.Y. Polit. Sci. Assn. Lutheran. Avocations: sports, antique collector, musician. Home: 813 Maple Pky Dover DE 19901-4238 Office: Del State Univ Dept History Polit Sci Dover DE 19901

HOFF, TIMOTHY, law educator, priest; b. Freeport, Ill., Feb. 27, 1941; s. Howard Vincent and Zillah (Morgan) H.; m. Virginia Nevill; children: Brian Charles, Morgan Witherspoon; stepchildren: Guy Baker, Katherine Baker. A.B., Tulane U., 1963, J.D., 1966; student U. London, 1961-62; LL.M., Harvard U., 1970. Bar: Fla. 1967, Ala. 1973, U.S. Dist. Ct. (mid. dist.) Fla. 1967. Assoc., Williams, Parker, Harrison, Dietz & Getzen, Sarasota, Fla., 1966-69; asst. legal editor The Fla. Bar, 1969; asst. prof. U. Ala., 1970-73, assoc. prof., 1973-75, prof. law, 1975-93, Gordon Rosen prof., 1993—; cons. Ala. Law Inst.; reporter Ala. Adminstrv. Procedure Act, 1977—; ordained priest Episcopal Ch. V.p., founding dir. Hospice of West Ala.; founding dir. Community Soup Bowl, Inc.; Episc. priest assoc. Canterbury Chapel U. Ala.; rector St. Michael's Episc. Ch., Fayette, Ala., 1988-96. Recipient Hist. Preservation Service award, 1976. Mem. ACLU, Maritime Law Assn. U.S., AAUP, Council on Religion and Law, Episc. Soc. for Ministry in Higher Edn., Phi Beta Kappa, Order of Coif, Omicron Delta Kappa, Eta Sigma Phi. Democrat. Club: University. Author: Alabama Limitations of Actions, 1984, 2d edit., 1992, Forms for Civil Trial Practice, 1991; contbr. articles to profl. jours. Home: 2601 Lakewood Cir Tuscaloosa AL 35405-2727 Office: U Ala Law Sch 101 Paul W Bryant Dr E Box 870382 Tuscaloosa AL 35487-0382

HOFFA, HARLAN EDWARD, retired university dean, art educator; b. Kalamazoo, June 23, 1925; s. Leolan William and Pearl (Foster) H.; m. Marian Perko, Aug. 10, 1946 (div. 1971); children: Kathryn Jane, Thomas Scott; m. Suzanne Aldridge Dudley, Sept. 11, 1971. BS, Wayne U., 1948, MEd, 1949; EdD, Pa. State U., 1959. Tchr. Evanston (Ill.) Pub. Schs., 1949-51; instr. art edn. Ohio State U., 1951-53; asst. prof. art State U. Coll. at Buffalo, 1953-59; assoc. prof. fine arts and edn. head dept. Boston U., 1959-65; art edn. specialist U.S. Office Edn., 1964-67; prof. edn. and fine arts, chmn. art edn. program Ind. U., 1967-70; prof., head dept. art edn. Pa. State U., 1970-76, head div. art and music edn., 1976-79, acting dir. Sch. Visual Arts, 1979-80, 84-85, assoc. dean for research and grad. studies Coll. Art and Architecture, 1985-90, ret., 1990, prof. emeritus, 1990—; assoc. dir. Ctr. Policy Studies in the Arts, 1989; Fulbright sr. lectr./researcher, Helsinki, Finland, Jan.-Jun., 1987. With AUS, 1943-45. Mem. Nat. Art Edn. Assn. (pres. 1971-73). Home: 1343 Penrose Cir State College PA 16803-3255

HOFFBERG, DAVID LAWRENCE, lawyer; b. N.Y.C., Jan. 8, 1932; m. Gwendolyn Dounce; children: Kevin, Claudia, Eric. A.B., Cornell U., 1953; LL.B., NYU, 1955. Bar: N.Y. 1956. Ptnr. Nixon, Hargrave, Devans & Doyle, LLP, Rochester, N.Y., 1965—; chmn. litigation/adminstrv. law sect. Nixon, Hargrave, Devans, & Doyle, Rochester, N.Y., 1990-92; mem. Com. to Advise N.Y. State Conf. on Civil Practice Law and Rules, 1968-70. Bd. dirs. GeVa Theatre, 1978-87, 97—, chmn. bd., 1980-82; bd. dirs. YMCA of Rochester and Monroe County, 1979-84, Rochester Area Crimestoppers, Inc., 1984-89, Arts for Greater Rochester, 1991-94; mem. Brockport Coll. Comty. Adv. Group, 1986-94; treas. Monroe County Dem. Com., 1978-82; pres. bd. dirs. Family Svc. of Rochester, 1970-73; mem. judicial screening com. Sen. Daniel Patrick Moynihan, 1983—; chmn. SUNY Brockport Coun., 1995—, chmn. presdl. search com., 1996-97. Fellow Am. Coll. Trial Lawyers, Am. Bar Found., N.Y. Bar Found.; mem. N.Y. State Bar Assn. (com. on jud. selection 1977-94, character com. appellate divsn. 4th dept. 1984-91, appellate divsn. jud. screening com. 1990-94, 97—), Monroe County Bar Assn. (chmn. judiciary com. 1973-76, trustee 1977-78, pres. 1983), Monroe County Bar Found. (bd. dirs. 1982-90, pres. 1987-89). Office: Nixon Hargrave Devans & Doyle LLP Clinton Sq PO Box 1051 Rochester NY 14603-1051

HOFFBERGER, JEROLD CHARLES, corporation executive; b. Balt., Apr. 7, 1919; s. Samuel H. and Gertrude (Miller) H.; m. Alice Berney, June 10, 1946; children: David B., Richard J., Carol S., Charles P. Grad., Tome Sch., 1937, U. Va., 1940. Pres., dir. Nat. Brewing Co., Balt., 1947-75; pres., chmn. bd., chief exec. officer Carling Nat. Breweries, Inc., Balt., 1975-78; bd. dir. Real Estate Holding Co., 1987; chmn., pres. Balt. Orioles, 1965-79, pres., 1979-83; owner Sunset Hill Farm, 1980-92; chmn. bd. dirs. Diversified Resource Mgmt. Ltd., 1978-90, Phoenix Health Corp., 1993—, Phoenix Bar Code Health Sys.; bd. dirs. Mchts. Terminal Corp. Past trustee United Jewish Appeal; vice chmn. bd. dirs. Hoffberger Found.; pres. Coun. Jewish Fedns. and Welfare Funds, 1975-78; chmn. United Israel Appeal, 1978-83; trustee Johns Hopkins Hosp., Balt., 1960-91; mem. adv. bd. Johns Hopkins Sch. Health and Pub. Hygiene, Balt.; bd. dirs. Ctr. for Pub. Policy in Israel; chmn. adv. coun. Wilmer Ophthalmol. Inst., 1990-93; hon. chmn. UIA, 1983—; chmn. bd. dirs. Jewish Agy., 1983-87, gov., 1975-92. Mem. U. Va. Alumni Assn., Nat. Steeplechase and Hunt Assn. (past steward), Suburban Country Club, Ctr. Club, Phi Epsilon Pi. Jewish. Office: 2624 LD Baltimore Rd Ste C Baltimore MD 21244

HOFFENBERG, MARVIN, political science educator, consultant; b. Buffalo, July 7, 1914; s. Harry and Jennie Pearl (Weiss) H.; m. Betty Eising Stern, July 20, 1947; children—David A., Peter H. Student, St. Bonaventure Coll., 1934-35; B.Sc., Ohio State U., 1939, M.A., 1940, postgrad., 1941. Asst. chief div. interindustry econs. Bur. Labor Statistics, Dept. Labor, 1941-52; cons. U.S. Mut. Security Agy., Europe, 1952, Statistik Sentralbyra, Govt. of Norway, Oslo, 1955; dir. research, econ. cons. dept. deVegh & Co., 1956-58; economist RAND Corp., 1952-56; staff economist Com. Econ. Devel., 1958-60; project chmn. Johns Hopkins U., 1960-63; dir. cost analysis dept. Aerospace Corp., 1963-65; Research economist Inst. Govt. and Pub. Affairs, UCLA, 1965-67, prof.-in-residence polit. sci., 1967-85, prof. emeritus, 1985—; dir. M.P.A. program, co-chmn. Interdepartmental Program in Comprehensive Health Planning UCLA, 1974-76. Author: (with Kenneth J. Arrow) A Time Series Analysis of Inter-Industry Demand, 1959; editor: (with Levine, Hardt and Kaplan) Mathematics and Computers in Soviet Economics, 1967; contbr. articles to profl. jours., chpts. to books. Mem. bd. advisers Sidney Stern Meml. Trust; bd. dirs. Vista del Mar Child Ctr., L.A. chpt. Am. Jewish Com., Reiss-Davis Child Study Ctr.; foreman L.A. County Grand Jury, 1990-91; commr. L.A. County Economy and Efficiency Commn., 1991-92. C.C. Stillman scholar; Littauer fellow Harvard U., 1946; recipient Disting. service award Coll. Adminstrv. Scis., Ohio State U., 1971. Fellow AAAS; mem. Am. Econ. Assn. Jewish. Office: U Calif Dept Polit Sci 4289 BuncheSci Los Angeles CA 90095

HOFFENBLUM, ALLAN ERNEST, political consultant; b. Vallejo, Calif., Aug. 10, 1940; s. Albert A. and Pearl Estelle (Clarke) H. BA, U. So. Calif., 1962. Mem. staff L.A. County Rep. Com., 1967-71; staff dir. Rep. Assembly Caucus Calif. legislature, Sacramento, 1973-75; polit. dir. Rep. Party of Calif., L.A., 1977-78; owner Allan Hoffenblum & Assocs., L.A., 1979—. Pub. Calif. Target Book, 1994—. Capt. USAF, 1962-67, Vietnam. Decorated Bronze Star medal. Mem. Internat. Assn. Polit. Cons., Am. Assn. Polit. Cons. Jewish. Office: 9000 W Sunset Blvd Ste 707 West Hollywood CA 90069-5807

HOFFER, ALMA JEANNE, nursing educator; b. Dalhart, Tex., Sept. 15, 1932; d. James A. and Mildred (Zimlich) Koehler; m. John L. Hoffer, Oct. 7, 1954; children: John Jr., James Leo, Joseph V., Jerome P. BS, Bradley U., 1970; MA, W. Va. Coll. Grad. Study Inst., 1975; EdD, Ball State U., 1981, MA, 1986. Reg. Nurse. Staff nurse St Joseph Hosp., South Bend, Ind., 1958-59, Holy Cross Cen. Sch., St Joseph Hosp., South Bend, 1959-63; sch. nurse South Bend Sch. Corp., 1970-72; faculty staff Morris Harvey Coll., Charleston, W.Va., W.Va. Inst. Tech., Montgomery, 1975-76; asst. prof. Ball State U., Ind., 1976-77, Ind. U.-Purdue U., Ft. Wayne, 1977-81; assoc. prof. U. Akron, Ohio, 1981-83, 91—, asst. dean, grad. edn., 1983-90, assoc. prof., 1991-93; prof., chair Dept. of Nursing St. Francis Coll., Fort Wayne, Ind., 1993-95; prin. investigator rsch. project Well Begun is Well Done Children's Med. Ctr. Women's Bd. Akron, 1995—; trustee Akron Child Guidance, 1983-88, 89—, chair planning com., 1988; nursing Blick Clin., Akron, 1988; rsch. cons. St. Joseph Hosp., Ohio, 1989; researcher, presenter in field. Contbg. author: Family Health Promotion Theories and Assessment, 1989, Nursing Connections, 1992. Task force mem. Gov. Celeste's Employee Assistance Program for State U. Campuses, Ohio, 1983-84, del. People to People Citizen Amb. Program to Europe, 1988. Mem. ANA, Nat. League for Nursing, Midwest Nursing Rsch. Soc., Transcultural Nursing Assn., Portage Country Club, Tippecanoe Country Club, Sigma Theta Tau. Republican. Roman Catholic. Avocations: tennis, golf, skiing. Office: PO Box 794 Bath OH 44210-0794

HOFFER, JAMES BRIAN, physicist, consultant; b. Madera, Calif., Aug. 2, 1956; s. Robert C. and Jane A. (Rylander) H.; m. Florina Bojeri, Aug. 20, 1983. BS in Physics and Math., Pacific Union Coll., 1977; MS in Physics, Mich. State. U., 1979, PhD in Physics, 1983. Vis. scientist Los Alamos (N.Mex.) Nat. Lab., 1981; instr. Mich. State U., East Lansing, 1983, rsch. assoc., nat. superconducting cyclotron lab., 1983; rsch. assoc., lab. for atmospheric and space physics U. Colo., Boulder, 1983-85; asst. scientist Applied Rsch. Corp., Landover, Md., 1985-86; pres. Hoffer and Assocs., Darnestown, Md., 1986-98, HofTek, Inc., Darnestown, 1998—; mem. tech. adv. com. Aviation Week, 1990-91. Author: Utilizing VAX/UMS Utilities and DCL, 1989; contbr. articles to sci. jours. Appointee Consumer Affairs Adv. Com., Montgomery County, Md., 1988-95; sci. fair judge, Fairfax, Va., 1989. Mem. Am. Astron. Soc., Sigma Pi Sigma. Achievements include development of technique to reduce computer time required for planetary ring model, of technique to reduce computer time required for modeling of gravitational interactions between pairs of binary stars. Home and Office: 15413 Deep Bottom Rd Darnestown MD 20874-3630

HOFFER, PAUL B., nuclear medicine physician, educator; b. N.Y.C., Apr. 9, 1939; m. Vicki Kornbluth; children: Marjorie, Joanne, Ilene, Suzanne, Alexandra. Student, Union Coll., 1956-59; M.D., U. Chgo., 1963; M.S., Yale U., 1977. Diplomate: Am. Bd. Radiology, Am. Bd. Nuclear Medicine. Resident in radiology U. Chgo., 1966-69, radiologist, 1969-70, dir. nuclear medicine, 1970-74; prof., dir. nuclear medicine U. Calif.-San Francisco, 1974-77; prof., dir. nuclear medicine Yale U., New Haven, 1977-96, prof., 1996—; mem. NIH Diagnostic Radiology Study Sect., 1984-86. Editor: Gallium 67 Imaging, 1978, Yearbook of Nuclear Medicine, 1981—, Diagnostic Nuclear Medicine, 1988; inventor radiation camera system, 1973. Served to lt. comdr. USN, 1964-66. Recipient Meml. medal Assn. Univ. Radiologists, 1968; James Picker Found. scholar, 1969-72. Mem. Soc. Nuclear Medicine (v.p. 1980-81), Am. Coll. Radiology, Am. Coll. Nuclear Physicians, Radiol. Soc. N.Am., AAAS. Jewish. Home: 48 Harbor Close New Haven CT 06519-2835 Office: Yale U Sch Medicine PO Box 208042 333 Cedar St New Haven CT 06510-3289*

HOFFER, ROY DANIEL, forensic electrical engineer; b. Lancaster, Pa., Jan. 1, 1957; s. Earl C. and Pearl H. BS in Physics magna cum laude, Millersville U., 1979; MSEE, U. Pa., 1981. Lic. profl. engr., Pa. Lighting rsch. engr. Armstrong World Industries, Lancaster, Pa., 1981-86; electronic design engr., project mgr. York (Pa.) Internat. Corp., 1986-91; supr. instrument engring. Datcon Instrument divsn. High Voltage Engring. Corp., Boston, 1991-93; tech. rep., applications engr. Consulting Engrs., Lancaster, 1993; calibration engr. Warner-Lambert Co., Morris Plains, N.J., 1994-96; forensic engr., expert witness, fire & accident investigator, safety engr., elec. and electronics design cons. Hoffer Engring., Lancaster, 1994—; mech. engring., physics and environ. sci. prof. Stevens Coll. of Tech., Lancaster, 1998—. Com. mem., vol. Redeemer Luth. Ch., Lancaster, 1986—, bd. dirs., 1992—; mem. Leadership Lancaster, 1992. Recipient Sojourners award USAR, 1976; Ashton fellow, 1979. Mem. IEEE, NSPE (bd. dirs., chair profl. engrs. in industry com., chair scholarships com. Lincoln chpt.), Instrument Soc. Am. (sr.), Nat. Fire Protection Assn., Pa. Assn. Arson Investigators, Lancaster Fire Safety Network, Lancaster Lebanon Sci. and Tech. Alliance (bd. dirs., treas.). Achievements include 17 patents for slow acting photocell lamp dimming control, power ltd. fluorescent lighting system, variable speed single and 3 phase AC motor drive systems.

HOFFERT, MARTIN IRVING, applied science educator; b. Bklyn., July 1, 1938; s. Solomon and Ceil (Hyman) H.; m. Linda Epstein, Sept. 4, 1960; 1 child, Eric; m. 2d, Iris E. Fierst, Jan. 29, 1965. BS in Aero. Engring., U. Mich., 1960, MS in Astronautics, 1964; PhD in Astronautics, Poly. Inst. Bklyn., 1967; MA in Liberal Studies, New Sch. for Social Research, 1969. Sr. scientist Gen. Applied Sci. Labs., Westbury, N.Y., 1962-67; research scientist NYU, 1967-68; sr. research scientist Advanced Tech. Labs., Westbury, 1968-69; mem. research staff Riverside Research Inst., N.Y.C., 1969-72; sr. research assoc. Goodard Inst. for Space Studies NASA, N.Y.C., 1972-74; sr. research scientist NYU, 1974-76, assoc. prof. applied sci., 1976-83, prof. applied sci., 1983-94, prof. physics, 1995—, chmn. applied sci., 1984-91; mgmt. ops. working group in planetary atmosphere NASA, Washington, 1986—; bilateral coop. working group VIII U.S. Del. Joint U.S.-USSR Commn., 1986—; cons. Exxon Rsch. & Engring., Annandale, N.J., 1986-95, Lawrence Livermore Nat. Lab., 1990—. Contbr. over 65 articles to profl. jour. and chpts. to books. Fellow AAAS; mem. AAIA, Am. Geophys. Union, Am. Metereol. Soc., Aspen Globet Change Inst. (adv. bd.). Democrat. Jewish. Avocations: bicycling, hiking, boating. Home: 12 Oak Dr Great Neck Long Island NY 11021 Office: NYU Dept Physics New York NY 10003

HOFFERT, PAUL WASHINGTON, surgeon; b. N.Y.C., Feb. 22, 1923; s. Charles and Rose (Isaacs) H.; m. Rosolyn Sheiman, Apr. 20, 1947; children: Marvin Jay, Renee Beth, Deborah Susan. AB with honors, Columbia U., 1942; MD, cum laude, Yale U., 1945. Diplomate Am. Bd. Surgery, Am. Bd. Abdominal Surgery. Intern New Haven (Ct.) Hosp., 1945-46; fellow radiology Hosp. U. Pa., 1948-49; resident surgery VA Hosp., Bronx, N.Y., 1949-53; pvt. practice medicine specializing in gen. and vascular surgery, Yonkers, N.Y., 1953—; attending surgeon Yonkers Gen. Hosp., 1953—, chief of surgery, 1987—; sr. gen. and vascular surgeon St. Joseph's Hosp., 1953—; assoc. vascular surgeon Montefiore Hosp., 1965—; asst. prof. surgery Albert Einstein Coll., 1955—. Contbr. articles to profl. jours. Capt. U.S. Army Med. Corps, 1946-48. Recipient citation Am. Cancer Soc., 1960. Fellow Am. Coll. Surgeons (pres. Westchester, N.Y. chpt.), Am. Coll. Angiology N.Y. Acad. Medicine, Westchester Acad. Medicine (charter), Clin. Soc. N.Y. Diabetes Assn.; mem. N.Y. Surgical Soc., N.Y. Soc. Cardiovascular Surgery, Am. Zionist Orgn. (life) (past pres. Lincoln Park, Yonkers region), Phi Beta Kappa, Alpha Omega Alpha, Phi Delta Epsilon, Masons. Home: 26 Indian Cove Rd Mamaroneck NY 10543-4439

HOFFHEIMER, DANIEL JOSEPH, lawyer; b. Cin., Dec. 28, 1950; s. Harry Max and Charlotte (O'Brien) H.; children: Rebecca, Rachel, Leah. Grad., Phillips Exeter Acad., 1969; AB cum laude, Harvard Coll., 1973; JD, U. Va., 1976. Bar: Ohio 1976, U.S. Dist. Ct. (so. dist.) Ohio 1976, U.S. Ct. Appeals (6th crct.) 1977, U.S. Ct. Appeals (D.C. and fed. crcts.) 1986, U.S. Ct. Internat. Trade 1986, U.S. Tax Ct. 1992, U.S. Supreme Ct. 1980, U.S. Tax Ct. 1992. Assoc. Taft, Stettinius & Hollister, Cin., 1976-84, ptnr., 1984—; lectr. law Coll. Law, U. Cin., 1981-83; trustee Judges Hogan & Porter Meml. Trust; mem. adv. bd. Ohio Dist. Ct. Rev. Editor-in-chief U. Va. Jour. Internat. Law, 1975-76; co-author: Practitioners' Handbook Ohio First District Court Appeals, 1984, 2d edit., 1991, Federal Practice Manual, U.S. 6th Circuit Court of Appeals, 1993, Manual on Labor Law, 1988; contbr. articles to profl. jours. Mem. Cin. Symphony Bus. Rels. Com., 1977-86, Cin. Composers Guild, 1988-93, Ohio Supreme Ct. Com. Racial Fairness, 1993—; trustee Underground R.R. Freedom Mus., 1994—; mem. adv. bd. for Consumer Protection, Cin., 1978-80, Hoxworth Blood Ctr. Univ. Cin. Hosp., 1994—; mem. bd. Hebrew Union Coll. Jewish Inst. Religion, 1994—, WGUC-FM Pub. Radio, 1988—, vice chmn., 1993-96, chmn., 1996—; trustee Cin. Chamber Orch., 1977-80, Seven Hills Sch., Cin., 1980-86, Internat. Visitors Ctr., Çin., 1980-84, Friends Coll. Conservatory of Music, Cin., 1985-86, Cin. Symphony Orch., 1988-94, 96—, sec., 1996—, Children's Psychiat. Ctr., Cin., 1986-89, treas., 1987-89; vice chmn. Jewish Hosp., Cin., 1989-92; Leadership Cin., 1989-90; sec., trustee Cin. Symphony Musicians Pension Fund, 1989—, Jewish Cmty. Rels. Coun., 1990-98, v.p., 1996-98; sec. Nat. Conf. Christians and Jews, 1992—; counsel Cin. AIDS Commn., 1991—, Cin. Inst. Fine Arts Govt. Affairs Com., 1993-94, B'nai B'rith Nat. Coun. Legacy Devel., 1996-97. Named Outstanding Young Man, U.S. Jaycees, 1984, 98. Life fellow Am. Bar Found., Ohio Bar Found., Am. Coll. of Trust & Estate Counsel; mem. ABA, Internat. Bar Assn., Internat. Trade Bar Assn., Internat. Arbitration Assn. (comml. arbitrator 1991-95), Fed. Bar Assn. (treas. 1984, sec. 1985, v.p. 1986-87, pres. 1987-88), Ohio State Bar Assn., Cin. Bar Assn. (trustee 1988-93, v.p. 1990-91, pres. 1992-93), Cin. Acad. Leadership for Lawyers 1998—), Harvard Club of Cin. (bd. dirs. 1980-88, v.p. 1983-86, pres. 1986-87). Democrat. Avocations: music, tennis, Chinese and Japanese art. Home: 3672 Willowlea Ct # A Cincinnati OH 45208-1816 Office: 1800 Star Bank Ctr 425 Walnut St Cincinnati OH 45202-3923 *The elusive meaning of life is really at our fingertips: to create and execute the purpose of making life better for others today and after. Felicitously, that is our joy.*

HOFFHEIMER, MINETTE GOLDSMITH, community service volunteer; b. Cin., May 1, 1927; d. Philip Hess and Cecile (Crager) Goldsmith; m. Arthur Hoffheimer Jr., June 16, 1948; children: Craig R., Roger Steven, James Martin, Mark Todd. Student, Conn. Coll. for Women, New London, 1945-48. Editor, prodr. (book in braille) Lilias Yoga and You, 1974, (poems) Marjorie's Book, 1974; editor: Lilias Yoga and Your Life, 1981; contbr. short story: (anthology) Cincinnati Short Story Winners, 1985. Trustee, sec. Cin. chpt. Nat. Coun. Jewish Women, 1966-73, chmn. and developer Large Type Program of Aid to Visually Handicapped, 1964-75, chmn. Angel Ball, 1968, on Angel Ball com. 1964-69, treas. thrift shop, 1965-67, auditor, mem. budget, ways and means, survey and evaluation coms., 1971; trustee Clovernook Home and Sch. for Blind, Cin., 1980-87; founder, 1st pres. Clovernook Assocs., Cin., 1981-85; trustee, chmn. edn. com., Boca Raton (Fla.) Mus. Art, 1996—; program developer, tchr. of Yoga to Blind, Cin., 1973-87;. Named Vol. of Yr. Clovernook Home and Sch. for Blind, 1976, Woman of Yr. Cin. Enquirer, 1983. Mem. Brandeis, Nat. Braille Assn. (After 4000 hours svc. award 1971, 15 yr. cert. svc. 1986), Cin. Yoga Tchrs. Assn., Life Long Learning Soc. Fla. Atlantic U., Friends of Boca Raton Mus. Art., others.

HOFFLEIT, ELLEN DORRIT, astronomer; b. Florence, Ala., Mar. 12, 1907; d. Fred and Kate (Sanio) H. *Maternal Grandfather: a Physics Professor at the University Gymansium, Königserg, E. Prussia, Paternal Grandfather: Real Estate, Friedland, E. Prussia. Parents married 1904 and came to America. After two World Wars, lost all contact with Germany. Brother Herbert B. Hoffleit, 1905-1981, a Professor of Classics, University of California, Los Angeles. Married Norfleet Daniel and has one daughter, Margaret who graduated from the University of California, Berkeley. Married Peter Doleman, Computer Scientist. They have two children Geoffrey, born in 1984 and Danielle born in 1986. These are Dorrit's only living relatives (The Dolemans).* AB, Radcliffe Coll., 1928, MA, 1932, PhD, 1938; DSc (hon.), Smith Coll., 1984, Ctrl. Conn. State U., 1998. From research asst. to astronomer Harvard Coll. Obs., 1929-56; mathematician Ballistic Research Labs., Aberdeen Proving Ground, Md., 1943-48; tech. expert, 1948-62; lectr. Wellesley Coll., 1955-56; mem. faculty Yale U., 1956—, sr. research astronomer, 1974—; dir. Maria Mitchell Obs., Nantucket, Mass., 1957-78; mem. Hayden Planetarium Com., N.Y.C., 1975-90; editor Meteoritical Soc., 1958-68. Author: Some Firsts in Astronomical Photography, 1950, Yale Bright Star Catalogue, 4th edit., 1982, Astronomy at Yale, 1701-1968, 1992; also rsch. papers. Recipient Caroline Wilby prize Radcliffe Coll., 1938, Grad. Soc. medal, 1964, cert. appreciation War Dept., 1946, alumnae recognition award Radcliffe Coll., 1983, George van Biesbroeck award U. Ariz., 1988, Glover award Dickinson U., 1995, Maria Mitchell Women in Sci. award, 1997; asteroid Dorrit named in her honor, 1987, Symposium in hon. of 90th birthday Yale U., 1997; inducted into Conn. Women's Hall of Fame, 1998. Fellow AAAS, Meteoritical Soc.; mem. Internat. Astron. Union, Am. Astron. Soc. (Annenberg award 1993), Am. Geophys. Union, Astron. Soc. New Haven (hon.), Am. Assn. Variable Star Observers (hon.), Am. Def. Preparedness Assn., N.Y. Acad. Scis., Conn. Acad. Arts and Scis., Nantucket Maria Mitchell Assn. (hon.), Nantucket Hist. Soc., Yale Peabody Mus. Assocs., Astron. Soc. Pacific, Phi Beta Kappa, Sigma Xi, Harvard Club of So. Conn. Office: Yale U Observatory PO Box 208101 New Haven CT 06520-8101 *The guiding motto of my life has been: Work for the work's sake and it will become a part of you. Work for the sake of worldly gain and you sell your soul to the Devil: Love for research and boundless perseverance have enabled me to achieve, not all that I might have wished, but far more than I would ever have dared to expect on the basis of mediocre high school grades.*

HOFFMAN, ALAN JAY, lawyer; b. Phila., Aug. 31, 1948; s. Heinz Julius and Sylvia (Wise) H.; children: Jennifer, Lauren, Allison. BBA, Temple U., 1970; JD, Villanova U., 1973. Bar: Pa. 1973, U.S. Dist. Ct. (ea. dist.) Pa. 1973, U.S. Dist. Ct. Del. 1973, U.S. Ct. Appeals (3rd cir.) 1973, Del. 1977, U.S. Supreme Ct. 1984, D.C. 1990. Asst. U.S. atty. U.S. Dept. Justice, Wilimington, Del., 1973-78; ptnr. Dilworth, Paxson, Kalish & Kauffman, Phila., 1979-92, mem. exec. mgmt. com., 1989-90, chmn. new bus. com.,

1990-91; ptnr. Blank, Rome, Comisky and McCauley, Phila., 1992—, mem. exec. mgmt. com., 1998—, co-chmn. atty. recruiting com.; adminstrv. ptnr. in charge Blank, Rome, Comisky and McCauley, Wilmington, Del., chmn. litigation and dispute resolution dept., 1996—; lectr. Widener Del. Law Sch., Wilmington, 1974. Contbg. co-editor Villanova Law Rev., 1972-73; contbr. articles to profl. jours. Bd. dirs. Men's Club Temple Adath Israel, Merion, Pa., 1993—. Recipient Atty. Gen.'s Spl. Commendation U.S. Dept. Justice, Washington, 1977. Mem. ABA, Pa. Bar Assn., Fed. Bar Assn., Phila. Bar Assn., Del. Bar Assn., Assn. Trial Lawyers Am., Del. Trial Lawyers Assn., Pa. Trial Lawyers Assn., White Manor Country Club (pres. 1993—, 1st v.p. 1990-93, bd. dirs. 1988-90, admissions chmn. 1989—). Avocation: golf. Office: Blank Rome Comisky & McCauley One Logan Sq Philadelphia PA 19103-6998

HOFFMAN, ALAN JEROME, mathematician, educator; b. N.Y.C., May 30, 1924; s. Jesse and Muriel (Schrager) H.; m. Esther Atkins Walker, May 30, 1947 (dec. July 1988); children: Eleanor, Elizabeth Hoffman Perry; m. Elinor Klausner Hershaft, Sept. 2, 1990. AB, Columbia U., 1947, PhD, 1950; DSc (hon.), Technion U., 1986. Mem. Inst. Advanced Study, Princeton, N.J., 1950-51; mathematician Nat. Bur. Standards, Washington, 1951-56; sci. liaison officer Office Naval Research, London, 1956-57; cons. Gen. Electric Co., N.Y.C., 1957-61; research staff mem. IBM Research Ctr., Yorktown Heights, N.Y., 1961—; fellow IBM Research Ctr., 1978—; vis. prof. Technion, Haifa, Israel, 1965, Stanford U., 1980-91, Rutgers U., 1990-96, Ga. Inst. Tech., 1992-93; adj. prof. CUNY, 1965-76, Yale U., 1976-85; Phi Beta Kappa lectr., 1989-90. With U.S. Army, 1943-46, ETO, PTO. Recipient von Neumann prize Ops. Rsch. Soc. and Inst. Mgmt. Sci., 1992. Fellow N.Y. Acad. Sci., Am. Acad. Arts and Scis.; mem. NAS, Am. Math. Soc. (coun. 1982-84). Office: IBM TJ Watson Rsch Ctr PO Box 218 Yorktown Heights NY 10598-0218

HOFFMAN, ALFRED JOHN, retired mutual fund executive; b. Amarillo, Tex., Apr. 16, 1917; s. Kurt John and Mabel (Beven) H.; m. Falice Mae Pittinger, Jan. 5, 1946 (dec. Feb. 1990); children: Susan Terry, John; m. Frances Ward, Sept. 15, 1990.. J.D., U. Mo., 1942. Atty. Prudential Ins. Co. Am., 1946-50, Kansas City Fire & Marine Ins. Co., 1950-59; CEO, founder Jones & Babson, Inc., Kansas City, 1959-85, vice chmn., 1985-93; pres., dir. Babson and UMB Mut. Funds, 1959-85, dir., 1985-93. Naval aviator USN, 1942-46. Mem. ABA, Mo. Bar Assn., Western Golf Assn. (bd. dirs.), Kansas City Golf Assn. (past pres., bd. dirs.), Kansas City Golf Found. (founder, chmn., bd. dirs.), Kansas City Srs. Golf Assn. (past pres., bd. dirs.), U.S. Golf Assn. (com.), Western Golf Assn. (past dir.). Home and Office: 6701 High Dr Shawnee Mission KS 66208-2260

HOFFMAN, ALICIA CORO, retired federal executive; b. Havana, Cuba, Mar. 28, 1937; d. Daniel P. and Alicia G. (Mignagaray) Camacho; m. Carlos J. Coro, May 1958 (dec. 1983); children: Alicia Biciocchi, Carlos M. Coro, Christina Kunowsky; m. Kenneth M. Hoffman, Mar. 1997. Tchg. diploma, U. Havana, 1961; MEd, U. Md., 1972. Tchr., supr. Montgomery County Pub. Schs., Rockville, Md., 1966-71; edn. spcialist U.S. Dept. Edn., Washington, 1971-80, dir. Horace Mann Learning Ctr., 1980-85, dep. asst. sec., acting asst. sec., Office for Civil Rights, 1985-87, dir. bilingual edn., 1987-88, dir. sch. improvement, 1988-96, sr. advisor, 1996-97; ret., 1997. Bd. dirs. Montgomery Pub. TV, 1984-94. Recipient Presdl. Meritorious Rank award, U.S. Sr. Exec. Svc., 1992, Hispanic Achievement award in Edn., Hispanic Orgns., 1992, named Hispanic Woman of Yr., 1986. Mem. Nat. Asns. Cuban Am. Educators (bd. dirs. 1992-98), Nat. Assn. Cuban Am. Women (advisor 1980-88). Roman Catholic. Home: 909 Parsons Dr Madison MD 21648-1103

HOFFMAN, ALLAN SACHS, chemical engineer, educator; b. Chgo., Oct. 27, 1932; s. Saul A. and Frances E. (Sachs) H.; m. Susan Carol Freeman, July 29, 1962; children: David, Lisa. BSChemE, MIT, 1953, MSChemE, 1955, ScDChemE, 1957. Instr. chem. engring. MIT, Cambridge, 1954-56; asst. prof. MIT, 1958-60, assoc. prof., 1965-70; research engr. Calif. Research Corp., Richmond, 1960-63; asso. dir. research Amicon Corp., Cambridge, 1963-65; prof. bioengring. and chem. engring. U. Wash., Seattle, 1970—; asst. dir. Center for Bioengring., 1973-83; cons. to various govtl., indsl. and acad. orgns., 1958—; UN adviser to Mexican govt., 1973-74. Author: (with W. Burlant) Block and Graft Copolymers, 1960; author numerous articles and book chpts. on chem. engring. and biomaterials; patentee in field. Kimberly Clark fellow, 1954-55, Visking fellow, 1955-56, Fulbright fellow, 1957-58, Battelle fellow, 1970-72; Festschrift in honor of 60th birthday 8 issues of Jour. Biomaterials Sci., Polymer Edn., 1993. 94. Mem. Am. Chem. Soc., Am. Inst. Chem. Engrs., Am. Soc. for Artificial Internal Organs, Internat. Soc. Artificial Internal Organs (trustee, bd. dirs. 1987-1990), Soc. for Biomaterials (pres. 1983-84, Clemson award for biomaterial sci. lit., 1985), Controlled Release Soc. (Excellence in Guiding Grad. Rsch. award 1989), Japan Biomaterials Soc. (Biomaterials Sci. prize 1990). Home: 7508 56th Ave NE Seattle WA 98115-6320 Office: U Wash Mail Box 352255 Seattle WA 98195-2255

HOFFMAN, ANDREW JAY, writer; b. Providence, R.I., Mar. 7, 1956; s. Melvin David and Elaine (Chandler) H.; m. Judith Ellen Gourse, May 28, 1988; children: Marcus, Alicia. BA, U. Pa., 1977; MA, U. Oreg., 1981; PhD, Brown U., 1988. Copy chief US Mag., N.Y.C., 1981-82; spl. asst. to the dean of grad. sch. Brown U., Providence, 1986-90, vis. scholar, 1992—; asst. prof. Ctrl. Conn. State U., New Britain, 1990-91. Author: Inventing Mark Twain, 1997, Beehive, 1992, Twain's Heroes, Twain's Worlds, 1988. Avocations: soccer, theatre. Home and Office: 76 Wilcox Ave Pawtucket RI 02860-5739

HOFFMAN, ANN FLEISHER, labor union official, lawyer; b. Phila., June 1, 1942; d. Willis Jr. and Mary (Leffler) Fleisher; m. Charles Stuart Hoffman Jr., June 7, 1964 (div. 1979); m. Arnold Perry Rubin, Jan. 1, 1985 (div. 1993). BA, Barnard Coll., 1964; JD, U. Md., 1972. Bar: Md., 1972, N.Y., 1978. Reporter, producer Sta. WBAL-TV, Balt., 1965-68; assignment editor, producer Sta. WJZ-TV, Balt., 1968-69; assoc. Edelman, Levy and Rubenstein, Balt., 1972-77; assoc. gen. counsel Internat. Ladies' Garment Workers Union, N.Y.C., 1977-79, dir. Profl. And Clerical Employees div., 1987-91; asst. dir. legis. dept. Internat. Ladies' Garment Workers Union, Washington, 1991-94, assoc. dir., 1994-95; exec. asst. to Atty Gen. U.S. Dept. Justice, Washington, 1979-81; counsel Dist. 1 Communications Workers Am., N.Y.C., 1981-85; adminstrv. asst. to v.p. Communications Workers Am., N.Y.C. and Cranford, N.J., 1985-87; assoc. legis. dir. Union of Needletrades, Indsl. and Textile Employees, 1995-96, legis. dir., 1997—; lectr. U. Md. Sch. of Law, Balt., 1972-77; adj. faculty Cornell U. Trade Union Women's Studies Program, N.Y.C., 1979-85; trustee Botto House Am. Labor Mus., Haledon, N.J., 1986-89. Author: (with others) Legal Status of Homemakers in Maryland, 1978, Bargaining for Child Care, 1985, 2d edit., 1991. Founding mem. Women's Law Ctr., Balt., 1971-77; mem. Balt. City Charter Review Commn., 1973-76; bd. dirs. ACLU Md. Chpt., Balt., 1975-77, Campfire Girls Chesapeake Council, Balt., 1976-77; co-chair Sachs for Atty. Gen., Md., 1976-77; pub. mem. N.Y. State Banking Bd., N.Y.C., 1984-85. Mem. ABA, Coalition of Labor Union Women (treas. N.Y.C. chpt. 1981-83), Nat. Network of Women Union Lawyers (founder), Lawyers and Legal Workers for Working Women (founder), Cornell U. Adj. Faculty Fedn., Friends of Earth (bd. dirs. 1996—), Order of Coif. Home: 2810 Mckinley St NW Washington DC 20015-1216 Office: Union Needletrades Indsl & Textile Employees 888 16th St NW Washington DC 20006-4103*

HOFFMAN, ARTHUR WOLF, English language educator; b. S.I., N.Y., Mar. 13, 1921; s. William Henry and Esther Matilda (Wolf) H.; m. Joyce Faythe Lake, Aug. 13, 1949; children: Ruth, Gail, Susan. B.A., Wesleyan U., 1942; M.A. in English, Yale U., 1949, Ph.D. in English, 1951. Instr. English Yale U., New Haven, 1949-53; asst. prof. English Syracuse U., N.Y., 1953-57, assoc. prof., 1957-62, prof., 1962-91, prof. emeritus, 1992—, chmn. dept. English, 1974-79. Author: John Dryden's Imagery, 1962; co-editor: Reading Poetry, 1968; author: Congreve's Comedies, 1993. Fellow Am. Council Learned Socs., 1961-62; Syracuse U. Humanities Research grantee, summer 1980. Lutheran. Office: Syracuse U Dept English 401 Hall of Langs Syracuse NY 13244-1170

HOFFMAN, AUREN, company executive. Student, U. Calif., Berkeley. CEO BridgePath, San Francisco. Author: Internet Economy, 1996 (Best Bus. Book award 1996). Mayor City of San Mateo, 1994-96. E-mail: mail@bridgepath.com. Office: BridgePath Ste 350 562 Mission St San Francisco CA 94105

HOFFMAN, BARBARA A., state legislator; d. Sidney Wolf and Eve (Simonoff) Marks; m. Donald Edwin Hoffman, 1960; children: Alan Samuel, Michael Stuart, Carolyn Mara. B.S., Towson State U., 1960; MLA, Johns Hopkins U., 1966. Secondary sch. tchr., Balt., 1960-63; supr. student tchrs. Morgan U., Balt., 1968-73; exec. dir. Md. Dem. Com., 1979-84; mem. Md. Senate, 1983—, chair budget and tax com. Bd. dirs. United Way Ctrl Md., U. Md. Med. Sys., Balt. Mus. Art, Living Classrooms Found. Recipient numerous awards and honors. Jewish. Office: Md Senate 733 W 40th St Ste 105 Baltimore MD 21211-2112 Other: 2905 W Strathmore Ave Baltimore MD 21209-3810

HOFFMAN, BARBARA JO, health and physical education educator, athletic director; b. Dayton, Ohio, Aug. 10, 1952; d. Harold Lee and Virginia May (Dafler) H. BA, Otterbein Coll., 1974; MEd, Ashland Coll., 1987. Tchr. Harrison Hills City Schs., Hopedale, Ohio, 1974—; coach volleyball, track, basketball Cadiz (Ohio) H.S., 1974-85, athletic dir., 1996—. Key advisor Ohio FHA/HERO, Columbus, 1990-96, mentor advisor, 1992. Recipient Golden Apple Achiever award Ashland Oil, Inc., 1989, Ohio Home Econs. Tchr. of Yr. award, 1991, Vocat. Home Econs. Program award, 1990, Pacesetter award, 1992, 93, 96, 97. Mem. NEA, AAHPERD, Nat. Interscholastic Athletic Adminstrs. Assn., Ea. Ohio Interscholastic Athletic Adminstrs. Assn. Republican. Methodist. Home: 647 Kerr Ave Cadiz OH 43907-1022 Office: Harrison Ctrl HS 440 E Market St Cadiz OH 43907-1297

HOFFMAN, BARRY PAUL, lawyer; b. Phila., May 29, 1941; s. Samuel and Hilda (Cohn) H.; m. Mary Ann Schrock, May 18, 1978; children: Elizabeth Barron, Hayley Rebecca. BA, Pa. State U., 1963; JD, George Washington U., 1968. Bar: Pa. 1972, Mich. 1983. Asst. U.S. Senator Wayne Morse, Oreg., Washington; spl. agt. FBI, Washington; asst. dist. atty. Phila. Dist. Atty.'s Office; exec. v.p., gen. counsel Valassis Communications, Inc., Livonia, Mich. 1st lt. U.S. Army, 1963-65, Korea. Home: 49933 Standish Ct Plymouth MI 48170-2882 Office: Valassis Communications Inc 19975 Victor Pkwy Livonia MI 48152-7001

HOFFMAN, BRENDA JOYCE, gastroenterology educator; b. Madisonville, Ky., Sept. 4, 1957; d. John Willis and Lavada Fae (Baxter) H. BS, Murray State U., 1979; MD, U. Ky., 1983. Diplomate Am. Soc. Gastroenterology and Internal Medicine. Resident Med. U. S.C., Charleston, 1983-86, chief med. resident, 1986-87, gastroent./internal medicine fellow, 1987-89, therapeutic fellow, 1989-90, clin. instr. medicine, 1990-91, asst. prof. medicine, 1991-95, assoc. prof. medicine, 1995—, chief endosonography, clin. dir., 1993—. Contbr. articles to profl. jours. Fellow ACP, Am. Coll. Gastroenterology; mem. Am. Gastroent. Assn., Am. Soc. Gastroenterology Examiners. Avocations: soccer, sailing, reading. Office: Med U SC 171 Ashley Ave Charleston SC 29425-0001

HOFFMAN, CARL H(ENRY), lawyer; b. St. Louis, May 28, 1936; s. Carl Henry and Anna Marie (Remlinger) H.; m. Pamela L. Polk, May 8, 1971 (div. Novl 1982); children: Kurt M., Jennifer K. BS, St. Louis U., 1958; postgrad., U. Mex., Mexico City, 1958, U. Nev., 1960-61, Tex. Technol. Coll., 1961-62; JD, Washington U., St. Louis, 1966. Bar: Mo. 1966, Fla. 1969, U.S. Supreme Ct. 1970; cert. civil trial adv. Nat. Bd. Trial Advocacy. Pilot Eastern Airlines, Inc., Miami, Fla.; assoc. Spencer & Taylor, Miami, Fla., 1969-70; pvt. practice, Miami, 1970-80; ptnr. Hoffman & Hertzig, P.A., Coral Gables, Fla., 1980—. Capt. USAF, 1958-63. Mem. ABA, ATLA, Fla. Bar (cert. civil trial lawyer, cert. bus. litigation lawyer, civil procedure rules com., chmn. aviation law com. 1997-98), Fla. Acad. Trial Lawyers, Am. Jurisprudence Soc., Greater Miami C. of C. (trustee). Office: Hoffman & Hertzig PA 241 Sevilla Ave Ste 900 Coral Gables FL 33134-6600

HOFFMAN, CHARLES FENNO, III, architect; b. Greenwich, Conn., May 28, 1958; s. Harrison Baldwin Wright and Louise Elkins (Sinkler) H.; m. Pia Christina Ossorio, Dec. 27, 1980; children: Wilhelmina C. L., Frederic W. S., Henry F., C. Fenno IV. BA in Environ. Design, U. Pa., 1983; MArch, U. Colo., 1986. Designer Fenno Hoffman & Assocs., Boulder, Colo., 1983—; pvt. practice designer Boulder, 1985; assoc. William Zmistowski Assoc. Architects, 1987—, Pellecchia-Olson Architects, Boulder, 1989—; prin. Fenno Hoffman Architects PC, Boulder, Colo., 1991—; cons. Summit Habitats, Inc., 1984—; design cons. The Denver Partnership, 1985, Downtown Denver, Inc., 1985; guest critic U. Colo., 1990—, guest lectr., 1991-92, 94, 95, 96, 97, design instr., 1995—; comml. cons. and design, comm. and software facilities, shopping malls, large scale, mixed use devel., urban renewal projects, 1997—. Prin. works include Ca'Venier Mus. for Venice Bienalle, 1985, Cleveland Pl. Connection, Denver, 1985 (1st prize 1985), hist. renovated house Boulder, 1986, 3 Gates 3 Squares, Denver, 1986, Geneva Ave. House, 1992, Jarrow Sch. master plan, 1994; numerous residential and multi-family projects, 1991—, Northeast Classroom, 1995, US Navy and Marine Corps. Facilities Assessments, 1996; author: Urban Transit Facility, A Monorail for Downtown Denver, 1985. Bd. dirs. Jarrow Sch. Mem. Am. Inst. Architects, Architects & Planners ofBoulder. Democrat. Episcopalian. Avocation: drawing, skiing, bicycling, computers. Office: 505 Geneva Ave Boulder CO 80302-7139

HOFFMAN, CHRISTIAN MATTHEW, lawyer; b. N.Y.C., Apr. 17, 1944; s. Christian Matthew and Nora Frances (Mulcahy) H.; m. Donna Nealon, Aug. 5, 1967; children: Kristen Anne, Jennifer Cara. BA, Boston Coll., 1966; JD, Harvard U., 1969. Bar: Mass. 1969, U.S. Dist. Ct. Mass. 1972, U.S. Ct. Appeals 1973, U.S. Claims Ct. 1984, U.S. Supreme Ct. 1993. Assoc. Foley, Hoag & Eliot, LLP, Boston, 1969-73, ptnr., 1974—. Mem. allocations coordinating com. United Way of Mass. Bay, 1980-86, policy rev. com., 1984-86. Mem. Harvard Club, Brae Burn Club (Newton, Mass.). Roman Catholic. Home: 17 Cliff Rd Weston MA 02493-1414 Office: Foley Hoag & Eliot LLP 1 Post Office Sq Ste 1700 Boston MA 02109-2170

HOFFMAN, CRAIG ALLAN, finance executive; b. Charleston, W.Va., Feb. 23, 1955; s. Maurice Louis and Roslyn Jean (Tesler) H.; m. Britta H. Hoffman; children: Elizabeth, Eric. BS in Fin. Ops., Syracuse U., 1977, MBA, 1978. CPA, Md. Fin. analyst Fairchild Industries, Germantown, Md., 1978-80; sr. cons. Ernst & Whinney, Balt., 1980-82; mgmt. cons. Control Data Corp., Balt., 1982-85; contr., treas. Deckel Corp., Columbia, Md., 1985-87; chief fin. officer, v.p. fin. Commerce Corp., Balt., 1987—. Avocations: chess, tennis, investments. Home: 12202 Velvet Hills Dr Owings Mills MD 21117-1227

HOFFMAN, DANIEL (GERARD), literature educator, poet; b. N.Y.C., Apr. 3, 1923; s. Daniel and Frances (Beck) H.; m. Elizabeth McFarland, May 22, 1948; children: Kate, Macfarlane. B.A., Columbia U., 1947, M.A., 1949, Ph.D., 1956. Instr. English Columbia U., 1952-56; vis. prof. Am. Lit. Faculté des Lettres, Dijon, France, 1956-57; asst. prof. to prof. English Swarthmore Coll., 1957-66; prof. English U. Pa., 1966-83, poet-in-residence, 1978-93, Felix E. Schelling prof. English lit., 1983-93, prof. emeritus, 1993—; fellow Ind. U. Sch. Letters, 1959; George Elliston lectr. poetry U. Cin., 1964; lectr. 6th Internat. Sch. Yeats Studies, Sligo, Ireland, 1965; poetry cons. Libr. of Congress, 1973-74, hon. cons. in Am. letters, 1974-77; poet-in-residence Cathedral Ch. of St. John the Divine, 1988—; vis. prof. English, King's Coll. London, 1991-92. Author: (poetry) An Armada of Thirty Whales, 1954, A Little Geste and Other Poems, 1960, The City of Satisfactions, 1963, Striking the Stones, 1968, Broken Laws, 1970, The Center of Attention, 1974, Able Was I Ere I Saw Elba, 1977, Brotherly Love, 1981, Hang-Gliding from Helicon, 1988, Middens of the Tribe, 1995; (criticism) Paul Bunyan: Last of the Frontier Demigods, 1952, The Poetry of Stephen Crane, 1957, Form and Fable in American Fiction, 1961, Barbarous Knowledge, 1967, Poe Poe Poe Poe Poe Poe Poe, 1972, Faulkner's Country Matters, 1989, Words to Create a World, 1993; editor: The Red Badge of Courage, 1957, American Poetry and Poetics, 1962, Ezra Pound and William Carlos Williams, 1983; editor, contbr.: (criticism) Harvard Guide to Contemporary American Writing, 1979. Served to 1st lt. USAAF, 1943-46. Decorated Legion of Merit; recipient U. Chgo. Folklore prize, 1949, Poetry Center Introductions prize, 1951, Yale Series of Younger Poets award, 1954, Ansley prize, 1957, Lit. award Athenaeum of Phila., 1963, 83, medal for excellence Columbia U., 1964, Nat. Inst. Arts and Letters award in poetry, 1967, meml. medal Hungarian PEN, 1980, Hazlett Meml. award for lit., 1984, Paterson Poetry prize, 1989; poetry grantee Ingram Merrill Found., 1971-72; fellow Am. Council Learned Socs., 1961-62, 66-67, NEH, 1975-76, Guggenheim Meml. Found., 1983-84. Mem. MLA, Assn. Literary Scholars and Critics, Acad. Am. Poets (chancellor 1973-97, chancellor emeritus 1997—), Authors Guild (council). Clubs: Century (N.Y.C.); Franklin Inn (Phila.). Office: Univ Pa Dept English Philadelphia PA 19104-6273

HOFFMAN, DANIEL STEVEN, lawyer, legal educator; b. N.Y.C., May 4, 1931; s. Lawrence Hoffman and Juliette (Marbes) Ostrov; m. Beverly Mae Swenson, Dec. 4, 1954; children: Lisa Hoffman Ciancio, Tracy Hoffman Cockriel, Robin Hoffman Black. BA, U. Colo., 1951; LLB, U. Denver, 1958. Bar: Colo. 1958. Assoc., then ptnr. Fugate, Mitchem, Hoffman, Denver, 1951-55; mgr. of safety City and County of Denver, 1963-65; ptnr. Kripke, Hoffman, Carrigan, Denver, 1965-70, Hoffman, McDermott, Hoffman, Denver, 1970-78; of counsel Hoffman & McDermott, Denver, 1978-84; mem. Holme Roberts & Owen, LLC, Denver, 1984-94; dean Coll. Law, U. Denver, 1978-84, dean emeritus, prof. emeritus, 1984—; ptnr. McKenna & Cuneo LLP, Denver, 1994—; bd. dirs. CLE in Colo., 1971-74; chmn., mem. Merit Screening Com. for Bankruptcy Judges, Denver, 1979-84; chmn. subcom. Dist. Atty.'s Crime Adv. Commn., Denver, 1984—; chmn. Senator Wirth's jud. nomination rev. com.; mem. Senator Campbell's jud. nomination rev. com. Contbr. chpts. to books. Mem. Rocky Mountain region Anti-Defamation League, Denver, 1985; bd. dirs. Colo. chpt. Am. Jewish Com., 1985, Legal Ctr., Denver, 1985—; mem. adv. com. Samaritan Shelter, Denver, 1985; chmn. Rocky Flats Blue Ribbon Citizens Com., Denver, 1980-83; mem. bd. visitors J. Reuben Clark Law Sch. Brigham Young U., 1986-88. With USAF, 1951-55. Recipient Am. Jewish Com. Nat. Judge Learned Hand award, 1993, Humanitarian award Rocky Mountain chpt. Anti-Defamation League, 1984, Alumni of Yr. award U. Denver Coll. Law, 1997. Fellow Am. Coll. Trial Lawyers (state chmn. 1975-76), Internat. Soc. Barristers, Colo. Bar. Found., Am. Bar Found.; mem. Colo. Bar. Assn. (pres. 1976-77, Young Lawyer of Yr. award 1965), Colo. Trial Lawyers Assn. (pres. 1961-62), Assn. Trial Lawyers Am. (nat. com. mem. 1962-63), Am. Judicature Soc. (bd. dirs. 1977-81), Order of Coif (hon.). Democrat. Jewish. Avocation: platform tennis. Office: McKenna & Cuneo LLP 370 17th St Ste 4800 Denver CO 80202-5648

HOFFMAN, DARLEANE CHRISTIAN, chemistry educator; b. Terril, Iowa, Nov. 8, 1926; d. Carl Benjamin and Elverna (Kuhlman) Christian; m. Marvin Morrison Hoffman, Dec. 26, 1951; children: Maureene R., Daryl K. BS in Chemistry, Iowa State U., 1948, PhD in Nuclear Chemistry, 1951. Chemist Oak Ridge (Tenn.) Nat. Lab., 1952-53; staff radiochemistry group Los Alamos (N.Mex.) Sci. Lab., 1953-71, assoc. leader chemistry-nuclear group, 1971-79, leader chem.-nuclear divsn., 1979-82, leader isotope and nuclear chem. divsn., 1982-84; prof. chemistry U. Calif., Berkeley, 1984-91, prof. emeritus, 1991-93, prof. grad. sch., 1993—; faculty sr. scientist Lawrence Berkeley (Calif.) Lab., 1984—; dir.'s fellow Los Alamos Nat. Lab., 1990—; dir. G.T. Seaborg Inst. for Transactinium Sci., 1991-96; panel leader, speaker Los Alamos Women in Sci., 1975, 79, 82, 97; mem. subcom. on nuclear and radiochemistry NAS-NRC, 1978-81, chmn. subcom. on nuclear and radiochemistry, 1982-84; titular mem. commn. on radiochem. and nuclear techniques Internat. Union of Pure and Applied Chem., 1983-87, sec., 1985-87, chmn., 1987-91, assoc. mem. 1991-93; organizer symposium Pacifichem Confs., 1984, 89, 95; lectr. Japan Soc. Promotion Sci., 1987; com. mem. Internat. Symposium on Nuclear and Radiochemistry, 1988; organizing com. Actinides, 1993; planning panel Workshop on Tng. Requirements for Chemists in Nuclear Medicine, Nuclear Industry, and Related Fields, 1988, radionuclide migration peer rev. com., Las Vegas, 1986-87, steering com. Advanced Steady State Neutron Source, 1986-90, steering com., panelist Workshop on Opportunities and Challenges in Rsch. with Transplutonium Elements, Washington, 1983; mem. energy rsch. adv. bd. cold fusion panel, Dept. Energy, 1989-90; mem. NAS separations subpanel of separations tech. and transmutation systems panel, 1992-94, NAS-NRC Bd. on Radioactive Waste Mgmt., 1994—. Contbr. articles to profl. jours. Sr. fellow NSF, 1964-65, Guggenheim Found. fellow, 1978-79; recipient Alumni Citation of Merit Coll. Scis. and Humanities, Iowa State U., 1978, Disting. Achievement award Iowa State U., 1986, IPRT Disting. Lectr., 1998, Berkeley citation U. Calif., 1996, U.S. Nat. Medal Sci., 1997, Leonard A. Ford Lectureship award Mankato State U., 1998, Soc. Cosmetic Chemists Frontiers Sci. award, 1998. Fellow AAAS (mem. coun. 1995-97), Am. Inst. Chemists (pres. N.Mex. chpt. 1976-78), Am. Phys. Soc.; mem. Am. Chem. Soc. (chmn. nuclear chemistry and tech. divsn. 1978-79, com. on sci. 1986-88, exec. com. divsn. nuclear chemistry and tech. 1987-90, John Dustin Clark award Ctrl. N.Mex. sect. 1976, Nuclear Chemistry award 1983, Francis P. Garvan-John M. Olin medal 1990), Am. Nuclear Soc. (co-chmn. internat. conf. Methods and Applications of Radioanalytical Chemistry 1987), Norwegian Acad. Arts and Scis., Am. Acad. Arts and Scis., U.S. Nat. Metal Sci., Sigma Xi, Phi Kappa Phi, Iota Sigma Pi (nat. hon. mem.), Pi Mu Epsilon, Sigma Delta Epsilon, Alpha Chi Sigma. Methodist. Home: 2277 Manzanita Dr Oakland CA 94611-1135 Office: Lawrence Berkeley Lab MS70A-3307 NSD Berkeley CA 94720

HOFFMAN, DAVID ALAN, lawyer; b. Balt., Jan. 3, 1947; s. Edward Joseph H. and Pauline (Narva) Jacobs; m. Marjorie Fox, Sept. 7, 1968 (div. 1978); m. Elisabeth Lawson Andrews, Sept. 27, 1980; children: Jessica, Jacob, Lily. AB summa cum laude, Princeton U., 1970; MA, Cornell U., 1974; JD magna cum laude, Harvard U., 1984. Bar: Mass. 1985, U.S. Dist. Ct. Mass. 1985, U.S. Ct. Appeals (1st cir.) 1985, U.S. Ct. Appeals (5th cir.) 1990, U.S. Supreme Ct. 1989. Instr. legal methods Harvard Law Sch., Cambridge, Mass., 1982-83; research asst. Harvard Law Sch., Cambridge, 1984; clk. 1st Cir. Ct. of Appeals, Boston, 1984-85; assoc. Hill & Barlow, Boston, 1985-92, mem., 1992—; adj. prof. law Harvard Law Sch., 1994-96, 1997—, Northeastern U., 1994-96; staff atty. Civil Liberties Union Mass., 1988-89; mem. Supreme Judicial Ct. Standing Com. on Dispute Resolution; mediator and arbitrator Mass. Office Dispute Resolution, Am. Arbitration Assn., Ctr. for Pub. Resources, Pvt. Adjudication Ctr. Co-author: Massachusetts Alternative Dispute Resolution, 1994; mem. editl. bd. Mass. Law Rev., 1987-89; contbr. articles to profl. jours. Bd. dirs. Walden Ctr. for Peace and Justice, Concord, Mass., 1987-89. Recipient Kennedy Prize for Best Thesis in English Dept., Princeton U., 1970. Mem. ABA (coun. mem., sect. individual rights and responsibilities, 1991-94, coun. mem. sect. dispute resolution), ACLU, Mass. Bar Assn. (commn. on the bicentennial the constitution 1986-88, chmn. individual rights and responsibilities sect. 1988-90), Boston Bar Assn. (chmn. ADR com. 1993-95), Nat. Lawyers Guild, Soc. Profls. in Dispute Rsolution (pres. N.E. chpt.), Soc. Profls. Dispute Resolution (pres. N.E. chpt.). Office: Hill & Barlow 100 Oliver St Boston MA 02110-2606

HOFFMAN, DAVID NATHANIEL, lawyer; b. N.Y.C., Aug. 10, 1960; s. Martin J. and Edith D. Hoffman; m. Joan Lynne Fiden, Feb. 18, 1990; children: Benjamin, Emily. JD, SUNY, Buffalo, 1986; cert. in bio-ethics, Columbia U., 1996. Bar: N.Y. 1997, U.S. Dist. Ct. (ea. dist.) N.Y. 1997, U.S. Dist. Ct. (so. dist.) N.Y. 1997. Litigation assoc. Martin, Clearwater & Bell, N.Y.C., 1986-88; assoc., then ptnr. Kanterman, Taub & Breitner, N.Y.C., 1988-94; founding ptnr. Breitner & Hoffman, N.Y.C., 1994-99, Law Offices of David N. Hoffman, P.C., N.Y.C., 1999—. Mem. Am. Soc. Law Medicine and Ethics, Nature Conservancy, Amnesty Internat., Habitat for Humanity, Assn. of Bar of City of N.Y. (legis. liaison com. on med. malpractice 1988-96, chmn. subcom. on organ donation 1996—, com. on bioethics). Avocations: sailing, SCUBA diving, woodworking, bicycling, philosophy. Office: 233 E 69th St New York NY 10021-5414

HOFFMAN, DONALD DAVID, cognitive and computer science educator; b. San Antonio, Dec. 29, 1955; s. David Pollock and Loretta Virginia (Shoemaker) H.; m. Geralyn Mary Souza, Dec. 13, 1986; 1 child from previous marriage, Melissa Louise. BA, UCLA, 1978; PhD, MIT, 1983. MTS and project engr. Hughes Aircraft Co., El Segundo, Calif., 1978-83; rsch. scientist MIT Artificial Intelligence Lab, Cambridge, Mass., 1983; asst. prof. U. Calif., Irvine, 1983-86, assoc. prof., 1986-90, prof., 1990-97; cons. Fairchild Lab. for Artificial Intelligence, Palo Alto, Calif., 1984; panelist MIT Corp. vis. com., Cambridge, 1985, NSF, Washington, 1988; conf. host IEEE Conf. on Visual Motion, Irvine, 1989; conf. host Office of Naval Rsch. Conf. on Vision, Laguna Beach, Calif., 1992; vis. prof. Zentrum für Interdisziplinäre Forschung, Bielefeld, Germany, 1995-96. Author: Visual Intelligence, 1998; co-author: Observer Mechanics, 1989; mem. editl. bd. Cognition, 1991—, Psychol. Rev., 1995-96; contbr. articles to profl. jours. Vol. tchr. Turtle Rock Elem. Sch., Irvine, 1988-90. Recipient Distinguished

Scientific award, Am. Psychol. Assn., 1989, Troland Rsch. award U.S. Nat. Acad. Scis., 1994; grantee NSF, 1984, 87. Mem. Am. Psychol. Soc. Avocations: running, swimming, racket sports, ice skating. Office: U Calif Dept Cognitive Sci Irvine CA 92697

HOFFMAN, DONALD M., lawyer; b. Los Angeles, Aug. 27, 1935; s. Henry Maurice and Viola Gertrude (Rothe) H. B.S., UCLA, 1957, LL.B., 1960. Bar: Calif. 1961. Pvt. practice L.A. County, 1961—; ptnr. firm Greenwald, Hoffman, Meyer & Montes, 1964—. Pres. L.A. Estate Planning Council. Served to 2d lt. U.S. Army. Mem. Am., Los Angeles County bar assns., Phi Alpha Delta, Beta Gamma Sigma. Club: Jonathan. Home: 3520 St Elizabeth Rd Glendale CA 91206-1226 Office: 500 N Brand Blvd Ste 920 Glendale CA 91203-1923

HOFFMAN, DONNA COY, learning disabilities educator; b. Cin., Apr. 18, 1940; d. Clifford Donovan and Dorothy (Roessler) Coy; m. Donald Edward Hoffman, June 17, 1961; children: David Clifford, Dawn Susan Hoffman Osha. BS in Edn., Miami U., Oxford, Ohio, 1961; MEd, Xavier U., 1989. Cert. profl. tchr., Ohio, N.J. English tchr. Oak Hills Local Sch. Dist., Cin., 1961-62; vis. tchr. Westfield (N.J.) Sch. Dist., 1974-77; teaching staff Fair Oaks Hosp., Summit, N.J., 1974-77; learning disabilities resource tchr. Finneytown Local Sch. Dist., Cin., 1979—; staff devel. com. Finneytown Schs., Cin., 1988-91; in-svc. com. Hamilton County Schs., Cin., 1988, 90. Deacon, chmn. Presbyn. Ch. of Wyoming, Cin., 1989-92; pres. Jr. Woman's Club Western Cin., 1966; founder, advisor Oak Hills Jr. Woman's Club, Cin., 1967. Named Outstanding Educator, Spl. Edn. Regional Resource Ctr. S.W. Ohio, 1988, Coun. for Econ. Edn., 1993. Mem. ASCD, Coun. for Exceptional Children (workshop speaker nat. meeting 1996), Orton Dyslexia Soc., Assn. on Handicapped Student Svcs. Programs in Postsecondary Edn., Transition and Comm. Consortium on Learning Disabilities (Ohio planning com. 1990-92). Republican. Avocations: music, needlework, travel. Office: Finneytown High Sch 8916 Fontainebleau Ter Cincinnati OH 45231-4898

HOFFMAN, DUSTIN LEE, actor; b. L.A., Aug. 8, 1937; s. Harry Hoffman; m. Anne Byrne, May 4, 1969 (div.); children: Karina, Jenna; m. Lisa Gottsegen, Oct. 21, 1980; children: Jacob, Rebecca, Max, Alexandra. Student, Santa Monica City Coll., Pasadena Playhouse. Stage debut: Sarah Lawrence Coll. prodn. of Yes Is For a Very Young Man; Broadway debut: A Cook for Mr. General, 1961; appeared in Endgame, The Quare Fellow, In The Jungle Of Cities, A Country Scandal, The Dumbwaiter, The Room, Waiting for Godot, Picnic on the Battlefield, Dirty Hands, The Cocktail Party, All Theatre Company of Boston, Three Men on A Horse, 1964, Harry, Noon and Night, 1965, The Journey of the Fifth Horse (Obie award 1966) 1966, Fragments, 1966, Eh? (Drama desk award 1967, Verna Rice award 1967, Thetre World award 1967), 1966, Jimmy Shine, 1968, Death of a Salesman, 1984, The Merchant of Venice, 1989; recorded: Death of a Salesman on Caedmon Records (Drama Desk award 1984); appeared in films: The Tiger Makes Out, 1967, The Graduate, 1967 (Acad. award nomination), Midnight Cowboy, 1969 (Acad. award nomination), John and Mary, 1969, Madigan's Millions, 1970, Little Big Man, 1970, Who Is Harry Kellerman and Why Is He Saying Those Terrible Things About Me?, 1971, Straw Dogs, 1971, Alfredo, Alfredo, 1973, Papillion, 1973, Lenny, 1974 (Acad. award nomination), All the President's Men, 1976, Marathon Man, 1976, Straight Time, 1978, Agatha, 1979, Kramer vs. Kramer, 1979, (Academy award for Best Actor, N.Y. Film Critics award), Tootsie, 1982, (Acad. award nomination, Golden Globe award), Ishtar, 1987, Rainman, 1988 (Academy Award for Best Actor), Family Business, 1990, Dick Tracy, 1990, Billy Bathgate, 1991, Hook, 1991, Hero, 1992, Outbreak, 1995, Sleepers, 1996, American Buffalo, 1996, Sphere, 1997, Mad City, 1997, Wag the Dog, 1998, Cosm, 1999, Joan of Arc, 1999; starred in TV prodn. of Death of a Salesman, 1985 (Emmy award nomination 1986). Recipient Golden Globe award, 1989; decorated officer Order of Arts and Letters (France), 1995, Golden Globe lifetime achievement award, 1997. Office: Punch Productions 1926 Broadway Ste 305 New York NY 10023-6915*

HOFFMAN, E. LESLIE, lawyer; b. Charleston, W. Va., Aug. 8, 1947; s. E. Leslie and Mary Jane (Lively) H.; m. Susan Sandy, Sept. 9, 1967 (div. 1983); children: Melissa North, Marc Clayton. BA Polit. Sci., West Va. U., 1969, JD, 1972. Bar: W.Va. 1972, U.S. Dist. Ct. (no. and so. dists.) W.Va. 1972, U.S. Ct. Appeals (4th crct.) 1973, U.S. Ct. Appeals (9th crct.) 1984. Asst. atty. gen. State W. Va., Charleston, 1972-76; asst. U.S. Atty. so. dist. W. Va., Charleston, 1976-81; asst. dir. atty. gen's. advocacy inst. U.S. Dept. Justice, Washington, 1982, trial atty. fraud sect., 1983-86; dep. sect. chief fraud sect. U.S Dept. Justice, Washington, 1987-88; counsel Pettit & Martin, Washington, 1988-90, ptnr., 1991-95; ptnr. Piper & Marbury, Washington, 1995—. Mem. ABA. Democrat. Episcopalian. Office: Piper & Marbury 1200 19th St NW Fl 7 Washington DC 20036-2430*

HOFFMAN, ELIZABETH PARKINSON, librarian; b. Pitts., Mar. 23, 1931; d. William Sterrett P. and Elizabeth Helen Hill; m. James William Hoffman, Apr. 2, 1944; childre; W. Sterrett, Elizabeth, Charles, Lloyd. BA, Dickinson Coll., 1942; MLS, Drexel U., 1941. Libr. coord. Haverford (Pa.) Twp. Sch. Dist., 1958-65; dir. divsn. libr. Pa. Dept. Edn., Harrisburg, 1965-75; chair dept. libr. sci. Villanova (Pa.) U., 1975-78; dir. Havertown (Pa.) Twp. Free Libr., 1979-91; cons. in field. Author 5 books. 8Mem.Llamerch Women's Club. Republican. Presbyterian. Avocations: travel, writing, needle work. Home: 805 Beechwood Rd Havertown PA 19083

HOFFMAN, ESTHER, pianist, educator; b. Toronto, Ont., Can., Sept. 30, 1922; d. Sidney and Annie (Wiseman) H.; m. Gerald Wexler, July 26, 1968. Grad. assoc. Toronto Conservatory Music, U. Toronto, 1939; diploma, Hebrew Union Coll., 1952. Faculty Toronto Conservatory of Music, 1941-44; piano faculty Mannes Coll., N.Y.C., 1962—. Recitalist Can. Broadcasting Corp.; recital and orch. appearances in Can. and the U.S. Mem. Music Tchrs. Nat. Assn. (cert.), Associated Music Tchrs. League (mem. exec. bd.), Piano Tchrs. Congress. Home: 124 W 79th St New York NY 10024-6446

HOFFMAN, FRED L., human resources professional; b. Wauseon, Ohio, Mar. 13, 1953; s. Lowell Max and Annabell (Whitmire) H.; m. Diane Patricia Pope, Sept. 19, 1975; Brandon C. BSBA, Bowling Green U., 1975. Asst. mgr. indsl. rels. Colonial Press div. Sheller-Globe Corp., Clinton, Mass., 1975-76; dir. human resources Leece-Neville div. Sheller-Globe Corp., Gainesville, Ga., 1976-88; v.p. human resources, staff ops. Golder Assocs., Atlanta, 1988—; bd. dirs. Hoffman-Rettig Foods, Inc., Maquoketa, Iowa, Golder Assocs. Corp., Atlanta. Guest columnist BG News, 1971-75. State dir. pub. rels. Ohio League of Coll. Reps., Columbus, 1974, 75; lt. col. aide-de-camp gov.'s staff Gov. Joe Frank Harris, Atlanta, 1983-91. Recipient disting. svc. award Bowling Green State U., 1975. Mem. Atlanta C. of C., Soc. Human Resources Mgmt., Antaen Soc. (pres. 1974-75), Pres.'s Club Bowling Green State U., Omicron Delta Kappa, Phi Delta Theta. Home: 235 Parian Run Duluth GA 30097-2418 Office: Golder Assocs Corp 3730 Chamblee Tucker Rd Atlanta GA 30341-4414

HOFFMAN, GENE D., food company executive, consultant; b. East St. Louis, Ill., July 29, 1927; s. Edmund H. and Bee (Hood) H.; m. Nancy P. Claney, Oct. 27, 1951; children: Kim Elizabeth, Keith Murdock. B.J. in Advt, U. Mo., 1948. Asst. advt. mgr. Montgomery Ward Co., 1948; copywriter, asst. mgr. advt. promotion Chgo. Tribune, 1949-50; mgr. promotion Phila. Bull., 1951-56; with The Kroger Co., 1956-77, gen. mgr. St. Louis div., 1956-61; dir. mktg. processed foods div., Cin., 1961-63, v.p., gen. mgr., 1964-66; corp. v.p. St. Louis, 1966, v.p. food mfg. divs., 1966-69; pres. Kroger Food Processing Co., 1969-72, Kroger Brands Co., 1972-74; sr. corp. v.p. parent co., 1974-75, corp. pres., bd. dirs. parent co., 1975-77; with Super Valu Stores, Inc., Mpls., 1977-88; pres. Super Valu Wholesale Food Cos., 1977-87, chmn., 1985-88; sr. corp. v.p. Super Valu Stores Inc.; chmn., chief exec. officer Food Giant, Inc.; pres., chief exec. officer Corp. Strategies Internat., Mpls., 1987—; pres. Mktg. Assocs., Inc., Mpls., 1987—; pres., chief exec. officer LeaderShape, Inc., Champaign, Ill., 1987—; chmn., bd. dirs. Quality Containers Internat., Inc., 1989—; bd. dirs. Novate Enterprise, Inc., Americana Mag., Rural Ventures, Inc., Lewis Grocer Co., Vital Resources, Inc., WestCoast Grocery Co., Paragon Trade Brands, Inc. Chmn. Leader Shape Inst.; chmn., bd. govs. ATO Found. Served with AC USNR, 1945-46. Mem. Am. Mgmt. Assn., Food Mktg. Inst., Greater Cin. C. of C. (v.p., dir.), AIM, Alpha Delta Sigma, Alpha Tau Omega. Episcopalian. Clubs: Interlachen Country (Mpls.), Comml., Cin., Hyde Park Golf and Country, Queen City, Bankers (Cin.); Tonka Racquets, Camargo Racquet. Office: Corp Strategies Internat 2859 Gale Rd Wayzata MN 55391-2623

HOFFMAN, GEORGE ALAN, consulting company executive; b. Albany, N.Y., May 16, 1937; s. Irving Marshall and Margaret (Coyne) H.; m. Kim Thi Nguyen, Oct. 10, 1971; children: Caroline, Christine. AB, U. Calif., Berkeley, 1980, MBA, 1982. Mgmt. analyst Am. Can Co., N.Y.C., 1966-69; cons. Vietnamese Air Force, Bien Hoa, Vietnam, 1970-74, Puslitbang, Jakarta, Indonesia, 1974-75; v.p. Union Bank, Oakland, Calif., 1987—. Author: Indonesian Production-sharing Oil Contracts, 1982, The Guns of T.E. Lawrence, 1996. Mem. Mensa. Club: Commonwealth (San Francisco). Avocation: mountaineering. Office: 460 Hegenberger Rd Oakland CA 94621-1404

HOFFMAN, GLENN JERRALD, agricultural engineering educator, consultant; b. Delaware, Ohio, Oct. 16, 1939; s. Herbert L. and Wilma (Lavender) H.; m. Maria Luisa Hunter; children: Kimberly, Karen, Sheryl. BS in agrl. engring., Ohio State U., 1963, MS, 1963; PhD, N.C. State U., 1967. Rsch. agrl. engr. USDA Rsch. Svc., Riverside, Calif., 1966-84; rsch. leader USDA Rsch. Svc., Fresno, Calif., 1984-89; dept. head U. Nebr., Lincoln, 1989—; consultant World Bank, Pakistan, 1996, Turkey, 1997, Assn. Regional Consortia, Argentina, 1997, China Agrl. Union, 1998. Lead editor: (monograph) Management of Farm Irrigation Systems, 1990; patentee in field; contbr. 168 articles to profl. jours.; developer models for predicting crop salt tolerance and determining leaching requirement for controlling soil salinity. Disting. alumnus Ohio State U., 1995. Fellow Am. Soc. Agrl. Engrs. (pres.'s citation 1994); mem. Internat. Com. on Irrigation and Drainage, Soil Sci. Soc. Am., Am. Soc. for Engring. Edn. Avocations: bridge, golf. Office: U Nebr 223 L W Chase Hall Lincoln NE 68583

HOFFMAN, GLORIA LEVY, communications executive; b. Norfolk, Va., Feb. 8, 1933; d. Maxwell Lewis and Jessie (Mashbitz) Levy; m. Frank Katz Hoffman (dec.); children: Daniel L., L. Stephen, Victoria Anne, Jonathan M. (dec.). BA in Speech and Radio, U. Wis., 1954. Pres. Creative Concepts in Comm., Ltd., Kansas City, Mo., 1984—, Peoplehood Products, Kansas City, 1987—. Author: I Belong to Me!: A Trip Thru Our Own Feelings, 1984, rev. edit., 1989, (catalog) Peoplehood-by-Mail, 1990; creator: The Super Sluggers, 1989, Captain Slug Slugs Drugs, 1990, Clown Around With Clancy, 1991, Sammy Slugger Slugs Drugs, 1993, rev. edit., 1993, I Slug Drugs apparel and buttons, 1993, Project Play-It-SAFE, 1994; creator, developer The Toddle Tent, 1996. Promotional and pub. rels. dir. Menorah Med. Ctr., Trans-Menorahs, Brandeis Books Drives; vol. Nelson Gallery Art, Kansas City Art Inst., Young Woman's Philharm., Children's Mercy Hosp. Recipient Commemorative Medal of Honor Hallmark, 1987; honored by Health Net Sr. Excel in its Sta. KMBZ-TV Amazing People series, 1999. Republican. Jewish. Home and Office: 212 E 130th Ter Kansas City MO 64145-1376

HOFFMAN, HEINZ JOSEPH, aerospace scientist, management consultant; b. Schifferstadt, Pfalz, Germany, Oct. 27, 1923; came to U.S., 1949; s. Theobald and Hermine (Kurz) H.; m. Irene C. Wickhorst, June 4, 1949 (dec. Jan. 1994); children: Paul, Kristina, Carla. DSc in Engring., Naval Acad. of Engring., Kiel, Germany, 1944; MS in Medicine, U. Mainz, Germany, 1949; EdD in Psychology, U. Sarasota, Fla., 1975. Cert. adult edn. educator N.Y. State Edn. Dept. Student intern South Nassau Cmty. Hosp., Rockville Ctr., N.Y., 1949-50; chief engr. Empire State Labs., Bellmore, N.Y., 1951-54; dir. value engring. Reeves Instrument Co., Garden City, N.Y., 1955-68; indsl. mgmt. cons. Internat. Mgmt. Consultants, Sarasota, 1969—; mem. Internat. Adv. Panel Shanghai Jiao Tong U., China; spkr. 1st Internat. Creative Study Conf., China; prin. spkr. Internat. Marine Engring. Conf., Internat. Creativ-Zentrum, Basel, Switzerland; prof. dept. edn. U. Sarasota, 1976, asst. to pres., founder univ. br. in Athens, Greece; tchr. Little Theater Dramatics, Massapequa, N.Y.; lectr., presenter numerous confs. in field. Author: (books) (in English) Cinematography: How to Produce Good Home Movies, 1959, Early Warning Radar Systems in Defense, 1959, High Power Resolution in Tracking Stars of the 7th Magnitude, 1960, Lunar Module Mission Simulator, Mechanical Moon Surface Support, 1961, Value Engineering for Quality and Profit, 1961, Davy Crockett, The First Atomic Infantry Rocket, 1963, Implementing the Teaching of Value Analysis, 1975, Applied Imagination in Education, 1975, Value Analysis for Staying Competetive and Improving Profits, 1985, The Germans of Today, The Offspring of Martin Luther, Karl Marx, Kaiser Wilhelm and Adolf Hitler, 1996, (in German) Wertanalyse, Grundlage der Rationalisierung, 1976, Wertanalyse, Ein Weg Zur Erschliesung Neuer Rationalisierungsquellen, 1978, Kreativitaetstechniken Fuer Manager, 1981, Brainstorming, Management Enzyklopaedie, 1982, Konstruktive Non-Konformitaet, Management Enzyklpaedie, 1983, Psychologie Der Wertanalyse, Management Enzyklopaedie, 1983, Kreativitaet, Die Chance Fuer Unsere Zukunhft, 1984, Kreativitaetstechniken Fuer Manager, 1986, Der Vitamin-Report, Gesundheit, Fittness Und Vitalitaet, 1990, Schach Der MS, Neue Strategie Gegen Multiple Sklerose, 1991, Wertanalyse, Die Westliche Antwort Auf Kaizen, 1994, Kreativitaet, Die Herausforderung An Geist Und Kompetenz, Handbuch, 1996, others; patentee in field; dir., prodr. TV films, plays for profl. and amateur theatre. Active Super Task Force to attract German firms, Greater Tampa Bay (Fla.) area. Mem. Soc. Am. Value Engrs., German Inst. Value Engring. (chmn. 1978-88). Achievements include development of REAC 500 Analog Computer used in design of Lunar Exc. Module for Apollo Space Program, Inertial Reference and Guidance Systems for various missile projects including Regulus and Regulus II; state of the art work for Sidewinder missile program, downrange tracking radar for Cape Canaveral, Verlort very long tracking radar, Davy Crockett, the first atomic warhead rocket, numerous star tracking systems for the military, Minitrack Calibration System, state of the art resolver used in many guidance systems, star tracker system for Mars program; contributions in medical field include participation in design of first artificial heart and first human centrifuge for testing all physiological parameters for astronauts and pilots. Home: 577 S Spoonbill Dr Sarasota FL 34236-1819

HOFFMAN, HOWARD STANLEY, experimental psychologist, educator; b. N.Y.C., May 23, 1925; s. Melvin Leo and Henrietta (Rosenthal) H.; m. Alice Marie Cruikshank, June 7, 1961; children: Randall, Gwendolyn, Russell, Franklin, Daniel, Martha. BA, New Sch. for Social Research, N.Y.C., 1952; MA, Bklyn. Coll., 1953; PhD, U. Conn., 1957. Rsch. fellow in auditory perception U. Conn., 1953-56, instr. dept. stats., 1956-57; asst. to prof. psychology Pa. State U., 1957-70; prof. psychology Bryn Mawr Coll., 1970-92, prof. emeritus, 1992—. Bd. editors: Jour. Exptl. Analysis Behavior, 1966-69, Jour. Exptl. Psychology, Animal Behavior Processes, 1974-84; reviewer: Jour. Comparative and Physiol. Psychology. Served with AUS, 1943-45. Fellow AAAS, Am. Psychol. Assn., Am. Psychol. Soc.; mem. Eastern Psychol. Assn., AAUP, Sigma Xi, Phi Kappa Phi, Psi Chi. Home: 3300 Darby Rd Apt 3211 Haverford PA 19041-1070 Office: Bryn Mawr Coll Dept Psychology Bryn Mawr PA 19010

HOFFMAN, IRA ELIOT, lawyer; b. Highland Park, Mich., Jan. 3, 1952; s. Maxwell Mordecai and Leah (Silverman) H.; m. Ruth Felsen, Aug. 19, 1975 (div. 1981); 1 child, Daniel Gideon; m. Meredith Lippman, Dec. 17, 1988; 1 child, Lauren Samantha. BA, U. Mich., 1973; MSc in Econs., London Sch. Econs., 1975; JD cum laude, U. Miami, 1983. Bar: Fla. 1983, U.S. Ct. Appeals (D.C. cir.) 1984, D.C. 1985, Md. 1991, U.S. Ct. Appeals (10th cir., 4th cir) 1992, U.S. Dist. Ct. (D.C. dist.) 1992, U.S. Dist. Ct. Md., 1992, U.S. Ct. Appeals (fed. cir.) 1994, U.S. Ct. Fed. Claims, 1998. Tchr. London Sch. Econs., 1975-77; rsch. assoc. Shiloah Ctr. Mid. East Studies, Tel Aviv U., 1978-80; staff atty. FTC, Washington, 1983; law clk. U.S. Ct. Appeals (D.C. cir.), Washington, 1983-84; assoc. Fried, Frank, Harris, Shriver & Jacobson, Washington, 1984-86, 87-88; counsel Ministry of Def. Mission to the U.S., Govt. of Israel, N.Y.C., 1986-87; counsel to vice chmn. U.S. Internat. Trade Commn., Washington, 1988-89; assoc. Howrey & Simon, Washington, 1989-91; pres. Israel Housing Investors, Inc., Rockville, Md., 1990-92; v.p. H.P.F. Prefab Constrn., Ltd., Givatayim, Israel, 1991-92; of counsel Savage & Schwartzman, Balt., 1992-94, McAleese & Assocs., P.C., McLean, Va., 1995-98, Grayson and Assocs. P.C., McLean, 1998—; pres. Smart Planet, LLC, Rockville, Md., 1998—. Translator: The Emergence of Pan-Arabism in Egypt, 1980; contbr. articles to profl. jours. Spl. counsel Nat. Sudden Infant Death Syndrome Found., Landover, Md., 1984-86; hon. counsel to chmn. Nat. Holocaust Meml. Coun., Washington, 1985. Mem. ABA. Jewish. Avocations: travel, sports, history. E-mail: hoffmani@erols.com.

HOFFMAN, IRWIN, orchestra conductor; b. N.Y.C., Nov. 26, 1924; s. Harry and Augusta (Cohen) H.; m. Esther Glazer, Feb. 21, 1946 (div. 1990); children: Joel H., Gary, Toby, Deborah; m. Maria Lourdes Lobo, 1990. Student, Juilliard Sch. Music, 1942-43, 45-48; MusD (hon.), U. Tampa, 1984. dir. music Orquesta Sinfonica de Chile, 1994-97. Condr. Phila. Orch. at Robin Hood Dell, summer 1942, Bronx (N.Y.) Symphony, 1948-52, Yonkers (N.Y.) Philharm., 1950-52, Westchester (N.Y.) Chamber Orch., 1950-52, for Martha Graham Dance Co., 1949-50; condr., mus. dir. Vancouver (B.C., Can.) Symphony Orch., 1952-64; assoc. condr. Chgo. Symphony Orch., 1964-68, acting music dir., 1968-69, condr., 1969-70, prin. condr. Grant Park, Chgo., 1965-73; permanent condr. Belgian Radio and TV Symphony Orch., 1973-76; music dir. Fla. Orch., 1968-87, music dir. laureate, 1987-95; music dir. Flagstaff (Ariz.) Festival of Arts, 1983-95; condr. St. Louis Little Symphony, summers 1959-64, lectr., condr., U. B.C., State Coll. Wash., 1958, guest condr. Toronto, Vancouver, Chgo., Israel Philharm., 1960, Dallas Symphony, 1962, Brazil, 1962, 78, St. Louis Symphony Orch., 1963, Miami and Tampa symphonies, 1967, protege of Serge Koussevitzky, Tanglewood, 1948-50, guest condr. BBC Symphony, Manchester, Eng., 1968, Brussels (Belgium), Radio Orch., 1968, Strasbourg (France) Radio Orch., 1968, BBC Welsh, 1969-82, BBC Scottish, 1971-82, BBC No. Orch., 1971-82, Orch. Nat., France, 1970, Orch. Philharmonique, France, 1970, Orch. Nat., Peru, 1970, Philharmonia Orch., Eng., 1971, Chgo., Vancouver symphonies, 1971, N.J., Denver, Costa Rica, 1977-78, Chgo., 1977, Montevideo (Uruguay) Nat., 1979, Buffalo symphonies, 1980-81, New Orleans Philharm., 1981, Winnipeg Symphony, 1985, Pitts. Symphony, 1986, Colorado Springs Symphony, 1989, Kitchener-Waterloo Symphony, 1989, music dir. Nat. Symphony Orch. of Costa Rica, 1987—; guest condr. Israel Chamber Orch., 1990, Jalapa Symphony, Mex., 1990, Phoenix Symphony, 1991, UNAM Mex., 1991, Orch. Symphonique Francaise, 1991, Orquesta Sinfonica, Caracas, 1992, 93, 94, Orquesta Sinfonica De Chile, 1992, 93, 94, music dir. 1995-97; guest condr. Orquesta Sinfonica de San Luis, Argentina, 1994, Orquesta de Sodre, Montevideo, Uruguay, 1994, Orquesta de Concepcion, Chile, 1995, Orquesta Sinfonica de Buenos Aires, 1996, 98, Taipei Symphony Orch., 1997, 98, 99, Orquesta Sinfonica de Bogotá, 1998, 99, Fla. Orch., 1999, Nat. Symphony Guatemala, 1998, Orquestra Sintonica Panama, 1999; composer two string quartets, violin sonata, Orquesta Filarmónica of Bogotá, Columbia, 1997, 98, others; collector autography music manuscripts, mus. memorablia. Served with AUS, 1943-45. Juilliard fellow, 1948. Home and Office: Orquesta Sinfonica Nacional, PO Box 1035-1000, San José Costa Rica

HOFFMAN, JAMES PAUL, lawyer, hypnotist; b. Waterloo, Iowa, Sept. 7, 1943; s. James A. and Luella M. (Prokosch) H.; 1 child, Tiffany K. B.A., U. No. Iowa, 1965, J.D. U. Iowa, 1967. Bar: Iowa 1967, U.S. Dist. Ct. (no. dist.) Iowa 1981, U.S. Dist. Ct. (so. dist.) Iowa 1968, U.S. Dist. Ct. (so. dist.) Ill, U.S. Tax Ct. 1971, U.S. Ct. Appeals (8th cir.) 1970, U.S. Supreme Ct. 1974. Sr. mem. James P. Hoffman, Law Offices, Keokuk, Iowa, 1967—; chmn. bd. Iowa Inst. Hypnosis. Fellow Am. Inst. Hypnosis; mem. ABA, Iowa Bar Assn., Lee County Bar Assn., Assn. Trial Lawyers Am., Ill. Trial Lawyers Assn., Iowa Trial Lawyers Assn. Democrat. Roman Catholic. Author: The Iowa Trial Lawyers and the Use of Hypnosis, 1980. Home and Office: PO Box 1087 Middle Rd Keokuk IA 52632-1087

HOFFMAN, JAMES R., bishop; b. Fremont, Ohio, June 12, 1932. Ed., Our Lady of Lake Minor Sem., Wawasee, Ind., St. Meinrad Coll., Mt. St. Mary Sem., Norwood, Ohio, Cath. U. Am. Ordained priest Roman Cath. Ch., 1957; ordained titular bishop of Italica and aux. bishop of Toledo, 1978; apptd. bishop of Toledo Roman Cath. Ch., Toledo, 1980. Address: Bishops Residence PO Box 985 Toledo OH 43697-0985*

HOFFMAN, JERRY IRWIN, dental educator; b. Chgo., Nov. 20, 1935; s. Irwin and Luba (Fox) H.; m. Sharon Lynn Seaman, Aug. 25, 1963; children: Steven Abram, Rachel Irene. Student, DePaul U., 1953-56; BS in Biology and Chemistry, Roosevelt U., 1956; DDS, Loyola U., Chgo., 1960; M of Health Care Adminstrn., Baylor U., 1972. Certificate, General Practice Residency, U.S. Army, 1978. Commd. officer U.S. Army, 1960 (served to 1962, returned 1964), advanced through grades to col., 1978; hdqrs. rep. local dental tng. confs. Europe U.S. Army, Garmisch, Fed. Republic Germany, 1965-67; cons. to Comdg. Gen. U.S. Army Med. Research and Devel. Command, Washington, 1972-76; cons. Office of Surgeon Gen. U.S. Army, Washington, 1972-76, liaison rep. to Nat. Adv. Council and Oral Biology and Medicine Study Sessions of the Nat. Inst. Dental Research and NIH, 1973-76; resident in Gen. Practice Residency U.S. Army, 1976-78; comdg. officer U.S. Army Dental Activity, Fort Monmouth, N.J., 1979-82; ret., 1982; pvt. practice dentistry Chgo., 1962-64; assoc. prof. operative dentistry Loyola U. Sch. Dentistry, Maywood, Ill., 1982-93, dir. gen. practice residency, 1982-85, coordinator extramural dental resources, 1983-85, assoc. dean for clin. affairs, 1985-93; dir. sci. programs Chgo. Dental Soc., 1993—; staff dentist Silas B. Hayes Army Hosp., Fort Ord, Calif., 1976-79, Patterson Army Hosp., Ft. Monmouth, 1979-82; lectr., presenter seminars in field. Contbr. articles, research papers to profl. jours. Decorated Legion of Merit, Meritorious Svc. Medal with oak leaf cluster. Fellow: Am. Coll. Dentists, Internat. Coll. Dentists; master: Acad. Gen. Dentistry; mem. ADA, Ill. Dental Soc., Chgo. Dental Soc., Am. Assn. Dental Schs., Am. Soc. Assn. Execs., Assn. Healthcare Execs., Profl. Conv. Mgmt. Assn., Omicron Kappa Upsilon.

HOFFMAN, JOEL ELIHU, lawyer; b. N.Y.C., Sept. 23, 1937; s. Samuel S. and Flora (Pasachoff) H.; m. Sandra Joyce Stone, June 3, 1962 (div. June 1985); children: Susanna Beth, Alexander Laurence, Jeremy Andrew; m. Katherine Louise Joss, Feb. 15, 1986. BA, NYU, 1957; LLB, Yale U., 1960. Bar: N.Y. 1960, D.C. 1963. Trial atty. antitrust div. U.S. Dept. Justice, Washington, 1960-63; assoc. Wald, Harkrader and Ross, Washington, 1963-68, ptnr., 1968-85; ptnr. Sutherland, Asbill and Brennan, Washington, 1985-99, of counsel, 1999—; adj. prof. law Franklin Pierce Law Sch., 1997—, Law Sch. George Mason U., 1998—. Mem. editorial adv. bd. Food Drug and Cosmetic Law Jour., 1981-89; contbr. articles to profl. jours. Mem. ABA (chmn. food and drug com. adminstrv. law sect. 1976-82, 95-99, vice chmn. consumer product regulation com. 1976—, coun. mem. 1973-76). Office: Sutherland Asbill & Brennan 1275 Pennsylvania Ave NW Ste 1 Washington DC 20004-2415

HOFFMAN, JOEL HARVEY, composer; b. Vancouver, B.C., Can., Sept. 27, 1953; came to U.S., 1964; s Irwin and Esther Beatrice (Glazer) H.; m. Dorotea Vittoria Vismara, Dec. 30, 1988. MusB summa cum laude, U. Wales, Cardiff, 1974; MusM, Juilliard Sch. Music, 1976, D of Mus. Arts, 1978. Prof. composition Coll./Conservatory Music U. Cin., 1978—; mem. faculty U. Cin.; artistic dir. Music Ninety-Nine Festival; resident composer MacDowell Colony Yaddo, Rockefeller Found., Camargo Found., Hindemith Found.; new music advisor Buffalo Philharm., 1991-92; composer-in-residence Nat. Chamber Orch., 1993-94. Composer: Sonata for Cello and Piano, 1982, Chamber Symphony, 1983, Double Concerto, 1984, Duo for viola and piano, 1984, Between Ten, 1985, Violin Concerto, 1986, The Hancock Trio, 1987, Fantasia Fiorentina for violin and piano, 1988, Crossing Points for string orch., 1990, Partenze for violin solo, 1990, Cubist Blues for piano trio, 1991, Music in Blue in Green for orch., 1991, Each for Himself/90? for piano solo, 1991, Metasmo for percussion trio, 1992, String Quartet No. 2, 1993, Self-Portrait with Mozart, 1994, Music for chamber orch., 1994, ChiaSsO for orch., 1995, L'Immensita dell'Attimo for voice and piano, 1995, The Music Within the Words, Part I for flute, oboe, cello and piano, 1996, Part II for viola, cello, harp and piano, 1996, Portogruaro Sextet for clarinet, horn, string trio, piano, 1996, l'Chaim Chantata, 1996, Stone Soup for violin and narrator, 1996, Millennium Dances for Orchestra, 1997, Self-Portrait with Gebirtig, 1998, Krakow Variations for viola sola, 1999, Reyzel, A Portrait for chamber ensemble, 1999; (recs.) Duo for Viola and Piano, CRI, 1991, Partenze for violin solo, Koch Internat., 1992, Music for Two Oboes, Centaur, 1995, Fantasy Pieces, Gasparo, 1996, Tum-Balalayke EMA Records, 1996; pianist in various recitals and solo concerts, Italy, France, Great Britain, U.S; pianist and arranger Trio Gebirtig. Recipient award Am. Acad.-Inst. Arts and Letters, 1987, commn. Nat. Endowment for the Arts, 1986, 91, Fromm Found., 1980, 82, Am. Harp Soc., 1982, Am. Music Ctr., 1991, Cin. Symphony Orch., 1993, Shanghai String Quartet, 1993, Nat. Chamber Orch., 1993; Ohio Arts Coun. fellow, 1983, 87, 91, 94,

96. Mem. ASCAP, Am. Music Ctr., Gruppo Aperto Musica Oggi, Coll. Music Soc., Composers Forum, Cin. Chamber Music Soc., U. Cin. Faculty Jewish Coun. (past pres.). Avocation: Chinese, Italian cooking. Fax: 513 556-0202; E-mail joel.hoffman@uc.edu. Office: U Cin Coll Conservatory Music Cincinnati OH 45221

HOFFMAN, JOHN D., engineering educator; b. Washington, Nov. 26, 1922. BS, Franklin and Marshall Coll., 1942; MS, Princeton U., 1948, PhD, 1949. Dir. Inst. Material Rsch.-Nat. Bur. Stds., 1967-82; prof., chmn. nuc. engrng. U. Md., 1982-85; dir., CEO, Mich. Molecular Inst., 1985-90, disting. rsch. fellow, 1990; rsch. prof. dept. materials sci. and engrng. Johns Hopkins U., Balt., 1990—. Recipient Pres.'s Meritorious Excellence award 1980. Fellow Am. Phys. Soc. (High Polymer Physics prize 1971); mem. NAE, ADA (hon.), Sigma Xi. *

HOFFMAN, JOHN ERNEST, JR., retired lawyer; b. N.Y.C., May 1, 1934; s. John E. and Effe K. (Dooling) H.; m. Jean Wheeler, Aug. 13, 1955; children: Jean E., John E., Katherine P., Carolyn W., Christine D. AB cum laude, Princeton U., 1955; JD, Harvard U., 1960. Bar: N.Y. 1961, U.S. Dist. Ct. (so. and ea. dists.) N.Y. 1963, U.S. Ct. Appeals (2d cir.) 1963, U.S. Supreme Ct. 1964, U.S. Ct. Appeals (3d cir.) 1974, U.S. Ct. Appeals (10th cir.) 1975, U.S. Ct. Appeals (6th cir.) 1986, U.S. Dist. Ct. (no. dist.) N.Y. 1989, U.S. Ct. Appeals (4th cir.) 1989. Assoc. Shearman & Sterling, 1960-68; ptnr. Shearman & Sterling, N.Y.C., 1968-92, ret., 1992. Co-author: American Hostages in Iran: The Conduct of a Crisis, 1985. Trustee Monadnock United Way, Monadnock Conservancy, Soc. for the Protection of N.H. Forests. 1st lt. U.S. Army, 1955-57. Fellow Am. Coll. Trial Lawyers. Congregationalist. Home: Seward Mt Farm Bowlder Rd PO Box 187 East Sullivan NH 03445-0187

HOFFMAN, JOHN FLETCHER, lawyer; b. N.Y.C., May 22, 1946; s. George Fletcher and Helen (Gilbert) H.; m. Coralie Tallman, June 29, 1969; children: Julie Gilbert, William Delano. BS, St. Lawrence U., 1969; JD, Washington and Lee U., 1975. Bar: N.Y. 1976, U.S. Dist. Ct. (so. dist.) N.Y. 1976, U.S. Dist. Ct. (ea. dist.) N.Y. 1978, U.S. Supreme Ct. 1980, U.S. Ct. Appeals (2d cir.) 1982, U.S. Dist. Ct. (no. dist.) Tex. 1988, U.S. Ct. Appeals (11th cir.) 1991. Assoc. Cadwalader, Wickersham & Taft, N.Y.C., 1975-83, ptnr., 1983-94; v.p., assoc. gen. counsel Schering-Plough Corp., Kenilworth, N.J., 1995—. Trustee First Unitarian Congl. Soc. Bklyn., 1980-83; trustee, treas. Bklyn. Children's Mus., 1985-95. Mem. ABA, Fed. Bar Coun., Order of Coif, Omicron Delta Kappa. Office: Schering Plough Corp 2000 Galloping Hill Rd Kenilworth NJ 07033-1328

HOFFMAN, JOHN RALEIGH, physicist; b. Evansville, Ind., July 7, 1926; s. John Henry and Ruth Margaret (Bryant) H.; m. Phyllis Christine Reindel, July 5, 1950; children: John Russell, Gary Paul. BS, U. Richmond (Va.), 1949; MS, U. Fla., 1951, PhD, 1954. Research asst. U. Fla., 1950-54; research scientist Sandia Corp., Albuquerque, 1954-57; project supr. Kaman Nuclear Co., Colorado Springs, 1957-68; v.p. Kaman Scis. Corp., Colorado Springs, 1968-86; sr. v.p. Kaman Scis. Corp., 1986-90, exec. v.p., 1990-92; gen. mgr. Kaman Instrumentation Corp., 1989-90; ret. Kaman Scis Corp., 1992; tech. and mgmt. cons., 1992—; bd. dirs. Red Spot Paint and Varnish Co., 1993—; mem. nominating commn. Colo. Supreme Ct., 1998. Served with USNR, 1944-46. Mem. Am. Phys. Soc., IEEE. Republican. Presbyterian. Home and Office: 5020 Lyda Ln Colorado Springs CO 80904-1008

HOFFMAN, JOSEPH FREDERICK, physiology educator; b. Oklahoma City, Mar. 7, 1925; s. Henry Raymond and Rena Virginia (Crossman) H.; m. Elena Citkowitz. BS, U. Okla., 1947, MS, 1948; MA, Princeton U., 1951, PhD, 1952. Lectr., rsch. asst. Princeton (N.J.) U., 1952-56; physiologist, sec. Nat. Heart Inst., Bethesda, Md., 1957-65; prof. physiology Yale U. Sch. Med., New Haven, 1965-74, chmn. dept. physiology, 1973-79; Eugene Higgins prof. cellular and molecular physiology Yale U. Sch. Med., New Haven, Conn., 1974—. Fellow AAAS, Am. Acad. Arts and Scis.; mem. NAS, Biophys. Soc. (pres. 1985-86), Soc. Gen. Physiologists (pres. 1975-76), Am. Physiol. Soc., Argentine Soc. Physiol Sci. (hon.). E-mail: joseph.hoffman@yale.edu. Office: Yale U Dept Cellular & Molec Phys 333 Cedar St New Haven CT 06510-3289

HOFFMAN, JUDY GREENBLATT, preschool director; b. Chgo., June 12, 1932; d. Edward Abraham and Clara (Morrill) Greenblatt; m. Morton Hoffman, Mar. 16, 1950 (div. Jan. 1983); children: Michael, Alan, Clare. BA summa cum laude, Met. State Coll., Denver, 1972; MA, U. No. Colo., 1976, MA in Spl. Edn. Moderate Needs, 1996. Cert. tchr., Colo. Presch. dir. B.M.H. Synagogue, Denver, 1968-70, Temple Emanuel, Denver, 1970-85, Congregation Rodef Shalom, Denver, 1985-88; tchr. Denver Pub. Schs., 1988—; bilingual tchr. adults in amnesty edn. Denver Pub. Schs., 1989-90. Author: I Live in Israel, 1979, Joseph and Me, 1980 (Gamoran award), (with others) American Spectrum Single Volume Encyclopedia, 1991. Coord. Douglas Mountain Therapeutic Riding Ctr. for Handicapped, Golden, Colo., 1985—; dir. Mountain Ranch Summer Day Camp for Denver Pub. Schs., 1989-91. Mem. Nat. Assn. Temple Educators. Democrat. Avocations: riding, writing, music.

HOFFMAN, JULIEN IVOR ELLIS, pediatric cardiologist, educator; b. Salisbury, South Rhodesia, July 26, 1925; came to U.S., 1957, naturalized, 1967; s. Bernard Isaac and Minrose (Bermant) H.; m. Kathleen Lewis, 1986; children: Anna, Daniel. B.Sc., U. Witwatersrand, Johannesburg, South Africa, 1944; B.Sc. Hons., 1945, M.B., B.Ch., 1949, M.D., 1970. Intern, resident internal medicine South Africa and Eng., 1950-56; research asst., postgrad. Med. Sch., London, 1956-57; fellow pediatric cardiology Boston Children's Hosp., 1957-59; fellow Cardiovascular Research Inst., San Francisco, 1959-60; asst. prof. pediatrics, internal medicine Albert Einstein Coll., N.Y., 1962-66; assoc. prof. pediatrics U. Calif. at San Francisco, 1966-70, prof., 1970—, prof. physiology, 1981-88, prof. emeritus, 1994; sr. mem. Cardiovascular Research Inst., U. Calif. at San Francisco, 1966—; mem. bd. examiners, sub-bd. pediatric cardiology Am. Bd. Pediatrics, 1973-78, subbd. pediatric intensive care, 1985-87; chmn. Louis Katz Award Com., Basic Sci. Council, Am. Heart Assn., 1973-74; George Brown Meml. lectr. Am. Heart Assn., 1977; George Alexander Gibson Meml. lectr. Royal Coll. Physicians (Edinburgh), 1978; Lilly lectr. Royal Coll. Physicians (London), 1981; Isaac Starr lectr. Cardiac Systems Dynamics Soc., Eng., 1982; John Keith lectr., 1985; Disting. Physiology lectr. Am. Coll. Chest Physicians, 1985; Nadas lectr. Am. Heart Assn., 1987; 1st Donald C. Fyler lectr. Children's Hosp., Boston, 1990. Recipient Bayer Cardiovascular Mentor award, 1989. Fellow Royal Coll. Physicians; mem. World Congress Pediatric Cardiology and Cardiac Surgery (hon. joint pres. Paris 1993), Am. Physiol. Soc., Am. Pediatric Soc., Soc. Pediatric Rsch. Extensive rsch. into congenital heart disease and coronary blood flow. Home: 925 Tiburon Blvd Belvedere Tiburon CA 94920-1525 Office: U Calif Med Ctr 1403 Hse Dept Pediats San Francisco CA 94143

HOFFMAN, KARLA LEIGH, mathematician; b. Paterson, N.J., Feb. 14, 1948; d. Abe and Bertha (Guthaim) Rakoff; m. Allan Stuart Hoffman, Dec. 26, 1971; 1 child, Matthew Douglas. BA, Rutgers U., 1969; MBA, George Washington U., 1971, DSc in Ops. Rsch., 1975. Ops. rsch. analyst IRS, Washington, 1970-72; rsch. asst. George Washington U., 1972-75, assoc. professional lectr., 1978-85; NSF postdoctoral rsch. fellow NAS, Washington, 1975-76; assoc. prof. sys. engrng. dept. George Mason U., Fairfax, Va., 1985-86; assoc. prof. ops. rsch. and applied stats. George Mason U., Fairfax, 1986-89, prof. ops. rsch., 1990—, disting. prof., 1989, interim dept. chmn., 1996-97, chmn., 1997-98, chmn. sys. engrng. and ops. rsch., 1998—; mathematician Nat. Bur. Stds., Washington, 1976-84; vis. assoc. prof. ops. rsch. U. Md., spring 1982; mng. ptnr. Optimization Software Assocs.; cons. to govt. agys., airline, telecom., and def. industries. Assoc. editor Internat. Abstracts of Ops. Rsch., The Math. Programming Jour., Series B, The Ops. Rsch. Soc. Jour. on Computing, Jour. Computational Optimization and Applications; contbr. articles to profl. jours. Recipient Applied Rsch. award Nat. Inst. Stds. and Tech., 1984, Silver medal U.S. Dept. Commerce, 1984. Mem. Ops. Rsch. Soc. Am. (sec.-treas. computer sci. tech. sect. 1979-80, vice chmn. sect. 1981, chmn. sect. 1982, vis. professional lectr. 1980—, chmn. tech. sect. com. 1983-86, coun. 1985-88, chmn. Lanchster Prize com. 1989, treas. 1993-94), Inst. Ops. Rsch. and Mgmt. Sci. (treas. 1995-96, exec. com. 1995-99, pres. 1998), Math. Programming Soc. (editor newsletter 1979-82, chmn. com. algorithms 1982-85, coun. 1985-88, exec. com. 1986-88, chmn. mem. com. 1988-89). Home: 6921 Clifton Rd Clifton VA 20124-1525

HOFFMAN, KENNETH MYRON, mathematician, educator; b. Long Beach, Calif., Nov. 30, 1930; s. Myron Grant and Madge (Harrison) H.; children: Donna, Laura, Robert; m. Alicia C. Coro, Mar. 1997. AA, John Muir Coll., 1950; AB, Occidental Coll., 1952; MA, UCLA, 1954, PhD, 1956. Instr. math. MIT, Cambridge, 1956-59, asst. prof., 1959-61, assoc. prof., 1961-63, prof., 1963-96, prof. emeritus, 1996—, chmn. pure math., 1968-69; chmn. Commn. on Edn., 1969-71, head dept. math., 1971-79; exec. dir. Commn. on Resources for Math. Sci., NRC, 1981-85, Math. Scis. Edn. Bd. NRC, Washington, 1989-91; assoc. exec. officer for edn. NRC, Washington, 1991-94; pres. MSTE Connection, Bethesda, Md., 1996—; chmn. adv. com. NSF Sci. and Engrng. Edn. Directorate, 1984-85; cons. Math. Scis. Edn. Bd. NRC, 1985-89; head, Office Govtl. and Pub. Affairs, Joint Policy Bd. for Math., 1984-89; chmn. Md. Math. & Sci. Coalition, 1996—; pres. Nat. Alliance State Sci. and Math. Coalitions, 1997—. Author: (with Ray Kunze) Linear Algebra, 1961, Fundamentals of Banach Algebras, 1962, Banach Spaces of Analytic Functions, 1962, Analysis in Euclidean Space, 1975; Contbr. (with Ray Kunze) articles to profl. jours. Mailing. Fellow Alfred P. Sloan Found., 1964-66. Mem. AAAS (council), Am. Math. Soc. (past mem. council), Math. Assn. Am., Nat. Council Tchrs. Math., Phi Beta Kappa. Office: MSTE.NET 4242 Est West Hwy Apt 504 Chevy Chase MD 20815

HOFFMAN, LARRY JAX, lawyer; b. N.Y.C., Aug. 20, 1930; s. Max and Pauline (Epstein) H.; m. Deborh E. Alexander, Oct. 2, 1954; children: Lisa, Ken, Heidi, Mark. AA, U. Fla.; JD, U. Miami. Bar: Fla. 1954. Chmn. Greenberg, Traurig, PA, Miami, 1968—; also bd. dirs. Greenberg, Traurig, Hoffman, Lipoff, Rosen & Quentel, PA, Miami. Mem. ABA, Fla. Bar Assn., Dade County Bar Assn. Avocations: music, art, tennis. Office: Greenberg Traurig 1221 Brickell Ave Miami FL 33131-3224

HOFFMAN, LINDA M., chemist, educator; b. N.Y.C., Dec. 18, 1939; d. Theodore and Esther (Schaefer) Weiss; m. Robert G. Hoffman, Feb. 2, 1958; 1 child, Samuel A. BS in Chemistry, Queens Coll., 1959; MS, NYU, 1967, PhD in Organic Chemistry, 1970. Postdoctoral fellow Sloan Kettering Inst. Cancer Research, N.Y.C., 1972-73; research assoc. Kingsbrook Jewish Med. Ctr., N.Y.C., 1973-77; asst. prof. Baruch Coll. CUNY, N.Y.C., 1977-79, assoc. prof., 1979-82, prof., 1982—, chair dept. natural scis., 1995-98; reviewer grant proposals NIH. Contbr. articles on Tay-Sachs disease and glycosphingolipids to profl. jours. Mem. edn. com. UN Internat. Sch., N.Y.C., 1981-84; bd. dirs. Forest Hills Gardens Corp. Recipient Moore award Am. Soc. Neuropathologists, 1981, 84, Founders Day award NYU, 1971, 112th Precinct Cmty. Coun. award, 1993. Mem. AAAS, Am. Chem. Soc., N.Y. Acad. Sci., Sigma Xi. Office: Baruch Coll Dept Natural Scis 17 Lexington Ave New York NY 10010-5518

HOFFMAN, LINDA R., social services administrator; b. New Haven, Conn., July 23, 1940; d. Bernard Harry and Sylvia (Paul) Rosenfield; m. Peter A. Hoffman, Sept. 25, 1965; 1 child, Tracie Lee. BA, Russell Sage Coll., 1962; MSW, Columbia U., 1968. Cert. social worker, N.Y. Case worker Conn. Dept. Welfare, New Haven, 1962-63; case worker N.Y.C. Bur. Child Welfare, 1963-65, supr., 1965-66; asst. to commr. program planning N.Y.C. Dept. Social Svcs., 1968-70; spl. asst. to commr. N.Y.C. Spl. Svcs. for Children, 1972-79; pres. N.Y. Found. Sr. Citizens, N.Y.C., 1979—; cons. USIA, Teheran, Iran, summer 1975; adj. prof., mem. dean's adv. coun. Columbia Sch. Social Work. Mem. Cmty. Bd. # 8, N.Y.C., 1981—; mem. pub. programs and policy com. United Jewish Appeal Fedn. N.Y., N.Y.C., 1982—; mem. YWCA/N.Y.C. Acad. Women Achievers, 1994, bd. dirs., 1995—, Women's Forum, 1998—. Recipient Presdl. Recognition award for Community Svc., 1983, East Manhattan C. of C. award for Disting. Civic Svc., 1990, award Mcpl. Art Soc., 1997, The Mcpl. Art Soc. of N.Y. award, 1997. Mem. Nat. Assn. Social Workers (cert.), Women's City Club of N.Y. Avocations: thoroughbred race horses, boating, fishing. Office: NY Found Sr Citizens 150 Nassau St Ste 1730 New York NY 10038-1516

HOFFMAN, LYNN RENEE, elementary education educator; b. Trenton, N.J., Apr. 19, 1957; d. Hugh L. and Thelma B. (Winner) H. BA in Theology, Immaculata Coll., 1983, BMus, 1985; postgrad., Gratz Coll., 1993; PhD, LaSalle U., 1995. Joined Sisters, Servants of Immaculate Heart of Mary, 1976; lic., nationally cert. massage therapist. Elem. tchr. Diocese of Arlington, Va., 1979-80, Diocese of Allentown, Pa., 1980-82, Archdiocese Phila., 1983-86, Diocese of Trenton, N.J., 1987-95; tchr. Abrahms Hebrew Acad., Yardley, Pa., Jewish Community Ctr., Belle Mead, N.J.; tchr. grade 3 Univ. Sch. Nova Southeastern U., Davie, Fla., 1995-96; therapist Am. Inst. Massage Therapy, Ft. Lauderdale, Fla., 1996-97; tchr. grade 5 Guilford County Sch. Dist., Greensboro, N.C., 1998—. Contbr. articles to children's publs. Moderator Young Astronauts, Trenton, 1987—; mem. Phila. Task Force, 1987—. Recipient Nat. Schs. Excellence award U.S. Dept. Edn., 1988. Mem. Nat. Cath. Ednl. Assn., The Smithsonian Assocs., Nat. Assn. Female Execs. Democrat. Avocations: tennis, softball, cross stitch, swimming. Office: Wiley Elem Sch Greensboro NC 27420

HOFFMAN, MALIZA MILDRED, interior designer; b. Vienna, Austria, Oct. 12, 1922; came to U.S., 1925; d. Morris and Sally (Flintenstein) Weinstock; children: Marla L. Hoffman, Jay Hoffman. BA, CCNY, 1956; Cert. Interior Design, N.Y. Sch. Interior Design, 1968. Interior designer Sachs-N.Y., N.Y.C. and Nassau County, 1967-82, Ethan Allen, Nassau County, L.I., 1983-85; lectr. in field. Mem. Womanspace, Great Neck, N.Y., 1997; one of founders Nat. women's Mus., Washington. Mem. Am. Soc. Interior Designers (profl. mem.). Avocations: playwriting, poetry. Home: 29 Leslie Ln New Hyde Park NY 11040-1836

HOFFMAN, MARC OLIN, state official; b. May 22, 1954. Grad. high sch., Trenton, Ill. Regional mgr. Ill. State Lottery Region 4, Cahokia. Supr., treas. Looking Glass Twp., New Baden, Ill.; bd. dirs. So. Ill. Law Enforcement Commn., Belleville, Ill., S.W. Planning Commn., Collinsville, Ill.; chmn. Clinton County Rep. Ctrl. Com., New Baden. Office: Ill Lottery Office Regional Mgr 3237 Mississippi Ave Cahokia IL 62206

HOFFMAN, MARIANNE MACINA, corporate relations administrator; b. N.Y.C., Apr. 29, 1951; d. Vito William Jr. and Frances (Florio) Macina; m. Neil Richard Hoffman, April 29, 1995. BS in Journalism, U. Fla., 1973; postgrad., U. London, 1973; AA in Advt. ARt, Inst. Atlanta, 1975. Writer Clearwater (Fla.) Sun, 1965-69; pub. rels., graphics specialist Hensley-Schmidt Engts., Atlanta, 1975-76; creative dir. Mackey Green & Assocs., Atlanta, 1976; assoc. editor So. Banker Mag., Atlanta, 1977-78; managing editor Pension World Mag., Atlanta, 1978-79; communications writer No. States Power Co., Mpls., 1979-80; advt. dir. Carlton Celebrity Dinner Theater, Bloomington, Minn., 1980-82; coord., mktg. svcs. St. Paul Cos. Inc., 1982-87; regional mgr. Western Ins. Info. Svc., Portland, Oreg., 1987-98; field corp. rels. mgr. Allstate Ins. Co., Bothell, Wash., 1998—; bd. dirs. Ins. Edn. Found. Oreg., Portland, 1989-98; mem. Wash. Ins. coun., 1999—, Oreg. Ins. Coun., 1998—, Idaho Ins. Adv. bd., 1998—. Exec. prodr.: (consumer videos) Preventing Home Burglary, 1988 (Gold medal 1990), Don't Give a Thief a Free Ride: Preventing Auto Theft, 1990, Bon Voyage: Tips for a Safe Vacation, 1993. Mem. task force Oreg. Juvenile Firesetter Edn., Salem, 1988-92; mem. Oreg. Coun. Against Arson, 1988-98, v.p., 1994, 95, 97, 98; mem. exec. bd. Crime Prevention Assn. Oreg., 1992-94, treas., 1995-97; bd. dirs. Oreg. Traffic Safety NOW, 1988-91, Keep Oreg. Green, 1999—; mem. steering com. Oreg. Safe Kids, 1997-98. Recipient Merit award Ins. Info. Inst., N.Y.C., 1989, Commendation award Oreg. Coun. Against Arson, 1989, Crime Prevention award Crime Prevention Assn. Oreg., 1990, Media award, 1989. Mem. Soc. Chartered Property Casualty Underwriters (Oreg. chpt. bd. dirs. 1990-92, new designee rep. we. region 1989-90, cert.). Republican. Roman Catholic. Avocations: tennis, golf, swimming, skiing, photography. Office: Allstate Ins Co Seattle Region 18911 North Creek Pkwy Bothell WA 98011

HOFFMAN, MARTIN LEON, psychology educator; b. Bayonne, N.J., Mar. 20, 1924; s. Nathan D. and Ann E. (Goldberg) H.; m. Lois Norma Wladis, June 24, 1951 (div. 1981); children: Amy, Jill; m. Elizabeth Ann Mercer, June 4, 1989. BSEE, Purdue U., 1945; MS in Psychology, U. Mich., 1948, PhD in Social Psychology, 1951. Asst. prof. Purdue U., Lafayette, Ind., 1949-53; sr. rsch. assoc. Merrill-Palmer Inst., Detroit, 1953-65; prof. U. Mich., Ann Arbor, 1965-85; prof. psychology NYU, 1985—. Editor: (series) Social and Emotional Development; co-editor: Review of Child Development Research, Vol. 1, 1964, Vol. 2, 1966 (Book of Yr. award Child Study Assn.); editor: Merrill-Palmer Quar., 1955-80, 80—; contbr. numerous articles to profl. jours. Ens. USN 1943-46. Founds. Fund for Psychiatry grantee, 1953-55, NIMH grantee 1957-70. Fellow APA (assoc. editor Devel. Psychology jour. 1980-82, editor Psychol. Rev. 1982-88), AAAS, Am. Psychol. Soc.; mem. AAUP, Soc. Rsch. in Child Devel. Office: NYU FAS Dept Psychology 6 Washington Pl Dept New York NY 10003-6634

HOFFMAN, MARY CATHERINE, nurse anesthetist; b. Winamac, Ind., July 14, 1923; d. Harmon William Whitney and Dessie Maude (Neely) H.; R.N., Methodist Hosp., Indpls., 1945; cert. obstet. analgesia and anesthesia, Johns Hopkins Hosp., 1949, grad. U. Hosp. of Cleve. Sch. Anesthesia, 1952; Staff nurse Meth. Hosp., 1945-49; research asst., then staff anesthetist Johns Hopkins Hosp., 1949-62; staff anesthetist Meth. Hosp., 1962-64, U. Chgo. Hosps., 1964-66; chief nurse anesthetist Paris (Ill.) Community Hosp., 1966-80; staff anesthetist Hendricks County Hosp., Danville, Ind., Ball Meml. Hosp., Muncie, Ind., 1981-86; instr.-trainer CPR, 1975-81; mem. Terr. 08 CPR Coordinating Com., 1975-80. Mem. Am. Assn. Nurse Anesthetists, Am. Heart Assn., Ind. Fedn. Bus. and Profl. Women's Clubs (Ill. dist. chmn. 1977-78, state found. chmn. 1978-79; found. award 1979). Republican. Presbyterian. Home: 1700 N Maddox Dr Muncie IN 47304-2674

HOFFMAN, MATHEW, lawyer; b. Bklyn., Mar. 9, 1954; s. S. David and Naomi B. (Brosterman) H.; m. Bracha Hoffman; children: Ari, Gavriel, Shelhevet, Miri, Shira, Tova. BA, U. Mich., 1974; JD, Columbia U., 1977. Bar: N.Y. 1978, U.S. Dist. Ct. (so. and ea. dists.) N.Y. 1978, U.S. Ct. Appeals (2d and 7th cirs.) 1980; ordained rabbi, 1988. Atty. Proskauer, Rose, N.Y.C., 1978-80, Gordon, Hurwitz, N.Y.C., 1980-85; ptnr. Koether, Harris & Hoffman, N.Y.C., 1985-89, Keck Mahin & Cate, N.Y.C., 1989-94, Rosen & Reade, N.Y.C., 1994-96; ptnr., head of litigation Todtman, Nachamie, Spizz & Hons, P.C., N.Y.C., 1997—. Contbr. articles to profl. jours. Mem. Jewish Flame (trustee 1979—). Home: 62 Rosehill Ave New Rochelle NY 10804-3615 Office: Todtman Nachamie Spizz & Johns PC 425 Park Ave New York NY 10022-3506

HOFFMAN, MERLE HOLLY, political activist, social psychologist, author; b. Phila., Mar. 6, 1946; d. Jack Rheins and Ruth (Dubow) H.; m. Martin Gold, June 30, 1979. BA magna cum laude in Psychology, Queens Coll., 1972; postgrad., CUNY, 1972-75. Founder, pres. Choices Women's Med. Ctr., Long Island City, N.Y., 1971—; family planning cons. Health Ins. Plan, N.Y.C., 1973-85; founder, pres. Ctr. for Comprehensive Breast Svcs., N.Y.C., 1979-82, Merle Hoffman Enterprises, N.Y.C., 1986—, Choices Mental Health Ctr., 1993—; speaker, debator on women's rights and polit. issues; founder, pres. Nat. Liberty Com., 1981. Cons. editor Female Health Topics and Diagnostic Reporter, 1979-81; editor, pub. On The Issues: The Progressive Woman's Quarterly; contbr. articles in field to various publs.; producer documentary film Abortion A Different Light; founder N.Y. Pro-Choice Coalition; host cable TV series MH: On the Issues, 1986. Mem. Nat. Assn. Abortion Facilities (co-founder, pres. 1976-77), Nat. Abortion Fedn. (co-founder, sec. 1977-78), Phi Beta Kappa. Office: Choices Women's Med Ctr Inc 29-28 41st Ave Long Island City NY 11101-3303

HOFFMAN, MICHAEL EUGENE, editor, publisher, museum curator; b. N.Y.C., July 5, 1942; s. Myron Block and Dorothy (Steinfeld) H.; m. Katharine Perkins Carter, Dec. 23, 1967 (dec.); children: Matthew, Sarah. BA in Religion and English with honors, St. Lawrence U., 1964. Exec. dir. Aperture Found., Inc., N.Y.C., 1965—, trustee, 1967—; curator Alfred Stieglitz Ctr., Phila. Museum Art, 1968—; exec. dir. Paul Strand Found., 1979-81. Dir. 50 maj. mus. exhbns. and over 300 publs. including Callahan, 1976, America and Lewis Hine, 1977, Interior America (photographs by Chauncey Hare), 1978, The Face of China, 1978, History of Photography Series: Erich Salomon and Clarence H. White, 1979, Lisette Model, 1979, Paul Strand, Manuel Alvarez Bravo, Roger Fenton, Dorothea Lange, 1987, From the Missouri West (photographs by Robert Adams) 1980, August Sander: Photographs of an Epoch 1904-1959, 1980, Ansel Adams: The Eloquent Light, 1980, Master of the Photographic Essay (photographs by W. Eugene Smith), 1981, American Frontiers: Photographs of Timothy O'Sullivan, 1981, Uncommon Places (photographs by Stephen Shore), 1982, Dorothea Lange: Photographs of a Lifetime, 1982, Tibet: The Sacred Realm (photographs 1880-1950), 1983, The Gardens at Giverny (photographs by Stephen Shore), 1983, Architecture and Community, 1983, Bill Brandt: Behind the Camera, 1984, The Golden Age of British Photography, 1984, Minor White: A Retrospective, 1984, Let Truth Be The Prejudice (W. Eugene Smith), 1985, Alvin Langdon Coburn, 1986, Andre Kertesz: Diary of Light 1912-1985, 1987, Samaras Photographs 1969-86, 1987, 1989; organizer photography exhbns. at the Alfred Steiglitz Ctr. at Phila. Mus. Art including Recent Acquisitions, 1979, Ansel Adams: 100 Photographs, 1980, The New Vision: 40 Years of Photography at the Institute of Design, 1980, Spirit of An American Place: Photographs by Alfred Stieglitz, 1980, The New West: Photographs by Robert Adams, 1981, Henri Cartier-Bresson: Photographer, 1981, American Frontiers: The Photographs of Timothy H. O'Sullivan 1867-1874, 1981, Frederick H. Evans: The Desired Haven, 1982, Danny Lyon: Pictures from the New World, 1982, Minor White Photographs, 1983, Tibet: The Sacred Realm Photographs 1880-1950, 1983, The Golden Age of British Photography, 1984, Let Truth Be the Prejudice: W. Eugene Smith, 1985, Minor White: A Retrospective, 1986, Alvin Langdon Coburn, 1986, Bill Brandt: Behind the Camera, 1986, with Arts Coun. of Gt. Britain Black Sun: The Eyes of Four, 1986-88, with Phila. Mus. Robert Adams: To Make It Home, 1989, Joseph Sudek A Life's Work, 1990, Nat. Gallery of Art The Paul Strand Centenary Exhbn, 1990, Phila. Mus., 1993, Workers, Sebastaio Salgado, 1993. Trustee, founder Internat. Photography Coun, London. 1st lt. U.S. Army, 1964-65. Recipient Fifty Best Books of Yr. award Am. Inst. Graphic Arts (9), Spl. award for Continued Excellence, Art Libraries Soc. Am., Periodical Aperture award Type Dir.'s Club, Creative Pub. citation Carey-Thomas, Citation of Commendation, Art Libraries Soc. N.Am. Mem. Soc. Photog. Edn., Pi Delta Epsilon. Office: Aperture 20 E 23rd St New York NY 10010-4463

HOFFMAN, MICHAEL JEROME, humanities educator; b. Phila., Mar. 13, 1939; s. Nathan P. and Sara (Perlman) H.; m. Margaret Boegeman, Dec. 27, 1988; children by previous marriage: Cynthia, Matthew. BA, U. Pa., 1959, MA, 1960, PhD, 1963. Instr. Washington Coll., Chestertown, Md., 1962-64; asst. prof. U. Pa., Phila., 1964-67; from asst. prof. to prof. U. Calif., Davis, 1967—, asst. vice chancellor acad. affairs, 1976-83, chmn. English dept., 1984-89, dir. Davis Humanities Inst., 1987-91, coord. writing programs, 1991-94, undergrad. coord., 1994-95, grad. advisor, 1995-98, dir. honors program, 1992-99; chmn. joint projects steering com. U. Calif.-Calif. State U., 1976-87; chmn. adv. bd. Calif. Acad. Partnership Program, 1985-87; dir. Calif. Humanities Project, 1985-91. Author: The Development of Abstractionism in the Writings of Gertrude Stein, 1965, The Buddy System, 1971, The Subversive Vision, 1972, Gertrude Stein, 1976, Critical Essays on Gertrude Stein, 1986, Essentials of the Theory of Fiction, 1988, rev. edit., 1996, Critical Essays on American Modernism, 1992. With USAR, 1957-61. Nat. Def. Edn. Act fellow U.S. Govt., 1959-62. Mem. Modern Lang. Assn. (Am. lit. group). Democrat. Jewish. Avocation: tennis. Home: 4417 San Marino Dr Davis CA 95616-5012 Office: U Calif Dept English Davis CA 95616

HOFFMAN, MICHAEL WILLIAM, lawyer, accountant; b. Bowling Green, Ohio, Feb. 5, 1955; s. Oscar William and Marie Louise (Carlson) H.; m. Lynne Ellen Steele, Aug. 31, 1975; children: Megan, Jessica, Kristine, Robert. BA in Acctg. summa cum laude, Bowling Green State U., 1976; JD, U. Toledo, 1981. Bar: Ohio 1981, Ga. 1983; CPA, Ga., Ohio. Acct. Ernst & Whinney, Toledo, 1976-81; acct., ptnr. Touche Ross & Co., Atlanta, 1981-86; v.p. Profl. Svcs. Network Inc., Atlanta, 1986; assoc. Chamberlain, Hrdlicka, White, Johnson & Williams, Atlanta, 1986-89; ptnr. Somers & Altenbach, Atlanta, 1989-91; atty. Hoffman & Assocs., Atlanta, 1991—; organizing dir. Paces Bank & Trust Co., Atlanta; spkr. in field. Author: RIA's U.S.A. News for the Inbound Investor, 1983. Treas. Friendship Force Internat., 1984; mem. troop com. Boy Scouts Am. Recipient Leadership award Boy Scouts Am., 1986. Mem. ABA, AICPA, State Bar Ga. (fiduciary law and tax sects.), State Bar Ohio, Ga. Soc. CPAs (chmn. estate, gift & trust sect.; Atlanta chpt. Estate, Gift and Trust sect., Disting. Com. Chair award 1998-99), Bowling Green State U.-Atlanta Alumni Assn. (pres. 1988-90), Atlanta Country Club (bd. dirs. 1998—), Serra. Republican. Roman Catholic. Avocations: golf, tennis, coaching Little League basketball. Email: mhoffman@avana.net. Home: 535 Willow Knolls Dr Marietta GA 30067-4647 Office: 6075 Lake Forrest Dr NW Ste 200 Atlanta GA 30328-3845

HOFFMAN, MITCHELL WADE, corporate executive; b. Newport News, Va., Sept. 27, 1954; s. Joseph and Sarah (Goldberg) H.; m. Patrice Lynn Bare, Dec. 2, 1978; 1 child, Loren Kimberly. BA in Psychol., U. Va., 1975; MBA, Coll. Wm. and Mary, 1978; MS in Fin., Va. Commonwealth U., 1988. Cert. purchasing mgr., Nat. Assn. Purchasing Mgmt. Sr. buyer Harvey Hubbell Inc., Christiansburg, Va., 1978-79; agt. purchasing Ingersoll Rand Inc., Roanoke, Va., 1979-82; supr. distbn. HoN Industries Inc., Richmond, Va., 1983; agt. capital purchasing Brockway Inc., Richmond, 1983-88; ops. fin. analyst Philip Morris, Inc., Richmond, 1988—; adj. prof. fin. Va. Commonwealth U., 1988—. Mem. Nat. Assn. Purshasing Mgmt., Nat. Assn. Fin. Mgmt., Alpha Iota Delta, Beta Gamma Sigma, Phi Kappa Phi. Avocations: reading, classical music, opera. Home: 4218 Brixton Rd Chesterfield VA 23832-7764

HOFFMAN, NANCY, art gallery director; b. N.Y.C., 1944. Wellesley Coll., 1964, Columbia U., 1966. Asst. registrar Asia House Gallery, N.Y.C., 1964-69; dir. Contemporary Gallery French & Co., N.Y.C., 1969-72; owner Nancy Hoffman Gallery, N.Y.C., 1972—; lectr., jury exhibitor throughout U.S. Contbr. chpt. to text. Office: Nancy Hoffman Gallery 429 W Broadway New York NY 10012-3799*

HOFFMAN, NANCY E., lawyer; b. N.Y.C., Mar. 19, 1944; d. Jack and Catherine (Wertheim) H.; m. Thomas G. Spagnoletti. BS in Indsl. and Labor Rels., Cornell U., 1966; MA in Am. History, N.Y.U., 1968; JD, St. John's U., 1973. Bar: N.Y. 1974, U.S. Dist. Ct. (so. and ea. dists.) N.Y. 1975, U.S. Dist. Ct. (we. and no. dists.) N.Y. 1984, U.S. Supreme Ct. 1975, U.S. Ct. Appeals (2d cir.) 1975. Asst. corp. counsel N.Y. Dept. Law, 1973-75; assoc. Plunkett & Jaffee, 1978-79; assoc. counsel Office Gen. Counsel N.Y. State United Tchrs., 1975-78, 79-84; asst. atty. gen. State of N.Y., Albany, 1984-85; dep. counsel div. legal affairs N.Y. State Dept. Social Svcs., 1985-86, first asst. counsel for fair hearings, 1986-89; gen. counsel Civil Svc. Employees Assn., Inc., 1989—. Recipient Disting. Svc. award Am. Arbitration Assn., 1997. Mem. ABA (labor/employment law sect., coun. mem., com. on state and local govt. bargaining, commn. on women in the profession), N.Y. State Bar Assn. (labor/employment law sect., future directions com., govt. bargaining com.), Women's Bar Assn. State of N.Y. Office: Civil Svc Employees Assn 143 Washington Ave Albany NY 12210-2303

HOFFMAN, NATHANIEL A., lawyer; b. Cin., Mar. 4, 1949; s. Ralph H. and Betty (Goldfarb) H.; m. Sara Naomi Fishman, Aug. 3, 1980; children: Joshua, Rebecca, Esther, David. BA, Yale U., 1971; JD, U. Mich., 1975. Bar: Calif. 1975, Wis. 1983. Assoc. McDonough, Holland & Allen, Sacramento, 1975-78, Herz, Levin, Teper, Sumner & Croysdale, Milw., 1982-85; ptnr. Michael, Best & Friedrich, Milw., 1985—; atty. N.Y.C. Pub. Devel. Corp., 1980-82. Mem. ABA, State Bar Wis., Milw. Bar Assn., State Bar Calif. Home: 3258 N 51st Blvd Milwaukee WI 53216-3236 Office: Michael Best & Friedrich 100 E Wisconsin Ave Ste 3300 Milwaukee WI 53202-4108

HOFFMAN, NEIL JAMES, academic administrator; b. Buffalo, Sept. 2, 1938; s. Frederick Charles and Isabella Dias (Murchie) H.; m. Sue Ellen Jeffery, Dec. 30, 1960; children: Kim, Amy, Lisa. B.S., SUNY-Buffalo, 1960, M.S., 1967. Chmn. unified arts dept. Grand Island Pub. Schs. (N.Y.), 1968-69; assoc. dean, assoc. prof. Coll. Fine and Applied Art Rochester Inst. Tech. (N.Y.), 1969-74; dir. program in artisanry Boston U., 1974-79; dean, chief adminstrv. officer Otis Art Inst., Parsons Sch. Design, Los Angeles, 1979-83; pres. Sch. Art Inst. Chgo., 1983-85, Calif. Coll. Arts and Crafts, Oakland, 1985-93, Otis Coll. Art and Design, L.A., 1993—; prof. photographer; mem. local arts couns. local arts orgns., state arts orgns., nat. arts orgns. Chair evaluation teams Western Assn. Schs. and Colls., 1982—; chmn. cultural planning process City of Oakland, 1986-91. Mem. Phi Delta Kappa. Office: Otis Coll Art and Design Office of President 9045 Lincoln Blvd Los Angeles CA 90045-3505

HOFFMAN, N.M., poet; b. Newburgh, N.Y., July 4, 1950; d. Charles Walter and Theresa Mary (Flannery) H. BA in English Lit., SUNY, Stony Brook, 1972; MA in English Lit., Portland State U., 1978; PhD in Poetics, N.Y. U., 1992. Instr. Clark Coll., Vancouver, Wash., 1983-85, Portland (Oreg.) C.C., 1983-85, N.Y. Univ., N.Y.C., 1990-93, 92nd St. Y, N.Y.C., 1993-98, Tai Chi Chu'an, Cloud Hands Manhattan; writer The Downtowner, Portland, 1985-86. Author numerous poems pub. in jours. in Can., U.S., and Eng.; lectr. and presenter at various events; collaborator with various painters, photographers, illustrators and composers. Mem. Amnesty Internat., N.Y.C., 1992—, mem. LWV, N.Y.C., 1990—. Anhinga Poetry award, Anhinga Press, 1986; Carnwath-Callendar fellow N.Y. Univ., 1990-91, Celia Siegel fellow N.Y. Univ., 1990-91, Edward Albee Found. Writing fellow Albee Found., 1988. Mem. ASCAP. Democrat. Roman Catholic.

HOFFMAN, OSCAR ALLEN, retired forest products company executive; b. Newark, Feb. 4, 1920; s. Ernest Benjamin and Edith Marie (Myers) H.; m. Carolyn Ruth Layman, May 10, 1947 (div.); children: Peter Miles, Jared Mark; m. Geri McReynolds, Aug. 21, 1956. A.B., Drew U., 1943; M.S., Syracuse U., 1945; Ph.D., Stanford U., 1948; postgrad., U.S. Naval War Coll., 1953. Sect. leader MIT-Naval Ops. rsch. group, Washington, 1948-54; mgr. ops. rsch. AMF, Greenwich, Conn., 1954-58; v.p., spl. asst. to pres. Champion Internat. Corp., Stamford, Conn., 1958-85; commr. fin. Stamford, 1978-82; chief ops. research Turkish Gen. Staff, Ankara, summer 1956. Republican. Episcopalian. Home: 1546 Georgetowne Ln Sarasota FL 34232-2014

HOFFMAN, PAUL FELIX, geologist, educator; b. Toronto, Ont., Can., Mar. 21, 1941; s. Samuel and Dorothy Grace (Medhurst) H.; m. Erica Jean Westbrook, Dec. 4, 1976; 1 child, Guy Samson. BS, McMaster U., 1964; MA, Johns Hopkins U., 1965, PhD, 1970. Lectr. Franklin & Marshall Coll., Lancaster, Pa., 1968-69; rsch. scientist Geol. Survey Can., Ottawa, Ont., 1969-92; lectr. U. Calif., Santa Barbara, 1971-72; prof. U. Victoria, B.C., Can., 1992-94; Stugis Hooper prof. geology Harvard U., Cambridge, Mass., 1994—; lectr. U. Calif., Santa Barbara, 1971-72; dist. lectr. Am. Assn. Petroleum Geologists, 1979-80; vis. prof. U. Tex., Dallas, 1978, Columbia U., 1990; adj. prof. Carleton U., 1989-92; mem. Internat. Union Geol. Scis. Commn. on Precambrian Stratigraphy, 1976, Internat. Commn. Lithosphere Working Group on Mobile Belts, 1986-90. Fairchild Found. vis. scholar Calif. Inst. Tech., 1974-75; recipient Bownocker medal Ohio State U., 1989. Fellow Royal Soc. Can. (Willet G. Miller medal 1997), Geol. Assn. Can. (past pres.' medal 1976, Logan medal 1992), Geol. Soc. Am.; mem. Am. Geophys. Union, Can. Soc. Petroleum Geologists (R.J.W. Douglas Meml. medal 1991), NAS U.S. (fgn. assoc.), Am. Acad. Arts and Sci. (fgn. hon.). Home: 1 Waterhouse St Apt 45 Cambridge MA 02138-3610 Office: Harvard U Dept Earth/Planetary Sci 20 Oxford St Cambridge MA 02138-2902

HOFFMAN, PENNY JOAN, adult nurse practitioner, administrator; b. Grand Rapids, Mich., Jan. 31, 1947. Diploma, Butterworth Hosp. Sch. Nursing, Grand Rapids, Mich., 1968; BSN, Mich. State U., 1972; MS in Edn., SUNY, Albany, 1978; MSN, U. Conn., 1995. Cert. in nursing adminstrn., adult nurse practitioner. Field tchr., pub. health nursing supr. Kent County Health Dept., Grand Rapids, 1972-74; pub. health staff nurse Greene County Pub. Health Nursing Svc., Cairo, N.Y.; staff nurse Vis. Nurse Assn. Albany, 1975-78; staff devel. coord. Washtenaw County Health Dept. and Vis. Nurse Assn., Ann Arbor, Mich., 1978-85; home care and hospice adminstr. United Hosp., Port Chester, N.Y., 1985-93; clin. supr., dir. patient care Vis. Nurse and Cmty. Care, Inc., Vernon, Conn., 1993-98; nurse practitioner Cons. Rheumatologists, Hartford, Conn., 1996-98, Advanced Practice Nursing Assocs., Rocky Hill, Conn., 1998—. Mem. ANA, Sigma Theta Tau. Office: 2138 Silas Deane Hwy Rocky Hill CT 06067

HOFFMAN, PHILIP GUTHRIE, former university president; b. Kobe, Japan, Aug. 6, 1915; s. Benjamin Philip and Florence (Guthrie) H. (Am. citizens); m. Mary Elizabeth Harding, Aug. 31, 1939; children: Philip Guthrie, Mary Victoria Hoffman Forsyth, Ruth Ann Hoffman Cabler, Jeanne Hoffman Camp. Student, George Washington U., 1936-37; A.B., Pacific Union Coll., 1938; M.A., U. So. Calif., 1942; Ph.D., Ohio State U., 1948; H.H.D. (hon.), Jacksonville U.; LL.D. (hon.), U. Americas, U. Akron; L.H.D. (hon.), Pikeville Coll., Marshall U., U. Houston, 1987; D.L. (hon.), Kyung Hee U., Korea; D.H.C. (hon.), Autonomous U., Guadalajara (Mex.); Litt.D. (hon.), U. St. Thomas, 1979. Credit mgr. Harding Sanitarium, Worthington, Ohio, 1938-40; instr. history Ohio State U. Columbus, 1946-49; asst. prof. history U. Ala., Tuscaloosa, 1949-51, assoc. prof., 1951-53, dir. arts and scis. extension services, 1949-53; dean, assoc. prof. history gen. extension div. Oreg. System Higher Edn., Portland, 1953-55; prof. history Portland State Coll., Oreg., 1955-57, dean faculty, 1955-57; v.p., dean faculties, prof. history U. Houston, 1957-61, pres., 1961-79, pres. emeritus, 1979—; cons. Mitchell Energy and Devel. Corp., Houston, 1980-81; pres. Tex. Med. Ctr. Inc., Houston, 1981-85; dir. Fed. Res. Bank Dallas. Mem. Nat. Commn. on Accrediting; mem. Am. Council on Edn., Coll. Entrance Exam. Bd. Lt. (j.g.) USNR, 1943-45. Recipient Centennial Achievement award Ohio State U., 1970, Merit award U. So. Calif., 1975. Mem. Tex. Hist. Assn., Gulf Hist. Assn., Am. Hist. Assn., Assn. Tex. Coll. and Univs. (pres.), Assn. Urban Univs. (pres. 1965-66), Nat. Assn. State Univs. and Land-Grant Colls. (dir. 1971-75), So. Univ. Conf. (pres. 1976-77), Phi Kappa Phi, Phi Alpha Theta (nat. pres. 1952-54), Omicron Delta Kappa. Clubs: Petroleum (Houston), Torch (Houston); Houston; River Oaks (Houston). Lodge: Rotary. Home: 2929 Buffalo Speedway Unit 2208 Houston TX 77098-1711

HOFFMAN, RICHARD BRUCE, lawyer; b. Columbus, Ohio, June 8, 1947; s. Marion Keith and Ruth Eileen (McLear) H.; m. Sandra Kay Schenkel, July 26, 1975; children: Kipp Hunter, Tyler Blake. BS in Gen. Engring., U. Ill., 1970; JD, DePaul U., 1973; LLM, John Marshall Sch. of Law, 1981. Bar: Ill. 1973, U.S. Dist. Ct. (no. dist.) Ill. 1973, U.S. Patent and Trademark Office 1973, U.S. Ct. Appeals (7th cir.) 1979, U.S. Ct. Appeals (fed. and 9th cirs.) 1982. Assoc. McCaleb, Lucas & Brugman, Chgo., 1973-76, ptnr., 1976-84; ptnr. Tilton, Fallon, Lungmus & Chestnut, Chgo., 1984—. Mem. ABA, Ill. Bar Assn., Chgo. Bar Assn., Intellectual Property Law Assn. Chgo., Am. Intellectual Property Law Assn., Internat. Trademark Assn., Legal Club Chgo., Union League-Chgo. Office: Tilton Fallon Lungmus & Chestnut 100 S Wacker Dr Ste 960 Chicago IL 60606-4002

HOFFMAN, RICHARD CURZON, IV, business administration educator; b. Balt., Aug. 10, 1947; s. Richard Curzon III and Cecile (de Poulpiquet) H.; m. Karin Saral, Nov. 27, 1976; 1 child, Hillary Elizabeth. BA, Trinity Coll., Hartford, Conn., 1970; MBA, U. Pa., Phila., 1973; PhD in bus., Ind. U., 1983. Asst. prof. Coll. William and Mary, Williamsburg, Va., 82-88, U. Del., Newark, 1988-93; assoc. prof. bus. adminstrn. Salisbury (Md.) State U., 1993—. Mem. editl. bd., assoc. editor Jour. African Fin. & Econ. Devel., 1990-94; mem. editl. bd. Jour. Managerial Issues, 1991-95, Jour. Bus. & Mgmt., 1993—; contbr. articles to profl. jours. Mem. long range planning com. Salisbury-Wicomico Arts Coun., 1994-96, chair, 1995-96; acad. adv. coun. Consorting U. for Internat. Bus. Studies, Clemson, S.C., 1991-93; bd. mem. Daily Record Co., Balt., 1973-77. With U.S. Army, 1970-76. Grantee Coll. William & Mary, Williamsburg, Va., 1985, U. Del., Newark, 1991, U.S. Dept. Edn., Washington, 1996-98. Mem. Strategic Mgmt. Soc., Acad. Mgmt., Acad. Internat. Bus. Avocations: jogging, skiing, reading, gardening, photography. Office: Salisbury State U 1101 Camden Ave Salisbury MD 21801-6837

HOFFMAN, RICHARD GEORGE, psychologist; b. Benton Harbor, Mich., Oct. 6, 1949; s. Robert Fredrick and Kathleen Elyce (Watts) H.; m. Julia Ann May, Dec. 18, 1970; children: Leslie Margaret, Michael Charles, Angela Lynn, Jennifer Elizabeth. BS with honors, Mich. State U., 1971; MA in Psychology, Long Island U., 1974, PhD in Clin. Psychology, 1980. Lic. con. psychologst. Instr. pediatrics U. Va., Charlottesville, 1977-80; asst. prof. pediatrics and family med. U. Kans., Wichita, 1980-84; asst. prof. behavioral sci. U. Minn., Duluth, 1984-90, assoc. prof. behavioral sci., 1990—, asst. dean for edn. and curriculum, 1997—, dir. neuropsychology lab., 1986—, co-dir. hypothermia and water safety lab., 1987—, co-dir. neurobehavioral toxicology lab., 1990—; vis. sr. fellow in human clin. neuropsychology U. Okla. Health Scis. Ctr., 1995-96; assoc. dir. Child Evaluation Ctr., Wichita, 1981-82; dir. adminstrn. Comprehensive Epilepsy Clinic, Wichita, 1983-84; cons. psychologist U. Assocs., P.A., Duluth, 1984—. contbr. articles to profl. jour. Pres. Home and Sch. Assn., St. Michael's Sch., Duluth, 1986. Rsch. grantee NIH, 1985, USCG, 1986, Sch. Medicine U. Kans., 1984, U. Minn., 1984, U.S. Army Med. Rsch. Command, 1988—, U.S. Naval Med. Rsch. Command, 1988, Gt. Lakes Protection Fund, 1991—, Agy. for Toxic Substances and Disease Registry, 1992-95, 95—. Fellow Am. Psychol. Soc., Am. Assn. Applied and Preventive Psychology; mem. APA, Nat. Acad. Neuropsychologists. Democrat. Roman Catholic. Avocations: bicycling, hiking. Home: 219 Occidental Blvd Duluth MN 55804-1365 Office: U Minn Dept Behavioral Scis Duluth MN 55812

HOFFMAN, RICHARD M., lawyer; b. N.Y.C., Oct. 22, 1942; s. Simon and Pearl (Lancet) H.; children—Mark, Michael. Grad., CCNY, 1964; LL.B., Bklyn. Law Sch., 1967. Bar: N.Y. 1968. Law clk. to U.S. Dist. Judge U.S. Dist. Ct. (ea. dist.) N.Y., N.Y.C., 1967-69; assoc. Kramer, Lowenstein, Nessen & Kamin, N.Y.C., 1969-73; various positions legal dept. Gen. Instrument Corp., N.Y.C., 1973-81, v.p., gen. counsel, 1981-86, v.p. gen. counsel, sec., 1986-91; pvt. practice, N.Y.C., 1991-94; sr. v.p., gen. counsel Coltec Industries Inc., N.Y.C., 1994-95; of counsel Rubin, Baum, Levin, Constant & Friedman, N.Y.C., 1995-99; ptnr. Friedman Kaplan & Seiler, N.Y.C., 1999—. Mem. ABA, Am. Corp. Counsel Assn., N.Y.C. Bar Assn. (com. corp. law depts. 1981-84). Home: 60 Brite Ave Scarsdale NY 10583-2328

HOFFMAN, RICHARD WILLIAM, banker; b. Rice Lake, Wis., Feb. 8, 1918; s. William A. and Anna (Amundson) H.; m. June M. Weink, June 27, 1948; children: William H., Stephen C. B.A., U. Wis., 1939; M.B.A., 1954; postgrad., Grad. Sch. Banking, U. Wis., 1952, BAI Sch. for Bank Auditors and Comptrollers, 1957; grad. certificate, Am. Inst. Banking, 1960. With First Wis. Nat. Bank Milw., 1939-83, asst. v.p., asst. comptroller, 1959-63, v.p., comptroller, 1963-70, 1st v.p., 1970-83; v.p. First Wis. Corp., 1965-83; instr. Duke U., 1943-45, Army Finance Sch., Ft. Benjamin Harrison, 1945, Am. Inst. Banking, 1946-62, U. Wis., 1946-62, BAI Sch. Bank Adminstrn., 1956-77. Mem. Polit. Edn. and Action League, 1962-68; adv. com. Pub. Expenditure Survey Wis., 1963-83; asso. div. chmn. Milw. County United Fund, 1960-63; mem. Milw. Am. Revolution Bicentennial Commn., 1975-76; exec. v.p. army fin. K.I.T., 1979—. Served to maj., Finance Corps AUS, 1941-46. Mem. Am. Inst. C.P.A.s, Am. Legion, Fin. Execs. Inst., Nat. Alumni Assn. Bank Adminstrn. Inst., Res. Officers Assn., Wis. Econ. Devel. Assn., Soc. Ret. U.S. Army Fin. Officers, Ala. Soc. CPA's, Beta Alpha Psi, Beta Gamma Sigma. Club: Wisconsin Alumni. Home: 6499 Eastwood Glen Dr Montgomery AL 36117-4713

HOFFMAN, ROBERT DEAN, JR., lawyer; b. New Orleans, Dec. 15, 1954; s. Robert Dean Sr. and Ruth Ann (Wheelahan) H.; m. Katherine Bel Thielen, 1987; children: Taylor Ann, R. Dean III. BS, Auburn U., 1975; JD, Loyola U., New Orleans, 1978; LLM in Taxation, Emory U., 1980. Bar: La. 1978, U.S. Dist. Ct. (ea. dist.) La. 1978, U.S. Ct. Appeals (5th cir.) 1979, U.S. Tax. Ct. 1981, U.S. Ct. Appeals (11th cir.) 1981, U.S. Dist. Ct. (mid. dist.) La. 1982, U.S. Dist. Ct. (we. dist.) La. 1995. Ptnr. Ballin & Hoffman, New Orleans, 1978-90; shareholder Burke & Mayer, 1994—; hearing com. mem. La. Atty. Disciplinary Bd., 1999—. Lanaza-Greco Meml scholar Loyola U., 1978. Fellow La. Bar Found.; mem. ABA, La. Bar Assn. Club: Over the Mountain Athletic (commr. 1985—, sportsmanship award 1986), Krewe of Olympia. Home: 12 Oaklawn Dr Covington LA 70433 Office: 1100 Poydras St Ste 2000 New Orleans LA 70163-1121

HOFFMAN, ROBERT HOWARD, investment banker; b. Stamford, Conn., Sept. 22, 1956; s. William Howard and Nancy Virginia (Robbins) H.; m. Katharine Nelson Rhodes, June 11, 1977 (div. Mar. 1986); 1 child, Julia Rhodes; m. Sandra Clinton Griffith, Aug. 22, 1987; children: Shena William, Brooks Lyon, Zephyr Griffith. BA with high honors, Coll. of Wooster, 1978; MBA, NYU, 1982. Rsch. asst. NERA, Inc., N.Y.C., 1978-80; asst. cons. Stone & Webster Mgmt. Cons., N.Y.C., 1980-81; pub. fin. officer Chase Manhattan Capital Markets, N.Y.C., 1982-83, asst. treas., 1983-86, 2d v.p., 1986-88; v.p. Chem. Securities, Inc., N.Y.C., 1988-89, Chase Securities, Inc., N.Y.C., 1990-91; assoc. Morgan Stanley/Dean Witter & Co., Inc., N.Y.C., 1991, v.p., 1992—, asset fin. group, 1996—. Mem. Beta Gamma Sigma. Office: Morgan Stanley & Co Inc Ste B3 1585 Broadway New York NY 10036-8293

HOFFMAN, ROBERT JAMES, retired electronics engineer; b. Portland, Oreg., Dec. 23, 1924; s. William Charles and Myra (Mayo) H. BS in Gen. Sci., MIT, 1951; MBA, Stanford U., 1956; postgrad., U. So. Calif., 1966. Lic. gen. radiotelephone FCC. Field engr. Western Elec. Co., Winston-Salem, N.C., 1951-53; engr. Lenkurt Elec. Co., San Carlos, Calif., 1956-58; group leader The Martin Co., Littleton, Colo., 1959-60; sr. reliability engr. Librascope, Glendale, Calif., 1962-68; proprietor Pinewood Electronics, LaPine, Oreg., 1977-81, Rideway, San Diego, 1990—; rschr. earthquake precursors, 1970—; inventor sewing machine empty bobbin alarm, 1984, telephone remote control, 1992. Pub.: (book) Semiconductor Data, 1962. Mem. Project Area Com., San Diego City Heights, 1993. With USN, 1943-46. Avocations: cycling, writing. Home: 5330 Orange Ave Apt 15C San Diego CA 92115-6045

HOFFMAN, ROBERT PHILLIP, legislative staff member. BA in Polit. Sci. magna cum laude, UCLA, 1988. Vol. casework asst. Office of U.S. Senator Pete Wilson, 1985-89; staff asst. Office of U.S. Senator Pete Wilson, Washington, 1989-90, legis. aide, 1990; speech writer Gov. Pete Wilson, Sacramento, 1990-91; dep. dir. Gov. Pete Wilson, Washington, 1993; legis. asst. Office of U.S. Senator John Seymour, Washington, 1991-92; legis. dir. Office of U.S. Senator Larry Pressler, 1992-93, 97, Office of U.S. Senator Mike DeWine, 1997—. Editor-in-chief Politicus, 1988. Mem. Phi Beta Kappa, Pi Sigma Alpha (pres. UCLA chpt.). Avocations: horse-back riding, long-distance running, reading. Office: 140 Russell Senate Office Washington DC 20510-3503

HOFFMAN, RONALD, historical institute administrator, educator; b. Balt., Feb. 10, 1941; s. Emanuel and Ethel (Lubin) H.; m. Sandra Zalma Rudman, Aug. 28, 1965; children: Maia, Barak. AA, Balt. C.C., 1963; BA, George Peabody Coll., 1964; MA, U. Wis., 1965, PhD, 1969. Asst. prof. history U. Md., College Park, 1969-74, assoc. prof., 1974-92, prof., 1992-95; dir. Omohundro Inst. Early Am. History and Culture, Williamsburg, Va., 1992—; prof. Coll. William and Mary, Williamsburg, 1993—; cons. Office Sec. Def., Washington, 1975—; symposia dir. U.S. Capitol Hist. Soc., Washington, 1977-93. Author: A Spirit of Dissension, 1973; co-author: The Pursuit of Liberty: A History of the American People, 1983; co-editor: Diplomacy and Revolution, 1971, Sovereign States in an Age of Uncertainty, 1982, Slavery and Freedom in the Age of the American Revolution, 1983, Arms and Independence: The Military Character of the American Revolution, 1983, An Uncivil War: The Southern Backcountry during the American Revolution, 1985, Peace and Peacemakers: The Treaty of 1783, 1985, The Economy of Early America: The Revolutionary Period, 1763-1790, 1989, We Call Overcome: Martin Luther King, Jr., and the Black Freedom Struggle, 1990, To Form a More Perfect Union: The Critical Ideas of the Constitution, 1992, Religion in a Revolutionary Age, 1994, Of Consuming Interests: The Style of Life in the Eighteenth Century, 1994, The Transforming Hand of Revolution, 1996, Launching the Extended Republic: The Federalist Era, 1996, The Bill of Rights: Government Proscribed, 1997; contbr. articles to hist. publs. 3d class petty officer USNR, 1959-61. Fellow Ford Found., 1967, Eleutherian Mills-Hagley Found., 1978; grantee NEH, 1977, Nat. Hist. Publs. and Records Commn., 1979—. Mem. Am. Hist. Assn., Orgn. Am. Historians, Assn. Documentary Editing, So. Hist. Assn., Va. Hist. Soc., Md. Hist. Soc. Democrat. Jewish. Home: 201 Palace Green St Williamsburg VA 23185-4238 Office: Omohundro Inst Early Am History and Culture PO Box 8781 Williamsburg VA 23187-8781

HOFFMAN, S. DAVID, lawyer, engineer, educator; b. N.Y.C., June 16, 1922; s. Joseph and Ida (Katz) H.; m. Naomi Barbara Brosterman, June 30, 1946; children: Mathew E., Robert Adam. BE in Elec. Engring., Yale U., 1945; JD, St. John's U., N.Y.C., 1955. Bar: N.Y. 1955, U.S. Supreme Ct. 1960, U.S. Ct. Mil. Appeals 1961, U.S. Patent Office 1964, Ill. 1981. Engr. Western Electric Co., N.Y.C., Newark, 1946-49; head elec. engring. Am. Nat. Stds. Inst., N.Y.C., 1949-66, resident legal counsel, 1955-66, dir. contracts and cert., 1955-66; v.p., gen. counsel Underwriters Labs. Inc., Northbrook, Ill., 1966-88; cons. counsel to the pres. Underwriters Labs. Inc., Northbrook, 1988-90; arbitrator Lake and Cook County (Ill.) Cts., 1989—; sec. U.S. nat. com. Internat. Electrotech. Commn., 1955-66; vol., cons. multimedia resource Highland Park (Ill.) H.S., 1990—; adj. prof. divsn. of indsl. and systems engring. dept. mech. engring. U. Ill., Chgo., 1974-92; vol. Internet tutor Highland Park Libr., 1996—; mgr. tech. activities Nat. Bur. Stds. for U.S. Consumer Products Safety Commn., 1970-71. Contbr. numerous articles to profl. jours. Mem. indsl. adv. bd. U. Ill., Chgo., 1974-95; commr. City of Highland Park (Ill.) Telecomms. Commn., 1998—; online instr. Sr. Net, 1998—. With USNR, 1942-46, 50-52, ret. comdr. JAG Corp. Recipient Achievement award U.S. Pres. Commn. on Exec. Interchange, 1973-74, Merit awards Am. Nat. Stds. Inst., Joint award ASTM-Stds. Engring. Soc., 1980, Margaret Dana award ASTM. Fellow IEEE (life), Stds. Engring. Soc. (Leo B. Moore medal 1980).

HOFFMAN, S. JOSEPH, advertising agency executive; b. Haverhill, Mass., Feb. 19, 1920; s. Joseph H. and Bessie (Milhendler) H.; m. Ruth V. Wicks, Nov. 17, 1951; children—Jane, David, Drew. Student, Boston U., 1940; BS, Ind. U., 1943. Pres. Duro Specialty Co., Lynn, Mass., 1945-50; with Ingalls Quinn & Johnson, Inc., Boston, 1950—; copywriter Ingalls Quinn & Johnson, Inc., 1950-56, copy chief, 1956-59, partner, 1959-64, prin., exec. v.p., 1964-78, pres., 1978-83, chmn., chief exec. officer, 1983-88, chmn. emeritus, 1989; pres. Adgroup Internat. Inc., Montreal, Que., Can., 1972-74; pres. Andover (Mass.) Liquors, Inc., The Vineyard, North Andover, Mass.; overseer rev. bd. Sta. WGBH-TV. Mem. Andover Devel. and Indsl. Commn., 1966—, Boston Civic Design Commn., 1988; ho. dels. Mass. Easter Seal Soc., pres., 1989—, Back Bay Assn. With AUS, 1942-44. Mem. New Eng. Broadcasters Assn., New Eng. Advt. Club, N.E. Advt. Hall of Fame, Lanam Club, Comml. Consul (Boston for Luxembourg). Home: 28 Hidden Way Andover MA 01810-4939 Office: Ingalls Quinn & Johnson Inc One Design Center Pl Boston MA 02210

HOFFMAN, SHARON LYNN, adult education educator; b. Chgo.; d. David P. and Florence (Soifer) Seaman; m. Jerry Irwin Hoffman, Aug. 25, 1963; children: Steven Abram, Rachel Irene. BA, Ind. U., 1961; M Adult Edn., Nat.-Louis Univ., 1992. High sch. English tchr. Chgo. Pub. Schs., 1961-64; tchr. Dept. of Def. Schs., Braconne, France, 1964-66; tchr. ESL Russian Inst., Garmisch, Fed. Republic Germany, 1966, 67; tchr. adult edn. Monterey Peninsula Unified Schs., Ft. Ord, Calif., 1977-79; tchr. ESL MAECOM, Monmouth County, N.J., 1979-80; lectr., tchr. adult edn. Truman Coll./Temple Shalom, Chgo.; tchr. homebound Fairfax County Pub. Schs., Fairfax, Va., 1976; entry operator Standard Rate & Data, Wilmette, Ill., 1986-87; rsch. editor, spl. projects editor Marquis Who's Who, Wilmette, 1987-92; mem. adj. faculty Nat.-Louis U., Evanston and Wheeling, Ill., 1993—; tutor coord., then coord. learning specialist Nat.-Louis U., 1993—; pres. Cultural Transitions, Highland Park, Ill., 1992—. Mem. ASTD, TESOL, Nat. Coun. Tchrs. English, Internat. Reading Assn., Chgo. Drama League. Home and Office: 2270 Highmoor Rd Highland Park IL 60035-1702

HOFFMAN, STANLEY MARC, editor; b. Cleve., 1959. BMus in Music Composition cum laude, Boston Conservatory of Music, 1981; MMus in Music Composition, New Eng. Conservatory of Music, 1984; PhD in Music Composition/Theory, Brandeis U., 1993. Engraver Scores Internat., Boston, 1990-98; editor ECS Pub., Boston, 1998—; vocalist Temple B'nai Torah High Holiday Choir, 1997—; condr. Temple Israel High Holidays Choir, Swampscott, Mass., 1988-96, Temple Emmanuel Choir, Newton, Mass., winter 1983. Composer: Three Short Piano Pieces, 1980, Two-part Invention (piano), 1980, The Man in the Street (cello), 1981, Romance for Orchestra (in C minor), 1982, Rondino (wind quintet), 1983, Little Sea Nocturne (orch.), 1982, Brass Sextet (2 trumpets, 2 horns, 2 trombones), 1984, Cycles (piano), 1985, Thirteen Ways of Looking at a Blackbird (BMI award 1984-85, mezzo soprano, string quartet), 1984, rev., 1993, Of All the Souls that Stand Create (baritone, piano), 1985, rev., 1993, An-im Zemiros (acapella choir), 1985, rev., 1993, String Quartet, 1987, rev., 1993, Poem and Lamentations (violin, piano), 1987, Piano Piece, 1986, Hymn of Glory (violas, cello), 1988, rev., 1994, Rain (acapella choir), 1988, rev., 1993, Nocturne for Nine Players (2 flutes, oboe, clarinet, bassoon, 2 horns, harp, percussion), 1992, Moulded Clay-Chiselled Rock (instrument in C, piano), 1994, Bagatelle (bassoon or bass trombone), 1994, A Song Without Words (horn), 1994, A Psalm Beyond the Silences (choir, piano), 1994, Lord of the World (acapella choir, 1994, A Pacific Prelude (brass quintet), 1995; There Is a Name (children's choir, guitar) 1995, Trio in One Movement (clarinet, viola, cello), 1995, Psalm 23 (acapella choir), 1998, Psalm 1 (a capella choir), 1998, Psalm 121 (a capella choir), 1998, The Writing of Autumn (choir, piano), 1999. Office: ECS Pub Co 138 Ipswich St Boston MA 02215-3534

HOFFMAN, STEVEN JAMES, historian, educator; b. Ft. Belvoir, Va., Oct. 28, 1959; m. Margaret A. Waterman. BA, Ga. State U., 1985, M of Heritage Preservation, 1987; PHD, Carnegie Mellon U., 1993. Adj. asst. prof. Bentley Coll., Waltham, Mass., 1993-95; lectr. in history Bradford (Mass.) Coll., 1993-95; asst. prof. S.E. Mo. State U., Cape Girardeau, 1995—. Contbr. articles, book revs. to profl. jours. Mem. Midwest Assn. for the Recognition and Recording of Ethnic Heritage (sec. 1997—). Office: SE Mo State U Dept History 1 University Plz Cape Girardeau MO 63701-4799

HOFFMAN, THOMAS EDGAR, mechanical engineer; b. Ashland, Ohio; s. Herbert Oscar and Ruth Mae (Semler) H.; m. Jill Ann Thompson, Oct. 13, 1956; 1 child, Betsy Sears Hoffman Hundahl. BS, U. Rochester, 1950; MS, MIT, 1951, ME, 1954. Registered profl. engr., Mass., Ariz. Draftsman F.E. Myers & Bros. Co., Ashland, 1944-49; rsch. asst. DAC Lab. MIT, Cambridge, Mass., 1950-56; staff engr. Arthur D. Little, Inc., Cambridge, 1956-64, sr. engr., 1978-86; chief engr. Smithsonian Astrophys. Obs., Cambridge, 1964-78; prin. Hoffman Design & Devel., Marblehead, Mass., 1986—; engring. cons. Kernco, Danvers, Mass., 1984—, MMT Obs., Amado, Ariz., 1983—, Maser Lab., S.A.O., Cambridge, 1992-96, others. Contbr. numerous articles to profl. publs. Charter mem. New Eng. Ski Mus., Franconia, N.H., 1982. With U.S. Army Air Corps, 1944-45. Recipient Group Achievement award NASA, 1977; Bur. Head's award Smithsonian Instn., 1978. Mem. ASME, AIAA, Optical Soc. Am., Ea. Yacht Club, Dolphin Yacht Club, Phi Beta Kappa, Tau Beta Pi. Republican. Avocations: skiing, sailing, officiating yacht racing, metalworking. Home: 18 Franklin St Marblehead MA 01945-3562

HOFFMAN, THOMAS EDWARD, dermatologist; b. L.A., Oct. 14, 1944; s. David Maurice and Ann (Corday) H.; m. Donna Madison, 1973 (div. 1977); m. Linda L., Feb. 20, 1979; children: David, Jay. AB, U. So. Calif., 1966; MD, Tulane U., 1970. Intern U. So. Calif. USC Med. Ctr., 1970-71; residency dermatology Stanford (Calif.) U., 1973-76, fellow dermatopathology, 1973-74; dermatologist pvt. practice, Menlo Park, Calif., 1976—; clin. assoc. prof. Stanford (Calif.) U., 1981-97, clin. prof. dermatology, 1997. With USPHS, 1971-73. Recipient Achievement award Tulane U., 1970. Fellow Am. Coll. Physicians, Am. Acad. Dermatology, Am. Soc. Dermatopathology, Am. Soc. Dermatologic Surgery, Am. Soc. Laser Medicine & Surgery. Avocations: tennis, skiing. Office: Menlo Dermatology Med Group 888 Oak Grove Ave Menlo Park CA 94025-4432

HOFFMAN, TREVOR WILLIAM, professional baseball player; b. Bellflower, Calif., Oct. 13, 1967. Student, U. Ariz. Pitcher San Diego Padres, 1993—. Office: San Diego Padres PO Box 2000 San Diego CA 92112-2000*

HOFFMAN, VALERIE JANE, lawyer; b. Lowville, N.Y., Oct. 27, 1953; d. Russell Francis and Jane Marie (Fowler) H.; m. Michael J. Grillo, Apr. 4, 1996. Student, U. Edinburgh, Scotland, 1973-74; BA summa cum laude, Union Coll., 1975; JD, Boston Coll., 1978. Bar: Ill. 1978, U.S. Dist. Ct. (no. dist.) Ill. 1978, U.S. Ct. Appeals (3rd cir.) 1981, U.S. Ct. Appeals (7th cir.) 1983. Assoc. Seyfarth, Shaw, Fairweather & Geraldson, Chgo., 1978-87, ptnr., 1987—; adj. prof. Columbia Coll., 1985. Contbr. articles to legal publs. Dir. Remains Theatre, Chgo., 1981-95, pres., 1991-93, v.p., 1991-95; dir. The Nat. Conf. for Cmty. and Justice, Chgo. Region, 1993—, nat. trustee, 1995—; trustee bd. advisors Union Coll., 1996—; dir. AIDS Found. of Chgo., 1997—, sec., 1999—; trustee Union Coll., 1999—. Mem. ABA, Chgo. Bar Assn., Law Club Chgo., Univ. Club Chgo. (bd. dirs. 1984-87), Phi Beta Kappa. Office: Seyfarth Shaw Fairweather & Geraldson 55 E Monroe St Ste 4400 Chicago IL 60603-5713

HOFFMAN, WAYNE MELVIN, retired airline official; b. Chgo., Mar. 9, 1923; s. Carl A. and Martha (Tamillo) H.; m. Laura Majewski, Jan. 26, 1946; children—Philip, Karen, Kristin. BA cum laude, U. Ill., 1943, J.D. with high honors, 1947. Bar: Ill. bar 1947, N.Y. bar 1958. Atty. I.C. R.R., 1948-52; with N.Y.C. R.R. Co., 1952-57, exec. asst. to pres., 1958-60, v.p. freight sales, 1960-61, v.p. sales, 1961-62, exec. v.p., 1962-67; chmn. bd. N.Y. Central Trans. Co., 1960-67, Flying Tiger Line, Inc. and Tiger Internat., Inc., 1967-86. Trustee McCallum Theatre, Palm Desert, Calif., Eisenhower Med. Ctr., Rancho Mirage, Calif. Served to capt. inf. AUS, World War II. Decorated Silver Star, Bronze Star with oak leaf cluster, Purple Heart with oak leaf cluster; Fourragere (Belgium). Mem. Bohemian Club (San Francisco), Vintage Club (Indian Wells), Phi Beta Kappa. Home: 74-435 Palo Verde Dr Indian Wells CA 92210-7367 Office: 2450 Montecito Rd Ramona CA 92065-1619

HOFFMAN, WILLIAM, author; b. Charleston, W.Va., May 16, 1925; s. Henry William and Margaret Julia (Beckley) H.; m. Alice Richardson, Nov. 13, 1924; children: Ruth Beckley, Margaret Kay. BA, Hampden-Sydney Coll., 1949, DLitt (hon.), 1980; postgrad., Washington & Lee U., 1949-50, DLitt (hon.), 1995; postgrad., State U. Iowa, 1950-51. Prof. English lit. Hampden-Sydney (Va.) Coll., 1952-59, writer-in-residence, 1964-71; bd. dirs. The Kay Co., Charleston. Author: The Trumpet Unblown, 1955, Days in the Yellow Leaf, 1958, A Place for My Head, 1960, The Dark Mountains, 1963, Yancey's War, 1966, A Walk to the River, 1970, A Death of Dreams, 1973, The Land That Drank the Rain, 1982, Godfires, 1985, Furors Die, 1990, Tidewater Blood, 1998, (short stories) Virginia Reels, 1978, By Land, by Sea, 1988, Follow Me Home, 1994, Best American Short Stories: Prize Stories The O. Henry A wards, Doors, 1999. With U.S. Army, 1943-46, ETO. Recipient Emily Clark Balch prize Va. Quar. Rev., 1988, Andrew Lytle prize The Sewanee Rev., 1989, Goodheart prize The Arthur and Margaret Glasgow Endowment Com., Washington and Lee U., 1989, Dos Passos prize, 1993, Hillsdale prize for fiction Fellowship So. Writers, 1995; named Cultural Laureate, State of Va., 1986; NEA fellow, 1976. Mem. Authors Guild, Fellowship of So. Writers. Republican. Presbyterian. Home: 280 David Bruce Ave Charlotte Court House VA 23923

HOFFMAN, WILLIAM KENNETH, retired obstetrician, gynecologist; b. Milw., Jan. 18, 1924; s. William Richard and Marian (Riegler) H.; m. Peggy Folsom, July 28, 1952; children: Janet Susan, Ann Elizabeth. Student, U. Wis., 1942-43, U. Pa., 1943-44; postgrad., U. Pa., 1954-55; MD, Marquette U., 1947. Intern Columbia Hosp., 1947-48, resident ob-gyn., 1948-49, mem. staff, 1949-91; ret., 1991; preceptor R.E. McDonald, MD, Milw., 1949-50; resident in ob-gyn U. Chgo., 1950-51; practice medicine specializing in ob-gyn, Milw., 1955-74; mem. staff, Columbia Hosp.; dir. health service U. Wis.-Milw., 1974-91, cons. Sch. Nursing, 1976-77, clin. assoc. prof., 1979-91, vice chmn., mem. instl. rev. bd., 1976-91, mem. instl. safety and health com., 1981-91, chmn., 1984-88. Recipient, Spaights Plaza Awd., U. Wisconsin-Milwaukee, 1998. Mem. ACOG, Am. Coll. Health Assn., Am. Coll. Sports Medicine, Royal Soc. Medicine, Am. Cancer Soc. (bd. dirs. Wis. divsn. 1983-88, pub. edn. com. Milw. divsn.). Home: 2023 E Trolley Ct Boise ID 83712-8445

HOFFMAN, WILLIAM M(OSES), playwright, editor; b. N.Y.C., Apr. 12, 1939; s. Morton and Johanna (Papiermeister) H. BA cum laude, CCNY, 1960. Asst. editor Hill & Wang Corp., N.Y.C., 1961-67, assoc. editor, drama editor, 1967-68; editor New American Play series, 1968-71; lit. adviser Scripts mag., N.Y.C., 1971-75; founder, dir. Wolf Company, 1968—; artist-in-residence Lincoln Center Student Program, 1971-72; artist-in-residence Changing Scene, 1972; playwright-in-residence American Conservatory Theatre, San Francisco, 1978; playwright-in-residence La Mama Experimenta Theatre Club, New York, 1978-79; vis. lectr. U. Mass. at Boston, 1973; adj. prof. playwriting Hofstra U., Hempstead, N.Y., 1980-86; adj. assoc. prof. U. Mich., 1988, New Sch., 1991-93, Juilliard Sch., 1991-93, Circle Repertory Co., 1993-94, Ariz. State U., 1994. Author: (plays) Thank You, Miss Victoria, 1965, Saturday Night at the Movies, 1965, Good Night, I Love You, 1966, Spring Play, 1967, Three Masked Dances, 1967, Incantation, 1967, Uptight, 1968, XXXXX, 1969, Luna, 1970, A Quick Nut Bread to Make Your Mouth Water, 1970, From Fool to Hanged Man, 1972, The Children's Crusade, 1972, I Love Ya, Ya Big Ape, 1973, Gilles de Rais, 1975, Cornbury, 1976, Shoe Palace Murray, 1978, Gulliver's Travels, 1978, A Book of Etiquette, 1978, As Is, 1985 (Tony award nomination best play 1986, Drama Desk award best play 1986, Obie award best play 1986), (with others) The Way We Live Now: American Plays and the AIDS Crisis, 1990, Riga, 1995; (operas) A Figaro for Antonia, 1983, The Ghosts of Versailles, 1991 (commd. by Met. Opera to write libretto); (TV scripts) Notes from the New World: Louis Moreau Gottschalk, 1976, Pink Panther's Magic Music Hall, 1977, The Last Days of Stephen Foster, 1977, Whistler: Five Portraits, 1978; (poetry) The Cloisters (song cycle), 1968, Fine Frenzy, 1972; (lyrics) Wedding Song, 1979; writer: (soap opera) One Life to Live; editor: New American Plays series, 3 vols., 1968-71, 31 New American Poets, 1970, Gay Plays, 1978; contbr. to profl. jours. Recipient Writers Guild award, 1992, Erwin Piscator award, 1994; MacDowell Colony fellow, 1971; Guggenheim fellow, 1974; NEA creative writing fellow, 1976; Playwriting fellow N.Y. Found. Arts, 1985, 94; Carnegie Fund for Authors grantee, 1972; PEN Am. Ctr. grantee, 1972; NEA grantee, 1975. Mem. ASCAP, Circle Repertory Co., PEN, Dramatists Guild, Writers Guild Am., Phi Beta Kappa. Office: ICM Christine Dahl 40 W 57th St New York NY 10019-4001*

HOFFMANN, CHARLES WESLEY, retired foreign language educator; b. Sioux City, Iowa, Nov. 25, 1929; s. John Wesley and Gertrude J. (Giessen) H.; m. Barbara Brandel Frank, Aug. 11, 1954; children: Eric Gregory, Karla Jennifer. B.A., Oberlin Coll., 1951; M.A., U. Ill., 1952, Ph.D., 1956. Fulbright fellow U. Munich, Germany, 1953-55; Instr. German UCLA, 1956-58, asst. prof., 1958-64; assoc. prof. Ohio State U., 1964-66, prof., 1966—, chmn. dept. German, 1969-77, 86-87. Author: Opposition Poetry in Nazi Germany, 1962, Survey of Research Tool Needs in German Language and Literature, 1978; also: articles on 20th Century German lit; adv. editor: Dimension, 1968-74. Recipient Disting. Teaching award UCLA, 1962, Lou Nemzer award for def. acad. freedom, 1982, Exemplary Faculty award Ohio State U., 1991; Fulbright grantee Germany, 1953-55, 1981. Mem. MLA, Am. Assn. Tchrs. German, ACLU, AAUP (pres. Ohio State U. 1984-86). Home: 291 Mccoy Ave Worthington OH 43085-3748 Office: Dieter Cunz Hall Columbus OH 43210

HOFFMANN, CHRISTOPH LUDWIG, lawyer; b. Elsterwerda, Germany, Oct. 9, 1944; came to U.S., 1965; s. Gunther and Ruth (Hornschuh) H.; m. Susan Magnuson, June 18, 1983. Student, Freie U. Berlin, 1964-65; BA, U. Wis., 1966; JD, Harvard U., 1969. Bar: Mass. 1969, R.I. 1977. Assoc. Bingham, Dana & Gould, Boston, 1969-76; asst. gen. counsel Textron Inc., Providence, 1976-83; v.p., gen. counsel, sec. Pneumo Corp., Boston, 1983-85; sr. v.p., gen. counsel, sec. Pneumo Abex Corp., Boston, 1985-91; v.p., sec., gen. counsel Raytheon Co., Lexington, Mass., 1991-94, sr. v.p. law, human resources and corp. adminstrn., sec., 1994-95, exec. v.p. law and corp. adminstrn., sec., 1995-98; ltd. ptnr. Carlisle 1999, L.P., 1998—; bd. dirs. Assoc. Industries Mass., 1994-98; trustee Deaconess Glover Hosp., 1994-98. Mem. ABA, New Eng. Legal Found. (bd. dirs. 1991—), Mass. Bar Assn., R.I. Bar Assn., Assn. Gen. Counsel.

HOFFMANN, DONALD, architectural historian; b. Springfield, Ill., June 24, 1933; s. George C. and Ines (Catron) H.; m. Theresa Cecelia McGrath, Apr. 12, 1958; children—George, Alan, Eric, Michael, Valerie. Student, U. Chgo., 1949-53, U. Kansas City, Mo., 1958. Mem. staff Kansas City (Mo.) Star, 1956-90, art critic, 1965-90; mem. journalism adv. com. Fulbright Scholarship Program, 1968-70. Editor: The Meanings of Architecture-Buildings and Writings by John Wellborn Root, 1967; author: The Architecture of John Wellborn Root, 1973, Frank Lloyd Wright's Fallingwater, 1978, 2d rev. edit., 1993, Frank Lloyd Wright's Robie House, 1984, Frank Lloyd Wright: Architecture and Nature, 1986, Frank Lloyd Wright's Hollyhock House, 1992, Understanding Frank Lloyd Wright's Architecture, 1995, Frank Lloyd Wright's Dana House, 1996, Frank Lloyd Wright, Louis Sullivan and the Skyscraper, 1998; asst. editor Jour. Soc. Archtl. Historians, 1970-72; contbr. articles to profl. jours. Younger Humanist fellow NEH, 1970-71; Art Critic's fellow-grantee Nat. Endowment for Arts, 1974. Mem. Soc. Archtl. Historians (bd. dirs. 1968-70), Am., Art Inst. Chgo. (life). Home: 6441 Holmes St Kansas City MO 64131-1110

HOFFMANN, FRANK WILLIAM, library science educator, writer; b. Geneva, N.Y., May 2, 1949; s. Frank Anton and Lydia Mae (Mayer) H.; m. Lee Ann Black, Jan. 5, 1980. BA, Ind. U., 1971, MLS, 1972; PhD, U. Pitts., 1977. Libr. Memphis Pub. Libr., 1972-74; grad. asst. Grad. sch. Libr. & Info. Sci. U. Pitts., 1974-77; libr. Woodville State Hosp., Carnegie, Pa., 1976-78; prof. Sam Houston State U., Huntsville, Tex., 1979—; part-time reference libr. Carlow Coll., Pitts., 1974-76, Northland Pub. Libr., Pitts., 1976-78; adj. prof. La. State U., 1980, U. Houston, 1985-88, U. Tex., Brownsville, 1996-97; editor Haworth Press, Binghamton, N.Y., 1990—, ABC-Clio, 1997. Author: The Literature of Rock, vol. 1, 1981 (Best Acad. Book, Choice Mag. N.Y.C. 1981), vol. 2, 1986, vol. 3, 1995, Popular Culture and Libraries, 1984, Intellectual Freedom & Censorship, 1988 (Best Acad. Book, Choice Mag. N.Y.C. 1988), Encyclopedia of Fads, vol. 1, 1990, vol. 2, 1991, vol. 3, 1992, vol. 4, 1993, American Popular Culture, 1995, Library Collection Development Policies, 1996, Guide to Popular U.S. Government Publication, 5th edit., 1998, Grantmanship for Schools and Public Libraries, 1998, Intellectual Freedom Bibliography, 1998; editor: Popular Culture in Libraries, 1993-96, Popular Culture Sourcebooks, 1990—; reviewer jours. in field; editor (book series) Popular Culture, 1977—; contbr. articles to profl. jours. Bd. trustees Montgomery County Pub. Libr. Sys., Conroe, Tex., 1990—; lay rep. Houston Area Librs., 1990—; automation consortium mem. North Harris C.C.- Montgomery Librs., Houston, 1994—. Mem. ALA, Spl. Libr. Assn. (Tex. chpt. bd. dirs. 1979-89), Popular Culture Assn., Beta Phi Mu. Democrat. Avocations: record collecting, weightlifting, cycling, reading. Home: 30 E Shadowpoint Cir The Woodlands TX 77381-5142 Office: Sam Houston State U Dept Libr Sci PO Box 2236 Huntsville TX 77341-2236

HOFFMANN, GREGG J., journalist, author; b. Oak Park, Ill., Feb. 23, 1949; s. Robert and Jeanine (Casper) H.; m. Pauline Ehlen, July 20, 1974. BA in Journalism, U. Wis., 1973; MA in Comm., U. Wis., Milw., 1985. Assoc. editor Burlington (Wis.) Std. Press, 1973-76; owner, operator M & T Comm., Whitefish Bay, Wis., 1976—; sr. lectr. U. Wis., Milw., 1987—; Milw. corr. Kenosha News, USA Today, Baseball Weekly, The Sporting News On-Line; sr. lectr. U. Wis., Milw., 1987—; bd. dirs. Internat. Soc. Gen. Semantics, Concord, Calif.; trustee Inst. Gen. Semantics, Englewood, N.J., 1991—; cons. in field. Author: The American Challenge, 1979, Media Maps and Myths, 1993, What You Can Do to Help the Hungry Feed Themselves, 1994, Mapping the Media, 1997, Down in the Valley: The History of Milwaukee County Stadium, 1999; contbr. articles to profl. jours. Recipient Enterpise Reporting award Wis. Newspaper Assn., 1973-74, Freedom Found. Honor medal, 1980, Top Journalism award Am. Planning Assn., 1980, Irving Lee award Inst. Gen. Semantics, 1997; Sanford Berman fellow Internat. Soc. Gen. Semantics, 1989; fellow Environ. Journalism Inst./ Knight Ctr. at Mich. State U. Mem. Midwest Soc. Gen. Semantics (founder), Assn. Educators Mass Communication, Soc. Profl. Journalists, Milw. Press Club, Soc. Environ. Journalists, Pro Basketball Writers Assn. Avocations: trout fishing, golf, hiking, reading. Home and Office: 4842 N Shoreland Ave Milwaukee WI 53217-5821

HOFFMANN, JOAN CAROL, retired academic dean; b. Cedarburg, Wis., Feb. 20, 1934; d. Frank Ernst and Althea Wilhelmina (Behm) H. Nursing diploma, Michael Reese Hosp., 1955; BS in Zoology, U. Wis., Madison, 1959; PhD in Physiology, U. Ill., Chgo., 1965. RN, Wis., Ariz. Sci. instr. Michael Reese Hsop., Chgo., 1959-62; USPHS trainee U. Ill., Chgo., 1962-64; NSF postdoctoral fellow Coll. de France, Paris, 1964-65; asst. prof. U. Rochester, N.Y., 1965-70; assoc. prof., prof. U. Hawaii, Honolulu, 1970-83; dean of students U. Mass. Med. Sch., Worcester, 1983-94; ret., 1994; chmn. anatomy U. Hawaii, 1973-80. Contbr. articles to sci. jours. NIH rsch. grantee, 1966-75. Mem. Endocrine Soc., Soc. for Study of Reprodn., Am. Assn. Anatomists, Women in Endocrinology (sec. 1978-79, pres. 1987-88), Am. Coun. Edn. (bd. dirs., Mass. chpt., network identification program 1993-94), Phi Beta Kappa, Sigma Xi. Avocations: gardening, needlework, wood turning, reading. Home: 77618 Malone Cir Palm Desert CA 92211

HOFFMANN, LOUIS GERHARD, immunologist, educator, sex therapist; b. Bloemendaal, Netherlands, July 12, 1932; came to U.S., 1950; s. Gerhard Hendrik and Louise Gertrude (Tobi) H.; m. Georgianna Grace Stracke, Nov. 4, 1955; children—Julianna Tobi, Eugenie Claire. B.A. with honors, distinction, Wesleyan U., 1953; Sc.M. in Hygiene, Johns Hopkins U., 1958, Sc.D., 1960. NSF postdoctoral fellow U. Calif., Berkeley, 1960-62; from instr. to asst. prof. microbiology Johns Hopkins U., Balt., 1962-64; asst. prof. U. Iowa, Iowa City, 1964-67, assoc. prof., 1967-74, prof., 1974-96, retired, 1996; pvt. practice sex therapy team, 1978—; Diplomate Am. Bd. Sexology. Contbr. articles to profl. jours. Mem. Democratic Central Com. Johnson County, Iowa, 1968-76. NIH fellow, 1962-63; grantee NIH, 1964-67, 80-83, NSF, 1968-74, Iowa Heart Assn., 1969-72, 77-79, Damon Runyon Meml. Fund, 1972-74. Home: 4 Timberwick Rd Santa Fe NM 87505-8908

HOFFMANN, MANFRED WALTER, consulting company executive; b. Bklyn., Apr. 21, 1938; s. Hermann Karl and Emilie (Talmon) H.; m. Barbara Ann Kenvin, Aug. 5, 1961; children: Lisa Joy, Lauren Kimberly, Kurt William. BS, Cornell U., 1960; MEd, Temple U., 1972, PhD, 1977. With Sun Oil Co., 1967-71; mgr. mktg. devel. Sun Oil Co., Rosemont, Pa., 1971-72; mgr. tng. Sun Oil Co., Rosemont, 1973-77, dir. orgn. and mgmt. devel., 1977-79; dir. human resources and adminstrn. Sun Prodn. Co., Dallas, 1979-83; dir. world wide human resources Sun Exploration & Prodn. Co., 1983-90; pres. Gyroscopic Mgmt. Inc., 1989—; lectr. Grad. Sch., U. Tex., Dallas, 1979—. Pres. PTA, bd. mem. Beechwood Sch., 1975-77; cons. exec. com. Orgns. Industrialization Congress Am., 1975-79; bd. dirs. Job Opportunity for Youth, 1980-81; bd. dirs. Dallas SER, 1986—. Served with USMCR, 1956-62. Mem. Am. Soc. Tng. and Devel., Am. Soc. Pers. Adminstrn., Dallas C. of C., Tex. Assn. Bus. Republican. Episcopalian. Home: 2112 Augusta Mc Kinney TX 75070-4300

HOFFMANN, MARTIN RICHARD, lawyer; b. Stockbridge, Mass., Apr. 20, 1932; m. Margaret Ann McCabe; children: Heidi H. Slye, William, Bern. AB, Princeton U., 1954; LLB, U. Va., 1961. Bar: D.C. 1961. Law clk. U.S. Ct. Appeals (4th cir.), 1961-62; asst. U.S. atty. Washington, 1962-65; minority counsel com. on judiciary Ho. of Reps., Washington, 1965-67; legal counsel to U.S. senator C. Percy Washington, 1967-69; asst. gen. counsel Univ. Computing Co., Dallas, 1969-71; gen. counsel Atomic Energy Commn., Washington, 1971-73; spl. asst. to sec. and dep. sec. def. Washington, 1973-74; gen. counsel Dept. Def., Washington, 1974-75; sec. Dept. Army, Washington, 1975-77; mng. ptnr. Gardner, Carton & Douglas, Washington, 1977-89; v.p., gen. counsel, sec. Digital Equipment Corp., Maynard, Mass., 1989-93; of counsel Skadden, Arps, Slate, Meagher & Flom, Washington, 1996—; sr. vis. fellow Ctr. for Policy, Tech. and Indsl. Devel., MIT, Cambridge, 1993-95; trustee Assn. U.S. Army, Washington; bd. dirs. Castle Energy, Phila., Sea Change Corp., Maynard, Mass., Mitretek Systems, Inc. Maj. USAR, 1954-73. Mem. Met. Club. Home: 1546 Hampton Hill Cir Mc Lean VA 22101-6021 Office: 1440 New York Ave NW Washington DC 20005-2111

HOFFMANN, MELANE KINNEY, marketing and public relations executive, writer; b. Baton Rouge, Jan. 25, 1956; d. Kenneth Lee and Louise (Walker) Kinney; m. R. Thomas Hoffmann, Oct. 10, 1981; children: Robert James II, Halloran Kinney, Richard Walker. BA, Am. U., 1977. Gen. mgr. Dance Project, Inc., Washington, 1979-81; account exec. J. Walter Thompson Advt., Washington, 1981-84; v.p., account supr. Ketchum Advt., Washington, 1984-88, Demaine Vickers Advt., Alexandria, Va., 1988-89; sr. counsel Porter/Novelli Pub. Rels., Washington, 1989—. Dir. Resolve, Washington, 1992-93; bd. dirs. nat. capital area YWCA, Washington, 1980-82. Mem. Am. Mktg. Assn. (mem. program com. 1990-92, co-chair), Ad Club Washington (mem. membership com. 1985-90, Addy award 1987). Presbyterian. Avocations: owning and riding horses, gardening, literacy tutoring. Office: Poter/Novelli 1120 Connecticut Ave NW Washington DC 20036-3903*

HOFFMANN, MICHAEL RICHARD, lawyer; b. Des Moines, Apr. 26, 1947; s. Robert Wyman and Margaret Inez Wagner (stepmother) H. and Patricia Hilliard; m. Amy Marie Gales; children: Kurt Michael, Kristen Elaine, Kevin Richard. BS in Chemistry and Zoology, U. Iowa, 1969; JD, Drake U., 1972; LLM in Patent and Trade Regulation, George Washington U., 1973. Bar: Iowa 1972, U.S. Ct. Customs and Patent Appeals 1972, U.S. Patent and Trademark Office 1973, U.S. Dist. Ct. (so. and no. dists.) Iowa 1974, U.S. Ct. Appeals (8th cir.) 1976, U.S. Supreme Ct. 1977. Clerk Jones, Hoffmann & Davison, Des Moines, 1970-73; assoc. Bacon and Thomas, Arlington, Va., 1973-74; assoc. Jones, Hoffmann & Davison, Des Moines, 1974-79, ptnr., 1979-83; pres. Michael R. Hoffmann, P.C., Des Moines, 1983-95; pvt. practice, 1995—; del. U.S./Japan Bilateral Session: A New Era in Legal and Econ. Relations, Tokyo, 1988; mem. Iowa Def. Counsel, Def. Research Inst., Inc. Recipient Am. Jurisprudence award Bancroft-Whitney Co. and Lawyers Coop. Pub. Co., 1970-72. Mem. Iowa State Bar Assn., ABA (sci. and tech. sect.), Iowa Patent Bar Assn. (charter mem.), Am. Patent Law Assn., Am. Judicature Soc., Polk County Bar Assn., Iowa Assn. Workers' Compensation Lawyers, Internat. Assn. Indsl. Accident Bds. and Commns., Prairie Club (pres. Des Moines chpt. 1993-94), Nat. Rifle Club (Washington). Office: 3708 75th St Des Moines IA 50322-3002

HOFFMANN, PETER CONRAD WERNER, history educator; b. Dresden, Germany, Aug. 13, 1930; came to Can., 1970; s. Wilhelm and Elfriede Frances (Müller) H.; m. Helga Luise Hobelsberger, July 22, 1959. Student, U. Stuttgart, 1953-54, U. Tübingen, 1954-55, U. Zurich, 1955, Northwestern U., 1955-56; PhD, U. Munich, 1961. William Kingsford prof. history McGill U., Montreal, Que., Can. Author: Die diplomatischen Beziehungen zwischen Württemberg und Bayern im Krimkrieg und bis zum Beginn der Italienischen Krise (1853-1858), 1963, Widerstand, Staatsstreich, Attentat: Der Kampf der Opposition gegen Hitler, 1969, Die Sicherheit des Diktators: Hitlers Leibwachen, Schutzmassnahmen, Residenzen, Hauptquartiere, 1975, The History of the German Resistance 1933-1945, 1977, Hitler's Personal Security, 1979, Widerstand gegen Hitler, 1979, German Resistance to Hitler, 1988, Claus Schenk Graf von Stauffenberg und seine Brüder, 1992, Stauffenberg: A Family History, 1905-1944, 1995, Stauffenberg und der 20 Juli 1944, 1998. Mem. Deutsche Schillergesellschaft, Can. Hist. Assn., Can. Com. History Second World War, Royal Soc. Can., Württembergischer Geschichts- und Altertumsverein, Am. Hist. Assn., German Studies Assn., Sigma Alpha Epsilon. Home: 4332 Montrose Ave. Montreal, PQ Canada H3Y 2A9

HOFFMANN, ROALD, chemist, educator; b. Zloczow, Poland, July 18, 1937; came to U.S., 1949, naturalized, 1955; s. Hillel and Clara (Rosen) Safran (stepson Paul Hoffmann); m. Eva Börjesson, Apr. 30, 1960; children: Hillel Jan, Ingrid Helena. BA, Columbia U., 1958; MA, Harvard U., 1960, PhD, 1962; D Tech. (hon.), Royal Inst. Tech., Stockholm, 1977; D.Sc. (hon.), Yale U., 1980, Columbia U., 1982, Hartford U., 1982, CUNY, 1983, U. P.R., 1983, U. Uruguay, 1984, U. La Plata, SUNY, Binghamton, 1985, Colgate U., Lehigh U., 1989, Carleton Coll., 1989; DSc (hon.), Ben Gurion U. of the Negev, 1989, U. Md., 1990, U. Athens, 1991; D.Sc. (hon.), U. Thessaloniki, Greece, 1991, U. Ariz., 1991, U. Cen. Fla., 1991, Bar Ilan U., 1991; DSc (hon.), U. St. Petersburg, Russia, 1991, U. Barcelona, 1992, Ohio State U., 1993; others. Jr. fellow Soc. Fellows Harvard, 1962-65; assoc. prof. Cornell U., Ithaca, N.Y., 1965-68; prof. Cornell U., 1968-74, John A. Newman prof. phys. sci., 1974-96, F.T. Rhodes prof. humane letters, 1996—. Author: (with R.B. Woodward) Conservation of Orbital Symmetry, 1970, Solids and Surfaces, 1988, (with V. Torrence) Chemistry Imagined; author: (poetry) The Metamict State, 1987, Gaps and Verges, 1990, The Same and Not the Same, 1995, (with S. Leibowitz Schmidt) Old Wine, New Flasks, 1997, Memory Effects, 1999. Recipient award in pure chemistry Am. Chem. Soc., 1969, Arthur C. Cope award, 1973, Fresenius award Phi Lambda Upsilon, 1969, Harrison Howe award Rochester sect. Am. Chem. Soc., 1970; ann. award Internat. Acad. Quantum Molecular Scis., 1970, Pauling award, 1974, Nobel prize in chemistry, 1981, inorganic chemistry award; Am. Chem. Soc., 1982, Nat. Medal of sci., 1983, Priestley medal, 1990, Centennial medal Harvard U., 1994, Jawaharlal Nehru Birth Centenary award, 1998. Mem. NAS (award in chem. scis. 1986), Am. Acad. Arts and Scis., Russian Acad. Scis. (N.N. Semenov Gold medal), Internat. Acad. Quantum Molecular Scis., Royal Soc. (fgn.), Indian Nat. Sci. Acad., Royal Swedish Acad. Scis., Finnish Acad. Arts and Letters. Office: Cornell U Dept Chemistry Ithaca NY 14853

HOFFMANN, ROBERT SHAW, museum administrator, educator; b. Evanston, Ill., Mar. 2, 1929; s. Robert Charles and Dorothy Elizabeth (Shaw) H.; m. Sally Ann Monson, June 17, 1951; children: Karl Robert, John Frederick, David Randolf, Brenna Elizabeth. BS, Utah State U., 1950; MA, U. Calif., Berkeley, 1954, PhD, 1955; DS (hon.), Utah State U., 1988. From instr. to prof. U. Mont., Missoula, 1955-68; prof., curator U. Kans., Lawrence, 1968-86, Summerfield Disting. prof., 1982; dir. Nat. Mus. Natural History, Washington, 1986-87; asst. sec. for rsch. Smithsonian Instn., Washington, 1988-92, asst. sec. sci., 1992-94, provost, 1994-95; acting dir. Nat. Air & Space Mus., Washington, 1995-96; sr. scientist Nat. Mus. Natural History, Washington, 1996—; gis. fellow Nat. Mus. Natural History, Washington, 1975-76; mem. U.S. Nat. Com. for INQUA, NAS, 1970-82, sec.-treas., 1972-

74, vice chmn., 1974-77, chmn., 1977-82, mem. adv. com. on USSR and Ea. Europe, 1970-75, mem. com. on Yellowstone Grizzlies, 1973-74, mem. ad hoc com. discussion group on US-USSR sci. policies, 1973; mem. mountain habitats com. Internat. Union for Conservation of Nature and Natural Resources, 1971—; mem. organizing com. First Internat. Theriological Congress, Moscow, 1974, mem. presidium, 1974-78; mem. Insectivore group, 1987—, Lagomorph Group, 1990—, Species Survival Commn.; mem. Soviet Union and Ea. Europe area com. Coun. Internat. Exch. Scholars, 1985-90; co-chair high latitude directorate U.S. Nat. Com. for Man and Biosphere, 1989-92; mem. com. on monographs and classification Systematics Agenda 2000, 1991; mem. adv. com. Internat. Sci. Found., 1992-94, chair biology III panel, 1993-94; cons. Faisalabad U., Pakistan, 1971—; adviser Inst. Arctic and Alpine Rsch., Boulder, Colo., 1980—, Quaternary Rsch. Ctr., Seattle, 1981—, and numerous others. Co-author: Mammals in Kansas, 1981, Mammals of the Northern Great Plains, 1983; coord., contbr. Mammal Species of the World, 1982, 93; also articles. NAS fellow, 1963-64; NSF grantee, 1957-87, and numerous other grants; recipient 30 Yr. medal U.S.-USSR Interacad. Exch., 1989. Fellow AAAS; mem. Internat. Coun. Mus. (mem. exec. coun. 1995-98, mem. ethics com. 1998—, U.S. Nat. Com. (bd. dirs. 1990-96), Am. Assn. Mus., Am. Assn. Quarternary Rsch., Am. Soc. Mammalogists (bd. dirs. 1965—, chmn. com. internat. rels. 1964-68, 72-78, 1st v.p. 1973-78, pres. 1981-82), Brit. Mammal Soc., Ecol. Soc. Am., Internat. Assn. Ecology, Internat. Mountain Soc., Soc. Systematic Biology (pres. 1988-89), Xerces Soc. (bd. dirs. 1992—), Russian Acad. Natural Scis. (fgn.), All-Union Theriological Soc. (hon.), ICOM (exec. council 1996-98, ethics com. 1997—), Sigma Xi, Phi Kappa Phi, Phi Sigma. Avocations: birdwatching, hiking, skiing, traveling. Office: NMNH Divsn Mammals Smithsonian Instn MRC 108 Washington DC 20560

HOFFMANN, THOMAS RUSSELL, business management educator; b. Milw., Sept. 10, 1933; s. Alfred C. and Florence M. (Morlock) H.; m. Lorna G. Gruenzel, Aug. 31, 1957; 1 child, Timothy Jay. BS, U. Wis., 1955, MS, 1956, PhD, 1959. Engring. trainee Allis-Chalmers Mfg. Co., 1956-59; asst. prof. U. Wis. Sch. Commerce, 1959-63; mem. faculty U. Minn. Sch. Mgmt., Mpls., 1963—; prof. U. Minn. Sch. Mgmt., 1965—, chmn. dept. mgmt. scis., 1969-78; dir. West Bank Computer Center, 1971-87; cons. to industry. Author: Production Management and Manufacturing Systems, 2 edit., 1967-71, (with others) Fortram 77: A Structured, Disciplined Style, 1978, 83, 88, Production and Inventory Management, 1983, 2d edit., 1991, Production and Operations Management, 1989; editor-in-chief Jour. Ops. Mgmt., 1993-95; contbr. articles to profl. jours. Chmn. long range planning com. Luth. Ch., 1971, pres., 1974, 89, treas., 1977-82, 93-98. Mem. Assn. Computing Machinery, Decision Scis. Inst., INFORMS, Am. Prodn. and Inventory Control Soc. (pres. Twin Cities chpt., 1970-71, pres. 1998). Home: 4501 Sedum Ln Edina MN 55435-4051 Office: U Minn Carlson Sch Mgmt Minneapolis MN 55455

HOFFMANN, WILLIAM FREDERICK, astronomer; b. Manchester, N.H., Feb. 26, 1933; s. Maurice and Charlotte (Hibbs) H.; m. Silke Elisabeth Margaretha Schneider, June 5, 1965; children: Andrea Charlotte, Christopher James. AB in Physics, Bowdoin Coll., 1954; PhD in Physics, Princeton U., 1962. Instr. physics Princeton (N.J.) U., 1958-61; rsch. assoc. NASA-GISS, N.Y.C., 1962, staff astronomer, 1965-73; instr. physics Yale U., New Haven, 1963-64; adj. assoc. prof. Columbia U., N.Y.C., 1970-73; prof. astronomy U. Ariz., Tucson, 1973-98, prof. emeritus astronomy, 1998—. Editor: (with H.Y. Chiu) Gravitation & Relativity, 1964. Pres. Spuyten Duyvil Assn., N.Y.C., 1971. NSF fellow, 1954; Danforth fellow, 1954-58. Fellow AAAS, Am. Physics Soc.; mem. Am. Astron. Soc., Sigma Chi, Phi Beta Kappa. Home: 4225 E Kilmer St Tucson AZ 85711-2825 Office: U Ariz Steward Obs Tucson AZ 85721

HOFFMASTER, BEVERLY ANN, elementary education educator. Tchr. Berkeley Hgts. Elem. Sch., Martinsburg, W.Va., 1989-98, specialist in elem. instrn., 1998—. Recipient State Tchr. of Yr. Elem. award W.Va., 1992. Office: Berkeley County Schs 401 S Queen St Martinsburg WV 25401

HOFFMEISTER, DONALD FREDERICK, zoology educator; b. San Bernardino, Calif., Mar. 21, 1916; s. Percival George and Julia Bell (Hillgartner) H.; m. Helen E. Kaatz, Aug. 11, 1938; m. 2d Florence Williamson, Aug. 15, 1995; children: James Ronald, Robert George. A.B., U. Calif.-Berkeley, 1938, M.A., 1940, Ph.D., 1944. Research, curatorial asst. Museum Vertebrate Zoology, U. Calif.-Berkeley, 1941-44, teaching asst. zoology, 1943-44; assoc. curator modern vertebrates Mus. Natural History, U. Kans., 1944-46, asst. prof. zoology, 1944-46; dir. Mus. Natural History, U. Ill., 1946-84, dir. emeritus, 1984—, mem. faculty univ., 1946—, prof. zoology, 1959-84, prof. emeritus, 1984—; research assoc. Mus. No. Ariz., 1969—. Author: Mammals, 1955, 1963, Fieldbook of Illinois Mammals, 1957, Zoo Animals, 1967, Mammals of Grand Canyon, 1971, Mammals of Ariz., 1986, Mammals of Illinois, 1989; also articles, reports. Fellow Ariz.-Nev. Acad. Sci.; mem. Am. Soc. Mammalogists (hon., sec. 1946-52, v.p. 1961-64, pres. 1964-66, Hartley H.T. Jackson award 1987), Midwest Mus. Conf. (hon., exec. v.p. 1962-63, pres. 1963-64), Am. Assn. Mus. (coun. 1973-76), Assn. Sci. Mus. Dirs. Home: 20 Fields E Champaign IL 61822-6129 Office: U Ill Mus Natural History Urbana IL 61801

HOFFMEISTER, JANA MARIE, cardiologist. MD, SUNY Upstate Med. Ctr., Syracuse, 1976. Diplomate Am. Bd. Internal Medicine, Am. Bd. Cardiovascular Diseases. Intern Albany (N.Y.) Med. Ctr., 1976-78, resident, 1978-80, fellow div. cardiology, 1981-83; fellow div. cardiology Emory U., Atlanta, 1984; fellow coronary angioplasty and interventional cardiology Emory U. Hosp., 1985-86; presenter numerous cardiology confs. Contbr. numerous articles to profl. jours. Mem. ACP, AMA, Cardiac Soc. Upstate N.Y., N.Y. State Soc. Internal Medicine, Am. Soc. Cardiovascular Intervention. Home: 7 Reddy Ln Albany NY 12211-1632

HOFFMEYER, WILLIAM FREDERICK, lawyer, educator; b. York, Pa., Dec. 20, 1936; s. Frederick W. and Mary B. (Stremmel) H.; m. Betty J. Hoffmeyer, Feb. 6, 1960 (divorced); 1 child, Louise C.; m. Karen L. Semmelman, 1985. AB, Franklin and Marshall Coll., 1958; JD, Dickinson Sch. Law, 1961. Bar: Pa. 1962, U.S. Dist. Ct. (mid. dist.) Pa. 1981, U.S. Supreme Ct. 1983. Pvt. practice law, 1962-81; sr. ptnr. Hoffmeyer & Semmelman, 1982—; adj. prof. real estate law York Coll. Pa., 1980-92, real estate law, paral legal program Pa. State U., 1978—. Author: The Abstractor's Bible, 1981, Pennsylvania Real Estate Installment Sales Contract Manual, 1981, Real Estate Settlement Procedures, 1982, Contracts of Sale, 1985, How to Plot a Deed Description, 1986; author, lectr., moderator and course planner numerous Pa. Bar Inst. CLE Programs. Recipient Disting. Svc. award Gen. Alumni Assn. of Dickinson Sch. Law, 1993, Pa. Bar medal, 1997. Mem. ABA, Pa. Bar Assn. (chmn., unauthorized practice of law com.), York County Bar Assn. (chmn. continuing legal edn. com., 1992-96), Am. Coll. Real Estate Lawyers, Lions (past pres. East York club), Masons (past pres. York County Shrine club), York Area C. of C. (chair small bus. support network 1997—). Address: 30 N George St York PA 17401-1214

HOFFNER, MARILYN, university administrator; b. N.Y.C., Nov. 16, 1929; d. Daniel and Elsie (Schulz) H.; m. Albert Greenberg, May 29, 1949; children: Doren Roe, Peter Cooper. BFA, Cooper Union. Art dir. Printers' Ink mag., N.Y.C., 1953-63; art dir. Print mag., N.Y.C., 1960-62; corp. art dir. Vision, Inc., Latin Am., 1963-75, 92-95; dir. alumni rels. and devel. Cooper Union, 1975-96, exec. dir. instnl. advancement, 1996—; project dir. Nat. Graphic Design Archives, 1990-97. Bd. dirs. Art Dirs. Club N.Y., 1973-75, 79-82, exec. sec., 1973-75, exec. treas., 1979-82; mem. Citizens Adv. Cultural Arts Com. Dutchess County, 1978-80. Named Alumnus of Yr., Cooper Union, 1968; recipient Gold medal Art Dirs. Club, 1979, N.Y. State Coun. of the Arts award, 1995. Mem. Cooper Union Alumni Assn. (editor-in-chief 1971-74, 1st v.p. 1974-75, pres. 1999—), Coun. Advancement and Support of Edn., Type Dirs. Club (numerous awards), Nat. Arts Club (exhbn. com.). Contbg. editor Print mag., Art Direction, Graphis mag.; designer mags., advt., books, exhbns. Home: 51 5th Ave New York NY 10003-4320 Office: 30 Cooper Sq New York NY 10003-7120

HOFFNUNG, AUDREY SONIA, speech and language pathologist, educator; b. N.Y.C., Mar. 15, 1928; d. Nathan and Gussie (Karp) Smith; BA cum laude, Bklyn. Coll., 1949; MA, Columbia U., 1950; PhD, City U. N.Y., 1974. Cert. and lic. speech pathologist, N.Y.; m. Joseph Hoffnung, Nov. 26, 1950; children: Bonnie Fern, Tami Lynn. Rehab. therapist Ridgewood Cerebral Palsy Ctr., 1949-50; dir. speech therapy Kingsbrook Med. Ctr., Bklyn., 1950-55; therapist and cons. Morris J. Solomon Clinic, Bklyn., 1956-58; therapist Speech and Hearing Ctr. Bklyn. Coll., 1958-62, 63-64; pvt. practice speech therapy Hewlett (N.Y.) Med. Ctr., 1961-63; pvt. practice speech therapy, Oceanside, N.Y., 1964-71; cons. on staff for aphasic patients Phys. Medicine and Rehab. Ctr., South Nassau Cmtys. Hosp., 1964-65; part-time lectr. Speech and Hearing Ctr., Queens (N.Y.) Coll., 1970-72; adj. lectr. dept. speech Bklyn. Coll., 1973-74, asst. prof. speech and lang. pathology, 1974-77; asst. prof. dept. speech comm. and theatre St. John's U., Jamaica, N.Y., 1977-80, assoc. prof., 1980-91, prof., 1991-98, chair, 1992-95, pvt. practice speech therapy, 1998—; guest lectr. N.Y. Orton Soc., 1979, Brookdale Med. Ctr., 1978, retired; mem. profl. adv. bd. Vis. Home Health Svcs. of Nassau County, 1973—. Author: (with Valletutti and McKnight) Facilitating communication in young children with handicapping conditions; (with Valletutti and Bender) A Functional Curriculum for Teaching Students With Disabilities Noverbal and Verbal Communication, 1996. Mem. Am. Speech-Lang.-Hearing Assn., N.Y.C. Speech, Hearing and Lang. Assn., N.Y. State Speech Lang. and Hearing Assn. (chairperson student activities 1978-79), L.I. Speech, Lang. and Hearing Assn., Nat. Student Speech-Lang.-Hearing Assn. (hon. advisor 1988), Aphasia Study Group of N.Y.C., N.Y. Acad. Scis. Contbr. articles on speech pathology to profl. jours. Home: 3282 Woodward St Oceanside NY 11572-4527

HOFFSTOT, HENRY PHIPPS, JR., lawyer; b. Pitts., Nov. 13, 1917; s. Henry Phipps and Marguerite (Martin) H.; m. Barbara Drew, Apr. 17, 1948 (dec. Sept. 1994); children: Thayer Hoffstot Drew, Henry Phipps III. AB, Harvard U., 1939, LLB, 1942. Bar: Pa. 1942. Assoc. Reed Smith Shaw & McClay, Pitts., 1946-55, ptnr., 1956-87, of counsel, 1987—; pres., dir. Pennsgrove Water Supply Co., 1967-84; bd. dirs. Landmarks Fin. Corp, Landmarks Real Estate Corp., 1991-95. Active Commn. for Study of Common Body of Knowledge for CPAs, N.Y., 1965-67, Nat. Pks. Centennial Commn., 1971-73; trustee Carnegie Libr., Pitts., 1966—, v.p., 1970—; trustee Carnegie Inst., 1966—, sec., 1968—; supervising com. Bellefield Boiler Plant, 1967—, chmn., 1978—; trustee Family and Children's Svc., 1962-68, 69-75, 77-83, pres., 1964-66; trustee Pitts. Regional Libr. Ctr., 1967-91; trustee St. Edmunds Acad., 1964-72, pres., 1968-70; bd. dirs. Cmty. Chest of Allegheny County, 1962-68, exec. com., 1968-69; bd. dirs. Mendelssohn Choir, Pitts., 1958-85, treas., 1959-61; bd. dirs. Pitts. Chamber Music Soc., 1968-90; bd. dirs. Vis. Nurse Assn. of Allegheny County, 1948-90, 98—, pres., 1957-60, 66-67, 79-83; mem. coun. Am. Mus. in Britain, 1979—; trustee Phipps Conservatory, Inc., 1985-98, pres., 1988-90; bd. dirs. Pitts. chpt. World Federalist Assn., 1967—; bd. dirs., Pitts. Opera Theatre Inc., chmn. 1992-94, 98—; trustee, sec. Vis. Nurse Found., Allegheny County, 1991-97, vice chmn., bd. trustees Pitts. History and Landmarks Found., 1995—; bd. dirs. U.S. Nat. Com. for the Internat. Coun. on Monuments and Sites, 1995-97; bd. advisors Women's Ctr. and Shelter, 1997—. With inf. AUS, 1942-46. Fellow Am. Bar Found.; mem. ABA, SAR (pres. Pitts. chpt. 1978-79), SAR Pa. Soc. (chancellor 1994—), Allegheny County Bar Assn., Am. Law Inst., Pa. Bar Assn., Duquesne Club. Presbyterian. Home: 5057 5th Ave Pittsburgh PA 15232-2128 Office: Reed Smith Shaw & McClay PO Box 2009 Pittsburgh PA 15230-2009

HOFKIN, GERALD ALAN, gastroenterologist; b. Balt., July 4, 1936; m. Phyllis Hofkin, Aug. 23, 1959; children: Leah, Stephen, Karen. AB, MA, Johns Hopkins U., 1957; MD, U. Md., 1961. Diplomate Am. Bd. Internal Medicine, Am. Bd. Gastroenterology. Intern U. Md. Hosp., Balt., 1961, resident in medicine, 1962-63, 64-65; resident in medicine Sinai Hosp., Balt., 1963-64, 65-66; resident in gastroenterology Letterman Hosp., San Francisco, 1966-67; pvt. practice Balt., 1969-91; staff Sinai Hosp., Balt., 1991-99; part-time pvt. practice Woodholme Gastroenterology Assocs., Balt., 1999—; chmn. med. exec. com. Sinai Hosp. Med. Staff, Balt., 1989, pres., 1992-93. Contbr. articles to profl. jours. Maj. U.S. Army, 1966-69. Named Disting. Physician, Sinai Hosp., 1992. Fellow ACP, Am. Coll. Gastroenterology; mem. Am. Soc. Gastroenterol. Endoscopy , Md. Soc. Gastrointesinal Endoscopy (pres. 1995-97), Balt. Amateur Radio Club (v.p. 1978-79), Balt. Radio Amateur TV Soc., Alpha Omega Alpha. Avocations: amateur radio, computers, bridge. Office: Woodholme Gastroenterology Assoc 1838 Greene Tree Rd Baltimore MD 21208

HOFLING, CHARLES ANDREW, anthropologist, linguist, educator; b. Biloxi, Miss., Mar. 9, 1953; s. Charles Kreimer and Madelyn (Laymon) H.; m. Lynne Elizabeth Turner, Sept. 22, 1978; children: Helen Elizabeth. BA, St. Louis U., 1975; MA, Washington U., St. Louis, 1978, PhD in Anthropology, 1982. Asst. prof. anthropology U. Ky., Lexington, Ky., 1984-91; vis. rsch. assoc. prof. U. Cin., Cin., 1991-96; asst. prof. So. Ill. U., Carbondale, Ill., 1996-99, assoc. prof., 1999—. Author: Itzá Maya Texts, 1991, Itzá, Maya Dictionary, 1997. Grantee NSF, 1991-93, 1995-97, NEH, 1993-95. Mem. Am. Anthrop. Assn., Linguistic Soc. Am., Soc. Applied Anthropology, Soc. for Study Indigenous Lang. of Am. Achievements include developing Reference Grammar, text collection, and Dictionary for Itzá, Maya. Office: Anthropology Dept Southern Illinois Univ Carbondale IL 62901

HOFMAN, KEN, professional sports team executive; b. Oakland, Calif.; m. Joan England; 2 children. Student, St. Mary's Coll.; grad., U.S. Merchant Marine Acad. Plastering contractor, 1948-51, home builder, 1951-57; founder Hofmann Co., 1957—; owner professional baseball team Oakland Athletics, 1995—. Regent emeritus, bd. trustees St. Mary's Coll.; fund-raiser Regional Theater for Arts in Walnut Creek, Mt. Diablo Med. Ctr. Master mariner, World War II. Named St. Mary's Alumnus of Yr., 1983. Mem. Nat. Assn. Home Builders, Local Bldg. Industry Assn. (pres., bd. dirs.), Alumni Assn. U.S. Merchant Marine Acad., Nat. Fish and Wildlife Found. (former dir.). Avocations: flying, golfing, hunting, fishing. Fax: 510-562-1633. E-mail: http://www.oaklandathletics.com. Office: Oakland Athletics 7677 Oakport St Ste 200 Oakland CA 94621

HOFMAN, LEONARD JOHN, minister; b. Kent County, Mich., Jan. 31, 1928; s. Bert and Dora (Miedema) H.; m. H. Elaine (Ryskamp) H., Aug. 19, 1949; children: Laurie, Janice, Kathleen, Joel. BA, Calvin Coll., 1948; BTh, Calvin Sem., 1951, MDiv, 1981. Pastor Wright Christian Reformed Ch., Kanawha, Iowa, 1951-54, Kenosha Christian Reformed Ch., Kenosha, Wis., 1954-59, North St. Christian Reformed Ch., Zeeland, Mich., 1959-65, Ridgewood Christian Reformed Ch., Jenison, Mich., 1965-77, Bethany Christian Reformed Ch., Holland, Mich.; pres. bd. trustees Christian Reformed Ch., Grand Rapids, Mich., 1977-82; gen. sec. Christian Reformed Ch. in N.Am., Grand Rapids, Mich., 1982-94, adminstrv. sec. for interchurch rels., 1995—. Sec. bd. trustees Calvin Coll., Grand Rapids, 1970-76. Recipient Oustanding Service award Calvin Alumni Assn., 1978. Mem. Nat. Assn. Evangelicals (bd. dirs. 1986-98, exec. com. bd. dirs. 1990-98, 2d vice chmn., bd. dirs. 1993-94, 1st vice chmn., bd. dirs. 1995-96, chmn. bd. dirs. 1997-98). Home and Office: 2237 Radcliff Cir SE Grand Rapids MI 49546-7725*

HOFMANN, DAVID JOHN, atmospheric science researcher, educator; b. Albany, Minn., Jan. 3, 1937; s. Gregory and Rose (Vos) H.; children: Gretchen, Jennifer, Karl. BS in Physics, U. Minn., 1961, MS in Physics, 1963, PhD in Physics, 1966. Grad. rsch. asst. Sch. Physics and Astronomy U. Minn., Mpls., 1961-65, postdoctoral rsch. assoc., 1965-66; asst. prof. physics dept. physics and astronomy U. Wyo., Laramie, 1966-70, assoc. prof., 1970-75, prof., 1975-91, dept. head, 1978-83; chief sci. Climate Monitoring and Diagnostics Lab. NOAA, Boulder, Colo., 1990-95, acting dir., 1995-96, dir., 1996—; prof. adjoint dept. astrophys., planetary and atmospheric scis. U. Colo., Boulder, 1991—; sci. Max Planck Inst. for Aeronomy, Lindau, Germany, 1973-74, Inst. Atmospheric Environ. Rsch., Garmisch-Partenkirchen, Germany, 1982, 89; mem. com. on atmospheric chemistry NRC, NAS, 1994-97, mem. polar rsch. bd., 1998—. Contbr. articles to profl. jours. Served USN, 1954-58. Alexander von Humboldt rsch. grantee Germany, 1989; recipient U.S. Antarctic Svc. medal, 1979, Sr. Sci. Humboldt prize Germany, 1992, Disting. Authorship award U.S. Dept. Commerce, 1990. Mem. Am. Geophys. Union (Excellence in Refereeing citation 1991, 94, Antarctic rsch. 1972-98), Sigma Xi (nat. lectr. 1985-88). E-mail: dhofmann@cmdl.noaa.gov. Office: NOAA Climate Monitoring & Diagnostic Lab Climate Monitoring & Dianostics Lab 325 Broadway St Boulder CO 80303-3337

HOFMANN, FRIEDER KARL, biotechnologist, consultant; b. Eppstein, Hessen, Germany, June 15, 1949; came to U.S., 1984; s. Friedrich Karl and Anna Johannette (Heist) H.; m. Sigrid Marianne Thomae, Sept. 5, 1975. MS, J.W. Goethe U., Frankfurt, Germany, 1977, PhD, 1981. Staff scientist, asst. prof. J.W. Goethe U., Frankfurt, 1977-81; sci. mgr. Brunswick Corp., Eschborn, Germany, 1982-84; tech. dir. Biotechnetics, San Diego, 1984-90; pres. ProCon Internat., Vista, Calif., 1990—, Ctr. for Continuous Edn., Vista, Calif., 1992—. Author: (with others) Scale-Up and Downstream Processing of rDNA Products, 1991, GMP Production of Monoclonal Antibodies, 1991; contbr. over 40 articles to profl. jours. Recipient Senckenberg prize Senckenberg Rsch. Soc., Frankfurt, 1977; Kirkpatrick Chem. Engring. Achievement Honor award Chem. Engring., 1989, Parenteral Drug Assn. Jour. award Parenteral Drug Assn., Pa., 1985. Mem. AIChE, Am. Chem. Soc., Tissue Culture Assn., European Soc. for Animal Cell Tech. Achievements include 6 patents for bioreactor and membrane technology; invention and development of tester for membrane filters, of first scalable membrane based animal cell reactor; first integration of upstream and downstream processes in bioreactor system; invention of formulation and procedure to grow animal cells in protein-free nutrient. Office: ProCon Internat 1773 Kings Rd Vista CA 92084-3640

HOFMANN, HUBERT FRANZ, management consultant; b. Wels, Oö, Austria, June 25, 1968; came to the U.S., 1995; s. Hubert and Elfriede (Ammeshofer) H.; m. Theresa Piotrowski, June 24, 1996. BSc, U. Linz, Austria, 1990; MBA and Computer Sci., U. Zürich & U. Linz, Austria, 1992. Project leader U. Zürich, 1991-92; mgr. enterprise solutions Aeroquip-Vickers, Inc., Ann Arbor, Mich., 1995-98; mgr. quality and methods ERIM Internat., Inc., Ann Arbor, Mich., 1999—; mgr. Union Bank Switzerland, Zürich, 1993-95. Author: Wirtschaftsinformatik, 1995; contbr. articles to profl. jours. Recipient Quality Recognition award Am. Soc. for Quality Control, 1996; Kurt Gödel scholar Austrian Ministry Sci., 1991. Mem. Strategic Leadership Forum. Avocations: soccer, biking, cooking. Office: ERIM Internat Inc PO Box 134008 Ann Arbor MI 48113-4008

HOFMANN, JOHN RICHARD, JR., lawyer; b. Oakland, Calif., June 24, 1922; s. John Richard and Esther (Starkweather) H.; m. Mary Macdonough, Feb. 6, 1954; children: John RichardIII, Gretchen Hofmann Will, Sarah Worthington Hack, John Macdonough Alexander. AB, U. Calif., Berkeley, 1943; JD, Harvard U., 1949. Bar: Calif. 1950. Assoc. Pillsbury, Madison & Sutro, San Francisco, 1949-58, ptnr., 1959-92, of counsel, 1992-96, ret. ptnr., 1996—; exec. v.p. MPC Ins., Ltd., 1988-96; city atty. City of Belvedere (Calif.), 1957-58. Mem. Calif. Bar Assn. Office: Pillsbury Madison & Sutro LLP PO Box 7880 San Francisco CA 94120-7880

HOFMANN, KARL HEINRICH, mathematics educator; b. Heilbronn, Fed. Republic Germany, Oct. 3, 1932; m. Isolde Hofmann, May 9, 1963; children: Claudia, Georg. PhD, U. Tubingen, Fed. Republic Germany, 1958. Prof. Tulane U., New Orleans, 1965-82, adj. prof., 1983—; prof. Techische Universitat, Darmstadt, Fed. Republic Germany, 1982—; vis. prof. Inst. Advanced Study, Princeton, N.J., 1967-68, U. Paris VI, 1973-74. Contbr. articles to profl. jours. Recipient E. Harris Harbison award Danforth Found., 1970; Alfred P. Sloan Found. fellow, 1966-68. Mem. Am. Math. Soc., Australian Math. Soc., Deutsche Mathematiker Vereinigung, Soc. Math. France. Office: Fachbereich Mathematik Technische, Fachbereich Math Tech U, Schlossgartenstr 7, D-64289 Darmstadt Germany

HOFMANN, PAUL BERNARD, healthcare consultant; b. Portland, Oreg., July 6, 1941; s. Max and Consuelo Theresa (Bley) H.; m. Lois Bernstein, June 28, 1969; children: Julie, Jason. BS, U. Calif., Berkeley, 1963, MPH, 1965, DPH, 1994. Research assoc. in hosp. adminstrn. Lab. of Computer Sci., Mass. Gen. Hosp., Boston, 1966-68; asst. dir. Lab. of Computer Sci., Mass. Gen. Hosp., 1968-69; asst. adminstr. San Antonio Community Hosp., Upland, Calif., 1969-70; assoc. adminstr. San Antonio Community Hosp., 1970-72; dep. dir. Stanford (Calif.) U. Hosp., 1972-74, dir., 1974-77; exec. dir. Emory U. Hosp., Atlanta, 1978-87; exec. v.p., chief ops. officer Alta Bates Corp., Emeryville, Calif., 1987-91; cons. Alta Bates Corp., Emeryville, 1991-92, Alexander & Alexander, San Francisco, 1992-94; disting. vis. scholar Stanford (Calif.) U. Ctr. for Biomed. Ethics, 1993-97; sr. fellow Stanford (Calif.) U. Hosp., 1993-94; sr. cons. strategic healthcare practice Alexander & Alexander Cons. Group, San Francisco, Calif., 1994-97; sr. v.p. strategic healthcare practice Aon Cons., San Francisco, 1997—; instr. computer applications Harvard U., 1968-69; lectr. hosp. adminstrn. UCLA, 1970-72, Stanford U. Med. Sch., 1972-77; assoc. prof. Emory U. Sch. Medicine, Atlanta, 1978-87. Author: The Development and Application of Ethical Criteria for Use in Making Programmatic Resource Allocation Decisions in Hospitals, 1994; contbr. articles to profl. jours. Served with U.S. Army, 1959. Fellow Am. Coll. Hosp. Adminstrs. (recipient Robert S. Hudgens meml. award 1976); mem. Am. Hosp. Assn., U. Calif. Alumni Assn.

HOFMANN, POLLY A., physiology educator; b. Dixon, Ill., July 8, 1960; married; 1 child. BS in Biology, U. Ill., 1982; PhD in Physiology, U. Pitts., 1987. Postdoctoral fellow dept. physiology U. Wis., Madison, 1987-91; asst. prof. dept. physiology and biophysics U. Tenn., Memphis, 1991-97, assoc. prof. dept. physiology, 1997—; mem. prof. search com. Dept. Physiology and Biophysics, U. Tenn., 1991-92, grad. program tng. com., 1992-93, 95—, student progress and promotions com. biomed. sci. Coll. of Medicine, 1992-94, chmn. search com. Dept. Preventive Medicine, 1993-94, chmn. grad. program tng. com. Dept. Physiology and Biophysics, 1993-95, student progress and promotions com. for biomed. sci. Coll. of Medicine, 1994-96, Alma and Hal Reagan fellowship selection com. Coll. Grad. Health Scis., 1994—, mem. conflict resolution coun. of student mistreatment program Coll. of Medicine, 1995—. Ad hoc reviewer Am. Jour. Physiology, Jour. Pharmacology and Exptl. Therapeutics; contbr. articles to profl. jours. Predoctoral fellow NIH, 1983-87, Postdoctoral fellow, 1989-92, grantee, 1992—; Postdoctoral fellow Am. Heart Assn., 1988-89, recipient Dave McClain Rsch. award, 1988, Established Investigator award, 1995, grantee, 1992-93. Mem. Am. Physiol. Soc. (career opportunities in physiology com. 1995—), Biophys. Soc., Internat. Soc. Heart Rsch. (Upjohn Young Investigator award 1990), Sigma Xi. Office: U Tenn Ste 426 894 Union Ave Dept & Memphis TN 38163-3514*

HOFMANN, THEO, biochemist, educator; b. Zurich, Switzerland, Feb. 20, 1924; emigrated to Can., 1964, naturalized, 1969; s. Edwin and Hedwig (Moos) H.; m. Doris Topham Forbes, July 15, 1953; children: Martin Ian, Tony David, Peter Adrian. Diploma chem. engring., Swiss Fed. Inst. Tech., Zurich, 1947, Dr. Sc. Tech., 1950. Research asst. U. Aberdeen, Scotland, 1950-52; sci. officer Hannah Dairy Research Inst., Ayr, Scotland, 1952-56; lectr. Sheffield (Eng.) U., 1956-64; prof. biochemistry U. Toronto, Ont., Can., 1964-89, emeritus prof. biochemistry, 1989—; vis. assoc. prof. U. Wash., 1962-63; vis. scientist Commonwealth Sci. and Indsl. Research Orgn., Sydney, Australia, 1971-72; vis. prof. divsn. natural scis. U. Calif.-Santa Cruz, 1981; vis. prof. physical chemistry, U. Lund, Sweden, 1987. Asso. editor: Can. Jour. Biochemistry, 1968-71; Contbr. numerous articles to profl. jours. Med. Rsch. Coun. (Can.) grantee, 1964-94. Mem. Can. Soc. Biochemistry and Molecular and Cellular Biology, Am. Soc. Biochemistry and Molecular Biology, Biochem. Soc. Rsch. in function and evolution of enzymes. Home: 199 Arnold Ave, Thornhill, ON Canada L4J 1C1 Office: U Toronto, Dept Biochemistry, Toronto, ON Canada M5S 1A8

HOFSOMMER, DONOVAN LOWELL, history educator; b. Ft. Dodge, Iowa, Apr. 10, 1938; s. Vernie George and Helma J. (Schager) H.; m. Sandra Louise Rusch, June 13, 1965; children: Kathryn Anne, Kristine Beret, Knute Lars. BA, U. Northern Iowa, 1960, MA, 1966; PhD, Okla. State U., 1973. Tchr. Fairfield (Iowa) High Sch., 1961-65; instr. U. Northern Iowa, Cedar Falls, 1965-66, Lea Coll., Albert Lea, Minn., 1966-70; teaching asst. Okla. State U., Stillwater, 1970-73; assoc. prof. and dept. head Wayland Coll., Plainview, Tex., 1973-81; corp. historian So. Pacific Co., San Francisco, 1981-85; hist. cons. Burlington No. Inc., Seattle, 1985-87; vis. prof. U. Mont., Missula, 1986-87; exec. dir. ctr. Western studies Augustana Coll., Sioux Falls, S.D., 1987-89; prof. history St. Cloud (Minn.) State U., 1989—; cons. Dyanelectron and Dynarail, Pueblo, Colo., 1979-81, Grand Trunk Corp., Detroit, 1988-95; mem. editl. bd. annals of Iowa, Iowa City, 1975-94, R.R. history, Akron, Ohio, 1975—. Author: Prairie Oasis, 1975, Katy Northwest, 1976, Southern Pacific 1901-1985, 1986; co-author: History of Great Northern Railway, 1988, Quanah Route, 1991, Grand Trunk Corp.,

1995; editor: Lexington Group Transport History, 1975—; mem. editl. bd. Annals of Iowa, Iowa City, 1975-92, R.R. History, Akron, Ohio, 1975—. With U.S. Army, 1960-66. Mem. Okla. Hist. Soc. (Wright Heritage award 1979), Ry. and Locomotive Hist. Soc. (Book award 1988, Sr. Achievement award 1995), Western History Assn., Orgn. Am. Historians, State Hist. Soc. Iowa, Am. Assn. for State and Local History. Democrat. Presbyterian. Home: 1803 13th Ave SE Saint Cloud MN 56304-2231 Office: St Cloud State U Dept History Saint Cloud MN 56301

HOFSTATTER, LEOPOLD, psychiatrist, researcher; b. Vienna, Austria, Mar. 11, 1902; came to U.S., 1938, naturalized, 1944; s. Leopold H. and Josefine (Eibuschuetz) H.; m. Lilli Schwarz, Apr. 16, 1930; m. Theresa Adams Mayer, Sept. 4, 1971. MD, U. Vienna, 1926. Demonstrator 1st Anat. Inst., U. Vienna, 1925-27; Intern Allgemeines Krankenhaus Wien, Vienna, 1927-28; resident, demonstrator 1st Surg. Clinic, Vienna, 1928-30; resident Maria Theresien Schloessel, 1930-33; rsch. fellow, fellow in neurosurgery Washington U., St. Louis, 1938-40; resident St. Louis State Hosp., 1941-42, asst. supt., 1942-62, chief gen. med., surg. divsn., 1960-62; mem. staff St. Vincent's Hosp., 1948-62, Deaconess Hosp., 1948-62; supt. St. Louis State Sch. and Hosp., 1962-67; sr. cons. resident tng. program Mo. Inst. Psychiatry, 1967-69, med. dir., 1972-74; supt. St. Louis State Hosp. Complex, 1970; clin. prof. psychiatry U. Mo. Sigma Xi fellow. Fellow AAAS, Am. Psychiat. Assn. (life); mem. Mo. Hosp. Physicians Assn. (past pres.), Sci. Rsch. Assn. Am., Ea. Mo. Psychiat. Soc., Goldenes Ehrenzeichen fuer Verdienste um das Land Wien (Austria), Sigma Xi. Home: 768 Glenvista Pl Saint Louis MO 63122-2020 Office: 5400 Arsenal St Saint Louis MO 63139-1403

HOFSTEAD, JAMES WARNER, laundry machinery company executive, lawyer; b. Jackson, Tenn., Feb. 3, 1913; s. Harry Oliver and Agnes Lucile (Blackard) H.; m. Ellen Frances Bowers, Dec. 27, 1940; 1 child, Eda Lucile. AB, Vanderbilt U., 1935, LLB, 1938. Bar: Tenn. Pvt. practice law; v.p. bd. dirs. United Tel. Co., 1969—; pres., dir. Wishy Washy, Inc., Nashville, 1946—; pres., dir. Wishy Sales Inc., 1959—. Capt. USMC, 1942-45. Mem. SAR (nat. committeeman, state pres. emeritus, nat. trustee), Vanderbilt Bar Assn. (pres. emeritus), So. Srs. Golf Assn., Soc. of the Cincinnati, English Speaking Union (chmn.), Soc. Colonial Wars (past gov. Tenn., deputy gov. gen.), C. of C., Belle Meade Country Club, 200 Club, Exch. Club, Eccentric Club (London), Gasparilla 48 Club, Cumberland Club (charter), Sons of Confederate Vets., Sigma Chi. Methodist. Home: 215 Deer Park Cir Nashville TN 37205-3324 Office: 3729 Charlotte Pike Nashville TN 37209-3734

HOFT, LYNNE ANN, educator, remedial specialist, educational consultant; b. Carroll, Iowa, Mar. 1, 1945; d. Norman North and Dorothy Mae (Dean) H.; 1 child, Timothy D. Cochran. BA, Briar Cliff Coll., 1971; MA in Spl. Edn., Ariz. State U., 1979; postgrad., U. Minn., 1989-92, U. St. Thomas, 1993—. Cert. elem. and spl. edn. tchr., Ariz., Minn.; lic. prin. K-12 and spl. edn. dir. Tchr. St. Edward Sch., Waterloo, Iowa, 1968-70, Chino Valley Sch., Ariz., 1971-77; program developer Chino Valley Sch., 1974-76; spl. edn. tchr. Tuba City Pub. Jr. H.S., Ariz., 1978-82; spl. edn. tchr., dept. chmn. Tuba City H.S., 1983-86, curriculum developer, 1984-85; remedial specialist Eagles' Nest Mid. Sch., 1986-88; spl. edn. coord. chpt. 1 Epsilon and Nexus programs Hopkins (Minn.) Pub. Schs., Hennepin County Home Sch., 1988-95, tchr. English, 1995—; founder, pres. Unltd. Learning Enterprises, Inc., Tuba City, 1983-85; trainer Empowering People/Positive Discipline, 1990—; invitational cons. Aim for Excellence, Mpls., 1990-91; cons./trainer Growth Essentials Model Programs, Health Realization, and Program Devel., 1994—. Probation aide Waterloo Juvenile Ct., 1970-71; vol. instr. Prescott Spl. Olympics, 1977-78; local coord. Tuba City Spl. Olympics, 1978-80. Recipient U.S. Dept. Edn. Sec. award, 1991. Mem. NEA, Minn. Edn. Assn., Hopkins Edn. Assn., Tuba City Unified Edn. Assn. (pres. 1985-86). Avocations: reading, piano, parenting.

HOGAN, BRIAN JOSEPH, editor; b. Aberdeen, S.D., Apr. 11, 1943; s. Arthur James and Magdalena (Frison) H.; m. Jamie Isabelle Schwingel, June 21, 1987. BS in Aerospace and Mech. Engring., U. Ariz., 1965, BS in Geophysics-Geochemistry, 1968; MS in Journalism, U. Utah, 1972. Rsch. asst. U. Va. Rsch. Labs for Engring. Scis., Charlottesville, 1965-66; exploration geophysicist Anaconda Co., Tucson, 1968-71; assoc. editor Benwill Pub. Co., Brookline, Mass., 1973-74; asst. editor Design News, Boston, 1974-75; midwest editor Design News, Chgo., 1975-87; sr. editor Design News, Newton, Mass., 1987-89, mng. editor, 1989-97; chief editor Mfg. Engring.-Soc. Mfg. Engrs., Dearborn, Mich. Author stage plays The Young O'Neil, 1983, Awakening, 1984. Precinct worker Cook County Rep. Com., Oak Park, Ill., 1986-87; interpreter Frank Lloyd Wright Home and Studio Found., Oak Park, 1981-87. Recipient numerous awards Am. Soc. Bus. Press Editors, Soc. Tech. Communication, Aviation Space Writers Assn. Mem. Am. Soc. Bus. Press Editors, Am. Hist. Print Collectors Soc. Republican. Roman Catholic. Avocations: photography, print collecting, cycling, hiking. Office: Mfg Engring 1 SME Dr PO Box 930 Dearborn MI 48121-0930

HOGAN, BRIGID L., molecular biologist; b. England, Aug. 28, 1943. BA, U. Cambridge, 1964, PhD, 1968. NATO rsch. fellow dept. biology MIT, 1968-70; lectr. biochemistry U. Sussex, England, 1970-74; sci. staff Imperial Cancer Rsch. Fund, Mill Hill, England, 1974-84; head lab. molecular embryology Nat. Inst. Med. Rsch., Mill Hill, England, 1985-88; prof. cell biology Vanderbilt Med. Sch., Nashville, 1988—; Hortense B. Ingram chair molecular oncology Howard Hughes Med. Inst., 1993—; vice chair Basement Membrane Gordon Conf., 1994, chair, 1996; co-chair sci. human embryo rsch. panel NIH, 1994; Jenkinson meml. lectr. U. Oxford, 1995; Margaret Pittman lectr. NIH, 1996. Mem. Br. Soc. Cell Biology (com. 1982-86), Br. Soc. Devel. Biology (com. 1984-88), NAS Inst. Medicine, European Molecular Biology Orgn. Office: Vanderbilt U Dept Cell Biology Med Ctr N Rm U2219 Nashville TN 37232-2175*

HOGAN, CURTIS JULE, union executive, industrial relations consultant; b. Greeley, Kans., July 25, 1926; s. Charles Leo and Anna Malene (Roussello) H.; m. Lois Jean Ecord, Apr. 23, 1955; children: Christopher James, Michael Sean, Patrick Marshall, Kathleen Marie, Kerry Joseph. BS in Indsl. Rels., Rockhurst Coll., 1950; postgrad., Georgetown U., 1955, U. Tehran, Iran, 1955-57. With Gt. Lakes Pipeline Co., Kansas City, Mo., 1950-55; with Internat. Fedn. Petroleum and Chem. Workers, Denver, 1955-85; gen. sec. Internat. Fedn. Petroleum and Chem. Workers, 1973-85; pres. Internat. Labor Rels. Svcs., Inc., 1976—; cons. in field; lectr. Rockhurst Coll., Kansas City, 1951-52. Contbr. articles to profl. pubs. Served with U.S. Army, 1945-46. Mem. Internat. Indsl. Rels. Assn., Indsl. Rels. Rsch. Assn., Oil Chem. and Atomic Workers Internat. Union. Home: 435 S Newport Way Denver CO 80224-1321 Office: Internat Fed Petroleum Chem Workers 435 S Newport Way Denver CO 80224-1321

HOGAN, EDWARD LEO, neurologist; b. Arlington, Mass., July 26, 1932; s. Patrick Francis and Margaret Mary (McSweeney) H.; m. Gail Manning, July 1, 1961; children: Patrick, Maryellen, Timothy, Maura, Michael. BS in Biochemistry, Tufts U., 1953, MD, 1957. Diplomate Am. Bd. Psychiatry and Neurology. Intern Barnes Hosp., St. Louis, 1957-58; resident in neurology Boston City Hosp., 1959-64; asst. in neurology Harvard U. Med. Sch., 1965-66; faculty U. N.C. Med. Sch., 1966-73, assoc. prof. neurology, 1969-73, assoc. prof. biochemistry, 1972-73, assoc. dir. neurobiology program faculty, 1971-73; prof. neurology, chmn. dept., prof. biochemistry Med. U. S.C., Charleston, 1973—; mem. merit rev. bd. neurobiology VA, 1976-79; mem. neurology B-1 study sect. NIH, 1981-85, chmn., 1983-85; mem. neuroscis. training com., NIH, 1989-93. Contbr. articles to profl. jours. Officer M.C. U.S Army, 1961-63. Fellow Am. Acad. Neurology; mem. Am. Neurol. assn., Assn. Univ. Prof. Neurology, Am. Soc. Biochemistry and Molecular Biology, Soc. Glycobiology, The Biochem. Soc. (U.K.), Am. Soc. Neurochemistry, internat. Soc. Neurochemistry, Soc. Neurosci., S.C. Neurol. Soc. (pres. 1978-79), Phi Beta Kappa, Alpha Omega Alpha. Roman Catholic. Home: 43 Hasell St Charleston SC 29401-1604 Office: Med U SC Dept Neurology 171 Ashley Ave Charleston SC 29425-0001

HOGAN, FRANCES L., executive; b. Boston, Apr. 12, 1969; d. Brian Russell and Carol Murray H. BA, Georgetown U., 1991; MA, Middlebury Coll., 1997. Pres., owner Resource Equipment Corp., Dedham, Mass., 1992—. Coun. mem. Assoc. Mems. Coun. Boston Athenaeum, 1994—. Office: Resource Equipment Corp 200 Milton St Dedham MA 02026

HOGAN, ILONA MODLY, lawyer; b. Erlangen, Fed. Republic of Germany, Nov. 23, 1947; came to U.S., 1951, naturalized, 1960; d. Stephen Bela and Gunda Pauline (Gastiger) Modly; m. Lawrence J. Hogan, Mar. 16, 1974; children: Matthew Lawrence, Michael Alexander, Patrick Nicholas, Timothy Stefan. Student, Marymount Coll., 1965-67; A.B. in Internat. Affairs, George Washington U., 1969; J.D., Georgetown U., 1974. Bar: D.C. 1975, Md. 1975. Intern and clk. AID, 1965-69; adminstrv. and legis. asst. to mem. Ho. of Reps., 1969-72; editor Legis. Digest, Ho. of Reps., Washington, 1972-73; asso. and law clk. firm Trammell, Rand, Nathan and Lincoln, Washington, 1972-74; mng. ptnr. firm Hogan and Hogan, Washington and Md., 1974-93; of counsel Venable, Baetjer, Howard & Civiletti, Washington, 1989-91; pres. Amcom Inc., 1978—; of counsel Salisbury & McLister, Frederick, Md., 1993—. Mem. Prince George's (Md.) Bd. Libr. Trustees, 1976-78, Prince George's County Econ. Devel. Adv. Com., 1979-82; co-chmn. Greater S.E. Cmty. Hosp. Ctr. for Aging, 1979-82; mem. Lawyers Steering com. for Reagan-Bush, 1980; nat. vice-chmn. Assn. Execs. for Reagan-Bush, 1984; mem. bus. and industry adv. com. 50th Am. Presdl. Inaugural, 1985; mem. Md. steering com. Bush for Pres., 1988, Gov.'s Higher Edn. Transition Team, 1988, Presdl. Personnel Adv. Com., 1989; v.p. St. John's Sch. Bd., 1987-88, pres. 1989; treas. U. Md. Bd. Regents, 1988-95; trustee St. James Sch., 1989-90; elected mem. County Commrs. of Frederick County, Md. 1994—. Mem. ABA, Md. Bar Assn., D.C. Bar. Republican. Roman Catholic. Home: 5614 New Design Rd Frederick MD 21703-7110 Office: Winchester Hall 12 E Church St Frederick MD 21701-5402

HOGAN, JAMES CARROLL, JR., public health administrator, research biologist; b. Milledgeville, Ga., Jan. 3, 1939; s. James C. and Leanna (Johnson) H.; m. Izola Stinson, Nov. 29, 1959; children: Pamela Renita, Gregory Karl, Jeffrey Darryl. BS, Albany State Coll., 1961; MS, Atlanta U., 1968; PhD, Brown U., 1972; postdoc. fellow, Yale U. Biology Dept., 1972-73. Rsch. assoc. Yale U. Sch. Medicine, New Haven, Conn., 1973-76; asst. prof. anatomy Howard U. Sch. Medicine, Washington, 1976-78; assoc. prof. U. Conn., Storrs, 1978-83; dir. minority student affairs U. Conn. Health Ctr., Farmington, 1983-87; chief clin. chemistry and hematology Conn. Dept. Health Svcs., Hartford, 1987—; mem. Community Svcs. Commn. and Bd. of Edn., 1994—, North Haven, Conn., 1989—; bd. dirs. Greater New Haven State Tchrs. Coll., 1989—, A Better Chance, Glastonbury, Conn., 1990—, Hartford (Conn.) Alliance for Sci. and Math. Edn., adv. com. Math. Connections. Contbr. articles to Jour. Ultrastructural Rsch., Jour. Protozoology, Jour. Embryology and Exptl. Morphology, Jour. Cell Biology, Jour. Nat. Tech. Assn., Jour. Pediatrics. Founder, pres. North Haven Assn. Black Citizens, 1988—, Chpt. Nat. Tech. Assn., 1990; coord. Martin Luther King Jr. annual luncheon Dept. Pub. Health, Conn., 1988—; active Dem. Town Com., North Haven, 1989—; com. chmn. Greater New Haveen chpt. NAACP. Josiah Macy Found. fellow, Marine Biol. Labs., 1978-80, Ford Found. postdoctoral fellow Marine Biol. Labs., 1980-81; vis. faculty fellow Yale U., 1984—. Mem. NAACP, Conn. Pub. Health Assn., Am. Soc. Cell Biology (Conn. chpt. pres.), Nat. Tech. Assn. (bd. dirs. Conn. chpt.), N.Y. Acad. Scis., Sigma Xi, Omega Psi Phi. Baptist. Achievements include first confirmation of Antigenic variation in Trypanosomes using the electron microscope, first confirmation of cytoplasmic markers in sex cells of killifishes using the electron microscope. Home: 51 Pool Rd PO Box 146 North Haven CT 06473-0146

HOGAN, JOHN DONALD, college dean, finance educator; b. Binghamton, N.Y., July 16, 1927; s. John D. and Edith J. (Hennessy) H.; m. Anna Craig, Nov. 26, 1976; children—Thomas P., James E. A.B., Syracuse U., 1949, M.A., 1950, Ph.D., 1952. Registered prin. Nat. Assn. Securities Dealers. Prof. econs., chmn. dept. Bates Coll., Lewiston, Maine, 1953-58; dir. edn. fin. research State of N.Y., 1959, chief mcpl. fin., 1960; staff economist, dir. research Northwestern Mut. Life Ins. Co., Milw., 1960-68; v.p. Nationwide Ins. Cos., Columbus, Ohio, 1968-76; dean Sch. Bus. Adminstrn. Central Mich. U., Mt. Pleasant, 1976-79; v.p. Am. Productivity Ctr., Houston, 1979-80; pres., chmn., chief exec. officer Variable Annuity Life Ins. Co., Houston, 1980-83; sr. v.p. Am. Gen. Corp., Houston, 1983-86; dean, prof. fin. Coll. Commerce U. Ill., Champaign, 1986-91; dean, prof. fin. and econs. Coll. Bus. Adminstrn. Ga. State U., Atlanta, 1991-97, prof. fin. and econs., 1998—; bd. dirs. Covenant Med. Ct., Champaign, 1986-92, Sinfonia da Camera, Champaign, Ga. Coun. on Econ. Edn., Pvt. Industry Coun., World Trade Ctr., Atlanta. Author: American Social Legislation, 1965, U.S. Balance of Payments and Capital Flows, 1967, School Revenue Studies, 1959, Fiscal Capacity of the State of Maine, 1958, American Social Legislation, 1973; editor: Dimensions of Productivity Research (2 vols.), 1981; contbr. articles to jours., abstracts to profl. meetings. Bd. dirs. Goodwill Industries, Columbus, 1972-76, chmn. capital fund drive, 1974-75; mem. Houston Com. on Fgn. Rels., 1980—, Chgo. Coun. on Fgn. Rels., 1986—, Chgo. com., 1987—. Served with U.S. Army, 1944-46, ETO; capt. (ret.) USAR. Maxwell fellow Syracuse U., 1950-52; recipient Best Article award Jur. Risk and Ins., Alumni Appreciation award U. Ill., 1991, 1964; Maxwell Centennial lectr. Maxwell Grad. Sch., Syracuse U., 1970. Mem. Acad. Mgmt., Am. Econ. Assn., Inst. Mgmt. Scis., Nat. Assn. Bus. Economists, Nat. Tax Assn. (dir. 1981-85, treas., exec. com. 1988—), Inst. Rsch. in Econs. of Taxation (dir. 1984—), Columbus C. of C. (chmn. econ. policy com. 1972-76), Phi Kappa Phi, Beta Gamma Sigma, Columbus Athletic Club, Heritage Club (Houston), Univ. Club (Chgo.), Lincolnshire Fields Country Club (Champaign), Commerce Club (Atlanta), World Trade Club (Atlanta, bd. dirs. 1993—). Clubs: Columbus Athletic; Heritage (Houston); University (Chgo.), Lincolnshire Fields Country (Champaign); Commerce Club (Atlanta). Office: Ga State U Coll Bus Adminstrn University Pl Atlanta GA 30303

HOGAN, J(OHN) PAUL, chemistry researcher, consultant; b. Lowes, Ky., Aug. 7, 1919; s. Charles F. and Alma (Wyman) H.; m. Glenda M. Moultrie, 1943; children: E. Fay Hogan Sweney, Kenneth B., Susan G. Hogan Lair. Student, U. Redlands, 1940-41; BS in Chemistry and Physics, Murray State U., 1942, DSc (hon.), 1971. Tchr. Mayfield (Ky.) High Sch., 1942-43; physics instr. Okla. State U., Stillwater, 1943-44; research chemist Phillips Petroleum Co., Bartlesville, Okla., 1944-48, group leader, 1948-60, polymer sci. sect. mgr., 1960-77, polymer sci. sr. research assoc., 1977-85, cons., 1985-86; cons. in field, 1986—; chmn. Northeast Okla. sect. Am. Chem. Soc., 1970. Patentee in field; contbr. chpts. to books. Recipient Creative Invention award Am. Chem. Soc., 1969, Perkin medal Soc. Chem. Industry, 1987, Heros in Chemistry award Am. Chem. Soc., 1998; named Disting. Alumnus, Murray State U., 1972, Inventor of Yr., Okla. Bar Assn. Copyright and Patent Sect., 1976, Polymeric Materials Man of Yr., Soc. Plastics Engrs., 1981; named to Hon. Order of Ky. Cols., 1972. Fellow Am. Inst. Chemists (Pioneer chemist award 1972). Republican. Baptist. Avocations: church work, fly fishing, chess, gardening. Home: 1049 SE Greystone Ave Bartlesville OK 74006-5010

HOGAN, JOHN TERRY, investment company executive. BS, Ohio State U., 1972; MBA, U. Dayton, 1975; PhD, Union Inst., 1992. Founder Dynamic Aviation, Inc., Belle Fontaine, Ohio, 1972-75; mfg. engring. mgr. Airstream, Inc., Jackson Center, Ohio, 1972-80; cons. Hogan & Assocs., DeGraff, Ohio, 1980-84; program mgr. NCR Corp., Dayton, Ohio, 1984-95; cons. Hogan & Assocs., Tipp City, Ohio, 1995-96; venture capitalist Blue Chip Venture Co., Cin., 1996—; assoc. adj. prof. Antioch U., Yellow Springs, Ohio, 1992—; bd. dirs. Miami Valley Venture Assocs., Dayton; investment policy bd. NCIC Capital Fund, Dayton, 1996—; bd. trustees Nat. Ctt. indsl. Competitivness, Dayton, 1997—. Mem. Am. Soc. Tng. & Devel., Coaching Club, Kappa Phi Kappa, Epsilon Pi Tau. Office: Hogan & Assocs 524 W Broadway Ave Tipp City OH

HOGAN, KENNETH JAMES, lawyer; b. Chgo., Apr. 22, 1970; s. James Kenneth and Marlene Ann (Beaman) H. BA, U. Ill., Urbana, 1992; JD, U. Ill., Champaign, 1995. Bar: Ill. 1995, U.S. Dist. Ct. (no. dist.) Ill. 1995. Legal advisor, hearing officer dept. adminstrv. hearings Office of Ill. Sec. of State, Joliet, Ill., 1996-98; staff atty. rsch. dept. Appellate Ct. of Ill. 3d Dist., Ottawa, Ill., 1998-99; appellate law clk. Justice Kent Slater Appellate Ct. of Ill. 3d Dist., Macomb, Ill., 1999—. Asst. to committeeman Orland Twp. Rep. Orgn., Orland Park, Ill., 1996-98; chmn. Ind. Leadership 2000, Orland Park, 1997. Republican. Roman Catholic. Home: 714 N Campbell St Apt C Macomb IL 61455 Office: Appellate Ct Ill 3d Dist 219 N Randolph St Macomb IL 61455

HOGAN, LORI ANN, finance director, accountant; b. Exeter, N.H., Sept. 11, 1969; d. Charles P. and Lyn P. (Sanderson) Heath; m. Gregory N. Hogan, Jan. 1, 1993; children: Britni N., Coleton N., Devyn R, Ryan J. BS in Accountancy, Bentley Coll., 1991. CPA, N.H. Auditor Arthur Andersen, Manchester, N.H., 1991-95; controller Eagle Mountain House, Jackson, N.H., 1996-97; dir. fin. The Mill at Loon Mountain, Lincoln, N.H., 1997—. Mem. Beta Gamma Sigma. Avocations: hiking, fishing, snowmobiling, skiing, waterskiing. Home: PO Box 379 Twin Mountain NH 03595-0379 Office: The Mill at Loon Mountain PO Box 537 Lincoln NH 03251-0537

HOGAN, MICHAEL RAY, diversified company executive; b. Newark, Ohio, Apr. 21, 1953; s. Raymond Carl and Mary Adele (Whalen) H.; m. Martha Ann Gorman, July 24, 1976; children: Colleen Michael, Patrick Gorman, Mary Kate, Andrei Sean. BA, Loyola U., Chgo., 1978; M in Mgmt. with distinction, Northwestern U., 1980. Cert. FLMI, HIA. Assoc. McKinsey & Co., Inc., Chgo., 1980-81, engagement mgr., 1982-83; sr. v.p., treas. FBS Ins. Co., Mpls., 1984-85; group v.p., gen. mgr. Gen. Am. Life Ins. Co., St. Louis, 1986, v.p., 1987-89, exec. v.p., 1990-95; pres., CEO Cova Corp., St. Louis, 1995-96; corp. v.p., controller Monsanto Co., St. Louis, 1996-99; v.p., CFO Sigma-Aldrich Corp., 1999—; cons. Swedish Trade Commn., Chgo., 1978, Lee Wards Creative Crafts Co., Elgin, Ill., 1979; chmn. Consultec, Inc., Atlanta, 1990-95, Cova Fin. Life Ins. Co., Oakbrook Terrace, 1995; chmn., CEO Genelco, Inc., St. Louis, 1990-95; mem. adv. bd. Integrated Hlth Svcs. Managed Care, Owings Mills, Md., 1994—; pres. GenCare Hlth Sys., Inc., 1990-95. Contb. articles to profl. jours. Active Experience St. Louis, 1986; mem. Leadership Ctr. of Greater St. Louis, 1987-95, bd. dirs., 1988-95, v.p. comms., 1989-90, pres., 1991-92; bd. dirs. Focus St. Louis, Inc., 1996—; treas., 1996-98; bd. dirs. Combined Health Appeal of Greater St. Louis, 1992-97, v.p. programs, 1992-94, pres., 1995-96; bd. dirs. St. Louis Coll. Pharmacy, 1995—, Wyman Ctr., 1997—, Combined Health Appeal of Am., 1997-98, United Way of Greater St. Louis, 1997—, vice-chmn., 1997—, Small World Adoption Found., 1998—. Scholar F.C. Austin Found., 1978-80, Phi Gamma Nu, 1980; recipient Nat. Vol. of Yr. award Combined Health Appeal of Am., 1996, Person of Yr. award Juvenile Diabetes Assn. St. Louis chpt., 1998, Gala Honoree, 1998, Health Citizen of Yr. award Combined Health Appeal Greater St. Louis, 1998, Corp. Leadership Divsn. award United Way Gtr. St. Louis, 1993, 95, Employee Divsn. award, 1997, 98. Mem. Beta Gamma Sigma. Roman Catholic. Avocations: reading, family, golf, travel. Home: 9368 Robyn Hills Dr Saint Louis MO 63127-1316

HOGAN, MICHAEL R(OBERT), judge; b. Oregon City, Oreg., Sept. 24, 1946; married; 3 children. A.B., U. Oreg. Honors Coll., 1968; J.D., Georgetown U., 1971. Bar: Oreg. 1971, U.S. Ct. Appeals (9th cir.) 1971. Law clk. to chief judge U.S. Dist. Ct. Oreg., Portland, 1971-72; assoc. Miller, Anderson, Nash, Yerke and Wiener, Portland, 1972-73; magistrate judge U.S. Dist. Ct. Oreg., Eugene, 1973-91, dist. judge, 1991—, chief judge, 1995—; bankruptcy judge U.S. Dist. Oreg., Eugene, 1973-80. Mem. ABA, Oreg. State Bar Assn. Office: US Courthouse 211 E 7th Ave Eugene OR 97401-2722*

HOGAN, NANCY KAY, elementary education educator; b. Auburn, Wash., Oct. 5, 1947; d. Henry Grant and Medora Ione (Elder) Kessner; m. David Allan Hogan, June 27, 1970; children: Jeffrey Allan, Jason Patrick, Jennifer Ann. BA in Edn., Western Wash. U., 1969; postgrad., U. Wash., 1973; M Ednl. Tech., City U., 1996. Cert. K-12 tchr., Wash. Tchr. kindergarten Kent (Wash.) Sch. Dist., 1970; elem. tchr. North Thurston Sch. Dist., Lacey, Wash., 1970-73; tchr. McLane Elem. Sch., Olympia, Wash., 1986-93, McKenny Elem. Sch., Olympia, 1993-94; tchr. Hansen Elem. Sch., Olympia, 1994—, also mem. tchr. support team. Mem. NEA, Internat. Reading Assn., Whole Lang. Umbrella, Wash. Edn. Assn., Olympia Edn. Assn., Dist. Inclusion Forum, Hansen Title I Team, Nat. Coun. Tchrs. English. Avocations: reading, boating, walking. Home: 3030 Aspinwall Rd NW Olympia WA 98502-1531 Office: Hansen Elem Sch 1919 Rd Sixty Five Olympia WA 98502

HOGAN, NEVILLE JOHN, mechanical engineering educator, consultant; b. Dublin, Ireland, Feb. 11, 1949; came to U.S., 1970; s. Walter Henry and Edna Constance (Liller) H.; m. Sara Jane Seiden; children: Alexandra, Brian, Amanda, Victoria. Diploma in engring. with honors, Coll. of Tech., Dublin, 1970; MS in Mech. Engring., MIT, 1973, mech. engring. degree, 1976, PhD in Mech. Engring., 1977; D (hon.), Tech. U. Delft, 1997. Product devel. and design engr. Donnelly Mirrors Ltd., Nass, Ireland, 1977-78; prof. MIT, Cambridge, 1978—; dir. Newman Lab., 1992—; cons. in phys. systems modeling, design and control and in biomed. engring. Contbr. numerous articles to profl. jours. TRW Found. fellow, Whitaker Health Scis. Fund fellow. Mem. AAAS, ASME, Sigma Xi.

HOGAN, ROBERT HENRY, trust company executive, investment strategist; b. N.Y.C., Apr. 12, 1926; s. Frederick Avertus and Carrie (Cronhardt) H.; m. Katherine Ann Wilkes, Feb. 9, 1957; children: Robert Wilkes, Mary Katherine, Margaret Ann, John William. Student, CCNY, 1943-44. Field rep. Moral Re-Armament, Inc., various locations, 1947-65; dir. Moral Re-Armament, Inc., N.Y.C., 1965-68; portfolio mgr. U.S. Trust Co., N.Y.C., 1969-72, asst. sec., 1972-78, asst. v.p., 1978-82, v.p., 1982-85, sr. v.p., 1985—. Mem. internat. adv. com. Up With People, Tucson, 1984—; mem. hon. bd. dirs. Uncommon Friends Found., Ft. Myers, Fla. M/sgt. U.S. Army, 1944-46, ETO. Mem. Assn. Investment Mgmt. and Rsch., N.Y. Soc. Security Analysts. Republican. Episcopalian. Avocations: philately, antiquarian books, fishing.

HOGAN, STEVEN L., lawyer; b. Los Angeles, Aug. 31, 1953; s. Kenneth Carlton Hogan and Ninon Michelle (Seigenberg) Kingsley; m. Debra Karen Garshfield, June 27, 1975; children: Rebecca Sarah, Cheryl Lee. AB magna cum laude, UCLA, 1975; JD, U. So. Calif., 1978. Assoc. Anderson, McPharlin & Conners, L.A., 1978-80; ptnr. Bryan Cave, L.A., 1980-95; shareholder Lurie & Zepeda, Beverly Hills, CA, 1995—. Mem. Los Angeles County Bar Assn., Order of Coif, Phi Beta Kappa, Phi Gamma Mu. Office: Lurie & Zepeda 9107 Wilshire Blvd Ste 800 Beverly Hills CA 90210-5533

HOGAN, THOMAS FRANCIS, federal judge; b. Washington, May 31, 1938; s. Bartholomew W. and Grace (Gloninger) H.; m. Martha Lou Wyrick, July 16, 1966; 1 son, Thomas Garth. A.B., Georgetown U., 1960, J.D., 1966; postgrad., George Washington U., 1960-62. Bar: Md. 1966, U.S. Dist. Ct. D.C. 1967, D.C. 1967, U.S. Ct. Appeals (D.C. cir.) 1972, U.S. Dist. Ct. Md. 1973, U.S. Supreme Ct. 1973. Law clk. to presiding judge U.S. Dist. Ct. D.C., 1966-67; counsel Nat. Commn. on Reform of Fed. Criminal Laws, Washington, 1967-68; ptnr. McCarthy & Wharton, Rockville, Md., 1968-75, Kenary, Tietz & Hogan, Rockville, 1975-81, Furey, Doolan, Abell & Hogan, Chevy Chase, Md., 1981-82; judge U.S. Dist. Ct. D.C., Washington, 1982—; asst. prof. Potomac Sch. Law, Washington, 1977-79; adj. prof. law Georgetown Law Ctr., 1985—. Pub. mem. Officer Evaluation Bd. U.S. Fgn. Service, 1973; chmn. Christ Child Inst. for Disturbed Children, 1975; bd. dirs. Providence Hosp., Washington, 1984-86. Recipient cert. recognition and appreciation for vol. services Montgomery County Govt., 1976; recipient cert. appreciation Christ Child Soc., 1976; St. Thomas More fellow Georgetown U. Law Ctr., 1965-66. Mem. ABA (Md. chmn. Drug Abuse Edn. Program, Young Lawyers sect. 1970-73, mem. Litigation sect.), Bar Assn. D.C. (mem. com. on D.C. cts.), Md. State Bar Assn. (Litigation sect.), Montgomery County Bar Assn. (chmn. legal ethics com. 1973-74, lawyer referral service com. 1974-75, adminstrn. justice com. 1979-82, bd. govs. 1977-78), Nat. Inst. for Trial Advocacy Assocs., Def. Research Inst., Md. Assn. Def. Trial Counsel, Md. Trial Lawyers Assn., Georgetown U. Alumni Assn., Smithsonian Assocs., John Carroll Soc., Knights of Malta. Clubs: Barristers, Chevy Chase, Lawyers. *

HOGAN, THOMAS HARLAN, publisher; b. Summit, N.J., July 8, 1944; s. Thomas John and Dorothy Ester (Bakker) H.; m. Mary Suzanne Howarth, Aug. 3, 1968; children: Thomas, Kathleen, Deborah. BA, LeMoyne Coll., 1966. Salesman Auerbach Pubs., Phila., 1968-69; mktg. mgr. IEEE, N.Y.C., 1969-70, BioSciences Info. Services, Phila., 1971-73; v.p. Data Courier Inc., Louisville, 1973-77; pres. Plexus Pub. Co., Medford, N.J., 1977—, Info. Today, Inc., Medford, 1980—. Co-author: Online Searching: A Primer,

1984, Proceedings of the National Online Meeting, 1980—; editor articles Information Today. Mem. Am. Soc. Info. Sci. (pres. 1987), Assn. Info. and Dissemination Ctrs. (pres. 1998-99). Democrat. Roman Catholic. Avocations: golf, sailing, skiing. Home: 3 Durwood Ct Medford NJ 08055-9123 Office: Info Today Inc 143 Old Marlton Pike Medford NJ 08055-8750

HOGAN, THOMAS VICTOR, insurance company executive; b. Jay, Okla., Feb. 1, 1936; s. Thomas Victor and Eula Mae (Cating) H.; m. Patsy Lynn Weir, June 12, 1955; children: Terry Michael, Jeffrey Robert. MS in Fin. Services, The Am. Coll., 1986. CLU, chartered fin. cons. Agent Northwestern Nat. Life, Wichita, Kans., 1955-61; field supr. Northwestern Nat. Life, Dallas, 1961-64; dist. mgr. Northwestern Nat. Life, Houston, 1964-67; mktg. mgr. Northwestern Nat. Life, St. Louis, 1967-72; supt. of agys. Northwestern Nat. Life, Mpls., 1972-75; br. mgr. Northwestern Nat. Life, Dallas, 1975-83; pres. Metroplex Fin. Services, Dallas, 1983-96, also bd. dirs.; v.p., mgr. employee benefits and fin. svcs. Roach Howard Smith & Hunter, Dallas, 1996—. Contbr. articles to profl. jours., tape series. Loan exec. United Way Mpls., 1973; treas. Royal Oaks Bapt. Ch., Dallas, 1979-87; bd. dirs. Carrollton Parks and Rec. Dept., 1993—, chmn., 1996-98; bd. dirs. DALU Found., 1994—. Merit scholar Phillips U., 1954. Mem. Am. Soc. CLUs and Chartered Fin. Cons. (pres. 1986, bd. dirs. 1983-89), Gen. Agts. and Mgrs. Assn. (bd. dirs. 1980-83), Dallas Estate Planning Coun. Republican. Avocations: golf, fishing, travel. Home: 2703 N Surrey Dr Carrollton TX 75006-4748 Office: Roach Howard Smith & Hunter 9330 Lbj Fwy Ste 1500 Dallas TX 75243-3449

HOGARTH, ROBIN MILES, business educator, university official; b. Simla, India, July 10, 1942; s. Robert Robison and Frances Mary Beryl (Prike) H.; m. Hélène Marie Jeanne Ballard, July 6, 1968; children: Marie-Anne, Claire, Paul. MBA, INSEAD, Fontainebleau, France, 1968; PhD, U. Chgo., 1972. Asst., then assoc. prof. INSEAD, 1972-79; assoc. prof. U. Chgo. Grad. Sch. Bus., 1979-82, prof., 1982—, dir. Ctr. Decision Rsch., 1983-94, Wallace W. Booth prof., 1989—, dep. dean, 1993—; vis. sr. lectr. London Bus. Sch., 1977-78. Author: Evaluating Management Education, 1979, Judgement and Choice, 1980, 87. Fellow Inst. Chartered Accts. (Eng. and Wales); mem. APA, Inst. Mgmt. Sci., Judgement and Decision-making Soc. (pres. 1992). Home: 5432 S East View Park Chicago IL 60615-5916 Office: U Chgo Grad Sch Bus 1101 E 58th St Chicago IL 60637-1511*

HOGARTY, RICHARD ANTHONY, political scientist, educator; b. Princeton, N.J., Sept. 26, 1933; s. James Robert and Marie Frances (Piscurick) H.; m. Ann Woodward Jeffers, May 5, 1956; children: Margaret, Michael, Susan, Ann, Peter, Timothy. AB, Dartmouth Coll., 1955; MGA, U. Pa., 1960; PhD, Princeton U., 1965. Adminstrv. asst. U.S. Senate, Washington, 1960-61; rsch. asst. Princeton U., 1961-65; asst. prof. Rider Coll., Lawrenceville, N.J., 1965-68; asst. prof., assoc. prof. U. Mass., Boston, 1968-78, prof., 1978—; dir. Gov.'s Task Force on Migrant Labor, Trenton, N.J., 1967-68; cons. N.J. Dept. Community Affairs, Trenton, 1967-68, New Eng. Regional Commn., Boston, 1972, Boston Pub. Schs., 1976, City of Boston, 1977-78. Author (case studies): N.J. Farmers and Migrant Housing Rules, 1966, Delaware River Drought Emergency, 1970, The Endangered Metropolis, 1986, The Search for Massachusetts Chancellor, 1988, Searching for a U. Mass. President, 1991, The Closing of Metropolitan State Hospital, 1995. Dir. Cranbury (N.J.) Housing Assocs., 1963-68, Citizens Coun. for Pub. Schs., Marblehead, Mass., 1969-72; vice-chmn. Dem. Town Com., Marblehead, 1970-80; sr. assoc. McCormack Inst. Pub. Affairs, Boston, 1988—. Lt. USMCR, 1955-57. Recipient William Addee Whitehead award N.J. Hist. Soc. 1967. Mem. ASPA, Am. Pol. Sci. Assn. Democrat. Roman Catholic. Avocations: tennis, cross-country skiing, woodworking. Home: 193 Green St Marblehead MA 01945-1511 Office: U Mass 100 Morrissey Blvd Boston MA 02125-3300

HOGBERG, CARL GUSTAV, retired steel company executive; b. Escanaba, Mich., July 19, 1913; s. Claus Emil and Anna C. (Franson) H.; BS in Metall. Engring., Mich. Coll. Mining and Tech., 1935, DEng (hon.) Mich. Tech. U., 1968; m. June Loraine Evans, June 10, 1935 (dec. Aug. 1991); children: David K., Janet H. (Mrs. Nicholas A. Matwiyoff). Blast-furnace apprentice South Chicago works, Carnegie-Ill. Steel Corp., 1935, various operating positions blast-furnace dept., 1935-39, sec. blast-furnace and coke-oven com., Pitts., 1939-41; asst. chmn. blast-furnace com. U.S. Steel Corp., Pitts., 1942-54, asst. to v.p. Mich. Limestone div., Detroit, 1955, asst. v.p., 1956, v.p., 1957-60, pres., 1960-63, v.p. raw materials service, parent co., 1964, pres. Orinoco Mining Co. subs., Caracas, Venezuela, 1965-70, v.p. internat. U.S. Steel Corp., 1970-73. Mem. AIME (J.E. Johnson, Jr. award 1945), Assn. Iron and Steel Engrs. (Kelly award 1950), Am. Iron and Steel Inst., Eastern Western States Blast Furnace and Coke Assns. Contbr. tech. articles trade publs. Home: 100 Norman Dr Apt 263 Cranberry Township PA 16066-4205

HOGE, JAMES CLEO, retired priest and school administrator; b. Charleston, W.Va., Nov. 28, 1916; s. James Cleo and Theresa (Bohnert) H. BA, Benedictine Coll., 1940; MA, St. Leo Coll., 1980. Joined Order St. Benedict, Roman Cath. Ch., 1938; ordained priest, 1943. Priest in charge Henando County Missions, Brooksville, Fla., 1944-48, 54-55; pastor Our Lady of Fatima Ch., Inverness, Fla., 1962-65, St. Benedict's Ch., Crystal River, Fla., 1969-89; pres. Cen. Cath. Sch. of Citrus County, Lecanto, Fla., 1985-91. Trustee St. Leo Coll., 1965-78; mem. sch. bd. Diocese St. Petersburg, Fla., 1983-88; pres. Citrus County Hist. Soc., 1994-95. Mem. North Suncoast Mins. Assn. (pres. 1974-75, 83-84), Rotary (pres. 1982-83, 90-91). Democrat. Home and Office: 5521 W Pine Cir Crystal River FL 34429-7518 *What is the most important reflection man can have on life? The Greek philospher Socrates said it first: "Knothe sou"—"Know thyself."*

HOGE, MICHAEL ALAN, psychologist; b. Lima, Ohio, Dec. 20, 1954; s. Ned William and Marilyn (Henkener) H.; m. Nancy Anderson, June 4, 1988; children: Christopher, Connor. BA summa cum laude, Kent State U., 1977, MA in Clin. Psychology, 1981, PhD in Clin. Psychology, 1984. Lic. psychologist, Conn. Psycholgy intern, dept. psychology Kent (Ohio) State Univ., 1980-81; psycholgy intern Columbiana County Mental Health Counseling Ctr., Lisbon, Ohio, 1981-82; psycholgy intern, Counseling and Group Resources Ctr. Kent (Ohio) State Univ., 1982-83; psychology fellow VA Med. Ctr., West Haven, Conn., 1983-84; instr. Yale Univ. Sch. Medicine, New Haven, Conn., 1984-85; asst. dir. Hill Mental Health Clinc, Conn. Mental Health Ctr., New Haven, 1984-85; asst. prof. psychology in psychiatry Yale U. Sch. Medicine, New Haven, 1985-91, assoc. prof., 1991—; dir. psychol. svcs. div. inpatient and partial hosp. Conn. Mental Health Ctr., New Haven, 1985-87, exec. dir. day hosp., 1987-90, dir. managed care system and asst. dir. edn. and tng., 1990-94, mem. exec. com. med. staff, 1989-94, acting v.p., 1990; dir. managed behavioral health svcs. devel. dept. psychiatry Yale U., 1995—; lectr., cons. and presenter in field. Contbr. reviews, chpts. to books and articles to profl. jours. Mem. Am. Assn. for Partial Hospitalization (bd. dirs. 1987-89, chair rsch. com. 1987-89, cons. rsch. com. 1989-93, chair continuing edn. com. 1987-89, pub. com. 1987-89, regional rep. for Conn. 1985-87), Partial Hospitalization Assn. Conn. (chair legis. and fin. com. 1985-86, v.p. 1985-86, pres. 1986-87), Am. Psychol. Assn., Consortium for Edn. in Groups and Orgns. (cons. 1988), Conn. Psychol. Assn., Nat. Alliance for the Mentally Ill, Catchment Area Coun., Phi Beta Kappa, and others. Office: Yale Univ Sch Medicine 25 Park St Fl 6 New Haven CT 06519-1110

HOGE, WARREN M., newspaper and magazine correspondent, editor; b. N.Y.C., Apr. 13, 1941; s. James F. Hoge and Virginia (McClamroch) Barber; m. Olivia Larisch, Nov. 21, 1981; 1 child, Nicholas; stepchildren: Christina, Tatjana. BA, Yale U., 1963; postgrad., George Washington U., 1964-65. Reporter Washington Star, 1964-66; bur. chief N.Y. Post, Washington, 1966-69; city editor, asst. mng. editor N.Y. Post, N.Y.C., 1970-75; dep. met. editor N.Y. Times, N.Y.C., 1976-78; fgn. corr. N.Y. Times, Rio de Janeiro, Brazil, 1979-83; fgn. editor N.Y. Times, N.Y.C., 1984-87, asst. mng. editor, 1987-90; asst. mng. editor and editor N.Y. Times Mag., N.Y.C., 1991-92, asst. mng. editor for culture, style, book rev., and recruitment of writers, 1993-96; chief London Bur., N.Y. Times, 1996—. Baptist. Home: 61 Eaton Pl, London SW1 8DF, England Office: NY Times, 66 Buckingham Gate, London SW1E 6AU, England

HOGENKAMP, HENRICUS PETRUS CORNELIS, biochemistry researcher, biochemistry educator; b. Doesburg, Gelderland, The Netherlands, Dec. 20, 1925; came to U.S., 1958; s. Johannes Hermanus and Maria Margaretha J. (Abeln) H.; m. Lieke Ter Haar, Apr. 25, 1953; children: Harry Peter, Derk John, Margaret Angelina. BSA, U. B.C., Vancouver, 1957, MSc, 1958; PhD, U. Calif., Berkeley, 1961. Rsch. biochemist U. Calif., Berkeley, 1961-62; assoc. scientist Fisheries Rsch. Bd. Can., Vancouver, B.C., 1962-63; asst. prof. U. Iowa, Iowa City, 1963-67, assoc. prof., 1967-71, prof., 1971-76; prof., head dept. biochemistry U. Minn., Mpls., 1976-92, prof. dept. biochemistry, 1992—; vis. prof. Australian Nat. U., Canberra, Australia, 1966-67, Philipps U., Marburg, Fed. Republic of Germany, 1986-87, 1988, 1990; guest scientist U. Calif. Los Alamos (N.Mex) Sci. Lab., 1974-75. Sgt. Royal Netherlands Army, 1946-50, Indonesia. Recipient Alexander von Humboldt-Stiftung award Philipps U.-Fachbereich Microbiology, Marburg, Fed. Republic of Germany, 1986-87; named to Minn. Acad. Medicine,Mpls., 1980-; Guggenheim fellow U. Iowa, Iowa City, 1974-75. Mem. AAAS, Am. Chem. Soc., Am. Soc. Biochemistry and Molecular Biology (mem. pub. affairs com. 1986-91), Assn. Med. Sch. Depts. Biochemistry, Internat. Union Biochemists (chmn. U.S. nominating com. 1988). Home: 2211 Marion Rd Saint Paul MN 55113-3805 Office: U Minn Med Sch Dept Biochem 4 225 Millard Hall 435 Delaware St SE Minneapolis MN 55455-0355*

HOGENSEN, MARGARET HINER, librarian, consultant; b. Ottawa, Kans., Oct. 11, 1920; d. Hebron Henry and Nellie Evelyn (Godard) Hiner; widowed. BA, U. Wichita, 1942; BS in Library Sci., U. Denver, 1945. Circulation librarian Boise (Idaho) Pub. Library, 1945-49, Pomona (Calif.) Pub. Library, 1950-51; reference librarian WFIL-TV, Phila., 1963-69; rsch. dir. Concept Films, Washington, 1969-72; ind. researcher, cons. Greenbelt, Md., 1973—. Bd. dirs. Greenbelt Homes, Inc., 1977-93, 98—, pres., 1983-88, treas. 1998—; past mem. bd. dirs. Greenbelt Consumer Coop., Nat. Coop. Bank, Nat. Coop. Bus. Assn.; pres. Ea. Coop. Housing Orgn., 1992-95. Mem. Nat. Assn. Housing Coops (bd. dirs. 1986-87, 1990-94). Democrat. Christian Scientist. Avocation: travel. Home: PO Box 218 Greenbelt MD 20768-0218

HOGG, DAVID CLARENCE, physicist; b. Vanguard, Sask., Can., Sept. 5, 1921; came to U.S., 1953, naturalized, 1964; s. Francis Sandison and Frances Katherine (Gadsby) H.; m. Jean E. MacMillan, Feb. 15, 1947; children—David Randal, Rebecca Jean. BSc, U. Western Ont. (Can.), London, 1949; MSc, McGill U., Montreal, Que., Can., 1951, PhD, 1953. With Bell Telephone Labs., 1953-77, head atmospheric physics research, 1966-72; head antenna and propagation research Bell Telephone Labs., Holmdel, N.J., 1972-77; chief environ. radiometry wave propagation lab. Environ. Research Lab., NOAA, Boulder, Colo., 1977-83, chief radio meteorology, 1983-86; lectr., adj. prof. U. Colo., Boulder, 1984—, lectr. ECE dept, 1989—; sr. scientist Colo. Inst. Research Environ. Scis., U. Colo., Boulder, 1986-89. Research, numerous publs. on microwaves, optics, satellite communications and remote sensing; patentee microwave antennas; composer vocal, choral, strings and piano classical music. Served with Can. Army, 1940-45. Recipient Silver medal U.S. Dept. Commerce, 1983, Composer's award Colo. Music Educators Assn., 1992. Fellow IEEE (founder Jersey Coast sect., Disting. Achievement award 1984); mem. NAE, Union Radio Scientifique Internat., Am. Music Ctr. Episcopalian. Home: 4978 Carter Ct Boulder CO 80301-3895

HOGG, JAMES HENRY, JR., retired education educator; b. Pleasantville, Pa., Aug. 15, 1926; s. James Henry and Carrie Ethel (Swan) H.; m. Elizabeth Beatrice George, Sept. 8, 1945 (dec. Feb. 1988); children: Carolyn Elizabeth, James Henry III; m. Reva Rowene Heffernan, Jan. 1, 1992. BA, Houghton Coll., 1951; MA, Allegheny Coll., 1961; EdD, Pa. State U., 1971. Cert. secondary tchr., Pa. Tchr. English and social studies Meadville (Pa.) Sr. H.S., 1962-67; instr. in secondary edn. Pa. State U., University Park, 1968-71, asst. prof., 1971-77, assoc. prof., 1977-91; ret., 1991; trustee Houghton Coll., 1964-67; Pa. State Adv. Bd., Mid. States Assn. Colls. and Schs., 1984-91 (chmn. evaluation teams, 1983-91). Contbr. articles to profl. jours. Councilman Cooperstown Borough, 1993-98. With U.S. Army, 1944-46, ETO. Named participant in 2d Inst. Am History Pa. State U., 1966, Assn. Tchr. Educators LaureATE, 1989; recipient cert. of appreciation U.S. House Reps. Page Sch., 1985. Mem. Nat. Assn. Tchr. Educators, Pa. Assn. Tchr. Educators, Phi Delta Kappa, Alpha Tau. Republican. Methodist. Avocations: hunting, fishing, bowling, chess. Home: Reisenman and Lakeview Drs Cooperstown PA 16317-0212

HOGG, JERRY D., federal judge; b. 1941. BS, W.Va. Tech. Inst., 1963; JD, U. W.Va., 1968. Pvt. practice, 1968-82; magistrate judge U.S. Dist. Ct. (so. dist.) W.Va., Charleston, 1982—. Office: US Dist Ct (so dist) WV 2000 A Fed Bldg 500 Quarrier St Charleston WV 25301-2130

HOGG, RICHARD, mineral/particle process engineering educator; b. Redcar, England, Jan. 6, 1938; married. BSc, U. Leeds, 1963; MS, U. Calif., Berkeley, 1965; PhD in Mineral Tech., U. Calif., 1970. From asst. prof. to assoc. prof. Pa. State U., 1969-79, prof. mineral processing, 1979—; asst. specialist mineral tech. U.Calif., Berkeley, 1966-69; mem. com. Comminution & Energy Consumption NAS, 1978-80. Recipient Antoine M. Gaudin award Soc. for Mining, Metallurgy & Exploration, 1994, Arthur F. Taggart award, 1997. Mem. AIME, Am. Filtration and Separations Soc., Sigma Xi. Research in fundamental basis of mineral processing operations; colloid and surface chemistry; mixing, segregation and flow of particulate solid materials; fine grinding processes. Office: Pa State Univ Mineral Procg Sect 115 Hosler Bldg University Park PA 16802-5000 Address: 1232 S Garner St State College PA 16801-6326

HOGG, ROBERT VINCENT, JR., mathematical statistician, educator; b. Hannibal, Mo., Nov. 8, 1924; s. Robert Vincent and Isabelle Frances (Storrs) H.; m. Carolyn Joan Ladd, June 23, 1956 (dec. June 1990); children: Mary Carolyn, Barbara Jean, Allen Ladd, Robert Mason; m. Ann Burke, Oct. 15, 1994. BA, U. Ill., 1947; MS, U. Iowa, 1948, PhD, 1950. Asst. prof. math. U. Iowa, Iowa City, 1950-56, assoc. prof., 1956-62, prof., 1962-65, chmn. dept. stats., prof. stats., 1965-83, 92-93, Hanson prof. mfg. productivity, 1993-95. Co-author: Introduction to Mathematical Statistics, 1959, 5th edit., 1995, Finite Mathematics and Calculus, 1974, Probability and Statistical Inference, 1997, 5th edit., 1992, Applied Statistics for Engineers and Physical Scientists, 1987, 2d edit., 1992; assoc. editor Am. Stats., 1971-74; contbr. articles to profl. jours. Vestryman local Episc. ch., 1958-60, 66-68, 91-92. With USNR, 1943-46. Grantee NIH, 1966-68, 75-78, NSF, 1969-74. Fellow Inst. Math. Stats. (program sec., bd. 1968-74), Am. Statis. Assn. (pres. Iowa sect. 1962-63, coun. 1965-66, 73-74, vis. lectr. 1965-68, 77-85, chmn. tng. sect. 1973, assoc. editor jour. 1978-80, pres.-elect 1987, pres. 1988, past pres. 1989, Founders award 1991); mem. Math. Assn. Am. (pres. Iowa sect. 1964-65, 95-96, bd. govs. 1971-74, visa. lectr. 1976-81, Outstanding Tchg. award 1993), Internat. Statis. Inst., Rotary (pres. Iowa City 1984-85), Sigma Xi (pres. Iowa dist. chpt. 1970-71), Pi Kappa Alpha. Home: 1241 Pheasant Valley St Iowa City IA 52246-8682 Office: U Iowa Dept Statis Acturial Sci Iowa City IA 52242

HOGG, SONJA, university athletics coach; b. Alexandria, La., Dec. 20; d. E.P. and Dorothy Chatelain. BS, MS, La. Tech. U. Tchr. jr. high sch. Alexandria, Baton Rouge; tchr., coach Ruston H.S., 1972-74; coach women's basketball La. Tech., 1974-84; v.p. for resource devel. Women's Basketball Hall of Fame, Little Rock, 1984-88; asst. athletic dir. mktg. and devel. U. Tex., Austin, 1988-90; coach Deer Park H.S., Austin; head coach Baylor U., Waco, Tex., 1994—. Mem. adv. bd. Naismith awards, Sports Found. Coun.; bd. dirs. Girl Scouts Am. Avocations: schnauzer dogs, community speaking, golf, hiking, skiing. Office: Baylor U 150 Bear Run Waco TX 76711-1267*

HOGG, STEPHEN P., otolaryngologist; b. Jackson, Ky., Feb. 14, 1921; s. Walter Scott and Jessie Lee (Stacy) H.; m. Mary Carldean Taylor, Sept. 9, 1944; 6 children. BS, U. Ky., 1941; MD, U. Louisville, 1944. Diplomate Am. Bd. Otolaryngology. Pres., founder Midwest Found. for Med. Care, 1971, Med Co-Peer Rev., 1974, CHOICECARE, 1979; v.p. Am. Assn. of Founds. for Med. Care, 1978-87. Lt. USN, 1944-47, PTO. Mem. Ohio State Otolaryngology Soc. (pres. 1964), Cin. Otolaryngology Soc. (pres. 1960), Cin. Acad. Medicine (pres. 1971). Home: 3327 Stettinius Ave Cincinnati OH 45208-2754

HOGGARD, LARA GULDMAR, conductor, educator; b. Kingston, Okla., Feb. 9, 1915; s. Calvin Peter and Eva Lillian (Smith) H.; m. Mildred Mae Teeter, Sept. 11, 1943; 1 dau., Susan. BA, Southea. Tchrs. Coll., 1934; MA, Columbia U., 1940, EdD, 1947. Supr. music Durant (Okla.) Pub. Schs., 1934-39; dir. choral activities, opera and oratorio U. Okla., 1940-43; assoc. founder, prin. instr. Waring Summer Choral Workshops, 1948-52; co-editor Shawnee Press, Del. Water Gap, Pa., 1946-52; dir. music and music edn. rsch. Indian Springs Sch., Ala. Edn. Found., Birmingham, 1955-60; founder Nat. Young Artist Competition, Midland-Odessa, 1962—; William Rand Kenan prof. music U. N.C., Chapel Hill, 1967-80, founder Carolina Choir, 1967—; founder N.C. Collegiate Choral Festival, 1969—; Fuller E. Callaway prof. music Columbus Coll., U. Ga., 1981-82. Condr.: NBC-USN Navy Hour, 1945; assoc. condr., Waring's Pennsylvanians, 1946-52; condr., dir.: Festival of Song, Civic Music and Nat. Concert Artists Corp., nat. touring concert group, 1952-53; founder, condr., musical dir., Midland-Odessa (Tex.) Symphony Orch. and Chorale, 1962-67; condr. numerous music festivals in Am., Europe; artistic dir., prin. condr. Festival of Three Cities, Vienna-Budapest-Prague, 1973, Jugendmusikfest in Wien, 1973, 74; guest lectr. and condr. at univs. and conservatories in Am. and Europe, dir., N.C. Summer Insts. In Choral Art, 1953-83; condr.: several mus. premieres, including Behold the Glory (Talmage Dean), with Louisville Orch., 1964, Light in the Wilderness (Dave Brubeck), Chapel Hill, 1968, new edit. Ein deutsches Requiem (Brahms) with N.C. Symphony, 1986, numerous others.; author: Improving Music Reading, 1947, Exploring Music, 1967; editor: an oratorio Light in the Wilderness (Dave Brubeck), 1968; composer-arranger-editor 37 choral publs.; editor: new English transl. and corr. orch. score and parts Ein deutsches Requiem (Brahms), 1983-89; composer: Le Jongleur, CBS-TV, 1951. Served to lt. (j.g.) USN, 1943-45, PTO. Recipient award for outstanding svc. to music in Ala., Ala. Fine Arts Festival, 1958, citation for outstanding svc. to fine arts in Tex., Tex. Senate and Gov., West Texan award, 1967, Tanner award U. N.C., 1972, Ten Best Profs. award, 1978, Order Long Leaf Pine Gov. N.C., 1980, Disting. Alumnus award Southeastern Okla. State U., 1981, Lara G. Hoggard endowed professorship named in his honor U. N.C., 1993. Mem. Music Educators Nat. Conf. (life; Master Builder), Am. Choral Dirs. Assn. (life, award for contbn. to music in N.C. 1976, citation for contbn. to music in Am., divsn. 5, 1986, award for excellence and lifelong commitment So. divsn. 1998), AAUP, N.C. Music Educators Assn. (hon. life), N.C. Lit. Soc. (life), Rotary, Phi Mu Alpha Sinfonia (nat. hon. life). Democrat. Presbyterian. *Creativity within the individual is our best weapon against total conformity and robotism. The arts challenge and elevate both the intellect and the spirit. Sensitivity and respect for the true, the good and the beautiful, stand in defiance of three attitudes which must not prevail, if civilization is to survive: bigotry, arrogant ignorance, and acceptance or approval of mediocrity.*

HOGGARD, LYNN, French and English language educator; b. Oakdale, La., July 19, 1944; d. Frank John Taylor Sr. (dec.) and Ruth Elizabeth (Bishop) Mott; m. Sylvestre Novak, July 1969 (div.); m. James Martin Hoggard, May 23, 1976; children: Jordan, Bryn. BA in English, Centenary Coll., 1966; MA in Comparative Lit., U. Mich., 1967; PhD in Comparative Lit., U. So. Calif., 1974. Vis. asst. prof. English Tex. Tech. U., Lubbock, 1974-76; instr. English Vernon Regional Jr. Coll., Wichita Falls, Tex., 1980-83; instr. English and French Midwestern State U., Wichita Falls, 1976-89, assoc. prof. French, 1989-91, Hardin prof., 1997—, coord. fgn. lang. program, 1991—. Author: Married to Dance: The Story of Irina and Frank Pal, 1995; translator: Sketch of a Serpent, 1989, Tent Posts, 1997; contbr. poetry to anthology. Bd. dirs. Wichita Falls Arts Coun., 1994-97; mem. collections com. Wichita Falls Museum and ARts Ctr., 1995-97. Grantee NEH, 1991. Mem. Am. Lit. Translators Assn., (pres. 1997—, mem. adv. bd. 1995—). Democrat. Methodist. Avocations: piano, jogging. Home: 111 Pembroke Ln Wichita Falls TX 76301-3941 Office: Midwestern State U 3410 Taft Blvd Wichita Falls TX 76308-2096

HOGGARD, MINNIE COLTRAIN, gifted education educator, consultant; b. Williamston, N.C.; d. Joshua Herbert and Nellie Mae (Wynne) Coltrain; m. Robert Lewis Hoggard; children: Robbin Lenora Hoggard Blake, Lewis Wynne Hoggard. BS, East Carolina U., 1975, MA in Ed., 1977, curriculum instrnl. specialist, 1988, EdS, 1991. Cert. reading specialist, instrnl. specialist, academically gifted tchr., supt., prin., N.C. Draftsman, bookkeeper East Coast Surveying Svc., Windsor, N.C., 1964-75; tcchr. reading Washington County Schs., Washington, N.C., 1975; elem. tchr. Martin County Schs., Williamston, 1975-85, tchr. academically gifted, 1985-93, academically gifted specialist, coord., 1993-97, cons. academically gifted local plan, 1996-97, mentor coord., 1998—, asst. prin., 1997-98, 98-99; supervising tchr. East Carolina U., Greenville, N.C., 1979-85; N.C. advisor Tar Heel Jr. Hist. Assn., Raleigh, 1986. Collaborating writer and tester elem. sch. curriculum in Can. for N.C. students; editor play Backwards into Time, 1986 (state award 1986). Pres. Windsor Jr. Woman's Club, 1969-71. Grantee Nat. Diffusion Network, 1986; recipient N.C. Advisor of Yr. award, 1986. Mem. Coun. for Exceptional Children, Nat. Assn. for Gifted Children. Democrat. Episcopalian. Avocations: recreational reading, walking, writing poetry, playing bridge, travel. Home: 302 Sutton Dr Windsor NC 27983-1324 Office: Martin County Schs 300 N Watts St Williamston NC 27892-2056

HOGGARD, SHARON RIDDICK, public relations executive; b. Portsmouth, Va., May 9, 1955; d. Leroy and Bessie Mills Riddick; m. Leroy Hoggard, Oct. 20, 1989; 1 child, Kendall Matthew. B of English & Journalism, Old Dominion U., 1979. Staff writer, photographer Jour. & Guide/Guide Pub. Co., Norfolk, Va., 1980-81; asst. graphic specialist Jour. & Guide/Hamptin Rds. Metro Weekender, Norfolk, Va., 1981-85, mng. editor, 1985-87; environ. inspector City of Portsmouth (Va.) Dept. Housing Svcs., 1987-88; housing counselor City of Portsmouth Dept Environ. Svcs., 1988-90; comm. coord. City of Portsmouth Pub. Info. Office, 1990-94; pub. info. coord. City of Chesapeake (Va.) Pub. Comm. Dept., 1994—; cons. in field. Coord. Black history Month Celebration, Windsor, Va., 1994—. Mem. Pub. Rels. Soc. Am. (job bank coord.). Baptist. Avocations: photography, writing, reading, sewing. Office: City of Chesapeake 306 Cedar Rd Portsmouth VA 23322

HOGGARD, WILLIAM ZACK, JR., amusement park executive; b. Albuquerque, Dec. 2, 1951; s. William Zack Sr. and Geneva Ruth (Garner) H.; m. Sandra K. Walker (div. 1989); children: Steven Wayne, Amanda Danielle; m. Deborah M. Neal, 1992; children: Roxanne A., Katrina K. Asst. mgr. Lone Star Amusements, Amarillo, Tex., 1969; gen. mgr. Golden Spread Amusements, Hedley, Tex., 1969-72; booking agt. Monte Young Shows, Provo, Utah, 1972; independent concessionaire Gene Ledel Shows, Ft. Worth, Tex., 1973; concession mgr. Schaffer Shows Unit 2, Dallas, 1974, Pearson Enterprises, Ft. Worth, 1975-76; gen. agt., concession mgr. Aero Space Shows, Dallas, 1977-80; western sales mgr., operating engr. Pretzel Ride Inc., Shiloh, N.J., 1981; broker, distributor of amusement rides, carnival operator Joshua, Tex., 1982—; chief exec. officer Phoenix Amusements (President's Park Amusement Park), Carlsbad, N.Mex., 1991-93; amusement ride inspector Beckman Ins. Agy., Brookfield, Wis., 1993—; loss control cons. Allied Speciality Ins. Co., St. Petersburg, Fla., 1985—, State Bd. of Ins., Austin, Tex., 1985—; cons. engr. Eli Bridge Co., Inc. Jacksonvil le, Ill., 1985-89, Pretzel Ride, Inc., Shiloh, N.J., 1981—; cons. Amusement Ride Safety Act 1982, State of Oklahoma. Carnival organizer and fund raiser, fair bds., numerous civic orgns., Tex., N.Mex. and Okla., 1969-89; CEO Phoenix Amusements (dba Presidents Park Amusement Park), Carlsbad, N.Mex., 1991-92; pres., CEO Hoggard Amusement Industries Inc., 1996—. Mem. Tex. Assn. Fairs and Expositions, Okla. Assn. Fairs and Festivals, Outdoor Amusement Bus. Assn., Nat. Assn. Amusement Ride Safety Officials, Lone Star Showmen's Club. Avocations: refurbishing used and antique amusement rides. Home and Office: PO Box 952 Joshua TX 76058-0952

HOGLE, JERROLD EDWIN, English language educator; b. L.A., May 15, 1948; s. Howard Clinton and Jane (Reynard) H.; m. Pamela Jean Wesp, Aug. 22, 1970; children: Karen, Joanne. BA summa cum laude, U. Calif., Irvine, 1970; MA, Harvard U., 1971, PhD, 1974. Tchg. fellow in humanities Harvard U., Cambridge, Mass., 1971-74; asst. prof. English U. Ariz., Tucson, 1974-80, assoc. prof. English, 1980-89, prof. English, 1989—, assoc. dean humanities, 1990-93, acting dean humanities, 1991, univ. disting. prof., 1996—, chair faculty, 1997—. Author: (book) Shelley's Process, 1988; editor: (book) Evaluating Shelley, 1996, mem. editl. bd. Keats Shelby jours.; mem. adv. bd. (website) Romantic Crossings, 1995—; mem. editl. adv. bd. Gothic Studies jour., 1999—; contbr. articles to essay collections, profl. jours. Pres. Butterfield Elem. PTO, Tucson, 1983-84; pres. Mountain View H.S. PTO, Tucson, 1989-90; local pres., state bd. dirs. Ariz. Assn. Gifted/Talented, Tucson, 1982-91; founder, Marana Found. for Edn., Tucson, 1991-92. Sgt. USAR, 1971-77. Guggenheim fellow, 1989-90, Mellon Huntington

Libr. fellow, 1990. Mem. MLA, N.Am. Soc. for Study of Romanticism (conf. chair 2000), Internat. Gothic Assn. (pres. 1995-97, past pres. 1997—), Keats-Shelley Assn. (mem. editl. adv. bd. 1989—). Democrat. Avocations: community service, school assistance. E-mail: hogle@u.arizona.edu. Office: U Ariz Dept English PO Box 210067 Tucson AZ 85721-0067

HOGLUND, FORREST EUGENE, petroleum company executive; b. Lawrence, Kans., July 1, 1933; s. Roy A. and Edna M. (McMichael) H.; m. Sally Sue Roney, June 19, 1956; children—Kelly M., Shelly L., Kristan K. BS in Mech. Engring, U. Kans., 1956. Registered profl. engr. Tex. With Exxon Corp., 1957-1977; v.p. ops. Exxon Corp. (Middle East), N.Y.C., 1973-75, v.p. gas, 1976-77; pres., chief oper. officer Tex. Oil and Gas, Dallas, 1977-83, pres., chief exec. officer, 1983-87; dir. USX Corp., Pitts., 1986-87; chmn., chief exec. officer Enron Oil & Gas Co. (subs. Enron Corp.), Houston, 1987—; mem. exec. com. U.S. Oil and Gas Assn., Houston; bd. dirs. Chase Bank Tex. Vice chmn. bd. visitors Univ. Cancer Found.--M.D. Anderson; area v.p. U. Kans. Endowment Assn.; former chmn. Houston Mus. Natural Sci. With C.E., U.S. Army, 1957-58. Mem. Am. Petroleum Inst., AIME, Soc. Petroleum Engrs., Ind. Petroleum Assn. Am., Tex. Ind. Producers and Royalty Assn., Petroleum Club, Dallas Country Club, River Oaks Country Club, Tau Beta Pi, Pi Tau Sigma, Sigma Tau, Omicron Delta Kappa. Office: Enron Oil & Gas Co 1400 Smith St Houston TX 77002

HOGLUND, JOHN ANDREW, lawyer; b. Cleve., July 19, 1945; s. Paul Franklin and Louise (Anderson) H.; m. Patricia Olwell, May 27, 1972; children: Britt Hannah, Maeve Olwell, Marc Paul-Joseph. BA, Augustana Coll., 1967; JD, George Washington U., 1972. Bar: Wash. 1973, U.S. Dist. Ct. (we. dist.) Wash. 1973, U.S. Ct. Appeals (9th cir.) 1973. Law clk. Wash. State Supreme Ct., 1973-74; assoc. Mooney, Cullen & Holm, Olympia, 1973-75; ptnr. Cullen, Holm, Hoglund & Foster, Olympia, 1975-81; pvt. practice Olympia, 1981—; pres. Hoglund Enterprises, 1987—; adj. prof. law sch. U. Puget Sound, Tacoma, Wash., 1989-90, trustee, 1984-92. Co-author: SKYCYL Practicing Law Manual, 1986-95, WSBA Book Automobile Negligence Law, 1988. Vice chmn. Group Health Coop., Olympia, 1978, Thurston County Dem. Cen. Com., Olympia, 1980; chmn. bd. dirs. S.W. Wash. Health Sys. Agy., 1979; alumni bd. dirs. George Washington U. Nat. Law Ctr., 1994-97, emeritus mem., 1997—. With U.S. Army, 1967-69. Named Boss of Yr. Thurston County Legal Secs. Assn., 1985. Mem. ABA, Thurston County Bar Assn. (trustee 1988-90, Svc. awards 1987, 90), ATLA, Wash. State Trial Lawyers Assn. (pres. 1983-84, Brandeis award 1980), Wash. State Trial Lawyers Found. (pres. 1985-87), Wash. State Bar Assn. (chmn. UPL com. 1979, CPR com., pub. rels. com., chmn. Lawyer Protection Fund com. 1991), Nat. Law Ctr. George Washington U. (alumni bd. 1994-97), Kiwanis (Disting. Pres. award 1980). Office: PO Box 7877 Olympia WA 98507-7877

HOGLUND, RICHARD FRANK, research and technical executive; b. Chgo., Mar. 22, 1933; s. Reuben Ture and Margaret Mabel (Thayer) H.; m. Arlene Diana Bieniasz, Jan. 7, 1956 (dec. Mar. 1986); children: Terrence, David, Mark; m. Susan Annette Vee, Feb. 10, 1987. Student, Valparaiso U., 1949-51; BS in Mech. Engring, Northwestern U., 1954, MS in Mech. Engring. (Gen. Electric fellow), 1955, PhD (Royal Cabell fellow), 1960. Dept. head Ford Aeronutronic, 1960-63; assoc. prof. aerospace engring., lab. dir. Purdue U., 1963-69; prof. aerospace engring. Ga. Inst. Tech., 1969; chief scientist Atlantic Research Corp., 1969-72; head ocean monitoring and control, chief advanced concepts tech. Def. Advanced Research Research Projects Agy., 1972-75; staff scientist Phys. Dynamics, Inc., Arlington, Va., 1975-77; v.p. Ops. Research, Inc., Silver Spring, Md., 1977; dep. asst. sec. of navy for research and advanced tech. and concepts Dept. Navy, Washington, 1977-80; sr. v.p. ORI, Inc., Silver Spring, Md., 1980-89; exec. v.p. Arete Assocs., Arlington, Va., 1989-90; staff v.p. undersea warfare Gen. Dynamics Corps., 1990-92; cons., 1993—. Contbr. articles to profl. jours.; editor: Energy Sources and Energy Conversion, 1967. Recipient Def. Meritorious Civilian Service medal Dept. Def., 1975. Home and Office: 7217 Kitchen Dr King George VA 22485-5227

HOGNESS, JOHN RUSTEN, physician, academic administrator; b. Oakland, Calif., June 27, 1922; s. Thorfin R. and Phoebe (Swenson) H. Student, Haverford Coll., 1939-42, D.Sc. (hon.), 1973; B.S., U. Chgo., 1943, M.D., 1946; D.Sc. (hon.), Med. Coll. Ohio at Toledo, 1972; LL.D., George Washington U., 1973; D.Litt., Thomas Jefferson U., 1980. Diplomate: Am. Bd. Internal Medicine. Intern medicine Presbyn. Hosp., N.Y.C., 1946-47; asst. resident Presbyn. Hosp., 1949-50; chief resident King County Hosp., Seattle, 1950-51; asst. U. Wash. Sch. Medicine, 1950-52, Am. Heart Assn. research fellow, 1951-52, mem. faculty, 1954-71, prof. medicine, 1964-71, med. dir. univ. hosp., 1958-63, dean, chmn. bd. health scis., 1964-69, exec. v.p. univ., 1969-70; dir. Health Scis. Ctr., 1970-71; pres. Inst. Medicine, Nat. Acad. Scis., 1971-74; prof. medicine George Washington U., 1972-74; pres. U. Wash., Seattle, 1974-79, pres. emeritus, 1979—; prof. medicine U. Wash., 1974-79; pres. Assn. Acad. Health Ctrs., 1979-88; disting. professorial lectr. dept. medicine Georgetown U., 1983-88; prof. Sch. Pub. Health, U. Wash., 1989-92; provost Hahnemann U., 1992-93; mem. commr.'s adv. com. on exempt orgns. IRS, 1969-71; mem. adv. com. for environ. scis. NSF, 1970-71, adv. com. to dir. NIH, 1970-71; mem. Nat. Cancer Adv. Bd., 1972-76, Nat. Sci. Bd., 1976-82; trustee China Med. Bd., 1965-92; mem. selection com. for Rockefeller pub. service awards Princeton U., 1976-82; chmn. med. injury compensation study steering com. Inst. Medicine, NAS; mem. council for biol. scis. Pritzker Sch. Medicine, U. Chgo., 1977-89; chmn. adv. panel on cost-effectiveness of med. techs. Office Tech. Assessment, U.S. Congress, 1978-80, chmn. study sect. for health care tech. assessment Nat. Ctr. for Health Svcs. Rsch. and Health Care Tech. Assessment, 1985-88; pres. Sun Valley Forum on Nat. Health, 1986-94; dir. Inst. for Health Policy Edn. and Rsch., U. Tex. Health Sci. Ctr., Houston, 1988; mem. Council Health Care Tech., HEW; adv. panel for study fin. grad. med. edn. Dept. Health and Human Services, 1980-87; chmn. com. to evaluate the artificial heart, Inst. Medicine, NAS, 1990-91. Contbr. articles to profl. jours. Trustee Case Western Res. U., 1972-73. Served with AUS, 1947-49. Johns Hopkins U. Centennial scholar, 1976; recipient Disting. Service award Med. Alumni Assn. U. Chgo., 1966, Profl. Achievement award Alumni Assn. U. Chgo., 1973; Convocation medal Am. Coll. Cardiology, 1973; Cartwright medal Columbia U. Coll. Physicians and Surgeons, 1978; Carel C. Koch Meml. award Am. Acad. Optometry, Toronto, 1986. Fellow AAAS, ACP (regent 1987-90), Am. Acad. Arts and Scis.; mem. NAS, Inst. Medicine, Assn. Am. Physicians, Assn. Am. Med. Colls. (exec. council, chmn.-elect coun. of deans 1968-69), Alpha Omega Alpha. Office: 514 Lost River Rd Mazama WA 98833-9700

HO-GONZALEZ, WILLIAM, lawyer; b. N.Y.C., Mar. 27, 1957; s. Jack Ho and Iluminada Gonzalez; m. Elizabeth Perez, June 8, 1985. BA, Columbia U., 1979; JD, Harvard U., 1982. Bar: N.Y. 1983, D.C. 1985, Va. 1985. Aeronautical atty. FAA, U.S. Dept. Transp., Washington, 1983-87; asst. U.S. atty. U.S. Atty.'s Office for D.C., Washington, 1987-92; spl. counsel immigration-related unfair employment practices Civil Rights divsn. U.S. Dept. Justice, Washington, 1992-96; sr. trial atty. criminal sect., civil rights divsn. U.S. Dept. Justice, Washington, 1996-98, spl. counsel office of atty. personnel mgmt., 1998—; mem. nat. adv. bd. Inst. for Puerto Rican Policy, Inc., 1985-91; mem. cmty. coun. WAMU-FM, 1997—. Mem. D.C. Cir. Task Force on Gender, Race and Ethnic Bias, Washington, 1993-94, Va. Commn. on Women and Minorities in Legal Profession, 1995—. Mem. Nat. Hispanic Bar Assn., Asian Pacific Am. Bar Assn., Hispanic Bar Assn. Commonwealth of Va. (founding, v.p. 1995-96, mem. bd. govs. 1996-97, pres. 1998—). Office: DOJ OAPM Rm 3521 950 Pennsylvania Ave NW Washington DC 20530-0001

HOGSTEL, MILDRED ONELLE, gerontology nursing consultant; b. Clifton, Tex., Aug. 22, 1929; d. Ole Gustav and Mable (Nelson) H. Assoc., Clifton Coll., 1948; BS in Nursing Edn., Baylor U., 1954; MSN, U. Tex., 1960; PhD, U. North Tex., 1974. RN, Tex.; cert. gerontol. nurse ANCC. Staff nurse Hendrick Hosp., Abilene, Tex., 1951-53, Baylor Hosp., Dallas, 1954; instr. Baylor U., Dallas, 1954-58, Tex. Christian U., Ft. Worth, 1959-63; staff nurse Seton Hosp., Austin, Tex., 1963-64; asst. prof., assoc. prof., prof. gerontol. nursing Tex. Christian U., Ft. Worth, 1964-94. Editor, author: Nursing Care of Older Adult, 1981, 2d edit., 1988 (Book of Yr. award Am. Jour. Nursing 1989), 3d edit., 1993, Geropsychiatric Nursing (Book of Year award Am. Jour. Nursing 1991), 2d edit., 1995, Clinical Manual of Gerontological Nursing, 1992; contbr. articles to profl. jours. Bd. dirs. Tarrant Area Cmty. of Chs., 1994—; mem. adv. coun. Area Agy. on Aging, 1994—. Recipient Disting. Alumni award Tex. Luth. Coll., 1989; named One of Great 100 Nurses, Dallas-Ft. Worth, 1992. Mem. ANA, Tarrant Area Gerontol. Soc., Sigma Theta Tau (Outstanding Nurse award Beta Alpha chpt. 1981, Pillar award 1995). Democrat. Lutheran. Avocations: genealogy, writing, walking.

HOGUE, CAROL JANE ROWLAND, epidemiologist, educator; b. Springfield, Mo., Dec. 11, 1945; d. Perry Albright and Lois Virginia (Spencer) Rowland; m. L. Lynn Hogue, May 28, 1966; 1 child, Elizabeth Rowland. AB summa cum laude, William Jewell Coll., Liberty, Mo., 1966; MPH, U. N.C., 1971, PhD, 1973. From rsch. assoc. to asst. prof. U. N.C. Sch. Pub. Health, Chapel Hill, 1969-77; asst./assoc. prof., dir. epidemiology prog. divsn. biometry U. Ark. for Med. Scis., Little Rock, 1977-82; br. chief pregnancy epidemiology br. Ctrs. Disease Control, Atlanta, 1983-88, dir. divsn. reproductive health, 1988-92; Terry prof. maternal and child health, prof. epidemiology Rollins Sch. Pub. Health, Emory U., Atlanta, 1992—; cons. FDA, Washington, 1978-80, EPA, Washington, 1980-81; vis. scientist Ctrs. Disease Control, Atlanta, 1982-83; fellow Environ. Health Inst., Pittsfield, Mass., 1990-97; mem. com. on unintended pregnancy Inst. Medicine, 1994-96; mem. regional adv. panel human reprodn. program WHO, 1991—, chmn., 1997—, mem. sci. tech. adv. group, 1998—. Contbr. articles to profl. jours., chpts. to books. Mem. nat. perinatal health promotion com. March of Dimes, White Plains, N.Y., 1990-93; priority one adv. coun. Kiwanis Internat., 1990-91. Fellow Am. Coll. Epidemiology; me. Soc. Epidemiologic Rsch. (pres. 1987-90), Am. Epidemiological Soc., Am. Pub. Health Assn. (program devel. bd. 1976-78), Population Assn. Am., Internat. Epidemiol. Assn., Nat. Med. Com., Planned Parenthood Fedn. Am. Democrat. Episcopalian. Avocations: sailing, hiking, reading. E-mail: chogue@sph.emory.edu. Office: 1518 Clifton Rd NE Atlanta GA 30322

HOGUE, DALE CURTIS, SR., lawyer; b. St. Louis, Feb. 11, 1942; s. William Curtis Hogue and Juanita Estel Bean; m. Alice Jeam Smith, 1963 (div. 1964); m. Carolyn Frances Jones, Oct. 24, 1965; children: Dale Curtis Jr., Sean Cyril Raymond, Stuart Ridgely. Student, U.S. Naval Acad., 1961; BS in Engring. Sci., Washington U., St. Louis, 1964; JD, Georgetown U., 1972. Bar: Va. 1972, D.C. 1973, N.C. 1990. Ptnr. Hogue, Rhodes & Boss, Washington, 1972-74, Cross, Murphy & Smith, Washington, 1974-77, Hogue, Crothers & Bernard, Washington, 1977-79; corp. sec., gen. counsel ADI, Las Vegas, Nev., 1979-81; pvt. practice Washington, 1981-88, Charlotte, N.C., 1988-89; atty. IBM, Charlotte, 1989-90; assoc. Pennie & Edmonds, Washington, 1990-92; ptnr. Mason, Fenwick & Lawrence (merged with Popham Haik Schnobrich & Kaufman 1994), Washington, 1992-95, Marks & Murase LLP, Washington, 1995-98, Kilpatrick & Cody, Washington, 1996-98, Coudert Bros., Washington, 1998-99, Antonelli, Terry, Stout & Kraus, LLP, Arlington, Va., 1999—; sec. Nat. Motor Vehicle Safety Adv. Coun., Dept. Transp., Washington, 1971-77. Author: (with others) Association of University Technology Managers Manual, 1992, 94. Minority opinion reporter Alexandria Va. Charter Rev. Commn. Capt. USAF, 1964-68, Vietnam. Mem. Am. Intellectual Property Law Assn., Internat. Fedn. of Intellectual Property Attys., Licensing Execs. Soc., Assn. of Univ. Tech. Mgrs., Internat. Fedn. of Indsl. Property Attys., Assn. of Univ. Tech. Mgrs. Republican. Episcopalian. Avocations: flying, golfing, sailing. Fax: 703-312-6666. E-mail: dhogue@antonelli.com. Office: Antonelli Terry Stout & Kraus LLP 1300 N Seventeenth St Ste 1800 Arlington VA 22209

HOGWOOD, CHRISTOPHER JARVIS HALEY, music director, educator; b. Nottingham, Eng., Sept. 10, 1941; s. Haley Evelyn and Marion Constance (Higgott) H. BA, Cambridge U., 1964, MA, 1969; postgrad., Charles U., Prague, Czechoslovakia, 1964-65; DMus (hon.), U. Keele, 1991. Founding mem. Early Music Consort of London, 1967-76; dir. The Acad. Ancient Music, London, 1973—; music faculty U. Cambridge, 1975—; artistic dir. Handel & Haydn Soc., Boston, 1986—; dir. music St. Paul Chamber Orch., 1987-92; prin. guest condr. St. Paul Chamber Orch., 1992-98; artistic dir. Summer Mozart Festival Nat. Symphony Orch. USA, 1993—; assoc. dir. Beethoven Academie, Antwerp, 1998—; hon. prof. music Keele (Eng.) U., 1986-89; internat. prof. early music performance Royal Acad. Music, London, 1992—; vis. prof. dept. music King's Coll., London, 1992-96. Author: Music at Court, 1977, The Trio Sonata, 1979, Haydn's Visits to England, 1980, Handel, 1984; editor Music in Eighteenth Century England, 1983, Holmes' Life of Mozart, 1991. Decorated comdr. Order of the Brit. Empire, 1989; recipient Willson Cobbett Medal Worshipful Co. Musicians, London, 1986, named Freeman, Worshipful Co., 1989, Disting. Musician award Inc. Soc. Musicians, 1997; hon. fellow Jesus Coll., Cambridge, 1989, Pembroke Coll., Cambridge, 1992. Home and Office: 10 Brookside, Cambridge CB2 1JE, England

HOHENBERG, JOHN, journalist, educator; b. N.Y.C., Feb. 17, 1906; s. Louis and Jettchen (Scheuermann) H.; m. Dorothy Lannuier, Oct. 16, 1928 (dec. Sept. 2, 1977); m. JoAnn Fogarty, Mar. 9, 1979; children: Pamela Jo, Eric. Student, U. Wash., 1922-24; Litt.B., Columbia U., 1927; postgrad., U. Vienna, 1928; LHD (hon.), Wilkes Coll., 1971. Reporter Seattle Star, 1923-24; writer N.Y. World, 1925; fgn. corr. N.Y. Evening Post, Vienna, Paris; asst. city editor N.Y. Evening Post, 1928-33; writer nat. politics N.Y. Jour.-Am., 1933-42; UN, Washington and fgn. corr. N.Y. Post, 1946-50; lectr. English Columbia, 1948, assoc. in journalism, 1949-50, prof. journalism, 1950-74, prof. emeritus, 1974—; Meeman lectr. U. Tenn., 1975, Meeman Disting. prof. journalism, 1976-77, 78-81, 87; Gannett profl. in residence U. Kans., 1977-78; Gannett disting. prof. journalism U. Fla., 1981-82; Nieman Found. lectr. Harvard U., 1981; vis. prof. U. Miami, 1982-83; Newhouse disting. prof. Newhouse Sch. Pub. Communications, Syracuse U., 1983-85; adminstr. Pulitzer Prizes and sec. Pulitzer Prize Bd., 1954-76, journalism juror, 1982, 83, 84; spl. cons. to Sec. USAF, 1953-63, to German Marshall Fund, 1980; Am. specialist lectr. State Dept. in 10 Asian countries, 1963-64; discussion leader Internat. Press Inst., New Delhi, 1966; sr. specialist East-West Center, Honolulu, 1967; mem. Japanese-Am. Assembly, Shimoda, Japan, 1967; vis. prof. Chinese U. of Hong Kong, 1970-71; lectr. 10 Asian countries for USIA, 1982. Author: The Pulitzer Prize Story, 1959, The Professional Journalist, 1960, rev. edit., 1968, 73, 78, 82, Foreign Correspondence--The Great Reporters and Their Times, 1964, 2d edit., 1995, The New Front Page, 1965, Between Two Worlds: Policy, Press and Public Opinion in Asian-American Relations, 1967, The News Media: A Journalist Looks at His Profession, 1968, Free Press/Free People: The Best Cause, 1971, New Era in the Pacific: An Adventure in Public Diplomacy, 1972, The Pulitzer Prizes: A History of the Awards in Books, Drama, Music and Journalism Based on Private Records over Six Decades, 1974, A Crisis for the American Press, 1978, The Pulitzer Prize Story II, 1980, The Parisian Girl, 1986, Concise Newswriting, 1987, The Bill Clinton Story: Winning the Presidency, 1994, The Pursuit of Excellence, an Autobiography, 1995, The Pulitzer Diaries, Inside America's Greatest Prize, 1996, Re-Electing Bill Clinton, 1997, Israel at 50, 1998; commentator ABC-TV series Century, 1999. Served with AUS, 1943-45. Recipient Pulitzer Prize Spl. award for services to Am. journalism, 1976; Disting. Service prizes for books: Foreign Correspondence, Between Two Worlds and A Crisis for the American Press, Sigma Delta Chi/Soc. Profl. Journalists, 1965, 68, 79; Sigma Delta Chi award for Most Disting. Teaching of Journalism, 1974; Gold Key award Columbia Scholastic Press Assn., 1974; inducted into Journalism Hall of Fame, Deadline Club of New York, 1981; Pulitzer traveling scholar Europe, 1927-28; research fellow Council Fgn. Relations in 10 Asian countries, 1964; Knight Found. grantee for free press study, 1969-70; Ford Found. travel study grantee Asia, 1971; Gannett Found. grantee for 1st amendment study, 1976-77. Mem. Am. Assn. Edn. Journalism, Internat. Press Inst., Columbia Journalism Alumni Assn. (pres. 1954), Authors League Am. Home: 7118 Sheffield Dr Knoxville TN 37909-2530

HOHENBERG, PIERRE CLAUDE, research physicist; b. Neuilly, Seine, France, Oct. 3, 1934; came to U.S., 1941; s. Eric and Hedwig (Bauer) H.; m. Barbara Blanchard, Dec. 18, 1965; 1 child, Laura Louise. AB, Harvard U., 1956, PhD, 1962. Prof. Tech. U., Munich, 1974-77; mem. tech. staff AT&T Bell Labs., Murray Hill, N.J., 1964-95; dep. provost for sci. and tech. Yale U., New Haven, Conn., 1995—. over 100 articles in field to profl. jours. Co-winner Fritz London prize for low temperature physics, 1990; recipient Max Planck medal German Phys. Soc., 1999. Fellow AAAS, Am. Phys. Soc., Am. Acad. Arts and Scis., N.Y. Acad. Scis.; mem. NAS. Office: Office of the Provost Yale Univ PO Box 208236 New Haven CT 06520-8236

HOHENBERGER, PATRICIA JULIE, fine arts and antique appraiser, consultant; b. Holyoke, Mass.; d. Ambrose Harrington and Irene Leo (Ducharme) Reynolds; m. John H. Hohenberger, June 27, 1953; children: Lisa Maria, Julie Suzanne, John Henry, James Reynolds, Patricia Antonia. BA in English, Coll. of New Rochelle, N.Y., 1950; MA in Folk Art Studies, NYU, 1983. Cert. elem. edn. tchr., Mass. Tchr. Hadley (Mass.) Pub. Schs., 1950-52, Springfield (Mass.) Pub. Schs., 1952-54; owner, dir. The Brown House Nursery Sch., Williamstown, Mass., 1962-64; tchr. Coindra Hall, Huntington, N.Y., 1970-71, St. Edward the Confessor, Syosset, N.Y., 1971-81; pres. Patricia Reynolds Hohenberger Appraisals, Northport, N.Y., 1983—; cons. Alexander-Benwood Co., Inc., Huntington, N.Y., 1991—; lectr. Folk Art Inst., N.Y., 1985, Symposium-Gen. Accident Ins., N.Y., 1994. Author: (monograph) Gentle Reminders of the Past, 1984. Recipient Recognition for Achievement award Alexander-Benwood Co., Inc., Huntington, N.Y., 1995. Mem. Nat. Trust for Historic Preservation, Nat. Mus. Women in the Arts (charter), New England Appraisers Assn. Roman Catholic. Avocations: collecting American decorative arts and antiques, photography. Home: 72 Burt Ave Northport NY 11768-2046

HOHENDAHL, PETER UWE, German language and literature educator; b. Hamburg, Fed. Republic Germany, Mar. 17, 1936; came to U.S., 1964; s. Wilhelm and Emilie (Uelschen) H.; m. Iky Maria Zoetelief, July 2, 1965; children: Deborah, Gwendolyn. Student, U. Bern, Switzerland, 1955, U. Hamburg, 1955-57, 59-63; PhD, U. Hamburg, 1964; postgrad., U. Goettingen, Fed. Republic Germany, 1958. Asst. prof. Pa. State U., 1965-68; assoc. prof. Washington U., St. Louis, 1968-69, prof., 1970-77, head dept., 1972-77; prof. comparative and German lit. Cornell U., Ithaca, N.Y., 1977—; chmn. dept. German Cornell U., Ithaca, 1981-86, Schurman prof. German and Comparative lit., 1985—; dir. Inst. for German Cultural Studies Cornell U., 1992—; Merton vis. prof. Berlin U., 1976; disting. vis. prof. Ohio State U., 1987; supr. Studien zur Literatur des 19, Jahrhunderts, 1993. Author: Literaturkritik und Oeffentlichkeit, 1974, Der Europaeische Roman der Empfindsamkeit, 1977, The Institution of Criticism, 1982, Literarische Kultur im Zeitalter des Liberalismus, 1985, A History of German Literary Criticism, 1988, Building a National Literature, 1989, Reappraisals: Shifting Alignments in Postwar Critical Theory, 1991, Heinrich Heine and the Occident: Multiple Identities, Multiple Receptions, 1991, Geschichte, Opposition, Subversion, Studien zur Literatur des 19, Jahrhunderts, 1993, Prismatic Thought: Theodor W. Adorno, 1995, others; mem. editl. bd. Studies in 20th Century Lit., 1979—, German Quar., 1983-88. Fellow Harvard U., 1964-65, fellow Ctr. for Interdisciplinary Rsch., Bielefeld, 1981, 87, Guggenheim Found., 1983-84. Mem. MLA, Am. Assn. Tchrs. German, N.Am. Heine Soc. (exec. coun. 1982—, pres. 1986-90), Zeitschrift fuer Germanistik (bd. dirs. 1990—). Home: 81 Genung Rd Ithaca NY 14850-9602 Office: Cornell U Dept of German Studies Ithaca NY 14853

HOHENEMSER, CHRISTOPH, physics educator, researcher; b. Berlin, May 29, 1937; came to U.S., 1947; s. Kurt H. and Katherine (Dietrich) H.; m. Anne S. Holland, June 20, 1960; children: Lisa, Julia. BA with honors, Swarthmore Coll., 1958; PhD, Washington U., St. Louis, 1963. Research assoc. Washington U., St. Louis, 1963-64; instr., asst. prof. Brandeis U., Waltham, Mass., 1964-71; assoc. prof. physics Clark U., Worcester, Mass., 1971-76, prof., 1976—; chmn. dept. physics Clark U., Worcester, 1979-83, chmn. sci., tech. and society program, 1971-84; chmn. environ., tech. and society program Clark U., 1984-92, dir. Ctr. for Tech., Environ. and Devel, 1983-84; vis. scientist U. Groningen, Netherlands, 1973-74, 78-79, U. Konstanz, Fed. Republic Germany, 1986, U. Calif., Berkeley, 1990-91. Co-author: Corporate Management of Health and Safety Hazards, 1988; co-editor: Risk in Technological Society, 1982, Perilous Progress, 1985; contbr. over 140 articles and chpts. on physics and tech. assessment to jours. and books. Recipient Bronze medal UN Environ. Programme, 1982; NSF research grantee, 1971-91. Fellow Am. Phys. Soc., Soc. Risk Analysis; mem. AAAS, Sigma Xi, Phi Beta Kappa. E-mail: chohenemser@clarku.edu. Home: 146 Mill Rd Littleton MA 01460-1548 Office: Clark U Dept Physics 950 Main St Dept Physics Worcester MA 01610-1473

HOHENRATH, WILLIAM EDWARD, retired banker; b. Sea Cliff, N.Y., Mar. 9, 1922; s. Daniel and Ethyle Josephine (Ziegler) H.; m. Vivian Haynes, Sept. 15, 1945 (div. Sept. 1967); 1 dau., Donna; m. Lois Pelletier, Mar. 8, 1969; stepchildren: Jeanne M., Renee T., Michelle A., Anthony J. Grad., Am. Inst. Banking, 1948; B.S. magna cum laude, N.Y. U., 1958, M.B.A., 1968. With Williamsburgh Savs. Bank, Bklyn., 1941—; v.p. Williamsburgh Savs. Bank, 1969-71, sr. v.p., 1971-88, ret., 1988. Mem. exec. com. Downtown Bklyn. Devel. Assn., govt./bus. joint econ. devel. com. of L.I., Nassau County Rep. Com., 1965-69; bd. dirs. Bklyn. Tb and Respiratory Disease Assn., 1970-85. Mem. Bklyn. Savs. Banks (chmn. mktg. com. 1972-74), Savs. Banks Assn. N.Y. State (exec. com. 1972-80), Am. Inst. Banking (pres. N.Y.C. chpt. 1966, chmn. trustees 1971-73, assoc. councilman 1969-74), Levittown C. of C. (pres. 1964-65), Bklyn. C. of C. (dir.). Home: PO Box 873 Greenport NY 11944-0868 Office: 1 Hanson Pl Brooklyn NY 11243-2907 *There are two things I try never to forget. 1. That all people do all things for some kind of self serving reason. This thought not only deflates ones own ego but helps one to understand another. 2. Failure to appreciate and put into perspective each of life's experiences, bitter or sweet, is only to cheat yourself.*

HOHL, CRAIG STEPHEN, risk management executive; b. Lake Worth, Fla., Nov. 13, 1963; s. Leo Stephen and Beverly Florence Hohl. BS in Aero. Scis./Bus. Mgmt., Embry-Riddle Aero. U., 1993. City mgr. Alamo Rent-A-Car, Ft. Lauderdale, Fla., 1994-96; regional sales dir. Nat. Auto Fin., Boca Raton, Fla., 1996-97; v.p. ops. First Fin., Ft. Lauderdale, 1997-98; bus. devel. Staff Leasing, Bradenton, Fla., 1998—. Lt. USN, 1987-93. Decorated 12 medals for heroism in Operation Desert Shield/Storm/Provide Comfort, U.S. Dept. Def., 1991-92. Mem. ASCA, ADPA, USGA, C. of C. Republican. Baptist. Avocations: flying, golf, softball, football, basketball. E-mail: cshohl@msn.com.

HOHN, DAVID, physician; b. Tucson, 1942. BS cum laude, U. Ill., 1964, MD, 1970. Intern Rush-Presbyn. St. Luke's Hosp., Chgo., 1970-71; resident in gen. surgery U. Calif., San Francisco, 1971-78, asst. prof. surgery, 1978-84, assoc. prof. surgery, 1984-87; assoc. prof. surgery U. Tex. Med. Sch., M.D. Anderson Cancer Ctr., 1987-90; prof. surgery U. Tex. Med. Sch., 1990-97; v.p. patient care M.D. Anderson Cancer Ctr.-U. Tex., Houston, 1993-97; pres., CEO Roswell Park Cancer Inst., 1997—. Mem. Assn. for Acad. Surgery, Am. Coll. Physician Execs., Am. Fedn. for Clin. Rsch., Am. Soc. for Clin. ONcology, Am. Assn. for Cancer Rsch., Surg. Infection Soc., Soc. of Surg. Oncology. Office: Roswell Park Cancer Inst Elm And Carlton St Buffalo NY 14263-0001*

HOHN, DAVID C., healthcare executive. MD, U. Ill., 1970. Pres., CEO Roswell Park Cancer Inst., 1997—. Mem. ACS. Office: Elm & Carlton Sts Buffalo NY 14263

HOHN, HARRY GEORGE, retired insurance company executive, lawyer; b. N.Y.C., Mar. 1, 1932; s. Harry George and Violia (Meehan) H.; m. Janet Jean LaRosa, June 19, 1954; children: Cynthia, Jennifer, Nancy, Patricia. BS, NYU, 1953, LLM, 1959; JD, Fordham U., 1956. Bar: N.Y. 1956, U.S. Supreme Ct. 1976. With N.Y. Life Ins. Co., N.Y.C., 1956—, sr. v.p., gen. counsel, 1977-82, exec. v.p., gen. counsel, 1982-83, exec. v.p., 1983-86, CEO, 1990-97, also chmn. bd. dirs., past vice chmn. bd. dirs., 1997—, ret. chmn., CEO, 1997; bd. dirs. Witco Corp., N.Y.C., Life and Health Ins. Med. Rsch. Fund, Million Dollar Roundtable Found.; chmn. bd. dirs. Life Ins. Coun. N.Y.; past chmn. Am. Coun. Life Ins.; mem. internat. adv. bd. Credit Comml. de France. Editor: Fordham Law Rev., 1955-56. Trustee Am. Coll., Com. Econ. Devel.; trustee emeritus Found. Ind. Higher Edn.; vice chmn., bd. trustees Nat. AIDS Fund; bd. govs. United Way of Tri-State. Fellow Am. Bar Found. (life); mem. Assn. Life Ins. Counsel (bd. govs.), Bus. Roundtable. Republican. Roman Catholic. Office: NY Life Ins Co 51 Madison Ave New York NY 10010-1603*

HOHN, WILLIAM J. (BILL HOHN), umpire; b. Butler, Pa., June 29, 1955; m. Grace Grippo, Dec. 26, 1983; 1 child, Meredith. Former umpire Gulf Coast League, Fla. Instrnl. League, Fla. State League, So. League, Puerto Rico Winter League, Pacific Coast League; umpire maj. league baseball Nat. League, N.Y.C., 1989—; with Umpires Union, Phila. Avocations: hunting, archery, reading. Office: Nat League 350 Park Ave New York NY 10022 also: Umpires Union 1735 Market St Philadelphia PA 19103

HOHNER, KENNETH DWAYNE, retired fodder company executive; b. St. John, Kans., June 24, 1934; s. Courtney Clinton and Mildred Lucile (Forrester) H.; m. Sherry Eloi Anice Edens, Feb. 14, 1961; children: Katrina, Melissa, Steven, Michael. BS in Geol. Engring., U. Kans., 1957. Geophysicist Mobil Oil Corp., New Orleans, Anchorage, Denver, 1957-72; sr. geophysicist Amerada Hess Corp., Houston, 1972-75, ARAMCO, London, 1975-79; far east area geophysicist Hamilton Bros., Denver, 1979-83; owner Hohner Poultry Farm, Erie, Colo., 1979-94; pres. Hohner Custom Feed, Inc., Erie, Colo., 1982-94. Mem. Soc. Exploration Geophysicists. Home: 1201 W Thornton Pkwy Denver CO 80260-5458

HOHNHORST, JOHN CHARLES, lawyer; b. Jerome, Idaho, Dec. 25, 1952; m. Raelene Casper; children: Jennifer, Rachel, John. BS in Polit. Sci./Pub. Adminstrn., U. Idaho, 1975, JD cum laude, 1978. Bar: Idaho 1978, U.S. Dist. Ct. Idaho 1978, U.S. Ct. Appeals (9th cir.) 1980, U.S. Ct. Claims 1983, U.S. Supreme Ct. 1987. Adminstrv. asst. to Sen. John M. Barker Idaho State Senate, 1975; ptnr. Hepworth, Lezamiz & Hohnhorst, Twin Falls, Idaho, 1978—. Contbr. articles to profl. jours. Mem. planning & zoning commn. City of Twin Falls, 1987-90. Mem. ABA, ATLA, Idaho State Bar (commr. 1990-93, pres. 1993), Idaho Trial Lawyers Assn. (regional dir. 1985-86), 5th Dist. Bar Assn. (treas. 1987-88, v.p. 1988-89, pres. 1989-90), Am. Acad. Appellate Lawyers, Greater Twin Falls C. of C. (chmn. magic valley leadership program 1988-89, bd. dirs. 1989-92), Phi Kappa Tau (Beta Gamma chpt., Phi award 1988). Office: Hepworth Lezamiz & Hohnhorst PO Box 389 133 Shoshone St N Twin Falls ID 83301-6150

HOI, SAMUEL CHUEN-TSUNG, art school dean; b. Hong Kong, Mar. 25, 1958; came to U.S., 1975; AB, Columbia Coll., 1980; JD, Columbia Law Sch., 1983; AAS, Parsons Sch. Design, N.Y.C., 1986. Dir. AAS program Parsons Sch. Design, N.Y.C., 1987-88; dir. parsons Parsons Sch. Design, Paris, 1988-91; dean Corcoran Sch. Art, Washington, 1991—. Mem., bd. dirs. Leadership Washington, 1996. Mem. Washington Area Lawyers for the Arts (bd. dirs.), Washington Area Arts Consortium (steering com.), Arlington Arts Ctr. (bd. dirs.), Assn. Ind. Colls. of Art and Design, Nat. Assn. Schs. Art and Design (bd. dirs.). Office: Corcoran Sch Art 500 17th St NW Washington DC 20006-4804*

HOIBY, LEE, composer, concert pianist; b. Madison, Wis., Feb. 17, 1926; s. Henry Bjorn and Violet Ethel (Smith) H. MusB, U. Wis., 1947; MA, Mills Coll., Oakland, Calif., 1952; cert., Curtis Inst., Phila., 1952; DFA (hon.), Simpson Coll., Indianola, Iowa, 1985. Composer (operas) The Scarf, 1955, Piano Concerto 1, 1957, A Month in the Country, 1964, Summer and Smoke, 1970, Something New for the Zoo, 1979, The Italian Lesson, 1980, The Tempest, 1985, This Is the Rill Speaking, 1992, (ballet) After Eden, 1967, (cantatas) Hymn of the Nativity, 1960, For You O Democracy, 1993, (oratorio) Galileo Galilei, 1975, Piano Concerto 2, 1979, (baritone and orch.) The Tides of Sleep, 1960, I Have A Dream, 1988, Serenade for Violin and Orch., 1987, Flute Concerto, 1994, also chamber, choral, vocal, theatre music. Recipient Am. Acad. Arts and Letters award, 1957; fellow Fulbright Found., 1952, Guggenheim Found., 1958, Nat. Endowment for the Arts, 1980, Rockefeller Found. grantee, 1979. Mem. ASCAP, Am. Guild Organists (hon.). Home: 800 Rock Valley Rd Long Eddy NY 12760-5225

HOINES, DAVID ALAN, lawyer; b. St. Paul, Oct. 18, 1946; s. Arnold H. and Patricia (Olson) H.; m. Bonnie K. Smith, June 4, 1983. BA, Calif. State U., San Jose, 1969; JD, Santa Clara U., 1972; LLM in Taxation, Boston U., 1973. Bar: Fla. 1975, Calif. 1975, N.Y. 1999, U.S. Dist. Ct. (so. dist.) Fla. 1975, U.S. Dist. Ct. (no. dist.) Calif. 1980, U.S. Dist. Ct. (mid. dist.) Fla. 1984, U.S. Dist. Ct. (ctrl. dist.) Calif. 1990, U.S. Ct. Claims 1980, U.S. Tax Ct. 1975, U.S. Ct. Appeals (fed. cir.) 1990, U.S. Ct. Appeals (4th cir.) 1985, U.S. Ct. Appeals (5th cir.) 1978, U.S. Ct. Appeals (9th cir.) 1980, U.S. Ct. Appeals (11th cir.) 1981, U.S. Supreme Ct. 1980, N.Y. 1999; cert. civil trial lawyer. Pvt. practice Ft. Lauderdale, Fla., 1975—; adj. instr. Nova U. Ctr. for Study of Law, 1977. Author: Taxman and the Textbook, The Ripon Forum, 1972. Mem. ABA, Assn. Trial Lawyers Am., Broward County Bar Assn., Fla. Bar Assn., Calif. Bar Assn., State Bar of N.Y., Hundred Club of Broward County, Tau Delta Phi. Avocations: ocean diving (free and scuba), snowskiing, running, boating, reading. Office: 1290 E Oakland Park Blvd Fort Lauderdale FL 33334-4443

HOKANA, GREGORY HOWARD, engineering executive; b. Burbank, Calif., 1944; s. Howard Leslie and Helen Lorraine H.; m. Eileen Marie Youell, 1967; children: Kristen Marie, Kenneth Gregory. BS in Physics, UCLA, 1966. Design engr. Raytheon Co., Oxnard, Calif., 1967-74; staff engr. Bunker Ramo Corp., Westlake Village, Calif., 1974-84; mgr. analog engring. AIL Systems, Inc., Westlake Village, 1984-91; mgr. product devel. Am. Nucleonics Corp., Westlake Village, 1991-93; tech. mgr. Litton Data Sys., Agoura Hills, Calif., 1994—. Mem. IEEE, Assn. Old Crows. Democrat. Methodist. Avocations: golf, swimming, photography. Home: 3485 Farrell Cir Newbury Park CA 91320-4333 Office: Litton Data Systems PO Box 6008 Agoura Hills CA 91376-6008

HOKE, EUGENA LOUISE, special education educator; b. Chgo., Feb. 26, 1949; d. Edward LaMar and Edna Lucille (Weikert) H. BS, Bowling Green State U., 1971; MEd, U. Maine, Orono, 1977. Cert. educator. Tchr. educable mentally retarded Marion Local Schs., Maria Stein, Ohio, 1971-73, Tri-Valley Local Sch., Dresden, Ohio, 1973-74; tchr. Edgewood Local Schs., Trenton, Ohio, 1974-78; learning disabilities tchr. Oak Hills Local Sch. Dist., Cin., 1978—; mem. prin.'s adv. com. C.O. Harrison Elem. Sch., Cin., 1987-88, 92-93, mem. tchr. asst. team, 1988-90; intervention inniatives team, 1998—, tech. team Venture Capital, 1996-98. Mem. Vol. in Parks, Hamilton County, Ohio, 1981-88; vol. Cin. Symphony Assn., 1988—, Friends of Pops, 1991—, Mus. Ctr., 1991, Aronoff Ctr. for the Arts, 1995—. Mem. NEA, Ohio Edn. Assn., Oak Hill Edn. Assn., Cin. Arts. Assn. Methodist. Avocations: photography, travel, hiking. Home: 5566 Biscayne Ave Cincinnati OH 45248-4225

HOKE, JUDY ANN, physical education educator; b. Mesa, Ariz., May 3, 1951; d. Jewell Juett and Margaret Lucille (Gibson) H. BA, Ariz. State U., 1973, MS, 1976. Cert. tchr. Ariz. Tchr., coach womens Tennis Tempe (Ariz.) Union High Sch. Dist., 1973—, chmn. Phys. Edn., 1978—; former co-chmn. sch. improvement com.; chmn. East Valley Women's Tennis Region; mem. Nat. Honor Soc. selection com., scholarship com. Mem. First Christian Ch., Phoenix Zoo. Named Outstanding Secondary Phys. Edn. Tchr. Yr. State of Ariz., 1991. Mem. NEA, AAHPERD, Ariz. Alliance Health Phys. Edn. Recreation and Dance, Tempe Secondary Edn. Assn., Women's Internat. Tennis Assn., U.S. Tennis Assn. Republican. Avocation: reading. Office: Marcos de Niza High Sch 6000 S Lakeshore Dr Tempe AZ 85283-3049

HOKE, MARTIN ROSSITER, former congressman; b. Lakewood, Ohio, May 18, 1952; s. George H. and Amalia (Vasu) H.; children: Elizabeth, Christopher, Peter. BA magna cum laude, Amherst Coll., 1973; JD, Case Western Res. Sch. Law, 1980. Atty. Seeley, Savage & Aussem, Cleve., 1980-90; founder, owner Red Carpet Airport Car Care, Cleve., 1980-89; pres., founder Red Carpet Cellular, Cleve., 1985—; mem. 103rd-104th Congress from 10th Ohio dist., Washington, D.C., 1993-96. Republican. Presbyterian. *

HOKE, SHEILA WILDER, retired librarian; b. Greensboro, N.C.; d. Herbert Bruce Wilder and Virginia Dare (Caylor) Wilder-Dell; m. Robert Edward Hoke, Nov. 22, 1958 (dec.); children: Raymond Fellow, Philip Wilder. Student, Montclair Coll., 1948; BA in History, U. Kans., 1950, postgrad., 1951, BS in Edn., 1952; postgrad., JOhn Hopkins U., 1955; MLS, U. Wis., 1955; MS in Edn., Southwestern Okla. State U., 1977; postgrad., Johns Hopkins U., Montclair State Coll. Tchr. history Fredonia (Kans.) High Sch., 1952-54; student asst. U. Wis., Madison, 1954-55; children's libr. BR Enoch Pratt Libr., Balt., 1955-58; libr. dir. U.S. Army Spl. Svcs., Bavaria, Fed. Republic Germany, 1958-59; libr. U.S. Army Dependent Schs., Straubing, Fed. Republic Germany, 1959-60; cataloger Southwestern Okla. State U. Libr., Weatherford, 1963-69, libr. dir., 1969-93; mem. spl. projects com. Okla. Dept. Edn., 1974, adv. com. Okla. State Regents Libr., 1975-77. Mem. Okla. State Regents for Higher Edn. Libr. Networking, 1989-93, 1st Bapt. Ch. Mem. ALA, AAUW (pres., state bd. dirs. 1980, Weatherford br. 1981-83), Okla. Libr. Assn. (chmn. tech. svcs. divsn. 1969-70, chmn. coll. and univ. divsn. 1972-73, chmn. adminstrs. workshop 1973, chmn. libr. edn. divsn. 1975-76, chmn. recruitment com. 1978, Archives com. 1980), Weatherford C. of C. (edn. com. 1974-75, cert. meritorious achievement from Gov. Nigh 1985), Custer County Hist. Soc., western Okla. Hist. Soc., Higher Edn. Alumni Coun. Okla., Delta Kappa Gamma (pres. Lambda chpt. 1980-82), Phi Alpha theta, Kappa Kappa Iota (pres. Lambda chpt. 1984-85). Democrat. Baptist.

HOKENSON, DAVID LEONARD, secondary school educator; b. Mpls., Nov. 9, 1950; s. Raymond Leonard and Barbara Jean (Hooker) H.; m. Cynthia Jane Luehmann, July 28, 1979. BA, St. Olaf Coll., 1972; postgrad., U. Minn., 1977, 78, 82. Lic. secondary sch. social studies and history tchr., Minn. Social studies tchr. Preston (Minn.)-Fountain Pub. Schs., 1972-93, Fillmore Ctrl. H.S., Harmony, Minn., 1993-95; Fillmore Ctrl. Mid. Sch., Preston, Minn., 1995—; mem. team evaluation State Dept. Edn., St. Paul, 1981, 83, 91, 98. Precinct chair Dem.-Farmer-Labor Party, Preston, 1990—; treas. Preston-Fountain Edn. Assn., 1987-93, negotiator, 1993-94; treas. Fillmore Ctrl. Edn. Assn., 1994; mem. evaluation team North Ctrl. Accreditation Assn., 1994; participant Project 120, 1995; mem. Nat. Trust for Hist. Preservation, Minn. Hist. Soc. Recipient scholarship Minn. Inst. for Advancement of Teaching, St. Paul, 1992, 97. Mem. Nat. Geog. Soc., Am. Scandinavian Found., Am.-Swedish Inst., Minn. Hist. Soc., Libr. of Congress. Office: Fillmore Ctrl Schs PO Box 50 Preston MN 55965-0050

HOKENSTAD, MERL CLIFFORD, JR., social work educator; b. Norfolk, Nebr., July 21, 1936; s. Merl Clifford and Flora Diane (Christian) H.; m. Dorothy Jean Tarrell, June 24, 1962; children: Alene Ann, Laura Rae, Marta Lynn. B.A. summa cum laude, Augustana Coll., 1958; Rotary Found. fellow, Durham (Eng.) U., 1958-59; M.S.W., Columbia U., 1962; Ph.D., Brandeis U., 1969, Inst. Ednl. Mgmt., Harvard U., 1977. With Lower East Side Neighborhood Assn., N.Y.C., 1962-64; community planning assoc. United Community Services, Sioux Falls, S.D., 1964-66; instr. Augustana Coll., Sioux Falls, 1964-66; research assoc. Ford Found. Project on Community Planning for Elderly, Brandeis U., Waltham, Mass., 1966-67; prof., dir. Sch. Social Work, Western Mich. U., Kalamazoo, 1968-74; prof., dean Sch. Applied Social Scis., Case Western Res. U., Cleve., 1974-83; Ralph and Dorothy Schmitt prof. Sch. Applied Social Scis., Case Western Res. U., 1983—, chmn. PhD program, 1990-94; prof. internat. health Sch. of Medicine, 1994—; vis. prof. Inst. Sociology, Stockholm U., 1978, Fulbright lectr., 1980; vis. prof. Nat. Inst. Social Work, London, 1981, Sch. Social Work, Stockholm U., 1982-86, Eotvos Lorand U., Budapest, Hungary, 1992, 95, 96, London Sch. Econs., 1994; Fulbright rsch. scholar Inst. Applied Social Rsch., Oslo, 1989; fellow U. Canterbury, Christchurch, New Zealand, 1994. Author: Participation in Teaching and Learning: An Idea Book for Social Work Educators; editor: Meeting Human Needs: An International Annual, Vol. V, Linking Health Care and Social Services: International Perspectives; editor-in-chief Internat. Social Work Jour., 1985-87; co-editor: Profiles in Internat. Social Work, 1992, Issues in International Social Work, 1997, (internat. issue) Jour. Gerontol. Social Work, 1988, (internat. mental health issue) Jour. Sociology and Social Welfare, 1990, Jour. Social Policy and Administration, 1993, Jour. Aging Internat., 1994, Jour. Applied Social Scis., 1996; contbr. articles to profl. jours., chpts. to books. Mem. alcohol tng. rev. com. Nat. Inst. Alcoholism and Alcohol Abuse, 1974-78; workshop leader Am. Assn. State Colls. and Univs., 1974; chmn. U.S. com. XVIII Internat. Congress Schs. Social Work, 1976; chmn. Kalamazoo County Cmty. Mental Health Svcs. Bd., 1971, vice chmn., 1972; mem. edn. and tng. task force Mich. Office Drug Abuse and Alcoholism, 1972-73; mem. Mich. Assn. Mental Health Bds., 1972; bd. dirs. Cleve. United Way Svcs., 1982-84, del. assembly, 1974-82, mem. periodic rev. oversight com., 1982, mem. leadership devel. com., 1978, cmty. resources com., 1988—; bd. dirs. Kalamazoo United Way, 1968-72; trustee Cleve. Internat. Program for Youth Workers and Social Workers, chmn. program com., 1985-87; mem. program devel. com. Cleve. Center on Alcoholism, 1976; trustee Alcoholism Services Cleve., Inc., 1977-86, v.p., 1982-85; trustee Cmty. Info./Vol. Action Ctr., 1982-88, chmn. leadership devel. com., 1984-86, chmn. unmet needs com., 1986-88, exec. com., 1985-88, v.p., 1986-88; exec. com. Western Reserve Geriatric Edn. Ctr., 1995—; mem. adv. com. Coun. for Internat. Exch. Scholars, 1991-93, Fedn. for Cmty. Planning Coun. on Older Persons, 1991—, chmn. caregiver support program initiative, 1995-96; mem. task force of social transition in Soviet Union, U.S. State Dept. Bur. Human Rights and Humanitarian Affairs; mem. UN NGO Com. on Aging, 1996—; mem. adv. coun. Cuyahoga County Dept. Adult and Sr. Svcs., 1998—; co-chmn. U.S. Com. for Internat. Yr. of Older Persons, 1999. Named Outstanding Alumnus, Augustana Coll., 1980, Ohio Soc. Worker of the Yr., 1992; Fulbright Research fellow; NIMH trainee, 1960-62; Vocat. Rehab. trainee, 1966; Gerontology trainee, 1967; Rotary Found. fellow, 1958-59. Mem. NASW (internat. com. 1989-93, chmn. 1992-93), Acad. Cert. Social Workers, Internat. Assn. Schs. Social Work (exec. bd. 1978-92, 98—, treas. 1978-86, v.p. N.Am. 1988-92, membership sec. 1996—), Internat. Coun. on Social Welfare (dir. U.S. com. 1982-92), Coun. on Social Work Edn. (del. 1972-75, 77-83, chmn. ann. program meeting 1973, chmn. com. on nat. legis. and adminstrv. policy 1975-79, mem. nominating com. 1978-81, internat. com. 1980-86, 96—, chmn. com. 1982-84, dir. 1979-82, exec. com. 1986-89, pres. 1986-89), Nat. Conf. on Social Welfare (bd. dirs. 1978-80, chmn. sect. V program com. 1977-78), World Future Soc. (area coord. 1972-74), Fulbright Assn. (v.p. N.E. Ohio chpt. 1990-91), Nat. Coun. on Aging (bd. dirs. 1991-97, internat. com. 1991-97, pub. policy com. 1992-97). Democrat. Episcopalian. Home: 2917 Weymouth Rd Cleveland OH 44120-2234 Office: Case Western Res U 10900 Euclid Ave Cleveland OH 44106-1712

HOKIN, LOWELL EDWARD, biochemist, educator; b. Chgo., Sept. 20, 1924; s. Oscar E. and Helen (Manfield) H.; m. Mabel Neaverson, Dec. 1, 1952 (div. Dec. 1973); children: Linda Ann, Catherine Esther (dec.), Samuel Arthur; m. Barbara M. Gallagher, Mar. 23, 1978 (div. July 1998); 1 child, Ian Oscar. Student, U. Chgo., 1942-43, Dartmouth Coll., 1943-44, U. Louisville Sch. Medicine, 1944-46, U. Ill. Sch. Medicine, 1946-47; MD, U. Louisville, 1948; PhD, U. Sheffield, Eng., 1952. Postdoctoral fellow dept. biochemistry McGill U., 1952-54, faculty, 1954-57, asst. prof., 1955-57; mem. faculty U. Wis., Madison, 1957—, prof. physiol. chemistry, 1961-68, prof. pharmacology, 1968-99, prof., chmn. pharmacology, 1968-93, prof. emeritus, 1999—. Contbr. numerous articles to tech. jours., chpts. to numerous books on phosphoinositides, biol. transport, the pancreas, the brain and lithium in manic-depression. With USNR, 1943-45. Mem. AAAS, Am. Soc. Biochemistry and Molecular Biology, Biochem. Soc. (U.K.), Am. Soc. Pharmacology and Exptl. Therapeutics, N.Y. Acad. Scis. Home: 5 Nokomis Ct Madison WI 53711-2710 Office: U Wis Med Sch Dept Pharm 1300 University Ave Madison WI 53706-1510

HOLABIRD, JOHN AUGUR, JR., retired architect; b. Chgo., May 9, 1920; s. John Augur and Dorothy (Hackett) H.; m. Donna Katharine Smith, Nov. 25, 1942 (div. 1969); children: Jean, Katharine, Polly, Lisa (dec.); m. Marcia Stefanie Fergestad, June 28, 1969 (dec. Mar. 1994); children: Ann, Lynn; m. Janet Nothhelfer Connor, May 7, 1996. BA, Harvard U., 1942, MArch, 1948. Archtl. designer Holabird & Root, Chgo., 1948-49, 55-64; assoc. firm Holabird & Root, 1964-70, ptnr., 1970-87; tchr. drama Francis Parker Sch., Chgo., 1949-55; stage designer NBC-TV, 1955. Major: archtl. works include Francis Parker Sch, Chgo., Ravinia Stage and Restaurant, Highland Park, Ill., 1970, Bell Telephone Labs, Naperville, Ill., 1975, Canal Bldg, Chgo., 1974. Pres. Park West Community Assn., 1962; dir. Lincoln Park Conservation Assn., 1960-64, Corlands, 1979-85; mem. Chgo. Commn. on Historic and Archtl. Landmarks, 1981-85; bd. dirs. Lincoln Park Community Conservation, 1964; trustee Francis Parker Sch., Ravinia Festival Assn., Ill. Inst. Tech., 1980-86. Served with U.S. Army, 1942-45. Decorated Silver Star, Bronze Star; Fourragère (Belgium); Order of William (The Netherlands). Fellow AIA (pres. Chgo. chpt. 1977-78); mem. Tavern Club, Harvard Club (dir. 1974-78), Phi Beta Kappa. Democrat. Home: 200 E Pearson St Apt 3W Chicago IL 60611-2352 Office: Holabird & Root 300 W Adams St Chicago IL 60606-5101

HOLBA, ANNETTE M., county detective, educator; b. Harrisburg, Pa., 1960; d. William S. and Elizabeth Umberger; m. Dennis Dale Holba, June 4, 1992; children: Michele Trivelli, Christina Trivelli. BA in Law and Justice, Rowan U., 1994; MA in Liberal Studies, Rutgers U., 1998. Detective Burlington County Pros.'s Office, Mt. Holly, N.J., 1989—; violinist in orhc. Mem. County Sex Crimes Investigators Assn. N.J. (chairperson 1992-94). Avocations: violin, chamber music. E-mail: quartet@skyhigh.com. Office: Burlington County Pros Office 49 Rancocas Rd Mount Holly NJ 08060

HOLBERTON, PHILIP VAUGHAN, entrepreneur, educator, professional speaker; b. N.Y.C., Sept. 29, 1942; s. Robert Maynard and Charlotte Metcalf (Stone) H.; m. Gale Russell, May 16, 1970 (div. 1980); children: Matthew Russell, Alexandra; m. Anne Meigs Blodget, June 6, 1987; 1 child, Philip Vaughan Jr., Tod. A.B. in Acctg., Franklin and Marshall Coll., Lancaster, Pa., 1964. CPA, N.Y. Auditor Hurdman and Cranstoun CPAs, N.Y.C., 1964-72; mgr. audit svcs. Peat Marwick CPAs, N.Y.C., 1975-79; investment profl. McDonald & Co., N.Y.C., 1972-75; asst. contr. Becton Dickinson & Co., Franklin Lakes, N.J., 1979-81; group contr. Becton Dickinson & Co., Paramus, N.J., 1981-85; v.p. fin. Gen. Cinema Theatres, Chestnut Hill, Mass., 1985-91; v.p. fin. and adminstrn., CFO Cambridge, Neuroscience, Inc., Cambridge, Mass., 1991-95; founder Holberton Group, Lincoln, Mass., 1995—; outside dir. Mgmt. Decision Lab., NYU, 1981-84; adj. faculty Northeastern U., Brandeis U. Chmn. strategic planning panel United Way of Bergen County, Paramus, 1983-85; dir. Poppenhusen Inst., College Point, N.Y., 1981-83; sr. warden St. Anne's in the Fields, Lincoln, Mass., 1994-96. Mem. AICPA, Fin. Execs. Inst. (pres. bd. dirs. Boston chpt. 1995-96), Nat. Spkrs. Assn., New Eng. Spkrs. Assn. (bd. dirs.). Office: Holberton Group PO Box 254 Lincoln MA 01773-0254

HOLBIK, KAREL, economics educator; b. Czech Republic, Sept. 9, 1920; came to U.S., 1948, naturalized, 1952; s. Karel and Catherine (Krouzel) H.; m. Olga Rehackova, Sept. 10, 1956; 1 son, Thomas. J.D., Charles U., Prague, 1947; M.B.A., U. Detroit, 1949; Ph.D., U. Wis., 1956. Researcher Bank of Am., San Francisco, 1951-53; teaching asst. in banking U. Wis., 1953-55; asst. prof. econs. Lafayette Coll., Easton, Pa., 1955-58; prof. econs. Boston U., 1958-86, prof. econs. emeritus, 1986—; cons. U.S. Naval War Coll., Newport, R.I., 1963-64; vis. prof. U. Brussels, 1969-70; vis. faculty Harvard U., 1981-98; chief sect. for devel. fin. instns. UN, 1976-80; Fulbright sr. scholar U. Tunis, 1983-84; internat. fin. cons., 1986—. Author: Italy in International Cooperation, 1959, Postwar Trade in Divided Germany, 1964, The United States, The Soviet Union and the Third World, 1968, Monetary Policy in Twelve Industrial Countries, 1973, Industrialization and Employment in Puerto Rico, 1975; others. Mem. Am. Econ. Assn., Am. Fin. Assn. Home: 313 Country Club Rd Newton MA 02459-3148 *It appears that America, more than any other country, challenges human capabilities and permits individual dreams to come true.*

HOLBROOK, ANNA, actress; b. Fairbanks, Alaska; m. Bruce Holbrook; 1 child. Student, U. Ariz., Trinity U. Actress: (TV) Dallas, 1981, Another World, 1988-91, 93-97, Law and Order, One Life to Live, Spin City, 1997, All My Children, 1997-98; (film) I Love Trouble, 1994, Force Majeure, 1998; (theatre) Blue Plains, Mr. Parnell, The Dolphin Position. Recipient Best Supporting Actress in Drama Series Daytime Emmy. Office: Another World 79 Madison Ave New York NY 10016-7802*

HOLBROOK, DONALD BENSON, lawyer; b. Salt Lake City, Jan. 4, 1925; s. Robert Sweeten and Kinnie Benson H.; m. Bety J. Gilchrist, Apr. 23, 1947; children: Mark, Thomas, Gregory, Mary.; Student, Colo. Coll., U. Utah; JD, U. Utah, 1952, PhD (hon.), 1990; PhD (hon.), HHD (hon.), Utah Valley C.C., 1990; DFA (hon.), 1990; DHL (hon.), Salt Lake City C.C. Bar: Utah 1953. Pres. Jones Waldo, Holbrook and McDonough, Salt Lake City, 1973-89; of counsel, 1995—; exec. v.p., legal officer Am. Stores Co., 1990-95; bd. dirs. Blue Cross/Blue Shield Utah, The Regence Group; commr. Utah Bar, 1983-87; bd. advs. Mountain Bell, 1974-84. Editor in chief: Utah Law Rev., 1951-52. Bd. dirs. Utah Ass. UN, 1963-64; bd. dirs., exec. com. Utah Coop. Assn., 1962-83, vice chmn., 1970-73, chmn., 1974-82, 83-85; chmn. Utah Partnership for Ednl. and Econ. devel., 1987-95; pres. and chmn. bd. Ballet West, 1982-84; bd. dirs. Utah Dem. Party, exec. sec., 1955-65, exec. com., 1956-65; chmn. antitrust and monopoly subcom. Western States Dem. Conf., 1962-66; campaign mgr. Gov. Calvin L. Rampton, 1964-68; candidate for U.S. Senate, 1964; commr. Western Interstate Commn. on Higher Edn., 1978-83, chmn., 1982. Recipient Disting. Alumni award U. Utah, 1985, Resolution of Appreciation Utah Ste Bd. Regents, 1990, Light of Learning award Utah State Bd. Edn., 1994; named Lawyer of Yr. Utah State Bar, 1990. Fellow Internat. Acad. Trial Lawyers, Am. Bar Found.; mem. U. Utah Coll. Law Alumni Assn. (pres. 1957), ABA (gen. chmn. Rocky Mountain region 1962, Utha chmn., mem. com. sect. corp., banking, bus. law 1962-95), Utah Bar Assn. (bd. commrs. 1982-87, chmn. com. World Peace Through Law 1964, pres. 1964-65), Order of the Coif (award for contbns. to law, scholarship and cmty. svc. 1968), Salt Lake City Country Club, Beta Theta Phi, Phi Kappa Phi, Delta Theta Phi (disting. alumni award 1967). Home: 1752 Laurelhurst Dr Salt Lake City UT 84108-3310

HOLBROOK, HAL (HAROLD ROWE HOLBROOK, JR.), actor; b. Cleve., Feb. 17, 1925; s. Harold Rowe and Aileen (Davenport) H.; m. Ruby Elaine Johnston, Sept. 22, 1945 (div.); children: Victoria, David; m. Carol Rossen (div.); 1 dau., Eve; m. Dixie Carter, May 27, 1984. Student, Suffield Acad., 1933-37, Culver Mil. Acad., 1938-42; B.A. with honors, Denison U., 1948. Played summer stock cos., 1947-53; organized (with wife) two-person stage prodn., touring high schs., clubs, univs., 1948-53, repertoire included a sketch based on Mark Twain's short story An Encounter with an Interviewer; appeared on TV as Abraham Lincoln, 1953; assembled solo show Mark Twain Tonight, 1953; night club performances, 1955-56; on tour U.S. TV appearances, 1954-59, in N.Y.C., 1959, 66, 76; on tour, 1960-63, TV spl., CBS, 1967; TV series, The Brighter Day, 1954-59, The Senator, 1970-71, Portrait of America (host), 1983-88, Evening Shade, 1990-94; rec. theatre presentation Mark Twain Tonight, 1959, 61, 67; concert engagements, U.S., Can., Vancouver Festival, Edinburgh Festival, Saudi Arabia, European tour auspices, Dept. State with ANTA, 1959-60; performed two-character play Do You Know the Milky Way, Vancouver, also N.Y.C., 1961, Am. Shakespeare Festival, Stratford, Conn., 1962; toured two-character play Mark Twain Tonight, 1964—(Tony award, Drama Critics Circle award 1966); appeared in play The Glass Menagerie, N.Y.C., 1965; also TV movies The Whole World is Watching, 1969, A Clear and Present Danger, 1970, Travis Logan, 1971, Suddenly Single, 1971, Goodbye Raggedy Ann, 1971, That Certain Summer, 1971-72 (Emmy nomination best actor in a drama), The Pueblo, 1973 (Emmy awards for best actor in a drama, actor of year in a spl.), Sandburg's Lincoln, 1974-75 (Emmy award outstanding lead actor in a ltd. series), Our Town, 1977 (Emmy nomination outstanding lead actor in a drama or comedy spl.), The Awakening Land, 1978 (Emmy nomination outstanding lead actor in ltd. series), When Hell Was In Session, 1979, The Senator, NBC, 1970-71 (Emmy award, Best actor in dramatic series), (miniseries) North and South, 1985, North and South: Book II, 1986, Dress Gray, 1986, The Fortunate Pilgrim, 1988; plays Abe Lincoln in Illinois, N.Y.C., 1963; appeared plays Tartuffe, Lincoln Center Repertory Co., 1963-65, the Apple Tree, N.Y.C., 1967, I Never Sang for My Father, 1968, Man of La Mancha, 1968, Does a Tiger Wear a Necktie, 1969, Lake of the Woods, 1972; appeared in motion picture The Group, 1966, Wild in the Streets, 1968, The People Next Door, 1970, The Great White Hope, 1970, They Only Kill Their Masters, 1972, Jonathan Livingston Seagull (voice only), 1973, Magnum Force, 1973, The Girl from Petrovka, 1974, Midway, 1976, All the President's Men, 1976, Julia, 1977, Capricorn I, 1978, Natural Enemies, 1979, The Fog, 1980, The Kidnapping of the President, 1980, Rituals, 1980, Creepshow, 1982, Star Chamber, 1983, Girls Nite Out, 1984, Wall Street, 1987, The Unholy, 1988, Fletch Lives, 1989, The Firm, 1993, Carried Away, 1996, Cats Don't Dance (voice only), 1997, Hercules (voice only), 1997; author: Mark Twain Tonight, 1959. Mem. com. on internat. cultural exchange Nat. Council on Arts and Govt. Served with C.E. AUS, 1943-46. Recipient Vernon Rice Meml. award, 1959, Outer Circle award, 1959; spl. citation for Mark Twain Tonight N.Y. Drama Critics Circle, 1966; Torch of Liberty award Anti-Defamation League B'nai B'rith, 1972. Mem. Mark Twain Meml. Assn. Club: Players (N.Y.C.).

HOLBROOK, JOHN SCOTT, JR., lawyer; b. Milw., Oct. 27, 1939; s. John Scott Holbrook and Francesca Marie (Eschweiler) Davidson; m. Mary Lynn Lorenz, June 13, 1980. BA, StanfordU., Palo Alto, Calif., 1961; JD, U. Mich., 1964. Bar: Wis. 1964. Ptnr. Quarles & Brady, Madison, Wis., 1964—. Mem. ABA, State Bar of Wis., Nat. Assn. of Bond Lawyers, Am. Coll. Bond Counsel. Office: Quarles & Brady 1 S Pinckney St Madison WI 53703-2892

HOLBROOK, MEGHAN ZANOLLI, fundraiser, public relations specialist, state pol. BS in English and Edn., U. Tenn., 1971, postgrad., 1978-83. Dir. ancillary svcs. Ridgeview Psychiat. Hosp., Oak Ridge, Tenn., 1971-83; therapist The Children's Ctr., Salt Lake City, 1985-86; mgr. corp. contbns. Sundance Inst. and Film Festival, Salt Lake City, 1989-91; fund raising and pub. rels. cons. Salt Lake City, 1992—. Fundraiser congl. campaign Wayne Owens, 1986, bus. liaison, 1986-88; fin. dir. gubernatorial campaign Ted Wilson, 1988, mayoral campaign Deedee Corradini, 1991; campaign mgr. gubernatorial campaign Stewart Hanson, 1991-92; del. Dem. Nat. Conv., 1996; chair Utah State Dem. Party, 1996—; mem. bd. dirs. Sundance Inst., 1989—, Inst. at Deer Valley, 1995—; mem. Utah Air Travel Commn., 1996—; mem. pres.'s adv. com. on arts Kennedy Ctr., Washington, 1996—. Mem. Assn. State Dem. Chairs (exec. com. 1998—). Home: 775 Hilltop Rd Salt Lake City UT 84103-3311 Office: 455 S 300 E Ste 102 Salt Lake City UT 84111-3222*

HOLBROOK, PATRICIA HOUSTON, counselor, psychotherapist; b. Shreveport, La., Sept. 12, 1947; d. Pickens Nolan and Ann (Park) Houston; m. Don Holbrook, May 17, 1979; children: Jennifer Lynn, Adam Christopher. BS, Va. Poly. Inst. and State U., 1973; MA, U. N.C., Charlotte, 1994. Lic. profl. counselor, N.C.; registered play therapist, N.C.; nat. cert. counselor, nat. cert. sch. counselor. Dir. women, infants and children program CPC, York, Pa., 1975-76; dir. food svc. hosps. and nursing home, Va., Pa., 1973-75, Md., 1977; acct. Reston (Va.) Home Owners Assn., 1977-84, Men's Apparel Club, Charlotte, 1985-94; sch. counselor Gaston County Schs., Gastonia, N.C., 1993-98; pvt. practice psychotherapy, Charlotte, 1998—. Mem. ACA, Am. Profl. Soc. on Abuse of Children, Assn. for Play Therapy, Phi Kappa Phi, Chi Sigma Iota. Presbyterian. Avocation: advocate for children. Home and Office: 308 Glencurry Dr Charlotte NC 28214-1180

HOLBROOK, ROBERT GEORGE, state legislator; b. Manchester, N.H., July 4, 1917; m. Helen E. Holbrook; 2 children. BS, Springfield Coll., 1939. Asst. treas. Mechanics Savs. Bank, Manchester, N.H., 1939-55; exec.v.p. City Savs. Bank, Laconia, N.H., 1955-79; former bank officer; mem. from dist. 7 N.H. State Ho. of Reps., mem. appropriations and fin. coms.; chmn. Oil Fund Disbursement Bd. Trustee Putnam Fund Lecture Series, Trust Funds City of Laconia; treas. City of Laconia; exec. v.p. City Savs. Bank, Laconia, 1955-79. Address: 1301 Old North Main St Laconia NH 03246-2667

HOLBROOK, SALLY DAVIS, author; b. L.A., July 2, 1932; d. Elias Kaylor and Elisabeth (Jackson) Davis; m. William Sumner Holbrook III, Sept. 22, 1956; children: William Sumner IV (dec.), Robert Davis. AB, Pomona Coll., Claremont, Calif., 1954. Author: Sun, Sand and Sausage Pie, 1992, Party Perfect and Pampered, 1995. Mem. Jr. League of Pasadena; assoc. Children's Hosp.-Pasadena Guild. Mem. The Town Club of Pasadena, The Valley Hunt Club. Republican. Episcopalian. Avocations: cooking, bridge, needlepoint, sailing, dollhouse miniaturist. Home: 1440 Vista Ln Pasadena CA 91103-1938 Address (summer): 1230 E Ocean Blvd Unit 303 Long Beach CA 90802-6907

HOLBROOK, SAMUEL, umpire; b. Lexington, Ky., July 7, 1965; married; 1 child. BA in Pub. Rels., E. Ky. U. Former umpire Appalachian League, Midwest League, Carolina League, Tex. League, Ea. League, Internat. League; umpire maj. league baseball Nat. League, N.Y.C., 1997—; with Umpires Union, Phila. Office: Nat League 350 Park Ave New York NY 10022 also: Umpires Union 1735 Market St Philadelphia PA 19103

HOLBROOK, STEPHEN EUGENE, printing executive; b. Warsaw, Ind., Sept. 15, 1952; s. Harold Eugene and Phyllis Jean (Grable) H.; m. Debra Jane Orr, Jan. 10, 1981; children: Chad Ryan, Kelly Nicole, Ryan Stephen. BS, Ind. U., 1974; MBA, Keller Grad. Sch., Chgo., 1998. Store mgr. Firestone Tire & Rubber Co., Akron, Ohio, 1974-78; customer svc. mgr. Donnite Corp., Plymouth, Ind., 1978-79; customer svc. rep. R.R. Donnelley & Sons, Warsaw, 1979-83; customer svc./dist. svc. supr. R.R. Donnelley & Sons, Dwight, Ill., 1983-94, human resources supr., 1994-95; customer svc. supr. R.R. Donnelley & Sons, Warsaw, 1995—; leader new product start-up R.R. Donnelley & Sons, Dwight, 1983-86, mem. joint mfg./sales team, Chgo., 1985-87, quality cons. bindery, Dwight, 1984-89. Vol. Am. Cancer Soc., Warsaw, 1997, Am. Heart and Lung Assn.; coach Warsaw Little League, bd. dirs. 1996; cons. Jr. Achievement, Ft. Wayne, Ind.; charter mem. Warsaw Cmty. Found. Pub. Edn., Inc.; coach Shorewood (Ill.) Soccer League, 1988-93, Troy Youth Baseball, Shorewood, 1990-94, Warsaw Youth Travel Roller Hockey Team, 1996-97, Troy All-Stars, 1994; mem. Dirs. Club--Wagon Wheel Playhouse Theatre. Mem. Ind. U. Alumni Assn. (life), Ind. U. Varsity Club, Assn. for Quality and Participation, Hoosiers for Higher Edn., Kiwanis (bd. dirs. Warsaw club 1993—, Dir. of Yr. 1993). Avocations: travel, clowning, youth activities, stock car racing. Home: 842 Lydia Dr Warsaw IN 46580-1949

HOLBROOK, THOMAS ALDREDGE, state legislator; b. St. Louis, Nov. 23, 1949. Ill. state rep. Dist. 113, 1995—. Office: 9200 W Main St Ste 4 Belleville IL 62223-1710

HOLBROOKE, RICHARD CHARLES ALBERT, ambassador, government official; b. N.Y.C., Apr. 24, 1941; s. Dan and Trudi (Moos) H.; children: David Dan, Anthony Andrew. B.A., Brown U., 1962; postgrad., Princeton, 1969-70. Joined Fgn. Service, 1962; served in Vietnam, 1963-66; mem. White House staff, 1966-67; assigned State Dept.; staff Paris (France) peace talks, 1968-69; dir. Peace Corps, Morocco, 1970-72; mng. editor Fgn. Policy mag., 1972-77; dir. publs. Carnegie Endowment for Internat. Peace, 1973-76; cons. Commn. Orgn. Govt. for Conduct of Fgn., 1974-75; contbg. editor Newsweek Internat., 1976; asst. sec. for East Asian and Pacific affairs Dept. State, Washington, 1977-81; v.p. Public Strategies, Washington, 1981-85; sr. advisor Lehman Bros., 1981-84; mng. dir. Shearson Lehman Bros., 1985—; columnist Asian Wall St. Jour., 1981—; U.S. amb. Federal Republic of Germany, 1993-94; asst. sec. state European and Can. affairs Dept. State, Washington, 1994-96; vice chmn. Credit Suisse First Boston, N.Y.C., 1996-99; U.S. amb. to U.N. N.Y.C., 1999—; chief negotiator Dayton Peace Accords, 1995; spl. presdl. emissary to Cyprus; etrustee Internat. Voluntary Services; mem. Trilateral Commn. Author: vol. The Pentagon Papers, 1967; Contbr. numerous articles to, N.Y. Times, Washington Post, Wall St. Jour., Atlantic, other mags. and jours. Bd. dirs. Internat. Rescue Com. Mem. Council Fgn. Relations, Inst. Strategic Studies. Office: US Mission to the UN 799 United Nations Plaza New York NY 10017-3505*

HOLBROW, CHARLES HOWARD, physicist, educator; b. Melrose, Mass., Sept. 23, 1935; s. Frederick and Florence Louisa (Gile) H.; m. Mary Louise Ross, June 17, 1956; children: Gwendolyn J., Elizabeth M., Alice J., Katherine A., Martha R. BA, U. Wis., Madison, 1955; AM, Columbia U., N.Y.C., 1957; MS, U. Wis., Madison, 1960; cert. Russian Inst., Columbia U., 1957; PhD, U. Wis., Madison, 1963. Asst. prof. Haverford Coll., 1962-65; research investigator U. Pa., 1965-66; assoc. editor Physics Today, N.Y.C., 1967; assoc. prof. Colgate U., Hamilton, N.Y., 1967-72, prof., 1972-86, Charles A. Dana prof. physics, 1986—, chmn. dept. physics and astronomy, 1978-81, 82-84, dir. div. natural scis. and math., 1985-88; vis. assoc. Calif. Inst. Tech., 1975-76; vis. physicist Brookhaven Nat. Lab., 1980-81; vis. prof. MIT, 1982, 88-89; guest scientist SUNY-Stony Brook, 1983-93; guest sci. investigator GSI Darmstadt, Germany, 1994-95; vis. rsch. scholar Harvard U., 1995. NSF coop. fellow, 1959-60; Am. Coun. Edn. acad. intern, 1972-73; NSF rsch. grantee, 1970-73, 83-97; NSF grantee, 1978; NSF faculty devel. grantee, 1981-82. Fellow Am. Phys. Soc.; mem. AAUP, Am. Assn. Physics Tchrs. Office: Colgate U Dept Physics and Astronomy Hamilton NY 13346

HOLCH, GREGORY JOHN, children's book editor, author; b. Tokyo, Nov. 19, 1952; (parents Am. citizens); s. Arthur Everett and Ellen Constance (O'Keefe) H.; m. Rhonda Lyn Brauer, Sept. 7, 1989; children: Jillian Brauer, Justin Brauer. BA in English, Manhattanville Coll., 1974; MA in Am. Civilization, NYU, 1984. Editl. asst. Globe Comm., Greenwich, Conn., 1977-78, Random House Student Book Clubs, N.Y.C., 1978-80, Bantam Books, N.Y.C., 1981-83; assoc. editor Scholastic, N.Y.C., 1983-85, editor, 1985-94, sr. editor, 1994—; guest editor Mademoiselle mag., 1974. Author: (novel) The Things with Wings, 1998; co-author: Jungle Jokes, 1979; author short stories; contbr. photographs in mags. Mem. Soc. Children's Book Writers and Illustrators, Am. Radio Relay League (life). Avocations: amateur extra class ham radio, photography. Office: Scholastic Inc 555 Broadway New York NY 10012-3919

HOLCK, FREDERICK H. GEORGE, priest, educator; b. Neuenburg, Germany, June 6, 1927; came to U.S., 1963, naturalized, 1968; s. Edward W. and Elizabeth L. (Luger) H.; m. Miriam I. Ahlgren, Jan. 23, 1954; children: Mark, Christopher, Thomas, David, Timothy. Student, U. Heidelberg, 1947-49, U. Tuebingen, 1949-52; Lic. Phil. in Philosophy summa cum laude, U. Salzburg, 1953, Ph.D. in Comparative Religion summa cum laude, 1954. Ordained to priesthood Anglican Ch. Diplomate Am. Bd. Counselors. Tutor Helsinki, 1954-56; sr. lectr. Peshawar U., Pakistan, 1957-59; parish minister in Can., 1960-62; prof. theology and history of religions Luth. Theol. Sem., Saskatoon, Sask., Can., 1962-63; asst. prof. religion and human devel. Lake Erie Coll., Painesville, Ohio, 1963-66; asst. prof. religion and Oriental philosophy Cleve. State U., 1966-68, assoc. prof., acting chmn. dept. philosophy and religion, 1968-70, prof., chmn. dept. religion, 1970-80, dir. Asian Studies Program, 1969-80, dir. Extended Campus Coll., 1982-85, prof. emeritus, 1987—; acad. v.p., dean coll. N.C. Wesleyan Coll., Rocky Mount, N.C., 1980-82. Editor: Ohio Jour. Religious Studies, 1972-80; Co-author, editor: Death and Eastern Thought, 1974, Ethics in World Religions: Systems and Sources, 1987; co-editor internat. editorial bd.: Ency. Hinduism, 1979-82; contbr. articles to profl. jours. and encys. Bd. dirs. Greater Cleve. Counseling, Inc., 1978-80, v.p., 1982-87; mem. adv. bd. World Fellowship Religions, 1978-82; bd. dirs. Polk County Hospice, 1991, v.p., 1993-95. Fellow Nat. Acad. Counselors and Family Therapists, Am. Coll. Counselors (founding); mem. Am. Acad. Religion, Ohio Acad. Religion (pres. 1974-75), Am. Philos. Assn., Nat. Alliance for Family Life (clin. mem., pres. S.E. region 1981-82), Rotary. Home: PO Box 1372 Tryon NC 28782-1372 Office: Cleve State U Dept Religion Cleveland OH 44115

HOLCOM, FLOYD EVERETT, international business consultant; b. Astoria, Oreg., Jan. 19, 1964; s. Edward Everett and Esther Jean (Wilkinson) H.; m. Sheryl Plagata, Dec. 1994; children: Nathaniel, Victoria Elizabeth. BA in Bus. Adminstrn., Oreg. State U., 1989; MBA, Portland State U., 1991. Sr. spl. ops. engr. Joint Spl. Forces Commd. Dept. Def.; dir. internat. trade field study program Internat. Trade Inst., Portland, Oreg.; internat. dir. The IBIS Group, 1991—; with Peratrovich, Nottingham & Drage Inc., Engring. Cons., Astoria, Oreg., 1997—; cons. Nike, Inc., 1991-93; spl. envoy State of Oreg. rep. to Fujian Provincial Govt., China, 1990; ind. retail co. with Unocal, 1979-89. Responsible for 1st U.S. comml. shipment to Vietnam since 1975, 1992. Adv. coun. Internat. Bus. Degree program Linfield Coll.; adv. bd. Open U. of Ho Chi Minh City, Vietnam. With U.S. Army, 1981-86, spl. forces res., 1986-94, spl. forces N.G., 1994—. Mem. Assn. Internat. Trade Specialists (past v.p., bd. dirs.), Japan-Am. Soc. Oreg., Pacific N.W. Internat. Trade Assn., Suzhou-Portland Sister City Assn. (bd. dirs.), N.W. Regional China Coun. (past chmn. fgn. hospitality com.), Soc. Am. Mil. Engrs., Army Engr. Assn., Spl. Forces Assn., World Affairs Coun. Oreg., World Trade Ctr. Portland, Columbia River Maritime Mus. Assn., Am. Philatelic Soc., Clatsop County Hist. Soc. (bd. dirs. 1998—). Republican. Episcopalian. Home: 367 Alameda Ave Astoria OR 97103-6201

HOLCOMB, CONSTANCE L., sales and marketing management executive; b. St. Paul, Oct. 28, 1942; d. John E. Holcomb and Lucille A. (Westerdahl) Hope; m. Walter D. Serwatka, May 1991. BS, U. Minn., 1965; MA in Intercultural Edn., U. of the Americas, Puebla, Mex., 1975. Rsch. analyst U.S. Dept. Def., Washington, 1965-66; br. gen. mgr. Berlitz Lang. Schs., Mexico City, 1966-68; pres., gen. mgr. Centro Lingüistico, Puebla, 1968-72; gen. mgr., prof. Lang. Ctr. Am. Sch. Found., Puebla, 1972-74; assoc. prof., dir. lang. programs U. of the Americas, Puebla, 1974-76; prof., dean faculty of langs. Nat. Autonomous U. Mex., Mexico City, 1976-78; dir. sales & mktg. Longman Pub. Co., N.Y.C., 1978-80, dir. internat. sales & mktg., 1980-84; mng. dir. ESL Pub. Div. McGraw-Hill Book Co., N.Y.C., 1984-85; dir. mktg. mgmt. McGraw-Hill Tng. Systems and Book Co., N.Y.C., 1985-86; dir. mktg. electronic bus. McGraw-Hill Book Co., N.Y.C., 1986-87; info. industry mgmt. cons., career mgmt. cons., ind. contractor, N.Y.C., 1987-91; mktg. cons. Sarasota, Fla., 1991—; v.p. MexTESOL, Mexico City, 1977-78. Editor: English Teaching in Mexico, 1975; contbr. articles to profl. jours. Bd. trustees, devel. com. mem. John and Mable Ringling Mus., 1993—; bd. dirs. Safe Place and Rape Crisis Ctr., Sarasota, 1997—; bd. dirs. Friends of Selby Pub. Libr., 1997-99. Mem. Assn. Am. Pubs. (com. chmn. internat. div. 1980-84, exec. com. 1980-84), Info. Industry Assn., Nat. Assn. Women Cons., Am. Soc. Profl. and Exec. Women. Office: 3555 Mistletoe Ln Longboat Key FL 34228-4103

HOLCOMB, DONALD FRANK, physicist, academic administrator; b. Chesterton, Ind., Nov. 8, 1925; s. Roger L. and Ethel (Frank) H.; m. Barbara Page, Aug. 26, 1950; children: Douglas Page, Jane D., Nancy M. A.B., DePauw U., 1949; M.S., U. Ill., 1950, Ph.D., 1954. Instr. U. Ill., 1954; mem. faculty Cornell U., 1954—, prof. physics, 1962—, dir. lab. atomic and solid state physics, 1964-68, chmn. dept. physics, 1969-74, 82-86, trustee, 1976-81; cons. Corning Glass Research Lab., 1959-64, Central Inst. Indsl. Research, Oslo, Norway, 1962. Contbr. profl. jours. Served with USNR, 1944-46. Sr. vis. fellow NATO, 1962; Guggenheim fellow, 1968-69; Sci. Research Council sr. fellow, 1978. Fellow Am. Phys. Soc., AAAS; mem. Am. Assn. Physics Tchrs. (pres. 1987, Oersted medal 1996), Sigma Xi. Presbyterian. Spl. rsch. solid state physics, chem. physics, coll. physics course devel. Home: 385 Savage Farm Dr Ithaca NY 14850-6505

HOLCOMB, DWIGHT A., city chief of police; b. Columbus, Ohio, May 2, 1955. AS in Law Enforcement Tech., Columbus (Ohio) State C.C., 1977; grad., FBI Nat. Acad., 163rd Session, Quantico, Va., 1990; B in Pub. Adminstrn. summa cum laude, Franklin U., 1995; FBI Acad., L.E.E.D.S. #36, 1998. Patrol officer patrol sect. Upper Arlington (Ohio) Divsn. Police, 1978-85, detective criminial investigation unit, 1985-87, sgt. patrol sect., 1987-94, sgt. tng. unit supr., 1994-95, chief of police, 1995—; student Ohio Peace Officers Tng. Acad., London, Ohio, 1986, 87, 91, 94. Inst. Police Tech. and Mgmt. U. North Fla., Jacksonville, Internal Affairs Investigation, 1995; assessor Commn. on Accreditation for Law Enforcement Agys., Fairfax, Va., Police Labor Rels. Com., 1989, 90, 91, Speed Measuring Device Com., 1991, City Health and Wellness Ins.. Com., 1991. Vol. Jr. Achievement, Upper Arlington, Upper Arlington Leadership Program, 1996, Leadership Ohio, 1997. Mem. Fraternal Order of Police (bargaining unit com. 1984, 85), FBI Nat. Acad. Assocs. (exec. bd. Ohio chpt. 1996, 97, 98, 99), Ohio Assn. Chiefs of Police, Internat. Assn. Chiefs of Police, Upper Arlington Rotary Club (program com. mem., sub-com. chair 1997, bd.dirs., 1998, 99). Office: City of Upper Arlington 3600 Tremont Rd Upper Arlington OH 43221

HOLCOMB, GRANT, III, museum director; b. San Bernardino, Calif., Sept. 30, 1944. BA, UCLA, 1967; MA, U. Del., 1970, PhD, 1972. Asst. prof. Mt. Holyoke Coll., South Hadley, Mass., 1972-80, SUNY, Stony Brook, 1980-81; curator San Diego Mus. Art, 1981-83; assoc. dir. TimKen Art Gallery, San Diego, 1983-85; dir. Meml. Art Gallery, Rochester, N.Y., 1985—. Author: (exhibit catalogue) John Sloan, The Gloucester Years, 1980, Wake of the Ferry, 1984; contbr. articles to profl. jours. Bd. dirs. BOA edits., 1991—, Conv. Vis. Bur., 1990—, Friends of Ganondagan, 1994—. Kress fellow Nat. Gallery Art, 1972; Am. Council Learned Socs. grantee, 1980. Mem. Assn. Art Mus. Dirs., Arts for Greater Rochester (bd. dirs. 1985—), Aesthetic Edn. Inst. (bd. dirs. 1985—). Office: Meml Art Gallery 500 University Ave Rochester NY 14607-1415

HOLCOMB, LYLE DONALD, JR., retired lawyer; b. Miami, Fla., Feb. 3, 1929; s. Lyle Donald and Hazel Irene (Watson) H.; m. Barbara Jean Roth, July 12, 1952; children: Susan Holcomb Davis, Douglas J., Mark E. BA, U. Mich., 1951; JD, U. Fla., 1954. Bar: U.S. Supreme Ct. 1966, U.S. Ct. Appeals (5th and 11th cirs.) 1981. Ptnr. Holcomb & Holcomb, Miami, 1955-72; assoc. Copeland, Therrel, Baisden & Peterson, Miami Beach, Fla., 1972-75; ptnr. Therrel, Baisden, Stanton, Wood & Setlin, Miami Beach, 1976-85; ptnr. Therrel Baisden & Meyer Weiss, Miami Beach, 1985-93; pvt. practice, Tallahassee, Fla., 1993-95; mem. organizing bd. Econ. Opportunities Legal Svcs. Program (now Legal Svcs. of Greater Miami, Inc.), 1965-75; organizing pres. So. Fla. Migrant Legal Svcs. Program (now Fla. Rural Legal Svcs.), 1966-68. Mem. exec. coun. So. Fla. coun. Boy Scouts Am., 1958-93; past pres. Miami chpt., past counselor state soc. Huguenot Soc. Fla. Served with USNR, 1947-53. Recipient Silver Beaver award So. Fla. coun. Boy Scouts Am., 1966. Fellow Am. Coll. Trust and Estate Counsel, 1980-94, Acad. Fla. Probate and Trust Litigation Attys., 1980-95; mem. Dade County Bar Assn. (dir. 1960-71, sec. 1963-71), Miami Beach Bar Assn. (pres. 1980), Estate Planning Council Greater Miami., Soc. Mayflower Descs. (past pres. Miami club, past counselor state soc.), SAR (past pres. Miami chpt.), Univ. Yacht Club. Republican. Mem. United Ch. of Christ. Home: 3538 Killarney Plaza Dr Tallahassee FL 32308-3491

HOLCOMB, RICHARD D., state commissioner. BA in Polit. Sci., Hampden Sydney Coll. Va., 1976; JD, U. Richmond, 1979. Chief staff U.S. Reps. John Linder, D. Slaughter, Jr., Craig T. James, 1989-94; commr. Va. Dept. of Motor Vehicles, Richmond, 1994—. Office: Va Dept of Motor Vehicles 2300 W Broad St Richmond VA 23269-0999

HOLCOMB, TERRI LYNN, computer graphic consultant; b. Fayetteville, Ark., July 27, 1963; d. John Wallace and Linda Merrell (Boals) H. AA, Tallahassee C.C., 1995; BA in Psychology, Fla. State U., 1997. Activity therapist South Ark. Regional Health Ctr., Camden, 1984-86; clk. typist Rep. Fin. Svcs., Atlanta, 1986-87; adminstrv. sec. Colquitt Mental Health Svcs., Moultrie, Ga., 1988-90; staff asst. Agy. Healthcare Adminstrn., Tallahassee, 1990-92; sec. Fla. Healthcare Purchasing Coop., Tallahassee, 1992-95; rsch. asst. Fla. Design Initiative, Tallahassee, 1996, web prodn. coord., 1997—. Mem. domestic violence task force NOW, Tallahassee, 1996—, sec., 1996—. Acad. scholar So. Ark. U. tech. br., 1981, Linda and Ray Patterson scholar, Tallahassee, 1994-95, Univ. Club, Tallahassee, 1997. Mem. AAUW, Golden Key. Office: Fla Design Initiative Fla A&M U Tallahassee FL 32307

HOLCOMB, WILLIAM A., retired oil and gas exploration, pipeline executive, retired real estate broker, consultant; b. Lockhart, Tex., Oct. 31, 1926; s. William A. and Annie O. (Pyl) H. B.B.A., U. Tex., 1949; J.D., U. Houston, 1963. Bar: Tex. bar 1963. Acctg. supr. Fireman's Fund-Am. Ins. Companies, 1950-51; mgr. ins. dept. Transcontinental Gas Pipe Line Corp., 1959-72; asst. treas.-asst. sec. Transco Companies, Inc., Houston, 1972-74; corp. sec. and/or asst. corp. sec. co. and various subsidiaries Transco Companies, Inc., 1977-82; cons., real estate broker, 1983-92, ret., 1992. Served with AUS, 1944-46. Life mem. Tex. Assn. Bus.; mem. State Bar Tex., Am. Mgmt. Assn., Am. Gas Assn., Interstate Natural Gas Assn., Am. Soc. Corp. Secs., Mus. Natural Sci., Houston Bd. Realtors, Houston C. of C. (past chmn. ins. com.), U. Tex. Ex-Students Assn. Home and Office: 1018 Townplace Houston TX 77057-1942

HOLCOMBE, RANDALL GREGORY, economics educator; b. Bridgeport, Conn., June 4, 1950; s. Lynn Montanye Holcombe and Gloria Gabriel (Rita) Ledbetter; m. Lora Hunt Pritchett, June 18, 1983. BS, U. Fla., 1972; MA, Va. Poly. Inst. and State U., 1974, PhD, 1976. Asst. prof. Tex. A&M U., College Station, 1975-77; prof. Auburn (Ala.) U., 1977-88, Fla. State U., Tallahassee, 1988—; mem. rsch. adv. coun. james Madison Inst., Tallahassee, 1987—, chmn., 1991—; mem. editorial bd. Rev. Austrian Econs., 1987-97, Pub. Fin. Rev., 1995—, Quar. Rev. Austrian Econs., 1998—; adj. scho lar Ludwig Von Mises Inst., 1982—. Author: Public Finance and the Political Process, 1983, An Economic Analysis of Democracy, 1985, Public Sector Economics, 1988, Economic Models and Methodology, 1989, The Economic Foundations of Government, 1994, Public Policy and the Quality of Life, 1995, Public Finance: Government Revenues and Expenditures in the United States Economy, 1996, (with R. Sobel) Growth and Variability in State Tax Revenue, 1997; contbr. articles to profl. jours. Scaife Found. fellow, 1972-73, H.B. Earhart Found. fellow, 1973-75; research grantee Earhart Found., 1979-80, 83, 89, 90, 98. Mem. Am. Econ. Assn., Pub. Choice Soc., So. Econ. Assn., Western Econ. Assn. Home: 3514 Limerick Dr Tallahassee FL 32308-3139 Office: Fla State U Dept Econs Tallahassee FL 32306

HOLDA, WILLIAM MICHAEL, academic administrator; b. Lafayette, Ind., June 14, 1949; s. Nicholas and Rosella Clark H.; m. Martha Sikora, July 1976; children: Patricia, John, Elizabeth, Nicholas. BA, St. Joseph's Coll., 1971; MusM, Ind. U., 1975; EdD, East Tex. State U., 1995. Instr. organ, piano, 1964-76, instr. voice, 1967-91; instr. St. joseph's Coll., Rensselaer, Ind., 1972-73; grad. teaching asst. Ind. U., Bloomington, 1973-75; instr. music, philosophy Kilgore (Tex.) Coll., 1975-90, dean admissions, registrar, 1990-96, pres., 1996—; mem. task force instl. effectiveness Tex. Higher Edn. Coord. Bd., 1993-94. Producer, dir. 7 Broadway musicals, 1975-84; conductor, performer 7 operas and concerts. Sponsor, moderator Kilgore Coll. Newman Club, 1976-86. Fellow St. joseph's Coll., 1974. Mem. Tex. Assn. C.C., Tex. Assn. Collegiate Registrars and Admissions Officers, Tex. Assn. Instl. Rschrs. Avocations: reading, music, woodworking, computers. Office: Kilgore Coll 1100 Broadway Kilgore TX 75662

HOLDAR, ROBERT MARTIN, chemist; b. Ozark, Ark., Feb. 10, 1949; s. Luther and Francess Ethyl (Briscoe) H.; m. Barbara Jean Sobczak, Jan. 5, 1985; children: Luther Edward, William Thomas, Frank King, Samuel Robert. BS in Chemistry, U. Ark., 1976; MS in Chemistry, Tex. A&M U., 1979; MBA, U. Dallas, 1996. Chemist Parkem Indsl. Svcs., LaPorte, Tex., 1979-80, Mohawk Labs div. NCH Corp., Irving, Tex., 1980—. Patentee in field. Chmn. Zoning Bd. Adjustments, Irving, 1991-95; mem. Local Emergency Planning Commn., Dallas, 1991-93; mem. bd. amortizations and appeals City of Irving, 1994; Grand Awards Judge, INTEL 49th Internat. Sci. Fair, 1998. With USAF, 1968-73. W.K. Noyce scholar U. Ark., 1975. Mem. Am. Chem. Soc., Nat. Assn. Corrosion Engrs., Am. Soc. Lubrication Engrs. (chmn. North Tex. sect. 1982-83), Irving Rep. Club (editor 1989-92, 94-97, treas. 1992-94), Irving Noon Toastmasters (pres. 1983, Accomplished Toastmaster award 1986). Avocations: snow skiing, scuba, gardening. Home: 2816 Brockbank Dr Irving TX 75062-4523 Office: NCH Corp Mohawk Labs 2730 Carl Rd Irving TX 75062-6405

HOLDAWAY, ERIC JOHN, military officer; b. Aurora, Colo., Apr. 13, 1964; s. Donald Melville and Doris Marangelo Holdaway; m. Suzanne Marie pace, Dec. 21, 1996. BA in Internat. Studies, U. Wash., 1986. Commd. 2d lt. USAF, 1987, advanced through grades to maj.; flight comdr. 6947 electronic security squadron USAF, Key West, Fla., 1987-89; officer in charge OL-TS 693d Intelligence Wing USAF, Shaw AFB, S.C., 1989-92; chief mission mgmt., 6975 electronic security squadron USAF, Saudi Arabia, 1990-91; aide to comndr., Air Force Intelligence Command USAF, Kelly AFB, Tex., 1994-97; ops. officr intelligence divsn., USAF Weapons Sch. USAF, Nellis AFB, Nev., 1997—. Decorated Bronze Star medal, 1991. Mem. VFW, Air Force Assn., U.S. Naval Inst., Assn. of Old Crows, U. Wash. Alumni Assn. (life). Home: 1924 Patagonia St Henderson NV 89012

HOLDAWAY, RONALD M., federal judge; b. Afton, Wyo.; m. Judy Janowski, Dec. 1958; children: Denise, Georgia. BA, U. Wyo., 1957, JD, 1959. Bar: Wyo. 1959, U.S. Dist. Ct. (Wyo.), U.S. Ct. Mil. Appeals, 1960, U.S. Army Ct. Mil. Rev., U.S. Supreme Ct., 1967. Commd. 2nd lt. U.S. Army., 1960, advanced through grades to brig. gen., 1989; legal staff officer U.S. Army, Ft. Lewis, Washington, 1960-63; legal staff instr. U.S. Army, Hawaii, 1963-66; instr. criminal law, Judge Advocate Gen.'s Sch. U.S. Army, Charlottesville, Va., 1966-69; staff judge advocate 1st cav. divsn. U.S. Army, Vietnam, 1969-70; chief govt. appellate divsn. U.S. Army, Washington, 1971-75, chief of pers., 1975-77; staff judge advocate U.S. Army, Stuttgart, Germany, 1978-80; exec. to judge advocate gen. U.S. Army, Washington, 1980-81, asst. judge advocate gen., 1981-83; judge advocate U.S. Army Europe, Heidelberg, Germany, 1983-87; chief judge Ct. Mil. Review U.S. Army, Washington, 1987-89; judge U.S. Ct. of Vets. Appeals, Washington DC, 1990—. Decorated Bronze Star, Legion of Merit, Disting. Svc. medal with Oak Leaf Cluster, Meritorious Svc. medal with Oak Leaf Cluster, Air medal, Nat. Def. Svc. medal, Vietnam Campaign medal with 4 campaign stars, Vietnam Svc. medal, Overseas medal (3). Mem. Wyo. State Bar Assn., Assn. U.S. Army, Ft. Myer Officers Club, Army Navy Club. Office: US Ct of Appeals for Vets Claims 625 Indiana Ave NW Ste 900 Washington DC 20004-2950

HOLDCRAFT, JANET R., academic administrator; b. Bridgeton, N.J., Sept. 30, 1940; d. Mulford M. and Sarah Hansel (Dilks) Rulon; m. E. Larry Holdcraft, Feb. 21, 1964 (wid. Sept. 1979); children: Larry B., Jodi Holdcraft Coates. BA, Glassboro State, 1962; MA, 1968; EdD, Seton Hall U., 1994. Tchr. fourth grade Glassboro (N.J.) Bd. Edn., 1962-67, tchr. devel. reading grade 7, 1967-68, tchr. corrective reading, grades 6-8, 1968-75, coord. Right-to-Read, 1975-77, tchr. compensatory edn. reading, 1977-80, Title I reading tchr. grades 7-8, 1980-84, BSI/lang. arts tchr., grades 7-8, 1984-93, tchr.

GED adult evening sch., 1988-89, head tchr., dir. student activities, 1988-93, asst. supt. curriculum and personnel, 1995—; prin. BSI Spl. Edn. program Glassboro Bd. Edn., summers 1991-93; prin. alt. evening h.s. Supr. Adult Cmty. Sch., Glassboro, 1993-94; dir. curriculum and instrn., Pennsville Sch. dist., N.J., 1994-95. Asst. leader Holly Shores chpt. Girl Scouts U.S., Franklinville, N.J., 1979-82; mem. Mothers Football Club, Delsea Regional H.S., Franklinville, 1979-80; mem. Ladies Rep. Club, Franklinville, 1980-83; chair Glassboro Mcpl. Alliance, 1995-97; mem. adv. bd. so. region N.J. Statewide Systemic Initiative, 1999—; mem. Franklinville United Meth. Ch. adminstrv. coun., budget com., pantry com., bd. dirs. Bright Promises Nursery Sch. Co-dir. reading grant U.S. Office of Edn., 1978-80; recognized by Gov.'s Tchrs. Recognition Program, State of N.J., 1988; recipient Elizabeth M. Bozarth scholarship N.J. Alpha Zeta, 1990. Mem. ASCD, N.J. Assn. Sch. Adminstrs., Reading Coun. of So. N.J. (bd. dirs. 1992—), N.J. Assn. Supervision and Curriculum (so. region bd. dirs. 1996—), Rotary Club Glassboro/Clayton/Elk Twp., Delta Kappa Gamma (Pi chpt. 1st v.p. 1990-92, rec. sec. 1988-90), Kappa Delta Pi (Xi Gamma chpt.). Methodist. Avocations: golf, reading, collecting salt and pepper shakers, the beach. Home: 589 Judy Ave Franklinville NJ 08322-3913 Office: Glassboro Pub Schs Glassboro NJ 08028

HOLDEN, BOB, state official; b. Kansas City, Mo.; m. Lori Hauser; children: Robert, John. BS in Polit. Sci., Southwest Mo. State; Degree Kennedy Sch. Govt. for Public Execs. and Flemming Fellow Leadership Inst., Harvard U. Former adminstrv. asst./liaison U.S. Congressman Richard Gephardt, St. Louis; mem. Mo. Ho. of Reps., 1983-89; now state treas. State of Mo., Jefferson City, 1993—; chmn. gen. approations com.; co-sponsor Excellence in Edn. Act; mem. Bd. Fund Commrs., Mo. State Employees Retirement System, Mo. Bus. Coun., Mo. Rural Opportunities Coun.; past chmn. Mo. Housing Devel. Commn. Dean Am. Legion Mo. Boy's State Legislative Sch.; mem. Holden Scholarship Fund, Leadership St. Louis; former mem. Confluence's Edn. Implementation, Tower Grove Hgts. Neighborhood Assn., Save the Children's Program; mem. Mo. Coun. Econ. Edn., Coun. State Govts.; vice-chair Mo. Cultural Trust. Mem. Nat. Assn. State Treas. (legis. chair). Office: St Treasurer PO Box 210 Jefferson City MO 65102-0210*

HOLDEN, FRED STEPHEN, industrial tree farmer; b. Seattle, Aug. 5, 1927; s. Charles Ray and Mary Frances (Hull) H.; m. Carole Kathryn Kronsteiner, Sept. 3, 1950; children: Lisl Kathryn, Miles Frederick. Student, Wash. State U., 1947-50, U. Oreg., 1950-51. Lumber buyer Bacon Lumber Co., Portland, Oreg., 1952-54; mill supt. Holden Lumber Co., Prescott, Oreg., 1955-58; timber broker Longview, Wash., 1958-67; real estate broker Ridgefield (Wash.) Agy., 1968-71; br. mgr. Tranasam. Title Ins. Co., Portland, 1972-76; lead examiner Tranasam. Title Ins. Co., Bellevue, Wash., 1977-89; owner, mgr. Pvt. Indsl. Tree Farm, Kirkland, Wash., 1983—. Author: Land and Trees, 1991. Ombudsman Wash. State Long-Term Care Ombudsman's Office, Seattle, 1992-98. With U.S. Army, 1946-47. Avocations: linguistics, Asian travel. Home and Office: 9821 Forbes Creek Dr Kirkland WA 98033-4476

HOLDEN, FREDERICK DOUGLASS, JR., lawyer; b. Stockton, Calif., Nov. 21, 1949; s. Frederick Douglass and Sarah Frances (Young) H.; m. Patricia Brierton, June 25, 1988; children: Elizabeth, Andrew. BA, U. Calif., Santa Barbara, 1971; JD, U. Calif., Davis, 1974. Bar: Calif. 1974, U.S. Dist. Ct. (no., cen., ea. and so. dists.) Calif. 1974, U.S. Ct. Appeals (9th cir.) 1974, D.C. 1996, U.S. Dist. Ct. D.C. 1996. Assoc. Brobeck, Phleger & Harrison LLP, San Francisco, 1974-81; ptnr. Brobeck, Phleger & Harrison, San Francisco, 1981—; mem. faculty Practising Law Inst., 1990; speaker Nat. Conf. Bankruptcy Judges, 1987, 91, Banking Law Inst., 1986, Calif. Continuing Legal Edn. of Bar, Calif., 1983-85, Calif. State Bar, 1993. Mng. editor U. Calif. Davis Law Rev., 1974. Mem. ABA (bus. bankruptcy com., spkr. 1991, 95), Calif. Bar Assn. (commendation 1983), San Francisco Bar Assn. (cert. appreciation 1985, 88, 90, 95), Turnaround Mgmt. Assn. (dir., sec. 1994-96), Am. Bankruptcy Inst., San Francisco Yacht Club, Sigma Pi (pres. 1970). Democrat. Avocations: triathlons, skiing, sailing. Home: 140 Bella Vista Ave Belvedere CA 94920-2466 Office: Brobeck Phleger & Harrison Spear St Tower 1 Market Plz Ste 341 San Francisco CA 94105-1193

HOLDEN, GEORGE FREDRIC, brewing company executive, public policy specialist, author; b. Lander, Wyo., Aug. 29, 1937; s. George Thiel Holden and Rita (Meyer) Zulpo; m. Dorothy Carol Capper, July 5, 1959; children: Lorilyn, Sherilyn, Tamilyn. BSChemE, U. Colo., 1959, MBA in Mktg., 1974. Adminstr. plastics lab. EDP, indsl chems. plant, prodn. process engring., tool control supervision, aerospace (Minuteman, Polaris, Sparrow), Parlin, N.J., Salt Lake City, Cumberland, Md., 1959-70; by-product sales, new market and new product devel., resource planning and devel. and pub. rels. Adolph Coors Co., Golden, Colo., 1971-76; dir. econ. affairs corp. pub. affairs dept., 1979-84, dir. pub. affairs rsch., 1984-86; owner Phoenix Enterprises, Arvada, 1986—; mgr. facilities engring. Coors Container Co., 1976-79; instr. brewing, by-products utilization and waste mgmt. U. Wis.; cons., speaker in field. Mem. bd. economists Rocky Mountain News, 1990—; mem. Heritage Found. Ann. Guide to Pub. Policy Expert, 1987—, Speakers Bur., Commn. on the Bicentennial U.S. Constitution, 1991-93; del. Colo. Rep. Conv., 1976—; adv. Cost of Govt. Day; bd. dirs. Colo. Pub. Expenditures Coun., 1983-86, Nat. Speakers Assn., Colo. Speakers Assn. (bd. dirs. 1987-90, 91-93), Nat. Assn. Bus. Economists, Colo. Assn. Commerce and Industry Execs. Ednl. Found. Sr. fellow budget policy Independence Inst. Colo. "ThinkTank". Mem. U.S. Brewers Assn. (chmn. by-products com. 1983-86, ednl. found. 1984-85, Hon. Gavel, 1975), Am. Inst. Indsl. Engrs. (dir. 1974-78), Washingtons Am. for Tax Reform Found. Co-author: Secrets of Job Hunting, 1972; The Phoenix Phenomenon, 1984; author: Total Power of One in America, 1991; contbr. articles to Chem. Engring. mag., 1968-76, over 400 published articles, white papers in field; over 900 speeches, 560 appearances on radio talk shows nationwide. Home: 6463 Owens St Arvada CO 80004-2732 Office: Phoenix Enterprises PO Box 1900 Arvada CO 80001-1900

HOLDEN, JAMES DANIEL, investment company executive; b. Chgo., May 22, 1940; s. William Hoyt and Bernice Elizabeth H.; children: Tracy, Stephanie, Christine. BSc, Millikin U., 1963. V.p. Morgan Stanley, N.Y.C., 1983-85, Kidder Peabody, N.Y.C., 1985-91, ABN-AMRO Corp., Chgo., 1991-95; dir. banking equity dept. Nomura Securities, N.Y.C., 1995-96; dir. investment banking Tradition North Am., N.Y.C., 1996-97; exec. v.p. USA Investments, Morristown, N.J., 1997-98; pres. Core Pacific Securities, N.Y.C., 1998—. Pres., exec. v.p. Oak Hill Assn., Middletown, N.J., 1974-76; dir. Barclay Farm Assn., Cherry Hill, N.J., 1976-78. Mem. The Cornell Club. Avocations: music, sports. Office: Core Pacific Securities 1 World Trade Ctr Ste 9145 New York NY 10048-1086

HOLDEN, LAURENCE PRESTON, artist; b. Grappenhall, Cheshire, Eng., Oct. 30, 1945; came to U.S., 1946; s. Roy Preston and Iris Doreen (Butterworth) H.; m. Carolyn Durant, Dec. 6, 1974. B.Visual Arts, Ga. State U., 1974, M.Visual Arts, 1979. part-time instr. grad. studies Ga. State U., Atlanta, 1993-95; adj. instr. Atlanta Coll. Art, 1991-93, Brenau Coll., Atlanta, 1991, Kenesaw (Ga.) State U., 1981-84. One man shows include Hambridge Ctr., Rabun Gap, Ga., 1986, O.K. Harris, N.Y.C., 1989, Berman Gallery, Atlanta, 1994, Macon & Co., Atlanta, 1998, Gwinnett Fine Arts Ctr., Atlanta, 1998; exhibited in group shows at High Mus., Atlanta, 1968, 1980, Albany (Ga.) Mus., 1981, Fla. Gulf Coast Art Ctr., Bellair, 1982, Tampa (Fla.) Mus., 1985, Knoxville (Tenn.) Mus., 1987, Mary Bell Gallery, Chgo., 1989, Eve Mannes Gallery, Atlanta, 1990, U. Mobile (Ala.), 1996, Addison/Ripley Gallery, Washington, 1999, Art Ctr., Navarre, Fla., 1998; represented in permanent collections Carnegie Ctr. Peace, Washington, State of Ga. Collection, City of Atlanta, IRS S.E. Svc. Ctr., Chamblee, Ga., Ga. State U., Atlanta, Hambidge Ctr., Rabun Gap, AT&T, Delta Airline, Cin. Airport, La Guardia Airport, N.Y., Hilton Hotel, Chgo., Saks 5th Ave., Houston, Hyatt Carlton Hotel, London, Ernst & Young, N.Y.C., Equifax Corp., Atlanta, Sheraton Hotel, Palm Beach, Fla., Kelsy-Seybold Hosp., Houston, Fisher Coll. Bus. Ohio State U., Columbus, Am. Airlines; contbr. articles to profl. jours. Recipient Award of Merit, Atlanta Arts Festival, 1969, High Mus. Art, Atlanta, 1968, Art in Pub. Places award City of Atlanta, 1977; Hambidge Ctr. fellow, 1984-97. Home: 1144 Hancock Dr NE Atlanta GA 30306-2514

HOLDEN, MARY GAYLE REYNOLDS, lawyer; b. Charlottesville, Va., Oct. 21, 1948; d. Bruce Dodson and Jane Rust (Monroe) R.; m. William L. Ashley III, June 7, 1970 (div. Dec. 1980); children: William Lloyd Ashley IV, David Monroe Ashley; m. Peter Randolph Holden, June 15, 1985; children: Peter Reynolds Holden, Benjamin Willson Holden. BA, Roanoke Coll., 1970; JD, U. Va., 1980. Bar: Va. 1980, U.S. Dist. Ct. (fed. dist.) 1980, U.S. Ct. Appeals (4th cir.) 1994. Assoc. McGuire, Woods, Battle & Boothe, Fairfax, Va., 1980-83; pvt. practice Sterling, Va., 1983-84; assoc. Frank, Bernstein, Conway & Goldman, McLean, Va., 1985; corp. counsel Crippen Cos., Gt. Falls, Va., 1986-88; assoc. Caligaro & Mutryn, Washington, 1988-89; ptnr. Leonard, Ralston & Stanton, Washington, 1990-97, Hopkins & Sutter, Washington, 1997—; Bd. dirs. Am. Cancer Soc., Loudoun County, Va., 1997—, Com. for Dulles, 1987-89, 98—, Jackson-Field Home for Girls, Jarrett, Va., 1988-89, Fairfax Choral Soc., 1983-89; mem. Loudoun Vol. Fin. Coun., 1994—, Loudoun County Leadership Ext. Coun., 1995—, Zonta Internat., 1997—. Mem. Loudoun County Affirmative Action Com., 1995—, chmn. 1995. Mem. Va. Bar. Assn., D.C. Bar Assn., Women in Tehc. (bd. dirs. 1999—), Reston C. of C., Dulles Area Transp. Assn., Loudoun County Transp. Assn. (bd. dirs. 1999—). Episcopalian. Avocations: skiing, Am. history.

HOLDEN, NATE, city councilman; div.;. BS, West Coast U., MS. Pres. Calif. Dem. Coun., 1970-74; asst. chief dep. to Kenneth Hahn, L.A. County Supr.; with Calif. State Senate Dist. 30, 1974-78; city councilman Dist. 10, L.A., 1987—, chmn. transp. com., vice chmn. pub. safety com.; mem. environ. quality and waste mgmt. com. L.A. City Coun.; bd. dirs. So. Calif. Rapid Transit Dist.. Mem. L.A. County Pub. Social Svc. Commn., U.S. Commn. on Govt. Procurement; alt. Colisum Commn.; founder 10th Councilmanic Dist. Athletic Found. With U.S. Army, WWII. Mem. NAACP, Nat. Contract Mgmt. Assn., Urban League, Crenshaw Neighbors. Office: City Hall East 20 N Main St Rm 403 Los Angeles CA 90012-4801*

HOLDEN, RAYMOND THOMAS, physician, educator; b. Washington, Apr. 11, 1904; s. Raymond Thomas and Celeste Selma (Moritz) H.; m. Mary Lightle, Oct. 9, 1958; 1 dau., Mary Elliott. Student, U. Notre Dame, 1922-24; M.D., Georgetown U., 1928, D.Sc. (hon.), 1980. Diplomate: Am. Bd. Obstetrics and Gynecology. Intern Providence Hosp., Washington, 1928-29; assoc., then attending obstetrician and gynecologist Providence Hosp., 1932-56, cons., 1956-60; resident Columbia Hosp. for Women, Washington, 1929-30; asst., asso., attending staff Columbia Hosp. for Women, 1933, chief med. staff, 1952-54, 62-64, acting adminstr., 1958-59; preceptorship Dr. R.Y. Sullivan Georgetown U. Sch. Medicine, 1930-32; assoc., attending obstetrics and gynecology D.C. Gen Hosp., 1932-47; asst., assoc., also attending obstetrics and gynecology Georgetown U. Hosp., 1933—; from clin. instr. to clin. prof. obstetrics and gynecology Georgetown U. Sch. Medicine, 1933-85, assoc. chmn. dept. ob/gyn, 1977-85, emeritus clin. prof., 1985—; cons. obstetrics and gynecology U.S. Naval Hosp., Bethesda, Md., 1948-68. Bd. dirs., exec. com. Tb Assn. D.C., 1947-49; bd. dirs., exec. com. D.C. divsn. Am. Cancer Soc., 1950-56; mem. Health Facilities Planning Coun., Washington, 1964-70; bd. dirs. D.C. chpt. ARC, mem. exec. com., 1975-86; trustee Columbia Hosp. for Women. Served to capt., M.C. USNR, 1942-46; rear adm. Res. Fellow ACS, Am. Coll. Obstetricians and Gynecologists; mem. AMA (D.C. mem. Ho. Dels. 1952-68, chmn. com. on human reproduction 1964-68, trustee 1968-77, vice chmn. 1974-75, chmn. 1975-77), D.C. Med. Soc. (chmn. exec. bd. 1951-52, pres. 1946-47), Washington Gynecology Soc. (sec. 1950-54, pres. 1956), So. Med. Assn., Assn. Profs. Gynecology and Obstetrics, Am. Legion, Alpha Omega Alpha. Clubs: Fifty Year of Am. Medicine (pres. 1979-80), Chevy Chase, Metropolitan. Home: 5120 Watson St NW Washington DC 20016-5340

HOLDEN, REBECCA LYNN, artist; b. Monterey, Calif., Nov. 29, 1952; d. Derrel Wayne and Zella Fay (Reed) H.; m. Mark Stuart Bales, June 3, 1971 (div. Nov. 1983); children: Shelly Dawn (dec.), Matthew Gregory; m. David Strong Taylor, Dec. 27, 1995. BA, U. Ark., 1995. Potter/owner Rebecca Holden Studio, Searcy, Ark., 1984-94; artist/owner Rebecca Holden's Red Lick Mountain Studio, Clarksville, Ark., 1994—. Potter, sculptor, artist specializing in speleo art forms. Recipient Art scholarship Susan Jones Rand Foun., 1992, 93. Avocations: caving, biking, boating.

HOLDEN, ROBERT WATSON, radiologist, educator, university dean; b. Brazil, Ind., Mar. 31, 1936; s. John William and Naomi Ellen (Watson) H.; m. Miriam Ann Bognanno, June 20, 1964; children: Anne, Robert II, Jennifer. BS in Pharmacy, Purdue U., 1958; MD, Ind. U., 1963. Diplomate Am. Bd. Radiology. Intern L.A. County Gen. Hosp., 1963-64; resident radiology Vanderbilt U., Nashville, 1970-73; asst. prof. Ind. U. Sch. Medicine, Indpls., 1973-77, assoc. prof., 1977-82, prof., 1982—, prof., chmn. dept. radiology, 1991-95, dean, 1995—; chief vascular and interventional radiology Wishard Meml. Hosp., Indpls., 1973-79, chief radiology, 1977-91; counselor NIH, 1990-94. Contbr. over 100 articles to profl. jours. Chmn. bldg. com. 1st United Meth. Ch., Mooresville, 1988-95. Capt. U.S. Army, 1964-66. Fellow Soc. Cardiovascular & Interventional Radiology, 1987; named Disting. Alumnus, Purdue U. Sch. Phharmacy, 1992. Mem. Am. Coll. Radiology (fellow 1988, counselor), Radiologic Soc. N.Am. (counselor), Ind. Roentgen Soc. (past pres.). Republican. Avocations: forestry, agriculture, tennis. Office: Ind U Sch Medicine fH 302 1120 S Drive Rm 302 Indianapolis IN 46202-5149

HOLDEN, TIM, congressman, protective official; b. St. Clair, Pa., Mar. 5, 1957; s. Joseph F. and Catherine Siney H.; m. Gwen Kieres. BA in Sociology, Bloomsburg State Coll., 1980. Ins. broker/real estate agent; probation officer Schuylkill County, Pa.; sgt.-at-arms Pa. Ho. of Reps.; sheriff Schuylkill County, Pa., 1985-93; mem. 103d-106th Congresses from 6th Pa. dist., Washington, 1993—; mem. agrl. com. Democrat. Roman Catholic. Office: US Ho of Reps 1421 Longworth HOB Washington DC 20515-3806*

HOLDEN, WILLIAM HOYT, JR., lawyer; b. Chgo.; s. William Hoyt and Bernice Elizabeth (McKenzie) H.; m. Mary Ann Kula, June 23, 1954 (div. June 1982); children: William, Christopher, Sarah, Peter. BS, U. Ill., 1954; JD, U. Md., Balt., 1965. Bar: Md. 1965, U.S. Supreme Ct. 1969. Assoc. Weinberg and Green, Balt., 1965-72, ptnr., 1973-83; sr. v.p. CRI, Inc., Rockville, Md., 1983-85; sr. advisor Legg Mason Wood Walker, Inc., Balt., 1985-86; pvt. practice Bethesda, Md., 1987—; pres., bd. dirs. Am. Franchise Cons., Inc., Bethesda, 1987—, Mid-Atlantic Title Closing, Inc. Capt. USNR, 1977, ret., 1982. Mem. Md. State Bar Assn., Order of Coif, Rotary. Republican.

HOLDEN, WILLIAM WILLARD, insurance executive; b. Akron, Ohio, Oct. 5, 1958; s. Joseph McCullem and Lettitia (Roderick) H.; m. Kim Homan, Aug. 31, 1985; 1 child, Jennifer Catharine. BA, Colgate U., 1981. Crime ins. trainee Chubb & Son, Inc., N.Y.C., 1981-82; exec. protection dept. mgr. Chubb & Son, Inc., San Jose, Calif., 1982-85, Woodland Hills, Calif., 1986-91; sr. v.p., mgr. Fin. Svcs. Group, Inc., Rollins, Hudig, Hall, Aon Fin. Svcs. Group, L.A., 1991—; tng. analyst Chubb & Son, Inc., Warren, N.J., 1985-86. Co-author manual: Chubb Claims Made Training, 1985; contbr. articles to Colgate alumni mag. Mgr., coach Campbell (Calif.) Little League, 1983-85; pres. Le Parc Homeowners Assn., Simi Valley, Calif., 1987-89; mem. Community Assn. Inst., L.A., 1986—; dir. Friends of the Vols. for L.A. Unified Sch. dist. Mem. Profl. Liability Underwriting Soc. (L.A. steering com.), Forum for Corp. Dirs. Republican. Avocations: golf, reading, running, swimming, skiing. Office: Aon Fin Svcs Group Inc 707 Wilshire Blvd Los Angeles CA 90017-3501

HOLDER, ANGELA RODDEY, lawyer, educator; b. Rock Hill, S.C., Mar. 13, 1938; d. John T. and Angela M. (Fisher) Roddey; 1 child, John Thomas Roddey Holder. Student, Radcliffe Coll., 1955-56; BA, Newcomb Coll., 1958; postgrad., Faculty of Law-King's Coll., London, 1957-58; JD, Tulane U., 1960; LLM, Yale U., 1975. Bar: La. 1961, S.C. 1960, Conn. 1981. Counsel Roddey, Sumwalt & Carpenter, Rock Hill, S.C., 1960-91; atty. criminal div. New Orleans Legal Aid Bur., 1961-62; counsel York County Family Ct., S.C., 1962-64; asst. prof. polit. sci. Winthrop Coll., Rock Hill, 1964-74; research assoc. Yale U. Law Sch., 1975-77, exec. dir. program in law, sci. and medicine, 1976-77; lectr. dept. pediatrics Yale U. Sch. Medicine, 1975-77, asst. clin. prof. pediatrics and law, 1977-79, assoc. clin. prof., 1979-83, clin. prof., 1983—; counsel for medicolegal affairs Yale-New Haven Hosp. and Yale Med. Sch., 1977-89. Author: The Meaning of the Constitution, 1968, 2d edit., 1987, 3d edit., 1997, Medical Malpractice Law, 1975, 2d edit. 1978, Legal Issues in Pediatrics and Adolescent Medicine, 1977, 2d edit., 1985, 3d edit., 1997; contbg. editor: Prism mag.; contbg. editor., AMA; mem. editorial bd.: IRB; Law, Medicine and Health Care, Jour. Philosophy and Medicine; contbr. articles to profl. jours. Mem. Rock Hill Sch. Bd., 1967-68; bd. dirs. Family Planning Clinic, chmn. 1970-73; bd. trustees Ednl. Commn. for Fgn. Med. Grads., 1990-97, exec. com., 1997; bd. dirs. Conn. Planned Parenthood, 1993-99, exec. com. 1996-99; mem. lawyers' rev. group Health Care Task Force, The White House, 1993; bd. trustees Cushing/Whitney Med. Libr. at Yale U., 1996—; ethics com. Leeway AIDS Hospice, New Haven, Conn., 1996—. Mem. ABA, S.C. Bar Assn. (medico-legal com. 1973—), La. Bar Assn., New Haven County Bar Assn., Am. Soc. Law and Medicine (treas. 1981-83, sec. 1983-85, pres. 1986-88, bd. dirs. 1977-91). Democrat. Episcopalian. Home: 23 Eld St New Haven CT 06511-3815 Office: Yale U School of Medicine 367 Cedar St New Haven CT 06510-3222

HOLDER, ANNA MARIA, holding company executive; b. Key West, Fla., Feb. 22, 1966; d. James Paul Yaccarino, Sr. and Carol (Joskey) McInerny; m. Harold D. Holder, 1996. AA, St. Petersburg Jr. Coll., 1989; BS, Eckerd Coll., 1991; MA, U. South Fla., 1994, postgrad., 1995—. Adminstr. Chase Bank Fla., Pinellas Park, 1989-91; substance abuse adminstr. Centurion Hosp., Tampa, 1992; staff writer, asst. features editor The Oracle, Tampa, 1992-93; v.p. The Holder Group, Inc., Tampa, 1994—; pres. Sun-Suns Trading Co., Inc., Tampa, 1996—. Author: Relationships Among Six Business Variables in the Black Press, 1994. Bd. dirs. Hillsborough County HealthCare Adv. Bd., 1996—; co-founder Friends of Hillsborough Health-Care, Inc., 19998; mem. Health Start Hillsborough, 1997—. Mem. LWV (pres. Hillsborough County (Fla.) chpt. 1995-96). Republican. Avocations: reading, skiing, walking. Fax: 813-222-8857. E-mail: holders@gte.net. Home: 5210 Interbay Blvd Apt 8 Tampa FL 33611-4145

HOLDER, BARBARA JUNE, educator in English and literature; b. Bklyn., June 24, 1941; d. Nathan and Sarina Kent; m. Alex A. Weiner, Dec. 9, 1963 (div. 1970); 1 child, Deborah Anne Goldman; m. Alan Holder, Sept. 12, 1972. BA magna cum laude, Columbia U., 1973, MA with hons., 1975, MPh, 1981. Pvt. practice dance tchr., 1970-78; adj. assoc. prof. Pace U., Pleasantville, N.Y., 1978-93; jour. cons. Dialogue House, N.Y.C., 1987-98; instr. in creative writing Ridgefield (Conn.) Adult Edn., 1998—; instr. lit. Ridgefield Libr., 1998; leader poetry workshops various librs., cultural ctrs., N.Y. 1990—, organizer and host poetry reading Pace U., Pleasantville, N.Y., 1981-90. Contbr. poems to numerous coll. and periodical anthologies. Recipient fellowships Columbia U., 1968-73, 1973-75. Mem. Poets and Writers Guild, Phi Beta Kappa. Home: 55 Gallow Hill Rd West Redding CT 06896

HOLDER, BEN R., protective services official; b. Dawson, Ga.; s. Leroy H.; m. Louise Grooms, Nov. 3, 1966; children: Rodney A., Kia Q. AA in Police Sci. and Adminstrn., Hillsborough C.C., Tampa, 1977; BA in Criminology, St. Leo Coll., 1989; LHD (hon.), Tampa Coll., 1993, DBA (hon.), 1994. Avaition mechanic USAF, Tampa, 1966-70; welder F.R. Strelow, Inc., Tampa, 1970-73; patrol officer Tampa Police Dept., 1973-75, vice detective, 1975-79, sgt., 1979-84, lt., 1984-86, capt., 1986-91, maj., 1991-93, police chief, 1993—. Mem. Fla. Assn. Chiefs Police, Internat. Assn. Chiefs Police. Office: Office of the Police Chief 411 N Franklin St Tampa FL 33602-2648*

HOLDER, DONALD, lighting designer. Grad., Yale Sch. of Drama. Lighting designer: (Broadway) The Lion King (Tony, Drama Desk, Outer Critics Cir. awards), Juan Darien (Tony, Drama Desk nominations), Hughie (Am. Theatre Wing nomination), Eastern Standard, Holiday, Solitary Confinement, (off-Broadway) Most Fabulous Story Ever Told, Sight Unseen, Three Days of Rain, After-Play, All My Sons, Communicating Doors, Caucasian Chalk Circle (Drama Desk nomination), Spunk, Avenue K, Fit to be Tied, From Above,, Richard II/III, Titus Andronicus, The Green Bird (American Theater Wing nomination), The Changeling, Jeffrey, Maiden's Prayer, Pterodactyls, many others; operas include: Salome; regional theatre includes Hartford Stage, Long Wharf, Mark Taper Forum, La Jolla Playhouse, American Repertory Theatre, Center Stage, many others; archtl. lighting includes Sony Plaza, Swiss Ctr. in N.Y. Winner 1998 Tony for Lion King lighting design. Office: Walt Disney Co 500 S Buena Vista St Burbank CA 91521*

HOLDER, ERIC H., prosecutor; b. N.Y.C., Jan. 21, 1951; s. Eric H. and Miriam R. (Yearwood) H. BA, Columbia Coll., 1973, JD, 1976. Bar: N.Y. 1977, D.C. 1980. Trial atty. pub. integrity sect. U.S. Dept. Justice, 1976-88; assoc. judge Superior Ct., Washington, 1988-93; U.S. atty. Dept. Justice, Washington, 1993-97, U.S. dep. atty. gen., 1997—. Mem. Concerned Black Men. Democrat. Office: Dep Atty Gen Dept Justice 950 Pennsylvania Ave NW Washington DC 20530-0001*

HOLDER, GEOFFREY LAMONT, dancer, actor, choreographer, director; b. Port-of-Spain, Trinidad, Aug. 1, 1930; s. Arthur and Louise (De Frense) H.; m. Carmen de Lavallade, June 26, 1955; 1 son, Leo. Ed., Queens Royal Coll., Port-of-Spain; student native dances in, W.Indies. Stage debut as mem. Roscoe Holder's Dance Co., Trinidad, 1942; formed own dance co., 1950; toured P.R. and the Caribbean, 1953, U.S. debut, 1953; Broadway debut: House of Flowers, 1954; solo dancer with Met. Opera, N.Y.C., 1956-57; dramatic debut Waiting for Godot, 1957; concerts with Geoffrey Holder Dance Co., N.Y.C., 1956-60; appeared at Festival of Two Worlds, Spoleto, Italy, 1958, Festividadi Ballet Hispanico, N.Y., 1979; dir., costume designer: The Wiz, Broadway, 1975-78, 78-84, 84 (Drama Desk award best costume design 1975, Tony award best costume design 1975, Tony award best director of musical 1975); dir., costume designer, choreographer: Timbuktu, 1978 (Tony award nomination outstanding costume design 1978); stage appearances as dancer include House of Flowers, 1954, Aida, 1956, La Perichole, 1956, Show Boat, 1957, Josephine Baker's Revue, 1964; stage appearances as actor Waiting for Godot, 1957, Twelfth Night, 1960, The Masque of St. George and the Dragon, 1973, From the Memoirs of Pontius Pilate, 1976, Night of One Hundred Stars Two, 1985, The Players Club Centennial Salute, 1989, Night of One Hundred Stars Three, 1990, Give My Regards to Broadway, 1991; choreographer Brouhaha, 1960, Mhil Daiim, 1964, Three Songs for One, 1964, I Got a Song, 1974, Fifty Golden Years of Showstoppers, 1982; costume designer The Twelve Gates, 1964, Three Songs for One, 1964; movie appearances include: All Night Long, 1961, Doctor Dolittle, 1967, Krakatoa, East of Java, 1969, Everything You've Always Wanted to Know About Sex, 1972, Live and Let Die, 1973, Swashbuckler, 1976, Annie, 1982, (narrator) Dance Black America, 1985, Boomerang, 1992; appeared in night clubs; TV appearances include: The Man Without a Country, 1973, John Grin's Christmas, 1986, Ghost of a Chance, 1987, (series) Chef du Jour, 1995; paintings exhibited, Barbados Mus., San Juan, P.R., Barone Gallery, N.Y.C., Gallery of Brooks Atkinson Theatre, N.Y.C., Gropper Gallery, Cambridge, Mass., Griffin Gallery, N.Y.C., Grinnel Galleries, Detroit; recorded albums of W. Indian songs and album of song stories; author: Black Gods, Green Islands, 1957, Geoffrey Holder's Caribbean Cookbook, 1974; contbr. articles to Playbill; others. Recipient United Caribbean Youth award, 1957, Monarch award Nat. Council Culture and Art, 1982, Ellis Island Medal of Honor, Nat. Ethnic Coalition of Organizations, 1986, Liberty award, N.Y.C., 1986; Guggenheim fellow, 1957. Mem. AFTRA, Screen Actors Guild, Actors Equity Assn., AGVA. Address: Donald Buchwald Assocs c/o Steve Kay 10 E 44th St New York NY 10017-3601*

HOLDER, GORDON S., career officer; b. Camden, N.J., July 21; m. Pat; children: Ann Marie, Jennifer Lynn. BA, Fla. State U., 1968; MS, Troy State U., 1980. Commd. ensign U.S. Navy, advanced through grades to rear admiral, 1993; served on USS Whidbey Island, 1987-89, stationed in Japan, 1989-91, stationed in Norfolk, 1992-97, served on USS Austin, 1992-93; comdr. Amphibious Group TWO, Norfolk, 1997-99, Mil. Sealift Command, Washington, 1999—. Decorated Legion of Merit, Bronze Star, Navy Commendation medal. Office: Mil Sealift Command 914 Charles Morris Ct SE WNY Washington DC 20398-5540

HOLDER, HAROLD DOUGLAS, SR., investor, industrialist; b. Anniston, Ala., June 25, 1931; s. William Chester and Lucile (Kadle) H.; m. Anna Maria Yaccarino, 1996; children: Debra Holder Carnaroli, Harold Douglas Jr. Student, Anniston Bus. Coll., 1949, Jacksonville State U., 1954-57, Druitt Sch. Speech, 1962. Dept. mgr. Sears, Roebuck & Co., Anniston, 1954-57; merchandising mgr. Sears, Roebuck & Co., Atlanta, 1957-59, dir. coll. recruiting, 1959-61, dir. exec. devel. program, 1961, asst. personnel dir., 1962-63; store mgr. Sears, Roebuck & Co., Cocoa, Fla., 1965-67, Ocala, Fla.,

1963-65; asst. zone mgr. Sears, Roebuck & Co., Atlanta, 1967-68, asst. gen. mgr. mdse., 1968-69, sales promotion mgr. So. area, 1968; pres., bd. dirs. Cunningham Drug Stores, Inc., Detroit, 1969-70; v.p. Interstate Stores, 1971; pres., bd. dirs. Rahall Communications Corp., 1971-73; chmn. bd., chief exec. officer, dir. Am. Agronomics Corp., 1973-86; pres. Harold Holder Leasing; mng. dir. The Holder Group, Inc., 1987—; CEO, bd. dirs. Cutler Mfg. Corp., 1989—, Atlas Aircraft Corp., 1987—; mem. exec. com., bd. dirs. Coastland Corp., Fla., 1979-84; pres., bd. dirs. Golden Harvest, Inc., 1976-88; bd. dirs., treas. Dome Products, Inc., 1989—. Author: Don't Shoot, I'm Only a Trainee, 1975. Chmn., bd. dirs. Miracle, Inc., Brevard County; chmn. United Appeal, Ocala, Fla., 1964, Cocoa, Fla., 1966; bd. dirs. United Way Hillsborough County (Fla.); chmn. Heart Fund Drive, Ocala, 1964, Marion (Fla.) Com. of 100; bd. dirs. So. Coll. Placement Assn., Am. Acad. Achievement; bd. dirs. Marion chpt. ARC, Opera Arts Assn.; exec. com. Share, U. Fla.; bd. trustees U. Tampa; chmn. bd. trustees, trustee emeritus Eckerd Coll. With USMC, 1950-53. Endowed Harold D. Holder chair of mgmt. Eckerd Coll. Recipient Disting. Service award Marion County 4-H Club, 1965, Golden Plate award, 1983, Champion of Higher Edn. award, 1982, Fla. NAACP Humanitarian award, 1984. Mem. Chief Execs. Forum, C. of C. (chmn. beautification com., retail bus. com.), Young Pres. Orgn. (past chmn. Fla. chpt.), Univ. Club, Tampa Yacht and Country Club. Episcopalian. Office: Holder Group Inc 201 N Franklin St Ste 2700 Tampa FL 33602

HOLDER, HOLLY IRENE, lawyer; b. Albuquerque, May 16, 1952; d. Howard George and Dorothy Evelyn (Doll) Holzum; m. William B. Holder Jr., June 4, 1974; 1 child, Eric James. BA with honors, U. Colo., 1974; JD with honors, U. Denver, 1980. Bar: Colo. 1980, U.S. Ct. Appeals (10th cir.) 1980. Chemist Indsl. Labs., Denver, 1974-76; law clk. to presiding justice Colo. Supreme Ct., Denver, 1979; assoc. Calkins, Kramer, Grimshaw and Harring, Denver, 1980-82, 84-88, McKenna, Conner & Cuneo, Denver, 1988-90, Saunders, Snyder, Ross & Dickson, Denver, 1990-93; pvt. practice Denver, 1993—. Mem. adv. com. Regional Coun. Govts. Water Resources Mgmt., 1984—; chmn. Chatfield Basin Assn., Denver, 1987, Chatfield Basin Master Plan Task Force, Denver, 1986—. Recipient Disting. Svc. award Denver Regional Coun. Govts., 1987. Mem. Colo. Bar Assn., Denver Bar Assn., Mensa, Denver Rotary. Republican. Avocations: golf, reading, book-collecting. Office: 17th St Ste 1500 Denver CO 80202-1202

HOLDER, HOWARD RANDOLPH, SR., broadcasting company executive; b. Moline, Ill., Nov. 14, 1916; s. James William and Charlotte (Bregal) H.; m. Clementi Lacey-Baker, Feb. 21, 1942; children: Janice Clementi Black, Susan Charlotte Holder, Marjory Estelle Holder, Howard Randolph Jr. BA, Augustine Coll., 1939. With radio stas. WHBF, Rock Island, Ill., 1939-41, WOC, Davenport, Iowa, 1945-47, WINN, Louisville, 1947, WRFC, Athens, Ga., 1948-56; pres. Clarke Broadcasting Corp., 1956-91, chmn., 1991—; chmn. WGAU and WNGC, Athens, 1956—, KVML and KZSQ, Sonora, Calif., 1987—, KVRQ, Atwater, Calif., 1995—, KTFN and KFMK, Merced, Calif., 1996—; mem. adv. bd. U. Ga. Coll. Journalism and Mass Comm., 1973-78, sec., 1973-74; pres. Mid-West Ga. Broadcasting, Inc., 1965-68; bd. dirs. AP Broadcasters, Inc., 1983-91. Author: Escape to Russia, 1995. Chmn. adv. bd. Salvation Army, 1962-63, life mem., 1952—; chmn. Athens Parks and Recreatoin Bd., 1952-62; chmn. Cherokee dist. Boy Scouts Am., 1966-67, bd. N.E. Ga. Eagle Scout Assn., 1989; mem. adv. bd. Clarke County Juvenile Ct., 1960-72, Athens-Clarke ARC, 1950-70; chmn. region IV Ga. divsn. Am. Cancer Soc., 1968; bd. dirs. Athens Crime Prevention Com., 1960-70; mem. Georgians for Safer Hwys., 1970; trustee Ga. Rotary Student Fund, Inc., 1969-90, trustee emeritus, 1990—; mem. Model Cities Policy Bd., 1970-71, Ga. Criminal Justice Coord. Com.; mem. Ga. Productivity Bd., 1984-85, hon. chmn. N.E. Ga. March of Dimes, 1996, 97, Walk Am., 1997; mem. bicentennial alumni activities com. U. Ga., 1982; co-pres. Friends U. Ga. Mus. Art, 1973-75; state bd. advisors Ga. Mus. Art, 1984—, life mem., 1997—; sec. adv. bd. Henry W. Grady Coll. Journalism and Mass Comm., U. Ga. adv. coun., 1990-92; mem. adv. group views for the nineties U. Ga., 1989-92; mem. fine arts task force, adv. com. for evaluation v.p. for svcs., U. Ga., 1989; mem. adv. com. Ga. Commn. for Nat. Bicentennial, 1976; bd. dirs. Rec. for the Blind, 1977-83, Athens Symphony, 1981-85, Quality Growth Task Force N.E. Ga., 1989-91; mem. Ga. Gov.'s Jail/Prison Overcrowding Com., 1982; mem. svcs. adv. coun. UGA, 1990—; mem. WWII Commemorative Com., 1993-95; trustee Clementi and Randolph Holder Girl Scout Trust, 1997—; dir. C&S Nat. Bank (now Nation's Bank), 1965-68; bd. dirs. Lyndon House Arts Ctr. Found., 1995-97. With AUS, 1941-46, ETO, maj. USAR ret.; hon. adm. Navy Supply Corps, 1997; col. R.I. Militia, 1997. Decorated Bronze Star with valor insignia; named Boss of Yr., Athens Jr. C. ofC., 1959, Broadcaster-Citizen of Yr., Ga. Assn. Broadcasters, 1962, Ga. Assn. Broadcasters Hall of Fame, 1993, Employer of Yr., Bus. and Profl. Women's Club, 1969, Athens Citizen of Yr., Rotary Club, 1971, Athens Woman's Club, 1971; recipient Silver Beaver award Boy Scouts Am., 1973, Inspiration award Athens Cmty. Coun. on Aging, 1990, Advt. Silver medal Am. Advt. Fedn., Liberty Bell award Athens Bar Assn., 1977, Robert Stolz medaille, 1973, Nat. DAR medal of Hon., 1983, Cert. of Merit United Daus. of the Confederacy, 1983, Disting. Citizen award Ga. Dept. Labor, 1994, George Washington Patriotic Achievement award Soc. of Cin. in the State of Ga., 1996, Outstanding Ga. Citizen Sec. of State, 1997, Gov.'s Outstanding Svc. award, 1997, Key to City, Athens/Clarke County, 1997; Paul Harris fellow, 1978, Will Watt fellow, 1984, Hue Thomas fellow, 1989, James E. West fellow, 1999; H. Randolph Holder Day proclaimed by the City of Athens, 1989, 98; named hon. admiral Navy Supply Corps, 1998, Key to Athens/Clarke, 1998, hon. col. R.I. Militia, 1998. Mem. Res. Officers Assn. (life, pres. Athens chpt. 1962), Am. Ex-Prisoners War (life), Ga. Assn. Broadcaster (pres. 1961), Athens Area C. of C. (pres. 1970), Ga. AP Broadcasters (pres. 1963), Augustana Coll. Alumni Assn. (bd. dirs. 1973-76, Outstanding Achievement award 1973), Golden Quill, Gridiron, Sigma Delta Chi, Alpha Psi Omega, Alpha Delta Sigma, Pi Gamma Kappa (Ga. Pioneer Broadcaster of Yr. award 1971, 91, Lamplighter award 1993), Phi Omega Phi (pres. 1938-39), Touchdown Club (pres. Athens club 1963-64), Rotary (pres. Athens club 1957-58, govt. dist. 692 1969-70, Rotary internat. pub. rels. com. 1987-90, W. Lee Arrandale Vocat. Excellence award 1992). Home: 383 Westview Dr Athens GA 30606-4635 Office: Clarke Broadcasting Corp 850 Bobbin Mill Rd Athens GA 30606-4208

HOLDER, JUDITH ANNE, guidance counselor; b. Sycamore, Ill., July 12, 1940; d. William Albert and Ruth Margaret (Wiedenhoeft) Healey; m. Donald Herman Holder, June 11, 1966; children: Krista Marie, Jason Matthew. BS in Home Econs., Iowa State U., 1962; MS in Guidance & Counseling, No. Ill. U., 1972. Tchr. home econs. Milw. Pub. Schs., 1962-63; flight attendent United Air Lines, Chgo., 1963; tchr. home econs. Maine East High Sch., Park Ridge, Ill., 1964-66, John Muir Jr. High Sch., Prince George County, 1966-68; guidance counselor Rockford (Ill.) Bd. Edn., 1972—. Sustaining mem. Jr. League Rockford, 1971—; vol. mem. Winnebago County Med. Alliance, Rockford, 1971—, St. Anthony Hosp. Aux., Rockford, 1971—. Golden Apple nominee, Rockford, Ill., 1997, 98. Mem. Ill. Assn. Coll. Admission Counselors, No. Ill. Counselors Assn., U.S. Tennis Assn., U.S. Assn. Ballroom Dance, Pi Beta Phi (Rockford alumnae club). Avocations: tennis, internat. travel, golf, skiing, ballroom dancing. Home: 3235 Andover Dr Rockford IL 61114-5413 Office: Rockford Bd Edn 201 N Madison St Rockford IL 61107 also: Guilford HS 5620 Spring Creek Rd Rockford IL 61114-6442

HOLDER, KATHLEEN, elementary education educator; b. Peoria, Ill., Jan. 19, 1942; d. Clifford B. and Margaret Anne (Bowker) Bourne; m. James Sherman Holder, Dec. 29, 1962; children: Laurie Lynn, Cheryl Anne. BS, Bradley U., 1965; MEd, Regents Coll., 1981; postgrad., SUNY, Cortland, 1990-91. Cert. elem. tchr., Ky., N.Y., Ga., Ill., tchr. birth-6 yrs., Am. Montessori Soc. Tchr. St. Philomena Sch., Peoria, Ill., 1962-63, Garfield Sch., Danville, Ill., 1964-67, St. David's Sch., Willow Grove, Pa., 1972-74, St. Austin Sch., Mpls., 1974-75, Knoxville (Tenn.) City Schs., 1977-79, Chenango Forks (N.Y.) Schs., 1985-92, Fayette County Schs., Lexington, Ky., 1992-96, Glynn County Schs., Brunswick, Ga., 1996-98; substitute tchr. Cedar Rapids, Iowa, 1999—; team coord. sci. impact project SUNY, Cortland, 1987-90, presenter tchrs. teaching tchrs., 1988, sci. insvc. workshops for tchrs. Fayette County Schs., 1994-96; team coord. Broome Tioga Boces Coop. Regional Curriculum Devel. Project. Author: Science Curriculum Resource Guide K-3, 1989. Hoyt Found. grantee, 1988. Mem. Nat. Reading Assn., Knoxville Reading Assn. (treas. 1978-79), Delta Zeta (Sec. 1977-79, Rose of Honor 1979), Sigma Alpha Iota. Lutheran. Avocations: singing, gardening, cooking, reading. Home: 500 Huntington Ridge Rd NE Cedar Rapids IA 52402-7304

HOLDER, LEE, educator and university dean emeritus; b. Upland, Calif., Jan. 19, 1932; s. Lee Newcomer and Mattie Beatrice (Richards) H.; m. Charlotte Rosa LaVars, Feb. 15, 1954; children: Lee Kurt, Liese Anne, Lawrence Keith, Lon Karl, Laurie Kristin. B.S., U. Calif.-Berkeley, 1953, M.P.H., 1958; postgrad., U. Wyo., 1961-63; Ph.D., U. Mich., 1968. With Oakland (Calif.) City Health Dept., 1956-57; dir. health edn. Monterey County (Calif.) Health Dept., 1958-59; asst. dir. health edn. Wyo. Health Dept., 1959-63; dir. community action studies project Nat. Commn. on Community Health Services; assoc. pub. health adminstrn. Johns Hopkins, 1963-66; assoc. prof. U. N.C., Sch. Pub. Health; dir. Planning and Evaluation Regional Med. Program N.C., 1968-71; dean coll. allied health professions, prof. cmty. medicine U. Tenn., Memphis, 1972-82; prof. health edn., adj. prof. health adminstrn. U. Okla., Oklahoma City, 1982-96; pres. Allied Health Internat., Inc., 1998—; adj. prof. polit. sci. Memphis State U., 1972-82; Cons. in health planning, Toledo, Idaho Falls, Idaho, Franklin, N.C.; cons. Gov.'s Task Force on Health, W.Va.; Chmn. Area-wide Council on Aging, 1974-76, Memphis Area Vocat. Tech. Edn. Coordinating Com., 1973-74; manpower cons. Nat. Assn. Partners of Ams., Caracas, Venezuela, 1976-82, Jordanian Royal Med. Services, Amman, 1977, U. Riyadh, Saudi Arabia, 1980-86; mem. Health Systems Agy. Contbr. articles to profl. jours. Chmn. Cmty. Planning Coun., Okla. Health Careers Coun., 1992-95; bd. dirs. Memphis United Way, United Health Svc. N.C., Vis. Nurses Assn. Memphis; past pres. Vol. Ctr. Memphis; pres. Okla. Ptnrs. of Ams., 1985-86; bd. dirs., 1st v.p. Okla. Alliance on aging, 1996—; bd. dirs. Areawide Aging Agy., 1997—, Okla. Pilot's Assn., 1997—. Col. AUS, ret.; with USAREUR 1954-55. Fellow Am. Pub. Health Assn., Soc. Pub. Health Educators, Royal Soc. Health, Am. Soc. Allied Health Professions (pres. 1979-80, dir., editorial bd. Jour. Allied Health 1973-80); mem. Council Edni. Instns. (chmn. 1976), Res. Officers Assn., Am. Legion, Mil. Order World Wars, VFW, SAR, Odd Fellow Club, Kiwanis (bd. dirs. 1998—), Phi Kappa Phi, Delta Omega, Alpha Eta (pres. 1978, 92-93). Home: 8674 N May Ave Oklahoma City OK 73120-4469 Office: 801 NE 13th St Oklahoma City OK 73104-5005

HOLDER, MIKE, coach; b. Odessa, Tex., Aug. 17, 1946; s. Burniss and Virginia Holder; m. Robbie Annette Yeates; 1 child, Michele. BS in mktg., Okla. State Univ., 1970, MBA, 1973. Head golf coach Okla. State Univ., 1974—. Office: Oklahoma State Univ 424 S Squires St Ste 200 Stillwater OK 74078-0300*

HOLDER, NEVILLE LEWIS, chemist; b. St. Joseph, Barbados, May 28, 1940; came to U.S., 1968, permanent resident, 1982; s. Cardon Elliot and Viola (Brathwaite) Tudor; m. Hyacinth Isoline Swaby, Sept. 4, 1965; children: Louis, Nadine, Nicole. BS with honors, U. West Indies, 1965, MS, 1969; PhD, U. Waterloo, 1973. Chemist Gillette Rsch. Inst., Rockville, Md., 1968-69, rsch. chemist, 1973-78; assoc. sr. investigator SmithKline Beecham Pharms., King of Prussia, Pa., 1978-92; sr. rsch. scientist Rhone-Poulenc Rorer Pharms., Collegeville, Pa., 1992-98, rsch. fellow, 1998—. Mem. editl. bd. Jour. Organic Chemistry, Carbohydrate Chemistry; contbr. more than 40 articles to profl. jours.; patentee in field. Mem. com. Boy Scouts Am., Cherry Hill, N.J., 1980-90. Recipient Barbadian Am. Alliance Accomplishment award, 1991; grad. scholar U. W.I., 1968-68, Ministry Edn. Bursary, Barbados Govt., 1961-64. Mem. Am. Chem. Soc., Nat. Orgn. Profl. Advancement Black Chemists & Chem. Engrs. (facilities chair Sci. Bowl Del. Valley chpt. 1990-98, scholarship & edn. coms. 1995—, v.p. 1996, v.p. Delaware Valley chpt. 1997-98, pres. Del. Valley chpt. 1998—, Corp. Liason award 1991), Phila. Organic Chemist Club, Toastmasters Internat. (charter, sergeant at arms 1990-91, treas. 1991-92, v.p. membership 1992, Compotent Toastmaster award 1989, Able Toastmaster award 1997). Episcopalian. Achievements include research in isolation and structure elucidation of natural products from the Jamaican cedar plant, synthesis of carbohydrate enones and their photochemical transformation to branched-chain monosaccharides, organic synthesis of drug substances, intermediates, isomers and potential impurities, chromatographic isolation and structure elucidation of impurities and decomposition products of drug substances and their synthetic intermediates, application of preparative HPLC using chiral and achiral stationary phases. Home: 13 Clemson Rd Cherry Hill NJ 08034-1213 Office: Rhone Poulenc Rorer Pharms 500 Arcola Rd Collegeville PA 19426-3930

HOLDER, RICHARD GIBSON, retired metal products executive; b. Paris, TN. BA, Vanderbilt U., 1953. With Reynolds Metals Co., Richmond, Va., 1953—, various mgmt. positions, 1953-78, v.p., gen. mgr. flexible packaging divsn., 1978-80, v.p., gen. mgr. flexible packaging & consumer products divsn., 1980-83, v.p. mill products divsn., 1983-84, exec. v.p., fabricating ops., 1984-86, exec. v.p., COO, 1986-88, pres., COO, 1988-92, chmn., CEO, 1992-96, also bd. dirs., 1996; bd. dirs. CPC Internat., Inc., Englewood Cliffs, N.J., Universal Corp., Richmond, Va.

HOLDER, SALLIE LOU, training and meeting management consultant; b. Cin., Jan. 25, 1939; d. David Clifford Austin and Ruth Margaret (Higby) Haver; m. Norman Horace Derwyn Holder, July 14, 1964 (div. Oct. 1975). Student, Duke U., 1957-59; BS in Home Econs. Edn., U. Md, 1962; MA in Human Resource Devel. and Edn., George Washington U., 1982. Tchr. Prince Georges County Schs., Md., 1962-66; home econs. tchr. La Reine Sr. High Sch., Suitland, Md., 1966-68; adult edn. Home econs. tchr. Suitland Sr. High Sch, 1969-73; mgr./asst. area sales mgr. The Fabric Tree, Hyattsville, Md., 1972-75; trainer Woodward & Lothrop, Washington and Prince Georges County, Md., 1975-79; conf. coord., non-credit short course coord. Univ. Coll. U. Md., College Park, 1979-87; analyst SYSCON, Washington, 1987-88; meeting mgmt. and tng. cons. Holder & Assocs., College Park, Md., 1988—; tng. specialist Fed. Deposit Ins. Corp., Washington, 1990; instr. Marymount U., Arlington, Va., 1990, Goucher Coll., Balt., 1991-93; facilitator New Beginnings, Takoma Park, Md., 1983-90, chmn. planning com., facilitator co-trainer, bd. dirs., 1983-84, chmn. facilitators, 1985-86. Mem. alumni bd. Coll. Human Ecology, U. Md., College Park, 1971-93, pres., 1973-74, 77-80, sec., 1985-86, v.p., 1988-90; bd. dirs., mem., cons. lay edn. com., cmty. edn. com. Pastoral Counseling and Consultation Ctrs., 1977-86; mem. seminarian com., search com., chmn. retreat com., vestry mem. Ch. of the Nativity, Camp Springs, Md., 1977-82; vestryman St. Andrews Episc. Ch., College Park, 1990-93, mem. Fisherfolk, 1993—, region 5 rep., 1997—, pledge sec., 1997—. Recipient Disting. Svc. award Alumni Bd. of Coll. Human Ecology, U. Md., 1981, Vol. award, 1991. Mem. ASTD (Washington chpt. employer coord. 1984-85, co-chmn. program com. 1986, chmn. meeting arrangements 1987-88, treas. 1989, ASTD day chmn., nat. issues chair 1990, chair scholarship com. 1992, coord. spl. interest group 1993, Spl. Achievement award 1987, 88, 90, Pres.'s award 1993), Soc. Govt. Meeting Planners (program commn. 1987-88, communication com., ann. conf. com. 1988-89, chmn. nominating com. 1990, ann. conf. presenter 1990, 93, 94, 98, bd. dirs. 1991-92, 95-97, chmn. edn. com. for 1992 ann. conf. 1995-97, newsletter editor), U. Md. Coll. Park Alumni Assn. (bd. govs. 1989-93), Assn. Meeting Profls., Profl. Conv. Mgrs. Assn., Md. Prince Georges Alumni assn. (v.p. 1994—), Coll. Park Bus. and Profl. Women, Women Bus. Owners Prince Georges County, Bus. Network Internat., Delmarva Depression Glass Club, Washington Met. Glass Club, Prince Georges Hist. Soc. Episcopalian. Home and Office: 9715 48th Pl College Park MD 20740-1404

HOLDER, TRUDY H., accounting director; b. Durham, N.C., June 3, 1965; d. Robert Lee and Patricia Ann (McLaurin) Hurt; m. Barry Lynn Holder, Sept. 24, 1983; children: Andrew Aaron, Alexander Rex. From mgr. acctg. to corp. controller Technology Planning & Mgmt. Corp., Durham, 1990-97; govt. contract acctg. mgr. to dir., div. acctg. Strategic Resource Solution, Cary, N.C., 1997—. Mem. Inst. Mgmt. Cons., Rsch. Triangle Park Deltek User's Group. Democrat. Baptist. Avocations: reading, outdoor sports, gardening.

HOLDERMAN, JAMES F., JR., federal judge; b. 1946. BS, U. Ill., 1968, JD, 1971. Judge U.S. Dist. Ct. (no. dist.) Ill., Chgo., 1985—; asst. U.S. atty. City of Chgo., 1972-78; ptnr. Sonnenschein, Carlin et al, Chgo., 1978-85; lectr. law U. Chgo., 1983—. Office: US Dist Ct US Courthouse 219 S Dearborn St Ste 2146 Chicago IL 60604-1801

HOLDERNESS, ALGERNON SIDNEY, JR., lawyer; b. Wilmington, Del., Mar. 31, 1938; s. Algernon Sidney and Mary Elizabeth (Crockett) H.; div.; children: Claire Crockett, Julia Simms. BA magna cum laude, Yale U., 1959, LLB cum laude, 1962. Bar: N.Y. Bar 1964, U.S. Dist. Ct. (so. and ea. dists.) N.Y. 1966, U.S. Ct. Appeals (2d cir.) 1966. Law clk. U.S. Ct. Appeals (2d cir.), 1962-63; asso. firm Milbank, Tweed, Hadley & McCloy, N.Y.C., 1964-72; ptnr. Milbank, Tweed, Hadley & McCloy, 1973-93, Andrews & Kurth L.L.P., Houston, 1994—. Author: (with others) N.Y. and Delaware Business Entities, 1997; editor: (with B. Wunnicke) Legal Opinion Letters Formbook, 1994; mem. bd. editors Yale Law Jour., 1960-62. Chmn. bd. mgrs. Bklyn. Cen. br. YMCA Greater N.Y., 1980-85, mem. exec. com. bd. dirs., 1982-95, chmn. exec. com. 1988-90; bd. govs. Bklyn. Heights Assn., 1979-88; mem. N.E. regional bd. YMCA of U.S.A., 1982-83, mem. east field com., 1983—, mem. nat. bd., 1984-89, exec. com., 1985-89. Mem. ABA (bus. law sect. legal opinion com., meetings com.), N.Y. State Bar Assn., Assn. of Bar of City of N.Y., Am. Coll. Investment Counsel (past trustee, pres. 1989-90), Am. Law Inst., N.Y. County Lawyers Assn. (Tri-Bar opinion com.), Downtown Assn., Yale Club (N.Y.C.), Grads. Club (New Haven), Order of Coif, Phi Beta Kappa. Office: Andrews & Kurth LLP 600 Travis St Ste 4200 Houston TX 77002-2910*

HOLDERNESS, SUSAN RUTHERFORD, at-risk educator; b. Cherokee, Iowa, Nov. 5, 1941; d. Parker William and Ruth Elvera (Peterson) Rutherford; m. Michael Aaron Holderness, Aug. 12, 1961; children: Lauren, Lisa, Jennifer, Joshua. BA in Edn., Wayne State U., Nebr., 1964; student, Iowa State U., 1960-61, Vocat. Cert., 1973. Tchr. various high schs. including Norwalk (Iowa) High Sch., 1968-78; tchr. South Alternative and East H.S., Des Moines, 1968-78; hist. site interpreter Salisbury House, Des Moines, 1971-78, 84-88, Minn. State Hist. Soc., St. Paul, 1978-84; cons. Profl. Match Cons., Des Moines, 1985-90; tour guide and conv. planner Des Moines Tour and Conv. Svcs., 1987-92; also dir. Christian edn. Douglas Ave. Presbyn. Ch., Des Moines; founding. mem. faculty Walnut Creek Campus H.S., 1995—; owner gourmet food shop, 1973. V.p. fundraising Des Moines Symphony Guild, 1990-92; bd. dirs., treas., sec. playground bldg. project Greenwood Sch. PTA, Des Moines, 1986-89; co-chmn. Civic Music Assn., Des Moines, 1987; pres., v.p., tour dir. St. Paul New Residents, 1980-83, others in past; bd. dirs. Ramsey County Friends of the Libr., 1981-83, Symphony Assn., mem., steering com. showhouse and ball, fundraising v.p.; with Des Moines Hist. Dist. Commn., 1998—. Mem. Iowa Victorian Soc., Compass Club (internat. pres. 1986-87), Internat. Platform Assn., Kappa Delta Pi, Gamma Phi Beta. Republican. Presbyterian. Avocations: tennis, water sports, gourmet cooking, volunteer work, art and theater. Office: Walnut Creek Campus 1101 5th St West Des Moines IA 50265-2608

HOLDING, LEWIS R., banker; b. 1927; married. B.S., U. N.C.; M.B.A., Harvard U. With First Citizens Bank & Trust Co., Raleigh, N.C., 1953—, former pres., chmn., dir., CEO, 1979—. Served with USAF, 1952-53. Office: First Citizens Banc Shares Inc PO Box 29549 Raleigh NC 27626-0549 also: 1st Citizens Bancshares Inc 20 E Martin St Raleigh NC 27601-1842*

HOLDING, R. EARL, oil company executive. Pres. Sinclair Oil Corp., Salt Lake City, bd. dirs., now CEO. Office: Sinclair Oil Corp 550 E South Temple Salt Lake City UT 84102-1098*

HOLDITCH, WILLIAM KENNETH, American literature educator; b. Ecru, Miss., Sept. 18, 1933; s. Sidney Wiliamson and Dora Faye (Dickerson) H. BA with honors, Southwestern at Memphis, 1955; MA in English, U. Miss., 1957, PhD in English, 1961. Instr. Am. lit. U. Miss., Oxford, 1957-59; asst. prof. U. New Orleans, 1964-69, assoc. prof., 1969-78, prof., 1978-90, rsch. prof., 1990-96, rsch. prof. emeritus, 1996—; bd. dirs. Tennessee Williams Festival, New Orleans, 1986-97, v.p., 1987—. Author numerous essays and short stories; editor: In Old New Orleans, 1983, The Tennessee Williams Journal, 1989—; co-editor: (with Mel Gussow) Two Tennessee Williams Volumes, Library of America; adv. editor: South Central Journal, 1990-93. Pres. Friends of U. New Orleans Libr., 1990-94; founder, bd. dirs. Pirate's Alley Faulkner Soc.; advisor Clarksdale Tennessee Wiliams Festival, 1992—. Named La. U. Tchr. of Yr. Amoco, 1980. Mem. MLA, South Cen. MLA. Avocations: walking, reading, collecting glass. Home: 732 Frenchmen St New Orleans LA 70116-1614 Office: U New Orleans Lakefront New Orleans LA 70148

HOLDREN, JOHN PAUL, energy and resource educator, researcher, author, consultant; b. Sewickley, Pa., Mar. 1, 1944; s. Raymond Andrew and Virginia June (Fuqua) H.; m. Cheryl Edgar, Feb. 5, 1966; children—John Craig, Jill Virginia. SB, MIT, 1965, SM, 1966; PhD, Stanford U., 1970; ScD (hon.), U. Puget Sound, 1975. Aerodyn. engr. Lockheed Missiles & Space Co., Sunnyvale, Calif., 1966-67; theoretical physicist Lawrence Livermore Lab., Calif., 1970-71; sr. research fellow Calif. Inst. Tech., Pasadena, 1972-73; asst. prof. energy and resources U. Calif.-Berkeley, 1973-75, assoc. prof. energy and resources, 1975-78, prof. energy and resources, 1978-96, Class of 1935 prof. energy, 1991-96, chmn. energy and resources, 1983-84; Teresa and John Heinz prof. environ. policy Harvard U., Cambridge, Mass., 1996—; dir. sci. tech. and pub. policy prog. Harvard U., Cambridge; cons. in fusion energy Lawrence Livermore Labs., 1974—; sr. investigator Rocky Mountain Biol. Lab., Crested Butte, Colo., 1974-88; vis. fellow East-West Ctr., Honolulu, 1979-80, Max-Planck-Gesellschaft, Starnberg, Fed. Republic Germany, 1987; vis. fellow arms control program MIT, 1988; vis. prof. physics U. Rome tor Vergata, 1987; vis. scientist Woods Hole Rsch. Ctr., 1992—; mem. Fusion Energy adv. com. Sec. of Energy, 1991-94. Co-editor: Man and the Ecosphere, 1971, Strategic Defences, 1987, The Cassandra Conference, 1988; co-author: Energy, 1971, Human Ecology, 1973, Ecoscience, 1977; co-editor: Earth and the Human Future, 1986; bd. editors Bull. of Atomic Scientists, Chgo., 1984-86. Mem. exec. com. Pugwash Confs. on Sci. and World Affairs, London and Geneva, 1982—, chmn., 1987—; chmn. U.S. Pugwash Com., Cambridge, Mass., 1983-95; mem. coun. Smithsonian Instn., 1988-91; bd. dirs. McArthur Found., 1991—; mem. Pres.'s Com. Advisors on Sci. and Tech., 1994—. Recipient Gustavsen lectureship U. Chgo., 1978; MacArthur Prize fellow MacArthur Found., Chgo., 1981-86; recipient Volvo Environ. Prize, 1993. Fellow AAAS, Am. Acad. Arts and Scis. (vice chmn. com. on internat. security 1983—, Kistiakowsky Meml. Lectureship 1986-87), Calif. Acad. Scis.; mem. NAS (com. internat. security and arms control 1992—, chmn. 1993—), Fedn. Am. Scientists (council, treas. 1979-80, vice chmn. 1981-84, chmn. 1984-86, bd. sponsors, 1986—, Pub. Service award 1979), Am. Phys. Soc. (Forum award 1995). Democrat. Office: Harvard U Kennedy Sch Govt Ctr Sci & Internat Affairs 79 JFK St Cambridge MA 02138-5801

HOLDREN, MURRAY F., municipal official; b. Mar. 18, 1931. Student, Bloomsburg U., 1948-95. Plant mgr. Pfaff & Kendall, Newark, 1960-71, Tire Kingdom, Phila., 1972-77; sec.-treas. Boro of Millville, Pa., 1991—. E-mail: murray1@postoffice.ptd.net. Home: 601 Old Berwick Rd Bloomsburg PA 17815

HOLDRIDGE, BARBARA, book publisher; b. N.Y.C., July 26, 1929; d. Herbert L. and Bertha (Gold) Cohen; m. Lawrence B. Holdridge, Oct. 9, 1959; 2 children. A.B., Hunter Coll., 1950. Asst. editor Liveright Pub. Corp., N.Y.C., 1950-52; co-founder Caedmon Records, Inc., N.Y.C., 1952; partner Caedmon Records, Inc., 1952-60, pres., 1960-62, treas., 1962-70, pres., 1970-75; founder Stemmer House Pubs. Inc., Owings Mills, Md., 1975; pres. Stemmer House Pubs. Inc., 1975—; co-founder, v.p. Shakespeare Rec. So., Inc., N.Y.C., 1960-70, Theatre Rec. Soc., Inc., N.Y.C., 1964-70; founder BEDE Prodns., 1984; co-founder History Rec. Soc., Inc., N.Y.C., 1964, pres., 1964-70; lectr. on Ammi Phillips, 1959; lectr. on book pub., 1992—; adj. prof. writing media Loyola Coll., Balt., 1987-91. Author: Ammi Phillips, 1968, Aubrey Beardsley Designs from the Age of Chivalry, 1983, Chinese Cut-Out Designs of Costumes, 1989; articles on Am. paintings. Recipient Am. Shakespeare Festival award, 1962, N.Y.C. certificate appreciation, 1972; named to Hunter Coll. Hall of Fame, 1972. Mem. 14 West Hamilton Street Club, Phi Beta Kappa Assn. of Greater Balt. (bd. dirs.). Office: 2627 Caves Rd Owings Mills MD 21117-2919

HOLDSWORTH, JOHN H., marketing professional; b. Hampton, Eng., Dec. 16, 1949. Student, U. London. With British Airways: sr. v.p. mktg. Utell Internat.; pres., COO Anasazi Travel Resources, Inc., 1992; exec. v.p. global accounts REZsolutions, Inc., Phoenix. Avocations: family, golf, football, baseball. Office: REZsolutions Inc 7500 N Dreamy Draw Dr #120 Phoenix AZ 85020

HOLDSWORTH, RAY W., architectural firm executive. Chmn., CEO Daniel Mann Johnson Mendenhall, L.A., 1989—. Office: Daniel Mann Johnson Mendenhall 3250 Wilshire Blvd Fl 4 Los Angeles CA 90010-1577*

HOLE, RICHARD DOUGLAS, lawyer; b. Auburn, N.Y., Aug. 23, 1949; s. Robert B. and Barbara (Swift) H.; m. Deborah Elizabeth Muldoon, Jan. 8, 1972; children: Emily, Brian, Jeffrey. BA, Hamilton Coll., 1971; JD, Syracuse (N.Y.) U., 1975. Bar: N.Y. 1976, U.S. Dist. Ct. (no. dist.) N.Y. 1976, U.S. Dist. Ct. (we. dist.) N.Y. 1980. Assoc. Bond, Schoeneck & King, Syracuse, 1976-83, ptnr., 1984—; pres. N.Y. Employee Benefits Conf., Rochester, 1987-88. Pres. Fayetteville-Manlius (N.Y.) Little League, Inc., 1988-93; pres. Eye Rsch. Inst. of Ctrl. N.Y., Syracuse, 1988-93; bd. dirs. Cystic Fibrosis Found., Syracuse, 1988-93; pres., bd. trustees United Ch. of Fayetteville, 1990-95, 98—; bd. dirs. Syracuse Symphony, 1995—. Mem. N.Y. State Bar Assn., Onondaga County Bar Assn., Nat. Assn. Coll. and Univ. Attys. Republican. Presbyterian. Office: Bond Schoeneck & King 18th Fl One Lincoln Ctr Syracuse NY 13202

HOLEC, ANITA KATHRYN VAN TASSEL, civic worker; b. Rahway, N.J., Nov. 11, 1947; d. Edward T. and Irene Eleanor (Barna) Van Tassel; m. Sidney W. Holec, Oct. 26, 1968. BS, U. Houston, 1969. Stockbroker Drexel Burnham Lambert, Inc., Miami, Fla., 1976-78, Merrill Lynch, Venice, Fla., 1979-80; fin. cons. Shearson Lehman Bros., Venice, 1981-87; owner, mgr. Closet Stretchers, Venice, 1987-89. Bd. dirs. Safe Place and Rape Crisis Ctr., Sarasota, 1987—, Womens Resource Ctr., Sarasota, 1981-86, 90-94, Friends Venice Libr., 1992-94, New Coll. Libr., 1991-94; mem. Leadership Sarasota, 1991-95, Jr. League of Sarasota, 1982—, Argus Found., 1982—. Avocations: reading, feminism. Home: 1708 Casey Key Rd Nokomis FL 34275-3370

HOLEY, BRETT ALLEN, television director, producer; b. Toledo, Aug. 31, 1960; s. Richard Allen and Ellen May (Long) H. BA, Cen. Mich. U., 1982. Prodn. asst. ABC News, N.Y.C., 1982-85; freelance dir., producer N.Y., 1982—; graphics producer ABC News Spl. Events, N.Y.C., 1987-88; producer, assoc. dir. ABC News, N.Y.C., 1988—. Recipient Emmy for Graphic Design for Primetime Live, 1990. Mem. NATAS, Internat. Radio & TV Soc., Alpha Epsilon Rho. Avocations: running, painting, photography, triathlons, writing. Home: 227 E 25th St New York NY 10010-3037 Office: ABC News 47 W 66th St Rm 800 New York NY 10023-6290

HOLFELD, DONALD RAE, railroad consultant; b. Lestock, Sask., Can., Apr. 10, 1947; came to the U.S., 1994; s. Alexander R. and Edith (Schwab) H.; m. Patricia Elizabeth Sewell, July 16, 1994. BS, U. Alta., 1973. Registered profl. engr. Assn. Profl. Engrs. B.C. Maintenance engr. CN Rail, Kamloops, B.C., 1977-80; track and roadway engr. CN Rail, Kamloops, 1980-81; planning engr. CN Rail, Montreal, 1981-82, track rsch. engr., 1982-83, sys. engr. tech., 1983-89, sys. dir. ops. tng., 1989-94; dir. tng. and engring. Zeta-Tech. Assocs., Inc., Cherry Hill, N.J., 1994—; aux. prof. McGill U., Montreal, 1988-94; lectr. in field. Inventor in field. Recipient Golden Spike awards Internat. Rwy. Tng. Assn., 1989-94. Mem. ASTD. Avocations: singing, jogging, travelling, reading, cooking. Office: Zeta-Tech Assocs Inc 900 Kings Hwy N Ste 208 Cherry Hill NJ 08034-1516

HOLFELDER, LAWRENCE ANDREW, pediatrician, allergist; b. Bklyn., June 7, 1939. MD, Albany Med. Coll., 1965. Diplomate Am. Bd. Pediats., Am. Bd. Allergy and Immunology. Intern St. Vincent's Med. Ctr., N.Y.C., 1965-66, resident, 1966-68, fellow in allergy and immunology, 1972; fellow in allergy and immunology U. Chgo. Hosps., 1970-71; now pvt. practice Tampa, Fla.; mem. staff St. Joseph's Hosp., Tampa; clin. prof. pediats. in allergy U. So. Fla. Mem. Am. Acad. Allergy and Immunology. Office: Harrelson Med Arts Bldg 3709 W Hamilton Ave Ste 1 Tampa FL 33614-4015

HOLGERS-AWANA, RITA MARIE, electrodiagnosis specialist; b. Chgo., Nov. 24, 1933; d. Joseph Theodore and Kathleen (Cooney) Konecny; m. Alan Miles Holgers, Aug. 8, 1960 (div. Sept. 1986); children: Dale, Ross; m. Benedict E.C. Awana, June 13, 1989 (dec. Feb. 1995). BS, N.Am. U., 1984, M of Nutripathic Sci., 1988, D of Nutripathy, 1988, PhD in Nutritional Philosophy, 1990. Nutritional cons. Vitality Testing, Phoenix, 1982-84; pres., CEO Vitality Testing, Glendale, Ariz., 1984-86, Zac Engring. Inc., Lombard, Ill., 1986—; credentials coord. Prin. Health Care, Oakbrook Terrace, Ill., 1995-98; spkr. women's coffee break group Harvard Ave. Free Evangelical Ch., 1997-98; spkr. Dowser's Club, 1997-98, spkr. in field; cons. Ubid, Inc., 1999—. Author: Me and My Non-Disease, 1983, Radiation, The Hidden Enemy, 1995; invention electronic water filter unit. Pres., v.p. S.W. Herbal Edn. Assn., Phoenix, 1984-85; sec. Better Breathers Club, Chula Vista, Calif., 1992-93, Concerned Citizens, Biggsville, Ill., 1975; co-founder, charter mem. Exec. Women's Coun., Moline, Ill., 1974; cub scout den leader Boy Scouts Am., Eldridge, Iowa, 1973; treas. food coop., Asuncion, Paraguay, 1958. With U.S. Fgn. Svc., 1956-61. Recipient Internat. Championship Golf Trophy, U.S. Dept. of State, 1959, Championship Golf trophy Hend-Co-Hills, 1974, 75, 77, Tai Chi Black Belt, Shingumatsu Martial Arts, 1993; named Woman of the Year, Internat. Biog. Ctr., Cambridge, Eng., 1998. Mem. Women in the Arts, Nat. Health Fedn., The Am. Dowsers Soc. (v.p. 1999), Computrek Computer Club, N.Am. Dowser's Club, Northern Ill. Am. Soc. Dowsers. Mem. Unity Ch. Avocations: golf, bowling, knitting, computer, martial arts. E-mail: docradrita@aol.com. Home and Office: Apt E 239 S Westmore Ave Lombard IL 60148-3066

HOLIDAY, EDITH ELIZABETH, former presidential adviser, cabinet secretary; b. Middletown, Ohio, Feb. 14, 1952; d. Harry Jr. and Kathlyn (Watson) H.; m. Terrence B. Adamson, June 8, 1985; children: Kathlyn Holiday Adamson, Elizabeth Holiday Adamson; 1 stepchild, Terrence Morgan Adamson. Student, Miami U., Oxford, Ohio, 1970-71; BS with honors, U. Fla., 1974, JD, 1977. Bar: Fla. 1977, D.C. 1978, Ga. 1984. Assoc. Read Smith Shaw & McClay, Washington, 1977-83, Dow Lohnes & Albertson, Atlanta, 1983-84; exec. dir. Commn. on Exec. Legis. and Jud. Salaries, Washington, 1984-85; spl. counsel polit. action com. Fund for Am. Future, Washington, 1985-87; dir. ops. George Bush for Pres., Inc., Washington, 1987-88; chief counsel, nat. fin. and ops. dir. Bush-Quayle 88, Washington, 1988; with legal svcs. staff George Bush for Pres. Compliance Com., Washington, 1988; asst. sec. for pub. affairs and pub. liaison, counselor to sec. Departmental Offices, U.S. Dept. Treasury, Washington, 1988; gen. counsel U.S. Dept. Treasury, Washington, 1989-90; asst. to U.S. pres., sec. of cabinet Washington, 1990-93; legis. asst. to U.S. Sen. Nicholas F. Brady, Washington, 1982-83; bd. dirs. Amerada Hess Corp., H.J. Heinz Co., Hercules, Inc., Bessemer Trust Co., N.A., 1993-96, Bessemer Trust Co. of N.J., 1993-96, Beverly Enterprises, Inc., Franklin Templeton Group Funds. Recipient Alexander Hamilton award Sec. of Treasury, 1991, spl. citation John Marshall Bar Assn. Mem. Phi Delta Phi, Kappa Tau Alpha.

HOLIK, BOBBY, professional hockey player; b. Jihlava, Czech Republic, Jan. 1, 1971. Left wing Hartford Whalers, 1989-92, New Jersey Devils, 1992—. Winner bronze medal with Czech Nat. Jr. team in 1990 World Championships; played in 1991 world Championships. Office: New Jersey Devils Continental Airlines Arena PO Box 504 East Rutherford NJ 07073-0504*

HOLL, JAMES ANDREW, prehospital care administrator; b. Jersey City, Sept. 15, 1961; s. Charles J. Jr. and Alice M. (Kearney) H. Cert. paramedic, N.J. Coll. Dentistry/Medicine, 1981; AS in Nursing, Atlantic C.C., 1986; BA in Nursing Mgmt., Stockton State Coll., 1991; postgrad. flight nurse prog., USAF Sch. Aerospace Medicine, 1993. Cert. emergency nurse, flight nurse. Firefighter, EMT instr., med. coord. Brigantine (N.J.) Fire Dept., 1979—, firefighter, instr. dep. coord emergency mgmt., 1987—; paramedic mobile intensive care West Jersey Health System, 1982-83, Underwood Meml. Hosp, 1980—; forensic med. investigator Atlantic County Med. Examiners Office, 1982-86; nurse dept. intensive care, emergency Shore Meml. Hosp., 1986-97. Mem. 714th Aeromed. Squad USAF, 1991—. Decorated USAF Commendation medal, 1997; recipient citation Senator Dan Dalton. Mem. Nat. Flight Nurses Assn., Nat. Registry Emergency Med. Technicians, N.J. State Emergency Med. Technician Instrs., Emergency Nurses Assn., Emergency Med. Svcs. Physicians Assn. (assoc.), Internat. Assn. Firefighters, Atlantic County Firefighters Assn. Office: 1417 W Brigantine Ave Brigantine NJ 08203-2147

HOLL, JOHN WILLIAM, engineering educator; b. Danville, Ill., Feb. 20, 1928; s. William Benjamin and Anna Marie (Waldo) H.; m. Antoinette Fillhouer, Aug. 20, 1950; children—Jessica, Vanessa, Melissa, Cassandra, Alyssa, Nathan, Zachary. BS in M.E. U. Ill., 1949, MS in M.E. 1951; PhD in M.E. Pa. State U., 1958, B of Music, 1996. Rsch. asst. in mech. engring. Engring. Experiment Sta. U. Ill., Urbana, 1949-51; rsch. assoc. Applied Rsch. Lab. Pa. State U., 1951-54, 56-58, asst. prof. engring. rsch., 1958-59, asso. prof. aerospace engring., 1963-67, prof., 1967-91, prof. emeritus, 1991—; asso. prof. mech. engring. U. Nebr., Lincoln, 1959-63; cons. in field. Mem. Lincoln Symphony Orch., 1960-63; mem. Nittany Valley Symphony Orch., State College, Pa., 1969—, State Coll. Mcpl. Band, 1977—; Trustee Unitarian Ch., Lincoln, 1961-62. Served with U.S. Army, 1955-56. Fellow ASME (R.T. Knapp award 1970, 91, Melville medal 1970, Centennial medallion 1980, dedicated service award 1985); assoc. fellow AIAA; mem. Internat. Clarinet Assn., Amateur Chamber Music Players, Sigma Xi, Phi Mu Alpha Sinfonia. Home: 1108 Mayberry Ln State College PA 16801-6952 Office: Pa State U Aerospace Engring University Park PA 16802

HOLL, WALTER JOHN, architect, interior designer; b. Richardton, N.D., May 14, 1922; s. John and Rose Mary Holl; m. Eleanor Mary Triervieler, Jan. 23, 1943; children: Mark Walter, Michael John, Randolph Gregory, Linda Michelle, Timothy James, John Walter. Student, Internat. Corr. Schs., 1946-47, 59, U. Nebr., 1976, Clarke Coll., 1981; student in photography, Clarke Coll., 1981. Licensed arch., Calif., interior designer, Ill.; cert. Nat. Coun. for Interior Design Qualifications. Steel detailer, estimator E.J. Voggenthaler Co., Dubuque, Iowa, 1941-42; engr., also methods developer Marinship Corp., Sausalito, Calif., 1942-44; ptnr. Holl & Everly, Dubuque, Iowa, 1946-47; prin. Holl Designing Co., also W. Holl & Assocs., Dubuque, San Francisco, 1947-87; prin. Walter J. Holl, Arch., Burlingame, Calif., 1987, 89, San Diego, Calif., 1989—, San Diego, 1989—; cons. Clarke Coll. Art Students, Dubuque, 1953-61; commd. arch., interior designer, constructor renovations and hist. preservation Dubuque County Courthouse, 1978-85; mem. convoy USCG Ofcl. Presdl. Security Patrol, 1979; oral exam commr. Calif. Bd. Archtl. Examiners, 1994—; cert. mem. Calif. State Office Emergency Svc.; participant The Brit. Coun.-Archs. Study Tour, Belfast, No. Ireland, 1995; juror Nat. Coun. for Interior Design Qualification, 1996, 98. Chmn. Dubuque Housing Rehab. Commn., 1976-77. With AUS, 1944-46, ETO. Decorated 2 bronze stars; recipient Nat. Bldg. Design awards, 1968, 69, 73, 94. Mem. AIA (bd. dirs. 1993—, pres.-elect north county sect. San Diego chpt. 1995, pres. 1996, bldg. codes and stds. com. San Diego chpt. 1998-99), USCG Aux. (comdr. 1975-78), Am. Soc. Interior Designers (profl.), Am. Arbitration Assn. (panel arbitrators), Inst. Bus. Designers (profl. Chgo. chpt.), Dubuque Golf and Country Club (bldg. commn. 1953-54), Julien Dubuque Yacht Club (commodore 1974-75), Mchts. and Mfrs. Club (Chgo.). Roman Catholic. Achievements include patent for castered pallet. Home and Office: Walter J Holl Architect Penthouse 126 11255 Tierrasanta Blvd San Diego CA 92124-2890

HOLLADAY, JAMES FRANKLIN, JR., minister; b. Meridian, Miss., May 23, 1951; s. James Franklin and Anne (Wedsworth) H.; m. Patricia Ann Martin, June 18, 1977; children: Meredith Anne, Emily Jean. BA, Samford U., 1973; MDiv, So. Bapt. Sem., Louisville, 1976, D Ministry, 1983. Ordained to ministry So. Bapt. Conv., 1976. Summer youth min. 1st Bapt. Ch., Chatsworth, Ga., 1972; campus min. Ky. Bapt. Conv., Middletown, 1974-76; program coord. East Bapt. Ch., Louisville, 1976-79, pastor, dir., 1979-92; pastor Clifton Bapt. Ch., Louisville, 1992—; bd. dirs. Office Ecumenical Affairs, Archdiocese of Louisville, 1985-91, 92-95; mem. pub. affairs com. Ky. Bapt. Conv., 1987-89, 93-94, adminstrn. com., 1996-97, exec. bd., 1994—, chair Missions & Evang. Commn., 1996-97. Chmn. Louisville Full Employment Task Force, 1976-78; sec. Kentuckiana Interfaith Comty. Louisville, 1979-80, v.p., 1980-81, pres., 1981-82, 94-96, bd. dirs. 1982—; mem. Kentuckiana Marriage Task Force, 1993-94; chmn. Hunger and Racial Justice Commn., treas., 1993-94; mem. Jefferson County Anti-Freeze Com., Louisville, 1980-81; pres. Phoenix Hill Assn., Louisville, 1981-83, bd. dirs., 1978-92; mem. steering com. Met. Louisville Interreligious Coalition on Civil Rights, 1987-93. Recipient Peace and Justice award Peace and Justice Commn., Archdiocese of Louisville, 1990, Vol. of Yr. award Phoenix Hill Assn., 1990. Mem. Interdenominational Ministerial Coalition of NAACP, Fedn. Ch. Social Agys. (pres. 1979-84), Long Run Bapt. Assn. (moderator), United Crescent Hill Ministries (bd. dirs. 1992—, v.p. 1993-94, pres. 1995-97), Omicron Delta Chi. Democrat. Home: 2817 Grinstead Dr Louisville KY 40206-2643 Office: Clifton Bapt Ch 1947 Frankfort Ave Louisville KY 40206-2000 *The prophet Micah reminds us that God desires three things of us: that we love mercy, do justice, and walk humbly with God. I suspect I will spend the rest of my life seeking to understand and practice those three simple admonitions.*

HOLLADAY, WILHELMINA COLE, interior design and museum executive; b. Elmira, N.Y., Oct. 10, 1922; d. Chauncy E. and Claire Elizabeth (Strong) Cole; m. Wallace Fitzhugh Holladay, Sept. 27, 1946; children: Wallace Fitzhugh, Scott Cole. BA, Elmira Coll., 1944; postgrad. art history, U. Paris, 1953-54, U. Va., 1960-61; PhD (hon.), Moore Coll. Art, 1988, Mt. Vernon Coll., 1988, Elmira Coll., 1989. Exec. sec. Howard Ludington, Rochester, N.Y., 1944-45, Chinese Embassy, Washington, 1945-48; staff Nat. Gallery of Art, Washington, 1957-59; dir. interior design div. Holladay Corp., Washington, 1970-95; dir. Adams Nat. Bank, 1978-86, chmn., 1978-86; founder, chmn., bd. dirs., creator art collection by women (Renaissance through contemp.), Nat. Mus. Women in Arts, 1982—. Founder archival libr. of periodicals, books, exhbn. catalogs on women's art for rsch. purposes; bd. durs. Am. Field Svc., 1964-80, Internat. Student House, 1973—, Leeds Castle Found.; mem. coun. Friends of Folger shakespeare Libr., 1978-82; mem. world svc. coun. YWCA; trustee Corcoran Gallery of Art, 1980-90; mem. Mayor's Blue Ribbon Com. Decorated Order of Merit (Norway); recipient Horizon's Theatre award, 1986, Anti-Defamation award, 1987, Thomas Jefferson award Am. Soc. Interior Designers, Disting. Woman's award Northwood Inst., 1987, Disting. Achievement award Nat. League Am. Pen Women, 1988, Women Achievers award Internat. Alliance, 1991, Woman That Makes a Difference award Intenat. Womens Forum, 1991, Women First award YWCA, 1993, Key to City of Kansas City, Fellows award for disting. svc. to arts New Orleans Mus. Art, 1997, Disting. Washingtonian award in lit. and the arts Univ. Club Washington, 1998; named Woman of Achievement, Washington Ednl. TV Assn., 1984, Woman of Distinction Coun. Ind. Colls., 1987, Birmingham So. Coll., 1991, Washingtonian of Yr., Washingtonian Mag., 1987, Hon. Citizen, State of Tex.; inducted into Nat. Women's Hall of Fame, 1996, fell. award Dist. Service to Arts, New Orleans Mus. Arts, 1997, Dist. Washingtonian Award, 1998. Mem. Am. Assn. Mus., Am. Fedn. Art, Women's Caucus for Arts, Mus. Modern Art, Art Libraries of N.Am., Archives Am. Art, Arttable, Smithson Soc., Internat. Women's Forum, Nat. Women's Econ. Alliance (bd. dirs. 1984—), Soaring Eagle award 1988). Episcopalian. Home: 3215 R St NW Washington DC 20007-2941 Office: Nat Mus Women Arts 1250 New York Ave NW Washington DC 20005-3970 *You haven't failed until you quit trying.**

HOLLAND, AGNIESZKA, film director, screenwriter; b. Warsaw, Poland, 1948; m. Laco Adamik. Editor FAMU Film Sch., Prague, Czechoslovakia; asst. to Krzysztof Zanussi X, Warsaw, 1973. Works include: (co-dir. with Jerzy Domaradzki and Pawel Kedzierski) Screen Test, 1977; (co-screenwriter) Rough Treatment, 1978; (worked on films) A Love in Germany, Man of Marble, Man of Iron, The Orchestra Conductor, Korczak, Danton, 1982; (screenwriter) Anna; (dir.) Provincial Actors, 1979, The Fever, 1980, The Lonely Woman, 1981, Angry Harvest, 1985, To Kill a Priest, 1988, Europa Europa, 1992, Oliver, Oliver, 1993, The Secret Garden, 1993, Washington Square, 1997, Total Eclipse, 1995; and numerous documentaries for French TV. Office: William Morris Agy Inc 151 S El Camino Dr Beverly Hills CA 90212-2775*

HOLLAND, AMY JEANETTE, psychiatrist; b. High Point, N.C., Jan. 25, 1964; d. Jefferson Dewey and Mary Esther (Marsh) H.; m. Dana Neal Martin, July 14, 1990; 1 child, Bradley Neal Holland Martin. BS magna cum laude, Wake Forest U., 1986; MD, East Carolina U., 1991. Cert. med. technologist. Med. technologist Humana Hosps., Greensboro, N.C., 1986-87; intern U. N.C. Hosps., Chapel Hill, 1991-92, resident in psychiatry, 1992-94; fellow in child psychiatry Emory U. Hosps., Atlanta, 1994-96. Mem. AMA, Am. Psychiat. Assn. (author, presenter poster nat. mtg. 1991), Am. Assn. Psychiatry and the Law, Ga. Med. Soc., Ga. Psychiat. Assn., Ga. Coun. on Child and Adolescent Psychiatry, Am. Acad. Child and Adolescent Psychiatry. Avocations: antique collecting, doll collecting, roller skating. Office: Whitlock Park Ctr 707 Whitlock Ave SW Bldg H Marietta GA 30064-3033

HOLLAND, BERNARD PEABODY, music critic; b. Norfolk, Va., Feb. 26, 1933; s. Bernard Peabody and Claudia Mildred (Emmerson) H.; m. Janet Carter, July 8, 1983 (div. July 1992); m. Elizabeth Wareham, Aug. 12, 1997. BA, U. Va., 1955. Tchr. of piano Pitts., 1966-81; music critic, writer Pitts. Post-Gazette, 1979-80; music critic N.Y. Times, N.Y.C., 1981—. Contbr. articles to N.Y. Times Mag., Harper's Mag., Saturday Rev. Mem. Century Assn., Phi Beta Kappa. Democrat. Episcopalian. Avocations: books, travel, all sports. Office: NY Times 229 W 43rd St New York NY 10036-3959

HOLLAND, BETH, actress; b. N.Y.C.; d. Samson and Florence (Liebman) Hollander; m. Louis L. Friedman, Aug. 28, 1953; children: Ellen Lynn, Cathy Jayne. Pvt. studies in acting, voice tng. Arts funding cons. N.Y. State Senate, 1974-89. Appeared in various roles on TV, film and theatre, also comedy video Your Favorite Jokes, 1988. Recipient Carbonell performance award Theatre League of South Fla., 1996. Mem. AFTRA (pres. N.Y. chpt. 1989-91, bd. dirs., trustee Health and Retirement Funds, past treas.), SAG, N.Y. TV Acad. (past bd. dirs.), Actors Equity Assn., Twelfth Night Club (bd. dirs.), Episcopal Actors Guild, Cath. Actors Guild, Players Club, Lambs Club. Avocations: travel, politics, arts. Home (winter): 146 Central Park W # 12F New York NY 10023-2005

HOLLAND, CHARLES EDWARD, medical products corporate executive; b. Pottstown, Pa., Aug. 31, 1940; s. Charles Edward and Ethel Viola (Ludwig) H.; m. Linda Beth VandeBerg, Nov. 20, 1982. Student, Messiah Coll., 1962-63; BS in Biology and Chemistry, Albright Coll., 1966; PhD in Zoology, Rutgers U., 1974. Clin. lab. technician Reading Hosp., West Reading, Pa., 1962-66; rsch. assoc. dept. biochemistry St. Louis U. Sch. Medicine, 1972-75; rsch. assoc. dept. pharmacology and surgery U. Ill.Med. Ctr., Chgo., 1975-77; clin. project mgr. Am. Critical Care (Am. Hosp. Supply), McGraw Park, Ill., 1977-81; asst./assoc. dir. clin. rsch. Glaxo Inc., Research Triangle Park, N.C., 1981-84; dir. planning and project mgmt. Glaxo Inc., Research Triangle Park, 1984-86, dir. human resources, 1986-87, dir. strategic planning, 1987-88, dir. dermatology bus. expansion, 1988-89, dir. dermatology bus. and product devel., 1989-91, group dir. dermatology bus. and product devel., 1991-95; pres. XPharm, Inc., Chgo., 1996—; sr. dir. licensing and tech. alliances Searle, Skokie, Ill., 1996—; bd. trustees Glaxo Bus. Sch., 1986-89, chmn. 1986-88. Contbr. articles to profl. jours. USPH fellow Rutgers U., 1966-71; grad. teaching fellow Rutgers U., 1971-72; NIH fellow St. Louis U. Sch. Medicine, 1973-75, U. Ill., 1975-77. Mem. Project Mgmt. Inst. (editor newsletter 1986-87), AAAS, Nat. Psoriasis Found., Soc. Investigative Dermatology, Am. Acad. Dermatology, Lic. Exec. Soc., Am. Cont. Dermatology Soc., Chgo. Biotech. Network (founder), Sigma Xi. Avocations: travel, nature, hiking, fishing.

HOLLAND, CHARLES R., military officer. BS in Aero. Engring., USAF Acad., 1968; grad., Squadron Officer Sch., 1974, Air Command and Staff Coll., 1975; MS in Bus. Mgmt., Troy State U., 1976; nat. security mgmt. course, 1982; grad., Indsl. Coll. of Armed Forces, 1986; program for sr. ofcls. in nat. security, Harvard U., 1990. Commd. 2d lt. USAF, 1968, advanced through grades to maj. gen., 1997; air ops. staff officer directorate of airlift Hdqs. U.S. Air Forces in Europe, Ramstein Air Base, West Germany, 1974-76; joint tng. exercise plans officer Mil. Airlift Ctr. Europe, Ramstein Air Base, 1976-77; chief space shuttle flight ops. br., exec. to comdr. L.A. Air Force Sta., 1979-83; comdr. 21st Tactical Airlift Squadron, Clark Air Base, The Philippines, 1983-85; dep. chief airlift and tng. divsn., mil. dep. acquisition Office of Asst. Sec. of Air Force, Washington, 1986-87, chief airlift and tng. divsn., mil. dep. acquisition, 1987-88; vice comdr., comdr. 1550th Combat Crew Tng. Wing, Kirtland AFB, N.Mex., 1988-91; comdr. 1st Spl. Ops. Wing, Hurlburt Field, Fla., 1991-93; dep. comdg. gen. Joint Spl. Ops. Command, Ft. Bragg, N.C., 1993-95; comdr. Spl. Ops. Command, Pacific, Camp H.M. Smith, Hawaii, 1995-97, Air Force Spl. Ops. Command, Hurlburt Field, 1997—. Decorated Def. Superior Svc. medal with 2 oak leaf clusters, Legion of Merit with oak leaf cluster, D.F.C., Meritorious Svc. medal with 2 oak leaf clusters. Office: AFSOC/CC CMD Ste 100 Bartley St Hurlburt Field FL 32544-5273

HOLLAND, CHRISTIE ANNA, biochemist, virologist; b. Newport News, Va., Aug. 25, 1950; d. Charles Everett and Helen (Bailey) Holland; m. Robert Keith Walty, June 24, 1989; children: Helen, Joshua. BS, U. Richmond, 1972; PhD, U. Tenn., 1977. Postdoctoral fellow Worcester Found. for Exptl. Biology, Shrewsbury, Mass., 1977-79, Ctr. for Cancer Rsch.-MIT, Cambridge, Mass., 1979-84; asst. prof. dept. radiation oncology U. Mass. Med. Ctr., Worcester, 1985-90, assoc. prof., 1990-91; dir. Ctr. for Virology, Immunology and Infectious Diseases Children's Nat. Med. Ctr., Washington, 1991—; assoc. prof. pediats., microbiology and biochemistry George Washington U. Med. Ctr., Washington, 1991-95, prof. pediats., assoc. prof. microbiology and biochemistry, 1995—. Mem. AAAS, Internat. Soc. Exptl. Hematology, Am. Soc. Cell Biology, Am. Soc. Virology. Home: 9105 Goshen Valley Dr Gaithersburg MD 20882-1447 Office: Childrens Nat Med Ctr 111 Michigan Ave NW Washington DC 20010-2916

HOLLAND, DAVID THURSTON, former editor; b. Phila., May 26, 1923; s. Rupert Sargent and Margaret Currier (Lyon) H. B.A., Harvard, 1944, M.A., 1946. Vice consul U.S. Fgn. Svc., Budapest, Hungary, 1945; teaching fellow Harvard U., Cambridge, Mass., 1946-49; coll. traveller Oxford U. Press, N.Y.C., 1953-54; asst. editor Harcourt Brace, N.Y.C., 1955-59; asst. editor Ency. Internat. Grolier Inc., N.Y.C., 1959-62, assoc. editor Ency. Americana, 1962-65, sr. editor, 1965-85; exec. editor, 1985; editor in chief Ency. Americana Grolier Inc., Danbury, Conn., 1985-91; ret., 1991. Democrat. Episcopalian.

HOLLAND, DAVID VERNON, minister; b. L.A., June 21, 1954; s. Walter Vernon H. and Wilma (McKenzie) Cowles; m. Dianne Sheri Cooper, July 17, 1976; children: Jessica, Lisa, Melinda, Justin. BTh, LIFE Bible Coll., 1979; postgrad., Gordon Conwell Sem., 1988—. Ordained to ministry, 1981. Youth pastor Angelus Temple, L.A., 1977-79; asst. pastor Bradford (Pa.) Foursquare Ch., 1979-81; pastor Easton (Mass.) Foursquare Ch., 1981—; div. supt. Northeast Div. Foursquare Chs., 1986—; pres. Emmaus Ministry Inst., Easton, 1983—; nat. cabinet mem., Internat. Ch. of Foursquare Gospel, L.A., 1990—; bd. dirs., Greater Boston Christian Alliance, 1990—; coun. mem., Boston Oper. Rescue, 1990—. Contbr. articles to profl. jours. Office: Foursquare Gospel Ch 421 Torrey St Brockton MA 02301-4617*

HOLLAND, DIANNA GWIN, real estate broker; b. Pueblo, Colo., Mar. 9, 1948; d. Everett Paul Gwin and Ava Mariea (Calvert) Johnson. Staff asst. The White House, Washington, 1971-77, exec. asst. to counsel, 1981-89; sales agt. Rand Real Estate, Alexandria, Va., 1977-79, Pagett Real Estate, Alexandria, 1979-81; assoc. broker WJD & Assocs., Alexandria, 1985-93; assoc. broker, asst. mgr. adminstrn. Long & Foster Realtors, 1993-96; prin. broker, v.p. Century 21 Campaigne, 1996-98; mng. broker Century 21 New Millennium, 1998—; exec. aide to chmn. Edward Lowe Industries, Inc., 1990-91. Del. Va. Republican Conv., 1981, 82, 84. Roman Catholic. Home: 311 Park Rd Alexandria VA 22301-2737

HOLLAND, EUGENE, JR., lumber company executive; b. Lincoln, Nebr., Dec. 13, 1922; s. Eugene and Louise (Bedwell) H.; m. Martha Randall, May 15, 1948; children: Diane Holland Drewry, Randall, Mary susan Boyd, Jean, Robert Lawrence. A.B., Princeton U., 1944. V.p., dir. Holland Lumber Co. Chmn. Chgo. bus. div. Am. Cancer Soc., 1961; dir. Kenilworth United Fund, 1961-63, Commerce and Industry div. Crusade of Mercy, 1972; Bd. dirs. Evanston Hosp. Served with USNR, 1943-46. Clubs: Princeton (Chgo.), Chicago (Chgo.); Princeton (N.Y.C.); Glen View. Home: 416 Sheridan Rd Kenilworth IL 60043-1221 Office: 231 S La Salle St Chicago IL 60604-1407

HOLLAND, GARY NORMAN, ophthalmologist, educator; b. Long Beach, Calif., July 30, 1953; s. Richard L. and Edith (Hewson) H. MD, UCLA, 1979. Diplomate Am. Bd. Ophthalmology, Nat. Bd. Med. Examiners; lic. MD, Calif., Ga. Intern in internal medicine UCLA, 1979-80; resident in ophthalmology Jules Stein Eye Inst., L.A., 1980-83; fellowship in uveitis rsch. Proctor Found. U. Calif. San Francisco, 1983-84; cornea fellowship Emory U. Med. Sch., Atlanta, 1984-85; prof. ophthalmology Jules Stein Eye Inst. UCLA, 1985—. Assoc. editor Am. Jour. Ophthalmology, 1993—. Mem. Am. Uveitis Soc. (chmn. edn. and rsch. com. 1994—). Office: UCLA 100 Stein Plz Los Angeles CA 90095-7065*

HOLLAND, H. RUSSEL, federal judge; b. 1936; m. Diane Holland; 3 children. BBA, U. Mich., 1958, LLB, 1961. With Alaska Ct. System, Anchorage, 1961, U.S. Atty.'s Office, Dept. Justice, Anchorage, 1963-65; assoc. Stevens & Savage, Anchorage, 1965-66; ptnr. Stevens, Savage, Holland, Erwin & Edwards, Anchorage, 1967-68; sole practice Anchorage, 1968-70; ptnr. Holland & Thornton, Anchorage, 1970-78, Holland, Thornton & Trefry, Anchorage, 1978, Holland & Trefry, Anchorage, 1978-84, Trefry & Brecht, Anchorage, 1984; judge U.S. Dist. Ct. Alaska, Anchorage, 1984—. Mem. ABA, Alaska Bar Assn., Anchorage Bar Assn. Office: US Dist Ct 222 W 7th Ave #54 Anchorage AK 99513-7501

HOLLAND, HAROLD HERBERT, banker; b. Clifton Forge, Va., Feb. 11, 1932; s. Tristum Shandy and Ida Blanche (Paxton) H.; m. Nellie Mae Thomas, Jan. 15, 1955; children: Richard Long, Michael Wayne. Student, Coll. of William and Mary, 1953-54; BA, George Washington U., 1957, MBA, 1958. Tech. asst. Fed. Res. Bd., Washington, 1959-61; v.p. Falls Church (Va.) Bank, 1961-67; exec. v.p. Bank of New River, Radford, Va., 1967-70; pres., CEO Farmers Nat. Bank, Salem, Va., 1970-75; chmn., pres., CEO, dir. Am. Nat. Holding Co., Kalamazoo, 1975-86, Am. Nat. Bank & Trust, Kalamazoo, 1975-86; chmn. bd., dir. Kalamazoo Econ. Devel. Corp., 1977-84; dir. Wynfield Prodns.; chmn. Old Kent Bank of Kalamazoo, 1986-87; cons. IMCOR, N.Y., 1989—; probate adv. Kalamazoo County Probate Ct. Exec. coun., v.p. S.W. Mich. coun. Boy Scouts Am., Kalamazoo, 1976-86, re-elected exec. coun., 1989—, pres., 1991-95; bd. dirs. Kalamazoo Conv. and Visitors Bur., 1981-82, Jobs for Mich. Grads., 1985-87, Downtown Tomorrow, Inc., 1985, West Mich. Telecom. Found., Blue Ridge Mountains coun. Boy Scouts Am., 1987-90, Jr. Achievement, 1994—; pres. Va. Mental Health Found., 1974-75; chmn. Kalamazoo 2000 Econ. Devel. Com., 1982; chmn., bd. dirs. Western Mich. U. Found., 1985-86; v.p., trustee I.S. Gilmore Found., Kalamazoo, 1976—, Arts Found. Mich.; trustee Borgess Hosp., 1986; chmn. Borgess Capital Campaign, 1986-87; county co-chmn. Gilmore for Congress, 1981; mem. City of Kalamazoo Pension Divestiture Study Com.; mem. campaign cabinet Goodwill Industries; probate adv. Kalamazoo County Probate Ct.; chmn., bd. trustees First United Meth. Ch., Kalamazoo, 1995-97. Recipient Disting. Service award U.S. Jaycees, 1965, Silver Beaver award Boy Scouts Am., 1985. Mem. Mich. Bankers Assn. (strategic planning com.), Mich. Coun. on Founds. (trustee 1994), Assn. of Bank Holding Cos. (dir. 1978-81), Kalamazoo County C. of C. (life, pres. 1981-83, chmn. strategic planning com. 1984), Mad Hatters (pres. Kaalamazoo), Rotary (Paul Harris fellow 1992). Republican. Methodist. Home: 901 Edgemoor Ave Kalamazoo MI 49008-2340

HOLLAND, HENRY NORMAN, marketing and management consultant; b. Norfolk, Va., Oct. 13, 1947; s. Henry Norman and Edith Leigh (O'Bryan) H.; m. Linda Diane Eggerking, June 1, 1968 (div. 1983); 1 child, Steven Frederick; m. Jane Elizabeth Bond, Dec. 27, 1983. BA, Chaminade Coll., 1972; MBA, U. Hawaii, 1977. Lic. ins. broker, Calif. Mgr. Chevron USA, Honolulu, 1965-75; dealer Dillingham Chevron, Honolulu, 1975-82; gen. mgr. Barcat Enterprises, San Francisco, 1982-85; counselor E.K. Williams of San Francisco, 1985; gen. mgr. Woodside (Calif.) Oil Co., 1985-88; cons. Holland Bus. Mgmt., San Francisco, 1989—; dir. Chevron Fed. Credit Union, Honolulu, 1971-75. Author: Make Yours Service, tng. seminars, newsletter, safety programs; contbr. articles to profl. jours. Loaned mgr. United Way, Honolulu, 1972; nation chief YMCA Indian Guides, Kailua, Hawaii, 1976-79. With U.S. Army, 1967-69, Vietnam. Mem. English Speaking Union, Met. League San Francisco Symphony, Golden Gate Nat. Parks Assn., Nat. Trust for Historic Preservation, San Francisco Mus. Soc., Chevron Adv. Coun., Nat. Assn. Enrolled Agts., Calif. Assn. Enrolled Agts., Sovereign Order of Saint John of Jerusalem Knights Hospitaller, VFW. Republican. Presbyterian. Avocations: travel, sports, bridge, cooking, reading.

HOLLAND, HUBERT BRIAN, lawyer; b. London, Eng., Mar. 28, 1904; came to U.S., 1915, naturalized, 1929; s. Charles Hubert and Lois Amy (Barber) H.; m. Gertrude Bancroft, Aug. 4, 1931 (dec. Dec. 1975); children: Alice Katharine, Charles Howard; m. Helen Buxton, Aug. 21, 1976 (dec. Feb. 1997). Student, Taft Sch., 1918-21; Ph.B., Yale, 1925; LL.B., Harvard U., 1928. Bar: Pa. 1929, Mass. 1935. Assoc. Williams, Brittain & Sinclair, Phila., 1928-30; atty. Dept. Justice, Washington, 1930-35; asst. atty. gen. Dept. Justice, U.S., 1953-56; asso. firm Ropes & Gray., Boston, 1935-42; partner Ropes & Gray., 1942-53, 56-76, of counsel, 1976—; lectr. Fed. Tax Inst. N.E., Inst. Fed. Taxation N.Y. U., 1950-51. Hon. trustee Kodaly Mus. Tng. Inst.; bd. dirs. Sharon (N.H.) Art Center, 1978-88. Fellow Am. Bar Found.; mem. Am. Law Inst., Am., Mass., Boston bar assns. Episcopalian. Home: Brookhaven at Lexington 1010 Waltham St Lexington MA 02421-8044 Office: 1 International Pl Boston MA 02110-2602

HOLLAND, ISABELLE CHRISTIAN, writer; b. Basel, Switzerland, June 16, 1920; d. Philip Edgar and Corabelle (Anderson) H. BA, Tulane U., 1942. Censor U.S. War Dept., New Orleans, 1942-44; corr. sec. Life Mag., N.Y.C., 1944-47; editl. asst. Nat. Coun. Protestant Episcopal Chs., N.Y.C., 1947-48; asst. editor Tomorrow Mag. Creative Age Press, N.Y.C., 1948-49; advt. copywriter Franklin Spier Advt. Agy., N.Y.C., 1949-53; assoc. editor McCall's Mag., N.Y.C., 1953-55; publicity dir. Crown Pubs., Lippincott Co., Delacorte Press, Harper's Mag., G.P. Putnam, Pubs., N.Y.C., 1956-69; writer, 1969—. Author: Cecily, 1967, Amanda's Choice, 1970, The Man Without a Face, 1972, (under name Francesca Hunt) The Mystery of Castle Renaldi, 1972, Heads You Win, Tails I Lose, 1973, Kilgaren, 1974, Journey of Three, 1974, Trelawny, 1976, Moncrieff, 1975, Of Love and Death and Other Journeys, 1975 (nominated Nat. Book award 1976), Darcourt, 1976, Grenelle, 1976, Alan and the Animal Kingdom, 1977, Hitchhike, 1977, The de Maury Papers, 1977, Dinah and the Green Fat Kingdom, 1978, Tower Abbey, 1978, The Marchington Inheritance, 1979, Counterpoint, 1980, Now Is Not Too Late, 1980, Summer of My First Love, 1981, The Lost Madonna, 1981, A Horse Named Peaceable, 1982, Abbie's God Book, 1982, Perdita, 1983, God, Mrs. Musket and Aunt Dot, 1983, The Empty House, 1983, After the First Love, 1983, Kevin's Hat, 1984, The Island, 1984 Green Andrew Green, 1984, A Death at St. Anselm's, 1984, Flight of the Archangel, 1985, Jenny Kiss'd Me, 1985, A Lover Scorned, 1986, Henry and Grudge, 1986, Toby the Splendid, 1987, Love and the Genetic Factor, 1987, The Christmas Cat, 1987, Bump in the Night, 1988, A Fatal Advent, 1989, Thief, 1989, The Easter Donkey, 1989, The Unfrightened Dark, 1989, The Journey Home, 1990, The Long Search, 1990, The Search, 1991, The House in the Woods, 1991, Behind the Lines, 1994, Family Trust, 1994, Promised Land, 1996. Mem. PEN, Authors Guild, Cosmopolitan Club (N.Y.C.). Avocation: cats. Address: care Elaine Markson Lit Agy 44 Greenwich Ave New York NY 10011-8347*

HOLLAND, JAMES PAUL, lawyer; b. Charleston, W.Va., Aug. 26, 1948; s. James Robert and Mary Lucille (Tonkin) H.; m. Betty Jane Robertson, May 31, 1971; 1 child, Marium Grace. BBA, Marshall U., 1972; JD, W.Va. U., 1975. Bar: W.Va. 1975. Atty. Columbia Gas Transmission Corp., Charleston, 1975-79, asst. gen. counsel, asst. sec., 1979-85, v.p., 1985-86, sr. v.p., 1986-88, pres., 1988-90, chmn. bd., chief exec. officer, 1990-96; pres. Columbia Gulf Transmission Co., Charleston, 1989-90, chmn. bd., chief exec. officer, 1990-96; of counsel Lewis, Friedberg, Glassr, Casey & Rollins, Charleston, 1997—; bd. dirs. W.Va. Oil and Natural Gas Assn., v.p., 1994-95, pres., 1995-96. With U.S. Army, 1968-70. Mem. ABA, W.Va. Bar Assn., Kanawha County Bar Assn., Fed. Energy Bar Assn., Ea. Mineral Law Found. (trustee 1979—, v.p. 1984-85, pres. 1985-86). Methodist.

HOLLAND, JAMES R., real estate corporation executive; b. St. Louis, Feb. 20, 1944; s. Randolph and Thelma (Robinson) H.; student Principia Coll., 1962-64; BFA, Ohio U., 1966; postgrad. U. Mo. Sch. Journalism, 1966; m. Helen M. Devine, Feb. 18, 1972; children: Danielle, James Randolph, Eric Marc. Photog. intern Nat. Geog. Soc., Washington, 1966, contract photographer for mag., 1967-68; film producer Christian Sci. Center, Boston, 1969-74; real estate developer, pres. Brownstone Properties, Inc., Boston, 1975-77; real estate broker Street & Co., Inc., Boston, 1978-82; pres. A Bit of Boston Real Estate, Inc., 1982—; photographs and films in permanent collections: Truman Libr., JFK Libr., Boston Pub. Libr., Ohio, Mo. univs., others. Active Neighborhood Assn. Back Bay, 1972—, Boston Home and Property Owners Assn.; assoc. Boston Pub. Libr.; lifetime Friend of Beverly Hills (Calif.) Pub. Libr., Dickerson Park Zoo, Mus. Ozarks History; mem. 10th Anniversary com. Boston U.'s Photographic Resource Ctr.; sponsor Babe Ruth Baseball League Team, 1992—. Recipient World Press Competition award, 1967, Newsweek/Bolex documentary film award, 1969, Indsl. Photography Film Competition award, 1970, Internat. Film and TV Festival of N.Y. bronze medal, 1971; named AAU Nat. Karate Champion, 1989; ranked 6th nationally in weapon's forms Reeves Sport Karate Ratings, 1989. Mem. Am. Soc. Mag. Photographers, Nat. Press Photographers (awards 1966, 67, 68), N.Am. Sport Karate Assn. (various awards). Author: The Amazon, 1971, Mr. Pops-Arthur Fiedler, 1972, Tanglewood (foreward Michael Tilson Thomas), 1973; illustrator-photographer Continental and Colonial Currency of Colonial America; contbr. Photojournalism-Principles and Practice (Clifton Edom), 2d edit., 1980; articles, photographs contbd. to various nat., internat. newspapers, mags., encys., video games, numerous textbooks; writer documentary film scripts; film work has appeared on NBC, ABC, CBS, PBS, BBC; producer limited edit. karate video tapes Twinkle Toes Videos. Office: A Bit of Boston Real Estate Inc 5 Brimmer St Boston MA 02108-1001

HOLLAND, JAMES RICKS, public relations executive, association executive; b. Savannah, Ga., Aug. 3, 1929; s. Francis Ross and Eleanor (Struck) H.; m. Paula Shepard, Feb. 14, 1959; children: Kristine, Carey, Jamie. A.B. in Journalism, U. Ga., 1954. V.p. advt. and pub. relations John Hancock Mut. Life Ins. Co., Boston, 1961-70; asst. postmaster gen. for communications U.S. Postal Service, Washington, 1970-73; dep. asst. sec. pub. affairs HEW, Washington, 1973-74, spl. asst. to sec., 1975-76; asst. press sec. to Pres. Ford, Washington, 1975-76; v.p. corp. affairs Miller Brewing Co., Milw., 1976-80; exec. v.p. corp. communications NBC, N.Y.C., 1980-82; pres. Holland Orgn., Bronxville, N.Y., 1982-85; dir. communications Am. Assn. Ret. Persons, Washington, 1985—. Served with USAF, 1950-52. Mem. Sigma Delta Chi. Home: 1913 23rd St NW Washington DC 20008-1632 Office: Am Assn Retired Persons 601 E St NW Washington DC 20049-0001

HOLLAND, JAMES TULLEY, plastic products company executive; b. Pikeville, Ky., May 24, 1940; s. Thomas Joseph and Mary Alta (Tulley) H.; m. Susan Ellen Joy, Jan. 10, 1943; children: James Christopher, Mary Kathleen. BA in Econs., U. Va., 1962; MBA, Am. U., 1969. With br. banking ops. United Va. Bank, Alexandria, 1965-67; with Booz Allen & Hamilton, Washington, 1967-76; treas., chief fin. officer O'Sullivan Corp., Winchester, Va., 1976-84, exec. v.p., 1984-86, pres., 1986—, CEO, 1995-98, ret., 1998, also bd. dirs.; bd. dirs. First Union Bank of Va.-Md.-D.C., Winchester Regional Health Sys. Corp. Capt. U.S. Army, 1963-65. Mem. Winchester Country Club (pres. 1988), Farmington Country Club (Charlottesville, Va.), Belle Haven Country Club (Alexandria). Roman Catholic. Avocations: golfing, reading. Home: 261 Merrifield Ln Winchester VA 22602-2306

HOLLAND, JEFFREY R., religious organization administrator; b. St. George, Utah, Dec. 3, 1940; s. Frank D. and Alice (Bentley) H.; m. Patricia Terry, June 7, 1963; children: Matthew, Mary, David. BS, Brigham Young U., 1965, MA, 1966; PhD, Yale U., 1973. Dean religious instrn. Brigham Young U., 1974-76; commr. Latter Day Saints Ch. Ednl. System, 1976-80; pres. Brigham Young U., 1980-89; gen. authority, mem. 1st Quorum of the 70 LDS Ch., 1989-94; Apostle Quorum of the Twelve, 1994—; dir. Deseret News Pub. Co., Key Bank of Utah, Key Bancshares of Utah, Inc. Mem. Am. Assn. Presidents of Ind. Colls. and Univs. (past pres.), Nat. Assn. Ind. Colls. and Univs. (former bd. dirs.), Am. Council Edn., Phi Kappa Phi. Office: LDS Church 47 E South Temple Salt Lake City UT 84150-1005*

HOLLAND, JIMMIE C., psychiatrist, educator; b. Forney, Tex., Apr. 9, 1928; m. James F. Holland; 5 children. BA, Baylor U., 1948, MD, 1952. Diplomate Am. Bd. Psychiatry, Am. Bd. Neurology. Instr. to prof. SUNY, Buffalo, 1956-73; assoc. prof., assoc. attending physician to asst. dir. cons.-liaison psychiatry Albert Einstein Coll. Medicine and Montefiore Med. Ctr., Bronx, N.Y., 1973-77; chair dept. psychiatry and behavioral Scis., Wayne E. Chapman prof. in psychiat. oncology Meml. Sloan Kettering Cancer Ctr., N.Y.C., 1977—; prof. dept. psychiatry Cornell U. Med. Coll., N.Y.C., 1977—; asst. attending physician to dir. dept. psychiatry E.J. Meyer Meml. Hosp./Erie County Med. Ctr., Buffalo, 1956-73; cons. NIMH-USSR joint schizophrenia study Psychiat. Rsch. Inst., Moscow, 1972-73, Nat. Inst. Drug Abuse and Alcoholism, Rockville, Md., 1973-75; chmn. psychiatry com. Cancer and Leukemia Group B Clin. Trials, Brookline, Mass., 1976—; cons. nat. adv. com. on hospice Robert Wood Johnson Found. and NIH, New Brunswick, N.J., 1980-84; mem. cancer control grant rev. com. Nat. Cancer Inst., Bethesda, Md., 1981-85; mem. com. study health consequences of stress of bereavement, Inst. of Medicine, Washington, 1983-84; chmn. task force on psychosocial oncology European Sch. Oncology, Venice, Italy, 1988-89; mem. Commn. on AIDS in N.Y. State Prisons, 1989. Editor: Handbook of Psycho-oncology: Psychological Care of the Patient with Cancer, 1989; editorial bd. Cancer Nursing Jour., 1977—, Oncology jour., 1980—; author, co-author 142 jour. articles, book chpts., monographs; cons., commentator film The DNR Dilemma, 1987. Bd. dirs. Cancer Care, Inc., 1979-81. Recipient Disting. Alumna award Baylor U., Waco, Tex., 1982; Am. Cancer Soc. Medal of Honor, 1994;. Fellow Am. Coll. Psychiatrists, Am. Psychiat. Assn., Acad. Psychosomatic Medicine (founding); mem. Am. Soc. Psychiat. Oncology/AIDS (pres. 1988—), Am. Cancer Soc. (nat. div. com. on rehab. 1979—, chair workshop psychol., social and behavioral medicine aspects of cancer, 1981, chair nat. com. psychosocial edn. and rsch., 1986—, del.-at-large 1986—), Am. Psychosomatic Soc., Soc. for Liaison Psychiatry (Spl. citation 1989), Am. Soc. Clin. Oncology, Internat. Psycho-oncology Soc. (founder, chair exec. com. 1984—). Office: Meml Sloan-Kettering Cancer Ctr 1275 York Ave New York NY 10021-6007

HOLLAND, JOHN BEN, clothing manufacturing company executive; b. Scottsville, Ky., Mar. 26, 1932; s. Elbridge Winfred and Lou May (Whitney) H.; m. Margaret Irene Pecor, Jan. 31, 1954; children: John Sandra, Robert. BS in Acctg., Bowling Green U., 1959. With Union Underwear Co., Inc., Bowling Green, Ky., 1961—, v.p. adminstrn., 1972-74, vice chmn., 1975, chmn., chief exec. officer, 1976-96; ret., 1996, cons., 1996—; bd. dirs. Dollar Gen. Corp., Farmers Nat. Bank. Bd. dirs. Ky. Coun. Econ. Edn., Louisville, 1981-90, Ky. Advocates for Higher Edn. Inc., 1985-93, Ky. C. of C., 1987-88, Camping World Inc., 1985-97, Associated Industries of Ky., Ireland-Am. Econ. Adv. Bd., Tech. Corp. Inc.; chmn. corp. coun. Western Ky. U., devel. steering com., 1985-96. Mem. Bowling Green-Warren County C. of C. (bd. dirs. 1981-85), Am. Arbitration Assn. (panel 1985-93). Office: Fruit of the Loom Inc PO Box 90015 Bowling Green KY 42102-9015

HOLLAND, JOHN JOSEPH, JR., economics educator; b. Hackensack, N.J., June 19, 1929; s. John Joseph and Marion Rita (Sexton) H.; m. Enda Mai Michelson, Aug. 5, 1978; 1 child, Marion Ada. BS in Econs., Villanova U., 1952; MBA, NYU, 1954, PhD, 1972. Credit analyst Fed. Res. Bank N.Y., N.Y.C., 1952-54; asst. loan officer Nat. Bank Detroit, 1954-57, Hanover Bank, N.Y.C., 1959-60; economist George G. Sharp, N.Y.C., 1961-68; prof. econs., chair Iona Coll., New Rochelle, N.Y., 1963-94; economist GRC Data, Inc., N.Y.C., 1968-72; vis. prof., acting chair Monmouth U., West Long Branch, N.J., 1994—; adj. prof. econs. Fordham U., N.Y.C., 1970-82, Pace U., N.Y.C., 1978-83; econs. cons. N.Y. State Legis., Albany, 1971-73; cons. in transp. field. Co-author: Role of Nuclear Power in Merchant Marine, 1964, Economic Reach of Port of Boston, 1969. econ. cons. N.Y. State Legis., Albany, 1971-73. NSF grantee, 1973, GE Found. grantee, 1974, Earhart Found. grantee, Ann Arbor, Mich., 1975-88. Mem. Am. Econ. Assn., N.Y. Acad. Scis., N.Y. State Econ. Assn., Ea. Econ. Assn., Met. Econ. Assn. Roman Catholic. Avocations: reading, walking, travel, writing. Home: 205 Morris Ave Spring Lake NJ 07762-1336 Office: Monmouth U Cedar Ave West Long Branch NJ 07764

HOLLAND, JOHN MADISON, family practice physician; b. Holden, W.Va., Oct. 7, 1927; s. Ophia I. and Lou V. (Elliott) H.; m. Mary Louise Bourne, Sept. 2, 1950; children—David, Stephen, Nancy. B.S., Eastern Ky. State U., Richmond, 1949; M.D., U. Louisville, 1952. Diplomate Am. Bd. Family Practice. Intern St. Joseph Infirmary, Louisville, 1952-53; gen. practice family medicine Physicians Group, Springfield, Ill., 1955-80; med. dir. St. John's Hosp., Springfield, 1971-94, St. John's Hospice, 1995—; clin. prof. family practice So. Ill. U., Springfield, 1978—. Served to capt. USAF, 1953-55. Mem. AMA, Am. Acad. Family Physicians, Am. Acad. Hospice/Palliative Medicine. Baptist. Home: 2131 Lindsay Rd Springfield IL 62704-3242 Office: 800 E Carpenter St Springfield IL 62702-5324

HOLLAND, JOSEPH DANIEL, psychologist, counselor; b. Boston, Aug. 20, 1946; s. Raymond and Marjorie (Leary) Holland; m. Elaine Marie Lonardo, Aug. 7, 1971; children: Christopher, Amanda. AB, Stonehill Coll., 1968; MA, Assumption Coll., 1971. Lic. ednl. psychologist. Tchr. math., social studies Franklin (Mass.) Sch. Dept., 1968-73; psychologist, counselor Palmer (Mass.) Pub. Schs., 1973—. Mem. Nat. Assn. Sch. Psychologists, Mass. Tchrs. Assn., Western Mass. Counselors Assn. (pres.). Avocations: sports, travel. Home: 2012 Wilbraham Rd Springfield MA 01129-1825 Office: Converse Mid Sch 24 Converse St Palmer MA 01069-1797

HOLLAND, JOSEPH JOHN, financial manager; b. New Brunswick, N.J., Nov. 7, 1927; s. Thomas Clifford and Ruth Elizabeth (Feaster) H.; m. Bernice T. Kearns, Jul. 1, 1984; B.S. magna cum laude, Mount St. Mary's Coll., 1952; M.B.A., Rutgers U., 1955; 1 son, Wayne Joseph. Sr. acct. Peat, Marwick, Mitchell & Co., Newark, 1952-61; plant controller, ops. auditor Crane Co., N.Y.C., 1961-65; fin. controller Ingersoll-Rand Co., U.K., 1965-68; v.p., controller PPD Corp., Newark, 1968-73; v.p. fin., treas. Edgcomb Steel & Aluminum Corp., Hillside, N.J., 1973-76; cons. in field, North Brunswick, N.J., 1978; v.p. fin., dir. Berry Solar Products, Edison, N.J., 1978-86; dir. fin. control Berger Industries, Maspeth, N.Y., 1986-88; cons. in field Milltown, N.J., 1988-96; ret. CPA, N.J., N.Mex.; Tex. Served with USN, 1946-48. Mem. Am. Inst. C.P.A.s. Clubs: Sales Execs. of N.J. (chmn. disting. salesman award 1978), Elks, Exchange (New Brunswick, N.J.). Home: 29 Highland Dr Milltown NJ 08850-1012

HOLLAND, KEN, sports team executive; b. Vernon, B.C., Can.; m. Cindy Holland; children: Brad, Julie, Rachel, Greg. Hockey player Medicine Hat, 1974-75, Toronto Maple Leafs, 1975-80, Hartford, 1980-83; hockey player Detroit Red Wings, 1983-84, Binghamton, Springfield; amateur scouting dir. Detroit Red Wings, asst. gen. mgr., gen. mgr., 1987—. Inductee Binghamton Hall of Fame, 1998. Office: c/o Detroit Red Wings 600 Civic Center Dr Detroit MI 48226*

HOLLAND, LYMAN FAITH, JR., lawyer; b. Mobile, Ala., June 17, 1931; s. Lyman Faith and Louise (Wisdom) H.; m. Leannah Louise Platt, Mar. 6, 1954; children: Lyman Faith III, Laura. BS in Bus. Adminstrn, U. Ala., 1953; LLB, 1957. Bar: Ala. 1957. Assoc. Hand, Arendall & Bedsole, Mobile, 1957-62; ptnr. Hand, Arendall, Bedsole, Greaves & Johnston, 1963-94, mem., 1995; mem. Hand Arendall LLC, 1996—. Mem. Mobile Hist. Devel. Com., 1965-69, v.p., 1967-68; bd. dirs. Mobile Azalea Trail, Inc., 1963-68, chmn. bd., 1963-65; bd. dirs. Mobile Mental Health Ctr., 1969-76, v.p., 1972, pres., chmn. bd., 1973; bd. dirs. Mobile chpt. ARC, 1969-89, 91-97, vice chmn., 1975-77, exec. vice chmn., 1978-80, chmn., 1980-82, life bd. dirs. emeritus, 1997—; bd. dirs. Deep South coun. Girl Scouts U.S., 1965-77, Gordan Smith Ctr. Inc., 1973, Bay Area Coun. on Alcoholism, 1973-76, Comty. Chest, Coun. of Mobile County, Inc., 1976-81; bd. dirs. Greater Mobile Mental Health-Mental Retardation, 1975-81, pres., 1975-77; mem. exec. com. Mobile Estate Planning Coun., 1988-97, pres., 1994-95. 1st lt. USAF, 1953-55; lt. col. USAF ret. Mem. ABA, Mobile County Bar Assn., Ala. State Bar (chmn. sect. corp., banking and bus. law 1978-80), Am. Counsel Assn., Am. Coll. Trust and Estate Counsel, Am. Coll. Trust and Estate Counsel Found. (bd. dirs. 1990-96), Ala. Law Inst. (coun. 1978—), Athleston Club (Mobile), Country Club of Mobile, Bienville Club, Lions, Pi Kappa Alpha, Phi Delta Phi. Baptist (deacon, ch. trustee 1968-73, chmn. trustees 1971-73). Home: 3606 Provident Ct Mobile AL 36608-1534 Office: Hand Arendall LLC PO Box 123 Mobile AL 36601-0123

HOLLAND, MARVIN A., federal judge; b. 1930. BA, Lafayette Coll., 1951; JD, Cornell U., 1954. Bar: N.Y. Ptnr. Holland & Zinlser, 1956-85; bankruptcy judge for ea. dist. N.Y., U.S. Bankruptcy Ct., Bklyn., 1985—. Office: US Bankruptcy Ct 75 Clinton St Brooklyn NY 11201-4201

HOLLAND, MAX, journalist; b. Providence, Dec. 9, 1950; s. Bernhard and Dora Holland. BA, Antioch Coll., Yellow Springs, Ohio, 1972. Newswriter Voice of Am., Washington, 1976; assoc. Ctr. for Internat. Policy, Washington, 1977-79; aide U.S. Rep. Toby Moffett-Conn., Washington, 1980; Washington rep. Am. Friends Svc. Com., Phila., 1980-82; columnist Nation mag., N.Y.C., 1982-86, contbg. editor, 1986—; contbg. editor Wilson Quar., Washington, 1992—. Author: When the Machine Stopped, 1989 (Bus. Week Top Ten award), The Leo Goes to Washington, 1994; contbr. articles to newspapers. Fellow Guggenheim Found., 1984, German Marshall Fund, 1986, NEH, 1990, Woodrow Wilson Internat. Ctr. for Scholars, 1991. Mem. Nat. Writers' Union, Nat. Book Critics Cir. Jewish. Home: 221 Constitution Ave NE Apt 23 Washington DC 20002-7332 Office: Nation Mag 110 Maryland Ave NE Washington DC 20002-5626

HOLLAND, MICHAEL FRANCIS, investment company executive; b. Cleve., July 8, 1944; s. Joseph Thomas and Mary Louise H.; m. Louise Grace, Aug. 20, 1966; children—Brian, Thomas, Joseph, Daniel, John, Michael Jr. AB, Harvard U., 1966; MBA, Columbia U., 1968. With Morgan Guaranty Trust Co., N.Y.C., 1968-80; investment mgr. Morgan Guaranty Trust Co., 1972-80, v.p., 1975-80; sr. v.p. investments Reliance Group, Inc., also Reliance Ins. Co., N.Y.C., 1980-83; pres. Holland & Co., Inc., 1983-84; pres., chief exec. officer First Boston Asset Mgmt. Corp., 1984-89; chmn., CEO Salomon Bros. Asset Mgmt., Inc., 1989-92; vice chmn. Oppenheimer & Co. Inc., 1992-94; dir., chmn. bd. dirs., chief exec. officer Global Growth and Income Fund, Inc., 1986-89; dir. The China Fund, Inc., 1992—; gen. ptnr. The Blackstone Group, 1994-95; chmn. Holland & Co. L.L.C., 1995—; dir. The Latin Am. Investment Fund, Inc., 1990-92; dir. ARM Fin. Group, Inc. Panelist: Wall Street Week with Louis Rukeyser, 1990—. Vice chrmn., Harvard Coll. Fund Assoc. Program, 1998—; mem. com. on univ. resources, com. on faculty selection Harvard U.; trustee Norwalk (Conn.) Hosp., 1990, vice chmn., 1996—; bd. trustees Vanguard Charitable Endowment Program, 1997—; memb. bd. fin. Town of New Canaan, Conn., 1997—. Mem. Harvard Club of N.Y.C. (bd. mgrs. 1998—). Clubs: Racquet & Tennis; Country of New Canaan, Winter (New Canaan); Harvard of Fairfield County. Home: 1 Greenley Rd New Canaan CT 06840-3513 Office: Holland & Co LLC 375 Park Ave New York NY 10152

HOLLAND, PHILLIP KENT, aerospace engineer; b. Wichita, Kans., Oct. 10, 1959; s. Phillip Norman and Lafreda Louise (Davenport) H.; m. Linda Kay Rosenbaum, June 27, 1980 (div. Dec. 1987); m. Delaine Marie Thompson, Mar. 17, 1989. BS in Aerospace Engring., Wichita State U., 1993. Seating engr. Raytheon Aircraft, Wichita, 1979-93; R&D group engr. Interiors and Seating Group Bombardier Learjet Inc., Wichita, 1993-99; pres. Millennium Concepts, Inc., Wichita, 1999—. *Mr. Holland has over twenty years of progressively responsible experience in Business Aircraft industry, in key decision making aircraft interiors, safety, and seat crashworthiness roles. He currently is president of Millennium Concepts, Inc., a company that specializes in aircraft interior design, engineering, and certification. He designed and certified the first crew seat to meet FAR Part 25.562 seat standards. He is the Vice-Chair on the SAE Seat Committee, which is responsible for the revision of all seat-related documents. He is a member of the SAE Seat Ad Hoc Committee, ARAC (Aviation Rulemaking Advisory Committee) and GAMA (General Aviation Manufacturers Association).* Mem. AIAA, Soc. Aerospace Engrs., (mem. AS8049 ad hoc com. 1990-97, vice chmn. SAE seat com. 1997—), GAMA (seat working group 1994—), Aviation Rulemaking Adv. Com. (AC25.562-1 seat working group 1994-96). Republican. Greek Orthodox. Achievements include design and certification engr. on aircraft seats and interiors. Home: 4206 Spyglass Cir Wichita KS 67226-3354 Office: Millennium Concepts Inc 1999 N Amidon Ste 230 Wichita KS 67203

HOLLAND, RANDY JAMES, state supreme court justice; b. Elizabeth, N.J., Jan. 27, 1947; s. James Charles and Virginia (Wilson) H.; m. Ilona E. Holland, June 24, 1972. B.A. in Econs., Swarthmore Coll., 1969; J.D. cum laude, U. Pa., 1972; LLM, Univ. Va., 1998. Bar: Del. 1972. Ptnr. Dunlap, Holland & Rich and predecessors, Georgetown, Del., 1972-80, Morris, Nichols, Arsht & Tunnell, Georgetown, Del., 1980-86; justice Supreme Ct. Del., Georgetown, 1986—; mem. Del. Bar Examiners, 1978-86; mem. Gov.'s Jud. Nominating Commn., 1978-86, sec., 1982-85, chmn., 1985-86; mem. Del. Supreme Ct. Consol. Com., 1985-86; pres. Terry-Carey Inn of Ct., 1991-94; v.p. Am. Inns of Ct., 1996—; co-chair Racial and Ethnic Task Force, 1995—; adj. prof. Widener U. Sch. Law, 1991—, U. Pa. Sch. Law, 1993-94; co-chair Del. Cts. Planning Com., 1996; chair nat. jud. adv. com. fed. Office of Child Support Enforcement; Jud. Ethics Adv. Commn., 1994—; del. Code Jud. Conduct Rev. Commn., 1991-94; del. Bar Bench Media Conf., 1990—. Mem. editorial bd. Del. Lawyer Mag., 1981-85; contbr. chpt. Del. Appellate Handbook, 1985—. Pres. adminstrv. bd. Ave. United Meth. Ch., Milford, Del. Bar Found.; hon. chmn. History of the Del. Bar in 20th Century, 1992—. Recipient Henry C. Loughlin prize for legal ethics U. Pa. 1972, St. Thomas More award, 1999; named Judge of the Yr. Nat. Child Support Enforcement Assn., 1992. Mem. ABA (standing com. on lawyer competence, nat. jud. coll. adv. commn. model rules jud. disclosure enforcement 1996), Am. Judicature Soc. (nat. trustee 1992—), Am. Inns of Ct. Found. (trustee 1992—, nat. trustee 1996—, v.p. 1996—), Am. Law Inst., Del. Bar Found., Am. Law Inst. Republican. Office: Del Supreme Ct Family Court Bldg 22 The Circle Georgetown DE 19947

HOLLAND, ROBERT CAMPBELL, anatomist, educator; b. Bushnell, Ill., Aug. 16, 1923; s. Harvey Howard and Lois Sarah (Campbell) H.; m. Hilda P. Burgi, Sept. 26, 1946 (dec. 1980); children: Jonathan Robert, Heather; m. Elaine M. Probst, Sept. 1, 1988; 1 child, Judith Ashley. BS, U. Wis., 1948, MS, 1949, PhD, 1955. Instr. Dental Sch. Northwestern U., 1949-51; asst. prof. anatomy Sch. Medicine U. N.D., 1955-60; assoc. prof. Sch. Medicine U. Ark., 1960-66; prof. chmn. dept. anatomy Mahidol U., Bangkok, 1966-76; prof., chmn. dept. anatomy Morehouse Sch. Medicine, Atlanta, 1976-90, prof. emeritus dept. anatomy, 1990—; mem. staff Rockefeller Found., 1966-76; vis. prof. UCLA Sch. Medicine, 1976. Author research pubs. on the brain. With M.C., U.S. Army, 1943-46. Fellow Wis. Alumni Rsch. Found., 1951-54, Nat. Found. for Infantile Paralysis, 1957-58; NIH grantee, 1959-88. Mem. Am. Assn. Anatomists, Am. Acad. Neurology, Soc. Exptl. Biology and Medicine, Soc. Neurosci., Sigma Xi.

HOLLAND, ROBERT CARL, economist; b. Tekamah, Nebr., Apr. 7, 1925; s. Carl Luther and Gretchen (Thompson) H.; m. DeEtte Harriet Hedlund, Sept. 7, 1947; children: Joan DeEtte Holland Geltz, Nancy Gretchen Holland Kerr, Timothy Robert. Student, U. Nebr., 1942-43, 46; BS in Fin., U. Pa., 1948, MA in Econs., 1949, PhD in Econs., 1959. Instr. money and banking U. Pa., 1948-49; with Fed. Res. Bank Chgo., 1949-61, v.p., 1959-61; with bd. govs. Fed. Res. System, 1961-76; mem. bd. govs. FRS, 1973-76, sec. of bd., 1968-71, exec. dir., 1971-73, sec. to fed. open market com., 1966-73; pres. Com. for Econ. Devel., Washington, 1976-90, sr. econ. cons., 1990-96; sr. fellow, bd. dirs. SEI Ctr. for Advanced Studies in Mgmt., U. Pa., 1990—; sr. fellow dept. Legal Studies, U. Pa., 1992—. With AUS, 1943-45. Mem. Am. Econ. Assn., Nat. Acad. Pub. Adminstrn., Internat. Soc. of Bus. Econs. and Ethics, Cosmos Club, Kenwood Country Club (Bethesda, Md.), Beta Theta Pi. Home: 5508 Cromwell Dr Bethesda MD 20816-2006

HOLLAND, ROBERT DEBNAM, SR., investment company executive; b. Norfolk, Va., Mar. 5, 1922; s. Ralph Frederick and Erma Gwendoly (Debnam) H.; m. Frances Lee Hodges, Dec. 26, 1943 (div. June 1984); children: Robert Debnam Jr., Elizabet Lee, William Peyton; m. Anne-Marie Lamb, Aug. 10, 1984. BA, U.S. Merchant Marine Acad., 1943, Centre Coll., Danville, Ky., 1949; postgrad., U. Va., 1950. Salesman IBM Corp., 1952-56; salesman Burroughs Corp., 1956-61, mgr. indsl. mktg., 1961-65; v.p. fin., pres. CIER, Inc., Washington, 1965-67; CEO Computer Leasing Co., 1967-74; pres. Photomatrics Corp., L.A., 1985-88; mng. ptnr. Transnat. Corp., Washington, 1975-85, Las Vegas, 1988—; bus. adv. U. Nev., Las Vegas, 1989—; treas., bd. dirsn. Internat. Label Co., Las Vegas, 1992—; chmn. exec. com. Network Recovery Sys., San Ramon, Calif., 1994—. Lt. comdr. USNR, 1942-55. Mem. AIM, Inst. Automation Rsch., Am. Mgmt. Assn., Sigma Chi, Omicron Delta Kappa, Phi Kappa Delta. Democrat. Episcopalian. Home: 3115 Pradera Cir Las Vegas NV 89121-3823 Office: U Nev 3720 Howard Hughes Pkwy Ste 130 Las Vegas NV 89109-5903

HOLLAND, ROBERT STEVENS, advertising executive, graphic designer; b. New Brunswick, N.J., Feb. 3, 1945; s. Ubert Cecil and Dorothy Teresa (Stevens) H.; m. Debra Ann Schlachman, June 21, 1969; children: David, Mairen. BFA, Md. Inst. Coll. Art, 1969. Asst. installationist The Balt. Mus. Art, 1969-72; art dir. Barton-Gillet, Balt., 1972-82; v.p., sr. art dir. Crowder Communications, Balt., 1982-84, ptnr., sr. art dir. R.S. Jensen, 1984-89; exec. art dir. William J. Kircher & Assocs., Washington, 1989-90; pres. Robert S. Holland Design, Ellicott City, Md., 1990—; mem. faculty Coll. Art, Md. Inst., 1993—; design cons. Michael David Brown, Inc., 1994—. Mem. Advt. and Graphic Arts Soc. Howard County (bd. dirs., pres. 1993-94), Am. Inst. Graphic Arts, Art Dirs. Club Met. Washington. Democrat.

HOLLAND, ROBIN JEAN, personnel company executive; b. Chgo., June 22, 1942; d. Robert Benjamin and Dolores (Levy) Shaeffer; 1 child, Robert Gene. BA in Pub. Rels. magna cum laude, U. So. Calif., 1977. Account exec. pub. rels. firm, 1977-79, Mgmt. Recruiters, 1979; owner, operator Holland Exec. Search, Marina Del Rey, Calif., 1979—; pres. Bus. Comm., Marina Del Rey, 1983—; cons. on outplacement to bus.; condr. seminars on exec. search; guest lectr. Active Ahead with Horses, Audubon Soc., conservation orgns. Recipient numerous local honors. Mem. Am. Coaster Enthusiasts, Mensa, Peruvian Paso Horse Owners and Breeders N.Am. Office: Holland Exec Search 4766 Admiralty Way Ste 9774 Marina Del Rey CA 90295

HOLLAND, ROSEMARY SHERIDAN, program evaluation consultant; b. Detroit, Oct. 15, 1939; d. Geoffrey Francis and Mary Ann (Beirne) Sheridan; m. Neal Holland, Sept. 1961 (div. Apr. 1968); 1 child, Daniel Holland; m. Fred Fechheimer, Nov. 29, 1974; 1 child, Steve Fechheimer. PhB, U. Detroit, 1961; MSW, U. Mich., 1969, MA, 1984, PhD, 1984. Tchr. Prince Georges County Bd. Edn., Seat Pleasant, Md., 1961-63; adminstrv. asst. Neighborhood Svc. Orgn., Detroit, 1969-73; dir. mental health planning Cmty. Health Planning Coun. S.E. Mich., Detroit, 1971-73; coord. adult mental health svcs. Detroit/Wayne County Comty. Mental Health Bd., 1973-76; pvt. practice Bloomfield Hills, Mich., 1976—; asst. prof. U. Detroit, 1984-89. Mem. NASW, APHA, APA. Avocations: walking, travel, reading.

HOLLAND, WILLARD RAYMOND, JR., electric utility executive; b. Springfield, Tenn., Apr. 22, 1936; s. Willard Raymond and Virginia (Byrum) H.; m. Mary Jean Fort; children: Willard Thomas, Lara Ann. BSEE, Rose Hulman Inst. Tech., 1965, MSEE, 1966. Registered profl. engr., Ohio, Mich. Assoc. engr. Detroit Edison Co., 1966-67, sales engr. comml. mktg., 1971-72, divsn. mgr. customer and mktg. svcs., 1972-74, mgr. thumb divsn., 1974-78, asst. mgr. prodn., 1979-80, mgr. nuclear ops., 1980-81, asst. v.p. & mgr. nuclear ops., 1981-82, v.p. nuclear ops., 1982-88, sr. v.p. nuclear ops., 1988-91; pres., COO Ohio Edison Co., Akron, 1991-93, pres., CEO, 1993-96, chmn., CEO, 1996-97; chmn., CEO FirstEnergy Corp., Akron, 1997—; chmn. bd. dirs. Pa. Power Co., New Castle; bd. dirs. A. Schulman, Inc., 1995—; bd. mgrs. Rose-Hulman Inst. Tech., 1996—. Trustee Akron Art Mus., 1992—, Akron Roundtable, 1993—, Leadership Akron, 1994—, Ohio Bus. Roundtable, Children's Hosp. Med. Ctr. Akron, 1992—, Akron Tomorrow, 1993—, Cleveland Tomorrow, 1998—; bd. dirs. Edison Elec. Inst., 1997—, Assn. of Edison Illuminating Coms., 1995—, Greater Cleveland Growth Assn, 1997—, Nuclear Energy Inst., 1998—. With U.S. Army, 1957-58. Mem. Akron City Club, Firestone Country Club, Portage Country Club. Avocations: photography, golf, hunting, fishing, antique cars. Office: FirstEnergy Corp 76 S Main St Akron OH 44308-1812

HOLLANDER, ANNE, writer; b. Cleve., Oct. 16, 1930; d. Arthur and Jean Hill (Bassett) Loesser; m. John Hollander, June 15, 1953 (div. 1977); children: Martha, Elizabeth; m. Thomas Nagel, June 26, 1979. BA, Barnard Coll., 1952. Author: Seeing Through Clothes, 1978, Moving Pictures, 1989, Sex and Suits, 1994, Feeding the Eye, 1999. Guggenheim fellow, 1975. Fellow N.Y. Inst. for the Humanities (interim dir. 1995-96); mem. Costume Soc. Am., College Art Assn., PEN Am. Ctr. (pres. 1995-96), Century Assn. *

HOLLANDER, DANIEL, gastroenterologist, medical educator; b. Mar. 3, 1939. Student, UCLA, to 1960; MD, Baylor U., 1964. Diplomate Am. Bd. Internal Medicine, Am. Bd. Gastroenterology. Intern Phila. Gen. Hosp., 1964-65; resident in internal medicine Med. Ctr., U. Kans., Kansas City, 1965-67; NIH rsch. fellow in gastroenterology U. Wash., Seattle, 1967-69; asst. prof. medicine Albany (N.Y.) Med. Coll., Union U., 1971-73, assoc. prof., 1973; assoc. prof. medicine, head div. gastroenterology Wayne State U., Detroit, 1973-77, prof. medicine, head div. gastroenterology, 1977-78; prof. medicine, head div. gastroenterology U. Calif., Irvine, 1978-94, prof. physiology and biophysics, 1981-94, assoc. dean for rsch. and program devel. Coll. Medicine, 1984-85, assoc. dean for acad. affairs, 1985-89, sr. assoc. dean for clin. affairs, 1989-91, chief gastroenterology Irvine Med. Ctr., 1979-94; exec. dean Sch. of Medicine U. Kans., Kansas City, 1994-95; chief med. officer Sierra Pacific Network, San Francisco, 1996-98; pres., CEO Harbor-UCLA, Rsch. and Edn. Inst., 1998—; prof. medicine UCLA, 1999—; attending physician, attending gastroenterologist Albany Med. Ctr. Hosp., 1971-73; chief gastroenterology svc., attending physician Harper Hosp., Detroit, 1973-78; cons. in gastroenterology Children's, Detroit Gen. and VA hosps., 1973-78; chief gastroenterology VA Med. Ctr., Long Beach, Calif., 1978-80; chmn.. Gastrointestinal Gerontology Rsch. Group, 1988-89; vis. scientist dept. molecular medicine U. Auckland, New Zealand, 1990-91; vis. prof., invited speaker numerous other univs., profl. meetings, confs.; prof. medicine U. Calif., San Francisco, 1996—. Author: (with G. Gitnick, N. Kaplowitz, I.M. Samloff, L.J. Schoenfield) Principles and Practice of Gastroenterology and Hepatology, 1988, (with A. Tarnawski) Gastic Cytoprotection—A Clinician's Guide, 1989, (with Porro G. Bianchi) Treatment of Digestive Disease with Sucralfate, 1989; mem. editl. bd., reviewer Can. Jour. Gastroenterology; contbr. numerous articles, revs. to profl. jours., book chpt. With USAF, 1969-71. Calif. Heart Assn. rsch. fellow, 1960; Fogarty Sr. Internat. fellow Oxford (Eng.) U., 1984-85; grantee NIH, Nat. Inst. on Aging, Nat. Insts. Arthritis, Metabolism and Digestive Diseases, Skillman Found., VA, Goldsmith Found., Internat. Pharm. Products. Mem. ACP (A. Blaine traveling scholar 1973), Am. Fedn. for Clin. Rsch. (pres. Midwestern sect. 1979-80), Am. Gastroent. Assn., Am. Physiol. Soc., Am. Soc. for Clin. Investigation, Orange County Gastroenterology Assn. (pres. 1986-87), Brit. Soc. Gastroenterology, European Assn. Gastroenterology, Western Assn. Physicians, Western Gut Club (pres. 1981-82), Alpha Omega Alpha. Office: Harbor-UCLA Rsch and Edn Inst 1124 W Carson St Torrance CA 90502-2006

HOLLANDER, EDWIN PAUL, psychologist, educator; b. Rochester, N.Y., Aug. 15, 1927; s. Victor and Lillian (Kravetz) H.; m. Patricia Ann Harrington, Apr. 18, 1959; 1 son, Peter Andrew. BS, Western Res. U., 1948; MA, Columbia U., 1950, PhD, 1952. Asst. prof. psychology Carnegie Inst. Tech., Pitts., 1954-58; asso. prof. psychology Washington U., St. Louis, 1958-60; asso. prof. internat. communication and social psychology Sch. Internat. Service, Am. U., Washington, 1960-62; prof. psychology SUNY-Buffalo, 1962-89, provost social scis. and adminstrn., 1971-73, dir. social psychology doctoral program, 1962-68, 73-76; vis. prof. Baruch Coll. and Univ. Grad. Ctr., CUNY, N.Y.C., 1987-89, Univ. Disting. prof. psychology, 1989—, prof. emeritus, 1999—; study dir. NAS, NRC, 1979-80; vis. faculty U. Istanbul, Turkey, 1957-58, U. Wis., 1961, Inst. Am. Studies, Paris, 1966-67, Harvard U., 1969-70, Oxford (Eng.) U., 1973; cons. NSF, 1965-68, HEW, 1967-72, NAS, NRC, Space Sci. Bd., 1969-70; prin. investigator research projects Office Naval Research, 1955-69, 76-79, NIMH, 1962-64. Author: Leaders, Groups and Influence, 1964, Principles and Methods of Social Psychology, 1967, 4th edit., 1981, Leadership Dynamics, 1978; co-editor: Current Perspectives in Social Psychology, 1963, 4th edit., 1976, Classic Contributions to Social Psychology, 1972; mem. editorial bd.: Jour. Abnormal and Social Psychology, 1962-64, Jour. Personality Social Psychology, 1965-67, Brit. Jour. Social and Clin. Psychology, 1967-79; Leadership Quarterly, 1989-91; editorial bd.: Sociometry, 1969-72, asso. editor, 1971-72; editorial bd., asso. editor: Internat. Rev. Applied Psychology, 1975-79; contbr. articles to profl. jours., chpts. to books, papers at internat. congresses and profl. meetings. Served with AUS, 1946-47; from ensign to lt. USNR, 1951-54. Fulbright fellow Turkey, 1957-58; NIMH sr. fellow Tavistock Inst. Human Rels., London, 1966-67; recipient Disting. Achievement award Psychol. Assn. Western N.Y., 1983, Kurt Lewin award social psychology N.Y. State Psychol. Assn., 1986. Fellow Am. Psychol. Soc., N.Y. Acad. Scis. (adv. com. psychology sect. 1990—), AAAS (sec. psychology sect. 1974-78), APA (chmn. com. psychology nat. internat. affairs 1962-63, coun. reps. 1965-66, 68-70, 79-81, 83-86, mem. bd. social and ethical responsibility for psychology 1975-78, com. on internat. rels. psychology 1981-84, pres. div. gen. psychology 1980-81), Soc. Indsl. and Orgnl. Psychol.; mem. AAUP (pres. Carnegie Tech. chpt. 1956-57), Soc. Exptl. Social Psychology (chmn. exec. com. 1969-70), Ea. Psychol. Assn. (bd. dirs. 1982-85, 91-94, pres. 1988-89), Soc. Psychol. Study Social Issues (coun. 1968-70), Internat. Assn. Applied Psychology (exec. com. 1975-86, U.S. treas. 1980-82), Internat. Soc. Polit. Psychology (gov. coun. 1985-87, v.p. 1988-90), Am. Assn. Univ. Adminstrs., Acad. Mgmt., Authors Guild, Sigma Xi, Omicron Delta Kappa, Psi Chi. Clubs: Cosmos (Washington), Harvard (N.Y.C.). Home: 330 E 39th St Apt 19L New York NY 10016-2122 Office: CUNY Baruch Coll & U Grad Ctr 17 Lexington Ave New York NY 10010-5518

HOLLANDER, GERHARD LUDWIG, computer company executive; b. Berlin, Feb. 27, 1922; s. Ernst Julius and Cacilie H.; m. Marianne Schempp, Dec. 24, 1957; children: Susan, Carolyn, Jeffrey. BS in Elec. Engring., Ill. Inst. Tech., 1947; MS, Washington U., St. Louis, 1948; EE, MIT, 1953. Registered profl. engr., Ill. Radio buyer Spiegel, Inc., 1940-42; rsch. engr. McDonnell Aircraft Co., 1947; asst. prof. engring. St. Louis U., 1948-49; sr. engr. servo lab. Raytheon Mfg. Co., 1949-51; mem. rsch. staff servomechanisms lab. MIT, Cambridge, 1952-54; sect. head data processing systems Clevite Rsch. Ctr., 1954-57; sect. mgr. computer systems Philco Corp., 1957-60; mgr. gen. purpose computer dept. Hughes Aircraft Co., 1960-61; pres., tech. dir. Hollander Assocs., Fullerton, Calif., 1961—; cons. govt. agys., indsl. firms, 1953—, Argonne Nat. Lab., 1957, USAF Hdqrs., 1959-60, IBM, 1976, Dept. Def., 1976-81, Social Security Adminstrn., 1975-79, Dept. of Energy, 1981-83; U.S. del. Internat. Fedn. of Automatic Control Congresses, Moscow, Russia, 1960; bd. dirs. WINCON, 1975-79, chmn., 1978-79; founding dir. Elec. and Electronics Exhibits, Inc., 1974. Fellow Inst. for Advancement Engring., Nat. Contract Mgmt. Assn. (vice chmn., program chmn. 1975-78), IEEE (chmn. computing devices com., vice-chmn. computer group, 1962-65, gen. chmn. joint nat. conf. maj. systems 1971, gen. chmn. Westex '86 Expert Systems conf., chmn. bd. dirs. Westex, 1986-90, Centennial medal 1984); mentor U. Calif., Irvine, 1995-97, adv. bd., 1997—; mem. Assn. Computer Machinery, Ops. Rsch. Soc. Am., Am. Fedn. Info. Processing Socs. (nat. joint computer com. 1959-61, dir. 1962-65, Cosati rep. NSF, 1965-68), Am. Automatic Control Coun. (control adv. com. 1960-62, mentor 1995-97, adv. bd. 1997—), Sigma Xi, Sigma Alpha Mu. Editor: Computers in Control, 1961; chmn. editorial bd. Computer Design, 1969-73; contbr. numerous articles to profl. jours.; patentee in field. Pioneer in hierarchical memory concept used in computers and packet switching in communications. Office: Hollander Assocs PO Box 2276 Fullerton CA 92837-0276

HOLLANDER, HERBERT I., consulting engineer; b. N.Y.C., July 23, 1924; s. Jacob and Saide (Sporer) H.; m. Evelyn V. Schovajsa, Sept. 4, 1949; children: Keith R., Janice G. BME, CCNY, 1955; MBA, Bernard Baruch Coll., 1963. Registered profl. engr., Conn., Fla., N.Y., Ohio, Maine, Va.; diplomate Am. Acad. Environ Engrs. (trustee). Dist. mgr. Detroit Stoker Co.-Div. United Indsl. Corp., N.Y.C., 1948-65; regional mgr. Riley Stoker Co., Worcester, Mass., 1965-69; prin. cons. Roy F. Weston Inc., West Chester, Pa., 1969-72, Gilbert Assocs., Inc., Reading, Pa., 1972-80; v.p. STV/Sanders & Thomas, Pottstown, Pa., 1980-88; prin. Hollander Assocs., Wyomissing, Pa., 1988—; presenter in field. Contbr. to Standard Handbook of Environmental Engineering; compiler, editor: ASTM Thesaurus on Resource Recovery Terminology; contbr. articles on indsl. and mcpl. waste-residue mgmt., fuel preparation and utilization, energy conversion, and power generation systems to confs., seminars and profl. jours. Mem. spring Twp. (Pa.) Zoning Bd., 1982-85. Fellow ASME (founding, past chmn. solid waste processing div., rsch. com. on indsl. and mcpl. wastes, Disting. medal of achievement 1990); mem. ASTM (founding mem. com. on resource recovery, com. on hazardous waste disposal, cert. of merit 1983, Frank W. Reinhart award 1984), Air and Waste Mgmt. Assn., Solid Waste Assn. N.Am., Am. Acad. Environ. Engrs. (trustee). Avocations: photography, golf. Fax: 610-678-2877. Home and Office: 1605 Sherwood Rd Reading PA 19610-1127

HOLLANDER, JOHN, humanities educator, poet; b. N.Y.C., Oct. 28, 1929; s. Franklin and Muriel (Kornfeld) H.; m. Anne Helen Loesser, June 15, 1953 (div. 1977); children: Martha, Elizabeth.; m. Natalie Charkow, Dec. 15, 1981. AB, Columbia U., 1950, AM, 1952; PhD, Ind. U., 1959; DLitt (hon.), Marietta Coll., 1982; LHD (hon.), Ind. U., 1990; DFA (hon.), Maine Coll. of Art, 1993. Jr. fellow Soc. Fellows, Harvard, 1954-57; lectr. English Conn. Coll., New London, 1957-59; instr. English Yale, 1959-61; asst. prof. English, fellow Ezra Stiles Coll., 1961-64, assoc. prof., 1964-66; prof. Hunter Coll., CCNY, 1966-77; prof. English Yale U., New Haven, 1977—, A. Bartlett Giamatti prof., 1987—, Sterling prof., 1995—; vis. prof. Linguistic Inst., Inc. U., 1964; mem. faculty Salzburg Seminar in Am. Studies, 1965; Christian Gauss seminarian Princeton U., 1962. Author: A Crackling of Thorns, 1958, The Untuning of the Sky, 1961, Movie-Going and Other Poems, 1962, Various Owls, 1963, Visions from the Ramble, 1965, The Quest of the Gole, 1966, Types of Shape, 1968, 2d edit., 1991, Images of Voice, 1970, The Night Mirror, 1971, Town and Country Matters, 1972, The Head of the Bed, 1973, Tales Told of the Fathers, 1975, Vision and Resonance, 1975, Reflections on Espionage, 1976, Spectral Emanations, 1978, In Place, 1978, Blue Wine, 1979, The Figure of Echo, 1981, Rhyme's Reason, 1981, 2d edit., 1989, Powers of Thirteen, 1983, (with Saul Steinberg) Dal Vero, 1983, In Time and Place, 1986, Some Fugitives Take Cover, 1988, Harp Lake, 1988, Melodious Guile, 1988, Tesserae, 1993, Selected Poetry, 1993, The Gazer's Spirit, 1995, The Work of Poetry, 1997, The Poetry of Everyday Life, 1998, Figurehead and Other Poems, 1999; editor: Poems of Ben Jonson, 1961, (with Harold Bloom) The Wind and the Rain, 1961, (with Anthony Hecht) Jiggery-Pokery, 1966, Poems of Our Moment, 1968, Modern Poetry: Essays in Criticism, 1968, American Short Stories Since 1945, 1968, (with Frank Kermode) The Oxford Anthology of English Literature, 1973, (with Reuben A. Brower and Helen Vendler) For I.A. Richards: Essays in His Honor, 1973, (with Irving Howe and David Bromwich) Literature as Experience, 1979, The Essential Rossetti, 1990, Animal Poems, 1994, Garden Poems, 1996, Committed to Memory, 1997, Marriage Poems, 1997, Marriage Poems, 1999; contbg. editor: Harper's mag, 1969-71; mem. editorial bd. Raritan, 1981—, Art and Lit., 1985—, Lit., 1989—; assoc. for poetry Partisan Review, 1959-65; mem. poetry bd. Wesleyan U. Press, 1959-62; contbr. poems, articles to various jours. Recipient Yale Younger Poets award, 1958, Poetry Chap Book award, 1962, award in lit. Nat. Inst. Arts and Letters, 1963, Levinson prize, 1974, Bollingen prize, 1983, Mina P. Shaughnessy award, 1963, Melville Cane award, 1990, Ambassador Book award, 1994, Gov.'s Arts award State of Conn., 1997, Robert Penn Warren-Cleanth Brooks award, 1998; Overseas fellow Churchill Coll., Cambridge (Eng.) U., 1967-68, sr. fellow NEH, 1973-74, Guggenheim fellow, 1979-80, MacArthur Found. fellow, 1990-95. Mem. Acad. Am. Poets (chancellor), Am. Acad. Arts and Letters, Am. Acad. Arts and Scis., Century Assn. Club (N.Y.C.), Phi Beta Kappa. Office: Yale U Dept English PO Box 208302 New Haven CT 06520-8302

HOLLANDER, LAWRENCE JAY, marketing executive; b. Chgo., Feb. 15, 1940; s. Harry and Ann Blanche (Rovner) H.; m. Sallie Sue Mines, June 21, 1964; children: Marla, Amy, Rebecca. BSBA, Roosevelt U., 1963. Dir. Far East ops. Indsl. & Sci. Conf. Mgmt., Chgo., 1972-77; dir. mktg. Far East ops. Clapp & Poliak, Inc., N.Y.C., 1978-81; pres. Expoconsul Internat. Inc., Princeton, N.J., 1981-95, EI Mktg., Inc., Princeton, 1987-94, Ctr. for Tech. Concepts, Inc., Princeton, 1988-92, Expoconsul Mktg. Group, Inc., Princeton, 1992-94; dir. corp. fin. J.S. Holdings Group, Inc., Bay Head, N.J., 1996; shareholder, investment banker J.S. Securities, Inc., Bayhead, N.J., 1995-96; pres. Entrepreneurial Mgmt. Group, Inc., Princeton, N.J., 1996—. Bd. dirs. Congregation Beth Chaim, West Windsor, N.J., 1984, Jewish Cmty. Ctr., of Delaware Valley, Ewing, N.J., 1987-96, v.p. 1990-92, pres. 1993-94; bd. dirs. Jewish Fedn. Mercer and Buck Counties, N.J., Pa., 1988-95, v.p., 1989-90; mem. planning bd. West Windsor Twp., N.J., 1997—. Mem. Rotary Club of the Princeton Corridor (charter mem. 1986—, sec. 1990-91, sgt.-at-arms 1991-92, 97-98, bd. dirs. 1992-93, 96—). Republican. Jewish. Avocations: weight-lifting, walking, tennis. Office: Entrepreneurial Mgmt Grp Inc PO Box 2231 Princeton NJ 08543-2231

HOLLANDER, MILTON BERNARD, corporate executive; b. Bayonne, N.J., Nov. 29, 1928; s. Harry and Lena (Hutner) H.; m. Betty Ruth Grodberg, June 8, 1952; children—Eva Lynn, J. Steven, Aaron Phillip, Joel Daniel. BS, Purdue U., 1951; MS, MIT, 1953; PhD, Columbia U., 1959. Dir. engring. ctr. Am. Machine & Foundry Co., Springdale, Conn., 1956-67; v.p. tech. Am.-Standard, Inc., N.Y.C., 1967-72; chmn. bd. Gulf & Western Invention Devel. Corp., N.Y.C., 1974-85; v.p. sci. and tech. Gulf & Western Industries, Inc., N.Y.C., 1972-85; ret., 1985; exec. v.p. Tech. Mgmt. Inc., Stamford, Conn., 1985—; chmn. bd., chief exec. officer Newport Electronics Inc., Stamford, 1989—; pres. Analog & Numeric Devices, Inc., Stamford, 1990—; cons. electronics lab. Columbia U., 1955-57; dir., tech. cons. Omega Engring. Inc., Stamford, Conn. Author tech. papers temperature measurement, metal cutting, instrumentation. Bd. dirs. Conn. Tech. Inst. Served with C.E. AUS, 1946-48, Korea. Recipient Outstanding Alumnus award Purdue U., 1972, Outstanding Mech. Engring. award, Purdue U., 1991; rsch. fellow MIT 1952-53; duPont rsch. fellow Columbia U., 1955-57; rsch. fellow Am. Soc. Tool and Mfg. Engrs., 1954-55; named Outstanding Young Man Am., 1965. Mem. ASME, Am. Welding Soc., Indsl. Research Inst. (bd. dirs.), Instrument Soc. Am., Soc. Mfg. Engrs., Sigma Xi. Patentee in field. Office: Newport Electronics 1 Omega Dr PO Box 4047 Stamford CT 06907-0047

HOLLANDER, ROBERT B., JR., Romance languages educator; b. N.Y.C., July 31, 1933; s. Robert B. and Laurene (McGookey) H.; m. Jean Haberman, Apr. 23, 1964; children: Cornelia Vanness, Robert B. III. A.B., Princeton U., 1955; Ph.D., Columbia U., 1962. Tchr. Latin and English, Collegiate Sch., N.Y.C., 1955-57; instr. English Columbia U., N.Y.C., 1958-62; mem. faculty dept. Princeton (N.J.) U., 1962—, prof. European lit., 1974—, chmn. comparative lit., 1994-98; mem. Nat. Coun. on Humanities, 1974-80, 87-92, vice chmn., 1978-80; mem. N.J. Com. for Humanities, 1980-86; dir. Dartmouth Dante Project, 1982—, Princeton Dante Project, 1997—; v.p. Assn. Internat. Studi de Lingua et Lett. Italiana, 1985-94; trustee La Scuola d'Italia, N.Y.C., 1986-92, Collegiate Sch., 1990-96, vice pres. bd., 1994-96, pres. bd., 98—. Author: Allegory in Dante's Commedia, 1969, Boccaccio's Two Venuses, 1977, Studies in Dante, 1980, Il Virgilio dantesco, 1983, Boccaccio's Last Fiction: Il Corbaccio, 1988, Dante's Epistle to Cangrande, 1993, Boccaccio's Dante and the Shaping Force of Satire, 1997; editor and translator: (with T. Hampton and M. Frankel) Amorosa Visione, 1986; co-editor: L'Espositione di Bernardino Daniello da Lucca sopra la Comedia di Dante, 1989. Trustee Nat. Humanities Ctr., 1981—, chmn. bd. trustees, 1988-91. Guggenheim fellow, 1970-71; NEH fellow, 1974-75, 82-83; recipient Gold medal of the City of Florence for work on behalf of Dante, 1988, Bronze medal of the City of Tours, 1993, John Witherspoon award in the Humanities, Com. for the Humanities, N.J., 1988, Internat. Nicola Zingarelli prize for Dantean philology and criticism, 1999; hon. citizen Ceutaldo, Italy, 1997. Mem. Dante Soc. Am. (mem. council 1976-85, pres. 1980-85), Am. Boccaccio Assn. Republican. Club: Cosmos (Washington). Office: Princeton U Dept of Romance Langs E Pyne Princeton NJ 08544

HOLLANDER, SAMUEL, economist, educator; b. London, Apr. 6, 1937; s. Jacob and Rachel-Leah (Bornstein) H.; m. Perlette Kéroub, July 20, 1959; children: Frances, Isaac. BSc in Econs, London Sch. Econs., 1959; MA, Princeton U., 1961, PhD, 1963. Asst. in instrn. Princeton U., 1962-63; asst. prof. econs. U. Toronto, Ont., Can., 1963-66, assoc. prof., 1966-70, prof., 1970-84, univ. prof., 1984-98, univ. prof. emeritus, 1998—; rsch. dir. U. Nice (CNRS), France, 1999—. Author: The Sources of Increased Efficiency, 1965, The Economics of Adam Smith, 1973, The Economics of David Ricardo, 1979, The Economics of J.S. Mill, 1985, Classical Economics, 1987, Ricardo: The 'New View'-Collected Essays I, 1995, The Economics of Thomas Robert Malthus, 1997, The Literature of Political Economy-Collected Essays II, 1998. Decorated officer Order of Can., 1998; Guggenheim fellow, 1968-69, Killam sr. fellow, 1973-75, Connaught sr. fellow, 1984-85, Social Sci. and Humanities Rsch. Coun. Can. fellow, 1981-84, 88-92, 93-96, 96-99, 99—. Fellow Royal Soc. Can. Jewish. Office: 150 St George St, Toronto, ON Canada M5S 1A1

HOLLANDER, STANLEY CHARLES, marketing educator; b. Balt., Aug. 2, 1919; s. Abraham A. and Selma (Langfeld) H.; m. Selma Dorothy Jacobs, Dec. 16, 1956. BS, NYU, 1941; MA, Am. U., 1946; PhD, U. Pa., 1954. Trainee, asst. mgr. Neisner Bros., various locations, 1941-43; analyst U.S. Office Price Adminstrn., Washington, 1943-45, cons., 1946; analyst Charles Stores Co., N.Y.C., 1945-47; instr. dept. mktg. U. Buffalo, 1947-49; instr. dept. mktg. U. Pa., Phila., 1949-54, assoc. prof., 1956-58; asst. prof. Sch. Bus. U. Minn., Mpls., 1954-56; assoc. prof. mktg. Mich. State U., East Lansing, 1958-59, prof., 1959-90, prof. emeritus, 1990—. Author: Retail Price Policies, 1958; Multinational Retailing, 1958; Restraints on Retail Competition, 1965; author (with D.J. Duncan) Modern Retailing Management, 1972, 77, (with R. Savitt), 83, (with R. Germain) Was There a Pepsi Generation Before Pepsi Discovered It?, 1992; editor: Exploration in Retailing, 1959; (with R. Moyer) Markets and Marketing in Developing Countries, 1968; (with J. Boddewyn) Public Policy Toward Retailing, 1972; Passenger Transportation, 1968; Business Consultants and Clients, 1963; Management Consultants and Clients, 1972, K. Rassuli) Marketing, 1993; also articles. Recipient NYU Inst. Retail Mgmt. award, 1964; named Disting. Scholar Mich. State U., 1982, Outstanding Mktg. Educator Acad. Mktg. Sci., 1991; essays written in honor of Stanley Hollander in Festschrift Historical Perspectives in Marketing, 1988. Mem. Am. Mktg. Assn., Am. Coll. Retailing Assn. (pres. 1986-88), Am. Econ. Assn., Acad. Mktg. Sci. (bd. govs. 1986-92), AAUP, Univ. Club (Lansing), Beta Gamma Sigma, Eta Mu Pi. Jewish. Office: Mich State U 305 North Bus Complex East Lansing MI 48824-1122

HOLLANDER, TOBY EDWARD, education educator; b. Queens, N.Y., June 21, 1931; s. David and Eve (Shroot) H.; m. Harriet Goldberg, June 14, 1953; children: Marc, Deborah. B.S. cum laude, NYU, 1952, M.B.A., 1953; Ph.D., U. Pitts., 1960. Instr. econs. U. Pitts., 1957-58; asst. prof. Duquesne U., 1958-59; prof. Baruch Coll., CUNY, 1963-67, dean, 1967-69, vice chancellor, 1969-71; dep. commr. higher edn. N.Y. State Edn. Dept., 1971-77; chancellor N.J. Dept. Higher Edn., Trenton, 1977-90; prof. Rutgers U., 1990—. Author books in field; contbr. articles to profl. jours. Served with U.S. Army, 1953-55. Mem. State Higher Edn. Exec. Officers Assn. (pres. 1977-78), Edn. Commn. of the States, Assn. Governing Bds. of Univs. and Colls. Home: 889 Lawrenceville Rd Princeton NJ 08540-4317 Office: Rutgers U Grad Sch Mgmt 92 New St Newark NJ 07102-1818

HOLLANDSWORTH, TODD MATHEW, baseball player; b. Dayton, Ohio, Apr. 20, 1973. Baseball player L.A. Dodgers, 1995—. Named Nat. League Rookie of the Yr. Baseball Writer's Assn. of Am., 1996. *

HOLLANS, IRBY NOAH, JR., retired association executive; b. Christiansburg, Va., Nov. 3, 1930; s. Irby Noah and Annie May (Lester) H.; m. Frances Jo Cox, June 21, 1957; children: Susan Frances, Carol Leigh, Irby Neil. B.S. in Gen. Bus. Adminstrn., Va. Poly. Inst. and State U., 1953. Mgr. promotion Sta. WRVA-Radio, Richmond, Va., 1956-64; editor bus. news Sta. WRVA-Radio, 1956-64; dir. travel devel. Va. State C. of C., 1964-70, asst. exec. dir., 1970-72; exec. dir. Optical Labs. Assn., Washington, 1972-96; instr. bus. Va. Commonwealth U., Richmond, 1965-71. Mem. Dulles (Va.) Internat. Airport Devel. Commn., 1968-76; mem. Va. Nat. Capital Airports Acquisition Study Commn., 1968-76; bd. dirs. Va. Thanksgiving Festival Inc., 1965-70, Keep Va. Beautiful, Inc., 1965-73, Central Va. Ednl. TV, 1970-72, Va. Travel Coordinating Com., 1964-72. Served to maj. USAF, 1953-72, Korea. Recipient Service award Va. Profl. Photographers Assn., 1966; Nat. award Profl. Photographers Assn. Am., 1970. Mem. Am. Soc. Assn. Execs. (cert.), Va. Pub. Rels. Conf., Nat. Assn. Wholesaler-Distbrs.-Pros Group, Am. Nat. Stds. Inst. (med. devices stds. mgmt. bd. 1973-80), Washington Soc. Assn. Execs., Va. C. of C., Vienna (Va.) Photog. Soc. (pres. 1990-92), Greater Washington Coun. Camera Clubs (exec. v.p. 1988-93), Rotary Internat. (exec. dir. 1996—). Home and Office: 5339 Cristfield Ct Fairfax VA 22032-3809

HOLLANSKY, BERT VOYTA, stock brokerage executive; b. Prague, Czech Republic, May 9, 1944; came to U.S., 1954.; BS, U. Ill., 1967; MBA, Am. Grad. Sch., Phoenix, 1969. Mgr. internat. devel. Cummins Engine Co., Columbus, Ind., 1969-81; v.p. Prudential Securities Inc., Columbus, 1981-89; v.p., stockbroker J.J.B. Hilliard W.L. Lyons Inc, Columbus, 1989—. Mem. Columbus C. of C., Hilliard Lyon's Dir.'s Club. Avocations: water skiing, family activities. Office: JJB Hilliard WL Lyons Inc PO Box 466 426 Washington St Columbus IN 47201-6758

HÖLLDOBLER, BERTHOLD KARL, zoologist, educator; b. Erling-Andechs, Germany, June 25, 1936; came to U.S., 1973; s. Karl and Maria (Russmann) H.; m. Friederike Probst, Feb. 9, 1980; children: Jakob, Stefan, Sebastian. Dr. rer. nat., U. Wurzburg, 1965; Dr. habil., U. Frankfurt a.M., 1969. Prof. zoology U. Frankfurt a.M., 1971-72; prof. biology Harvard U., Cambridge, Mass., 1973-90, Alexander Agassiz prof. zoology, 1982-90; prof. U. Wurzburg, Germany, 1989—; adj. prof. U. Ariz., Tucson; rsch. assoc. Harvard U. Author: (with Edward O. Wilson) The Ants, 1990 (Pulitzer Prize for gen. non-fiction 1991), (with E.O. Wilson) Journey to the Arts, (Shortlisted for the Rhone-Poulenc Sci. Book prize, 1995, Phi Beta Kappa prize, 1995). John Simon Guggenheim fellow, 1980; recipient Sr. Scientist award Alexander von Humboldt Found., 1986-87, Gottfried Wilhelm Leibniz prize, 1989, Phi Beta Kappa prize (with E.O. Wilson) 1995, Karl Ritter von Frisch medal and Sci. prize, German Zool. Soc., 1996, Körber-prize for European Sci., 1996, Benjamin Franklin, Wilhelm v. Humboldt Prize of the German Amer. Acad. Counc. (GAAC), 1999. Fellow AAAS, Am. Animal Behavior Soc.; mem. Nat. Acad. of Sci. (fgn. mem.), Am. Acad. Sci., German Acad. der Naturforscher Leopoldina, Bayerische Acad. der Wissenschaften, Acad. Europaea, Berlin-Brandenburgische Acad., Am. Philos. Soc. (fgn. mem.). Office: Biozentrum Am Hubland, D-97074 Würzburg Germany

HOLLE, REGINALD HENRY, retired bishop; b. Burton, Tex., Nov. 21, 1925; s. Alfred W. and Lena (Nolte) H.; m. Marla C. Christianson, June 16, 1949; children: Todd, Joan. BA, Capital U., 1946, DD (hon.), 1979; MDiv, Trinity Luth. Sem., 1949; D of Ministry, Ohio Consortium Religious Stdy, 1977; DD (hon.), Wittenberg U., 1989. Ordained minister Evang. Luth. Ch. Am., then bishop. Assoc. pastor Zion Luth. Ch., Sandusky, Ohio, 1949-51; sr. pastor Salem Meml. Luth. Ch., Detroit, 1951-72, Parma Luth. Ch., Cleve., 1973-78; bishop Mich. dist. Am. Luth. Ch., Detroit, 1978-87; bishop NW Lower Mich. Synod Evang. Luth. Am., Lansing, 1988-95; bd. dirs. Aubsburg Fortress Pub. House, Wittenberg U. Author: Planning for Funerals, 1978; contbr. to Augsburg Sermon Series. Bd. dirs. Ronald McDonald House Ctrl. Mich., 1995—, Planned Giving Luth. Social Svcs. Mich., 1995—. Recipient Pub. Svc. citation Harper Woods City Coun., 1976, Recognition for Community Svc., Detroit Pub. Schs., 1974.

HOLLEB, ARTHUR IRVING, surgeon; b. N.Y.C., Apr. 1, 1921; s. Simon and Kate (Liss) H.; m. Carolyn R. Oglesby, June 16, 1951; children: Susan Jane and David Gene (twins). AB, Brown U., 1941; MD, NYU, 1944. Diplomate: Am. Bd. Surgery. Intern Queens Gen. Hosp., Jamaica, N.Y., 1944-45; resident tumor surgery and pathology Meadowbrook Hosp., Hempstead, N.Y., 1945-46, chief resident gen. surgery, 1948-50, asst. dir. tumor svc., 1954-56; mem. staff Meml. Hosp., N.Y.C., 1950-67, assoc. chief med. officer, 1966-67, cons. breast svc. surgery dept., 1968-95; assoc. vis. surgeon James Ewing Hosp., N.Y.C., 1966-67; mem. rsch. staff M.D. Anderson Hosp. and Tumor Inst., Houston, 1967-68, cons. breast cancer study sect., 1968-88; sr. v.p. med. affairs and rsch., chief med. officer Am. Cancer soc., N.Y.C., 1968-88; from instr. to clin. assoc. prof. surgery Med. Coll. Cornell U., 1965-67; assoc. clinician Sloan-Kettering Inst., 1961-67; assoc. prof. surgery U. Tex. M.D. Anderson Hosp. and Tumor Inst., 1967-68, assoc. dir. edn., 1967-68; James Ewing Meml. lectr. Soc. Surg. Oncology, 1980; Wendell Scott Meml. lectr. Am. Coll. Radiology, 1978; mem. evaluation panel, sr. clin. traineeships in surgery, cancer control br. USPHS, 1965-68; mem. cancer control adv. com. diagnostic rsch. adv. group and therapy com. Nat. Cancer Inst., NIH, 1972-82. Editor in chief: Jour. CA; editorial adv. bd. Am. Jour. Preventive Medicine. With USNR, 1946-48. Recipient W.W. Keen Disting. Svc. award Brown U., 1977, Disting. Alumnus award Meml. Sloan Kettering Cancer Ctr., 1989. Mem. ACS, AMA, Am. Assn. Cancer Edn., Am. Assn. Cancer Rsch., Am. Cancer Soc. (bd. dirs. N.Y.C. chpt. 1964-67), Am. Radium Soc. (v.p. 1969-70), Assn. Am. Med. Colls., Assn. Hosp. Dirs. Med. Edn. (chmn. surg. edn. com. 1965-67), Harris County Med. Soc., Am. Soc. Clin. Oncology, James Ewing Soc. (pres. 1972-73), N.Y. Acad. Medicine, N.Y. County Med. Soc., N.Y. Acad. Scis., N.Y. Cancer Soc. (pres. 1971), N.Y. Surg. Soc., Brown U. Club. Home and Office: 3 Highridge Rd Larchmont NY 10538-1409

HOLLEB, DORIS B., urban planner, economist; b. N.Y.C., Oct. 26, 1922; m. Marshall M. Holleb, Oct. 15, 1944; children: Alan, Gordon, Paul. BA magna cum laude, Hunter Coll., 1942; MA, Harvard U., 1947; postgrad. U. Chgo., 1959-60, 65-66. Economist Fed. Res. Bd., Washington, 1943-44; freelance journalist, 1945-63; econ. cons. Chgo. Dept. City Planning, 1963-64; rsch. assoc. Ctr. Urban Studies, U. Chgo., 1966-78, sr. rsch. assoc., 1978-88, dir. Met. Inst., 1973-84, professorial lectr., 1979—; chmn., Francis W. Parker Sch. Ednl. Coun., 1963-80; cons., 1980-92; bd. dirs. Adlai E. Stevenson Inst., 1972-79; mem. adv. coun. Ctr. for the Study Democratic Inst., 1975-79; bd. dirs. Inter. Am. Found., 1980-84, Pacific Basin Inst., 1981-98; mem. nat. adv. com. White House Conf. on Balanced Nat. Growth and Econ. Devel., 1978; mem. Northea. Ill. Planning Commn., 1973-77; mem. Chgo. Met. Area Transp. Coun., 1980-84; mem. adv. coun. to Nat. Ctr. Rsch. on Vocat. Edn., Dept. Edn., 1979-82, Dept. State adv. com. internat. investment, tech. and devel., 1979-81; commr. Chgo. Plan Commn., 1986—; bd. dirs. Internat. Ctr. for Rsch. on Women, 1985-91, Nat. Coun. on Humanities, 1998—. Author: Social and Economic Information for Urban Planning, 1968, Colleges and the Urban Poor, 1972; contbr. articles to profl. jours.; v.p. editl. bd. Illinois Issues, 1977—. Mem. Am. Inst. Cert. Planners, Am. Planning Assn., Am. Econ. Assn., Arts Club, Univ. Club, Quadrangle Club, Harvard Club N.Y.C., Phi Beta Kappa, Nat. Phi Beta Kappa Assocs. (dir. 1997—), Lambda Alpha.

HOLLEMAN, PAUL DOUGLAS, lawyer; b. Okmulgee, Okla., May 18, 1931; s. Paul and Mary Anne (Douglas) H.; m. Mary W. Dreier, Oct. 4, 1958; children—Martha Anne, Paul Frederick, Andrew Douglas. B.A. magna cum laude, U. Ky., 1953; LL.B., Harvard U., 1958. From assoc. to ptnr. Holme Roberts & Owen LLC, Denver, 1958-69, mem., 1972—; pres. Inter-Am. Petroleum Corp., Denver, 1969-72; chmn. 28th Ann. Rocky Mountain Mineral Law Inst., Colo., 1982. Contbr. articles to profl. jours. Trustee Disciples of Christ Ch., 1993—. 1st lt. U.S. Army, 1951-53. Mem. Colo. Bar Assn. (chmn. mineral law sect. 1975-76), Denver Bar Assn., ABA (chmn. natural resource sect. workshop on fed. oil and gas leasing and ops. 1983-85), Phi Beta Kappa. Republican. Avocations: golf; travel; reading. Office: Holme Roberts & Owen LLC 1700 Lincoln St Ste 4100 Denver CO 80203-4541

HOLLEMAN, SANDY LEE, religious organization administrator; b. Celina, Tex., June 6, 1940; d. Guy Lee and Gustine (Kirby-Sheets) Luna; m. Allen Craig Holleman, June 5, 1959. Cert., Eastfield Coll., 1979. With Annuity Bd. So. Bapt. Conv., Dallas, 1958—, mgr. personnel, 1983-85, dir. human resources, 1985-91, v.p. human resources, 1991-99; ret., 1999—. Mem. Am. Mgmt. Soc. (dir. salary surveys local chpt. 1986—, v.p. chpt. svcs. 1987—), Dallas Soc. Human Resource Mgmt., Soc. Human Resource Mgmt., Diversity Club Dallas (program chmn. 1976, v.p. 1977), Order Ea. Star, Daus. of Nile. Baptist. Avocations: needlepoint, genealogy, decorating, doll collecting. Home: 4524 Sarazen Dr Mesquite TX 75150-2348 Office: Annuity Bd So Bapt Conv 2401 Cedar Springs Rd Dallas TX 75201-1427

HOLLENBAUGH, H(ENRY) RITCHEY, lawyer; b. Shelby, Ohio, Nov. 12, 1947; m. Diane Robinson Nov. 21, 1973 (div. 1989); children: Chad Ritchey, Katie Paige; m. Rebecca U., Aug. 8, 1995. BA, Kent State U., 1969; JD, Capital U., 1973. Bar: Ohio 1973, U.S. Dist. Ct. (so. dist.) Ohio 1974, U.S. Ct. Appeals (6th cir.) 1976, U.S. Supreme Ct. 1978. Investigator Ohio Civil Rights Com., Columbus, Ohio, 1969-72; legal intern City Atty.'s Office, Columbus, Ohio, 1972-73, asst. city prosecutor, 1973-75, sr. asst. city atty., 1975-76; ptnr. Hunter, Hollenbaugh & Theodotou, Columbus, Ohio, 1976-85, Delligatti, Hollenbaugh, Briscoe & Milless, Columbus, Ohio, 1985-91, Climaco Seminatore Delligatti & Hollenbaugh, Columbus, 1991-93, Delligatti, Hollenbaugh & Briscoe, Columbus, 1993-95; Draper, Hollenbaugh & Briscoe, 1996-; mem. Ohio Pub. Defender Commn., 1988-94; chmn. Franklin County Pub. Defender Commn., 1986-92. Treas. The Gov's. Com., 1987-96, Friends With Celeste, Friends of Gov's. Residence, 1987-92, Participation 2000, 1987-91. Fellow ABA Found. (chair commn. on advt. 1993-97, ho. of dels. 1993—); mem. Ohio State Bar Assn. (bd. govs. 1989-94, pres. 1992-93), Columbus Bar Assn. (pres. 1987-88), Nat. Conf. Bar Pres., Nat. Assn. Criminal Def. Lawyers, Capital Club. Democrat. Methodist. Avocations: golf, politics. Home: 8549 Glenalmond Ct Dublin OH 43017-9737 Office: Draper Hollenbaugh Briscoe Yashko & Carmany 175 S 3rd St Columbus OH 43215-5134

HOLLENBECK, DOROTHY ROSE, special education educator; b. Yakima, Wash., May 8, 1941; d. George Milford and Blance Mary (McCarthy) Hollenbeck; BS in Speech and Lang. Therapy, Marquette U., 1964; MA in Spl. Edn., San Francisco State U., 1969; m. Thomas M. Chambers, Aug. 14, 1971; adopted children—David, Monique, Christopher, George, Elizabeth. Speech pathologist Mpls. Pub. Schs., 1964-65, Milbrae (Calif.) Sch. Dist., 1965-68; reading specialist Dept. Def., Landstuhl, Germany, 1970-71; tchr. children with extreme learning problems Portland (Oreg.) Public Schs., 1971-80, ednl. diagnostician, spl. edn., 1980-84, program specialist program devel., 1984-86, diagnostic specialist assessment program spl. edn., 1986-94, speech and lang. pathologist, 1994-95; spch. and lang. pathologist, spl. edn. tchr., Chinacum, Washington Sch. Dist. 1995 —; cert. instr. develop. therapy U. Ga., 1982; instr. Portland State U., D.C.E., 1982, 83. HEW Dept. Rehab. fellow, 1969. Mem. Am. Speech and Hearing Assn. (cert. in clin. competence), Common Cause, Cousteau Soc., NEA, Oreg. Edn. Assn., Nat. Council Exceptional Children (presenter nat. conv. 1984). Democrat. Roman Catholic. Author: PEACHES (Pre-Sch. Ednl. Adaptation for Children Who Are Handicapped), 1978. Home: 505 Garfield St Port Townsend WA 98368-4405 Office: Chinacum Pub Schs PO Box 278 Chimacum WA 98325-0278

HOLLENBERG, PAUL FREDERICK, pharmacology educator; b. Phila., Sept. 18, 1942; s. Frederick Henry and Catherine (Dentzer) H.; m. Emily Elizabeth Vanootighem, May 6, 1967; children: Kathryn Mary, David Paul. BS in Chemistry, Wittenberg U., 1964; MS in Biochemistry, U. Mich., 1966, PhD in Biochemistry, 1969. Postdoctoral fellow U. Mich., Ann Arbor, 1969, U. Ill., Urbana, 1969-72; asst. prof. Northwestern U., Chgo., 1972-81, assoc. prof., 1981-84, prof. pathology and molecular biology, 1984-87; prof. pharmacology, chmn. dept. Wayne State U. Sch. Medicine, Detroit, 1987-94, U. Mich. Med. Sch., Ann Arbor, 1994—; mem. pharmacology test com. Nat. Bd. Med. Examiners; mem. Chem. Pathology Study Sect. NIH, 1987-91. Co-founder, assoc. editor Chem. Rsch. in Toxicology, 1988—; assoc. editor Jour. Pharmacology and Exptl. Therapeutics; mem. editl. bd. Drug Metabolism and Disposition. Schweppe Found. research fellow, 1974-77; NIH research grantee, 1974—. Mem. Am. Chem. Soc., Am. Soc. Biochemists and Molecular Biologists, Am. Soc. Pharmacology and Exptl. Therapeutics (sec./treas. 1998-99), Am. Assn. for Cancer Rsch., Soc. Toxicology, Internat. Soc. for Study of Xenobiotics. Avocations: reading, running, golf. Home: 1968 Woodlily Ct Ann Arbor MI 48103-9728 Office: Univ Mich 2301 MSRB III Sch Medicine 1150 W Medical Center Dr Ann Arbor MI 48109-0632*

HOLLENSHEAD, ROBERT EARL, judge; b. St. Louis, July 24, 1940; s. Earl Finley and Marguerite Louise (Milburn) H.; m. Cil Gee, Apr. 24, 1999; children by previous marriage: Cynthia Estelle, David Hugh. BA, U. Mich., 1963, JD, 1966. Bar: Mich. 1967, U.S. Dist. Ct. (ea. dist.) Mich. 1967, U.S. Dist. Ct. (ea. dist.) Mich. 1972. Law clk., assoc. Langs, Molyneau & Armstrong, Detroit, 1966-67; assoc. firm Strommel Sharp Walsh O'Sullivan Beauchamp & Edson, Port Huron, Mich., 1971-72; adminstrv. law judge Mich. Pub. Svc. Commn., Lansing, 1972—; adj. prof. Cooley Law Sch., Lansing, 1977; faculty advisor Nat. Jud. Coll., 1982, 90. Capt. JAGC, U.S. Army, 1967-71. Mem. State Bar Mich. (coun. adminstrv. law sect. 1976-84, pub. utility law com., adminstrv. law judges com.), Mich. Assn. Adminstrv. Law Judges (v.p. 1975-76, pres.-elect 1991, pres. 1992-93), Nat. Assn. Regulatory Utility Commrs. (staff subcom. on adminstrv. law judges 1984-89), Phi Alpha Delta. Home: 6068 Columbia St Haslett MI 48840 Office: Mich Pub Svc Commn PO Box 30221 6545 Mercantile Way Lansing MI 48911-5990

HOLLER, RITA ATWELL, photojournalist; b. Cumberland, Md., Sept. 7, 1941; d. Victor Birnet Atwell and Irene Josephine (Burkholder) Hite; m. Lloyd Luther Holler, Apr. 23, 1960; children: Lloyd Victor, Kevin Scott (dec.), David Kyle, Kent Alan. AA in Letters, Arts and Scis., Pa. State U., 1989; AS in Radio and TV, York Coll. Pa., 1992. Freelance photojournalist York, 1978—; pub. rels. rep. press releases York Dispatch, 1997. Contbr. articles, photojournalist various popular and religious publs. Active Gideon Ladies Aux., YCAT, Mgmt. Assn. York County. Named Most Well-Known Bus. Woman from York, Apprise mag., Hershey, Pa., 1996. Mem. Pa. Women's Press Assn. Avocations: hunting, bicycling, swimming.

HOLLERAN, JOHN W., lawyer; b. Poughkeepsie, N.Y., June 17, 1954. BA, Gonzaga U., 1976, JD, 1979. Bar: Wash. 1979, Idaho, 1980, Calif. 1987. Counsel Boise (Idaho) Cascade Corp., 1979-83, assoc. gen. counsel, 1983-91, v.p., gen. counsel, 1991-96, sr. v.p., gen. counsel, 1996—; chmn. Fibre Box Assn. Legal adv. com., 1989-91; bd. advisors Gonzaga U. Sch. Law, 1991—; mem. Idaho Vol. Lawyers Program Policy Coun., 1991—. Mem. ABA, Wash. State Bar Assn., Boise Bar Assn., Idaho State Bar, State Bar Calif., Am. Corp. Counsel Assn. Office: Boise Cascade Corp PO Box 50 1111 W Jefferson St Boise ID 83728-0001*

HOLLERBACH, PAULA ELIZABETH, demographer, researcher; b. Elizabeth, N.J., Jan. 14, 1945; d. George Henry Sr. and Norma Pierron Hollerbach; m. Rolland Glen Hass; 1 child, Erik Glen. BA in Sociology cum laude, Cornell U., 1966; MA in Sociology, Duke U., 1968, PhD in Sociology, 1991; postgrad., Columbia U. Lectr. sociology Duke U., Durham, N.C., 1970-71; asst. prof. sociology Queens Coll. CUNY, Flushing, 1971-76, assoc. prof. sociology, 1976-78; assoc. The Population Coun., N.Y.C., 1978-90; adj. prof. sociology Hunter Coll. CUNY, N.Y.C., 1991; rsch. officer Family Health Internat., Arlington, Va., 1992-95; sr. rsch. and evaluation officer Acad. for Ednl. Devel., Washington, 1992-95; cons. to family planning programs in Mexico, Jamaica and Colombia, The Population Coun., N.Y.C., 1983-87; sr. assoc. cons. Sociomed. Resource Assocs., Westport, Conn., 1995. Author: (with S. Diaz-Briquets) Fertility Determinants in Cuba, 1983. Grantee Ford Found., N.Y.C., 1984-85, Nat. Inst. Child Health and Human Devel., Washington, 1984-85, Rockefeller Found., N.Y.C., 1984-85; fellow NIH Tng. Grant, Duke U., Durham, 1966-69. Mem. Internat. Union for the Sci. Study Population, Population Assn. Am. (bd. dirs. 1988-90). Democrat. Avocation: reading. E-mail: Phollerb@aed.org. Fax: 202-884-8879. Office: Acad for Ednl Devel 1825 Connecticut Ave NW Washington DC 20009-5721

HOLLERMAN, CHARLES EDWARD, pediatrician; b. Turtle Creek, Pa., Apr. 22, 1929; s. Harry R. and Lena F. H.; m. Catharine, Aug. 22, 1953; children: James, Karen, Jeffrey, Pamela. BS in Chemistry, Allegheny Coll., 1951; MD, Cornell U., 1955. Lic pediatrician, Pa., Va., Ohio. Intern York County (Pa.) Hosp., 1955-56; resident U.S. Navy Sch. Aviation Medicine, Pensacola, Fla., 1957; pvt. practice Cochranton, Pa., 1959-60; pediatric resident Children's Hosp., Buffalo, 1960-62; fellow in clin. nephrology SUNY, 1962-65, instr. pediatrics, 1965-66; asst. prof. pediatrics Georgetown U., 1966-69, asso. prof., 1969-74, prof., 1974-75; prof. U. S.D., Vermillion, 1976-82; asst. dean clin. services U. S.D.; acting dean, exec. dean U. S.D. Sch. Medicine, 1977-79, dean, 1979-82, v.p. health affairs, 1979-82; chmn. dept. pediatrics Mercy Hosp., Pitts., 1982-86, v.p. med. affairs, 1985-92; v.p. med. affairs St. Joseph's Mercy Hosps., Clinton Twp., Mich., 1992-95; regional v.p. physician and clin. integration Mercy Health Ptnrs. Southwest Ohio, Cin., 1995—. Author: Pediatric Nephrology-Medical Outline Series, 1979; contbr. in field. Served with USN, 1956-59. Fellow Am. Coll. Physician Execs. (cert. physician); mem. AMA, Am. Acad. Pediats., Phi Beta Kappa (cert. pediatrician, pediat. nephrologist, med. mgr.). Home: 2457 Cardinal Hill Ct Cincinnati OH 45230-1476 Office: Mercy Health Ptnrs Ste 100 4340 Glendale-Milford Rd Cincinnati OH 45242

HOLLETT, GRANT T., career officer; b. Ishpeming, Mich.; m. Lynn Conrad; children: Kristin Lieb, Traci, G.T. Commd. ensign U.S. Navy, 1964, advanced through grades to rear admiral, dir. plans total, quality leadership adv., asst. dep. commdr.; asst. dep. logistics U.S. Navy, Washington; gen. mgr., group v.p. Vickers Electronic Sys., TRINOVA Corp., Cin.; dir. Electronic Sys., 1996; policy bd. res. forces Sec. Def. Dean's coun. Duke U., former dir. Urban League Lexington, Ky. Decorated Legion of Merit. Office: Vickers Electrnic Sys 1151 Mason Morrow Rd Lebanon OH 45036-9687*

HOLLEY, CYRUS HELMER, management consulting service executive; b. Chgo., June 14, 1936; s. Cyrus Howell and Elizabeth Fay (Helmer) H.; m. Shirley Marquitta Cannon, Aug. 31, 1957; children—Barrett Cannon, Russell William. BS in Chem. Engring., Tex. A&M U., 1957; LLD (hon.), Bloomfield (N.J.) Coll., 1998. Registered profl. engr. Vice pres. indsl. chems. BASF Wyandotte Corp., Parsippany, N.J., 1976-79; sr. v.p. minerals & chem. div. Engelhard Corp., Edison, N.J., 1979-81, v.p., exec. v.p., 1981-83, v.p., pres., chief operating officer metals div., 1983-84, sr. v.p., pres. chem. div., 1984-85, exec. v.p., chief operating officer, 1985-91; pres. Mgmt. Cons. Svcs., Grapevine, Tex., Iselin, N.J., 1991—; CEO Oakmont Enterprises, Inc., 1993—; bd. dirs. Kerns Oil & Gas. Contbr. articles to profl. jours. Trustee Bloomfield (N.J.) Coll., 1988-97, trustee emeritus, 1997—; dir. Nat. Assn. Ptnrs. in Edn., 1990-95, Tex. Assn. Ptnrs. in Edn., 1991-99, N.J. Assn. Ptnrs. in Edn., 1991-99, Tex. Bus. & Edn. Coalition, 1992-96; chair Ind. Coll. Fund. N.J., 1990-92; bd. dirs. Tex. Ind. Coll. Fund, 1998—. Mem. AICE. Republican. Presbyterian. Avocations: reading; golf; music. Office: Mgmt Cons Svcs 1701 W Northwest Hwy Grapevine TX 76051-8105

HOLLEY, EDWARD GAILON, library science educator, former university dean; b. Pulaski, Tenn., Nov. 26, 1927; s. Abe Brown and Maxie Elizabeth (Bass) H.; m. Robbie (Bobbie Lee) Gault, June 19, 1954; children: Gailon Boyd, Edward Jens, Beth Alison, Amy Lin Holley. BA magna cum laude, David Lipscomb Coll., Nashville, 1949; MA, George Peabody Coll., 1951; PhD, U. Ill., 1961. Asst. libr. David Lipscomb Coll., 1949-51; mem. staff U. Ill., 1951-62, libr. edn., philosophy and psychology libr., 1957-62; dir. librs. U. Houston, 1962-72; dean Sch. Libr. Sci. Sch. Library Sci., U. N.C. at Chapel Hill, 1972-85, prof., 1985-89, William Rand Kenan, Jr. prof., 1989-95; prof. emeritus U. N.C. at Chapel Hill, 1996—; vis. lectr. U. Wis., Madison, summer 1968; vis. prof. North Tex. State U., summer 1970, UCLA, fall 1986; mem. adv. coun. libr. resources U.S. Office Edn., 1968-71; cons. various librs. Tex., Ill., S.C. bd. higher edn., NEH, U.S. Dept. Edn. Author: Charles Evans, American Bibliographer, 1963, Raking the Historic Coals, 1967, (with Don Hendricks) Resources of Texas Libraries, 1968, ALA at 100, 1976, Resources of South Carolina Libraries, 1976; co-author: The Library Services and Construction Act, 1983; contbr. articles to profl. jours. Trustee Disciples of Christ Hist. Soc., 1973-85; mem. governing bd. U. N.C. Press, 1975-95, chmn., 1989-93; trustee OLC, Inc., 1985-94, chmn., 1989-92. Lt. USNR, 1953-56. Coun. on Libr. Resources fellow, 1971. Mem. ALA (pres. 1974-75, chmn. pub. bd. 1972-73, Scarecrow Press award 1964, Melvil Dewey medal 1983, Lippincott award 1987), Assn. for Libr. and Info. Sci. Assn. (Profl. Edn. award 1998), Tex. Libr. Assn. (pres. 1971), Southea. Libr. Assn. (Rothrock award 1992), N.C. Libr. Assn. (Disting. Svc. award 1995), Assn. Coll. and Rsch. Librs. (editor monographs 1969-72, Rsch. Libr. of Yr. award 1988), Spl. Librs. Assn. (hon.), Phi Kappa Phi, Kappa Delta Pi, Beta Phi Mu (pres. 1984-86, award 1991, Alise award 1998). Democrat. Mem. Ch. of Christ. Address: 1508 Ephesus Church Rd Chapel Hill NC 27514-2551

HOLLEY, IRVING BRINTON, JR., historian, educator; b. Hartford, Conn., Feb. 8, 1919; s. Irving B. and Mary L. (Sharp) H.; m. Janet Carlson, Oct. 9, 1945; children: Janet Turner Holley Wegner, Jean Carlson Holley Schmidt, Susan Sharp Holley. B.A. cum laude, Amherst Coll., 1940; M.A. (Brooker scholar), Yale U., 1942, Ph.D., 1947; student, Oxford U., summer, 1937. Instr. dept. history Duke U., Durham, N.C., 1947-51; asst. prof. Duke U., 1952-54, asso. prof., 1955-61, prof., 1962-89, prof. emeritus, 1989—; vis. prof. U.S. Mil. Acad., 1974-75, Nat. Def. U., 1978-79; cons. to Army Research Office, 1963-73; mem. U.S. Commn. on Mil. History, 1974—; occasional lectr. Army War Coll., USAF Acad., Inf. Sch., Air War Coll., Command and Gen. Staff Coll.; chmn. adv. com. on history Sec. Air Force, 1970-79; mem. adv. com. on history NASA, 1974-81. Author: Ideas and Weapons, 1953, Buying Aircraft, 1964, Development of Aircraft Gun Turrets in the AAF, 1917-1944, Evolution of the Liaison Type Airplane, 1917-1944, 1946, An Enduring Challenge: The Problem of Air Force Doctrine, 1974, General John M. Palmer, Citizen Soldiers, and the Army of a Democracy, 1982; contbr. articles on mil. history to scholarly publs.; editor: The Transfer of Ideas: Historical Essays, 1968, editorial adviser various jours. Trustee Air

Force Hist. found., 1973—. Served with USAAF, 1942-47, to maj. gen. Res., 1947-81. Decorated D.S.M., Legion of Merit; recipient Outstanding Civilian Service to the Army medal, 1975, Exceptional Civilian Service to the Air Force medal., 1979. Fellow AIAA (assoc.); mem. Am. Hist. Assn., Soc. History of Tech., Soc. Mil. History, Phi Delta Theta. Episcopalian. Home: 2701 Pickett Rd Apt 3028 Durham NC 27705-5651 Office: Duke Univ Dept History Durham NC 27708

HOLLEY, LAWRENCE ALVIN, retired labor union official; b. Elkhart, Ind., Nov. 7, 1924; s. Olin Coet and Carrie (Erwin) H.; m. Joyce Reed, Mar. 5, 1946 (dec. Jan. 1997); 1 child, Claudia Joyce. Student public schs., Elkhart. Bus. rep. Vancouver (Wash.) Aluminum Trades Council, 1951-57; pres. Wash. State Card and Label Council, 1952-57; internat. rep. Aluminum Workers Internat. Union, St. Louis, 1957-65, wage engr., 1965, research and ednl. dir., 1967-75; dir. Region 5 Aluminum Workers Internat. Union, Vancouver, Wash., 1975-77; pres. Aluminum Workers Internat. Union (now Aluminum, Brick and Glass Workers Internat. Union), St. Louis, 1977-85; farmer La Center, Wash., 1985—; v.p. Union Label and Service Trades Dept., AFL-CIO, 1980-85, exec. bd. Maritime Trades Dept., 1981-85, Garde de la Porte, 1986-87, elected chief, 1989-90, Box Car, 1987-88, state chmn. 1987-89, dir., Washington, 1988-89,; chief De Train Voiture, Clark County, Wash., 1989—, Grand chief de Train, 1991-92, elected Grand chef De Gare Du Washington, 1992-93. Served with U.S. Army, 1943-46, PTO. Decorated Bronze Star with oak leaf cluster. Mem. DAV (life), China Burma India (life), Elks, Voyageur 40/8 Club, Eagles Lodge (life). Democrat. Office: Chef de Gare La Center WA 98629 *Don't worry half of your troubles won't happen.*

HOLLEY, MARIE THERESA, medical/surgical nurse; b. Washington, Apr. 25, 1953; d. Thomas Jeremiah and Pauline Theresa (Conley) Shea; m. Arthur W. Holley, Mar. 22, 1986; children: Theresa Marie, Arthur Thomas. AAS, No. Va. C.C., Annandale, 1980; BSN cum laude, Marymount Coll. Va., 1982, MSN, 1983; postgrad., U. Md., 1987—. RN, Va., Md., D.C.; cert. CPR instr. Staff nurse Sibley Meml. Hosp., Washington, 1980-84; staff nuse health ctr. Marymount Coll. Va., Arlington, 1981-82, grad. asst., 1982-83; instr./asst. prof. Marymount U., Arlington, 1983-89; edn. specialist Hebrew Home Greater Washington, Rockville, Md., 1989-90; staff nurse NIH, Rockville, 1990-92; dir. inpatient surg. nursing Bon Secours Hosp., Balt., 1992-94; dir. med.-surg. nursing Dorchester Gen. Hosp., Cambridge, Md., 1994-95, nursing supr., 1995-98, patient care facilitator, 1998—; PRN nursing supr. Salisbury (Md.) Nursing and Rehab. Ctr., 1995—; clin. instr. Salisbury State U., 1995-96. Mem. ANA, Alzheimers Assn. Ea. Shore (chmn. edn. com. 1994), Delta Epsilon Sigma, Sigma Theta Tau (Eta Alpha chpt. sec. 1984-86). Home: 6371 Whitman Rd Parsonsburg MD 21849-2145

HOLLEY, SYLVIA A., state legislator; b. Rutland, Vt., Apr. 7, 1942; married; 2 children. BS, Rivier Coll., 1983. Ret. video teleconf. specialist Digital Corp.; mem. N.H. Ho. of Reps.; exec. dept. and adminstrn. com. Bd. dirs. ARC, Nashua, state rels. officer; sec. LWV; cons. Everywoman's Ctr. YWCA, Manchester; gift shop vol. Cath. Med. Ctr. Avocations: singing, traveling. Office: 6 Benton Dr Nashua NH 03060-1622*

HOLLEY, TAMMY D. FENNELL, critical care nurse; b. Rockmart, Ga., Mar. 29, 1967; d. Ira Eugene and Barbara Ann (Sprayberry) Fennell; m. Jonathan Olin Holley, Dec. 23, 1989; children: Jonathan Olin Adam, Jacob Emery Aaron. ASN, Floyd Coll., Rome, Ga., 1987. Cert. ACLS. Med.-surg./telemetry unit nurse Paulding Meml. Med. Ctr., Dallas, Ga., 1986-88; staff nurse, relief charge nurse CCU Floyd Med. Ctr., Rome, Ga., 1988—, CCU charge nurse, utilization rev. nurse, 1994—. Home: 930 Lowery Rd Rockmart GA 30153-3416

HOLLI, MELVIN GEORGE, history educator; b. Ishpeming, Mich., Feb. 22, 1933; s. Walfred and Sylvia (Erickson) H.; m. Betsy Biggar, Aug. 12, 1961; children: Susan, Steven. Student, Suomi Coll., 1952-54; BA, North Mich. U., 1957; MA, U. Mich., 1958, PhD, 1969. Curator manuscripts Bentley Libr., U. Mich., Ann Arbor, 1962-64; asst. prof., assoc. prof. history U. Ill., Chgo., 1965, prof., 1975—, chmn. dept., 1991-94; Fulbright prof. U. Finland, 1978, 89-90. Author: Reform in Detroit, 1969, Detroit, 1975, Ethnic Chicago, 1981, 3d edit., 1995 (Nonfiction prize Soc. Midland Authors 1985, Best book award Ill. Polit. Sci. Assn. 1985), Bashing Chicago Traditions, 1989, Restoration: Chicago Elects a New Daley, 1991, The Mayors: The Chicago Political Tradition, 1995, The American Mayor: The Best and Worst Big City Leaders, 1999; (with Paul M. Green) From Mid Century to Millennium: A View From Chicago's City Hall, 1999; bd. editors: Urban Affairs Quar., 1992-95; editor: U. Ill. Press Ethnic History in Chicago book series. Bd. dirs. Scandinavian Ctr., North Park Univ., Chgo., 1997—. Woodrow Wilson fellow, 1957-58; recipient Disting. Alumni award No. Mich. U., 1985. Mem. Am. Hist. Assn., Orgn. Am. Historians, Swedish Am. Hist. Soc. (mag. bd. 1990-93), Soc. Midland Authors (bd. dirs. 1989-93, 94—). Home: 1311 Ashland Ave River Forest IL 60305-1029 Office: Dept History U Ill Chicago IL 60607

HOLLIDAY, ALBERT EDWARDS, publisher; b. Oswego, N.Y., June 25, 1934; s. Faval and Hilda Margaret (Karpinski) H.; m. Joan Marie Davis, Aug. 17, 1956; children: Edwards, Matthew. BA, Mich. State U., 1960, MA, 1964. Speech correctionist St. Johns (Mich.) Pub. Schs., 1960-64, dir. of info., 1962-64; coord. sch. pub. rels. Fairfax (Va.) County Pub. Schs., 1964-67; assoc. dir. Project Pub. Info., Madison, Wis., 1967-68; dir. info. and publs. Pa. Dept. Edn., Harrisburg, 1968-73; pres. cons. firm Ednl. Comm. Ctr., Camp Hill, Pa., 1973-81, publ., editor, 1975—. Author: Speak For Your Life and Leisure, 1975; co-editor: Putting Words and Pictures About Schools into Print, 1960; editor, publ. Jour. of Ednl. Rels., 1975—, (mag.) Pennsylvania mag., 1981—. With U.S. Army, 1956-57. Home and Office: Ednl Comm Jour Ednl Publ 1830 Walnut St Camp Hill PA 17011-3974

HOLLIDAY, BERTHA GARRETT, psychologist; b. Kansas City, Mo., Nov. 15, 1947; d. Harold L. Sr. and Margaret L. (Garrett) H. BA, U. Chgo., 1969; EdM, Harvard U., 1970; PhD, U. Tex., 1978; postgrad., Cornell U., 1982-83. Counselor Inst. for Pupil Study, Kansas City, 1970-71; sr. project mgmt. specialist Model Cities Dept., Kansas City, 1971-74; asst. prof. Vanderbilt U., Nashville, 1978-85; Congl. Sci. fellow Senate Dem. Policy Com., Washington, 1985-86; nat. mgr. program evaluation Cities in Schs., Inc., Washington, 1986-87; chief program evaluation D.C. Commn. on Mental Health, Washington, 1988-94; dir. ethnic minority affairs APA, Washington, 1994—; ind. cons. Abt Assocs., HiTech Internat., Kaufman Found., Washington and Kansas City, 1986—; mem. D.C. State Mental Health Planning Com., Washington, 1997. Editor Communique, 1994—; contbr. chpts. to books and articles to profl. jours. Recipient Howell Murray award U. Chgo., 1969; rsch. grantee Nat. Inst. Gen. Med. Scis., Washington, 1996—, U.S. Ctr. Mental Health Svcs., 1995—; Fgn. Study scholar Am. Field Svc., N.Y.C., 1964; grad. fellow Danforth Found., St. Louis, 1974; postdoctoral fellow Ford Found., N.Y.C., 1982. Mem. APA, Assn. Black Psychologists, Met. Women's Dem. Club, Delta Sigma Theta (co-chair Self-Awareness Self Esteem Project 1988-92). Avocations: African art, reading, gardening, sewing, travel. Office: APA 750 1st St NE Washington DC 20002-4241

HOLLIDAY, CHARLES O., JR., chemical company executive; b. Nashville, Tenn., Mar. 9, 1948; s. Charles O. Sr. and Ann (Hunter) H.; m. Ann Blair, June 27, 1970; children: Scot, Chad. BS in Indsl. Engring., U. Tenn., 1970; postgrad., U. Pa., 1985. Registered profl. engr., Tenn. Indsl. engr. E.I. DuPont de Nemours & Co., Nashville, 1970-72, mfg. supr., 1972-74; bus. analyst E.I. DuPont de Nemours & Co., Wilmington, Del., 1974-77; mfg. mgr. E.I. DuPont de Nemours & Co., Charleston, S.C., 1977-80; fin. and planning mgr. E.I. DuPont de Nemours & Co., Martinsville, Va., 1980-82; asst. plant mgr. E.I. DuPont de Nemours & Co., Seaford, Del., 1982-84; planning mgr. E.I. DuPont de Nemours & Co., Wilmington, Del., 1984-86, bus. mgr., 1986—; CEO E.I. DuPont de Nemours & Co., 1998—. Contbr. articles to profl. jours. fin. leader Boy Scouts Am., Seaford, Del., 1982; sunday sch. tchr. United Meth. Ch., Seaford, 1982. Mem. Inst. Indsl. Engrs. (sr., chpt. officer 1972-74, program dir. Charleston, S.C. 1977-79). Republican. Club: Radley Run Country. Office: E I Du Pont de Nemours 1007 Market St Wilmington DE 19801-1227

HOLLIDAY, JOHN MOFFITT, insurance company executive; b. Kansas City, Mo., June 11, 1935; s. Joseph W. and Olive (Moffitt) H.; m. Betty Branson, Jan. 25, 1964 (div.); children: John Jr., Christopher, Hadley; m. Cecile Seraphim, Jan. 24, 1986; children: George, Paul, Philip. BA, Dartmouth Coll., 1957; MBA, U. Pa., 1959. Asst. treas. Employees Reinsurance Co., Kansas City, 1961-67, v.p., treas., 1967-74; v.p. dir. investments Kansas City (Mo.) Life Ins. Co., 1974-78; v.p. Waddell and Reed, Inc., Kansas City, 1978-83, sr. v.p., 1983—. State rep. Mo. Gen. Assembly, Jefferson City, 1963-64. Mem. Fin. Analyst Soc. (past pres. 1969), Fin. Exec. Inst., Kansas City Country Club, Hallbrook Country Club. Episcopalian. Avocations: hunting, fishing, skiing, tennis. Home: 11705 High Dr Leawood KS 66211-2227 Office: Waddell & Reed Inc 6300 Lamar Ave Shawnee Mission KS 66202-4200

HOLLIDAY, PATRICIA RUTH MCKENZIE, evangelist; b. Jacksonville, Fla., Nov. 17, 1935; d. Robert Irving and Leona Adele (Bell) McKenzie; m. Jan. 20, 1965; children: Connie, Katheryn, Alexander. Student, Massey Bus. Coll., 1969, Luther Rice Sem., 1976; DD, Southeastern Theol. Sem., 1986, ThD, 1989, PhD, 1992. Sec. Delta Drug Corp., Jacksonville, 1965—; pres. Microfilm Ctr., Jacksonville, 1974—, Miracle Outreach Ministry, Jacksonville, 1974—; pastor Miracle World Outreach, Jacksonville; prof. Southeastern Theol. Sem., Jacksonville, 1992—. Author: Holliday for the King, 1978, Be Free, 1979, Only Believe, 1980, Born Anew, 1981, The Walking Dead, 1982, Anointing Power, 1982, Signs, Wonders and Reactions, 1984, Dealing with Heresies, 1986, Marriage Answers, 1992, Solitary Satanist, 1993, Entertaining Angels of Light, 1993, The Plan: Ascended Masters, 1994, The New World Aftershock, 1994, Can. Women Preach?, 1995, New Creations, 1995, From Curses to Blessings Vols. 1, 2 & 3, 1995, Angel Fire, 1995, Can Witches Be Saved, 1996, Spirit of Idolatry, 1996, Is Halloween Pagan?, 1996, Gods of the Stars, Astrology, 1997, Gifts of the Holy Spirit, 1997, Baptism of the Holy Spirit, 1997, Deliverance Manuals, Vols. 1, 2 & 3, 1997, Spiritual Welfare Army, 1997, Spiritual Warfare - Weapons, 1997, Healing & Miracles, 1998, The Spiritual Armor of God, 1998, Children of the New Age, 1998, Prayer Warriors, 1998, Battling Territorial Spirits, 1998, New Age Inner Healing, 1999, Demons Tremble, 1999, Transference of Spirits, 1999; columnist Christian Courier. Sec. Four Found., Inc.; Rep. candidate Fla. Ho. of Reps., 1972; mem. Fla. Rep. Com., 1976-80; lobbyist Fla. Legislature, 1978-80; hostess Pat Holliday TV Show, Jacksonville. Mem. Minutewomen of Fla. Club (founder) Univ. Women Club, Ponte Vedra Women's Club. Home: 9252 San Jose Blvd Apt 2804 Jacksonville FL 32257-9205

HOLLIDAY, PETER OSBORNE, JR., dentist; b. Macon, Ga., July 9, 1921; s. Peter Osborne and Martha Elizabeth (Riley) H.; m. Mary Lucille Dozier, Nov. 12, 1949; children: Peter III, Lucy, Lindsay, Mary. DDS, Emory U., 1945; postgrad., U. Mich., 1947-48. Pvt. practice dentistry Macon, 1947—; mem. Gov. Carter's Dental Adv. Com., Atlanta, 1972. Head dental div. United Givers Fund, Macon, 1956; mem. bicycle com. Macon-Bibb County Planning & Zoning Commn., 1995—. With USNR Dental Corps, 1945-47, China. Fellow Am. Coll. Dentists, Internat. Coll. Dentists (dep. regent for Ga. 1983-85); mem. ADA (alt. del. 1978), Ga. Dental Assn. (sec.-treas. 1971-76, v.p. 1977, pres. 1978-79), Ga. Acad. Dental Practice (charter), Hinman Dental Soc., Ctrl. Dist. Dental Soc. (pres. 1963, Dentist of Yr. 1962), Pierre Fauchard Acad., League of Am. Wheelmen, So. Bicycle League. Democrat. Unitarian. Home: 744 Forest Hill Rd Macon GA 31210-4202 Office: Holliday Dental Assocs 360 Spring St Macon GA 31201-6789

HOLLIDAY, POLLY DEAN, actress; b. Jasper, Ala., July 2, 1937; d. Ernest Sullivan and Velma Mabell (Cain) H. B. Music Edn., Ala. State Women's Coll. (now U. Montevallo), 1959; postgrad., Fla. State U., 1960; D.H.L. hon., Mt. St. Mary's Coll., 1982. Tchr. music Sarasota (Fla.) public schs., 1961. Appeared with Asolo Theatre Repertory Co., Sarasota, 1962-72; appeared in Off-Broadway, Wedding Band, 1972; Quarrel of Sparrows, 1993, Broadway shows All Over Town, 1975, Arsenic and Old Lace, 1986-87, Cat on a Hot Tin Roof, 1990 (Tony nomination), Picnic, 1994; appeared in plays The Glass Menagerie, Tyrone Guthrie Theatre, Mpls., 1988; appeared as Flo on CBS-TV series Alice, 1976-80 (4 Emmy nominations), Flo, 1981 (Emmy nomination); appeared in CBS-TV series The Client, 1995-96, Golden Girls, 1986, Amazing Stories, 1986, Home Improvement, 1993, 94; appeared in TV movies You Can't Take It With You, 1981, The Shadyhill Kidnapping, 1981, All the Way Home, 1981, Missing Children, 1982, A Gift of Love, 1983; PBS Wonderworks series Konrad, 1985, (TV movies) Triumph of the Heart, 1991; appeared in feature films All The Pres.'s Men, 1975, The One and Only, 1977, Gremlins, 1984, Moon Over Parador, 1987, Mrs. Doubtfire, 1993, Mr. Wrong, 1996, The Parent Trap, 1998. Recipient Golden Globe award for best supporting actress on TV series, 1978, 79. Episcopalian. Office: Lantz Office 888 7th Ave New York NY 10106*

HOLLIDAY, ROBERT KELVIN, retired state senator, former newspaper executive; b. Logan, W.Va., Feb. 11, 1933; s. James Kelvin and Helen Kathleen (Harris) H.; children: Kelvin Edward, Kathleen Holliday Eddy, Stephen Kerr, Robert L., Jeffrey, Tracey, Brandon. BA, W.Va. Tech., 1954; MA, Marshall U., 1955. Co-owner, editor Montgomery (W.Va.) Herald, 1955-85; co-owner, editor Meadow River Post, 1960-85; Co-owner, editor Meadow River Post, Rainelle, W.Va., 1966-85; mem. W.Va. Ho. of Dels., 1963-68, W.Va. Senate, 1968-72, 80-96; adj. polit. sci. instr. W.Va. Inst. Tech., 1994, W.Va. State Coll., 1997-98, Bluefield State Coll. and Greenbrier C.C. Author: Test of Faith, About Montgomery, Our Chat, A Portrait of Fayette, Politics in Fayette County. Mem. W.Va. State Dem. Exec. Com., 1978-80; pres. Fayette Needy Assn. Served with U.S. Army. Recipient Gov.'s Living Dream award Martin Luther King Jr., 1988, Outstanding Leadership award W.Va. NAACP, 1988, award Kanawha-Fayette Cmty. Svc., Inc., 1985, 88, 89, 91, 92, 93, 94, 95, 96, 97, 98. Mem. W.Va. Mental Health Assn. (past dir.), Fayette Mental Health Assn. (past pres.), W.Va. Edn. Assn. (Pearl S. Buck award 1982), Rehab. Assn. (Structural Barriers award 1988), W.Va. Trial Lawyers Assn. (Outstanding Legislator 1988, 92), Masons (32-degree). Presbyterian.

HOLLIDAY, THOMAS EDGAR, lawyer; b. Ft. Hood, Tex., July 3, 1948; s. William Lamont and Eileen (Fiebig) H.; m. Linda Loudon, May 7, 1988; children: Devon M., Trey S. BA, Stanford U., 1971; JD, U. So. Calif., 1974. Bar: Calif. 1974. Assoc. Gibson, Dunn & Crutcher LLP, L.A., 1974-81; ptnr. Gibson, Dunn & Crutcher, L.A., 1981—. Editor: (book, desk edition) Antitrust and Trade Regulations. Trustee S.W. Mus., L.A., 1981—, Found. for People, L.A., 1985-90; mem. L.A. Police Dept. Meml. Found. Bd. Fellow Am. Coll. Trial Lawyers; mem. Fed. Bar Assn. (exec. com. L.A. chpt. 1990, pres.-elect 1997). Avocation: collecting Southwestern art. Office: Gibson Dunn & Crutcher LLP 333 S Grand Ave Ste 4400 Los Angeles CA 90071-3197*

HOLLIEN, HARRY FRANCIS, speech and communications scientist, educator; b. Brockton, Mass., July 16, 1926; s. Henry Gregory and Alice Bernice (Coolidge) H.; m. Patricia Ann Milanowski, Aug. 26, 1969; children: Karen Ann, Kevin Amory, Keith Alan, Brian Christopher, Stephanie Ann, Christine Ann. BS, Boston U., 1949, MEd, 1951; MA, U. Iowa, 1953, PhD, 1955. Asst. prof. Baylor U., 1955-58, U. Wichita, 1958-62; assoc. prof. speech U. Fla., Gainesville, 1962-68; prof. U. Fla., 1968-98, prof. linguistics, 1976-98, prof. criminal justice, 1979-98, assoc. dir. communication scis. lab., 1962-68, dir., 1968-75; dir. Inst. Advanced Study of Communication Processes, 1975-98, prof. emeritus, 1998—, assoc. dir. linguistics, 1989-91; vis. prof. Inst. Telecommunications and Acoustics, Wroclaw Tech. U., Poland, 1974; adj. prof. Juilliard Sch. Music, N.Y.C., 1973-84; rsch. assoc. Gould Research Lab., 1958; vis. sci. Speech Transmission Lab., Royal Inst. Tech., Stockholm, 1970, U. Trier, Fed. Republic of Germany, 1987; fencing coach U. Iowa, 1953-55; mem. communication sci. study sect. NIH, 1963-67; mem. neurobiology merit rev. bd. VA, 1969-74; pres. Hollien Assocs., 1966—; cons. in field. Author: Current Issues in Phonetic Sciences, 1978, Acoustics of Crime, 1990; assoc. editor Jour. Speech and Hearing Rsch., 1967-69; editor The Phonetician, 1975-92, Jour. Voice, 1987—; mem. edtl. bd. Jour. Comm. Disorders, 1980-91, Jour. Rsch. in Singing, 1980-83, Jour. Phonetics, 1982-85, Studia Phonetica Posnan, 1985—, Speech, Language and the Law, 1993—. Chmn. bd. Unitarian Fellowship, Waco, Tex., 1956-58; chmn. bd. Wild Animal Retirement Village, 1981-90. Served with USN, 1944-46; with USNR, 1946-75. Recipient Garcia/Sandoz prize Internat. Assn. Logopedics and Phoniatrics, 1971, Gould award Wm. and Harrett Gould Found., 1975, Gutzmann medal Union European Phoniatrists, 1980; NIH career fellow, 1965-70, Fulbright scholar, 1987. Fellow Am. Speech and Hearing Assn., AAAS, Acoustical Soc. Am., Internat. Soc. Phonetic Scis. (pres. 1989-98, sec.-gen. 1975-89, exec. v.p. 1983-89, Kay Elemetrics prize 1987, S. Smith prize 1991, Soc. Honors 1998), Am. Acad. Forensic Sci. (John R. Hunt award 1988), Inst. Acoustics; mem. SAR (v.p. local chpt. 1998—), Am. Assn. Phonetic Scis. (pres. 1973-75, editor 1976-79, exec. com. 1979-82), Acad. for Forensic Application of Communication Scis. (editor 1975-80, exec. com. 1976-93, mem. sci. coun. 1975-76, chmn. 1985-93), Japan Soc. Phonetic Scis. (hon. v.p. 1989-97), World Congress Phoneticians (permanent coun.), Voice Found. (sci. bd., merit awards 1981, 93), Internat. Assn. Forensic Phonetics, Fla. Acad. Scis., Mayflower Descendents (dep. gov. local chpt. 1999—), Sigma Xi. Republican. E-mail: Hollien@Grove.ufl.edu. Achievements include patent for apparatus using radiation sensitive switch for signalling and recording data. Home: 229 SW 43rd Ter Gainesville FL 32607-2270 Office: U Fla Inst Advanced Study Comm Processes 46 Dauer Hall Gainesville FL 32611

HOLLIGER, FRED LEE, oil company executive; b. Kansas City, Mo., Feb. 4, 1948; s. Ronald and Margorie (Klein) H.; m. Susan Lynn Harris, Oct. 6, 1972; children: Meredith, Allison, Lauren. BS in Petroleum Engring., U. Mo., Rolla, 1970; postgrad., U. Mich., 1978. Petroleum engr. Transok Pipeline Co., Tulsa, 1971; reservoir engr. No. Natural Gas Co., Omaha, 1972-73; project mgr. No. Natural Gas Co., Lyons, Kans., 1974-76; area mgr. No. Natural Gas Co., Great Bend, Kans., 1977-79; gen. mgr. mktg. No. Natural Gas Co., Omaha, 1980-83, v.p. gas supply, 1984-85, v.p. mktg., 1986, pres., COO, 1987-88; exec. v.p., COO Giant Industries, Scottsdale, Ariz., 1989—, Giant Exploration and Prodn. Co., Scottsdale, 1993—; dir. Giant Industries. Mem. Nat. Petroleum Refining Assn. (dir. 1990—), Desert Highlands Golf Club. Office: Giant Industries 23733 N Scottsdale Rd Scottsdale AZ 85255-3466*

HOLLIN, SHELBY W., lawyer; b. Varilla, Ky., July 29, 1925; s. Herbert and Maggie Hollin; m. Martha Jane Fisch, Nov. 27, 1948; children—Sheila K, Henry T., Richard G., Roberta E., Nathan W., Jacob C. B.B.A., St. Mary's U., 1965, J.D., 1970. Bar: Tex. 1969, U.S. Supreme Ct. 1974, U.S. Claims, 1978, U.S. Ct. Appeals 1981, Ky. 1990. Sole practice, San Antonio, 1969—; mem. nat. bd. advisors Am. Biog. Inst. Served with USAF, World War II. Decorated Air medal, Air Force Commendation medal with oak leaf cluster; recipient award for fighting discrimination Govt. Employed Mejures, 1981, others. Mem. Tex. State Bar, San Antonio Bar Assn., Res. Officers Assn. (life), Air Force Assn. (life), VFW (life), DAV (life), Am. Legion, Mil. Order World Wars. Baptist. Home and Office: 7710 Stagecoach Dr San Antonio TX 78227-3430

HOLLINGER, CHARLOTTE ELIZABETH, medical technologist, tree farmer; b. Meadville, Miss., June 29, 1951; d. John Fielding and Irene Elizabeth (Mullins) H. BS in Biology, U. So. Miss., 1973. Cert. med. Technologist ASCP. Staff med. technologist U. Miss. Med. Ctr., Jackson, 1974-76, Grady Hosp., Atlanta, 1976, Atlanta ARC, 1976-78; staff med. technologist I Emory U. Hosp., Atlanta, 1978-85, staff med. technologist II, 1985-88, asst. chief technologist, 1988-94; del. Blood Bank Del. to People's Republic China, People-to-People, Seattle, 1988. Supporter numerous civic orgns. including World Wildlife Fund, AmFAR, HSUS, Open Hand Project, Atlanta Humane Soc. Mem. Am. Assn. Blood Banks, Am. Soc. Clin. Pathologists, NOW, Forest Farmers Assn., Habitat for Humanity, People for Ethical Treatment Animals, People-to-People, Miss. Forestry Assn., Cousteau Soc., Ga. Pub. TV, U. So. Miss. Alumni Assn., Atlanta Zool. Soc., Delta Zeta, Pi Tau Chi. Roman Catholic. Avocations: reading, needlework, traveling, swimming, camping. Home: 2490 Silver King Dr Grayson GA 30017-1470

HOLLINGER, MANNFRED ALAN, pharmacologist, educator, toxicologist; b. Chgo., June 28, 1939. BS, North Park Coll., Chgo., 1961; PhD, Loyola U., Chgo., 1967. Postdoctoral fellow Stanford U., Palo Alto, Calif., 1967-69; prof. U. Calif., Davis, 1969—, chmn. dept. med. pharmacology and toxicology, 1990—. Author: Respiratory Pharmacology and Toxicology, 1985, Yearbook of Pharmacology, 1990, 91, 92; asst. editor, field editor Jour. Pharm. Exptl. Therapy, 1978—; cons. editor CRC Press, Boca Raton, Fla., 1989—. Mem. Yolo County Grand Jury, Woodland, Calif.; bd. dirs. Davis Little League. Burroughs-Wellcome fellow Southampton U., U.K., 1986; Fogarty sr. fellow NIH, Heidelberg (Germany) U., 1988. Office: U Calif Sch Med Dept of Med Pharm/Toxicol 4453 Tupper Hall Davis CA 95616*

HOLLINGS, ERNEST FREDERICK, senator; b. Charleston, S.C., Jan. 1, 1922; s. Adolph G. and Wilhelmine D. (Meyer) H.; m. Rita Louise Liddy, Aug. 21, 1971; children by previous marriage—Michael Milhous, Helen Hayne, Patricia Salley, Ernest Frederick III. B.A., The Citadel, 1942, LL.D. (hon.), 1960; LL.B., U. S.C., 1947, LLD (hon.), 1980. Bar: S.C. 1947, U.S. Supreme Ct. 1952, U.S. Ct. Appeals (D.C.) 1989. Mem. S.C. Ho. of Reps., 1948-54, speaker pro tem, 1951-54; lt. gov. of S.C., 1955-59, gov., 1959-63; practiced in Charleston, 1963-66; U.S. senator State of S.C., 1966—; ranking mem. commerce sci. and transp. com., commerce justice state judiciary and related agys. subcom., sr. mem. budget com.; mem. Hoover Comm. on Intelligence Activities, 1954-55, Pres.'s Adv. Comm. on Intergovtl. Rels., 1959-63, on Federalism, 1981—; chmn. Legis. Coun., 1955-59, Regional Adv. Coun. on Nuclear Energy; mem. adv. com. Nat. River and Harbors Congress; del. Law of Sea Conf.; appropriations com., senate Dem. policy com., senate Dem. Tech. & Comms. com. Author: The Case Against Hunger: A Demand for a National Policy, 1970. Served to capt. U.S. Army, 1942-45, ETO, NATOUSA. Recipient Founders award S.C. Com. for Tech. Edn., 1963, Nat. Vet. award, 1968, Friend of Edn. award S.C. Edn. Assn., 1974, Neptune award Am. Oceanic Orgn., 1978, James Woodruff award Assn. U.S. Army, 1980, Nat. Future award Am. Space Found., 1984, S.C. Disting. Pub. Svc. award, 1983, Consumer Fedn. of Am. Disting. Pub. Svc. award 1985, Govt. Social Responsibility award Martin Luther King Jr. Ctr., 1986, Golden Bulldog award Watchdogs of the Treasury, 1988, Outstanding Leadership award Nat. Assn. Black-owned Broadcasters, 1988, Disting. Health Svcs. award, 1988, The Sound Dollar award, 1988-90, Hall of Leaders award Nat. Travel Industry, 1990, Disting. Svc. award Nat. Assn. Ind. Colls. and U., 1990, Nat. Security Indsl. Assn., 1990, Congl. award Nat. Coalition for Cancer Rsch., 1992, Sgt. Jasper Freedom award S.C. C. of C., 1992, No. 1 Govtl. Friend of Tourism, SE Tourism Soc., 1993, Spl. Health Recognition award N.H. Assn. Cmty. Health Ctrs., 1994; named one of Ten Outstanding Young Men U.S. Jr. C. of C., 1954, and numerous other awards. Mem. ABA, Charleston County Bar Assn., S.C. Bar Assn., Assn. Citadel Men, Hibernian Soc., Am. Legion, Univ. S.C. Law Fedn., St. Andrews Soc. Democrat. Lutheran. Lodges: Elks, Masons. Office: US Senate 125 Russell Senate Bldg Washington DC 20510*

HOLLINGSWORTH, ABNER THOMAS, university dean; b. Wilmington, Del., Mar. 19, 1939; s. Abner and Dorothy Elizabeth (Dunn) H.; m. Jacqueline Manning, Mar. 19, 1966; children: Alexander, Thomas. BSin BA, U. Del., Newark, 1964; MBA, Mich. State U., 1966, PhD, 1969. Asst. prof. mgmt. So. Ill. U., Carbondale, 1969-71, Fla. Atlantic U., 1971-73; assoc. prof. mgmt. U. S.C., 1973-77, prof. mgmt., 1977-80; prof. mgmt. U. Petroleum and Minerals, Dhahran, Saudi Arabia, 1980-82; prof. mgmt., chmn. mgmt. dept. U. N.C., Asheville, 1983-87; dean Sch. Bus. Adminstrn. Monmouth Coll., 1987-88, prof. mgmt., 1988; prof. mgmt. and dir. Bus. Rsch. Inst. St. John's U., 1988-90; prof. mgmt. and dean Sch. Bus. Fla. Inst. Tech., Melbourne, 1990—; cons. in field; conductor numerous tng. programs. Author: (with Richard Hodgetts) Readings in Basic Management, 1975, (with H. H. hand) A Practical Approach to the Management of Small Business, 1979, Readings in Small business Management, 1979, Supervisory Behavior, 1974, (with R. Howell and R. Hodgetts) A Reader, Study Guide in Basic Management, 1979, others; assoc. editor Jur. Bus. Rsch., 1984-87; editorial bd. Jour. Mgmt., 1977-79, book reviewer for Acad. Press, Bus. Pubs., Inc., Wiley/Hamilton, many others; contbr. articles to profl. jours. Bd. dirs. Holmes Regional Med. Ctr. & Health First, Inc., Melbourne, Jr. Achievement of Ea. Ctrl. Fla., United Way. Rsch. grantee, Inst. Pub. Utilities, Mich. State U., 1967, Fla. Atlantic U., 1972, U. S.C., 1975, Social Security Adminstrn., 1977, others. Avocations: scuba diving, sailing, reading. Office: Fla Inst Tech Sch Bus 150 W University Blvd Melbourne FL 32901-6975

HOLLINGSWORTH, GARY MAYES, Internet access provider company; b. Mexico, Mo., June 1, 1944; s. Allan Dee and Mabel Etta (Mayes) H.; m. Theresa Ann LaRoche, June 30, 1984; children: Lisa Marie, Allan Dee, Sarah Elizabeth. BS, Truman State U., 1972; MA, Webster U., St. Louis, 1982. CPA, Mo. Staff announcer Sta. KXEO-KWWR-FM, Mexico, 1962-64, news dir., 1964-65, program dir., account exec., 1969-72; sr. acct. KPMG Peat, Marwick, St. Louis, 1972-75; audit mgr. T.G. Bancshares Co., St. Louis, 1975-76; group contr. Wetterau Inc., St. Louis, 1976-80; chief fin. officer Gen. Grocer Co., St. Louis, 1980-84; v.p., sec., bd. dirs. Dana Brown Pvt. Brands, Inc., St. Louis, 1984-92; exec. v.p., gen. mgr. Private Brands Coffee & Tea Co., St. Louis, 1992-93; nat. sales mgr. store brands Chock Full O' Nuts Corp., N.Y.C., 1993-96; exec. v.p. Inlink Comm., St. Louis, 1996—; mem. adj. faculty Maryville U., St. Louis, 1982-83, The Dive Shop of St. Louis, 1990—; bd. dirs. Phythe Group, Ltd., St. Louis. Mem. Zoning Bd. of Adjustment, Olivette, Mo., 1992-97; city clk. City of Olivette, Mo., 1997, Olivette, mem. city coun., 1997—; mem. devel. bd. PARA QUAD, Inc., 1990-93; pres., trustee Bon Aire Subdivsn., 1990. Capt. U.S. Army. Mem. AICPA, Mo. Soc. CPAs, Fin. Exec. Inst. (bd. dirs. St. Louis chpt. 1988-94, pres. 1993-94), Profl. Assn. Dive Instrs. (cert.), Clayton Jaycees (pres. 1979), M.C. Investment Club (pres. 1991-92), Masons. Methodist. Avocations: scuba diving, reading, golf. Home: 14 Bon Aire Dr Saint Louis MO 63132-4301 Office: Inlink Comm Inc 443 N New Ballas Rd Saint Louis MO 63141-6800

HOLLINGSWORTH, JACK WARING, mathematics and computer science educator; b. South Haven, Kans., Mar. 3, 1924; s. Virgil Braxton and Ethel (Waring) H.; m. Nancy Lee Harris, Sept. 14, 1950; children: Joel, Priscilla, Seth (dec.). B.S. in Engring. Physics, U. Kans., 1948, B.A., 1949; M.S., U. Wis., 1951, Ph.D., 1954. Teaching asst. U. Kans., 1947-49; teaching asst. U. Wis., 1949-50, computing asst., 1950-54; gen. sci. aide U.S. Naval Ordnance Lab., 1950; mathematician Gen. Electric Co., 1954-57; mem. faculty Rensselaer Poly. Inst., 1957-79, prof. math., 1961-79, supr. computer lab., 1957-70, chmn. interdisciplinary com. computer sci., 1967-73; prof. Sch. Computer Sci. and Tech./Rochester Inst. Tech., N.Y., N.Y., 1979-86; dir. Sch. Computer Sci. and Tech./Rochester Inst. Tech., N.Y., 1980-82; prof. math. Rochester Inst. Tech., 1986-96, prof. emeritus, 1996—; mem. Bd. Coop. Ednl. Services, Saratoga-Warren Counties, 1970-79. Served to 1st lt. USAAF, 1943-45. Decorated D.F.C., Air medal with 4 oak leaf clusters, Purple Heart; Jack Hollingsworth Prize in Computer Sci. established in his honor Rennselaer Poly. Inst. Mem. Assn. Computing Machinery (treas. spl. interest group of univ. computing centers 1964-70), Am. Math. Soc., Soc. Indsl. and Applied Math., Math. Assn. Am., Sigma Xi, Tau Beta Pi, Omicron Delta Kappa, Kappa Eta Kappa. Mem. Reformed Ch. (elder). Lodge: Mason. Home: 55 Crestview Dr Pittsford NY 14534-2242

HOLLINGSWORTH, JOHN ALEXANDER, retired science and mathematics educator, writer, consultant; b. Owego, N.Y., Sept. 25, 1925; s. John Alexander Sr. and Florence Eve (Haley) W.; m. Winifred Louise Stoelting Hollingsworth. BS in Agr., N.C. A&T State U., 1950, MS in Adult Edn., 1985; MS in Biology, N.C. Ctrl. U., 1960; postgrad., Cornell U., 1962-63. Staff sgt. U.S. Army, 1943-46, advanced through grades to capt., 1949-57; tchr. sci. Fayetteville (N.C.) City Schs., 1959-73, coord. sci., 1968-83, coord. math., 1973-83; cons., author, artist Cherokee Village, Ark., 1985—; dir. Emergency Sch. Assistance Act Pilot Project, Fayetteville, 1972-80; grants writer Title I and Emergency Sch. Assistance Act Pilot Project, Fayetteville, 1972-80. Co-author: (booklet) The Improvement of High School Research Through the Research Participation Program, 1968. Active Ecology Action/Common Ground, Willits, Calif.; active, charter mem. Nat. Mus. of the Am. Indian. Mem. NEA (life), Nat. Ret. Tchrs. Assn., N.C. Sci. Tchrs. Assn. (state pres. 1971-73), N.C. Assn. Educators (pres. Fayetteville unit 1970-71), N.C. Ret. Sch. Pers., N.C. Ret. Govtl. Employees Assn. Avocations: watercolor painting, genealogy, gardening. Home: 61 Otalco Dr Cherokee Village AR 72529

HOLLINGSWORTH, MARTHA LYNETTE, secondary school educator; b. Waco, Tex., Oct. 9, 1951; d. Willie Frederick and Georgia Cuddell (Bryant) J.; m. Roy David Hollingsworth, Dec. 31, 1971; children: Richard Avery, Justin Brian. A.A., McLennan Community Coll., 1972; B.B.A., Baylor U., 1974, MS in Ednl. Administrn., 1992. Tchr., Connally Ind. Sch. Dist., Waco, 1974—; with Adult Edn. Night Sch., 1974-78; chairperson for Area III leadership conf. Vocat. Office Careers Clubs Tex., Waco, 1985—; active Lakeview Little League Booster Club, 1985—. Mem. PTA (hon. life), Vocat. Office Edn. Tchr.'s Assn. Tex., Assn. Tex. Profl. Educators (v.p. local chpt. 1988-90), Future Homemakers Am. Area VIII (hon.), Tex. Future Farmers Am. (hon.), Delta Kappa Gamma. Baptist. Office: Connally Vocat Dept 715 N Rita St Waco TX 76705-1140

HOLLINGSWORTH, PIERCE, publishing executive. Pub. Real Estate Bus., Wheaton, Ill., Real Estate Profiles, Wheaton, 1998—. Office: Hollingsworth Group 213 W Wesley St Ste 202 Wheaton IL 60187-5135*

HOLLINGSWORTH, SAMUEL HAWKINS, JR., bassist; b. Birmingham, Ala., June 29, 1922; s. Samuel Hawkins and Bennie Louise (Brown) H.; m. Patricia Ann Patton, Apr. 1, 1957 (div. 1967); children: Priscilla P., Samuel Hawkins III; m. Elizabeth Mary Malezi, Dec. 31, 1974. Student, Juilliard Sch. Music, N.Y.C., 1940-42, George Peabody Coll. Tchrs., Nashville, 1953-54. Prin. bassist Nashville Symphony, 1946-65, Chamber Symphony of Phila., 1966-68, Dallas Symphony, 1968-70; prin. bassist Pitts. Symphony, 1970-92, prin. emeritus, 1992-95; retired, 1995. Mem. governing bd. dirs. Nashville Symphony Orch., 1960-63; chmn. Dallas Symphony Orth Players, 1969-70. Home: 1111 Pinewood Dr Pittsburgh PA 15243-1809

HOLLINGTON, RICHARD RINGS, JR., lawyer; b. Findlay, Ohio, Nov. 12, 1932; s. Richard Rings and Annett (Kirk) H.; m. Sally Stecher, Apr. 4, 1959; children: Florence A., Julie A., Richard R. III. Peter S. BA, Williams Coll., 1954; JD, Harvard U., 1957. Bar: Ohio 1957. Ptnr. Marshman, Hornbeck & Hollington, Cleve., 1958-67, McDonald, Hopkins, Hardy & Hollington, Cleve., 1967-69; law dir. City of Cleve., 1971-72; sr. ptnr. Baker & Hostetler, Cleve., 1969-71, 73—; chmn. bd. dirs. The Ohio Bank, 1985—. Mem. Ohio Gen. Assembly, 1967-70, Cuyahoga County Rep. Ctrl. Com., 1962-66; exec. com. Ohio Rep. Fin. Com., 1971—, Cuyahoga County Rep. Orgn., 1968—, Geauga County Rep. Orgn., 1998—; trustee Cleve. State U., 1970-73, Greater Cleve. Hosp. Assn., 1976-82, Cleve. Mus. Natural History, 1969-81, Cleve. Zool. Soc., 1970—, N.E. Ohio Regional Sewer Dist., 1972-73, Cuyahoga County Hosp. Found., 1968-73, Cleve. 500 Found., 1990-95, U. Findlay, 1991—, others; bd. commrs. grievance and discipline Ohio Supreme Ct. Mem. ABA, Ohio Bar Assn., Greater Cleve. Bar Assn., Sixth Cir. Jud. Conf. (life), Eighth Dist. Ohio Jud. Conf. (life), Ct. Nisi Prius, Union Club (Cleve.), The Country Club (Pepper Pike), Pepper Pike Club, Roaring Gap (N.C.) Club, Rolling Rock (Pa.) Club. Home: 13792 County Line Rd Chagrin Falls OH 44022-4008 Office: Baker & Hostetler 3200 National City Ctr 1900 E 9th St Ste 3200 Cleveland OH 44114-3475

HOLLINGWORTH, ROBERT MICHAEL, toxicology researcher; b. Yorkshire, England, Oct. 4, 1939; married; 1961; 2 children. BSc, Univ. Reading, 1962; PhD, Univ. Calif., 1966. Asst. prof. to prof. insect toxicology Purdue Univ., West Lafayette, Ind., 1966-87; dir. Pesticide Rsch. Ctr., prof. entomology, zoology Mich. State Univ., 1987-98; dir. Nat. Food Safety Toxicol. Ctr., 1991—; vis. prof. Stauffer Chem. Co., 1974-75. Mem. Toxicology Study Sect, NIH, 1976-80; Environ. Protection Agy., sci. adv. panel, Fifra, 1982-84; chmn. Divsn. Pesticide Chem. Am. Chem. Soc., 1984. Fellow Am. Chem. Soc., Soc. Toxicology, Entomology Soc. Am., Am. Coun. Sci. Health; mem. AAAS, Soc. Risk Analysis. Achievements include research on metabolism and mode of action of insecticides and related chemicals. Office: Mich State U Nat Food Safety Toxicol Ctr 165 Food Safety & Biog Bldg East Lansing MI 48824-1302*

HOLLINS, DAVID MICHAEL, professional baseball player; b. Buffalo, May 25, 1966. Student, U. S.C. With Phila. Phillies, 1990-95, Boston Red Sox, 1995, Minn. Twins, 1996, Seattle Mariners, 1996, Anaheim (Calif.) Angels, 1997—; designated hitter Toronto (Ont., Can.) Blue Jays, 1999—; mem. Nat. League All-Star Team, 1993. Player World Series Team, 1993. Office: Toronto Blue Jays Skydome, 1 Blue Jays Way Ste 3200, Toronto, ON Canada M5V 1J1*

HOLLINS, MITCHELL LESLIE, lawyer; b. N.Y.C., Mar. 11, 1947; s. Milton and Alma (Bell) H.; m. Nancy Kirchheimer, Mar. 27, 1977 (div. 1999); children: Herbert K. II, Dorothy Ann. BA, Case Western Res. U., 1967; JD, NYU, 1971. Bar: Ill. 1971, U.S. Dist. Ct. (no. dist.) Ill. 1971. Assoc. Sonnenschein Nath & Rosenthal, Chgo., 1971-78, ptnr., 1978—; asst. sec., dir. Jr. Achievement Chgo., 1980—; bd. dirs. Young Men's Jewish Coun., 1973-75; bd. dirs. young people's div. Jewish United Fund Met. Chgo., 1972-76; bd. dirs. Med. Rsch. Inst. Coun. Mem. exec. com., 1979-92, sec., 1981-82, gen. counsel, 1983-86, vice chmn., 1987-92, chmn. jr. bd., 1978-79. Editor NYU Jour. Internat. Law and Politics, 1970-71. Asst. sec., dir. Jr. Achievement Chgo., 1980—; bd. dirs. Young Men's Jewish Coun., 1973-75; bd. dirs. young people's divsn. Jewish United Fund Met. Chgo., 1972-76; bd. dirs. Med. Rsch. Inst. Coun., mem. exec. com., 1979-92, sec., 1981-82, gen. counsel, 1983-86, vice chmn., 1987-92, chmn. jr. bd., 1978-79. Mem. ABA, Am. Coll. Investment Counsel, Chgo. Bar Assn., Standard Club, Lake Shore Country Club (mem. bd. govs. 1984-92, sec. 1985-92), Legal Club, Law Club. Republican. Office: Sonnenschein Nath & Rosenthal 8000 Sears Tower Chicago IL 60606

HOLLINSHEAD, ARIEL CAHILL, research oncologist, educator; b. Allentown, Pa., Aug. 24, 1929; d. Earl Darnell and Gertrude Loretta (Cahill) H.; m. Montgomery K. Hyun, June 12, 1957; children: William C., Christopher C. Student, Swarthmore Coll., 1947-48; AB, Ohio U., 1951, DSc (hon.), 1977; MA, George Washington U., 1955, PhD, 1957. Asst. prof., fellow in virology Baylor U. Med. Ctr., 1958-59; asst. prof. pharmacology George Washington Med. Ctr., 1959-61, asst. prof. medicine, 1961-64, assoc. prof. medicine, head lab. virus and cancer rsch., 1964-73, prof., dir. lab. virus and cancer rsch., 1974-89; on sabbatical leave 1990, prof. medicine emeritus, 1991—; pres. HT Virus and Cancer Rsch., 1991—; clin. rschr. trials in oncology and virology; cons. to biotech. cos. and FDA panel; panelist FDA and NIH. Contbr. over 270 articles on active immunotherapy and immunochemotherapy of cancer and virus diseases to sci. jours. Bd. dirs. Nat. Women's Econ. Alliance, Ohio U., Med. Coll. Pa.,1980—, Women's Inst., 1995-97. Named Med. Woman of Yr. Joint Bd. Am. Med. Colls., 1975-76, one of Outstanding Woman of Am., 1987, Outstanding Alumnus of Yr., Ohio U., 1990; recipient Cert. merit Med. Coll. Pa., 1975-76, Marion Spencer Fay Med. Woman Year award Med. Coll. Pa.; decorated Star of Europe, 1980. Fellow AAAS, Washington Acad. Sci. N.Y. Acad. Scis.; mem. Grad. Women in Sci. (nat. pres. 1985-86, bd. dirs. 1986-92), Internat. Soc. Preventive Oncology, Nat. Soc. Exptl. Biology and Medicine (Disting. Scientist award 1985, Disting. Scientist emeritus award for Outstanding Career in Tchg. and Rsch. in Medicine 1996, past pres. Greater Washington chpt.), Am. Soc. Microbiology, Am. Assn. Cancer Research, Am. Assn. Immunologists, Clin. Immunology Soc., Internat. Soc. Antiviral Research, Am. Soc. Clin. Oncology, Internat. Assn. Study Lung Cancer, Internat. Union Against Cancer, Am. Med. Writers Assn., Phi Beta Kappa (alumnus 1990). Clubs: Kenwood Country, Blue Ridge Mountain Country, Washington Forum (pres. 1987, 91). Achievements include being first to purify, develop and test cancer gene products which induce long-lasting cell-mediated immunity, development of and patent for new form of HIV and AIDS immunochemo-therapy; patentee in field. Home: 3637 Van Ness St NW Washington DC 20008-3130 *The Latin phrase "Carpe diem", meaning seize the day, or, guard the moment: my first discovery for effective viral disease treatment was the use of purine, pyrimidine and sulfur-containing analogues, one of which was used to attenuate virulent polioviruses: another discovery was the first non virion antigen to block virus-induced animal tumors: my first discovery for effective cancer immunotherapy was the separation of active peptides from cell membranes and the first proof of their efficacy in tumor prevention in animals and in man. I discovered that little pieces of these active proteins (called epitopes) not only were useful for monitoring tumor progression U.S. patent received but were the oncogene products for even better polyvalent therapies in the future. With Dr. T.H.M. Stewart, established the first identification of induced dormancy in human lung cancer patients in USA and Canada receiving our vaccines and, greater than 12 year survival free of lung cancer.*

HOLLINSHEAD, EARL DARNELL, JR., lawyer; b. Pitts., Aug. 1, 1927; s. Earl Darnell and Gertrude (Cahill) H.; m. Sylvia Antion, June 29, 1957; children: Barbara, Kim, Earl III, Susan. AB, Ohio U., 1948; LLB, U. Pitts., 1951. Bar: Pa. 1952, U.S. Ct. Mil. Appeals 1954, U.S. Dist. Ct. (we. dist.) Pa. 1955, U.S. Supreme Ct. 1956, U.S. Ct. Appeals (3d cir.) 1959, U.S. Dist. Ct. (ea. dist.) Ohio 1978. Sole practice Pitts., 1955-70; ptnr. Hollinshead and Mendelson, Pitts., 1970-89, Hollinshead, Mendelson, Bresnahan & Nixon, P.C., Pitts., 1990-97; sole practitioner Pitts., 1997—; mem. Pitts. Estate Planning Council. Contbr. articles to profl. jours. Served to lt. USNR, 1951-55. Fellow Pa. Bar Found. (life); mem. Pa. Bar Assn. (chmn. real property divsn. 1983-85, real property, probate and trust sects. 1985-86), Allegheny County Bar Assn. (chmn. real property sect. 1975-76), Pa. Bar Inst. (lectr., planner, bd. dirs. 1988-94), Am. Coll. Real Estate Lawyers. Home: 2535 Windgate Rd Bethel Park PA 15102-2730 Office: 630 Grant Bldg Pittsburgh PA 15219-2105

HOLLIS, BRUCE WARREN, experimental nutritionist, industrial consultant; b. Elyria, Ohio, May 29, 1951; s. Warren Eugene and Evelyn Katherine (Jabbusch) H.; m. Betsy Eberle Yount, Aug. 16, 1980. B.S., Ohio State U., 1973, M.S., 1976; Ph.D., U. Guelph, Ont., 1979. Postdoctoral fellow Case Western Res. U., Cleve., 1979-82, asst. prof. nutrition, 1982-86; assoc. prof. pediatrics Med. U. S.C., Charleston, 1986-94; assoc. prof. biochemistry and molecular biology, 1989-94, dir. gen. clin. rsch. ctr. lab., 1990-95, prof. pediatrics, biochemistry and molecular biology, 1994—. Med. researcher, indsl. cons. Contbr. chpts. to books, articles to sci. jours. Recipient NIH awards, 1980, 82, Mead Johnson Nutritionals award The Am. Inst. of Nutrition, 1991, Disting. Alumni award Ohio State U., 1996. Mem. Endocrine Soc., Am. Soc. Bone and Mineral Research, Am. Inst. Nutrition, Sigma Xi. Republican. Home: 906 Kushiwah Cr Ct Charleston SC 29412-4938 Office: U SC Med Dept Pediatrics Charleston SC 29425

HOLLIS, CHARLES EUGENE, JR., savings and loan association executive; b. Daytona Beach, Fla., Sept. 14, 1948; s. Charles Eugene and Betty Lou (Beech) H.; m. Carol Repass, Mar. 20, 1971 (div. Nov. 1993); children: Stephanie Dyane, Charles Preston, Robin Jene. AA, Dayton Beach Jr. Coll., 1968; BA, U. South Fla., 1972. CPA, Fla. Asst., Deloitte Haskins & Sells, Tampa, Fla., 1972-73, sr. asst., 1973-75, sr., 1975-78, mgr., 1978-82; audit mgr. Jack Eckerd Corp., Clearwater, Fla., 1982-85; v.p. fin., contr. Freedom Savs. and Loan Assn., Tampa, 1985-87, sr. v.p., chief fin. officer, treas., 1987-88, exec. v.p., 1988-89; exec. v.p. CenTrust Fed., Miami, Fla., 1990; supervisory fin. instn. specialist Resolution Trust Corp., Atlanta, 1990-95; exec. v.p. Beech Mgmt. Group, Inc., 1996—. City councilman City of Temple Terrace, Fla., 1976-86, vice mayor, 1981-82; chmn. fin. and taxation com. Fla. League Cities, Tallahassee, 1979-81; mem. fin. com. Nat. League Cities, Washington, 1980-86, code enforcement bd. City of Temple Terrace, 1986-91; treas. Christ Our Redeemer Luth. Ch., 1984-86, pres. 1987-88; treas. Fla. Synod-Evangelical Luth. Ch. in Am., 1988-92—; trustee Univ. Community Hosp., 1987-91; charter mem., treas. Northeast Sertoma, 1989-90. Recipient Disting. Service award, U. South Fla. Coll. Bus., 1972, Outstanding Alumnus award Beta Alpha Psi, 1983. Mem. Am. Inst. CPAs, Fla. Soc. CPAs, Fin. Mgrs. Soc., Tampa C. of C. (Leadership Tampa 1987-88), Beta Alpha Psi. Republican. Home and Office: 985 Gardendale Dr Columbia SC 29210-4906

HOLLIS, DARYL JOSEPH, judge; b. Pitts., Oct. 22, 1946; s. Joseph and Margaret Clara (Meszar) H.; m. Linda Eardley, July 18, 1970. BS in Edn., Pa. State U., 1968, MEd in Remedial Reading, 1971; JD, Cath. U. Am., 1984. Bar: Pa. 1987, D.C. 1989. Law clk. D.C. Office of Employee Appeals, Washington, 1984-85, adminstrv. law judge, 1985-97, sr. adminstrv. law judge, 1997—; lectr. D.C. Bar Assn. Pro Bono Svcs., Washington, 1985—; mem. Transplant Recipients Internat. Orgn., Nat. Capital Area Chpt., 1993—. Mem. Columbia Pines Citizens Assn., 1993—. Mem. Transplant Recipients Internat. Orgn. Democrat. Roman Catholic. Avocations: woodworking, hiking, Civil War, baseball history, sports. Home: 4002 Rose Ln Annandale VA 22003-1943

HOLLIS, DONALD ROGER, banking consultant; b. Warren, Ohio, Mar. 4, 1936; s. Louis and Lena (Succo) H.; m. Marilyn G. Morganti, Aug. 23, 1958; children—Roger, Russell Kirk, Gregory, Heather. B.S., Kent State U., 1959. Regional mgr. Glidden Corp., San Francisco, 1959-65; dir. mgmt. info. services Glidden Corp., Cleve., 1965-68, SCM Corp., N.Y.C., 1968-71; v.p. Chase Manhattan Bank, N.Y.C., 1971-81; sr. v.p. First Chgo. Corp., 1981-85, exec. v.p., 1986-95, head systems, data processing, cash mgmt. and security products and quality programs, 1986-95; pres., CEO DRH Strategic Cons., Chgo., 1995—; bd. dirs. Deluxe Corp. Open Port Tech. Teltrend, Inc, Edify Corp., Information Advantage Inc.; mem. governing coun. Good Shepherd Hosp. Bd. dirs. Advocate Health Sys.; mem. exec. com. Ill. Inst. Tech. Bd. Trustees; mem. Ill. Inst. Tech. Rsch. Inst. @D. Office: 20 S Clark St Ste 620 Chicago IL 60603-1803

HOLLIS, JAN MICHAEL, astrophysicist, scientific computer analyst; b. Martinsburg, W.Va., June 5, 1941; s. Delbert Irvin and Betty (Collier) H.; m. Carol Ann Getz, Feb. 1, 1964 (div. Oct. 1993); children: David Collier, Mary Morgan; m. Joan Ellen Isensee, Nov. 8, 1995. AB in Math., Duke U., 1963; MA in Astronomy, U. Va., 1972, PhD in Astronomy, 1976. Submarine officer USN, 1963-69; sci. computer analyst Nat. Radio Astronomy Obs., Tucson, 1973-79; space telescope data mgr. NASA, Greenbelt, Md., 1979-82; head sci. ops. br. NASA, Greenbelt, 1982-88, asst. chief earth and space data computing divsn., 1988—; mem. Internat. Halley Watch Sci. Working Group, NASA, Greenbelt, 1981, mem. Hubble Space Telescope Image Processing Sci. Working Group, 1990. Contbr. over 70 articles to profl. jours. Trustee Glenelg (Md.) United Meth. Ch., 1997—. Lt. USN, 1963-69. Fellow Royal Astron. Soc.; mem. Am. Astron. Soc. (Van Biesbroeck Award com. 1997—), Internat. Astron. Union. Democrat. Avocations: astronomy, model trains, tennis, hiking, peanut butter fudge. Office: NASA Goddard Space Flight Ctr Code 930 Greenbelt MD 20771

HOLLIS, JOE, coach; b. Lawrenceburg, Tenn., July 13, 1947; m. Carole Antley; children: Joseph, William, Cole. BS in Secondary Edn., Auburn U., 1969. Asst. coach offense Troy State U., 1972-77; coach offensive line Auburn U., 1978-79; coord. offense U. Tulsa, 1980-83; head coach football Jacksonville State U., 1984; asst. coach offense U. Ga., 1985-90; coach offensive line Ohio State U., 1991-96; head coach football Ark. State U., State University, 1997—. Avocations: fishing, golf, travel. Office: Ark State Univ PO Box 1000 State University AR 72467-1000*

HOLLIS, JUDY WILSON, curriculum resource educator; b. Columbus, Ga., Dec. 20, 1945; d. Clarence and Beatrice (Grant) Wilson; m. Harold Hollis, June 20; children: Bridget, Antoinette. BS, Savannah State U., 1968; MS, Fort Valley State U., 1972; reading specialist, Ctrl. Conn. U., 1976; Degree in Ednl. Specialist, Nova Southeastern U., 1996; PhD, Jacksonville (Fla.) Theol. Seminary, 1998; D in Theology, Jacksonville Theol. Sem., 1998. Cert. reading, elem. edn. and ednl. specialist, Fla. Fifth grade tchr. Bibb County Pub. Schs., Macon, Ga., 1968-72; kindergarten tchr. Muscogee County Schs., Columbus, 1972-73; resource tchr. Canton (Conn.) Pub. Schs., 1973-75; reading specialist Balt. Pub. Schs., 1975-78, Bethlehem (Pa.) Pub. Schs., 1978-84; fifth grade tchr. Orla Vista, Orlando, Fla., 1984-85; reading specialist Seminole C.C., Sanford, Fla., 1986-87, Oak Ridge H.S., Orlando, 1987-90; curriculum resource tchr. Rock Lake, Orlando, 1990—; mem. Future Tchrs., Savannah, 1967-68, Early Childhood Devel. Com., Orlando, 1996-97; chairperson Staff Devel. Com., Orlando, 1990-95. Homeless counselor Orlando Rescue Union, 1995—; pres. hands-on ministries E.C. Reems Women's Internat. Ministries, 1995—; vol. jail ministries Orange County Fla. Corrections Inst., 1996—; women Sunday sch. tchr. Life Ctr. Ch., Eatonville, Fla. Recipient Virginia McIntyre award Virginia McIntyre Orgn., Orlando, 1994, Achievement honor Fla. Assn. Dist. Supts., Orlando, 1996; Reading grantee Orange County Pub. Schs., Orlando, 1993, Math Reading grantee Darden, Inc., Orlando, 1997. Mem. PTA, Internat. Reading Assn. Avocations: rugmaking, walking, reading, antiques. Home: 8737 Alegre Cir Orlando FL 32836-5453 Office: Orange County Pub Schs 445 W Amelia St Orlando FL 32801-1128

HOLLIS, JULIA ANN ROSHTO, critical care and medical/surgical nurse; b. Monroe, La., June 25, 1945; d. Joseph Edward and Mary Eleanor (Coverdale) Roshto; m. William Davis Hollis, Mar. 2, 1964; children: David Terrel, Julia Allison. BSN, N.E. La. U., 1976. RN, La., Ala., Miss.; cert. BCLS, ACLS. Staff nurse to head nurse E.A. Conway Hosp., Monroe, 1977-84; staff nurse, charge nurse ICU, critical care North Monroe Community Hosp., Monroe, 1984-87; staff nurse neurotrama surg. ICU U. South Ala. Med. Ctr., Mobile, 1988-89; staff nurse, charge nurse Norrell Health Care, Mobile, 1990—, Medforce Internat., New Orleans; owner Resource Mgmt., 1997. Chpt. leader Nurses for Christ, Inc. Mem. AACN, AAUW, Ala. Nurses Assn., Met. Writer's Guild. Home: 5073 Dawes Lane Ext Theodore AL 36582-9627

HOLLIS, LINDA EARDLEY, urban planning consultant; b. Washington, Feb. 1, 1948; d. Edward Pixton and Margy (Anderson) Eardley; m. Daryl Joseph Hollis, July 18, 1970. BA, Pa. State U., University Park, 1968; M in Regional Planning, U. N.C., 1979. Planning analyst First-Citizens Bank, Raleigh, N.C., 1973-76; rsch. assoc. ctr. for urban regional studies U. N.C., Chapel Hill, 1978-79; rsch. assoc. The Osprey Co., Tallahassee, 1980-81, Patrick H. Hare Planning and Design, Washington, 1982-83; cons. Tischler & Assocs., Inc., Bethesda, Md., 1983-96; analyst dept. fiscal svcs. Md. Gen. Assembly, Annapolis, 1988-89; dir. devel. policy Urban Land Inst., Washington, 1997-99; ind. cons., 1999—. Rep. Mason dist. Fairfax County Commn. on Organ and Tissue Donation and Transplantation, 1995-97, vice chmn., 1996-97. Mem. Am. Planning Assn. (nat. bd. dirs., regional rep. 1986-88, chmn. nat. state policy coordinating com. 1987-88). Democrat. Avocations: music, reading, traveling. Home and Office: 4002 Rose Ln Annandale VA 22003-1943

HOLLIS, LOIS B., history and political science educator; b. May 6, 1939. MA, Atlanta U., 1963, PhD, 1975. Prof. pub. adminstrn., program coord. Albany (Ga.) State U., 1983-98, interim chair, pub. adminstrn. program coord., 1998—. E-mail: lhollis@asurams.edu. Office: 427 Poinciana Ave Albany GA 31705

HOLLIS, LOUCILLE, risk control administrator, educator; b. Ft. Myers, Fla., Feb. 16, 1949; d. Luke Sr. and Louise (Wilcox) Black; m. Benjamin L. Hollis, Jr., Sept. 26, 1985. BS, N.Y. Inst. Tech., 1982, MBA, 1984. Staff asst. Equitable, N.Y.C., 1977-79, budget analyst, 1979-81, fin. analyst, 1981-85, mgr. operational planning, 1985-87, mgr. expense control, 1987-88; project leader L.I. R.R. Co., Jamaica, N.Y., 1988-91, asst. risk mgr., 1991-97; specialist in risk coverage Met. Transp. Authority, N.Y.C., 1997—; comml. arbitrator Am. Arbitration Assn. Bronx fundraiser Cancer Fund Am., Knoxville, Tenn., 1991, 92; mem. bd. placement project United Way Linkage; literacy vol. Recipient Psychology award N.Y. Inst. Tech., 1981, acad. scholarship Ft. Myers Bd. Edn., 1977; honoree LIRR Women's History Celebration. Mem. NAFE, Nat. Black MBA Assn., Risk and Ins. Mgmt. Soc., RR Ins. Mgmt. Assn., Conf. Minority Transp. Ofcls., Psi Nat. Honor Soc. Democrat. Avocations: reading, personal computers, phys. fitness. Office: Met Transp Authority 347 Madison Ave New York NY 10017-3706

HOLLIS, MARY FERN CAUDILL, nurse educator, music educator; b. Augusta, Ga., Mar. 13, 1942; d. Robert Paul and Fern (Alderton) Caudill; children: Harry N. III (dec.), Mary Melissa, H. Newcombe IV. B in Music Edn., U. Louisville, 1964; AS in Nursing, Tenn. State U., 1980; postgrad., Nashville Tech. Inst., 1987—. RN, Tenn. Staff nurse oncology and med.-surg. units St. Thomas Hosp., Nashville, 1981-82; staff oncology nurse Alive Hospice, Nashville, 1982-83; scheduling coord. HCA Parkview Med. Ctr., Nashville, 1987-88; nurse, staff relief coord. Partners Home Health, Nashville, 1989-90; nursing supr. Kimberly Quality Care Staffing, Nashville, 1991-92; RN coord. on call MedPartners Nursing Svc. of Mid. Tenn., Nashville, 1994-95; profl. vocal soloist; tchr. piano, music edn., music theory, voice, 1962—. Author: Out of My Suffering: Reflections of a Hospice Nurse, 1984. Mem. Music Tchrs. Nat. Assn., Tenn. Music Tchrs. Assn., Nashville Area Music Tchrs. Assn., Am. Coll. Musicians, Nat. Guild Piano Tchrs., Sigma Alpha Iota, Gamma Phi Beta.

HOLLIS, REGINALD, archbishop; b. Eng., July 18, 1932; emigrated to Can., 1954; s. Jesse Farndon and Edith Ellen (Lee) H.; m. Marcia Crombie, Sept. 7, 1957; children—Martin, Hilda, Aidan. BA, Cambridge U., Eng., 1954; MA, Cambridge U., 1958; BD, McGill U., Montreal, 1956; DD (hon.), U. South, 1977, Montreal Diocesan Theol. Coll., 1975. Ordained to ministry Anglican Ch. as deacon, 1956, as priest, 1956. Chaplain Montreal Diocesan

Theol. Coll.; also chaplain to Anglican students McGill U., 1956-60; asst. St. Matthias Parish, Westmount, Que., 1960-63; incumbent St. Barnabas Ch., Roxboro, Que., 1963-66; rector St. Barnabas Ch., 1966-71, Christ Ch., Beaurepaire, Que., 1971-74; dir. parish and diocesan services Diocese Montreal, 1974-75, bishop, 1975-90; archbishop of Montreal Met. of the Ecclesiastical Province of Can., 1989-90; asst. bishop Diocese of Ctrl. Fla., Orlando, 1990-94; episc. dir. Anglican Fellowship of Prayer, 1990-94; rector St. Paul's Ch., New Smyrna Beach, Fla., 1994-97; ret., 1997. Author: Abiding in Christ, 1987. Home: ste 203, 250 Douglas St, Victoria, BC Canada V8V 2P4

HOLLIS, SHEILA SLOCUM, lawyer; b. Denver, July 15, 1948; d. Theodore Doremus and Emily M. (Caplis) Slocum; m. John Hollis; 1 child, Windsong Emily Lanford. BS in Journalism with honors, U. Colo., 1971, BS in Gen. Studies cum lau, 1971; JD, U. Denver, 1973. Bar: Colo. 1974, D.C. 1975, U.S. Supreme Ct. 1980. Trial atty. Fed. Power Commn., Washington, 1974-75; assoc. firm Wilner & Scheiner, Washington, 1975-77; dir. office enforcement Fed. Energy Regulatory Commn., Washington, 1977-80; pvt. practice, 1980-87; ptnr. Vinson & Elkins, Washington, 1987—; sr. ptnr. Metzger, Hollis, Gordon & Alprin, Washington, 1992-97; ptnr. in charge, chair energy practice Duane, Morris & Heckscher, LLP, Washington, 1997—; professorial lectr. in energy law George Washington U., 1980—. Co-author: Energy Decision Making, 1983, Energy Law and Policy, 1989; mem. editl. bd. Oil and Gas Reporter, Pub. Utility Fortnightly; contbr. articles to profl. publs. Established and developed enforcement program Fed. Energy Regulatory Commn.; mem. adv. bd. Pub. Utility Ctr., N.Mex. State U., 1986-94, Gas Industry Stds. Bd., 1998—; pres. Women's Coun. Energy and Environ., 1997—; mem. bd. dirs. Nat. Assn. Vets. Health Care. U. Denver scholar, 1972-73. Fellow ABA (mem. ho. of dels., vice chair sect. environ., energy and resources, chair coord. group energy law 1989-92, 95-97, chair standing com. environ. law 1997—); mem. Internat. Bar Assn., Am. Law Inst., Nat. Gas Inst. (chmn. 1983-90), Fed. Energy Bar Assn. (pres. 1991-92), Oil and Gas Ednl. Inst. (v.p.), Southwestern Legal Found. (trustee), Colo. Bar Assn., D.C. Bar Assn., Women's Bar Assn. D.C., Nat. Press Club, Cosmos Club, George Washington U. Club. Roman Catholic. Office: Duane Morris & Heckscher LLP 1667 K St NW Ste 700 Washington DC 20006-1608

HOLLIS, SUSAN TOWER, college dean; b. Boston, Mar. 17, 1939; d. James Wilson and Dorothy Parsons (Moore) Tower; m. Allen Hollis, Nov. 10, 1962 (div. Feb. 1975); children: Deborah Durfee, Harrison. AB, Smith Coll., 1962; PhD, Harvard U., 1982. Cert. cmty. coll. instr. history and humanities. Asst. prof. Scripps Coll., Claremont, Calif., 1988-91; prof. Coll. of Undergrad. Studies The Union Inst., L.A., 1991-93; dean of the college and prof. humanities Sierra Nev. Coll.-Lake Tahoe, Incline Village, Nev., 1993-95; ind. scholar, cons. Reno, 1995-96; ctr. dir., assoc. dean Ctrl. N.Y. Ctr. SUNY Empire State Coll., Syracuse, 1996—. Author: The Ancient Egyptian " Tale of Two Brothers", 1990; editor: Hymns, Prayers and Songs: Anthology of Ancient Egyptian Lyrics & Poetry (by John L. Foster), 1996; asst. editor: Working With No Data, 1987; co-editor: Feminist Theory and the Study of Folklore, 1993; mem. adv. bd. KMT, A Modern Jour. of Ancient Egypt, 1991—; contbr. articles to profl. jours. Music vol. Open Readings, Belmont, Mass., 1982-88; vol. Sierra Club, 1988—; problem capt. Odyssey of the Mind, Nev., 1994-95, judge, 1997-98; crew chief Tahoe Rim Trail, 1994-96; active Masterworks Chorale, N.Y., 1996—. Mem. Am. Acad. Religion, Am. Assn. Higher Edn., Am. Folklore Soc., Am. Oriental Soc., Am. Rsch. Ctr. Egypt, Egyptological Soc. N.Y., Internat. Assn. Egyptologists, Soc. for Study Egyptian Antiquities, Soc. Bibl. Lit. (co-chair Egyptology and Ancient Israel Group 1995-96, chair 1996—), Appalachian Mountain Club (co-leader 1987-88), N.Y. Acad. Scis., Incline Village/Crystal Bay C. of C. (sec. and bd. dirs. 1994-95), Adirondack Mountain Club (1996—), Ka-na-wa-ke Canoe Club (bd. dirs. 1998—). Democrat. Home: 48A Ponderosa Dr Syracuse NY 13215-1607 Office: SUNY Empire State Coll 219 Walton St Syracuse NY 13202-1226

HOLLIS, TIMOTHY MARTIN, bank executive; b. Marietta, Ga., Nov. 13, 1962; s. Milton Joel and Mary Syvila (Skanner) H. BSBA in Mgmt., Shorter Coll., 1986. Desk supr. front desk Wyndham Hotel Co., Atlanta, 1986-87; personal banker C&S/Sovran Corp., Atlanta, 1987-90, sr. personal banker, 1990-91; asst. br. mgr., banking officer NationsBank of Ga., N.A., Atlanta, 1991-92, banking ctr. mgr., 1992-95; sales mgr. First Union Nat. Bank Ga., Atlanta, 1995-97; fin. specialist AVP, 1997—. Treas., mktg. chairperson, fin. com., bd. trustees Choral Guild of Atlanta, 1991; mem. Buckhead Young Reps., Atlanta, 1989-92; bd. dirs. Artcare, Inc., Atlanta, 1991-94; docent, vol., mem. Friends of Zoo Atlanta; mem. steering com. First Night Atlanta, 1993-99, 1994 class Atlanta Midtown Leadership Program, Atlanta Midtown Alliance, 1992—, Human Rights Campaign Fund, 1992—, GAPAC, 1993-95; mem. adv. bd. Atlanta Exec. Network, 1993-96, Joining Hearts, Inc., 1994-99; steering com. Aids Walk Atlanta, 1995-97; bd. dirs. Positive Impact, 1996-97, Pets are Lovin Support, Inc., 1997-99; co-chair Young Profls. of Atlanta Exec. Network, 1996-98; conf. chair First Night Internat., 1998—; bd. dirs. AIDS Treatment Initiatives, 1997—, pres., 1998—. Mem. Atlanta Track Club (vol.). Methodist. Avocations: running, singing, working-out, volunteering. Home: 28 Finch Trl NE Atlanta GA 30308-2418 Office: First Union Nat Bank Ga 1605 Monroe Dr NE Atlanta GA 30324-5003

HOLLIS, WALTER WINSLOW, government official; b. Braintree, Mass., Nov. 13, 1926; s. Ralph C. and Ella May (McKean) H.; m. Dorcas Ann Meanear, Aug. 21, 1949 (dec.); children: Nancy Ann, Jeffrey Lee, David Michael, Susan Jane. B.A., Northeastern U., 1949; postgrad., Boston U., 1950-51, Nat. War Coll., 1972-73; M.S., George Washington U., 1973. Optical designer, optical engr., fire control systems engrng. Frankford Arsenal, 1951-65, chief Combat Vehicle & Gen. Instruments Fire Control Lab., 1965-68; sci. advisor U.S. Army Combat Devels. Experimentation Command, Ft. Ord, 1968-73, U.S. Army Operational Test and Evaluation Agy., 1973-80; dep. under sec. for ops. research Dept. Army, Dept. Def., Washington, 1980—. Served with U.S. Army, 1945-46. Recipient Presdl. Disting. Exec. award, Allen R. Matthews award Internat. Test and Evaluation Assn., 1992, Presdl. Meritorious Exec. award, DA Exceptional Civilian Svc. award. Avocations: woodworking; horticulture. Office: Dep Under Sec of the Army 102 Army Pentagon Washington DC 20310-0102

HOLLIS, WILLIAM FREDERICK, information scientist; b. Cleve., May 25, 1954; s. Raymond Frederick and Elizabeth (Meyer) H.; m. Jo Anne Kohlenberg, June 25, 1977; children: George Anthony, Dawn Elizabeth. BS, Bowling Green State U., 1976; MLS, Kent State U., 1979, EdD, 1992. Cert. chemisty/physics educator Ohio. Info. specialist B.F. Goodrich Rsch. & Devel. Ctr., Brecksville, Ohio, 1979-82; instr. libr. and info. sci. Coll. Wooster (Ohio), 1982-84; sr. info. specialist GenCorp Rsch., Akron, 1984, acting head tech. info., 1985, head tech. info ctr., 1986—; instr. sci. & tech. Stark Tech. Coll., Canton, Ohio, 1983-84. Elder United Ch. of Christ, Suffield, Ohio, 1986-89. Mem. Am. Chem. Soc., Am. Inst. Physics, Am. Soc. Info. Sci., Assn. Ednl. Communications & Tech. Home: 1547 Suffield Oaks Ln Mogadore OH 44260-8890 Office: GenCorp Tech Ctr 2990 Gilchrist Rd Akron OH 44305-4418

HOLLIS-ALLBRITTON, CHERYL DAWN, retail paper supply store executive; b. Elgin, Ill., Feb. 15, 1959; d. L.T. and Florence (Elder) Saylors; stepparent Bobby D. Hollis; m. Thomas Allbritton, Aug. 10, 1985. BS in Phys. Edn., Brigham Young U., 1981; cosmetologist, 1981. Retail sales clk. Bee Discount, North Riverside, Ill., 1981-82, retail store mgr., Downers Grove, Ill., 1982, Oaklawn, Ill., 1982-83, St. Louis, 1983; retail tng. mgr. Arvey Paper & Office Products (divsn. Internat. Paper), Chgo., 1984, retail store mgr., Columbus, Ohio, 1984—. Republican. Mem. LDS Ch. Avocations: writing, reading, travel. Office: Arvey Paper & Office Products 431 E Livingston Ave Columbus OH 43215-5533

HOLLISTER, DEAN, publishing company executive; b. Allentown, Pa., July 16, 1948; s. Charles and Mary-Jane (Marsteller) H.; m. Sylvia Reubens, Sept. 11, 1976; children: Peter, Daniel. BA, Washington & Lee U., 1970; MPhil, Columbia U., 1976. With Reed Reference Pub., New Providence, N.J., 1976—; now v.p. database production Reed Elsevier-New Providence, 1993—. Republican. Lutheran. Office: Reed Elsevier-New Providence 121 Chanlon Rd New Providence NJ 07974-1541*

HOLLISTER, LEO EDWARD, physician, educator; b. Cin., Dec. 3, 1920; s. William Baker and Ruth Victoria (Appling) H.; m. Louise Agnes Palmieri, Feb. 1, 1950 (div. Oct. 1966); children: Stephen, David, Cynthia, Matthew. BS, U. Cin., 1941, MD, 1943. Diplomate Am. Bd. Internal Medicine. Intern Boston City Hosp., 1944; residence in medicine VA Med. Ctr., San Francisco, 1947-49; chief med. service VA Med. Ctr., Palo Alto, Calif., 1953-60, assoc. chief staff, 1960-70, med. investigator, 1970-82, sr. med. investigator, 1982-86; prof. medicine Stanford U., Palo Alto, 1970—; dir. U.S. Pharmacopeia, Rockville, Md. Mem. editorial bd. Clin. Pharmacology Therapeutics, 1962-85; author: Chemical Psychoses, 1968, Clinical Use of Psychotherapeutic Drugs, 1972, Clinical Pharmacology Psych Drugs, 1978; numerous articles. Served to comdr. USNR, 1945-46, 50-52. Recipient Meritorious Service award VA, 1960, Middleton award VA, 1966. Fellow ACP (Menninger award 1985); mem. Am. Soc. Clin. Pharm. Therapeutics (pres. 1972), Am. Coll. Neuropsychopharmacology (pres. 1974), Coll. Internat. Neuropsychopharmacology (pres. 1978). Presbyterian. Avocations: art collecting, sports. Home: 1111 Bering Dr Unit 1304 Houston TX 77057-2334 Office: Harris County Psychiat Ctr PO Box 20249 Houston TX 77225-0249

HOLLISTER, NANCY, state legislator. Lt. gov. State of Ohio, 1995-98, rep. Ho. of Reps., 1999—. Office: State House 77 S High St Columbus OH 43266*

HOLLISTER, WILLIAM GRAY, psychiatrist; b. Lincoln, Nebr., July 21, 1915; s. Vernon Leo and Lela Gretchen (Pilcher) H.; m. Frances Flora Scudder, Mar. 23, 1940; children—David W., Robert Michael, Alan Scudder, Frances Virginia. A.B. in Anthropology, U. Nebr., 1937, B.S. in Psychology, 1940, M.D., 1941; M.P.H. (Rockefeller fellow), Johns Hopkins U., 1947; postgrad., Washington Psychoanalytic Inst., 1958-65. Diplomate Am. Bd. Psychiatry and Neurology, Am. Bd. Preventive Medicine. Intern Grady Hosp., Atlanta, 1941-42; resident in psychiatry Bishop Clarkson Meml. Hosp., Omaha, 1942-43, USPHS Hosp., Fort Worth, 1947-49; supr. venereal disease control Miss. Bd. Health, Jackson, 1943-46; psychiat. cons. Region IV USPHS, Atlanta, 1949-56; nat. sch. mental health cons. NIMH, Bethesda, Md., 1956-61; chief br. community research and services NIMH, 1962-65; prof. psychiatry, dir. cmty. psychiatry U. N.C., Chapel Hill, 1965-86, prof. emeritus, 1988—; cons. in occupational psychiatry IBM, Research Triangle Park, N.C., 1965-85; nat. mental health chmn. Nat. Congress PTA, 1958-62, 65-69. Author: Experiences in Rural Mental Health, 1974, Alternative Services in Community Mental Health: Programs and Processes, 1985; (with E. M. Bower) Behavior Science Frontiers of Education, 1967; composer, librettist (opera) Inca's Chosen Bride, 1997. Served with NIMH, 1943-65. Fellow Am. Psychiat. Assn., Am. Public Health Assn. (Disting. Service medal 1964); mem. AMA. Unitarian. Home: 750 Weaver Dairy Rd Apt 134 Chapel Hill NC 27514-1481

HOLLISTER, WINSTON NED, pathologist; b. Milw., Mar. 23, 1942; s. Harold Arthur and Jeannette Clara (Gastrav) H.; m. Carol Jean Potter, Dec. 7, 1963 (div. May 1978); children: Timothy Carl, David Andrew, Charles Davis; m. Margaret Ravenel Papen, Oct. 29, 1988. BS in Physics, U. Wis., 1964; MD, Med. Coll. Wis., 1971. Diplomate Am. Bd. Internal Medicine, Am. Bd. Pathology. Staff pathologist St. Joseph's Hosp., Milw., 1976—; pres., CEO Franciscan Shared Lab, Wauwatosa, Wis., 1988-90; med. dir., chmn. bd. dirs. Med. Sci. Labs., Wauwatosa, 1989—; cons. in field. Contbr. articles to profl. jours. Vestry mem. St. Paul's Episcopal Ch., Milw., 1978-83. Lt. USN, 1964-67. Recipient Houghton & Houghton award Med. Soc. Wis., 1971. Fellow Coll. Am. Pathologists (clin. practice com. 1984-87); mem. ACP, Am. Pathology Found. (pres. 1994—), River Tennis Club (bd. dirs., pres. 1978—), The Milw. Club, Univ. Club Milw. Republican. Episcopalian. Avocations: sailing, skiing, tennis, travel, music. Home: 7749 W Hawthorne Rd Mequon WI 53097-2007 Office: Med Sci Labs 11020 W Plank Ct Wauwatosa WI 53226-3279*

HOLLMAN, BARBARA CAROL, psychoanalyst, psychotherapist, consultant; b. N.Y.C., July 18, 1941; d. Samuel and Lillian (Verlin) Malkin; 1 child, Lee Jeffrey. BA, CUNY, 1964; MA, NYU, 1965; MSW, Adelphi U., 1985; postgrad., Manhattan Inst. Psychoanalysis, N.Y.C., 1995—. Cert. social worker, N.Y. Tchr. Syosset (N.Y.) Schs., 1966-70; social work technician Variety Pre Schooler's Workshop, Syosset, 1976-83; psychotherapist Cen. Nassau Guidance, Hicksville, N.Y., 1985-86, Melillo Ctr. for Mental Health, Glen Cove, N.Y., 1987—; pvt. practice, Hicksville, Glen Cove, 1985—, Teaneck, N.J., 1995—; speaker in field. Contbr. articles to profl. jours. Bd. dirs. The Family Exch. Ctr., 1978-83; parent mem. Com. on Handicapped, 1982-83. Fellow Soc. Clin. Social Workers; mem. NASW, Acad. Cert. Social Workers. Office: 175 Cedar Ln Teaneck NJ 07666-4315 Mailing Address: PO Box 39 Sea Cliff NY 11579-0039

HOLLMAN, CHARLOTTE ANDERSON, pediatric neurologist; b. Phila., Mar. 20, 1953; d. Richard Davis and Jeanette (Olliver) Anderson; m. Jay Lynn Hollman, May 31, 1986; children: David Scott, Peter John, James Andrew. MD, La. State U., New Orleans, 1977. Diplomate Am. Bd. Pediatrics; diplomate in child neurology Am. Bd. Psychiatry and Neurology; diplomate Am. Bd. Qualification in EEG. Resident and chief resident in pediatrics Baylor Coll. Medicine, Houston, 1977-80; fellow in child neurology U. Minn., Mpls., 1980-83; med. missionary Taitung, Taiwan, 1983; asst. prof. neurology Case Western Res U./Metro Gen. Hosp., Cleve., 1986-90; pvt. practice Neuromed. Ctr., Baton Rouge, La., 1983-86, 90—. Mem. adv. bd. Parents for Exceptional Progress, 1995—, therapeutic Horse Back Riding Program, 1995, La. Epilepsy Assn., 1984-86. Phi Mu Found. schoalr, 1975. Fellow Am. Acad. Pediatrics; mem. Child Neurology Soc., Am. Acad. Neurology, Christian Med. Dental Soc. Avocations: travel, reading, camping, biking, cross-stitch. Home: 4412 Lake Lawford Ct Baton Rouge LA 70816 Office: Neuromed Ctr 7777 Hennessy Ste 10000 Baton Rouge LA 70808

HOLL-MATTHEWS, DEE LYNN, career counselor, psychotherapist, personal development and success coach; b. Lima, Ohio, Mar. 8, 1949; d. James Adam Holl and Eileen (Gross) Parker; m. David William Dingledine (div. 1974); children: Jeffrey, Jennifer Holl Flowers. BA, U. Houston, 1985; MA, Amber U., 1993. Lic. profl. counselor. Human resources generalist Omniplan, Houston, 1986-87; plant pers. mgr. Digital Equipment, Greenville, S.C., 1987-90; sr. human resources cons. Digital Equipment, Dallas, 1990-93; cons. Drake, Beam, Morin, Dallas, 1993-95; sr. human resources mgr. Stream Internat., Dallas, 1995; site mgr., career counselor, profl. coach CDS/Mobil Oil, Dallas, 1995—; personal devel. and success coach; conf. spkr. Visions, Dallas, 1995. Vol. counselor AIDS Interfaith Coun., Dallas, 1994. Recipient plaque Johnson Space Ctr., 1984. Mem. ACA, ASTD, IACMP (Internatl. Assn. of Career Mgmt. Profls.), (pres.-elect, conf. spkr. Dallas 1996). Office: Career Devel Svcs Mobil Pl 3000 Pegasus Park Dr Dallas TX 75247-6204

HOLLOMAN, MARILYN LEONA DAVIS, nurse nonprofit administrator; b. Bklyn., Oct. 6, 1952; d. Leon Courbourne and Gwendolyn Omega (Crichlow) Davis; m. Theodore Albert Holloman, July 30, 1971 (div. Apr. 1975); children: Tedette Ann (dec.), Amina Omega Suedi. AAS in Nursing, Queensboro C.C., Bayside, N.Y., 1973; FNP, U. Miami, 1980. Founder, pres., CEO Women and Children 1st Inc., Miami, 1992—; allocations panel mem. United Way, Dade County, Fla., 1989-96; mem. at large Switchboard of Miami, 1992, treas., 1993-94, sec., 1994-95; fellow common ground Kellogg Found./U. Miami, 1993-95; primary cand. 1996 (Fla. House Rep., Dist 101). Author: Melody's of Life, 1982; editor Health Plan Baby Book, 1985; editor, pub. Legislative Update Women and Children 1st Inc., 1994—. Former pres. Dem. Black Caucus-Dade County chpt., 1991-92; Dem. candidate Fla. Ho. Reps., 1996. Mem. ANA (cert. specialist family nurse practitioner), Fla. Nurses Assn. (legis. dist. coord. 1984—), Nat. Assn. Parliamentarians, Miami Parliamentary Law Unit (pres. 1993-95, v.p. 1995-97). Democrat. Avocations: drama, reading, dance, travel. Home and Office: 3575 Barrel Springs Dr Orange Park FL 32073

HOLLOMAN, PATRICIA LEO, nurse; b. Bklyn., June 26, 1933; d. Henry Frederick Tatje and Ruth Rose Green; m. Thomas P. Leo, June 19, 1959; m. John Lawrence Sullivan Holloman Jr., May 20, 1969; children: Charlotte, Paul, Karin, Laura, Ellen. BSN, St. Johns U., Queens, N.Y., 1956. RN, N.Y. Staff nurse Kings County Hosp., Bklyn., 1953-55, educator, 1955-56, supr. cardiac oper. room, 1956-58, asst. supt. nursing, 1959-60; spl. asst. USPHS, Washington, 1966-67; spl. asst., exec. dir. APHA, Washington, 1967-69; staff nurse Mt. Sinai Med. Ctr., N.Y.C., 1976—; vice-chmn. coun. nursing practice Mt. Sinai Med. Ctr., N.Y.C., 1986—. Mem. ANA (cert., chmn. inst. collective bargaining, 1996-98, dir. ar large, 1998—, Shirley Titus award 1998), AACN. Assn. Oper. Room Nurses (cert.), N.Y. State Nurses Assn. (cert. of Appreciation 1990-97). Democrat. Home: 27-40 Ericsson St East Elmhurst NY 11369 Office: Mt Sinai Med Ctr 1 Gustave Levy Pl New York NY 10029

HOLLORAN, THOMAS EDWARD, business educator; b. Mpls., Sept. 27, 1929; s. Edward Francis and Florence G. (Loftus) H.; m. Patricia M. Holloran, June 26, 1954; children: Mary Patricia Harley, Anne Florence. BS, U. Minn., 1951, JD, 1955. Bar: Minn. 1955, Fed. 1955. Ptnr. Wheeler and Fredrikson, Mpls., 1955-67; exec. v.p. Medtronic, Inc., Mpls., 1967-73; pres. Medtronic, Inc., 1973-75; chmn., chief exec. officer Inter-Regional Fin. Group, Inc. (renamed Dain Rauscher Corp), Mpls., 1976-85; prof. Grad. Sch. Bus. U. of St. Thomas, St. Paul, 1985—; bd. dirs. ADC Telecomms., Inc., Mpls., Malt-O-Meal Co., Flexsteel Industries, Inc., Dubuque, Iowa, Medtronic, Inc., MTS Systems Corp., Mpls., Nat. city Bank Mpls., Nat. City Bancorp., Mpls. Spl. judge Mcpl. Ct. of Shorewood, Excelsior, Tonka Bay, Greenwood and Deephaven, Minn., 1961-65; Mayor, City of Shorewood, 1971-74; chmn. Urban Coalition, Mpls., 1977-78, City of Mpls. Task Force on Tech., 1983-84; mem. Mpls.-St. Paul Met. Airports Commn., 1974-82, vice chmn., 1976-82, chmn., 1989-91; bd. trustees Coll. St. Scholastica, 1971-81, chmn., 1979-81; trustee Coll. St. Thomas, 1979-88, U. Minn. Found., 1983-85, Bush Found., 1982—, chmn. 1991-96; trustee Mpls. Art Inst., 1986-93, Mpls. Children's Health Ctr., 1983-84; pres. Upper M.W. Coun., Mpls., 1978-80; bd. dirs. InterStudy, Excelsior., 1975-85, Minn. Press Coun., 1982-87, mem. corp. bd. Cath. Archdiocese Mpls. and St. Paul, 1990—. With USN, 1952-54, Korea. Mem. ABA, Minn. State Bar Assn. Roman Catholic.

HOLLOWAK, THOMAS LEO, archtitist, historian; b. Balt., Feb. 4, 1954; s. Stanley Adam and Martha Lee (Murphy) H. BA in History, U. Md., Balt., 1984; MA in History, U. Md., College Park, 1990. Libr. asst. Peabody Libr., Balt., 1978-84; city archivist, records mgmt. officer City of Balt., 1985-89; archivist U. Balt., 1990—; rschr. on Md.'s Polish cmty.; foudner Historyk Press. Author: Index to Marriages and Deaths in the (Baltimore) Sun, 1837-1850, 1978, Index to Marriages in the (Baltimore) Sun, 1851-1860, 1978, index to Obituaries and Death Nitoces Appearing in the Jednosc-Polonia, 1926-1946, 1983, Index to Obituaries in the Dziennik Chicagoski, 1984, 2d edit., 1987, Index to Obituaries in the Dziennik Chicagoski, 1910-1920, 1987, Longevity: An Index to the List of Decendents, Aged Seventy Years and Upwards appearing in the Annual Reports of the Board of Health for Baltimore City, 1880-1889, 1986, Faith, Work, Struggle: A History of Baltimore Polonia, 1988, Baltimore's Past: A Directory of Historical Sources, 1995, Polish Heads of Household in Maryland: An Index to the 1910 Census, 1990, Births From the Baptismal Register, St. Stanislaw Kostka, 1779-1889, 1992, Polonians Listed in the Baltimore City Directories, 1875-1895, 1992, Baltimore's Polish Language Newspapers: Historical and Genealogical Abstracts, 1891-1925, 1992, A Chronicle of War of 1812 Soldiers, Seamen and Marines, 1993, Baltimore's Polonia: A Brief History, 1995, A History of Polish Longshoremen and Their Role in the Establishment of a Union at the Port of Baltimore, 1996. Archivist Edgar allan Poe Soc. Md., Samuel Ready found., Inc., Gen. Soc. Colonial Wars. Grantee Md. Humanities Coun., 1989; Pabish Meml. scholar, 1984. Mem. Am. Records Mgrs. Assn. (v.p. Md. chpt. 1980-89), Balt. History Network (organizer), Md. Geneal. Soc. (chmn. publs. com. 1977-80), Polish Heritage Assn. Md. (editor, mem. exec. bd. 1981-85), Md. Hist. Soc. (mem. genealogy com. 1988—, 1st pl. Norris Harris Source Record Contest 1977-78, Hon. Mention 1983-84), Balt. Bibliophiles, Polish Am. Hist. Soc., Phi Alpha Theta. Avocations: sailing, swimming, travel, reading. Office: U Balt 1420 Maryland Ave Baltimore MD 21201-5706

HOLLOWAY, BRUCE KEENER, former air force officer; b. Knoxville, Tenn., Sept. 1, 1912; s. Frank P. and Elizabeth (Keener) H.; m. Frances Purdy, Oct. 14, 1944; children: Candace, Taylor, Amy. Student, U. Tenn., 1930-31; B.S., U.S. Mil. Acad., 1937; student, Calif. Inst. Tech., 1941; grad., Nat. War Coll., 1951. Commd. 2d lt. U.S. Cavalry, 1937; 2d lt. U.S. Army Air Corps, 1938; advanced through grades to gen. USAF, 1965; comdr. fighter aviation 14th Air Force, China Theater, 1942-43, 1st Fighter Group, March AFB, Calif., 1946; various staff assignments Air Def. Command, 1947-50; dep. dir. requirements Hdqrs. USAF, 1951-55; dep. comdr. 9th Air Force, Shaw AFB, S.C., 1955-57, 12th Air Force, Waco, Tex., 1957-59; dir. requirements USAF; also mem. mil. liaison com. USAF, AEC, 1959-61; dep. comdr. in chief U.S. Strike Command, MacDill AFB, Fla., 1961-65; comdr. in chief USAF in Europe, comdr. 4th Allied Tactical Air Force, 1965-66; vice chief of staff (Dept. Air Force), 1966-68; comdr. in chief SAC, chmn. joint strat. targeting planning staff Offutt AFB, Nebr., 1968-72; ret., 1972; acting assoc. adminstr. for aeronautics and space tech. NASA, Washington, 1973-74; cons. aerospace industry, 1974—; pres. U.S. Strategic Inst., 1974-75, 82—; bd. dirs. Sierra Rsch. Corp., 1980-84. Trustee N.Y. Inst. Tech., 1972-86, Nova U., Ft. Lauderdale, Fla., 1973-82. Decorated D.S.M., Silver Star, D.F.C., Legion of Merit, Air medal, also decorations from China, Thailand, S. Vietnam, Brazil, France, Germany. Mem. Def. Preparedness Assn., 14th Air Force Assn., Ret. Officers Assn., Am. Fighter Aces Assn., Order Daedalians, SAR, Phi Gamma Delta. Presbyterian. Home: 5124 Belleville Ave Orlando FL 32812-1001 Office: US Strategic Inst PO Box 618 Kenmore Station Boston MA 02215

HOLLOWAY, CHARLES ARTHUR, public and private management educator; b. Whittier, Calif., May 28, 1936; s. Heber H. and Theodosia S. (Stephens) H.; m. Christina Ahlm, July 11, 1959; children: Deborah, Susan, Stuart. BSEE with honors, U. Calif., Berkeley, 1959; MS, UCLA, 1963, PhD in Bus. Adminstrn. with distinction, 1969. Sr. engr. Bechtel Corp., San Francisco, 1964-65; teaching fellow UCLA, 1965-66; asst. prof. to prof. Stanford (Calif.) U., 1968—, Herbert Hoover prof. pub. and pvt. mgmt., 1980-91, assoc. dean acad. affairs Grad. Sch. Bus., 1980-87, 90-91, Kleiner Perkins Caufield and Byers prof. mgt., 1991—; dir. Axicon, The E-Greetings Network, CMC Industries, Kana Com. Author: Decision Making Under Uncertainty: Models and Choices, 1979, Perpetual Enterprise Machine: Seven Keys to Corporate Renewal, 1994. Bd. dirs. League to Save Redwoods. Served with USN, 1959-63. Fellow Ford Found., 1966-68. Mem. Inst. Mgmt. Sci., Ops. Rsch. Soc. Am., Stanford Integrated Mfg. Assn. (co-chair 1991-95, co-chair Stanford Ctr. for Entrepreneurial Studies 1995—). Home: 730 Santa Maria Ave Palo Alto CA 94305-8438 Office: Stanford U Grad Sch Bus Stanford CA 94305

HOLLOWAY, DAVID JAMES, political science educator; b. Dublin, Ireland, Oct. 13, 1943; came to U.S., 1983; s. James Joseph and Gertrude Mary (Kennedy) H.; m. Arlene Jean Smith, June 12, 1976; children: James, Ivor. MA, PhD, Cambridge (Eng.) U., 1964. Asst. lectr. U. Lancaster (Eng.), 1967-69; rsch. assoc. Inst. for Strategic Studies, London, 1969-70; lectr. U. Edinburgh (Scotland), 1970-84, reader, 1984-86; prof. Stanford (Calif.) U., 1986—, co-dir. Ctr. Internat. Security and Arms Control, 1991-97, Raymond A. Spruance prof. in internat. history, 1997—, assoc. dean humanities and scis., 1997-98, dir. Inst. for Internat. Studies, 1999—; dir. internat. rels. program Stanford U., 1989-91. Author: The Soviet Union and the Arms Race, 1983, Stalin and the Bomb, 1994; co-author: (with S. Drell and P. Farley) The Reagan Strategic Defense Initiative, 1985. Bd. dirs. Ploughshares Found., San Francisco, 1989—. Mem. Am. Polit. Sci. Assn., Am. Assn. for the Advancement of Slavic Studies. Avocations: opera, reading. Home: 710 Torreya Ct Palo Alto CA 94303-4160 Office: Stanford U Ctr Internat Security Arms Control 320 Galvez St Stanford CA 94305-6105*

HOLLOWAY, DONALD PHILLIP, lawyer; b. Akron, Ohio, Feb. 18, 1928; s. Harold Shane and Dorothy Gayle (Ryder) H.; BS in Commerce, Ohio U., Athens, 1950; JD, U. Akron, 1955; MA, Kent State U., 1962. Bar: Ohio 1955. Title examiner Bankers Guarantee Title & Trust Co., Akron, 1950-54; acct. Robinson Clay Product Co., Akron, 1955-60; librarian Akron-Summit Pub. Library, 1962-69, head fine arts and music div., 1969-71, sr. librarian, 1972-82; pvt. practice law, Akron, 1982—. Payroll treas. Akron Symphony Orch., 1957-61: treas. Friends Library Akron and Summit County, 1970-72. Mem. Music Library Assn., ABA, Ohio Bar Assn., Akron Bar Assn., Ohio Library Assn., ALA, Nat. Trust for Hist. Preservation, Internat. Platform Assn., Soc. Archtl. Historians, Coll. Art Assn., Art

Libraries North Am., Akron City Club, North Coast Soc. Republican. Episcopalian. Avocations: art and architecture, music, travel. Home: 601 Nome Ave Akron OH 44320-1682

HOLLOWAY, EDGAR AUSTIN, retired diversified business executive; b. Anguilla, Miss., Mar. 29, 1925; s. Tom W. and Lillie (Martin) H.; m. Bettye Jo Marmor, Oct. 3, 1947; 1 child, Janis Lynn (Mrs. Fichlie). BS, U. Louisville, 1947. C.P.A., Ohio, Miss., Ky., Ariz. Acct. Deloitte & Touche, Louisville, 1947-49, Cin., 1957-59; C.P.A. Coopers & Lybrand, Louisville, 1949-51; asst. treas. Diamond Crystal Salt Co., St. Clair, Mich., 1951-57; controller Diamond Internat. Corp., 1959-66; corp. controller Cudahy Co., Phoenix, 1966-68; v.p., controller Cudahy Co., 1968-72, The Clorox Co., Oakland, Calif., 1972-73; v.p. fin. The Clorox Co., 1973-79; v.p. fin., treas. Three Phoenix Co., 1979-85, cons., 1985-91. City treas., Jeffersontown (Ky.), 1943-47; bd. dirs. YMCA. Served to lt. (j.g.) USNR, 1944-47. Mem. AICPA, Fin. Execs. Inst. (nat. dir. Western area 1978-79, sec. San Francisco chpt. 1977, treas. 1978, 2d v.p. 1979, dir. Ariz. chpt. 1980-81). Clubs: Orinda (Calif.); Country (fin. com. 1977-78), Rotary. Home: 3227 Brookwood Dr Edgewood KY 41017-3208 Office: 21639 N 14th Ave Phoenix AZ 85027-2805

HOLLOWAY, EDWARD OLIN, human services manager; b. Rochester, N.Y., July 3, 1944; s. Charles Robert and Chrystal Gertrude (Darling) H.; m. Hama Elizabeth Farris, Dec. 23, 1967. AA, Palm Beach Jr. Coll., Lakeworth, Fla., 1964; BA, Lenoir Rhyne Coll., 1967; MS in Pub. Health, U. N.C., 1975. From sanitarian I to sanitarian supr. I Palm Beach County Health Dept., West Palm Beach, Fla., 1969-73; from emergency med. svcs. coord. to exec. dir. dist. IX Health Planning Coun., Inc., West Palm Beach, 1975-89; sr. health and human svcs. planner bd. county commrs. Palm Beach County Dept. Community Svcs., West Palm Beach, 1989—; mem. faculty Pub. Health Physician Residency Program, 1990—; mem. 1998 accreditation for five yrs., U. Miami; mem. steering com. Fla. Atlantic U. Inst. Govt., 1992—, vice chmn., 1994—. Chmn. dist. 9 adv. coun. Dept. Helath and Rehab. Svcs., West Palm Beach, 1990-92; pres. Fla. Assn. Health Planning Agys., Inc., 1984-89; mem. planning unit steering com. Leadership Palm Beach County, 1991; chmn. health care dist. feasibility subcom. Palm Beach County, 1989-90; mem. Palm Beach County data collection com. Health and Human Svcs. Planning Assn., 1992-98; mem. Interagy. Planning Group, 1994—; mem. Palm Beach Gardens Cmty. H.S. Adv. Com., 1994—; appointee for customer svc. West Palm Beach U.S. Dept. Vet. Affairs Med. Ctr., 1997—; mem. Palm Beach County Partnership for Aging program United Way, 1998—. With U.S. Army, 1967-69, Vietnam. Decorated Bronze Star, Purple Heart, Army Commendation medal, Cross of Gallantry (Vietnam); recipient Outstanding Svc. award Fla. Assn. Health Planning Agys., 1989, Outstanding Achievement award Bd. County Commrs. Palm Beach County Citizens Adv. Com. on Health and Human Svcs., 1995; planning grantee Regional Emergency Med. Svcs., 1975; recipient Letters of Commendation, CDC, 1980, Gov. of State of Fla. Lawton Chiles, 1998. Mem. ASPA (chpt. 102 coun. mem. 1989-98), APHA, Nat. Environ. Health Assn., U. N.C. Sch. Pub. Health Alumni Assn. (bd. dirs. 1994—). Democrat. Lutheran. Avocations: reading, target and skeet shooting, machairology. Office: Bd County Commrs Palm Beach Dept Community Svcs 810 Datura St West Palm Beach FL 33401-5204

HOLLOWAY, GORDON ARTHUR, lawyer; b. Wichita, Kans., July 27, 1938; s. George Arthur and Margurite (Bondurant) H.; m. Carol H. Criss, Sept. 1, 1960; children: Gregory Arthur, Suzanne Criss, Garrett Austin. BBA, U. Tex., 1960, JD, 1963. Bar: Tex. 1963, Colo. 1993. Assoc. McGregor, Sewell, Junell & Riggs, Houston, 1963-71; ptnr. Sewell and Riggs, Houston, 1971-93, Holloway & Rowley, 1994—. Staff sgt. Air N.G., 1964-71. Mem. Am. Bd. Trial Advocates (diplomate), Nat. Assn. Railroad Trial Counsel, Internat. Assn. Defense Counsel, Tex. Bd. Legal Specialization (cert. personal injury, civil trial law), Houston Club, Intertel. Office: Holloway & Rowley P C 1415 Louisiana St Ste 2550 Houston TX 77002-7360

HOLLOWAY, HILIARY HAMILTON, retired lawyer, banker; b. Durham, N.C., Mar. 7, 1928; s. Joseph Sim and Zelma (Slade) H.; m. Beatrice Gwen Larkin, Dec. 22, 1951; children: Hiliary H., Janis L. BBA, N.C. Central U., 1949; EdM, Temple U., 1956, JD, 1964. Bar: Pa. 1965, U.S. Dist. Ct. (ea. dist.) Pa. 1967, U.S. Supreme Ct. 1977. Bus. mgr. St. Augustine's Coll., Raleigh, N.C., 1950-53; nat. exec. dir. Kappa Alpha Psi, Phila., 1953-65; assoc. Hazell & Bowser, Phila., 1965-68; asst. counsel Fed. Res. Bank, Phila., 1968-72, v.p., gen. counsel, 1973-82, sr. v.p., gen. counsel, 1982-89; ptnr. Marshall, Dennehey, Warner, Coleman & Goggin, Phila., 1990-99; ret.; arbitrator Am. Arbitration Assn.; cons. U. Pa., Phila., 1976; chmn. Urban Edn. Found., Phila., 1986-89; bd. dirs. Mellon PSFS Bank, Berean Fed. Savings Bank; mem. adv. coun. NIH, 1989-93; CEO, chmn. New Atlantic Bank, Norfolk, Va., 1989-93. Chmn. oversight commn. overseeing fin. for City of Phila., Pa. Inter-govtl. Coop. Authority, 1993-95. Recipient Disting. Cmty. Svc. award Chapel of Four Chaplains, Phila., 1975, Martin Luther King award Educator's Roundtable, Phila., 1977, Laurel Wreath award Kappa Alpha Psi, Detroit, 1982, Disting. Alumni award N.C. Ctrl. U., 1986. Mem. ABA, Nat. Interfrat. Conf. (pres. 1996).

HOLLOWAY, JAMES LEMUEL, III, foundation executive, retired naval officer; b. Charleston, S.C., Feb. 23, 1922; s. James Lemuel and Jean Gordon (Hagood) H.; m. Dabney Hix Rawlings, Dec. 14, 1942; children: Lucy Dabney Lyon, Jane Meredith. BSEE, Naval Acad., Annapolis, 1942. Cert. naval aviator, naval nuclear reactor operator. Commd. ensign USN, 1942; served in destroyers USN, Atlantic, Pacific World War II, 1942-45; carrier jet fighter pilot USN, Korea, 1951-53; comdr. 1st nuclear carrier Enterprise USN, Vietnam, 1965-67; advanced through grades to adm. USN, 1973; comdr. carrier striking force U.S. 6th fleet, Ea. Mediterranean, 1970; comdr. U.S. 7th fleet USN, Vietnam, 1971-73; vice chief naval ops. USN, 1973-74, mem. Joint Chiefs of Staff, Dept. Def., 1974-78, chief naval ops., 1974-78, ret., 1978; pres. Coun. Am.-Flag Ship Operators, Washington, 1981-88; pres. Naval Hist. Found., Washington, 1982-98, chmn., 1998—; def. and fgn. policy cons. Paine Webber, Inc., 1980-88; bd. dirs. Statia Terminals Inc., Deerfield, Fla.; chmn. Dept. of Def. Spl. Rev. Group investigating Iranian hostage rescue, 1981; exec. dir. Presdl. Task Force on Combatting Terrorism, 1985; spl. envoy V.P. Bush to Middle East, 1986; commr. Predl. Blue Ribbon Commn. on Def. Mgmt., 1985, congl. Commn. on Mcht. Marine and Def., 1987-88, Presdl. Commn. on Long Term Integrated Strategy, 1987-88; U.S. rep. to South Pacific Commn., 1990-94. Tech. advisor: (film) Top Gun, 1985; contbr. articles to mags. Trustee St. James Sch., Md., 1962—, pres., 1989—, chmn. 1996; bd. dirs. Olmsted Found., Washington, 1978—; mem. bd. advisors The Citadel, 1981-86; chmn. adv. bd. U.S. Naval Acad., 1983-91; chmn. Hist. Annapolis Found., Inc., 1986-96, chmn. emeritus, 1996—; pres., chmn. Naval Acad. Found., 1994—; trustee George Marshall Found., 1988-96; dir. Atlantic Coun., 1987-96; bd. visitors and govs. St. John's Coll., 1995, Bd. Mariners Mus., Newport News, Va., 1995—. Decorated Bronze Star (4), Air medals (2), Legion of Merit, DFC, Def. DSM with 2 oak leaf cluster, Navy DSM with 4 oak leaf clusters, Order of Rising Sun (Japan), Grand Cross (Fed. republic Germany), Legion of Honor (France), Rank of Commandeur, 31 others; recipient Triennial Modern Patriot award SAR, 1994, Disting. Patriot award, 1999, Disting. Pub. Svc. award Navy League, 1996, Disting. Patriot award SAR, 1999; elected Nat. Wrestling Hall of Fame, 1998. Mem. Assn. Naval Aviation (chmn. 1985-91), Met. Club (Washington gov. 1988—, pres. 1992), Brook Club (N.Y.C.), N.Y. Yacht Club (N.Y.C.), Md. Club (Balt.), Annapolis Yacht Club, Soc. Cin., Alfalfa Club (Washington). Republican. Episcopalian. Avocation: sailing. Home: 1694 Epping Farms Rd Annapolis MD 21401-6672 Office: Naval Hist Found Washington Navy Yard Naval Hist Found Bldg 57 Washington DC 20374

HOLLOWAY, JEROME KNIGHT, publisher, former military strategy educator, retired foreign service officer; b. Phila., May 8, 1923; s. Jerome Knight and Emily Margaret (Ennis) H.; m. Gertrud Harms, Apr. 16, 1953 (dec. Jan. 1976); children—Jerome Knight III, Karen M., Nicholas H. A.B., Cath. U., 1947; M.A., U. Mich., 1959; lang. student, Tokyo, Japan, 1958-60; fellow, Harvard, 1968-69. Joined U.S. Fgn. Service, 1947, ret., 1975; 3d sec. Rangoon, Burma, 1947-49; vice-consul Shanghai, China, 1949-50, Bremen, Germany, 1950-52; consul Hong Kong, 1952-57; 2d sec. Tokyo, 1960-61; assigned State Dept., Washington, 1961-64, 69-70; 1st sec. Stockholm, Sweden, 1964-65; counselor, 1965-68; consul gen. Osaka-Kobe, Japan, 1970-74; state dept. adviser to pres. U.S. Naval War Coll., Newport, R.I., 1974-75; prof. strategy U.S. Naval War Coll., 1976-90; pub. Hanlin Press, Newport, R.I., 1990—. Served to lt. (j.g.) USNR, 1942-46. Mem. U.S. Naval Inst., Assn. Asian Studies. Home: 72 Webster St Newport RI 02840-4080

HOLLOWAY, JOHN THOMAS, physicist; b. Cape Girardeau, Mo., June 19, 1922; s. Herbert Henry and Addie Mae (Cahill) H.; m. Kay Vickers, Nov. 11, 1965; children—Linda, Kim (dec. Jan. 1999). A.B., Millikin U., Decatur, Ill., 1943; Ph.D., Iowa State U., 1957. With nuclear physics br. Office Naval Research, Washington, 1946-53; head br. Office Naval Research, 1951-52; research asst. Ames Lab., AEC, Iowa, 1954-57; with Office Dir. Def. Research and Engring., Washington, 1958-61; dep. dir. Office of Sci. Dir. Def. Research and Engring., 1959-61; with NASA, 1961-68, dep. dir. grants and research contracts, 1961-67, chief advanced programs and tech., space applications div., 1967-68; dir. Nat. Hwy. Safety Research Center, Dept. Transp., 1968-69; v.p. research Ins. Inst. Hwy. Safety, 1969-72; asso. dir. ops. Interdisciplinary Communications Program, Smithsonian Instn., 1972-77, program mgr. internat. program population analysis, 1972-77, research and devel. cons. in hwy. safety, biomed. electronics, energy conservation, 1977-78; sr. staff officer bd. on radioactive waste mgmt. Nat. Acad. Scis.-NRC, 1978-85; cons. on radioactive waste mgmt., hwy. safety, 1985—; mem. conf. com. Nat. Conf. Advancement Research, 1971-75. Author papers in field; adviser documentary films. Served with USNR, 1944-46. Mem. Am. Phys. Soc., Sigma Xi. Clubs: Cosmos (Washington); Army-Navy Country (Arlington, Va.). Home: 2220 Cathedral Ave NW Washington DC 20008-1504

HOLLOWAY, JULIA BOLTON, professor emerita, theologian; b. London, England, Apr. 14, 1937; Arrived in US Dec. 1953.; d. John Robert Glorney and Sybil Margaret (Rutherford) B.; m. Halbert Harold, (separated 1967); children: Richard, Colin, Jonathan. BA in English, San Jose State, Calif., 1954-57; MA in English, U. Calif., Berkeley, 1966-67; PhD in English, U. Calif., 1974. Asst. tchr. U. Calif., Berkeley, 1967-71; asst. prof. Quincy Coll., Ill., 1971-74; assoc. master Princeton Inn Coll., N.J., 1974-76; asst. prof. Princeton U., 1974-81, U. Colo., Boulder, 1981-87; vis. prof. So. Meth. U., 1987, 91; assoc. prof. U. Colo., Boulder, 1987, 91; acting curator Casa Guidi, Florence, Italy, 1987-88; dir. Medieval Studies U. Colo., Boulder, 1988-92; prof. emerita, 1992—; novice Cmty. of the Holy Family, 1992-96, acting libr., 1993-96. Author: Bibliography of Latini, 1986, The Pilgrim and the Book: Dante, Langland, Chaucer, 1986, Latini, Il Tesoretto, 1981, Equally in God's Image: Women in the Middle Ages, 1990, Gregersson, Gascoigne, Life of Saint Birgitta of Sweden, 1991, Saint Bride and Her Book: Birgitta of Sweden's Revelations, 1992, Twice-Told Tales: Brunetto Latino Dante Alighieri, 1992, Elizabeth Barrett Browning, Aurora Leigh and Other Poems, 1995, The Julian Library Portfolio, 1996, The Julian Website, 1996; contbr. articles to profl. jours. Bd. dirs. Colo. Endowment for the Humanities, 1983-86, Rocky Mountain Peace Ctr., 1983-86; mem. Quaker Del. to Heads of State, 1980; vice-chmn. Colo. Women's Agenda, 1988. Recipient Summer Seminar, Summer Stipend awards NEH; AAUW Founders fellow, 1987-88. Mem. MLA, Early English Text Soc., Medieval Acad., Bronte Soc., Browning Inst. Avocation: bookbinding.

HOLLOWAY, MARVIN LAWRENCE, retired automobile club executive, ranch and grove owner; b. Gordon, Ga., May 27, 1911; s. Percy Thomas and Lillie Mae (Bozeman) H.; m. Elizabeth Kirkland, Feb. 14, 1948. BA magna cum laude, Wofford Coll., 1933. Sec., mgr. AAA Auto Club South (formerly Peninsula Motor Club), Tampa, Fla., 1938-53, pres., 1953-76, chmn. bd., CEO, 1976-90, ret., 1990; bd. dirs. Am. Automobile Assn., Falls Church, Va., 1975-86, sec., 1985-86; bd. dirs. AAA Found. for Traffic Safety, 1970-88; chmn. Ea. Conf. AAA Motor Clubs, 1960-62, Southeastern Conf., 1974; pub. AAA Going Places mag. Recipient Achievement award U. Tampa, 1955, Top Mgmt. award Sales and Mktg. Execs. of Tampa, 1983, Dynamic Leadership award Southeastern Conf. AAA Clubs, 1983, Disting. Svc. award Wofford Coll., 1983, Disting. Svc. award Fla. Sheriffs' Assn., 1984; named Mr. Motorist AAA Clubs Fla., 1982. Mem. Blue Key, Scabbard and Blade, Sr. Order Gnomes, Phi Beta Kappa, Pi Kappa Phi. Republican. Avocation: hunting. Home: 29244 Whipporwill Ln Wesley Chapel FL 33543-4327

HOLLOWAY, OTHELLE JUNE, elementary school educator; b. Holdenville, Okla., Mar. 26, 1939; d. William Otho and Berniece E. (Floyd) French; m. Philip Lee Holloway, Dec. 23, 1960. BS, Oklahoma City U., 1962. Tchr. Oklahoma City Sch. Sys., 1962-72, Heritage Hall Sch., Oklahoma City, 1972-98. Mem. Alpha Delta Kappa. Democrat. Avocations: reading, arts and crafts, antiques, tennis. Home: 6223 N Utah Ave Oklahoma City OK 73112-1362

HOLLOWAY, PAUL FAYETTE, retired aerospace executive; b. Hampton, Va., June 7, 1938; s. Eldridge Manning and Minnie Powell H.; m. Barbara Jane Menetch, June 23, 1956; children: Paul Manning (dec.), Eric Scott. BS, Va. Poly. Inst. and State U., 1960; postgrad., U. Va., 1961, Coll. William and Mary, 1962-63; grad. advanced mgmt. program, Harvard U., 1988; PhD (hon.), Old Dominion U., 1994. With NASA Langley Rsch. Ctr., Hampton, Va., 1960-97; aerospace technologist NASA Langley Rsch. Ctr., 1960-69, space shuttle task group, 1969, chief space sys. divsn., 1972-75; acting dep. assoc. adminstr. Office Aeronautics and Space Tech., 1977, dir. for space, 1975-85, dep. dir., 1985-91, dir., 1991-96, acting dep. adminstr., 1992-93, ret., 1997; cons. in field. Mem. editl. bd. Jour Spacecraft and Rockets, 1972-77, editor in chief, 1978-80; contbr. articles to profl. jours. Mem. Poquoson (Va.) Planning Commn.; v.p. local PTA; mem. coll. bd. Thomas Nelson C.C., 1997—. Recipient Outstanding Leadership medal NASA, 1980, Exceptional Svc. medal, 1981; Presdl. Rank award for meritorious exec., 1981, Presdl. Rank award for disting. exec., 1987, 93, Equal Opportunity medal, 1992, Disting. Svc. medal, 1992; named Peninsula Engr. of Yr., Peninsula Engrs. Club, 1996. Fellow AIAA (v.p. publs. 1991-94), Am. Astronautical Soc.; mem. Fed. Exec. Inst. Alumni Assn., Sr. Execs. Assn., Internat. Acad. Astronautics, Sigma Gamma Tau, Phi Kappa Phi. Methodist. Home: 16 N Westover Dr Poquoson VA 23662-1424

HOLLOWAY, PAUL HOWARD, materials science educator; b. Marion, Ind., Oct. 31, 1943; s. Charles D. and Pauline (Poe) H.; m. Bette Lorraine Zubrod, Jan. 10, 1943; children: Michael, Brian, Kimberly. BS, Fla. State U., 1965, MS, 1966; PhD, Rensselaer Poly. Inst., Troy, N.Y., 1972. Metallurgist Gen. Electric Co., Schenectady, 1966-69; staff mem. Sandia Nat. Lab., Albuquerque, 1972-78; assoc. prof. dept. materials sci. and engring. U. Fla., Gainesville, 1978-81, prof. dept. materials sci. and engring., 1981—, rsch. prof., 1997-99; dir. MICROFABRITECH, Gainesville; statewide coord. Advanced Microelectronics and Materials Program, Tampa, 1988-91. Editor: Compound Semiconductor Growth, Processing Devices, 1988, Characterizatin of Metals and Alloys, 1993, Handbook of Compound Semiconductors, 1995, Critical Revs. in Solid State and Materials Scis.; contbr. chpts. to books, articles to profl. jours. Mem., chmn. Alachua County 4-H Adv. Coun., Gainesville, 1986-88, 95—; mem Alachua County Extension Office Adv. Coun., Gainesville, 1986-91. Recipient Muller award U. Wis.-Milw., 1988; named Tchr. of Yr. Coll. Engring. U. Fla., Gainesville, 1988. Fellow Am. Vacuum Soc. (hon., pres. 1987, Albert Nerken award 1999); mem. ASTM (vice-chmn. 1983-86), Am. Soc. Metals, The Mining, Metallurgy, Materials Soc., Alpha Sigma Mu. Office: U Fla Dept Materials Sci Gainesville FL 32611

HOLLOWAY, RALPH LESLIE, anthropology educator; b. Phila., Feb. 6, 1935; s. Ralph L. and Marguerite (Grugan) H. BS in Geology, U. N.Mex., Albuquerque, 1959; PhD in Anthropology, U. Calif., Berkeley, 1964. Asst. prof. Columbia U., N.Y.C., 1964-69, assoc. prof., 1969-73, prof., 1973—. Editor: Primate Aggression, Territoriality and Xenophobia: A Comparative Perspective, 1974; contbr. numerous articles to profl. jours. Guggenheim Found. fellow, 1974; NSF grantee, 1984. Fellow AAAS, N.Y. Acad. Sci.; mem. Am. Anthrop. Assn., Am. Assn. Phys. Anthropologists, Soc. for Neurosci., Sigma Xi, Phi Beta Kappa. Office: Columbia U Dept Of Anthropology New York NY 10027

HOLLOWAY, RICHARD LAWRENCE, marriage-family therapist, college official; b. Buffalo, May 18, 1949; s. Robert Lee and Aurelia (Muresan) H.; m. Julie Ann Sianko, Sept. 26, 1987; children: Evan Richard, Kendall Marie. AB in Speech and Theater, Heidelberg Coll., Tiffin, Ohio, 1971; MS in Instrnl. Des. Devel. and Evaluation, Syracuse U., 1974, PhD in Instrnl. Des. Devel. and Evaluation, 1976; postgrad. in marriage and family therapy, Coll. Medicine Baylor U., 1987-90. Asst. prof. ednl. measurement Coll. Pharmacy U. Minn., Mpls., 1977-78, asst. prof. family medicine Sch. Medicine,, 1978-82, assoc. prof., 1982-84; assoc. prof., head com. resources Minn. Ext. Svc., St. Paul, 1985-86; prof. Baylor Coll. Medicine, Houston, 1986-91, prof., rsch. dir., 1991-92; prof., assoc. dean student affairs, vice chair, divsn. chief Med. Coll. Wis., Milw., 1992—, assoc. dean for student affairs, 1996—; vis. prof. Syracuse (N.Y.) U., 1981. TV host Campus Closeup, One Step Ahead, Mpls., 1984-86; contbr. chpts. to books, articles to profl. jours. Bd. dirs. Milw. Ave. Homeowners Assn., Mpls., 1976-83. Recipient E.B. Knight Jour. award NACTA, 1977; vis. scholar U. Mich., 1983. Mem. APA, Am. Assn. Marriage and Family Therapy, Am. Ednl. Rsch. Assn. (Recognition award 1985), Soc. Tchrs. Family Medicine (bd. dirs. 1989-95, pres. 1993-94, Recognition award 1982). Democrat.

HOLLOWAY, ROBERT CHARLES, orchestrator, arranger, composer; b. Balt., June 20, 1927; s. George Albert and Edna Mildred (Smith); m. Leslee R. Seymour, June 4, 1960; children: Bruce, Collin, Christy, Heather, Deven, Duana. Grad., Balt. Poly. Inst., 1947. Arranger, orchestrator Alvin Ailey Dance Co., 1987; pres. Chelsea Music Svc., Inc., N.Y.C., 1990-92; v.p. St. Croix Records, 1961—. Arranger, orchestrator for ABC-TV, CBS Radio, NBC Tonight Show, Radio City Music Hall, USN Band, Boston Pops Orch., San Antonio Symphony, Denver Symphony; orchestrator Le Ballet de Coeurs commd. by San Francisco Ballet; (Broadway musicals) Odyssey, Barnum, Peter Pan, Sophisticated Ladies, On Your Toes, Jerome Robbins Broadway; (performers) Skitch Henderson, Enrique Madriguera, Richard Hayman, Tommy Tune, Betty Carter, Eddie Fisher, Caterina Valente, Connie Francis, Raquel Bitton; composer: Prelude, Busybody, Celebration, Southern Suite, Improvisations in Jazz, Celebration. With USN, 1944-46, USNR, 1946-54. Mem. ASCAP, Am. Soc. Music Arrangers, Am. Fedn. Musicians. Home: Rte 123 East Alstead NH 03602

HOLLOWAY, SHIRLEY J., state agency administrator. BA in Speech Pathology, Lewis and Clark Coll.; BS in Spl. Edn., Ea. Wash. U.; BS in Edn., Western Wash. U.; PhD in Ednl. Leadership, Gonzaga U. Cons. Alaska Dept. Edn., Juneau, 1971, commr. of edn., 1994—; spl. edn. dir. Alaska's State Operated Schs., 1972; prin., asst. supt. North Slope Borough (Alaska) Sch. Dist., 1975-90, supt., 1987-90; supt. Nine Mile Falls Sch. Dist., Wash., 1992-94; former speech and hearing clinician, tchr. hearing impaired students, Wash.; vis. prof. pub. sch. adminstrn. U. Alaska, Anchorage, 1990-92; past pres. Arctic Sivunmun Ilisagvik Coll., Major's Workforce Devel. Program, Barrow (Alaska), North Slope Borough. Vol. civic and profl. assns., task forces and adv. groups. Office: 801 W 10th St Ste 200 Juneau AK 99801-1823

HOLLOWAY, WILLIAM JIMMERSON, retired educator; b. Smithfield, Va., May 6, 1917; s. Arnett Jimmerson and Lucy Pernell (White) H.; m. Julia Naomi Edmundson, June 17, 1944; children: Wendell, Arnett, Lynn. B.S. with honors, Hampton Inst., 1940; M.A., U. Mich., 1946; Ed.D., U. Ill., 1961; postgrad., Harvard U., 1950. Prin. Union Sch., Hampton, Va., 1946-47; dean students Savannah State Coll., 1947-55; prin. Ligon High Sch., Raleigh, N.C., 1956-57; counselor N.C. Central U., Durham, 1959-61; supt. Va. State Sch., Hampton, 1961-65; edn. program officer U.S. Office Edn. Washington, 1965-70; vice provost Ohio State U., Columbus, 1970-78; prof. edn. Ohio State U., 1970-82, prof. emeritus, 1982—; dir. Nigerian edn. program, Ohio State U., 1980-82; pres. Internat. Ednl. and Service Inst., Inc., Raleigh, N.C., 1981-88; disting. prof. edn. St. Augustine's Coll., Raleigh, 1983-87. Author: The Education of Blacks in Virginia Before the Civil War, 1619-1860, 1993; editl. bd. The Negro Educational Review, 1972, editor-in-chief, 1995. Trustee Freedoms Found., 1974, St. Augustines Coll., 1968-77. Recipient Freedoms Found. medal, 1954, Superior Accomplishment award HEW, 1968, Disting. Alumni award Hampton Inst., 1970, award Nat. Press Inst., 1972, Outstanding Citizen award Ohio Gen. Assembly, 1978, Outstanding Achievement award Ohio State U., 1978, Disting. Service award Ohio State U., 1984, Community Leadership award Capital U., 1978, Nat. Disting. Service award United Negro Coll. Fund, 1979, Excellence in Internat. Edn. award Govt. of Nigeria, Disting. Career award Negro Ednl. Rev., 1984, Outstanding Achievement award U. Mich., 1987; Harvard Far Eastern Studies fellow, 1956. Mem. Am. Assn. Higher Edn., Am. Personnel and Guidance Assn., Alpha Kappa Delta, Phi Delta Kappa, Kappa Delta Pi. Democrat. Presbyterian (elder). Clubs: Lions (pres. 1975); Cosmos (Washington). Home: 4450 S Park Ave Apt 309 Chevy Chase MD 20815-3633 *As an educator I have worked to develop sensitivity to the needs, hopes, and aspirations of all people, particularly those at the bottom of the socio-economic ladder. With youth and adults I have labored to kindle sparks of brotherhood leading to harmony. I feel that our survival on this planet is linked with our capacity to use cultural differences in creative and constructive ways.*

HOLLOWAY, WILLIAM JUDSON, JR., federal judge; b. 1923. AB, U. Okla., 1947; LLB, Harvard U., 1950; LLD (hon.), Oklahoma City U., 1991. Ptnr. Holloway & Holloway, Oklahoma City, 1950-51; atty. Dept. Justice, Washington, 1951-52; assoc., ptnr. Crowe and Dunlevy, Oklahoma City, 1952-68; judge U.S. Ct. Appeals (10th cir.), Oklahoma City, 1968-84, chief judge, 1984-91, sr. judge, 1992—. Mem. ABA, Fed. Bar Assn., Okla. Bar Assn., Oklahoma County Bar Assn. Office: US Ct Appeals 10th Cir PO Box 1767 Oklahoma City OK 73101-1767

HOLLOWELL, MONTE J., engineer, operations research analyst; b. Helena, Ark., Dec. 30, 1949; s. Jerry B. and Imogene (Hartsfield) H.; m. Jan Bennett, Nov. 19, 1972; children: J. Brett, Matt J. BS in Math., BA in Physics, Ouachita Baptist Univ., 1972; MS in Indsl. Engring., U. Tex., El Paso, 1978. Air def. officer U.S. Army, 1972-80; industrial engr. PPG Industries, Wichita Falls, Tex., 1980-82; industrial engr. U.S. Army Missile Command, Redstone Arsenal, Ala., 1982-85, gen. engr., 1985—. Mem. Redstone Arsenal Military Ops. Rsch. Soc., Air Def. Artillery Assn. (U.S. rep. to NATO panel 10 concerned with long-term rsch. in air def.). Home: 12038 Chicamauga Trl SE Huntsville AL 35803-1546 Office: Advanced Systems Concepts Redstone Arsenal AL 35898-5242

HOLLOWS, GREGORY G., federal judge; b. 1947. JD, Loyola U., 1979. With Gibson, Dunn & Cautcher, 1979-82; asst. U.S. atty., 1982-88, asst. U.S. atty. chief civil divsn., 1988-90; apptd. magistrate judge ea. dist. U.S. Dist. Ct. Calif., 1990, chief magistrate judge, 1997. With USMC, 1969-74. Fax: (916) 491-3915. Office: US Courthouse 8th Fl 530 I St Sacramento CA 95814-4708

HOLLY, LAUREN, actress; b. 1964; d. Grant and Michael Holly; m. Danny Quinn (div.); m. Jim Carrey. Grad., Sarah Lawrence Coll. Appeared in TV series Spenser: For Hire, All My Children, 1986-89, The Antagonists, 1991, Picket Fences, 1992, Fantasy Island; TV films include Love Lives On, 1985, Archie: To Riverdale and Back Again, 1990, Fugitive Among Us, 1992, Dangerous Heart, 1994, Vig, 1998; appeared in films Seven Minutes in Heaven, 1985, Band of the Hand, 1986, The Advantures of Ford Fairlane, 1990, The Bruce Lee Story, 1993, Dumb and Dumber, 1994, Sabrina, 1995, Beautiful Girls, 1996, Down Periscope, 1996, Turbulence, 1997, A Smile Like Yours, 1997, No Looking Back, 1998, Entropy, 1999, Any Given Sunday, 1999. *

HOLLYER, A(RTHUR) RENE, lawyer; b. Wycoff, N.J., July 28, 1938; s. Richard W. and Florence (Vervaet) H.; m. Lauraine Dennis, Apr. 8, 1978; children: James Richard, Jennifer Ashley. BA, Williams Coll., 1961; MPA, Woodrow Wilson Sch., Princeton, 1963; LLB, Columbia U., 1966. Bar: N.J. 1966, U.S. Dist. Ct. N.J. 1966, N.Y. 1968, U.S. Dist. Ct. (so. and ea. dists.) N.Y. 1969, U.S. Ct. Appeals (3rd cir.) 1970, U.S. Ct. Appeals (2d cir.) 1971, D.C. 1972, U.S. Supreme Ct. 1974. Law sec. to judge chancery divsn. N.J. Superior Ct., Newark, 1966-67; assoc. Olwine, Connelly, Chase, O'Donnell & Weyher, N.Y.C., 1968-70, 72-74; asst. U.S. atty. Dist. N.J., 1970-71; ptnr. Hollyer, Brady, Smith, Troxell, Barret, Rockett, Hines & Mone, L.L.P. and predecessor firms, N.Y.C., 1974—. Mem. N.Y. State Bar Assn., Assn. of Bar of City of N.Y. (profl. discipline com. 1990-92, 95-98, chmn. complaint mediation panel 1991-92, 95-98, ethics com. 1992-95, profl. responsibility com. 1998—). Home: 50 Hamilton Rd Glen Ridge NJ 07028-1109 Office: Hollyer Brady Smith Troxell Barrett Rockett Hines & Mone LLP 551 5th Ave New York NY 10176-0001

HOLLYFIELD, JOHN SCOGGINS, lawyer; b. Harlingen, Tex., Aug. 20, 1939; m. Penny Pounds, Dec. 27, 1962; children: Jon Scott, Courtney. Bar: Tex. 1968;. Assoc. Fulbright & Jaworski, Houston, 1968-75, ptnr., 1975—. Lt. USNR, 1961-65. Recipient Pres.'s award Houston Bar Assn., 1986. Mem. ABA (coun. real property sect. 1986-93, sec. 1993-94, vice chair real property divsn. 1994-96, chair elect 1996-97, chair 1997-98, ho. of dels. 1999—), Am. Coll. Real Estate Lawyers (pres. 1990-91), Anglo-Am. Real Property Inst. (gov. 1986—). Office: Fulbright & Jaworski LLP 1301 Mckinney St Houston TX 77010-3031

HOLM, SIR IAN, actor; b. Sept. 12, 1931; s. James Harvey and Jean (Wilson) Cuthbert; m. Lynn Mary Shaw, 1955 (div. 1965); m. Sophie Baker, 1982 (div. 1986); m. Penelope Wilton, 1991. Student, Royal Acad. Dramatic Art, 1950-53. Actor with Shakespeare Mem. Theatre, 1954-55; in repertory, 1956; toured in Titus Andronicus, 1957; numerous roles Royal Shakespeare Co. including Henry V, Romeo and Richard III, 1958-67; plays include Moonlight, 1993, Landscape, 1994, King Lear, 1997 (Evening Std. award for Best Actor); film appearances include Young Winston, Alien, Chariots of Fire (named Best Supporting Actor, Cannes Film Festival, 1981, Brit. Acad. Film and TV Arts, 1982, Acad. Award nomination Best Supporting Actor, 1982), Greystoke, Brazil, Dance With A Stranger, 1985, Wetherby, 1985, Dreamchild, 1985, Another Woman, 1988, Henry V, 1990, Hamlet, 1990, Kafka, 1991, The Naked Lunch, 1992, Blue Ice, 1992, Hour of The Pig, 1993, The Madness of King George, 1994, Lochness, 1994, Mary Shelley's Frankenstein, 1995, Big Night, 1995, Night Falls on Manhattan, 1995, The 5th Element, 1996, A Life Less Ordinary, 1996, The Sweet Hereafter, 1996 (Genie Best Actor award), Existenz, 1998, The Hunted, 1998, Simon Magus, 1998; others; TV appearances include The Lost Boys (Best Actor award Royal TV Soc., 1979), Strike, 1981, (miniseries) Game, Set and Match, 1988, The Last Romantics, 1991, (series) The Borrowers, 1992-93, The Match, 1998, Esther Kahn, 1999, Joe Gould's Secret, 1999, Beautiful Joe, 1999; others; TV appearances include Landscape, BBC, 1995, King Lear, BBC, 1997, Alice Through the Looking Glass, Channel 4, 1998. Awarded Knighthood by Queen of Eng., 1998; recipient Tony award for Best Supporting Actor, 1967, Evening Std. award, 1967. Office: care Julian Belfrage Assocs, 46 Albemarle St, London W1X 4PP, England

HOLM, JOHN ALEXANDER, linguist, educator; b. Jackson, Mich., May 16, 1943; s. James P. and Leah (Reisbig) H. BA in English, U. Mich., 1965; MA in Tchg. English as a Fgn. Lang., Columbia U., 1968; PhD in Linguistics, U. London, 1978. Tchr. English U. Los Andes, Bogotá, Colombia, 1965-66; tchr. English and German Detroit Inst. of Tech., 1971-73; tchr. of English Kollegium Sarnen, Switzerland, 1973-75; lectr. in linguistics Coll. of the Bahamas, Nassau, 1978-80; prof. English Hunter Coll., CUNY, 1980-98; prof. linguistics Grad. Ctr., CUNY, 1989-98; chair English linguistics U. Coimbra, Portugal, 1998—. Editor: (with F. Byrne) Atlantic Meets Pacific, 1993; editor: Central American English, 1983; author: (with A. Shilling) Dictionary of Bahamian English, 1982, Pidgins and Creoles, 1988-89 (2 volumes), Introduction to Pidgins and Creoles, 1999; bd. editors Jour. of Pidgin and Creole Langs. Fulbright scholar U. Coimbra, Portugal, 1993-94, U. London, 1986-87, Excellence in scholarship Hunter Coll., 1988; rsch. grantee NEH, 1973-84, U. Papua New Guinea, 1989, tchg./travel grantee Brazilian Linguistics Assn., 1999; Woodrow Wilson fellow, 1967-68. Mem. Soc. for Pidgin and Creole Linguistics (pres. 1993-95), Am. Speech Assn., Creole Lang. Libr. (bd. editors). Avocations: traveling, speaking fluent German, French, Spanish, Portuguese. Office: Grupo Estudos Anglo Am, U Coimbra Faculdade Letras, 3049 Coimbra Portugal

HOLM, JOY ALICE, psychology educator, art educator, artist, goldsmith; b. Chgo., May 21, 1929; d. Alvin Herbert and Willette Eugenia (Miller) H. BFA, U. Ill., 1952; MS in Art Edn. Inst. Design, Ill. Inst. Tech., 1956; PhD in Edn., U. Minn., 1967. Tchr. art, Eng. West Chgo. H.S., 1952-54; instr., tchr. art J.S. Morton H.S. & Jr. Coll., Cicero, Ill., 1954-65; asst. prof. art & design Mankato (Minn.) State U., 1965-66; asst. prof. art Ill. State U., Normal, 1966-69; assoc. prof. art & design So. Ill. U., Edwardsville, 1969-71; assoc. prof. art, art edn. Winona (Minn.) State U., 1971-75; assoc. prof., chmn. dept. art St. Mary's Coll. of Notre Dame, Ind., 1975-76; assoc. prof. art & design, secondary, continuing edn. U. Wis., Eau Claire, 1976-78; assoc. prof. art & design Sch. Art & Design Kent (Ohio) State U., 1978-80; lectr. Jungian studies C.G. Jung Inst., Evanston, Ill., 1980-82; adj. assoc. prof. art edn. Sch. Art and Design, Sch. Edn. U. Ill., Chgo., 1981-82; lectr. U. Calif. Ext., Santa Cruz, 1983—; adj. prof. art edn., design San Jose (Calif.) State U., 1983-84; owner bus. designer-goldsmith Oak Park, Ill., 1980-82, Carmel, Calif., 1982-87; owner bus. designer-goldsmith Atelier XII, Winona, 1988—; curriculum cons. North Ctrl. Assn. Accreditation Team State of Ill., Edwardsville, 1970; regional cons. Supt. Pub. Instrn., Springfield, Ill., 1970; juror exhbns.; panelist, spkr., presenter confs., meetings. Contbr., cons. Alternative Medicine: A Definitive Guide, 1994; contbr. articles to profl. jours; one-woman shows: J. Sterling Morton H.S. & Jr. Coll., 1963, Russell Art Gallery, Bloomington, 1968, Owatonna (Minn.) Art Ctr., 1980, 86; exhbns. include La Grange (Ill.) Art League (Best of Show, 1st Place award prints), 1963, 64, Minn. Mus. Art, 1974, 75, Craft & Folk Art Mus., L.A., 1978, The Gallery Kent State U., 1978, 79, Saenger Nat. Small Sculpture and Jewelry Exhibit, 1978, Diamonds Internat., N.Y., 1978, Inst. Design Alumni, 1988, Internat. Biographical Ctr. Congress Exhbn., Edinburgh, Scotland, 1994, others. Fellow World Lit. Acad.; mem. AAUP, Nat. Art Edn. Assn. (rep. Wis. Women's Caucus Houston Conf. 1978, higher edn. divsn. 1961—), Am. Assn. Higher Edn., Coll. Art Assn., Soc. N.Am. Goldsmiths, Internat. Sculpture Ctr., Gemological Inst. Am., C.G. Jung Inst. (Chgo.), Hon. Soc. Illustrators (hon.), Internat. Soc. Study of Subtle Energies and Energy Medicine, Assn. Transpersonal Psychology, Inst. Noetic Scis., Alpha Lambda Delta (hon.), Phi Kappa Phi (hon.). Methodist. Office: Atelier XII PO Box 183 Winona MN 55987-0183

HOLM, RICHARD HADLEY, chemist, educator; b. Boston, Mass., Sept. 24, 1933; m. Florence L. Jacintho, June 8, 1958; children—Sharon, Eric, Christian, Marg. B.S., U. Mass., 1955; Ph.D., Mass. Inst. Tech., 1959. Instr., then asst. prof. chemistry Harvard U., 1959-65, prof., 1980—; asso. prof. U. Wis., 1965-67; prof. chemistry Mass. Inst. Tech., 1967-75, Stanford U., 1975-80. Sloan Found. fellow, 1964-67. Mem. Am. Acad. Arts and Scis., NAS (Chem. Scis. award 1993), Am. Chem. Soc., Chem. Soc. London. Home: 483 Pleasant St Apt 10 Belmont MA 02478-3266 Office: Harvard U Dept Chemistry Cambridge MA 02138

HOLM, ROY K., church administrator; b. Palmer, Nebr., May 4, 1936; s. Bruno G. and Elizabeth (Muellenhoff) H.; m. Maxine E. Baase, June 26, 1960; children: Sherri, Debra, Gina, Michael, David. BA, Concordia Sem., 1957, grad., 1960, DD, 1989. Ordained pastor Luth. Ch. Parish pastor various churches including St. Peter's, Estevan, Sask., Can., St. Luke's, Midale, Sask., St. John's, Outram, Sask., 1960-78; dist. pres. Luth. Ch.-Mo. Synod, Manitoba-Sask. Dist., 1978-88, Ctrl. Dist. Luth. Ch.-Can., 1988—; chmn. Coun. Pres., Luth. Ch.-Can., 1988—. Chmn. bd. regents Concordia Coll., Edmonton, Alta., Can., 1993—; trustee Luth. Found., Regina, Sask., 1986—. Decorated 125th Commemorative medal, Can., 1993. Avocation: tennis. Office: Ctrl Dist Luth Ch Canada, 1927 Grant Dr, Regina, SK Canada S4S 4V6

HOLM, VANJA ADELE, developmental pediatrician, educator; b. Kiruna, Sweden, Oct. 5, 1928; came to U.S, 1955.; d. C.V. Hjalmar and Elma Adele (Nystrom) H.; m. Carl Holm, June 15, 1952; children: Ingrid Adele, Erik Carl Anders. Med. Kand., Karolinska Inst., Stockholm, 1950, MD, 1955. Intern Swedish Hosp., Seattle, 1955-56; resident in pediatrics U. Wash. Sch. Medicine, Seattle, 1956, 62-64, fellow in devel. pediatrics, 1964-65, instr. pediatrics, 1965-69, asst. prof. pediatrics, 1969-81, assoc. prof. pediatrics, 1981-96, prof. emeritus, 1996—; attending pediatrician Children's Orthopedic Hosp., Univ. Hosp. Editor: Early Intervention: A Team Approach, 1978 (Am. Med. Writers award 1979), The Prader Willi Syndrome, 1981; contbr. some 60 articles to profl. jours. Fellow Am. Acad. Pediatrics, Am. Acad. Cerebral Palsy and Devel. Medicine, Am. Assn. Mental Retardation; mem. Soc. Devel. Pediatrics, Wash. State Med. Assn. (Aesculapius award 1979), Soc. Behavioral Pediatrics. Democrat. Office: U Wash CHDD PO Box 357920 Seattle WA 98195-7920

HOLMAN, ARTHUR STEARNS, artist; b. Bartlesville, Okla., Oct. 25, 1926; s. Newton Davis and Barbara (Hendry) H. BFA, U. N.Mex., 1951; postgrad., Hans Hofmann Sch., 1951, Calif. Sch. Fine Arts, San Francisco, 1953. One-man shows include Esther Robles Gallery, L.A., 1960, David Cole Gallery, San Francisco, 1962, 80, De Young Mus., San Francisco, 1963, San Francisco Mus., 1963, Gumps Gallery, San Francisco, 1964, 65, 66, 69, 87, Marin Civic Ctr. Gallery, 1970, 95, William Sawyer Gallery, San Francisco, 1971, 73, 74, 76, John Bolles Gallery, Santa Rosa, Calif., 1982, Braunstein, Quay Gallery, San Francisco, 1992; group exhbns. include San Francisco Mus., 1960-76, Downey Mus., L.A., 1961, 50 Calif. Artists, Whitney Mus., N.Y.C., Walker Art Ctr., Albright-Knox Gallery, Des Moines Art Ctr., 1962, U. N.C. Annual, 1965, Smithsonian Instn., Washington, 1977, Coll. of Marin, 1983, Hall of Flowers, San Francisco, 1985, 86, 20th Century Landscape Drawings, De Young Mus., San Francisco, 1989, Jan Holloway Gallery, San Francisco, 1989, Bolinas (Calif.) Mus., 1997; represented in permanent collections, San Francisco Mus., Oakland Mus., Mills Coll., Stanford U., Eureka Coll., Achenbach Found., San Francisco. Served with USAAF, 1945-46. Address: PO Box 72 Lagunitas CA 94938-0072

HOLMAN, BILL, composer. Student, U. Colo., 1944-45, UCLA, 1947, Westlake Coll. Music, 1948-50. Mem. Lighthouse All Stars, 1950-51, Conte Candoli, 1955, Shelley Manne, 1955, Shorty Rogers, 1957. Recs. include Kenton Presents: The Bill Holman Octet, 1954, The Fabulous Bill Holman, 1957, In a Jazz Orbit, 1958, Jive for five, 1958, Bill Holman's Great Big Band, 1960, The Bill Holman Band, 1988, A View From the Side (Grammy award for Best Instrumental Composition 1996), Brilliant Corners, 1997; composer for various artists including Count Basie, Louis Bellson, Natalie Cole, Maynard Ferguson, Woody Herman, Peggy Lee, Carmen McRae, Diane Schuur, Sarah Vaughn, Joe Williams, Doc Severinsen, others. Recipient Grammy award for Best Instrumental Arrangement, 1987, 97; named Best Arranger by Jazz Times Readers Poll, 1990, 95, 98, 99, Arranger of Yr. Downbeat Readers' Poll and Critics Poll, 1998. Office: Open Door Mgmt 865 Via de la Paz Ste 365 Pacific Palisades CA 90272

HOLMAN, BOB, poet; b. LaFollette, Tenn., Mar. 10, 1948; s. R. Merwin Holman and Sally Ruth Schoenbachler; m. Elizabeth Murray, Oct. 22, 1982; children: Dakota Sunseri, Sophia Murray Holman, Daisy Sally Murray Holman. AB, Columbia U., 1970; student, St. Marks Poetry Project, N.Y.C., 1974-80. Co-dir. The Nuyorican Poets Cafe, N.Y.C., 1989-96; creator, prodr. The U.S. Poetry, N.Y.C., 1991-96; tchr. The New Sch., N.Y.C., 1993-95; founder Mouth Almighty Records, N.Y.C., 1995-98; guide The Mining Co., N.Y.C., 1996—; prodr. The World of Poetry, N.Y.C., 1997—; prof. Bard Coll., Annandale-on-Hudson, N.Y., 1998—; slammaster Nuyorican Poets Cafe, N.Y.C., 1989-96; bd. dirs. A Gathering of Tribes, N.Y.C., Poets House, N.Y.C. Author: The Collect Call of the Wild, 1995 (Next Mags. Drop Kick in the NEXT Millenium award 1995); co-editor: ALOUD! Voices from the Nuyorican Poets Cafe, 1994 (Am. Book award 1994); poet (CD) In With the Out Crowd, 1998. Fax: 212-334-6415. E-mail: bholman@washingtonsquarearts.com. Office: Washington Sq Arts 12 E 10th St New York NY 10003

HOLMAN, BUD GEORGE, lawyer; b. N.Y.C., June 30, 1929; s. Harry and Fannie Abrams (Bass) H.; m. Kathleen Barbara McLean, Sept. 1, 1961; children: Jennifer Jean, Wayne George. BBA, CCNY, 1950; LLB, Yale U., 1956. Bar: N.Y. 1956, Conn. 1979, D.C. 1982. Law sec. to judge N.Y. Ct. Appeals, 1956-58; practice in N.Y.C., 1958—; ptnr. Kelley Drye & Warren (and predecessor firms), 1965—; pres., chmn. bd. dirs. Sixty Sutton Corp., 1969-97; lectr. Practising Law Inst., Wage Price Inst., Young Pres. Orgn. Editor: The Bar, 1949-50, Yale Law Jour., 1955-56. Trustee U.S. Naval Acad. Found., 1978-85; bd. dirs. USO Met. N.Y. Mem. Naval Res. Assn. (pres. 3d naval dist. chpts. 1973-75, mem. nat. adv. coun. 1975-94), Am. Arbitration Assn. (bd. dirs., mem. exec. com.), Army and Navy Union, Naval Order U.S., Navy League (bd. dirs. coun. N.Y. chpt. 1979-99), Yale U. Law Sch. Assn. (mem. exec. com. 1987-90, 93-96, bd. dirs.), Met. Club, Yale Club, Beta Gamma Sigma. Democrat. Presbyterian. Home: 60 Sutton Pl S New York NY 10022-4168 Office: Kelley Drye & Warren LLP 101 Park Ave New York NY 10178-0002

HOLMAN, DONALD REID, lawyer; b. Astoria, Oreg., Jan. 30, 1930; s. Donald Reuben and Hattie Laveda (Card) H.; m. Susan Muncy Morris, Aug. 31, 1956; children: Donald Reid, Laura Morris Holman O'Brien, Douglas Edward. B.A., U. Wash.-Seattle, 1951, J.D., 1958; postgrad., U. Oreg.-Eugene, 1955-57. Bar: Oreg. Assoc. Miller, Nash, Wiener, Hager & Carlsen, Portland, 1958-63, ptnr., 1963-93, mng. ptnr., 1987-90; sr. counsel, 1994—; bd. dirs. Byers Industries, Inc., Portland, Copeland Lumber Yards Inc., Portland, Huntair Inc., Portland. Lt. (j.g.) USN, 1951-55; capt. JAGC USNR, 1977-90, ret. Fellow Am. Bar Found.; mem. Multnomah County Bar Assn., Oreg. State Bar Assn., Order of Coif, Multnomah Athletic club (trustee 1983-85, v.p. 1985-86), Waverley Country Club, Phi Delta Phi. Republican. Avocations: tennis, golf, squash. Home: 8040 SW Broadmoor Ter Portland OR 97225-2121 Office: Miller Nash Wiener Hager & Carlsen 111 SW 5th Ave Ste 3500 Portland OR 97204-3699

HOLMAN, HALSTED REID, medical educator; b. Cleve., Jan. 17, 1925; s. Emile Frederic and Ann Peril (Purdy) H.; m. Barbara Marie Lucas, June 26, 1949 (div. July 9, 1982); children: Michael, Andrea, Alison; m. Diana Barbara Dutton, Aug. 10, 1985; 1 child, Geoffrey. Student, Stanford U., 1942-43, UCLA, 1943-44; MD, Yale U., 1949. Med. resident Montefiore Hosp., N.Y.C., 1952-55; staff physician Rockefeller Inst., N.Y.C., 1955-60; prof. medicine Stanford (Calif.) U., 1960—, chmn. dept. medicine, 1960-71, co-chief, divsn. family and community medicine, 1987—, dir. clin. scholar program, 1969-97, dir. Multipurpose Arthritis Ctr., 1977-97, co-chief, divsn. immunology and rheumatology, 1997—, dir. Stanford Program for Mgmt. of Chronic Disease, 1997—; pres. Midpeninsula Health Svc., Palo Alto, Calif., 1975-80; mem. adv. bd. Calif Health Facilities Commn., Sacramento, 1978-81, Office Tech. Assessment, U.S. Congress, 1979-81, Inst. Advancement of Health, N.Y.C., 1982-90; Guggenheim prof. medicine, 1960—. Author 2 books; assoc. editor Arthritis and Rheumatism, 1995—; contbr. articles to profl. jours. Recipient Bauer Meml. award Arthritis and Rheumatism Found., N.Y., 1964. Master Am. Coll. Rheumatology; fellow ACP (Laureate award no. Calif. chpt. 1994), AAAS (coun. 1974-79); mem. Assn. Am. Physicians, Am. Soc. Clin. Investigation (pres. 1970), Western Assn. Physicians (pres. 1966), Arthritis Found. (Hero Overcoming Arthritis 1998). Democrat. Home: 747 Dolores St Stanford CA 94305-8427 Office: Stanford U Divsns Fam/Cmty Med/Immunol 1000 Welch Rd Ste 203 Palo Alto CA 94304-1808

HOLMAN, HARLAND EUGENE, retired motion picture company executive; b. Waupaca, Wis., Oct. 4, 1914;]; s. Clair R. and Elizabeth (Anderson) H.; m. Evelyn June Hooper, Dec. 24, 1940; children: John H., June Elizabeth (Mrs. Jon D. Huss), Catherine Ellen (Mrs. John F. Chavez). B.A., U. Wis., 1936. C.P.A., Wis., Calif. Auditor Gen. Mills, Inc., 1936-42; v.p. finance Aviation Maintence Corp., Van Nuys, Calif., 1946-48; studio mgr., COO Warner Bros. Pictures, Inc., 1948-70; v.p. fin., treas. A.J. Industries, Inc., L.A., 1970-92, ret., 1992. Served to lt. comdr. USNR, 1942-46; rear adm. Res. Decorated commendation USMC; recipient Civilian commendation Vice Pres. U.S., 1967; Minuteman award Treasury Dept., 1967. Mem. AICPA, Calif. Soc. CPAs, Navy league, Phi Beta Kappa. Presbyterian (elder). Home: 5011 Hayvenhurst Ave Encino CA 91436-1114

HOLMAN, JAMES, allergist, immunologist; b. Jacksonville, Tex., Aug. 13, 1921. MD, U. Tex. Southwest, 1945. Diplomate Am. Bd. Allergy and Immunology. Intern Parkland Meml. Hosp., Dallas, 1945-46; resident in allergy U. Va., Charlottesville, 1947-48; fellow in medicine U. Tex. Southwest, Dallas, 1946-47, 48-50; with Presbyn. Hosp., Dallas, 1966—; asst. clin. prof. pharmacology U. Tex. Southwest Med. Sch., 1950-83, clin. assoc. prof. internal medicine, 1981-88. Fellow Am. Acad. Allergy, Asthma and Immunology, Am. Coll. Allergy, Asthma and Immunology, Am. Coll. Clin. Pharmacology and Chemotherapy. Office: Presbyn Prof Bldg 8210 Walnut Hill Ln Ste 818 Dallas TX 75231-4421

HOLMAN, JAMES LEWIS, financial and management consultant; b. Chgo., Oct. 27, 1926; s. James Louis and Lillian Marie (Walton) H.; m. Elizabeth Ann Owens, June 18, 1948 (div. 1982); children: Craig Stewart, Tracy Lynn, Mark Andrew; m. Geraldine Ann Wilson, Dec. 26, 1982. BS in Econs. and Mgmt., U. Ill., Urbana, 1950, postgrad., 1950; postgrad. Northwestern U., 1954-55. Traveling auditor, then statistician, asst. controller parent buying dept. Sears, Roebuck & Co., Chgo., 1951-54; asst. to sec.-treas. Hanover Securities Co., Chgo., 1954-65; asst. to controller chem. ops. div. Montgomery Ward & Co. Inc., Chgo., 1966-68; controller Henrotin Hosp., Chgo., 1968; bus. mgr. Julian, Dye, Javid, Hunter & Najafi, Associated, Chgo., 1969-81, cons. 1981-84; vol. cons., adminstrv. asst. Fiji Sch. Medicine, Suva, 1984-86, cons., 1987-89; vol. bus. cons. U.S. Peace Corps, Honduras, 1989, cons., 1989—; cons., dir., sec.-treas. Comprehensive Resources Ltd., Glenview (Ill.), Wheaton (Ill.) and Walnut Creek, Calif., 1982; bd. dirs., sec.-treas. Medtran, Inc., 1980-83; sec. James C. Valenta, P.C., 1979-82; sponsored project adminstr. Northwestern U., Evanston, Ill., 1984. Sec., B.R. Ryall YMCA, Glen Ellyn, Ill., 1974-76, bd. dirs., 1968-78; trustee Gary Meml. United Meth. Ch., Wheaton, 1961-69, 74-77; bd. dirs. Goodwill Industries Chgo., 1978-79, DuPage (Ill.) Symphony, 1954-58, treas., 1955-58. Served with USN, 1944-46. Baha'i. Mem. Kiwanis (bd. dirs. Chgo. 1956-60, bd. dirs. youth found. 1957-60, pres. 1958-60). Home and Office: 1571 Burr Oak Ct # B Wheaton IL 60187-2709

HOLMAN, J(OHN) LEONARD, retired manufacturing corporation executive; b. Moose Jaw, Sask., Can., Aug. 30, 1929; s. Charles Claude and Lillian Kathleen (Haw) H.; m. Julia Pauline Benfield, July 18, 1953; children: Nancy Jane, Sally Joan. B.S. in Civil Engring., U. Alta., 1953. Pres. Consolidated Concrete Ltd., Calgary, Alta., Can., 1969-72; dir., pres. BACM Industries Ltd., Calgary, 1972-76; exec. v.p. Genstar Corp., Calgary, 1976-79, San Francisco, 1980-87; dir. several subs. cos. Genstar Corp.; pres., chief exec. officer CBR Cement Corp., San Mateo, Calif., 1986-88, chmn. bd., 1988-89, ret., 1990; bd. dirs., officer several nat. trade assns. Mem. Assn. Profl. Engr. Alta., Calgary Exhbn. and Stampede (hon. life., dir.), Calgary Golf and Country Club, Bernardo Heights County Club. Home: 111 Country Club Estates, 111-5555 Elbow Dr SW, Calgary, AB Canada T2V 1H7

HOLMAN, JOSEPH S., automotive sales executive. Chmn. bd. Holman Enterprises, Pennsauken, N.J., 1946—. Office: Holman Enterprises 7411 Maple Ave Pennsauken NJ 08109-2946*

HOLMAN, KERMIT LAYTON, chemical engineer; b. Morris, Minn., Nov. 16, 1935; s. Melvin Martinous and Jennie Ethel (Erickson) H.; m. Audrey Mae Redwing, Nov. 21, 1959; children: Erik, Jennifer, Peter. Student, St. Olaf Coll., 1953-54; B.S., U. N.D., 1957; M.S., U. Idaho, 1961; Ph.D., Iowa State U., 1964. Tape devel. engr. 3M Co., St. Paul, 1957-60; sr. chem. engr. Dow Chem. Co., Golden, Colo., 1964-65; mem. faculty dept. chem. engring. N.Mex. State U., Las Cruces, 1965-76; prof. N.Mex. State U., 1976—; prof., chmn. dept. chem. engring. U. Idaho, Moscow, 1976-81; tech. assoc. Weyerhaeuser, Tacoma, 1981-85, sr. engring. specialist, 1985-97, engring. advisor, 1997—; chmn. Forest products Divsn., 1996-97; cons. in field. Mem. Am. Inst. Chem. Engrs., Tech. Assn. Pulp and Paper Industry, Sigma Xi, Tau Beta Pi. Republican. Lutheran. Home: 31619 37th Ave SW Federal Way WA 98023-4008 Office: Weyerhaeuser Tech Ctr PO Box 2999 Tacoma WA 98477-2999

HOLMAN, MARK, state official; b. Pitts., Oct. 14, 1957; children: Jennifer, Sarah Jane. BS in Polit. Sci., Indiana U. Pa., 1979. Staff asst. Senator J. Heinz, 1980-82; adminstrv. asst. Congressman T. Ridge, 1983-91; exec. dir. Fund for Pa. Leadership, 1991-93; chief of staff Office of the Gov. of Pa., 1995—. Office: Office of Gov State Capital Bldg Rm 225 Harrisburg PA 17120

HOLMAN, RALPH THEODORE, biochemistry and nutrition educator; b. Mpls., Mar. 4, 1918; s. Alfred Theodore and May Carlia Anna (Nilson) H.; m. Karla Calais, Mar. 26, 1943; 1 child, Nils Teodor. AA, Bethel Jr. Coll., 1937; BS, U. Minn., 1939; MS, Rutgers U., 1941; PhD, U. Minn., 1944. Instr., div. of biochemistry U. Minn., Mpls., 1944-46; NRC-Nat. Acad. Scis. fellow Med. Nobel Inst., Stockholm, Sweden, 1946-47; Am. Scandinavian Found. fellow U. Uppsala, Sweden, 1947; assoc. prof. biochemistry and nutrition Tex. A&M U., College Station, 1948-51; assoc. prof. biochemistry Hormel Inst., U. Minn., Austin, 1951-56, prof., 1956-88, exec. dir., 1975-85; emeritus prof. Hormel Inst., U. Minn., 1988—; also adj. prof. of biochemistry Mayo Med. Sch., Rochester, Minn., 1977—; mem. nutrition study sect. NIH, 1959-63; pres., organizer Golden Jubilee Internat. Congress on Essential Fatty Acids and Prostaglandins, 1980; mem. adv. bd. Deul. Conf. on Lipids, 1960-86; Sinclair Meml. lectr. Third Internat. Congress on Essential Fatty Acids and Eicasanoids, Adelaide, 1992. Founding editor Progress in Lipid Research, 1951—; editor Lipids, 1974-85; mem. editl. bd. Jour. Nutrition, 1962-66; contbr. 400 publs. on nutritional biochemistry of lipids; current rsch. on essentiality of omega 3 fatty acids. Pres. Mower County Coun. Churches., Austin, 1953-57; mem. Hormel Found., Austin, 1979-86. Recipient Fachini award Italian Oil Chemists, Milan. Fellow Am. Inst. Nutrition (Borden award 1966); mem. NAS, Am. Chem. Soc., Am. Oil Chemists Soc. (pres. 1974-75, Lipid Chemistry award 1979), Am. Soc. Biol. Chemists, Am. Orchid Soc. (rsch. com. 1980-85), Am. Heart Assn. (bd. dirs. Minn. affiliate 1991-93). Democrat. Congregationalist. Avocations: writing history, gardening, orchid culture, research on orchid fragrances, constrn. Home: 1403 2nd Ave SW Austin MN 55912-1609 Office: U Minn Hormel Inst 801 16th Ave NE Austin MN 55912-3679*

HOLMAN, WILLIAM BAKER, surgeon, coroner; b. Norwalk, Ohio, Mar. 22, 1925; s. Merlin Earl and Rowena (Baker) H.; m. Jane Elizabeth Henderson, June 24, 1951; children: Craig W., Mark E., John S. BS, Capital U., 1946; MD, Jefferson Med. Coll., 1950. Intern, St. Luke's Hosp., Cleve., 1950-51, resident in gen. surgery, 1951-52, 55-57; practice medicine specializing in surgery, Norwalk, 1957-92; coroner Huron County, Norwalk, 1962-95, health commr., 1985-95; asst. clin. prof. surgery Med. Coll. Ohio at Toledo, 1984-92; Bd. dirs. REMSNO, Toledo, 1974-92, Norwalk Profl. Colony, 1983-92 ; mem. exec. com. Huron County Republican Com., Norwalk, 1980; bd. dirs. Fisher-Titus Med. Ctr., 1977-82, chmn., 1982; bd. dirs. Norwalk Area Health Svcs., Inc., 1987-92, 94—; mem. Norwalk City Sch. Bd. Edn., 1962-78, pres., 1964, 67-71, 78. Served to 1st lt. U.S. Army, 1952-54; Korea. Fellow ACS; mem. AMA, Ohio State Med. Assn., Huron County Med. Soc. (pres. 1978), Ohio State Coroners Assn., Nat. Assn. Med. Examiners. Lutheran. Avocations: boating; photography; stamp collecting; gun collecting. Home: 39 Warren Dr Norwalk OH 44857-2447

HOLMBERG, ALBERT WILLIAM, JR., publishing company executive; b. Orange, N.J., Sept. 18, 1923; s. Albert William and Margaret (Flanagan) H.; m. Dorothy McCollum, Oct. 27, 1945 (div. Apr. 1972); children—Jeanne (Mrs. Fletcher J. Johnson, Jr.), Margaret D. (Mrs. Roy D. Duckworth III), Ellen T.; m. Ruth Sulzberger Golden, May 26, 1972. B.S. in Bus. Adminstrn, Lehigh U., 1947. With N.Y. Times, 1947-70, circulation mgr., 1964-70; pres. Chattanooga Times Co., 1970—; pres., dir. Times Pub. Co. Served to 1st lt. USAAF, World War II. Clubs: Rotary (Chattanooga), Mountain City (Chattanooga). Home: 1108 Cumberland Rd Chattanooga TN 37419-1006 Office: Times Printing Co PO Box 951 100 E 10th St Chattanooga TN 37401-0951*

HOLMBERG, RUTH SULZBERGER, publishing company executive; b. N.Y.C., Mar. 12, 1921. A.B., Smith Coll., 1943. Pub. Chattanooga Times Co., 1965-92, chmn. bd. dirs., 1992—; bd. dirs. N.Y. Times Co. Bd. dirs. Hunter Mus. Art, Pub. Edn. Found., Smithsonian Nat. Bd. Mem. Jr. League (sustaining). Office: Times Printing Co 100 E 10th St PO Box 951 Chattanooga TN 37401-0951*

HOLMBERG, SHARON K., psychiatric mental health and geriatrics nurse, researcher, educator; b. Lynch, Nebr., Oct. 26, 1945; d. Harry Theodore and Helen Elizabeth (Shearon) H. BSN, U. Nebr., Omaha, 1967; MSN, NYU, 1972; Cert., Stockholm U., 1979; PhD, U. Rochester, 1994. RN, Conn., N.Y., Ind. Staff and head nurse coronary care Mt. Sinai Hosp., N.Y.C., 1967-69; head nurse psychiat. rsch. NYU Med. Ctr., N.Y.C., 1969-72; staff nurse geriatrics Ulleråkers Hosp., Uppsala, Sweden, 1977; dir. supportive care svcs. Manchester (N.H.) Mental Health Ctr., 1973-76; clin. nurse specialist Conn. Mental Health Ctr., New Haven, 1979-89; psychiat. nursing faculty Yale U. Sch. Nursing, New Haven, 1979-89; psychiat. nursing cons. St. John's Nursing Home, Rochester, N.Y., 1990-95; postdoctoral fellow U. Rochester, 1994-95; assoc. prof. Ind. U., Indpls., 1995—. Author: (chpts.) Mental Health Psychiatric Nursing, 1984, 88, 93; contbr. articles to profl. jours. Mem. State Planning Conf. on Elderly, Concord, N.H., 1975; bd. dirs. Continuum of Care, New Haven, 1980-89. Recipient Swedish Inst. grant, 1977-78, Rsch. Found. for Mental Hygiene grant, Walter Cancer Found. grant, Annie W. Goodrich award Yale U. Sch. Nursing, 1989,

Predoctoral fellowship NIMH, 1992-94. Mem. APHA, ANA, Nat. League for Nursing, Soc. for Edn. and Rsch. in Psychiat. Nursing, Midwest Nursing Rsch. Soc., Sigma Theta Tau (Rsch. grant 1993-94). Avocations: Scandinavian folk dancing, cross-country skiing, rowing. Office: Indiana U Sch Nursing 1111 Middle Dr Indianapolis IN 46202-5243

HOLME, RICHARD PHILLIPS, lawyer; b. Denver, Nov. 6, 1941; s. Peter Hagner Jr. and Lena (Phillips) H.; m. Barbara June Friel, July 17, 1944; children: Daniel Friel, Robert Muir. BA, Williams Coll., Williamstown, Mass., 1963; JD, U. Colo., 1966. Bar: Colo. 1966, U.S. Dist. Ct. Colo. 1966, U.S. Ct. Claims 1990, U.S. Ct. Appeals (10th cir.) 1966, U.S. Ct. Appeals (1st cir.) 1980, U.S. Dist. Ct. D.C. 1988, U.S. Ct. Appeals (D.C. cir.) 1988, U.S. Ct. Appeals (4th cir.) 1989, U.S. Ct. Appeals (fed. cir.) 1995, U.S. Supreme Ct. 1975. Assoc. Davis, Graham & Stubbs, Denver, 1966-68, ptnr., 1972-87, 91—; mng. ptnr., D.C. office Davis, Graham & Stubbs, Washington, 1987-91; dep. Denver Dist. Atty., 1969-71; grievance com. Colo. Supreme Ct., Denver, 1979-85, civil rules com., 1994—, civil justice com., 1998—. Fellow Am. Coll. Trial Lawyers (Colo. state chair 1994-96); mem. ABA, Colo. Bar Assn. (bd. govs. 1974-76, 85-87, 95-99), Denver Bar Assn. (trustee 1977-80, 1st v.p. 1997-98), Pinehurst Country Club, Order of Coif. Republican. Presbyterian. Office: Davis Graham & Stubbs PO Box 185 370 17th St Ste 4700 Denver CO 80202-5682

HOLMEN, REYNOLD EMANUEL, chemist; b. Essex, Iowa, Oct. 23, 1916; s. John Algott and Clara Amelia (Christensen) H.; m. Betty Jane Heginbottom, June 20, 1942 (dec. 1990); children: Karen C., John R., Robert C.; m. Johnnie Mae Leak, Nov. 20, 1993. AB, Augustana Coll., Ill., 1936; MS, U. Mich., 1937, PhD, 1949. Rsch. chemist DuPont Co., Phila., also Flint, Mich., 1937-46; sr. rsch. chemist ctrl. rsch. dept. 3M Co., St. Paul, 1948-55, sect. mgr. tech. info. and patient liaison, 1955-57, sect. mgr. inorganic sect., 1957-62, organic scouting mgr., 1959-62, mgr. R&D Lab., Reflective Product divsn., 1962-71, lab. mgr. R&D spl. enterprises dept., 1971-82; v.p. R&D KEMSERCH, Inc., Onamia, Minn., 1984-96. Author: Kasimir Fajans: The Man and His Work, 1990. With med. corps. U.S. Army, 1941. Rackham scholar U. Mich., 1936-37. Mem. Am. Chem. Soc., AAAS, Phi Lambda Upsilon, Sigma Gamma Epsilon. Lutheran. Achievements include 20 U.S. patents; development of first catalytic dehydration of lactic acid to acrylic acid, first catalytic dehydrochlorination of alphachloropronic acid to acrylic acid, (with other) first sealed polycellular cubecorner retroreflective sheet, first conterfeit-resistant driver's license adopted by a state. Home: 2225 Lilac Ln White Bear Lk MN 55110-3824

HOLMER, ALAN FREEMAN, trade association executive, lawyer; b. N.Y.C., July 24, 1949; s. A. Freeman and Marcia K. (Wright) H.; m. Joan Mary Ozark, June 30, 1973; children—Scott, Joy. A.B., Princeton U., 1971; J.D., Georgetown U., 1978. Bar: D.C., Oreg. Adminstrv. asst. Senator Bob Packwood, Washington, 1972-78; assoc. Steptoe & Johnson, Washington, 1978-81; dep. asst. to pres. for intergovtl. affairs The White House, Washington, 1981-83; dep. asst. sec. for import adminstrn. Dept. Commerce, Washington, 1983-85; gen. counsel Office of U.S. Trade Rep., Washington, 1985-87; amb. Dep. U.S. Trade Rep., Washington, 1987-89; ptnr. Sidley & Austin, Washington, 1989-96; pres. Pharm. Rsch. and Mfrs. Am., Washington, 1996—; adj. prof. Georgetown U. Law Ctr., Washington, 1990; amb. and chmn. U.S. del. to Bonn Econ. Conf., 1990. Author: (with Judith H. Bello) The Antidumping and Countervailing Duty Laws: Key Legal and Policy Issues, 1987, Guide to the U.S.-Canada Free-Trade Agreement, 1990; contbr. numerous articles to profl. jours. Mem. Svcs. Policy Adv. Com., 1991-94; mem. adv. coun. Korea Econ. Inst. Am., 1992-96; trustee Met. D.C. chpt. Cystic Fibrosis Found., 1984-96, pres., 1991-94); bd. dirs. Coun. on Family Health, 1996—, Friends of the Nat. Libr. of Medicine, 1996—, Nat. Health Coun., 1999—. Recipient Disting. Cmty. Svc. award Princeton Club Washington, 1992. Mem. Internat. Fedn. of Pharm. Mfrs. (mem. coun. 1996—), Health Care Quality Alliance (bd. dirs., treas. 1996—). Republican. Office: Pharm Rsch and Mfrs Am 1100 15th St NW Washington DC 20005-1707

HOLMES, ALBERT WILLIAM, JR., physician; b. Chgo., Feb. 3, 1932; s. Albert William and Eleanor Muir H.; m. Lois Ann Geiger, Sept. 4, 1954; children: Nancy, William, Elizabeth, Robert. Student, U. Chgo., 1947-49; BA, Knox Coll., 1952; MD, Western Res. U., 1956. Diplomate Am. Bd. Internal Medicine. Intern Presbyn. Hosp., Chgo., 1956-57; resident Presbyn.-St. Luke's Hosp., Chgo., 1957-59, 61-62; instr. U. Ill., Chgo., 1961-62, asst. prof., 1963-65, assoc. prof., 1966-68, prof. medicine, 1968-70; prof. medicine and microbiology Rush Med. Coll., Chgo., 1971-75; dir. sect. hepatology Rush-Presbyn.-St. Luke's Med. Center, Chgo., 1966-75; asso. chmn. dept. medicine Rush-Presbyn.-St. Luke's Med. Center, 1972-75, acting v.p. research affairs, 1973-74; prof., chmn. dept. internal medicine Tex. Tech U., Lubbock, 1975-83, prof. medicine, 1983-85; prof., chmn. dept. medicine U. Ill., Peoria, 1985-89; prof. medicine U. Calif., San Francisco, 1990-96, prof. emeritus medicine, 1996—; chief medicine Valley Med. Ctr., 1990-96. Contbr. articles in field to profl. jours. Served with U.S. Army, 1959-61. Recipient Alumni Achievement award Knox Coll., 1976; NIH spl. fellow, 1963-66. Fellow ACP; mem. Am. Assn. Study Liver Diseases, Ctrl. Soc. Clin. Rsch., Alpha Omega Alpha. Presbyterian. Home: 1137 W Escalon Ave Fresno CA 93711-2018 Office: Dept of Med University Medical Ctr Fresno CA 93702

HOLMES, ANN HITCHCOCK, journalist; b. El Paso, Apr. 25, 1922; d. Frederick E. and Joy (Crutchfield) H. Student, Whitworth Coll., 1940, So. Coll. Fine Arts, 1944. With Houston Chronicle, 1942—, fine arts editor, 1948-89, critic-at-large, 1989-98. Author: Presence, The Transco Tower, 1985, Joy Unconfined—Robert Joy in Houston: A Portrait of Fifty Years, 1986, Alley Theater: Four Decades in Three Stages, 1986. Mem. Houston Mcpl. Art Commn., 1965-74; mem. fine arts adv. coun. U. Tex., Austin, 1967—; bd. dirs. Rice Design Alliance, Houston, 1988-91, Alliance Francaise, Houston, 1989-93, Bus. Arts Fund, Houston, 1993-96. Recipient Ogden Reid Found. award for study of arts in Europe, 1953; Guggenheim fellow, 1960-61; recipient Ford Found. award, 1965, John G. Flowers award archtl. writing Tex. Soc. Architects, 1972, 74, 77, 80. Mem. Am. Theater Critics Assn. (exec. com. 1975—, co-chmn. 1987-88). Home and Office: 10807 Beinhorn Rd Houston TX 77024-3008

HOLMES, ANNA-MARIE, ballerina, ballet mistress; b. Mission City, B.C., Can., Apr. 17, 1946; came to U.S., 1981; d. George Henery and Maxine Marie (Botterill) Ellerbeck; m. David Holmes, 1962; 1 child, Lian-Marie. Student, U. B.C.; diploma, Royal Conservatory of Music. lectr. in field. Appeared in Swan Lake, Cinderella, Romeo and Juliet, Sleeping Beauty, Bayadere, Laurencia, Paquita, Graduation Ball, Les Sylphides, Prince Igor, Giselle, Nutcracker, Firebird, Raymonda; guest appearances at numerous theatres, including: Berlin Staarts Opera, Royal Albert Hall, London, Roy Alex, Toronto, Ont., Royal Festival Hall, London, Teatro Colon, Buenos Aires, Covent Garden, London; danced with Kirov Ballet, Leningrad, 1963; featured ballerina in dance films including Tour En L'Air, Ballet Adagio, Don Juan, Chinese Nightengale; numerous appearances on European and North Am. TV; artistic dir., prin. choreographer Tenn. Festival Ballet, Oak Ridge, 1981—; staged ballets Am. Ballet Theatre, Dance Theatre of Harlem, Boston Ballet, 1984; ballet mistress Ballet Theatre Francais, 1985; tchr. Boston Ballet Co., 1985; set Giselle for Boston Ballet, 1987, full length Don 2, 1989; mng. dir. Performing Arts/Dance Ctr., Oak Ridge, 1982-85; co-dir. ballet co. Massimo Opera Theatre, Palermo, Italy, 1982-83; appt. asst. to artistic dir. Boston Ballet, 1989, appt. dean ctr. for dance edn., assoc. dir., 1993, artistic dir., 1997—; guest tchr. Nervi Festival, Genoa, Italy; prodr. film documentation of Kirov Vagonova Tchg. system; artistic dir. Jackson Internat. Competition Sch., 1990, Internat. Ballet Competition Sch., 1994; staged full length Swan Lake, Tokyo, 1991, Sleeping Beauty Act III Boston Ballet, 1991, Giselle, 1991, full length Sleeping Beauty, Boston Ballet, 1993, 96, Tokyo, 1996. Office: Boston Ballet 19 Clarendon St Boston MA 02116-6100

HOLMES, BARBARAANN KRAJKOSKI, secondary education educator; b. Evansville, Ind., Mar. 21, 1946; d. Frank Joseph and Estella Marie (DeWeese) Krajkoski; m. David Leo Holmes, Aug. 21, 1971; 1 child, Susan Ann Sky. BS, Ind. State U., 1968, MS, 1969, specialist cert., 1976; postgrad. U. Nev., 1976-78. Acad. counselor Ind. State U., 1968-69, halls dir., 1969-73; dir. residence halls U. Utah, 1973-76; sales assoc. Fidelity Realty, Las Vegas, Nev., 1977-82. cert. analyst Nev. Dept. Edn., 1981-82; tchr. Clark County Sch. Dist., 1982-87, computer cons., adminstrv. specialist instructional mgmt. systems, 1987-91, chair computer conf., 1990-92, adminstrv. specialist K-6, 1990-93, dean of students summer sch. site adminstr. Eldorado H.S., 1991-96; asst. prin. Garrett Middle Sch., Boulder City, Nev., 1997—; mem. leadership design team Clark County Sch. Dist., 1996-98. Named Outstanding Sr. Class Woman, Ind. State U., 1969; recipient Dir's. award U. Utah Residence Halls, 1973, Outstanding Sales Assoc., 1977; Tchr. of Month award, 1983, Dist. Outstanding Tchr. award, 1984, Dist. Excellence in Edn. award, 1984, 86, 87, 88. Mem. AAUW, Am. Assn. Women Deans, Adminstrs. and Counselors, Am. Personnel and Guidance Assn., Am. Coll. Personnel Assn., Alumnae Assn. Chi Omega (treas. Terre Haute chpt. 1971-73, pres., bd. officer Las Vegas 1977-81), Clark County Panhellenic Alumnae Assn. (pres. 1978-79), Computer Using Educators So. Nev. (sec. 1983-86, pres.-elect 1986-87, pres. 1987-88, state chmn. 1988-89, conf. chmn. 1989-92, sec. 94-96, Hall of Fame 1995), Job's Daus. Club (guardian sec. 1995—), Order Ea. Star, Phi Delta Kappa (Action award 1990-96, newspaper editor 1992-93). Developed personal awareness program U. Utah, 1973-76. Home: 1227 Kover Ct Henderson NV 89015-9017 Office: Garrett Middle Sch 1200 Avenue G Boulder City NV 89005-2921

HOLMES, BERT OTIS E., JR., retired newspaperman; b. Milan, Tenn., Sept. 20, 1921; s. Otis E. and Mary (Lassiter) H.; m. Marian Bush, June 10, 1942 (dec. Nov. 1964); children: Bert Otis E., Richard Bush; m. Helen Hankins, July 24, 1965; children: Chris, David. AA, Magnolia A. and M. Jr. Coll., 1940; BS, So. Meth. U., 1942. Successively copy reader, makeup editor, state editor, city staff reporter, city editor Dallas Times Herald, 1946-56, news editor, 1956-60, asst. mng. editor, 1960-64, exec. editor, 1964-65, assoc. editor, 1965-90. Pres. Family Svc. Agy., 1963-68, Tex. United Community Svcs., 1970-72, Sr. Citizens of Greater Dallas, 1995-96; bd. dirs. Dallas United Fund, Dallas Community Coun. With AUS, 1942-46, PTO. Mem. Dallas Assembly, Sigma Delta Chi, Dallas Press Club (pres. 1957, 78-79). Methodist. Home: 4515 W Lawther Dr Dallas TX 75214-1935

HOLMES, BRADLEY PAUL, information technology management consultant; b. Boston, Sept. 14, 1953; s. Melvin Felix and Sadako Ruth (Sato) H. BA, Dartmouth Coll., 1975; JD, Georgetown U., 1978. Bar: N.Y. 1979. Assoc. Windels Marx Davies & Ives, N.Y.C., 1978-79; law clk to Hon. Mary Johnson Lowe U.S. Dist. Ct. (so. dist.) N.Y., 1979-81; assoc. Skadden, Arps, Slate, Meagher & Flom, N.Y.C., 1981-84; legal advisor to commr. FCC, Washington, 1984-86, chief policy and rules divsn. Mass Media Bur., 1986-89; U.S. Amb., Asst. Sec. for internat. comms. and info. policy Dept. State, Washington, 1989-93; pres. Bradley P. Holmes and Assocs., Info. Tech. Cons., Vienna, Va., 1993-94; mng. dir., ptnr. Global Telecomms. Group, Coopers & Lybrand, L.L.P., Washington, 1994-96; pres. Bradley P. Holmes & Assocs., Info. Tech. Cons., Washington, 1997-98; exec. v.p. CTR Group, Ltd., Woodcliff Lake, N.J., 1998-99; pres. Project OXYGEN Network Ltd., Hamilton, Bermuda, 1999—. Mem. ABA. Republican. Episcopalian. Avocations: golf, skiing, tennis. Home: 1813 Parkside Dr NW Washington DC 20012-2201 Office: 1 Parliament St Hamilton NJ 07675-7654

HOLMES, BROOX GARRETT, lawyer; b. Mobile, Ala., Nov. 15, 1932; s. Williams Coghlan and Philomene (Boogaerts) H.; m. Laura Claire Hays, Feb. 21, 1955; children: Broox Garrett, Dupree Hays, Williams Coghlan II. B.A., U. Ala., 1954, J.D., 1960. Bar: Ala. 1960. Since practiced in Mobile; mem. firm Armbrecht, Jackson, DeMouy, Crowe, Holmes & Reeves, 1960—. Trustee St. Paul's Episcopal Sch., chmn. bd., 1980-83. Served to capt. USMCR, 1954-58. Fellow Am. Coll. Trial Lawyers (state chmn. 1991-92), Am. Bar Found.; mem. ABA, Ala. State Bar (bd. commrs. 1987-93, chmn. litigation sect. 1991, pres. 1994-95), Mobile Bar Assn. (exec. com. 1987-93), Nat. Assn. R.R. Trial Counsel, Internat. Assn. Def. Counsel, Am. Law Inst., Ala. Law Inst., Ala. Def. Lawyers (pres. 1977-78), Mobile Country Club (pres. 1983-84), Mobile Touchdown Club, Athelstan Club, Delta Kappa Epsilon, Phi Delta Phi. Episcopalian. Home: 609 Fairfax Rd E Mobile AL 36608-2939 Office: Armbrecht Jackson DeMouy Crowe Holmes & Reeves PO Box 290 Mobile AL 36601-0290

HOLMES, CECILE SEARSON, religion editor; b. Columbia, S.C., Jan. 6, 1955; d. James Gadsden and Anne Keene (Searson) Holmes. BA in Journalism magna cum laude, U. S.C., 1977; fellow, U. N.C., 1982; MA in Liberal Studies, U. N.C., Greensboro, 1994. Religion writer Greensboro News and Record, 1984-87; religion writer Houston Chronicle, 1987-89, sect. editor, 1989—; mem. faculty summer journalism workshop Houston Chronicle, 1988-92; co-dir. minority journalism workshop News and Record, 1988. Author: Witnesses to the Horror: North Carolinians Remember the Holocaust, 1988; contbr. articles, book revs. to profl. jours. Mem. N.C. Episcopal Diocese Hunger Commn., 1980s; vol. Greensboro Urban Ministry, 1983-86; moderator NCCJ Forum, 1985, Ethics of Humane Care, Greensboro, 1986; mentor Edn. for Ministry, Houston, 1989—; advisor United Way Campaign for Homeless, Houston, 1991. Recipient award Piedmont Bapt. Assn., 1984, Community Journalism award N.C. A&T State U., 1984, Pub. Svc. award N.C. Press Assn., 1985, Wilbur award Religious Pub. Rels. Coun., 1986, others. Mem. Soc. Profl. Journalists (chpt. pres. and v.p., coord. registration nat. conv. 1989), Religion Newswriters Assn. (treas. 1990-92, 2d v.p. 1992-94, 1st v.p. 1994-96, pres. 1996—, 2d place award ann. contest 1989, 92, 1st place award religion sect. 1994), Houston Press Club, Beta Sigma Phi (past v.p. Greensboro chpt., Woman of Yr. award), Kappa Tau Alpha, Omicron Delta Kappa. Avocations: gardening, photography, reading, antiques. Office: Houston Chronicle 801 Texas St Houston TX 77002-2996*

HOLMES, CHARLES EVERETT, lawyer; b. Wellington, Kans., Dec. 21, 1931; s. Charles Everett and Elizabeth Francis (Bergin) H.; m. Lynn Lacy, Jan. 2, 1954; children: Anne Lacy, Charles Everett, Rebecca. BA, Wichita U., 1953; LLB, U. Okla., 1961. Bar: Okla. 1961. Practice, Tulsa, after 1961; sec. Sinclair Oil & Gas Co., Sinclair Can. Oil Co., Mesa Pipeline Co., Border Pipe Line Co., Sinclair Transp. Co., Ltd.; ptnr. Rogers, Bell & Robinson, Tulsa, 1969-71; v.p. Nat. Bank of Tulsa, 1971-78; atty. Petro-Lewis Corp., Denver, 1978-87; v.p. Freeport-McMoRan Oil & Gas Co., 1987-92; v.p. FM Properties, Inc., 1992-95; ret., 1995; pvt. practice, Denver, 1996—. Served with USAF, 1954-56, 61-62. Mem. ABA, Okla. Bar Assn., Colo. Bar Assn., Denver County Bar Assn. Roman Catholic. (del. Okla. Council Cath. Diocese 1966—, chmn. Cath. Parish Governing Body 1968—, bd. dirs. Youth Services, Travelers Aid, Com. Fgn. Relations).

HOLMES, CHARLOTTE AMALIE, English educator; b. Augusta, Ga., Apr. 26, 1956; d. Harold H. and Annie Davis Holmes; m. James E. Brasfield, Mar. 7, 1983; 1 child, Williamson Stanhope. BA in English, La. State U., 1977; MFA, Columbia U., 1980. Editl. asst. Paris Rev., N.Y.C., 1979-80; assoc. editor Ecco Press, N.Y.C., 1980-82; instr. West Carolina U., Cullowhee, N.C., 1984-87; asst. prof. Pa. State U., University Park, 1987-93, assoc. prof. English, 1993—. Author: Gifts and Other Stories, 1994; contbr. to book: The Family Track, 1998. Pa. Arts Coun. grantee, 1989, 93; Stegner fellow Stanford U., 1982-83; writers exch. fellow Poets & Writers, 1993. Mem. Associated Writing Programs. Democrat. E-mail: cxh18@psu.edu. Office: Pa State U English Dept Borrowes Bldg University Park PA 16802

HOLMES, COLGATE FREDERICK, hotel executive; b. Passaic, N.J., Aug. 21, 1935; s. Colgate and Orva Della (Gough) H.; m. Elizabeth Ann Troughton, June 6, 1959; 1 dau., Elizabeth Colgate. BS, Cornell U., Ithaca, N.Y., 1956; postgrad., Harvard U. Sch. Bus., 1958-59. Chgo. sales rep., asst. dir. catering Palmer House, Hilton Hotels, 1956-58; dir. food and beverage Caribe Hilton, Hilton Internat. Co., San Juan, P.R., 1963-64; gen. mgr. V.I. Hilton, St. Thomas, 1964-66; regional dir. V.I. Hilton, Philippines, Guam, Australia; gen. mgr. Manila Hilton, Philippines, 1966-70; regional dir. S.Am. Manila Hilton; gen. mgr. Sao Paulo (Brazil) Hilton, Brazil, 1970-71; mgr. conv. and group sales InterContinental Hotels, 1959-60; corp. dir. sales InterContinental Hotels, N.Y.C., 1960-62; exec. asst. mgr. Hotel Indonesia, Djakarta, 1962-63; v.p. Pacific, gen. mgr. Ala Moana Hotel, Americana Hotels, 1972-73; regional v.p., gen. mgr. Hyatt Regency-Chgo., Hyatt Corp., 1973-79; exec. v.p. Hyatt Internat. Corp., 1979-81, pres., 1981-82; from pres. to vice-chmn. Ritz-Carlton Hotel Co., 1982-89, vice chmn., 1987-89; chmn. Holmes Hotel Co., 1989—; pres., CEO Rockresorts, Inc., 1988-89; chmn., CEO Biltmore Hotel Co., 1990-95, Grand Wailea Resort, Maui, 1993-95, Sovereign Hotel Group, Ltd., 1994—; mng. dir. Signature Hotel Group, Kuala Lumpur, Malaysia, 1996-98, vice-chmn., 1998-99; pres., CEO World-Span Hospitality, 1999—; lectr. modern hotel ops. and food and beverage Sch. Hotel Adminstrn., Cornell U.; lectr. Philippine Inst. Hotel Mgmt.; bd. dirs. Better Bus. Bur. Chgo., Country Hts. Holdings, Bhd, Kuala Lumpur; bd. dirs., exec. com. Chgo. Conv. and Tourism Bur. Adv. bd. Hotel & Motel Mgmt. Mag. Mem. Chaine des Rotisseurs, Cornell Soc. Hotelmen, Am. Hotel Assn., Chgo. Hotel Assn. (dir.), V.I. Hotel Assn. (v.p. 1965-66), Chgo. Hotel-Motel Assn. (pres. 1979), Hotel and Restaurant Assn. Philippines (v.p. 1968-69), Skal Club Internat., Am. Soc. Travel Agts., Alpha Chi Rho. Clubs: Manila Yacht; University Yacht (Atlanta); Atletico de São Paulo. Address: 1720 N La Salle Dr Apt 19 Chicago IL 60614-5847

HOLMES, DARRELL, travel consultant; b. Angola, Ind., May 28, 1921; s. G.W. and Catharine (Conrad) H.; m. Eleonore Hohmann, Nov. 20, 1943; children: Kip Lee, Jeffrey, Lynn Ellen, Mary Ann; m. Phyllis Brock, Dec. 31, 1989. B.A., Ohio State U., 1941, M.A., 1948, Ph.D., 1950. Research asst. bur. ednl. research Ohio State U., 1949-50; asst. prof. Muskingum Coll., New Concord, Ohio, 1950-52; asst. prof. San Diego State Coll., 1952-54, assoc. prof., 1955-58, exec. dean, 1958-64; pres. U. No. Colo., Greeley, 1964-71, East Stroudsburg (Pa.) State Coll., 1971-80, Internat. Ctr. Ednl. Svcs., 1981-89, Ctr. for Study of Retirement Issues, 1989-91; tourism cons. Malaysia, Taiwan, Mexico, 1990—; sr. mgmt. cons. Easter Seal systems Nat. Easter Seal Soc., 1993—; pres. Southwestern Research Assocs., Inc., 1957-64; dir. First Nat. Bank, Greeley, Colo.; adj. prof. biology San Diego State U., 1984-85. Contbr. articles to profl. jours. Mem. Commn. Internat. Edn., 1969—; mem. nat. adv. com. Air Force ROTC, to sec. air force, 1965-69; trustee Calif. Western Sch. Law, 1985-87. Served from pvt. to 2d lt., C.E. AUS, 1942-45. Mem. Am. Council Edn. (dir. 1967-70), AAAS, Am. Statis. Assn., Am. Edn. Research Assn., Am. Assn. State Colls. and Univs. (dir. 1967-71, pres. 1971-72), Pa. Assn. Colls. and Univs. (dir. 1973-78, v.p. 1976, pres. 1977). Club: Rotarian (dir.). Home: PO Box 187 Blanco TX 78606-0187 *Until excellence is confronted, mediocrity is master....The search is a lifetime; this thought, the North Star.*

HOLMES, DAVID L., religion educator. BA in English, Mich. State U.; MA in English, Columbia U.; MA, PhD in Religion, Princeton U.; postgrad., Columbia U., Union Theol. Sem., NYU, Duke U. Div. Sch. Prof. religion Coll. of William and Mary, 1965—; instr. Carnegie-Mellon U.; vis. prof. U. Va. Author: A Brief History of the Episcopal Church, 1993, Devereux Jarratt: An Autobiography, 1995, George Washington Memorial Oration, 1999, A Nation Mourns, 1999, others; ch. revs. editor: Anglican and Episcopal History; contbr. articles to profl. jours. Mem. Am. Soc. Ch. History (mem. exec. coun.), Hist. Soc. Episcopal Ch. (exec. bd. dirs.), Am. Acad. Religion, Ptnrs. for Sacred Places, Episcopal Guild of Scholars, James Madison Soc., Phi Beta Kappa. Democrat. Episcopalian. Office: Coll William & Mary Dept Religion Sir Christopher Wren Bldg Williamsburg VA 23187-8795

HOLMES, DAVID LEO, recreation and leisure educator; b. Hammond, Ind., Jan. 4, 1943; s. Leo Victor and Hannah Marget (Robertson) H.; m. Barbara Ann Krajkoski, Mar. 21, 1971; 1 child, Susan Ann Sky. AA, Vincennes U., 1967; BS, Ind. State U., 1969, MS, 1970; PhD, U. Utah, 1976. Tchr., dir. sch. recreation and outdoor edn. Rockville (Ind.) Jr. Ctr., Ind. State Dept. Corrections, 1970-72; instr. Nat. Outdoor Leadership Sch., Washington, Conn., 1972; teaching fellow U. Utah, Salt Lake City, 1973-76; from asst. to prof. program coord. sport and leisure dept. U. Nev., Las Vegas, 1976-91, prof. dept. leisure studies, 1991—; adj. asst. prof. dept. recreation Ind. State U., Terre Haute, 1972-73; lectr. in field. Contbr. more than 125 articles to profl. jours.; author 5 monographs; editor 6 jours. Active State Comprehensive Outdoor Recreation Planning Com., Nev., 1988; planning team Clark Country Nev. Sch. Dist., 1987-88; adv. bd. Clark Country Nev. Parks and Recreation, 1979-88, vice-chmn., 1984. Officer USMCR, Desert Storm, 1990-91. Recipient Pacemaker award, Faculty Citation Vincennes U., 1990, Spl. Pres. award Nat. Assn. Country Parks & Recreation Officials, 1986; named Outstanding Alumni U. Utah, 1987; recipient Spl. Recognition award Ind. State U., 1987, Hon. Mem. Wings, Blue Parachute Team, # 1 USAF Acad., 1982; grantee various institutions. Mem. AAHPERD (life, Cmty. Svc. award 1987), Nev. Recreation and Park Soc. (Excellence award 1995), Am. Assn. for Leisure and Recreation (bd. dirs. 1981-82, v.p. recreation S.W. dist. 1981), Nev. Parks and Recreation Soc., Nev. State Parks Coop. Assn. (bd. dirs. 1991-92, 93-94), Nev. Assn. for Health, Phys. Edn. and Recreation (pres. 1979-80, Profl. of Yr. 1983-84), Armed Forces Recreation Soc. (v.p. 1998), U. Nev. Alumni Assn. (Prof. Worthy of Recognition 1995). Methodist. Avocations: skydiving, running, weightraining. Home: 1227 Kover Ct Henderson NV 89015-9017 Office: U Las Vegas Leisure Studies Program Dept Tourism/Conv Adminstrn 4505 S Maryland Pky Las Vegas NV 89154-9900

HOLMES, DEBBIE, nurse; b. Toledo, May 11, 1948; d. George and Betty Jane (Purney) Tighe; m. Rodney Holmes, Sept. 3, 1977; children: Kelly, Kevin, Keith, Jimmy, George. Diploma in bus., Stautzenberger Bus. Coll., Toledo, 1967; A in Med. Assistance, U. Toledo, 1988, ADN, 1992. RN; cert. med. asst., 1989. Nurse critical care and ICCU unit Med. Coll. Hosp., Toledo. Mem. Phi Theta Kappa, U. Toledo Alumni Assn. Home: 4417 Walker Ave Toledo OH 43612-1859

HOLMES, DOLORIS GRANT (DOLORIS SCHWERNER), writer, social worker, theater director; b. Manchester, Conn., Feb. 7, 1929; d. George Joseph and Dorothy Josephine (Grant) H.; m. Monte Bliss (wid. 1959); m. Armand Schwerner (dec. Feb. 1999); children: Adam, Ari (dec.). BA, U. Conn., 1952; M of Social Svcs., Boston U., 1957. Social worker S.I. Hosp., 1971-80; med. social worker Maimonides Hosp., Bklyn., 1980-81; dir. youth art NYC Youth Bd., L.I.; dir., performer White Mask Theatre, 1975—; interviewee for Archives of Am. Art, Anais Nin; mem. Barry Harris Jazz Chorus. Author: The Lady of the Grape Arbor, 1993; dir., writer play Goddess of Red Mud; dir., writer, producer, performer When All the Saints Sing, 1992; active in prodns. Fish-Joy, Soho 20, 1973, Fish-Joy, White Mask Theatre, 1977, Fish-Joy and Goddess of Red Mud, White Mask Theatre, 1990, Searching for the Women of the Left Bank, 1995; contbr. to various publs. including Art Work, No Comml. Value, Am. Poetry Rev., Unbuilt Am., Anais Nin, a Woman Speaks, Wellspring; writer (short stories) Upbeat Triangles, 1996, Poems on the Brain and Red Feet Too, 1996, Big Mo and Little Clo, 1997; videos of plays Lucille L'Ortel Film/Video Arts, Lincoln Ctr. Performance Arts, N.Y.C. Grantee Poets and Writer, 1999—, N.Y. State Coun. on the Arts, 1972, 77; finalist Louis Comfort Tiffany award, 1969, N.Y.C. Dept. of Cultural Affairs, 1974; recipient Golden Poetry award World of Poetry, 1987, 88, silver Poetry awards, 1986, 89. Mem. Poets and Writers (N.Y.C.), Women in Limbo (N.Y.C.), Dramatists Guild, Filmmakers Coop. Archives.

HOLMES, DWIGHT ELLIS, architect; b. Ashville, N.C., Nov. 8, 1938; s. John Dwight and Leymon (Butler) H.; m. Mary Rose Speer; children—Sheryl, John, Scott. B.S. in Architecture, Ga. Inst. Tech., 1960; B.Arch., N.C. State U., 1962. Registered architect, Fla. Architect Mark Hampton, Architect, Tampa, Fla., 1961-72; architect Rowe Holmes Assocs. Architects, Inc., Tampa, Fla., 1972-84, The Design Arts Group, Inc., Tampa, 1984-85, Rowe Holmes Hammer Russell Architects, Inc., Tampa, 1986-92, Holmes, Hepner & Assocs. Architects, Tampa, 1992—. Contbr. articles to profl. jours. Mem. State of Fla. Smart Schs. Clearinghouse, 1997—. Recipient numerous awards Am. Assn. Sch. Adminstrs., Am. Plywood Assn., Archtl. Record, Council Ednl. Facilities Planners, Fla. Concrete and Products Assn., Inc., Fla. Growers' Assn., Hillsborough County Planning Comm., Owens Corning Co., Fla. Solar Energy Ctr., Hillsborough County Hist. Preservation Bd., State of Fla. Fellow AIA (medal of honor Fla. Central chpt. 1980, award of honor Fla./Caribbean region 1982, numerous other awards). Republican. Episcopalian. Clubs: University, Tampa Yacht and Country. Home: 5800 S Gordon Ave Tampa FL 33611-4768 Office: Holmes Hepner & Assocs Architects 100 W Kennedy Blvd Tampa FL 33602-5180*

HOLMES, ERLINE MORRISON, retired educational administrator, consultant; b. Newark, Aug. 31, 1922; d. Samuel A. and Levada (Thurman) Morrison; m. William C. Holmes, Aug. 19, 1943 (dec. 1968); 1 child, William C. Jr. BS, Newark State Tchrs. Coll., 1943; MA, Seton Hall U., 1970. Cert. elem. and secondary social studies tchr., prin., sch. adminstr., N.J. Dir. employer women and working teens YWCA, Germantown, Pa., 1943-46; elem. tchr. Orange (N.J.) Bd. Edn., 1950-64; remedial and lang. arts tchr. South Orange (N.J.) Bd. Edn., 1965-66; secondary social studies tchr. Orange

H.S., 1966-69, vice prin., 1969-72, prin., 1973-75; asst. supt. Orange Bd. Edn., 1975-90, interim supt., 1990; ret., 1990; mem. N.J. Study Commn. on Adolescent Edn., 1976-77; cons. Nat. Inst. Edn., Washington, 1982, site evaluator, cons., Paterson and Newark, N.J. Dept. Edn., Trenton, 1990-96; site evaluator N.J. Coun. on Arts, 1993. Pres., bd. dirs. YWCA of Essex and West Hudson, Orange, 1978; pres. N.J. Alliance Black Sch. Educators, 1984-86; treas. Arts Coun. Essex Area, 1986-88; v.p. Family Svc. and Child Guidance Ctr., Orange, 1992-96; Orange Bd. Adjustment, 1986-97, chmn., 1997—. Cited for Outstanding Achievement in Edn., Negro Bus. and Profl. Women, 1979; recipient Cmty. Svc. award United Way of Essex, 1983-84, 84-85. Mem. Nat. Alliance Black Sch. Educators (life), Phi Delta Kappa. Presbyterian. Avocations: bowling, travel, reading, researching family history.

HOLMES, FRANCIS WILLIAM, plant pathologist; b. Yonkers, N.Y., May 21, 1929; m. Helen M. Bequaert, June 7, 1953; children: Peter, Sarah, Joseph. AB in Botany and Zoology, Oberlin Coll., 1950; PhD in Plant Pathology, Cornell U., 1954. Asst. prof. shade tree labs. U. Mass., Amherst, 1954-61; assoc. prof. U. Mass., 1961-70, prof., 1970-91, dir. shade tree labs., 1973-88, extension prof., 1988-91, prof. emeritus, 1991—; pvt. practice Amherst, 1991—; NSF sr. postdoctoral fellow U. Utrecht, Baarn, The Netherlands, 1962-63; lectr. U. Novi Sad, U. Belgrad and U. Sarajevo, 1971; sr. fellow Agrl. U., Wageningen, Netherlands, 1984-85; guest investigator New Zealand Forest Rsch. Inst., 1986. Incorporator, treas. Amherst Human Rels. Coun., 1968-70; active Boy Scouts Am., 1942-70; libr. New Eng. Quaker Rsch. Libr., 1965-85. Recipient Pub. Svc. award Nat. Arbor Day Found., 1980, Environ. Merit award EPA, 1980; Fulbright travel grant, Netherlands, 1962-63, 70-71, Am. Philos. Soc. grant, 1984-85; Internat. Agrarisch Centrum Wageningen fellow, 1985. Mem. Am. Phytopath. Soc., Can. Phytopath. Soc., Internat. Soc. Plant Pathology, Internat. Soc. Arboriculture (treas. New Eng. chpt. 1979-84, membership sec. 1985-96, chair ISA rsch. com. 1979-93, author award 1980, award of merit 1993, hon. life 1990), Royal Dutch Bot. Soc. (corr.), Mass. Tree Wardens and Foresters Assn. (hon. mem., advisor, disting. svc. award 1986, George E. Stone award 1991), Mass. Arborists Assn. (hon.), Assn. for Women in Arboriculture. Quaker. Home and Office: 24 Berkshire Ter Amherst MA 01002-1302

HOLMES, FREDERIC LAWRENCE, science historian; b. Cin., Feb. 6, 1932; m. Harriet Holmes, 1959; 3 children. B.S., MIT, 1954; M.A., Harvard U., 1958, Ph.D., 1962. Asst. prof. history of sci. MIT, 1962-64; asst. prof. to assoc. prof. Yale U., New Haven, 1964-72, prof., chmn. sect. history of medicine, 1979—, master Jonathan Edwards Coll., 1982-87; prof. history of sci., chmn. dept. history of medicine and sci. U. Western Ont., 1972-79; Dept. of Hist. of Med. Yale U Schl Med, New Haven, CT, 1979—. Author: Claude Bernard and Animal Chemistry, 1974, Lavoisier and the Chemistry of Life, 1985, Eighteenth Century Chemistry as an Investigative Enterprise, 1989, Hans Krebs: The Formation of a Scientific Life, 1991, Hans Krebs: Architect of Intermediary Metabolism, 1993, Antoine Lavoisier-The Next Crucial Year: or the Souras of His Quantitative Method in Chemistry, 1998; contbr. articles to profl. jours. Rsch. grantee NIH, 1963-67, NSF, 1968-70, 88—, Can. Coun., 1973-74. Mem. History of Sci. Soc. (pres. 1981-83), Am. Assn. History Medicine, Can. Soc. Hist. and Philos. Sci. Office: Yale U Sch Medicine Dept Hist Med PO Box 208015 New Haven CT 06520-8015

HOLMES, GARY LEE, medical/surgical nurse; b. Garden City, Kans., Aug. 30, 1951; s. Vern Lynn and Phyllis Ann (Vincent) H.; m. Margaret Emily Holmes, Jan. 10, 1973; children: Gary Lee Jr., Andrew Martin. BSN, Spalding U., 1985. RN, Ky., 1985, Ind., 1992; BCLS instr. CPR. Staff nurse burn unit Humana Hosp. U. Louisville (Ky.), 1982-85, staff nurse CRN, 1986-87, staff nurse emergency rm., 1987-88, staff nurse, 1989-92; staff nurse CRN, telemetry Humana Hosp. Audubon, Louisville, 1992; infusion therapy, med.-surg. RN Kinberly Quality Care, Jeffersonville, Ind., Louisville, 1992-95; night shift supr. Hillcreek Manor Nursing Home Rehab. Facility, 1997—; nurse Prime Stat and Star Med. Health Profls., 1997—. With USN, 1969-85. Mem. Spalding U. Nursing Students. Home: 5418 Ripple Ln Louisville KY 40218-4224

HOLMES, GENTA HAWKINS, diplomat; b. Anadarko, Okla., Sept. 3, 1940. BA, U. So. Calif., 1962. Jr. officer U.S. Embassy, Abidjan, Ivory Coast, 1964-66; with office spl. assistance to Sec. of State for Refugee Affairs, 1966-68; spl. asst., youth officer U.S. Embassy, Paris, 1968-71; with N.Y. regional office OEO, 1972-73; with office devel. fin., econ. bur. U.S. Dept. State, 1973-74; chief econ. and commercial sect. U.S. Embassy, Bahamas, 1974-77; congl. fellow Am. Polit. Sci. Assn., 1977-78; with bur. congl. rels. U.S. Dept. State, 1978-79; asst. adminstr. legis. affairs AID, 1979-82; mem. 25th Exec. Seminar in Nat. and Internat. Affairs, 1982-83; mem. bd. examiners, 1983-84; dep. chief of mission U.S. Embassy, Lilongwe, Malawi, 1984-86, Port-au-Prince, Haiti, 1986-88, Pretoria, South Africa, 1988-90; U.S. amb. to Namibia, 1990-92; dir. gen. fgn. svc., dir. pers. U.S. Dept. State, Washington, 1992-95; diplomat in residence U. Calif., Davis, 1995-97; U.S. amb. to Australia, 1997—. Office: US Embassy Canberra APO AP 96549

HOLMES, GEORGE EDWARD, molecular biologist, educator; b. Chgo., May 8, 1937; m. Norreen Ruth Petersen, Mar. 12, 1967; children: George Petersen, Norreen Eliza. BS in Biology and Chemistry, Wiley Coll., 1960; MS in Natural Sci., Chgo. State U., 1967; postgrad., U. Calif., Davis, 1967-68; PhD in Molecular Biology, U. Ariz., 1973. Med. technologist DePaul Hosp., St. Louis, 1961, Chgo. Hosp., 1961-67; tchr. Chgo. Bd. of Edn., 1965-67; rsch. assoc. Rockefeller U., N.Y.C., 1973-74; asst. prof. dept. microbiology Coll. of Medicine Howard U., Washington, 1974-82, assoc. prof., 1982—. Contbr. articles to Nature, Jour. Virology, Virology, Molecular and Gen. Genetics, Jour. Gerontology, Jour. Mutation Rsch. NIH fellow in molecular biology, 1968-73; Nat. Inst. on Aging grantee, 1982-87, Am. Soc. Biol. Chemistry and Molecular Biology Travel grantee, 1990. Mem. AAUP (chpt. pres., chair faculty grievance commn. 1994—, pres. D.C. Conf., pres. D.C. conf.), Am. Soc. Biochemistry and Molecular Biology (invitee The Gordon Conf. on Biology of Aging 1986), Am. Soc. Virology, Am. Inst. Chemists, Am. Men and Women in Sci. and Medicine, Gerontol. Soc. Am. Lutheran. Achievements include research in molecular and general genetics, nature, mutation, virology and gerontology. Fax: 410-381-0222. E-mail: gholmes@fac.howard.edu. Office: Howard U Coll of Medicine Dept Microbiology Washington DC 20059

HOLMES, GRACE ELINOR, pediatrician; b. Crookston, Minn., Mar. 27, 1932; d. William August and Anne Erika (Ermisch) Foege; m. Frederick Franklin Holmes, June 26, 1955; children: Heidi, Cindy, Lisa, Theodore, Julia, Andrew. BA, Pacific Luth. U., 1953; MD, U. Wash., 1957. Diplomate Am. Bd. Family Practice. Missionary physician Luth. Ch. Clinics, Malaysia, 1959-63; pediat. cons. Kilimanjaro Christian Med. Ctr., Tanzania, 1970-72; instr. pediat. Med. Ctr. U. Kans., Kansas City, 1967-69, asst. prof., 1969-70, 72-80, assit. prof. preventive medicine, 1978-80, assoc. prof. depts. pediat. & preventive medicine, 1980-87, full prof. depts. pediat. & preventive medicine, 1987—. Author: Whither Thou Goest, I Will Go, 1992. Recipient Humanitarian Svc. award Med. Alumni Assn. U. Wash. Sch. Medicine, 1995; named Alumna of Yr. Pacific Luth. U., 1988. Avocations: writing, music, photography. Home: 4701 Black Swan Dr Shawnee KS 66216-1234 Office: U Kans Med Ctr 4004 Robinson Hall 3901 Rainbow Blvd Kansas City KS 66160-0001*

HOLMES, HARRY DADISMAN, health facility administrator; b. Houston, Aug. 8, 1944; s. Harry Newton and Ruth Eleanor (Dadisman) H.; m. Patricia Ann Hunt, Aug. 23, 1969; children: Hillary Hunt, Ashley Elizabeth. BA, Rice U., 1966; MA, La. State U., 1968; PhD, U. Mo., 1973. Asst. prof. urban devel. U. Tenn., Knoxville, 1973-76; asst. to exec. v.p. Tex. Med. Ctr., Inc., Houston, 1976-80; dir. govt. affairs, orgnl. liaison U. Tex. System Cancer Ctr., Houston, 1980-90, asst. to pres., 1981-90; assoc. v.p. gvtl. rels. U. Tex. M.D. Anderson Cancer Ctr., Houston, 1990—; mem. Cancer Ctrs. Adminstrs. Forum, 1994—; mem. select com. on pub. issues Greater Houston Hosp. Coun., 1983-94; mem. exec. adv. bd. White, Petrov and McHone, 1987-95; mem. pub. rels. adv. coun. Tex. Med. Ctr., 1985—; chair South Tex. Legis Conf., 1985, 87; founder Biotech. Assn., 1986; mem. exec. com. Nat. Cancer Ctr. Networks, 1998—. Mem. adminstrv. bd. St. Luke's Meth. Ch.; mem. Mayor's Task Force on Pvt. Sector Initiatives for Houston, 1981-82, Houston C.C. Found. Bd., 1992—, Greater Houston Partnership State and Fed. Com., 1989—; mem. U. Tex. Tex./Mex. Border Health Task Force, 1989—, exec. com., 1989—; pres. Houston Higher Edn. Fin. Corp., 1989—; mem. Rice U. Fund Coun., 1991-94, Nat. Cancer Ctrs. Task Force, 1991—; mem. exec. bd. Leadership Houston, 1983-86, Houston Ctr. for Humanities, 1983-86; mem. govt. rels. com. Greater Houston Hosp. Coun., 1985-95; mem. com. Instnl. Task Force on Oncology in Chile, 1986-87; exec. com. Instnl. Strategic Planning Com., 1986-95; divsn. chmn. United Way of Houston, 1983; com. to evaluate the status of minority and women faculty, faculty adminstrs. and adminstrv. staff U. Tex., M.D. Anderson Cancer Ctr., 1990. White fellow U. Mo., 1972. Mem. Am. Assn. Cancer Insts. (mem. govt. rels. com. 1998—), Houston C. of C. (co-chmn. govt. rels. com. 1982-83), Rice U. Alumni Assn. (exec. bd., chmn. publs. com. 1982-83), Phi Alpha Theta. Home: 5642 Cedar Creek Dr Houston TX 77056-2310 Office: U Tex MD Anderson Cancer Ctr 1515 Holcombe Blvd Houston TX 77030-4009

HOLMES, HELEN BEQUAERT, project director; b. Boston, Sept. 6, 1929; d. Joseph Charles and Frances Alice (Brown) Bequaert; m. Francis William Holmes, June 7, 1953; children: Peter Alan, Sarah Ruth, Joseph Mark. AB, Oberlin Coll., 1951; MS, Cornell U., 1953; PhD, U. Mass., 1970. Cert. secondary tchr., Mass. Sci. tchr. Northampton (Mass.) Sch. for Girls, 1965-67; asst. prof. biology Springfield (Mass.) Tech. Community Coll., 1971-73, Russell Sage Coll., Troy, N.Y., 1976-78; vis. lectr. genetics Tufts U., Medford, Mass., 1978-80; rsch. assoc. Fedn. of Orgns. for Profl. Women, Washington, 1978-82; vis. scholar Spelman Coll., Atlanta, 1982-83; vis. scientist U. Groningen, The Netherlands, 1984-85; scholar assoc. Women's Rsch. Inst. Hartford (Conn.) Coll. for Women, 1986-88, 90-91; assoc. fellow Inst. for Advanced Study in Humanities U. Mass., Amherst, 1988-90; rsch. assoc. Nat. Women's Studies Assn., College Park, Md., 1992; coord. Ctr. for Genetics, Ethics and Women, Amherst, 1992—; con. U.S. Congress Office of Tech. Assessment, Washington, 1987. Editor: Birth Control and Controlling Birth, 1980, The Custom Made Child?, 1981, Feminist Perspectives in Medical Ethics, 1992, Issues in Reproductive Technology I: An Anthology, 1992; mem. editorial bd. Bioethics, 1986—, Hypatia, 1987—; contbr. articles to profl. jours. Mem. Pub. Transp. Com., Amherst, Mass., 1989-91, Srs. and Law Together (SALT) Com., Amherst, 1993-97; organizer nat. conf. Women and Genetics in Contemporary Soc., 1996. Grantee NSF, 1978-81, 82-83, NIH, 1995-96; recipient Fulbright award Coun. for Internat. Exchange of Scholars, U. Waikato, 1986-87. Mem. Soc. for Women in Philosophy (organizer, regional conf. 1989), Feminist Approaches to Bioethics (co-founder), Phi Beta Kappa, Sigma Xi. Mem. Soc. of Friends. Avocations: hiking, canoeing, reading. Home and Office: 24 Berkshire Ter Amherst MA 01002-1302

HOLMES, HENRY, literary agent, book publicist, writer and editor, advertising and marketing consultant; b. Fall River, Mass., June 30, 1935. AS in Broadcast Journalism, Grahm Coll., 1961; Cert. in Leadership, Dale Carnegie, 1962; postgrad. in non-fiction writing, Famous Writers Sch., Westport, Conn., 1966-69; (hon.) degree, Grahm Coll., 1970. News prodr./sports prodr. Report on Sports WHDH-TV-Radio (CBS); asst. pub. rels. dir. Doherty, Clifford, Steers & Shenfield, Inc., N.Y.C. and Boston, 1962-64; sports dir. WCEE-TV (CBS), Rockford, Ill.; news dir. WRLH-TV (NBC), Hanover, N.H.; media comms./mktg. Boston Red Sox, 1961-62, 73-75; sports dir. WRLM-FM, Providence; mktg. prof. Zayre Corp., Natick, Mass., 1984-86; mktg./sales promotion McGraw Hill Corp., Heightstown, N.J., Castle Harlan, Inc., N.Y.C.; project coord. Addison Wesley Publ. Co., Reading, Mass.; broadcast instr. Career Acad., Boston; advt. instr. Fisher Coll., Fall River, Mass., 1976; announcer Avco Pro Golf Classic, 1969; (with Bruce Martin) Voice of Detroit Red Wings and Detroit Lions; speaker in field. Documentary writer, prodr. JFK assassination spl., 1963; narrator Election Capsule '68, Big Eight Football TV spl. with Pro Football Hall of Famer Elroy Hirsch, 1970, Best in Sports interviews, 1961; anchor Heartbeats in Sports Headlines pre-game sports features WSAR-AM. Fundraiser Jerry Lewis Telethon, Rockford, United Cerebral Palsy, Rockford, Internat. Club for Physically Handicapped, Rockford, Beloit (Wis.) Jaycees, WBEL Community Charity Drive, Beloit. With USN, 1956-58. Avocations: nonfiction writing, general research, interviewing, current events, professional and college sports. Home and Office: PO Box 433 Swansea MA 02777-0433

HOLMES, HENRY ALLEN, government official; b. Bucharest, Rumania, Jan. 31, 1933 (parents Am. citizens); s. Julius Cecil and Henrietta (Allen) H.; A.B., Princeton U., 1954; certificat d'etudes politiques (Woodrow Wilson fellow) U. Paris, 1958; m. Marilyn Janet Strauss, July 25, 1959; children: Katherine Anne, Gerald Allen. Intelligence research analyst Dept. State, 1958-59; commd. fgn. service officer Dept. State, 1959; assigned to Am. embassy, Yaounde, Cameroun, 1959-61, Dept. State, Washington, 1961-63, 67-70, Am. embassy, Rome, 1963-67, counselor polit. affairs Am. Embassy, Paris, 1970-74; sr. exec. Seminar in Fgn. Policy, Washington, 1974-75; assigned as dir. Office NATO and Atlantic polit. mil. affairs Bur. European Affairs, Washington, 1975-77; dep. chief of mission U.S. embassy, Rome, 1977-79; prin. dep. asst. sec. state for European affairs, Washington, 1979-82; ambassador to Portugal, 1982-85; asst. sec. Bur. Politico Military Affairs, U.S. Dept. State, Washington, 1986-89; amb. at large for burdensharing, 1989-93, asst. sec. def. for spl. ops. and low-intensity conflict, 1993—. Served as capt. USMCR, 1954-57. Mem. Am. Fgn. Service Assn., Council Fgn. Relations. Episcopalian. Club: Met. (Washington). Office: US Dept of Defense Special Ops & Low Intensity Conflict 2500 Defense Pentagon Washington DC 20301-2500

HOLMES, IRVIN R., JR., marketing professional. V.p. mktg. Del Monte Foods, San Francisco. Office: Del Monte Foods 1 Market Plz San Francisco CA 94105-1420

HOLMES, JAMES, investment company executive; b. Eng., Oct. 24, 1919; s. David T. and Emily (Hill) H.; m. Mildred Alice Deans, July 14, 1943; children: David Caird, Barbara Mary. B.Sc. in Econs, U. London, 1949. With Can. Pacific Ltd., Montreal, Que., Can., 1949-70; sr. research economist Can. Pacific Ltd., 1960-61, spl. asst. fin. dept., 1961-63, asst. treas., 1963, treas., 1964-69, dir. fin. planning, 1969-70; dir. fin. Falconbridge Nickel Mines Ltd., Toronto, Ont., Can., 1970; v.p. fin. Falconbridge Nickel Mines Ltd., 1971-76, Falconbridge Dominicana (C por A), 1970-76; chmn. bd., chief exec. officer Electrohome Ltd., Kitchener, Ont., 1977-80, dir., 1977-81; chmn. bd., dir. Central Ont. TV Ltd., 1977-80; chmn. bd., chief exec. officer Homeware Industries Ltd., Homeware Ltd., 1980-82; pres. Holmes and Co., Toronto, 1983—, Caird Holmes Mgmt. Ltd., 1984—, Bartam Holmes Inc., 1992—. Served with RAF, 1940-46. Mem. Can. Mfrs. Assn. (dir. 1980-84). Office: 2170 Marine Dr Unit 1005, Oakville, ON Canada L6J 2L5

HOLMES, JAMES HILL, III, lawyer; b. Birmingham, Ala., Sept. 10, 1935; s. Houston Eccleston and Celia Lindsey (Wearn) H.; m. Julia (Judy) Ryman, Aug. 17, 1963; children: James H. IV, Randell Ryman, Tucker Malone. BBA, So. Meth. U., 1957, LLB, 1959. Bar: Tex. 1959, U.S. Dist. Ct. (no. dist.) Tex. 1963, U.S. Dist. Ct. (ea. dist.) Tex. 1966, U.S. Dist. Ct. (we. dist.) Tex. 1979, U.S. Ct. Appeals (5th and 11th cirs.) 1981, U.S. Ct. Mil. Appeals 1960, U.S. Supreme Ct. 1974. Ptnr. Burford & Ryburn, Dallas, 1962—; spkr. State Bar Tex. Profl. Devel. Program, 1987-93; mock trial participant Tex. Nurses Assn., 1978-86; co-chair Supreme Ct. Adv. Com. on Professionalism for Supreme Ct. Tex., 1989-90. Contbr. articles to profl. jours. Past mem. University Park (Tex.) Bd. Adjustment; chmn. University Park Planning and Zoning Commn., 1988-94; city councilman City of University Park, 1994, mayor pro tem, 1998-99; past. dir. Child Guidance Clinic; past dir., pres. All Sports Assn., Dallas, 1977; pres. University Park Cmty. League, 1987-88; past bd. dirs. Park Cities Town North YMCA; numerous other offices in civic orgns. With USAF, 1959-62. Recipient Presdl. Citation State Bar of Tex., 1995. Fellow Am. Coll. Trial Lawyers, Tex. Bar Found.; mem. ABA, Dallas Assn. Def. Counsel (chmn. 1984-85), Tex. Assn. Def. Counsel (pres. 1992-93, Founder's award 1997), Assn. Def. Trial Attys., Internat. Assn. Def. Counsel, Def. Rsch. Inst., Dallas Bar Assn. (numerous offices and coms.), Tex. Bar Assn., Am. Bd. Trial Advocates (sec.-treas., pres.-elect Dallas chpt. 1999), Patrick E. Higginbotham Am. Inn of Ct. (master 1989-95), State Bar Coll. (Tex.), Blue Key, Phi Alpha Delta, Phi Delta Theta. Episcopalian. Avocations: jogging, spectator sports, outdoors. Home: 3804 Lovers Ln Dallas TX 75225-7101 Office: Burford & Ryburn LLP 3100 Lincoln Pla 500 N Akard St Ste 3100 Dallas TX 75201-6697

HOLMES, JEAN LOUISE, real estate investor, Holocaust scholar, educator; b. Butler, Mo., Dec. 9, 1943; d. Victor Julius and Helen Emilia (Knapheide) Witte; m. Eugene Philmore Carter Jr., Aug. 21, 1965 (div. Aug. 1992); children: Kristin, Lance; m. Reed M. Holmes, Jan. 26, 1993. AA, Graceland Coll., Lamoni, Iowa, 1963; BA, Iowa State U., 1965; postgrad., U. Paris, 1965, Tufts U., 1973; MA in Judaic Studies magna cum laude, Hebrew Coll., Brookline, Mass., 1989; postgrad., Ratisbonne Ctr. of Judaic Studies, Jerusalem, 1993-95, Hebrew U., 1992, 95. Lic. bldg. constrn. supr., Mass. Tchr. French Iowa, Mass.; 1966-69; tchg. English lang. and lit. Iowa, 1966-67; real estate broker Carter Realty, Pepperell, Mass., 1975—; pres., mgr. Viewpax Mondiale, Independence, Mo., 1982—; pres. Keshet Hashalom, Jerusalem, 1989—; clk. Ctrl. Middlesex Multiple Listing Svc., Concord, Mass., 1980-81, v.p., 1982, pres., 1983; lectr. Internat. Holocaust Scholars Conf., Berlin, 1994, Mpls., 1996; dir., adj. prof. student intercultural travel to Israel, Jordan, Egypt, Park Coll., Mo., Graceland Coll., 1982—. Mem. adv. bd. Peace Ctr., Independence, 1989-91. Recipient Friendship award Israel Ministry of Tourism, Jerusalem, 1992. Mem. Greater Lowell (Mass.) Bd. Realtors. Avocations: photography, archaeology, adventure travel, literature. Home: PO Box 680 Pepperell MA 01463-0680 Office: Holmes Mgmt 76 Main St Pepperell MA 01463-1561

HOLMES, JERRY DELL, retired organic chemist; b. Mt. Vernon, Tex., Nov. 30, 1935; s. W.L. and Amie E. (Marshall) H.; m. Margaret L. King, June 22, 1957; children: Lisa, Melinda, Jerry D. Jr., James. BS, East Tex. State U., 1956; PhD, U. Tex., 1964; postgrad. in Advanced Mgmt., Harvard U., 1991. Chemist Am. Oil Co., Texas City, Tex., 1956-60; chemist, then sr. chemist Tex. Eastman Co., Longview, 1963-74, div. dir., 1974-80; staff asst. research and devel. Chem. Div. Eastman Kodak Co., Kingsport, Tenn., 1980-82; dir. research and devel. Tex. Eastman Co., Longview, Tex., 1982-84; dir. devel. Chems. div. Eastman Kodak Co., Kingsport, 1984-88, acting dir. R&D, 1988, assoc. dir. research, chem. div., 1988-89, dir. rsch., chem. div., 1989-90; v.p. rsch. Eastman Chem. Co., Kingsport, 1990-95; v.p. R&D, 1995-97, ret., 1997; bd. dirs. Reilly Industries, Inc.; lectr. in field of rsch. and devel. Contbr. articles to profl. jours.; patentee in field. Mem. Am. Chem. Soc., Indls. Rsch. Inst. Presbyterian. Achievements include research and lectures in field of doubling the output of research using TQM.

HOLMES, JOHN LEONARD, chemistry educator; b. London, Nov. 29, 1931; came to Can., 1958; s. Leonard Thomas and Jessie Ethel (Doble) H.; m. Una Jane Watts, Dec. 12, 1958 (div. 1993); children: Susan P., Jonathan B.; m. Sheila Jean Robertson, Apr. 13, 1994; stepchildren: John Fergus, Isobel Clare. BSc, London U., 1954, PhD, 1957, DSc, 1983. Postdoctoral fellow NRC, Ottawa, Can., 1958-60; I.C.I. fellow Edinburgh U., Scotland, 1960-61, lectr., 1961-62; asst. prof. U. Ottawa, 1962-65, assoc. prof., 1965-73, prof., 1973-97, emeritus prof., 1997—; Nuffield vis. prof. U. Ghana, 1971, Overbeek vis. prof. U. Utrecht, The Netherlands, 1979, Disting. vis. scholar U. Adelaide, Australia, 1984; vis. fellow Australian Nat. U., Canberra, 1993; internat. sci. exchange fellow U. Bern, 1993. Editor Organic Mass Spectrometry jour., 1976-93, European Mass Spectrometry jour., 1994—; contbr. over 250 articles to profl. jours. Recipient Barringer Rsch. award Can. Spectroscopy Soc., 1980, Herzberg award Can. Spectroscopy Soc., 1990. Fellow Chem. Inst. Can. (medal 1989), Royal Soc. Can.; mem. Am. Soc. Mass Spectrometry, Brit. Soc. Mass Spectrometry (life), Internat. Yacht Racing Union (judge 1986-99), Can. Yachting Assn., Royal Yachting Assn. Clubs: Britannia Yacht (Ottawa). Home: 121 Buell St Unit 58, Ottawa, ON Canada K1Z 7E7 Office: U Ottawa, Chem Dept, Ottawa, ON Canada K1N 6N5

HOLMES, JOHN RICHARD, physicist, educator; b. Chula Vista, Calif., Sept. 24, 1917; s. Robert and Mary Elizabeth (Burns) H.; m. Louise Murphy, 1951 (dec. Oct. 1989); children: Susan Diana, Ronald John, Sandra Kathleen. AB in Physics, U. Calif., Berkeley, 1938, MA, 1941, PhD, 1942. With radiation lab. U. Calif., 1942-45; mem. faculty physics U. So. Calif., Los Angeles, 1945-63, prof., 1954-63, chmn. dept. physics, 1956-62; prof. U. Hawaii, Honolulu, 1963—, chmn. physics dept., 1963-72, emeritus prof. physics, 1989—; Fulbright lectr. U. Madrid, 1962-63; cons. Autonetics Corp., Anaheim, Calif., Douglas Aircraft, Santa Monica, Calif., Electro-Optical Sys., Pasadena, Calif.; lectr. Edwards AFB, Loyola U., L.A.; UNESCO cons., Argentina, 1970. mem. internat. adv. bd. Optica Pura y Aplicada, Madrid. Whiting fellow in physics U. Calif., Berkeley, 1938. Fellow Am. Phys. Soc., Optical Soc. Am.; mem. AAAS. Address: Sun Lakes Country Club 1590 Crystal Downs St Banning CA 92220-6614

HOLMES, KATHLEEN MARIE, secondary education educator; b. Buffalo, N.Y., July 31, 1956; d. Ernest Leonard and Kathryn Ann (Malovich) H. BS, Westminster Coll., Salt Lake City, 1978; MS in Edn., Buffalo State Coll., 1985, MS in Creativity, 1994. Cert. English and social studies tchr., N.Y. Adult basic edn. tchr. Kearns (Utah) Cmty. Sch., 1978-81; English/social studies tchr. St. Mary's H.S., Lancaster, N.Y., 1981-85; humanities instr. Orchard Park (N.Y.) H.S., 1985—, coord. Japan home stay program, 1995—; creativity/leadership tng. cons., Orchard Park, 1990—. Mem. St. Mary's H.S. Found. bd., capital campaign co-chair, 1993-97. Mem. Nat. Coun. Tchrs. English, N.Y. State English Coun. Roman Catholic. Avocations: genealogy, reading, biking, hiking, travel. Office: Orchard Park High Sch 4040 Baker Rd Orchard Park NY 14127-2052

HOLMES, KEITH, professional boxer; b. Washington. Named WBC Middleweight Champion, 1996, 98, lost WBC Middleweight Champ. in 12th rnd. to Hassine Cherifi. Achievements include record of 30 wins and 2 losses, with 20 knock-outs. *

HOLMES, KING KENNARD, medical educator; b. St. Paul, Sept. 1, 1937. AB, Harvard Coll., 1959; MD, Cornell U., 1963; PhD in Microbiology, U. Hawaii, 1967. Diplomate Am. Bd. Internal Medicine, infectious diseases. Resident U. Wash., Seattle, 1967-68, chief resident, 1968-69, from instr. to assoc. prof. medicine, 1969-78, vice chmn. dept. medicine, 1984-89, prof. medicine, 1978—, dir. Ctr. AIDS and Sexually Transmitted Diseases, 1989—; head divsn. pulmonary diseases USPHS Hosp., Seattle, 1969-70, asst. chief dept. medicine, 1969-83, head divsn. infectious diseases, 1970-83; dir. Sexually Transmitted Disease Clinic, Harborview Med. Ctr., 1972-79, chief med., 1984-89; mem. numerous adv. coms. Nat. Inst. Allergy & Infectious Diseases, NIH, USPHS, WHO, NAS; prin. investigator NIH, Nat. Cancer Inst., Nat. Inst. Allergy & Infectious Diseases, Nat. Inst. Child Health & Human Devel., Ctrs. Disease Control, 1983—. With USN, 1965-67. Recipient Squibb award Infectious Disease Soc. Am., 1978, Thomas Parran award Am. Veneral Disease Assn., 1983. Fellow ACP, Royal Coll. Physicians Eng.; mem. AMA, Inst. Medicine-NAS, Assn. Am. Physicians, Am. Epidemiol. Soc., Am. Fedn. Clin. Rsch. Office: U Wash Str AIDS & STDs 1001 Broadway Ste 215 Seattle WA 98122-4381*

HOLMES, LARRY, JR., retired professional boxer; b. Cuthbert, Ga., Nov. 3, 1949; s. John and Flossie Holmes; children: Listy, Lisa. Ed. public schs. Formerly worked in car wash, quarry, rug mill, foundry, profl. boxer, 1973—. Heavyweight champion World Boxing Council, 1978-83, Internat. Boxing Fedn., 1983-85. Won 19 of 22 amateur fights. Undefeated for a record 13 years. Office: Larry Holmes Enterprises 704 Alpha Bldg Easton PA 18042*

HOLMES, LOIS REHDER, composer, piano and voice educator; b. Canton, Ill., Jan. 8, 1927; d. John and Elizabeth Mary Grace (Staton) Kleinsteiber; div.; 1 child, Jessica Regina. BA in Sociology, Ill. Wesleyan U., 1949, MusB in Voice, Organ & Piano, 1950; MS in Reading, Western Ill. U., 1981. Cert. tchr., Ill. Libr. worker Withers Pub. Libr., Bloomington, Ill., 1950-51; music tchr. Toledo (Ill.) Schs., 1951-52; music and art librarian Hutchinson (Kans) Pub. Libr., 1952-53; pvt. practice piano & voice tchr. various cities, Ill., 1955—; tchr. 1st & 2d grades South Fulton Sch., Havana, Ill., 1972-81. Composer: Musical Notions, 1991, Seascape, 1993, Divertimento, 1995, Bittersweet, 1996, Buglers at Sunrise, 1997, Dream Catcher, 1998, Fourteen New Christmas Carols for the 21st Century, 1999, others. Organist/choir dir. Ctrl. Christian Ch., Havana, 1974-79; vol. March of Dimes, Chgo., 1997—, Amnesty Internat. USA, Chgo., 1993—. Mem. Nat. Guild Piano Tchrs. (adjudicator internat. piano composition contest 1996—), Hymn Soc. U.S. and Can., Phi Kappa Phi. Home: 116 E Adams St Havana IL 62644-1411

HOLMES, MARJORIE ROSE, author; b. Storm Lake, Iowa; d. Samuel Arthur and Rosa (Griffith) H.; m. Lynn Mighell, Apr. 9, 1932; children—Marjorie Mighell Croner, Mark, Mallory, Melanie Mighell Dimopoulos; m. George P. Schmieler, July 4, 1981. Student, Buena Vista Coll., 1927-29, DLitt (hon.), 1976; BA, Cornell Coll., 1931, LHD (hon.), 1998. Tchr. writing Cath. U., 1964-65, U. Md., 1967-68; mem. staff Georgetown Writers Conf., 1959-81. Free-lance writer short stories, articles, verse for mags. including McCall's, Redbook, Reader's Digest; bi-weekly columnist: Love and Laughter, Washington Evening Star, 1959-75; monthly columnist: Woman's Day, 1971-77; author: World By the Tail, 1943, Ten O'Clock Scholar, 1946, Saturday Night, 1959, Cherry Blossom Princess, 1960, Follow Your Dream, 1961, Love is a Hopscotch Thing, 1963, Senior Trip, 1962, Love and Laughter, 1967, I've Got to Talk to Somebody, God, 1969, Writing the Creative Article, 1969, Who Am I, God?, 1971, To Treasure Our Days, 1971, Two from Galilee, 1972, Nobody Else Will Listen, 1973, You and I and Yesterday, 1973, As Tall as My Heart, 1974, How Can I Find You God?, 1975, Beauty in Your Own Back Yard, 1976, Hold Me Up a Little Longer, Lord, 1977, Lord, Let Me Love, 1978, God and Vitamins, 1980, To Help You Through the Hurting, 1983, Three from Galilee—The Young Man from Nazareth, 1985, Writing the Creative Article Today, 1986, Marjorie Holmes' Secrets of Health, Energy and Staying Young, 1987, The Messiah, 1987, At Christmas the Heart Goes Home, 1991, The Inspirational Writings of Marjorie Holmes, 1991, Gifts Freely Given, 1992, Writing Articles From the Heart, 1993, Second Wife, Second Life!, 1993, Still by Your Side-How I Know a Great Love Never Dies, 1996; contbg. editor Guideposts, 1977—; bd. dirs. The Writer, 1975—. Bd. dirs. Found. Christian Living, 1975—. Recipient Honor Iowans award Buena Vista Coll., 1966, Alumni Achievement award Cornell Coll., 1963, Woman of Achievement award Nat. Fedn. Press Women, 1972; Celebrity of Yr. award Women in Communications, 1975; Woman of Yr. award McLean Bus. and Profl. Women, 1976; award Freedom Found. at Valley Forge, 1977; gold medal Marymount Coll. Va., 1978. Mem. Am. Newspaper Women's Club, Nat. Fedn. Press Women, Author's Guild, Washington Nat. Press Club. *Talent imposes 2 responsibilities: to use it, and to use it for good.*

HOLMES, MELVIN ALMONT, insurance company executive; b. West New York, N.J., Jan. 2, 1919; s. Edward L. and Sarah J. (Brown) H.; m. Clare G. White, May 30, 1943; children: Clare Ann, Karen, Joan, Patricia, Catherine, Donald, Jacqueline. Student in bus. adminstrn., NYU; L.H.D. (hon.), Coll. of Ins., 1976. C.P.C.U., 1955. With Frank B. Hall & Co., Inc., Briarcliff Manor, N.Y., 1937-84; asst. mgr. liability dept. Frank B. Hall & Co., Inc., 1945-52, asst. v.p., 1952-56, v.p., 1956-68, chief exec. officer, pres., 1968-73, vice chmn., 1973-79, cons., dir., 1979-84; Chmn. bd. trustees Coll. of Ins., 1974-76. Hon. trustee Valley Hosp., Ridgewood, N.J. Served to capt. C.E., U.S. Army, 1941-46. Recipient Good Scout award Boy Scouts Am., 1975; Free Enterprise award Ins. Fedn. N.Y., 1975. Mem. Nat. Assn. Ins. Brokers (past pres.), Ins. Soc. N.Y., Soc. C.P.C.U.s (Eugene A. Toale Meml. award 1976), Ins. Inst. Am., Am. Inst. Property and Liability Underwriters Inc. (past trustee), Ins. Fedn. N.Y. (past pres.). Clubs: Tequesta Country. Home: 275 Beach Rd Apt A101 Tequesta FL 33469-2802

HOLMES, MICHAEL GENE, lawyer; b. Longview, Wash., Jan. 14, 1937; s. Robert A. and Esther S. Holmes; children: Helen, Peyton Robert. AB in Econs., Stanford U., 1958, JD, 1960. Bar: Oreg. 1961, U.S. Dist. Ct. Oreg. 1961, U.S. Ct. Appeals (9th cir.) 1961, Temp. Emergency Ct. Appeals 1976, U.S. Supreme Ct. 1976. Assoc. Spears, Lubersky, Bledsoe, Anderson, Young & Hilliard, Portland, 1961-67, ptnr., 1967-90; ptnr. Lane Powell Spears Lubersky, Portland, 1990-95, of counsel, 1995; mem. Oreg. Joint Com. of Bar, Press & Broadcasters, 1982-85, sec., 1983-84, chmn. 1985. Author Survey of Oregon Defamation and Privacy Law, ann., 1982-95. Trustee Med. Rsch. Found. Oreg., Portland, 1985-94, exec. com., 1986-94; hon. trustee Oreg. Health Scis. Found., 1995—; trustee Portland Civic Theatre, 1962-66. Mem. Oreg. Bar Assn., Phi Beta Kappa.

HOLMES, MIRIAM H., publisher; b. Bavaria, Germany, June 2, 1951; came to U.S., 1952; d. Max J. and Mala (Rosenwasser) H.; m. Stephen H. Gelb, June 25, 1995. BA, Queens Coll., 1972; JD, Yeshiva U., 1987. Bar: N.Y. 1988. Pres. Holmes & Meier Pub., N.Y.C., 1990—. Mem. Assn. Jewish Book Pub. (exec. com.), Jewish Book Coun. (exec. com.), Women's Nat. Book Assn. Office: East Bldg 160 Broadway New York NY 10038-4201

HOLMES, NANCY ELIZABETH, pediatrician; b. St. Louis, Aug. 3, 1950; d. David Reed and Phyllis Anne (Hunger) Holmes; m. Arthur Erwin Kramer, May 15, 1976; children: Melanie Elizabeth Kramer, Carl Edward Kramer. BA in Psychology, U. Kans., 1972; MD, U. Mo., 1976. Diplomate Am. Acad. Pediatrics. Intern., resident in pediatrics St. Louis Children's Hosp., Washington U., St. Louis, 1976-81; pediatrician Ctrl. Pediatrics, St. Louis, 1981—; sch. physician Sch. Dist. Clayton, Mo., 1985-92; asst. prof. clin. pediatrics Washington U., St. Louis, Mo., 1993—; cons. 1st. Congregational Preschool, Clayton, 1984-86, Jewish Hosp. Daycare Ctr., St. Louis, 1993—, Flynn Park Early Edn. Ctr., Un.iv. City, Mo., 1994—, community outpatient experience Preceptor Hosp., St. Louis Children's Hosp., 1991-93, 94—; mem. med. exec. com. St. Louis Children's Hosp., 1992-94. Elder Trinity Presbyn. Ch., University City, 1989-92, 96—; vol. reading tutor Flynn Park Sch., University City, 1992-98; cub scout leader Flynn Park Sch., 1993-98; bd. dirs. Children's Hosp. Care Group. Fellow Am. Acad. Pediatrics; mem. AMA, Mo. State Med. Assn., St. Louis Metro. Med. Soc, St. Louis Pediatric Soc. Presbyterian. Avocations: reading, gardening, photography, travel. Office: Ctrl Pediatrics Inc 8888 Ladue Rd # 130 Saint Louis MO 63124-2090*

HOLMES, PAUL KINLOCH, III, prosecutor; b. Newport, Ark., Nov. 10, 1951; s. Paul K. Jr. and Virginia (Harrison) H.; m. Katherine Hewitt, July 28, 1978; children: Christopher, Stephen. BA, Westminster Coll., 1973; JD, U. Ark., Fayetteville, 1978. Bar: Ark. 1978. Ptnr. Warner & Smith Attys. at Law, Ft. Smith, Ark., 1978-93; U.S. atty. Western Dist. Ark., Ft. Smith, Ark., 1993—. Office: US Courthouse 6th and Rogers Fort Smith AR 72901

HOLMES, RANDALL KENT, microbiology educator, physician, university administrator; b. Muskegon, Mich., Nov. 7, 1940; s. Scott Travis and Helen Marie (Rosell) H.; m. Kathryn Louise Voelker, June 16, 1962; children: Rebecca Kathryn, Elisabeth Marie. AB, Harvard U., 1962; MD, PhD in Microbiology, NYU, 1968. Diplomate Am. Bd. Internal Medicine, Am. Bd. Infectious Diseases. Intern, then resident Beth Israel Hosp., Boston, 1968-70; research assoc. NIH, Bethesda, Md., 1970-72; instr. medicine U. Tex. Southwestern Med. Sch., Dallas, 1972-73, asst. prof., 1973-75, assoc. prof., 1975-76; prof., chmn. microbiology and immunology Uniformed Services U. Health Scis., Bethesda, 1976-95, assoc. dean for acad. affairs, 1984-93, acting chmn. biochemistry, 1993-95; prof., chmn. microbiology U. Colo. Sch. Medicine, Denver, 1995—; mem. adv. com. vaccines and related biol. products Nat. Ctr. for Drugs and Biologics, Bethesda, 1983-87; mem. cholera panel NIH, 1987-92; mem. bacteriology and mycology 1 study sect. NIH, 1993-95; chair VA-DOD Rsch. Program on Mechs. of Emerging Pathogens Rev. Panel, 1997. Contbr. articles to profl. jours. Served to surgeon USPHS, 1968-70. Recipient Research Career Devel. award NIH, 1975-76. Fellow ACP, Infectious Diseases Soc. Am.; mem. Am. Acad. Microbiology (bd. govs. 1992-95, com. on awards 1995—), Am. Soc. for Clin. Investigation, Am. Soc. for Microbiology (editorial bd. Infection and Immunity 1978-86, Microbiol. Revs. 1983-88, mem. steering com. postdoctoral rsch. assoc. program Nat. Ctr. for Infectious Disease 1993-95, chmn. 1996—), Nat. Bd. Med. Examiners (mem. microbiology test com. 1984-86, chmn. 1987-93, mem. U.S. med. licensing exam. step I com. 1990-92, mem. U.S. med. licensing exam. composite com. 1992-95), Phi Beta Kappa, Alpha Omega Alpha. Republican. Avocations: reading, hiking, camping, swimming. Office: U Colo Health Scis Ctr Dept Microbiology Campus Box B 175 4200 E 9th Ave Denver CO 80262

HOLMES, RICHARD ALBERT, software engineer, consultant; b. Santa Barbara, Calif., May 7, 1958; m. Janet M. Dunbar; children: Brian D., Kevin M. AA in Music summa cum laude, City Coll. San Francisco, 1987; BS in Computer Sci. summa cum laude, Nat. U., 1991; postgrad., Stanford U., 1993—. Ind. software cons. San Francisco, 1986-88; software quality assurance contractor Oxford & Assocs., Mountain View, Calif., 1988-89; microkernel diagnostics engr. Apple Computer, Cupertino, Calif., 1990-93, file system engr., 1994-96; operating sys. engr. Hewlett Packard, Cupertino, Calif., 1996-99; staff engr. Veritas, Mountain View, Calif., 1999—. CCSF tchr. & faculty scholar, 1986, 87, Alpha Gamma Sigma scholar, 1987. Mem. IEEE, Assn. for Computing Machinery, Alpha Gamma Sigma (treas. 1986-87). Avocations: playing classical guitar, gem & mineral collecting, computer music and sound generation, music improvisation and composition. Office: Hewlett-Packard Co MS 47LA1 19447 Pruneridge Ave Cupertino CA 95014-0683

HOLMES, RICHARD BROOKS, mathematical physicist; b. Milw., Jan. 7, 1959; s. Emerson Brooks Holmes and Nancy Anne Schaffter; m. Sandra Lynn Wong, June 27, 1998. BS, Calif. Inst. Tech., 1981; MS, Stanford (Calif.) U., 1983. Sr. sys. analyst Comptek Rsch., Vallejo, Calif., 1982-83; staff scientist Western Rsch., Arlington, Va., 1983-85; sr. scientist AVCO Everett (Mass.) Rsch. Lab., 1985-88; prin. rsch. scientist North East Rsch. Assocs., Woburn, Mass., 1988-90; sr. mem. tech. staff Rocketdyne divsn. Rockwell Internat., Canoga Park, Calif., 1990-95; sr. staff scientist Lockheed Martin Rsch. Labs., Palo Alto, Calif., 1995-98; pres. Nutronics, Inc., Carson City, Nev., 1998—; cons. North East Rsch. Assocs., 1990. Contbr. Matched Asymptotic Expansions, 1988; contbr. articles to Phys. Rev. Letters, Phys. Rev., Jour. of the Optical Soc. Am. and IEEE Jour. of Quantum Electronics. Mem. No. Calif. Scholarship Founds., Oakland, 1977; mem. Wilderness Soc., Washington, 1989. Stanford fellow Stanford U., 1982; fellow MIT, 1990; recipient Presdl. Medal of Merit, 1992. Mem. AAAS, SPIE (conf. organizer 1995—), Am. Phys. Soc., Optical Soc. Am. Achievements include patents for means for photonic communication, computation, and distortion compensation; discovery of spin-two phonons. Office: Nutronics Inc 1668 E Clearview Dr Carson City NV 89701-6572

HOLMES, RICHARD DALE, secondary education educator, historical consultant; b. Sandown, N.H., Sept. 6, 1945; s. John B. Jr. and Marjorie A. (Andrews) H.; m. Carol A. Martineau, Dec. 19, 1970; children: John B. III, Leah K. BEd, Keene (N.H.) State Coll., 1968; MA, Rivier Coll., Nashua, N.H., 1980. Cert. tchr., N.H. Tchr. social studies Pelham (N.H.) Meml. Sch., 1968—, chmn. dept., 1975—; hist. cons., rschr. Sandown Mus., 1980-88, Chester (N.H.) Hist. Soc., 1989—. Author: View from Meeting House Hill, 1988, Derry, 1995, Chester Revisited, 1997. Pres. Old Meeting House Assn., Sandown, 1987—; trustee Bicentennial Mus., Derry, N.H., 1989—; mem. Derry Hist. Dist. Commn., 1988—, chmn. 1998—. With U.S. Army, 1969-71, Vietnam. Decorated Cross of Gallantry with palm, Civic Action medal 1st class (Vietnam). Mem. NEA, Pelham Edn. Assn. (v.p. 1976-77), N.H. Hist. Soc., Sandown Hist. Assn. (hist. cons., rschr. 1980-88, pres. 1986-87), Derry Hist. Soc., Nat. Fedn. Blind. Congregationalist. Avocations: collecting books, public speaking, research. Home: 33 Hillside Ave Derry NH 03038-2215 Office: Pelham Meml Sch 59 Marsh Rd Pelham NH 03076-3160

HOLMES, RICHARD WINN, lawyer, retired state supreme court justice; b. Wichita, Kans., Feb. 23, 1923; s. Winn Earl and Sidney (Clapp) H.; m. Gwen Sand, Aug. 19, 1950; children—Robert W., David K. B.S., Kans. State U., 1950; J.D., Washburn U., 1953, LLD (hon.), 1991. Bar: Kans. 1953, U.S. Dist. Ct. 1953. Practice law Wichita, Kans., 1953-77; judge Wichita Mcpl. Ct., 1959-61; instr. bus. law Wichita State U., 1959-60; justice Kans. Supreme Ct., 1977-90, chief justice, 1990-95; ret., 1995; of counsel Goodell, Stratton, Edmonds & Palmer, Topeka, 1995—. Served with USNR, 1943-46. Mem. ABA, Kans., Topeka, Wichita bar assns., Am. Judges Assn. (founder, bd. govs. 1980-88). Home: 2535 SW Granthurst Ave Topeka KS 66611-1271 Address: 515 S Kansas Ave Topeka KS 66603-3415

HOLMES, ROBERT EDWARD, photographer; b. Ilkeston, Derbyshire, Eng., Mar. 21, 1943; came to the U.S., 1979; s. Maurice E. and Marjorie E. (Jones) H.; m. Barbara Jane Perez, Aug. 16, 1979; children: Emma S., Hannah S. BS, U. London, 1964; diploma in town planning, Nottingham (Eng.) Coll. Art, 1967. Dep. planning officer Broxtowe Dist. Coun., Nottinghamshire, Eng., 1971-79; freelance photographer and writer Calif., 1979—; bd. mem. Survival Internat., London, 1973-79; pres. Am. Soc. Media Photographers, N.Y., 1984-85. Author, photographer: Thomas Cook Guide to California, 1993, Thomas Cook Guide to New England, 1994, Thomas Cook Guide to Hawaii, 1995; photographer: (series) Day in the Life, 1990-96, Spirits in Stone, 1993. Named Travel Photographer of Yr., Soc. Am. Travel Writers, 1990, 92. Fellow Royal Geog. Soc.; mem. Reform Club (London). Avocations: wine and food, mountaineering, jazz, painting. Home: PO Box 556 Mill Valley CA 94942-0556 Office: Robert Holmes Photography 3000 Bridgeway Sausalito CA 94965-1489

HOLMES, ROBERT EUGENE, state legislative consultant, journalist; b. Shelbyville, Ind., June 5, 1928; s. Eugene Lowell and Sarah Lucinda (Hughes) H.; m. Retha Carolyn Richey, June 27, 1955 (div. Sept. 1966); children: Enid Adair Offley, William Houstoun (dec.), Holly Ann Holmes. BA in Polit. Sci., DePauw U., 1950; MA in Journalism, Ind. U., 1953; MA in Communs. and Urban Affairs, Stanford U., 1976. Staff reporter Elkhart, Ind. Truth, 1954-57; city editor, investigative editor Press-Enterprise, Riverside, Calif., 1957-70; sr. cons. Calif. State Senate Dem. Caucus, Sacramento, 1971-74, dep. dir., 1978-79; press sec. Lt. Gov. of Calif., Sacramento, 1975-77; project dir. Border Area Devel. Study, U.S. Econ. Devel. Adminstrn., Sacramento, 1978; staff dep. dir. Calif. Senator Robert Presley, Sacramento, 1979-83; chief cons. Joint Legis. Ethics Com., Calif. Legislature, Sacramento, 1981-82; staff dir. Joint Com. on Prison Constrn. and Ops., Calif. Legislature, Sacramento, 1983-94; rsch. cons. Calif. Rsch. Bur., Calif. State Libr., Sacramento, 1991-92; cons. Calif. Hist. State Capitol Commn., 1995-96. Author, editor rschr. legis. reports; contbg. editor creative writing quar. Noah's Hotel, Inverness, Calif., 1991-98; editor/pub. sports newsletter weekly Big Red Ramblings, 1997—; contbr. articles to mags., short stories, 1961—. Pres., Golden Bear Dem. Club, Sacramento, 1972-74; media dir. Lt. Gov. Campaign, Sacramento and L.A., 1974. Sgt. USMC, 1951-53. Recipient Silver Gavel award ABA, 1969, 1st Place media award Calif. State Bar Assn., 1968, 1st Place award Calif. Newspaper Pubs. Best Series, 1969, 70, 71; Am. Polit. Sci. Assn. Ford Found. fellow Stanford U., 1970. Mem. NAACP, ACLU, Calif. Writers Club, Common Cause. Democrat. Avocations: bicycling, racquetball, world travel, short story writing. Home: 416 Florin Rd Sacramento CA 95831-2007

HOLMES, ROBERT WAYNE, service executive, consultant, biological historian; b. Brush, Colo., July 16, 1950; s. George William Jr. and Reba Mary (Sandel) H. BA, Western State Coll., 1972. Exec. Rose Exterminator Co., San Francisco, 1986-92; founder, owner BFE Cons., 1992—. Author: The Killing River, Countdown. Mem. Smithsonian Instn., Washington, 1986, Sta. KRMA-TV-PBS, Denver, 1987, Ft. Morgan (Colo.) Heritage Found., 1988, Ctr. for Study of Presidency, Wilson Ctr., Nat. Mus. Am. Indian, Nat. Trust for Hist. Preservation, 1994-95. Mem. AAAS, N.Y. Acad. Scis., Acad. Polit. Sci., Wilson Ctr. Assoc. Ctr. for Study of the Presidency, Am. Mus. Natural History, Nat. Trust for Hist. Preservation, Denver Mus. Natural History, Nat. Mus. Am. Indian, Nature Conservancy, FPCN, SoAm. Explorers Club.

HOLMES, ROSCETTE YVONNE LEWIS, organizational development and training consultant; b. Portland, Oreg., Dec. 1, 1944; d. Roscoe Warfield and Burnadine (Langston) Lewis; m. Johnny Mason Holmes, Jr., July 28, 971; children: Roderick Earl, Andriette Yvonne. BS, Tex. So. U., 1965, MS, 1970, EdD, 1991; postgrad., U. Houston, 1979. Cert. in adminstrn. and supervision; cert. family, civil and adolescent mediator. With Houston Ind. Sch. Dist., 1965-96, sch. tchr. E.O. Smith Jr. H.S., 1965-69, tchr. biology, coord. sch. sci. fair Madison Sr. H.S., 1970-74, mem. sci. content team Emergency Sch. Aid Act, 1974-76, staff. devel. specialist for tchr. tng., 1976-78, instrnl. specialist for sci. Area I, 1978-81, asst. prin. Hogg Mid. Sch., 1981-84, dir. chpt. I, 1984-90, asst. prin. Fleming Fine Arts Mid. Sch., 1990-96; owner, pres., CEO (tng. and orgnl. devel. consulting firm) Roscette's Diversified Svcs. and Assocs., Houston, 1996—; cons. Prairie View, Tchr. Corp, Peace Corps, 1976-78; cons. Ednl. Leadership Inst., Prescription Learning Inc.; endl. cons. North Forest Ind. Sch. Dist.; mem. Tex. adv. coun. Dept. Human Resources Adv. Bd., Tex., vice chair Tex. Adv. Coun. Social Work Cert. NSF grantee, 1968-70. Mem. ASCD, Houston Profl. Adminstrs., Experiment in Internat. Living, Top Ladies of Distinction Inc., Delta Sigma Theta (voter registration, Sch. After Sch. Project, hypertension screening, v.p., dean of probates 1967, v.p. 1980-81, pres. Suburban Houston-Ft. Bend Alumnae chpt. 1981-83, nat. membership intake trainer, nat. scholarship and standards com. 1997—), Phi Delta Kappa. Democrat. Episcopalian. Address: RDS & Assocs Orgnl Devel and Tng Cons 7919 Oakington Dr Ste D Houston TX 77071-2028

HOLMES, STEPHANIE ELEANOR, music educator, violinist; b. Frankfurt, Germany, Sept. 30, 1966; d. Thomas Gordon and Iramtroud Margerita (Klenk) H. BS in Sci. Edn., Va. Tech. Inst., 1988, MA in Music Edn., 1991; MMus in Orchestral Conducting, James Madison U., 1998. Cert. tchr., Va. Violinist, orch. libr. Virginia Beach (Va.) Symphony Orch., 1991-95; violinist Commonwealth Musical Stage, Virginia Beach, 1992-95, Hotel Paradise Roof Garden Orch., Norfolk, Va., 1992-96, Lynchburg (Va.) Symphony Orch., 1996—; orch. dir./strings specialist Tallwood H.S., Virginia Beach, 1992-95; asst. dir. orchs./grad. tchg. asst. James Madison U., 1995-97; dir. orchs. Lake Braddock Secondary Sch., Va.; mem. faculty string edn. George Mason U. Guest conductor Spring String Thing, Harrisonburg, 1996, 97, Virginia Beach All City Orch, 1997, Jr. Regional Orch. S.E. Dist. of Va., Virginia Beach, 1996, Norfolk All City Orch., 1995, 96. Powel Tchr.'s scholar State of Va., 1988. Mem. NEA, Nat. Sch. Orch. Assn. (sec. 1995-97), Music Educators Nat. Conf., Va. Band and Orch. Dir.'s Assn. Democrat. Avocations: painting, acting. Office: Lake Braddock Secondary Sch 9200 Burke Lake Rd Burke VA 22015-1682

HOLMES, STEPHEN T., political science and law educator; b. 1948. BA, Denison U., 1969; MA, Yale U., 1974, MPhil, 1975, PhD, 1976. From asst. to assoc. prof. Harvard U., 1979-85; prof. polit. sci. and law U. Chgo., 1985-96; prof. law Sch. Law NYU, 1996—; prof. polit. sci. Princeton (N.J.) U., 1996—. Office: NYU Sch Law 110 W 3d St New York NY 10012

HOLMES, SUE ELLEN, library director; b. Lawrence, Mass., Oct. 4, 1950; d. Francis Augustine and Katherine Elizabeth (Gallagher) H. MLS, U. R.I., 1977. Dir. children's svcs. Stevens Meml. Libr., North Andover, Mass., 1977-90; libr. dir. Stevens Meml. Libr., North Andover, 1990—. Mem. ALA, New Eng. Libr. Assn., Mass. Libr. Assn. Roman Catholic. Office: Stevens Meml Libr 345 Main St North Andover MA 01845-2636

HOLMES, SUZANNE MCRAE, nursing supervisor; b. Birmingham, Ala., June 23, 1952; d. Paul Bickman and Mabel E. (Tyler) McRae; m. Bryan Thomas Holmes, Jan. 14, 1989; 1 child, Meredith Rae. ADN, Jefferson State Coll., Birmingham, 1988. RN, Ala.; cert. BCLS instr.; cert. asthma educator, Am. Lung Assn. Staff nurse burn unit The Children's Hosp., Birmingham, 1988-89; staff nurse dept. medicine The Kirklin Clinic at U. Ala.-Birmingham, 1989-90, head nurse gen. medicine clinic, 1990-91, head nurse allergy clinic, 1991—; facilitator and spkr. on nursing edn. at asthma workshops Rorer Pharms., Collegeville, Pa., 1994—; mem. faculty Genecom, N.Y.C., 1994—; operator 1-800 Allergy Info. Svc., 1991-92. Editor Allergy Update, 1991-92. Mem. Am. Coll. Allergy and Immunology, Am. Acad. Allergy, Asthma and Immunology,mem. Am. Lung Assn. (cert. asthma educator), Asthma and Allergy Found. Am. (charter bd. dirs. Ala. chpt.). Presbyterian. Avocations: baking, sewing, gardening. Office: The Kirklin Clinic Allergy Clinic 4th Fl 2000 6th Ave S Birmingham AL 35233-2110

HOLMES, SUZON TROPEZ, financial analyst; b. New Orleans, Apr. 13, 1949; d. Maxwell Sterling and Ethel (Ross) Tropez; m. Mahlon Holmes, Sept. 19, 1969 (div. Mar. 1993); children: Sterling Christopher, Leslie Corine. BA in Biology, U. N.C., Greensboro, 1972; BS in Acctg., N.C. A&T State U., 1988; postgrad., St. Edwards U., 1997—. Med. technologist Moses Cone Hosp., Greensboro, 1972-73, Gate City Ob-Gyn. Office, Greensboro, 1973-75; charge technologist L. Richardson Hosp., Greensboro, 1976-79; lab. mgr. N.C. A&T STate U., 1979-87; acctg. aid John P. McDonald, CPA, 1987-88; lab technologist Ramsey County Hosp., St. Paul, 1989-91; acct. 3M Co., St. Paul, 1989-91; fin. analyst 3M Co., Austin, 1991—; med. technologist S. Austin Med. Ctr., 1993-97. leader Girl Scouts U.S., Greensboro, 1979-85; bd. dirs. Bell House Cerebral Palsy Home, Greensboro, 1981-84; adv. bd. health com. N.C. A&T State U., Greensboro, 1981-85; dir. choir Clev. United Meth. Ch., St. Paul, 1990-91; cons. Jr. Achievement Am., St. Paul, Austin, 1990-97; adv. bd. sch. bus. Austin C.C., 1996—. Mem. Am. Inst. CPA (bd. dirs. minority affairs), Nat. Assn. Black Accts. (pres. 1996—), Inst. Mgmt. Accts. (exam adminstr. 1992-95), Am. Soc. Clin. Pathologist. Avocations: reading, piano, needlepoint. Home: 311 Hunters Glen Dr Plainsboro NJ 08536

HOLMES, SVEN ERIK, federal judge; b. Grand Junction, Colo., Feb. 13, 1951; s. Clifford Newton and Ruth (Bradley) H.; m. Lois Romano, Oct. 31, 1983; children: Kristen Elizabeth Romano, Virginia Morgan Romano. AB, Harvard U., 1973; JD, U. Va., 1980; LLM, Georgetown U., 1987. Bar: Okla. 1980, D.C. 1985, U.S. Dist. Ct. D.C. 1985, U.S. Dist. Ct. (no., ea. and we. dists.) Okla. 1985, U.S. Ct. Appeals (10th and D.C. cirs.) 1985, U.S. Tax Ct. 1985, U.S. Ct. Claims 1985, U.S. Supreme Ct., 1994. Campaign coord. David L. Boren for Gov., Oklahoma City, 1975; adminstrv. asst. to gov. State of Okla., Oklahoma City, 1975-77; law clk. to judge U.S. Dist. Ct. (no. dist.) Okla., Tulsa, 1980-81; assoc. Doerner, Stuart, Saunders, Daniel & Anderson, Tulsa, 1981-83; exec. dir., counsel Dems. for "80's", Washington, 1983-85; spl. tax counsel senator David L. Boren, Washington, 1985; from assoc. to ptnr. Williams & Connolly, Washington, 1985-87, 89-95; designated liaison staff mem. Senate Select Com. on Secret Mil. Assistance to Iran, Washington, 1987; gen. counsel, staff dir. Senate Select Com. on Intelligence, Washington, 1987-89; v.p. Balt. Orioles, 1989-93. Mem. Okla. Bar Assn., D.C. Bar Assn. Lutheran. Avocations: reading, tennis. Office: US Dist Ct 411 US Courthouse 333 W 4th St Tulsa OK 74103-3839

HOLMES, TYRONE ANTHONY, performance consulting company executive, educator; b. Camden, N.J., Nov. 28, 1961; s. Coleman Anthony and Charlotte Louise (Pounds) H.; m. Angela T. Fowler, July 5, 1997. BS, Pa. State U., 1984, MEd, 1986, EdD, 1996; MS, SUNY, Oswego, 1989. Lic. profl. counselor, Mich. Coord. residence hall programs Pa. State U., State College, 1985-86, grad. tchg. asst., 1992-94; asst. dir. Hewitt Union, SUNY, Oswego, 1986-89; human resource mgr. Amerisure Cos., Jericho, N.Y., 1990-92; asst. prof. Eastern Mich. U., Ypsilanti, 1994-96, Wayne State U., Detroit, 1996—; pres. T.A.H. Performance Cons., Inc., Farmington Hills, Mich., 1996—. Contbr. chpts. to books. Mem. ACA, ASTD, Soc. for Human Resource Mgmt., Am. Coll. Pers. Assn. (exec. coun. rep. 1992—, Grad. Student award 1995, Annuit Coeptus award 1996), Nat. Career Devel. Assn., Mich. Career Devel. Assn. (post-secondary rep. 1995-97, pres. 1997—). Methodist. Avocations: running, reading, watching movies. Home and Office: 24907 Woodridge End Farmington Hills MI 48335

HOLMES, WALTER JOHN, public relations consultant, author; b. N.Y.C., June 9, 1906; s. William Henry and Anna Katherine (McArdle) H.; m. Ellen Irene Jennings, Nov. 5, 1938 (dec. Sept. 1975); 1 child, Ellen Misita; m. Grace Ellen Pritchard, Dec. 8, 1990. Grad. high sch., N.Y.C. With adv. dept. N.Y. Morning World, N.Y.C., 1921-22; printing pressman Henleo Press, N.Y.C., 1922-31; chief radio announcer Sta. WBNX - Voice of Bronx, N.Y.C., 1932-47; v.p. Bronx C. of C., N.Y.C., 1947-54; pub. rels. asst. Compt. of City of N.Y., 1954-63, 66-70; pub. rels. dir. Empire State C. of C., Albany, N.Y., 1963-66; pub. rels. asst. to compt. Audit and Control State of N.Y., Albany, 1971-79; pvt. practice Albany, 1979—; mem. faculty Northeastern Inst. Commerce & Trade Execs., Yale U., 1957; acting pub. rels. dir. Schenectady (N.Y.) County C.C., 1979-81; pub. rels. cons. N.Y. State Tchrs. Retirement Sys., Albany, 1983-87. Author: Essays & Poems of Walter J. Holmes, 1988. Publicity dir. Svc. Corps Retired Execs., Albany; sr. mem. Hudson Valley Writers Guild; life mem. Men's Garden Club Albany; assoc. mem. First Ch. in Albany (Reformed). Recipient Nat. Assn. Broadcasters award, 1945. Mem. Lions Club (life, pres. Bronx chpt. 1948-49, dist. gov. and internat. coun. 1950-51, internat. counselor Albany chpt. 1963—, Melvin Jones fellow), N.Y. Press Club, Am. Acad. Poets, Amherst Assn. Nat. Poetry Libr., Soc. of Silurians, Knight of Pythias, Elks (Troy bull. editor 1978, Disting. Citizens award 1985), Univ. Club Albany (poet-in-residence), Adirondack Mt. Club. Avocations: reading, writing, travel. Home and Office: 72 Pleasant View Ave Albany NY 12203-3215

HOLMGREN, MIKE, professional football coach; b. San Francisco, June 15, 1948; m. Kathy Holmgren; children: Gretchen, Emily, Jenny and Calla (twins). BS in Bus. Fin., U. So. Calif., 1970. Coach Lincoln High Sch., San Francisco, 1971-72, Sacred Heart High Sch., 1972-74, Oakgrove High Sch., 1975-80; quarterbacks coach, offensive coord. San Francisco State U., 1981-82; quarterbacks coach Brigham Young U., 1982-85; quarterbacks coach San Francisco 49ers, 1985-89, offensive coord., 1989-92; head coach Green Bay

Packers, 1992-98, Seattle Seahawks, 1999—. Office: Seattle Seahawks Kingdome 11220 NE 53rd St Kirkland WA 98033-7595*

HOLMGREN, MYRON ROGER, social sciences educator; b. Willmar, Minn., Mar. 19, 1933; s. Alfred and Cleora Victora (Scott) H.; m. Ellen Mary Shaheen, June 9, 1957; children: Brian, Mary Jo Haas. BA, Mankato State U., 1958; MA, No. Colo. State U., 1959. Instr. Grinnell (Iowa) H.S., 1959-62, Joliet (Ill.) Jr. Coll., 1962-66; instr., fin. advisor Am. Express Fin. Advisors, Joliet, 1966-72; instr. Benedictine Coll., Atchison, Kans., 1973, Moraine Valley C.C., Palos Hills, Ill., 1974-75; isntr. Minooka (Ill.) H.S., 1974—; dept. chmn. Minooka H.S., 1984-87, local dir. Xerox Award in Humanities, 1988-93, dir., coach Scholastic Bowl Team, 1976-93, chmn. philosophy & goals North Etrl. Accreditation, 1987-88. Author: Profitable Pricing Techniques, 1973; contbr. articles to profl. jours. Block chmn. March of Dimes, Am. Cancer Soc., 1989, 92-93; treas. bd. dirs. The Family Counseling Agy. of Will and Grundy Counties, 1996—. Asian Found. grantee, 1962. Mem. NEA, Ill. Edn. Assn., Ill. Assn. Econ. Tchrs., Ill. Consumer Edn. Assn., Internat. Platform Assn. Republican. Episcopal. Avocations: reading, writing, travel, gourmet cooking, market analysis. Home: 1314 Douglas St Joliet IL 60435-5814

HOLMGREN, PAUL, professional hockey coach; b. St. Paul; m. Doreen Holmgren; children: Jason, Kirsten, Wes, Greta. Student, U. Minn. Player Phila. Flyers, 1975-84, asst. coach, 1985-88, head coach, 1988-91; head coach Hartford Whalers, 1992-97; player Minn. North Stars, Mpls., 1984-85; dir. player personnel Phila. Flyers, 1997—. Office: Phila Flyers First Union Ctr 3601 S Broad St Philadelphia PA 19148*

HOLMQUEST, DONALD LEE, physician, astronaut, lawyer; b. Dallas, Apr. 7, 1939; s. Sidney Browder and Lillie Mae (Waite) H.; m. Ann Nixon James, Oct. 24, 1972. B.S. in Elec. Engring., So. Meth. U., 1962; M.D., Baylor U., 1967, Ph.D. in Physiology, 1968; J.D., U. Houston, 1980. Student engr. Ling-Temco-Vought, Dallas, 1958-61; electronics engr. Tex. Instruments, Inc., Dallas, 1962; intern Meth. Hosp., Houston, 1967-68; pilot tng. USAF, Williams AFB, Ariz., 1968-69; scientist-astronaut NASA, Houston, 1967-73; research assoc. MIT, 1968-70; asst. prof. radiology and physiology Baylor Coll. Medicine, 1970-73; dir. nuclear medicine Eisenhower Med. Ctr., Palm Desert, Calif., 1973-74; assoc. dean medicine, assoc. prof. Tex. A&M U., College Station, 1974-76; dir. nuclear medicine Navasota (Tex.) Med. Ctr., 1976-84, Med. Arts Hosp., Houston, 1977-85; ptnr. Wood Lucksinger & Epstein, Houston, 1980-91, Holmquest & Assocs., Houston, 1991—; v.p. legal affairs N.Am. Med. Mgmt., Inc., Nashville, 1995-96; asst. prof. internal medicine Baylor Coll. Medicine, Houston, 1999—. Contbr. articles to med. jours. Mem. Soc. Nuclear Medicine, Am. Coll. Nuclear Physicians, Tex. Bar Assn., Am. Fighter Pilots Assn., Sigma Xi, Alpha Omega Alpha, Sigma Tau. Home and Office: Holmquest and Assocs 109 Marrakech Ct Bellaire TX 77401-5117

HOLMSTEAD, JEFFREY RALPH, lawyer; b. American Fork, Utah, June 20, 1960; s. R. Kay and Mary L. (Gillison) H.; m. Elizabeth Tisdel, Aug. 17, 1985; children: Emily Kay, Eric Noble, Elizabeth Anne, Eli Jeffrey. BA, Brigham Young U., 1984; JD, Yale U., 1987. Bar: Pa. 1988, D.C. 1998. Jud. clk. to Hon. Douglas H. Ginsburg D.C. Cir. Ct. Appeals, Washington, 1987-88; assoc. Davis Polk & Wardwell, Washington, 1988-89; asst. counsel to Pres. of U.S. The White House, Washington, 1989-90, assoc. counsel, 1990-93; assoc. Latham & Watkins, Washington, 1993-95, ptnr., 1996—. Republican. Mem. LDS Ch. Office: Latham & Watkins Ste 1300 1001 Pennsylvania Ave NW Washington DC 20004-2585

HOLNESS, GORDON VICTOR RIX, engineering executive, mechanical engineer; b. London, Sept. 6, 1939; came to U.S., 1969; s. Ernest Arthur and Ivy A. (Rix) H.; m. Susan F. Sage (dec.); m. Audrey A. Bezz, Apr. 18, 1984. Cert., Croydon Tech. Coll., Surrey, Eng., 1962; diploma in environ. engring., Nat. Coll., London, 1964. Registered profl. engr. Mich., Minn., Tex., Conn., Calif., Kans., Colo., Fla., Ariz., N.Y., D.C., Ala., N.C., Ky., Ohio, Mo., Tenn., Ill., Ont., Can. Design engr. West Sussex County Coun., Chichester, Sussex, Eng., 1956-59, C. McKechnie Jarvis & Ptnrs., London, 1959-64, Barlow Leslie & Ptnrs., Croydon, 1964; sr. engr. R. J. Tamblyn & Ptnrs., Toronto, Ont., Can., 1964-66; asst. chief engr. Giffels Assocs., Windsor, Ont., Can., 1966-69; from asst. chief engr. to pres. and CEO, bd. dirs. Albert Kahn Assocs. Inc., Detroit, 1969—, also bd. dirs. Contbr. articles to profl. jours. Bd. dirs. YMCA, Mt. Clemens, Mich., 1980-82. Fellow ASHRAE (chmn. energy mgmt. com. 1987, chmn. govt. affairs com. 1989); mem. NSPE, Am. Cons. Engrs. Coun., Chartered Inst. Bldg. Svcs. of Eng., Engring. Soc. Detroit, Mich. Soc. Profl. Engrs. (v.p. 1986, fellow 1998), Detroit Econ. Club (bd. dirs.). Republican. Presbyterian. Avocations: golf, tennis, racquetball, chess, sailing. Home: 55 S Edgewood Dr Grosse Pointe MI 48236-1226 Office: Albert Kahn Assocs Inc 7430 2nd Ave Ste 800 Detroit MI 48202-2798

HOLOD, RENATA, historian; b. Sept. 6, 1942. BA with hons., U. Toronto, 1964; AM, U. Mich., 1965; PhD, Harvard U., 1972. Prof. U. Pa., Phila., 1972-77, 80—. Recipient Agakhan award for arch., Geneva, 1977-80. E-mail: rholod@sas.upenn.edu. Office: History Art Dept Univ Pa 3405 Woodland Walk Philadelphia PA 19104-6208

HOLONYAK, NICK, JR., electrical engineering educator; b. Zeigler, Ill., Nov. 3, 1928; s. Nick and Anna (Rosoha) H.; m. Katherine R.A. Jerger, Oct. 8, 1955. BS, U. Ill., 1950, MS, 1951, PhD (Tex. Instruments fellow), 1954; DSc (hon.), Northwestern U., 1992; DEng. (hon.), Notre Dame U., 1994. Mem. tech. staff Bell Telephone Labs., Murray Hill, N.J., 1954-55; physicist, unit mgr., mgr. advanced semiconductor lab. Gen. Electric Co., Syracuse, N.Y., 1957-63; prof. elec. engring. and materials research lab. U. Ill., Urbana, 1963—, John Bardeen chair prof. elec. & computer engring. & physics, 1993—; mem. Center Advanced Study, 1977—; series editor Prentice-Hall, Inc., 1962—; cons. Monsanto Co., 1964-89, Nat. Electronics Co., 1963-70, Skil Corp., 1967, GTE Labs. Tech. Adv. Council, 1973, Xerox, 1983-87, Ameritech, 1985-86. Author: (with others) Semiconductor Controlled Rectifiers, 1964, Physical Properties of Semiconductors, 1989. Served with U.S. Army, 1955-57. Recipient Cordiner award GE, 1962, John Scott medal City of Phila., 1975, GaAs Conf. award with Welker medal 1976, Monie A. Ferst award Sigma Xi, 1988, Nat. Medal Sci. NSF, 1990, NAS award Indsl. Application Sci., 1993, ASEE Centennial medal, 1993, 50th Ann. award Am. Elec. Assn., 1993, Japan Prize, 1995. Fellow. IEEE (life, Morris Liebmann award 1973, Jack A. Morton award 1981, Edison medal 1989), Am. Acad. Arts and Scis., Am. Phys. Soc., Am. Optical Soc. (Charles H. Townes award 1992), Internat. Engring. Consortium; mem. AAAS, NAE, NAS (Indsl Application of Sci. award 1993), Electrochem. Soc. (Solid State Sci. and Tech. award 1983), Math. Assn. Am., Ioffe Inst. (hon. 1992), Minerals, Metals and Materials Soc. (John Bardeen award 1995), Russian Acad. Scis. (fgn. mem.), Eta Kappa Nu (Karapetoff Eminent Mems. award 1994, eminent mem. 1998), Tau Beta Pi (Outstanding Alumnus award 1999). Home: 2212 Fletcher St Urbana IL 61801-6915 Office: U Ill Dept Elec/ Computer Engring 1406 W Green St Urbana IL 61801-2918

HOLOUBEK, JOE, physician; b. Clarkson, Nebr., Sept. 9, 1915; s. Joe and Marie (Kucera) H.; m. Alice Baker, July 18, 1939; children: Mary Josephine, Brian, Robert, Martha Alice. BS, U. Nebr., 1937, MD, 1938. Diplomate Am. Bd. Internal Medicine. Intern Univ. Hosp., Omaha, 1938-39; fellow dept. medicine La. State U. Sch. Medicine, New Orleans, 1939-41; clin. assoc. prof. medicine La. State U. Sch. Medicine, Shreveport, 1958-68, 68-72, clin. prof. medicine, 1972-90, clin. prof. emeritus, 1990—; del. task force on aging State of La. from Diocese of Shreveport, 1986-88; mem. com. on aging La. Interfaith Conf., 1988—. Assoc. editor: The Linacre Quarterly, 1967-78. Maj. U.S. Army med. corps, 1941-46. Recipient Diocesan medal of honor Bishop William B. Friend, 1995; appt. to Knight Comdr. of Order of St. Gregory the Great by Pope John XXIII, 1962, Knight of the Equestrian Order of the Holy Sepulchre of Jerusalem by Pope Paul VI, 1978, Knight Comdr. of the Order by Pope John Paul II, 1983, Knight Commander with Star, 1988, Knight of the Grand Cross of the Order, 1993, Knight Commander with Star of Order of St. Gregory the Great, Pope John Paul II, 1999. Fellow Am. Coll. Cardiology, Am. Coll. Physicians Laureate award 1987), Coun. Clin. Cardiology, N.Y. Acad. Scis.; mem. AMA, AHA (bd. dirs. 1955-58, Disting. Achievement award 1970), So. Med. Assn., La. Heart Assn. bd. dirs. 1950-70, pres. 1956), Shreveport Med. Soc. (Disting. Svc. award 1967), La. State Med. Assn., Nat. Fedn. Cath. Physicians Guilds (del. 1952-65, 70—, 2d v.p. 1957-59, v.p. 1959-61, pres. 1961-63), Am. Fedn. Clin. Rsch. (sr. mem.), So. Soc. Geriatric Medicine (founding mem.), Knights of St. Gregory the Great (pres. La. Conf. 1989-90), Cath. Acad. of Scis. of U.S. of Am. (academician 1990—), Nu Sigma Nu, others.

HOLOVAK, MIKE, sports association executive; b. Lansford, PA; m. Pauline Holovak; children: Michelle, Cindy. Student, Boston Coll. Football player Los Angeles Rams, Los Angeles, CA, 1946, Chicago Bears, Chicago, IL, 1947-48; coach jr. varsity Boston College, MA, 1949-50; head coach Boston College, MA, 1951-59; dir. player pers. Boston Patriots (now New England Patriots), Foxboro, MA, 1959-61, head coach, 1961-68, gen. mgr., 1964-68, pers. asst., 1977, dir. coll. scouting, 1978; with San Francisco 49ers, San Francisco, CA, 1969-70, Oakland Raiders, 1971, N.Y. Jets, 1972-76; various positions including dir. player pers., asst. gen. mgr. Tenn. Oilers (formerly Houston Oilers), 1981-89, exec. v.p., gen. mgr., 1989-1992, exec vp., gen. manager, 1992-97; v.p., dir. regional scouting Houston Oilers, 1997—. Inductee State of Pa. Hall of Fame, 1983, Orange Bowl Hall of Honor, 1984. Office: Tenn Titans Bapt Sports Pk 7640 Hwy 70 S Nashville TN 37221*

HOLQUIST, JAMES MICHAEL, Russian and comparative literature educator; b. Rockford, Ill., Dec. 20, 1935; s. Leonard and Billye Alverta (Appleby) H.; m. Lydia Landis, July 30, 1960 (div. Dec. 1972); children: Peter Isaac, Benjamin Michael, Joshua Appleby; m. Katerina Clark, Apr. 15, 1974 (separated May 1998); children: Nicholas Manning, Sebastian. B.A. with highest honors, U. Ill., 1963; Ph.D., Yale U., 1968. Asst. prof. Yale U., New Haven, 1968-72, assoc. prof., 1972-75; assoc. prof., dept. chmn. U. Tex., Austin, 1976-78, prof., 1978-80; prof. Slavic langs. and lit. dept., chmn. Ind. U., Bloomington, 1981-85; prof. comparative lit., dir. lit. major Yale U., New Haven, 1986-91; chair coun. on Russian and East European studies Yale U., 1992-98, chair Dept. Comparative Lit., 1998—; Gauss lectr. Princeton U., 1991; exchangee Soviet Acad. Scis., 1983; mem. exec. com. and editl. bd. PMLA. Author: (with Kernan and Brooks) Man and His Fictions, 1973, Dostoevsky and the Novel, 1977, reprinted, 1986; editor: (co-translator) The Dialogic Imagination: Four Essays by M.M. Bakhtin, 1981, (with Katerina Clark) Mikhail Bakhtin, 1984, Dialogism: The World of Mikhail Bakhtin, 1990, Philosophy of the Act, 1993; editor-in-chief: Tex. Slavic Studies, 1980; co-editor: Ind. Soviet Studies, 1982; editorial bd.: Yearbook of Comparative and Gen. Lit., 1982, Slavic Rev., 1983. Served with U.S. Army, 1958-61. Rockefeller Humanities fellow, 1983; vis. scholar Phi Beta Kappa, 1984-85; grantee NEH, 1979, 94, Morse fellow Yale U., 1970. Mem. MLA, Am. Assn. Advancement of Slavic Studies, Internat. Bakhtin Soc. (newsletter editor 1982—), Internat. Dostoevsky Soc., Am. Assn. Tchrs. Slavic and East European Langs., Grotesque Club, Mory's Assocs., Elizabethean Club. Democrat. Home: 180 Linden St Apt H3 New Haven CT 06511-2459

HOLROYD, MICHAEL, author; b. London, Aug. 27, 1935; s. Basil and Ulla (Hall) H.; m. Margaret Drabble. Author: Lytton Strachey, 1968, 2d edit., 1994 (filmed as Carrington), Augustus John, 1975, 2d edit., 1996, Bernard Shaw, 1988-93, abridged edit., 1997. Mem. PEN (pres. Eng. chpt. 1986-88), Soc. Authors (chmn. 1973-74), Arts Coun. of Eng. (chmn. lit. panel 1992-95), Royal Soc. of Lit. (chmn. 1998—). Office: care Lescher & Lescher Ltd 47 E 19th St New York NY 10003-1323

HOLROYD, RICHARD ALLEN, research scientist; b. Jamestown, N.Y., Dec. 31, 1930; s. Edmond W. and Effie I. (Carlson) H.; m. Dwana C. Holroyd, May 11, 1957; children: Thomas, Scott. BA, Wooster Coll., 1952; PhD, Rochester U., 1956. Asst. prof. UCLA, Jogjakarta, Indonesia, 1957-59; researcher Mellon Inst., Pitts., 1959-64, Atomics Internat., Canoga Park, Calif., 1964-69, Brookhaven Nat. Lab., Upton, N.Y., 1969—; sr. scientist, 1989—. Contbr. numerous articles about radiation chemical effects in nonpolar liquids to profl. jours. Recipient Humboldt award Germany, 1975. Office: Brookhaven Nat Lab Bldg 555 Upton NY 11973

HOLSAPPLE, LINDA HARRIS, retired editor; b. New Rochelle, N.Y., Nov. 20, 1948; d. Herbert Barney and Elizabeth (Curren) Harris; m. Earle Taylor Holsapple III; children: Elizabeth, John. BS in Intermediate Edn., Loyola U., Chgo., 1971; MA in Higher Edn. Adminstrn., Cath. U., 1973; postgrad., U. Va., 1975. Classroom tchr., admissions counselor various colls., 1971-78; comm. specialist, editor Rutgers Cmty. Health Plan, New Brunswick, N.J., 1978-85; ret. Editor Rutgers Cmty. Health Plan Member News, 1979-85. leader, cons. Warren (N.J.) Girl Scouts, 1987-96; leader Warren Cub Scouts, 1993-97. Mem. PTO (chair nomination com.). Avocations: nature hiking, leading school and scout hikes. Home: 281 Kercheval Ave Grosse Pointe MI 48236-3105

HOLSCHER, ROBERT F., county official. Dir., ceo Kenton County Airport Bd, Hebron, Ky., 1961—. Office: Kenton County Airport Bd PO Box 752000 Cincinnati OH 45275-2000 also: Cin/NoKY Internat Airport Terminal 1 2939 Terminal Dr Hebron KY 41048*

HOLSCHUH, JOHN DAVID, federal judge; b. Ironton, Ohio, Oct. 12, 1926; s. Edward A. and Helen (Ebert) H.; m. Carol Eloise Stouder, May 25, 1952; 1 child, John David Jr. BA, Miami U., 1948; JD, U. Cin., 1951. Bar: Ohio 1951, U.S. Dist. Ct. (so. dist.) Ohio 1952, U.S. Ct. Appeals (6th cir.) 1953, U.S. Supreme Ct. 1956. Atty. McNamara & McNamara, Columbus, Ohio, 1951-52, 54; law clk. to Hon. Mell. G. Underwood U.S. Dist. Ct., Columbus, 1952-54; ptnr. Alexander, Ebinger, Holschuh, Fisher & McAlister, Columbus, Ohio, 1954-80; judge U.S. Dist. Ct. (so. dist.) Ohio, 1980—, chief judge, 1990-96; adj. prof. law Ohio State U. Coll. Law, 1970; mem. com. on codes of conduct Jud. Conf. U.S., 1985-90. Pres. bd. dirs. Neighborhood House, Columbus, 1969-70; active United Way of Franklin County, Columbus. Fellow Am. Coll. Trial Lawyers; mem. Order of Coif, Phi Beta Kappa, Omicron Delta Kappa. Home: 2630 Charing Rd Columbus OH 43221-3628 Office: US Dist Ct 109 US Courthouse 85 Marconi Blvd Rm 109 Columbus OH 43215-2823

HOLSCHUH, JOHN DAVID, JR., lawyer; b. Columbus, Ohio, Dec. 21, 1955; s. John D. and Carol Elouise (Stouder) H.; m. Wendy G. Ellis, Sept. 22, 1984; children: Heather Elyse, John David III, Jacob Alexander. BS, Miami U., Oxford, Ohio, 1977; JD, U. Cin., 1980. Bar: Ohio 1980, U.S. Dist. Ct. (so. dist.) Ohio 1980, U.S. Ct. Appeals (6th cir.) 1986, U.S. Supreme Ct. 1986, U.S. Dist. Ct. (ea. dist.) Ky. 1987, Ky. 1991. Assoc. Santen, Shaffer & Hughes, Cin., 1980-87, ptnr., 1987-89; ptnr. Santen & Hughes, Cin., 1989—; pros. atty. City of Loveland, Ohio, 1987-92, magistrate, 1992—; mem. faculty Nat. Inst. Trial Advocacy, 1990, 91, 96; participant Pretrial Civil Litigation Skills Workshop, 1991. Author: Medical Malpractice, 1986, Tort Reform Pleading, 1987, Civil Procedure, 1986, rev. edit., 1989, Damages for Plaintiff and Defense Attorneys in Ohio, 1990, 2d edit., 1991, Tort Reform Update, 1990. Recipient Merit award Ohio Legal Ctr. Inst., 1986. Mem. ATLA, Ohio Acad. Trial Lawyers (trustee 1991-95, 1998—), Ohio State Bar Assn., Hamilton County Trial Lawyers (pres. 1990-92), Cin. Bar Assn. (chmn. common pleas ct. 1991-93, trustee 1995—, co-chmn. bench-bar conf. 1997-98, sec. 1999—), 6th Cir. Jud. Conf. (del. 1983-88, life mem.), Potter Stewart Inns of Ct. (emeritus mem.), Order of Barristers. Avocations: sports, travel. Office: Santen & Hughes 312 Walnut St Ste 3100 Cincinnati OH 45202-4044

HOLSEN, JAMES NOBLE, JR., retired chemical engineer; b. Palo Alto, Calif., June 20, 1924; s. James N. and Esther (Giltrud) H.; m. Nancy Schwankhaus, Feb. 24, 1950 (div.); children—James Noble III, David Edwards; m. Margot Meyer Best, Nov. 11, 1977; stepchildren—Victoria, Christopher, John. B.S., Princeton U., 1948; D.Sc., Washington U., St. Louis, 1954. Registered profl. engr., Mo. Chem. engr. Olin Mathieson Chem. Corp., 1954-55; asst. prof. chem. engring. Washington U., 1955-58, assoc. prof., 1958-61, prof., 1961-73; prof. chem. engring. U. Mo.-Rolla, 1973-74, vis. prof. engring. mgmt., 1974-75; program mgr. McDonnell Douglas Corp., St. Louis, 1977-92; ret., 1992; cons. chem. engring. and aerospace scis.; vis. prof. engring. Kabul U., Afghanistan, 1963-64, 69-73; mem. U.S. Engring. Team, Kabul, 1963-64, 69-73. Served with AUS, 1942-46. Fellow AIAA (assoc.); mem. Am. Inst. Chem. Engrs. (chmn. St. Louis sect. 1962), Am. Chem. Soc., Am. Soc. Engring. Edn., AAAS, Ethical Soc. Sigma Xi, Tau Beta Pi. Club: Princeton Quadrangle. Achievements include research on gas phase reaction kinetics, gaseous transport properties, materials processing in space, satellite components and structure, thermodynamics. Active in environmental affairs with St. Louis Audubon Soc. Home: 419 E Argonne Dr Kirkwood MO 63122-4523

HOLSEN, ROBERT CHARLES, accountant; b. Manitowoc, Wis., Nov. 10, 1913; s. Herman J. and Lilly (Krumm) H.; m. Constance Weber, Nov. 18, 1938; children: Robert Charles, Catherine Jane. Ph.B., U. Wis., 1938. C.P.A., Wis. Staff accountant Ernst & Ernst, Chgo., 1938-56; partner Ernst & Ernst (Nashville office), 1956-62; partner Ernst & Ernst (Cleve. office), 1962-76, cons., 1976—. Served to lt. comdr. USNR, 1944-46. Mem. Am. Inst. C.P.A.s (com. on auditing procedure, spl. com. on quality control, spl. com. on equity funding), Ohio Soc. C.P.A.s. Club: Masons. Home: 182 Valley Frg Nashville TN 37205-4706 Office: 414 Union St Ste 2100 Nashville TN 37219-1779*

HOLSINGER, JAMES WILSON, JR., physician; b. Kansas City, Kans., May 11, 1939; s. James Wilson and Ruth Leona (Reitz) H.; m. Barbara Jenn Craig, Dec. 28, 1963; children: Anna Elizabeth, Martha Ruth, Sarah Frances, Rachel Catherine. Student Duke U., 1957-60, MD, 1964, PhD, 1968; MS, U. S.C., 1981, B.A. U. Kentucky, 1997, D.S. (hon.), Pikeville Coll., 1996. Intern, Duke U. Hosp., Durham, N.C., 1964, resident in surgery, 1965, fellow in thoracic surgery, 1966; fellow in anatomy Duke U., Durham, 1966-68; resident in surgery U. Fla., Gainesville, 1968-70, fellow in cardiology, 1970-72; with VA, 1969-94, chief of staff VA Med. Ctr., Augusta, Ga., 1978-81; dir. VA Med. Ctr., Richmond, Va., 1981-90, Lexington, Ky., 1993-94; chief med. dir. Dept. Vets.' Affairs, Washington, 1990-93; under Sec. Health, 1992-93; prof. medicine and anatomy Med. Coll. Ga., Augusta, 1978-81; prof. medicine and health adminstrn. Med. Coll. Va., Richmond, 1981-93; asst. v.p. health scis. Va. Commonwealth U., Richmond, 1985-90; chancellor med. ctr. U. Ky., Lexington, 1994—, prof. medicine, surgery and anatomy coll. medicine, 1994—; prof. health care adminstrn. Coll. Allied Health Profls., 1994—. Author, editor med. and religious books; contbr. articles to med. and religious publs. Mem. com. evangelism N. Ga. conf. United Meth. Ch., 1980-81; mem. com. 80, World Meth. Coun., 1981—, mem. bd. discipleship Va. Conf., 1982-86, lay mem., 1984-93, assoc. dist. lay leader, 1983-84, dist. lay leader, 1984-86, conf. lay leader, 1986-92, conf. chmn. health and welfare minisitries, Ky., 1996—, Ky. conf. lay mem., 1996—, del. gen. conf., 1988, 92, 96, del. S.E. jurisdictional conf., 1988, 92, 96; mem. exec. com. World Meth. Coun., 1986—, treas. 1993—, mem. gen. coun. on ministries United Meth. Ch., 1988—, mem. Gen. Bd. Pubs., 1992-96, bd. dirs. United Methodist Pub. House, 1996—; commr. Joint Commn. on the Accrediation of Healthcare Orgns, 1996—. Maj. gen. M.C., USAR, 1989-92. Fellow ACP, Am. Coll. Cardiology, Am. Coll. Healthcare Execs. (Gold Medal award 1993); mem. Am. Assn. Anatomists, Am. Heart Assn. (fellow clin. coun.), Soc. Med. Adminstrs., Internat. Brotherhood Magicians (order of Merlin), Ret. Officers Assn. (bd. dirs. 1998—). Republican. Home: 4705 Waterside Ct Lexington KY 40513-1424 Office: U Ky Chandler Med Ctr Office of Chancellor A-301 Kentucky Clinic Lexington KY 40536-0284

HOLSINGER, WAYNE TOWNSEND, retail executive, retired; b. Trafford, Pa., Apr. 9, 1931; s. John C. and Cora I. (Brethauer) H.; m. Marilyn Kay Wynn, May 25, 1957; 1 child, Deborah Kay. EdB, S.W. Mo. Univ., 1958. With Sears Roebuck & Co., 1956-86, v.p. wearing apparel, 1976-81, sr. exec., v.p. sales and mktg., 1981-86; owner, chief exec. officer Washington Apparel Group, Inc., Franklin, Ky., 1986-91, ret., 1991; Mem. Fathers Day Coun. div. Am. Inst. Mens and Boyswear. Former bd. dirs. Chgo. Boys Club; dir. Better Bus. Bur., 1981-96. With USN, 1950-54. Mem. Men's Fashion Assn. Republican. Mem. Ch. of Christ. Home: 3525 S Cass Ct Oak Brook IL 60523-2633

HOLST, SANFORD, strategic consulting executive, author; b. Batavia, N.Y., Nov. 4, 1946; s. William Walker and Catherine (Loggie) H.; children: Suzanne, Kristina. BS in Aero., Astronautics, MIT, 1968; MBA, UCLA, 1970. Engr. advanced design group Lockheed Aircraft Corp., Los Angeles, 1968-71; analyst UCLA, Los Angeles, 1972-73, So. Calif. Assn. Govts., Los Angeles, 1973-78; systems analyst Northwest Industries, Los Angeles, 1978-80; v.p. computer systems dept. Parsons Corp., Pasadena, Calif., 1980-93; pres. The Holst Group, L.A., 1993—. Author: Kombucha Phenemenon, 1995; editor Taurus mag., 1971-72; contbr. articles to profl. jours. Vice chmn. Beverly Hills (Calif.) Bicentennial Com., 1976. Mem. Phi Kappa Sigma (pres. Alpha Mu chpt. 1967-68). Office: Holst Group 14755 Ventura Blvd Ste 413 Sherman Oaks CA 91403-3669

HOLSTAD, SCOTT CAMERON, writer, network specialist; b. Beverly, Mass., Sept. 19, 1966; s. Vernon Floyd and Nancy Elizabeth (Lipscomb) H.; m. Lisa Mary Lundgren, Jan. 8, 1994. BA in English, U. Tenn., Knoxville, 1990; MA in English, U. Calif., Long Beach, 1994. Instr. Calif. State U., Long Beach, 1992-94; editl. coord. TSI Inc., L.A., 1994-96, internet svcs. architect, 1995-96; assoc. prof. DeVry Inst., Pomona, Calif., 1995; tech. writer, editor Earthlink Network, Pasadena, Calif., 1996-97, documentation specialist, 1997, sr. documentation specialist, 1997—; cons. Wireme Cons., L.a., 1995—. Author: Junction City, 1993, Distant Visions, 1994, Binge, 1994, Places, 1995 (Pulitzer prize nomination 1996). Mem. PEN, Soc. Tech. Commn. (v.p. 1996—), Author's Guild, Acad. Am. Poets, Soc. Computer Profls., Usenix. Avocations: writing, computer games, mountain biking, reading. E-mail: schewell.com. Home: PO Box 10608 Glendale CA 91209

HOLSTEAD, JOHN BURNHAM, lawyer; b. Dallas, Mar. 5, 1938; s. J.B. and Maurice (Cook) H.; m. Marilyn Morris, Nov. 23, 1963; children: Will, Rand, Scott. B.A., La. Tech. U., 1959; LL.B., U. Tex.-Austin, 1962. Bar: Tex., U.S. Dist. Ct. Tex. 1965, U.S. Ct. Appeals (5th cir.), U.S. Ct. Appeals (loth cir.), U.S. Supreme Ct. 1974. Briefing clk. Tex. Sup. Ct., 1962-63; assoc. Vinson & Elkins, Houston, 1965-72, ptnr., 1972—; dir. Goodwill Industries of Houston, Inc.; speaker civil litigation and bus. disputes. Fellow Internat. Soc. Barristers, Houston Bar Found., Tex. Bar Found.; mem. ABA, Tex. Bar Assn., Houston Bar Assn. Episcopalian. Club: River Oaks Country. Office: Vinson & Elkins 3200 First City Tower 1001 Fannin St Ste 3300 Houston TX 77002-6760

HOLSTEIN, DAVID, psychotherapist, management consultant, educator; b. N.Y.C., Apr. 9, 1934; s. Morris and Esther (Newman) H.; m. Anita Elizabeth Morell, Sept. 8, 1957; children: Gregory Andrew, Christopher Daniel, Carrie Jacqueline. BA, CCNY, 1955; MA, Lehigh U., 1957. Nat. cert. counselor, clin. hypnotherapist, Ericksonian clin. therapist. With IBM, 1957-87; numerous mktg. and product devel. positions IBM, White Plains, 1957-70; dir. planning system corp. staff IBM, Armonk, N.Y., 1971-72; dir. planning, market devel., product evaluation IBM, White Plains, 1973-75, dir. market research Gen. Bus. Group, 1975-79, dir. strategic mgmt. Gen. Bus. Group, 1980-81, dir. organ and exec. rsch. ISCG, 1982-85; v.p. mgmt. services Entry Systems div. IBM, Boca Raton, Fla. and Montvale, N.Y., 1985-86; dir. Somers project office Infosystem and Support Group IBM, White Plains, 1987; bus. cons. White Plains, 1987-88; founder, pres., exec. dir. The Hudson Ctr., Cornwall-on-Hudson, N.Y., 1988—; prof. counseling Long Island U., 1997—. Author: (books) Management Systems, 1976, Digital Computers in Engring., 1977; Contbr. articles to profl. jours. Pres., trustee Cornwall Bd. of Edn., Cornwall, N.Y., 1976-78; trustee Mt. St. Mary Coll., Newburgh, N.Y., 1978-85, Orange County Hospice, Goshen, N.Y., 1985—, Orange County Family Counseling, Newburgh, 1986—. Mem. Am. Assn. for Counseling and Devel., Am. Psychol. Assn. Democrat. Roman Catholic. Avocation: jogging, reading. Home: 3 Idlewild Park Dr Cornwall On Hudson NY 12520-1047 Office: Hudson Ctr 276 Hudson St Cornwall On Hudson NY 12520-1016

HOLSTEIN, JAY ALLEN, Judaic studies educator; b. Phila., Mar. 22, 1938; s. Jules B. and Belle (Kellman) H.; m. Ellen Susanne Holstein, Oct. 5, 1997; children: Sarah Abigail, Joshua Saul. AB, Temple U., 1960; B in Hebrew Lit., Hebrew Union Coll., N.Y.C., 1962, M in Hebrew Lit., 1966; PhD, Hebrew Union Coll., Cin., 1970. Ordained rabbi, 1966. J.J. Mallon prof. Judaic studies Sch. Religion U. Iowa, Iowa City, 1970—, endowed chair Judaic studies, 1976; mem. faculty Senate, 1995—. Author: The Jewish Experience, 1989; contbr. articles to profl. publs.; mem. editorial bd. Counseling and Values, 1984—. Recipient Collegiate Teaching award, 1991. Democrat. Avocations: marathon running, tae kwon do. Home: 540 West Side Dr Iowa City IA 52246-4353 Office: U Iowa Sch Religion 404 Gilmore Hall Iowa City IA 52242-1320

HOLSTEIN, JOHN CHARLES, state supreme court judge; b. Springfield, Mo., Jan. 10, 1945; s. Clyde E. Jr. and Wanda R. (Polson) H.; m. Mary Frances Brummell, Mar. 26, 1967; children: Robin Diane Camacho, Mary Katherine Link, Erin Elizabeth. BA, S.W. Mo. State Coll., 1967; JD, U. Mo., 1970; LLM, U. Va., 1995. Bar: Mo. 1970. Atty. Moore & Brill, West Plains, Mo., 1970-75; probate judge Howell County, West Plains, 1975-78, assoc. cir. judge, 1978-82; cir. judge 37th Jud. Cir., West Plains, 1982-87; judge so. dist. Mo. Ct. Appeals, Springfield, 1987-88, chief judge so. dist., 1988-89; judge Supreme Ct. Mo., Jefferson City, 1989—, chief justice, 1995-97; instr. bus. law S.W. Mo. State Coll., 1976-77. Lt. col. USAR, 1969-87. Office: Supreme Ct Mo PO Box 150 Jefferson City MO 65102-0150

HOLSTEIN, WILLIAM KURT, business administration educator; b. Stamford, Conn., Nov. 19, 1936; s. Kurt Edward and Doris Christiana (Werner) H.; m. Audrey Louise Bedford, Aug. 15, 1959; children: Kurt Edward II, William Kurt Jr., Catherine Louise. BChE, Rensselaer Poly. Inst., Troy, N.Y., 1958; MS in Indsl. Mgmt., Purdue U., 1959, PhD in Econs., 1964. Instr., then asst. prof. indsl. mgmt. Purdue U., 1959-64; asst. prof., then assoc. prof. Harvard U. Grad. Sch. Bus. Adminstrn., 1964-72; prof. SUNY, Albany, 1972—, disting. svc. prof., 1991—, dean sch. of bus., 1972-81, 86-87, exec. dir. Inst. for Study of Info. Sci., 1988—; dir. Ctr. for Pvt. Enterprise Devel., Budapest, Hungary, 1991-93; dir. exec. devel. programs in Singapore, Taiwan and Central Am., 1969—, cons. to industry and govt.; vis. prof. IMEDE, Lausanne, Switzerland, 1983-85. Co-author: Production Planning and Control, 1963, Casebooks in Production Management, 1968, BASIC: Concepts and Applications, 1987; author articles in field. Trustee Upsala Coll., 1969-72; mem. accreditation com., editorial adv. com., visitation teams Am. Assembly of Collegiate Schs. of Bus., 1972-81; mem. exec. com. Middle Atlantic Assn. Schs. Bus. Adminstrn., 1976-81, pres., 1980; bd. dirs. Albany Symphony Orch., 1976—; bd. dirs., treas., v.p. adminstrn. Parsons Child and Family Center, Albany, 1977-94 , pres., 1989-92; chmn. Metro 2000 Project, 1979; mem. com. on computer-aided mfg. Nat. Acad. Scis., 1980-83. Mem. Inst. Mgmt. Scis., Am. Prodn. and Inventory Control Soc. (hon.), Delta Sigma Pi, Beta Gamma Sigma. Lutheran. Home: 10 Chestnut Hill Rd N Loudonville NY 12211-1664 Office: SUNY at Albany Sch Bus Albany NY 12222

HOLSTI, KALEVI JACQUE, political scientist, educator; b. Geneva, Apr. 25, 1935; s. Rudolf Woldemar and Liisa Anniki (Franssila) H.; children: Liisa, Matthew, Karina. B.A., Stanford U., 1956, M.A., 1958, Ph.D., 1961. Mem. faculty U. B.C., Vancouver, 1961—; U. Killiam prof. polit. sci. U. B.C.; vis. prof. McGill U., Montreal, 1972-72, Kyoto (Japan) U., 1977, Hebrew U., Jerusalem, 1978, Internat. U. Japan, 1988, 92, 94; vis. fellow Australian Nat. U., 1983; cons. in field. Author: International Politics: A Framework for Analysis, 7th edit., 1994, Why Nations Realign, 1982, The Dividing Discipline: Hegemony and Pluralism in International Theory, 1985, Peace and War: International Order and Armed Conflict, 1648-1989, 1991, Change in the International System: Essays on the Theory and Practice of International Relations, 1991, The State, War, and the State of War, 1996; editor: Internat. Studies Quar., 1970-75; co-editor: Can. Jour. Polit. Sci., 1978-81. Recipient Killam Rsch. prize, 1992; Fulbright scholar, 1959-60; Can. Coun. leave fellow, 1967, 72, 78, Can. Coun. Killam Rsch. fellow, 1987-89; named Univ. Killam Prof., 1997. Fellow Royal Soc. Can.; mem. Internat. Studies Assn. (pres. 1986-87), Can. Polit. Sci. Assn. (pres. 1984-85). Office: U BC, Dept Polit Sci, Vancouver, BC Canada V6T 1Z1

HOLSTI, OLE RUDOLF, political scientist, educator; b. Geneva, Aug. 7, 1933; came to U.S., 1940, naturalized, 1954; s. Rudolf Waldemar and Liisa (Franssila) H.; m. Ann Wood, Sept. 20, 1953; children: Eric Lynn, Maija. B.A. with highest honors, Stanford U., 1954, Ph.D., 1962; M.A.T., Wesleyan U., Middletown, Conn., 1956. Instr., asst. prof. polit. sci., research coordinator Stanford U., 1962-67; assoc. prof. U. B.C., Vancouver, Can., 1967-71; prof. U. B.C., 1971-74; George V. Allen prof. polit. sci. Duke U., 1974—, chmn. dept. polit. sci., 1977-83; prof. Dept. Polit. Sci. U. Calif., Davis, 1978-79; Mem. adv. com. on hist. diplomatic documentation U.S. Dept. State, 1983-86; mem. oversight com. NSF, 1981-84; co-dir. Triangle Univs. Security Sem. Duke U., 1983-98. Author: (with others) Content Analysis: A Handbook with Application for the Study of International Crisis, 1963, (with D.J. Finlay and R. R. Fagan) Enemies in Politics, 1967, Analysis of Communication Content: Developments in Scientific Theories and Computer Techniques, 1969, Content Analysis for Social Sciences and Humanities, 1969, Crisis Escalation War, 1972, Unity and Disintegration in International Alliances: Comparative Studies, 1973, Change in the International System, 1980, American Leadership in World Affairs: The Vietnam and Breakdown of Consensus, 1984, Public Opinion and American Foreign Policy, 1996; contbg. author numerous books including International Crises, 1972, Political Science Annual, 1975, Thought and Action in Foreign Policy, 1975, The Behavior of Nations, 1976, World Politics, 1976, Diplomacy, 1979, Challenges to America, 1979, Containment, 1986, Behavior, Society and Nuclear War, 1989, Soviet-American Relations after the Cold War, 1991, Explaining the History of American Foreign Relations, 1991, Psychological Dimensions of War, 1991, Diplomacy, Force and Leadership, 1993; Encyclopedia of U.S. Foreign Relations, 1997—, assoc. editor Western Polit. Quar., 1970-79, Jour. Conflict Resolution, 1967-72; bd. editors Computer Studies in the Humanities and Verbal Behavior, 1968-76, Am. Jour. Polit. Sci., 1975-80; Internat. Interaction assoc.; Am. Review of Politics: editor then bd. editors Internat. Studies Quar., 1970—, Jour. Politics, 1991—; adv. bd. Univ. Press Am. 1976—; corr. editor Running Jour.; corr. Racing South.; contbr. numerous articles to profl. jours. Served with AUS, 1956-58. Recipient Nevitt Sanford award, 1988, Disting. Tchrs. award Howard Johnson, 1990, Runner of Yr. award CGTC, 1985, Alumni Disting. Undergrad. Tchg. award, 1995; GE Found. Owen D. Young fellow, 1960-61, Haynes Found. Rsch. fellow, 1961-62, Can. Coun. Leave fellow, 1970-71, Ctr. Advanced Study in Behavioral Sci. fellow, 1972-73, Ford Found. Faculty Rsch. fellow, 1972-73, Guggenheim fellow, 1981-82, Pew Faculty fellow Harvard U., 1990; grantee Can. Coun. Rsch., 1969, NSF, 1975-77, 79-81, 83-85, 88-90, 92-95, 96-98; mem. Nat. Champion Cross Country Team (men 50-59), 1985, 88, champion, 1988; champion Tar Heel Running Tour, 1987, champion, Triple Crown Race, 1992-93; named Runner Yr. Carolina Godiva Track Club, 1993. Mem. Internat. Studies Assn. (pres. west region 1969-70, south region 1975-77, nat. pres. 1979-80), Internat. Soc. Polit. Psychology (coun. 1990-92, v.p. 1993-95, Nev. H. Sanford award 1988), Internat. Peace Sci. Soc. (pres. so. sect. 1975-76), Am. Polit. Sci. Assn. (coun. 1982-84, adminstrn. com. 1982-85), Can. Polit. Sci. Assn., Western Polit. Sci. Assn. (exec. coun. 1971-74, Best Dissertation award 1964), Phi Beta Kappa, Duke Faculty Club, Duke Master Runners Club, Carolina Godiva Track Club (Runner of Yr. award 1985, 93), Fleet Feet Running Club. E-mail: holsti@acpub.duke.edu. Home: 608 Croom Ct Chapel Hill NC 27514-6706 Office: Duke U Dept Polit Sci PO Box 90204 Durham NC 27708-0204

HOLSTON, SHARON SMITH, government official; b. Cleve., Dec. 15, 1945; d. Charles Coolidge and Eva Mae (Hall) Smith; m. Joseph Holston, Jr., Dec. 22, 1973; children: Joseph Ikaweba, Eve Denise. AB, Columbia U., 1967; M in Pub. Adminstrn., Harvard U., 1986. Personnel mgmt. specialist U.S. Commn. Civil Rights, 1967-70, HEW, 1970-72; EEO officer FDA, Rockville, Md., 1972-74, personnel mgmt. specialist, 1975-77, acting exec. officer, 1977-79, spl. asst. to assoc. commr. mgmt. and ops., 1979-80, dep. assoc. commr. mgmt. and ops., 1980-88, acting assoc. commr. mgmt. and ops., 1986-88, assoc. commr. mgt. and ops., 1988-93, assoc. commr. mgt. and sys., 1993—. Recipient Award of Merit, FDA, 1982, 87, also commr.'s spl. citation, 1985-94; Sr. Mgmt. citation HHS, 1988, Presdl. Meritorious Rank award, 1992. Rec. sec., mem. Jack & Jill of Am.; active Mt. Calvary Bapt. Ch. Office: FDA Mgmt and Sys 5600 Fishers Ln Rm 1495 Rockville MD 20857-1750*

HOLT, BERTHA MERRILL, state legislator; b. Eufaula, Ala., Aug. 16, 1916; d. William Hoadley and Bertha Harden (Moore) Merrill; m. Winfield Clary Holt, Mar. 14, 1942; children: Harriet Wharton Holt Whitley, William Merrill, Winfield Jefferson. AB, Agnes Scott Coll., 1938; LLB, U. Ala., 1941; grad., Sch. Creative Leadership, Greensboro, N.C., 1992. Bar: Ala. 1941. With Treasury Dept., Washington, 1941-42, Dept. Interior, Washington, 1942-43; mem. N.C. Ho. of Reps. from 22d Dist., 1975-80, 25th Dist., 1980-94, chmn. select com. govtl. ethics, 1979-80, chmn. constl. amendments com., 1981, 83, mem. joint commn. govtl. ops., 1982-88, chmn. appropriation com. justice and pub. safety, 1985-88, co-chair House appropriation sub-com. transp., 1991-92, co-chair appropriation sub-com. Justice and Pub. Safety, 1993—. Pres., Democratic Women of Alamance, 1962, chmn. hdqrs., 1964, 68; mem. N.C. Dem. Exec. Com., 1964-75, 95—; pres. Episcopal Ch. Women, 1968; mem. coun. N.C. Episcopal Diocese, 1972-74, 84-87, 95—; chmn. budget com. 1987; chmn. fin. dept., 1973-75, parish grant com., 1973-80, mem. standing com., 1975-78; chmn. Alamance County Social Svcs. Bd., 1970; mem. N.C. Bd. Sci. and Tech., 1979-83; chair Legis. Women's Caucus, 1991-94; past bd. dirs. Hospice N.C.; bd. dirs. State Coun. Social Legis., pres. SCSL 1996-97, State Conf. Social Work, N.C. Epilepsy Assn., N.C. Pub. Sch. Forum, 1989, U. N.C. Sch. Pub. Health Adv. Bd., Salvation Army Alamance County, N.C., Nursing Found., 1989, Epilepsy Found., 1989; bd. Alternatives for Status Offenders Burlington, N.C., Sch. Pub. Health Adv. Bd.; bd. dirs. N.C. ACLU, Partnership For Chioldren (N.C.), 1993-98. Recipient Outstanding Alumna award Agnes Scott Coll., 1978, Legis. award for svc. to elderly Non-Profit Rest Home Assn., 1985, health, 1986, ARC, 1987, Faith Active in Pub. Affairs award N.C. Coun. of Chs., 1987, Ellen B. Winston award State Coun. For Social Legis., 1989, Disting. Svc. award Alamance County, 1992, Chi Omega award Women in Leadership, 1st ann. Hallie Ruth Allen Dem. Women award Alamance County, 1992; named One of 5 Distinguished Women of N.C. (Govt.), 1991. Mem. AAUW, NOW, N.C. Women's Forums, Law Alumni Assn. U. N.C. Chapel Hill (bd. dirs. 1978-81, 1994-98), N.C. Bar Assn. (bd. dirs. sr. lawyers sect.), English Speaking Union, N.C. Hist. Soc., Soc. Wine Educators, Les Amis du Vin, Pi Beta Phi, Phi Kappa Gamma (hon.), Century Club. Address: PO Box 1111 Burlington NC 27216-1111*

HOLT, CHARLES ASBURY, economics educator; b. Richmond, Va., Oct. 2, 1948; s. Charles Asbury and Josephene (Hannah) H.; children: Abbi Anne, Sarah Holliday. BA, Washington and Lee U., 1970; MS, Carnegie-Mellon U., 1974, PhD, 1977. Asst. prof. econs. U. Minn.-Mpls., 1976-82, assoc. prof., 1982-83; assoc. prof. U. Va., Charlottesville, 1983-90, prof., 1990—, Bankard prof. econs., 1996—, dir. undergrad. studies in econs., 1984-86, dir. grad. studies, 1989-92, chmn. dept. econs. 1996—; cons. FTC, Washington, 1982-92; vis. scholar U. Barcelona, 1986-88, Stanford (Calif.) U., 1996; bd. dirs. Thomas Jefferson Ctr. Polit. Econ., 1993-96. Author: Experimental Economics, 1993; editor: Exptl. Econs., 1997—; assoc. editor Internat. Jour. Game Theory, Econ. Theory, 1995—; contbr. articles to profl. jours., chpt. to book. Served to E4 USNR, 1971-73. Recipient Savage Dissertation award NBER-NSF, 1977, Henderson Dissertation award Carnegie-Mellon U., 1977; Nat. Sci. Found. grantee, 1980—; U.S.-Spain Joint Com. Post Doctoral Rsch. grantee 1987. Mem. Am. Econ. Assn., Atlantic Econ. Assn., So. Econ. Assn. (1st v.p. 1994), Western Econ. Assn., Econ. Sci. Assn. (pres. 1991-93). Home: 1641 Oxford Rd Charlottesville VA 22903-1329 Office: U Va Dept Econ Rouss Hall # 114 Charlottesville VA 22903-3288

HOLT, DENNIS F., media buying company executive. Student, U. So. Calif. Salesman RKO, L.A.; founder, pres., CEO, chmn. Western Internat. Media Corp., L.A. Office: Western Internat Media Corp 8544 W Sunset Blvd West Hollywood CA 90069-2310

HOLT, DONALD A., university administrator, agronomist, consultant, researcher; b. Minooka, Ill., Jan. 29, 1932; s. Cecil Bell and Helen (Eickoff) H.; m. Marilyn Louise Jones, Sept. 6, 1953; children: Kathryn A. Holt Stichnoth, Steven Paul, Jeffrey David, William Edwin. BS in Agrl. Sci., MS in Agronomy, U. Ill.; PhD in Agronomy, Purdue U. Farmer Minooka, Ill., 1956-63; instr., asst. prof., assoc. prof. then prof. agronomy Purdue U., West Lafayette, Ind., 1964-82; prof., head dept. agronomy U. Ill., Urbana-Champaign, Ill., 1982-83, dir. Ill. Agr. Expt. Sta., assoc. dean Coll. Agr., 1983-96, sr. assoc. dean Coll. Agr., cons. environ. sci., 1996—; cons. Deere and Co., Ottumwa, Iowa, 1978, NASA, Houston, 1979, Control Data Corp., Mpls., 1978-79, EPA, Corvallis, Oreg., 1981—. Town Bd. commr., Otterbein, Ind., 1972-76. Fellow AAAS, Am. Soc. Agronomy (pres. 1988), Crop Sci. Soc. Am.; mem. Agrl. Rsch. Inst. (pres. 1991), Am. Forage and Grassland Coun., Ill. Forage and Grassland Coun., Gamma Sigma Delta (internat. pres. 1974-76). Republican. United Methodist. Home: 1801 Moraine Dr Champaign IL 61822-5261 Office: U Ill Office of the Dean 170 EA5B 1101 W Peabody Dr Urbana IL 61801-4723

HOLT, DONALD DALE, magazine editor; b. Chgo., Mar. 31, 1936; s. Edward Joseph and Elsie Edith (Matthies) H.; m. Lolita Saranne Larson, Aug. 15, 1959; children: Lisa, Bradley, Dawn, Courtney. B.A., Wheaton (Ill.) Coll., 1957; postgrad., U. Chgo., 1960-61, Roosevelt U., 1963-64. Reporter, asso. editor Press Publs., Elmhurst, Ill., 1958-61; reporter Chgo. Daily News, 1961-64; corr. Newsweek mag., N.Y.C., 1964-66, Chgo. Bur. chief, 1966-71, news editor, 1971-75, mng. editor internat. edit., 1975-77, sr. editor, 1977-79; bd. editors Fortune mag., 1979-81, internat. editor, 1981-94; gen. editor, 1994-95; editor, sr. v.p. Jour. of Commerce, 1995—. Author: The Justice Machine, 1972. Served as 1st lt. AUS, 1958. Recipient Robert F. Kennedy Journalism award, 1971, Gavel award Am. Bar Assn., 1972, Page One award New York Newspaper Guild, 1972. Office: Two World Trade Ctr New York NY 10048

HOLT, EDWARD THOMAS ROBERT, retired physician; b. London, July 18, 1924; arrived in U.S., 1968; s. Albert Edward and Anne Maude (Gilbert) H.; m. Betty Frances Michell, Mar. 28, 1948 (div. 1971); 1 child, Elizabeth; m. Jill Maureen Welbourn, Oct. 10, 1975; children: Tracey, Trudi. Student, Camberwell Coll. Art, 1938-41, London U., 1948-53; MB BS, St. Thomas's Hosp., London, 1953; MD, 1968. Diplomate Am. Bd. Ob-Gyn., Royal Coll. Ob-Gyn. Med. practitioner Southend on Sea, Eng., 1954-64, Hamilton, New Zealand, 1964-65; gen. practice New Zealand, 1964-65, Sydney, NSW, Australia, 1965-68; assoc. dir. Pfizer, Groton, Conn., 1969-71; pres. Thameside Ob-Gyn. Centre, Groton, 1971—; cons. gynecologist Coast Guard Acad., Groton, 1976-79; cons. ob/gyn. L.B.J. Tropical Med. Ctr., Am. Samoa, 1980, 82. Rep. Town Coun., Groton, 1985. Lt. Royal Navy Vol. Res., 1942-46. Recipient pers. coat of arms Queen Elizabeth II, 1993. Fellow Am. Coll. Ob.-Gyn., Royal Soc. of Medicine; mem. Am. Med. Illustrators (assoc.). Avocations: watercolor, sculpture, sailing, flying. Home: 145 Military Hwy Groton CT 06340-2407 Office: Thameside Ob-Gyn Ctr 495 Gold Star Hwy Groton CT 06340-6228

HOLT, EDWIN JOSEPH, psychology educator; b. Shreveport, La.; s. James S. and Sammie L. (Draper) H.; m. Essie Williams; children: Lisa Michelle, Rachelle Justine. BA, Cen. State U., Wilberforce, Ohio, 1958; MS, Ind. U., 1962; EdD, U. Ark., 1972; postgrad., U. Tenn., 1976. Cert. lic. profl., La. Tchr. Caddo Parish Sch. System, Shreveport, 1959-67, guidance counselor, 1967-68, asst. prin., 1968-71, prin., 1971-74, dir. spl. services, 1974-80, asst. supt., 1980-90; now assoc. prof. psychology La. State U., Shreveport, 1990—; adj. asst. prof. La. State U., Baton Rouge, 1972, N.E. La. U., Monroe, 1973, La. Tech. U., Ruston, 1974, Grambling (La.) State U., 1974-84. Vice-pres. N.W. La. United Way, 1987; dir. Summer Youth Program, Trinity Bapt. Ch., 1980-90; activie Shreveport Clean Community Commn., 1981-85, Shreveport Youth Enrichment Program, 1986-90, La. Parental Involvement Task Force, 1987, Shreveport Task Force on Housing, 1984, Caddo Community Coun. of Parents and Educators, 1984-90; bd. dirs. Am. Heart Assn., 1991-92, Norwella Coun. Boy Scouts Am., 1983-87; fin. chmn. Carver br. YMCA Bd. Mgmt., 1983-88; cultural arts chmn. Caddo Dist. PTA Bd. Mgrs., 1981-90. Nat. Sci. Found. fellow, So. Fund fellow, NDEA fellow; recipient Nat. Council of Negro Women's award, 1984, 85, Nat. Univ. Women's Council award, 1984, 85. Mem. NEA, ACA, La. Edn. Assn., Am. Assn. Sch. Adminstrs., Caddo Assn. Educators, Kappa Delta Pi, Sigma Pi Phi. Baptist. Avocations: bowling, swimming, jogging, reading. Home: 208 Plano St Shreveport LA 71103-2057 Office: La State U Dept Psychology One University Pl Shreveport LA 72225

HOLT, GERALD WAYNE, retired counseling administrator; b. Woodbury, Tenn., July 17, 1935; s. Slaughter L. and Pearl (Simmons) H.; m. May Jane Neely, Aug. 28, 1955; children: Lucinda Jane, Cheryl Kay, Beth Ann. BS, Ball State U., 1957, MA, 1959, postgrad., 1960-61. Tchr. social studies Union City (Ind.) schs., 1957-60, Storer Jr. High Sch., Muncie, Ind., 1960-69; asst. prin. Storer Middle Sch., Muncie, 1969-78; prin. Franklin Middle Sch., Muncie, 1978-79; Christian edn. dir. Glad Tidings Ch., Muncie, 1975-78, 81-84; tchr. social studies Storer Middle Sch., Muncie, 1979-88; Christian edn. dir. Calvary Christian Ctr., Muncie, 1985-87; guidance dir. Northside Middle Sch., Muncie, 1988-99. Bd. dirs. Sch. Employees Credit Union, Muncie, 1987-94; treas. Glad Tidings Ch., Muncie, 1961-72, trustee, 1974-83; trustee Calvary Christian Ctr., Muncie, 1984-88, 90-98. Mem. Muncie Tchrs. Assn., Am. Assn. Counseling and Guidance, Elem. Sch. Guidance and Counseling, NEA, Ind. Tchrs. Assn., Assn. for Supervision and Curriculum Devel., Phi Delta Kappa, Lions. Assemblies of God. Avocations: golf, bowling, photography, collecting political buttons. Office: Northside Mid Sch 1120 W Yale Ave Muncie IN 47304

HOLT, GLEN EDWARD, library administrator; b. Abilene, Kans., Sept. 14, 1939; s. John Wesley and Helen Laverne (Schrader) H.; m. Leslie Edmonds, Jan. 29, 1994; children from previous marriage: Kris, Karen, Gordon. BA, Baker U., 1960; MA, U. Chgo., 1965, PhD, 1975. From instr. to asst. prof. Wash. U., St. Louis, 1968-82; dir. honors div. Coll. Liberal Arts, U. Minn., 1982-87; exec. dir. St. Louis Pub. Libr., 1987—; cons. Chgo. Hist. Soc., 1976-79, Mo. Hist. Soc., St. Louis, 1979-87, NEH, Washington, 1980-82; mem. Online Computer Libr. Ctr. Pub. Libr. Adv. Com., 1991-95. Co-editor: St. Louis, 1975; co-author: Chicago, A Guide to the Neighborhoods, 1979. Bd. dirs. U. Mo. Sch. Libr. and Info. Sci., 1987—. Named Woodrow Wilson Found. fellow, 1963-64, Danforth fellow, 1963-68. Mem. Am. Libr. Assn., Pub. Libr. Assn., Spl. Librs. Assn. (St. Louis com. on fgn. rels.), Media Club. Avocations: photography, collecting paperweights, books and midwestern art. Home: 4954 Lindell Blvd Apt 4W Saint Louis MO 63108-1520 Office: St Louis Pub Libr 1301 Olive St Saint Louis MO 63103-2389

HOLT, HOMER A., JR., urologist, educator; b. Ashland, Ky., July 6, 1938; s. Homer A. Holt; m. Virginia Cayce, Nov. 22, 1962; children: Kathryn Holt Kerpestein, Kimberly, Homer A. III. BA, Vanderbilt U., 1960; MD, U. Louisville, 1965. Diplomate Am. Bd. Urology. Straight surg. intern U. Louisville Sch. Medicine, 1965-66, resident in gen. surgery, 1966-67, resident in urology, 1968-71, chief resident in urology, 1971-72, clin. prof. surgery (urology), 1972—; pvt. practice, Louisville, 1972—; cons. dept. surgery (urology) VA Med. Ctr., Louisville; mem. active staff Norton Hosp.; mem. active staff, bd. dirs. Alliant Med. Pavilion; mem. courtesy staff Kosair Children's Hosp., Columbia Hosps., Bapt. Hosp. East, Caritas Med. Ctr.; pres. med. staff Meth. Evang. Hosp., 1989-90. Contbr. articles to med. jours. Capt. M.C., USAF, 1967-69. Fellow ACS (com. on applicants for Ky. 1982-98, chmn. com. 1988-98); mem. Am. Urol. Assn., Southeastern Sect. Am. Urol. Assn., Am. Lithotripsy Soc., Ky. Med. Assn., Ky. Urol. Assn. (pres. 1979-80), Jefferson County Med. Soc. (editor bull. 1978-79, treas. found. bd. 1984-86). Home: 5805 Keewood Ct Louisville KY 40222 Office: Gray Street Med Bldg 210 E Gray St Ste 1000 Louisville KY 40202

HOLT, JAMES FRANKLIN, retired numerical analyst, scientific programmer analyst; b. Alexander, Ark., Aug. 24, 1927; s. Edward Warbritton and Etta Turner (Ludi) H.; m. Gloria Anne Gaishin, May 5, 1963; children: Gregory James, Elizabeth Diana, Debora Anne. BA in Math., UCLA, 1953. With Pacific Mutual Ins. Corp., L.A., 1953-54; assoc. engr. Lockheed Aircraft Corp., Burbank, Calif., 1954-58; mem. tech. staff Space Tech. Labs., El Segundo, Calif., 1958-61, Aerospace Corp., El Segundo, 1961-91. Author: (play) To Play's the Thing, 1963 (French Grand Prix award); author: Anthony Bacon a.k.a. William Shakespeare, 1994; internat. expert zeros of arbitrary functions, eigenvalues, non linear boundary value problems, differential algebraic equations, numerical integration methods; papers in field. Mem. Univ. Recreation Assn. UCLA (pres. 1952-53), UCLA Student Exec. Council, Young Reps., L.A., 1960-66. Cpl. USAF, 1945-48. Mem. Aerospace Profl. Staff Assn. (1st v.p. 1985-87), Shakespeare Authorship Roundtable, Alliance of L.A. Playwrights. Avocations: chess, research on chaos, fractals, Mandelbrot set, Shakespeare authorship and identity of Jack the Ripper, bowling, writing; 8th Air Force chess champion 1948 (undefeated). Home: 3534 Mandeville Canyon Rd Los Angeles CA 90049-1022

HOLT, JAMES THEODORE, nursing educator; b. Phila., Nov. 24, 1941; s. Francis Downey and Genevieve Marie (Walters) H. ADN, Prince Georges C.C., Largo, Md., 1976; BA, Glassboro (N.J.) State Coll., 1990. Supr. infirmary State of Md., Jessup, 1982-84; med. coord. Beacon Hall, Berlin, N.J., 1984-85; head nurse Ancora State Hosp., Hammonton, N.J., asst. risk mgr., 1990-94; client svcs. rep. N.J. Dept. Human Svcs., Hammonton, 1985-90; pvt. practice Blackwood, N.J. With USN, 1960-62. Home: 134 Madison Ave W Magnolia NJ 08049-1308

HOLT, JOHN MANLY, retired corporate lawyer; b. Chgo., July 15, 1925; s. Newton Ormand and Annie Marie (Hoover) H.; m. Barbara Lenfesty, Dec. 23, 1950; children: Mark B., Susan Holt Braun, Brent D. AB, DePauw U., 1950; JD, Ind. U., Indpls., 1956. Bar: Ind., D.C., U.S. Supreme Ct. Indsl. engr. Eli Lilly & Co., Indpls., 1952-54, pers. rep., 1954-55, supr., 1955-56, atty., 1956-64, asst. counsel, 1964-69, sr. counsel, 1969-77, sec., gen. counsel Pharm. divsn., 1977-87; ret., 1987; cons. Nat. Commn. on Marijuana & Drug Abuse, Washington, 1971-73; trustee Food and Drug Law Inst., Washington, 1976-87; chmn. adv. com. Ind. divsn. Addiction Svcs., 1976-82; mem. Ind. Prescription Abuse Study Commn., 1988. Mem. bd. visitors Ind. U. Sch. Law, Indpls., 1991-98, vice chmn. 1997-98, chmn. 1999; mem. Pepper Com., City/County Govt., Indpls., 1989, Tax Adjustment Bd. of Marion County, Indpls., 1989-94; bd. dirs. Indpls. Park Found., 1992-98; dir. Ctrl. Ind. Coun. on Aging, 1994-98, vice chair 1997-99. Served with U.S. Army, 1943-46, 1950-52. Named Sagamore of the Wabash by Gov. of Ind., 1988; recipient Spirit of Philanthropy award Ind. U./Purdue U., 1991, Order of Constantine, Internat. Sigma Chi, 1989, Disting. Alumni Svc. award Ind. U. Sch. Law, Indpls., 1992. Mem. Ind. Bar Assn., Indpls. Bar Assn., D.C. Bar Assn., Svc. Club Indpls., Columbia Club Indpls., Indpls. Alumni Assn. (dir. Ind. U. Sch. Law-Indpls. 1968-71, v.p. 1997—, pres. 1998), Sigma Chi (pres. Indpls. alumni chpt. 1964, chmn., 1985-96, chmn. emeritus 1997-98), Phi Delta Phi. Republican. Presbyterian. Avocations: photography, biking, gardening, travel, fishing. Home: 3421 Bay Road North Dr Indianapolis IN 46240-2970

HOLT, JONATHAN TURNER, public relations executive; b. New Haven, Jan. 8, 1949; s. Frederick Burton and Thelma (Turner) H.. BA, Drew U., 1971. Chief adminstrv. officer Office of Policy and Analysis, FEA, Washington, 1973-76; chmn. bd. dirs. Holt, Ross Inc., Gladstone, N.J., 1977—; pres. Environ. Affairs Inst., 1991—; cons. U.S. Dept. Energy Regional polit. dir. Pres. Ford Com., Washington, 1976. Vice-chmn. Westfield (N.J.) Town Rep. Com., 1980-84; mem. Delaware River Basin Water Resources Assn., 1979—; vice chmn. bd. visitors, Drew U., 1998—. NSF fellow, 1971. Mem. N.J. State C. of C., Am. Water Works Assn., N.J. Audubon Soc., Am. Assn. Polit. Cons., Pub. Rels. Soc. Am. (bd. dirs. N.J. chpt.), Nature Conservancy (trustee N.J. chpt.). Republican. Office: Holt & Ross Inc 205 Main St Gladstone NJ 07934-2059

HOLT, LEON CONRAD, JR., lawyer, business executive; b. Reading, Pa., June 19, 1925; s. Leon Conrad and Elizabeth (Bright) H.; m. June M. Weidner, June 30, 1947; children: Deborah Holt Weil, Richard W. BS cum laude in Metall. Engring, Lehigh U., 1948; JD, U. Pa., 1951. Bar: N.Y. 1952. With firm Mudge, Stern Williams & Tucker (attys.), N.Y.C., 1951-53; atty. Am. Oil Co. (and predecessor co.), N.Y.C., 1953-57; gen. atty. Air Products & Chems., Inc., Allentown, Pa., 1957-61; v.p. Air Products & Chems., Inc., 1961-76, v.p. adminstrn., 1976-78, gen. counsel, 1961-78, vice chmn. bd., chief adminstrv. officer, 1978-90, also dir., mem. exec., finance, pub. policy coms.; bd. dirs. VF Corp., also mem. exec. fin. and audit coms., 1983-98. Vice chmn. Lehigh Centennial Fund, 1964-65; chmn. Allentown Bd. Ethics, 1970-74; bd. dirs. Lehigh County United Fund, 1971-83, mem. exec. com., 1971-74, campaign chmn., 1972; bd. dirs. Allentown YMCA, 1965-69, trustee, 1972-79; trustee Allentown Art Mus., pres., 1988-92; mem. Allentown Sch. Dist. Authority, 1978-86; trustee Mfrs. Alliance for Productivity and Innovation, 1981-91; mem. adv. bd. Inst. Law and Econs., U. Pa., bd. overseers Law Sch., 1985-94; trustee Dorothy Rider-Pool Health Care Trust, 1982-96, chmn., 1990-96, Rider-Pool Found., Com. Econ. Devel.; dir. Pa. chpt. Nature Conservancy, Pocono Lake Preserve, Pennsylvanians for Modern Cts.; co-chmn. Partnership for Comty. Health, 1991-94. Lt. (j.g.) USNR, 1943-46. Mem. ABA, Pa. Soc., Assn. Bar N.Y.C., Allentown C. of C. (gov. 1965-68), Tunkhannock Creek Assn., Alpha Tau Omega, Lehigh Country Club (bd. govs. 1970-77). Republican. Episcopalian. Home: 3003 Parkway Blvd Allentown PA 18104-5384 Office: 1611 Pond Rd Ste 300 Allentown PA 18104-2258

HOLT, LESLIE EDMONDS, librarian; b. Mpls.; d. Peter Robert and Elizabeth Knox (Donovan) Edmonds; m. Glen Edward Holt, Jan. 29, 1994. BA, Cornell Coll., 1971; MA, U. Chgo., 1975; PhD, Loyola U.,

Chgo., 1984. Asst. children's libr. Indian Trails Libr. Dist., Wheeling, Ill., 1972-73; libr. Erikson Inst. for Early Edn., Chgo., 1973-75; youth svcs. libr. Rolling Meadows (Ill.) Libr., 1975-82; libr. multicultural head start resource ctr. Chgo. Pub. Libr., 1982-84; asst. prof. grad. sch. libr. and info. sci. U. Ill., Urbana, 1984-90, assoc. dean, 1988-89; dir. youth svcs. and family literacy St. Louis Pub. Libr., 1990—; pre-sch. advisor Rolling Meadows (Ill.) Park Dist., 1978-85; cons. to reading program The Latin Sch., Chgo., 1980-82; vis. lectr. Loyola U. of Chgo., 1980-84, U. Ill. Extension, Belleville, 1992; product mgr. Mister Anderson's Co., McHenry, Ill., 1981-84; instr. Nat. Coll. Edn., Evanston, Ill., 1982-84, Webster U., Webster Groves, Mo., 1991; cons. for libr. devel. Ill. Math. and Sci. Acad., Aurora, Ill., 1986-90; peer reviewer, advisor U.S. Dept. Edn. Office Edn. Rsch. and Improvement, 1987-89; libr. cons. Reading Rainbow Resources Guide, Sta. WNET-TV, N.Y.C., 1987, 88; adj. instr. U. Mo., Columbia, 1991, 92, 93; literary advisor Grace Hill Neighborhood Svcs., 1991-95; cons. Paschen-Tishman-Jahn, 1988; presenter in field. Author: An Investigation of the Effectiveness of an On-Line Catalog in Providing Bibliographic Acccess to Children in a Public Library Setting, 1989, Family Lieracy Programs in Public Libraries, 1990; contbr. articles to profl. jours. Mem. Success by Six Com., United Way of Met. St. Louis, 1993—. Grantee in field. Mem. ALA (mem. Carroll Preston Baber award jury 1992-94, World Book award 1986), Nat. Assn. Edn. Young Children, Internat. Reading Assn., Mo. Libr. Assn. (mem. summer reading program com. 1991, mem. Mark Twain award com. 1992), USA Toy Libr. Assn. (charter mem.), Assn. Libr. Svc. to Children (mem. toys, games and realia evaluation com. 1983-85, chair local arrangements 1984-85, chair rsch. com. 1985-88, mem. Randolph Caldecott com. 1987, mem. software evaluation 1988-89, mem. svc. to children with spl. needs 1989-91, chair Charlemae Rollins pres. program 1990-91, active, 1991, chair edn. com. 1991-93, 93—, bd. dirs. 1993-96, v.p., pres.-elect 1997-98, pres. 1998-99, past pres. 1999-2000), Children's Reading Round Table (mem. spl. award com. 1987-88). Office: St Louis Pub Lib 1301 Olive St Saint Louis MO 63103-2325

HOLT, LINDA FITZGERALD, elementary education educator; b. Ft. Benning, Ga., Apr. 10, 1956; d. Donald Carl and Bobbie Jane (Oliver) Fitzgerald; m. James Anthony Holt, Aug. 16, 1975 (div. June 1991); 1 child, Laura Leigh. AA, Hopkinsville (Ky.) C.C., 1976; BS, Western Ky. U., 1979; MA, Murray (Ky.) State U., 1984. Cert. elem. tchr., Ky. Math/sci. demonstration tchr. K-12 Hopkins County Schs., Madisonville, Ky., 1979-97; gifted/talented resource tchr. Caldwell County Schs., 1997—; math. cons. K-12, workshop presenter Hopkins County Sch. Sys., Madisonville, 1980-97, Badgett Ctr. Ednl. Enhancement; tchr. trainer Ky. K-8 Math. Specialist Program and 4-5 Sci. Specialist Program, 1990-93. Grantee NSF, 1990, 93. Mem. Nat. Coun. Tchrs. Math. (presenter regional conf. Paducah 1993), Nat. Sci. Tchr. Assn., Internat. Reading Assn., Ky. Coun. Tchrs. Math. (conf. presider 1990), Ken-Lake Coun. Tchrs. Math., Western Ky. Math.-Sci. Alliance (bd. dirs., elem. rep.). Democrat. Baptist. Avocations: arts and crafts, reading, rock hunting. Home: 681 Pidcock Rd Princeton KY 42445 Office: Caldwell County Bd Edn PO Box 229 Princeton KY 42445-0229

HOLT, MARJORIE SEWELL, lawyer, retired congresswoman; b. Birmingham, Ala., Sept. 17, 1920; d. Edward Rol and Juanita (Felts) Sewell; m. Duncan McKay Holt, Dec. 26, 1946; children: Rachel Holt Tschantre, Edward Sewell, Victoria. Grad., Jacksonville Jr. Coll., 1945; JD, U. Fla., 1949. Bar: Fla. 1949, Md. 1962. Pvt. practice Annapolis, Md., 1962; clk. Anne Arundel County Circuit Ct., 1966-72; mem. 93d-99th Congresses from 4th Dist. of Md., 1973-86; armed services com.; vice-chmn. Office Tech. Assessment, 1977; chmn. Republican Study com., 1975-76; of counsel Smith, Somerville & Case, Balt., 1986-90; supr. elections Anne Arundel County, 1963-65; del. Rep. Nat. Conv., 1968, 76, 80, 84, 88; mem. Pres.'s Commn. on Arms Control and Disarmament; mem. ind. commn. USAR; bd. dirs. Annapolis Fed. Savs. Bank; mem. adv. bd. Crestar. Co-author: Case Against The Reckless Congress, 1976, Can You Afford This House, 1978. Bd. dirs. Md. Sch. for the Blind, Hist. Annapolis Found. Recipient Disting. Alumna award U. Fla., 1975, Trustees award U. Fla. Coll. Law, 1984, Alumnae Outstanding Achievement award, 1997. Mem. ABA, Md. Bar Assn., Anne Arundel Bar Assn., Phi Kappa Phi, Phi Delta Delta. Presbyterian (elder 1959).

HOLT, MICHAEL BARTHOLOMEW, lawyer; b. Jersey City, July 10, 1956; s. William A. and Grace (Donohue) H.; m. Mary Patricia Butler, Aug. 14, 1982; children: Melissa Aislynn, Scott Michael, Eric Michael. BA magna cum laude, Providence Coll., 1978; JD, Seton Hall U., 1982. Bar: N.J. 1982, U.S. Dist. Ct. N.J. 1982, U.S. Dist. Ct. (ea. and so. dists.) N.Y. 1985, U.S. Ct. Appeals (3d cir.) 1985, U.S. Supreme Ct. 1986, N.Y. 1990. Assoc. Keane, Brady & Hanlon, Jersey City, 1982-84, Waters, McPherson, McNeill P.A., Secaucus, N.J., 1984-87; ptnr. O'Halloran, Holt and Assocs., Bayonne, N.J., 1987-89, Carroll & Holt, Secaucus, 1989-91; pvt. practice Secaucus, 1991-95; corp. counsel NYK Lines (N.Am.) Inc., Secaucus, 1995—. Mem. ABA, N.J. State Bar Assn., N.Y. State Bar Assn. (corp. counsel com.). Home: 9 Melrose Ave North Arlington NJ 07031-5917 Office: NYK Line Inc 300 Lighting Way Secaucus NJ 07094-3679

HOLT, MICHAEL KENNETH, management and finance educator, consultant; b. Jackson, Tenn., Apr. 13, 1961; s. Kenneth Harvey and Dorothy (Price) H.; m. Carol Lynn Walls, Aug. 13, 1983; children: Mitchell Harris, Marleigh Alyson. BS, Union U., 1983; MS, La. State U., 1985; PhD, U. Memphis, 1999. CPM. Broker First Nat. Bank of Commerce, New Orleans, 1985-86; mgr. Invest at Jackson (Tenn.) Nat. Bank, 1986-87; stock broker Merrill Lynch, Jackson, Tenn., 1987-89; prof. Union U., Jackson, Tenn., 1989—; chmn. bd. Leaders Credit Union, Jackson, Tenn.; cons. Best Home Ctr., Jackson, Tenn., 1994-97, mem. regional planning commn., 1996—; cons. Quaker Oats, Jackson, 1991, Memphis Cablevision, Memphis, 1990; nominee bd. dirs. Fed. Res. Bank St Louis, 1997. Editor: Jour. Industry and Commerce, 1993-94, Update, 1990—; contbr. articles to profl. jours. Recipient Instrnl. Innovation award Union U., 1995. Office: Union U 1050 Union University Dr Jackson TN 38305-3697

HOLT, NANCY IRENE, elementary education educator; b. Mpls., Feb. 27, 1948; d. Donald Freeman and Mildred Florence (Kragskow) Kendall; m. Henry Highum Holt, June 26, 1971 (div. Apr. 1994); 1 child, Allison. BS, U. Minn., 1970; MA, Coll. St. Catherine, St. paul, 1996. Tchr. Franklin Pierce Pub. Schs., Tacoma, 1976-78, Panama City (Fla.) Pub. Schs., 1979-80, Great Falls (Mont.) Pub. Schs., 1984-90, Christian Heritage Acad., Burnsville, Minn., 1993-95; elem. tchr. St. Paul Pub. Schs. Dist. 625, 1995—. Singer, bd. dirs. City of Lakes Sweet Adelines, Mpls., 1990—. Office: St Paul Pub Schs Dist 625 360 Colborne St Saint Paul MN 55102-3228

HOLT, PAUL DECOURCY, III, city planner; b. Norfolk, Va., Sept. 27, 1971; s. Paul deCourcy Jr. and Carol Reams (Paulette) H. BA in Econs., Va. Poly. Inst. and State U., 1993; M.City and Reg. Planning, Clemson U., 1996. Planning intern Pickens County, S.C., 1995-96; sr. planner James City County, Williamsburg, Va., 1996—. Mem. Am. Planning Assn., Nature Conservancy, Nat. Trust for Hist. Preservation. Office: James City County 101 Mounts Bay Rd Bldg E Williamsburg VA 23185-6569

HOLT, PETER M., sports team executive. Pres., CEO Holt Co. of Ohio, San Antonio; chmn. bd. San Antonio Spurs. Office: San Antonio Spurs PO Box 207916 San Antonio TX 78220-7916*

HOLT, PETER ROLF, physician, educator; b. Berlin, Sept. 8, 1930; s. Arthur and Ruth H.; m. Joyce Weil, May 15, 1979; children: Rachel Janna, Shawn David, Tamara Naomi. BSc, U. London, 1949, MB, BS with honors, 1954. Intern London Hosp., 1954-55; asst. resident in medicine St. Luke's Hosp. Center, N.Y.C., 1957-59; tng. fellow in medicine Mass. Gen. Hosp., Boston, 1959-61; chief gastroenterology med. Service St. Luke's Hosp. Center, N.Y.C., 1961-96; attending physician Service St. Luke's Hosp. Center, 1971—, Presbyn. Hosp., N.Y.C., 1988; chief gastroenterology St. Luke's-Roosevelt Hosp. Ctr., N.Y.C., 1996—; research collaborator Brookhaven Nat. Lab., Upton, N.Y., 1973-79; mem. faculty dept. medicine Coll. Physicians and Surgeons, Columbia U., N.Y.C., 1961—, prof., 1975—; mem. Bio-enging. Inst., Columbia U., 1975—, Inst. Human Nutrition, 1978—, Comprehensive Cancer Ctr.; mem. 12th work group on clin. research Nat. Commn. on Digestive Disease, 1977-79; mem. nat. sci. adv. com., nat. rev. com. Nat. Found. for Ileitis and Colitis, 1976-88, also chmn. research tng. awards com.; vis. investigator Meml. Sloan-Kettering Cancer Ctr., 1988-89; lectr. Trevor Howell Lecture British Geriatrics Soc., 1992, Dorothy Ewerson Lectr., Univ. Pisa, 1999. Author, contbr. chpts. to books, articles to med. jours. Served to maj. Brit. Royal Army M.C., 1955-57. NIH grantee.; Recipient William H. Rorer award in Gastroenterology, 1965. Fellow ACP (gov.'s com. 1978-81); mem. AAAS, N.Y. Gastroent. Assn. (chmn. com. rsch. 1973-74, chmn. com. on aging 1982-86, chmn. admissions com. 1985-86, ethics com. 1997—), Intersoc. Com. Clin. Investigation in Digestive Disease (chmn. 1975-79), Am. Assn. Study of Liver Diseases, Am. Fedn. Clin. Rsch., Am. Physiol. Soc., Am. Soc. Clin. Investigation, Am. Soc. Clin. Nutrition, Am. soc. Cancer Rsch., N.Y. Acad. Sci., Gerontol. Soc. Am., Harvey Soc., Organisation Mondiale de Gastro-Enterologie (chair nominating com. 1990-94, nomenclature com. and rsch. com.). Office: St Luke's Roosevelt Hosp Ctr 1111 Amsterdam Ave New York NY 10025-1716

HOLT, PHILETUS HAVENS, III, architect; b. Summit, N.J., Aug. 19, 1928; s. Robert Sherman and Alice Kathleen (Gallwey) H.; m. Nancy deFreest Brownley, June 16, 1950; children—Alexandra Foster, Robert Stephen. A.B. with honors, Princeton U., 1950, M.F.A., 1952. Registered architect, N.J., N.Y., Conn., Mass., Maine, Vt., Pa., Md., Calif.; lic. profl. planner, N.J. Designer W.F.R. Ballard, Architect, N.Y.C., 1952-55; designer, assoc. C.K. Agle, Architect, Princeton, N.J., 1955-65; ptnr. Holt & Morgan, Princeton, 1965-72; prin. Holt Morgan Russell Architects, P.A., Princeton, 1972—; v.p. Architects Housing Co., Trenton, N.J., 1976-90; mem. State Rev. Bd. for Historic Sites, N.J., 1983—, vice chmn., 1989-97, chmn. 1997—; guest lectr. U. Pa., Phila., 1972—. Architect Douglass & Cook Colls. (hon. mention Am. Inst. Steel Constrn. 1979), 1977, Batsto Visitors Ctr., 1982, (restoration and preservation) Drumthwacket Gardens, 1983; illustrator book: Gardens of Illusion (Alice Davis Hitchcock award 1982), 1982. Trustee, Arts Council of Princeton, 1970-82, pres., 1972; mem. Mayor's Adv. Com. for Downtown, Princeton, 1971-72. Recipient Design awards N.J. Soc. Architects/AIA, 1970, 71, 73, 75, N.J. Hist. Preservation award, 1995. Mem. AIA (medal 1952), Hist. Soc. of Princeton (former trustee, pres. 1980-82), Soc. Archtl. Historians. Club: Corinthians (N.Y.C.). Home: 3472 Lawrenceville Rd Princeton NJ 08540-4718 Office: Holt Morgan Russell Architects 350 Alexander St Princeton NJ 08540-7106

HOLT, RICHARD DUANE, lawyer; b. Champaign, Ill., Aug. 1, 1942. BS, Eastern Ill. U., 1964; JD, U. Fla., 1969. Bar: Fla. 1970. Ptnr. Gunster, Yoakley, Valde-Fauli & Stewart, PA, West Palm Beach, Fla. Mem. ABA, Fla. Bar, Palm Beach County Bar Assn., Phi Delta Phi. Office: Phillips Point Ste 500 E 777 S Flagler Dr West Palm Beach FL 33401-6161*

HOLT, ROBERT EZEL, data processing executive; b. Red Bay, Ala., May 8, 1957; s. Robert E. Sr. and Ruby (Weathers) H.; m. Elizabeth Ann Simmons, May 19, 1978; children: Robert E. III, James Michael. AA, N.E. Community Coll., 1977; BS, Miss. State U., 1980. Operator, programmer Watkins, Ward & Stafford, CPA, West Point, Miss., 1978-81; computer programmer Gen. Tire Corp., Inc., Columbus, Ohio, 1981-83; programmer, analyst Arvin Industries, Inc., Starkville, Miss., 1983-84; analyst, data processing mgr. Data Systems Mgmt., Inc., Columbus, Miss., 1984—; data processing cons., West Point, 1983. Deacon, chmn. Calvary Bapt. Ch., West Point, 1990-91; mem. West Point Follies, 1991. Recipient Deacon Cert., Calvary Bapt. Ch., West Point, 1986. Democrat. Baptist. Avocations: golf, hunting, fishing, gardening. Home: 1190 Lone Oak Park West Point MS 39773-9792 Office: Data Systems Mgmt Inc Ste 300 Court Square Towers Columbus MS 39701-5733

HOLT, ROBERT THEODORE, political scientist, dean, educator; b. Caledonia, Minn., July 26, 1928; s. Oscar Martin and Olga Linnea (Mattson) H.; m. Shirley J. Russell, Dec. 14, 1957; children: Susan Jane, Ann Carol, Sharon Linnea. AB magna cum laude, Hamline U., 1950; MPA, Princeton U., 1952, PhD, 1957. Instr. dept. polit. sci. U. Minn., Mpls., 1956-57, asst. prof., 1957-60, assoc. prof., 1960-64, prof., 1964—, chmn. dept., 1978-81, dir. Ctr. for Comparative Studies in Tech. Devel. and Social Change, 1967-80, dir. rsch. devel. Coll. Liberal Arts, 1975-78, dean Grad. Sch., 1982-91, chair rsch. exec. coun., 1988-91, interim dean Coll. Liberal Arts, 1996; bd. dirs. Coun. Grad. Schs., 1984-90, chair, 1989-90; mem. Assembly Social and Behavioral Scis., NAS, 1972-75. Author: Radio Free Europe, 1958, (with F.W. Van de Velde) Strategic Psychological Operations, 1960, The Soviet Union: Paradox and Change, 1962, (with J.E. Turner) The Political Basis of Economic Development, 1966, The Methodology of Comparative Research, 1970, Political Parties in Action, 1971, (with Turner and Chase) American Government in Comparative Perspective, 1979. With U.S. Army, 1953-55. Fellow Ctr. for Advanced Studies in Behavioral Scis., 1961-62. Mem. Am. Polit. Sci. Assn., Internat. Studies Assn., Mid West Polit Sci. Assn., Assn of Grad. Schs. (exec. com. 1985-88, chair grad. student fin. assistance com. 1986-91), 39er's Club. Episcopalian. Office: U Minn Polict Sci Dept 1414 Social Sci Tower 267 19th Ave S Minneapolis MN 55455

HOLT, RONALD LAWRENCE, anthropologist, educator; b. Sweetwater, Tex., Dec. 3, 1949; s. William Hazelwood and Minnie Louise (Crider) H.; children: Ian Ari, Robin Nikko, Melody Louisa. BA, Tex. Tech U., 1974, MA, 1976; PhD, U. Utah, 1987. Tchr. So. Utah U., 1981-82; T U. Utah, 1983-86; dir. of honours, full prof. anthropology Weber State U., Ogden, Utah, 1986—. Author: Beneath These Red Cliffs: An Ethnohistory of the Utah Pointes, 1992. Founding trustee Utah Dem. Leadership Coun., 1995; Dem. candidate U.S. Congress, 1992. Mem. Am. Anthrop. Assn., Nat. Collegiate Honors Assn., Exchange Club. Buddhist. Avocation: martial arts. Office: Weber State University 2904 University Cir Ogden UT 84408-2904

HOLT, RUSH DEW, congressman, physics educator, researcher, consultant; b. Weston, W.Va., Oct. 15, 1948; s. Rush Dew and Helen (Froelich) H.; m. Margaret Lancefield, 1985. BA, Carleton Coll., 1970; MS, NYU, 1975, PhD, 1981. Am. Phys. Soc. Congl. fellow U.S. Congress, Washington, 1982-83; vis. scientist High Altitude Obs., Boulder, Colo., 1984; asst. prof. physics dept. Swarthmore (Pa.) Coll., 1980-88; sci. analyst U.S. Dept. State, 1987-89; asst. dir. Plasma Physics Lab. Princeton (N.J.) U., 1989-98; mem. U.S. Congress from 12th N.J. dist., 1999—. Patentee in field. Mem. Am. Phys. Soc., Am. Assn. Physics Tchrs., AAAS, Sigma Xi. Five time winner "Jeopardy". Office: Ho of Reps 1630 Longworth HOB Washington DC 20515*

HOLT, SIDNEY CLARK, journalist; b. St. Louis, Sept. 7, 1955; s. Noel Clark and Rosalee (Powell) H.; m. Jill Brodsky, Nov. 16, 1991; children: Elizabeth Summers, Victoria Edmunds. BA, Columbia U., 1979. Editor Simon & Schuster Inc., N.Y.C., 1979-84; asst. editor Rolling Stone, N.Y.C., 1984-85, assoc. editor, 1985-87, sr. editor, 1987-89, asst. mng. editor, 1989-90, mng. editor, 1990-97; editl. dir. US mag., N.Y.C., 1995-97; v.p. Wenner Media, Inc., N.Y.C., 1996-97; exec. v.p., editor-in-chief Ad Week Mags., N.Y.C., 1988—. Editor: The Rolling Stone Interviews: The 1980s, 1989. Bd. dirs. Fedn. Protestant Welfare Agys., N.Y.C., 1994—. Mem. Am. Soc. Mag. Editors. Democrat. Methodist. Home: PO Box 839 Rhinebeck NY 12572-0839 Office: AdWeek Magsne 1515 Broadway New York NY 10036-8901

HOLT, STEPHEN S., astrophysicist; b. N.Y.C., May 17, 1940; s. Aaron J. and Faye E. (Schwartz) Holtz; m. Carol Ann Weissman, June 3, 1961; children: Peter David, Eric Lawrence, Laura Kimberly. BS, NYU, 1961, PhD in Physics, 1966. Instr. physics N.Y. U., 1964-66; astrophysicist Goddard Space Flight Center, Greenbelt, Md., 1966—; chief high energy astrophysics NASA Hdqrs., 1980-81; dir. Lab. for High Energy Astrophysics Goddard Space Flight Ctr., Greenbelt, Md., 1983-90; dir. space scis. Goddard Space Flight Ctr., 1990—; lectr. physics U. Md., 1967-87, adj. prof. astronomy, 1988—. Contbr. articles to profl. jours. Recipient medal for exceptional sci. achievement NASA, 1977, 80, medal for outstanding leadership, 1991, Presdl. meritorious exec. award, 1992, John C. lindsay Meml. award outstanding scientific achievement, 1993. Fellow Am. Phys. Soc. (councillor divsn.); mem. Am. Astron. Soc. (chair div.), Sigma Xi, Tau Beta Pi, Sigma Pi Sigma. Home: 1207 Mimosa Ln Silver Spring MD 20904-1448 Office: Goddard Space Flight Ctr Mail Code 600 Greenbelt MD 20771 *The most important intrinsic requisites for success in experimental science are probably imagination and diligence. Very few individuals possess these in sufficient quantities to dominate the extrinsic variables which shape their careers in research, however. I consider myself fortunate to have been able to capitalize on whatever talent I possess by having my research interests aligned with funding priorities, and by being blessed with the cooperation of unselfish and stimulating colleagues.*

HOLT, WILLIAM E., lawyer; b. Phila., Aug. 31, 1945. BBA, U. Iowa, 1967, JD with distinction, 1970. Bar: Iowa 1970, Wash. 1971. Law clk. to Hon. William T. Beeks U.S. Dist. Ct. (we. dist.) Wash., 1970-71; mem., chmn. Gordon, Thomas, Honeywell, Malanca, Peterson & Daheim, Tacoma; adj. prof. U. Puget Sound Law Sch., 1974-75. Note editor Iowa Law Rev., 1969-70. Mem. ABA, Wash. State Bar Assn. (exec. com. real property, probate and trust sect. 1987-89), Phi Delta Phi. E-mail: holtw@gth-law.com. Office: Gordon Thomas Honeywell Malanca Peterson & Daheim PO Box 1157 Ste 2200 Tacoma WA 98401-1157

HOLT, WILLIAM HAROLD, JR., film producer, consultant; b. Evergreen Park, Ill., Aug. 22, 1949; s. William Harold and Thalma Grace (Bowyer) H.; m. Kelly Colleen Simmert, June 17, 1978; children: Eric William, Megin Colleen. Student, U. Ill., 1974. Exec. producer Salvation Army, Chgo., 1975-80; ops. mgr. Audio Visual Requirements, Chgo., 1980-82; account exec. Rent Com., Inc., Schiller Park, Ill., 1982-88; prin., prodr. Willow Assocs., Downers Grove, Ill., 1988—; actor Cmty. Theatre, Chgo., 1970-80; stage dir. Salvation Army, Chgo., 1972-80; chmn. judging U.S. Festivals Assn., Elmhurst, Ill., 1977—; stage dir. pvt. practice, Chgo., 1980—; prodr. Electrosonic Sys., Mpls., 1987—, Pioneer Display Systems Divsn. Comm. Am., Upper Saddle River, N.J., 1990—. With (multi-image) Centenary, 1978, Midway Airlines, 1985, Amoco at 100 Meeting, 1989, INFOCOMM Internat. War of the Walls, 1990—, Amoco Corp. Meeting Prodn., 1990-94; prodr. Pressroom of the Future, Komori America, 1997. Mem. Internat. Video Signage Assn., Am. Film Inst., Audio Engrng. Soc., Chgo. Audio-Visual Prodrs., Chgo. Film/Video Coun. (v.p. 1985-86, pres. 1987-88, treas. 1991-92). Salvation Army. Avocations: music, railroading, photography. Home and Office: Willow Assocs 4061 Glendenning Rd Downers Grove IL 60515-2228

HOLTBY, KENNETH FRASER, manufacturing executive; b. Escanaba, Mich., May 18, 1922; s. David William and Nina Kate (Hemenway) H.; m. Bettie Roberts, June 11, 1943; children—Michael Earle, Tracy Linda Buren, Jeffrey Thomas, Kristen Ann Buren, Matt Fraser. BSME, Calif. Inst. Tech., 1947; SM in Indsl. Mgmt., MIT, 1961. Aerodynamicist Boeing Co., Seattle, 1947, various mgmt. positions, 1953-82, sr. v.p., 1982-87; bd. dirs. Keytronics Corp., Spokane. Found. mem. Pacific Sci. Ctr., Seattle, 1974—. Served to lt. USAF, 1943-46. Fellow Brit. Royal Aero. Soc., AIAA (hon., Aircraft Design award 1984); mem. NRC, U.S. Nat. Acad. Engrng. Avocations: tennis; skiing; sailing. Address: 2907 Croatian Way Anacortes WA 98221

HOLTE, DEBRA LEAH, investment executive, financial analyst; b. Madison, Wis.; d. Daniel Kenneth and Marian Anne Reitan. BA, Concordia Coll., Moorhead, Minn., 1973. Chartered Fin. Analyst, Cert. Divorce Planner. Capital markets specialist 1st Bank Mpls., 1981-83; v.p. Allison-Williams Co., Mpls., 1983-86, Nelson, Benson & Zellmer, Denver, 1986-90; exec. v.p. Hamil & Holte Inc., Denver, 1990-93; pres. Holte & Assocs., Denver, Taos, N.Mex., 1993—. Active Denver Jr. League, Western Pension Com., 1986—; bd. dirs. Denver Children's Home, 1987—, treas., 1987-91, chmn. fin. com., 1987-91, v.p., 1990—, chmn. nominating com., 1991—, pres.-elect, 1994-95, bd. pres., 1995—; adv. bd. Luth. Social Svcs., 1987; co-chair U.S. Ski Team Fundraiser; bd. dirs. Minn. Vocat. Edn. Fin., Mpls., 1984-86; bd. dirs. Colo. Ballet, 1988-93, chair nominating com., 1991-93, v.p., 1992-93, chmn. bd., 1993; mem. Fin. Analyst Nat. Task Force in Bondholder Rights, 1988-90; bd. dirs. Ctrl. City Opera Guild, 1994-95, Western Chamber Ballet, 1994-96, Taos Humane Soc., 1997—; social co-chmn. The Arapahoe Fox Hunt, 1993-94. Mem. Fin. Analysts Fedn., Denver Soc. Security Analysts (bd. dirs. 1990-97, chair ethics and bylaws com. 1987—, chair edn. com. 1988, chair membership com. 1989, rec. sec. 1990, sec. 1991, treas. 1992, program chair 1993, pres. 1994-95, dir. 1995-96). Office: PO Box 2491 Taos NM 87571-2491

HOLTEN, JOHN V., food products executive; b. 1956. Degree, Harvard U., 1982. Mng. dir. DNC Capital Corp., N.Y., 1981-86; chmn., CEO Holberg Industries, Inc., Greenwich, 1986—. Office: Holberg Industries Inc 545 Steamboat Rd Greenwich CT 06830-7170*

HOLTER, DON WENDELL, retired bishop; b. Lincoln, Kans., Mar. 24, 1905; s. Henry O. and Lenna (Mater) H.; m. Isabelle Elliott, June 20, 1931; children: Phyllis Holter Dunn, Martha Holter Hudson (dec.), Heather Holter Ellis. BA, Baker U., 1927, DD, 1948; postgrad., Harvard U., 1928; BD, Garrett Theol. Sem., 1930; PhD, U. Chgo., 1934; LLD, Dakota Wesleyan U., 1969; DD, St. Paul Sch. Theology, 1973, Westmar Coll., 1976. Ordained to ministry Meth. Ch. as elder, 1934. Asst. minister Euclid Meth. Ch., Oak Park, Ill., 1930-34; missionary in Philippines, 1935-45; minister Central Ch., Manila, 1935-40; interned with family by the Japanese, Santo Tomas Internment Camp, Manila, 1942-45; prof. Union Theol. Sem., Manila, 1935-40; pres. Union Theol. Sem., 1940-45; minister Hamline Meth. Ch., St. Paul, 1946-49; prof. Garrett Theol. Sem., 1949-58; founding pres. St. Paul Sch. Theology, 1958-72; bishop Nebr. area United Meth. Ch., 1972-76; del. Internat. Missionary Conf., India, 1938; spl. study mission, Africa, 1958; rep., mem. pers. com. Meth. Bd. of Global Ministries, 1964-72; chmn. commn. ministry Gen. Conf., 1968-70, mem. gen. bd. higher edn. and ministry, 1972-76, chmn. div. ordained ministry, 1972-76, del. gen. and jurisdictional confs., 1964, 66, 68, 70, 72. Author: Fire on the Prairie, Methodism in the History of Kansas, 1969, Flames on the Plains, A History of United Methodism in Nebraska, 1983, The Lure of Kansas, The Story of the Evangelicals and United Brethren, 1853-1968, 1990. Trustee St. Paul Sch. Theology. Home: 7725 Briar St Shawnee Mission KS 66208-4331

HOLTER, ROBERT M., federal judge; b. Williston, N.D., Mar. 13, 1927. BS, U. Mont., JD, 1954. Bar: Mont. 1954. Legal practice Bozeman, from 1956; county atty. Gallatin County, 1961-62; judge Mont. Dist. Ct. (19th dist.), from 1977; magistrate judge U.S. Dist. Ct. Mont., Great Falls; chmn. Mont. Criminal Jury Instrn. commn., 1980-92, Mont. Child Support Enforcement Commn., 1985-87, Mont. Dist. Ct. Com., 1979-85; mem. faculty Nat. Jud. Coll., 1985-88. Served with U.S. Army, 1945-46, 1st lt. USAF, 1954-56. Recipient Nat. Patrolman award, Nat. Ski Patrol award. Mem. State Bar Mont., Mont. Judges Assn. (pres. 1986-87), Rotary Club, Masons. Episcopalian. Avocations: skiing, antique collecting, flying, golf. Address: PO Box 2386 Great Falls MT 59403-2386

HOLTGREWE, HENRY LOGAN, urologist; b. Springfield, Ill., Nov. 25, 1930; s. Edgar Henry and Harriet (Logan) H.; m. Virginia Ann Lightfoot, Aug. 25, 1954; children: Kent Logan, Sally Ann Welch. BA, Kans. U., 1951, MD, 1955. Diplomate Am. Bd. Urology. Intern Hosp. of U. Pa., Phila., 1955-56; asst. resident gen. surgery Duke U. Hosp., Durham, N.C., 1956-57; resident in urology Kans. U. Med. Ctr., Kansas City, 1959-62; mem. med. staff Anne Arundel Med. Ctr., Annapolis, Md., 1962—; chief urology Anne Arundel Med. Ctr., Annaplis, Md., 1966-76, pres. med. staff, 1973-75; assoc. prof. urology Johns Hopkins U. Sch. Medicine, Balt.; pres.-elect, sec.-treas. Am. Bd. Urology, 1992—; mem. Nat. Kidney and Urol. Disease Info. Clearing House, NIH, Bethesda, Md., urology program group to Nat. Inst. Diabetes and Digestive and Kidney Diseases; mem. panel Agy. for Health Care Policy and Rsch., USPHS, Washington; mem. internal sci. com. on benign prostatic hypertrophy WHO, Paris, chmn. com. on internat. econs. benign prostatic hypertrophy; presenter, lectr. in field. Contbr. numerous articles to profl. publs., chpt. to books. Treas. Am. for Urol. Disease, 1986-91, bd. dirs. 1992-93; chmn. judiciary selection comm. Anne Arundel County, 1988; bd. trustees Anne Arundel Med. Ctr., Annapolis, Md., 1973-81. With USNR, 1957-59. Recipient William P. Burpeau award Acad. Medicine N.J., 1993. Fellow ACS; mem. AMA, Am. Urol. Assn. (bd. dirs. 1984-94, chmn. arrangements ann. meeting in Spain, 1973, sec. Mid-Atlantic sect. 1976-81, exec. com. 1984-86, treas. 1986-91, mem. adv. com. on urology Am. Coll. Surgeons 1986-93, pres. elect. 1991-92, pres. 1992-93, chair health policy coun. 1994—) Am. Assn. Genitourinary Surgeons (trustee), Am. Assn. Clin. Urologists, Soc. Internat. D'Urologie, Md. Urol. Assn. (pres. 1970-75), Anne Arundel Med. Soc. (pres. 1966-68), Med. Surg. Faculty Md., Ala. Urol. Soc. (hon.), Fla. Urol. Soc. (hon.), Sigma Nu, Nu Sigma Nu, Alpha Omega Alpha. Avocations: model railroading, scuba diving, marine biology, underwater photography. Home: 473 Fair Oaks Dr

Severna Park MD 21146-3107 Office: Conte Bldg 116 Defense Hwy Ste 200 Annapolis MD 21401-7045

HOLTHAUSEN, MARTHA ANNE, interior designer, painter; b. Columbus, Ohio, Oct. 28, 1934; d. Clyde Aloysius and Olive Letitia (Marlowe) Gloeckner; m. Don Trudeau Allensworth, Aug. 14, 1960 (div. 1976); 1 child, Karen Ayn; m. Ernest Arthur Holthausen, Dec. 9, 1989. BFA cum laude, Ohio State U., 1956; postgrad., Baldwin-Wallace Coll., 1959, Mt. Vernon Coll., Washington, 1980, 81. Fashion illustrator The Marston Co., San Diego, 1956-57, The Higbee Co., Cleve., 1957-58; instr. art Lakewood (Ohio) Pub. Schs., 1958-60; tchr. Princes Georges County (Md.) Pub. Schs., 1960; account exec. Stansbury Design, Inc., Prince Georges County, Md., 1975-76; interior designer Berwin Interiors, Bethesda, Md., 1977-79, W. & J. Sloane, Inc., Washington, 1980-84; pres., interior designer Martha Allensworth Interior Design, Inc., Falls Church, Va., 1984—; guest artist-in-residence Nat. Park Svc., Yosemite Nat. Park, Calif., summer 1988, 89, 91, 95. Watercolor and oil paintings in pvt. collections. Bd. dirs. C. of C. Herndon, Va., 1985-86; v.p. Montgomery County (Md.) Art Assn., 1962-63. Mem. AAUW, Vienna (Va.) Arts Soc. Episcopalian. Avocations: gardening, bicycling. Office: Martha Allensworth Interior Design Inc Ste 900 N 7799 Leesburg Pike Falls Church VA 22043-2413

HOLTKAMP, JAMES ARNOLD, lawyer, educator; b. Albuquerque, Apr. 4, 1949; s. Clarence Jules and Karyl Irene (Roberts) H.; m. Marianne Coltrin, Dec. 28, 1973; children: Ariane, Brent William, Rachel, Allison, David Roberts. BA, Brigham Young U., 1972; JD, George Washington U., 1975. Bar: Utah 1976, U.S. Dist. Ct. Utah 1977, U.S. Ct. Appeals (10th cir.) 1979, Colo. 1995. Mem. staff U.S. Senate Watergate Com., Washington, 1974; atty.-advisor Dept. Transp., Washington, 1975; atty. Dept. Interior, Washington, 1975-77; assoc. Van Cott, Bagley, Cornwall & McCarthy, Salt Lake City, 1977-81, ptnr., 1981-89; ptnr. Davis, Graham & Stubbs, Salt Lake City, 1989-92, Stoel Rives, Salt Lake City, 1992-97, LeBoeuf, Lamb, Greene & MacRae, Salt Lake City, 1997—; adj. prof. Law Sch., Brigham Young U., Provo, Utah, 1979-97, Coll. Law U. Utah, 1995—. Co-author: Utah Environmental and Land Use Permits and Approvals Manual, 1981; contbr. articles to legal jours. Missionary LDS Ch., 1968-70; active Gt. Salt Lake coun. Boy Scouts Am., 1977—; trustee Coalition for Utah's Future, 1996—. Mem. ABA (vice-chmn. air quality commn. 1985-89), Utah State Bar (chmn. energy and natural resources sect. 1984-85, chmn. pub. utilities law com. 1990-93, Lawyer of Yr. award 1981), Utah Mining Assn., Utah Petroleum Assn., George Washington Law Assn. (nat. bd. dirs. 1999—). Home: 3221 Da Vinci Dr Salt Lake City UT 84121-5764 Office: LeBoeuf Lamb Greene & MacRae 136 S Main St Ste 1000 Salt Lake City UT 84101-1665

HOLTKAMP, SUSAN CHARLOTTE, elementary education educator; b. Houston, Feb. 23, 1957; d. Clarence Jules and Karyl Irene (Roberts) H. BS in Early Childhood Edn., Brigham Young U., Provo, Utah, 1979, MEd, 1982. Cert. tchr., Utah. 2d grade tchr. Nebo Sch. Dist., Spanish Fork, Utah, 1979-84, kindergarten tchr., 1984-85; tchr. 2d grade DODDS, Mannheim, Fed. Republic Germany, 1985-86; tchr. 3d grade Jordan Sch. Dist., Salt Lake City, 1987-92, tchr. 5th grade, 1992—. Mem. NEA, JEA, Utah Edn. Assn., ASCD.

HOLTMEIER, ROBERT J., accountant; b. Cin., Apr. 17, 1924; s. Elmer J. and Hilda M. Holtmeier; m. Anna Marie Holtmeier, Sept. 4, 1948; 1 child, Teresa Ann. MBA, U. Cin., 1978. CPA, Ohio. Contr., asst. treas. Aluminum Industries, Cin., 1947-59; v.p. fin. Merry Mfg. Co., Cin., 1958-69, Denby Ltd., Cin., 1969-74; sec., treas. Porter Precision Products, Cin., 1974-86; owner Robert J. Holtmeier CPA, Cin., 1986—. Author: Business Forecasting in Today's World, 1955. Sgt. USAF, 1942-46, ETO. Mem. Ohio Soc. CPAs. Avocations: golf, painting in oil, model building.

HOLTON, GERALD, physicist, science historian; b. Berlin, Germany, May 23, 1922; s. Emanuel and Regina (Rossmann) H.; m. Nina Rossfort, Sept. 12, 1947; children: Thomas, Stephan. Nat. certificate elec. engring., Sch. Tech., Oxford, Eng., 1940; B.A., Wesleyan U., 1941, M.A., 1942, D.H.L. (hon.), 1981; M.A., Harvard U., 1946, Ph.D., 1948; D.Sc. (hon.), Grinnell Coll., 1967, Kenyon Coll., 1977, Bates Coll., 1979; LL.D. (hon.), Duke U., 1981. Instr. Wesleyan U., 1941-42, Brown U., 1942-43; staff, officers radar course and OSRD Harvard, 1943-45, various faculty positions, 1945—; Mallinckrodt prof. physics and prof. history of sci.; exchange prof. Harvard-Leningrad U., 1962; vis. mem. Inst. Advanced Study, Princeton, 1964; fellow Center Advanced Study in Behavioral Scis., Stanford, 1975-76; vis. prof. MIT, 1976-94; Herbert Spencer lectr. Oxford U., 1979; Morris Loeb lectr. Harvard U., 1993; Rothschild lectr. Harvard U., 1997; Jefferson lectr. in humanities, 1981; John Simon Guggenheim fellow, 1980-81; mem. com. scholarly comm. with People's Republic of China, NAS, 1967-72, mem. com. conduct of sci., 1989-91; mem. U.S. Nat. Commn. on UNESCO, 1975-80, U.S. Nat. Commn. of IUHPS, 1982-89, Coun. of Scholars, Libr. of Congress, 1980—, U.S. Nat. Commn. on Excellence in Edn., 1981-83; mem. adv. com. for sci. and engring. edn. NSF, 1985-93, chair, 1986-89; mem. selection bd. Albert Einstein Peace Prize, 1980—; mem. German Am. Acad. Coun. Kuratorium, 1997—. Author: Introduction to Concepts and Theories in Physical Science, 1952, 2d edit., 1985, (with D.H.D. Roller) Foundations of Modern Physical Science, 1958, Science and the Modern Mind, 1958, Science and Culture, 1965, (with others) The Project Physics Course, 1970, 75, 81, The 20th Century Sciences: Studies in Intellectual Biography, 1971, Thematic Origins of Scientific Thought: Kepler to Einstein, 1973, 2d edit., 1988, The Scientific Imagination: Case Studies, 1978, 98, (with others) Limits of Scientific Inquiry, 1979, Albert Einstein, Historical and Cultural Perspectives, 1982, 97, The Advancement of Science and Its Burdens, 1986, 98, Science and Anti-Science, 1993, Einstein, History and Other Passions, 1995, (with Gerhard Sonnert) Gender Differences in Science Careers: The Project Access Study, 1995, Who Succeeds in Science? The Gender Dimension, 1995; editor-in-chief Daedalus, 1957-61; mem. editl. com., editl. adv. bd. The Collected Papers of Albert Einstein, 1980—; contbr. articles to profl. jours. Recipient J.D. Bernal prize Soc. Social Studies Sci., 1989, Joseph Priestley medal Dickinson Coll., 1994. Fellow AAAS (bd. dirs. 1967-71), Am. Philos. Soc., Am. Acad. Arts and Sci. (editor 1957-63, exec. bd. 1970-78, coun. 1991-95), Am. Phys. Soc. (chmn. divsn. history of physics 1992-93), Internat. Acad. History of Sci. (v.p. 1981-89), Deutsche Acad. Naturforscher-Leopoldina, Internat. Acad. Philosophy of Sci.; mem. Am. Inst. Physics (governing bd. 1968-74, Andrew Gemant award 1989), Am. Assn. Physics Tchrs. (Robert A. Millikan medal 1967, Oersted medal 1980), History Sci. Soc. (pres. 1983-84, George Sarton meml. lectr. 1962, George Sarton medal 1989, Joseph H. Hazen Edn. prize). Office: Harvard U Jefferson Phys Lab Cambridge MA 02138

HOLTON, GRACE HOLLAND, accountant; b. Durham, N.C., Sept. 14, 1957; d. Samuel Melanchthon and B. Margaret (Umberger) H. BS in Math., Univ. N.C., Greensboro, 1978; MBA, Univ. N.C., Chapel Hill, 1984; M.Acctg. Sci., U. Ill., 1993. CPA N.C.; cert. mgmt. acct. Indsl. engr. Burlington Industries, Inc., Mayodan, N.C., 1978-79; plant indsl. engr. Burlington Industries, Inc., Stoneville, N.C., 1979-80; methods indsl. engr. Blue Cross and Blue Shield of N.C., Durham, 1980-82; fin. analyst R.J. Reynolds, Inc., Winston-Salem, N.C., 1984-85; accounting cons. Ryder Truck Rental, Inc., Miami, Fla., 1985-88; controller Ryder Jacobs (div. Ryder Distbn. Resources), Jessup, Md., 1988-90; grad. asst. in acctg. U. Ill., Urbana, 1990-93; contr. Salem NationaLease, Winston-Salem, N.C., 1993-94; dir. fin. Chapel Hill-Carrboro City Schs., 1994—. KPMG-Peat Marwick scholar, 1991-92. Mem. AICPAs, Inst. Mgmt. Accts., N.C. Soc. CPAs. Democrat. Methodist.

HOLTON, HELEN LARA, city official, marketing professional; b. Norfolk, Va., Aug. 18, 1960; d. Hiram Holton and Barbara Marie Goodwin Cuffie. Student, Morgan State U., Balt., 1977-80; BS, U. Balt., 1982; MS in Bus., Johns Hopkins U., 1995. CPA, Md. Sr. acct. USF&G, Balt., 1985-86; lead fin. adminstr. Westinghouse, Linthicum, Md., 1986-93; contr. Excelsior Cos., Silver Spring, Md., 1993-94; cons. Resource One Mgmt. Group, Balt., 1994-97; mktg. dir. Bolton Offutt Donovan, Inc., Balt., 1997—; mem. Balt. City Coun., 1995—. Treas., Civic Works, Inc., Balt., 1996—; treas. Black Jewish Forum of Balt., 1991-96. Recipient 1st place award Nat. Black MBA Assn. Competition, 1994; named among Top 100 Women of Md., Warfields/The Daily Record, 1997. Mem. AICPA, NAACP (life), Delta Sigma Theta (Verda Freeman Welcome Polit. award 1997). Democrat. Avocations: golf, theatre, museums, fine dining, shopping for antiques. Office: Balt City Coun 100 Holliday St Ste 518 Baltimore MD 21202-3417*

HOLTON, J(ERRY) THOMAS, concrete company executive; b. Middletown, Ohio, June 7, 1932; s. Joseph Walton and Elizabeth (Fagaly) H.; m. Annie Lou Dearborn, Sept. 26, 1958; children: Elizabeth, Luanne, Ruth, Catherine, J. Thomas Jr. BSE, Princeton U., 1954; MBA, Harvard U., 1959. V.p. Sherman Concrete Pipe Co., Birmingham, Ala., 1959-66, pres., 1966-74; pres. Sherman Industries, Birmingham, 1974-84; pres., chmn. Sherman Internat. Corp., Birmingham, 1984—; bd. dirs. Fed. Res. Bank Atlanta, Robin-Morton Corp., KSA, Inc., Sciotoville, Ohio, The Shaw Group Ltd., Halifax, N.S., Stockham Valve & Fittings Co. Inc. Pres. coun. U. Ala. Birmingham, 1984-92; mem. exec. bd. Boy Scouts Am., Birmingham, 1985—; chmn., Salvation Army, Birmingham; elder Briarwood Presbyn. Ch., Birmingham, 1968—. Lt. comdr. Civil Engring. Corp. USN, 1954-57. Mem. Birmingham Country Club, Shoal Creek, The Club, Summit Club. Home: 10 Ridge Dr Birmingham AL 35213-3632 Office: Sherman International Inc 402 Office Park Dr Ste 100 Birmingham AL 35223-2435

HOLTON, RAYMOND WILLIAM, botanist, educator; b. Riverside, Calif., Apr. 30, 1929; s. Homer Hopkins and H. Charlotte (Hall) H.; children: Betsey Diane, Nancy Joann, William Louis, Thomas Raymond. B.A., Pomona Coll., 1951; M.S., U. Mich., 1954, Ph.D., 1958. Instr. botany U. Mich.-Flint Coll., 1957-59, asst. prof., 1959-61; research asso. U. Tex., 1961-62, USPHS trainee, 1962-63; asst. prof. botany U. Tenn., 1963-64, assoc. prof., acting head botany, 1964-65, prof., head botany, 1965-72, 73-85, prof. botany, 1985-96, prof. emeritus, 1997—, co-dir., 1984-86, acting dir. biology consortium, 1992-93; sr. Fulbright lectr. dept. botany U. Durham, Eng., 1972-73; vis. prof. U. Groningen, The Netherlands, 1987, 94. Mem. Bot. Soc. Am., Am. Soc. Plant Physiologists, Phycol. Soc. Am., Internat., Brit. phycol. socs., AAAS. Phylogenetic and biochem. research on algae, particularly cyanobacteria and fresh water rhodophyta. Home: 118 Greenbrier Dr Knoxville TN 37919-4165 Office: U Tenn Dept Botany 437 Hesler Biology Bldg Knoxville TN 37996-1100

HOLTON, ROBERT PAGE, publishing executive; b. St. Paul, Jan. 18, 1938; s. Robert Henry and Grace (Page) H.; m. Sandra Janice Heyl, July 16, 1960. B.S. in Indsl. Distbn., Clarkson Coll., 1960. Asst. editor McGraw-Hill Indsl. Distbn., N.Y.C., 1960-61; dist. mgr. McGraw-Hill Indsl. Distbn., Chgo., 1963-65, McGraw-Hill-Textile World, Phila., 1965-71, McGraw-Hill-Chem. Engring., Pitts., 1971-76; mktg. service dir. McGraw-Hill-Chem. Engring., N.Y.C., 1976-81; sr. v.p., pub., Marine Engring./Log Simmons-Boardman, N.Y.C., 1981-85; pub. PennWell Publ.-Computer Graphics World mag., 1985-94; pres. Robert Holton Assocs., 1994—; group pub. Computer Graphics World, Computer Artist, Computer Graphic World Buyers Guide, Computer Graphics World-Asia Pacific, Electronic Pub., Color Pub., 1991-94. Assoc. pub., advt. dir. USA Lawyers Weekly Pubs., 1997-98; contbr. articles to profl. jours. Recipient Order of Merit Boy Scouts Am., 1969; recipient Silver Beaver Boy Scouts Am., 1975. Mem. Assoc. Bus. Pubs. (pub. com. 1989-92).

HOLTON, WALTER CLINTON, JR., lawyer; b. Winston-Salem, N.C.; s. Walter Clinton and Mabel (Hartsfield) H.; m. Lynne Rowley. BA in Polit. Sci., U. N.C., 1977; JD, Wake Forest U., 1984. Bar: N.C. 1984, U.S. Dist. Ct. (mid. dist.) N.C. 1986, U.S. Ct. Appeals (4th cir.) 1990, U.S. Supreme Ct., 1996. Asst. dist. atty. Office 21st Jud. Dist. Atty., Winston-Salem, 1985-87; assoc. White & Crumpler, Winston-Salem, 1987-88; pvt. practice Winston-Salem, 1989; ptnr. Holton & Menefee, Winston-Salem, 1989-92, Tisdale, Holton & Menefee, PA, Winston-Salem, 1992-94; U.S. atty. Office U.S. Atty. Mid. Dist. N.C., Greensboro, N.C., 1994—. Democrat. Office: Office US Atty PO Box 1858 Greensboro NC 27402-1858

HOLTON, WILLIAM, artist; b. Knoxville, Tenn., 1966. Student, U. Ariz., 1987-88; BFA, Atlanta Coll. Art, 1991. Intern Rolling Stone Press, Atlanta, 1989; assistant Atlanta Arts Festival, 1991. One-man shows include Anthony Ardavin Gallery, Atlanta, 1994, TVUUC Gallery, Knoxville, 1999; two-person shows include Anthony Ardavin Gallery, Atlanta, 1995, 97, 99; group shows include Anthony Ardavin Gallery, Atlanta, 1993, Atlanta Coll. Art Gallery, 1993, Southeastern Ctr. Contemporary Art, Winston-Salem, N.C., 1997, Zoe Gallery, Louisville, Ky., 1998, 99; contbg. artist: Drawing, Space, Form and Expression, 1988. Recipient Merit award Magic City Arts Festival, 1991, Best of Show award ARTFEST, 1994; Regional Visual Arts fellow Southeastern Arts Fedn./Nat. Endowment Arts, 1996.

HOLTON, WILLIAM COFFEEN, electrical engineering executive; b. Washington, July 24, 1930; s. William B. and Esther (Coffeen) H.; m. Mary Schaeffer, Aug. 5, 1953; children: Elizabeth Ashe, William Andrew, Sarah Anne. BS in Physics, U. N.C., 1952; PhD in Physics, U. Ill., 1960. Tech. staff corp. rsch. lab. Tex. Instruments, Dallas, 1960-65; mgr. quantum electronics Tex. Instruments, 1965-72, dir. advanced components lab., 1972-78, dir. R & D semicondr. group, 1978-82, mgr. strategic planning, 1982-83; dir. Semiconductor Rsch. Corp., Research Triangle Park, N.C., 1984-88, sr. dir., 1989-90, v.p., 1990-95; prof. N.C. State U., Raleigh, 1996—. Lt. (j.g.) USN, 1952-54. Union Carbide fellow, 1959; recipient Dept. of Energy award, 1997. Fellow IEEE (Phillips award 1998), Am. Phys. Soc., Electron. Device Soc. of IEEE (governing bd. 1975-98, chmn. internat. electron device meeting 1975); mem. Phi Beta Kappa, Phi Eta Sigma. Presbyterian. Home: 601 Brookview Dr Chapel Hill NC 27514-1401 Office: NC State Univ Box 8617 234B Engring Grad Rsch Ctr Raleigh NC 27695-7911

HOLTON, WILLIAM MILNE, English language and literature educator; b. Charlotte, N.C., Nov. 4, 1931; s. William Hubon and Mary (Milne) H.; m. Sylvia Wallace, July 3, 1964. AB cum laude, Dartmouth Coll., 1954; LLB, Harvard U., 1957; MA, Yale U., 1959, PhD, 1965. Bar: Tenn. 1957, U.S. Supreme Ct. 1965. Atty. Roberts & Weil, Chattanooga, Tenn., 1957, Nat. Edn. Assn., Washington, 1958; instr. English U. Md., College Park, 1961-65, asst. prof., 1966-72, assoc. prof., 1972-78, prof., 1978—; Fulbright lectr. Uppsala U., Sweden, 1965-66; vis. prof. Cyril & Methodius U., Skopje, Yugoslavia, 1970; lectr. Dept. State Czechoslovakia, Yugoslavia, Poland, Sweden, 1965-84, various other orgns.; del. various internat. meetings. Author: Cylinder of Vision, 1972; co-author: Private Dealings, 1970, 74; editor, translator: The Big Horse, 1974; co-editor: The New Polish Poetry, 1978; co-editor, translator: Reading the Ashes, 1977 (Golden Pen award), Austrian Poetry Today, 1985; co-author: Serbian Poetry from the Beginnings to the Present, 1989, The Songs of the Serbian People, 1997; contbr. articles to profl. jours. IREX fellow, 1980; grantee NEH, 1980, U. Md., 1967, 69, 74, 76, 78, 85, 88; recipient Amicus Poloniae medal, 1981. Mem. PEN, Stephen Crane Soc., James Joyce Found., Phi Beta Kappa. Democrat. Episcopalian. Home: 517 A St SE Washington DC 20003-1140 Office: Univ of Md Dept English College Park MD 20472

HOLTZ, CAROLYN A., medical/surgical nurse; b. Madisonville, Ky., Oct. 20, 1952; d. Charles H. and Betty J. (Lee) Walker; children: Kara Megan, Jace Ashley. ADN, U. Evansville, 1977, BSN, 1989. Staff nurse Deaconess Hosp., Evansville, Ind., 1977—.

HOLTZ, EDGAR WOLFE, lawyer; b. Clarksburg, W.Va., Jan. 18, 1922; s. Dennis Drummond and Oleta (Wolfe) H.; m. Alberta Lee Brinkley, May 6, 1944; children: Diana Hilary, Heidi Johanna. BA, Denison U., 1943; JD, U. Cin., 1949. Bar: Ohio 1949, U.S. Supreme Ct. 1957, D.C. 1961. Assoc. firm Matthews & Matthews, Cin., 1949-53; asst. dean Chase Law Sch., Cin., 1952-55; asst. solicitor City of Cin., 1950-55; asst. chief office of opinions and rev. FCC, Washington, 1955-56; dep. gen. counsel FCC, 1956-60; mem. firm Hogan & Hartson, Washington, 1960—. Trustee Denison U., Granville, Ohio, 1974—; chmn. bd. Ctr. for the Arts, Vero Beach, Fla., 1995-97; bd. dirs. Cultural Coun. Indian River County, 1998—. Served to 1st lt. USAAF, 1943-45. Decorated D.F.C., Air medal with 2 clusters, 8 Battle Stars; recipient Alumni citation Denison U., 1993. Fellow Am. Bar Found.; mem. ABA (standing com. on gavel awards), Ohio Bar Assn., D.C. Bar Assn., Fed. Comms. Bar (pres. 1977-78), Am. Juicature Soc., Newcomen Soc. N.Am., Moorings Club (Vero Beach, Fla.), Met. Club (Washington, George Town Club (Washington). Republican. Methodist. Office: Hogan & Hartson 555 13th St NW Ste 800E Washington DC 20004-1161

HOLTZ, GLENN EDWARD, band instrument manufacturing executive; b. Detroit, Jan. 15, 1938; s. Edward Christian and Evelyn Adele (Priehs) Foutz H.; m. Mary Eleanor Russell, Nov. 25, 1981; children by previous marriage: Robert, Kimberly, Rene, Letitia, Kimberly, Pamela. B in Music Edn., U. Mich., 1960, M in Music Edn., 1964; cons. motivation student, Pers. Dynamics, Mpls., 1980. Music tchr. Middleville H.S., Mich., 1960-62; dist. mgr. Selmer Co., Elkhart, Ind., 1965-74; sales mgr. Selmer Co., Elkhart, 1974-76; pres. Knapp Mus. Co., Grand Rapids, Mich., 1976-80; v.p. mktg. sales Gemeinhardt/CBS, Elkhart, 1981-83; pres., CEO Gemeinhardt Co., Inc., 1983—; pres., bd. dirs., trustee Vandercook Coll. Mus. Dist. gov. Lion's Internat., Jackson, Lansing, Battle Creek, Mich., 1970-71; pres. Middleville Bd. Edn., 1964-66; bd. dirs., treas. Midwest Band and Orch.; mem. bd. music Ind. Coun., pres. Music Industry Conf. Recipient Disting. award Lion's Internat., Mich., 1971. Mem. Nat. Assn. Band Instrument Mfrs. (pres. 1986-88), Am. Music Conf. (bd. dirs. 1987—, past pres. nat. Fla. ind. coun.), Nat. Assn. Music Merchants (bd. dirs., Disting. Music Industry award), Music Industry Conf. Bd. (pres. 1998—). Republican. Office: Geminhardt PO Box 788 Elkhart IN 46515-0788

HOLTZ, JOSEPH NORMAN, marketing executive; b. Matawan, N.J., Oct. 11, 1930; s. Joseph Antone and Catherine Martina (Crosby) H.; m. Irene Strano, July 15, 1951; children: Joseph Jr., Karl, Gary, Robert, Eric. AA, De Vry Tech. Inst., 1954; student, Monmouth Coll., 1955-56; BBA, Nat. U., 1988, MBA, 1989; grad., Realtor Inst. Lic. real estate broker Calif., Cert. Factoring Specialist designation Internat. Factoring Inst., Cert. Mortgage Investor designation Nat. Mortgage Investors Inst. Engr. Bendix Aviation, Red Bank, N.J., 1952-56, Hughes Aircraft Co., L.A., 1956-73; pres. Jo-Rene Assocs., Orange, Calif., 1973-86; asst. v.p. Builders Sales Corp., Santa Ana, Calif., 1986-87; exec. v.p. The Lehnert Group, Irvine, Calif., 1987-88; pres. J.N. Holtz Assocs., Orange, 1988—; CEO Holtz Funding Group, Orange, 1994—; v.p., corp. broker Mortgage Outlet Corp., 1992-94; corp. broker Shancie Real Estate Corp., 1992-94. Com. mem. United Way, Santa Ana, 1987-97. Mem. IEEE, Inst. Residential Mktg., Sales and Mktg. Coun., Nat. Assn. Factoring Profls., Nat. Real Estate and Mortgage Investors Assn., Phoenix Club, Am. Soc. for Quality Control. Republican. Avocations: computer programming, travel. Home: 5045-2 E Almond Ave Orange CA 92869-4245 Office: J N Holtz Assocs PO Box 10014 Santa Ana CA 92711-0014

HOLTZ, LAURENCE, artisan, photographer; b. Spangler, Pa., Jan. 9, 1949; s. Paul Omer and Helen Zita (McCombie) H.; m. Priscilla Suzanne Adsit, May 17, 1981; 1 child, Samara Adsit. BA, LaSalle Coll., Phila., 1974. Hand weaver Hardwick, Vt., 1987—. Contbr. short story and poetry to Coldspot, 1998. Mem. Ctrl. Vt. Regional Planning Commn., Montpelier, 1982, Plainfield (Vt.) Planning Commn., 1982; vol. Vt. Dept. Corrections Northeast Regional Correctional Facility, St. Johnsbury, 1998—; mem. Reparative Probation Bd., Barre Office, 1998—. Mem. New England Antiquities Rsch. Assocs., Vt. Weaver's Guild. Avocations: instrumental music, creative writing. Office: PO Box 51 Hardwick VT 05843-0051

HOLTZ, LOUIS LEO, former college football coach, sports commentator; b. Follansbee, W.Va., Jan. 6, 1937; m. Beth Barcus, July 22, 1961; children: Luanne, Skip, Kevin Richard, Elizabeth. BA, Kent State U., 1959; MA, U. Iowa, 1961. Asst. football coach U. Iowa, Iowa City, Coll. William and Mary, Williamsburg, Va., U. Conn., Storrs, U. S.C., Columbia, Ohio State U., Columbus; head football coach Coll. William and Mary, 1969-71, N.C. State U., Raleigh, 1972-75; coach N.Y. Jets, 1976; head football coach U. Ark., Fayetteville, 1977-83, U. Minn., Mpls., 1983-85, Notre Dame U., Ind., 1986-96; analyst Coll. Football Today CBS, N.Y.C., 1997—; motavational spkr. Author: Kitchen Quarterback, Fighting Spirit. Named NCAA Dist. Coach of Yr., 1973, Nat. Coach of Yr. Football Writers, Sporting News, 1977; S.W. Conf. Coach of Yr. AP, UPI, 1979; team Nat. Champions, 1988, longest consecutive winning streak (23), 1988-89; named Nat. Coach of Yr., 1988. Roman Catholic. Office: CBS Sports care Coll. Football Today 524 W 57th St New York NY 10019-2924*

HOLTZ, MICHAEL P., hotel executive. Pres., CEO Amerihost Properties, Inc., Des Plaines, Ill. Office: Amerihost Properties Inc 2400 E Devon Ave Ste 280 Des Plaines IL 60018-4625*

HOLTZ, SARA, lawyer, consultant; b. L.A., Aug. 7, 1951. BA, Yale U., 1972; JD, Harvard U., 1975. Bar: D.C. 1975, Calif. 1982. Assoc. Brownstein, Zeidman & Schomer, Washington, 1975-77; dep. asst. dir. FTC, Washington, 1977-82; divsn. counsel Clorox Co., Oakland, Calif., 1982-90; v.p., dep. gen. counsel Nestle U.S.A., Inc., San Francisco, 1990-94; prin. Client Focus, 1996—. Mem. Am. Corp. Counsel Assn. (bd. dirs. 1986-95, chmn. 1994-95). Office: 9407 Swan Lake Dr Granite Bay CA 95746-7205

HOLTZ, SIDNEY, publishing company executive; b. N.Y.C., Mar. 24, 1925; s. Jacob and Rose (Cholmar) H.; m. Florence Fogel, Sept. 6, 1952; children: Jeffrey, Clifford, Linda. BS, LIU, 1949; MS, NYU, 1950; BPA (hon.), Brooks Inst., 1973. Tchr. pub. schs. N.Y.C., 1951-53; advt. sales rep. N.Y. Herald Tribune, 1953-58; with Ziff-Davis Pub. Co., N.Y.C., 1958-85; mem. sales staff Popular Photography, 1958-60, advt. dir., 1960-67, assoc. pub., 1967-68, pub., 1968-85, corp. v.p., 1972-85; pres. Holtz Assocs., 1985—; bd. dirs. Photographic Adminstrs. Inc.; worldwide exhibit dir. Conservation Edn. Diving Archeology Mus., 1990; dir. photographic workshop electronic imaging New Sch. for Social Rsch. With U.S. Army, 1943-46. Mem. Internat. Photography Hall of Fame (chmn. emeritus), Photog. Art and Sci. Found., Internat. Photog. Coun., Photog. Adminstrs., Inc. (1st v.p., bd. dirs.), Ardsley Country Club, The Dutch Treat Club, Nat. Arts Club. Home and Office: 206 Palisade Ave Dobbs Ferry NY 10522-3514

HOLTZ, TOBENETTE, aerospace engineer; b. Rochester, N.Y., June 20, 1930; d. Marcus and Leah (Cohen) H.; m. Joseph Laurinovics, Dec. 25, 1964. BS in Aeronautical Engring., Wayne State U., 1958; MS in Aero/Astro Engring., Ohio State U., 1964; PhD, U. So. Calif., L.A., 1974. Sr. engr. North Am. Aviation, Columbus, Ohio, 1954-59; rsch. assoc. Ohio State U., Columbus, 1959-60; sr. engr. U. So. Calif. Rsch. Found., Pt. Mugu, 1960-62, Northrop Corp., Hawthorne, Calif., 1962-67; engring. specialist McDonnell Douglas Corp., Huntington Beach, Calif., 1967-75; staff engr. Acurex Corp., Mountain View, Calif., 1975-76; project mgr. Aerospace Corp., El Segundo, Calif., 1976-82; tech. mgr. TRW, Inc., San Bernardino, Calif., 1982—. Contbr. articles to profl. jours. Assoc. fellow AIAA (sect. vice chair 1980-82, 91-92, nat. tech. com. 1991—, organizer nat. confs. 1979, 86, 88, 94, 96, 98, 99 Disting. Svc. award 1983). Office: TRW Inc PO Box 1310 San Bernardino CA 92402-1310

HOLTZCLAW, DIANE SMITH, elementary education educator; b. Buffalo, May 26, 1936; d. John Nelson and Beatrice M. (Salisbury) Smith; m. John Victor Holtzclaw, June 27, 1959; children: Kathryn Diane, John Bryan. BS in Edn. magna cum laude, SUNY, Brockport, 1957, MS with honors, 1961; postgrad., SUNY, Buffalo, 1960-65, Canisus Coll., 1979, Nazareth Coll., 1981-82. Tchr. Greece Cen. Sch., Rochester, N.Y., 1957-60; supr. SUNY, Brockport, 1960-64, assoc. prof. edn., 1960-64; dir. Early Childhood Ctr., Fairport, N.Y., 1968-80; tchr. Fairport Cen. Schs., 1971—; ednl. cons. in field; specialist child devel. Ch. music dir., Rochester, N.Y., 1983—; pres. bd. dirs. Downtown Day Care Ctr., Rochester, 1974-83; mem. exec. bd. Rochester Theatre Organ Soc., 1988—. Mem. Fairport Edn. Assn. (exec. bd. 1982-83, del. 1983), N.Y. State United Tchrs., AAUW (exec. bd. 1973-74, 77-79, 83-84, pres. Fairport br. 1971-73), Internat. Platform Assn., Kappa Delta Pi. Home: 1455 Ayrault Rd Fairport NY 14450-9301 Office: Fairport Cen Schs 38 W Church St Fairport NY 14450-2130

HOLTZCLAW, MARK ALEXANDER, social worker; b. Guantanamo Bay, Cuba, Feb. 27, 1961; s. James Calvin and Virginia Maree Holtzclaw; m. Kellie Elizabeth Helsley, Apr. 14, 1988; children: Fred, Alexander, Erica. AA, Sante Fe C.C., Gainesville, Fla., 1984; BS, Fla. State U., 1989, MSW, 1996. Social worker Fla. Dept. Health and Rehab. Svcs., Gainesville, 1990-95; program specialist Divsn. Disease Control, Tallahassee, 1996-98; health edn. program mgr. Office Tobacco Control, Tallahassee, 1998—. Named Teen of Yr., Fla. Elks, 1979, Davis Productivity award Fla. TaxWatch, 1993. Mem. NASW, ASPA, Pub. Adminstrn. Grad. Assn., Phi Alpha. Republican. Episcopalian. Office: Office of Tobacco Control 725 S Calhoun St G-14 Bloxham Bldg Tallahassee FL 32301

HOLTZMAN, ARNOLD HAROLD, chemical company executive; b. Phila., May 11, 1932; s. William and Rae (Shapiro) H.; m. Phyllis Raskow, June 26, 1955; children: Rosalind Ann, Linda Susan, William Lewis. BS, Drexel Inst., 1954; MS, Lehigh U., 1956, PhD, 1957. Asst. metallurgist J. Bishop & Co., Malvern, Pa., 1954; with duPont Co., various locations, 1957-89; rsch. mgr., dist. sales mgr. polymer intermediates dept. duPont Co., Wilmington, Del., 1973-76; mgr. new bus. programs, ctrl. R&D dept. duPont Co., Wilmington, 1976-78, mgr. health products, 1980-81, dir. devel. divsn. ctrl. R&D dept., 1982-89, cons., 1989—; pres. Action Games, Inc., 1988—; bd. dirs. Alzheimer's Assn. (Del. chpt.), 1992-97, pres., 1992-95; rsch. assoc. Elwyn, Inc, 1997—. Recipient John Price Wetherill medal Franklin Inst., 1969. Fellow Am. Soc. Metals; mem. Sigma Xi. Achievements include patentee in processing of metals and non metals. Home and Office: 208 Stonecrop Rd Wilmington DE 19810-1320

HOLTZMAN, ELLEN A., foundation executive; b. N.Y.C., Mar. 5, 1952; d. Jerome and Corinne (Weinbaum) H.; m. Michael P. Bloom, June 18, 1978 (div. 1983); m. Robert S. Evans, Aug. 8, 1986. BA in Art History, George Washington U., 1973; MA in Art History, U. Calif., Santa Barbara, 1975. Cert. tchr., Calif. Asst. to dir. Bklyn. Mus., 1980-82, asst. mgr. pub. programs and media, 1983-85; asst. dir. Queens Mus., Flushing, N.Y., 1985-88; mng. dir. New Mus. Contemporary Art, N.Y.C., 1988-92; program dir. for arts Henry Luce Found., Inc., N.Y.C., 1992—; adj. faculty Bank St. Coll. Edn., N.Y.C., 1990; participant exec. mgmt. workshop NYU, 1986. Exec. com. N.Y.C. Arts Coalition, 1988-92; mem. N.Y. Hist. Soc. Cmty. Adv. Bd., 1994. Mem. Am. Assn. Mus. (surveyor mus. assessment program 1990—), N.Y. Archival Soc., Art Table, Grantmakers in the Arts. Avocation: travel. Office: Henry Luce Found Inc 111 W 50th St New York NY 10020-1202

HOLTZMAN, GARY YALE, administrative and financial executive; b. N.Y.C., Aug. 7, 1936; s. Abram and Pearl (Kashetsky) H.; m. Alice A. Lang, Sept. 5, 1958; children: Bruce, Sheri, Michele. BBA, CCNY, 1958. Exec. v.p. control and ops. Jordan Marsh Co., Miami, Fla., 1967-87; sr. v.p. ops. and stores L. Luria & Sons Inc., Miami, 1987-93; exec. dir. Mar Jewish Community Ctr., Greater Miami, Fla., 1993-95; TSR-Social Security Adminstrn., 1995—; bd. advisers Universal Nat. Bank. Bd. dirs. Dade County Safety Coun., Miami, 1978-85, Jewish Cmty. Ctr. Greater Miami, 1983-88, Fla. Bus. Roundtable, 1975-80, Anti-Defamation League of B'nia B'rith, 1983-87; bd. advisers Opportunities Industrialization Ctr., 1982-84; pres. Michael Ann Russell Jewish Cmty. Ctr., 1984-86, bd. dirs., 1980—; life bd. dirs. Temple Beth Torah Adath Yeshurun, 1969-75, 96—, Temple B'nai Aviv, 1984-86; active Miami Jewish Fedn.; com. chmn. United Way of Dade County. Lt. U.S. Army, 1958-59; capt. USAR, 1959-65. Recipient Americanism award Anti-Defamation League, 1983; recipient Adath Yeshurun Man of Yr. award, 1978. Mem. Greater Miami C. of C., Fla. Retail Fedn. Democrat. Home: 2019 Cove Ln Weston FL 33326-2336

HOLTZMAN, JOAN KING, musician, composer; b. Aberdeen, S.D., Aug. 14, 1925; d. James Wilfred and Miriam Hughes (Evans) K.; m. Wayne Harold Holtzman, Aug. 23, 1947; children: Wayne Jr., James, Scott, Karl. B in Music Edn., Northwestern U., 1947; EdMA, Stanford U., 1948. Pres. Jojo's Prodns., Austin, Tex., 1991—. Author: (with Leslie Holtzman) The Fat Rat and This and That, 1997, (with Rosario Ahumada de Diaz) Happy Times with English, 1987; composer, pianist, singer children's cassettes Jo Jo's Songs for Growing Up, 1991, Beasts, Veggies and Sospetigious Things, 1993; composer melodies song book and cassette Symphony for Simple Simon, 1984 (award of excellence Am. Symphony Orch. League, 1984); composer numerous songs. Active Save Children Fedn., 1954—, pres. 1958; vol. Austin Cerebral Palsy Ctr., 1955-59; mem. Pan Am. Round Table, 1958—, sec. 1965-66; co-founder Internat. Hospitality Com. Austin, 1960—, chmn. host families, 1960-62; pres. PTA Austin H.S., 1972; mem. Austin Arts Commn., 1977-83; mem. nat. adv. coun. Nat. Sch. Vol. Program, Washington, 1976-91; mem. adv. com. Austin Ind. Sch. Dist., 1983-91, forming future com., 1982; mem. arts plan task force City of Austin, 1985; docent, gov. mansion, 1983—; nat. class rep. Northwestern U. Sch. Music, 1977-91; mus. vol. Austin State Hosp., 1967-83; sec, bd. dirs. Austin Symphony Orch. Soc., 1968—; state bd. dirs. Very Special Arts - Tex., 1987-91; bd. dirs, chmn. coms. Child and Family Svcs., Austin, 1965-82. Named Outstanding Fundraiser Austin Symphony Devel. fund drive, 1981; Festival Favorite New Tex. Choral Music Festival, Austin, 1995, Yellow Rose Tex., Tex. Gov., 1995, Vol. of Yr., 1995. Mem. Women's Symphony League Austin (pres. 1958-59, charter mem., Woman of Yr. award 1991), Austin Jr. League (Vol. Extraordinaire award 1985), Mortar Bd. U. Tex. Austin (Citation award 1976), Playhouse Singers, Settlement Club, Austin Woman's Club, Univ. Ladies Club (pres. 1971-72), Sigma Alpha Iota (charter mem., pres. 1972-73, Rose of Honor award 1976). Office: Jojo's Prodns 3300 Foothill Dr Austin TX 78731-5823

HOLTZMAN, ROBERT ARTHUR, lawyer; b. L.A., July 17, 1929; s. Ruben and Bertha (Dembowsky) H.; m. Barbara Polis, June 26, 1954 (dec. 1985); children: Melinda, Mark, Bradley; m. Liliane Gurwith Endlich, July 6, 1986. BA, UCLA, 1951; LLB, U. So. Calif., 1954. Bar: Calif. 1955, U.S. Dist. Ct. (cen. dist.) Calif. 1955, U.S. Ct. Appeals (9th cir.) 1958. Assoc. Gang, Tyre & Brown, L.A., 1954; assoc. Loeb and Loeb, L.A., 1956-63, ptnr., 1964-95; of counsel, 1996—; judge pro tem Mcpl. Ct. L.A. Jud. Dist.; lectr. Calif. Continuing Edn. of Bar. Contbr. articles to legal publs. With U.S. Army, 1954-56. Mem. ABA (dispute resolution sect., vice-chmn. arbitration com.), Calif. Bar Assn. (chmn. com. on adminstrn. of justice 1984-85), L.A. County Bar Assn., Am. Arbitration Assn. (panel arbitrators 1974—, panel mediators 1992—, arbitrator large complex case program 1993—). Office: Loeb & Loeb LLP 1000 Wilshire Blvd Ste 1800 Los Angeles CA 90017-2475

HOLTZMAN, ROBERTA LEE, French and Spanish language educator; b. Detroit, Nov. 24, 1938; d. Paul John and Sophia (Marcus) H. AB cum laude, Wayne State U., 1959, MA, 1973; MA, U. Mich., 1961. Fgn. lang. tchr. Birmingham (Mich.) Sch. Dist., 1959-60, Cass Tech. H.S., Detroit, 1961-64; from instr. to prof. French and Spanish, Schoolcraft Coll., Livonia, Mich., 1964-84, chmn. French and Spanish depts., 1984—. Trustee Cranbrook Music Guild, Ednl. Community, Bloomfield Hills, Mich., 1976-78. Fulbright-Hays fellow, Brazil, 1964. Mem. AAUW, NEA, MLA, Nat. Mus. Women in Arts (co-founder 1992), Am. Assn. Tchrs. of Spanish and Portuguese, Am. Assn. Tchrs. of French, Mich. Edn. Assn. Avocations: swimming, book collecting, photography, travel. Office: Schoolcraft Coll 18600 Haggerty Rd Livonia MI 48152-3932

HOLTZMAN, WAYNE HAROLD, psychologist, educator; b. Chgo., Jan. 16, 1923; s. Harold Hoover and Lillian (Manny) H.; m. Joan King, Aug. 23, 1947; children: Wayne Harold, James K., Scott E., Karl H. BS, Northwestern U., 1944, MS, 1947; PhD, Stanford U., 1950; LHD (hon.), Southwestern U., 1980. Asst. prof. psychology U. Tex., Austin, 1949-53, assoc. prof., 1953-59, prof., 1959—, dean Coll. Edn., 1964-70, Hogg prof. psychology and edn., 1964—; assoc. dir. Hogg Found. Mental Health, 1955-64, pres., 1970-93, spl. counsel, 1993—; dir. Social Sci. Rsch. Coun., 1957-63, Centro de Investigationes Sociales, Mex., 1960-70; cons. USAF, also mem. sci. adv. bd., 1969-71; mem. com. basic rsch. com. NRC, 1968-71; mem. behavioral sci. study sect. USPHS, 1957-59, mem. mental health study sect., 1960, chmn. personality and cognition rsch. rev. com., 1968-72; mem. rsch. adv. panel Soc. Security Adminstrn., 1961-62; mem. L.Am. adv. bd. IBM, 1985-89; dir. WHO Collaborating Ctr. in Mental Health for Tex. and Mex., 1993—. Author: (with B.M. Moore) Tomorrow's Parents, 1964, Computer Assisted Instruction Testing and Guidance, 1971, (with R. Diaz-Guerrero and J. Swartz) Personality Development in Two Cultures, 1975, Introduction to Psychology, 1978; (with K.A. Heller and S. Messick) Placing Children in Special Education, 1982, (with T. Bornemann) Mental Health of Immigrants and Refugees, 1990, School of the Future, 1992; editor: Jour. Ednl. Psychology, 1966-72. Trustee Ednl. Testing Service, Princeton, 1972-74, 77-80, 83-86, J.W. and Cornelia Scarborough Found., 1977-82, Ctr. for Applied Linguistics, 1978-80, Salado Inst. Humanities, 1980-85, Population Inst., 1979-85, Menninger Found., 1982—, Population Resource Ctr., 1980—, chmn. bd. dirs.; dir. Sci. Rsch. Assocs., 1975-88; pres., bd. dirs. S.W. Ednl. Devel. Lab., 1974-75; mem. adv. com. computing activities NSF, 1970-73; mem. computer sci. and engring. bd. NAS, 1971-73, chmn. panel on selection and placement of mentally retarded students, 1979-82; chmn. interdisciplinary cluster on social and behavioral devel. Pres.'s Biomed. Research Panel, 1975-76; bd. dirs. Found.'s Fund for Rsch. in Psychiatry, 1973-77, chmn., 1976-77; dir. Conf. of S.W. Found., 1976-84, pres., 1978-79; mem. nat. adv. mental health coun. Alcohol, Drug Abuse, and Mental Health Adminstrn., 1978-81; mem. acad. info. sys. adv. coun. IBM, 1982-85; chmn. bd. dirs. The Menninger Clinic, 1993-97, The Learning Initiative, 1995—. Lt. (j.g.) USNR, 1944-46. Faculty Research fellow Social Sci. Research Council, 1953-54; Faculty Research fellow Center Advanced Study Behavioral Scis., 1962-63. Fellow APA, AAAS; mem. Tex. Psychol. Assn. (pres. 1957), S.W. Psychol. Assn. (pres. 1958), Am. Statis. Assn., InterAm. Soc. Psychology (pres. 1966-67), Am. Ednl. Rsch. Assn., Internat. Union Psychol. Scis. (sec.-gen. 1972-84, pres. 1984-88, exec. com. 1972-92), Philos. Soc. Tex. (pres. 1982-83), Sigma Xi. Methodist. Home: 3300 Foothill Dr Austin TX 78731-5823

HOLTZMANN, HOWARD MARSHALL, lawyer, judge; b. N.Y.C., Dec. 10, 1921; s. Jacob L. And Lillian (Plotz) H.; m. Anne Fisher, Jan. 14, 1945 (dec. Aug. 1967); children: Susan Holtzmann Richardson, Betsey; m. Carol Ebenstein Van Berg, Dec. 23, 1972. AB, Yale Coll., 1942, JD, 1947; LittD (hon.), St. Bonaventure U., 1952; LLD (hon.), Jewish Theol. Sem., N.Y.C., 1990. Bar: N.Y. 1947. Atty. Colorado Fuel & Iron Corp., Buffalo, N.Y., 1947-49; ptnr. Holtzmann, Wise & Shepard, N.Y.C., 1949-95; judge Iran-U.S. Claims Tribunal, The Hague, Netherlands, 1981-94; arbitrator and dispute resolution cons., 1994—; arbitrator Claims Resolution Tribunal for Dormant Accounts, Zurich, Switzerland, 1998—; U.S. del. UN Commn. on Internat. Trade Law, 1975—, Hague Conf. on Pvt. Internat. Law, 1985; advisor U.S.A. Arbitration agreements with USSR, Russian Fedn., China, Hungary, Bulgaria, Czechoslovakia, Poland and German Dem. Republic. Author, editor: A New Look at Legal Aspects of Doing Business with China, 1979; co-author: A Guide to the Unicitral Model Law on International Commercial Arbitration—Legislative History and Commentary, 1988 (cert. of merit Am. Soc. Internat. Law 1991); contbr. chpts. to books and articles to law jours. Mem. governing coun. Downstate Med. Sch. SUNY, Bklyn., 1961-78; trustee St. Bonaventure U., Olean, N.Y., 1968-90, trustee emeritus, 1990—; chmn. bd. Jewish Theol. Sem., N.Y.C., 1983-85, hon. chmn., 1985—; trustee Inst. Internat. Law, Pace U. Sch. Law, 1992—. Mem. ABA (chmn. com. code ethics comml. arbitrators 1973-77), Internat. Council for Comml. Arbitration (hon. vice chmn.), Am. Arbitration Assn. (hon. chmn., adv. bd. Bahrain arbitration ctr., adv. bd. Stockholm arbitration inst., Gotshal Internat. Arbitration award 1980), Internat. Arbitration Commn. (chmn.), Internat. C. of C. (vice chmn. arbitration commn. 1979—), Am. Bar Found., N.Y. County Lawyers Assn., Internat. Law Assn., Am. Fgn. Law Assn. (v.p. 1995, dir. 1995—), Internat. Bar Assn., N.Y. State Bar Assn., Assn. of Bar of City of N.Y., Am. Soc. Internat. Law (cert. merit 1991), Soc. Profls. in Dispute Resolution, Indsl. Relations Research Assn., N.Y. Law Inst., Am. Judicature Soc., Am. Assn. for Internat. Commn. of Jurists.

HOLUB, BARBARA ANN, rehabilitation nurse; b. South Euclid, Ohio, Mar. 29, 1961; d. Peter Cyril Anthony Dominic and Kathleen Theresa (Horner) McHale; m. Thomas John Joseph Holub, June 1, 1991; children: Colleen Marie, Ryan Thomas. ASN, Mattatuck C.C., 1985, Assoc. Liberal Arts, 1983. RN, Conn.; cert. rehab. nurse; cert. ins. rehab. specialist. Rehab. nurse Yale New Haven Hosp., 1985-89, Hosp. St. Raphael, New Haven, 1989-96, Grant St. Health and Rehab. Ctr., Bridgeport, Conn., 1996-97, Cedar Ln. Health & Rehab. Ctr., Waterbury, Conn., 1997—. Mem. Assn. Rehab. Nurses (v.p. 1992-93, pres. 1993-94, bd. dirs. 1995—). Republican. Roman Catholic. Avocations: decorating, crafts, travel, outdoors, financial management. Home: 1 Farrell Dr Ansonia CT 06401-2809 Office: Cedar Ln Health and Rehab Ctr 128 Cedar Ave Waterbury CT 06705-2700

HOLUB, JEANNE HELEN, English language educator; b. Davenport, Iowa, Sept. 6, 1949; d. Ralph L. and Corinne R. (Jansen) Judge; m. Terry L. Holub, Apr. 14, 1973 (div. Dec. 1986); children: Edward, Sarah, Katherine. Bachelor's degree, Marycrest Coll., 1971. Tchg. cert., Iowa. Tchr. Ft. Madison (Iowa) H.S., 1971-73; feature reporter Waterloo (Iowa) Courier, 1973-75; comms. dir. Hawkeye C.C., Waterloo, 1975-77; tchr. Waterloo Comty. Schs., 1977—. Mem. NEA, Nat. Coun. Tchrs. English, Iowa Coun. Tchrs. English, Iowa Edn. Assn., Waterloo Edn. Assn. (former pres.). Roman Catholic. Avocations: reading, needlepoint. Office: West H S 425 E Ridgeway Ave Waterloo IA 50702-5043

HOLUB, MARTIN, architect; b. Prague, Czechoslovakia, Dec. 11, 1938; came to U.S., 1970; naturalized, 1977; s. Jan and Miloslava (Jerabkova) H. MS, Czech Tech. U., 1963; PhD, Acad. Art, Prague, 1966. Registered architect N.Y., N.J., Tenn., Fla., Conn. Designer Konstruktiva, Prague, 1963-67; asst. architect Greater London Coun., 1967-68; sr. designer R. Seifert and Ptnrs., London, 1968-69, Kahn and Jacobs, N.Y.C., 1970-71; prin. Martin Holub Architects and Planners, N.Y.C., 1971—. Prin. works includes Rokeby Apts., Nashville (Design award 1976). Mem. AIA, Am. Arbitration Assn., Archtl. League N.Y. Avocations: skiing, art. Home: 500 E 77th St Apt 1529 New York NY 10162-0019 Office: 116 W 72nd St Fl 16 New York NY 10023-3338

HOLUM, JOHN D., federal agency administrator; b. Highmore, S.D., Dec. 4, 1940; m. Barbara Pedersen; 1 child, Tracy Lynn. BA in Math. and Phys. Scis., No. State Teachers Coll., S.D.; JD with honors, George Washington U., 1970. Legis. dir. Senator George McGovern, 1965-79; with policy planning staff Dept. of State, 1979-81; mem. campaign Senator Gary Hart, 1984, 88; mem. potential exploratory com. Gov. Bill Clinton, 1987; exec. dir. platform drafting com., platform com. Dem. Nat. Conv., 1992; def. and fgn. policy adviser Clinton Presdl. Campaign, 1992; practicing atty. O'Melveny & Myers, 1981-93; dir. U.S. Arms Control and Disarmament Agy., Washington, 1993-97; sr. advisor, nominated to be undersec. of state Arms Control and Internat. Soc., Washington, 1997-99, 99—. Fellow Harvard U. Mem. Coun. Fgn. Rels. Avocations: flying, sailing, scuba diving, playing bluegrass and country music. Office: Office of Undersecretary 2201 C St NW Rm 7208 Washington DC 20520-0001*

HOLUTIAK-HALLICK, STEPHEN PETER, JR., retired career officer, businessman, educator; b. N.Y.C., May 3, 1945; s. Stephen and Hope (Kukura) H.; m. Ann Marie Bazycki, July 29, 1972; children: Larissa Ann, Christine Michelle, Stephen Michael III. BA in Russian, Penn State U., 1967; MA in Slavic Studies, U. Manitoba, Winnipeg, Can., 1969; AS in Bus. Mgmt., C.C. of Allegheny County, 1977; MBA in Internat. Bus., Mercer U., 1992; cert. in Russian area studies, Pa. State U. With USAR, 1967-95, advanced through grades to lt. col., 1970-71, 85-95; translator, interpretor, mgr. Russian translation dept. Pullman-Swindell, Inc., Pitts., 1972-76; inspector mech. engring. dept. Robert W. Hunt, Co., Pitts., 1977-79; adminstr., procurement svcs. KHD, Humboldt of Wedag, N.Y.C., Montreal, Atlanta, 1979-82, adminstr., project mgmt. svcs., 1982-84, cvr. expediting and subcontracts adminstrn., 1984-85; staff intelligence officer Forces Command Hdqs., U.S. Army, 1985-90; asst. prof. mil. sci. Clemson (S.C.) U., 1990-92; mem. INF. Treaty inspection team U.S. Army, 1988, inspector gen. 95th Divsn., 1992-95; ret.; adj. instr. Park Coll., Tinker AFB, Okla., 1993-95, Am. Coll., Atlanta, 1997; pres. TATO's Choice, Duluth, Ga., 1995—; cons. doing bus. in former USSR. Author: Slavic Toponymic Atlas of the United States, Vol. 1, Ukrainian, 1982, Dictionary of Ukrainian Surnames in the United States, 1994; mem. editl. bd. Rudnyckiana, 1986-92, chmn., 1993-95; contbr. articles to profl. jours. Organizer St. Andrew's Ukrainian Orthodox Mission Parish, Atlanta; vol. instr. English Tchrs. for Ukraine, 1996-99. Decorated Army Commendation medal (2), Meritorious Svc. meda. (3); recipient Danforth Leadership award, 1963, Wasyl Swystun prize of Ukrainian Studies, U. Man., 1967-68, grad. assistantship, 1968-69, Cert. of Appreciation, DAV, 1985-97, Am. Soc. Blind, 1985; Senatorial grantee Pa. State U., 1963-67. Mem. Res. Officers Assn. of U.S., Am. Security Coun. (U.S. Congl. adv. bd.), Atlanta Com. of Internat. Rels., Am. Name Soc. Home: 2755 Kenwood Ct Duluth GA 30096-3683

HOLWAY, ELLEN TWOMBLY HAY, primary education educator; b. Summit, N.J.; d. Allan and Ellen Clark (Twombly) Hay; m. William Crocker Holway III; children: Julie Ellen, Suzanne Clark, Cammy Twombly, Amy Hay, Daniel Hitchcock, Joanna Howland. AB in Psychology cum laude, Colby Coll., 1953; MEd, U. Lowell, 1975; postgrad., U. Mass., Lowell, 1987—, Boston U., 1978, Cen. New Eng. Coll., 1987. Cert. elem. tchr. and prin., perceptually handicapped, gen. supr., supt./asst.supt., Mass.; asst. psychologist, psychometrist, child welfare worker, pub. assistance caseworker, Maine. Asst. psychologist, acting dept. head Pineland Hosp. and Tng. Ctr., 1953-55; elem. tchr., specialist Odenton, Md., 1955-57; primary tchr., prof. devel. team leader Horace Mann, Maynard, Mass., 1972—; elem. asst. prin., elem. prin. Green Meadow Sch.; mem. adj. faculty dept. bus. and career edn. Boston U. Grad. Sch. Edn.; freelance editor, cons. pilot program liaison D.C. Heath Pub. Co.; developer, coord. Acton-Boxborough Student Activities Fund, numerous others; cons. Technol. R & D Corp.; mem. Mass. Math. Adv. Com., Mass. Sci. Adv. Com.; lead tchr. New Standards Project. Chmn. Acton and Acton-Boxborough Regional Sch. Com., Acton 250th Celebration; mem. MASC Assessment Com.; charter mem., bd. dirs., mem. pub. rels. com. Acton Hist. Soc.; jr. leader, coord. summer camp Girl Scouts U.S.A.; counselor citizenship badge, Eagle advisor Boy Scouts Am., Acton and Maynard; tchr., supr. ch. sch., numerous others. Mem. NEA, ASCD, Am. Ednl. Rsch. Assn., Nat. Sch. Bd. Assn., Nat. Career Edn. Assn (charter), Mass. ASCD, Mass. Assn. Sch. Coms., Mass. Tchrs. Assn., Maynard Edn. Assn., LWV (charter, v..p., chmn. pub. rels.), Yarmouth Hist. Soc. (life), Phi Beta Kappa, Pi Lambda Theta, Pi Gamma Mu. Home: 48 Alcott St Acton MA 01720-5539 Office: Green Meadow Sch 12 Bancroft St Maynard MA 01754-2017

HOLWAY, JAMES MICHAEL, regional planner, state agency administrator; b. Balt., Aug. 22, 1958; m. Rita Jo Anthony; 1 child, Joseph. BA in Polit. Sci., Cornell U., 1981; M in Regional Planning, U. N.C., 1987, PhD in Environ. Planning, 1990. Cert. planner. Asst. dir. Ariz. Dept. Water Resources, 1996—; faculty assoc. Ariz. State U., Tempe, 1993—, mem. external adv. bd. Herberger Ctr. for Design Excellence, 1996—. Mem. adv. com. City of Phoenix Sonoran Preserve, 1994—. Mem. Am. Planning Assn., Ariz. Planning Assn., Ariz. Hydrolic Soc., Am. Water Works Assn., Lambda Alpha Internat.

HOLYDAY, DOUGLAS CHARLES, city councillor; b. Etobicoke, Ont., Can., July 31, 1942; s. Arthur John and Anne H.; m. Franca Palma Pellizzari, Aug. 16, 1969; children: Stephen, David. Formerly ward 6 councillor Etobicoke City Coun.; past chmn. Etobicoke Bd. Health; mayor City of Etobicoke, 1994-97; councillor City of Toronto, 1999—; former pres., owner Holyday Ins. Brokers, Inc., Etobicoke. Founding chair Etobicoke Lakeshore Oldtimers Hockey Tournament; chair Etopicoke red shield appeal campaign Queensway Gen. Hosp., 1990-99; chair cmty. appeals com. 1991-92. Mem. Kingsway Kiwanis Club (past pres., past chair youth svcs. com., past dir. music festival). Anglican. Avocations: golf, hockey, reading. Office: City Hall 2d Fl. 100 Queen St W. Toronto, ON Canada M5H2N22

HOLYER, ERNA MARIA, adult education educator, writer, artist; b. Weilheim, Bavaria, Germany, Mar. 15, 1925; d. Mathias and Anna Maria (Goldhofer) Schretter; AA, San Jose Evening Coll., 1964; student San Mateo Coll., 1965-67, San Jose State U., 1968-69, San Jose City Coll., 1980-81; DLitt, World U., 1984; DFA (hon.), The London Inst. Applied Rsch., 1992; m. Gene Wallace Holyer, Aug. 24, 1957. Freelance writer under pseudonym Ernie Holyer, 1960—; tchr. creative writing San Jose (Calif.) Met. Adult Edn., 1968—; artist, 1958—. Exhibited in group shows Crown Zellerbach Gallery, San Francisco, 1973, 74, 76, 77; I.B.C. Gallery, San Francisco, 1978 (medal of Congress, 1988, 89, 92, 94, Congress Challenge trophy, 1990), L.A., 1981, Cambridge, Eng., 1992, Cambridge, Mass., 1993, San Jose, Calif., 1993, Edinburgh, 1994, San Francisco, 1996. Recipient Woman of Achievement Honor cert. San Jose Mercury-News, 1973, 74, 75, Lefoli award for excellence in adult edn. instrn. Adult Edn. Senate, 1972, Women of Achievement awards League of Friends of Santa Clara County Commn., San Jose Mercury News, 1987, various art awards. Mem. N.L.A.P.W. Inc., World Univ. Roundtable (doctoral). Author: Rescue at Sunrise, 1965; Steve's Night of Silence, 1966; A Cow for Hansel, 1967; At the Forest's Edge, 1969; Song of Courage, 1970; Lone Brown Gull, 1971; Shoes for Daniel, 1974; The Southern Sea Otter, 1975; Sigi's Fire Helmet, 1975; Reservoir Road Adventure, 1982, Wilderness Journey, Golden Journey, California Journey, 1997; contbr. articles to various mags., newspapers, and anthologies. Home and Office: 1314 Rimrock Dr San Jose CA 95120-5611

HOLYFIELD, EVANDER, professional boxer; b. Atlanta, Oct. 19, 1962. Winner unanimous decision vs. Ray Mercer, 1995, defeated Mike Tyson to win WBC Heavyweight Title, 1996, defended title successfully winning over Lennox Lewis, 1999. Winner Bronze medal 1984 summer Olympics, World Boxing Assn. cruiserweight title, 1986, Internat. Boxing Fedn. cruiserweight title, 1987, World Boxing Coun. cruiserweight title, 1988, Internat. Boxing Fedn. heavyweight championship, 1997; undisputed heavyweight world champion, 1990-92, 93-94. Office: Main Event 811 Totowa Rd # 100 Totowa NJ 07512-1207*

HOLZ, ARNOLD G., federal agency administrator; b. May 18, 1937. BS in Acctg., U. Balt., 1959; postgrad., Georgetown U. CPA, Md.; cert. govt. fin. mgr. Acct. Deloitte & Touche, 1960-73; dir. gen. acctg. State of Md.-Asst. State Comptr., 1973-94; CFO NASA, Washington, 1994—. Mem. AICPA, Md. Assn. CPA, CFO Coun. U.S. (charter), Govt. Fin. Officers Assn. (past pres.), Md. Pub. Fin. Officers Assn. (past pres.). Office: NASA 300 E St SW Washington DC 20546

HOLZ, GEORGE G., IV, research scientist, medicine educator; b. Santa Monica, Calif., May 8, 1953; s. George G. and Mignon M. (Kiproff) H. BS, Cornell U., 1975; PhD, U. Ill., 1984. Rsch. fellow Tufts U. Med. Sch., Boston, 1984-89; rsch. assoc. Howard Hughes Med. Inst., Boston, 1990-93; instr. medicine Mass. Gen. Hosp.-Harvard Med. Sch., Boston, 1990-93, asst. prof. medicine, 1994-98; assoc. prof. physiology and neurosci. NYU Med. Sch., N.Y.C., 1998—. Corp. mem. Marine Biol. Lab., Woods Hole, Mass. Recipient Rsch. award Am. Diabetes Assn., 1996; N.Y. State Regents scholar Cornell U., 1971-75; rsch. grantee NIH. Mem. AAAS, Soc. for Neurosci., Endocrine Soc., Soc. Gen. Physiologists, Am. Diabetes Assn., Boston Area Neuroscis. Group. Home: PO Box 288 West Falmouth MA 02574-0288

HOLZ, HAROLD A., chemical and plastics manufacturing company executive; b. N.Y.C., June 26, 1925; s. Herman A. and Genevieve (Murphy) H.; m. Joanne Axtell, Oct. 3, 1953; children: Gretchen, Timothy. BS, Stevens Inst. Tech., 1946, ME, 1947. Tech. rep. Union Carbide Corp., N.Y.C., 1947-49, Hartford, Conn., 1949-52, St. Louis, 1952-58; asst. regional mgr. Union Carbide Corp., Chgo., 1958-64; regional mgr. Union Carbide Corp., 1964-65; account exec. Union Carbide Corp., N.Y.C., 1965-85; v.p. sales, new product devel. Marval Industries, Inc., 1986-97; cons. Chappaqua, N.Y., 1997—. Mem. nat. bd. govs. Nat. Plastics Ctr. and Mus., Leominster, Mass., 1995—. Served to lt. (j.g.) USNR, 1943-50. Mem. The Plastics Acad. (bd. dirs. 1996—, adminstr. Plastics Hall of Fame), Soc. Plastics Engrs. (disting. mem., pres. 1975-76), Plastics Pioneers Assn. (bd. govs. 1981-85, sec. 1989-91, v.p. 1991-93, pres. 1993-95), Plastics Inst. Am. (trustee 1995—), Union Carbide Retiree Corps. (pres. Lower Westchester County chpt. 1996-97), Chappaqua (N.Y.) Club, Swim and Tennis Club. Home: 35 Ridge Rd Chappaqua NY 10514-2508 Office: 315 Hoyt Ave Mamaroneck NY 10543-1836

HOLZ, ROBERT KENNETH, geography educator; b. Kankakee, Ill., Nov. 3, 1930; s. Harry H. and Margaret (Conway) H.; m. Joyce F. Harpin, May 19, 1951; 1 child, Eric R. BA in Zoology, So. Ill. U., 1958, MA in Geography, 1959; PhD in Geography, Mich. State U., 1963. Asst. prof. U. Tex., Austin, 1962-67, assoc. prof., 1967-72, prof., 1972—, dir. ctr. for Middle Eastern Studies, 1991-95, Eric W. Zimmerman Regents prof., 1994-99, Eric W. Zimmerman Regents prof. emeritus, 1999—; cons. in field. Co-author: Mendes I, 1980; author, editor: The Surveillant Science, 2d edit., 1985. Staff sgt. USAF, 1951-55. Recipient Group Achievement award NASA, 1974, Urban Achievement award L.B.J. Sch. Pub. Affairs, 1984. Mem. Assn. Am. Geographers (chmn. remote sensing specialty group 1980-82, chmn. southwest div. 1971-72, medal for outstanding contbns. to remote sensing Remote Sensing Specialty Group 1998), Am. Soc. Photogrammetry, Tex. Assn. Coll. Tchrs., Am. Congress of Surveying and Mapping. Roman Catholic. Avocations: hunting, fishing, squash. Home: 2610 Fiset Dr Austin TX 78731-5614 Office: U Tex Dept Geography Austin TX 78712

HOLZBACH, JAMES FRANCIS, civil engineer; b. Elizabeth, N.J., July 26, 1936; s. Norman Bernard and Mary Elizabeth (Devine) H.; m. Juliette Horwitz, May 21, 1977. BSCE, U. Notre Dame, 1960. Registered profl. engr., N.Y. Commd. ensign C.E. Corps USN, 1960, advanced through grades to lt. comdr., 1967, resigned, 1970; contract adminstr. Teetor-Dobbins Cons. Engrs., Rochester, N.Y., 1970-72; assoc. engr. Monroe County Dept. Engring., Rochester, 1972-90, acting chief constrn., 1990-92, mng. engr., 1993—. Contbr. articles to profl. jours. Active Dispute Rev. Bd. Found. Mem. ASCE, Am. Underground Constrn. Assn. Home: 50 Westminster Rd Rochester NY 14607-2231 Office: Monroe County Divsn Engring 50 W Main St Rochester NY 14614-1228

HOLZBACH, RAYMOND THOMAS, gastroenterologist, author, educator; b. Salem, Ohio, Aug. 19, 1929; s. Raymond T. and Nelle A. (Conroy) H.; m. Lorraine E. Cozza, May 26, 1956; children—Ellen, Mark, James. BS, Georgetown U., 1951; MD, Case Western Res. U., 1955. Diplomate Nat. Bd. Med. Examiners, Am. Bd. Internal Medicine. Intern, asst. resident U. Ill. Research and Edn. Hosps., Chgo., 1955-56; sr. asst. resident medicine Cleve. Met. Gen. Hosp., 1959-60; asst. chief gastroenterology Case Western Res U., 1961-63; physician Gastroenterology Unit U. Hosps. of Cleve., 1961-63; instr. medicine Case Western Res. U. Sch. Medicine, Cleve., 1961-64; clin. instr. medicine Case Western Res. U. Sch. Medicine, 1964-71; head gastrointestinal research unit, assoc. physician div. medicine St. Luke's Hosp., Cleve., 1967-73; dir. div. gastroenterology St. Luke's Hosp., 1970-73; head gastrointestinal research unit dept. medicine Cleve. Clinic Found., 1973—; vis. prof. numerous instns. including Mayo Med. Sch., 1974, U. Calif., San Diego, 1977, U. Heidelberg, 1978, U. Pa., 1979, U. Zurich, 1980, U. Munich, 1982, U. Minn. Med. Ctr., 1985, med. ctrs., numerous Japanese univs., 1985, 92, Karolinska Inst., 1986, Royal Soc. London, 1987, Pa. State U. Sch. Med., U. Helsinki, RWTH-Aachen, Düsseldorf, Fed. Republic of Germany, U. Groningen, Utrecht, U. Amsterdam, The Netherlands, 1989, U. Perugia, Italy, Va. Commonwealth U.-Med. Coll. Va., Richmond, Christ Ch. Sch. Medicine, U. Otago, New Zealand, SUNY, Buffalo Sch. Medicine, 1990, Pontifical/Cath. U. Chile Sch. Medicine, 1991, Hiroshima U. Sch. Medicine, 1992, Kyoto U. Sch. Medicine, 1992, Sch. Medicine U. Jikei, Tokyo, 1992, Tel Aviv U., Israel Sch. Medicine, 1995, U. Leipzig, Germany, 1996, U. Heidelberg, Germany, 1996; lectr. in field. Mem. editl. bd. Gastroenterology jour., 1984-89; contbr. revs. and articles to med. jours. Served to capt. USAF, 1957-59. Recipient Alexander von Humboldt Found. Spl. Program award, 1978, 82. Fellow ACP; mem. ABA, Am. Gastroent. Assn. (rsch. com. 1976-79), Ctrl. Soc. Clin. Rsch., Am. Assn. for Study of Liver Diseases, AAAS, Am. Soc. Biol. Chemists, Am. Physiol. Assn., Biophys. Soc., Internat. Assn. Study of Liver, Am. Fedn. Clin. Rsch., Midwest Gut Club, Am. Soc. Clin. Nutrition, Ohio State Med. Assn., Sigma Xi. Unitarian. Home: 39251 Lander Rd Chagrin Falls OH 44022-2146 Office: Cleve Clin Found 9500 Euclid Ave Cleveland OH 44195-0001

HOLZBAUR, ERIKA L., medical educator. BS in Chemistry and History with honors, Coll. William and Mary, 1982; PhD in Biochemistry, Pa. State U., 1987. Rsch. fellow, teaching asst. Dept. Molecular and Cell Biology, Pa. State U., 1982-87, postdoctoral scientist, 1987-88; asst. prof. Dept. Animal Biology, Sch. Vet. Medicine, U. Pa., Phila., 1992-98; assoc. prof. biochemistry Dept. Animal Biology, Sch. of Vet. Medicine, U. Pa., Phila., 1998—. Contbr. articles to profl. jours., chpts. to books. Grad. Sch. fellow Pa. State U., 1984-85, 85-86; Postdoctoral fellow NIH, 1988-92; recipient Established Investigator award Am. Heart Assn., 1996. Mem. Am. Soc. Cell Biology, Pa. Muscle Inst., U. Pa. Cancer Ctr., Phi Beta Kappa, Phi Zeta. Office: U Pa 143 Rosenthal Bldg 3800 Spruce St Philadelphia PA 19104-6008*

HOLZENDORF, KING, JR., city councilman; m. Betty Holzendorf; children: King L. III, Kevin, Kessler, Kim Lockley. BS, Edward Waters Coll., Jacksonville, Fla. City councilman City of Jacksonville, 1995—, vice chmn. Recreation and Cmty. Devel. Com., mem. Land Use and Zoning Com., mem. Pub. Health and Safety Com., 1998—, vice chair pub. health and safety, 1998—; dir. Ct. Svc. Unit, River Regional Human Svc. Inc.; bd. dirs. Fla. Martin Luther King Jr. Inst. Nonviolence. Sgt. 1st class, Fla. N.G., ret. Mem. NAACP. Democrat. Office: 117 W Duval St Ste 425 Jacksonville FL 32202-3700*

HOLZER, EDWIN, advertising executive; b. June 22, 1933. MusB, Yale U., 1954, MusM, 1955; postgrad., Ind. U., 1956. Acct. exec. Benton & Bowles Inc., N.Y.C., 1959-62; account supr. William Esty Co., N.Y.C., 1962-66; account supr. Grey Advt. Inc., N.Y.C., 1966-68, mgmt. supr., 1968-70; exec. v.p. Grey Inc., N.Y.C., 1970-73; pres., CEO, COO Grey-North Inc., Chgo., 1973-85; chmn., CEO, Grey Chgo. (name changed to LOIS/GGK 1988), 1988; chmn., CEO LOIS/EJL (formerly Lois/USA), Chgo., 1988—. Office: LOIS/EJL 111 E Wacker Dr # 600 Chicago IL 60601-2101

HOLZER, HAROLD, public information officer, historian, writer; b. Bklyn., Feb. 5, 1949; s. Charles and Rose (Last) H.; m. Edith Spiegel, Feb. 27, 1971; children: Remy, Meg. BA, CUNY, Queens, 1969; diploma (hon.), Lincoln Meml. U., 1988, Lincoln Coll., 1992. Editor Manhattan Tribune, N.Y.C., 1969-73; dir. spl. projects Dept. Civic Affairs, City of N.Y., 1973-75; press sec. to Congresswoman Bella Abzug N.Y.C., 1975-77; communications specialist Sec. of State office, N.Y., 1978; dir. pub. affairs Sta. WNET (PBS), N.Y.C., 1978-84; v.p. pub. affairs Javits Conv. Ctr., N.Y.C., 1984-85; exec. v.p. pub. affairs Urban Devel. Corp., State of N.Y., 1985-92; chief comm. officer Met. Mus. Art, N.Y.C., 1992-96, v.p., 1996—. Co-author: The Lincoln Image, 1984, Changing the Lincoln Image, 1985, The Confederate Image, 1987, The Lincoln Family Album, 1990, Lincoln on Democracy, 1990, Mine Eyes Have Seen the Glory, 1993; author: The Lincoln-Douglas Debates, 1993, Washington and Lincoln Portrayed, 1993, Dear Mr. Lincoln: Letters to the President, 1993, Witness to War: The Civil War, 1996, The Civil War Era, 1996; The Lincoln Mailbag: America Writes to the President, 1998; contbr. more than 275 articles on Lincoln and the Civil War to popular mags., scholarly jours.; contbr. chpts. in books; columnist Antique Trader, 1985-95; contbg. editor: Americana Mag., 1991-93; writer various pamphlets on Abraham Lincoln; contbg. historian various CD-ROMS, TV spls. on C-SPAN, A&E, The History Channel, NBC, ABC, PBS. Lectr. on Lincoln and Civil War before various hist. groups; co-organizer 3 traveling exhbns. on Lincoln and Civil War; trustee N.Y. State Archives Partnership Trust, 1994—. Recipient Barondess/Lincoln award Civil War Round Table of N.Y., 1984, 91, 94, George Washington medal Freedom Found. Valley Forge, 1988, Writer of Distinction award Internat. Reading Assn., 1989, award Manuscript Soc. Am., 1996. Mem. Abraham Lincoln Assn. (bd. dirs. 1988-95, Achievement award 1991), Lincoln Group of N.Y. (v.p. 1979-90, pres. 1990-96, Achievement award 1988, 93), State Coun. for Humanities (bd. dirs. 1991-93), Ulysses S. Grant Assn. (bd. dirs. 1996—), The Lincoln Forum (vice chmn. 1996—). Office: Met Mus of Art 1000 5th Ave New York NY 10028-0113

HOLZER, JENNY, artist; b. Gallipolis, Ohio, July 29, 1950; d. Richard Vornholt and Virginia (Beasley) H.; m. Michael Andrew Glier, May 21, 1984; 1 child. Student, Duke U., 1968-70, U. Chgo., 1970-71; BFA, Ohio U., 1972, DA (hon.), 1994; MFA, R.I. Sch. Design, 1977; postgrad., Whitney Mus. Am. Art, 1977. One-woman shows include Rüdiger Schöttle Gall, Münich, 1980, Barbara Gladstone Gallery, N.Y.C., 1983, 86, 94, Kunsthalle, Basel, Switzerland, 1984, Dallas Mus. Art, 1986, Des Moines Art Ctr., 1986, Aspen Art Mus., 1986, Artspace, San Francisco, 1986, Mus. Contemporary Art, Chgo., 1986, MIT, Cambridge, 1986, Rhona Hoffman Gallery, Chgo., 1987, Inst. Contemporary Art, London, 1988, Bklyn. Mus., N.Y.C., 1988, DIA Art Found., N.Y.C., 1989, Guggenheim Mus., N.Y.C., 1989, Des Moines Art Ctr., Galerie Monika Spruth, Cologne, Germany, 1998, Am. Pavillion, 44th Biennale, Venice, Italy, 1990, Laura Carpenter Fine Art, Santa Fe, 1991, La. Mus., Humlebaek, Denmark, 1991, Albright-Knox Art Gallery, Buffalo, 1991, Walker Art Gallery, Mpls., 1991, Ydessa Hendeles Art Found., Toronto, 1992, Dallas Mus. of Art, 1993, Haus der Kunst, Munich, 1993, Bergen Mus. Art, Norway, 1994, Art Tower Mito, Japan, 1994, Williams Coll. Mus. Art, Williamstown, Mass., 1995, Monika Sprüth Galerie, Cologne, Germany, 1995, Kunstmus. Kartause Ittingen, Kanton Thurgau, Warth, Switzerland, 1996, Galerie Rähnitzgasse, Dresden, 1996, Contemporary Art Mus., Houston, 1997, Index Gallery, Osaka, Japan, 1997, Yvon Lambert Gallery, Paris, 1998, Inst. Cultural Itau, São Paulo, Brazil, 1998, others; exhibited in group shows at Mus Fridericianum Orangerie and Neue Gall, Kassel, Germany, 1982, Mus. Art Carnegie Inst., Pitts., 1985, Israel Mus., Jerusalem, 1986, Frankfurter Kunstverein, Frankfurt, Germany, 1986, Europa/Amerika Mus. Ludwig, Koln, 1986, Sonsbeck: Internat. Sculpture Exhbn., Arnheim, The Netherlands, Whitney Mus. Am. Art, N.Y.C., 1989, Mus. Contemporary Art, L.A., 1989, Mus. Modern Art, N.Y.C., 1988, 90, 96, Mus. Fridericianum, Kassel, Germany, 1987, Ctrl. Mus., Utrecht, The Netherlands, 1991, Kunsthalle, Basel, Switzerland, 1992, Ujazdowski Caste, Warsaw, Poland, 1993, Guggenheim Mus., Soho, N.Y.C., 1993, 96, Lenbachhaus, Munich, 1994, SITE Santa Fe, 1995, Pompidou Ctr., Paris, 1996, Joseph Helman Gallery, N.Y., 1997, Kunsthalle Wien, Vienna, Austria, 1998, Nat. Gallery Australia, Canberra, 1998, Rhona Hofman Gallery, 1998. Recipient Golden Lion award for best pavillion 44th Venice Biennale, 1990,, Planet of Europe, gold medal for title, gold medal for design Art Dirs. Club Europe, 1993, Skowhegan medal for installation Skowhegan Sch. Painting and Sculpture, N.Y., 1994, Crystal award for outstanding contbn. to cross-cultural understanding, World Econ. Forum, Cologny-Geneva, Switzerland, 1996. Avocations: reading, riding. *

HOLZER, MARC, public administration educator; b. Bronx, N.Y., Feb. 28, 1945; s. Philip and Ann Lee (Blinder) H.; m. Madeleine Fuchs, Aug. 31, 1969; children: Matthew, Benjamin. BA in Polit. Sci., U. Rochester, 1966; MPA, U. Mich., 1967, PhD in Polit. Sci., 1971. Asst. prof. govt. and pub. adminstrn. John Jay Coll. Criminal Justice, CUNY, 1971-74, assoc. prof., 1975-79, prof., 1980-89; prof. pub. adminstrn. Rutgers U., Newark, 1989—; founder, exec. dir. Nat. Ctr. for Pub. Productivity, 1975—; founder, chmn. Internat. Productivity Network, 1988—; cons. internat. and fed. depts. agys., city, state and county agys.; dir. numerous funded projects in field; mem. Croton-Harmon Bd. Edn., 1984-87, pres. 1986-87; adv. acad. bd./bd. trustees Campus Arts & Scis., Athens. Mem. Am. Soc. Pub. Adminstrn. (chmn. nat. tng. com. 1981-82, 83-84, nat. coun. 1982-85, chairperson mgmt. sci. sect. 1981-82, 89-90, pres. N.Y Met. chpt. 1978-79, 79-80, chairperson sect. humanistic, artistic and reflective expression 1993-95, chair publs. com. 1993-94, N.Y. Met. Outstanding Acad. award 1985, N.J. Outstanding Achievement award 1992, Nat. ASPA: vice-pres, 1998-99, pres-elect, 1999-2000, pres, 2000-01; Nat. ASPA, Donald C. Stone award 1994); founder, co-chairperson Pub. Adminstrn. Teaching Roundtable, 1980—. Author: (with others) Managing for Improved Productivity, 1981; (with Arie Halachmi) Public Sector Productivity, 1988; (with Virginia Cherry) Public Administration Research Guide, 1991; editor: Productivity in Public Organizations, 1976, Public Productivity Handbook, 1991; (with K. Morris and W. Ludwin) Literature in Bureaucracy: Readings in Administrative Fiction, 1979; (with Ellen D. Rosen) Current Cases in Public Administration, 1981; (with Stuart Nagel) Productivity and Public Policy, 1984; (with Arie Halachmi) Strategic Issues in Public Sector Productivity, 1986, Competent Government, 1995; (with Vatche Gabrielian) Case Studies in Productive Public Management, 1995; (with Kathie Callahan and Joseph Delorio) Reinventing New Jersey, 1995, (with Kathie Callahan) In Defense of The Public Service, 1997; founder, editor-in-chief Public Productivity and Mgmt. Rev., 1975—, Public Voices, 1994—; assoc. editor: Internat. Ency. Pub. Policy and Adminstrn.; mem. editorial bd. Internat. Jour. Pub. Adminstrn., Pub. Adminstrn. Quar., Pub. Budgeting and Fin. Mgmt., The Pub. Mgr. (formerly The Bureaucrat), Jour. of Non-Profit and Pub. Sector Mktg., Jour. Mgmt. History, Internat. Jour. Orgnl. Theory and Behavior, ASPA Classics, Korean Rev. Pub. Adminstrn., Pub. Adminstrn. Rev., Pub. Adminstrn. and Mgmt.; contbr. numerous chpts. to books, articles to profl. jours. Sr. Fellow Rockefeller Inst. Gov., 1986-87. Home: 4 Giglio Ct Croton On Hudson NY 10520-2005 Office: Rutgers U Hill Hall 7th Fl 360 King Blvd Newark NJ 07102-1801

HOLZER, THOMAS E., physicist. PhD, U. Calif., San Diego, 1970. Sr. scientist High Altitude Obs., Nat. Ctr. for Atmospheric Rsch., Boulder, Colo., 1978—, dir., 1990-95. Fellow Am. Geophys. Union (James B. MacElwane award 1978); mem. Norwegian Acad. Sci. and Letters, Internat. Astron. Union, Am. Astron. Soc., Internat. Union of Radio Scis. Office: High Altitude Obs/NCAR 3450 Mitchell Ln Boulder CO 80301-2260

HOLZER, THOMAS LEQUEAR, geologist; b. Lafayette, Ind., June 26, 1944; s. Oswald Alois and Ruth Alice (Lequear) H.; children: Holly Christine, Elizabeth Alice. BSE, Princeton U., 1965; MS, Stanford U., 1966, PhD, 1970. Asst. prof. geology U. Conn., Storrs, 1970-75; adj. environmentalist Griswold & Fuss, Manchester, Conn., 1973-75; research geol. U.S. Geol. Survey, Menlo Park, Calif., 1975-82, rsch. geologist, 1984-88, 93—; dep. asst. dir. rsch. U.S. Geol. Survey, Reston, Va., 1982-84, chief br. engring. seismology and geology, 1989-93; cons. assoc. prof. geology and environ. sci. Stanford U., 1994—. Contbr. numerous articles to profl. jours. Coach Am. Youth Soccer Orgn., Palo Alto, Calif., 1979-82. Recipient Superior Svc. award U.S Geol. Survey, 1981, Outstanding Pub. Svc. award U.S. Geol. Survey, 1991. Fellow Geol. Soc. Am. (chmn. engring. geology divsn. 1988-89, councilor 1995-97, Disting. Svc. award hydrogeology divsn. 1995, Richard H. Jahns Disting. Lectr. 1998); mem. AAAS, Am. Geophys. Union, Assn. Groundwater Scientists and Engrs., Earthquake Engring. Rsch. Inst., Sigma Xi. Republican. Presbyterian. Avocation: tennis. Home: PO Box 851 Palo Alto CA 94302-0851 Office: US Geol Survey 345 Middlefield Rd Menlo Park CA 94025-3591

HOLZINGER, BRIAN, professional hockey player; b. Parma, Ohio, Oct. 10, 1972; s. Harry and Peggy Holzinger. Student, Bowling Green State U., 1991—. Center Buffalo Sabres, 1995—; participant U.S. Olympic Festival, St. Louis, 1994,. Bookreader 6th grade class Kenwood Elem. Sch., Bowling Green, 1995. Named Most Valuable Player U. Toronto Cross Border Challenger, Badger Hockey Showdown, Milw., Player of Yr. CCHA, Hockey News Collegiate, Hockey Digest Collegiate; recipient Jim Sears award, 1992-93, Sam Cooper Trophy, 1992-93, 93-94, Hobey Baker Meml. award, 1995; named to All-Tournament team Dexter Hockey Classic, 1993, All-Tournament team Great Alaska Face-Off, 1992, All-CCHA Second Team, 1992-93, Tital West First-Team All American, 1994-95. Mem. Assn. Systems Mgmt. Office: Buffalo Sabres Marine Midland Arena One Seymour H Knox III Plz Buffalo NY 14203*

HOLZMAN, D. KEITH, record company executive, producer, arts consultant; b. N.Y.C., Mar. 22, 1936; s. Jacob Easton and Minnette Cathryn (Sternberger) H.; m. Jo Susan Handelman, Nov. 16, 1971; children: Susanne Carla, Lucas Jon, Rebecca Leigh. BA, Oberlin (Ohio) Coll., 1957; MFA, Boston U., 1959. Asst. to gen. mgr. and stage mgr. N.Y.C. Light Opera, 1959, 62-64; dir. prodn. Elektra Records, N.Y.C., 1964-70; v.p. prodn. and mfg. Elektra/Asylum/Nonesuch Records, Los Angeles, 1970-81; sr. v.p. prodn. and mfg. Elektra/Asylum/Nonesuch Records, 1981-84; pres. ROM Records, 1987—; producer, arts cons. Treasure Trove, Inc., 1984—; mng. dir. Discovery Records, Santa Monica, Calif., 1991-98; prin. Keith Holzman Solutions Unltd., 1998—; pres. Treasure Trove Inc.; dir. Nonesuch Records, 1980-84; music supr. Witches of Eastwick, Warner Bros., Los Angeles, 1986; bd. dirs. Plumstead Theatre Soc., Los Angeles, 1985—, Early Music Acad., Los Angeles, 1983-86, Assn. Classical Music, N.Y.C., 1983-86. Served with AUS, 1960-62. Mem. Audio Engring. Soc., Early Music Acad. (bd. dirs.) Nat. Acad. Rec. Arts and Scis., Assn. Classical Music (bd. dirs.), Plumstead Theatre Co. (bd. dirs.). Avocation: flying.

HOLZMAN, ESTHER ROSE, perfume company executive; b. Frankfurt, Germany; d. Fred and Anna Marie (Zell) Wetmore; m. Nicholas J. Holzman; 1 child, Stephanie Maria. M Organic Chemistry, Pvt. Sch. Dr. Binder, Stuttgart, Germany. Exec. asst. Bosch G.M.B.H., Stuttgart; owner, chief exec. officer Holzman & Stephanie Perfumes, Inc., Lake Forest, Ill., 1986—; normal control, pioneering rsch. studies in nuclear medicine under Phillip H. Henneman, M.D., Seton Hall U., Jersey City, N.J.; normal control, diabetes rsch. under Phillip H. Henneman, M.D. Organizer campaign to rescind cutbacks in fed. funding for med. rsch., 1969, 70. Recipient award for historic restoration of residential bldgs., Village of Oak Park, Ill., 1974, 76. Roman Catholic. Avocations: fashion, home design, knitting, botany, needlepoint. Office: PO Box 921 Lake Forest IL 60045-0921

HOLZMAN, FRANKLYN DUNN, economics educator; b. Bklyn., Dec. 31, 1918; s. Abraham and Mollie (Mandel) H.; m. Mathilda Sara Wiesman, Dec. 14, 1946; children—Thomas Ludwig, David Carl, Miriam Alexandra. B.A., U. N.C., 1940; M.A., Harvard, 1948, Ph.D., 1952. Economist Dept. Treasury, 1947-48, cons., 1949-52; research fellow Russian Research Center, Harvard, 1949-52, research asso., 1961—; prof. econs. U. Wash., 1952-61; prof. econs. Tufts U., mem. faculty Fletcher Sch. Law and Diplomacy, 1961-92; vis. prof. UCLA, 1956, Stanford U., 1957, Columbia U., 1961, MIT, 1963; cons. U.S. Dept. Treasury, 1950, 51, UN, 1963-64, 89, ACDA, 1964-73, Joint Econ. Com., U.S. Congress, 1959, 73, 81, U.S. Commn. on Trade and Investment Policy, 1971, U.S. Dept. Commerce, 1972, 75-78, Stockholm Internat. Peace Rsch. Inst., 1978, Brookings Instn., 1978; Am. co-dir. Joint U.S.-Hungarian Ann. Econ. Confs. and Rsch. Effort, 1973-86. Author: Soviet Taxation: The Fiscal and Monetary Problems of a Planned Economy, 1955, Foreign Trade under Central Planning, 1974, Financial Checks on Soviet Defense Expenditures, 1975, International Trade Under Communism-Politics and Economics, 1976, Soviet Economy: Past, Present and Future, 1982, Economics of Soviet Bloc Trade and Finance, 1987; contbr. 125 articles to scholarly jours. Served to staff sgt. USAAF, 1942-45. Co-winner Furth Internat. Ruble Convertibility competition, 1990; honored by publ. Econ. Adjustment and Reform in Ea. Europe and the Soviet Union: Essays in Honor of Franklyn D. Holzman, edited by Josef C. Brada, Ed A. Hewett and Thomas Wolf, 1988. Mem. Am. Econ. Assn. (chmn. com. on US-USSR Confs., 1985-87), Am. Assn. Advancement of Slavic Studies (exec. com. 1964-65), Am. Assn. Study of Soviet-Type Economies (exec. com. 1966-67), Econometric Soc., Assn. for Comparative Econ. Studies (pres. 1976-77). Home: 33 Peacock Farm Rd Lexington MA 02421-6341

HOLZMAN, MALCOLM, architect; b. Newark, Sept. 26, 1940; s. Herman and Bertie (Hollander) H.; m. Andrea Lea Landsman, Mar. 15, 1985; children: Maxwell, Samuel. BArch, Pratt Inst., 1963. Registered architect, Alaska, Ariz., Conn., D.C., Fla., Hawaii, Minn., Nebr., N.J., N.Y., Ohio, S.C., Tex., Utah, Va., Wis. Architect John Graham & Co., N.Y.C., 1963-64; assoc. Hugh Hardy & Assocs., N.Y.C., 1964-67; founding ptnr. Hardy Holzman Pfeiffer Assocs., N.Y.C., L.A., 1967—; John R. Emens Disting. Prof. Ball State U., Muncie, Ind., 1993; Saarinen chair Yale U., New Haven, Conn., 1987-88, Davenport chair Yale U., New Haven, 1976-77; Eschweiler chair U. Wis., Milw., 1977-79; vis. prof. Coll. Architecture and Design, Lawrence Tech. U., Southfield, Mich., 1991. Author: Reusing Railroad Stations, 1976; researcher: Movie Palaces, 1982; prin. works include bldgs. at Madison Civic Ctr., 1980 (AIA honor 1981), BEST Products Corp. Hdqs. (Phase I) (AIA honor 1983), The Willard Hotel, Washington, 1983, Sta. WCCO-TV Comm. Ctr. and Hdqs., Mpls., 1983; West Wing, Va. Mus. Fine Arts, Richmond, 1985, Ctr. for Arts, Middlebury Coll., 1992, Fine Arts Edn. Bldg., U. Nebr., Omaha, 1992, Dillingham Hall, L.A. Pub. Libr. Ctrl. Libr., 1993, Punahou Sch., Honolulu, 1994, David Saul Smith Union, Bowdoin Coll., 1995, Temple Israel, Ohio, 1995, Hawaii Theater Ctr., Honolulu, 1996, Cleve. Pub. Libr., Yulman Theater, Union Coll., 1995, Lied Edn. Ctr. for the Arts, Creighton U., Nebr., 1996, Hendrix Student Ctr., Clemson U., Berrie Ctr. for the Performing and Visual Arts Ramapo Coll., Mahwah, N.J., Music and Fine Arts Edn. Ctr. U. North Tex., Denton, Walsh Ctr. for Performing Arts, Tex. Christian U., Ft. Worth, San Angelo (Tex.) Mus. of Fine Arts and Edn. Ctr., Internat. Mus. Ceramic Art Alfred U., Dining Hall U. of the South, Lucille Little Theater, Transylvania U., Salisbury (Md.) Upper Sch. Trustee AmonCarter Mus., Ft. Worth, 1981-91, Pratt Inst., 1991-94. Recipient Disting. Alumni award Pratt Inst., 1988 (mem. bd. trustees 1991-94); Arnold W. Brunner prize in Architecture, Nat. Inst. of Arts and Letters, 1974. Fellow AIA (Firm of the Yr. award 1981); mem. N.Y. State Assn. Architects, N.Y.C. AIA (Medal of Honor 1978), Archtl. League, Mcpl. Art Soc. Office: Hardy Holzman Pfeiffer Assocs 902 Broadway Fl 19 New York NY 10010-6082*

HOLZMAN, PHILIP SEIDMAN, psychologist, educator; b. N.Y.C., May 2, 1922; s. Barnet and Natalie (Seidman) H.; m. Hannah Abarbanell, Sept. 18, 1946; children: Natalie Kay, Carl David, Paul Benjamin. BA, CCNY, 1943; PhD, U. Kans., 1952. Diplomate: Am. Bd. Examiners Profl. Psychology. Psychology intern Topeka VA Hosp., 1946-49; psychologist Topeka State Hosp., 1949-51, cons., 1951-58; psychologist Menninger Found., Topeka, 1949-68; dir. research tng. Menninger Found., 1963-68; prof. psychiatry and psychology U. Chgo., 1968-77; prof. psychology dept. psychology Harvard U., 1977-92; prof. dept. psychiatry Med. Sch., 1977-92; Esther and Sidney R. Rabb prof. psychology Harvard U., 1984-92, prof. emeritus, 1992; chief Lab. of Psychology McLean Hosp., Belmont, Mass., 1977—; tng. and supervising psychoanalyst Boston Psychoanalytic Soc. and Inst., 1977—; vis. prof. U. Minn., 1965, U. Kans., 1966, Boston U., 1973, Jefferson Med. Coll., 1981, U. Pa., 1987; Thomas William Salmon lectr. N.Y. Acad. Medicine, 1994; mem. small grants com. NIMH, 1960-64, clin. projects research rev. com., 1964-68, clin. program projects research rev. com., 1970-74, treatment devel. and assessment rev. com., 1982-86; cons. Ill. State Psychiat. Inst., 1970-77; mem. adv. coms. classification of mental disorders WHO. Author: (with others) Cognitive Control, 1959, Psychoanalysis and Psychopathology, 1970, (with Karl Menninger) The Theory of Psychoanalytic Technique, rev. edit, 1973; editor: (with Merton M. Gill) Psychology Versus Metapsychology, 1975, (with Mary Hollis Johnston) Assessing Schizophrenic Thinking, 1979; bd. editors: Psychol. Issues, 1968—, Contemporary Psychology, 1969-76, Bull. of Menninger Clinic, 1961—, also Psychoanalysis and Contemporary Thought, Jour. Psychiat. Rsch., 1980-92; assoc. editor Schizophrenia Bulletin, Schizophrenia Rsch., Harvard Review of Psychiatry, Harvard Mental Health Letter; contbr. articles to profl. jours. Mem. Topeka Mayor's Com. on Human Rels., 1963-68; chmn. bd. dirs. Founds.' Fund for Rsch. in Psychiatry; mem. program adv. com. MacArthur Found., sci. adv. bd. NIMH, 1986-92; bd. trustees Menninger Found., 1978—; mem. sci. coun. Nat. Alliance Rsch. Schizophrenia and Depression, 1989—. With AUS, 1943-46. Recipient Career Scientist award NIMH, 1974-77, 92—; Stanley Dean award Am. Coll. Psychiatrists, 1984, Lieber prize Nat. Alliance for Rsch. in Schizophrenia and Depression, 1988, Joseph Zubin award Soc. Rsch. in Psychopathology, 1994; Townsend Harris medal CCNY, Gold medal for lifetime achievement APA, 1997, William K. Warren award Internat. Congress on Schizophrenia Rsch., 1997. Fellow APA, AAAS, Am. Acad. Arts and Scis., Am. Coll. Neuropsychopharmacology; mem. Am. Psychoanalytic Assn., Boston Psychoanalytic Soc., Am. Psychopath. Assn., Inst. Medicine of NAS, Soc. for Rsch. in Psychopathology (pres. 1997-98). Office: Harvard U William James Hall Cambridge MA 02138 also: McLean Hosp Lab Belmont MA 02178

HOLZMAN, SANDRA, artist, educator; b. Rockville Centre, N.Y., Oct. 28, 1951; d. Irving Charles and Ida Rebecca (Mishkin) H.; m. Thomas G. Grubb, Sept. 9, 1989 (div. Nov. 1997). Student, Phila. Coll. Art; BFA, Sch. Visual Arts, N.Y.C., 1976. Owner, mgr. Sandra Holzman, textiles, N.Y.C., 1977-99; a founder, instr. Santa Fe Sch Art and Enlightenment, 1999—; asst. to graphic arts instr. Sch. Visual Arts, 1976-77; instr. Bklyn. Friends Sch., 1980, YWCA-Craft Students League, N.Y.C., 1981, 90, RISD, Providence, 1982, Parrish Art Mus., Southampton, N.Y., 1984-86, East Hampton (N.Y.) Hist. Soc., 1985, Brookfield (Conn.) Craft Ctr., 1985-95, Women's Studio Workshop, N.Y., 1988, Peters Valley Craft Ctr., N.J., 1988-91, Ctr. for Book Arts, N.Y.C., 1989-91, Taos (N.Mex.) Sch. Art, 1989-94, Woodstock (N.Y.) Guild, 1989-95, Rensselaer County Coun. for Arts, Troy, N.Y., 1990-92, N.J. Ctr. for Visual Arts, 1991-97, Summit, Old Church Cultural Ctr. Sch. Art, Demarest, N.J., 1995-97, Taox Inst. Art, 1989-99. One-woman shows South St. Seaport Mus., N.Y.C., 1974, Unicorn Gallery, N.Y.C., 1977, Temperance Hall Gallery, Bellport, N.Y., 1986, Babylon (N.Y.) Pub. Libr., 1986, Washington Art Gallery, Washington Station, Conn., 1989, Greene County Coun. for the Arts, Catskill, N.Y., 1994, 97, N.J. Ctr. for Visual Arts, Summit, 1995, Hunter (N.Y.) Mt. Gallery, 1995; exhibited in group shows throughout U.S. and Can., including South Street Seaport Mus., N.Y.C., 1974, Unicorn Gallery, N.Y.C., 1977, Phila. Mus., 1979, Lincoln Ctr., N.Y.C., 1980, Elements Gallery, Greenwich, Conn., 1982, Fordham U., N.Y.C., 1985, Temperance Hall Gallery, Bellport, N.Y., 1986, Riverhead (N.Y.) Pub. Libr., 1986, Babylon (N.Y.) Pub. Libr., 1986, Gayle Willson Gallery, Southampton, 1988, Washington Art Gallery, Washington Station, Conn., 1989, Nicoyalsen Mus., Capser, Wyo., 1992, Mus. Fine Arts, San Francisco, 1992, Greene County Coun. on Arts, Windham, N.Y., 1993, 96, Montreal (Que., Can.) Contemporary Mus., 1994, Acnthus Gallery, Saugerties, N.Y., 1994, N.J. Ctr. for Visual Arts, 1995, Amrita Club Gallery, Poughkeepsie, N.Y., 1995, Elaine Benson Gallery, Bridgehampton, N.Y., 1996; represented permanent collections Parrish Art Mus., Southampton, N.Y., South St. Seaport Mus., N.Y.C., Greene County Coun. on the Arts, Catskill, Taos (N.Mex.) Inst. Art; contbr. articles to various publs.; work featured in Archtl. Digest, Designers West, House & Garden, Fiber Arts mag. Mem. visual arts com. Greene County Arts Coun., 1988-94; mgr. Greene Food Coop., Greenville, N.Y., 1990-97. Mem. Open Space Gallery. Avocations: gardening, hiking, kayaking, cross-country skiing. E-mail: sandrasilk@roadrunner.com.

HOLZNER, BURKART, sociologist, educator; b. Tilsit, Germany, Apr. 28, 1931; came to U.S., 1957, naturalized, 1965; s. Hans Otto and Brigitte (Prenzel) H.; children by previous marriage: Steven, Daniel, Claire; m. Leslie Salmon-Cox; stepchildren: Sara Ruth Salmon-Cox, Weir Becket Strange. Student, U. Munich, 1949-52, 53-54, U. Wis., 1952-53; postgrad., U. Wis., 1957-59; Diplom Psychologe, U. Bonn, 1957, Dr.Phil., 1958. Grad.

asst., acting instr. U. Wis., 1958-60; asst. prof. U. Pitts., 1960-63, assoc. prof., 1963-65, prof., chmn. sociology dept., 1966-80, dir. bd. visitors field staff Learning Research and Devel. Center, 1964-66, 71-78, dir. Univ. Center for Internat. Studies, 1980—, prof. Univ. Ctr. for Internat. Studies., 1998—, also sr. research assoc.; assoc. sociologist, assoc. dir. Social Sci. Rsch. Inst., U. Hawaii, 1965-66; vis. prof. sociology, dir. Social Rsch. Centre, Chinese U. of Hong Kong, 1969-70, external examiner in sociology, 1995-98; vis. prof. U. Augsburg, 1977, Chinese Acad. Social Scis., Beijing, 1979, 80; cons. Nat. Inst. Edn., Westinghouse Electric Corp.; mem. exec. com. Pa. Coun. for Internat. Edn., 1980-89, chmn., 1980-83, 88-89. Author: Amerikanische und deutsche Psychologie, 1958, Völkerpsychologie, 1960, Reality Construction in Society, rev. edit, 1972, (with John Marx) Knowledge Application: The Knowledge System in Society, 1979; editor: (with Roland Robertson) Identity and Authority, Explorations in the Theory of Society, 1980, (with Jiri Nehnevajsa) Organizing for Social Research, 1981, (with Zdenek Suda) Directions of Change: Modernization Theory, Research and Reality, 1981, (with Andrew Dinniman) Education for International Competence in Pennsylvania, 1988; co-editor Knowledge: Creation, Distribution, Utilization, 1985, Knowledge in Society, 1987-89. Mem. dist. export council U.S. Dept. Commerce. Recipient Philip R.A. May award for internat. svc., 1991; named hon. citizen of Johnstown, Pa., hon. mem. U. Augsburg, 1990. Mem. Am. Sociol. Assn., North Central Sociol. Assn., Pa. Sociol. Assn., Sociol. Rsch. Assn., Sozialwissenschaftlicher Studienkreis für Internationale Probleme, Internat. Soc. for Comparative Study of Civilizations (mem. U.S. coun., v.p. 1977-79), Assn. Internat. Edn. Adminstrs. (exec. com. 1986—, pres. 1990-91), World Federalist Assn. Pitts. (pres. 1996—). Home: 1700 Grandview Ave Apt 801 Pittsburgh PA 15211-1006 Office: U Pitts U Ctr Internat Studies 4G40 Forbes Quadrangle Pittsburgh PA 15260-7454

HOLZRICHTER, FRED WILLIAM, foundation executive; b. Chgo., Mar. 10, 1944; s. Hugo and Elsie (Bonk) H.; m. Margaret Ann Boicourt, Mar. 19, 1966; children: Mark, Sara, Emily. BA in English, Wartburg Coll., Waverly, Iowa, 1970. Cert. fund-raising exec. Acct. exec. Iowa Credit Union League, Des Moines, 1971-75; mgr. svc. corp. Ill. Credit Union League, Bensonville, 1975-78; pres. The Holzrichter Co., Chgo., 1978-82; dir. instnl. advancement Morgan Park Acad., Chgo., 1982-89; dir. devel. Brescia Coll., Owensboro, Ky., 1989-96; exec. sec. Joliet (Ill.) Jr. Coll. Found., 1996—; dir. advancement Jane Addams Coll., Chgo., 1999—; Creator: (broadcast series) Good News America. Blue and gold officer U.S. Naval Acad., Annapolis, Md., 1992—; campaign staff Citizens for Thompson, Chgo., 1976; cmty. leadership sch. Joliet C. of C., 1997. With U.S. Army, 1967-69. Recipient Commandant's award U.S. Naval Acad., 1994. Mem. Nat. Soc. Fund Raising Execs., Coun. for Advancement and Support of Edn. (bd. dirs. 1993-96), Assn. of Luth. Devel. Execs. Home: 1618 Autumn Dr Joliet IL 60431-8532

HOM, RICHARD YEE, research engineer; b. Phoenix, July 26, 1950; m. Kathleen Chien; 1 child, Matthew Richard Chien. BS in Engring. Sci. and Aero. and Aerospace Tech., Ariz. State U., 1973. Asst. engr. Sperry Flight System, Phoenix, 1973; sr. engr., composite tool engring. Boeing Comml. Airplane Co., Seattle, 1973-84, specialist engr., 1984-88; sr. specialist engr. R&D, metall. processing and advanced projects Boeing Aerospace Co., 1984-90, also automation tech.; with customer svcs. and airline support Boeing Comml. Airplace Group, 1990-91; prin. rsch. engr. metallics R&D Boeing Def. and Space Group, 1991—. Mem. AIAA, SMA, Air Force Assn., Soc. Mfg. Engrs., Aircraft Owners and Pilots Assn., ASM Internat. Home: 28704 15th Ave S Federal Way WA 98003-3161 Office: Boeing Def and Space Group M/S 8J-74 PO Box 3999 Seattle WA 98124-2499

HOMAN, J. MICHAEL, library administrator; b. Portland, Oreg., Aug. 16, 1947; s. Gerald B. and Beverly J. Homan. BA, Lewis and Clark Coll., 1969; MA, U. Chgo., 1971; cert. advanced study, UCLA, 1972. MEDLARS analyst UCLA, 1972-74, head info. svcs., 1974-79; head info. svcs. Upjohn Co., Kalamazoo, Mich., 1979-88; asst. univ. libr. scis. U. Calif., Irvine, 1988-94; dir. libs. Mayo Found./Mayo Clinic, Rochester, Minn., 1994—. Author: (book chpts.) Management of Scientific and Technical Libraries, 1986, Introduction to Reference Sources in the Health Sciences, 1984. USPHS fellow U. Chgo., 1969-71, UCLA, 1971-72. Mem. ALA, Med. Libr. Assn. (bd. dirs. 1987-89, editor bull. 1995—, mng. editor of books 1990-95), Assn. Acad. Health Sci. Libr. Dirs. (bd. dirs. 1991-94), Spl. Librs. Assn., Am. Med. Informatics Assn., Coalition for Networked Info. (rep.). Episcopalian. Avocations: music, opera, traveling, reading. Office: Mayo Clinic 200 1st St SW Rochester MN 55905-0002

HOMAN, KENNETH LEWIS, auditor; b. Bridgeton, N.J., Feb. 8, 1949; s. Lewis and Brenda Homan. BA, Colo. State U., 1971; BS, Edison State Coll., 1981; AS, Camden County Coll., 1984. Cert. mcpl. fin. officer N.J. Dept. Cmty. Affairs. Social worker Cumberland County Bd. Social Svcs., Vineland, N.J., 1972-74; planning coord. Cumberland County Bd. Freeholders, Bridgeton, N.J., 1974-78; staff auditor Bowman & Co., CPA's, Voorhees, N.J., 1979; coord. Morris County Bd. Freeholders, Morristown, N.J., 1979-80; prin. acct. Camden (N.J.) County Bd. Freeholders, 1980-82, asst. comptr., 1982-84, prin. auditor, 1984-96; prin. auditor Camden County Bd. Social Svcs., 1997—. Sec. Somerdale (N.J.) Planning Bd., 1992—. Mem. Assn. Govt. Accts. (cert. govt. fin. mgr.), N.J. Govt. Fin. Officers Assn., N.J. County Fin. Officers Assn., N.Y./N.J. Intergovernmental Audit Forum. Home: PO Box 121 Somerdale NJ 08083-0121 Office: Camden County Bd Social Svcs 600 Market St Camden NJ 08102-1249

HOMAN, RALPH WILLIAM, finance company executive; b. Wilkes-Barre, Pa., June 7, 1951; s. Norman Ryan and Adelaide Bernice (Sandy) H.; m. Donna Marie Webb, Jan. 25, 1975. *Ralph was named after his paternal grandfather who was from Bloomsburg, Pa., and was an executive with Magee Carpet. He invented the Automatic Thread Selecting Machine that for the first time enabled carpet manufacturers to make products by machine with patterns and colors. He married Joyce Dewey of Enfield, England shortly after meeting during World War I. Their one child, Norman, born in 1921 married Adelaide Sandy of Chicago in 1944. They had two children, Marjorie in 1948, and Ralph II in 1951. Ralph married Donna Marie Webb of Pittsburgh in 1974. They had no children by choice.* BS in Acctg., Wheeling Coll., 1977; MBA in Mktg., Nat. U., 1986. Paymaster Dravo Corp., Pitts., 1974-75; tax preparer H&R Block, Wheeling, W.Va., 1977; fin. services exec. NCR Credit Corp., Sacramento, 1977-84; leasing exec. CSB Leasing, Sacramento, 1984-85; pres. Convergent Fin. Svcs., Colorado Springs, Colo., 1985—; bd. dirs. Concord Coalition, Colorado Springs. *Ralph began the marketing department for NCR Credit Corporation in 1980 when it was a new subsidiary. It was the first captive lessor in the computer industry. He won a corporate productivity award while there, and designed its sales territories and marketing materials. He later started CFS Leasing (FKA Convergent Financial Services) in 1985. He created an automated lease document processing system as well as LeasQuot software for his vendors' use. This led to service superiority that lessors much larger could not match, thus giving CFS a competitive edge. He kept the company small for an even greater service advantage.* cons. Jr. Achievement, 1990—. Co-winner Name the Plane Contest Pacific Southwest Airlines, 1984; recipient Businessperson of Yr. award, Colo. Springs chpt. Future Bus. Leaders Am., 1995. Mem. The 30/40 Something Social Club (founder, pres. Sedona chpt.), Am. Assn. Boomers (pres. Pikes Peak chpt. 1992-93), Toastmasters (treas. Oak Creek chpt. 1988-89), Kiwanis (sec. 1988-89, founder, chmn. adult soccer league), Concord Coalition (bd. dirs., pres. Colorado Springs chpt.). Avocations: photography, camping, off-road motorcycling, woodworking. Home and Office: Convergent Fin Svcs 5720 Escapardo Way Colorado Springs CO 80917-3340

HOMAN, RICHARD WARREN, physician, educator; b. N.Y.C., July 28, 1940; s. H. Frank and Irmgard Homan; m. Katherine Poulos, June 16, 1963; children: Gregory William, Christopher Allen. BA, Colgate U., 1962; MD, SUNY, 1966. Diplomate Am. Bd. Psychiatry and Neurology, Am. Bd. Clin. Neurophysiology; cert. Nat. Bd. Med. Examiners. Resident in neurology UCLA, 1970; fellow in neurophysiology Albert Einstein Coll. Medicine, Bronx, N.Y., 1972-74; asst. prof. neurology U. Tex., Southwestern Med. Sch. and Dallas VA Med. Ctr., 1974-82, assoc. prof. neurology, chief neurology svc., 1982-89; prof., chmn. neurology Med. Coll. Ohio, Toledo, 1989-94; prof., chmn. neurology Tex. Tech. U. Health Sci. Ctr., Lubbock, 1994-97, prof. neuropsychiatry and behavioral medicine, pharm. practice, pharm. scis., dir. Ctr. Neuropsychiat. Studies, 1997—; examiner Am. Bd. Clin. Neurophysiology, 1981-94; cons. Tex. State Bd. Med. Examiners, Austin, 1995—. Editor (collected sci. manuscripts) Rational Polypharmacy, 1996; contbr. chpts. to books. Mem. profl. adv. bd. Dallas Epilepsy Found., 1985-87, Epilepsy Found. N.W. Ohio, Toledo, 1989-94; mediator South Plains Ctr. for Dispute Resolution, Lubbock, 1998. Fellow Am. Electroencepalographic Soc., Am. Acad. Neurology; mem. Am. Epilepsy Soc., Phi Beta Kappa. Avocations: scuba diving, playing harp. E-mail: neurwh@ttuhsc.edu. FAX: 806-745-9720. Home: 109 S Lakeshore Ransom Canyon TX 79366 Office: Dept Neuropsychiatry 3601 4th St Lubbock TX 79430

HOMANS, PETER, psychology and religious studies educator; b. N.Y.C., June 24, 1930; s. Howard Parmalee and Dora (Parker) H.; m. Celia Ann Edwards, Feb., 1958; children: Jennifer, Patricia, Elizabeth. Lectr. Trinity Coll., U. Toronto, Ont., Can., 1962-64; asst. prof. Hartford (Conn.) Sem. Found., 1964-65; asst. prof. psychology and religious studies U. Chgo., 1965-68, assoc. prof., 1968-78, prof., 1978-97, prof. emeritus, 1997—, vis. prof., 1997—; mem. tchg. faculty Chgo. Ctr. for Psychoanalysis. Author: Theology After Freud, 1970, Jung in Context, 1979, 2d edit., 1995 (translated into Italian and Japanese), The Ability to Mourn: Disillusionment and the Social Origins of Psychoanalysis, 1989; editor: The Dialogue Between Theology and Psychology, 1968, Childhood and Selfhood: Essays on Erik Eriksons Psychology, 1978; editor, contbr.: Morning, Monuments, and the Experience of Loss: Essays on Coming to Terms with the Past at Century's End, 1999. Soc. for Values in Higher Edn. grantee, 1973-74, Am. Theol. Soc. grantee 1978, Nat. Inst. Humanities summer seminar grantee, 1982, rsch. and travel grantee Am. Coun. Learned Socs., 1983. Mem. APA, Am. Acad. Religion, Am. Hist. Assn., Am. Acad. Psychoanalysis (sci. assoc.). Office: U Chgo Divinity Sch 1025 E 58th St Chicago IL 60637-1509

HOMB, SCOTT MICHAEL, rehabilitation services professional; b. Monroe, Wis., Apr. 13, 1951; s. Wesley C. and Dolores L. Homb. MA, U. South Fla., 1972; PhD, Pacific Western U., 1993. Cert. rehab. counselor; cert. med. case mgr.; cert. vocat. evaluation specialist. Area counseling supr. State of Fla., St. Petersburg, 1978-79; dir. rehab. Nat. Rehab. Assocs., St. Petersburg, 1980-85; sr. med. case mgr. State of Fla., St. Petersburg, 1987-96, brain and spinal cord injury program supr., 1996—.

HOMBURGER, FREDDY, physician, scientist, artist; b. St. Gall, Switzerland, Feb. 8, 1916; came to U.S., 1941, naturalized, 1952; s. Ludwig and Cécile (Gaille) H.; m. Regina Thürlimann, Nov. 8, 1939. Student, U. Vienna, Austria, 1936-37; MD, U. Geneva, Switzerland, 1941. Diplomate Nat. Bd. Med. Examiners., Am. Bd. Toxicology. Rsch. fellow, intern pathology Yale Med. Sch. and New Haven Hosps., 1941-43; intern, rsch. fellow in medicine Harvard Med. Sch., Thorndike Meml. Lab., Boston City Hosp., 1943-45; fellow in medicine Meml. Hosp., N.Y.C., 1946-48; chief clin. investigation Sloan-Kettering Inst. Cancer Research, N.Y.C., 1945-48; instr. medicine Cornell U. Med. Coll., 1946-48, rsch. prof. medicine; dir. cancer rsch. and control unit Tufts U. Sch. Medicine, Boston, 1948-57; mem. courtesy staff Mt. Desert Island Hosp., Bar Harbor, Maine, 1955-73, Eastern Meml. Hosp., Ellsworth, Maine, 1957-60; sci. assoc. Jackson Lab., Bar Harbor, 1951-60; rsch. prof. oncology, div. basic scis. Sch. Grad. Dentistry, Boston U., 1973—; rsch. prof. pathology Sch. Medicine, 1974—; mem. sci. staff Mallory Inst. Pathology, Boston City Hosp., 1979—; mem. Grad. Sch. Faculty Boston U., 1981—; Mem. corp. Gesell Inst. Child Devel., 1960-78; chmn. adv. com. Am. Students U. Geneva; pres., dir. Bio-Research Inst., Inc., 1957-90, Bio-Research Cons., Inc., 1957-95 ; pres. Trenton Exptl. Lab. Animal Co., Bar Harbor, 1969-81; treas., dir. Cambridge Coordinating Com. Drugs, 1972-74; hon. consul of Switzerland in Boston, 1964-86; neutral mem. mixed med. commn. War Dept., 1944-46. Author: The Medical Care of the Aged and Chronically Ill, 3d edit., 1973, The Biological Basis of Cancer Management, 1957; editor: The Physiopathology of Cancer, 3d edit., 1974-76, Progress in Experimental Tumor Research, vols. I-XXXII, 1960-89, The Rational Use of Advanced Medical Technology With the Elderly, 1994; sr. editor: Symposia on Research Advances Applied to Medical Practice, Current Concepts in Toxicology; exhibited paintings in one-man shows, N.Y.C., Paris, Zurich, Geneva, Boston, Portland, Maine. Mem. overseers com. to visit Harvard U., 1965-71, 76-82; bd. dirs. Cambridge Soc. Early Music, 1970—; trustee Opera Co., Boston, 1967-84; chmn. Friends Busch-Reisinger Mus., 1974-85; visitor paintings Boston Mus. Fine Arts, 1974-91; mem. adv. bd. Lachaise Found.; bd. overseers Mt. Desert Island Biol. Lab., 1985-88, trustee 1988-98; bd. dirs. Copley Soc. Boston, 1986-91, Longy Sch. Music, Cambridge, 1984-93, Coun. for the Arts at MIT, 1991-94; exec. sec. Friends of Switzerland, Boston, 1986—. Recipient Julius Adams Stratton prize for cultural achievement, 1991. Fellow AAAS, N.Y. Acad. Scis. (ednl. adv. com. 1967), Acad. Toxicol. Scis.; mem. Nat. Hypertension Assn. (nat. adv. council 1978—), AMA, Endocrine Soc., Am. Assn. Cancer Research, Am. Fedn. Clin. Research, N.Y. Acad. Medicine, Soc. Exptl. Biology and Medicine, Am. Assn. Pathologists, Soc. Toxicology, Am. Soc. Pharmacology and Exptl. Therapeutics, Royal Soc. Health, Brit. Soc. Toxicology, Soc. Pharmacol. and Environ. Pathologists, Endocrine Soc., New Eng. Soc. Pathologists, Cambridge C. of C. (dir. 1969-73), Sigma Xi. Clubs: Harvard (Boston); Cosmos (Washington). Home: 25 Marion St Apt 12 Brookline MA 02446-4966 Office: 675 Massachusetts Ave Cambridge MA 02139-3309

HOMER, BARRY WAYNE, lawyer; b. Junction City, Kans., Jan. 13, 1950. BA, U. Kans., 1972; JD, U. Chgo., 1975. Bar: Calif. 1975, U.S. Dist. Ct. (no. dist.) Calif. 1975, U.S. Tax Ct. 1980. Assoc. Brobeck, Phleger & Harrison, San Francisco, 1975-82, ptnr., 1982—. Co-author: Attorney's Guide to Pension and Profitsharing Plans, 1985, Compensating the Executive with Stock: Some Planning Possibilities and the Effect of the Parachute Provisions, 1986; contbr. articles to profl. jours. Mem. ABA (employee benefits com. tax sect. 1978—), Western Pension & Benefits Conf. Office: Brobeck Phleger & Harrison Spear St Tower 1 Market Plz Ste 341 San Francisco CA 94105-1193

HOMER, DAVID ROBERT, federal judge; b. 1947. BA, Brown U., 1969; JD, Syracuse U., 1975. Bar: N.Y. Trial atty. criminal divsn. U.S. Dept. Justice, 1975-79; asst. U.S. atty. for no. dist. N.Y., U.S. Dept. Justice, Albany, 1979-95; magistrate judge for no. dist. N.Y., U.S. Magistrate Ct., Albany, 1995—. Office: Foley Courthouse 445 Broadway Ste 441 Albany NY 12207-2926

HOMER, RAYMOND RODNEY, film producer, director; b. Bronx, N.Y., Dec. 9, 1926; s. Jermone and Dorothy (Schick) H.; m. Anne Marie Hearn, Sept. 27, 1952 (div.); children: Jeffrey John, Mark Norbert, Scott Daniel, Bruce Raymond; m. Nancy Carman Reisner, 1964; m. Beverly June Elam, Oct. 30, 1983; children: Kelly Ray, Casey Wade. BFA in Art, Morgan Sch. Art, 1949. Pres. Creative Color Inc., N.Y.C., 1959-72, Durham Prodns. Inc., N.Y.C., 1972-86, Raymond R. Homer Prodns., N.Y.C., 1986—; artistic dir. Vandam Theater, N.Y.C., 1988; pres. Trilateral Pictures, 1991-98, Pavilion Pictures, 1998; dir. Western Eagle Humanitarian Found., World Children's Peace Found. Producer films including American Gothic, 1988, The Pawn, 1980, Rip-Off, 1977, Dream City, 1976, Death Rage, 1975, Queen of Diamonds, 1974, The Inheritance, 1973, Swiss Conspiracy, 1972; dir. plays, N.Y. including Six O'Clock Boys, 1986, Two, 1984, One Night Stand, 1982. Seaman USN, 1944-46. Mem. Dirs. Guild Am. Republican. Methodist. Avocations: horseback riding, flying, scuba diving. Home: 5335 Oak Park Ln Apt 136 Agoura Hills CA 91377-5411

HOMER, WILLIAM INNES, art history educator, art expert, author; b. Merion, Pa., Nov. 8, 1929; s. Austin and Evelyn (Innes) H.; 1 child, Stacy Innes; m. Christine D. Hyer, Aug. 24, 1986. A.B., Princeton U., 1951; postgrad., N.Y.U., 1952-53; M.A., Harvard U., 1954; Ph.D., 1961. Instr. dept. art and archeology Princeton, 1955-59, lectr., 1959-61, asst. prof., 1961-64; assoc. prof. history of art Cornell U., 1964-66; prof. U. Del., Newark, 1966—, chmn. dept. art history, 1966-81, 86-93; dir. index of dissertations and theses in Am. art Archives of Am. Art, Washington; vis. fellow Princeton U., 1972-73; assoc. fellow Center for Advanced Studies, Nat. Gallery of Art, 1980-81; mem. Del. Arts Council, 1969-70, New Castle County Beautification Bd., 1967-70; adv. screening com. (overseas) Fulbright-Hays Fellowship Awards, 1970-72, chmn., 1971-72; mem. sr. fellowship panel Nat. Endowment for Humanities, 1970; mem. exhbn. com. Del. Art Mus., 1968-73, chmn. accessions com., 1974-78. Author: Seurat and the Science of Painting, 1964, Robert Henri and His Circle, 1969, Alfred Stieglitz and the American Avant-Garde, 1977, The Photographs of Gertrude Käsebier, 1979, Alfred Stieglitz and the Photo-Secession, 1983, Pictorial Photography in Philadelphia, 1984; co-author Albert Pinkham Ryder: Painter of Dreams, 1989, Thomas Eakins, His Life and Art, 1992; mem. editorial bd. Am. Art Jour., 1970—, Winterthur Portfolio, 1978-80; sr. editor Am Art Rev., 1992—. Mem. adv. com. Am. Studies Inst., Lincoln U., 1967-76; mem. corp. Mus. Am. Art, Ogunquit, Maine, 1958-92; regional adv. com. Archives Am. Art, 1979—; trustee Am. Friends Nat. Portrait Gallery, London, 1995—, Sewell C. Biggs Mus. Am. Art, 1994-97; bd. dirs. Ctr. Advanced Studies in Visual Arts Nat. Gallery Art, 1994-98. Council of Humanities fellow Princeton U., 1962-63; Am. Council Learned Socs. fellow, 1964-65; Guggenheim fellow, 1972-73; Nat. Endowment for Humanities fellow, 1980-81; Ctr. for Advanced Study U. Del. fellow, 1985-86. Fellow Royal Soc. Arts (London), New Pictorialist Soc. (dir. 1981—); mem. Coll. Art Assn. Am., Pictorial Photographers Am., Royal Photog. Soc., Welcome Soc. of Pa., Phi Kappa Phi. Clubs: Princeton (N.Y.C.); Nat. Arts., Cosmos. Home: PO Box 3595 Wilmington DE 19807-0595 Office: U Del Dept Art History Newark DE 19716

HOMESTEAD, SUSAN (SUSAN FREEDLENDER), psychotherapist; b. Bklyn., Sept. 20, 1937; d. Cy Simon and Katherine (Haas) Eichelbaum; m. Robert Bruce Randall, 1956 (div. 1960); 1 child, Bruce David; m. George Gilbert Zanetti, Dec. 13, 1962 (div. 1972); m. Ronald Eric Homestead, Jan. 16, 1973 (div. 1980); m. Arthur Elliott Freedlender, Apr. 1, 1995. BA, U. Miami-Fla., 1960; MSW, Tulane U., 1967. Diplomate Am. Bd. Clin. Social Work; Acad. Cert. Social Workers, 1971, LCSW, Va., Calif. Psychotherapist, cons., Richmond, Va., 1971—, Los Altos, Calif.; pvt. practice, Homestead Counseling, Richmond, Piedmont Psychiatric Ctr., P.C. (formerly Psychol. Evaluation Rehab. Cons., Inc.), Lynchburg, Va., 1994-97; cons. Family and Children's Svcs., Richmond, 1981—, Richmond Pain Clinic, 1983-84; Health Internat. Va., P.C., Lynchburg, 1984-86, Franklin St. Psychotherapy & Edn. Ctr, Santa Clara, Calif., 1988-90; pvt. practice, 1971—; Santa Clara County Children's Svc., 1973-75, 86-88; co-dir. asthma program Va. Lung Assn., Richmond, 1975-79, Loma Prieta Regional Ctr.; chief clin. social worker Med. Coll. Va., Va. Commonwealth U., 1974-79; field supr. 1980 Census, 1981-87. Contbr. articles to profl. jours. Active Peninsula Children's Ctr., Morgan Ctr., Coun. for Community Action Planning, Community Assn. for Retarded, Comprehensive Health Planning Assn. Santa Clara, Mental Health Commn., Children and Adolescent Target Group Calif., Women's Com. Richmond Symphony, Va. Mus. Theatre, mem. fin. com. Robb for Gov.; mem. adv. com. Va. Lung Assn.; mem. steering com. Am. Cancer Soc.(Va. div.), Epilepsy Found., Am. Heart Assn. (Va. div.), Cen. Va. Guild for Infant Survival. Mem. NASW, Va. Soc. Clin. Social Work, Inc. (charter mem., sec. 1975-78), Internat. Soc. Communicative Psychoanalysis & Psychotherapy, Am. Acad. Psychotherapists, Internat. Soc. for the Study of Dissociation, Am. Assn. Psychiatric Svcs. for Children.

HOMICK, DANIEL JOHN, lawyer, financial executive; b. Cleve., Nov. 10, 1947; s. John and Frances (Ziherl) H.; m. Victoria Frances Majoros, Sept. 1, 1974; children: Alexandra Victoria, Christopher Daniel, Andrew William, Elizabeth Irene. AB, John Carroll U., 1969, MA, 1971; diploma, U. Vienna, Strobl, Austria, 1972; JD, Capital U., 1978. Bar: Ohio, 1978. Asst. mgr. Shaker Heights (Ohio) Theatre, 1968-71; teaching assoc. John Carroll U., Univ. Heights, Ohio, 1969-71; dept. chmn. Magnificat High Sch., Rocky River, Ohio, 1972-73; asst. to dir. Dept. Human Resources and Econ. Devel. City of Cleve., 1973-75; acting state dir., program officer U.S. Govt. ACTION, Columbus, Ohio, 1975-79; assoc. gen. counsel Am. Invsco, Atlanta and Chgo., 1980-82; program mgr. Mortgage Guaranty Ins. Corp., Milw., 1982-86, v.p. mortgage securities, 1986-87; sr. v.p. capital markets and mktg. CenTrust Savs. Bank, Miami, 1987-89; v.p. negotiated transactions, capital markets Gen. Electric Mortgage Securities Corp., Raleigh, N.C., 1989-93; registered rep. GECC Capital Mkts., Inc., 1990-96; v.p. structured transactions GE Capital Mortgage Svcs., Inc., Raleigh, N.C., 1993-94; v.p. direct placements GE Capital Mortgage Corp., 1994-96; v.p. structured finance, registered rep. Berean Capital Inc., Raleigh, N.C., 1996—; prin., v.p. Berean Capital Ptnrs., Inc., 1998—; pvt. practice law, Columbus, 1978-79; instr., tng. cons. Columbus Tech. Inst., 1978-79. Mem. fin. devel. com. Raleigh Boychoir, 1998—; mem. Ctrl. YMCA Long Bow Coun., 1996—; bd. dirs. Mental Health Assn. Dade County, Miami, 1987-89, Cherrywood Villlage Condominium Assn., Brown Deer, Wis., 1983-84, Summit Chase Condominium Assn., Columbus, Ohio, 1979-80; campaign coord. Andrew Young for Mayor, Atlanta, 1982. Mem. ABA (chmn. mortgage guaranty ins. subcom. 1985-87, chmn. securitization mortgages subcom. 1987-93, chmn. securitization com. 1987-94, ad hoc com. on ctrl. and ea. European law initiative 1991-93, financing affordable housing com. 1991—, internat. investment in real estate com. 1991-95, ad hoc com. on tech. asst. to emerging econs. 1993—, co-chair conf. The Evolving Worldwide Legal and Regulatory Climate for Securitization, Brussels 1993, standing com. on CLE 1993-97, group chair real estate and mortgage investment coms. 1994-95, coun. real property, probate and trust law sect. 1995-98, standing com. on membership 1995—, co-chair 1998—, standing com. on publs. 1995-97, standing com. on goal IX/Diversity 1997—, task force on securitization of assets 1996-98, com. fed. regulation of securities 1996—, task force on fin. svcs. and European Cmty. 1996—, com. internat. bus. law 1996—, subcom. fgn. investments in U.S. 1996—, com. internat. real property fin. and secured transactions 1998—, com. newly ind. states of the former Soviet Union 1998—, subcom. securitization of assets 1998—, subcom. multinat. merger and acquisitions 1998—), Mortgage Banker's Assn. (comml. real estate fin. com. 1990-92, secondary market and securitization subcom. 1990-92), Am. Assn. Advancement Slavic Studies, Delta Sigma Rho, Phi Alpha Theta. Avocations: Russian history, travel. Home and Office: 8608 Cold Springs Rd Raleigh NC 27615-3107

HOMMES, FRITS AUKUSTINUS, biology educator; b. Bellingwolde, Netherlands, May 28, 1934; came to U.S., 1979; s. Aukustinus and Anje (Wester) H.; m. Grietje Renes, June 14, 1958; children: Peter, Anneliek. M.Sc. in Chemistry, U. Groningen, Netherlands, 1958; Ph.D., U. Nijmegen, Netherlands, 1961. Diplomate Am. Bd. Med. Genetics. Research asst. dept. biochemistry U. Nijmegen, 1959-61; instr. U. NiJmegen, 1963-66; postdoctoral fellow dept. biochemistry and biophysics U. Pa., Phila., 1961-63; head lab. dept. pediatrics U. Groningen, 1966-72, assoc. prof., 1972-79; prof. dept. biochemistry and molecular biology Med. Coll. Ga., Augusta, 1979-93, dir. biochem. genetics lab., 1980-93; dir. biochem. genetics lab. NYU, 1993-96, prof. dept. pediat., 1993-96; dir. biochem. genetics lab. N.Y. Med. Coll., Valhalla, 1996—, prof. dept. pathology, pediat., biochem., 1996—; cons. genetic diseases Dutch Health Council, 1974-79, FDA, 1992—; chmn. Dutch Bioenergetics Study Group, 1975-77.. Author: Inborn Errors of Metabolism, 1973, Normal and Pathological Development of Energy Metabolism, 1975, Models for the Study of Inborn Errors of Metabolism, 1979, Techniques in Human Diagnostic Biochemical Genetics, A Laboratory Manual, 1990; mem. editorial bd. Nutrition and Metabolism, 1975—; contbr. articles to profl. jours.; patentee in field. Chmn. Groningen chpt. Round Table, 1970-71; chmn. No. Dist., Netherlands, 1973-75, mem. nat. bd., 1974-75. Fulbright fellow, 1961-63; recipient medal City of Milan, 1987, Disting. Svc. award SERGG, 1993. Fellow Am. Coll. Med. Genetics; mem. AAAS, European Soc. Pediatric Rsch., Soc. Study of Inborn Errors of Metabolism, Soc. Inherited Metabolic Disease (bd. dirs. 1993-95), Am. Soc. Human Genetics (chmn. com. biochem. genetics 1990-91), N.Y. Acad. Sci., Soc. Pediatric Rsch., Am. Soc. Biol. Chemists. Roman Catholic. Office: NY Med Coll Dept Pathology, Pediat, Biochem Valhalla NY 10595

HON, JOHN WINGSUN, physician; b. Canton, China, Aug. 21, 1947; s. Yuen-Pak and Yuk-Ying (Chan) H. BA, CUNY, 1972; MA, SUNY, Buffalo, 1975; DO, Kirksville Coll. Medicine, 1979. Diplomate Am. Coll. Emergency Physicians; bd. cert. emergency medicine and family practice. Enlisted U.S. Army, 1975, advanced through ranks to capt., 1979; intern, resident Tripler Army Med. Ctr., Honolulu, 1979-80; gen. med. officer U.S. Army Med. Corps, Honolulu, 1979-80; intern Tripler Army Med. Ctr., Honolulu, 1979-80; gen. med. officer U.S. Army Med. Corps, Korea, 1980-81, U.S. Mil. Acad., West Point, 1981-83; attending physician Woodhull Hosp., Bklyn., 1983-86; pvt. practice Woodside, N.Y., 1983—, Elmhurst, N.Y., 1993—; attending physician Bronx Lebanon Hosp., 1987-91, Astoria (N.Y.) Gen. Hosp., 1983—, St. John Hosp., Elmhurst, N.Y., 1992—, N.Y. Hosp. Dept. Medicine, 1996; clin. asst. prof. family practice N.Y. Coll. Osteo. Medicine, 1994—. Fellow Am. Coll. Emergency Physicians; mem. Am. Osteo. Assn., N.Y. State Osteo. Med. Soc., Chinese Am. Med. Soc. (life). Avocations: photography. Home: 148 Cat Rock Rd Cos Cob CT 06807-1302 Office: 30-96 51st St Flushing NY 11377-1457 also: 86-08 Elmhurst Ave Elmhurst NY 11373

HONAHAN, H(ENRY) ROBERT, motion picture theatre executive; b. N.Y.C., June 26, 1937; s. Henry Walter and Mary (Kovac) H.; children: Sara Anne, Robert Jeremiah. BBA, U. San Jose; postgrad., UCLA, 1968. Div. mgr. Loews Theatres, Los Angeles, 1968-73; gen. mgr. ABC Theatres, San Francisco, 1971-73, asst. to pres., 1973-76; asst. to pres. United Artists Communications, San Francisco, 1976-80; v.p. Honahan Entertainment, Ft. Lauderdale, Fla.; cons., motion picture exec. producer Ft. Lauderdale, 1981—; pub. Honahan Newsletter Bus. and Film, Ft. Lauderdale, 1988—; pres., CEO Famous Artists Movie Entertainment, Ft. Lauderdale, Fla. Author: Basic Theatre Operation, 1967; exec. producer (films) The World Without Me, 1999, Race to Triumph, 1999, The Dave Lindsey Story, 1999. Recipient Citizen Community Svc. award City of Los Angeles, 1972, Best Subject Live Action award Ft. Lauderdale Film Festival, Film Prodr. of Yr. award, 1992. Office: Honahan Entertainment Group Maj Motion Picture Prodns 2001 NW 9th Ave Fort Lauderdale FL 33311-4052

HONAKER, CHARLES RAY, health facility administrator; b. Charleston, W.Va., Jan. 13, 1947; s. Charles Frederick and Avis Linda (McCarthy) H.; m. Sarah Powers, Aug. 30, 1969; children: Charles Erik, Cara Powers, Katherine Powers, Erin Powers. BA, U. Del., 1977; M in Health Sci., Johns Hopkins U., 1981. Cert. nursing home adminstr., healthcare exec.; diplomate Am. Coll. Healthcare Execs. Dir. residential treatment Gov. Bacon Health Ctr.-State of Del., Delaware City, 1975-80; sr. health planner State of W.Va., Charleston, 1980-83; assoc. hosp. adminstr. Pinecrest State Hosp., Beckley, W.Va., 1983-84; nursing home adminstr. Arthur B. Hodges Ctr., Charleston, W.Va., 1984-86, Carondelet Holy Family Ctr., Tucson, 1986-89; hosp. adminstr. Carondelet Holy Cross Hosp., Nogales, Ariz., 1989-96; CEO St. Thomas More Health Sys., Canon City, Colo., 1996—; bd. mem., v.p. So. Ariz., Am. Cancer Soc., 1989-94; chair, bd. mem. Office of Rural Health, U. Ariz., Tucson, 1990—; chmn. bd. Ariz. Rural Health Assn., Phoenix. Bd. dirs. Sahuarita (Ariz.) Unified Sch. Dist., 1987-91, C. of C., Nogales, 1995, St. Scholastica Acad., Canon City, 1998—, Fremont County, Colo. Econ. Devel. Coun., 1998—. Fellow Am. Acad. Med. Adminstrs., Am. Coll. Health Care Adminstrs.; mem. U.S.-Mex. Border Health Assn., Ariz.-Mex. Commn. (pub. health coms.). Republican. Roman Catholic. Avocations: dog breeding and showing, Arabian horse breeding, shooting, hunting. Home: PO Box 2136 Canon City CO 81215-2136 Office: St Thomas More Health Sys 1338 Phay Ave Canon City CO 81212-2302

HONAKER, JIMMIE JOE, lawyer, ecologist; b. Oklahoma City, Jan. 21, 1939; s. Joe Jack and Ruby Lee (Bowen) H.; children: Jay Jimmie, Kerri Ruth. BA, Colo. Coll., 1963; MA, U. No. Colo., 1991; JD, U. Wyo., 1966, MS, 1995; postgrad., Utah State U., 1995—. Bar: Colo. Bar, U.S. Ct. Appeals (10th cir.), 1982. Pvt. practice Longmont, Colo., 1966-91. Incorporator Longmont Boys Baseball, 1969; chmn. Longmont City Charter Commn., 1973; chmn. ch. bd. 1st Christian Ch., Longmont, 1975, 76; chmn. North Boulder County unit Am. Cancer Soc., 1978, 79. Recipient Disting. Svc. award Longmont Centennial Yr., 1971; named Outstanding Young Man, Longmont Jaycees, 1973. Mem. ABA, Colo. Bar Assn. (interprofl. com. 1972-91, environ. law sect. 1999—), Denver Bar Assn., Christian Legal Soc., Internat. Assn. Approved Basketball Ofcls. (cert.), Nat. Eagle Scout Assn., Ecol. Soc. Am., Colo. Mountain Club, Uintah Mtn. Club, Phi Alpha Delta, Alpha Kappa Psi, Xi Sigma Pi. Avocations: private pilot, mountain climbing. Address: Utah State U Box 1320 Logan UT 84322-0199

HONAMAN, J. CRAIG, health facility administrator; b. Montclair, N.J., June 15, 1943; s. Richard Karl and Gloria (McElwain) H.; m. Dee Dee Toerpe, Dec. 31, 1971; children: Justin Craig Jr., Garman Grayson. BS, N.C. State U., 1965; MS, U. Ala., 1971. Sr. v.p. Bapt. Hosp., Pensacola, Fla., 1970-79; exec. v.p. Tallahassee (Fla.) Meml. Hosp., 1979-89; adminstr. Quorum Health Resources/Leesburg (Fla.) Regional Med. Ctr., 1989-91; v.p., adminstrn. home health care Meth. Med. Ctr., Jacksonville, Fla., 1991-92; pres. Kellogg Healthcare, Inc., Jacksonville, 1992-93, KNH Healthcare, Jacksonville, 1993-95; exec. dir. HomeCare Alliance of Ga., Inc., Atlanta, 1994-98; sr. v.p. Hanev & Assocs., Atlanta, 1998—; cons. in field, Jacksonville, Fla., 1991—. Contbr. articles to profl. jours. Active Boy Scouts Am., ARC, Am. Cancer Soc., Ronald McDonald House. Capt. U.S. Army, 1966-69, Vietnam. Recipient Nat. Golden Hour award MBB Helicopter, 1988. Fellow Am. Coll. Healthcare Execs. (cert. health care mgr.), Rotary. Episcopalian. Avocations: golf, running. Office: Hanev & Assocs 560 Cambridge Way NE Ste 101 Atlanta GA 30328-1007

HONAN, WILLIAM HOLMES, journalist, writer; b. N.Y.C., May 11, 1930; s. William Francis and Annette (Neudecker) H.; m. Nancy Burton, June 22, 1975; children: Bradley, Daniel, Edith. BA, Oberlin (Ohio) Coll., 1952; MA, U. Va., 1955. Editor The Villager (weekly newspaper), N.Y.C., 1957-60; asst. editor New Yorker mag., 1960-64; freelance writer nat. mags., 1964-68; asso. editor Newsweek, 1969; asst. editor N.Y. Times mag., 1969-70, travel editor, 1970-72, 73-74, arts and leisure editor, 1974-82, culture editor, 1982-88, chief cultural corr., 1988-93; nat. higher edn. corr., 1993—; mng. editor Saturday Rev., 1972-73. Author: Greenwich Village Guide, 1959, Ted Kennedy: Profile of a Survivor, 1972, Bywater: The Man Who Invented the Pacific War, Brit. edit., 1990, Visions of Infamy: The Untold Story of How Journalist Hector C. Bywater Devised the Plans That Led to Pearl Harbor, 1991, Remember, Japanese edit., 1991, Treasure Hunt: A New York Times Reporter Tracks the Quedlinburg Hoard, 1997, (play) Zingers, 1999, (pamphlet) Another La Guardia, 1960; compiler, editor: Fire When Ready, Gridley: Great Naval Stories From Manila Bay to Vietnam, 1993; contbr. articles to nat. mags. and profl. jours. Served with AUS, 1956-57. Office: NY Times 229 W 43rd St New York NY 10036-3959

HONDERICH, JOHN ALLEN, newspaper publisher; b. Toronto, Ont., Can., July 6, 1946; s. Beland Hugh and Florence Rene (Wilkinson) H.; m. Katherine Mary Govier, Feb. 27, 1981 (sep.); children: Robin Christian, Emily Rose. BA in Polit. Sci. and Econs. with honors, U. Toronto, 1968, LLB, 1971. Bar: Ont., 1973. Reporter The Ottawa (Ont.) Citizen, 1973-76; mem. Ottawa Bur. The Toronto Star, 1976-79; Ottawa bur. chief The Toronto Star, Toronto, 1979-80; Washington bur. chief The Toronto Star, Toronto, Can., 1980-82; dep. city editor The Toronto Star, Toronto, 1982-84, bus. editor, 1984-86, editorial page editor, 1987-88, editor, 1988-94, pub., 1994—. Author: Arctic Imperative: Is Canada Losing the North?, 1987. Mem. Can. Press, Can. Daily Newspaper Assn., Commonwealth Press Union, Can. Newspaper Assn. Office: Toronto Star, 1 Yonge St, Toronto, ON Canada M5E 1E6*

HONE, RANDOLPH COOPER, architect; b. Tulsa, July 9, 1949; s. Herbert Miles and Ruth (Cooper) H. BS in Architecture, Okla. State U., 1972. Registered arch., Mo. Arch. John M. Taylor, Springfield, Mo., 1975; arch. Esterly, Carvers & Assocs., Springfield, 1976-77, Marshall, Waters, Woody, Springfield, 1978-79, Paul Rich, Arch., Springfield, 1980-81, SMBC, Springfield, 1982; prin. Randolph Cooper Hone, Arch., Turners, Mo., 1983—. Archtl. work published in Log Home Living, 1996, Country Heart mag., 1997, Better Homes & Gardens Home Plan Ideas, 1988. Rep. for motorcycle safety Traffic Safety Alliance of the Ozarks, Springfield, 1992-97. Mem. BMW Motorcycle Owners of Am. (pres. chpt. 8 Springfield BMW Road Riders 1996), BMW Riders Assn. Republican. Avocations: restoring motorcycles, cross-country motorcycle touring. Home and Office: PO Box 125 Turners MO 65765-0125

HONEA, FLOYD FRANKLIN, lawyer; b. Dallas, May 20, 1950; s. Floyd Franklin and Gloria Anne H. BS, North Tex. State U., 1973; JD, U. Tex., 1976. Bar: Tex. 1976, U.S. Supreme Ct., U.S. Ct. Appeals (5th and 10th cirs.), U.S. Ct. Claims, U.S. Dist. Ct. (no., ea. and we. dists.) Tex. Ptnr. Payne & Vendig, Dallas, 1976-97; shareholder Winstead Sechrist & Minick, P.C., Dallas, 1997—. Mem. Dallas Hist. Soc., 1978—; mem. Rep. Nat. Com. Rep. party Tex., 1979—; Keeton fellow, mem. dean's coun. U. Tex. Sch. Law; active Dallas Zool. Soc., 1986—, Dallas Symphony Assn.; sponsor Kimbell Art Mus., Smithsonian Inst., WMS Civic Trust, Dallas Mus. Art. Mem. ABA, State Bar Tex., Dallas Bar Assn., The 500, Inc., Crescent Club Dallas. Baptist. Home: 8865 Flint Falls Dr Dallas TX 75243-7542 Office: 5400 Republic Nat Bank Towe Dallas TX 75201

HONEA, JOYCE CLAYTON, critical care nurse; b. San Antoino, Oct. 4, 1952; d. Leslie James and Shirley Louis (Steinfeldt) Clayton; m. Bertrand N. Honea III, May 1, 1982; children: Matt Baker, Elissa Baker. BS in Nursing, Loretto Heights Coll., 1976; MS, Cen. Mich. U., 1990. Nursing faculty Front Range C.C., Ft. Collins, Colo., 1990—; family nurse practitioner U. No. Colo., 1999. Mem. ANA (sec. 1985-87).

HONEMANN, DANIEL HENRY, lawyer; b. Balt., Oct. 20, 1929; s. Henry Letcher and Maude Elizabeth (Wilson) H.; m. Rose Ann Clark, Mar. 23, 1974; children by previous marriage: Deborah, Dori, Daniel, Donna. AB, Western Md. Coll., Westminster, 1951; JD, U. Md., 1956. Bar: Md. 1956. Practice law Balt.; partner firm Clapp, Somerville, Honemann & Beach, 1962-85, Whiteford, Taylor & Preston, 1986—; asst. U.S. atty. Dist. Md., 1960-61. Author: (with others) Robert's Rules of Order Newly Revised, 9th edit. Served to 1st lt. inf. AUS, 1951-53. Decorated Bronze Star, Combat Inf. badge. Fellow Am. Coll. Trust and Estate Counsel, Md. Bar Found.; mem. ABA (ho. of dels. 1978-80), Md. Bar Assn. (sec. 1977-84, bd. govs. 1975-84), Balt. Bar Assn. Home: 2318 Harcroft Rd Lutherville Timonium MD 21093-2638 Office: 7 Saint Paul St Ste 1400 Baltimore MD 21202-1654

HONER, RICHARD JOSEPH, surgeon; b. Ottawa, Ill., 1953. MD, U. Ill., 1979. Diplomate Am. Bd. Surgery, Am. Bd. Colon and Rectal Surgery. Intern St. Marys Hosp., Grand Rapids, Mich., 1979-80, resident in surgery, 1980-84; fellow in colon and rectal surgery Ferguson Hosp., Grand Rapids, 1984-85; with Winter Haven (Fla.) Hosp., 1985—. Office: Gessler Clinic 635 1st St N Winter Haven FL 33881-4191*

HONEY, RICHARD CHURCHILL, retired electrical engineer; b. Portland, Oreg., Mar. 9, 1924; s. John Kohnen and Margaret Fargo (Larrison) H.; m. Helen Waugaman, June 8, 1952 (div. Feb. 1980; children: Leslie, Steven, Laura, Janine; m. Jo Anne Kipp, Jan. 11, 1993. BS, Calif. Inst. Tech., 1945; EE, Stanford U., 1950, PhD, 1953. Research asst. Stanford U., 1948-52; sr. research engr. microwave group Stanford Research Inst., 1952-60; tech. program coordinator Electromagnetic Techniques Lab., 1960-64, lab. dir., 1964-70, staff scientist, 1970-89, sr. prin. scientist, 1989-93; dir. ILC Tech.; mem. Army Sci. Bd., 1978-84. Contbr. articles to books, encyc., profl. jours. Served with USN, 1943-46. Fellow IEEE, Optical Soc. Am.; mem. Optical Soc. No. Calif., Coyote Point Yacht Club, Sigma Xi. Patentee in field. Office: SRI Internat 333 Ravenswood Ave Menlo Park CA 94025-3453

HONEYCHURCH, DENIS ARTHUR, lawyer; b. Berkeley, Calif., Sept. 17, 1946; s. Winston and Mary Martha (Chandler) H.; m. Judith Ann Poliquin, Oct. 5, 1969; children: Sean, James, Thomas. BA, UCLA, 1968; JD, U. Calif., San Francisco, 1972. Bar: Calif. 1972, U.S. Dist. Ct. (no. dist.) Calif. 1972, U.S. Ct. Appeals (9th cir.) 1972. Dep. pub. defender Sacramento County Calif., Sacramento, 1973-75; supervising asst. pub. defender Solano County, Fairfield, Calif., 1975-78; ptnr. Honeychurch & Finkas and predecessor firm, Fairfield, 1978—. Bd. dirs. Fairfield-Suisun Unified Sch. Dist., Fairfield, 1979-83, Solano Coll., Fairfield, 1985—; chmn. bd. dirs. Downtown Improvement Dist., Fairfield, 1980-82; mem. Dem. Ctr. Com. Solano County, 1994-98. Mem. ABA, Nat. Assn. Criminal Def. Lawyers, Calif. Attys. Criminal Justice, Calif. Pub. Defenders Assn., Solano County Bar Assn. (pres. 1991), Calif. Bd. Legal Specialization (cert.), Nat. Bd. Trial Advocacy (cert.). Democrat. Office: Honeychurch & Finkas 823 Jefferson St Fairfield CA 94533-5591

HONEYCUTT, BRENDA, secondary education educator. Tchr. sci. Fort Mill (S.C.) Middle Sch.; chmn. sci. dept.; rep. Nat. Mid. Sch. Conf. Recipient hon. mention Outstanding Earth Sci. Tchr. award Nat. Assn. of Geology Teachers, 1992, S.C. Earth Sci. Tchr. Yr., 1992. Office: Fort Mill Middle Sch 200 Hwy 160 BYP Fort Mill SC 29715-2209

HONEYCUTT, GEORGE LEONARD, photographer, retired; b. High Point, N.C., Jan. 5, 1936; s. Leonard Franklin and Pearl (Reynolds) H.; m. Sandra Spencer, Mar. 29, 1955; children: George Keith, Stephen Kurt, Kevin Spencer. Student, Sch. Modern Photography, N.Y.C., 1954. Photographer Charlotte (N.C.) News, 1959-62; Staff photographer Houston Chronicle, 1963, dir. photography, 1963-97, retired, 1997. Served with AUS, 1955-57. Recipient awards AP, awards UP, awards Headliners; 4-time winner Profl. Football Hall of Fame. Mem. Nat. Press Photographers Assn. (named Nat. Newspaper Photographer of Yr. 1962). Methodist. Office: 801 Texas St Houston TX 77002-2906

HONEYCUTT, VAN B., computer services company executive; b. 1945. With Computer Scis. Corp., El Segundo, Calif., 1975—, v.p., pres. industry svcs. group, chmn., pres., CEO, 1996—. Office: Computer Scis Corp 2100 E Grand Ave El Segundo CA 90245-5024*

HONEYSTEIN, KARL, lawyer, entertainment company executive; b. N.Y.C., Jan. 10, 1932; s. Herman and Claire (Rosen) H.; m. Buzz Halliday, Sept. 14, 1965 (div. Dec. 1978); 1 child, Gail. BA, Yale U., 1953; JD, Columbia U., 1959. Bar: N.Y. 1959. Assoc. Greenbaum, Wolff & Ernst, N.Y.C., 1959-62; v.p. Ashley Famous Agy., N.Y.C., 1962-69, Internat. Famous Agy., N.Y.C., 1969-71; exec. v.p. The Sy Fischer Co., N.Y.C. and L.A., 1971-80; exec. v.p., chief operating officer The Taft Entertainment Co., Los Angeles, 1980-88; pres. K.H. Strategy Corp., Los Angeles, 1988—; lectr. law Bklyn. Law Sch., N.Y.C., 1973-75. Served to lt. j.g. USNR, 1953-56. Fellow Internat. Coun. NATAS; mem. Friars Club, Regency Club.

HONG, GREGORY LEONG, bank executive; b. N.Y.C., Mar. 26, 1964; s. Franklin Leong and Lorraine Leiko (Miyahara) H.; m. Diane Grace Seitz, Apr. 9, 1994. BA, NYU, 1986; MBA, Fordham U., 1989. Assoc. corp. fin. Long-Term Credit Bank Japan, Ltd., N.Y.C., 1989-91, asst. v.p., 1991-93, v.p., 1993-98; sr. v.p. LTCB Trust Co., N.Y.C., 1998—. Mem. NYU Alumni Assn., Fordham MBA Alumni Assn. Avocations: tennis, running. Home: 16 Saint Claire Ave Old Greenwich CT 06870-1922 Office: Long-Term Credit Bank 165 Broadway Fl 49 New York NY 10006-1480

HONG, HOWARD VINCENT, library administrator, philosophy educator, editor, translator; b. Wolford, N.D., Oct. 19, 1912. BA, St. Olaf Coll., 1934; postgrad., Wash. State Coll., 1934-35; PhD, U. Minn., 1938; postgrad., U. Copenhagen, 1938-39; D.Litt. (hon.), McGill U., Montreal, 1977; D.D. (hon.), Trinity Sem., Columbus, Ohio, 1983; D.H.L. (hon.), Carleton Coll., 1987; ThD (hon.), U. Copenhagen, 1992. With English dept. Wash. State Coll., 1934-35; with Brit. Mus., 1937; mem. faculty dept. philosophy St. Olaf Coll., Northfield, Minn., 1938-78, asst. prof. philosophy, 1940-42, assoc. prof., 1942-47, prof., 1947-78, chmn. Ford Found. self-study com., 1955-56, dir. Kierkegaard Library, 1972-84; vis. lectr. U. Minn., 1955; mem. Nat. Lutheran Council Scholarship and Grant Rev. Bd., 1958-66; lectr. Holden Village, Washington, 1963-70; mem. Minn. Colls. Grant Rev. Bd., 1970. Author, editor, contbr.: Integration in the Christian Liberal Arts College, 1956, books most recent This World and the Church, 1955; editor, contbg. author: Christian Faith and the Liberal Arts, 1960; co-editor, translator: (with Edna H. Hong) works by Gregor Malantschuk, numerous works by Soren Kierkegaard, Soren Kierkegaard's Journals and Papers, Vol. I, 1968 (Nat. Book award for transl. 1968), Søren Kierkegaard's Journals and Papers, Vol. II, 1970, Søren Kierkegaard's Journals and Papers, Vol. III-IV, 1975, Søren Kierkegaard's Journals and Papers, V-VII, 1978, The Controversial Kierkegaard (Gregor Malantschuk), 1980, Two Ages (Søren Kierkegaard), 1978, The Sickness unto Death (Søren Kierkegaard), 1980, The Corsaair Affair (Søren Kierkegaard), 1981, Fear and Trembling-Repetition, 1983, Philosophical Fragments-Johannes Climacus, 1985, Either/Or, 1987, Stages on Life's Way, 1988, The Concept of Irony, 1989, For Self-Examination and Judge for Yourself!, 1990, Eighteen Upbuilding Discourses, 1990, Practice in Christianity, 1991, Concluding Unscientific Postscript, 1992, Three Discourses on Imagined Occasions, 1993, Upbuilding Discourses in Various Spirits, 1993, Works of Love, 1995, Without Authority, 1997, Point of View, 1998, The Moment and Late Writings, 1998, The Book on Adler, 1998; gen. editor Kierkegaard's Writings, 1972—. Field sec. War Prisoners Aid, U.S., Scandinavia, and Germany, 1943-46; sr. rep. Service to Refugees, Luth. World Fedn., Germany and Austria, 1947-49; sr. field officer refugee div. World Council Chs., Germany, 1947-48. Decorated Order of Dannebrog (Denmark), Order of the Three Stars, Latvia; recipient award Minn. Humanities Commn., 1983; fellow Am.-Scandinavian Found.-Denmark, 1938-39, Am. Council Learned Socs., 1952-53, Rockefeller Found., 1959, sr. research fellow Fulbright Commn., 1959-60, 64, sr. fellow NEH, 1970-71; grantee NEH, 1972-73; publ. grantee Carlsberg Found., 1974, 86, 88, editing-translating grantee NEH, 1978-90, 95-98. Home: Old Dutch Rd Northfield MN 55057 Office: St Olaf Coll Kierkegaard Libr Northfield MN 55057

HONG, JAMES MING, industrialist, venture capitalist; b. Macao, Portuguese Colony, Oct. 1, 1946; came to U.S., 1956; s. William L.T. and Siu Jung H.; children: Diana, Paula, Susanna, Jonathan Ming. BBA in Acctg., Pace U., 1965, PhD (fellow) in Econs., Mktg., Internat. Bus., 1973; MBA in Fin. NYU, 1966; PhD in Econs., Mktg., Internat. Bus., 1973. Sr. corp. planning and devel. mgr. Mobil Corp., N.Y.C., 1965-70; dir. fin. systems and planning McGraw Hill Inc., N.Y.C., 1970-72, dir. fin. and systems, 1972-74; v.p., corp. controller Beverage Mgmt. Inc., Columbus, Ohio, 1974-75, v.p. fin., treas., chief fin. officer, 1976-79; sr. exec. v.p., chief fin. officer Mid Atlantic Coca Cola Bottling Co., Inc., Harrisburg, Pa., 1980-87, pres. chmn., chief exec. officer Sav-A-Stop Inc., Orange Park, Fla., 1987-88; chmn., pres., chief exec. officer Hong Capital and Mgmt. Corp., 1980—; pres., chmn., chief exec. officer The Odyssey Group, Inc., Cin., 1991-92; chmn., CEO Reliance (USA) Inc., Cin., 1992—; sr. chmn., CEO Sci-Lab Group Inc.; chmn., dir. First Jardin Group, Hong Kong; bd. dirs. Simpson-York Ltd., Reliance (USA) Inc., Scioto Corp., Wood-Bradley Group, Inc. Bd. dirs. Va. Council Econ. Edn., Va. Commonwealth U., United Coll. Fund, Soc. Prevention Blindness, Richmond Symphony, Red Cross Va. Recipient Woodrow Wilson fellow, Regent scholar NYU, Trustee fellow. Office: Hong Capital and Mgmt Corp PO Box 11431 Richmond VA 23230-1431

HONG, RICHARD, pediatrician, educator; b. Danville, Ill., Jan. 10, 1929; s. William and Louise (See) H.; m. Marion Shaw Taylor, May 31, 1952; children—Susan, Steven, Andrew, Laura. B.S., U. Ill., 1949, M.D., 1953. Diplomate Am. Bd. Pediats., Am. Bd. Allergy and Immunology. Intern Cook County Hosp., Chgo., 1953-54; resident Children's Hosp., Cin., 1957-60; research asso. immunology dept. pediatrics Coll. Medicine, U. Cin., 1957-65; asst. prof. peddiatrics U. Minn., 1965-67, prof., 1967-69; prof. pediatrics U. Wis. Med. Sch., Madison, 1969-92; assoc. dean U. Wis. Med. Sch., 1971-75; prof. pediatrics U. Vt. Med. Sch., Burlington, 1992—. Served with USAF, 1954-57. Recipient Immune Deficiency Found.'s Outstanding Achievement award, 1995. Mem. Soc. Pediatric Rsch., Am. Assn. Immunologists, Am. Soc. Clin. Investigation, Am. Pediatric Soc., Soc. for Exptl. Hematology, Reticuloendothelial Soc., Clin. Immunology Soc., Ctrl. Soc. for Clin. Rsch. Midwest Soc. for Pediatric Rsch., Phi Beta Kappa, Phi Kappa Phi. Home: 537 Stockbridge Rd Charlotte VT 05445-9354 Office: Vt Regional Cancer Ctr U Vt Genetics Lab 32 N Prospect St Burlington VT 05401-3338

HONG, SE JUNE, computer engineer; b. Seoul, Republic of Korea, May 5, 1944; came to U.S., 1965; s. Eo Kil and Oak Soon (Sohn) H.; m. Karen Fay McCully, Aug. 31, 1968; 1 dau., Kessely Corea. BSEE, Seoul Nat. U., 1965; MSEE, U. Ill., 1967, PhDEE, 1969. Staff engr. Sys. Devel. Lab., IBM, Poughkeepsie, NY, 1969-73, adv. engr., 1973-78, sr. engr., 1978; mem. rsch. staff T.J. Watson Rsch. Ctr., IBM, Yorktown Heights, NY, 1978—, mgr., 1981-82, sr. mgr., 1982-91, 92-94, sr. staff office rsch. divsn., v.p. plans and controls, 1991-92; vis. prof. Korea Advanced Inst. Sci. and Tech., Seoul, 1980, POSTECH, Pohang, summer 1999; vis. assoc. prof. U. Ill., 1974-75; chmn. standing sci. com. Pacific Rim Internat. Conf. on Artificial Intelligence, 1992-94. Author: Converstaional English, 1963; contbr. articles to profl. jours.; patentee in field. Bd. dirs. Mid-Hudson Arts and Sci. Ctr., Poughkeepsie, N.Y., 1972-78; bd. dirs. Dutchess County United Way, 1972-74, Dutchess County Family Counseling Svc., 1973-78, Univ. Ill. Elec. and Computer Engring. Dept. Alumni Assn., 1995—. Recipient Honorable Mention award for Outstanding Young Elec. Engr. Eta Kappa Nu, 1975, Disting. Service award NY State Jaycees, 1976, Disting. Alumnus award U. Ill., 1989, various awards IBM. Fellow IEEE (chmn. E. Peori award com. 1991-92, Disting. Visitor 1972-75), Internat. Fedn. of Info. Processing Socs. (U.S. del. tech. com. on artificial intelligence 1990-94, vice chmn. 1992-94); mem. Assn. Computing Machinery, Am. Assn. Artificial Intelligence, Nat. Acad. Engring. Korea (fgn.), Korean Scientists and Engrs. in Am., Sigma Xi. Democrat. Methodist. Home: 1374 Whitehill Rd Yorktown Heights NY 10598-3643 Office: TJ Watson Rsch Ctr IBM PO Box 218 Yorktown Heights NY 10598-0218

HONG, WAUN KI, medical oncologist, clinical investigator; b. Kyung gi Do, South Korea, Aug. 13, 1942; naturalized Sept. 17, 1976; s. Sung Ku and Bok Young; m. Mi Hwa Yoo, Sept. 9, 1969; children: Edward, Burton James. Student, Yon-Sei U., 1963, MD, 1967. Diplomate Am. Bd. Internal Medicine in Medical Oncology. Rotating intern Bronx-Lebanon Hosp., N.Y.C., 1970-71; jr. med. resident Boston Vets. Affairs Med. Ctr., 1971-72, sr. med. resident, 1972-73, chief of medical oncology, 1975-84, program dir. hematology/oncology tng. program, 1982-84; teaching assoc. Sch. Medicine Boston U., 1971-73, asst. prof. medicine, 1975-79, assoc. prof. medicine, 1980-84; clin. instr. medicine Cornell U., 1973-75; attending physician in medicine Boston City Hosp., 1978-84; clin. assoc. prof. pharmacology Northeastern U., Boston, 1980-84; internist, prof. medicine M.D. Anderson Cancer Ctr., U. Tex., Houston, 1984—, chief sect. thoracic med. oncology, 1987-88; chief sect. head, neck and thoracic med. oncology M.D. Anderson Cancer Ctr., U. Tex., 1988-92, chmn. dept. thoracic/head and neck med. oncology, 1993—; mem. sci. adv. bd. U. Ala. Birmingham Comprehensive Cancer Ctr., 1998—, Roy Castle Lung Cancer Found., 1997—, U. Calif. San Diego Cancer Ctr., 1997—, Shanghai (China) 2d Med. U. Joint Ctr. Clin. Rsch., 1997—, Fox Chase Cancer Ctr. Population Sci. Program, 1997, Kimmel Found. on Cancer Rsch., 1996—, Yale Cancer Ctr., 1996—, Vanderbilt Cancer Ctr., Seoul Nat. U. Cancer Ctr., 1996—; Baylor Coll. Medicine SPORE program, 1995—, The Cancer Inst. of N.J., 1993-98, The San Antonio Cancer Inst., 1993—; cons. Battelle Pharms., 1997—, Taiho Pharms., 1997—, Trilex Pharms., 1996—, Sequus Pharms., 1996—, Ho-En Ctrl. Rsch. Inst., 1996—, Ilex Oncology, 1995—; Houston Vet. Affairs Med. Ctr., 1992—; adj. prof. medicine Baylor Coll. Medicine, Houston, 1991—; vis. prof. Meml. Sloan-Kettering Cancer Ctr., 1998, Boston U. Cancer Ctr., 1997, Boston VA Med. Ctr., 1997, Nat. Cancer Inst. Intramural Program, 1996, U. Minn. Cancer Ctr., 1994, Tufts U. Sch. Medicine, 1993, Dana-Farber Cancer Ctr., 1993, Johns Hopkins Oncology Ctr., 1993, Tex. Tech. U. Sch. Medicine, 1992; lectr. in medicine Tufts U., 1975-84; Am. Cancer Soc. clin. rsch. prof., 1996—; Gen. Motors Found. vis. prof. Editor: (with others) Chemoimmuno Prevention of Cancer, 1991, The Biology and Prevention of Aerodigestive Tract Cancer, 1992, Advances in the Diagnosis and Therapy of Lung Cancer, 1993, Retinoids in Oncology, 1993, Early Detection of Cancer: Molecular Markers, 1994, Head and Neck Cancer: Basic and Clinical Aspects, 1995, Head and Neck Cancer: A Multidisciplinary Approach, 1996, Lung Cancer, 2d edit., 1998, Internat. Jour. Oncology, 1996—; dep. editor Clin. Cancer Rsch., 1996—; sr. editor Clinical Cancer Research, 1994—, Jour. Molecular and Cellular Differentiation, 1992—, Cancer Rsch., 1993-97; mem. editl. bd. The Cancer Jour., 1998—, Cancer Therapeutics, 1997—, PDQ Screening and Prevention, NCI, 1993-95, Annals of Surg. Oncology, 1993—, Cancer Rsch. Therapy and Ctrl., 1993-96, Jour. Clin. Oncology, 1992-95, Cancer Prevention, 1990-93; mem. editl. adv. bd. Cancer Epidemiology, Biomarkers and Prevention, 1994-96, Jour. Nat. Cancer Inst., 1990—. Served as flight surgeon South Korean Air Force, 1967-70. Recipient AACR 17th Ann. Richard and Hinda Rosenthal Found. award, 1993, pres. citation Am. Soc. for Head and Neck Surgery, 1991; Jr. Med. Oncology fellow Meml. Sloan-Kettering Cancer Ctr., 1973-74, Sr. Med. Oncology fellow Cornell U., 1974-75, ACS Disting. Svc. award, 1993, ASCo 3d Ann. Am. Cancer Soc. lectureship award, 1995, Ho-Am prize in medicine Sam-Sung Found., 1994—, M.D. Anderson faculty achievement award in cancer prevention, 1993, Milken Family Found. Cancer Rsch. award, 1990, numerous others; also numerous federal, industry, and found. grants. Fellow AAAS; mem. AMA, ACP, Am. Radium Soc., Am. Fedn. Clin. Rsch., Assn. Am. Physicians, Am. Assn. Cancer Rsch. (bd. dirs. 1996—, publs. com. 1996—, ogram com., subcom. on clin. investigations 1993-94, cancer prevention 1993-94, mem. task force clin. investigations 1990—, chmn. com. on clin. cancer rsch. 1995), Am. Cancer Soc. (clin. rsch. prof. 1996—, mem. med. affairs adv. group on professorships in clin. oncology, mem. nat. conf. clin. trials 1992, profl. edn. subcom. on profs. clin. oncology 1990—), Am. Soc. Clin. Oncology (vice chair cancer prevention and control com. 1995-96, mem. cancer edn. com. 1995-96, mem. edn. com. 1994-96, chmn. cancer prevention and ctrl. com. 1994), Nat. Cancer Inst. (mem. adv. com. to dir. 1997—, extramural bd. sci. advisors 1996—, cancer ctrs. rev. working group 1995-96, mem. pres.'s cancer panel 1994, mem. interim combined ad hoc bd. sci. counselors 1995), Tex. Med. Assn., Radiation Therapy Oncology Group (mem. med. oncology com. 1989—, head and neck com. 1989—), Harris

County Med. Soc., Soc. Head and Neck Surgeons. Office: U Tex MD Anderson Cancer Ctr 1515 Holcombe Blvd Houston TX 77030-4009

HONHART, FREDERICK LEWIS, III, academic director; b. San Diego, Oct. 29, 1943; s. Frederick Lewis Jr. and Rossiter (Hyde) H.; m. Barbara Ann Baker, Aug. 27, 1966; children: David Frederick, Stephen Charles. BA, Wayne State U., 1966; MA, Case-Western Res. U., 1968, PhD, 1972. Cert. archivist. Field rep. Ohio Hist. Soc., Columbus, 1972-73; asst. dir. univ. archives & hist. collections Mich. State U., East Lansing, 1974-79, dir., 1979—; mem. adv. bd. Mich. Nat. Hist. Publs. & Records Commn., Lansing, 1979—; cons. in field. Creator: (microcomputer sys.), MicroMARC:amc, 1986 (Coker prize 1988), MicroMARC for Integrated Format, 1995; contbr. articles to profl. jours. Mem. Soc. Am. Archivists, Mich. Archival Assn. (pres. 1984-86), Midwest Archives Conf. (chair program com. 1982, 94). Avocations: reading, sports. Office: Mich State U 101 Conrad Hall East Lansing MI 48824-1327

HONIG, ARNOLD, physics educator, researcher; b. N.Y.C., Feb. 28, 1928; s. Ralph and Margaret (Gershman) H.; m. Alice Sterling, Oct. 3, 1947 (div. Nov. 1977); children—Lawrence, Madeleine, Jonathan; m. Dolly Komar, Jan. 6, 1979; stepchildren—Arne, Tanya. B.A., Cornell U., 1948; M.S., Columbia U., 1950, Ph.D., 1953. Research asst. microwave spectroscopy Columbia U., N.Y.C., 1951-53; research physicist solid state physics U. Calif.-Berkeley, 1953-54; research fellow molecular physics Ecole Normale Superieure, Paris, 1954-56; asst. prof. physics Syracuse U., N.Y., 1956-59, assoc. prof., 1959-62, prof., 1962—; cons. ITT Labs., 1960-63, Gen. Atomics, 1993-96, Oxford Instruments, 1997—; ptnr., owner Sci.-Art Systems Co., N.Y.C., 1968-78; vis. prof. Hebrew U., Jerusalem, 1962; vis. scientist Com. a l'Energie Atomique, Saclay, France, 1965. Contbr. articles to profl. jours.; patentee infrared image transducer, matrix piano keyboard, prodn. spin-polarized fuels, multi-chronal fluorescence microscope. Pres. Oran Meml. Park Assn., N.Y., 1981-83. Recipient Glover Meml. award Dickinson Coll., 1966, Chancellor's citation for exceptional acad. achievement, 1999, numerous research grants, NSF, Dept. Energy, others. Mem. Am. Phys. Soc., Fedn. Am. Scientists, AAAS. Avocations: music; farming. Office: Syracuse U Dept Physics Syracuse NY 13244

HONIG, EDWIN, comparative literature educator, poet; b. N.Y.C., Sept. 3, 1919; s. Abraham David and Jane (Freundlich) H.; m. Charlotte Gilchrist, Apr. 1, 1940 (dec. 1963); m. Margot S. Dennes, Dec. 15, 1963 (div. 1978); children: Daniel D., Jeremy D. A.B., U. Wis., 1941, A.M., 1947; M.A. (hon.), Brown U., 1958. Instr. English Purdue U., 1942-43, N.Y.U. and Ill. Inst. Tech., 1946-47, U. N.Mex., 1947-48, Claremont Coll., summer 1949; instr. English Harvard U., 1949-52, Briggs-Copeland asst. prof. English, 1952-57; mem. faculty Brown U., 1957-82, prof. English, 1960-82, chmn. dept., 1967, prof. comparative lit., 1962-82; vis. prof. U. Calif. at Davis, 1964-65; Mellon prof. Boston U. intersession, 1977. Author: García Lorca, rev. edit, 1963; poems The Moral Circus, 1955; criticism Dark Conceit: The Making of Allegory, 1959; poems The Gazabos: 41 Poems, 1960, Survivals, 1964, Spring Journal: Poems, 1968, Four Springs, 1972, Shake a Spear With Me, John Berryman, 1974, At Sixes, 1974; criticism Calderón and The Seizures of Honor, 1972; play/libretto Calisto and Melibea, 1972; poems The Affinities of Orpheus, 1976, Selected Poems (1955-1976), 1979, Interrupted Praise, 1983, Gifts of Light, 1983, The Imminence of Love: Poems 1962-92, 1993; stories Foibles and Fables of an Abstract Man, 1979; (with Jean Zaleski) art book Cow/Lines, 1982, (with Walter Feldman) God Talk, 1993; plays Ends of the World and Other Plays, 1983; criticism The Poet's Other Voice: Conversations on Literary Translation, 1985; translations Calderón: 4 Plays, 1961, Cervantes' Interludes, 1964, Calderón's Life Is A Dream, 1970, Fernando Pessoa's Selected Poems, 1971, Keeper of Sheep, 1986, Poems, 1986, García Lorca's Diván and Other Writings, 1974, Fernando Pessoa's Always Astonished: Selected Prose, 1988, Miguel Hernández's The Unending Lightning, 1990, Garcia Lorca's The Divan poems, puppet plays and newly discovered play, 1990, Calderón: Six Plays, 1993; (with Oscar Williams) anthologies The Mentor Book of Major American Poets, 1961, The Major Metaphysical Poets, 1968, Spenser, 1968; translation (with A.S. Trueblood) Lope de Vega's La Dorotea, 1985; plays, Cambridge, Mass., The Widow, 1953, N.Y.C., Washington and Denver, The Phantom Lady, 1964, Stanford Summer Festival, Calisto and Melibea, 1966, BBC Radio, London, Life Is A Dream, 1970; prod. opera (with Jerome Rosen), Davis, Calif., Calisto and Melibea, 1979, Life Is a Dream, 1988, Los Angeles, 1991. Decorated Order of St. James of the Sword (Portugal); recipient Golden Rose award New Eng. Poetry Club, 1961; grantee Nat. Acad. Arts and Letters, 1966; Poetry prize Sat. Rev., 1956; Phi Beta Kappa poet Brown U., 1961, 82; Guggenheim fellow, 1948, 62; Amy Lowell traveling poetry fellow, 1968; R.I. Gov.'s award for excellence in arts, 1970; Nat. Endowment for Humanities fellow for ind. study, 1975; grantee, 1977-80; Nat. Endowment for Arts fellow in creative writing, 1977; fellow in opera libretto, 1979; recipient Nat. Endowment for arts PEN fiction project award, 1983; Transl. award Poetry Soc. Am., 1984; Nat. award Transl. Ctr. Columbia U., 1985. Office: Brown U English Dept PO Box 1852 Providence RI 02912-1852 *Being young and old at the same time; having little concern for past accomplishments, great concern for new possibilities; distrusting all dogmas; valuing friendship and solitude; becoming yourself through others; honoring trees, bridges, natural skies, water and fire; taking air freely and escaping finally into it.**

HONIG, GEORGE RAYMOND, pediatrician; b. Chgo., May 5, 1936; s. Joseph C. and Raymonde S. (Moses) H.; m. Karen R. Jacobson, Dec. 18, 1960 (dec.); children: Sharon, Debra, Robert; m. Olga M. Weiss, May 24, 1998. BS in Liberal Arts and Sci., U. Ill., 1959, MD, 1961, MS in Pharmacology, 1961; PhD in Biochemistry, George Washington U., 1966. Diplomate Am. Bd. Pediatrics, Nat. Bd. Med. Examiners. Intern Johns Hopkins Hosp., Balt., 1961-62, fellow in pediatrics, 1961-63, asst. resident in pediatrics, 1962-63; rsch. assoc. Nat. Cancer Inst. NIH, 1963-66; fellow in pediatric hematology U. Ill., Chgo., 1966-68, asst. prof. pediatrics, 1968-69, assoc. prof., 1969-74, prof., 1974-75, attending physician, 1968-75, dir. pediatric hematology svc., 1972-75, prof., head dept. pediatrics Coll. Medicine, 1984—; prof. pediatrics Northwestern U., Chgo., 1975-83; attending physician, dir. div. hematology Children's Meml. Hosp., Chgo., 1975-83. Contbr. numerous articles to profl. jours. Mem. AAUP, Am. Acad. Pediatrics, Am. Assn. Cancer Rsch., Am. Soc. Biochemistry and Molecular Biology, Am. Soc. Hematology, Am. Pediatric Soc., Soc. Pediatric Rsch., Alpha Omega Alpha. Office: U Ill Coll Medicine 840 S Wood St Chicago IL 60612-7317

HONIGBERG, CAROL CROSSMAN, lawyer; b. Salina, Kans., Sept. 23, 1955; d. Robert Denfield and Barbara Jane (Eckberg) Crossman; m. Paul Mark Honigberg, Aug. 18, 1979; children: Michael Crossman, Margaret Ann. AB, Duke U., 1977; JD, Vanderbilt U., 1980. Bar: Va. 1980. Assoc. Hazel & Thomas, P.C., Alexandria, Va., 1980-86; propr. Hazel & Thomas, P.C., Falls Church, Va., 1986—. Mem. ABA, Nat. Assn. Bond Lawyers, Comml. Real Estate Women (pres. No. Va. chpt. 1998-99). Office: Hazel & Thomas PC 3110 Fairview Park Dr Ste 1400 Falls Church VA 22042-4503

HONKANEN, JARI OLAVI, electrical engineer; b. Uurainen, Finland, June 3, 1964; came to U.S., 1988; s. Eero Olavi and Aino Inkeri (Kuusisto) H. MS, Helsinki U. Tech., Finland, 1989; MBA, So. Meth. U., 1993. Engr. Ericsson Network Sys., Richardson, Tex., 1988-91, sr. engr., 1991-94; sr. software engr. Sprint, Irving, Tex., 1994-95, DSC Comms. Corp., Plano, Tex., 1995; pres. Odin TeleSystems Inc., Dallas, 1995—; also bd. dirs. Odin Telesystems, Inc., Dallas. Sgt. Finnish Air Force, 1983-84. Mem. IEEE, Assn. Computing Machinery, Beta Kappa Sigma. Avocations: weight lifting, biking, rollerblading, tennis, travel. Office: Odin TeleSystems Inc PO Box 59686 Dallas TX 75229-1686

HONNOLD, JOHN OTIS, law educator; b. Kansas, Ill., Dec. 5, 1915; s. John Otis and Louretta (Wright) H.; m. Annamarie Kunz, June 26, 1939; children: Carol Honnold Davidon, Heidi Honnold Spencer, Edward. B.A., U. Ill., 1936; J.D., Harvard U., 1939; LLD (hon.), Capital U., 1991, Pace U., 1997. Bar: N.Y. 1940, Pa. 1953, U.S. Supreme Ct 1953. Atty. firm Wright, Gordon, Zachry & Parlin, N.Y.C., 1939-41, SEC, 1941; chief ct. rev. br. OPA, 1942-46; mem. faculty U. Pa. Law Sch., 1946-69, 74-84, prof. law, 1952-69, 74-84, prof. emeritus, 1984—; Arthur Goodhart prof. sci. of law. U. Cambridge, 1982-83; mem. vis. faculty U. Beijing, 1984, U. Hawaii, 1986, U. Fla., 1988; Canterbury vis. fellow, N.Z., 1986; lectr. UN seminar, Moscow, 1990, U. Stockholm, 1990; chief internat. trade law br. UN; sec. UN Commn. on Internat. Trade Law, 1969-74; mem. faculty law sessions Salzburg (Austria) Seminar Am. Studies, 1960, chmn., 1963, 66; chief counsel Miss. Office, Lawyer's Com. for Civil Rights under Law, 1965; U.S. del., mem. drafting com. diplomatic conf. preparing uniform law for internat. sales of goods, The Hague, Holland, 1964; U.S. del UN Commn. Internat. Trade Law, 1969, 77; U.S. del. diplomatic confs. Conv. Carriage of Goods by Sea, Hamburg, 1978, Contracts for Internat. Sale of Goods, Vienna, 1980; gen. reporter 12th Internat. Congress Comparative Law, 1986. Author: (with C. Mooney, S. Harris, C. Reitz) Sales and Secured Financing, 6th edit., 1993, The Life of the Law, 1964, (with E.L. Barrett, Jr. and P.W. Bruton) Cases and Materials on Constitutional Law, 3d edit., 1968, (with others) Commercial Law, 5th edit., 1993, Uniform Law for International Sales under the 1980 UN Convention, 1982, 3rd edit., 1999, 1991, Spanish edit., 1987, Security Interests in Personal Property, 1985, Korean edit., 1998, (with S. Harris and C. Mooney) 2d edit., 1992, Documentary History, Uniform Law for International Sales, 1989, (with C. Reitz) Sales Transactions: Domestic and International, 1992, (with others) United Nations Legal Order, 1995; contbr. articles to profl. jours.; bd. editors: Am. Jour. Comparative Law, 1959-70, 76-84. Guggenheim fellow, 1958; Fulbright sr. research scholar U. Paris, 1958; recipient Theberge award for contbn. to Pvt. Internat. Law, ABA, 1986; Lincoln Laureate, 1992.

HONOR, NICHOLAS KELLY, disc jockey, accountant; b. San Mateo, Calif., Jan. 4, 1969; s. Ricardo Honor and Frances Oliden. AA in Bus. Adminstrn., Coll. of San Mateo, 1992; BSBA, Calif. Poly. State U., 1995. Disc jockey Sound Experience, San Francisco, 1989-92, KCPR, San Luis Obispo, Calif., 1993-95, Tortilla Flats, San Luis Obispo, Calif., 1995-96, Soundsation, San Mateo, 1992—. Author: The Essence of Honor, 1994, 3rd Times a Charm, 1995, Judg This Cover by the Book, 1995, A Wonderful Collection of Poetry, 1996. Mem. Phi Sigma Kappa (recruitment com. 1993-96). Libertarian. Avocations: skateboarding, mountain bike riding, poetry, travelling. Office: Soundsation 2 Claremont Ct Millbrae CA 94030-1010

HONOUR, LYNDA CHARMAINE, research scientist, educator, psychotherapist; b. Orange, N.J., Aug. 9, 1949; d. John Henry, Jr. and Evelyn Helena Roberta (Pietrowski) H. BA, Boston U., 1976; MA, Calif. State U., Fullerton, 1985, UCLA, 1989; PhD, U. So. Calif., 1997. Lic. marriage, family and child psychotherapist and psychologist, Calif. Prof. psychology Pepperdine U., Malibu, Calif., 1989-95; pvt. practice mind-body behavioral medicine, including clin. psychoneuroimmunology and psychoneuroendocrinology, West L.A., Calif., 1991—; clin. and vis. prof. throughout so. Calif., including Calif. Sch. Profl. Psychology, Calif. State U., Long Beach, 1989—, Calif. State U., Northridge; rsch. scientist in neuroendocrinology and neurochemistry in numerous labs.; condr. rsch. Neuropsychiat. Inst., Brain Rsch. Inst., Mental Retardation Rsch. Ctr., UCLA, Tulane U. Med. Sch., V.A. Med. Ctr., New Orleans, Salk Inst. Biol. Studies; rsch. cons. U. Calif. Med. Ctr., Irvine; cons. in rsch. or psychotherapy, 1976—. Contbr. articles to Hosp. Practice, Peptides, Physiology and Behavior, Pharmacology, Biochemistry and Behavior, also others. Rsch. grantee Organon Internat. Rsch. Group, The Netherlands, 1984-88. Mem. AAAS, APA, Am. Psychological Soc., Soc. for Neurosci., Calif. Assn. Marriage, Family and Child Psychotherapists, N.Y. Acad. Scis., Sons and Daus. of Pearl Harbor Survivors, Psi Chi. Roman Catholic. Achievements include identification of a peptide which facilitates and another peptide inhibits learning and memory task performance permanently in a developmental paradigm in mice, and facilitation peptide can permanently reverse induced learning/memory deficit, with implications for mental retardation treatment; member research team which isolated and characterized corticotropic hormone releasing factor; delineated various effects of peptides on behavior. Avocations: professional musician, artist, mind-related issues, time-space travel involving the unified field theory, metaphysics.

HONSA, VLASTA, retired librarian; b. Žilina, Czechoslovakia, Sept. 1, 1924; came to U.S., 1951; d. František Petr and Marie (Širkova) Petrova; m. Vladimir Honsa, June 26, 1948; children: Patricia, Eva Honsa-Hogg. *Husband, Vladimir Honsa is a retired professor of linguistics and Spanish dialectology. He received his Ph.D from the University of Michigan in 1957 and his teaching career included the following universities: Marquette, Southern California, Indiana and the University of Nevada, Las Vegas and as Fulbright Professor in Colombia, Uruguay and Panama. Daughter, Patricia Honsa, is an Environmental Scientist for the Environmental Protection Agency. Daughter, Eva Honsa-Hogg, served as an Educational Consultant, Texas and Republic of Korea, Family Advocacy Outreach Manager, USAF, School Counselor and Teacher, Nevada. She coauthored Cooperative Learning and Critical Thinking: A Winning Combination. Eva and husband, Wayne Hogg, have two children.* BA, Charles U., Prague, 1947; MLS, Ind. U., 1968. Gifts libr. Ind. U. Libr., Bloomington, 1968-70; head reference dept. Clark County Libr., Las Vegas, Nev., 1970-80; asst. adminstr. Clark County Libr., Las Vegas, 1980-94; ret., 1994; coord. Found. Collection, part of the Found. Ctr.'s Cooperating Collections network, Clark County Libr., 1979-94. Author: Nevada Foundation Directory, 1984, 2d edit., 1989, 3rd edit., 1994. Bd. dirs. So. Nev. Musical Arts Soc., Las Vegas, 1989-92; organized and presented fundraising workshops for cmty. fund raisers sponsored by Las Vegas-Clark County Libr. Dist., 1979-94. Recipient Ind. U. grant-in-aid to conduct rsch. of publs. in cen. Am. univs. and nat. librs., 1970, Champion award Las Vegas-Clark County Libr. Dist., 1985. Mem. ALA, AAUW, Nev. Libr. Assn., Univ. Nevada Las Vegas Faculty Club. Roman Catholic. Avocations: reading, music, arts, travel. E-Mail: honsa@worldnet.att.net. Home: 2680 Congress Ave Las Vegas NV 89121-1316

HOOD, DENISE PAGE, federal judge; b. 1952. BA, Yale Univ., 1974; JD, Columbia Sch. of Law, 1977. Asst. corp. counsel City of Detroit, Law Dept., 1977-82; judge 36th Dist. Ct., 1983-89, Recorder's Ct. for the City of Detroit, 1989-92, Wayne County Circuit Ct., 1993-94; district judge U.S. Dist. Ct. (Mich. ea. dist.), 6th circuit, 1994—. Recipient Judicial Service award Black Women Lawyers Assn., 1994. Mem. Am. Bar Assn., State Bar of Mich., Detroit Bar Assn. (Chmn. of Yr. award 1988), Assn. of Black Judges of Mich., Mich. Dist. Judges Assn., Am. Inns of Ct., Wolverine Bar Assn. (bd. of dirs.), Women Lawyers Assn. of Mich., Fed. Bar Assn., Nat. Assn. of Women Judges, Nat. Bar Assn. Judicial Coun., Mich. Judicial Inst. Office: US Courthouse 231 W Lafayette Blvd Rm 235 Detroit MI 48226-2779*

HOOD, EARL JAMES, lawyer, state legislator; b. Spearfish, S.D., Apr. 28, 1947; s. Earl Kenneth and Florence Lorraine (Castor) m. Judith G. Witzel, June 2, 1968 (div. Sept. 1974); children: Jason, Jared Jon; m. Kathleen Gay Donahue, Sept. 13, 1975; 1 child, Stewart Lee. BS, Black Hills State Coll., 1969; JD, U. S.D., 1972. Assoc. Richards Law Firm, Spearfish, 1972-74; ptnr. Richards and Hood, Spearfish, 1974-78, Richards, Hood and Brady, P.C., Spearfish, 1979-90, Richards, Hood, Brady & Nies, P.C., Spearfish, 1990-95; mem. S.D. Ho. of Reps., Pierre, 1983-92; speaker pro tem Pierre, 1989-90; speaker of the house S.D. Ho. of Reps., Pierre, 1991-92; officer, dir., shareholder Richards, Hood & Nies, P.C., 1995—; city atty. City of Spearfish, 1972-76, 87—. Chief Spearfish Vol. Fire Dept., 1982-83; pres. Black Hills State Coll. Found., Inc., Spearfish, 1986; mem. S.D. Pvt. Industry Coun., 1993-94; mem. S.D. Quality Govt. Commn., 1993-94; chair Kids Voting, Spearfish, 1993-95, bd. dirs., 1994-95; chair Workforce Devel. Coun. S.D., 1994-95. Recipient Vigil Honor Order of Arrow, BSA, 1965, Disting. Alumnus award Black Hills State U., 1990; named S.D. Firefighter of Yr. Keep S.D. Green Assn., 1984, Friend of Edn. S.D. Edn. Assn., 1990. Mem. S.D. Bar Assn., S.D. Trial Lawyers Assn., Lions, Masons (Spearfish Lodge #18), Order Eastern Star (Queen City chpt #89), Black Hills Scottish Rite, Naja Shrine. Republican. Avocations: reading, golf. Home: 101 S 5th St PO Box 611 Spearfish SD 57783-0611 Office: Richards Hood & Nies PO Box 759 Spearfish SD 57783-0759

HOOD, EDWARD EXUM, JR., retired electrical manufacturing company executive; b. Boonville, N.C., Sept. 15, 1930; s. Edward Exum and Nellie (Triplett) H.; m. Kay Transou, Dec. 30, 1950; children: Lisa Kay, Molly Ann. M.S. in Nuclear Engring., N.C. State U., 1953. Registered profl. engr., Ariz. Powerplant design engr. Gen. Electric Co., 1957-62, mgr. supersonic transport engine project, 1962-67, v.p., gen. mgr. comml. engine div., from 1968, v.p., group exec. internat. group, 1972-73, v.p., group exec., power generation group, 1973-77, sr. v.p., sector exec. tech. systems and materials sector, from 1977, vice-chmn. and exec officer, 1979-93, also bd. dirs. Served with USAF, 1952-56. Fellow AIAA; mem. Nat. Acad. Engring., Aerospace Industries Assn. (chmn. 1981). Home: 11674 Lake House Ct No Palm Beach FL 33408-3318 Office: GE PO Box 8300 260 Long Ridge Rd Stamford CT 06927-9100

HOOD, ERNEST ALVA, SR., pharmaceutical company executive; b. East St. Louis, Ill., July 10, 1910; s. Orestes Rastus and Daisy Ernestine (Eslick) H.; m. Taeko Haruta; children: Ernest Jr., Dharathula (Hood) Harris, Daisy. CEO Cophtra Ltd., N.Y.C., 1950—; power maintainer Con Edison, N.Y.C., 1952-72; N.Y. rep. Coastal Pharm. Co. Ltd., Norfolk, Va., Ghana, 1974-76; cons. Coastal Pharm. Co. Ltd., Bklyn., Ghana, 1976—; cons. Uchi Ichi Shoji Ltd., Japan, 1946—, Jaiama Tayorma Natural Scrap Exch., Freetown, Sierra Leone, Lome Natural Scrap Exch., Lome, Togo, 1994—, Abua Farms and Industries, Ashanti, 1996—, Buckberra Trading Co., Okyere Bour & Co., Ashanti, Two Worlds Mfg. Co.; advisor Cophtra Ltd. Author: (autobiography) Hoodisan-1910-1994. Bd. dirs., Cen. Bklyn. Coord. Coun. 1st lt. U.S. Army. Recipient Ulchii award, Republic South Korea. Mem. VFW, Vets. Assn. Home: 8025 Hickory Ave Gary IN 46403-2265 Office: Cophtra Ltd 550 Green Ave Brooklyn NY 11216-5710

HOOD, JOHN B., lawyer; b. Morgantown, W.Va., Jan. 10, 1944; m. Bonnie Russell, Nov. 22, 1962; children: John Jr., David, Brian. BA, Amherst Coll., 1966; LLB, U. Va., 1969. Bar: N.Y. 1970, Pa. 1979. Ptnr. Nixon, Hargrave, Devans & Doyle, Rochester, N.Y., 1969—. Mem. N.Y. State Bar Assn., Monroe County Bar Assn., Am. Coll. Real Estate Lawyers, Inst. of Property Taxation. Avocations: golf, travel, skiing. Office: Nixon Hargrave Devans Doyle Clinton Sq PO Box 1051 Rochester NY 14603-1051*

HOOD, JOSEPH M., federal judge; b. 1942. BS, U. Ky., 1965, JD, 1972. Law clk. U.S. Dist. Ct. (ea. dist.) Ky., 1972-76, magistrate, 1976-90, judge, 1990—. Active United Cerebral Palsy Ea. Ky.; bd. trustees Alice LLoyd Coll. Decorated Bronze Star with V device and 4 oak leaf clusters. Mem. YMCA, Rotary, Bellefonte Country Club. Office: US Dist Ct 354 Federal Bldg 330 W Broadway St Frankfort KY 41601*

HOOD, LAMARTINE FRAIN, agriculture educator, former dean; b. Johnstown, Pa., Feb. 25, 1937; s. Lamartine and Marion Camm (Frain) H.; m. Emeline Rose Harpster, June 18, 1960; children: Thomas Gregory, Christopher Michael, Sandra Beth. BS, Pa. State U., 1959, PhD, 1968; MS, U. Minn., 1963. Asst. prof. Cornell U., Ithaca, N.Y., 1968-74, assoc. prof., 1974-80, prof. food sci., 1980-86, assoc. dir. Agr. Experiment Station, 1980-83, assoc. dir. office of rsch., 1980-86; dir. N.Y. State Agr. Experiment Sta. Cornell U., Geneva, N.Y., 1983-86; dean Coll. Agr. Sci., dir. Agr. Expt. Sta., dir. Coop. Ext. Pa. State U., University Park, 1986-95, prof., 1986—; mem. adv. bd. Chase Lincoln Bank, Geneva, 1984-86; chmn. bd. dirs. ADEC, 1994-95. Author/editor: Carbohydrates & Health, 1977; contbr. articles to profl. jours. and chpts. for books. Fellow Inst. Food Technologists; mem. Am. Assn. Cereal Chemists (William F. Geddes Meml. Lectureship award 1984, pres. 1987-88, chmn. bd. 1988-89), Ithaca Geneva, State Coll. Rotary Club, Gamma Sigma Delta, Phi Lambda Upsilon. Home: 1694 Princeton Dr State College PA 16803-3257 Office: Pa State U 106 Agrl Adminstrn Bldg University Park PA 16802

HOOD, LEROY EDWARD, molecular biologist, educator; b. Missoula, Mont., Oct. 10, 1938; s. Thomas Edward and Myrtle Evylan (Wadsworth) H.; m. Valerie Anne Logan, Dec. 14, 1963; children: Eran William, Marqui Leigh Jennifer. B.S., Calif. Inst. Tech., 1960, Ph.D. in Biochemistry, 1968; M.D., Johns Hopkins U., 1964. Med. officer USPHS, 1967-70; staff scientist Pub. Health Svc., Bethesda, Md., 1967-70; sr. investigator Nat. Cancer Inst., 1967-70; asst. prof. biology Calif. Inst. Tech., Pasadena, 1970-73, assoc. prof., 1973-75, prof., 1975-92, Bowles prof. biology, 1977-92, chmn. div. biology, 1980-89; Gates prof. molecular biotech., chmn. bd. U. Wash. Sch. Medicine, Seattle, 1992—; dir. NSF Sci. and Tech. Ctr. for Molecular Biotech., 1989—. Author: (with others) Biochemistry, a Problems Approach, 1974, Molecular Biology of Eukaryotic Cells, 1975, Immunology, 1978, Essential Concepts of Immunology, 1978, The Code of Codes: Scientific and Social Issues in the Human Genome Project, 1992; co-editor: Advances in Immunology, 1987. Co-recipient, Albert Lasker Basic Medical Research Award, 1987, recipient Scientist of the Year Award, 1993, R&D Magazine. Mem. NAS, Am. Assn. Immunologists, Am. Assn. Sci., Am. Acad. Arts and Scis., Sigma Xi. Avocations: mountaineering, rockclimbing, photography. Office: U of Washington Molecular Biotechnology Box 35 7730 Seattle WA 98195-7730*

HOOD, LUANN SANDRA, special education educator; b. Bklyn., Jan. 10, 1955; d. Louie A. and Sylvia M. (Hall) Mayo; m. Stephen J. Hood. BA, St. Joseph's Coll., Bklyn., 1976; MS in Edn., Bklyn. Coll., 1979. Cert. tchr. N, K, 1-6, spl. edn., N.Y.C. lic. Edn. counselor adolescents Am. Indian Comty. House, Inc., N.Y.C., 1977-79; tchr. children with retarded mental devel. Pub. Sch. 273, Bklyn., 1979-83; tchr. early childhood Pub. Sch. 128, Bklyn., 1983-94; tchr. emotionally handicapped Pub. Sch.215, Bklyn., 1994-95; tchr. learning disabled Pub. Sch. 101, Bklyn., 1995—. Exec. sec. bd. trustees Am. Indian Comty. House, Inc., N.Y.C., 1980-91. Recipient Regents scholarship N.Y. State Edn. Dept., 1972; grantee: Indian League of the Americas, Inc. 1972, 73, 74, 75, Thunderbird Am. Indian Dancers, Inc., 1972, 73, 74, 75, Internat. Order of King's Daughters and Sons, 1976. Mem. N.Y. State Tchrs. of Handicapped. Democrat. Roman Catholic. Avocation: photography.

HOOD, NICHOLAS, councilman; b. Detroit, Oct. 25, 1951; m. Denise Page; children: Nathan, Noah. BA, Wayne State U., 1973; MDiv, Yale U., 1976. Assoc. min. Plymouth United Ch. of Christ, Detroit, 1976-84; interim min. Plymouth United Ch. of Christ, 1984-86, sr. min., 1985—; city councilman City of Detroit, 1993—; bd. trustees United Ch. of Christ, 1991; mem. Health Occupations Coun., Mich., 1991. Author: Five Growing Black Churches, United Church Board for Homeland Ministries, 1983. bd. dirs. Conf. Consultations, Plymouth Non-Profit Housing Corp.; chmn. bd. Plymouth Day Care Ctr./Day Sch. Office: Detroit City Coun 1340 City Coun Bldg Detroit MI 48226*

HOOD, ROBERT HOLMES, lawyer; b. Charleston, S.C., Oct. 5, 1944; s. James Albert and Ruth (Henderson) H.; m. Mary Agnes Burnham, Aug. 5, 1967; children: Mary Agnes, Elizabeth, Robert Holmes Jr., James Bernard. BA, U. of the South, 1966; JD, U. S.C., 1969. Bar: U.S. Supreme Ct. 1969, S.C. 1969, U.S. Dist. Ct. S.C. 1969, U.S. Ct. Appeals (4th cir.) 1969. Asst. atty. gen. State of S.C., Columbia, 1969-70; ptnr. Sinkler, Gibbs & Simons, Charleston, 1970-85; prin. Hood Law Firm, Charleston, 1985—. Mem. Assn. Def. Trial Attys. (pres. 1985-86), Am. Bd. Trial Advs. (diplomate, pres. Charleston chpt. 1997), Internat. Assn. Def. Counsel, Def. Rsch. and Trial Inst. (bd. dirs. 1987-90), Fedn. Ins. and Corp. Counsel (state chmn. 1997—), S.C. Def. Trial Attys. Assn. (pres. 1980-81), Network of Trial Law Firms. Episcopalian. Office: 172 Meeting St Charleston SC 29401-3126

HOOD, RONALD CHALMERS, III, historian, writer; b. Florence, Ala., Apr. 2, 1947; s. Ronald Chalmers II and Elizabeth Woods (Craig) H.; m. Lucile O'Connor, Dec. 20, 1969; children: Ronald Chalmers IV, Reed Cathleen. BS, U.S. Naval Acad., 1969; MA, U. Maine, Orono, 1972; PhD, U. Md., 1979. Commd. 2d lt. USMC, 1969, advanced through grades to capt., 1973, resigned, 1982; historian, writer Johns Hopkins U., Balt., 1982—, George Mason U., Fairfax, Va., 1982—, U. Md., College Park, 1982—; lectr. Smithsonian Instn., Washington, 1988; speaker Conf. on Strategic Studies, Washington, 1985; co-chair Muscle Shoals Revisited Conf. on Future of Tenn. Valley, 1993; theatre and arts critic The Prince William Jour. Author: (history monograph) Royal Republicans, 1985; co-author: (mil. history) Military Effectiveness, 1987, Body, Mind, Spirit: 75 Years of Camp Hazen YMCA, 1995; contbr. editorial columns to Washington Post, Richmond Times-Dispatch, Potomac News, articles to profl. jours.; theater and arts cr itic Prince William Jour. Asst. scoutmaster Boy Scouts Am., Woodbridge, Va., 1989—; advisor County Sch. Bd., Prince William County, Va., 1991; instr. ARC, Prince William County, 1982—. Samuel Eliot Morison fellow U. Maine, Orono, 1971-72, Grad. Sch. fellow U. Md., 1975, fellow Am. Philos. Soc., 1998. Mem. AAUP, Writers' Ctr., Smithsonian Instn., Nat. Geographic Soc. Avocations: travel, acting, bike riding, aquatic activities, cross-country skiing. Fax: (703) 497-9578. Home and Office: 12317 Oakwood Dr Woodbridge VA 22192-1911

HOOD, THOMAS GREGORY, minister; b. Stamford, Conn., Mar. 26, 1948; s. George E. and Shirley W. (Brundage) H.; m. Esther A. Whitcomb, July 1, 1967; children: Thomas G., Sarah D. BA, Johnson State Coll., 1984; MDiv, Covington Sem., Rossville, Ga., 1986, PhD in Counseling, 1988. Ordained to ministry Fellowship of Christian Assemblies, 1969, Am. Bapt. Chs. in U.S.A., 1984. Asst. pastor Bethel Full Gospel Ch., Barton, Vt., 1968-71; pastor Lyndonville (Vt.) Full Gospel Ch., 1969-71, Sheffield (Vt.) Fed. Ch., 1971-74, Sutton (Vt.) Bapt. Ch., 1972-84, Adams Center (N.Y.) Bapt. Ch., 1984—; del. Am. Bapt. Conv., N.Y., 1984—; presenterAdams, N.Y. pub. schs., 1986—. Author: The Lord's Prayer, 1986, A Theology of Victory, 1987, Biblical Principles, 1988; composer religious songs. Mem. Am. Bapt.Mins. Coun. Republican. Home: 13463 US Rt 11 Adams Center NY 13606 *It is impossible to forgive ourselves for our failures if we are unwilling to forgive others theirs. The rule we use to judge others will always reflect back on ourselves.*

HOOD, WILLIAM BOYD, JR., cardiologist, educator; b. Sylacauga, Ala., Mar. 25, 1932; s. William Boyd and Katherine Elizabeth (Anderson) H.; m. Katherine Candace Todd, May 5, 1972; 1 son, Jefferson Boyce. B.S. summa cum laude, Davidson Coll., 1954; M.D., Harvard U., 1958. Intern Peter Bent Brigham Hosp., Boston, 1958-59, resident in internal medicine, 1959-60, 62-63; from asst. prof. to assoc. prof. medicine Harvard U., 1967-71; from assoc. prof. to prof. medicine Boston U., 1971-82; chief cardiology Boston City Hosp., 1973-82; prof. medicine U. Rochester (N.Y.), 1982—; head cardiology unit Strong Meml. Hosp., Rochester, 1982-98; cons. NIH, 1975—, NASA, 1994—. Mem. editorial bd. New Eng. Jour. Medicine, 1974-81, Circulation, 1980-83, Circulation Research, 1982-89, Jour. Clin. Investigation, 1984-89, Cochrane Collaboration Heart Group, 1997—; contbr. articles, revs. and editorials on cardiovascular physiology to profl. jours., chpts. to books. Served to capt. USAF, 1963-65. Research grantee NIH, 1971-98; grantee Am. Heart Assn., 1971-76. Fellow ACP; mem. Am. Soc. Clin. Investigation, Assn. Am. Physicians, Am. Heart Assn., Am. Physiol. Soc., Assn. Profs. Cardiology (past pres.), N.Y. Cardiol. Soc. (past pres.), Phi Beta Kappa, Alpha Omega Alpha. Achievements include studies on experimental and clinical myocardial ischemia and infarction, and congestive heart failure.

HOOD, WILLIAM WAYNE, JR., lawyer; b. Tulsa, July 22, 1941; s. William Wayne and Alys (Charles) H.; m. Nancy Raynolds; children—W. Wayne III, Kristina L. B.A., U. Okla., 1963; LL.B., U. Tulsa, 1966. Bar: Okla. 1966, U.S. Dist. Ct. (no. dist.) Okla. 1966. Diplomate Am. Coll. Matrimonial Trial Lawyers. Pvt. practice, Tulsa, 1966-70; pub. defender Tulsa County, 1966-68; ptnr. Hood & Lindsey, Tulsa, 1970-87, Hood & Raynolds, 1989—. Served to maj. JAGC, USAR, 1966-84. Fellow Am. Acad. Matrimonial Lawyers (v.p. 1985-88, pres. Okla. chpt. 1991-93), Internat. Acad. Matrimonial Lawyers (bd. govs. Am. chpt. 1987-91); mem. Okla. Bar Assn. (dir. continuing legal edn.-family law 1980-84, chmn. family law sect. 1975-77, 80-82), Tulsa County Bar Assn. (exec. com. 1979). Republican. Roman Catholic. Office: Hood & Raynolds 1914 S Boston Ave Tulsa OK 74119-5217

HOOE, LYNN V., federal judge; b. 1927. BA, U. Pitts., 1951; LLB, Wayne State U., 1955. Pvt. practice, 1957-81; magistrate judge U.S. Dist. Ct. (ea. dist.) Mich., Detroit, 1981—. Office: US Dist Ct Ea Dist Mich 619 US Courthouse 231 W Lafayette Blvd Detroit MI 48226

HOOFARD, JANE MAHAN DECKER, elementary education educator; b. Grand Junction, Colo., Apr. 29, 1946; d. Nat Don and Bernita Margaret (Williams) Mahan; m. William Edward Hoofard, Mar. 6, 1982; children: Lynna Kay Decker, Keith Dale. BA, Ft. Lewis Coll., 1968. Cert. tchr., Calif. Tchr. 3rd, 6th grades Shasta Lake Union Sch. Dist., Summit City, Calif., 1968-73; tchr., MGM cons., coord., brain drain writer Shasta County Schs., Redding, Calif., 1975-81; tchr. 2nd, 3rd grades Manton (Calif.) Joint Union Sch. Dist., 1987-89; elem. and mid. sch. tchr. Mineral (Calif.) Elem. Sch. Dist., 1989—. Writer, editor, pub. AAUW. Mem. Calif. Tchrs. Assn., Shasta Lake Tchrs. Assn. (past pres.). Home: PO Box 104 Mineral CA 96063-0104 Office: Mineral School PO Box 130 Mineral CA 96063-0130

HOOG, MARJORIE, architect; b. Paris, Feb. 28, 1947; came to U.S., 1951; d. Armand and Marie Jacques (Debrix) H.; m. John L. Young, Nov. 2, 1974 (div. 1984); stepchildren: Marcolm, Lila, Anina, Dara; 1 child, Madeleine Hoog-Crellin. Student Cooper Union, N.Y.C., 1966-68; BA, NYU, 1969; MArch, Harvard U., 1972; MBA, Columbia U., 1992. Registered architect, N.Y. Designer, Ulrich Franzen & Assoc., N.Y.C., 1971-73; architect Urban Deadline Architects, N.Y.C., 1974-76; prin. Marjorie Hoog Architect, N.Y.C., 1976-81; assoc. Prentice & Chan, Ohlhausen, N.Y.C., 1981-86; propr. Marjorie Hoog Architect, 1986-91; assoc. ptnr. Herbert Beckhard-Frank Richlan & Assocs., N.Y.C., 1987-95; prin. Helpern Architects, N.Y.C., 1995-96; proj. mgr. F.G. Assocs. Contractors, 1996-97; project mgr. Surtsey Realty, N.Y.C., 1997—; co-founder Archive Women in Architecture, N.Y.C., 1974; coord. Women's Sch. Planning and Architecture, Bristol, R.I., summer 1978; vis. asst. prof. Pratt Inst., N.Y.C., fall 1983; guest lectr., panelist in field. Appeared in show Firing the Imagination, Urban Ctr., N.Y.C. and Bennington (Vt.) Coll., 1988. Named co-leader del. Archtl. Soc. China, 1977, 80. Mem. Alliance Women in Architecture (co-founder), China Study Group on Environ. Issues (co-founder), Archtl. League, AIA, NOW. Home: 128 W 82nd St New York NY 10024-5527 Office: Surtsey Realty 2130 Broadway New York NY 10023-1722

HOOG, THOMAS W., public relations executive. Chief of staff Gary Hart, Washington, 1975-80; pres., CEO Hoog & Assocs., 1980-90; chmn. pub. affairs Hill & Knowlton Worldwide, 1990-96; pres., CEO Hill & Knowlton, U.S., 1996—. Bd. dirs. Smithsonian Air & Space Mus., Wolf Trap Found. for Performing Arts, Am. Fedn. of Aging Rsch., New Deal Inc., Up With People. Office: Hill & Knowlton 466 Lexington Ave New York NY 10017-3140

HOOGESTRAAT, THOMAS JOHN, human services professional; b. Carroll, Iowa, Mar. 30, 1946; s. John Carl Hoogestraat and Lorraine Ann (Bruggeman) Hunter; m. Diana Elizabeth Stienkamp, June 13, 1970; children: Christopher, Sarah, Heather. BA, U. Nebr., Omaha, 1975. Social worker Glenwood (Iowa) State Hosp. Sch., 1975-80, unit dir., dept. head, 1980-86, asst. supt. treatment program svcs., 1986—. Sec. Mills County Econ. Devel., Glenwood, 1996. Served with USN, 1965-69. Mem. VFW (quartermaster). Avocations: fishing, horseback riding, travel. Office: Glenwood State Hosp Sch 711 S Vine St Glenwood IA 51534-1927

HOOGLAND, ROBERT FREDERICS, lawyer; b. Paterson, N.J., Apr. 3, 1955; s. Robert J. and Lucretia H.; m. Diane Wood, Sept. 21, 1983 (div. Mar. 1985). BA, U. Fla., 1976; MBA, Rollins Coll., 1977; JD, U. Fla., 1982. Bar: Fla. 1983, U.S. Dist. Ct. (mid. dist.) Fla. 1989. Assoc. Giles, Hedrick & Robinson, Orlando, Fla., 1983-89; ptnr. Hoogland & Durket, P.A., Longwood, Fla., 1989-92, Robert F. Hoogland, P.A., Altamonte Springs, Fla., 1992—. Mem. ABA, Fla. Bar Assn., Orange County Bar Assn., Seminole County Bar Assn., Winter Park C. of C., Phi Delta Phi. Republican. Roman Catholic. Avocations: tennis, golf, fishing. Home: 139 Olive Tree Cir Altamonte Springs FL 32714-3240 Office: PO Box 160021 Altamonte Springs FL 32716-0021

HOOK, HAROLD SWANSON, management consulting executive; b. Kansas City, Mo., Oct. 10, 1931; s. Ralph C. and Ruby (Swanson) H.; m. Joanne T. Hunt, Feb. 19, 1955; children: Karen Anne, Thomas W., Randall T. BS in Bus. Adminstrn., U. Mo., 1953, MA in Acctg., 1954; grad., So. Meth. U. Inst. Ins. Mktng., 1957; postgrad., NYU, 1967-70; LLD (hon.), U. Mo., 1983, Westminster Coll., 1983. CLU, FLMI. Mem. faculty U. Mo. Sch. Bus., 1953-54; asst. to pres. Nat. Fidelity Life Ins. Co., Kansas City, Mo., 1957-60, dir., 1959-66, adminstrv. v.p., 1960-61, exec. v.p., investment com., 1961-62, pres., exec. com., 1962-66; sr. v.p. U.S. Life Ins. Co., N.Y.C., 1966-67, dir., 1967-70, exec. v.p., mem. exec. com., 1967-68, pres., 1968-70; pres. Calif.-Western States Life Ins. Co., Sacramento, 1970-75, chmn., 1975-79, sr. chmn., 1979-91, also bd. dirs.; mem. exec. com. Am. Gen. Corp., Houston, 1975-97, pres., 1975-81, chmn., chief exec. officer, 1978-96, also bd. dirs., chmn., 1996-97; founder, pres. Main Event Mgmt. Corp., Houston, 1971—; bd. dirs. Duke Energy Corp.,Charlotte, N.C., Sprint Corp., Kansas City, Mo., Cooper Industries, Inc., Houston, Chase Manhattan Corp., N.Y.C., Chase Manhattan Bank, N.Y.C., Chase Bank ofTex., Houston. Founder, mem. Naval War Coll. Found.; trustee, Baylor Coll. Medicine, Houston; coun. overseers Jesse H. Hones Grad. Sch. Adminstrn., Rice U., Houston; pres. nat. exec. bd. Boy Scouts Am., 1988-90, now mem. nat. adv. coun. Boy Scouts Am., mem. adv. bd. Sam Houston Area coun.; past pres. Houston Commerce, bd. dirs., Greater Houston Partnership (formerly Houston C. of C.), Director Emeritus. Recipient Citation of Merit U. Mo. Alumni Assn., 1965, Faculty-Alumni award U. Mo., 1978; Silver Beaver award Boy Scouts Am., 1974, Disting. Eagle Scout award, 1976, Silver Antelope award, 1989, Silver Buffalo award, 1990; Chief Exec. Officer award Fin. World mag., 1979, 82, 84, 86; named Man of Yr., Delta Sigma Pi, 1969, Outstanding Chief Exec. Officer in Multiline Ins. Industry, Wall Street Transcript, 1981-87. Fellow Life Mgmt. Inst.; mem. Mgmt. Exec. Soc., Philos. Soc. Tex., Tex. Assn. Taxpayers (bd. dirs.), Nat. Assn. Life Underwriters, Houston Assn. Life Underwriters, Forum Club (bd. govs. 1983-93), River Oaks Country Club, Petrolum Club, Econ. Club N.Y.C., Eldorado Country Club, Rotary, Beta Gamma Sigma (dirs. table 1976, nat. honoree 1984). Presbyterian. Office: Main Event Mgmt Corp PO Box 3665Pky Houston TX 77253-3665 also: PO Box 3247 Houston TX 77253-3247*

HOOK, JERRY B., pharmaceutical company executive; b. Elk City, Okla., Sept. 7, 1937; m. Jacqueline H. Smith; children: Bruce, Marilyn. BS, B in Pharmacy with honors, Wash. State U., Pullman, 1960; MS, U. Iowa, 1964, PhD, 1966; DSc (hon.), John Jay Coll. Criminal Justice, CUNY, 1989. Diplomate Am. Bd. Toxicology. Assoc. prof. pharmacology Mich. State U., East Lansing, 1971-75, prof. of pharmacology, 1975-78, prof. pharmacology and toxicology, 1978-83, dir. ctr. for environ. toxicology, 1980-83; v.p. preclin. R & D Smith Kline & French Labs. Phila., King of Prussia, Pa., 1983-87, v.p. preclin. R & D worldwide, 1987-88, v.p. devel., R & D, 1988-89; v.p. devel., R & D SmithKline Beecham Pharms., King of Prussia, 1989-90, sr. v.p., dir. devel. R & D, 1990-93; pres., chief exec. officer Lexin Pharm. Corp., Horsham, Pa., 1993-96; pres., CEO Sparta Pharm., Inc., Horsham, Pa., 1996-98, chmn., pres., CEO, 1998—; Burroughs-Wellcome vis. prof. U. N.D., 1981; vis. scientist Fed. Am. Soc. for Exptl. Biology Vis. Scientists for Minority Instns. Program, U. P.R. Med. Sch., 1984, Herbert H. Lehman Coll. of City U., 1985, Calif. State U., 1988, Pembroke State U., 1989; mem. adv. com. to bd. sci. counselors Nat. Toxicology Program, 1982-86; chmn. peer rev. panel of experts Nat. Toxology Program; vis. scientist John Jay Coll. Criminal Justice CUNY, 1987, mem. adv. bd. Toxicology Rsch. and Tng. Ctr., 1986-93. Author 225 publs. peer-reviewed lit., 60 book chpts., published symposia, reviews, symposia presentations. Bd. dirs. Montgomery County Community Coll. Found., 1987-89. Fellow Am. Coll. Clin. Pharmacology (hon.); mem. AAAS, Am. Soc. for Pharmacology and Exptl. Therapeutics, Internat. Union of Pharmacology (vice chmn. toxicology sect. 1987-90, chmn. toxicology sect. 1990-94), Internat. Union of Toxicology (1st v.p. 1989-92), Mid-Atlantic Chpt. Soc. of Toxicology, Soc. of Toxicology (councillor 1983-85, v.p. elect 1985-86, v.p. 1986-87, pres. 1987-88, past pres. 1988-89, IUTOX councillor). Office: Sparta Pharm Inc Pennsylvania Bus Campus Rock Plz III/111 Rock Rd Horsham PA 19044-2310

HOOK, JOHN BURNEY, investment company executive; b. Franklin, Ind., Sept. 6, 1928; s. Burney S. and Elsie C. (Hubbard) H.; m. Georgia Delis, Feb. 8, 1958; children—David, Deborah. BS, Ind. U., 1956, MBA, 1957. CPA, Ohio.; cert. fin. analyst. Store mgr. Goodman-Jester, Inc., Franklin, Ind., 1949-50; auditor Ernst & Ernst, Indpls., 1953-56; financial analyst Eli Lilly & Co., Indpls., 1957-59; gen. ptnr. Ball, Burge & Kraus, Cleve., 1966-72; pres., dir. Cuyahoga Mgmt. Corp., 1966-81; mng. ptnr. Hook Ptnrs., Cleve., 1984—. Mem. AICPA, Am. Inst. CFAs, Cleve. Athletic Club, Union Club (Cleve.), Westwood Country Club. Republican. Methodist. Home: 435 Bates Dr Cleveland OH 44140-1422 Office: Hook Ptnrs 647 Huntington Bldg Cleveland OH 44115

HOOK, RALPH CLIFFORD, JR., business educator; b. Kansas City, Mo., May 2, 1923; s. Ralph Clifford and Ruby (Swanson) H.; m. Joyce Fink, Jan. 20, 1946; children—Ralph Clifford III, John Gregory. BA, U. Mo., 1947, MA, 1948; PhD, U. Tex., 1954. Instr. U. Mo., 1947-48; asst. prof. Tex. A&M U., 1948-51; lectr. U. Tex., 1951-52; co-owner, mgr. Hook Buick Co., also Hook Truck & Tractor Co., Lee's Summit, Mo., 1952-58; assoc. prof. U. Kansas City, 1953-58; dir. Bur. Bus. Research and Services, Ariz. State U., 1958-66, prof. mktg., 1960-68; dean Coll. Bus. Adminstrn., U. Hawaii, 1968-74; prof. mktg. U. Hawaii, 1974-96, prof. mktg. emeritus, 1996—; vis. distinguished prof. N.E. La. U., 1979; dir. Hook Bros. Corp., Family Bus. Ctr. Hawaii, Pan Pacific Inst. Ocean Scis., Mauna Loa Macadamia Ptnrs., ltd. partnerships. Author: (with others) The Management Primer, 1972, Life Style Marketing, 1979, Marketing Service, 1983; contbr. (with others) monograph series Western Bus. Roundup; founder, moderator Western Bus. Roundup radio series, 1958-68. Bd. dirs. Jr. Achievement Hawaii. 1st lt. F.A., AUS, 1943-46; col. Res. Recipient alumni citation of merit U. Mo. Coll. Bus. and Pub. Adminstrn., 1969; Distinguished Service award Nat. Def. Transp. Assn., 1977, God and Service award United Meth. Ch./Boy Scouts Am., 1986; named to Faculty Hall Fame Ariz. State U. Coll. Bus. Assn., 1977, Hawaii Transp. Hall of Fame, 1986; named Educator of Yr., Western Mktg. Educators' Assn., 1998. Fellow Internat. Coun. for Sml. Bus. (pres. 1963); mem. Hawaii World Trade Assn. (pres. 1973-74), Am. Mktg. Assn. (v.p. 1965-67, pres. Cen. Ariz. chpt. 1960-61, pres. Honolulu chpt. 1991-92, Wayne A. Lemberg award for disting. svc. 1995), Western Assn. Collegiate Schs. Bus. (pres. 1972-73), Sales and Mktg. Execs. Internat. (life), Nat. Def. Transp. Assn. (Hawaii v.p. 1978-82), Newcomen Soc. N.Am. (Hawaii chmn.), Pi Sigma Epsilon (v.p. for edn. programs 1990-94), Mu Kappa Tau (pres. 1996-98), Beta Gamma Sigma, Omicron Delta Kappa, Beta Theta Pi, Delta Sigma Pi (gold coun.). United Methodist. Home: 311 Ohua Ave Apt 1104D Honolulu HI 96815-3636 Office: U Hawaii Coll Bus Adminstrn 2404 Maile Way Bldg C Honolulu HI 96822-2223

HOOK, VIVIAN YUAN-WEN HO, biochemist, neuroscientist; b. Oakland, Calif., Mar. 21, 1953; d. Timothy T. and Cheng-Ping (Wang) Ho; m. Gregory R. Hook, July 9, 1976; children: Lisa, Michelle. AB, U. Calif., Berkeley, 1974; PhD, U. Calif., San Francisco, 1980. From postdoctoral fellow to sr. scientist NIMH, NIH, Bethesda, Md., 1980-85; asst. prof. Uniformed Svcs. U., Bethesda, 1986-90, assoc. prof., 1991-94; assoc. prof. U. Calif., San Diego, 1994-95, prof., 1996—; biochemistry and neuroscience study sect. Nat. Inst. Drug Abuse, Bethesda, 1989-92. Contbr. articles to profl. jours. NIH grantee, 1987—; Wellcome Sr. Scientist fellow NIH, 1983-86, Pharmacology Rsch. Assoc. fellow, 1980-82; recipient Ind. Scientist award NIH, 1994—. Mem. Soc. for Neurosci., Am. Soc. Biochemistry and Molecular Biology, Endocrinology Soc. Achievements include research in proteases required for synthesis of peptide neurotransmitters and hormones.

HOOK, WILLIAM FRANKLIN, retired radiologist; b. Williston, N.D., May 26, 1935; s. Charles Ellis and Ann (Franklin) H.; m. Margo Joanne Booth, June 21, 1958 (div. Sept. 1968); children: William, Christopher, Paul; m. Merry Jean Schimke, Nov. 26, 1968 (div. 1987); 1 child, Kari Ann; m. Linda Marie Rohrich, Aug. 18, 1988. AB, Stanford U., 1957; MD, Jefferson Med. Coll., 1961. Diplomate Am. Bd. Radiology, Am. Bd. Nuclear Medicine. Staff radiologist O&R Clinic, Bismarck, N.D., 1969-74; dir. nuclear radiology O&R Clinic, Bismarck, 1983-98, chmn. dept. radiology, 1990-98; chief dept. radiology Bismarck Hosp., 1970-74; dir. dept. radiology Mandan (N.D.) Hosp., 1974-81; staff radiologist Meth. Hosps., Dallas, 1981-83, Med. Ctr. One, 1984-98; co-dir. Regional MRI Ctr., Bismarck, 1987-92; asst. clinical prof. U. N.D., 1978—. Author: Common Sense and Modern First Aid, 1967; contbr. articles profl. jours. Lt. USNR, 1961-64, col. Res. ret.; comdr. USAR hosp., Persian Gulf, 1991-92. Mem. AMA (Physician's Recognition award 1983-86, 86-92), Am. Coll. Radiology, Soc. Nuclear Medicine, N.D. State Radiol. Soc., 6th Dist. Med. Soc. Lutheran. Avocations: hunting, golf, aviation. Address: PO Box 2424 36636 N Mule Train Carefree AZ 85377

HOOKE, MICHAEL PETER, secondary education educator; b. San Francisco, Nov. 6, 1965; s. Dennis Michael and Jacklyn Ellen Hooke. BA, Gonzaga U., 1987; Master Catechist, Diocese of Oakland, 1990; MA in Systematic Theology, Dominican Sch. Philosophy and Theology, Berkeley, Calif., 1991. Educator St. Joseph Notre Dame H.S., Alameda, Calif., 1988—, religion dept. chair, 1996—; theater dir. St. Joseph Notre Dame H.S., Alameda, 1991—, bookstore mgr., 1996—; guest lectr. Roman Cath. Diocese of Oakland, 1988—. Mem. KC, ASCD, Nat. Cath. Ednl. Assn., Nat. Assn. of Social Studies Tchrs., Nat. Thespian Soc. Democrat. Roman Catholic. Avocations: theater, camping, gardening, reading, ethnic events. Office: St Joseph Notre Dame HS 1011 Chestnut St Alameda CA 94501-4315

HOOKE, ROGER LEBARON, geomorphology and glaciology educator; b. Glen Ridge, N.J., Jan. 3, 1939; s. Robert Gay and Katharine Mary (Glidden) H.; m. Ann Peck, Sept. 2, 1961; children: Bruce, Lyn. BA, Harvard U., Cambridge, Mass., 1961; PhD, Calif. Inst. Tech., Pasadena, 1965. Asst. prof. geomorphology U. Minn., Mpls., 1965-70, assoc. prof. geomorphology, 1970-80, prof. geomorphology, 1980—; assoc. dir. glaciological rsch. Tarfala Rsch. Sta., U. Stockholm, 1981-95. Contbr. articles to profl. jours. Fellow Geol. Soc. Am.; mem. Internat. Geol. Soc. Unitarian. Home: PO Box 640 Deer Isle ME 04627-0640 Office: U Minn Dept Geology Geophysics Minneapolis MN 55455

HOOKER, JAMES TODD, manufacturing executive; b. Ashland, Ohio, Dec. 21, 1946; s. Melvin Todd and Harriett (Lutz) H.: m. Sallie Foulkrod Utz, Feb. 22, 1975; 1 child, Stephanie Rae. BSBA magna cum laude, Ashland U., 1973. Advt. mgr. The Gorman-Rupp Co., Mansfield, Ohio, 1974-76, mfg. engr., 1976-79; asst. service mgr. The Gorman-Rupp Co., Mansfield, 1979-80, gen. service mgr., 1980-86, asst. sales mgr., 1986-90; mgr. mfg. The Gorman-Rupp Co., Mansfield, Ohio, 1990-95, dir. mfg., 1995-98, v.p. mfg. and facilities, 1998—. Solicitor United Way, Mansfield; moderator, bd. deacons Presbyn. Ch., 1988-89, elder, mem. Session; chmn. bd. Trustees Richland County Leadership Unltd.; mem. Heritage Found.; plank owner USN Meml. Found.; chmn. bd. Mansfield Richland County Chamber Edn. Found. Decorated Vietnamese Gallantry Cross. Mem. Omicron Delta Epsilon. Republican. Home: 1090 Trout Dr Mansfield OH 44903-9144 Office: The Gorman-Rupp Co 305 Bowman St Mansfield OH 44903-1600

HOOKER, JO, interior designer; b. Evanston, Ill., Dec. 13, 1932; d. Armand Francis and Josephine Margaret (Daus) Conto; m. Donald E. Hooker, Feb. 11, 1956 (div. 1975); children: Elizabeth Ann Hooker Gilbertson, Kathryn Maura Hooker. BFA, U. Ill., 1955; postgrad., Ariz. State U., 1972-76. Cert. Nat. Coun. for Interior Design Qualification, 1980; ASID. Interior designer Barrows Design Studio, Phoenix, 1976-94; interior designer, owner Jo Hooker Interior Design, Scottsdale, Ariz., 1994—. Designer showcases for Phoenix Home and Garden, 1986, 87, 91, Phoenix Mag., 1999. Mem. Am. Soc. Interior Designers (cert. profl., bd. dirs. Ariz. North chpt. 1996-98, ethics chair 1994-99, hist. com. 1996-97, Design Excellence award Ariz. North chpt. 1985, NCIDQ juror 1997, chair North design awards excellence competition), Soc. Illustrators, U. Ill. Scholastic Honorary. Office: Jo Hooker Interior Design 6615 N Scottsdale Rd Scottsdale AZ 85250-4421

HOOKER, MARY KATHERINE, librarian; b. Jan. 14, 1942. BA, Our Lady of the Lake U., 1963; MLS, U. Calif., Berkeley, 1965; MA, Tex. A&M U., 1983. Libr. sys. dir. City of El Paso, 1992—. Office: 501 N Oregon El Paso TX 79901

HOOKER, MICHAEL KENNETH, university chancellor; b. Richlands, Va., Aug. 24, 1945; s. Aaron Kenneth and Margaret (Smith) H.; m. Anna Hostettler, Dec. 22, 1966 (div. 1992); 1 child, Alexandra Christine; m. Carmen Buell, Dec. 18, 1993. BA, U. N.C., 1969; MA, U. Mass., 1972, PhD, 1973; LittD (hon.), Drexel U., 1988., 1986-92; asst. prof. Harvard U., Cambridge, Mass., 1973-75; asst. prof. philosophy Johns Hopkins U., Balt., 1975-77, asst. dean, 1977-78, assoc. dean, 1978-80, dean, 1980-82; pres. Bennington (Vt.) Coll., 1982-86, U. Md., Balt. County, 1986-92, U. Mass. Sys., Boston, 1992-95; chancellor U. N.C., Chapel Hill, 1995—; chmn. biotech. adv. com. Office Tech. Assessment U.S. Congress, Washington, 1981-83; bd. dirs. Centura Banks, Inc., 360 Degrees Comm., Luminex, Inc. Editor: Descartes, 1978, Leibniz, 1982. Recipient Homewood award John Hopkins U., 1980, Chancellor's medal U. Mass., 1989; Woodrow Wilson fellow, 1972-73, Harvard U. faculty rsch. fellow, 1974. Mem. Leibniz Soc. (bd. dirs. 1979-83), Internat. Berkeley Soc. (v.p. 1978-79), Am. Philos. Assn. Soc. (chmn. com., bd. officers 1977-82). Home: 1001 Raleigh Rd Chapel Hill NC 27514-4418 Office: U NC CB 9100 Chapel Hill NC 27599-9100*

HOOKER, OLIVIA J., psychologist, educator; b. Muskogee, Okla., Feb. 12, 1915; d. Samuel David and Anita Juliette (Stigger) H. BS, Ohio State U., 1937; MA, Columbia U., 1947; PhD, U. Rochester, N.Y., 1962. Cert. sch. psychologist, N.Y. Elem. tchr. Columbus (Ohio) Pub. Schs., 1937-45; clin. psychologist dept. mental hygiene State of N.Y., Albion, 1948-51, Bedford Hills, 1951-57, Rochester, 1955-57; research psychologist dept. mental hygiene State of N.Y., Letchworth Village, 1957-61; sch. psychologist Bur. Child Guidance, N.Y.C., 1951-52; psychologist Kennedy Child Studies Ctr., N.Y.C., 1961-64, dir. psychol. svcs., 1964-83; assoc. prof. Fordham U., Bronx, N.Y., 1974-85; cons. St. Benedict's Day Care Ctr., N.Y.C., 1976—, Fred S. Keller Sch., Yonkers, N.Y., 1987—. Trustee Terence Cardinal Cooke Health Svcs. Coun., N.Y.C., 1984-96; mem. adv. bd. Child Life program Westchester County Med. Ctr., Valhalla, N.Y., 1985—; v.p. White Plains NAACP, 1985-87, White Plains Sr. Pers. Employment Coun., 1987-96; tutor Literacy Vols. Am., 1987—; bd. dirs. White Plains Child Day Care Assn., 1988—, Vis. Nurse Assn. Westchester, 1988-94; chmn. adminstrv. bd. Trinity United Meth. Ch., 1985-87. Served with women's res. USCG, 1945-46. U. Rochester fellow, 1955-56; recipient Women's award Women's History Assn., 1986. Fellow APA (div. on devel. disability), Am. Assn. Mental Retardation. Avocations: creative writing, gardening, music. Office: Fordham U Dept Psychology Bronx NY 10458

HOOKER, RENÉE MICHELLE, postanesthesia and perinatal nurse; b. Kansas City, Mo., June 26, 1965; d. Roland Edward and Loretta Mae (Rathbun) Woods; m. Joel Thomas Hooker, Sept. 17, 1988; children: Andrew, Catherine, Rebekah. BSN, U. Kans., 1987. RN, Tex., Calif.; cert post anesthesia nurse, inpatient obstetric nurse ANCC; cert. ACLS, neonatal resuscitation; cert. BLS instr. Am. Heart Assn. Staff med.-surg. nurse Desert Hosp., Palm Springs, Calif., 1987-88; staff nurse neonatal ICU Santa Rose Children's Hosp., San Antonio, 1988; staff obstetrics nurse, supr. post anesthesia care unit McKenna Meml. Hosp., New Braunfels, Tex., 1988—; prepost anesthesia care nurse mgr. McKenna Meml. Hosp., New Braunfels, 1999. Mem. Assn. Women's Health, Obstet. and Neonatal Nursing, Tex. Assn. Post Anesthesia Nurses, Am. Soc. Post Anesthesia Nurses, Assn. Oper. Room Nurses. Republican. Roman Catholic. Avocations: reading, cooking, travel, child advocacy. Office: McKenna Meml Hosp 600 N Union Ave New Braunfels TX 78130-4191

HOOKER, RICHARD ARTHUR, computer scientist; b. Syracuse, N.Y., Mar. 11, 1951; s. William and Josephine (Barbera) H.; children: Elizabeth, Sara, Richard, Rana, Jeremy. AS in Computer Sci., Harvard U., 1975; BSEE cum laude, SUNY, Utica, Rome, 1979; postgrad., Harvard U. Biomed. engr. Squibb Med., Syracuse, N.Y., 1979-82; applications engr. NEC, Boston, 1982-87, INMOS/SGS, Boston, 1988-91; engr.-scientist IBM, Waltham, Mass., 1991—. Patentee in field; author: Power PC Compiler Writers' Manual, 1995, Performance Analysis, Planning and Engineering, 1996, Multimedia Benchmarking, 1997—. Home: 7 Belmont Cir Belmont MA 02451-8713

HOOKER, ROBERT, automotive executive; b. 1932. With Import Motors, Inc., Grand Rapids, Mich., 1977—; CEO Transnational Motors, Grand Rapids, 1994—. Office: PO Box 2008 Grand Rapids MI 49501-2008*

HOOKER, ROBERT WRIGHT, journalist; b. New Haven, July 11, 1947; s. Charles Wright and Elma (Black) H.; m. Ellen Ann McMackin, Apr. 13, 1974; 1 child, Matthew Wright. BA in History, Davidson (N.C.) Coll., 1969; MA in History, Vanderbilt U., 1971. Reporter St. Petersburg (Fla.) Times, 1971-78, polit. editor, 1978, night city editor, 1979, projects editor, 1979-87, Tampa city editor, 1987, state editor, 1987-90, bus. editor, 1990-96, metropolitan editor, 1996, asst. mng. editor, 1997—; bd. dirs. Trend Mag., Inc., St. Petersburg, 1991-97. Author: The Times and Its Times: 1884-1984, 1984. 1st lt. USAR, 1971. Recipient Nat. Edn. Reporting award, Edn. Writers of Am., 1983, Best Investigative Reporting award, Am. Sports Editors Assn., 1983. Home: 2982 60th Ave S Saint Petersburg FL 33712-4524 Office: St Petersburg Times PO Box 1121 Saint Petersburg FL 33731-1121

HOOKER, VAN DORN, architect, artist; b. Carthage, Tex., Sept. 22, 1921; s. Van Dorn and Anne (Wylie) H.; m. Marjorie Mead, June 14, 1947;

children: Ann, Van Dorn III, John Hardy. Student, Coll. of Marshall, Tex., 1938-40; BArch, U. Tex., 1947; postgrad., U. Calif.-Berkeley, 1950-51. Registered architect, N.Mex., Tex. Architect, ptnr. McHugh & Hooker-Bradley P. Kidder & Assocs., Santa Fe, 1956-63; univ. architect U. N.Mex., Albuquerque, 1963-87; univ. architect emeritus U. N.Mex., 1987—, assoc. prof. architecture, 1971-87; assoc. prof. architecture emeritus, 1987—. architect numerous bldgs.; one-man show, Bradywine Gallery, Albuquerque, 1973, group shows include, Mus. of N.Mex., 1963, 1979; represented permanent collection, Mus. N.Mex.; author: Centuries of Hands, 1996, N.Mex., 2000; contbr. articles to various publs. Trustee Albuquerque Acad., 1972-82; bd. dirs. Corrales Land Trust, 1991—. Recipient Regents medal U. N.Mex. Fellow AIA (pres. Albuquerque chpt. 1971, Silver medal We. Mountain region), Assn. Univ. Architects (pres. 1971); mem. N.Mex. Architecture Found. (pres. 1987), Santa Fe Chamber Music Festival (bd. dirs.), N.Mex. Soc. Architects (honor and merit awards, pres. 1973, Appreciation award 1987). Address: PO Box 10149 Albuquerque NM 87184-0149

HOOKER, WADE STUART, JR., lawyer; b. Brockton, Mass., Sept. 23, 1941; s. Wade S. and Eleanor M. (Tolan) H.; m. Susan M. Levine, May 20, 1984; children: Thomas A., Richard P. BA, Harvard Coll., 1963; LLB, U. Va., 1966. Bar: N.Y. 1969. Assoc. Casey, Lane & Mittendorf, N.Y.C., 1968-77; ptnr. Burlingham Underwood LLP, N.Y.C., 1979—; spkr. in field. Contbr. articles to profl. jours. Maxwell fellow Syracuse U., Resident scholar Indian Law Inst., New Delhi, 1966-67. Mem. ABA, Assn. Bar City of N.Y., Computer Law Assn., Inc., Internat. Bar Assn., Maritime Law Assn. U.S. (chair com. maritime regulation and promotion 1990-94), Mensa. Office: Burlingham Underwood LLP One Battery Pk Plaza New York NY 10004

HOOKER, WILLIAM, administrative services officer; b. Grand Rapids, Mich., Aug. 19, 1942. BA, Western Mich. U., 1971. Adminstr. City of Grand Rapids, 1973-83, adminstrv. svcs. officer, 1983—. Office: City of Grand Rapids Community Development Dept 300 Monroe Ave NW Grand Rapids MI 49503-2281*

HOOKHAM, ELEANOR KING, painter; b. Marlow, Okla., Apr. 5, 1909; d. William Frank Sr. and Sara Caroline (Smith) King; m. George Lawrence Salley, July 9, 1934 (div. Mar. 1940, dec. Aug. 1989); 1 child, Jane King; m. Robert Ernest Hookham, Nov. 5, 1943; children: Tarrant King, Robert Peyton. Student, Oklahoma City Coll.; D Art (hon.), Elmhurst (Ill.) Coll., 1987; hon. D, Cultural Acad. France, Paris, 1980, Internat. Sem. Modern Art, Terme, Italy, 1982. Founder, chmn. Elmhurst Art Mus., 1997—; tchr. art, Elmhurst, 1946-83. One-woman shows include Montross Gallery, N.Y.C., 1939-41, Galerie Internat., N.Y.C., 1962-63, 64, 65, Pensacola (Fla.) Art Mus., Galerie Marcel Bernheim, Paris, 1965-84, Galerie Bernheim Jeune, 1980-82, Elmhurst Art Mus., 1998; exhibited in group shows at Leonard Clayton Gallery, N.Y.C., 1938, Johnson Gallery, Chgo., 1959, 60, 61, Ill. State Art Mus., Chgo., 1964, Internat. Fedn. Culturelle Feminine, 1968, Musée d'Art Modern, Athens and Paris, 1969, Goblein, Paris, 1969; author: Creative Art and the Subconscious, 1979, Compilation of My Color Theory, Color-La Couleur; represented in permanent collections at George Pompido U., Paris, Musée D'Art Moderne Ville de Paris, Am. univs. and museums. Chmn. bd. Elmhurst Fine Arts & Civic Ctr. Found., 1974. Recipient medaille vermail Encouragement Au Progre, Paris, 1981, medal L'Academie de Lutece, Paris, 1979, gold medal Mus. in Sony Bldg., Osaka, Japan, 1980, gold grand priz Humanitaire de France, Paris, 1984, Palme D'or, Paris Critiques, 1981, medaille vermeil Aarts Sci. et Lettres, Paris, 1989, award of merit Am. Legion, Elmhurst, 1989, Civic Hall of Fame award Elmhurst C. of C., 1993, lifetime achievement award Ill. Arts Alliance, Chgo., 1995; named Woman of Yr. in art YWCA, DuPage County and Chgo., 1985. Mem. DAR (regent 1961-62), Elmhurst Artsits' Guild (hon. life, pres. 1951-53, 71-73), Colonial Dames Am., Nat. Soc. Arts and Letters (Chgo. chpt.). Episcopalian. Avocations: golf, swimming. Home: 289 Adelia St Elmhurst IL 60126-3537

HOOKS, GEORGE BARDIN, state senator, insurance and real estate company executive; b. Americus, Ga., May 9, 1945; s. Thomas Bardin III and Rose Mary (Fay) H.; m. Gail Ann Goen, Aug. 30, 1975; children: George Bardin Jr., Mary Ann. BA, Auburn U., 1970; postgrad., Princeton U. V.p. southeast region Alliance of Am. Insurers, Atlanta, 1972-77; pres. Hooks Agy. Inc., Americus, Ga., 1977—; rep. State of Ga. House Reps., 1980-90; sen. State of Ga. Senate, 1990—; floor leader for Gov. Ga. House Reps., 1988-90, chair rules com., 1992-93, appropriations com., 1993—. Active bd. dirs. Ft. Valley State U., 1992—, Mercer U., 1997—. Named Legislator of Yr., Mcpl. Assn., 1992, County Com. Assn., 1993. Mem. Ga. Assn. Ins. Agts. (bd. dirs. 1978-80. legis. dir. 1974, Pres. Citation 1974, 80), Ga. C. of C. (leadership Ga. 1982), Americus C. of C. (legis. chmn.), Rotary, Kappa Alpha. Democrat. Baptist. Home: 145 Taylor St Americus GA 31709-4056 Office: PO Box 928 Americus GA 31709-0928*

HOOKS, MARY LINDA, adult education educator; b. Albany, Ga., Apr. 22; d. Tobe Sr. and Linda (Anthony) Cain; m. Arthur Franklin Hooks; children: Angela, Darryl, Stanley, Ashia. BS, Albany (Ga.) State Coll., 1961; MS, Fla. State U., 1985. Tchr. bus. subjects Chgo., 1961-64; course writer, instr. McNamara Skills Ctr., Detroit, 1964-74; course designer, instr. YWCA, Detroit, 1965-66; continuing edn. instr. Mary Grove Coll., Detroit, 1974-75; tchr. math. Pinetta Jr. High Sch., Madison, Fla., 1976—; tchr. math/job skills Jefferson County High Sch., Monticello, Fla., 1977-78; tchr. reading/kindergarten Jefferson Elem. Sch., Monticello, 1978-79; coord., facilitator, instr. bus. edn. and adult edn. Jefferson County Adult Sch., Monticello, 1979—; with MAL Found., Tallahassee, Fla., 1999—; cons. Edwards Enterprise Sch., Albany, 1989-91; owner pvt. edn. svc., MAL Found. Inc., Tallahassee. cons. Youth Street (television show). Judge, vol. 4-H Jefferson County, Monticello, 1985—; bd. dirs. Greenville (Fla.) Day Care Ctr., 1988-90, corr. sec., 1988-90; candidate for Supt. Pub. Schs., Monticello, 1988; mem. adv. bd. United Found., Detroit, 1969-74; vol. Youth Ctr., Greenville City Hall, 1988-90; charter mem. Fla. Adult Literacy Resource Ctr., 1993—. Recipient Dedication/Appreciation award McNamara Skills Ctr., Detroit, 1973-74, Jefferson County 4-H, 1985-91, others. Mem. LINK-Progressive Women's Club, Fla. Adult Literacy Resource Ctr. Ptnrs. (charter), Internat. Platform Assn., Kiwanis, Fla. Adult Assn. Avocations: researching herbs, collecting antiques, gardening, needlework, spectator sports. Office: Jefferson County Adult Sch 760 E Washington St Monticello FL 32344-2549

HOOKS, VENDIE HUDSON, III, surgeon; b. Metter, Ga., Nov. 1, 1948; s. Vendie Hudson Jr. and May (Jones) H.; m. Carolyn Anderson Braithwaite, Nov. 1, 1974; children: Hudson, Susanna, David, Katherine. BS, U. Ga., 1970; MD, Med. Coll. Ga., 1974. Diplomate Am. Bd. Surgery, Am. Bd. Colon and Rectal Surgery. Intern surgery Med. Coll. Ga. Hosps., Augusta, 1974-75; resident gen. surgery Med. Coll. Ga. Hosps., 1975-78, chief resident gen. surgery, 1978-79; G.I. surgery fellow gen. infirmary U. Leeds (Eng.), 1979-80; colon and rectal surgery fellow U. Minn. Hosps., 1982-83; asst. prof. surgery, asst. chief sect. GI surgery Med. Coll. Ga., Augusta, 1980-85; dir. colon/rectal surgery clinic Med. Coll. Ga., 1980-85; attending in surgery VA Hosp., Augusta, 1980-85; asst. clin. prof. surgery Med. Coll. Ga., Augusta, 1985-94; assoc. clin. prof. surgery, 1994—; staff surgeon Univ. Hosp., Augusta, 1985—, St. Joseph Hosp., Augusta, 1985—; attending colon/rectal surgery endoscopy Univ. Hosp., Augusta, 1986—; dir. Southeastern Familial Polyposis Registry; bd. dirs. Richmond-Columbia County unit Am. Cancer Soc., v.p. medicine, 1985-91; mem. Ethicon Colon and Rectal Adv. Panel, 1988, Panel Specialist-Surgery, Vocat. Rehab., 1980—; mem. interview com. for med. sch. admissions Med. Coll. Ga., 1981-82, 84-85, mem. tissue com., 1983-85; chmn. familial polyposis registry com. U. Hosp. Augusta, 1986—; assoc. examiner Am. Bd. Colon and Rectal Surgery, 1995-98, mem., 1998—. Co-author: Textbook of Gastroenterology, 1984, Clinical Management of Gastrointestinal Cancer, 1984; contbr. articles to profl. jours.; book reviewer and abstractor in field; reviewer Gastrointestinal Endoscopy, 1985-88. Pres. med. staff U. Hosp., Augusta, Ga., 1999, Richmond County Hosp. Authority, Augusta, 1998-02. Recipient Continuing Med. Edn. award Am. Soc. Colon and Rectal Surgeons, 1984, 87, Spl. award for colorectal cancer control Am. Cancer Soc., 1987, Cert. of Appreciation, Am. Cancer Soc., 1991-92, Award of Excellence, Am. Cancer Soc., 1992-93; grantee Am. Soc. Hosp. Pharmacists, 1981, Smith Kline & French Labs., 1981, Merck Sharp & Dohme, 1984. Fellow ACS, Southeastern Surg. Congress, Am. Soc. Colon and Rectal Surgeons; mem. AMA (Physician Recognition award 1984-89, 1990-93, 93-96, 97-00), Med. Assn. Ga., Richmond County Med. Soc., So. Med. Assn., Moretz Surg. Soc., Assn. for Acad. Surgeons, Ga. Gastroenterologic and Endoscopy Soc., Am. Soc. for Gastrointestinal Endoscopy, Soc. Am. Gastrointestinal Endoscopic Surgeons, Ga. Surg. Soc., Piedmont Soc. Colon and Rectal Surgeons (pres. 1992-94), Soc. Surgery Alimentary Tract, Phi Beta Kappa, Phi Kappa Phi. Methodist. Avocations: golf, hunting. Office: Colon and Rectal Surgery Assocs PC 820 Saint Sebastian Way Ste 7C Augusta GA 30901-2641

HOOLEY, DARLENE, congresswoman, county commissioner; b. Williston, N.D., Apr. 4, 1939; d. Clarence Alvin and Alyce (Rogers) Olsen; m. John Hooley; children: Chad, Erin. BS in Edn., Oreg. State U., 1961, postgrad., 1963-65; postgrad., Portland State U., 1966-67. Tchr. Woodburn (Oreg.) & Gervais Sch., 1962-65, David Douglas Sch. Dist., Portland, Oreg., 1965-67, St. Mary's Acad., Portland, 1967-69; mem. West Linn (Oreg.) City Coun., 1976-80; state rep. Oreg. State Ho. of Reps., 1980-87; county commr. Clakamas County (Oreg.) Bd., 1987-96; mem. 105th-106th U.S. Congress from 5th dist. Oreg., 1996—. Vice-chair Oreg. Tourism Alliance, Portland, 1991—. bd. dirs. Pub. Employees Ret. Bd., Portland, 1989—, Cmty. Corrections Bd., Oregon City, 1990—, Providence Med. Ctr., Portland, 1989—; acting chair Oreg. Trail Found. Bd., Oregon City, 1991—; mem. Urban Growth Policy Adv. Com., Portland, 1991—. Named Legislator of the Year Oreg. Libr. Assn., 1985-86, Oreg. Solar Energy Assn., 1985; recipient Spl. Svc. award Clackamas City Coun. for Child Abuse Prevention, 1989. Mem. LWV, Oreg. Women's Polit. Caucus (Women of the Yr. 1988). Democrat. Office: 1419 Longworth Bldg Washington DC 20515-3705*

HOOLEY, JAMES ROBERT, oral and maxillofacial surgeon, educator, dean; b. Stillwater, Minn., Nov. 5, 1932; s. Robert Joseph and Dorothy Agnes (Goss) H.; m. Margaret Ann Sullivan, Aug. 22, 1959; children: Michael, Mary, Grace, Thomas. D.D.S., St. Louis U., 1957; postgrad., New York Med. Coll., 1957-59; Harvard U. Program in Health Systems Mgmt., 1978; certificate in oral surgery, U. Pa., 1960. Diplomate: Am. Bd. Oral and Maxillofacial Surgery. Practice dentistry, specializing in oral and maxillofacial surgery Seattle, 1963-81; instr. dept. oral and maxillofacial surgery U. Wash. Sch. Dentistry, 1963-65; chief U. Wash. Hosp. Dental Service, 1964-72; asst. dean U. Wash. Hosp. Dental Service (Sch. Dentistry), 1966-71, assoc. prof., 1968-72, prof., chmn. dept., 1972-80; dean Sch. Dentistry, UCLA, 1981-86; acting chmn. dept. oral and maxillofacial surgery Naval Dental Sch., Bethesda, Md., 1990-92; oral and maxillofacial surgeon U.S. Navy, 1992—. Author: Hospital Dentistry, 1970, A Self-Instructional Guide to Oral Surgery in General Dentistry, 1978, Hospital Dental Practice, 1979. Sect. editor: Jour. of Oral Surgery, 1972-76. Democratic precinct committeeman 43d Dist., Seattle, 1979. Served to capt. U.S. Army, 1960-62; to capt. Dental Corps USN Res., 1963—. Recipient Alumni Merit award St. Louis U., 1987; Internat. Coll. Dentists fellow 1987, Am. Coll. Dentists fellow 1992. Mem. ADA, Internat. Assn. Oral and Maxillofacial Surgeons, Brit. Assn. Oral and Maxillofacial Surgeons, Am. Assn. Oral and Maxillofacial Surgeons, European Assn. Cranio-Maxillary Surgery. Roman Catholic. Office: 15915 Asilomar Blvd Pacific Palisades CA 90272

HOOPER, ANNE DODGE, pathologist, educator; b. Groton, Mass., July 16, 1926; d. Carroll William and Bertha Sanford (Wiener) Dodge; m. William Dale Hooper, June 17, 1952; children: Elizabeth Anne, Joan Elaine, Caroline Mae. AB, Washington U., St. Louis, 1947, MD, 1952. Diplomate in pathologic anatomy, clin. pathology and forensic pathology Am. Bd. Pathology. Rotating intern Virginia Mason Hosp., Seattle, 1952-53; resident in internal medicine St. Francis Hosp., Hartford, Conn., 1953-54; resident in pathologic anatomy and clin. pathology New Britain (Conn.) Gen. Hosp., 1954-57, Presbyn. Hosp., Phila., 1957-58; resident in forensic pathology Office Med. Examiner, Phila., 1958-60; from pathologist to acting chief lab svc. VA Hosp., Coatesville, Pa., 1960-66; dir. lab. St. Albans (Vt.) Hosp., 1966-69, Kerbs Hosp., St. Albans, 1966-71, Williamson Appalachian Regional Hosp., South Williamson, Ky., 1971-73, Beckley (W.Va.) Appalachian Regional Hosp., 1974-76; asst. prof. pathology W.Va. Sch. Osteo. Medicine, Lewisburg, 1977, assoc. prof. pathology, 1978-97, cons. in pathology, 1997—; lab. accreditation insp. CAP, 1982-00, Am. Osteo. Assn., 1996-98. Contbr. articles to profl. jours. Pres. local elem. sch. PTA, St. Albans, 1967-68; pres. Greenbrier unit Am. Cancer Soc., Lewisburg, 1989-93, bd. dirs. W.Va. div., Charleston, 1987-94, profl. edn. com. W.Va. div., 1982-94. Fellow Coll. Am. Pathologists, Am. Acad. Forensic Scis.; mem. AMA, W.Va. Med. Soc., Raleigh County Med. Soc., Am. Soc. Clin. Pathologists, Internat. Acad. Pathologists, Nat. Assn. Med. Examiners, Am. Osteo. Coll. Pathologists (assoc.). Avocation: playing violin and viola. Office: WVa Sch Osteo Medicine 400 N Lee St Lewisburg WV 24901-1128

HOOPER, BILLY ERNEST, retired medical association administrator; b. Pawnee City, Nebr., June 22, 1931; s. James Ernest and Beulah Edith (Thiemann) H.; m. Janice Jewell, Apr. 17, 1954; children: Roger William, Robin Suzanne. BS in Agr., DVM, U. Mo., 1961; MS, Purdue U., 1963, PhD, 1965. Diplomate Am. Coll. Vet. Patholoigsts. From asst. prof. to assoc. prof. Purdue U., Lafayette, Ind., 1965-68, assoc. dean, 1973-86; assoc. prof. U. Mo., Columbia, 1968-71; prof. U. Ga., Athens, 1971-73; exec. dir. Assn. Am. Vet. Med. Colls., Washington, 1986-92; assoc. dean Coll. Vet. Medicine Okla. State U., Stillwater, 1992-97; ret., 1997; bd. dirs. Pew Nat. Vet. Edn. Program, Phila. Bd. dirs. United Way, Lafayette, 1983-86. Sgt. USMC, 1949-52. Named Alumnus of Yr. Sch. Vet. Medicine, U. Mo., 1988. Mem. AVMA (mem., chair coun. on edn., com. on animal tech. 1980-86).

HOOPER, CARL GLENN, civil engineer, software author, contractor; b. Granville, N.Y., Apr. 6, 1936; s. W. Glenn and Alma (Osborne) H.; m. Priscilla Anne Hall, June 15, 1957; children: Martin Eric, Diane Elizabeth, Lynn Louise, Charles Douglas, Julie Anne. BSCE, Norwich U., 1958. Registered profl. engr., Vt., Fla., N.C. Mng. ptnr. Hooper Constrn. Co., Canton, N.C., 1960—; town auditor Town of Poultney (Vt.), 1964-67; pres. Hooper Constrn. Products Corp., Granville, N.Y., 1969-76; project dir. Briley, Wild & Assocs., Ormond Beach, Fla., 1977-88; dir. community svcs., city engr. City of Daytona Beach Shores (Fla.), 1988-96; pres. Bent Tree Software Inc., Canton, 1990—. Author computer programs for personal fin. and real estate program, others. 1st lt. C.E., U.S. Army, 1958-60. Mem. ASCE. Republican. Methodist. Avocations: gourmet cooking, computer programming. Home and Office: 496 Burnette Cove Rd Canton NC 28716-5511

HOOPER, CATHERINE EVELYN, senior development engineer; b. Bklyn., Nov. 10, 1939; d. Frederick Charles Jr. and Catherine Veronica (Heaney) Podeyn; m. Melvyn Robert Lowney, Nov. 30, 1957 (div. 1970); children: Denise Lowney Andrade, Michele Lowney Budris; m. William White Hooper, Sept. 21, 1974. Student, San Jose (Calif.) City Coll., 1969, De Anza Coll., 1980. Insp. Amelco Semiconductor, Mountain View, Calif., 1966-68; lab. technician Fairchild R & D, Palo Alto, Calif., 1968-73; sr. lab. technician Varian Cen. Rsch., Palo Alto, 1973-84; sr. devel. engr. Hughes Rsch. Labs., Malibu, 1984—. Contbr. articles to profl. jours. Pres. Conejo Valley chpt. Nat. Women's Polit. Caucus., 1994. Mem. Am. Vacuum Soc., Materials Rsch. Soc., Grad. Women in Sci. (L.A. pres. 1990-92), Internat. Soc. Optical Engrs., Sigma Xi (sec. 1987-90, 94). Office: HRL Labs LLC 3011 Malibu Canyon Rd Malibu CA 90265-4797

HOOPER, DONALD ROBERT, retired corporate chief executive; b. Deer Island, N.B., Can., Apr. 17, 1935; came to U.S., 1954; s. Raymond Wendall and Norma (Doughty) H.; m. Peggy DeForest, June 28, 1958 (div. 1974); children: Diane Evelyn, John Gregory, Suzanne Carole, Donald Robert II; m. Susan Paula Amenta, May 22, 1987. BTh, Ea. Christian Inst., Orange, N.J., 1957; LLB, LaSalle U., Chgo., 1963; BS in Profl. Meteorology, U. Md., 1964; DD (hon.), Univ. of West, Pasadena, Calif., 1978. founder Am. Soc. Profl Supts., 1978. Author: Weather and Flight Patterns of Europe, 1963 (award 1963), Blueprint Reading Made Easy, 1979, Weather of North Polar Regions, 1968, Visual Poetry and How It's Done, 1995. Mem. Rep. Nat. Com., Washington, 1990-99; mem. The Presdl. Trust, Washington, 1991-92; life mem. Air Force Aid Soc., Washington, Yosemite Assn. Staff sgt. USAF, 1955-67. Decorated Air Force Commendation medal; recipient Cert. of Recognition, Rep. Nat. Com., Washington, 1991. Fellow Am. Soc. Profl. Supts.; mem. Internat. Soc. Exptl. Artists, Internat. Soc. Visual Poetry Artists (dir. emeritus), Acad. Am. Poets, Air Weather Assn. (life). Mem. Ch. of Christ. Avocations: commercial aviation pilot, poetry, photography, North Polar exploration, meteorology. Home: 56 Goodwin Dr Somers CT 06071-0852

HOOPER, EDWIN BICKFORD, physicist; b. Bremerton, Wash., June 18, 1937; s. E.B. and Elizabeth (Patrick) H.; m. Virginia Hooper, Dec. 28, 1963; children: Edwin, Sarah, William. SB, MIT, 1959, PhD, 1965. Asst. prof. applied sci. Yale U., New Haven, 1966-70; physicist, asst. dep. assoc. dir. Lawrence Livermore (Calif.) Nat. Lab., 1970—. Contbr. articles to profl. jours. Pres. Danville (Calif.) Assn., 1982-84; pres. Friends Iron Horse Trail, 1984-86; v.p. San Ramon Valley Edn. Found., 1989-90; dir. leadership, San Ramon Valley, 1990-92. Fellow Am. Phys. Soc. (bd. dirs. div. Plasma Physics 1990-91); mem. AIAA (sr.), Am. Assn. for Advancement Sci. Office: Lawrence Livermore Nat Lab L-637 Livermore CA 94550-4436

HOOPER, GERRY DON, information systems specialist, consultant; b. Durant, Okla., Aug. 11, 1941; s. Carrell and Edith Pauline (Hancock) H.; m. Patricia Ann Reynolds, July 9, 1960; children: Lisa Dawn, Lauri Anne. BS, Southeastern Okla. State U., 1963, postgrad., 1963. Cert. tchr. Tex. Tchr. Amarillo (Tex.) Ind. Sch. Dist., 1963-66; systems analyst VA, Austin, Tex., 1966-68, Svc. Bur. Corp., Dallas, 1968; systems rep. IBM, Dallas, 1968-80, adv. industry specialist, 1980-85; sr. mgmt. cons. IBM, Atlanta, 1985-98. Mem. Am. Prodn. and Inventory Control Soc. Baptist. Avocations: skiing, travel, camping, restoring cars.

HOOPER, HENRY OLCOTT, academic administrator, physicist; b. Washington, Mar. 9, 1935; s. Olcott Lorin and Eleanor (Drew) H.; m. Donna Faulkingham, June 10, 1956 (div. 1992); children: Deborah, Bruce, Katherine, Michael, Andrew; m. Jeanne Riley Hughes, Mar. 2, 1996. B.S. in Engring. Physics, U. Maine, 1956; M.S. in Physics, Brown U., 1959, Ph.D., 1961. Asst. prof. Brown U., Providence, 1961-64; asst. prof. physics Wayne State U., Detroit, 1964-66, assoc. prof., 1966-70, prof., 1970-73; prof., chmn. dept. physics U. Maine, Orono, 1973-76, dean Grad. Sch., 1977-80, v.p. acad. affairs, 1979-80; assoc. v.p. acad. affairs, dean Grad. Coll. No. Ariz. U., Flagstaff, 1981-97, interim v.p. acad. affairs, 1993-95, assoc. provost rsch. and grad. studies, 1995-96, prof. physics, dir. Bilby Rsch. Ctr., 1997—; dir. sci. and math. Learning Ctr., 1998—; cons. NASA, Huntsville, Ala., 1967-68; mem. rev. panel div. ednl. programs Argonne (Ill.) Nat. Lab., 1982-84; mem. exec. bd. Assoc. Western Univs., 1991-97, chair 1995-96; v.p. Nat. Coun. Univ. Rsch. Adminstrs., 1991-92, pres., 1992-93. Author: College Physical Science, 3d edit., 1974, Physics and the Physical Perspective, 1977, 2d rev. edit., 1980; editor: Conf. Procs. Amorphous Magnetism, 1973. Fellow Am. Phys. Soc.; mem. AAAS, Am. Assn. Physics Tchrs. E-mail: henry.hooper@nau.edu. Home: 1300 W University Heights Dr S Flagstaff AZ 86001-8526 Office: No Ariz U PO Box 6013 Flagstaff AZ 86011-4085

HOOPER, IAN (JOHN DEREK GLASS), marketing communications executive; b. London, Sept. 8, 1941; came to U.S., 1979; s. John Desmond Glass and Moira Elizabeth (White) H. Student, Coll. Distributive Trades, London, 1960-62, 65-67, Harvard U., 1979. With S. H. Benson, London, 1960-62, 65-67, Nairobi, Kenya, 1962-64; with McCann-Erickson Advt., London, 1967-79; sr. v.p., group account dir. McCann-Erickson, N.Y.C., 1979-85; exec. v.p., mng. dir. McCann Direct, N.Y.C., 1985-90; sr. v.p., worldwide account dir. Young & Rubicam, N.Y.C., 1990-91; sr. v.p., account dir. Brouillard Communications, N.Y.C., 1991-94; sr. v.p., mktg. dir. DeVries Pub. Rels., N.Y.C., 1994—. Home: 1049 Park Ave New York NY 10028-1061 Office: DeVries Pub Rels 30 E 60th St New York NY 10022-1008

HOOPER, JAMES WILLIAM, educator; b. Tuscumbia, Ala., June 13, 1937; s. John Albert and Stella (Tompkins) H.; m. Mona Elaine Nading, Dec. 27, 1959; children: Bruce, Stacey, Blaine. BS in Math., Florence (Ala.) State Coll., 1959; MS in Math., Auburn (Ala.) U., 1960; MS in Computer Sci., U. Mo., Rolla, 1971; PhD in Computer Info. Sci., U. Ala., Birmingham, 1979. Instr. math. Florence State Coll., 1960-62; data systems analyst NASA Marshall Space Flight Ctr., Huntsville, Ala., 1962-74, data systems engr., 1974-80; assoc. prof. computer sci. U. Ala., Huntsville, 1980-88, prof. computer sci., 1988-93; dir. Ctr. for Environ., Geotech. and Applied Scis. Marshall U., Huntington, W.Va., 1993—, prof., Arthur and Joan Meyer Weisberg Chair software engring, 1991—, exec. dir. Office Rsch. and Econ. Devel., 1996-98, v.p. rsch., 1998—, dean grad. sch. info. tech. and engring., 1998—; mem., bd. dirs. Marshall U. Rsch. Corp., 1993-96, pres., 1996—; cons. computer sci. and software engring.; reviewer jours. and funding agys. Author: (with Rowena O. Chester) Software Reuse: Guidelines and Methods, 1991. Elder Jordan Park Ch. of Christ, Huntsville, 1984-93, 26th St. Ch. of Christ, Huntington, 1994—; bd. dirs. Ann. Nat. Conf. on Software Tech., pres., 1993-94. Recipient Exceptional Svc. medal NASA, 1977; grantee U.S. govt. agys. and several cos., 1983—. Mem. IEEE (Outstanding Educator of Yr., Huntsville sect. 1986-87), IEEE Computer Soc. (pres. Huntsville chpt. 1987-88), Assn. Computing Machinery, Soc. Am. Mil. Engrs., Soc. Computer Simulation, Internat. Assn. Mgmt. Tech., Phi Kappa Phi, Kappa Mu Epsilon, Upsilon Pi Epsilon. Mem. Ch. of Christ. Home: 148 Honeysuckle Ln Huntington WV 25701-4726 Office: Marshall U Marshall U Huntington WV 25755

HOOPER, JOHN ALLEN, retired banker; b. Danbury, Conn., Dec. 9, 1922; s. Kenneth Malcolm and Grace Lillian (Jardon) H.; m. Susanne Leona Sipperly, Nov. 27, 1948; children: Judith Elaine, John Nash. B.B.A., U. Mich., 1947, M.B.A., 1948. With Chase Manhattan Bank, N.Y.C., 1948-85; exec. v.p. Chase Manhattan Bank, 1972-85, sr. v.p., 1964-71, mem. mgmt. com., 1975-85, vice-chmn. bd., 1983-85; chmn. bd., chief exec. officer Bank of the Commonwealth, Detroit, 1971-72. Served with AUS, 1943-46. Decorated Army Commendation medal; named Man of Year, Inst. Human Relations, 1974. Mem. Patterson Club, Wilderness Country Club, Royal Poinciana Golf Club. Home: 100 Tall Pine Ln Apt 2101 Naples FL 34105-2614

HOOPER, JOHN DAVID, coast guard officer; b. Cleveland Heights, Ohio, Jan. 19, 1954; s. George John and Grace Isabelle (Maloney) H.; m. Patricia Ann Boucher, May 13, 1979; children: Katherine Ann, Robert John, Christopher John. AS in Math., Lorain C.C., 1975; BS in Marine Sci., Mass. Maritime Acad., 1979; MS in Nat. Security Affairs, U.S. Naval War Coll., 1994; MA in Mil. Studies, Am. Mil. U., 1999. Lic. deck watch officer afloat, 2d mate unlimited, USCG. Commd. ens. USCG, 1979; marine safety officer USCG, Toledo, 1979-80; divsn., deck watch, boarding officer CGC Bibb, New Bedford, Mass., 1980-82; chief planning-marine info. sect. 7th Coast Guard Dist. (Aids to Navigation Br.), Miami, Fla., 1987-90; civilian staff officer fleet ops., deck-navigation inspector Military Sealift Command Atlantic USN, Bayonne, N.J., 1982-87; exec. officer USCG Res. Unit CGC Gallatin, Gov.'s Island, N.Y., 1983-87; exec. officer, commanding officer USCG Res. Unit CGC Dallas, Gov's Island, N.Y., 1990-95; damage control officer USN, Freehold, N.J., 1990—; Coast Guard Res. liaison, staff officer Coast Guard Atlantic Area-Cutter Mgmt., Portsmouth, Va., 1995-98; instr. CG liaison USN Tactical Tng. Group, Atlantic Dam Neck, Va., 1998—. Lt. USCG, 1979-82. Inductee Naval Order of U.S., 1994. Mem. U.S. Naval Inst., Res. Officers Assn., Naval War Coll. Found., Mass. Maritime Acad. Alumni Assn. Republican. Roman Catholic. Avocations: sailing, tennis. Home: 25 Newbury Rd Howell NJ 07731-2109 Office: USN Military Sealift CMD Tng Ctr-E 1029 State Route 33 Freehold NJ 07728-8440

HOOPER, JOHN EDWARD, retired physicist, researcher; b. Edmonton, Alberta, Can., Dec. 25, 1926; arrived in Denmark, 1952; s. Percival Ralph and Mary Michelina Grant (Ferguson) H.; m. Lizzie Trolle, Sept. 24, 1955 (dec. Apr. 1990); children: Alasdair, Angus. BSc with honors, St. Andrews U., Scotland, 1949; PhD, Bristol U., Eng., 1953. Rsch. visitor Cern Theory Study Group, Copenhagen, 1952-53; Churchill scholar Niels Bohr Inst., Copenhagen, 1954-55, Rask-Oersted scholar, 1955-56, asst., 1957-71; lectr. Neils Bohr Inst., Univ. Copenhagen, Copenhagen, 1972-92; project leader Danish-Swedish Spiral Reader, Stockholm, 1968-71; sci. assoc. Cern, Geneva, 1985-86; ret., 1993; vis. Univ. Tenn., Knoxville, 1961-62. Co-author: The Cosmic Radiation, 1958; designer: (software, specifications) A Spiral Reader for Bubble Chamber Film; designer: Development Plant for Nuclear Emulsions; contbr. articles to profl. jours. Dep. Dansk Magisterforening, Copenhagen, 1972-84. Fellow Soc. Antiquaries Scotland; mem. Am. Phys. Soc., N.Y. Acad. Sci., The Tweeddale Soc. (coun. mem. 1994-99), The Civic Soc., Peeblesshire Archaeol. Soc. (treas. 1994-96, chmn. 1997-99). Avocations: archaeology, early medieval history, geneaology. Home: 38 George St, Peebles EH45-8DL, Scotland

HOOPER, JOSH, screen actor, director, producer, writer; b. Pa., 1952; s. Henry Lloyd and Mary Katherine H.; m. Cynthia Yeiser; children: Spencer, Mason. BA, Franklin & Marshall Coll., 1974. Tchr. Lower Dauphin Sch. Dist., Hummelstown, Pa., 1974-76; prodn. mgr. Sta. WLYH-TV, Lebanon, Pa., 1976-79; producer PM Mag. Sta. WTVH-TV, Syracuse, N.Y., 1979-80; co-host, producer PM Mag. Sta. WGAL-TV, Lancaster, Pa., 1980-83; pres. Josh Hooper Prodns., Inc., Harrisburg, Pa., 1983-94; actor-dir., pres. A Different Look, L.A., 1983-92; broadcast advt. dir. The Bon Ton, York, Pa., 1992-94; pres., creative dir. Zero Gravity Films, Harrisburg, Pa., 1994—; theater dir., N.Y., Pa., Calif., 1974—; co-host Sta. WITF Auction, Hershey, Pa., 1982, 83, Easter Seals Telethon, Harrisburg, 1983, Children's Miracle Network, Lancaster, 1983; directing fellow Am. Film Inst., L.A., 1988-89; improv comedian L.A. Connection, 1989, Public Nuisance, L.A., 1989-92. producer, dir. (TV program) Suite 10:15, 1977; exec. producer (TV kids mag.) Thresholds, 1978; actor (play) Waiting for Godot, 1985, The Winter's Tale, 1986 (film) Station to Freedom, 1987, (TV film) Lucy and Desi: Before The Laughter, 1991; dir. (short film) Collared, 1988, The Point, 1989, Bumper to Bumper, 1989. Mem. Common Cause, Washington, 1980-90; chmn. comms. Three Mile Island Pub. Interest Resource Group, Harrisburg, 1982-84; comm. chair Fox Ridge Neighbors, 1985-87; active Ctr. for Def. Info.; charter mem. Franklin and Marshall Coll. Pres.'s Farwest Adv. Coun.; bd. dirs. Children's Playroom Parent Edn. Ctrs.; mem. Envision Capital Region Task Force. Recipient Addy award Am. Advt. Fedn., 1987, Addy award Cen. Pa. Advt. Fedn., 1985, 87, 88, Telly award, 1987, 88, 89, Gold award Creativity '96; Film Grants Panelist NEH, 1990, Vision award, Mobius award, 1997. Mem. Am. Film Inst. Alumni Assn. (past pres.), SAG, Ctrl. Pa. Ad Club (bd. dirs. 1994, 95), Capital Area Assn. for the Edn. Young Children, Success by Six. Democrat. Episcopalian. Avocations: running, swimming, bicycling, boating.

HOOPER, MARCIA SARITA, pediatric critical care nurse; b. Detroit, Dec. 31, 1954; d. Alphonso and Annie M. (Garland) H. BSN, Mercy Coll. Detroit, 1977; MSN, U. Phoenix, 1998. RN, Mich.; CCRN; cert. pediatric nurse practitioner, clin. nurse mgr.; cert. PALS instr., BCLS instr. Staff nurse Children's Hosp. of Mich., Detroit, 1977-91, preceptor, 1991-98. Mem. AACN (cert. critical care nurse).

HOOPER, PATRICIA, writer; b. May 4, 1941. BA, U. Mich., 1963, MA, 1964. Author: Other Lives, 1984, A Bundle of Beasts, 1987, The Flowering Trees, 1995, At the Corner of the Eye, 1997.

HOOPER, ROBERT ALEXANDER, television producer, international educator; b. Annapolis, Md., Apr. 13, 1947; s. P. Alexander and Louise (Hickey) H.; m. Virginia L. Gordon. BA in Econs., U. Calif., San Diego, 1969; JD, U. Calif., Davis, 1974; MFA in Motion Picture and TV, UCLA, 1982. Bar: Calif. 1975. Film prodr. Scripps Inst. of Oceanography, La Jolla, Calif., 1978-79, EPA, Washington, 1979-81; ind. film prodr. with ABC-TV and CBC, Del Mar, Calif., 1981-84; tv prodr. Sta. KUAC-TV, Fairbanks, Alaska, 1984-86; asst. prof. comm. Boston U., 1986-87; assoc. prof. comm. Loyola Marymount U., L.A., 1987-98; exec. prodr. KPBS-TV, San Diego, 1997—; vis. assoc. prof. U. Calif., San Diego, 1993, 97; cons. CBC, Toronto, 1982-83, Radio-TV Malaysia, 1998, Asia-Pacific inst. for Broadcasting Devel., 1998-99, Fiji TV, 1996; Fulbright sr. scholar comm. program U. Sains Malaysia, Penang, 1989-90, U. South Pacific, Fiji, 1994; tng. adviser Am. Samoa Govt.-Sta. KVZK-TV, 1992—; acad. specialist U. Papua New Guinea, 1995; Eisenhower fellow, Malaysia, 1996, course dir., Asia-Pacific Inst. for Broadcasting Devel., Malaysia, 1998—. Prodr., dir. (documentaries) Voices From Love Canal, 1978, Decisions at 1000 Fathoms, 1981, Battle at Webber Creek, 1985 (Press Club award), Alaska's Killer Whales, 1989 (Cine Golden Eagle and Silver Apple award); segment prodr. (ABC 20/20) The Deep, 1983; exec. prodr. Nature's Classic, 1998 (Press Club award, four Emmy nominations), Afoot and Afield, 1998, The Impossible Railroad, 1999; op.-editor writer, L.A. Times, San Diego Union-Tribune, 1999. Eisenhower fellow, Malaysia, 1996; recipient Hennessy trophy Internat. Environ. Film Festival, Paris, 1983. Mem. NATAS, Calif. Bar Assn., Eisenhower Fellows Assn., Sigma Delta Chi. Democrat. Avocation: underwater photography. Office: KPBS-TV 5200 Campanile Dr San Diego CA 92182-5400

HOOPER, ROGER FELLOWES, architect, retired; b. Southampton, N.Y., Aug. 18, 1917; s. Roger Fellowes and Justine Van Rensselaer (Barber) H.; m. Patricia Bentley, Aug. 10, 1946; children: Judith Bayard Teresi, Rachel Bentley Zingg, Roger Fellowes III. AB, Harvard U., 1939, MArch, 1948. Ptnr. Malone & Hooper, San Francisco, 1949-60; ptnr., pres. Hooper Olmsted & Emmons, San Francisco, 1964-79; chmn. Hooper Olmsted & Hrovat, San Francisco, 1980-94, retired, 1994. Bd. mgr. Marin YMCA, San Rafael, Calif.; bd. dirs., pres. Marin Conservation League, San Rafael. Lt. comdr. USNR, 1941-45, WWII. Mem. AIA.

HOOPER, ROY B., home health consultant, insurance broker, lobbyist; b. Lawton, Okla., Mar. 19, 1947; s. Roy Basil and Frances (Castle) H.; m. Lawanna Sue James, Aug. 2, 1969; children: Blake, Mark. BS, Cameron U., 1971. Registered lobbyist GTE S.W. for Okla., Okla. Youth Svcs., Okla. Ind. Auto Dealers Assn., Southwestern Med. Ctr. Healthback. Real estate broker Lawton, 1968-90; rep. State of Okla., Lawton, 1974-86, senator, 1986-94; ins. broker Lawton, 1966—; dir. managed care Southwestern Med. Ctr., Lawton, 1994-99, HealthBack, Oklahoma City, 1999—. Pres. Cameron Former Students Assn., Lawton, 1974, Lawton Crimestoppers Orgn., 1996, S.W. chpt. Am. Heart Assn., 1995-96, Lawton Pub. Sch. Found., 1998; v.p. Lawton Bd. Realtors, 1974, KTRO, Lawton Pub. Schs. Found., Pres.'s Ptnrs. Cameron U.; councilman Ward 2, Lawton, 1972-74. Sgt. USAR, 1968-74. Democrat. Baptist. Avocations: hunting, fishing, golf, horse back riding, gardening. Office: PO Box 425 Lawton OK 73502-0425

HOOPER, STEVEN W., communications executive. D in Civil Engring., Seattle U.; MBA, Wharton Sch. Asst. v.p., mgr. internal fin. consulting Seattle First Nat. Bank; corp. contr., treas. McGraw, 1982-86, exec. v.p., chief operating officer of cable divsn.; pres. Cellular One's Pacific Northwest/Rocky Mountain region AT&T Wireless Svcs. Inc., chief fin. officer; pres., chief exec. officer AT&T Wireless Svcs. Inc., Kirkland, Wash., until 1996; co-CEO Teledesic, Kirkland, 1997—; chmn., CEO NEXTLINK Comm. Inc., 1999—; bd. dirs. U. Prep, Seattle U. MBA Program; chair. U. Prep Fin. Com.; active Seattle U. Mentor Program. Office: Teledesic 2300 Carillon Pt Kirkland WA 98033-7353*

HOOPER, TOBE, film director; b. Austin, Tex., 1943. Asst. dir. dept. film U. Tex. Dir.: (films) The Texas Chainsaw Massacre, 1974, Eaten Alive, 1977, The Funhouse, 1981, Poltergeist, 1982, Lifeforce, 1985, Invaders from Mars, 1986, The Texas Chainsaw Massacre II, 1986, (TV film) Salem's Lot, 1979. Office: care Internat Creative Mgmt 3100 N Damon Way Burbank CA 91505-1015*

HOOPER, WAYNE NELSON, clergy member; b. Toronto, Ont., Can., May 25, 1944; s. Earl Edward and Ruby Evelyn (Nelson) H.; m. Diane Elizabeth, Aug. 24, 1968; children: Tanya Joy, Craig Nelson. BA, McMaster U., 1967; MDiv, Gordon-Conwell Theol. Sem., 1970. Ordained to ministry Baptist Ch., 1970. Asst. pastor Emmanuel Bapt. Ch., Cambridge, Mass., 1967-68, First Bapt. Ch., Braintree, Mass., 1968-70; pastor Uxbridge (Ont.) Bapt. Ch., Can., 1970-73; founding pastor Credit Valley Bapt. Ch., Mississauga, Ont., Can., 1973-79; sr. pastor First Bapt. Ch., Orillia, Ont., Can., 1979-83, Avenue Rd. Bapt. Ch., Cambridge, Ont., Can., 1986-98; asst. sec. dept. Can. Missions Bapt. Conv. Ont. and Que., 1983-86; sr. pastor First Baptist Dartmouth Ch., Nova Scotia, Can., 1998—. Contbr. articles to profl. jours. Mem. recruitment com. Bapt. Conv. Ont. and Que., 1973-75, mem. planning com., 1978-80, mem. coun., 1976-82, mem. exec. com., 1977-78, ctrl. sect. rep., 1982-83; conv. staff rep. Ottawa and N.W. Assns., 1983-86; Bapt. Conv. Ont. and Que. rep. to Inter-Church Regional Planning Assn., 1983-86; mem. Canadian Baptist Ministries Coun., 1995—. Mem. Can. Bapt. Fedn. (v.p. 1988-91, pres. 1991-94). Avocations: sports, boating, skiing, tennis, golf. Home: PO Box 186 Dartmouth, Nova Scotia, ON Canada B2Y 3Y3*

HOOPER, WILLIAM EDWARD, broadcast journalist; b. Tampa, Fla., Mar. 10, 1964; s. Dennis William and Doris Jean (Burkhart) H. Student, U. Tenn., 1984-87; degree cert., Profl. Acad. Broadcasting, Knoxville, Tenn., 1988. Traffic reporter K-Trans, Knoxville, 1987-93; news dir. Sta. WNOX-FM, Knoxville, 1988-90, Sta. WWZZ-FM, Knoxville, 1991-93; news reporter Sta. WKXT-TV, Knoxville, 1993-96; creator, editor Tenn. Online, 1996—; editor Tenn. Star Jour., Pigeon Forge, Tenn.; host, writer Radio Appalachia, Knoxville, 1987-92, Celebrate Knoxville, 1991, WKXT's Tenn. Bicentennial Minute, 1995; feature writer Foothills mag., Knoxville, 1993; host, prodr. Viewpoint Talkshow, 1994-96, freelance writing, 1998—. Author: (broadcast reports) Public Access Denied: Tennessee Statute 40-23-116; syndicated columnist Banjo Newsletter, 1981; author Looking Back Column, 1997—; guest columnist So. Partisan mag., Appalachian Quar. mag.; ednl. cons. Treas. Knoxville Juvenile Diabetes Assn., 1989; trustee Nat. Medal of Honor Mus. of Mil. History, Chattanooga, 1998—; project mgr. The South Found., 1997—; bd. dirs. Tenn. Civil War Preservation Assn., 1998—. Recipient Cert. of Appreciation, Knoxville Transit Co., 1993, Cert. of Merit, Tenn. Hist. Commn., So. Journalism award 1996, Tenn. Jefferson Davis Media award 1996, Cert. of Appreciation City of Knoxville, 1996, Robert E. Lee Media award Tenn. divsn. SCV, 1996, Merit award Tenn. Gov., 1996, Cmty. Svc. award Knox County Commn., 1996, Horace V. Wells Cmty. Svc. award East Tenn. Soc. Profl. Journalists, 1996, Cert. of Merit, Tenn. Hist. Commn., 1996, 97, 98, Hist. Preservation award West Tenn. Sons Confederate Nat. Pk., 1997, SCV Commander's Awd. for historical preservation, 1999, Golden Press Card Investigative Reporting, 1999, Golden Press Card Gen. News Reporting, 1999, Comdr.'s award SCV, 1999, Cert. of Merit, Tenn. Hist. Commn., 1999, Pub. Svc. in Journalism award Tenn. Press Assn., 1999. Mem. Soc. Profl. Journalists (1st pl. award for radio feature reporting Atlanta chpt. 1990, Investigative Reporting award Atlanta chpt. 1994, TV-Feature Reporting award 1995, TV Deadline News award 1995, So. Journalist award 1996), East Tenn. Soc. Profl. Journalists (1st place Investigative Reporting award 1999, 1st place Gen. News Reporting award 1999, 2d place Deadline Photography award 1999), Investigative Reporters and Editors, Masons (historian Knoxville 1990—, Meritorious cert. 1991, 92). Avocations: musician, horseback riding, whitewater caneoing, hunting, archaeology. Office: WE Hooper and Assocs 920 Yarbrough Ln Gatlinburg TN 37738-3442

HOOPES, FARREL G., secondary education educator. Tchr. Star Valley H.S., Afton, Wyo. Recipient Tchr. Excellence award Internat. Tech. Edn. Assn., 1992. Office: Star Valley HS PO Box 8000 Afton WY 83110*

HOOPES, JANET LOUISE, educator, psychologist; b. Phila., Mar. 5, 1923; d. Raymond Talmage and Pearl H. (Jacobs) H.; m. John E. Gausmann, June 11, 1977; children: Lenoir Gausmann Heilman, Eric J. AB, Bryn Mawr Coll., 1944, PhD, 1965; M in Clin. Psychology, U. Mich., 1948. Jr. psychologist Rochester (N.Y.) Guidance Ctr., 1948-51; psychologist Children's Aid Soc. Pa., Phila., 1951-58, chief psychologist, 1958-70; prof. edn. and child devel. Bryn Mawr (Pa.) Coll., 1970-85, prof. emeritus, 1985—; bd. dirs. Hill Top Prep. Sch., Rosemont, Pa., 1971—. Author: An Infant Rating Scale: Its Validation and Usefulness, 1967, A Follow-Up Study of Adoptions: The Functioning of the Children, 1970, Prediction in Child Development: A Longitudinal Study of Adoptive and Non-Adoptive Families-The Delaware Family Study, 1982, Identity Formation in the Adopted Adolescent, 1985, Adoption & Identity Formation, 1990, Formal Adoption of the Developmentally Vulnerable African-American Child: Ten-Year Outcomes, 1997. Bd. dirs. Children's Aid Soc. Pa., Phila., 1987. Served as ensign Med. Service Corps, USNR, 1944-46. Mem. APA, Pa. Psychol. Assn., Orton Dyslexia Soc., Lansdowne Symphony Orch. Assn. (bd. dirs. 1989—). Presbyterian (elder 1967—). Home: 173 Marlyn Rd Lansdowne PA 19050-1807 Office: Bryn Mawr Coll West House Bryn Mawr PA 19010

HOOPES, TOWNSEND WALTER, business consultant, former government official; b. Duluth, Minn., Apr. 28, 1922; s. Henry Townsend and Edna Andrea (Mortrued) H.; m. Ann Merrifield, Oct. 17, 1964; 1 dau., Andrea; children by previous marriage: Townsend Walter III, Peter Schmidt; stepchildren: Marsha, Cecily, Briggs, Thomas. Grad., Phillips Acad., Andover, Mass., 1940; AB in Econs., Yale U., 1944. Editl. writer Buffalo Evening News, 1946; asst. to chmn. com. armed svcs. Ho. of Reps., Washington, 1947-48, asst. to sec. def., 1948-53; student Nat. War Coll., 1950-51; dep. asst. sec. def. internat. security affairs Dept. Def., Washington, 1965-66, prin. dep. asst. sec. def. internat. security affairs, 1966-67, undersec. air force, 1967-69; asst. to pres. Spencer Chem. Co., 1953-55; assoc. J.H. Whitney & Co., 1955-57; ptnr. Cresap, McCormick & Paget, 1958-64, v.p., dir. Washington office, 1969-71; also corporate dir.; pres. Assn. Am. Publishers, Washington and N.Y.C., 1973-86; vice chmn. AIDS Therapy Inst., 1995—; cons. on orgn. NSC, 1954, Dept. State Dept. Def., 1957; sec. mil. panel spl. studies project Rockefeller Bros. Fund, 1957-58; cons. Pres.'s Com. on USIA Abroad, 1960. Co-prodr. mus. theatrical co. Hoopes Troupe, 1985—; author: The Limits of Intervention, 1970, The Devil and John Foster Dulles, 1973, Townsend Hoopes on Arms Control, 1987; co-author: Eye Power, 1979, Driven Patriot: The Life and Times of James Forrestal, 1992, FDR and the Creation of the UN, 1997; contbr. articles to profl. jours. Bd. dirs. Com. for Nat. Security, 1978-88, Am. Com. on U.S.-Soviet Rels., Washington, 1980-92. With USMC, 1943-46. Named Disting. Internat. Exec., U. Md., 1991; fellow Woodrow Wilson Internat. Center Scholars, 1971-73. Mem. Coun. Fgn. Rels., Yale Club, Century Club (N.Y.C.), Chevy Chase Club (Md.), Fed. City Club (Washington), Fairfield Country Club (Conn.).

HOOPLE, SALLY CROSBY, retired humanities and communications educator; b. Dansville, N.Y., Oct. 23, 1930; d. Thomas Joseph and Lucille Esther (Rex) Crosby; m. Donald G. Hoople, June 3, 1951; children: Nancy, Anne Ralte, Douglas, David. BA, Syracuse U., 1952, MA, 1953; MA, NYU, 1971; PhD, Fordham U., 1984. Tchr. ESL, citizenship Adult Edn., Syracuse, N.Y., 1953-56, Oneida, N.Y., 1956-62; tchr. ESL Cambridge Bus. Sch., N.Y.C., 1962-63; tchr. English White Plains (N.Y.) H.S., 1963-86; prof. humanities and comms. Maine Maritime Acad., Castine, 1986-96; ret., 1996; fgn. expert tchg. history and composition Henan Normal U., Xinxiang, China, 1997-98, China Agrl. U., Beijing, 1999. Contbr. Dictionary of Literary Biography, 1994, Oxford Companion to Women's Writing in the U.S., 1994, Dictionary of Art, 1996, articles to profl. jours., newletters. Mem. Am. Lit. Soc., NCTE (chair com. pub. doublespeak 1996-99), Melville Soc., MLA, Phi Beta Kappa. Democrat. Episcopalian. Avocations: music, reading, hiking, boating, bicycling, swimming. Home: PO Box 184 Castine ME 04421-0184

HOOPS, ALAN, health care company executive; b. 1947. Asst. administr. Long Beach Mem. Hosp., 1973-77; v.p. PacifiCare Health Sys. Inc., Cypress, Calif., 1977-85, sec., from 1982, sr. v.p., 1985-86, COO, exec. v.p., 1986-93, chmn., CEO, 1993—. Office: Pacificare Health Systems Inc PO Box 25185 Santa Ana CA 92799-5186*

HOOPS, WILLIAM JAMES, clergyman; b. Welch, Okla., June 10, 1957; s. Paul Raymond and Bertha Lue (Stillwell) H.; m. Susan Denise Towers, May 12, 1983; 1 child, Robert Paul. BA, Okla. Bapt. U., 1983; MDiv, Golden Gate Sem., 1987. Ordained to ministry So. Bapt. Ch., 1987. Ministerial intern 1st Bapt. Ch., Concord, Calif., 1984-87; pastor 1st Bapt. Ch., Marina, Calif., 1987-91; chaplain USAFR, Travis AFB, Calif., 1975—; instl. min. Fed. Bur. Prisons, Fed. Correctional Instn., Lompoc, Calif., 1991-99, Intensive Confinement Ctr., Lompoc, 1996-99, Fed. Correctional Instn., Allenwood, Pa., 1999—. Producer TV documentary Insights, 1986-87. Bible tchr. 1st So. Bapt. Ch., Lompoc, 1991-99. Capt. USAFR, 1975—. Mem. Air Force Assn., Res. Officers Assn., Calif. So. Bapt. Conv. (revival steering com. 1988-90), Ctrl. Coast Bapt. Assn. (vice moderator 1987-88, dir. evangelism 1988-91), Pacific Coast Bapt. Assn., Lompoc Fed. Correctional Instn. Employees Club (sec. 1991-92), Ctrl. Coast Ministrial Alliance (pres. 1988-89), Calif. Campers on Mission (pres. 1995-98, v.p. 1998-99). Avocation: recreational vehicle camping.

HOORNSTRA, EDWARD H., retail company executive; b. Sault Ste Marie, Mich., 1921; married. Pres. Pik-N-Pak Food Stores, 1952-65; pres. Li'l Gen. Stores, 1965-69; with Gen. Host Co., Stamford, Conn., 1968—, v.p. ops., 1968-70, pres., 1970-74, vice chmn., 1974-87; pres. Del-Tem Investments, Clearwater, Fla., 1987—; dir. Gen. Host Corp., Stamford, Conn. Served with U.S. Army, 1940-45. Lodges: Shriners; Masons. Home: 2321 Kent Pl Clearwater FL 33764-7566

HOORT, STEVEN THOMAS, lawyer; b. Grand Rapids, Mich., Sept. 18, 1949; s. Allard Hoort and Margaret J. (Vanderkooy) Koens; m. Nancy E. Redmon, Mar. 18, 1978; 1 child, Kendra. BA with high honors, Grand Valley State Coll., Allendale, Mich., 1972; JD magna cum laude, U. Mich., 1975. Bar: Mich. 1977, U.S. Dist. Ct. (ea. dist.) Mich. 1977, Mass. 1978, U.S. Dist. Ct. Mass. 1978, U.S. Ct. Appeals (1st cir.) 1978, U.S. Dist. Ct. (we. dist.) Mich. 1993. Law clk. U.S. Dist. Ct. (ea. dist.) Mich., Bay City, Mich., 1975-78; assoc. Ropes & Gray, Boston, 1978-84, ptnr., 1984--. Mem. ABA (bus. law sect.), Boston Bar Assn., Order of Coif. Office: Ropes & Gray 1 International Pl Boston MA 02110-2602

HOOTMAN, HARRY EDWARD, retired nuclear engineer, consultant; b. Oak Park, Ill., June 5, 1933; s. Merle Albert and Rachel Edith (Atkinson) H.; m. Linda P. Smith, Nov. 23, 1963; children: David, Holly, John. BS in Chemistry, Mich. Technol. U., 1959, MS in Nuc. Engring., 1962; LLB, LaSalle Ext. U., 1971, MA in English Lit., U. S.C., 1999. Registered profl. engr., S.C. Rsch. assoc. Argonne (Ill.) Nat. Lab., 1959-62; process engr. Savannah River Plant, Aiken, S.C., 1962-65; rsch. assoc. reactor physics group, nuclear engring. div. Savannah River Lab., Aiken, 1965-87; with New Reactor Devel. Group, 1987-92, adv. engr. Planning, Studies and Analysis, 1992-95; ret., 1995; cons. transuranic waste disposal and incineration, radioisotope prodn., separation and shielding; instr. Math. and Engring. Dept. U. S.C., Aiken, 1979-80, 90-94. Inventor alpha waste incinerator. Bd. dirs. Central Savannah River Area Sci. and Engring. Fair, Inc., Augusta, Ga., 1972-91. Served to sgt. USAF, 1953-57. Mem. Am. Acad. Environ. Engrs., Nat. Soc. Profl. Engrs. (local chmn. 1978-79), Am. Nuclear Soc. (local chmn. 1979-80), Am. Phys. Soc., Sigma Xi. Baptist. Home: 820 Brandy Rd Aiken SC 29801-7281

HOOTS, CHARLES WAYNE, principal; b. Pittsfield, Ill., Nov. 17, 1953; s. Merle Wayne and Shirley Mae (Saling) H.; m. Diane Kay Sawyer, Aug. 21, 1976; 1 child, Elizabeth Anne. AA, Lewis & Clark Coll., 1973; BA, Blackburn Coll., 1976; MA, U. Ill., Springfield, 1983; postgrad., Western Ill. U., 1995—. Tchr. Porta Jr.-Sr. H.S., Petersburg, Ill., 1977-78; tchr. New Berlin (Ill.) H.S., 1978-80, dean of students, 1980-84, asst. prin., 1984-85, prin., 1985-92; asst. prin. Glenwood H.S., Chatham, Ill., 1992-95; prin. Glenwood H.S., Chatham, 1995—; presenter in field. Author: Alternative to Suspension, 1995. Mayor Village of New Berlin, Ill., 1989-93, trustee, 1996—. Mem. ASCD, Nat. Assn. Sch. Adminstrs., Nat. Assn. Secondary Sch. Prins, Ill. Prins. Assn., Phi Kappa Phi. Episcopalian. Home: 123 Heritage Pt New Berlin IL 62670-6409 Office: Glenwood HS 595 Chatham Rd Chatham IL 62629-8000

HOOVER, BETTY-BRUCE HOWARD, private school educator; b. Wake County, N.C., Mar. 20, 1939; d. Bruce Ruffin and Mary Elizabeth (Brown) Howard; m. Herbert Charles Marsh Hoover, Sept. 3, 1961; children: David Andrew, Howard Webster, Lorraine Hoover Clark. BA, Wake Forest U., 1961; MA, U. South Fla., 1978. Tchr. English Greensboro (N.C.) Sr. H.S., 1961-62, Lindley Jr. H.S., Greensboro, 1963, Bekeley Prep. Sch., Tampa, Fla., 1976—; chmn. English dept. Bekeley Prep. Sch., Tampa, 1977-85, dir., dean upper divsn., 1984—, chmn. curriculum com., 1982-86. Author: Resources in Education, 1992. Pres., Suncoast Midshipmen Parents Club, Tampa Bay Area, 1983-84. Mem. ASCD, Nat. Coun. Tchrs. English, Sociedad Honoraira Hispanica, The Nat. Coun. States, Wake Forest U. Alumni Assn., DAR, Hillsborough County Bar Aux., Cum Laude Soc. (sec. 1981—), Nat. Honor Soc., Phi Beta Kappa, Phi Sigma Iota, Sigma Tau Delta, Kappa Kappa Gamma. Republican. Episcopalian. Avocations: sewing, gardening. Home: 11902 Wandsworth Dr Tampa FL 33626-2611 Office: Berkeley Preparatory Sch 4811 Kelly Rd Tampa FL 33615-5020

HOOVER, CAROL FAITH, publisher; b. Eagle Grove, Iowa, Jan. 24, 1921; d. Calvin Bryce and Faith Sprole Hoover; 1 child, Sheila Faith. BA, Duke U., 1940; MSSW, U. N.C., 1947; DSW, Cath. U., 1973. Pres. Ariadne Press, Washington and Rockville, Md., 1976—. Editor: Write an Uncommonly Good Novel, 1990 (Fiction prize 1993). Pres. Self Help for Equal Rights, 1973-76, Women's Coun. NIMH, 1980's. Mem. Writers Mentor Group. Democrat. Episcopalian. Home: 4817 Tallahassee Ave Rockville MD 20853

HOOVER, DAVID CARLSON, lawyer; b. Waterville, Maine, Apr. 22, 1950; s. Jack Cauldwell and Mary Elizabeth (Donavan) H.; m. Kathleen Delia Powell, June 28, 1981; children: Maegan Elizabeth, Peter Daniel, Christian Shaw. BA, U. N.H., 1972; JD cum laude, Suffolk U., 1976. Bar: Mass. 1977, U.S. Dist. Ct. Mass. 1982, U.S. Supreme Ct. 1982, U.S. Ct. Appeals (1st cir.) 1983. Atty. advisor NOAA, Washington, 1976-79; gen. counsel Mass. Div. Marine Fisheries, Boston, 1979-83; spl. asst. atty. gen. Mass. Dept. Atty. Gen., Boston, 1980—; gen. counsel Mass. Dept. of Fisheries, Wildlife and Environ. Law Enforcement, Boston, 1983—; adminstrv. law judge Commonwealth of Mass., 1979; lectr. Franklin Pierce Law Ctr., Concord, N.H., 1984. Mem. editorial bd. Territorial Sea Jour., U. of Maine Sch. of Law; contbr. articles to profl. jours. Ch. lector; tchr. Cath. Youth Orgn.; vol. New England Shelter for Homeless Vets.; exec. dir. Mass. Wildcats AAU Basketball Club. Recipient Am. Jurisprudence award Lawyers Cooperative Pub. Co. Mem. Mass. Bar Assn., Com. on Chemical Dependency, Atty. advisor to Mock-Trial Tournament, Law Related Edn. Com., Lawyers Concerned for Lawyers, Internat. Assn. of Approved Basketball Offcls. Avocations: miniaturist, woodworking, civil war history, coaching youth basketball. Home: 808 Watertown St Newton MA 02465-2116 Office: Dept Fisheries Wildlife and Environ Law Enforcement 100 Cambridge St Rm 1901 Boston MA 02202-0044

HOOVER, DAVONNA MARIA, primary education educator; b. Hagerstown, Md., Aug. 5, 1937; d. David Hildebrand and Frances Elizabeth (Moore) H. BEd in Elem. Edn., Coll. Notre Dame Md., 1970; MEd in Elem. Edn., Loyola Coll., Balt., 1985. Joined Sch. Sisters of Notre Dame, Balt., 1955-86; profl. cert. in religion. Tchr. grades 1-2 St. Gerard's Cath. Sch., Ft. Oglethorpe, Ga., 1957-58; tchr. grades 2-3 Sacred Heart of Jesus, Balt., 1958-68; tchr. grade 3 Our Lady of Perpetual Help Acad., Ybor City, Tampa, Fla., 1968-75; tchr. phys. edn. and art grades 1-5 Holy Spirit Cluster-Lower, Balt., 1975-79; tchr. grade 3 St. Augustine's Sch., Elkridge, Md., 1979-82; tchr. grade 3 Madonna Cath. Sch., Balt., 1982—, vice prin., 1990-94. Volleyball City Tampa (Fla.) Recreation Dept., 1971-75, softball, 1974-75. Named Outstanding Elem. Tchr. Am., Washington, 1975; Valley Forge (Pa.) Freedom Found. grantee, 1975. Mem. ASCD, Nat. Cath. Edn. Assn., Va. Geneal. Soc., Germanna Colony Va. (life). Roman Catholic. Avocations: percussionist folk mass, amateur genealogist, before sch. care provider, elem. sch. choir dir.

HOOVER, DEBORAH, critical care, medical and surgical nurse; b. Bay St. Louis, Miss., Apr. 1, 1958; d. Donald Terence and Mary Mauvereen (Graham) Ball; m. Harold Hoover, Jan. 16, 1982; children: Harold Ryan, Carolyn Mauvereen. BSN, Miss. Coll., Clinton, 1991; LPN, Jones Jr. Coll., Ellisville, Miss., 1980; AA, Jones Jr. Coll., 1982. Pvt. duty nurse Upjohn Health Care, Baton Rouge, 1984; charge nurse Zachary (La.) Manor Nursing Home, 1984; staff nurse Hinds Gen. Hosp., Jackson, Miss., 1982-83, Jones County Community Hosp., Laurel, Miss., 1979-82; 3-11 supr. Clinton (Miss.) Country Manor, 1983-84, 85-86; charge nurse Tracehaven Nursing Home, Vicksburg, Miss., 1986-87; staff nurse Vicksburg (Miss.) Med. Ctr., 1987-91; nurse mgr. ICU Vicksburg Med. Ctr., 1991—, nurse dir. emergency rm., 1992—, asst. chief nursing officer, critical care dir., 1994, critical care and emergency dept. dir., 1996—, pain mgmt. dir., 1999—; acute care nurse practitioner grad. program UMC Sch. Nursing. Mem. AACN, ANA, Miss. Nurses Assn., Student Nurses Assn., Emergency Nurses Assn., Miss. Coll. Nursing Honor Soc., C. of C. (amb.), Lions, Sigma Theta Tau, Alpha Chi. Baptist. Home: 120 Post Oak Ln Vicksburg MS 39180-7686

HOOVER, DONALD LEROY, construction executive; b. Lancaster, Pa., May 28, 1952; s. E. Leroy and Arlene M. (Pickel) H.; m. Sharon Lee Horne, Aug. 15, 1973; children: Steven, Andrew. Student, Millersville U., 1970-71, U. Wis., 1977. Analyst materials Schick Inc., Lancaster, 1970-75; mgr. bus. Reitz Concrete Constrn., Neffsville, Pa., 1976-77; pres. Hoover-Kemp Inc., Lancaster, 1977-83; sec./treas. Oberholtzer Constrn. Inc., East Petersburg, Pa., 1987-88; pres. Indsl. Restorations Ltd., East Petersburg, 1983-92, Donald L. Hoover, Lancaster, 1992—; dir. Teen Challenge Tng. Ctr.,

Rehresburg, Pa., 1983-98, sec., mem. vice-chmn. exec. com., 1989-98; mem. adv. bd. High Constrn., Inc., Lancaster, 1987-88. Treas. New Life Assembly of God, Lancaster, 1982-86, 88-94, also bd. dirs., 1987-88, 92-94; exec. v.p. Strasburg-Willow St. Baseball/Softball Assn. Mem. Meadia Heights Golf Club, Strasburg Athletic Assn. (pres., bd. dirs. 1994-97). Republican. Avocations: coaching baseball, travel. Home: 1909 Edisonville Rd Strasburg PA 17579-9622 Office: 203C Greenfield Rd Lancaster PA 17601-5816

HOOVER, GEORGE SCHWEKE, architect; b. Chgo., July 1, 1935; s. George Milton and Antoinette (Schweke) H.; children: Sandra Jean, Ranya Sue; m. Mary Elizabeth Benoit, June 6, 1987. BArch., Cornell U., 1958. Registered architect, Colo., Calif., Tex., Minn., Ala., Tenn. Draftsman Holabird Root and Burgee, Chgo., 1957, Designer James Sudler Assocs., Denver, 1961-62; architect Ream, Quinn Assocs., Denver, 1962-65, Muchow Assocs., Denver, 1965-76; prin. Hoover Berg Desmond, Denver, 1976—; tenured prof. arch. U. Colo. Coll. Arch. and Planning, chmn. dept. arch., 1997—; vis. lectr. U. N.Mex., Okla. State U., Harvard U., Miami U. Prin. works include Douglas County Adminstrn. Bldg., Light of the World Cath. Ch., U. Colo. Bldg., Denver, Denver Diagnostic and Reception Ctr., Labs for Atmospheric and Space Physics, U. Colo., Boulder, Colo. Acad. Master Plan, U. Ariz. Engring. Complex Master Plan, Multipurpose Arena, Nat. Western Stockshow, Nat. Wild Animal Rsch. Ctr., Colo. State U. Conf. Ctr., Storage Tech. Corp., Aerospace & Mech. Engring. Bldg. U. Ariz., Environ. and Natural Resources Bldg. U. Ariz., Master Plan Cummins Power Generation Group Hdqs., Fridley, Minn., Master Plan Fleetguard and Mfg. Plant, Cookeville, Tenn.; finalist Denver Cen. Libr. Competition, 1991; exhbn. Gund Hall Gallery, Grad. Sch. Design, Harvard U., 1986; mem. editl. bd. Avant Garde. Lt. (j.g.) USN, 1958-61. Recipient 1st Design award Progressive Arch., 1972, Citation, 1974, Design award, 1984, 87, Charles Goodwin Sands Medal for excellence in design Tau Beta Pi, Fed. Design Achievement award, 1984, Honor award Interfaith Forum on Religion, Art, and Arch., 1986, Tau Sigma Delta medal, 1991; named Outstanding Young Architect, Archtl. Record, 1974,. Fellow AIA (steering com., Pitts. Corning award 1989, Nat. Honor award 1975, 83, 90, Firm of Yr. award Colo. chpt. 1991, Regional Firm of Yr. award 1992, Architect of Yr. award Colo. chpt. 1995), Nat. Acad. Design.; mem. Nat. Com. Design (steering com., chmn. awards task group 1989-92), Nat. Com. Archtl. Edn. (steering com. 1990-92). Episcopalian. Home: 320 Humboldt St Denver CO 80218-3934 Office: Art Hoover Desmond Arch 1645 Grant St Denver CO 80203-1601 also: U Colo 1250 14th St Denver CO 80202-1712*

HOOVER, JOHN ELWOOD, former military officer, consultant, writer; b. Timberville, Va., Apr. 28, 1924; s. Saylor Cornelius and Ruby Mae (Brill) H.; m. Mary Jo Cox, May 17, 1953; children: Mary Kathryn, Holly Bullock. Student, Bridgewater (Va.) Coll., 1941-43, Amherst (Mass.) Coll., 1943-44; BS, U.S. Mil. Acad., 1947; MA, Georgetown U., 1955; postgrad., Columbia U., 1955-56, U.S. Army Command and Gen. Staff Coll., Ft. Leavenworth, Kans., 1958-59, U.S. Army War Coll., Carlisle Barracks, Pa., 1962-63. Commd. 2d lt. U.S. Army, 1947, advanced through grades to maj. gen., 1971; with 24th Inf. Div., Japan and Korea, 1948-51, Ft. Gordon, Ga., 1951-53; faculty dept. social scis. U.S. Mil. Acad., 1955-58; bn. comdr. U.S. Army, Fed. Republic of Germany, 1959-60, Hdqrs. U.S. Army Europe, Fed. Republic of Germany, 1961-62; with Office Asst. Sec. Def. for Internat. Security Affairs, Washington, 1963-66; chief communications plans Hdqrs. Pacific Command, Hawaii, 1966-69, group comdr. Vietnam, 1969-70; exec. officer, then dir. communications systems, then dep. asst. chief staff for communication-electronics Hdqrs. Dept. Army, Washington, 1970-73; dep. comdg. gen. U.S. Army Communications Command, Ft. Huachuca, Ariz., 1973-74; dir. Joint Tactical Communications Office, Office Sec. Def., Ft. Monmouth, N.J., 1974-78; ret., 1978; cons. command, control, communications and mgmt.; historian emeritus U.S. Army Signal Rgt.; author and speaker on U.S. mil. communications history. Decorated D.S.M., Legion of Merit with oak leaf cluster, Bronze Star with oak leaf cluster, Meritorious Svc. medal, Air medal with oak leaf cluster, Joint Svc. Commendation medal; Staff Svc. medal (Republic of Vietnam); Vietnam Gallantry Cross with palm; Order Mil. Merit (Republic of Korea). Mem. Assn. Grads. U.S. Mil. Acad., Signal Corps Assn., Warner Robins Rotary.

HOOVER, KENNETH RAY, political science educator, writer; s. Lee Armstrong and Margaret Anne Hoover; m. Judith Ann Maybee; children: Andrew, Erin. BS, Beloit (Wis.) Coll., 1962; MS, U. Wis., 1965, PhD, 1970. Asst. prof. U. Wis., Whitewater, 1964-70; assoc. prof. Coll. of Wooster, Ohio, 1970-78, U. Wis.-Parkside, Kenosha, 1978-88; prof. Western Wash. U., Bellingham, 1988—; chair dept. polit. sci. Western Wash. U., 1988-95, pres. faculty senate, 1995-96. Co-author: Conservative Capitalism, 1989, Ideology and Political Life, 2d edit., 1994, Elements of Social Science, 6th edit., 1995, The Power of Identity, 1997. Mem. sr. commons room St. Catherine's Coll., Oxford, 1997. Recipient Best Article award Utopian Studies Jour., 1994; hon. fellow U. Southampton Internat. Ctr., 1987-88. Avocations: sailing, cross-country skiing, woodworking. Office: Dept Polit Sci Western Wash U Arntzen Hall 415 MS 9082 Bellingham WA 98225

HOOVER, LYNN DI SHONG, psychotherapist, health care consultant; b. Oakland, Calif., Nov. 11, 1949; d. John J. and Phyllis (Beard) Field; m. James A. Hoover III, Apr. 4, 1956; children: Rebecca D., Jeffrey A. BA, U. Md., Balt., 1975, MSW, 1976; postgrad., U. Pa., 1982. Cert. social worker; lic. social worker, Md. Coord. clin. svcs. Big Bros./Big Sisters of Del., 1976-80; dist. supr. Md. Children and Family Svcs., 1980-83; clin. mem. Am. Assn. for Marriage and Family Therapy, 1983—; pvt. practice, 1984—; prin. The Hoover Assocs., Wexford, Pa., 1997-99. Author, prodr., actor: Julian's Revelations, 1996; contbr. articles to profl. jours. Lector, eucharistic minister, organizer prayer ministry, children's svcs. Sts. John and Paul Cath. Ch., Sewickley, Pa., 1994-99. Mem. Assn. Ind. Info. Profls., Collaborative Family Healthcare Coalition. Avocations: writing, horseback riding, walking, reading. Home and Office: Healthy Concepts Consultations 173 Georgetown Rd Boxford MA 01921

HOOVER, OLIVER D., classics scholar; b. Brantford, Ont., Can., Jan. 13, 1972; s. David Lloyd and Jean Margot (Goetz) H. BA in History/Classics, McMaster U., Hamilton, Ont., 1994, MA in Ancient History, 1996. Grad. asst. NYU, N.Y.C., 1996—; excavator Aphrodisias Excavations, NYU, Turkey, 1998. Contbr. articles to profl. jours. Mem. Am. Philol. Assn., Am. Numismatic Soc., Am. Assn. Greek and Latin Epigraphy, Classical Assn. of Atlantic States.

HOOVER, PAUL, poet; b. Harrisonburg, Va., Apr. 30, 1946; s. Robert and Opal (Shinaberry) H.; m. Maxine Chernoff, 1974; children: Koren, Philip, Julian. BA cum laude, Manchester Coll., 1968; MA, U. Ill., 1973. Asst. editor U. Ill. Press, Champaign, 1973-74; prof. English Columbia Coll., Chgo., 1974—; co-founder Poetry Ctr., Sch. of Art Inst. of Chgo., 1974, bd. mem. 1974-87, pres. 1975-78; editor OINK!, 1971-85; co-founder, editor New Am. Writing, 1986. Author: Letter to Einstein Beginning Dear Albert, 1979, Somebody Talks a Lot, 1983, Nervous Songs, 1986, Idea, 1987 (Carl Sandburg award Friends of Chgo. Pub. Libr. 1987), Saigon, Illinois, 1988, The Novel: A Poem, 1990, Totem and Shadow: New and Selected Poems, 1999; editor: Postmodern American Poetry, 1994, Viridian, 1997 (Georgia prize 1997), Totem and Shadow, 1999; contbr. to various periodicals including New Yorker, Partisan Rev., New Directions, Sulfur, Chgo. Rev., Triquarterly, Am. Poetry Rev., New Republic; author: (screenplay) Viridian, 1994. Nat. Endowment for Arts fellow, 1980; Ill. Arts Coun. fellow, 1983, 84, 86; recipient General Electric Found. award for Younger Writers, 1984. Mem. MLA. Office: Columbia Coll Dept of English 600 S Michigan Ave Chicago IL 60605-1900 Home: 369 Molino Ave Mill Valley CA 94941-2767*

HOOVER, PEARL ROLLINGS, nurse; b. LeSueur, Minn., Aug. 24, 1924; d. William Earl and Louisa (Schickling) Rollings; m. Roy David Hoover, June 19, 1948 (dec. Mar. 1987); children: Helen Louise, William Robert (dec.). Grad. in nursing, U. Minn., 1945, BS in Nursing, 1947; MS in Health Sci., Calif. State U., Northridge, 1972. Dir. affiliate nursing sch. Mooselake (Minn.) State Hosp., 1948-49; nursing instr. Anchor Hosp., County Hosp., St. Paul, 1949-51; student nurse supr. and instr. Brentwood VA Hosp., L.A., 1951-52; sch. nurse L.A. Unified City Schs., 1963-91, substitute sch. nurse, 1991-96. Camp nurse United First Meth. Ch., winter and summer past 35 yrs.; rec. sec. Reseda Women's Club; courtesy chmn. First United Meth. Women. Mem. L.A. Coun. Sch. Nurses, Calif. Sch. Nurses Orgn. Democrat. Methodist. Home: 17851 Lull St Reseda CA 91335-2237

HOOVER, RICHARD, set designer. Prodn. designer films including: It Takes Two, 1988, Feeling 109, 1988, Torch Song Trilogy, 1988, Bob Roberts, 1992, Storyville, 1992, Dream Lover, 1994, Panther, 1995, Dead Man Walking, 1995, The Blackout, 1997, Apt Pupil, 1998, The Cradle Will Rock, 1999, Payback, 1999; designer TV movies: Family of Spies, 1990, Heat Wave, 1990, Zooman, 1995, (TV series) Twin Peaks, 1990; art dir.: Somewhere Tomorrow, 1983, Checking Out, 1989, Cradle Will Rock, 1999; set decorator: Wisdom, 1986, In the Mood, 1987; visual cons. Ed Wood, 1994; set designer: Sweet Lorraine, 1987; visual effects supr.: Armageddon, 1998, Freejack, 1992. Winner 1999 Tony award for best set design for Not About Nightingales, Evening Standard award, London Critics' Cir. award, Drama Desk award, Outer Critics Cir. award; nominated for Oscar for best effects for Armageddon, 1998, also Golden Satellite Award nomination, 1999. Office: c/o IATSE Local 847 13949 Ventura Blvd #301 Sherman Oaks CA 91423*

HOOVER, ROBERT ALLAN, university president; b. Des Moines, May 9, 1941; s. Claude Edward and Anna Doris H.; m. Jeanne Mary Hoover, Feb. 22, 1968; children: Jennifer Jill Jacobs, Suzanne Elizabeth. BS, Ariz. State U., 1967, MA, 1969; PhD, U. Calif., Santa Barbara, 1973. Instr. polit. sci. Utah State U., Logan, 1971-73, asst. prof. polit. sci., 1973-79, assoc. prof. polit. sci., chair polit. sci. dept., 1979-84, prof. polit. sci., 1984-91, dean Coll. Humanities, Arts and Social Scis., 1984-91; v.p. for acad. affairs U. Nev., Reno, 1991-96; pres. U. Idaho, Moscow, 1996—. Author: The Politics of MX: A New Direction in Weapons Procurement?, 1982, The MX Controversy: A Guide to Issues and References, 1982, Arms Control: The Interwar Naval Limitation Agreements, 1980. Bd. dirs. United Way, Reno, 1994-96, Channel 5, Reno, 1991-95, St. Scholastica Acad., Canon City, Colo., 1991-96. Avocations: skiing, jogging, camping. Office: Univ Idaho Adminstrn Bldg Rm 105 Moscow ID 83844-3151

HOOVER, ROBERT CLEARY, retired bank executive; b. Highland Park, Ill., July 26, 1928; s. Howard Earl and Dorothy (Higgs) H.; m. Beatrice Leona Borroughs, June 21, 1949 (div.); children: Catherine, Robert C. II, Holly; m. Nancy Ellen Pitman, July 25, 1959 (div.); children: John, Elizabeth, Courtney; m. Cecilia Susan Flournoy, July 3, 1981; 1 child, Whitney Suzanne. BA, U. Calif., Berkeley, 1950. Asst. advt. mgr. Hoover Co., North Canton, Ohio, 1951-54; v.p., asst. gen. mgr. Golden State Linen Svc., Oakland, Calif., 1954-61; asst. mgr. Wells Fargo Bank, San Francisco, 1961-66; v.p. Bank Calif. Assn., San Francisco, 1966-84, v.p., spl. asst. to chmn. bd. and chief exec. officer, 1984-94; ret. Bd. mem. Providence Hosp., Oakland, 1985-91, Bay Area Tumor Inst., 1975—. Mem. Am. Inst. Banking, Naval War Coll. Found. (life), Navy League United States (life), Naval Order U.S. (life), Bohemian Club, Claremont Country Club, Pacific Union Club. Republican. Episcopalian. Avocations: swimming, antique collecting, travel, art, skeet and trap. Home: 46 Sotelo Ave Piedmont CA 94611-3535

HOOVER, ROLAND ARMITAGE, publisher, printer; b. Buffalo, Jan. 14, 1929; s. John Frank and Constance (More) H.; m. Cynthia Lee Adams, July 14, 1962; children: Sarah Adams, Emily Armitage. B.S., Yale U., 1949. Mgmt. trainee Cleve. Electric Illuminating Co., 1949-50; graphic designer studio of Hubert Leckie, Washington, 1955-56; supr. tech. reports Atomic Energy div. Allis-Chalmers Mfg. Co., Washington, 1956-63; editor-in-charge Publs. Office, Research and Engring. Support div. Inst. for Def. Analyses, 1963-65; exec. editor Brookings Instn., Washington, 1965-67; dir. publs. Brookings Instn., 1967-84; univ. printer Yale U., New Haven, 1984-94, pursuivant of arms, 1989—; sr. critic in graphic design Yale Sch. Art, New Haven, 1991-94; propr. pvt. press, free lance typographer, 1958—. Served from ensign to lt. (j.g.) USNR, 1951-53. Fellow Davenport Coll., Yale U., 1985—. Mem. Am. Printing History Assn., Yale Sherlock Holmes Soc., Elizabethan Club (Yale U.), Sigma Xi, Tau Beta Pi. Democrat. Episcopalian. Home: 5505 Pembroke Ter Bethesda MD 20817-6318

HOOVER, WILLIAM LEICHLITER, forestry and natural resources educator, financial consultant; b. Brownsville, Pa., July 29, 1944; s. Aaron Jones and Edith (Leichliter) H.; B.S., Pa. State U., 1966, M.S., 1971; Ph.D., Iowa State U., 1977; m. Peggy Jo Spangler, Aug. 30, 1976; children: Jennifer Mary, Monica Susan, Samuel Spangler. Research asst. Pa. State U., Iowa State U., 1970-74; asst. prof. Purdue U., West Lafayette, Ind., 1974-79, assoc. prof. dept. forestry and natural resources, 1980-85, prof., 1986—. asst. dept. head and extension coord.; mem. Boy Scouts Am. Served to 1st lt., C.E., U.S. Army, 1967-69. Decorated Bronze Star. Mem. Internat. Soc. Ecol. Economics, Forest Products Soc., Soc. Am. Foresters. Republican. Presbyterian. Author: A Guide to Federal Income Tax for Timber Owners, Timber Tax Management; contbg. editor taxes Tree Farmer Mag. Home: 206 Connolly St West Lafayette IN 47906-2724 Office: Purdue U Dept Forestry West Lafayette IN 47907

HOPCROFT, JOHN EDWARD, dean, computer science educator; b. Oct. 7, 1939. BS in EE, Seattle U., 1961; MS in EE, Stanford U., 1962, PhD in Elec. Engring., 1964. Asst. prof. Princeton (N.J.) U., 1964-67; assoc. prof. Cornell U., Ithaca, N.Y., 1967-71, prof., 1972-85, Joseph C. Ford prof., 1985—, chmn. computer sci. dept., 1987-92, assoc. dean coll. affairs Coll. Engring., 1992-93, dean Coll Engring., 1994—; vis. prof. Stanford U., Calif., 1970-71; mem. Info. Sci. and Tech. Office Def. Advanced Rsch. Projects Agy. (DARPA) (chair robotics working group); chmn. adv. bd. NSF, 1987-90; mem. computer sci. and telecomm. bd. NAS/NRC, 1988—, adv. com. for David and Lucille Packard Fellowships in Sci. and Tech., 1991—; mem. sci. adv. bd. USAF, Inst. for Def. Analysis, David and Lucille Packard Found., NSF. Co-author: Formal Languages and Their Relation to Automata, 1969, The Design and Analysis of Computer Algorithms, 1974, Introduction to Automata Theory, Language, and Computation, 1979, Data Structures and Algorithms, 1983, Planning, Geometry and Complexity of Robot Motion, 1987. NSF Grad. fellow, 1961-64. Fellow IEEE, AAAS, Am. Acad. Arts and Scis.; mem. NAE (mem. acad. adv. bd. 1992-95), Nat. Sci. Bd., Inst. for Def. Analysis Supercomputing Rsch. Ctr., Assn. Computing Math. (Turing award 1986), Soc. for Indsl. and Applied Math., Ctr. Excellence Space Data and Info. Sci. (interim dir. 1987-88). Office: Cornell U Coll Engring Deans Office 242 Carpenter Hall Ithaca NY 14853-2201*

HOPE, BOB, actor, comedian; b. Eltham, Eng., May 29, 1903; m. Dolores Reade, Feb. 19, 1934; children: Linda, Anthony, Kelly, Nora. Ed. pub. schs., Cleve.; DFA (hon.), Brown U., Jacksonville (Fla.) U.; LHD (hon.), Quincy (Ill.) Coll., Georgetown U., So. Meth. U., Dallas, Ohio State U., Ind. U., John Carroll U., U. Nev., Monmouth Coll., Whittier Coll., Pa. Mil. Coll., Miami U., Oxford, Ohio, U. Cin., Calif. State Colls., Mercy Coll., N.J., Coll. of Desert, Baldwin-Wallace Coll., St. Louis U., Oral Roberts U., U. Charleston; LLD (hon.), U. Wyo., Northwestern U., Evanston, Ill., St. Bonaventure U., Pace Coll., Pepperdine U., U. Scranton, Western State U., Calif.; HHD (hon.), Ohio Dominican Coll., Bowling Green U., Santa Clara U., Fla. So. Coll., Wilberforce U., Northwood Inst., Mich., Norwich U., Bethel Coll., Tenn., Utah State U., St. Anselm's Coll., N.H., Washington U., St. Louis; D of Internat. Relations (hon.), Salem Coll.; D of Pub. Service (hon.), St. Ambrose Coll.; D of Humane Service (hon.), Drury Coll.; D of Humane Humor (hon.), Benedictine Coll., Kans.; D of Performing Arts (hon.), Dakota Wesleyan U.; LittD (hon.), Gonzaga U. Entertained Svc. Forces overseas and in U.S. Began in vaudeville and also appeared on stage; now in motion pictures, TV, radio; actor: (stage) Ballyhoo, 1932, Roberta, 1933, Ziegfeld Follies, 1935, Red Hot and Blue, 1936, (films) Going Spanish, 1934, The Old Grey Mayor, 1935, Thanks for the Memory, 1938, College Swing, 1938, Give Me a Sailor, 1938, The Big Broadcast of 1938, 1938, Never Say Die, 1939, Some Like It Hot, The Cat and the Canary, 1939, The Road to Singapore, 1940, The Ghostbreakers, 1940, Caught in the Draft, 1941, Nothing But the Truth, 1941, Road to Zanzibar, 1941, Louisiana Purchase, 1941, Road to Morocco, 1942, My Favorite Blonde, 1942, Star Spangled Rhythm, 1942, They Got Me Covered, 1943, Let's Face It, 1943, The Princess and the Pirate, 1944, The Road to Utopia, 1945, Monsieur Beaucaire, 1946, My Favorite Brunette, 1947, Where There's Life, 1947, Road to Rio, 1948, Paleface, 1948, Sorrowful Jones, 1949, The Great Lover, 1949, Fancy Pants, 1950, Lemon Drop Kid, 1951, My Favorite Spy, 1951, Greatest Show on Earth, 1952, Son of Paleface, 1952, Road to Bali, 1953, Off Limits, 1953, Here Come the Girls, 1953, Casanova's Big Night, 1954, 7 Little Foys, 1955, That Certain Feeling, 1956, Iron Petticoat, 1956, Beau James, 1957, Paris Holiday, 1958, Alias Jesse James, 1959, The Facts of Life, 1960, Bachelor in Paradise, 1961, Road to Hong Kong, 1962, Critic's Choice, 1963, Call Me Bwana, 1963, A Global Affair, 1964, I'll Take Sweden, 1965, Boy, Did I Get a Wrong Number!, 1966, Eight on the Lam, 1967, The Private Navy of Sargeant O'Farrell, 1968, How to Commit Marriage, 1969, Cancel My Reservation, 1972, The Muppet Movie, 1979, Spies Like Us, 1985, Radio Star-die AFN-Story, 1994; also TV variety shows including The Bob Hope Christmas Special, 1987, The Bob Hope Birthday Special, 1988, Bob Hope's Yellow Ribbon Party, 1991, Bob Hope: A 90th Birthday Celebration, 1993, Bob Hope: Laughing with the Presidents, 1996; TV movies include A Masterpiece of Murder, 1986; author: They Got Me Covered, 1941, I Never Left Home, 1944, So This is Peace, 1946, Have Tux, Will Travel, 1954, I Owe Russia, 1963, Five Women I Love, 1966, The Last Christmas Show, 1974, Road to Hollywood, 1977, (with Melville Shavelson) Confessions of a Hooker-Lifelong Love Affair with Golf, 1985, Don't Shoot It's Only Me, 1990. Decorated Hon. Comdr., Order of Brit. Empire; recipient 4 Spl. Acad. awards, Emmy award, 3 People's Choice awards for best male entertainer, 1975-76, People to People award Pres. Eisenhower, Congrl. Gold medal Pres. Kennedy, Medal of Freedom Pres. Johnson, Peabody award, Jean Hersholdt Humanitarian award, Criss award, Disting. Service medals from all branches of Armed Forces, Poor Richard award, Kennedy Ctr. Honors award, 1985, numerous others; fellow Westminster (N.J.) Choir Coll.; named Most Decorated Entertainer, Guiness Book of World Records, Honored Entertainer, Guiness Book of Records. Home: Hope Enterprises Prodn 3808 W Riverside Dr Burbank CA 91505-4325*

HOPE, CHRISTOPHER LAWRENCE, middle school educator; b. Buffalo, May 25, 1969; s. Lawrence Erwin and Lorraine Marion (Frank) H. BS in Elem. Edn., SUNY, Buffalo, 1991; MS in Reading Edn., Canisius Coll., 1993. Cert. elem. tchr., reading and math. tchr., N.Y. 6th - 8th grade reading tchr. Our Mother of Good Counsel Sch., Blasdell, N.Y., 1993—; moderator 1st local N.Y. State Champion Stock Market Game, 1996-97, WNY Stock Market Game, 1998, Mid. Sch. WNY Stock Market Game Champions, 1998; mem. adv. bd. for ednl. affairs Buffalo News, 1998. Mem. Ken-Bailey Neighborhood Housing Svcs., Buffalo, 1990—; pres. Thornton Ave. Block Club, Buffalo, 1993-95. Named Power Tchr., USA Today Newspaper, 1996, Influential People of 20th Century, 1998. Mem. Nat. English Tchrs. Coun., Western N.Y. Umpires Assn., Western N.Y. Girls Basketball Ofcls. (bd. dirs., banquet chmn.), Western N.Y. Girls Soccer Ofcls. (bd. dirs.), Western N.Y. Boys Volleyball Ofcls. (election chmn.), Western N.Y. Girls Volleyball Ofcls. Democrat. Roman Catholic. Avocations: sporting events, entertaining, travel. Home: 125 Sundown Trl Williamsville NY 14221-2222 Office: Our Mother of Good Counsel Sch 15 Oakwood Ave Blasdell NY 14219-1230

HOPE, ELLEN, pathologist, educator; b. N.Y.C., Apr. 25, 1942. AA, Lasell Jr. Coll., Auberndale, Mass., 1961; BS with honors, N.Y. Inst. Tech., 1976; MS with honors, SUNY, Stony Brook, 1987. Med. technologist New Eng. Deaconess Hosp., Brookline, Mass., 1962-64; rsch. asst. pathology lab. Cancer Rsch. Inst., Brookline, Mass., 1964-66; lab. supr. North Shore Univ. Hosp. Cornell Med. Ctr., Manhasset, N.Y., 1973-84; asst. prof. med. tech. SUNY, Stony Brook, N.Y., 1984-90; prof., coord. MS in Clin. Sci. program Calif. State U., Dominguez Hills, Calif., 1990—; clin. adj. faculty L.I. U., Greenvale, N.Y., 1979-84, N.Y. Inst. Tech., Old Westbury, 1979-84; judge Health Occupations Students of Am., Nat. Competitive Events; dir. CSUDH Study and Cultural program, Eng., 1991, dir. Internat. Health Seminar, Australia, 1989; co-dir. study and cultural program U. Uppsala Karolinska Inst., Sweden, U. Oslo, Norway, 1988; presenter at numerous confs. and convs. Contbr. numerous articles to profl. jours. Cmty. leader Campaign to Prevent Handgun Violence Against Kids, 1996—; mentor Calif. Acad. Math & Scis., 1990-95; univ. rep. Long Beach (Calif.) Pub. Safety Summit, 1995—; mem. nat. com. World Food Day, 1991-94; vol. Long Beach Civic Light Opera, 1994-95; mem. vol. Long Beach Symphony Guild, 1994—; mem. docent Long Beach Mus. Art, 1996—; mem. L.A. World Affairs Coun., 1996—. Recipient numerous grants. Fellow Royal Soc. Arts; mem. AAUW, Am. Soc. Sch. Allied Health Professions, Am. Soc. Clin. Pathologists (specialist in hematology, regional assoc. mem. award 1998), Calif. Assn. Med. Lab. Tech., Am. Assn. for World Health, Coalition for Allied Health Leadership, Alpha Eta (pres. chpt. 1996—, bd. dirs. 1991—). E-mail: ehope@research.csudh.edu. Office: Calif State U Dept Clin Scis Sch of Health 1000 E Victoria St Carson CA 90747-0001

HOPE, GEORGE MARION, vision scientist; b. Waycross, Ga., Jan. 24, 1938; s. George Marion and Jessie Candler (Norman) H.; m. Dorothy Marie Hendrix, Aug. 4, 1956; 1 child, Steven Richard. AB, Mercer U., 1965; MA, U. Fla., 1967, PhD, 1971. Asst. prof., rsch. assoc. U. Louisville, 1972-80; assoc. rsch. scientist U. Fla., Gainesville, 1980—; dir. low vision svc. U. Fla. Eye Ctr., U. Fla. Coll. Medicine, 1980—; co-dir. low vision clinic Dept. Ophthalmology U. Louisville, 1972-79. Contbr. numerous articles to profl. jours. Nat. Eye Inst. NIH grantee, 1975-78, 83-87. Mem. AAAS, Assn. Rsch., Vision and Ophthalmology (placement svc. 1972-84), Sigma Xi. Avocations: photography, camping, nature study. Office: U Fla PO Box 100284 Gainesville FL 32610-0284

HOPE, GERRI DANETTE, telecommunications management executive; b. Sacramento, Feb. 28, 1956; d. Albert Gerald and Beulah Rae (Bane) Hope. AS, Sierra Coll., Calif., 1977; postgrad. Okla. State U., 1977-79. Instructional asst. II San Juan Sch. Dist., Carmichael, Calif., 1979-82; telecomm. supr. Delta Dental Svc. of Calif., San Francisco, 1982-85; telecomm. coordinator Farmers Savs. Bank, Davis, Calif., 1985-87; telecomm. officer Sacramento Savs. Bank, 1987-95; owner GDH Enterprises, 1993-97; telecomm. analyst II contractor dept. ins. State Calif., 1995—; sr. telecomms. engr. Access Health, Inc., Rancho Cordova, Calif., 1996-97, Any Time Access, Sacramento, 1997-98, GDH Enterprises, North Highlands, 1993-97; employment devel. dept. assoc., info. systems analyst specialist State of Calif., 1998—; founder Custom Label Designer, Sacramento, 1993-96; mem. telecomm. adv. panel Golden Gate U., Sacramento; lectr. in toll fraud prevention and network security. Mem. Telecomm. Assn. (v.p. membership com. Sacramento Valley chpt., 1993, v.p. dir. programs 1997-98, corp. conf. com. programs bd. 1997-99, v.p. pub. rels. bd.), Am. Philatelic Soc., Sacramento Philatelic Assn., Errors, Freaks and Oddities Club, Philatelic Collectors. Republican. Avocations: writing, computers, philately, animal behavior, participating in Christian ministry. Home: 3025 U St Antelope CA 95843-2513 Office: GDH Enterprises Telecom Unit Project Mgmt PO Box 512 North Highlands CA 95660-0512

HOPE, JAMES FRANKLIN, mayor, civil engineer, consultant; b. Toledo, Aug. 2, 1917; s. George Thomas and Alice Mae (Martin) H.; m. Virginia Lee Mountjoy, June 10, 1944; children: James F. Jr., Virginia Lee BeVille. BCE magna cum laude, U. Toledo, 1939. Registered profl. engr., Ohio, Va.; registered profl. surveyor, Ohio. Field engr., asst. supt. Art Metal Constrn. Co., Jamestown, N.Y., 1939-40; asst. to chief engr. Doyle and Russel and Wise Constrn. Co., Richmond, Va., 1940-41; exec. engr. Doyle and Russell, Norfolk, Va., 1941-43; pres. Reid & Hope, Inc. Contractors & Engrs., Suffolk, Va., 1946-83; bd. dirs. Old Dominion Investors Trust, Inc., 1952—, pres. 1965—; cons. engr. for comml., indsl. and condominium projects, 1984—. Mem. Suffolk City Coun., 1963-78, 90-94; vice mayor City of Suffolk, 1965, mayor, 1966-78, 90-92; exec. com., bd. dirs. Va. Mcpl. League, 1966-78; mem. Bldg. Codes Bd. of Adjustments and Appeals, 1963-90, chmn. 1985-90; mem. Affordable Housing Com., SE Va. Planning Dist. Commn., 1963-78, chair 1967-68, v. chair 1965-66, Hampton Roads Area Com., 1966-82, chair 1978-82, SE Va. Water Authority, 1970-78, v. chair 1975, chair 1976, Jail Study Com.; chmn. Suffolk 1980 Census Com., Southeastern Tidewater Manpower Authority, 1973-78; trustee, chmn. comm. fin., past chmn. Oxford Meth. Ch.; bd. dirs. Old Dominion coun. Boy Scouts Am., and others. Lt. USN, 1943-46, PTO. Recipient Disting. Svc. medal and plaque Cosmopolitan Club, 1973, Disting. Alumni award U. Toledo Coll. Engring., 1983, Gold T award U. Toledo Alumni Assn.; inducted Hall of Fame, Calvin M. Woodward High Sch., 1985; Paul Harris fellowship Rotary, 1996. Mem. NSPE, Soc. Am. Mil. Engrs., Associated Gen. Contractors of Am. (bd. dirs. Va. br., pres. Va. br. 1959, Constrn. Man of Yr. award), Va. Soc. Profl. Engrs. (bd. dirs. Tidewater chpt. 1960-63), Ea. Va. Assn. Contractors, State Registration Bd. for Contractors (past. chmn., past vice chmn.), Va. State C. of C., Suffolk-Nansemond C. of C. (bd. dirs. 1956-57), Lions (pres., bd. dirs. 1961-62, Melvin Jones fellow 1997), Rotary (Paul Harris fellow 1998). Republican. Home: 704 Jones St Suffolk VA 23434-4951

HOPE, JUDITH H., Democrat party chairman; b. Warren, Ark., Nov. 2, 1939; d. Carroll Charles and Mayme (Stevens) Hollensworth; m. Thomas A. Twomey, Jr.; children: Leif Erling, Nisse Elizabeth. *Judith Hope was born in Warren, Arkansas. Father Carroll Hollensworth served in the State Legislature for several decades and became Speaker of the Assembly. Mother Mayme Hollensworth was a writer and radio talk show host who devoted much of her later years to helping at the Little Rock Children's Hospital. Daughter Nisse Hope designs and creates flower gardens in East Hampton. Son Erling Hope is a fine wood-working craftsman. He is married to Alice Moore Hope, and they have a six-year old daughter, Soren. Judith is married to Tom Twomey, and East Hampton attorney, who is a member of Who's Who in America.* Student, Gulf Park Coll. for Women, 1956-57, U. Ark., 1957-60, Tobe Coburn Sch., N.Y., 1960-61. Town supr. East Hampton, N.Y., 1974-76, 84-88; appointments officer to N.Y. Gov. Hugh L. Carey, 1976-79; spl. asst. to Gov. for L.I., 1979-81; mem. Dem. Nat. Com., 1989-92; 1st vice chairwoman N.Y. State Dem. Party, 1989-92; mem. exec. com. Dem. Nat. Com., 1997; chairwoman N.Y. State Dem. Party, 1995—; mem. N.Y. Bldg. Codes Coun. *In 1973, Hope was the first woman elected Town Supervisor in the history of Suffolk County. Thereafter, served in the cabinet of Governor Hugh Carey and was in charge of all appointments to State agencies and boards. In 1983, was elected to two further terms as East Hampton Town Supervisor. In 1995, elected New York State Democratic Committee Chair and led the grassroot, statewide campaigns resulting in President Clinton's record-breaking 1996 win 52 out of 62 counties; in 1997, the defeat of 217 incumbent Republican office-holders; and, in 1998, winning 3 out of 4 statewide races.* Mem. N.Y. State Women's Dem. Leadership Coun., 1990-95; dir. Planned Parenthood of Suffolk County, 1988—; vice chmn. South Fork Nature Conservancy; founding mem. East End Women's Network; mem. N.Y. State Ctr. for Women in Govt., L.I. LWV. Recipient Woman of Yr. award Suffolk County Human Rights Commn., 1986, Woman of Yr. award East Hampton Assn. Univ. Women, 1988, Pres.'s Pub. Svc. award Nature Conservancy, 1988, Environ. Roll of Honor, Group for the South Fork, 1990, Cmty. Svc. award Apple Inst., 1992. Mem. Pi Beta Phi. Office: 60 Madison Ave Ste 1201 New York NY 10010-1600*

HOPE, MARGARET LAUTEN, civic worker; b. N.Y.C.; 1 son, Frederick H., III. *Maternal grandfather Henry G.F. Lauten and wife, Lillie Falls Weiss Lauten. Mrs. Lauten's parents were George Weiss and Elizabeth O'Donnell Weiss of Staten Island, N.Y. Mr. and Mrs. Henry G.F. Lauten resided in Long Island, N.Y. and Palm Beach, FL. Mr. Lauten wrote the Worth Street Rules that govern the textile industry. He was also with the cotton textile merchants and on the arbitration council. Paternal grandfather Dr. Fritz J. Swanson Sr. resided in Westerly, R.I. at Shelter Harbor. He was knighted by the King of Sweden and given the title, Count of Vasa.* Privately educated. Mem. ball coms. various charity fund raising events. Named Internat. Woman of Yr., Internat. Biog. Ctr., Cambridge, Eng., 1996-97. Mem. Jr. League N.Y.C., Everglades Club, Sailfish Club (Palm Beach), Women's Nat. Rep. Club (N.Y.C.), St. James Club (London). Address: PO Box 601 Palm Beach FL 33480-0601

HOPE, MARK ALAN, soft drink company executive; b. Lawrence, Kans., Jan. 21, 1960; s. Lowell Wayne and Marilyn Rose (Fogle) H.; m. Linda Carol LaRue, Dec. 18, 1982; children: Bradley, Jessica, Scott. BA, Campbell U., 1985. Enlisted U.S. Army, 1977, advanced through grades to 1st lt., 1987, resigned, 1988, mem. Elite Delta Force, 1982-85; prodn. supr. Coca-Cola Co., Atlanta, 1988-89; maintenance supr., prodn. mgr. Perrier Group, Poland, Maine, 1989; br. mgr. Perrier Group, Miami, Fla., 1989-90; ops. mgr. Dr. Pepper/Seven-Up Cos., Dallas, 1990-92; pres., CEO Water Point Systems Inc., Ft. Worth, 1992-94; mgr. strategic planning The Coca-Cola Co., Vienna, Austria, 1995-96; region mgr. The Coca-Cola Co., Bucharest, Romania, 1997-98, Budapest, Hungary, 1999—. Decorated Meritorious Svc. medal. Republican. Methodist. Home: CC 817-2 PO Box 311 Mendham NJ 07945-0311 Office: Coca-Cola Carpathian Region, Nemedi ut 104, 2330 Dunaharszti Hungary

HOPE, SAMUEL HOWARD, accreditation organization executive; b. Owensboro, Ky., Nov. 5, 1946; s. James Russell and Lorraine (Jones) H.; m. Judy Bucher, June 24, 1978. B.Mus., Eastman Sch. Music, Rochester, N.Y., 1967; M.Music Arts, Yale U., 1970; pupil of, Nadia Boulanger, France, 1966, 67. Dean, composer-in-residence Atlanta Boy Choir Sch. Music, 1970-73, trustee, 1973—; vis. instr. Lee Coll., Cleveland, Tenn., 1973-74; exec. dir. music alumni, asso. dir. grad. profl. programs Campaign for Yale Yale U., 1974-75; exec. dir. Nat. Assn. Schs. Music, Nat. Assn. Schs. Art and Design, Reston, Va., 1975—, Joint Commn. on Dance and Theatre Accreditation, 1978-83, Nat. Assn. Schs. Theatre, 1980—, Higher Edn. Arts Data Services, 1981—, Nat. Assn. Schs. Dance, 1981—, Working Group on Arts in Higher Edn., 1982—, Coun. of Arts Accrediting Assns., 1988—; chmn. assembly of specialized accrediting bodies Council on Postsecondary Accreditation, 1979-82, bd. dirs., 1992-93; bd. dirs. Council Specialized Accrediting Agys., 1978-81, sec.-treas., 1979-81; mem. com. recognition Council Postsecondary Accreditation, 1984-88; chmn. adminstv. com. Found. Advancement Edn. in Music., 1986-90. Composer Piano Sonata I, 1968, II, 1971; motet Solus Ad Victimam Procedis, Domine, 1970, Blessed Be Thou Lord, 1976, Trio for Oboe, Cello and Piano, 1970, Cantata I, 1973, Cantata II, 1975, Symphonia: Psalm 145, 1982, Toccata: Psalm 117 for Organ, 1993; exec. editor Arts Edn. Policy Rev. mag., 1984—. Chmn. govt. relations com. Nat. Music Council, 1976-79, bd. dirs., 1978-84; mem. exec. com. Am. Soc. Univ. Composers, 1977-83; nat. alumni council Eastman Sch. Music, 1975-78, chmn., 1976-77; bd. dirs. Am. Music Conf., 1978-82; trustee Am. Acad. for Liberal Edn., 1997—. Recipient Composition prize Yale U., 1968, 69, 70. Mem. Am. Music Center, Coll. Music Soc., Music Educators Nat. Conf., Am. Inst. Graphic Artists, Music Tchrs. Nat. Assn., Am. Assn. for Theatre in Higher Edn., Am. Alliance for Theatre and Edn. Episcopalian. Club: Yale (N.Y.C. and Washington). Home: 10717 Rosehaven St Fairfax VA 22030-2826 Office: 11250 Roger Bacon Dr Ste 21 Reston VA 20190-5202

HOPE, THOMAS WALKER, marketing professional; b. St. Paul, May 19, 1920; s. Joseph Nathaniel and Alma (Ryden) H.; m. Mabeth Sue Stewart, Apr. 30, 1949; children: Vincent W., Stephen D., Dana R. Student, U. Minn., 1937-39; BA, U. Tex., El Paso, 1942. Mgr. film dept. Gen. Mills, Inc., Mpls., 1945-54; asst. advisor for nontheatrical films Eastman Kodak Co., Rochester, N.Y., 1954-65; market analyst E.K. Co., Rochester, 1965-70; founder, pres. Hope Reports, Inc., Rochester, 1970-87, chmn., chief exec. officer, 1987—; founder, v.p. Council on Internat. Nontheatrical Events, Washington, 1956-86; cons. Marshall Plan, Govt. of France, Paris, 1952, various other corps., 1970—. Author: Hope Reports AV-USA, 1970-72, 74—, (with others) Dollars and Sense of Business Films, 1955; producer 66 indsl. films and tng. media; exec. producer Lone Ranger television series; contbr. Ency. Britannica Yearbook, 1975—; contbr. articles to profl. jours. Mem. Otetiana Council, Boy Scouts Am., Rochester, 1954—. Capt. Signal Corps, U.S. Army, 1942-45, ETO. Decorated Bronze Star, Can. Parachute Wings with Silver Maple leaf, 1998; recipient Silver Beaver award Boy Scouts Am., 1960. Life fellow Soc. Motion Picture and TV Engrs. (gov.); mem. Comm. Media Mgmt. Assn. (founder), Univ. Film and Video Assn. (life, mem. adv. council 1970—), Nat. Council Chs. (mem. communications commn. 1980-91), Internat. Communications Industries Assn., Internat. TV Assn., Phi Kappa Tau (pres. U. Tex. El Paso chpt. 1941-42). Presbyterian. Fax: (716) 442-1725.

HOPE, WILLIAM DUANE, zoologist, curator; b. Fort Collins, Colo., June 7, 1935; s. William Earl and Lois Howe (Burnett) H.; m. Colleen Bryan, Dec. 23, 1956 (div.); children: Pamella Kay, Karen Gail, Linda Michelle. B.S., Colo. State U., 1957, M.S., 1960; Ph.D., U. Calif., Davis, 1965. Systematic zoologist. dept. invertebrate zoology Nat. Mus. Natural History, Smithsonian Instn., Washington, 1964-69; curator Nat. Mus. Natural History, Smithsonian Instn., 1969-75, chmn. dept., 1976-81. Contbr. articles to profl. jours. Mem. Am. Assn. Zool. Nomenclature, Am. Micros Soc., Biol. Soc. Washington, Helminthological Soc. Washington, Soc. Nematologists, Soc. Systematic Zoology, Internat. Assn. Meiobenthologists. Republican. Avocations: hiking, biking, flyfishing, bird watching. Office: Smithsonian Instn Nat Mus Natural History Dept Invertebrate Zoology Washington DC 20560

HOPEN, ANTON JOHN, lawyer; b. Phila., Aug. 31, 1969; s. John Hopen and Joan Girard; m. Lisa Michelle Nicholson, May 27, 1995; 1 child, Anna Noel. BA in Biology, U. South Fla., 1991; JD, U. Fla., 1995. Bar: Fla. 1995, U.S. Dist. Ct. (mid. dist.) Fla. 1997, (no. dist.) Fla. 1999, U.S. Patent and Trademark Office 1998, U.S. Dist. Ct. (so. dist.) Fla. 1999, U.S. Ct. Appeals (fed. cir.) 1999, (11th cir.) 1999. Asst. state atty. 6th Jud. Cir., Clearwater, Fla., 1995-98; registered patent atty. Lott & Friedland, Coral Gables, Fla., 1998-99; ptnr. Smith & Hopen, Clearwater, 1999—; lectr. forensic DNA, Fla. Dept. Law Enforcement, Tallahassee, 1998—; trial judge U. Miami Coll. Law, 1998-99. Mem. Am. Intellectual Property Law Assn., Patent Law Assn. South Fla. (officer 1998-99). Republican. Avocations: golf, saltwater fishing. Fax: 727-507-8668. E-mail: ajhopen@baypatents.com. Office: Smith & Hopen PA Ste 220 15950 Bay Vista Dr Clearwater FL 33760

HOPEN, HERBERT JOHN, horticulture educator; b. Madison, Wis., Jan. 7, 1934; s. Alfred and Amelia (Sveum) H.; m. Joanne C. Emmel, Sept. 12, 1959; children: Timothy, Rachel. BS, U. Wis., 1956, MS, 1959; PhD, Mich. State U., 1962. Asst. prof. U. Minn., Duluth, 1962-64; prof. U. Ill., Urbana, 1965-85, prof., acting head, 1983-85; prof. horticulture U. Wis., Madison, 1985-97, prof. emeritus, 1997, chmn. dept. horticulture, 1985-91. Mem. Am. Soc. for Hort. Sci., Weed Sci. Soc. Am., North Ctrl. Weed Sci. Soc., Yggdrasil, Sigma Xi. Avocations: reading, gardening. Office: U Wis Dept Hort 1575 Linden Dr Madison WI 53706-1514

HOPEN, WILLIAM DOUGLAS (BILL HOPEN), sculptor; b. N.Y.C., Apr. 13, 1951; s. Harold M. and Mary R. Hopen; m. Olga E. Gioulis; children: Gabriel, Moriah. Student, CUNY, 1968-72; BA, W.Va. State Regents, 1985. Prin. works include sculptures at Harrison County Libr., Clarksburg, W.Va., 1979, Internat. Stone Sculptors Symposium, Balt., 1980, St. Paul's Cath. Ch., Wierton, W.Va., 1981, Mother's Day Shrine, Grafton, W.Va., 1982, St. Stephen Cath. Ctr., Ona, W.Va., 1982, Dicean Chancery, Wheeling, W.Va., 1983, St. Mary's Cath. Ch., Wheeling, 1983, High Knob Ch., Sutton, W.Va., 1984, State Capitol Grounds, Charleston, 1985, 89, Harrison County Courthouse, Clarksburg, 1985, St. Michael's Cath. Ch., Vienna, W.Va., 1986, St. Francis Hosp., Charleston, 1986, Sunrise Mus., Charleston, 1987, St. Joseph Hosp., Parkersburg, W.Va., 1988, Our Lady of the Lake Med. Ctr., Baton Rouge, 1989, City Pk., Gallipolis, Ohio, 1990, St. Margaret-Mary Ch., Parkersburg, 1992, Davis and Elkins (W.Va.) Coll. Libr., 1993, Wheeling Jesuit Coll., 1993, Cath. H.S., Baton Rouge, 1993, St. Vincent's Children's Svcs., Bklyn., 1994, St. James Cath. Ch., Clarksburg, 1994, Tamarack Pavilion, Beckly, W.Va., 1995, State Capitol Rotunda, Charleston, 1996, St. Vincent's Hosp., Indpls., 1997, The Adorers Chapel, Wichita, Kans., 1998; represented in permanent collections Tamerack Pavilion, Beckly, Sunrise Mus., Charleston, W.Va. Culture and History Sculpture Garden, Charleston, Steifle Fine Arts Ctr., Wheeling, Sleethe Gallery W.Va. Wesleyan Coll., Buckhannon, Wheeling Jesuit Coll., Potomac State Coll., Kaiser, W.Va., Davis and Elkins Coll., Dryfus Energy Ltd., Singapore, pvt. collections. Avocations: wilderness camping, hiking, canoeing, cycling. Office: Hopen Studio 266 N Hill Rd # A Sutton WV 26601-1230

HOPF, FRANK RUDOLPH, dentist; b. N.Y.C., Sept. 1, 1920; s. Rudolph Aldridge and Jennie Victoria (Fusco) H.; B.S., Purdue U., 1942; postgrad. Middlesex U. Sch. Medicine, 1943-44; D.D.S., N.Y. U., 1953, postgrad., 1957-61; M.A., Columbia, 1953, M.P.H., 1955; m. Elsie Hedlund, Sept. 10, 1949; children—Christine, Frank, Victoria, William, Robert. Asst. dir. Bur. Dental Health, N.Y. State Dept. Health, Albany, 1956-57, regional dental dir., White Plains, 1967-90; pvt. practice dentistry specializing in periodontics, Rye, 1957—. Research asso. dept. periodontics, N.Y. U. Coll. Dentistry, 1958-61; clin. asst. prof. dept. periodontics N.J. Coll. Medicine and Dentistry, Jersey City, 1962-67; adj. asst. prof. dept. community dentistry Columbia Sch. Dental and Oral Surgery, N.Y.C., 1971-76; vis. prof. dept. preventive dentistry, Pitts. U. Sch. Dentistry, 1967-72. Pres., Country Ridge Home Owners Assn., Rye Brook, N.Y., 1960-62. Served with USNR, 1944-46. NIH grantee, 1957. Fellow Am. Public Health Assn., Am. Sch. Health Assn., N.Y. Acad. Dentistry, Am. Coll. Dentists; mem. ADA, N.Y. State Public Health Assn. (pres. 1970-72), Westchester Shore Dental Study Club (pres. 1960-61), Royal Soc. Health, North Eastern Soc. Periodontics, AAAS, Westchester Acad. Medicine, Am. Soc. Dentistry for Children, Federation Dentaire Internationale. Roman Catholic. KC (4 deg.). Club: Westchester Country (Rye, N.Y.). Contbr. articles to profl. publs. Home: 42 Rockinghorse Trl Rye Brook NY 10573-1038 Office: 33 Cedar St Rye NY 10580-2031

HOPF, HAROLD HERBERT, retired chemical engineer; b. Ware, Mass., Apr. 21, 1936; s. Herbert Henry and Lottie Maud (Senecal) H.; m. Winifred Ann Dorsey, June 29, 1957; children: Peter Harold, William David, Susan Elizabeth Haryasz. BSChemE, U. Mass., 1958, MSChemE, 1970. Registered profl. engr., N.Y. Devel. engr. Monsanto Co., Indian Orchard, Mass., 1961-82, corp. fellow, 1982-98; ret., 1998; CEO U.S. Wave Energy, Inc., Longmeadow, Mass., 1995—; pres. Polystress Co., Longmeadow, 1988—. Author: (software), tech. editor: Stress/Strain in Polymers, 1993; patentee ocean wave power generators, polymer processing systems. Children's story author/reader Pub. Libr., Longmeadow, 1989, Shriners Hosp., Springfield, Mass., 1989. Recipient Centennial award Boston Edison, 1986. Mem. Soc. Am. Inventors. Avocation: computer software devel. Home: 65 Pioneer Dr Longmeadow MA 01106-2805

HOPFENBECK, GEORGE MARTIN, JR., lawyer; b. N.Y.C., Mar. 1, 1929; s. George Martin and Margaret Spencer (Felt) H.; m. Ruth Elizabeth Allen, June 27, 1953; children: Ann Elizabeth, James Allen. BA, Williams Coll., 1951; JD, Yale U., 1954. Bar: Colo., 1955. Assoc. Davis, Graham & Stubbs and predecessor Lewis, Grant & Davis, Denver, 1954-59, ptnr., 1959-92, of counsel, 1993—. Bd. dirs. Am. Cancer Soc. Inc., Colo. divsn., Denver, 1966-90, chmn., 1975-77; bd. dirs. Colo. Regional Cancer Ctr. Inc., Denver, 1974-81, pres., 1975-77; bd. dirs. Am. Cancer Soc. Inc., Atlanta, 1984-90, Denver Parks and Recreation Found., 1966-75; bd. dirs. Boys and Girls Clubs of Metro Denver, Inc., 1993—, chmn., 1998—; mem. Colo. State Pers. Bd., Denver, 1971-75, chmn., 1971-72; mem. Denver Bd. Parks & Recreation, 1961-69; trustee Kent Sch. for Girls, Denver, 1970-73; chmn. campaign com. for Gov. Love, Colo., 1966, campaign com. for McKevitt for Congress, Denver, 1970. Recipient St. George medal Am. Cancer Soc., 1982. Mem. ABA, Colo. Bar Assn., Denver Country Club (bd. dirs. 1967-70), University Club (Denver) (bd. dirs. 1973-82). Republican. Episcopalian. Home: 450 Race St Denver CO 80206-4121 Office: Davis Graham & Stubbs PO Box 185 370 17th St Ste 4700 Denver CO 80202-5682 also: 333 Logan St Ste 108 Denver CO 80203-4089

HOPFIELD, JOHN JOSEPH, biophysicist, educator; b. Chgo., July 15, 1933; s. John Joseph and Helen (Staff) H.; children: Alison, Jessica, Natalie; m. Mary Waltham, 1996. AB, Swarthmore Coll., 1954; PhD, Cornell U., 1958; DSc (hon.), Swarthmore Coll., 1992. Mem. tech. staff ATT Bell Labs., 1958-60, 73-89; vis. rsch. physicist Ecole Normale Superieure, Paris, France, 1960-61; asst. prof., then asso. prof. physics U. Calif. at Berkeley, 1961-64; prof. physics Princeton U., 1964-80, Eugene Higgins prof. physics, 1978-80; Dickinson prof. chemistry and biology Calif. Inst. Tech., Pasadena, 1980-96; prof. molecular biology Princeton (N.J.) U., 1997—. Trustee Battelle Meml. Inst. Guggenheim fellow, 1969, MacArthur Prize fellow, 1983; recipient Michelson-Morley prize, 1988, Wright prize, 1989; named Calif. Scientist of Yr., 1991, Neural Net Pioneer award IEEE, 1997. Fellow Am. Phys. Soc. (Oliver E. Buckley prize 1968, Biol. Physics prize 1985); mem. NAS, Am. Acad. Arts and Scis., Am. Philos. Soc., Phi Beta Kappa, Sigma Xi. Office: Princeton U Dept Molecular Biology Princeton NJ 08544

HOPGOOD, JAMES F., anthropologist; b. Cape Girardeau, Mo., Apr. 18, 1943; s. Finley Marshall and Marjorie Louise (Schneider) H.; m. Esther Berg, Jan. 29, 1966; 1 child, Myka Lynn. BA, U. Mo., 1965, MA, 1969; MPhil, U. Kans., 1971, PhD, 1976. Asst. prof. anthropology No. Ky. U., Highland Heights, 1973-76, assoc. prof., 1976-90, prof., 1990—, chmn. dept. sociology, anthropology and philosophy, 1984-98, mem. exec. com. faculty senate, 1978-80; vis. instr. Washburn U., Topeka, 1969; vis. prof. Instituto Tecnologico y de Estudios Superiores de Monterrey, Mex., 1971, U. Monterrey, 1980; profl. assoc. Asian studies devel. program East-West Ctr. and U. Hawaii, summers, 1991, 93, 94. Author: Bajavista: Urban Adaptation in a Mexican Squatter Settlement, 1979; editorial bd. Jour. of Third World Studies; contbr. articles, reports to profl. jours. Mem. edn. com. Cin. Mus. Natural History, 1992-94. Jewish Chautauqua Soc. scholar in residence No. Ky. U., 1988-98; recipient Sasakawa fellowship San Diego State U., summer 1996. Fellow Am. Anthrop. Assn. (mem. exec. com. 1996-98—); mem. Ky. Acad. Sci. (bd. gov. 1995-98), Ctrl. States Anthropol. Soc. (pres. 1996-97), Sigma Xi, Lambda Alpha. Home: 4918 Corn Row Ct Independence KY 41051-8101 Office: No Ky U Dept Sociology Anthrop Ph Highland Heights KY 41099

HOPKINS, ALBEN NORRIS, lawyer; b. Ripley, Miss., Feb. 14, 1941; s. Lloyd Carter and Reba Genova (Norris) H.; m. Ruth Boyd, May 31, 1963; children: Ashley Anne, A. Norris. BA, Delta State Coll., 1963; JD, U. Miss., 1965; BA, William Carey Coll., 1985; student, Blue Mountain Coll. Bar: U.S. Dist. Ct. (so. dist.) Miss. 1966, U.S. Dist. Ct. (no. dist.) Miss. 1970, U.S. Ct. Appeals (5th cir.) 1972, U.S. Supreme Ct. 1972, U.S. Ct. Appeals (11th cir.) 1981, U.S. Ct. Mil. Appeals 1986. Assoc. Daniel, Coker & Horton, Jackson also Gulfport, Miss., 1965-67; ptnr. Daniel, Coker & Horton, Jackson also Gulfport, 1967-69, resident ptnr., 1969-77; sr. ptnr., mng. ptnr. Hopkins, Crawley, Bagwell, Upshaw & Parsons, Gulfport, 1977—. Bd. dirs. Delta State U. Found., 1991-94, pres., 1994; bd. dirs. USO, 1974-75, 83—, Gulf Pines Coun. Girl Scouts U.S.A., 1974-82, 85—, United Way Harrison Coutny; bd. dirs., chmn. planned giving com., dist. dir. Am. Heart Assn.; asst. chmn. State Heart Fund, 1983, chmn., 1985; asst. adjutant gen. State of Miss., 1991-95, chief judge Mil. Ct. Appeals, 1996—. Served to maj. gen. U.S. Army N.G., 1965-95, ret. Fellow Miss. Bar Found.; mem. Internat. Assn. Def. Counsel, Fedn. Ins. Counsel, Maritime Law Assn. U.S., Southeastern Admiralty Assn., Hinds County Bar Assn., Harrison County Bar Assn. (v.p. 1976-77), Miss. Bar Assn. (mem. jud. selection com. 1978-79), ABA, Lamar Order, Fed. Bar Assn. (bd. dirs. 1979-82), Kappa Alpha, Pi Kappa Delta, Phi Alpha Delta, Omicron Delta Kappa, Broadwater Country Club, Windance Country Club, Gulfport Yacht Club, Univ. Club, Masons, Shriners, YorkRite, others. Republican. Baptist. Office: PO Box 1510 Gulfport MS 39502-1510*

HOPKINS, SIR ANTHONY (PHILIP), actor; b. Port Talbot, South Wales, U.K., Dec. 31, 1937; s. Richard Arthur and Muriel Annie (Yeates) H.; m. Petronella Barker, 1967 (div. 1972); 1 child, Abigail; m. Jennifer Ann Lynton, Jan. 13, 1973. Student, Welsh Coll. Music and Drama, Cardiff, Wales, 1954-56, Royal Acad. Dramatic Art, London, 1961-63; DLitt (hon.), Wales, 1988; Fellow (hon.), St. David's Coll., Lampeter, Wales, 1992. Ind. stage, screen, TV actor, 1963—. Made London stage debut in Julius Caesar, 1964; mem. Nat. Theatre Co., 1966-73; appeared in Juno and the Paycock, 1966, A Flea in Her Ear, 1966, Three Sisters, 1967, The Dance of Death, 1967, As You Like It, 1967, The Architect and the Emperor of Assyria, 1971, A Woman Killed with Kindness, 1971, Coriolanus, 1971, The Taming of the Shrew, 1972, Macbeth, 1972, Equus (Best Actor award N.Y. Drama Desk, Best Actor award Outer Critics Circle, Best Actor award Am. Authors Celebrities Forum), N.Y.C., 1974-75, (L.A. Drama Critics award), Los Angeles, 1977, The Tempest, Los Angeles, 1979, Old Times, N.Y.C., 1983, The Lonely Road, London, 1985, Pravda, Nat. Theatre, London, 1985-86 (Olivier award 1985, Stage Actor award Variety Club), King Lear, Nat. Theatre, London, 1986-87, Anthony & Cleopatra, Nat. Theatre, London, 1987, M Butterfly, Shaftesbury Theatre, London, 1989, (also director) August, 1994; films include (debut) The Lion in Winter, 1968, Hamlet, 1969, The Looking Glass War, 1970, When Eight Bells Toll, 1971, Young Winston, 1972, A Doll's House, 1973, The Girl from Petrovka, 1974, Juggernaut, 1974, A Bridge Too Far, 1977, Audrey Rose, 1977, International Velvet, 1977, Magic, 1978, The Elephant Man, 1979, A Change of Seasons, 1980, The Bounty, 1984 (Film Actor award Variety Club), The Good Father, 1985, 84 Charing Cross Road, 1986 (Best Actor award Moscow Film Festival 1987), The Dawning, 1987, A Chorus of Disapproval, 1988, Desperate Hours, 1989, The Silence of the Lambs, 1991 (Acad. award for Best Actor, 1992, Best Actor award Chgo. Film Critics 1992, Best Actor award Boston Film Critics 1992, Best Actor award N.Y. Film Critics 1992, Film Actor award Variety Club 1992, Best Film Actor award BAFTA 1992), Freejack, One Man's War, 1990, Spotswood/The Efficiency Expert, 1990, Howard's End, 1991, Bram Stoker's Dracula, 1992, Chaplin, 1992, Remains of the Day, 1993 (Acad. award nominee for Best Actor 1994, Best Actor award L.A. Film Critics Assn. 1993, Best Actor award Nat. Soc. Film Critics (U.S.A.) 1993, BAFTA UK best film actor award, Guild of Regional Film Writers UK Best Actor award, Variety Club UK Film Actor award 1993, Japan Critics Best Actor in a Fgn. Film award), Shadowlands, 1993 (Best Actor award Nat. Bd. Rev. 1993, Best Actor award L.A. Film Critics Assn. 1993, Best Actor award Nat. Soc. Film Critics (U.S.A.) 1993), The Trial, 1993, The Road to Welville, 1993, Legends of the Fall, 1994, The Innocent, 1995, Nixon, 1995 (Acad. award nominee for Best Actor 1996), August, 1996, Surviving Picasso, 1996, The Edge, 1997, Amistad, 1997, The Mask of Zorro, 1998, Meet Joe Black, 1998; BBC-TV series War and Peace (Best TV Actor award Soc. Film and TV Arts), 1972; TV shows include A Heritage and Its History, 1968, Vanya, Hearts and Flowers, Three Sisters, The Peasants' Revolt, Dickens, Danton, The Poet Game, Vanya, Hearts and Flowers, Decision to Burn, War and Peace, Cuculus Canorus, Lloyd George, Q.B. VII, 1971, Find Me, A Childhood Friend, Possessions, All Creatures Great and Small, 1975, The Lindbergh Kidnapping Case, 1976 (Emmy award), Victory at Entebbe, 1976, Dark Victory, Mayflower: The Pilgrim's Adventure, 1979, The Bunker, 1980 (Emmy award), Peter and Paul, 1980, Othello, BBC, 1981, Little Eyolf, BBC, 1981, The Hunchback of Notre Dame, 1982, A Married Man, 1984, The Arch of Triumph, CBS, 1984, Hollywood Wives, ABC, 1984, Guilty Conscience, CBS, 1984, Blunt, BBC, 1985, The Tenth Man, CBS, 1988, Across the Lake, BBC, Heartland, BBC, Great Expectations, 1989, Disney Primetime, To Be The Best, 1990, others. Decorated Comdr. of Order of Brit. Empire, 1987, Knights Bachelor, 1993, Comdr. of Order of Arts & Letters, France, 1996. Office: CAA 9830 Wilshire Blvd Beverly Hills CA 90212-1804

HOPKINS, BERNARD (THE EXECUTIONER HOPKINS), professional boxer; b. Phila., Jan. 15, 1965. IBF middleweight champion, 1995. Now 34-2-1 with 26 knockouts, 1998.

HOPKINS, CASSANDRE' F., land use planner; b. Ahookie, N.C., Nov. 11, 1968; d. Willie Lee and Mildred Elaine (Ward) H. B, N.C. Cen. Univ., 1993, MPA, 1996, postgrad., 1998—. Mem. NCAPA, APA, NFBPA. Home: 6837 Coventry Ridge Rd Raleigh NC 27616-3501 Office: City Sanford Cmty Devel 1601 Hillcrest St Sanford NC 27330

HOPKINS, DAVID MOODY, geologist; b. Nashua, N.H., Dec. 26, 1921; s. Donald Wheeler and Henrietta (Moody) H.; m. Joan Prewitt, Dec. 27, 1949 (dec. Sept. 1955); children: Dana, Chindi Ann; m. Martha Bryant, Sept. 25, 1957 (div. June 1970); 1 child, Alexander Carrier Hopkins; m. Rachel Chouinard Stanley, Aug. 23, 1970. BS, U. N.H., 1942; MS, Harvard U., 1948, PhD, 1955. From geologist to sr. rsch. geologist U.S. Geol. Survey, Washington, 1942-55, Menlo Park, Calif., 1955-84; disting. prof. U. Alaska, Fairbanks, 1985-94; ret., 1994; dir. Alaska Quaternary Ctr., 1984-89; cons. U.S. Nat. Park Svc., Anchorage, 1986—, Alaska Divsn. Geol. and Geophys. Surveys, 1995-97. Editor, contbr. The Bering Land Bridge, 1967; co-editor, contbr. Paleoecology of Beringia, 1982; contbr. articles to profl. jours. With USAF, 1945-47. Recipient Franklin Burr award Nat. Geographic Soc., 1993. Fellow Geol. Soc. Am. (chmn. Geomorphology and Quaternary Geology divsn. 1969-70, Archaeol. Geology divsn. 1984-85, Kirk Bryan award 1968, Career award in Geoarcheology 1990, Career award in Quaternary Geology and Geomorphology 1995), Arctic Inst. N.Am. (editl. bd. 1979—), Calif. Acad. Sci.; mem. Am. Quaternary Assn. (pres. 1974, Career award in Quaternary studies 1998), Soc. Am. Archaeology (Fryxell award 1988). Democrat. Avocations: railfan, photography. Home: 40 Steelhead Rd Fairbanks AK 99709-3201

HOPKINS, DONALD J., lawyer; b. Long Beach, Calif., Jan. 9, 1947; m. Ellen Colokathis, Aug. 29, 1970; children: Melanie J., Shannon R., Christopher S. AB, Stanford U., 1968; JD, Harvard U., 1971. Bar: Mass. 1971, Colo. 1974, U.S. Dist. Ct. Colo. 1974. Mem. firm Holme Roberts & Owen LLP, Denver, 1973—. Fellow Am. Coll. Trust and Estate Counsel. Office: Holme Roberts & Owen LLP 1700 Lincoln St Ste 4100 Denver CO 80203-4541

HOPKINS, DONALD ROSWELL, public health physician; b. Miami, Fla., Sept. 25, 1941; s. Joseph Leonard and Iva (Major) H.; m. Ernestine Mathis, June 24, 1967. BS, Morehouse Coll., 1962; MD, U. Chgo., 1966; MPH, Harvard U., 1970; DSc (hon.), Morehouse Coll., 1988, Emory U., 1994; LHD (hon.), U. Mass., Lowell, 1997. Intern San Francisco Gen. Hosp., 1966-67; resident U. Chgo. Hosps., 1970-72; med. officer program planning and evaluation Ctrs. for Disease Control, Atlanta, 1972-74, dep. chief environ. health service div., 1974, asst. dir. ops., 1977-80, asst. dir. internat. health, 1980-84; sr. cons. Global 2000 Inc., Carter Presdl. Ctr., Atlanta, 1987-97; dep. dir. Ctrs. for Disease Control, 1984-87; cons. Carter Ctr. Global 2000 Program, Atlanta, 1987-97; assoc.exec. dir. The Carter Ctr., Inc., 1997—; asst. prof. tropical pub. health Harvard U., Boston, 1974-77; chmn., advisor on internat. health research Dr. Peter Bourne, White House, Washington, 1977; mem. U.S. del. World Health Assembly, Geneva, Switzerland, 1977-78, 80-86; mem. global adv. group on immunization WHO, Geneva, 1978-79, mem. steering com. epidemiology working group, 1980-83. Author: Princes and Peasants-Smallpox in History, 1983. Recipient Commd. Corps Disting. Service medal USPHS, 1986, Joseph Mountin Lecture award Ctrs. for Disease Control, 1981, John Snow award APHA, 1997; named knight Nat. Order of Mali, 1998, Order of Bifurcated Needle WHO, 1977, MacArthur fellow, 1995. Fellow Am. Acad. Arts & Scis.; mem. Am. Soc. Tropical Medicine and Hygiene, Inst. Medicine Nat. Acad. Sci., Phi Beta Kappa. Democrat. Episcopalian. Office: Carter Presdl Ctr Inc One Copenhill Bldg 453 Freedom Pkwy Atlanta GA 30058*

HOPKINS, EARL NORRIS, metallurgist; b. Calico Rock, Ark., July 15, 1930; s. Earl L. and Roxie M. (Norris) H.; m. Elizabeth E. Walkup, Aug. 9, 1952; children: Stephanie, Stephen, Elizabeth, Patrick, Kathleen, Jennifer. BS, Rockhurst Coll., 1952. Metallographer Westinghouse Elec. Corp., Kansas City, Mo., 1952-59; metallurgist Olin Corp., Independence, Mo., 1995—; assoc. scientist Ames Lab. Iowa State U., 1959-66; sr. scientist Continental Can Co., Chgo., 1966-72; chief metallurgist Midland Ross Corp., Melrose Park, Ill., 1972-79, TRW Corp., Lebanon, Tenn., 1979-93. Contbr. articles to profl. jours. Leader Boy Scouts Am., Lombard, Ill., 1965-73. Mem. Am. Soc. Metals. Achievements include discovery and development of low temperature electropolishing for electron microscopy; pioneered use of digital computers for control of heat treat processes; development of methods for thin film electron microscopy for rare earth metals. Avocations: historical research, golf. Home: 1325 Dickinson Rd Independence MO 64050-1366 Office: Olin Corp PO Box 250 Independence MO 64051-0250

HOPKINS, ESTHER ARVILLA HARRISON, retired chemist, patent lawyer; b. Stamford, Conn., Sept. 18, 1926; d. George Burgess and Esther (Smalls) Harrison; m. John Payne Mitchell, Dec. 27, 1952 (div.); 1 child, Susan Weamah Emma; m. Thomas Ewell Hopkins, Jan. 20, 1959; 1 child, Thomas Ewell Jr. AB, Boston U., 1947; MS, Howard U., 1948, Yale U., 1962; PhD, Yale U., 1967; JD, Suffolk U., Boston, 1977. Bar: Mass. 1977; registered patent atty. Patent and Trademark Office, Dept. Commerce. Instr. chemistry Va. State Coll., Petersburg, 1949-52; research chemist New Eng. Inst. Med. Research, Ridgefield, Conn., 1955-59, Am. Cyanamid Corp., Stamford, 1959-61; scientist Polaroid Corp., Cambridge, Mass., 1967-73, jr. patent atty., 1973-78, sr. project adminstr., 1979-86, tech. liaison mgr., 1986-88; dep. gen. counsel dept. environ. protection Commonwealth of Mass., Boston, 1989—. Contbr. articles to profl. jours. Trustee Boston U., 1985—, bd. visitors, pres. Boston U. Alumni, 1985-87; bd. dirs. YMCA USA, Chgo.; clk. Clara Barton Camp for Girls with Diabetes Inc., North Oxford, Mass., 1985-90; chair, clk. fin. com. Town of Framingham, Mass., selectman, 1999—; commr. Framingham Tercentennial; sec. Soc. Promoting Theol. Edn., Boston; mem. bd. overseers Regional Lab. for Ednl. Improvement of the N.E. and the Islands, Andover, Mass.; mem. adv. com. MetroWest Health, Inc.; mem. nomination evaluation com. Nat. Medal of Tech. Named Woman of Achievement, Mass. Fedn. Bus. and Profl. Women, 1979, Leading Woman Patriots Tr. Coun. Girl Scouts U.S. Mem. Am. Chem. Soc. (chair com. profl. rels., chair northeastern sect. 1983, mem. coun. policy com.), Phi Beta Kappa, Sigma Xi, Sigma Pi Sigma, Beta Kappa Chi, Alpha Kappa Alpha. Unitarian-Universalist. Avocations: music, money. Home: 1550 Worcester Rd Apt 524 Framingham MA 01702-8937

HOPKINS, GEORGE MATHEWS MARKS, lawyer, business executive; b. Houston, June 9, 1923; s. C. Allen and Agnes Cary (Marks) H.; m. Betty Miller McLean, Aug. 21, 1954; children: Laura Hopkins Corrigan, Edith Hopkins Collins. Student, Ga. Tech., 1943-44; BSChemE, Ala. Poly. Inst., 1944; LLB, JD, U. Ala., 1949; postgrad., George Washington U., 1949-50. Bar: Ala. 1949, Ga. 1954; registered patent lawyer, U.S.; registered profl. engr., Ga.; Can. qualified deep-sea diver. Instr. math. U. Ala., 1947-49; assoc. A. Yates Dowell, Washington, 1949-50, Edward T. Newton, Atlanta, 1950-62; ptnr. Newton, Hopkins and Ormsby (and predecessor), Atlanta, 1962-87; sr. ptnr. Hunt, Richardson, Garner, Todd & Cadenhead, Atlanta, 1987-91; ptnr. Hopkins & Thomas, 1991-95; ret., 1996; spl. asst. atty. gen. State of Ga., 1978; chmn. bd. Southeastern Carpet Mills, Inc., Chatsworth, Ga., 1962-77, Thomas-Daniel & Assocs., Inc., 1981-85, Ea. Carpet Mills, Inc., 1983-87; CEO, Airamar Chem. Engring., Inc., Doraville, Ga., 1997—; asst. dir. rsch., legal counsel Auburn (Ala.) Rsch. Found., 1954-55; spl. asst. atty. gen. State of Ga., 1978; chmn. bd. S.E. Carpet Mills, Inc., Chatsworth, Ga., 1962-77, Thomas-Daniel & Assocs., Inc., 1981-85, Ea. Carpet Mills, Inc.; dir. Xepol Inc. Served as lt., navigator, Submarine Service USNR, 1944-46, 50-51. Mem. ABA, Ga. Bar Assn. (chmn. sect. patents 1970-71), Atlanta Bar Assn., Am. Intellectual Property Law Assn., Am. Soc. Profl. Engrs., Submarine Vets. World War II (pres. Ga. chpt. 1977-78), Phi Delta Phi, Sigma Alpha Epsilon, Atlanta Lawyers Club, Phoenix Soc., Cherokee Town and Country Club, AtlantaSoc. Episcopalian. Home: 795 Old Post Rd NW Atlanta GA 30328-4758*

HOPKINS, GERALD FRANK, trade association administrator; b. La Grande, Oreg., Dec. 6, 1943; s. Albert Benjamin and Phyllis Nadine (Munn) H.; m. Mary Martha Abbott, June 9, 1967; children: Angela, Ann. BS, Ea. Mont. Coll., 1966, MS, 1967; postgrad., U. So. Calif., 1973. Grad. asst. Ea. Mont. Coll., Billings, 1966-67; tchr., adminstr. Elysian Schs., Billings, 1967-69; adminstrv. asst. Internat. Schs., Bangkok, 1969-73; prin. Nashua (Mont.) Pub. Schs., 1973-76, Roundup (Mont.) Pub. Schs., 1976-86; owner, operator Town Pump, Billings, 1986-90; exec. dir. La Grande/Union County C. of C., 1990-92; tchr., adminstr. Huntington (Oreg.) Pub. Schs., 1992—; project coord. Title I, 1996-97. Author: BJ & Boz, 1989, Humor in the Classroom, 1995; contbr. articles to profl. jours. Bd. dirs. Family Crisis Intervention, Roundup, 1983-86, Sr. Citizens Vol. Program, Roundup, 1983-86, State Reading Assn., Roundup, 1986-88, Continuing Edn. Coun., La Grande, 1990, Oreg. Trail Days., Continuing Counsel Higher Edn.; mem. Coop. Community Exch. Coun., 1983-86, hist. validation com Airport Svc. Coun., La Grande, 1991. Recipient State Disting. Title I. award, Nat. Disting. Title I program, 1996-97, Oreg. Small Sch. Innovative Program, 1997, Internat. Pres. Humanitarian award, 1998. Mem. Small Bus. Adminstrn., Nat. C. of C., Elem. Adminstrs. Assn. (dir. ea. dist. 1988-90), Lions (internat. officer 1973-95, Outstanding Achievement award 1986, bd. dirs. La. Grande Club, Roundup of Lion Yr. 1977, 78, 79, 2d Internat. Pres.'s Humanitarian award 1978), Ambs. (assoc.). Home: 68068 Hunter Rd Summerville OR 97876-8133

HOPKINS, GROVER PREVATTE, lawyer; b. Jacksonville, Fla., Sept. 2, 1933; s. John Taylor and Capitola (Prevatte) H.; m. Ann Hutchinson, Oct. 16, 1965 (dec.); children: John, George, James, Corbin; m. Connie Jefferys, June 7, 1973. AB, Fla. State U., 1958; JD, U.N.C., 1971. Bar: N.C. 1971, U.S. Dist. Ct. (ea. dist.) N.C. 1971, Fla. 1972, U.S. Ct. Appeals (4th cir.) 1974, U.S. Supreme Ct. 1974, D.C. 1981; cert. mediator N.C. Cts., 1997. Announcer, Sta. WTAL, Tallahassee, 1951-54; pub. rels. dir. Inter-Am. U., San Germán, P.R., 1958-60; pers. mgr. Northridge Knitting Mills, San Germán, 1960-62; cons. bus. and pers., Mayagüez, P.R., and Miami, Fla., 1963-69; mem. Weeks & Muse, Tarboro, N.C., 1971-73, Hopkins & Assocs., Tarboro, 1973—. Served with U.S. Army, 1954-57. Mem. ABA, N.C. Bar Assn., D.C. Bar Assn., Inter-Am. Bar Assn. (sec. gen. 1989-91). Republican. Episcopalian. Office: Hopkins & Assocs 212 N Main St Tarboro NC 27886-5008

HOPKINS, HENRY TYLER, museum director, art educator; b. Idaho Falls, Idaho, Aug. 14, 1928; s. Talcott Thompson and Zoe (Erbe) H.; children—Victoria Anne, John Thomas, Christopher Tyler. BA, Sch. of Art Inst., Chgo., 1952, MA, 1955; postgrad., UCLA, 1957-60; PhD (hon.), Calif. Coll. Arts and Crafts, 1984, San Francisco Art Inst., 1986. Curator exhbns., publs. Los Angeles County Mus. of Art, 1960-68; dir. Fort Worth Art Mus., 1968-74, San Francisco Mus. of Modern Art, 1974-86; chmn. art dept. UCLA, 1991-94, dir. F.S. Wight Gallery, 1991-95, dir. Armand Hammer Mus. Art and Cultural Ctr., 1994-99, prof. art, 1999—; lectr. art history UCLA Ext., 1994-99; instr. Tex. Christian U., Ft. Worth, 1968-74; dir. U.S. representation Venice (Italy) Bienniel, 1970; dir. art presentation Festival of Two Worlds, Spoleto, Italy, 1970; co-commr. U.S. representation XVI Sao Paulo (Brazil) Biennale, 1981; cons. NEA, mem. mus. panel, 1979-84, chmn., 1981; cons., mem. mus. panel NEH, 1976. Contbr. numerous articles to profl. jours., also numerous mus. publs. Served with AUS, 1952-54. Decorated knight Order Leopold II, Belgium); recipient special internat. award, Art L.A., 1992. Mem. Assn. Art Mus. Dirs. (pres. 1985-86), Coll. Art Assn., Am. Assn. Museums, Western Assn. Art Museums (pres. 1977-78). Home: 939 1/2 Hilgard Ave Los Angeles CA 90024-3032 Office: UCLA Art Dept 405 Hilgard Ave Los Angeles CA 90024

HOPKINS, JACK WALKER, former university administrator, environmental educator; b. Fitzgerald, Ga., Feb. 16, 1930; s. Milton Newton and Hattie Lee (Walker) H.; m. Katherine Lee Arthur, Apr. 20, 1957; children—David Arthur, Mark Steven, Susan Kay. Student, North Ga. Coll., 1947-48; B.A., U. N.C., 1951; M.A., Emory U., 1962; Ph.D., U. Fla., 1966. Asst. prof. polit. sci. Ga. Inst. Tech., 1965-66, Ga. State Coll., Atlanta, 1966-67; assoc. prof. Emory U., Atlanta, 1967-71; prof., chmn. dept. Tex. Tech U., Lubbock, 1971-75; prof. pub. and environ. affairs Ind. U., Bloomington, 1975—; provost Malaysia Program, Ind. U., Shah Alam, Malaysia, 1985-86; assoc. dir. Ind. Ctr. on Global Change and World Peace, 1992-94, dir., 1994-95; research cons. Inst. Pub. Adminstrn. (Peru), N.Y.C., 1964-65. Author: The Government Executive of Modern Peru, 1967, Latin America in World Affairs, 1976; editor: Latin America and Caribbean Contemporary Record, (4 times) 1982-86, Latin America: Perspectives on a Region, 1987, 2d edit., 1998, The Eradication of Smallpox, 1989, Policymaking for Conservation in Latin America, 1995. Dist. chmn. Dem. Ctrl. Com., DeKalb, Ga., 1970; del. Dem. Nat. Conv., 1976; mem. Bloomington Common Coun., 1991-95, pres., 1993. Fulbright lectr. to Argentina, 1968; NASPAA/ASPA pub. adminstrn. fellow, 1970-71; Rockefeller found. scholar, 1982. Mem. Latin Am. Studies Assn. Democrat. Avocations: sailing, hiking. Home: 2618 Covenanter Ct Bloomington IN 47401-5408 Office: Ind U Sch Pub and Environ Affairs Bloomington IN 47405

HOPKINS, JAN, journalist, news anchor; b. Warren, Ohio, May 22, 1947; d. Walter Charles and Lois Avelene (Botroff) Reed; m. Walter Hopkins, June 14, 1969 (div. Nov. 1981); m. Richard Trachtman, Nov. 8, 1986. Dir. news Sta. WTCL, Warren, Ohio, 1973-75; reporter, anchor Sta. WERE, Cleve., 1975-77; reporter Sta. WKBN-TV, Youngstown, Ohio, 1977-80; reporter, anchor Sta. WLWT-TV, Cin., 1980-82; assignment editor CBS News, N.Y.C., 1983; reporter, prodr. ABC News, N.Y.C., 1983-84; anchor bus. news CNN, N.Y.C., 1984—. Author: (chapter) Knight Bagehot Guide to Business Journalism, 1990. Trustee Hiram Coll., 1988-94; adv. bd. Knight Bagehot program jouralism Columbia U., N.Y.C., 1994. Recipient Peabody award U. Ga., 1988, Front Page award Newswomen Club N.Y., 1988; Knight Bagehot fellow Columbia U. Sch. Journalism, 1982-83; named to Hall of Excellence Ohio Found. Ind. Colls., 1993, Warren, Ohio, H.S. Disting. Alumni Hall of Fame, 1995. Mem. Econ. Club N.Y. Office: CNN Bus News 5 Penn Plz Fl 20 New York NY 10001-1810

HOPKINS, JEANNETTE ETHEL, book publisher, editor; b. Camden, N.J., Dec. 7, 1922; d. Carleton Roper and Gladys Eugenia (Hull) H. BA, Vassar Coll., 1944; MS, Columbia Sch. Journalism, 1945. Asst. to Sunday editor New Haven Register, 1945-46; reporter Providence Evening Bull., 1946-50, Oklahoma City Times, 1950-51; sr. editor Beacon Press, Boston, 1951-56, Harcourt Brace, N.Y.C., 1956-64, Harper & Row, N.Y.C., 1964-73; v.p. Met. Applied Res. Ctr., N.Y.C., 1970-72, cons. editor, 1973-80, 89—; dir. Wesleyan Univ. Press, Middletown, Conn., 1980-89; adj. prof. English Wesleyan U., 1987-89, U. N.H., 1989; propr. Portsmouth Athenaeum, 1991. Author: Books That Will Not Burn, 1952, 14 Journeys to Unitarianism, 1951, (with K.B. Clark) Relevant War Against Poverty, 1968, Legacy: A History of the South Church Endowment, 1995. Mem. coun. Inst. Religion in an Age of Sci., 1968-72, 80-82, 88-91; mem. bd. Unitarian UN Office, 1977-80; mem. Commn. on Appraisal, Unitarian Universalist Assn., 1976-78; bd. dirs. ACLU, 1970-79, mem. nat. adv. coun., 1986—; bd. govs. Comty. Ch. N.Y., 1960-66, Unitarian-Universalist Ch., Portsmouth, 1990-93, lay min., 1991-95; trustee South Ch. Endowment Fund, 1996-99; v.p. Unitarian Fellowship for Social Justice, 1958-62. Louise Hart Van Loon fellow, Vassar Coll., 1944; recipient Disting. Alumni award Columbia Sch. Journalism, 1981. Democrat. Unitarian. Home and Office: 39 Pray St Portsmouth NH 03801-5226

HOPKINS, JEFFREY P., federal judge; b. 1960. JD, Ohio State U., 1985. Law clk. to Hon. Alan E. Norris U.S. Ct. Appeals (6th cir.), 1985-87; assoc. Squire, Sanders & Dempsey, 1987-90; asst. U.S. atty. U.S. Dist. Ct. (so. dist.) Ohio, 1990-96; bankruptcy judge U.S. Dist. Ct. (so. dist.) Ohio, Cin., 1996—. Fax: (513) 684-2028. Office: US Dist Ct So Dist Ohio US Bankruptcy Ct Ste 800 221 E 4th St Atrium 2 Cincinnati OH 45202

HOPKINS, JOHN DAVID, lawyer; b. Memphis, Feb. 8, 1938; s. John and Helen (Sweeney) H.; m. Evelyn Harry, June 8, 1963 (div. Feb. 1985); children: John David III, Katharine Jane, Matthew Joseph; m. Laurie Eileen House, June 3, 1987. BA, Vanderbilt U., 1959; LLB, U. Va., 1965. - Bar: Ga. 1966, D.C. 1979. From assoc. to ptnr. King & Spalding, Atlanta, 1965-93; exec. v.p., gen. counsel Jefferson-Pilot Corp., Greensboro, N.C., 1993—; bd. dirs., mem. exec. com. Rock-Tenn Co., Atlanta; mem. Guilford Coll. Bd. of Visitors, 1994—; bd. dirs. Univ. N.C. at Greensboro Excellence Found. Bd. dirs. Atlanta Ballet, 1991-93, Greensboro United Arts Coun., 1994-97; trustee Children's Sch., Inc., Atlanta, 1971-79, 88-89, Nat. Assn. Children's Hosps. and Related Instns., Alexandria, Va., 1973-79. Lt. USN, 1959-62. Mem. ABA, Ga. Bar Assn. (chmn. corp. code revision com., corp. and banking sect. 1970-79), D.C. Bar Assn., Atlanta Lawyers Club, Greensboro Country Club, Cherokee Town and Country Club (Atlanta), Order of Coif, Omicron Delta Kappa. Democrat. Episcopalian. Office: 100 N Greene St Greensboro NC 27401-2507

HOPKINS, JOHN KENDALL, college administrator, architect; b. Auckland, New Zealand, Nov. 18, 1954; arrived in New Zealand, 1982; s. Kendall Edward and G. Joy (Clark) H.; m. Karen Fay Shears, June 20, 1982; children: Kendall Blair, Klara Stafford. BSc in Architecture, U. Newcastle, NSW, Australia, 1978, BArch with honors, 1981; MArch, UCLA, 1991. Registered architect, NSW. Archtl. draftsman Piper & Ptnrs. Architects, Auckland, 1973-76; architect Noel Bell-Ridley Smith Architects, Sydney, NSW, 1981-82; assoc. prof. architecture Andrews U., Berrien Springs, Mich., 1982-95; cons., photographer Hopkins Studio, Berrien Springs, 1995—; prof., dir. architecture program Judson Coll., Elgin, Ill., 1996—; vis. lectr. U. Newcastle, 1990; adj. prof. architecture U. Notre Dame, South Bend, Ind., 1996, 97; architecture edn. cons. Judson Coll., Elgin, 1995-96; awards jury chmn. AIA, S.W. Mich., Kalamazoo, 1992, 93, 94. Contbr. articles to profl. jours. Recipient rsch. award Progressive Architecture, 1991, award invited architecture competition Australasian Conf. Assn., Newcastle, Australia, 1993, Image of Yr. award Berrien Springs Camera Club, 1994, 95. Mem. Royal Australian Inst. Architects (N.B. Pitt-Hardie scholarship 1981), Illuminating Engring. Soc. (mem. rsch. com.), Internat. Assn. Lighting Designers (mem. rsch. com.), Soc. Bldg. Sci. Educators. Avocations: architecture, landscape and portrait photography. Home: 211 S Kimmel St Berrien Springs MI 49103-1272 Office: Judson Coll Divsn Art Design Architec 1151 N State St Elgin IL 60123-1404

HOPKINS, JUDITH OWEN, oncologist; b. Norfolk, Va., Sept. 6, 1952; d. Austin and Edythe Owen; m. Marbry Benjamin Hopkins, III; 1 child, Benjamin Owen Hopkins. BS magna cum laude, Westhampton Coll., 1974; D of Medicine, U. Va., 1977. Diplomate Am. Bd. Internal Medicine, Am. Bd. Internal Medicine-Oncology. Resident in internal medicine Bowman Gray Sch. Medicine, N.C. Baptist Hosp., Winston-Salem, 1977-80, oncology fellowship, 1980-82; pvt. practice Winston-Salem, 1984—; clin. asst. prof. medicine Bowman Gray Sch. Medicine, Winston-Salem, 1984-92, asst. prof. medicine, 1982-84; clin. assoc. prof. medicine Bowman Gray Sch. Medicine, 1992—. Contbg. author: Tumors of the Central Nervous System, 1982; contbr. articles to profl. jours and abstracts. Bd. dirs. Hospice of Winston-Salem/Forsyth County, 1988-92, mem. profl. adv. com., 1982-92; preceptor for alt. curriculum Bowman Gray Sch. Medicine, 1988; mem. speakers bur. Am. Cancer Soc., 1982-92, chmn. profl. edn. com., 1982-85. Mem. ACP, Am. Soc. Internal Medicine, N.C. Soc. Internal Medicine, N.C. Med. Soc., Forsyth-Davie-Stokes County Med. Soc., Am. Soc. Clin. Oncology, Piedmont Oncology Assn., Southeastern Cancer Control Consortium, N.C. Oncology Soc. (chmn. clin. practices com. 1991-92, co-prin. investigator 1995—), Phi Beta Kappa, Alpha Omega Alpha. Episcopalian. Avocations: athletics, religion, camping. Home: 313 Susanna Dr Kernersville NC 27284-2161 Office: 2825 Lyndhurst Ave Ste 103 Winston Salem NC 27103-4146

HOPKINS, KAREN BROOKS, performing arts executive; b. 1951; d. Howard and Paula Brooks; divorced; 1 child, Matthew. BA in Theater Arts with honors, U. Md., 1973; MFA, George Washington U., 1980. Mem. group sales staff Am. Theater, Washington, 1973; cmty. rels. dir. Qwindo's Windo Dance Trouing Co., Washington, 1975; theater mgr., asst. dir. Chelm Players Touring Co., 1975-76, prodr., 1975-78; theater dir. Jewish Cmty. Ctr. of Greater Washington, 1976-78; devel. dir. The New Playwright's Theatre, Washington, 1978-79; devel. officer Bklyn. Acad. of Music, 1979-81, v.p. planning and devel., 1981-88, exec. v.p., 1988-98, COO and exec. v.p., 1998-99, pres., 1999—; adj. prof. program for arts adminstrn. Bklyn. Coll., 1980-84. Author: Successful Fundraising for Arts and Cultural Organizations, 1989, 2d edit., 1997. Fundraising cons. art instns., 1979—; chmn. Performing Arts Ctrs. Consortium, 1995-97. Recipient King Olav medal Norwegian Nat. Ballet, 1982, Dramaten medal, 1995. Office: Brooklyn Acad Music 30 Lafayette Ave Brooklyn NY 11217-1430

HOPKINS, LEE BENNETT, writer, educator; b. Scranton, Pa., Apr. 13, 1938; s. Lee Hall and Gertrude (Thomas) H. BA, Kean Coll., 1960; MS, Bank St. Coll., 1964; profl. diploma, Hunter Coll., 1966; LLD (hon.), Kean Coll., 1980. Elem. tchr. Fair Lawn (N.J.) Pub. Schs., 1960-66; lang. arts supr. Bank St. Coll., N.Y.C., 1966-68; curriculum specialist Scholastic, Inc., N.Y.C., 1968-75; pvt. practice author Scarborough, N.Y., 1975—; cons., vis. prof. various U.S. and Can. colls. and univs.; bd. dirs. Soc. Sch. Librs. Internat.; lit. cons. Random House Achievement Program in Lit.; chmn. Nat. Coun. Tchrs. English poetry award com. Author: Been to Yesterdays: Poems of a Life, 1996 (The Christopher Book award and Golden Kite Honor Book award), numerous children's and junior books, poetry (awards include Nat. Coun. Tchrs. English, Tchrs. Choice award, Pa. Keystone to Reading award, Am. Inst. Graphic Arts award); contbr. articles, texts, and curriculum materials to mags., profl. jours. Recipient Lasting Contbn. to Field Children's Lit. awad U. So. Miss., 1989, Manhattan Coun. Literacy award Internat. Reading Assn., 1983, Ednl. Leadership award Phi Delta Kappa, 1980; named Keystone (Pa.) Author of Yr.; established Lee Bennett Hopkins Poetry award in conjunction with Children's Lit. Coun. Pa. State U., 1993—, Lee Bennett Hopkins Promising Poet award in conjunction with Internat. Reading Assn., 1995—. Avocations: reading, travel. Home and Office: 307 Kemeys Cove Briarcliff Manor NY 10510-2050*

HOPKINS, LEWIS DEAN, planner, educator; b. Lakewood, Ohio, Feb. 20, 1946; s. W. Dean and Harriet (Painter) H.; m. Susan Brewster Cocker, Aug. 24, 1968; children: Joshua, Nathaniel. BA, U. Pa., 1968, postgrad., 1968-69, M of Regional Planning, 1970, PhD, 1975. Asst. prof. landscape arch. Inst. Environ. Studies/U. Ill., Urbana-Champaign, 1972-79, assoc. prof. landscape arch., urban and regional planning, 1979-84, prof., head dept. urban and regional planning, 1984-97, prof. landscape arch., 1984—; vis. lectr. dept. town and regional planning U. Sheffield, Eng., 1980; coord. grad. program in landscape arch. U. Ill., 1976-79, chair search com. for head dept. landscape arch., 1985, chair com. to evaluate dir. Inst. Environ. Studies, 1990, com. pub. adminstrn. program, 1990, campus budget strategies com., 1991-94, chancellors strategic planning com., 1993-95, campus senate, 1976-79, 82-84, chair ednl. policy com. 1978-79, senate coun. 1978-79, 82-83, budget com. 1984-86; project dir. Ill. Streams Info. sys., 1981-90; fellow Com. Instnl. Coop. Acad. Leadership Program, 1989-90; external site visit team dept. landscape arch. and environ. planning, Ariz. State U., 1990; rsch. adv. com. Ill.-Ind. Sea Grant Program, 1991—; exec. com. Office of Solid Waste Rsch., 1992-95; Fulbright sr. scholar to Nepal, 1997-98. Co-editor: (with Gill-Chin Lim) Jour. Planning Edn. and Rsch., 1987-91; mem. editl. bd. Jour. Planning Lit., Computers, Environment and Urban sys., Urban and Regional Info. Sys. Assn. Jour., Jour. Planning Edn. and Rsch., others; reviewer: European Jour. Ops. Rsch., Geographical Analysis, Internat. Regional Sci. Rev., Landscape Jour., Mgmt. Sci., Transp. Rsch., others; contbr. articles to profl. jours. Mem. AAUP (pres. campus chpt. 1983-84), Am. Planning Assn. (chair nominating com. Ill. chpt. 1988), Am. Inst. Cert. Planners, Assn. Collegiate Schs. of Planning (regional rep. to exec. bd. 1989-91), Inst. Mgmt. Scis., Regional Sci. Assn., Urban and Regional Inf. Sys. Assn. for Planning Accreditation Bd. (chair site visit teams 1988, 92, 94, team mem. 1995, com. on dual degree programs 1992-93), Planning Accreditation Bd. (chair 1997—). Achievements include research in human and computer problem solving processes for incompletely defined spatial problems; land and water resources management, information, and decision support systems; comprehensive planning processes and institutions. Office: U Ill Urbana-Champaign Dept Urban/Regional Plan 611 E Taft Dr Champaign IL 61820-6921*

HOPKINS, LINDA ANN, school psychologist; b. Bristol, Va., Aug. 23, 1937; d. James Robert and Trula Mae (Mink) Broce; AB, King Coll., 1959; MA, East Tenn. State U., 1977, postgrad., 1977-79; postgrad. Radford U., 1978-79, U. Va., 1980-89; m. James Edwin Hopkins, Oct. 8, 1960; children: James Edwin, David Lawrence. Nat. cert. sch. psychologist. Social worker Washington County Welfare Dept., Abingdon, Va., 1959-61; social worker Bristol (Va.) Welfare Dept., 1963-65, Washington County Welfare Dept., 1965-68, Bristol Meml. Hosp., 1968-72; psychologist Washington County Public Schs., Abingdon, 1978-87; pvt. practice sch. psychology, Abingdon, 1987-91; sch. psychologist Georgetown (S.C.) Dist. Pub. Schs., 1991—; adj. prof. East Tenn. State U., 1989-91. Active Pawleys Island Rescue Squad Midway Fire Dept. Mem. Nat. Assn. Sch. Psychologists, Phi Kappa Phi. Methodist. Home: 64 Osprey Way Georgetown SC 29440-8504 Office: Georgetown County Pub Sch Dist 305 Front St Georgetown SC 29440-3733

HOPKINS, MARJORIE JOHNSON, writer; b. Potter, Nebr., Oct. 8, 1926; d. Clarence William and Edith C. (Challburg) Johnson; m. Don Lee Hopkins, Apr. 11, 1953; children: Paula, Lisa (dec.), Mark. BA, Nebr. Wesleyan U., 1949; postgrad., U. Va., 1967-68. Adminstrv. sec. Amb. Joseph C. Grew, Washington, 1950-54; supervisor performing arts & cmty. svcs. Arlington (Va.) County Dept. Recreation & Parks, 1955-62; dir, co-owner Camp-at-Mayfield, Herndon, Va., 1962-69; dir. adminstrn. Air Conditioning & Refrigeration Inst., Arlington, 1970-88; co-owner Compu-Help, Arlington, 1983-91. Author: Private Lies, 1997. Bd. dirs. Sunrise Preservation Group. Mem. Pinehurst Investment Club, N.C. Writers Network, Southeast N.C. Radio Reading Svc., PEO. Presbyn. Home: 5 Salem Dr Pinehurst NC 28374-8503

HOPKINS, MARTHA JANE, education educator; b. Astoria, Oreg., Mar. 21, 1938; d. Willie Lester and Della May (Solmon) H. BA, N.W. Nazarene Coll., 1959; MS, Ind. U., 1961; EdD, U. Idaho, 1971. Tchr. Lynch Elem. Sch., Portland, Oreg., 1959-60, Corvallis (Oreg.) High Sch., 1961-64, Bethany (Okla.) Nazarene Coll., 1964-66; athletic dir. N.W. Nazarene Coll., Nampa, Idaho, 1984-87, acad. dean, 1987-89, prof. health and phys. edn., 1966—, chair dept. bus., 1992-95; chmn. Div. Profl. Studies, Nampa, 1985-96, chair dept. kinesiology, 1997—. Bd. dirs. Coll. Ch. of Nazarene, Nampa, 1989. Named to Idaho New Agenda Hall of Fame, 1988, NAIA Coaches Hall of Fame, 1982, N.W. Nazarene Coll. Athletic Hall of Fame, 1990. Mem. AAHPERD, Am. Assn. for Higher Edn., Idaho Assn. Health Phys. Edn. and Dance (pres. 1971-72), DAR (chair nat. def. com. EEDAHHOW chpt. 1989-97), Nat. Wellness Inst., IAHPER (disting. svc. award 1996). Avocations: genealogy, racquetball, skiing, crafts, reading. Home: 204 Mirage Ave Nampa ID 83651-2282 Office: NW Nazarene Coll Holly St Nampa ID 83686

HOPKINS, MURIEL-BETH NORBREY, lawyer; b. Fredericksburg, Va., June 29, 1951; d. Maurice D. and Grace (Hill) Norbrey; m. L. David Hopkins, Dec. 28, 1973; children: David, Michelle. BA cum laude, Wake Forest U., 1973; JD, Coll. William and Mary, 1977. Bar: Va. 1977, N.C. 1984. Assoc. Tucker & Marsh Law Firm, Richmond, Va., 1977-78; asst. atty. gen. Commonwealth of Va., Richmond, 1978-80; asst. U.S. atty. U.S. Dept. Justice, Richmond, 1980-82, Shreveport, La., 1982-83; mgr. small bus. group Winston-Salem (N.C.) C. of C., 1985; asst. counsel Wake Forest U., Winston-Salem, 1985-91; adj. prof. sch. law Wake Forest U., 1986, adj. prof. history, 1997—; bd. dirs. Carolina Medicorp, Inc., 1989. Sec. Sawtooth Ctr. Visual Design, Winston-Salem, 1987-88; mem. Bus. & Tech. Ctr., Winston-Salem, 1987-88, Carolina Medcorp. Inc., 1989; mem. campaign cabinet

United Way, 1989; bd. dirs. Urban League, Richmond, Va., 1980-82, Winston-Salem, 1985-89, Brenner Children's Hosp., 1992-95, Tanglewood Found., 1993-95; chmn. fundraiser United Negro Coll. Fund, 1992, 94. Mem. ABA (assoc. editor young lawyer's affiliate outreach pub.), Winston-Salem/Forsyth County Bar Assn. (exec. com. 1987-88), N.C. Bar Assn. (cle com.), The Links, Jack & Jill, N.C. Assn. Black Lawyers, Nat. Bar Assn. (continuing legal edn. com.). Baptist. Avocations: tennis, Civil War museums, college football. Office: Wake Forest U PO Box 7656 Winston Salem NC 27109-7656

HOPKINS, P. JEFFREY, Asian studies educator, author, translator; b. Providence, Sept. 30, 1940; s. Charles Edwin and Ora Ruth (Adams) H. BA magna cum laude, Harvard U., 1963; PhD, U. Wis., 1973. Asst. prof. U. Va., Charlottesville, 1973-77, assoc. prof., 1977-89, prof., 1989—, dir. Ctr. for South Asian Studies, 1979-82, 85-94; vis. prof. U. B.C., Vancouver, Can., 1983-86; Numata Disting. prof. Buddhist studies U. Hawaii, 1995; chief interpreter into English for His Holiness the Dalai Lama on tours to N.Am., Gt. Britain, Europe, S.E. Asia and Australia, 1979-89; pres. Inst. for Asian Democracy, Washington, 1994—; organizer, dir. Nobel Peace Laureates Conf., U. Va., 1998. Author or translator over 20 books on Tibetan Buddhism; contbr. articles to profl. jours. Fulbright scholar, India and Germany, 1971-72, India, 1982. Mem. Internat. Assn. Buddhist Studies (bd. dirs. 1986-89), Am. Acad. Religion, Tibet Soc., Tibetan Studies Inst. (pres. 1987—). Office: U Va Dept Religious Studies 104 Cocke Hall Charlottesville VA 22903-3281

HOPKINS, PHILIP JOSEPH, journalist, editor; b. Orange, Calif., Dec. 10, 1954; s. Philip Joseph and Marie Elizabeth Hopkins; m. Susan Lisa Ingman, Oct. 5, 1991; 1 child, Robin Genevieve Hopkins. BA in Journalism, San Diego State U., 1977; cert. tissue therapist, Ctr. for Decubitis Ulcer Rsch., 1981. Reporter La Jolla (Calif.) Light & Jour., 1973; editl. cons. San Diego Union, 1974; asst. prodr. Southwestern Cable TV, San Diego, 1974; corr. Mission Cable TV, San Diego, 1975; photojournalist United Press Internat., San Diego, 1976; editor Rx Home Care mag., L.A., 1981, Hosp. Info. Mgmt. mag., 1981; editor, assoc. pub. Arcade mag., 1982; mng. editor Personal Computer Age, L.A., 1983-84; bur. chief Newsbytes syndicated column, 1985-86; v.p. Humbird Hopkins Inc., L.A., 1978-89; writer, editor, rschr. Ind. Rsch. and Info. Svc., 1988-90; writer, analyst Geneva Bus. Rsch., 1990; sci. writer The Cousteau Soc., 1990; pub. cons. U. So. Calif., 1989-90; mgr. KP-IT Kaiser Permanente, 1991—. Co-author: The Students' Survival Guide, 1977, 78; photographs have appeared in Time and Omni mags., The Mythology of Middle Earth, Parenting Your Aging Parents, Beginners Guide to the SLR, NBC-TV's Saturday Night Live. Pres. Ind. Writers of So. Calif., 1988. Recipient 1st and 4th place awards Nikon, Inc., Photo Contest, 1974, 3rd prize Minolta Camera Co. Creative Photography awards, 1975, Best Feature Photo award Sigma Delta Chi Mark of Excellence contest, 1977. Mem. Healthcare Info. and Mgmt. Sys. Soc., Computer Press Assn. (life, hon.). Office: Kaiser Permanente 393 E Walnut IT/992 Pasadena CA 91188

HOPKINS, RAYMOND FREDERICK, political science educator; b. Cleve., Feb. 15, 1939; s. William Edward Hopkins and Ada Elizabeth (Cornwall) Lewis; m. Carol Lynnette Robinson, June 5, 1962; children—Mark Raymond, Kathryn Carol. BA, Ohio Wesleyan U., 1960; postgrad., Yale Divinity Sch., New Haven, 1960-61; MA, Ohio State U., 1963; PhD, Yale U., 1968. Instr. polit. sci. Swarthmore Coll., Pa., 1968-69, assoc. prof., 1973-78, prof., 1978—, chmn. dept. polit. sci., 1983-84, 87-91; dir. pub. policy Swarthmore Coll., 1990-96; rsch. assoc. Univ. Coll., Dar es Salaam, 1965-66; vis. scholar U. Mich., summer 1968; vis. scholar Weatherhead Ctr. for Internat. Affairs, Harvard U., summer 1969, 75, 98; rsch. assoc. Ind. U., 1970-71, U. Nairobi, 1971; vis. scholar Food Policy Rsch. Inst., Stanford U., Calif., 1982-83; vis. fellow Internat. Food Policy Rsch. Inst., Washington, 1984-86; cons. AID, Food and Agr. Orgn., Rome, World Food Programme, Rome, Dept. State, Washington, World Bank, Washington. Author: Political Roles in a New State, 1971, Structures and Process in International Politics, 1973, Global Political Economy of Food, 1979, Global Food Interdependence, 1980; contbr. numerous articles to profl. jours. Mem. property com. bd. mgrs. Swarthmore Coll., 1979-86; chmn. Swarthmore Democratic Com., 1978-82; ruling elder Swarthmore Presbyterian Ch., 1981-86; del. World Food Summit, 1996; pres. Internat. Svc. Cmty. Inc., 1995—. Fellow NDEA, 1961-63, Social Sci. Rsch. Coun., 1969, NEH, 1973, Guggenheim Found., 1974, Woodrow Wilson Internat. Ctr., 1975, Rockefeller Found., 1979, German Marshal Found., 1986, Pew fellow, Harvard, 1993; Fulbright disting. chair Italy, 1995; Yale Internat. Rels. grantee; recipient Heinz endowment, 1982. Mem. AAUP (pres. Swarthmore chpt. 1971-72), Am. Polit. Sci. Assn. (exec. coun.), Internat. Studies Assn., African Studies Assn.. Home: 308 Ogden Ave Swarthmore PA 19081-1413 Office: Swarthmore Coll Dept Polit Sci Swarthmore PA 19081

HOPKINS, ROBERT ARTHUR, retired industrial engineer; b. Youngstown, Ohio, Dec. 14, 1920; s. Arthur George and Margaret Viola (Brush) H.; m. Mary Madelaine Bailey, Apr. 6, 1946; 1 child, Marlaine Hopkins Kaiser. BBA, Case Western Reserve U., 1949; cert. loss control engr., U. Calif., Berkeley, 1969. Ins. agt. Nat. Life and Accident Ins. Co., Lorain, Akron, Ohio, 1951-56, San Mateo, Calif., 1951-56; ins. agt., engr. Am. Hardware Mt. Ins. Co., San Jose, Fresno, Calif., 1956-60; loss control engr. Manhattan Guarantee-Continental Ins. Co., Calif., 1967-77. Organizer Operation Alert DC, Lorain, 1951-52; prin. spkr. DC, Fresno, 1957; active Pleasant Hill (Calif.) Civil Action Com., 1981-83; civilian coord. Office Emergency Svcs., Pleasant Hill, 1983-85; advisor, coord. airshows and warbird aircraft, 1980—; chmn. bd. Western Aerospace Mus., Oakland, Calif., 1988; ops. asst. for tower and ops. 50th Anniversary Golden Gate Bridge, San Francisco, 1987; advisor, coord. Travis AFB Air Expo '90, 1990; advisor Air Expo '96, NAS Alameda (Calif.) 50th Anniversary, 1990; advisor NAS Moffett Field Air Show, 1990, 92, Calif. Coast Air Show, Half Moon Bay, 1993-94, Dixon May Fair honoring WWII 50th anniversary, 1995; warbird coord. Port of Oakland Airshow, 1987; warbird advisor/coord. Beale AFB, 1993—; mem. Smithsonian Mus, Smithsonian Air & Space Mus; charter mem. Nat. Mus. of Am. Indian, Am. Air Mus. Britain; life mem. Western Aerospace Mus. Served with USAAC, 1942-46. Recipient Letter of Appreciation Fresno DC, 1957, cert. of appreciation City of Pleasant Hill, 1986, cert. of recognition and spl. citizenship award Calif. State Senate, 1995. Mem. No. Calif. Safety Engrs. Assn. (v.p., pres., chmn. 1974-77), Confederate Air Force (mem. staff, leader Pacific wing 1980—), Nat. Aero. Assn., Aero. Club No. Calif., Hamilton Field Assn. (dir. ops. Wings of Victory Air Show 1987, coord. 1988, 89—, asst. to pres. 1989—, advisor contr. 1990—), VFW (life, state civil disaster chmn. Area 5 Calif. 1991), Air Force Assn., Kiwanis (chpt. sec.-treas.), Am. Air Mus. in Britain. Republican. Roman Catholic. Avocations: fishing, reading, writing, aircraft restoration. Home: 48 Mazie Dr Pleasant Hill CA 94523-3310

HOPKINS, ROBERT ELLIOTT, music educator; b. Greensboro, N.C., Oct. 2, 1931; s. Julian Setzer and Elizabeth Stewart (Daniel) H. MusB, U. Rochester, 1953; MusM, 1954, D Mus. Arts, 1959; postgrad., Acad. for Music, Vienna, Austria, 1959-60. Instr. Mars Hill Coll., 1954-57, 60-63; prof. music Youngstown (Ohio) State U., 1963-93; prof. emeritus, 1993—. Editor: Alexander Reinagle: The Philadelphia Sonatas, 1978; contbr. New Grove Dictionary of Music and Musicians, 1980, New Grove Dictionary of American Music, 1987, New Grove Dictionary of Opera, 1992. Music dir. various chs., N.C. and Ohio, 1954-81; chmn. Nat. Piano Concerto Competition, Youngstown Symphony Soc., 1986-90. Recipient Disting. Prof. award Youngstown State U., 1990; Fulbright-Hays grantee, 1959-60, rsch. grantee Youngstown State U., 1969-70, 83. Fellow Am. Guild. Organists (dean Youngstown chpt. 1968-69, 73-74, S. Lewis Elmer award 1962, 66); mem. Am. Musicological Soc., Am. Matthay Assn.

HOPKINS, SALLYE F., women's health nurse; b. Waco, Tex., Jan. 17, 1928; d. Gerald P. and Birdie Mae (Peters) Ferguson; m. Aeron Hopkins, Aug. 22, 1950 (dec.); children: Cathy (dec.), Eddie, Beth. Diploma, Hillcrest Meml. Hosp., 1948; student, Baylor U. Health nurse Tri-County Health Nurse, Newton, Tex.; shift supr., labor/delivery Hillcrest Med. Ctr., Waco; dir. nurses Merryville (La.) Gen. Hosp.; staff nurse Newton (Tex.) County Meml. Hosp., 1990. Baptist. Home: PO Box 12 Newton TX 75966-0012

HOPKINS, SAMUEL, retired investment banker; b. Highland, Md., Oct. 18, 1913; s. Samuel Harold and Roberta (Smith) H.; m. Winifred Holt Bloodgood, Oct. 15, 1938 (dec. Oct. 1954); children: Samuel, Henry; m. Anne E. Dankmeyer, Oct. 21, 1955; children: Robert, Frederick. B.S., Johns Hopkins U., 1934; LL.B., U. Md., 1938. With Fidelity & Deposit Co. of Md., 1934-69, asst. to treas., 1934-50, asst. treas., 1950-54, sec., 1954-67, v.p., sec., dir., 1967-69; dir., mem. trust com. Equitable Trust Co., Balt., 1954-81; sec., dir. Md. Life Ins. Co., 1963-69; gen. partner Alex. Brown & Sons (investment bankers), Balt., 1970-75; ltd. partner Alex. Brown & Sons (investment bankers), 1976-87; bd. dirs. Am. Maritime Cases, Inc. Mem. adv. com. housing for elderly U.S. Housing and Fin. Agy., 1956-60; mem. Balt. Bd. Recreation and Parks, 1965-77, pres., 1965-67, 74-77, v.p., 1968-74; Rep. candidate for Congress, 1952; mem. Md. Ho. of Dels., 1950-54; Rep. candidate for mayor, Balt., 1955; del. Rep. Nat. Conv., 1976; trustee Balt. Mus. Art, Peale Mus., Sheppard and Enoch Pratt Hosp., 1972-89; trustee, v.p. State Colls. Md., 1963-70; mem. Balt. City Planning Commn., 1985-95. Lt. USNR, 1942-45. Mem. ABA, Balt. Security Analysts Soc., Md. Hist. Soc. (treas. 1956-69, pres. 1970-75, chmn. bd. trustees 1988-90), Inst. Chartered Security Analysts. Episcopalian. Home: 45 Warrenton Rd Baltimore MD 21210-2924

HOPKINS, STEPHEN, film director, producer. Motion picture dir., prodr. Exec. prodr. film Crossworlds, 1996; prodr., dir. Lost in Space, 1998, Under Suspicion, 1999; dir. films Nightmare on Elm St. 5: The Dream Child, 1989, Predator 2, 1990, Dangerous Game, 1991, Judgement Night, 1993, Blown Away, 1994, The Ghost and the Darkness, 1996, Tube Tales, 1999; dir. T.V. series Tales from the Crypt, 1989. Office: c/o DGA 7920 Sunset Blvd Los Angeles CA 90046*

HOPKINS, THEODORE MARK, minister, guidance counselor; b. Vermontville, Mich., Jan. 2, 1926; s. Donald James and Alice (Truman) H.; m. Ruth Ann Allspaw, Oct. 10, 1954; children: Sarah, Phoebe, Martha, Rebekah. BA, Taylor U., 1954; MRE, No. Bapt. Theol. Sem., Lombard, Ill., 1957; BD, No. Bapt. Theol. Sem., 1958; MDiv (converted from BD), 1971. Ordained to ministry Bapt. Ch., 1958; cert. tchr., high sch. counselor. Pastor First Bapt. Ch., Darlington, Wis., 1958-60, Lexington, Ill., 1960-61; pastor Killdeer (N.D.) Bapt. Ch., 1961-65, First Bapt. Ch., Hardin, Mont., 1965-66, Centerville (S.D.)-Wakonda Bapt. Chs., 1966-68, Liberty Union Bapt. Ch., Milan, Mo., 1995—; interim pastor Meml. Bapt. Ch., Chambers, Nebr., 1969-70; bi/voacat. pastor First Bapt. Ch., Mercer, Mo., 1976-78, Blythedale, Mo., 1979-90; guidance counselor public schs., Lineville, Iowa, 1976-88; pastor-counselor to Am. Bapt. Men Janesville Bapt. Assn., 1959-60, Am. Bapt. Men of Mont., 1965-66; chmn. Christian edn. N.D. Bapt. Conv. 1962-64, leadership edn., 1964-65; rep. N.D. Bapt. Conv. Open Theol. Conf., Greenlake, Wisc. 1964, S.D. Bapt. Conv., 1968; chmn. Fergus Falls, Minn. Child Evangelism Com., 1972-73; dir. music North Grand River Bapt. Assn., 1986-95, , dir. discipleship tng., 1993-95; dir. music North Ctrl. Bapt. Assn., Mo., 1966-99. Sec. Centerville Ambulance Svc., 1967-68; served two terms pres. Lineville Edn. Assn.; vol. Centerville chpts. Alcoholics Anonymous; dir. of music North Grand River (Mo.) Bapt. Assn., 1986-95. With USN, 1944-46, PTO, 1951-52, Korea; with USNR, 1946-51, 52-54. Republican. Avocations: music, walking, photography, reading. Home: Box 68 305 E Monroe St Corydon IA 50060-1632 *I have found the greatest satisfaction and happiness in life comes through being of service to others, even when that service is not always appreciated.*

HOPKINS, THOMAS MATTHEWS, former naval officer; b. Balt., Feb. 3, 1927; s. John Howard and Grace Marie (Martin) H.; m. Marjorie Kendall Leonard, Apr. 8, 1950; children: Margaret, Karen, Annette. B.S. in Mech. Engring, Cornell U., 1948; naval engr. degree, M.I.T., 1955. Commd. ensign U.S. Navy, 1948, advanced through grades to rear adm., 1977; project officer, submarines Bur. Ships and subsequently Naval Ship Systems Command, 1964-68; force maintenance officer U.S. Submarine Force, U.S. Atlantic Fleet, 1968-71; project mgr. Naval Sea Systems Command, Attack Submarine (SSN) Acquisition Project, 1972-76; fleet maintenance officer U.S. Atlantic Fleet, 1977-80; dep. comdr. for ship systems Naval Sea Systems Command, Washington, 1980-82, ret., 1982; exec. cons. Harbridge House, Inc., Washington, 1982-84, U.S. Maritime Adminstrn., Washington, 1982-84; ind. cons. in naval architecture and marine engring. with emphasis on submarines and ship survivability, 1984—; adj. rsch. staff mem. Inst. for Def. Analyses,. 1995—. Decorated Meritorious Service medal (2), Legion of Merit. Mem. ASTM (bd. dirs. 1988-90, F-25 com. on ships and marine tech.), Am. Soc. Naval Engrs., Soc. Naval Archs. and Marine Engrs., Internat. Orgn. for Standardization (tech. com. on ships and marine tech., secretariat for piping and machinery subcom. 1995—). Episcopalian. Home: 1113 Carper St Mc Lean VA 22101-2109

HOPKINSON, SHIRLEY LOIS, library and information science educator; b. Boone, Iowa, Aug 25, 1924; d. Arthur Perry and Zora (Smith) Hopkinson; student Coe Coll., 1942-43; AB cum laude (Phi Beta Kappa scholar 1944), U. Colo., 1945; BLS, U. Calif., 1949; MA (Honnold Honor scholar 1945-46), Claremont Grad. Sch., 1951; EdM, U. Okla., 1952, EdD, 1957 Tchr. pub. sch. Stigler, Okla., 1946-47, Palo Verde High Sch., Jr. Coll., Blythe, Calif., 1947-48; asst. librarian Modesto (Calif.) Jr. Coll., 1949-51; tchr., librarian Fresno, Calif., 1951-52, La Mesa, Cal., 1953-55; asst. prof. librarianship, instructional materials dir. Chaffey Coll., Ontario, Calif., 1955-59; asst. prof. librarian ship, San Jose (Calif.) State Coll., 1959-64; assoc. prof., 1964-69, prof., 1969—; bd. dirs. NDEA Inst. Sch. Librs., summer 1966; mem. Santa Clara County Civil Service Bd. Examiners. Recipient Master Gardner cert. Oreg. State U. Extension Svc. Book reviewer for jours. Mem. ALA, Calif. Library Assn., Audio-Visual Assn. Calif., NEA, AAUP, AAUW (dir. 1957-58), Bus. Profl. Women's Club, Sch. Librs. Assn. Calif. (com. mem., treas. No. sect. 1951-52), San Diego County Sch. Librs. Assn. (sec. 1945-55), Calif. Tchrs. Assn., LWV (bd. dirs. 1950-51, publs. chmn.), Phi Beta Kappa, Alpha Lambda Delta, Alpha Beta Alpha, Kappa Delta Pi, Phi Kappa Phi (disting. acad. achievement award 1981), Delta Kappa Gamma (sec. 1994-96, legis. liaison, 1996—). Author: Descriptive Cataloging of Library Materials; Instructional Materials for Teaching the Use of the Library. Contbr. to profl. publs. Editor: Calif. Sch. Libraries, 1963-64; asst. editor: Sch. Library Assn. of Calif. Bull., 1961-63; book reviewer profl. jours. Office: 1340 Pomeroy Ave Apt 408 Santa Clara CA 95051-3658

HOPP, ANTHONY JAMES, advertising agency executive; b. Detroit, Jan. 31, 1945; s. William J. and Beverly (Gildea) H.: m. Nancy Jane Dunckel, Nov. 11, 1969; children: Beth, Michael. BA in Advt./Mktg., Mich. State U., 1967, MA in Advt./Psychology, 1968. Asst. account exec. Campbell-Ewald Adv., Warren, Mich., 1968-70; account exec. Lintas Campbell-Ewald, Warren, Mich., 1970-74, account supr., 1974-75, v.p., account supr., 1975-79, sr. v.p., mgmt. supr., 1979-85, group sr. v.p., group mgmt. supr., 1985-88, exec. v.p., account dir., 1988-93, pres., 1993-95, vice chmn., 1995—, also bd. dirs.; bd. dirs. C-E Comm., Warren, Lintas Ams. Recipient Robert E. Healy award Interpublic Group of Cos., 1989. Mem. Adcraft, Hunters Creek, Bloomfield Hills Country Club, Pine Lake Country Club. Avocations: golf, hunting, boating. Office: Campbell-Ewald Adv 30400 Van Dyke Ave Warren MI 48093-2368*

HOPP, DANIEL FREDERICK, manufacturing company executive, lawyer; b. Ann Arbor, Mich., Apr. 14, 1947; s. Clayton A. and Monica E. (Williams) H.; m. Maria G. Lopez, Dec. 20, 1968; children: Emily, Daniel, Melissa. BA in English, U. Mich., 1969; JD, Wayne State U., 1973. Bar: Ill. 1974, Mich. 1980. Atty. Mayer, Brown and Platt, Chgo., 1973-79; atty. Whirlpool Corp., Benton Harbor, Mich., 1979-84, asst. sec., 1984-85, sec., asst. gen. counsel, 1985-89, v.p., gen. counsel, sec., 1989-98, sr. v.p., corp. affairs and gen. counsel, 1998—; past co-chmn. Conf. Bd. Legal Quality Coun. Mem. City of St. Joseph (Mich.) Planning Comm.; bd. dirs. Lakeland Regional Health Sys., Joseph, Mich. With U.S. Army, 1969-71. Mem. Am. Soc. Corp. Secs. (past pres., bd. dirs. Chgo. chpt.), Mich. Bar Assn. (mem. Open Justice Commn.), Ill. Bar Assn., Berrien County Bar Assn. Republican. Mem. Ch. of Christ. Avocation: golf. Office: Whirlpool Corp Adminstrv Ctr 2000 N M 63 Benton Harbor MI 49022-2692*

HOPPE, ARTHUR WATTERSON, columnist; b. Honolulu, Apr. 23, 1925; s. Arthur Scrivner and Margaret Elizabeth (Watterson) H.; m. Gloria Mary Nichols, Apr. 27, 1946; children—Leslie, Andrea, Arthur, Prentiss. B.A. cum laude, Harvard U., 1949. Reporter San Francisco Chronicle, 1950-60, columnist, 1960—. Author: The Love Everybody Crusade, 1960, Dreamboat, 1962, The Perfect Solution to Absolutely Everything, 1968, Mr. Nixon and My Other Problems, 1971, Miss Lollipop and the Doom Machine, 1973, The Tiddling Tennis Theorem, 1977, The Marital Arts, 1985, Having a Wonderful Time, 1995. Served with USNR, 1942-46, PTO. Avocations: tennis, golf. Office: Chronicle Pub Co 901 Mission St San Francisco CA 94103-2905

HOPPE, BARBARA G., historic site administrator; b. Alexandria, La., Sept. 24, 1961. BA, U. N.C., Wilmington, 1984. Mus. shop mgr. Fort Fisher State Hist. Site, Kure Beach, N.C., 1985-97, site mgr., 1997—. Office: Fort Fisher State Historic Site PO Box 169 Kure Beach NC 28449*

HOPPE, DAVID RUTLEDGE, writer; b. Evanston, Ill., Dec. 28, 1950; s. John and Edmar (von Henke) H.; m. Mary Helen Schaaf, June 10, 1983; 1 child. BA, Macalester Coll., 1973; MA, U. Minn., 1976; MFA, Bennington Coll., 1986. From audio-visual dir. to asst. dir. Michigan City (Ind.) Pub. Libr., 1980-88; resource ctr. dir. Ind. Humanities Coun., Indpls., 1988-94; creative dir. 2d Globe, Indpls., 1994-98; dir. Nuvo Cultural Inst., Indpls., 1998—; writer Nuvo Newsweekly, Indpls., 1998—; writer-in-residence Ball State U., Muncie, Ind., 1994; fellow Butler Univ. Writer's Studio, 1994. Editor: Where We Live, 1989, Hard Pieces: Dan Carpenter's Indiana, 1993; contbr. popular publs. Project dir. Wordstruck Festival, Indpls., 1991, 93, Libr. Literacy Program, Michigan City, 1988. Home: 6001 Broadway St Indianapolis IN 46220-1807

HOPPE, LEA ANN, elementary education educator; b. Birmingham, Ala., Mar. 20, 1959; d. George Carson and Annie Merle (Carleton) Jones; m. David Thomas Hoppe, Nov. 21, 1983; children: Kathryn Ann, Emily Louise. BS in Edn., Samford U., Birmingham, 1981; MA in Edn., U. Ala., Tuscaloosa, 1986. Cert. tchr., Ala. Reading tutor Pearson's Reading & Math. Ctr., Birmingham, 1979-81; kindergarten tchr. Scottsboro (Ala.) City Schs.-Brownwood, 1981-86; pre-kindergarten tchr., ctr. dir. First Bapt. Learning Ctr., Scottsboro, 1986-89; kindergarten tchr. Covenant Weekday Kindergarten, Huntsville, Ala., 1990-95, Randolph Sch., Huntsville, 1995—; chmn. bd. dirs. First Bapt. Child Devel. Ctr., Huntsville, 1992—; conf. leader Samford U., Birmingham, 1993, Farley Elem. Parents Orgn., Huntsville, 1994. Author: (children's activity books) A Child For All Seasons: Volume 1, 1994, Volume 2, 1994. Children's choir dir. First Bapt. Ch., Huntsville, 1991—, children's Sunday Sch. tchr., 1993—. Mem. Nat. Assn. Edn. Young Children, So. Early Childhood Assn., Ala. Assn. Young Children, Delta Omicron (life), Kappa Delta Pi, Kappa Delta Epsilon, Pi Gamma Mu, Omicron Delta Kappa. Republican. Baptist. Avocations: singing, playing the trombone, children's literature. Home: 2911 Barcody Rd SE Huntsville AL 35801-2218 Office: Randolph Sch 1005 Drake Ave SE Huntsville AL 35802-1099

HOPPE, PETER CHRISTIAN, biologist, geneticist; b. Long Beach, Calif., Feb. 16, 1942; s. John Calvin and Venetia Bodell (Mortensen) H.; m. Linda Lee Peters, June 14, 1963; children—Tina Christine, Kirk Christian, Todd Christopher. B.S., Calif. State Poly. U., 1964; M.S., Kans. State U., 1966, Ph.D., 1968. Asso. staff scientist The Jackson Lab., Bar Harbor, Maine, 1970-73; staff scientist The Jackson Lab., 1973-81, sr. staff scientist, 1981-95, emeritus, 1995—; vis. prof. U. Geneva, 1979-80. Contbr. articles to profl. jours. Named Disting. Alumnus Calif. State Poly. U., 1981; Am. Cancer Soc. Eleanor Roosevelt fellow, 1979-80. Office: The Jackson Lab Bar Harbor ME 04609

HOPPEL, ROBERT GERALD, JR., lawyer; b. Scranton, Pa., Dec. 26, 1921; s. Robert Gerald and Ellen Amelia (Casey) H. B.S., U. Scranton, 1950; J.D., Georgetown U., 1954. Bar: D.C. 1955, U.S. Ct. Appeals (D.C. cir.) 1955, U.S. Supreme Ct. 1974. Supervising auditor GAO, Washington, 1950-57; ptnr. Coles & Goertner, Washington, 1957-82; ptnr. Hoppel, Mayer & Coleman, Washington, 1982-84; sole practice, 1984—. Served to cpl. USAAF, 1943-45. Mem. ABA, Maritime Adminstrv. Bar Assn., D.C. Bar, Bar Assn. D.C., Internat. Platform Assn., Am. Legion, Nat. Lawyers Club. Republican. Roman Catholic. Clubs: Propellor (Washington). Office: 3600 Massachusetts Ave NW Washington DC 20007-1449

HOPPENSTEADT, FRANK CHARLES, educator, mathematician, university administrator; b. Oak Park, Ill., Apr. 29, 1938; s. Frank Carl and Margaret Hoppensteadt; children: Charles, Matthew, Sarah. BA, Butler U., 1960; MS, U. Wis., 1962, PhD, 1965. Instr. math. U. Wis., Madison, 1965; asst. prof. math. Mich. State U., East Lansing, 1965-68, dean Coll. Natural Sci., 1986-95; dir. sys. sci. engr. rsch., prof. math. and elec. engring. Ariz. State U., Tempe, 1995—; assoc. prof. NYU-Courant, N.Y.C., 1968-76; prof., 1976-79; prof. U. Utah, Salt Lake City, 1977-86, chmn. dept. math., 1982-85. Author: Mathematical Methods in Population Biology, 1982, An Introduction to Mathematics of Neurons, 1986, 2d edit., 1997, Mathematics in Medicine and the Life Sciences, 1991, Analysis and Simulation of Chaotic Systems, 1993, Weakly Connected Neural Networks, 1997. Mem. Am. Math. Soc. (chmn. applied math. com. 1976-80), Soc. Indsl. and Applied Maths., Sigma Xi. Office: Ariz State U Dir SSERC Box 7606 Tempe AZ 85287-7606

HOPPENSTEADT, JON KIRK, law librarian; b. Milw., Feb. 24, 1959; s. George Arthur and Sheila Ann (Doyle) H. BA, U. Nev., 1980, '81; MA, Denver U., 1984; JD, U. Minn., 1989. Asst. mgr. Farwell & Mikkelson, Reno, 1976-83; rschr., abstractor TrendTrack, Boulder, Colo., 1983; reference libr. intern Denver U., Englewood (Colo.) Pub. Libr., 1984; indexer, abstractor Info. Access Co., Foster City, Calif., 1984-86; pub. libr. intern Mpls. Pub. Libr., 1987-88; student dir. Legal Assistance to Minn. Prisoners, Mpls., 1988-89; reference libr. U. Minn. Law Libr., Mpls., 1988-91; victims' rights advocate Rohnert Park, Calif., 1992-96, Palm Harbor, Fla., 1996—; with Wear Its At, Palm Harbor, Fla., 1997-98. Cataloger Westlaw Legal Database Catalog, 1991. Mem. Nat. Orgn. for Victim Assistance, Washington, 1992; founder Profls. for Access, Santa Rosa, Calif., 1993; mem. Nat. Victim Ctr., Ft. Worth, 1993—. Democrat. Lutheran. Avocations: photography, drawing, hiking. Home and Office: 2890 Spring Oak Ct Palm Harbor FL 34684-1662

HOPPENSTEIN, ABRAHAM SOLOMON, investment and merchant banker, consultant; b. Benoni, Republic of South Africa, Oct. 9, 1931; came to U.S., 1976; s. Charles and Rachel (Diner) H.; m. Taubene Judith Frank, Jan. 19, 1954; children: Rachelle Schlosberg, Joel, Saul, Deborah Zucker. B in Commerce, Witwatersrand U. Law Sch., Johannesburg, Republic of South Africa, 1951, LLB, 1955. Barrister of Supreme Ct. Republic of South Africa, High Ct. of Swaziland. Chmn., chief exec. officer Abrubhill Investments Ltd. Chartrex Internat. Ltd., 1956, Fairdeal Investments (PTY) Ltd., Selcourt Centre Ltd., Selcourt Fin. Corp. Ltd., South Africa; trade commr. South African Embassy, Tel Aviv, Israel, 1975; counsellor polit. affairs South African Embassy, Washington, 1976-77, consul gen., 1979-80; consul gen. South African Consulate Gen., N.Y.C., 1980-86; pres., CEO Chartrex Internat. Ltd., N.Y.C., 1993—, AHI West Side Creek Inc., AHI Equinox Inc.; v.p. internat. affairs Allen & Co. Inc., N.Y.C., 1986-92; pres. Chartrex, Inc., 1986—. Contbr. articles to profl. jours. Mem. steering com. Global Econ. Action Inst., N.Y.; mem. exec. com. South African Jewish Bd. Deps., South African Zionist Fedn., 1978-79; trustee Temple Israel, White Plains, N.Y., 1988-90; bd. dirs. Helen Keller Internat., 1997—. Aspen Inst. for Humanities fellow, 1988. Mem. East Rand Attys. Assn. (chmn. 1969-70), N.Y. C. of C. (hon. mem.), Lions Internat. (hon. mem. 1980), Econ. Club. N.Y., Fgn. Policy Assn., Polo Club of Boca Raton (gov. 1998—). Avocations: golf, tennis, swimming, photography, travel. Fax: 561-999-0588. Office: Chartrex Internat Ltd PO Box 812373 Boca Raton FL 33481-2373

HOPPER, ARTHUR FREDERICK, biological science educator; b. Plainfield, N.J., Sept. 7, 1917; s. Arthur Frederick and Catherine (Hoenig) H.; m. Amy Patricia Hull, Dec. 28, 1940 (dec. Nov. 1982); children: Arthur Frederick, Geoffrey Victor, Christopher James, Gregory Lorton; m. Patricia Ann Vennett, Sept. 6, 1986. AB, Princeton U., 1938; MS, Yale U., 1942; PhD, Northwestern U., 1948. Instr. Northwestern U., Evanston, Ill., summer 1948; asst. prof. Wayne U., Detroit, 1948-49; asst. prof. to prof. Rutgers U., New Brunswick, N.J., 1949-80, dir. biol. scis. grad. program, 1973-75; rsch. assoc. Brookhaven (N.Y.) Nat. Lab., 1961-68; visiting prof. U. Liège Med. Sch., Belgium, 1967-68; prof. emeritus Rutgers U., New Brunswick, 1980—; rsch. assoc. Detroit Cancer Inst., 1948-49; scientist aboard Columbia U. R/V "Vema", summer, 1955, 58; vis. investigator Battelle

N.W., Richland, Wash., summer 1970, Jackson Meml. Lab., Bar Harbor, Maine, summers, 1971, 73. Author: Foundations of Animal Development, 1st ed. 1979, 2nd ed. 1985; contbr. articles to profl. jours. Chmn. troop 53 Boy Scouts Am., Bedminster, N.J., 1953-58; v.p., pres. Bedminster Bd. Edn., 1957-63; coach, mgr. Far Hills Little League Baseball, 1954-56; pres. Somerset County Bd. Edn., Somerville, N.J., 1960-63; coord. radiology def. Somerset County, 1959-63; bd. dirs. Palm Beach County Kidney Assn., Lake Worth, Fla., 1988-90, mem. med. adv. bd., 1993—. 1st lt. USAAF, 1943-46; lt. col. USAFR, 1946-68. Rsch. grantee NSF, USPHS, Am. Cancer Soc., Lalor Found, Rutgers U. Rsch. Coun., 1950-80. Mem. AAAS, Soc. Integrative and Comparative Biology, Soc. Devel. Biologists, Sigma Xi. Home: 231 Cocoanut Row Palm Beach FL 33480-4132

HOPPER, CAROL, meeting and trade show administrator; b. Montreal, Que., Can., Apr. 23, 1952; m. Cedric Heimrath; stepchildren: Natasha, Erik. Student, McGill U., 1972; cert., Canadian Inst. Orgnl. Mgmt., 1991. Asst. Ben Fuller Assocs., 1973-89; show dir. Nat. Ski Industries Assn., Montreal, 1989-91, exec. dir., 1991-96, dir. show svcs., 1997-98; meeting planner Chateau Travel, 1998—; mem. adv. com. sporting goods bus. program Sir Sandford Fleming Coll., 1994-98. Mem. Can. Assn. Exposition mgrs., Jr. League Montreal (bd. dirs., chmn. coms. 1987-92). Avocations: skiing, golf, reading, travel, sports. Home: 302 Perrault, Rosemere, PQ Canada J7A 1B9

HOPPER, DAVID HENRY, religion educator; b. Cranford, N.J., July 31, 1927; s. Orion Cornelius and Julia Margaret (Weitzel) H.; m. Nancy Ann Nelson, June 10, 1967 (div. June 1984); children: Sara Elizabeth, Kathryn Ann, Rachel Suzanne. BA, Yale U., 1950; BD, ThM, Princeton Theol. Sem., 1953, ThD, 1959. Ordained Presbyn. minister, 1961. Asst. prof. Macalester Coll., St. Paul, 1959-67, assoc. prof., 1967-73, James Wallace prof. of religion, 1973—. Author: Tillich: A Theological Portrait, 1967 (N.J. Authors award 1968), A Dissent on Bonhoeffer, 1975, Technology, Theology, and the Idea of Progress, 1991. With USN, 1945-46. Recipient Newberry ACM Faculty fellow, 1992-93, Templeton Found. Sci./Religion Course award, 1996. Mem. Am. Acad. Religion, Internat. Bonhoeffer Soc., Hist. of Sci. Soc., Kierkegaard Soc. Home: 1757 Lincoln Ave Saint Paul MN 55105-1954 Office: Macalester Coll Dept Religious Studies 1600 Grand Ave Saint Paul MN 55105-1801

HOPPER, DENNIS, actor, writer, photographer, film director; b. Dodge City, Kans., May 17, 1936; m. Brooke Hayward; daughter: Marin; m. Doria Halprin; daughter: Ruthana; m. Katherine LaNasa, June, 1989; son: Henry Lee. Ed., San Diego pub. schs. Numerous TV appearances include Loretta Young Show, 1954; appeared in films: Rebel Without a Cause, 1955, Jagged Edge, 1955, I Died A Thousand Times, 1955, Giant, 1956, The Steel Jungle, 1956, Story of Mankind, 1957, Gunfight at the O.K. Corral, 1957, From Hell to Texas, 1958, The Youngland, 1959, Key Witness, 1960, Night Tide, 1963, The Sons of Katie Elder, 1965, Queen of Blood, 1966, The Trip, 1967, Glory Stompers, 1967, Hang 'Em High, 1968, Cool Hand Luke, 1967, True Grit, 1969, Easy Rider, 1969, The Last Movie, 1971, Kid Blue, 1973, Hex, 1973, The Sky is Falling, 1975, James Dean-The First American Teenager, Mad Dog Morgan, 1976, Tracks, 1976, American Friend, 1978, Apocalypse Now, 1979, Wild Times, 1980, Out of the Blue, 1980, King of the Mountain, 1981, Renacer, 1981, Human Highway, 1981, Rumble Fish, 1983, The Osterman Weekend, 1983, Slagskämpen, 1984, My Science Project, 1985, O.C. & Stiggs, 1985, White Star, 1985, The Texas Chainsaw Massacre Part 2, 1986, Blue Velvet, 1986 (Montreal World Film Festival award 1986), Hoosiers, 1986 (Acad. award nomination 1987), River's Edge, 1987, Black Widow, 1987, Pick-up Artist, 1987, Straight to Hell, 1987, Riders of the Storm, 1988, Let it Rock, 1988, Blood Red, 1989, Flashback, 1990, Motion & Emotion, 1990, Chattahoochie, 1990, Superstar: Life and Times of Andy Warhol, 1990, Backtrack, 1991, Sunset Heat, 1991, Schneeweissrosenrot, 1991, Indian Runner, 1991, Hearts of Darkness, 1991, Paris Trout, 1991, Eye of the Storm, 1991, Super Mario Brothers, 1993, Boiling Point, 1993, True Romance, 1993, Red Rock West, 1993, Speed, 1994, Chasers, 1994, Waterworld, 1995, Search and Destroy, 1995, Carried Away, 1996, Last Days of Frankie the Fly, 1996, Cannes Man, 1996, Basquiat, 1996, Top of the World, 1997, Road Ends, 1997, Good Life, 1997, Star Truckers, 1997, Blackout, 1997, Tycus, 1998, Meet the Deedles, 1998, Sources, 1999, Lured Innocence, 1999, Justice, 1999, Jesus' Son, 1999, Bad City Blues, 1999, EdTV, 1999, Straight Shooter, 1999; writer, dir. Easy Rider 1969 (Cannes Film Festival Best New Dir. award 1969), The Last Movie, 1971, Out of the Blue, 1980, Chasers, 1994,Colors, 1988, The Hot Spot, 1990, Paris Trout, 1991, Double Crossed, 1991, Sunset Heat, 1992, Nails, 1992; TV movies include The Heart of Justice, 1993, Samson and Delilah, 1996, Marlon Brando: The Wild One, 1996, The Last Days of Frankie the Fly, 1996, James Dean: A Portrait, 1996; exhibited photographs at Fort Worth Art Mus., Denver Art Mus., Wichita Art Mus., Cochran Art Mus., Spileto Mus., Parco Gallery, Tokyo, Osaka, Kumatomo, Japan; author: (photographic book) Out of the Sixties, 1986. Recipient Best Film award Venice Film Festival, 1971, Best Film award Cannes Film Festival, 1980. Office: care Creative Artists Agy 9830 Wilshire Blvd Beverly Hills CA 90212-1804*

HOPPER, PEGGY F., education educator; b. Clarksdale, Miss., Nov. 19, 1955; d. John Hart and Peggy Sue (Foard) Fondren; m. George Martin Hopper, Nov. 23, 1976; children: Benjamin George Hopper, Summer LeMett Hopper. BS in Liberal Arts, Miss. State U., 1977; MS in Curriculum and Instrn., U. Memphis, 1986, EdS, 1991; PhD in Holistic Tchg./Learning, U. Tenn., 1996. Asst. to dir. U. of Memphis Grad. Ctr., Jackson, 1987; tchr. U. Sch. of Jackson, Tenn., 1987-89; coord. for young adult lit. Jackson/Madison County Libr., 1990; instr. Jackson State C.C., 1989-91; assoc. prof. Walters State C.C., Morristown, Tenn., 1992—; adj. instr. U. Tenn., Knoxville, 1996—; adv. bd. Coll. of Edn. Admissions, U. Tenn., 1995. Contbr. articles to profl. jours., articles to profl. newsletters. Pres. Gen. Fedn. of Women's Club - Jr. Chilhowee Club, Maryville, Tenn., 1998; bd. dirs. Blount County Jr. Playhouse, 1997—, Boys and Girls' Clubs of Blount County, 1998—. Grantee Nat. Assn. Developmental Edn., 1997. Mem. Tenn. Assn. Developmental Edn. (pres. 1996-97), Nat. Assn. Developmental Edn. (liaison 1996-97), Internat. Reading Assn., Phi Lambda Theta, Phi Kappa Phi, Kappa Delta Pi. Avocations: travel, reading, gardening. Office: Walters State Cmty Coll 500 S Davy Crockett Pkwy Morristown TN 37813-1908

HOPPER, SALLY, state legislator; widowed; children: Nancy, Joan, Caroline, Anne. BA, U. Wyo., 1956. Mem. Colo. Senate, Denver, 1987-99; chair Senate Health, Environ., Welfare and Insts. com.; chair Criminal Justice Commn, mem. Judiciary com. Mem. nat. bd. Ptnrs. for Access to the Woods; mem., bd. dirs. Spalding Cmty. Found.; bd. dirs. Easter Seals of Colorado. Mem. Kappa Kappa Gamma. Republican. Episcopalian. Home: 21649 Cabrini Blvd Golden CO 80401-9487

HOPPER, STEPHEN RODGER, hospital administrator; b. Chgo., Aug. 28, 1949; s. Rodger Patterson and Dorothy Ann (Newberg) H.; m. Janet Sue Waddill, June 10, 1972; children: Nathan John, Amanda Sue. BA, Ill. Coll., 1971; MHA, U. Minn., 1974. Adminstrv. resident Rochester (Minn.) Meth. Hosp., 1973-74; dir. support svcs. Jennie Edmundson Hosp., Council Bluffs, Iowa, 1974-78; asst. adminstr. Trinity Meml. Hosp., Cudahy, Wis., 1978-83, sr. v.p. med. svcs., 1983-84; pres., chief exec. officer McDonough Dist. Hosp., Macomb, Ill., 1985—; bd. dirs. Midamerica Nat. Bank, Canton, Ill. Bd. dirs. Macomb Area Indsl. Devel., 1985—, Wesley Village, 1988—; bd. dirs. YMCA, Macomb, 1987-94, also past pres.; chmn. staff parish com. Wesley United Meth. Ch., Mcomb, 1990-92; dist. chmn. Medicine Lodge dist. Illowa coun. Boy Scouts Am., 1997-99. Fellow Am. Coll. Healthcare Execs.; mem. Ill. Hosp. Assn. (past pres. region 1-B, bd. dirs. 1991-95), Macomb C. of C. (bd. dirs. 1990-94), Rotary (pres.-elect Macomb 1995-96, pres. 1996-97). Avocations: golf, reading, computers, travel. Home: 112 W Totem Trl Macomb IL 61455-1272 Office: McDonough Dist Hosp 525 E Grant St Macomb IL 61455-3318

HOPPER, VANESSA J., oncological nurse; b. Port Hueneme, Calif., Feb. 6, 1955; d. Richard E and Ruth Ellen (Ober) Bird; m. Bennie J. Hopper, Jr., Dec. 8, 1984; 1 child, Bennie J. III. BSN, U. Tex., San Antonio, 1978. RN, Tex.; cert. in ACLS; cert. oncology nurse. Staff nurse Met. Gen. Hosp., San Antonio; head nurse S.W. Oncology Assocs., P.A., San Antonio, 1982-95; nurse South Tex. Oncology and Hematology, P.A., San Antonio, 1995-96; nurse mgr. Tex. Oncology, P.A., San Antonio, 1996-97; nurse mgr., oncology unit St. Luke's Bapt. Hosp., San Antonio, 1997—. Mem. Oncology Nurses Soc. (bd. dirs., sec.). Home: 5915 Woodridge Cv San Antonio TX 78249-3115 Office: St Luke's Bapt Hosp 7930 Floyd Curl Dr San Antonio TX 78229-3903

HOPPER, WALTER EVERETT, lawyer; b. Houghton, Mich., Oct. 29, 1915; s. Walter E. and Maude (Crum) H.; m. Jeannette Ross, Aug. 23, 1941 (dec. 1947); 1 dau., Nancy Cameron Hopper Marcovici; m. Diana Kerensky, Sept. 24, 1958; 1 stepdau., Nicole Sudrow Hopper Neilan. A.B., Cornell U., 1937, J.D., 1939; grad., Command and Gen. Staff Sch., Indsl. Coll. Armed Forces. Bar: N.Y. 1939, U.S. Supreme Ct. 1946, D.C. 1959. Practice in Ithaca, 1939-42, N.Y.C., 1946—; mobilization designee, office dep. chief of staff mil. ops. Dept. of Army, 1952-67; chmn., chief exec. officer Fort Amsterdam Corp., 1973-81; dir. Davis Brake Beam Co. Chmn. trustees Loyal Legion Found.; trustee Inst. on Man and Sci., 1969-71, Signal Hill Edni. Ctr.; bd. dirs. U.S. Flag Found. Lt. col., inf. ETO, col. AUS (ret.). Decorated Army Commendation medal with oak leaf cluster; N.Y. State Conspicious Service Cross with Maltese Cross; Order Ruben Dario Nicaragua; comdr. Order Orange-Nassau, Netherlands; Order St. John of Jerusalem. Mem. Internat. Assn. Protection Indsl. Property (exec. com. Am. group 1958-71), Internat. Fiscal Assn., British Fifth Army Old Comrades Assn., Nat. Fgn. Trade Council (mem. coms.), Internat. C. of C. (rep. internat. conf. revision internat. conv. protection indsl. property 1958, U.S. council 1949-71, mem. coms.), Am. Arbitration Assn. (panelist), U.S. Trademark Assn. (past v.p., dir., chmn. internat. com.), UN Assn. (dir. N.Y. chpt. 1964-66), Holland Soc. (pres. 1966-71), Loyal Legion (comdr.-in-chief 1964-67), Assn. Bar City N.Y., N.Y. State Criminal Bar Assn., Res. Officers Assn. (pres. N.Y. State 1949), Confrerie des Chevaliers du Tastevin, Pilgrims, Soc. War 1812, Founders and Patriots of Am., Mayflower Descs., Soc. Colonial Wars, St. Nicholas Soc. (pres. 1982-84), S.R., Huguenot Soc. Am. (pres. 1972-75), Mil. Order Fgn. Wars, Soc. of Cin., St. Andrews Soc., Explorers Club (N.Y.C.), Univ. Club (N.Y.C.), Met. Club (Washington), Army-Navy Club (Washington). Home: 715 Park Ave New York NY 10021-5047 *The key to success in human endeavor is determination.*

HOPPING, RICHARD LEE, college president emeritus; b. Dayton, Ohio, July 26, 1928; s. Lavon Lee and Dorothy Marie (Anderson) H.; m. Patricia Louise Vance, June 30, 1951; children: Ronald, Debra, Jerrold. Student, Chaffey Coll., 1947-48, U. Dayton, 1948-49, Sinclair Coll., 1948-49; BS, So. Coll. Optometry, 1952, OD, 1952, DOS (hon.), 1972; DSc (hon.), SUNY, 1995. Practice optometry Dayton, Ohio, 1953-73; pres. So. Calif. Coll. Optometry, Fullerton, 1973-97, pres. emeritus, 1997—; mem. Nat. Acads. of Practice, 1983—; chmn. Nat. Acad. Practice in Optometry, 1985-89; chmn. 13th dist. med. quality rev. com., State of Calif. Bd. Med. Quality Assurance, 1985-93; member St. Jude Hosp. Adv. Bd., 1985—; nat. spokesperson Better Vision Inst., 1988—; cons. in field. Contbr. numerous articles on vision and health care to profl. publs. V.p. Orange County (Calif.) coun. Boy Scouts Am., 1977-79, mem. adv. coun., 1979-94; mem. Coun. Assocs. of Red Cross, North Orange County Svc. Ctr., 1978-80; mem. adv. coun. YWCA, North Orange County, 1984-92. Named Optimist of Yr. Dayton View Optimists, 1956; recipient Orange County Retinitis Pigmentosa award of Excellence in field of vision care, 1988, award of Excellence VisionAmerica, 1991, Dirs. Choice award Optical Labs. Assn., 1995, Leo award of Excellence in Global Eye Care Nat. Eye Rsch. Found., 1995, People of Vision award Prevent Blindness Am., 1997. Fellow APHA (Vision Care Disting. Achievement award 1984), Am. Acad. Optometry (chmn. primary care optometry sect. 1973-79, chmn. awards com. 1981-90); mem. Am. Optometric Assn. (pres. 1971-72, chmn. profl. enhancement adv. com. 1982-89, Optometrist of Yr. 1988, AOA Nat. Optometerist of Yr. 1988, chair industry rels. com. 1989-95, chair nat. ednl. summit conf. 1990-91, chair Nat. Optometric Edn. Summit com. 1991-92, chair centennial adv. com. 1996—, Scope of Optometric Practice Conf. 1992, Dr. Raymond I. Meyers award 1990, Disting. Svc. award 1993), Calif. Optometric Assn. (hon. life, jud. coun., Optometrist of Yr. 1988, Paul Yarwood Meml. award 1997), Assn. Ind. Calif. Colls. and Univs. (trustee 1973—), Optometric Ext. Programs Found. (hon. life), Assn. Schs. and Colls. of Optometry (pres. 1983-85), Ohio Optometric Assn. (pres. 1964-65, Optometrist of Yr. 1962, hon. life), Retinitis Pigmentosa Internat. (adv. exec. com. 1984-88), Dayton C. of C. (Man of Yr.), Lincoln of Orange County Club (chmn. ethics com. 1988-92, lifetime achievement awd. SCO, 1997). Office: So Calif Coll Optometry 2575 Yorba Linda Blvd Fullerton CA 92831-1615*

HOPPING, WILLIAM RUSSELL, hospitality industry consultant and appraiser; b. Balt., May 3, 1947; s. Russell Leroy and Janet Louise (Cloud) H.; m. Catherine Wilson; 1 child, William Alexander. BS in Hotel Adminstrn., Cornell U., 1969; MBA, U. Denver, 1978. Mgr. Sylvania (Ohio) Country Club, 1972-77; sr. cons. Pannell Kerr Forster, Denver, 1978-82; cons. Ginther Wycoff Grp., Denver, 1982-85; pres. W.R. Hopping & Co., Inc., Denver, 1985—; mem. adv. bd. travel and tourism dept. Arapahoe C.C., 1998. Vol., Big Bros., Inc., Denver, 1990—; chmn. adv. bd. U. Denver Profl. Career Devel. Prog., 1987-88, chmn. task force, Career and Placement Ctr., 1989. 1st lt. U.S. Army, 1970-72. Mem. Appraisal Inst., Internat. Soc. Hospitality Cons. (pres. 1990-91, chmn. 1991-93, chmn. emeritus, 1993—), Cornell Soc. Hotelmen (pres. Rocky Mountain chpt. 1984-85), Counselors of Real Estate. Avocations: bicycling, skiing. Office: W R Hopping & Co Inc 6334 S Yates Ct Littleton CO 80123-6738

HOPPLE, JEANNE M., adult nurse practitioner; b. Pitts., Nov. 2, 1955; d. John Andrew and Esther Ruth (Seitz) Dethis; m. William H. Hopple II, May 21, 1977; children: Mary Christine, Melissa Jeanne, Matthew John. BSN, U. Pitts., 1977; MSN, U. South Fla., 1993. RN, Fla.; cert. adult nurse practitioner, acute care nurse practioner, cardiovascular clin. specialist, cardiology acute care nurse practitioner, case mgr. in cardiovascular surgery, critical care nurse. Staff nurse CCU, med. ICU S.W. Fla. Regional Med. Ctr. and Healthpark Med. Ctr.-Lee Meml. Hosp., Ft. Myers; clin. educator angioplasty and med. critical care S.W. Fla. Regional Med. Ctr., Ft. Myers, cardiac patient educator; edn. specialist in med. nursing, dept. ednl. svcs. Lee Meml. Hosp., Ft. Myers; clin. specialist, acute care practitioner, case mgr. Charlotte Regional Med. Ctr., Punta Gorda, Fla., 1995-97; mem. Lipid Nurse Task Force. Mem. AACCN (past local treas.), Fla. Nurses Assn., Advanced Practice Nursing Coun. S.W. Fla., Masters RN Group, Sigma Theta Tau. Home: 23381 Van Buren Ave Pt Charlotte FL 33980-5939 Office: SW Fla Heart Group 8540 College Pky Fort Myers FL 33919-5143

HOPPLE, RICHARD VAN TROMP, JR., advertising agency executive; b. Cin., Mar. 20, 1947; s. Richard Van Tromp and Marie (Mitchell) H.; m. Patricia Spalt, July 16, 1972; children: Peter Van Tromp, Richard Halstead, Brooks McNeil. BS, Northwestern U., 1969. Acct. exec. Dancer-Fitzgerald-Sample, N.Y.C., 1969-72; sr. v.p. Benton & Bowles, Inc., N.Y.C., 1972-85, D'Arcy-Masius-Benton & Bowles, Inc., N.Y.C., 1985-86; with Wells, Rich, Greene Worldwide, N.Y.C., 1986-91, formerly pres. East, then pres. Worldwide; from vice-chmn. to pres. Darcy Masius Benton & Bowles, N.Y.C., 1992-96; CEO Unicast Comm., 1996—. Bd. dirs. (Conn.) Wilton United Way, 1979. Mem. Racquet and Tennis (N.Y.C.), Am. Rivers (bd. dirs.), City Ctr. of N.Y. (bd. dirs.). Office: Unicast Communications 650 Fifth Ave New York NY 10019

HOPPS, RAYMOND, JR., film producer, lawyer; b. Balt., July 26, 1949; s. Raymond Hopps Sr. and Ella Louise Dixon. BA cum laude, Howard U., 1971; JD, Loyola U., Chgo., 1974. Bar: Ill. 1975. CEO, art atty. Cmty. Legal Counsel, Chgo., 1972; staff and adminstr. Chgo. Vol. Legal Svcs., 1972-74; assoc. Archie B. Weston Sr. Ltd., Chgo., 1975-77; pvt. practice Chgo., 1977-78, film prodr., 1978; prodr. N.Y. Film Colony, 1979; with svc. work Internat. Econs.; owner, prodr., artist Am. Oriental Internat. Ltd., Balt., 1980—; staff rschr. Task Force for Cmty. Broadcasting, Chgo., 1973-78; atty. cons. Assn. of Audio-Visual Prodrs., Chgo., 1978; coord. N.Y. Film Colony, 1979; staff atty. Ebony Talent Assocs., Chgo. Composer: Concerto Impossible, 1987, For Your Eyes Only, 1981, Victory for the Free Planet, 1991; author: (prose) Master E, 1986; composer, author: Free Planet, 1991; writer, film prodr. for screen. Staff artist Eubie Blake Cultural Ctr., Balt., 1990—; assoc. Nat. Football League and Balt. Ravens. With USAF, 1968-91, brig. gen. Res. Mem. NAACP, Internat. Mid. East Assn., Am. Mgmt. Assn., Equal Opportunity Found., Jim Straw Heritage Exch., WFI Corp. Democrat. Avocations: music, dancing, films, walking. Office: AMI Ltd Motion Pictures PO Box 67585 Baltimore MD 21215-0016 also: 2806 Garrison Blvd Apt 1 Baltimore MD 21216-1846

HOPSON, EDWIN SHARP, lawyer; b. Louisville, Apr. 23, 1945; s. Henry Dockins and Martha (Linton) H.; m. Jane Mayo Fitzpatrick, July 20, 1968; children: Edwin Hopson Jr., Martha. BSL, U. Louisville, 1967, JD, 1969; LLM, George Washington U., 1971. Bar: Ky. 1969, Fla. 1969, U.S. Supreme Ct. 1972, U.S. Dist. Ct. (we. dist.) Ky. 1974, U.S. Ct. Appeals (6th cir.) 1977. Atty. Solicitor's Office, U.S. Dept. Labor, Washington, 1969-72; field atty. NLRB, Balt., 1972-74; assoc. Tarrant, Combs, Blackwell & Bullitt, Louisville, 1974-77; ptnr. Tarrant, Combs & Bullitt, Louisville, 1977-80, Wyatt, Tarrant & Combs, Louisville, 1980—. Editor Ky. Bench & Bar, 1989-91; chpt. editor: How Arbitration Works, 1989, 2d edit., 1991; contbr. articles to profl. jours. Bd. dirs. Bellewood Presbyn. Children's Home, Louisville, 1988-96, pres., 1991-93; bd. dirs. Louisville Ballet, 1991—, v.p., 1992-93, pres., 1993-94; bd. dirs. Bellewood Children's Found., 1995—, pres., 1995-96. Fellow Coll. Labor & Employment Lawyers, Inc.; mem. ABA (co-chmn. future directions of arbitration subcom. 1989-94), FBA (chpt. pres. 1991-92), Louisville Bar Assn. (co-chmn. labor and employment law sect. 1982-83), Ky. Bar Assn. (co-chmn. labor and employment law sect. 1987-89, mem. ho. of dels. 1996—). Republican. Presbyterian. Avocations: flying, various sports, reading. Home: 3003 Lightheart Rd Louisville KY 40222-6138 Office: Wyatt Tarrant & Combs Citizens Plz Louisville KY 40202

HOPSON, JAMES WARREN, publishing executive; b. St. Louis, May 24, 1946; s. David Warren and Ruth L. (Dierkes) H.; m. Julie Ann Eastlack, Dec. 21, 1968; children: John, Benjamin, Gillian. BJ, U. Mo., 1968; MBA, Harvard U., 1973. Project mgr. Des Moines Register & Tribune, 1973-76, dir. ops., 1976-78, circulation dir., 1978-79; gen. mgr. Corpus Christi (Tex.) Caller Times, 1979-82; pub. Middlesex News, Framingham, Mass., 1982-88; pres. N.E. Group-Harte-Hanks Comms., Framingham, 1984-88; pub. The Press of Atlantic City, N.J., 1989-94; pres. Community Newspaper Co., Boston, 1994-95, Thomson Ctrl. Ohio, Newark, 1995—. Pres. Vol. Ctr. Atlantic County, 1992—; treas. DeCordova Mus., Lincoln, Mass., 1983-89, dir., 1983-89; sec. Family Health Svc. Cen. Ohio, 1997—. 1st lt. U.S. Army, 1968-73, Vietnam. Mem. New Eng. Newspaper Assn. (chmn. circulation com. 1986-88), Mass. Newspaper Pub. Assn. (dir. 1984-88), Metrowest C. of C. (chmn. 1987-88). Office: Thomson-Ctrl Ohio 15 N 3rd St Ste 4 Newark OH 43055-5555

HOPTON, JANICE, elementary school principal. Prin. Skyway Elem. Sch., Opa Locka, Fla., 1987—. Office: Skyway Elem Sch 4555 NW 206th Ter Opa Locka FL 33055-1299*

HOPWOOD, VICKI JEANE, medical center official; b. Oskaloosa, Iowa, Dec. 23, 1967; d. Jerry Lynn and Mary Gaynelle (Emerson) Hopwood. AS in Bus. Adminstrn., Abraham Baldwin Coll., Tifton, Ga., 1988, AS in Polit. Sci., 1989; BBA, Ga. Southwestern U., 1992. Med. records clk. Tift Gen. Hosp., Tifton, Ga., 1986-88; data processing clk. Tift Gen. Hosp., Tifton, 1989-90, utilization rev. clk., 1990-93, transciptionist, 1993-94; legal sec. Simpson, Gray & Carter, Tifton, 1994; med. staff asst. St. Francis Hosp., Columbus, Ga., 1994-95; med. staff asst. S.E. Ga. Regional Med. Ctr., Brunswick, 1995-96, med. staff office mgr., 1996-98, mgr. managed care svcs., 1998—. Mem. Nat. Assn. Med. Staff Svcs. (cert. provider credentialing specialist, cert. med. staff coord.), Ga. Assn. Med. Staff Svcs., Ga. Soc. for Managed Care. Office: SE Ga Regional Med Ctr 2415 Parkwood Dr Brunswick GA 31520-4211

HOR, JOHNSON, contractor; b. San Francisco, Oct. 13, 1972; s. George Chen and Denise Hor. BSBA, San Francisco State U., 1995; MS, U. Phoenix, 1998; postgrad., New Coll. Sch. Law, 1998—. Sub-dealer, cons. Infinitel.Inginex, San Francisco, 1992-99; bus. rep., lobbyist Associated Students, Inc., San Francisco, 1993-95; transp. analyst, sr. sed. Levi Strauss & Co., San Francisco, 1995-97; contractor Chevron Products Co., San Francisco, 1998; with MEDWEB, San Francisco, 1998-99. Chief tech. officer Curtin Pacific Inst. Criminal Justice, San Francisco, 1998-99. Mem. Nat. Assn. Black Accts., San Francisco Trial Lawyers Assn., Platinum Guild Internat., Pi Kappa Phi. Avocations: investments, immigratino legal advocate, laser tag. Home: 170 Montgomery St Ste 111 San Francisco CA 94111 Office: MEDWEB 667 Folsom St San Francisco CA 94107

HORAHAN, EDWARD BERNARD, III, lawyer; b. Drexel Hill, Pa., Dec. 30, 1951; s. Edward Bernard and Ann Veronica (Schneeweis) H.; m. Rebecca Joy Fusco, Mar. 13, 1976; 1 child, Elizabeth Joy. BA, LaSalle Coll., Phila., 1973; JD, Yale U., 1976. Bar: D.C. 1976. Staff atty. office of gen. counsel SEC, Washington, 1976-78; staff atty. office of solicitor, plan benefits security div. U.S. Dept. Labor, Washington, 1978-80; assoc. Arter & Hadden, Washington, 1980-84; ptnr. Parker, Chapin, Flattau & Klimpl, Washington, 1984-88, Stroock & Stroock & Lavan, Washington, 1988-93; pvt. practice Law Offices of Edward B. Horahan III, Washington, 1993-96; counsel Groom Law Group, Washington, 1996—. Mem. ABA. Office: Ste 1200 1701 Pennsylvania Ave NW Washington DC 20006-5805

HORAK, JAMES ALBERT, materials scientist, nuclear engineer, educator; b. Plainfield, N.J., Oct. 28, 1931; s. John Sr. and Florence Gladys (Newman) H.; m. Diane Judy Herman, July 9, 1954; children: Ralph James, Kendell John, Gregory Eugene. BS in Metall. Engring., U. Ill., 1958; MS in Materials Sci., Northwestern U., 1963, PhD in Materials Sci., 1966. Reg. nuclear engr., Calif. Mem. staff Argonne (Ill.) Nat. Lab., 1958-68, Los Alamos (N.Mex.) Nat. Lab., 1968-69, Sandia Labs., Albuquerque, 1969-74; assoc. prof. nuclear engring. U. N.Mex., Albuquerque, 1969-74, prof., 1974; mem. staff Lockheed-Martin Energy Sys., Oak Ridge, Tenn., 1974-93; group leader Lockheed-Martin Energy Sys., Oak Ridge, 1993—. With USAF, 1953. Am. Nuclear Soc. fellow, 1979. Home: 304 Calloway Cir Lenoir City TN 37772-5964 Office: Lockheed Martin Energy Sys PO Box 2009 Oak Ridge TN 37831-2009

HORAK, JAN-CHRISTOPHER, film studies educator, curator; b. Bad Münstereifel, Fed. Republic Germany, May 1, 1951; came to U.S., 1951; s. Jerome V. and Giselle (Offermanns) H.; m. Martha F. Schirn, May 17, 1988; 1 child, Gianna. BA, U. Del., 1973; MS, Boston U., 1975; PhD, Westfälische Wilhelms-U., Münster, Germany, 1984. Intern Internat. Mus. Photography, Rochester, N.Y., 1975-76, assoc. curator George Eastman House, 1984-87, curator film, 1987-90, sr. curator, 1990-94; asst. prof. film studies U. Rochester, 1985-90, assoc. prof., 1990-93, prof., 1994; dir. Münchner Filmmuseum, Munich, Germany, 1994-98; prof. Hochschule f. Fernsehen u. Film, 1995-98; dir. archives and collections Universal Studios, L.A., 1998—; prof. UCLA, 1999—; panelist, chmn. film panel N.Y. State Coun. of Arts, N.Y.C., 1986-89; cons. USIA, 1988-90; archivists adv. bd. The Film Found., N.Y.C., 1990-94; v.p., pres. Assn. Moving Image Archivists, 1991-93; exec. com. Internat. Fedn. Film Archives, 1993-95, Kuratorium Junger Deutscher Film, 1995-97. Author: Anti-Nazi Filme der Emigration, 1984, Fluchtpunkt Hollywood, 1986, The Dream Merchants, 1989, Lovers of Cinema: The First American Film Avant-Garde, 1995, Berge, Licht und Traum: Arnold Fanck und der deutsche Bergfilm, 1997, Making Images Move: Photography and Avant-Garde Cinema, 1997; editor: Film und Foto der 20er Jahre, 1979, Helmar Lerski, 1982; contbr. articles to profl. jours. Recipient Louis B. Mayer award Mayer Found., Am. Film Inst., 1975; Heinrich Herz Stiftung fellow, 1979-81. Mem. Soc. Cinema Studies, Assn. Moving Image Archivists, Domitor, Soc. Exile Studies, Internat. Assn. Audio-Visual Media and History. Avocations: travel, skiing, swimming. Office: Universal Studios Inc 100 Universal City Plz Universal City CA 91608

HORAKOVA, ZDENKA ZAHUTOVA, retired toxicologist, pharmacologist; b. Jindrichuv Hradec, Czechoslovakia, Apr. 6, 1925; came to U.S., 1968, naturalized, 1974; d. Josef and Aloisie (Sohajova) Zahut; m. Vaclav Horak, Sept. 26, 1949; 1 child, David. M Pharmacy, Charles U., Prague, Czechoslovakia, 1949, D of Natural Scis., 1952; PhD in Pharmacology, Czechoslovakian Acad. Scis., Prague, Czechoslovakia, 1962. Sustantant pharmacy Kostelec Nad Orlici, Czechoslovakia, 1945-47; teaching asst. dept. pharmacology med. faculty Charles U., Prague, 1949-50; rsch. pharmacologist, head pharmacology dept. Rsch. Inst. Pharmacy and Biochemistry, Prague, 1950-68; rsch. pharmacologist exptl. therapeutics br. Nat. Heart and Lung Inst., NIH, Bethesda, Md., 1969-74; rsch. pharmacologist sect. on molecular pharmacology Nat. Heart, Lung and Blood Inst., NIH, Bethesda, 1974-77, rsch. pharmacologist Lab. Cellular Metabolism, 1977-78; toxicologist residue evaluation and surveillance div. Food Safety and Quality Svc.,

U.S. Dept. Agr., Washington, 1978-81; toxicologist residue evaluation and planning div. Sci., Food Safety and Inspection Svc., U.S. Dept. Agr., Washington, 1981-87; toxicologist forest pest mgmt. Forest Svc., U.S. Dept. Agr., Washington, 1987-93, ret., 1993; vis. guest Zambon Pharm. Rsch. Inst., Bresso-Milano, Italy, 1968; vol. work in profl. field. Contbr. articles to profl. jours. Recipient award Patent and Invention Office, Prague, 1960; WHO fellow Milan, Rome, 1961. Mem. Am. Soc. Pharmacology and Exptl. Therapeutics, Soc. Toxicology, Internat. Union Pharmacology, Internat. Soc. for Study Xenobiotics, Internat. Soc. Biochem. Pharmacology, Internat. Inflammation Club, European Biol. Rsch. Assn., Inflammation Rsch. Assn., Soc. Exptl. Biology and Medicine, Cell and Molecular Biology in Space, Toxicology Forum, Immunotoxicology Discussion Group, Archeol. Inst. Am., Czechoslovak Soc. Arts and Scis., Internat. Assn. Med. Assistance to Travelers, Smithsonian Assocs. Democrat. Roman Catholic. Avocations: art, sports, travel. Home: 5508 Oakmont Ave Bethesda MD 20817-3528

HORAN, HAROLD EUGENE, university administrator, former diplomat; b. Houston, June 16, 1927; s. Eugene F. and Bessie (Bain) H.; m. Bonnie McLeroy, Aug. 25, 1950; children: Elizabeth, Tessa, James. Student, Rice U., 1944-45, U. Paris, 1950-51; B.B.A., U. Houston, 1950, J.D., 1953. Bar: Tex. 1953. Asst. county atty. Harris County, Tex., 1953-54; atty. FTC, Washington, 1954-57; fgn. service officer U.S. Dept. State, from 1957; U.S. ambassador to Malawi Lilongwe, 1978-80; dep. asst. sec. state U.S. Dept. State, 1980-81; now dir. programs Inst. for Study of Diplomacy Georgetown U., Washington; sr. advisor for, Africa, Nat. Security Council, 1973-76. Served with USAAF, 1945-46. Recipient Bates Legal Scholar award, 1953; Meritorious Service award FTC, 1955; Meritorious Service award Dept. State, 1968. Mem. Am. Fgn. Service Assn., Tex. Bar Assn. Methodist. Home: 230 S Carolina Ave SE Washington DC 20003-1940

HORAN, JOSEPH PATRICK, interior designer; b. Waterloo, Iowa, Feb. 9, 1942; s. Raymond John and Anna Louise Horan. BS in Applied Art, Iowa State U., 1964. Cert. interior designer, Calif. Interior designer L.S. Ayres & Co., Indpls, 1964-70, W. & J. Sloane, Inc., San Francisco, 1970-82; prin., owner Joseph Horan Interior Design, San Francisco, 1982—; adv. bd. Interiors and Sources Mag., 1990—. Work represented in Better Homes and Gardens, San Francisco mag., Designers West mag., Christian Sci. Monitor, Interior Visions book, 1988, New Decorating Book, 1990, 100 Designers Favorite Rooms, 1993, Design Sense, 1996. Mem. organizing com., com. chmn. beaux arts ball San Francisco Mus. Modern Art, 1984-88, 90-91; mem. organizing com. San Francisco chpt. Design Industry Found. for AIDS, 1986-88. Fellow Am. Soc. Interior Designers (profl., bd. dirs. Calif. North chpt. 1983-84, 87, v.p. 1985-86, 88, pres. 1989-91, 1st prize ASID/ Flexalum Design With Blinds 1980, nat. bd. dirs. 1991-94, nat. v.p. programs 1995-96); mem. Nat. Trust Hist. Preservation (design assoc.), Calif. Coun. for Interior Design Certification. E-mail: sandyhoran@aol.com. Fax: (415) 922-0719. Office: 3299 Washington St San Francisco CA 94115-1666*

HORAN, JUSTIN THOMAS, retired association executive; b. Manchester, N.H., Feb. 6, 1927; s. Richard and Helen (Lenihan) H.; m. Helen Raymah Cook, Mar. 20, 1952; children: Catherine Helen, Carol Ann, Justin Thomas, Steven Edward, Daniel Kevin, Mark Gregory, Virginia Louise, Paul David. B.S., U. N.H., 1950; postgrad., Yale U., 1958, Syracuse U., 1961, Mich. State U., 1964. Asst. v.p. Manchester C. of C., 1955-57; exec. v.p. Newton (Mass.) C. of C., 1957-66, Greater Lawrence (Mass.) C. of C., 1966-69; pres. Greater Waterbury (Conn.) C. of C., 1969-75, Greater Pitts. C. of C., 1975-94; chmn. bd. regents Inst. Orgn. Mgmt., 1966—. Contbr. articles to profl. publs. Met. chmn. Western Conn., Nat. Alliance Businessmen, 1973-75; mem. Mayor's Com. on Econ. Devel., Pitts., 1976—; vice chmn., trustee LaRoche Coll.; mem. corp. North Hills Passavant Hosp. Served to capt. U.S. Army Res., 1950-59. Mem. Am. C. of C. Execs. (dir., vice chmn. 1981-82, chmn. 1983-84), New Eng. Assn. C. of C. Execs. (past pres.), Mass. Assn. C. of C. Execs. (past pres.). Clubs: Duquesne (Pitts.), Allegheny (Pitts.). Home: 103 Camden Ct Pittsburgh PA 15237-2331

HORAN, LEO GALLASPY, physician, educator; b. New Augusta, Miss., Sept. 17, 1925; s. Leo and Kate B. (Gallaspy) H.; m. Nancy Carolyn Flowers, July 23, 1966; children: David, Tracey, Paige. B.S., Tulane U., 1947, M.D., 1949. Intern Salt Lake County Gen. Hosp., Salt Lake City, 1949-50; resident in medicine Charity Hosp., New Orleans, 1952-56; asst. prof. medicine Tulane U., New Orleans, 1958-61; asso. prof. medicine U. Tenn., Memphis, 1961-67; prof. medicine Med. Coll. Ga., Augusta, 1967-73; prof., chmn. dept. medicine U. Louisville, 1973-82; prof. medicine Eastern Va. Med. Sch., Norfolk, 1983-84; prof. medicine Med. Coll. Ga., Augusta, 1984-93, prof. emeritus, 1994—; joined Cardiovascular Assocs. of Savannah, 1993-95; prof. medicine Mercer U. Sch. Medicine, 1998—; chief med. svc. VA Hosp., Augusta, 1967-73, chief cardiologist, 1984-93; chief med. svc. Louisville Gen. Hosp., 1973-82; assoc. chief of staff for rsch. VA Med. Ctr., Hampton, Va., 1983-84. Mem. editorial bd.: Jour. Electrocardiology, 1968—, Jour. Am. Coll. Cardiology, 1986-90; contbr. articles to profl. jours. Served with USNR, 1950-52. USPHS grantee, 1965-93; Am. Heart Assn. grantee, 1963-66. Fellow A.C.P., Am. Coll. Cardiology, Am. Coll. Chest Physicians; mem. Am. Soc. Clin. Investigation, Central Soc. Clin. Research, Assn. Profs. Medicine, Assn. Am. Physicians, Assn. Univ. Cardiologists. Democrat. Presbyterian. Address: 10 Topsail Ct Savannah GA 31411-1729

HORAN, MARY ANN THERESA, nurse; b. Denver, July 4, 1936; d. John Paul and Lucille (Somma) Perito; m. Stephen F. Horan, Sr., Dec. 28, 1957; children: Seanna, Dana, Michelle, Annette, Stephen Jr., Christine, David. BSN, Loretto Heights Coll., Denver, 1958; postgrad, Pima Community Coll., 1982. RN, Ala. Staff nurse Med. Ctr. Hosp., Huntsville, Ala., 1978-79, Crestwood Hosp., Huntsville, 1980-81, St. Joseph Hosp. Eye Surgery, Tucson, 1981—; v.p. Success Achievement Ctr., Tucson, 1987—; Shaklee distbr., 1996—. Contbr. articles to nursing jours., poetry to lit. jours. Republican. Roman Catholic. Home: 8311 E 3rd St Tucson AZ 85710-2550

HORAN, MARY JO, adult education educator, consultant; b. Annapolis, Md., Mar. 16, 1937; d. Thomas Lawrence and Eleanor Marie (Counihan) Greene; children: Richard Jr., Thomas, Christopher, Mary Catherine, Megan, Patrick. BA, Saint Mary's Coll., 1959; MA, Ctrl. Mich. U., 1982; PhD, Va. Tech. U., 1988. Dist. mgr. U.S. Census Bur., Alexandria, Va., 1979-80; spl. asst. Dept. Interior, Washington, 1983; rsch. asst. Va. Tech. U., Falls Church, 1982-86, Naval Surface Weapons Command, Dahlgren, 1986-87; assoc. prof. Dokuz Eylul U., Izmir, Turkey, 1989; instr. European divsn. U. Md., 1989-90; assoc. prof. Troy State U., Ft. Myers, Va., 1991-96; adj. prof. George Mason U., Fairfax, Va., 1983-85, Am. Mil. U., Manassas, Va., 1997—; cons., trainer USAF, Europe, 1989. Mem. ASTD, ASPA. Avocations: tennis, travelling, movies, antiques, reading.

HORAN, PATRICK M., English educator; b. Phillipsburg, N.J., July 27, 1958; s. Edward R. and Marguerite (De Lorenzo) H. BA in English, Montclair State Coll., 1980; MA in English, NYU, 1985; doctoral student, Drew U. Cert. tchr., N.J. English tchr. Sacred Heart Sch., Dover, N.J.; tchr. English, music, Latin, French Morris Cath. High Sch., Denville, N.J.; adj. prof. Rutgers U., Newark, Bergen Community Coll., Paramus, N.J. Mem. Nat. Coun. Tchrs. English. Home: 62 Spring St Apt 6 Williamstown MA 01267-2851

HORCHOW, S(AMUEL) ROGER, marketing consultant; b. Cin., July 3, 1928; s. Reuben and Beatrice (Schwartz) H.; m. Carolyn Pfeifer, Dec. 29, 1960; children: Regen Horchow Fearon, Elizabeth Horchow Routman, Sally. BA, Yale U., 1950. Buyer Foley's, Houston, 1953-60; v.p. Neiman-Marcus, Dallas, 1960-68, 69-71; pres. Design Research, Cambridge, Mass., 1968-69, Kenton Collection, Dallas, 1971-73; chmn. Horchow Collection, Dallas, 1973-90. Author: Elephants in Your Mailbox, 1979, Living in Style, 1981; producer Crazy for You, 1991-95. Bd. dirs. Am. Inst. Pub. Svc., Ctr. for Human Nutrition, Yale Art Galley, Mus. Modern Art, N.Y.C., Dallas Symphony, Better Bus. Bur., Pub. Radio Internat., Up with People, Friends of Art and Preservation of Embassies, Delia's, World Wildl. Mem. Yale Club (N.Y.C.), Nantucket Yacht Club, Knickerbocker Club. Office: 5722 Chatham Hill Rd Dallas TX 75225-3208

HORE, JOHN EDWARD, commodity futures educator; b. Dec. 13, 1929; s. Ernest and Doris Kathleen (Horton) H.; m. Diana King, May 3, 1958; children: Edward John Bruce, Celia Kathleen Hore Milne, Timothy Frank. BA with honors, King's Coll., Cambridge, Eng., 1952, MA, 1957. Chartered fin. analyst. Asst. sales mgr. Borthwicks, London, 1952-54; security analyst Dominion Securities, Toronto, Ont., Can., 1955-57; asst. mktg. mgr. Rio Algom, Toronto, 1957-61; dir. Bell, Gouinlock & Co., Toronto, 1961-75; v.p., dir. futures Can. Securities Inst., Toronto, 1979-94, seminar leader, 1980—; investment edn. cons., 1995—; cons. Can. Dept. Agr., 1993; founding sec. Can. Nuclear Assn.; past v.p. Brit. Can. Trade Assn.; chmn. 1st Can. Internat. Futures Rsch. Seminar, 1985, also editor Proc., 2 vols., 1986; spkr. Can.-Am. Inst. Conf. on Fin. Svcs. at Detroit-Windsor, 1989, compliance seminar Futures Industry Assn. at Alexandria, Va., 1990; chmn. Can. Futures Conf., 1986; chmn. 3d, 4th, 5th and 6th Can. Internat. Futures Conf. and Rsch. Seminars, 1987, 88, 89, 90, mng. editor Selected Papers 1988-91. Author: Trading on Canadian Futures Markets, 1984, 5th edit., 1993; co-author: Association for Investment Management and Research Standards of Practice Handbook, 1982 (Pres. Reagan Citation 1984); co-editor: Canadian Securities Course, 1980-94. Gov. Montcrest Sch., 1970-73; mem. Commodity Futures Adv. Bd., Ont., 1989-95; apptd. mem. internat. com. Futures Industry Assn., Washington, 1988-91, rowing com. Upper Can. Coll., Toronto, 1982-86; pres. St. George's Soc. Toronto, 1978-80, chmn. edn. com., 1987. With Royal Army Ednl. Corps, 1948-49, Singapore. Mem. Toronto Soc. Fin. Analysts (bd. dirs. 1968-71), Assn. for Investment Mgmt. and Rsch. (formerly Fin. Analysts Fedn., bd. dirs. investment analysis stds. 1974-85, emeritus 1985), Univ. Club (bd. dirs. 1980-83), Arts and Letters Club, Leander Club (assoc.) (Henley-on-Thames), Hurlingham Club, Royal Overseas League (pres. Ont. chpt., chmn. Toronto round table 1999—) (London). Anglican. Avocations: historical research, squash, choral music, poetry. Office: 185 Carlton St, Toronto, ON Canada M5A 2K7

HORECKER, BERNARD LEONARD, retired biochemistry educator; b. Chgo., Oct. 31, 1914; s. Paul and Bessie (Bornstein) H.; m. Frances Goldstein, July 12, 1936; children: Doris Colgate, Marilyn Diamond Schnell, Linda Lally. B.S., U. Chgo., 1936, Ph.D., 1939; Laureate honoris causa in Biol. Scis., U. Urbino (Italy), 1982. Rsch. assoc. chemistry U. Chgo., 1939-40; examiner U.S. Civil Svc. Commn., 1940-41; biochemist USPHS, NIH, Bethesda, Md., 1941-59; chief lab. of biochemistry and metabolism Nat. Inst. Arthritis and Metabolic Disease, 1956-59; professorial lectr. enzyme chemistry George Washington U., 1950-57; guest rsch.-worker Pasteur Inst., Paris, 1957-58; prof. microbiology, chmn. dept. NYU Coll. Medicine, 1959-63; prof. molecular biology, chmn. dept. Albert Einstein Coll. Medicine, 1963-72, assoc. dean for sci. affairs, 1971-72; mem. Roche Inst. Molecular Biology, Nutley, N.J., 1972-84; head Lab. Molecular Enzymology, Roche Inst. Molecular Biology, 1977-84; adj. prof. Cornell U. Med. Coll., 1972-84, prof. biochemistry, 1984-89, prof. emeritus biochemistry, 1989, dean Grad. Sch. Med. Sci., 1984-92; vis. prof. Albert Einstein Coll. Medicine, 1972-84; vis. prof. biochemistry U. Calif., 1954, U. Parana, Brazil, 1960, 63; vis. lectr. U. Ill., 1956; Ciba lectr. Rutgers U., 1962; Phillips lectr. Haverford Coll., 1965; vis. prof. Kyoto (Japan) U., 1967; vis. prof. biochemistry and molecular biology Cornell U., 1965; vis. prof. U. Ferrara, Italy; Reilly lectr. Notre Dame U., 1969; vis. lectr. U. Rotterdam, 1970; prof. honoris causa Fed. U. Parana, Curitiba, Brazil, 1981—; mem. sci. adv. bd. Roche Inst. Molecular Biology, Nutley, N.J., 1967-72, chmn., 1971-72; dir. Academic Press, Inc., 1968-73; mem. Research Career Award com. Nat. Inst. Gen. Med. Scis., 1966-70; mem. personnel com. Am. Cancer Soc., 1968-72, mem. sci. adv. com. for biochemistry and chem. carcinogenesis, 1974-78, mem. Council for Research and Clin. Investigation Awards, 1984-88; mem. biology div. adv. com. Oak Ridge Nat. Lab., 1976-80; mem. Med. Scientist Tng. Program Sect. NIH, 1970-72. Editor Biochem. and Biophys. Rsch. Communications, 1959-89, Current Topics in Cellular Regulation, 1969-89, Archives Biochemistry and Biophysics, 1960-68; chmn. editorial bd. Archives of Biochemistry and Biophysics, 1968-84; contbr. articles to sci. publs. Recipient Paul Lewis Labs. award in enzyme chemistry, 1952, Superior Accomplishment award Fed. Security Agy., 1952, Rockefeller Pub. Svc. award, 1957, Hillebrand prize Am. Chem. Soc., 1954, Award in Biol. Scis., Washington Acad. Scis., 1954, Fulbright Travel award, 1963; Commonwealth Fund fellow, 1967. Fellow AAAS, Am. Acad. Arts and Scis.; mem. NAS, Am. Chem. Soc. (vice chmn. div. biol. chemistry 1975-76, chmn. 1976-77), Biochem. Soc. (Eng.), Swiss Biochem. Soc. (hon. mem.), Spanish Biochem. Soc., hon. mem.), Japanese Biochem. Soc. (hon. mem.), Hellenic Biochem. and Biophys. Soc. (hon. mem.), Am. Soc. Biol. Chemists (pres. 1967-68, chmn. editorial com. 1962-63, Merck award 1981), Virchow-Pirquet Med. Soc. (Neuburg medal 1981), Harvey Soc. (v.p. 1969-70, pres. 1970-71), Brazilian Acad. Sci. (hon.), PanAm. Assn. Biochem. Socs. (vice chmn. 1971, chmn. 1972, mem. exec. com. 1971-78), Indian Nat. Acad. Sci., Argentine Acad. Sci. (corr.), Phi Beta Kappa, Sigma Xi. Home: 16517 Cypress Villa Ln Fort Myers FL 33908

HORGAN, DENIS EDWARD, journalist; b. Boston, Nov. 27, 1941; s. Cornelius Leonard and Anne Marie (Grigalus) H.; m. Patricia Jeanne Alerding, Nov. 26, 1967; children: Denis, Timothy, Daniel. BA in Journalism, Northeastern U., 1964; postgrad., U. Tex., 1964-65. Copyboy Boston Globe, 1960-63, reporter, 1963-64, 65-66; editor, pub. Bangkok (Thailand) World, 1968-71; editor, columnist Washington Star, 1971-81, Hartford (Conn.) Courant, 1981—; adv. com. journalism dept. So. Conn. State U., New Haven, 1986—; instr. in journalism U. Hartford, 1990-92; bd. dirs. Latinos Contra SIDA, Hartford. Author: Sharks in the Bathtub, 1986. Coach West Hartford (Conn.) Travel Baseball League, 1990—. Capt. U.S. Army, 1966-68. Recipient Columnist of Yr. award UPI, 1987, Column of Yr. award Sigma Delta Chi, 1988, 90, other local and regional awards. Roman Catholic. Avocation: Boston Red Sox. Home: 45 Riggs Ave West Hartford CT 06107-2740 Office: Hartford Courant 285 Broad St Hartford CT 06115-2510

HORGER, EDGAR OLIN, III, obstetrics and gynecology educator; b. Eutawville, S.C., May 30, 1937; s. Edgar Olin Jr. and Frances Durant (Jordan) H.; m. Polly Jo Collins, May 29, 1960; children: Edgar Olin IV, David Collins, Patricia Bowen. BS, Furman U., 1959; MD, Med. Coll. S.C., 1962. Intern Med. U. Hosp., Charleston, S.C., 1962-63; resident in ob-gyn Med. U. Hosp., 1963-67; NIH fellow U. Pitts., 1967-68, asst. prof., 1968-69; asst. prof. Med. U. S.C., Charleston, 1969-71, assoc. prof., 1971-76, prof., 1976-90, dir. maternal-fetal medicine, 1973-90; prof. ob-gyn. U. S.C. Sch. Medicine, Columbia, 1990—, chmn., 1993—; mem. S.C. Bd. Med. Examiners, 1985-87. Contbr. articles to profl. jours. Mem. adv. bd. Charleston chpt. March of Dimes, 1984-90. Served to capt. AUS, 1963-66. Recipient Fellowship award U.S. Pub. Health Service, 1967-68, Disting. Alumnus award Med. U. S.C., 1995. Mem. AMA, S.C. Med. Assn., Am. Coll. Obstetricians and Gynecologists (Outstanding Faculty award Dist. IV 1988, vice chmn. S.C. sect. 1993-96, chmn. 1996-98, treas. dist. IV 1997—), Coun. Res. Edn. ObGyn, South Ctrl. Ob-Gyn. Soc., South Atlantic Assn. Ob-Gyn. (exec. com. 1983-94, sec. 1987-90, v.p. 1990-91, pres.-elect 1991-92, pres. 1992-93), So. Perinatal Assn. (dir. Mid-Atlantic region 1974-76), Soc. Perinatal Obstetricians (dir. 1977-78), Am. Gynecol. Obstet. Soc., Am. Assn. Ob-Gyn., S.C. Ob-Gyn. Soc. (pres. 1991-92), Columbia Med. Soc., Assn. Profs. Gynecology and Obstetrics (Excellence in Tchg. award 1992), S.C. State Bd. Med. Examiners (bd. dirs. 1985-87), Alpha Omega Alpha. Clubs: Carolina Yacht, Summit. Home: 125 Holliday Rd Columbia SC 29223-3108 Office: U SC Sch Medicine Dept Ob-Gyn 2 Richland Medical Park Dr Columbia SC 29203-6864

HORII, NAOMI, editor; b. West Lafayette, Ind., Jan. 12, 1968; d. Yoshiyuki and Nobuko Ruth (Abe) H. BS, U. Colo., 1989; MA, U. Mo., 1993. Editor MYU Pub., Tokyo, 1989-91; tchr., talented and gifted program Boulder, Louisville, Colo., 1994-95; editor Many Mountains Moving, Boulder, 1994—; also bd. dirs. Many Mountains Moving; editor English sect. Rocky Mountain Jiho, 1996—. Vol. Takarazuka Exch. Program, Boulder, 1993—, Nightwalk Women's Safety Program, Boulder, 1987-89. Rocky Mountain Women's Inst. fellow, 1996-97; Gary Higa Found. Meml. scholar, 1988; recipient Anheuser-Busch award, 1997. Mem. NAFE, Rocky Mountain Book Pub. Assn., Visiones. Avocations: camping, hiking, reading, writing, music. Office: Many Mountains Moving 420 22nd St Boulder CO 80302-7909

HORISBERGER, DON HANS, conductor, musician; b. Millersburg, Ohio, Mar. 2, 1951; s. Hans and Jeannette (Grossniklaus) H. MusB, Capital U., 1973; MusM, Northwestern U., 1974, MusD, 1985. Dir. music 1st Presbyn. Ch., Waukegan, Ill., 1976-88; with Chgo. Symphony Chorus, 1977—, sect. leader, 1984-91, asst. condr., 1990-98, assoc. conductor, 1998—; dir. Waukegan Concert Chorus, 1979-97; organist/choirmaster Ch. of the Holy Spirit, Lake Forest, Ill., 1988—; lectr. in music Capital U., Columbus, Ohio, 1974-75; asst. to lang. coach Chgo. Symphony Chorus, 1978—. Fulbright-Hayes grantee 1975. Mem. Am. Choral Dirs. Assn. (chair community choruses cen. div. spl. interest 1988-91), Assn. Profl. Vocal Ensembles (chorus Am.).

HORKEY, WILLIAM RICHARD, retired diversified oil company executive; b. Tulsa, Apr. 22, 1925; s. William Edward and Clara Doris (Rice) H.; m. Barbara Jeanne Williamson, Oct. 18, 1952; children: Elaine Gail, Edward Richard, Ellen Beth. BA, State U. Iowa, 1947; LLB, U. Okla., 1950; grad., Advanced Mgmt. Program, Harvard U., 1962. Bar: Okla. 1950. With Gulf Oil Corp., 1950-51, Skelly Oil Co., 1951-55, Helmerich & Payne, Inc., Tulsa, 1955-90; sec., legal counsel Helmerich & Payne, Inc., 1955-64, v.p., 1960-64, exec. v.p., 1964-87, sr. v.p., 1987-90, bd. dirs., 1957-90; chmn. Grand River Dam Authority, Okla. Ordinance Works Authority, Woolslayer Cos. Inc., EnviroFuels Inc.; bd. dirs. The Great Eastern Shipping Co. London. Bd. dirs. Tulsa United Way, 1978-88; chmn. S.E. Tulsa YMCA, 1970-72; pres. Met. Tulsa YMCA, 1972-73, Tulsa Bus. Health Group 1978-96; chmn. Tulsa chpt. ARC, 1987-88; dir. Tulsa Emergency Med. Authority, 1977-95, chmn., 1981-95; pres. Tulsa Cmty. Found., for Indigent Health Care, 1980—. Mem. ABA, Okla. Bar Assn., Tulsa County Bar Assn., Order of Coif, So. Hills Country Club, Mid-Continent Harvard AMP (Tulsa) (pres. 1969-75), Phi Delta Phi, Phi Delta Theta. Presbyterian (deacon and elder). Home: 5686 S Evanston St Tulsa OK 74105 Office: 5416 S Yale Ave Ste 350 Tulsa OK 74135-6241

HORKOWITZ, SYLVESTER PETER, chemist; b. Lansford, Pa., Sept. 7, 1921; s. Simeon and Mary (Leshefka) H.; m. Olga Assaf, Sept. 12, 1964. Student, Kans. State Coll., Pittsburg, 1948-51. Chemist Spencer Chem. Co., Pittsburg, 1946-51; chief chemist Spencer Chem. Co., Vicksburg, Miss., 1951-56; rsch. mgr. Spencer Chem. Co., Orange, Tex., 1956-61; v.p. Spencer Chem. Far East, Tokyo, 1961-65; chem. mgr. Far East Gulf Oil Corp., Tokyo, Singapore, Bangkok, 1965-72; cons. chemist New Orleans, 1972—; cons. chemist New Orleans, 1972—; bd. dirs.; chmn. A-Jin Chem. Co., Pusan, Republic of Korea, 1965-68; adv. bd. Pertamina Gulf, Djakarta, Indonesia, 1969-71; bd. dirs. chmn. Gulf Plastics-Singapore. Contbr. articles to profl. jours. With U.S. Army, 1942-46. Mem. ASTM, Am. Oil Chemists Soc., Soc. Plastics Engrs., Am. Chem. Soc. Republican. Byzantine Catholic Ch. Achievements include patents for ethylene/acrylate co-polymers, deconyl peroxide-free radical polymerization initiator, ammonium nitrate prilling tower process. Home and Office: 5700 Ruth St Metairie LA 70003-2330

HORLICK, GARY NORMAN, lawyer, legal educator; b. Washington, Mar. 12, 1947; s. Reuben S. and Gertrude V. (Cooper) H.; m. Kathryn L. Mann, June 1, 1986. AB, Dartmouth Coll., 1968; BA, MA, Diploma in Internat. Law, Cambridge (Eng.) U., 1970; JD, Yale U., 1973. Bar: Conn. 1974, U.S. Ct. Appeals (D.C. cir.) 1975), D.C. 1977, U.S. Supreme Ct. 1977, U.S. Ct. Internat. Trade 1979, U.S. Ct. Customs and Patent Appeals 1980. Asst. to rep. Ford Found., Santiago, Chile, 1973-74; asst. rep. Ford Found., Bogota, Colombia, 1974-76; assoc. Steptoe & Johnson, Washington, 1976-80; internat. trade counsel U.S. Senate Fin. Com., Washington, 1981; dep. asst. sec. U.S. Dept. Commerce, Washington, 1981-83; ptnr. O'Melveny & Myers, Washington, 1983—; lectr. law Yale U., New Haven, 1983-86; adj. prof. Georgetown U. Law Ctr., Washington, 1986—; lectr. various orgns.; adv. com. U.S. Ct. Internat. Trade, 1993-97; mem. permanent group of experts World Trade Orgn., chmn., 1996-97. Mem. ABA (chmn. standing com. on customs law 1993), Coun. Fgn. Rels., Internat. Law Assn. (mem. exec. coun. Am. br. 1983—), Internat. Bar Assn. (vice chmn. antitrust and trade law 1987-89), D.C. Bar Assn. (chmn. internat. divsn. 1984-85), Am. Soc. of Internat. Law (exec. coun. 1998—). Office: O'Melveny & Myers 555 13th St NW Ste 500W Washington DC 20004-1159

HORMAN, KAREN LOEB, elementary education educator; b. Norfolk, Va., July 26, 1947; d. Joseph Arthur and Ruth Helen (Goldstein) Loeb; m. Neil Paul Rosenthal, Dec. 16, 1967 (div. 1984); children: Josh Scott, Karen; m. Richard Elliot Horman, Oct. 27, 1985 (dec.). BS, U. Md., 1969. Tchr. Brown Sta. Elem. Sch., 1969-72, Cold Spring Elem. Sch., Potomac, Md., 1972-73, Montgomery County Pub. Schs./Fallsmead Elem. Sch., Rockville, Md., 1973-93, Brown Sta. Elem. Sch., 1969-72, Thurgood Marshall Elem. Sch., Gaithersburg, Md., 1993—; tchr. math. Montgomery County Pub. Schs., Md., 1980-86. Bd. dirs. Tourette's Syndrome of Am., Bayside, N.Y., 1988-90; antique dealer Frederick, Md. Jewish. Avocations: travel, antiques. Office: Thurgood Marshal Elem Sch McDonald Chapel Way Gaithersburg MD 20878

HORMATS, ROBERT DAVID, economist, investment banker; b. Balt., Apr. 13, 1943; s. Saul and Ruth H. B.A., Tufts U., 1965; M.A., Fletcher Sch. Law and Diplomacy, 1966, M.A. in Law and Diplomacy, 1967, Ph.D., 1970. Research asst. Fletcher Sch. of Law and Diplomacy, 1968-69; research asso. Univ. Coll., Dar-es-Salaam, Tanzania, 1967-68; staff mem. internat. econ. affairs Nat. Security Council, 1969-73, sr. staff mem., 1974-77; sr. dep. asst. sec. for econ. and bus. affairs Dept. State, 1977-79; ambassador and dep. U.S. trade rep., 1979-81, asst. sec. state for econ. and bus. affairs, 1981-82; v.p. Goldman, Sachs and Co., 1982, mng. dir., 1998—; vice chmn. Goldman Sachs (Internat.), 1987—; guest scholar Brookings Instn., 1973-74; vis. lectr. Princeton U., 1983; mem. internat. capital markets com. N.Y. Stock Exch.; bd. dirs. U.S. Russia Investment Fund, Engelhard Hanovia, Inc., Human Genome Scis., Inc.; mem. Econ. Club of N.Y. Author: Making U.S. International Economic Policy, 1984, Reforming the International Monetary System, 1987, Am. Albatross: The Foreign Debt Dilemma, 1988, The Global Economy: America's Role in the Decade Ahead, 1989; mem. editorial bd. Fgn. Policy mag., Internat. Economy mag. Bd. overseers Tufts U.; bd. dirs. Coun. on Fgn. Rels. Decorated Legion of Honor (France); Shell Oil Co. fellow, 1967-68; Council on Fgn. Relations fellow, 1973-74; Recipient Arthur Flemming award, 1978. Mem. Econ. Club of N.Y. (bd. dirs.), US-ASEAW Bus. Coun. (bd. dirs.). Home: 55 East End Ave Apt 8A New York NY 10028-7949 Office: Goldman Sachs & Co 85 Broad St New York NY 10004-2456

HORN, ANDREW WARREN, lawyer; b. Cin., Apr. 19, 1946; s. George H. and Belle (Collin) H.; m. Melinda Fink; children: Lee Shawn, Ruth Belle. B.B.A. in Acctg., U. Miami, 1968, J.D., 1971. Bar: Fla. 1971, Colo. 1990, U.S. Dist. Ct. (so. dist.) Fla. 1972, U.S. Tax Ct. 1974. Ptnr. Gillman & Horn P.A., Miami, Fla., 1973-74; pvt. practice Miami, 1974—. Active civic coun. Children's Hosp., Miami. Recipient Am. Jurisprudence award Lawyers Coop. Pub. Co., 1970. Mem. ABA, Fla. Bar, Assn. Trial Lawyers Am., Acad. Fla. Trial Lawyers.

HORN, BERNARD, English language educator, writer; b. Bklyn., Mar. 6, 1944; s. Harry and Bella (Shell) H.; m. Linda L. Watson, Aug. 24, 1980; children: Gabriella Klein, Hedya Klein, Rebecca. BSChemE, MIT, 1965; PhD in English, U. Conn., 1977. Rsch. engr. Shell Oil Co., Deer Park, Tex., 1965-66; English prof. No. Essex C.C., Haverhill, Mass., 1971-84, Framingham (Mass.) State Coll., 1984—; cons., tech. writer Cybermation, Medford, Mass., 1983-84, Computervision, Bedford, Mass., 1989-91, InContext Enterprises, Harvard, Mass., 1995-96; presenter in field. Author: Facing the Fires: Conversations with A.B. Yehoshua, 1997; contbr. articles to profl. jours.; author numerous poems. Fellow NEH, 1978-79, 80, 85, 90, 95. Mem. MLA, Assn. for Jewish Studies, Nat. Assn. Profs. Hebrew. Democrat. Jewish. Home: 1195 Concord St Framingham MA 01701-4517

HORN, BRENDA SUE, lawyer; b. Beech Grove, Ind., Apr. 22, 1949; d. Donald Eugene Horn and Barbara Joyce (Waggoner) Christie. AB with distinction, Ind. U., 1971; MS, Purdue U., 1975; JD summa cum laude, Ind. U., 1981. Bar: Ind. 1981, U.S. Dist. Ct. (so. dist.) Ind. 1981. Assoc. Ice Miller Donadio & Ryan, Indpls., 1981-87, ptnr., 1988—. Assoc. editor Ind. Law Rev., 1980-81. Bd. dirs. Ballet Internationale, 1995—, treas., 1996—; pres. Greenleaf Cmty. Ctr., 1992-93, 95-98, v.p., 1991, sec., 1990; bd. dirs., v.p. Cmty. Alliance for the Far East Side, 1997-99; bd. dirs. Big Sisters of Ctrl. Ind., 1995-98, hon. dir., 1998—. Named among Influential Women in Indpls., Ind. Lawyer and Indpls. Bus. Jour., 1998. Mem. ABA, Am. Coll. Bond Counsel (bd. dirs., v.p. 1995-98, pres. 1998—), Ind. Bar Assn., Indpls. Bar Assn. (bd. mgrs. 1992), Ind. Mcpl. Lawyers Assn., Nat. Assn. Bond

Lawyers, Phi Beta Kappa. Office: Ice Miller Donadio & Ryan Box 82001 One American Sq Indianapolis IN 46282

HORN, CARL, III, federal judge; b. 1951. BA with honors, U. Va., 1973; JD, U. S.C., 1976. Bar: N.C. 1976. Assoc. Grier, Parker, Poe, Thompson, Bernstein, Gage & Preston, Charlotte, N.C., 1976-79; legal counsel, instr. Wheaton Coll., 1979-82; spl. asst. civil rights divsn. U.S. Dept. Justice, Charlotte, 1982-83, chief asst. U.S. atty. for western dist. N.C., 1987-93; ptnr. Horn & Conrad and predecessor, Charlotte, 1984-87; chief magistrate judge for western dist. N.C., U.S. Magistrate Ct., Charlotte, 1993—. Author: Fourth Circuit Criminal Handbook, 1994—, Horn's Federal Jury Instructions for the Fourth Circuit: Criminal Edition, 1997, Federal Civil Practice in the Fourth Circuit, 1997, The Law for Doctors, 1999; editor: The Battle for Morality in Pluralistic America, 1985; contbr. articles to law jours. Office: 401 W Trade St Ste 238 Charlotte NC 28202-1619

HORN, CAROL GARVER, foundation administrator; b. Lodi, Ohio, May 21, 1942; d. Jesse Gale and Ruth Marie Garver; m. Dennis D. Horn, June 6, 1964; childen: Angela Beth, Bryon Geoffrey. BS, Manchester Coll., 1964; MS, Ind. U., 1966. Tchr. Wabash (Ind.) City Schs., 1964-68, 77-90; exec. dir. Edn. for Conflict Resolution, Inc., North Manchester, Ind., 1990-98, Cmty. Found. of Wabash County, North Manchester, 1991—; dir. sch. svcs. Edn. for Conflict Resolution, Inc., North Manchester. Trustee Manchester Coll., North Manchester, Ind., 1980-90, 95—. Mem. Ch. of the Brethren. Office: Cmty Found of Wabash County PO Box 98 North Manchester IN 46962-0098

HORN, CHARLES F., state senator, lawyer, electrical engineer; b. Bellefontaine, Ohio, July 20, 1924; s. Huber H. and Mary C. Horn; m. Shirley E. Horn, Aug. 1, 1953; children: Holly E., Charles J., Heidi E. BSEE, Purdue U., 1949; LLB, Cleve. State U., 1954. Application engr. Westinghouse Electric, Cleve., 1949-51; engr. Hertner Electric Co., Cleve., 1951-53; owner, engr. Lease Equipment Engring., Cleve., 1953-61; owner, ptnr. IRBATCO, Cleve., 1953-61; atty. Dayton, Ohio, 1961—; city coun. mem. City of Kettering, Ohio, 1963-69, mayor, 1969-80; county commr. Montgomery County, Ohio, 1980-84; mem. Ohio State Senate, Columbus, 1985—; adv. panel Office of Sci. and Tech.; chair Econ. Devel., Tech. and Aerospace Com.; senate rep. Thomas Edison Tech. Bd., Devel. Financing Policy Bd., Ohio Indsl. Tng. Program Bd.; 3-term chair Fed. Labs Consortium Adv. Bd., 1980-83; cons. NSF; participant U.S. Conf. Mayors.; chair Ohio Econ. Study, 1997, 98, 99. Organizer Miami Valley Coun. Govts., Montgomery County; trustee Nat. Aviation Hall of Fame, Cox Arboretum, Cmty. Devel. Corp.; past trustee Grandview Hosp., Kettering C. of C., Dayton Area Sr. Citizens, Kidney Soc., Leukemia Soc., Pub. Opinion Ctr.; founder, chmn. Camp for Kids Who Can't; past adv. bd. Kettering Meml. Hosp.; past chmn. mcpl. sect. United Way Campaign; promoter formation of Wright Tech. Network; founder and past chair of Regional Econ. Strategies Forum. Served with U.S. Army Air Corps, 1942-45, CBI Theatre. Recipient numerous awards including Michael A. DeNunzio award U.S. Conf. of Mayors, 1980, Citizen award Pub. Children Svc. Assn. Ohio, 1988, Legislator of Yr. award Nat. Assn. Social Workers, 1989, Tech. award Dayton Area Tech. Network, 1989, Disting. Legis. Svc. award Ohio Human Svcs. Dirs. Assn., 1989, Pub. Svc. award Quality Dayton, 1990, Tom Bradley Regional Leadership award Nat. Assn. Regional Coun., 1989, Vol. of Yr. award Camp Kern YWCA, Pub. Svc. award Ohio Computer Tech. Ctr., 1990, Topcat Tech. award State of Ohio, 1997, Guardian of Small Bus. award Nat. Fedn. of Ind. Bus., 1998. Mem. Eta Kappa Nu, Tau Beta Pi. Republican. Avocations: tennis, golf, bicycling, horticulture. Office: Horn Coen & Rife 2344 W Schantz Kettering OH 45409 also: State Senate Ohio Senate Bldg Ste 222 Statehouse Columbus OH 43215

HORN, CHARLES M., lawyer; b. Boston, Sept. 28, 1951; s. Garfield Henry and Alexandra (Matz) H.; m. Jane Charlotte Luxton, May 29, 1976; children: Andrew L., Caroline C. AB magna cum laude, Harvard Coll., 1973; JD, Cornell Law Sch., 1976. Bar: D.C. 1976, U.S. Dist. Ct. D.C. 1977, U.S. Ct. Appeals (D.C. cir.) 1977, U.S. Supreme Ct. 1980. Atty. U.S. Securities and Exchange Commn., Washington, 1976-82, br. chief divsn. enforcement, 1982-83; asst. dir. securities and corp. practices Office Comptroller of Currency, Washington, 1983-86, dir. securities and corp. practices, 1986-89; ptnr. Stroock & Stroock & Lavan, Washington, 1989-92, Mayer, Brown & Platt, Washington, 1992—; mem. faculty Am. Bankers Assn. Nat. Grad. Compliance Sch., 1991-92, 94, Fed. Fin. Instns. Exam. Coun. (programs off-balance-sheet risk, Trust Exams. Sch.); lectr. in field. Edit. adv. bd. Bank Acctg. and Fin., 1993—; contbr. articles to profl. jours. Mem. ABA (Banking law com., subcom. securities, com. fed. regulation securities, subcom. securities activities banks, fiduciaries), D.C. Bar Assn., Harvard Club Washington, Washington Golf and Country Club. Home: 1918 Massachusetts Ave Mc Lean VA 22101-4907 Office: Mayer Brown & Platt 2000 Pennsylvania Ave NW Washington DC 20006-1812

HORN, CHRISTIAN FRIEDRICH, venture capital company executive; b. Dresden, Germany, Dec. 23, 1927; came to U.S., 1954, naturalized, 1959; s. Otto Hugo and Elsa H.; m. Christa Winkler, Feb. 13, 1954; 1 child, Sabrina. MS, Technische Hochschule, Dresden, 1951; PhD, Technische Hochschule, Aachen, Germany, 1958. Rsch. scientist German Acad. Sci., Berlin, 1951-53, Farbwerke Hoechst, Germany, 1953-54; rsch. mgr. Union Carbide, N.Y.C., 1954-65; pres. Polymer Tech. Inc., N.Y.C., 1965-74; v.p. W.R. Grace & Co., N.Y.C., 1974-81, sr. v.p., 1981-95, also bd. dirs.; pres. Horn Venture Ptnrs. (formerly Grace Horn Ventures), Cupertino, Calif., 1983—, mng. ptnr., 1987—; pres. Horn Investment Corp., Cupertino, 1996—; bd. dirs. Cardiopulmonary, Timothy's Coffees of the World, Rosti Inc. Patentee in field. With German Army, 1944-45. Decorated Iron Cross. Lutheran. Office: Horn Venture Ptnrs 20300 Stevens Creek Blvd Cupertino CA 95014-2240

HORN, DONALD HERBERT, lawyer; b. Bronx, N.Y., Nov. 22, 1945; s. Herbert H. and Alice (Entwistle) H.; m. Marcia Thomas, Oct. 10, 1971. BA cum laude, Queens Coll., 1966; JD, Harvard U., 1969; postgrad. pub. exec., Carnegie-Mellon U., 1981. Bar: N.Y. 1970, D.C. 1975. Sr. trial atty. Bur. Operating Rights CAB, Washington, 1969-76, atty.-advisor Office Gen. Counsel, 1976-80, assoc. gen. counsel for pricing and entry, 1980-84; dep. asst. gen. counsel for internat. law U.S. Dept. Transp., Washington, 1985-88, asst. gen. counsel for internat. law, 1988—. Chmn. transp. Forest Hills Citizens Assn., Washington, 1983-97. Recipient Sec. Transp. Gold medal award granted to Office Internat. Law, 1995. Mem. Fed. Bar Assn., Harvard U. Law Sch. Assn., Queens Coll. Alumni Assn., Phi Beta Kappa, Omicron Delta Epsilon. Office: US Dept Transp 400 7th St SW Washington DC 20590-0001

HORN, DOREEN T., critical care nurse; b. Syracuse, N.Y., July 18, 1964; d. George J. Podolak and Theresa E. (Florczyk) Waite; children: Jaclyn Marie, Daniel Joseph. Diploma, St. Elizabeth Hosp., Utica, N.Y., 1985; postgrad., Community Gen. Hosp., Syracuse. RN, N.Y.; cert. ACLS and PALS. Sr. staff nurse coronary-telemetry unit Community Gen. Hosp., to 1992, emergency nurse, 1992—. Mem. Am. Heart Assn. Home: 205 Lawdon St Syracuse NY 13212-2022

HORN, FLOYD P., federal agency administrator; b. Winchester, Mass., Dec. 24, 1943. Adminstr. dept. agrl. rsch., edn. and econs. Agrl. Rsch. Svc., Washington, 1995—. Office: Agrl Rsch Svc Dept Agr Rsch Edn & Econs 1400 Independence Ave SW Washington DC 20250

HORN, KENNETH LEROY, editor; b. Richmond, Calif., July 13, 1947; s. Leroy Kenneth and Rose Adelaide (Corey) H.; m. Peggy Louise Paul, May 19, 1973. BS, Bethany Coll., 1970; postgrad., Golden Gate Bapt. Theol. Sem., Mill Valley, Calif., 1976-78; MA summa cum laude, Simpson Coll., San Francisco, 1978; DMin, Calif. Grad. Sch. Theology, Glendale, 1981. Assoc. pastor Bethel Temple, Walnut Creek, Calif., 1970-73; sr. pastor Evangel Assembly, Healdsburg, Calif., 1974-77; assoc. pastor Trinity Christian Life Ctr., Pacifica, Calif., 1978-80; theology instr. Simpson Coll., San Francisco, Sacramento, 1978-79, 81-83; sr. pastor Davis (Calif.) Christian Assembly, 1981-88; minister-at-large Assemblies of God, 1988-92; sr. pastor Ashland (Oreg.) Christian Ctr., 1992-97; mng. editor Pentecostal Evangel Assemblies of God, Springfield, Mo., 1997—. Contbr. articles to profl. jours.; TV host: Give the Wind a Mighty Voice. Nat. chmn. Ministries Behind the Iron Curtain, Sacramento, 1985-88; bd. dirs. Ch. Care Am., Springfield, 1990-92; sect. rep. Assemblies of God, Contra Costa/Capital, Calif., spokesman ministers groups; chaplain Convoy of Hope, Springfield, 1997—. Avocations: fishing, outdoors, reading, church history. Office: Pentecostal Evangel 1445 N Boonville Ave Springfield MO 65802-1894

HORN, MARIAN BLANK, federal judge; b. N.Y.C., June 24, 1943; d. Werner P. and Mady R. Blank; m. Robert Jack Horn; children: Juli Marie, Carrie Charlotte, Rebecca Blank. AB, Barnard Coll., 1962; student, Cornell U., Columbia U., 1965, NYU, 1965-66; JD, Fordham U., 1969. Bar: N.Y. 1970, D.C. 1973, U.S. Supreme Ct. 1973. Asst. dist. atty. Bronx County, N.Y., 1969-72; assoc. Arent, Fox, Kintner, Plotkin & Kahn, 1972-73; project mgr. Am. U. Law Sch. study on alts. to conventional criminal adjudication U.S. Dept. Justice, 1973-75; litigation atty. Fed. Energy Adminstrn., 1975-76; sr. atty. office gen. counsel strategic petroleum res. br. Dept. Energy, 1976-79, dep. asst. gen. counsel for procurement and fin. incentives, 1979-81; dep. assoc. solicitor div. surface mining Dept. Interior, 1981-83, assoc. solicitor div. gen. law, 1983-85, prin. dep. solicitor, acting solicitor, 1985; judge U.S. Ct. of Federal Claims, 1986—; adj. prof. law Washington Coll. Law, Am. U., 1973-76, George Washington U. Sch. Law, 1992—. Office: US Ct Fed Claims 717 Madison Pl NW Washington DC 20005-1011*

HORN, MARTIN F., state agency administrator; b. N.Y.C., June 26, 1948; s. Sidney and Zenith Horn; m. Janis Mostow, Feb. 1, 1970; children: Joanna, David. BA, Franklin & Marshall Coll., 1969; MA, CUNY, 1973. Parole officer N.Y. State Divsn. of Parole, N.Y.C., 1969-74; sr. parole officer N.Y. State Dept. Correctional Svcs., N.Y.C., 1974; asst. prof. SUNY-Utica/Rome, 1975-77; dir. temporary release Dept. Correctional Svcs., Albany, N.Y., 1977-79, asst. to commr., 1979-81, asst. commr., 1981-84; supt. Hudson (N.Y.) Correctional Facility, 1984-85; dir. ops. Divsn. of Parole, Albany, 1985-91, exec. dir., 1991—. Office: Divsn of Parole 97 Central Ave Albany NY 12206-3001

HORN, MYRON KAY, consulting petroleum geologist, author, educator; b. Miami, Fla., Jan. 28, 1930; s. Harry I. and Sykes K. (Kaplan) H.; m. Barbara DeCasseres Rothschild, Apr. 9, 1955; children: Lisa, Marc, Nina. B.S., U. Colo., 1952; M.S., U. Houston, 1958; Ph.D., Rice U., 1964. Sr. research geologist Pure Oil Co., Crystal Lake, Ill., 1960-64; group leader geophys. research Cities Service Co., Tulsa, 1964-65; mgr. geol. research Cities Service Co., 1965-70, dir. exploration and prodn. rsch., 1970-83, dir. applied rsch. and tech. ops., 1983-1987; ret., 1987; pvt. practice cons. Tulsa, 1987—; mem. U.S. sci. adv. com. Joint Oceanographic Inst., 1983-87; editor Circum-Pacific Meeting, Am. Assn. Petroleum Geologists, Singapore, 1986, lectr., China and Hungary, Japan, 1986-90, Saudi Arabia, 1993; founder, pres. BXK Graphics, 1997—. Contbr. articles to profl. jours. Served to lt. (j.g.) U.S. Navy, 1952-55. Mem. Am. Assn. Petroleum Geologists (hon., editor 1979-83, exec. com., disting. service award 1986). Home: 5919 S Gary Pl Tulsa OK 74105-7427

HORN, PAUL ERVIN, minister; b. Grinnell, Iowa, Mar. 24, 1919; s. Harry Edgar and Florence Henrietta (Bump) H.; m. Elvis Devlin, Dec. 21, 1940; children: Sandra, Larry, Cynthia. BA, San Jose State U., 1942; MDiv, Berkeley Bapt. Div. Sch., 1945; PhD, Calif. Grad. Sch. Theology, 1973. Ordained to ministry Conservative Bapt. Assn. Am., 1945. Pastor Elmhurst Bapt. Ch., Oakland, Calif., 1945-55, Bell Bapt. Ch., Cudahy, Calif., 1955-66, 1st Bapt. Ch., Montclair, Calif., 1966-77, Calvary Bapt. Ch., Hemet, Calif., 1977-83, 1st Bapt. Ch., Wrightwood, Calif., 1984-90; bd. dirs. Conservative Bapt. Assn. So. Calif., Anaheim, 1956-88, pres., 1959-60, min. at large, 1990—; bd. dirs. Conservative Bapt. Home Mission Soc., Wheaton, Ill., 1960-66; parliamentarian Conservative Bapt. Assn. Am., Wheaton, 1950-85, v.p. western chpt., 1967-74. Mem. Conservative Bapt. Fgn. Mission Soc. (sec. 1988-91). Republican. Avocation: photography. Address: PO Box 1422 Yucaipa CA 92399-1422

HORN, PAUL JOSEPH, musician; b. N.Y.C., Mar. 17, 1930; s. Jack L. and Frances (Sper) H.; m. Tryntje; children: Marlen L., Robin F. Mus.B., Oberlin Conservatory Music, 1952; Mus.M. (fellow), Manhattan Sch. Music, 1953; student, Acad. Meditation, Himalayas, India, 1967, 68; PhD (hon.), U. Victoria, Canada, 1999. Tchr. system transcendental meditation UCLA (also at Berkeley and centers throughout U.S. and Can.); Mem. Sauter-Finigan Band, 1956-57, Chico Hamilton Quintet, 1957-58, NBC Staff Orch., Hollywood, Calif., 1960; free-lance studio work, 1960-70; formed Paul Horn Quintet, 1959, Golden Flute Records, 1982. Rec. artist for, Dot, World Pacific, HiFi, Columbia, RCA Victor records, producer, artist, Epic Records, Kuckuck Records, concerts throughout U.S. and Europe, 1957—, tours to People's Republic China, 1978, 81, concert tour of USSR, 1983, 86, 88, Nepal and Tibet, 1998; guest speaker, performer jazz clinics at numerous univs., 1961—; producer: TV documentary Paul Horn in China; (Recipient Grammy nomination 1966, 87, 2 Grammy awards 1966), motion picture appearances; guest TV performer; star: TV series The Paul Horn Show; made solo flute recs. in Taj Mahal, (Inside), 1968, 89; in Gizeh pyramids, (Inside the Great Pyramid), in Lithuania (Inside the Cathedral, Inside Canyon de Chelly), in Lhasa, Tibet (Inside the Potala), Mushroom Records, 1976, Golden Flute Records, 1984, Kuckuck Records, 1986, Canyon Records, 1997; author: (autobiography) Inside Paul Horn, 1990. Bd. dirs. Victoria Symphony Orch., Performing Rights Orgn. Can., Pro Can. Served with AUS, 1953-56. Also awards from Jazz Polls; also awards from Downbeat mag., awards from Playboy mag. Address: PO Box 6193 Sta C, Victoria, BC Canada V8P 5L5

HORN, RALPH, bank executive; b. Corinth, Miss., Feb. 16, 1941. BS, Miss. State U., 1963; Mgmt. degree, Harvard U., 1992. Mgmt. trainee 1st Tenn. Bank N.A., Memphis, 1963, mgr. bank's bond divsn., 1976; pres., COO, dir. 1st Tenn. Nat. Corp., Memphis, 1991; vice chmn., dir. 1st Tenn. Bank N.A. (subs. 1st Tenn. Nat. Corp.), 1991—, CEO, chmn., 1994, chmn. bd. dirs., 1996—; past bd. dirs., past chmn. bd. Mcpl. Securities Rulemaking Bd. Mem. adv. bd. Anthony Commn. Tax Reform. Mem. Pub. Securities Assn. (past bd. dirs., past chmn. bd.), Regional Mcpl. Securities Assn. (co-founder, past co-chmn.), Dealer Bank Assn. (past chmn. fed. affairs com., past bd. dirs.), Bankers Roundtable (bd. dirs.), Tenn. Bankers Assn. (past bd. dirs.). Office: 1st Tennessee Nat Corp PO Box 84 Memphis TN 38101-0084*

HORN, RUSSELL EUGENE, engineering executive, consultant; b. Yoe, Pa., May 4, 1912; s. Eugene M. and Charlotte (Snyder) H.; m. Eleanor B. Baird, Jan. 12, 1934; children: Russell Eugene, Ralph Elliot, Rosalind Emily (Mrs. Lee Kunkel), Robert Errol. BS, Pa. State U., 1933. Foreman Pa. Dept. Hwys. dist. office, York, Pa., 1933-35; draftsman, supr., designer C.S. Buchart, architect, 1935-41; exec. v.p., chief engr. Buchart Engring., 1945-59, pres., chief engr., 1959-61; pres., chief engr. Buchart-Horn, Inc., cons. engrs., 1961-72, chmn. bd. dirs., 1972—; pres. PACE Resources, Inc., 1970-87, chmn. bd. dirs., 1970—, chief exec. officer, 1987-88; dir. emeritus Dauphin Deposit Bank and Trust Co.; dir. emeritus adv. bd. So div. Dauphin Deposit Bank & Trust Co.; bd. dirs. AAA White Rose Motor Club, chmn., 1975-78; bd. dirs. Auto Club So. Pa.; bd. dirs. emeritus Retirement Homes of Meth. Ch., 1978—. Served to col. AUS, 1940-45. Mem. Soc. Am. Mil. Engrs., NSPE, Pa. Soc. Profl. Engrs. (pres. Lincoln chpt. 1961), Pa. Assn. Cons. Engrs. (pres. 1965, bd. dirs. 1966), Pa. Hwy. Information Assn. (bd. dirs.), Am. Soc. Hwy. Engrs. (nat. pres. 1962), Tech. Socs. Council Southeastern Pa. (chmn. 1963), Engring. Soc. York, Profl. Engrs. Pvt. Practice, Am. Concrete Inst., Assn. Pa. Constructors, Assn. Hwy. Ofcls. N. Atlantic States, Assn. U.S. Army, Res. Officers Assn., ASCE, VFW, Cons. Engrs. Council, Am. Legion, Pa. State U. Alumni Club York County. Clubs: Univ., Lake, Exchange (Golden Deeds award 1979), Mt. Nittany Soc. Pa. State U. Lodges: Masons (32 deg.; Order of the Double Eagle award, 1983, Legion of Freedom award 1986, outstanding engring. alumnus, 1987), York County Agrl. Soc. (life), Moose. Home: 1270 Brockie Dr York PA 17403-4448 Office: Pace Resources Inc 40 S Richland Ave York PA 17404-3470

HORN, RUSSELL EUGENE, JR., business executive; b. York, Pa., Sept. 15, 1934; s. Russell Eugene and A. Eleanor (Baird) H.; m. Franziska Kathe Kastner (dec. 1995); children: Silvia S., Russell E. III, Monika K., Ursula F., John D. Sgt. 1st class U.S. Army Security Agy., 1952-62; sales trainee, sales rep. Print-O-Stat, Inc., York, Pa., 1962-63; mgr. Print-O-Stat, Inc., York, 1970-73, exec. v.p., 1976-77, pres., 1977-96; mgr. Print-O-Stat, Inc., Towson, Md., 1963-70; v.p. Print-O-Stat, Inc., Md., Del., 1973-76; office of pres. Pace Resources, Inc., York, Pa., 1987-96; pres., ceo Pace Resources, Inc., York, 1999—; also bd. dirs.; bd. dirs. Buchart-Horn, Inc., others; mem. adv. bd. Dauphin Deposit Bank-York Region, 1984-98; also officer, advisor, exec. various corps. Active various edn., charitable activities. Mem. York Area C. of C. Home: 120 Leeds Rd York PA 17403-3814 Office: Pace Resources Inc 40 S Richland Ave York PA 17404-3470

HORN, SAMUEL EDGAR, academic administrator; b. New Zealand, Oct. 24, 1964; s. Clive Redwood and Anita (Maldonado) H.; m. Bethanie Joy Davenport, Dec. 15, 1986; 1 child, Robert Douglas. BA, Bob Jones U., Greenville, S.C., 1986, MA, 1988, PhD, 1995. Prof. Bob Jones U., Greenville, 1987-96, dir. extended edn., 1991-94; v.p. acad. affairs Northland Bapt. Bible Coll., Dunbar, Wis., 1996—; cons. T & H Consulting, Greenville; bd. dirs. Worldwide Tentmakers, Inc., Greenville, Arimethea Found., Greenville, Acts Ministries, Greenville. Editor Integrity, 1997—. Avocation: harbor lighthouse collector. Office: Northland Bapt Bible Coll W10085 Pike Plains Rd Dunbar WI 54119-9285

HORN, SHIRLEY, vocalist, pianist; b. Washington; 1 dau., Rainy. Student, Howard U. Albums include Cat on a Hot Fiddle, 1959, Embers And Ashes, 1960, Live at the Village Vanguard, 1961, Loads of Love, 1963, Shirley Horn with Horns, 1963, Travelin' Light, 1965, For Love of Ivy, 1968, A Dandy in Aspic, 1968, Where Are You Going?, 1972, A Lazy Afternoon, 1979, All Night Long, 1982, Violets For Your Ears, 1983, The Sentimental Touch (titled Songbirds in U.S.), 1985, I Thought About You, 1987, Softly, 1988, Close Enough for Love, 1988, Tune in Tomorrow, 1990, You Won't Forget Me, 1991, Dedicated to You-Tribute to Sarah Vaughan with Carmen McRae, 1991, Here's to Life, 1992 (Grammy nomination, Best Jazz Vocal for "Light Out of Darkness", 1994), Violets for Furs, 1994, I Love You Paris, 1994, All Night Long, 1994, (with Charles Ables, Billy Hart) At Northsea, 1996, Jazz Round Midnight, 1998 (Grammy). Office: Verve Records Worldwide Plaza 825 8th Ave Fl 23 New York NY 10019-7472*

HORN, STEPHEN, congressman, political science educator; b. San Juan Bautista, Calif., May 31, 1931; s. John Stephen and Isabelle (McCaffrey) H.; m. Nini Moore, Sept. 4, 1954; children: Marcia Karen, John Stephen. AB with great distinction, Stanford, 1953, postgrad., 1953-54, 55-56, PhD in Polit. Sci. 1958; M in Pub Adminstrn., Harvard, 1955. Congl. fellow, 1958-59; adminstrv. asst. to sec. labor Washington, 1959-60; legislative asst. to U.S. Senator Thomas H. Kuchel, 1960-66; sr. fellow The Brookings Instn., 1966-69; dean grad. studies and research Am. U., 1969-70; pres. Calif. State U., Long Beach, 1970-88, Trustee prof. polit. sci., 1988-93; mem. 103rd-106th Congress from 38th Calif. dist., 1993—; chmn. subcom. govt. mgmt., info. & tech. 103rd-105th Congress from 38th Calif. dist.; mem. govt. reform, transp. & infrastructure com. &; sr. cons., host The Govt. Story on TV, The Election Game (radio series), 1967-69, vice chmn. U.S. Commn. on Civil Rights, 1969-80 (commr. 1980-82); chmn. Urban Studies Fellow Adv. Com., U.S. Dept. HUD, 1969-70; mem. Law Enforcement Ednl. Prog. Adv. Com., U.S. Dept Justice, 1969-70; adv. bd. Nat. Inst. Corrections, 1972-88 (chmn. 1984-87),. Author: The Cabinet and Congress, 1960, Unused Power: The Work of the Senate Committee on Appropriations, 1970, (with Edmund Beard) Congressional Ethics: The View from the House, 1975. Active Pres.-elect Nixon's Task Force on Orgn. Exec. Br., 1968, Kutak Found.; vice chmn. Long Beach Area C. of C., 1984-88; co-founder Western U.S. Com. Arts and Scis. for Eisenhower, 1956; chmn. Am. Assn. State Colls. and Univs., 1985-86; mem. Calif. Ednl. Facilities Authority, 1984-93. USAR, 1954-62. Fellow John F. Kennedy Inst. Politics Harvard U., 1966-67. Fellow Nat. Acad. Pub. Adminstrn.; mem. Stanford Assocs., Stanford Alumni Assn. (pres. 1976-77), Phi Beta Kappa, Pi Sigma Alpha. Republican. Office: US Ho of Reps 2331 Rayburn Ho Office Bldg Washington DC 20515-0538

HORN, THOMAS JOSEPH, JR., educator; b. Albany, Jan. 6, 1953; s. Thomas Joseph and Antoinette (Bologna) H.; m. Dawn Marie Kerr, June 28, 1980 (div. Jan. 1983); children: Thomas Matthew; m. Elizabeth Lynn Chase, Aug. 31, 1993; 1 stepchild, Stephanie Blair. BA, SUNY, 1975, MS, 1982. Clerical, computer FBI, Albany, 1976-83; tchr. computers Mohonasen High Sch., Schenectady, N.Y., 1983-85; coord. computers Fort Edward (N.Y.) Pub. Schs., 1985—. Author: Windows and Nine Applications Made Easy, 1994. Tchr. Sacred Heart Ch., Troy, N.Y., 1985—, Ch. of Immaculate Conception, Schenectady, 1996—. Regents scholar, 1971. Mem. Assn. Rsch. Enlightenment. Roman Catholic. Avocations: running, computers, music. Home: 23 Blue Barns Rd Rexford NY 12148-1114 Office: Fort Edward Pub Schs 220 Broadway Fort Edward NY 12828-1520

HORN, VICKIE LYNN, medical/surgical nurse, educator; b. Bloomfield, Iowa, Sept. 7, 1955; d. Paul Nelson and Norcita Janice (Glasgow) Seals; 1 child, Braden Seth. BSN, N.E. Mo. State U., Kirksville, 1977; MS, Coll. St. Francis, Joliet, Ill., 1988. Cert. ACLS. House supr. Burlington (Iowa) Care Ctr.; float staff nurse Burlington Med. Ctr.; operating room nurse clinician Ottumwa (Iowa) Regional Health Ctr., perioperative nurse clinician. Mem. Am. Assn. Operating Room Nurses.

HORNACEK, JEFFREY JOHN, professional basketball player; b. Elmhurst, Ill., May 3, 1963. Student, Iowa State. With Phoenix Suns, 1986-92; guard Phila. 76ers, 1992-94, Utah Jazz, 1994—. Named NBA All-Star, 1992. Office: Utah Jazz 301 W South Temple Salt Lake City UT 84181*

HORNAK, ANNA FRANCES, library administrator; b. College Station, Tex., June 3, 1922; d. Josef and Anna (Drozd) H. B.A., U. Tex., Austin, 1944; B.L.S., U. Ill., Champaign-Urbana, 1945; Ed.M., U. Houston, 1956. Children's librarian Schenectady Pub. Library, N.Y., 1945-47; children's librarian Pasadena Pub. Library, Calif., 1947-49; supr. Juvenile Div. Houston Pub. Library, 1949-57, asst. dir., 1957-89, ret., 1989. Named Outstanding Woman, YWCA of Houston, 1977; Outstanding Houston Profl. Woman, Fed. Houston Profl. Women, 1982. Avocations: collecting miniature books; collecting Bohemian red glass; restoring antique furniture. Home: 2217 Woodhead St Houston TX 77019-6820

HORNAK, THOMAS, retired electronics company executive; b. Bratislava, Slovakia, Oct. 14, 1924; came to U.S., 1968; s. Stefan and Elisabeth (Meer) H.; m. Vera Lautner, Mar. 15, 1958; 1 child, Thomas. MSEE, Tech U., Bratislava, 1947; PhD in Elec. Engring., Tech U., Prague, Czech Republic, 1966. Sect. mgr. Tesla Radio Research Lab., Prague, 1947-61; sci. advisor Computer Research Inst., Prague, 1962-68; mem. tech. staff Hewlett Packard Labs., Palo Alto, Calif., 1968-73, mgr. research dept., 1973-91, prin. engr., 1991-99, ret., 1999. Contbr. articles to profl. jours. Patentee in field. Fellow IEEE (assoc. editor Jour. Solid State Cirs. 1986-88, chmn. solid state cirs. and tech. com. 1979-81).

HORNBACK, JOSEPH HOPE, mathematics educator; b. Nevada, Mo., Apr. 20, 1910; s. Joseph Thomas and Geordia (Munn) H. A.B., Central Coll., 1932; M.A., Harvard, 1933; Ph.D., U. Ill., 1952; postgrad., U. Chgo., 1933-34, 41-42, 46-49. Tchr. math. Calumet City (Ill.) High Sch., 1934-37, U. Chgo. Lab Sch., 1937-42; asst. prof. math. U. Ala., 1952-57, asso. prof., 1957-63, prof., 1963-80, prof. emeritus, 1980—; vis. scientist to high schs. for Ala. Acad. Sci. Chmn. gen. bd. 1st Christian Ch., Tuscaloosa, Ala., 1974-76; mem. world outreach com. Christian Chs. of Ala., 1973-75. Served as lt. USNR, 1942-46. Mem. Am. Math. Soc., Math. Assn. Am., Sigma Xi, Phi Kappa Phi. Club: Mason. Office: PO Box 151 Nevada MO 64772-0151

HORNBAKER, ALICE JOY, author; b. Cin., Feb. 3, 1927; children: Christopher Albert, Holly Jo, Joseph Bernard III. BA cum laude and honors in Journalism, U. Calif., San Jose, 1949. Asst. woman's editor San Jose Mercury-News, 1949-55; columnist Life After 50, Cin. Post newspaper, 1993—; free-lance writer, Cin.; writer, broadcaster The Alice Hornbaker Show Sta. 89.3 WMKK-FM, 1996—; owner, mgr. Frisch's Big Boy Restaurant, Cin., 1955-68; dir. pub. relations Children's Home Soc. Calif., Santa Clara, 1968-71; asst. dir. pub. relations United Fund Calif., Santa Clara, 1971—; editor Tristate Sunday Enquirer mag., 1986-89, columnist Generations Tristate mag.; editorial dir. Writers Digest Sch., Cin., 1971-75; columnist, critic, mag. writer, reporter, copy editor Tempo sec. Cin. Enquirer, 1975-93 , also book editor and critic, columnist for Aging, feature writer Tempo sect.; reporter news segments on aging Sta. WKRC-TV; tchr. adult edn. Forest Hills Sch. Dist., Thomas More Coll., 1973—; reporter, specialist on aging for Cin. Enquirer, 1989-93, commentator on aging Sta. WMLX-AM, 1991-93; broadcaster, writer Sta. WMKV-FM, 1996—. Author: Preventive Care: Easy Exercise Against Aging, 1974; byline in People, Modern Maturity, St. Anthony Messenger, N.Y. Times Sun. mag., Ohio Heritage mag. and others; contbr. fiction to Enquirer mag.; freelance mag. writer. Recipient Bronze award in Am. health journalism Am. Chiropractic Assn., 1977, 78, Golden Image award Assn. Ohio Philanthropic Homes, 1989; 1st pl. for feature writing Cin. Editors Assn., 1983, 1st and 3rd pl. feature writing awards Ohio Profl. Writers, Inc., 1992, Journalist of Yr. award Ohio chpt. Am. Coll. Health Care Adminstrs., 1993, Journalism award Greater Cin. Joint Coun. on Geriat. Care, 1993. Mem. Blue Pencil of Ohio State U. (pres. 1981-82), Women in Comm., Ohio Newspaper Women's Assn. (v.p. 1981-83, 1st pl. human interest story 1977-85, 2d pl. column award 1979, Tops in Ohio award 1982, M.M. McMullen 2d pl. award, 1982, Recognition award 1985, 4th pl. on aging Nat. Legacies contest 1994), Soc. Profl. Journalists (treas. 1981-82), Ohio Press Women, Inc. (1st and 3d pl. awards for feature writing 1992). Office: CW Post 125 E Court St Cincinnati OH 45202-1212

HORNBECK, HAROLD DOUGLAS, psychotherapist; b. Ashtabula, Ohio, Dec. 12, 1952; s. Harold Garnet and Garnet Jean (Osburn) H. BS, Ohio State U., 1977; MS in Social Adminstrn., Case Western Res. U., 1987. ACSW, LISW, QCSW; diplomate NASW; cert. Cleve. Ctr. for Cognitive Therapy. Child life worker Rainbow Babies and Children's Hosp., Cleve., 1977-85; psychotherapist Cmty. Counseling Ctr., Ashtabula, 1985-88, Riverview Psychiat. Assocs., Ashtabula, 1988-98, UHHL Laurelwood Counseling Ctr., 1998—; adj. faculty Ursuline Coll., Pepperpike, Ohio, 1989; clin. dir. Critical Incident Stress Mgmt. Team, Ashtabula, 1993—; chmn. Ohio Children's Trust Fund LAB, Ashtabula, 1988—; v.p. bd. HIV/AIDS Task Force Ashtabula County, 1989—; bd. dirs. Homesafe Shelter for Battered Women, Ashtabula, 1988-92. Camp dir. Matthew Salem Camp for Cystic Fibrosis, Lakewood, Ohio, 1993—, bd. trustees, 1993—; vice pres., 1993-94, pres., 1996—, counselor, 1978—, v.p., 1994-96, pres., 1996—; bd. trustees Matthew Salem Camping Found., 1993-96, v.p., 1996—, pres.; bd. dirs. Early Childhood Intervention Project, Ashtabula, 1988-93; advisor Jr. Achievement, Ashtabula, 1992-94; group leader HIV/AIDS Support Group, Ashtabula County, Lake County, Geauga County, 1993—; mentor Ashtabula City Schs., 1993; facilitator I Can Cope Am. Cancer Soc., Ashtabula, 1988—, bd. dirs. We-Can-Week-End, Columbus, Ohio, 1990-94; bd. dirs. Ashtabula County Cmty. Housing Devel. Orgn., Inc., 1996—. Recipient Recognition of Excellence award Ashtabula County Med. Ctr., 1990, Vol. of Yr. award Ashtabula chpt. ARC, 1995, Golden Role award nomination J.C. Penny, 1999. Mem. NASW, Acad. Cert. Social Workers, Assn. for Care Children's Health, Ohio Soc. for Clin. Social Work (v.p. bd. Cleve. chpt. 1995-96, pres. 1996—, state level sec. 1996-97, state bd. dirs. 1996—), Intenrat. Critical Incident Stress Found. Democrat. Methodist. Avocations: collecting miniatures, restoring furniture, Bonsai. Home: 3603 Silvius St Ashtabula OH 44004-4140

HORNBEIN, THOMAS FREDERIC, anesthesiologist; b. St. Louis, Nov. 6, 1930; s. Leonard and Rosalie (Bernstein) H.; m. Gene Schwartz (div. 1968); children: Lia, Lynn, Cari, Andrea, Robert; m. Kathryn Mikesell, Dec. 24, 1971; 1 child, Melissa. BA, U. Colo.; MD, Wash. U. Diplomate Am. Bd. Anesthesiology. Intern King County Hosp., Seattle; resident in anesthesiology Wash. U., St. Louis, USPHS postdoctoral residency; instr. anesthesiology div. Wash. U., 1960-61; asst. prof. U. Wash., Seattle, 1963-67, assoc. prof., 1967-70, prof., 1970—; vice chmn. Dept. Anesthesiology, U. Wash., Seattle, 1972-74, asst. chmn. research 1974-77, chmn. 1978-93, research affiliate Primate Ctr., 1980. Author: Everest the West Ridge, 1966. Mem. bd. trustees Little Sch., Bellevue, Wash., 1982-89. Served to lt. comdr. USN, 1961-63. Recipient George Norlin award U. Colo., Denver, 1970, Alumni Centennial Symposium award 1975, Disting. Teaching award U. Wash., 1982; Fellow AAAS; mem. Am. Physiol. Soc. (editor 1967-73), Am. Soc. Anesthesiologists (Rovenstine lectr. 1989), Assn. Univ. Anesthetists (treas. 1969-72, pres. 1974-75), Soc. Acad. Anesthesia Chairmen, Inst. of Medicine, Phi Beta Kappa, Alpha Omega Alpha. Avocation: mountaineering. Office: U Wash Sch Medicine Dept Anesthesiology PO Box 356540 Seattle WA 98195-6540

HORNBERGER, GEORGE MILTON, environmental science educator; b. Fountain Springs, Pa., June 22, 1942; s. George Vincent and Olive Mae (Delcamp) H.; m. Joan Marie Zackey, Aug. 28, 1965; children: Rachel Joan, George Zackey. BSCE, Drexel U., 1965, MSCE, 1967; PhD, Stanford U., 1970. Asst. prof. U. Va., Charlottesville, 1970-75, assoc. prof., 1975-84, prof., 1984—, disting. prof., 1991—, Ernest H. Ern prof., 1993—; vis. fellow Australian Nat. U., Canberra, 1977-78; vis. scientist Inst. Hydrology, Wallingford, Eng., 1980, U.S. Geol. Survey, 1990-91; hon. vis. prof. U. Lancaster (Eng.), 1984-85, Stanford U., 1990-91, U. Colo., 1997-98; mem. bd. Radioactive Waste Mgmt. of NAS, 1986-91, chmn. Commn. on Geoscis., Environment and Resources, 1996—. Author: Numerical Methods in Subsurface Hydrology, 1971, Elements of Physical Hydrology, 1998; assoc. editor Am. Geophys. Union, 1980-84; N.Am. editor John Wiley & Sons, Eng., 1986-92; editor-in-chief Water Resources Rsch., Am. Geophys. Union, 1993-96. Recipient John Wesley Powell award U.S. Geol. Survey, 1995, First Biennial medal for natural systems Australian Simulation Soc., 1995; elected to NAE, 1996; grantee NSF, Army Rsch. Office, EPA, Nat. Park Svc., NATO, Dept. Energy. Fellow Am. Geophys. Union (Robert E. Horton award hydrology sect. 1993, Excellence in Geophys. Edn. award 1999), Assn. for Women in Sci.; mem. NAE, Geol. Soc. Am., Sigma Xi. Home: 308 Farm Ln Charlottesville VA 22902-5324 Office: U Va Dept Environ Sci Clark Hall Charlottesville VA 22903-3188

HORNBERGER, ROBERT HOWARD, psychologist; b. Trenton, N.J., Jan. 26, 1933; s. Jennings Howard and Leah Margaret (Lewis) H.; m. Anne Deshon Lyman, June 11, 1958; children: Lynn Diane, Todd Lyman. BA, Amherst Coll., 1954; MA, U. Iowa, 1957, PhD, 1957. Lic. psychologist, Fla. Instr. to assoc. in med. psychology U. Nebr. Coll. Medicine, Omaha, 1958-62; staff psychologist Nebr. Psychiat. Inst., Omaha, 1958-62; chief psychologist Drs. Young, Wigton & Aita, Omaha, 1962-65; dir. Eastern Maine Guidance Ctr., Bangor, 1965-68; assoc. dir. The Counseling Ctr., Bangor, 1968-69; lectr. in psychology U. Maine, Orono, 1966-69; dir. psychology tng. VA Med. Ctr., Gainesville, Fla., 1969-81; asst. to assoc. adj. prof. U. Fla., Gainesville, 1969—; staff psychologist VA Med. Ctr., Gainesville, 1981—; bd. advisors Fla. Mental Health Inst., Tampa, 1987-95; psychologist pvt. practice, Gainesville, 1976-85, 90-98. Contbr. articles to profl. jours. Founder, 1st pres. Sugarfoot Cmty. Improvement Assn., 1972; pres. Mental Health Assn. Alachua County, Gainesville, 1981, Mental Health Assn. Fla., Tallahassee, 1987, Planned Parenthood Nebr., Omaha, 1963; comdr. Gainesville Power Squadron, 1995-96. Mem. Fla. Psychol. Assn. (pres. north ctrl. Fla. chpt. 1996). Democrat. Unitarian. Avocations: sailing, bridge, bicycling, travel. Home: 4056 NW 23rd Cir Gainesville FL 32605-2683 Office: DVA Med Ctr Psychology Svc # 116B Gainesville FL 32608

HORNBERGER, SUSAN J., critical care nurse, educator; b. Wichita, July 25, 1947; d. Dwight C. and Helen J. Hornberger. Diploma, Wesley Sch. Nursing, Wichita, 1968; BSN, Wichita State U., 1985, MSN, 1991. ACLS, BCLS; cert. advanced registered nurse practitioner. Sr. team leader CCU Marin Gen. Hosp., Greenbrae, Calif.; charge nurse emergency room Wesley Med. Ctr., Wichita; patient care supr. cardiac ICU St. Francis Regional Med. Ctr., Wichita, staff nurse cardiac ICU; critical care clin. nurse specialist St. Joseph Med. Ctr., Wichita; owner Nursing Practice Consultations; nurse mgr. post anesthesia care/pre-operative holding units Columbia Med. Ctr.-East, El Paso. Mem. AACN, Sigma Theta Tau. Home: 945 S Mesa Hills Dr Apt 3806 El Paso TX 79912-5158

HORNBLASS, BERNICE MIRIAM, educational evaluator, reading and learning disabilities specialist; b. N.Y.C., Sept. 12, 1951; d. Max and Sydell (Strickman) Brooks; m. Albert Hornblass, Dec. 23, 1973; children: David, Moshe, Elana. BA, Barnard Coll., Columbia U., 1973; MA, Tchrs. Coll., 1975; postgrad., NYU, 1976-79; cert. in interior design, 1985-87; EdM in Reading and Learning Disabilities, Columbia U., 1994. Cert. real estate salesman, N.J., N.Y., reading tchr., learning disabilities specialist, N.J. Tchr. CAlhoun Sch., N.Y.C., 1974-75; art therapist Carrier (N.J.) Clinic, 1976; with For Children Only, N.J., 1983-85; owner, mgr. Bernice-Hornblass-Interior Design, Englewood, N.J., 1987—; reading and learning specialist Manhattan Day Sch., 1992—; asst. dir. special edn. dept., 1996-99. Exhibited in group shows N.J. Pub. Library, 1986, Jewish Community Ctr. on Palisade, 1986. Dir. sabbath community visitation program Meml. Slan-Kettering Meml. Hosp., N.Y.C., 1977—; mem. visitation program Englewood Hosp., 1986—; mem. program com. Amit-Am. Mizrachi Women, 1986-87. Recipient 10 yr. vol award Meml. Sloan-Kettering Hosp., 1987. Republican. Jewish. Avocations: skiing, swimming. Home and Office: 156 Maple St Englewood NJ 07631-3630

HORNBY, DAVID BROCK, federal judge; b. Brandon, Manitoba, Can., Apr. 21, 1944; s. William Ralph Hornby and Retha Patricia (Fox) Sword; m. Helaine Cora Mandel, Oct. 9, 1946; children: Kirstin, Zachary. BA, U. Western Ont., 1965; JD, Harvard U., 1969. Bar: Va. 1973, Maine 1974, U.S. Supreme Ct. 1980. Law clk. U.S. Ct. Appeals, New Orleans, 1969-70; assoc. prof. U. Va. Sch. Law, Charlottesville, 1970-74; ptnr. Perkins, Thompson, Hinckley & Keddy, Portland, Maine, 1974-82; U.S. magistrate Dist. Maine, Portland, 1982-88; assoc. justice Maine Supreme Jud. Ct., Portland, 1988-90; judge U.S. Dist. Ct. Maine, 1990—; chief judge, 1996—; mem. Fed. Jud. Ctr.'s Com. on Dist. Judge Edn., 1994-98, chair 1995-98; com. on ct. adminstrn. and case mgmt. Jud. Conf. of the U.S., 1990—, chair 1997—. Contbr. articles to profl. jours.; editor, officer Harvard Law Rev., 1967-69. Fellow Am. Bar Found.; mem. ABA, Am. Law Inst., Maine State Bar Assn., Maine Bar Found. (bd. trustees 1990-94), Cumberland County Bar Assn. Office: US Dist Ct Edward T. Gignoux Courthouse 156 Federal St Portland ME 04101-4152

HORNBY, ROBERT RAY, mechanical engineer; b. La Crosse, Wis., Dec. 2, 1958; s. William James and Nancy Kay Hornby; m. Michal Rae Berrey, Aug. 2, 1980; children: Tabitha Kay, Maria Rae, Felicia Anne, Belinda Jo. BS in Mech. Engring., U. of Wis., Platteville, 1981. Registered profl. engr., Wis. Engring. cons. Geoscan Svcs. Co., Tulsa, Okla., 1983-84; sr. project engr. Howard Rotavator Co., Inc., Muscoda, Wis., 1984; mech. design engr. Rayovac, Portage, Wis., 1984-85; designer Gilman Engring. Co., Janesville, Wis., 1985-86; assoc. mech. design engr. Gilman Engring. Co., Janesville, 1986-87; mech. design engr. Giddings Lewis, Janesville, 1987-89, sr. mech. design engr., 1989-92, project mgr., 1992-95; sr. engr. NIMCO Corp., Crystal Lake, Ill., 1995-96; asst. project engr. Lamb Assembly & Test, Rockford, Ill., 1996-97, project engr., 1997—. Edn. chmn. Good Shepherd Luth. Ch., Janesville, 1985-88, religious counselor, 1992—; com. chmn. Explorer post 400 Boy Scouts Am., Janesville, 1985-91, scoutmaster troop 516, Janesville, 1985-95, asst. scoutmaster, 1995—, also commr. Koshkonong dist., Janesville. Recipient Scoutmaster award of merit Boy Scouts Am., 1990, Dist. Award of Merit, 1992, Silver Beaver award Boy Scouts Am., Janesville, 1998, 99; named Outstanding Leader Exploring Koshkonong Dist. Boy Scouts Am., Janesville, 1991, 93. Mem. ASME, NSPE, Soc. Mfg. Engrs. Achievements include development of math. model to predict lateral movement of oil well drill bit while drilling; patent applied for modular machine that welds plastic caps to gable top cardboard cartons. Home: 2135 Morningside Dr Janesville WI 53546-1121 Office: Lamb Assembly & Test 2140 12th St Rockford IL 61104-7351

HORNBY-ANDERSON, SARA ANN, metallurgical engineer, marketing professional; b. Plymouth, Devon, Eng., Apr. 17, 1952; came to U.S., 1986; d. Foster John and Joanna May (Duncan) Hornby; m. John Victor Anderson, Sept. 2, 1978 (div. May 1987). BSc in Metallurgy with honors, Sheffield (Eng.) City Poly., 1973, PhD in Indsl. Metallurgy, 1980. Chartered engr. Metallurgist Joseph Lucas Rsch., Solihull, Eng., 1970, William Lee Maleable, Dronfield, Eng., 1972; tech. sales specialist Applied Rsch. Labs, Luton, Beds, Eng., 1973-74; quality assurance metallurgist Firth Brown Tools, Sheffield, 1974-75, rsch. metallurgist high speed steel, 1975; lectr. Sheffield City Poly., 1975-78; grad. metallurgist, strip devel. metallurgist British Steel Corp., Rotherham, Eng., 1978-80; program mgr. Can. Liquid Air, Montreal, 1980-85; group mktg. mgr. Liquid Air Corp., Countryside, Ill., 1986-90; tech. mgr. Liquid Air Corp., Walnut Creek, Calif., 1990-93; bus. devel. mgr.-metals and materials Can. Liquid Air, Toronto, Ont., 1993-97, N.Am. steel tech. mgr., 1995-97; dir. steelmaking tech., dir. ops. Goodfellow Techs. Inc., Mississauga, Ont., 1997—; dir. ops. Goodfellow Techs. Inc., Mississauga, 1997-99; mgr. bus. devel. Stantec Global Techs. Ltd. (formerly Goodfellow Techs. Inc.), 1999—; bd. dirs., chmn. R & D com., mem. publs. com., chmn. promotions and mktg. com. INvestment Casting Inst., Dallas; presenter to confs. in field. Contbr. articles to profl. jours.; patentee in field of metallurgy. Mem. AIME, Inst. Metals (young metallurgists com. 1974-80), Sheffield Metall. Soc. Inst. Metals (sec. 1978-80), Am. Soc. Metals, Am. Foundry Soc., Powder Metals Soc., Am. Iron & Steel Soc. (steering com. 1987—, chmn. topics com. 1988—, sec. 1992, vice chair 1993, chmn. 1994, bd. dirs., strategic planning com. 1995-98, internat. affairs com., chmn. 1998, bd. dir. Ad-hoc com. on Internat. Affairs). Mem. Ch. of Eng. Avocations: scuba diving, horseback riding, swimming. E-mail: sara.hornby@sympatico.ca.

HORNE, GRANT NELSON, public relations consultant; b. Salt Lake City, Jan. 14, 1931; s. Joseph Feramorz and Ida Verene (Nelson) H.; m. Georgia Henry, July 6, 1957 (div. Feb. 1977); 1 child, Mary Corneille. BA magna cum laude, Yale U., 1952; MA, U. Utah, 1954. Instr. Gunnery Sch., Washington, Conn., 1955-57, Great Books Found., N.Y.C., 1958-61; dir. pub. relations Edison Electric Inst., N.Y.C., 1961-72; sr. v.p. Underwood Jordan Assocs., N.Y.C., 1972-79; retired v.p. corp. comms. Pacific Gas and Electric Co., San Francisco, 1980-96; past chmn. Pub. Rels. Seminar. Bd. dirs. Patrons the Vatican Mus.; bd. govs. San Francisco Symphony; active Knights of Malta. Mem. Arthur W. Page Soc., Yale Club (N.Y.C.), Villa Taverna Club (San Francisco), Alta Club (Salt Lake City), Commonwealth Calif. Club. Roman Catholic. Avocations: chamber music, classical piano. Office: Pacific Gas & Electric Co 77 Beale St San Francisco CA 94105-1814

HORNE, JOHN R., farm equipment company executive; b. Gary, Ind., 1938. Grad., Purdue U., 1960, Bradley U., 1964. Group v.p., gen. mgr. Navistar Internat. Transp. Corp.; pres., COO, now CEO Navistar Internat. Corp., also bd. dirs., pres., CEO, 1995—. Mem.Soc. Automotive Engrs. (chmn. fin. com.). Office: Navistar Internat Corp 455 N Cityfront Plaza Dr Chicago IL 60611-5503

HORNE, LENA, singer; b. Bklyn., June 30, 1917; d. Gail Lumet Buckley; m. Lennie Hayton, Dec. 1947 (dec. 1971). Degree (hon.), Howard U., Spelman Coll. Dancer, Cotton Club, 1934; toured, recorded with Noble Sissle Orch., 1935-36, Charlie Barnet's Band, 1940-41; became cafe soc. singer; starred in: motion pictures Cabin in the Sky, Stormy Weather, Death of a Gunfighter, Thousands Cheer, I Dood It, Swing Fever, Broadway Rhythm, Two Girls and a Sailor, Ziegfield Follies, Panama Hattie, Till the Clouds Roll By, Words & Music, Duchess of Idaho, Meet Me in Las Vegas, others; singer popular music ; TV appearances include spl. Harry and Lena, 1970, series Cosby Show, Sanford and Son; theatrical appearances in Dance with Your Gods, Blackbird, The Lady & Her Music, 1984; albums: Lena Goes Latin, 1987, Stormy Weather, The Men in My Life, 1989, Greatest Hits, 1992, At Long Last Lena, 1992, Best of Lena Horne, 1993, We'll Be Together Again, 1994, Lena Horne Christmas, 1995, Lena Sings Hollywood, 1996, Whispering, 1996, Lena Soul, 1996, More Than You Know, 1997; author: (with Richard Schickel) Lena, 1965. Recipient Page One award N.Y. Newspaper Guild, Lifetime Achievement award Ebony Mag., Antoinette Perry Spl. award, 1981, Spingarn award NAACP, 1983, Kennedy Ctr. honor for lifetime contributions to the arts, 1984, Paul Robeson award Actor's Equity, 1985, Pied Piper award ASCAP, 1987, 2 Grammy awards; named to Black Filmmakers Hall of Fame. Office: care Edward White & Co 21700 Oxnard St Ste 400 Woodland Hills CA 91367-7559*

HORNE, MICHAEL STEWART, lawyer; b. Mpls., May 10, 1938; s. Owen Edward and Adeline (DiGeorgio) H.; m. Martha Brean, Sept. 11, 1965; children: Jennifer, Katherine, Sarah, Owen. BA, U. Minn., 1959; LLB, Harvard U., 1962. Bar: D.C. 1963, U.S. Ct. Appeals (D.C. cir.) 1964, U.S. Supreme Ct. 1968, U.S. Ct. Appeals (6th cir.), 1966, U.S. Ct. Appeals (9th cir.) 1978, U.S. Ct. Appeals (4th cir.) 1979, U.S. Ct. Appeals (5th cir.), 1979, U.S. Ct. Appeals (2d cir.) 1980, U.S. Ct. Appeals (11th cir.) 1983, U.S. Ct. Appeals (8th cir.) 1984, U.S. Ct. Appeals (10th cir.), 1997. Assoc. Covington & Burling, Washington, 1964-71, ptnr., 1971—. Mem. D.C. Bar Assn., ABA, FCC Bar Assn., Am. Judicature Soc. Democrat. Home: 9008 Levelle Dr Bethesda MD 20815-5608 Office: Covington & Burling 1201 Pennsylvania Ave NW PO Box 7566 Washington DC 20044-7566

HORNE, THOMAS LEE, III, entrepreneur; b. Athens, Ga., Dec. 21, 1950; s. Thomas Lee and Roberta Eldridge (Brunby) H.; m. Karen Blair, 1972 (div. 1980); m. Skeater Jane Doster, 1982 (div. 1985). BA, Stetson U., 1972. Mechanic Durham Motors, New Orlrans, 1973-74; parts man Ferguson Pontiac, Daytona Beach, Fla., 1976-80; salesman Rooks Salvage, Orlando, Fla., 1980-84; owner, mgr. Dourphous Enterprises, Orlando, 1980—; pres. Brumby Enterprises, Franklin, La., 1992—; mgn. ptnr. Horne Partnership, Franklin, 1992—; trustee Brumby Family Trust, Franklin, 1985—; treas. Riggs Land Corp., Franklin, 1992—; dir. Emerald Land Corp., Berwick, La. Mem. Loyal Order Moose. Liberatarian. Unitarian. Avocations: windsurfing, camping, travel. Office: Dourphous Enterprises PO Box 5349 225 Main St Ste 12 Destin FL 32541-2562 also: Dourphous Enterprises 1803 Crown Way PO Box 547881 Orlando FL 32854-7881 also: Aycock Horne 519 Main St PO Box 999 Franklin LA 70538-0999

HORNER, ALTHEA JANE, psychologist; b. Hartford, Conn., Jan. 13, 1926; d. Louis and Celia (Newmark) Greenwald; children: Martha Horner Hartley, Anne Horner Benck, David, Kenneth. BS in Psychology, U. Chgo., 1952; PhD in Clin. Psychology, U. So. Calif., 1965. Lic. psychologist, N.Y., Calif. Tchr. Pasadena (Calif.) City Coll., 1965-67; from asst. to assoc. prof. Los Angeles Coll. Optometry, 1967-70; supr. Psychology interns Pasadena Child Guidance Clinic, 1969-70; pvt. practice specializing in psychoanalysis and psychoanalytic psychotherapy. N.Y.C., 1970-83; supervising psychologist dept. psychiatry Beth Israel Med. Ctr., N.Y.C., 1972-83, coordinator group therapy tng., 1976-82, clinician in charge Brief Adaptation-Oriented Psychotherapy Research Group, 1982-83; assoc. clin. prof. Mt. Sinai Sch. Medicine, N.Y.C., 1977-91, adj. assoc. prof., 1991—; mem. faculty Nat. Psychol. Assn. for Psychoanalysis, N.Y.C., 1982-83; sr. mem. faculty Wright Inst. Los Angeles Postgrad. Inst., 1983-85; pvt. practice L.A., 1983—; clin. prof. dept. Psychology UCLA, 1985-95. Author: (with others) Treating the Neurotic Patient in Brief Psychotherapy, 1985, Object Relations and the Developing Ego in Therapy, 1979, rev. edit., 1984, Little Big Girl, 1982, Being and Loving, 1978, 3d edit. 1990, Psychology for Living (with G. Forehand), 4th edit., 1977, The Wish for Power and the Fear of Having It, 1989, The Primacy of Structure, 1990, Psychoanalytic Object Relations Therapy, 1991, Working With the Core Relationship Problem in Psychotherapy, 1998, Chrysalis, 1999; mem. editorial bd. Jour. of Humanistic Psychology, 1986—, Jour. of the Am. Acad. of Psychoanalysis; contbr. articles to profl. jours. Mem. AAAS, APA, Calif. State Psychol. Assn., Am. Acad. Psychoanalysis (sci. assoc.), So. Calif. Psychoanalytic Soc. and Inst. (hon.). Office: 3579 E Foothill Blvd # 256 Pasadena CA 91107-3119

HORNER, BOB, broadcast executive. Pres. NBC News Channel 6, Charlotte. Office: care NBC News Channel 6 1001 Woodridge Center Dr Charlotte NC 28217-1986*

HORNER, CARL MATTHEW, chemistry educator; b. Cicero, N.Y., June 4, 1930; s. Oscar Wendell and Gladys Cecilia (Horner) H. BS, LeMoyne Coll., 1952; MS, Syracuse U., 1958, PhD, 1965. Asst. prof. analytical chemistry SUNY-Oneonta, 1958-61, assoc. prof., 1961-64, prof., 1964-97, prof. emeritus, 1998—; coord. ann. instrumental chemistry workshops, 1986—. NSF CAUSE grantee, 1979-82; NSF CSIP grantee, 1986-88; Walter B. Ford Found. grantee, 1980, 83. Mem. Am. Chem. Soc., Soc. Applied Spectroscopy, AAAS, N.Y. Acad. Scis. Avocations: scuba diving, underwater photography. Achievements include: research in infrared spectroscopy and laboratory robotics. Home: 24 Suncrest Ter Oneonta NY 13820-4632

HORNER, CONSTANCE JOAN, federal agency administrator; b. Summit, N.J., Feb. 24, 1942; d. David Earl and Cecelia (Murphy) McN.; m. Charles Edward Horner, May 7, 1965; children: David Bayer, Jonathan Purcell. BA in English Lit., U. Pa., 1964; MA in English Lit., U. Chgo., 1967. Dep. asst. dir. policy planning and evaluation ACTION Agy., Washington, 1981-82, acting assoc. dir. domestic & anti-poverty ops., 1982-83, dep. assoc. dir. for VISTA & service-learning, 1982-83; assoc. dir. for econs. & govt. Office of Mgmt. and Budget, Washington, 1983-85; dir. Office of Pers. Mgmt., Washington, 1985-89; deputy sec. HHS, 1989-91; asst. to pres. and dir. presdl. pers. The White House, Washington, 1991-93; mem. U.S. Commn. on Civil Rights, Washington, 1993-98; commr. The White House Fellows Commn., Washington, 1985-89; guest scholar The Brookings Inst., Washington, 1993—; vis. faculty Princeton (N.J.) U., 1994; fellow, lectr. Johns Hopkins U., 1994-95. Bd. dirs. Annie E. Casey Found., Baltimore, Md., 1994—. Fellow Nat. Acad. Pub. Adminstrn.; mem. Cosmos Club. Republican. Home: 3171 Porter St NW Washington DC 20008-3210 Office: Brookings Inst 1775 Massachusetts Ave NW Washington DC 20036-2188

HORNER, ELAINE EVELYN, secondary education educator; b. Portales, N.Mex., Feb. 26, 1941; d. Carlton James and Clara C. (Roberson) Carmichael; m. Bill G. Horner, Feb. 2, 1959; children: Billy G. Jr., Frances E. Moreau, Aaron J. BA, Ea. N.Mex. U., 1973, MEd, 1978. Tchr. Artesia (N.Mex.) Jr. High Sch., 1973-98, ret., 1998. Recipient Honor of Excellence award Navajo Refining, 1993. Mem. NEA, Nat. Coun. Tchrs. Math., N.Mex. Coun. Tchrs. Math., Artesia Edn. Assn. (v.p. 1987-88), Delta Kappa Gamma (treas. 1988—). Democrat. Baptist. Avocations: reading, golf. Home: 2406 N Haldeman Rd Artesia NM 88210-9435

HORNER, HARRY CHARLES, JR., sales executive, theatrical and film consultant; b. Pitts., Oct. 30, 1937; s. Harry Charles and Sara Marie (Hysong) H.; m. Patricia Ann Hagarty, June 15, 1965 (div. 1981); m. Sharon Kae Wyatt, Dec. 30, 1983; children: Jeffrey Brian, Jennifer Leigh, Mark Gregory. BFA, U. Cin., 1963; postgrad., Xavier U., Cin., 1963-64. Mgr. Retail Credit Co., Atlanta, 1964-68; ops. mgr. Firestone Tire and Rubber Co., L.A., 1968-80; exec. v.p. Romney/Ford Enterprises Inc., Scottsdale, Ariz., 1980-85; sales mgr. Environ. Care Inc., Calabassas, Calif., 1985-93; ops. v.p. Albuquerque (N.Mex.) Grounds Maintenance, Inc., 1993—; pres., chief exec. officer The Cons. Group Cos. Ltd., Palm Desert, Calif., 1984—; pres. E. Valley Theatre Co., Chandler, Ariz., 1984-86. Cons. Ariz. Commn. on Arts, Phoenix, 1983-84. Republican. Mem. LDS Ch. Avocations: flying, model railroads. Office: Albuquerque Grounds Maintenance Inc 8442 Washington Pl NE Albuquerque NM 87113-1671

HORNER, JAMES, composer; b. 1953. Works include: composer (film scores) Battle Beyond the Stars, 1980, Humanoids from the Deep, 1980, Deadly Blessing, 1981, The Hand, 1981, The Pursuit of D.B. Cooper, 1981, Wolfen, 1981, Star Trek II: The Wrath of Khan, 1982, 48 Hours, 1982, Brainstorm, 1983, Gorky Park, 1983, Something Wicked This Way Comes, 1983, Space Raiders, 1983, Testament, 1983, Uncommon Valor, 1983, The Stone Boy, 1984, (with Chris Young) Barbarian Queen, 1985, Cocoon, 1985, Heaven Help Us, 1985, The Journey of Natty Gann, 1985, Volunteers, 1985, Wizard of the Lost Kingdom, 1985, In Her Own Time, 1985, An American Tail, 1986 (Grammy award nominee for best album of original instrumental score 1987), The Name of the Rose, 1986, Off Beat, 1986, Where the River Runs Black, 1986, *batteries not included, 1987, P.K. & the Kid, 1987, Project X, 1987, Cocoon: The Return, 1988, Red Heat, 1988, Vibes, 1988, Willow, 1988, The Land Before Time, 1988, Dad, 1989, Field of Dreams, 1989 (Acad. award nominee for best original score 1989), Glory, 1989 (Grammy award for best album of original instrumental score 1990), Honey, I Shrunk the Kids, 1989, In Country, 1989, I Love You to Death, 1990, Another 48 Hours, 1990, (with Ernest Troost) Andy Colby's Incredibly Awesome Adventure, 1990, Class Action, 1991, My Heroes Have Always Been Cowboys, 1991, Once Around, 1991, The Rocketeer, 1991, An American Tail: Fievel Goes West, 1991, Patriot Games, 1992, Sneakers, 1992, Thunderheart, 1992, Unlawful Entry, 1992, House of Cards, 1993, Jack the Bear, 1993, Swing Kids, 1993, A Far Off Place, 1993, Once Upon a Forest, 1993, Searching for Bobby Fischer, 1993, The Man Without a Face, 1993, Bopha!, 1993, We're Back!: A Dinosaur's Story, 1993, The Pelican Brief, 1993, The Pagemaster, 1994, Clear and Present Danger, 1994, Legends of the Fall, 1994, Apollo 13, 1995 (Acad. award nominee for best original dramatic score 1996), Braveheart, 1995 (Acad. award nominee for best original dramatic score 1996), Casper, 1995,The Devils' Own, 1997, Titanic, 1998 (Oscar & Grammy, 1998), Mighty Joe Young, 1998, The Mask of Zoro, 1998, Deep Impact, 1998; (film songs) (from An American Tail) Somewhere Out There, 1986 (Acad. award nominee for best original song 1986, Grammy awards for song of yr. and best song written for motion picture 1987), (from The Land Before Time) If We Hold on Together, 1988, (from An American Tail: Fievel

Goes West) Way Out West, 1991, Dreams to Dream, 1991, The Girl I Left Behind, 1991; (film shorts scores) Tummy Trouble, 1989, (TV movie scores) Angel Dusted, 1981, A Few Days in Weasel Creek, 1981, Rascals and Robbers-The Secret Adventures of Tom Sawyer and Huck Finn, 1982, A Piano for Mrs. Cimino, 1982, Between Friends, 1983, Surviving, 1985, Extreme Close-Up, 1990; music adaptor, composer: (film score) The Lady in Red, 1979; music condr., composer: (film score) The Dresser, 1983; music designer, composer: (film score) Krull, 1983; music dir., composer: (film score) Star Trek III: The Search for Spock, 1984; music prodr., composer: (film score) Commando, 1985; music condr., arranger, composer: (film score) Aliens, 1986 (Acad. award nominee for best original score 1986, Grammy award nominee for best instrumental composition 1986). Office: Gorfaine Schwartz Agency 13245 Riverside Dr Ste 450 Sherman Oaks CA 91423-2172*

HORNER, JENNIE LINN, retired educational administrator, nurse; b. Memphis, Tex., Feb. 27, 1932; d. Lester C. and Cecil T. (Knight) Linn; m. Billy A. Gooch, June 4, 1951 (dec.); children: Brenda Michael, Patricia Lynn Magneson, Robert Allen; m. 2d Donald M. Horner, July 26, 1975. RN, U. Tex., 1955; BS, No. Ariz. U., 1977, MA, 1978, EdD, 1984. Cert. tchr., registered nurse, Ariz., Tex. Indsl. nurse Lipton Tea Co., Galveston, Tex., 1955-56; head nurse U. Tex. Med. Br., Galveston, 1956-58; sch. nurse Wash. Sch. Dist., Phoenix, 1970-77; tchr. middle sch., 1977-80; asst. prin. Murphy Sch. Dist., Phoenix, 1980-82; assoc. prin. middle sch. Madison Sch., Phoenix, 1982-84; lang. arts coordinator Madison Sch. Dist., Phoenix; prin. Dysart Unified Sch. Dist., El Mirage, Ariz., 1984-87; adminstr. for ednl. svcs., 1987-91, ret., 1991; med. cons. Medahab, Phoenix. Mem. Assn. Supervision and Curriculum Devel., Sch. Nurses Orgn. Ariz. (past pres.), Am. Vocat. Assn., Am. Sch. Health Assn., Nat. Assn. Sch. Nurses, Nat. Assn. Elem. Sch. Prins., Nat. Sch. Health Assn., Ariz. Sch. Health Assn. (bd. dirs.), Ariz. Adminstrs. Assn., Aware West, Phi Delta Kappa. Democrat. Home: 186 Rainbow Dr PMB 8648 Livingston TX 77399-1086

HORNER, JOHN ROBERT, paleontologist, researcher; b. Shelby, Mont., June 15, 1946; s. John Henry and Miriam Whitted (Stith) H.; m. Virginia Lee Seacotte, Mar. 30, 1972 (div. 1982); 1 child, Jason James; m. Joann Katherine Raffelson, Oct. 3, 1986 (div. 1994); m. Celeste Claire Roach, Jan. 21, 1995. DSc (hon.), U. Mont., 1986. Rsch. asst. dept. geology Princeton (N.J.) U., 1975-82; curator paleontology Mus. of the Rockies, Mont. State U., Bozeman, 1982—; adj. prof. biology and geology dept. geology Mont. State U., 1982—; rsch. scientist Am. Mus. Nat. History, N.Y.C., 1980-82. Co-author: Maia: A Dinosaur Grows up, 1985, Digging Dinosaurs, 1988 (N.Y. Acad. Sci. award 1989), Digging Up Tyrannosaurus Rex, 1993, The Complete T-Rex, 1993, Dinosaur Lives, 1997; contbr. articles to profl. jours. With USMC, 1966-68; Vietnam. MacArthur fellow, 1986. Discovered a new genus of duckbilled dinosaur, Maiasaura; accomplishments include: the theory of endothermic metabolism in dinosaur development, of parental nurture of new-born hatchlings, that Tyrannosaurus rex was a scavenger; excavator of the Egg Mountain cache of dinosaur nests. Home: 310 Hoffman Dr Bozeman MT 59715-5724 Office: Mont State U Mus Of The Rockies Bozeman MT 59717

HORNER, MATINA SOURETIS, retired college president, corporate executive; b. Boston, July 28, 1939; d. Demetre John and Christine (Antonopoulos) Souretis; m. Joseph L. Horner, June 25, 1961; children: Tia Andrea, John, Christopher. AB cum laude, Bryn Mawr Coll., 1961; MS, U. Mich., 1963, PhD, 1968; LLD (hon.), Dickinson Coll., 1973; LLD, Mt. Holyoke Coll., 1973; LLD (hon.), U. Pa., 1975, Smith Coll., 1979, Wheaton Coll., 1979, U. Mich., 1989; LHD (hon.), U. Mass., 1973, Tufts U., 1976, U. Hartford, 1980, U. New Eng., 1987, Bentley Coll., 1989, New Eng. Coll., 1989, Pine Manor Coll., 1989, Am. Coll. Greece, 1990; DLitt (hon.), Claremont U. Ctr. and Grad Sch., 1988, Hellenic Coll., 1990; LHD (hon.), Colby Sawyer Coll., 1991. Teaching fellow U. Mich., Ann Arbor, 1962-66, lectr. motivation personality, 1968-69; lectr. social relations Harvard U., Cambridge, Mass., 1969-70, asst. prof. clin. psychology, 1970-72, assoc. prof. psychology, 1972-89, cons. univ. health svcs., 1971-89; pres. Radcliffe Coll., Cambridge, 1972-89, pres. emerita, 1989—; exec. v.p. TIAA-CREF, N.Y.C., 1989—; bd. dirs. Neiman Marcus Group, Boston Edison Co. Co-author: The Challenge of Change, 1983; contbr. psychol. articles on motivation to profl. jours. and chpts. to books. Mem. adv. coun. NSF, 1977-87, chair, 1980-86; bd. trustees Twentieth Century Fund, 1973—, Am. Coll. of Greece, 1983-90, Mass. Eye and Ear Infirmary, 1986-90, Com. for Econ. Devel., 1988—, vice-chmn., 1992-98; bd. trustees Mass. Gen. Hosp., Inst. Health Professions, 1988—, vice chmn., 1994, chair, 1995; bd. dirs. Coun. for Fin. Aid to Edn., 1985-89, Beth Israel Hosp., 1989-95; bd. dirs. Revson Found., 1986-92, chmn., 1992-97; bd. dirs. Women's Rsch. and Edn. Inst., 1979—, chair rsch. com., 1982—; mem. Coun. on Fgn. Rels., 1984—; exec. com. ACE Bus. Higher Edn. Forum, 1984-86; exec. com. New Eng. Colls. Fund, 1980—, 2d v.p., 1984-85, 1st v.p., 1985-88, pres., 1988-89; mem. nat. panel to study declining test scores Coll. Entrance Exam. Bd., 1976-77; exec. com., chair task force Pres.'s Commn. for Nat. Agenda for 1980s, 1979-80; adv. com. Women's Leadership Conf. on Nat. Security, 1982—; exec. com. Coun. on Competitiveness, 1986-89; chair task force on health care Challenge to Leadership Conf., 1987-89; bd. dirs. Greenwall Found., 1997, Fund for City of N.Y., chair, 1997. Recipient Roger Baldwin award Mass. Civil Liberties Union Found., 1982, citation of merit Northeast Region NCCJ, 1982, Career Contbn. award Mass. Psychol. Assn., 1987, Disting. Bostonian award, 1990, Ellis Island medal, 1990. Mem. NOW (nat. corp. adv. bd. of legal def. and edn. fund 1984—), Am. Laryngol. Voice Rsch. and Edn. Found. (pres.), Nat. Inst. Social Scis. (medal for outstanding svc. 1973), Phi Beta Kappa, Phi Delta Kappa, Phi Kappa Phi.

HORNER, RUSSELL GRANT, JR., energy and chemical company executive. BA, U. Okla., 1961, LLB, 1963. Bar: Okla. 1963. Ptnr. Kerr-Davis, 1963-69; div. counsel Kerr-McGee Corp., Oklahoma City, 1969-75, sr. v.p., gen. counsel, corp. sec., 1997—; v.p. land Transworld Drilling Co., 1975-82, exec. v.p., 1982-86, v.p. gen counsel, 1986-87. Office: Kerr McGee Corp PO Box 25861 Oklahoma City OK 73125-0861

HORNER, SANDRA MARIE GROCE (SANDY HEART), educator, poet, songwriter, lyricist; b. Dallas; d. Larnell and Lee Ella (Lacy) Groce; divorced; 1 child, Danielle Marie. BA in Sociol./Philosophy with honors, Calif. State U., Dominguez Hills, 1980; postgrad., UCLA, 1978, 82-83, Consumnes River Coll., 1987, Nat. U., 1991, So. Utah U., 1993. Cert. elem. edn. K-8, Nev., K-A Occ. Std.: Bus. and Office Occupations; cert. instr. credential Calif.; cert. lifetime tchg. credential bus., Calif. Prodn. asst., sec. Paramount Pictures Corp., Hollywood, Calif., 1968-74; instr. L.A. C.C. Dist., 1976-78; tchr. Verbum Dei H.S., L.A., 1977-79; tchr., dept. chair L.A. Unified Sch. Dist., 1975-83; tchr. Sacramento (Calif.) City Unified Sch. Dist., 1985-87; editor, pub. Multi-Family Publs., Sacramento, 1986-89; tchr. Clark County Sch. Dist., Las Vegas, Nev., 1991-98; adj. instr. C.C. So. Nev., Las Vegas, 1988-95; radio broadcast interview Poetry Today with Ken Lerch WRTN 93.5 FM, N.Y.C., 1997. Editor: (books/newsletters) Groce Family Newsletter, 1986; recording contracts Hilltop Records, 1996, 97, AME Record Recording Co., 1997, Hollywood Artists Record Co., 1997; author numerous poems; albums include America, Hill Top Country, Star Route USA, Music of America. Recipient Nat. History recognition award Soc. History Rsch. and Preservation, 1989, Editor's Choice awards Nat. Libr. of Poetry, 1996; inducted into Internat. Poetry Hall of Fame, 1996. Mem. AAUW, AAUP, Internat. Soc. Poets (Disting. Mem.), Am. Bus. Women's Assn., Internat. Platform Assn. Democrat. Avocations: literature, music, history, art, antiques. Office: PO Box 56392 Sherman Oaks CA 91413-1392

HORNER, WINIFRED BRYAN, humanities educator, researcher, consultant, writer; b. St. Louis, Aug. 31, 1922; d. Walter Edwin and Winifred (Kinealy) Bryan; m. David Alan Horner, June 15, 1943; children: Winifred, Richard, Elizabeth, David. AB, Washington U., St. Louis, 1943; MA, U. Mo., 1961; PhD, U. Mich., 1975. Instr. English U. Mo., Columbia, 1966-75, asst. prof. English, 1975-80, chair lower div. studies, dir. composition program, 1974-80, assoc. prof., 1980-83, prof., 1984-85, prof. emerita, 1985—; prof. English, Radford chair rhetoric and composition Tex. Christian U., Ft. Worth, 1985-93, Cecil and Ida Green disting. prof. emerita, 1993-97. Editor: Historical Rhetoric: An Annotated Bibliography of Selected Sources in English, 1980, The Present State of Scholarship in Historical Rhetoric, 1983, Composition and Literature: Bridging the Gap, 1983, Rhetoric and Pedagogy: Its History, Philosophy and Practice, 1995; author: Rhetoric in a Classical Mode, 1987, Nineteenth-Century Scottish Rhetoric: The American Connection, 1993, Life Writing, 1996; co-author Harbrace Coll. Hancbook, 11th edit., 1990, 12th edit., 1994, 13th edit., 1998. Named Disting. prof. Tex. Woman's U., 1999; Inst. for the Humanities fellow U. Edinburgh, 1987; NEH grantee, 1976, 87. Mem. Internat. Soc. for History Rhetoric (exec. coun. 1986), Rhetoric Soc. Am. (bd. dirs. 1981, pres. 1987), Nat. Coun. Writing Program Administrs. (v.p. 1977-85, pres. 1985-87), Coll. Conf. on Composition and Communication (exec. com.), Modern Lang. Assn. (mem. del. assembly 1981). Fax: (573) 445-6896. E-mail: engwin@showme.missouri.edu. Home and Office: 1904 Tremont Ct Columbia MO 65203-5467

HORNICK, RICHARD BERNARD, physician; b. Johnstown, Pa., Jan. 27, 1929; s. Paul Steven and Gertrude (Cowan) H.; children: Douglas, Thomas, Marcie, Blaine; m. Susan Finnegan. A.B., Johns Hopkins U., 1951, M.D., 1955. Diplomate: Am. Bd. Internal Medicine. Intern Johns Hopkins Hosp., Balt., 1955-56, resident in medicine, 1956-57; mem. faculty U. Md. Med. Sch., 1959-78, head infectious diseases, 1963-78; prof. U. Rochester, N.Y., 1979-87, chmn. dept. medicine, 1979-85, assoc. dean affiliated hosps. and external rels., 1985-87; v.p. med. edn. Orlando (Fla.) Regional Healthcare System, 1988—; cons. WHO, mem. Armed Forces Epidemiol. Bd. Contbr. articles to med. jours. Served with U.S. Army, 1957-59. Fellow ACP (bd. govs., regent); mem., Am.Soc. MIcrobiology, Am. Fedn. Clin. Rsch., Am. Soc. Clin. Investigation, Am. Clin. and Climatol. Assn., Assn. Am. Physicians, Infectious Disease Soc., Coun. of Med. Specialties Soc. Home: 75 Palmer Ave Winter Park FL 32789-2529 Office: Orlando Regional Healthcare System 1414 Kuhl Ave Orlando FL 32806-2093

HORNICK, SUSAN FLORENCE, secondary education educator, fine arts educator; b. Aug. 29, 1947. MS in Art Edn., Queens Coll., 1973; permanent N.Y. state reading cert., Hunter Coll., 1984, prof. diploma advanced cert., 1996. Fine arts tchr. Hillcrest H.S., Jamaica, N.Y., 1973-74, Ea. Dist. H.S., Bklyn., 1974-75, Tottenville H.S., S.I., N.Y., 1975-76; fine arts tchr., title 1 reading tchr. Prospect Heights H.S., Bklyn., 1976-78; fine arts tchr. Grover Cleveland H.S., Ridgewood, N.Y., 1978—; dept. coord. Grover Cleveland H.S., Ridgewood, 1986-87. Home: 46-05 Hanford St Douglaston NY 11362

HORNIK, JOSEPH WILLIAM, civil engineer; b. N.Y.C., May 7, 1929; s. Joseph and Josephine (Nemecek) H.; B.C.E., Cooper Union, 1952; grad. studies Columbia U., 1955-61; m. Barbara Joan Simko, Nov. 16, 1957; children: Heidi Josepha, Joseph Jared, Jason William, Heather Justine. Field engr. Stone & Webster Engring. Corp., Roanoke Rapids, N.C. and Portsmouth, Va., 1952-54; sr. engr. Howard, Needles, Tammen & Bergendoff, Jersey City, 1954-56; resident engr. Edwards & Kelcey, Bridgeport, Conn., 1956-59; project engr., project supt. The Austin Co., Bklyn. and San Juan, P.R., 1959-62; resident engr. Seelye, Stevenson, Value & Knecht, Whitehall, N.Y., 1962-65; county engr., county supt. hwys. County of Rockland, New City, N.Y., 1965-90; cons. engr., West Nyack, N.Y., 1967—; assoc. Hudson Internat. Group, Wayne, Pa., 1993-98; assoc. Internat. Environ. Svcs., Wayne, 1995-98; village engr. Village of Sloatsburg, N.Y., 1972-81, 85-88, Village of Haverstraw, N.Y., 1982-83, Village of Monroe, N.Y., 1984-92, Village of New Hempstead, N.Y., 1988-90, Village of Nyack, N.Y., 1988-94. Mem. Rockland County Planning Bd., 1972-90, Rockland County Drainage Agy., 1972-90, Rockland County Soil and Water Conservation Agy., 1972-90, Rockland County Traffic Safety Bd., 1979-90, Nat. Com. on Uniform Traffic Control Devices, 1985—. Lic. profl. engr., N.Y., Conn., Fla., P.R.; lic. land surveyor, N.Y. Fellow ASCE; mem. NSPE, N.Y. State County Hwy. Supts. Assn. (dir. 1975-87, v.p. 1980-81, pres. 1982), N.Y. State Soc. Profl. Engrs., Nat. Assn. County Engrs. (dir. 1984-90), Nat. Assn. Counties, Am. Rd. and Transp. Builders Assn., Rockland County Assn. Hwy. Supts. (pres. 1979), Inst. Engrs., Architects and Surveyors of P.R., Soil and Water Conservation Soc. Am., Omega Delta Phi. Clubs: West Nyack Swim and Tennis, West Rock Tennis. Home and Office: 2 Dearborn Rd West Nyack NY 10994-1104

HORNING, ROBERT ALAN, securities broker; b. Bristol, Tenn., Jan. 8, 1954; s. Sanford Lee and Pauline Stern (Marks) H.; m. Phyllis Ann Bockian, Apr. 12, 1981; children: Aaron Marks, Rachel Michelle. BA, U. Tenn., 1976, MA, 1979. Edn. specialist Knoxville (Tenn.) Police Dept., 1979-80; security cons. Sonitrol of Knoxville, 1980-81; sales rep. Guardsmark, Inc., Charleston, W.Va., 1981-84; mgr. in charge Guardsmark, Inc., L.A., 1984-88; v.p. mktg.-western region Fed. Armored Express, L.A., 1988-92; ptnr. Upton Affiliates, L.A., 1993—. Bd. dirs. B'Nai Tikvah Congregation, L.A., 1989—, v.p. membership, 1991, v.p. ritual com.; governance coun. Paseo Del Rey Natural Sci. Magnet Sch., 1996—. Mem. Am. Soc. Indsl. Security (chmn. L.A. chpt. 1990), Internat. Platform Assn., Phi Beta Kappa, Omicron Delta Kappa. Democrat. Jewish. Avocation: reading. Home: 7911 Denrock Ave Los Angeles CA 90045-1112

HORNS, HOWARD LOWELL, physician, educator; b. Buffalo, N.D., July 11, 1912; s. Otto and Crystal Belle (Sherwin) H.; m. Edith Marie Frostenson, Sept. 22, 1940; children—James S., Susan M. Horns Kolstad, William H. B.A., U. Minn., 1940, B.S., 1942, M.B., 1943, M.D., 1944. Intern U. Minn. Hosp.; resident in internal medicine; mem. faculty U. Minn. Med. Sch., 1947—, asst. dean, 1949-55, clin. prof. medicine, 1955—; staff physician Nicollet Clinic, Mpls., 1955—; pres. Minn. Bd. Med. Examiners, 1970, Fedn. State Med. Bds. U.S., 1974-75; mem. Nat. Bd. Med. Examiners, 1975—, Liaison Com. Continuing Med. Edn., 1975—. Contbr. articles to med. jours. Bd. dirs. Eitel Hosp., Mpls., 1956—, Met. Vis. Nurses Assn., 1984—, Nat. Commn. on Cert. of Physicians Assts., Inc., 1986—. Served with M.C. AUS, 1953-55. Fellow A.C.P. (gov. 1970-74); mem. AMA, Minn., Mpls. socs. internal medicine, Alpha Omega Alpha. Unitarian. Home: 100 Melbourne Ave SE Minneapolis MN 55414-3516 Office: 2001 Blaisdell Ave Minneapolis MN 55404-2414

HORNSBY, BRUCE RANDALL, composer, musician; b. Richmond, Va., Nov. 23, 1954; s. Robert Stanley and Lois (Saunier) H.; m. Kathy Yankovich, Dec. 31, 1983. BA, U. Miami, Coral Gables, Fla., 1977. Recording artist; albums include The Way It Is, 1986 (double platinum award, gold award Eng., Platinum award Can., gold award Germany, gold award Australia), Scenes from the Southside, 1988 (platinum award, gold award Eng., platinum award Can.), A Night on the Town, 1990 (gold award Can., silver award Eng.), Harbor Lights, 1993 (gold award), Hot House, 1995, Spirit Trail, 1998; composer numerous songs including The Way It Is (Song of Yr. ASCAP 1987), Mandolin Rain, Jacob's Ladder, Every Little Kiss, Valley Road, Look Out Any Window, Defenders of the Flag, On the Western Skyline, The End of Innocence, Across the River, Lost Soul, Fields of Gray, Rainbow's Cadillac, Walk in the Sun, Spider Fingers, (with E-40) Things'll Never Change, 1997; performed on records by Bob Dylan, The Grateful Dead, Rock and Roll Hall of Fame Concert Album, 1996, Tin Cup soundtrack, Bonnie Raitt, Bob Seger, Squeeze, Cowboy Junkies, Huey Lewis, Nitty Gritty Dirt Band, Chaka Khan, others; performed the Nat. Anthem, World Series Game 5, 1997. Recipient Best New Artist Grammy award, 1986, Best Bluegrass Rec. Grammy award, 1989, Best Pianist Keyboard Mag., 1987, 88, 89, 90, 91, 93; Best Song of Yr. Grammy nomination, 1989, Record of Yr. Grammy nomination, 1989, Best Performance by a Duo or Group Grammy nomination, 1990, Best Original Score Emmy award, 1987, Best Pop Instrumental Grammy award for "Barcelona Mona" with Branford Marsalis, 1994, Best Pop Instrumental Grammy nomination for "Star Spangled Banner" with Branford Marsalis, 1995, Best Pop Instrumental Grammy nomination for "Song B", 1995, Best Song Written for a Motion Picture "Love Me Still" with Chaka Khan Grammy nomination, 1995; winner Best Beyond album Downbeat Reader's Poll, 1994. Home: 311 Indian Springs Rd Williamsburg VA 23185*

HORNSTEIN, MARK, financial executive; b. N.Y.C., Dec. 7, 1947; s. Joseph and Anne (Fox) H.; BBA, Pace U., 1969; postgrad. N.Y.U., 1973. Staff acct. Peat, Marwick, Mitchell & Co., N.Y.C., 1969-70; sr. acct. Robert J. Cofini & Co., N.Y.C., 1972-74; asst. v.p. United Va. Factors Corp., N.Y.C., 1974-77; asst. v.p., adminstrv. head mortgage loan div. James Talcott, Inc., N.Y.C., 1977-78; loan adminstrn. officer Aetna Bus. Credit, Inc., East Hartford, Conn., 1978-79; asst. v.p. A.J. Armstrong Co. Inc. (now Bankamerica Bus. Credit, Inc.), N.Y.C., 1979-83; v.p. Leucadia Nat. Corp., N.Y.C., 1983—; treas. Am. Investment Co., St. Louis, 1984—; asst. v.p. Cardiff Equities Corp. (merger Leucadia Nat. Corp.), La Jolla, 1984-86; v.p. Charter Nat. Life Ins. Co., St. Louis, 1985-93, PHLCORP, Inc. (formerly Baldwin United Corp.), Phila., 1987—; sec. Bolivian Power Co., Ltd., LaPaz, Bolivia, 1988-94; v.p. Transp. Capital Corp., N.Y.C., 1992-94, chmn., pres., 1994-96. Served with USNR, 1970-72. Home: 25 Sutton Pl S New York NY 10022-2441 Office: 315 Park Ave S New York NY 10010-3607

HORNYAK, EUGENE AUGUSTINE, bishop; b. Kucura, Backa, Yugoslavia, Oct. 7, 1919; emigrated to U.S., 1948, naturalized, 1955, emigrated to Eng., 1961; s. Peter and Juliana (Findrik) H. Ph.B., Pontifical U., Rome, 1941, S.T.D., 1947; J.C.B., Gregorian U., Rome, 1947. Ordained priest Roman Catholic Ch. (Byzantine rite), 1945; asst. priest Struthers and Warren, Ohio, 1948-49; adminstr. St. Michael's Ch., Newton Falls, Ohio, 1949-50; prof. moral theology, canon law, liturgy, also spiritual dir. Sts. Cyril and Methodius Byzantine Seminary, Pitts., 1950-55; spiritual dir. St. Basil's Ukrainian Minor Seminary, Stamford, Conn., 1958-61; entered Order St. Basil the Great, Can., 1956-57; master novices, also superior St. Josaphat's Monastery, Glen Cove, L.I., 1961; apptd. titular bishop Hermonthis; also aux. to Cardinal Godfrey (for Ukrainian Catholics in Eng. and Wales), London, 1961-63; bishop-apostolic exarch for Ukrainian Catholics in Eng. and Wales, 1963-87, for Ukrainians in Scotland, 1968-87; mem. Pontifical Commn. of Ea. Code of Canon Law, Rome, 1977-90; consultor Sacred Congragation for Ea. Cath. Chs., Rome, 1978-94. Home and Office: St Olga's House, 14 Newburgh Rd, Acton, London W3 6DQ, England *Our earthly life comes, grows and fades away; it has God's support, it has its aims and its destiny. As a Christian, a monk and a Catholic bishop, I am endeavouring to attain those aims, reach that destiny, and be instrumental in helping and guiding my fellowmen to do likewise, according to the teachings and example of Christ, God incarnate, as faithfully transmitted to us by his Church.*

HOROSZEWICZ, JULIUSZ STANISLAW, oncologist, cancer researcher, laboratory administrator; b. Warsaw, Poland, Jan. 4, 1931; came to U.S., 1961; s. Tytus Michal and Stefania (Domanska) H.; m. Hanna Urszula Kubik, Jan. 12, 1969; children: Nike Joanna, Peter Juliusz. D of Medicine summa cum laude, Acad. of Medicine, Lodz, Poland, 1954, DMSc, 1960. Teaching asst. dept. bacteriology Acad. of Medicine, Lodz, 1950-55, asst. prof., 1955-59, assoc. prof., 1959-61; cancer rsch. scientist Roswell Park Meml. Inst., Buffalo, 1962-64, sr. cancer rsch. scientist, 1964-67, assoc. cancer rsch. scientist, 1967-76, prin. cancer rsch. scientist, 1976-86; assoc. chief oncological urology rsch. N.Y. State Dept. Health, Roswell Park Meml. Inst. Div., Buffalo, 1986-88; dir. exptl. cancer ctr. Millard Fillmore Hosp., Buffalo, 1988—; dir. electron microscopy lab. viral oncology, 1963-66, dir. human fibroblast interferon program Roswell Park Meml. Inst., 1976-82; chmn. Pleuro-Pneumonia Like Organisms subcom. human cancer virus task force Nat. Cancer Inst., Bethesda, Md., 1963-64, mem. Nat. Prostatic Cancer Project working cadre, 1972-74; assoc. rsch. prof. microbiology SUNY, Buffalo, 1966—; rsch. prof. biology Canisius Coll., Buffalo, 1968—, Niagara U., Niagara Falls, N.Y., 1968—; sci. cons. Cytogen Corp., Princeton, N.J., 1990—, Pacific NW Rsch. Found., Seattle, 1993—. Mem. editl. bd. The Prostate, 1994—; contbr. more than 100 articles to profl. jours.; patentee on specific monoclonal antibody for diagnosis and treatment of human prostate cancer. Rockefeller Found. fellow, 1961-62; Rsch. grantee Nat. Cancer Inst., 1979-82, Phi Beta Psi, 1987—; named Citizen of Yr. Am.-Polish Eagle, Buffalo, 1967. Mem. AAAS, Am. Assn. Cancer Rsch., Am. Soc. Microbiology, Polish Soc. for Bacteriology, Am. Cancer Soc., Am. Assn. for Clin. Rsch., N.Y. Acad. Scis. Roman Catholic. Achievements include patent on specific monoclonal antibody for diagnosis and treatment of human prostate cancer. Avocations: fishing, bridge, classical music, chess. Home: 2210 N Forest Rd Williamsville NY 14221-1357 Office: Millard Fillmore Hosp 3 Gates Cir Buffalo NY 14209-1194

HOROVITZ, ADAM, recording artist; b. N.Y.C., Oct. 31, 1967. Founder, mem. Young and the Useless, 1981-83; mem. The Beastie Boys, 1983—; owner Grand Royal, Grand Royal mag., 1984—. Albums include Licensed to Ill, 1986, Paul's Boutique, 1989, Check Your Head, 1992, 94, Ill Communication, 1994, Some Old Bullshit, 1994, In Sound from Way Out, 1996, Def & Dumb, 1996, (singles) Jimmy James, 1992, Gratitude, 1992, So What'cha Want, 1992, Sabotage, 1994, Hey Ladies, 1997, (extended play singles) Pollywog Stew, 1982, Cooky Puss, 1983, Rock Hard, 1984, Tour Shot, 1994, Sure Shot, 1994, Get It Together, 1994, Root Down, 1995, Aglio E Olio, 1995, (video) Skills to Pay the Bills, 1992; rap artist Heart of Soul, 1988, Rap's Biggest Hits, 1990, Rap Rap Rap, 1996, Rap: Most Valuable Players, 1996; vocals Rap's Biggest Hits, 1990; prodr. Cb4, 1993, Rebirth of Cool (vol. 3), 1995, Music for Our Mother Ocean, 1996, Rap Rap Rap, 1996, Rap: Most Valuable Players, 1996. Office: care Grand Royal/Capitol Records 1750 Vine St Los Angeles CA 90028-5209*

HOROVITZ, ISRAEL ARTHUR, playwright; b. Wakefield, Mass., Mar. 31, 1939; s. Julius Charles and Hazel (Solberg) H.; m. Doris Keefe, Dec. 25, 1959 (div. 1974); children: Rachael Keefe, Matthew Keefe, Adam Keefe; m. Gillian Adams, July, 1981; children: Hannah Rebecca and Oliver Adams (twins). Fellow, Royal Acad. Dramatic Art, London, 1961-63; postgrad. in English, CUNY, 1972-77, MA in English, 1977; PhD (hon.), Mass. State, 1991. Am. playwright-in-residence Royal Shakespeare Co., London, 1965; lectr., 1961-75; Fanny Hurst prof. theatre arts Brandeis U., 1974-75; artistic dir. N.Y. Playwrights Lab., 1975—; founder, artistic dir. Gloucester (Mass.) Stage Co., 1980—. Author: (plays) The Comeback, 1958, The Death of Bernard the Believer, 1960, This Play is About Me, 1961, The Hanging of Emanuel, 1962, Jump, 1962, Hop and Skip, 1963, The Killer Dove, 1963, The Indian Wants the Bronx, 1964-66, It's Called the Sugar Plum, 1965, Line, 1967, Rats, 1967, The Honest-to-God Schnozzola, 1968, Chiaroscuro (or Morning), 1968, The World's Greatest Play, 1968, First Season; collection of plays, 1968, Leader, 1969, Morning, Noon and Night, (with others), 1969, Acrobats, 1971, Play for Germs (TV), 1972, Dr. Hero, 1972, Shooting Gallery, 1972, The Wakefield Plays; 7-play cycle including The Alfred Trilogy: Part 1-Alfred the Great, Part 2-Our Father's Failing, Part 3-Alfred Dies, 1972-77 and The Quannapowitt Quartet: Part 1-Hopscotch, Part 2-The 75th, Part 3-Stage Directions, Part 4-Spared, 1971-79; Cappella (novel), 1973; Uncle Snake, 1975, The Great Labor Day Classic, 1979, The Primary English Class, 1975, The Bottom, 1975-76, Mackerel, 1977, Sunday Runners in the Rain, 1979-80, Nobody Loves Me; (novella), 1975, The Reason We Eat, 1976; adaption Ionesco's l'homme aux Valises: Man with Bags, 1977; adaptation from Melville's Bartleby, The Scrivener, 1978; The Former One-On-One Basketball Champion; teleplays Today I Am A Fountain Pen, 1977, A Rosen by Any Other Name, 1979, The Chopin Playoffs, 1978, adaptation from Mailer's The Deer Park, 1979-80; (plays) The Good Parts, 1979—, adaptation from Dickens- Scrooge and Marley, 1980-81, Park Your Car in Harvard Yard, 1980-83, The Widow's Blind Date, 1985-88, Henry Lumper, 1984-87, Year of the Duck, 1984-87, Firebird at Dogtown, 1984-85, North Shore Fish, 1985-87, Faith, 1988, Fighting Over Beverley, 1988-93, Strong-Man's Weak Child, 1988-90, Unexpected Tenderness, 1993-94, Barking Sharks, 1995, The Chips are Down (BBC radio), 1995, Lebensraum, 1996, My Old Lady, 1996, Captains and Courage, 1996, Free Gift, 1996, One Under, 1997, Phone Tag, 1997, Speedbag, 1999; (stage adaptations) Today I Am a Fountain Pen, A Rosen by Any Name, The Chopin Playoffs, 1986; (films) Park Your Car in Harvard Yard, 1991—, Fast Eddie, 1980, The Strawberry Statement, 1971, Believe in Me, 1972, Author! Author!, 1982, Fell, 1982-83, Berta, 1982-83, Light Years, 1985-86, Wedlock, 1985-86, (with Diane Kurys) A Man in Love, 1987-88, Payofski's Discovery, 1987-88, The Deuce, 1988-90, The Pan, 1989-91, Letters to Iris, 1989-90, The Quiet Room, 1990, Strong Man, 1991-93, James Dean, 1993—, Without A Word, 1994, A Star is Born (remake), 1994—, The Lounge Player, 1995—, The Widow's Blind Date, 1995, North Shore Fish, 1995, Captains and Courage, 1996, (with Istvan Szabo) The Taste of Sunshine, 1997, 300 Boys, 1999; contbr. to nat. mags, plays translated, pub. and performed in more than 20 langs. Recipient Vernon Rice award, 1967-68, Drama Desk award, 1967-68, Jersey Jour. best play award, 1968, Obie award, 1967-68, 68-69, French Critics prize, 1974, Christopher award, 1975, Emmy award, 1975, prix Italia-Silver Palm, 1982, L.A. Weekly Critics prize, 1984, 95, Commendation Gov. of Mass., 1984, Eliot Norton prize, 1986, Best Play award Boston mag., 1987, Lifetime Achievement award B'nai Brith, 1996, Washington Coll. Literary prize, 1996, Boston Pub. Libr. Literary Lights award, 1997; Rockefeller fellow, 1968-69, Nat. Endowment for Arts fellow, 1974, Fulbright fellow, 1975-76, Guggenheim fellow, 1977-78. Mem. Actors Studio, New Dramatists Com., Eugene O'Neill Found., Authors' League Am. (exec. council). Nationally ranked masters track and road runner; most produced Am. playwright in French language. Office: William Morris Agy 1350 Avenue Of The Americas New York NY 10019-4702 also: care Jim Crabbe William Morris Agy 151 S El Camino Dr Beverly Hills CA 90212-2704 also: Voyez

Mon Agent, 10 Av George V, 75008 Paris France also: Felix Bloch Erben, Hardenberg Strasse 6, D-10623 Berlin Germany

HOROVITZ, ZOLA PHILIP, pharmaceutical company executive; b. Pitts., Oct. 12, 1934; s. Reuben and Jean (Liff) H.; m. Marlene C. Davis, Aug. 24, 1958; children: Bonna Lynn, Reid Alan. BS in Pharmacy, U. Pitts., 1955, MS in Pharmacy, 1958, PhD in Pharmacology, 1960. Researcher Vets. Rsch. Labs., Pitts., 1958-60; sr. rsch. investigator Squibb Inst. Med. Rsch., Princeton, N.J., 1959-64, med. monitor, 1964-66, dir. pharmacology, 1967-72, assoc. rsch. dir., 1972-78, assoc. dir. devel., 1978-82, v.p., 1982-89; v.p. licensing Bristol-Myers Squibb Corp., Princeton, 1990-91, v.p. bus. devel. and planning, 1991-94; cons. to biotech. and pharm. industry, 1994—; bd. dirs. Procept Corp., Cambridge, Mass., Diacrin Inc., Charlestown, Mass., Phyton Inc., Ithaca, N.Y., BioCryst Pharm., Birmingham, Ala., Magainin Pharm., Plymouth Meeting, Pa., Synaptic Pharm., Paramus, N.J., Roberts Pharm., Eatontown, N.J., Clinicor, Austin, Tex., Avigen, Alameda, Calif. Editor: Angiotensin Conversion Enzyme Inhibition, 1983. Pres. Princeton Jewish Ctr., 1980-82; mem. East Brunswick (N.J.) Bd. Edn., 1965-69, N.J. Cancer Rsch. Commn., 1989-95. Recipient rsch. award Soc. Biol. Psychiatry, 1965. Fellow Am. Pharm. Assn., Acad. Pharm. Scientists; mem. Am., Brit. Pharmacology Socs. Jewish.

HOROWITZ, BARRY ALLAN, music company executive; b. N.Y.C., June 21, 1948; s. Henry and Tania (Aisenfeld) H.; m. Maida Barbara Schwartzberg, Oct. 9, 1977 (dec. Oct. 1994); children: Jessica, Jared. BA, Hofstra U., Hempstead, N.Y., 1971. From sales staff to sr. dir. ops. Sam Ash Music Corp., Hicksville, N.Y., 1971-95, v.p. purchasing and merchandising, 1995—. Avocations: running, skiing. Office: Sam Ash Music Corp 278 Duffy Ave Hicksville NY 11801-3605

HOROWITZ, BARRY MARTIN, systems research and engineering company executive; b. Bklyn., Apr. 20, 1943; s. Isaac Harry and Clara Fireda (Weintraub) H.; m. Sheryl Robin Lang, Jan. 24, 1965; children: Hillary, Charles. BSEE, CCNY, 1965; MSEE, NYU, 1967, PhDEE, 1969. Asst. project engr. Bendix Corp., 1965-66, sr. project engr., 1967-69; project engr. Gen. Precision, 1966-67; tech. staff MITRE Corp., McLean, Va., 1969-71, group leader, 1971-74, dept. head, 1974-79; dir. spl. studies MITRE Corp., Bedford, Mass., 1979-80, tech. dir., 1980-84, v.p. strategic programs, 1984-85, v.p. programs, 1985-86, sr. v.p., gen. mgr., 1986, group v.p., gen. mgr., 1986-87, exec. v.p., chief oper. officer, also dir.; now chmn., CEO Concept Five Tech, McLean, 1996—; cons. sci. adv. bd. USAF, Pentagon, Washington, 1982—, Def. Sc. Bd., Pentagon, 1988—. Contbr. articles to profl. jours. Mem. IEEE, AIAA, Armed Forces Communications and Electronics Assn. (pres. 1987-88, pres.-elect 1990, Gold medal for Engring. 1990), Ctr. Sci. and Internat. Affairs., Eta Kappa Nu, Tau Beta Pi. Avocation: musician. Home: 9900 Windy Hollow Rd Great Falls VA 22066-3549 Office: Concept Five Tech 7525 Colshire Dr Mc Lean VA 22102-7508*

HOROWITZ, BEN, medical center executive; b. Bklyn., Mar. 19, 1914; s. Saul and Sonia (Meringoff) H.; m. Beverly Lichtman, Feb. 14, 1952; children: Zachary, Jody. BA, Bklyn. Coll., 1940; LLB, St. Lawrence U., 1940; postgrad. New Sch. Social Rsch., 1942. Bar: N.Y. 1941. Dir. N.Y. Fedn. Jewish Philanthropies, 1940-45; assoc., ea. regional dir. City of Hope, 1945-50, nat. exec. sec., 1950-53, exec. dir., 1953-85, gen. v.p., bd. dirs., 1985—, bd. dirs. nat. med. ctr., 1980—; bd. dirs. Beckman Rsch. Inst., 1980—. Mem. Gov.'s Task Force on Flood Relief, 1969-74. Bd. dirs., v.p. Hope for Hearing Found., UCLA, 1972-96; bd. dirs. Forte Found., 1987-92, Ch. Temple Housing Corp., 1988-93, Leo Baeck Temple, 1964-67, 86-89, Westwood Property Owners Assn., 1991—. Recipient Spirit of Life award, 1970, Gallery of Achievement award, 1974, Profl. of Yr. award So. Calif. chpt. Nat. Soc. Fundraisers, 1977; Ben Horowitz chair in rsch. established at City of Hope, 1981. City street named in his honor, 1986. Jewish. Formulated the role of City of Hope as pilot ctr. in medicine, sci., and humanitarianism, 1959. Home: 221 Conway Ave Los Angeles CA 90024-2601 Office: City of Hope 208 W 8th St Los Angeles CA 90014-3208

HOROWITZ, CAROLE SPIEGEL, interior designer; b. Pitts., Mar. 24, 1940; d. Alvin Duane and Leah (Greenstein) Spiegel; m. Don Roy Horowitz, Jan. 31, 1960; children: Cindy H. Urbach, Thomas Samuel. Student, Carnegie Mellon U., 1958-61. Cert. interior horticulturist, landscape profl. Owner Carole Horowitz Interior Design, Pitts., 1965-72; pres. Plantscape, Inc., Pitts., 1973—. Chmn. U. Pitts. Small Bus. Com., 1986-92; bd. dirs. United Way Allegheny County, Pitts., 1991-94, Jr. Achievment Allegheny County, Pitts., 1985-95, Vocat. Rehab. Ctr., Pitts., 1989-91. Recipient Nat. Landscape award White House and Am. Assn. Nurseryman, 1990, YWCA Entrepreneur Leadership award, 1990; named Entreprenuer of Yr. Ernst & Young & Inc. Mag., 1988, Pa.'s Best 50 Women in Bus. award 1997. Mem. Interior Plantscape Assn. (sec., v.p., 1982-85), Associated Landscape Contractor of Am. (cert.), Internat. Facility Mgmt. Assn., Rivers Club, Pitts., Westmoreland Country Club, Export, Pa., Rotary (sec. Downtown Pitts. chpt.). Jewish. Avocations: travel, golf. Office: Plantscape Inc 3101 Liberty Ave Pittsburgh PA 15201-1400

HOROWITZ, DAVID CHARLES, consumer commentator, newspaper columnist; b. Bronx, N.Y., June 30, 1937; s. Marcus Lazar and Dorothy (Lippman) H.; m. Suzanne E. McCambridge, Aug. 26, 1972; 2 daus. BA, Bradley U., 1959; MS in Journalism, Northwestern U., 1961; CBS fellow, Columbia U., 1962-63. Editor in chief Tazewell County (Ill.) Newpaper, 1956; reporter Peoria (Ill.) Jour. Star, 1957-60, Lerner Newspapers and Chgo. City News Bur., 1959-60; newscaster Sta. KCCI Radio-TV, Des Moines, 1960-62; newswriter-producer ABC Radio Network, N.Y.C., 1963; Far East corr. NBC News, 1963-64; pub. affairs dir. Sta. WMCA, N.Y.C., 1964-66; corr., edn. editor, consumer commentator NBC News, Los Angeles, 1966-92; consumer affairs specialist CBS (KCBS-TV) News, 1993-96; syndicated columnist Creators Syndicate, L.A.; creator, host, exec. producer syndicated TV show Fight Back! with David Horowitz, L.A., 1977-92; pres. Fight Back! Found. For Consumer Edn.; syndicated commentator Fight Back! Radio Reports, 1989—; commentator Sta. CNBC, 1990-96. Author: Fight Back and Don't Get Ripped Off, 1979, Business of Business, 1989, Fight Back! For Your Medical Health, vols. 1-4, 1993, Fight Back at Work, 1994; host, exec. prodr. Best Defense, 1993; exec. prodr. Fight Back at Work, 1994, CBS-TV Spl. Frog Girl: The Jenifer Graham Story (Genesis Animal Rights award 1990). Patron Los Angeles County Art Mus.; bd. dirs. Nat. Broadcast Editorial Conf., Am. Cancer Soc.; bd. advisers Los Angeles Jewish Home for Aged, Calif. div. Am. Cancer Soc.; adv. bd. Am. Heart Assn. Los Angeles County, UCLA Publs.; adv. bd. to Los Angeles County Dist. Atty.; bd. dirs. City of Hope; founder, bd. dirs. Fight Back! Found.; mem. charitable adv. com. City of L.A., 1991—; hon. mayor Brentwood Cmty., L.A., 1991-98. With USNR, 1954-62. Recipient Los Angeles City and County citation for pub. svc., 1979, 80, 81, 82, 83, 89, 92, Calif. State Legislature pub. svc. citation, 1980, 81, 82, 83, 91, 92, Spirit of Life award City of Hope, 1979, 1983, Chief U.S. Postal Insp.'s award, 1981, 93, Emmy awards for consumer reporting NATAS, 1974, 76-77, 81-86, 89, 90-95, L.A. Press Club award for consumer reporting, 1991, News Reporting award UPI, 1983, 94, Pub. Svc. award Social Security Adminstrn., 1987, medals N.Y. Internat. Film and TV Festival, 1984-86, Golden Mike award, 1986, 94, Armed Forces TV Network Svcs. award, 1988, Toastmasters Internat. Leadership award, 1991, Community Svc. award SBA, 1991, Excellence in Journalism award Nat. Homecare Assn., 1992, Disting. Alumni award Northwestern U., 1994, Cmty. Svc. award UCLA Ctr. Aging, 1995, AP News Reporting award, 1995, Angel award Excellence in Media, 1998, Golden Halo award Motion Picture Coun. So. Calif., 1998, Quality of Life award Proctor Health Care Found., 1998, Lifetime Achievement award Kern County Law Enforcement Found., 1999; named to Journalism Hall of Achievement, Northwestern U., 1997, L.A. Press Club Best TV Feature Reporting award, 1997. Mem. ASCAP, AFTRA, SAG, BMI, Am. Assn. Travel Agts. (Travelers Adv. award 1991), Broadcast Music, Inc., Internat. Radio-TV Soc., Radio-TV News Dirs. Assn., The Guardians, Soc. Consumer Affairs Profls., Nat. Futures Assn. (adv. bd.), Child Passenger Safety Assn., Ill. Broadcasters Assn. (Disting. Svc. award 1986), Screen Actors Guild, Newspaper Feature Creator's Assn., Writers Guild Am., Medill Journalism Sch. Alumni Assn. (pres. 1990-98), Friars Club, Overseas Press Am. Club (N.Y.C.), Alpha Epsilon Pi, Sigma Delta Chi, Phi Delta Kappa, Omicron Delta Kappa. Avocations: writing, gardening, theater, collecting serious music, collecting contemporary art. Home: PO Box 49915 Los Angeles CA 90049-0915 *Life is full of compromise, but to compromise principle is to give up your self-respect. I don't want anyone to take me for a sucker, and I don't like to see anyone else taken, either. A lot of things are unfair in life. It's tough; that's the way it is. But, by heaven, if you can do something about it, do it.*

HOROWITZ, DON ROY, landscape company executive; b. Pitts., Mar. 12, 1930; s. Samuel and Clara (Aberman) H.; m. Carole Spiegel, Jan. 29, 1960; children—Cindy Urbach, Thomas. B.S., U. Pitts., 1952. Editor Pitts. Spectator mag., 1951-52; writer Fairchild Publs., 1952-53; pub. relations dir. Dubin. Feldman & Kahn. Inc., 1955-58; pres. Carlton Advt., Pitts., 1959-71, Corp. Communications Counselors, Pitts., 1962-71, Defensive Instruments, Inc., Tulsa, 1968-74; v.p. Defensive Instruments, Inc., 1974-77; pres. Mut. Advt. Agy. Network, Mpls., 1969-70, Homehelp Unlimited, Inc., Pitts., 1969-73, Flashguard, Inc., Pitts., 1971-76, Showrooms-On-Wheels, Inc., 1976-77; v.p. Normda Industries, Inc., San Diego, 1969-72, Ednl. Crime Prevention Programs, Inc., Pitts., 1974-77, Plantscape, Inc., Pitts., 1987-96; bd. dirs., v.p. Lawrenceville Devel. Corp., Pitts.; bd. dirs., tres., Phipps Conservatory, Pitts. Chmn. Plants for Clean Air Coun., Reston, Va., 1988—. Mem. Associated Landscape Contractors Am. (co-chmn., interior plantscape div. 1988-90, chmn. 1992-93). Club: Westmoreland (Pitts.), Rivers (Pitts.). Home: 5464 Darlington Rd Pittsburgh PA 15217-1506 Office: 3101 Liberty Ave Pittsburgh PA 15201-1415

HOROWITZ, DONALD LEONARD, lawyer, educator, researcher, political scientist, arbitrator; b. N.Y.C., June 27, 1939; s. Morris and Yetta (Hibscher) H.; m. Judith Anne Present, Sept. 4, 1960; children: Marshall, Karen, Bruce. AB, Syracuse U., 1959, LLB, 1961; LLM, Harvard U., 1962, AM, 1965, PhD, 1967. Bar: N.Y. 1962, D.C. 1979, U.S. Ct. Appeals (D.C., 6th, 7th and 10th cirs.) 1970, U.S. Supreme Ct. 1969. Law clk. U.S. Dist. Ct. (ea. dist.), Pa., 1965-66; rsch. assoc. Harvard U. Ctr. Internat. Affairs, 1967-69; atty. Dept. Justice, Washington, 1969-71; fellow Coun. on Fgn. Rels./Woodrow Wilson Internat. Ctr. Scholars, Washington, 1971-72; rsch. assoc. Brookings Instn., Washington, 1972-75; sr. fellow Rsch. Inst. on Immigration and Ethnic Studies/Smithsonian, Washington, 1975-81; prof. law and polit. sci. Duke U., Durham, N.C., 1980—; Charles S. Murphy Prof. Duke U., Durham, 1988-93, James B. Duke prof., 1994—; vis. prof. Charles J. Merriam scholar U. Chgo. Law Sch., 1988; vis. fellow Cambridge U., Eng., 1988; Sticerd Disting. Vis. London Sch. Econs., 1998-2000; vis. scholar Universiti Kebangsaan Malaysia Law Faculty, 1991; cons. Ford Found., 1977-82; mem. internat. adv. com. Office of the High Rep., Bosnia, 1998—; McDonald-Currie Meml. lectr. McGill U., Montreal, Que. Can., 1980; mem. Coun. on Role of Cts., 1978-83. Author: The Courts and Social Policy (Nat. Acad. Public Adminstrn. Louis Brownlow prize for best book in pub. adminstrn. 1977), 1977; The Jurocracy: Government Lawyers, Agency Programs and Judicial Decisions, 1977; Coup Theories and Officers' Motives, 1980, Ethnic Groups in Conflict, 1985, A Democratic South Africa? Constitutional Engineering in a Divided Soc., 1991 (Am. Polit. Sci. Assn. Ralph J. Bunche award for best book in ethnic and cultural pluralism, 1992); mem. editl. bd. Ethnicity, 1974-82, Law and Soc. Rev., 1979-82, Law and Contemporary Problems, 1983-84, 89—, Jour. Democracy, 1993—. Guggenheim fellow, 1980-81; Nat. Humanities Ctr. fellow, 1984. Fellow Am. Acad. Arts and Scis. Office: Duke University School Law Durham NC 27706

HOROWITZ, FRANCES DEGEN, academic administrator, psychology educator; b. Bronx, N.Y., May 5, 1932; d. Irving and Elaine (Moinester) Degen; m. Floyd Ross Horowitz, June 23, 1953; children: Jason Degen, Benjamin Meyer. BA, Antioch Coll., 1954; EdM, Goucher Coll., 1954; PhD, U. Iowa, 1959. Tchr. elem. sch. Iowa City, 1954-56; grad. rsch. asst. Iowa Child Welfare Sta., U. Iowa, 1956-59; asst. prof. psychology So. Oreg. Coll., Ashland, 1959-61; asst. prof. home econs. U. Kans., Lawrence, 1961-62, USHPS rsch. fellow, 1962-63, assoc. prof. dept. human devel. and family life, 1964-69, prof. dept. human devel. and family life, psychology, 1969—, chmn. dept., 1969-75, rsch. assoc., 1964-75, assoc. dean, 1975-78, vice chancellor rsch., grad. studies and pub. svc., also dean grad. sch., 1978-91, dir. Infant Rsch. Lab., 1964-91; pres. Grad. Sch. and Univ. Ctr. CUNY, 1991—; bd. dirs. Feminist Press; guest rsch. assoc. Bur. Child Rsch. U. Kans., and Parsons (Kans.) State Hosp. and Tng. Ctr., summer 1960; vis. prof. dept. psychology Tel Aviv U., 1973-74; guest rschr. dept. pediat. Kaplan Hosp., Rehovot, Israel, 1973-74; vis. lectr. dept. psychology Hebrew U., Jerusalem, 1976, cons. rsch. programs in early edn., 1980—; pres. Ctr. for Rsch., Inc., Lawrence, 1978-91; cons. OAS, 1971, U.S. Office Edn., 1969-73, NIMH, 1979; cons. to early infant stimulation program, Caracas, Venezuela, 1976; lectr. infant devel., day care to local and regional cmty. groups, 1966—; mem. adv. com. Carolina Inst. on Early Edn. of the Handicapped, 1978-83; reviewer NSF, 1978-91; mem. U. Kans. del. to Peoples Republic China, 1980; guest lectr. various profl. groups, univs., 1964—; exch. scholar Chinese Acad. Scis., People's Republic China, 1982; mem. Office Sci. Integrity Rev. Adv. Com. PHS, 1991-93; nominating com. Weizmann Women in Sci. award Am. Com. Weizmann Inst. Sci., 1994; mem. Nat. Task Force Grad. Edn., 1994—; mem. workforce devel. subcom. N.Y.C. Partnership, 1994—; mem. U.S. Nat. Com. for the Internat. Union of Psychol. Sci., 1995-97; mem. overseers' com. to visit dept. psychiatry Harvard U.; mem., founding adv. bd. Sackler Inst. for Human Brain Devel.; bd. dirs. Nat. Coun. for Rsch. on Women. Co-editor science watch sect. Am. Psychologist, 1993—; mem. editorial bd. Jour. Devel. Psychology, 1969-75, Early Childhood Edn. Quar., 1974—, Devel. Rev., 1981—, Infant Behaviour & Development, 1984—; contbr. articles to profl. jours. Trustee Antioch Coll., 1987-91, L.I. Univ., 1992—; bd. dirs. Cmty. Children's Ctr., 1965-68, Douglas County Vis. Nurse Assn., 1968-69; mem. workforce devel. subcom., N.Y.C. Partnership; mem. coun. advisors, Nat. Ctr. for Children in Poverty; mem. commn. on women in higher edn. Am. Coun. on Edn. Recipient Trustees award medal Cherry Lawn Sch., Conn., 1971, Outstanding Educator of Am. award, 1973, Disting. Psychologist in Mgmt. award Soc. for Psychologists in Mgmt., 1993; named to Women's Hall of Fame U. Kans., 1974; Ford Found. fellow, 1954, Ctr. for Advanced Studies Behavioral Scis. fellow, Stanford U., 1983-84. recipient Rebecca Rice Alumni award Antioch Coll., 1996. Fellow APA (mem. divsn. devel. psychology, pres. divsn. devel. psychology 1977-78, mem. publs. bd. 1985-91, chief sci. adviser 1989-93, pres. 1991-94, Centennial award 1992, pres. 1991-94), AAAS; mem. Soc. Rsch. in Child Devel. (editor monographs 1976-83, pres. 1997—), Am. Assn. on Mental Deficiency, North Ctrl. Accrediting Assn. (bd. commrs. 1977-80), Am. Psychol. Found. (pres. 1991-94), Coun. Rsch. Polic and Grad. Edn. (chair, mem. exec. com.), Assn. Grad. Schs. (mem. exec. com.), N.Y. Women's Forum (bd. dirs. 1995—), Nat. Assn. of State Univs. and Lnd-Grant Colls. (chair commn. on human resources and social change, bd. dirs. 1999—), Sigma Xi, Phi Beta Kappa (hon.). Home: 145 Central Park W Apt 4A New York NY 10023-2004 Office: CUNY Grad Sch and U Ctr 365 5th Ave New York NY 10016-4309

HOROWITZ, FRED LEE, dentist, administrator, consultant; b. Chgo., June 10, 1954; s. Jacob and Celia (Morgenstern) H. BA, Washington U., St. Louis, 1976, DMD, 1979; cert. of residency, Sinai Hosp. Detroit, 1980. Gen. practice dentistry Chgo., 1981-92; chief dental cons. Charter Barclay Hosp., Chgo., 1985-89; mem. med. teaching staff Ravenswood Hosp., Chgo., 1983-92, Michael Reese Hosp., Chgo., 1984-90; mem. med. staff St. Francis Hosp., Evanston, 1987-91; exec. v.p. Dental Benefit Providers, Bethesda, Md., 1995-97; pres. Affiliated Network Svcs., Chgo., 1998—; pres., CEO, TDC, Chgo. and St. Louis, 1987-94; v.p. Employers Health Ins. Co., Green Bay, Wis., 1995; cons. Humana HMO, 1992-94; trustee Coun. on Dental Benefit Processing Stds., 1992; CEO The Amherst Group, Ltd., 1993-94; bd. dirs. The Morgen Group, Chgo.; chmn. bd. trustees Dental Benefit Svcs. Ill., 1997; chmn. Affiliated Network Svcs., LLC, 1998-99. Contbg. author: EDI Primer for the Dental Office, 1995, The Managed Healthcare Handbook, 1996; contbr. articles to Ravenswood Hosp. publs. Treas. Chgo. Homes of Dearborn Park, 1998; chmn. bd. dirs. NADP Found., Dallas, 1997—; trustee Congregation Kol Ami, Chgo., 1998. Recipient Gabryl award Nat. Assn. Dental Plans, 1998. Mem. ADA, Health Ins. Assn. of Am. (dental rels com. 1995-96), Acad. Gen. Dentistry, Chgo. Dental Soc., Nat. Assn. Prepaid Dental Plans (bd. dirs., treas. 1994, vice-chair 1995, chmn. pub. rels. commn. 1996, chmn. found. 1996-99), No. Ill. Practice Assn. (dir. 1998—), Ill. Ambs., Alpha Omega (Leadership award 1979). Office: Affil Network Svcs 211 W Wacker Dr Ste 1100 Chicago IL 60606

HOROWITZ, GAYLE LYNN, physical education educator; b. Flushing, N.Y., Apr. 29, 1971; d. Robert and Ruth Lois (Brokowsky) H.; m. Chris Topping, Dec. 25, 1993. BS in Physical Edn., Queens Coll., 1993; MS in Physical Edn., Hofstra U., 1993. Lic. tchr. N.Y.C., N.Y.; certified profl. tennis instr., U.S. Nat. Tennis Acad. Teaching asst. Queens Coll., Flushing, N.Y., 1990; team sports activites splst. Pub. Sch. 219, Flushing, 1990-91; health phys. edn. tchr. Franklin K. Lanc HS, Bklyn., 1993-95, William C. Bryant H.S., Queens, 1995-96, John Bowne H.S., Queens, 1996—; asst. jr. varsity volleyball coach John Bowne HS, Flushing, 1991; guest lectr. circus arts Hofstra U., 1993—, AIDS edn. Franklin K. Lane HS, 1994—. Auxiliary police officer, N.Y.C. Police Dept., Queens, 1988-92; faculty co-advisor Bisexual, Gay, Lesbian Student Union. Mem. United Federation Tchrs., Kissena Cycling Club (sec.). Democrat. Avocations: judo, bicycling, aikido, weight training. Office: John Bowne HS 63-25 Main St Flushing NY 11367

HOROWITZ, GEDALE BOB, investment banker; b. N.Y.C., June 13, 1932; s. Abraham and Florence (Bob) H.; m. Barbara Silver, Aug. 17, 1958; children: Ruth Ellen, Seth Robert. A.B., Columbia U., 1953, J.D., 1955. Bar: N.Y. 1956. With Salomon Bros., N.Y.C., 1955-67, gen. ptnr., 1967-81, mng. dir., 1981-87; exec. v.p., dir. Salomon, Inc., N.Y.C., 1981-97; sr. mng. dir. Salomon Smith Barney, 1997—. Vice chmn. bd. trustees Barnard Coll., 1976—; trustee and vice chmn. L.I. Jewish Hosp., 1982-98, chhmn., 1995-98; dir. Mspl. Assistance Corp., City of N.Y., 1989-94; bd. dirs. Jewish Cmty. Rels. Coun. on N.Y., Inc., 1989—, pres., 1998—; bd. dirs. Statue of Liberty-Ellis Island Found., Inc., 1999—; chmn. N.Y. State Local Govt. Assistance Corp., 1991-94; trustee, chmn. emeritus, exec. com. mem. North Shore/L.I. Jewish Health Sys., 1998—. Served with U.S. Army, 1956-58. Mem. Bond Market Assn. (chm. 1978-79), Securities Industry Assn. (treas. 19 87, chmn. 1991), Mcpl. Securities Rulemaking Bd. (chmn. 1977-78), Mcpl. Bond Club N.Y. (pres. 1982-83), The Bond Club of N.Y., Inc. (pres. 1994-95). Office: Salomon Smith Barney 7 World Trade Ctr Fl 46 New York NY 10048-4697

HOROWITZ, HAROLD, architect; b. Chgo., Sept. 6, 1927; s. Samuel and Anna (Miller) H.; m. Clara Marie Stastny Bentz, Sept. 1, 1950 (dec. Aug. 1996). B.A. in Architecture, Ill. Inst. Tech., 1950; M.Arch., Mass. Inst. Tech., 1951. Registered architect, Md. Research architect Bldg. Research Labs., S.W. Research Inst., Princeton, N.J., 1953-55; tech. dir. Bldg. Research Inst., Nat. Acad. Scis.-NRC, Washington, 1955-63; supervisory architect NSF, Washington, 1963-75; program mgr. div. advanced tech. applications NSF, 1972, program mgr., div. advanced energy research and tech., 1973-75; program mgr. div. solar research Energy Research and Devel. Agy., 1975; dir. research Nat. Endowment for Arts, 1975-88; ind. cons., 1988—; mem. UNESCO Working Group on Cultural Stats., 1979-85; mem. adv. com. State of the Arts Report to Congress, 1988; mem. program com. Internat. Conf. on Cultural Econs. and Planning, 1984, 86, 88, 90, lectr., cons. in field. Author: The American Jazz Music Audience, 1986, Status of Artists in the U.S.A., 1992, UNESCO Report on the Conditions of American Artists, 1993; co-editor: Paying for the Arts, 1987. Served with AUS, 1946-48. Recipient nat. and internat. awards. Mem. AIA (emeritus, rsch. com. 1965-70), Internat. Inst. for Audio-Visual Comm. and Cultural Devel. (extraordinary mem.), Assn. Higher Edn. Facilities Officers (hon.), Washington Print Club Inc. (bd. dirs. 1988-92, editl. com. 1990—). Home: 4 Barkwood Ct Rockville MD 20853-2308

HOROWITZ, HARRY I., podiatrist; b. Astoria, N.Y., Nov. 8, 1915; s. Jacob and Fannie (Singer) H.; m. Sylvia Glaser, Feb. 11, 1940; children: Marc, Susan. Student, CCNY, 1932-34; Pod.G, First Inst. Podiatry, N.Y.C., 1937; D in Podiatry, L.I.U., 1946; D.P.M., N.Y. Coll. Podiatric Medicine, 1967; LHD (hon.), 1982. Diplomate Am. Bd. Ambulatory Foot Surgery (hon.). Pvt. practice specializing in podiatry Astoria, N.Y., 1937-76, Belleair, Fla., 1976-95; ret., 1995; mem. podiatry practice com. Workmen's Compensation Bd. N.Y. State, 1953-66, chmn. com., 1966-76; dir. Foot Clinics of N.Y., 1970-71; chmn. bd. Suncoast Orthotic Labs., Clearwater, Fla., 1978-83; podiatry panel Dept. Welfare N.Y.C.; arbitrator between Am. Bd. Foot Surgery and Am. Bd. Ambulatory Foot Surgery, 1982; cons. Sch. Podiatric Medicine Barry U., 1988-89. With citizens com. Union Free Sch. Dist. 29, Merrick, N.Y., 1957; mem. library com. dist. 29, 1964; founder Fund for Advancement Podiatry Edn., 1958; hon. pres. Fund for Podiatry Edn. and Rsch., 1963-94, sec., 1963-66; chmn. Task Force on Podiatry, Health and Hosp. Corp., N.Y.C., 1976-78; trustee N.Y. Coll. Podiatric medicine, 1973-74, cons., 1981-84; chmn. Commn. to Study and Evaluate Foot Clinics of N.Y., 1980-81; chmn. ADL, Clearwater Lodge, 1985-87, B'nai Brith, Fla. vol. tutor North Sch. Pinellas County Schs., Fla., 1987-98. With U.S. maritime Svc., 1943-45. Recipient award Jour. Podiatry, 1948, Apple from the Tchr. award Pinellas Classroom Tchrs., 1989, 90; Podiatrist of Year Queens County Podiatry Soc., 1956, 71, Podiatry Soc. State N.Y., 1957, 61, testimonial N.Y. Coll. Podiatric Medicine, 1971; named Disting Practitioner, Nat. Acads. Practice, 1992. Mem. APHA, Am. Civil Liberies Union, Am. Podiatric Med. Assn. (exec. coun., trustee 1955-62, award 1963, Disting. Svc. award 1982, Spl. Svc. award 1983), Am. Assn. Hosp. Podiatrists, Fla. Pub. Health Assn. (chmn. podiatric sect. 1983-85), Acad. Podiatry, Physicians for Social Responsibility, Nat. Peace Found. Clubs: Masons, B'nai B'rith (outstanding svc. award 1988). Home: 100 Oakmont Ln Clearwater FL 33756-1984

HOROWITZ, HERBERT EUGENE, educator, consultant, former ambassador; b. Bklyn., July 10, 1930; s. Max and Jean (Pomerantz) H.; m. Lenore Joan Glasser, Jan. 6, 1963; children: Jason, Richard. B.A., Bklyn. Coll., 1952; M.A., Columbia U., 1964, Fletcher Sch. Law & Diplomacy, 1965; diploma, Nat. War Coll., 1972. Econ. officer Am. Embassy, Taipei, Taiwan, 1957-62; chief China econ. unit U.S. Consulate, Hong Kong, 1965-69; chief comml. and econ. sect. U.S. Liaison Office, Beijing, 1973-75; dir. Office for Rsch. of East Asia Dept. State, Washington, 1975-78; dir. Office East-West Econ. Policy Dept. Treasury, Washington, 1979-80; consul gen. U.S. Consulate Gen., Sydney, Australia, 1981-84; dep. chief of mission U.S. Embassy, Beijing, Peoples Republic of China, 1984-86; amb. to Republic of Gambia, 1986-89; cons. Washington, 1990—; lectr. George Mason U. Mem. Am. Fgn. Svc. Assn., Dacor-Bacon House. Home and Office: 2737 Devonshire Pl NW # 111 Washington DC 20008-3454

HOROWITZ, IRA R., gynecologic oncologist; b. Bklyn., Dec. 17, 1954; s. Benjamin and Frieda Horowitz; m. Julie A. Wood; children: Andrea, Rebecah. BA in Biology, U. Rochester, 1976; MD, Baylor U., 1980. Diplomate Am. Bd. Ob/Gyn. Resident to chief resident Baylor Coll. Medicine, Houston, 1980-84; gynecologic oncology fellow Johns Hopkins Med. Inst., Balt., 1985-87; clin. instr. ob-gyn. Baylor Coll. Medicine, 1984-85; instr. ob-gyn. Johns Hopkins U. Sch. Med., 1985-87, asst. prof. ob-gyn., oncology, 1987-92; assoc. prof. ob-gyn. Emory U. Sch. Medicine, Atlanta, 1992—, Emory U. Sch. Medicine, Winship Cancer Ctr., Atlanta, 1993—; asst. prof. Emory U. Sch. Medicine, Ctr. Clin. Evaluation, Atlanta, 1995—. Co-editor: Plantao em ginecologia e obstetricia, 1995, Obstetrics & Gynecology On Call, 1st edit., 1993, Advances in Obstetrics and Gynecology, vol. 3, 1996, Advances in Obstetrics & Gynecology, vol. 4, 1997. Fellow ACOG, ACS, Internat. Soc. Study Vulvovaginal Disease; mem. Soc. Gynecologic Oncologists, Soc. Gynecologic Surgeons, Soc. Surg. Oncology. Avocations: camping, travel. Office: Emory U Sch Medicine GYN/OB 1639 Pierce Dr Atlanta GA 30322

HOROWITZ, IRVING LOUIS, publisher, educator; b. N.Y.C., Sept. 25, 1929; s. Louis and Esther (Tepper) H.; m. Ruth Lenore Horowitz, 1950 (div. 1964); children: Carl Frederick, David Dennis; m. Mary Curtis Horowitz, 1979. BSS, CCNY, 1951; MA, Columbia U., 1952; PhD, Buenos Aires U., 1957; fellow, Brandeis U., 1958-59. Asst. prof. sociology Bard Coll., 1960; assoc. prof. social theory Buenos Aires U., 1955-58; chmn. dept. sociology Hobart and William Smith Colls., 1960-63; from assoc. prof. to prof. sociology Washington U., St. Louis, 1963-69; chmn. dept. sociology Livingston Coll., Rutgers U., 1969-73; prof. sociology grad. faculty Rutgers U., 1969—, Hannah Arendt prof. social and polit. theory, 1979—, Bacardi chair Cuban studies, 1992—; vis. prof. sociology U. Caracas, Venezuela, 1957, Buenos Aires U., 1959, 61, 63, SUNY, Buffalo, 1960, Syracuse U., 1961, U. Rochester, fall 1962, U. Calif., Davis, 1966, U. Wis., Madison, 1967, Stanford U., 1968-69, Am. U., 1972, Queen's U., Can., 1973, Princeton U., 1976, U. Miami, 1992; vis. lectr. London Sch. Econs. and Polit. Sci., 1962; prin. investigator for numerous sci. and rsch. projects; chmn. bd. dirs., editor-in-chief Transaction/Soc. Author: Idea of War and Peace in Contemporary Philosophy, 1957, Philosophy, Science and the Sociology of Knowledge, 1960, Radicalism and the Revolt Against Reason: The Social Theories of Georges Sorel, 2d edit., 1968, The war Game: Studies of the New Civilian Militarists, 1963, Historia y Elementos de la Sociologia del Conocimiento, 1963, Professing Sociology: The Life Cycle of a Social Science,

1963, The New Sociology: Essays in Social Science and Social Values in Honor of C. Wright Mills, 1964, Revolution in Brazil: Politics and Society in a Developing Nation, 1964, The Rise and Fall of Project Camelot, 1967, rev. edit., 1976, Three Worlds of Development: The Theory and Practice of International Stratification, 1966, rev. edit., 1972, Latin American Radicalism: A Documentary Report on Nationalist and Left Movements, 1969, Sociological Self-Images, 1969, The Knowledge Factory: Masses in Latin America, 1970, Cuban Communism, 1970, 9th edit., 1998, Foundations of Political Sociology, 1972, Social Science and Public Policy in the United States, 1977, Dialogues on American Politics, 1979, Taking Lives: Genocide and State Power, 1979, 4th edit., 1996, Beyond Empire and Revolution, 1982, C. Wright Mills: An American Utopian, 1983, Winners and Losers, 1985, Communicating Ideas, 1987, Daydreams and Nightmares, 1990 (winner best biography Nat. Jewish Book Award), The Decomposition of Sociology, 1993, Behemoth: Main Currents in the History and Theory of Political Sociology, 1999. Chmn. bd. Hubert H. Humphrey Inst. Ben Gurion U. Recipient Harold D. Lasswell award Policy Sci. Orgn. Fellow AAAS; mem. AAUP, USIA (bd. advisors), Am. Polit. Sci. Assn., Nat. Assn. Scholars (bd. dirs.), Authors Guild, Ctr. for Study The Presidency, Coun. Fgn. Rels., Internat. Soc. Polit. Psychology (founder), Soc. Internat. Devel., U.S. Gen. Acctg. Office (exec. adv. bd.), U.S. Info. Agy. (exec. adv. bd. Radio and TV Marti), Nat. Assn. Scholars (bd. dirs.), Inst. for a Free Cuba. Subject of Festschrift: The Democratic Imagination, 1994. E-mail: ihorowitz@www.transactionpub.com. Fax #: (732) 445-3138. Home: 1247 State Rd # Rt206 Princeton NJ 08540-1619 Office: Rutgers U Transaction Pubs Bldg 4051 New Brunswick NJ 08903

HOROWITZ, ISAAC M., control research consultant, writer; b. Safed, Galilee, Israel, Dec. 15, 1920; Came to U.S., 1951; s. Yeshayahu Y. Horowitz and Feige Loberboim; m. Chana Shankman, Sept. 15, 1945 (div. Dec. 1984); children: Sharon, Ruth, David, Dafna; m. Gloria T. August, Dec. 24, 1984; children: Matanya, Benyakir. BSc with honors, U. Man., Can., 1944; BEE, MIT, 1948; MEE, Poly. Inst. N.Y., 1953, DEE, 1956. Design engr. Taller & Cooper, Bklyn., 1948; electronic engr. Israel Def. Army, Haifa, 1948-50, Halross Instruments, Winnipeg, Can., 1950-51; from instr. to asst. prof. Poly. Inst. Bklyn., 1951-58; sr. staff Hughes Res. Labs., Malibu, Calif., 1958-62; sr. scientist Hughes Aircraft Co., Culver City, Calif., 1962-67; prof. U. Colo., Boulder, 1967-85, U. Calif., Davis, 1985-91; cons. and writer Boulder, 1991—; cons. Israel Aircraft Co., Lod, 1969-72, Flight Dynamics Lab., WPAFB, Dayton, Ohio, 1983-92, Sandia Nat. Labs., Livermore, Calif., 1991—; Prof. Cohen Chair, Weizmann Inst. Sci., Rehovot, Israel, 1969-85; dist. vis. prof. Air Force Inst. Tech., WPAFB, 1983-92. Author: Synthesis of Feedback Systems, 1963, Quantitative Feedback Design Theory, 1993. Recipient Best Paper award Nat. Electronics Conf., 1956, Rufus Oldenberger medal ASME, 1992; rsch. grantee NASA, NSF, AFOSR, 1967-91. Fellow Internat. Elec. and Electronics Engrs. Republican. Hebrew. Achievements include patents in magnetic amplifiers, phase-locked loop; founder and developer of quantitative feedback theory (QFT). Home: 660 S Monaco Pky Denver CO 80224-1229*

HOROWITZ, JACK, biochemistry educator; b. Vienna, Austria, Nov. 25, 1931; came to U.S., 1938; s. Joseph and Florence (Gutterman) H.; m. Carole Ann Sager, June 11, 1961; children—Michael Joseph, Jeffrey Frederick. B.S., CCNY, 1952; Ph.D., Ind. U., 1957. Rsch. assoc. Columbia U., N.Y.C., 1957-61; asst. prof. biochemistry Iowa State U., Ames, 1961-65, assoc. prof. biochemistry, 1965-71, prof. biochemistry, 1971-95, univ. prof., 1995—, chmn. dept. biochemistry, 1971-74, chmn. molecular, cellular and devel. biology program, 1977-80; vis. scholar Rockefeller U., N.Y.C., 1968; vis. prof. Yale U., 1974-75; vis. scientist MIT, 1990-91; program dir. biophysics and biochemistry NSF, 1993-94. Contbr. articles to profl. jours. NSF fellow, 1952-54, 57-59; NIH and NSF grantee, 1961—; recipient faculty citation Iowa State U., 1989. Mem. RNA Soc., Am. Soc. Biochemistry and Molecular Biology, AAAS, Phi Beta Kappa, Sigma Xi, Phi Kappa Phi. Jewish. Home: 2014 Country Club Blvd Ames IA 50014-7013 Office: Iowa State U Dept Biochemistry Bioph Ames IA 50011

HOROWITZ, KENNETH A., communications executive, entrepreneur. AB cum laude, Cornell U., 1973. One of original founders Cellular One; lead investor S. Fla. Soccer, L.L.C., Ft. Lauderdale; owner, operator various cellular phone bus. ventures, U.S.; banking, real estate, comm. and tech. entrepreneur; bd. dirs. pvt. and pub. cos. Achievements include pioneer work in the wireless telephone industry. Fax: 954-733-6105. Office: care Miami Fusion FC 2200 W Commercial Blvd Ste 104 Fort Lauderdale FL 33309-3058*

HOROWITZ, MARY CURTIS See **CURTIS, MARY ELLEN**

HOROWITZ, MICHAEL DORY, cardiothoracic surgeon; b. Dec. 1, 1954. BS, U. Miami, 1977, MD, 1981. Diplomate Am. Bd. Surgery, Am. Bd. Thoracic Surgery. Resident in surgery then surgeon U. Miami/Jackson Meml., 1981-86, 88-92; fellow in thoracic and cardiovascular surgery Alton Ochsner Med. Found., New Orleans, 1986-88; asst. prof. surgery U. Miami, 1988-92; med. dir. cardiac surgery Singing River Hosp., Pascagoula, Miss., 1993—. Office: 4211 Hospital Rd Ste 302 Pascagoula MS 39581

HOROWITZ, MORRIS A., economist; b. Newark, Nov. 19, 1919; s. Samuel and Anna (Litwin) H.; m. Jean Ginsburg, July 12, 1941; children—Ruth, Joel. BA in Econs., NYU, 1940; PhD in Econs., Harvard U., 1954. Mem. faculty Northeastern U., Boston, 1956—, prof. econs., chmn. dept., 1959-90, emeritus prof., 1992—; vice-chmn. Mass. Joint Labor-Mgmt. Com. for Mcpl. Police and Fire, 1980—; ad hoc labor arbitrator, manpower cons. Home: 5 Riedesel Ave Cambridge MA 02138-2211 Office: Northeastern U 5 Riedesel Ave Cambridge MA 02138-2211

HOROWITZ, RAYMOND J., lawyer; b. N.Y.C., May 7, 1916; s. Israel S. and Sadye (Freiman) H.; m. Margaret Goldenberg, Sept. 22, 1940; 1 dau., Judith. A.B., Columbia U., 1936, LL.B., 1939. Bar: N.Y. 1939. Pvt. practice N.Y.C., 1939-41; asst. corp. counsel City of N.Y., 1941-43; assoc. Meyer, Wallach & Silverson, N.Y.C., 1943-46; ptnr. McGoldrick, Dannett, Horowitz & Golub (and predecessors), N.Y.C., 1946-69; former mem., now of counsel firm Graubard, Mollen & Miller (and predecessors), 1969—; cons. Nat. Housing Agy, 1946-47, Office Housing Expediter, 1947, Temporary State Housing Rent Commn., 1950-51. Author: (with others) Building Regulation in New York City, 1944. Chmn. trustees' vis. com. on Am. paintings and sculpture Met. Mus. Art; trustee Archives of Am. Art; commr. Nat. Mus. Am. Art; mem. trustees' coun. Nat. Gallery of Art. Mem. Assn. Bar City N.Y., N.Y. County Lawyers Assn., Phi Beta Kappa. Clubs: Century Assn. Home: 930 5th Ave New York NY 10021-2651 Office: Graubard Mollen & Miller 600 3rd Ave New York NY 10016-1901

HOROWITZ, SAMUEL BORIS, biomedical researcher, educational consultant; b. Perth Amboy, N.J., Aug. 26, 1927; s. Sol and Lillian (Levine) H.; m. Joan Hughes, June 15, 1956 (div. 1971); m. Marian Sylvia Herman, May 23, 1973 (div. 1986); 1 child, Ann Julia. A.B., Hunter Coll., N.Y.C., 1951; Ph.D., U. Chgo., 1956. Research assoc. Eastern Pa. Psychiat. Inst., Phila., 1958-62; vis. investigator Inst. Physiol. and Med. Biophysics U. Uppsala, Sweden, 1962-63; head lab. A. Einstein Med. Ctr., Phila., 1963-72; chief cellular physiology lab. Mich. Cancer Found., Detroit, 1972-93, chmn. dept. biology, 1975-78, chmn. dept. physiology and biophysics, 1981-93. Contbr. articles to profl. jours. Served with U.S. Army, 1946-47. Fellow AAAS; mem. Am. Assn. Cancer Research, Am. Soc. Cell Biology, Sigma Xi. Home and Office: 4159 Woodland Dr Ann Arbor MI 48103-9775

HOROWITZ, STANLEY H., electrical engineer. Cons. Electrical Power Systems. Editor Computer Applications Mag. Mem. Nat. Acad. Engrs. Home: 3143 Griggsview Ct Columbus OH 43221-4612*

HOROWITZ, WINONA LAURA See **RYDER, WINONA**

HOROWITZ, ZACHARY I., entertainment company executive; b. N.Y.C., Apr. 27, 1953; s. Ben and Beverly (Lichtman) H.; m. Barbara J. Natterson; children: Jennifer Lily, Charles Samuel. BA summa cum laude, Claremont Mens Coll., 1975; JD, Stanford U., 1978. Bar: Calif. 1978. Assoc. Kaplan, Livingston, Goodwin, Berkowitz & Selvin, Beverly Hills, Calif., 1978; from sr. atty. to dir. bus. affairs West Coast CBS Records, L.A., 1978-83; v.p. bus. and legal affairs MCA Records, Universal City, Calif., 1983-84, sr. v.p. bus. and legal affairs, 1984-88; from sr. v.p. bus. and legal affairs to COO Universal Music Group, Universal City, 1986-95, pres., 1995-98, pres., COO, 1999—; bd. dirs. Universal Victor Japan; mem. op. com. Motown Recording Co., L.A., 1988-93. Mem. bd. editors Stanford Law Rev., 1977-78. Nat. bd. dirs. City of Hope, 1989—, vice chmn. Music Industry chpt., 1985-86, chmn. maj. gifts com., 1986-90, nat. campaign co-chmn., 1990-91, pres., 1991-92, chmn., 1993-94, endowment chair, 1995-97, major gifts choir, 1997—, adv. bd. Nashville Celebrity Baseball Game, 1995—. Mem. NARAS (presdl. adv. com. 1996—), Record Industry Assn. Am. (bd. dirs. 1990—, fin. com. 1993—). Office: Universal Music Group 70 Universal City Plz North Hollywood CA 91608-1011

HORR, WILLIAM HENRY, lawyer; b. Portsmouth, Ohio, Sept. 23, 1914; s. Charles Chick and Effie (Amberg) H.; m. Marjorie Bell Marshall, Aug. 31, 1940; children—Robert W., Thomas M., Catherine, James C., Elizabeth; m. 2d Wilma Crawford, Mar. 12, 1988. A.B., Ohio Wesleyan U., 1936; J.D., U. Cin., 1939. Bar: Ohio 1939. Practice in Portsmouth, 1939-42, 45—; atty. Skelton, Kahl, Horr, Marshall & Burton, 1939-42, 45-78; spl. agt. FBI, Louisville, Indpls., Newark, 1942-45; substitute judge Mcpl. Ct., Portsmouth, 1955-80; gen. counsel Ohio Wesleyan U., 1966-70. Mem. Portsmouth Bd. Edn., 1947- 60; pres. Portsmouth YMCA.; trustee Ohio U. Portsmouth Br., Shawnee State Coll., 1955-80, Ohio Wesleyan U., 1953-68; chmn. bd. Hill View Retirement Ctr., 1973-85. Recipient Disting. Svc. award Portsmouth Jr. C. of C., 1947. Mem. Ohio Bar Assn. (past mem. exec. com.), Portsmouth Bar Assn. (past pres.), Phi Delta Phi, Phi Kappa Psi, Omicron Delta Kappa, Rotary. Republican. Methodist. Home: 1732 Hillview Cir Portsmouth OH 45662-2673 Office: 602 Chillicothe St Ste 206 Portsmouth OH 45662-4066

HORRELL, JEFFREY LANIER, library administrator; b. Carbondale, Ill., Sept. 19, 1952; s. C. William and Ettelye M. (Hanser) H. BA, Miami U., Oxford, Ohio, 1975; AM in Libr. Sci., U. Mich., 1976, MA, 1978; PhD, Syracuse U., 1995. Libr. intern Nat. Gallery of Art, Washington, 1977; asst. libr. art and architecture U. Mich., Ann Arbor, 1977-80; libr. Sherman Art Libr./Dartmouth Coll. Libr., Hanover, N.H., 1981-86; Coun. Libr. Resources libr. mgmt. intern Syracuse (N.Y.) U. Libr., 1986-87, asst. to univ. libr. for planning, 1987-88, asst. univ. libr. pers., budget and planning, 1988-92; libr. Fine Arts Libr. Harvard Coll. Libr., Cambridge, 1992-98; assoc. libr. Harvard Coll. Collections, Cambridge, 1998—; pres. ARLIS/Wash. 1987. Author: Treasures of the Hood Museum of Art, 1985; contbr. articles to profl. publs. Mem. ALA, Coll. Art Assn., Art Libr. Soc. N.Am. (pres. 1987-88), U. Mich. of Info. Studies Alumni Soc. (pres. 1997-98). Avocations: travel, photography. Office: Harvard Coll Libr Rm 193 Widener Library Cambridge MA 02138

HORRELL, KAREN HOLLEY, insurance company executive, lawyer; b. Augusta, Ga., July 10, 1952; d. Dudley Cornelius and Eleanor (Shouppe) Holley; m. Jack E. Horrell, Aug. 14, 1976. B.S., Berry Coll., 1974; J.D., Emory U., 1976. Bar: Ohio 1977, Ga. 1977. Corp. counsel Great Am. Ins. Co., Cin., 1977-80, v.p., gen. counsel, sec., 1981-85, sr. v.p., gen. counsel, sec., bd. dirs., 1985—; pres. corp. svcs. Great Am. Ins. Property & Casualty Group, 1999—; counsel Am. Fin. Corp., 1980-81; gen. counsel numerous subsidiaries Great Ins. Co.; sec., asst. sec. numerous other fin. and ins. cos.; bd. dirs. Tri-Health, Inc., Bethesda, Inc. Trustee Cmty. Chest, 1987-91, Seven Hills Schs., 1991—, v.p., 1995—; mem. cabinet United Appeal, 1984; bd. dirs. YWCA, 1984-90, v.p. fin., 1986-89; mem. Hamilton County Blue Ribbon Task Force on Child Abuse and Neglect Svcs., 1989-91; trustee Ohio Ins. Inst., 1994—, chair 1996-99, Bethesda Hosp. Inc.; chair Ohio Joint Underwriting Assn., 1992-97; trustee Berry Coll., 1999—. Mem. ABA, Cin. Bar Assn. (admissions com. 1978-91, nominating com. 1987-90). Democrat. Home: 2355 Easthill Ave Cincinnati OH 45208-2608 Office: Great Am Ins Co 580 Walnut St Cincinnati OH 45202-3110

HORROCKS, NORMAN, library science educator, editor; b. Manchester, Eng., Oct. 18, 1927; s. Edward Henry and Annie (Barnes) H.; m. Sandra Sheriff, Feb. 3, 1967; children: Julie Carol, Carl Scott, Gina Louise, Anne Patricia, Sarah Helen. FLA, Sch. Librarianship, Manchester, 1950; ALAA, Libr. Assn. Australia, 1957; BA, U. Western Australia, 1960; MLS, U. Pitts., 1964, PhD, 1971. Asst. librarian Manchester pub. libraries, 1943-45, 50-53; librarian Brit. Council, Cyprus, 1954-55; tech. librarian State Library Western Australia, 1956-61; teaching fellow U. Pitts., 1963-64, instr., 1964-69, asst. prof., 1969-71; assoc. prof. Sch. Library Service, Dalhousie U., 1971-73, prof., 1973-86, dir. sch., 1972-86, dean Faculty Mgmt. Studies, 1983-86; adj. prof. Dalhousie U., 1995-98, prof. emeritus, 1999—; v.p. editorial Scarecrow Press, Metuchen, N.J., 1986-95; editl. cons. Scarecrow Press, Lanham, Md., 1995—; vis. lectr. Perth Tech. Coll., 1961-63; ext. lectr. Pa. State Libr., 1966-70; vis. lectr. U. Hawaii, 1969; adj. prof. Rutgers U., 1987-95; chmn. Overseas Book Ctr., Halifax, 1980-83; mem. adv. bd. sci. and tech. info. Nat. Rsch. Coun. Can., 1980-86; mem. adv. bd. com. on bibliog. svcs. Nat. Libr. Can., 1980-86; mem. promotion and distbn. panel Can. Coun. Editor: North Western Newsletter, 1952-53, Jour. Edn. for Librarianship, 1971-76; asso. editor: Govt. Publ. Rev., 1973-81; contbr. articles to profl. jours. Bd. visitors Pratt Inst. Rutgers U. Served with Brit. Army, 1945-48. Recipient merit award Atlantic Provinces Libr. Assn., 1979, Disting. Alumnus award U. Pitts., 1982, Hon. Alumni award Rutgers U., 1995. Fellow The Libr. Assn. (U.K.) (hon.); mem. ALA (coun. 1972-81, 83-95, exec. bd. 1977-81, various coms., Lippincott award 1995), Am. Soc. for Info. Sci. (various coms.), Am. Inst. Parliamentarians, Archons of Colophon (convenor 1992), Can. Libr. Assn. (2d v.p. 1978-80, various coms., Outstanding Svc. to Librarianship award 1995), Halifax Libr. Assn., Can. Coun. Libr. Schs. (chmn. 1974-76), Assn. Libr. and Info. Sci. Edn. (v.p., pres. 1985-86, svc. award 1990, profl. contributions award 1996), Assn. Am. Libr. Schs. (chmn. editl. bd. 1971-76), N.S. Libr. Assn. (life), Australian Libr. and Info. Assn., N.J. Libr. Assn. (Disting. Svc. award coll. and univ. sect. 1995), Bibliosmiles, Intelligence Corps Assn. (life), Progressive Librs. Guild, Beta Phi Mu (pres. 1991-93). Home: 2 Casavechia Ct, Dartmouth, NS Canada B2X 3G6 Office: PO Box 440, Dartmouth, NS Canada B2Y 3Y5

HORSBRUGH, PATRICK, architect, educator, environologist; b. Belfast, No. Ireland, June 21, 1920; came to U.S., 1960; s. Charles Bethune and Marion Rose (McQueen) H. Diploma with honors, Archtl. Assn. Sch. Architecture, 1949; diploma city planning, U. London, 1951. With Raglan, Squire and Ptnrs., London, 1956-57; vis. critic Harvard Grad. Sch. Design, 1956; with depts. architecture, planning and landscape architecture univs. Ill., N.C., 1957-58; dep. dir., then dir. Hamilton-Wentworth (Ont.) Planning Area Bd., 1958-60; vis. prof. architecture U. Nebr., 1960-65, U. Tex., 1965-67; prof. architecture U. Notre Dame, 1967-84, prof. emeritus, dir. grad program environic studies, 1970-80; founder, chmn. bd. Environic Found. Internat., Inc., 1970-94; cons. environ. and planning issues, ednl. and design practices; adj. prof. dept. architecture Andrews U., Mich. Designer: High Paddington Project, London, 1951; co-designer: New Barbican Com. Project, London, 1954; contbr: Winston Churchill Meml. in the U.S. commemorating the Iron Curtain Speech given in Fulton, Mo.; author: High Buildings in the United Kingdom, 1952, Pittsburgh Perceived, The Form, Features and Feasibilities of the Prodigious City, 1963; editor: The Texas Conference on Our Environmental Crisis, 1966. Co-chmn. Internat. Earth Day, 1978; v.p. Channel Tunnel Assn., 1974-94; mem. Ind. curriculum adv. coun. Ind. Bd. Edn., 1986. With Royal Arty., 1938-41; with RAF Vol. Res., 1941-46. Bernard Webb fellow Academica Britannica, Rome, 1950; B.Y. Morrison Meml. lectr. U.S. Dept. Agr., 1969. Fellow AIA (regional and urban design com.), Royal Soc. Arts, Royal Geog. Soc., Brit. Interplanetary Soc.; mem. Royal Inst. Brit. Architects, Royal Town Planning Inst., Am. Planning Assn., Ancient Monument Soc., Soc. Indsl. Archaeology, Soc. Protection Ancient Bldgs, Georgian Group, Nat. Trust (Gt. Britain), Am. Soc. Landscape Architects (hon.), Am. Soc. Interior Designers (hon.), Irish Georgian soc., Ry. Devel. Soc., Christopher Wren Soc. (founder, London 1995), No. Ireland Partnership. Address: 916 Saint Vincent St South Bend IN 46617-1443

HORSCH, KATHLEEN JOANNE, social services administrator, educator, consultant; b. Mpls., June 27, 1936; d. Clement Nicholas and Delta Jesse (Steckman) Simmer; m. Lawrence Leonard Horsch, Aug. 25, 1956; children: Daniel L., Timothy J., Christopher G., Catherine J., Sarah E. Student, U. Minn., 1967-73. Various positions local, state and nat. levels Am. Cancer Soc., Mpls., 1965—, pres. Hennepin County bd. dirs., 1978, hon. life mem. Hennepin Unit bd., 1992—, chmn. bd. dirs. Minn. divsn., 1984-86, hon. life mem. Minn. divsn., 1993—; sec. nat. bd. Am. Cancer Soc., N.Y.C., 1982-85, vice-chmn. nat. bd., 1985-87, chmn. nat. bd. Am. Cancer Soc., Atlanta, 1987-89, dir. nat. bd., 1992-97, hon. life mem., 1997—, chair Lan W. Adams award com., 1993-98; pres. Dynamics of Vol. Effectiveness, Inc., Mpls., 1985-95; mem. faculty Met. State U., St. Paul, 1982-94, U.S. Nat. Com./Internat. Union Against Cancer UICC, Washington, 1989-94. Adv. bd. Look Good Feel Better, 1986—, Drucker Found. Non-Profit Mgmt., 1992—; mem. Joint Commn. Health, 1989; bd. govs. United Way Am., 1990-96, St. Croix area United Way, 1996—, vice-chair, 1997; bd. govs. Youth for Understanding Internat. Exch., 1992—, vice-chair, 1997, chair, 1998—; bd. govs. Courage Ctr., 1993—, vice-chair, 1996—. Recipient Svc. to Mankind award. Mem. Internat. Cancer Union (coun. 1990-94), Campaign Orgn., Pub. Edn. and Svc. Program (chair 1990-94), Josephson Inst. Ethics (bd. dirs. 1991-96), bd. govs. Nat. Assembly 1995—, Minikahda Club. Avocations: gardening, boating, piano, swimming, hiking.

HORSCH, LAWRENCE LEONARD, venture capitalist, corporate revitalization executive; b. Mpls., Dec. 2, 1934; s. Leonard Charles and Cecilia May (Chamberlain) H.; m. Kathleen Joanne Simmer, Aug. 25, 1956; children: Daniel Lawrence, Timothy John, Christopher Girard, Catherine Jessica, Sarah Elisabeth. BA with honors, Coll. St. Thomas, 1957; MBA, Northwestern U., 1958. Investment banker Paine Webber Jackson & Curtis, Mpls., 1961-67; v.p. N.Am. Fin. Corp., Mpls., 1967-71; pres. Eagle Investment Corp., Mpls., 1971-87; chmn., chief exec. officer Munsingwear Inc., Mpls., 1987-90; chmn. bd. Eagle Mgmt. & Fin. Corp., Mpls., 1990—; chmn. bd. dirs. Sci. Med. Life Sys., Maple Grove, Minn., 1971-94; bd. dirs. Boston Sci. Corp., Leuthold Funds, Inc. 1st lt. USAF, 1959-61. Mem. Fin. Analysts Fedn., Mpls. Athletic Club, Minikahda Country Club. Home: 1404 Hilltop Rdg Saint Joseph WI 54082-2013 Office: Eagle Mgmt & Fin Corp PO Box 235 Stillwater MN 55082-0235

HORSEMAN, BARBARA ANN, church musician, voice educator; b. Clinton, Iowa, Nov. 29, 1935; d. Ted Rex and Lillian Mae (Bean) Smith; m. William F. Horseman, Dec. 26, 1963; children: Megan, Jill. Diploma, Cottey Jr. Coll. for Women, Nevada, Mo., 1955; MusB, U. Mo., Kansas City, 1957, MusM, 1958, postgrad., 1958-61. Dir. chancel choir Zion United Ch. of Christ, Kansas City, Kans., 1957—, dir., founder 4 handbell choirs, 1989—, founding mem., officer 3-C Circle, 1981-83, mem., past pres. adult fellowship, 1963-93, co-sponsor youth group, 1981-83, dir. jr. and sr. high sch. choirs, 1979-80, supt. Sunday sch., 1986-88; pvt. tchr. voice and piano, Kansas City, 1963—; pre-school tchr., Kansas City, 1991—; vocal and keyboard tchr. Hill Top Dance Ctr., 1992—; dir. children's chors Kansas City Dance Theatre Co., 1992—; vocal, keyboard tchr. Starstruck Dance Studio, Tonganoxie, Kans., 1997—. Pres. Philharm. Aux., Kansas City, 1975-76; pres. Creative Experiences, Kansas City, 1983; pres. PTA, 1970-72, bd. dirs., 1973-81, now life mem. Mem. Am. Guild English Handbell Ringers, Choristers Guild, Cottey Coll. Alumnae Assn. (bd. dirs. 1963-75, nat. pres. 1973-74), Mozart Music Club, P.E.O. (pres. Kansas City 1975-77), Mu Sigma Epsilon, Delta Psi Omega, Sigma Alpha Iota. Home: 3233 N 85th Pl Kansas City KS 66109-1024 Office: Zion United Ch of Christ 2711 N 72nd St Kansas City KS 66109-1738

HORSEY, DAVID, editorial cartoonist; b. Evansville, Ind., Sept. 13, 1951; m. Nole Ann Ulery; children: Darielle Jean, Daniel Rayden. BA in Comms., U. Wash., 1976; MA in Internat. Rels., U. Kent, Canterbury, Eng., 1986. Formerly govt. reporter, polit. columnist Wash. State Capitol; polit. reporter, columnist, editl. cartoonist Daily Jour.-Am., Bellevue, Wash., 1976-79; editl. cartoonist, columnist, mem. editl. bd. Seattle Post-Intelligencer, 1979—; syndicated Tribune Media Svcs., 1986-89, King Features/N.Am. Syndicate, N.Y.C., 1988—; instr. Acad. Realist Art, Seattle, 1998; propr. Horsey-Words and Pictures, Seattle, 1993—. Author: Politics and Other Perversions, 1974, Horsey's Rude Awakenings, 1981, Horsey's Greatest HIts of the '80s, 1989, The Fall of Man, 1994; co-editor: (anthology) Cartooning AIDS Around the World, 1992; exhibited cartoons at Art Inst. Seattle, 1992, Michael Pierce Gallery, Seattle, 1997, Shoreline C.C., 1999, others. Asst. coach North Ctrl. Little League Baseball, 1992-94; youth coach Woodland Soccer Club, 1989-98; chmn. campaign for excellence St. Benedict Elem. and Mid. Sch., 1991-93, pres. sch. commn., 1993-95. Recipient 1st place Best of the West Journalism Competition, 1995, Environ. Media award, 1995, Global Media award Population Inst., 1991, Berryman award Nat. Press Found., 1998, Pulitzer prize for editl. cartooning, 1999, numerous others. Mem. Soc. Profl Journalists (12 1st place regional awards, Susan Hutchinson Bosch award 1999), Assn. Am. Editl. Cartoonists (pres.-elect 1999—). Office: Seattle Post Intelligencer PO Box 1909 101 Elliott Ave W Seattle WA 96111

HORSFALL, SARA, sociology educator; b. Cherokee, Iowa, Oct. 3, 1946; d. Edward and Florence (Tow) Towe; m. John Muir Horsfall; 1 child, Nathan Rongopai. BSc, Mont. State U., 1969; PhD, Tex. A&M U., 1996. Stringer, journalist News World-India, N.Y.C. and Bombay, 1975-78; London bur. chief N.Y.C. Tribune, 1978-82; London corr./office mgr. Mid. East Times, 1982-85; grad. asst. Tex. A&M U., College Station, 1992-96, lectr., 1993-96, vis. scholar, 1997; lectr. Walls Unit, Lee Coll., Huntsville, Tex., 1997; vis. asst. prof. Stephen F. Austin State U., Nacogdoches, Tex., 1997-98; asst. prof. sociology Tex. Wesleyan U., Ft. Worth, 1998—; 68914ger, journalist News World-India, N.Y.C. and Bombay, 1975-78; active Inter-univ. Consortium for Polit. and Social Rsch., Ann Arbor, Mich., 1995; presenter in field; pvt. piano and guitar instr., 1987—; guitar instr. Univ. Plus, Tex. A&M U., 1987-95; pres., CEO Habersham at Northlake Condominiums, Inc., 1998—. English editor: Budgeting and Investment Planning in Bogota, Colombia, 1993; editor: Race and Ethnic Studies Inst., 1992; referee jours. in field; co-editor: Chaos, Complexity and Sociology, 1997; contbr. articles, features, revs. to newspapers and profl. publs. Mem. liberal arts coun. Tex. A&M U., 1991-93, liberal arts awards com., 1993; mem. editl. adv. bd. Collegiate Press, Calif., 1997; organizer, dir., tchr. Ch. Family Summer Camp, 1991, 92, 93, 95, 96; organizer, sponsor Anandaloy: Elem. Sch. for Slum Dwellers, Calcutta, 1978; choir dir. St. Anthony's Cath. Ch., 1986-92. Mem. Assn. for Sociology of Religion, Soc. for Sci. Study of Religion, Am. Sociol. Assn., S.W. Sociol. Assn., Brazos Valley Guitar Soc. (founder, pres. 1986-97), Phi Kappa Phi. Avocations: classical guitar, crafts, thinking, poetry. Office: Tex Wesleyan U 1201 Wesleyan Fort Worth TX 76105

HORSFALL, WILLIAM ROBERT, educator; b. Mountain Grove, Mo., Jan. 11, 1908; s. Frank and Margaret Atwood (Vaulx) H.; m. Annie Laurie Ellis, Sept. 7, 1930. BS, U. Ark., 1928; MS, Kans. State U., 1929; PhD, Cornell U., 1933. Lt. col. USAR, 1943-45, ret. Recipient Hoogstraal medal Am. Soc. Tropical Medicine, 1990. Fellow Ent. Soc. Am.; mem. Am. Mosquito Control Assn. (Nat. Svc. award 1985). Avocations: wood carving, painting. Office: Univ Ill Dept Entomology 320 Morrill Hall 505 S Goodwin Ave Urbana IL 61801-3707

HORSLEY, ERNEST, city administrator; b. Cleve., Dec. 18, 1950. BA, Fla. Internat. U., 1973. Recreation ctr. dir. City Hialeah, Fla., 1973-80, recreation supr., 1980-94, supt. sts., 1986-94, dir. leisure svcs. & sts., 1994—. Mem. Fla. Parks & Recreation Assn., Parks & Recreation Assn. Office: City Hialeah 5601 E 8th Ave Hialeah FL 33013-1397*

HORSLEY, JACK EVERETT, lawyer, author; b. Sioux City, Iowa, Dec. 12, 1915; s. Charles E. and Edith V. (Timms) H.; m. Sallie Kelley, June 12, 1939 (dec.); children: Pamela, Charles Edward; m. Bertha J. Newland, Feb. 24, 1950 (dec.); m. Mary Jane Moran, Jan. 20, 1973; 1 child, Sharon. AB, U. Ill., 1937, JD, 1939. Bar: Ill. 1939. Ptnr. Craig & Craig, Mattoon, Ill., 1939—, sr. atty.-of counsel, 1983—; vice-chmn. bd. dirs. Ctrl. Nat. Bank, 1976-91, chmn. trustee com., mem. exec. com., 1986-91, dir. emeritus; mem. Harlan Moore Heart Rsch. Found., 1968—, asst. treas., 1996—; mem. lawyers adv. coun. U. Ill. Law Forum, 1960-63; lectr. Practicing Law Inst., N.Y.C., 1967-73, U. Ill., Champaign, 1974, Ct. Practice Inst., Chgo., 1974—, Coll. Law Inst. Continuing Legal Edn. U. Mich., 1967, Bankers' Seminar, 1992; vis. lectr. Orange County (Fla.) Med. Soc., 1985, San Diego Med. Soc., 1970, U. S.C., 1976, Duquesne Coll., 1970, U. Ill. Law Forum, 1972, alumni adv. com., 1991—; vis lectr. trial practice NYU Coll. Law, 1972; faculty banker seminar Wis. Med. Assn., Lake Geneva, 1997; lectr. med./legal seminars on tour Chgo., Cleve., Pa., Orlando, 1995; chmn. rev. bd. Ill. Supreme Ct. Disciplinary Commn., 1973-76, adv. cons., 1976—; lectr. Cleve.

Hosp., Shelby, N.C., 1976; legal cons. Cenbank Trust Co., 1992-95; vis. prof. trial practice Fordham Law Sch., N.Y.C., 1998. Narrator Poetry Interludes, Sta. WLBH-FM, 1977-91; author: Trial Lawyer's Manual, 1967, Voir Dire Examinations and Opening Statements, 1968, Current Development in Products Liability Law, 1969, Illinois Civil Practice and Procedure, 1970, The Medical Expert Witness, 1973, Testifying in Court, 1973, 5th edit., 1997, supplement 4th edit., 1993, The Doctor and the Law, 1975, The Doctor and Family Law, 1975, The Doctor and Business Law, 1976, The Doctor and Medical Law, 1977, Anatomy of a Medical Malpractice Case, 1984, 3rd edit., 1993, History of Craig & Craig, Attorneys, 1968-89, 1990, supplement, 1993, 2nd edit., 1994, Municipals: G.O. of Revenue, 1992, World War II, D-Day, 1st edit., 1994, 2nd edit., 1998, Trial Techniques, 1995, Legal Liability Exposure of Trust Co. Officers, 1996, On Trust Dept. Guide-lines and Risks, 1996, On Federal Evidence and Examination, 1995, 96, 97, Memories of World War II In the European Theater, Purple Heart, 1997, History of the Bar in East Central Illinois, 1997, Remembrances: An Autobiography, 1998; co-author: RN Legally Speaking, 1998, Mathew Bender Forensic Sciences, 1999; editor Med. Econs., 1969—, Fifty Eight Years as Attorney, 1997, 2nd edit., 1998; legal cons. Mast-Head, 1972; contbr. A.L.L. Life, Stafford, Va., 1988—, Fed. Evidence Rules, 1996, Cross-Exam. Techniques and Potential Traps, 1996, Forensic Scis. on Texts and Treatises, 1981, 2d edit. 1999, Christianity: Creationism vs. Darwinism, 1999; cons., reviewer Civil Practice State and Fed. Cts., 1998-99; contbr. articles to profl. jours. Alt. del. to Rep. Platform Com., 1992; active Senatorial Reelection Com., 1993; mem. exec. com. Ill. Rep. Election Campaign, 1997; founding mem. U.S. Air Mus., Am. Air Mus.; pres. bd. edn. sch. dist. 100, 1946-48; bd. dirs. Harlan Moore Heart Rsch. Found., 1968-91, hon. dir., 1991—; vol. reader in rec. texts Am. Assn. for Blind, 1970-72; chmn. exec. com. U. Ill. Law Forum, 1990-91; pres. Res. Officers Assn. East Cen. Ill., 1988-89; founder Bertha Newland Horsley award St. John's Coll. Nursing, Springfield, Mary Jane Horsley award trophy Mattoon (Ill.) H.S.; mem. exec. com. Ill. Rep. Election Campaign, 1997. Col. U.S. Army, 1942-46, ETO, USA JAGD (hon., ret., promoted hon. full col., 1997). Decorated Purple Heart. Recipient Disting. Svc. award U. Ill., 1995. Fellow Am. Coll. Trial Lawyers (co-chair membership commn. 1998); mem. ABA, Ill. Bar Assn. (exec. coun. ins. law 1961-63, com. chmn. banking law 1972, lectr. law course for attys. 1962, 64-65, sr. counsellor 1989—, Disting. Svc. award 1982-83), Assn. of Bar of City of N.Y. (non-resident), Coles-Cumberland Bar Assn. (v.p. 1968-69, pres. 1969-70, chmn. com. jud. inquiry 1976-80, chair meml. com. 1989—, mem. exec. com. 1998, sr. counsellor 1989, co-author Forensic Scis. Jour. 1991, 2d edit. 1999), Am. Arbitration Assn. (nat. panel arbitrators, counsel advisor hearing officers in Ill. 1996-97), U. Ill. Law Alumni Assn. (life mem., pres. 1966-67, Alumni of Month Sept. 1974, exec. com. 1990-91), Ill. Appellate Lawyers Assn., Soc. Legal Scribes, Ill. Def. Counsel Assn. (pres. 1967-88), Soc. Trial Lawyers (chmn. profl. activities 1960-61, bd. dirs. 1966-67), U.S. Supreme Ct. Hist. Soc. (co-chmn.), Adelphic Debating Soc., Assn. Ins. Attys., Internat. Assn. Ins. Counsel, Am. Judicature Soc., Res. Officers Assn. (pres. 1997-98, chair exec. com., pres. emeritus 1999), U. Ill. Alumni Assn. (exec. com. 1990-91), Soc. Legal Scribes, Masons (Sr. Master award 1992), Delta Phi (exec. com. alumni assn. 1960-61, 67-68), Sigma Delta Kappa. Lutheran. Home: 913 N 31st St Mattoon IL 61938-2271 Office: Craig & Craig 1807 Broadway PO Box 689 Mattoon IL 61938-0689 also: 227 1/2 S 9th St PO Box 1545 Mount Vernon IL 62864-0030 *Constant study and learning are essential to success. Not to learn is not to live.*

HORSLEY, RICHARD DAVID, banker; b. 1942. With FDIC, Washington, 1964-66, Ernst and Ernst, N.Y.C., 1966-72; compt. 1st Ala. Bancshares Inc., Montgomery, 1972-77, v.p., compt., 1977-82; vice chmn., exec. fin. officer Regions Fin. Corp., Birmingham, Ala., 1982—, also bd. dirs. Office: Regions Fin Corp 417 20th St N Birmingham AL 35203-3203*

HORSLEY, WALLER HOLLADAY, lawyer; b. Richmond, Va., July 2, 1931; s. John Shelton Jr. and Lilian (Holladay) H.; m. Margaret Stuart Cooke, Dec. 3, 1955; children: Margaret Terrell, Stuart W., John Garrett. BA with distinction, U. Va., 1953, LLB, 1959. Bar: Va. 1959, U.S. Dist. Ct. (ea. dist.) Va. 1959, U.S. Tax Ct. 1959, U.S. Ct. Appeals (4th cir.) 1959, U.S. Supreme Ct. 1969. Ptnr. Hunton & Williams, Richmond, 1965-92; Horsley & Horsley, Richmond, Va., 1992—; lectr. taxation U. Va. Law Sch., 1961-65, 69. Mem. adv. coun. Sch. Bus., Va. Commonwealth U., 1983-91; sr. warden St. Stephen's Episcopal Ch., 1977-79; gen. conv. dep. Diocese of Va., 1979, 85; pres. Richmond Tennis Patrons Assn., 1969, Va. Silver Star Found., 1985-86; mem. bd. visitors U. Va., 1988-92. With USN, 1953-56; to lt. comdr. USNR, 1956-62. Recipient Algernon Sydney Sullivan award, 1953; named Outstanding Young Man of Yr. Richmond Jr. C. of C., 1965. Fellow Am. Bar Found., Va. Bar Found.; mem. ABA, Va. State Bar (pres. 1982-83), Va. Bar Assn., Am. Coll. Trust and Estate Counsel (pres. 1990), Country Club of Va., Bull and Bear Club, Westwood Racquet Club, Omicron Delta Kappa, Phi Beta Kappa, Order of Coif. Democrat. Episcopalian. Mem. editorial bd. Taxation for Lawyers, 1975-86, Probate Lawyer, 1976-87, Probate Notes, 1976-87, editor, 1986-87; bd. advisors Va. Tax Rev., 1981—; contbr. articles to legal jours. Office: Horsley & Horsley 5020 Monument Ave Fl 2 Richmond VA 23230-3620

HORSLUND, JENS-OTTO, diplomat; b. Goedvad, Denmark, June 12, 1960; s. Jens Peter Horslund Pedersen and Gudrun Horslund; m. Githa Birkegaard, June 22, 1985; children: Matias, Oliver, William. Studnet, Whittier Coll., 1985-86; MA in Polit. Sci. and Pub. Adminstrn., U. Aarhus, Denmark, 1988. Sect. head Ministry of Fin., Copenhagen, 1987-88; desk officer Asian desk Ministry Fgn. Affairs, Copenhagen, 1988-89, sect. head EEC policy, 1989-90, sect. head planning, 1990-91, sect. head NATO policy, 1994-97; first sec. Royal Danish Embassy, Riyadh, Saudi Arabia, 1991-94; first polit. sec. Royal Danish Embassy, Washington, 1997—. Lutheran. Avocations: squash, soccer, drums, rock and roll, chess. E-mail: horslund@erols.com and jehors@wasus.um.dk. Home: 11104 Bowen Ave Great Falls VA 22066 Office: Royal Danish Embassy 3200 Whitehave St NW Washington DC 20008

HORST, BRUCE EVERETT, manufacturing company executive; b. Three Rivers, Mich., Feb. 17, 1921; s. Walter and Genevieve (Turner) H.; m. Patricia Kranish, Oct. 4, 1969; children: Michael, Diane, Mark. BS in Bus. and Engring. Adminstrn, Mass. Inst. Tech., 1943. With Barber-Colman Co., Rockford, Ill., 1946-76, pres., 1965-75, vice chmn. bd., 1975-76; pres. Mid-States Screw Corp., 1976—. Bd. dirs. Rockford YMCA, 1964-75, pres., 1965-67. Served to 1st lt. USAAF, 1943-45. Decorated Air medal. Mem. Rotary, Univ. Club (Rockford), Forest Hills Country Club (Rockford) (past sec.), Moorings Country Club (Naples), Yacht Club at Lake Geneva (Wis.). Home: 2625 Harlem Blvd Rockford IL 61103-4117 Office: Mid-States Screw Corp 1817 18th Ave Rockford IL 61104-7399

HORST, DEENA LOUISE, state legislator; b. Sacramento, Feb. 14, 1944; s. Orlo John and Louise Helena (Schultz) Poovey; m. Gordon Lee Horst, 1966; children: Randall, Rebecca. BSE, Emporia State U., 1966, MA, 1972; postgrad., Kans. State U., 1993—. Elem. tchr. Peabody Sch., 1966-68; mid. sch. art tchr., dept. chmn. South Mid. Sch., Unified Sch. Dist. # 305, 1968—; mem. from dist. 69 Kans. State Ho. of Reps., 1995—. State and nat. ofcl. U.S. Jaycee Women, 1968-84; sec. Saline County Rep. Ctrl. Com., Kans., 1992-95. Named Outstanding State Pres., U.S. Jaycee Women, 1979-80; co-recipient Master Tchr. award State of Kans., 1991. Mem. C. of C., Phi Alpha, Alpha Theta Rho, Phi Delta Kappa, Epsilon Sigma Alpha (Zone Outstanding Sister award 1990). Address: 920 S 9th St Salina KS 67401-4806

HORST, PAMELA SUE, medical educator, family physician; b. Hershey, Pa., Jan. 23, 1951; d. Ralph H. and Helen (Fry) H.; m. Thomas H. Dennison, Feb. 6, 1982; 1 child, Elizabeth Dennison. BS, Pa. State U., 1972; MD, Pa. State U., Hershey, 1976. Diplomate Am. Bd. Family Practice. Resident in family practice Shadyside Hosp., Pitts., 1979; family physician North Jefferson Health Svcs., Clayton, N.Y., 1979-82; physician emergency rm. Geisinger Med. Ctr., Philipsburg, Pa., 1982-84; asst. prof. family medicine Albany (N.Y.) Med. Coll., 1984-88; assoc. prof. health sci. ctr. SUNY, Syracuse, 1988—; med. dir. family practice ctr. St. Joseph's Hosp. Health Ctr., Syracuse, 1989—, assoc. residency dir. family practice residency, Syracuse, 1990—; chmn. St. Joseph's Health Alliance, 1995-97, SyraHealth, IPA, 1997-98. Author: (with others) Ambulatory Medicine, 1993, Manual of Family Practice, 1996; reviewer Am. Family Physician, Jour. Family Practice. Mem. pub. issues com., bd. dirs. ctrl. N.Y. chpt. Am. Cancer Soc.; past v.p. bd. dirs. Home Aides Ctrl. N.Y., Syracuse. Mem. Am. Acad. Family Physicians (instr. advanced life support in obstetrics 1992—), Soc. Tchrs. Family Medicine. Avocations: gardening, reading. Office: St Joseph's Health Ctr Family Practice Residency 301 Prospect Ave Syracuse NY 13203-1899*

HORSTMANN, DOROTHY MILLICENT, retired physician, educator; b. Spokane, Wash., July 2, 1911; d. Henry J. and Anna (Hunold) H. AB, U. Calif., 1936, MD, 1940; DSc (hon.), Smith Coll., 1961; MA (hon.), Yale, 1961; D Med. Scis. (hon.), Women's Med. Coll. of Pa., 1963. Intern San Francisco City and County Hosp., 1939-40, asst. resident medicine, 1940-41; asst. resident medicine Vanderbilt U. Hosp., 1941-42; Commonwealth Fund fellow, sect. preventive medicine Sch. Medicine, Yale U., New Haven, 1942-43; instr. preventive medicine Sch. Medicine, Yale U., 1943-44, 45-47, asst. prof., 1948-52, assoc. prof., 1952-56, assoc. prof. preventive medicine and pediatrics, 1956-61, prof. epidemiology and pediatrics, 1961-69, John Rodman Paul prof. epidemiology, prof. pediatrics, 1969-82; John Rodman Paul prof. epidemiology, prof. pediatrics emeritus, sr. research scientist Sch. Medicine Yale U., 1982; instr. medicine U. Calif., San Francisco, 1944-45. Recipient Albert Coll. award, 1953, Gt. Heart award Variety Club Phila., 1968, Modern Medicine award, 1974; James D. Bruce award ACP, 1975, Thorvald Madsen award State Serum Inst. (Denmark), 1977, Maxwell Finland award Infectious Disease Soc.-Am., 1978, Disting. Alumni award U. Calif. Med. Sch., 1979, NIH fellow Nat. Inst. Med. Rsch., London, 1947-48. Master ACP; fellow Am. Acad. Pediatrics (hon.); mem. NAS, Infectious Disease Soc. Am. (pres. 1975), Am. Soc. Clin. Investigation, Am. Epidemiol. Soc. (v.p. 1974-75), Am. Pediatric Soc., Am. Soc. Virology (coun. 1983-84), Soc. Epidemiol. Rsch., Internat. Epidemiol. Assn., Royal Soc. Medicine (hon., epidemiology/preventive medicine sect.), Conn. Acad. Sci. and Engring., European Assn. Against Virus Diseases, South African Soc. Pathologists (hon.), Cuban Soc. Hygiene & Epidemiology (hon.), Sigma Delta Epsilon (hon.). Home: 11 Autumn St New Haven CT 06511-2220 Office: Yale U Sch Medicine Epidemiology and Pub Health PO Box 208034 New Haven CT 06520-8034*

HORSTMANN, JAMES DOUGLAS, college official; b. Davenport, Iowa, Oct. 2, 1933; s. Leonard A. and Agnes A. (Erhke) H.; m. Carol H. Griffiths, Sept. 8, 1956; children: Kent, Karen, Diane. BA, Augustana Coll., 1955. C.P.A., Ill., Wis. Staff acct., auditor Arthur Andersen & Co., Chgo., 1955-61; v.p., controller Harry S. Manchester, Inc., Madison, Wis., 1961-65; sr. v.p. fin., treas. H. C. Prange Co., Sheboygan, Wis., 1965-83; also dir. H. C. Prange Co.; dir. planned giving Augustana Coll., Rock Island, Ill., 1983-85, v.p. for devel., 1985-93, v.p. planned giving, 1993-98, v.p. emeritus, 1998—; pres. Schonstedt Instrument Co., 1993-95; chmn. Wis. Mchts. Fedn.; dir. First Wis. Nat. Bank, Fond du Lac. Chmn. Sheboygan County (Wis.) Republican Party, 1969-70; vice chmn. Wis. 6th Congl. Dist., 1972-73; del. Nat. Rep. Conv., 1976; campaign chmn. Sheboygan United Way, 1977, treas., 1973-75, v.p., 1975-78, pres., 1978-79; bd. dirs. Public Expenditure Survey Wis., 1981-83; bd. dirs. Rock Island YMCA, 1986-87; v.p. Sheboygan Arts Found., 1973-75; v.p., bd. dirs. Sheboygan Retirement Home, 1977-83; bd. dirs. Franciscan Mental Health Ctr., 1984-94, pres., 1985-88; bd. dirs. Franciscan Health Care Systems, 1988-92; bd. trustees Friendship Manor, 1993—, Coun. on Children at Risk, 1989—, Franciscan Med. Ctr., 1990-92. With USN, 1955-57. Named Outstanding Fund Raising Exec. Nat. Soc. Fund Raising Execs., 1992; recipient Outstanding Svc. award Augustana Coll., 1979. Mem. Am. Cancer Soc. (bd. dirs. Rock Island unit 1992—), Wis. Inst. CPAs, Ill. Soc. CPAs, Sheboygan County Assn. CPAs, Fin. Execs. Inst. (dir.), Quad-City Estate Planning Coun., Augustana Coll. Alumni Assn. (pres. 1970-71), Rock Island Arsenal Golf Club, Econ. Club Sheboygan (pres. 1976-77), Kiwanis. Lutheran. Home: 1245 36th Ave Rock Island IL 61201-6022 Office: Augustana Coll 639 38th St Rock Island IL 61201-2210

HORTEN, CARL FRANK, textile manufacturing company executive; b. Fort Lauderdale, Fla., Aug. 19, 1914; s. Joseph Frederick and Phyllis (Gregory) H.; m. Alice Jeannette Yereance, June 8, 1940; children—Bruce Carl, Lynn Alice, Heather Belle. B.S., Geneva Coll., 1936; M.B.A., Harvard, 1938; grad. exec. program, U. N.C., 1959. Sales corr. L. Sonneborn Sons, 1938-40; asst. controller Nashua Mfg. Co., 1940-47; controller Textron So., Inc., 1947-49; with Springs Mills, Inc., Ft. Mill, S.C., 1949—; v.p. Springs Mills, Inc., 1964-66, treas., 1967—, exec. v.p., 1966—, sec., 1969, also dir.; chmn. bd. Lancaster Internat. Sales Corp., S.C.; treas., dir. Boundsgreen Co. Ltd., Bermuda; dir. Carolina Carpet Co., Daralon Textile Mfg. Corp., Jakarta, Indonesia. Served to lt. (j.g.) USNR, 1943-46. Home: Presbyterian Home E-217 Clinton SC 29325 Office: Springs Mills Inc Fort Mill SC 29715

HORTIS, ATHENA MARIA, physical education educator; b. Charlotte, N.C., Feb. 2, 1965; d. Michael Thomas and Elaine Audry (Chamberlain) H. BS, U. S.C., 1990; postgrad., Furman U., Greenville, S.C., 1996—. Phys. edn. sci. tchr. Ben Hagood Elem., Pickens, S.C., 1990-91; phys. edn. tchr. Shannon Forest Sch., Greenville, S.C., 1991-93; phys. edn. tchr. Christ Ch. Episcopal Sch., Greenville, 1992—, tennis coach girls, 1992-98, track coach girls, 1992-98, C-team girls basketball coach, 1992-95, jr. varsity girls basketball coach, 1996, girls varsity basketball coach, 1997-98, girls golf coach, 1997-98, dept. chmn., 1997-98; tchr. phys. edn. Greenville County Schs., 1998—; coach clinics Furman U., Greenville, 1993; coach swim team Greenville Country Club/Silverleaf, 1987-96; owner Pool Mgmt. Co., Pool Watch, Inc., 1997-98; coach Southside Pub. H.S., Greenville. Named Track Coach of Yr. Northwestern Regional 1-A Coaches Conf. Affiliated, 1992-98, Region II A Girls Track Coach of Yr., 1997-98, Region II A Girls Basketball Coach of Yr. Republican. Presbyterian. Home: 5033 Maplewood Dr Greenville SC 29615-3829 Office: Christ Ch Episcopal Sch 245 Cavalier Dr Greenville SC 29607-4265

HORTMAN, DAVID JONES, secondary education educator; b. Washington, Aug. 12, 1954; s. Jack Doyle and Elizabeth (Jones) H.; m. Ellen Shea Johnston, Aug. 28, 1976; children: Melissa, Gregory, Jeffrey. BS, Millersville U., 1976. Tchr. Kennard Dale H.S., Fawn Grove, Pa., 1976-79; designer Gichner Mobile Sys., Dallastown, Pa., 1979-81; tchr. York (Pa.) County Vocat.-Tech. Sch., 1981, Susquehannock H.S., Glen Rock, Pa., 1982—, York (Pa.) Tech. Inst., 1988-91; cons. in field. Pres. Dallastown (Pa.) Jaycees, 1983-84, active, 1982-85. Recipient Tchr. Excellence for Pa. award Internat. Tech. Edn. Assn., 1992. Mem. Internat. Tech. Edn. Assn. (Tchr. Excellence award 1993), Tech. Edn. Assn. Pa. (Tchr. Excellence award 1992-93), York County Tech. Edn. Assn. (pres. 1991-92). Republican. Methodist. Avocations: gardening, sports, travel. Home: 264 W High St Red Lion PA 17356-1528 Office: Susquehannock HS PO Box 128 Glen Rock PA 17327-0128*

HORTON, CLAUDE WENDELL, physicist, educator; b. Cherryvale, Kans., Sept. 23, 1915; s. Roy Wesley and Marie (Terwilleger) H.; m. Louise Walthall, Nov. 23, 1938; children: Claude Wendell, Margaret Elaine. B.A. with honors in Physics, Rice Inst., 1935, M.A. in Physics, 1936; postgrad., Princeton U., 1937-38; Ph.D. in Physics, U. Tex., 1948. Asst. seismologist Shell Oil Co., 1936-37, party chief field crew, 1938-43; research asso. underwater sound lab. Harvard, 1943-45; research physicist def. research lab. U. Tex., Austin, 1945—; prof. physics U. Tex., 1953-71, acting chmn. dept., 1956-57, chmn. dept., 1957-62, prof. geology, 1965-71; Mem. Corp. Woods Hole (Mass.) Oceanographic Instn., 1966-84. Assoc. editor: Underwater Sound, Jour. Acoustical Soc. Am., 1982-86. Fellow Acoustical Soc. Am. (Pioneers of Underwater Acoustics medal 1980), Am. Phys. Soc.; mem. Am. Geophys. Union, Soc. Exploration Geophysicists. Home: Brighton Gardens Marriott Box 232 4401 Spicewood Springs Rd Austin TX 78759-8589

HORTON, DEBBI-JO, accountant; b. Providence, R.I., Aug. 30, 1961; d. Peter Albert and Susan Lee (Berwick) Abrams; divorced; children: Samantha Barth, Ryan William. BS, Bryant Coll., 1988. CPA. Co-owner Wm Abrams & Sons, Rehoboth, Mass., 1979-82; staff acct. Ernst & Young, Providence, 1986-89; owner, CPA DJ Horton & Assocs., East Providence, 1989—; taxation com. chair SBANE, Waltham, Mass., 1995-97; legis. com. mem. SBA Adv. Coun., Providence, 1996—; New England tax implementation com. White Conf. on Small Bus., Washington, 1995—, R.I. taxation chair, 1995-97, R.I. del., 1995-97. Recipient Woman of Achievement award Bus. and Profl. Women, 1995, Leadership award Bryant Coll. Alumni Assn., 1997; named Young Careerist, 1994. Mem. AICPA (small bus. tax. com. 1997—), R.I. Soc. of CPAs (legis. com. mem. 1996-97), Very Small Bus. Resource Network (steering com.), No. R.I. Chamber (chair small bus. com.). Office: DJ Horton & Assocs PO Box 14288 East Providence RI 02914-0288

HORTON, EDWARD CARL, retired military officer, public administrator; b. Syracuse, N.Y., Sept. 5, 1950; s. Carl and Marjorie Lucille (Clark) H.; m. Chong Sun Kim, Aug. 23, 1980; children: Paul E., David S. BS, U.S. Mil. Acad., 1972; MS in Pers. Mgmt., Troy State U., 1980; MPA, U. Mont., 1983; diploma, U.S. Army War Coll., 1994-96. Commd. 2d lt. U.S. Army, 1972, advanced through grades to lt. col., 1990; platoon leader, exec. officer Co B, 1-506 Infantry, 101st Airborne divsn., Ft. Campbell, Ky., 1973-74, scout platoon leader, support platoon leader, 1974-75; detachment comdr. 2d Replacement Detachment, 2d Infantry divsn., Camp Casey, Korea, 1975-76; co. comdr., instr., asst. chief Benning Ranger divsn. U.S. Army Ranger Sch., Ft. Benning, Ga., 1977-80; asst. prof. mil. sci. U. Mont., Missoula, 1980-83; with 193d Infantry Brigade, Ft. Clayton, Panama, 1983-86; staff officer Office Tech. Advisor and Army Initiatives Group, Washington, 1987-90; comdr. 5th Battalion, 87th Infantry, 193d Infantry Brigade, Ft. Davis, Panama, 1990-92, Yakima (Wash.) Tng. Ctr., 1992-94; chief spl. studies, sr. planner Office of Asst. Chief Staff for Installation Mgmt., 1994-97; dist. adminstr. Fla. Dept. of Children and Families, Palm Beach County, 1997—; mem. policy com. Cultural and Natural Resources Fed. Adv. Panel, Yakima, Wash., 1992-94. Mem. Palm Beach County Juvenile Justice Coun., Gov.'s Commn. on Child Welfare Stds. and Tng. Children's Svcs. Coun., Palm Beach County Health and Human Svcs. Planning Assn., Dist. IX Health and Human Svcs. Bd.; mem. regional workforce devel. bd. dirs. WAGES Coalition; mem. sch. health task force Palm Beach Spl. Task Force Sch. Readiness; chmn. Fla. State Employees Charitable Campaign; active United Way. Mem. Assn. U.S. Army, Am. Pub. Human Svcs. Assn., Am. Humane Assn., Internat. City/County Mgmt. Assn., Ellensburg C. of C., Greater Yakima C. of C. (ex officio bd. dirs. 1992-94), Rotary. Home: 10129 Caoba St Palm Beach Gardens FL 33410-5121

HORTON, ELLIOTT ARGUE, JR., lawyer, business consultant; b. Rochester, N.Y., May 8, 1926; s. Elliott Argue and Alice Marion (Ernisse) H.; m. Flaminia Maria Serafini, Oct. 10, 1951 (dec. Oct. 1983); children: Philip A., Christopher T., Thomas F., Jonathan A. BA, Yale U., 1946; LLD, Harvard U., 1950. Bar: N.Y. 1951, D.C. 1972, U.S. Tax Ct. 1965, U.S. Ct. Appeals (2d and D.C. cirs.) 1972. Assoc. Harris, Beach, Wilcox, Keating & Linowitz, Rochester, 1952-60, ptnr., 1960-77; gen. counsel Rank Xerox, Ltd., London, 1977-83; dir. govt. affairs Xerox Corp., Stamford, Conn., 1983-84, v.p. pub. affairs, 1985-87; cons. Harwich Port, Mass., 1987-90; adj. prof. anti-trust law Syracuse U., N.Y., 1975-76; lectr. anti-trust law Fed. Legal Pubs., Washington and San Francisco, 1976-78;. Served as ensign USNR, 1946-47, PTO. Fellow Am. Bar Found.; mem. Monroe County Bar Assn. (pres. elect 1976-77), Coun. Fgn. Rels., Fgn. Policy Assn. (bd. dirs. 1984-90), Kent Club. Democrat. Avocations: tennis, swimming, gardening. Home: 2512 Main St South Chatham MA 02659-1307

HORTON, FINIS GENE, financial services company executive; b. Batesville, Ark., Jan. 3, 1953; s. Allie George and Zelda (Brooks) H. BA, Ark. Coll., 1974; postgrad., Ark. State U., 1974-75, U. Cen. Ark., 1976. Asst. v.p., cost mgr. Worthen Bank, Little Rock, 1975-81; contr. First Fed. Bank of Morrilton, Ark., 1981-82; bank auditor Superior Fed. Bank, Little Rock, Ft. Smith, Ark., 1982-91; mng. dir. Audit Svcs. Group, Little Rock, 1991-95; pres., owner Corp. Bus. Svcs., Conway, Ark., 1991—; bd. dirs. Corp. Bus. Svcs. Am. Inc. Mem. Nat. Fin. Assocs., Kiwanis (pres. Little Rock 1978-79, bd. dirs. 1979-81). Avocation: sports. E-mail: fghorton@yahoo.com. Mailing: PO Box 1352 Conway AR 72032 Office: PO Box 1352 Conway AR 72033-1352

HORTON, FRANK, former congressman, lawyer; b. Tex., Dec. 12, 1919; s. Frank and Mary (Hathcox) H.; m. Nancy Richmond, Dec. 14, 1980; children by previous marriage: Frank J., Steven W. BA, La. State U., 1941; LLB, Cornell U., 1947; LHD (hon.), Rochester Inst. Tech., 1990; LLD (hon.), U. Rochester, 1993. Bar: N.Y. 1947. Assoc. Johnson, Reif & Mullan (and predecessor firm), Rochester, N.Y., 1947-52; ptnr. Johnson, Reif & Mullan (and predecessor firm), 1952-69; mem. 88th-102nd Congresses from 29th dist., 1963-93; ranking minority mem. com. govt. ops., legis. and nat. security subcoms., post office and civil service com., exec. com. Ho. com. on coms., mem. joint com. on atomic energy, 1975-77; lawyer Venable, Baetier Howard & Civiletti, Washington, 1993—; mem. exec. bd. Congl. Arts Caucus; former exec. v.p., atty. Internat. Baseball League; participant U.S.-Can. Interparliamentary Conf., Ottawa, Ont., 1969, Washington, 1973; chmn. Commn. on Fed. Paperwork; co-chmn. Northeast-Midwest Congl. Coalition; mem. North Atlantic Assembly, 1981-93; mem. Congl. Travel and Tourism Caucus. Congl. Steel Caucus, Congl. Human Rights Caucus, Congl. Post Caucus, Congl. Space Caucus, congl. adv. Pres's Commn. Nat. Agenda for Eighties; mem. Presdl. Adv. Commn. on Federalism; rep. of U.S. Ho. Reps. at dedication Israeli Knesset, 1966; others. Co-author: How to End the Draft-A Case for an All Volunteer Army, 1967, A Study of Urban Education in America, 1968, A Study of Air Safety, 1969; author: Election Reform: Remedy for an Impending Crisis, 1969, The Public's Right to Know, 1972, A Blueprint for Regulatory Reform, 1976. Mem. exec. com. Seneca dist. Otetiana council Boy Scouts Am., 1955—; pres. Rochester Community Baseball, Inc., 1957-62; councilman-at-large Rochester City Council, 1955-61; bd. visitors U.S. Naval Acad. Served to maj. AUS, 1941-46. Mem. ABA, N.Y. (exec. com. young lawyers sect. 1952), Rochester (sec. 1953-57), Fed., Western N.Y. (pres. 1956-57), D.C. bar assns., Res. Officers Assn. (past pres.), VFW, Am. Legion, Cornell Law Assn. (exec. com.), N.Y. Conservation Council, Order Coif, Phi Kappa Phi. Presbyterian (elder, trustee). Clubs: Jesters, Capitol Hill. Lodges: Masons (33 deg.); Shriners. Office: Venable Baetjer Howard & Civiletti 1201 New York Ave NW Ste 1000 Washington DC 20005-6197

HORTON, FRANK ELBA, university official, geography educator; b. Chgo., Aug. 19, 1939; s. Elba Earl and Mae Pauline (Prohaska) H.; m. Nancy Yocom, Aug. 26, 1960; children: Kimberly, Pamela, Amy, Kelly. BA, Western Ill. U., 1963; MS, Northwestern U., 1964, PhD, 1966. Faculty U. Iowa, Iowa City, 1966-75; prof. geography U. Iowa, 1966-75; dir. Inst. Urban and Regional Research, 1968-72, dean advanced studies, 1972-75; v.p. acad. affairs, research So. Ill. U., Carbondale, 1975-80; prof. geography and urban affairs, chancellor U. Wis., Milw., 1980-85; prof. geography, pres. U. Okla., Norman, 1985-88; prof. geography, higher edn. adminstrn., pres. U. Toledo, 1988-98, pres. emeritus, 1999—; prin. Horton & Assocs., Denver, 1999—; mem. commn. on leadership devel. and acad. adminstrn. Am. Coun. on Edn., 1983-85; mem. presdl. adv. com. Assn. on Governing Bds., 1986—; dir. 1st Wis. Nat. Bank of Milw., 1980-85, Liberty Nat. Bank, Oklahoma City, 1986-89, Trustcorp. Bank, 1989-90; bd. dirs. Interstate Bakeries. Author, editor: (with B.J.L. Berry) Geographic Perspectives on Urban Systems - With Integrated Readings, 1970, Urban Environmental Management - Planning for Pollution Control, 1974; editor: (with B.J.L. Berry) Geographical Perspectives on Contemporary Urban Problems, 1973; editorial adv. bd.: (with B.J.L. Berry) Transportation, 1971-78. Co-chmn. Goals for Milw. 2000, 1981-85, Greater Milw. Com., 1980; mem. bus. devel. sub-com. Okla. Coun. Sci. and Tech., 1985-88; mem. Harry S. Truman Library Inst., 1985-88, William Rockhill Nelson Trust, 1985-88; bd. govs. Am. Heart Assn., Wis., 1980-85, Ohio Supercomputer Ctr., 1993—; mem. exec. com. Okla. Acad. State Goals, 1986-88; trustee Toledo Symphony Orch., 1989—, Toledo Hosp., 1989—, Pub. Broadcasting Found. Northwest Ohio, 1989-93, Key Bank, 1990—, Ohio Aerospace Inst., 1990—; chair Inter-Univ. Coun. Pres. of Ohio Public Univs., 1992-93; mem. exec. com. Com. of 100, Toledo, 1989-92. Served with AUS, 1957-60. Mem. AAAs (nat. coun. 1976-78), Assn. Governing Bds. (mem. presdl. adv. commn. 1986—), Assn. Am. Geographers, nat. Assn. State Univs. and Land Grant Colls. (chair urban affairs div. 1983-85, chmn. Coun. of Pres. 1987-88, exec. com. 1983-88), Nat. Hwy. Rsch. Soc., Okla. Coun. on Sci. and Tech., MidAm. State Univs. Assn. (pres. 1987-88), Ohio Supercomputer Ctr. (bd. govs. 1993), Ohio Aerospace Inst. (trustee 1990—), Okla. Acad. State Goals (pres. 1987-88), Okla. State C. of C. and Industry (v.p. 1987-88), Toledo Area C. of C. (vice chmn. bd. dirs. 1991-93). Home: 288 River Ranch Cir Bayfield CO 81122-8774 Office: U Toledo 2801 W Bancroft St Toledo OH 43606-3328

HORTON, GARY J., advertising executive. Student, Grand Rapids C.C., 1960; BA, Mich. State U., 1962. Pub. rels. officer GM, Detroit, 1962-65;

creative dir. Leo Burnett, Chgo., 1966-79; ran internal co. Concepts Young & Rubicam, N.Y.C., 1979-81; chief creative officer DMB&B, Chgo., 1981-96; dep. mng. dir., chief creative officer DMB&B, Detroit, 1996—. Office: DMB&B Detroit PO Box 5012 3310 Big Beaver Rd Troy MI 48007-5012

HORTON, GLORIA ANN, English educator; b. Birmingham, Ala., June 24, 1942; d. Richard Lewis and Evelyn Mae (Trevarthen) Peterson; m. Thomas J. Horton, Apr. 6, 1974; children: Eve Ann, Richard Evan (twins). BS in Edn., U. Ala., Tuscaloosa, 1964, MA in English, 1969; postgrad., U. Ala., 1970-71. Cert. tchr., Ala. Tchr. Woodlawn H.S., Birmingham, 1964, Glen Iris Elem. Sch., Birmingham, 1965-67; instr. Livingston (Ala.) U., 1970-71; tchr. Avondale Sch., Birmingham, 1970, Scottsboro (Ala.) City Schs., 1976-79; instr. MP Sch., Fort McClellan, 1985-86; adj. instr. English Jacksonville (Ala.) State U., 1987-89, instr. English, 1989—, co-dir., interim inst. dir. writing project, 1995—; sec. Ala. Writing Project Network, 1996—. Co-author: Exploring Descriptive Grammar, 1995; contbr. articles to profl. jours. Pres. Oxford Arts Coun., 1995-97. Mem. Nat. Coun. Tchrs. English (bd. dirs. 1996—), Ala. Coun. Tchrs. English (bd. dirs. 1994—, membership chair 1995-97, v.p., pres.-elect 1997—, Disting. Svc. award 1996), Assn. Coll. English Tchrs. Ala. (bd. dirs. 1996—, liaison officer 1996—), Europa Club (pres. 1992-96). Methodist. Avocations: reading, traveling. Home: 1927 Little John Dr Oxford AL 36203-3315 Office: Jacksonville State U English Dept 214 Stone Ctr Jacksonville AL 36265

HORTON, GRANVILLE EUGENE, occupational medicine physician, retired air force officer; b. Jean, Tex., July 2, 1927; s. James Granville and Etna (Boyle) H.; m. Mildred Helen Veale, June 13, 1953; children: Linda Kay, Kevin Bruce, Carson Scott. BA, Tex. Technol. Coll., 1950; MD, U. Tex., 1954; tng. in radioactive isotope techniques, Oak Ridge Inst. Nuc. Studies, 1958; postgrad., U.S. Air Force Sch. Aerospace Medicine, 1975. Intern Detroit Receiving Hosp., 1954-55; practice medicine, 1955-56, Outlar-Blair Clinic, Wharton, Tex., 1956-72; dir. dept. nuc. medicine Nightingale Hosp., El Campo, Tex., 1973-75; mem. staff Horton Med. Clinic, El Campo, 1972-75; commd. col. U.S. Air Force, 1975; chief aeromed. services Brooks AFB, Tex., 1976-82; ret. USAF, 1982; part-time rsch. assoc. radioisotope dept. Meth. Hosp., Houston, 1961-66; mem. med. adv. com. and sec. med. staff Caney Valley Meml. Hosp., Wharton, 1956-72; clin. dir. Wharton County TB Assn., 1957-67. Bd. dirs. Wharton County divsn. Am. Cancer Soc., pres., 1960-61; dir. 8th dist. Tex., Citizens Com. for Hoover Report, 1957-58. With USN, 1946-47. Fellow Am. Coll. Angiology (state gov. 1979), Am. Coll. Nuc. Medicine; mem. AMA, AAAS, Am. Nuc. Soc., Am. Coll. Emergency Physicians, Soc. Nuc. Medicine, Tex. Assn. Physicians Nuc. Medicine, Law Enforcement Officers Tex. (assoc.), Tex. Med. Found., Tex. Med. Assn. (ho. of dels. 1959-61), Wharton C. of C. (dir., v.p. 1960-61), El Campo C. of C., Elks Lodge, Phi Chi. Republican. Episcopalian. Home: 15102 Oakmere St San Antonio TX 78232-4623 Office: Concentra Med Ctrs Ste 200 10200 Broadway St San Antonio TX 78217-4434

HORTON, HORACE ROBERT, biochemistry educator; b. St. Louis, Aug. 26, 1935; s. Horace Reade and Martha Elizabeth (Gorg) H.; m. Roberta Alanne Geehan, Jan. 31, 1959; Robert Reade, Michael Edward, Richard Ashley, Rebecca Alanne. B.S., Mo. Sch. Mines and Metallurgy, 1956; M.S., U. Mo., 1958, Ph.D., 1962. Nat. Acad. Sci. fellow Brookhaven Nat. Lab., Upton, N.Y., 1961-62, research assoc., 1962-64; asst. prof. chemistry and biochemistry N.C. State U., Raleigh, 1964-67, assoc. prof. biochemistry, 1967-72, prof., 1972-81, Alumni Disting. prof., 1979, William Neal Reynolds Disting. prof., 1981-95, prof. emeritus, 1996—; vis. prof. biochemistry Lund U., Sweden, 1974. Author: Principles of Biochemistry, 1993, 2d edit., 1996; co-author: Biochemistry, 2d edit., 1994; contbr. articles to profl. jours. Bd. dirs. Wake Blood Plan, 1980-95. Danforth assoc., 1968; NSF fellow, 1959-61; grantee NIH, 1966-72, 82-86, NSF, 1972-80. Mem. Am. Soc. Biochem. and Molecular Biology, N.C. State Acad. Outstanding Tchrs. (exec. bd. 1980-82, 94-96), Sigma Xi, Phi Kappa Phi (pres. N.C. State U. chpt. 1989-90). Presbyterian. Office: NC State U Box 7601 Raleigh NC 27695-7622*

HORTON, JAMES WRIGHT, retired lawyer; b. Belton, S.C., Dec. 24, 1919; s. John Aiken and Emmae (Tate) H.; m. Eunice Rice, Nov. 20, 1948; children—James Wright, Max Rice, Rex Rice. B.A., Furman U., 1942; J.D., Harvard U., 1948. Bar: S.C. 1948. Ptnr. Nettles & Horton, Greenville, S.C., 1948-52; ptnr. Rainey, Fant & Horton, Greenville, S.C., 1952-70, Horton, Drawdy, Marchbanks, Ashmore, Chapman & Brown, Greenville, S.C., 1970-78, Horton, Drawdy, Ward & Johnson, Greenville, S.C., 1978-91; ret., 1992. Pres. United Fund Greenville County, 1959; mem. Greenville County Sch. Trustees, 1964-70, vice chmn., 1969; pres. Greenville Family and Children's Service, 1954-55, 68-70; bd. dirs. Salvation Army, 1969—, treas., 1970-71; bd. dirs. Family and Children's Service, Greenville Mental Health Clinic, 1956-59, Greater Greenville Community Found., 1981. Col. USMCR, ret. Decorated Silver Star. Mem. Greenville County Bar Assn. (pres. 1981). Baptist (deacon 1964-69, 71-72, 86-88). Home: 2 Osceola Dr Greenville SC 29605-3013

HORTON, JARED CHURCHILL, retired corporation executive; b. Greenwich, Conn., Oct. 8, 1924; s. Frederic Jared and Marcelene (Churchill) H.; m. Pauline Elizabeth Finn, June 14, 1947; children: Janette Elizabeth Hall, Cynthia Joan Carpenter, Allison Jane Riecker, Juliana Ruth. Student, Yale U., 1942; grad., Packard Jr. Coll., 1948. With PM Industries, Stamford, Conn., 1948-54; with Alleghany Corp., N.Y.C., 1954-88, treas., 1956-88, sec., 1959-61, 63-88, v.p., 1967-88. Served to 1st lt. AUS, 1942-46. Episcopalian. Home: Coachlamp Ln Greenwich CT 06830

HORTON, JEANETTE, municipal government official; b. Paterson, N.J., Dec. 1, 1938; d. David and Mary (Carpenter) Potash; m. Troy Horton, Oct. 31, 1958 (dec. May 1990); m. Christos Prousalis, June 29, 1991. Student, Broward C. C., 1970-72, Barry U., 1982, Fla. Atlantic U., 1983-84, Fla. State U., 1985. Cert. mcpl. clk., Fla. Bookkeeper Fla. Housewares, Miami, Fla., 1961-65; asst. to comptroller Gulf Stream Press, Miami, 1965-70; comptroller Chrysler Plymouth, Miami, Fla., 1970-75; mcpl. clk., fin. dir. Village of Biscayne Park, Fla., 1975-91, Bal Harbour (Fla.) Village, 1991—. Commr. Cooper City, Fla., 1971-73. Mem. Fla. Assn. City Clks. (scholarship 1985-87, scholarship chmn. 1988-89), Am. Bus. Woman of Yr. award 1985, pres., v.p. 1985-87), Dade/Broward City Clks. and Fin. Dirs. (pres. 1992-93), Fla. City and County Mgrs. Assn., Bus. and Profl. Women (pres. 1981), Internat. Mcpl. Clks. Assn., Pers. Mgmt. Assn., Acad. for Advanced Edn. of Mcpl. Clk. Cert. Lic. Ofcl. Democrat. Roman Catholic. Avocation: reading. Home: 19245 NW 14th St Hollywood FL 33029-4506 Office: Village of Bal Harbour 655 96th St Bal Harbour FL 33154-2428

HORTON, JERRY SMITH, minister; b. Columbus, Miss., Oct. 6, 1941; s. William Robert and Sarah Elizabeth (Smith) H.; m. Patricia Jan Taylor, May 30, 1964; children: Thomas Christian, William Andrew. AA, Wood Jr. Coll., 1963; BA in Edn., U. Miss., 1968; MDiv, Emory U., 1972. Ordained to ministry United Meth. Ch., 1973. Min. various chs. in Miss. and Ga., 1962-72; assoc. min. Southaven (Miss.) 1st United Meth. Ch., 1972-74; min. Minor Meml. United Meth. Ch., Walls, Miss., 1974-81; parish dir. Iuka (Miss.) 1st United Meth. Ch., 1981-84; min. Belzoni (Miss.) 1st United Meth. Ch., 1984-91, Fulton (Miss.) 1st United Meth. Ch., 1991-92, Holly Springs (Miss.) 1st United Meth. Ch., 1992-95, Long Beach (Miss.) 1st United Meth. Ch., 1995—; mem. bd. diaconal ministries No. Miss. Conf., United Meth. Ch., 1972-74, mem. commn. on equitable salaries, 1981-90, conf. ins. com., 1990-94; head chaplain vol. chaplaincy program in local hosp. Bd. dirs. Habitat for Humanity, Marshall County; active Vol. Chaplaincy Program in local hosp., North Miss. chpt. Emmaus Walk Cmty. in Miss., Citizen Vols. Against Crime, 1994 Class Competitive Cmty. Program, Marshall County; trustee Rust Coll., 1992-95; trustee Internat. Seamen and Trucker Ctr., Gulfport, 1996—. Named one of Outstanding Young Men of Am., Internat. Jaycees, 1976, Top Evangelistic Pastor of Conf., 1981; honored with Spl. Proclamation, Mayor of Iuka; Estaral scholar. Mem. Rotary. Avocations: hunting, scuba diving, fishing, youth work, writing devotions. Office: 1st United Meth Ch 208 Pine St Long Beach MS 39560-6041 *The real test of a truly great minister is not that his members will think about him, but that those members will be lead to remember what he said and will think more about Jesus.*

HORTON, JOHN EDWARD, periodontist, educator; b. Brockton, Mass., Dec. 30, 1930; s. Harold Ellsworth and Anita Helen (Samuelson) H.; children—m. Jacqueline A. Hansen, June 10, 1951; John Edward, Janet Elaine, James Elliot, Jeffrey Eugene, Joseph Everett; m. Susan Drake, Aug. 4, 1984. B.S., Providence Coll., 1952; D.M.D., Tufts U., 1957; M.S.D., Baylor U., 1965; M.A., George Washington U., 1978. Commd. 1st lt. U.S. Army, 1957, advanced through grades to col., 1972; cons. to surgeon U.S. Army, Europe, 1967-70; guest scientist dept. immunology Nat. Inst. Dental Research, Bethesda, Md., 1970-73; chief depts. microbiology and immunology Inst. Dental Research U.S. Army, 1973-77, ret., 1977; lectr. Johns Hopkins U. Sch. Pub. Health, 1975-79; asst. professorial lectr. George Washington U., Washington, 1972-74, assoc. professorial lectr., 1974-76, professorial lectr., 1976-77; assoc. prof., chmn. program dir. dept. periodontology Harvard U. Sch. Dental Medicine, 1977-81; prof., chmn., program dir. dept. periodontology Ohio State U. Coll. Dentistry, Columbus, 1981—; cons. VA Med. Ctr., West Roxbury and Brockton, Mass., 1978-81; cons. div. research grants NIH, 1973-86, VA Out-Patient Ctr., Columbus, U.S. Air Force Med. Ctr., Wright Patterson AFB, U.S. Army Inst. Dental Research. Editor: Mechanisms of Localized Bone Loss, 1978. Contbr. numerous articles to profl. jours. Decorated Commendation medal, Meritorious Service medal, Legion of Merit, Outstanding Internatl. Scholar Awd., Alpha Epsilon Chapter. Fellow AAAS, Am. Coll. Dentists, Am. Pub. Health Assn., Internat. Coll. Dentists, Royal Soc. Health; mem. Turkish Soc. Periodontology (hon.), Omicron Kappa Upsilon, Assn. Gnathology (hon., Taiwan), Phi Delta Kappa, Sigma Xi, Phi Beta Delta. Office: Ohio State U Coll Dentistry Dept Periodontology 305 W 12th Ave Columbus OH 43210-1267*

HORTON, JOSEPH JULIAN, JR., academic dean, educator; b. Memphis, Nov. 7, 1936; s. Joseph Julian and Nina (Williams) H.; m. Linda Anne Langley, May 30, 1964; children: Joseph Julian, Anne Adele, David Douglas. AA, Lon Morris Jr. Coll., 1955; BA, N.Mex. State U., 1958; MA, So. Meth. U., 1965, PhD, 1968; postgrad. Harvard U., 1970-71. Claims examiner Social Security Adminstrn., Kansas City, Mo., 1958-60, claims authorizer, 1960-61; with FDIC, Washington, 1967-71, fin. economist, 1967-69, coordinator merger analysis, 1969-71; prof., chmn. dept. econs. and bus. Slippery Rock State Coll. (Pa.), 1971-81; vis. fin. economist Fed. Home Loan Bank Bd., Washington, 1978-79; prof., chmn. commerce div. Bellarmine (Ky.) Coll., 1981-82, dean W. Fielding Rubel Sch. Bus., 1982-86; dean Sch. Mgmt. U. Scranton, Pa., 1986-96; dean Coll. Bus. Adminstrn., U. Cen. Ark., 1996—; asst. prof. George Washington U., Washington, 1968-69, U. Md., College Park, 1969-70; pres. Pa. Conf. Economists, Internat. Acad. Bus. Disciplines, Congress of Polit. Economists, U.S.A. Bd. editors Eastern Econ. Jour.; contbr. to profl. jours. Recipient Cokesbury award So. Meth. U., 1965; NSF Grad. fellow, 1964-66, Ford Found. Dissertation fellow, 1966-67, Harvard U. Research fellow, 1970-71, Bank Adminstrn. Inst. Clarence Lichtfeldt fellow, 1981, Burk fellow. Mem. Am. Econ. Assn., Am. Fin. Assn., Internat. Acad. Bus. Disciplines (pres.), N. Am. Econs. and Fin. Assn. (bd. dirs., v.p., pres.), Eastern Econ. Assn. (v.p.). Office: U Cen Ark Office of Dean Coll Bus Adminstrn Conway AR 72035-0001

HORTON, JOSEPH MATTHEW, college dean, humanities educator; b. Pittsfield, Mass., Oct. 20, 1955; s. John Gerald and Lucille Rita (Roy) H.; m. Susan Raye Berthiaume, June 20, 1981; children: Brian Joseph, Benjamin Matthew. BS, St. Anselm Coll., 1977; MS, Mich. State U., 1978; EdD, Vanderbilt U., 1988. Lectr. in criminal justice St. Anselm Coll., Manchester, N.H., 1979—, lectr. in humanities, 1981—, dean of students, 1990—; programs evaluation specialist N.H. Crime Commn., Concord, N.H., 1979; asst. dean St. Anselm Coll., 1980-84, dir. phys. plant, 1984-90; mem. student affairs think tank New Eng. Resource Ctr. Higher Edn., Boston, 1996—. Bd. dirs., chmn. St. Catherine Sch., Manchester, 1987—; bd. dirs. Greater Manchester chpt. ARC, 1995—. Fulbright scholar, 1995. Mem. Nat. Assn. Student Personnel Adminstrs., Assn. Integrative Studies, Alpha Phi Sigma. Avocations: reading, traveling, exercising. Home: 817 Maple St Manchester NH 03104-3214 Office: St Anselm Coll 100 Saint Anselms Dr Manchester NH 03102-1308

HORTON, KATHRYN LYNNE, marketing executive; b. Troy, Ohio, Sept. 12, 1950; d. Fred and Bonnie June (Perry) Nolls; m. Brad VanDyck, Dec. 25, 1978 (div. June 1985); children: Scott Allen, Geoffrey Randall. BA in Bus., ITO, L.A., 1985, mktg. specialist, 1986. Customer svc. rep. Nationwide Ins., Akron, Ohio, 1974-76, Polymetrics, Santa Clara, Calif., 1976-79; fin. dir. SCS, Santa Clara, 1979-85; mktg. mgr. Ch. of Scientology Internat., L.A., 1985-90; customer svc. rep. Steven Tomczak & Assocs., Burbank, Calif., 1990-92; sr. mktg. v.p. Exec. Software, Glendale, Calif., 1992-94; owner The Mktg. Biz, La Crescenta, Calif., 1994—. Mem. NAFE. Office: The Mktg Biz 143 S Glendale Ave Ste 208 Glendale CA 91205-1137

HORTON, KENNETH, investor; b. Newport, Nebr., May 11, 1921; s. Fred and Clara E. (Cottrel) H.; m. Evelyn H. Shafer, Dec. 29, 1939 (div. 1961); children: Kenneth Eugene, Helen Clara Catherine; m. Arlene J. Mitchell, July 23, 1962. AA, Valley Coll., San Bernardino, Calif., 1951; grad., Law Enforcement Officers Tng. Sch., San Bernardino, Calif., 1957. Crew leader 1st suppression fire crew Civilian Conservation Corp, Glendora, Calif., 1937-39; journeyman R.R. Car Shop/Santa Fe R.R., San Bernardino, 1940-44; boy's counselor San Bernardino County Juvenile Hall, 1948-53; supr. state champion drill team Calif. Youth Authority, Whittier, 1954; layout carpenter Bectal Constrn. Co., Oro grande, Calif., 1954-55; patrolman, vice officer Police Dept., San Bernardino, 1956-66; ind. investor Thousand Oaks, Calif., 1950—. Sustaining mem. Rep. Nat. Com., Washington, 1978—. With U.S. Army, 1944-45. Decorated Combat Infantryman medal, Bronze Star medal; recipient Letter of Appreciation for apprehending holdup man Security Pacific Bank, 1974. Lutheran. Avocations: maker of fine furniture, 1st edition book collection, antique automobiles. Address: PO Box 1432 Thousand Oaks CA 91358

HORTON, LAWRENCE STANLEY, electrical engineer, apartment developer; b. Hanston, Kans., July 25, 1926; s. Gene Leigh and Retta Florene (Abbott) H.; m. Margaret Ann Cowles, Nov. 26, 1946 (dec. 1964); children: Craig, Lawrence Stanley, Steven J.; m. Julia Ann Butler Wirkkula, Aug. 15, 1965; stepchildren: Charles Wirkkula Horton, Jerry Higginbotham Horton. BSEE, Oreg. State U., 1949. Elec. engr. Mountain States Power Co., Calif. Oreg. Power Co., Pacific Power and Light Co., 1948-66; mgr. Ramic Corp., 1966-69; cons. elec. engr. Marquess and Assocs., Medford, Oreg., 1969-85, sec., bd. dirs.; pres., owner Medford Better Housing Assn., 1985—; ptnr. Terpening Terrace, T'Morrow Apts., Johnson Manor, Champion Pk.; bd. dirs. People's Bank of Commerce; former bd. dirs. Valley of Rogue Bank, developer various apt. complexes and retirment communities, 1969—, Northwood Apts., Horton Plz., Fountain Plz., Anna Maria Creekside, Terpening Ter.; bd. dirs. Medford Hist. Commn. Active Medford Planning Commn., Archtl. Review Commn., Housing Authority, Peoples Bank Commerce; bd. govs. State of Oreg. Citizens Utility; pres. United Fund, 1963-64. With USN, 1945-46. Named Rogue Valley Profl. Engr. of Yr., 1969. Mem. IEEE, Nat. Soc. Profl. Engrs., Profl. Engrs. of Oreg., So. Oreg. Rental Owners Assn. (pres.), Rogue Valley Geneol. Soc. (pres.), Medford C. of C. (dir.), Rogue Valley Yacht Club (commodore 1974-75, dir., local fleet capt., champion), Rogue Valley Knife and Fork (past pres.), San Juan 21 Fleet Assn. (western vice commodore, Top Ten San Juan Sailor West Coast, 1980), Jackson Toastmasters (founder 1957), Medford Rotary, Kiwanis (life, pres. Crater Golden 1990-91). Republican. Methodist. Grad. instr. Dale Carnegie course, 1955, 56; contbr. elec. articles to profl. assns., 1956-61. Office: Medford Better Housing Assn 1118 Spring St Medford OR 97504-6272

HORTON, LINDA RAE, lawyer; b. Louisville, Dec. 1, 1946; d. Raymond Thomas and Marcia Bryan Horton; m. Henry Ninghan Ho (dec. Jan. 1987); 1 stepchild, Michael Ho; m. Carl V. Nelson Jr.; children: Jonathan Horton, Colleen Horton, Cassandra Nelson, Douglas Nelson. BA, U. Ky., 1968; JD, George Washington U., 1975; LLM, Georgetown U., 1997. Bar: Md., D.C., U.S. Supreme Ct. Mgmt. intern FDA, Arlington, Va., 1968-69; legis. asst. FDA, Rockville, Md., 1970-74; chief legis. br. FDA, Rockville, 1974-75, trial atty., 1975-76, assoc. chief counsel, 1976-79, dep. chief counsel, 1979-93, dir. internat. policy, 1993—; adj. prof. George Washington U. Sch. Law, Washington, 1983-85, Georgetown U. Sch. Law, Washington, 1999—; bd. dirs. Am. Nat. Stds. Inst., N.Y.C. Chair editl. bd. Food and Drug Law Jour., 1985-86; contbr. chpts. to books and articles to profl. jours. Precinct capt. Dem. Party Ky., Jeffersontown, 1968, del. state pres. conv., Louisville, 1968; PTA fgn. lang. coord. Montgomery County Schs., Potomac, Md., 1986-89; dep. mgr., parent swim team Montgomery Swim League, Rockville, Md., 1988-90. Recipient Disting. Svc. award Dept. Health Human Svc., Washington, 1989, Meritorious Svc. award Am. Nat. Stds. Inst., 1997. Mem. ABA, Md. Bar Assn., D.C. Bar Assn., Supreme Ct. Bar, Nat. Cooperation Lab. Accreditation (bd. dirs. 1997—). Presbyterian. Avocations: travel, bridge, reading, hiking, writing. E-mail: lhorton@oc.fda.gov. Office: FDA HF-23 Rm 15-74 5600 Fishers Ln Rockville MD 20857

HORTON, MICHAEL, public affairs executive, information specialist; b. Montreal, Can., Mar. 10, 1918; s. Irving and Anne (Spector) H.; m. Lydia Franklin Wells, June 14, 1947; children: Hilary, Christopher, Lydia, Cleveland. BA, Bishop's U., Quebec, 1939; postgrad., Columbia U., 1940. News editor Sta. WMCA, N.Y.C., 1939-40; reporter Buffalo Evening News, 1940-41; news editor Washington-Times Herald, Washington, 1941-42; editor, columnist N.Y. Herald Tribune, Paris, 1946-52; chief French press br. Marshall Plan, Paris, 1952-53; dir. pub. rels. div. NBC, 1953-58; dir. info. CBS, N.Y.C., 1958-61; dir. pub. rels. div. CPC Internat., Zurich and Brussels, 1961-79; prin. Michael Horton Assocs., Brussels and Brunswick, Maine, 1979—. Author: (with others) Developing the Corporate Image, 1960. With MIS, 1942-46. Mem. Internat. Pub. Rels. Assn. (coun. mem. 1965—), Pub. Rels. Soc. Am., Nat. Press, Overseas Press. Unitarian. Avocations: photography, tennis, music. Home and Office: 17 Cleaveland St Brunswick ME 04011-2109

HORTON, MICHAEL L., mortgage company executive, publishing executive; b. Pasadena, Calif., Oct. 19, 1961; s. Jerry S. and Mary L. Horton. BA in Bus. Econs., Claremont McKenna Coll., 1983. Lic. real estate broker. Gen. mgr. I.W.S., Pasadena, 1976-80; proprietor NBB Svcs. Orgn., Upland, Calif., 1980-85; regional mgr. Sycamore Fin. Group Inc., Rancho Cucamonga, Calif., 1984-87; CEO, pres. Boulder Fin. Corp., Rancho Cucamonga, 1987—, M.C.M. Pub. Corp., Rancho Cucamonga, 1992—; pres., CEO Sandstone Realty Group, Inc., 1995—; chm. C.H.A.M.P. Inc., 1996—. Author: A Real Estate Professional's Guide to Mortgage Finance, 1985; author Mortgage Fin. Newsletter, 1984—; author fin. workshop. Mem. Rep. State Ctrl. Com., Calif., 1980—, Bldg. and Industry Assn., Rancho Cucamonga, 1988—, Res Publica Soc., Claremont, Calif., 1986—; donor mem. L.A. World Affairs Coun., 1988—. Claremont McKenna Coll. scholar, 1981-83; recipient Dons D. Lepper Meml. award Exec. Women Internat., 1981, So. Calif. Edison Bus. Competition award, 1979, 81. Mem. Nat. Assn. Realtors, Inland Empire West Bd. Realtors. Avocations: basketball, racquet sports, water sports. Office: Boulder Fin Corp 9121 Haven Ave Ste 180 Rancho Cucamonga CA 91730-5453

HORTON, ODELL, federal judge; b. Bolivar, Tenn., May 13, 1929; s. Odell and Rosa H.; m. Evie L. Randolph, Sept. 13, 1953; children: Odell, Christopher. AB, Morehouse Coll., 1951; cert., U.S. Navy Sch. Journalism, 1952; JD, Howard U., 1956; HHD (hon.), Miss. Indsl. Coll., 1969; LLD (hon.), Morehouse Coll., 1983. Bar: Tenn. 1956. Pvt. practice law Memphis, 1957-62; asst. U.S. atty. Western Dist. Tenn., Memphis, 1962-67; dir. div. hosp. and health services City of Memphis, 1968; judge Criminal Ct. Shelby County, Memphis, 1969-70; pres. LeMoyne-Owen Coll., Memphis, 1970-74; commentator Sta. WREC-TV (CBS), Memphis, 1972-74; judge U.S. Dist. Ct. (we. dist.) Tenn., 1980—, chief judge, 1987; mem. Jud. Conf. of U.S. Com. on Defender Svcs.; chair com. to establish a Death Penalty Resource Ctr., Nashville. Bd. mgrs. Meth. Hosp., Memphis, 1969-79; bd. dirs. Family Svc. Memphis, United Negro Coll. Fund, N.Y.C., 1970-74. With USMC, 1951-53. Recipient Disting. Alumni award Howard U., 1969, L. M. Graves Meml. Health award Mid-South Med. Ctr. Coun., Memphis, 1969, Bill of Rights award West Tenn. chpt. ACLU, 1970, Disting. Service award Mallory Knights Charitable Orgn., 1970, Disting. Service award Smothers Chapel C.M.E. Ch., 1971, Outstanding Citizen award Frontiers Internat., 1969, Ralph E. Bunche Humanitarian award Boy Scouts Am., 1972, Outstanding Educator and Judge award Salem-Gilfield Bapt. Ch., 1973, Spl. Tribute award A.M.E. Ch., 1974, United Negro Coll. Fund award, 1974, Humanities award Citizens Com. Coun. of Memphis, 1969, Shelby County Penal Farm award, 1974, Disting. Service award LeMoyne-Owen Coll., 1974, Disting. Service award Lane Coll., 1977, Dedicated Community Service award Christian Meth. Episc. Ch., 1979. Mem. NAACP, ABA (sr., chair conf. fed. trial judges, jud. adminstrn. divsn., chair exec. com. nat. conf. fed. trial judges 1994-95). *

HORTON, PATRICIA MATHEWS, artist, violist and violinist; b. Bklyn., Mar. 6, 1932; d. Edward Joseph and Margaret (Briggs) Mathews; m. Ernest H. Horton Jr., Mar. 6, 1982; 1 stepchild, Carol Horton Tremblay. Student in viola, William Primrose Master Class, 1980; student, Glendale (Calif.) C.C., 1981-90, 93, Art Ctr. Coll. Design, Pasadena, Calif., 1988-93; student in painting composition, Peter Liashkov, L.A., 1993-97. Profl. musician on violin and viola, 1951-86; musician on tour U.S., Can., Cuba, 1952-57. Played with New Orleans Philharm., 1959-61, U.S. Tour of San Francisco Ballet, 1965, L.A. Civic Light Opera, 1974-80; played L.A. engagements of Bolshoi Ballet Co., 1975, Am. Ballet Theatre, 1974-80, N.Y.C. Opera, 1974-80, Royal Ballet of London, 1978, Alicia Alonzo's Cuban Ballet, 1979, Harlem Ballet, 1984, Deutsche Oper Berlin, 1985; played on motion picture and TV soundtrack recs., through 1986; one-woman shows include Claremont (Calif.) Sch. Theology, 1997, Pasadena First United Meth. Ch., 1997, 99. Active Dem. Nat. Com., Women's Caucus for Art. Mem. Am. Fedn. Musicians (life), Alpha Gamma Sigma. Avocation: hiking local mountains, desert and beaches.

HORTON, PAUL BRADFIELD, lawyer; b. Dallas, Oct. 19, 1920; s. Frank Barrett and Hazel Lillian (Bradfield) H.; m. Susan Jeanne Diggle, May 19, 1949; children: Bradfield Ragland, Bruce Ragsdale. B.A., U. Tex., Austin, 1943, student Law Sch., 1941-43; LL.B., So. Methodist U., 1947. Bar: Tex. 1946. Ptnr. McCall, Parkhurst & Horton, Dallas, 1951—; lectr. mcpl. bond law and pub. finance S.W. Legal Found.; drafter Tex. mcpl. bonds legislation, 1963—. Mem. Gov.'s Com. Tex. Edn. Code, 1967-69. Served to lt. USNR, 1943-46. Mem. ABA, Dallas Bar Assn., Southwestern Legal Found., Nat. Water Resources Assn., Tex. Water Conservation Assn., Govt. Fin. Officers Assn., The Barristers, Dallas Country Club, Crescent Club, Tower Club, Delta Theta Phi, Beta Theta Pi. Home: 5039 Seneca Dr Dallas TX 75209-2219 Office: McCall Parkhurst & Horton 717 N Harwood St Ste 900 Dallas TX 75201-6586

HORTON, PAUL CHESTER, psychiatrist; b. Cin., Jan. 29, 1942; s. Paul Chester Sr. and Elizabeth Pauline (Rice) H.; m. JoAnn Alice Baker, Aug. 30; children: Paul Andrey, Alexander Robert. BA, U. Minn., 1964; MD, &, 1968. Diplomate Am. Bd. Psychiatry and Neurology. Rotating intern U. Cin., 1969; resident in psychiatry Yale U., New Haven, 1972; staff psychiatrist Guidance Clinic of Camden County, West Collingswood, N.J., 1972-74, Milford (Conn.) Family and Child Guidance Clinic, 1974-77; mem. faculty Sch. Medicine Yale U., New Haven, 1974-76; pvt. practice Meriden, 1974—; cons. psychiatrist Child Guidance Clinic Cen. Conn., Meriden, 1980—; med. dir., 1994—; mem. faculty U. Conn. Sch. Medicine, Farmington, 1978-79; cons. Caring for Children, San Francisco, 1989—; reviewer Am. Jour. Psychiatry, 1980—, and others. Author: Solace, 1981, Solace, paperback edit. 1983, Solace, Japanese edit., 1985; sr. editor: The Solace Paradigm, 1988; contbr. articles to profl. jours. Big Brother Big Bros. Orgn., Mpls., 1964-68. Lt. comdr. USN, 1972-74. Mem. Am. Psychiat. Assn., Meriden Wallingford Med. Assn., Gridiron Club. Home: 18 Metacomet Dr Meriden CT 06450-3568 Office: 234 Hobart St Meriden CT 06450-4380

HORTON, SIR ROBERT BAYNES, railroad company executive; b. Bushey, Eng., Aug. 18, 1939; s. William H. Horton and Dorothy Joan (Baynes) Dunn; m. Sally Doreen Wells, July 28, 1962; children: Simon, Ruth. BSME, U. St. Andrews, Scotland, 1960; MS, MIT, 1971; LLD (hon.), Dundee U., 1988; DCL (hon.), Kent U., 1990; DBA (hon.), North London U., 1991; DSc (hon.), Cranfield Inst. Tech., 1992; LLD (hon.), Aberdeen U., 1992; DSc (hon.), Kingston U., 1993; DUniv (hon.), Open U., 1993. With Brit. Petroleum Ltd. (now BP plc), London, 1957-86, 88-92; gen. mgr. BP Tankers, London, 1975-76, gen. mgr. corp. planning, 1976-79; mng. dir., CEO BP Co. plc, 1979-83, chmn., 1990-92; chmn., CEO Standard Oil Co., Cleve., 1986-88; chmn. Railtrack plc, 1993—, JXX Oil & Gas plc, 1995-97; bd. dirs. Emerson Electric Co., Partnerre, Premier Farnell Plc.; pres. Beso, U.K., 1993—; vice-chair BIM, 1984-90, ABSA, 1992—; dir. ICL plc, 1982-84, Pilkington Bros., 1985-86, Emerson Electric, 1987—, Ptnr. Re, 1993—, Farnell Electronics plc, 1995—. Chmn. Sloan Sch. Vis. Com., 1987-

95; chancellor U. Kent at Canterbury, Eng., 1990-95; gov. King's Sch., Canterbury, 1984—; chair Bus. in the Arts Tate Gallery Found., 1988-92. Fellow Inst. Chem. Engrs., Royal Soc. Arts, City and Guilds of London, Athenaeum Club (London), Leander Club (Henley). Anglican. Avocations: music, country activities, reading. Fax: 0171-567 9120.

HORTON, ROBERT CARLTON, geologist; b. Tonopah, Nev., July 25, 1926; s. Frank Elijah and Eathel Margaret (Miller) H.; m. Beverly Jean Burhans, Dec. 5, 1952; children: Debra, Robin, Cindy. B.S., U. Nev., 1949, D.Sc. (hon.), 1985, Geol. Engr., 1966. Assoc. dir. Nev. Bur. Mines, Reno, 1956-66; cons. Reno, 1966-76; dir. geology div. Bendix Field Engring Corp. (Grand Junction), Colo., 1976-81; dir. U.S. Bur. Mines, Washington, 1981-87; dir. strategic materials rsch. U. Nev., Reno, 1987-90, assoc. dean MacKay Sch. Mines, 1989-90, assoc. dean emeritus, 1990—; mem. Nev. Gov.'s Mining Adv. Com., 1966-72. Author: Barite Deposits of Nevada, 1962, Fluorspar Deposits of Nevada, 1963, History of Nevada Mining, 1963. Republican candidate for Congress from Nev., 1958. Served to lt. USNR, 1944-46, 53-56, PTO. Kennecott scholar, 1948; named Engr. of Yr. Reno chpt., NSPE, 1967; recipient Outstanding Alumnus John Mackay medal, Mackay Sch. Mines, 1991. Mem. AIME (subsect. chmn. Reno 1962-63), Soc. Econ. Geologists, Mining and Metall. Soc. Am. Methodist. Office: U Nev-Reno Mackay Sch Mine Reno NV 89557

HORTON, SHERMAN D., JR., state supreme court justice; b. 1931. AB, Dartmouth Coll.; LLB, Harvard U. Assoc justice. N.H. Supreme Ct., Concord, NH, 1990—. Office: NH Supreme Court One Noble Dr Concord NH 03301-6160*

HORTON, TERESA EVETTS, municipal official; m. Ronnie Horton; children: Joey, Brandon, Jessica, Morgan. Student, Tenn. State U., Austin Peay State U. Adminstrv. asst. dept. personnel City of Nashville, 1972-80, developer, coord. pers. programs, 1980-85; bus. mgr. Nashville Convention Ctr., 1985-91, exec. dir., 1991—. Mem. Mayor's Econ. Devel. Planning Com., Nahsville Downtown Partnership; mem. bd. Goodwill Industries. Mem. NAFE, Internat. Assn. Assembly Mgrs., Nashville YWCA/Cable, Nashville Hotel/Motel Assn., Internat. Assn., Exposition Mgrs., Nashville Area C. of C. Office: Nashville Convention Ctr 601 Commerce St Nashville TN 37203-3707*

HORTON, THOMAS EDWARD, JR., mechanical engineering educator; b. Houston, Jan. 12, 1935; s. Thomas Edward and Minnie Tolula (Sloan) H.; m. Bobbie Jean Newcomb, June 8, 1963; children—Holly Anne, Thomas Edward. BS, U. Tex., 1957, PhD, 1964; MS (Caterpillar rsch. fellow), Stanford U., 1958. Jr. mech. engr. Shell Devel. Co., Houston, 1957-58; tchg. asst., rsch. asst., rsch. scientist U. Tex., Austin, 1959-62; rsch. engr. Jet Propulsion Lab. Calif. Inst. Tech., Pasadena, 1962; sr. rsch. engr. Jet Propulsion Lab. Calif. Inst. Tech., 1963-66; asso. prof. mech. engring., rsch. engr. U. Miss., 1966-71, prof., rsch. engr., 1971-94, emeritus prof., 1994—; dir. U.S. Army Laser Sci. Lab., Redstone Arsenal, Ala., 1975-76, Reiton Corp. of Houston; cons. Army Research Office, Jet Propulsion Lab., Marathon Oil Co., Shell Devel. Co., Exxon, Chevron, Mobil, Texaco. Contbr. articles to profl. jours. Fellow AIAA (assoc.; mem. tech. coms.); mem. ASME (life; mem. tech. coms.), Am. Phys. Soc., Am. Soc. Engring. Edn. (research award Southeastern sect. 1971), Sigma Xi (pres. local chpt.), Tau Beta Pi (student adviser), Pi Tau Sigma, Phi Eta Sigma. Republican. Methodist. Patentee in field. Home: 209 Saint Andrews Cir Oxford MS 38655-2518 Office: U Miss Dept Mech Engring University MS 38677

HORTON, THOMAS ROSCOE, business advisor; b. Fort Pierce, Fla., Nov. 17, 1926; s. Charles Montraville Horton and Ruby Mae (Swain) Warren; m. Marilou Deeming, Dec. 19, 1947; children—Susan, Jean, Marilyn. BS, Stetson U., 1949, LHD (hon.), 1982; MS, U. Fla., 1950, PhD, 1954; LLD (hon.), Pace U., 1976; DLitt (hon.), U. Charleston, 1980. Instr., asst. headmaster Bolles Sch., Jacksonville, Fla., 1950-52; with IBM Corp., Armonk, N.Y., 1954-82; pres., chief exec. officer Am. Mgmt. Assn., N.Y.C., 1982-89, chmn., chief exec. officer, 1989-91, chmn., 1991-92; advisor Stetson U., DeLand, Fla., 1992-96; bd. dirs. Enesco Group, Inc., 1998—, Stanhome, Inc., 1991-98, The Comml. Bank, Am. Precision Industries, 1990-95, Charlesbridge Pub. Co., 1983-91, Perrigo Corp., 1987-88; mem. adv. bd. Who's Who in Fin. and Industry, 1988—. Author: What Works for Me, 1986, Beyond the Trust Gap, 1990, The CEO Paradox, 1992; editor: Traffic Control - Theory and Implementation, 1965; columnist Mgmt. Rev., 1982-92, Dirs. & Bds., 1998—; assoc. prodr. SHO Entertainment, Inc., 1997—. Life mem. Salvation Army; trustee Bethune-Cookman Coll., Daytona Beach, Fla., 1971-82, hon., 1982—; trustee Pace U., N.Y.C., 1975-92, emeritus trustee, 1992—; trustee Am. Grad. Sch. Internat. Mgmt., Glendale, Ariz., 1982-92, Stetson U. Bus. Sch. Found., 1992—; mem. econ. devel. com. City of DeLand (Fla.), 1992—; trustee emeritus Stetson U., 1996—; bd. dirs. Kids Voting USA, 1991—, chair, 1992-98; adv. bd. Am. C. of C. of Cuba in U.S., 1996—. With U.S. Army, 1944-46, ETO. Fellow Acad. Mgmt., Internat. Acad. Mgmt. (vice chancellor); mem. European Found. for Mgmt. Devel., Japan Mgmt. Assn. (hon.), Korean Mgmt. Assn. (hon.), Pres.' Assn. N.Y.C. (chmn. 1982-91), Nat. Assn. Corp. Dirs. (faculty mem., bd. dirs. 1996—, chair 1999—), Internat. Coun. for Innovation in Higher Edn., Assn. Internat. des Etudiants en Scis. Econs. et Commls. (hon. dir. 1990—), Russian Econs. Soc. (hon.), Mgmt. Exec. Soc., Conf. Bd. (sr.), DeLand Country Club, Lake Beresford Yacht Club. Methodist. Office: Stetson U PO Box 8395 Deland FL 32720

HORTON, W. MIKE, financial company executive; b. Greenville, Miss., July 28, 1941; s. W.F. and Ruth Kain H.; m. Pamela Gene Steen, July 21, 1967; children: Lacy, Michael. BS in Mktg., Miss. State U., Starkville, 1971. Acctg. mgr. Mr. Quik Stores, Inc., Indianola, Miss.; dir. acctg. Sunflower Stores, Inc., Indianola; asst. controller The Lewis Grocer Co., Indianola, controller, CFO, treas.; dist. controller Supervapu, Inc., Indianola, Hammond, La.; cons. in field. Mem. Greenville Yacht Club (commodore 1986—). Roman Catholic. Avocations: boating, traveling, music. E-mail: PAMH@TEAINFO.com. Home: 507 Mimosa Ave Indianola MS 38751

HORTON, WILFRED HENRY, mathematics educator; b. Newark, Nottingham, Eng., May 27, 1918; s. Henry and Alice M. (Spence) H.; m. Margaret E. Haskard; children: Richard, Sheila, David, Jennifer. BSc in Math. with honors, U. Coll., Nottingham, 1940; Engr., Stanford U., 1959. With De Havilland Aircraft Co., Hatfield, Eng., 1940-45, Percival Aircraft, Luton, Eng., 1945-50; sr. sci. officer Royal Aircraft Establishment, Farnborough, Eng., 1950-54, prin. sci. officer, 1954-57; assoc. prof. Stanford (Calif.) U., 1959-67; prof. Ga. Inst. Tech., Atlanta, 1967-84; prof. emeritus U. System Ga., 1985—; cons. various orgns. Contbr. articles to profl. jours. and encys. Achievements include design of test facilities for supersonic aircraft, hypersonic wind tunnel.

HORTON, WILLIAM RUSSELL, retired utility company executive; b. Toronto, Ont., Can., Aug. 25, 1931; s. Russell Burton and Freda Catherine (Middleton) H.; m. Dorothy Viva Rye, Nov. 27, 1954; children: William Russell, Robert Freeman, Douglas Lloyd, Ronald Edward. BA Sci. in Mining Engring., U. Toronto, 1955. Engr. Imperial Oil Ltd., Calgary and Camrose, Alta., Can., 1955-56; engr., mgr. Black Sivalls & Bryson Ltd., Edmonton, Alta., 1956-65; v.p. Gamma Engring. Ltd., Edmonton, 1965-68; pres. Horton Engring. Ltd., Edmonton, 1968—, also bd. dirs.; mem. Alta. Pub. Utilities Bd., Edmonton, 1973-76, chmn., 1976-83; exec. v.p. Can. Utilities Ltd., Edmonton, 1984-90; bd. dirs. Can. Utilities Ltd., Alta. Power Ltd.; mem. Centre for Study Regulated Industries McGill U.; hon. mem. Can. Assn. Members Pub. Utility Tribunals. Mem. Assn. Profl. Engrs. Geologists and Geophysicists Alta. (life), Northwest Electric Light and Power Assn. (hon. life). Avocations: sports, music, reading. Home: 17490 Coral Beach Rd, Winfield, BC Canada V4V 1C1 Office: Can Utilities Ltd, 1500-909 11th Ave SW, Calgary, AB Canada T2R 1N6

HORVAT, SARAH KOBS, museum adminstrator; b. Ft. Atkinson, Wis., July 17, 1972. Adminstrv. asst. Charles Allis Art Mus., Milw., 1995-97; program and promotions coord. Charles Allis Art Mus., 1997—. Office: Charles Allis Art Mus 1801 N Prospect Ave Milwaukee WI 53202-1933*

HORVÁTH, CSABA, chemical engineering educator, researcher; b. Szolnok, Hungary, Jan. 25, 1930; came to U.S., 1963; s. Gyula and Róza (Lányi) H.; children: Donatella, Katalin. Diploma in Chem. Engring., U. Tech. Scis., Budapest, Hungary, 1952, Dr. (hon.), 1986; PhD, J.W. Goethe U., Frankfurt-Main, Germany, 1963; MA (hon.), Yale U., 1979. Asst. in chem. tech. U. Tech. Scis., Budapest, 1952-56; chem. engr. Hoechst AG, Frankfurt am Main, 1956-61; research fellow Harvard U., Cambridge, Mass., 1963-64; research assoc. Yale U. Sch. Medicine, New Haven, 1964-69, assoc. prof., 1970-79, prof. chem. engring., 1979—, chmn. dept. chem. engring., 1987-93; prof. chem. engring. Llewellyn West Jones Jr., 1993-98, Roberto C. Goizueta, 1998—; cons. various govt. and indsl. orgns. Co-author: Introduction to Separation Science, 1973; editor: Series High Performance Liquid Chromatography, 1981—; mem. editl. bd. 9 sci. periodicals; contbr. more than 290 rsch. papers and articles to sci. publs. Recipient S. Dal Nogare award Delaware Valley Chromatography Forum, 1978, Tswett medal 15th Internat. Symposium on Advances in Chromatography, 1979, Humboldt sr. U.S. scientist award Humboldt Found., Fed. Republic of Germany, 1982, EAS Chromatography award, 1986, Van Slyke award N.Y. Metro Sect. Am. Assn. Clin. Chemists, 1992, A.J.P. Martin award Chromatography Soc. U.K., 1994, Disting. Contbn. in Separation Sci. award Calif. Separation Sci. Soc., 1995, Nat. award N.E. Region Chromatography Discussion Group, 1997, Halász medal award Hungarian Separation Sci. Soc. Funding, 1997, Golay award 21st Internat. Symposium on Capillary Chromatography and Electrophoresis, 1999. Fellow AIChE, Am. Inst. Med. and Biomed. Engrs. (founding); mem. AAAS, Deutsche Gesellschaft fuer Chemisches Apparatewesen, Chemische Technik und Biotechnologie e.v., Am. Chem. Soc. (nat. chromatography award 1983), Am. Ceramic Soc., Hungarian Chem. Soc. (hon.), Hungarian Acad. Scis. (external), Conn. Acad. Sci. and Engring., Conn. Acad. Arts and Scis., Inst. Food Technologists, Sigma Xi. Home: PO Box 605 41 Temple Ct New Haven CT 06511-6820 Office: Yale U PO Box 208286 9 Hillhouse Ave New Haven CT 06511-6815

HORVATH, DAVID BRUCE, computer consultant, writer, educator; b. Phila., Jan. 3, 1963; s. Ernest O. Jr. and E. Roberta (Lock) H.; m. Mary E. Geno, May 23, 1987. AS in Engring., Delaware County C.C., 1985; BA in Computer and Info. Scis., Temple U., 1985; MS in Organizational Dynamics, U. Pa., 1998. Cert. computer profl. Inst. for Cert. of Computing Profls. Sr. cons., sys. analyst GE Cons./Aerospace, Phila., 1985-91; ind. cons. Cooperative Bus. Solutions, Phila., 1991-93; sr. cons. Alternative Resources Corp. (formerly CGI Sys. Inc.), Phila., 1993—; instr. Delaware County C.C., Media, Pa., 1992; sr. adj. instr. Burlington County Coll., Pemberton, N.J., 1988-90; adj. instr. Goldey-Beacom Coll., Wilmington, Del., 1994-95, Camden County Coll., Blackwood, N.J., 1990—; mem., treas. participant steering com. dynamics orgn. U. Pa., Phila., 1990-93; software metrics cons. Australian Stock Exch., Sydney, NSW, 1993; founding mem. GE Cons.-Tng. Focus Group, Phila., 1988-91; presenter and lectr. in field. Author: UNIX for the Mainframer, 1996; editor newsletter News of Chester Twp., 1994-97, (with others) UNIX Unleashed, 2d edit., 1997, 3rd edit., 1998, (with others) Red Hat Linux Unleashed, 2nd edit., 1998, Using UNIX, 2nd edit., 1998; contbr. articles to profl. jours. Mem. alumni 25th anniversary planning com. Delaware County C.C., 1992; del. 1st internat. conf. Jeanne Suavé Found., Montreal, Que., Can., 1992; judge, chair judges Delaware Valley Sci. Fairs, Phila., 1990—; participant weather spotter program NOAA, Phila., 1988—; bd. dirs. Inst. Certification Computing Profls. Edn. Found., 1998—; mem. computer sci. adv. coun. Camden County Coll., 1995—. Mem. Internat. Freelance Photographers Orgn., Internat. Function Point Users Group, Mensa, Digital Equipment Computer User Soc., HTML Authors Guild, Del. Valley Oracle Users Group (spkr.), The Authors Guild, Del. Valley Micro Focus Users Group (spkr.). Republican. Episcopalian. Avocations: camping, photography, gardening, international travel. Office: Alternative Resources Corp 504 Longbotham Dr Aston PA 19014-2502

HORVÁTH, MICHAEL JOSEPH, curator; b. Zágráb, Hungary, June 30, 1915; came to U.S., 1963; s. Michael and Leona (Csincsak) H.; m. Margaret Julie Pázmándy, May 9, 1970. PhD in Law, U. Budapest, Hungary, 1933; MSLS, Western Mich. U., 1964. curator, founder Cardinal Mind, Port Orange, 1979—. Author: Hungarian Civilization, 1995. Founder Hungarian Folk Art Mus. Home: 546 Ruth St Port Orange FL 32127-4361

HORVATH, TERRI LYNN, writer, publishing company executive; b. Indpls., Feb. 26, 1953; d. Lawrence Norman and Frances Lorraine (Switzer) Vernon; m. Dennis Emery Horvath, June 15, 1975. BA, Butler U., 1975. Prodn. mgr. Topics Newspapers, Indpls., 1976-79; publs. coord. Resort Condominiums Internat., Indpls., 1979-80; freelance writer and photographer, Indpls., 1980-91; owner Publishing Resources, Indpls., 1991—; bd. dirs. The Network of Women in Bus., Indpls., 1993-95. Author: Spread the Word, 1995, Fund=raising Success, 1996; co-author: Cruise In, 1997. Chair VIP hospitality World Gymnastics Championships, Indpls., 1991; chair pub. rels. The Julian Ctr., Indpls., 1994-96. Office: Publishing Resources 9220 N College Ave Indianapolis IN 46240-1031

HORVITZ, HOWARD ROBERT, biology educator, researcher; b. Chgo., May 8, 1947; s. Oscar and Mary Horvitz; m. Martha Constantine-Paton, May 2, 1993; 1 child, Alexandra Constantine. BS in Math., BS in Econs., MIT, 1968; MA in Biology, Harvard U., 1972, PhD in Biology, 1974. Postdoctoral fellow Med. Rsch. Coun. Lab. Molecular Biology, Cambridge, Eng.; asst. to assoc. prof. biology MIT, Cambridge, 1978-86, prof., 1986—, career devel. assoc. prof. biology, Whitehead Inst., 1982-85, mem. sci. adv. bd. Howard Hughes program in neurosci., 1984-88, investigator Howard Hughes Med. Inst., 1988—; neurobiologist (neurology), geneticist (medicine) Mass. Gen. Hosp., Boston, 1989—; advisor dept. biochemistry and molecular biology Harvard U., 1984-90; mem. neurobiology adv. bd. Cold Spring Harbor Lab., 1984—; mem. sci. adv. bd. Hereditary Disease Found., 1987-93, collaborative rsch. group adv. com., 1988-93, cure HD initiative adv. com., 1996—; mem. sci. adv. bd., Jane Coffin Childs Meml. Fund for Med. Rsch., 1989-97; sci. adv. bd. Com. on Scholarly Comm. with People's Rep. of China, U.S. NAS, 1987-93, Ain-Shams Med. Genetics Ctr. Cairo, 1990-91; co-organizer Gordon Conf. on Devel. Biology, 1985; organizer biennial meeting Cold Spring Harbor Internat. Conf., 1985, coms., 1981, 87; mem. organizing com. biennial meeting Ea. Coast C. Elegans, Cambridge, 1988, 90; mem. sci. rev. com. Amyotrophic Lateral Sclerosis Assn., 1990-95, co-chair meetings 1991, 93; lectr. Harvey Soc., 1989; macrofil steering com. spl. programme for esch and tng. in tropical diseases, WHO, 1992-95; adv. bd. Umea (Sweden) Ctr. Molecular Pathogenesis, 1993-96; co-chair working group on preclin. models for cancer Nat. Cancer Inst., NIH, 1996—; mem. adv. coun. Nat. Ctr. for Human Genome Rsch., NIH, 1996—; mem. sci. adv. group Sanger Ctr., Cambridgeshire, Eng., 1994—; chair devel. biology review com. Swedish Found. for Strategic Rsch., 1996; mem. sci. adv. bd. Umea (Sweden) Ctr. Molecular Pathogenesis, 1993-96; external review bd. dept. molecular, cellular and devel. biology U. Colo., Boulder, 1996; mem. sci. adv. group U. Pa. Med. Ctr. Inst. Aging, 1995—; cons. sci. adv. bd. Axys Pharms. Inc., 1998—, New England BioLabs Inc., 1998—. Author: (with others) The Role of Intercelluar Signals: Navigation, Encounter, Outcome, 1979, Genetic Maps, Vol. 1, 1980, Nematodes as Biological Models, 1980, Development of the Nervous System, 1981, Repair and Regeneration of the Nervous System, 1982, The Nematode Caenorhabditis elegans, 1988; mem. editl. bds. Jour. Neurogenetics, 1982-88, Jour. Neurosci., 1984-89, Devel. Biology, 1985-95, Genes and Devel., 1986-98, Cell, 1987-99, Trends in Genetics, 1987—, Neuron, 1987-90, The New Biologist, 1989-92, Genetic Analysis: Techniques and Applications, 1990-95, Current Opinion in Neubiology, 1990—, Current Biol., 1992-95, Annual Rev. Genetics, 1993-97, Cell Death & Differentiation, 1994—, Neurobiology of Disease, 1994—, Jour. Exptl. Therapeutics and Oncology, 1995—, Invertebrate Neurosci., 1994—, Devel., 1986-93, Cancer Rsch., 1995-2001, Procs. of the NAS, 1997-99, Jour. Cell Biology, 1997-2000; patentee in field; contbr. numerous articles to profl. jours. Mem. adv. bd. World Health Orgn. Spl. Programme for Rsch. and Tng. in Tropical Diseases, Microfil steering com., 1992-95. Recipient Rsch. Career Devel. award NIH, 1981-86, Spencer award in Neurobiology, Columbia U., 1986, Warren Triennial prize Mass. Gen. Hosp., 1986, Molecular Biology award U.S. Steel Found., 1988, Method to Extend Rsch. in Time award NIH, 1991, V.D. Mattia award Roche Inst. Molecular Biology, 1993, Hans Sigrist award, 1994, Charles A. Dana award for pioneering achievements in health and edn. Inst. Medicine NAS, 1995, Ciba-Drew award for biomed. sci., 1996, Rosenstiel award Brandeis U., 1998, Passano award for the advancement med. sci., 1998, Alfred P. Sloan Jr. prize GM Cancer Rsch. Found., 1998, Gairdner Found. Internat. award, 1999; Woodrow Wilson fellow, 1968, NSF predoctoral fellow, 1968-72, Muscular Dystrophy Assn. postdoctoral fellow, 1974-77. Fellow AAAS, Am. Acad. Arts and Scis., Am. Acad. Microbiology, Am. Acad. Microbilogy; mem. Am. Assn. Cancer Rsch., U.S. Nat. Acad. Scis., Genetics Soc. Am. (membership com. 1984-86, bd. dirs. 1990-92, 94-96, organizer ann. meeting 1989, v.p. 1994, pres. 1995), Soc. Devel. Biology (nominations com. 1989), Soc. Nematologists, Soc. Neurosci. (pub. info. com. 1993-95), Am. Soc. Cell Biology (organizing com. ann. meeting 1992, pub. policy com. 1993-96, joint steering com. pub. policy 1994-97, exec. com. 1995—), Am. Soc. Microbiology, Helminthological Soc. Washington. Office: MIT Dept Biology 68-425 77 Massachusetts Ave Dept 68-425 Cambridge MA 02139-4307

HORVITZ, MICHAEL JOHN, lawyer; b. Cleve., Feb. 15, 1950; s. Harry Richard and Lois Joy (Unger) H.; m. Jane Rosenthal, Aug. 25, 1979; children: Katherine R., Elizabeth R. BS in Econs., U. Pa., 1972; JD, U. Va., 1975; LLM in Taxation, NYU, 1980. Bar: Ohio 1975, Fla. 1976. Assoc. Hahn, Loeser, Freedheim, Dean & Wellman, Cleve., 1975-78; counsel Hollywood, Inc., Fla., 1978-79; assoc. Jones, Day, Reavis & Pogue, Cleve., 1980-85, ptnr., 1985—; mem. adv. bd. Kirtland Capital Ptnrs., L.P., 1992—; chmn. Parkland Mgmt. Co., 1992—; vice chmn. Horvitz Newspapers, Inc., 1994—; pres. H.R.H. Family Found., 1992—; chmn. H.R.H. Family Trust, 1992—; bd. dirs. Zephyr Mgmt., Inc. Trustee Jewish Cmty. Fedn. Cleve., 1993—, Case Western Res. U., Musical Arts Assn., 1992—, Cleve. Ctr. Econ. Edn., 1992-95, Am. Cancer Soc., Cuyahoga County unit, 1989-95, Hathaway Brown Sch., Mt. Sinai Med. Ctr., Cleve. chpt. Am. Jewish Com., 1984-95, Montefiore Home for the Elderly, 1982-90, Health Hill Hosp. for Children, 1982-95, bd. pres., 1987-89; bd. dirs. Cleve. Mus. Art, 1991—, pres. bd., 1996—. Office: Jones Day Reavis & Pogue 901 Lakeside Ave E Cleveland OH 44114-1116 also: Parkland Mgmt Co 1001 Lakeside Ave E Ste 900 Cleveland OH 44114-1172

HORVITZ, PAUL MICHAEL, finance educator; b. Providence, Aug. 6, 1935; s. Abraham and Rose (Gershkoff) H.; m. Carol Broomfield, Nov. 17, 1955; children: Marcia Ellen, Steven Jay. BA, U. Chgo., 1954; MBA, Boston U., 1956; PhD in Econs., MIT, 1958. Fin. economist Fed. Reserve Bank of Boston, 1957-60; asst. prof. Boston U., 1960-62; sr. economist, compt. of currency, Washington, 1963-66; dir. rsch. FDIC, 1967-77; Judge James A. Elkins prof. banking and finance U. Houston, 1977—; bd. dirs., Bank United, Houston. Mem. Am. Econ. Assn., Am. Fin. Assn, Shadow Fin. Regulatory Com. Author: Management of Bank Funds, 1981, Monetary Policy & the Financial System, 6th edit., 1987; co-editor Jour. Fin. Services Research; contbr. articles to profl. jours. Home: 150 Sugarberry Cir Houston TX 77024-7244 Office: U Houston Coll Bus Adminstrn Houston TX 77204-6282

HORVITZ, SUSAN SMITH, educator; b. Fall River, Mass., Feb. 19, 1953; d. Henry Edward and Ann Frances (Lilley) Smith; m. Stewart Marc Horvitz, Apr. 4, 1976; children: Andrew, Sarah, Emily. BA, Skidmore Coll., 1974; MEd, R.I. Coll., 1983; postgrad., Bridgewater State Coll., 1990—. Cert. tchr., Mass. Tchr. bilingual edn. Fall River (Mass.) Pub. Schs., 1974-76, tchr. French, Spanish, 1976-80, tchr. reading, 1980-85, curriculum resource tchr., 1985—; instr. U. Mass., Dartmouth, 1997—; mem. Mass. Ednl. Assessment Program Curriculum Adv. Com.-Social Studies, 1992-96; presenter at profl. confs. Author: (monograph) Interdisciplinary Units, 1991; contbr. articles to profl. jours. Pres. BMC Durfee High Sch. Class of 1971, Fall River, 1971—; v.p. Somerset (Mass.) Jr. High Sch. PTO, 1990-91, pres. 1991-93; active Supts.' Parents' Adv. Coun., Somerset, 1991-93; mem. Southeast Regional Reading Coun., 1996—. Mem. Delta Kappa Gamma (pres. Beta chpt. 1994-98). Avocations: skiing, swimming, reading, cooking, horseback riding. Home: 10 Brewster Dr Somerset MA 02726-4709 Office: Fall River Pub Schs Fall River MA 02720

HORWICH, ALLAN, lawyer; b. Des Moines, Apr. 8, 1944; s. Joseph Maurice and Bernice (Davidson) H.; m. Carolyn Ruth Allen, Feb. 28, 1975; children: Benjamin, Diana, Eleanor, Flannery. AB, Princeton U., 1966; JD, U. Chgo., 1969. Bar: Ill. 1969, U.S. Dist. Ct. (no. dist.) Ill. 1969, U.S. Ct. Appeals (7th cir.) 1971, U.S. Ct. Appeals (10th cir.) 1983, U.S. Supreme Ct. 1976, U.S. Dist. Ct. (ctrl. dist.) Ill. 1990, U.S. Dist. Ct. (ea. dist.) Wis. 1995, U.S. Dist. Ct. (ea. dist.) Mich. 1995, U.S. Ct. Appeals (6th cir.) 1996. Assoc. Schiff Hardin & Waite, Chgo., 1969-74; ptnr. Schiff Hardin and Waite, Chgo., 1975—, vice-chmn., 1989-95; adj. prof. law Northwestern U. Sch. Law, 1999—. Mem. Metropolitan Club. Home: 216 W Concord Ln Chicago IL 60614-5743 Office: Schiff Hardin & Waite 6600 Sears Tower Chicago IL 60606

HORWICH, GEORGE, economist, educator; b. Detroit, July 23, 1924; s. Charles and Rose (Katzman) H.; m. Geraldine Lessans, Dec. 27, 1953; children: Ellen Beth, Karen Louise, Robert Lloyd, Susan Jean. Student, Wayne State U., 1942-43, 46, Ind. U., 1943-44; AM, U. Chgo., 1951, PhD, 1954. Lectr. econs. Extension Ctrs. Ind. U., Gar and Calumet, 1949-52; instr. econs. Ind. U., Bloomington, 1952-55; rsch. assoc. Nat. Bur. Econ. Rsch., N.Y.C., 1955-56; from asst. prof. to prof. econs. Purdue U., West Lafayette, Ind., 1956—, chmn. econs. dept., 1974-78; Burton D. Morgan prof. for study pvt. enterprise Purdue U., 1981-94; sr. rsch. assoc. Brookings Instn., Washington, 1958-62; sr. economist U.S. Dept. Energy, Washington, 1978-80; spl. asst. for contingency planning U.S. Dept. Energy, 1984; adj. scholar Am. Enterprise Inst., 1984—; collaborating scientist energy divsn. Oak Ridge Nat. Lab., 1988-94; mem. U.S. Treasury Cons. Group, Washington, 1969; cons. Fed. Res. Bank, Chgo., 1971; vis. prof. econs. U. Calif., San Diego, 1971-72, People's Univ. of China, Beijing, 1992, Kobe (Japan) U. Commerce, 1996-97, Victoria U., Wellington, New Zealand, 1997; staff Ind. Coun. Econ. Edn., West Lafayette, 1974—, Ctr. Pub. Policy and Pub. Adminstrn., Purdue U., West Lafayette, 1977—; advisor Econ. Inst. Rsch. and Edn., Boulder, Colo., 1977—; cons. U.S. Dept. Energy, 1980-88, Fortune 500 cos., 1965—, U.S. Dept. State, Washington, 1982, 92, Hudson Inst., 1991. Author: Money, Capital and Prices, 1964; (with others) Costs and Benfits of a Protective Tariff on Refined Petroleum Products After Crude Oil Decontrol, 1980, Energy: An Economic Analysis, 1983; (with D.L. Weimer) Oil Price Shocks, Market Response and Contingency Planning, 1984; Responding to International Oil Crises, 1988; editor: Monetary Process and Policy, 1967, (with P.A. Samuelson) Trade, Stability, and Macroeconomics, 1974; (with J.P. Quirk) Essays in Contemporary Fields of Economics, 1981; (with E.J. Mitchell) Policies for Coping with Oil-Supply Disruptions, 1982, Energy Use in Transportation Contingency Planning, 1983; (with G.J. Lynch) Food, Policy and Politics, 1989; contbr. articles to profl. jours. With U.S. Army, 1943-46, ETO. NSF grantee; Fulbright rschr., 1996-97. Mem. Internat. Assn. Energy Econs., Am. Econ. Assn., Midwest Econs. Assn., Mont. Pelerin Soc., Nat. Assn. Scholars, Phila. Soc., Assn. Pub. Policy Analysis and Mgmt. Home: 120 Seminole Dr West Lafayette IN 47906-2116 Office: Purdue U Dept Econs West Lafayette IN 47907-1310

HORWIN, LEONARD, lawyer; b. Chgo., Jan. 2, 1913; s. Joseph and Jennie (Fuhrmann) H.; m. Ursula Helene Donig, Oct. 15, 1939; children—Noel Samuel, Leonora Marie. LLD cum laude, Yale U., 1936. Bar: Calif. 1936, U.S. Dist. Ct. (cen. dist.) Calif. 1937, U.S. Ct. Appeals (9th cir.) 1939, U.S. Supreme Ct. 1940. Assoc., Lawler, Felix & Hall, 1936-39; ptnr. Hardy & Horwin, Los Angeles, 1939-42; counsel Bd. Econ. Warfare, Washington, 1942-43; mem. program adjustment com. U.S. War Prodn. Bd., 1942-43; attache, legal advisor U.S. Embassy, Madrid, Spain, 1943-47; sole practice, Beverly Hills, Calif., 1948—; dir., lectr. Witkin-Horwin Rev. Course on Calif. Law, 1939-42; judge pro tempore Los Angeles Superior Ct., 1940-42; instr. labor law U. So. Calif., 1939-42. U.S. rep. Allied Control Council for Ger., 1945-47; councilman City of Beverly Hills, 1962-66, mayor, 1964-65; chmn. transp. Los Angeles Goals Council, 1968; bd. dirs. So. Calif. Rapid Transit Dist., 1964-66; chmn. Rent Stabilization Com., Beverly Hills, 1980. Fellow Am. Acad. Matrimonial Lawyers; mem. ABA, State Bar Calif., Order Coif, Balboa Bay Club, Aspen Inst., La Costa Country Club. Author: Insight and Foresight, 1990, Plain Talk, 1931—; contbr. articles to profl. jours. E-mail address: lhorwin@mindspring.com. Office: 121 S Beverly Dr Beverly Hills CA 90212-3002

HORWITZ, BARBARA ANN, physiologist, educator, consultant; b. Chgo., Sept. 26, 1940; d. Martin Horwitz and Lillian (Knell) bloom; m. John M. Horowitz, Aug. 17, 1970. BS, U. Fla., 1961, MS, 1962; PhD, Emory U., 1966. Asst. rsch. physiologist U. Calif., Davis, 1968-72, asst. prof. physiology, 1972-75, assoc. prof., 1975-78, prof., 1978—, chair animal physiology, 1991-93, chmn. neurobiology, physiology and behavior dept., 1993-98; cons. Am. Inst. Behavioral Rsch., Palo Alto, Calif., 1980, Am. Inst. Rsch., Washington, 1993—, NSF, Washington, 1981-84, NIH, Washington, 1995-99. Contbr. articles to profl. jours. Recipient Disting. Tchg. award, 1982, Pres.'s award for Escellence in fostering Undergrad. Rsch., 1995; named Arthur C. Guyton Physiology Tchr. of Yr., 1996; USPHS postdoctoral fellow, 1966-68. Fellow AAAS; mem. Am. Physiology Soc. (edn. and program coms., coun. 1993-96), Am. Soc. Zoologists, N.Y. Acad. Scis., N.Am. Assn. for Study of Obesity (exec. coun. 1988-92, pres.-elect 19996), Soc. Exptl. Biol. Medicine (exec. coun. 1990-94), Phi Beta Kappa (pres. Davis chpt. 1991-92), Sigma Xi (pres. Davis chpt. 1980-81), Phi Kappa Pi, Phi Sigma (v.p. Davis chpt. 1983—, nat. v.p. 1989—). Office: U Calif Dept Neurobiology Phys Davis CA 95616

HORWITZ, DAVID A., physician, scientist, educator. BA, U. Mich., 1958; MD, U. Chgo., 1962. Intern, resident Michael Reese Hosp., Chgo., 1966; rheumatology fellow Southwestern Med. Sch. U. Tex., 1969; instr. internal medicine Southwestern Med. Sch. U. Tex., Dallas, 1968-69; from asst. prof. to assoc. prof. medicine Sch. Medicine U. Va., Charlottesville, 1969-79, prof. medicine, 1979-80; prof. medicine and microbiology, chief divsn. rheumatology and immunology sect. Sch. Medicine U. So. Calif., L.A., 1980—; vis. prof. Clin. Rsch. Ctr., Harrow, Eng., 1976-77; vis. investigator Inperial Cancer Rsch. Fund, London, 1988-89. Contbr. articles to profl. jours. Achievements include research in elucidation of lymphocytes, cytokines and immunologic circuits involved in the regulation of antibody production, characterization of pathologic abnormalities in immune regulation in subjects with Systemic Lupus Erythematosus; use of novel strategies to treat patients with autoimmune disease. Office: U So Calif Divsn Rheumatology & Immunology 2011 Zonal Ave # 711 Los Angeles CA 90033-1034

HORWITZ, DONALD PAUL, lawyer; b. Chgo., Feb. 5, 1936; s. Theodore J. and Lillian H. (Shlensky) H.; m. Judith Robin, Aug. 23, 1964; children: Terry Robin Kass, Linda Diane, Gail Elizabeth. BS, Northwestern U., 1957; JD, Yale U., 1960. Bar: Ill. 1961, D.C. 1961, U.S. Supreme Ct. 1966; CPA, Ill. With atty. gen.'s honors program Dept. Justice, 1961-63; atty. Gottlieb & Schwartz, Chgo., 1963-66; with Arthur Young & Co. CPAs, Chgo., 1966-72; ptnr. Arthur Young & Co. CPAs, 1971-72; exec. v.p., sec., dir. McDonald's Corp., Oak Brook, Ill., 1972-90; ptnr. Sonnenschein, Nath & Rosenthal, Chgo., 1990—; lectr. Northwestern U. Law Sch., Grad. Sch. Commerce, DePaul U., Chgo.; bd. dirs. Bernard Tech. Inc., 1997—, chmn. bd., 1998—; sec. System Capital Corp, 1996. Contbr. articles to profl. jours. Trustee Goodman Theatre/Chgo. Theatre Group, 1993-96, Evans Scholars Found., Western Golf Assn., 1984-87; pres., bd. dirs. Briarwood Country Club, 1972-73; caucus nominating com. Village of Glencoe, Ill., 1975-78, vice-chmn., 1988-89; bd. dirs. Chgo. Med. Sch./U. Health Scis., 1989-93, 99—, Northwestern Healthcare Network, 1990-94; vice-chmn., bd. dirs., chmn. bd. Highland Park Hosp., Lakeland Health Ventures and Northwestern Network, bd. govs., 1994—; adv. coun. Northwestern U. Kellogg Bus. Sch.; chmn. Midwest region Anti-Defamation League, 1994-95; mem. nat. commn., 1994—. Mem. ABA, Ill. Bar Assn., Chgo. Bar Assn., Chgo. Bar Found. (trustee 1990-97), Standard Club, Econs. Club, Northmoor Country Club, Chgo. Yacht Club.

HORWITZ, ELEANOR CATHERINE, information and education official; b. N.Y.C., Dec. 21, 1941; d. Fritz and Hedwig E.F. (Kramer) Jahoda; m. Paul Horwitz, Aug. 15, 1964; children: Gregory Douglas, Catherine Helen, Laura Elizabeth. BA, Swarthmore Coll., 1962; MA, NYU, 1967; MS, Cornell U., 1969; postgrad., Oreg. State U., 1969-70. Sci. tchr. New Lincoln Sch., N.Y.C., 1962-67; coordinator outdoor edn. Lane County Int. Edn. Dist., Eugene, Oreg., 1969-70; staff writer Billerica (Mass.) Banner, 1971-72; instr., writer Mass. Audubon Soc., Lincoln, 1972-75; pub. use specialist U.S. Fish and Wildlife Service, Concord, Mass., 1975; staff writer Soc. Am. Foresters, Washington, 1975-76; chief info. and edn. Mass. Div. Fisheries and Wildlife, Westborough, 1977—; mem. Mass. Gov.'s Forestry Rev. Bd., Boston, 1976-77; mem. steering com. Sec.'s Adv. Group on Environ. Edn. Exec. Office of Environ. Affairs, Commonwealth of Mass., 1990—, co-chair, 1992-97, chair, 1997-98; bd. dirs. Mass. Wildlife Fedn., 1986—, v.p., 1989-95, 97—, pres., 1995-97. Author: Clearcutting, A View from the Top, 1974; author, editor: Ways of Wildlife, 1977 (ACI Book award 1978); editor: (mag.) Massachusetts Wildlife, 1977—; contbr. articles to popular mags. Active Concord Natural Resources Commn., 1976-82, chmn. 1979-80; trustee Concord Land Conservation Trust, 1988—, trustee Holbrook Island Trust, 1995—. Recipient R.E. Dimmick award Oreg. Wildlife Soc., 1970, citation Worcester County League Sportsmen's Clubs, 1987, citation Minutemen chpt. Ducks Unltd., 1987, Conservation award Mahar Fish & Game Assn., 1991, Woman of Yr. award N.E. County Quabbin Anglers Assn., 1991, Sposrtsman of Yr. New England Outdoor Writers, 1998. Mem. Outdoor Writers Assn., New Eng. Outdoor Writers Assn. (membership sec. 1987-90, bd. dirs. 1987—, sec. 1990-93, v.p. 1993-94, pres. 1994-95), Am. Forestry Assn. (life), New Eng. Conservation Info. and Edn. Assn. (chmn. 1986-87, 90-91, Conservation Communicator of Yr. 1999), Wildlife Soc. (profl. cert., cmn. edn. com. 1974-76, 84-87, nominating com. 1990-91, mem. Leopold award com. 1996-98, cert. of recognition 1978), Nashoba Sportsmen's Club, Concord Rod and Gun Club, Maynard Rod and Gun Club (hon.). Mem. United Ch. of Christ. Office: Mass Divsn Fisheries and Wildlife Westborough MA 01581

HORWITZ, IRWIN DANIEL, otolaryngologist, educator; b. Chgo., Mar. 31, 1920; s. Sol and Belle (Stern) H.; m. Isabel Morwitz, July 23, 1944; children—Steven, Judd, Clare. B.S., U. Ill., 1941, M.D., 1943. Intern Cook County Hosp., Chgo., 1944; resident Ill. Eye and Ear Infirmary, Chgo., 1946-48; practice otolaryngology Chgo., 1948—; clin. prof., head div. otolaryngology Chgo. Med. Sch., 1969; prof. Rush Med. Sch., 1976—; formerly chief div. otolaryngology Mt. Sinai Hosp., former pres. med. staff. Contbr. articles profl. jours. Served to capt., M.C. AUS, 1944-46. Fellow A.C.S.; mem. AMA, Chgo. Otol. and Laryngol. Assn., Am. Acad. Ophthalmology and Otolaryngology, Ill., Chgo. med. socs. Home: 6431 N Knox Ave Lincolnwood IL 60646-3420 Office: 8 S Michigan Ave Chicago IL 60603-3357

HORWITZ, MARCIA J., fundraiser, writer; b. Bklyn., Dec. 21, 1951; d. Harold Horwitz and Sylvia (Dunn) Rothstein; m. Wallace V. Calvert, Aug. 17, 1986 (div. Oct. 1991); 1 child, David W. Calvert. BA, Clark U., 1973. Tchg., acting dir., asst. dir. Worcester (Mass.) Cmty. Sch. of Performing Arts, 1972-76; pub. rels. asst. Hartt Coll. Music, Hartford, Conn., 1976; exec. dir. Nat. Guild Comm. Schs./Arts, N.Y.C., 1976-80; dir. concerts and cmty. rels. 3d St. Music Sch., N.Y.C., 1980-82; dir. devel. Richmond (Va.) Children's Mus., 1986-92; dir. devel. Lewis Ginter Bot. Garden, 1992-97, mgr. pub. info., grant writer, 1997—. Columnist For Kids Sake mag., Richmond Parents mag., Richmond News Leader, others, 1989—; musician Klezm'or'amim, Klezmor or Less. Mem. adv. panel Nat. Endowment for the Arts, Washington, 1978-79. Mem. Va. Assn. Fundraising Execs. (pres. 1995-96). Jewish. Office: Marcy Horwitz & Assocs 3824 Garden Rd Richmond VA 23235-1236

HORWITZ, ORVILLE, cardiologist, educator; b. Strafford, Pa., Nov. 20, 1909; s. George Quintard and Marian (Newhall) H.; m. Nataline B. Dulles, Sept. 15, 1934; children: Marian Newhall Horwitz Parmenter, George Dulles, Jonathan. BS, Harvard U., 1932; MD, Johns Hopkins U., 1936; MA (hon.), U. Pa., 1971. Diplomate Am. Bd. Internal Medicine. Intern Pa. Hosp., 1938-40, chief med. resident, 1940-41, fellow in cardiology, 1942; mem. faculty U. Pa. Med. Sch., 1941—, prof. medicine, 1970-85, prof. pharmacology, 1973-85, emeritus prof., 1985—; chief vascular clinic Hosp. U. Pa., 1966-69, chmn. com. patient care, 1973-75; cons. NASA, 1946-69; founder, pres. Vascular Hypertension Research., 1971-91, pres. emeritus, 1991—. Author: Cardiac and Vascular Diseases, 1971, Index of Suspicion in Treatable Diseases, 1975, Diseases of Blood Vessels, 1985, From Mount Olympus to the Moon, 1998; contbr. over 200 articles, abstracts on cardiovascular disease. Mem. Legion of Honor The Chapel of The Four Chaplains, Phila., 1979—. Served to lt. comdr. M.C., USNR, 1942-46, USMC, 1944-46. Grantee NIH, 1950-81. Fellow ACP (dir. courses 1972, 76, assoc. editor bull. 1950-56); mem. Am. Coll. Cardiology (dir. course 1976), Am. Physiol. Assn., Microcirculatory Conf., Am. Clin. and Climatol. Assn. (v.p. 1982-83), Am. Heart Assn. (chmn. coun. on circulation 1966-68, chmn. sci. couns. 1973-75), Pa. Med. Soc. (award for 50 yrs. of med. practice 1988), Shakespeare Soc. Phila., Phila. Club, Faculty U. Pa. Club, Athenaeum Club, Gulph Mills Golf Club (dir. 1965-66). Democrat. Episcopalian. Home and Office: 2 Private Way Wayne PA 19087-2646 *In the past half century technology has far outdistanced philosophy and good will. The bomb, the box, the machine, and the pill are each responsible for a revolution of their own. Only by understanding ourselves and others will we be able to deal with scientific advances of such magnitudes.*

HORWITZ, PAUL, physicist; b. N.Y.C., Dec. 4, 1938; s. Louis David and Sylvia Helen (Laibman) H.; m. Eleanor Catherine Jahoda, Aug. 15, 1964; children: Gregory Douglas Lee, Catherine Helen, Laura Elizabeth. AB, Harvard U., 1960; MS, Columbia U., 1963; PhD, NYU, 1967. Rsch. assoc. Cornell U., Ithaca, N.Y., 1967-69, U. Oreg., Eugene, 1969-71; prin. rsch. scientist Avco Everett Rsch. Lab., Everett, Mass., 1971-79; sr. scientist Bolt, Beranek & Newman Inc., Cambridge, Mass., 1979-91; divsn. scientist Bolt, Branek & Newman Inc., Cambridge, Mass., 1991-94; prin. scientist, 1994-97; sr. scientist The Concord Consortium, 1997—. Contbr. articles to profl. jours. Recipient Founders Day award NYU, 1969, 2 EDUCOM Nat. awards for ednl. software, 1992; Am. Phys. Soc. Congl. fellow, 1975-76; GM Corp. scholar Harvard U., 1960. Mem. Am. Ednl. Rsch. Assn. Home: 32 Riverside Ave Concord MA 01742-3020 Office: 70 Fawcett St Cambridge MA 02138-1110

HORWITZ, RITA, outpatient surgery nurse, educator; b. St. Louis, May 25, 1933; d. Meyer and Sophie (Waldman) H. Diploma, Jewish Hosp. Sch. Nursing, St. Louis, 1954; BSN cum laude, St. Louis U., 1980; MA in Edn. and Human Resource Mgmt., Washington U., St. Louis, 1984. Supr. med. div. Jewish Hosp., St. Louis; in charge cardiovascular surgery St. Louis U. Med. Ctr.; coord. pediatric surgery Barnes Hosp., St. Louis, nurse, outpatient surgery ctr., nurse, ophtholmology operating room, 1993-98, nurse, operating rm. urology holding area, 1997-98; ret., 1998. Contbr. articles to profl. jours. Mem. edn. and devel. program Jewish Fedn. Mem. ASTD, Am. Soc. Ophthalmic RNs, St. Louis Writers Guild, Chesterfield C. of C., Nat. Coun. Jewish Women, AORN, Jewish Hosp. Sch. Nursing Alumni Assn. (bd. dirs. 1987-89), St. Louis Women's Commerce Assn., Assn. Therapeutic Humor, Hadassah Nurses' Coun., Sigma Theta Tau. Home: 13131 Royal Pines Dr # 7 Saint Louis MO 63146

HORWITZ, RONALD M., business administration educator; b. Detroit, June 25, 1938; s. Harry and Annette (Levine) H.; m. Carol Bransky, Mar. 30, 1961; children: Steven, Michael, David, Robert. BS, Wayne State U., 1959, MBA, 1961; PhD, Mich. State U., 1964. CPA, Mich. Prof. fin. U. Detroit, 1963-73, 75-79; healthcare cons., dir. personnel devel. Arthur Young & Co., Detroit, 1974-75; prof. fin., dean Sch. Bus. Adminstrn. Oakland U., Rochester, Mich., 1979-90, acting v.p. for acad. affairs, 1992-93, prof. fin., 1991-92, 93—; bd. dirs. United Am. Healthcare corp. Contbr. articles to profl. jours. Bd. dirs. Providence Hosp. and Med. Ctr., 1995—, The Roeper Sch., 1996—; pub. mem. Greater Detroit Health Coun., 1980—; mem. audit com. Daus. of Charity Nat. Health System, 1988-93, mem. fin. com. 1999—; mem. adv. bd. Providence Hosp., Southfield, 1980-95. Stonier fellow Am. Bankers Assn., 1963. Mem. Healthcare Fin. Mgmt. Assn. (bd. dirs. 1976-80), Mich. Assn. CPA's (grantee 1960), Fin. Mgmt. Assn., Am. Acctg. Assn., Acctg. Aid Soc. Detroit (founder), Mich. Bridge Assn. (pres. 1974-76). Avocation: bridge (life master). Office: Oakland U Sch Bus Adminstrn Rochester MI 48309-4493

HORWITZ, WILLIAM J., treasurer; b. St. Louis, Jan. 10, 1946; s. Harold S. and Henrietta B. Horwitz; children: Harris Saul, Pallas Hannah Eleanor. AB, Harvard U., 1967; MPhil, Yale U., 1969, PhD, 1971. Assoc. prof. classics dept. U. Okla., Norman, 1971-79; treas. Bride's House, St. Louis, 1979—. Contbr. articles to profl. jours. Recipient Woodrow Wilson fellowship, 1967, John Harvard Hon. scholarship, 1964, 66. Mem. Harvard Club of St. Louis (v.p. 1988-90, chmn. various coms. 1986-88), Yale Club of St. Louis. Office: Bride's House 1010 Locust St Saint Louis MO 63101-1306

HOSEA, JULIA HILLER, communications executive, paralegal; b. Cin., Oct. 19, 1952; d. Clifford John and Nancy Carol (Elberg) Hiller; m. Jon Michael Ausman, Nov. 3, 1973 (div. 1978); m. Robert Arthur Hosea, Mar. 22, 1987. BA, Allegheny Coll., 1975; cert., Inst. Paralegal Tng., Phila., 1975. Gen. paralegal Pettigrew & Bailey, Miami, Fla., 1975-76, Joseph J. Weisenfeld Law Offices, Miami, 1976-81; corp. paralegal Wood & Lamping, Cin., 1981-85; pension specialist Katz, Teller Brant & Hild, Cin., 1985-89; owner, mgr. Chrysalis Communications, Cin., 1989-90, The Hosea Group, Grand Junction, 1990-95; owner Ruby Canyon Textiles, Grand Junction, 1996—; adj. instr. Coll. Mt. St. Joseph, Cin., 1984-90. Contbr. articles to profl. publs. Mem. Cin. Paralegal Assn. (pres. 1984-85), Nat. Fedn. PAralegal Assn. (chmn. pension sect. 1986-87, editor Nat. Paralegal Reporter 1988-92).

HOSEK, JAMES ROBERT, economist; b. Evanston, Ill., Aug. 31, 1944; s. Walter Frank and Frances Miriam (Hoffman) H.; m. Susan DeWire, Sept. 10, 1966; children: Katherine, Adrienne, Peter. BA, Cornell U., 1966; MA, U. Chgo., 1970, PhD, 1975. Rsch. analyst Nat. Bur. Econ. Rsch., New Haven, 1970-73; assoc. economist RAND, Santa Monica, Calif., 1973-79, economist, 1979-83, sr. economist, 1983—, dir. def. manpower rsch. ctr., 1981-85, head dept. econs. and stats., 1985-90, corp. rsch. mgr., human capital, 1990-94, human capital and material resource policy, 1994-96; mem. panel NAS, Washington, 1988; mem., chair econ. adv. coun. Calif. Inst. Fed. Policy Rsch., 1994—; founding mem. Advanced Transp. Industry Consortium, 1997—. Editor RAND Jour. of Econs., 1988—; assoc. editor Abstracts of Working Papers in Econs., 1986-96; contbr. articles to profl. jours. Recipient numerous rsch. grants. Fellow Interuniversity Sem. on Armed Forces and Soc.; mem. Am. Econ. Assn., Western Econ. Assn., Phi Eta Sigma. Avocations: bicycling, photography, hiking.

HOSEK, JOHN JUDE, planning organization executive; b. Cleve., Oct. 1, 1949; s. Norbert James and Elizabeth H.; m. Sharon Marie Hamilton, Nov. 30, 1996; children: Brian Avon, Matthew Avon. BA, Cleve. State U., 1974; MA in Managerial Econs., Case Western Res. U., 1986. Dir. NE Ohio Areawide Coord. Agy., Cleve., 1984—; adj. faculty Meyers Coll., Cleve., 1984-92. Vol. Normandy Nursing Home, Rocky River, Ohio, 1997. Recipient Greater Cleve. Pub. Works Performance award Cleve. State U., 1994. Mem. Ohio Assn. Regional Couns. (chair transp. com. 1997, 98). Avocations: writing, music, walking, hiking. Home: 16 Pond Dr Rocky River OH 44116-1064

HOSEMAN, DANIEL, lawyer; b. Chgo., Aug. 18, 1935; s. Irving and Anne (Pruzansky) H.; m. Susan H. Myles, Aug. 7, 1960; children: Lawrence N., Joan E., Jonathan W. B.A., U. Ill., 1956, J.D., 1959. Bar: Ill. 1959, U.S. Dist. Ct. (no. dist.) Ill. 1960, U.S. Ct. Appeals (7th cir.) 1967, U.S. Supreme Ct. 1976. Sole practice, Chgo., 1959—; mem. panel pvt. atty. trustees U.S. Bankruptcy Ct. No. Dist. Ill., 1979—; arbitrator Cir. Ct. Cook County. Trustee Ill. Legal Svcs. Fund, 1978—; v.p. Allied Jewish Sch. Bd. Met. Chgo., 1977—; v.p. United Synagogue Am., 1978—. Served with USAFR, 1959-65. Mem. Am. Bankruptcy Inst., Advs. Soc., Decalogue Soc. Lawyers (pres. 1981-82, award of merit 1979-80), Ill. Bar Assn. (gen. assembly, long-range planning com.), Lake County Bar Assn. (com. on bankruptcy 1980—), Chgo. Coun. Lawyers, Comml. Law League Am., Am. Bankruptcy Inst., Nat. Assn. of Bankruptcy Trustees. Home: 2151 Tanglewood Ct Highland Park IL 60035-4231 Office: 77 W Washington St Ste 1220 Chicago IL 60602-2901

HOSEMANN, C. DELBERT, JR., lawyer; b. New Orleans, June 30, 1947; s. Charles D. and Patricia H.; m. Mary Lynn Lagen; children: Kristen Cullen, Charles Delbert III, Mark Mansfield. BBA, U. Notre Dame, 1969; JD, U. Miss., 1972; LLM in Taxation, NYU, 1973. Assoc. Dossett, Magruder & Montgomery, Jackson, Miss., 1973-78; ptnr. Magruder, Montgomery, Brocato & Hosemann, Jackson, 1978-88, Phelps Dunbar, L.L.P., Jackson, 1988—. Contbr. articles to profl. jours.; speaker in field. Mem. Miss. del. southeast regional employee benefits liaison com. EP/EO Atlanta, 1986—, chmn., 1992-93; mem. Leadership Jackson, 1991-92, bd. dirs., 1995-96; pres. Miss. Blood Svcs., Inc., 1994-95; Rep. nominee U.S. Congress 4th Congl. Dist., 1998. Mem. ABA (employee benefits com., taxation sect., continuing legal edn. com. budget and fin. com.), Hinds County Bar Assn. (sec. 1980), Miss. State Bar Assn. (dir. young lawyers sect. 1976-78, taxation com.), Jackson Young Lawyers Assn. (pres. 1977-78). Office: Phelps Dunbar 200 S Lamar St Ste 500 Jackson MS 39201-4013

HOSENPUD, JEFFREY, cardiovascular physician; b. Nov. 21, 1951; m. Janet Robbins, June 10, 1979; children: Jessica Sydney, Nathaniel Louis. BA with high honors, U. Calif., San Diego, 1973; MD, UCLA, 1977. Diplomate in internal medicine and cardiovascular medicine Am. Bd. Internal Medicine; diplomate Nat. Bd. Med. Examiners. Intern U. Wash., Seattle, 1977-78, resident in medicine, 1978-79; resident in medicine Med. Coll. Wis., Milw., 1979-80; fellow in cardiology Oreg. Health Scis. U., Portland, 1980-82, instr. medicine, 1982, instr.medicine, 1982, asst. prof. medicine, 1983-88, assoc. prof., 1988-93, prof., 1993-94; prof., chief divsn. cardiovascular medicine Med. Coll. Wis., Milw., 1994-98, Northwest Nut. Life prof. medicine, 1994—. Contbr. articles to profl. jours.; referee jours. USPHS fellow, 1981-83; Oreg. Heart Assn. rsch. fellow, 1981; NIH grantee; N.L. Tartar rsch. fellow, 1981, 82, other grants and awards. Fellow Am. Coll. Cardiology (coun. on clin. cardiology); mem. Am. Fedn. for Clin. Rsch., Internat. Soc. for Heart Transplantation, Western Soc. for Clin. Investigation, Pacific N.W. Transplant Soc., Am. Soc. Transplant Physicians, United Network for Organ Sharing, Trasnplantation Soc., Alpha Omega Alpha. Office: Med Coll Wis Cardiovascular Medicine Froedtert East FM Lit East 9200 W Wisconsin Ave Milwaukee WI 53226-3522

HOSEY, SHERYL LYNN MILLER, editor; b. Phila., May 15, 1968; d. Roger Lee and Janice Catherine (Myers) M.; m. John William Hosey, July 8, 1994. AA, Bucks County C.C., Newtown, Pa., 1989; BFA summa cum laude, Va. Commonwealth U., 1992, MA, 1997. Cert. secondary sch. tchr., Pa. Instr. drama Va. Commonwealth U., Richmond, 1989-92; program support technician Va. Commonwealth U./Med. Coll. Va., Richmond, 1992-97; proofreader, editor. Mem. Nat. Coun. Tchrs. English, Phi Kappa Phi. Avocations: acting, singing, reading, designing and making clothes, attending plays, symphony and ballet. E-mail SHosey@Meniscus.com. Home: 1159 Valley Stream Dr Perkiomenville PA 18074 Office: Meniscus Ltd 9 Presidential Blvd Bala Cynwyd PA 19004

HOSHAW, LLOYD, historian, educator; b. Benton, Ind., May 9, 1924; s. Walter and Gladys Ethel (Blue) H.; m. Evelyn F. Tyler, Dec. 24, 1954; children: Linda, John, James, Walter, David, Paul. BA, Goshen Coll., 1949; MA, Ind. U., 1951. Tchr. Winamac (Ind.) High Sch., 1952-55; instr. LaSalle(Ill.)-Peru-Oglesby Jr. Coll., 1955-65; history prof., dept. chair Rock Valley Coll., Rockford, Ill., 1965-88; history prof. Rock Valley Coll., Rockford, 1988—. Author: A History of Eastern Civilizations, Vol I., 1994, Vol. II, 1995. With USN, 1944-45. Mem. AAUP, Archeol. Inst. Am. (Rockford chpt.), Asia Soc., Ill. State Hist. Soc., Rockford Hist. Soc. Baptist. Avocations: photography, travel. Home: 1860 Charlotte Dr Rockford IL 61108-6508

HOSHIELD, SUSAN LYNN, pediatric nurse practitioner. AA, North Cen. Mich. Coll., 1972, ADN, 1978; BSN, Lake Superior State U., 1990; MSN, U. Mich., 1993. RN, PNP. Sales mgr. Petoskey Floral & Bridal, Petoskey, Mich., 1968-77; staff nurse NICU No. Mich. Hosp., Petoskey, 1978-88, primary nurse II/NICU, 1989-90, regional perinatal coord., 1990-95, infant apnea nurse coord., 1990-95; nursing faculty Lake Superior State U., Sault Ste. Marie, Mich., 1995-96; pediatric nurse practitioner Burns Clinic Med. Ctr., Petoskey, Mich., 1996-98; primary nurse NICU and pediactrics No. Mich. Hosp., Petoskey, Mich., 1999—, Wellness Inst. for Wholistic Living, Harbor Springs, Mich., 1999—; adv. bd. Mich. SIDS Alliance, Lansing, 1993—, vice chair, 1996-97, chair, 1997-98; chairperson Children's Health Fair, Petoskey, 1991-95; adj. faculty Lake Superior State U., Sault Ste Marie, Mich., 1994. Author: (pamphlet) Infant Apnea Clinic, 1994. Adv. bd. sex edn. curriculum Harbor Springs, Mich., 1992-98; mem. Immunization Task Force, Charlevoix, Mich., 1994; adv. com. Mich. State U. Coop. Ext., Petoskey, 1992-95, Adolescent Health, Charlevoix, 1990-93; mem. Harbor Springs Cmty. Band, 1996—. Vol. Spotlight, Mich. SIDS Alliance, 1994; hon. chairperson March of Dimes WalkAmerica, 1994, 95. Mem. AWHONN, Perinatal Assn. of Mich. (bd. dirs., sec. 1993-95), Mich. Assn. Apnea Profls., Nurses Assn. Pediat. Nurses and Practitioners, Mich. Nurses Assn. of Pediat. Nurses and Practitioners, Petoskey Area Bus. and Profl. Women (rec. sec. 1998—). Avocations: quilting, alternative health care practices, healing touch and therapeutic touch. E-mail: shosh@northlink.net. Home: 421 Emmet St Petoskey MI 49770-2603

HOSHINO, YOSHIRO, industrial technology critic; b. Tokyo-Shi, Tokyo-Hu, Japan, Jan. 13, 1922; s. Teruoki and Matsue Hoshino; m. Kumiko Serizawa, July 7, 1954; children: Syuichiro, Kenjiro, Chieko, Tetsuro. B, Tokyo Inst. Tech., 1944, Dr., 1980. Asst. tech. staff Agy. of Tech., Tokyo, 1944-45, critic, 1945-62; prof. Ritsumeikan U., Kyoto, 1962-68, cirtic, 1968-81; prof. indsl. tech. Teikyo U., Tokyo, 1981-97, critic, 1997—; hon. prof. N.E. U., Shenyang, Republic of China, 1985—. *His works on Chinese technologies were the result of joint research with professors of N.E.U. In 1992, Chinese philosophers selected him as one of the thirty representative Japanese philosophers at the present time. They wrote: "On the other hand, he was a historian and a critic." His Collected Works were composed of philosophical, historical and critical essays on modern technologies. He began to do comparative studies of technology, economy and politics among Japan, China and Europe from the 13th century to the 19th century. These papers appeared in English in the Teikyo University Economic Review in 1996 and 1997.* Author: Collected Works of Yoshiro Hoshino, 1977-79, Future of Civilization, 1980, Fundamental Problems on Latest Technology, 1986, Technology, Economy and Politics—Japan and China, 1945-1991, 1993. Bd. dirs. Japanese Soong Ching-ling Meml. Found., Tokyo, 1988—. Avocation: driving. Home: 908019 Chiyogaoka Asao-ku, Kawasaki-shi, Kanagawa-ken 215-0005, Japan

HOSICK, HOWARD LAWRENCE, cell biology educator, academic administrator; b. Champaign, Ill., Nov. 1, 1943; s. Arthur Howard and Eunice Irma (Miller) H.; m. Cynthia Ann Jacobson, June 15, 1968; children: Steven Cameron, Anna Elise, Rachel Victoria. BA, U. Colo., 1965; PhD, U. Calif., Berkeley, 1970. Postdoctoral fellow Karolinska Inst., Stockholm, 1970-72; assoc. research biochemist U. Calif., Berkeley, 1972-73; asst. prof. Wash. State U., Pullman, 1973-78, assoc. prof., 1978-83, prof. cell biology, 1983—, chmn. dept. zoology, 1983-87, chmn. dept. genetics and cell biology, 1987-91; vis. scientist U. Reading, Eng., 1978; disting. scientist Aichi Cancer Ctr., Nagoya, Japan, 1986; vis. scholar Cambridge U., 1994; rsch. com. Am. Heart Assn., 1989; grant rev. com. Nat. Cancer Inst., 1993—. Rev. editor In Vitro Cellular and Molecular Biology, 1986—; contbr. articles to profl. jours. Bd. govs. Internat. Assn. Breast Cancer Rsch., 1993—. Recipient H.S. Boyce award, 1981, Shell Faculty Devel. award, 1984, Cancer Rsch. award Eagles Club, 1989, G. and L. Pfeiffer Rsch. Found. award, 1992; fellow NIH, NSF, Am. Cancer Soc., Damon Runyan-Walter Winchell Cancer Fund, Fogarty Internat. Ctr., 1968—; grantee NIH, NSF, Am. Cancer Soc., Am. Inst. Cancer Rsch., Pfeiffer Found., 1973—, U.S. Army. Mem. Am. Soc. Cell Biology, Tissue Culture Assn., Am. Assn. Cancer Research, Internat. Assn. Breast Cancer Research. Democrat. Buddhist. Lodge: Rotary. Avocations: running, woodworking, model aviation. Home: 1185 NE Lake St Pullman WA 99163-3869 Office: Wash State U Dept Zoology Pullman WA 99164-4236

HOSIER, LINDA G., educator; b. Somerville, N.J., Mar. 15, 1948; d. Louis S. and Linda Julia (Braun) Grube; m. David Keith Short, Aug. 1, 1970 (div. Apr. 1986); children: Kristi Elizabeth, Andrew Alan; m. Robb R. Hosier, July 25, 1998; children: Robb R. Jr., Scott J., Timothy I., James E., Sherry H. BA, Pfeiffer Coll., 1970; MEd, U. N.C., 1973. Tchr. English Lexington (N.C.) City Schs., 1970-71; tchr. lang. arts, social studies Kannapolis (N.C.) City Schs., 1971-73; tchr. English, history Franklinton (N.C.) City Schs., 1973-74; tchr. English Bristol (Tenn.) City Schs., 1976-77; tchr. lang. arts, social studies High Point (N.C.) City Schs., 1983; tchr. acad. gifted lit., math. Stokes County Schs., Danbury, N.C., 1983—; tchr. lang. arts and social studies Guilford County Schs., 1995—; coord. childrens ministries Cathedral of Praise Ch., Greensboro, N.C., 1993—; missionary to Haiti, the Sioux Indian Nation, Mex. Mem. NEA, N.C. Edn. Assn., N.C. Assn. of Gifted, N.C. Tchrs. of English. Avocations: reading, travel, writing, gardening, singing. Home: 9027 Ambridge Ln Kernersville NC 27284-9267 Office: Northwest Mid Sch 5300 NW School Rd Greensboro NC 27409-9799

HOSKIE, LORRAINE, consumer products representative, poet; b. Nansemond County, Va., Aug. 26, 1953; m. Eddie Lewis Hoskie, July 7, 1972 (div. Oct. 1980); children: Jacqueline Marie, Quinton Lewis. BS, Va. Commonwealth U., 1977. Clk. Christian Children's Fund, Richmond, 1977-79, corr. rsch. clk., 1979-80; eligibility worker City of Richmond, 1982-83; substitute tchr. Sch. Bd., Richmond, 1983-86; telemarketer Energy Savs. Exterior, Richmond, 1995-96; CRT operator Snelling Pers. Svcs., Richmond, 1996; mail clk. Abacus, Richmond, 1997; office worker Kelly Svcs., Richmond, 1997; remittance processor Calipher, Inc., Richmond, 1997—; substitute tchr. Sch. Bd. of Franklin, Va., 1987; ch. sec. SDA-Ephesus, Richmond, 1981-82; vol. worker Bapt. Student Union Va. Commonwealth U., Richmond, 1971-72, math. tutor Spl. Svcs. Program, 1972. Sec. Ephesus Prison Ministry, 1996—; team sec. Ephesus Va. Dept. Correction, 1993-94. Named Golden Poet, World of Poetry, Sacramento, 1990, recipient award of merit cert., 1990; recipient Poet of Merit award Am. Poetry Assn., 1988, Appreciation award VA Dept. Corrections, 1994. Democrat. 7th Day Adventist. Avocations: crocheting, creative writing, music, poetry writing. Home: 4673 Briary Dr Apt H Richmond VA 23224-3020

HOSKINS, ALEXANDER L. (PETE HOSKINS), zoological park administrator; b. Woodland, Calif., Sept. 1, 1947; s. Edgar and Betty (Stoner) H.; m. Sharon Paula Barr, May 19, 1990; children: Emily, David, Adam. BA in Polit. Sci., San Jose State U., 1969; MA in Pub. Adminstrn., U. Minn., 1971. Asst. to city mgr. City of Foster City, Calif., 1971-72; mgmt. analyst Mng. Dir.'s Office, City of Phila., 1972-80, exec. dir. Fairmount Park., 1980-88, commr. of streets, 1988-93; pres., CEO, Zool. Soc. Phila., 1993—. Contbr. articles to various publs. Exec. v.p. Chestnut Hill Cmty. Assn., 1974-76; trustee Cmty. Leadership Seminars, 1978-80, Unitarian Soc. Germantown, 1985-87; chmn. Delaware Valley Regional Horticulture Industry Coun., 1985-86, Phila. Independence Marathon, 1985-88;. Recipient ann. award for meritorious mcpl. svc. Ctrl. Phila. Devel. Corp., 1986, honor award for restoration and revitalization Pa.-Del. chpt. Am. Soc. Landscape Architects, 1986, govt. svc. award Phila. sect. ASCE, 1990, govt. award for excellence in pub. adminstrn. Phila. regional chpt. ASAP, 1991, award for engring. excellence Cons. Engrs. Coun. N.J., 1991, William V. Donaldson award for civic price PhilaPride, 1992. Mem. Am. Pub. Works Assn. (Delaware Valley exec. com. 1992—). Office: Phila Zoo Garden 3400 W Girard Ave Philadelphia PA 19104-1196*

HOSKINS, BARBARA R(UTH) WILLIAMS, elementary educator, elementary principal; b. Pineville, Ky., June 7, 1945; d. John and Patsy Ann (Buell) Williams; m. Teddy Michael Hoskins, Dec. 12, 1961; children: Susan Ann Hoskins Brown, Shelia Marie Hoskins Key. BS, Union Coll., 1977, MA, 1978, postgrad., 1980-89; postgrad., U. Ky., 1990. Cert. elem. edn., elem./secondary principalship, elem./secondary supervision, dir. pupil pers., Ky. Tchr. Bell County Bd. Edn., Pineville, 1977—, prin., 1997—; edn. instr. S.E. C.C., Middlesboro, Ky., 1987—; BLS instr. Am. Heart Assn., Corbin, Ky., 1990—. Co-author: History of Bell County, 1994. Active Bell County Hist. Soc., 1992—, Laubach Literary Action Agy., Bell County, 1991—, Nat. Arbor Day Found., Nebr., 1995. Mem. Bell County Edn. Assn., Upper Cumberland Edn. Assn., Ky. Edn. Assn., NEA, Nat. Alliance Tchrs. Math. and Sci., Bell County Extension Coun., Iota Sigma Nu. Republican. Baptist. Avocations: walking, jogging, science and math activities, local history research. Home: RR 1 Box 69 Pineville KY 40977-9712 Office: Arjay Elem Sch HC69 Rte 120 Arjay KY 40902

HOSKINS, BOB (ROBERT WILLIAM HOSKINS), actor; b. Bury St. Edmunds, Suffolk, Eng., Oct. 26, 1942; s. Robert and Elsie Lillian Hoskins; m. Jane Livesey (div.); 2 children: Alex, Sarah; m. Linda Banwell, 1984; 2 children: Jack, Rosa. Student, Stroud Green Sch. Stage debut in Romeo and Juliet, Victoria Theatre, Stoke-on-Trent, 1968; joined Royal Shakespeare Co., 1976; stage appearances include Pygmalion, Albery, Eng., 1974, Aldwych, 1976, The World Has Turned Upside Down, 1978, Has Washington Legs?, 1978, True West, 1989, Guys and Dolls, 1981, Old Wicked Songs, 1996-97, Stage, 1996-97; TV appearances include On The Move, 1976, Pennies From Heaven, 1978, (miniseries) Flickers, 1980, Othello, 1981, The Dunera Boys, 1986, The Changeling, 1993, World War II: When The Lions Roared, 1994; film appearances include Zulu Dawn, 1980, The Long Good Friday, 1981, Cotton Club, 1984, Mona Lisa (Best Actor award Cannes Festival, Nat. Soc. Film Critics, 1987), Who Framed Roger Rabbit?, 1988, Mermaids, 1990, Heart Condition, 1990, Shattered, 1990, The Favor the Watch, 1990, The Projectionist, 1990, Hook, 1991, Passed Away, 1991, Super Mario Bros., 1992, Nixon, 1995, Michael, 1996, Cousin Bette, 1996, Twenty-Four/Seven, 1997, 1 Inch Over the Horizon, 1997, others; (films) actor, writer, director The Raggedy Rawney, 1988; actor, director The Rainbow, 1994; actor, prodr. The Secret Agent, 1995. Avocations: photography, gardening, playgoing. Office: Internat Creative Mgmt Ltd, Oxford House 76 Oxford St, London W1N 0AX, England

HOSKINS, CARLTON L., career military officer; b. Owensboro, Ky., Mar. 8, 1971; s. Robert Martin and Marylou (Graham) H. BS in Polit. Sci., USAF Acad., 1994. Btn. intelligence officer Counterintelligence Support Btn., Ft. Meade, 1995; exec. officer 902nd Mil. Intelligence Group, Ft. Meade, 1996; counterintelligence officer 716th Mil. Intelligence Btn., Ft. Meade, Md., 1996-97; adjutant Allied Mil. Intel Btn., Sarajevo, Bosnia, 1997-98; comd. of intelligence Def. Spl. Weapons Agy., Washington, 1998—; social aide to U.S. Pres. The White Ho. Mil. Office, Washington, 1997—. Mem. Army-Navy Club (mem. polo team 1996—), Mil. Polo Team. Home: 326 North Carolina Ave SE Washington DC 20003-2023

HOSKINS, JOHN HOWARD, urologist, educator; b. Breckenridge, Minn., Mar. 18, 1934; s. James H. and Ruth (Johanson) H.; m. Nancy Weih, Aug. 3, 1957; children: William, James, Laura, Sara. BA in History, U. Iowa, 1956; BS in Medicine, U. S.D., 1959; MD, Temple U., 1961. Diplomate Am. Bd. Urology. Practice medicine specializing in urology Sioux Falls, S.D., 1966-96; head sect. urology U. S.D. Sch. Medicine, Vermillon, 1977-93; ret., 1997. Maj. M.C. U.S. Army, 1967-69, Vietnam. Fellow ACS; mem. AMA, Am. Urol. Assn., Augustana Fellows, Masons, Shriners, Rotary. Republican. Methodist.

HOSKINS, MABLE ROSE, secondary education educator, English language educator; b. Natchez, Miss., May 23, 1945; d. Johnny and Josephine (Jones) Reynolds; m. Charles Hoskins, Dec. 23, 1973 (div. Dec. 5, 1989). BA in English, Jackson State Coll., 1967; MED, Miss. State U., 1979, Ednl. Specialist, 1982. Tchr. English Natchez (Miss.) Pub. Schs., 1968-70, Quitman (Miss.) Consol. Schs., 1971-81, Meridian (Miss.) Schs., 1981—; bd. dirs. Pub. Employee's Retirement Sys., Jackson, 1988-92, Meridian Bonita Lakes Authority. Co-author: (teaching units) Miss. Writers Teaching Units for Secondary English, 1988; consulting editor: (book) Mississippi Writers-An Anthology, 1991. Newsletter editor, co-editor Assn. of Meridian Educators, 1988-92; mistress of ceremonies Alpha Kappa Alpha Sorority, Meridian, 1985-90; Children's Discovery, vol. coord. Meridian Coun. for the Arts, 1990. Named S.T.A.R. tchr. Miss. Econ. Coun., 1980, Tchr. of Yr., Meridian Pub. Schs., 1988, 94, finalist Miss. Hall of Master Tchrs., 1994. Mem. NEA, Miss. Assn. Educators (Mem. of Yr. 1988, bd. dirs. 1990-93), Miss. Coun. Tchrs. English, Nat. Coun. Tchrs. English, Phi Kappa Phi, Phi Delta Kappa. Baptist. Avocations: reading, listening to music. Home: 1402 39th Ave Meridian MS 39307-6001 Office: Meridian H S 2320 32nd St Meridian MS 39305-4657

HOSKINS, RICHARD JEROLD, lawyer; b. Ft. Smith, Ark., June 19, 1945; s. Walter Jerold and Emma Gladys (Gaither) H.; m. Kristine Orr; children: Stephen Weston, Philip Richard. B.A., U. Kans., 1967; J.D., Northwestern U., 1970. Bar: N.Y. 1971, Ill. 1976, U.S. Supreme Ct. 1982. Assoc. Davis Polk & Wardwell, N.Y.C., 1970-73; asst. U.S. atty., So. Dist. N.Y., 1973-76; assoc. Schiff Hardin & Waite, Chgo., 1976-77, ptnr., 1978—; adj. prof. U. Va. Law Sch., 1980-83, Northwestern U. Law Sch., 1992-98, sr. lectr., 1999—. Contbr. articles to profl. jours. Mem. vis. com. U. Chgo. Div. Sch.; bd. trustees Seabury-Western Theol. Sem.; Chancellor Episcopal Diocese of Chgo. Fellow Am. Coll. Trial Lawyers, Am. Bar Found.; mem. ABA, Ill. State Bar Assn., Chgo. Bar Assn., 7th Cir. Bar Assn., Assn. of Bar of City of N.Y., Chgo. Coun. Lawyers, Law Club Chgo., Met. Club (Chgo.), Univ. Club (Chgo.). Office: 6600 Sears Tower Chicago IL 60606

HOSKINS, WILLIAM JOHN, obstetrician, gynecologist, educator; b. Harlan, Ky., May 10, 1940; s. Lonnie S. and Joanne (Huff) H.; m. Betty Jean Gay, Sept. 10, 1960 (div. 1985); children: Tonya J., William John Jr.; m. Iffath Abbasi Ahson, Nov. 9, 1985; children: Ahad A., Mariya A. BA, U. Tenn., Knoxville, 1962; MD, U. Tenn., Memphis, 1965. Diplomate Am. Bd. Ob-Gyn., Am. Bd. Gynecol. Oncology. Commd. lt. USN, 1966, advanced through grades to capt.; intern Jacksonville (Fla.) Naval Hosp., 1966-67; med. officer Destroyer Squadron 8 USN, Mayport, Fla., 1967-68; resident in ob-gyn Oakland (Calif.) Naval Hosp., 1968-71; mem. staff, dept. ob -gyn Pensacola (Fla.) Naval Hosp., 1971-74; fellow in gynecol. oncology U. Miami, Fla., 1974-76; dir. Gynecol. Oncology Nat. Naval Med. Ctr., Bethesda, Md., 1976-86; assoc. prof. ob-gyn Uniformed Svcs. U., Bethesda, 1976-86; ret. USN, 1986; assoc. chief gynecology svc. Meml. Sloan-Kettering Cancer Ctr., N.Y.C., 1988-90, chief gynecology svc., 1990—, 1990—; assoc. prof. ob-gyn Cornell U. Med. Ctr., N.Y.C., 1986-90; prof. ob-gyn. Cornell U. Med. Coll., N.Y.C., 1990-94, vice chmn. protocol com. gynecol. oncology group, 1993-94, vice chmn. gynecologic oncology group, 1993—; Avon chair gynecologic oncology rsch. Meml. Sloan-Kettering Cancer Ctr., N.Y.C., 1995-96, dep. physician in chief disease mgmt. teams, 1996—; chmn. ovarian com. Gynecol. Oncology Group, Phila., 1984-89. Editor: Principles and Practice of Gynecology and Oncology, 1992, 2d edit., 1996, Cancer of the Ovary, 1993, Cervical Cancer and Perinvasive Peoplasia, 1996, Cancer Management: A Multidisciplinary Approach, 1996; contbr. 224 articles to profl. jours., also chpts. to books. Fellow Am. Coll. Obstetricians and Gynecologists (v.p. Navy sect. 1982-83), ACS; mem. Am. Gynecol. and Obstet. Soc., Soc. Gynecol. Oncologists (sec.-treas. elect 1992, sec.-treas. 1994—, coun. mem. 1988-91), Soc. Gynecol. Surgeons, Internat. Gynecol. Cancer Soc., Am. Radium Soc., Am. Assn Cancer rsch., 1996—. Republican. Muslim. Office: Meml Sloan-Kettering Cancer Ctr 1275 York Ave Dept Obg New York NY 10021-6007

HOSKINS, WILLIAM KELLER, pharmaceutical executive, mediator/ arbitrator, lawyer; b. Cin., Feb. 22, 1935; s. John Hobart and Gertrude Louise (Keller) H.; m. Elizabeth Ann Grimm, Aug. 5, 1961; children: Bruce, Andrew, John, Elizabeth, Allison. BA, Yale U., 1956; LLB, Harvard U., 1962. Bar: Ohio 1962, U.S. Dist. Ct. (so. dist.) Ohio 1963, U.S. Tax Ct. 1963, U.S. Ct. Appeals (6th cir.) 1964, N.Y. 1982, Mo. 1983. Assoc. Frost & Jacobs, Cin., 1962-68; gen. counsel Drackett Co., Cin., 1968-71, v.p., gen. counsel, 1971-81; assoc. gen. counsel Bristol Myers Co., N.Y.C., 1981, spl. counsel, 1982; v.p., gen. counsel, sec. Hoechst Marion Roussell (formerly Marion Labs. Inc.), Kansas City, Mo., 1982-97; gen. ptnr. Hoskins Group, Boston, 1998—; pres. Hoskins & Assocs., Boston, 1998—; chmn. household div. Soap and Detergent Assn., N.Y.C., 1978-79, chmn. Chem. Spltys. Mfg. Assn., Washington, 1982; bd. dirs. Copley Pharm., Canton, Mass., Am. Arbitration Assn., N.Y.C.. Mem. Hamilton County Rep. Ctrl. Com., Ohio, 1970-81; sec.-treas. Marion Labs. Polit. Action Com., 1982-89; sec.-treas. polit. action com. Mid-Am. Com. Sound Govt., Lake Quivira, Kans., 1982-86; bd. dirs. Landmark Legal Found., Kansas City, 1995—. Lt. (j.g.) USN, 1956-59. Mem. ABA, Mo. Bar Assn., Ohio Bar Assn., N.Y. Bar Assn., Cin. Bar Assn., Harvard Law Sch. Alumni Assn. (bd. dirs. 1991-95). Roman Catholic. Fax: 617-742-2368. Home: 85 E India Row Apt 20B Boston MA 02110-3397 Office: Hoskins and Assocs 85 E India Row # 20b Boston MA 02110-3320

HOSLER, CHARLES LUTHER, JR., meteorologist, educator; b. Honey Brook, Pa., June 3, 1924; s. Charles Luther and Miriam Deichley (Stauffer) H.; m. Gladys Cheesbrough, 1947 (div.); children:Sharon Elizabeth, David Charles, Lynn Rebecca, Peter William; m. Anna R. Stahel, 1971. Student, Bucknell U., 1943-44, MIT, 1944-45; B.S., Pa. State U., 1947, M.S., 1948, Ph.D., 1951. Faculty Pa. State U., University Park, 1948—; prof. meteorology Pa. State U., 1960—, head dept., 1961-65, dean Coll. Earth and Mineral Scis., 1965-85, sr. v.p. rsch., dean Grad. Sch., 1985-92; hydrographer Pa. Dept. Forests and Waters, 1949-59; meteorol. cons., 1950—, vis. prof. colls., lectr. civic and profl. groups; condr. daily TV weather program, 1957-67; spl. rsch. microphysics of clouds; chmn. bd. atmospheric scis. and climate Nat. Acad. Scis., 1984-86; mem. Nat. Sci. Bd., 1985-94; mem. nat. adv. com. on oceans and atmosphere; chmn. bd. trustees Univ. Corp. for Atmospheric Rsch., Boulder, Colo., 1981-85. Contbr. articles to profl. jours. Served to lt. (j.g.) USNR, 1943-46; lt. comdr. Res. Fellow Am. Meteorol. Soc. (councilor, pres. 1976); mem. Nat. Acad. Engring., Am. Geophys. Union Am. Chem. Soc. (regional lectr. 1971-72), AAAS, Sigma Xi (pres. Pa. State U. 1958, nat. lectr. 1972), Tau Beta Pi. Home: 1229 Smithfield Cir State College PA 16801-6426 Office: Pa State U 617 Walker Bldg University Park PA 16802-5014

HOSLER, RUSSELL JOHN, retired education educator; b. DuPont, Ohio, Apr. 2, 1906; s. John Henry and Etta (Spitznaugle) H.; m. Hilda Elizabeth Weible, Dec. 25, 1927 (dec. Oct. 1966); children: Philip Eugene, Helen Hosler Daggett, Russell John Jr.; m. Mary Margaret O'Connell, Aug. 23, 1968. AB, Defiance Coll., 1932; MA, Toledo U., 1941; EdD, Ind. U., 1946. Tchr. high sch. Montpelier, Ohio, 1927-34, Fostoria, Ohio, 1934-38; Tchr. high sch. Libbey High Sch., Toledo, 1938-42; asst. prof. commerce Ind. U., 1942-46; faculty U. Wis., Madison, 1946—, prof., 1953-76, emeritus, 1976—, chmn. dept. edn., 1955-59. Co-author: Gregg Shorthand for Colleges, rev. edit, 1958, 65, 73, Gregg Transcription for Colleges, 1959, rev. edit., 1966, 75, Programmed Gregg Shorthand, 1969, Personal Typing, 1979; co-author: (with M. Hosler) The History of the National Business Education Association, 1993; contbr. articles to profl. mags. Recipient John Robert Gregg award, 1966. Mem. Nat. Bus. Edn. Assn (pres. 1968-69), Nat. Bus. Tchrs. Assn. (pres. 1955), Nat. Assn. Bus. Tchr. Edn. (pres. 1959-61). Home: 8011 Hwy KK Milton WI 53563-9801

HOSLEY, MARGUERITE CYRIL, volunteer; b. Houston, July 29, 1946; d. Frederick Willard and Marguerite Estella (Arisman) Collister; m. Richard Allyn Hosley II, July 18, 1968; children: Richard A. III, Sean Frederick, Michelle Cyril. BS in Edn., U. Houston, 1968; postgrad., Tex. A&M U., 1970-71. Cert. tchr., Tex. Tchr. Sharpstown H.S., Houston, 1968-69, Bryan (Tex.) H.S., 1969-71; ins. asst. Farmers Ins., Stafford, Tex., 1981-83; adminstrv. asst., fin. asst. Christ United Meth. Ch., Sugarland, Tex., 1984-92; mem. planning and zoning commn. City of Sugarland, 1995-98; mem. Sugarland City Coun., 1998—. Pres. bd. dirs. Ft. Bend Boys Choir, 1984-85; docent Bayou Bend Collection and Gardens, Houston Mus. Fine Arts, 1994—, day chair, 1997-98; with Imag Hogg Ceramic Circle, 1994—, social chmn., 1997-98; bd. dirs. Am. Cancer Soc., 1990-97; pres. Am. Cancer Soc. League, 1993-94; mem. Lone Staar Stomp com. Ft. Bend Mus. Assn., 1991-97; parent vol. Ft. Bend Ind. Schs., 1980-94; raffle chmn. Ft. Bend Drug Alliance Gala, 1989; newsletter chmn. Am. Heart Assn. Guild, 1990-91, v.p., 1992-93. Named Ft. Bend Outstanding Woman, Ft. Bend County, 1992. Mem. Houston Ladies' Tennis Assn. (team capt.), Ft. Bend Mus., Sweetwater Country Club (bd. govs. 1990-93), Sweetwater Women's Assn. (treas. 1985-87, pres. 1987-88), Friends of Casa (charter mem.), Aggie Moms Club, Chi Omega Alumnae. Republican. Methodist. Avocations: tennis, dancing, reading, continuing education classes. Home: 427 W Alkire Lake Dr Sugar Land TX 77478-3527

HOSMAN, SHARON, elementary education educator; b. Springfield, Mo., May 20, 1939; d. Charles E. and Jewell A. (Allgood) Beckerdite; m. Ralph W. Hosman, Jan. 1, 1980; children: Kevin Cook, Melissa Cook, Shawn Cook. BS, SW Mo. State U., 1964, MS, 1980. Tchr. music Pleasant Hope (Mo.) Sch., 1964-66; elem. tchr. Willard (Mo.) Pub. Schs., 1966-93. Mem., piano player Preston/Urbana United Meth. Ch. Mem. Internat. Reading Assn., Am. Fedn. Tchrs. Methodist. Home: HC 80 Box 782 Camdenton MO 65020-8612

HOSMAN, SHARON LEE, music educator; b. Bisbee, Ariz., Nov. 2, 1943; d. Roy Lee and Virginia Baldwin (Bandel) H. BA, Loretto Heights Coll., 1965; MA, U. No. Colo., 1979. Tchr. Livermore (Calif.) Sch. Dist., 1965-66, Jefferson County Pub. Schs., Golden, Colo., 1966-97; faculty rep. North Area Citizens Adv. Com., Arvada, Colo., 1979-81, S.I.P.C., Arvada, 1982-83, North Area Sch. Improvement Process Com., Arvada, 1984-91, North Area Accountability com., 1991-92. Piano accompanist for sch. groups, 1965-97. Mem. NEA, DAR, Jefferson County Edn. Assn., Colo. Edn. Assn., Music Tchrs. Nat. Assn., Colo. State Music Tchrs. Assn., Denver Area Music Tchrs. Assn., Musicians' Soc. Denver, Am. Guild Organists, Hereditary Order of First Families of Mass., Smithsonian, Denver Rescue Mission, Denver Dumb Friends League, St. Luke's Hosp. Aux. (life). Republican. Episcopalian. Avocations: art, music, drama, reading, gardening.

HOSMAN-NELSON, JILL MARIE, special education educator; b. Salem, Mass., Oct. 11, 1972; d. Thomas Joseph and Elizabeth Ann (Crowdis) H. BS, Bridgewater State Coll., 1995; MEd, Salem State Coll., 1999. Tchr. adapted phys. edn. Kennedy Day Sch., Brighton, Mass., 1995—, coord. after sch. program, 1995-97, adaptive design cons., 1997—; instr. Kidsfit, Youth SPARC, Boston, 1995—. Mem. AAHPERD, Mass. Alliance for Health, Phys. Edn., Recreation and Dance. Home: 41 Linwood St Haverhill MA 01830-6525

HOSMER, PHILIP, writer, communications professional; b. Liverpool, Eng., July 30, 1962; s. Howard Jr. and Dorothy (Addison) H.; m. Gina Ann Kazimir, Jan. 16, 1993. BS, U. Md., 1984. Reporter Montgomery Jour., Rockville, Md., 1984-88; writer/editor Washington Bus. In Formation, Arlington, Va., 1988-90; reporter The Courier News, Bridgewater, N.J., 1990-93; contbg. writer The Balt. Sun, 1993-96; writer/editor Balt. City C.C., 1993-96; lectr./instr. Catonsville (Md.) C.C., 1995—; pubs. coord. St. Joseph Med. Ctr., Towson, Md., 1996-98; sr. writer United Way Ctrl. Md., Balt., 1998—. Bd. dirs. FISH Homeless Program, Somerville, N.J., 1992, vol. host, 1991-93; organizer Amnesty Internat., College Park, 1981-84; vol. Pets on Wheels, Inc., Balt., 1994—. Recipient First Place in Interpretive Writing, N.J. Press Assn., 1993, award of Merit, Dalton Pen Comm., 1997, Best in Md. award for annual reports Pub. Rels. Soc. Am., 1997, Best in Md. award for newsletters Pub. Rels. Soc. Am., 1997; Knight Ct. for Specialized Journalism fellow, 1993. Avocations: travel, bicycling, soccer. Home: 349 Delmar Ct Abingdon MD 21009-2904

HOSOKAWA, DAVID, advertising executive. CEO TMP Worldwide, Inc., N.Y.C., vice chmn. Office: TMP Worldwide Inc 1633 Broadway Fl 33 New York NY 10019-6781*

HOSPERS, JOHN, philosophy educator; b. Pella, Iowa, June 9, 1918; s. John G. and Dena (Verhey) H. B.A., Central Coll., 1939, D.Litt., 1962; M.A., State U. Iowa, 1941; Ph.D., Columbia U., 1944. Instr., Columbia U., 1946-48; asst. prof., assoc. prof. U. Minn., 1948-56; prof. Bklyn. Coll., 1956-66, Calif. State U., Los Angeles, 1966-68; prof. philosophy U. So. Calif. Sch. Philosophy, Los Angeles, 1968-88; Fulbright research scholar U. London, 1954-55; vis. prof. UCLA, 1960-61, 64. Author: Meaning and Truth in the Arts, 1946, (with W. Sellars) Readings in Ethical Theory, 1970, Introduction to Philosophical Analysis, 1967, 4th edit., 1997, Human Conduct, 1961, 3d edit., 1996, Readings in Introductory Philosophical Analysis, 1968, Introductory Readings in Aesthetics, 1969, Artistic Expression, 1971, Libertarianism, a Political Philosophy for Tomorrow, 1971, Understanding the Arts, 1982; editor The Personalist, 1968-78, Philosophical Quar., 1978-83, The Monist, 1983-92. Mem. Am. Soc. Aesthetics (pres. 1983-85). Home: 8229 Lookout Mountain Ave Los Angeles CA 90046-1546

HOSSAIN, MURSHED, physicist; b. Pathaliakandi, Homna, Comilla, Bangladesh, Nov. 21, 1950; came to U.S., 1979; s. Mohammad Abdul Alim and Mehar Nigar; m. Sufia Khatun, July 25, 1982; children: Chintan, Chetak. BSc with honors, Dacca U., Bangladesh, 1975, MSc, 1976; MS, Coll. William & Mary, 1981; PhD, Coll. William & Mary, Va., 1983. Jr. rsch. officer Forest Rsch. Inst., Chittagong, Bangladesh, 1977-78; sci. officer AEC, Dhaka, Bangladesh, 1978-79; staff scientist Inst. for Computer Applications in Sci. & Engring. NASA Langley Rsch. Ctr., Hampton, Va., 1983-85; assoc. rsch. scientist Courant Inst. Math. Scis., NYU, 1985-88; rsch. scientist Bartol Rsch. Inst., U. Del., Newark, 1988-91, sr. rsch. scientist, 1991-97; adj. faculty Rowan U., Glassboro, N.J., 1995-97, asst. prof. dept. chemistry and physics, 1998; postdoctoral fellow, clin. resident Thomas Jefferson U. Hosp., Phila., 1998—; mem. mng. com. B.G. Press H.S., Tejgaon, Dhaka, Bangladesh, 1974-77; v.p. Dacca U. Physics Assn., 1975-76; joint sec. Sr. Forrest Rsch. Officers Assn., Forest Rsch. Inst., 1977-78. Contbr. articles to Jour. Plasma Physics, Physics Fluids, Phys. Rev. Letters, Plasma Physics and Controlled Fusion, Astrophys. Jour., Physics Letters, Computer Physics Comm., Phys. Rev., Physics Edn. Mem. Am. Assn. of Physicists in Medicine. Achievements include research on effects of the coupling of plasma diffusion and heat flow in transport, on astrophysical convection, on fluid and magnetofluid turbulence theory and simulation. Home: 15 Berks Ct New Castle DE 19720-3752 Office: Thomas Jefferson U Hosp Dept Radiation Oncology 111 S 11th St Philadelphia PA 19107-5084

HOSSEINIYAR, MANSOUR M., software engineer, financial consultant; b. Tehran, Iran, Jan. 18, 1957; came to U.S., 1976; s. Ali and Maryam Hosseiniyar. AS, Delta Coll., Univ. Ctr., Mich., 1978; BS, Calif. State U., Fresno, 1980; MS, U. So. Calif., L.A., 1984, Engr. in Elec. Engring. Degree, 1988; PhD, U. S. Calif., 1988. Cert. Nat. Assn. Realtors, Calif. Assn. Realtors. Asst. prof. Delta Coll., 1976-78, Calif. State U., Fresno, 1979-80; tech. staff, software engr. Versys Corp., Torrance, Calif., 1981-83; rsch. assist. U. So. Calif., 1983-89; tech. staff, software engr. Teledyne Corp., L.A., 1985-88; tech. staff, engr. Rockwell Corp., Canoga Park, Calif., 1989-95; mem. tech. staff, engr. Jet Propulsion Lab., Calif. Inst. Tech., Pasadena, 1995-96, MICROPOLIS Corp., Chatsworth, Calif., 1996-97; sr. software engr. XYLAN Corp., Calabasas, Calif., 1997—; corp. officer, broker, Equal Financial, Encino, Calif., 1992-97, Capital Financial, Tarzana, Calif., 1990-97. Precinct officer nat. election, Calabasas, Calif., 1996. Mem. IEEE, Nat. Assn. Securities Dealers (cert.), Southland Regional Assn. Realtors. Democrat. Moslem. Avocations: mountain hiking, jogging, swimming, finance. Home: 24763 Via Del Llano Calabasas CA 91302-3020 Office: XYLAN Corp 26679 Agoura Rd Calabasas CA 91302-1900

HOSSLER, DAVID JOSEPH, lawyer, law educator; b. Mesa, Ariz., Oct. 18, 1940; s. Carl Joseph and Elizabeth Ruth (Bills) H.; m. Gretchen Anne, Mar. 2, 1945; 1 child, Devon Annagret. BA, U. Ariz., 1969; JD, 1972. Bar: Ariz. 1972, U.S. dist. ct. Ariz. 1972, U.S. Supreme Ct. 1977. Legal intern to chmn. FCC, summer 1971; law clk. to chief justice Ariz. Supreme Ct., 1972-73; chief dep. county atty. Yuma County (Ariz.), 1973-74; ptnr. Hunt and Hossler, Yuma, Ariz., 1974—; instr. in law and banking, law and real estate Ariz. Western Coll.; instr. in bus. law, mktg., ethics Webster U; co-chmn. fee arbitration com. Ariz. State Bar, 1990—; instr. agrl. law U. Ariz. Mem. precinct com., Yuma County Rep. Cen. Com., 1974-98, vice chmn., 1982; chmn. region II Acad. Decathalon competition, 1989; bd. dirs. Yuma County Ednl. Found., Yuma County Assn. Behavior Health Svcs., also pres., 1981; coach Yuma High Sch. mock ct. team, 1987—; bd. dirs. Friends of U. Med. Ctr. With USN. Recipient Man and Boy award Boys Clubs Am., 1979, Freedoms Found. award Yuma Chpt., 1988, Demolay Legion of Honor, 1991; named Vol. of Yr., Yuma County, 1981-82. Mem. Assn. Trial Lawyers Am., Am. Judicature Soc., Yuma County Bar Assn. (pres. 1975-76), Navy League, VFW, Am. Legion, U. Ariz. Alumni Assn. (nat. bd. dirs., past pres., hon. bobcat 1996, Disting. Citizen award, 1997, Rotary (pres. Yuma club 1987-88, dist. gov. rep. 1989, dist. gov. 1992-93, findings com. 1996, dist. found. chair 1996—, Van Houton award 1996, Rotary Found. citation for Meritorious svc.). Editor-in-chief Ariz. Adv., 1971-72. Episcopalian (vestry 1978-82). Home: 2802 S Fern Dr Yuma AZ 85364-7909 Office: Hunt and Hossler 330 W 24th St Yuma AZ 85364-6455 also: PO Box 2919 Yuma AZ 85366-2919

HOST, STIG, oil company executive; b. Copenhagen, Denmark, Sept. 26, 1926; came to U.S., 1941; s. Thorkil and Eli (Stallknecht) H.; m. Jeanne Grinnell, Feb. 24, 1951; children: N. George, Alexander (dec.), Christian T., T. Amory. AB in Econs., Harvard U., 1951; postgrad. in Bus., NYU, 1952-53. Bunker sales agt. Cory Mann George Corp., N.Y.C., 1950-53; cargo sales asst. Mobil Internat., N.Y.C., 1953-57; dir. cargo sales, Europe and North Africa Mobil Supply Co., Ltd., London, 1957-59; mng. dir. Mobil Sales (Internat.), Tokyo, 1959-61; v.p. crude and product sales Mobil Sales and Supply Corp., N.Y.C., 1961-65, exec. v.p. marine, indsl. and govt. sales, 1965-68; pres., gen. mgr. Mobil Oil Italiana, Rome, 1968-72; v.p., bd. dirs. Mobil Europe, Inc., London, 1972-73; vice-chmn., chief exec. officer Skaarup Shipping Corp., Greenwich, Conn., 1973-79; chmn., bd. dirs. Internat. Energy Corp., Stamford, Conn., 1979—; chmn., bd. dirs. Internat. Marine Sales, Inc., Stamford, 1979—, Kriti Exploration, Inc., Houston, 1980—, Kriti Properties and Devel. Corp., Houston, 1985—; bd. dirs. Fla. Fuels, Inc., Miami, Fla.; mem. exec. and audit coms., bd. dirs. DeVegh Mut. Fund, N.Y.C., 1977-86; trustee, mem. exec. com. and audit coms. Alliance Internat. Fund, N.Y.C., 1980—; trustee Winthrop Focus Funds, N.Y.C., 1986—, Alliance Global Environ. Fund, 1990—, Alliance New Europe Fund, 1990—, Alliance All Asia Investment Fund, 1994—; chmn. Alexander Host Found., 1984—; exec. trustee Am. Scandinavian Found., 1987—; overseer Tufts U. Coll. Engring., 1990-93. Mem. Fulbright Commn., Rome, 1969-71; trustee Temple U., Rome, 1971-72, Overseas Sch. of Rome, 1968-71. Served as mcht. marine officer, 1943-46, ETO. Decorated Order of Grande Ufficiale, Govt. of Italy, 1970. Mem. Am. Petroleum Inst. (25 yr. club), Harvard U. Alumni Assn. (bd. dirs., chmn. communications com., mem. continuing edn. com., nominations overseers and dirs. com., 1985-89). Republican. Episcopalian. Clubs: Harvard of N.Y. (chmn. long range planning 1978-82), N.Y. Yacht; Indian Harbor Yacht (Greenwich) (bd. dirs., audit com. 1973-78); Royal Automobile (London); Tokyo. Home: 103 Oneida Dr Greenwich CT 06830-7127 Office: Kriti Mgmt Inc 345 E 37th St Rm 312 New York NY 10016-3256

HOSTETLER, DEAN BRYAN, industry environmental compliance consultant; b. Newport, R.I., Oct. 25, 1953; s. Dean Herman and Amarina (Negri) H.; m. Marilyn C. Sullivan, Nov. 3, 1979; children: Courtney Marie, Devon Mary, Caitlin Ruth. BS, Maine Maritime Acad., 1977. Tug pilot, capt.-master, 1981—; pres. Pro Mar, Inc., Portsmouth, R.I., 1988—, profl. maritime cons., 1988—; curriculum devel., mtg. mgr., cons. Jamestown Marine Svcs., Jamestown, R.I., 1992-93; gen. mgr., cons., mgr. salvage action response team Weeks Jamestown, Inc., Cranford, N.J., 1993-98; owner, pres. Pro-mar; bd. dirs. Global Ops., Firefighters and Rescue Svcs.; cons. in field. Author, editor, cons.: Emergency Towing Procedures and Safety Manual, 1994. Mem. Area Contingency Plan Com., Marine Safety Office, Providence, 1992—; pres. Portsmouth Pirates Soccer Club, 1994-96; dir. R.I. Olympic Devel. Girls Soccer Program, 1995—. Mem. Maine Maritime Alumni Assn., Narragansett Bay Maritime Assn. (adminstr. 1993—), Portsmouth Pirates Soccer Club (v.p., pres., dir. coaches 1993-99), FC Greater Boston Bolts (team mgr. 1997—), R.I. Lady Stingrays (pub. rels. 1999—), Port of Providence Propeller Club, MSO Providence and Long Island Sound Area Contingency Plan Com., MSO port of Providence Marine Firefighting, mem. subcom. ops. Avocations: avid sailor, skiing, soccer. Fax: (401) 683-3283. Office: Pro-Mar Inc 30 Miller Rd Portsmouth RI 02871-1900

HOSTETLER, JOHN JAY, systems consultant; b. Hutchinson, Kans., Nov. 20, 1957; s. Melvin C. and Bette Jane (Hall) H.; m. Kay Charisse Siemens Ward, June 27, 1981 (div. Mar. 1992); children: Holden, Jordan; m. Renny Ann Justice, Sept. 11, 1992; children: Nichole, Keith. BA in Clin. Psychology, Wichita (Kans.) State U., 1980; MA in Psychology, Clayton U., St. Louis, 1989. Cert. lead assessor SEI/CMM Framework, Carnegie Mellon U. Computer programmer Boeing Computer Svcs., Wichita, 1983-85, program mgr., 1985-86; sr. systems analyst Pizza Hut, Inc., Wichita, 1986-89, mgr., 1989; systems cons. Boeing Comml. Airplane, Wichita, 1989—; coaching cons. SEI/CMM (Boeing, Carnegie Mellon U.), Wichita, 1992—, Kans. State Legis.; instr., tchr. Boeing Edn. & Tng., 1989—. Author, editor: Whispers From the Past, 1991, A Christmas Spirit, 1995, A Quality Roadmap for Boeing Wichita Information Systems, 1997, Boeing Wichita's Software Improvement Story, 1998. Recipient Alumni award Hutchinson C.C., 1992. Mem. Andover Cmty. Theater, Project Mgmt. Inst., Wichita State U. Alumni Assn., Turpentine Creek Wildlife Ranch Found., Phi Kappa Phi, Psi Chi (v.p. 1979-82). Republican. Presbyterian. Avocations: songwriting, tennis, running, basketball, kid activities. Home: 1 Swallow Ln Wichita KS 67230-6619 Office: Boeing Co 4200 Southeast Blvd Wichita KS 67210-1618

HOSTETTER, AMOS BARR, JR., cable television executive; b. N.Y.C., Jan. 12, 1937; s. Amos Barr and Leola (Conroy) H. BA cum laude, Amherst Coll., 1958; MBA, Harvard U., 1961. Asst. to v.p. fin. Am. & Fgn. Power Co., N.Y.C., 1958-59; investment analyst Cambridge (Mass.) Capital Corp., 1961-63; co-founder, exec. v.p. Continental Cablevision, Inc., Boston, 1963-80, pres., chief exec. officer, 1980-85, chmn., chief exec. officer, 1985-96; CEO MediaOne, Inc., Boston, 1996—; chmn., CEO Continental Cablevision, Inc. (named changed to Media One), 1985—; founder, bd. dirs. Cable Satellite Pub. Affairs Network, 1979—; bd. dirs. Commodities Corp., Princeton, N.J.; trustee various mut. funds Mass. Fin. Services, 1985—; bd. dirs. Corp. Pub. Broadcasting, Washington, 1975-79, The Walter Kaitz Found., 1981—; trustee Children's TV Workshop, N.Y.C., 1980—, New Eng. Med. Ctr. Hosp., Boston, 1981—, Nantucket Conservation Found., 1986—; corporator Perkins Sch. for Blind, Watertown, Mass, 1982—; bd. overseers Mus. Fine Arts, Boston, 1987—. Named Man of Yr., Cablevision Mag., 1972. Mem. Nat. Cable TV Assn. (nat. chmn. 1973-74, dir. 1968-75, 82—, Larry Boggs award 1975), Amherst Coll. Soc. Alumni (pres. 1982-84, exec. comm. 1982—, chmn. 1987—), Internat. Radio and TV Soc. Office: The Pilot House Lewis Wharf Boston MA 02110*

HOSTETTLER, JOHN N., congressman; b. Evansville, Ind., July 19, 1961; s. Earl Eugene and Esther Aline (Hollingsworth) H.; m. Elizabeth Ann Hamman, Nov. 12, 1983; children: Matthew, Amanda, Jaclyn. BSME, Rose-Hulman Inst. Tech. Reg. profl. engr. Engr. So. Ind. Gas and Electric, Evansville, 1986-94; Congressman U.S. Congress, Washington, 1995—; mem. Agriculture and National Security coms. Deacon 12th Avenue Gen. Baptist, 1986—. Republican. Baptist. Office: HS Ho of Reps 431 Cannon HOB Washington DC 20515-0601*

HOSTETTLER, STEPHEN JOHN, naval officer; b. Evansville, Ind., Aug. 23, 1931; s. Ernest Hoffman and Frances Reitz (Bays) H.; m. Lucy Ann Ingalls, June 10, 1953; children: Kathryn Ann, Stephen John Jr. B.S., U.S. Naval Acad., 1953; M.S.E.E., U.S. Naval Postgrad. Sch., 1960; P.M.D., Harvard Bus. Sch., 1969. Commd. ensign USN, advanced through grades to rear adm.; comdr. USS Halsey CG 23; program mgr. medium-range missile systems Naval Sea Systems Commnad, 1974-76; comdr. U.S. Naval Forces, Republic of Korea; sr. mem. Mil. Armistice Commn., UN Command, Republic of Korea, 1979-81; dir. surface combat systems div. Office Chief Naval Ops., Washington, 1981-82; dir. Joint Cruise Missile Office, Washington, 1982-86, ret., 1986; v.p., gen. mgr. Va. propulsion div. Atlantic Research Corp., Alexandria, Va., 1986-92; ret., 1992—. Decorated Bronze Star medal., Def. Superior Svc. medal, Def. D.S.M., Legion of Merit.

HOSTLER, CHARLES WARREN, international affairs consultant; b. Chgo., Dec. 12, 1919; s. Sidney Marvin and Catherine (Marshall) H.: 1 son, Charles Warren, Jr. B.A., U. Calif. at Los Angeles, 1942; M.A., Am. U., Beirut, Lebanon, 1955, Georgetown U., 1950; Ph.D., Georgetown U., 1956. Commd. 2d lt. U.S. Air Force, 1942, advanced through grades to col.; ret., 1963; dir. internat. ops. McDonnell Douglas Corp., Middle East, N.Africa, Beirut, 1965-67; mgr. internat. ops. McDonnell Douglas Corp., Paris, 1963-65; mgr. internat. mktg., missiles and space McDonnell Douglas Corp., 1967-69; pres. Hostler Investment Co., Newport Beach, Calif., 1969-74; chmn. bd. Irvine (Calif.) Nat. Bank, 1972-74; dir. Wynn's Internat., Inc., Fullerton, Calif., 1971-74; dep. asst. sec. for internat. commerce, dir. Bur. Internat. Commerce, U.S. Dept. Commerce, Washington, 1974-76; regional v.p. Mid-East and Africa, E-Systems Inc., Cairo, Egypt, 1976-77; pres. Pacific SW Capital Corp., San Diego, 1977-89; ambassador U.S. Govt., Bahrain, 1989-93; hon. consul gen. State of Bahrain, 1993—; adj. prof. Sch. Internat. Svc., Am. U., Washington, 1955-63; pres. San Diego Consular Corps. Author: Turkism and the Soviets, 1957, The Turks of Central Asia, 1993; contbr. articles to econ., comml. and mil. jours. Chmn. Calif. Contractors State Lic. Bd., 1973-79, San Diego County Local Agy. Formation Commn., 1979-89; chmn. Calif. State Park and Recreation Commn., 1983-89; pres. San Diego Consular Corps, 1996-98. Decorated Legion of Merit; recipient Fgn. Affairs award for pub. svc. U.S. State Dept. Mem. Am. Polit. Sci. Assn., Am. Ordnance Assn., Middle East Inst. (bd. govs. 1962-80, 93—). Office: # 302 1101 First St Coronado CA 92118-1474

HOSTNIK, CHARLES RIVOIRE, lawyer; b. Glen Ridge, N.J., Apr. 8, 1954; s. William John and Susan (Rivoire) H. AB, Dartmouth Coll., 1976; JD, U. Puget Sound, 1979. Bar: Wash. 1980, U.S. Dist. Ct. (we. dist.) Wash. 1980, U.S. Dist. Ct. (ea. dist.) Wash. 1982, U.S. Ct. Appeals (9th cir.) 1983, Hoh Tribal Ct. 1984, Nisqually Tribal Ct. 1984, Puyallup Tribal Ct. 1984, Shoalwater Bay Tribal Ct. 1984, Skokomish Tribal Ct. 1984. Asst. atty. gen. Atty. Gen.'s Office State of Wash., Olympia, 1980-84; assoc. Kane, Vandeberg, Hartinger & Walker, Tacoma, 1984-87; ptnr. Anderson, Burns & Hostnik, Tacoma, 1988—; trial and appellate judge N.W. Intertribal Ct. Sys., Edmonds, Wash., 1986—. Author: (chpt.) Washington Practice, 1989. Com. mem. to re-elect Justice R. Guy, Olympia and Tacoma, 1990. Mem. N.W. Tribal Ct. Judges Assn. Office: Anderson Burns & Hostnik Ste A-1 6915 Lakewood Dr West Tacoma WA 98467

HOSTON, GERMAINE ANNETTE, political science educator; b. Trenton, N.J.; d. Walter Lee and Veretta Louise H. AB in Politics summa cum laude, Princeton U., 1975; MA in Govt., Harvard U., 1978, PhD in Govt., 1981. Rsch. asst. Princeton (N.J.) U., 1973-75; teaching asst. Harvard U., Cambridge, Mass., 1977-78; asst. prof. polit. sci. Johns Hopkins U., Balt., 1980-86, assoc. prof. polit. sci., 1986-92; prof. polit. sci. U. Calif., San Diego, 1992—, dir. Ctr. for TransPacific Studies Values, Culture, Politics, 1993—; vis. prof. L'Ecole des Hautes Etudes en Scis. Sociales, Paris, 1986, Osaka City U., Japan, 1990, U. Tokyo, 1991; faculty advisor Chinese lang. program Johns Hopkins U., 1981-92, mem. undergrad. ethics bd., 1980-83, pub. interest investment adv. com., 1982-83, 84-85, undergrad. admissions com., 1983-84, 86-87, 88-89, pres.'s human climate task force, 1987, dir. undergrad. program, 1987, 88-89, mem. com. undergrad. studies, 1987-91, organizer comparative politics colloquium, 1987-89, dept. colloquium, 1987-89, 91-92; mem. Japanese studies program com. U. Calif., San Diego, 1992—, mem. Chinese studies program, 1994—, field coord. comparative politics, 1994—, dir. grad. studies comparative politics, 1997-98; bd. dirs. Inst. East-West Security Studies, N.Y.C., 1990-97; mem. Am. adv. com. The Japan Found., 1992—; mem. Edn. Abroad Program (EAP) com. U. Calif., 1996—; mem. adv. com. Calif. Ctr. Asia Soc.; mem. com. tech. comms. Inst. East West Security Studies, 1997—; participant numerous workshops and seminars; lectr. in field. Author: Marxism and the Crisis of Development in Prewar Japan: The Debate on Japanese Capitalism, 1986, The State, Identity, and the National Question in China and Japan, 1994, (with others) The Biographical Dictionary of Neo-Marxism, 1985, The Biographical Dictionary of Marxism, 1986, Culture and Identity: Japanese Intellectuals During the Interwar Years, 1990, The Routledge Dictionary of Twentieth-Century Political Thinkers, 1992; mem. editl. bd. Jour. Politics, 1997—; contbr. articles and book revs. to profl. jours.; pub. numerous papers. Active Md. Food Com., 1983-92, program concepts subcom. CROSS ROADS Com., Diocese of Md., 1987-88, outreach com. St. David's Episcopal Ch., Balt., standing commn. human affairs Gen. Conv. of the Episcopal Ch., 1991-97; chair peace and justice commn. Episcopal Diocese Md., 1984-87, co-chair companion diocese com., 1987-92, chair CROSS ROADS program bd., 1988-92; exec. bd. dirs. Balt. Clergy and Laity Concerned, 1985-86; alternate, regular lay del. 69th Gen. Conv. of The Episcopal Ch., Detroit, 1988; trustee Va. Theol. Sem., 1988—; lay del. 70th Gen. Conv. of The Episcopal Ch., Phoenix, Ariz., 1991; dep. Nat. Conv. Episcopal Ch., 1988-93. Am. Legion Aux. scholar, 1972, Am. Logistical Assn. scholar, 1972-76; fellow Harvard U., 1975-77, NSF, 1975-77; Lehman fellow Harvard U., 1978-79, Fgn. Lang. and Area Studies fellow, 1978-79; fellow Am. Assn. Univ. Women Ednl. Found., 1979-80; Fgn. Rsch. scholar U. Tokyo, 1979, 82, 84, 85, 86, 91; Travel grantee Assn. Asian Studies, Japan-U.S. Friendship Commn., 1981; Internat. fellow Internat. Fedn. Univ. Women, 1982, 83; Postdoctoral grantee Social Sci. Rsch. Coun., 1983; fellow NEH, 1983; Kenan Endowment grantee Johns Hopkins U., 1984-85; fellow Rockefeller Found. Internat. Rels., 1985-88; Travel grantee Assn. Asian Studies, 1991; grantee Japan-U.S. Friendship Commn., 1997; rsch. grantee Acad. Senate Com. on Rsch., 1996. Mem. Asia Soc. (trustee 1994—), Am. Polit. Sci. Assn. (mem. coun. 1991-93, mem. com. on internat. polit. sci. 1997—, v.p. 1998—), Assn. Asian Studies (mem. N.E. Asia coun. 1992-95, vice-chair N.E. Asia coun. 1993—, editor Jour. Asian Studies 1994—, mem. coun. on fgn. rels. 1990—), Internat. Platform Assn., Pacific Coun. on Internat. Policy, Women's Fgn. Policy Group. Democrat. Episcopalian. Avocations: reading, cooking, sailing, tennis, working out. Office: U Calif San Diego Dept Polit Sci 0521 301 Social Sci Bldg 9500 Gilman Dr La Jolla CA 92093-5003

HOTCHKIN, JOHN FRANCIS, church official, priest; b. Chgo., Feb. 3, 1935; s. John Edward and Sarah Jane (Cure) H. BA, St. Mary of Lake Sem., Mundelein, Ill., 1954; STL, Pontifical Gregorian U., Rome, 1960, STD cum laude, 1966; DHL (hon.), Cath. U. Am., 1997, LLD (hon.), 1997. Ordained priest Roman Cath. Ch., 1959. Assoc. pastor Christ the King Parish, Chgo., 1960-64, St. Therese Parish, Chgo., 1966; assoc. dir. bishop's com. for ecumenical and interreligious affairs Nat. Conf. Cath. Bishops, Washington, 1967-71, exec. dir., 1971—; consultor Pontifical Coun. for Promoting Christian Unity, 1972—, Vatican Secretariat for Non-Christians, 1985-90. Recipient award Cath. Press Assn., 1969, Fitzgerald award Nat. Assn. Diocesan Ecumenical Officers, 1990; named Joseph Cardinal Bernardin Laureate for Ecumenical and Interreligious Affairs, Archdiocese of Chgo., 1997. Mem. Cath. Theol. Soc. Am., N.Am. Acad. Ecumenists, Ecumenical Officers Assn. Office: Nat Conf Cath Bishops 3211 4th St NE Washington DC 20017-1106

HOTCHKISS, ANDRA RUTH, lawyer; b. Beloit, Wis., Aug. 6, 1946; d. Hilton Delos and Katherine Ruth (Huffer) H.; m. Robert K. Byron, May 31, 1977 (dec. 1978); m. Gerald Thomas Marsischky, Feb. 25, 1990. BA cum laude, Oberlin Coll., 1968; JD, Harvard U., 1971. Bar: Mass. 1971, Calif. 1982, U.S. Dist. Ct. Mass. 1975, U.S. Ct. of Fed. Claims 1987. Dep. gen. counsel Mass. Dept. Pub. Health, Boston, 1971-78; asst. atty. gen. Mass. Dept. Atty. Gen., Boston, 1978-85; assoc. Behar & Kalman, Boston, 1985-88; assoc. Sullivan & Worcester, Boston, 1989-92, ptnr., 1992-97, of counsel, 1997—; instr. legal writing Harvard U., Cambridge, Mass., 1984, 85. Mem. adv. com. Robert K. Byron Pub. Svc. award, 1978—; elected rep. Oberlin Coll. Nat. Alumni Coun., 1973-83, reunion gift com. co-chair, 1993. Mem. ABA, Mass. Bar Assn., Boston Bar Assn., Am. Health Lawyers Assn., Women's Bar Assn. Mass., Civil Liberties Union Mass. Avocations: flute, cross country skiing, gardening, cats, travel. Office: Sullivan & Worcester One Post Office Sq Boston MA 02109*

HOTCHKISS, EUGENE, III, retired academic administrator; b. Berwyn, Ill., Apr. 1, 1928; s. Eugene and Jeanette (Kennan) H.; m. Suzanne Ellen Troxell, Nov. 17, 1962; 1 dau., Ellen Sinclair. AB, Dartmouth Coll., 1950; PhD, Cornell U., 1960; LLD (hon.), Ill. Coll., 1976, Lake Forest Coll., 1993. Asst. to dean Dartmouth Coll., 1953-54, asst. dean, 1954-55, asso. dean, 1958-60; asst. dean Cornell U., Ithaca, N.Y., 1955-58; dean students, lectr. history Harvey Mudd Coll., Claremont, Calif., 1960-63; dean coll. Harvey Mudd Coll., 1962-68; exec. dean Chatham Coll., Pitts., 1968-70; pres. Lake Forest (Ill.) Coll., 1970-93, pres. emeritus, 1993—; sr. fellow Assn. of Governing Bds., 1995—, Found. for Ind. Higher Edn., Chgo., 1993—. Lt. (j.g.) USNR, 1950-53. Mem. Chgo. Coun. Fgn. Rels., Econ. Club, Chgo. Onnentsia Club, Caxton Club, Phi Beta Kappa, Phi Kappa Phi, Chi Phi. Office: Lake Forest Coll 555 N Sheridan Rd Lake Forest IL 60045-2338

HOTCHKISS, HARLEY N., professional hockey team owner; b. Tillsonburg, Ont., Can.. BS in Geology, Mich. State U. CEO, gov. Calgary Flames, owner, gov.; bd. dirs. Conwest Exploration Co. Ltd., Nova Corp., Mich. State U. Found., Telus Corp.; chmn. NHL Bd. Govs., 1995—. Past chmn. Foothills Hosp. Bd.; vice chmn. Foothills Hosp. Found.; co-chmn. Pntrs. in Health Campaign. Office: Calgary Flames, PO Box 1540 Sta M, Calgary, AB Canada T2P 3B9*

HOTCHKISS, HENRY WASHINGTON, real estate broker and financial consultant; b. Meshed, Iran, Oct. 31, 1937; s. Henry and Mary Bell (Clark) H. BA, Bowdoin Coll., 1958. French tchr. Choate Sch., Wallingford, Conn., 1959-62; v.p. Chem. Bank, N.Y.C., 1962-80, v.p. Chem. Bank International, San Francisco, 1973-80; dir. corp. rels., mgr. Crédit Suisse, San Francisco, 1980-87, fin. cons., 1989—; with Dan Mello Real Estate, 1994—; bd. dirs. Calif. Coun. Internat. Trade, 1976-87; dir. Indonesia-U.S. Bus. Seminar, Los Angeles, 1979. Assoc. bd. regents L.I. Coll. Hosp., 1969-71, pres., 1971, bd. regents, 1971-73; bd. dirs. Gordonstown Am. Found., 1986—, pres., 1986-99; chmn. Captain Joshua Slocum Centennial Com. of Fairhaven, Mass., 1995-98; bd. dirs. Joshua Slocum Soc. Internat., Inc., 1998—. Capt. USAR, 1958-69. Mem. Mayflower Soc., SAR, Soc. of the Cin., Explorers Club N.Y. (treas. no. Calif. chpt. 1984-86), St. Francis Yacht Club (San Francisco). Home: 80 Fort St Fairhaven MA 02719-2812

HOTCHKISS, VIVIAN EVELYN, employment agency executive; b. Fulda, Germany, May 5, 1956; came to U.S., 1957; d. Fred Roy and Rosemary Krug. Student, Pierce Coll., 1974-75, Calif. State U., Northridge, 1976, UCLA, 1991—. Adminstrv. sec. Taurus Fin. Corp., Hollywood, Calif., 1976-79; adminstrv. asst. Peoples Fin. Corp., Encino, Calif., 1979-81, Thor Employment Agy., L.A., 1981-83, Creative Capital Corp., L.A., 1983—; owner, pres. Bus. Systems Staffing & Assocs., L.A., 1985—; exec. dir. Edn. Counseling & Placement Program, L.A., 1990-95. Author: (newsletter) The Leader; contbr. articles to newspaper, 1996-97. Mem. Execs. Assn. L.A. (membership dir. 1989-96, Member of Yr. 1990), Exec. LeTip of West L.A. (membership inspector 1996-98, program dir., 1997-98, bd. dirs., mem.-at-large 1998—). Avocations: wine enthusiast, photography, travel, computers, animals. Office: Bus Sys Staffing & Assocs Inc 10680 W Pico Blvd Ste 210 Los Angeles CA 90064-2223

HOTCHKISS, WINCHESTER FITCH, retired investment banker; b. N.Y.C., Jan. 24, 1928; s. Horace Leslie and Alta Jane (Fitch) H.; m. Jane Hutchinson Ellsworth, June 10, 1955; children: Winchester Fitch, Leslie Ellsworth, Mary Stevens. Student, Yale, 1952. Advt. mgr. Intercontinental Hotels Corp., N.Y.C., 1957-59; employed various investment banking firms, 1959—: with Stone & Webster Securities Corp., N.Y.C., 1967-75; v.p. Stone & Webster Securities Corp., 1969—. Mem. promotion com. Citizens for Eisenhower, 1956; mem. N.J. Rep. Fin. Com., 1976—; trustee Westminster Sch., Simsbury, Conn.; v.p. Morristown Meml. Hosp., 1976-87. With AUS, 1946-48, ETO. Mem. Securities Industry Assn. (mem. syndicate com. 1971). Clubs: Bond (N.Y.C.), River (N.Y.C.) (gov. 1972-91, sec. 1978-91); Somerset Hills (N.J.) Country (gov., sec. 1974, pres. 1983-90). Home: 154 S Beach Rd Hobe Sound FL 33455-2436

HOTCHNER, AARON EDWARD, author; b. St. Louis, June 28, 1920; s. Samuel and Sally (Rossman) H.; children: Timothy, Holly, Tracy. AB, LLB, Washington U., St. Louis, 1941, LHD (hon.), 1992. Bar: Mo. 1941. Practiced law in St. Louis, 1941-42; articles editor Cosmopolitan mag., 1948-50; v.p., treas. Newman's Own, Inc.; v.p. Hole in the Wall Gang Camp. Freelance writer short stories and articles in various mags. including Sat. Eve. Post, Esquire, Readers Digest, 1950—; TV playwright Playhouse 90, 1958-60; adapted major Hemingway works for TV including For Whom The Bell Tolls, 1958, The Killers, 1959; writer screenplay Adventures of a Young Man, 1961; author: The Dangerous American, 1958, Papa Hemingway: A Personal Memoir, 1966, revised, 1999, Treasure, 1970, King of the Hill, 1972, Looking for Miracles, 1974, Doris Day, 1976, Sophia, Living and Loving, 1979, The Man Who Lived at the Ritz, 1981, Choice People, 1984, Hemingway and His World, 1989, Blown Away, 1990, Louisiana Purchase, 1996; playwright: The Short Happy Life, 1961, The White House, 1964, The Hemingway Hero, 1967, Do You Take This Man?, 1970, Sweet Prince, 1980, Let 'Em Rot, 1987, Welcome to the Club, 1989, Courtroom Cantata, 1995, Exactly Like You, 1996, Papa Hemingway (rev.), 1999, Exactly Like You, 1999. Founding dir. Hole in the Wall Gang Fund. Served to maj. USAAF, 1942-46, NATOUS. Recipient Disting. Alumni award Law Sch., Washington U., 1992. Mem. Mo. Bar Assn., Writers Guild Am., Dramatists Guild, PEN, Authors Guild, Authors Guild Found. (bd. dirs.), Century Club. Address: 14 Hillandale Rd Westport CT 06880-5225

HOTCHNER, HOLLY, curator, museum director. BA in Art History and Studio Art, Trinity Coll., 1973; MA in Art History, diploma conservation, NYU, 1982; student Mus. Mgmt. Inst., U. Calif., Berkeley, 1992. Exhbns. cataloguer, collections cataloguer Mus. Modern Art, N.Y.C., 1973-76; chief conservator N.Y. Hist. Soc., N.Y.C., 1984-88, dir. mus., 1984-95; pres. Holly Hotchner Fine Arts Mgmt., N.Y.C., 1995-96; dir. Am. Craft Mus., N.Y.C., 1996—; mem. com. for Sonny Sloan endowment fund, 1994-95, Lit. Vols.; chmn. bd. 235 E. 73rd Owners Corp., 1994-98; mem. edn. com. Whitney Mus. Am. Art, 1994-98; mem. bd. trustees N.Y. Landmarks Conservancy, 1996-98; lectr., panelist, juror in field. conservation projects include Met. Mus., N.Y., 1979-80, The Green Room, Lincoln Ctr., 1980, The Ch. of Ascension, N.Y., 1987-88. Conservation Ctr. scholar Inst. Fine Arts, 1979-82; grantee for vis. scholars Brit. Coun., 1981-82; grantee Nat. Mus. Arts, 1982-83; Travel grantee Met. Mus., 1983-84; Sherman Fairchild Conservation fellow Met. Mus., 1983-84; grantee Samuel H. Kress Found., 1983-84. Fellow Internat. Inst. Conservation, Am. Inst. Conservation; mem. Am. Assn. Mus., Art Table, Phi Beta Kappa. Office: Am Craft Mus 40 West 53rd St New York NY 10019

HOTELLING, HAROLD, law and economics educator; b. N.Y.C., Dec. 26, 1945; s. Harold and Susanna Porter (Edmondson) H.; m. Barbara M. Anthony, May 4, 1974; children: Harold, George, James, Claire, Charles. AB, Columbia U., 1966; JD, U. N.C., 1972; MA, Duke U., 1975, PhD, 1982. Bar: N.C. 1973. Legal advisor U. N.C., Chapel Hill, 1972-73; instr. bus. law U. Ky., Lexington, 1977-79, asst. prof., 1980-84; asst. prof. dept. econs. Oakland U., Rochester, Mich., 1984-89; assoc. prof. econs. Lawrence Technol. U., Southfield, Mich., 1989—; chmn. dept. humanities social scis. and comm. Lawrence Technol. U., Southfield, 1994—. Contbr. articles to profl. jours. Episcopalian. Home: 2112 Bretton Dr S Rochester Hls MI 48309-2952 Office: Lawrence Technol U Dept Humanities Southfield MI 48075

HOTH, STEVEN SERGEY, lawyer; b. Olewein, Iowa, Jan. 30, 1941; s. Donald Leroy and Ina Dorothy (Barr) H.; m. JoEllen Maly, July 29, 1967; children: Andrew Steven, Peter Lindsey. AB, Grinnell Coll., 1962; JD, U. Iowa, 1966; postgrad. U. Pa., 1968, Oxford (Eng.) U., 1973. Bar: U.S. Ct. Appeals (8th cir.) 1966, U.S. Tax Ct. 1967, U.S. Ct. Claims 1967, U.S. Dist. Ct. Iowa 1968, U.S. Dist. Ct. N.D. 1968, U.S. Dist. Ct. S.D. 1968, U.S. Supreme Ct. 1973, U.S. Ct. Appeals (7th cir.) 1982. Law clk. to chief justice U.S. Ct. Appeals (8th cir.), Fargo, N.D., 1967-68; assoc. Hirsch, Adams, Hoth & Krekel, Burlington, Iowa, 1968-72, ptnr., 1972-91; private practice, Burlington, 1992—; asst. atty. Des Moines County, Burlington, 1968-72, atty., 1972-83; alt. mcpl. judge, Burlington, 1968-69; lectr. criminal law Southeastern Community Coll., West Burlington, 1972-82; assoc. prof. polit. sci. Iowa Wesleyan Coll., Mt. Pleasant, 1981-82; pres., Iowa Truck Rail; pres. Burlington Truck-Rail; pres. Family Commn. Southeast Iowa, Burlington Short Line RR. Inc., Iowa Internat. Investments; sec. Burlington Loading Co. Chmn. Des Moines County Civil Service Commn.; trustee Charles H. Rand Lecture Trust; mem. Des Moines County Conf. Com., Des Moines County Conf. Bd.; dir. Burlington Med. Ctr. Staff Found.; moderator 1st Congl. Ch., Burlington; bd. dirs. UN Assn.; bd. dirs. Burlington Med. Ctr. Staff Found.; clerk Burlington North Bottoms Levy and Drainage Dist., bd. mem., pres. Burlington Cmty. Sch. Dist. Bd. Edn., chmn. commn. on ministry, mem. exec. com. Nat. Assn. Congl. Christian Chs.; moderator Nat. Assn. Congl. Christian Chs.; treas. 1st dist. Dem. Com.; bd. dirs. Legal Aid Soc. Planned Parenthood Des Moines County. Reginald Heber Smith fellow in legal aid Cheyenne River Indian Reservation, Eagle Butte, S.D., 1967-68; recipient chmn.'s award ARC, 1980. Mem. ABA (internat. sect., tax sect.), Iowa State Bar Assn., Des Moines County Bar Assn., Am. Judicature Soc., Agrl. Law Com., Iowa Def. Council, Grinnell Coll. Alumni Assn. (bd. dirs.), Burlington-West Burlington C. of C. (bd. dirs.), Nat. Assn. Congrl. Christian Chs. Clubs: Burlington Golf, New Crystal Lake (Burlington) (pres.). Lodges: Elks, Eagles, Masons, Rotary (Burlington). Contbr. numerous articles to profl. jours. Office: PO Box 982 Hoth Bldg 200 Jefferson St Burlington IA 52601

HOTHERSALL, LORETTA ANNE, family nurse practitioner; b. Bklyn., July 13, 1952; d. Edward Alfred and Rose (Laurino) O'Donnell; m. John Hothersall, Mar. 11, 1972; children: Margaret, John, Colleen. Diploma in nursing, Kings County Hosp. Ctr., Bklyn., 1972; paralegal cert., L.I. U., 1989; BS in Profl. Arts, St. Joseph's Coll., Windham, Maine, 1993; grad., Simmons Coll., Boston, 1996; postgrad. cert., Simmons Coll., 1997. RN; cert. BLS, Maine; RN, N.Y., Maine; cert. bereavement counselor, N.Y., cert. inpatient obstetrics. Staff nurse premature nursery Kings County Hosp., 1972-76; staff nurse NICU Maimonides Med. Ctr., Bklyn., 1979-86; staff nurse maternal child Luth. Med. Ctr., Bklyn., 1987-88, staff nurse spl. care nursery, 1988-90; staff nurse maternity Maine Med. Ctr., Portland, 1990-91, clin. level III nurse, 1991-92, asst. head nurse, 1992-94, coord. H.O.M.E. care early discharge program, 1994-95, staff nurse maternity, 1995—, nurse practitioner-diabetes, 1996—; instr. obstet. teen clinic Maine Med. Ctr., 1990—, BLS instr., 1991—, coord. antepartum support group, 1991—; with bereavement group-maternity Maine Med. Ctr. and Luth Med. Ctr., 1990—. Vol. blood drive ARC, Maine, 1992. Mem. AWHONN (legis. chairperson 1994-96), Coalition Maine Nurses Orgn. (rep. from AWHONN 1994-96). Avocations: flower arranging, gardening, reading. Home: 4 Scabbard Rd Scarborough ME 04074-9332 Office: Maine Ctr for Endocrinology and Diabetes 100 US Rt 1 Scarborough ME 04074

HOTMIRE, ERIK JOSEPH, press secretary; b. Paulding, Ohio, Mar. 2, 1973. BA in Polit. Sci., Taylor U., 1995. Sports announcer, on-air personality, asst. news dir., WERT AM-FM, Van Wert, Ohio, 1988-92, 93, 94; news dir. WERT AM-FM, Van Wert, 1988-92, 93, 94; on-air personality WAJI-FM, Ft. Wayne, Ind., 1994-95, WLAB-FM, Ft. Wayne, 1995; assignment editor WPTA-TV (ABC), Ft. Wayne, 1995; dep. press sec. Office of U.S. Senator Dan Coats, Washington, 1996-98; press sec. Office of U.S.

Senator Sam Brownback, Washington, 1998—. Office: 303 Hart Senate Office Bldg Washington DC 20510-1604

HOTTINGER, JAY, state legislator; m. Cheri Moss, May 21, 1994. BA, BS summa cum laude, Capital U., Columbus, Ohio, 1992. Mgr. Jay Co.; city councilman City of Newark, Ohio, 1992-94; pres. pro tem Newark City Coun., 1994; rep. dist. 77 Ohio Ho. of Reps., Columbus, 1995-98; senator, 1998—. Bd. dirs. East Mound Comty. Devel. Corp., Am. Cancer Soc. (Newark). Named Outstanding Young Man of Licking County, 1992. Mem. Police Athletic League, Newark Area C. of C. Office: 042 State House Senate Bldg Columbus OH 43215-6108*

HOTTINGER, JOHN CREIGHTON, state legislator, lawyer; b. Mankato, Minn., Sept. 18, 1945; s. Raymond Creighton and Hilda (Baker) H.; m. Miriam Jean Willging, Oct. 31, 1971; children: Julie, Creighton, Janna. BS, Coll. St. Thomas, St. Paul, 1967; JD, Georgetown U., 1971. Bar: Minn. 1972, U.S. Dist. Ct. Minn. 1977, U.S. Dist. Ct. (no. dist.) Ohio 1981, U.S. Ct. Appeals (5th cir.) 1991, U.S. Supreme Ct. 1992. Legis. asst. Hon. Donald M. Fraser, Washington, 1968-69, Dem. Study Group, Washington, 1969-73; ptnr. Farrish, Johnson, Maschka & Hottinger, Mankato, 1973-85; sr. ptnr. Hottinger Law Offices, Mankato, 1985-91; ptnr. Gislason, Dosland, Hunter & Malecki, Mankato, 1991-95; sr. ptnr. Hottinger Law Office, Mankato, 1995—; of counsel MacKenzie and Gustafson, St. Peter, 1997—; mem. Minn. Senate, 1991—, asst. majority whip, 1993-95, majority whip, 1996—, chair health and family security com., 1997—; chair Bd. of Govt. Innovation and Cooperation, 1995. Dem. candidate for Minn. Senate, 1982, for U.S. Ho. of Reps., 1994. Mem. ABA, 5th Dist. Bar Assn., Minn. Bar Assn. Roman Catholic. Avocation: computer ops., writing. Office: Hottinger Law Office Box 3183 Mankato MN 56002-3183

HOTZ, HENRY PALMER, physicist; b. Fayetteville, Ark., Oct. 17, 1925; s. Henry Gustav and Stella (Palmer) H.; m. Marie Brase, Aug. 22, 1952; children: Henry Brase, Mary Palmer, Martha Marie. B.S., U. Ark., 1948; Ph.D., Washington U., St. Louis, 1953. Asst. prof. physics Auburn U., Ala., 1953-58, Okla. State U., Stillwater, 1958-64; assoc. prof. Marietta Coll., Ohio, 1964-66; physicist, scientist-in-residence U.S. Naval Radiol. Def. Lab., San Francisco, 1966-67; assoc. prof. U. Mo., Rolla, 1967-71; physicist Qanta Metrix div. Finnigan Corp., Sunnyvale, Calif., 1971-74; sr. scientist Nuclear Equipment Corp., San Carlos, Calif., 1974-79, Envirotech Measurement Systems, Palo Alto, Calif., 1979-82, Dohrmann div. Xertex Corp., Santa Clara, Calif., 1982-86; sr. scientist Rosemount Analytical Div. Dohrmann, 1983-91; cons. Burlingame, Calif., 1991—; cons. USAF, 1958-62; mem. lectr. selection com. for Hartman Hotz Lectrs. in law, liberal arts U. Ark. Served with USNR, 1944-46. Mem. Am. Phys. Soc., Am. Assn. Physics Tchrs., AAAS, Phi Beta Kappa, Sigma Xi, Sigma Pi Sigma, Pi Mu Epsilon, Sigma Nu. Methodist. Lodge: Masons. Home: 290 Stilt Ct Foster City CA 94404-1323 Office: Hotz Assocs 525 Almer Rd Apt 201 Burlingame CA 94010-3955

HOTZ, ROBERT LEE, science writer, editor; b. Hartford, Conn., Mar. 7, 1950; s. Robert B. and Joan (Willison) H.; m. Jennifer Hall Arlen, May 21, 1988; children: Michael Arlen, Robert Arlen. BA magna cum laude, Tufts U., 1973, MA, 1973. Tech. editor Intermetrics, Inc., Cambridge, Mass., 1973-76; reporter The News-Virginian, Waynesboro, 1976-79, The Pitts. Press, 1979-84; sci. writer The Atlanta Jour.-Constn., 1984-90, projects editor, 1991-93; sci. editor, 1993; sci. writer The L.A. (Calif.) Times, 1993—; participant NSF Antarctica Expeditions, 1987, 95. Author: Designs on Life: Exploring the New Frontiers of Human Fertility, 1991; contbr. articles to profl. publs. Recipient Sci. Journalism award AAAS, 1977, 88, 97, Ga. Best Reporting award AP, 1986, Metro Staff Pulitzer Prize spot news, 1995, Walter Sullivan award Am. Geophys. Soc., 1995, Journalism award ASCE, 1995, Media award Nat. Mental Health Assn., 1996. Mem. Nat. Assn. Sci. Writers (bd. dirs.), Soc. Profl. Journalists (Ray Sprigle Meml. award 1982, 84), Nat. Press Club. Episcopalian. Home: 236 21st St Santa Monica CA 90402-2416 Office: The LA Times Times Mirror Sq Los Angeles CA 90012

HOUBOLT, JOHN CORNELIUS, physicist; b. Altoona, Iowa, Apr. 10, 1919; s. John H. and Hendreika (Van Ingen) H.; m. Mary Morris, June 14, 1949; children: Mary Cornelia, Joanna, Julie. BS, U. Ill., 1940, MS, 1942; PhD, Swiss Fed. Inst. Tech., Zurich, 1958, hon. doctorate, 1975; hon. doctorate, Clarkson U., 1990. Bridge engr. I.C. R.R., 1940; city engr. Waukegan, Ill., 1941; aero. research scientist NASA, Hampton, Va., 1942-49; asso. chief dynamic loads div. NACA-NASA, 1949-62; chief theoretical mechanics div. NASA, 1962-63; sr. v.p., dir. Aero Research Asso. Princeton Inc., N.J., 1963-76; chief scientist Langley Research Center, Hampton, Va., 1976-85; cons. and adviser to govt. agys. and industry, 1985—; instr. grad. extension div. U. Va., 1944—, Va. Poly. Inst., 1958—; exchange scientist Royal Aircraft Establishment, Eng., 1949; dir. Doweave, Inc., Walker-Gordon Labs.; Mem. Air Force Scientific Adv. Bd. Asso. editor: Jour. Spacecraft and Rockets. Recipient Rockefeller Pub. Svc. award, 1956, Exceptional Sci. Achievement award NASA, 1963, Structures, Structural Dynamics and Materials award AIAA, 1967, Disting. Civil Enging. Alumni award U. Ill., 1969, Illini Achievement award U. Ill., 1970, Dryden Rsch. lectr. award, 1972, Space Act award NASA, 1983, Pa. Engr. of Yr. award, 1989, U. Ill. Alumni award, 1997. Fellow AIAA (hon. v.p. tech.); mem. Nat. Acad. Engrs., Tau Beta Pi, Chi Epsilon, Phi Kappa Chi, Sigma Xi. Rsch., numerous reports in aeros., aeroelasticity, structures, atmosphere turbulence, space flight and landing. Home: 51 Winster Fax Williamsburg VA 23185-5543 Office: Langley Rsch Ctr NASA Hampton VA 23665

HOUCHEN, CONSTANCE ELAINE, nursing administrator; b. Jamaica, W.I., Aug. 25, 1941; d. Leslie Percival and Olive Isabelle Lobban; m. Dave Houchen (dec.); children: Trevor, Adrian, Diedre. AAS, N.Y.C. Community Coll., 1968; BSN, CCNY, 1977; MSN, U. Fla., 1996. Supr. Hollis Park Gardens Nursing Home, Queens, N.Y., 1974-78; operating room nurse VA Med. Ctr., Northport, N.Y., 1979-81; operating room nurse VA Med. Ctr., Gainesville, Fla., 1981-85, night supr., 1986-95, head nurse, 1995—. Mem. Nat. Black Nurses Assn. (NBNA), Sigma Theta Tau. Home: 4607 NW 32nd Ave Gainesville FL 32606-6026

HOUCHIN, JOHN FREDERICK, SR., human services administrator; b. Oak Park, Ill., Nov. 1, 1945; s. O. Boyd and Mary Ruth (Schroke) H.; m. Bette Louise Arnold, July 9, 1969; children: John Jr., David Locke. AA, Kemper Mil. Sch. & Coll., Boonville, Mo., 1966; BS, Ohio State U., 1968; EdD, U. Mass., 1987. Prog. dir. Cuyahoga County Assn. Retarded Citizens, Cleve., 1973-75; resdl. dir., asst. supt. Ohio Dept. Mental Health & Retardation, Broadview Devel. Ctr, Broadview Hts., Ohio, 1975-80; reg. mental retardation coord. Mass. Dept. Mental Health, Region IV A, Watertown, Mass., 1980-83; dir. devel. svcs. Mass. Dept. Mental Health, Belchertown State Sch., 1983-86; asst. reg. dir. Conn. Dept. Retardation, Region 6, Waterford, 1986-91; CEO G.B. Cooley Svcs. for Retarded Citizens, West Monroe, La., 1991-97; regional dir. Conn. Dept. of Mental Retardation, 1997—; lectr. in field. Contbr. book: Supported Employment Implementation, 1988. State adv. coun. Conn. Dept. Rehab. Svcs., Hartford, 1988-91; regional adv. coun. Region 8 Office Mental Retardation, 1992-94, chmn., 1993; mem. Monroe Beautification Bd., 1996-97; mem. Twin Cities Mayors Com. on Disabled, 1994-97; bd. dirs. Eastern Conn. Regional Transp. Consortium, 1997—. Capt. U.S. Army, 1969-72. Mem. Internat. Platform Assn., Internat. Freelance Photographer Assn., Monroe C. of C., N.E. La. Camera Club (pres. 1993-94), Waterford Rotary Internat. Episcopalian. Avocation: photography. Office: Ea Region Dept Mental Retardation 401 W Thames St Unit 202 Norwich CT 06360-7155

HOUCHIN, LAURA BRAXTON, oncology nurse clinician; b. Tampa, Fla., June 1, 1948; d. Thomas Elword and Donnadeen Elaine (Neal) Braxton; m. Dennis Roy Houchin, Aug. 23, 1969; children: Brian Thomas, Keith Patrick, Alison Colleen. Diploma in Nursing, Michael Reese Hosp. & Med. Ctr, Chgo., 1970; BSN, Barton Coll., Wilson, N.C., 1990. Cert. oncology nurse. Staff nurse St. Margaret's Hosp., Hammond, Ind., 1970-82; utilization rev. nurse Calumet Found., Highland, Ind., 1982-83; med. specialist Intra Corp., Raleigh, N.C., 1983-85; staff nurse Rex Hosp., Raleigh, 1985-90; oncology nurse clinician, asst. nurse mgr. Duke Med. Ctr., Durham, N.C., 1990—; chmn. Cancer Survivor's Day, Duke Cancer Ctr., Durham, 1994—; spkr. Glaxo-Wellcome, Research Triangle Park, N.C., 1995—, Duke Oncology Consortium, Durham, 1996—, Eli Lilly Pharms., Indpls., 1998. Author Oncology Nursing Forum, 1994—. Mem. Oncology Nursing Soc. (leadership fellowship 1996), N.C. Triangle Oncology Nursing Soc. (program chair 1994, pres. 1996), Sigma Theta Tau. Office: Duke Med Ctr Box 3877 Durham NC 27710

HOUCHIN, SUSAN KAY, social services administrator; b. Kearney, Nebr., Sept. 14, 1949; d. Charles Andrew and Audrey Lavon (Wood) H.; m. Wilfredo Azul La Luz, Apr. 26, 1980 (div. 1989); 1 child, Susana Blanca. BA in Edn., U. Nebr., 1971; MEd, Boston U., 1975. English/speech tchr. Lincoln (Nebr.) Pub. Schs., 1971-73; head tchr. U.S. Army Pre-Discharge Edn. Program, Stuttgart, Germany, 1973-75; exec. dir. human devel. ctr. YMCA of San Diego County, 1976-82; asst. dir. Lancaster County Mental Health Ctr., Lincoln, 1982-83; exec. dir. Youth Svc. System, Lincoln, 1983-86; exec. dur. Girls Inc. Sioux City, Iowa, 1986-90; dir. svc. ctrs. Indpls., 1990—; cons. Arthur D. Little, Inc., Yuma, Ariz., 1980-82, Aspen Svcs. Corp., Washington, 1976-83, Office Human Devel. U.S. Dept. HHS, Washington, 1983-97; bd. dirs. Nat. Network for Youth, Washington, 1985-86. Author: (manual) The Art of Trusteeship, 1995; contbr. chpts. to books and manuals. Mem. edn. com. Children's Mus., Indpls., 1990-92; bd. dirs. Ctr. for Women, Sioux City, 1988-90; mem. Mayor's Adv. Com. on Youth, Lincoln, 1983-86; chair San Diego County Delinquency Prevention Commn., 1979-82. Recipient Outstanding Svc. award MINK Youth Svc. Network, 1991, Woman of Excellence award Women Aware, 1989. Democrat. Episcopalian. Avocations: reading, writing fiction, sailing, canoeing, quilting.

HOUCK, CHARLES WESTON, federal judge; b. Florence, S.C., Apr. 16, 1933; s. William Stokes and Charlotte Barnwell (Weston) H.; children from previous marriage: Charles Weston, Charlotte Elizabeth. Grad., U. N.C., 1954; LLB, U. S.C., 1956. Bar: S.C. Mem. firm Willcox, Hardee, Houck, Palmer & O'Farrell, 1956, 58-70;; ptnr. Houck, Clarke & Johnson, 1971-79; judge U.S. Dist. Ct. S.C., Florence, 1979—, now chief justice. Mem. S.C. Ho. of Reps., 1963-66; chmn. Florence City-County Bldg. Commn., 1968-76. Served with AUS, 1957-58. Mem. ABA, S.C. Bar Assn. Episcopalian. Office: US Dist Ct PO Box 2317 Florence SC 29503-2317*

HOUCK, JOHN ROLAND, clergyman; b. Balt., Apr. 15, 1923; s. Walter Webb and Wilhelmina Anna (Pfaff) H.; m. Minerva Arline Wiessinger, Nov. 28, 1947; children—John Roland, James Michael, David Walter, Paul Harold. B.A. cum laude, Capital U., Columbus, Ohio, 1947, D.D. (hon.), 1976; B.D., Evang. Lutheran Sem., Columbus, 1950. Ordained to ministry Am. Luth. Ch., 1950; pastor St. Michael Luth. Ch., Perry Hall, Md., 1950-60; regional dir. bd. Am. missions Am. Luth. Ch., Washington, 1960-67; exec. dir. bd. Am. missions Am. Luth. Ch., Mpls., 1970-73; dir. div. service and mission in Am. Am. Luth. Ch., 1974-79; asso. exec. sec. div. mission service Luth. Council U.S.A., N.Y.C., 1967-70; gen. sec. Luth. Council U.S.A., 1979-87; pastor emeritus St. Michael's Luth. Ch., Perry Hall, Md., 1988—. Democrat. Home: 8810 Walther Blvd Apt 2309 Baltimore MD 21234-0025 Office: St Michaels Luth Churc Baltimore MD 21236

HOUCK, WILLIAM RUSSELL, bishop; b. Mobile, Ala., June 26, 1926. Student, St. Bernard Jr. Coll., Cullman, Ala., St. Mary's Sem. Coll., St. Mary's Sem., Balt., Cath. U. Ordained priest Roman Cath. Ch., 1951. Titular bishop of Alessano and auxiliary bishop Jackson, Miss., 1979-84, bishop, 1984—. Address: PO Box 2248 237 E Amite St Jackson MS 39225*

HOUGEN, JON TORGER, physical chemist, researcher; b. Sheboygan, Wis., Oct. 23, 1936; s. Edward Thomas and Mildred (Dulmes) H.; m. Ruth Marie Sandham, Aug. 24, 1954 (div. Apr. 1969); 1 child, Torger Jon; m. Zhi Jun Duan, Feb. 16, 1997. B.S., U. Wis.-Madison, 1956; A.M., Harvard U., 1958, Ph.D., 1960. Postdoctoral fellow NRC of Can., Ottawa, Ont., 1960-62, assoc. research officer, 1963-66; physicist Nat. Bur. Standards, Gaithersburg, Md., 1967-68, chief molecular spectroscopy sect., 1969-73, research scientist, 1974-85, sr. fellow, 1985—. Mem. editorial adv. bd. Jour. Molecular Spectroscopy, 1967—; contbr. articles to profl. jours. Recipient Coblentz award Coblentz Soc., 1968, Silver medal Nat. Bur. Standards, 1974, Gold medal Nat. Bur. Standards, 1980. Fellow Am. Phys. Soc. (Plyler prize 1984); mem. Optical Soc. Am. (Lippinott award 1984). Avocation: foreign language study. Home: 13022 Thyme Ct Germantown MD 20874-2008 Office: Nat Inst Stds and Tech Optical Tech Divsn Gaithersburg MD 20899-8441*

HOUGH, AUBREY JOHNSTON, JR., pathologist, physician, educator; b. Little Rock, July 20, 1944; s. Aubrey Johnston and Thelma Willeen (Miller) H.; m. Linda Ann Yaeger, June 10, 1968; children: Charles Prentiss, Robert Page. BA, Hendrix Coll., 1966; MD, Vanderbilt U., 1970. Diplomate Am. Bd. Pathology. Resident dept. pathology Vanderbilt U., Nashville, 1970-72, chief resident, 1974-75, asst. prof. dept. pathology, 1975-78, asst. prof. dept. orthopedics, 1977-78, assoc. prof. depts. pathology and orthopedics, 1978-80; prof. and vice chmn. dept. pathology U. Ark. for Med. Scis., Little Rock, 1980-81, prof., chmn. dept. pathology, 1981—; Disting. Prof. Nat. Inst. Arthritis & Metabolic Disease, Bethesda, 1972-74; clin. assoc. Nat. Inst. Arthritis & Metabolic Disease, Bethesda, Md., 1972-74; chief of staff U. Ark. Hosp., Little Rock, 1986-88; pres. Ark. Acad. Pathology, Little Rock, 1982-86, Coun. of Dept. Chmn. U. Ark. Coll. of Medicine, Little Rock, 1987-88; chief of staff U. Hosp. of Ark., 1986-88, 98-2000; mem. pathology test com. Nat. Bd. Med. Examiners, 1989-92, chmn., 1993-95, comp II com., 1992-95; mem. Nat. Bd. Med. Examiners, 1996-99; mem. residency rev. com. for pathology Accreditation Coun. Med. Edn., 1990-96. Author: Tumors of the Adrenal Gland, 1987; contbr. numerous articles on orthopedic diseases to profl. jours, chpts. to books; assoc. editor Human Pathology, 1988-97; editorial bd. Am. Jour. Pathology. Alumni fund rep. Hendrix Coll., Conway, Ark., 1983-86; chmn. Shideler Chemistry Edn. Endowment, 1991-97. Served as surgeon USPHS, 1972-74. Basic Sci. Grantee Nat. Inst. Gen. Med. Studies, 1978, Altheimer Found., 1984, Nat. Inst. Arthritis, 1988; recipient Dirs. Commendation VA, 1980, Disting. Svc. award U. Ark., Little Rock, 1985, Disting. Alumni Hendrix Coll., 1999. Fellow Coll. Am. Pathologists (field inspector 1977-88); mem. AMA, AAUP, U.S.-Can. Acad. Pathology, Am. Soc. Clin. Pathologists, Am. Soc. Investigative Pathology, Assn. Clin. Scientists (Brown Meml. lectr 1986), Arthur Purdy Stout Soc., Assn. Pathology Chmn. (mem. publ. affairs com. 1985—, chmn. 1993-96), Orthopedic Rsch. Soc., History of Medicine Assocs. (bd. dirs. 1986-88), Assn. Am. Med. Colls. (mem. coun. academic soc. Washington 1985-89). Democrat. Clubs: Bapt. Med. Dental (Memphis) (program chair 1983-84). E-mail: houghaubreyJ@exchange.uams.edu. Home: 23 Lorine Cir Little Rock AR 72205-2530 Office: U Ark for Med Scis 4301 W Markham St # 517 Little Rock AR 72205-7101

HOUGH, EDYTHE S. ELLISON, dean. BS in Nursing cum laude, U. Conn., 1961; MS in Psychiat. Nursing, Yale U., 1963; EdD in Early Childhood & Devel. Studies, UCLA, 1979; cert., Harvard U., 1984, Albert Einstein Med. Sch. Leadership Inst., 1984. Instr. sch. nursing U. Conn., Storrs, 1964-65; instr. sch. nursing UCLA, 1965-68, asst. prof., 1968-69; asst. prof. dept. nursing Mt. St. Mary's Coll., L.A., 1972-75; asst. prof. dept. psychosocial nursing U. Wash., Seattle, 1978-84, assoc. prof. dept. psychiatry & behavioral sci., 1984-85; fellow Harborview Med. Ctr., Seattle, 1984-85; assoc. prof., head dept. psychiat. nursing U. Ill., Chgo., 1985-86, chief psychiat. clin. svcs., 1985-86, assoc. dean acad. affairs Coll. Nursing, 1986-87, assoc. prof., 1987-88; assoc. v.p., assoc. dean Coll. Nursing Rush-Presbyn.-St. Luke's Med. Ctr., Chgo., 1988-92; assoc. dean edn. Coll. Nursing Rush Univ., 1991, prof. dept. med. nursing, 1992-93; prof. Coll. Nursing Wayne State U., Detroit, 1993—; dean Rush U., 1993-97; cons. Brentwood VA Hosp., L.A., 1969, Martin Luther King Hosp., L.A., 1973, Am. Inst. Rsch. Behavioral Scis., Palo Alto, Calif., 1977, YMCA Latchkey Child program, Seattle, 1978, King's Fund Ctr. King Edward's Hosp. Fund, London, 1983, Coll. Nursing Rush U., 1987; presenter in field. Contbr. articles to profl. jours. Mem. gov. bd. Cmty. Psychiat. Clinic, 1979-84, v.p., 1983-84, chair long-range planning com., 1983-84; gov. bd. Keystone Resources, 1982-84, Arbor Housing Assocs., 1983-84; mem. Wash. State Social Skills Consortium, 1983-85, Fourth Presbyn. Ch. Literacy Tutoring project, 1986-89, Women's Health Exec. Network, 1991-92, Sch. Medicine Charter Com. Ctr./Inst. Health Care Effectiveness, 1994—; bd. trustees Detroit Visiting Nurses Assn.; bd. dirs. Visiting Nurse Assn. Southeast Mich., 1993—, Greater Detroit Area Health Coun., Inc., 1993—. Recipient Nat. Rsch. Svc. award, 1978, Child Mental Health Faculty Devel. award NIMH, 1984, Women's Action New Direction award Women Healing the World, 1995; UCLA grantee, 1977. Fellow Am. Acad. Nursing; mem. NOW (Chgo. chpt.), ANA (coun. nurse rschrs., coun. nursing adminstrn.), Am. Psychiat. Nurses Assn., Ill. Orgn. Nurse Execs., Mich. Assn. Colls. Nursing (treas. 1993—), Mich. Nurses Assn., Midwest Nursing Rsch. Soc., Sigma Theta Tau, Soc. Edn. Rsch. Psychiat. Nursing, Transcultural Nursing Soc. Home: 2831 Thaxton Ln Oakton VA 22124-3021

HOUGH, J. MARIE, real estate company official; b. Trenton, N.J., Oct. 15, 1940; d. Michael J. and Evelyn M. (Klink) Mazur; m. Gary T.M. Hough, Apr. 7, 1990. Degree in bus. adminstrn., Rider Bus. Coll., 1964; AA, L.A. City Coll., 1967; BEd, Cin. Coll., 1970; MEd, Azusa Pacific U., 1982. Cert. tchr., Calif. Vocat. tchr. Papua New Guinea Inst., 1972-80; adminstrv. asst. Princeton (N.J.) U., 1980-82; bus. instr. Criss Coll., Anaheim, Calif., 1983-87; instr. office occupations Regional Occupational Program, Santa Ana, Calif., 1987-90; bus. instr. Somos Hermandas Unidas, Anaheim, 1991-92; office tech. instr. United Cambodian Community Vocat. Ctr., Long Beach, Calif., 1992-93; bus. mgr. Hough Enterprises, San Clemente, Calif., 1993-95; realtor First Team Real Estate, Mission Viejo, Calif., 1995, The Prudential Calif. Realty, Mission Viejo, 1995-96, Prudential-Jon Douglas Realty Co., Laguna Niguel, Calif., 1996-97, The Prudential Calif. Realty, San Clemente, 1997-98, Del Mar Realty, San Clemente, 1998-99, Profl. Real Estate/Better Homes & Gardens, San Juan Capistrano, Calif., 1999—. Ind. rep. Nat. Telephone and Comms., Inc., Irvine, 1996—; singer Capistrano Chorale, San Juan Capistrano, Calif. Mem. Am. Vocat. Assn. Avocations: aquadynamics, aerobics, singing, photography, traveling. Home: 32302 Alipaz St Spc 261 San Juan Capistrano CA 92675-4163 Office: Profl Real Estate/Better Homes & Gardens # 103 32332 Camino Capistrano San Juan Capistrano CA 92672-4094

HOUGH, JACK VAN DOREN, otologist; b. Lone Wolf, Okla., Sept. 12, 1920; s. Chapman Ernest and Hazel (Van Doren) H.; m. Joan Ingle, Dec. 29, 1943; children: Ted Chapman, Jack Van Doren Jr., Timothy Ingle, David Alliston. BS, Southeastern State U., 1939; MD, U. Okla., 1943. Diplomate Am. Bd. Otorhinolaryngology. Intern USN Hosp., Farragut, Idaho, 1944; resident, then fellow in otolaryngology U. Okla. Hosps., Oklahoma City, 1946-50; clin. instr. otorhinolaryngology U. Okla. Health Scis. Ctr., Oklahoma City, 1950-51; now clin. prof. otorhinolaryngology, head and neck surgery U. Okla. Health Scis. Ctr.; pvt. practice Oklahoma City, 1951—; bd. dirs. MAP Internat., Inc.; developer surg. techniques and instruments for hearing restoration and middle ear reconstrn., electromagnetic hearing devices, cochlear implants. Contbr. sci. articles and textbook chpts. to med. publs. Past ruling elder, Cen. Presbyn. Ch., Oklahoma City; founder, Covenant Community Ch. Oklahoma City, 1980, now session moderator. Decorated Bronze Star, recipient Presdl. Unit citation, Navy Dept. citation for heroism; recipient Harris P. Mosher award Triologic Soc., numerous awards from profl. orgns.; inducted into Okla. Hall of Fame, 1991. Mem. AMA, Am. Bd. Otolaryngology, Am. Acad. Otolaryngology-Head and Neck Surgery, Am. Otological Soc. (past pres., award of merit), Head and Neck Surgery of Am., Am. Triological Soc., Oklahoma County Med. Assn., Okla. Med. Assn., Okla. Acad. Medicine, Osler Soc., Am. Acad. Ophthalmologic and Otolaryngologic Allergy, Christian Med. Soc., Christian Soc. Otolaryngology-Head and Neck Surgeons (founder, past pres.), MAP Internat. (founder), Otosclerosis Study Group (past pres.), Audiology Soc., Von Bekesy Soc. (past pres.), Pan-Am. Assn. Otorhinolaryngology and Bronchoesophagology, Politzer Soc., Am. Sci. Affiliation, numerous other profl. orgns. Home: 9117 SW 22nd St Oklahoma City OK 73128-4918 Office: Hough Ear Inst 3400 NW 56th St Oklahoma City OK 73112-4404

HOUGH, JANET GERDA CAMPBELL, research scientist; b. Glen Ridge, N.J., Dec. 22, 1948; d. Ralph William and Gerda Lydia (Baarck) Campbell; m. John Harrison Hough, Oct. 1, 1966 (div.); 1 child, Laura Leigh. Student Temple U. and Tyler Sch. Art, Phila., 1970-72, Pa. Acad. Fine Arts, 1972, Camden County Coll., Blackwood, N.J., 1973-75; B.S., Thomas Jefferson U., 1977. Lab. animal technician Inst. Med. Rsch., Camden, N.J., 1972-75; rsch. technician dept. biochemistry Thomas Jefferson U., Phila., 1976, phlebotomist, hematology technician, 1976-78, med. technologist spl. hematology, 1978-79, rsch. technician dept. med. genetics, 1979-80; with micromedic systems Rohm & Haas, Horsham, Pa., 1981-85; micromedic Internat. Clin. Nuclear Inc., Costa Mesa, Calif., and Horsham, 1985-91. Collaborator, editor textbook Hematology for Medical Technologists, 1983; poet, illustrator Thought Progressions, 1984. Charter mem. Nat. Rep. Presdl. Task Force, 1984—, Nat. Rep. Senatorial Com., 1984—, Rep. Presdl. Citizen's Adv. Commn., 1989-91, Nat. Rep. Congl. Com., 1992—. Mem. Internat. Soc. Poets, Am. Poetry Assn. (pub. anthologies 1986-90), Nat. Libr. Poetry (pub. anthology 1992). Roman Catholic. Avocations: drawing, painting, long-distance walking.

HOUGH, JOHN DENNIS, public relations executive. BA, Gonzaga U., 1968. Chief of staff Office of Gov. Cecil Andrus, Boise, Idaho, 1974-77; dir. field offices U.S. Dept. of Interior, 1977-80; regional mgr. ITT Corp., Seattle, 1980-84; exec. v.p. First Interstate Bank, 1984-90; co-pres. Rockey Co., Inc., Seattle, CEO, 1998—. Office: The Rockey Co Inc 2121 5th Ave Seattle WA 98121-2510*

HOUGH, LAWRENCE A., former financial organization executive. In enging., Stanford U.; grad., Sloan Sch. of Mgmt., MIT. Fin. analyst Stanford U.; with Student Loan Mktg. Assn., Washington, D.C., 1973-77, 79—, exec. v.p., mktg. svcs. and systems, now, pres., chief exec. officer, 1990-96; pres., CEO Albert Lord, 1996—; chmn. bd. Shakespeare Theater, Washington. also: Shakespeare Theatre 516 Eighth St SE Washington DC 20003-3808*

HOUGH, LESLIE SELDON, educational administrator; b. Springfield, Ohio, Oct. 2, 1946; s. Donald Woodrow and Stella Alta (Finney) H.; m. Sharon Ann Cornell, May 31, 1969; children: Amity Melinda, Amanda Michelle, Leslie Elizabeth. BA, Olivet Nazarene U., 1969; MA, U. Va., 1973, PhD, 1977. Co-dir. Ohio labor history project Ohio Hist. Soc., Columbus, 1975-77; dir. archives labor urban affairs Walter P. Reuther Libr. Wayne State U., Detroit, 1992-97; dir. spl. collections Ga. State U., Atlanta, 1977-92, dir. W.J. Usery Jr. Ctr. for the Workpl., 1997—; cons. Clayton County Water Authority, Riverdale, Ga., 1988-90, Equifax, Inc., Atlanta, 1990-92. Mem. adv. bd. Mich. Hist. Records, Lansing, 1993-97; bd. dirs. Ga. Humanities Coun., Atlanta, 1988-92. With U.S. Army, 1970-71. Democrat. Presbyterian. Avocation: running. Home: 4283 Russert Ct Lilburn GA 30047 Office: Ga State Univ WJ Usery Jr Ctr for Workpl Atlanta GA 30303

HOUGH, M. CATHERINE, nursing educator; b. Susquehanna, Pa., Apr. 14, 1949; d. Frederick G. and Catherine T. (Arnold) H. Diploma, Binghamton State Hosp., 1972; BS in Nursing, U. North Fla., 1987, MS, 1990; PhD, Fla. State U., 1999. Critical care clin. supr. St. Vincent's Med. Ctr., Jacksonville, Fla., dir. cardiovascular nursing, dir. critical care nursing, nursing adminstrv. coord. Mem. AACN (Jacksonville chpt.), Fla. Nurses Assn., Sigma Theta Tau Internat. (Lambda Rho chpt.).

HOUGH, RICHARD T., chemical company executive; b. Evanston, Ill., Nov. 5, 1923; s. William J. and Helen (Trevellyan) H.; m. Nancy Rambeau, Nov. 4, 1944; children: William R., David R., Janet H. Folley. Student, Cornell U., 1942-43; BA, Lake Forest Coll., 1948. With Chemcentral Corp., Chgo., 1948-88; pres. Chemcentral Corp., 1965-87, also bd. dirs., 1954-98, chmn. bd. dirs., 1975-98. With USAF, 1943-45. Mem. Indian Hill Country Club (Winnetka, Ill.). Republican. Home: 913 Barkclay Cir Lake Forest IL 60045-4212

HOUGH, ROBERT ALAN, civil engineer; b. East Orange, N.J., Aug. 6, 1959; s. Robert Elmer and Margaret (Dean) H. AB in Civil Enging., Lafayette Coll., 1981; MBA in Mgmt., Fairleigh Dickinson U., 1995. Registered profl. engr., N.J. Project mgr. water/wastewater engring. dept. Van Note-Harvey Assocs., Princeton, 1981—, head dept., 1994—; twp. engr. Twp. of Woolwich, Gloucester County, N.J., 1993—. Class rep. Pingry Sch. Alumni Assn., 1977—, bd. dirs., 1981—; bd. dirs., pony league dir., mgr., coach Springfield Jr. Baseball League, Inc., 1985—, pres., 1989-90; mem. bd. Union County Regional H.S. Dist. No. 1, 1997. Mem. NSPE, ASCE, Am. Water Works Assn., N.J. Soc. Profl. Engrs., Water Environ. Fedn., N.J. Assn. Environ. Authorities, N.J. Soc. Mcpl. Engrs. Roman Catholic. Avocations: softball, golf. Home: 38 Tudor Ct Springfield NJ 07081-3023 Office: Van Note-Harvey Assocs 77 Alexander Rd Princeton NJ 08540-6300

HOUGH, STEVEN HEDGES, lawyer; b. Cleve., May 24, 1938; s. William Rockwell and Virginia Hull (Olds) H.; m. Carolyn Millicent Day, July 29, 1968 (dec. July 1981); children: Glenn, Holly, Heather. BSBA, Chico State Coll., 1961; JD, U. Calif., San Francisco, 1964. Bar: Calif. 1966, U.S. Dist. Ct. (no. dist.) Calif. 1966, U.S. Ct. Appeals (9th cir.) 1966, U.S. Supreme Ct. 1975. Trial atty. L.A. County Pub. Defender, L.A., 1966-76, head dep., 1976—; pres. Criminal Cts. Bar Assn., L.A., 1984; asst. presiding referee state bar ct. State Bar Calif., L.A., San Francisco, 1985-91, chair standing com. on delivery of legal svcs. to criminal defendants, 1978-79; bd. govs. Long Beach (Calif.) Bar Assn., 1990, 91; instr., lectr., panelist trial advocacy clinic, day in ct. program; mtgs. L.A. County Pub. Defenders, marshal program Calif. Youth Authority, Long Beach Police Dept., other orgns. Mem. First Congregational Ch., Santa Ana, Calif., deacon, 1985-87, 91-93, 96—; mem. PTA several schs.; referee, coach, bd. dirs. region 5 Am. Youth Soccer Orgn.; referee, coach North Huntington Beach Soccer Club, Coast Soccer League; treas. Orange County Soccer Referees Assn., 1986; sustaining mem. Boy Scouts Am., Girl Scouts U.S.; mem. Westhaven Homeowners Assn., Gifted Children's Assn. Orange County; life mem. So. Calif. Acro Team; fund raising solicitor United Way Crusade, Brotherhood Crusade. Recipient Charitable Giving Hon. award Brotherhood Crusade, 1982. Mem. ABA (criminal law sect.), Criminal Cts. Bar Assn., Calif. Pub. Defenders Assn., Calif. Attys. for Criminal Justice, S.E. Bar Assn., Calif. State Bar Assn., Long Beach Bar Assn. (bd. govs. 1990, 91), South Bar Bar Assn., U.S. Supreme Ct. Bar Assn., Nat. Coll. Criminal Def. Lawyers and Pub. Defenders, Nat. Assn. Criminal Def. Lawyers, Am. Judicature Soc., Am. Contract Bridge League (Bronze life master), Mission Viejo Country Club, Hastings Alumni Assn., Univ. Sch. Alumni Assn., Lambda Chi Alph. Republican. Avocations: golf, bridge, soccer, travel. Office: LA County Pub Defenders Office 210 W Temple St Fl 19 Los Angeles CA 90012-3210

HOUGHTALING, PAMELA ANN, technology writer, consultant; b. Catskill, N.Y., July 8, 1949; d. Stanley Kenneth and Mildred Edythe (Fyfe) H. BA, Princeton U., 1971; cert. Russian Inst., Columbia U., 1976, M in Internat. Affairs, 1974. Internat. rels. analyst Libr. of Congress, Washington, 1974-75, U.S. GAO, Washington, 1976-77; pub. affairs specialist IBM Corp., Washington, 1977-81; sr. external programs analyst IBM World Trade Americas/Far East Corp., North Tarrytown, N.Y., 1981-82; mgr. labor affairs/bus. practices U.S. Coun. Internat. Bus., N.Y.C., 1982-84; communications specialist-advt. IBM Corp., Boca Raton, Fla., 1984-86; staff communications specialist IBM Corp., White Plains, N.Y., 1986-88; communications cons., 1988-90; sr. mktg. specialist Wang Labs., Bethesda, Md., 1990-93; pub. rels. dir. STG Mktg. Comm., 1993-94; mgr. mktg. comm. Cable & Wireless, Inc., Vienna, Va. 1994-95; tech. comms. cons., 1995-98; contractor to Applied Physics Lab. Johns Hopkins U., Old Dominion Sys., Inc., 1998—. Mem. Am. Mktg. Assn., Armed Forces Comms. and Electronics Assn.

HOUGHTON, ALAN NOURSE, association executive, educator, consultant; b. Hartford, Conn., Jan. 17, 1924; m. Elizabeth T. Jones, Mar. 30, 1946; children: Alan Nourse, Elizabeth Boardman, John Barnard, Suzanne Tolles. AB cum laude, Harvard U., 1946, AM, 1951; postgrad., Columbia U., 1951, U. Conn., 1961, 62-63. Faculty Groton (Mass.) Sch., 1946-51; chmn. classics dept. Loomis Sch., Windsor, Conn., 1951-55; headmaster Pine Point Sch., Stonington, 1955-67, Renbrook Sch., West Hartford, 1967-73; exec. dir. Conn. Assn. Ind. Schs., 1974-89; ednl. cons. Madison, 1989-94. Mem. Sch. Bldg. Com., Lyme, Conn., 1959, Zoning Bd. Appeals, 1959-61, Zoning and Planning Commn., 1963-65, Bd. Fin., 1971-75, Lyme Dem. Town Com., 1957-63; trustee Blair Acad., Blairstown, N.J., Pine Point Sch., Stonington, Conn., Renbrook Sch., Country Sch., Madison, Conn.; corporator Hartford Hosp. 1st lt. USAAF, 1943-45. Decorated D.F.C., Air medal with three oak leaf clusters; Houghton Wing named for him at Pine Point Sch. Mem. Conn. Assn. Ind. Schs. (tchrs. edn. and profl. stds. rep. 1963-66, v.p., pres.), Classical Assn. New Eng., Mile Creek Beach Club (bd. govs. 1958-73), Harvard Club (N.Y.C.), Madison Winter Club, Phi Delta Kappa, Pi Eta. Home: 26 Sylvan Rd Madison CT 06443-3303

HOUGHTON, AMORY, JR., congressman; b. Corning, N.Y., Aug. 7, 1926; m. Priscilla Dewey Houghton; 4 children. BA, Harvard U., 1950, MA, 1952; hon. docotorate, Alfred U., 1963, Albion Coll., 1964, Cen. Coll., 1966, Clarkson Coll. Tech., 1968, Elmira Coll., 1982, Hartwick Coll., 1983, Houghton Coll., 1983. Exec. officer Corning Glass Works, 1951-86; mem. 100th-106th Congresses from 31st (fomerly 34th) N.Y. dist., Washington, 1987—; mem. ways and means com.; mem. Grace Commn., Bus. Council N.Y. State, Bus. Adv. Commn. for Gov. N.Y., Labor-Industry Coalition for Internat. Trade. Trustee Brookings Instn. Served with USMC, 1945-46. Mem. Corning C. of C. Republican. Lodge: Rotary. Office: US Ho of Reps 1110 Longworth Bldg Washington DC 20515-3231*

HOUGHTON, ANTHONY, physics educator, research scientist; b. Heanor, Eng., Oct. 4, 1935; came to U.S., 1963; s. George and Florence G. (Frost) H.; m. Patricia Sanchez-Cerani, July 15, 1961. BSc, U. Birmingham, Eng., 1956, PhD, 1959. Rsch. physicist McMaster U., Hamilton, Ont., Can., 1960-63; asst. prof. physics Brown U., Providence, 1963-67, assoc. prof., 1967-71, prof., 1971—, chmn. dept. physics, 1992-98; postdoctoral fellow Carnegie Inst. Tech., 1959-60, U. Calif., San Diego, 1959-60; vis. prof. Oxford (Eng.) U., 1970, U. Paris at Orsay, 1970, U.K. AEC, Harwell, Eng., 1971, U. So. Calif., 1975-76, Manchester (Eng.) U., 1976, U. Sussex, Eng., 1977, U. Heidelberg, Germany, 1977, 78, Dalhousie U. Halifax, N.S., Can., 1979, Imperial Coll., London, 1982-83, U. Calif., San Diego, 1989-90, numerous others; cons. Los Alamos Nat. Lab., 1988—. Contbr. numerous articles to profl. jours. Recipient rsch. grants. Fellow Am. Phys. Soc. Home: 173 Mathewson Rd Barrington RI 02806-4426 Office: Brown U Dept Physics Providence RI 02912

HOUGHTON, ARTHUR A., professional society administrator; b. N.Y.C., May 6, 1940. BA, Harvard U., 1963, MA, 1981; MA, Am. U. Beirut, 1966. Fgn. svc. officer Dept. of State, Washington, 1966-79; acting curator J. Paul Getty Mus., Malibu, Calif., 1982-86; fgn. policy coord. White House Office Nat. Drug Policy, Washington, 1988-95; pres. Arthur Houghton Assocs., Washington, 1995—. Author 2 books; contbr. over 30 articles to profl. jours. Recipient Harriman award U.S. Fgn. Svc. Assn., 1974. Fellow Royal Numismatic Soc.; mem. Soc. Francaise Numismatique, Swiss Numismatic Soc., Met. Club (Washington). Office: Ste 230 1100 Connecticut Ave NW Washington DC 20036-1648*

HOUGHTON, CHARLES NORRIS, stage director, author, educator; b. Indpls., Dec. 26, 1909; s. Charles D. Mansfield and Grace (Norris) H. AB, Princeton, 1931; DFA (hon.), Denison U., 1959; HHD (hon.), U. Louisville, 1983; LHD (hon.), Lynchburg Coll., 1987; DFA (hon.), Miami (Ohio) U., 1991. Lectr. drama, dir. dramatics Princeton, 1941-42; guest prof. drama Smith Coll., 1947; lectr. comparative lit. Columbia, 1948-54; producer, dir. television CBS, 1951-52; adj. prof. drama Barnard Coll., 1954-58; co-mng. dir. Phoenix Theatre, N.Y.C., 1953-63; adj. prof. drama, guest dir. Exptl. Theatre, Vassar Coll., 1959-60; prof. drama, dir. Exptl. Theatre, 1962-67; dean div. theatre arts State U. N.Y. Coll., Purchase, 1967-75; prof. State U. N.Y. Coll., 1967-80; bd. dirs. Theatre, Inc., N.Y.C., 1946-73; Berg. vis. prof. English N.Y. U., 1976, 80-81; Bingham prof. humanities U. Louisville, 1979. Stage mgr. on, Broadway, 1933-37; stage designer: Broadway prodns. Whiteoaks, How to Get Tough About It, 1937-38, Dame Nature, Waltz in Goosestep, Good Hunting, 1939-40, The Sleeping Prince, 1956; art dir., St. Louis Mcpl. Opera, 1939-40, dir., Elitch's Gardens Theatre, Denver, 1948-49, Macbeth, London, 1947, Broadway, 1948, Kansas City, 1982, Clutterbuck, 1949, Billy Budd, Broadway, 1951, Julius Caesar, Louisville, 1982, Misalliance, Sarasota, 1983, Lynchburg, 1984; dir. Romeo and Juliet, 1984, The Misanthrope, 1986; author: Moscow Rehearsals, 1936, Advance from Broadway, 1941, But Not Forgotten, 1951, Return Engagement, 1962, The Exploding Stage, 1972, Entrances and Exits, 1991; editor: Masterpieces of Continental Drama, 3 vols, 1963, Great Russian Short Stories, 1958, Great Russian Drama, 1960; assoc. editor: Theatre Arts Mag, 1945-48; contbr. to nat. theatrical mags. Vice chmn. panel Am. Council on Arts in Edn., 1975-77; v.p. Arts, Edn. and Americans, Inc., 1977-84. Guggenheim fellow, 1934, 35, 60-61. Fellow Am. Acad. Arts and Scis., Am. Theatre Assn.; mem. Nat. Coun. Chs. Christ (chmn. adv. com. on drama 1954-57), Nat. Theatre Conf. (pres. 1968-69), Am. Coun. Arts in Edn. (pres. 1973-75), Inst. Advanced Studies in Theatre Arts (mem. adv. coun.), Theatre Devel. Fund (bd. dirs. 1990-93), Coll. of Fellow of Am. Theatre, Century Assn. (N.Y.C.), Phi Beta Kappa. Home: 11 E 9th St New York NY 10003-5946

HOUGHTON, DAVID DREW, meteorologist, educator; b. Phila., Apr. 26, 1938; s. Willard Fairchild and Sara Nancy (Holmes) H.; m. Barbara Flora Coan, June 22, 1963; children: Eric Brian, Karen Jeanette, Steven Andrew. BS, Pa. State U., 1959; MS, U. Wash., 1961, PhD, 1963. Rsch. scientist Nat. Ctr. Atmospheric Rsch., Boulder, Colo., 1963-68; exch. scientist USSR Acad. Scis., Moscow, 1966; vis. scientist Courant Inst. Math. Scis., N.Y.C., 1966; asst. prof. dept. meteorology U. Wis., Madison, 1968-69, assoc. prof., 1969-72, prof., 1972—, chmn. dept., 1976-79, 91-94; scientist Internat. Sci. and Mgmt. Group for Global Atmospheric Research Program, Bracknell, Eng., 1972-73; lectr. Nanjing U., People's Republic of China, 1980 ; vis. sr. scientist Nat. Meteorol. Ctr., Washington, 1988; vis. scientist Inst. of Atmospheric Physics, Acad. of Scis., Beijing and Nanjing U., Nanjing, People's Republic of China, 1989; vis. cons. World Meteorol. Orgn., Geneva, 1997; vis. prof. Clark Atlanta U., 1998. Contbr. articles to profl. jours.; editor-in-chief: Handbook of Applied Meteorology. Vice chmn. Planning Commn., Town of Dunn, Wis., 1977-81. NSF fellow, 1960-63. Fellow AAAS, Am. Meteorol. Soc. (chmn. edn. and human resources commn. 1987-93, pres. 1995-96); mem. Phi Beta Kappa, Sigma Xi, Phi Kappa Phi. Quaker. Office: U Wis Dept Atmos and Ocean Sci Madison WI 53706

HOUGHTON, JAMES RICHARDSON, retired glass manufacturing company executive; b. Corning, N.Y., Apr. 6, 1936; s. Amory and Laura (Richardson) H.; m. May Tuckerman Kinnicutt, June 30, 1962; children: James DeKay, Nina Bayard. AB, Harvard U., 1958, MBA, 1962. With Goldman, Sachs & Co., N.Y.C., 1959-61; with Corning Glass Works (name changed to Corning Inc. 1989), 1962-96; European area mgr. Corning Glass Works, Zurich, Switzerland, 1964-68; v.p., gen. mgr. consumer products divsn. Corning Glass Works, 1968-71, vice chmn. bd., dir., chmn. exec. com., 1971-83, chmn. bd., CEO, 1983-96; bd. dirs. Met. Life Ins. Co., J.P. Morgan Co., Inc., Exxon Corp.; mem. Harvard Corp. Trustee Corning Inc. Found., Corning Mus. Glass, Pierpont Morgan Libr., N.Y.C., Met. Mus. Art; mem. Trilateral Commn., Bus. Coun. With U.S. Army, 1959-60. Episcopalian. Clubs: Corning Country; River, Harvard, Univ., Links (N.Y.C.); Brookline (Mass.) Country; Tarratine (Dark Harbor, Maine); Augusta (Ga.) Nat. Golf; Rolling Rock, Laurel Valley Golf (Ligonier, Pa.). Office: Corning Inc 80 E Market St Ste 201 Corning NY 14830-2722

HOUGHTON, KATHARINE, actress; b. Hartford, Conn., Mar. 10, 1945; d. Ellsworth Strong and Marion Houghton (Hepburn) Grant. BA, Sarah Lawrence Coll., Bronxville, N.Y., 1965. Founding mem. Pilgrim Repertory Co. (Shakespeare touring co. sponsored by Ky. Arts Commn.), 1971-72, S.C. Arts Commn., 1972, Miss. Arts Commn., 1973, Conn. Arts Commn., St. Joseph Coll., 1974. Debut on Broadway stage in A Very Rich Woman, 1965; appeared in stage plays Charley's Aunt, New Orleans Repertory, 1966, The Front Page, Broadway, 1968, Ten O'Clock Scholar, Royal Poinciana Playhouse, Fla., 1969, The Private Ear/The Public Eye, Sullivan, Ill., 1969, Sabrina Fair, Ivoryton Playhouse, 1968, The Miracle Worker, Sullivan, Ill., A Scent of Flowers (Theatre World award), Off Broadway, 1969, Misalliance, Hartford Stage Co., 1970, The Taming of the Shrew, Actors Theatre, Louisville, 1970, Poor Richard, Tartuffe, 1970, Ring Around the Moon, Hartford Stage Co., 1970, Major Barbara, The Glass Menagerie, Actors Theatre of Louisville, 1971, Play It Again Sam, Actors Theatre of Louisville, 1971, Suddenly Last Summer, Ivanhoe, Chgo., 1973, The Prodigal Daughter, Kennedy Center, Washington, 1973, Bell, Book and Candle, Pensacola, Fla., 1974, The Rainmaker, Ind. Repertory Co., 1975, Spiders Web, Atlanta, 1977, Hedda Gabler, Nashville, 1978, Dear Liar, Dayton, Ohio, 1978, 13 Rue de L'Amour, Ind. Repertory Co., 1978, Antigone, Nashville, 1979, Uncle Vanya, Acad. Festival Theatre, Lake Forest, 1979, Forty Carats, Radford U. Theatre, Va., 1979, A Doll's House, St. Edward's U. Theatre, Tex., 1979, The Sea Gull, Pitts. Public Theatre, 1979, The Glass Menagerie, Pa. Stage Co., 1980, Taming of the Shrew, Pa. State Festival, 1980, Terra Nova, Actors Theatre of Louisville, 1980, The Merchant of Venice, South Coast Repertory, Costa Mesa, Calif., 1981, A Touch of the Poet, Yale Repertory Theatre, 1983, To Heaven in a Swing, Am. Place Theatre, N.Y.C., tour various theaters, 1983-85, Sally's Gone She's Left Her Name, Am. Festival Theatre, N.H., 1984-86, Vivat, Vivat Regina, Mad Woman of Chaillot, The Time of Your Life, Children of the Sun, Mirror Repertory Co., N.Y.C., 1985, A Bill of Divorcement, Westport Country Playhouse, Conn., 1985, One Slight Hitch, Charlotte Repertory Co., 1986, To Heaven in a Swing, Amherst Coll., Bowdoin Coll., 1986, and Bronson Alcott Centennial Celebration, 1988, The Hooded Eye, West Bank Downstairs Theatre Bar, 1987, Ivoryton Playhouse, 1987, Murder in the Cathedral, West Point Cadet Chapel, 1987, The Leaves of Vallombrosa, 1988, Our Town, Broadway, 1988-89, Love Letters, Ivoryton Playhouse, 1989, To Kill A Mockingbird, Paper Mill Playhouse, N.J., 1991; motion pictures include Guess Who's Coming to Dinner, 1967, The Gardener, 1972, Eyes of the Amaryllis, 1981, Mr. North, 1987, Billy Bathgate, 1990, Ethan Frome, 1992, The Night We Never Met, 1992, Kalamazoo, 1993, Let It Be You, 1994; TV series The Adams Chronicles, 1975; TV mini-series I'll Take Manhattan, 1986; appeared on TV in Legacy of Fear, 1974, The Color of Friendship, 1981, (daytime serials) One Life to Live, 1989, All My Children, 1992; toured in Sabrina Fair, 1975, The Mousetrap, Arms and the Man, Dear Liar, 1976, The Streets of New York, Westport, Conn., Guildford, N.H., Dennis, Mass., Denver, 1980; appeared in To True to Be Good, Acad. Festival Theatre, Lake Forest, Ill., 1977, Spingold Theatre, Waltham, Mass., 1977, Annenberg Center, Phila., 1977; author: (plays) To Heaven in a Swing, 1982, Merlin, 1984, Buddha, On The Shady Side, The Right Number, 1986, (book) The Marry Month of May, 1988; (stage prodns.) Phone Play, 1988, Good Grief, 1988, Mortal Friends, 1988 (stage prodn. premiere 1988), The Lick Penny Lover, 1988, Only Angels, 1997, (screenplays) The Heart of the Matter, 1989, Journey to Glasnost, 1990, Good Grief, 1991, Motherman, 1993, Acting in Concert, 1994, Spot, 1996, (play) Best Kept Secret, A Dangerous Liaison in the Cold War, 1998; co-author: Two Beastly Tales, 1975; editor: MHG: A Biography, 1989. Mem. Dramatists Guild.

HOUGHTON, MYRON JAMES, theology educator; b. Schenectady, N.Y., July 26, 1941; s. William James and Louise J. (Dlubac) H. Diploma, Moody Bible Inst., 1962; BA, Pillsbury Coll., 1964; BDiv, Grand Rapids Bapt. Sem., 1967; M Liberal ARts, So. Meth. U., 1971; MA, St. Thomas Theol. Sem., 1977; ThD, Concordia Sem., St. Louis, 1986; PhD, Dallas Theol. Sem., 1993. Ordained Bapt. Ch., 1966. Mem. faculty, chair theology dept. Denver Bapt. Bible Coll., 1971-83, Faith Bapt. Theol. Sem., Ankeny, Iowa, 1986—; mem. faculty theology dept. Faith Bapt. Bible Coll., Ankeny, 1983-86; interim pastor Berean Bapt. Ch., Boulder, 1972-73, South Holly Bapt. Ch., Littleton, Colo., 1975-76, 80. Contbr. articles to profl. publs. Mem. Evang. Theol. Soc. Office: Faith Bapt Theol Sem 1900 NW 4th St Ankeny IA 50021-2152

HOUGHTON, RAYMOND CARL, JR., computer science educator; b. Greenfield, Mass., May 26, 1947; s. Raymond Carl and Phyllis Irene (Richason) H.; m. Jan Marie Laws, Sept. 22, 1973; children: Raymond James, April Monica, Amy Rose. BS in Math., Norwich U., 1969; MS in Computer Sci., George Washington U., 1975; MSEE, Johns Hopkins U., 1980; PhD in Computer Sci., Duke U., 1991. Computer operator Norwich U., Northfield, Vt., 1967-69; specialist programmer power transformer dept. GE Co., Pittsfield, Mass., 1969-70; mathematician armament dept. GE Co., Burlington, Vt., 1972-73; mem. tech. staff Computer Scis. Corp., Silver Spring, Md., 1974-75; data systems analyst computer security applications div. Nat. Security Agy., Ft. Meade, Md., 1975-78; computer scientist Inst. Computer Scis. and Tech./Nat. Bur. Standards, Gaithersburg, Md., 1978-83; instrnl. rsch. asst. dept. computer sci. Duke U., Durham, N.C., 1984-91; assoc. prof. dept. math. and computer sci. Augusta (Ga.) Coll., 1987-93; lectr. Skidmore (N.Y.) Coll., 1993-95; pres. Cyber Haus Learning Ctrs., Delmar, N.Y., 1995—; bd. advisers, columnist Software Engring: Tools, Techniques, Practice, 1990-94; spkr. at profl. confs.; adj. prof. Sch. Bus. SUNY, Albany, 1997—. Contbr. to profl. publs. 1st lt. U.S. Army, 1971-72, Vietnam. Recipient Certs. of Recognition, U.S. Dept. Commerce, 1981, 83, Letter of Appreciation, Defence Comms. Agy., 1976. Mem. IEEE, N.Y. Acad. Scis., Assn. Computing Machinery. Democrat. Lutheran. Achievements include description of software development tools. Office: Cyber Haus 159 Deleware Ave Delmar NY 12054-0418

HOUGHTON, ROBERT CHARLES, secondary education educator; b. Dover, N.H., Apr. 12, 1958; s. Raymond David and Barbara Jean (Lyle) H. Student, USCG Acad., New London, Conn., 1976-77; BA with honors, U. Calif., Riverside, 1987, postgrad., 1987-89. Teaching credential, Calif. Various teaching positions, 1977-80; pharmacy technician Anaheim (Calif.) Meml./Brea (Calif.) Cmty., 1980-85; teaching asst. U. Calif., Riverside, 1988-90; instr. Mt. San Jacinto (Calif.) Coll., 1989-90; tchr. Desert Sands Unified, Indio, Calif., 1990—, interim asst. prin., 1997-98; MA ednl. administrn. Chapman U., 1999; counselor Chem. Awareness Network, Indio, Calif., 1990—; computer cons. Desert Sands Unified Sch. Dist., Indio, 1994—; resident tchr. Calif. State U., San Bernardino, 1994-95; asst. tour dir. Lakeland Tours, Washington, 1991-98. Mem. NEA, Nat. Coun. Social Studies, Nat. Geographic Soc., Calif. Tchrs. Assn., Nat. Trust Historic Preservation, Civil War Trust. Republican. Avocations: travel, photography, reading, hiking, camping. Home: 79320 Port Royal Ave Indio CA 92201-1262 Office: 81195 Miles Ave Indio CA 92201-2807

HOUGLAND, VIRGINIA LEE, mathematics educator; b. Ft. Hancock, N.J., Feb. 7, 1944; d. Kenneth Murray and Virginia Francis (Lawrence) Smith; m. James Warren Hougland, July 3, 1964 (dec. June 1994); children: Victoria, Jeffrey. BA in Math., Wash. State U., 1968; MA in Counseling, Ball State U., 1974; tchg. cert., Murray State U., 1987. Tchr. El Paso C.C., Duluth & Colorado Springs, Minn. & Colo., 1976; tchr. math., sci., psychology Thomas Sumter Acad., Dalzell, S.C., 1979-82; chair mid. sch. math. Embry-Riddle U., Ft. Campbell, Ky., 1982-89; tchr. math., dir. upper sch. Univ. Heights Acad., Hopkinsville, Ky., 1982-88; mem. math. faculty Hopkinsville C.C., Ft. Campbell, 1987-89; tchr. math. Madisonville (Ky.) North Hopkins H.S., 1988—; leader math. dist. cluster Ky. Dept. Edn., Frankfurt, 1997. Mem. NEA, Nat. Coun. Tchrs. Math., Ky. Edn. Assn.,Ky. Acad. Assn. (acad. team coach 1984—), Hopkins County Edn. Assn., Delta Kappa Gamma. Episcopalian. Avocation: needlework. Home: 113 S Sunset Cir Hopkinsville KY 42240-3833 Office: Madisonville North Hopkins H S 4515 Hanson Rd Madisonville KY 42431-6151

HOUK, BENJAMIN NOAH, artistic director, choreographer; b. Seattle, Apr. 4, 1962; s. Robert Louis Houk and Marilyn Joan (Haugen) Sundin; children: Marissa, Skylar; m. Lauri-Michelle Rohde, July 11, 1991; children: Madeline, Katherine. Studied dance, Amherst Ballet Acad., 1978, Jan Collum Sch. Ballet, 1979, Jo Emery Sch., 1979-80, N.Y. studios, 1980-83, Robert Joffrey Workshop, 1981, Am. Ballet Ctr., 1980-83, Pacific NW Ballet, 1983—; student, U. Wash., 1988—. Prin. dancer Pacific Northwest Ballet, Seattle, 1983—; asst. dir. Bravo Ballet Arts in Edn. Program, Seattle, 1993-96; with Pacific Northwest Ballet, Seattle, 1987-89, soloist, 1987—, prin. dancer, 1989-96; M.C., coord. Joffrey, N.Y.C., 1983; artistic dir., choreographer Nashville Ballet, 1996—; guest artist Orange County Ballet, Ithaca, N.Y., 1981, Koslovs and Friends, San Francisco, 1985, Ballet Oreg., Portland, 1988, Ballet Chgo., 1989, Nev. Dance Theatre, Las Vegas, 1990, Tacoma Perf. Dance Co., 1980, Nevada Festival Ballet, 1993-94, Maui Ballet Co., 1994; dance instr., lectr., 1984—. Significant ballet roles with Pacific Northwest Ballet include Romeo in The Tragedy of Romeo and Juliet, Sigfried in Swan Lake, Franz in Coppelia, The Prince in The Nutcracker; others include Albrecht in Giselle, Othello in The Moor's Pavane; choreographer: Capriole Suite, 1988, By When, 1989, Shard, 1990, First Light, 1992, Schubert 2-4-5, 1994, Bete Noir, 1993, Across and Back, 1994, Nutcracker, 1995, Open Water, 1995, Aida, 1997, Passage, 1998, Swan Lake (after Petipa), 1998; TV appearance on Disney Presents Bill Nye the Science Guy, 1994. Artistic dir. Benefit for the Homeless, Everett, Wash., 1990-91. Grantee Tacoma (Wash.) Arts Coun., 1986. Mem. Am. Guild Mus. Artists. Avocations: reading, windsurfing, pottery, mountaineering, painting. Office: Nashville Ballet 2976 Sidco Dr Nashville TN 37204-3715*

HOUK, JAMES CHARLES, physiologist, educator; b. Northville, Mich., June 3, 1939; s. James Charles and Elowene (Tower) H.; m. Antoinette Iacuzio, Dec. 28, 1963; children: Philip, Nadia, Peter. BSEE, Mich. Tech. U., 1961; MSEE, MIT, 1963; PhD, Harvard U., 1966. Instr. Harvard U. Med. Sch., 1967-69, asst. prof., 1969-73; lecturer Mass Inst. Tech., 1971-73; assoc. prof. Johns Hopkins U. Med. Sch., 1973-78; adjunct assoc prof. Univ. of North Carolina, 1975; prof., chmn. dept. physiology Northwestern Univ. Med. Sch., 1978—. Co-author: Medical Physiology 14th edit., 1980, Handbook of Physiology--The Nervous System II, 1981, Encyclopedia of Neuroscience, 1987, Models of Information Processing in the Basal Ganglia, 1995; contbr. chpts. to books. Recipient Javits award NIH, 1984-92. Mem. IEEE, AAAS, Soc. for Neurosci., Am. Physiol. Soc., European Neurosci. Assn., Assn. of Chmn. of Dept. of Physiology, Internat. Neural Network Soc. Office: Northwestern U 303 E Chicago Ave Chicago IL 60611-3093

HOUK, KENDALL NEWCOMB, chemistry educator; b. Nashville, Tenn., Feb. 27, 1943; s. Charles H. and Janet Houk; 1 child, Kendall M.; m. Robin L. Garrell. AB, Harvard U., 1964, MS, 1966, PhD, 1968. Asst. prof. chemistry La. State U., Baton Rouge, 1968-72, assoc. prof., 1972-75, prof., 1975-80; prof. U. Pitts., 1980-86; prof. UCLA, 1986-91, chmn. dept. chemistry and biochemistry, 1991-94; dir. chemistry div. nat. sci. Found., 1988-90. Contbr. numerous articles to profl. jours. Recipient Schrodinger medal World Assn. Theoretically Oriented Chemists, 1998. Fellow AAAS; mem. Am. Chem. Soc. (Cope Scholar award 1988, James Flack Norris award in physical organic chemistry 1991). Office: UCLA Dept Chemistry and Biochemistry 405 Hilgard Ave Dept And Los Angeles CA 90095-9000

HOUK, MARGARET, writer; b. Grand Rapids, Mich., Jan. 8, 1932; d. Albert Louis and Ruth Kenyet (Schwartz) Petzold; m. John Peter Houk, Aug. 16, 1952; children: Cynthia Whitney, Deborah Peterson, Susan Pierquet, Kenneth Katchenago. BS in Home Econs. with honors, Valparaiso U., 1953. Writer, self-employed Appleton, Wis., 1971—; writer, photographer Network Health Plan, Appleton, 1987-89; writer Valleysun weekly newspaper, Menasha, Wis., 1989; tchr. writing U. Wis.-Fox Valley, Menasha, 1989—, G.L. Christian Writer's Conf., Green Lake, Wis., 1991, U. Wis., Oshkosh, 1992, Fox Valley Tech. Coll., Appleton, 1987-89; spkr. in field. Contbr. more than 700 articles to comml. jours.; author: (books) That Very Special Person - Me!, 1990, 100 Easy Ways to Teach/Child to Love God's World, 1994, Lighten Up and Enjoy Life More, 1996; contbg. writer: (anthology) Almost Every Answer to Practically Any Teacher!, 1992. Pres. Appleton Area Ecumenical Network, Fox Valley, 1984-88, 94-96; addiction interventionist Addiction Intervention Ministry, Fox Valley, 1991—; residential chmn. Am. Cancer Soc., Appleton, 1970; bd. dirs. Family Svcs. and Youth Svcs. Assns., 1970s. Recipient writing award Mich. State Bar Assn. contest, 1949. Mem. Evangel. Press Assn., Associated Ch. Press (mem. and conv. coms. 1995-97), Wis. Regional Writers Assn. (recipient writing awards 1986, 87, 91), Word and Pen Christian Writers Club (treas. 1997-99), Fox Valley Writers Club, Writers Info. Network, Prince of Peace WELCA (v.p. 1998, pres. 1999). Lutheran. Avocations: singing, camping, travel, gardening, needlework. Home: W2355 Valleywood Ln Appleton WI 54915-8712

HOULE, JEFFREY ROBERT, lawyer; b. Biddeford, Maine, July 27, 1965; s. Marcel Paul and Lois Marie (Jackson) H.; m. Lorren Johnston Houle, Oct. 11, 1997; 1 child, Grace Morgan. AB, Boston Coll., Chestnut Hill, Mass., 1987; JD, Western New Eng. Coll., Springfield, Mass., 1991; LLM in Taxation, Cert. in Employee Benefits Law, Georgetown U., Washington, 1992, LLM in Securities Regulation, 1995. Bar: D.C., N.Y., Conn., Mass., Maine. Pres. A.F.I. Investments, Springfield, Mass., 1988-91, Washington Capital Ventures, LP, Washington, 1995-98; law clk. Stones Solicitors, Exeter, Devon, Eng., 1989; jud. intern to the Hon. Joan Glazer Margolis U.S. Magistrate Judge, New Haven, Conn., 1990; legal intern Office of Atty. Gen. Robert Abrams, N.Y.C., 1990; analyst The Bur. of Nat. Affairs, Inc., Washington, 1992; assoc. Andros, Floyd & Miller PC, Hartford, Conn., 1992-94, Elias, Matz, Tiernan & Herrick LLP, Washington, 1994-98; ptnr. Greenberg Traurig, McLean, Va., 1998—. Contbr. articles to profl. jours. With U.S. Army, 1984-86. Mem. ABA, The Army and Navy Club, The Federalist Soc.,The Tower Club, Phi Alpha Delta. Republican. Roman Catholic. Avocations: hiking, swimming, horseback riding, travel. Home: 444 New Jersey Ave SE Washington DC 20003-4003 Office: Greenberg Traurig 1300 Connecticut Ave NW Washington DC 20036

HOULE, JOSEPH ADRIEN, orthopedic surgeon; b. Ft. Saskatchewan, Alta., Can., Nov. 3, 1928; came to U.S., 1978; s. Adelard Houle and Bertha (Durocher) Guay; divorced; children: Valerie, Diane, Lorraine, Louis, Doreen, Ludmilla, Virginia; m. Marjorie Elizabeth Tuhy. BSc, cert. in premed., U. Ottawa, 1955; MD, Laval U., 1960, Licentiate Med. Council of

Can., 1960. Cert. specialist orthopaedic surgery, Quebec, Can. Intern Hotel Dieu Hosp., Quebec City, Can., 1959-60; resident in gen. surgery St. Vincent de Paul Hosp., Sherbrooke, Que., Can., 1960-61, St. Vincent's Hosp., Bridgeport, Conn., 1961-62; resident in orthopaedic surgery Montreal Children's Hosp., Montreal Gen. Hosp. and Queen Mary's Vet. Hosp., 1962-65; practice medicine specializing in orthopaedic surgery Montreal, Can., 1965-78; chief of orthopaedic surgery Thomas Davis Med. Ctr., Tucson, 1978-95, ret., 1995. Produced film Mechanical Knee, 1969. Mem. Bd. Med. Examiners of Ariz., 1978. Served to capt. Royal Can. Forces, 1956-67. Mem. AMA, Can. Orthopaedic Assn., Ariz. Orthopaedic Assn., Pima County Med. Soc. Roman Catholic. Avocations: photography, flying, woodworking. Home: PO Box 11225 Casa Grande AZ 85230-1225 Office: Thomas Davis Med Ctrs 1789 E Hatfield Rd Casa Grande AZ 85222-1225

HOULE, JOSEPH E., mathematics educator; b. Hartford, Conn., Oct. 11, 1930; s. Joseph E. and Rena (Cyr) H.; m. Constance Deschamps, June 19, 1954; children—Marie, Joseph, Celia, Elizabeth, Amy, Bernice. A.B., Cath. U. Am., 1952, M.A., 1954, Ph.D., 1959. From instr. to assoc. prof. math. Georgetown U., 1953-62; assoc. prof. Seton Hall U., 1962-63; prof. math. Pace U., N.Y.C., 1963-94, chmn. dept., 1963-70, dean Dyson Coll. Arts and Scis., 1971-90, vice provost, 1987-90; dir. Ctr. for Applied Ethics, 1982-93, emeritus, 1994—; Internat. Exec. Svc. Corps. vol. exec. Ministry of Edn., Budapest, Hungary, 1991. Fellow N.Y. Acad. Scis. (chmn. sect. math. 1968-69); mem. Math. Assn. Am., Phi Beta Kappa Assocs., Phi Beta Kappa, Sigma Xi. Roman Catholic. Home: A188 Harrogate 400 Locust St Lakewood NJ 08701-7411

HOULIHAN, GAIL LANIER, child advocate, educator; b. Mt. Vernon, N.Y., Sept. 15, 1936; d. Fred K. Houlihan and Burniece Ruth Oliver Phillips; m. Raymond D'Arsey Houlihan, Jr., May 16, 1959 (div. July 1997); children: Jeffrey John, Raymond D'Arsey III, Michael William, Pamela Lanier, Sean Patrick. BA in English, Douglass Coll., New Brunswick, N.J., 1958. With exec. mgmt. trainee program Doubledy Pub. Co., N.Y.C., 1958-59; elem. sch. tchr. Pennsauken (N.J.) Sch. Dist., 1959; conf. coord. for nat. conf. Nat. Assn. Foster Care Reviewerw, 1991-92. Mem. Gov.'s Com. for Children, Youth and Families, 1978-82; mem. township com. Bordentown (N.J.) Twp. Govt., 1982-88, dep. mayor, 1985, 87, mauor, 1986; mem. Bordentown Twp. Planning Bd., 1986-88; founding mem. Bordentown Sewerate Authority, 1986, vice chmn., 1986, chmn., 1987, 91, bd. dirs., 1986-92; coord. Bordentown Twp. Emergency Mgmt., 1987-91; mem. State Helath Planning Bd., 1994—; active N.J. State Adv. Coun., Trenton, 1979—, mem. exec. com., 1979-86; trustee Assn. for Children of N.J., Newark, 1980—, treas., 1989-91, adminstrv. v.p., 1995-97; bd. dirs. Comty. Concerts of Bordentown, 1980-91, pres., 1986-88; bd. dirs. Prevention Edn., Inc., Lawrence Twp., N.J., 1990-92; vice chmn. Children's Interagy. Coordinating Coun., Mt. Holly, N.J., 1993-97, chmn., 1997—; bd. dirs. Morris Hall St. Lawrence Rehab. Ctr., 1993—. Home: 119 Chatsworth Ave Beach Haven NJ 08008-1538

HOULIHAN, GERALD JOHN, lawyer; b. Cortland, N.Y., Aug. 26, 1943; s. Robert Emmett and Helen (Corsi) H.; m. Claudia C. Kitchens; children: Andrea, Gerald Jr., Maureen, Katherine, Colleen. BS, U. Notre Dame, 1965; JD, Syracuse U., 1968. Bar: N.Y. 1968, U.S. Dist. Ct. (we. dist.) N.Y. 1968, U.S. Ct. Appeals (2nd cir.) 1972, U.S. Supreme Ct. 1980, U.S. Ct. Appeals (5th cir.) 1981, U.S. Ct. Appeals (11th cir.) 1981, Fla. 1985, U.S. Dist. Ct. (so. dist.) Fla. 1985, U.S. Dist. Ct. (so. dist.) N.Y. 1986, U.S. Dist. Ct. (no. dist.) Fla. 1986, U.S. Ct. Appeals (4th and D.C. cirs.) 1987, U.S. Dist. Ct. (middle dist.) Fla., 1987. Assoc. Harris, Beach, Keating et al., Rochester, N.Y., 1968-72; asst. U.S. atty. U.S. Atty.'s Office, Rochester, 1972-81; sr. litigation counsel U.S. Dept. Justice, Rochester, 1981-82; chief asst. U.S. atty. U.S. Atty.'s Office, Miami, Fla., 1982-85; ptnr. Steel Hector & Davis, Miami, 1985-91; mem. Greenberg, Traurig, Hoffman, Lipoff, Rosen & Quentel, P.A., Miami, 1991-95; ptnr. Houlihan & Ptnrs., P.A., 1995—. Advocate Am. Bd. Trial Advocates. Belle L. Landry scholar Syracuse Soc. Mem. Fed. Bar Assn. (pres. 1993-94, bd. dirs. Miami chpt. 1988—), Order of Coif. Democrat. Roman Catholic. Home: 5191 SW 76th St Miami FL 33143-6015 Office: Houlihan & Ptnrs PA 2600 S Douglas Rd Ste 600 Miami FL 33134-6125

HOULIHAN, HILDA IMELIO, physician; b. Buenos Aires, June 20, 1937; came to U.S., 1964, naturalized, 1968; d. Luis and Elvina (Bertolini) Imelio; m. Thomas Brendon Houlihan, Apr. 24, 1965; children: Ingrid, Erika. BA, Liceum # 1 Figueroa Alcorta, Buenos Aires, 1954; MD, Nat. U. Buenos Aires, 1963. Diplomate Am. Bd. Family Practice. Assoc. resident in ob-gyn. Durand Hosp., Buenos Aires, 1963-64; intern Balt. Women's Hosp., 1964-65; assoc. resident in anesthesiology U. Md. Hosp., Balt., 1965-66, sr. resident in anesthesiology, 1966-67, 68-69, fellow in anesthesiology, 1967-68; chief med. svcs. Somerset/Worcester Counties Unity Eastern Shore State Hosp., Cambridge, Md., 1969-70, acting chief anesthesia and physician in charge, 1970-71, chief anesthesiology svcs., 1971-73; med. dir. Holly Ctr., Salisbury, Md., 1973-85; pvt. practice specializing in family medicine Salisbury, 1985—; cons. Salisbury Pub. Health Dept. Named Profl. of Yr., Wicomico Assn. for Retarded Citizens. Fellow Am. Acad. Family Practice, Royal Soc. Medicine (London); mem. AMA, Md. Acad. Family Practice, Med. and Chirurg. Faculty Md. (alt. del. to AMA, mem. coun. for Wicomico County, various coms.), Rotary Club Wicomico County, Wicomico County Med. Soc. (sec.-treas. 1986, v.p. 1987, pres. 1988), Green Hill Yacht and Country Club, Wicomico Hunt Club. Republican. Roman Catholic. Avocations: fox hunting, travel, piano, oil painting. Home: 1318 Toadvine Rd Salisbury MD 21804-9245 Office: 1405 S Division St Salisbury MD 21804-7232

HOULIHAN, JAMES WILLIAM, criminal justice educator; b. Chgo., Aug. 3, 1939; s. James William and Julia Dorothy (Nash) H.; m. Patricia Louise Halper, Apr. 11, 1964; 1 child, Erin Candice. BSBA in Fin. and Mgmt., Loyola U., Chgo., 1968; MBA in Econs. and Mgmt., DePaul U., Chgo., 1971; EdD, No. Ill. U., 1996; grad., USAF Command and Staff Coll., 1979, Air War Coll., 1988, Nat. Def. U., 1978. Spl. agt. Criminal Investigation divsn. U.S. Treasury Dept., Chgo., 1963-91, dir. tng., 1984-91, spl. staff asst. to chief, 1988-90; various positions U.S. Army/U.S. Army Res./N.G., various locations, 1962-69, USAF/USAFR, various locations, 1969-92; comdr. USAF Intelligence Command, Glenview, Ill., 1988-92; prin. E.C. Cons., St. Charles, Ill., 1991—; prof. Lewis U., Romeoville, Ill., 1990—; adj. mgmt. prof. Elgin (Ill.) C.C., 1977—, mem. adv. com., mgmt. program, 1982—; adj. mgmt. prof. Ctrl. Tex. Coll., 1988—, Vincennes U., 1991—, Lewis U., Romeoville, 1995—; mem. adv. com. criminal justice program St. Xavier U., Chgo., 1973—; mem. adminstrv. rev. bd. Ill. Dept. of Corrections, 1995—. Mem. Inst. on Edn. and Athletics, U. Chgo., 1983-89; mem. Roosevelt Inst. on Pub. Policy Studies, U. Ill., Chgo., 1986-88; mem. Pres.'s Club, St. Ignatius Coll. Prep., Chgo., 1989—. Recipient George Washington Honor medal Freedoms Found. at Valley Forge, 1977, 80, 81, 86, 92, Albert Gallatin award Sec. of U.S. Treasury, 1991, Outstanding Faculty award Lewis U., 1996; named Disting. LaSallian Educator, 1997. Mem. Am. Legion (exec. com.), Res. Officers Assn., Air Force Assn., Air War Coll. Alumni Assn., Am. Assn. Adult and Continuing Edn. Roman Catholic. Avocation: volunteer work. Office: Lewis U Rte 53 Box 1029 Romeoville IL 60446

HOULIHAN, PATRICK THOMAS, museum director; b. New Haven, June 22, 1942; s. John T. and Irene (Rourke) H.; m. Betsy Eliason, June 19, 1965; children: Mark T. and Michael D. (twins). BS, Georgetown U., 1964; MA, U. Minn., 1969; PhD, U. Wis., Milw., 1971. Asst. commr. N.Y. State Mus., Albany, 1980-81; dir. Heard Mus., Phoenix, 1972-80, S.W. Mus., L.A., 1981-87, Millicent Rogers Mus., 1988-93; writer, rschr. Ugo Prodns., L.A., 1993—

HOUMES, BLAINE V., emergency physician; b. Sept. 13, 1952. MD, U. N.D., 1988. Diplomate Am. Bd. Emergency Medicine. Intern Cook County Hosp., Chgo., 1988-89, resident, 1989-92; mem. staff Mercy Med. Ctr., Cedar Rapids, Iowa, 1992—. Mem. Am. Coll. Emergency Physicians, Am. Acad. Emergency Medicine, Iowa Med. Soc. Office: Linn County Emergency Medicine 701 10th St SE Cedar Rapids IA 52403-1251

HOUNSFIELD, GODFREY NEWBOLD, radiation scientist; b. Aug. 28, 1919; s. Thomas H. Ed., City and Guilds Coll., London; diploma, Faraday House Elec. Engring. Coll., London; MD (hon.), U. Basel, 1975; DSc (hon.), City U., 1976, U. London, 1976; DTech (hon.), U. Loughborough, 1976; D honoris causa, Cambridge U., 1992. Joined EMI Ltd., Hayes, Middlesex, Eng., 1951, head med. systems sect., cen. research labs., 1972-76, sr. staff scientist, 1977—; professional fellow in imaging scis. Manchester U., 1978-86. Contbr. articles to sci. jours. Recipient Nobel prize in Physiology or Medicine, 1979; MacRobert award, 1972; Wilhelm-Exner medal Austrian Indsl. Assn., 1974; Ziedses des Plantes medal Physikalishe Medizinische Gesellschaft, Würzburg, 1974; Prince Philip Medal award CGLI, 1975; ANS Radiation Industry award Ga. Inst. Tech., 1975; Lasker award Lasker Found., 1975; Duddell Bronze medal Inst. Physics, 1976; Golden Plate award Am. Acad. Achievement, 1976; Reginald Mitchell Gold medal Stoke-on-Trent Assn. Engrs., 1976; Churchill Gold medal, 1976; Gairdner Found. award, 1976; decorated comdr. Order Brit. Empire, 1976, knight, 1981. Fellow Royal Soc. Led design team for 1st large all-transistor computer to be built in Gt. Britain; invented EMI-scanner computerized transverse axial tomography system for X-ray exam.; developed new X-ray technique (EMI-scanner system). Office: Ctrl Research Labs EMI Group, Dawley Rd, Hayes Middlesex UB3 1HH, England

HOUPIS, CONSTANTINE HARRY, electrical engineering educator; b. Lowell, Mass., June 16, 1922; s. Harry John and Metazia (Gourokous) H.; m. Mary Stephens, Aug. 28, 1960; children: Harry C., Angella S. Student, Wayne U., 1941-43; BS, U. Ill., 1947, MS, 1948. Spl. rsch. asst. U. Ill., 1947-48; devel. elec. engr. Babcock & Wilcox Co., Alliance, Ohio, 1948-49; instr. elec. engring. Wayne State U., 1949-51; prin. elec. engr. Battelle Meml. Inst., Columbus, Ohio, 1951-52; prof. elec. engring. Air Force Inst. Tech., Wright-Patterson AFB, Ohio, 1952-96, prof. emeritus, 1997—; guest lectr. Nat. Tech. U. Athens, 1958, U. Patras, 1984, Weizmann Inst. Sci., 1984, U. Strathclyde, 1995, Binghampton U., 1996; sr. rsch. assoc. Air Force Flight Dynamics Directorate, 1981-97, sr. rsch. assoc. emeritus, 1997—. Author: (with J.J. D'Azzo) Feedback Control System Analysis and Synthesis, 1960, 2d edit., 196; Principles of Electrical Engineering: Electric Circuits, Electronics, Energy Conversion, Control Systems Computers, 1968; Linear Control Systems Analysis and Design: Conventional and Modern, 1975, 4th edit., 1995; (with J. Lubelfeld) Outline of Pulse Circuits; (with G.B. Lamont) Digital Control Systems: Theory Software, Hardware, 1985, 2d edit., 1992; (with S. Rasmussen) Quantitative Feedback Theory: Theory and Application, 1999, also articles on automatic controls in profl. jours. in U.S., U.K. and Greece. Served with AUS, 1943-46. Recipient Outstanding Engr. award Dayton Area Nat. Engrs. Week, 1962. Fellow IEEE; mem. Am. Soc. Engring. Edn., Am. Hellenic Edn. Progressive Assn., Tau Beta Pi, Eta Kappa Nu. Greek Orthodox. Home: 1125 Brittany Hills Dr Dayton OH 45459-1415 Office: Air Force Inst Tech 2950 P St Bldg 642 Dayton OH 45433-7765

HOUPT, JAMES EDWARD, lawyer; b. Calif., 1951; m. Leslie Ann Jones Houpt. BA with distinction, Calif. State U., Chico, 1976; JD cum laude, Harvard U., 1992. Bar: Va. 1992, D.C. 1992, Md. 1993, U.S. Ct. Appeals (4th cir.) 1992, Calif. 1997, U.S. Ct. Appeals (9th cir.) 1997. News dir. Sta. KNVR-FM, Paradise, Calif., 1978-80; anchor, reporter Sta. KHSL-AM-TV, Chico, 1980-85; sr. reporter Sta. KOLO-TV, Reno, 1985-89; assoc. Baker & Hostetler, Washington, D.C., 1992-97, Orrick, Herrington & Sutcliffe LLP, Sacramento, Calif., 1997—; lectr. journalism Calif. State U., 1981, 85; adj. prof. law sch. U. Calif., Davis, vis. prof., 1999. Author: (booklet) Access to Electronic Records, 1990, The Libel Curtain: A Comparison of Canadian & American Libel Law, 1994, Going On-Line: Is the World Wide Web a Web for the Unwary?, 1996, Boarding a Moving Bus: Developing an Internet Risk Management Strategy, 1997; contbr. articles to legal and gen. interest publs. With USN, 1970-74. Recipient Cert. of Merit, Calif.-Nev. AP TV-Radio Assn., 1983, 84, 86. Mem. ABA, Va. State Bar Assn., D.C. Bar, Calif. Bar Assn., VFW. Avocations: photography, hiking. Office: Orrick, Herrington & Sutcliffe LLP 400 Capitol Mall Ste 3000 Sacramento CA 95814-4421

HOUPT, JEFFREY LYLE, psychiatrist, educator; b. Phila., Aug. 13, 1941; s. H. Lyle and Elizabeth (McAlpine) H.; m. Corinne A. Anderson, Dec. 28, 1964; childrens Brian Jeffrey, Eric Robert. BS in Zoology, Wheaton Coll., 1963; MD, Baylor Coll. Medicine, 1967. Diplomate Am. Bd. Psychiatry and Neurology. Intern Boston City Hosp., 1967-68; resident in psychiatry Yale U., New Haven, 1968-71; staff med. officer Oak Knoll Naval Hosp., Oakland, Calif., 1971-73; adj. asst. prof. psychiatry Presbyn. Hosp., San Francisco, 1973-75; asst. prof. to prof. psychiatry Duke Med. Ctr., Durham, N.C., 1975-83; prof. psychiatry, chmn. dept. Emory U. Sch. Medicine, Atlanta, 1983-90; dean Sch. Medicine Emory U., Atlanta, 1988-96; dean Sch. Medicine, vice chancellor for med. affairs U. N.C., Chapel Hill, 1997—; CEO U. N.C. Health Sys., Chapel Hill, 1998—. Author: The Importance of Mental Health Services for General Health Care, 1979; contbr. articles to med. jours. Lt. comdr. USN, 1971-73. Fellow Am. Coll. Psychiatry (pres.), Am. Psychiat. Assn. Home: 51319 Eastchurch Chapel Hill NC 27514-8302 Office: Univ North Carolina at Chapel Hill School of Medicine Chapel Hill NC 27599

HOURANEY, WILLIAM GEORGE, marketing and public relations executive; b. Altoona, Pa., Dec. 11, 1945; s. William George and Elizabeth (Ajay) H.; m. Joan Buttleman, Mar. 28, 1969 (div. Feb. 1975); 1 child, Steven David; m. Jill Christine Harth, Feb. 4, 1979. Founder, chmn. bd. Am. Dream Ent. Corp. and predecessor cos., Boca Raton, Fla., 1966—; chmn., founder Am. Dream Festival, Boca Raton, 1984—. Office: American Dream Ent Corp PO Box 273527 Boca Raton FL 33427-3527*

HOURANI, LAUREL LOCKWOOD, epidemiologist; b. Carmel, Calif., Sept. 10, 1950; d. Eugene Franklin and Katherine Ruth (Miller) Betz; m. Ghazi Fayez Hourani, Feb. 28, 1984; children: Nathan, Danna, Lisa. BA, Chico State U., 1977; MPH, Am. Univ. Beirut, 1983; PhD, U. Pitts., 1990. Prog. evaluator Community Hosp. Monterey Peninsula, Carmel, Calif., 1978-81; instr./researcher Am. Univ. Beirut, 1981-85; predoctoral fellow U. Pitts., 1985-89; researcher, cons. V.A. Med. Ctr., Pitts., 1988-90; dir., tumor registry Med. Ctr. U. Calif. Irvine, Orange, 1990-92; epidemiologist Naval Health Rsch. Ctr., San Diego, 1993-95; head divsn. health scis., 1995—; cons. Nat. Devel. Commn. South Lebanon, 1981-83. Author: No Water, No Peace, 1985; contbr. articles to profl. jours. Bd. dirs. Am. for Justice in Middle East, Beirut, 1982-85, Nat. Devel. Com., South Lebanon, 1983-85. Recipient grant V.A., Pitts., 1989, rsch. grant U. Rsch. Bd., Beirut, 1985. Mem. Am. Psychol. Assn., Am. Pub. Health Assn., Soc. for Epidemiologic Rsch. Office: Naval Health Rsch Ctr Divsn Epidemiology PO Box 85122 San Diego CA 92186-5122

HOUSE, CHARLETTA, librarian; b. Mobile, Ala., July 9, 1937; d. Charlie and Nevada (Travis) H. BS, Ala. State U., 1959; MLS, U.Md., 1973; MEd, Salisbury State U., 1993. Acquisitions asst. libr. Ala. A&M Libr., Normal, Ala., 1963-68; asst. libr. circulation dept. U. Md. Eastern Shore, Princess Anne, 1968-71, head circulation dept., 1972-83; circulation, reference libr. Salisbury (Md.) State U., 1984-86, reference, spl. collection libr., 1986—. Mem. Wicomico County Commn. of Women, Dem. Club of Wicomico County. Mem. AAUW, LWV, NAACP, Nat. Polit. Congress of Black Women, Md. Libr. Assn., Nat. Women of Achievemnt, Inc., The Links, Inc., Kappa Delta Pi, Delta Sigma Theta Sorority, Inc. Methodist. Avocation: reading. Office: Salisbury State Univ Blackwell Libr 1101 Camden Ave Salisbury MD 21801-6837

HOUSE, DAVID L., electronics components company executive; b. 1943. With Raytheon, 1965-69, Honeywell, 1969-72, Microdata, 1972-74; v.p., gen. mgr. Intel Corp., 1974-96; chmn., pres., CEO Bay Network Computers, Santa Clara, 1996; now sr. v.p. Intel Corp., 1996-98; pres. Nortel Network, Santa Clara, 1998. Address: Nortel Network Bay Network Computers 4401 Great America Pkwy Santa Clara CA 95052-8185*

HOUSE, DONALD LEE, SR., software executive, private investor, management consultant; b. Covington, Ga., Aug. 7, 1941; s. Ben Luther and Almeda (Johnson) H.; m. Nickie Fargason, Oct. 19, 1962; children: Donald Lee Jr., Danielle Elizabeth. BS, Ga. Inst. Tech., 1963, MS, 1967. Process engr. E.I. Dupont, Chattanooga, 1966-68; asst. to pres. Jefferson (Ga.) Mills Inc., 1968; exec. v.p. Mgmt. Sci. Am. Inc., Atlanta, 1968-87; investor, bus. cons. Atlanta, 1987-99; chmn. Clarus Corp., Atlanta, 1992-97; also bd. dirs.; bd. dirs. BT Squared Techs., Expeditor Sys., Transnexus Technologies, Melita Internat., Inc., Telinet Technologies, Carreker-Antinori, Inc.; mem. Ga. Tech. Adv. Bd. 1st lt. U.S. Army, 1963-65. Mem. Tech. Assn. Ga. (bd. dirs.). Republican. Club: Cherokee Town and Country (Atlanta). Avocation: reading, horse farm. Home: 2480 Spalding Dr Atlanta GA 30350-3600 : 3970 Johns Creek Ct Suwanee GA 30024-1265

HOUSE, JAMES STEPHEN, social psychologist, educator; b. Phila., Jan. 27, 1944; s. James Jr. and Virginia Miller (Sturgis) H.; m. Wendy Fisher, May 13, 1967; children: Jeff, Erin. BA, Haverford Coll., 1965; PhD, U. Mich., 1972. From. instr. to assoc. prof. sociology Duke U., Durham, N.C., 1970-78; assoc. prof. sociology/assoc. rsch. scientist Survey Rsch. U. Mich., Ann Arbor, 1978-82, assoc. chair dept. sociology, 1981-84, prof. sociology, rsch. scientist Survey Rsch. Ctr., 1982—, chair dept. sociology, 1986-90, dir. Survey Rsch. Ctr., Inst. Social Rsch., 1991—. Author: Work Stress and Social Support, 1981; co-editor: Sociological Perspectives on Social Psychology, 1995; assoc. editor Social Psychology Quar., 1988-91, N.Am. editor Work and Stress, 1985-88, Jour. Health & Social Behavior, 1997—; contbr. articles to profl. jours., chpt. to book. Guggenheim fellow, 1986-87. Fellow AAAS, Am. Acad. Arts and Scis., Soc. Behavioral Medicine; mem. Am. Sociol. Assn., Acad. Behavioral Medicine Rsch., Soc. for Psychol. Study of Social Issues, Soc. for Epidemiol. Rsch. Office: Univ Mich Inst Social Rsch PO Box 1248 Ann Arbor MI 48106-1248

HOUSE, JOHN WILLIAM, otologist; b. L.A., July 12, 1941; s. Howard and Helen House; m. Barbara Breithaupt, Mar. 28, 1993; children: Hans, Chris, Kurt, Steven, Kevin. BS, U. So. Calif., 1964, MD, 1967. Intern L.A. County-U. So. Calif. Med. Ctr., 1967-68; resident Glendale (Calif.) Adventist Hosp., 1971-72, L.A. County Med. Ctr., 1972-74; fellow Otologic Med. Group, L.A., 1974, pvt. practice, 1975—; pres. House Ear Inst., L.A., 1987—. Mem. editorial bd. Am. J. Otology, 1986—; contbr. articles to jours. in field. Admissions com. interviewer, U. So. Calif. Sch. Medicine, Los Angeles, 1976—; mem. Los Angeles County Sheriff's Res. Med. Co. Capt. U.S. Army, 1969-71. Recipient Hocks Meml. award Am. Tinnitus Assn., 1988; named Tchr. of Yr., U. So. Calif. Family Practice Dept., 1987. Fellow Am. Acad. Otolaryngology/Head and Neck Surgery; mem. AMA, Am. Neurotology Soc. (program chmn. 1976—, pres. 1998-99), Am. Soc. Mil. Otolaryngologists, Pan-Am. Assn. Otorhinolaryngology Broncho Esophagology, Jonathan Club (Los Angeles). Avocations: skiing, computers, running, swimming. Office: House Ear Clinic Inc 2100 W 3rd St Fl 1 Los Angeles CA 90057-1922

HOUSE, KAREN ELLIOTT, company executive, former editor, reporter; b. Matador, Tex., Dec. 7, 1947; d. Ted and Bailey Elliott; m. Arthur House, Apr. 5, 1975 (div. Sept. 1983); m. Peter Kann, June 4, 1984; children: Hillary, Petra, Jason, Jade. BJ, U. Tex., 1970; postgrad. Inst. Politics, Harvard U. Edn. reporter Dallas Morning News, 1970-71, with Washington bur., 1971-74; regulatory corr. Wall Street Jour., Washington, 1974-75, energy and agr. corr., 1975-78, diplomatic corr., 1978-84; fgn. editor Wall Street Jour., N.Y.C., 1984-89; v.p., Internat. Group Dow Jones & Co., 1989-95, pres. Internat. Group, 1995—; trustee Boston U.; mem. adv. bd. Ctr. Strategic Internat. Studies; mem. vis. com. Harvard U. Ctr. Internat. Affairs. Recipient Edward Weintal award for Diplomatic Reporting, Georgetown U., 1980-81, Edwin Hood award for Diplomatic Reporting Nat. Press Club, 1982, Disting. Achievement award U. So. Calif., 1984, Pulitzer prize for Internat. Reporting, 1984, Overseas Press Club Bob Considine award, 1984, 88; Harvard fellow, 1982. Fellow Nat. Acad. Arts and Scis. Home: 58 Cleveland Ln Princeton NJ 08540-3077 Office: Dow Jones & Co 200 Liberty St Fl 11 New York NY 10281-1099

HOUSE, KAY SEYMOUR, editor; b. Payson, Ill., May 18, 1924; d. Emil Aaron and Mary Gaskin (Seymour) H.; m. Ralph Barr McReynolds, Sept. 22, 1945 (div. June 1958); children: Barr, Kirk. BA, U. Ill., 1945; MA, Washington U., 1946; PhD, Stanford U., 1963. Acting instr. Ohio State U., Columbus, 1946-47; instr. Stanford (Calif.) U., 1961-63; prof. San Francisco State U., 1963-88, chair English dept., 1987-88; sr. lectr. Fulbright Program, Italy, 1968-69; resident dir. program in Italy Calif. U., Florence, 1972-74; editor-in-chief Works of J.F. Cooper, Worcester, Mass., 1990—; cons. univ presses, Calif., Mass., Mo., 1965—; chair screening commn. Fulbright Hays Scholars, Washington, 1974-77. Author: Cooper's Americans, 1965, (chpt. in book) Sphere History of Literature, 1975, 87, American Novelists Revisited, 1982; editor: The Pilot and Satanstoe, 1986, 90. V.p. Hist. Soc. Adams County, Quincy, Ill., 1989-96. Mem. MLA, Assn. Italiana di Studi Americani, Toscani Internat. del Mondo, Am. Antiquarian Soc. (fellowship 1978), Assn. Lit. Scholars and Critics, Nat. Assn. Scholars, Nat. Alumni Forum. Avocations: promoting excellence in the fine arts, golf, wildlife preservation.

HOUSE, ROBERT WILLIAM, technology management educator; b. Wellsville, Ohio, May 31, 1927; s. Kenneth Edgar and Florence Margaret (McIntosh) H; m. Pauline Mae Krebs, Sept. 4, 1948; children: Tamara Lynn, Deborah Jo, Linda Kay, Pamela Mae, Karen Ann. BS with high honor, Ohio U., Athens, 1949, MS, 1952; PhD, Pa. State U., 1959; grad. Program Mgmt. Devel., Harvard Bus. Sch., 1966. Mathematician U.S. Naval Proving Grounds, Dahlgren, Va., 1950-51; electronic scientist Wright-Patterson AFB, Dayton, Ohio, 1951-54; instr., asst. prof. Pa. State U., 1954-59; sr. fellow Battelle Meml. Inst., Columbus, Ohio, 1959-66, mgr., 1966-74; presdl. exec. U.S. State Dept., Washington, 1974-75; prof. Vanderbilt U., Nashville, 1975-81, dean, Grad. Sch., 1981-84, Ingram Disting. prof., dir. mgmt. tech. program, 1984-90, Ingram Disting. prof. engring. mgmt. emeritus, 1990, prof. elec. engring. emeritus, 1990—; adj. prof. math. Ohio State U., 1962-68; cons. Gov. of Brazil, Sao Paulo, 1975-83. Patentee spl. purpose computers, 1968. With USN, 1945-46. Recipient Achievement award Pres. Gerald Ford, 1975. Fellow IEEE (dir. 1973-76, Centennial medal, 1984), IEEE Systems, Man & Cybernetics Soc. (pres. 1965), IEEE Engring Mgmt. Soc. Avocations: travel, photography. Home: 1800 Kingsbury Dr Nashville TN 37215-5708 Office: Vanderbilt Univ Box 6188 Sta B Box 6188 Sta B Nashville TN 37235

HOUSE, STEPHEN EUGENE, information systems consultant; b. Pueblo, Colo., July 18, 1951; s. Floyd Eugene and Jewell (Brame) H.; m. Cheryl Virginia Ashby, Mar. 15, 1975; children: Deborah Lynne, Mark Stephen. BS in Bus. Info. Systems, West Coast U., 1992. Programmer Calif. Sch. Employees Assn., San Jose, 1976-79; programmer/analyst Marysville (Calif.) Joint Unified Sch. Dist., 1979-80; tech. lead Mervyns, Hayward, Calif., 1980-85, Lucky Stores, Inc., Dublin, Calif., 1985-87; project lead Northrop, Pica Rivera, Calif., 1987-92; tech. cons. Computer Profls. Inc., Charlotte, N.C., 1992-97; sys. cons. Sys. and Programming Cons., Charlotte, 1997—.

HOUSE, W(ILLIAM) MICHAEL, lawyer; b. Birmingham, Ala., Dec. 19, 1945; s. B. William and Kathryn Regina (Cantrell) H.; m. Kathryn House, Sept. 30, 1969; children: Tanner, Slade, Kate. BS, Auburn U., 1968; JD, U. Ala., 1971. Bar: Ala. 1971, D.C. 1992. Legal asst. to Congressman James M. Collins, Washington, 1971-72; atty. Ala. Supreme Ct., Montgomery, 1972-76; assoc. Odom, Argo, Enslen, Montgomery, 1976-79; chief of staff Sen. Howell Helfin, Washington, 1979-86; of counsel McNair Law Firm, Washington, 1986-88; ptnr. Shaw, Pittman et al, Washington, 1988-91; ptnr. Hogan & Hartson, Washington, 1991—, chair legis group. Pres. Ala. Young Lawyers, 1976; chmn. Ala. Citizens Conf., Ala. State Courts, 1974-75; co-chmn. Potomac Group Dem. Nat. Com., 1987-93; mem. bus. adv. coun. Auburn Sch. Bus., 1990-93. Capt. U.S. Army, 1971-80. Named Ala. Outstanding Young Man Ala. JC's, 1979. Mem. Ala. Bar Assn. (award of merit 1974), Am. Judicature Soc. (bd. dirs.), Am. Counsel Bus. Fellows (bd. dirs.), Pi Kappa Alpha (bd. dirs. Meml. Found. 1980-86). Avocations: tennis, reading, skiing. Office: Hogan & Hartson 555 13th St NW Ste 800E Washington DC 20004-1161

HOUSE-HENDRICK, KAREN SUE, nursing consultant; b. San Francisco, July 16, 1958; d. Mathas Dean and Marilyn Frances (Weigand) House. Casa Loma Coll., 1985; AS in Nursing, SUNY at Albany, 1987. Psychiat. charge nurse Woodview Calabasas (Calif.) Hosp., 1985-87, Treatment Ctrs. Am., Van Nuys, Calif., 1987-88; cons., RN Valley Village Devel. Ctr., Reseda, Calif., 1988; plastic surg. nurse George Sanders, M.D., Encino, Calif., 1986—; nurse New Image Found., 1989—, Mid Valley Youth Ctr., 1991—; dir. nursing Encino Surgicenter (Sanders), 1992—; dir. nursing Devel. Tng. Svcs. for Devel. Disabled, 1988—; nurse cons. New Horizons for Developmentally Disabled, 1993. Instr. vol. ARC. Recipient Simi Valley Free Clinic Scholarship. Mem. Encino C. of C. Home: 2526 Gayle Pl Simi

Valley CA 93065-2338 Office: 16633 Ventura Blvd Ste 110 Encino CA 91436-1834

HOUSEL, DAVID, athletic director; b. York, Oct. 18, 1946; m. Susan McIntosh. BA, Auburn U., 1969. News editor Huntsville (Ala.) News, 1969-70; from adminstrv. asst. athletic office Auburn (Ala.) U., 1970-72, instr. journalism, advisor newspaper, 1972-80, asst. dir. sports info., dir., asst. athletic dir., 1980-94, athletic dir., 1994—. Author: Saturdays to Remember, Fram the Desk of David Housel--A Collection of Auburn Stories. Mem. Phi gamma Delta, Omicron Delta Kappa, Sigma Delta Chi. Office: Auburn Univ Athletic Dept PO Box 351 Auburn AL 36831-0351

HOUSEL, DONNA JANE, artist; b. Cumberland, Md., July 21, 1949; d. Donald Glenn and Eleanor Jane (Swauger) Whitford; m. Benjiman Harry Housel, Mar. 1, 1969; 1 child, Benjiman Aaron. Grad. H.S., Hyndman, Pa. Owner West Straub Art Studio, Buffalo Mills, Pa., 1992—; instr. Allegany Arts Coun., Cumberland, Md., 1997. Vol. Red Ribbon campaign Twin Lakes Drug and Alcohol Rehab. Ctr., Somerset, Pa., 1997. Recipient 1st pl. Bird, 1995, 1st pl. Oil, 1997. Mem. Somerset County Artist Assn. (pres. 1996-97), Bedford County Arts Coun., Allegany Art Coun., Colored Pencil Soc. Am., Pa. Soc. Ornithology. Republican. Lutheran. Home and Studio: 422 Ridge Rd Buffalo Mills PA 15534-8803

HOUSEL, JERRY WINTERS, lawyer; b. Cripple Creek, Colo., Aug. 9, 1912; s. James Robert and Emma (Winters) H.; m. Mary Elaine Bever, July 8, 1941; children: James Robert, Jerry Laine, John Ora, Peter Elliott. BA, U. Wyo., 1935, JD, 1936; PhD, Am. U., 1941; HD (hon.), U. Wyo., 1996. Bar: Wyo. 1936. Assoc. Arnold and Arnold, Laramie, 1936; teaching fellow Am. U. Grad. Sch., 1937; asst. to U.S. Senator Schwartz, 1937-40; atty. FTC, 1941, War Relocation Authority, 1942; practiced in Cody, Wyo., 1946—; past owner Cody Trading Co. and Bar TL Ranch; past pres., mem. Wyo. Bd. Law Examiners, 1956-70; past chmn., dir. Key Bank formerly The Bank of Greeley, Colo.; past chmn. dir. Cmty. First Bank (formerly Key Bank-Cody); past dir. Key Bancshares Wyo. formerly 1st Wyo. Bancorp; chmn. Frosh LLC. Mem. Cody City Coun., 1950; past dem. nat. committeeman, Wyo. With USNR, 1943-46. Mem. ABA (ho. of dels. 1965-67, 76-94, bd. govs. 1989-92), Am. Judicature Soc. (bd. dirs. 1967), Wyo. State Bar (pres. 1964), Cody C. of C. (pres. 1953), Am. Legion (comdr. Cody post 1951). Office: 1100 Rumsey Ave Cody WY 82414-3606

HOUSEL, NATALIE RAE NORMAN, physical therapist; b. Syracuse, N.Y., July 25, 1959; d. Rudolf Anthony and Pauline Mary (Proia) Norman; m. Thomas Hugh Housel, June 25, 1988; children: Heather, Tommy and Tiffany (twins). BS in Phys. Therapy, Ithaca Coll., 1981; MA in Applied Psychology, Fairfield U., 1986; student, UCF-FGCU, 1998—. Cert. geriatric clin. specialist Am. Bd. Phys. Therapy Specialties. Staff phys. therapist N.Y., 1981-85; sr. phys. therapist Rome (N.Y.) Devel. Ctr., 1987-89; asst. dir. phys. therapy Tioga (N.Y.) Gen. Hosp. and Nursing Home, 1989-91, Corning (N.Y.) Hosp., 1991-92; asst. dir. rehab. svcs. Arnot Ogden Med. Ctr., Elmira, N.Y., 1992-93; sch. phys. therapist Collier County Pub. Schs., Naples, Fla., 1993-94; pvt. practice phys. therapist Ft. Myers, Fla., 1995-96; dir. phys. therapy Beverly Enterprises, Ft. Myers, Fla., 1995-96; therapy supr. Lee Meml. Health Sys. Health Park Care Ctr., Ft. Myers, Fla., 1996-97; rehab. mgr. occupl., speech and phys. therapy Lee Meml. Home Health, Fort Myers, Fla., 1997-98; instr phys. therapy assts. Broome C.C., 1989, wound care nutrition for Hosp. Food Adminstrs., 1997; oral examiner for phys. therapy licensees N.Y. State, Albany, 1988-90. Adult group leader Family Faith Formation, St. Columbkill Ch., Ft. Myers, Fla., 1996-97. Fellow Am. Acad. Wound Mgmt. (cert. wound care specialist); mem. APA, Am. Phys. Therapy Assn., Am. Soc. on Aging. Avocations: flute, piano, swimming. Home: 1626 N Hermitage Rd Fort Myers FL 33919-6409

HOUSER, DONALD RUSSELL, mechanical engineering educator, consultant; b. River Falls, Wis., Sept. 2, 1941; s. Elmont Ellsworth and Helen (Bunker) H.; m. Colleen Marie Collins, Dec. 30, 1967; children: Kelle, Kerri, Joshua. BS, U. Wis., 1964, MS, 1965, PhD, 1969. Registered profl. engr., Ohio. Instr. U. Wis., Madison, 1967-68; from asst. prof. to prof. Ohio State U., Columbus, 1968—, dir. Gear Dynamics and Gear Noise Rsch. Lab., 1979—, dir. Ctr. for Automotive Rsch., 1994—; v.p. Gear Rsch. Inst., State Coll., Pa., 1990—. Author: Gear Noise, 1991; contbg. editor Sound and Vibration mag., 1988-96; assoc. editor Jour. Mech. Design, 1993-94; mem. adv. bd. JSME Internat. Jour.; contbr. articles to profl. jours. Elder St. Andrews Presbyn. Ch., Columbus, 1972-75. Fellow ASME (legis. liaison Ohio coun. 1976-80, Century II medallion 1980); mem. Am. Gear Mfrs. Assn. (acad.), Soc. Automotive Engrs., Am. Helicopter Soc. Roman Catholic. Achievements include development of technology for measuring gear transmission error under load. Office: Ohio State U 206 W 18th Ave Columbus OH 43210-1189

HOUSER, GORDON SINCLAIR, editor; b. Emporia, Kans., Aug. 22, 1953; s. Robert Carol and Mildred Olive (Benedict) H.; m. Theresa Jeanne Schuler; children: Ethan, Abri. BA, Wichita (Kans.) State U., 1976. Editl. asst. The Mennonite, Newton, Kans., 1978-84; asst. editor The Mennonite, Newton, 1984-92, editor, 1992—. Chmn. bd. dirs. Newton Area Peace Ctr., 1984-87. Recipient Seaton award Kans. Quar., 1986, 3d pl. critical rev. award Evang. Press Assn., 1990, 3d pl. editl. award, 1993, hon. mention editl. award Associated Ch. Press, 1993. Mem. Meetinghouse (treas. 1993-99), Coun. on Ch. and Media. Mennonite. Avocations: writing fiction, book reviewing, biking, preaching. Home: 417 W 11th St Newton KS 67114-1717 Office: The Mennonite 722 N Main St Newton KS 67114-1819

HOUSER, HAROLD BYRON, epidemiologist; b. North Liberty, Ind., Nov. 22, 1921; s. Edgar Allen and Gladys Chloe (Stillson) H.; m. Clara Jane Goin, Sept. 18, 1944; children: Cristene, Edgar, John, Susan, James. AB, Ind. U., 1942, MD, 1944. Intern U.S. Marine Hosp., New Orleans, 1944-45; resident Crile VA Hosp., Cleve., 1947-49; asst. prof. medicine SUNY, Syracuse, 1952-58; asst. prof. medicine and community health Case Western Res. U., 1958-64, assoc. prof., 1965-74, prof. epidemiology, 1974-92, prof. emeritus, 1992—, chmn. dept. biometry, 1975-85, chmn. dept. epidemiology and biostats., 1985-92; cons. in field. Contbr. numerous articles to profl. jours. Served with U.S. Army, 1945-47, 49-52. Recipient Group Lasker award Am. Pub. Health Assn., 1954, Disting. Civilian award Dept. Def., 1973. Fellow Infectious Diseases Soc.; mem. Am. Epidemiol. Soc. (pres. 1991). Home: 10409 E Windflower Ct Sun Lakes AZ 85248-9289

HOUSER, NATHAN, philosophy educator; b. Auburn, Ind., May 10, 1944; s. Frank F. and Viola M. (Hose) H.; m. Aleta Halme, Dec. 12, 1975; children: Jesse, Ezra. PhD, U. Waterloo, 1985. Asst. prof. philosophy Ind. U., Indpls., 1986-91, assoc. prof. philosophy, 1991-97, prof. philosophy, 1997—; assoc. editor Writings of Charles S. Peirce, Indpls., 1983-85, assoc. editor, 1985-93, gen. editor, 1993—; dir. Peirce Edition Project, 1993—. Adv. bd. Modern Logic Pub., 1993—; mem. editl. bd. Internat. Jour. Applied Semiotics, 1994—; co-editor: Essential Peirce, 1992, vol. 2, 1998, Studies in the Logic of Charles Sanders Peirce, 1997; adv. bd. Centro Interamericano de Semiotica C.S. Peirce. V.p. Centro Interamericano de Semiótica C.S. Peirce. Fulbright-Hays fellowship, 1978; devel. grant Prince Charatible Trusts, 1996, grant for collaborative rsch. Nat. Endowment for Humanities, 1997. Mem. Am. Philos. Assn., Soc. Advancement Am. Philosophy, Charles S. Peirce Soc., History of Sci. Soc., Semiotic Soc. Am., Assn. Documentary Editing. Office: CA545 IUPUI 425 University Blvd Indianapolis IN 46202-5148

HOUSER, RONALD EDWARD, lawyer, mediator; b. Fairbury, Nebr., Aug. 11, 1949; s. Edward Erle and Lois Charlotte (Dux) H.; m. Linda Marie Webber, June 13, 1971 (div. 1985); children: Angela Marie, Brian Edward, Darren James; m. Beatrice Virginia McMullen Bupp, July 24, 1993. DVM, U. Mo., 1974; MS, Ohio State U., 1979; JD, U. Ga., 1990. Bar: Ga. 1990, U.S. Dist. Ct. (mid., no. and so. dist.) Ga. 1990, U.S. Ct. Appeals (11th cir.) 1990, U.S. Ct. Mil. Appeals 1993, U.S. Supreme Ct. 1993. Asst. instr. Univ. Nebr., Lincoln, 1979-83; owner, mgr. Lincoln Animal Health Clinic, 1983-85; atty. Cook, Noell, Tolley, Bates & Michael, Athens, Ga., 1990—. Contbr. articles to profl. jours. Mem. Nebr. State Bd. Health, 1980-84. Mem. Nat. Lawyers Assn., Nebr. Vet. Med. Assn. (dist. pres. 1979-81), Christian Legal Soc., Res. Officers Assn., Am. Legion, Phi Alpha Delta, Sigma Xi. Avocations: sports, reading, gardening. Home: PO Box 502 Athens GA 30603-0502 Office: Cook Noell Tolley Bates & Michael LLP 304 E Washington St Athens GA 30601-2751

HOUSER, RUTH G., data communications manager; b. Virginia Beach, Va., Feb. 25, 1953. BS in Acctg. cum laude, Wheeling Coll., 1975. CPA, Fla., Ga., W.Va. Sr. acct. Price Waterhouse, Pitts., 1975-79; mgr. internal control Lockheed Space Opers. Co., Cape Canaveral, Fla., 1980-84; mgr. info. systems AT&T, Orlando, Fla., 1984-85; mgr. data systems group AT&T, Morristown, N.J., 1985-86, mgr., CFO systems architecture, 1986-87; fin. dir. France and Italy AT&T, Paris, 1987-89; mgr. acctg. policy AT&T, Morristown, 1989-90; dir. billing svcs. AT&T, Bridgewater, N.J., 1990-92; controller, Network Wireless Systems AT&T, Morristown, N.J., 1992-93; fin. mgr., leader billing team WorldPartners/WorldSource AT&T, Bridgewater, N.J., 1993-95; cons. AT&T Solutions, 1995; dist. mgr. Lucent Technologies Intellectual Property, Coral Gables, Fla., 1995-98; revenue assurance mgr. Data Networking Svcs., St. Petersburg, Fla., 1998-99; CFO, data networking, mergers, acquisitions strategy & implementation Lucent Technologies, St. Petersburg; tax cons., Atlanta, 1979-83; fin. cons. Wheeling Coll., 1975; dir. CPA forum AT&T CFO, Morristown, 1988-90. Vol. C. Dillon Libr., Bedminster, N.J., 1985, v.p. bd. trustees, 1988-92; sec., trustee Friends of C. Dillon Libr., 1992-95; committeewoman Somerset County Reps. Dist. 5, Bedminster, 1993-95, Bedminster Twp., 1995. Mem. AICPA, FICPA. Avocations: internat. travel, theatre, reading, sports. Home: 1100 Pinellas Bayway S Apt H3 Tierra Verde FL 33715-2102 Office: Lucent Technologies Room 2A118 11399 16th Ct N Saint Petersburg FL 33716-2328

HOUSER, THOMAS HENRI, voice educator; b. Hopewell, Va., June 30; s. H.J. and Mary Lee (Thrift) H.;. Cert. in voice, Peabody Conservatory of Music; BA, Goddard Coll.; MA, Norwich U.; PhD, Fairfax U., London; adv. study, Accademia Musicale, Chigiana Siena, Italy, Alexander Inst., London. Voice tchr. Peabody Inst., Balt., NYU, N.Y.C., Cath. U., Washington; dir. vocal pedagogy Marywood U., Scranton, Pa., 1986—; pvt. tchr. New Holland, Pa., N.Y.C.; cons. in U.S., Can., Europe, Asia and Africa. Author: The Gift of Voice, Articulation: The Dance of Sound, Poets, Painters, and Poulenc; Movement and Awareness, The Gift of Voice: A History of Voice Teaching. Recipient Adv. Study award Govt. Italy, Adv. Study award Monte dei Paschi Banko, Italy, Charles Purcell award N.Y. Studio of the Theatre, Lillie Lehmann award, Jean de Reszke award, Van L. Lawrence fellow of The Voice Found. Mem. Nat. Assn. Tchrs. Singing, N.Y. Singing Tchrs. Assn., Voice and Speech Trainers Assn., Voice Found.

HOUSEWORTH, RICHARD COURT, state agency administrator; b. Harveyville, Kans., Jan. 18, 1928; s. Court Henry and Mabel (Lynch) H.; m. Laura Louise Jennings, Nov. 1, 1952; children: Louise, Lucile, Court. B.S., U. Kans., 1950. Mgmt. trainee Lawrence Nat. Bank, Kans., 1951-52; pres. 1st Nat. Bank, Harveyville, 1952-55; exec. v.p. Ariz. Bank, Phoenix, 1955-87, cons., 1987-88; dir. Export-Import Bank of the US, Washington, 1988-91; alt. U.S. exec. dir. The Inter-American Devel. Bank, Washington, 1991-93; supt. of banks, Banking Dept. State of Ariz., 1993—; chmn. Conf. of State Bank Suprs., Washington. Past pres. Better Bus. Bur., Tucson; past chmn. bd. Pacific Coast Banking Sch. U. Wash.; past pres. Barrow Neurol. Inst. of St. Joseph's Hosp.; past chmn. Valley of the Sun Visitors and Conv. Bur. Served with U.S. Army, 1946-48. Recipient 1st Disting. Service award Scottsdale Jaycees, 1962. Mem. Ariz. C. of C. (1st pres., dir.), Tucson C. of C. (past pres.), Am. Inst. Banking (past pres. Maricopa chpt.), Ariz. Bankers Assn. (past pres.), Urban League of Phoenix (past chmn.), Paradise Valley Club, Met. Club, Phi Delta Theta. Republican. Episcopalian. Home: 83 Colonia Miramonte Paradise Valley AZ 85253 Office: Supt of Banks 2910 N 44th St Ste 310 Phoenix AZ 85018-7256

HOUSMAN, ARNO DAVID, urologist; b. Mar. 4, 1951. BS, Cornell U., 1973; MD, SUNY, Bklyn., 1980. Diplomate Am. Bd. Urology. Resident in surgery, asst. instr. dept. surgery SUNY Downstate Med. Ctr., Bklyn., 1980-83; asst. resident in urology Yale-New Haven (Conn.) Hosp., 1983-85, chief resident in urology, 1986; instr. dept. surgery Yale U. Sch. Medicine, New Haven, 1986-87; sr. attending Phelps Meml. Hosp. Ctr., Sleepy Hollow, N.Y., 1986—; asst. attending Westchester County Med. Ctr., Valhalla, N.Y., 1986—; vis. attending Yale-New Haven Hosp., 1988—; asst. attending Cornell-N.Y. Hosp., N.Y.C., 1989—; courtesy staff Cmty. Hosp. Dobbs Ferry, N.Y., 1989—; asst. attending St. Agnes Hosp., White Plains, N.Y., 1993—; v.p. med. staff Phelps Meml. Hosp. Ctr., 1995-97; mem. Castle Connolly Med. Ltd. Contbr. articles to profl. jours. Mem. Am. Urol. Assn., Am. Assn. Clin. Urologists, N.Y. Med. Soc., N.Y. State Urologic Assn., Westchester Med. Soc., Yale Urologic Soc., Hudson Ind. Practice Assn. (bd. dirs.). Office: Arno D Housman MD 325 S Highland Ave Briarcliff Manor NY 10510

HOUSNER, GEORGE WILLIAM, retired civil engineering educator, consultant; b. Saginaw, Mich., Dec. 9, 1910; s. Charles and Sophie Ida (Schust) H. BSCE, U. Mich., 1933; PhD, Calif. Inst. Tech., 1941. Registered profl. engr., Calif. Engr. U.S. Corps Engrs., Los Angeles, 1941-42; ops. analyst 15th Air Force, Libya and Italy, 1943-45; prof. engring. Calif. Inst. Tech., Pasadena, 1945—, now prof.emeritus; earthquake engring. cons. Pasadena, 1945—; mem. Gov.'s Earthquake Coun., 1971-76, L.A. County Earthquake Commn., 1971-72; mem. adv. panel on Earthquake Hazard Nat. Acad. Scis., 1981-83; chmn. com. on earthquake engring. NRC, 1983-92, com. on internat. decade natural hazard reduction, 1986-88; chmn. seismic adv. bd. CALTRANS, 1990-94. Author 3 textbooks; contbr. articles to profl. jours. Recipient Disting. Civilian Svc. award U.S. War Dept., 1945, Bendix Rsch. award Am. Soc. Engring. Edn., 1967, Nat. medal Sci., 1988, The Washington award Western Soc. Engrs., 1995. Mem. NAE (Founders award 1991), NAS, Seismol. Soc. Am. (pres. 1977-78, medal 1981), ASCE (von Karman medal 1972, Newmark medal 1981), Internat. Assn. Earthquake Engring. (pres. 1969-73), Earthquake Engring. Rsch. Inst. (pres. 1954-65), Japan Acad. Office: Calif Inst Tech Dept Engring 211 Thomas Lab Pasadena CA 91125

HOUSNER, JEANETTE ANN, artist, jeweler; b. Richland Center, Wis., Oct. 9, 1940; d. Richard Edward and Ardyce Evelyn (Kotvis) H.; m. Christos John Papadopoulos, Oct. 12, 1964 (div. Aug. 1988); children: Rachel, Sarah. BA, Milw.-Downer Coll., 1962; MFA, Cranbrook Acad. Art, 1964. Instr., office clk. Indian Arts and Crafts Bd., Sitka, Alaska, 1965-66; instr. jewelry Cen. Wash. U., Ellensburg, Wash., 1967-78; bus. mgr. Laughing Horse Summer Theatre, Ellensburg, 1992-93; owner, artist Jewelry, Metalsmithing, Ellensburg, 1966—. Jewelry represented on slides in permanent collection Cranbrook Acad. Art; evening bag Art to Wear, Larson Gallery, Yakima, Wash., 1990 (Best of Accessories award), pendant 21st Kittitas County Show, Gallery One, Ellensburg, 1991 (Outstanding 3-Dimensional award), pin 40th Cen. Wash. Exhbn., Larson Gallery, Yakima, 1996 (hon. mention), pendant 26th Kittitas County Show, Gallery One, Ellensburg, 1997 (hon. mention); exhibited in numerous group shows, 1962—. Office worker Habitat for Humanity, Ellensburg, 1994-96. Mem. AAUW, NOW, LWV, Soc. N.Am. Goldsmiths, Coll. Art Assn., Am. Craft Coun., Larson Gallery Guild. Home and Office: PO Box 636 Ellensburg WA 98926-0636

HOUSTON, ALFRED DEARBORN, energy company executive; b. Quincy, Mass., Aug. 14, 1940; s. Alfred Dearborn and Merriland (Westwood) H.; m. Patricia Selko, Oct. 23, 1965; children—Melissa, Sherriden. BS in Econs., U. Pa., 1962; AMP, Harvard U., 1982. With New Eng. Electric System and subs., 1962—, treas., 1983-84; exec., CFO New Eng. System and subs., 1984-98; CFO, v.p. fin. New Eng. Electric System and subs., 1985-87, sr. v.p., 1987-93, exec. v.p., 1994-98, chmn., 1998—; v.p. New Eng. Power Service Co., 1975-76, pres., 1993—; v.p., dist. mgr. Narragansett Electric Co., Providence, 1976-77, v.p., treas., 1977-98; v.p. New Eng. Power Co., 1983-98; dir. Arkwright Ins. Co., 1998—, Mass. Bus. Round Table. Active United Way So. New Eng., 1976-78; trustee Boston Ballet, 1994—, Nichols Coll., 1994—, Mass. Taxpayers Found., 1994—. Mem. U. Pa. Club Boston (past pres., trustee). Office: New England Electric System 25 Research Dr Westborough MA 01582-0001

HOUSTON, ALLAN WADE, professional basketball player; b. Louisville, Apr. 4, 1971; married. BA in African-Am. Studies, U. Tenn., 1993. Guard Detroit Pistons, 1993-96, New York Knicks, 1996—. Achievements include NBA Draft first round eleventh pick, 1993. Office: New York Knicks Madison Square Garden 2 Penn Plz New York NY 10121-0001*

HOUSTON, ALMA FAYE, psychiatrist; b. Chgo., Oct. 4, 1944; d. Harlan Eugene and Ruth Viola (Minster) H. BA, U. Ark., 1966; BSM, MD, U. Ark., Little Rock, 1969, JD, 1980. Diplomate Am. Bd. Psychiatry and Neurology. Child psychiatrist Akron Child Guidance Ctr. Republican. Baptist. Avocation: percussionist in a folk music band. Office: Akron Child Guidance Ctr 87 N Canton Rd Akron OH 44305

HOUSTON, BILL, state commissioner. BS in Bus. Adminstrn., U. Ark., 1960; cert., Rutgers U., 1968. From bank examiner to regional dir. Memphis Region Fed. Deposit Ins. Corp., Washington, 1960-93; ret., 1993; pres., prin. owner Banctactics, Inc., Maryville, Tenn., 1994-95; dep. commr. State Tenn. Dept. Fin. Instns., Nashville, 1995-96, commr., 1996—; instr. FDIC Tng. Ctr., 1982-93, asst. dir., 1984-85; instr. Mid-South Sch. Banking, U. Memphis, 1994—; bd. mem., treas. Conf. State Bank Suprs., Washington, 1997—; state liaison com. Fed. Fin. Instns. Examination Coun., Washington, 1997—; bd. dirs. Collateral Pool Bd., Nashville; spkr. in field. Sr. exec. fellow Harvard U., Cambridge, Mass., 1982. Office: Fin Instn Dept 500 Charlotte Ave Fl 4 Nashville TN 37243-1401*

HOUSTON, CAROLINE MARGARET, editor; b. Harrogate, Eng., May 8, 1964; came to U.S., 1975; d. William H. and Sylvia (Fineron) H. BA in Internat. Studies and Mid East Studies, George Mason U., 1989, postgrad., 1990—. Cert. fluency in Farsi and French; cert. diamontologist and gemologist Diamond Coun. Am.; lic. pvt. pilot. Editor Maxim Techs., Vienna, Va., 1988-89; sec. Am. Near East Refugee Aid, Washington and Israel, 1989-90; asst. sec., treas. World Resources Inst., Washington, 1990-91; asst. dir. client svcs. Britches of Georgetowne, McLean, Va., 1991-92; reference copyright sr. clk., preservation technician Libr. Congress, Washington, 1992-95, copyright office automation asst., 1995—; devel. cons. Legacy Internat., Jerusalem, 1990-91. Violinist with semi-profl. orchs., 1972-84. Mem. NOW, Amnesty Internat.; chmn., treas. Episcopal Ch. of Va., No. Va. Chpt. Holy Land Com. Mem. NAFE, Internat. Studies Assn., Mid. East Inst., Libr. Congress Profl. Assn. (chair membership com., co-chair pub. affairs com.), Atlantic Coun. U.S. Avocations: study of languages, piloting, martial arts, computer programs. Home: 8174 Peakwood Ct Apt 6 Manassas VA 20111-2143

HOUSTON, C(LARENCE) STUART, radiologist, educator; b. Williston, N.D., Sept. 26, 1927; s. Clarence Joseph and Sigridur (Christianson) H.; m. Mary Isabel Belcher, Aug. 12, 1951; children: Stanley, Margaret, David, Donald. MD, U. Man., Winnipeg, Can., 1951; DLitt, U. Sask., Saskatoon, Can., 1987. Demonstrator in anatomy U. Sask., 1960-61, teaching fellow in radiology, 1963-64, lectr., 1964-65, asst. prof., 1965-67, assoc. prof., 1967-69, prof., 1969-95, emeritus prof., 1995—, head dept. med. imaging, 1982-87. Author: To the Arctic by Canoe, 1974, Pioneer of Vision, 1980, Arctic Ordeal, 1984, R.G. Ferguson, Crusader, 1991, Arctic Artist, 1994; editor jour. Can. Assn. Radiologists, 1976-81. Recipient Roland Michener Conservation award Can. Wildlife Fedn., 1986, Douglas H. Pimlott Conservation award Can. Nature Fedn., 1988, Ralph D. Bird award Man. Naturalists' Soc., 1989, Doris Huestis Speirs award Soc. Can. Ornithologists, 1989, Eugene Eisenmann medal Linnean Soc. N.Y., 1990, Sask. Order of Merit, 1992, Officer of Order of Can., 1993. Mem. Can. Soc. for History of Medicine (pres. 1987-89), Royal Coll. Physicians and Surgeons (mem. coun. 1984-90, chmn. specialty com. 1984-88), Am. Ornithologists' Union (mem. coun. 1978-80, chmn. memls. com. 1984—, v.p. 1990-91). Avocations: bird banding. Home: 863 University Dr, Saskatoon, SK Canada S7N 0J8 Office: U Hosp Dept Med Imaging, 103 Hospital Dr, Saskatoon, SK Canada S7N 0W8

HOUSTON, DAVID WINSTON, federal judge; b. 1944. BBA, U. Miss., 1966, JD, 1969. Spl. agt. FBI, 1969-72; ptnr. Houston, Chamberlin & Houston, 1972-83; asst. dist. atty. U.S. Ct. Appeals (1st cir.), 1975-76; atty. gen. City of Aberdeen, Miss., 1976-83; former mcpl. judge City of Aberdeen; chief bankruptcy judge U.S. Dist. Ct. (no. dist.) Miss., Aberdeen, 1983—. Mem. ABA, Fed. Bar Assn., Nat. Conf. Bankruptcy Judges (bd. govs. 1984-87, 89-91, pres. 1993-94), Am. Coll. Bankruptcy, 1st Jud. Dist. Bar Assn., Miss. Bar Assn. (bd. bar commrs. 1982-85), Monroe County Bar Assn. Fax: (601) 369-2635. Office: US Dist Ct (no dist) Miss Fed bldg 301 W Commerce St Aberdeen MS 39730

HOUSTON, DOROTHY MIDDLETON, elementary education educator; b. LaGrange, Ga., Oct. 23, 1936; d. Robert Meriwether and Marie Elizabeth (Davis) Middleton; m. Richard Gray Houston Sr., June 3, 1956; children: Jean, Ann, Richard Jr., Thomas Sandy. BS in Edn., U. Ga., 1958, MEd, 1970. Tchr. Auburn (Ga.) Elem. Sch., 1958-59; instr. women's dept. phys. edn. U. Ga., Athens, 1970-71; tchr. phys. edn. Woodstock (Ga.) Elem. Sch., 1971-72, Brumby Elem. Sch., Marietta, Ga., 1972-77, Murdock Elem. Sch., Marietta, Ga., 1977-81; tchr. Teasley Elem. Sch., Smyrna, Ga., 1981-95; retired, 1995. Childcare program adminstr. Internat. Student Conf., Toccoa, Ga., 1986; tchr. tng. Pub. Schs. Ga., 1969-92. Mem. Phi Kappa Phi. Baptist. Avocations: fitness, recreational crafts, cooking, gardening. Home: 1849 SErvice Dr NE Marietta GA 30066-1917

HOUSTON, E. JAMES, JR., bank officer; b. Highland Park, Mich., Sept. 25, 1939; s. Ernest James and Frieda Mary (Milligan) H.; m. Ann Draper, Dec. 16, 1961; children: James Lee, Jay Douglas. B.S. in Finance, Wayne State U., 1964, M.B.A., 1967. Asst. v.p. Bank of the Commonwealth, Detroit, 1957-69; v.p. Birmingham Bloomfield Bank, Mich., 1969-70; pres. Birmingham Bloomfield Bank, 1970-71; exec. v.p. Fidelity Bank Mich., Birmingham, 1971; pres. Houston & Assos., Inc., Birmingham, 1971-91; mgr. loan rev. Republic Bancorp Inc., Ann Arbor, Mich., 1991-93, mgr. loan control, 1993-94, loan control officer, 1994-95, v.p. loan control, 1995—; lectr. fin. Wayne State U. Sch. Bus. Adminstrn., Detroit, 1971—. Active Bloomfield Hills Hockey Assn.; pres. pro tem Village of Bingham Farms Village Council; chmn. Southfield Twp. Citizens' Com.; v.p. Hickory Hollow Homeowners Assn.; trustee Southeastern Oakland County Water Authority; mem. Community House Assn., Birmingham; bd. dirs. CATV, Birmingham YMCA; mem. parents council Brookside Sch., Cranbrook, Mich.; pres. Brookside Sch. Dads Club; mem. Cranbrook Arena Com. Mem. Birmingham-Bloomfield C. of C., Greater Detroit C. of C. Republican. Presbyterian. Club: Wayne State U. Alumni; Lodge: Rotary. Home: 2807 Charter Dr Apt 203 Troy MI 48083-1324 Office: Republic Bancorp Inc 1700 N Woodward Ave Bloomfield Hills MI 48304-2211

HOUSTON, ELIZABETH REECE MANASCO, correctional education consultant; b. Birmingham, Ala., June 19, 1935; d. Reuben Cleveland and Beulah Elizabeth (Reece) Manasco; m. Joseph Brantley Houston; 1 child, Joseph Brantley Houston III. BS, U. Tex., 1956; MEd, Boston Coll., 1969. Cert. elem. tchr., Calif., cert. spl. edn. tchr., Calif., cert. community coll. instr., Calif.; cert. adminstr., Calif. Tchr., elem. Ridgefield (Conn.) Schs., 1962-63; staff, spl. edn. Sudbury (Mass.) Schs., 1965-68; staff intern Wayland (Mass.) High Sch., 1972; tchr., home bound Northampton (Mass.) Schs., 1972-73; program dir. Jack Douglas Ctr., San Jose, Calif., 1974-76; tchr. specialist spl. edn., coord. classroom svcs., dir. alternative schs. Santa Clara County Office Edn., San Jose, Calif., 1986-94; instr. San Jose State U., 1980-86, U. Calif., Santa Cruz, 1982-85, Santa Clara U., 1991-94; cons. Houston Rsch. Assocs., Saratoga, Calif., 1981—. Author: (manual) Behavior Management for School Bus Drivers, 1980, Classroom Management, 1984, Synergistic Learning, 1986, Learning Disabilities in Psychology for Correctional Education, 1992. Recipient President's award Soc. Photo-Optical Instrumentation Engrs., 1979, Classroom Mgmt. Program award Sch. Bds. Assn., 1984, Svc. to Youth award, Juvenile Ct. Sch. Adminstrs. of Calif., 1989-94; grantee Santa Clara County Office Edn. Tchr. Advisor Program U.S. Sec. Edn., 1983-84. Home: 12150 Country Squire Ln Saratoga CA 95070-3444

HOUSTON, FRANK MATT, dermatologist; b. New Orleans, Dec. 15, 1939; s. Matt Francis and Amanda Vallie (Welch) H.; m. Helen Butler, Apr. 24, 1965; children: F. Matt, Catherine E.C., Amanda J.B. BS, La. State U., 1960, MD, 1964. Diplomate Am. Bd. Dermatology. Intern Johns Hopkins U., Balt., resident; physician, dermatologist Greensboro (N.C.) Dermatology Assocs., 1970—; cons. Moses H. Cone Hosp., Greensboro, N.C., Wesley Long Hosp. Greensboro, 1970—; adj. asst clin. prof. dermatology U. N.C.

Sch. of Medicine, Chapel Hill, 1980—. Bd. dirs. Greensboro Hist. Mus., Greensboro Preservation Soc., Greensboro Symphony Soc., Greensboro Opera Co. Capt. U.S. Army, 1965-71. Fellow Am. Acad. Dermatology; mem. AMA. N.C. Soc. Medicine, Royal Coll. of Physicians, Am. Coll. Physicians, Am. Skin Assn. (scientific adv. com. to bd. dirs.), Greensboro City Club (bd. dirs.). Republican. Episcopalian. Avocations: travel, aerobics, music. Office: Greensboro Dermatology 2704 Saint Jude St Greensboro NC 27405-3670

HOUSTON, GEORGE R., college president. BSBA, Georgetown U. 1st in class, 1961; MBA, George Washington U., 1967; DHH (hon.), Georgetown U., 1982. CPA, D.C. Acct. Schumaker & Yates CPAs, Washington, 1961-66; asst. prof. acctg. Georgetown U., Washington, 1966-92, disting. prof., 1992-94, treas., 1970-92, v.p. for fin. affairs and treas., 1974-90, sr. v.p. and treas., 1990-92, mng. dir. endowment fund, 1992-94; pres. Mt. St. Mary's Coll., Emmitsburg, Md., 1994—; site visitor Middle States Assn. Acad. Accreditation Svc., 1974-89, fin. cons., 1991-93, fin. reviewer, 1993; mem. bd. cons. Riggs Nat. Bank; sr. exec. adv. coun. Met. Washington Minority Bus. Enterprises; mem. Pres.' Commn. on White House Fellowships Selection Panel. Contbr. articles to profl. jours.; presenter papers to ednl. and fin. confs. Mem. Holy Trinity Ch. Adminstrv. Coun., Nat. Com. of Arts for the Handicapped, Woodstock Theol. Ctr.; adj. lectr. in acctg. Georgetown U., 1962-66. Mem. AICPA, D.C. Inst. CPA's (1st place achievment award 1961), Nat. Assn. Coll. and Univ. Officers, Georgetown U. Alumni Assn. (ann. award 1976), C. of C. Frederick County, Beta Gamma Sigma (hon.), Phi Lambda Theta (hon.). Office: Mount St Mary's Coll Office of Pres 16300 Old Emmitsburg Rd Emmitsburg MD 21727*

HOUSTON, GERRY ANN, oncologist; b. Baldwyn, Miss., July 16, 1953; d. Jeff Davis and Frances Holland (Agnew) Goodson; m. Terry L. Houston, Dec. 18, 1976 (dec. May 1987); 1 child, Claire Holland; m. Abe John Malouf, July 23, 1988. BA, U. Miss., 1974, MD, 1978. Diplomate Am. Bd. Internal Medicine, Am. Bd. Medical Oncology, Am. Bd. Hospice and Palliative Care. Intern U. Med. Ctr., Jackson, Miss., 1978-79, resident, 1979-81, fellow oncology, 1981-83; ptnr. Jackson (Miss.) Oncology Assocs., 1987—; staff physician Miss. Bapt. Med. Ctr., Jackson, 1983—, Meth. Med. Ctr., Jackson, 1983—, St. Dominic Hosp., Jackson, 1983—, River Oaks Hosp., Jackson, 1983—, Univ. Med. Ctr., Jackson, 1983—; med. dir. Hospice of Ctrl. Miss., Jackson, 1989—; mem. exec. com. Baptist Med. Ctr., 1994; med. dir. Bapt. Comprehensive Breast Ctr., 1997—. Contbr. articles to profl. jours. Chmn. exec. com. Miss. divsn. Am. Cancer Soc., 1993-95, pres., bd. dirs., 1989-93. Clin. rsch. fellow Am. Cancer Soc. Fellow ACP; mem. AMA, Nat. Hospice Orgn., Acad. Hospice Physicians, So. Assn. Oncology, Am. Soc. Clin. Oncology, Alpha Omega Alpha. Episcopalian. Avocations: jogging, reading, snow skiing. Office: Jackson Oncology Assocs 1190 N State St Ste 501 Jackson MS 39202-2413

HOUSTON, IVAN JAMES, insurance company executive; b. Los Angeles, June 15, 1925; s. Norman Oliver and Doris Talbot (Young) H.; m. Philippa Elizabeth Jones, July 15, 1946; children—Pamela, Kathleen, Ivan Abbott. B.S., U. Calif. at Berkeley, 1948; postgrad., U. Man., 1948-49; LLD, U. La Verne, 1993. With Golden State Mut. Life Ins. Co., Los Angeles, 1948—; v.p., actuary Golden State Mut. Life Ins. Co., 1962-66, sr. v.p., actuary, 1966-70, pres., chief exec. officer, 1970-77, chmn., pres., 1977-80, chmn., chief exec. officer, 1980-90, chmn., 1990—; dir. First Interstate Bank Calif., Pacific Telesis Corp., Family Savs. Mem. L.A. World Affairs Coun., 1970—; chmn. ctrl. region United Way, Inc., L.A., 1973-75, mem. corp. bd. dirs., 1973-80, v.p., 1973-75; bd. dirs. M & M Assn., L.A. Urban League, pres., 1977—; bd. fellows Claremont U. Ctr., 1972-80; bd. regents Loyola Marymount U., 1972-75, 79-82; bd. visitors Anderson Grad. Sch. Mgmt., UCLA, 1990-93; pres. City of L.A. Human Rels. Commn., 1993-95. With Inf. AUS, 1944-45. Decorated Purple Heart, Bronze Star; knight comdr. Order St. Gregory the Great. Fellow Life Office Mgmt. Inst.; mem. Am. Acad. Actuaries, Am. Soc. Pension Actuaries, Internat. Actuarial Assn., Los Angeles Actuarial Club, Conf. Cons. Actuaries (assoc.), Am. Coun. Life Ins. (dir.), Life Office Mgmt. Assn. (dir., mem. exec. com. 1972-75, chmn. 1979), Calif. C. of C. (dir.), Los Angeles Area C. of C. (dir.), Town Hall, Calif. Club, Cosmos Club, Kappa Alpha Psi, Sigma Pi Phi. Roman Catholic. Club: Calif. (Los Angeles). Home: 5111 S Holt Ave Los Angeles CA 90056-1117 Office: 1999 W Adams Blvd Los Angeles CA 90018-3500

HOUSTON, JAMES D., writer; b. San Francisco, Nov. 10, 1933; s. Albert Dudley and Alice Loretta (Wilson) H.; m. Jeanne Wakatsuki, Mar. 27, 1957; children: Corinne, Joshua, Gabrielle. BA in Drama, San Jose (Calif.) State U., 1956; MA in Lit., Stanford U., 1962. Lectr. in writing Stanford U., 1968-69; lectr. in writing U. Calif., Santa Cruz, 1969-83, vis. prof., 1987-93; disting. vis. writer U. Hawaii, Honolulu, 1983-84; Allen T. Gilliland chair in telecomm. San Jose State U., 1985-86; vis. writer U. Mich., Ann Arbor, fall 1985, U. Oreg., Eugene, 1994; mem. adv. bd. Squaw Valley Cmty. of Writers, Calif., 1990—, Tandy Beal Dance Co., Santa Cruz, 1985—, Santa Cruz Actors Theatre. Author: (novels) Between Battles, 1968, Gig, 1969 (Joseph Henry Jackson award 1967), Continental Drift, 1978, Love Life, 1985, The Last Paradise, 1998 (Am. Book award 1999), others; (non-fiction) Californians: Searching for the Golden State, 1982 (Am. Book award 1983), In the Ring of Fire: A Pacific Basin Journey, 1997, others; co-author: (with Jeanne Wakatsuki Houston) Farewell to Manzanar, 1973, (with John R. Brodie) Open Field, 1975; films include Li'a, The Legacy of a Hawaiian Man, 1988, Listen to the Forest, 1991, The Hawaiian Way: The Art and Family Tradition of Slack Key, 1993, Words, Earth and Aloha: The Sources of Hawaiian Music, 1995 (Silver Maile award 1995), (with Jeanne Wakatsuki Houston and John Korty) Farewell to Manzanar, 1976 (NBC World Premiere movie 1976, Humanitas prize 1976); contbr. numerous articles to popular jours. Mem. Calif. Coun. for Humanities, San Francisco, 1983-87, cons., 1988—; mem. steering com. Pacific Rim Film Festival, Santa Cruz, 1988—. Wallace Stegner Writing fellow Stanford U., 1966-67, rsch. fellow East-West Ctr., Honolulu, 1984, Resident fellow Rockefeller Found., Bellagio, Italy, 1995. Mem. PEN West, Western Am. Lit. Assn. (Disting. Achievement award 1999), Calif. Studies Assn. Avocations: bluegrass music, ragtime piano, hatha yoga. Home and Office: 2-1130 E Cliff Dr Santa Cruz CA 95062

HOUSTON, JAMES GORMAN, JR., state supreme court justice; b. Eufaula, Ala., Mar. 11, 1933; s. James Gorman and Mildred (Vance) H.; m. Martha Martin, Dec. 3, 1955; children: Mildred Vance, J. Gorman III. BS, Auburn U., 1955; LLB, U. Ala., 1956, JD, 1969. Bar: Ala. 1956. Law clk. to chief justice Ala. Supreme Ct., Montgomery, 1956-57; ptnr. Houston & Martin, P.C., Eufaula, 1960-85; assoc. justice Ala. Supreme Ct., Montgomery, 1985—; county atty. Barbour County, Clayton, Ala., 1961-79. Contbr. numerous opinions to So. Reporter; contbr. articles to profl. jours. Mayor pro tem, alderman City of Eufaula, 1964-70; pres. Heritage Assn., Eufaula, Ala., 1979-82; mem. Ala. Commn. on Uniform State Laws. 1st lt. JAGC, USAF, 1957-60. Named Citizen of Yr., City of Eufaula, 1979; recipient Alumni Achievement in Humanities award Auburn Univ., 1993. Fellow Am. Bar Found.; mem. ABA, Ala. Bar Assn., Ala. State Bar (examiner 1979-82, disciplinary commn. 1984-85, state bar commr. 1982-85), Barbour County Bar Assn. (pres. 1975), Eufaula C. of C. (pres. 1974). Republican. Methodist. Office: Ala Supreme Ct 300 Dexter Ave Montgomery AL 36104-3741

HOUSTON, JANICE LYNN, employment counselor; b. Atlantic City, Nov. 22, 1972; d. Jimmy Lee Snyder and Cheryl Rae Geary; m. Steve Martin Houston, Apr. 12, 1996. BA in Polit. Sci., Colo. State U., 1995. Cert. employment counselor State Wyo. Dept. Edn. Fin. aid technician Colo. State U., Ft. Collins, 1996-97; employment specialist State Wyo. Dept. Employment, Cheyenne, 1997-98; placement specialist Job Corps, Cheyenne, 1998—; awards com. chair Internat. Assn. Pers. in Employment Security-Wyo. chpt., Cheyenne, 1997-98. Vol. big sister Campus Club Colo. State U., Ft. Collins, 1994-95; vol. Wyo. Rep. Party, Cheyenne, 1996. Mem. Greater Cheyenne C. of C. (edn. com. mem. 1998—), Colo. State U. Alumni, Lambda Delta Sigma. Mem. LDS Ch. Office: Job Corps Office Admissions Placement 1111 E Lincolnway Ste 101 Cheyenne WY 82001

HOUSTON, JOSEPH BRANTLEY, JR., optical instrument company executive; b. Birmingham, Ala., June 15, 1934; s. Joseph Brantley and Inez (Graben) H.; m. Elizabeth Reece Manasco; 1 child, J. Brantley III. AB in Astronomy, U. Tex., 1956; MS, Northeastern U., 1969. Commd. 2d lt. C.E., U.S. Army, 1956, advanced through grades to capt., 1968; optical engr. Perkin-Elmer, Wilton, Conn., 1961-64; mgr. massive optics, chief engr. underwater optical sys. Itek Corp., Lexington, Mass., 1964-71; asst. to pres. Kollmorgen E-O Divsn., Northampton, Mass., 1971-73; v.p. advanced devel. and spl. projects Itek Corp., Sunnyvale, Calif., 1973-81; founder Houston Rsch. Assocs., Saratoga, Calif., 1981—, Houston Tech. Internat., Inc., San Jose, Calif., 1991-97; founder, exec. dir. Forum for Mil. Applications of Directed Energy, Huntsville, Ala., 1989-96. Contbr. articles to profl. jours.; inventor. Recipient Outstanding Civilian Svc. medal U.S. Army, 1987. Fellow Internat. Soc. Optical Engring. (life; pres. 1977-78, advanced tech. advisor 1981—, Goddard award 1982); mem. Optical Soc. Am. (founder, chair Fabrication and Testing Tech. Group, editor Optical Workshop Notebook). Office: 12150 Country Squire Ln Saratoga CA 95070-3444

HOUSTON, PAUL DAVID, school association administrator; b. Springfield, Ohio, Apr. 10, 1944; s. Paul Doran and Irene Almeda (Sansom) H.; m. Marilyn Kay Bowyer, Aug. 27, 1966 (div. July 1986); children: Lisa Lenore, Suzanne Elizabeth, Caroline Michelle; m. Jovel Kane, June 27, 1988 (div. Aug. 1997). BA, Ohio State U., 1966; MAT, U. N.C., 1968; cert. advanced study, Harvard U., 1971, EdD, 1973; D (hon.), Duquesne U., 1997. Tchr. Chapel Hill (N.C.) City Schs., 1968-70; prin. Summit (N.J.) City Schs., 1972-74; asst. supt. Birmingham (Ala.) City Schs., 1974-77; supt. Princeton (N.J.) Regional Schs., 1977-86, Tucson Unified Sch. Dist., 1986-91, Riverside (Calif.) Unified Schs., 1991-94; exec. dir. Am. Assn. Sch. Adminstrs., Arlington, Va., 1994—; vis. prof. Brigham Young U., Princeton U.; pres. S.W. Regional Labs. Bd., 1989-90. Author: Articles of Faith and Hope for Public Education, 1997; co-author: Exploding the Myths, 1993; contbr. articles to profl. jours. Pres. N.J. Interscholastic Assn.; bd. dirs. Princeton and Tucson Libr., 1977-87, YMCA, 1977-87. Finis E. Engleman scholar, 1972; recipient Richard Green Leadership award Coun. of Great City Schs., 1991; named Exec. Educator of the Month Exec. Educator, 1985, 100 Outstanding Exec. Educators in N.Am., 1984, 93. Mem. Rotary (pres. 1983-84), Phi Delta Kappa. Home: 401 12th St S Apt 1822 Arlington VA 22202-4237 Office: Am Assn Sch Adminstrs 1801 N Moore St Arlington VA 22209-1813

HOUSTON, SAMUEL ROBERT, statistics educator, consultant; b. L.A., May 20, 1935; s. Samuel James and Myrtle Lenore (Baker) H.; m. Judith Ann Jackson, May 20, 1963; children: Michael (dec.), Cathleen, Karen. BA cum laude, UCLA, 1957; MA, Calif. State U., Los Angeles, 1961; MS, U. Oreg., 1964; PhD, Colo. State Coll., 1967. Ordained to ministry Western Orthodox Ch. in Am., 1985. Instr. math. L.A. Unified Sch. Dist., 1957-65; program assoc. and rsch. specialist C.F. Kettering Found., Denver, 1966-68; prof. math. and applied stats. U. No. Colo., Greeley, 1968-92, chmn. math. and applied stats. dept., 1988-92, prof. and chair emeritus, 1992—; postdoctoral scholar UCLA, 1967-68; adj. prof. Pepperdine U., 1972-75; vis. prof. U. Wyo., 1979-80, U. Ga., 1985-86. Author: Judgment Analysis: Tool for Decision Makers, 1974; editor: Jour. Exptl. Edn., 1975-78; reviewer Computer Revs., N.Y.C., 1990-94; mem. editorial bd. Multiple Linear Regression Viewpoints, Akron, Ohio, 1986-94; contbr. articles to profl. publs. Served with USAF, 1958-59. Fellow NSF, 1960-64; Nat. Cancer Inst. postdoctoral fellow Yale U. Sch. Medicine, 1973-74. Mem. Am. Statis. Assn. (Colo.-Wyo. chpt.), Am. Ednl. Research Assn. (pres. spl. interest group 1970-71), Rocky Mountain Ednl. Research Assn., Am. Inst. Cancer Research, AERA Evaluation Network, Sigma Xi, Phi Delta Kappa. Home: 3711 W 230th St Apt 136 Torrance CA 90505-3823

HOUSTON, SANDRA LEE, nurse educator, medical/surgical nurse, ambulatory surgical nurse; b. Wilmington, Del., Dec. 16; d. Jepther N. Sr. and Mary Frances (Edelin) Pollard; m. Charles Houston Jr., Sept. 6. Diploma in nursing, Jewish Hosp./Med. Ctr. Bklyn., 1980; BSN, Medgar Evers Coll., Bklyn., 1989; MA in Nursing, NYU, 1995. RN, N.Y., Del., Mass. Oper. rm. RN Interfaith Med. Ctr., Bklyn., 1980—; instr. LPN program USAR; adj. prof. nursing edn. Medgar Evers Coll., CUNY. Rsch. on What Are the Perceived Financial Rewards for Registered Nurses Pursuing a BSN Degree?. Capt. USAR, 1988—. Mem. ANA, Rsch. Officers Assn., N.Y. State Nurses Assn., Assn. Oper. Rm. Nurses, Alumni Assn. NYU Medgar Evers Coll., Jewish Hosp. and Med. Ctr. Sch. Nursing. Office: 555 Prospect Pl Brooklyn NY 11238-4204

HOUSTON, WHITNEY, vocalist, recording artist; b. East Orange, N.J., Aug. 9, 1963; d. John R. and Cissy H.; m. Bobby Brown, July 18, 1992; 1 child, Bobbi Kristina Houston Brown. HHD (hon.), Grambling U. Trained under direction of mother; mem. New Hope Bapt. Jr. Choir, 1974; background vocalist Chaka Khan, 1978, Lou Rawls, 1978, Cissy Houston, 1978, appeared in Cissy Houston night club act; record debut (duet with Teddy Pendergrass) Hold Me, 1984; albums include Whitney Houston, 1985, Whitney, 1986, I'm Your Baby Tonight, 1990, My Love Is Your Love, 1999; songs include Greatest Love of All, Saving My Love For You, Didn't We Almost Have It All, You're Still My Man, I'm Your Baby Tonight, 1991; (duet with Mariah Carey from Prince of Egypt soundtrack) When You Believe, 1998; appeared in HBO TV spl. Welcome Home, Heroes, With Whitney Houston, 1991; fashion model Glamour Mag., Seventeen mag., 1981; actress (movie) The Bodyguard, 1992, Waiting To Exhale, 1995, The Preacher's Wife, 1996. Recipient Grammy award, 7 Am. Music awards, 4 #1 Single Record awards; named Artist of Yr. Billboard mag., 1986. Grammy award for Best Female Pop Performance, 1985, 4 nominations, 1994, 87; Winner Am. Music award, 1985 (2), 1986 (5), 1988 (2). Office: care John Houston Nippi Inc 2160 N Central Rd Fort Lee NJ 07024-7547*

HOUSTON, WILLIAM ROBERT MONTGOMERY, ophthalmic surgeon; b. Mansfield, Ohio, Nov. 13, 1922; s. William T. and Frances (Hursh) H.; B.A., Oberlin Coll., 1944; M.D., Western Res. U., 1948; m. Marguerite LaBau Browne, Apr. 25, 1968; children: William Erling Tenney, Marguerite Elisabeth LaBau, Selby Cabot Truitt Vanderbilt. Intern, Meth. Hosp. Bklyn., 1948-49, Ill. Eye and Ear Infirmary, Chgo., 1949-50; resident N.Y. Eye and Ear Infirmary, 1950-52; practice medicine specializing in ophthalmic surgery, Mansfield, 1952—; fellow retinal vascular disease NYU, 1968-69; mem. staffs Mansfield Gen. Hosp., Mansfield, N.Y. U. Bellevue Med. Center, N.Y.C.; assoc. prof. clin. ophthalmology N.Y. U. Sch. Medicine. Pres. Mansfield Symphony Soc., 1965-68, Mansfield Civic Music Assn., 1965; mem. Mansfield City Sch. Bd., 1962-65, v.p., 1965. Served to capt. M.C. USAF, 1952-55. Diplomate Am. Bd. Ophthalmology. Recipient Honor award Acad. Ophthalmology. Fellow Internat. Coll. Surgeons; mem. SR (color guard 1961-71), Nat. Geneal. Soc. (award of Merit), Ohio Hist. Soc. (life), Western Res. Hist. Soc. (life fellow), N.Y. Geneal. and Biog. Soc. (life), Ohio Geneal. Soc. (trustee 1955—). Editor, Ohio Records and Pioneers Families, 1970—. Address: 456 Park Ave W Mansfield OH 44906-3118

HOUTCHENS, BARNARD, lawyer; b. Johnstown, Colo., Aug. 5, 1911; s. Everet Harrison and Evelyn Mary (Barnard) H.; m. Margaret Belle Colvin, Dec. 28, 1940; children: John Barnard, Marilyn (dec.). B.A., U. Nebr., 1933, LL.B., 1935; LL.D., U. No. Colo. at Greeley, 1963. Bar: Colo. 1935. Practiced in Greeley, 1935-90; ret., 1990; city atty. Greeley, 1941-47, 49-50; mem. bar com. Colo. Bd. Law Examiners, 1947-81, chmn., 1968-81. Trustee State Colls., Colo., 1948-65, pres. bd., 1964-65; nat. sec.-treas. Assn. Gov. Bds. State Univs. and Allied Instns., 1960-62; bd. dirs. U. No. Colo. Found., 1975-79, pres., 1978-79. Fellow Am. Coll. Trial Lawyers; mem. ABA, Colo. Bar Assn., Weld County Bar Assn. (pres. 1946-47), Greeley Jr. C. of C., Greeley C. of C. (pres. 1951-52), Blue Key, Sigma Chi. Clubs: Rotary, Elks (past exalted ruler Greeley), Masons. Home: 1020 48th Ave Greeley CO 80634-2316

HOUTCHENS, ROBERT AUSTIN, JR., biochemist; b. Denver, Mar. 31, 1953; s. Robert A. and Lorna G. (Smyth) H.; m. Cynthia Susan Barth, July 24, 1976; children: Hilary, Graham. BS in Engring. Sci., Colo. State U., 1975, PhD, 1980. Grad. research asst. biochemistry dept. Colo. State U., Ft. Collins, 1976-80; sr. research chemist Dow Chem. Co., Midland, Mich., 1980-84, project leader, 1984-89; project leader DowElanco, 1989-90; sr. rsch. scientist BIOPURE Corp., Boston, 1990-94, tech. mgr., 1994-96, sr. tech. mgr., 1996-97, assoc. dir. process devel., 1997—. Contbr. articles on biochemistry to profl. jours. Patentee in field. Fellow Boettcher Found. Mem. Am. Chem. Soc., AAAS, Sigma Xi, Tau Beta Pi. Home: 22 Briar Dr Milford MA 01757-1069 Office: BIOPURE Corp 11 Hurley St Cambridge MA 02141-2110

HOUTZ, DUANE TALBOTT, hospital administrator; b. Kansas City, Mo., Apr. 28, 1933; s. Dudley and Helen (Talbott) H.; m. Margaret McNiel; children: Erik Siegfried, Jamie Houtz Harvey. BS, U. Kans., 1955; MHA, Washington U., St. Louis, 1960. Asst. dir. Shands Teaching Hosp. and Clinics, Gainesville, Fla., 1961-65; asst. prof. Ctr. for Health and Hosp. Adminstrn., U. Fla., Gainesville, 1964-65; adminstr., exec. v.p. Baptist Med. Ctr., Montclair-Birmingham, Ala., 1965-75; hosp. dir. Alton Ochsner Med. Found., New Orleans, 1975-77; pres. Morton F. Plant Hosp., Clearwater, Fla., 1977-92, pres. emeritus, 1992—; nat. advisor to the health care industry Pershing Yoakley & Assocs., P.C., 1995—; chmn. Southeastern Hosp. Conf., 1986-87; chmn., pres. SunHealth Care Plans Fla., 1986-87; bd. dirs. SunHealth Enterprises Inc., SunHealth Corp. Contbr. articles to profl. jours. Chmn. alt. revenue com. Pinellas County Emergency Med. Svcs. Adv. Coun., Fla., 1982; bd. dirs. Cmty. Svc. Coun., Birmingham, 1972-75, United Way of Pinellas County, 1987-93, campaign chmn. med. divsn., 1992-94; bd. dirs. Fla. League for Nursing, 1989-98, Bay Area Hosp. Coun./Tampa Bay Hosp. Coun., 1990-95, Morton Plant Found., 1990-96; mem. Fla. Geriatric Rsch. Bd., 1993—; mem. adv. bd. Jr. League Pinellas County, 1993-94; mem. Vets. Affairs Mgmt. Assistance Coun., 1996—; vice chmn. Sun Coast Health Coun., 1998. Capt. USAF, 1955-58. Recipient Acad. award USAF Basic Flight Sch., 1956, award of merit Fla. Hosp. Rsch. and Edn. Found., 1993, Washington U. Hosp. Adminstrn. Program Alumni of Yr. award, 1996; fellow Birmingham Bapt. Hosp. Found., 1985. Fellow Am. Coll. Healthcare Execs. (Regents award 1992); mem. Nat. League Nursing (bd. dirs.), Am. Hosp. Assn. (vice chmn. council nursing 1983 research com.), Assn. Voluntary Hosps. Fla. (bd. dirs. 1979-83, pres. 1979-80), Fla. Hosp. Assn. (trustee, bd. dirs. 1979-82), Greater Clearwater C. of C. (Outstanding Citizen selection com. 1982, bd. govs. 1984-87, bd. govs. 1987-88), Pinellas Suncoast C. of C. (adv. council 1984-87), Phi Delta Theta (Birmingham chpt. pres. 1970-71). Lodge: Kiwanis. Office: Pershing Yoakley & Assocs 400 Cleveland St Clearwater FL 33755-4041

HOUX, MARY ANNE, investments executive; b. Kansas City, Mo., Aug. 16, 1933; d. Rial Richardson Oglevie and Geraldine Marie (McHale) Oglevie; m. Phillip Clark Houx, May 12, 1962 (dec. Dec. 1974); 1 child, Clark Oglevie. BS in Edn., U. Kans., 1954. Tchr. Kirkwood (Mo.) Pub. Schs., 1954-55, Kansas City (Kans.) Pub. Schs., 1955-57; asst. to v.p. Woolf Bros., Kansas City, Mo., 1957-59; Midwest dir. C.A.R.E., Inc., Kansas City, 1959-62; legal sec. Phillip C. Houx, Chico, Calif., 1962-74; owner Mary Anne Houx Investments, Chico, 1974—. Trustee Chico Unified Sch. Dist. Bd., 1977-90; coun. person City of Chico, 1990-91; 3rd dist. supr. County of Butte, Calif., 1991—. Mem. Calif. Sch. Bds. Assn. (pres. 1987-88), Greater Chico C. of C. (Athena award 1993). Republican. Roman Catholic. Office: PO Box 1087 Chico CA 95927-1087

HOVANESSIAN, SHAHEN ALEXANDER, electrical engineer, educator; b. Tehran, Iran, Sept. 6, 1931; came to U.S., 1949; s. Alexander and Jenik (Thadeus) H.; m. Mary Mashourian, Sept. 17, 1960; children: Linda Larsen and Christina Tchaparian (twins). BSEE, UCLA, 1954, MSME, 1955, PhDEE, 1958. Registered profl. engr., Calif. Research scientist Chevron Research Corp., La Habra, Calif., 1958-63; sr. scientist Hughes Aircraft Co., El Segundo, Calif., 1963-86; sr. tech. specialist Aerospace Corp., El Segundo, Calif., 1986-96; lectr. UCLA, 1962—; cons. engr. L.A., 1996—; mem. adv. group for aerospace R & D NATO, 1985-87. Author: (with Louis A. Pipes) Matrix—Computer Methods in Engineering, 1969; Digital—Computer Methods in Engineering, 1969; Radar, Detection and Tracking Systems, 1973; Computational Mathematics in Engineering, 1976; Synthetic Array and Imaging Radars, 1980; Radar System Design and Analysis, 1984; Introduction to Sensor Systems, 1988; (with Khalil Seyrafi) Introduction to Electro-Optical Imaging and Tracking Systems, 1993; editor Computers and Elec. Engring., 1973-76. Inventor radar computer. Fellow IEEE (U.S. del. Moscow 1973, disting. lectr.); mem. ASME, Sigma Xi, Tau Beta Pi. Democrat. Roman Catholic. Avocations: investments; real estate. Home: 3039 Greentree Ct Los Angeles CA 90077-2020

HOVANNISIAN, RICHARD G., Armenian and Near East history educator; b. Tulare, Calif., Nov. 9, 1932; s. Kaspar and Siroon (Nalbandian) H.; m. Vartiter Kotcholosian, Mar. 2, 1957; children: Raffi, Armen, Ani, Garo. BA in History, U. Calif., Berkeley, 1954, MA in History, 1958; cert. in Armenian, Coll. Arménien, Beirut, 1956; PhD in History, UCLA, 1966; hon. doctorate, Erevan State U., Armenia, 1994, Artsakh State U., Armenia, 1997. cert. tchr., Calif. Tchr. Fresno (Calif.) City Schs., 1958-62; lectr. Armenian UCLA, 1962-69, prof. Armenian and Near Ea. history, 1969—; chair modern Armenian history Armenian Ednl. Found., 1987—; assoc. dir. G.E. von Grunebaum Ctr. Near Ea. Studies UCLA, 1979-95; assoc. prof. history Mt. St. Mary's Coll., L.A., 1965-69; advisor Calif. Bd. Edn., Sacramento, 1984-85, 86-88; cons. on multicultural edn.; lectr. to univ. and cmty. groups and profl. confs. worldwide; mem. U.S.-USSR commns. Am. Coun. Learned Socs., 1985-91, U.S. project coord. for study contemporary ethnic processes in U.S. and USSR. Author: Armenia on the Road to Independence, 1967, 4th edit., 1984, The Republic of Armenia, vol. I, 1971, vol. II, 1982, vols. III-IV, 1996, The Armenian Holocaust, 1980, The Armenian Genocide in Perspective, 1986, The Armenian Genocide: History, Politics, Ethics, 1992, The Armenian People form Ancient to Modern Times, vol. I, The Dynastic Periods: From Antiquity to the Fourteenth Century, vol. II, Foreign Dominion to Statehood: The Fifteenth to Twentieth Century, 1997, Remembrance and Denial: The Case of the Armenian Genocide, 1998; author: (with others) Transcaucasia: Nationalism and Social Change, 1983, Le Crime de Silence: Le Génocide des Arméniens, 1984, A Crime of Silence, 1985, Toward the Understanding and Prevention of Genocide, 1984, Genocide: A Critical Bibliographic Review, 1988, Embracing the Other: Philosophical, Psychological, and Historical Perspectives on Altruism, 1992, Diasporas in World Politics, 1993, Genocide and Human Rights, 1993, Genocide: Conceptual and Historical Dimensions, 1994, The Legacy of History in Russia and the New States of Eurasia, 1994; editor: The Armenian Image in History and Literature, 1981, Islam's Understanding of Itself, 1983, Ethics in Islam, 1985, Poetry and Mysticism in Islam: The Heritage of Rumi, 1994, The Thousand and One Nights in Arabic Literature and Society, 1997, The Persian Presence in Islam, 1998, Religion and Culture in Medieval Islam, 1999, Enlightenment and Diospora: The Armenian and Jewish Cases, 1999; chmn. editorial bd. Armenian Rev., Ararat, Haigazian Armenological Rev., Mitk, Human Rights Rev.: Jour. of Soc. for Armenian Studies; contbr. numerous articles to profl. jours. Calif. rep. Western Interstate Commn. for Higher Edn., 1978-94; bd. dirs. Facing History and Ourselves Found., Internat. Alert, Found. for Rsch. on Armenian Architecture, Internat. Inst. Holocaust and Genocide Studies, Armenian Assembly of Am., Ctr. for Comparative Genocide Studies, Sydney, Australia, Armenian Ctr. for Nat. and Internat. Studies, Armenia. Recipient Nat. Svc. award Armenian Nat. Com. of Am., 1978, Man of Yr. award Armenian Profl. soc., 1980, Citizen of Yr. award Armenian Am. Citizens League, 1981, Citizen of Yr. award United Armenian Cultural Assn. of Chgo., 1981, Recognition award Armenian Cultural Assn., Fresno, Calif., 1982, Man of Yr. award Rep. Assembly Armenian Ch. Am., 1983, Recognition award Armenian Ednl. Found., 1984, Mesrop Mashdots medal and citation Catholicos of Cilicia, Lebanon, 1984, Person of Yr. award Armenian Cultural Assns. Western U.S., 1985, Disting. Scholar award and medal Armenian Cultural Assns. U.S. and Can., 1986, Recognition Program award Armenian Assembly and Hamazkaine, Nor Seroont and Tekeyan Cultural Assns., 1987, Humanity award Facing History and Ourselves Found., 1988, Dadian award for advancement of Armenian culture Armenian Students Assn. Am., 1990, Disting. Svc. award Armenian Nat. Com. Western U.S., 1996, Disting. Achievement award Internat. Soc. for Traumatic Stress Studies, 1998, Mouses Khorenatsi award and medal Republic Armenia, 1998, also other citations and recognitions; grantee NEH, 1981-82, Calif. Coun. Humanities, 1985-86; Humanities Inst. fellow, 1972, Guggenheim fellow, 1974-75. Fellow Middle East Studies Assn. (mem. editorial bd.), Am. Assn. Advancement of Slavic Studies; mem. Armenian Acad. Sci. (academician), Am. Hist. Assn., Soc. for Armenian Studies (founder, pres. 1974-75, 90-92, book rev. editor jour., mem. editorial bd.), Oral History Assn., Nat. Assn. Armenian Studies (hon.). Armenian Apostolic. Office: UCLA Dept History PO Box 951473 Los Angeles CA 90095-1473

HOVE, ANDREW CHRISTIAN, federal agency administrator; b. Minden, Nebr., Nov. 9, 1934; s. Andrew C. and Rosalie (Vopat) H.; m. Ellan Matzke, June 12, 1956; children: Catherine Breen, Peter, Nancy, Graul. BS, U. Nebr., 1956; postgrad., U. Wis., 1960-63. Chmn., chief exec. officer Minden Exec. Bank and Trust Co., 1960-90; vice chmn. FDIC, Washington, 1990-92, chmn., 1992-94, vice chmn., 1994-97, 98—, chmn., 1997-98. Lt. USN, 1956-60. Office: FDIC 550 17th St NW Washington DC 20429-0001

HOVEL, ESTHER HARRISON, art educator; b. San Antonio, Tex., Jan. 12, 1917; d. Randolph Williamson and Carrie Esther (Clements) Harrison; m. Elliott Logan Hovel, Sept. 30, 1935; children: Richard Elliott, Dorothy Auverne. BA, Incarnate Word Coll., 1935; postgrad., Oxford U., 1979, British Inst. Art, Florence, Italy, 1980. Civil svc. auditor U.S. Govt. Office of Price Adminstrn., San Antonio, 1942-44; interior decorator Parkway Interior Design Studio, El Paso, Tex., 1968-72; instr. stained glass and sculpture El Paso Mus. Art, 1972-78; tchr. sculpture Albuquerque Sr. Ctrs., 1983-85; docent El Paso Mus. Art, 1972-82. Exhibited sculpture Museo De Artes, Juarez, Mexico, 1981 (1st place 1981). Bd. dirs. YMCA, Albuquerque, 1963-64 (plaque 1964); charter mem. and bd. dirs. Contact Lifeline Internat., Albuquerque, 1982-92 (2 plaques 1986, 90); mem. Com. on Bicentennial of U.S. Constitution, Washington and N.M., 1987-89. Recipient 2 medals Exxon Corp., 1986, 89, Medal of Merit Pres. Ronald Reagan, 1987; grantee Exxon Corp., 1986, 90. Mem. Jr. League Internat. (various offices 1948-97), Rotary "Anns" (various offices). Republican. Mem. Christian Ch. Avocations: sculpture, stained glass, oil painting, travel, volunteerism. Home: 7524 Bear Canyon Rd NE Albuquerque NM 87109-3847

HOVER, JOHN CALVIN, II, banker; b. Orange, N.J., May 13, 1943; s. John Curry and Edith Margaret (Hopkins) H.; 1 child, Margaret Biddle. BA in English Lit., U. Pa., 1965, MBA in Mktg., 1967; postgrad., Aspen Inst., 1988. With Chem. Bank, 1968-76; with corp. banking and personal banking U.S. Trust Co. of N.Y., N.Y.C., 1976-80, sr. v.p., div. mgr., pvt. banking, 1980-91, exec. v.p., 1991-98; retired, 1998; chmn. UST Pvt. Equity Investors Fund, Inc.; bd. dirs. New Hope & Ivyland R.R., Pa.; chmn. bd. overseers, U. Mus., Phila. Trustee U. Pa., Phila., Brick Presbyn. Ch., N.Y.C. Mem. St. Nicholas Soc., 1st Troop Phila. City Cav., Soc. Colonial Wars, St. Andrews Soc., Most Venerable Order of Hosp. of St. John of Jerusalem, Knickerbocker Club, Univ. Club, Psi Upsilon. Avocations: railroadiana. Home: 47 E 64th St New York NY 10021-7044

HOVERSTEN, ELLSWORTH GARY, insurance executive, producer; b. Minneota, Minn., Jan. 1, 1941; s. Emmanuel and Frieda Louise (Fligge) H.; m. Lillie Mae Jones, Oct. 29, 1965; children: Athena Marie, Dionne Shawn. LLB, LaSalle Ext. U., 1971. CPCU, CIC. Teller First. Nat. Bank, Ivanhoe, Minn., 1960-68; ins. mgr. First State Ins., Ivanhoe, 1968-87; ins. mng. v.p. Community Ins. Inc., Ivanhoe, 1987—; contact person Epilepsy Founds. Minn., Ivanhoe, 1980—. EMT Ivanhoe Ambulance, 1967-84; sec., treas. Ivanhoe Fireman and Relief Assn., 1969-84, Lions, 1968-83; CPR instr. Ivanhoe, 1980-83; treas. Mulder for State Rep., Ivanhoe, 1992, 94, 96, 98; treas. Lincoln County Salvation Army; pres. Ivanhoe Housing Bd., 1993—, dir., 1980—. With USAF, 1962-66. Mem. Soc. CPCUs, Soc. Cert. Ins. Counselors (cert.), Am. Legion (adjutant 1988—), Rotary (pres. 1991-92), Lions (sec., treas. Ivanhoe 1968-83), Rotary Found, Paul Harris fellow. Avocations: reading, wood working, gardening. Office: Community Ins Inc 323 N Norman Box L Ivanhoe MN 56142-0150

HOVEY, GRAHAM BILLINGS, public affairs journalist; b. Cedar Falls, Iowa, Jan. 18, 1916; s. Leroy Dana and Lois Stella (Graham) H.; m. Mary Jean Landgraf, June 20, 1941; 1 child, Thomas Dana. BA, U. Minn., 1939, MA, 1953. Reporter Waterloo (Iowa) Daily Courier, 1938-40, Internat. News Svc., Detroit, Kansas City, Dallas, Tulsa, Chgo., N.Y.C., 1940-42; war corr. Internat. News Svc., Africa and Europe, 1942-44; Washington corr. AP, Washington, 1944-46; asst. editor The New Republic, Washington, 1946-47; lectr. in journalism U. Minn., 1947-49; asst. then assoc. prof. journalism U. Wis., Madison, 1949-56; editl. writer, UN corr. Mpls. Star-Tribune, 1956-59; European corr. Mpls. Star-Tribune, London, 1959-65; mem. editl. bd. fgn. affairs analyst The N.Y. Times, 1965-76; fgn. affairs reporter The N.Y. Times, Washington, 1977-80; prof. comm., dir. Mich. Journalism Fellows program U. Mich., Ann Arbor, 1980-86, prof. emeritus of comm., 1986—; vis. prof., lectr. U. Calif., Berkeley, U. Ind., U. Iowa, U. Minn., U. Wis., SUNY. Contbr.: My First Year as a Journalist, 1995. Chmn. Detroit Com. on Fgn. Rels., Detroit, 1988-90; mem. Coun. on Fgn. Rels., N.Y.C., 1968-96, Newspaper Guild, N.Y., 1945-80. Recipient U. Wis. award for Disting. Svc. in Journalism, 1978, Annual Achievement award U. No. Iowa, 1981, Page One award Newspaper Guild of Twin Cities, 1961, Best Press Interpretation of Fgn. Affairs award Overseas Press Club Am., 1958, Outstanding Achievement award U. Minn., 1985, others; Fulbright rsch. grantee, Italy, 1953-55. Avocations: classical music and opera, reading, walking, hiking, international travel. Home: 800 Hausman Rd Apt 170 Allentown PA 18104-8497

HOVIN, ARNE WILLIAM, agronomist, educator; b. Norway, Dec. 30, 1922; came to U.S., 1952, naturalized, 1957; s. Einar Lauritz and Aslaug Hovind; m. Carol Helen Frink, Oct. 24, 1953; children: Randi Ann, Leif Erik. B.S., Agrl. U. of Norway, 1949; Ph.D., UCLA, 1957. Research geneticist USDA Regional Pasture Research Lab., University Park, Pa., 1958-64; investigation leader Forage Br., Beltsville, Md., 1964-69; prof. agronomy and plant genetics U. Minn., St. Paul, 1969-81; assoc. dir. Mont. Agrl. Expt. Sta., Bozeman, 1981-87; prof. emeritus agronomy Mont. State U., Bozeman, 1987—; chmn. Nat. Grass Variety Rev. Bd., 1968-69; sec. Grass Breeders Work Planning Conf., 1973-75, v.p., 1975-77, pres., 1977-79; sec., chmn. Regional Tech. Coms. on Forage Crop Breeding. Contbr.: chpts. to Turfgrass Science, 1969, Hybridization of Crop Plants, 1980; sci. articles to profl. jours. Served with Norwegian N.G., 1943-46. Mellon-King travel grantee Australia, 1970; Fulbright-Hays sr. research scholar Norway, 1978. Mem. Am. Forage and Grassland Council (Merit cert. 1975), Am. Soc. Agronomy, Crop Sci. Soc. Am., Alpha Zeta, Gamma Sigma Delta. Office: Mont State U Dept Plant Sci Bozeman MT 59717

HOVIND, DAVID J., manufacturing company executive; b. 1940. BA, U. Wash., 1964; postgrad., Stanford U., 1984. With PACCAR Inc., Bellevue, Wash., 1964—, sr. v.p., 1986-87, exec. v.p., 1987-93; now pres. PACCAR Inc., 1993—. Office: PACCAR Inc PO Box 1518 777 106th Ave NE Ste B Bellevue WA 98004-5017*

HOVING, JOHN HANNES FORESTER, consulting firm executive; b. N.Y.C., July 18, 1923; s. Hannes and Mary Alma (Gilbert) H.; m. Anne Fisher Spiers, Feb. 1, 1958; children: Christopher, Karen Anne, Katherine Jean. BA in History, U. Chgo., 1947. Radio news editor, reporter Milw. Jour., Capital Times, Madison, Wis., 1947-51; asst. to chmn. Democratic Nat. Com., 1952-54; exec. positions Kefauver, Stevenson, Johnson, Humphrey, Sanford presdl. campaigns; asst. to presdl. asst. for trade policy 1962; v.p. exec. action Air Transp. Assn. Am., Washington, 1956-64; propr. cons. firm Washington, 1964-72; sr. v.p. Federated Dept. Stores, Inc., Cin., 1972-82; pres. The Hoving Group (cons. firm), Washington, 1982—. Chmn. Washington Theol. Consortium, 1993-96; mem. adv. bd. Fashion Inst. Design Merchandising; past dep. chmn. planning Dem. Nat. Com. With AUS, 1943-46. Decorated Purple Heart, Bronze Star. Mem. Am. Assn. Polit. Cons., Met. Club, Nat. Press Club, Nat. Capital Dem., Queen City Club (Cin.), Lotos Club (N.Y.C.). Home: 4831 Albemarle St NW Washington DC 20016-4346

HOVING, RAYMOND HOWARD, consultant; b. Ann Arbor, Mich., Dec. 6, 1947; m. Linda D. Somerville, May 20, 1972; children: Katy, Nell, Wesley. BS in Indsl. Engring., Lehigh U., 1969, MS in Mgmt. Sci., 1971. Mgr. bus. info. systems Air Products & Chems., Inc., Allentown, Pa., 1979-84, dir. emerging info. tech., 1984-89, dir./ MIS process systems group, 1989-94, dir. info. tech. svcs., 1994-97; pres. Ray Hoving & Assocs., New Tripoli, Pa., 1997—; adj. prof. Lehigh U., Bethlehem, Pa., 1995; lectr. in field. Mem. Soc. Info. Mgmt. (mem. exec. bd., v.p. issues advocacy 1996-97, pres.-elect).

HOVING, THOMAS, museum and cultural affairs consultant, author; b. N.Y.C., Jan. 15, 1931; s. Walter and Mary (Osgood Field) H.; m. Nancy Melissa Bell, Oct. 3, 1953; 1 dau., Petrea Bell. BA, Princeton U., 1953, MFA, 1958, PhD, 1959, HHD (hon.), 1968; LHD (hon.), Hofstra U., 1966; LLD (hon.), Pratt Inst., 1967; DFA (hon.), NYU, 1968; LittD (hon.), Middlebury Coll., 1968. Staff Medieval Met. Mus. Art and The Cloisters, 1959-65, curator, 1965-66; commr. parks N.Y.C., 1966-67; adminstr. Dept. Recreation and Cultural Affairs, 1967; dir. Met. Mus. Art, 1967-77; pres. Hoving Assocs., Inc.; museum and cultural affairs cons. firm Hoving Assocs., Inc., N.Y.C., 1977—; pres. spl. mus. exhibitions The Planning Corp., 1983-91; arts and entertainment corr. ABC-TV show 20/20, 1978-84; editor Connoisseur mag., 1981-91. Author: Guide to the Cloisters, 1964, The Chase, The Capture, 1975, Kuerners and Olsons; exhbn. catalogue, 1976, Two Worlds of Andrew Wyeth: A Conversation with Andrew Wyeth, 1978, Tutankhamun, The Untold Story, 1978, King of the Confessors, 1981, Masterpiece, 1986, Discovery, 1989, Making the Mummies Dance, 1993; co-author: Andrew Wyeth: Autobiography, 1995, False Impressions, The Search for Big Time Art Fakes, 1996, Greatest Works of Art of Western Civilization, 1997; contbr. articles on art, parks and recreation to profl. publs., mags. and newspapers. Past trustee Inst. Fine Arts NYU. Lt. USMC, 1953-55. Decorated knight Legion of Honor France; recipient Bronze medal Citizens Budget Com., 1966, Cue mag. award, 1966, Disting. Achievement award Advt. Club Am., 1966, Disting. Contbn. award Park Assn. N.Y.C., 1967, Elsie de Wolfe award Am. Inst. Interior Designers, 1967, Woodrow Wilson award Princeton U., 1977. Mem. AIA (hon.). Office: Hoving Assocs Inc 150 E 73rd St New York NY 10021-4362

HOVIS, ROBERT HOUSTON, III, lawyer; b. Washington, Apr. 19, 1942; s. Robert Houston and Lera Frances (Robbins) H.; m. Mary Ann Jennings, Dec. 27, 1965. BS, U. Tenn., 1964, JD, 1966. Bar: Tenn. 1967, Va. 1967, U.S. Dist. Ct. (ea. dist.) Va. 1973. Asst. commonwealth atty. Fairfax County, Va., 1969-71; pvt. practice law Fairfax County, Fairfax County, 1971—; prin. Robert H. Hovis III PC, Annandale, Va.; commr. in chancery Circuit Ct. Fairfax County, 1969—; commr. in chancery Cir. Ct. Fairfax County, 1969—. Mem. adv. coun. Salvation Army, Annandale, 1984—; bd. dirs. Annandale C. of C., 1984. With U.S. Army, 1967-69, Germany. Mem. ATLA (cert. Nat. Coll. Advocacy 1981, cert. Med. Malprctice Advanced Coll. 1983), Va. Trial Lawyers Assn. (profl. negligence sect.), Va. State Bar, Fairfax County Bar Assn., Trial Lawyers for Pub. Justice (Va. state coord. 1993—), Fairfax County Cir. Ct. (ind. case evaluator), Ethridge Soc., Rotary (pres. 1983-84). Mem. ATLA (cert. Nat. Coll. Advocacy 1981, cert. Med. Malpractice Advanced Coll. 1983), Va. Trial Lawyers Assn. (profl. negligence sect.), Fairfax County Bar Assn., Va. State Bar, Trial Lawyers for Pub. Justice (Va. state coord. 1993—), Fairfax County Cir. Ct. (ind. case evaluator), Ethridge Soc., Million Dollar Advocates Forum. Democrat. Methodist. Lodge: Rotary (pres. 1983-84). Home: 2700 Green Holly Springs Ct Oakton VA 22124-1457 Office: 4544 John Marr Dr Annandale VA 22003-3308

HOVMAND, SVEND, chemical engineer, engineering executive; b. Nakskov, Denmark, Jan. 3, 1939; came to U.S., 1977; s. Eyvind Frederic and Yrsa (Petersen) H.; m. Beverly Ann Cocozella, Dec. 17, 1966; children: Peter, Lars. MSCE, The Tech. U. Copenhagen, 1961; PhD in Chem. Engring., U. Cambridge, 1968. Postdoctoral resident asst. U. Cambridge, Eng., 1968-69; R&D mgr. Niro Atomizer, Copenhagen, 1970-77; v.p. Niro Atomizer Inc., Columbia, Md., 1977-89; pres. Bowen Engring., Summerville, N.J., 1982-89, Niro Ceramic Inc., Columbia, 1983-89; pres., gen. mgr. Crossville (Tenn.) Ceramics, 1989—. Patents in the field. Mem. Ctr. for Profl. Advancement (dir. indsl. drying course 1989), Tile Coun. of Am. (bd. dirs. 1990—, mem. exec. com. 1992-96, pres. 1994-95), Ceramic Tile Edn. Found. (bd. dirs. 1996-98). Office: Crossville Ceramics 346 Sweeny Dr Crossville TN 38555-5459

HOWALD, JOHN WILLIAM, lawyer; b. St. Louis, Dec. 21, 1935; s. Herbert John and Irene Dorothy (Weber) H.; m. Nina M. Zierenderg, June 15, 1957 (div. 1970); children: Deborah A., Catherine A., Laura A., John William; m. Betty L. Curtis, Feb. 14, 1971; 1 stepchild, Tracy L. BS, U. Mo., 1957; JD, St. Louis U., 1962. Bar: Mo. 1962, U.S. Dist. Ct. (ea. dist.) Mo. 1962, U.S. Ct. Appeals (8th cir.) 1965, U.S. Supreme Ct. 1985. V.p. sales Eureka Svc. and Equip. Co., Eureka, Mo., 1959-62; ptnr. Sheehan, Furtaw & Howald, Hillsboro, Mo., 1963-64, Thurman, Nixon, Smith & Howald, Hillsboro, 1964-70, Thurman, Nixon, Smith, Howald, Weber & Bowles, Hillsboro, 1970-80, Thurman, Smith, Howald, Weber & Bowles, Hillsboro, 1989-91, Thurman, Howald, Weber, Bowles & Senkel, Hillsboro, 1991-95, Thurman, Howald, Weber, Senkel & Norrick, L.L.C., Hillsboro, 1995—; bd. dirs. LaBarque Ent. of Jefferson County, Hillsboro, 1965—, Rustic Hills Resort Ltd., Hillsboro, 1968—. Mem. Mo. Ethics Commn., 1994-98, vice-chmn., 1995-96, chmn., 1996-98. Lt. (j.g.) USN, 1957-59. Recipient Spl. award, Meramec Basin Assn., 1967, 69. Fellow Am. Bar Found., Am. Coll. Trust and Estate Counsel (Mo. chmn. 1987-92); mem. ABA, Estate Planning Coun. St. Louis (pres. 1990-91), Mo. Bar Assn. (bd. govs. 1975-87, Pres. Spl. award 1979), Jefferson County Bar Assn. (pres. 1963-64). Avocations: travel, golf. Home: 3360 Franks Ct House Springs MO 63051-1005 Office: Thurman Howald Weber Senkel & Norrick LLC PO Box 800 One Thurman Ct Hillsboro MO 63050

HOWARD, ALEX T., JR., federal judge; b. 1924. Student, U. Ala., 1942, U. Ala., 1946, Auburn U., 1942-44; JD, Vanderbilt U., 1950. U.S. probation officer Mobile, Ala., 1950-51; ptnr. Johnstone, Adams, Howard, Bailey & Gordon, Mobile, 1951-86; U.S. commr. U.S. Dist. Ct. (so. dist.) Ala., 1956-70; judge U.S. Dist. Ct. (so. dist.) Ala., Mobile, 1986—, chief judge, 1989-94; assoc. editor Am. Maritime Cases for Port of Mobile. Served to 2d lt. U.S. Army, 1943-46. Mem. ABA, Internat. Soc. Barristers, Internat. Assn. of Ins. Counsel, Maritime Law Assn. of U.S., Southeastern Admiralty Law Inst. (dir. 1978-80), Ala. Bar Assn., Ala. Def. Lawyers Assn. (dir. late 1950's), Mobile Bar Assn. (pres. 1973). Office: US Courthouse 113 Saint Joseph St Mobile AL 36602-3606

HOWARD, ANGELA KAY, lawyer, accountant; b. Tripoli, Libya, May 29, 1964; d. Laydell Ronnie and Thelmarie (Harris) H. BS magna cum laude, Va. State U., 1986; JD, DePaul U., 1989. Bar: Ill. 1989, U.S. Dist. Ct. (no. dist.) Ill. 1989, D.C. 1991. Mortgage compliance officer Cmty. Bank of No. Va., Sterling, Va. Mem. ABA, Ill. Bar Assn., Chgo. Bar Assn., D.C. Bar, Nat. Assn. Black Accts. Avocations: travel, play, reading. Home: 10660 Blendia Ln Apt #6 Manassas VA 20109 Office: Cmty Bank of No Va 107 Free Ct Sterling VA 20164

HOWARD, ANN HUBBARD, insurance agency executive; b. Dorchester, Md., July 2, 1938; d. Sherwood Marcus and Irene Meade (Cannon) Hubbard; m. Luke Vincent Howard Sr., Oct. 20, 1956; children: Annette H. Mitchell, Diana H. Johnson, Luke V. Jr., Peter Martin, Angela M. Pugh, Joseph Richard. Grad. high sch., Easton, Md. Cert. health cons.; CLU, Life Underwriters Tng. Coun. Fellow. Libr. aide Talbot County Bd. of Edn., Easton, 1973-74; advt. mgr. Talbot Banner Newspaper, Easton, 1974-77; regional mgr., account exec. Blue Cross-Blue Shield, Easton, 1977-87; agt. N.Y. Life Ins., Easton, 1987-88, Guardian Life Ins. Co., Easton, 1988-99; pres., broker Ann H. Howard and Assocs. Inc., Easton, 1986—; owner Shorewoman Mag., 1980-83; Nat. Assn. Securities Dealers lic. registered rep. Guardian Investors Svcs. Corp., 1988-99, Park Ave. Securities, 1999—. Coord. Talbot Community Health Fair, Easton, 1984-85; bd. dirs. For All Season's Meml. Hosp. at Easton, Inc. Planned Gifts Com.; pres. Easton Bus. Mgmt. Authority. Life Underwriters Tng. Coun. fellow, 1993. Mem. NAFE, Chesapeake Assn. Life Underwriters (pres. 1982-83), Md. State Assn. Life Underwriters (pres. 1997-98), C. of C. (bd. dirs. 1973-86, pres. 1980, Businesswoman of Yr. award 1989). Democrat. Roman Catholic. Office: PO Box 2220 Easton MD 21601-2220

HOWARD, ARTHUR ELLSWORTH DICK, law educator; b. Richmond, Va., July 5, 1933; s. Thomas Landon and Marie Antoinette (Dick) H. BA, U. Richmond, 1954; LLB, U. Va., 1961; BA with honors, Oxford U., 1960, MA, 1965; LLD (hon.), James Madison U., 1983, U. Richmond, 1984, Campbell U., 1986, Coll. William and Mary, 1991. Bar: Va., D.C. 1961. Asso. Covington & Burling, Washington, 1961-62; law clk. to Supreme Ct. Justice Hugo L. Black, Washington, 1962-64; assoc. prof. law U. Va., Charlottesville, 1964-67, prof., 1967-76, White Burkett Miller prof. law and public affairs, 1976—, assoc. dean, 1967-69, dir. Ctr. for Pub. Svc., 1988-89; counsel sessions Gen. Assembly Va., 1969, 70. Author: Commentaries on the Constitution of Virginia, 2 vols., 1974 (Phi Beta Kappa prize), The Road from Runnymede: Magna Carta and Constitutionalism in America, 1968, (with Baker and Derr) Church, State and Politics, 1982, Democracy's Dawn, 1991, Constitution-Making in Eastern Europe, 1993, Magna Carta: Text and Commentary, 1998; bd. editors The American Oxonian, 1968—, The Wilson Quar., 1977—. Chmn., exec. dir. Va. Commn. on Constl. Revision, 1968-69; chmn. Va. Commn. on Bicentennial of U.S. Constn., 1985-92; mem. Va. Ind. Bicentennial Commn., 1966-83; vice chmn. Magna Carta Commn. Va., 1965-66; Va. sec. Rhodes Scholarship Trust, 1970—; counselor to Gov. of Va., 1982-86; bd. dirs. James Madison Meml. Found. With U.S. Army, 1954-56. Recipient Disting. Prof. award U. Va., 1981, Randa medal Czech Republic, 1996; fellow Woodrow Wilson Internat. Center for Scholars, Smithsonian Instn., Washington, 1974-75, 76-77; fellow Ctr. Advanced Studies U. Va., 1970-71, 76-77, 82-83; Rhodes scholar Oxford U., 1958-60. Mem. Va. Bar Assn. (v.p. 1970-71), Va. Acad. Laureates (chmn. 1981-92), Cosmos Club (Washington), Oxford and Cambridge Club (London). Episcopalian. Home: 627 Park St Charlottesville VA 22902-4654 Office: U Va Sch Law 580 Massie Rd Charlottesville VA 22903-1738

HOWARD, BARBARA SUE MESNER, artist; b. Princeton, N.J., Aug. 6, 1944; d. Maximilian Hutchinson and Ethel Gertrude (Vieten) Mesner; m. James Scott Howard, Dec. 26, 1967. Sculpture study, H.I. Gates, sculptor, Washington, 1965-66; BA, Hood Coll., Frederick, Md., 1966; postgrad., Rutgers U., 1967-69. Cert. tchr., N.J. Asst. buyer Jordan Marsh, Boston, 1966-67; sculpture instr. Princeton Art Assn., 1968-71, 77-78; art tchr. N.J. Pub. Schs., 1967-70; chmn. art dept. Stuart Country Day Sch., Princeton, 1970-76; artist Hightstown, N.J., 1977—. Exhibited in group shows Art Cons., Princeton, 1974, 75, 78, Gallery 100, Princeton, 1975, Betty Parson Gallery, N.Y.C., 1975, Hunterdon Art Ctr., Clinton, N.J., 1977, Squibb Gallery, Princeton, 1973, 82, Art Masters Gallery, Princeton, 1984, Trenton City Mus., 1984, Grippi Gallery, N.Y.C., 1984, 85, 86, Gourgaud Gallery, 1986, N.J. Ctr. Visual Arts, Summit, 1987, Morris Mus., Morristown, N.J., 1987, A.D. Gallery, N.J. 1989-99, Artworks Gallery, Art Ctr. Trenton, 1989, Williams Collection Gallery, Princeton, 1991, 92; Hood Coll. Centennial Alumnae Art Exhbn., 1993; Women's Studies Gallery Princeton U., 1995-96; represented in numerous pvt. collections. Fellow Mixed Media N.J. State Council on the Arts, 1985; recipient Purchase award Mercer County Artists Exhibition, 1983. Mem. Artworks, Artists Equity, Mus. Modern Art, Smithsonian Assocs., Met. Mus. Art, Internat. Sculpture Ctr., Nat. Mus. Women in Arts (charter). Avocations: long distance swimming, biking. Studio: 451 S Main St Hightstown NJ 08520-3405 also: Eable Crag Lk Piercefield NY 12973

HOWARD, BETTIE JEAN, surgical nurse; b. Balt., Sept. 26, 1926; d. Milton James and Elizabeth Maria (Morgan) Knight; m. Stanley Lewis Howard; children: Amanda J. Scott, Sarah L. Howard, Mary McK. Strobel, Elizabeth M. Shaner, Roderick S. Diploma, Church Home and Hosp., Balt., 1947. RN, Md.; cert. bd. gastroenterology nurse. Head nurse med.-surg. unit Church Home & Hosp., Balt., 1947-48; surg. pediat. staff nurse Johns Hopkins Hosp., Balt., 1948-51, surg. pediat. acting head nurse, 1951-52, otolaryngology endoscopy head nurse, 1952-56; pediat. emergency rm. triage nurse U. Md. Hosp., Balt., 1966-68; head nurse surg. endoscopy nurse U. Md. Med. Ctr., Balt., 1968—; mem. adv. bd. Astra Merck for Patient Self Mgmt. Programs; spkr. Soc. Internat. Gastroent. Nurses and Endoscopy Assocs. VIth Internat. Congress, Paris, 1996, VII Internat. Congress, Vienna, 1998. Contbr.: (book chpt. sect.) Policy and Politics for Nurses, 1993; contbr. articles to profl. jours. Chmn. Digestive Disease Nat. Coalition, Washington, 1993-95; mem. coord. exec. panel Nat. Digestive Disease Info. Clearinghouse, NIH, Bethesda, Md., 1992—; mem. adminstrv. bd. Grace United Meth. Ch., Balt., 1993-95. Mem. Soc. Gastroenterology Nurses and Assocs., Inc. (pres. 1988-89, Gabriele Schindler award 1991), Soc. Internat. Gastroenterol. Nurses and Endoscopy Assocs. (charter, spkr. 1998), Chesapeake Soc. Gastroenterology Nurses and Assocs. (charter, pres. 1981-83), Certifying Bd. Gastroenterology Nurses and Assocs. Inc. (pres. 1992-93). Republican. Avocations: reading, interior decorating, sewing, Native-American collection. Home: 905 Saxon Hill Dr Cockeysville MD 21030-2905 Office: U Md Med Ctr 22 S Greene St Baltimore MD 21201-1544

HOWARD, BLAIR DUNCAN, Lawyer; b. Alexandria, Va.; s. T. Brooke and Elizabeth Duncan H.; m. Catherine Cremins; children: Thomas Brooke II, Caitlin Margaret. BA, U. Va., 1960; LLB, American U., 1963. Ptnr. Howard, Leino & Howard, Alexandria, Va., 1966—. Capt. USA, 1963-65. Named One in Best Lawyers of America (book), 1989—, Superstar Ohio Assn. Criminal Defense Lawyers, Columbus, 1994, One of Top Lawyers in Met. Washington, Washingtonian Mag. article, 1997. Fellow Am. Coll. Trial Lawyers; mem. ABA, ATLA, Alexandria Bar Assn., Va. State Bar Assn. (faculty professionalism course 1990-93). Office: Howard Leino & Howard 19 Culpeper St Warrenton VA 20186-3319

HOWARD, BRADFORD REUEL, travel company executive; b. Honolulu, Aug. 6, 1957; s. Joseph DeSylva and Marguerite Evangeline (Barker) H.; m. Marcia Andresen, June 23, 1985; children: Evan DeSilva Andresen, Blair Marguerite. BS in Bus., U. Calif., Berkeley, 1979. Owner, operator Howard Janitorial Svcs., Oakland, Calif., 1970-80; prodn. mgr. Oakland Symphony Orch., 1976-80; brand mgr. The Clorox Co., Oakland, 1980-85; gen. mgr., corp. sec. Howard Tours, Inc./Howard Enterprises, Oakland, 1985—; co-owner Howard Mktg. Cons., Oakland, 1985—; cons. Marcus Foster Found., Oakland, 1984-85; pres., gen. mgr. Piedmont (Calif.) Community Theater, 1976-92. Mem. Calif. Alumni Assn. (bd. dirs. 1991-95), U. Calif. Bus. Alumni Assn. (v.p. 1986-88, pres. 1988-89, Bay Area chpt. 1983-84), U. Calif. Devel. Coun., Oakland-Sunrise Rotary (sec. 1985-87, pres. 1987-88), Lake Merrit Breakfast Club. Avocations: theater, athletics, wine appreciation. Office: Howard Tours Inc 516 Grand Ave Oakland CA 94610-3598

HOWARD, CARL (MICHAEL), lawyer; b. Chgo., July 23, 1920; m. Kathleen Agnes Costello, May 10, 1953; 1 child, Carl Michael. AB, DePauw U., 1942; JD, U. Calif., San Francisco, 1949. Bar: Calif. 1951. Supervising dep. corps. commr. State of Calif., San Francisco, 1951-69; supervisory asst., asst. house counsel Fed. Home Loan Bank of San Francisco, 1970-75; legal counsel Home Fed. Savs. and Loan Assn., San Francisco, 1976-88, chmn. bd. dirs., 1985-86; assoc. Kerner, Colangelo & Imlay, 1976-86; sole practice, 1987-95. Lt. USNR, 1942-46, PTO. Mem. State Bar Calif., Am. Legion. Republican. Roman Catholic. Avocations: walking, golfing, bicycling. Home: 2450 Quintara St San Francisco CA 94116-1139

HOWARD, CAROLE MARGARET MUNROE, retired public relations executive; b. Halifax, N.S., Can., Mar. 5, 1945; came to the U.S., 1965; d. Frederick Craig and Dorothy Margaret (Crimes) Munroe; m. Robert William Howard, May 15, 1965. BA, U. Calif., Berkeley, 1967; MS, Pace U., 1978. Reporter Vancouver (Can.) Sun, 1965; editl. assoc. Pacific N.W. Bell, Seattle, 1967-70, employee info. supr., 1970-72, advt. supr., 1972, project mgr. EEO, 1972-73, mktg. mgr., 1973, info. mgr., 1974-75; dist. mgr. media rels. AT&T, N.Y.C., 1975-77, dist. mgr. planning, 1977-78, dist. mgr. advt., 1978-80; media rels. mgr. Western Electric, N.Y.C., 1980-83; divsn. mgr. regional pub. rels. AT&T Info. Sys., Morristown, N.J., 1983-85; v.p., dir. pub. rels. and comm. policy The Reader's Digest Assn., Inc., Pleasantville, N.Y., 1985-95; ret.; mem. summer faculty profl. pub. course Stanford U., 1993-95; bd. dirs. Andrew Corp. Author: (with Wilma Mathews) On Deadline: Managing Media Relations, 1985, 2nd edit., 1994; contbg. author: Communicators' Guide to Marketing, 1987, Experts in Action: Inside Public Relations, 2d edit., 1988, Travel Industry Marketing, 1990, The Business Speakers Almanac, 1994; newsletter editor Wash. State Rep. Ctrl. Com., 1973-74; contbg. editor Pub. Rels. Quar.; pres. The Reader's Digest Found.; adv. bd. Pub. Rels. News, Pub. Rels. Rev., Jour. Employee Comm. Mgmt., Ragan Pub. Rels. Jour. Mem. corp. adv. bd. Caramoor Ctr. for Music and the Arts; bd. dirs. The Hundred Club of Westchester, Inc., The Lila Acheson Wallace Fund for Met. Mus. of Art, Madison Square Boy's and Girl's Club of N.Y.C. Mem. Women in Comm. (bd. dirs. Wash. state 1973), Internat. Assn. Bus. Communicators, Pub. Rels. Soc. Am., Nat. Press Women, Wash. Press Women (bd. dirs. 1972), Issues Mgmt. Assn., Pub. Rels. Seminar, Am. Cancer Soc., Arthur Page Soc., Wisemen, The Aspen Club, La Paloma Country Club, Gray Wolf Ski Club, San Juan Outdoor Club, Pagosa Springs Arts Coun., Pi Beta Phi. Anglican. Home and Office: PO Box 5499 Pagosa Springs CO 81147-5499

HOWARD, CAROLYN J. B., state legislator; b. Deland, Fla.; married; 3 children. BS, Fla. A&M U.; MEd, Bowie State Coll. Supr. Chapt. I program Prince George's County; del. Dist. 24 Md. State Delegation, 1988-90, 91—, mem. ways and means com., mem. joint budget and audit com., vice chair county affairs com., chair transp. and telecomm. com., chair county affairs com., 1994-98; chair Ho. Dem. Caucus, 1999—, Md. Legis. Block Caucus, 1999—. Del. Dem. Nat. Conv., 1984, 92; dir. Dist. 3 Nat. Black Caucus of State Legislators. Named Disting. Alumni Nat. Assn.

Equal Opportunity, 1983, 88; recipient Counselor's Adv. award PGMACD, 1988. Mem. NEA, ASCD, Md. State Tchrs. Assn., Prince George's County Educators Assn. (Outstanding Svc. in Politics award 1983), Nat. Coun. Negro Women (life), Bus. and Profl. Women's Club, Delta Sigma. Office: Md Ho of Reps Ste 204 State Capitol Annapolis MD 21401*

HOWARD, CECIL BYRON, pediatrician; b. Wallins, Ky., Apr. 16, 1927; s. William Knott and Maggie (Cawood) H.; m. Rebekah Ann Buckley, Mar. 4, 1931; children: Mark Byron, Sally Ann Howard Truxal, Maggie Elizabeth Howard Ray. BA, Vanderbilt U., 1949, MD, 1953. Intern U. Va. Hosp., Charlottesville, 1953-54; resident U. Tex. Med. Br., Galveston, 1954-56; pediatrician pvt. practice, Maryville, Tenn., 1956—. Dir. Christian Ch. Found. Handicapped, 1983—; elder 1st Christian Ch., Maryville, 1961—; scoutmaster Boy Scouts Am., 1964-79, chmn. Tuckaleechee Dist. Great Smoky Mountain Coun., 1973-75; mem. Blount County D.H.S. Child Abuse Rev. Team, 1965—. With U.S. Army, 1945-47. Fellow Am. Acad. Pediatrics; mem. Blount County Med. Soc. (pres. 1973), Maryville Optimist Club (pres. 1973). Republican. Avocations: jogging, hiking, piano. Office: 1103 E Lamar Alexander Pkwy Maryville TN 37804-5130

HOWARD, CHARLENE, community health nurse, administrator; b. Beaumont, Tex., Dec. 29, 1949; d. Henry and Hattie Mae (Cruse) Collins; m. Edward C. Howard, Oct. 21, 1989; children: Wednesday, Edward V. III. Diploma, Bapt. Hosp. Sch. Nursing, Beaumont, 1974; BSN, Lamar U., Beaumont, 1983. Cert. women's health advanced nurse practitioner; recert. Head nurse Women's and Children's Hosp., Beaumont; clin. supr. Port Arthur (Tex.) Health Dept., asst. DON; DON Grayson County Health Dept., Sherman, Tex. Mem. Tex. Pub. Health Assn.

HOWARD, CHRISTY J., actuary; b. Evanston, Ill., Oct. 6, 1954; d. Coydel Sandford and Ethel Marie (Franklin) Howard; children: Raymond Christopher Gunn, Justin Howard Gunn. BA, Oberlin Coll., 1976; MS in Stats., Carnegie Mellon U., 1979, MS in Pub. Policy and Mgmt., 1979. Analyst CNA, Chgo., 1979-83, mgr. comml. property pricing, 1983-85, mgr. profl. liability res. and ops. analysis, 1985-92, asst. v.p. splty. lines reserving and ops. analysis, 1993-96, v.p. and chief actuary property/casualty valuation and fin. analysis, 1996-99; sr. v.p., chief actuary CNA E&S, Chgo., 1999—. Trustee Prairie State Coll., 1992-95. Fellow Casualty Actuarial Soc.; mem. Am. Acad. Actuaries. Office: CNA CNA Plaza Chicago IL 60685

HOWARD, CLARICE HARDEE, special education educator; b. Baxley, Ga., May 29, 1962; d. Frank D. and Beth (Fulghum) Hardee; m. Jarrett Mayes Howard, June 24, 1989. BS in Edn., U. Ga., 1984; MEd, Ga. State U., 1989; Edn. Specialist Degree, West Ga. Coll., 1993. Tchr. mentally handicapped Glynn County Middle Sch., Brunswick, Ga., 1984-86, Lee St. Elementary Sch., Jonesboro, Ga., 1986-87, Richards Middle Sch., Lawrenceville, Ga., 1987, Flat Rock Middle Sch., Fayetteville, Ga., 1990-91; tchr. handicapped presch., presch. coord., spl. edn. dir.'s adminstrv. asst. Oak Grove Elem. Sch., 1991-97; spl. ednl. cons. Fayette County, 1997—; conductor workshops in field; cons. in field. Youth counselor St. Simons Meth. Ch., 1985-86, vacation Bible tchr.; mem. Boy Scouts Am., Handicapped, 1986-89. Named Atlanta Jour. Honor Tchr., 1991, P.L.A.C.E. Educator of Yr., 1996. Mem. ASCD, Coun. for Exceptional Children, Assn. for Severely Handicapped.

HOWARD, CLIFTON MERTON, psychiatrist; b. Quincy, Mass., Aug. 11, 1922; s. Clifton Merton and Ruth Gilkey (Henderson); m. Margaret Carroll, June 16, 1951 (div. Aug. 1964); children: Kristen, Lauren, Siri; m. Susan D. Krex., May 30, 1965; children: Michael Scott, Jonathan, Robert. SB, Harvard U., 1944, AM, 1947; MD, Columbia U., 1963. Diplomate Am. Bd. Med. Examiners. Rsch. physicist divsn. of Atomic Energy Com. Brookhaven Nat. Lab., 1947-48; founder Waveforms, Inc., 1951-53; pres., CEO Electronic Workshop Sales Corp., 1951-59, Sound Workshop, Inc. and E.W. Assocs., Inc., 1953-59; intern Mt. Sinai Hosp., N.Y.C., 1963-64; resident in psychiatry Columbia-Presbyn. Med. Ctr., 1964-65, N.Y. State Psychiat. Inst., N.Y.C., 1965-66; sr. psychiat. resident Drug Rsch. Svc., 1966-67; dir. evening Psychiat. Clinic, Mt. Carmel Guild, Union City, N.J., 1964-67; asst. attending psychiatrist Vanderbilt Clinic, Columbia Presbyn. Med. Ctr., 1969-75; cons. in psychiatry Columbia Presbyn. Med. Ctr., 1969-75, assoc. attending psychiatrist, psychiat. drug rsch. unit, 1971-75; pvt. practice N.Y.C., 1967-98, N.J., 1980—; instr. engring. dept., Harvard Coll., 1946; instr. physics dept. CCNY, 1948-50, NYU, 1948-54, instr. psychiatry dept. Columbia Coll. of P&S, 1967-71, assoc. in psychiatry dept., 1971-75. Staff writer APPLE computer mag., 1982-85; founder, pres., CEO S&H Software, Inc.; Apple computer cert. software developer lic. to Reader's Digest, D.C. Heath Co., John T. Wiley & Sons, and others. Lt. USNR, 1943-46, PTO. Mem. APA, Ams. of Armorial Ancestry, Ancient and Hon. Artillery Co. of Mass., Baronial Order of Magna Charta, Flagon and Trencher, Gen. Soc. Mayflower Descs. (surgeon gen. N.J. soc. 1978-84), Jamestowne Soc., New Eng. Hist. and Geneal. Soc., Old Bridgewater Hist. Soc., Order Founders and Patriots of Am., Order of the Crown of Charlemagne, Soc. Descs. of Colonial Clergy, Soc. Ams. Royal Descent, Descs. of Illegitimate Sons and Daus. of Kings and Queens of England (aka Royal Bastard Soc.), Soc. Colonial Wars, Sons of Revolution, SAR. Avocations: genealogy, computers, medieval history, gardening. Home and Office: 105 Lakeview Dr Old Tappan NJ 07675-7071

HOWARD, CONSTANCE ADAIR, bank officer; b. Savannah, Ga., Oct. 2, 1964; d. Frank Roy and Bette Adair (Moore) Hurst; m. Joseph Michael Howard, May 19, 1990; children: Justin Michael, Joseph Hunter Howard, Benjamin Parker Paige. Student, South Coll., Savannah, 1985, Armstrong State Coll., 1988. Cert. fin. advisor series 7, 63 licenses. Fin. advisor Prudential Securities, Savannah, 1991-94; registered rep. A.G. Edwards & Sons, Inc., Savannah, 1994-96; investment adv. mktg. dir. Cornerstone Fin., Atlanta, 1996—; banking officer, br. mgr. med. arts br. 1st Liberty Bank, Savannah, 1997—; fin. spkr., instr. to pub. sch. students, Savannah, 1992—; fin. spkr. to local bus. orgns., Savannah, 1992—; fin. instr. Savannah Tech. Inst., 1993—; fin. guest spkr. Sta. WSAV-TV, Savannah, 1993—; instr. fin. classes Carroll Tech., 1996. Fin. columnist: The Richmond Hill Bryan County News, 1993—, The Ga. Guardian, 1993—, The Savannah Parent, 1993, The Knowledge Exch., 1993, Times-Georgian, 1996; co-prodr., host fin. talk show Money Talks, Savannah, 1994—; prodr., host radio program Community Closeup WBMQ talk radio, WIXV I-95, Savannah. Internship mentor Savannah H.S. Program, 1993; mem. bus. adv. Coun. C. of C., 1998-99, Leadership Savannah, 1998—; adv. coun. First Steps Meml., 1998-99. Mem. Am. Bus. Women's Assn., Small Bus. Chamber (bd. dirs., treas. 1993—), Savannah C. of C. (bus. advisory com. 1997-99). Avocations: tennis, painting. Office: Investment Adv Mktg Dir First Liberty Bank 5110 Waters Ave Savannah GA 31404

HOWARD, DAVID, ballet school administrator; b. London, June 14, 1937; came to U.S., 1966; s. Walter and Dorothy (Fell) Edwards. Grad., Arts Edn. Sch., London, 1955; D (hon.), Oklahoma City U., 1998. Mem. faculty Sch. Ballet, Harkness House for Ballet Arts, N.Y.C., 1966—; prin. tchr. Harkness Ballet Co., N.Y.C., 1967—; dir. Sch. Ballet Harkness House for Ballet Arts, N.Y.C., 1969—; founder David Howard Sch. Ballet, N.Y.C., 1977; company teacher Am. Ballet Theater, 1990—; Am. adjudicator 1st Internat. Ballet Competition, Miss., 1979; co-dir., co-founder Northeastern Ballet Summer Sch., Bard Coll., 1979; assoc. artistic dir. Catskill Ballet Theatre, 1980; founded David Howard Dance Ctr., N.Y.C., 1986—; mem. founding bd. Swiss Profl. Sch., Zurich; guest tchr. Royal Ballet, 1986-87, 93, 95, San Francisco Ballet, Juilliard Sch.; guest tchr., coach Am. Ballet Theatre, 1990-93, Bejart Ballet, 1992-94; author 23 albums of music for ballet class, 65 CD's; artistic advisor Nat. Dance Co. Mex., Mexico City, 1996-97; artistic assoc. Marin Dance Theatre, San Rafael, Calif., 1996-97; tchr. trainer David Howard Found., Seattle, Tulsa, Dallas, Erie, Pa., Boston, N.Y.C., 1990-96; tchr. steps Broadway Dance Ballet Acad., East N.Y.C., 1996—; tchr. N.Y. On The Rd., 1996—; tchr. tng. program Internat. Ballet Competition, Jackson, Miss., 1998. Prin. dancer, London Palladium, 1955-57, with, Royal Ballet Eng., 1957-63, soloist, 1958-63, Nat. Ballet Can., 1963-64; appeared in: musical Little Me, London, 1964-66; collaborator double album ballet music, 1981, with Royal Ballet, 1991-92, 97—, Finnish Nat. Ballet, 199%, Royal Swedish Ballet, 1977—; choreographer: Rachmaninoff Suite, 1971, Divertissement D'Adam, 1971, Rossini Variations, 1973, Designs in Shades of Baroque, 1974, Fantasy, 1980; teaching record albums include David Howard in Class, various others; rec. video tapes; rec. 70 CDs. Recipient Dance Master of Am. ann. award, 1983. Mem. Regional Dance Am. (dir. pres.), royal Acad. Dancing, London Actors Equity (Adeline Genee Silver medal for male dancers 1954), Brit. Actors Equity. *I have followed with great enthusiasm the growth of dance in the United States and want to dedicate myself to the development of ballet training in America and bring it to a higher level. I have devoted my time and effort to Regional Dance America, which reflects and contributes to the ever increasing size of ballet audiences across America. With this happening, no longer will the dancers who are developed each year have to seek employment within the long established European system of state-supported ballet houses.*

HOWARD, DAVID E., artist; b. N.Y.C., Jan. 25, 1952; s. John C. and Florence (Martino) H. Student, Ohio U., 1969-71; MFA, San Francisco Art Inst., 1974. Comml. photographer Athens, Ohio, 1969-71; tchr. photography San Francisco Ctr. for Visual Studies, 1971-74, visual artist in photography, 1975—, dir., 1975—; vis. instr. City Coll. San Francisco; grad. isntr. San Francisco Art Inst. Author: Photography for Visual Communicators, Objective Reality, 1972, monographs Realities, 1976, Perspectives, 1978, American Artist, 1990, Illusionistic Perceptions; photography numerous periodicals including Village Voice, N.Y.C., San Francisco Chronicle, Artweek, N.Y. Art Revs., 1990, L.A. Reader, Tribal Arts, 1998, Filipinas, 1998, TV Documentary series; one-man shows include G. Ray Hawkins Gallery, Images Gallery N.Y.C., U. Calif. Extension, John Bolles Gallery, San Francisco, Hirshhorn Mus., Smithsonian Instn., Washington, San Francisco Art Inst., Ohio U., Athens, Thomas J. Crowe Gallery, L.A., Madison (Wis.) Art Ctr., Lehigh U., Pa., Fourth Street Gallery, N.Y.C., Intersection Gallery, San Francisco, Third Eye Gallery, N.Y.C., Ctr. for Visual Studies, San Francisco, Hutchinson Community Coll., Kans., Hank Baum Gallery, San Francisco, Martin Webber Gallery, 1986, Marc Richards Gallery, L.A., 1987, E.Z.T.V., L.A., 1987, 88, G. Ray Hawkins Gallery, L.A., 1988, Fine Arts Mus. L.I., 1989, Phila. Mus. Art, 1990; numerous group shows including Art Commn. Gallery, San Francisco, DeYoung Mus., San Francisco, Oakland (Calif.) Mus., Palace of Fine Arts, San Francisco, Camera Work, L.A., Erie (Pa.) Art Ctr., Vorpal Gallery, 1985, Cal. State U., 1988, San Francisco Pub. Libr., 1987, Video Refuses, 1986, Hadley Martin Gallery, San Francisco, 1987, Fine Art Mus. L.I., 1989, Chandler Gallery, Seattle, 1991; represented in collections Mus. Modern Art, N.Y.C., Oakland (Calif.) Mus., San Francisco Mus. Modern Art, City of San Francisco, De Saisset Art Gallery, Santa Clara, Calif., Whitney Mus. Am. Art, Hirshhorn Mus., Smithsonian Instn., Art Ctr., Waco, Tex., Memphis Brooks Mus., Memphis, Akron (Ohio) Art Mus., Am. Mus. Natural History, N.Y.C.; pvt. collections; prodr. videotape New York's East Village Art Scene, 1985, California's Art Scene, 1986, others; prodr. exptl. films: Analysis of Realities, 1974, Levels of Consciousness, 1976, Levels of Reality; prodr., dir. Art Seen, TV comml. documentary series on contemporary art televised in N.Y.C., L.A., San Francisco, Miami, Fla., Portland, Oreg., New Orleans, San Francisco, aired PBS, 1994, T.V. show Keith Haring: Artist at Work, selected segments shown Whitney Mus., Hirschhorn-Smithsonian Instn.; internat. exhbns. 10th and 13th Internat. Exhbns. Contemporay Art, Royan, France, 34thand 41st Internat. Salons of Japan, Tokyo, and 5 cities, Mex. Exhbn., Ex Convento de Carman, Guadalajara, 31st Cork Film Festival, 1986, Chgo. Film Festival, 1986, 42nd San Francisco Internatl. Film Fest., 1999, Presidio Earth Days Fest., 1999; other mus., galleries, univs. in U.S. and Europe; produced and directed films New York's East Village Art Scene, 1985, California's Art Scen, Parts 1 & 2, Levels of consciousness, Levels of Reality; presenter weekly cable TV series; Blackstar syndicated photographer, N.Y.C. Recipient San Francisco Art Festival award. E-mail: artseen@sirius.com. Home and Office: Visual Studies 49 Rivoli St San Francisco CA 94117-4306

HOWARD, DEAN DENTON, electrical engineer, researcher, consultant. B.S.E.E., Purdue U., 1949; M.S.E.E., U. Md., College Park, 1951. Elec. engr. Naval Research Lab., Washington, 1949-84; cons. in elec. engring. Kaman Corp., Alexandria, Va., 1984-94; cons. in field, 1994—; instr. George Washington U., Washington, 1983-94. Author: (with others) Radar Handbook, 1990; co-author: Radar Handbook, 1970, Airborne Radar, 1961; contbr. articles to IEEE jour.; patentee (multiple) in monopulse radar and related fields. Served with USN, 1945-46. Recipient Radar Devel. award U.S. Navy, 1978, Meritorious Civilian Service award, 1980. Fellow IEEE; mem. Research Soc. Am. Avocation: ham radio W3PRH.

HOWARD, DESMOND KEVIN, professional football player; b. Cleveland, OH, May 15, 1970. BA Comm. Studies, U. Mich. Wide receiver Washington Redskins, 1992-94; wide receiver, kick returner Jacksonville Jaguars, 1995, Green Bay Packers, 1996-97, Oakland Raiders, 1997—. Named College Football Player of the Year, The Sporting News, 1991; recipient Heisman Trophy, 1991, Maxwell award, 1991, MVP Super Bowl XXXI, 1997. Office: Oakland Raiders 1220 Harborbay Pkwy Alameda CA 94502*

HOWARD, DONALD SEARCY, banker; b. Leadville, Colo., Aug. 13, 1928; s. Paul Parker and Amanda Jane (Searcy) H.; m. Phyllis Havey, Oct. 1, 1955; children: Steven, Julie, Rebecca, Martin. BSBA, Northwestern U., 1950; MBA, Harvard U., 1955. Rsch. assoc. Bus. Sch., Harvard U., Boston, 1955-57; ofcl. asst. overseas div. Citibank, London, 1957; asst. cashier Citibank, N.A., N.Y.C., 1959-60; asst. v.p. Citibank, N.A., 1960-63, v.p., 1963-69, dep. comptroller, 1969-72; sr. v.p.-fin. Citicorp-Citibank, 1972-79, exec. v.p., chief fin. officer, 1980-88; chief fin. officer Salomon Inc., N.Y.C., 1988-93; mem. fin. acctg. stds. adv. com. Fin. Acctg. Found., Stamford, Conn., 1985-88; mem. Internat. Acctg. Stds. Adv. Commn., London, 1986-93; dir. Bank Leumi N.Y. Trust Co., 1994—, Green Garden, Inc., Bedford, Pa., 1996—, Consolidated Purchasing Svcs., Bernardsville, N.J., 1987—. Co-Author: Managing The Liability Side of the Balance Sheet, 1976, Evolving Concepts of Bank Capital Management, 1980. Chair emeritus trustees Cornerstone Sch., Jersey City, 1993—; trustee Vis. Nurse Assn. Ctrl. N.J., 1995-97. Lt. comdr. USNR, 1950-57, Korea. Mem. Am. Bankers Assn. (chief fin. officer's exec. com. 1984-87). Presbyterian.

HOWARD, EDWARD FRANCIS, lawyer; b. New Brighton, Pa., Oct. 4, 1942; s. Allen Michael and Mary Rosalie (Herbulock) H.; m. Eleanor Elizabeth Harding, Dec. 28, 1968. BA, Geneva Coll., 1966; JD, Harvard U., 1969. Bar: U.S. Dist. Ct. D.C. 1970, U.S. Supreme Ct. 1970. Legis. asst. U.S. Rep. Spark Matsunaga, Washington, 1970-75; gen. counsel U.S. Select Com. on Aging, Washington, 1975-79, Nat. Council on Aging, Washington, 1979-82; counsel for social security U.S. House. Select Com. on Aging, Washington, 1982-83; coord. pub. policy Villers Found., Washington, 1983-89; gen. counsel U.S. Bipartisan Commn. on Comprehensive Health Care, Washington, 1989-90; exec. v.p. Alliance for Health Reform, 1991—; adj. faculty New Sch. for Social Rsch., 1980; ofcl. observer White House Confs. on Aging, 1981, facilitator, 1995. Contbr. articles to profl. jours. Chair pub. policy com. Am. Soc. on Aging, 1984-86, bd. dirs., 1986-88; mem. primary care journalism award selection com. Pew Health Professions Commn., 1995—. With U.S. Army, 1961-63. Hunter Coll. fellow, 1987. Mem. ABA (commn. on legal problems of the elderly 1979-86), Nat. Acad. Social Ins. Roman Catholic. Avocation: basketball.

HOWARD, ELIZABETH, corporate communications and marketing executive; b. Littleton, N.H., Apr. 24, 1950; d. Ellis Woodruff and Elizabeth (Millar) H. BA, U. N.H., 1972; MS, Pratt Inst., 1985. Dir. corp. comm. Nat. Distillers Chem. Corp, N.Y.C., 1978-85; dir. pub. rels. Transway International Corp., White Plains, N.Y., 1985; pres. Corp. Communications Group Millennium Inc., N.Y.C., 1986; pres. Elizabeth Howard & Co., N.Y.C., 1987—; instr. Columbia U. Sch. Internat. and Pub. Affairs; publ. and editor-in-chief Observations. Contbr. articles to profl. mags. Pres. Katherine Gibbs Sch. Scholarship found., 1987-88, 94-96, bd. dirs.; bd. dirs. Brenda Daniels Dance Com., 1993-95, Hamilton-Madison Settlement House, N.Y.C., 1984-89, pres., 1987-89; mem. com. YMCA Greater N.Y., 1993-94. Mem. Global Econ. Action Inst., Women Execs. Pub. Rels. (bd. dirs. 1984-87), Fin. Women's Assn. (bd. dirs. 1994), Carnegie Coun., Women's Fgn. Policy Assn., Urban Land Inst., Ricardo O'Gorman Libr.; founding mem. Crusade, Inc. Home: 152 E 94th St Apt 8B New York NY 10128-2578 Office: 156 W 56th St New York NY 10019-3800

HOWARD, ELIZABETH ANN BLANTON, courier service executive; b. Spindale, N.C., Mar. 14, 1934; d. John Lloyd and Monnie Clare (Geer) Blanton; m. Bill O. Howard, Aug. 13, 1950; children: Deborah Monnette Howard Gustafson, Michael Ray. Grad. H.S., Rutherfordton, N.C.; real estate student, U. S.C., 1965. Sales rep. Reserve Life Ins. Co., Rutherfordton, N.C., 1956-63; sec., salesperson Johnny Barker Real Estate, Columbia, S.C., 1963-65; sec. A.M. Pullen & Co., Columbia, 1963-65; owner, mgr. Ann's Sample Shop, Columbia, S.C., 1965-81; pres. Modubilt Corp., Columbia, 1965-75, First Comml. Assocs., Inc., Columbia, 1965-75, Ann's Rag Time Van, Columbia, 1979-88; sec., treas. Howard's Courier Svc., Inc., Rutherfordton, N.C., 1990—; bldg. project mgr. Gen. Svc. Adminstrn., 1960's. Contbg. editor: Creative Ways to Raise Funds and Activate Alumni, 1995; contbr. History Book for Spindale United Meth. Ch. Pres. Spindale Elem. PTA, 1956, Belvedere Elem. PTA, Columbia, S.C., 1963-66; bd. dirs. Rutherfordton, N.C. C. of C., 1991-92, 96-99, Rutherford County Concert Assn., Habitat. Named Sec. of Yr. WIOS Radio, Columbia S.C., 1967; recipient Charles Z. Flack award, Rutherfordton, N.C., 1992, award for svc. Am. Cancer Soc., 1996. Mem. Sears Coun. of Career Women (charter), Rutherfordton Hist. Soc., Rutherfordton Ctrl. H.S. Alumni Assn. (pres., All Class Reunion award 1992). Democrat. Methodist. Avocations: travel, rehabilitation of older homes, reading, grandchildren. Home: 1198 Oak Springs Rd Rutherfordton NC 28139-8099 Office: PO Box 475 Spindale NC 28160-0475

HOWARD, ELSIE STERLING, marketing executive; b. Phila., June 30, 1946; d. Julian Alexander and Reba (Shaffer) S.; m. Eugene Jay Howard, Mar. 9, 1969; children: Heidi, Elizabeth. BA, U. Pa., 1968. Mgr. spl. events Miami Heart Assn., Miami Beach, Fla., 1986-91; mktg. cons. Temple Beth Sholom, Miami Beach, 1991-92, Women's Healthcare Svc., Miami Beach, 1992-93; spl. events cons. Sylvester Comp. Cancer Ctr., Miami, Fla., 1991-92; pres. Sterling Pub. Rels., Miami Beach, 1993—; bd. dirs. Bankers Trust Co. of Fla., Children's Home Soc., 1996—. Active Citizens Commemorative Coin Adv. Com., U.S. Mint, 1994—; founding mem. Trustees' Coun. of Penn Women, 1986—, chair, 1994—; assoc. trustee U. Pa., 1987-91, founding mem. pres.'s coun., 1983—, so. regional alumni trustee, 1991—, overseer Sch. of Veterinary Medicine, 1992—, dir. Inst. Contemporary Arts, 1991—, trustee, 1990—, pres. Gen. Alumni Soc., 1995—; mem. Commn. on Status of Women, City of Miami Beach, 1992—, vice chair, 1993; founding mem. devel. coun. Sylvester Comprehensive Cancer Ctr., U. Miami Sch. Medicine, 1993—, chair spl. events task force, 1993—, vice chair devel. coun., 1995—; mem. Police Sub-Com. Task Force, City of Miami Beach, 1993—. Recipient Ivory Lady award NFIC, 1986, Women of Charity award Am. Cancer Soc., 1986, Love and Hope Rose award Juvenile Diabetes, 1985. Mem. Am. Numismatic Assn. (Pres. award 1995), Brickell Ave. Literary Soc., U. Pa. Gen. Alumni Soc. (mem. exec. com. 1991—), U. Pa. Dade Alumni Club (founding pres. 1982-85, secondary sch. chmn. 1988-90), U. Pa. Faculty Club, Westview Country Club, Foundlings Club. Democrat. Avocations: scuba diving, power walking, reading. Home: 4825 Lakeview Dr Miami FL 33140-2634

HOWARD, FRANK JOSEPH, JR., public relations company executive; b. San Francisco, Sept. 27, 1957; s. Frank Joseph and Carolyn Merced (Samish) H.; m. Cynthia Anne Fox, Sept. 6, 1997. BA in L.Am. Studies, St. Mary's Coll. Calif., MOraga, 1979; MA in Edn., U. San Francisco, 1996. Over the counter trader Shearson-Lehman Bros., San Francisco, 1987-88; field rep. to Senator Pete Wilson, U.S. Senate, San Francisco, 1988; pres., CEO, FJH & Assocs., San Francisco, 1989-92; comm. specialist Rep. Nat. Com., Washington, 1992; in-country rep., comm. officer Internat. Rep. Inst., Phnom Penh, Cambodia, 1993; mng. dir., sr. v.p. Nat. Grassroots & Comm., Alexandria, Va., 1994-95; pres. Howard Cons. Group, Bethesda, Md., 1995—. Mem. Rep. Nat. Com., 1992—; bd. dirs. Summer Opera Theater Co., Washington, 1998-99. Mem. Am. Assn. Polit. Cons., Internat. Assn. Polit. Cons., Md. C. of C., Washington Bd. Trade, Mongolian Bus. Coun., Russian-Am. Bus. Coun. Roman Catholic. Avocations: rugby, sailing, art appreciation, travel. Office: Howard Cons Group 5225 Pooks Hill Rd Bethesda MD 20814

HOWARD, GENE CLAUDE, lawyer, former state senator; b. Perry, Okla., Sept. 26, 1926; s. Joe W. and Nell L. (Brown) H.; m. Belva J. Prestidge, Dec. 28, 1979; children: Jean Ann Howard, Joe Ted, Belinda Janice. LLB, U. Okla., 1951. Bar: Okla. 1950, U.S. Ct. Mil. Appeals 1956, U.S. Supreme Ct. 1956. Ptnr. Howard & Widdows (now Howard, Widdows, Buffogle & Vaughn PC), Tulsa, 1952—; mem. Okla. Ho. of Reps., 1958-62; mem. Okla. Senate, 1964-82, pres. pro tem, 1974-81; bd. dirs. Roseland Oil and Gas, Inc., Local Am. Bank; trustee Phila. Mortgage Trust; mem. exec. com. Coun. State Govts., 1976-82, bd. trustees Okla. Coll. Savings Plan; chmn. Okla. State and Edn. Employees Group Ins. Bd. Pres. Okla. Jr. Dems., 1954; del. Dem. Nat. Conv., 1964; mem. So. Growth Policy Bd., 1972-76. With U.S. Army, 1944-46, PTO, lt. col. USAF, 1961-62. Mem. Okla. Bar Assn., Tulsa County Bar Assn. (Outstanding Young Atty. 1953), Phi Delta Phi. Mem. Christian Ch. (Disciples of Christ). Home: 2404 E 29th St Tulsa OK 74114-5619 Office: Howard Widdows Bufogle & Vaughn PC 1500 Nations Bank Ctr 15W6 Tulsa OK 74119

HOWARD, GEORGE, JR., federal judge; b. Pine Bluff, Ark., May 13, 1924. Student, Lincoln U., 1951; B.S., U. Ark., J.D., 1954; LL.D., 1976. Bar: Ark. bar 1953, U.S. Supreme Ct. bar 1959. Pvt. practice law Pine Bluff, 1953-77; spl. assoc. justice Ark. Supreme Ct., 1976, assoc. justice, 1977; justice U.S. Ct. Appeals, Ark., 1979-80; U.S. dist. judge, Eastern dist. Little Rock, 1980—; Mem. Ark. Claims Commn., 1969-77; chmn. Ark. adv. com. Civil Rights Commn.. Recipient citation in recognition of faithful and disting. svc. as mem. Supreme Ct. Com. of Profl. Conduct, 1980, disting. jurist award Jud. Coun. Nat. Bar Assn., 1980, Wiley A. Branton Issues Symposium award, 1990; voted outstanding trial judge 1984-85 Ark. Trial Lawyers Assn.; inducted Ark.'s Black Hall of Fame, 1994; recipient keepers of the spirit award Univ. Ark., Pine Bluff, 1995, quality svc. award Ark. Dem. Black Caucus, 1995. Mem. ABA, Ark. Bar Assn., Jefferson County Bar Assn. (pres.). Baptist. *

HOWARD, GEORGE HARMON, management consultant; b. St. John, Wash., Nov. 14, 1934; s. George Philip and Corrinne Cadwallader (Rippeteau) H.; m. Elizabeth Ann Ogden, Dec. 22, 1956 (dec. July 1991); children: Debra Ann, Keith Philip, Corrie Lou Govostis, Stacia Elizabeth. BA, Wash. State U., 1957; MBA, Harvard U., 1967. Sales rep. Burroughs Corp., Spokane, Wash., 1957; various positions USAF, 1958-77; vice commdr. AF Contract Mgmt. Div., Kirtland AFB, N.Mex., 1978; mgr. corp. devel. Leisure Dynamics, Evergreen, Colo., 1978-80; pres. HBK Assocs., Inc., Evergreen, 1981-87; dir. ops. ILX Lightwave Corp., Bozeman, Mont., 1988-89; sr. cons. Matrix Mgmt. Group, Seattle, 1990-94; pres. HBK Assocs. Inc., Auburn, Wash., 1994—; pres. Howard Farms, Inc., St. John, Wash., 1986—. Co-author: TFX Acquisition, 1966. Instr. Red Rocks Community Coll., Denver, 1986-87; del. Colo. Rep. Conv., Denver, 1984. Recipient Outstanding Sr. award Wash. State U., 1957, Legion of Merit award USAF, 1978, Bronze star USAF, 1968. Mem. Shrine, York Rite Bodies, Masonic Lodge, Order of Eastern Star, Wheatland Grange, Air Force Assn., The Ret. Officers Assn. Republican. Episcopalian. Avocations: computers, boating, fishing. Home: 6358 S 298th Pl Auburn WA 98001-3040 Office: HBK Assocs 6358 S 298th Pl Auburn WA 98001-3040

HOWARD, GEORGE TURNER, JR., retired surgeon; b. Harlan, Ky., May 31, 1913. MD, Harvard U., 1937; LLD, L.M.U., 1996. Diplomate Am. Bd. Surgery. Intern, then resident in surgery Boston City Hosp., 1937-41; resident in surgery Meml. Hosp. Cancer and Allied Disease, N.Y.C., 1941-42; mem. staff St. Mary's Hosp., Ft. Sanders Hosp., U. Tenn. Meml. Hosp., Children's Hosp., East Tenn. Bapt. Hosp.; ret., 1982. *Dr. Howard received an honorary doctor of law degree at the centennial commencement ceremony of Lincoln Memorial University. Howard is a descendant of General Oliver Otis Howard, its founder. Dr. Howard graduated from Harvard Medical School, 1937, and has worked at Boston and New York hospitals.He was written numerousarticles on surgical treatments and published three books. Howard pioneered the first injected administration of penicillin in Knoxville in the 1940s. He was president of Knoxville Symphony and helped found the University of Tennessee chapter of Phi Beta Kappa and Knoxville Racquet Club. He and his wife, Sue (Crizer) Howard, have four children.* Fellow ACS, AIM, Southeastern Surg. Congress. Home: 1209 Scenic Dr Knoxville TN 37950

HOWARD, GERALD KELLY, county official; b. Greenville, S.C., Dec. 25, 1953; m. Jeannie Edwards Howard, July 7, 1979; children: Kelly, Kristen. BS in Econs., Clemson U., 1976. V.p. econ. devel. C. of C., Greenville, S.C., 1986-97; dir. econ. devel. Anderson (S.C.) County Govt., 1997—. Office: Anderson County Econ Devel 5805 Airport Rd Anderson SC 29626-5303

HOWARD, GLEN SCOTT, foundation executive, lawyer; b. Birmingham, Ala., May 28, 1950; s. Jack and Bernice (Koffman) H.; m. Lauren Oldak, Sept. 2, 1978; 1 chld, Gregory Alan. AB cum laude, Harvard Coll., 1971; JD, U. Chgo., 1974. Law clk. to chief judge U.S. Dist. Ct., Altanta, 1974-76; assoc. Sutherland, Asbill & Brennan, Washington, 1976-81, ptnr., 1981-86; gen. counsel, COO Fannie Mae Found., Washington, 1996-97, sr. advisor, 1997—; lectr. energy policy issues. Performer radio show and record album: Classics Illustrated, 1984; contbr. articles to profl. jours. Bd. dirs. Davis Meml. Goodwill Industries, Washington, Greater D.C. Cares, Washington; gen. counsel Cares at Law, Washington, Leadership Washington, 1997—; active Nat. Petroleum Council's Natural Gas Study, 1990-92; chair Greater Washington Bus. Philanthropy Summit, 1999; tchr. Temple Sinai Religious Sch., 1997—. Mem. ABA, Choral Arts Soc. Democrat. Avocations: choral music, tennis, cooking. Office: Fannie Mae Found 4000 Wisconsin Ave NW Washington DC 20016-2800

HOWARD, HARRY CLAY, lawyer; b. Rockwood, Tenn., May 1, 1929; s. Harry Clay and Julia Roe (Cannon) H.; m. Mary Helen Harrison, June 12, 1951 (dec. Dec. 1997); children: Helen Howard Porter, Anne Howard Freihofer; m. Telside Matthews Strickland, Dec. 15, 1998. BA, Vanderbilt U., 1951; LLB, Emory U., 1955. Bar: Ga. 1955. Sr. ptnr. King & Spalding, Atlanta, 1956-92, ret. ptnr., 1993—; bd. dirs. Avondale Mills Inc. Mem. coun. Emory Law Sch., 1975-85, chmn., 1976-77; bd. dirs. Cen. Atlanta Progress Inc., 1981-85, Wesley Woods Geriatric Hosps., 1987-93, chmn., 1988-92; trustee Wesley Homes Inc., 1961-93, chmn., 1981-86; past trustee Oglethorpe U., The Lovett Sch. 1st lt. USMC, 1951-53. Mem. Am. Law Inst., State Bar Ga., Atlanta Bar Assn., Lawyers Club Atlanta, Piedmont Driving Club, Commerce Club, Peachtree Golf Club, Phi Beta Kappa, Omicron Delta Kappa. Office: King & Spalding 191 Peachtree St NE Atlanta GA 30303-1740

HOWARD, HENRY, state legislator; m. Earnestine. Owner Howard Enterprises; mem. Ga. Ho. of Reps., Atlanta, 1990—; vice chmn. indsl. rels. com., mem. banks and banking, state planning and cmty. affairs com. Past city commr., Augusta, Richmnod County. Democrat. Baptist. Office: United States Information Agency 301 4th St SW Washington DC 20547-0009 also: PO Box 2182 Augusta GA 30903-2182

HOWARD, HUBERT WENDELL, English language educator, academic administrator, choral conductor; b. Anderson, Ind., Sept. 22, 1927; s. Karl Fuller and Mary (Conley) H.; Rosemary Becker, July 18, 1956; children: Mary, Catherine, Mark. AB, DePauw U., 1949; MA, Stanford U., 1952; diploma in voice, Juilliard Sch., 1958; PhD, U. Minn., 1971. Free lance profl. singer N.Y.C., 1955-60; instr. English U. Minn., Mpls., 1960-64; asst. to assoc. prof. English St. John Fisher Coll., Rochester, N.Y., 1964-74, prof., 1974—, dean of coll., 1980-84, provost, 1984-88, dir. Glee Club, 1966—, dir. honors program, 1989-97, faculty coord. Weekend Coll., 1997—; voice and diction coach Xerox Corp., Stas. WXXI, WOKR-TV, WTROC-TV, 1979—; choir dir. St. Michael's Ch., Rochester, 1968-80; adjudicator N.Y. State Saengerbund, Troy and Binghamton, 1983-86. Author poems, satires, essays, gen. ednl. articles. Nat. treas. Indian Guides YMCA, Rochester, 1968-70; dir. creative writing Girl Scouts U.S.A., Rochester, 1971-72; bd. dirs. Young Audiences, Rochester, 1973-79; mem. scholarship com. Alliance Tool & Die Co., Rochester, 1980-86. Served with U.S. Army, 1952-54. Rector scholar DePauw U., 1945-49, Hoover scholar Stanford U., 1950-52; recipient Teaching Excellence award Winton Found., Mpls., 1962. Mem. MLA, N.Y. Coll. English Assn., N.E. Am. Soc. for 18th Century Studies, Delta Phi Lambda affiliate Am. Acad. Poets, Delta Epsilon Sigma, Phi Mu Alpha, Lambda Chi Alpha. Republican. Roman Catholic. Avocations: walking, travel. Home: 46 Torrington Dr Rochester NY 14618-2010 Office: St John Fisher Coll 3690 East Ave Rochester NY 14618-3597*

HOWARD, J. WOODFORD, JR., political science educator; b. Ashland, Ky., July 5, 1931; s. J. Woodford and Florence Alberta (Stephens) H.; m. Valerie Hope Barclay, Apr. 10, 1960; 1 child, Elaine Howard Christ. B.A. summa cum laude, Duke U., 1952; M.P.A., Princeton U., 1954, M.A., 1955, Ph.D., 1959. Instr. Lafayette Coll., Easton, Pa., 1958-59; postdoctoral fellow Harvard Law Sch., 1961-62; asst. prof. Lafayette Coll., 1959-62; asst. prof. Duke U., 1962-66, assoc. prof., 1966-67; assoc. prof. Johns Hopkins U., 1967-69; prof. polit. sci. Johns Hopkins U., Balt., 1969-75, Thomas P. Stran prof., 1975-96, prof. emeritus, 1996—, chmn. dept., 1973-75. Author: Mr. Justice Murphy: A Political Biography, 1968, Courts of Appeals in the Federal Judicial System, 1981 (cert. merit ABA 1982); mem. editl. bd. Law and Soc. Rev., 1975-76, 78-82, Am. Polit. Sci. Rev., 1977-81, Jour. Politics, 1979-93, Johns Hopkins U. Press, 1991-93; contbr. articles to profl. jours. Mem. history program adv. com. Fed. Jud. Ctr., 1989-95; mem. fine arts accessions com. Balt. Mus. Art; mem. music com. Balt. Symphony Orch.; bd. dirs. Shriver Hall Concert Series; vestryman Ch. of Redeemer, Balt., 1988-90. Lt. USAF, 1955-57. Recipient Outstanding Tchr. awards Lafayette Coll., 1960, Duke U., 1966, Johns Hopkins U., 1969, 70, 93. Mem. Am. Polit. Sci. Assn., So. Polit. Sci. Assn., Nat. Capitol Area Polit. Sci. Assn. (coun. 1986-89), Am. Judicature Soc., Law and Soc. Assn., Supreme Ct. Hist. Soc., 14 Hamilton St. Club (Balt.), Princeton Club (N.Y.C.), Phi Beta Kappa, Omicron Delta Kappa. Office: Johns Hopkins U Dept Polit Sci Baltimore MD 21218-2685

HOWARD, JACK, labor relations consultant; b. Santa Ana, Calif., Aug. 26, 1924; s. Floyd Willie and Inez (Cooley) H.; m. Margaret Anne McKinnon, Aug. 25, 1950 (dec.); children: Marc, Anne. AB, U. Calif., Berkeley, 1948; MA, UCLA, 1952. Reporter Springfield (Ohio) Daily News, 1949-51; labor editor San Francisco Chronicle, 1952-60; chief investigator govt. information subcom. U.S. Ho. of Reps., 1960-63; spl. asst. to undersec. of Labor, 1963-64; adminstr. Neighborhood Youth Corps, 1964-66, Bur. of Work Programs, 1966-67; exec. asst. to Sec. Labor, 1968; v.p. Ednl. Scis. Programs, Inc., N.Y.C., 1969-71; sec.-treas., cons. William Benton Found., N.Y.C., 1971-80; asst. to pub. Ency. Brit., N.Y.C., 1971-73; asst. dir. Twentieth Century Fund, N.Y.C., 1974-76; asst. to pres. Am. Fedn. State, County and Mcpl. Employees AFL-CIO, 1976-97; ind. cons., 1997—; internat. v.p. Am. Newspaper Guild-AFL-CIO, 1957-60. With AUS, 1943-46. Congl. fellow Am. Polit. Sci. Assn., 1957-58; Recipient Distinguished Svc. award Dept. Labor, 1965. Mem. ACLU. Home: 219 5th St NE Washington DC 20002-5919

HOWARD, JACK BENNY, chemical engineer, educator, researcher; b. Tompkinsville, Ky., Oct. 16, 1937; s. Harley Hugh and Opal Mae (Branstetter) H.; m. Carolyn Butler, Jan. 4, 1969; children: Courtenay Bine, Jonathan David. BS, U. Ky., 1960, MS, 1961; PhD, Pa. State U., 1965. Asst. prof. MIT, Cambridge, 1965-72, assoc. prof., 1972-75, prof., 1975—; Wilhelm lectr. Princeton U., 1977; Oblad lectr. U. Utah, 1989. Author: New Energy Technology, 1971; contbr. numerous articles to profl. jours.; patentee in field. Mem. Govt. Panels on Energy Tech., Washington, 1970—. Mem. AAAS, Am. Chem. Soc. (chair fuel chemistry div. 1983-84, Storch award 1983), Am. Inst. Chem. Engrs., Combustion Inst. (program chair 1982, Silver medal 1984, Bernard Lewis Gold medal 1992). Office: MIT 77 Massachusetts Ave Rm 66-454 Cambridge MA 02139-4307

HOWARD, JAMES JOSEPH, III, utility company executive; b. Pitts., July 1, 1935; s. James Joseph Jr. and Flossie (Wenzel) H.; m. Donna J. Fowler; children: James J. IV, Catherine A., Christine A., William F. BBA, U. Pitts., 1957; MS, MIT, 1970. With Bell Telephone of Pa., Pitts., 1957-78, v.p., gen. mgr., 1976-78; v.p. ops. Wis. Telephone Co., Milw., 1978-79, exec. v.p., chief operating officer, 1979-81, pres., chief exec. officer, 1981-83, chmn., chief exec. officer, 1983; pres., chief operating officer Ameritech, Chgo., 1983-87, dir.; pres., chief exec. officer No. States Power Co., Mpls., 1987—, chmn., 1988—; bd. dirs. Walgreen Co., Deerfield, Ill., No. States Power Co., Mpls., Honeywell, Mpls., Fed. Res. Bank of Mpls., Ecolab, St. Paul, ReliaStar Fin., Mpls., Edison Electric Inst., Electric Power Rsch. Inst., chmn. Nuclear Energy Inst. Trustee U. St. Thomas, St. Paul. Sloan fellow MIT, 1969. Mem. Conf. Bd. N.Y. *

HOWARD, JAMES KENTON, university administrator, journalist; b. June 30, 1943; s. Arthur R. and Dora G. (Utt) H.; m. Lynn M. Marsh, Sept. 23, 1982; children: Lara L., James M. BA, U. Okla., 1965, MA, 1979; Inst. Ednl. Mgmt., Harvard U., 1991. Asst. dean students U. Okla., Norman, 1965-67, asst. to pres., 1967-68, asst. to v.p. for univ. rels. and devel., 1978; editor Northland Press, Flagstaff, Ariz., 1972-77; cons. Okla. Dept. Public Safety, Oklahoma City, 1977; asst. dean student affairs Northeastern State U., Tahlequah, Okla., 1978-79, dir. univ. svcs., 1979-82, asst. prof. journalism, 1979—, v.p. adminstrn., 1982-91, v.p. bus. and devel., 1991—, trustee NSU Found., 1981-90, 92—; mem. Coun. Bus. Officers, Okla. State Regents for Higher Edn., 1982—; adv. dir. BancFirst, 1995—. Author: Ten Years With the Cowboy Artists of America, 1976. Bd. dirs. Friends of Mus. No. Ariz., 1974-77; chmn. No. Ariz. campaign March of Dimes, 1973-74; No. Ariz. coord. Babbit for Atty. Gen. Campaign, 1974; grustee Flagstaff-Coconino County Pub. Libr., 1976-77, chmn. bd. trustees, 1976-77; pres. Indian Nations Soccer Coun., 1981-82; bd. dirs. Indian Nations coun. Boy Scouts Am., 1990-94; trustee Tahlequah Pub. Schs. Found., 1990—, chair, 1992-98; bd. dirs., exec. com. Leadership Okla., 1990—, pres., 1994-95, mem. Class II, 1988-89, bd. dirs., Okla. Assn. of Coll. and Univ. Bus. Offices, 1993-98, pres., 1996-97; bd. dirs., exec. com. Okla. Acad. for State Goals, 1993, chair, 1999; bd. dirs. Okla. Found. for Excellence, 1996—, Okla. Arts Inst., 1997—; pres. Boys and Girls Club of Tahlequah, 1996—; chair Cherokee County Cmty. Sentencing Coun., 1997—. Adv. Dir., BancFirst, 1995—, pres., Coll. Assn. of Liability Mgmt., 1997-98, bd. dirs., Okla. Arts Inst., 1997—; chair, Cherokee County Commty. Sentencing Counc., 1997—, With USAF, 1968-72. Recipient Eason Book Collection award, 1965, Book Design award Rounce and Coffin Club of L.A., 1974-75, Citation of Profl. Merit Northeastern State U., 1991, Excellence in Okla. Leadership award, 1995, Disting. leadership award Nat. Assn. Cmty. Leadership, 1995-96. Mem. U. Okla. Assn. (life), Okla. Assn. Coll. and Univ. Bus. Officers (bd. dirs. 1993-98, pres. 1996-97), Nat. Cowboy Hall of Fame and Western Heritage Ctr. (life), Tahlequah Area C. of C. (bd. dirs. 1985-88), Mensa, Rotary (past pres., Paul Harris fellow), Sigma Delta Chi, Kappa Tau Alpha, Lambda Chi Alpha. Office: Northeastern State U Adminstrn Bldg Ste 109 Tahlequah OK 74464

HOWARD, JAMES WEBB, investment banker, lawyer, engineer; b. Evansville, Ind., Sept. 17, 1925; s. Joseph R. and Velma (Cobb) H.; m. Phyllis Jean Brandt, Dec. 27, 1948; children: Sheila Rae, Sharon Kae. BS in Mech. Engring, Purdue U., 1949; postgrad., Akron (Ohio) Law Sch., 1950-51, Cleve. Marshall Law Sch., 1951-52; MBA, Case Western Res. U., 1962; J.D., Western State Coll. Law, 1976. Registered profl. engr., Ind., Ohio. Jr. project engr. Firestone Tire & Rubber Co., Akron, 1949-50; gen. foreman Cadillac Motor Car div. GM, 1950-53; mgmt. cons. M.K. Sheppard & Co., Cleve., 1953-56; plant mgr. Lewis Welding & Engring. Corp., Ohio, 1956-58; underwriter The Ohio Co., Columbus, 1959; chmn. Growth Capital, Inc., Chgo., 1960-98; pvt. practice law San Diego, 1979-85; pres. Meister Brau, Inc., Chgo., 1965-73, The Home Mart, San Diego, 1974-82; mng. agt., fin. instn. specialist FDIC/RTC, 1985-90; specialist in charge Office of FDIC-DOL, Portland, Oreg., 1986-87. Developer of "Lite" beer. Co-chmn. Chgo. com. Ill. Sesquicentennial Com., 1968. Served with AUS, 1943-46. Decorated Bronze Star, Parachutist badge, Combat Inf. badge. Mem. ASME, Nat. Assn. Small Bus. Investment Cos. (past pres.), State Bar Calif., Grad. Bus. Alumni Assn. Western Res. U. (past gov.), Masons, Tau Kappa Epsilon, Pi Tau Sigma, Beta Gamma Sigma. Methodist.

HOWARD, JANE OSBURN, educator; b. Morris, Ill., Aug. 12, 1926; d. Everett Hooker and Bernice Otilda (Olson) Osburn; BA, U. Ariz., 1948; MA, U. N.Mex., 1966, PhD, 1969; m. Rollins Stanley Howard, June 5, 1948; children: Ellen Elizabeth, Susan Nuttall. Instr. U. N.Mex. Sch. Medicine, Albuquerque, 1968-70, mem. staff pediatrics, deaf blind children's program, Albuquerque, 1971-72, asst. dir. N.Mex. programs for deaf blind children, 1972-74, instr. psychiatry, instr. pediatrics, coordinator deaf-blind children's program, 1972-76, edn. cons., 1976—, publicity and pub. relations cons., 1983—; Cons. Mountain-Plains Regional Ctr. for Services to Deaf-Blind Children, Denver, 1971-74, Bur. Indian Affairs, 1974. Active Cystic Fibrosis, Mother's March, Heart Fund, Easter Seal-Crippled Children. Recipient fellowships U. N.M., 1965-68, U. So. Calif. John Tracy Clinic, 1973. Fellow Royal Soc. Health; mem. Council Exceptional Children, Am. Assn. Mental Deficiency, Nat. Assn. Retarded Children, AAUW, Pi Lambda Theta, Zeta Phi Eta, Alpha Epsilon Rho. Republican. Methodist. Home: 615 Valencia Dr SE Albuquerque NM 87108-3742

HOWARD, JEAN E., English educator; b. Houlton, Maine, Oct. 20, 1948; d. Ralph Woodrow and Eleanor (Ross) H.; m. James M. Baker, Sept. 30, 1972; children: Katherine Howard, Caleb Howard. BA, Brown U., 1970; MPhil, U. London, 1972; PhD, Yale U., 1975. Asst. prof. Syracuse (N.Y.) U., 1975-81, assoc. prof., 1981-88; prof. English, Columbia U., N.Y.C., 1988—. Author: Shakespeare's Art of Orchestration, 1984, The Stage and Social Struggle in Early Modern English, 1994; co-author: Engendering A Nation, 1997; co-editor: The Nation Shakespeare; mem. editl. bd. Shakespeare Quar., Shakespeare Studies, Renaissance Drama. Folger fellow Folger Shakespeare Libr., 1996; sr. scholar NEH, 1997. Mem. MLA (exec. com. Shakespeare divsn. 1995-00), Shakespeare Assn. Am. (pres.-elect 1999-00). Home: 430 W 116th St Apt 7C New York NY 10027 Office: Columbia U Dept English 602 Philosophy Hall New York NY 10027

HOWARD, JEFFREY HJALMAR, lawyer; b. N.Y.C., Aug. 23, 1944; s. Virgil Edward and Margaretta E. H.; m. Brenda H. Howard, June 19, 1966; children: Taggart Harrison, Brooke Kennedy. BA in Philosophy, Randolph-Macon Coll., 1966; postgrad. (English Speaking Union scholar) U. Edinburgh (Scotland), 1965; LLB, U. Va., 1969. Bar: D.C. 1970, U.S. Sup. Ct. 1978, Va. 1987. Law clk. Circuit Ct., Montgomery County, Md., 1969-70; assoc. Covington & Burling, Washington, 1970-74; assoc. gen. counsel for toxics, pesticides and solid waste U.S. EPA, Washington, 1974-76; ptnr. Crowell & Moring, 1989—; lectr. antitrust and environ. law U. Va. 1976-89; lectr. environ. law Peking U., Peoples Republic of China, 1986. Mem. ABA, D.C. Bar Assn., Va. Soc. Fellows, Order Coif, Alpha Psi Omega, Alpha Epsilon Pi, Delta Sigma Rho-Tau Kappa Alpha, Omicron Delta Kappa. Editorial bd. Va. Law Rev., 1967-69; contbr. chpts. to books and articles to profl. jours. Home: 1021 Duchess Dr Mc Lean VA 22102-2007 Office: 1001 Pennsylvania Ave NW Washington DC 20004-2505

HOWARD, JOHN ADDISON, former college president, institute executive; b. Evanston, Ill., Aug. 10, 1921; s. Hubert Elmer and Edith (Sackett) H.; m. Janette Marie Nobis, Aug. 11, 1951; children: Marie Starr, Steven Lamson, Martha Nobis, Katherine Louise. Student, Princeton U., 1939-42; B.S., Northwestern U., 1947, M.A., 1949, Ph.D., 1962; LL.D., Grove City Coll., 1972, Brigham Young U., 1976, Rockford Coll., 1980. Instr. French Palos Verdes Coll., Rolling Hills, Calif., 1947-49; dean students Palos Verdes Coll., 1949-51, v.p., 1950-51, pres., 1951-55; exec. vice chmn. Pres.'s Com. on Govt. Contracts, 1956-57; pres. Rockford (Ill.) Coll., 1960-77; dir. Rockford Coll. Inst., 1977-80; pres. The Rockford Inst., 1980-86, counselor, 1986-97; sr. fellow The Howard Ctr. Religion, Family & Soc., 1997—. Contbg. author: Dilemmas Facing the Nation, 1979. Mem. U.S. Commn. on Marijuana and Drug Abuse, 1971-73, Pres.'s Task Force on Priorities in Higher Edn., 1969-70; pres. Ingersoll Found., 1983—. Served to 1st lt. AUS, 1942-45. Decorated Silver Star with oak leaf cluster, Purple Heart with oak leaf cluster; Recipient Horatio Alger award, 1967; Educator of Yr. Religious Heritage Am., 1980. Mem. Am. Assn. Pres. Ind. Colls. and Univs. (pres. 1969-72), Phila. Soc. (pres. 1979-81), Rockford Country Club, Univ. Club Chgo., Rotary, Phi Beta Kappa. Home: 1802 Birchwood Ln Rockford IL 61107-1866

HOWARD, JOHN BRIGHAM, lawyer, foundation executive; b. Edgewood, Pa., June 9, 1912; s. Lemuel Frederic and Anna (Kimm) H.; m. Dorothy Koch, June 5, 1937 (dec. Oct. 1966); children: Elizabeth K., Frederic K., Theodore B., Catherine M.; m. Margaret Betz, Sept. 12, 1970. B.S. summa cum laude, Harvard U., 1933, Ph.D., 1936; postgrad., Calif. Inst. Tech., 1933-34; J.D. cum laude, U. Chgo., 1942. Bar: Ill., D.C., Supreme Ct. bars. Jr. Harvard Soc. Fellows, 1936-39; asst. legal adviser Dept. State, 1946-47; adviser U.S. delegation to U.N. Atomic Energy Commn., 1946; counselor Am. Mission Aid to Greece, 1947, dep. chief, 1948; cons. Congl. relations ECA, 1948-49; special asst. to sec. of state, 1949-50; regional planning adviser Nr. East, S. Asia, Africa affairs Dept. State, 1950-51; dep. dir., dir. ovserseas activities Ford Found., 1952-54, dir. internat. tng. and research, 1955-67; pres., trustee Internat. Legal Center, 1967-77; trustee Internat. Center for Law in Devel., 1978-84. Contbr. articles to profl. jours. Mem. Council on Fgn. Relations, Am. Soc. Internat. Law, Soc. Internat. Devel., Phi Beta Kappa, Phi Delta Phi. Home: 1 Hillside Pl Chappaqua NY 10514-3701*

HOWARD, JOHN LINDSAY, lawyer, forest industry company executive; b. Drumheller, Alta., Can., Nov. 18, 1931; s. Lindsay Lee and Nancy (Martin) H.; m. Jeannette Huguenin, Nov. 21, 1969. B.Comm., U. B.C., 1959, LL.B., 1961; LL.M., Harvard U., 1968; postgrad., McGill U., Montreal, Can., 1967. Bar: B.C. 1962, Que. 1967, Fed. Queen's Counsel 1977. Mem. Brahan, Dickerson & Howard, Vancouver, B.C., 1962-67, Tansey, de Grandpre, Montreal, 1968-71; asst. dep. minister Fed. Dept. Consumer and Corp. Affairs, Ottawa, Ont., 1971-79; sr. v.p. law and corp. affairs MacMillan Bloedel Ltd., Vancouver, 1979-96, cons., corp. dir., 1996—. Co-author: Proposals for a New Corporation Law for Canada, 1971, Proposals for a Securities Market Law for Canada, 1979. Home: PO Box 1132, Sooke, BC Canada V0S 1N0

HOWARD, JOHN LORING, retired trust banker; b. Auburn, N.Y., Apr. 12, 1935; s. Chauncey Frisbie and Ruth Dorothea (Burrows) H.; m. Catherine Edith Swaffin, July 1, 1961; children: John Loring, Jr., Sarah Catherine. BS, Cornell U., 1957; postgrad., NYU, 1961-62; grad. with distinction, Southwestern Grad. Sch. Banking, 1970. V.p. Chase Manhattan Bank, New York, 1961-77; sr. v.p., div. mgr. RepublicBank Houston, 1978-82; sr. v.p., group mgr. RepublicBank Trust Co., Houston, 1983-87, NCNB Tex. Nat. Bank, Dallas, 1988-91; sr. v.p., group mgr. NationsBank of Tex., N.A., Dallas, 1992-95, v.p., 1996-99; ret., 1999. Elder Munn Avenue Presbyn. Ch., East Orange, N.J., 1963-64; chmn. troop com. Boy Scouts Am., New Providence, N.J., 1975-77, chmn. Polaris dist. Friends of Scouting, Houston, 1980-82, vice chmn. North Trail dist. com., Dallas, 1990-93, chmn., 1994-95, mem. Arrowhead dist. com., Austin, 1998—; mem. fin. com. Spring Woods United Meth. Ch., Houston, 1981-84. 1st lt. USMC, 1957-60. Mem. Am. Soc. Corp. Secs. (sec. S.W. regional group 1984-85), Govt. Fin. Officers Assn. Republican. Home: 10676 Bramblecrest Dr Austin TX 78726-1906

HOWARD, JOHN MALONE, surgeon, educator; b. Autaugaville, Ala., Aug. 25, 1919; s. Fontaine Maury and Mary Lorena (O'Brien) H.; m. Nina Lyman Abernathy, Dec. 22, 1943; children: John Malone Jr., Robert Fontaine, Nina Louise, George Glenn, Susan Elaine, Laura Leigh. BS, Birmingham So., 1941; MD, U. Pa., 1944. Resident in surgery U. Pa., 1944-50; mem. faculty Baylor U., Houston, 1950-55; prof., chmn. Emory U., Atlanta, 1955-57; chair surgery Hahnemann Med. Coll., Phila., 1958-62; dir. emergency med. svcs. Med. Coll. Ohio, Toledo, Ohio, 1974-78, prof. surgery, 1974—; prof. emeritus Med. Coll. Ohio, Toledo; pvt. practice surgery Toledo, 1990—; dir. U.S. army surg. rsch. team Korean War. Editor: Studies of Battle Casualties in Korea, vol. III, 1953, vol. I, 1955, vol. II, 1955, vol. IV, 1955 (with others) Surgical Diseases of the Pancreas, 1960, 3rd edit., 1997, The Chemistry of Trauma, 1963, Cardiovascular Surgery-Supplement to Circulation, 1963, Septic Shock. Clinical and Experimental Experiences, 1964, Studies of Ultraviolet Irradiation: Its Efficiency in Preventing Infections in Operative Wounds, 1964; contbr. chpts. to books, more than 400 articles to profl. jours. Capt. U.S. Army Med. Corps., 1951-53. Decorated Legion of Merit; recipient Distinction award Nat. Rsch. Coun., Disting. Achievement award Am. Trauma Soc. Mem. Royal Coll. Surgeons Edinburgh (hon.), Brazilian Coll. Surgeons (fgn.). Avocations: fishing, boating, history, gardening. Home: 11004 Winslow Rd Whitehouse OH 43571-9643*

HOWARD, JOSEPH B. (JOE HOWARD), actor; b. Yonkers, N.Y., Nov. 24, 1948; s. Joseph Bernard and Mary Irene (Crimmins) H.; m. Sharon Atkinson Hess, Nov. 29, 1975; children: Jeremy Patrick, Julia Rosamond. BA, Hamilton Coll., 1970. Pvt. investigator Pinkerton's Nat. Detective Agy., Albany, N.Y., 1970-71; profl. actor, 1971—; tchr. music Antilles Sch., St. Thomas, V.I., 1972-73; bd. dirs and gen. dir. Theatre of Light, Inc., L.A., 1977-82; bd. dirs. Robinson's Books & Creative Arts, Ventura, Calif., 1982-92; founder and bd. dirs. All Am. Entertainment Cluster, L.A., 1996-98. Appeared in Broadway plays So Long, 174th St., 1976, Shenandoah, 1976-77; (TV series) MATHNET, 1987-94; (film) Grumpy Old Men, 1994, Minnesota Dreamers, 1999. Founder and dir. Citizens Alliance for Responsible Edn., Eden Prairie, Minn., 1993-94; campain mgr. sch. bd. election, Eden Praire, 1994. Mem. SAG (vol. income tax asst., L.A. 1997), AFTRA, Actors Equity Assn. Avocations: fishing, folk singing, folk guitar. Home and Office: 13610 Valley Vista Blvd Sherman Oaks CA 91423-4344

HOWARD, JOSEPH HARVEY, retired librarian; b. Olustee, Okla., Jan. 15, 1931; s. William Lester and Letitia Browder (Dickey) H.; m. Patricia Shaughnessy Schiebel, Apr. 10, 1980. B in Mus. Edn., U. Okla., 1952, MLS, 1957. Assoc. dir. pub. svcs. U. Colo. Libr., Boulder, 1960-63; vol. Peace Corps, Kuala Lumpur, Malaysia, 1963-65; head catalog dept. Washington U., St. Louis, 1956-67; asst. chief descriptive cataloging divsn. Libr. of Congress, Washington, 1967-68; chief descriptive cataloging divsn. Libr. of Congress, 1968-72, chief serial record divsn., 1972-75, asst. dir. (cataloging) processing dept., 1975-76, asst. libr. for processing svcs., 1976-83; dir. Nat. Agrl. Libr., Beltsville, Md., 1983-94, ret., 1994. Author: Malay Manuscripts—A Bibliographical Guide, 1966. Served with AUS, 1952-54. Recipient Outstanding Svc. to Librarianship award U. Okla., 1979. Mem. ALA (Melvil Dewey medal 1985).

HOWARD, JUWAN, professional basketball player; b. Chgo., Feb. 7, 1973. Student, U. Mich., 1994. Forward Washington Wizards (fomerly Washington Bullets), Landover, Md., 1994—. Vol. From the Heart. Named H.S. player of year Ill., 1991, Rookie of Month, NBA, Feb. 1994. Office: Washington Wizards MCI Ctr 601 F St NW Washington DC 20004-1605*

HOWARD, KAREN LYNN, marketing executive; b. Goldsboro, N.C., Oct. 17, 1967; d. Charles Ty and Beverly Ann (Schmidt) H. BA with honors in Bus. Adminstrn., U. Puget Sound, 1990; MBA, Duke U., 1995. Sales assoc. Best Products, Aurora, Colo., 1983-84; spl. projects asst. to pres. KRM Software Devel. Co., Englewood, Colo., 1984-89; mktg. asst. Riviera Fin. Svcs., Seattle, 1989; adminstrv. coord. Fin. Insights, Tacoma, 1990; devel. excellence ops. trainee Seafirst Nat. Bank, Seattle, 1990, programmer, analyst, 1991, project mgr., 1992-93; customer loyalty mgr. Sprint, 1995-96; sr. mktg. mgr. Sprint PCS, 1996-98, Siemens Information & Communiaction Networks, 1998-99; strategic alliance mgr. Oracle Corp., 1999—. Agy. coord. Seafirst Adopt-A-Family Program, 1990; dept. coord. Food Lifeline Food Drive, Seattle, 1991; div. coord. Seafirst campaign drive United Way, 1991, 92; v.p., bd. dirs. Pathways for Women, Edmonds, Wash., 1991-92, pres., bd. dirs., 1993. Recipient Disting. Svc. award Alpha Kappa Psi, 1990; dean's scholar U. Puget Sound, 1990; named Seafirst Outstanding Vol. of Yr., 1992; named to Outstanding Young Women of Am., 1991. Mem. Am. Mktg. Assn., Kappa Alpha Theta, Alpha Kappa Psi. Avocations: skiing, photography, golf, gourmet cooking, tennis. Home: 528 Shorebird Cir Unit 8204 Redwood City CA 94065-1047 Office: Oracle Corp 500 Oracle Pkwy Redwood Shores CA 94065

HOWARD, KATHLEEN, computer company executive; b. Norman, Okla., Nov. 3, 1947; d. Robert Adrian and Jane Elizabeth (Morgens) H.; m. Lawrence W. Osgood, Aug. 10, 1968 (div. Sept. 1970); m. Norman Edlo Gibat, Oct. 15, 1971. Student U. Okla., 1966-68. Typesetter, Selenby Press, Norman, 1968-72; owner, pres. Noguska Industries, Fostoria, Ohio, 1973—; co-founder Home Wine Mchts., Chgo., 1976; cons. Bechtel Corp., Ann Arbor, Mich. and Gaithersburg, Md., 1980—; chairperson Am. Software Project, 1985; ptnr. Popular Topics Pubs., 1993—. Author: All You Need to Know About MSDOS, 1993; co-author, illustrator: Lore of Still Building, 1972; co-author: Making Wine, Beer and Merry, 1973, Computer Comix Mag., 1986; pres. Popular Topics Press, Inc., also jours. and bus. mgmt. software. Treas. United Way of Fostoria, 1986-88, 2d v.p. 1988-90; bd. dirs. Pvt. Industry Coun., 1988-90. Recipient Founders award Home Wine and Beer Trade Assn. Chgo., 1976. Mem. Better Bus. Bur., Nat. Fedn. Ind. Bus., C. of C. (bd. dirs. 1986-92), Employer's Assn. Toledo, Altrusa Internat. Club (sec. Fostoria chpt. 1984-85, pres. 1986-88, editor dist. #5 1988-90). Avocations: painting, printing, travel, reading. Office: Noguska Industries 735 N Countyline St Fostoria OH 44830-1586

HOWARD, KATSUYO KUNUGI, counselor, educator, consultant; b. Kushigata, Yamanashi, Japan, Apr. 9, 1945; came to U.S., 1972; m. John P. Howard, Feb. 14, 1976; children: Shinichi, Keiko. BS, Chiba (Japan) U., 1968; MA in Linguistics, Calif. State U., Fresno, 1976, MA in Counseling, 1979; EdD, U. San Francisco, 1996. Lic. marriage, family and child counselor, Calif.; cert. tchr., community coll. credential, adult edn., Calif. Instr. Fresno City Coll., 1976-80; advisor Internat. Student Counseling, Calif. State U., Fresno, 1978-80, counselor, 1980-86; coord. SE Asian Student Svcs., Calif. State U., Fresno, 1986—; pvt. practice and cons., Fresno, Calif., 1992—; presenter in field. Author: Passages: An Anthology of the Southeast Asian Refugee Experience, 1990; prodr.: (video) Pathfinders: Hmong Refugees in Higher Education, 1987, Voices of Challenge: Hmong Women in Transition, 1997. Bd. dirs. The East-/west Ctr. Assn. East-West Community Svcs. Mem. Soc. for Intercultural Edn., Tng. and Rsch., Nat. Assn. for Fgn. Student Affairs, Cen. Valley Asian Pacific Women (bd. dirs.), Japanese Am. Citizen League, Calif. Assn. Marriage and Family Therapists, Cen. Valley Refugee Forum, Am. Assn. for Counseling and Devel., Am. Coll. Pers. Assn., Hmong Am. Women Assn., Asian & Pacific Americans in Higher Edn. Office: Calif State U Fresno 5150 N Maple Ave # Ms62 Fresno CA 93740-8026

HOWARD, KENNETH IRWIN, psychology educator; b. Chgo., Oct. 19, 1932; s. Simon and Florence (Bergman) H.; m. Michele R. Krauss, Oct. 1, 1995; children by previous marriage: Deborah, Peter, Lisa, David, Rebecca, Matthew. BA, U. Calif., Berkeley, 1954; PhD, U. Chgo., 1959. Prof. psychology Northwestern U., Evanston, Ill., 1967—. Contbr. over 150 articles to profl. publs.; author 5 books in field. 1st lt. U.S. Army, 1954-56. NIMH rsch. scientist, 1991-96; recipient Disting. Rsch. Career award Soc. for Psychotherapy Rsch., 1991, Disting. Contbn. Profession Psychology award Ill. Psychol. Assn., 1994, Disting. Profl. Contbns. to Knowledge award Am. Psychol. Assn., 1995. Democrat. Jewish. Office: Northwestern U Dept Psychology Evanston IL 60208

HOWARD, LAWRENCE E., federal judge; b. 1934. BS, U. Notre Dame, 1958, JD, 1961. Pvt. practice Grand Rapids, Mich., 1961-76; chief bankruptcy judge U.S. Dist. Ct. (we. dist.) Mich., Grand Rapids, 1976—. With U.S. Army, 1954-56. Fax: (616) 456-2425. Office: US Bankruptcy Ct We Dist Mich 766 Fed Bldg Grand Rapids MI 49503

HOWARD, LEE MILTON, international health consultant; b. India, Nov. 9, 1922; s. John A. and Grace Mary (Lemen) H.; m. Maxwell C. Croft, June 22, 1946; children: Regan Ellis, Christine Baker, Kirk Anderson, Gene Reid. B.Sc., Baylor U., 1945; M.D., Johns Hopkins U., 1947, M.P.H., 1958, Dr.P.H., 1959. Diplomate: Am. Bd. Preventive Medicine. Med. and surg. resident Church Home Hosp., Balt., 1947-50; mem. med. staff Clough Meml. Hosp., Ongole, Andhra, India, 1950-53; dir. Victoria Meml. Hosp., Warangal, Andhra, India, 1953-56; physician Med. Care Clinic, Johns Hopkins Hosp., 1957; U.S. adviser on malaria Philippines, 1960-62; U.S. regional malaria adviser Far East AID, 1962-64; chief malaria br. health div. AID, Washington, 1964-66; dep. dir. health svc. Office Tech. Coop. and Rsch., 1966-67, dir., 1967; dir. Office Health, Devel. Support Bur., 1967-80; mem. expert co. on malaria WHO, 1966-79, chmn. com., 1970, adviser parasitic diseases, 1970; mem. U.S. del. World Health Assembly, 1969-79, WHO cons. on resource moblzn., 1979-81; AID devel. fellow, 1979-80; vis. asso. prof. parasitology Inst. Hygiene, U. Philippines, 1960—; vis. lectr. Johns Hopkins U. Sch. Pub. Health, Harvard Sch. Pub. Health, Yale U., Boston U., Tulane U.; vis. fellow Inst. Devel. Studies, U. Sussex, 1979; mem. U.S. del., PAHO directing coun.; chief office resource mblzn. PAHO, 1981-82, office of external affairs, 1982-87; cons. to AID, WHO, World Bank, 1987—; sec., mem. exec. com. Gorgas Meml. Inst., 1972; mem. U.S. Sr. Exec. Svc. Recipient Superior Honor award AID, 1974, Disting. Career Svc. award AID, 1987; rsch. fellow U.S. Armed Forces Epidemiol. Bd., 1958-59. Fellow Am. Pub. Health Assn., Royal Soc. Tropical Medicine and Hygiene; mem. Am. Soc. Tropical Medicine and Hygiene, Philippine Pub. Health Assn., Johns Hopkins U. Sch. Pub. Health Soc. Alumni (pres. 1984-85), Soc. Scholars (Johns Hopkins U.), Nat. Coun. Internat. Health (charter mem.). Club: Cosmos (Washington). Home: 647 Azalea Dr Apt 1 Rockville MD 20850-2012

HOWARD, LEWIS SPILMAN, lawyer; b. Knoxville, Tenn., Oct. 10, 1930; s. Frank Catlett and Lillian (Spilman) H.; m. Anne Robinson, Dec. 26, 1953 (div. 1976); children: Catherine C., Martha S., Lewis S. Jr., Laura A. BSBA, U. Tenn., 1953, JD, 1953. Bar: Tenn. 1953, U.S. Ct. Mil. Appeals 1954, U.S. Dist. Ct. Ga. 1954, U.S. Dist. Ct. Tenn. 1956, U.S. Ct. Appeals (6th cir.) 1959. Ptnr. Kennerly, Montgomery, Howard & Finley, Knoxville, 1957-84, Howard & Ridge, Knoxville, 1984—; gen. counsel Coal Creek Mining and Mfg. Co., Knoxville, 1969—, pres., 1971—. Vice chmn. Knoxville Bd. Edn., 1968-71. Capt. JAGC, USAR, 1953-56. Mem. ABA, Tenn. Bar Assn., Knoxville Bar Assn., Cherokee Country Club, Club LeConte. Republican. Presbyterian. Avocation: boating. Home: 1604 Kenesaw Ave Knoxville TN 37919-7863 Office: Howard & Ridge First Tennessee Tower #1304 Knoxville TN 37929

HOWARD, LOUIS NORBERG, mathematics educator; b. Chgo., Mar. 12, 1929. AB in Physics, Swarthmore Coll., 1950; MA in Math. Physics, Princeton U., 1952, PhD in Math. Physics, 1953. Higgins lectr. in math. Princeton U., 1953-55; asst. prof. math. MIT, 1955-59, assoc. prof. math., 1959-64, prof. math., 1964-84, prof. emeritus, 1984; prof. math. Fla. State U., 1981-86, McKenzie prof. math., 1986-96, prof. emeritus, 1996—; rsch. assoc. in math. and aero. Caltech, 1955. Mem. editl. bd. Advances in Applied Math., Studies in Applied Math. Guggenheim Found. fellow, 1961, Sloan Found. fellow, 1962; Fairchild scholar Calif. Inst. Tech., 1976. Fellow Am. Phys. Soc. (coun. mem. fluid dynamics divsn. 1983, Fluid Dynamics prize 1997); mem. Am. Math. Soc. (sci. policy com. 1983-87), Math. Assn. Am., Soc. for Indsl. and Applied Math. Office: Dept Math Fla State Univ Tallahassee FL 32306-3027*

HOWARD, LOUNITA COOK, nonprofit executive director; b. Lebanon, Tenn., July 30, 1962; d. Gordon Lew and Sandra Marie (Davis) Cook; m. Bobby Le Howard, Feb. 19, 1983. BS, Middle Tenn. State U., 1985. Intern The Bus. Jour., Nashville, 1985; staff writer The Nashville Bus. Jour., 1985-86; staff writer The Lebanon Democrat, 1986-89, news editor, 1989-98; exec. dir. United Way of Wilson County, Lebanon, Tenn., 1998—. adv. coord. Wilson County United Way, 1990, mem. comms. com., 1991-92; mem. adv. bd. March of Dimes, Wilson County, 1991; grad. Leadership Wilson, 1995. Recipient Appreciation plaques Wilson County Edn. Assn., 1988, Enhanced 911 Wilson County, 1990; Sch. Bell award Tenn. Edn. Assn., 1988-89, Cert. of Recognition, 1990, Cert of Appreciation, March of Dimes, 1991, Mng. Editors awards Tenn. Assoc. Press. Mem. Tenn. Press Assn. (1st pl. award 1989-91, 95, 97-98), Soc. Profl. Journalists, Lebanon Bus. and Profl. Women's Club (2d v.p. 1993-94, 1st v.p. 1994-95, pres. 1995-96, Woman of Yr. 1994-95, Young Careerist 1990). Baptist. Avocations: home renovation, remodeling, gardening, reading. Office: United Way of Wilson County 114 E Main St PO Box 3541 Lebanon TN 37088-3541

HOWARD, LYN JENNIFER, medical educator; b. Buxton, U.K., Jan. 19, 1938; came to U.S., 1965; naturalized, 1971; d. Peter and Bess (Donnelly) Marsh; m. Burtis Howard, Mar. 13, 1965 (div. 1988); children: Peter Howard, Thia Howard; m. Jack Alexander, Sept. 10, 1995. BA, Oxford U., 1960, MA, BM, BCh, 1964. Diplomate Am. Bd. Internal Medicine. Intern London Hosp., 1964-65; intern Kans. City Med. Ctr., 1965-66, resident, 1966-70; fellow in clin. nutrition and gastroenterology Vanderbilt Hosp., 1971-73; dir. clin. nutrition program Albany (N.Y.) Med. Coll., 1973-80, asst. prof. medicine, pediat., 1973-76, assoc. prof. medicine, pediat., 1977-84, prof. medicine, 1984—, head divsn. clin. nutrition, 1986—; asst. dir. Clin. Studies Ctr., Albany Med. Ctr., 1973-78; attending physician Albany Med. Ctr. Hosp., 1973—; attending physician, cons. clin. nutrition Albany VA Hosp., 1973—; cons. pediat. gastroenterology St. Peter's Hosp., Albany, 1974—; med. dir. Albany Home Health Resources, 1991-92; mem. working group Nat. Commn. Digestive Diseases, 1977; mem. NIH Consensus Devel. Conf., 1978, nutrition rsch. directions, 1979, spl. study sect. clin. nutrition rsch. units, 1980, nutrition study sect., 1989-93; cons. AMA Drug Evaluations, 1982, Medicare, Blue Cross/Blue Shield S.C., 1987—; keynote spkr. Australian Soc. Parenteral and Enteral Nutrition, Perth, 1993, 1st Clin. Nutrition Symposium, Kuala Lumpor, Malaysia, 1994. Contbg. editor Nutrition Reviews, 1981-87, 89; mem. editl. bd. Jour. Drug-Nutrient Interactions, 1984, Contemporary Issues in Clin. Nutrition, 1985, Jour. Am. Soc. Parenteral and Enteral Nutrition, 1987-90; contbr. articles, abstracts to profl. jours., chpts. to books. Exec. dir. Oley Found. for Home Parenteral and Enteral Nutrition, 1983-87, pres., 1987-91, med. dir., 1991; pres. Camphill Found., Pa., 1994. Recipient Clifton C. Thorne Cmty. Svc. award, 1990, Physician of Yr. award Albany chpt. Crohn's Colitis Found. Am., 1991; elected 1st woman mem. Great Lakes Interurban Club, 1990; Major County scholar, 1956; grantee Nutrition Found., 1973-79, U.S. Dept. Agriculture, 1978-81, William F. Donner Found., 1983, Oley Found. for Home Parenteral and Enteral Nutrition Patients, 1983—, Home Health Care of Am., 1983-88, Hosp. for Incurables Found., 1987-88, 91, Schaeffer Found. for Faculty Devel., 1988. Fellow Royal Coll. Physicians, Am. Coll. Physicians, Am. Coll. Nutrition (dir. 1985-88); mem. Am. Bd. Nutrition (dir. 1980, pres. 1982-84), Brit. Med. Assn., Am. Soc. Parenteral and Enteral Nutrition (abstract selection com. 1980, nutrition support standards com. 1984, future directions com. 1991, OASIS working group 1991-92, award 1992), Am. Soc. Clin. Nutrition (rsch. com. 1978, edn. com. 1979, councilor 1982-85, chair post grad. clin. nutrition tng. com. 1983-88, clin. practice in health and disease 1991), Am. Inst. Nutrition, Am. Gastroent. Assn. (co-organizer post grad. tng. course 1987, tng. and edn. com. 1988-91, abstract selection com. 1989), N.Am. Soc. Pediat. Gastroenterology, Am. Fedn. Clin. Rsch. (abstract selection com. 1986), Alpha Omega Alpha. Office: Albany Med Coll Albany NY 12208

HOWARD, MALCOLM JONES, federal judge; b. Kinston, N.C., June 24, 1939; s. Clayton and Thelma (Jones) H.; m. Eloise McGinty, Nov. 24, 1964; children: Shannon Lea, Joshua Brian. BS, U.S. Mil. Acad., 1962; JD, Wake Forest U., Winston Salem, N.C., 1970. Bar: N.C. 1970, U.S. Ct. Appeals (4th cir.) 1973. Sec. Judge Adv. Gen. Sch., Charlottesville, Va., 1970-71; legis. counsel to sec. U.S. Army, Washington, 1971-72; asst. U.S. atty. Ea. Dist. N.C., Raleigh, 1972-73; dep. spl. counsel to Pres. U.S. Washington, 1974; sr. ptnr. Howard Browning Sams & Poole, Greenville, S.C., 1974-88; U.S. dist. judge Ea. Dist. N.C., Greenville, 1988—. With U.S. Army, 1962-82. Office: US Dist Ct PO Box 5006 Greenville NC 27835-5006*

HOWARD, MELVIN, financial executive; b. Boston, Jan. 5, 1935; s. John M. and Molly (Sagar) H.; m. Beverly Ruth Kahan, June 9, 1957; children: Brian David, Marjorie Lyn. BA, U. Mass., 1957; MS, Columbia U., 1959. Fin. exec. Ford Motor Co., Dearborn, Mich., 1959-67; v.p. adminstrn. Shoe Corps. of Am., Columbus, Ohio, 1967-70; contr., sr. v.p. fin., chief fin. officer Xerox Corp., 1970-84, exec. v.p., chmn. fin. svcs., 1984-86, vice chmn. of bd., 1986-90, bd. dirs., 1982-90; pres., CEO Ehrlich Bober Fin. Corp., 1990-92; mng. dir. Taurus Adv. Group, 1993-94; bd. dirs. Gould Pumps, Inc., Sector Mgmt., Inc. Trustee Nursing and Home Care, Commonwealth Coll. 1st lt. AUS, 1957. Mem. Birchwood Country Club, Frenchman's Creek Country Club, Beta Gamma Sigma. Home: 3139 Miro Dr S Palm Beach Gardens FL 33410*

HOWARD, MICHAEL EARL, clinical research specialist; b. Phila., Nov. 8, 1959; s. Jerome Jr. and Juanita (Sullivan) H.; m. Regina Maria Smith, Sept. 8, 1990; children: Tamira, Shannon, Alexis, Michael Earl. BS, East Stroudsburg (Pa.) U., 1982; MBA, St. Joseph U., Phila., 1996. Analytical chemist Rorer Pharm., Inc., Ft. Washington, Pa., 1982-87; sr. clin. rsch. specialist, project leader Rhone-Poulenc Rorer Pharm., Collegeville, Pa., 1987—. Recipient Excellence in Chemistry award Am. Chem. Soc., 1976. Mem. AAAS, Assocs. of Clin. Pharmacology, Drug Info. Assn., Urban League, Kappa Alpha Psi. Avocations: track and field, distance running, photography. Home: 111 Progress Dr Conshohocken PA 19428-1277 Office: Rhone-Poulenc Rorer Pharm 500 Arcola Rd Collegeville PA 19426-3930

HOWARD, MICHAEL ELIOT, historian, educator; b. London, Nov. 29, 1922; s. Geoffrey Eliot and Edith Julia Emma (Edinger) H. MA, U. Oxford, 1948, LittD, 1976; LittD, Leeds (Eng.) U.; DLitt, U. London, 1988. Asst. lectr. history Kings Coll. U. London, 1947-53, lectr. war studies, 1953-62; prof. war studies U. London, 1963-68; fellow higher defence studies All Souls Coll., Oxford, 1968-77; prof. history of war U. Oxford, 1977-80, regius prof. modern history, 1980-89; prof. history Yale U., New Haven, 1989-93; pres. Internat. Inst. Strategic Studies, London. Author: The Franco Prussian War, 1961 (Duff Cooper Prize, 1962), Grand Strategy, vol. IV, 1971 (Wolfson award for history); many others. Served to capt. Brit. Army, 1942-45. Decorated Mil. Cross His Majesty King George VI, 1943; named Knight Bachelor Her Majesty Queen Elizabeth II, 1986, Commdr. of the Brit. Empire, 1987; recipient Atlantic award NATO, 1989. Fellow Brit. Acad., U.S. Acad. Arts and Scis., Athenaeum Club, Garrick Club (London). Anglican.

HOWARD, MICHAEL JOSEPH, communications executive, real estate developer; b. Detroit, Oct. 26, 1951; s. Thomas Angel and Margaret Jane (Uttenweiler) H.; divorced; children: Jennifer Paula, Daniel Joseph. Student, Schoolcraft Coll., 1971. Lic. real estate broker, Mich.; lic. residential builder, Mich. Mem. field svc. staff ITT, Southfield, Mich., 1971-81; pres. Howard Properties, Inc., Southfield, 1988—, Allied Alarm Systems, Inc., Southfield, 1988—, Allied Communications, Inc., Southfield, 1979—. Commr. Downtown Devel. Authority, Southfield, 1989—. Mem. Nat. Assn. Home Builders, Nat. Fedn. Ind. Bus., Mich. Assn. Home Builders, Mich. Pay Telephone Assn. (treas. 1986), Southfield C. of C., Optimist Club (charter). Republican. Roman Catholic. Avocations: numismatics, classic cars, boating. Office: Allied Communications Inc 17600 Northland Park Ct Southfield MI 48075-4321

HOWARD, MILDRED, sculptor; b. San Francisco, 1945. AA, cert. in fashion arts, Coll. Alameda, 1977; MFA in Fiberworks, John F. Kennedy U., 1985. One-woman shows include Mill Valley (Calif.) Old Post Office, 1984, Dade County Libr., Miami, Fla., 1985, Calif. State U., Hayward, 1987, Headlands Ctr. for the Arts, Sausalito, Calif., 1991, San Francisco Art Inst., 1991, Gallery Paule Anglim, San Francisco, 1991, 93, INTAR, N.Y.C., 1992, U. Art Gallery, Sonoma State U., Rohnert Park, Calif., 1992, San Jose (Calif.) Mus. Art, 1994, Hammonds House Galleries, Atlanta, 1994, Capp St. Project, San Francisco, 1994; group exhbns. include Security Pacific Gallery, San Francisco, 1992, Lew Allen Gallery, Santa Fe, 1992, Shea & Bornstein Gallery, Santa Monica, 1992, Creative Time, N.Y.c., 1992, Berkeley Art Ctr., 1992, Nina Nielsen Gallery, Boston, 1993, New Mus. Contemporary Art, N.Y.C., 1993, Calif. Crafts Mus., San Francisco, 1994, U. Calif. Berkeley Mus. Art, Sci. and Culture, 1994, Laney Coll., Oakland, Calif., 1994, The Mus. at Blackhawk, Danville, Calif., 1994, Hampton (Va.) U. Mus., 1994, Gallery Resche, Paris, 1994, Yerba Buena Ctr. for the Arts, San Francisco, 1994, Installation Gallery, San Diego, 1994, Jewett Hall Gallery, U. Maine, Augusta, 1994, CCAC, Oakland, 1994, Oakland Mus., 1994, Louis Stern Fine Arts, L.A., 1995, Gallery Concord, 1995, others; represented in permanent collections Oakland Mus., Wadsworth Athaneum, Hartford, Conn., Rene and Veronica di Rosa Found., Napa, Calif., pvt. collections. Recipient Bank of Am. award, San Francisco, 1975, Small Projects award Inter Arts Marin, San Rafael, Calif., 1984, Adaline Kent award San Francisco Art Inst., 1991; fellow in mixed media Calif. Arts Coun., 1990, Lila A. Wallace/Reader's Digest Internat. Traveling fellow, 1992-93. Office: c/o Porter Troupe Gallery 301 Spruce St San Diego CA 92103-5626*

HOWARD, M(OSES) WILLIAM, JR., minister, seminary president; b. Americus, Ga., Mar. 3, 1946; s. M. William and Laura (Turner) H.; m. Barbara Jean Wright, July 11, 1970; children: Matthew Weldon, Adam Turner, Maisha Wright. B.A., Morehouse Coll., 1968, L.H.D., 1984; M.Div., Princeton Theol. Sem., 1972; D.D., Miles Coll., 1979, Central Coll., 1980. Ordained to ministry Am. Baptist Ch., 1974; exec. dir. Black Council, Ref. Ch. in Am., N.Y.C., 1972-92; pres. N.Y. Theol. Sem., N.Y.C., 1992—; bd. dirs. Nat. Conf. Black Churchmen, 1975-80; moderator Commn. of World Council Chs. Program to Combat Racism, 1976-78; bd. dirs. Nat. Media Found.; pres. Nat. Council Chs., 1979-81; condr. Christmas services for hostages Am. embassy, Tehran, 1979; chmn. UN Seminar on Bank Loans to South Africa, Zurich, 1981; chmn. ecumenical delegation to Syria, 1984, instrumental (with Rev. Jesse Jackson) in obtaining release of Lt. Robert O. Goodman, USN; chair religious com. to welcome Nelson Mandela to U.S.A., 1990. Researcher: Born to Rebel - Autobiography of Benjamin Elijah Mays, 1967; editor: monthly newsletter Black Caucus RCA, 1973-92; pub., producer ann. lectureship, 1975-92. Active YMCA; trustee Trenton State Coll., 1981-82, Nat. Urban League; bd. dirs. Children's Def. Fund, The Independent Sector, founding mem. People for Am. Way; pres. Am. Com. on Africa, 1987-92; mem. coun. Fgn. Rels., 1997—. Recipient Disting. Service award as chmn. Commn. on Justice, Liberation and Human Fulfillment, Disting. Alumnus award Princeton Theol. Sem., 1984; decorated comdr. Order Knights of Holy Sepulchre. Mem. NAACP, Assn. Theol. Schs. in U.S. and Can. (sec. 1998—), Sigma Pi Phi. Office: NY Theol Sem 5 W 29th St New York NY 10001-4501 *Perhaps the greatest challenge to humanity today is to see that our moral and ethical development catches up, and keeps pace with, our advances in technology.*

HOWARD, NANCY E., lawyer; b. Ft. Wayne, Ind., Aug. 13, 1951. BA, Stanford U., 1973, JD, 1977. Bar: Calif. 1977. Mem. Tuttle & Taylor, L.A., 1977—. Contbr. articles to profl. jours. Mem. Order of Coif., Phi Beta Kappa. Office: Tuttle & Taylor 355 S Grand Ave 40th Fl Los Angeles CA 90071-3176

HOWARD, NATHAN SOUTHARD, investment banker, lawyer; b. Marysville, Ohio, May 4, 1941; s. Cone Howard Jr. and Catherine (Southard) H.; divorced; children—Ercil Coleman, Lyndsay Christine. B.A., William and Mary Coll., 1962, J.D., 1965. V.p. White Weld & Co., N.Y.C., 1972-75; v.p. Prudential-Bache Securities, Inc., N.Y.C., 1975-80, assoc. dir., 1980-82, mng. dir., 1985-89; dir. energy and utilities group Barclays de Zoete Wedd Corp. Fin., N.Y.C., 1990-93; v.p. energy divsn. Bank of N.Y., N.Y.C., 1993—. Bd. dirs. People Symphony Concerts, N.Y.C., 1982—. Mem. ABA, N.Y. State Bar, N.Y. Soc. Securities Analysts, Bond Club N.Y., Univ. Club (N.Y.C.). Office: Bank of NY 19th Fl 1 Wall St Fl 19 New York NY 10005-2500

HOWARD, PATRICK GENE, marine corps officer; b. Wheeling, Va., Nov. 28, 1945; s. Gene Edward and Margaret Anna (Fry) H.; m. Paula Lee Oberle, May 25, 1969; children: Brian, Michael, Marc. BS, U.S. Naval Acad., Annapolis, Md., 1967; MS in Pub. Adminstrn., Shippensburg U., 1987. Commd. USMC, advanced through grades to maj., 1995; comdg. officer 2d Bn., 10th Marines, 1981; head policy sect., exec. asst. Hqrs. Marine Corps; comdr. 11th Marines, 1990-92; sec. gen. staff Asst. Commandant Marine Corps Office, 1992-93; dir. pers. mgmt. divsn. Manpower and Res. Affairs Dept. Hdqs. Marine Corps, Washington, 1993-95; comdg. gen. Marine Corps Base, Camp Lejeune, N.C., 1995-97, dep. comdg. gen., 1997—. Decorated Legion of Merit with Combat V and gold star, Def. Meritorious Svc. Medal, Meritorious Svc. medal with gold star. Roman Catholic. Avocation: golf. Office: Marine Corps Base PSC Box 20004 Quantico VA 22134*

HOWARD, PIERRE, state official; m. Nancy Elizabeth Barnes; children: Christopher, Caroline. Grad., U. Ga., 1965, JD, 1968. Former mem. Ga. Senate, Atlanta, former asst. floor leader, former chmn. human resources com.; lt. gov. State of Ga., Atlanta, 1991-98; ptnr. Spl. Corp. Strategies, Atlanta, 1999—. Recipient Nathan Davis award AMA, 1996. Mem. Phi Beta Kappa. Office: Spl Corporate Strategies 2451 Cumberland Pky 3431 Atlanta GA 30339*

HOWARD, RICHARD JAMES, mycology researcher; b. Appleton, Wis., May 29, 1952; s. Robert Stanley and Ruth Virginia (Hale) H.; m. Mary Elizabeth Weinberg, Aug. 17, 1979; children: Robinson, Cameron. BS, U. Wis., 1974; MS, Cornell U., 1977, PhD, 1980. Postdoctoral fellow Washington U., St. Louis, 1979-80; rsch. biologist biochemicals dept. DuPont Co., Wilmington, Del., 1980-83, sect. rsch. biologist dept. agrl. products, 1983-85, prin. investigator Ctrl. R&D, 1986-97; rsch. assoc. agrl. products DuPont Co., Wilmington, 1997—. Contbr. articles to profl. jours. Bd. dirs. Birth Ctr. Found., Greenville, Del., 1986-90. NSF fellow, 1980. Mem. Mycol. Soc. Am. (mem. coun., treas. 1996—), assoc. editor Mycologia, Alexopoulos award 1990). Office: Ctrl R&D Dupont Exper Stn E402 Wilmington DE 19880-0402

HOWARD, RICHARD RALSTON, II, medical health advisor, researcher, financier; b. Winnfield, Kans., May 26, 1948; s. Richard Ralston and Ione (Mayer) H. BBA, Loyola U., New Orleans, 1970; MPH, Tulane U., 1977, MS, 1984, DrPH, 1988. Researcher Loyola U., 1973; educator Dominican Coll., New Orleans, 1977; educator Sch. Pub. Health Tulane U., New Orleans, 1978-82, researcher Sch. Medicine, 1979-88; med. health advisor Howard Med. Clinic, Slidell, La., 1982-91; founder The Inst. Econ. Tech. Rsch., New Orleans, 1993—. NIH grantee, 1979; VA grantee, 1984. Mem. Internat. Platform Assn., Am. Assn. Individual Investors, Beta Beta Beta. Achievements include research on the impact of the health food industry on nutrition awareness, cocaine testing through quantitative tear analysis, vitamin C and ophthalmic wound healing. Home: 3531 Nashville Ave New Orleans LA 70125-4339

HOWARD, RICHARD TURNER, construction company executive; b. Rock Hill, S.C., Jan. 3, 1935; s. Paul Noble and Pauline (Sugg) H.; children: Richard Turner, James Fowles, George Anderson; m. Elizabeth Hall, 1993. B.S., U. S.C., 1957. Vice-pres. Howard Constrn. Co., 1957-72; exec. v.p. Paul N. Howard Co., Greensboro, N.C., 1972-77; pres., chief exec. officer Paul N. Howard Co., 1977-85; chmn., chief exec. officer Howard Mgmt. Group, Inc., 1985—; bd. dirs. N.C. Licensing Bd. for Gen. Contractors, 1989-94. Bd. dirs. Greensboro C. of C., 1972-78, Greensboro Devel. Co., 1982—, Green Hill Art Gallery, 1984-86; trustee U. N.C., Greensboro, 1983-87, Nat. Conf. Christians and Jews, 1978-88; bd. visitors Guilford Coll., 1986-94, 95-98; vice-chmn. First Flight Centennial Commn., 1994—, pres. first Flight Centennial Found.; mem. Centennial of Flight Commn. Mem. Greensboro C. of C., Figure Eight Yacht Club, Greensboro Country Club. Republican. Presbyterian. Home: 1907 Lafayette Ave Greensboro NC 27408-7203 Office: 812 N Elm St Greensboro NC 27401-1511

HOWARD, ROBERT ELLIOTT, former federal official, consultant, educator; b. Staten Island, N.Y., Feb. 19, 1933; s. David and Helen (Gresser) H.; m. Bulbul Batra, Mar. 24, 1957; children: Nina Howard Regan, Nicholas, Sarah. AB, Columbia U., 1952; DPhil, Oxford U., Eng., 1957. Rsch. fellow in physics Carnegie Inst. Tech., Carnegie-Mellon U., Pitts., 1958-60; rsch. physicist Nat. Bur. Standards, Washington, 1960-67; mem. profl. staff Office Mgmt. and Budget, Washington, 1968-87, dep. assoc. dir. for nat. security, 1987-90, assoc. dir. for nat. security and internat. affairs, 1990-93; vis. prof. Nat. Defense Univ., Washington, 1993-95; pres. R.E. Howard Assocs., 1995; adj. prof. nat. security studies Georgetown U., Washington, 1993—; vis. rsch. physicist U.K. Atomic Energy Authority, Harwell, Eng., 1962; pres. R.E. Howard Assocs., 1995—. Contbr. numerous articles to profl. jours. Recipient Presdl. Meritorious Exec. award, 1987, Presdl. Disting. Exec. award, 1990; Fulbright fellow Indian Inst. Tech., New Delhi, 1966. Fellow Am. Phys. Soc. Republican. Avocations: walking, reading, arts.

HOWARD, ROBERT FRANKLIN, observatory administrator, astronomer; b. Delaware, Ohio, Dec. 30, 1932; s. David Dale and Clarine Edna (Morehouse) H.; m. Margaret Teresa Farnon, Oct. 4, 1958; children—Thomas Colin, Alan Robert, Moira Catharine. BA, Ohio Wesleyan U., 1954; PhD, Princeton U., 1957. Carnegie fellow Mt. Wilson and Palomar Obs., Pasadena, Calif., 1957-59; staff mem. Mt. Wilson and Palomar Obs., 1961-81; asst. prof. U. Mass., Amherst, 1959-61; asst. dir. for Mt. Wilson Mt. Wilson & Las Campanas Obs., Pasadena, 1981-84; dir. Nat. Solar Obs., Tucson, 1984-88, astronomer, 1988-98, astronomer emeritus, 1998—. Editor: Solar Magnetic Fields, 1971; editor: (jour.) Solar Physics, 1987-98; contbr. articles to profl. jours. Mem. Am. Astron. Soc., Internat. Astron. Union. Office: Nat Solar Obs PO Box 26732 950 N Cherry Ave Tucson AZ 85719-4933

HOWARD, ROBERT STAPLES, newspaper publisher; b. Wheaton, Minn., Oct. 23, 1924; s. Earl Eaton and Helen Elizabeth (Staples) H.; m. Lillian Irene Crabtree, Sept. 2, 1945; children: Thomas, Andrea, William, David. Student, U. Minn., 1942, 45. Pub. various daily, weekly newspapers, 1946-55; pub. Chester, Pa. Times, 1955-61; Pres. Howard Publs. (18 daily newspapers), 1961—. With AUS, 1942-43; 2d lt. USAAF, 1944-45. Home: PO Box 1337 Rancho Santa Fe CA 92067-1337 Office: PO Box 570 Oceanside CA 92049-0570

HOWARD, RON, director, actor; b. Duncan, Okla., Mar. 1, 1954; s. Rance and Jean Howard; m. Cheryl Alley, June 7, 1975; 4 children: Bryce, Jocelyn and Paige (twins), Reed. Student, U. So. Calif., Los Angeles Valley Coll. Co-chmn. Imagine Films Entertainment, L.A. Actor: (theatre) The Seven Year Itch, 1956, Hole in the Head, 1963; (films) The Journey, 1959, Five Minutes to Live, 1959, Music Man, 1962, The Courtship of Eddie's Father, 1963, Village of the Giants, 1965, Wild Country, 1971, Happy Mother's Day... Love George, 1973, American Graffiti, 1973, The Spikes Gang, 1974, The First Nudie Musical, 1976, Eat My Dust, 1976, The Shootist, 1976, Grand Theft Auto (also dir.) 1977, More American Graffiti, 1979, The Magical World of Chuck Jones, 1992, (TV, host/narrator) Frank Capra's American Dream, 1997; dir.: Night Shift, 1982, Splash, 1984, Cocoon, 1985, Gung Ho, (also exec. prodr.) 1986, No Man's Land, (also exec prodr.) 1987, Willow, 1988, Parenthood (also co-author) 1989, Backdraft, 1991, Far and Away (also co-prodr., co-author) 1992, The Paper, 1994, Apollo 13, 1995 (Outstanding Directorial Achievement in Motion Picture award Dir. Guild Am. 1996), Ransom, 1996, Edtv, 1999; exec. prodr.: Clean and Sober, 1988, Vibes, 1988, Closet Land, 1991, Inventing the Abbotts, 1997, Hiller and Diller (TV, exec.), 1997, From the Earth to the Moon (mini series), 1998, Sports Night (TV series, exec.), 1998, Felicity (TV series, exec.), 1998, Student Affairs (TV), 1999, How to Eat Fried Worms, 1999, Detox, 1999, The PJs (TV series, exec.), Edtv, 1999; regular TV series The Andy Griffith Show, 1960-68, The Smith Family, 1971-72, Happy Days, 1974-80; other TV appearances include New Breed, Wonderful World of Disney, Gentle Ben, Laverne and Shirley, Twilight Zone, Danny Kaye Show, Fugitive, Dennis the Menace, Bonanza, Five Fingers, Gunsmoke, The F.B.I., 11th Hour, (TV movies) The Migrants, 1974, Locusts, 1974, Huckleberry Finn, 1975, Cotton Candy (co-writer, dir.) 1978, Act of Love, 1980, Bitter Harvest, 1981, Fire on the Mountain, 1981, Skyward (dir., co-exec. prodr.) 1981, Through the Magic Pyramid (dir., exec. prodr.) 1981, When Your Lover Leaves (co-exec./prodr.) 1983, Return to Mayberry, 1986. Mem. AFTRA, SAG, Acad. Motion Picture Arts and Scis. Office: care of Peter Dekom Bloom DeKom & Hergott 150 S Rodeo Dr Beverly Hills CA 90212-2408 also: Imagine Entertainment 1925 Century Park E Ste 230 Los Angeles CA 90067-2702*

HOWARD, RUSTIN RAY, corporate executive; b. Eugene, Oreg., Oct. 18, 1956; s. Ray L. and Dorothy V. (Johnson) H.; m. Maureen W. Howard, Dec. 17, 1979; children: Matthew, Aubrey, Danielle, Travis. BS, Brigham Young U., 1987; MBA, Cornell-Johnson Grad. Sch., Ithaca, N.Y., 1989. Missionary LDS Porto Alegre Mission, Rio Grande Do Sul, Brazil, 1976-78; ptnr. Solar Farms, Rupert, Idaho, 1979-87; with SROne Venture Capital, Ithaca, 1988-89; prin. H&H Techs., Ithaca, 1988-91; pres. Phyton Catatytic, Inc., Ithaca, 1990-94; CEO, chmn. bd. dirs. Phyton Catalytic, Inc., Ithaca, 1990-93; pres., CEO, BioWorks, Inc., Geneva, N.Y., 1993-97; chmn. bd. dirs. Innovative Dynamics, Inc., Ithica, N.Y., 1995—; CEO Sage Corp., Trumansburg, 1998—. Contbr.: International Mergers and Acquisitions, 1990. Scoutmaster troop 67 Boy Scouts Am., Ithaca, 1993-96; mem. adv. bd. biotech. dept. Cornell U., 1992-97; mem. adv. bd. Tompkins County Trust Co., 1990-95. Mem. Aircraft Owners and Pilots Assn., N.Y. Biotech. Assn. (legis. com.), Cornell Alumni Assn. (pres. 1994-96, Johnson Grad. Sch. Mgmt. bd. 1994—). Republican. LDS Ch. Avocations: basketball, flying, golf, skiing, science. Office: Innovative Dynamics Inc 2560 N Triphammer Rd Ithaca NY 14850-9726

HOWARD, STEPHEN WRIGLEY, telecommunications executive; b. Buffalo, Sept. 7, 1940; '. Norman Wrigley and Vesta (Gow) H.; m. Eileen F. O'Neill (div. 1973); children: Elizabeth Anne, Amy Lindsay; m. Dimiti Ann Stegeman; 1 child, Sarah Winsome. BLS, Boston U., 1981. Underwriter Aetna Life & Casualty Co., Boston, 1963-66; mem. sales and mktg. staff New Eng. Telephone Co., Boston, 1966-82; mgr., cons. liaison AT&T, Morristown, N.J., 1983; ptnr. Howard Assocs., Lebanon, Maine, 1983—; adj. faculty Boston U., 1982—, St. Joseph's Coll., Standish, Maine, 1995—; lectr., Software Inst., Andover, Mass., 1984-88. Author software. Mem. York County Citizens' Alliance, Lebanon, 1987—, Boston U. Alumnae Sch. Com., 1987—. Republican. Episcopalian. Avocations: tennis, forestry, trap and skeet.

HOWARD, SUSANNE C., lawyer; b. White Plains, N.Y., July 14, 1951; d. Leonard F. and Trudy Howard. AB in History, Washington U., St. Louis, 1973; JD, Cath. U., Washington, 1977. Bar: Mass. 1978, U.S. Dist. Ct. Mass. 1978, U.S. Ct. Appeals (1st cir.) 1979. Researcher Environ. Law Inst., Washington, 1976-77; mng. ptnr. Thomas & Howard, Cambridge, Mass., 1977-80; sr. assoc. Choate, Hall & Stewart, Boston, 1981-86; v.p., asst. gen. counsel Aldrich, Eastman & Waltch, Inc., Boston, 1986-87; sr. assoc. Csaplar & Bok, Boston, 1987-88; counsel Warner & Stackpole, Boston, 1988-92; New England regional counsel Trust for Public Land, Boston, 1992-94; pres. Consensus Capital, Inc., Cambridge, Mass., 1995-99; pres. L.F. Howard Assocs., Inc., N.Y.C., 1998—, also bd. dirs.; mem. faculty Mass. Continuing Legal Edn. Programs, Boston, 1988-92. Contrb. articles to profl. jours. Mem. Environ. Adv. Com. to Atty. Gen., Mass., 1990-95; bd. dirs. Cambridge YWCA, 1987-93, pres., 1991-92. Mem. Boston Bar Assn. (mem. steering com. environ. sect. 1987-91, chair wetlands and waterways com. 1989-91), Women's Bar Assn. Mass. (bd. dirs. 1981-83, co-chair legis. policy com. 1979-81, Pub. Svc. to Bar and Cmty. award 1991). Office: LF Howard Assocs Inc 60 E 42nd St New York NY 10165

HOWARD, TERRY THOMAS, obstetrician/gynecologist; b. Cleve., May 14, 1943; s. Henry and Paula H.; m. Phyllis C. Schaevitz, Aug. 21, 1965; children: Jennifer, Jason, Brian. AB magna cum laude, Columbia U., 1965; MD, Harvard Med. Sch., 1969. Diplomate Am. Bd. Ob-Gyn. Intern, resident gen. surgery Beth Israel Hosp., Boston, 1969-71; resident ob-gyn Boston Hosp. for Women, 1971-74; physician Chelmsford (Mass.) Med. Assocs., 1974-88, Harvard Cmty. Health Plan, Chelmsford, 1988-97, Harvard Vanguard Med. Assocs. (formerly Harvard Cmty. Health Plan), Chelmsford, 1998—; trustee Lowell (Mass.) Gen. Hosp., 1987—. Bd. dirs. Friends of the Children Concert Band, Chelmsford, 1981—; trustee Congregation Shalom, Chelmsford, 1993-96. Fellow Am. Coll. Obstetrics & Gynecology, Am. Coll. Surgeons; mem. Am. Soc. Reproductive Medicine. Office: Harvard Vanguard Med Assocs 228 Billerica Rd Chelmsford MA 01824-3604

HOWARD, VICTOR, management consultant; b. Montreal, Que., Can., Aug. 12, 1923; s. Thomas and Jean (Malkinson) H.; BA, Sir George Williams U., 1947; BSc, 1948; PhD, Mich. State U., 1954; m. Dorothy Bode, Dec. 25, 1953. Mech. design engr. Canadian Vickers Ltd., Montreal, 1942-46; with Aluminum Co. Can., 1946-48, E.B. Badger Co., Boston, 1948-50; asst. prof. Mich. State U., 1952-56; social scientist Rand Corp., 1956-58; staff exec., personnel dir. System Devel. Corp., Santa Monica, Calif., 1958-66; staff cons. Rohrer, Hibler & Replogle, San Francisco, 1966-69; mng. dir. Rohrer, Hibler & Replogle Internat., London and Brussels, 1969-74, ptnr. 1974, mgr. San Francisco, 1974-88, dir., 1979-88; pres. V. Howard and Assocs., 1988—, The Inst. on Stress and Health in the Work Place, 1988—; vice chair State Bd. Psychology, 1989-93. Fellow Brit. Inst. Dirs.; mem. Am. Psychol. Assn., Western Psychol.Assn., U.S. Power Squadrons (comdr. Sequoia Squadron 1981, dist. comdr. 1987), Calif. State Mil. Res. (col. 1984), Reform Club, Hurlingham (London) Club, Thames Motor Yacht Club (Molesey, Eng.), Order of St. John of Jerusalem (chevalier)Sovereign Mil. Order of the Temple (prior Priory of St Francis, Grand Cross), Masons (33 degree), Shriners, Sigma Xi. Home and Office: 530 Los Altos Ct Santa Rosa CA 95403-1329

HOWARD, WALTER BURKE, chemical engineer; b. Corpus Christi, Tex., Jan. 22, 1916; s. Clement and Nell (Smith) H.; m. Virginia Kentucky Freeman, Feb. 14, 1942; children—Thomas Clement, Virginia Ann. B.A., U. Tex., 1937, B.S. in Chem. Engring, 1938, M.S., 1940, Ph.D., 1943. Registered profl. engr., Tex.; chartered engr., U.K. From asst. to sr. chem. engr. Bur. Indsl. Chemistry, U. Tex., Austin, 1939-52; from sr. engr. to scientist Monsanto Chem. Co., Texas City, Tex., 1952-64; mgr. process safety, sci. fellow to disting. fellow Monsanto Co., St. Louis, 1965-81; process safety tech. cons., 1981—. Contbr. chpts. to books, articles to profl. jours. Patentee in field. Vice-pres. Texas City Sch. Bd., 1963-64; chmn. bd. dirs. Mainland Opportunity Sch., 1958-61; mem. area council Boy Scouts Am., 1958-60; active P.T.A.; trustee Austin Presbyn. Theol. Sem., 1961-64. Fellow Brit. Instn. Chem. Engrs., Am. Inst. Chem. Engrs. (dir., Walton/Miller award 1987, Ann. Inst. lectr. 1987), Am. Chem. Soc., Combustion Inst. Internat., Nat. Fire Protection Assn. (Disting. Svc. award 1984), Austin Engrs. Club (past dir.), Phi Beta Kappa, Sigma Xi, Phi Lambda Upsilon. Presbyterian (elder). Address: 1415 Bopp Rd Saint Louis MO 63131-4135

HOWARD, WILLIAM GATES, JR., electronics company executive; b. Boston, Nov. 6, 1941; s. William Gates and Mary Louise (Creager) H.; m. Kathleen Louretta Shipp, June 4, 1983. B.E.E. with distinction, Cornell U., 1964, M.S., 1965; Ph.D., U. Calif.-Berkeley, 1967. Asst. prof. dept. elec. engring. and computer scis. U. Calif.-Berkeley, 1967-69; group ops. mgr. Motorola Semicondr. Group, Mesa, Ariz., 1969-76; v.p., dir. tech. and planning Motorola Semicondr. Sector, Phoenix, 1976-83; v.p., dir. research and devel. Motorola Inc., Schaumburg, Ill., 1983-87; sr. fellow Nat. Acad. of Engring., Washington, 1987-91; dir. BEI Techs., Inc., Ramtron Internat Corp., VLSI Techs., Inc. Xilinx, Inc., Sandia Corp., Lockheed-Martin Energy Rsch. Co., Lockheed-Martin Idaho Techs. Co.; chmn. semicondr. tech. adv. com. U.S. Dept. Commerce, 1978-83; chmn. adv. group on electron devices Dept. Def., 1982—, mem. def. sci. bd., 1996—; mem. study com. on tech. and implications of VLSI, NAS, 1980; chmn. vis. com. on advanced tech. Nat. Inst. Stds. and Tech., 1988-92; chmn. Def. Sci. Bd. Task Force on Microelectronics Rsch. Facilities, 1991-92; mem. Sandia Pres. Adv. Coun., Oak Ridge Nat. Lab. Adv. Coun.; chmn. bd. dirs. Credence Sys., Inc. Author: (with D.J. Hamilton) Basic Integrated Circuit Engineering, 1976, (with B. Guile) Profiting from Innovation, 1992; patentee (with J.B. Cecil) improved reference current source, ladder termination circuit, three terminal zener diode. Fellow AAAS, IEEE (vice chmn. circuits and systems soc. 1976-78); mem. Nat. Acad. of Engring., Sigma Xi, Phi Kappa Phi, Eta Kappa Nu, Tau Beta Pi. Office: 10642 E San Salvador Dr Scottsdale AZ 85258-6114

HOWARD, WILLIAM MATTHEW, educator, lawyer, arbitrator, author; b. Oak Park, Ill., Dec. 16, 1934; s. William and Martha Geraldine (Herlock) H.; children: Matthew William, Stephanie Sue. BSBA, U. Mo., 1956, JD, 1958; postgrad., U. Nice, France, 1976, U. London, 1977; PhD, Ariz. State U., 1995. Bar: Mo. 1958, U.S. Supreme Ct. 1986; cert. mediator and arbitrator, Fla. Supreme Ct. Jr. ptnr. Bryan, Cave, McPheeters & McRoberts, St. Louis, 1958-66; asst. to pres. Granite City (Ill.) Steel Co., 1966-69; pres. Thomson Internat. Co., Thibodaux, La., 1969-70; founder, pres., chmn. bd. The Catalyst Group, Phoenix, 1970-97; dean, ctr. adminstr. The Union Inst., San Diego, 1997—; mem. adj. faculty U. Mo., Columbia, 1956-58, St. Louis U., 1958-61, Ariz. State U., 1994-96, Ottawa U., 1994-96, Nova Southeastern U., 1996-97; chmn. unauthorized practice law com. Mo. Bar, St. Louis, 1964-65; chmn. bd. N.V. Vulcaansoord, Terborg, The Netherlands, 1975-78, E. Chalmers Holdings, Ltd., Glasgow, Scotland, 1977-78; exec. com. Chem. Bank, Irvine, Calif., 1985-90; vis. lectr. UCLA, 1987; arbitrator Am. Arbitration Assn., N.Y.C., 1987—, N.Y. Stock Exch., 1987—, Nt. Assn. Securities Dealers, Chgo., 1987—, Nat. Futures Assn., Chgo., 1988—, Am. Stock Exch., N.Y.C., 1988; hearing officer Mo. Dept. Natural Resources, Jefferson City, 1987-89, Internat. Ct. Arbitration, 1993, Inter-Am. Comml. Arbitration Commn., 1993—; mem. Fla. Automobile Arbitration Bd., 1997—; bd. dirs. Xeric Corp., Denver. Editor newsletter Extras, 1970—; exec. producer: (motion picture) Twice a Woman, 1979; contbr. numerous articles and revs. to various jours. Bd. dirs. U. Mo. Alumni Assn., 1986, Breckenridge (Colo.) Film Festival, 1989, Actors Theatre Phoenix, 1990; mem., pres.' club adv. bd. Phoenix Art Mus., 1990; dir. Scottsdale Cultural Coun., 1991. Mem. Am. Arbitration Assn. (regional adv. com.), Soc. Profls. in Dispute Resolution, Fla. Acad. Mediators, Nat. Inst. Dispute Resolution, Mensa, Order of Coif. Avocations: literature, travel, theatre, visual arts, skiing. Office: The Union Inst 2878 Camino Del Rio S Ste 115 San Diego CA 92108-3870

HOWARD, WILLIAM PERCY, physician; b. Canton, Miss., Dec. 29, 1947; s. John Wesley Griffin and Ann (Wallace) H.; m. Nancy Rose Moyers, May 25, 1980; children: John W.G. II, Ann Skidmore, Ashley Elizabeth. BS in Chem. Engring., Miss. State U., 1970; MD, U. Miss., 1979. Chem. engr. Miss. Chem. Corp., Yazoo City, 1970-75; resident U. Med. Ctr., JAckson, Miss., 1979-82; staff physician emergency physician MEA Med. Sys., JAckson, Miss., 1982-90, clin. staff physician, 1990—; chmn. bd. dirs. 1st Intermed Corp., 1997—, Miss. Emergency Assn., 1997—; mem. physicians adv. com. Blue Cross-Blue Shield, 1993—. Named Madison County Cattleman of Yr., Miss., 1991. Fellow Am. Acad. Family Practitioners; mem. AMA, Am. Angus Assn., Miss. State Med. Assn. Republican. Methodist. Avocations: antiques, history, architecture, cattle farming. Office: MEA Med Clinic 5606 Old Canton Rd Jackson MS 39211-4217

HOWARD, WILLIAM S., federal judge. Apptd. bankruptcy judge ea. dist. U.S. Dist. Ct. Ky., 1990. Fax: (606) 233-2604. Office: 100 E Vine St Ste 300 Lexington KY 40507-1432

HOWARD-HILL, TREVOR HOWARD, English language educator; b. Wellington, New Zealand, Oct. 17, 1933; came to U.S. 1972; s. Roland Henry and Dulcie Helena (Howard) Hill; children: Miranda Caroline, Victoria, Penelope Anne Din, Christopher John, Dorothy Disterheft. BA, Victoria U., Wellington, N.Z., 1955; MA, Victoria U., 1957, PhD, 1960; DPhil, U. Oxford, Eng., 1971. Head cataloguing Alexander Turnbull Libr., Wellington, 1961-63; sr. rsch. fellow Oxford U. Computing Lab., 1965-70; lectr. English Univ. Coll., Swansea, Wales, 1970-72; assoc. prof. English U. S.C., Columbia, 1972-77; prof English U. S.C., 1977-90, chmn. dept. English, 1990-91, C. Wallace Martin prof. English, 1990—; coll. dir. S.C. Coun. Tchrs. English, 1982-85; bibliography/access panelist NEH, 1984, 86. Author: Ralph Crane, 1972, Literary Concordances, 1979, Middleton's Vulgar Pasquin: Essays on a Game of Chess, 1995, editor: Sir John van Olden Barnavelt, 1980, The Book of Sir Thomas More: Essays, 1989, A Game of Chess, 1990, Thomas Middleton's A Game of Chess, 1993, Middleton's Bridgewater Manuscript of A Game of Chess, 1995; mem. editl. bd. Lit. Rsch., 1986-94, Rev., 1992—, Shakespeare Notes, 1996—; compiler: Oxford Shakespeare Concordances, 1969-73, Index to British Literary Bibliography, 7 vols., 1969—; editor Papers of the Bibliog. Soc. Am., 1994—. Recipient Russell award for rsch. U. S.C., 1988; U. New Zealand fellow, 1958-59, NIRNS fellow Oxford U., 1966-67, fellow H.E. Huntington Libr., 1975, NEH, 1979, Guggenheim fellow, 1989, fellow Folger Shakespeare Libr., 1993, Brit. Libr. Ctr. for Book, 1994-95. Mem. MLA, Modern Humanities Rsch. Assn., Malone Soc., Soc. for Textual Scholarship, Renaissance Soc. Am., Shakespeare Assn. Am., New Zealand Libr. Assn., Bibliog. Soc. London, Bibliog. Soc. Oxford, Bibliog. Soc. Am. (coun. 1994—), Southeastern Renaissance Conf. (pres. 1995-96). Home: 823 Poinsettia St Columbia SC 29205-2039 Office: U SC Dept English Columbia SC 29208

HOWARD-PEEBLES, PATRICIA N., clinical cytogeneticist; b. Lawton, Okla., Nov. 24, 1941; d. J. Marion and R. Leona (prestidge) Howard; m. Thomas M. Peebles, Aug. 16, 1975. BSEd, U. Ctrl. Okla., 1963; student, Randolph-Macon Coll. Women, 1964; PhD in Zoology (Genetics), U Tex. at Austin, 1969. Diplomate Am. Bd. Med. Genetics; cert. clin. cytogeneticist, med. geneticist. Sci. and history tchr. Piedmont (Okla.) Pub. Schs., 1963-64; biochem. technician biochemistry sect. biology divsn. Oak Ridge (Tenn.) Nat. Lab., 1964-66; instr. rsch. pediatrics dept. pediatrics, instr. cytotech. U. Okla. Health Scis. Ctr., Oklahoma City, 1971-72; asst. prof., dir. Cytogenetics Lab. U. So. Miss., Hattiesburg, 1973-77, assoc. prof., dir. Cytogenetics Lab., 1977-80; assoc. prof. dept. pub. health, staff Lab. Med. Genetics U. Ala., Birmingham, 1980-81; assoc. prof., dir. Cytogenetics Lab. dept. pathology U. Tex. Health Sci. Ctr., Dallas, 1981-85, prof., dir. Cytogenetics Lab., 1985-87; prof. dept. human genetics Med. Coll. Va., Richmond, 1987—; clin. cytogeneticist, dir. Cytogeneticist lab. Genetics & IVF Inst., Fairfax, Va., 1987—; Am. Cancer Soc. postdoctoral fellow dept. human genetics U. Mich. Med. Sch., Ann Arbor, 1969-70, dept. human genetics and devel. Coll. Physicians and Surgeons, Columbia U., N.Y.C., 1970-71; genetic cons. Ellisville (Miss.) State Sch., 1973-80; attending staff dept. pathology Parkland Meml. Hosp., Dallas County Hosp. Dist., 1981-87; mem. sci. adv. com. Fragile X Found., 1985—; mem. Internat. Standing Com. on Human Cytogenetic Nomenclature, 1991-96. Contbr. articles to profl. jours., chpts. to books; reviewer Am. Jour. Human Genetics, Am. Jour. Med. Genetics, Clin. Genetics, Human Genetics. Fellow Am. Coll. Med. Genetics (founding mem.); mem. AAAS, Am. Soc. Human Genetics, Assn. Genetic Technologists, Tex. Genetics Soc. (chmn. planning com. ann. meeting 1984), Delta Kappa Gamma, Sigma Xi. Baptist. Office: Genetics & IVF Inst 3020 Javier Rd Fairfax VA 22031-4609

HOWARDS, STUART S., physician, educator; b. Milw., Mar. 29, 1937; s. Harvey H. and Anne (Levin) H.; m. Carter N. Howards, Aug. 20, 1966; children: Penelope P., Hugh N. BA, Yale U., 1959; MD, Columbia U., 1963. Intern in surgery Peter Bent Brigham Hosp., Boston, 1963-64, resident in urology, 1968-71; resident in surgery Childrens Hosp., Boston, 1964-65; rsch. assoc. NIH, Bethesda, Md., 1965-68; asst. prof. urology and physiology U. Va., Charlottesville, 1971-74, assoc. prof., 1974-76, prof., 1976—, chief divsn. pediat. urology, 1986—; chmn. exam com. Am. Bd. Urology, 1985-91, trustee, 1986-92, pres., 1992-93, exec. sec., 1997—. Editor: Infertility in the Male, 1991, 3d edit., 1997, Adult and Pediatric Urology, 1991, 3d edit., 1995; editor Jour. Urology, 1983—. Maj. USPHS, 1965-68. Recipient Career Investigation award NIH, 1973-78. Fellow Am. Acad. Pediats.; mem. Am. Urologic Assn. (Golden Cystoscope award 1981, Scott award 1990, Hugh Young award 1991), Clin. Soc. Genitourinary Surgeons, Am. Fertility Soc. (bd. dirs. 1994-96, treas. 1996—), Soc. Andrology, Genitourinary Surgeons, Am. Assn. Genito-Urinary Surgeons (sec.-treas. 1992-97), Am. Soc. Reproductive Medicine (bd. dirs. 1993-96). Home: 1150 W Leigh Dr Charlottesville VA 22901-7706 Office: U Va Hosp Jefferson Park Ave Charlottesville VA 22908

HOWARTH, DAVID H., retired bank executive; b. Lafayette, Ind., Apr. 3, 1936; s. C.H. and Dorothy H.; m. Mary Alice Fisher, Nov. 22, 1960 (dec. Oct. 1998); children: Lynn Howarth Easton, David P. Student, Wabash Coll., 1955-56; BS in Indsl. Econs., Purdue U., 1958; postgrad. banking, U. Wis., 1970; grad. exec. program, Columbia U., 1975. With INB Nat. Bank, N.W., 1958-61, 64-92, pres., 1978-83, chmn., CEO, 1983-92; bd. dirs. Lafayette Life Ins. Co.; chmn., bd. dirs. Union Bank & Trust, Delphi, Ind., 1997-98. Mem. Ind. Econ. Devel. Coun., Indpls., First Christian Ch.; bd. dirs. North Cen. Health Svcs., YWCA Found.; bd. dirs. Comty. Found. Greater Lafayette, pres., 1988, 89; chmn. Purdue Adv. Coun. for Econ. Edn., 1987; chmn. NCHS and Lafayette Home Hosp., Inc., 1984; campaign chmn. United Way, 1982; pres. Lafayette Parks Found., 1993-97. Named Sagamore of the Wabash Govt. Ind., 1986, 93. Mem. Ind. Bankers Assn. (conv. chmn. 1983, v.p. 1984-85, pres. 1985-86, bd. dirs. 1987, trustee, chmn. long-range planning com. 1987-91), Greater Lafayette C. of C. (pres. 1976-77, Marquis de Lafayette award 1992), Ind. State C. of C. (bd. dirs.), Purdue U. Alumni Assn. (citizenship award 1985), Masons. Avocation: golf. Home: 5016 E Oriole Dr Monticello IN 47960-7265

HOWARTH, WILLIAM (LOUIS), education educator, writer; b. Mpls., Nov. 26, 1940; s. Nelson Oliver and Mary Watson (Prindiville) H. BA with highest distinction, U. Ill., 1962; MA, U. Va., 1963, PhD, 1967. Instr. Princeton (N.J.) U., 1966-68, asst. prof., 1968-73, assoc. prof., 1973-81, prof. English, 1981—; mem. exec. com. Princeton Environ. Inst.; advisor Program in Environ. Studies, Program in Am. Studies Princeton (N.J.) U.; cons. Ctr. for Edts. of Am. Authors, 1974, Rockefeller Bros. Fund, 1976, Geraldine W. Dodge Found., 1981, Nat. Geog. Soc., 1984, Corp. for Pub. Broadcasting, 1986, NEH, 1987, Nat. Rural Studies Coun., 1988, Atlantic Ctr. for Arts, 1990, Sante Fe Environ. Coun., 1991, ALA, 1993, Assn. for the Study of Lit. and Environment, 1994. Author: Nature in American Life, 1972, The John McPhee Reader, 1976, The Book of Concord, 1982, Thoreau in the Mountains, 1982, Traveling the Trans-Canada, 1987, Mountaineering in the Sierra Nevada, 1989; author book chpts.; editor-in-chief: The Writings of Henry D. Thoreau, 1972-80; mem. numerous editorial bds.; editorial adviser numerous jours. and publs.; contbr. articles to profl. jours. Woodrow Wilson Found. fellow, 1966, Henry E. Huntington Libr. fellow, 1968, NEH fellow, 1977, John E. Annan BiCentennial Preceptor, Princeton, 1973. Mem. MLA, Am. Studies Assn., Thoreau Soc. Am. (pres. 1975-76), Am. Soc. Environ. History, Am. Lit. Assn., Nat. Geographic Soc. (contract writer 1978—), Nat. Rural Studies Coun. (assoc.), Assn. for the Study of Lit. and Environ. (adv. bd.), Am. Soc. Environ. History (adv. bd.), Ctr. for Am. Places, Phi Beta Kappa. Office: Princeton U 22 McCosh Hall Princeton NJ 08544-5627

HOWAT, JOHN KEITH, museum executive; b. Denver, Apr. 12, 1937; s. James Bowcott and Nancy Selden (Skinker) H.; grad. Phillips Exeter Acad., 1955; B.A., Harvard, 1959, M.A., 1962; Ford fellow N.Y.U. Inst. Fine Arts, 1965-66; m. Anne Hadley, Jan. 21, 1958; children—Karen Louise, Laura Anne. Curator, Hyde Collection, Glens Falls, N.Y., 1962-64; asst. curator dept. Am. paintings and sculpture Met. Mus. Art, N.Y.C., 1967-68, assoc. curator-in-charge, 1968-70, curator, 1970-82, chmn. depts. Am. art, 1982—. Mem. adv. com. archives Am. art Smithsonian Instn., 1969—; trustee Archives of Am. Art, 1988—. Chester Dale fellow Met. Mus. Art, 1966-67. Clubs: Union, Century Association. Author exhbn. catalog, John Frederick Kensett 1816-1872, 1968; co-author: 19th Century America: Paintings and Sculpture (exhbn. catalog), 1970; The Hudson River and Its Painters, 1972; co-author: John Frederick Kensett: An American Master, 1985, An American Paradise: The World of The Hudson River School, 1987. Home: 1100 Park Ave New York NY 10128-1202 Office: Met Mus Art Fifth Ave # 82nd St New York NY 10028

HOWAT, KEVIN JOHN, publishing executive; b. Turtle Creek, Pa., May 22, 1953; s. Jack William and Julia (Green) H.; m. Jane Elizabeth Townsend, Sept. 30, 1984; children: Lucy, Sophia Jane. BA cum laude, Franklin & Marshall Coll., 1975. Exec. editor, pub. Internat. Thomson, Wadsworth, Belmont, Calif., 1979-88; new products mgr. The Learning Co., Fremont, Calif., 1988-90; sr. acquisitions editor Addison-Wesley Edn. Software, Redwood City, Calif., 1990-92; dir. strategic mktg., bus. devel. Macromedia Inc., San Francisco, 1992-94; v.p. product devel., pub. Simon & Schuster Pub., N.Y.C., 1994-98; v.p., bus. devel., brand mgmt. Time Inc. New Media, N.Y.C., 1998—; founder, adv. bd. New Media Ctrs., San Francisco, 1993-94;. Pub. numerous CD-ROM software (various awards). Program com. EDUCOM (Educational Comp. Conf.), Washington, 1990-93. Recipient Ednl. Software Product award Softward Pub. Assn., 1990. Avocations: music, mountain biking, theater, running. Home: 200 Crow Hill Rd Mount Kisco NY 10549-3804 Office: Time Inc New Media 1271 Ave Americas New York NY 10020

HOWBERT, EDGAR CHARLES, lawyer; b. Detroit, June 29, 1937; s. Edgar Cowgill and Martha Viola (Brekke) H.; m. Susan Bartlett Rumsey, July 24, 1974; children: John Edgar, Dana Elizabeth. AB, Princeton U., 1959; LLB, Harvard U., 1965. Bar: Mich. 1966. Assoc. Dickinson & Wright, Detroit, 1965-72, ptnr., 1972—. Pres. Franklin Wright Settlements, Inc., Detroit, 1984, Friends Sch. in Detroit, 1986. Lt. USN, 1959-62; trustee Univ. Liggett Sch., 1991-97. Mem. Detroit Bar Assn., Am. Bankruptcy Inst., Turnaround Mgmt. Assn. (bd. dirs. 1989-91, 92—), Country Club of Detroit. Office: Dickinson Wright PLLC 500 Woodward Ave Ste 4000 Detroit MI 48226-3416

HOWDEN, FRANK NEWTON, Episcopal priest, humanities educator; b. Phila., Mar. 23, 1916; s. John George and Sarah Harvey (McFarlane) H.; m. Cornelia Jane Fenton, Oct. 7, 1943 (dec. Aug. 1981); children: Robert Newton, William John McFarlane, Susan Catherine Victoria Howden Blanchard, Sarah Jane Fenton; m. Mary Valerie Clark, Apr. 23, 1983. *Reverend Frank Newton Howden's father was born in Edinborough, Scotland, April 19, 1876. He was secretary and treasurer of Clyde Dock Company from 1902-1909. In 1910 he emigrated to Philadelphia, Pennsylvania, and worked for the Rapid Transport until 1918. Thereafter, his family lived in various parts of the Catskill Mountains in the state of New York. He died in 1954. The Reverend's mother, Sarah Harvey McFarlane, was born in Glasgow, Scotland, March 1, 1875, and died in September of 1964.* AB, U. of the South, 1940; STB, Gen. Theol. Sem., N.Y.C., 1943; MS, Ctrl. Conn. U., 1968; postgrad., McGill U., Montreal, Can., 1953-56. Ordained priest Episcopal Ch.; cert. tchr., Conn. Curate St. Peter's Ch., Auburn, N.Y., 1943-44, All Angels Ch., N.Y.C., 1944-45; priest in charge (vicar) St. John's Ch., Sewaren and Fords, N.J., 1945-48; rector St. Luke's Ch., St. Albans, Vt., 1951-56, Trinity Ch., Waterbury, Conn., 1956-66; history tchr. Woodbury (Conn.) H.S., 1966-69; prof. humanities Waterbury State Tech. Coll., 1970-82; rector Trinity Ch., Lime Rock, Conn., 1969-85, elected rector emeritus, 1985—; pres. Priests' Fellowship, Conn., 1958-59; archdeacon New Haven County, Diocese of Conn., 1963-66, dean Litchfield Deanery, 1984-85. *Since retirement, the Reverend Frank Newton Howden has been busy writing his latest manuscript, Life of Christ.* Author: A Rule of Life, 1954, Life Here and Hereafter, 1992. 1st lt. Chaplain Corps, U.S. Army, 1948-51, chaplain Vt. Nat. Guard, 1952-56. Mem. St. Margaret's Soc. (assoc.), Over-Seas League (London), English-Speaking Union. Democrat. Avocations: photography, audio-visual presentations, preaching and taking services in Anglican churches. Home: 9 Argyle Rd Southborough, Tunbridge Wells TN4 0SU, England

HOWE, ART (ARTHUR HENRY HOWE, JR.), professional baseball manager; b. Pitts., Dec. 15, 1946; m. Elizabeth Louise Falconio, Aug. 16, 1969; children: Stephanie Lynn, Gretchen Leigh, Matthew Louis. BS, BA, U. Wyoming, 1969. Computer programmer Westinghouse Corp., 1969-70; player Carolina League, Salem, 1971, International League, Charleston, WV, 1972-75, Pittsburg Pirates, Pittsburg, PA, 1974, 75, International League, Memphis, TN, 1976, Houston Astros, Houston, TX, 1976-83, St. Louis Cardinals, St. Louis, MO, 1984-85; coach Texas Rangers, Arlington, TX, 1985-88; mgr. Houston Astros, Houston, TX, 1988-93; mgr. Puerto Rican League, Bayamon, PR, winters 1979, 80, 82, Ponce, PR, winter 1985; mgr. Oakland Athletics, 1996—; hitting coach Colo. Rockies, 1995. Named Mgr. of Yr. P.R. League, 1980, Dominican Rep. La Romana, 1994-95. Office: Oakland Athletics 7677 Oakport St Ste 200 2d Fl Oakland CA 94621-1933*

HOWE, CON EDWARD, city manager; b. St. Louis, Oct. 23, 1949. BA, Yale U., 1972; MA in City Planning, MIT, 1975. Exec. dir. Mass. Land Bank; with Gov.'s Office Mass.; dir. Manhattan Office N.Y. City Planning Dept., 1982-87, exec. dir., 1987-91; dir. planning City of L.A., 1992—. Mem. Am. Planning Assn., Urban Land Inst. Office: Planning Dept City of Los Angeles 221 N Figueroa St Ste 1640 Los Angeles CA 90012-2639

HOWE, CRAIG WALTER SANDELL, medical organization executive, internist; b. Mpls., Apr. 11, 1948; s. Walter A. and Essie Marie (Sandell) H.; m. Susan Kay Hansen, Apr. 21, 1969; 1 child, Elsbeth Marie. BS, U. Minn., 1969; PhD, Cambridge (Eng.) U., 1974; MD, Cornell U., N.Y.C., 1978. Diplomate Am. Bd. Internal Medicine, Am. Bd. Med. Oncology. Rsch. assoc. Meml. Sloan-Kettering Cancer Ctr., N.Y.C., 1974-76; intern, resident in internal medicine Barnes Hosp., St. Louis, 1978-81; fellow in hematology Harvard U. Med. Sch., Boston, 1981-83; asst. prof. U. Iowa Med. Sch., Iowa City, 1983-86; assoc. prof., dir. bone marrow transplantation Med. Coll. Va., Richmond, 1986-92; CEO, Nat. Marrow Donor Program, Mpls., 1992—; chmn. steering com. for T-cell depletion trial Nat. Heart, Lung and Blood Inst., Bethesda, Md., 1994—. Editor: Immunobiology of Trophoblast, 1974; contbr. articles to med. and sci. jours. Mem. task force Minn. Dept. Health, 1994. Mem. Am. Soc. Blood and Marrow Transplantation, Am. Soc. Clin. Oncology. Home: 5020 Fremont Ave S Minneapolis MN 55419-1158 Office: Nat Marrow Donor Program 3433 Broadway St NE Ste 500 Minneapolis MN 55413-1763

HOWE, DANIEL WALKER, historian, educator; b. Ogden, Utah, Jan. 10, 1937; s. Maurice Langdon and Lucie (Walker) H.; m. Sandra Fay Shumway, Sept. 3, 1961; children: Rebecca, Christopher, Stephen. AB magna cum laude, Harvard U., 1959; MA, Oxford (Eng.) U., 1965; PhD, U. Calif., Berkeley, 1966. From instr. to assoc. prof. history Yale U., 1966-73; assoc. prof. history UCLA, 1973-77, prof., 1977-92, chmn. dept., 1983-87; Harmsworth vis. prof. Am. history, Oxford (Eng.) U., 1989-90, Rhodes prof. Am. history, 1992—. Author: The Unitarian Conscience, 1970, The American Whigs: An Anthology, 1973, Victorian America, 1976, The Political Culture of the American Whigs, 1979, Making the American Self, 1997. Served to lt. U.S. Army, 1959-60. Kent fellow Danforth Found., 1964-66; Charles Warren Center for Studies in Am. History fellow, 1970-71; NEH fellow, 1975-76; Guggenheim fellow, 1984-85; Huntington Libr. fellow, 1992, 94. Mem. Am. Hist. Assn., Orgn. Am. Historians, Soc. Am Historians, Oxford and Cambridge Club (London). Episcopalian. Home: 3814 Cody Rd Sherman Oaks CA 91403-5019 Office: St Catherine's Coll, Oxford England

HOWE, DRAYTON FORD, JR., lawyer; b. Seattle, Nov. 17, 1931; s. Drayton Ford and Virginia (Wester) H.; m. Joyce Arnold, June 21, 1952; 1 son, James Drayton. AB, U. Calif., Berkeley, 1953; LLB, U. Calif., San Francisco, 1957. Bar: Calif. 1958. CPA Calif. Atty. IRS, 1958-61; tax dept. supr. Ernst & Ernst, San Francisco, 1962-67; ptnr. Bishop, Barry, Howe, Haney & Ryder, San Francisco, 1968—; lectr. on tax matters U. Calif. extension, 1966-76. Mem. Calif. Bar Assn., San Francisco Bar Assn. (chmn. client relations com. 1977), Calif. Soc. CPA's. Office: Bishop Barry Howe Haney & Ryder 44 Montgomery St Ste 1300 San Francisco CA 94104

HOWE, EDWIN A(LBERTS), JR., lawyer; b. Cleve., Jan. 21, 1939; s. Edwin Alberts and Helen Dorothy (Beck) H.; m. Margaret Joan Webber, Sept. 12, 1964; children: Christopher, Melissa, Katie. BA, Yale U., 1961; JD with honors, U. Mich., 1964. Bar: N.Y. 1965, U.S. Supreme Ct. 1976. Assoc. Devevoise and Plimpton, N.Y.C., 1964-70; ptnr. Howe & Addington LLP, N.Y.C., 1970—. Trustee Garden City (N.Y.) Pub. Libr., 1982-86, chmn., 1986-88; trustee Village of Garden City, 1988-89; mem. Garden City Environ. Adv. Bd., 1994-98; mem. Westport Land Acquisitions Com., 1999—. Fellow Inst. Dirs.; mem. ABA, Internat. Fiscal Assn., Counselors of Real Estate, Urban Land Inst., Nat. Real Estate Forum (chmn. 1996—), Assn. of Bar of City of N.Y., N.Y. State Bar Assn., Internat. Bar Assn., Internat. Law Assn. (Am. Br.), Am. Soc. Internat. Law, Am. Fgn. Law Assn., Sky Club, Yale Club, Netherland Club, No. Lake George Yacht Club, Lake George Assn., Rogers Rock Club. Republican. Episcopalian. Avocation: fishing, golf, reading, theatre, languages. Home: 164 Roseville Rd Westport CT 06880 Office: Howe & Addington LLP 450 Lexington Ave New York NY 10017-3911

HOWE, FANNY QUINCY, poet; b. Buffalo, Oct. 15, 1940; d. Mark Dewolfe and Mary Manning H.; m. Carl Francisco Senna, Oct. 28, 1968 (div. Nov. 1978); children: Annelucien Senna, Danzy Senna, Maceo Senna. Student, Stanford U., 1958-61. Lectr. Tufts U., Medford, Mass., 1968-71, Columbia U., N.Y.C., 1975-78, MIT, Cambridge, Mass., 1978-87; assoc. dir. Edn. Abroad-UC, London, 1993-95; prof. U. Calif., San Diego, 1987—. Author of poems and novels. Fellow NEA, 1969, 91, St. Botolph, 1976, Calif. Coun. Arts, 1993. Fellow Bunting Inst. Democrat. Roman Catholic. Avocation: swimming. Home: 5580 La Jolla Blvd #31 La Jolla CA 92037 Office: U Calif Gilman Dr 0410 La Jolla CA 92093-0410

HOWE, FISHER, management consultant, former government official; b. Winnetka, Ill., May 17, 1914; s. Lawrence and Hester (Davis) H.; m. Deborah Froelicher, June 4, 1945; children: Elizabeth, Shippen. A.B., Harvard, 1935; student, Nat. War Coll., 1948. Salesman Coats & Clarks Thread Co., N.Y.C., 1935-40, Patons & Baldwins, Ltd., Yorkshire, Eng., 1936-37; mem. staff Office of Dir., OSS, Washington, London, Mediterranean, Far East, 1941-45; fgn. svc. officer Dept. State, 1945-68, spl. asst. under sec. of state, econ. affairs, 1945-46, dep. dir. Bur. Intelligence and Rsch., exec. sec., dir. exec. secretariat, 1956-58; dep. chief of mission and charge Am. Embassy, Oslo, Norway, 1958-62, The Hague, The Netherlands, 1962-65; mem. policy planning coun., 1965-68; exec. dir., asst. dean Johns Hopkins U. Sch. Advanced Internat. Studies, 1968-72; dep. exec. dir. Commn. on Orgn. of Govt. for Conduct of Fgn. Policy, Washington, 1973-75; sec., gen. adv. com. Energy R & D Adminstrn., 1975-77; dir. instl. rels. Resources for the Future, Inc., 1978-82; ptnr. Lavender/Howe & Assocs., Washington, 1982—. Author: Computer and Foreign Affairs, 1968, Fund Raising and the Nonprofit Board Member, 1988, Board Member's Guide to Fund Raising, 1991, Welcome to the Board, 1995, Board Member's Guide to Strategic Planning, 1997. Trustee Fountain Valley Sch., Colorado Springs, Colo., Pilgrim Soc., Plymouth, Mass., Support Ctr. Washington, Inst. Circadian Physiology, Boston. Served to lt. USNR, 1943-44, overseas svc. Mem. Metropolitan Club (Washington), Mill Reef. Address: 2015 48th St NW Washington DC 20007-1553

HOWE, FLORENCE, English educator, writer, publisher; b. N.Y.C., Mar. 17, 1929; d. Samuel and Frances (Stilly) Rosenfeld. A.B., Hunter Coll., 1950; A.M., Smith Coll., 1951; postgrad., U. Wis., 1951-54; D.H.L. (hon.), New Eng. Coll., 1977, Skidmore Coll., 1979, DePauw U., 1987, SUNY Coll. Old Westbury, 1992. Teaching asst. U. Wis., 1951-54; instr. Hofstra Coll., 1954-57; lectr. English Queens Coll., 1956-57; asst. prof. English Goucher Coll., 1960-71; prof. humanities and Am. studies SUNY-Old Westbury, 1971-87; prof. English City. Coll. and Grad. Sch., CUNY, 1987—; pres., dir. The Feminist Press at CUNY, 1970—; vis. prof. U. Utah, 1973, 75, U. Wash., 1974, John F. Kennedy Inst. Am. Studies Free U. Berlin, 1978, Oberlin Coll., 1978, Denison U., 1979, MLA Summer Inst. U. Ala., 1979, Coll. Wooster, 1980, Grad. Sch. Dept. English CUNY, 1986-87. Author: The Conspiracy of the Young, 1970, Seven Years Later: Women's Studies Programs in 1976, 1977, Myths of Coeducation: Selected Essays, 1964-1984, 1984; editor: (with Ellen Bass) No More Masks! An Anthology of Poems by Women, 1973, Women and the Power to Change, 1975, (with Nancy Hoffman) Women Working: An Anthology of Stories and Poems, 1979, (with Suzanne Howard, Mary Jo Boehm Strauss) Everywoman's Guide to Colleges and Universities, 1982, (with Marsha Saxton) With Wings: An Anthology of Literature by and About Disabled Women, 1987, An Anthology of 20th Century American Women Poets, (with John Mack Faragher) Women and Higher Education in American History, 1988, Tradition and the Talents of Women, 1991, No More Masks, 1993; mem. editl. bd. Women's Studies: An Interdisciplinary Jour., 1971—, SIGNS: Women in Culture and Society, 1974-80, Jour. Edn., 1976—, The Correspondence of Lydia Marie Child, 1977-81, Research in the Humanities, 1977—; contbr. essays to profl. jours. Recipient Mina Shaughnessy award Fund for Improvement of Post-Secondary Edn., 1982-83; NEH fellow, 1971-73; Ford Found. fellow, 1974-75; Fullbright fellow, India, 1977; Mellon fellow Wellesley Coll., 1979, Rockefeller Found. fellowship T. Bellagio, 1997; U.S. Dept. State grantee, 1983, 93. Office: The Feminist Press at CUNY 365 5th Ave New York NY 10016

HOWE, GORDON, former professional hockey player, sports association executive; b. Saskatoon, Sask., Can., Mar. 31, 1928; came to U.S., 1944; s. Albert Clarence and Katherine (Schultz) H.; m. Colleen Janet Joffa, Apr. 15, 1953; children: Marty Gordon, Mark Steven, Cathleen Jill, Murray Albert. Profl. hockey player with Detroit Red Wings Hockey Club (Nat. Hockey League), 1944-73, player, pres.; with Houston Aeros (World Hockey Assn.), 1971-73, New Eng. Whalers (World Hockey Assn.), Hartford, Conn., 1977-78, Hartford Whalers, NHL, 1980-82; spl. asst., mng. ptnr. Hartford Whalers, 1982-92. Co-author: Gordie Howe, No. 9, (with Colleen Howe and Charles Wilkens) After the Applause, 1989, (with Colleen Howe) And...Howe!, 1995. Recipient Order of Can. medal, 1971; named Canada's Athlete of Year, 1963; holder Hart Meml. Trophy, Art Ross Trophy, Lester Patrick Trophy; 12-time mem. NHL 1st All-Star Team; 9-time mem. NHL 2d All-Star Team; named Most Valuable Player and to 1st All-Star Team World Hockey Assn., 1974. Mem. Nat. League Hall of Fame, Mich. Sports Hall of Fame, Omaha Sports Hall of Fame. Congregationalist. Address: Power Play Internat Inc 6645 Peninsula Dr Traverse City MI 49686-1737*

HOWE, GRAHAM LLOYD, photographer, curator; b. Sydney, N.S.W., Australia, Apr. 18, 1950; came to U.S., 1976; s. Raymond R. and Gwendoline B. Howe; m. Karen Bowers, 1989; 1 child, Rebecca Raine. Diploma in art and design, Prahran Coll. Advanced Edn., Melbourne, Australia, 1971; M.A., UCLA, 1978, M.F.A., 1979. Dir. Australian Centre for Photography, Sydney, 1974-75; curator Graham Nash Collection, Los Angeles, 1976-89; dir. Curatorial Assistance, Pasadena, Calif., 1987—. Author: (catalogue) Paul Outerbridge, Jr., 1976, Paul Outerbridge, Jr.: Photographs, 1980, Sir John Herschel and the Camera Lucida, 1990, Eikoh Hosoe: Meta, 1991, "Nudi"-Paul Outerbridge, 1996; co-author: A Day in The Life of Australia, 1981, Paul Outerbridge, Jr.: A Singular Aesthetic, 1982 (catalogue) Two Views of Manzanar, 1978; editor: New Photography Australia-A Selective Survey, 1974, Aspects of Australian Photography, 1974, The Graham Nash Collection, 1978, 10 Photographers-Olympic Images, 1984. Grantee NEA, 1982; grantee Ford Found., 1978; UCLA Art Council scholar, 1977. Mem. Soc. for Photog. Edn. Home: 113 E Union St Pasadena CA 91103-3927*

HOWE, HAROLD, II, academic administrator, former foundation executive, educator; b. Hartford, Conn., Aug. 17, 1918; s. Arthur and Margaret Marshall (Armstrong) H.; m. Priscilla Foster Lamb, Sept. 4, 1940; children: Catherine Howe Short, Merrill Howe Leavitt, Gordon Armstrong. BA, Yale U., 1940; MA in History, Columbia U., 1947; postgrad., Harvard Grad. Sch. Edn., 1958-59, U. Cin., 1953-55; LLD (hon.), Adelphi U., 1966, U. St. Louis, 1967, U. Notre Dame, 1967, Princeton U., 1968, CUNY-Hunter Coll., 1981, U. Hartford, 1982; LL.D. (hon.), Tulane U., 1991. Tchr. history Darrow Sch., New Lebanon, N.Y., 1940-41, Phillips Acad., Andover, Mass., 1947-50; prin. jr. and sr. high schs. Andover, Mass., 1950-53; prin. Walnut Hills H.S., Cin., 1953-57, Newton (Mass.) H.S., 1957-60; supt. schs. Scarsdale, N.Y., 1960-64; dir. Learning Inst. N.C., 1964-65; U.S. Commr. of Edn., Washington, 1966-68; program advisor on edn. in India Ford Found., 1969-70; v.p. for edn. Ford Found., N.Y.C., 1971-81; sr. lectr. Harvard U. Grad. Sch. Edn., 1982-95. Author: Picking Up the Options, 1968, Thinking About Our Kids, 1993. Trustee Yale U., 1962-68, Vassar Coll., Taft Sch., Coll. Entrance Exam. Bd., John Hay Whitney Found., 1973-81; bd. dirs. Kennedy Ctr., Washington, 1967-68; mem. Commn. on Humanities, Am. Coun. Learned Socs., 1962-63; mem. Nat. Coun. on Edn. Rsch., 1978-82, chmn., 1980-82; chmn. bd. dir. Inst. Ednl. Leadership, 1982, 88; trustee Ednl. Testing Svcs., 1986-95, chairperson, 1990-92. With USNR, 1942-45. Recipient Gold medal for public service NYU, 1968, James Bryant Conant award Edn. Commn. of States, 1986, Harold W. McGraw, Jr. Prize in Education, 1994. Home: 80 Lyme Rd Hanover NH 03755-1218

HOWE, HERBERT MARSHALL, JR., political science educator; b. Providence, June 17, 1945; s. Herbert Marshall Sr. and Evelyn Grace Mitchell Howe. BS, U. Wis., 1970; MA, Fletcher Sch. Law & Diplomacy, 1973; PhD, Harvard U., 1978. Cert. EMT, Washington. Writer W.W. Norton, N.Y.C., 1977-79; freelance corr. Phila. Inquirer, 1979-80; policy analyst Libr. Congress, Washington, 1980-82; program officer Inst. Internat. Edn., Washington, 1982-84; rsch. prof. Georgetown U., Washington, 1984—, dir. African studies, 1989-97; cons. Amnesty Internat., Eng., 1998; vis. rschr. U. London, 1999; cons. in field. Author Do Not Go Gentle, 1980, Paxafricana, 1999. Vol. U.S. Peace Corps, Nigeria, Jamaica, 1966-68; pres. Nigeria-Biafra Aid Com., Madison, Wis., 1968. Mem. Royal African Soc., African Studies Assn., Washington Canoe Club. Democrat. Episcopalian. Avocations: canoe racing, masters swimming, emergency medicine. E-mail: howeh@gunet.georgetown.edu. Office: Sch Fgn Svc Georgetown Univ 37th O St NW Washington DC 20057

HOWE, JAMES TARSICIUS, retired insurance company executive; b. Calcutta, India, Nov. 20, 1924; came to U.S., 1975; s. Joseph Ne-Ching and Anna Su-Cheng (Huang) Hou; m. Juliana Wong, Feb. 8, 1948; children: Christopher, Celine, Catherine, Charles, Caroline. *James Howe's son Christopher is a Barrister-at-Law and banker in New York City. Son Charles is a medical doctor in Indiana. Daughter Celine is in insurance service in New York City. Daughter Catherine is a computer software executive in Florida and daughter Caroline is a banking executive in Chicago. His grandson Justin has an MPA from Cornell University. Grandson Jason attends University of Massachusetts, and grandson Julien attends Columbia University in New York City. Grandson Reuben attends Indiana U. and grandson Robin attends Pennington, New Jersey.* Diploma in bus. adminstrn., Chinese U., Hong Kong, 1969; postgrad. in advanced mgmt., Lingnam Inst. Bus. Adminstrn., Hong Kong. Trainee Bank of China, Calcutta, 1942-45; various managerial positions Bank of China, Calcutta and, Pakistan, 1945-51; mng. ptnr. import and export firm Karachi, Pakistan, 1951-54; various exec. positions Am. Internat. Underwriters (Pakistan) Ltd., 1954-65, Am. Internat. Underwriters (Far East) Inc., 1965-73; pres., mng. dir. Am. Internat. Underwriters, Hong Kong, 1973-75; from asst. treas. to v.p. Am. Internat. Group, Inc., N.Y.C., 1975-92; ret., 1992; bd. dirs., chmn. audit and conduct coms. A.I.G. Life Co. Ltd., Can.; bd. dirs. numerous corps.; bd. dirs., v.p., treas. Starr Equipment Corp.; bd. dirs., vice chmn. A.I. Credit Corp., AICCO; bd. dirs., sec., treas. Starr Land Co.; bd. dirs., treas Starr Realty Corp., Hunter Lyon Inc.; asst. treas. Paul Napolitan, Inc.; treas. C.V. Starr & Co., Inc., also numerous other subs. Named hon. Ky. col., 1979; Knight of Holy Sepulchre of Jerusalem, Roman Cath. Ch. Mem. Am. Mgmt. Assn., Nat. Assn. Corp. Treas., Nat. Assn. Rev. Appraisers and Mortgage Underwriters (sr.), Internat. Real Estate Inst., Chinese Cath. club (life), Royal Hong Kong Golf Club (life absent mem.), Am. Club Hong Kong (life absent mem.), Royal Hong Kong Jockey Club (past pres.), Serra Club (N.Y.C.), Rotary, KC (grand knight Short Hills coun.). Home: Palace Place Suite #3601, No 1 Palace Pier Ct, Etobicoke, ON Canada M8V 3W9

HOWE, JAS. MURRAY, lawyer; b. Daytona Beach, Fla., July 13, 1924; s. James M. Jr. and Rosina (Jacocks) H.; m. Barbara Burleigh, Sept. 2, 1949; children: James M. Jr., Sylvia Howe Thompson, John B., Samuel M., Peter J. AB magna cum laude, Harvard U., 1947, LLB cum laude, 1950. Bar: Mass. 1950. Assoc. Choate, Hall & Stewart, Boston, 1950-53; assoc., then ptnr. Sullivan & Worcester, Boston, 1954-62; exec. v.p., dir. Boston Capital Corp., 1963-70; ptnr. Sullivan & Worcester, Boston, 1970-92, of counsel, 1993—; bd. dirs. Schooner Capital Corp., Boston, Schooner Asset Mgmt. Co., LLC; sec. bd. dirs. Iron Mountain Inc., Boston; trustee N.E. Investors Trust, Boston, 1986—, The Trustees of Reservations, Beverly, Mass., 1990—. Pres. Harvard Law Sch. Assn., 1984-86. Capt. arty. U.S. Army, 1943-46, ETO; col. USAR, ret. 1965. Mem. ABA, Boston Bar Assn., Phi Beta Kappa. Republican. Episcopalian. Home: 42 W Cedar St Boston MA 02114-3302 Office: Sullivan & Worcester 1 Post Office Sq Ste 2300 Boston MA 02109-2129

HOWE, JOHN KINGMAN, manufacturing, sales and marketing executive; b. Everett, Wash., Nov. 7, 1945; s. John Cutler and Nancy Carpenter (Kingman) H.; m. Loretta Kerr, Aug. 27, 1966; children: Steven Cutler, Nancy Kingman. Student Ohio State U., 1963-65. Field technician Data Corp., Dayton, Ohio, 1965-66; letter carrier U.S. Post Office, Dayton, 1966; sales rep. E.S. Klosterman Co., Dayton, 1966-71, v.p. 1971-72; v.p. sales, dir. Springfield Binder Corp., Ohio, 1981-84, dir., pres., chief exec. officer, 1984-95; dir., pres. The John K. Howe Co., Inc., Dayton, Ohio, 1972-87, chmn., chief exec. officer, dir. 1987—; pres. Cutler-Kingman, Inc. div. Thump Properties, Cin., 1979-86, owner, 1986—; gen. ptnr. H&B Enterprises, Dayton, 1977-86, Design Investment Properties, Dayton, 1979-86, BMR Properties, Ltd., Dayton, 1979-82; adminstr. John K. Howe Co./Profit Sharing, Cin., 1973—, John K. Howe Co./Pension Plan, 1976—; owner Androscoggin Designs, Dayton, 1979-86. Pres. South Dixie Bus. Assn., Kettering, Ohio, 1978-82; mem. design review com. Lincoln Park Owner's Assn., 1989-91, chmn., 1992-94; pres. Woods of Lincoln Park Homeowner's Assn., 1992-94, mem. Fraze Pavilion fund raising com., 1991-92; mem. Confrerie de la Chaines de Rotisseurs Bailliage de Cin., 1993—; chmn. ops. com. Adams Place Homeowners Assn., Inc., 1996-98, v.p., bd. mgrs. 1998—. Mem. Cin. C. of C., Dayton C. of C. Republican. Presbyterian. Office: The John K Howe Co Inc 400 Pike St Fl 6 Cincinnati OH 45202-4237

HOWE, JOHN PRENTICE, III, health science center executive, physician; b. Jackson, Tenn., Mar. 7, 1943; s. John Prentice and Phyllis (MacDonald) H.; children: Lindsey Warren, Brooke Olmsted, John Prentice IV. BA, Amherst Coll., 1965; MD, Boston U., 1969. Diplomate Am. Bd. Internal Medicine, internal medicine and cardiovascular disease. Research assoc. cellular physiology Amherst Coll., 1963-64; research assoc. cardiovascular physiology Boston U. Sch. of Medicine, 1966-67, lectr. medicine, 1972-73; intern Boston City Hosp., 1969-70, asst. resident, 1970-71; research fellow in medicine Harvard U., 1971-73, Peter Bent Brigham Hosp., 1971-73; survey physician Framingham Cardiovascular Disease Study, Nat. Heart and Lung Inst., 1971; asst. clin. prof. medicine U. Hawaii, 1973-75; asst. prof. medicine U. Mass., 1975-77, assoc. prof., 1977-85, vice chmn. dept. medicine, 1975-78, asst. dean continuing edn. for physicians, 1976-78, assoc. dean profl. affairs and continuing edn., 1978-80, acad. dean, 1980-85, vice chancellor, 1980-85, acting chmn. dept. anatomy, 1982-85; pres., prof. medicine U. Tex. Health Scis. Ctr., San Antonio, 1985—; assoc. chief div. medicine U. Mass. Hosp., 1975-78, dir. patient care studies dept., 1975-80, chief of staff, 1978-80. Mem. editorial bd. Archives Internal Medicine, 1991—; contbr. numerous articles to profl. jours., chpts. to books. Trustee S.W. Found. for Biomed. Rsch., San Antonio Med. Found., S.W. Rsch. Inst. Maj. M.C, U.S. Army, 1973-75. Alfred P. Sloan scholar Amherst Coll., 1962-65; recipient Ruth Hunter Johnson award Boston U. Sch. of Medicine, 1969. Fellow ACP, Am. Coll. Cardiology, Am. Coll. Chest Physicians; mem. AMA (del. ho. of dels. 1995—, coun. on sci. affairs 1993—), Am. Heart Assn. (fellow coun. clin. cardiology), Tex. Med. Soc. (coun. med. edn. 1986—, ho. of dels. 1989—, pres.-elect 1997—), Tex. Soc. Biomed. Rsch. (past pres.), Bexar County Med. Soc. (exec. com. 1985—, pres. 1996), Alpha Omega Alpha, Omicron Kappa Epsilon. Avocations: tennis; skiing. *

HOWE, JOHN THOMAS, film director, educator; b. Toronto, Ont., Can., Aug. 30, 1926; s. Thomas and Margret Ogilvy (Manzie) H.; m. Beverley Jean Luchuck, Oct. 23, 1974; children: Natalie Elaine, Nicholas Thomas (dec.). BA, U. Toronto, 1950. Freelance radio, TV staff producer Can. Broadcasting Corp., 1945-55; staff mem. Can. Repertory theatre, 1950-51; dir., producer Nat. Film Bd. Can., 1955-83; prof. dept. cinema-TV U. So. Calif., L.A., 1983-96. Dir., composer feature film Why Rock the Boat?, 1974; producer, dir., editor, composer feature film A Choice of Two, 1981; dir., producer numerous feature documentaries, theatrical shorts, TV dramas, others. Capt. Royal Can. Arty., 1944-46, ETO. Mem. Assn. Can. TV and Radio Artists, Dir.'s Guild Am., Soc. Filmmakers (past pres.), Soc. Composers, Authors, and Music Pubs. Can., Can. Coun. Film Orgns. (past pres.), Syndicat Gen. Cinema (past pres.). Office: Sch Cinema Univ So Calif University Park Los Angeles CA 90007

HOWE, JOHN WADSWORTH, bishop; b. Chgo., Nov. 4, 1942; s. John Wadsworth Howe and Shirley Anita (Hansen) H.; m. Karen Louise Elvgren, Sept. 1, 1962; children: Katherine Janet Howe Rickwald, John Wadsworth III, Jessica Ruth Howe. BA, U. Conn., 1964; MDiv, Yale U., 1967; DD (hon.), Berkeley-Yale, 1989, U. of the South, Tenn., 1990, Naskota House, 1991. Ordained to ministry Episcopal Ch. as deacon, 1967, as priest 1968, as bishop, 1989. Chaplain Loomis Sch., Windsor, Conn., 1967-69, Miss Porter's Sch., Farmington, Conn., 1969-72; assoc. rector St. Stephen's Episcopal Ch., Swickley, Pa., 1972-76; rector Truro Episcopal Ch., Fairfax, Va., 1976-89; bishop coadjutor Diocese of Cen. Fla., Orlando, 1989-90, Episcopal bishop, 1990—; founder Sharing of Ministries Abroad. Author: Which Way? 1972, Our Anglican Heritage, 1976, Sex: Shall We Change the Rules, 1991; contbr. articles to mags; co-author Resolution and the Sanctity of Human Life adopted by 69th Gen. Conv. Episcopal Ch., Detroit. Mem. Nat. Orgn. of Episcopalian for Life (chmn. bd.), Fellowship of Witness (former pres.). Home: 5583 Jessamine Ln Orlando FL 32839-2023 Office: Diocese Office 1017 E Robinson St Orlando FL 32801-2023

HOWE, JONATHAN THOMAS, lawyer; b. Evanston, Ill., Dec. 16, 1940; s. Frederick King and Rosalie Charlotte (Volz) H.; m. Lois Helene Braun, July 12, 1963; children: Heather C., Jonathan Thomas Jr., Sara E. BA with honors, Northwestern U., 1963; JD with distinction, Duke U., 1966. Bar: Ill. 1966, U.S. Dist. Ct. (no. dist.) Ill. 1966, U.S. Ct. Appeals (7th cir.) 1967, U.S. Tax Ct. 1968, U.S. Supreme Ct. 1970, U.S. Ct. Appeals (D.C. cir.) 1976, U.S. Ct. Appeals (9th cir.) 1980, U.S. Ct. Appeals (4th, 5th, 11th dirs.) 1983, U.S. Claims Ct. 1990. Ptnr. Jenner & Block, Chgo., 1966-85, sr. ptnr. in charge assn. and adminstrv. law dept., 1978-85; founding and sr. ptnr., pres. Howe & Hutton, Chgo., Washington, 1985—; exec. and adv. coms. to Ill. Sec. of State to revise the Ill. Not for Profit Act, 1983-86; dir. Pacific Mut. Realty Investors, Inc., 1985-86; dir. cable TV options for public Chgo. Access Corp., 1995-97. Contbg. editor Ill. Inst. for Continuing Legal Edn., 1973—, Sporting Goods Bus., 1977-91, Meeting News, 1978-88, Meetings Mgr., 1988—, Meetings and Convs., 1991—; contbr. articles to profl. jours.; legal editor Meetings and Convs., 1990—. Mem. Dist. 27 Bd. Edn., Northbrook, Ill., 1969-89, sec., 1969-72, pres., 1973-84; chmn. bd. trustees Sch. Employee Benefit Trust, 1979-85; founding bd. dirs., pres. Sch. Mgmt. Found. Ill., 1976-84; mem. exec. com. Northfield Twp. Rep. Orgn., 1967-71; bd. deacons Village Presbyn. Ch. Northbrook, 1975-78, trustee, 1981-83; mem. Arts and Music Forum, 4th Presbyn. Ch., Chgo., 1990-93; spl. advisor Pres.'s Coun. Phys. Fitness and Sports, 1983-87, Duke Univ. Sch. of Law Bd. of Visitors (life mem.). Named Industry Leader of Yr., Meeting Industry, 1987, Sch. Bd. Mem. Yr. (twice) , Ill. State Bd. Edn.; recipient Internat. Found. PaceSetters award Hospitality Sales Mktg. Assn., 1996. Fellow Internat. Forum of Travel and Tourism Advs., Am. Soc. Assn. Execs. (vice-chmn. legal com. 1983-86); mem. Internat. Assn. Conv. and Hosp. Indsl. Attys. (founder), ABA (antitrust sect. Nat. Inst. com., trade assn. law com. corp. banking and bus. law sect., sect. on litigation, adminstrv. law sect.; mem. internat. law com., continuing edn. com., tort and ins. practice, vice-chmn. com. sports law 1986—, standing com. meetings and travel 1988-93, spl. advisor 1993—), Task Force on Membership Benefits for Disabled Lawyers, Ill. Bar Assn. (antitrust sect., civil practice sect., sch. law sect., adminstrv. law sect.; co-editor Antitrust Newsletter 1986-70), Chgo. Bar Assn. (def. of prisoners com. 1966-83, antitrust law com. 1971—, continuing edn. com. 1977—, chmn. assn. and non-profit soc. law com. 1984-86), Am. Soc. Assn. Execs. (vice-chmn. legal com., founding mem. legal sect.), Assn. Hospitality Industry Attys. (founder, bd. dirs. 1994—), Nat. Sch. Bds. Assn. (nat. bd. dirs. 1979-89, exec. com. 1981-89, sec.-treas. 1983-85, 2d v.p. 1985-86, pres.-elect 1986-87, chmn. devel. com. 1982-87, pres. 1987-88), D.C. Bar Assn., Am. Judicature Soc., Ill. Assn. Sch. Bds. (pres. 1977-79, bd. dirs. 1971-88), Chi Bar Found. (life), Assn. Forum Chicagoland (assoc., formerly Chgo. Soc. Assn. Execs.), Nat. Sch. Bds. Assn. Found. (pres./trustee 1995—), Greater Washington Soc. Assn. Execs., Legal Club, Law Club,

Mid-Am. Club, Tower Club, Univ. Club Chgo., Psi Upsilon. Home: 126 W Delaware Pl Chicago IL 60610-3252 Office: 20 N Wacker Dr Ste 4200 Chicago IL 60606-3103 also: 1899 L St NW Washington DC 20036-3804

HOWE, KIMBERLY PALAZZO, critical care nurse; b. Youngstown, Ohio, Nov. 25, 1958; d. Joseph A. and Josephine A. (Mele) Palazzo; m. Jeffrey Lawrence Howe, Sept. 11, 1982. AAS, Youngstown State U., 1979, BSN, 1987; MS in Nursing, Case Western Res. U., 1990. Cert. critical care nuse, ACLS, BLS, clinical nurse specialist. Staff nurse, ICU Western Res. Care System/Northside Med. Ctr., Youngstown, 1979-87, staff educator, 1987-90, critical care clin. nurse specialist, 1990—. Contbr. articles to profl. jours. Mem. mem. adv. coun. Youngstown State U., 1989—. Mem. AACN (grantee 1989), N.Am. Nursing Diagnosis Assn., Am. Heart Assn., Soc. Critical Care Nursing, Ohio Nurses Assn., Sigma Theta Tau. Home: 2951 Belmar Dr Youngstown OH 44505-2107

HOWE, LISA MARIE, veterinarian, educator; b. Wichita Falls, Tex., Feb. 11, 1961; d. Charles Edward and Frances Elizabeth (Crabtree) Butler; m. Michael Wayne Howe, Jan. 16, 1993. AS, Cisco (Tex.) Jr. Coll., 1981; student, Abilene (Tex.) Christian U., 1981-83; BS, Tex. A&M U., 1985, DVM, 1987, PhD, 1993. Diplomate Am. Coll. Vet. Surgeons. Vet. intern U. Mo. Coll. Vet. Medicine, Columbia, 1987-88; vet. clin. assoc. Tex. A&M U. Coll. Vet. Medicine, College Station, 1988-91, clin. asst. prof. vet. medicine, 1993-95, asst. prof. vet. medicine, 1995—; mem. pub. rels. com. Am. Coll. Vet. Surgeons, 1994—. Contbr. articles to profl. jours. Mem. Am. Vet. Med. Assn., Am. Assn. Vet. Clinicians, Internat. Alliance Tchr. Scholars, Brazos Valley Vet. Med. Assn. Mem. Ch. of Christ. Avocations: motorcycling, reading, Net surfing, gardening. Office: Tex A&M U Coll Vet Medicine Dept Sm Animal Med & Surg College Station TX 77843

HOWE, LYMAN HAROLD, III, chemist; b. Wilkes-Barre, Pa., Nov. 5, 1938; s. Lyman Harold and Esther Madeline (Smith) H.; m. Mary Louise Reinhart, June 16, 1962; 1 child, Jennifer. B.S., Duke U., 1960; M.S., Emory U., 1961; Ph.D., U. Tenn., 1966. Rsch. assoc. Emory U., 1960-61; rsch. and teaching assoc. U. Tenn., 1962-66; rsch. chemist water mgmt. TVA, Chattanooga, 1966-97. *Thirty-one years experience in (1) defining chemical analysis work and costs, (2) providing how-to analytical methodology, (3) finding contact laboratories, (4) solving chemical problems, (5) invoking basic principles of chemistry to solve problems, (6) designing and reviewing collaborative test plans and results, (7) developing and executing project plans involving physical and chemical measurements for customers, (8) evaluating and developing analytical chemistry techniques, (9) designing and conducting special air and water chemistry studies, and (10) making recommendations.* Co-author publs. in field. Fellow ASTM (water com. results advisor 1976-97, Max Hecht award 1985, Award of Merit 1993); mem. Am. Chem. Soc., Nat. Mgmt. Assn., Am. Contact Bridge League (Ace of Clubs award, third place Chattanooga Club Master of Yr. award 1989, reviewer environ. sci. and tech. 1989), U.S. Chess Fedn. Clubs: Torch (1st v.p. chpt. 1981, pres. 1982-83, 2d v.p. 1984-88), The Nost. Presbyterian. Home: 1241 Mountain Brook Cir Signal Mountain TN 37377-2127

HOWE, MARTHA MORGAN, microbiologist, educator; b. N.Y.C., Sept. 29, 1945; d. Charles Hermann and Miriam Hudson (Wagner) M.; m. Terrance Gary Cooper. A.B., Bryn Mawr Coll., 1966; Ph.D., MIT, 1972. Postdoctoral fellow Cold Spring Harbor Lab, N.Y., 1972-74; asst. prof. bacteriology U. Wis., Madison, 1975-77, assoc. prof., 1977-81, prof., 1981-84, Vilas prof., 1984-86; Van Vleet prof. virology U. Tenn., Memphis, 1986—; mem. genetic biology rev. panel NSF, 1980-82; mem. gen. rsch. support rev. com. NIH, Bethesda, 1982-86, mem. microbial physiology and genetics 2 study sec., 1997—; mem. sci. adv. com. instnl. rsch. grants Am. Cancer Soc., 1991-94. Assoc. editor Virology, 1983-92, Genetics, 1994; mem. editorial bd. Jour. Bacteriology, 1985-90; contbr. articles to profl. jours. and books. Recipient Rsch. Career Devel. award NIH, 1978; H.I. Romnes Faculty fellow U. Wis., 1981; Amoco Teaching award U. Wis., 1981. Fellow Am. Acad. Microbiology (bd. govs. 1991—); mem. Am. Soc. Microbiology (chmn. divsn. H 1983, councillor divsn. H 1989-91, chmn. com. on awards 1990-96, pres.-elect 1999—, Eli Lilly award 1985, ASM Founders Disting. Svc. award 1999), Am. Soc. Biochemistry and Molecular Biology, Genetics Soc. Am. (bd. dirs. 1989-91, program com. 1989-90). Office: U Tenn Dept Microbiology and Immunology 858 Madison Ave Memphis TN 38163

HOWE, MARVINE HENRIETTA, newspaper reporter; b. Shanghai, China, Dec. 3, 1928; parents Am. citizens; d. James Lewis and Mary Scott (West) H. BLitt, Rutgers U., 1950. News broadcaster Radio Maroc, Rabat, Morocco, 1951-55; contbr. Brit. Broadcasting Corp., Rabat, 1952-55, McGraw-Hill World News, Morocco, 1958-62; stringer Time-Life, Algiers, Rabat, Lisbon, 1956-65, N.Y. Times, Algiers, Rabat, Lisbon, 1957-71; bur. chief N.Y. Times, Rio de Janeiro, 1972-75; corr. N.Y. Times, Portugal and Angola, 1975-76; bur. chief N.Y. Times, Beirut, Ankara, Athens, 1977-84; reporter Met. staff N.Y. Times, N.Y.C., 1984-94; freelance writer, 1995—; lectr. Lycee, Fez, Morocco, 1950-51, Univ. Ctr., Va., 1959, Rutgers U. Journalism Sch., 1991; del. Internat. Women's Media Conf., Washington, 1986. Author: The Prince and I or One Woman's Morocco, 1956; author travel articles; contbr. to travel guidebooks; contbr. articles to The Monitor, Scholastic, Middle East Jour., The Nation, New Republic, Africa Report, Internat. Herald Tribune, Washington Report on Middle East Affairs, others. Recipient Poetry award Douglass Coll., 1950; Adalaide Zagoren fellow Rutgers U., 1991. Mem. AAUW, Silurians. Democrat. Presbyterian. Avocations: theater, classical music, ballet, travel. Home: 203 S Jefferson St Lexington VA 24450-2028 Office: Alto Da Barra, 38 Bloco D-4D, 2780 Oeiras Portugal

HOWE, PATRICIA MOORE, adult education educator; b. Woodside, N.Y., Oct. 10, 1938; d. James Preston and Florence (McGowen) Moore; m. Douglas C. Howe, Aug. 2, 1958; children: William, David, Timothy. BS in Lit., SUNY, Oneonta, 1972, MS in Edn., 1975. Cert. elem. and adult edn., Del. Tchr. Cecil County Bd. Edn., Elkton, Md., 1979-80; beginning reading instr. Chesapeake Job Corps Ctr., Port Deposit, Md., 1980-85; coord. adult programs U. Del., Newark, 1987-97, acad. coord., 1993-98, ret., 1998; owner Edn. Works. Home: 23 Acorn Dr Elkton MD 21921-3209

HOWE, RICHARD CUDDY, state supreme court chief justice; b. South Cottonwood, Utah, Jan. 20, 1924; s. Edward E. and Mildred (Cuddy) H.; m. Juanita Lyon, Aug. 30, 1949; children: Christine Howe Schultz, Andrea Howe Reynolds, Bryant, Valerie Howe Winegar, Jeffrey, Craig. B.S., U. Utah, 1945, J.D., 1948. Bar: Utah. Law clk. to Justice James H. Wolfe, Utah Supreme Ct., 1949-50; judge city ct. Murray, Utah, 1951; individual practice law Murray, 1952-80; assoc. justice Utah Supreme Ct., Salt Lake City, 1980—, justice, chief justice; mem. Utah Constnl. Revision Commn., 1976-85. Chmn., original mem. Salt Lake County Merit Coun.; mem. Utah Ho. of Reps., 1951-58, 69-72, Utah Senate, 1973-78. Named Outstanding Legislator Citizens' Conf. State Legislatures, 1972. Mem. ABA, Utah Bar Assn., Sons of Utah Pioneers. Mem. LDS Ch. Office: Utah Supreme Ct 450 S State St PO Box 140210 Salt Lake City UT 84114-0210*

HOWE, RICHARD RIVES, lawyer; b. Portland, Oreg., Dec. 21, 1942; s. Hubert Shattuck Jr. and Anna Gertrude (Moody) H.; m. Elizabeth Anne Crowell, Aug. 29, 1964; 1 child, Richard Rives Jr. BA, Yale U., 1964; JD, Harvard U., 1967. Bar: N.Y. 1968, U.S. Ct. Appeals (2d cir.) 1973, U.S. Dist. Ct. (so. and ea. dists.) N.Y. 1973, U.S. Supreme Ct. 1973. Assoc. Sullivan & Cromwell, N.Y.C., 1967-74, ptnr., 1974—. Bd. dirs. Peoples' Symphony Concerts, N.Y.C., 1983—, Bar Assurance and Reinsurance Ltd., Bermuda, 1994—, Nat. Com. Am. Fgn. Policy, Inc., 1999—. Mem. ABA (mem. com. on corp. practice, bus. law sect.), N.Y. State Bar Assn. (mem. exec. com. 1982-99, chmn. 1992-93, bus. law sect., chmn. securities regulation com. 1982-86), Assn. Bar City of N.Y., Phi Beta Kappa, Pi Sigma Alpha. Democrat. Home: 86 Woodfield Dr Short Hills NJ 07078-1654 Office: Sullivan & Cromwell 125 Broad St Fl 28 New York NY 10004-2489

HOWE, ROGER EVANS, mathematician, educator; b. Chgo., May 23, 1945; s. John Perry and Marilyn (Leilani) (Evans) H.; m. Carolyn (Rutter) Read Howe, Sept. 9, 1967; Nicholas Read, Katherine Joanna. BA, Harvard Coll., 1966; PhD in Math., U. Calif., Berkeley, 1969. Asst. prof. SUNY, Stony Brook, 1969-72, assoc. prof., 1972-74; prof. Yale U., New Haven, 1974—; vis. mem. Inst. for Advanced Study, Princeton, N.J., 1971-72; guest prof. U. Bonn, Germany, 1973-74; vis. prof. Oxford U., Eng., 1978, Rutgers U., New Brunswick, N.J., 1989-90, U. Paris VII, 1996; fellow Inst. for Advanced Studies, Hebrew U. of Jerusalem, 1988; bd. dirs. Conn. Acad. Edn. in Math., Sci. and Tech., Math. Scis. Edn. Bd. Co-author: Non-abelian Harmonic Analysis, 1992; advisor Jour. die reine und angewandte Mathematik, 1985-97; editor Bull. Am. Math. Soc., 1988-90; mem. editl. bd. Math. Rsch. Letters, Hong Kong, 1993-96, Advances in Math., 1995—, Transformation Groups, 1995—; contbr. articles to profl. jours. Guggenheim Found. fellow, 1983, Japan Soc. Promotion of Sci., Tokyo, 1993. Fellow Am. Acad. Arts and Scis., Conn. Acad. Sci. and Engring., Nat. Acad. Sci.; mem. Am. Math. Soc. (editor 1989-92), Math. Assn. Am. (com. Lester R. Ford award), Nat. Coun. Tchrs. Math. Office: Yale U PO Box 208283 New Haven CT 06520-8283*

HOWE, RONALD EVANS, minister; b. Charles City, Iowa, Feb. 17, 1945; s. Evans R. and Elizabeth (Atchison) H.; m. M. Kristin Petersmith, Aug. 16, 1970; children: Sarah Elizabeth, Rachel Ellen, Michael Evans. Cert., Moody Bible Inst., 1966, AB, 1969; AB, U. Iowa, 1968, JD, 1972; ThM, Dallas Theol. Sem., 1975. Lic. to ministry Ind. Mission Ch., 1966, ordained Evang. Free Ch. Am., 1990. Bar: Iowa 1972, Tex. 1973, U.S. Tax Ct. 1974. Atty. Lawn Offices of Gordon Macdowell, Dallas, 1972-75; sr. min. Elim Chapel, Winnipeg, Man., Can., 1975-85, Evang. Free Ch., Fresno, Calif., 1985—; broadcaster weekly radio program Free to Live, 1985—; owner, pres. Elim Place, Inc.; adj. prof. Winnipeg Theol. Sem., 1975-85, Briercrest Grad. Sch., Caronport, Sask, Can., 1985-87; bd. dirs. Haggai Inst., Winnipeg, 1977-85, Link Care Ctr., Fresno, 1985—; bd. govs. Winnipeg Bible Coll. and Sem., 1982-85; mem. exec. com. Fresno Christian Sch., 1985—; cons. Evangelical Ministries Found., Fresno, 1999—; lectr. in field. Author: (booklet) Breakfast of Champions, 1984. Exec. dir. Comty. Advocacy Found., Fresno, 1999—. Recipient Mayor's Commendation for 10 Yrs. of Contbn. in Leadership to City of Fresno, 1995, Outstanding Bus. award for leadership in edn. Compact Fresno, 1998. Mem. North Fresno Rotary. Republican. Office: Evang Free Ch 3438 E Ashlan Ave Fresno CA 93726-3506 *The greatest challenge of my life is to be alert daily to the struggle of maintaining integrity between what I say and what I practice. This authenticity or lack thereof will impact my personal, family and professional life.*

HOWE, SANDRA JO, library director; b. St. Louis, Sept. 30, 1960; d. Raymond Lee and Elizabeth Ann Griffin; m. Steven Howe, June 24, 1977 (div. Nov. 1978); children: Beth Marie Howe, Ricky A. Rudd. Student, Culver-Stockton Coll., 1999—. Pharmacy technician Grand Leader Pharmacy, Canton, Mo., 1981-87; mgr., cons. Mo. Pizza Co., Canton, 1993-96; asst. libr. Canton Pub. Libr., 1996-97, dir., 1997—. Mem. ALA, AAUW, Mo. Libr. Assn., Students in Free Enterprise, Phi Beta Lambda. Avocations: reading, promoting literacy, nature walks, gardening. Office: Canton Pub Libr 409 Lewis St Canton MO 63435

HOWE, SUSAN LEONE, artist, printmaker, design consultant; b. Sarasota, Fla., June 16, 1947; d. James Leo and Mary Jeanne (Johnson) Lefholz; m. Kenneth J. Campagna, Dec. 12, 1970 (div. 1985); m. William Clarence Howe, Apr. 23, 1987. BA, San Jose State U., 1973. Art dir. Scale Models Unltd., Menlo Park, Calif., 1969-78; pres., owner Campagna & Assocs., Palo Alto, Calif., 1978-87; artist, printmaker Two Hat Studios, Aptos, Calif., 1987—. One-woman shows include Maturango Mus., Ridge Crest, Calif., 1994, Santa Cruz (Calif.) County Bldg., 1994, U. Calif. YWCA, Berkeley, 1995; exhibited in group shows at Matrix Gallery, Sacramento, 1990, U. Hawaii, 1993, San Bernardino (Calif.) County Mus., 1993, ARC, Chgo., 1994, St. Francis Found., San Francisco, 1996, State of the Arts, Oakland, Calif., 1996, Atelier Gallery, Santa Cruz, 1996, Desert Art, Palm Desert, Calif., 1996-97, Takara Gallery, Houston, 1997, Hewletpackard, Santa Clara, Calif., 1997-98, Paper Inparticular, Columbia, Mo., 1998. Mem. Arts Guild Santa Cruz County, Arts Guild Sonoma. Avocation: garden and landscape designing. Office: Two Hat Studios 1570 Cox Rd Aptos CA 95003-9779

HOWE, VERNON WESLEY, mathematics educator; b. Burundi, Aug. 4, 1942; came to U.S., 1945; s. Parshall L. and Adelia F. (Swingle) H.; m. Winona R. Scott, July 25, 1965; children: Andrew, Stephanie. MA in Math., U. Calif., Berkeley, 1966; PhD in Math., Dartmouth Coll., 1971; MS in Computer Sci., Calif. State U., Fullerton, 1986. Instr. math. Atlantic Union Coll., South Lancaster, Mass., 1966-67; asst. prof. math. U. Ark., Fayetteville, 1971-74; prof. math. and computing La Sierra U., Riverside, Calif., 1974—; vis. prof. math. Colgate U., Hamilton, N.Y., 1982-83; cons. computing Comarco Corp., Anaheim, Calif., 1985-90. Recipient G.T. Anderson award for teaching La Sierra U., 1994, Zapara award for coll. teaching, 1986, Tchr. of Yr. award Loma Linda U., 1976. Mem. Am. Math. Soc., Math. Assn. Am., Soc. Indsl. and Applied Math., Assn. for Computing Machinery, Am. Birding Assn. Seventh-day Adventist. Avocation: birdwatching. Home: 11238 Rogers St Riverside CA 92505-2628 Office: La Sierra U 4700 Pierce St Riverside CA 92505-3332

HOWE, WARREN BILLINGS, physician; b. Jackson Heights, N.Y., Oct. 25, 1940; s. John Hanna and Francelia (Rose) H.; m. Hedwig Neslanik, Aug. 7, 1971; children: Elizabeth Rose, Sarah Billings. BA, U. Rochester, 1962; MD, Washington U., St. Louis, 1965. Diplomate Am. Bd. Family Practice with CAQ in Sports Medicine, Nat. Bd. Med. Examiners. Intern Phila. Gen. Hosp., 1965-66; resident physician Highland Hosp./U. Rochester, 1969-71; family physician Family Medicine Clinic of Oak Harbor (Wash.), Inc., PS, 1971-92; student health physician, univ. team physician We. Wash. U., Bellingham, 1992—; team physician Oak Harbor High Sch., 1972-92; head tournament physician Wash. State High Sch. Wrestling Championships, Tacoma, 1989—; attending physician Seattle Goodwill Games, 1990; clin. asst. prof. U. Wash. Sch. Medicine, 1975-82. Contbr. articles to profl. jours. and chpts. to books; editl. bd. The Physician and Sports Medicine Jour., 1984—. Bd. dirs. Oak Harbor Sch. Dist. #201, 1975-87; chmn. Oak Harbor Citizen's Com. for Sch. Support, 1988-90. Lt. comdr. USN, 1966-69, Vietnam. Recipient Disting. Svc. award City of Oak Harbor, 1984; Paul Harris fellowship Oak Harbor Rotary Club. Fellow Am. Coll. Sports Medicine (chair membership com. 1986-95), Am. Acad. Family Physicians; mem. Wash. State Med. Assn., Am. Med. Soc. for Sports Medicine, Am. Coll. Health Assn. Presbyterian. Home: 4222 Northridge Way Bellingham WA 98226-7804 Office: WWU Student Health Ctr 25 High St Bellingham WA 98225-9112

HOWE, WESLEY JACKSON, medical supplies company executive; b. Jersey City, June 7, 1921; s. Wesley Veith and Phyllis (Jackson) H.; m. Suzanne Rodrock, July 20, 1946; children: Marc Edward, Richard Douglas, Suzanne. ME, Stevens Inst. Tech., Hoboken, N.J., 1943, MS, 1953; DEng (hon.), Stevens Inst. Tech., 1981; LHD, U. N.J. Medicine & Dentistry (hon.), 1988. With Becton, Dickinson and Co., Franklin Lakes, N.J., 1949-92; group v.p., then exec. v.p. Becton, Dickinson and Co., Rutherford, N.J., 1970-72, pres., chief exec. officer, dir., 1972-80, chmn. bd., 1980-92, exec. chmn. bd. emeritus, 1992—, chief exec. officer, dir., 1980-89, pres., 1983-87; dir., former chmn. N.J. Mfrs. Ins. Co.; chmn. Re-Ins. Co., N.J. Bus. and Industry. Chm. emeritus bd. trustees Stevens Inst. Tech. 1st lt. AUS, 1944-46, '51-52. Mem. N.J. C. of C. (dir.), Arcola Country Club.

HOWE, WILLIAM HUGH, artist; b. Stockton, Calif., June 18, 1928; s. Edwin Walter and Eugenia (Mercante) H. AB, Ottawa (Kans.) U., 1951. Illustrator Western Auto Supply, Kansas City, Mo., 1952, Kansas City Mdse. Mart, 1953-56; comml. artist U.S. Army C.E., Kansas City, 1958-64, Howard Needles Tammen & Bergendoff Cons. Engrs., Kansas City, 1964-68, Urban & Regional Planning, 1968-70; freelance artist, 1970—. Exhibited paintings of butterflies Philbrook Art Ctr., Tulsa, Ft. Worth Children's Mus., Montserrat Gallery, N.Y.C., Witte Meml. Art Mus., San Antonio, Anthropology Mus., Chapultepec Park, Mexico City; represented in permanent collections: Smithsonian Instn., Washington, Franklin Mint (Pa.), Cranbook Inst., Bloomfield HIlls, Mich., U. Mich. Exhibits Mus., Ann Arbor, Oak Knoll Mus., Clayton, Mo., Am. Mus. Natural History, N.Y.C., Denver Mus. Natural History, Am. Baptist Assembly, Green Lake, Wis., Mowbray Union, Ottawa U., Kans., Cen. Mo. State Coll., Warrensburg, Mich. State U., East Lansing, U. Wyo. Art Mus., Laramie, San Diego Mus. Nat. History, Balboa Park, U. Ariz., Tuscon, Ill. State Mus. Art, Springfield, Mont. Hist. Soc., Helena, Wyo. State Art Mus., Cheyenne, Ariz. State U., Tempe, Milw. Pub. Mus., State Capitol Bldg., Denver, Denver Pub. Libr., Kansas City (Mo.) Mus. History Sci., Presdl. Palace, Tamazunchale, San Luis Potosi, Mexico, Ottawa (Kans.) Jr. H.S., others; Am. Heritage Wildlife cards Am. Butterflies, 1983, U. Kans., 1994, U. Calif. Berkeley, Allyn Mus. Entomology, Sarasota, U. Colo., Colo. State U., Calif. Acad. Scis., San Francisco, Oakland (Calif.) Mus., James Ford Bell Mus., U. Minn. (Mpls), Coutts Art Mus., 1997; Author-artist: Our Butterflies and Moths, 1964, The Butterflies of North America, 1975, Butterfly Chart of North America, 1979, Butterfly sect. Readers Digest North American Wildlife, 1980; co-author (with Carlos R. Beutelspacher Baights), U.N.A.M., Mexico City, 1984; one man show Caroline Kingcade Gallery, North Kansas City, Mo., 1988, Coutts Mus. of Art, El Dorado, 1997, Dallas Mus. Natural History, Fair Park, 1999, George P. Spiva Art Ctr., Joplin, Mo., 1999; TV show Hoy Mismo, 1986. Mem. Ottawa Community Arts Coun., Leavenworth Arts. Coun.; mem. Larry Hatteberg's "Kans. People" KAKE-TV, Wichita. Named Am. Artist Am. References, 1990. Mem. Jour. Lepidopterists Soc., Burroughs Nature Club, Audubon Soc. Mo., Central States Entomo. Soc., Los Angeles County Mus., Spiva Art Ctr., Dallas Mus. Natural History, Mus. Culture and Natural History, Harvard Botanical Mus.. Democrat. Episcopalian. Avocation: collecting butterflies in Mexico and Guatemala. Home and Studio: 822 E 11th St Ottawa KS 66067-3138

HOWELL, ALLEN WINDSOR, lawyer; b. Montgomery, Ala., Mar. 10, 1949; s. Elvin and Bennie Merle (Windsor) H.; m. Donna K. Graffander, Sept. 2, 1989; children: Christopher Darby, Joshua Darby, Jeremiah Graffander. BA, Huntington Coll., 1971; JD, Jones Sch. Law, 1974. Bar: Ala. 1974, U.S. Supreme Ct. 1977, U.S. Ct. Appeals (fed. cir.) 1983, U.S. Ct. Appeals (11th cir.) 1981, U.S. Tax Ct. 1979, U.S. Claims Ct. 1982, U.S. Dist. Ct. (mid. dist.) Ala. 1975, U. Dist. Ct. (so. dist.) Ala. 1978. Archivist Hist. Rsch. Ctr. Air U., Maxwell AFB, Ala., 1972-75; pvt. practice Montgomery, 1975-82, 83—; adj. prof. Faulkner U., Montgomery, 1975—, law sch. 1983-85; asst. atty. gen., chief legal sect. Ala. Medicaid Agy., Montgomery, 1982-83. Author: Alabama Civic Practice Forms, 1986, 3d edit., 1992, Alabama Torts Case Finder, 1988, Alabama Personal Injury and Torts, 1996, Trial Handbook for Alabama Lawyers, 2d edit., 1998. Hon. lt. col., aide de camp Gov. Ala., 1974. Mem. ABA (contbr. editor profl. liability newsletter, litigation sect. 1990-92), Assn. Trial Lawyers Am., Montgomery County Bar Assn. (newsletter editorial com. 1984-85), Nat. Bd. Trial Adv. (cert. civil litigation 1981, 86, 91, examiner ethics, evidence and civil procedure). Mem. Ch. of Christ. Office: PO Box 70367 Montgomery AL 36107-0367

HOWELL, BENJAMIN FRANKLIN, JR., geophysicist, educator; b. Princeton, N.J., June 12, 1917; s. Benjamin Franklin and Claire M. (Mead) H.; m. Constance M. Benson, June 30, 1943 (dec.); children: Barbara Carolyn, Catherine Ann (dec.), Bonnie Andrea, James Benjamin. A.B., Princeton U., 1939; M.S., Calif. Inst. Tech., 1942, Ph. D., 1949. Research engr. div. war research U. Calif. at San Diego, 1942-45; geophysicist United Geophys. Co., 1946-49; faculty Pa. State U., 1949—, prof. geophysics, 1953—, head dept. geophysics and geochemistry, 1949-63; asst. dean Pa. State U. (Grad. Sch.), 1968-70, assoc. dean, 1970-82, dean emeritus, 1982—; Chief cons. seismologist Vibratech Engring. Co., Hazleton, Pa., 1955-69. Author: Introduction to Geophysics, 1959, Earth and Universe, 1972, Introduction to Seismological Research: History and Development, 1990; Editor: Contributions in Geophysics in Honor of Beno Gutenberg, 1958. Fellow Am. Geophys. Union (sec. sect. tectonophysics 1956-59, sect. seismology 1959-63), Geol. Soc. Am.; mem. soc. Exploration Geophysics, Seismol. Soc. Am. (pres. 1963-64), Phi Beta Kappa, Sigma Xi. Baptist. Home: 1143 Smithfield Cir State College PA 16801-6424 Office: 406 Deike Bldg University Park PA 16802-2713

HOWELL, BRADLEY SUE, librarian; b. McKinney, Tex., July 15, 1933; d. Jessie Leonard and Carrie Pearl (Nickerson) LaFon; m. Richard Dunn Howell, May 18, 1957; children: Mark Richard, Celeste Ella, Jane Elizabeth. BS in Edn., So. Meth. U., 1955; MS in Libr. Sci., East Tex. State U., 1968. Tchr. J.B. Hood Jr. High Sch., Dallas, 1955-56, Mineral Wells (Tex.) Jr. High Sch., 1957-58; libr. Ascher Silberstein Sch., Dallas, 1963, San Jacinto Sch., Dallas, 1960-62, 65-81, Woodrow Wilson High Sch., Dallas, 1981—. Pres. tex. United Meth. Hist. Soc., 1980-84; sec. South Ctrl. Jurisdiction, Archives and history of United Meth. Ch., 1980-88, v.p. local ch. sect. The United Meth. Hist. Soc., 1989-95, chmn., 1995—; pres. PTA, Woodrow Wilson High Sch., 1983-84; leader Camp Fire, Inc., 1970—. Recipient Wakan award Camp Fire, Inc., 1976, Hilteni award, 19782, Sawnequas award, 1988, Golich Vol. award, 1998, Terrific Tchr. award Tex. PTA, 1984, Jim Collin sOutstanding award, 1986, Honor award Nat. Sch. Pub. Relation Assn., 1986, Dallas Positive Parents award, 1987, Golden Flame award, 1990. Mem. Dallas Assn. Sch. Librs. (pres. 1975-76), Tex. Assn. Sch. Librs., Tex. Libr. Assn. (chmn. archives and history roundtable 1990-92), Am. Libr. Svcs. to Children (Newbery com. 1980), Freedoms Found. at Valley Forge (pres. Dallas chpt. 1997—), Delta Kappa Gamma (state achievement award 1988, Golden Gift Leadership Mgmt. award 1985), Alpha Delta Pi, Phi Delta Kappa, Delta Psi Kappa, Pi Lambda Theta. Democrat. Home: 722 Ridgeway St Dallas TX 75214-4453 Office: Woodrow Wilson High Sch 100 S Glasgow Dr Dallas TX 75214-4518

HOWELL, BRUCE INMAN, academic administrator; b. Roanoke Rapids, N.C., Mar. 12, 1942; s. Leroy Inman and Pauline (Massey) H.; m. Mable Lea Smith, Aug. 22, 1965; children: Bruce Inman Jr., Virginia Lea. BS in English and History, East Carolina U., 1964, MA in History and Sch. Adminstrn., 1965; postgrad., N.C. State U., 1971, 84, Mich. State U., 1971, Duke U., 1976, N.C. Bank Dirs. Coll., 1999. Cert. grad. tchr., prin., supr., N.C., investment banker, stock exchange and brokerage office procedures. Instr., grad. asst. East Carolina U., Greenville, N.C., 1964-65; stockbroker Interstate Securities Corp., Charlotte, N.C., 1968-70; dean continuing edn. Lenoir C.C., Kinston, N.C., 1970-75; pres. Sampson Tech. Coll., Clinton, N.C., 1975-80, Wake Tech. C.C., Raleigh, N.C., 1980—; adj. prof. dept. adult and C.C. edn. N.C. State U., 1982—, gen. adv. com., 1982; mem. Wake County-Raleigh Pvt. Industry Coun., 1983-94, Raleigh Econ. Devel. Roundtable, 1984—, exec. com.; adv. N.C. govt. agys., Wake Co. Communities in Schs., 1990—; adv. Cen. Carolina Consortium, 1993-97, pres., 1996-97; mem. numerous ednl. commns. and task forces. Author: Debasement: A Problem of Imperial Rome, 1966, The Lenoir County Story, 1968; editorial bd. Community Coll. Review, N.C. State U., 1982-93; contbr. articles to profl. jours. Mem. Lenoir County Schs. Vocat. Adv. com., 1972-75, Econ. Devel. Com., Fuguay-Varina; bd. dirs. Lenoir County Heart Fund, 1972, Lenoir County Fair Assn., 1970, Branch Banking & Trust Co., Cary, N.C., 1980-98; chmn. bd. dirs. Crescent State Bank, 1998—; mem. Wake County Interagy. Coord. Coun., 1981; membership com. N.C. Lit. and Hist. Assn., 1978; mem. adminstrv. bd. Westminster United Meth. Ch., 1973-76; active First United Meth. Ch., Clinton, 1977-81, chmn. adminstrv. bd., 1978-80, White Plains, 1981—, trustee, 1997—. Grad. fellow East Carolina U., 1964-65; Kellogg Community Svcs. fellow, Lenoir Community Coll., 1971; named one of Outstanding Young Men Am., 1975, 77, 78, Jacyee of Yr., 1967, Outstanding Old Jaycee of Yr., 1971; recipient Chief Exec. Officer award So. Region Assn. Community Colls., 1989. Mem. Am. Coun. on Edn., Nat. Coun. Cmty. Svcs. Continuing Edn., Nat. Coun. Resource Devel., So. Assn. Colls. and Schs. (evaluation com. 1982, 90, 92-94), N.C. Assn. Colls. and Univs. (mem. govtl. agys. liaison com. 1983-90, pres. 1993), N.C. C.C. Adult Edn. Assn., N.C. Assn. Pub. C.C. Pres. (numerous com. assignments, pres. 1986-87), N.C. Employees Assn., Nat. Geneal. Soc. (N.C. chpt.), Am. Numismatic Assn., Greater Raleigh C. of C. (mem. adv. com. manpower resource devel. program 1980, leadership round table 1983—, higher edn. roundtable 1986—), Cary C. of C. (econ. devel. com. 1983—, edn. task force com. 1987—, pres.-elect 1998), Fuquay-Varina C. of C. (bd. dirs. 1987-90), Execs. Club of Raleigh (pres. 1996-98), Cary Rotary (pres. 1999—), Phi Delta Kappa, Kappa Delta Pi. Avocations: antiques, furniture refinishing, gardening, numismatics. Home: 1105 Queensferry Rd Cary NC 27511-6426 Office: Wake Tech Community Coll 9101 Fayetteville Rd Raleigh NC 27603-5655

HOWELL, CATHERINE JEANINE, retired secondary education educator; b. Benton, Ill., Apr. 15, 1935; d. Lloyd William Reed and Lena Pearl (Armstrong) Goodin; m. Charles Lindy Barnfield, Apr. 13, 1950 (div. Apr. 23, 1973); m. Charles E. Howell, June 28, 1975; children: Alan Reed, Robert, Timothy Michael Barnfield; stepchildren: Crystal Lea, Carla Sue. A in Technol., So. Ill. U., 1962, BA, 1968, MS in Edn., 1976, postgrad. specialist, 1986. Cert. educator and supr., Ill. Clk. Kroger, Benton, Ill., 1957-60; elem. tchr. Benton Elem. Sch. Dist. 47, 1968-70; secondary art tchr. Marion (Ill.) Cmty. Unit Sch. Dist. 2, 1970-94; ret., 1994; instr. art John A. Logan C.C., Carterville, Ill., 1975-89, 97-98, instr. vocat. edn., 1992, part-time acad. instr. art, 1997-98; cons. in field. Prin. work includes Strings of Creation, 1988, Portrait Sketch of Brenda Edgar, 1991. Art judge DuQuoin

(Ill.) State Fair, 1990-91; mem. Ill. State Bd. Edn. Leadership Canf., 1989-98; co-founder Downstate Art Educator's Assn. Recipient Award of Excellence Ill. State Bd. Edn., 1988, Sch. Bell award Williamson Co. ESR, 1988-89, Outstanding Art Educator award Ill. Alliance for Arts Edn., 1988, Ill. Art Educator award, 1989, Nat. Ill. Art Educator award, 1990, Senate Resolution Senator James Rea, 1989, Proclamation Gov. James Thompson, 1990; Ill. Tchr. of the Yr., State of Ill., 1989. Mem. AAUW, Ill. Art Edn. Assn. (sec. dir. 1990), Little Egypt Arts Assn., Ill. Ret. Tchrs. Assn.,So. Ill. U. Alumni Life, Downstate Art Edn. (life), Elk Ladies, Delta Kappa Gamma, Phi Kappa Phi, Beta Sigma Phi. Avocations: graphic art, computer graphics. antique dealer, network marketing. Home: 3000 W Woodlawn Pl Marion IL 62959-5541

HOWELL, CHARLES MAITLAND, dermatologist; b. Thomasville, N.C., Apr. 14, 1914; s. Cyrus Maitl and Lilly Mae (Ammons) H.; m. Betty Jane Myers, Feb. 12, 1949; children—Elizabeth Myers, Pamela Jane. B.S., Wake Forest U., Winston-Salem, N.C., 1935; M.D., U. Pa., 1937. Intern Charity Hosp., New Orleans, 1937-38; resident in medicine Burlington County Hosp., Mt. Holley, N.J., 1938-39; sch. physician Lawrenceville (N.J.) Sch., 1939-42; resident in pathology N.C. Baptist Hosp., Winston-Salem, 1947-48; resident in dermatology Columbia-Presbyn. Med. Ctr., N.Y.C., 1948-50; resident in allergy Roosevelt Hosp., N.Y.C., 1950-51; practice medicine specializing in dermatology Winston-Salem, 1951—; mem. staff N.C. Bapt., Forsyth Meml. hosps.; mem. faculty Bowman Gray Sch. Medicine, Wake Forest U., 1951-86, head. sect., 1984-86, prof. dermatology, 1967-84, prof. emeritus, 1984, head sect., 1961-86, acting head sect., 1984-86. Served as officer M.C. AUS, 1942-46. Fellow Am. Acad. Dermatology, Am. Acad. Allergy; mem. N. Am. Clin. Dermatol. Soc., N.Y. Acad. Scis. Democrat. Baptist. Clubs: Old Town (Winston-Salem); Bermuda Run Country (Clemmons, N.C.). Home: 1100 E Kent Rd Winston Salem NC 27104-1116 Office: 340 Pershing Ave Winston Salem NC 27103-2513

HOWELL, CHERIE ANN, volunteer recruitment coordinator, educator; b. Natrona Heights, Pa., Apr. 20, 1973; d. Stewart Blake and Rosalie Ann (Durci) H. BA in English, Mt. Union Coll., 1996. Cert. tchr., Ohio, Pa. Spl. events coord. Americorps, Family Svc. Corps. Butler County, Slippery Rock, Pa., 1996; substitute tchr. South Butler County Sch. Dist., Saxonburg, Pa., 1997—; vol. recruitment coord. Big Bros. Big Sisters of Butler County, 1997—. Newsletter editor Family Svc. Corps of Butler County, 1997. Mem. Nat. Coun. Tchrs. English., Family Svc. Corps Improvement Team. Avocations: scrapbooks, reading, organizing. Home: 206 Rachel Dr Saxonburg PA 16056-9408

HOWELL, CHRISTOPHER ALLEN, technical writer; b. Columbus, Ohio, Oct. 12, 1957; s. Arthur and Betty Jean (Anthony) H.; m. Charlotte Lewis Wells, Sept. 25, 1995. BA in Journalism, Ohio State U., 1988; student, U. Ctrl. Fla., 1999—. Prodr., reporter Sta. WBZS Radio, Orlando, 1990-91; announcer, music host Sta. WMFE Radio, Orlando, 1991-93, prodr., 1995—; editor, writer Total Graphic Svcs. Inc., Orlando, 1991-94; freelance tech. writer, web designer, pub. Author (newsletter) Graphics Graffiti, 1991-94. Avocations: reading, computers, auto racing.

HOWELL, CONNIE RAE, critical care nurse; b. St. Charles, Ill., July 13, 1952; d. George and Genevieve B. (Zornow) H. Diploma, Evangelical Sch. Nursing, Oak Lawn, Ill., 1973. Cert. critical care nurse. Staff nurse U. Utah Hosp., Salt Lake City, 1977-79, U. Wash. Hosp., Seattle, 1979-83, Sherman Hosp., Elgin, Ill., 1983-87, Univ. Hosp. and Clinics, Madison, Wis., 1987-90, Sherman Hosp., Elgin, Ill., 1991—. Mem. AACN, Evangelical Sch. Nursing Alumnae Assn.

HOWELL, DONALD LEE, lawyer; b. Waco, Tex., Jan. 31, 1935; s. Hilton Emory and Louise (Hatchett) H.; m. Gwendolyn Avera, June 13, 1957; children: Daniel Liege, Alison Avera, Anne Turner. BA cum laude, Baylor U., 1956; JD with honors, U. Tex., 1963. Bar: Tex. 1963. Assoc. Vinson & Elkins, Houston, 1963-70, ptnr., 1970—, mem. mgmt. com., 1980—. Capt. USAFR, 1956-59. Fellow Am. Bar Found., Tex. Bar Found., Houston Bar Found., Am. Law Inst.; mem. ABA, Am. Coll. Bond Counsel, Houston Bar Assn., Nat. Assn. Bond Lawyers (pres. 1981-82, bd. dirs. 1979-83), Attys. Liability Assurance Soc. (Bermuda bd. dirs. 1992—, U.S. bd. dirs. 1992—), Houston Club, Houston Ctr. Club, Order of Coif, Phi Delta Phi. Democrat. Episcopalian.

HOWELL, EMBRY MARTIN, researcher; b. Bethesda, Md., Nov. 18, 1945; d. David Grier and Louise (McMichael) Martin; m. Joseph Toy Howell III, Dec. 28, 1965; children: Andrew Martin, Jessica Ramsey. AB, Barnard Coll., 1968; MSPH, U. N.C., 1972; PhD, George Washington U., 1991. Computer programmer Corp. Trust Co., N.Y.C., 1968; computer programmer dept. city and regional planning U. N.C., Chapel Hill, 1969-70; summer intern State Bd. Health, Raleigh, N.C., 1972; rsch. asst. dept. ob-gyn Georgetown U. Hosp., Washington, 1972-73; health planner, biostatistician Health Systems Agy. No. Va., Falls Church, 1973-75; biostatistician Nat. Capital Med. Found., Washington, 1975-79; dir. SysteMetrics, Inc., Washington, 1979-92; v.p. Mathematica Policy Rsch., Washington, 1992—; dir. Nat. Evaluation Healthy Start Program; sprk. in field. Contbr. numerous articles to profl. jours. Vol. Children's Hosp. Hospice. USPHS trainee, 1971-72; recipient Agy. for Health Care Policy and Rsch. Dissertation Rsch. grant, 1990-91. Mem. Am. Pub. Health Assn., Assn. for Social Scis. in Health, Assn. for Pub. Policy Analysis and Mgmt., Am. Evaluation Assn., Phi Beta Kappa. Avocations: singing, tennis, swimming.

HOWELL, FRANCIS CLARK, anthropologist, educator; b. Kansas City, Mo., Nov. 27, 1925; s. Edward Ray and Myrtle Marie (Clark) H.; m. Betty Ann Tomsen, June 17, 1955; children—Brian David, Jennifer Clare. PhB, U. Chgo., 1949, MA, 1951, PhD, 1953. Instr. anatomy Washington U., St. Louis, 1953-55; asst. prof. to prof. anthropology U. Chgo., 1955-70; prof. anthropology U. Calif.-Berkeley, 1970-91, emeritus prof., 1991—. Contbr. numerous articles on human biol. and cultural evolution to profl. jours. Trustee L.S.B. Leakey Found., 1969—. Served with USN, 1944-46. Recipient Franklin L. Burr prize, Nat. Geographic Soc., 1993. Fellow Am. Acad. Arts and Scis.; mem. Nat. Acad. Scis., Am. Philos. Soc., AAAS, Calif. Acad. Sci. (trustee 1975—), Acad. des Scis., Inst. de France. Home: 1994 San Antonio Ave Berkeley CA 94707-1620 Office: Univ of Calif Mus Vertebrate Zoology Berkeley CA 94720

HOWELL, GEORGE BEDELL, equity investing and managing executive; b. Schenectady, Sept. 19, 1919; s. Jesse M. and Grace (Gerhaeusser) H.; m. Mary Barbara Crohurst, July 10, 1944; children: Raymond Gary, Terry Barbara, Janice Patricia, Nancy Jo, George Bedell Jr. BS in Adminstrv. Engring., Cornell U., 1942. With GE, 1946-59; v.p. mfg. Leece Neville Co., Cleve., 1959-61, Royal Electric Co., Pawtucket, R.I., 1961-62; dir. ops. packaging equipment and product devel. Acme Steel Co. (merged with Interlake Steel Corp. 1965), 1962-64; v.p. adminstrv. svc. Interlake Steel Corp., Chgo., 1964-66; v.p. internat. divsn., v.p. Acme Products divsn. Interlake Steel Corp., 1966-70; CEO Golconda Corp., Chgo., 1970-72; v.p. devel. Internat. Minerals & Chems. Corp., 1972-73, sr. v.p., pres. industry group, 1974-77, exec. v.p., 1977-81; pres., CEO Wurlitzer Co., 1982-86, chmn., pres., CEO, 1986-87, vice chmn., 1987-88; prin. Mid West Ptnrs., Chgo., 1988-89; gen. ptnr. Pfingsten Ptnrs., Chgo., 1989-94, ptnr., 1994—; chmn. Hallcrest Holding Corp., 1992-97, dir., 1998—. Chmn. bd. trustees Village of Oak Brook, Ill., 1965-73, pres., 1973-79; trustee Christ Ch., Oak Brook, vice chmn., 1992-97, trustee emeritus, 1998. N.Y. State and Univ. scholar Cornell U., 1942. Mem. McGraw Wildlife Found., Chgo. Athletic Assn., Medinah Country Club, Econ. Club (Chgo.), Ocean Reef Club (Fla.). Home: 5 Brighton Ln Oak Brook IL 60523-2323 Office: 520 Lake Cook Rd Ste 375 Deerfield IL 60015-5632 *Trust in God. Balance family, work, church and government service. Live every day of your life.*

HOWELL, GEORGE COOK, III, lawyer; b. New Orleans, June 27, 1956; s. George C. Jr. and Billie Grace (Webb) H.; children: Margaret Sloan, George C. IV. AB magna cum laude, Princeton U., 1978; JD, U.Va., 1981. Bar: Va. 1981, U.S. Dist. Ct. (ea. dist.) Va. 1982, U.S. Ct. Appeals (4th cir.) 1982. Law clk. U.S. Dist. Ct. (ea. dist.) Va., Alexandria, 1981-82; assoc. Hunton & Williams, Richmond, Va., 1982-89, ptnr., 1989—. Contbr. Va. Law Rev., 1980; editor-in-chief Va. Tax Rev., 1980-81; articles editor The Tax Lawyer, 1983-86, mng. editor, 1987-89. Mem. usher's guild 1st Presbyn. Ch., Richmond, 1986-90; participant Leadership Metro Richmond, 1987-88. Mem. ABA (taxation sect. chmn. remic task force 1987-88, chmn. mini-program on mortgage-backed securities 1988, chmn. subcom. on asset securitization 1988-90, vice chmn. com. on fin. trans. 1990-92, chmn. com. on fin. trans. 1992-94, sec. taxation 1995-97, mem. sect. taxation coun., 1997—), Princeton Assn. Va. (treas. 1987-89, pres. 1989-91), Order of Coif, Phi Beta Kappa. Republican. Avocations: golf, tennis, basketball, running, the stock market. Office: Hunton & Williams 951 E Byrd St Richmond VA 23219-4040

HOWELL, GEORGE WASHINGTON, lawyer, consultant; b. Fairfield, Ala., Jan. 11, 1927; s. George Washington and Margaret Lorraine (Hamric) H.; m. Joan Cotty White, Sept. 4, 1954 (dec. Mar. 1993); children: Jeffrey Page, Jennifer Margaret; m. Patricia Van Metre Minkler, Oct. 24, 1993. Student, Emory U., 1944-45, U. S.C., 1945-46; B.S. in Math., U. Ala., 1948, J.D., 1951. Bar: Ala. 1951, Miss. 1961. Atty. U.S. Steel Corp. TCI div., Fairfield, Ala., 1951-57; atty. Ingalls Shipbldg. Corp., Pascagoula, Miss., 1957-62, gen. counsel, 1962-66, v.p., gen. counsel, 1966-70; v.p., gen. counsel Litton Industries, Inc. Marine Group, Pascagoula, Miss., 1970-87, sr. counsel, 1988-92; cons. on litigation State of Wash., Olympia, 1982-85; chmn. taxation commn. Shipbuilder's Council Am., Washington, 1966-70; dir. Miss. Econ. Council, Jackson, 1972-73; adj. prof. law U. Miss., Oxford, 1973-82. Originator Young Leaders Camps at Kanuga for At Risk Children, 1993; pres. South Miss. Festival of Arts, Pascagoula, 1962; mem. Miss. Com. for Humanities, Jackson, 1973-82; mem., pres. Pascagoula Sch. Bd., 1981-86; mem. Miss. Research and Devel. Council, Jackson, 1979-83; mem., vice chmn. Gov.'s Commn. on Efficiency and Economy in State Govt., 1970; mem. Gov.'s Adv. Com. on Edn. Conf., Jackson, 1972, Gov.'s Task Force on Pub. Edn. Reform, 1982, Govs's. Private Sector Council, Jackson, 1984-86; pres. Community Concert Assn., Pascagoula, 1981-83; Asheville Cmty. Hero Torch Bearer Olympic Games, 1996. Served to comdr. USNR, 1944-87. Recipient Outstanding Contbn. award Miss. R & D Ctr., 1984, Merit award Pascagoula C. of C., 1966; mem. U. Ala. Baseball Team of Century award, 1993. Mem. ABA, Miss. Bar Assn., Birmingham Jr. C. of C. (pres. 1956), Pi Mu Epsilon, Omicron Delta Kappa, Pi Kappa Alpha. Episcopalian. Avocations: gardening; tennis; riding; camping. Home and Office: RR 2 Box 80A Horse Shoe NC 28742-9802

HOWELL, HARLEY THOMAS, lawyer; b. Chgo., June 5, 1937; s. Harley W. and Geneva (Engelmann) H.; m. Aliceann A. McLaughlin, Apr. 23, 1983; children by previous marriage: Shelley A. Young, Rebecca L., Emily S. AB, Princeton U., 1959; JD, Yale U., 1962. Bar: Md. 1962, U.S. Supreme Ct. 1966, D.C. 1972. Law clk. to chief judge U.S. Ct. Appeals (4th cir.) 1962-63; assoc. Semmes, Bowen & Semmes, Balt., 1966-72, ptnr., 1972-92; ptnr., Howell, Gately, Whitney & Carter LLP, Towson, Md., 1992-98, counsel, 1998-99; ptnr. Howell & Gately, Towson, Md., 1999—; mem. Gov.'s Commn. to Revise Annotated Code Md., 1975-85; mem. standing com. on rules of practice and procedure Ct. Appeals of Md., 1985—. Bd. dirs. Balt. Symphony Orch., 1975—, sec., 1986—; trustee Sheppard & Enoch Pratt Hosp., Towson, Md., 1991—. Served to capt. JAG Corps, U.S. Army, 1963-66. Decorated Army Commendation medal. Fellow Am. Coll. Trial Lawyers, Am. Acad. Appellate Lawyers, Md. Bar Found.; mem. ABA, Md. State Bar Assn., Bar Assn. Balt. City, Balt. County Bar Assn., D.C. Bar Assn., Fed. Bar Assn., Wine and Food Soc., Wranglers Law Club (Balt.). Home: 1012 Chestnut Ridge Dr Lutherville Timonium MD 21093-1716 Office: Howell & Gately, Court Towers, Suite 240 Ste 240 210 W. Pennsylvania Ave. Baltimore MD 21204-4821

HOWELL, HILTON HATCHETT, JR., business executive; b. Waco, Tex., Mar. 25, 1962; s. Hilton Hatchett Sr. and Donna (Massingill) H.; m. Robin Mary Robinson, June 15, 1991; children: Hilton Hatchett III, Alston Elizabeth. BA, Baylor U., 1984, JD cum laude, 1988; MBA, U. Tex., 1990. Bar: Ga. 1993, Tex. 1988. Atty. Liddell, Sapp, Zivley, Hill & Laboon, Houston, 1989-91; exec. v.p., dir. Delta Life Ins. Co., Delta Fire and Casualty Ins. Co., Atlanta, 1991—; exec. v.p., dir. Atlantic Am. Corp., Atlanta, 1991-95, pres., CEO, 1995—; v.p., sec., dir. Bull Run Corp., Atlanta, 1993—; dir. Am. So. Ins. Cos., Atlanta, Gray Comm. Sys., Atlanta. Bd. dirs. Ga. Dept. Human Resources, Atlanta, 1993-97; trustee Woodruff Arts Ctr., Inc., 1998—; mem. bd. regents Univ. Sys. of Ga., 1997—. Mem. Piedmont Driving Club, Capital City Club, Diplomats, Benedicts, Hedonia Club, Young Pres.'s Orgn. Baptist. Avocations: golf, hunting. Office: Atlantic Am Corp 4370 Peachtree Rd NE Atlanta GA 30319-3023

HOWELL, JAMES EDWIN, economist, educator; b. Sterling, Colo., Mar. 6, 1928; s. James William, Jr. and Lois (Brown) H.; m. Linda Leinbach, 1965; children: Kenneth E., William J., Jan E., Caitlyn B. BA, Fresno State Coll., 1950; MA, U. Ill., 1951, Yale U., 1953; PhD, Yale U., 1955. Instr. econs. and stats. Yale U., 1954-56; mem. staff Ford Found., 1956-58, 62, cons., 1958-72; Theodore J. Kreps prof. econs. Stanford U., 1958—, asso. dean Grad. Sch. Bus., 1965-70; vis. prof. econs. London Bus. Sch., 1992; dir. gen. Internat. Inst. Mgmt. and Adminstrn., Berlin, 1970-72; dir. Stanford-Insead Advanced Mgmt. Program, European Inst. Bus. Adminstrn., France, 1979-81; sometime prof., lectr. U. Hawaii, U. Calif.-Berkeley, Stanford in Vienna, U. Pa., Nat. U. Singapore, London Bus. Sch.; vis. prof. Humboldt U., Berlin, 1995; cons. U.S. and Europe; dir., v.p. Ann. Revs. Inc. Author/co-author: Higher Education for Business, 1959, European Economics-East and West, 1967, Mathematical Analysis for Business Decisions, 1963, 2d edit., 1971, (with G. L. Bach) Economics, 11th edit., 1987. Served with AUS, 1946-47. Ford Found. faculty fellow Harvard U., 1959-60; NSF sr. postdoctoral fellow London Sch. Econs., 1963-64; recipient Davis award for lifetime achievement Stanford U., 1996. Club: University (N.Y.C.). Home: 96 Serrano Dr Atherton CA 94027-3934 Office: Stanford U Grad Sch Bus Stanford CA 94305

HOWELL, JAMES TENNYSON, allergist, immunologist, pediatrician; b. Memphis, Jan. 25, 1944. MD, U. Ark., 1970. Diplomate Am. Bd. Allergy & Immunology, Am. Bd. Pediatrics. Intern Tampa Gen. Hosp., 1970-71; resident in pediatrics Children's Med. Ctr., Dallas, 1973-76; fellow in allergy and immunology Tex., Galveston, 1976-78; with St. Edwards Mercy Med. Ctr., Ft. Smith, Ark., 1976-78. Fellow Am. Coll. Allergy, Asthma and Immunology; mem. AMA, Am. Acad. Pediatrics. Office: Cooper Clinic 6801 Rogers Ave Fort Smith AR 72903-3296

HOWELL, JEANETTE HELEN, retired cultural organization administrator; b. Portsmouth, Hampshire, Eng., June 2, 1925; came to U.S., 1976; d. Henry Augustus and Mary Scott (Randall) Butler-Frere; m. Reginald Robert Howell, Aug. 14, 1948; children: Josephine Thalia Howell, Robert Henry Adam Howell, Matthew Charles Howell. Student, High Wycombe Coll. Art, 1967-71, Sutton Sch. Art. Dir./owner Bourne End (pre-sch.), Bucks, Eng., 1965-69; adminstr. Historic Denver, Denver, 1980-83; mgr. II Bur. Conservation, State of Maine, Thomaston, 1987-90; dir. Lincoln County Hist. Assn., Wiscasset, Maine, 1990-93; ret., 1993. Founder Decorative and Fine Arts N.J., pres., 1997; co-founder Decorative and Fine Arts Soc. U.K., 1966, Decorative and Fine Arts Soc. ednl. lectrs. and seminars (pres. 1977); bazaar chmn. St. John's Cathedral, Denver, 1981; pres. Damariscotta (Maine) Arts Coun., 1984-86; sr. warden St. Andrew's Ch., Newcastle, Maine, 1992-96; co-founder Friends of Colonial Pemaquid (Maine), 1993. Nurse emergency med. hosp., Weymouth, Dorset, Eng., 1942-48. Recipient Americans-By-Choice Outstanding Svc. award Citizenship Day com., Denver, 1983, Appreciation award Maine Vols. in Parks, 1997. Avocations: gardening, archaeology, history rsch., literature. Home: 534 Harrington Rd Pemaquid ME 04558-4214

HOWELL, JOEL DUBOSE, physician, educator; b. Tex., May 11, 1953; s. Wilson and Nora (Levitas) H.; m. Linda C. Samuelson, June 26, 1976; children:Jonathan Samuelson, Benjamin Samuelson. BS, Mich. State U., 1975; MD, U. Chgo., 1979; PhD in History and Sociology of Sci., U. Pa., 1987. Intern, resident in internal medicine U. Chgo., 1979-82; Robert Wood Johnson clin. scholar U. Pa., Phila., 1982-84; instr. U. Mich., Ann Arbor, 1984-86, asst. prof., 1986-90, assoc. prof., 1990-97, prof., 1997—. Editor: Technology and American Medical Practice: 1880-1930, 1988, Medical Lives and Scientific Medicine at Michigan; author: Technology in the Hospital, 1995. Henry J. Kaiser Family Fedn. Faculty scholar, 1989-92, Charles E. Culpeper Found. Med. Humanities scholar, 1992-96. Fellow ACP, Am. Assn. for History Medicine, Am. Osler Soc.

HOWELL, JOHN A., television station executive; b. Florence, S.C., Dec. 12, 1924. V.p., gen. mgr. WPXI TV Cox Enterprises, Inc., Pitts., 1987—. Office: Cox Enterprises Inc 11 Television Hill Pittsburgh PA 15214-4025*

HOWELL, JOHN FLOYD, insurance company executive; b. Mt. Juliet, Tenn., Dec. 24, 1932; s. Robert Lee and Rachel Mae (Draper) H.; m. Margaret Ann Herring, Dec. 27, 1955; children: John Floyd, Leigh Ann, Stephen Donelson. Student, Vanderbilt U., 1951-53; B.A., U. Iowa, 1955, postgrad., 1955-56. Actuarial asst. Nat. Life & Accident Ins. Co., Nashville, 1963-64, asst. actuary, 1964-65, 2d v.p., 1965-71, v.p., 1971-81, sr. v.p., 1981-83, also dir.; v.p., chief actuary Ind. Life & Accident Ins. Co., 1984-88, sr. v.p., chief actuary, 1989-96, ret., 1996. Bd. dirs. Vol. Jacksonville, 1984-89, Mental Health Resource Ctr., Jacksonville, 1987-90, Fla. Meth. Bd. Pensions, 1988-96, Jacksonville Urban League, 1992-95. Fellow Soc. Actuaries; mem. Am. Acad. Actuaries, Richland Country Club (Nashville), Epping Forest Yacht Club (Jacksonville). Methodist. Home: 74 Ravenwood Hills Cir Nashville TN 37215-6167

HOWELL, JOHN MCDADE, retired university chancellor, political science educator; b. Five Points, Ala., Jan. 28, 1922; s. John William and Bettie Mae (Lee) H.; m. Gladys Evelyn David, Aug. 9, 1952; children: David Noble, Joseph Lee. A.B., U. Ala., 1948, M.A., 1949; Ph.D., Duke U., 1954. Instr. U. Idaho, 1950; instr. Randolph-Macon Woman's Coll., Lynchburg, Va., 1951-52, Duke U., 1952-53; asst. prof. Sweet Briar Coll., Lynchburg, 1953-54, Memphis State U., 1954-57; assoc. prof. East Carolina U., Greenville, N.C., 1957-61; prof. East Carolina U., 1961-87, chmn. polit. sci. dept., 1963-66, dean Coll. Arts and Scis., 1966-69, dean Grad. Sch., 1969-73, vice chancellor for acad. affairs, 1973-79, chancellor, 1982-87. Author: (with others) Conflict of International Obligations and State Interests, 1972; Contbr.: (with others) chpts. to The International Law Standard and Commonwealth Developments, 1966, De Lege Pactorum, 1970; articles to profl. jours. Served with USAAF, 1942-45. Decorated Bronze Star medal. Mem. Phi Beta Kappa, Phi Kappa Phi, Pi Sigma Alpha. Home: 1953 Quail Ridge Rd Apt E Greenville NC 27858-5599

HOWELL, JOHN REID, mechanical engineering educator; b. Columbus, Ohio, June 13, 1936; s. Frederick Edward and Hilma Lavilla (Kief) H.; m. Arlene Elizabeth Pollitt, June 20, 1959 (div. 1974); m. Susan Gooch Conway, May 20, 1979; children: John Reid Jr., Keli Dianne, David Lee. BSChemE, Case Inst. Tech., 1958, MSChemE, 1960, PhD, 1962. Registered profl. engr. Aerospace engr. NASA Lewis Research Ctr., Cleve., 1961-68; assoc. prof. U. Houston, 1969-73, prof., 1973-78; dir. Energy Inst. U. Houston, 1975-78; vis. prof. mech. engring. U. Tex., Austin, 1978-79, prof., 1979-82, E.C.H. Bantel prof., 1982-90, Baker-Hughes prof., 1990—, chmn. mech. engring. dept., 1986-90, dir. Ctr. for Energy Studies, 1988-91, assoc. dean for rsch. Coll. Engring., 1996-99; dir. thermal transport and thermal processing program NSF, 1994-95. Co-author: Thermal Radiation Heat Transfer, 1981, 3d edit., 1992, Design of Solar Thermal Systems, 1984, Fundamentals of Engineering Therdynamics, 1987, 2d edit., 1992; editor: Journal of Heat Transfer, 1995—; also numerous articles. Commr. Renewable Energy Resources Commn., Austin, 1980-81. Served to 1st lt. USAF, 1962-65. Recipient Spl. Svc. award NASA, 1965, Ralph Coats Roe award Am. Soc. Engring. Edn., 1987, Max Jakob award AIChE/ASME, 1998; named to Hon. Order Ky. Cols., 1980. Fellow ASME (Heat Transfer Meml. award 1991), AIAA (Thermophysics award 1990). Office: U Tex Dept Mech Engring Etc 7 # 142D Austin TX 78712

HOWELL, JOSEPH TOY, company owner; b. Nashville, Apr. 1, 1942; s. Joseph and Carroll (Toy) H.; m. Embry, Dec. 28, 1965; children: Andrew, Jessica. BA, Davidson Coll., 1964; MA, Union Theol. Seminary, N.Y.C., 1968, U. N.C., 1970. Rsch. asst. Ctr. for Urban and Regional Planning U. N.C., Chapel Hill, 1969; rsch. assoc. U. N.C., 1970-72; planning intern Rsch. Triangle Planning Commn., Research Triangle Park, N.C., 1970; assoc. Gladstone Assocs., Washington, 1972-74; dir. of housing devel. Episcopal Diocese of Washington, 1974-78; dir. of devel. Nat. Corp. for Housing Ptnr., Washington, 1978-81; pres. Howell Assocs., Washington, 1981—; bd. dirs. D.C. Community Humanities Coun., Washington; loan com. mem. Patrician Mortgage, Washington, 1985-97. Author: (books) Hard Living on Clay Street, 1973, Real Estate Development Syndication, 1983. Avocations: photography, tennis, sailing, travel. Office: Howell Assocs 815 15th St NW Ste 830 Washington DC 20005-2201

HOWELL, JULIUS AMMONS, plastic surgeon; b. Thomasville, N.C., Apr. 14, 1914; s. Cyrus Maitland and Lillie Mae (Ammons) H.; m. Octavia Anne Southern, Oct. 20, 1951; children: Anne, Karen, Robin. LLB, Wake Forest U., 1935, BS, 1940; MD, U. Pa., Phila., 1943. Diplomate Am. Bd. Plastic & Reconstructive Surgery, Am. Bd. Otolaryngology. Chief plastic surgery sect. Bowman Gray Sch. Medicine, Winston Salem, N.C., 1959-84, prof. emeritus plastic surgery, 1984—; lectr. Sch. Law Wake Forest U., Winston Salem, N.C., 1978-94; pvt. practice Winston Salem, N.C., 1984—; mem. medico-legal com. N.C. Med. Soc., Raleigh, 1960-93, South Soc. Plastuc Surgery; mem. adv. com. N.C. Indsl. com., Raleigh, 1976-86; trustee Blue Cross/Blue Shield, Chapel Hill, 1964-68. Co-author: Plastic Surgery, 1979. Julius Ammons Howell Endowed Chair Surgery named in his honor Bowman Gray Sch. Medicine, 1995. Mem. ACS; Am. Soc. Plastic & Reconstructive Surgery (medicolegal com.), Am. Assn. Plastic Surgeons. Baptist. Office: 480 Forsyth Med Pk Winston Salem NC 27103

HOWELL, KEVIN L., hotel executive. V.p. Nat. 9 Inns, Salt Lake City, 1987—. Office: Nat 9 Inns 2285 S Main St Ste 9 Salt Lake City UT 84115-2640*

HOWELL, MARY ELLEN HELMS, nursing educator, neonatal nurse; b. Florence, S.C., Jan. 13, 1960; d. Ernest Little Jr. and Sara (Amaryllis) Helms; m. David Alexander Howell; 1 child, Sara Ashley. BSN, Clemson U., 1982; M in Nursing, U. S.C., 1987. RN, S.C. Nursing intern McLeod Regional Med. Ctr., Florence, 1982, staff nurse I in neonatal ICU, 1982-83, staff nurse II in neonatal ICU, 1983-87, asst. head nurse neonatal ICU, 1987; nursing instr. Florence(S.C.)-Darlington Tech. Coll., 1987-91; unit dir. newborn and spl. care nursery The Women's Ctr., 1992-93; mem. faculty nursing Florence Darlington Tech. Coll., 1993-98; nursing instr. Med. U. S.C.; instr. Am. Lung Assn. on Asthma Awareness, McLeod's Women's Resource Ctr. on Sibling Preparation Classes and Infant Care; nursing instr. Med. U. S.C., 1998—. mem. infant mortality task force, 1992—. Mem. NAACOG (cert. in high risk neonatal nursing 1989), Nat. League of Nursing, S.C. Perinatal Assn., Latta Jr. Charity League, Dillon Med. Aux., Sigma Theta Tau, Alpha Xi. Baptist.

HOWELL, MICHELLE ELANE DAVIS, educator; b. Washington, Ohio, Feb. 16, 1958; d. Roger Gilbert Davis and Norma Jane (Brill) Wolfe; m. Christopher Lee Howell; children: Nathanial Webster, Rachel Colleen, Adrianne Leigh. BS, Ohio U., 1988; MEd, Miami U., 1994. Reference asst. Carnegie Pub. Libr., Washington, Ohio, 1979-88; tchr. 1st grade Clinton Massie Sch. Dist., Clarksville, Ohio, 1989; instr. lang. arts East Clinton Sch. Dist., Lees Creek, Ohio, 1989—; chair, faculty advisor East Clinton Mid. Sch., New Vienna, Ohio, 1997-98; presenter in field. Author of poems, short stories. Mem. NEA, Nat. Coun. Tchrs. English, Ohio Edn. Assn., Ohio Writing Project, Advanced Ohio Writing Project, East Clinton Edn. Assn., Leadership Clinton, Phi Kappa Phi. Democrat. Roman Catholic. Hme: 154 Creek Rd Clarksville OH 45113-9318 Office: East Clinton Mid Sch 204 S 2nd St New Vienna OH 45159

HOWELL, PAUL NEILSON, oil company execuitve; b. Gulfport, Miss., Sept. 13, 1918; s. Posey N. and Eva Meredith (Colmer) H.; m. Evelyn Marie Edmiston, June 7, 1947; children: Steven K., Douglas W., David L., Bradley N. BSChemE, La. State U.; DCL honoris causa, The Univ. of the South, 1988. Engr. Esso Standard Oil Co., Baton Rouge, La., 1946-51; pres. La. Tank Lines, Inc., New Orleans, 1953-55, Howell Refining Co., San Antonio, 1955-69; chmn., CEO Howell Corp., Houston, 1969-95, pres., CEO, 1995-97, bd. dirs., 1997—; chmn. Howell Petroleum Corp., 1981-84; chmn. 11th dist. Fed. Res. Br. Bank, Houston, 1983-84. Chmn. S.W. Rsch. Inst., 1968-70, U.S. Navy Meml. Found., 1988-96; bd. dirs. Tex. Med. Ctr., 1976—, Houston Advanced Rsch. Ctr., 1982-90; vice chmn. Trinity U., San Antonio, 1971-73; gov. Rice U., Houston, 1979-86; chmn. adv. bd. Salvation Army, Houston, 1990-93, dir. nat. adv. bd., 1989—; regent U. of South, Sewanee, Tenn., 1990-94. Comdr. USNR, 1941-46, 51-53, PTO, Korea; rear adm.

USNR (ret.). Mem. NAM (dir. 1964-70), Nat. Petroleum Refiners Assn. (chmn. 1966-68), Am. Petroleum Inst. (bd. dirs. 1966-68, 85-95), U.S. C. of C. (bd. dirs. 1984-87). Republican. Episcopalian. Clubs: River Oaks Country. Home: 3711 San Felipe St Unit 15F Houston TX 77027-4040 Office: Howell Corp 1111 Fannin 1500 Howell Bldg Houston TX 77002-6923*

HOWELL, RALPH RODNEY, pediatrician, educator, geneticist; b. Concord, N.C., June 10, 1931; s. Fred Lee and Grace Mary (Blackwelder) H.; m. Sarah Vosburg Esselstyn, Nov. 19, 1960 (dec.); children: Grace Meyer, Elizabeth Eriksson, John Esselstyn. BS, Davidson Coll., 1953; MD, Duke U., 1957. Intern Duke U., 1957-58, resident in pediatrics, 1958-59, research fellow in pediatrics and medicine, 1959-60; clin. assoc. and staff NIH, Bethesda, Md., 1960-64; assoc. prof. pediatrics Johns Hopkins U., Balt., 1964-72; pediatrician-in-chief Univ. Children's Hosp. at Hermann, Houston, 1972-87; chmn. med. bd. Univ. Children's Hosp. at Hermann, 1972-87; David Park prof. U. Tex. Med. Sch., Houston, 1972-89, chmn. dept. pediatrics, 1972-87; prof., chmn. dept. pediatrics U. Miami Sch. Medicine, 1989—; sec. med. staff Jackson Meml. Hosp., Miami, 1992-93, v.p. med. staff, 1993-97, pres. med. staff, 1997—; cons. pediatrics M.D. Anderson Hosp. and Tumor Inst., 1972-89; mem. metabolism study sect. NIH, 1973-77, chmn. maternal and child health adv. com., 1983-86; mem. exec. com. Nat. Practitioner Data Bank, 1995-98; mem. nat. clin. adv. com. Nat. Found. March of Dimes, 1973-79; mem. nat. med. adv. bd., bd. dirs. Muscular Dystrophy Assn., chmn. sci. adv. bd.; vis. prof. Inst. Molecular Genetics, Baylor Coll. Medicine, Houston, 1988; chief pediatrics Jackson Childrens Hosp., U. Miami-Jackson Meml. Med. Ctr., 1989—. Author: (with G.H. Thomas) Selected Screening Tests for Genetic Metabolic Diseases, 1973, (with F.H. Morriss, L.K. Pickering) Role of Human Milk in Infant Nutrition, 1986; contbr. articles to profl. jours. Trustee Jackson Lab. Bar Harbor, Maine; dir. Rip van Winkle Found., Claverack, N.Y., 1987-92, pres., 1992—; bd. dirs. Congl. Ch. Found., Coconut Grove, Fla. Served to sr. surgeon USPHS, 1960-64. Fellow AAAS, Am. Acad. Pediatrics (com. on genetics); mem. AMA (ho. of dels. 1996—), Am. Pediatric Soc., Soc. Pediatric Rsch., Houston Pediatric Soc. (pres. 1978-79), Tex. Med. Assn., Soc. Inborn Errors of Metabolism (pres. 1981), Miami Pediatric Soc., Fla. Med. Assn., Am. Coll. Med. Genetics (bd. dirs. 1991—, treas. 1995-96, pres.-elect 1997-98, pres. 1999—), Nat. Human Genome Rsch. Inst. (chmn. ethical, social and legal issues rev. group 1996—), Coconut Grove (Fla.) Sailing Club, Pi Kappa Alpha, Cosmos Club (Washington). Home: L'Hermitage Villa 66 2000 S Bayshore Dr Miami FL 33133-3256 Office: U Miami Sch Medicine Dept Pediatrics D-820 PO Box 16820 Miami FL 33101-6820

HOWELL, ROBERT EDWARD, hospital administrator; b. Marietta, Ohio, Jan. 19, 1949; married; 3 children. BS, Muskingham Coll., 1971; MS in Hosp. and Health Svcs. Adminstrn., Ohio State U., 1977. Assoc. dir. U. Minn. Hosps. and Clinics, Mpls., 1980-86; exec. dir. Med. Coll. Ga. Hosps. and Clinics, Augusta, 1986-94; dir., CEO, U. Iowa Hosps. and Clinics, Iowa City, 1994—; mem. exec. com. Accreditation Coun. for Grad. Med. Edn. Mem. Coun. Tchg. Hosps. (past chmn.), Am. Assn. Med. Colls. (exec. com.), Am. Hosp. Assn. (coord. com. med. edn.), Univ. Health System Consortium (exec. com.). Office: U Iowa Hosps and Clinics 200 Hawkins Dr Iowa City IA 52242-1009*

HOWELL, R(OBERT) THOMAS, JR., lawyer, former food company executive; b. Racine, Wis., July 18, 1942; s. Robert T. and Margaret Paris (Billings) H.; m. Karen Wallace Corbett, May 11, 1968; children: Clarinda, Margaret, Robert. AB, Williams Coll., 1964; JD, U. Wis., 1967; postgrad., Harvard U., 1981. Bar: Wis. 1968, Ill. 1968, U.S. Dist. Ct. (no. dist.) Ill. 1968, U.S. Tax Ct. Assoc. Hopkins & Sutter, Chgo., 1967-71; atty. The Quaker Oats Co., Chgo., 1971-77, counsel, 1977-80, v.p., assoc. gen. corp. counsel, 1980-84, v.p., gen. corp. counsel, 1984-96, corp. sec., 1994-96; of counsel Seyfarth, Shaw, Fairweather & Geraldson, Chgo., 1997—; bd. dirs. Ill. Inst. of Continuing Legal Edn. Editor: (mags.) Barrister, 1975-77, Compleat Lawyer, 1983-87. Bd. dirs. Metro. Family Svcs.; bd. dirs. Chgo. Bar Found., 1987—, pres., 1991-93; trustee 4th Presbyn. Ch., Chgo., 1989-92, pres., 1994-96; bd. dirs. Chgo. Equity Fund, 1992-96. Capt. USAR, 1966-72. Mem. ABA, Ill. Bar Assn., Wis. Bar Assn., Chgo. Bar Assn. (bd. mgrs. 1977-79, chmn. young lawyers sect. 1974-75), Food and Drug Law Inst. (bd. dirs. 1986—), LawClub Chgo., Econ. Club Chgo., Univ. Club Chgo. (bd. dirs. 1982-85, 87-88, v.p.). Presbyterian. Home: 853 W Chalmers Pl Chicago IL 60614-3233 Office: Seyfarth Shaw Fairweather & Geraldson 55 E Monroe St Ste 4200 Chicago IL 60603-5863

HOWELL, TALMADGE RUDOLPH, radiologist; b. Pikeville, N.C., May 2, 1933. MD, Duke U., 1958. Diplomate Am. Bd. Radiology. Intern Brooke Gen. Hosp., San Antonio, 1958-59; resident in radiology Med. Coll. Va., 1963-66, clin. prof. radiology; fellow in pediat. radiology Cin. Children's Hosp., 1967-69; chmn. dept. radiology Children's Hosp., Richmond, Va. Fellow Am. Coll. Radiology; mem. AMA, AAUP, So. Med. Assn. (editl. bd.), Soc. Pediat. Rsch., Radiol. Soc. North Am., Assn. Mil. Surgeons U.S. C-Mail: thowell@vcu.org. Address: 2924 Brook Rd Richmond VA 23220-1215

HOWELL, TERRY ALLEN, agricultural engineer; b. Dallas, Sept. 7, 1947; s. Levi Lowe III and Lila Lee (Allen) H.; m. Mary Sue Parkerson, Feb. 22, 1969; children: Terry A. Jr., Lisa K. Dreibrodt, Michael S. BS, Tex. A&M U., 1969, MS, 1970, PhD, 1974. Rsch. asst. Tex. A&M U., College Station, 1969-70, rsch. assoc., 1971-74; asst. prof. N.Mex. State U., Las Cruces, 1975, Tex. A&M U., College Station, 1976-79; agr. engr. USDA ARS, Fresno, Calif., 1979-83, Bushland, Tex., 1983--. Co-author: Irrigation of Agricultural Crops, 1991, Design and Operation of Farm Irrigation Systems, 1980, Limitations to Effective Water Use in Crop Production, 1983, Modification of the Aerial Environment Crops, 1979; co-editor, co-author: Management of Farm Irrigation Systems, 1991. Tchr. Paramount Bapt. Ch., Amarillo, 1985-94, deacon, 1987—; troop com. chmn. Boy Scouts Am., Amarillo, 1991-93. Fellow ASAE (chmn. soil and water divsn. 1987-88, Paper award 1972, 74, 80, soil and water divsn. editor 1993-97); mem. ASCE (chmn. irrigation water requirements com. 1990-93, Tipton award 1997), Am. Soc. Agronomy (A-3 divsn. chair-elect 1998—), Soil Sci. Soc. Am., Irrigation Assn. (person of yr. award 1995), Coun. for Agrl. Sci. and Tech., Tex. Agrl. Irrigation Assn. Office: USDA ARS Drawer 10 PO Drawer 10 Bushland TX 79012-0010

HOWELL, THOMAS, history educator; b. Houston, Jan. 20, 1944; s. John Thomas and Hazel (Hall) H.; m. Donna Jo Walker, Aug. 14, 1971; children: Catherine Jewel, Judith Hazel. BA, La. Coll., 1964; MA, La. State U., 1966, PhD, 1971. Instr. La. State U., 1967-68; instr. La. Coll., Pineville, 1968-70, asst. prof., 1970-72, assoc. prof., 1972-77, prof., 1977, Crowell prof., 1984—, chmn. dept. history and polit. sci., 1975-95, chmn. div. social and behavioral scis., 1995—; lectr. La. Coun. for Humanities, 1983, 86, 87, 90-96; project dir. La. Endowment for Humanities, 1989. Mem. La. Elections Integrity Commn., 1980-86, vice chmn., 1981; coord. La. Civitan Youth Citizenship Seminar, 1975-76; commr. Gulf Coast Athletic Conf., 1981—; mem. NAIA Nat. Eligibility Commn., 1983—, chmn., 1995—; mem. hearing com. disciplinary bd. La. Bar Assn. Mellon summer fellow, 1981; Fulbright lectr. U. Iceland, 1986-87. Mem. La. Hist. Assn., So. Hist. Assn., SW Assn. Pre-Law Advisers, Orgn. Am. Historians, Alpha Chi, Omicron Delta Kappa. Baptist. Home: 216 Myrtle St Pineville LA 71360-5164 Office: La Coll Dept History Pineville LA 71359

HOWELL, WILLIAM ASHLEY, III, lawyer; b. Raleigh, N.C., Jan. 2, 1949; s. William Ashley II and Caroline Erskine Greenleaf; m. Esther Holland, Dec. 22, 1973. BS, Troy State U., 1972; postgrad. U. Alabama, Birmingham, 1974-75; JD, Birmingham Sch. Law, 1977. Bar: Ala. 1977, U.S. Dist. Ct. (no. dist.) Ala. 1977, U.S. Ct. Appeals (5th cir.) 1977, U.S. Supreme Ct. 1982, U.S. Ct. Appeals (11th cir.) 1983, U.S. Dist. Ct. (mid. dist.) Ala. 1987. Atty. pub. defender div. Legal Aid. Soc. of Birmingham, 1977-78, civil divsn. Legal Aid Soc. Birmingham, 1978-81; dist. office atty. SBA, Birmingham, 1980-82, supervising atty. Ala. Dist., 1982—; spl. asst. U.S. Atty. (Middle Dist.), Ala., 1988—; part-time instr. legal and social environ. and human resources mgmt. Jefferson State C.C., Birmingham, 1993. Contbr. articles to profl. jours. Bd. dirs. Hoover Homeowners Assn., 1977-81, Southside Ministries, Inc., 1990-91, v.p. bd. dirs., 1990-91; bd. dirs. SafeHouse of Shelby County, Inc., 1990-93, vice chmn., 1991-93; mem. outreach commn., Episc. Ch. of St. Francis of Assisi, Pelham, Ala., 1992, 95, 97; del. State Conv., alternate del., 1993, 94; vol. reader Radio Reading Svc. Network for Blind, 1991-93; active Shelby County Econ. Devel. Coun., 1993-94. Recipient Am. Jurisprudence Criminal Procedure Book award. Mem. ABA (sect. corporation, banking and bus. law), Nat. Parks and Conservation Soc. (life), Fed. Bar Assn. (sec. Birmingham chpt. 1980-81, del. nat. conv. 1993, 94, del. mid year meeting, 1994-95), Ala. Bar Assn. (com. on future of the profession 1978-81, 83-84, com. on quality of life 1992-93, sect. bankruptcy and corp. law, sect. bankruptcy and comml. law, sect. corp. counsel, sect. banking and bus. law), Nature Conservancy (life), Birmingham Bar Assn., Birmingham Venture Club, Sierra Club (life), Sigma Delta Kappa (v.p., Outstanding Sr. award 1977). Episcopalian. Office: US SBA 2121 8th Ave N Ste 200 Birmingham AL 35203-2326

HOWELL, WILLIAM PAGE, real estate executive; b. Carnegie, Okla., July 27, 1952; s. Herman Glen and Muriel Joyce (Raby) H.; 1 child, Blake Alexander Sewell-Howell. BS, Southwestern U., Weatherford, Okla., 1975; MS, U. Okla., 1976. Chief exec. officer, pres. Howell Assocs., Norman, Okla., 1976-84; dir. Saudi Arabian Investment Corp., Dallas, London, 1984-87; dir. acquisitions Mitsui Fudosan (N.Y.) Inc., N.Y.C., 1987-93; prin., ptnr. Peninsula Mgmt. Corp., N.Y.C., 1993—; pres. Howell Assocs. of N.Y., N.Y.C., 1993—; mng. ptnr. Cushman Peninsula Asset Mgmt. Group, N.Y.C., 1993—; mng. dir. Unique Hotels and Resorts, N.Y.C., 1998—; chmn., CEO, H.A.I. Investment Advisors, N.Y.C., 1999—; dir. adv. bd. Comml. Property News, N.Y.C., 1990—. Demographics coord. Dem. Nat. Com., Atlanta, 1976-77. Mem. Urban Land Inst., Assn. Fgn. Investors in U.S. Real Estate, Fedn. Internat. Adminstrs. de Bein Conseils Immobiliers, Japan Soc., N.Y. Real Estate Club, Internat. Devel. Rsch. Coun. Avocations: flying, skiing, skydiving, fishing, golf. Home: 111 E 30th St Apt 10A New York NY 10016-7352

HOWELL, WILLIAM ROBERT, retail company executive; b. Claremore, Okla., Jan. 3, 1936; s. William Roosevelt and Opal Theo (Swan) H.; m. Judy Howell; children: Ann Elizabeth, Teresa Lynn. BBA, U. Okla., 1958. With J.C. Penney Co., Inc., 1958—; store mgr. J.C. Penney Co., Inc., Tulsa, 1968-69; dist. mgr., dir. Treasury Stores subs., Dallas, 1969-71; div. v.p., dir. domestic devel. Treasury Stores subs., N.Y.C., 1973-76, regional v.p., western regional mgr., 1976-79, sr. v.p., dir. merchandising, mktg. and catalog, 1979-81, exec. v.p., 1981-82, vice chmn. bd. dirs, 1982-83, chmn., chief exec. officer, 1983-97; chmn. emeritus J.C. Penney Co., Inc., Plano, Tex., 1997—; bd. dirs. Exxon Corp., Warner-Lambert Corp., Bankers Trust Co., Halliburton Co., The Williams Cos., Ctrl. and S.W. Corp. Trustee Nat. Urban League. Mem. Am. Mgmt. Assn., Bus. Coun., Nat. Retail Fedn. (bd. dirs.), Am. Soc. of Corp. Execs., Dirs.' Table, Delta Sigma Pi, Beta Gamma Sigma. Baptist.

HOWELLS, MURIEL GURDON SEABURY (MRS. WILLIAM WHITE HOWELLS), volunteer; b. White Plains, N.Y., May 3, 1910; d. William Marston and Katharine Emerson (Hovey) Seabury; m. William White Howells, June 15, 1929; children: Muriel Gurdon Howells Metz, William Dean. Founder Brit. War Relief Soc., Madison, Wis., 1941, pres., 1941-43; apptd. visitor, dept. decorative arts and sculpture Boston Mus. Fine Arts, 1955-72, dept. am. decorative arts, 1972-97; ladies com. Inst. Contemporary Art, Boston, 1955-68; co-founder, trustee Strawbery Banke Mus., Inc., Portsmouth, N.H., 1958-75, overseer, 1975-81, hon. overseer, 1981—; co-founder, steering com. Guild, 1959-91; bd. dirs. Garden Club Am., 1959-62, nat. chmn. medal award com., 1962-65, judge flower arrangements; pres. Piscataqua Garden Club, 1952-54; mem. Harvard Solomon Islands Expdn., Malaita, 1968; 1st chmn. Boston chpt. Venice Com., Internat. Fund for Monuments (now Save Venice Inc.), 1970-71, vice-chmn. Boston chpt., 1971-77, mem. exec. com., 1971-89, hon. chmn., 1989—. Awarded King's medal for Svc. in the Cause of Freedom (Britain), 1946; recipient Hist. Preservation award zone 1 Garden Club Am., 1976. Mem. Nat. Soc. Colonial Dames N.H., Soc. Preservation New England Antiquities (mem. Maine coun. 1976-78), Mayflower Soc., Women's Travel Club (pres. 1967-69), Chilton Club, Colony Club. Address: 11 Lawrence Ln Kittery Point ME 03905-5104

HOWELLS, R. TIM, professional sports team executive; m. Patty Howells; four children. Grad., U. Utah, 1968. With Howells, Inc., Salt Lake City, 1968-82; v.p., co-owner, pvt. investor Howells, Inc., from 1982; gen. mgr. Utah Jazz NBA, 1989—. Office: Utah Jazz 301 W South Temple Salt Lake City UT 84101-1216*

HOWELLS, WILLIAM WHITE, anthropology educator; b. N.Y.C., Nov. 27, 1908; s. John Mead and Abby MacDougall (White) H.; m. Muriel Gurdon Seabury, June 15, 1929; children—Gurdon Howells Metz, William Dean. SB, Harvard U., 1930, PhD, 1934; DSc (hon.), Beloit Coll., 1975, U. Witwatersrand, 1985. From asst. prof. to prof. anthropology U. Wis., 1939-54, prof. integrated liberal studies, 1948-54; prof. anthropology Harvard U., 1954-74, prof. emeritus, 1974—; hon. fellow Sch. Am. Research, 1975. Author: Mankind So Far, 1944, The Heathens, 1948, Back of History, 1954, Mankind in the Making, 1959, rev. edit., 1967, The Pacific Islanders, 1973, Cranial Variation in Man, 1973, Evolution of the Genus Homo, 1973, Skull Shapes and The Map, 1989, Getting Here: The Story of Human Evolution, 1993, Who's Who in Skulls, 1995; editor: Early Man in the Far East, 1949, Ideas on Human Evolution, 1962, Paleoanthropology in the People's Republic of China, 1977, Am. Jour. Phys. Anthropology, 1949-54; assoc. editor Human Biology, 1955-74. Served as lt. USNR, 1943-46. Recipient Viking Fund medal in phys. anthropology, 1954. Fellow AAAS, Indian Anthrop. Assn. (fgn.), Am. Acad. Arts and Scis., Am. Anthrop. Assn. (pres. 1951, Disting. Service award 1978), Soc. Antiquaries London; mem. NAS, Austrian Acad. Scis., Mass. Hist. Soc., Am. Assn. of Physical Anthropologists (sec., treas. 1939-41, Charles R. Darwin Lifetime Achievement award 1992); corr. mem. Geog. Soc. Lisbon, Anthrop. Soc. Paris (Broca prix du Centenaire 1980), Anthrop. Soc. Vienna, Royal Soc. South Africa (fgn.), Soc. for Biol. Anthropology Spain (corr.). Clubs: Somerset, Tavern (Boston); Harvard Faculty. Home: 11 Lawrence Ln Kittery Point ME 03905-5104

HOWENSTEIN, MARK STEPHEN, law educator; b. Sept. 7, 1955. MA, U. Calif., Berkeley, 1989, PhD, 1993; JD, Tulane U., 1981. Law clerk 22d Jud. Cir. Mo., St. Louis, 1981-84; atty. Klutho, Cody, Kilo & Flynn, St. Louis, 1984-86; assoc. prof. Ramapo Coll. N.J., Mahwah, 1993—; tchg. asst. U. Calif., Berkeley, 1986-93. E-mail: mhowenst@ramapo.edu. Office: Ramapo Coll Dept Am Internat Studies 505 Ramapo Valley Rd Mahwah NJ 12457

HOWER, DONNA WILSON, elementary education educator; b. Petaluma, Calif., Sept. 9, 1948; d. Loran Richard and Marie Libby (Turner) Wilson; m. John C. Hower, July 14, 1973; 1 child, Alaina Marie. BA, U.S. Internat. U., 1970. Calif. gen. elem. tchg. credential. Tchr. Juarez-Lincoln Elem., Chula Vista, Calif., 1970-73, Hillsborough (Calif.) City Schs., 1974—; computer mentor, tchr. Hillsborough (Calif.) Schs., 1985-87, grant writer, 1990-91; regional fellow Calif. Ctr. for Sch. Restructuring, 1992—. Pres. Hillsborough Tchrs. Assn., 1979. Recipient Kent awards San Mateo County Bd. Edn., 1990, Golden Bell award Calif. State Sch. Bds. Assn., 1991. Mem. ASCD, Nat. Coun. Tchrs. Math., Calif. Math. Coun., Calif. League Middle Schs., Calif. Tchrs. Assn. (local pres. 1978-79). Avocations: golfing, water skiing, snow skiing. Office: Crocker Middle Sch 2600 Ralston Ave Hillsborough CA 94010-6544

HOWER, FRANK BEARD, JR., retired banker; b. Louisville, Nov. 26, 1928; s. Frank Beard and Katharine (Coffman) H.; m. Virginia W. Barker, Dec. 30, 1954; children: Frank Beard III, William. AB, Centre Coll., Danville, Ky., 1950. With Liberty Nat. Bank, Louisville, 1950-90, exec. v.p., 1967-71, pres., 1971-90, CEO, chmn. bd. dirs., 1973-90, ret., 1990; bd. dirs. Falls City Industries, Inc., Louisville, Bank One, Ky., Alliant Health Sys., Inc., Am. Life and Accident Ins. Co., Churchill Downs Inc., Anthem Inc.; chmn. Norton Kosair Childrens Hosp., Inc., 1983-84. Trustee J. Graham Brown Found., U. Louisville; chmn. regional adv. bd. Comptr. of Currency, 1976; mem. Ky. Registry of Election Finance, 1966-70, Ky. Econ. Progress Commn., 1964-70; vice chmn. Ky.-Tenn. Export Coun.; gen. chmn. United Appeal, 1969; chmn. Greater Louisville Fund for the Arts, 1976; v.p. Louisville Philharm. Orch., 1974-75; chmn. Regional Airport Authority of Louisville and Jefferson County, Louisville Devel. Com.; bd. dirs., chmn. U. Louisville; trustee, chmn. Ky. Ind. Coll. Found.; trustee Centre Coll.; mem. Actors Theatre Bd. 2nd lt. USMCR, 1951-52, Korea. Mem. Am., Ky. bankers assns., Robert Morris Assos., Assn. Res. City Bankers, Louisville C. of C. (pres. 1973). Republican. Episcopalian. Office: Bank One Ky 416 W Jefferson St Louisville KY 40202-3202

HOWER, PAUL H., hotel executive. Exec. v.p. ops. Prime Hospitality Corp., Fairfield, N.J., 1993—. Office: Prime Hospitality Corp PO Box 2700 700 Route 46 E Fairfield NJ 07004-1532*

HOWES, ALFRED S., business and insurance consultant; b. Troy, N.Y., Sept. 10, 1917; s. Alfred G. and Frances (Youngs) H.; m. Elizabeth Hoffner, Oct. 10, 1942; children: Wendy, Mary Lee, Constance Ellen. Student, Brown U., 1934-35, U. Ala., 1935-36, Syracuse U., 1943-44. Cert. agt., advanced underwriting cons. for N.Y. and Vt. With Conn. Mut. Life Ins. Co.; owner bus. cons. co., 1946; pres. Employee Incentive Plans of Am., Inc.; chmn. bd. Utica Duxbak Corp., 1956-86; dir. Hyden, Inc., Outdoor Outfitters, 1960-86; pres., dir. Hyden, Inc. and Wood Realty Inc., 1970-80; bd. dirs. Bering Trading Corp., Employee Incentive Plans, Inc., Killip Svcs., Inc., SVM Inc., Nursing Homes, Inc., Emerson Plastics Corp., Insulating Shapes Inc., Scotsmoor Co. Inc., Smiley Bros., Inc., Pub. Gray Letter, Century Planning Co., Inc., Hurd Shoe Co., Wood & Hyde Co., ApMew, Inc., Am. Paper Machinery, Inc.; purchasing agt. for neutral nations. Contbr. articles on taxes to profl. jours. Past sec., bd. dirs. N.Y.C. Estate Planning Coun.; bd. dirs. Placid's Parkas, Inc., 1956-82, Winchestor Knitting Mills, Inc., 1960-75, J.A. Firsching & Son, Inc., 1976-85, Triple A Aircraft Corp.; mem. N.Y. State Temporary Commn. on Banking, Ins. and Fin. Svcs., 1983-84. With U.S. Army, 1943-46, ETO. Mem. Nat. Assn. Life Underwriters (pres. N.Y. chpt. 1965-66, life, pub. rels. chmn.), N.Y. State Assn. Life Underwriters (chmn. com. to revise laws concerning decedents and their estates, pres. 1966-67), N.Y.C. Assn. Life Underwriters (bd. dirs., pres.), Am. Philatelic Soc., Assn. for Advanced Life Underwriting (pres. 1970-71), Million Dollar Roundtable, Collectors Club, Brown Club, Fort Schuyler Club, Princeton Club, Ft. Orange Club. Home: 42 Fenimore Rd Scarsdale NY 10583-2252 Office: 530 5th Ave Fl 11 New York NY 10036-5101

HOWES, EDWARD HERBERT, educator; b. Aug. 12, 1920. AB in History, Knox coll., 1943; MA in History, U. Calif., Berkeley, 1947, PhD in History, 1955. From instr. to prof. history Calif. State U., Sacramento, Calif., 1952-85, chmn. history dept., 1960-61, 76-78, prof. emeritus, 1985—; pres. Far West Intercollegiate Athletic Conf., 1965-66. With USAF, 1943-45. Home: 8225 Lake Forest Dr Sacramento CA 95826-2957

HOWES, JAMES GUERDON, airport director; b. Balt.; s. James Harold and Edna Esther (Lowman) H. BS, U. Md., 1967, MBA, 1969. Staff asst. U.S. Senate, Washington, 1965-68; regional mktg. adminstrn. Hertz Corp., Balt., 1972-75; commr. aviation Dutchess County, Poughkeepsie, N.Y., 1975-80; airport dir. St. Petersburg-Clearwater (Fla.) Internat. Airport, 1980—. Producer radio programs Choral Masterpieces, 1985-95, King of Instruments, 1983-95, Sacred Classics, 1995—. Committeeman Rep. Nat. Com. Campaign, Washington, 1974-84, Riverside Ch., N.Y.C., 1976-80; v.p. Boy Scouts Am., Largo, Fla., 1987-91, nat. coun. rep., 1992-96. Capt. USAF, 1969-72. Recipient So. divsn. Airport of Yr. Safety award, 1998. Mem. Am. Assn. Airport Execs., Southeastern Airport Mgrs. Assn. (pres. 1993-94), Airports Coun. Internat. (internat. air svc. com. 1994—), Belleair Country Club. Methodist. Avocations: flying, scuba diving, classical music, photography, white water rafting. Home: 41 Pine Wood Cir Safety Harbor FL 34695-5421 Office: St Petersburg Clearwater Internat Airport Terminal Bldg Ste 221 Clearwater FL 33762

HOWES, JONATHAN B., planning and public policy educator. BA, Wittenberg U., 1959; MRP, U. N.C., 1961; MPA, Harvard U., 1966. Various planning positions U.S. Dept. HUD, Washington, 1961-70; coun. mem. Chapel Hill, N.C., 1975-87; mayor Chapel Hill, 1987-91; dir. Ctr. for Urban and Regional Studies U. N.C., N.C., 1970-93; prof. planning U. N.C., Chapel Hill, 1970-93, prof. planning and pub. policy, spl. asst. to chancellor, 1997—; sec. N.C. Dept. Environ., Health and Natural Resources, 1993-97. Fellow Nat. Acad. Pub. Adminstrn. (chmn., bd. trustees 1997—); mem. Am. Inst. Cert. Planners, Cosmos Club. Home: 108 Cedar St Chapel Hill NC 27514

HOWES, LORRAINE DE WET, fashion designer, educator; b. Port Elizabeth, South Africa, Dec. 24, 1933; came to U.S., 1957; d. Jacobus Egnatius and Johanna Elizabeth (Lowenburg) de W. Student, Sch. Fashion Design, Boston, 1957-58. Apprentice Jonathan Logan & Adam Leslie, Johannesburg, South Africa, 1953-55; apprentice, wookroom asst., model Norman Hartnell, designer to the Queen, London, 1955-57; model Peter Lumley Agy., London, 1955-57; designer, dept. mgr. Design Rsch. Inc., Cambridge, Mass., 1957-59; model Hart Agy., Boston, 1957-76; designer, mgr. Estabrook & Newell, Boston, 1959-62; designer, owner Lorraine de Wet, Boston, 1962-79; from asst. prof. apparel design to assoc. prof. R.I. Sch. Design, Providence, 1976-82, prof., 1988—, acting head dept. apparel design, 1976-79, head dept. apparel design, 1979—; adj. faculty apparel design R.I. Sch. Design, Providence, 1972-76; designer, cons. apparel industry and theatre, 1979—; dir. Hamilton Cornell Mass., 1986—; design and tech. edn. cons. apparel and textiles Hangzhou Econ. Commn., China, 1986-88; individual grants panel Nat. Endowment for Arts, 1994. Named Faculty Mem. of Yr., RISD Alumni Assn., 1984-85; recipient John R. Frazier Excellence in Tchg. award RISD, 1993, Hon. Alumna award RISD, 1995; champion R.I. Pub. Links, 1983, 84. Mem. Fashion Group, Costume Soc. Am., Fashion Inst. Tech. Design Lab. Avocation: golf. Office: RISD Dept Apparel Design 2 College St Providence RI 02903-2784

HOWES, MELINDA SUE, marketing executive; b. Weston, W.Va., Nov. 16, 1947; d. John Everett and Eloise (McNemar) H. BA in Communications, Columbia Union Coll., Takoma Park, 1969. Assoc. program dir. WGTS-FM Radio, Takoma Park, Md., 1967-69; asst. pub. rels. dir. Nat. Recreation & Parks Assn., Washington, 1970-71, Washington Med. Ctr., 1971-72; dir. pub. rels. and audiovisual communication Washington Adventist Hosp., Takoma Park, 1972-74; news reporter WTAP-TV & Radio, Parkersburg, W.Va., 1974-76; features editor The Daily Times, Marietta, Ohio, 1976-79; v.p. mktg. Fla. Hosp. Med. Ctr., Orlando, 1979-82; pres., owner Mktg. Support Group, Orlando, 1982—. Chair promotion com. Fla. Hosp. Capital Campaign, Orlando, 1991-96; mem. pres.'s coun. Fla. Hosp. Found., Orlando, 1988-96, mem. Golden Circle of Friends, 1983-96. Recipient Telly award, 1990, Addy award, 1982, 89, 90, Touchstone award Am. Hosp. assn. Mktg. and Pub. Rels. Soc., 1985, 86, MacEachern award Am. Hosp. Assn., 1982, Nurse Recruiting Retention award, 1981, many others for articles, reports. Mem. Orlando Area Ad Fedn. Republican. Seventh-day Adventist. Avocations: reading, writing, sports, photography. E-mail: mshowes1@aol.com. Home: PO Box 113 West Union WV 26456-0113 Office: PO Box 113 West Union WV 26456-0113

HOWES, MICHAEL, sculptor, educator; s. Emmett and Mildred Howes; m. Eleanor Dean Barnett, Sept. 7, 1968; 1 child, Michael Andrew. BFA in Sculpture, La. State U., Baton Rouge, 1971; MFA, U. Ala., Tuscaloosa, 1974. Dir. Absolutely Art, Baton Rouge, La., 1975—; from instr. to prof. art Nicholls State U., Thibodaux, La., 1977-99; artist rep. Baton Rouge Gallery, Baton Rouge, La., 1995—; artist rep. Ward-Nasse Gallery, N.Y.C., 1995—, Bienville Gallery, New Orleans, 1981-94. Artist/designer: 50th Meml. Nicholls State U., 1999, Saltminer Meml., St. Mary Parish Tourist Ctr., 1997, Seedling, Monroe (La.), City Hall, 1996; work in permanent sculpture collections St. Albans Ctr., La. State U., Baton Rouge, 1967, Charleston (S.C.) Coll., 1993, Longman Collection, 1998. Mem. La. Metalsmiths Assn., Internat. Sculpture Ctr. Avocation: metalsmithing glass slumping. Home: 1505 Stuart Ave Baton Rouge LA 70808-3775 Office: Nicholls State Univ Dept Art Box 2025 Thibodaux LA 70310

HOWES, SOPHIA DUBOSE, writer; b. Balt., Apr. 20, 1954; d. John Carleton and Marie Josephine (Meeth) Jones; m. Edward Phillip Howes, Jan. 26, 1996; 1 child, Michael Laurence. Student, Barnard Coll., 1972-75; BFA with honors, NYU, 1982, MFA, 1994; postgrad. in law, Fordham U., 1999—. Mktg. asst. Stewart Tabori & Chang/Welcome Enterprises, N.Y.C., 1982-83; supr. word processing Harcourt Brace Jovanovich, N.Y.C., 1983-84; legal asst. Skadden, Arps, Slate, Meagher & Flom, N.Y.C., 1984-93; script reader Haft Nassiter Co., N.Y.C., 1994; editl. assoc. Matthew Bender & Co. Inc., N.Y.C., 1994-97; extern Fodham U. Sch. Law, Surrogate's Ct., N.Y.C., 1999. Author one act plays, including Better Dresses, Rosetta's Eyes, 1988, 1988, Adamov, 1992, two act play Harps in the Wind, 1994. Recipient

Grad. award in playwriting, NYU-Tisch Sch. Arts, 1994, Seidman awrd for talent, 1982. Mem. The Dramatists Guild. Avocation: mountain climbing.

HOWES, THEODORE CLARK, claims examiner; b. Ridgefield, Conn., Dec. 25, 1929; s. Robert Clark and Phyllis Evelyn (Greene) H.; m. Anne Christine Tourgee, Sept. 28, 1968. BS, Springfield (Mass.) Coll., 1956. Cert. tchr., Mass. Claims examiner Geico, Chevy Chase, Md., 1967-78, U.S. Dept. Labor, Washington, 1978—. Innovator in use of laser for mil. application. Sgt. USAF, 1948-52. Mem. Soc. Mayflower Descendants, Alden Kindred Am., Am. Legion. Republican. Congregationalist. Avocations: hunting, fishing, gardening, horseback riding, antiques. Home: Fox Meadow Farm 17110 Bollinger School Rd Emmitsburg MD 21727-8721 Office: US Dept Labor 200 Constitution Ave NW Washington DC 20210-0001

HOWES, WILLIAM CRAIG, English educator; b. Huntsville, Ont., Can., Feb. 23, 1955; came to U.S., 1977; s. William Hay and Merle Eleanor (Luck) H.; m. Sara Lois Collins, July 1, 1979; 1 child, William Seth. BA with honours, U. Toronto, 1977; MA, Princeton U., 1978, PhD, 1980. Asst. prof. English U. Hawaii, Honolulu, 1980-87, assoc. prof., 1987-94, prof., 1994—; bd. dirs. Poets in the Schs., Honolulu, Ctr. for Biographical Rsch., 1998—. Author: Voices of the Vietnam POWs, 1993; editor: Biography: An Interdisciplinary Quarterly, 1994—; contbr. articles to profl. jours. Bd. dirs. Poets in the Schs., Honolulu, 1985—. Recipient Pres. citation for teaching, 1986, Regents medal for Tchg., 1998. Mem. Coun. Editors Learned Jours. (v.p. 1996-97, pres. 1998-99), Hawaii Lit. Arts Coun. (pres. 1982—, Elliott P. Cades award Lit. 1994), Modern Lang. Assn. Avocations: acting, running, softball. Office: U Hawaii Dept English 1733 Donaghho Rd Honolulu HI 96822-2315

HOWETH, LYNDA CAROL, small business owner; b. Okemah, Okla., Sept. 19, 1949; d. Clyde Leon and Hattie Arlene (Hymer) Williamson; children: Amanda B. Knowles, Harold W., Jennifer M. Student, Okla. State Tech. U., 1969, South Okla. City C.C., 1974. Mgr. five stores European Flower Markets, Oklahoma City, 1972-76; dist. sales rep. Profl. Office Systems, Inc., Oklahoma City, 1976-81; exec., owner Bus. Med. Systems, Inc., Oklahoma City, 1981—. V.p. dist. 41 Sch. Bd. Western Heights, Oklahoma City, 1991-94, pres., 1994-98; founding mem. steering com. Okla. Bus. Health Inst., 1994. Mem. Nat. Sch. Bd. Assn., Okla. State Sch. Bd. Assn., Vital Info. Profls. (v.p., treas. 1988-90), Med. Tips Club (v.p., treas. 1990-91). Democrat. Avocations: reading, walking. Home: 3328 SW 47th St Oklahoma City OK 73119-4325 Office: Bus Med Systems Inc Bldg A-200 1601 SW 89th St Ste A200 Oklahoma City OK 73159-6365

HOWETT, JOHN CHARLES, JR., lawyer; b. Tampa, Fla., Feb. 11, 1946; s. John Charles and Martha Carlton (Durrance) H.; m. Mary K. Sheehan, Oct. 12, 1974; children: Timothy S., Julia K. BA, U. Pa., 1968; JD, Dickinson Sch. of Law, 1974. Bar: Pa. 1974, U.S. Supreme Ct. 1979. Law clk. Hon. Roy Wilkinson Commonwealth Ct. Pa., Harrisburg, 1974-75; sr. ptnr. Howett, Kissinger & Miles, P.C., Harrisburg, 1975—. Contbr. articles to profl. jours. 1st lt. U.S. Army, 1968-71, Vietnam. Mem. Pa. Bar Assn. (chmn. family law sect. 1995-96, bd. govs. 1978-81, 88-91, pres. young lawyers divsn. 1979-80), Am. Acad. Matrimonial Lawyers (pres. Pa. chpt. 1999—), Dauphin County Bar Assn. (pres. 1994-95, chmn. family law sect. 1990-91), Internat. Acad. Matrimonial Lawyers. Office: Howett Kissinger & Miles PC PO Box 810 130 Walnut St Harrisburg PA 17101-1612

HOWETT, MARK WILLIAM, kinesiotherapy; b. Brookville, Ohio, June 29, 1924; s. Mark and Reatha (McKelly) H.; m. Virgaina Aileen Lowe, June 11, 1950; three children. BS, Ohio State U., 1951. From staff therapist to chief corrective therapy VA Med. Ctr., Dayton, Ohio, 1952-87; bd. dirs., therapist Brookville Enterprises, Inc., Brookville, Ohio, 1973—. Mem. Ohio Kinesiotherapy Assn. Home: 313 Maple St Brookville OH 45309-1712

HOWEY, JOHN RICHARD, architect; b. New Haven, Jan. 13, 1933; s. Joseph Herman and Dorothy Pauline (Good) H.; m. Maria Andrea Hatges, Sept. 8, 1968; children: John Michael, Dorothy Anne. Student, Wooster Coll., 1951-52; BS, Ga. Inst. Tech., 1956, BArch, 1957. Registered architect Fla., N.C. With various archtl. firms, Fla. and Ga., 1958-61; project architect Harvard & Jolly, Architects, St. Petersburg, Fla., 1961-63; pres. John Howey, Architect, AIA, Tampa, Fla., 1963-73, John Howey Assocs., Tampa, Fla., 1973—; pres. Baypark, Inc., Tampa, 1988—. Prin. works include coll. bldgs. U. So. Fla., 1975, Louis Pappas Restaurant, Tarpon Springs, Fla., 1975 (honor design award AIA 1976), office bldg. 101 S. Franklin St., Tampa, 1980 (Fla. Preservation award 1984), Williers Residence, Tampa, 1980 (honor design award AIA 1981), modular urban transit shelters, 1977 (U.S. patent 1980, honor design award AIA 1985), Tehran, Iran Libr. Project, 1978, Baypark Pl. apt. bldgs., Tampa, 1989 (honor design award AIA 1989), others; author: The Sarasota School of Architecture, 1995. With U.S. Army Corps of Engrs., 1957-58. Fellow AIA (Fla./Caribbean region Design Excellence Honor award 1985, Fla. ctrl. chpt. Medal of Honor 1986); mem. Sertoma Club (bd. dirs. 1970-73), Exch. Club. Episcopalian. Avocations: photography, painting. Home: 2538 W Palm Dr Tampa FL 33629-7314 Address: John Howey Assocs 121 W Whiting St Tampa FL 33602-5136

HOWIE, ELIZABETH JANE (BETSY HOWIE), writer, actress; b. Ann Arbor, Mich., June 6, 1962; d. Charles Randall and Mary Lou (Hutzel) H.; m. Frederick John Tetzeli (div.). BFA in Acting, NYU, 1983. Author: (musical) Cowgirls, 1996, (novel) Snow, 1998; actress Cowgirls, 1996. Mem. AFTRA, SAG, Actor's Equity, Dramatists Guild. Office: Elaine Markson Agy 44 Greenwich Ave New York NY 10011-8347

HOWIE, JOHN ROBERT, lawyer; b. Paris, Tex., June 29, 1946; s. Robert H. and Sarah Francis (Caldwell) H.; m. Evelyn Eileen Yates, May 3, 1969; children: John Robert, Ashley Elizabeth, Lindsey Leigh. BBA, North Tex. State U., 1968; JD, So. Meth. U., 1976. Bar: Tex. 1976, U.S. Dist. Ct. (no. dist.) Tex. 1977, U.S. Ct. Appeals (5th, 9th, 10th and 11th cirs.), U.S. Supreme Ct. 1985, U.S. Dist. Ct. (so., ea., and we. dists.) Tex. 1987; cert. in personal injury trial law Tex. Bd. Legal Specialization, 1982. Law Offices of Windle Turley, Dallas, 1976-88, Misko & Howie, 1988-95, ptnr. Howie & Sweeney, LLP, 1995—; adj. prof. trial advocacy So. Meth. U. Sch. Law, 1988-89, 92—, So. Meth. Sch. Law exec. brd. mem., mem. exec. com. Editor The Verdict, 1981-87. Lt. comdr. USN, 1968-73. Fellow So. Trial Lawyers Assn., Roscoe Pound Found. Civil Trial Adv.-Nat. Bd. Trial Adv. (cert. civil trial law), Internat. Acad. Trial Lawyers; mem. Tex. Trial Lawyers Assn. (bd. dirs. 1983—, chmn. product liability com. 1988-89), Dallas Trial Lawyers Assn. (sec.-treas. 1984, v.p. 1985, pres. 1986), Assn. Trial Lawyers Am. (vice chmn. aviation sect. 1984-85, chmn. 1986, Wiedemann Wysocki award 1990), Am. Bd. Trial Advocates (sec. Dallas chpt. 1988, pres. 1989), ABA (vice chmn. aviation law sect. 1986-91, chair 1992), State Bar Tex. (aviation law sect. coun. 1994—, personal injury trial specialist), Lawyer/Pilots Bar Assn., Flight Safety Found, Million Dollar Advs. Forum, Trial Lawyers for Pub. Justice Found., Ark. Trial Lawyers Assn., Ga. Trial Lawyers Assn., Com. for a Qualified Judiciary, Safe Communities Exec. Adv. Com., So. Meth. U. Jour. Air Law and Commerce (bd. advs.), fellow Tex. Bar Found., rsch. fellow Southwestern Legal Found., fellow Dallas Bar Found., Internat. Soc. Air Safety Investigators (contbr. Million Dollar Argument series 1989), Pres.'s Coun. U. North Tex. Democrat. Presbyterian. Home: 6508 Turtle Creek Blvd Dallas TX 75205-1248 Office: Howie & Sweeney LLP 2911 Turtle Creek Blvd Ste 1400 Dallas TX 75219-6258

HOWIE, PHILIP WESLEY, sculptor; b. Boston, Sept. 14, 1960; s. John and Beverly (Watson) H.; m. Alexandra Chermayeff, May 10, 1992; children: Phineas, Olivia. BA, Rhodes Coll., 1982; postgrad., N.Y. Studio Sch., 1983-86. Sculptor N.Y.C. and Catskill, 1986—; sculpture technician N.Y. Studio Sch., N.Y.C., 1991-96; invited guest of Edna St. Vincent Millay Colony for the Arts, Austerlitz, N.Y., 1991. One person exhbn. AAA Gallery, N.Y.C., 1999; group exhibns. include Nat. Arts Club(award of distinction), 1985, N.Y. Study Sch. Gallery, N.Y.C., 1994, Monique Knowlton Gallery, Kent, Conn., 1994, 55 Mercer, N.Y.C., 1994, Greene County Coun. Arts, 1996, Achim Moeller Fine Art, 1999; particpant in Art Show at Armory, N.Y.C.; represented in permanent pvt. collections. Recipient Spaventa Award scholarship N.Y. Studio Sch.. 1984-86. Home: 882 W Main St Catskill NY 12414-5111

HOWITT, ARNOLD MARTIN, university researcher, administrator, educator; b. N.Y.C., Jan. 6, 1947; s. Wilfred D. and Mildred (Wolch) H.; m. Maryalice Sloan; children: Matthew, Molly, Alexandra, Mark. BA, Columbia U., 1969; MA, Harvard U., 1971, PhD, 1976. Asst. prof. Brown U., Providence, 1974-76; asst. prof. Harvard U., Cambridge, Mass., 1976-80, assoc. prof., 1980-82, assoc. dir. Taubman Ctr. State and Local Govt., Kennedy Sch. Govt., 1983-93, exec. dir. Taubman Ctr. State and Local Govt., Kennedy Sch. Govt., 1993—; exec. dir. coop. mobility rsch. program MIT, Cambridge, 1998—; cons. in field; part-time lectr. SUNY, Albany, 1984-92, U. Wash., Seattle, 1988—. Author: Managing Federalism, 1984; co-author, editor: Perspectives on Management Capacity Building, 1986; contbr. articles to profl. jours. Office: Harvard U Kennedy Sch Govt 79 JF Kennedy St Cambridge MA 02138-5801

HOWITT, DAVID ANDREW, human resources executive; b. N.Y.C., Feb. 11, 1953; s. George and Naomi Doris (Rubenstein) H.; m. Leigh Ann Louise Kulp, Jan. 31, 1976; children: Jennifer Elizabeth, Caitlin Rachel. BS in Bus. and Econs., Lehigh U., 1975. Cert. sr. profl. in human resources. Pers. rep. Mutual Benefit Life Ins. Co., Newark, 1975-80; mgr. human resources C-E Lummus, The Lummus Co., Bloomfield, N.J., 1980-83; dir. human resources Pubrs. Phototype, Inc., Carlstadt, N.J., 1983-85; v.p. human resources Fireman's Fund Ins. Co., Novato, Calif., 1985-97; sr. cons. IBM, San Francisco, 1998—. Mem. of corp. United Way of Morris County, Cedar Knolls, N.J., 1986-89; pres. Bay Area Outreach and Recreation Program, 1993—; bd. dirs. Edn. Found. Orinda, 1994-97; trustee Orinda Union Sch. Dist., 1997—. Mem. Soc. for Human Resources Mgmt., No. Calif. Human Resources Coun., Assn. Human Resources Systems Profls. Democrat. Office: IBM Corp 425 Market St San Francisco CA 94105

HOWLAND, BETTE, writer; b. Chgo., Jan. 28, 1937; d. Sam and Jessie (Berger) Sotonoff; m. Howard C. Howland (div.); children—Frank, Jacob. BA, U. Chgo., 1955. Assoc. prof. com. social thought U. Chgo., 1993-97. Author: W-3, 1974, Blue in Chicago, 1978 (1st prize Friends of Am. Writers), Things to Come and Go, 1983, Trial, 1998, Calm Sea and Prosperous Voyage, 1999. Fellow Rockefeller Found., 1969, Marsden Found., 1971, Guggenheim Found., 1978, Nat. Endowment for the Arts, 1981, MacArthur Found., 1984. Jewish. Address: PO Box 405 Union Pier MI 49129-0405

HOWLAND, JOAN SIDNEY, law librarian, law educator; b. Eureka, Calif., Apr. 9, 1951; d. Robert Sidney and Ruth Mary Howland. BA, U. Calif., Davis, 1971; MA, U. Tex., 1973; MLS, Calif. State U., San Jose, 1975; JD, Santa Clara (Calif.) U., 1983; MBA, U. Minn., 1997. Assoc. librarian for pub. svcs. Stanford (Calif.) U. Law Library, 1975-83, Harvard U. Law Library, Cambridge, Mass., 1983-86; dep. dir. U. Calif. Law Library, Berkeley, 1986-92; dir. law libr., Roger F. Noreen prof. law, dir. info. tech. U. Minn. Sch. of Law, 1992—. Questions and answers column editor Law Libr. Jour., 1986-91; memt. column editor Trends in Law Libr. Mgmt. & Tech., 1987-94. Mem. ALA (chmn. cultural diversity com. 1995-97), Am. Assn. Law Librs. (chmn. edn. com. 1987-90, 95-97), Am. Assn. Law Schs. (libr. tech. com. 1998—), Am. Indian Libr. Assn. (treas. 1992—), Am. Law Inst. Office: U Minn Law Sch 229 19th Ave S Minneapolis MN 55455-0400

HOWLAND, KRISTINE KAY, college administrator; b. Plymouth, Wis., May 11, 1947; d. Merland Walter and Harriet Mae (Radloff) Nelson; m. Robert Vaughn Howland, Dec. 30, 1977. AAS, SUNY, 1968; BS, Cornell U., 1978; MBA, Plymouth State Coll., 1989. Cert. advanced profl. studies. Mgr., buyer John Lewton Apparel, Ithaca, N.Y., 1969-70; purchasing sec. Ithaca Coll., 1970-71, adminstr. for spl. events, 1971-74; conf. coord. Cornell U., Ithaca, 1974-79; sales rep. trainee The Travelers Ins. Co., Inc., Syracuse, 1979-80; spl. projects coord. Groton (Conn.) Resources Organized Inc., 1980-81; dir. sales Sheraton Inn-Norwich, Conn., 1982-83, Norwich Inn & Spa, 1983-84; program coord. Keene State Coll., 1984-85, asst. to the pres., 1985-88, dir. of devel. and alumni affairs, 1988-94, dir. institutional advancement; v.p. for devel. Tiffin (Ohio) U., 1994-95; dir. major and planned gifts Goucher Coll., Balt., 1995—; v.p. N.H. Women in Higher Edn. State Planning Bd., 1991-93. Adult vol. and mem. Girl Scouts Am., 1954—; chair group travel devel. Southeastern Conn. Tourism Dist., Mystic, Conn., 1982-83, chair advt. com., 1983-84; mem. public rels. com. Greater Keene C. of C., 1984-94; mem. Corp. Child Care Group, Inc., Keene, 1985-89, v.p., 1987-89; mem. ednl. programs com. N.H. Coun. on Fund Raising, 1991-94; chair membership com. Chesapeake Planned Giving Coun., 1997-98; founding mem., bd. dirs. Southeastern Conn. Tourism Dist., East Lyme, Conn., 1982-84. Recipient Judith A. Sturnick award N.H. Women in Higher Edn. Assn., 1993; named Founding Mem. of Major Gifts Exch. Md. chpt. Nat. Soc. of Fund Raising Execs., 1996-97. Mem. AAUW (pres. 1992-94), Chesapeake Planned Giving Coun., Cornell Club of Md., Cornell Club of N.Y., Coun. for Advancement and Support of Edn., Nat. Assn. of Women in Edn., Nat. Soc. for Fund Raising Execs., Md. Assn. of Women in Edn. Episcopalian. Avocations: reading, hiking, cooking. Office: Goucher Coll 1021 Dulaney Valley Rd Baltimore MD 21204-2753

HOWLAND, L.R., protective services official. Grad., U. Va., Nat. Exec. Inst., Harvard U., U.S. Secret Svc. Sch., Oreg. Exec. Devel. Inst., Oreg. State Police Acad. Trooper Oreg. State Police, 1967-72, detective, 1972-78, corp., 1978-81, sgt., 1981-83, lt., 1983-86, capt., 1986-88, maj., 1988-90, dep. supt., 1990-93, supt., 1993—. Office: Oreg. State Police 400 Public Service Bldg Salem OR 97310*

HOWLAND, RICHARD HUBBARD, architectural historian; b. Providence, Aug. 23, 1910; S. Carl Badger and Cora Augusta (Hubbard) H. A.B., Brown U., 1931, also hon. doctor's degree; A.M., Harvard U., 1933; Ph.D., Johns Hopkins U., 1946. Fellow Agora excavations, Athens, Greece, 1936-38; instr. Wellesley Coll., 1939-42; chief pictorial records sect. OSS, 1943-44; founder dept. history art Johns Hopkins, 1947, chmn. dept., 1947-56; pres. Nat. Trust for Historic Preservation, 1956-60; chmn. dept. civil history Smithsonian Instn., Washington, 1960-67; spl. asst. to sec. Smithsonian Instn., 1968-85; trustee Am. Sch. Classical Studies, Athens; founding mem. Am. Com. Internat. Commn. Historic Sites and Monuments. Author: (with Eleanor Spencer) Architecture of Baltimore, 1954, Greek Lamps and Their Survivals, 1958. Trustee Sotterley Found., Accokeek Found., Inc., Irish Georgian Soc. Evergreen Found. Recipient O.B.E. award Queen Elizabeth, 1991; named Order of Geo I., Greece; mem. U.S. Order of St. John of Jerusalem. Fellow Royal Soc. of the Arts, Phila. Athenaeum; mem. Fellows in Am. Studies, Soc. Archtl. Historians (founding mem.), English Speaking Union, Soc. Cincinnati (hon.), Md. Soc. Colonial Wars, Victorian Soc. in Am. (former pres.), Century Assn., Knickerbocker Club, 14 West Hamilton St. Club, Cosmos Club, Arts Club, Dacor-Bacon Club, City Tavern Club, Phi Gamma Delta. Home: 3900 Cathedral Ave NW Apt 712A Washington DC 20016-5299

HOWLAND, RICHARD MOULTON, lawyer; b. Glen Cove, L.I., N.Y., Jan. 2, 1940; s. Richard Moulton and Natalie (Fuller) H.; m. Julie Rose Keschl, Sept. 28, 1974 (div.); children: Kimberly Merrill, Gillian Fuller. BA, Amherst Coll., 1961; JD, Columbia U., 1968. Bar: Mass. 1968. Assoc. firm Nutter, McLennen & Fish, Boston, 1968-69, DiMento & Sullivan, Boston, 1969-70; atty. for students U. Mass., Amherst, 1970-74; practice law Amherst, 1974—; Legal Infirmary Amherst, 1997—; adj. prof. U. Mass., 1972-76, Western New Eng. Coll. Sch. Law, 1993-94; vis. lectr. Amherst Coll., 1983, mock trial team coach, 1989-98; mock trial team coach Tufts Coll., 1998, Deerfield Acad., 1999—. Co-editor Mass. Lawyers Weekly, 1979-94, emeritus, 1994; statistician New England Blizzard, 1996-98, Springfield Sirens Pro Soccer, 1999—. Asst. moderator Town of Leverett, 1988-93, moderator, 1993-96; mem. Leverett Sch. Bldg. Com., 1988-89; trustee Art Inst. Boston, 1990-92, Greenfield C. C. Found., 1991-97, Amherst Regional High Sch. Coun., 1993-95; trustee Amherst Hist. Soc., 1990-95; pres. Leverett PTO, 1981-85; mem. devel. com. Pioneer Valley High Sch. of the Performing Arts, 1996-97; pres. Interfaith Housing Corp., Amherst, 1984-93; bd. dirs. Leverett Craftsmen and Artists, Inc., 1986—, treas., 1988-89, v.p., 1988-89, pres., 1989—; bd. dirs. Community Multisvc. Inc., Northampton, Mass., 1987-93; trustee Wildwood Cemetery Assn., 1987—; bd. dirs., sec. Responsible Hospitality Inst., 1990-95; mem. host com. Russia-Amherst Exchange City of Petrozavadsk, 1988—; del. rep. Town of Amherst to Sister City, Kanegasaki, Japan, 1992-95; chair Amherst-Kanegasaki Sister Com., 1994-95; mem. bd. career com., Hampshire-Franklin Sch., 1995—; cert. ofcl. U.S. Assn. Track and Field, 1996—; Western Mass. track and field ofcl., 1995—; We. Mass. football ofcl., 1995—; referee FIFA Soccer, 1997—; collegiate water polo ofcl., 1997—; asst. coach varsity girls soccer Amherst Regional H.S., 1995—. Lt. (j.g.) USNR, 1961-65. Mem. ABA (chmn. profl. liability com. Gen. Practice Sect. 1987-90, chmn. certification and specialization com. Gen. Practice Sect. 1992-95, chmn. family law com. 1995-96, chmn. certification, specialization and law sch. curriculum com. 1996-98, mem. coun. 1997—), Mass. Bar Assn. (chmn. com. on chem. dependency, Mass. Community Svc. award 1984), Franklin Bar Assn., Hampshire Bar Assn. (del. to Mass. Bar Assn., sec., v.p. 1986), Mass. Acad. Trial Lawyers, Amherst C. of C. (pres. 1985-93, Dakin medallion 1995), Nat. High Sch. Slavic Honor Soc. (hon.), Amherst Alumni Athletic Assn. (bd. dirs. 1995—), Skating Club (past v.p., treas. 1987-96, Amherst). Democrat. E-mail: howland@crocker.com. Home: 326 N Pleasant St Amherst MA 01002-1706

HOWLAND, RONALD L., federal judge. Magistrate judge U.S. Dist. Ct. (we. dist.) Okla., Oklahoma City. Office: 1305 US Courthouse 200 NW 4th St Oklahoma City OK 73102-3026

HOWLAND, WILLARD J., radiologist, educator; b. Neosho, Mo., Aug. 28, 1927; s. Willard Jay and Grace Darlene (Murphy) H.; m. Kathleen V. Jones, July 28, 1945; children: Wyck, Candice, Charles, Thomas, Heather. AB, U. Kans., 1948, MD, 1950; MA, U. Minn., 1958; DSc (hon.), Coll. Med. N.E. Ohio, 1990. Intern U.S. Naval Hosp., Newport, R.I., 1950-51; pvt. practice medicine Kans., 1951-55; resident Mayo Clinic, Rochester, Minn., 1955-58; radiologist Ohio Valley Gen. Hosp., Wheeling, W.Va., 1959-67; prof., dir. diagnostic radiology Med. Units U. Tenn., Memphis, 1967-68; dir., chmn. dept. radiology Aultman Hosp., Canton, Ohio, 1968-87; pres. med. staff Aultman Hosp., Canton, 1978; prof., chmn. radiology coun. Coll. Medicine N.E. Ohio U., Rootstown, 1976-87, program dir. integrated radiology residency, 1976-87. Author, co-author three books and rsch. papers in field. With U.S. Army, 1945-46, USN, 1950-51. Fellow Am. Coll. Radiology; mem. AMA, Radiol. Soc. N.Am., Am. Roentgen Ray Soc., Ohio State Radiol. Soc. (pres. 1980-81), Masons. Republican. Presbyterian. Office: 1405 Harbor Dr NW Canton OH 44708-3098

HOWLETT, D(ONALD) ROGER, art gallery executive, art historian; b. Syracuse, N.Y., Mar. 27, 1945; s. Donald Bliss and Dorothy Irene (Trautman) H. BA, Hamilton Coll., 1966; MA, SUNY, Cooperstown, 1967; postgrad., Yale U., 1968-69. Mem. curatorial dept. Garvan Coll., Yale U. Art Gallery, New Haven, 1967-68; mem. painting dept. Childs Gallery, Boston, 1970—, v.p., ptnr., 1972-83, pres., 1983—; pres. Childs Gallery, N.Y.C., 1983-91; councilor Emerson Gallery, Hamilton Coll., Clinton, N.Y., 1985—; trustee Lyme Acad. of Fine Arts, Old Lyme, Conn., 1992—. Author: Sculpture of Donald De Lue, 1990, William Partridge Burpee, 1991, The Lynn Beach Painters, 1998; collections arranged: George Luks (author catalog), 1973-74, Molly Luce: Eight Decades of the American Scene (author catalog), 1983. Mem. Am. Assn. Mus., Soc. for Propatating the Gospel Among the Indians and Others in N.Am., St. Botolph Club, Boston Athenaeum. Avocation: watercolorist. Home and Office: Childs Gallery 169 Newbury St Boston MA 02116-2834

HOWLETT, STEPHANIE ANN, home care equipment sales representative, nurse; b. Kansas City, Kans., Dec. 23, 1957; d. Wayne Stewart and Anna Marie (Barancik) H. AA, Kansas City Community Coll., 1979; student, Colo. Ctr. for The Blind, 1995-96. RN. Critical care nurse Providence-St. Margarets Health Ctr., Kansas City, Kans., 1979-82; primary pvt. duty nurse Quality Care In, Kansas City, Mo., 1980-81; dir. nursing Profl. Nursing Service, Kansas City, Mo., 1981-86; med. services cons. Crawford Health and Rehab. Services, Kansas City, Mo., 1986; sales rep. HOMEDCO, Lenexa, Kans., 1986-92, mem. presidents adv. coun., 1986-92; mem. adv. bd. Olsten Health Care Svcs., Kansas City, Mo., 1986-92, utilization rev. com., 1986-92, budget com., 1987-92. Mem. Jr. League, Wyandotte and Johnson County, 1988-91; vol. Vis. Nurses Assn., 1997-98, Network Rehab. Svcs., 1998-99. Named one of Outstanding Young Women Am., 1987. Mem. NAFE, Nat. Rehab. Assn., Assn. Rehab. Nurses, Support Hospice Oncology Profls., Kansas City Met. Discharge Coords., Kansas City Regional Homecare Assn. (edn. com., infusion therapy com.), Kiwanis Club of Lenexa (bd. dirs.), Bi Partisian. Avocations: travel, reading, exercise, learning adaptability to blinded skills. Home: 10507 College Ave Kansas City MO 64137-1763

HOWLEY, JAMES MCANDREW, lawyer; b. Dunmore, Pa., Oct. 3, 1928; s. Joseph Austin and Mary Helene (Ruddy) H.; m. Mary McDade; 1 child, Maura. BS, U. Scranton, 1952; LLB, U. Pa., 1955. Bar: Pa. 1956, U.S. Dist. Ct. (mid. dist.) Pa. 1956, U.S. Ct. Appeals (3d cir.) 1960. Pvt. practice Scranton, Northeastern Pa., 1956—; panel mem. and speaker at various legal symposiums; chmn. and commr. Pa. State Ethics Commn.; chmn. Gov.'s Spl. Trial Ct. nomination commn., Lackawanna County, Pa., 1987; disciplinary bd. Supreme Ct. Pa. hearing com., 1987; lawyer's adv. com. U.S. Ct. Appeals (3d cir.), 1983-86, U.S. Dist. Ct. (mid. dist.) Pa., 1981-86. Chmn. and trustee Marywood Coll., trustee St. Mary's Villa. Fellow Am. Coll. Trial Lawyers; mem. ABA, Pa. Bar Assn., Pa. Def. Inst., Pa. Trial Lawyers Assn., Am. Bd. Trial Advs. (cert.), Lackawanna County Bar Assn., Scranton C. of C. (bd. dirs.), Country Club of Scranton (pres. 1974-79), Friendly Sons of St. Patrick (pres. 1986). Roman Catholic. Avocations: golf, tennis. Home: 115 Maple Ave Clarks Summit PA 18411-2513 Office: 1000 Bank Towers 321 Spruce St Scranton PA 18503-1400

HOWLEY, PETER ANTHONY, communications executive; b. Phila., Mar. 5, 1940; s. Frank Leo and Edith Jenkins (Cadwallader) H.; m. M. Mavin Renz, June 25, 1966; children: Tara Noel, Christina Maeve, Sean-Francis Cadwallader. B in Indsl. Engring., NYU, 1962, MBA in Mktg., 1970. Mem. mgmt. staff AT&T, White Plains, N.Y., 1965-73, MCI, Inc., N.Y.C., 1973-76; v.p., gen. mgr. Citizens Utilities Co., Kingman, Ariz., 1976-85; chmn., pres., CEO Centex Telemgmt., Inc., San Francisco, 1985-94; founder, chmn., pres., CEO, Air Power Comm., Inc., San Francisco, 1995-96; chmn. Western Ventures, San Francisco, 1994-98; founder, pres., CEO IPWireless, Inc., Mill Valley, Calif., 1998—; bd. dirs. FaxSAV Corp., Woodbridge, N.J., SOS Wireless Comms., Irving, Calif., Exodus Comm., Inc., Santa Clara, Calif., Worldport Comms., Inc., Houston; mem. adv. bd. NASDAQ Corp., 1992-94. Contbr. to numerous profl. publs. Capt. USAF, 1962-65, 68-69. Mem. Am. Bus. Conf. Roman Catholic. Avocations: skiing, tennis, running, sailing. Home: 25 Cornwall St Mill Valley CA 94941-1730 Office: 101 California St Ste 4225 San Francisco CA 94111-5845

HOWLEY, PETER MAXWELL, pathology educator; b. New Brunswick, N.J., Oct. 9, 1946; s. Bartholomew Maxwell and Grace (Size) H.; m. Ann Margaret McElwee, Aug. 23, 1969; children: Cristin, Megan, Maura. AB, Princeton U., 1968; M Med. Sci., Rutgers U., 1970; MD, Harvard U., 1972. Diplomate Am. Bd. Pathology. Intern Mass. Gen. Hosp., Boston, 1972-73; commd. lt. USPHS, 1973, advanced through grades to capt., 1985; rsch. assoc. NIH, Bethesda, Md., 1973-75; resident in pathology Nat. Cancer Inst., Bethesda, 1975-77, prin. investigator, 1977-84, lab. chief, 1984-93; ret., 1993; George Fabyan prof. comparative pathology, chmn. dept. Harvard Med. Sch., Boston, 1993—; mem. sci. adv. bd. ONYX Pharm. Co., Richmond, Calif., 1992-97, Baxter Internat., Deerfield, Ill., 1995—; chair Nat. Cancer Policy Bd., 1997—. Editor: The Molecular Basis of Cancer, 1996, Virology, 3d edit., 1995; contbr. over 190 articles to med. jours. Recipient Wallace P. Rowe award Nat. Inst. Allergy and Infectious Diseases, 1986, Meritorious Svc. award USPHS, 1989, Paul Ehrlich-Ludwig Darmstaedter prize Govt. of Germany, 1994. Fellow Am. Acad. Microbiology; mem. NAS, Inst. Medicine, Am. Acad. Arts and Scis. Achievements include patent for Recombinant DNA Process Utilizing Papillomavirus DNA as a Vector. Office: Harvard Medical Sch Bldg D2-Rm 629 200 Longwood Ave Boston MA 02115-5701*

HOWORTH, DAVID, producer, director; b. N.Y.C., Aug. 30, 1941; s. Marion Beckett and Dorothy Huldah (Cowing) H.; m. Bea Borges, May 6, 1967. AA, Santa Barbara (Calif.) C.C., 1970; student, UCLA, 1977, Am. Film Inst., L.A., 1982. V.p., co-owner Golden Coast Films, Santa Barbara, 1971-82, owner, prodr., dir., 1982—. Software developer, prodr.: (CD-ROM/Internet series) Career Link, 1996, Wildlife/Nature series, 1993; prodr., dir.: Careers: Nursing, 1993; co-prodr., co-writer: (ednl. picture) Just Beer, 1983. With USMCR, 1960-65. Recipient awards Columbus Internat. Film/Video Festival, 1993, Nat. Mental Health Assn., 1981, Excellence-

Suitable for Family Viewing, No. Calif. Motion Picture and TV Coun., 1975. Mem. NATAS, AMA (acad. med. films), Internat. Interactive Comms. Soc., Greater Santa Barbara Advt. Club (pres. 1972). Avocations: historical films, records, swimming, boating. E-mail: gcf@silcom.com. Office: Golden Coast Films 2020 Alameda Padre Serra Santa Barbara CA 93103-1756

HOWORTH, DAVID BISHOP, lawyer; b. Temple, Tex., Feb. 6, 1947; s. Marion Beckett and Mary Hartwell (Bishop) H.; m. Martha Ellen Peacock, Aug. 29, 1970; children: Katherine Somerville, Emily Hartwell. BA, Yale U., 1971; JD, U. Miss., 1975. Bar: N.Y. 1976, U.S. Dist. Ct. (so. and ea. dists.) N.Y. 1977, U.S. Ct. Appeals (2d cir.) 1984, Oreg. 1990, U.S. Dist. Ct. Oreg. 1990, U.S. Ct. Appeals (9th cir.) 1991, Wash. 1996. Assoc. Dewey Ballantine, N.Y.C., 1975-77, 78-83, ptnr., 1984-90; asst. prof. law U. Miss., University, 1977-78; ptnr. Foster, Pepper & Shefelman, Portland, Oreg., 1990—. Mem. ABA, N.Y. State Bar Assn., Assn. Bar City of N.Y. Home: 01960 SW Palatine Hill Rd Portland OR 97219-7950 Office: Foster Pepper & Shefelman 101 SW Main St Fl 15 Portland OR 97204-3292

HOWREY, EUGENE PHILIP, economics educator, consultant; b. Geneva, Ill., Dec. 1, 1937; s. Eugene Edgar and Ellen Pauline (Boord) H.; children: Patricia Marie, Richard Philip, Margaret Ellen, Mark McCall. A.B., Drake U., 1959; Ph.D., U. N.C., 1964; M.A. (hon.), U. Pa., 1972. Asst. prof. econs. Princeton U., N.J., 1963-69; assoc. prof. econs. U. Pa., Phila., 1969-73; prof. econs. U. Mich., Ann Arbor, 1973—; prof. stats. U. Mich., 1978—; cons. Mathematica, Inc., Princeton, 1965-75; guest lectr. Inst. Advanced Studies, Vienna, 1974, 76. Contbr. articles to profl. jours. Research grantee NSF, 1975, 79, 84. Mem. Ann Arbor Velo Club, Ann Arbor Bicycle Touring Club (pres. 1979-80), Phi Beta Kappa. Democrat. Roman Catholic. Avocation: bicycling. Home: 2152 Overlook Ct Ann Arbor MI 48103-2336 Office: U Mich Dept Econs Ann Arbor MI 48109

HOWROYD, JANICE BRYANT, personnel placement executive; b. Tarboro, N.C. Pres., CEO, prin. ACT 1 Pers. Svcs., Torrance, Calif., 1978—. lectr. in field. mem. Minority Bus. Opportunity Day trade fair, LA, Jr. Achievement of Ctrl. Ariz. Inc., 1992-93, Project Life; bd. dirs. L.A. Urban League, St. Anne's Maternity Home, Internat. Visitors coun. for city of L.A., L.A. Urban League. Recipient Minority Enterprise Devel. Week Achievement award U.S. Dept. of Commerce, Ceert. of Achievement award No. Calif. Regional Purchasing coun., 1992, Entertainment and Bus. Cmty Achievement award NAACP Legal Def. Fund. 1992, Distinguished Svc. award Joint Conf., Inc., 1993, Nat. Minority Supplier of the Year award Nat. Minority Supplier Devel. coun., 1993, Black Women of Achievement AT & T Entrepreneur of the Year, 1994. Mem. Nat. Assn. of Women Bus. Owners; bd. dirs. Greater L.A. African Am. C. of C.; adv. bd. mem. Northrop-Rice Aviation Inst. of Technol. Office: ACT 1 Pers Svc 5334 Torrance Blvd Torrance CA 90503-4012

HOWSON, AGNES WAGNER, health educator; b. Lebanon, Pa., May 9, 1940; d. Lester Frederick and Mary Elizabeth (Engle) Wagner; m. Robert Douglas Howson, Mar. 25, 1961; children: R. Douglas, Geoffrey F., Eric M., Stephen M. AS, Becker Jr. Coll., 1960; AA in Edn., Brookdale C.C., 1971, AAS in Nursing, 1975; BS in Human Svcs., Thomas A. Edison State Coll., N.J., 1988; MA in Edn., Georgian Ct. Coll., 1995; PhD in Natural Health, Clayton Coll., Birmingham, Ala., 1998. RN, N.J.; cert. health edn. specialist. Substitute sch. nurse Middletown Twp. (N.J.), 1976-82; staff nurse Riverview Hosp., Red Bank, N.J., 1977-78, 80-81; clinic supr., counselor Planned Parenthood of Monmouth County, Shrewsbury, N.J., 1978, 87; staff cmty. health nurse MCOSS Nursing Svcs., Red Bank, N.J., 1983-89; nurse health educator Family Health Resource Ctr. Riverview Med. Ctr., Red Bank, N.J., 1989-92; health educator Blue Cross/Blue Shield Health Ctr., Eatontown, N.J., 1994-95; RN, diabetes educator Wellness Ctr. Jersey Shore Med. Ctr., Neptune, N.J., 1996-97; adj. prof. health studies Monmouth U., West Long Branch, N.J., 1998—. Mem. Am. Holistic Nurses Assn., Am. Assn. Health Educators. Home: 128 Bruce Rd Red Bank NJ 07701-5605

HOWZE, JOSEPH LAWSON EDWARD, bishop; b. Daphne, Ala., Aug. 30, 1923; s. Albert Otis and Helen Artamesa (Lawson) H. B.S., Ala. State U., 1948; postgrad. in bus. mgmt., Phillips Coll., Gulfport, Miss., 1980; LL.D. (hon.), U. Portland, 1974, St. Bonaventure U., 1977, Manhattan Coll., N.Y.C., 1979; H.H.D. (hon.), Sacred Heart Coll., Belmont, N.Y., 1977; HHD (hon.), The Lift Bible Crusade Coll., 1987. Ordained priest Roman Catholic Ch., 1959; pastor chs. Charlotte, Southern Pines, Durham, Sanford, Asheville, all N.C., 1959-72; aux. bishop of (Diocese of Natchez-Jackson), Miss., 1972-73; bishop (Diocese of Natchez-Jackson), 1973-77, Diocese of Biloxi, Biloxi, 1977—. Trustee Xavier U., New Orleans; mem. Miss. Health Care Commn.; mem. adminstrv. bd., vacation com. NOCB/USCC; mem. edn. com. USCC, mem. social devel. and world peace com.; liaison com. to Nat. Office of Black Catholics, NCCB.; bd. dirs. Biloxi Regional Med. Ctr. Democrat. Clubs: K.C, Knights of St. Peter Claver. Address: PO Box 1189 120 Reynoir St Biloxi MS 39530-4130*

HOWZE, KAREN AILEEN, newspaper editor, lawyer, multi-cultural communications consultant; b. Detroit, Dec. 8, 1950; d. Manuel and Dorothy June (Smith) H.; children: Charlene Marie-Aileen, Karie JoAnn, Lucinda Gloria Patrice. B.A. in Journalism, U. So. Calif., 1972; J.D., Hastings Coll. Law, San Francisco, 1977. Bar: Md. 1989, D.C. 1990. Intern Detroit Free Press, 1971; reporter San Francisco Chronicle, 1972-78; asst. editor Newsday, L.I., 1978-79; asst. mng. editor Rochester Times Union, N.Y., 1979-80; Sunday features editor Rochester Democrat & Chronicle, N.Y., 1980-81; mng. editor systems USA Today, Arlington, Va., 1981-86, mng. editor internat. edit., 1986-88; editor, dir. corp. news systems newspaper div. Gannett Co. Inc., Washington, 1988-90; prin. Howze & Assocs., Washington, 1990—, Karen Aileen Howze, P.C., Washington, 1990—; lectr. comm. Am. U., Washington, Howard U., Washington; presenter Am. Press Inst., Poynter Inst. Media Studies, Maynard Inst. Journalism Edn. Author: Making Differences Work: Cultural Context in Abuse and Neglect Practice for Attorneys and Judges, 1996; editor: People & Product, 1993-95. Bd. dirs. N.Am. Coun. Adoptable Children, 1990-97, Maat Inst., 1990-97, The Chelsea Sch., 1991—; pres., founder Adoption Support Inst., Washington, 1990. Mem. Nat. Assn. Black Journalists (bd. dirs. 1975-81, sec., parliamentarian, ANPA vice chair minority opportunity com. 1986), Am. Soc. Newspaper Editors (chair press rm. convention, mem. pres. and bar com.). Roman Catholic. Clubs: Capital Press, Washington Press. Avocations: painting; piano; house renovations and real estate. Office: Karen Aileen Howze PC PO Box 1127 Silver Spring MD 20910-0127

HOXIE, FREDERICK EUGENE, history educator; b. Hoolehua, Hawaii, Apr. 22, 1947; s. John Wadman and Catherine (Agee) H.; m. Elizabeth Anne Schroder, July 11, 1970 (dec. Dec. 1983); children: Silas, Charles; m. Holly Frances Hanscom, Jan. 3, 1986; stepchildren: Stephen Hoskins, Philip Hoskins. BA, Amherst Coll., 1969, PhD in Humane Letters (hon.), 1994; MA, Brandeis U., 1976, PhD, 1977. Tchr. Phila. Pub. Schs., 1969-70; high sch. tchr. Punahou Sch., Honolulu, 1970-72; asst. prof. Antioch Coll., Yellow Springs, Ohio, 1977-82, assoc. prof., 1982-83; dir. D'Arcy McNickle Ctr. for Am. Indian History, Newberry Libr., Chgo., 1983-94, v.p. rsch. and edn., 1994-98; Swanlund prof. history U. Ill., Urbana, 1998—; cons. Cheyenne River Sioux Tribe, Eagle Butte, S.D., 1977-78, U.S. Senate Com. on Indian Affairs, Washington, 1989-90, Little Big Horn Coll., Crow Agency, Mt., 1990-98, Nat. Park Svc., Denver Support Ctr., 1997-98. Author: A Final Promise, 1984, Parading Through History, 1995; editor: Indians in American History, 1988, 2d edit., 1997, Ency. of North American Indians, 1996. Bd. dirs. Ill. Humanities Coun., Chgo., 1997—; trustee Nat. Mus. Am. Indian, Smithsonian, 1990-95. Humanities fellow Rockefeller Found., 1984-85, fellow NEH, 1990-91. Mem. Am. Hist. Assn. (program chmn. 1992), Am. Soc. for Ethnohistory (pres. 1995-96), Orgn. Am. Historians (exec. bd. 1997—). Avocations: running, tennis. E-mail: hoxie@uicu.edu. Office: U Ill Dept History 309 Gregory Hall 810 S Wright St Urbana IL 61801

HOXIE, JOEL P., lawyer; b. Waterloo, Iowa, Dec. 4, 1948; s. Wirt Pierce and Jeanne (Ogle) H.; m. Cynthia Ann Mast, Aug. 12, 1978; children: Robert Lewis, Laura Ann. AB, Princeton U., 1971; JD, U. Iowa, 1978. Atty. Snell & Wilmer, Phoenix, 1978—. Trustee Heard Mus., Phoenix, 1990—, v.p., 1990-95, pres., 1995-97, pres. bd. trustees; pres. Princeton Alumni Assn. No. Ariz., Phoenix, 1990—. Lt. USN, 1971-75. Mem. Nat. Bar Assn., Ariz. State Bar Assn., County Bar Assn., Securities Industry Assn. (legal and compliance divsn. 1992—), Phoenix Country Club. Methodist. Avocations: golf, tennis, swimming, hiking. Home: 5301 E Mariposa St Phoenix AZ 85018-3029 Office: Snell & Wilmer 1 Arizona Ctr Phoenix AZ 85004

HOXIE, RALPH GORDON, educational administrator, author; b. Waterloo, Iowa, Mar. 18, 1919; s. Charles Ray and Ada May (Little) H.; m. Louise Lobitz, Dec. 23, 1953 (dec. 1992); m. Ada B. Edgerton, June 21, 1997. BA, U. No. Iowa, 1940; MA, U. Wis., 1941; PhD, Columbia, 1950; LLD (hon.), Chung-ang U., 1965; LittD (hon.), D'Youville Coll., 1966; grad., Air War Coll., 1971; LHD (hon.), Gannon U., 1988, Wesley Coll., 1989, U. No. Iowa, 1990, Shepherd Coll., 1992, Teikyo Post U., 1994, Long Island U., 1995, Fitchburg State Coll., 1997. Roberts fellow Columbia, 1946-47, Roberts travelling fellow, 1947-48, asst. to provost, 1948-49; asst. prof. history, gen. editor Social Sci. Found.; asst. to chancellor U. Denver, 1950-53; project asso. Columbia Bicentennial History, 1953-54; dean Coll. Liberal Arts and Scis., L.I. U., 1954-55; acting dean C. W. Post Coll., 1954-55, dean, 1955-60, provost, 1960-62, pres., 1962-68; chancellor L.I. U., 1964-68, cons., 1968-69; pres. Center for Study of Presidency, 1969-95; chmn. Ctr. for Study of Presidency, 1995-96, pres., chmn. emeritus, 1997—; pub. mem. Fgn. Svc. officer selection bd. U.S. Dept. State; vis. lectr. U. Ala., U. Calif., Irvine, Columbia U., U. Colo., Colo. State U., U. Wyo., Chapman Coll., U. No. Colo., Colo. Coll., Gannon U., Gettysburg Coll., Heidelberg Coll., U. Kans., Muskingum Coll., Post Coll., St. Francis Coll. N.Y., USAF Acad., Naval War Coll., Nat. Archives, Nat. War Coll., Oglethorpe U., U. Genoa, Italy, U. Pitts., U. Tex., El Paso, U Wis., Northwestern U., U. No. Iowa; bd. govs. Banque Continentale br. Franklin Nat. Bank. Author: John W. Burgess, American Scholar, 1950, Command Decision and the Presidency, 1977, (with others) A History of The Faculty of Political Science, Columbia University, 1955, Organizing and Staffing the Presidency, 1980; editor: Frontiers for Freedom, 1952, The White House: Organization and Operations, 1971, The Presidency of the 1970's, 1973, The Presidency and Information Policy, 1981, The Presidency and National Security Policy, 1984 ; editor Presdl. Studies Quar., 1970-95; contbg. author: (with others) Freedom and Authority in Our Time, 1953, The Coattailless Landslide, 1974, Power and the Presidency, 1976, Classics of the American Presidency, 1980, The Blessings of Liberty, 1987, Popular Images of American Presidents, 1988, Rating Game in American Politics, 1988, Science and Technology Advice to the President, Congress, and Judiciary, 1988, The American Presidency: Historical and Contemporary Perspectives, 1988, Points of View, 1988, The Presidency in Transition, 1989, Dictionary of American History, 1996, Points of View, 1998; contbr. articles to profl. jours. and encys. Bd. dirs. United Fund L.I., Bklyn. Inst. Arts and Scis., Tibetan Found., L.I. Coun. Alcoholism, Bklyn. chpt. ARC Greater N.Y.; chmn., pres. bd. dirs. Am. Friends Chung-ang U.; pres. Pub. Mems. Assn. Fgn. Svc.; trustee Air Force Hist. Found., U. No. Iowa Found., Nat. Inst. Social Scis., Kosciuszko Found. N.Y., Mackinac Coll., North Shore chpt. Am. Assn. UN, Downtown Bklyn. Assn., Coun. Higher Ednl. Instns. N.Y.C.; mem. adv. bd. L.I. Air res. Ctr.; mem. adv. coun. Robert A. Taft Inst. Govt.; sec. Nassau County Commn. on Govt. Revision; co-chmn. Nassau-Suffolk Conf. Christians and Jews; dir., pres. Great-N.Y. Coun. Fgn. Students; bd. govs. Human Resources Ctr., N.Y. Korean Vets. Meml. Commn. Served to capt. USAAF, 1942-46; brig. gen. USAF ret. Decorated Meritorious Svc. medal, Legion of Merit, Korean Cultural medal, numerous other medals; recipient Disting. Svc. medal City N.Y., 1965, Alumni Achievement award U. No. Iowa, 1965, Alumni Achievement award Columbia U., 1997, Columbia award for Disting. Achievment, 1997; named Man of Yr. Paderewski Found., 1966, Man of Yr. Eloy Alfaro Found., 1966. Fellow Am. Studies Assn. Met. N.Y.; mem. Am. Hist. Assn., Internat. Assn. Univ. Pres., Am. Polit. Sci. Assn., Acad. of Polit. Sci., Navy League, Air Force Assn., Res. Officers Assn. (pres. Mitchel chpt.), V.F.W., Am. Legion, L.I. Assn. (dir.), Am. Polar Soc., Kappa Delta Pi, Pi Gamma Mu, Alpha Sigma Lambda, Delta Sigma Pi, Gamma Theta Upsilon. Episcopalian. Clubs: Century Assn., Met., Columbia Univ. Faculty House (N.Y.C.); Met. (Washington); Bklyn., Montauk (Bklyn.); Old Westbury Golf and Country and Mill River (hon.). Home: PO Box 248 Oyster Bay NY 11771-0248 Office: 208 E 75th St New York NY 10021-2925 *Each day I seek to ask how I can better serve others. Assuredly, in so serving, ours will be the richest of dividends and life takes on an ever-fuller meaning.*

HOXMEIER, MARLETTE MARIE, nurse educator; b. Anoka, Minn., May 14, 1953; d. Kenneth A. and Laurel (Edeburn) Nelson; m. Kenneth J. Hoxmeier, Apr. 16, 1977; children: Nicholas Nelson, Joseph Simon. Diploma, St. Cloud Sch. Nursing, 1974; BS in Health Arts, Coll. of St. Francis, Joliet, Ill., 1992, postgrad., 1995—. RN, Mn.; cert. in low risk neonatal nursing AAWONN. Staff nurse St. Paul Ramsey Hosp., 1974-79; nurse instr. Regional Kidney Disease Program, Mpls., 1979-83; staff nurse preceptor Mpls. Children's Med. Ctr., 1983-87; asst. head nurse St. Joseph's Hosp./Healtheast, St. Paul, 1987-97; computerized documentation educator Healtheast, St. Paul, 1997—; neonatal resuscitation instr. Am. Acad. Pediatrics, 1990—. Mem. Minn. Neonatal Nurses and Mgrs. (v.p. 1987-93). Democrat. Lutheran. Avocations: reading, doll making, collecting dolls. Home: 4174 Oakcrest Dr Vadnais Hts MN 55127-7977 Office: Healtheast Midway Healthcare Campus 1700 University Ave Saint Paul MN 55104

HOXTER, CURTIS JOSEPH, international economic adviser, public relations and affairs counselor; b. July 20, 1922; s. Jacob and Hanna (Katzenstein) H.; m. Grace Lewis, Feb. 4, 1945 (dec.); children: Ronald Alan, Victoria Ann, Audrey Theresa; m. Allegra Branson, Jan. 2, 1981. AB, NYU, 1948, MA, 1950. Staff contbr. AUFBAU-Reconstn., N.Y.C., 1939-40; feature writer, reporter L.I. (N.Y.) Daily Press, 1940-42; editor, writer, reporter Office War Info., N.Y.C., 1943-45; pub. info. officer Dept. State, 1945-47; dir. pub. rels. Internat. C. of C., 1948-53; info. cons. Econ. Cooperation Agy., Washington, 1950-55; exec. v.p. George Peabody and Assocs., Inc., 1953-56; pvt. practice, 1956—; pub. rels. cons. various cos.; columnist Scripps-Howard Newspapers; adviser U.S. Com. for UN Day, Internat. Economy mag., on internat. econ. and fin. problems to govt. agys., U.S. Del. Disarmament Conf., London; mem. internat. adv. bd. Bus. Week Chief Exec. Roundtable. Contbr. and commentator articles to nat. mags. and newspapers. With AUS, World War II. Decorated Order of Merit of the Republic of Austria, 1991. Mem. Met. (N.Y.C.), Overseas Press (N.Y.C. chpt.), Nat. Press, Econ. Club N.Y., Leewood Country Club, Coral Beach and Tennis. Office: 380 Lexington Ave New York NY 10168-0002

HOY, CHARLES WILLIAM, III, electrical controls company executive; b. Bossier City, La., July 2, 1953; s. Charles W. and Patsy Louise (Herring) H.; m. Susan Lynette Wagoner, Sept. 29, 1979; children: Charles Christopher, Phillip Henry. Student, La. State U., Shreveport, 1971-76. Field engr. Appleton Elec., Dallas, 1980-84; sales mgr. S.W. region Hazlux Lighting, Houston, 1984-89, O-Z/Gedney Co., Houston, 1989-93; gen. mgr. controls O-Z/Gedney Co., Tulsa, 1993-95, market mgr., 1995-97, also chmn. adv. bd.; tech. sales egr. KSI, Inc., Skiatook, Okla., 1997—. Scoutmaster, commr. Boy Scouts Am., Okla. and Tex., 1979—; vol. various youth activities Bapt. Ch., Okla., Tex. and La., 1971—. Recipient Dist. award of merit Boy Scouts Am., 1991. Mem. IEEE, Intertribal Indian Club of Tulsa (scholar), Shriners, Masons (32d degree). Republican. Avocations: scouting, bluegrass music, fishing, family. Home: 15100 N Peoria Ave Skiatook OK 74070-3258

HOY, CYRUS HENRY, language professional, educator; b. St. Marys, W.Va., Feb. 26, 1926; s. Albert Pierce and Marie Dorothy (West) H. B.A., U. Va., 1950, M.A., 1951, Ph.D., 1954. Instr. English U. Va., 1954-56; asst. prof. Vanderbilt U., 1956-60, asso. prof., 1960-64; prof. English U. Rochester, N.Y., 1964-76, John B. Trevor prof. English and comparative lit., 1976-94, John B. Trevor prof. emeritus, 1994—, chmn. dept. English, 1984-88. Author: The Hyacinth Room, An Investigation Into the Nature of Comedy, Tragedy, and Tragicomedy, 1964; author: intro., notes and commentaries to The Dramatic Works of Thomas Dekker, 4 vols., 1980; mem. editl. bd. Shakespeare Quar., 1968-90, Medieval and Renaissance Drama, 1980-92; gen. editor: Regents Renaissance Drama Series, 1964-76; co-editor Dramatic Works in the Beaumont and Fletcher Canon, Vol. 1, 1966, Vol. 2, 1970, Vol. 3, 1976, Vol. 4, 1979, Vol. 5, 1982, Vol. 6, 1984, Vol. 7, 1989, Vol. 8, 1992, Vol. 9, 1994, Vol. 10, 1996; contbr. articles to profl. jours. Fulbright scholar, 1952-53; Guggenheim fellow, 1962-63. Democrat. Presbyterian. Home: 70 Oliver St Rochester NY 14607-1609 Office: U Rochester Dept English Rochester NY 14627

HOY, GEORGE PHILIP, clergyman, food bank executive; b. Indpls., Feb. 5, 1937; s. Clarence Augustus Hoy and Margaret Louise (Etter) Wooley; m. Barbara J. Turpen, Aug. 11, 1957 (dec. Feb. 1987); children: Rene Hoy Riegle, Sherri Hoy Haas, Matthew Philip; 1 foster child, Richard H. Johnson; m. Margie S. Cissell (div.). BA, Ky. Wesleyan Coll., 1958; MDiv, So. Bapt. Theol. Sem., Louisville, 1962. Ordained to ministry United Ch. of Christ, 1962, Nat. Bapt. Conv. 1997. Pastor Union United Ch. of Christ, Evansville, Ind., 1962-72, Faith United Ch. of Christ, Ft. Wayne, Ind., 1975-80, St. Matthew's United Ch. of Christ, Evansville, 1981-87; dir. Youth Svc. Bur., Evansville, 1972-75; pastor St. Peter's United Ch. of Christ, Evansville, 1987-94; mem. faculty Brescia Coll., Owensboro, Ky., 1970-72; chaplain Evansville State Hosp., 1966-72, Fraternal Order Police, Evansville, 1982-92, chaplain, life mem.; dir. Tri-State Food Bank, Evansville, 1987—; del. gen. synod Ind.-Ky. Conf., United Ch. of Christ, 1978-81. Religion columnist Evansville Press, 1983-93. Vol. Habitat for Humanity, Americus, Ga., 1980-81; mem. City-County Human Rels. Commn., Evansville, 1984-93; bd. dirs. Leadership Evansville, 1987-92, Outreach Ministries, Evansville, 1987-93; mem. regional bd. advisors Ch. World Svc., 1987—; mem. Ill. and Ind. Hunger Coalitions; mem. Bread for the World, Amnesty Internat., Food Rsch. and Action, Police Athletic League; mem. Vanderburgh County Coun., 1992—, pres., 1994-95, v.p., 1997; v.p. Vanderburgh County Coun., 1997; mem. Soil and Water Conservation Dist. Bd.; bd. dirs. Repertory People of Evansville, St. Anthony Ctr. for Family Life, Southwestern Ind. Regional Coun. on Aging; mem. instnl. rev. bd. U. So. Ind.; mem. cmty. adv. coun. Evansville Ctr. for Med. Edn.; mem. Local Emergency Planning Com.; assoc. supr. Vanderburgh County Soil and Water conservation Dist.; chair fin. Pigeon Creek Greenway; assoc. pastor First Ebenezer Bapt. Ch.; chmn. hunger walk CROP; mem. disaster resistant com. Vanderburgh County; walk coord., com. mem. Evansville Stand for Children. Recipient ecumenical award Evansville Area Coun. of Chs., 1987, Native Am. award Coun. of Bear, Evansville, 1988; named to CROP Honor Roll, 1997, Hon. Order Ky. Cols. Mem. NAACP, ACLU, Internat. Brotherhood Magicians, Ind. Psychol. Assn., Tri-State Pastors Circle (pres. 1984-85), Northside Ministerial Assn., Evansville Tri-State Assn. (pres. 1972-75), Isaac Walton League, Greenpeace. Democrat. Avocations: music, art, drama, dance performing, model railroading. Home: 217 Cherry St Evansville IN 47713-1242

HOY, HAROLD HENRY, artist; b. Spokane, Wash., May 16, 1941; s. James K. and Rose Hoy; m. Pei-In Kathy Chen, Arp. 5, 1942. BA, Ctrl. Wash. State U., Ellensburg, 1965; MFA in Painting, U. Oreg., 1967, MFA in Sculpture, 1969. Art instr. Lane Cmty. Coll., Eugene, Oreg., 1970—; lectr. U. Oreg., Eugene, 1974, Lower Columbia Coll., Longview, Wash., 1979, Eastern Wash. U., Cheney, 1979, U. Kans., Lawrence, 1982. One-man shows include William Sawyer Gallery, San Francisco, 1979, U. Oreg. Art Mus., Eugene, 1979, Eastern Wash. U., Cheney, 1979, Blackfish Gallery, Portland, Oreg., 1981, Jackson St. Gallery, Seattle, 1982, Northwest Artists Workshop, Portland, 1982, Project Space Gallery, Eugene, 1982, 84, New Zone Gallery, Eugene, 1985, Internat. Firehouse Cmty. Ctr., Portland, 1987, U. No. Iowa, Cedar Falls, 1989, Portland State U., 1991, Hunt Ctr. Performing Arts, Eugene, 1991, Quartersaw Gallery, Portland, 1991, 93, 95, others; exhibited in group shows at Jackson St. Gallery, Seattle, 1983, Northwest Artists Workshop, Portland, 1983, Project Space Gallery, Eugene, 1983, Artquake, Portland, 1983, 84, Oreg. State U., Corvallis, 1983, Marylhurst (Oreg.) Coll., 1983, Weber State Coll., Ogden, Utah, 1983, Wing Lake Meml. Mus., Seattle, 1984, Pub. Image Gallery, N.Y.C., 1984, Portland Art Mus., 1985, U. Hawaii, Honolulu, 1985, Clark Coll., Vancouver, Wash., 1986, New Zone Gallery, Eugene, 1984, 85, 86, 88, 90, 91, 92, Lane Cmty. Coll., Eugene, 1983, 86, 88, 91, Blackfish Gallery, Portland, 1984, 86, Thinking Eye Gallery, L.A., 1987, Newport (Oreg.) Art Mus., 1984, Kerns Art Ctr., Eugene, 1989, Erb Meml. Union Gallery, U. Oreg., Eugene, 1988, 89, Clackamas Cmty. Coll., Oregon City, Oreg., 1987, 90, Corvallis (Oreg.) Art Ctr., 1989, 90, Art Gallery U. Hawaii, Honolulu, 1991, 94, William Sawyer Gallery, San Francisco, 1993, Hult Ctr. for Performing Arts, Eugene, 1986, 88, 89, 93, 94, Maude Kerns Art Ctr., Eugene, 1985, 87, 88, 90, 92, 94, 95, others. Co-founder, bd. dirs. New Zone Gallery, Eugene, 1984-87; founder, bd. mem. Project Space Gallery, Eugene, 1980-83. Recipient Individual Artist fellowships Oreg. Arts Commn., 1971, 77. Democrat. Office: Lane Cmty Coll 4000 E 30th Ave Eugene OR 97405-0640

HOY, HAROLD JOSEPH, marketing educator, retail executive, management consultant, author, military officer; b. Pine Grove, Pa., Jan. 10, 1934; s. Harold Jefferson and Naomi E. (Fehr) H.; m. Z. Jane Brown, July 2, 1960; children: Kathryn Burgess, Elisabeth Wermuth, Suzanne Hoy-Wong, Kristen Shugrue. BS, Pa. State U., 1955; MBA, U. Hartford, 1973; postgrad., U. Conn., 1981, Harvard U., 1986, Pa. State U., 1990; PhD candidate, U. Bradford., Eng., 1998. Gen. mgr. Montgomery Ward & Co., Chgo., 1963-67, D & L Stores, New Britain, Conn., 1967-81; prof. mktg. Ctrl. Conn. State U., New Britain, 1974-79, U. Conn., Storrs, 1977-79, Pa. State U., 1979-91; pres. H.J. Hoy Assocs. Mgmt. Cons., Pine Grove, Pa., 1979-99; mem. Woodrow Wilson Inst. Internat. Scholars, Washington, 1994-95; founder, dir. Pa. State U. Small Bus. Devel. Ctr., U.S. Small Bus. Inst., Pa. State U., Harrisburg; dir. internat. rsch. scholars Harvard U., 1997. Editl. reviewer various coll. book pubs. and acad. mgmt. and mktg. jours; contbr. articles to profl. jours. Capt. 1st co. Gov.'s Foot Guard Ct. Army N.G., Hartford, Conn. 1st lt. Fin. Corps, U .S. Army. Named Wisdom Hall of Fame fellow, 1997. Mem. Am. Mktg. Assn., Acad. Mktg. Sci., Acad. Internat. Bus., Internat. Coun. for Small Bus., Masons (32 deg.). Avocations: photography, international tourism, philately.

HOY, JAMES F., folklorist; b. Wichita, Kans., Dec. 15, 1939; s. Kenneth L. and Marteil (Rice) H.; m. Catherine J. Thompson, Mar. 13, 1965; children: Farrell, Joshua. BS, Kans. State U., 1961; MA, Kans. State Tchrs. Coll., 1965; PhD, U. Mo., 1970. Instr. English El Dorado (Kans.) Jr. H.S., 1963-65; vis. prof. English Idaho State U., Pocatello, 1975; prof. English Emporia (Kans.) State U., 1970—. Author: The Cattle Guard, 1982, Prairie Poetry, 1995, Cowboys & Kansas, 1995; co-author: Plains Folk, 1987, Plains Folk II, 1992. Bd. dirs. Kans. State Hist. Soc., Topeka, 1992—; trustee Am. Folklife Ctr., Washington, 1996—. Recipient Season award for nonfiction Kans. Quar., 1981. Mem. Am. Assn. Australian Lit. Studies, Western History Assn., Mid-Am. Medieval Assn. (pres. 1980, 96), Medieval Acad. Am., Am. Folklore Soc., Kans. Folklore Soc. (pres. 1974, 85). Avocations: ranching, cowboying, travel, camping. Home: 938 County Rd 130 Emporia KS 66801 Office: Emporia State U 1200 Commercial St Emporia KS 66801-5087

HOY, MARJORIE ANN, entomology educator; b. Kansas City, Kans., May 19, 1941; d. Dayton J. and Marjorie Jean (Acker) Wolf; m. James B. Hoy; 1 child, Benjamin Lee. AB, U. Kans., 1963; MS, U. Calif., Berkeley, 1966, PhD, 1972. Asst. entomologist Conn. Agrl. Expt. Sta., New Haven, 1973-75; rsch. entomologist U.S. Forest Svc., Hamden, Conn., 1975-76; asst. prof. entomology U. Calif., Berkeley, 1976-80, assoc. prof. entomology, 1980-82, prof. entomology, 1982-92, prof. emeritus, 1992—; Fischer, Davies and Eckes prof., dept. entomology and nematology U. Fla., Gainesville, 1992—; chmn. Calif. Gypsy Moth Sci. Adv. Panel, 1982—; mem. genetics resources adv. com. USDA, 1992—; F.E. Guyton disting. lectr. Auburn (Ala.) U., 1997. Editor, co-editor: Genetics in Relation to Insect Managment, 1979, Recent Advances in Knowledge of the Phytoseiidae, 1982, Biological Control of Pests by Mites, 1983, Biological Control in Agricultural IPM Systems, 1985, Insect Molecular Genetics, 1994, The Phytoseiidae as Biological Control Agents of Pest Mites and Insects: A Bibliography, 1996, Managing the Citrus Leafminer, 1996; mem. editorial bd. Exptl. and Applied Acarology, Biol. Control, Biocontrol Sci. and Tech.; contbr. articles to profl. jours. Recipient citation for outstanding achievments in regulatory entomology Fla. Divsn. Plant Industry, 1995, USDA honor award Sec. of Agr., 1996, award for sci. Nat. Agri-Mktg. Assn., 1998, sr. faculty award U. Fla. chpt. Gamma Sigma Delta, 1998. Fellow AAAS, Royal Entomol. Soc. London, Entomol. Soc. Am. (mem. Pacific br. governing bd. 1985, Bussart award 1986, Founder's Meml. award 1992); mem. Am. Genetic Assn., Internat. Orgn. Biol. Control (v.p. 1984-85), Am. Inst. Biol. Scis. (adv. coun. 1996-98, governing bd. 1999—), Acarological Soc. Am. (governing bd. 1980-84, pres. 1992), Soc. for Study of Evolution, Fla. Entomological Soc. (Team Rsch. award 1997, Outstanding Tchg. award 1999), Phi Beta Kappa, Sigma Xi (chpt. sec. 1979-81, Sr. Faculty Rsch. award 1996). Avocations: hiking, gardening, snorkeling. Home: 4320 SW 83rd Way Gainesville FL 32608-4131 Office: U Fla Dept Entomology and Nematology PO Box 110620 Gainesville FL 32611-0620

HOY, WILLIAM, film editor. Prin. works include films The Philadelphia Experiment, 1984, No Way Out, 1986, Silent Assassins, 1986, Best of the Best, 1988, Dances with Wolves, 1990, Star Trek VI: The Undiscovered Country, 1992, Patriot Games, 1992, Sliver, 1993, Judicial Consent, 1994, Outbreak, 1995, Seven, 1995, The Eighteenth Angel, 1996, Man in the Iron Mask, 1998, The Bone Collector, 1999. Office: Broder Kurland Webb & Uffner 9242 Beverly Blvd Ste 200 Beverly Hills CA 90210*

HOY, WILLIAM IVAN, minister, educator; b. Grottoes, Va., Aug. 21, 1915; s. William I. and Ileta (Root) H.; student Lees-McRae Coll., 1933-34; BA, Hampden-Sydney Coll., 1936, DD, 1997; BD, Union Theol. Sem., 1942; STM, Bibl. Sem. N.Y., 1949; PhD, U. Edinburgh, 1952; m. Wilma J. Lambert, Apr. 29, 1945; children: Doris Lambert Hoy Bezanilla, Martha Virginia. Tchr. high sch., Va., 1936-39; interim pastor Asheboro (N.C.) Presbyn. Ch., 1948, 52-53; asst. prof. Bible, Guilford Coll., 1947-48; asst. prof. religion U. Miami, from 1953, prof., 1963-81, chmn. dept. religion, 1958-79, prof. religion emeritus, 1981—; cons. World Coun. Christian Edn., Lima, Peru, 1971. Moderator, Presbytery of Everglades, 1960-61, stated clk., 1968-73, 78-79; interim stated clk. Presbytery of Tropical Fla., 1991-93; moderator Synod of Fla., 1985-86; pres. Greater Miami Ministerial Assn., 1964, 80-82; mem. bd. Christian edn. Presbyn. Ch. U.S., 1969-73, mem. Gen. Assembly Mission Bd., 1978-88; bd. dirs. Met. Fellowship Chs., 1970—, v.p., 1972-73, exec. sec., 1974-76, mem. Task Force on World Hunger, 1978-81; trustee Davidson Coll., 1975-87, trustee South Fla. Ctr. Theol. Studies, 1985-96; participant profl. internat. confs., Barcelona, Lausanne, Rome, Sydney, Goettingen, others, and three White House confs. for religious leaders. Served to comdr. USNR, ret. Decorated Purple Heart; awarded keys of Cities of Miami Beach (twice) and Coral Gables, 1987; named to Honorable Order of Ky. Colonels. Fellow Soc. Sci. Study Religion; mem. Internat. Assn. Historians Religion, Soc. Bibl. Lit., Am. Acad. Religion, Am. Soc. Ch. Hist., Studiorum Novi Testamenti Societas, Scottish Ch. History Soc., Religious Rsch. Assn., Internat. Conf. Sociology of Religion, Am. Oriental Soc., Internat. Sociol. Assn., Res. Officers Assn. (past nat. chaplain, nat. councilman 1965-66, pres. Fla. dept. 1965-66, v.p. for navy dept. Fla.), Seabee Vets. Am., Iron Arrow, Am. Legion, Rotary (pres. S. Miami club 1991-92, Paul Harris fellow (2)), Phi Kappa Phi, Omicron Delta Kappa (province dep., mem. gen. coun. 1971-76, Disting. Svc. Key 1976, Robert L. Morlan Faculty Sec. nat. award 1990), Lambda Chi Alpha Alumni Hall of Fame, 1996, Alpha Psi Omega, Theta Delta, Omega. Co-author: History of the Chaplains Corps, USN, Volume 6; also articles and book revs. in various publs. Home: 5881 SW 52nd Ter Miami FL 33155-6330 Office: PO Box 248348 Miami FL 33124-8348 *It is better to fail at a worthy cause than to succeed at an unworthy one.*

HOYAS, RAYMOND T., state senate official; b. Providence, Feb. 20, 1959. AA, C.C. of R.I., 1981. Clk. R.I. State Senate, Providence, 1989—. Office: RI State Senate State House Rm 114 Providence RI 02903

HOYE, ROBERT EARL, systems science educator; b. Warwick, R.I., Jan. 12, 1931; s. S. Earl and Alice (Landry) H.; m. Patricia Buswell, Aug. 20, 1955; children: Robert Earl Jr., Joanne D., Peter M., Kathleen B. BA, Providence Coll., 1953; MS, St. John's U., N.Y.C., 1955; PhD, U. Wis., Madison, 1973. Instr. St. John's U., 1953-55; dir. guidance Middleboro (Mass.) Pub. Schs., 1955-56, Rutland (Vt.) Pub. Schs., 1956-57; dean Champlain (Vt.) Coll., 1957-58; supt. Frontier Regional Sch. Dist., Deerfield, Mass., 1958-60; New Eng. dir. Sci. Rsch. Assocs. subs. IBM, Chgo., 1960-65; nat. dir. Learning Systems div. Xerox Corp., N.Y.C., 1965-66; dir. Instrnl. Media Lab. U. Wis., Milw., 1966-73; asst. v.p. U. Louisville, 1974-81, prof. cmty. health Sch. Medicine, 1981-92, prof. urban policy, coord. grad. program in health systems, 1981-95, prof. edn., 1992-95, prof. emeritus, 1995—; cons. to mgmt., Louisville, 1966—; prof. health svcs. Walden U., 1988—; vis. prof. exec. leadership U. Sarasota, 1995—; bd. dirs. Alliant Home Health Agy. Author: Index to Computer Based Learning, 1973; co-author: Home Health, 1996; editor Edn. Jour., 1968-73; also articles. Recipient cert. of merit San Diego State U., 1983, Grad. Teaching Excellence award U. Louisville, 1984, gold medal Project Innovation, 1984. Fellow Am. Acad. Med. Adminstrs. (diplomate, chmn. editl. bd. 1986-94), Royal Soc. Health (Statesman in Healthcare Adminstrn. award 1992). Democrat. Roman Catholic. Home: 2238 Wynnewood Cir Louisville KY 40222-6342

HOYE, WALTER BRISCO, retired college administrator; b. Lena, Miss., May 19, 1930; s. William H. and LouBertha (Stewart) H.; m. Vida M. Pickens, Aug. 28, 1954; children—Walter B. II, JoAnn M. B.A., Wayne State U., 1953. Sports/auto editor Detroit Tribune, 1958-65; sports editor Mich. Chronicle, 1965-68; assoc. dir. pub. relations San Diego Chargers Football Co., 1968-76; media liason NFL, 1972-75; community services officer San Diego Coll. Dist., 1976-78; placement officer Ednl. Cultural Complex, San Diego, 1978-80, info. officer, 1980-82, placement officer, adminstrv. asst., 1982-83, placement/program support supr., 1983-91, supr. program support svcs., 1989—; cons. in field. Bd. dirs. San Diego County ARC; active San Diego Conv. and Tourist Bur., Joint Ctr. Polit. Studies, Am. Cancer Soc., San Diego Urban League, Neighborhood Housing Assn., Public Access TV. Named San Diego County Citizen of Month, May, 1979; recipient United Way Award of Merit, 1974. Mem. Internat. Assn. Auditorium Mgrs., Am. Personnel and Guidance Assn., San Diego Career Guidance Assn., Nat. Mgmt. Assn., Assn. Calif. Community Coll. Adminstrs., Calif. Community Coll. Placement Assn., Rocky Mountain Assn. Student Fin. Aid Adminstrs. Home: 6959 Ridge Manor Ave San Diego CA 92120-3146

HOYER, LEON WILLIAM, physician, educator; b. Mpls., Mar. 6, 1936; s. Ludolf J. and Inez (Fuglesteen) H.; m. Diane Desmond Lawrence, Dec. 30, 1960; children: Helen Kristin, Sharon Anne, Erik William. AB, Harvard U., 1958; MD, U. Minn., 1962. Diplomate Am. Bd. Internal Medicine, Nat. Bd. Med. Examiners. Intern and asst. resident in medicine Presbyn. Hosp., N.Y.C., 1962-64; assoc. resident in medicine, fellow in hematology, asst. prof. medicine Strong Meml. Hosp.-U. Rochester Med. Ctr., 1966-70; prof. medicine, head hematology div. U. Conn. Sch. Medicine, Farmington, 1970-85; dir., v.p. rsch. Holland Lab., ARC Biomed. Svcs., Rockville, Md., 1985—; adj. prof. genetics George Washington U., Washington, 1988—, prof. medicine, 1995—; chmn. med. and sci. adv. com. Nat. Hemophilia Found., N.Y.C., 1982-85; mem. hematology study sect. NIH, Bethesda, Md., 1976-80, 87-91. Editor: Factor VIII Inhibitors, 1984, Recombinant Technology in Hemostasis and Thrombosis, 1991, Inhibitors to Coagulation Factors, 1995; contbr. numerous articles and revs. to profl. publs., chpts. to books. J. Macy Found. faculty scholar, 1978-79, Murry Thelin Rsch. award Nat. Hemophilia Found., 1981, grantee Nat. Heart, Lung and Blood Inst., 1968—. Fellow ACP; mem. Am. Soc. Hematology (chair publs. com. 1990-96, councillor 1996-98), Am. Soc. Clin. Investigation, Internat. Soc. Thrombosis and Hemostasis (sci. and standardization com. 1985-90, v.p. XVIIth congress Washington 1999). Achievements include establishment and expansion of largest blood research institute in U.S.; research on the nature of hemophilia and Von Willebrand's disease. Home: 6 Bolling Ln Bethesda MD 20817-4004 Office: Holland Lab 15601 Crabbs Branch Way Rockville MD 20855-2736

HOYER, MARY LOUISE, social worker, educator; b. Wausau, Wis., Dec. 4, 1925; d. Jacob and Julia (Anderson) Stuhlfauth; m. William Henriksen Hoyer, June 30, 1948; children: Mark Charles, Gail Maren. BS in Biochemistry, U. Minn., 1948; MSW, Cath. U., 1985, D of Clin. Social Work, 1994. Lic. cert. clin. social worker, Md.; bd. cert. diplomate in clin. social work. Rsch. biochemist NIH, Bethesda, Md., 1948-50; dir. Teller Tng. Ctr. Internat. Telephone and Telegraph, Washington, 1967-69; specialist employee devel. Civil Svc. Commn., Washington, 1969-75, supr. sys. sect., 1975-78; mgr. agy. assistance divsn. Office Pers. Mgmt., Washington, 1978-82; vol. counselor Comty. Crisis Ctr., Bethesda, 1980-82; classroom and field instr. Cath. U., Washington, 1986-91; clin. social worker St. Francis Ctr., Washington, 1985-88; pvt. practice as clin. social worker Bethesda, 1987—; dep. exec. dir. task force on exec. devel. in sr. exec. svc.: Policy Initiatives for Reform of Civil Svc., Office of Pers. Mgmt., Washington, 1978-79. Contbr. rsch. articles to profl. jours. Precinct chairperson Dem. Action Group, Bethesda, 1962-66; fin. cons. Sch. Bd., Hamilton, Mont., 1950-54; cons. Internat. Visitors Info. Svc., Washington, 1962-66; vol. Md. Fair Housing, Bethesda, 1962-66. Legis. fellow U.S. Congress, Washington, 1980. Mem. NASW, Greater Washington Soc. Clin. Social Workers. Democrat. Lutheran. Home and Office: 5901 Lone Oak Dr Bethesda MD 20814-1845

HOYER, STENY HAMILTON, congressman; b. N.Y.C., June 14, 1939; s. Steen T. and Jean Baldwin (Slade) H.; m. Judith Elaine Pickett, June 17, 1961 (dec. Feb. 1997); children: Susan, Stefany, Anne. BS, U. Md., 1963; LL.B., Georgetown U., 1966. Bar: Md. 1966. Exec. asst. to U.S. senator, 1962-66; mem. Haislip & Yewell, Marlow Heights, Md., 1966-69, Hoyer & Fannon, District Heights, Md., 1969-81; pvt. practice law, 1981—; mem. 97th-106th Congresses from 5th Md. dist., 1981—; mem. appropriations com. 97th-105th Congresses from 5th Md. dist.; chmn. House Dem. Caucus 97th-103rd Congresses from 5th Md. dist., 1989—; mem. Ho. Oversight com. 97th-101st Congresses from 5th Md. dist.; ranking mem. Commn. on Security and Coop. in Europe; mem. appropriations com., oversight com. 105th Congress from 5th Md. Dist.; mem. Md. Senate, 1966-78, pres., 1975-78, chmn. Prince George's County del., mem. fin., joint budget and audit coms., 1968, chmn. joint commn. on intergovtl. cooperation, 1971. Mem. Md. Bd. Higher Edn., 1978-81; mem. Balt. Council Fgn. Relations; bd. visitors U. Md. Sch. Pub. Affairs. Mem. U. Md. Alumni Assn. (trustee), Phi Sigma Alpha, Omicron Delta Kappa, Delta Theta Phi, Sigma Chi. Home: 970 Parlett Morgan Rd Mechanicsville MD 20659-4708 Office: US House of Reps 1705 Longworth HOB Washington DC 20515

HOYLE, SIR FRED, astronomer, mathematician; b. Gilstead, Bingley, Yorks, June 24, 1915; s. Ben and Mabel (Pickard) H.; m. Barbara Clark, 1939; 2 children. MA, Emmanuel Coll. and St. John's Coll., Cambridge U., 19. Fellow St. John's Coll., 1939-72, hon. fellow, 1973—; univ. lectr. math. Cambridge U., 1945-58; staff mem. Mount Wilson and Palomar Obs., Calif., 1956-62; Plumian prof. astronomy and exptl. philosophy Cambridge U., 1958-72, dir. Inst. Theoretical Astronomy, 1966-72; vis. prof. astrophysics Calif. Inst. Tech., 1958—; hon. prof. physics and astronomy Manchester U., 1973—; vis. prof. at large Cornell U., 1973-79; hon. research prof. Cardiff U., 1975—; prof. astronomy Royal Instn., 1969-72. Author: Recent Research in Solar Physics, 1949; Nature of the Universe, 1950; Decade of Decision, 1953; Frontiers of Astronomy, 1955; The Black Cloud, 1957; Ossian's Ride, 1958; A for Andromeda, 1962; Astronomy, 1962; Of Men and Galaxies, 1964; Galaxies, Nuclei and Quasars, 1965; October First is too late, 1966; Man in the Universe, 1966; (with Geoffrey Hoyle) Fifth Planet, 1963, Rockets in Ursa Major 1969, Seven Steps to the Sun, 1970, The Molecule Man, 1971, From Stonehenge to Modern Cosmology, 1972, The Inferno, 1972, Nicolaus Copenicus, 1973, Into Deepest Space, 1974, The Incandescent Ones, 1977, The Westminster Disaster, 1978; Action at a Distance in Physics and Cosmology, 1974, Highlights in Astronomy (U.S.)/Astronomy Today (U.K.), 1975, Astronomy and Cosmology, 1975, Ten Faces of the Universe, 1977, On Stonehenge, 1977, Energy of Extinction: the case for Nuclear Energy, 1977; (with N. C. Wickramasinghe) Lifecloud, 1978, Diseases from Space, 1979, Space Travellers, the Origins of Life, 1980, Evolution from Space; (with J. V. Narlikar) Physics-Astronomy Frontier, 1980; Ice: The Ultimate Human Catastrophe, 1981; Author: (with Geoffrey Hoyle) The Giants of Universal Park, The Frozen Planet of Azuron, The Energy Pirate, The Planet of Death, 1982; Author: The Intelligent Universe, 1983, Comet Halley, 1985, The Small World of Fred Hoyle, 1986, (with N.C. Wickramasingue) Cosmic Life Force, 1988, The Theory of Cosmic Grains, 1991, Our Place in the Cosmos, 1990, Home is Where the Wind Blows, 1993. Recipient Mayhew prize, 1936; Smith's prize, 1938; Goldsmith Exhibitioner, 1938, Sr. Exhibitioner Royal Commn. of 1851, 1938; Kalinga prize, 1968; Gold medal Royal Astron. Soc., 1968, Bruce medal Astron. Soc. of the Pacific, 1970, Royal medal Royal Soc., 1974, Dorothea Klumpke Roberts award Astron. Soc. Pacific, 1977, Dag Hammarskjold Gold medal Academie Diplomatique de la Paix, 1986, Balzan prize, 1994, Karl Schwarzchild medal German Astron. Soc., 1992, Annenberg Astronomy Edn. award Am. Astron. Soc., 1996, Crafoord prize Royal Swedish Acad. Scis., 1997; Hon. fellow Emmanuel Coll., Cambridge, 1983; hon. mem. Am. Acad. Arts and Scis., 1964, Royal Irish Acad., Mark Twain Soc. Fellow Inst. Astronomy Cambridge U. (hon.); mem. Am. Philos. Soc. (fgn.). Fgn. assoc. Nat. Acad. Scis., 1969. Avocations: music; mountaineering. Address: The Royal Soc, 6 Carlton House Terr, London SWIY 5AG, England

HOYLE, WILLIAM VINTON, JR., lawyer; b. Newport News, Va., Apr. 8, 1949; s. William Vinton and Nancy Nelson (Granberry) H.; children: Tiffany Lynn, Suzanne Michelle. BA, Coll. of William and Mary, 1972; JD, U. Richmond, 1982; postgrad. in internat. law, Cambridge U., Eng., 1979. Bar: Va. 1982, U.S. Dist. Ct. (ea. and we. dists.) Va. 1982, U.S. Ct. Appeals (4th cir.) 1982, U.S. Supreme Ct. 1987. Journalist Newport News (Va.) Daily Press, Norfolk Virginian=Pilot, Richmond Times=Dispatch, 1970-79; ptnr. Hoyle, Corbett, Hubbard & Smith, Newport News, 1982-88, Hoyle & Allen, P.C., Newport News, 1989-91; pvt. practice Newport News, 1991—; frequent planner, author, editor, lectr. Va. State Bar profl. seminars. Co-editor, contbg. author: Employment Law in Virginia, 1997—. Bd. dirs. Peninsula Legal Aid Ctr., Inc., 1990—. Mem. Assn. Trial Lawyers Am., Va. Trial Lawyers Assn., Va. Bar Assn., Va. State Bar, Newport News Bar Assn., Nat. Employment Lawyers Assn. Avocations: hunting, sailing, travel, writing.

HOYLES, JOHN D.V., company executive; b. Val D'Or, Que., Can., Oct. 16, 1950; s. Newman John Sankey and Elizabeth Esther (Delamere) H.; m. Sally Ann Kilgour, Aug. 13, 1977; children: Julie, Lesley. BA, U. Ottawa, Ont., 1972; LLB, York U., Toronto, Ont., 1975. Ptnr. Smith & Hoyles, New Liskeard, Ont., 1977-79; dir. of tour Office of the Prime Min., Ottawa, 1979-80; founding ptnr. Byck, Hoyles & Grant, New Liskeard, 1980-90; exec. dir. GST Consumer Info. Office, Ottawa, 1990-91; exec. v.p., gen. mgr. Nat. Capital Commn., Ottawa, 1991-96; exec. dir. Can. Bar Assn., Ottawa, 1996—. Chmn. fundraising Gloucester (Ont.) Arts Ctr., 1995-96. Mem. Camelot Golf and Country Club (corp. sec. 1995-96, bd. govs., pres. 1997—). Home: 13 Diceman Crescent, Gloucester, ON Canada K1B 3Y2 Office: Can Bar Assn Ste 902, 50 O'Connor St, Ottawa, ON Canada K1P 6L2

HOYME, CHAD EARL, packaging company executive; b. Sioux Falls, S.D., Nov. 6, 1933; s. Knute Odell and Martha (Johnson) H.; m. Carolyn Ella Robson, June 21, 1958; children: Christopher, Beth, Amy, Tod. B.S. in Bus. Adminstrn., U. S.D., 1956. Acctg. mgr. Cargill Inc., Mpls., 1956-63; chief acct. Northwest Paper Co., Cloquet, Minn., 1963-65; budget dir. Potlatch Corp., Lewiston, Idaho, 1965-67; corp. controller Potlatch Corp., 1968-72, gen. mgr. folding carton operations, 1972-75; owner Morris Floral Co., Minn., 1975-78; gen. mgr. Consol. Packaging Corp., Clinton, Miss., 1978-82, v.p. paper converting group, 1982-84; gen. mgr. folding carton ops. Manville Forest Products Corp., Clinton, Miss., 1985; v.p., gen. mgr. carton products div. Riverwood Internat. Corp., 1986-91; pres., chief exec. officer Corson Mfg. Co., Lockport, N.Y., 1991-98, chmn., bd. dirs., 1999—; bd. dirs. Cinema 360, Inc.; chmn. bd. dirs. Paperboard Packaging Coun., 1992-94. Bd. dirs. Lockport YMCA, 1994—, Big Bros. Big Sisters of Niagara County, 1995—; mem. Rep. State Ctrl. Com. Idaho, 1968-72; elder Presbyn. Ch., 1989-91. 2d lt. AUS, 1956. Lodges: Elks, Rotary. Home: PO Box 266 Olcott NY 14126-0266 Office: Corson Mfg Co 2024 Michigan St Lockport NY 14094

HOYNES, LOUIS LENOIR, JR., lawyer; b. Indpls., Sept. 23, 1935; s. Louis L. and Catharine (Parker) H.; m. Judith E. Kass, Oct. 12, 1958 (div. 1979); children: Thomas M., William D., Ellen B.; m. Virginia Devin, Dec. 9, 1979. AB, Columbia U., 1957; JD cum laude, Harvard U., 1962. Bar: N.Y. 1963, U.S. Supreme Ct. 1967, U.S. Dist. Ct. (so. dist.) N.Y., U.S. Ct. Appeals (2d, 7th and 9th cirs.). Assoc. Willkie, Farr & Gallagher, N.Y.C., 1962-68, ptnr., 1969-90; counsel Nat. League Profl. Baseball Clubs, 1970-90; sr. v.p., gen. counsel Am. Home Products Corp., 1990—; lectr. law Columbia U., N.Y.C., 1982-91; bd. dirs. Cytec Industries Inc.; trustee Food and Drug Law Inst. Served to lt. USNR, 1957-59, PTO. Mem. ABA, N.Y. State Bar Assn., Assn. of City of Bar of N.Y., The Assn. Gen. Counsel. Home: 47 Cornwells Beach Rd Sands Point NY 11050-1305

HOYT, ANTHONY S., publishing executive; b. N.Y.C., Nov. 3, 1938; s. Everett W. and Elizabeth Alice (Sayer) H.; m. Judith Mervine (div.); m. Kathleen Brown (div.); children: Elizabeth Dow, Robert Everett. Student, U. Va., 1957-60. Account exec. Doherty, Clifford Steas & Shenfield, N.Y.C., 1961-64; account supr. Fuller & Smith & Ross, N.Y.C., 1964-68; sales rep. Time Mag., N.Y.C., 1968-71; account supr. Rumoill-Hoyt, N.Y.C., 1971-73; advt. dir. New York/New West Mags., L.A., 1973-77; prin. Tony Hoyt & Assocs., L.A., 1977-79; assoc. pub. Calif. Mag., L.A., 1979-84; sales mgr./pub. Hearst Mags., L.A., N.Y.C., 1984-95; sr. v.p., pub. Nat. Enquirer/Star, N.Y.C., 1995—. Mem. N.Y. Ad Club. Avocations: golf, tennis. Office: Am Media 415 Madison Ave Fl 15 New York NY 10017-1111*

HOYT, BRADLEY JAMES, financial advisor; b. Spokane, Wash., Sept. 26, 1949; s. Delmar W. and Katherine (Bjerke) H.; m. Carolyn Nirk (div.); 1 child, Bret; m. Christine M. Loomis, Nov. 28, 1977 (div.); 1 child, Harley. BA in Bus. Adminstrn., Eastern Wash. U., 1976; cert., Coll. Fin. Planning, 1987. Adminstrv. asst. Boise Cascade Homes, Post Falls, Idaho, 1976-77, dealer, coordinator, 1977-78; direct sales rep. Boise Cascade Homes, Boise, 1978-80, territorial sales mgr., 1980-81; v.p., office mgr. Cascade Homes, Post Falls, 1981-82; sr. fin. advisor Waddell & Reed, Spokane, 1982-84, sr. acct. exec., 1984—; mem. Pres.'s Coun., Waddell & Reed, 1990-92; pres. Hoyt Ranch, Inc., Spokane, 1978—. Mem. N.W. Natural Resources Bd., 1993—. Mem. Inst. CFPs, Spokane C. of C. (mem. prodn. com. 1987—, 1st v.p. 1988, pres. Ag Expo 1989, chairperson Ag bur. 1994-95). Avocation: motorcycles. Office: Waddell & Reed 11707 E Sprague Ave Spokane WA 99206-6110

HOYT, CHARLEE VAN CLEVE, management executive; b. Bluefield, W.Va., May 21, 1936; d. Charles Ives Van Cleve and Kathryn Margarete (Harden) Perrow; m. Ronald Reiner Hoyt, 1959 (div. 1983); children: Dean Christopher, Jason Allen. BA in Edn., U. Fla., 1959, MEd, 1962, postgrad., 1963-64. Cert. spl. edn. tchr. Tchr. Amherst County Schs., Elon, Va., 1958; tchr. spl. edn. Marion County Schs., Ocala, Fla., 1959-61; counselor Univ. Counseling Ctr., Gainesville, Fla., 1962-63, Sunland Tng. Ctr., Gainesville, 1963; mem. community faculty Minn. Met. State Coll., Mpls., 1972-83; mem. council City of Mpls., 1975-86; ptnr. Van Cleve Assocs., 1980-87, 91—; pres. Van Cleve, Doran & Bruno, Inc. 1987-91; corp. officer BAM Leasing Co., Inc., 1987-97; dir. human resources Pascua Yagu Tribe, 1988-95; adj. faculty U. Phoenix, Tucson, 1995—; vis. tchr. Tucson Unified Sch. Dist., 1995—; pres. Van Cleve Assocs., 1991—; bus. mgr. An Actor's Studio, 1996-98; mem. faculty Govt. Tng. Service, St. Paul, 1978-86, Ariz. Govt. Tng. Services; pres. Minn. Women in City Govt., St. Paul, 1978-79; mem. Met. Land Use Adv. Bd., St. Paul, 1978-83; bd. dirs. Transp. Adv. Bd., St. Paul, 1979-81; mem. conf. faculty League of Minn. Cities, St. Paul, 1979-82; bd. dirs. Met. Council Criminal Justice Adv. Bd., St. Paul, 1979-82; pres. Women in Mcpl. Govt., Nat. League of Cities, Washington, 1980-81, founder minority caucus coalition, 1982, dir., 1982-84; curriculum cons. Nat. Women's Edn. Fund, Washington, trainer, 1982-86; officer JTPA Grantee Orgn. Region IX, 1994—; commr. Pima County/Tuscon Women's Commn. Presenter numerous workshops; contbr. articles to profl. jours. Mem. Women Helping Women YWCA, 1987—; various offices with Republican Party, Minn., 1970-86 ; pres. Burroughs Elem. Sch. PTA, Mpls., 1973-74; panelist White House Conf., 1981; chmn. Senator Durenburger's Task Force on Women's Issues, Mpls., 1981-84; bd. dirs. Nat. Conf. Rep. Mayors and Council Mems., 1984-85; mem. Senator Durenburger's Intergovtl. Relations Adv. Com., Mpls., 1984-86; bd. dirs. Twin Cities Internat. Program, Mpls., 1983-86; participant Women's Dialogue US/USSR, Moscow, 1985; trustee Council Internat. Programs, Cleve., 1985-90; bd. dirs. At the Foot of the Mountain Theater, Mpls., 1985-86, Tucson Ctrs. for Women and Children, 1988-92; bd. dirs. GOP Feminists, Hamline U. Ctr. for Women in Govt.; mem. Nat. Women's Polit. Caucus, Hennepin County Women's Polit. Caucus; mem. Tucson Support for Success Team, 1986-92, Tuscon YWCA Women Helping Women; bd. dirs. Tucson Ctrs. Women and Children. Mem. Am. Soc. Training and Devel., Minn. Women Elected Ofcls. (pres. 1983-85), Izaak Walton League, Tucson C. of C. Methodist. Club: Remington Investment (pres. 1968-70) (Mpls.). Avocations: lapidary, music, handwork, camping, science fiction. Home: 6932 E 2nd St Tucson AZ 85710-1222

HOYT, CHARLES KING, architect, editor; b. Lakehurst, N.J., Apr. 23, 1938; s. Charles Freeland Hoyt and Maude Leslie King. BArch, U. Pa., 1961. Registered arch., N.Y., Conn. Arch. Harrison & Abromovitz, N.Y.C., 1963-66, Edward Larrabee Barnes, N.Y.C., 1966-69; archtl. dir. N.Y. State Urban Devel. Corp., N.Y.C., 1969-73; sr. editor Archtl. Record, 1972-97; pvt. practice house design and renovation Lyme, Conn., 1997—. Author: Buildings for Commerce and Industry, 1978, Public, Municipal and Community Buildings, 1980, Interior Spaces Designed by Architects, 1981, Cities, 1982, More Places for People, 1983; contbr. articles to profl. jours., encys. Fellow AIA (past chair Haskell awards com., N.Y.C. chpt. hist. bldgs. com.); mem. Mcpl. Arts Soc. Hist. Preservation, Profl. Svcs. Mgmt. Assn. (awards jury 1991), Soc. Mktg. Profl. Svcs. (awards jury 1982), Soc. Archtl. Historians, Nat. Trust, Nature Conservancy, Wilderness Soc., Civitas, Smithsonian Instn. Republican. Home and Office: 484 Joshuatown Rd Lyme CT 06371-3034

HOYT, CLARK FREELAND, journalist, newspaper editor; b. Providence, Nov. 20, 1942; s. Charles Freeland and Maude Leslie (King) H.; m. Jane Ann Hauser, Sept. 30, 1967 (div. Jan. 1978); m. Linda Kauss, Aug. 22, 1988. AB, Columbia Coll., 1964. Research asst. to U.S. Senator, Washington, 1964-66; reporter Lakeland (Fla.) Ledger, 1966-68; politics writer Detroit Free Press, 1968-70; Washington corr. Miami Herald, 1970-73; nat. corr. Knight Newspapers, Washington, 1973-75; news editor Washington bur. Knight Newspapers, 1975-77; bus. editor Detroit Free Press, 1977-79, conv. editor, 1979-80, asst. to exec. editor, 1980-81; mng. editor Wichita Eagle-Beacon, Kans., 1981-85; news editor Washington Bur., Knight-Ridder Newspapers, 1985-87, bur. chief, 1987-93, v.p. news, 1993-99, Washington editor, 1999—. Recipient Pulitzer prize nat. reporting, 1973. Mem. Nat. Press Club (fin. sec., bd. govs. 1975), Gridiron Club. Home: D-1004 2440 Virginia Ave NW Washington DC 20037 Office: 700 National Press Bldg Washington DC 20045

HOYT, COLEMAN WILLIAMS, postal consultant; b. N.Y.C., Nov. 11, 1925; s. Colgate and Muriel (Williams) H.; m. Cecilia Lucia Guarana, Oct. 21, 1972; children: Coleman Williams, Andrew Erskine, Stephen Tecumseh. B of Naval Sci., Tufts U., 1945; BS, Yale U., 1948. With Reader's Digest Assn., Pleasantville, N.Y., 1948-87; mgr. book prodn. Reader's Digest Assn., Pleasantville, 1950-61, mgr. book subscription svc., 1961-63, mgr. subscription svc. RCA Victor Record Club, 1963-65, mgr. corp. distbn., 1965-76, v.p., dir. distbn., 1976-87; pvt. practice cons. Woodstock, Vt., 1987—; mem. Postmaster Gen.'s Mailers Tech. Adv. Com., 1968—, chmn., 1971-73. Pub. mem. USIA inspection team, Lebanon, 1971; nat. trustee Outward Bound, Inc., 1972-88; trustee Vt. Land Trust, 1988-93, vice chmn., 1989-92; mem. dir. coun. Nat. Postal Mus., Smithsonian, Washington, 1995—. Ensign USNR, 1943-46. Recipient Disting. Svc. award U.S. Postal Svc., 1973, Donald Mumma award Graphics Comm. Assn., 1987, Miles Kimball award Mail Advt. Svc. Assn., 1987. Mem. Mag. Pubs. Assn. (chmn. postal com. 1974-80), Direct Mktg. Assn. (bd. dirs. 1973-79, chmn. govt. affairs com. 1983-86), Assn. Am. Pubs., Pub. Mems. Assn. of Fgn. Svc., Advt. Mail Mktg. Assn. (bd. dirs. 1982—), Yale Club of N.Y., Squadron A Club, Lakota Club. Republican. Episcopalian. Home and Office: Saddlebow Farm 2351 N Bridgewater Rd Woodstock VT 05091-9670

HOYT, DON, SR., home builder, former association executive; b. North Adams, Mich., Mar. 28, 1930; s. George Washington and Frances (Monroe) H.; m. Dorothy Hess, Mar. 7, 1947 (div. Oct. 1952); m. Ella Mae Lake, Dec. 20, 1952; children: Peggy, Jerry, Linus, Don Jr., Becky, Barbara. Pres. Nat. Trappers Assn., Bloomington, Ill., 1977-85; lic. home builder, 1985—; co-owner Hoyt's Adult Foster Care Home, 1992-98. Mem. Nat. Trappers Assn., Mich. Trappers Assn. (life), NRA (endowment), NRA-ILA (sustaining). Author: Traplines West, 1994. Home: 15412 Tau Rd Marshall MI 49068-9530 Office: 216 N Center St # Bloomington IL 61701-3901

HOYT, HERBERT AUSTIN AIKINS, television producer; b. Buffalo, June 20, 1937; s. John Davidson Hill and Amie Dean (Aikins) H. BA, Yale U., 1959. Reporter Niagara Falls (N.Y.) Gazette, 1963-64; prodr., exec. prodr. WGBH Ednl. Found., Boston, 1965—. Prodr. TV programs including The Advocates, 1969-74, Enterprise: The Wildcatter, 1981, Vietnam: A Television History, Tet 1968, LBJ Goes to War, 1964-65 (Emmy, Writers Guild of Am. awards), Reagan's New Federalism: Shift or Shaft?, 1983, The Nuclear Age, 1989; exec. prodr. Zoom, 1974-75, In Search of the Real America, 1975-78, Frontline Special Report: Crisis in Central America, 1984-85, Mexico, 1988, Korea: The Unknown War, 1990, The American Experience: Eisenhower, 1993, The Windsors, 1994, The Churchills, 1996, The American Experience: Carnegie, The Richest Man in the World, 1997, Reagan, 1998, Mac Arthur, 1999. Mem. Yale Club (N.Y.C.). Office: WGBH 125 Western Ave Boston MA 02134-1098

HOYT, IRVIN N., judge; b. Cavalier, N.D., July 23, 1941; s. Earl and Susie (Steely) H.; m. Charlotte J. Anderson, Dec. 2, 1988; children: Stephan, Tracy, Stacey. BS in Bus. Adminstrn., U. S.D., 1963, JD, 1965. Bar: S.D. 1965, U.S. Dist. Ct. S.D. 1968. Assoc., ptnr. Churchill Sauer Manolis & Hoyt, Huron, S.D., 1965-70; ptnr. Hoyt & Hoyt, Huron, 1970-75; judge Cir. Ct. State of S.D., Huron, 1975-87; judge dist. S.D. U.S. Bankruptcy Ct., Pierre, 1987—; dir. Great Plains Bankruptcy Inst., 1992—; faculty advisor Nat. Coll. State Trial Judges, Reno. States atty. Beadle County, Huron, 1972-74. Mem. Nat. Conf. Bankruptcy Judges, State Bar S.D., S.D. Judges Assn. (pres.). Democrat. Methodist. Avocations: hunting, fishing, tennis. Home: 204 Colony Loop Fort Pierre SD 57532-2223

HOYT, J. BRIAN, light manufacturing company logistics executive; b. Flint, Mich.; s. Harry Dale and Charlene Francis (Smith) H. BSBA, Mich. Technol. U., 1974; MBA, U. Mich., 1976. From ops. rsch. analyst Whirlpool Corp., Benton Harbor, Mich., 1976—. Bd. dirs. First Resource Fed. Credit Union; bd. trustees Mich. Tech. Fund. Mem. Am. Mktg. Assn., Coun. Logistics Mgmt., First Resource Fed. Credit Union (bd. dirs.), Mich. Tech Fund (bd. trustees). Avocations: running, boating, photography. Home: 4970 Notre Dame Ave Stevensville MI 49127-9214 Office: Whirlpool Corp 150 Hilltop Rd # Md7520 Saint Joseph MI 49085-2388

HOYT, JAMES JOHN, educator; b. Apr. 26, 1947. MS, Columbia U., 1973; PhD, NYU, 1989. Counselor Nassau C.C., Garden City, N.Y., 1973—, vice chair faculty senate, 1989-97. E-mail: hoytj@sunynassau.edu. Home: 135 Lido Blvd Lido Beach NY 11561

HOYT, JAMES LAWRENCE, journalism educator, athletic administrator; b. Wausau, Wis., July 18, 1943; s. Lawrence Beryl and Eleanor (Kischel) H.; m. Cheryl Johannes, July 23, 1966; children: Randall James, Rebecca Cheryl, Diane Caroline. BS, U. Wis., 1965, MS, 1967, PhD, 1970; postgrad., U. Pa., 1967-68. Reporter Sta. WTMJ-TV, Milw., 1965-67; prof. journalism Ind. U., Bloomington, 1970-73; writer, editor NBC News, Washington, 1972; prof. journalism U. Wis., Madison, 1973—; dir. U. Wis. Sch. Journalism, Madison, 1981-91; chmn. athletic bd., faculty rep. NACC Big Ten Conf. Western Collegiate Hockey Assn., U. Wis., Madison, 1991—. Author: Mass Media in Perspective, 1984, Writing News for Broadcast, 1994; contbr. articles to profl. jours. Mem. Assn. for Edn. in Journalism and Mass Comm., Radio-TV News Dirs. Assn., Broadcast Edn. Assn., Internat. Radio-TV Soc. Methodist. Avocation: ice hockey. Home: 4709 Fond Du Lac Trl Madison WI 53705-4812 Office: U Wis Sch Journalism 821 University Ave Madison WI 53706-1412

HOYT, JOHN ARTHUR, humane society executive; b. Marietta, Ohio, Mar. 30, 1932; s. Claremont Earl and Margaret Adeline (Hawkins) H.; m. Gertrude Ellen Mohnkern, June 7, 1957; children: Margaret Rose, Karen Elizabeth, Anne Christine, Julie Kay. BA, Rio Grande Coll., 1954, DD, 1968; MDiv, Colgate Rochester Div. Sch., 1958; Dr honoris causa, U. Bucharest, Romania, 1995; LHD (hon.), St. Thomas U., Miami, Fla., 1998, U. St. Petersburg, Russia, 1997. Ordained to ministry Baptist Ch., 1957; pastor Allen Park (Mich.) Bapt. Ch., 1958-60, First Presbyn. Ch., Leroy, N.Y., 1960-64; sr. minister Drayton Ave. Presbyn. Ch., Ferndale, Mich., 1964-68, First Presbyn. Ch., Fort Wayne, Ind., 1968-70; pres. Humane Soc. U.S., Washington, 1970-91, chief exec., 1992-97; pres. emeritus, 1997—; pres. Humane Soc. Internat., Washington, 1991-94; pres., dir. Humane Soc. of Can., Toronto, 1994-98; vice chmn. bd. dirs. EarthKind Internat., Washington, London, 1991-98; pres. Earthkind, U.S., Washington, 1994-97. Author: Animals in Peril: How "Sustainable Use" is Wiping Out the World's Wildlife, 1994. Pres. Nat. Assn. for Humane and Environ. Edn., East Haddam, Conn., 1970-94, chmn. bd. dirs. 1973-95; trustee Rio Grande (Ohio) Coll., 1979-86, Lake Erie Coll., Painesville, Ohio, 1986-88; bd. dirs. The Am. Fondouk, Boston, 1986-97, Earth Day 1990, 1989-90, Global Tomorrow Coalition, 1989-94; pres. World Soc. for Protection of Animals, London, 1986-90, v.p., 1990-98; pres. dir. Ctr. for Respect Life and Environment, Washington, 1986-98; pres., dir. Internat. Ctr. Earth Concerns, Calif., 1994-98; dir. Grupo de los Cien, Mex., 1994-98, Counterpart Internat., Washington, 1997—; mem. Earth Charter Commn.; v.p. Internat. Devel. Conf., Washington, 1997-99. Recipient Disting. Alumnus award Rio Grande Coll., Founders award for Humane Excellence ASPCA, 1991, George T. Angell Humanitarian award Mass. SPCA, 1992, Pres.'s Disting. Ministry award Sch. of Theology at Claremont, Calif., 1995, Reverence for Life Commendation Albert Schweitzer Inst. for the Humanities, 1998. Home: 320 Bear Castle Dr Bumpass VA 23024-4925 Office: Humane Soc US 2100 L St NW Washington DC 20037-1525

HOYT, KENNETH BOYD, educational psychology educator; b. Cherokee, Iowa, July 13, 1924; s. Paul Fuller and Mary Helen (Tinker) H.; m. Phyllis June Howland, May 25, 1946; children: Andrew Paul, Roger Alan, Elinore Jane. B.S., U. Md., 1948; M.A., George Washington U., 1950; Ph.D., U. Minn., 1954; Ed.D. (hon.), Crete Coll., 1981. Tchr., counselor Northeast (Md.) High Sch., 1948-49; dir. guidance Westminster (Md.) High Sch., 1949-50; tchg. asst. U. Minn., 1950-51, instr. ednl. psychology, 1951-54; asst. prof. U. Iowa, Iowa City, 1954-57; assoc. prof. U. Iowa, 1957-60, prof. edn., 1961-69; dir. Splty. Oriented Student Research Program, prof. edn. U. Md., Silver Spring, 1969-74; dir. office career edn. U.S. Office Edn., 1974-82; disting. vis. scholar Embry Riddle Aero. U., 1982-84; Univ. Disting. prof. edn. Kans. State U., 1984—; dir. counseling high skills vo-tech career options program Kansas State U., 1993-98; cons. Ordnance Civilian Personnel Agy., 1954-60, Iowa Dept. Pub. Instrn., 1954-69, U.S. Dept. Labor, 1956-68, 65—, U.S. Office Edn., 1958—, Nat. Inst. Edn., 1973—. Author: (with L.A. Van Dyke) The Drop-Out Problem in Iowa High Schools, 1958, (with C.P. Froehlich) Guidance Testing, 1960, Selecting Employees for Developmental Opportunites and Guidance Services; Suggested Policies for Iowa Schools, 1963, Career Education: Contributions to an Evolving Concept, 1976, Career Education: Where It Is and Where It Is Going, 1981; co-author: Career Education: What It Is and How To Do It, 1972, Career Education and the Elementary School Teacher, 1973, Career Education in the Middle Junior High School, 1973, Career Education for Gifted and Talented Students, 1974, Career Education in the High School, 1977; Editor: Counselor Education and Supervision, 1961-65; Mem. editorial bd.: Personnel and Guidance Jour, 1960-63; Contbr. articles to profl. jours. Served with AUS, 1943-46. Fellow APA (divsn. 17); mem. Am. Counseling Assn. (pres. 1966-67, Arthur Hitchcock Outstanding Disting. Profl. Svc. award, 1994), Am. Vocat. Assn. (Outstanding Svc. award 1972), Assn. Counselor Edn. and Supervision (Disting. Svc. award 1965, Outstanding Career award 1990), Nat. Career Devel. Assn. (Eminent Career award 1981, pres. elect 1991-92, pres. 1992-93), Am. Sch. Counselors Assn., Am. Ednl. Rsch. Assn., Nat. Assn. for Industry Edn. Cooperation (vice-chmn. 1992—), Phi Delta Kappa. Home: 149 N Dartmouth Dr Manhattan KS 66503-3021 Office: Kans State U Coll of Edn 369 Bluemont Hall Manhattan KS 66506-5300

HOYT, KENNETH M., federal judge; b. 1948. AB, Tex. So. U., 1969, JD, 1972. Mem. firm Wickliff, King, Hoyt & Jones, 1972-75, Anderson, Hodge, Jones & Hoyt, 1975-79, Webster & Andrews, 1979-81; presiding judge 125th Civil Dist. Ct., 1981-82; pvt. practice law Kenneth M. Hoyt & Assocs., 1983-85; justice U.S. Ct. Appeals (1st cir.), 1985-88; judge U.S. Dist. Ct. (so. dist.)Tex., Houston, 1988—; faculty trial advocacy program South Tex. Coll., 1981-82; adj. prof. Thurgood Marshall Sch. Law, 1983-84. Contbr. articles to profl. jours. Former bd. dirs. Bus. and Profl. Men's Club; judge trial advocacy program U. Houston, 1982-84, 87-88; former mem. Juvenile Justice & Delinquency Prevention Adv. Bd., Blue Ribbon Commn., Rev. Criminal Justice Corrections System, Referendum Force, Selection of Judges; former mem. adv. bd. Parents of Murdered Children and Coalition of Victims Rights; formerly active Salvation Army; former chmn. Capital Devel. Com., Wheeler Ave. Bapt. Ch.; past dir. Houston Lawyer's Referral Svc. With USNG, 1972-78. Decorated Am. Spirit medal; recipient Outstanding Community Svc. award Kendleton, Tex., Ethel Ranson Art & Literary Club award, Outstanding Acheivement award Thurgood Marshall Sch. Law Alumni Assn., 1986; named one of Most Outstanding Black Rep. South Tex. Mem. Nat. Bar Assn., State Bar Tex. (task force, minimum continuing legal edn.). Office: US District Courthouse 9513 US Courthouse Houston TX 77002 Office: US District Courthouse Suite 11144 515 Rusk St Houston TX 77002-2605*

HOYT, MARY FINCH, author, editor, media consultant, former government official; 2 children. Free-lance mag. writer, speechwriter, formerly with Ladies' Home Jour. mag.; info. officer Peace Corps; pres. sec. to Mrs. Edmund Muskie, 1968, pres. sec. to Mrs. George McGovern, 1972, former ptnr. McClure, Schultz and Hoyt (pub. rels.).; press sec. to Mrs. Rosalynn Carter and East Wing coord. The White House, Washington, 1977-81; dir. communications Nat. Trust for Hist. Preservation, Washington, 1989-93; author, editor, media cons., 1993—. Author: American Women of the Space Age, 1966, (with Eleanor McGovern) Uphill: A Personal Story, 1974. Mem. Presdl. Commn., 1977. Democrat.

HOYT, MONT POWELL, lawyer; b. Oklahoma City, Apr. 3, 1940; s. Lester Dean and Paula (Powell) H.; m. Alice Nathalie Ryan, June 15, 1974; children: Mont Powell Jr., Kathleen, Michael, Caroline. B.A., Northwestern U., 1962; J.D., Okla. Law Sch., 1965; M in Comparative Law, U. Chgo., 1968. Bar: Okla. 1965, Tex. 1968, D.C. 1991. Law clk. U.S. Dist. Ct., Oklahoma City, 1965; stagiaire to French advocat Paris, 1967-68; assoc. Baker & Botts, Houston, 1968-75, ptnr., 1975-92; shareholder Verner, Liipfert, Bernhard, McPherson & Hand, Houston, 1993-94; ptnr. Hughes & Luce, Houston, 1994—; adj. prof. U. Houston, 1970-76;. Contbr. articles to profl. jours. Bd. dirs. French Am. Found., N.Y.C., 1979-85, Mexican Cultural Inst., 1991-95, Fgn. Policy Assn., 1991-93; mem. Latin Am. adv. bd. Americas Soc., 1992—; elder Meml. Drive Presbyn. Ch., 1973-76, 83-86. Mem. ABA (chmn. sect. internat. law and practice 1984-85), Internat. Bar Assn. (coun. sect. of energy and nat resources law 1983-86), Am. Law Inst., Am. Soc. Internat. Law, Am. Arbitration Assn., German Am. C. of C. (bd. dirs. 1978-94), InterAm. C. of C. (bd. dirs. 1991-99, chmn. 1996-98), U. Chgo. Law Sch. Alumni Assn. (v.p. 1990-91), Coun. on Fgn. Rels. (chmn. Houston 1991-92), Houston Country Club (Houston), Met. Club (Washington). Avocations: Spanish language study, running, international affairs, ham radio. Office: PO Box 131026 Houston TX 77219-1026

HOYT, NELLY SCHARGO (MRS. N. DEMING HOYT), history educator; b. Nicolaev, USSR, Jan. 15, 1920; came to U.S., 1941, naturalized, 1946; d. Simon S. and Vera (Rivkind) Schargo; m. N. Deming Hoyt, Sept. 7, 1946; children: Susan, Victor. Bacc. es Lettres, Musee de l'Homme, 1939, certificate Anthropologie, 1940; B.A., Smith Coll., 1943; M.A., Columbia U., 1944, Ph.D., 1946. Research analyst U.S. Mission to UN, 1946-48; cons. research in comtemporary cultures Columbia U. Mus. Natural History, 1949-53; prof. dept. history Smith Coll., 1949-90, Achilles prof. history, 1974-90, Achilles prof. emeritus history, 1990—, chmn. dept., 1977-79, dir. Jr. Yr. in Geneva program, 1983-84; exchange prof. Hamburg U. Hist. Seminar, Apr.-July 1985, 88; dir. Jr. Yr. in Hamburg program, 1991-92. Editor: Smith Coll. Studies in History, 1961-83; author: (with T. Cassirer) Selections from Diderot's Encyclopedia, 1965, History in the Encyclopédie, 2d edit., 1970, Study of Culture at a Distance, 1950; contbr. (with T. Cassirer) articles to profl. jours. Bd. dirs. Alumnae Assn., chmn. assn. edn. com., 1972-79; cons. Mus. Fine Arts, Springfield, Mass., 1979-80. Mem. Société du Dixhuitième Siècle. Home: 11 Jewett St Northampton MA 01060-2807

HOYT, RICHARD COMSTOCK, economics consulting company executive; b. St. Paul, Sept. 30, 1939; s. Charles Richardson and Minnie (Comstock) H.; BS, Kans. State U., 1961; MS, U. Minn., 1968, PhD, 1972; m. Ingrid Langensiepen, Oct. 24, 1964; children: Monika Anna, Derek Richard. Milling engr. Tennant & Hoyt Co., Lake City Minn., 1971-72, pres., 1972; rsch. asst. U. Minn., 1968-71; pres. Analytics, Inc., Excelsior, Minn., 1973—; lectr. in field; adj. prof. law U. Minn., 1998. Founder, exec. dir. Youth Hunting Club, Minn., 1993. Served with C.E., U.S. Army, 1962-65. Mem. Am. Econ. Assn., Am. Agrl. Econ. Assn., Am. Coll. Forensic Examiners, Am. Law & Econ. Assn., Nat. Assn. Forensic Econs., Mgmt. Sci. Assn. Republican. Contbr. articles in field to profl. jours. Home: 5710 Ridge Rd Excelsior MN 55331-9147 Office: 464 2nd St Excelsior MN 55331-1963

HOYT, ROSEMARY ELLEN, tax accountant; b. Iowa City, Iowa, Apr. 12, 1949; d. Joseph Asa Hoyt and Mary Jane (Brobst) Vandermark; m. Louis O. Scott, Oct. 16, 1965 (div. Nov. 1968); children: Wayne L. Lawson, Jo Anna Jane Kollasch; m. David K. Duckworth, July 23, 1983 (div. Dec. 1994); 1 child, Mary Rose Duckworth. Cert. in applied banking/consumer credit, Am. Inst. Banking, 1988; BBA, So. Calif. U., 1992, MBA, 1997. Cert. in trust adminstrn; cert. trust ops. specialist; cert. in trust tax. Teller Community Bank of Fla., St. Petersburg, 1973-75; bookkeeper Chevron Svc. Sta., St. Petersburg, 1975-77, Landmark Bank, St. Petersburg, 1977-80; teller First Nat. Bank of Ely, Nev., 1981, Nev. Bank and Trust, Ely, 1982; asst. v.p. and trust officer First Nat. Bank Farmington, N.Mex., 1983-96; tax acct. Bank One, Westerville, Ohio, 1997—; pres., founder Day Camp Southside, St. Petersburg, 1976-77. Planning chmn. terr. 5 ann. meeting ARC, Farmington, 1990-91, babysitting instr., 1990-96, basic aid tng. instr., 1992, Project Read instr., 1994; coord. United Way, 1997. Recipient Appreciation award ARC, 1991. Mem. Fin. Women Internat. (by-laws com. 1990-91, treas. 1993-94), Nat. Assn. Trust Ops. Specialists (bd. dirs. 1992), Am. Bus. Women's Assn. (v.p. 1991, pres. 1992, Appreciation award 1989, Woman of Yr. 1995). Republican. Methodist. Avocations: crocheting, cooking, gardening. Office: Bank One 774 Park Meadow Rd Westerville OH 43081-2871

HOYT, WILLIAM, city planner; b. Cleve., Ohio, Aug. 19, 1942. BA, Ohio State U., 1965, MA, 1970, PhD, 1980. Planning supr. City of Columbus, Ohio, 1975-85; dir. planning dept. City of Grand Rapids, Mich., 1985—. Office: City of Grand Rapids Planning Dept 300 Monroe Ave NW Grand Rapids MI 49503-2281

HOYT, WILLIAM LLOYD, chief justice; b. St. John, N.B., Can., Sept. 13, 1930; s. Lloyd Albert and Dorothy Alice Ruth (Fraser) H.; m. Joan Elizabeth Millier, Sept. 4, 1954; children: Martha, Janet, Susan. BA, Acadia U., Wolfville, N.S., Can., 1952, MA, 1952; BA in law, U. Cambridge, Eng., 1956. Bar: N.B., 1957. Lawyer Hoyt, Mockler, Allen & Dixon, Fredericton, N.B., 1957-81; judge Ct. of Queen's Bench of N.B., St. John, 1981-84; judge Ct. of Appeal of N.B., Fredericton, 1984-93, 98—, chief justice of N.B., 1993-98; mem. Fredericton Barristers' Soc., 1957-81, pres., 1970-71; mem. N.B. Barristers' Soc., 1957-81, coun., 1970-72, 75-79, chmn. profl. conduct com., 1971-72, 77-79, course leader civil litigation bar admission course, 1972-77; mem. Can. Inst. for Advanced Legal Studies, Cambridge, Eng., 1979, 89; mem. N.B. Fed. Jud. Appointments Com., 1988-90, chmn., 1988-90; lectr. in field. Bd. govs. Beaverbrook Art Gallery, Fredericton, 1979-87, chmn. acquisitions com., 1980-87. Recipient Queen Elizabeth II's Silver Jubilee medal, 1977, 125th Anniversary of Can. Confedn. medal, 1992. Mem. Can. Bar Assn. (nat. coun. 1973-79, pres. N.B. br. 1975-77, com. on the Can. constn. 1977-78), Can. Inst. for the Adminstrn. of Justice (dir. 1979-83), Can. Judges Conf. (dir. 1985-89), N.B. Jud. Coun. (vice-chmn. 1988—), Can. Inst. Internat. Affairs (pres. Fredericton br. 1970-71). *

HOZESKI, BRUCE WILLIAM, English language and literature educator; b. Grand Rapids, Mich., Feb. 28, 1941; s. Gerard Thadeus and Dorothy Elizabeth (Platschore) H.; m. Kathleen Antoinette Tuma, Sept. 9, 1967; 1 child, Alison Michelle. AA, St. Peter's Coll., Balt., 1961; BA, Aquinas Coll., 1964; MA, Mich. State U., 1966, PhD, 1969. Instr. Lansing (Mich.) Community Coll., 1967-69; grad. asst. Mich. State U., East Lansing, 1964-69; from asst. prof. to prof. English Ball State U., Muncie, Ind., 1969—; dir. grad. programs in English Ball State U., 1999—. Author: Hildegard of Bingen's Scivias, 1986, Hildegard of Bingen's Liber Vitae Meritorum, 1993, Hildegard of Bingen: The Book of the Rewards of Life, 1997, Hildegard von Bingen's Mystical Visions, 1998; bibliographer: (with Lorrayne Y. Baird-Lange and Bege K. Bowers) An Annotated Chaucer Bibliography, 1989, 90, 91, 92, Studies in the Age of Chaucer; contbr. An Annotated Chaucer Bibliography, 1993, 94, 95, 96, 97, 98, Studies in the Age of Chaucer; mem. editl. bd. Classical and Modern Lit., A Quar., 1988—; editor-in-chief, mng. editor Ball State U. Forum, 1984-90; contbr. chpts. to books, articles to profl. jours. Mem. Medieval Acad. Am., Early English Text Soc., New Chaucer Soc., The Medieval and Renaissance Drama Soc., Medieval Assn. Midwest (editor 1982-85), Internat. Soc. Hildegard (exec. coun. 1989—, pres. 1984-89), Lambda Iota (exec. sec., treas.). Roman Catholic. Avocations: tennis, flower gardening. Home: 7404 W Augusta Blvd Yorktown IN 47396-9353 Office: Ball State U Dept English 2000 W University Ave Muncie IN 47306-0460

HOZUMI, MOTOO, medical educator, medical researcher; b. Fukushima, Japan, Mar. 12, 1933; s. Akiine and Fumi Hozumi; m. Sakiko Wakabayashi, May 4, 1963; children: Yuko, Masamichi, Ayako. BSc, Tokyo U. Edn., 1956, MSc, 1958, Dsc, 1961. Rsch. mem. Nat. Cancer Ctr. Rsch. Inst., Tokyo, 1962-64, chief ctrl. lab., 1964-75; dir. dept. chemotherapy Saitama (Japan) Cancer Ctr. Rsch. Inst., 1975-93, dir., 1990-93; spl. rsch. Saitama (Japan) Cancer Ctr., 1993-96; rsch. mem. Roswell Park Meml. Inst., Buffalo, N.Y., 1965-67; vis. prof. Showa U. Med. Sch., Tokyo, 1988—; cons. Japan Immunoresearch Inst., Takasaki, Japan, 1993-98. Author: Advances in Cancer Research, 1983, Ciba Foundation Symposium, 1990, Status of Differentiation Therapy, 1991, (rev. jour.) CRC Critical Rev. Oncol./Hematol., 1985. Recipient Princess Takamatsu Cancer Rsch. Found. prize, 1974. Mem. AAAS, Japanese Cancer Assn. (councilor 1973-98), Japan Hematol. Soc. (councilor 1992-98), Am. Assn. for Cancer Rsch., N.Y. Acad. Scis. Avocation; music. Home: 12-288 Fukasaku, Omiya Saitama 330, Japan

HRABOWSKI, FREEMAN ALPHONSA, III, university president; b. Birmingham, Ala., Aug. 13, 1950; s. Freeman A. II and Maggie (Geeter) H.; m. Jacqueline Coleman, Aug. 29, 1970; 1 child, Eric. BA, Hampton (Va.) Inst., 1970; MA, U. Ill., 1971, PhD, 1975. Asst. dean student svcs., vis. asst. prof. U. Ill., Champaign-Urbana, 1974-76; assoc. dean grad. studies Ala. A&M U., Normal, 1976-77; v.p. for acad. affairs, dean arts and scis. Coppin State Coll., Balt., 1977-87; exec. v.p. U. Md. Baltimore County, Balt., 1987-92, interim pres., 1992-93, dir. Meyerhoff scholarship program, 1989-93, pres., 1993—. Co-author: Beating the Odds, 1998. mem. Md. Gov.'s commn. on State taxes and Tax Structure, Annapolis, 1990, co--chair Md. Gov.'s Transition Policy Group on Edn., 1994-95; chair Md. Humanities Coun., Balt., 1991; bd. dirs. U. Md. Med. Sys., Balt. Gas and Electric Co., Balt. Equitable Soc, France/Merrick Found., McCormick & Co., Mercantile Safe Deposit & Trust Co., Md. Acad. of Scis., Greater Balt. Com., Loyola Coll. of Md., 1994-97, Balt. Community Found., Joint Ctr. for Polit. and Econ. Studies. Recipient 20 Yr. Outstanding Alumnus award Hampton U., 1990. Baptist. Home: 18 Aston Ct Owings Mills MD 21117-1439 Office: U Md Balt County Office of President 1000 Hilltop Cir Baltimore MD 21250-0001*

HRACHOVINA, FREDERICK VINCENT, osteopathic physician and surgeon; b. St. Paul, Minn., Sept. 2, 1926; s. Vincent Frank and Beatrice (Funda) H.; m. Joan Halverson, July 2, 1955. BA in Chemistry, Macalester Coll., St. Paul, 1948; DO, Kirksville Coll. Osteo. Med., Mo., 1956. Chemist Mpls.-St. Paul area, 1948-51; intern Clare Gen. Osteo. Hosp., Mich., 1956-57; pvt. practice Mpls. Minn., 1957-84; asst. prof. osteo. principles and practices Southeastern Coll. Osteo. Medicine, North Miami Beach, Fla., 1985-88; founder, pres. Physician Placement Svc., Fla. and Minn., 1973—; med. dir. Associated Bioscience, Inc., Mpls., 1992, Sera-Tec Biologicals Inc., Jacksonville, Fla., 1993-94; staff physician Allegheny Biologicals, Inc., Jacksonville, 1995-96; med. dir. Serologicals, Jacksonville, 1996; med. ins. examiner Hooper Holmes, Inc., St. Petersburg, Ft. Myers, Fla., 1997—; ins. med. examiner Examination Mgmt. Svcs., Inc., Tampa, Ft. Myers, Fla., 1998—; lectr. Internat. Acad. Osteo. Medicine, Brussels, 1984; mem. Northlands Regional Med. Program, Inc., 1971-73; mem. Health Svcs. Devel. Com., Regional Adv. Group; founder, faculty advisor Fla. Acad. Osteopathy Student Assn., Southeastern Coll. Osteo. Medicine, North Miami Beach, Fla., 1987; staff physician Centeon Bio-Svcs. Plasma Corp., St. Paul, Mpls., summer, 1998. Author: Microscopic Anatomy, 1952; Methods of Development of New Osteopathic Medical Colleges in the Next Millennium, 1977. Contbr. articles to profl. jours. Mem. Crow Wing County (Minn.) Portage-Crooked Lake Preservation Soc., 1977—, Sr. Citizen Assn., Garrison, Minn., 1991—, Deerwood Civic and Commerce Assn., Deerwood, Minn., 1992—; chmn. street lights program Pinebrook South, Venice, Fla. Grantee Smith Kline & French Labs., 1973, 89, Hill Labs, Gusman Med. Equipment, 1987. Mem. Am. Coll. Osteo. Family Practice, Am. Osteo. Assn. (life, coun. fed. health programs, drug enforcement adminstrn. prescribers working com. 1974-75), Am. Acad. Osteopathy (life), Am. Assn. Sr. Physicians, Am. Osteo. Acad. Sports Medicine (life), Am. Blood Resources Assn., Am. Assn. Blood Banks, Gulf Coast Hibiscus Soc. (presdl. liason to Venice C. of C. 1996), Minn. Osteo. Assn. (life, pres. 1965-66, exec. dir. 1966-74, pub. rels. dir. 1974-75), Assn. Osteo. State Exec. Dirs. (pres. 1970-71, dir. 1971-74, founder nat. legis. sem. 1974), Fla. Soc. Coll. Osteopathic Family Practice (lectr. Mo. soc.), Fla. Acad. Osteopathy (bd. trustees, chmn. audit and membership com.), Fla. Osteo Found. (v.p.), Ga. Osteopathic Med. Assn. (chmn. Olympic com. 1995-96), Fla Osteo. Med. Assn. (Dade county chpt. chmn. osteo. lit. com., conv. chmn. dist. two 1994, dist. #7 Sarasota County, chmn. legis. com. dist. 11), Fla. Osteopathic Med. Soc. (dist. 5, 7, 11), Internat. Acad. Osteo. Medicine (bd. trustees), Minn. Gymnastic Assn. (founder 1962-72), Fla. Acad. Osteopathy Student Assn. at Southeastern Coll. Osteopathic Medicine (originator, advisor), Dade-Broward Osteopathic Med. County Soc., Duval County Osteopathic Soc., Sarasota County Osteo. Soc., Twin-City Model A Ford Club, Pierce Arrow Soc. (sec. Fla. region 1988, news reporter Arrow Driver Midwest region, Mpls., life, founder Midwest region, 1983, dir./treas., 1983-84, gen. chmn. Midwest region swapmeet, Golden Valley, MN, 1990, nat. dir. 1983-84, contbr. articles to Arrow Jour.), Venice C. of C. (mem. membership com., mem. amb. com.), Cadillac LaSalle Club (founder 1978, treas. North Star region 1978-83), Classic Car Club Am. (life, membership chmn. Minn. upper midwest region 1977, sec. 1978, Gold Coast region-Fla.), Antique Auto Club. Am. (life, news reporter St. Paul chpt., Minn. region, Ft. Lauderdale region, Jacksonville region, Venice chpt., Lemon Bay region, judge at nat. meet Venice, Fla. 1997), Breakfast club Mpls., Y.E.S. Club 1st Nat. Bank Deerwood (Minn.), Scottish Rite, Valley of St. Paul, Lions (Bay Lake, Minn. del. to internat. conv., Miami, Fla., 1989), Optimist Club (dir. Mpls. 1959-62, 69-72, pres. 1970-71, gen. chmn. fl. exercise Olympic gynmastic program 1959-65), Masons (life, Capitol City #217, St. Paul), Shriners (life mem. Zuhrah Shrine Temple, Mpls., fund raising com.), Phi Sigma Gamma (life, nat. pres. 1987-89, pres. grand coun. and found. 1987-89, grand coun. advisor and chmn. bd.), Arlington Shrine Club (Jacksonville), Cummer Gallery of Art and Gardens (Jacksonville), Arlington Preservation Soc. (Jacksonville), Venice Shrine Club (Fla.), Aadzuhma Shrine Club (Brainerd, Minn.). Home: 1238 Lucaya Ave Venice FL 34292-1407

HRANIOTIS, JUDITH BERINGER, artist; b. N.Y.C., Jan. 11, 1944; d. Richard Frederick and Barbara Ann (Blight) Beringer; children: Anthony J. Bellantoni, Robert John Bellantoni; m. Peter Hraniotis; stepchildren: Christine Hraniotis, Terry Hraniotis, Helen Finn. Student, Sch. Visual Arts, N.Y.C., 1962, NYU, 1994; studied with, John Hamburger. Exhibited in group, juried shows at Hudson Valley Art Assn., 1998, 99, White Plains, N.Y., 1990, 91, 97, 98, Milford (Conn.) Arts Ctr. 1991-95, The Am. Artists Profl. League, N.Y.C., 1991, 95, 96, Catharine Lorillard Wolfe Art Club, N.Y.C. 1991, 92, 95, 96, 97, 98, 99, Kent (Conn.) Art Assn., 1991, 92, 93, 94, 95, 96, 97, 98, 99, Ridgewood (N.J.) Art. Inst., 1992, 1999, Mt. St. Mary Coll., Newburgh, N.Y., 1993, 96, Arts. Coun., Orange County, Middletown, 1994, Mamaroneck Artist Guild at Westbeth Gallery, N.Y.C., 1994, Green County Coun. on the Arts, N.Y., 1996, Salmagundi Club, 1997, CLWAC-Broome St. Gallery, N.Y.C., 1999. Recipient 1st Pl. Graphics award Mt. St. Mary Coll., 1994, 96, Newburgh, 1990, 91, Grumbacher Silver medal Mt. St. Mary Coll., 1993, 1st Pl. Graphics award Ann. Open Art Exhibit, Arts Coun. of Orange County, 1994, Dutchess County Art Assn., 1995, 97. Fellow Am. Artist Profl. League, Catherine Lorillard Wolfe Art Club (bd. dirs., asst. treas.); mem. Nat. Mus. of Women in the Arts, Kent Art Assn. (bd. dirs., rec. sec. 1993-95, 96, 97, 98, 99, Cert. of Merit, 1991, 96), Hudson Valley Art Assn. (elected), Woodstock Art Assn. (Prof. Active Artist), Scenic Hudson, Sierra Club, Salmagundi Club N.Y.C. Republican. Avocations: perennial gardening, local history, international cooking, amateur naturalist. Home: 245 Browns Rd Walden NY 12586-3027

HRANITZKY, RACHEL ROBYN, lawyer; b. Irving, Tex., Mar. 16, 1968; d. Dennis Rogers and Jeanne Beverly (Crooks) H. BA, Tex. Christian U., 1987, U. Tex., 1988; JD, So. Meth. U., 1995. Bar: Tex. 1995, U.S. Dist. Ct. (no. dist.) Tex. 1997, U.S. Dist. Ct. (ea. dist.) Tex. 1999. Tchr. Grapevine (Tex.) H.S., 1988-92; clk. to Hon. Candace Tyson, 44th Dist. Ct., Dallas, 1993; assoc. coun. Mesa, Inc., Dallas, 1995; assoc. Hiersche, Martens, Hayward, Drakeley & Urbach, Dallas, 1996—; rsch. asst. William V. Dorsaneo, III, 1993-95; clinic atty. So. Meth. U. Legal Clinics, Dallas, 1995. Mem. ABA, ATLA, Dallas Bar Assn., Delta Theta Phi. Avocations: art, music, sports, cooking, dancing. Home: 5400 Preston Oaks Rd #2021 Dallas TX 75240 Office: 15303 Dallas Pkwy Ste 700 LB-17 Dallas TX 75248

HRENOFF, NATALIA OLYMPIADA, nurse; b. San Francisco, Sept. 1, 1948; d. Arseny Konstantinovich and Olympiada Michielovich (Osetinsky)

H. BA, U. Calif., Berkeley, 1971. Med. asst., operating technician St. Joseph's Hosp., San Francisco, 1972-78; RN U. Calif. San Francisco Med. Ctr., 1981-83, Leigh Meml. Hosp., Virginia Beach, Va., 1985-86; RN, mother/baby dyad program Sharp Meml., San Diego, 1986-89; with Scripps Meml. Dialysis Ctrs., La Jolla, Calif., 1989-96; dialysis RN Gambro Healthcare Svcs., Escondido, Calif., 1996—, TRC Dialysis, Oceanside, Calif., 1996—; faculty U. Calif.-San Diego. Advocate Gay and Lesbian Rights. Served to lt. (j.g.) USN, 1983-85. Mem. Greenpeace, Animal Rights. Democrat. Avocations: music (piano and guitar), gardening, skiing, jogging, hiking. Home: 2935 Segovia Way Carlsbad CA 92009-8231

HRIC, JOAN ESTHER, English educator, writer; b. Highland, Ill., Jan. 27, 1951; d. Samuel Earl Douglas and Eileen Rose (Gibbs) Korte; 1 child, Amanda Joanne Branham Albers; m. Raymond Joseph Hric, June 20, 1986. BSBA, U. Mo., 1991, MA in English, 1994, cert. writing, 1991. Clk. typist Security Divsn. Civil Svc., Granite City Army Depot, Ill., 1969-71; steno clk. Eustis Directorate Civil Svc., Ft. Eustis, Va., 1974-76; steno clk. Mapping Divsn. Civil Svc., St. Louis, 1982-87, steno clk. Software Divsn., 1987-88; peripheral operator, jr. sect. chief Dow Jones/The Wall Street Jour., Highland, Ill., 1976-77; sec. leadership dept. Jewish Fedn. St. Louis, 1981-82; English instr. Learning Ctr. Jefferson Coll., Hillsboro, Mo., 1994; English instr. Midlands Tech. Coll., Columbia, S.C., 1994-99, mgr. Writing Ctr., 1995-99; tchr. computer tech. Dutch Fork Mid. Sch., Ballantine, S.C., 1999—; mem. English 100 Com., Columbia, 1995—; cons. MTO Speciality Shop, Gaston, S.C., 1995—. Author poems. V.p. Friends of the Gaston Libr., 1996—. Recipient Editor's award Nat. Libr. Poetry in Best Poems of 1995, 1995, Faraway Places, 1995, Best Poems of 1997, Choice award Best Poems of Horizons, 1997, 1st Pl. award The Quill, 1996, , 2nd place, 1995, others. Mem. S.C. Writing Ctrs. Assn., S.C. Writers Workshop, Gaston Writers Cir., Jefferson Mo. Writers Guild. Office: Dutch Fork Mid Sch 1528 Old Tomah Rd Irmo SC 29063

HRINAK, DONNA JEAN, ambassador; b. Sewickley, Pa., Mar. 28, 1951; d. John and Mary (Pukach) H.; m. Gabino (Lou) Flores, July 15, 1977; 1 child, Wyatt A. Flores. BA, Mich. State U., 1972. State dept. officer Am. Embassy, Bogota, Colombia, 1979-81; former dep. prin. officer Am. Embassy, Warsaw, Poland, 1977-79, Mexico City, 1974-81; former min. counselor Am. Embassy, Teguciagalpa, Honduras, 1989-91; regional affairs officer for C.Am. Dept. State, Washington, 1982-84, dep. asst. sec. for inter-Am. affairs, 1991-93; dep. prin. officer U.S. Consultate Gen., Sao Paulo, Brazil, 1984-87; coord. Policy for Summit of Ams. 1994, 1993-94; amb. to Dominican Republic Santo Domingo, 1994-97; amb. to Bolivia-La Paz, 1998—. Named one of Ams. Ten Outstanding Young Working Women, Glamour mag., 1985. Mem. Am. Fgn. Svc. Assn., Exec. Women in Govt., Inter-Am. Dialogue Fgn. Policy Assn. Avocations: reading mysteries, playing tennis, watching baseball. Office: US Embassy La paz US Dept State Washington DC 20521*

HRISKEVICH, MICHAEL EDWARD, oil and gas consultant; b. Timmins, Ont., Can., Mar. 7, 1926; s. Elio and Antonina I. (Pashkevich) H.; m. Mary Ann Ban, May 10, 1947; children: Michael, Brian, Brenda, Shirley. BS, Queens U., 1947, MS, 1949; PhD, Princeton U., 1952. Exploration mgr. Banff Oil Ltd., Calgary, Alta., 1965-69, tech. coordinator, 1969-71; exploration mgr. Aquitaine Co. of Can., Ltd., Calgary, 1971-76, v.p. exploration, 1976-80, sr. v.p. exploration, 1980-81; sr. v.p. corp. affairs and spl. projects Canterra Energy Ltd., Calgary, 1981-83, ret., 1983; oil and gas cons., 1983—; pres. Banaqu Exploration Ltd., 1983—. Contbr. articles to profl. jours. Segsworth scholar, 1943; Major Rattray scholar, 1947; Research Council Can. grantee, 1948-49. Mem. Can. Soc. Petroleum Geologists (pres. 1969), Am. Assn. Petroleum Geologists (sec. 1987-88), Geol. Soc. Am., Assn. Profl. Engrs., Geologists and Geophysicists of Alta., Calgary Petroleum Club, Glencoe Club, Earl Grey Golf Club, Sigma Xi. Roman Catholic. Home: 608 Stratton Terr SW, Calgary, AB Canada T3H 1M6

HRITZ, GEORGE F., lawyer; b. Hyde Park, N.Y., Aug. 28, 1948; s. George F. and Margaret M. (Callahan) H.; m. Mary Elizabeth Noonan; 1 child, Amelia C. Hritz. AB, Princeton U., 1969; JD, Columbia U., 1973. Bar: N.Y. 1974, D.C. 1978, U.S. Supreme Ct. 1979. Law clk. U.S. Dist. Ct. (ea. dist.) N.Y., N.Y.C., 1973; assoc. Cravath, Swaine & Moore, N.Y.C., 1974-77; counsel U.S. Senate Select Com. Ethics Korean Inquiry, Washington, 1977-78; ptnr. Moore & Foster, Washington, 1978-80, Davis, Weber & Edwards, N.Y.C., 1980—; assoc. ind. counsel Washington, 1986-89; mem. adv. com. U.S. Dist. Ct. (ea. dist.) N.Y., 1990—. Trustee Fed. Bar Found., 1998—; bd. dirs. gen. counsel exec. com. Internat. Rescue Com., 1982—; chmn. planning bd. Village of Sleepy Hollow, N.Y., 1993-97. Mem. Fed. Bar Coun., D.C. Bar Assn. Home: 505 Cognewaugh Rd Greenwich CT 06807-1110 Office: Davis Weber & Edwards 100 Park Ave Ste 3200 New York NY 10017-5516

HRNA, DANIEL JOSEPH, pharmacist, lawyer; b. Taylor, Tex., March 19, 1940; s. Stephan Peter and Anna Ludmilla (Baran) H.; BS, U. Houston, 1963, JD, 1970; m. Velma Isobel Lesson, Sept. 3, 1963 (dec. Jan. 1994); children: Anna Marie, Daniel Steven, Brian Keith. Bar: Tex. 1972. In mgmt., Gunning-Casteel Co., El Paso, Tex., 1963-65; dir. pharmacy svcs. Tex. Inst. Rehab. & Rsch., Houston, 1966-79; dir. pharmacy Alief Gen. Hosp., Belhaven Hosp., Houston, 1979-85, West Houston Med. Ctr., 1985-88; mem. faculty Baylor U. Coll. Medicine, 1977-79, Sharpstown Gen. Hosp., 1988-94; with Owen Healthcare, Inc. at Sharpstown Gen. Hosp., 1990-94; pvt. practice, 1994—; pres. Rx-IBR Corp. Mem. ABA, Am. Pharm. Assn., Tex. Pharmacy Assn., State Bar Tex., Tex. Soc. Hosp. Pharmacists, Am. Soc. Pharmacy Law, Am. Hosp. Assn., Harris County Pharm. Assn., Houston Bar Assn., Galveston-Houston Pharm. Hosp. Assn., Czech Heritage Soc. Tex. (legal adv., trustee), Profl. Photographers Guild Houston (hon.), Delta Theta Phi, Kappa Psi, Phi Delta Chi. Roman Catholic. Office: 11920 Beechnut St Houston TX 77072-4034

HRONES, JOHN ANTHONY, mechanical engineering educator; b. Boston, Sept. 28, 1912; s. Emil and Olga Victoria (Cech) H.; m. Margaret Baylis, June 17, 1938; children: Janet H. Roach, Stephen Baylis, Mary H. Parsons, John Anthony. S.B., MIT, 1934, S.M., 1936, Sc.D., 1942. Asst. factory mgr. Coldwell Lawnmower Co., Newburgh, N.Y., 1937-39; asst. mech. engring. dept. MIT, 1934-36, instr., 1936-37, 39-41, asst. prof., 1941-45, asso. prof., 1945-57, prof. mech. engring., 1948, head machine design div., 1946, dir. Dynamic Analysis and Control Lab., 1950; v.p. acad. affairs Case Inst. Tech., Cleve., 1957-67; provost Case Inst. Tech., 1964-67; provost sci. and tech. Case-Western Res. U., 1967-76, provost emeritus, prof. engring., 1976—; pres. A.I.T. Found., Inc., 1969-91, dir., 1969—; cons. automatic control and machine design, 1939—; chmn. Univ. Circle Rsch. Ctr. Corp., 1967-73; pres. ChiCorp., 1967-68, chmn., 1967-77; rsch. adv. com. AID, 1978-82. Author: (with Nelson) Analysis of the Four Bar Linkage, 1951; contbr. articles to engring. publs. Trustee Asian Inst. Tech., Cleve. Mus. Nat. History. Mem. ASME, NAE, Am. Soc. Engring. Edn., Am. Acad. Arts and Scis., Inst. for Def. Analyses (trustee 1958-85), Sigma Xi, Tau Beta Pi, Pi Tau Sigma. Clubs: Cleveland Skating (trustee 1970-73), MIT Club of S.W. Fla. (pres.). Home: 9397 Midnight Pass Rd Apt 306 Sarasota FL 34242-2949

HRONES, STEPHEN BAYLIS, lawyer, educator; b. Boston, Jan. 20, 1942; s. John Anthony and Margaret (Baylis) H.; m. Anneliese Zion, Sept. 11, 1970; children: Christopher, Katja. BA cum laude, Harvard U., 1964; postgrad., U. Sorbonne, Paris, 1964-65; JD, U. Mich., 1968. Bar: Iowa 1969, Mass. 1972, U.S. Dist. Ct. Mass. 1973, U.S. Ct. Appeals (1st cir.) 1979, U.S. Tax Ct. 1985, U.S. Supreme Ct. 1991. Pvt. practice Heidelberg, Germany, 1970-72, Boston, 1973-86; ptnr. Hrones and Harwood, Boston, 1986-90, Hrones and Garrity, Boston, 1990—; clin. assoc. Suffolk U. Law Sch., Boston, 1979-82; faculty advisor Harvard Law Sch., 1988—; instr. Northeastern Law Sch., 1998. Author: How To Try a Criminal Case, 1982, Criminal Practice Handbook, 1995; contbr. articles to profl. jours. Trustee Orgn. for Assabet River; mem. schs. and scholarship com. Harvard U.; fundraiser Harvard Coll. Fund, 1985—; candidate for bd. overseers Harvard U., 1999. Fulbright scholar, 1968-69. Mem. Nat. Assn. Criminal Def. Lawyers, Mass. Assn. Criminal Def. Lawyers, Mass. Bar Assn., Boston Bar Assn., Nat. Lawyers Guild. Democrat. Avocations: squash, skiing, windsurfing, vegetable gardening. E-mail: Azhro@aol.com. Home: 39 Winslow St Concord MA 01742-3817 Office: Hrones and Garrity Lewis Wharf Bay 232 Boston MA 02110

HRUBY, VICTOR JOSEPH, chemistry educator; b. Valley City, N.D., Dec. 24, 1938; s. Victor John and Helen (Berube) H.; m. Patricia Ann McGovern, Aug. 1, 1966; children: Timothy Joseph, Stephen Michael, Patrick Andrew. BS, U. N.D., 1960, MS, 1962; PhD, Cornell U., 1965; D Honorus Causa, Free U. of Brussels, Belgium, 1989. Instr. med. coll. Cornell U., N.Y.C., 1965-67; rsch. assoc. Cornell U., Ithaca, N.Y., 1967-68; asst. prof. chemistry U. Ariz., Tucson, 1968-72, assoc. prof., 1972-77, prof., 1977—, prof. biochemistry, 1978—, prof. Ariz. Rsch. Labs., 1981—, prof. neurosci., 1988—, Regents prof., 1989—; guest worker NIH, Bethesda, Md., 1975-76; vis. prof. Harvard U., Cambridge, Mass., 1984-85, Calif. Inst. Tech., Pasadena, 1993; rector's lectr. Free U. Brussels, 1979; Blomquist lectr. Cornell U., 1996. Editor International Jour. of Peptide and Protein Rsch., 1988-96, Jour. of Peptide Rsch., 1997—; editor: Peptides: Structure and Function, 1983; The Peptides: Conformation in Biology and Drug Design, 1985; patentee in field. Served with USAR, 1955-58. Recipient Javits award USPHS, 1987, merit award NIH, 1988, Pierce award Am. Peptide Soc., 1993; fellow Fulbright-Hays Found., 1979, John Simon Guggenheim Found., 1984; sr. scientist Humboldt award, 1999—. Fellow AAAS, N.Y. Acad. Scis., Am. Inst. Chemists; mem. Am. Chem. Soc. (pres. SAAS 1974, councilor MCS 1993-97), Am. Peptide Soc. (pres. 1990-91), Am. Soc. Biochemistry and Molecular Biology, Biophysics Soc., Protein Soc., Sigma Xi. Avocations: philosophy, sociology, ethics, sports. Office: U Ariz Dept Chemistry Tucson AZ 85721

HRUSKA, ALAN J., lawyer; b. N.Y.C., July 9, 1933. B.A., Yale U., 1955, LL.B., 1958. Bar: N.Y. 1959, U.S. Supreme Ct. 1970. Assoc. firm Cravath, Swaine & Moore, N.Y.C., 1958-67; ptnr. Cravath, Swaine & Moore, 1968—; chmn. planning and program com. 2d Circuit Jud. Conf., 1974-80; co-chmn. 2d Circuit Commn. Reduction of Burdens and Costs in Civil Litigation, 1977-80; commr. N.Y. State Exec. Adv. Commn. on Adminstrn. of Justice, 1981-83; chmn. bd. SoHo Press, Inc., 1986—. Author: Borrowed Time, 1984. Mem. ABA, Am. Coll. Trial Lawyers, N.Y. State Bar Assn., Assn. of Bar of City of N.Y. (sec. 1965-66), Fed. Bar Coun. (trustee 1976—, pres. 1984-86), Inst. Jud. Adminstrn. (trustee 1978-92, pres. 1982-85, bd. dirs. 1992—), Ctr. for Pub. Resources (exec. com. 1984—), Fund for Modern Cts. (bd. dirs. 1994—). Office: Cravath Swaine & Moore 825 8th Ave Fl 38 New York NY 10019-7475

HRUSKA, FRANCIS JOHN, marine surveyor, consultant; b. Trnovec N/V, Czechoslovakia, Jan. 19, 1935, came to U.S., 1977; s. Ferdinand and Julia (Klepanec) H.; m. Ludmila Liptak, Apr. 19, 1958; children—Zuzana, Daniela, Martin. Grad. with honors, Nautical Sch. for Inland Waterways, Czechoslovakia, 1952, State Nautical Sch., Poland, 1955; student Walsey Hall Corr. Coll., Oxford, Eng., 1973-74. Cert. master mariner, 1961, marine pilot, 1969. Ships nautical officer Czechoslovak Ocean Shipping, Prague, 1955-62; exec. nautical engr. State Nautical Authority, Czechoslovakia, 1962-66; master C.S.P.D. Sea Branch, Czechoslovakia, 1966-68; marine pilot Ghana Rys. and Ports, 1968-72, Nat. Port Authority, Liberia, 1972-75; harbour master, chief marine officer, 1975-77; marine surveyor Nautech, Inc., Latham & Assocs., Master Marine Cons., Inc., New Orleans, 1978-82; pres. Plimsoll Marine Surveyors, Inc., Covington, La., 1983—; chmn. exam. bd. for pilots Nat. Port Authority, Monrovia, Liberia, 1975-77; nautical advisor Govt. of Liberia, 1975-77; cons. Comprehensive Study for Devel. of Port of Monrovia, 1975-77, Elbe-Oder-Danube Waterways System, Czechoslovakia, 1963-66. Contbr. articles to profl. jours. Office: Plimsoll Marine Surveyors Inc PO Box 8528 Mandeville LA 70470-8528

HRYCAK, PETER, mechanical engineer, educator; b. Przemysl, Poland, July 8, 1923; came to U.S., 1949, naturalized, 1956; s. Eugene and Ludmyla (Dobrzanska) H.; m. Rea Meta Limberg, June 13, 1949; children: Maria (dec.), Michael Paul, Orest W.T., Alexandra Martha. Student, U. Tubingen, Germany, 1946-48; BS with honors, U. Minn., 1954, MS, 1955, PhD, 1960. Registered profl. engr., N.J. Adminstrv. asst. French Mil. Govt. in Germany, 1947-49; instr. mech. engring. U. Minn., Mpls., 1955-60; mem. tech. staff Bell Telephone Labs., Murray Hill, N.J., 1960-65; sr. project engr. Curtiss-Wright Corp., Woodridge, N.J., 1965; assoc. prof. mech. engring. N.J. Inst. Tech., 1965-68, prof., 1968-93, prof. emeritus, 1993—, dir. jet rsch. lab., 1966-93; Participant in Internat. Conf. on Engring. and Applied Sci. *Looking back over my professional career, it seems to me that there is no substitute for interest in, and curiosity for, new developments, and hard work to generate new ideas and to update oneself in the rapidly shifting environment of today. First comes, however, one's responsiblity to maintain one's body in good mental and physical health. This may be achieved through a life filled with physical activities and hobbies, but also through an ability to "take it easy" at times, to recover from life's strain and to contemplate. All that should be filled with feelings for social justice and awareness of one's social responsibility which, in itself, may temper and blunt the inevitable desires, conflicts, and frustrations of the highly competitive modern life. Last but not least is perhaps the ability to laugh at oneself and be able to see both sides of the story. In 1958 at the University of Minnesota, Peter Hrycak worked under Professor J. J. Ryan, the inventor of the "Black Box" for airplanes, on the design of a hydraulic bumper able to safely stop passenger cars hitting barriers at up to 40 MPH. From 1961-62, he designed an instrument package for a solar-powered communications satellite able to maintain room temperature in orbit for a period of time. He also recently wrote articles on the integration of Ukraine into the family of world nations, using topics from technology, sociology, and history.* Contbr. articles to profl. jours.; one of original Telstar designers. Bd. dirs. Ukrainian Congress Com. Am., Mpls., 1956-60, Plast Camp, East Chatham, N.Y., 1963-68; v.p. Ukrainian Music Found., 1977-97; pres. assn. Peremyschyna, 1993-99. NASA grantee, 1967-68; NSF grantee, 1982-84. Mem. AIAA (sr.), AAUP, ASME, Inst. Environ. Scis. (sr.), Ukrainian Engrs. Soc. Am. (pres. 1966-67), Am. Geophys. Union, Nat. Ukrainian Acad. Engring. Scis., Shevchenko Sci. Soc., Ukrainian Acad. Arts and Scis. in U.S.A., Sigma Xi, Pi Tau Sigma, Tau Beta Pi. Home: 19 Roselle Ave Cranford NJ 07016-2532 Office: NJ Inst Tech 323 Martin Luther King Jr Blvd Newark NJ 07102-1824

HRYCIK, PAULINE EMILY, educator; b. Buffalo, Sept. 23, 1946; d. Roman and Isabelle Mary Waleszczak. BA in English, Edn., Niagara U., 1973; MS in Edn., Canisius Coll., 1976; postgrad., SUNY, Buffalo, 1983, 84. Cert. elem. tchr., secondary English, SAS administrv., drug educator. Itinerant tchr. Buffalo Pub. Schs., 1979; prin. K-8 Diocese of Buffalo, 1974-79; tchr. English, gifted-talented, adminstrv. asst, team leader Royalton-Hartland Sch. Dist., Middleport, N.Y., 1980-88; 8th grade English tchr. Medina (N.Y.) Cen. Sch. Dist., 1988—. Contbr. articles to profl. jours. Named Outstanding Tchr. of English N.Y. State Coun. Tchrs. English. Mem. Nat. Coun. Tchrs. English, N.Y. State Coun. Tchrs. English, AGATE, N.Y. State Mid. Sch., Medina Tchrs. Assn. (peer mediation trainer, conf. planning com., N.Y. state tchr. exam. grader 1993—). Home: 33 Garnet Rd Buffalo NY 14226-2505

HRYNKOW, SHARON HEMOND, federal government administrator, researcher. BA in Biology, R.I. Coll., 1983; PhD in Neurosci., U. Conn., 1990; postdoctoral studies, U. Oslo, Norway, 1990-92. Sci. officer U.S. Dept. State, Washington, 1992-95; sci. policy analyst Fogarty Internat. Ctr., NIH, Bethesda, Md., 1995-97, spl. asst. office of dir., 1997-99, dir. divsn. internat. rels., 1999—; mem. adv. bd. Nat. Coun. for Internat. Health, Washington, 1997. Contbr. articles to profl., peer-reviewed jours. includng Jour. Neurosci., Developmental Brain Rsch., and others; chief drafter on strategy and policy toward internat. HIV/AIDS, State Dept. U.S. Recipient Lette N. Sangstad award (rsch. stipend) Oslo, Norway, 1990-92. Mem. AAAS (Diplomacy fellowship 1992-94), Coun. on Fgn. Rels., Am. Scandinavian Assn., Norwegian Soc. of Washington, Am. Pub. Health Assn., Soc. for Neurosci., Women in Neurosci. Office: Fogarty Internat Ctr NIH Bldg 31 Rm B2C02 Bethesda MD 20892

HSI, DAVID CHING HENG, plant pathologist and geneticist, educator; b. Shanghai, China, May 17, 1928; came to U.S., 1948, naturalized, 1961; s. Yulin and Sue Jean (King) H.; m. Kathy S.W. Chiang, 1952; children: Andrew C., Steven D. BSA, St. John's U., Shanghai, 1948; MS, U. Ga., 1949; PhD, U. Minn., 1951. Grad. teaching asst. U. Minn., St. Paul, 1950; postdoctoral fellow U.S. Cotton Field Sta., Sacaton, Ariz., 1951-52; mem. faculty N.Mex. State U., Las Cruces, 1952—, prof. plant pathology and genetics, 1968-92, prof. emeritus, 1992—; cons. AID, Pakistan, 1970; coord. external evaluation panel Peanut Collaborative Rsch. Support Program, U.S.A., West Africa, S.E. Asia, 1993-95; acad. exch. People's Republic China, 1978, 84, 85, Republic China, 1979, 81, 82, Brazil and Argentina, 1980, Australia, 1983, South Africa, 1981; judge sr. botany N.Mex. Sci. and Engring. Fair, 1979—. Author rsch. papers in field; co-developer new crop cultivars. Past bd. dirs., treas. Carver Pub. Libr., Clovis, N.Am.; elder 1st Presbyn. Ch., Albuquerque, workship com. chmn., 1981-82, adult edn. com. chmn., 1988-91, pers. com., 1995—; mem. nat. adv. coun. discipleship and worship Gen. Assembly United Presbyn. Ch. U.S.A., 1978-81, mem. nat. theol. reflections working group, 1980-81, mem. ednl. and congl. nurture unit, 1991-93, N.Mex. Child Abuse Neglect Prevention Implementation Task Force, 1993—; mem. bd. edn. Albuquerque Pub. Schs., 1982, sec. bd. edn., 1983, v.p., 1984; bd. dirs. Mid. Rio Grande Coun. Govts., 1983, 84; chair Albuquerque Sisters Cities Bd., 1986-88; 1st v.p. Albuquerque Sister Cities Found., 1995-96, pres., 1996-98; mem. com. higher edn. Gen. Assembly The Presbyn. Ch. (U.S.A.), 1991-93, preparation ministry com., Presbytery Santa Fe, 1993—, chair, 1996-97; co-chair N.Mex. Advocates for Children and Families, 1993-95, vice chair, 1995-98; bd. dirs. Greater Albuquerque Vol. Adminstrs., 1992-95, Project Change, 1994—, v.p., 1996—; v.p. Albuquerque Edn. Retirees, 1995-96, pres., 1996—; v.p. Edn. Success Alliance, 1996-98. Recipient Disting. Rsch. award Coll. Agr. and Home Econs. N.Mex. State U., 1971, Disting. Svc. award, 1985; inducted into Sr. Citizen's Hall of Fame, 1993. Fellow AAAS (hon., coun. mem. 1998—, Southwestern and Rocky Mountain divsn., exec. com. 1993-95, pres.-elect 1995-96, pres. 96-97); mem. Internat. Soc. Plant Pathology, Am. Phytopath. Soc. (judge Internat. Sci. and Engring. Fair 1983), Nat. Sweet Potato Collaborators Group (chmn. sprout prodn. and root piece propagation com. 1982-84), Nat. Geog. Soc., Am. Peanut Rsch. and Edn. Soc. (chmn. site selection com. 1981, award com., pres.-elect 1981, pres. 1982), N.Mex. Acad. Sci. (chmn. com. 1980, pres. 1981, 82, treas. 1984-92, dist. scientist award 1984), Nat. Assn. Acad. Sci. (pres.-elect 1992-93, pres. 1993-94), N.Mex. Chinese Assn. (pres. 1983-84, 92-93, treas. 1985-86, bd. dirs. 1998—), Chinese Am. Citizens Alliance (v.p. Albuquerque lodge 1988-92), Albuquerque Coun. for Internat. Visitors (v.p. 1988, pres. 1989-91), Sigma Xi (life, N.Mex. coord. centennial celebration), Kiwanis Internat. (past pres. Clovis, past chmn. spl. program com., bd. dirs. Albuquerque). Home and Office: 2504 Griegos Rd NW Albuquerque NM 87107-2870 *In grateful appreciation of my God-given talents and opportunities, my privileged academic trainings in China and U.S.A., and my professional experience and associations with world-wide scientists, I shall continue to contribute to the scientific advancement and practice, and to promote human understanding and international cooperation for the betterment of mankind and for the glorification of my Creator.*

HSI, MORRIS YU, mechanical engineer, applied researcher; b. Taipei, Taiwan, Aug. 23, 1951; s. En Sui and I Hsian (Wang) H.; m. Linda Syau Lin Chang, Aug. 28, 1982. BSME with honors, Nat. Cheng Kung U., Tainan, Taiwan, 1974; MSME, Iowa State U., 1979; PhD in Applied Mechanics, U. Mich., 1987. Registered profl. engr., Mich. Mech. engr. Taiwan Power Co., Keelung, 1976-77; product design engr. Ford Motor Co., Dearborn, Mich., 1987-92, tech. specialist, 1992-97; tech. specialist Ford Visteon Automotive Sys., Plymouth, Mich., 1997—; reviewer, evaluator of tech. pubs. profl. socs. Contbr. articles to profl. jours. 2d lt. Taiwanese Army, 1974-76. Recipient Henry Ford Technol. award Ford Motor Co., 1990, Mich. Outstanding Engr. in Industry Am. Consulting Engrs. Coun. Mich. and Mich. Soc. Profl. Engrs., 1999. Mem. NSPE, Soc. Automotive Engrs. (noise and vibration gen. com.), Mich. Soc. Profl. Engrs. (dir. Detroit Metro chpt. 1999—). Achievements include pioneering in application of computational aeroacoustics to automotive projects; pioneering in application of computational fluid dynamics to analyze and design vehicle's underhood thermal environment; patents pending on noise control of automotive climate control systems. Avocations: painting, swimming. Home: 46922 Elmsmere Dr Northville MI 48167-1034 Office: Ford Visteon Automotive Sys 45000 Helm St Plymouth MI 48170-6046

HSIA, DAVID, health services researcher, administrator; b. N.Y.C., Nov. 22, 1950; s. David Yi-Yung and Hsio Hsuan (Shih) H.; m. Susie Q. Lew, Nov. 12, 1991; children: Julie Lew Hsia, Katie Lew Hsia. BA, Haverford Coll., 1972; JD, Yale U., 1975; MD, U. Ill., 1984; MPH, Harvard U., Boston, 1982. Atty. Fed. Reserve Bd., Washington, 1975-79; intern VA Med. Ctr., Washington, 1984-85; resident Johns Hopkins, Balt., 1985-87; med. officer HHS Office of Inspector Gen., Washington, 1987-92, HHS Agy. for Health Care Policy and Rsch., Rockville, Md., 1992—; detailee Nat. Performance Review, Washington, 1993—. Contbr. articles to profl. jours. including New Eng. Jour. Medicine, JAMA, Annals of Internal Medicine, Am. Jour. Pub. Health. Office: HHS-AHCPR 2101 E Jefferson St Rockville MD 20852-4908

HSIA, FRANKLIN WEN-HAI, computer programmer, systems analyst, consultant; b. Taipei, Taiwan, Feb. 27, 1966; came to U.S., 1976; s. John and Daisy Chen-Chieh (Yu) H. BA in Computer Sci., U. Buffalo, 1990. Program designer N.Y. State Sch. Bds. Assn., Albany, 1991-92; sr. computer programmer analyst N.Y. State Dept. Taxation and Fin., Albany, 1992-94; sr. computer programmer analyst N.Y. State Dept. Health, Albany, 1994-95, assoc. computer programmer analyst, 1995-98, data comm. specialist, 1998—; exec. cons. Get Connected!, Clifton Park, N.Y., 1996—. Cons. United Cerebral Palsy N.Y., Albany, 1995-96; mem. Sierra Club, Albany, 1996—. Recipient Best Practice award N.Y. State Forum Info. Resource Mgmt., 1996. Office: N Y State Dept Health Empire State Plz C 146 Concourse Albany NY 12237

HSIANG, JOHN, neurosurgeon; b. Hong Kong, Nov. 15, 1958; came to U.S., 1978; m. Lena Hsiang, June 25, 1983; children: Ida, Eugene. BSc, U. Iowa, 1981; PhD, U. Chgo., 1986, MD, 1988. Diplomate Am. Bd. Neurol. Surgery. Assoc. prof. in neurosurgery Prince of Wales Hosp., Hong Kong, 1994-97; attending neurosurgeon Virginia Mason Med. Ctr., Seattle, 1997—; editl. reviewer Hong Kong Med. Jour., 1998—. Fellow Hong Kong Med. Acad.; mem. Am. Assn. Neurol. Surgery, Congress Neurol. Surgery, Hong Kong Coll. Surgeons. Avocations: boating, swimming. E-mail: nsrjnh@vmmc.org. Office: Virginia Mason Med Ctr 1100 9th Ave Seattle WA 98101

HSIAO, CHIE-FANG, neuroscientist; b. Chi-Yei, Taiwan, Jan. 15, 1945; came to U.S., 1983; s. Zu-Chin and Chiao (Ching) H.; m. Shu-Lan Lin, Jan. 29, 1976; children: Kathryne, Amy. BS in Pharmacology, Taipei (Taiwan) Med. Coll., 1976; PhD in Med. Sci., Osaka (Japan) U., 1983. Rsch. assoc. SUNY, Stony Brook, 1983-85, U. Colo., Boulder, 1985-89; rsch. instr. U. Mo., Kansas City, 1989-92; neuroscientist U. Calif., L.A., 1992—; lectr. U. Mo., Kansas City, 1988-89; rsch. instr. Osaka U. Med. Sch., 1981-83, U. Calif., L.A., 1992—. Advisor Taipei Med. Sch. Alumni, Calif., 1993, Taiwanese Assn., Colo., 1985. Recipient Nat. Rsch. Svc. award NIH, 1992, fellowship Fight for Sight Inc., 1984, scholarship Japan Rotary, 1982. Mem. AAAS, Soc. for Neurosci., Naturalistic Soc. USA. Avocations: reading, singing, swimming, yoga, tennis. Home: 1835 Camden Ave Apt 102 Los Angeles CA 90025-4470 Office: Univ Calif 405 Hilgard Ave Los Angeles CA 90095-9000

HSIAO, JACK NAI-CHANG, physician; b. Taipei, Taiwan, Nov. 9, 1969; came to U.S., 1984; s. Chung-Cheng and Yin-Mei (Lan) H. BA, Boston U., 1992, MD, 1995. Pres. Esplanade Newsline, Inc., Cambridge, Mass., 1994—; PhD candidate Boston U. Sch. Med., 1995—. Publisher (online newsletter) Esplanade Newsline, 1994—. Chmn. New England Rep. China Student & Scholar Acad. Forum; gen. mgr. Boston U. Softball Team, 1995—; bd. dirs. Taiwan C. of C. Recipient Excellence in Leadership award Taipei Econ. and Cultural Office, Boston, 1997. Mem. AMA, Mass. Med. Soc., New England Assn. Chinese Professionals (v.p.), New England-Taiwan C. of C. (bd. dirs.). Avocations: softball, computers, golf, travel. Home: 75 Cambridge Pkwy Cambridge MA 02142-1229

HSIAO, KWANG-JEN, genetics and biochemistry educator; b. Canton, Guangdong, China, Dec. 14, 1948; s. Mong-Neng and Wan-Chieng (Chu) H.; m. Yuh-Yeh Yang, Jan. 20, 1973; children: Hann C., Yi-Ching. BSc in Chemistry, Chung-Yuan U., Republic of China, 1971; PhD in Biomed. Scis., CUNY, 1978. Assoc. prof. biochemistry Nat. Yang Ming U. (formerly Nat. Yang Ming Med. Coll.), Taipei, Taiwan, 1979-80, prof. Inst. of Genetics, 1989—, dean gen. affairs, 1990-93; vis. assoc. investigator Vets. Gen. Hosp., Taipei, Taiwan, 1980-81, assoc. investigator, 1981-83, investigator dept. med. rsch., 1983—, dir. biochem. genetic lab., 1984—; dir. pedt. rsch. resources Nat. Health Rsch. Insts., Taipei, 1996-98; cons. in clin. biochemistry Cancer

Soc. Republic of China, Taipei, 1985-87; dep. sec. 4th Asian Pacific Congress of Clin. Biochemistry, Hong Kong, 1985-88; mem. internat. organizing com. 5th and 6th Internat. Congress of Inborn Errors of Metabolism, Asilomar, Calif., 1989-90, Milan, Italy, 1993-94; cons. Neonatal Screening Ctr. Maternal and Child Health Assn., Taipei, 1993—, Neonatal Screening Ctr., Guangzhou, Canton, 1994—; vis. prof. Shanghai Second Med. U., 1995—; hon. prof. Rsch. Inst. Clin. Med., China-Japan Friendship Hosp., Beijing, 1995—. Mem. editorial bd. Advances in Clin. Chemistry, 1992—; contbr. articles to profl. publs. Named Outstanding Svcs. Pers. VA, Republic of China, 1986, Outstanding Rsch. Scientist, Nat. Sci. Coun., 1989, 90, 91, Outstanding Edn. Pers., Ministry of Edn., 1993; recipient Health Medal of 2d Order, Dept. Health, Republic of China, 1998. Fellow Nat. Acad. Clin. Biochemistry, Australasian Coll. Biomed. Scientists; mem. Preventive Medicine Found. (pres. 1987—), Chinese Assn. Clin. Biochemistry (pres. 1992-94), Assn. Lab. Medicine (exec. dir. 1991-97), Internat. Fedn. Clin. Chem. (awards com. 1997—), Internat. Soc. Clin. Enzymology, Asian Pacific Fedn. Clin. Biochemistry (sci. com. 1988-95), Internat. Soc. for Neonatal Screening, Internat. Fedn. Clin. Chemistry (awards com. 1997—), Am. Assn. Clin. Chemistry, Assn. Clin. Biochemists London, Chinese Biochem. Soc., Australian Assn. Clin. Biochemists, Chinese Chem. Soc., Chinese Soc. Microbiology, Chinese Toxicol. Soc., Endocrine Soc. Republic of China, Formosan Med. Assn., Nat. Pub. Health Assn., Soc. Inherited Metabolic Disorders, Soc. Study Inborn Errors Metabolism. Avocations: classical Chinese furniture, classical Chinese folk arts and works of art.

HSIAO, MING-YUAN, nuclear engineer, researcher; b. Kaohsiung, Taiwan, Feb. 23, 1954; came to U.S., 1978; s. Fei and Hwang-Fang H.; m. Shwu Chuen Lee. MS, U. Ill., 1980, PhD, 1983. Postdoctoral fellow Los Alamos (N.Mex.) Nat. Lab., 1983-84; asst. prof. Pa. State U., University Park, 1984-90; sr. engr. Commonwealth Edison Co., Chgo., 1990—. Author, reviewer jour. publs.; contbr. articles to profl. jours. including Physics of Fluids, Nuclear Fusion, Nuclear Tech., Fusion Tech., Computer Physics Comm., Nuclear Engring. and Design. Univ. fellow U. Ill., 1981-83, Profl. Devel. fellow U.S. Dept. Energy, 1987; recipient Faculty Summer Rsch. award Argonne (Ill.) Nat Lab., 1986-89. Mem. Am. Nuclear Soc. (Mark Mills award 1984), Sigma Xi, Phi Tau Phi. Achievements include identification of and studies on velocity space particle loss mechanism in field reversed configurations; research in fusion plasma theory and engineering, computational physics and engineering, and nuclear fuel management. Office: Commonwealth Edison Co 1400 Opus Pl Ste 400 Downers Grove IL 60515-1198

HSIEH, DIN-YU, applied mathematics educator; b. Jiangsu, Peoples Republic of China, Mar. 25, 1933; arrived in the U.S., 1955; s. K.S. and C. (Wei) H.; m. Lily Kwang-Fei Chow, Dec. 26, 1958; children: Paul, Daniel. BS, Nat. Taiwan U., 1954; MS, Brown U., Providence, 1957; PhD, Calif. Inst. Tech., Pasadena, 1960. Rsch. fellow Calif. Inst. Tech., 1960-63, asst. prof., 1963-68; assoc. prof. Brown U., 1968-78, prof., 1978—; prof., head dept. math. Hong Kong U. Sci. & Tech., 1990-96, acting dean sci., 1990-91, 92; cons. Jet Propulsion Lab. Pasadena, 1963-67; advisor Ningbo (Peoples Republic of China) U., 1986—. Author: Asymptotic Methods, 1983, Fluid Dynamics, 1987, America, America, 1990, Amid Hills, by the Lake, 1991, Contemplating China, 1991, Wave and Stability in Fluids, 1994, Swallow Flying, 1998. Mem. Am. Phys. Soc., Hong Kong Math. Soc., Edn. and Sci. Soc. (pres. 1987-90), Hong Kong Soc. Theoretical and Applied Mechanics (founding pres. 1996-97). Avocation: swimming. Office: Brown U Divsn Applied Maths Providence RI 02912

HSIEH, MICHAEL THOMAS, venture capitalist; b. Hong Kong, Mar. 9, 1958; came to U.S., 1968; s. Ching Chi and Za Za (Suffiad) H.; m. Tonia Chao, Sept. 6, 1987. BA, Harvard U., 1980, MBA, 1984. Analyst Merrill Lynch Capital Markets, N.Y.C., 1980-81; assoc. Sun Hung Kai Securities, N.Y.C., 1981-82; asst. v.p. Chappell and Co., San Francisco, 1984-86; pres. LF Internat. Inc., San Francisco, Calif., 1986—; bd. dirs. Wilke Rodriguez, N.Y.C., Li & Fung (Trading) Ltd., Hong Kong, The Original San Francisco Toymakers, Danskin, Inc., N.Y.C., Wood Assocs., Santa Clara, Minami Internat., N.Y. Exec. dir. Ctr. for Pacific Rim, U. San Francisco. Mem. Harvard Club (dir.), San Francisco Tennis Club, Olympic Club. Office: LF Internat Inc 360 Post St Ste 705 San Francisco CA 94108-4903

HSU, CHENG, decision sciences and engineering systems educator; b. Taipei, Republic of China, May 11, 1951; came to U.S., 1976; s. Chung-Yu and Te-Zeng (Yeh) H.; m. Ihsin Lydia Wu, Oct. 24, 1979; 1 child, Diana. BS in Indsl. Engring., Tunghai U., Taichung, Republic of China, 1973; MS, Ohio State U., 1978, PhD, 1983. Info. engr. China Tech. Cons., Inc., Taipei, 1975-76; grad. rsch. asst. Ohio State U., Columbus, 1977-80, grad. teaching assoc., 1980-82; asst. prof. decision scis. and engring. systems Rensselaer Poly. Inst., Troy, N.Y., 1982-88, assoc. prof., 1988-96, dir. undergrad. programs, 1989-91, dir. doctoral program, 1994—, prof., 1996—; cons. Coopers & Lybrand, Albany, N.Y., 1988, Digital Equipment Corp., Nashua, N.H., 1991, Gen. Electric R&D, Schenectady, N.Y., 1995—; patentee in field. Author: Enterprise Integration and Modeling: The Metadatabase Approach, 1996, internet Enterprises Planning 2000, 1999. Grantee GM, CED, Johnson & Johnson, 1986-89, Aluminum Co. Am., Digital Equipment Corp., 1992-95, GM, IBM, 1986-95, AT&T, 1987, NATO, 1988, State of N.Y., 1988, NSF, 1991-96, Samsung, 1995—, U.S. Army, 1995-96, N.Y. State Dept. Transp., 1997—. Mem. IEEE (sr.), ACM, Inst. Mgmt. Sci., Ops. Rsch. Soc. Am., Soc. Mfg. Engrs. (sr.), Prodn. and Ops. Mgmt. Soc., N. Am. Chinese Bus. Educators Assn. (bd. dirs. 1988-90). Republican. Home: 5 Christine Ct Latham NY 12110-3734 Office: Rensselaer Poly Inst 5219 CII Troy NY 12180-3590

HSU, CHENG-TZU THOMAS, civil engineering educator; b. I-Lan, Taiwan, Republic of China, Dec. 18, 1941; came to U.S., 1969; s. Moun-Chun Chung and A-Mei Hsu; m. Ursula Cruz Trivino; children: Anthony Trivino, Jennifer M.T. BSE, Cheng-Kung U., Tainan, Taiwan, 1964; MSc, Coll. Chinese Culture, Taipei, Taiwan, 1967, Yale U., 1972; MEngring., PhD, McGill U., Montreal, Que., Can., 1969, 74. Registered profl. engr., Taiwan, Que., Ont. Bridge design engr. Beauchemin-Beaton-Lapointe, Inc., Montreal, 1974; civil engring. specialist Bechtel and Co., Montreal and Toronto, 1974-78; asst. prof. N.J. Inst. Tech., Newark, 1978-83, assoc. prof., 1983-86, prof. civil engring., 1986—, assoc. chmn. grad. studies, 1988-93; cons. engr. Paulus, Sokolowski & Sartor, Inc., Warren, N.J., 1980-81; cons. Shih Engring. Co., Fairfield, N.J., 1982, Samuel M. Ruth & Assocs., Newark, 1984; hon. prof. Wuhan (China) U. Tech., 1992. Editor: Advances in Structural Concrete Design, 1983; contbr. over 100 articles to profl. jours. and conf. procs. 2d lt. Republic of China Army, 1964-65. Yale U. fellow, 1969-71, Miron fellow McGill U., Montreal, 1971-73. Fellow ASCE (Raymond C. Reesersch. prize 1987), Am. Concrete Inst. (com. mem. 1979—); mem. Sigma Xi, Chi Epsilon, Tau Beta Pi. Roman Catholic. Achievements include research in limit analysis-RC beams and frames, moment-curvature for reinforced concrete, load-deformation of RC columns, load-deformation of steel fiber RC beams. Office: NJ Inst Tech Dept Civil & Environ Engring 323 King Blvd Newark NJ 07102-1824

HSU, CHIEH SU, applied mechanics engineering educator, researcher; b. Soochow, Kiangsu, China, May 27, 1922; came to U.S., 1947.; s. Chung yu and Yong Feng (Wu) H.; m. Helen Yung-Feng Tse, Mar. 28, 1953; children—Raymond Hwa-Chi, Katherine Hwa-Ling. BS, Nat. Inst. Tech., Chungking, China, 1945; MS, Stanford U., 1948, PhD, 1950. Project engr. IBM Corp., Poughkeepsie, N.Y., 1951-55; assoc. prof. U. Toledo, 1955-58; assoc. prof. Univ Calif.-Berkeley, 1958-64, prof., 1964—, chmn. div. applied mechanics, 1969-70; mem. sci. adv. bd. Alexander von Humboldt Found. of Fed. Republic Germany, Bonn, 1985—; mem. U.S. nat. com. theoretical and applied mechanics U.S. Nat. Acad. Scis., 1985-90. Author: Cell-to-Cell Mapping, 1987; contbg. author: Thin-Shell Structures, 1974, Advances in Applied Mechanics, vol. 17, 1977; tech. editor Jour. Applied Mechanics, N.Y.C., 1976-82; assoc. editor profl. jours.; author of over 106 tech. papers. Recipient Alexander von Humboldt award Fed. Republic Germany, 1986; Guggenheim Found. fellow, 1964-65; Miller research prof., U. Calif.-Berkeley, 1973-74. Fellow ASME (Centennial award 1980, N.O. Myklestad award 1995) Am. Acad. Mechanics; mem. Acoustical Soc. Am., Soc. Indsl. and Applied Math., U. S. Nat. Acad. Engring., Acad. Sinica, Sigma Xi. Office: U Calif Dept Mech Engring Berkeley CA 94720-1740

HSU, CHO-YUN, history educator; b. Amoy, China, July 10, 1930; came to U.S., 1970; s. Feng-chao and Ying (Tsang) H.; m. Man-li Sun, Feb. 9, 1969; 1 child, Leo. BA, Nat. Taiwan U., 1953, MA, 1956; PhD, U. Chgo., 1962. Asst. rsch. fellow, 1956-62; assoc. research fellow Academia Sinica, Taiwan, 1962-67; rsch. fellow Inst. History and Philology, Academia Sinica, Taiwan, 1967-70; assoc. prof. Nat. Taiwan U., 1962-65, prof., 1965-70, chmn., 1963-70; prof. history and sociology U. Pitts., 1970-83, Univ. prof., 1983-98; Weilun chair, prof. hist. Chinese U. of Hong Kong, 1991-98, hon. prof., 1998—; John Burns prof. U. Hawaii, 1996; Semans vis. prof. Duke U., 1999—. Author: Introduction to Historical Research, 1965, Anthology of Studies in Ancient China, 1967, Ancient China in Transition, 1968, Han Agriculture, 1980, History of Western Chou Period, 1984, Western Chou Civilization, 1988; columnist various newspapers; contbr. articles to profl. jours. Bd. dirs. Chiang Ching-Kuo Found., 1989—. Recipient Asian Studies Program award UCIS, U. Pitts., 1967; Fulbright-Hays research fellow, 1978. Mem. Academia Sinica Taiwan, Coun. Academie Sinica, Assn. Asian Studies, Am. Assn. Chinese Studies (pres. 1985-87), Phi Beta Kappa. Avocation: reading. Office: U Pitts Dept History 3M36 Forbes Quad Pittsburgh PA 15260

HSU, IMMANUEL CHUNG YUEH, history educator; b. Shanghai, China, May 6, 1923; came to U.S., 1949, naturalized, 1962; s. Thomas K.S. and Mary (Loh) H.; m. Dolores Menstell, Apr. 14, 1962; 1 child, Vadim Menstell. B.A., Yenching U., China, 1946; M.A., U. Minn., 1950; Ph.D. (Harvard-Yenching fellow), Harvard U., 1954. Postdoctoral research fellow Harvard U., 1955-58; vis. asso. prof. history, vis. prof. Harvard Summer Sch., 1961, 64, 68, 75; asst. prof. history U. Calif. at Santa Barbara, 1959-60, asso. prof., 1960-65, prof., 1965—, chmn. history dept., 1970-72; faculty rsch. lectr., 1971; mem. del. to Chinese Acad. Scis., Beijing, spring 1979, 80; vis. prof. Hamburg U., Germany, spring 1973, Stockholm U., 1990; Fulbright lectr., 1973. Author: Intellectual Trends in the Ch'ing Period, 1959, China's Entrance into the Family of Nations, 1960, The Ili Crisis: A Study of Sino-Russian Diplomacy, 1871-1881, 1965, The Rise of Modern China, 1970, 2d edit., 1975, internat. edit., 1975-76, 3d edit., 1983, 4th edit., 1990, 5th edit., 1995 (Commonwealth Lit. priz of Calif. 1971); editor: Readings in Modern Chinese History, 1971, Late Ch'ing Foreign Relations, 1866-1905, in The Cambridge History of China, Vol. 11, 1980, China Without Mao, 1983, 2d edit., 1990. Guggenheim fellow, 1962-63; Nat. Acad. Scis. disting. scholar to China, spring 1983. Mem. Am., Pacific hist. assns., Assn. Asian Studies, Assn. Ch'ing Studies. Office: U Calif Dept History Santa Barbara CA 93106

HSU, JOHN CHAO-CHUN, retired pediatrician; b. China, 1916. MD, U. Peiping Union Med. Coll., 1942; MPH, U. MIch., 1948. Diplomate Am. Bd. Pediatrics. Physician Nat. Inst. Health, Chungking, China, 1943-45; attending physician The 5th Mcpl. Hosp., Shanghai, China, 1946-47; postgrad. rsch. fellow Columbia U./Mt. Sinai Hosp., N.Y.C., 1948; rotating intern St. Elizabeth Hosp., Dayton, Ohio, 1950-51; resident in pediatrics Kaiser Found. Hosp., Oakland, Calif., 1953-54, Beth El Hosp., Bklyn., 1954-55; chief resident in pediatrics Royal Alexandra Hosp., Edmonton, Can., 1956-57; rsch. fellow Children's Hosp., L.A., 1958-59; pvt. practice specializing in pediatrics, L.A., 1959—. Fellow Royal Soc. Health (London), Royal Soc. Tropical Medicine and Hygiene (London), Am. Acad. Pediat.; mem. AMA, APHA, Med. Coun. Can. (lic.). Home: PO Box 22683 San Francisco CA 94122-0683

HSU, KYLIE, language educator. BA, U. Mich., 1980; MA, Calif. State U., Northridge, 1994; PhD, UCLA, 1996. Lang. and math. instr. U. Mich., Ann Arbor, 1976-80; asst. to pres. Am. GNC Corp., Chatsworth, Calif., 1980-86, exec. v.p., 1986-93; instr. in Chinese UCLA, 1994-95; dir. lang. inst. Pacific States U., L.A., 1996-97; asst. prof. Calif. State U., L.A., 1997—; vis. asst. prof. UCLA, 1999; manuscript evaluator Edwin Mellen Press, Lewiston, N.Y., 1998—; editor-in-chief Pacific States U. Newsletter, 1997; judge Chinese Poetry Recital Contest, L.A., 1997; conf. chair Eng. Lang. Tchg. Conf., L.A., 1996. Author: Discourse Analysis, 1998; contbr. articles to profl. jours. Presdl. fellow/rsch. grantee U. Calif., Berkeley, 1996-97; James B. Angell scholar, 1979-80. Mem. IEEE (exhibits chair 1993), Modern Langs. and Lits. (curriculum com. chair 1998), Am. Coun. on Tchg. of Fgn. Langs. (panel chair 1997), Am. Assn. for Applied Linguistics (session chair 1995), Assn. for Linguistic Typology (scholar), Phi Beta Kappa. E-mail: kyliehsu@msn.com. Office: Calif State U LA 5151 State University Dr Los Angeles CA 90032-8112

HSU, MING CHEN, federal agency administrator; b. Beijing, China, Sept. 14, 1924; came to U.S., 1944; d. Chin-Men and Mary Sung Yung (Chu) Chen; 1 child, Victoria W. BA summa cum laude, George Washington U., 1949; LLD (hon.), Ramapo Coll., 1988, Kean Coll., 1989. Market rsch. analyst NBC Corp., N.Y.C., 1953-57; mg. market rsch. RCA Internat. Div., N.J., 1957-69; dir. internat. market RCA Corp., N.Y.C., 1969-78, staff v.p. for internat. trade, 1978-82; spl. trade rep. Gov. Tom Kean, Newark, 1982-90; dir. N.J. Div. Internat. Trade, Newark, 1982-90; commr. Fed. Maritime Commn., Washington, 1990—; speaker, lectr. on nat. and internat. affairs on numerous network and local TV programs. Author: American Arbitration Journal, 1956; editor: Suggested Amendments to the United Nations, 1960, Enabling Instruments of the United Nations, 1961; contbr. articles to jours. in field. At-large del to Rep. Nat. Conv., 1984, 88; mem. Def. Adv. Com. on Women in the Svcs., 1989, Nat. Commn. on Observance of Internat. Women's Yr., N.J. Adv. Coun. Channel Thirteen/WNET, U.S. Commn. on Civil Rights, U.S. Sec. Commerce's Adv. Com. on East-West Trade, Sec. Commerce's Export Now Adv. Com., Svc. Policy Adv. Com.; trustee Newark Mus.; bd. dirs. Com. of 100; mem. U.S. Holocaust Meml. Coun. Com. on Conscience Nat. Adv. Forum. Recipient Spl. award Women's Equity Action League, 1978, Alumni Achievement award George Washington U., 1983, Woman of Achievement award, N.J. Fedn. Bus. and Profl. Women, 1985, Achievement award Career Women's Achievement Network, 1986, Philbrook award Women's Polit. Caucus, 1989, N.J. Pride award for econ. devel., 1989, Paul L. Troast award, N.J. Bus.and Industry, 1989, Woman on the Move award, Bus. Jour. N.J., 1989; named Woman of Yr., Asian-Am. Profl. Women's Assn., 1983. Mem. Phi Beta Kappa. Avocations: rsch. projects on China during WWII, collecting antiques, Chinese and English silver, reading mystery novels. Office: FMC 800 N Capitol St NW Washington DC 20002-4244

HSU, MING-YU, engineering educator; b. Kweiyang, Kweichow, China, Dec. 4, 1925; s. Pei-Kung and Wan-Ju (Hsiao) H.; m. Chih-Ju Yao, Jan. 1, 1952; children: Chi-Hsing, Chi-Yun, Chi-En, Chi-Che, Chi-Cheng. BE, Nat. Kweichow U., 1948; Dipl.Engr., Delft Tech. U., The Netherlands, 1959. Registered profl. engr., Ill., Ga., Fla., S.C. Prof. Cheng-Kung U., Tainan, Taiwan, 1960-68; dir. Land Devel. Commn., Taipei, 1960-68; engring. cons. Ministry of Housing & Utilities, Sehba, Libya, 1968-71; sr. engr. Philipp Holzmann Ag., Hamburg, Fed. Republic of Germany, 1971-74, Weber, Griffith & Mellican, Galesburg, Ill., 1974-80; chief engr. Chatham Engring. Co., Savannah, Ga., 1980-82; sr. cons. Hussey, Gay, Bell & DeYoung, Inc., Savannah, 1982—; prof. Savannah Coll. of Art and Design, 1986—; designed and constructed numerous indsl. office, apt. and comml. bldgs., marine structures including docks, loading platforms, marinas, shipyards and water and waste water treatment structures. Contbr. articles on structural engring. to profl. jours. Mem. Nat. Soc. Profl. Engrs., ASCE. Home: 1115 Wilmington Island Rd Savannah GA 31410-4508 Office: Hussey Gay Bell & DeYoung 329 Commercial Dr Savannah GA 31406-3630

HSU, SAMUEL, music history educator, concert pianist; b. Shanghai, June 20, 1947; naturalized U.S. citizen, 1980; s. John and Dorothy (Wong) H. B.S., Phila. Coll. Bible, 1969, B.Mus., 1969; Ph.D., U. Calif., Santa Barbara, 1972; postgrad. with Rosina Lhevinne, Juilliard Sch. Music, 1972-76. Ordained deacon Presbyterian Ch., 1984, ordained elder, 1991. Isntr. piano Westmont Coll., Montecito, Calif., 1971-72; instr. music history and piano Phila. Coll. Bible, 1972-74, asst. prof., 1974-76, chmn. dept. piano, 1976—, assoc. prof., 1976-80, prof., 1980-99, chmn. honors program, disting. prof., 1999—; keyboardist Trenton Symphony Orch., 1983-84. instr. piano Csehy Summer Sch. Music, 1974—, bd. dirs., 1982—, dean faculty, 1999—. Numerous solo and ensemble performance appearances including Kennedy Ctr., Washington, Phila. Acad. Music, Martin Luther King Chapel, Atlanta. Pillsbury Found. grantee. Mem. Phila. Music Tchrs. Assn. (bd. dirs. 1976—, 2d v.p. 1980-82), Am. Musicol. Soc., Delta Epsilon Chi, Pi Kappa Lambda. Office: PO Box 2340 Philadelphia PA 19103-0340

HSU, STEPHEN MING, materials scientist, chemical engineer; b. Shanghai, China, Nov. 20, 1943; s. Chu-chen and Man-Yeo Hsu; m. Stella P. Lee, Sept. 8, 1968; children: Stephanie C., Vivian C. BSChemE, Va. Polytechnic Inst. State U., 1968; MSChemE, Pa. State U., 1972, PhD in Chem. Engring., 1976. Project engr. Dorr Oliver, 1968; rsch. engr. Amoco, 1974-78; group leader Nat. Inst. Stds. and Tech., Gaithersburg, 1978-85, chief ceramics divsn., 1985-92, group leader surface properties ceramics divsn., 1992—; vis. prof. chem. engring. Pa. State U., 1991-92, adj. prof. chem. engring., 1983-97; adj. prof. materials scis. U. Md., 1994-98; Eshbach vis. fellow Ctr. for Engring. Tribology, Northwestern U., 1992; postdoctoral rsch. advisor NRC, 1980; panelist nat. materials adv. bd., Nat. Acad. Scis., 1985; chmn. Gordon Rsch. Conf. on Tribology, 1988, lectr., 1980, 84, 86, 88, 92; mem. Nat. Steering Com. on Superconductivity Rsch. for Power Transmission, 1987-91; mem. com. on ceramic tribology, nat. materials adv. bd. Nat. Acad. Sci., 1986-87; chair numerous confs. Contbr. articles to profl. jours. Recipient Capt. Alfred E. Hunt meml. medal, 1980, Al Sonntag award 1991, Soc. of Tribologists and Lubricating Engrs.; Diamond Shamrock grad. fellow, 1971, Bronze medal for Superior Fed. Svc., Dept. Commerce, 1983, Silver medal for Meritorious Fed. Svc., 1990. Mem. AICE, TMS ASME (rsch. com. on tribology 1984-92), ASTM (mem. recycled oil p roducts 1979-87, chmn. 1983-85, mem. automotive products 1979-92, mem. analytical methods 1979-92, mem. oxidation methods 197-92, mem. petroleum products 1978-92, chmn. additive response of oils 1984-88), Am. Ceramics Soc. (mem. tribology working group 1985-86, dir. program on phase diagrams 1989-91), Soc. Automotive Engrs., Soc. Tribologists and Lubricating Engrs. (dir. 1987-94, membership com. 1987-90, chmn. ann. meeting program com. 1986, analytical com. 1985-86, chmn. paper solicitation 1983, lubrication fundamentals com., paper solicitation chmn. com. 1984, steering com. mem. Wear Conf. 1995-97, sec., treas. Weer Materials Conf., 1997—), Orgn. Chinese Am. (founding pres. Chgo. chpt. 1976), Editl. bd., Tribology Letters, 1995—, Tech. dir., Biomaterials Consortium, 1996—. Asian Pacific Am. Coun. (award 1987), Phi Kappa Phi, Phi Lambda Upsilon. Avocations: tennis, reading, bridge. Office: Nat Inst Stds and Tech I-270 & Quince Orchard Gaithersburg MD 20899

HSU, THOMAS TSENG-CHUANG, civil engineer, educator; b. Swatow, China, July 28, 1933; came to U.S., 1958; s. Benjamin D.H. and Lucy S.K. (Ma) Zi; m. Laura H.N. Ling, July 20, 1963; children: Lynne Ling, Mia Ming. BS, Harbin (China) Poly. U., 1957; MS, Cornell U., 1960, PhD, 1962. Engr. structural rsch. lab. Portland Cement Assn., Skokie, Ill., 1962-68; assoc. prof. structural engring. U. Miami, Coral Gables, Fla., 1968-73, prof., 1973-79, dept. chmn., 1974-78; vis. prof. dept. civil engring. Nat. Taiwan U., Taipei, 1979-80; prof. structural engring. U. Houston, 1980—, chmn., 1980-84, Moores univ. scholar, 1998—; Eshbach disting. vis. prof. Tech. Inst., Northwestern U., 1991-92; prin. investigator NSF, Washington, 1970—; cons. Kaiser Transit Group, Dade County, Fla.; 1977-79. Author: Torsion of Reinforced Concrete, 1984, Unified Theory of Reinforced Concrete, 1993; contbr. articles to profl. jours. Recipient Rsch. medal Am. Soc. Engring. Edn., 1969, Award of Excellence, Halliburton Found., 1990; named Hon. Disting. Prof., Harbin Inst. Civil and Archtl. Engring., China, 1993. Fellow ASCE (Walter L. Huber Rsch. prize 1974), Am. Concrete Inst. (Leonard C. Wason medal 1965, Arthur R. Anderson award 1990). Home: 5034 Glenmeadow Dr Houston TX 77096-4212 Office: U Houston Dept Civil Environ Engring Houston TX 77204-4791

HSU, YU KAO, aerospace scientist, mathematician, educator; b. Wukang, Hunan, China, Apr. 24, 1922; s. Ming Yung and Zhu Ching (Liu) H.; came to U.S., 1956, naturalized, 1972; Ph.D., Rensselaer Poly. Inst., 1966; m. Martha Tih Wang, Dec. 11, 1965; children: Timothy, Melinda. Rsch. asst. Rensselaer Poly Inst., Troy, N.Y., 1962-66; asst. prof. aerospace engring. W.Va. U., Morgantown, 1966-71; asso. prof. math. Univ. Coll., U. Maine, Orono, 1971-83, prof., 1983-93, prof. emeritus, 1993—; inst. guest MIT, 1978; vis. fellow Princeton (N.J.) U., 1993; presented paper to NASA, 1993. Author: Two Phase Laminar Film Condensation; Applied Mathematics for Engineering Technology; contbr. articles to profl. jours. Recipient Faculty award W.Va. U., 1971; U. Maine Summer Faculty Rsch. awards, 1976, 80, 90; summer faculty fellow Goddard Space Flight Ctr., 1987, 88, NASA Langley Rsch. Ctr., 1989. Mem. Am. Math. Soc., AIAA, Soc. Indsl. and Applied Math., Acad. Mechanics, Sigma Xi. Roman Catholic. Research, publs. in pressure field caused by cone rotating in non-Newtonian liquid, also supercaritating hydrofoil, also non-steady molecular beam of strong shock structure problem, laminar film condensation. Home: 121 Juniper St Bangor ME 04401-4155

HSUEH, CHUN-TU, political scientist, historian, foundation executive; b. Canton, China, Dec. 12, 1922; came to U.S., 1949, naturalized, 1960; m. Cordelia Teh-hua Huang, Dec. 13, 1952. Cert., China Sch. Jornalism, Hong Kong, 1939; LL.B., Chaoyang U., China, 1946, Raffles Coll., Singapore, 1946-49; M.A., Columbia U., 1953, Ph.D., 1958; hon. doctorate, U. San Martín de Porres, Lima, Peru, 1984. Research assoc. polit. sci. Stanford U., 1959-62; lectr. history U. Hong Kong, 1962-64; vis. assoc. prof. SUNY, Plattsburgh, 1964-65; assoc. prof. U. Md., College Park, 1965-68; prof. politics U. Md., 1968-92; pres. Huang Hsing Found., Md., 1990—; prof. Columbia U., summer 1969, 89; sr. assoc. mem. St. Antony's Coll., Oxford U., 1969; vis. prof., acting dir. Free U. Berlin, 1970; prof. Harvard U., summer 1979, 84; vis. scholar Peking U., 1983, Hebrew U., Jerusalem, 1984; disting. vis. prof. Zhongshan U., Guangzhou, China, 1983—, Wuhan U., 1984—, Peking U., 1989—, Zhejiang U., 1992—, Hunan U., 1996—, Shandong U., 1999—; adv. prof. Fudan U., Shanghai, 1985—; vis. fellow Australian Nat. U., Canberra, 1985; rsch. assoc. Ctr. for Chinese Studies U. Calif., Berkeley, 1985-86; chmn. Washington and S.E. Regional Seminar on China, 1974-81; exec. dir. Asian Polit. Scientists Group in U.S.A., 1975—; mem. vis. com., dept. internat. rels. Lehigh U., 1979-85; pres., chmn., Huang Hsing Found., Md., 1990—; vis. prof. U. Hong Kong, Trinity term, 1985, hon. prof., 1991—; hon. prof. People's U., China, 1993—, Fgn. Affairs Coll., Beijing, 1996—, Jianghan U., Wuhan, China, 1987—, Ningxia U., 1992—, Nanjing Normal U., 1996—, Chinese Acad. Social Scis., 1998—, The Confucius Acad., Shandong, 1998—; trustee Jinan U., Guangzhou, China, 1989—, Nanjing U., 1998—; advisor Sun Yat-sen Found., Guangzhou, 1992—; bd. dirs. Atalntic Coun. U.S., Washington, 1994—; bd. dirs. Russian Rsch. Ctr. Chinese Acad. Social Scis., 1996—; hon. pres. Internat. Studies Assn., 1998—; advisor Churchill Coll., U. Cambridge, 1998—, mem. exec. com.; mem. Atlantic Coun. Found., 1999—. Author: Huang Hsing and the Chinese Revolution, 1961, Chinese edit., 1980; editor, contbr.: Revolutionary Leaders of Modern China, 1971, French edit., 1973, Dimensions of China's Foreign Relations, 1977, Asian Political Scientists in North America: Professional and Ethnic Problems, 1977, China's Foreign Relations: New Perspectives, 1982, Traditional Government in Imperial China: A Critical Analysis, 1982, The Chinese Revolution of 1911: New Perspectives, 1986; author/editor of books in Chinese (English title): People, Places and Politics, 1991, New Dimensions of China's Diplomacy, 1997, The New Russia: Politics, Economics and Diplomacy, 1997, Modernization of the Legal System and China's Economic Development, 1997, Confucianism and Modernization of Chinese Culture, 1998, trade and Economic Relations Between China and Russia, 1999, China and Central Asia, 1999, Central and Eastern Europe in Transition, The Cradle of Modern Chinese Jurisprudence: A History Chaoyang University, 1999, Sun Tzu's Art of War and the International Security of the New Century, 1999, Chai Zemin: The First PRC Ambassador to the U.S. Mem. Nat. Bicentennial Ethnic-Racial Coun., 1974-76, Nat. Com. on U.S.-China Rels., 1976—; mem. adv. com. Md. Bicentennial Commn., 1975-76; mem. nat. exec. com. Caucus for New Polit. Sci., 1973-75. Mem. Assn. for Asian Studies (chmn. com. on scholars of Asian descent 1981-84), Western Returned Scholars Assn. (Beijing; overseas hon. v.p., hon. chmn. Fund 1994—), Am. Polit. Sci. Assn., Internat. Studies Assn. Office: 14017 Wagon Way Silver Spring MD 20906-2065

HU, CHENMING, electrical engineering educator; b. Beijing, China, July 12, 1947; came to U.S., 1969; m. Margaret Hu, Feb. 14, 1972; children: Raymond, Jason. BS, Nat. Taiwan U., Taipei, 1968; MS, U. Calif., Berkeley, 1970, PhD, 1973. Asst. prof. MIT, 1973-76; prof. U. Calif., Berkeley, 1976—, Chancellor's prof., 1998—; mgr. nonvilatile memory devel. Nat. Semicondr., Santa Clara, 1980-81; hon. prof. Beijing U., 1988, Tsing Hwa U., 1991, Chinese Acad. Sci., 1991; dir. Joint Svcs. Electronics Program, 1989-92, Indsl. Liaison Program, 1992-95. Co-author: Solar Cells, 1983, Advanced MOS Device Physics, 1989, Nonvolatile Semiconductor Memory, 1991; patentee solid state devices and tech.; contbr. over 500 articles to profl. jours. Chmn. bd. East Bay Chinese Sch., Oakland, Calif.,

1989-91. Recipient Design News Excellence in Design award, 1991, Semiconductor Rsch. Corp. Tech. Excellence award, 1992, Outstanding Inventor award, 1993, R&D 100 award, 1996, Monie Ferst award Sigma Xi, 1998, W.Y. Pang Found. award for rsch. excellence, 1999. Fellow IEEE (editl. bd. Trans. on Electronic Devices 1986-88, Jack Morton award 1997), NAE., Inst. Physics. Office: U Calif Dept Elec Engring and Computer Sci Berkeley CA 94720

HU, CHEN-SIEN, surgeon; b. Taiwan, Mar. 11, 1949; came to U.S. Aug., 1976; m. Li Ling; children: Jessica, Johnathan. MD, Taipei (Taiwan) Med. Sch., 1974; M in Pub. Health, Johns Hopkins U., 1977. Diplomate Am. Bd. Surgery, Am. Bd. Colon Rectal Surgery. Surgical resident Union Meml. Hosp., Balt., 1977-82; vascular fellow Tex. Heart Inst., Houston, 1982-83; colon-rectal resident U. Tex., Houston, 1983-84; pvt. practice Fla., 1984—; chief surgery Columbia HCA Hosp., New Port Richey, Fla., 1993—. Fellow Am. Coll. Surgeons, Am. Soc. Colon Rectal Surgery; mem. Soc. Laprascopic Surgeons, Soc. Am. Gastrointestinal Endoscopic Surgeons. Office: 5719 High St New Port Richey FL 34652-4036

HU, EDNA GERTRUDE FENSKE, pediatrics nurse; b. Arlington, S.D., June 11, 1922; d. Walter O. and Therese (Kautz) Fenske; m. Patrick P.C. Hu, Nov. 26, 1954; children: Lou Anne Hu Yee, Mark C., Lawrence P. BS in Nursing, U. Colo. Sch. Nursing, 1954. RN, Colo. Staff pediatrics nurse Colo. Gen. Hosp., Denver, 1954-63, night nursing supr., 1963-65; staff nurse alcohol withdrawal unit Denver Gen. Hosp., 1971-73; staff surg. nurse Fitzsimons Army Hosp., Denver, 1973-79; staff nurse VA Hosp., Allens Pk., Mich., 1979-81, Drug and Alcohol Withdrawal and Rehab. Ctr., Ft. Dodge, Iowa, 1981-83; researcher Ft. Collins, Colo., 1988—; researcher effects on memory following long term residence in another culture; instr. English, health care, Asia. Recipient Disting. Alumna award Class of 1954. Mem. ANA, Colo. Nurses Assn., Non-practicing and Part-time Nurses Assn. Home: 2518 Timber Ct Fort Collins CO 80521-3120

HU, JOHN CHIH-AN, retired chemist, research engineer; b. Nanzhang, Hubei, China, July 12, 1922; came to U.S., 1954; naturalized, 1965; s. Zi-Zing and Zhao-Xian (Zeng) H.; m. Betty Siao-Yung Ho, Oct. 26, 1957; children: Arthur, Benjamin, Carl, David, Eileen, Franklin, George. *Mr. Hu, the eldest of seven children, was born in the city of Nanzhang, a city where fourteen generations of his family lived for almost 400 years. He and his wife, Betty, a chemist, also have seven children; six sons and one daughter. Four of his sons received their degrees from MIT while his three other children received their degrees from Stanford University. Although all of his seven children chose engineering as their careers, they are all musically talented and each plays violin as a hobby.* BS in Chemistry, Nat. Ctrl. U., Nanjing, China, 1940; MS in Organic Chemistry, U. So. Calif., 1957, postgrad., 1957-61; PhD (hon.), Marquis Giuseppe Scicluna Internat. U. Found., 1985. Cert. profl. chemist. Dir. rsch. dept. Plant 1, Taiwan Fertilizer Mfg. Co., Chilung, 1947-54; rsch. assoc. dept. chemistry U. So. Calif., L.A., 1957-61; rsch. chemist Chem. Seal Corp. Am., L.A., 1961-62, Products Rsch. and Chem. Corp., Glendale, Calif., 1962-66; sr. rsch. engr. materials and tech. unit Boeing Co., Seattle, 1966-71; specialist engr. Quality Assurance Labs., Seattle, 1971-90, ret., 1990; cons. UN; lectr. profl. confs., China. *Mr. Hu is a Certified Professional Chemist, inventor and author. He was a Boeingengineer for 24 years, until his retirement in 1990. His professional interests lie in the fields of organic chemistry, polymeric materials technology, liquid and gas chromatography, mass spectrometry, and analytical pyrolysis. His career history had made him an expert in adhesion science and polymer technology. He was also engaged in the development of new analytical methods for chemical characterization of polymeric materials. Mr. Hu also developed the method of pyrolysis-mass spectrometry, which is the procedure for rapid analysis of high polymers.* Author: Analytical Approach, 1983, Advances in Chromotography, vol. 23, 1984; editor Puget Sound Chemist, 1984-92; referee profl. jours. Analytical Chemistry, Analytica Chimica Acta, Am. Chem. Soc., short courses; contbr. articles on analytical pyrolysis, gas chromatography, mass spectrometry, polymer characterization, chemistry and tech. of sealants and adhesives to profl. pubs. in Chinese and English; patentee in chromatopyrography. Fellow Am. Inst. Chemists; mem. Am. Chem. Soc. (chmn. Puget Sound sect. 1988, councilor 1989-92), Royal Soc. Chemistry (London), N.Y. Acad. Scis., Phi Lambda Upsilon. Achievements include research in field of new alaytical methods for chemical characterization of polymeric materials; development of method of pyrolysis-mass spectrometry. Home: 2813 Whitworth Ave S Renton WA 98055-5008

HU, JOSEPH KAI MING, insurance company executive; b. Hong Kong, Oct. 3, 1953; came to the U.S., 1963; s. Hon Wai and Kwan Yee H.; m. Donna Taeko, Mar. 31, 1984; 1 child, Jennifer Chiemi. BBA in Mktg., U. Hawaii, 1980. CPCU. Sales rep. Bankers Life Nebr., Honolulu, 1980-82; comml. lines mgr. Royal Ins. Agy., Honolulu, 1982-86; account exec. Frank B. Hall of Hawaii Inc., Honolulu, 1986-87, Jardine Ins. Brokers Inc., Honolulu, 1987-88; sr. v.p. Am. Ins. Agy. Inc., Honolulu, 1988—. Mem. Chartered Property and Casualty Underwriters (pres. Hawaii chpt. 1990-91, dir. Hawaii chpt. 1995—), Profl. Ins. Agts. Assn. (dir. Hawaii chpt. 1988—, pres. Hawaii chpt. 1993-94), Internat. Ins. Soc., Hong Kong Bus. Assn. Hawaii, Chinese Chamber Hawaii, Waikiki Rotary (treas. 1991-92). Office: Am Ins Agy Inc 900 Fort St Mall Ste 500 Honolulu HI 96813-3717

HU, LI, art educator; b. Shanghai, China, Sept. 16, 1950; s. Renzhi Hu and Keren He; m. Ping Li, Feb. 22, 1988; children: Yichen Hu, Elina Hu. BFA, Shanghai U., 1986; MFA, U. S.D., 1993. Art designer Xiechang Sewing Machine Co., Shanghai, 1977-83; asst. prof. Shanghai U., 1986-89, U. Wis., Oshkosh, 1993—. Solo shows include Colo. State U., Ft. Collins, 1998, Coker Coll., Hartsville, S.C., 1998, Linfield State Coll., McMinnville, Oreg., 1998, McHenry County Coll., Crystal Lake, Ill., 1998, Chadron State Coll., Nebr., 1997, Kansas City Artists Coalition, Kansas City, Mo., 1997, Mont. State U., Billings, 1996, Corvallis Arts Ctr., Oreg., 1996, Minnetonka Ctr. for the Art, Wayzata, Minn., 1995, Bloominton Art Ctr., Minn., 1995, others; group shows include Leslie Powell Gallery, Lawton, Okla., 1997, Smithtown Twp. Arts Coun., St. James, N.Y., 1997, Korean Cultural Ctr., L.A.,, 1996, Medici Art Ctr., Phila., 1996, San Francisco State U. Student Ctr. Art Gallery, Calif., 1995, Berkeley Art Ctr., Calif., 1995, others; work collected at Sioux City Art Ctr., Iowa, U. S.D., Vermillion, Coal and Oil Corp., Ji Lu, Japan, Art Corp. of Japan-China, Kobe, Japan. Recipient Hon. Mention Okla.: Centerfold, Seventh, Leslie Powell Gallery, Lawton and the U. of Sci. and Art, Chickacha, 1997, Faculty Devel. Rsch. grant U. Wis., Oshkosh, 1996, 1995, Juror's award Berkeley Art Ctr. Assn., Calif., 1995, others. Home: 604 W 20th Ave Oshkosh WI 54901-6824

HU, LINCOLN, media technology executive, computer scientist; b. Taipei, Taiwan. BS in Computer Sci., Columbia U., 1982, MS in Computer Sci., 1985. Rsch. staff assoc. Columbia U., N.Y.C., 1982-85; dir. tech. devel. Indsl Light & Magic, Lucasfilm Ltd., San Rafael, Calif., 1986-96; chief tech. officer Sony Pictures/Imageworks, Culver City, Calif., 1996—. Mem. Acad. Motion Picture Arts and Scis. (digital imaging tech. awards com. 1995—, sci. engring. award 1995, Tech. Achievement award 1996), Assn. for Computing Machinery. Office: Sony Pictures/Imageworks 9050 Washington Blvd Culver City CA 90232-2518

HU, SUE KING, elementary and middle school educator; b. Prince Frederick, Md., Nov. 7, 1938; d. James Elliott and Anna Irene (Hutchins) King; m. Richard Chee Chung Hu, July 2, 1960; children: Stephen Tse Wen, Sharon Yen Mei. BS, Towson (Md.) State U., 1960; MA, Marymount U., Arlington, Va., 1987. Cert. tchr., Va. Elem. tchr. Arlington (Va.) County Pub. Schs., 1977-90, elem. sch. rep., 1986-90, tchr. sci. mid. sch., 1990-94; environ. edn. cons., instr. Phoebe Knipling Outdoor Edn. Lab., Broad Run, Va., 1994—; workshop presenter Nat. Wildlife Fedn., Vienna, Va., 1989, 90; ednl. cons. Greenhouse Crisis Found., Washington, 1989-91; adj. prof. George Mason U., 1991, 94-95, instr. in environ. sci. Audubon Naturalist Soc., Chevy Chase, Md., 1990—; presenter children's workshops Fairfax County Schs., 1990—. Writer children's newspaper Sci. Weekly, 1990-91. chair edn. com. Fairfax (Va.) Audubon Soc., 1987-92, bd. dirs., 1988-92, v.p. natural history and edn., 1990-92. Recipient cert. of accomplishment Arlington County Pub. Schs., 1989, svc. award Fairfax Aududon Soc., 1992; named Notable Woman of Arlington, Arlington Commn. on the Status of Women, 1993. Mem. ASCD, Nat. Assn. Biology Tchrs. (elem.-mid. sch. chair 1988-89, presenter conf. 1986-89), Nat. Sci. Tchrs. Assn. (presenter conf. 1988-89), Coun. Elem. Sci. Internat., , Va. Assn. Sci. Tchrs., Delta Epsilon Sigma, Kappa Delta Pi. Democrat. Methodist. Avocations: hiking, birdwatching, cooking. Home: 2524 Leeds Rd Oakton VA 22124-1406

HUANG, CHANG-SHAN, landscape architect, educator; b. Fushun, China, Feb. 28, 1959; came to U.S., 1985; s. Wei-Guo Huang and Shu-Mei Chen; m. Ying Shan, Feb. 10, 1985; 1 child, Kerry. B in Architecture, Tsinghua U., 1983; MLA, Pa. State U., 1992; MA, PhD, U. Pa., 1995. Registered landscape architect, Tex. Instr. Tsinghua U., Beijing, 1983-85; landscape arhcitect John Rahenkamp Cons., Inc., Phila., 1988-91; cmty. planner Michael Cabot Assn., Stroudsburg, Pa., 1992-95; asst. prof. landscape architecture Tex. A&M U., College Station, 1995—. Mem. Am. Inst. Cert. Planners, Am. Soc. Landscape Architects, Am. Planning Assn., Phi Beta Delta. Avocations: landscape drawing, watercolor, photography, music, travel. Home: 803 Royal Adelade Dr College Station TX 77845-4441 Office: Tex A&M U Coll Architecture College Station TX 77843

HUANG, CHIEN CHANG, electrical engineer; b. Nanking, Peoples Republic of China, Feb. 16, 1931; came to U.S., 1957; s. Ling-Kuo Huang and Yi-Ching Liu; m. Li-May Tsai, June 2, 1962; children: Frederick G., Lewis G. BSEE, Taiwan Coll. Engring., Tainan, 1954; MSEE, U. Ill., 1959; postgrad., U. Pa., 1960-62. Engr. Burrough Corp., Paoli, Pa., 1960-64; sr. staff engr. Unisys Corp., San Diego, 1974—; sr. engr. Philco Ford Corp., Blue Bell, Pa., 1965-69; staff engr. Fairchild Semiconductor, Mountain View, Calif., 1969-71; sr. staff engr. Am. Micro Systems, Santa Clara, Calif., 1971-74. Contbr. articles to profl. jours. Home: 14481 Maplewood St Poway CA 92064-6446 Office: Unisys Corp 10850 Via Frontera San Diego CA 92127-1788

HUANG, DENIS KUO YING, chemical engineer, consultant; b. Canton, China, May 14, 1925; came to U.S., 1948; s. Shui Fu and Wai Men Wong; married; 1 child, Lloyd K. BS in Math., St. John's U., 1944; BSChemE, U. Calif., Berkeley, 1950; MSChemE, U. Maine, Orono, 1951; DChemE, Poly. Inst. Bklyn., 1958. Head chemist Internat. Paper Co., Phila., 1958-62; sr. rsch. chemist Simoniz Co., Chgo., 1962-65; sr. rsch. engr. Westvaco Corp., Laurel, Md., 1965-78; process engring. cons. Fed. Paper Bd., Augusta, Ga., 1978-90; UNIDO tech. expert to India, 1971; OAS tech. cons. to Argentina, 1972; UNDP cons. to China, 1983. Patentee in field; contbr. articles to ency., profl. jours. Mem. TAPPI, Sigma Xi, Phi Lambda Upsilon. Avocations: body building, tennis. Home: 426 SW Fairway Lndg Port Saint Lucie FL 34986-2163

HUANG, DONGZHOU, civil engineering educator, scientist, engineer; b. Ruijin, China, Nov. 5, 1949; came to U.S., 1990; s. Ziquan and Youdi (Zhu) H.; m. Yingying Shu, Feb. 10, 1979; 1 child, Yicheng. BS, Tongji U., 1974, MS, 1985, PhD, 1989. Asst. prof. Tongji U., Shanghai, China, 1980-88, assoc. prof., 1989—; rsch. assoc. prof. Fla. Internat. U., Miami, 1990-95, rsch. prof., 1995-97; engr. Fla. Dept. Transp., Miami, 1997—; assoc. dir. of bridge rsch. ctr. Tongji U., 1986-90. Co-author: Stability and Vibration of Bridge Structures, 1991 (1st Prize for Best Publs. in China 1993); contbr. books and articles to profl. jours. Mem. Am. Soc. of Civil Engrs., N.Y. Acad. Sci., Portland Cement Assn. (cement industry adv. bd.). Achievements include development of methods for analyzing dynamic responses/impact factors of multi-girder bridges, box girder bridges, curved girder bridges and cable-stayed brides due to moving vehicles and found the basic relationship between static and dynamic responses as well as the relationship between impact factor and lateral load distribution factor; developed finite element methods for analyzing elastic and inelastic lateral buckling of truss and trussed-arched bridges, as well as for static and dynamic analysis of curved box girder bridges; developed a practical method for determining lateral load distribution factors of arch bridges. Home: 18255 SW 89th Ct Miami FL 33157-5917

HUANG, ENG-SHANG, virology educator, biomedical engineer; b. Chia-Yi, Taiwan, Republic of China, Mar. 17, 1940; came to U.S., 1968; s. Juong-Sun and King-fa (Ong) H.; m. Shu-Mei Huong, Dec. 26, 1965; children: David Y., Benjamin Y. BS, Nat. Taiwan U., Taipei, Taiwan, 1962, MS, 1964; PhD, U. N.C., 1971. Asst. prof. U. N.C., Chapel Hill, 1973-78, assoc. prof., 1978-86, prof., 1986—; virology program leader Cancer Rsch. Ctr., Chapel Hill, 1979-91; mem. virology study sect. DRG/NIH, Bethesda, Md., 1978-82; mem. AIDS basic rsch. rev. com. Nat. Inst. Allergy & Infectious Diseases/NIH, 1988-90; chmn. Internat. Sci. Promotion Com., U.S. chpt., 1988—. Contbr. articles to Molecular Biology of Human Cytomegalovirus, Devel. Abnormality Induced by Cytomegalovirus Infection, Interaction between Cytomegalovirus and Human Immunodeficiency Virus. Chmn. membership com. Soc. Chinese Bioscientists in Am., Washington, 1988-89, coun. mem., 1993-96. Lt. ROTC, 1964-65. NIH fellow, 1971-73, Rsch. Career Devel. award NIAID, NIH, 1978-83; grantee in field. Mem. AAAS, Am. Soc. Microbiology, N.Y. Acad. Sci., Am. Assn. Cancer Rsch. Democrat. Achievements include development of mouse model to study the developmental abnormality induced by cytomegalovirus infection in humans; research in inhibition of human cytomegalovirus DNA replication by ganciclovir (DHPG). Office: U NC CB#7295 Lineberger Cancer Ctr Chapel Hill NC 27599-7295

HUANG, EUGENE YUCHING, civil engineer, educator; b. Changsha, China, Nov. 28, 1917; came to U.S., 1948, naturalized, 1962; s. Sam and Yi Yun (Chao) H.; m. Helen M. Woo, Aug. 20, 1955; children: Martha, Pearl, William, Mary, Priscilla, Stephen. M.S., U. Utah, 1950; D.Sc., U. Mich., 1954. Registered profl. engr., Ill., Mich. Asst. engr. Chinese Nat. Hwy. Adminstrn., 1941-45, asso. engr., 1945-48; research asst. Engring. Research Inst., U. Mich., 1953-54; research asst. prof. civil engring. U. Ill., Urbana, 1954-58; asso. prof. U. Ill., 1958-63; prof. transp. engring. Mich. Tech. U., Houghton, 1963-84; acting head dept. civil engring., 1979-80; acting dean of grad. studies Mich. Tech. U., Houghton, 1981-83, prof. emeritus transp. engring., 1984—; cons. transp. systems design, soil mechanics, 1954—. Author: Overview of the American Transportation System, 1976; contbr. numerous articles on transp. design systems and research on materials for pavement to profl. jours. Recipient Faculty Research award Mich. Tech. U., 1967. Fellow ASCE; mem. AAAS, ASTM, NRC (transp. rsch. bd. 1954), Am. Soc. Engring. Edn., Assn. Asphalt Paving Technologists, Inst. for Opns. Rsch. and the Mgmt. Scis., Am. Ry. Engring. Assn., Sigma Xi, Chi Epsilon, Tau Beta Pi, Phi Tau Phi. Episcopalian. Home: 400 Garnet St Houghton MI 49931-1420

HUANG, FAN-H FRANK, materials scientist, researcher; b. Taiwan, May 13, 1940; came to U.S., 1966; BS, Taiwan Normal U., 1965; PhD, Rensselaer Poly. Inst., Troy, N.Y., 1973. Rsch. assoc. Cornell U., Ithaca, N.Y., 1973-77; prin. scientist Westinghouse Hanford Co., Richland, Wash., 1977-94, Kaiser Hanfor Co., Richland, 1994-96, Fluor Daniel N.W., Inc., Richland, 1996—. Author: Fracture Properties of Irradiated Alloys, 1995; contbr. articles to profl. jours. Mem. ASTM, Am. Nuclear Soc. Avocations: swimming, hiking, fishing. Office: Fluor Daniel Northwest Inc PO Box 1050 Richland WA 99352-1050

HUANG, FRANCIS FU-TSE, mechanical engineering educator; b. Hong Kong, Aug. 27, 1922; came to U.S., 1945, naturalized, 1960; s. Kwong Set and Chen-Ho (Yee) H.; m. Fung-Yuen Fung, Apr. 10, 1954; children: Raymond, Stanley. BS, San Jose State Coll., 1951; MS, Stanford U., 1952; Profl. M.E., Columbia U., 1964; Cultural Doctorate in Energy Sci. (hon.), World U., Ariz., 1990. Design engr. M.W. Kellogg Co., N.Y.C., 1952-58; faculty San Jose (Calif.) State U., 1958—, assoc. prof. mech. engring., 1962-67, prof., 1967-91, prof. emeritus, 1991, chmn. dept., 1973-81; hon. prof. heat power engring. Taiyuan (People's Republic of China) U. Tech., 1981—. Author: Engineering Thermodynamics—Fundamentals and Applications, 1976, 2d edit., 1988. Capt. Chinese Army, 1943-45. Recipient Disting. Teaching award Calif. State Coll. System, 1968-69; named Outstanding Prof. of Yr., Tau Beta Pi, 1967, 76, Prof. of Yr., Pi Tau Sigma, 1985; NSF faculty fellow, 1962-64. Mem. AAAS, ASME, AIAA, AAUP, Am. Soc. Engring. Edn., N.Y. Acad. Scis., Sigma Xi. Home: 1259 Sierra Mar Dr San Jose CA 95118-1235 Office: San Jose State U Dept Mech Engring San Jose CA 95192

HUANG, HERMAN FU, transportation researcher; b. Iowa City, Iowa, May 19, 1966. BS, Case Western Res. U., 1987; MS, Ind. U., 1990; PhD, U. N.C.-Chapel Hill, 1995. Rsch. asst. Hwy. Safety Rsch. Ctr., U. N.C., Chapel Hill, 1991-95, rsch. assoc., 1996—. Contbr. articles to profl. jours. Mem. Am. Planning Assn., Inst. Transp. Engrs. (assoc.), Transp. Rsch. Bd. (individual affiliate). Avocations: fitness, travel. Office: Univ of North Carolina 730 Airport Rd Chapel Hill NC 27514-5738

HUANG, JACOB CHEN-YA, physician, city official; b. Chia-Yi, Taiwan, Dec. 25, 1937; came to U.S., 1966, naturalized, 1974; s. Chang-Chiang and Agenes Cheng-Jen H.; m. Vivian Lin, Oct. 3, 1970; children: Phyllis, Albert, Edward. Intern, Taipei City Hosp., 1964-65, house officer in pediatrics, 1965-66; fellow in clin. pathology Albert Einstein Coll. Medicine-Lincoln Hosp., 1968-70; chief drug diagnostic sect. N.Y.C. chief med. examiner, 1968-79; resident in family medicine Lutheran Med. Center, N.Y.C., 1970-71; clin. asso. prof. NYU, 1972-76; dist. health dir. N.Y.C., Dept. Health, 1971-76; med. dir. Paterson City (N.J.) Health Dept., 1977—; chmn. dept. family practice Dover (N.J.) Gen. Hosp. and Med. Center, 1980—; trustee N.J. Passaic PRO, 1987—; bd. dirs. ambulatory care adv. bd. Beth Israel Hosp., N.Y.C., 1972-76, cmty. adv. bd. ambulatory svcs. St. Vincent Med. Ctr., N.Y.C., 1972-76, COMED-IPA Inc., N.J., 1980—; bd. dirs. Mount Olive City (N.J.) Bd. of Health, 1993—. Recipient Physician's Recogniation award AMA. Diplomate Am. Bd. Family Practice. Fellow Am. Coll. Preventive Medicine, Am. Acad. Family Physicians; mem. Am. Public Health Assn., Am. Chinese Med. Assn. N.J. (pres., founder), N.J. Am. Acad. Family Physicians (trustee 1994—, bd. dirs. 1994—, exec. bd. dirs. 1995—), Chinese Am. Med. Soc. (bd. dirs.), Chinese Am. Physicians Network of N.J. (pres. 1997—), Columbia U. Sch. Pub. Health Alumni Assn. (exec. bd. 1992—). Home: 3 Walnut Hill Dr Chester NJ 07930-3006 Office: Bartley Sq Rte 206 Flanders NJ 07836

HUANG, JIA-HONG, materials science educator; b. Taipei, Taiwan, May 21, 1958; s. Wen-Su and Lee-Chun (Lee) H.; m. Lih-Hwa Fuh, Jan. 1, 1987; children: Evelyn, Johnny Huang. BS, Nat. Tsing Hua U., Hsinchu, Taiwan, 1980, MS, 1984; PhD, U. Ill., Urbana-Champaign, 1989. Rsch. asst. U. Ill., Urbana-Champaign, 1985-89; assoc. prof. nuclear engring. Nat. Tsing Hua U., 1989-94, prof. nuclear engring. and engring. physics, 1994-97, prof. engring. and system sci., 1997—; rsch. scholar U. Ill., Urbana-Champaign, 1997-98. Editor jour. Chinese Corrosion Engring., 1994—; contbr. articles to profl. jours. Mem. ASM Internat., Minerals, Metals and Materials Soc., Chinese Soc. Materials Sci., Phi Tau Phi, Phi Kappa Phi. Avocations: swimming, traveling, classical music. Office: Nat Tsing Hua U Dept Engring & System Sci, 101 Kuang Fu Rd Sect 2, Hsinchu 300, Taiwan Address: 100-20 Chein Chung Rd, Hsinchu Taiwan 300, TAIWAN

HUANG, KERSON, physics educator; b. Nan Ning, Kwangsi, Peoples Republic of China, Mar. 15, 1928; came to U.S., 1947; s. Horton T. and Shi (Ng) H.; m. Julia M. Sheng, Sept. 9, 1956 (div. 1971); m. Rosemary E. Verducci, May 19, 1979; 1 child, Kathryn Camille. SB, MIT, 1950, PhD, 1953. Instr. MIT, Cambridge, 1953-55, asst. prof. physics, 1957-61, assoc. prof., 1961-66, prof., 1966—; fellow Inst. for Advanced Study, Princeton, N.J., 1955-57; hon. prof. Fudan U., Shanghai, Peoples Republic of China, 1980. Author: Quarks, Leptons and Guage Field, 1982, Statistical Mechanics, 1987, I Ching, 1987, Quantum Field Theory, 1998; cons. editor: World Sci. Pub., Singapore, 1981—. Fellow Alfred P. Sloan Found., 1961-62, Guggenheim Found., Geneva, 1962, sr. fellow Fulbright Founf., Santiago, Chile, 1974. Fellow Am. Acad. Arts and Scis., Am. Phys. Soc. Office: MIT 77 Massachusetts Ave Rm 6309 Cambridge MA 02139-4307

HUANG, KUN LIEN, software engineer, scientist; b. Nantou, Taiwan, Jan. 20, 1953; came to U.S., 1984; S. Chai-Chang and Fei-Chei (Chi) H.; m. Sue Hui Lee, Mar. 24, 1981; 1 child, Wayne. BS, Nat. Taipei Inst. Tech., Taiwan, 1973, N.D. State U., 1986; MS, U. Mo., 1988. Mech. engr. Ta Tung Aluminum Co., Taipei, 1975-76; rsch. mgr. Ta Tung Aluminum Co., Tapei, 1976-77, prodn. tech. mgr., 1977-79, quality control mgr., 1979-84; computer programmer U. Mo., Columbia, 1988; systems analyst, programmer NCR Corp., San Diego, 1989-92; database cons. Gamma-Metrics, 1992-93; software engr. Sci. Applications Internat. Corp., 1993-95; Unix adminstr. Gen. Instrument Corp., 1995-98; sr. database mgr. Indusoft, Inc., 1998—; cons. Computing Ctr., U. Mo., Columbia, 1987-88. Recipient Nat. scholarship Republic China Jaycees, Taipei, 1972. Mem. AAAS, San Diego Taiwanese Cultural Assn. Republican. Avocation: fishing. Home: 8939 Adobe Bluffs Dr San Diego CA 92129-4400

HUANG, MEI QING, physics educator, researcher; b. Wuhan, Hubei, People's Republic China, Jan. 20, 1942; came to U.S., 1988; parents Gong Li and Hui Qin Xia Huang; m. Jin Song Chen, Jan. 6, 1938; children: Qun Chen, Li Chen. Grad. dept. physics, U. Sci. and Tech. China, Beijing, 1964. Asst. prof. dept. physics U. Sci. and Tech. China, 1964-70; asst. prof. dept. physics U. Sci. and Tech. China, Hefei, 1970-78, instr., 1978-87, assoc. prof., 1987—, head div. magnetism, 1986-88; rsch. assoc. dept. MEMS Carnegie-Mellon U., Pitts., 1983-85, 88-91, rsch. scientist in advanced materials, 1991—; participant Chinese-Am. coop. program in atomic, molecular and condensed matter physics Chinese Acad. Sci. and Am. Physics Soc., 1988; presenter at nat. and internat. confs., including 5th, 6th, 30th, 34th, 35th, 36th, 37th, 38th, 40th, 41st Ann. Conf. on Magnetism and Magnetic Materials, Internat. Conf. on Rare Earth Applications and Devels., 11th and 12th Internat. Workshop on Rare Earth Magnets and Their Applications. Contbr. articles to Physica, Jour. Appleid Physics, Jour. Magnetism and Magnetic Materials, Jour. Less Common Metals. Recipient 3d prize of sci. and tech. Acad. Sci. China, 1988. Mem. Chinese Phys. Soc., Am. Phys. Soc. Achievements include patent pending for Cerium-free Mischmetal Fe-B-o Permanent Magnets; research on magnetic properties and structure of magnetic recording powder using magnetic measurements, electron microscopic investigation and Mossbauer spectrum analysis, magnetic properties and structure of rare earth intermetallic properties using X-ray diffraction and magnetic measurement, influence of hydrogen on the magnetic characteristics of R2Fe14B system, magnetic and structural properties of R2Fe17Nx, R2(Fe, Co)17Nx, (Sm, R)2Fe17Nx nitrides, Fe16N2, RC013-xSix, sintering studies of permanent magnet materials, metal bonded Sm2Fe17Nx type magnets, synthesis and characterize structure and magnetic properties of Fe-Co alloy nanoparticles. Home: 5 Bayard Rd Apt 409 Pittsburgh PA 15213-1905 Office: Carnegie Mellon Rsch Inst PO Box 2950 700 Technology Dr Pittsburgh PA 15219-3124

HUANG, MILTON PEECHUAN, physician, researcher, educator; b. Mar. 3, 1963. BSEE, BA in Psychology, Stanford U., 1986; MD, U. Tex., 1990. Med. lic. Tex., Mich.; bd. cert. gen. psychiatry. Intern U. Mich. Hosps., Ann Arbor, 1990-91, resident, 1991-94, fellow in psychiat. informatics, 1994-96, lectr., 1996—; chief resident U. Mich., Ann Arbor, 1993; asst. dir. psychiat. informatics program U. Mich., Ann Arbor, 1996—. Contbr. articles to profl. jours., chpts. to books. Mem. Am. Psychiat. Assn., Am. Med. Informatics Assn., Mich. Psychiat. Soc., Psychiat. Soc. Informatics (sec.-treas. steering com. 1996—, chair info. sec. and confidentiality com. 1997). Office: U Mich Dept Psychiatry Box 0390 1500 E Medical Center Dr Dept Ann Arbor MI 48109-0390

HUANG, PAN MING, soil science educator; b. Pu-tse, Taiwan, Sept. 2, 1934; arrived in Can., 1965; s. Rong Yi and Koh (Chiu) H.; m. Yun Yin Lin, Dec. 26, 1964; children: Daniel Chian Yuan, Crystal Ling Hui. BSA, Nat. Chung Hsing U., Taichung, Taiwan, 1957; MSc, U. Man., Winnipeg, Can., 1962; PhD, U. Wis., Madison, 1966. Cert. prof. agrologist. Asst. prof. soil sci. U. Sask., Saskatoon, Can., 1965-71, assoc. prof., 1971-78, prof., 1978—; nat. vis. prof., head dept. soil sci. Nat. Chung Hsing U., 1975-76; mem. agr. adv. bd. Lewis Pubs., 1991—; hon. prof. Huazhong Agr. U., 1992—, Guanxi Agrl U., 1993—, Henan Agrl. U., 1996—; acad. advisor Chinese Acad. Scis., 1996—. Author: Soil Chemistry, 1991; mem. editl. bd. Chemosphere, 1987-97, Pedosphere, 1990—, Trends in Agr. Sci., 1991-95, Advances in Environ. Sci., 1993—, Geodema, 1994—, Soil Sci. Plant Nutrition, 1998—, Water, Air, and Soil Pollution, 1998, Humic Substances in the Environment, 1998; editor 9 books; spl. editor, mem. editl. bd. Water Pollution Rsch. Jour. Can., 1983-89, 91-93, Agro's Ann. Rev. Crop Ecology, 1995—; mem. editl. adv. bd. Trends in Soil Sci., 1995—; contbr. over 200 articles to profl. jours., chpts. to books. Bd. dirs. Saskatoon Chinese Mandarin Sch., 1977-79, Saskatoon Soc. for Study Chinese Culture, 1983—. 2d lt. Taiwan Mil. Tng. Corps, 1957-59. Recipient Disting. Rschr. award U. Sask., 1997; grantee The UN Environment Programme, Nat. Scis. and Engring. Rsch. Coun. Can. and numerous other agys., 1965—. Fellow AAAS, Can. Soc. Soil Sci., Soil Sci. Soc. Am. (rep. Clay Minerals Soc. 1979-83, chmn. divsn. S-9, 1983-84, bd. dirs. 1983-84, assoc. editor 1987-92, editor spl. publ. 1986, 98, rep. to Internat. Union Pure and Applied Chemistry 1990—, Internat. Soil Sci.

award com. 1986-87, Marion L. and Christie M. Jackson Soil Sci. award com. 1990—, fellow com. 1992—, chmn.-elect divsn. S-2, 1993-94, chmn. 1994-95,, past chmn. 1995-96, bd. dirs. 1995-96, spl. awards com. 1995-96, chair nominations com. divsn. s-2 1995-96), Am. Soc. Agronomy; mem. Internat. Soc. Soil Sci. (chmn. working group MO 1990—), Am. Chem. Soc., N.Y. Acad. Scis., Internat. Union Pure and Applied Chemistry (assoc., commn. environ. analytical chemistry 1993-95, titular mem. comm. fundamental environ. chemistry 1995-97), Internat. Assn. Study Clays (treas. 1993—), Chinese Acad. Scis. (acad. com. 1988-94, adv. com. 1997—), Internat. Human Substances Soc. (leader Can. nat. chpt. 1992—), Can. Network Toxicology (team on metal speciation 1993-96), Sigma Xi. Avocations: music, reading. Home: 130 Mount Allison Cres, Saskatoon, SK Canada S7H 4A5 Office: U Sask Dept Soil Sci, Campus Dr 51, Saskatoon, SK Canada S7N 5A8

HUANG, PETER HENRY, law educator; b. Pitts., Dec. 6, 1958. AB, Princeton U., 1976; MS, Harvard U., 1978, PhD, 1984; JD, Stanford U., 1997. Economist F.T.C., Washington, 1984-85; assoc. Sullivan & Cromwell, L.A., 1996; asst. prof. U. Pa. Law Sch., Phila., 1997—; vis. asst. prof. U. Calif. Econs. Dept., Berkeley, 1989, UCLA, L.A., 1990, 91, Stanford U. Econs. Dept., Palo Alto, Calif., 1994; vis. lectr. U. So. Calif., L.A., 1995, 96. Mem. Phi Beta Kappa. Office: U Pa Law Sch 3400 Chestnut St Philadelphia PA 19104-6204

HUANG, PIEN CHIEN, biochemistry educator, scientist; b. Shanghai, China, July 13, 1931; came to U.S., 1955, naturalized, 1969; s. C. Hwa and H. (Tong) H.; m. Ru chih Chow, June 10, 1956; children: Suber S., Suzanne S. B.S., Nat. Taiwan U., 1953; M.S., Va. Tech. U., 1956; Ph.D., Ohio State U., 1960. Research fellow Calif. Inst. Tech., 1960-65; asst. prof. dept. biochemistry Johns Hopkins U., 1965, assoc. prof., to 1976, prof., 1976—; prof. biomed., chair life sci. dept., dean Coll. Life. Sci. Nat. Tsing Hua U., 1993-96; vis. scholar Med. Rsch. Coun. Molecular Biology Lab., Cambridge, Eng., 1972; vis. prof. Acad. Sinica, 1987-88; program dir. NSF, 1996—. Editor: (with Cohen, Lillienfeld) Genetic Issues in Public Health and Medicine; (with Kuo and Wu) Genetic Engineering Techniques: Recent Advances, (with Chang, Lin) Molecular Biology of Neoplasia, contbr. articles to profl. jours. Fellow NIH, Fogarty Sr. Internat. Mem. Am. Soc. Biol. Chemists, Genetics Soc. Am., Am. Soc. Biophysics, Soc. Cell Biology, Academia Sinica. Office: Johns Hopkins U Dept Biochemistry 615 N Wolfe St Baltimore MD 21205-2103

HUANG, SUNG-CHENG, electrical engineering educator; b. Canton, China, Oct. 26, 1944; came to U.S., 1967; s. Hip-chung Wong and Chi-hung Chung; m. Caroline S. Soong, Sept. 4, 1971; children: Michael, Dennis. BSEE, Nat. Taiwan U., Taipei, 1966; DSc, Wash. U., 1973. Rsch. assoc. biomed. computer lab. Wash. U., St. Louis, 1973-74; project engr. Picker Corp., Cleve., 1974-77; asst. prof. UCLA Sch. Medicine, 1977-82, assoc. prof., 1982-86, prof., 1986—; Edward Farber lectr. U. Chgo., 1986. Mem. editl. bd. Jour. Nuc. Medicine, 1997—, Jour. Cerebral Blood Flow, 1989-92; dep. chief editor Jour. Cerebral Blood Flow and Metabolism, 1993—; contbr. over 200 articles to profl. jours. Recipient George Von Hevesy prize World Congress of Nuclear Medicine and Biology, 1982; grantee U.S. Dept. Energy, 1977—, NIH, 1977—. Mem. AAAS, IEEE, Soc. Nuclear Medicine, Soc. Cerebral Blood Flow. Achievements include patent for spread beam overlap method; development of various tracer techniques used for positron emission tomographic (PET) studies in nuclear medicine; research in computer tomographic image construction technique. Office: UCLA Sch Medicine Divsn Nuclear Medicine and Biophysics 10833 Le Conte Ave Los Angeles CA 90095-3075

HUANG, THOMAS SHI-TAO, electrical engineering educator, researcher; b. Shanghai, China, June 26, 1936; came to U.S., 1958; s. Chien Liang and Allen (Chien) H.; m. Margaret Y. Nee, Apr. 4, 1959; children: Caroline B., Marjorie A., Thomas T., Gregory T. BS, Nat. Taiwan U., Taipei, 1956; MS, MIT, 1960, ScD, 1963. Asst. prof. MIT, Cambridge, Mass., 1963-67, assoc. prof., 1967-73; prof. Purdue U., West Lafayette, Ind., 1973-80; prof. U. Ill., Urbana, 1980—, William L. Everitt Disting. Prof., 1996—; vis. prof. Swiss Inst. Tech., Zurich, U. Hannover, Federal Republic of Germany, U. Que., Can., others; cons. IBM, AT&T Bell Labs., MIT Lincoln Lab., Kodak, others. Author 2 books; editor 10 books; contbr. more than 300 articles to tech. jours. Recipient A. V. Humboldt U.S. Sr. Scientist award Alexander V. Humboldt Found., 1976-77; Guggenheim fellow, 1971-72; fellow Japan Assn. for Promotion of Sci., 1986. Fellow IEEE (Signal Processing Soc. Tech. Achievement award 1987, Soc. award 1991), Optical Soc. Am., Internat. Assn. for Pattern Recognition, Internat. Optical Engring. Soc. Office: Univ Ill Coordinated Sci Lab 1308 W Main St Urbana IL 61801-2307

HUANG, THOMAS WEISHING, lawyer; b. Taipei, Taiwan, Feb. 1, 1941; came to U.S., 1967; s. Lienden and Helen (Yen) H. BA, Taiwan U., 1964; JD magna cum laude, Ind. U., Indpls., 1970; LLM, Harvard U., 1971, SJD, 1975. Bar: D.C. 1975, Mass. 1976, U.S. Dist. Ct. Mass. 1976, U.S. Ct. Appeals (1st cir.) 1978, N.Y. 1980. Judge adv. Chinese Army, Taiwan, 1964-65; legal officer Treaty and Legal Dept., Ministry of Fgn. Affairs, Taiwan, 1966-67; assoc. Chemung County Legal Svcs., Elmira, N.Y., 1975-76; assoc. law firm Taylor Johnson & Wieschhoff, Marblehead, Mass., 1980; prin. Reiser & Rosenberg, Boston, 1982-86, Huang & Assocs., Boston, 1987-88, Hale, Sanderson, Byrnes & Morton, Boston, 1988-96; of counsel Chin, Wright & Branson P.C., Boston, 1996-97; shareholder Sherburne, Powers & Needham, P.C., Boston, 1997-98, ptnr. Holland & Knight, LLP, Boston, 1998—; exec. v.p. Excel Tech. Internat. Co., Brunswick, N.J., 1982-88; bd. dirs. Asian Am. Bank & Trust Co., Boston, exec. com., clk., 1993—; legal counsel Nat. Assn. Chinese Ams., Washington, 1979-80. Mem. editl. staff Ind. Law Rev., 1969-70; contbr. articles to legal jours. Bd. dirs. Chinese Econ. Devel. Coun., Boston, 1978-80; mem. Gov.'s Adv. Coun. on Guangdong, 1984-87; mem. minority bus. task force Senator Kerry's Office, 1988—. Mem. Boston Bar Assn. (mem. internat. law sect. steering com. 1979-90, mem. ad hoc com. on code of profl. conducts), Nat. Assn. Chinese Ams. (v.p. Boston chpt. 1984-86, pres. 1986-88, 1st. v.p. nat. assn. 1994-97), Taiwan C. of C. in New Eng. (clk., bd. dirs. 1996—). Democrat. Home: 30 Farrwood Dr Andover MA 01810-5233 Office: Holland & Knight LLP One Beacon St Boston MA 02108

HUANG, TING-CHIA, chemical engineering educator, researcher; b. Tainan, Taiwan, June 1, 1932; s. Tzuo and Nai (Yeh) H.; m. Juei-Chin Wan, Jan. 19, 1958; children: Ling-Yuang, Ling-Huei, Ping-Hsien, Chao-Cheng. BS, Nat. Cheng Kung U., Tainan, 1955; D Engring., U. Tokyo, 1979. Tchg. asst. dept. chem. engring. Nat. Cheng Kung U., 1956-60, instr., 1960-65, assoc. prof., 1965-68, prof., 1968—, chmn., dir. dept., 1981-87, v.p., 1995-97, acting pres., 1996-97; nat. chair prof. Ministry of Edn., 1997—; IAEA rsch. fellow Japan Atomic Energy Rsch. Inst., Tokai-mura, Ibaraki-Ken, 1962; rsch. assoc. U. Houston, 1969-70; tech. cons. ChiMeng Indsl. Co., Ltd., Hsin-Hua, Taiwan, 1979—; cons. Ministry Edn., Taipei, Taiwan, 1988-94, Kang Hsiang Lan Pharmaceutice Co., Ltd., Yung-Kan Ind. Park, Tainan Syan, Taiwan, 1989—. Author: Experimental Physical Chemistry, 1963, 20th edit., 1987, Chemical Engineering Thermodynamics, 1971, Physical Chemistry, 1978, 84, 5th edit., 1990, Experiments in Physical Chemistry, 1983, 3d edit., 1988; regional editor Waste Mgmt. jour.; contbr. over 180 articles to profl. jours. Recipient Engring. Sci. award Hsu's Found., 1975, Engring. Acad. award Ministry Edn., 1979, outstanding rsch. awards Ministry Edn., 1983, 84, Nat. Sci. Coun., 1986-94; named Outstanding Invited Rschr. Nat. Rsch. Coun., 1995—. Mem. AIChE, Chinese Inst. Engrs. (best paper award 1975, 85, 96, Outstanding Engring. Prof. award 1991), Chinese Inst. Chem. Engrs. (assoc. editor-in-chief jour. 1986—, Chin Kai-Ying award 1991, best paper award 1994, 95, Chem. Engr. Inst. prize 1997), Chinese Chem. Soc., Soc. Chem. Engrs. Japan, Chinese Inst. Mining Engring. (best paper award 1989, 95), Phi Tau Phi. Avocations: reading, inventing, writing, music, table tennis. Address: 4th fl 23 Alley 17 Ln 133, Sec 2 Chong Hua E Rd, Tainan 70104, Taiwan Office: Nat Cheng Kung U, No 1 Ta-Siue Rd, Tainan 70101, Taiwan

HUANG, VICTOR TSANGMIN, food scientist, researcher; b. Republic of China, Dec. 12, 1951; came to U.S., 1975; s. Shen Tan and Yeh Gee (Lai) H.; m. Jean Fong Chen, June 9, 1978; children: Hank Su, Andrea Su. BS, Hsing-Hua U., Hsin-Chu, Republic of China, 1973; MS, U. Chgo., 1977; PhD, Ohio State U., 1981. Teaching asst. U. Chgo., 1975-77; rsch. assoc. Ohio State U., Columbus, 1977-81; food scientist Pillsbury Co., Mpls., 1981—; presenter dairy, baby and bakery product formulation field, 1977-94. Contbr. articles to profl. jours.; patentee frozen desserts and microwave food formulation fields in U.S. and Europe. Vice pres. Minn. Taiwanese Assn., Mpls., 1985. 2d lt. Taiwan Army, 1973-75. Mem. Am. Dairy Sci. Assn., Inst. Food Technologists, Am. Assn. Cereal Chemists, Am. Chem. Soc., Toastmasters (pres. Mpls. 1988). Office: Pillsbury Tech Ctr 330 University Ave SE Minneapolis MN 55414-1779

HUANG, WEN-XIANG, artist, educator; b. Wu Hu, An-Hui, China, Nov. 21, 1929; came to the U.S., 1989; s. Jin-Tanw and De-Xian Huang; three children. Grad., Chinese Fine Artist's Acad., ZheKiang Province Art Inst. Assoc. prof. Shanghai Internat. Studies U., 1953-89; lectr. Tokyo Shan-Lin Inst. Calligraphy, 1989; instr. Syi-Lai Buddhist Temple, Hacienda Heights, Calif., 1990-91; painting instr. L.A. City Coll., 1996-98; art editor Shanghai Fgn. Lang. Press, 1980-89; advisor Chinese Artists Assn., Chinese Calligraphy and Painting Assn., L.A., N.Y. Ctr. for Internat. Art and Culture. Works exhibited at The Confucius Temple, Qufu, China, 1985, JAGDA Peace Posters Internat., Tokyo, 1987, The Forest of Stone Tablets, Hanguan, China, 1988, The Chinese Am. Cultural Ctr., L.A., 1990-92, Hollywood Bowl Art Show, 1991-92, Pacific Asia Mus., 1993. Recipient awards Pacific Asia Mus. Calif., Hollywood Arts Affair, Glendale Art Assn., L.A. Mem. World Assn. Chinese Artists, Shanghai Artist Assn. (v.p.). Home: 1261 N St Andrews Pl Hollywood CA 90038

HUANG, YUNG-HUI, chemical engineer; b. Taipei, Taiwan, July 20, 1953; came to U.S., 1979; s. Lien-chih and Yu-Pei (Tsai) H.; m. I-Hung Huang, May 15, 1992. BS, Nat. Ctrl. U., Chung-Li, Taiwan, 1976; MS, U. S.C., 1982; PhD, U. Fla., 1986. Rsch. assoc. Auburn (Ala.) U., 1987-88, Mich. Molecular Inst., Midland, 1988-90; sys. engr. S3 Technologies, Columbia, Md., 1990-92; sr. process engr. Formosa Plastics Corp., Livingston, N.J., 1992-95; sr. project engr. J.M. Huber Corp., Havre de Grace, Md., 1995—; vis. scholar Tech. U. Denmark, Lynby, 1984; organizer Polymer Symposium '95 Sci., Engring. and Tech., Houston, 1995. Contbr. articles to profl. jours. 2d lt. Chinese Army, 1976-78. Mem. AIChE, Soc. Plastics Engrs., Soc. for Advancement of Materials and Process Engring., Sigma Xi. Achievements include 2 patents in field; avocations: basketball, tennis, music, literature, computer. Home: 963 Redfield Rd Apt I Bel Air MD 21014-4685 Office: J M Huber Corp 907 Revolution St Havre De Grace MD 21078

HUARD, JEFFREY SCOTT, community planner; b. Grosse Pointe, Mich., Nov. 26, 1967; s. Dennis John and Beverly Jean (Carlson) H.; m. Suzanne Marie Schmidt, Dec. 4, 1993; children: Andrew, Alex. BS, No. Mich. U., Marquette, 1989. Planner Delta Charter Twp., Lansing, Mich., 1990—. Mem., sec. Planning Commn., City of Grand Ledge, Mich., 1997—. Mem. Am. Inst. Cert. Planners, Profl Cmty. Planners in State of Mich. Avocation: basketball coaching. Home: 218 E Main St Grand Ledge MI 48837-1659 Office: Delta Charter Twp 7710 W Saginaw Hwy Lansing MI 48917-8974

HUBAN, CHRISTOPHER M., retail buyer, manager; b. Milton, Mass., Sept. 22, 1964; s. Marvin Frank Huban and Joan Beverly Reilly; m. Lisa Corsini; children: Emily Grace, Hannah Rose, Hope MacKenzie. BS in Bus. Adminstrn., Northeastern U., 1988. Buyer Hills Dept. Stores, Canton, Mass., 1989-91, 93—, Fair Stores, Auburn, Mass., 1991-93, Ann & Hope Stores, Cumberland, R.I., 1993-99; sales mgr. Syroco, Inc., Peabody, Mass., 1999—. Chmn. Milton Rep. Town Com., 1995—; town meeting mem. Milton Govt., 1995—. Mem. Chetolah Yacht Club (fleet capt. sunfish class). Episcopalian. Avocation: sailing. Home: 41 Magnolia Rd Milton MA 02186-3204

HUBAND, FRANK LOUIS, educational association executive; b. Washington, July 12, 1938; m. Carol Singer. BS, Cornell U., 1961, PhD, 1967; JD, Yale U., 1975. Bar: D.C. 1975, U.S. Patent Office, 1977; registered prof. engr., Tex. Asst. prof. elec. engring. and math. scis. Rice U., Houston, 1966-72; owner, pres. Engring. Systems, Houston, 1972-73; atty., advisor FEA, Washington, 1975-76; div. dir. NSF, Washington, 1976-90; exec. dir. Am. Soc. for Engring. Edn., Washington, 1990—; cons. Tex. Instrument, 1968-75; lectr. George Mason U., Fairfax, Va., George Washington U. Author: Protection of Computer Systems and Software, 1986. Mem. ABA, IEEE. Office: Am Soc for Engring Edn 1818 N St NW Ste 600 Washington DC 20036-2476

HUBBARD, ARTHUR THORNTON, chemistry educator, electro-surface chemist; b. Alameda, Calif., Sept. 17, 1941; s. John White and Ruth Frances (Gapen) H.; children: David A., Lynne F. BA, Westmont Coll., 1963; PhD, Calif. Inst. Tech., 1967. Prof. chemistry U. Hawaii, Honolulu, 1967-76, U. Calif., Santa Barbara, 1976-86; Ohio eminent scholar and prof. chemistry U. Cin., 1986-99, dir. Surface Ctr., 1986-99; dir. Santa Barbara Sci. Project, 1999—; chmn. Ohio Sci. and Engring. Roundtable, 1990-95. Co-editor Jour. Colloid and Interface Sci., 1993—. Mem. Am. Chem. Soc. (assoc. editor jour. Langmuir 1984-90, vice chair surface and colloid div. 1999, Kendall award 1989), Electrochem. Soc. (David C. Grahame award 1993), Am. Phys. Soc. Office: Santa Barbara Sci Project PO Box 42530 Santa Barbara CA 93140-2530

HUBBARD, CARL AUBREY, aerospace engineer, management consultant; b. Denver, Oct. 4, 1940; s. Howard Henry and Genevieve Ruth (Claxton) H.; m. Georgeanne Dorothy Lively, Mar. 13, 1964; children: Suzanne Michelle, Carl Aubrey Jr. BS in Gen. Sci., Oreg. State U., 1963; MS in Applied Sci., Augustana Coll., 1978. Mil. officer U.S. Army, 1963-80; program mgr. AMI Industries Inc., Colorado Springs, Colo., 1980-81; project leader Martin Marietta Corp., Long Beach, Calif., 1981-85; project engr. Martin Marietta Corp., Long Beach, 1985-89; sr. staff systems engr. Martin Marietta Corp., Denver, 1989-93; mgmt. cons. Ctr. for Systems Mgmt., San Jose, Calif., 1993-94; program mgr. Lockheed-Martin Corp., Reston, Va., 1994-96; project engr. Lockheed-Martin Corp., Reston, 1996—. Inventor in field. Leader Boy Scouts Am., Colorado Springs, 1979-81, leader, commr., L.A., 1981-89. Maj. U.S. Army, 1963-80; lt. col. USAR, 1980-93. Mem. Assn. U.S. Army, Internat. Coun. on Systems Engring. Avocations: stamp collecting, model railroading. Home: 12526 Chasbarb Ter Oak Hill VA 20171-2468

HUBBARD, DANIEL T., JR., public information officer. BS in Broadcast Journalism, U. Kans., 1995. Asst. press sec. U.S. Senator Christopher S. "Kit" Bond, 1996, 96-98, dep. comm. dir., 1998; comm. dir. Dole/Kemp Campaign, 1996; press and rsch. dir. Missourians for Kit Bond, 1998—. Office: 274 Russell Senate Office Washington DC 20510-2503

HUBBARD, DEAN LEON, university president; b. Nyssa, Oreg., June 17, 1939; s. Gaileon and Rhodene (Barton) H.; m. Aleta Ann Thornton, July 12, 1959; children: Melody Ann, Dean Paul John, Joy Marie. BA, Andrews U., 1961, MA, 1962; diploma in Korean Lang., Yunsei U., Seoul, Korea, 1968; PhD, Stanford U., 1979. Dir. English Lang. Schs., Seoul, 1966-71; asst. to pres. Loma Linda U., Calif., 1974-76; acad. dean Union Coll., Lincoln, Nebr., 1976-80, pres., 1980-84; pres. NW Mo. State U., Maryville, 1984—; chair Acad. Quality Consortium, 1993-96; examiner Malcolm Baldridge Nat. Quality Award, 1993-96; judges panel Mo. Quality Award, 1994-96; adv. coun. edn. statistics U.S. Dept. Edn., 1997—. Mem. ACE Leadership Devel. Coun., 1996—. Avocation: classical music. Office: NW Mo State U Office of President Maryville MO 64468-6001*

HUBBARD, DONALD, marine artist, writer; b. Bronx, N.Y., Jan. 15, 1926; s. Ernest Fortesque and Lilly Violet (Beck) H. (div.); children: Leslie Carol, Christopher Eric, Lauren Ivy, Carmeron C. McNail; m. Kay Frances Boldt, Oct., 1998. Student, Brown U., 1944-45; AA, George Washington U., 1959, BA, 1958; student, Naval War Coll., 1965-66. Commd. ensign U.S. Navy, 1944, advanced through grades to comdr., 1965, served as naval aviator, 1944-67, ret., 1967; founder, operator Ocean Ventures Industries, Inc., Coronado, Calif., 1969-77, Sea Eagle Pubs., Coronado, 1988; lectr. on marine art; SCUBA instr. Author: Ships-in-Bottles, 2d edit., 1988, A How To Guide to a Venerable Nautical Craft, 1971, Buddleschiffe: Wie Macht Man Sie, 1972, The Complete Book of Inflatable Boats, 1979, Where to Paddle in San Diego County and Nearby Mexico, 1992, Days of Yore: Rhymes and Other Writings, 1995, Neptune's Table: Cooking the Sea Food Exotics, 1997; editor The Bottle Shipwright, works featured in American Artist of the Bookplate, 1970-90; contbr. articles to various publs.; featured on House and Garden TV show, What's My Hobby?. Decorated Air medal, U.S. Navy. Mem. Ships-in-Bottles Assn. (pres. N. Am. divsn. 1982—), Nature Printing Soc., Am. Soc. Bookplate Collectors and Designers, San Diego Watercolor Soc. (bd. dirs. 1981-82), San Diego Maritime Assn. E-mail: hubbarddon@aol.com. Home and Office: 1022 Park Pl Coronado CA 92118-2822

HUBBARD, ELIZABETH, actress; b. N.Y.C.; d. Benjamin Alldritt and Elizabeth (Wright) H.; divorced; 1 son, Jeremy Danby Bennett. A.B. cum laude, Radcliffe Coll.; postgrad., Royal Acad. Dramatic Art, London. Leading role: CBS daytime TV serial As the World Turns, 1984— (8 Emmy nominations for Best Leading Actress), NBC daytime TV serial The Doctors; appeared on Broadway in Present Laughter, Joe Egg, Time for Singing, Look Back in Anger, I Remember Mama (musical), others; appeared in off-Broadway prodn. Boys from Syracuse, Threepenny Opera (musicals); movie appearances include I Never Sang for My Father, The Bell Jar, Ordinary People; frequent guest TV talk shows. Bd. dirs. Found. in Motion, Immigration and Refugee Svcs. of Am., U.S. Com. for Refugees. Recipient Clarence Derwent award for The Physicists, 1965; Emmy award for best actress in The Doctors, 1974, Emmy award for best actress in First Ladies Diaries: Edith Bolling Wilson, 1976. Mem. AFTRA (nat. bd. dirs.),.

HUBBARD, ELIZABETH LOUISE, lawyer; b. Springfield, Ill., Mar. 10, 1949; d. Glenn Wellington and Elizabeth (Frederick) H.; m. A. Jeffrey Seidman, Oct. 27, 1974 (div. May 1982). B.A., U. Ky., 1971; JD with honors, Ill. Inst. Tech.-Chgo. Kent Coll. Law, 1974. Bar: Ill. 1974, U.S. Dist. Ct. (no. dist.) Ill. 1974, U.S. Ct. Appeals (7th cir.) 1976, U.S. Supreme Ct. 1984. Atty. Wyatt Co., Chgo., 1974-75, Gertz & Giampietro, Chgo., 1975-76, Baum, Sigman, Gold, Chgo., 1976-81, Elizabeth Hubbard, Ltd., 1981-98, Hubbard & O'Connor, Ltd., 1998—; legal counsel NOW, Chgo., 1978-94, sec., 1977. Editor Chgo. Kent Law Rev., 1970; supplement editor Litigating Sexual Harassment and Sex discrimination Cases, 1997, 98, 99. Bd. dirs., mem. The Remains Theatre, 1985-94. Mem. Chgo. Bar Assn. (fed. civil procedure com.), Ill. State Bar Assn., Nat. Employment Lawyers Assn. (chair Ill. chpt. 1992-95, sec.-treas. 1997—). Home: 420 W Grand Ave Apt 4A Chicago IL 60610-4087 Office: 55 E Monroe St Chicago IL 60603-5713

HUBBARD, HAROLD MEAD, retired research executive; b. Beloit, Kans., Apr. 16, 1924; s. Clarence Richard and Elizabeth (Mead) H.; m. Doreen J. Wallace, Aug. 13, 1948 (div. 1975); children: Stuart W., David D.; m. Barbara Bell Czarnecki, May 9, 1976 (div. 1987); m. Betty A. Martin, Oct. 9, 1991 (div. 1997). B.S., U. Kans., 1948, Ph.D., 1951; DSc (hon.), Regis U., 1984. Instr. chemistry U. Kans., Lawrence, 1949-51; rsch. chemist, rsch. mgr., lab. mgr. E. I. DuPont de Nemours & Co., Inc., Wilmington, Del., 1951-69; dir. phys. sci. Midwest Rsch. Inst., Kansas City, Mo., 1970-75, v.p. rsch., 1976-78, sr. v.p. ops., 1979-82, exec. v.p., 1983-90; dir. Solar Energy Rsch. Inst., 1982-90; Spark M. Matsunaga disting. fellow in energy and environ. U. Hawaii at Manoa, 1991-96; pres., CEO Pacific Internat. Ctr. for High Tech. Rsch., Honolulu, 1992-95; vis. sr. fellow Resources for the Future, 1990-91; bd. dirs. Guaranty State Bank; chair Nat. Rsch. Coun. bd. on energy and environ. sys., 1991-96. With U.S. Army, 1942-45. Mem. Mo. Acad. Sci. (councillor at large 1977-80), Tech. Transfer Soc. (v.p. 1978-79), Am. Chem. Soc., AAAS, N.Y. Acad. Scis., Am. Solar Energy Soc., Colo. Renewable Energy Soc. (pres. 1996-97), Sigma Xi, Delta Upsilon, Cosmos Club. Home: 1889 Denver West Dr Apt 1524 Golden CO 80401-3138

HUBBARD, HARVEY HART, aeroacoustician, noise control engineer, consultant; b. Swanton, Vt., June 17, 1921; s. Horace Waite and Elbie (Hart) H.; m. Sadie Margaret Miller; children: Thomas W., Susan H., Pamela L., Walter R. BSEE, U. Vt., 1942. Engr. Westinghouse Mfg. Co., Pitts., 1942; br. chief NASA, Hampton, Va., 1945-59, asst. div. chief, 1959-80; sr. rsch. assoc. Coll. William and Mary, Williamsburg, Va., 1981-85; cons. Bionetics Inc., Hampton, 1985-87, Planning Rsch. Corp., Hampton, 1987—. Author over 130 book chpts. and tech. reports in aeroacoustics rsch. and noise control engring., 1949-92. Lt. col. USAF, 1942-45, PTO. Recipient Sonic Boom Rsch. award, 1968, Medal for Exceptional Sci. Achievement, 1969, NASA, medal for Disting. Pub. Svc., 1992. Fellow AIAA (assoc., Aeroacoustics medal 1979), Acoustical Soc. Am. (pres. 1989-90, Silver medal in noise 1978); mem. Inst. of Noise Control Engring. (pres. 1979). Presbyterian. Home: 325 Charleston Way Newport News VA 23606-1174

HUBBARD, HERBERT HENDRIX, lawyer; b. Balt., Sept. 20, 1922; s. Amberson Hardy and Louise Virginia (Hendrix) H.; m. Joanne Hileman Nottingham, June 5, 1948; children: Melissa Hubbard O'Donnell, Alison Hubbard. JD, U. Md., Balt., 1950. Bar: Md. 1950, U.S. Dist. Ct. Md. 1950, U.S. Ct. Appeals (4th cir.) 1953, U.S. Supreme Ct. 1963. Clk. to dist. judge U.S. Dist. Ct. Md., Balt., 1950-51; assoc. France, Rouzer & Harris, Balt., 1951-52, 54-59; asst. U.S. atty. Dist. Md., Balt., 1952-53, dep. U.S. atty., 1953-54; atty., sr. mem. Saul Ewing Weinberg & Green (formerly Weinberg and Green LLC), Balt., 1959—; founding dir. Devel. Credit Fund, Inc., Balt., 1984-96. Chmn., corp. devel. coun. Sheppard & Enoch Pratt Hosp., Balt., 1978-86. Mem. ABA, Md. Bar Assn. (founding, chmn. profl. liability ins. com. 1976-82), Bar Assn. Ins. Trust (trustee 1976-88), Legal Mut. Liability Ins. Soc. Md. (sr. v.p., gen. counsel, bd. dirs., exec. com. 1986—, founding dir.), Order of Coif. Episcopalian. Avocation: tennis, bridge, golf. Home: 6 Upland Rd Apt D2 Baltimore MD 21210-2242 Office: Saul Ewing Weinberg & Green 100 S Charles St Ste 1500 Baltimore MD 21201-2770

HUBBARD, HOWARD JAMES, bishop; b. Troy, N.Y., Oct. 31, 1938; s. Howard James and Elizabeth D. (Burke) H. BA, St. Joseph's Sem., Yonkers, N.Y., 1960; STL, Gregorian U., Rome, 1964; DD (hon.), Siena Coll., 1977; LHD (hon.), Coll. St. Rose, 1977. Ordained priest Roman Catholic Ch., Rome, 1963; bishop of Albany Diocese of Albany, N.Y., 1977—; former parish priest St. Joseph's Ch., Schenectady, 1964; parish priest Cathedral Parish, Albany, 1964-65; asst. dir. Cath. Charities, Schenectady, 1966; chaplain Convent of the Sacred Heart, Kenwood, Albany, 1966; dir. Providence House, Albany, 1966; vicar gen. Diocese of Albany, 1976; dir. Cath. Interracial Coun.; coord. Urban Apostolate, from 1972; dir. Office of Pastoral Planning, Albany, 1974-76; diocesan consultor Diocese of Albany, 1976-77. Pres. Urban League. Office: Bishop of Albany Pastoral Ctr 40 N Main Ave Albany NY 12203-1410 Address: 125 Eagle St Albany NY 12202-1718*

HUBBARD, JEFFREY CHARLES, educational administrator; b. L.A., Jan. 26, 1957; s. Jack L. and Donna Bernice (Johnson) H.; m. Lori Ellen Blinzler, Jan. 7, 1979 (div. June 1994); children: Jordan Earl, Kevin Dean. BA in Drama, Calif. State U., San Bernardino, 1981; MA in Edn., U. Redlands, 1991; postgrad., U. S.C. Tchr. high sch. Rim of the World Unified Schs., Lake Arrowhead, Calif., 1983-92, prin. elem. sch., 1992-95, dir. personnel, 1995—; prof. U. Redlands (Calif.), 1994—; motivational speaker. Bd. dirs. Arrowhead United Way, 1996-98. Acad. Rsch. fellow U. Redlands, 1991. Mem. ASCD, Calif. Assn. Bus. Educators, Assn. Calif. Sch. Adminstrs. Democrat. Avocations: computers, horse race handicapping, camping, reading. Office: Rim of the World Unified Sch Dist PO Box 430 Lake Arrowhead CA 92352-0430

HUBBARD, JOHN MORRIS, golf course executive; b. Beech Creek, Pa., Feb. 13, 1916; s. Morris R. and Ina May (Putman) H.; m. Virginia A. Nelson, June 4, 1938; children: Robert, Nancy. Student, Gen. Motors Engring. and Mgmt. Inst., 1938, U. Detroit, 1939. Sr. engr. Fisher Body, Warren, Mich., 1935-74; retired, 1974; pres. Oxford Hills Golf and Country Club, Pontiac, Mich., 1974—; advisor Ferris State Coll., Big Rapids, Mich., 1960-74; instr. math. U. Indpls., summer 1991; designed and constructed Oxford Hills Golf Course, 1961. Mem. Soc. Engring. Illustrators (bd. dirs., Outstanding Achievement award 1981). Republican. Lodges: Rotary (bd. dirs. Oxford club 1981-82), Elks, Masons (master mason 1960-61). Home: 350 E Drahner Rd Oxford MI 48371-5306 Office: Oxford Hills Golf and Country Club 300 E Drahner Rd Oxford MI 48371-5306

HUBBARD, JOHN RANDOLPH, university president emeritus, history educator, diplomat; b. Belton, Tex., Dec. 3, 1918; s. Louis Herman and Bertha (Altizer) H.; m. Lucille Luckett, Jan. 29, 1947 (div. Dec. 1983); children: Elisa, Melisse, Kristin. A.B., U. Tex., 1938, A.M., 1939, Ph.D., 1950; L.H.D., Hebrew Union Coll., Los Angeles, 1971, Westminster Coll., Fulton, Mo., 1977; LL.D., Sch. of Ozarks, 1973, U. So. Calif., 1980. Pvt.

sec. to ICC commr., 1939-41; teaching fellow U. Tex., 1946-48; vis. asst. prof. Brit. history La. State U., 1948; asst. prof. European history Tulane U., 1949-52, asso. prof., 1953-58, prof., 1958-65; dean Newcomb Coll., 1953-65; vis. asst. prof. European history Yale, 1952-53; chief edn. adviser U.S. AID, India, 1965-69; v.p. for acad. affairs, provost U. So. Calif., Los Angeles, 1969-70; pres. U. So. Calif., 1970-80, pres. emeritus, 1980—, John R. Hubbard Chair Brit. history, 1980—; U.S. amb. to India, 1988-89; co-chmn. Indo-U.S. Subcommn. on Edn. and Culture, 1982—. Contbr.: articles and revs. to Jour. Modern History; other ednl. jours. Mem. bd. Tulane-Lyceum Assn., 1953-65, Isidore Newman Sch., 1953-65; mem. Region 12 selection com. Woodrow Wilson Fellowship Program, also chmn., 1955-65; mem. bd. U.S. Edn. Found., India; mem. Indian adv. bd. Women's Coll. Faculty Exchange program; pres. bd. Am. Internat. Sch., New Delhi; mem. So. Calif. adv. bd. Inst. Internat. Edn.; trustee Scholarships for Children of Am. Mil. Personnel; bd. dirs. Community TV So. Calif., Los Angeles. Served as an aviator in USN, 1941-46; flight instr. and patrol plane comdr. Atlantic and Pacific fleets; lt. comdr. Res. Decorated D.F.C., Air medals (4); chevalier des Palmes Académiques; Stella della Solidarietá Italiana Italy; Order of Taj 3d degree Iran; recipient Disting. Services to Higher Edn. in U.S. award Tulane U., New Orleans, 1976; Air U. award, 1976; Disting. Alumnus award U. Tex., Austin, 1978, Alben W. Barkley medal for disitng. svc., 1989. Mem. Am., Miss. Valley hist. assns., So. Hist. Soc. (exec. council 1954-56), Anglo-Am. Hist. Soc., Assn. Ind. Calif. Colls. and Univs. (trustee), Am. Council Edn. (commn. on fed. relations 1975-77), Assn. Am. Univs. (council on fed. relations 1975-79), Orgn. Am. Historians, Conf. Brit. Studies, Am. Council Learned Socs., Phi Beta Kappa, Phi Delta Kappa, Alpha Kappa Psi, Delta Kappa Epsilon, Omicron Delta Kappa. Clubs: Royal Aero (London), Athenaeum (London); Los Angeles Country; California (Los Angeles); University (N.Y.C.); Cosmos (Washington). Office: U So Calif Dept History Los Angeles CA 90089 *The fear of false knowledge is the beginning of wisdom.*

HUBBARD, KENNETH GENE, climatologist; b. Bridgeport, Nebr., Mar. 21, 1949; s. Harold D. and Bessie B. (Arrants) H.; m. Susan Elizabeth Alcorn, Aug. 15, 1971; children: Carter M., Benjamin W. MS, S.D. Sch. Mines and Tech., 1973; PhD, Utah State U., 1982. Meteorologist Geophys. Fluid Dynamics Lab., Princeton, N.J., 1973-74, Utah Water Rsch. Lab., Logan, 1974-77; climatologist Utah Dept. Agriculture, Logan, 1977-81, U. Nebr., Lincoln, 1981—; dir. High Plains Climate Ctr., Lincoln, 1987—. Co-author: Automated Weather Station Networks, 1993; contbr. chpts. to books, articles to publs. Fellow Ctr. for Great Plains Studies; mem. AAAS, Am. Soc. Agronomy, Am. Meteorol. Soc. (com. agrl. and forest meteorology 1986-89), Am. Assn. State Climatologists (pres. 1985-86), World Meteorol. Orgn. (rapporteur 1992-96). Achievements include rsch. in automated weather data network devel. Office: U Nebr 242 Chase Hall Lincoln NE 68583

HUBBARD, LINCOLN BEALS, medical physicist, consultant; b. Hawkesbury, Ont., Can., Sept. 8, 1940; s. Carroll Chauncey and Mary Lunn (Beals) H.; came to U.S., 1957; m. Nancy Ann Krieger, Apr. 3, 1961; children: Jill, Katrina. B.S. in Physics, U. N.H., 1961; Ph.D., MIT, 1967. Diplomate Am. Bd. Radiology; cert. health physicist Am. Bd. Health Physics. Postdoctoral appointee Argonne Nat. Lab., 1966-68; asst. prof. math. and physics Knoxville Coll. (Tenn.), 1968-70; asst. prof. physics Furman U., Greenville, S.C., 1970-74; chief physicist Mt. Sinai Hosp., Chgo., 1974-75, 79—, Cook County Hosp., Chgo., 1975-88; ptnr. Fields, Griffith, Hubbard & Broadbent, Inc., 1978-93; pres. Hubbard, Broadbent & Assoc., Ltd., 1993—; assoc. prof. med. physics, Rush U., 1986— . Mem. Am. Assn. Physicists in Medicine, Am. Coll. Radiology, Am. Phys. Soc. Author: (with S.S. Stefani) Mathematics for Technologists, 1979, (with G. B. Greenfield) Computers in Radiology, 1984. Home and Office: 4113 W End Rd Downers Grove IL 60515-2307

HUBBARD, MICHAEL JAMES, lawyer; b. N.Y.C., Dec. 8, 1950; s. William Neil and Elizabeth (Terleski) H. AB, U. Mich., 1976; JD, Marquette U., 1979. Bar: Wis. 1980, Mich. 1980. Assoc. Kidston, Peterson P.C., Kalamazoo, 1980, Barbier, Goulet & Petersmarck, Mt. Clemens, Mich., 1981; pvt. practice Detroit, 1982-86, Belleville, Mich., 1990-98; assoc. Lawrence J. Stockler, P.C., Southfield, Mich., 1987; staff atty. Hyatt Legal Svcs., Southgate, Mich., 1988; assoc. Dunchock, Linden & Wells, Coruna, Mich., 1989. Mem. Mich. Trial Lawyers Assn., State Bar Mich. Republican. Avocations: reading, racquetball.

HUBBARD, PAUL LEONARD, company executive; b. Cin., Oct. 31, 1942; 1 child, Paul Anthony. BS in Bus. Edn., Ohio U., 1965; MSW, Wayne State U., Detroit, 1971. Instr. Stowe Adult Edn., Cin., 1965; tchr. data processing Detroit Pub. Sch., 1967-74, bus. edn. tchr., 1965-71; assoc. dir. Downriver F.N.S. of Wayne County, Detroit, 1971-74; dir. cmty. self-determination New Detroit, Inc., 1974-79, asst. v.p., 1979-82, sr. v.p., 1985-89, pres., 1989-94; commr. dept. of neighborhoods City of Toledo, Ohio, 1994-98, acting dir. econ. devel., 1996-97; com. builder Dept. HUD, 1998—; cons. to black studies Wayne County Community Coll., Detroit, 1971-74. Contbr. articles to profl. jours. Chmn. Mich. Bell Consumer Adv. Bd., 1984. Recipient Community Svc. award, Detroit St. Svcs., 1978; named Alumni of the Yr., Assn. Black Social Workers, 1981; recipient Outstanding Svc. award, McDonald's, Detroit, 1982, Appreciation award, Gentlemen of Wall St., 1984, Mayor's award Spirit of Toledo, 1997. Mem. League Goodwill (bd. dirs.), Nat. Assn. Black Social Workers (pres. 1987-88), Internat. Exchange Bd., Masons, Alpha Phi Alpha. *

HUBBARD, PETER LAWRENCE, lawyer; b. Syracuse, N.Y., Apr. 4, 1946; s. Bardwell B. and Barbara (Bowen) H.; m. Hannah R., June 21, 1967; 1 child, Brian C. BA, Syracuse U., 1968, JD, 1971; postgrad., Judge Advocate Gen.'s Sch., Charlottesville, Va., 1976. Bar: N.Y. 1972, U.S. Dist. Ct. (no. and we. dists.) N.Y. 1972, U.S. Ct. Appeals (2d cir.) 1983. Assoc. Smith & Sovik, Syracuse, N.Y., 1971-72; asst. dist. counsel U.S. SBA, Syracuse, 1972-80; ptnr. Menter, Rudin & Trivelpiece, Syracuse, 1980—; lectr. in field. Contbr. articles to profl. jours. Pres. Reachout Inc., County Drug Rehab. Agy., Syracuse, 1979. Office: Menter Rudin & Trivelpiece 500 S Salina St Ste 500 Syracuse NY 13202-3300

HUBBARD, ROBERT GLENN, economics educator; b. Apopka, Fla., Sept. 4, 1958; s. Charles Whistnant and Myrtle Jean (Dabbs) H. BA, BS, U. Cen. Fla., 1979; AM, Harvard U., 1981, PhD, 1983. Prof. econs. Northwestern U., Evanston, Ill., 1983-87; Russell L. Carson prof. econs. and fin. Columbia U., N.Y.C., 1988—; dep. asst. sec. U.S. Dept. Treasury, Washington, 1991-92; John M. Olin fellow, Nat. Bur. Econ. Rsch., Cambridge, Mass., 1987-88; cons., U.S. Dept. State, Dept. Energy, Internat. Trade Commn., Social Security Adminstrn., Nat. Petroleum Coun., numerous pvt. corps. Editor: Asymmetric Information, Corporate Finance and Investment, 1989; contbr. numerous articles to profl. jours. Grantee, NSF, 1983—. Mem. Am. Econ. Assn., Econometric Soc., Royal Econ. Assn., Am. Fin. Assn. Republican. Presbyterian. Avocations: reading, theater, travel. Office: Columbia U Grad Sch Bus 609 Uris Hall New York NY 10027

HUBBARD, RUTH, biology educator; b. Vienna, Austria, Mar. 3, 1924; came to U.S., 1938; d. Richard and Helene (Ehrlich) Hoffmann; m. Frank Twombly Hubbard, Dec. 26, 1942 (div. 1951); m. George Wald, June 11, 1958; children: Elijah, Deborah Hannah. AB, Radcliffe Coll., 1944, PhD, 1950; DSc (hon.), Macalester Coll., 1991, U. Toronto, Ont., Can., 1991, So. Meth. U., 1997; LHD (hon.), So. Ill. U., Edwardsville, 1991. Lab. technician Tenn. Pub. Health Service, Chattanooga, 1945-46; fellow U. Coll. Hosp. Med. Sch., London, 1948-49; Guggenheim fellow Carlsberg Lab., Copenhagen, Denmark, 1952-53; research fellow Harvard U., Cambridge, Mass., 1950-52, 54-58, research assoc., lectr., 1958-74, prof., 1974-90, prof. emerita, 1990—; vis. prof. M.I.T., Cambridge, 1972; cons. Boston Women's Healthbook Collective 1982—. Author: (with Margaret Randall) The Shape of Red: Insider/Outsider Reflections, 1988; author: The Politics of Women's Biology, 1990, (with Elijah Wald) Exploding the Gene Myth, 1993, 97, 99, Profitable Promises: Essays on Women, Science and Health, 1995; editor: Women Look at Biology Looking at Women, 1979, Genes and Gender II, 1979, Biological Woman--The Convenient Myth, 1982, Woman's Nature: Rationalizations of Inequality, 1983, Reinventing Biology: Respect for Life and the Creation of Knowledge, 1995; contbr. more than 150 articles on sci. and women's issues to profl. and lay books and jours. Adv. coun. mem. Nat. Women's Health Network, Washington, 1980—; bd. dirs. Coun. Responsible Genetics, Boston, 1982—, Boston Women's Health Book Collective, 1998—; mem. adv. bd. Boston Women's Fund, 1983-85; mem. adv. bd. Civil Liberties Union of Mass., 1990-91, 95—, bd. dirs., 1991-95. Recipient Paul Karrer medal Swiss Chem. Soc., 1967, Peace and Freedom award Women's Internat. League for Peace and Freedom, 1985, Feminist Marathoner award Boston chpt. NOW, 1991, Disting. Svc. award Am. Inst. Biol. Sci., 1992. Fellow AAAS; mem. Marine Biol. Lab. (trustee 1973-78, trustee emerita 1990—), Soc. Biol. Chemists, Nat. Women's Studies Assn., Phi Beta Kappa, Sigma Xi. Avocations: reading, music, yoga, swimming. Home: 21 Lake View Ave Cambridge MA 02138-3325

HUBBARD, STANLEY STUB, broadcast executive; b. St. Paul, May 28, 1933; s. Stanley Eugene and Didrikke A. (Stub) H.; m. Karen Elizabeth Holmen, June 13, 1959; children: Kathryn Elizabeth Hubbard Rominski, Stanley Eugene II, Virginia Anne Hubbard Morris, Robert Winston, Julia Didrikke Coyte. BA, U. Minn., 1955; hon. doctorate, Hamline U., 1995. With Hubbard Broadcasting, St. Paul, 1951—, pres., 1967—, chmn., CEO, 1983—; bd. dirs. Minn. Bus. Partnership, U.S. Satellite Broadcasting Co., Inc.; mem. broadcast adv. com. to comm. subcom. Ho. of reps., 1977-79; mem. FCC Adv. Com. on Advanced TV, 1988-95; mem. U.S. Nat. Inf. Infrastructure Adv. Coun., 1994-96. Contbr. articles to profl. jours. Chmn. St. Croix Valley Youth Ctr., 1968—; trustee Hubbard Found.; bd. dirs. U. Minn. Found., Mpls., Am. Friends of Jamaica, Assn. Maximum Svc. TV, U. St. Thomas, Bapt. Hosp. Fund Sponsor Bd., Broadcast Pioneers Libr., Minn. Bus. Partnership; past advisor Gov.'s Crime Commn., Ramsey County Ice Arena Com.; past bd. dirs. The Guthrie Theater, The Psychoanalytic Found. of Minn., Sci. Mus. of Minn., Minn. Internat. Ctr.; past mem. Hazelden Adv. Com.; mem. Met. Airports Pub. Found. Adv. Bd. Recipient Mitchell Charnley award Northwest Broadcast News Assn., 1991, Internat. Humanitarian award Am. Friends of Jamaica, 1989, Arthur C. Clarke award Satellite Broadcasting and Comm. Assn., 1994, DreamMaker award Children's Cancer Rsch. Fund, 1994, Disting. Svc. award Nat. Assn. Broadcasters, 1995, Spurgeon award Boy Scouts Am., 1985, Avatar award Broadcast Cable and Fin. Mgmt., 1995, Human Rights award Am. Jewish Com., 1995, Cmty. Leadership award Mpls./St. Paul chpt. Alzheimer's Assn., 1995, Most Innovative Product award Minn. High Tech. Coun., 1995, Journalism Innovator award U. Nebr., 1996, Minn. Family Bus. award U. St. Thomas, 1996, Disting. Alumnus award Breck Sch., 1996, Minn. and Dakotas Entrepreneur of Yr. award, 1996, Heritage award U.S. Hockey Hall of Fame, 1996, U. Minn. M Club Hall of Fame Lifetime Achievement award, 1996, Broadcasters' Found. Golden Mike award, 1997, Acad. of Achievement's Golden Plate award, 1997; named to Broadcasting and Cable Hall of Fame, 1991, Soc. Satellite Profls. Internat. Space Hall of Fame, 1992, Acad. Achievement's Golden Plate award, 1997, Broadcast Pioneer award Minn. Broadcasters Assn., 1998. Mem. NATAS (chmn. bd. Trustees.), Broadcast Pioneers, Internat. Radio and TV Soc., M. Avocations: sailing and boating, reading, photography. Office: Hubbard Broadcasting Inc 3415 University Ave W Saint Paul MN 55114-2099

HUBBARD, STEVAN RALPH, biophysicist, educator; b. Sioux Falls, S.D., Dec. 19, 1957; s. Robert Earl and Joanne Marie (Lindgren) H.; m. Elizabeth Jane Albert, Dec. 27, 1986. BS, Cornell U., 1980; PhD, Stanford U., 1988. Postdoctoral rsch. scientist Columbia U., N.Y.C., 1988-93, assoc. rsch. scientist, 1993-95; asst. prof. pharmacology NYU, N.Y.C., 1995—. Achievements include determination of the three-dimensional structures of protein molecules by x-ray crystallography.

HUBBARD, SUSAN MARY, writer, English educator; b. Syracuse, N.Y., Sept. 6, 1951; d. Middleton John Schwartz and Dorothy Katharine Long; m. J. T. W. Hubbard, June 16, 1979 (div. Aug. 1994); children: Katherine Ada, Clare Adrienne; m. Robley Wilson, June 17, 1995. BA, Syracuse U., 1974, MFA, 1984. Reporter, columnist Evening Press, Binghamton, N.Y., 1974-76, Evening Sentinel, Ansonia, Conn., 1976-78; investigative reporter Jour.-Courier, New Haven, 1978; reporter Herald-Jour., Syracuse, 1979-80; tchg. asst. Syracuse U., 1981-84, instr., 1984-88; project editor ERIC Clearinghouse, 1986-87; sr. lectr. Cornell U., Ithaca, N.Y., 1988-95; writer in residence Pitzer Coll., Claremont, Calif., 1995; assoc. prof. U. Ctrl. Fla., Orlando, 1995—. Author: Walking on Ice, 1990 (Assoc. Writing Programs prize 1989), Blue Money, 1999. Fellow Yaddo, 1999; recipient Master Writer's award Nat. Writer's Voice, 1997; fellow Aspen Writers' Conf., 1987; Writer's fellow Montolieu Writers' Workshop, 1998. Mem. Associated Writing Programs (mem. exec. bd. 1999—), Fla. Coll. English Assn. (mem. exec. sec. 1998—). Office: U Ctrl Fla PO Box 161346 Orlando FL 32816

HUBBARD, WALTER BRYAN, engineer, consultant; b. Lawton, Okla., Oct. 14, 1954; s. Elise B. (Stakely) H.; m. Jana Sue Buchner; children: Kelli Krystin, Ashely Nicole. BS in Chemistry, North Tex. State U., 1983. Engring. technician Mostek Corp., Carollton, Tex., 1977-80; sr. engring. assoc. Texas Instruments, Dallas, 1980-83; photo/etch engr. VLSI, Inc., San Jose, Calif., 1983-84; etch/photo engr. Signetics Corp., Sunnyvale, Calif., 1984-85; dist. applications engring. mgr. Canon, USA, Irving, Tex., 1985-93; photolithography staff engr. VLSI, Inc., San Antonio, 1993—; R&D cons. engr. Piedra Drilling, Englewood, Colo., 1992—; cons. online entertainment Glitchmaster, Englewood, 1994—. Contbr. articles to profl. jours. Mem. Beta Sigma Phi. Achievements include patent and patent pending for semiconductor, photolithography technologies, innovations in laterial acoustical drilling detection and angular deflection; avocation: antiques. Home: 8510 Timber Ldg San Antonio TX 78250-4168 Office: VLSI Tech Inc 9651 Westover Hls San Antonio TX 78251-2701

HUBBARD, WILLIAM BOGEL, planetary sciences educator; b. Liberty, Tex., Nov. 14, 1940; s. William Bogel and Marie Hubbard; m. Jean North Gilliland, June 8, 1963; children: Lynne Marie, Laurie North. BA, Rice U., Houston, 1962; PhD, U. Calif., Berkeley, 1967. Rsch. fellow Calif. Inst. Tech., Pasadena, 1967-68; asst. prof. astronomy U. Tex., Austin, 1968-72; assoc. prof. planetary scis. U. Ariz., Tucson, 1972-75, dir. Lunar and Planetary Lab., 1977-81, prof., 1975—; cons. Lawrence Livermore (Calif.) Nat. Lab., 1972-86, NASA, 1994—; prin. investigator NASA, 1974—, NSF, 1970, 79, 83, 86-93; exch. scientist USSR Nat. Acad. Sci., 1973, mem. com. div. for planetary scis., 1985-88. Contbr. articles to profl. jours.; assoc. editor: Icarus, 1980—. Fellow Japan Soc. for Promotion of Sci., Am. Geophys. Union; mem. AAAS, Am. Astron. Soc., Internat. Astron. Union, Am. Hereford Assn., Nat. Cattlemen's Beef Assn., Sigma Xi. Democrat. Episcopalian. Home: 2618 E Devon St Tucson AZ 85716-5506 Office: U Ariz Lunar & Planetary Lab Tucson AZ 85721-0092

HUBBARD, WILLIAM JAMES, library director; b. Grand Rapids, Mich., July 17, 1941; s. Willard Wright and Sara (Rast) H.; m. Barbara Ockun, Sept. 8, 1962; children: William, Thomas, James, Gregory. Engr., supr. Rochester (N.Y.) Telephone Corp., 1963-71; contract libr. Xerox Corp., Webster, N.Y., 1971-72; libr. circulation SUNY, Fredonia, 1973-75; libr. user svcs. Va. Poly. Inst. and State U., Blacksburg, 1975-80; dir. libr. svcs., dir.automation-networks, act. state libr. Va. State Libr., Richmond, 1980-88; univ. libr. Jacksonville (Ala.) State U., 1988—. Author: Stack Management, 1981; assoc. editor Ala. Librarian; contbr. articles to profl. jours. Mem. Am. Soc. Info. Sci., Ala. Libr. Assn., Nat. Assn. of Scholars. Office: State U Univ Libr Jacksonville AL 36265

HUBBARD, WILLIAM KEITH, government executive; b. Rocky Mount, N.C., Jan. 12, 1949; s. Ryan Buckhannon and Maple Eliza (Moore) H.; m. Bobbie Norris Sutton Hubbard, Feb. 5, 1975; children: Helen Elizabeth, Erin Katherine, William Andrew. BA, U. N.C., 1970; MA, Am. U., 1976. Assoc. commr. for policy FDA, Washington, 1991-99, acting dep. commr. for policy, 1999—. Office: Dept Health & Human Services U.S. Food & Drug Administration 5600 Fishers Ln Rockville MD 20852-1750*

HUBBARD, WILLIAM NEILL, JR., pharmaceutical company executive; b. Fairmont, N.C., Oct. 15, 1919; s. William Neill and Mary Emma (Fenegan) H.; m. Elizabeth Terleski, Dec. 28, 1945 (dec. Mar. 1984); children—William Neill III, Michael J., Mary E., Elizabeth A., Susan E.; m. Joyce Elaine Wixson, Apr. 3, 1987. A.B., Columbia, 1942; postgrad., U. N.C. Sch. Medicine; M.D., N.Y. U., 1944. Mem. house staff 3d med. div. Bellevue Hosp., N.Y.C., 1944-50; instr. medicine N.Y. U., 1950-53, asst. prof., 1953-59; asst. dean, then assoc. dean N.Y. U. Coll. Medicine, 1951-59; dean U. Mich. Med. Sch., 1959-70, assoc. prof. internal medicine, 1959-64, prof., 1964-70; dir. U. Mich. Med. Center, 1969-70; gen. mgr. pharm. div., v.p. Upjohn Co., 1970-72, exec. v.p., 1972-74, pres., 1974-84, dir., 1968-91; dir. Johnson Controls, Inc., Consumers Power; bd. dirs. Pharm. Mfrs. Assn., 1978-80, 81-84, chmn. bd., 1980-81; chmn. coun. health care tech. Inst. Medicine of NAS, 1986-90; cons. USPHS; trustee N.Y. Acad. of Medicine, 1994—; bd. dirs. Pan-Am. Health and Edn. Found., 1996—. Mem. Nat. Adv. Commn. on Libraries, 1966-68; med. adv. com. W.K. Kellogg Found., 1959-67, trustee, 1979-92; mem. Gov.'s Adv. Com. on Edn. Health Care, 1965-69; trustee Bronson Meth. Hosp., 1970-84; chmn. Gov.'s Action Com. on Corrections, 1972-73; mem. panel ednl. consultants Commn. on Edn. for Health Adminstrn., 1973-75; mem. com. on med. edn. Brown U., 1974-77; mem. nat. sci. bd. NSF, 1974-80, cons. to bd., 1980-83; bd. dirs. Family Health Internat. (formerly Internat. Fertility Research Program), 1981-90; mem. bd. sci. and tech. for internat. devel. Nat. Acad. Scis., 1978-80, Council on Sci. and Tech. for Devel., 1978-83; bd. visitors in East Asian studies U. Mich., 1976-80; bd. overseers Morehouse Coll., 1976-81; bd. dirs. Nat. Med. Fellowships, Inc., 1973-75, Nat. Fund. Med. Edn., 1962-75; trustee Kalamazoo Coll., 1973-78, Columbia U., N.Y.C., 1981-89; mem. bd. regents Nat. Library of Medicine, 1963-67, 72-76, chmn., 1965-67, 74-76, cons., 1976-84; bd. dirs. Am. Near East Refugee Aid, 1977-82; dir. devel. council U. Mich., 1979-87; mem. population adv. panel Office of Technology Assessment, U.S. Congress, 1979-81; chmn. bd. visitors Med. Ctr. U. Mich., 1989—; bd. visitors U. Mich. Sch. of Nursing, 1995-98, Columbia U. Sch. Nursing, 1990—. Fellow ACP, Am. Acad. Arts and Scis., Royal Soc. Medicine; mem. AMA, Inst. Medicine of NAS, Harvey Soc., N.Y. Acad. Medicine, Soc. Alumni Bellevue Hosp., Mich. Med. Soc. (coun. 1960-62), Kalamazoo Acad. Medicine, Am. Soc. Clin. Pharmacology and Therapeutics, Assn. Am. Med. Colls. (pres. 1966-67), Jamestown Soc., Sigma Xi, Alpha Omega Alpha. Fax #: (616) 372-9305. Home: 3634 Woodcliff Dr Kalamazoo MI 49008

HUBBE, HENRY ERNEST, financial forecaster, funds manager; b. Hamburg, Germany, Aug. 13, 1932; came to U.S., 1958; s. H.V. and Ingeborg M. (Schroeder) H.; m. Mary E. Wylie, 1961; children: John, Michael. BA, NYU, 1971, MBA, 1974. Area adminstr. Bank of Am. NT&SA, San Francisco, 1958-63; asst. v.p. Citibank N.Am., N.Y.C., 1963-74; sr. v.p. European Am. Bank, N.Y.C., 1974-84; pres. Internat. Treasury Cons., N.Y.C., 1984-94; mng. dir. Fintech (UK) Ltd., London, 1985-96, Fintech Asset Mgmt., London, 1985-96; pres. HEHH Software Corp., Mamaroneck, N.Y., 1978—, Fintech (USA) Ltd., N.Y.C., N.Y., 1996—; mem. faculty Am. Inst. Banking, N.Y.C., 1974-83; guest speaker internat. confs., profl. orgns.; panel mem. Bus. Internat., London. Contbr. articles to profl. jours.; patentee in field. Mem. Beta Gamma Sigma (v.p. 1971—). Avocation: golf.

HUBBEL, MICHAEL ROBERT, insurance company executive, educator; b. Grand Rapids, Mich., June 5, 1954; s. Robert Lewis and Irene Rose (Socha) H. AA, Lansing Community Coll., 1974; BA, Mich. State U., 1976; MBA, Coll. of Ins., 1994. CPCU. Rsch. analyst Farm Bur. Ins. Group, Lansing, Mich., 1971-81; sr. rsch. analyst Hastings (Mich.) Mut. Ins. Co., 1981-85; assoc. prof. ins., dir. ins. program Olivet (Mich.) Coll., 1985-89; v.p. informational resources Pioneer State Mut. Ins. Co., Flint, Mich., 1989-93; assoc. dir. Ctr. for Profl. Edn. Coll. of Ins., N.Y.C., 1993-95; assoc. prof. ins., dir. ins. Olivet (Mich.) Coll., 1995—, chair dept. bus. and econs., 1996—; instr. risk mgmt. Lansing C.C., 1991, ins. Mich. State U. Coll. Bus., East Lansing, 1983-84, 88-89, continuing edn., 1985-92; mem. Mich. Ins. Bur. Agts. Edn. Adv. Coun., 1992-93, 95—; writer property-casualty test devel. panels Mich. Ins. Bur., 1989, 91; book reviewer Ins. Inst. Am., 1987, 90. Editor, creator monthly trade newsletter Third Thursday, 1981-82; contbr. articles to trade jours. and newsletters. Explorer advisor, mem. com. Chief Okemos coun. Boy Scouts Am., 1987-89; v.p. Grand Ledge Jaycees, 1982-83; mem. ins. adv. bd. Olivet Coll., 1990-92, Northwestern Mich. Coll., 1992; adminstr. Mich. Ins. Hall of Fame. Recipient Presdl. award Olivet Coll., 1988, 90. Mem. Soc. CPCUs (chpt. bd. dirs. 1989-90), Cen. Mich. Underwriters Assn. (pres. 1982-83), 1752 Club, Gamma Iota Sigma (assoc., advisor 1986-89, 95—, mem. nat. bd. trustees, v.p. 1990-92, pres. 1992-95). Lutheran. Avocations: sailing, skiing, golf, reading, writing. E-mail: mhubbel@olivenet.edu. Office: Olivet Coll Mott 406 Olivet MI 49076

HUBBELL, BILLY JAMES, lawyer; b. Pine Bluff, Ark., May 21, 1949; s. Arley E. and Mary M. (Duke) H.; m. Judy C. Webb, Feb. 21, 1981; children: Jennifer Leigh, William Griffin. BE, U. Cen. Ark., 1971; JD, U. Ark, Little Rock, 1978. Bar: Ark. 1978, U.S. Dist. Ct. (ea. dist.) Ark. 1978, U.S. Ct. Appeals (8th cir.) 1987. Tchr. Grady (Ark.) High Sch., 1971-78; assoc. Smith and Smith, McGehee, Ark., 1978-79; ptnr. Smith, Hubbell and Drake, McGehee, 1979-86, Griffin, Rainwater & Draper, P.A., Crossett, Ark., 1987-90; dep. prosecuting atty. Ashley County, Ark., 1989-90; mcpl. judge Crossett, 1991—, pvt. practice, 1991—. Candidate Ark. Ho. of Reps., Lincoln County, 1984, 10th Jud. Dist. Cir./Chancery Judge, 1998. Sgt. USAR, 1970-76. Mem. Ark. Bar Assn., S.E. Ark. Legal Inst. (chmn. 1984-85, Ashley County Bar Assn. (past pres.), Ark. Trial Lawyers Assn. Democrat. Seventh Day Adventist. Avocations: jogging, computers. Office: PO Box 574 Crossett AR 71635-0574

HUBBELL, DAVID SMITH, surgeon, educator; b. Dallas, Aug. 29, 1922; s. Jay Broadus and Lucinda (Smith) H.; m. Barbara Baynard, July 3, 1947; children: Katherine, Lawrence, Daniel. AB, Duke U., 1943, MD, 1946. Diplomate Am. Bd. Surgery, Am. Bd. Thoracic Surgery. Pathologist U.S. Army Tripler Hosp., Honolulu, 1947-49; resident and Am. Cancer Soc. fellow in surgery Yale U. Hosp., New Haven, 1949-54; attending surgeon Bayfront and St. Anthony's Hosp., St. Petersburg, Fla., 1955-85; prof. depts. surgery and anatomy. U. So. Fla., Tampa, 1985—. Capt. M.C., U.S. Army, 1947-49. Recipient award for outstanding rsch. Moffitt Cancer Soc., Tampa, 1994. Fellow Am. Cancer Soc. (life mem.); mem. ACS (pres. Fla. chpt. 1973-74), Fla. Assn. Thoracic Surgeons (pres. 1980-81), Pinellas County Med. Soc. (pres. 1969-70), Rotary. Republican. Presbyterian. Avocations: tennis, collecting and speaking on 1st editions by Mark Twain. Office: Moffitt Cancer Ctr 12902 Magnolia Dr Tampa FL 33612-9416

HUBBELL, ELIZABETH WOLFE, English language educator; b. Chgo., Mar. 10, 1940. BA, Wellesley Coll., 1962; MA in Tchg. Secondary English, U. N.H., 1988. English tchr. Masconomet Regional Jr. Sr. H.S., Topsfield, 1987-88, Hovnanian Armenian Sch., New Milford, N.J., 1989-91, Cecils Coll., Asheville, N.C., 1991-99. Named Tchr. of the Yr., N.C. Assn. Schs. and Colls., 1993. Presbyterian.

HUBBELL, ERNEST, lawyer; b. Trenton, Mo., Aug. 28, 1914; s. Platt and Maud Irene (Ray) H.; m. Nevah Smith, Apr. 25, 1943; 1 child, Platt Thorpe. AA, North Cen. Mo. Coll. (formerly Trenton Jr. Coll.), 1934; JD, Georgetown U., 1938. Bar: D.C. 1937, Mo. 1938, U.S. Supreme Ct. 1946. Practiced in Trenton, 1938-39, Jefferson City, Mo., 1939-42; pvt. practice, Kansas City, Mo., 1947-52; ptnr. Hubbell, Sawyer, Peak, O'Neal & Napier (formerly Hubbell, Lane & Sawyer), Kansas City, 1952—; asst. atty. gen. Mo., 1939-42; first chmn. bench, bar com. 16th Jud. Cir. Ct., Kansas City, 1964-69, mem 16th Cir. Jud. Nominating Commn., 1970-75; mem. U.S. Cir. Judge Nominating Commn., 1977-80. Trustee Legal Aid and Defender Soc. Greater Kansas City, 1964-73; mem. Law Found. U. Mo. Kansas City, 1966-71; chmn. Nat. Council on Crime and Delinquency, 1966-76; pres. Hubbell Family Hist. Soc., 1981-85; mem. Soc. Fellows Nelson Art Gallery. With USAAF, 1942-44, capt. JAGC, 1944-46. Mem. ABA, Kansas City Met. Bar Assn. (pres. 1963-64, ann. Achievement award 1974, 1st ann. Litigator Emeritus award), Mo. Bar Assn., Assn. Trial Lawyers Am. (assoc. editor R.R. law sect. of jour. 1951—), Mo. Assn. Trial Attys. (pres. 1954, editor bull. 1955), Lawyers Assn. Kansas City, Lawyers Assn. St. Louis, Archeol. Inst. Am., Sierra Club (life). Episcopalian. Democrat. Club: Kansas City. Home: 1210 W 63d St Kansas City MO 64113-1513 Office: Hubbell Sawyer Peak O'Neal & Napier Power and Light Bldg 106 W 14th St Fl 12 Kansas City MO 64105-1914

HUBBELL, FLOYD ALLAN, physician, educator; b. Waco, Tex., Nov. 13, 1948; s. F.E. and Margaret (Fraser) H.; m. Nancy Cooper, May 23, 1975; 1 child, Andrew Allan. BA, Baylor U., 1971, MD, 1974; MS in Pub. Health, UCLA, 1983. Diplomate Am. Bd. Internal Medicine. Intern, then resident Long Beach med. program U. Calif., Irvine, 1975-78, asst. prof. medicine, 1981-89, assoc. prof. medicine and social ecology, 1989-97; prof. medicine and social ecology, 1997—; dir. primary care internal medicine residency U. Calif., Irvine, 1992—, chief divsn. gen. internal medicine and primary care,

1992—, dir. Ctr. for Health Policy and Rsch., 1993—. Contbr. articles to profl. jours. Recipient Outstanding Tchr. award U. Calif., Irvine, 1985, 89. Fellow ACP; mem. APHA, Soc. Gen. Internal Medicine, Physicians for Social Responsibility. Democrat. Avocations: reading, skiing, water sports. Office: U Calif Irvine Health Policy and Rsch 100 Theory #110 Irvine CA 92697-5800

HUBBELL, JOHN HOWARD, radiation physicist; b. Ann Arbor, Mich., Apr. 9, 1925; s. Howard Adams Hubbell and Mildred Jeanetta (Lipe) Hubbell Dyson; m. Jean Garber Norford, June 11, 1955; children: Anne Virginia Hubbell Cooper, Shelton Eric, Wendy Jean Hubbell Carballo. BS in Engring. Physics, U. Mich., 1949, MS in Physics, 1950; doctor honoris causa, U. Cordoba, 1996. Researcher x-ray crystal diffraction group Nat. Bur. Standards (name now Nat. Inst. Standards & Tech.), Washington, 1950-51, researcher thermodynamics sect., 1951, researcher radiation theory group, 1951-62; dir. x-ray and ionizing radiation data ctr. Nat. Bur. Standards (name now Nat. Inst. Standards & Tech.), Washington & Gaithersburg, Md., 1963-81; researcher Ctr. for Radiation Rsch. Nat. Bur. Standards (name now Nat. Inst. Standards & Tech.), Gaithersburg, 1982-88, researcher, cons. Photon and Charged Particle Data Ctr., 1988—; mem. cross sect. evaluation working group Brookhaven (N.Y.) Nat. Lab., 1965—; cons. Lawrence Livermore (Calif.) Nat. Lab., 1966—, Lawrence Berkeley (Calif.) Lab., 1981—, Internat. Atomic Energy Agy., Vienna, 1987—, WHO, Geneva, 1989—; sec. task force on x-ray absorption coefficients Internat. Union Crystallography, 1979—; lectr. USSR Acad. Scis., 1979, People's Republic of China State Bur. Metrology, 1987, 93, India Under Indo-U.S. Spl. Fgn. Currency Program, 1972, 74, 90; invited lectr. Japanese Soc. Radiol. Tech., Nagoya Ann. Conf., Kyoto, Osaka, 1995; vis. prof. U. Cordoba, Argentinia, 1996. Author: Photon Cross Sections, Attenuation Coefficients and Energy Absorption Coefficients, 1969 (citation classic awards 1982, 89, 90); editor Jour. Applied Radiation and Isotopes, 1988-92; editor-in-chief Radiation Physics and Chemistry, 1992—; contbr. articles to profl. jours. and ency., chpt. to book. Scoutmaster, Boy Scouts Am., Washington, 1953-60; ch. sch. tchr. Foundry United Methodist Ch., Washington, 1963-78. With U.S. Army, 1943-45, ETO. Decorated Bronze Star; recipient Faculty medal Tech. U. Prague, 1982; named Outstanding Alumnus U. Mich. Nuclear Engring. Dept., 1995. Fellow Am. Nuclear Soc. (Radiation Industry award 1985, Profl. Excellence award 1990), Health Physics Soc. (chmn. gen. radiation protection sect., stds. com. 1984-90); mem. Am. Phys. Soc., Soc. Nuclear Medicine (Paul C. Aebersold award 1985), Internat. Radiation Physics Soc. (exec. councillor 1985-91, v.p. for N.Am. 1991-94, pres. 1994-97, chmn. adv. bd. 1997—), Hubbell Family Hist. Soc., Internat. Higher Edn. Acad. Scis. Achievements include development of computationally tractable solutions for the (now called) Hubbell rectangular source integral and Epstein-Hubbell generalized elliptic-type integral. Avocations: eclipse chasing, playing harmonica. Home: 11830 Rocking Horse Rd Rockville MD 20852-2322 Office: Nat Inst Standards and Tech Radiation Physics Buil Gaithersburg MD 20899 *In this later stage of my life I view my global science connections more and more as an opportunistic tool toward realizing, incrementally at least, Teilhard de Chardin's envisioned "noosphere" (humanity as a caring communicating "thinking skin" of the earth), declaring the pragmatic and compelling authenticity of the option of a friendly cosmos as not only a place in which to live, but also to bravely wear as a suit of clothes, in contrast to the hostile and judgmental cosmos envisioned, dwelt in, and worn by many.*

HUBBELL, KATHERINE JEAN, marketing consultant; b. Norfolk, Va., Mar. 5, 1951; d. Lester Earle and Katherine Jean (Bush) H.; m. Daryl Paul Domning, July 10, 1987; 1 child, Charlotte Roxanna Domning. BA in English, BS in Math., Clemson U., 1974; MBA in Mktg., Va. Polytech. Inst. & State U., 1991. Info. systems engr. MITRE Corp., McLean, Va., 1975-79; mem. tech. staff MITRE Corp., Bedford, Mass., 1980-81; design engr. GE, Wilmington, Mass., 1979-80; budget assoc. nat. hdqrs. ARC, Washington, 1982-92; mktg. cons. Dominion Group, Vienna, Va., 1993-98; with Nat. Found. Women Bus. Owners, Silver Spring, Md., 1999—; adv. com. The Arc of Montgomery County, 1998—. Recreation vol. ARC, Bethesda Naval Hosp., 1976-79; vol. Holy Cross Hospice, 1984-87; strategic planning com. Christian Life Cmtys. Mid-Atlantic Region, 1989-90, co-chairperson, 1995—; database mgr. Christian Life Cmtys. U.S., 1993-97; allocations com. United Way Nat. Captiol Area, 1989-91. Mem. Am. Mktg. Assn., Assn. Part-Time Profls., Soc. Competitive Intelligence Profls. Home: 9211 Wendell St Silver Spring MD 20901-3533 Office: Nat Found Women Bus Owners 1100 Wayne Ave Ste 830 Silver Spring MD 20910

HUBBS, CLARK, zoologist, researcher; b. Ann Arbor, Mich., Mar. 15, 1921; s. Carl Leavitt and Laura Cornelia (Clark) H.; m. Catherine Vickery Symons; children: Laura Ellen Hubbs Tait, John Clark, Ann Frances Hubbs Weissman. BA, U. Mich., 1942; PhD, Stanford U., 1951. Instr. zoology U. Tex., Austin, 1949-52, asst. prof., 1952-57, assoc. prof., 1957-63, prof., 1963-88, Regents prof., 1988-91, Regents prof. emeritus, 1991—, chmn. biology dept., 1974-76, chmn. zoology dept., 1978-86, with grad. faculty dept. marine sci., 1987-91; curator ichthyology Tex. Meml. Mus., 1978—; vis. prof. U. Okla., Kingston, 1970-84; bd. dirs. Hubbs/Sea World Rsch. Inst., San Diego; faculty advisor U. de Nuevo Leon, Monterey, Mex., 1985-87; biology advisor Bd. Higher Edn., Little Rock, 1987, Jackson, Miss., 1983; leader Rio Grande Fishes Recovery Team, U.S. Interior Dept., Albuquerque, 1978—; mem. adv. com. Fish, Wildlife and Parks, U.S. Interior Dept., Washington, 1975-77; mem. sci. adv. com. Bass Anglers Sportsmans Soc., Montgomery, Ala., 1974-92; mem. sci. adv. bd. Tex. Utilities, Dallas, 1971—; chmn. inland task force, power plant sitting com., Office of Gov., Austin, Tex., 1971-72; mem. nuclear power adv. com. Tex. Energy Adv. Council, Austin, 1978-80; U.S. rep. European Ichthyological Congress, 1985-88; bd. dirs. Nature Conservancy of Tex., 1988-94; mem. rev. com. USDI, San Juan, P.R. Mng. editor Copeia, 1971-84; author over 300 sci. articles on fish biology. Mem. NRC Com. on Glen Canyon Releases in to the Colorado River, 1991-96; bd. dirs. Tex. Environ. Def. Fund, 1997—. Served with U.S. Army, 1942-46, PTO. Named Educator and Researcher of Yr., Tex. chpt. Am. Fisheries Soc., 1978; recipient Excellence, Golden and Hon. awards Am. Fisheries Soc., 1988; Clark Hubbs Endowed Professorship in Zoology established in his honor, Dept. Zoology, Clark Hubbs Aquarium named in his honor. Mem. Am. Soc. Ichthyologists and Herpetologists (pres. 1987, lifetime achievement award 1992), Am. Inst. Fish Rsch. Biol. (pres. 1995-98), Tex. Acad. Scis. (pres. 1972-73, Disting. Scientist of Yr. 1998), S.W. Assn. Naturalists (pres. 1966-67, W.F. Blair Eminent Naturalist 1990, George M. Sutton award 1996), Sociedad Iotiológica Mexicana Asociación Cientifica (hon.). Office: U Tex Dept Zoology Austin TX 78712*

HUBBS, DONALD HARVEY, foundation executive; b. Kingman, Ariz., Jan. 3, 1918; s. Wayne and Grace Lillian (Hoose) H.; m. Flora Vincent, June 14, 1945; children: Donald Jr., Susan Tyner, Diane Schultz, Wayne, David, Adrienne Busk. BA in Edn., Ariz. State U., 1940; JD, Southwestern U., 1956. Bar: Calif., 1956; CPA. Acct. Wright and Hubbs, L.A., 1945-67; pvt. practice atty. L.A., 1956-81; pres., dir. Conrad N. Hilton Found., L.A., 1981-98, chmn. bd., CEO, 1998—; bd. dirs. Trans World Airlines, 1977; regent Mt. St. Mary's Coll., 1983-98; bd. councilors U. So. Calif. Law Sch., 1992—. Hon. chief of the tribes, Oku Ghana, West Africa. 1st lt. (inf.) U.S. Army. Decorated Purple Heart. Mem. State Bar of Calif., So. Calif. Assn. for Philanthropy (pres. 1985-86), Riviera Country Club, L.A. Country Club. Avocations: cattle ranching, hunting, fishing, golfing. Home: 1658 San Onofre Dr Pacific Palisades CA 90272-2735 Office: Conrad N Hilton Found 10100 Santa Monica Blvd Ste 740 Los Angeles CA 90067-4100

HUBEL, DAVID HUNTER, physiologist, educator; b. Windsor, Ont., Can., Feb. 27, 1926; s. Jesse Hervey and Elsie (Hunter) H.; m. Shirley Ruth Izzard, June 20, 1953; children: Carl Andrew, Eric David, Paul Matthew. BSc, McGill U., 1947, MD, 1951, DSc (hon.), 1978; AM (hon.), Harvard U., 1962; DSc (hon.), U. Man., 1983; DHL (hon.), Johns Hopkins U., 1990; DSci, U. Western Ont., 1993; DSc, Oxford U., 1994, Gustavus Adolphus Coll., 1994, Ohio State U., 1995; D honoris causa, U. Madrid, 1997; JD honoris causa, Dalhousie U., 1998. Intern Montreal Gen. Hosp., 1951-52; asst. resident neurology Montreal Neurol. Inst., 1952-53, fellow clin. neurophysiology, 1953-54; asst. resident neurology Johns Hopkins Hosp., 1954-55; rsch. fellow Walter Reed Army Inst. Rsch., Washington, 1955-58; sr. fellow neurol. scis. group Johns Hopkins U., 1958-59; faculty Harvard U. Med. Sch., 1959—, George Packer Berry prof. physiology, chmn. dept., 1967-68, George Packer Berry prof. neurobiology, 1968-82, John Franklin Enders univ. prof., 1982—; George H. Bishop lectr. exptl. neurology Washington U., St. Louis, 1964; Jessup lectr. biol. scis. Columbia, 1970; James Arthur lectr. Am. Mus. Natural History, 1972; Ferrier lectr. Royal Soc. London, 1972; Harvey lectr. Rockefeller U., 1976; Weizmann meml. lectr. Weizmann Inst. Sci., Rehovot, Israel, 1979; George Eastman prof. Oxford, Eng., 1991-92; Eastman prof., Oxford, Eng., 1991-92; Fenn lectr. 30th internat. congress Internat. Union Psychol. Sci., Vancouver, B.C., Can., 1986; rschr. brain mechanisms in vision; bd. syndics Harvard U. Press, 1979-83; Brookhart lectr. Oreg. Health Scis., 1992, Murlin lectr. U. Rochester, 1992, Thurston lectr. Washington U., 1992; 1st ann. George A. Miller lectr. Cognitive Neurosci. Soc., 1995; keynote spkr. plenary session Am. Assn. for Lab. Animal Sci., Balt., 1995; Hoyt lectr. U. Calif. Sch. Medicine, San Francisco, 1995. Speaker in field. Served with AUS, 1955-58. Recipient Trustees award Rsch. to Prevent Blindness, 1971, Lewis S. Rosentiel award for disting. work in basic med. rsch., 1972, Karl Lashley prize Am. Philos. Soc., 1977, Louisa Gross Horwitz prize Columbia U., 1978, Dickson prize in medicine U. Pitts., 1979, Ledile prize Harvard U., 1980, Nobel prize, 1981, Outstanding Sci. Leadership award Nat. Assn. for Biomed. Rsch., 1990, City of Medicine award, 1990, Glen A. Fry medal Coll. Optometry, Ohio State U., 1991, Charles F. Prentice medal Am. Acad. Optometry, 1993, Helen Keller prize Helen Keller Eye Rsch. Found., 1995; fellow Harvard Soc. Fellows, 1971—, Royal Soc. Medicine, 1991, First Ann. George A. Miller lectr. Cognitive Neurosci. Soc., Gerald award Soc. Neurosci., 1993, Hon. mem. Spanish Soc. Opth., 1997, Dr. Honoris Causa U. Madrid, 1997. Fellow AAAS, Am. Acad. Arts and Scis.; mem. NAS, Am. Physiol. Soc. (Bowditch lectr. 1966), Deutsche Akademie der Naturforscher Leopoldina, Soc. for Neurosci. (Grass lectr. 1976, Gerard award 1993), Assn. for Rsch. in Vision and Ophthalmology (Friedenwald award 1975), Johns Hopkins U. Soc. Scholars, Am. Philos. Soc. (Karl Spencer Lashley prize 1977), Royal Soc. London, Spanish Soc. Ophthalmology (hon.), Academica Europaea (fgn. mem.), Sigma Xi. Home: 98 Collins Rd Waban MA 02468-2235 Office: Harvard U Med Sch Dept Neurobiology 220 Longwood Ave Boston MA 02115-5701

HUBEL, DENNIS JAMES, judge; b. N.Y.C., Nov. 3, 1947. BS in Electrical Engring., Cornell U., 1969; postgrad., U. Wash., 1972-73; JD cum laude, Lewis & Clark Coll., 1976. Bar: Oreg. 1976, Wash. 1985, U.S. Dist. Ct. Oreg., U.S. Dist. Ct. (ea. and we. dists.) Wash., U.S. Ct. Appeals (9th cir.), U.S. Supreme Ct. Judge U.S. Magistrate, Portland, 1998—; adj. prof. Lewis & Clark Coll., Portland, Oreg., 1980-82. Mem. Am. Bd. Trial Advs., Oreg. State Bar Assn. (chmn. jury instrn. com. 1988-91, chmn. procedure & practice com. 1991-93). Office: 927 US Courthouse 1000 SW Third Ave Portland OR 97204

HUBEN, BRIAN DAVID, lawyer; b. Inglewood, Calif., May 14, 1962; s. Michael Gerald and Dorothy (Withers) H.; m. Kathy Henson Johnson, Apr. 6, 1991; children: Kaitlin Johnson, Mariana Johnson. BA, Loyola Marymount U., 1984; JD, Loyola Law Sch., 1987. Bar: Calif. 1988, U.S. Dist. Ct. (no., ce., ea. and so. dists.) Calif. 1988, Ariz., 1994, U.S. Ct. Appeals (9th cir.) 1988, D.C. 1989, U.S. Supreme Ct. 1996. Assoc. Steinberg, Nutter & Brent, Santa Monica, Calif., 1988-89, Smith & Hilbig, Torrance, Calif., 1989-95, Robie & Matthai, L.A., 1995—; spl. master State Bar of Calif., 1995-99; del. L.A. County Bar Assn. State Conv., 1990—. Mem. instl. rev. bd. Torrance Meml. Med. Ctr., 1990-95. Mem. Calif. Bar Assn., D.C. Bar Assn., L.A. County Bar Assn., Loyola Marymount Univ. Alumni Assn. (dir., bd. dirs. 1995—). Democrat. Roman Catholic. Avocations: travel, sports, current events. Office: Robie & Matthai 500 S Grand Ave 15th Fl Los Angeles CA 90071-2609

HUBER, SISTER ALBERTA, college president; b. Rock Island, Ill., Feb. 12, 1917; d. Albert and Lydia (Hofer) H. BA, Coll. St. Catherine, St. Paul, 1939; MA, U. Minn., 1945; PhD, U. Notre Dame, 1954. Mem. faculty Coll. St. Catherine, 1940—, prof. English, 1953-97; prof. emerita, 1997; chmn. dept. Coll. St. Catherine, 1960-63, acad. dean, 1962-64, pres., 1964-79. Trustee Avila Coll., Kansas City, Mo., 1986-97, St. Joseph's Hosp., St. Paul, 1971-80; pres. UN Assn. Minn., 1980-81; bd. dirs. St. Paul YMCA, 1986-92. Decorated Chevalier, Ordre des Palmes Acad.; recipient Outstanding Achievement award U. Minn. Alumni Assn., 1981. Mem. Phi Beta Kappa, Pi Gamma Mu. Office: 1724A Munster Ave Saint Paul MN 55116-3031

HUBER, ANN CERVIN, nurse; b. Balt., Dec. 1, 1941; d. John and Rose (Kortus) Cervin; m. Frank H. Huber, Sept. 26, 1964; children: Holly Ann, Joann Františka. Diploma, Union Meml. Hosp. Sch. Nursing, 1963; BSN, U. Md., 1994. RN, Md.; cert. community health nurse. Staff nurse Union Meml. Hosp., Balt., clin. nurse, 1963-74; pub. health nurse Balt. City Health Dept., 1975-79; community health nurse Harford County Health Dept., Bel Air, Md., 1979-94; coord. and AIDS case mgr. Harford County, 1994—. Active Czech and Slovak Heritage Assn. Md. Recipient Govs. Citation, 1990, Unsung Hero award Harford Con. Cmty. Svcs., 1996, Heart to Heart award Harford County, 1997. Mem. ANA, Assn. Nurses AIDS Care, Md. Nurses Assn. (chmn. sunshine com.), Md. Classified Employees Assn. (treas. 1986-88), SOKOL (pres. 1986-88, 1994-96, v.p. 1991-94, 96-97, bd. dirs. 1988-90), Sigma Theta Tau.

HUBER, CLAYTON LLOYD, marketing professional, engineer; b. Corpus Christi, Tex., May 4, 1955; s. James Lloyd and Lealla Jean (Snyder) H.; m. Verna Marlene May, Aug. 16, 1975; children: Konstanze Marlena, James Clayton, Katerina Nicole, Kassandra Kay. BS in Chem. Engring., W.Va. Inst. Tech., 1978. Registered profl. engr., W.Va.; cert. energy mgr. Project engr. Am. Cyanamid Co., Willow Island, W.Va., 1978-80; process engr. Mobay Chem. Corp., New Martinsville, W.Va., 1980-82; process design engr. Mobay Chem. Corp., Charleston, S.C., 1982-85; indsl. utilization specialist Hope Gas, Inc., Clarksburg, W.Va., 1985-88; mgr. mktg. tech. svc. Hope Gas, Inc., Parkersburg, W.Va., 1988-89; mgr. indsl. and tech. mktg. Hope Gas, Inc., Clarksburg, W.Va., 1989-95, mgr. residential, comml., tech. mktg., 1995—. Mem. W.Va. 4-H Club All Stars, Jacksons Mill, 1974—, Clarksburg Madrigal Singers; elder Ch. of Christ; steering com. W.Va. Clean State Program. Mem. NSPE, AIChE, Soc. Plastics Engrs., Assn. Energy Engrs., Am. Chem. Soc., Environ. Engrs. and Mgrs. Inst. of Assn. Energy Engrs. (charter), Nat. Coun. on Weights and Measures, W. Va. Natural Gas Vehicle Coalition (chair mktg. and devel. com.), W. Va. Environ. Inst., W. Va. Soc. Profl. Engrs. (pres. T. Moore Jackson chpt., state chmn. membership com., state bd. dirs.), Am. Assn. Cost Engrs. (bd. dirs.). Democrat. Avocations: racquetball, softball, fishing, hunting, golf. Home: 225 Paula Blvd Clarksburg WV 26301-3940 Office: Hope Gas Inc PO Box 2868 805 Bank One Ctr W Clarksburg WV 26301

HUBER, CLAYTON SHIRL, university dean; b. LaPoint, Utah, Feb. 28, 1938; s. LeRoy and Vera Johanna (Taylor) H.; m. Beth briggs, July 25, 1963; children: Kerry, Philip, LaNae, Douglas, LeAnn, Brad, Kevin. BS, Utah State U., 1962, MS, 1963; PhD, Purdue U., 1968. Lab. instr. Utah State U., Logan, 1962-63; rsch. asst. Purdue U., West Lafayette, Ind., 1965-68; sr. scientist Kraftco, Glenview, Ill., 1968; mgr. Technology Inc., Houston, 1968-75; scientist Am. Potato Co., Blackfoot, Idaho, 1975-76; dept. chair Brigham Young U., Provo, Utah, 1976-88, dean, 1988—; chmn. adv. com. NASA Ctr., Purdue U., West Lafayette, 1990-95; cons. to food industry, 1976—; mem. exec. com. Thrasher Rsch. Found., Salt Lake City, 1994—. Mem. editl. bd. Comtex Sci., 1982; contbr. articles to profl. jours.; patentee in field. Dist. chmn. Boy Scouts Am., Houston, 1974-75; voting dist. chmn. Rep. Party, Provo, 1979-82, county and state del. 1st lt. U.S. Army, 1963-65. Decorated Army Commendation medal; recipient Snoopy award Astronaut Office/NASA, 1970, NASA's Sci. and Tech award, 1971; named Virginia Cutler Lecture, Brigham Young U. Fellow Inst. Food Technologists (Tex. sect. chmn. 1972-73, chmn. Bonneville sect. 1980-81), Poultry Sci. Assn. (com. chmn. 1980-81). Republican. LDS. Avocations: backpacking, fishing, oil painting. Home: 189 E 4380 N Provo UT 84604-5008

HUBER, COLLEEN ADLENE, artist; b. Concordia, Kans., Mar. 30, 1927; d. Claude Irve and Freda (Trow) Baker; m. Wallace Charles Huber, Oct. 18, 1945 (dec.); children: Wallace Charles II (dec.), Shawn Dale, Devron Kelly (dec.), Candace Lynette, Melody Ann. Student, UCLA, 1974-78; BA cum laude, Calif. Poly. U., 1983. Co-owner, artist The Rocket (community newspaper), Garden Grove, Calif., 1955-58; quick sketch artist Walt Disney Prodn. Co., Burbank, Calif., 1958-59; v.p., art dir. Gray Pub. Co., Fullerton, Calif., 1968-76; tchr. North Orange County Sch. Dist., La Palma, Calif., 1974-76; art dir. Shoppers Guide, Upland, Calif., 1979-81; pub., owner Community Woman/Huber Ad Agy., Anaheim, Calif., 1976-79; artist Bargain Bulletin Pub., Fallbrook, Calif., 1979-82; graphic artist, designer Van Zyen Pub., Fallbrook, 1982-83; cons. sales East San Diego Mag./Baker Graphics, Rancho San Diego, Calif., 1978-88; owner, artist Coco Bien Objet d'Art, Laguna Beach, Calif., 1986-92; instr. Camp Fire Inc., 1990-92; instr. Coco Bien Objet d'Art, Temecula, Calif., 1992-93, Sun City, Calif., 1993—, Castle Rock, Wash., 1993—; dir. edn. Art Acad., Orange County, 1992-94; instr. Lake Elsinore Community Ctr., 1992—, San Jacinto C.C., 1997-98; 2nd v.p. Fine Art Inst., San Bernadina Mus., San Bernardino, Calif. Author: Gail, 1980 (1st Pl. award 1981, 2d Pl. award 1981); artist: Yearlings (2d Pl. award 1985), Penning (1st Pl. award 1987). Participant Art-A-Fair, Laguna Beach Festival Show. Recipient certs. North Orange County ROP, 1976-77, 2d pl. San Bernardino Art Show, 1995, Hon. Mention Nat. Orange Show, 1996, City of Lake Elsinore, 1997, 1st pl. award FAI San Bernardino Mus., 1999. Fellow Zonta (2d v.p. 1990-91), Laguna Beach C. of C. (docent gallery night 1988); mem. Exec. Women, Calif. Press Women Assn. (chmn. jr. journalism contest Orange County chpt. 1985-86, pres. 1986-87; yearly chair Taste of Valley art show 1997), Wildlife Art Assn. Republican. Roman Catholic. Avocations: baseball fan, golf, swimming, dancing, theatre.

HUBER, DAVID LAWRENCE, physicist, educator; b. New Brunswick, N.J., July 31, 1937; s. Howard Frederick and Katherine Teresa (Smith) H.; m. Virginia Hullinger, Sept. 8, 1962; children: Laura Theresa, Johanna Jean, Amy Louise, William Hullinger. BA, Princeton U., 1959; MA, Harvard U., 1960, PhD, 1964. Instr. U. Wis., Madison, 1964-65, asst. prof., 1965-67, assoc. prof., 1967-69, prof., 1969—; dir. Synchrotron Radiation Ctr., 1985-97, Phys. Scis. Lab, Stoughton, Wis., 1992—; disting. vis. prof. U. Mo., Kansas City, 1988. A.P. Sloan fellow, 1965-67, Guggenheim fellow, 1972-73, Nat. Assn. State Univs. and Land Grant Colls. fellow Office of Sci. and Tech. Policy, 1990-91. Fellow Am. Phys. Soc.; mem. AAAS, Sigma Xi. Office: Univ Wis Phys Scis Lab 3725 Schneider Dr Stoughton WI 53589-3034

HUBER, DON LAWRENCE, publisher; b. Milw., Aug. 17, 1928; s. Wallace Fred and Florence (Bleck) H.; m. Joan Mac Monnies, June 23, 1951. Student, Carthage (Ill.) Coll., 1946-48; B.S. in English, Northwestern U., 1950. Sales exec. sta. WOR (radio), N.Y.C., 1957-58; owner, gen. mgr. Sta. KALE-Radio, Pasco, Washington, 1958-60; mgr. advt. Standard Rate and Data Service, N.Y.C., 1961-70; v.p., pub. Computer and Communication Decisions, Hayden, N.J., 1970-87, VNU Bus. Press.; pvt. practice specializing in bldg. pvt. homes, 1990—. Served with USN, 1946-48. Mem. Sales Execs. N.Y., Navy League. Club: Northwestern University (N.Y.C.). Home and Office: 24 Rolling Dr Glen Head NY 11545-2613

HUBER, DONALD MARK, protective services official; b. Newark, Mar. 2, 1956; s. Donald Millard and Cecelia Madeline (Cicalese) H.; m. Carol Ann Milito, Sept. 8, 1996; 1 child, Erich Christian. N.J. cert. EMT, uniform fire code inspector, fire/arson investigator, uniform code fire ofcl.; USAF crash rescue specialist. Fire fighter Irvington (N.J.) Fire Dept., 1980-87, fire lt., 1987-91, fire capt., 1991-95, dep. fire chief, 1995, dir., chief, 1995—; pres. N.J. State Firemen's Mutual Benevolent Assn. Local #14, Irvington, 1984-87, chmn. legis. affairs, Rahway, N.J., 1993-95; trustee Irvington Mental Health Assn., 1995—. Author: 100 Year History of the Irvington Fire Department (1894-1994), 1995; editor-in-chief (monthly) N.J. State Firemen's Mutual Benevolent Assn. Bull., 1983-93. CPR instr. Am. Heart Assn., 1980—; legis. aide to assemblyman James Zangari 28th Legis. Dist., 1985-94; hon. dep. sheriff Essex County Sheriff's Office, 1996—; active Warren Twp. Hist. Soc., Compassion Internat., Christian Applachian Project. Sgt. USAF, 1976-80. Recipient Legis. commendation N.J. State Gen. Assembly, Trenton, 1990; named Fire Fighter of Yr., Irvington C. of C., 1990. Mem. Internat. Assn. Fire Fighters (pres. local #2004 1993-95), Internat. Assn. Arson Investigators, Internat. Assn. Fire Chiefs, Nat. Fire Protection Assn., N.J. State Dep. Chiefs Assn., N.J. State Career Fire Chiefs Assn., Firemen's Mutual Benevolent Assn.. Roman Catholic. Home: 103 Reinman Rd Warren NJ 07059-5737 Office: Irvington Fire Dept Civic Square Irvington NJ 07111

HUBER, DONALD SIMON, physician; b. Clarendon, Pa., Apr. 18, 1929; s. Walter Casper and Mary Agnes (Earley) H.; m. Mary Hanks, Sept. 6, 1958; children: Donald Scott, Mark Walter, Mary Lisa. BA, Duke U., 1951, MD, 1954. Diplomate Am. Bd. Internal Medicine, Am. Bd. Allergy and Immunology. Intern Charity Hosp., New Orleans, 1954-55; resident internal medicine Tulane U. Hosp., New Orleans, 1955-56, 58-60; pvt. practice Huntsville, Ala., 1960-96 (ret. 1996); clin. assoc. prof. medicine Sch. Primary Med. Care, Huntsville, 1985—; med. dir. Cmty. Free Clinic. Lt. commdr. USN, 1956-58, USNR, 1958-60. Fellow Am. Coll. Allergists; mem. AMA, Am. Acad. Allergy and Immunology, Ala. Soc. Allergy and Immunology (pres. 1985), Huntsville Rotary Club (bd. dirs. 1978). Republican. Methodist. Avocations: raquet ball, traveling. Home: 502 Eustis Ave SE Huntsville AL 35801-4112

HUBER, DOUGLAS CRAWFORD, pathologist; b. S. Charleston, W.Va., June 11, 1939; s. Abram Paul and Mary Ashley (Grow) H.; m. Deena Rae Freedman, Aug. 8, 1969; children: Adam Crawford, Laura Kristen; m. Angelika Madelon Pohl, June 3, 1961 (div. 1965); 1 child, Heidemarie Jutta. Student, Harvard U., 1958, 59; AB, Emory U., Atlanta, 1960; MD, Emory U. Sch. of Med., Atlanta, 1964. Cert. anatomic and clin. pathology, dermatopathology Med. Assn. Ga. Assoc. pathologist Baldwin County Hosp., Milledgeville, Ga., 1971-72, Leary Lab., Boston, 1972-73; lab. dir. Homer D. Cobb Mem. Hosp., Phenix City, Ala., 1973-79; gen. practitioner Leonard Morse Hosp., Natick, Mass., 1979-80; lab. dir. WellStar Douglas Hosp., Douglasville, Ga., 1980—; med. dir. Roche Biomedical Lab., Atlanta Div., Tucker, Ga., 1989-93; deputy state commr. Coll. Am. Pathologists Lab. Inspection Program, Skokie, Ill., 1976-79; v.p. Ala. Assn. Pathologists, Birmingham, 1979; with WellStar Northwest Physicians Group, 1996—. Pres. Nam Vets of Ga., 1982-85; capt. with U.S Army, 1965-67. Fellow Coll. Am. Pathologists, Am. Soc. Clinical Pathologists.

HUBER, EVELYNE, political science educator; b. Zurich, Switzerland. Degree in social psychology, U. Zurich, 1972; MA in Polit. Sci., Yale U., 1973, PhD in Polit. Sci., 1977. Vis. asst. prof. polit. sci. U. R.I., 1976-77; lectr. polit. sci. U. Wis., Milw., 1978-79; asst. prof. polit. sci. Coll. of the Holy Cross, 1979-85; from asst. prof. to assoc. prof. polit. sci. U. Calif., Irvine, 1985-87; from assoc. prof. to prof. Northwestern U., Evanston, Ill., 1987-92; Morehead alumni disting. prof. polit. sci. U. N.C., Chapel Hill, 1992—; dir. Inst. Latin Am. Studies, Duke U./U. N.C. programs, U. N.C.; mem. joint com. Latin Am. Social Sci. Rsch. Coun./ACLS, 1995—, regional advice panel Latin Am.; editl. bd. Polit. Power and Social Theory, 1990—; mem. Inst. Advanced Study, Princeton, 1998-99. Author: The Politics of Workers' Participation: The Peruvian Approach in Comparative Perspective, 1980; co-author: Democratic Socialism in Jamaica: The Political Movement and Social Transformation in Dependent Capitalism, 1986, Capitalist Development and Democracy, 1992 (co-winner outstanding book award Am. Sociol. Assn. 1991-92); co-editor: States Versus Markets in the World System, 1985. Grantee Fulbright Found. 1981, NSF, 1991-93, UN Rsch. Inst. for Social Devel.; ffellow German Acad. Exch. Svc., 1991. Office: Inst of Latin Am Studies Univ NC at Chapel Hill Chapel Hill NC 27599-3205 Office: U NC Dept Polit Sci Chapel Hill NC 27599-3265*

HUBER, FRITZ GODFREY, physical education educator, exercise physiologist; b. Wauseon, Ohio, Nov. 24, 1955. BEd, U. Toledo, 1978; MS, U. Okla., 1985; EdD, U. No. Colo., 1991. Head coach Am. Turners, Toledo, 1976-78; tchr., coach St. Wendelin Sch., Fostoria, Ohio, 1978-79; head gymnastics coach Sally Stanley Acad., Perry, Ga., 1980-83, Gymnest Sch. Gymnastics, Macon, Ga., 1985-87; grad. asst. U. Okla., Norman, 1983-85, U. No. Colo., Greeley, 1987-88; prof. phys. edn. Oral Roberts U., Tulsa, 1988—; chmn. health, phys. edn. and recreation dept., Oral Roberts U., chairperson U. Faculty Rsch. com.; clinic adviser Am. Running and Fitness Assn., Bethesda, Md., 1991—; coach, referee Spl. Olympics, Tulsa, 1988, 89, 90. Mem. AAHPERD, Am. Coll. Sports Medicine, Okla. Assn. Health, Phys. Edn., Recreation and Dance, Nat. Strength and Conditioning Assn. (cert.), U.S. Gymnastic Fedn., Am. Running and Fitness Assn. Office: Oral Roberts U 7777 S Lewis Ave Tulsa OK 74171-0001

HUBER, JAY D., state agency administrator; b. Oswego, N.Y., Sept. 27, 1936. Dir. airport ops. Md. Aviation Adminstrn., Balt., 1997—. Office: Md

Aviation Adminstrn Balt-Washington Internat PO Box 8766 Baltimore MD 21240-0766

HUBER, JOAN ALTHAUS, sociology educator; b. Bluffton, Ohio, Oct. 17, 1925; d. Lawrence Lester and Hallie (Althaus) H.; ; m. William Form, Feb. 5, 1971; children: Nancy Rytina, Steven Rytina. B.A., Pa. State U., 1945; M.A., Western Mich. U., 1963; Ph.D., Mich. State U., 1967. Asst. prof. sociology U. Notre Dame, Ind., 1967-71; asst. prof. sociology U. Ill., Urbana-Champaign, 1971-73; assoc. prof. U. Ill., 1973-78, prof., 1978-83, head dept., 1979-83; dean Coll. Social and Behavioral Sci., Ohio State U., Columbus, 1984-92; coordinating dean Coll. Arts and Sciences, Ohio State University, Columbus, 1987-92, provost, 1992-93; sr. v.p., provost emeritus prof. Sociology emeritus, 1994. Author: (with William Form) Income and Ideology, 1973, (with Glenna Spitze) Sex Stratification, 1983. Editor: Changing Women in a Changing Society, 1973, (with Paul Chalfant) The Sociology of Poverty, 1974, Macro-Micro Linkages in Sociology, 1991. NSF research awardee, 1978-81. Mem. Am. Sociol. Assn. (v.p. 1981-83, pres. 1987-90), Midwest Sociol. Soc. (pres. 1979-80). Home: 2880 N Star Rd Columbus OH 43221-2959 Office: Ohio State U Dept Sociology 300 Bricker Hall 190 N Oval Mall Columbus OH 43210-1321

HUBER, JOHN MICHAEL, lumber executive; b. N.Y.C., Oct. 13, 1958; s. Edward F. and Mary Elizabeth (Fallon) H. BA with honors in Philosophy, Boston U., 1981. Lumber broker Mor-Wood, Inc., Morehead, Ky., 1981-84; chmn., CEO Acorn Industries, Inc., Morehead, 1984-95; v.p. Pallet & Pallet, Inc., Toronto, Ont., Can., 1995-97; CEO Diamond Forest Resources, Inc., Clearfield, Ky., 1986—; CFO Clearcreek Hardwoods, Grayson, Ky., 1988—; co-founder H & M Investments LLC, 1995. Active Rowan County Learning Found., Morehead, 1989—, Am. Heart Found., St. Jude's Children's Hosp., Sloan Kettering Cancer Inst.; bd. dirs. Rowan County Adult Basic Edn. and Literacy Adv. Bd., 1994-96. Named to the Hon. Order of Ky. Col's. Mem. Citizens Against Govt. Waste (sustaining mem., cert. appreciation 1988, 89, 90), Nat. Congl. Rep. Com. (cert. appreciation 1988, 89, 90), Nat. Wooden Pallet and Container Assn. (bd. dirs. 1995-97), Internat. Assn. Pallet Recyclers (bd. dirs. 1992-94, pres. 1994, past pres. 1995), Masons. Roman Catholic. Avocations: outdoor sports, cooking, golf. Office: Diamond Forest Resources Inc 2 Acorn Ln Morehead KY 40351

HUBER, MICHAEL FREDERICK, journalist, educator; b. Oklahoma City, Okla., Dec. 4, 1952; s. James Arnold and Mary Frances (Kaho) H.; m. Cynthia Christine Morris, May 14, 1983; children: Eric William, Samuel James, Nicholas Andrew, Todd Michael. BA, Ind. U., Bloomington, 1974, MA, 1977. Reporter, editor The Chgo. Sun-Times, Chgo., 1977-79, The Courier-Journal, Louisville, Ky., 1979-82; night city editor The Miami Herald, 1982-86; exec. editor Review Publs., Miami, 1986-89; bus. writer The Miami Herald, 1989-91; asst. prof. Fla. Internat. U., Miami, 1992-; cons., Miami, 1991-; asst. dir. The Journalism Writing Project, Miami, 1992-; v.p. The Word Assn., Inc., Miami, 1995-. Co-author: (book) Words Into Flesh, 1994. Recipient award Ill. Assn. Press Editors, 1978, award Ill. Press Assn., 1978. Presbyterian. Home: 11100 Griffing Blvd Miami FL 33161-7250

HUBER, PAUL WILLIAM, biochemistry educator, researcher; b. Medford, Mass., July 23, 1951; s. William Francis and Catherine (Sheridan) H. BS, Boston Coll., 1973; PhD, Purdue U., 1978. NIH postdoctoral fellow U. Chgo., 1979-81, rsch. assoc., 1982-85; asst. prof. U. Notre Dame, Ind., 1985-92, assoc. prof., 1992—, assoc. chmn., 1993-97; vis. fellow Yale U., 1997. Contbr. articles to profl. jours. Mem. AAAS, Am. Soc. Biochemistry and Molecular Biology. Home: 1215 E Irvington Ave South Bend IN 46614-1417 Office: U Notre Dame Dept Chemistry/Biochemistry Notre Dame IN 46556

HUBER, RICHARD GREGORY, lawyer, educator; b. Indpls., June 29, 1919; s. Hugh Joseph and Laura Marie (Becker) H.; m. Katherine Elizabeth McDonald, June 21, 1950; children: Katherine, Richard, Mary, Elizabeth, Stephen, Mark. BS, U.S. Naval Acad, 1942; JD, U. Iowa, 1950; LLM, Harvard U., 1951; LLD (hon.), New England Sch. Law, 1985, Northeastern U., 1987, Roger Williams U., 1996. Instr. law U. Iowa, 1950; assoc. prof. law U. S.C., 1952-54; assoc. prof. Tulane U., 1954-57; assoc. prof. Boston Coll., 1957-59, prof., 1959-90, dean, 1970-85; disting. prof. Roger Williams U., Bristol, R.I., 1993-95; prof. New England Sch. Law, Newton, Mass., 1995-99; adj. faculty Boston Coll., 1999—. Contbr. articles and book revs. to profl. jours. Past chairperson pers. and fin. coms. Mass. chpt. Multiple Sclerosis Soc.; past pres. bd. trustees Beaver Country Day Sch. With USN, 1941-47, 51-52. Mem. ABA (bd. dels., mem. coun. legal edn. 1981-85, trustee law sch. admissions coun 1983-85), Soc. Am. Law Tchrs., Assn. Am. Law Schs. (pres. 1988-89), Coun. Legal Edn. Opportunity (pres. 1975-79), Am. Judicature Soc., Mass. Bar Assn., Mass. Bar Found. Democrat. Roman Catholic. Home: 406 Woodward St Waban MA 02468-1523 Office: 885 Centre St Newton MA 02459-1154

HUBER, RICHARD LESLIE, insurance company executive; b. Brevard, N.C., Nov. 2, 1936; s. William Worden and Marion (Griffith) H.; m. Roberta Palmer, June 10, 1960; children—Benjamin Philip, Alexander Leslie, Marcus Sebastian. BA, Harvard U., 1958. V.p. Citibank, N.A., Sao Paulo, Brazil, 1973-77; sr. v.p. Citibank, N.A., Tokyo, 1977-82; group exec. Citibank, N.A., N.Y.C., 1982-87; exec. v.p. Chase Manhattan Bank, N.Y.C., 1988-90; vice chmn., bd. dirs. Continental Bank Corp./Continental Bank, N.A., Chgo., 1990-94; pres., COO Grupo Wasserstein Perella, N.Y., 1994-95; vice chmn. strategy, finance and adminstrn. Aetna Inc. (formerly Aetna Life & Casualty), Hartford, Conn., 1995-97, pres., CEO, 1997—, chmn. bd. dirs., 1998—; bd. dirs. Re Corp. Dir. Hartford Ballet; Trustee Mark Twain House, Hartford. Lt. USCG, 1959-60. Mem. Coun. on Fgn. Rels. (N.Y.C.), Harvard Club N.Y.C. Office: Aetna Inc 151 Farmington Ave Hartford CT 06101-5900*

HUBER, RICHARD MILLER, American studies consultant; b. Ardmore, Pa., July 27, 1922; s. John Y. Jr. and Caroline (Miller) H.; divorced; children: Cintra Hutchinson Huber McGauley, Richard Miller Jr., Casilda Carter. BA, Princeton U., 1945; PhD, Yale U., 1953. Mem. faculty Princeton (N.J.) U., 1950-54; pres. Princeton Manor Constrn. Co., 1958-62; producer, moderator Sta. WHWH-AM-FM, Princeton, 1965-67; corr. Sta. WNET-TV, N.Y.C., 1967-68; dean Sch. Gen. Studies Hunter Coll., N.Y.C., 1971-77, exec. dir. div. continuing edn., 1977-82; asst. dir. TV and radio Nat. Endowment for the Humanities, Washington, 1983-84, spl. asst. to chmn., 1984-85; pres. Huber Assocs., Washington, 1985—; pres. Prodn.-in-Progress, Inc., Washington, 1986-89; cons. Am. studies Dept. State and U.S. Info. Agy., 1989—. Author: Big All The Way Through: The Life of Van Sandvoord Merle-Smith, 1952, The American Idea of Success, 1971, rev. edn., 1987, How Professors Play the Cat Guarding the Cream: Why We're Paying More and Getting Less in Higher Education, 1992; editor: (with Wheaton J. Lane) New Jersey Historical Series, 31 vols., 1965. Mem. Coun. of Friends, Princeton U. Libr. 2nd lt. USAAF, 1942-45, Italy. Decorated Air medal; recipient N.J. Hist. Soc. award, 1965, award of merit Am. Assn. State and Local History, 1965, Author's award N.J. Assn. Tchrs. of English, 1965, award of recognition N.J. Hist. Commn., Trenton, 1983. Mem. Soc. Am. Historians, Am. Studies Assn. Republican. Episcopalian. Avocations: tennis, jogging, swimming. Office: Huber Assocs Ste 926 2950 Van Ness St NW Washington DC 20008-1120

HUBER, ROBERT, biochemist, educator; b. Munich, Feb. 20, 1937; s. Sebastian and Helene (Kebinger) H.; m. Christa Huber, 1960; children: Ulrike, Martin, Robert, Julia. Diploma, Tech. Universität Munich, 1960, PhD, 1963, Habilitation, 1968; D (hon.), Louvain, Belgium, 1987, U. Ljubljana, Slovenia, 1989; D for Medicine and Surgery (hon.), U. 'Tor Vergata', Rome, 1991. External prof. Tech. U. Munich, 1976; prof., dir. Max-Planck-Inst. for Biochemistry, Martinsried, Germany, 1972—. Editor Jour. Molecular Biology. Decorated grosse Verdienstkreuz mit Stern und Schulterband, Order for Merit for Sci. and Arts (Germany); recipient E.K. Frey medal Gesellschaft für Chirurgie, 1972, Otto Warburg medal Gesellschaft für Biologische Chemie, 1977, Emil van Behring medal U. Marburg, 1982, Keilin medal Biochem. Soc. London, Richard Kuhn medal Soc. German Chemists, 1987, E.K. Frey-E. Werle meml. medal, 1989, Kone award Assn. Clin. Biochemists, 1990, Sir Hans Krebs medal, 1992, Bayerischer Maximilianorden für Wissenschaft und Kunst, 1993, Linus Pauling medal, 1993, 94, Disting. Svc. award Miami Biotech. Winter Symposia, 1995, Max Tishler prize Harvard U., 1997, Max Bergmann medal U. Tübingen, 1997, co-recipient Nobel prize for chemistry, 1988. Fellow Royal Soc. London, Third World Acad. Scis., Am. Acad. Microbiology; mem. NAS (U.S.A.) (fgn. assoc.), European Molecular Biology Orgn. (coun. mem.), Japanese Biochem. Soc. (hon.), Deutsche Chemische Gesellschaft, Gesellschaft für Biologische Chemie, Am. Soc. Biol. Chemists (hon.), Swedish Soc. Biophysics (hon.), Bayerische Acad. der Wissenschaften, Deutsche Acad. der Naturforscher Leopoldina, Croatian Acad. Scis. and Art (corr.), Acad. Nazionale der Lincei, European Molecular Biology Orgn. Office: Max Planck Inst Biochem, Am Klopferspitz 18A, Martinsried Munich 82152, Germany

HUBER, THOMAS MARTIN, container company executive; b. Highland, Ill., Nov. 4, 1919; s. Martin J. and Ida R. (Burke) H.; m. Martha A. Kaseberg, Aug. 15, 1942; children: Timothy B., Martha A. Huber Scavone. B.S., U. Ill., 1941; student, Northwestern U. Grad. Sch. Bus.-Inst. Internat. Mgmt., 1970. With Owens-Ill. Inc., 1946-84, v.p., gen. mgr. Cuban ops., 1957-60; v.p. internat. div. for industry relations, area mgr. Owens-Ill. Inc., N. Am., Caribbean, Far East, 1960-61; v.p., gen. mgr. Belgian ops. Owens-Ill. Inc., 1961-65, v.p., gen. mgr. Venezuelan ops., 1965-68, v.p., gen. mgr. European ops., 1968-73; corp. v.p., gen. mgr. European div. Owens-Ill. Inc., Toledo, 1973-80; gen. mgr. worldwide bus. devel. Owens-Ill. Inc., 1980-81, sr. v.p., 1981-84; pvt. practice mgmt. cons., 1984—; pres. Kimble Italiana S.P.A., Italy, 1968-80, Owens-Ill. Internat. S.A., Switzerland, 1968-80, Durobor S.A., Belgium, 1968-80; vice chmn. Hellenic-Owens Glass Co., Greece, 1968-80; dir. United Glass Ltd., U.K., 1968-80, Gerresheimer Glass GMBH, Germany, 1968-80, Giralt La Porta, S.A. Spain, 1968-80. Served to maj. C.E. AUS, 1941-45. Republican. Roman Catholic. Club: Bermuda Run Country. Home: 2323 Bermuda Vlg Advance NC 27006-9476

HUBER, VIDA S., nursing educator; b. West Liberty, Ohio, Mar. 27, 1937; d. L.L. and Nanna V. (Bender) Swartzentruber; m. Harold E. Huber, June 6, 1970; 1 child, Heidi Marie. Diploma, Milford Meml. Hosp., 1959; BSN, Eastern Mennonite Coll., 1961; MA in Nursing Edn., Columbia U., Tchrs. Coll., 1966, EdD, 1970. Staff nurse Milford Meml. Hosp., Del., 1959-60; nursing supr. County Rest Home, Greenwood, Del., 1959-60, 61-65; instr. nursing Milford Meml. Hosp., Del., 1961-64, ednl. dir., 1964; chmn., prof. Eastern Mennonite Coll., Dept. Nursing, Harrisonburg, Va., 1967-84; vis. prof. U. Va. Sch. Nursing, Charlottesville, Va., 1984-86; exec. dir. Va. Soc. Profl. Nurses, Harrisonburg, Va., 1987-88; prof., dept. head nursing James Madison U., Harrisonburg, Va., 1988—; speaker in field; bd. dirs. County Rest Home, Greenwood, Del., 1970-81, pres., 1980-81. Contbr. articles to profl. jours. Named Outstanding Young Women Am., 1973, Outstanding Educator AM. 1973, 75; recipient Women's Caucus Award for Svc., 1992. Mem. ANA, Am. Assn. Colls. Nursing, Nat. League Nursing, Va. Assn. Colls. Nursing, Mennonite Nurses Assn. (project dir. 1988), Kappa Delta Pi, Pi Delta Kappa, Pi Lambda Theta.

HUBERMAN, BENJAMIN, technology consultant; b. Havana, Cuba, Jan. 25, 1938; came to U.S., 1946; s. Henry and Marcella (Waisman) H.; m. Gisela Bialik, Oct. 13, 1963; children: Jonathan, Martin. AB, Columbia Coll., 1959; BS, Columbia U., 1960; diploma of Imperial Coll., U. London (Eng.), 1962. Sr. official Arms Control & Disarmament Agy., Washington, 1966-73, Nat. Security Coun., Washington, 1973-75; dir., policy evaluation Nuclear Regulatory Commn., Washington, 1975-77; sr. official Office Sci. and Tech. Policy, Washington, 1977-81; dep. sci. advisor to pres. White House, Washington, 1981; v.p. Cons. Internat. Group, Inc., Washington, 1982-88, pres., 1988-90; pres. Huberman Cons. Group, Washington, 1990—; bd. dirs. Muse Techs. Inc., Albuquerque, AETC Inc., San Diego. Lt. USN, 1960-66. Fulbright scholar, London, 1960-61. Mem. Coun. Fgn. Rels., Met. Club, Cosmos Club (Washington). Home: 3907 S Ocean Blvd Highland Bch FL 33487-3305 Office: Huberman Cons Group 1090 Vermont Ave NW Ste 800 Washington DC 20005-4905

HUBERMAN, JEFFREY ALLEN, architect; b. Boston, Jan. 2, 1942; s. Sidney H. and Miriam (Walker) H.; m. Barbara Kemp, May 16, 1964 (div.); children: Amy Beth, Marc Walker. BArch, U. Fla., 1964. Designer Odell Assocs., Charlotte, N.C., 1964-67, Wolf-Johnson Assocs., Charlotte, 1967-69; designer, architect Wolf Assocs., Charlotte, 1970-71; ptnr. Gantt Huberman Architects, Charlotte, 1971—; mem. N.C. Bd. Architecture, 1995—, sec., 1996-97, treas., 1997—; bd. dirs. Green Hill Ctr. N.C. Art. chmn. annual fund drive Charlotte-Mecklenburg Arts and Sci. Coun., 1975-81, v.p., 1977-78, bd. dirs., 1977; bd. dirs. Charlotte Opera Assn., 1966-82, pres., 1979-81; pres. Children's Theatre, 1984-85, bd. dirs., 1981-87; bd. dirs. Temple Beth El, 1968-83, Charlotte-Mecklenburg Community Rels. Com., 1974-84, Planned Parenthood of Greater Charlotte, 1978-80, Charlotte Jr. Soccer Found., 1978-82, Tarradiddle Players, 1986-87; chmn. Charlotte Clean City Com., 1975-77; youth soccer coach, 1975-84; com. mem. Performing Arts Ctr. Adv. Ctr., 1983-85; adv. com. Charlotte/Douglas Internat. Airport, 1987-88, art adv. com., 1992—. Fellow AIA (chmn. honor awards com. 1972, treas. Charlotte, N.C. sect. 1976-77, chmn. audit com. 1987, bd. dirs. 1987-92, long range planning com. 1990, component resources com. 1992, pres. N.C. chpt. 1991, N.C. Archtl. Found. 1994), Nat. Coun. Archtl. Registration Bd. (juror divsns. B and C archtl. registration exam. 1984-86, chmn. divsn. B graphic 1989, mem. master jurors com. 1986, mem. archtl. registration exam. com. 1996-97, interim devel. program com. 1998-99). Office: Gantt Huberman Architects 500 N Tryon St Charlotte NC 28202-2232

HUBERT, FRANK WILLIAM RENE, retired university system chancellor; b. Milam County, Tex., June 2, 1915; s. Jonce Sherod and Lura Gertrude (White) H.; m. Mary Julia Glidden, June 15, 1940; children: Frank William Rene, Mary Katherine. B.A., U. Tex., 1938, M.A., 1946, Ph.D., 1950; LL.D., Baylor U., 1979; LLD, Tex. Coll., 1992. Dir. Lutcher Stark Boys, Inc., Orange, Tex., 1938-44; prin., dir. secondary edn. Stark Sr. High Sch., Orange, 1946-48; research fellow, curriculum and instrn. U. Tex., 1948-49; adminstrv. asst. Found. Sch. Program Act div. Tex. Auditor's Office, Austin, 1949-50; dir. div. Found. Sch. Program Act div. Tex. Auditor's Office, 1949-50; dir. div. profl. standards, also div. tchr. edn. Tex. Edn. Agy., Austin, 1950-55; supt. schs. Orange Ind. Sch. Dist., 1955-59; dean Sch. Arts and Scis., Tex. A&M U., College Station, 1959-65; dean Coll. Liberal Arts Tex. A&M U., 1965-69, dean Coll. Edn., 1969-79, dir. basic div., 1959-60, chancellor, 1979-82, chancellor emeritus, 1983—; exec. sec. Tex. Bd. Exam. Tchr. Edn., 1952-55; mem. com. 75 U. Tex.; pres. Tex. Conf. Tchr. Edn., 1959; mem. Nat. Council Accreditation Tchr. Edn., 1953-55; v.p. S.W. Ednl. Devel Corp., 1966-67, pres., 1967-68; mem. Nat. Adv. Commn. on Mexican-Am. Edn., U.S. Office Edn., 1967-69; adv. council U.S. Command and Gen. Staff Coll., 1972-75; pres. Corp. Research and Engring. in Edn., 1969—; mem. bd. cons. Center for Research and Edn. Free Enterprise, 1977-80; mem. Tex. Adv. Com. Tech.-Vocat. Edn., 1978-80, Gov.'s Com. Pub. Edn., 1966-69. Mem. Charter Change Commn., Orange, 1958; trustee Tex. Coll., 1974-84. Served with AUS, 1944-46. Mem. NEA, Orange Edn. Assn. (pres. 1943-44), Assn. Tex. Colls. and Univs. (pres. 1965-66), Am. Tex. Assns. Sch. Adminstrs., Am. Acad. Polit. and Social Sci., Philos. Soc. Tex., Tex. Tchrs. Assn. (chmn. com. tchr. edn. and profl. standards 1955-60), Sons Republic Tex., Coushatta Camellia Soc. (pres. 1991-92), Am. Camellia Soc. (edn. com. 1991-93). Home: 2404 Morris Ln Bryan TX 77802-2327

HUBERT, HELEN BETTY, epidemiologist; b. N.Y.C., Jan. 22, 1950; d. Leo and Ruth (Rosenbaum) H.; m. Carlos Barbaro Arostegui, Sept. 11, 1976 (div. May 1987); 1 child, Joshua Daniel Hubert. BA magna cum laude, Barnard Coll., 1970; MPH, Yale U., 1973, MPhil, 1976, PhD, 1978. Rsch. assoc. Yale U., New Haven, 1977-78; rsch. epidemiologist Nat. Heart, Lung and Blood Inst., Bethesda, Md., 1978-84; rsch. dir. Gen. Health, Inc., Washington, 1984-87; sr. rsch. scientist Stanford (Calif.) U., 1988—. Peer rev. Am. Jour. Epidemiology, Am. Jour. Pub. Health, Chest, Jour. AMA (JAMA), Archives Internal Medicine; contbr. articles to profl. jours., chpts. to books. NIH grantee, 1997—. Mem. Am. Coll. Epidemiology, Soc. Epidemiol. Rsch., Assn. Rheumatology Health Profls., Phi Beta Kappa, Sigma Xi (grant-in-aid for rsch. 1978). Avocations: swimming, hiking. Office: Stanford Univ Med Ctr Ste 3305 701 Welch Rd Palo Alto CA 94304

HUBERT, JEAN-LUC, chemicals executive; b. Metz, Moselle, France, Mar. 13, 1960; s. Andre and Franziska (Schmidt) H. Diplome Ingenieur, Ecole Centrale Paris, 1982, Diplome Detudes Approfondies, 1982; MS in Mech. and Nuclear Engring., Northwestern U., 1985; M in Project Mgmt. with distinction, Keller Grad. Sch., 1996. Simulation engr. Didier Werke, Wiesbaden, Fed. Republic Germany, 1981; engr. Iron and Steel Rsch. Inst., Metz, France, 1983; cryogenic applications engr. L'Air Liquide, Paris, 1985-86; R&D mgr. cryogenic refrigeration processes Liquid Air Corp., Countryside, Ill., 1986-89, project mgr. new processes devel. group, 1989-93; concurrent multi project mgr., primary metals and combustion, mktg. and applications group Air Liquide America Corp, Countryside, Ill., 1993-95; applied tech. engrng. dept. mgr. Air Liquide Am. Corp., Countryside, Ill., 1995-99; mgr. bus. devel. ctrl. engrng. dept. Air Liquide Am. Corp., Countryside, 1999—; new process devel. cons. Liquid Air Corp./Energy Systems, Lake Charles, La., 1987-90, BIG3/INS, Houston, 1990-91, exceptional ops. mgr., coord. subcontractors, regional svc. and sales coord. applications unit, 1992-93. Patentee cryogenic food freezing, cryogenic embrittlement processes, pipeline rehab. processes, multi-step combined mech./thermal stripping processes, supercritical chemical extraction processes, ozone based food sanitizing processes. 2d lt. French Navy, 1982-83. Tuition fellow Georges Lurcy Found., 1984, Henri Blanchenay fellow French Inst., 1984, Bieneck/Didier fellow, Fed. Rep. Ger., 1984, Northwestern U. Rsch. assistantship, 1984. Mem. ASME, Inst. Food Technologists (profl.), Internat. Inst. Refrigeration, Iron and Steel Soc. Achievements include 6 US, Canadian and 2 European patents for High Efficiency Linear Freezer, for Method and Apparatus for Enhancing Production Capacity and Flexibility of a Multi-tier Refrigeration Tunnel, for Process and Apparatus for Embrittling and Subsequently Removing an Outer Protective Coating of a Pipe or Pipeline, and for Efficiency Process and Apparatus for same and for a fast efficient, low-cost stripping process of non-metallic layers from steel substrates, for supercritical CO2 pressure swing absorption based cleaning methods and systems and for process and equipment for sanitizing food using ozone. Avocations: continuing education and intellectual enrichment, classical music, computers, horsemanship, 20th Century history. Home: 253 Woodstock Ave Clarendon Hills IL 60514-2822 Office: Air Liquide Am Corp 5230 East Ave La Grange IL 60525-3133

HUBLER, JULIUS, artist; b. Granite City, Ill., Dec. 11, 1919; s. Voyle and Marie (Lewedag) H.; m. Loretta Lanter, Apr. 26, 1943; children: Stuart Alden, Ann Marlowe McClure. B.S., S.E. Mo. U., 1943; M.A., Ed.D., Columbia U., 1951. Sci. tchr. Wibaux High Sch., Mont., 1942-43, Ashton High Sch., Idaho, 1943-45; art instr. CCNY, 1946-48; prof. art SUNY-Buffalo, 1948-82; freelance artist Buffalo, 1982—; painter, graphic designer, sculptor, photographer. One-man exhbn. Albright-Knox Mus., Buffalo, 1991, Rodman Hall Nat. Exhbn. Ctr., St. Catharines, Ont., Can., 1991; exhibited in group shows Taipei Mus. Fine Arts, 1983-88, 94, Internat. Miniature Print Biennial, 1989, Salon de Peiture et d'Estambe Montreal, Que., Can., Silvermine, New Canaan, Conn., 1994; contbr. articles to profl. publs. Mem. Western N.Y. Peace Ctr. Deans scholar; State U. Iowa grad. scholar, 1944; Arthur W. Dow scholar Columbia U., 1947; disting. service awardee U. Buffalo, 1958; recipient Silvermine award, 1999. Mem. AAUP (bd. dirs., pres. N.Y. state chpt. 1956-60), Soc. Am. Graphic Artists (Warren Mack Meml. purchase award 1962), NAD (assoc., Samuel F.B. Morse medal 1977, Anonymous prize 1980, Leo Meissner prize 1989), Amnesty Internat., Brit.-N.Am. Philatelic Assn., Buffalo Stamp Club, Helvetia Am. Club. Clubs: Buffalo Stamp, Helvetia Am. Address: 9855 Hollingson Rd Clarence NY 14031-1595 *One is in debt to an endless number of people living and dead. Many have paid a horrible price. Change and, hopefully progress, are rarely welcome. Products of imagination testify to the necessary sacrifice, dedication, strength and vision. It is not a matter of formal education but vigilant attention to life, beliefs and purposes.*

HUBLEY, CAROLE FIERRO, family nurse practitioner; b. New Brunswick, N.J., Dec. 16, 1945; d. John Frank and Elizabeth Emma (Vayda) Fierro; m. Gordon Grant Hubley, May 17, 1976; 1 child, Georgina Grant. Nursing diploma, County Hosp. Sch. of Nursing, Hagerstown, Washington County, Md., 1966; BS, George Washington U., 1981; nurse practitioner-health care scis., George Washington Sch. Medicine and Health Care Scis., 1981. RN, Md.; lic. family nurse practitioner, Md. Staff nurse in pediatrics Frederick (Md.) Meml. Hosp., 1966-67; chief clin. nurse allergy clinic U. Md., College Park, 1967-79; nurse practitioner nursing supr. U. Md. Sch. of Medicine, Balt., 1982-83; nurse, case mgr. Gateway II project Anne Arundel County Dept. Health, Annapolis, 1984-88, primary care provider sexually transmitted diseases clinic, 1987-91; dir. health ctr. peer educator progam Hood Coll., Frederick, Md., 1992-94; primary care provider 2100 Med. Group, Balt., 1994—; advisor Baccus chpt. Hood Coll., Frederick, 1993-94, mem. ADAPT com., 1992-94, staff devel. com. 1993-94; preceptor U. Md. Sch. Nursing, 1995. Vol. ARC, College Park, 1972, 8th grade catechist St. Andrew by the Bay Ch., Annapolis, 1992-94; vol tchrs.' aide Cape St. Claire Elem. Sch., Annapolis, 1987; substitute tchr. sci. and social studies Broadneck H.S., Annapolis, 1998—. Recipient Svc. award for disaster relief ARC College Park, 1972. Mem. ANA, Md. Nurses Assn. (legis. com. 1985), Nurse Practitioners Assn. Md., Am. Coll. Nurse Practitioners, Md. Coll. Health Nurses Assn. (pres. 1978-79), Am. Coll. Health Assn., Assn Reproductive Health Profls. Roman Catholic. Home: 2014 Chesapeake Rd Annapolis MD 21401-5715 Office: Ste 225 10457 Mill Run Cir Owings Mills MD 21117

HUBLEY, REGINALD ALLEN, publisher; b. New Rochelle, N.Y., Aug. 21, 1928; s. Reginald McDonald and Eleanor Francis (Stock) H.; m. Karleen J. Smith, Apr. 7, 1979; children: Brandon, Caroline, Matthew. B.S. in Commerce and Fin., Bucknell U., 1952. Salesman McGraw Hill Pub. Co., N.Y.C., N.J., 1952-54; dist. mgr. Elec. Constrn. and Maintenance, and Elec. Wholesaling publs., Cleve., 1954-59; sales mgr. Elec. Constrn. and Maintenance, and Elec. Wholesaling publs., N.Y.C., 1959-63; pub. Elec. Constrn. and Maintenance, and Elec. Wholesaling publs., 1963-69, Nucleonics Week, Nucleonics & Sci. Research, N.Y.C., 1966-69, Aviation Week and Space Tech., N.Y.C., 1969—, Am. Machinist, N.Y.C., 1976—; v.p. European ops. McGraw-Hill Pub. Co., London, 1979-87, v.p. internat., 1987-88, ret., 1988; cons. British Aerospace, The Economist London, Nikkei Bus. Pub. Tokyo, 1988-90. Served with USN, 1946-48, PTO. Fellow Inst. of Dirs., London; mem. Internat. Fedn. Periodical Pubs. (exec. com.), Aviation Hall of Fame (bd. nominations 1971—). Republican.

HUBNER, ROBERT WILMORE, retired business machines company executive, consultant; b. Seattle, Mar. 21, 1918; s. Robert G. and Thurza (Wilmore) H.; m. Katherine L. Huick, Apr. 4, 1942 (dec. June 1996); children: Melissa, Robert Wilmore; m. Patricia Craig, Jan. 24, 1997. Grad., U. Wash., 1941. With IBM, 1941-43, 43-78, dir. recruitment, 1956, exec. asst. to exec. v.p., 1957, sales mgr. data processing div., 1957-59, exec. asst. to chmn. bd., 1959-61, dir. mktg., 1961-65, v.p. mktg., 1965-68, v.p., group exec., 1968-71, sr. v.p., mem. mgmt. com., 1972-78, ret., 1978. Mem. emeritus adv. bd. Grad. Sch. Bus., U. Wash.; trustee emeritus South Street Seaport, N.Y.C., Nat. Trust for Historic Preservation; trustee Maritime Ctr. at Norwalk, Conn.; past trustee Edgartown (Mass.) Reading Rm. Mem. N.Y. Yacht Club (N.Y.C., past trustee), Wee Burn Club, Edgartown Yacht Club (Mass., past commodore), Edgartown Golf Club, Riomar Country Club (Vero Beach, Fla.), Cruising Club Am. (past trustee), Pilgrims Club. Home: 911 Greenway Ln Vero Beach FL 32963-2109

HUCHEL, FREDERICK M., historian, writer, consultant, speaker, educator; b. Brigham City, Utah, Aug. 28, 1947; s. John L. and Mary L. (Andersen) H. BS, Brigham Young U., 1975. Dir. Railroad Village Mus., Corinne, Utah, 1965; asst. ch. history dept. Brigham Young U., Provo, Utah, 1970-75; translation exegesis specialist LDS Ch., Salt Lake City, 1975-76; dir. Brigham City Mus. Gallery, 1977-82; pres. Sequitur Computer Systems, Brigham City, 1983-91; asst. dir. for bus. rels. Utah State U. Bus. Coll., Logan, 1991-94; staff dir. Utah Biomed. Industry Coun., Salt Lake City, 1994-95; pres. FMH Cons. Svcs., Brigham City, 1995—; chmn. Brigham City Art Week, 1977-82, Beersheba Exhibit Com., 1979; site chmn. Utah Statehood Day, 1982; bd. dirs. Internat. Archaeol. Rsch. Inst., 1986; dir. Utah Internat. Med. Device Congress Steering Com., 1994-95; rsch. historian multi-vol. series The Work and the Glory, 1989—; faculty Brigham U., 1996—, Logan L.D.S. Inst. of Religion, 1999. Author: Utah State Centennial History of Box Elder County, 1999; editor Utah Internat. Med. Device Congress Proc., 1992-94; contbr. articles and revs. to hist. and profl. jours. and newspapers. Advisor Gov.'s Golden Spike Centennial Com., 1965-66; mem. Brigham City Comty. Theatre Bd., 1970; bd. dirs. Golden Spike Assn., 1964-96, v.p., 1969-96, mem. Golden Spike Re-enactment cast, 1969-96. Office: 13 N 2d E Brigham City UT 84302

HUCHRA, JOHN PETER, astronomer, educator; b. Jersey City, N.J., Dec. 23, 1948; s. Mieczyslaw Piotr and Helen Ann Huchra; m. Rebecca M. Henderson; 1 child, Harry Matthew. BS, MIT, 1970; PhD, Calif. Inst. Tech., 1976. Ctr. fellow Ctr. for Astrophysics, Cambridge, Mass., 1976-78; astronomer Smithsonian Astrophys. Obs., Cambridge, Mass., 1978-89, sr. astronomer, 1989—; lectr. Dept. Astronomy, Harvard U., Cambridge, Mass., 1979-84, prof., 1984—; assoc. dir. Ctr. for Astrophysics, Cambridge, Mass., 1987-98; dir. F.L. Whipple Observatory, 1994-98; coun. mem. Space Telescope Sci. Inst., Balt., 1987-95; chmn. working group on galaxy radial velocities Internat. Astron. Union, Paris, 1988—; chmn. large astron. data base working group NASA/IPAC, Washington, 1988-92; mem. astronomy and astrophysics survey Optical Panel, NAS, NRC, 1989-90; adv. bd. and vis. com. Arecibo Obs., Ithaca, N.Y., 1989-92; users com. Cerro Tololo Inter-Am. Obs., La Serena, Chile, 1989-91; vis. com. ESO, 1993-97; mem. NRC Com. on Astronomy and Astrophysics, 1994, co-chmn. 1997—; mem. AURA, bd. dirs. 1995—. Contbr. more than 230 articles to profl. jours. Rsch. grantee, NASA, 1979—, Smithsonian Inst., 1980, NSF, 1984-89. Fellow AAAS (Newcomb Cleve. award 1990), Am. Phys. Soc. (pub. policy com. 1988-95); mem. NAS, Am. Astron. Soc. (pub. bd. chmn., 1986-88, councilor 1998-2001, sci. editor Astrophys. Jour. 1998-2000), Royal Astron. Soc., Astron. Soc. of the Pacific, Am. Phys. Soc. Astrophysics Disn. (exec. com. 1996-97), Nat. Environ. Leadership Coun., Wilderness Soc., Nat. Audubon Soc., Mass. Audubon Soc., Union of Concerned Scientists, Nature Conservancy, Trustees of Reservations, Appalachian Trail Conf., Am. Contract Bridge League, Greenpeace, Green Mtn. Club, Appalachian Mtn. Club, Sierra Club, Sigma Xi, Gamma Nu. Achievements include discovery of Comet Huchra, of nearest gravitational lens; revision of cosmic distance scale; completion of first Center for Astrophysics Redshift Survey; measurement of infall of our Milky Way Galaxy into the Virgo Cluster; discovery of Great Wall of galaxies. Office: Harvard-Smithsonian Ctr Astrophysics 60 Garden St Cambridge MA 02138-1516

HUCHTEMAN, RALPH DOUGLAS, lawyer; b. Garland, Tex., Oct. 8, 1946; s. Ray Edwin and Hazel Laverne (Clark) H.; m. Sherry Lynn Horner, Mar. 12, 1994; children: Lara Victoria, Brett Norman, Bryan Randolff. AA, Okla. Mil. Acad., 1966; BA in Polit. Sci., Okla. State U., 1969; JD, Okla. U., 1972. Bar: Okla. 1972, U.S. Dist. Ct. (we. dist.) Okla. 1972. Ptnr. Doak & Huchteman, Oklahoma City, 1972-73, Wolf & Wolf P.C. (formerly Wolf, Wold, Huchteman & Graven), Norman, Okla., 1982-88; prin. Huchteman Law Offices, Norman, 1989-98; staff atty. Legal Svcs. of Eastern Okla., Inc., Bartlesville, 1998-99, mng. atty., 1999—; assoc. mcpl. judge, Noble, Okla., 1990-98, Blanchard, Okla., 1992-98; vis. asst. prof. Coll. Bus., Okla. U., 1972-73; temporary justice Okla. Ct. Appeals, Oklahoma City, 1982-83. State exec. sec. Student Lobby for Higher Edn., Stillwater, Okla., 1968-69. 1st lt. U.S. Army, 1973. T.A. Shadid scholar Okla. U., 1969; recipient A.C. Hunt Practice award Okla. U., 1972. Mem. ATLA, Okla. Bar Assn., Okla. Trial Lawyers Assn. Democrat. Office: Legal Svcs Eastern Okla 217 S Choctaw Bartlesville OK 74003

HUCHTHAUSEN, DAVID RICHARD, sculptor, real estate developer; b. Wisconsin Rapids, Wis., Mar. 25, 1951; s. Richard Leeland and Irma Ruth (Fehrmann) H. BA, U. Wis., Wausau, 1972; BS, U. Wis., 1974; MFA, Ill. State U., 1977. Instr. Ill. State U., Bloomington, 1975-77, Royal Coll. Art, London, 1977; artist-in-residence J. and L. Lobmetr, Vienna, Austria, 1977-78; design dir. Milropa Studios, N.Y.C., 1979-80; prof. art Tenn. Tech. U., Cookeville, 1980-89; mng. ptnr. W/H Properties, Seattle, 1989—; pres. Somerset Properties Inc., Seattle, 1994—; curatorial cons. Woodson Art Mus., Wausau, Wis., 1976-90. One man shows include Habatat Galleries, Detroit, 1978-98, Miami, Fla., 1984-98, Chgo., 1988, Boca Raton, Fla., 1990, 92, Pontiac Mich., 1995, Heller Gallery, N.Y.C., 1979, 82, 83, 85, 88, St. Louis Art Mus., 1984, Traver Gallery, Seattle, 1984, 87, William Traver Gallery, Seattle, 1990, 92, 95, Leo Kaplan Modern, 1992, 94, 96, Galerie L, Hamburg, Germany, 1994, 96; exhibited in group shows at Bloomingdales, N.Y.C., 1975, Mus. fur Kuntshandwerk, Frankfurt, West Germany, 1976, Huntington (W.Va.) Galleries, 1976, U. Wis., Madison, 1976, Habatat Galleries, Detroit, 1976-79, 80, 83, 86, 87, 88, 90, 91, U. Kans., Lawrence, 1977, Ill. State Mus., Springfield, 1977, Little Rock Art Ctr., 1978, J. & L. Lobmer Galleries, Vienna, Austria, 1980, Det. Inst. Art, 1981, 82, 87, Hastings (Nebr.) Coll., 1982, Huntsville (Ala.) Mus. Art, 1982, Am. Craft Mus., 1982, Heller Gallery, N.Y.C., 1984-88, Huntington Mus., 1984, 86, Boise (Idaho) Mus. Art, 1984, Nippon Gakki, Tokyo, 1984, Toledo Mus. Art, 1988, 92, Darmstadt Mus. Art, West Germany, 1988, Corning (N.Y.) Mus., 1988, 90, Bellevue (Wash.) Art Mus., 1991, Hokkaido Mus. Art, Sapporo, Japan, 1991-92, Tamayo Mus., Mexico City, 1992, Marco Mus., Montreay, Mex., 1992; represented in permanent collections Met. Mus. Art N.Y.C., Smithsonian Inst., Washington, L.A. County Mus., High Mus., Atlanta, Corning Mus., Am. Craft Mus., N.Y.C., Hokkaido Mus. Art, Sapporo, Japan, Art Mus., Dusseldorf, Germany, Det. Inst. Art, Indpls. Mus. Art, Toledo Mus. Art, Mus. fur Kunst und Gerwerbe, Hamburg, Germany, Rockwell Mus., Corning, Huntington Mus. Art, Ill. State Mus., Normal, St. Louis Mus. Art, Mus. Decorative Arts, Prague, Czechoslovakia, JB Speed Mus., Louisville, Birmingham (Ala.) Mus. Art. Author: Americans in Glass, 1981, 84. Chair exec. com. Greater Duwamish Com., Seattle, 1995—; mem. South Downtown Bus. Group, Seattle, 1995—, Trust for Hist. Preservation. Rsch. grant Woodson Found., 1973-74; Stein fellowship Ill. State U., 1976; Fulbright scholar U. Applied Arts, 1977-78. Mem. Am. Craft Coun., Glass Art Soc., Classic Yach Assn., Sodo Bus. Assn. (Seattle). Avocations: historic preservation, antique collecting, yachting. Office: Somerset Properties Inc 3911 Airport Way S Seattle WA 98108-5237

HUCHTON, PAUL JOSEPH, JR., pediatrician; b. El Paso, Tex., Mar. 15, 1934; s. Paul Joseph Sr. and Eugenia Cregor (Kimbrough) H.; m. Sheila Ann Borsian, June 1, 1963; children: Hadley Ann Bernhard, David Morgan, Amy H. Anderson, Karen. BA, U. Tex., 1954; MD, Vanderbilt U., 1958. Diplomate Am. Bd. Pediat. Intern Vanderbilt U. Hosp., Nashville, 1958-59; resident U. Chgo., 1959-60; from resident to chief resident U. Colo., Denver, 1960-61; pvt. practice specializing in pediat., El Paso, 1963—; mem. staff Providence and Sierra Med. Ctr., El Paso; med. dir. Prudential Health, El Paso. Mem Tex. Med. Assn. (del., counsellor 1970-93), El Paso County Med. Soc. (pres. 1985), Rotary Club El Paso (pres. 1980, Paul Harris award 1983). Republican. Episcopalian. Avocations: long distance cycling, computers. Office: 1515 N Oregon St El Paso TX 79902-4042

HUCK, JOHN LLOYD, pharmaceutical company executive; b. Bklyn., July 17, 1922; s. John Lloyd and Adrienne (Warner) H.; m. Dorothy Bertha Foehr, Nov. 20, 1943; children: Lloyd E., Jeanne Huck Leslie-Hughes, Virginia Huck Stalcup. B.S. in Chemistry, Pa. State U., 1946. Research chemist Hoffmann-LaRoche, Nutley, N.J., 1946, sales rep., 1948, dir. sales tng., 1951, asst. gen. sales mgr., 1955, dir. product devel., 1958; dir. mktg. Merck Sharp & Dohme Div., West Point, Pa., 1958; v.p. mktg. planning MSD div., 1966, v.p. sales and mktg., 1968, exec. v.p., 1969, exec. v.p., gen. mgr., 1972, pres., 1973; sr. v.p. Merck & Co., Rahway, N.J., 1975, exec. v.p., 1977, dir., 1977-86, pres., chief operating officer, 1978-85; chmn. bd. Merck & Co., 1985-86; chmn. bd., chief exec. officer Nova Pharm. Corp., Morristown, N.J., 1986-88; chmn. bd. Nova Pharm. Corp., 1988-91. Patentee in field. Trustee Pa. State U., 1977-92, v.p., 1985-88, pres. bd., 1988-91; trustee Morristown Meml. Health Found., Inc., N.J., 1979-96, chmn. bd., 1986-88; trustee Geraldine R. Dodge Found. 1st lt. USAAF, 1942-46. Alumni fellow Coll. Medicine Pa. State U., 1980, Coll. of Sci., 1983. Mem. Morris County Golf Club, Piper's Landing Golf Club. Republican. Presbyterian. Home: 1 Carriage Hill Dr Morristown NJ 07960-6994

HUCK, LEWIS FRANCIS, lawyer, real estate consultant and developer; b. Bklyn., Mar. 19, 1912; s. Frank and Jessie (Green) H.; LLB, St. John's U., 1938, LLM, 1939; m. Rosemay Ahearn, Jan. 5, 1940 (dec. 1949); children: Janet Ahearn, L. Francis, William G. (dec.); m. Frances M. Love, Jan. 7, 1950 (dec. 1985); children: Robert L., James J.; m. Virginia I. Reid, Apr. 18, 1987. Bar: N.Y. 1939, Tex. 1975, Mass. 1947, U.S. Dist. Ct. (so. dist.) Tex. 1992, U.S. Ct. Appeals (1st and 3d cirs.) 1996, U.S. Supreme Ct., 1996. Practice law, 1939—; with trust dept. Guaranty Trust Co. N.Y., 1929-41; atty. Gen. Electric Co., Schenectady, 1945-47, chem. counsel, 1947-48, atomic energy counsel, 1948-51, gen. mgr., Richland, Wash., 1951-55; asst. to exec. v.p. Gen. Dynamics Corp., 1955-57; lawyer, real estate cons. and developer, 1957-68; v.p., dir., cons. real estate devel. Eastern Airlines, Inc., 1968-88; pres. Huck Enterprises Co. Inc., 1980—; bd. dirs. Sea-Air Shuttle Corp. Served maj. AUS, 1941-45. Democrat Home: 15084 Kimberley Ln Houston TX 77079-5125

HUCKABEE, HARLOW MAXWELL, lawyer, writer; b. Wichita Falls, Tex., Jan. 22, 1918; s. Edwin Cleveland and Gladys Idella (Bonney) H.; m. Gloria Charlotte Comstock, Jan. 10, 1942; children: Bonney M., David C., Stephen M. BA, Harvard U., 1948; JD, Georgetown U., 1951. Bar: U.S. Dist. Ct. D.C. 1952, U.S. Ct. Appeals (D.C. cir.) 1952. Cashier br. office Columbian Nat. Life Ins. Co., Boston, 1935-40; lawyer Fed. Housing Adminstrn., Washington, 1955-56; trial lawyer, criminal sect., tax divsn. U.S. Justice Dept., Washington, 1956-63; lawyer IRS, Washington, 1963-67; trial lawyer organized crime and racketeering sect. U.S. Justice Dept., Washington, 1967-68, trial lawyer criminal sect., tax divsn., 1968-80. Author: Lawyers, Psychiatrists and Criminal Law, 1980; contbr. articles to profl. jours. and legal publs. including Diminished Capacity Dilemma in the Federal System, 1991. Maj. U.S. Army, 1940-45, 48-55, ETO, Korea; lt. col. USAR, 1961. Methodist. Home: 5100 Fillmore Ave Apt 913 Alexandria VA 22311-5048

HUCKABEE, MICHAEL DALE, governor; b. Hope, Ark., Aug. 24, 1955; m. Janet McCain, May 25, 1974; children: John Mark, David, Sarah. BA in Religion magna cum laude, Ouachita Bapt. U., Arkadelphia, Ark., 1976; postgrad., Southwestern Bapt. Theol. Sem., Ft. Worth, 1976-77. Ordained to ministry So. Bapt. Conv., 1974. Pastor Walnut Street Bapt. Ch., Arkadelphia, 1974-75, Immanuel Bapt. Ch., Pine Bluff, Ark., 1980-85; evangelist various Christian ministries; pastor Beech Street 1st Bapt. Ch., Texarkana, Ark., 1986—; Lt. Gov. State of Ark., 1993-96, governor, 1996—; founder, past pres. Am. Christian TV Sys., Pine Bluff; pres. Ark. Bapt. Conv., 1989—; mem. adv. bd. So. Bapts. for Life; numerous others. Weekly newspaper columnist Positive Alternatives. Former bd. govs. Ark. Boys State; former county coord. Unborn Child Amendment Com., Pine Bluff; former pres., bd. dirs. Jefferson County unit Am. Cancer Soc., pres., 1984-85; former participant, bd. dirs. Leadership Pine Bluff; bd. dirs. B.O.N.D., bus. orgn. for new downtown, Texarkana, Friendship Ctr., Texarkana; mem. allocations com., vol. United Way Texarkana; mem. citizen's adv. com. Texarkana Sch. Bd.; spkr. to numerous chs., schs. and bus. orgns.; mem. procedures rev. com. St. Michael Hosp., 1988-90; chmn. Texarkana Easter Seals Telethon, 1993-94; pres. Ark. Bapt. State Conv., 1989-91. Mem. Nat. Religious Broadcasters, Texarkana Ministerial Alliance (TV chmn.), Texarkana C. of C. Home: 1800 Center St Little Rock AR 72206-1418 Office: Office of the Gov State Capitol Rm 250 Little Rock AR 72201-1088*

HUCKABY, GARY CARLTON, lawyer; b. Lanett, Ala., July 12, 1938; s. Carl Walker and Mary Evelyn (Meriwether) H.; m. Jeanne Davey Huckaby, Feb. 23, 1963; children: Gary Jr., John Stephen, Michael Stewart. BA, U. Ala., 1960, JD, 1962. Bar: U.S. Supreme Ct. 1963, U.S. Ct. of Mil. Appeals 1963, U.S. Ct. Appeals (5th and 11th cirs.) 1963, U.S. Dist. Ct. (no., middle and so. dists) Ala. 1963. Law clk. to chief justice Ala. Supreme Ct., Montgomery, 1962-63; asst. U.S. Sen. Lister Hill, Washington, 1963; ptnr. Smith, Huckaby & Graves, Huntsville, Ala., 1966-85, Bradley, Arant, Rose & White, Huntsville, 1985—; dir. Am. Coll. of Trial Lawyers Ala. Ctr. for Law & Civic Edn., 1992—. Dir. coun. Internat. Visitors of Huntsville-Madison County, 1983-89, Tenn. Valley Boy Scouts Am., 1975-79, Mental Health Assn. Madison County, 1970-78, Ala. Law Sch. Found., 1981—; pres. Huntsville-Madison County Mental Health Bd., 1977-80, Madison County Heart Assn., 1968; active Citizens Com. on Higher Edn. of Ala. Legis., 1976, judicial sect. of Huntsville-Madison County Local Govt. Study Com., 1969. Capt. USAF, 1963-66. Fellow Am. Bar Found.; mem. ABA (bd. govs. 1990-91, house of delegates, chmn. standing com. on lawyer referral and info. services 1982-85, chmn. spl. com. on delivery of legal services 1976-79, standing com. on lawyers pub. service responsibility 1987-90, consortium on legal services and the pub. 1976-79, task force on pub. edn. 1978, standing com. on lawyers in the armed forces 1971-73), Ala. State Bar (pres., bd. commrs. 1981-87, exec. com. 1982-83, 84-85, 87-88, chmn. governance com. 1986-87, action group on professionalism, disciplinary bd. 1981-87; recipient award of merit 1986), Huntsville-Madison County Bar Assn. (pres. 1977-78, chmn. grievance com. 1976, bench and bar relations 1981, convention host com. 1971, law day com. 1968), Am. Judicature Soc. (bd. dirs.), Rotary. Democrat. Episcopalian. Home: 701 Greene St SE Huntsville AL 35801-4232 Office: Bradley Arant Rose & White 200 Clinton Ave W Ste 900 Huntsville AL 35801-4900

HUCKABY, MARK ANSON, paramedic, educator, emergency medical services specialist; b. Columbia, Tenn., Aug. 25, 1965; s. Paul and Mildred Louise (Tomlin) H. Cert. paramed. tech., Vol. State Community Coll., Gallatin, Tenn., 1986. Lic. paramedic, Tenn; cert. EMT/paramedic, Tex, adv. EMS instr., Tex., ACLS/BCLS instr., advanced BTLS instr. Firefighter/paramedic Maury Co., Tenn., 1981; pub. safety operator/dispatcher Williamson County, Tenn., 1990; supr. paramedics The General Jackson, Opryland USA, Inc., Opryland Hotel, The Grand Ole Opry, Nashville, 1986; sr. emergency med. technician, paramedic Nashville Fire Dept., 1987; EMS del. to U.S.S.R./Europe Citizen Ambassador program; paramed. tech. preceptor Vol. State C.C., Gallatin, Tenn., 1989; supr. health and emergency med. svcs. Fiesta Tex. Theme Park, San Antonio, 1991; EMS educator MEDIC Inc., San Antonio, 1994, Allied Health, San Antonio Coll.; tech. resource specialist Tex. Dept. Health, Bur. Emergency Mgmt., 1996, assoc. dir. EMS, 1997, EMS specialist, 1998; corp. mgr. health svcs. Six Flags Theme Pk. Staff writer EMS Messenger, mem. conf. staff and faculty, mem. leadership acad. faculty; text reviewer Appleton and Lange Pub., Jones and Bartlett Pub.; mem. editl. rev. bd., advanced CISD team mem. Tex. EMS mag. Mem. med. com. Tex. Spl. Olympics. Mem. ARC, ASTM (f-30 EMS com.), Am. Heart Assn., Nat. Assn. EMTs, Nat. Paramedic Soc., Nat. Assn. EMS Educators, Nat. Assn. EMS Quality Profls., Nat. Assn. EMS Physicians, Tenn. Paramedic Soc., Tex. Assn. EMTs, United Paramedics (Nashville chpt.), Internat. Assn. Fire Fighters, Internat. Assn. Fire Chiefs (EMS sect., Indsl. sect.).

HUCKEBY, KAREN MARIE, graphic arts executive; b. San Diego, June 4, 1957; d. Floyd Riley and Georgette Laura (Wegimont) H. Student Coll. of Alameda, 1976; student 3-M dealer tng. program, St. Paul, 1975. Staff Huck's Press Service, Inc., Emeryville, Calif., 1968—, v.p., 1975—. Mem. Rep. Nat. Task Force, 1984—; bd. dirs. CitiArts Benefactors, Concord, Calif., 1990-93, v.p., treas., 1991-93. Recipient service award ARC, 1977. Mem. East Bay Club of Printing House Craftsman (treas. 1977-78), Oakland Mus. Soc., Nat. Trust Historic Preservation, Smithsonian Inst., San Francisco Mus. Soc., Internat. Platform Assn., Am. Film Inst., Commonwealth Club. Home: 1054 Hera Ct Hercules CA 94547 Office: Staff Huck's Press Svc Inc 691 S 31st St Richmond CA 94804-4022

HUCKINS, HAROLD AARON, chemical engineer; b. Cambridge, Mass., Nov. 28, 1924; s. Harold Aaron and Julia E. (Nugent) H.; m. Elizabeth L. Kearns, Nov. 15, 1952; children: Richard W., Robert M., Christopher N., Patricia A., Leslie K. BSChemE, Northeastern U., 1945; ASME, Lowell Inst., 1946; postgrad., Boston U., 1947-49, U. Pitts., 1950-52. Chem. process engr., asst. project mgr. Monsanto Chem. Co., Boston-Everett, Mass., 1945-49; sr. process engr., group leader Koppers Co. Chem. Div., Pitts., 1949-53; mgr. pilot plants, project mgr. Sci. Design Co., Inc., N.Y.C., 1953-66; v.p. tech. ops. Oxirane Chem. Co., Princeton, N.J., 1966-73; v.p. tech. assessment Halcon SD Group, N.Y.C., 1973-85; pres. Princeton Advanced Tech., Inc., 1985—; dir. Assn. Cons. Chemists and Chem. Engrs. div., N.Y.C., 1990-93, program chair, 1992-93; dir. Materials Tech. Inst., St. Louis, 1976-85. Coauthor: The Chemical Plant, 1966; contbr. articles to profl. jours. Fellow AIChE (chair ctrl. Jersey sect. 1976-77, dir mgmt. divsn. 1981-82, dir. materials engring. and sci. divsn. 1992-93, chmn. chem. tech. materials com. 1983-84, chmn. John Fritz medal commn. 1989, chmn. entrepreneurial forum 1994—, Chem. Engring. Practice award 1994); mem. Am. Soc. Materials, Am. Chem. Soc., Am. Ceramic Soc. Nat. Assn. Corrosion Engrs. (conf. chmn. 1984), Comml. Devel. Assn., Mensa Internat., Country Club of Hilton Head Island, Port Royal Racquet Club, Hilton Head Ski Club (bd. dirs.). Achievements include 9 U.S. patents for chemical process technology. Fax: (843) 689-9212. Office: Princeton Advanced Tech Inc 4 Bertram Pl Hilton Head Island SC 29928-3936

HUCKMAN, MICHAEL ANDREW, reporter; b. Jan. 16, 1962. BA, U. So. Calif., 1983. Reporter, anchor KRTV-KTVQ, Great Falls, Billings, Mont., 1983-85; reporter KBCI-TV, Boise, Idaho, 1985-88, KGUN-TV, Tucson, 1988-91, WXYZ-TV, Southfield, Mich., 1991—. E-mail: mikeh4usc@aol.com.

HUCKMAN, MICHAEL SAUL, neuroradiologist, educator; b. Newark, Aug. 20, 1936; s. Louis Fillmore and Mollie (Lehman) H.; m. Beverly Joy Blachman, Aug. 2, 1964; children: Andrew Garfield, Robert Steven. A.B., Princeton U., 1958; M.D., St. Louis U., 1962. Rotating intern, then resident in radiology Phila. Gen. Hosp., 1962-63, 65-68; fellow in neuroradiology Edward Mallinckrodt Inst. Radiology, Washington U., St. Louis; also univ. instr. radiology Edward Mallinckrodt Inst. Radiology, Washington U., 1968-70; mem. faculty Rush Med. Coll., Chgo., 1970—; prof. radiology Rush Med. Coll., 1978—; dir. sect. neuroradiology Rush-Presbyn.-St. Luke's Med. Center, 1970—; mem. faculty Cook County Grad. Sch. Medicine, 1972-91; cons. Nat. Ctr. for Health Care Tech., 1980-81; sec.-gen. XVI Symposium Neuroradiologicum, 1994-98. Mem. editorial bd. Jour. Computer Assisted Tomography, 1976-94, Radiographics, 1983-87, Applied Radiology, 1987-89; cons. editor Am. Jour. Roentgenology, 1990-91; contbr. articles to med. jours. Served with USNR, 1963-65. Spl. fellow Nat. Inst. Neurol. Diseases and Blindness, 1968-70. Fellow Am. Coll. Radiology; mem. AMA, Am. Soc. Neuroradiology (sec. 1980-83, pres. elect 1986-87, pres. 1987-88, editor-in-chief Am. Jour. Neuroradiology 1989-97, editor emeritus 1998—, archivist 1998—, Gold medal 1999), Radiol. Soc. N.Am., Am. Soc. Head and Neck Radiology, Am. Roentgen Ray Soc., Assn. Univ. Radiologists, Soc. Magnetic Resonance Imaging, World Fedn. Neuroradiol. Socs. (historian 1993-97, v.p. 1997—, pres.-elect 1998), Ill. Med. Soc., Ill. Radiol. Soc., Chgo. Med. Soc., Blockley Radiol. Soc., Soc. for Scholarly Publ., Coun. Biology Editors, Soc. Fifth Line, Sigma Xi, Phi Delta Epsilon. Jewish. Clubs: Princeton Alumni of Chgo. (trustee 1982-84), Caxton. Home: 175 E Delaware Pl Apt 7401 Chicago IL 60611-1731 Office: 1753 W Congress Pky Chicago IL 60612-3809

HUCKS, CYNTHIA STOKES, university finance officer, accountant; b. Oklahoma City, Apr. 6, 1961; d. Richard Glenn and Myrtle Beatrice (Crisp) Stokes; m. Donald Lester Hucks, June 14, 1980; children: Catherine Diane, Sara Caitlin. BS in Accountancy, U. N.C., Wilmington, 1994. CPA, N.C. Budget systems mgr. U. N.C., Wilmington, 1995-97, dir. resource mgmt., 1997—. Mem. Internat. Mgmt. Accts., Phi Kappa Phi, Beta Gamma Sigma. Avocations: reading, gardening. Office: U NC Wilmington Provost's Office 601 S College Rd Wilmington NC 28403-3297

HUCKSHOLD, WAYNE WILLIAM, elementary education educator; b. St. Louis, Mar. 5, 1952; s. Albert Clarence and Jane Martha (Stewart) H.; m. Paula Louise Ransin, June 14, 1977 (div. Apr. 1982); 1 child, Kristen Louise. BS in Edn., U. Mo., 1976, MEd, 1977. Cert. elem. edn. K-8, phys. edn. K-9, health edn. K-12, sci. 7-9, Mo.; Nat. Coun. Accreditation of Tchr. Edn.; cert. personal trainer Am. Coun. Exercise. Tchr. grade 3 Camdenton (Mo.) R-III, 1977-81, coach football, track and cross country, 1978-81; fitness instr., athletic trainer Columbia (Mo.) Sports Medicine, 1981-84; student athletic trainer U. Mo., Columbia, 1983-84, grad. tchg. asst., 1984-85; elem. tchr. Francis Howell Sch. Dist., St. Charles, Mo., 1985-91, elem. tchr. phys. edn., 1991—, mem. supt.'s comm. coun., 1992-93; master's swim coach West County YMCA, Chesterfield, Mo., 1991—, personal trainer, 1992—; level 2 swim coach Am. Swimming Coaches Assn., 1997—; head women's varsity swim coach Francis Howell H.S., 1998-99; asst. head coach U.S.S. Swim Team, St. Peter's Rec-Plex; new tchr. mentor Francis Howell S.D., 1996—. Named YMCA Endurance Athlete of Yr., YMCA, St. Louis, 1990; grantee Union Electric Co., St. Louis, 1989; fellow Tchrs. Acad. Class 1994, Network for Ednl. Devel., Danforth Found., 1993-94. Mem. NEA, AAHPERD, Mo. Edn. Assn., Francis Howell Edn. Assn., Mo. Alliance for Health, Phys. Edn., Recreation and Dance, U.S. Phys. Edn. Assn., Nat. Assn. for Sport and Phys. Edn., Assn. for Advancement Health Edn. Avocations: running, swimming, biking, triathlons, spending time with family and friends. Home: 1549 Milbridge Dr Chesterfield MO 63017-4611 Office: Francis Howell School Dist 4545 Central School Rd Saint Charles MO 63304-8618

HUCKSTEAD, CHARLOTTE VAN HORN, retired home economist, artist; b. Garwin, Iowa, Jan. 13, 1920; d. George Loren and Esther Olive (Carver) Van Horn; m. Lowell Raine Huckstead (dec.); children: Karen C., Roger H., Martha E., Paul R., Sarah S. BS, U. Wisc., 1942; BFA, Boise (Idaho) State U., 1989. Merchandising Montgomery Ward, Chgo. and Santa Monica, Calif., 1941-42; "Rosie the Riveter" WWII, Chgo. and Beloit, Wis., 1942-46; woman's editor Dairyland News, Milw., 1950-54; interior designer, cons., tchr. South Bend, Marshfield, Wis., Merced, Calif., 1952-69; extenion home economist U. Minn., Rochester, 1973-78; dir. food svcs. Milton (Wisc.) Sch. Dist., 1978-85; artist, 1952—. Painting and sculpture. Bd. dirs. Rock County Hist. Soc., Janesville, Wis., 1979-84, Milton Hist. Soc., 1979-85; vol. Idaho Genealogy Libr., 1994-96; treas. Wis. Food Svc. Assn., 1980-85; leader/mem. Girl Scouts Am., 1934-78. Mem. AAUW, Nature Conservancy, Idaho Hist. Soc. (vol. 1985-99), Idaho Centennial Art Group (sec. 1991, show chmn. 1992, historian 1993-95), Idaho Water Color Soc., Morrison Ctr. Aux. (vol. 1986-99, bd. dirs. 1992-93, 97-99, Auxilian of Yr. 1995), Boise State Alumni Assn., Audubon Soc., Ch. Women United (editor 1985-86), Sierra Club, Boise Art Mus., Wis. Alumni Assn., Friends of Hist. Mus. Boise. Protestant. Avocations: reading, history, archaeology, theatre, travel. Home: 10507 Irving Ct Boise ID 83704-8054

HUDAK, JOSEPH DAVID, state police investigator, educator, forensic engineer; b. Pottstown, Pa., Feb. 11, 1956; s. Joseph Andrew and Eleanore Barbara (Pierzchala) H.; children: Meredith Rebecca, Jonathan Michael, Wesley Robert; m. Joann Marie Kempf. BS in Civil Engring. with honors, Drexel U., 1979. Accredited accident reconstructionist Accreditation Commn. for Traffic Accident Reconstruction. Civil engr. IU Conversion Systems, Horsham, Pa., 1980-82, VFL Tech., Malvern, Pa., 1982-84; state trooper Pa. State Police, Harrisburg, 1984—; adj. faculty Tex. A&M U., 1995—; pres., forensic engring. cons. iE Forensic Cons., Inc., Newfoundland, Pa., 1997—; alternate rep. ACTAR bd. dirs., 1995—. Contbr. articles to profl. publs.; presenter in field of traffic homicide investigations. Mem. ASCE (assoc.), Soc. Automotive Engrs. (assoc.), Nat. Assn. Traffic Accident Reconstructionists and Investigators, Md. Assn. Traffic Accident Invesigators, Fraternal Order Police, Rotary, Tau Beta Pi, Chi Epsilon. Avocations: reading, sports, martial arts, stone masonry, weight training. Home: RR 1 Box 167C Newfoundland PA 18445 Office: Pa State Police HC 6 Box 6810 Hawley PA 18428-9013

HUDAK, PAUL ALEXANDER, retired engineer; b. Youngstown, Ohio, Oct. 8, 1930; s. Paul and Elizabeth (Hoffman) H.; m. Ingrid Gertrud Matzke, June 6, 1964; children: Frank, David, Greta. BS in Math., Youngstown U., 1958. Reliability/safety engr. N.Am. Aviation, L.A. and Downey, Calif., 1958-64, Douglas Aircraft, Long Beach, Calif., 1964-73, Chrysler Def., Sterling Heights, Mich., 1973-77, Boeing Airplane Co., Seattle and Everett, Wash., 1977-85, Mare Island Naval Shipyard, Vallejo, Calif., 1985-93; ret., 1993. Cpl. USMC, 1951-53. Mem. IEEE. Achievements include proposal for tech. ctr. to integrate edn. and work creation; proposal for devel. of world village of UN to meet social needs and promote world order. Home: 220 Bluebell Pl Vallejo CA 94589-1837

HUDAK, THOMAS F(RANCIS), finance company executive; b. Donora, Pa., Jan. 29, 1942; s. Thomas Joseph and Ann Marie (Petrus) H.; m. Dorothy Ann Palko, July 27, 1963; children: Diana Lynn, Debra Ann, Thomas David. B.S., St. Vincent Coll., 1963; M.B.A., Ohio State U., 1968. Bar: C.P.A., Ohio. Accountant Coopers & Lybrand, Columbus, Ohio, 1963-65; dept. mgr., data processing Western Electric Corp., Columbus, 1965-66; fin. controls mgr. Indsl. Nucleonics Co., Columbus, 1966-69; sr. v.p. fin., chief fin. officer G.C. Murphy Co., McKeesport, Pa., 1969-85, chmn. bd., 1981-85; pres. Hudak & Assocs.; treas. Mack Realty Co., McKeesport, Murphy Devel. Corp., Court House Village Co., Spotsylvania Realty Co.; bd. dirs., pres. Terry Farris Stores, Inc.; mem. adv. bd. Liberty Mut. Ins. Co.; corp. comptr. PPG Industries, Inc., Pitts., 1986-89; chmn. bd. dirs., pres. Continental Plastics, Inc., 1989-95; bd. dirs. RXI Corp. Bd. dirs., pres. G.C. Murphy Co. Found. Mem. AICPA, U.S. C. of C., Fin. Execs. Inst. (dir. Pitts. chpt. 1982-85), Risk and Ins. Mgmt. Soc., Nat. Retail Mchts. Assn. (dir. fin. div. 1982-85), Nat. Assn. Corp. Dirs., Machinery and Allied Products Inst. (fin. coun.), Assn. Spice Traders, Assn. Dressings and Sauces, Peanut Butter and Nut Processors Assn.

HUDDLE, FRANKLIN PIERCE, JR., diplomat; b. Providence, May 9, 1943; s. Franklin Pierce and Clare (Scott) H.; m. Chanya Sawangrot, May 13, 1988; 1 child, Pavarage. BA, Brown U., 1965; postgrad., Columbia U.,

1965-66; MA, Harvard U., 1970, PhD, 1978. Coord. Arabic affairs Peace Corps, Bisbee, 1968-69; instr. Harvard U., Cambridge, Mass., 1970-74; with Dept. of State, Washington and abroad, 1974—; charge d'affaires Dept. of State, Rangoon, Burma, 1990-94; dir. Pacific Island Affairs, 1994-96; consul gen. Bombay, India, 1996-99, Toronto, 1999—. Author: Libyan Arabic, 1966; author, editor: Let's Go Europe, 1971; co-author: Nationalities of the USSR, 1975; photography shows in Thailand, Nepal and Washington, 1980, 81, 84; patentee rocket coatings, 1960. Recipient Rivkin award; Ford Found. grantee; Wayland scholar. Mem. Phi Beta Kappa. Democrat. Unitarian. Avocations: piano, chess, ice skating. Office: Dept of State 2201 C St NW Washington DC 20521

HUDDLESON, EDWIN EMMETT, III, lawyer; b. Washington, Oct. 20, 1945; s. Edwin Emmett and Mary (Taeusch) H.; m. Andra Nan Oakes, July 8, 1978; children: Michael, Jonathan. BS, Stanford U., 1967; JD, U. Chgo., 1970. Bar: Calif. 1970, D.C. 1977. Law clk. to Judge Charles M. Merrill U.S. Ct. Appeals 9th cir., 1970-71; civil div. U.S. Dept. Justice, Washington, 1971-77. Author: Waiver of Miranda Rights, 1969, Confidentiality for Editorial Process, 1978, UCC Transaction Guide Leasing, 1989—, Appellate Advocacy, 1991, New Developments Leasing, 1993; Environmental Law Protections for Lenders, 1994; mem. U. Chgo. Law Rev., 1968-70, comment editor, 1969-70; contbr. articles on comml. law, First Amendment, appellate advocacy to law jours. Fellow Am. Bar Found.; mem. ABA, FBA, Charles Fahy Am. Inns. of Ct. (master). Home: 1962 Upshur St NW Washington DC 20011-5354 Office: Driscoll & Draude 1230 31st St NW Washington DC 20007-3400

HUDDLESTON, CHARLES B., surgeon, educator; b. Sedalia, Mo., Nov. 18, 1952; s. Charles M. and Dorothy G. Huddleston; m. Elizabeth Benson, May 20, 1978; children: Laura, Rachel, Alexander. BA, U. Mo., 1974; MD, Vanderbilt U., 1978. Diplomate Am. Bd. Surgery, Am. Bd. Thoracic Surgery. Intern in internal medicine Vanderbilt Med. Ctr., Syracuse, 1978-79, resident in gen. surgery, 1979-86, resident in CT surgery, 1986-88; fellowship in pediat. CT surgery Hosp. for Sick Children, London, 1988-89; assoc. prof. surgery SUNY Health Sci. Ctr., Syracuse, 1989-90, Washington U. Sch. Medicine, St. Louis, 1990—; dir. heart transplant program, dir. lung transplant program, dir. heart-lung transplant program, chief pediat. surgery St. Louis Children's Hosp., 1994—. Capt. USNR, 1994—. Mem. Phi Beta Kappa. Methodist. Home: 1132 Conwyck Ln Saint Louis MO 63131

HUDDLESTON, EUGENE LEE, retired American studies educator; b. Ironton, Ohio, Jan. 29, 1931; m. Mary Lou Fishbeck, June 17, 1961; 1 son, John. A.B., Marshall U., 1953; M.A., Ohio U., 1956; Ph.D., Mich. State U., 1965. Asst. prof. Ind. State U., Terre Haute, 1962-66; asst. prof., assoc. prof. Mich. State U., East Lansing, 1966-77; prof. Am. thought and lang. Mich. State U., 1977-93; ret., 1993. Author: (with Douglas A. Noverr) The Relationship of Literature and Painting: A Guide to Information Sources, 1978; (with A. Staufer and P. Shuster) C&O Power: Steam and Diesel Locomotives of the Chesapeake and Ohio Railway, 1900-1965, 1965, 7th reprint, 1984; Thomas Jefferson: A Reference Guide, 1982; (with T.W. Dixon, Jr.) The Allegheny-Lima's Finest, 1984, reprint, 1997; (with R. LeMassena) Norfolk and Western Railway, Vol. 1, 1985; The Van Sweringen Berkshires, 1986; (with C.W. Turner and T.W. Dixon, Jr.) Chessie's Road, 2d edit., 1986; World's Greatest Mallets, 1986; Riding That New River Train, 1989; Appalachian Crossing: The Pocahontas Roads, 1989; (with E. Young and J. Joseph) Chesapeake & Ohio, Coal, and Color, 1997; (with Kevin EuDaly) Chesapeake and Ohio, Vol. 1, 1999; contbr. articles to jours., photographs to pubs. Recipient Norman Foerster award, 1966. Mem. Chesapeake and Ohio Hist. Soc., Ry. and Locomotive Hist. Soc., Nat. Ry. Hist. Soc. Home: 3926 Raleigh Dr Okemos MI 48864-3642

HUDDLESTON, FOREST WILLIS, retired mental healing counselor; b. Kingsburg, Calif., Oct. 3, 1915; s. John Samuel and Myra Jennie (Beaver) H.; m. Allene Moore, June 3, 1944 (div. 1979); children: June M., Ralph Reed, Virginia Marie; m. Jacqueline Louise Barber, Sept. 3, 1986. Student, Redley (Calif.) City Coll., 1934-36, U. Puget Sound, 1936-38, Fresno State Coll., 1940-41, 47-48. Ordained to ministry Universal Life Ch., 1978. Mem. sales staff various furniture stores, Sacramento, 1959-70; research dir. Allied Research and Counseling, Sacramento, 1970-76, Huddleston Claibourne Counseling Ctr., Sacramento, 1983-84; ret., 1984. Developer Huddleston Method treatment for mental illness. Asst. dir. Oak Park Youth Band, Sacramento, 1968-70; active various community service orgns., Sacramento, 1958-. Sgt. USAF, 1942-45. Nominated Nobel Peace Prize, 1992. Avocation: coin collecting. Home and Office: 5965 E Shields Ave Unit 160 Fresno CA 93727-8060

HUDDLESTON, JOHN FRANKLIN, obstetrics and gynecology educator; b. Jacksonville, Fla., June 26, 1942; s. Paul Mc Kisson and Mary Rebecca (Robinson) H.; m. Kathryn Ann Welch, Dec. 30, 1982; children: Suzanne Marie, Edward Ryan, John Stuart, Mary Kathryn, Ryan Mc Kisson. BS, U. Fla., Gainesville, 1963; MD, Duke U., 1967. Diplomate Am. Bd. Ob-Gyn, Am. Bd. Maternal-Fetal Medicine. Dir. maternal-fetal medicine Sch. of Medicine, U. Ala., Birmingham, Ala., 1963-86; pvt. practice Jacksonville, Fla., 1986-89; prof., dir. maternal-fetal medicine Sch. of Medicine, Emory U., Atlanta, 1989-96, Coll. of Medicine, U. Fla. Sch. of Medicine, Jacksonville, 1997—. Contbr. to profl. jours., articles, and book chpts. Surgeon USPHS, 1969-71. Mem. Ctrl. Assn. Obstetricians and Gynecologists, Am. Gynecologic and Obstetrics Soc., Soc. Perinatal Obstetricians, South Atlantic Assn. Obstetricians and Gynecologists. Avocations: computers, skiing, camping, canoeing. Office: U Fla Health Scis Ctr Dept Ob/Gyn 653-1 W 8th St Jacksonville FL 32209-6511

HUDDLESTON, JOSEPH RUSSELL, judge; b. Glasgow, Ky., Feb. 5, 1937; s. Paul Russell and Laura Frances (Martin) H.; m. Heidi Wood, Sept. 12, 1959; children: Johanna, Lisa, Kristina. AB, Princeton U.; JD, LLM, U. Va. Bar: Ky. 1962, U.S. Ct. Appeals (6th cir.) 1963, U.S. Supreme Ct. 1970. Ptnr. Huddleston Bros., Bowling Green, Ky., 1962-87; judge Warren Cir. Ct. Divsn. I, Bowling Green, Ky., 1987-91, Ky. Ct. appeals, Bowling Green, Ky., 1991—; mem. Adv. Com. for Criminal Law Revision, 1969-71; mem. exec. com. Ky. Crime Commn., 1972-77. Named Ky. Outstanding Trial Judge, 1990. Mem. ABA, Ky. Bar Assn. (ho. of dels. 1971-80), Assn. Trial Lawyers Am. (state del. 1981-82), Ky. Acad. Trial Attys. (bd. govs. 1975-87, pres. 1978), Bowling Green Bar Assn. (pres. 1972), So. Ky. Estate Planning Coun. (pres. 1983), Bowling Green-Warren County C. of C. (bd. dirs. 1987-91), Port Oliver Yacht Club (Comodore). Democrat. Episcopalian. Home: 644 Minnie Way Bowling Green KY 42101-9210 Office: 1945 Scottsville Rd Ste 101 Bowling Green KY 42104-5824

HUDEC, MARY SUZANNE, nursing and patient services administrator; b. Cleve., Nov. 29, 1944; d. John A. and Rita C. (Burns) H. BSN, Coll. of Mt. St. Joseph, Cin., 1966; MSN, U. Calif., San Francisco, 1973. Charge nurse Parma (Ohio) Community Hosp., 1969; staff nurse VA Med. Ctr., Cleve., 1969-70; head nurse/staff nurse VA Med. Ctr., San Francisco, 1970-72; assoc. chief, nursing svc. VA Med. Ctr., Martinez, Calif., 1973-75, Palo Alto, Calif., 1975-79; chief, nursing svc. VA Med. Ctr., Dayton, Ohio, 1979-81; chief, nursing svc. VA Med. Ctr., Washington, 1981—, assoc. dir. patient svcs.; presenter in field. Lt. USNR, 1966-69. Recipient Outstanding Vietnam Vet. award, 1979. Mem. Am. Orgn. Nurse Execs. (treas. nat. capitol area 1985, pres.-elect 1986-87, pres. 1987-88, 93-94, bd. dirs. 1994-96), Am. Coll. Healthcare Execs., U. Calif. San Francisco Alumni Assn. Office: Vets Affairs Med Ctr 50 Irving St NW Washington DC 20422-0001*

HUDEC, ROBERT EMIL, lawyer, educator; b. Cleve., Dec. 23, 1934; s. Emil and Mary (Tomcho) H.; m. Marianne Miller, Sept. 8, 1956; children: Michael Robert, Katharine Wright. B.A., Kenyon Coll., 1956, LL.D. (hon.), 1979; M.A., Cambridge U., 1958; LL.B., Yale U., 1961. Bar: D.C. 1963, Minn. 1974. Law clk. to Mr. Justice Potter Stewart, U.S. Supreme Ct., 1961-63; asst. gen. counsel Office Spl. Rep. for Trade Negotiations, Exec. Offices, 1963-65; Rockefeller Found. research fellow, 1965-66; asso. prof. law Yale U. Law Sch., 1966-72; prof. law U. Minn. Law Sch., Mpls., 1972—, Melvin C. Steen prof. law, 1986—. Author: The Gatt Legal System and World Trade Diplomacy, 1975, 2d edit., 1990, Developing Countries in the Gatt Legal System, 1987, Enforcing International Trade Law: The Evolution of the Modern GATT Legal System, 1993, Essays on the Nature of International Trade Law, 1999; contbr. articles to profl. jours. Mem. Am. Law Inst., Minn. Bar Assn. Office: U Minn Law Sch Minneapolis MN 55455

HUDES, NANA BRENDA, marketing professional; b. N.Y.C., Nov. 25; d. Harry and Anita Lorraine (Seiken) Richter; m. Barton Hudes, Sept. 2, 1958 (div. Sept. 1972); children: Layne A., Michael F., Meredith A. Student, Skidmore Coll.; BA magna cum laude, Pace U., 1974; MS with honors, Coll. of New Rochelle, 1976. Dir. mail mktg. mgr. Pergamon Press, Elmsford, N.Y., 1979-80, spl. sales mgr., 1980-81; mktg. mgr. Knowledge Industry Publs., White Plains, N.Y., 1981-82; mktg. mgr. Grolier Electronic Pub., Danbury, Conn., 1982-84, dir. mktg., 1984-86; mktg. mgr. R.R. Bowker, New Providence, N.J., 1986-88, mktg. dir., 1988-91, sr. dir. mktg., 1991-99; tchr. social studies Rye Neck (N.Y.) Mid. Sch., 1978-79. Dist. leader, county committeeperson Dem. Party, Matawan Twp., N.J., 1964. Home: 233 E 69th St New York NY 10021-5414

HUDGENS, SANDRA LAWLER, retired state official; b. New Orleans, Feb. 15, 1944; d. Avril Lawler and Peggy V. (Crager) Kelly; m. Adolfo DiGennaro, Oct. 20, 1967 (div. 1970); 1 child, Daniel Darryn DiGennaro; m. Stanley Dalton Hudgens, Feb. 17, 1973; children: Stephanie Hudgens Cap, Richard Stanley, Michael Shane. Student, U. Nev., 1962-64, U. Grenoble, France, 1964-65, U. Aix-Marseille, Nice, France, 1965, U. Nev., Las Vegas, 1980—. Traffic ct. clk. III Clark County Juvenile Ct. Svcs., Las Vegas, 1965-71; planning commr. City of Las Vegas, 1988-92, chmn. planning commn., 1991-92; br. mgr. registration divsn. Dept. Motor Vehicles and Pub. Safety, State of Nev., Las Vegas, 1971-96; rep. Weststar FCU, Las Vegas, 1988-96; advocate State of Nev. Employees Assn., Las Vegas, 1971-96; coord. State of Nev. team City of Las Vegas Corp. Challenge, 1987-90; dir. so. chpt. Am. Fedn. State, County and Mcpl. Employees/State Nev. Employees Assn. retirees AFL/CIO. Past treas., sec. Las Vegas Civic Ballet Assn., Las Vegas, 1987-93; treas. Women's Dem. Club Clark County, Las Vegas, 1996-97, pres., 1998; chmn., vice-chmn. United Blood Svcs. Adv. Coun., Las Vegas, 1993-96; chmn. 1st Ann. Flood Awareness Week, mem. adv. coun. Clark County Regional Flood Dist., Las Vegas, 1987-88; treas., sec., badge and advancement counselor Boy Scouts Am., Las Vegas, 1976-90. Mem. Am. Bus. Women's Assn. (chmn. souvenir program Western Regional Conf. 1997). Democrat. Episcopalian. Avocations: hunting, knitting, photography, RVing, biking. Home: 3840 Russet Falls St Las Vegas NV 89129-7644

HUDGINS, CATHERINE HARDING, business executive; b. Raleigh, N.C., June 25, 1913; d. William Thomas and Mary Alice (Timberlake) Harding; m. Robert Scott Hudgins IV, Aug. 20, 1938; children: Catherine Harding Adams, Deborah Ghiselin, Robert Scott V. BS, N.C. State U., 1929-33; grad. tchr. N.C. Sch. for Deaf, 1933-34. Tchr. N.C. Sch. for Deaf, Morganton, 1934-36, N.J. Sch. for Deaf, Trenton, 1937-39; sec. Dr. A.S. Oliver, Raleigh, 1937, Robert S. Hudgins Co., Charlotte, N.C., 1949—, v.p., treas., 1960—, also bd. dirs. Mem. Jr. Svc. League, Easton, Pa., 1939; project chmn. ladies aux. Profl. Engrs. N.C., 1954-55, pres., 1956-57; pres. Christian High Sch. PTA, 1963; program chmn. Charlotte Opera Assn., 1959-61, sec., 1961-63; sec. bd. Hezekiah Alexander House Restoration, 1949-52, Hezekiah Alexander House Aux., 1975—, treas., 1983-84, v.p., 1984-85, pres., 1985-89; sec. Hezekiah Alexander Found., 1986—; past chmn. home missions, annuities and relief Women of Presbyn. Ch., past pres. Sunday Sch. class; mem. Heritage Foun. Press. Club, 1995—, Empower Am., 1995—. Named Woman of Yr. Am. Biographical Soc., 1993. Mem. N.C. Hist. Assn., English Speaking Union, Internat. Platform Assn., Mint Mus. Drama Guild (pres. 1967-69), Internat. Biog. Ctr. Eng. (dep. dir. gen.), Heritage Found. (pres. club, 1994), Empower Am. (leadership coun. 1995), Daus. Am. Colonists (state chmn. nat. def. 1973-74, corr. sec. Virginia Dare chpt. 1978-79, 84-85, state insignia chmn. 1979-80), DAR (mem. nat. chmn.'s assn., rec. sec. nat. officers club 1990—, chpt. regent 1957-59, chpt. chaplain 1955-57 N.C. program chmn. 1961-63, state chmn. nat. def. 1973-76, state rec. sec. 1977-79, hon. state regent for life, chmn. N.C. Geneal. Register 1982, nat. vice chmn. S.E. region Am. Indians 1989—, rec. sec. Nat. Officers Club 1990-92, v.p. N.C. State Officer's Club 1991-92, pres. 1992-94), Children Am. Revolution (N.C. sr. pres. 1963-66, sr. nat. corr. sec., 1966-68, sr. nat. 1st v.p. 1968-70, sr. nat. pres. 1970-72, hon. sr. nat. pres. life 1972—, 2d v.p. Nat. Officers Club, 1st v.p. 1977-79, pres. 1979-81), Huguenot Soc. N.C., Carmel Country Club (Charlotte), Viewpoint 24 Club, (v.p. 1986, pres. 1987). Home: 1514 S Wendover Rd Charlotte NC 28211-1726 Office: Robert S Hudgins Co PO Box 17217 Charlotte NC 28227-0099

HUDGINS, LOUISE NAN, art educator; b. Ft. Worth; d. Joe Wallace and Lillian Frances (Taylor) H. BA, U. North Tex., 1960, postgrad., 1965. Cert. tchr. art, Tex. Fine arts supr. Dallas Ind. Sch. Dist., 1981-82; tchr. art Lida Hooe Elem. Sch., Dallas, 1966-81, Greiner Arts Acad., Dallas, 1982-86, Hotchkiss Montessori Acad., Dallas, 1986-94, Dealey Montessori Acad., Dallas, 1994—; state textbook com. Tex. Edn. Agy., Austin, 1981-82, com. mem., cons., 1984-85, workshop presenter U. Tex., 1989-91, Montessori Certification Program, Dallas, 1992-95, Pine Bluff, Ark., 1995, 98, Pensacola, Fla., 1998; mem. com. Tex. Art Assessments Study, Richardson, 1993. Co-author: (tchr. textbook) Through Their Eyes, 1989; contbg. author: (student textbooks) Inside Art, 1992. Named Elem. Tchr. of Yr. Oak Cliff C. of C., Dallas, 1980. Mem. ASCD, Nat. Art Edn. Assn., Tex. Art Edn. Assn. (chair elem. divsn. 1983-84, rep. assembly 1987-89, Elem. Art Educator of Yr. 1988), Dallas Art Edn. Assn. (pres. 1988-89). Home: 1451 Winding Brook Cir Dallas TX 75208-2912

HUDIAK, DAVID MICHAEL, academic administrator, lawyer; b. Darby, Pa., June 27, 1953; s. Michael Paul and Sophie Marie (Glowaski) H.; m. Veronica Ann Barbone, Aug. 28, 1982; children: David Michael, Christopher Andrew, Jonathan Joseph. BA, Haverford Coll., 1975; JD, U. Pa., 1978. Bar: Pa. 1979, U.S. Dist. Ct. (ea. dist.) Pa. 1979, N.J. 1981, U.S. Dist. Ct. N.J. 1981. Assoc. Jerome H. Ellis, Phila., 1978-79, Berson, Fineman & Bernstein, Phila., 1979-80; pvt. practice Aldan, Pa., 1980-81; dir. tng. paralegal program PJA Sch., Upper Darby, Pa., 1982—, acting dir., 1983-89, dir., 1989—; v.p. The PJA Sch., Inc., 1989—, bd. dirs.; v.p., sec.-treas., bd. dirs. 7900 West Chester Pike Corp., 1994—; mem. staff Nat. Ctr. Ednl. Testing, Phila., 1982-87; instr. Villanova (Pa.) U., 1985. Mem. Havertown Choristers; active U. Pa. Light Opera Co., 1977-84. Mem. ABA, Pa. Bar Assn., Founders Club Haverford Coll. Office: PJA Sch 7900 W Chester Pike Upper Darby PA 19082-1917

HUDICK, ANDREW MICHAEL, II, finance executive; b. Holly Springs, Miss., May 11, 1958; s. Joseph Frank and Marie Carmella (Peters) H.; m. Anne-Marie Gwynn, Oct. 3, 1998. BSCE, U. Va., 1980; Cert. fin. planner, Coll. for Fin. Planning, 1982, MS in Retirement Planning, 1991. Registered investment advisor, U.S., Va. Engr. Norfolk & Western Rwy., Roanoke, Va., 1980-81; prin., founder, head Fee-Only Fin. Planning, L.C., Roanoke, 1981—; adj. faculty Va. Polytech. and State U., 1994-96. Fin. planning columnist Blue Ridge Bus. Jour., 1989-94, Va. Skyline, 1986-89; contbr. articles to profl. jours. Bd. dirs. Assn. Retarded Citizens, Roanoke, 1985, Mental Health Assn. Roanoke, 1984-86, treas. 1986; chmn. speaker's bur. United Way Roanoke Valley, 1985-86. Recipient Disting. Svc. award Mental Health Assn., 1984, 86, Outstanding Svc. award United Way Roanoke Valley, 1986; named Outstanding Vol., Va. Skyline Girl Scout Coun., Salem, 1986, one of Top 60 Fin. Advisors, Worth Mag., 1994, one of Top 200 Fin. Advisors, Worth Mag., 1996, one of Top 250 Fin. Advisors, Worth Mag., 1997, one of Top 300 Fin. Planners, Worth Mag., 1998, One of Top 120 Fin. Advisors for Physicians, Med. Econs. mag., 1998. Mem. Inst. Cert. Fin. Planners (cert.), Nat. Assn. Personal Fin. Advisors (bd. dirs., v.p. 1993, treas. 1994, pres. 1995-96), Internat. Assn. Fin. Planning (pres. 1987-88), Internat. Bd. Stds. and Practices for Cert. Fin. Planners (bd. examiners 1989-93), Toastmasters (advanced speaking cert., treas. Roanoke 1984-85, pres. 1985, gov. dist. 66 1986). Avocations: handball, croquet, bridge. Office: Fee-Only Financial Planning LC 355 Campbell Ave SW Roanoke VA 24016-3624

HUDIK, MARTIN FRANCIS, hospital administrator, educator, consultant; b. Chgo., Mar. 27, 1949; s. Joseph and Rose (Ricker) H.; m. Eileen Hudik; 1 child, Theresa Margaret. BS in Mech. and Aerospace Engring., Ill. Inst. Tech., 1971; BPA, Jackson State U., 1974; MBA, Loyola U., 1975; postgrad., U. Sarasota, 1975-76. Cert. health care safety mgr., hazard control mgr., hazardous materials mgr., OSHA hazardous materials response instr., hazardous materials incident comdr., disaster coord., police instr., Ill., security cert. instr., Ill. With Ill. Masonic Med. Ctr., Chgo., 1969-94, dir. risk mgmt., 1974-79, asst. adminstr., 1979-94; facilities mgr. Bethany/Adv. Hosp., 1997-98; capt. tng. divsn. Cicero (Ill.) Police Dept., tng. and internal affairs divsn., 1971—; instr. Nat. Safety Coun. Safety Tng. Inst., Chgo., 1978-85; cons. em. Coun. Tech. users Consumer Products, Underwriters Labs., Chgo., 1977-96; instr., lt. U.S. Def. Civil Preparedness Agy. Staff Coll., Battle Creek, Mich., 1977; liaison officer to Cook County, asst. dir. Emergency Svcs. and disaster Agy. Town of Cicero, 1988-97; pres., bd. dirs. Cook County Emergency Mgmt. Coun., 1991-92; bd. dirs. Cook County Emergency Mgmt. Agy., 1992-97, Cmty. Fed. Credit Union, 1992-93; exec. bd., pres. Postal Svc. Postal Customer Adv. Coun., Cicero, 1996—; bd. dirs. Chicagoland Postal Adv. Cooun., 1998—. Pres. sch. bd. Mary Queen of Heaven Sch., cicero, 1977-79, 84-86; pres. Mary Queen of Heaven Ch. Coun., 1979-81, 83-86, St. Leonard Parish Coun., 1998—; pres. I.M.M.C. Employee Club, 1983-86. Ill. State scholar, 1969-71; recipient Meritorious Svc. award Town of Cicero, 1990, Spl. Svc. award Underwriters Lab., 1992, Cook County Sheriffs Dept., 1993, medal of Merit Town of Cicero, 1996, Excellence in Svc. award U.S. Postal Svc., 1997, Emergency Svcs. Achievement award Town of Cicero, 1997 Outstanding Effort award U.S. Postal Svc., 1998, Police Achievement award Town of Cicero, 1998, Outstanding Svcs. award Cicero Postal Coun., 1998, Svc. Recognition award U.S. Postal Svc., 1999. Mem. Am. Coll. Healthcare Execs., Am. Soc. Hosp. Risk Mgmt., Nat. Fire Protection Assn., Am. Soc. SafetyEngrs. (profl.), Am. Soc. Law and Medicine, Ill. Hosp. Security and Safety Assn. (co-founder 1976, founding pres. 1976-77, hon. dir. 1977-82), Cath. Alumni Club Chgo. (bd. dirs. 1983-84, 86), Mensa, Masons (Berwyn, Ill. chpt.), Pi Tau Sigma, Tau Beta Pi, Alpha Sigma Nu. Republican. Roman Catholic. Home: 2116 S 51st Ct Cicero IL 60804-2345 Office: Ill Masonic Med Ctr 2116 S 51st Ct Chicago IL 60804-2345

HUDLER, GEORGE, plant pathologist, educator. Prof. plant pathology Cornell U., Ithaca, N.Y. Recipient Excellence in Teaching award, 1992. Office: Cornell U 315 Plant Science Building Ithaca NY 14853-5904

HUDNALL, JARRETT, JR., management and marketing educator; b. Rhome, Tex., Oct. 6, 1931; s. Jarrett and Katherine (Wilson) H.; m. Sarah Ruth Warren, Nov. 24, 1955; children: Jarrett Joseph, William Warren, Katherine Lee, Thomas Wilson. Student, Arlington (Tex.) State Coll., 1948-50; BBA, U. Tex., Austin, 1953, MBA, 1956; PhD, U. Ala., 1966. Lectr. U. Tex., 1955-56; asst. prof. Arlington State Coll., 1956-58; instr. U. Ala., 1958-61; asst. prof. La. Tech. U., 1961-62, assoc. prof. mktg., 1962-67, prof., head dept. bus., 1967-77; exec. Superior Supply Co., Inc., 1978-83, P&A div. Ciba-Geigy, 1983-84; v.p. Rohcar, Inc., 1984-90; prof. mgmt. and mktg. Stephen F. Austin State U., Nacogdoches, Tex., 1985-92; dean coll. bus. and commerce Livingston (Ala.) U., 1992-94; prof. mktg. Miss. U. for Women, Columbus, 1994—; v.p. Ctrl. Asian Consultants, LLC; bd. dirs. SBI; cons. firms in chem. fertilizer, petroleum, farm equipment mfg., bus.; cons. agrl. and econ. devel. products W. Republic of Uzbekistan, 1995. Author: (with A.L. Seeyle) Compensation of Retail Department Store and Specialty Store Salesman in Major Texas Cities, 1957, Attitudes of Gulf Service Station Dealers Toward Minor Tuneup and Repair Work, 1963, An Economic Analysis of Income and Employment in a Four-State Deep South Region, 1950-60, 1966. Lt. AUS, 1953-55. Gulf Oil Corp. fellow, 1963. Mem. Am., So. mktg. assns., S.W. Fedn. Allied Disciplines, Am. Collegiate Retailing Assn., So. and Southwestern Bus. Dean's Assn., Small Bus. Inst. Dirs.' Assn., Sigma Iota Epsilon, Beta Gamma Sigma, Alpha Kappa Psi, Kappa Delta Pi. Democrat. Baptist. Home: 1003 Lakeview Dr Ruston LA 71270-5233 Office: PO Box 940 Columbus MS 39703-0940

HUDNER, PHILIP, lawyer, rancher; b. San Jose, Calif., Feb. 24, 1931; s. Paul Joseph and Mary E. (Dooling) H.; m. Carla Raven, Aug. 6, 1966; children: Paul Theodor, Mary Carla. B.A. with great distinction, Stanford U., 1952, LL.B., 1955. Bar: Calif. 1955. Lawyer Pillsbury, Madison & Sutro, San Francisco, 1958—, ptnr., 1970—; rancher San Benito County, Calif., 1970—. Asst. editor: Stanford Law Rev., 1954-55; author articles on estate and trust law. Pres. Soc. Calif. Pioneers, 1976-78; bd. of regents St. Mary's Cathedral, San Francisco; trustee, sec. Louise M. Davies Found., 1974—; pres. Drum Found., 1985—. Served with U.S. Army, 1956-58. Fellow Am. Bar Found.; mem. Internat. Acad. Estate and Trust Law (steering com. 1974-75, exec. coun. 1980-85), San Benito County Saddle Horse Assn., Order of Malta, Phi Beta Kappa, Pacific Union Club, Lagunitas Country Club, Frontier Boys, Bohemian Club, Rancheros Visitadores. Democrat. Roman Catholic. Office: Pillsbury Madison & Sutro 235 Montgomery St Fl 16 San Francisco CA 94104-3074

HUDNUT, DAVID BEECHER, retired leasing company executive, lawyer; b. Cin., Feb. 21, 1935; s. William Herbert and Elizabeth Allen (Kilborne) H.; m. Robin Fraser, Apr. 12, 1958; children: David Beecher, Marjorie Elizabeth, Joshua Fraser, John Marshall, Benjamin Parker. AB, Princeton U., 1957; JD, Cornell U., 1962. Bar: N.Y. 1962, U.S. Supreme Ct. 1967. Assoc., Hughes, Hubbard & Reed, N.Y.C., 1962-67; with Ind. and chem. products div. Ford Motor Co., 1967-69; v.p. U.S. Leasing Internat., Inc., San Francisco, 1969-76, sr. v.p., 1976-90; bd. dirs. Gary D. Nelson Assocs., Inc., 1995—, Bread and Roses, 1995—, chmn., 1999—, Cameron House Found., 1979-98, pres., 1980-92; bd. dirs. Svcs. for Srs., 1970-96, pres. 1990-92, No. Calif. Presbyn. Homes, 1971-77, chmn., 1973-76, 79-86; bd. dirs. Edgewood Children's Ctr., 1979-86, Ind. Colls. No. Calif., 1981-84, Exec. Svc. Corps, 1991-93, adv. bd. Alumnae resources, 1982-94, Calif. Hist. Soc., 1986-92, pres. 1989-91. Home: 9 Via Capistrano Belvedere Tiburon CA 94920-2030

HUDNUT, ROBERT KILBORNE, clergyman, author; b. Cin., Jan. 7, 1934; s. William Herbert and Elizabeth (Kilborne) H.; m. Mary Lou Lundell; children by previous marriage: Heidi, Robert Kilborne, Heather, Matthew. B.A. with highest honors, Princeton, 1956; M.Div., Union Theol. Sem., N.Y.C., 1959. Ordained to ministry Presbyn. Ch., 1959; asst. minister Westminster Presbyn. Ch., Albany, N.Y., 1959-62; minister St. Luke Presbyn. Ch., Wayzata, Minn., 1962-73, Winnetka (Ill.) Presbyn. Ch., 1975-94; exec. dir. Minn. Pub. Interest Research Group, 1973-75; Co-chmn. Minn. Joint Religious Legis. Coalition, 1970-75. Author: Surprised by God, 1967, A Sensitive Man and the Christ, 1971, A Thinking Man and the Christ, 1971, The Sleeping Giant: Arousing Church Power in America, 1971, An Active Man and the Christ, 1972, Arousing the Sleeping Giant: How to Organize Your Church for Action, 1973, Church Growth Is Not the Point, 1975, The Bootstrap Fallacy: What The Self-Help Books Don't Tell You, 1978, This People-This Parish, 1986, Meeting God in the Darkness, 1989, Emerson's Aesthetic, 1996, Call Waiting, 1999. Pres. Greater Met. Fedn. Twin Cities, 1970-72; chmn. Citizens Adv. Com. on Interstate 394, 1971-75; nat. chmn. Presbyns. for Ch. Renewal, 1971; Chmn. Democratic Party 33d Senatorial Dist. Minn., 1970-72, Minnetonka Dem. Party, 1970-72; fusion candidate for mayor, Albany, 1961; Bd. dirs. Minn. Council Chs., 1964-70; trustee Princeton U., 1972-76, Asheville (N.C.) Sch., 1979—. Rockefeller fellow, 1956; named Outstanding Young Man Minnetonka, 1967; recipient Distinguished Service award Minnetonka Tchrs. Assn., 1969. Mem. Phi Beta Kappa. Home and Office: 7145 65th St S Cottage Grove MN 55016-1130

HUDNUT, WILLIAM HERBERT, III, senior resident fellow, political scientist; b. Cin., Oct. 17, 1932; s. William Herbert Jr. and Elizabeth (Kilborne) H.; m. Beverly Guidara; children: Michael Conger, Laura Anne, Timothy Norton, William Herbert IV, Theodore Beecher, Christopher Shew. BA magna cum laude, Princeton, 1954; MDiv summa cum laude, Union Theol. Sem., N.Y.C., 1957; DD (hon.), Hanover Coll., 1967, Wabash Coll., 1969; LLD (hon.), Butler U., 1980, Anderson Coll., 1982, Franklin Coll., 1983, Millikin U., 1987, Ind. U., 1994, Elmhurst Coll., 1996; LittD (hon.), U. Indpls., 1981; DPS (hon.), Blackburn Coll., 1987. Ordained to ministry Presbyn. Ch., 1957; asst. minister Westminster Ch., Buffalo, 1957-60; pastor 1st Presbyn. Ch., Annapolis, Md., 1960-63; dir. Westminster Found., Annapolis, 1960-63; sr. minister 2d Presbyn. Ch., Indpls., 1963-72; mem. 93d Congress from Ind., 1973-74; dir. dept. community affairs Ind. Central U., Indpls., 1975; mayor City of Indpls., 1976-91; fellow Inst. Politics Harvard U., 1992; sr. fellow Hudson Inst., Indpls., 1992-94; pres. Civic Fedn., Chgo., 1994-96; sr. resident fellow The Urban Land Inst., Washington, 1996—; mem. Presdl. Adv. Com. on Federalism, 1981-84. Author: Minister/Mayor, 1987, The Hudnut Years in Indianapolis, 1976-1991, 1995, Cities on the Rebound, 1998; editor: Union Sem. Quar. Rev., 1956-57; contbr. sermons, articles to profl. publs. Mem. Bd. Pub. Safety, Indpls., 1970-71, Rep. Nat. Com., 1987; pres. Anne Arundel County Mental Health Assn., 1961-63; pres., bd. dirs. Marion County Mental Health Assn., 1966-68, Westminster Found., Purdue U., 1969-73; bd. dirs. Cmty. Svc. Coun. Met. Indpls., 1964-68, Family Svc. Assn., 1966-72, Flanner House,

1968-72; pres. trustees Darrow Sch., New Lebanon, N.Y., 1968-75; Task Force on Fed. Deficit, 1981; mem. Adv. Commn. on Intergovtl. Rels., 1984-90; bd. dirs. Indpls. Ctr. for Adv. Rsch., 1976-91, Humane Soc., 1983-91; trustee Roosevelt Ctr. Am. Policy Studies, Washington, 1984-87; Pleasant Run Children's Home Found. bd., 1992-94, Children's Home & Aid Soc. Ill., 1994-96; co-vice chmn. Alliance for Redesigning Govt., 1992—; mem. Police Found. Bd., 1997—; mem. Nat. Assn. Securities Dealers Regulation Bd., 1996-98, Nat. Adjudicatory Coun., 1998; mem. accreditatio bd. Am. Planning Assn., 1998—. Recipient William Booth award Salvation Army, 1984, Russell G. Lloyd disting. svc. award Ind. Assn. Cities and Towns, 1985, Rosa Parks award Am. Assn. for Affirmative Action, 1992, Woodrow Wilson award Princeton U., 1986, disting. urban mayor award Nat. Urban Coalition, 1987; named All-Pro City Mgmt. Team, City and State mag., 1986, 89, 92; fellow Nat. Acad. Pub. Adminstrn., 1994—. Mem. Columbia Club Indpls. (bd. dir. 1994-96), Kiwanis, Masons (33 deg.), Phi Beta Kappa. Office: The Urban Land Inst 1025 Thos Jefferson St NW Washington DC 20007-5201 *Life is relationships, and whatever we can do to enlighten and strengthen each other, in the family circle, among our friends, in business, in society at large, will help. This requires ardor and self-surrender, faith, hope and humor.*

HUDSON, ALAN ROY, neurosurgeon, medical educator, hospital administrator; b. Cape Town, South Africa, Mar. 16, 1938; s. John George H.; m. Susan Elizabeth Hurd, 1962; children: Jean, Katherine, Erin, Roy. MB ChB of Surgery, U. Cape Town, 1960. Intern Groote Schuuv Hosp., Cape Town; prof. neurosurgery U. Toronto; James Wallace McCutcheon chair, surgeon in chief Toronto Hosp.; pres., CEO Toronto Hosp. (name now Univ. Health Network), 1991-99; CEO Princess Margaret Hosp., Toronto, 1996-99; pres., CEO U. Health Network, 1999—. Contbr. numerous articles, chpts. to profl. jours. Fellow Royal Coll. Surgeons Can., Royal Coll. Surgeons Edinburgh, Royal Coll. Surgeons South Africa (hon.); mem. World Fedn. Neurosurg. Soc. (hon. pres., congress). Avocation: yachting. Office: Toronto Gen Hosp, 585 University Ave BW 1-658, Toronto, ON Canada M5G 2C4

HUDSON, ANTHONY WEBSTER, retired federal agency administrator, minister; b. Durham, N.C., Mar. 23, 1937; s. Emanuel and Adele (Nixon) H.; m. Glenda Buchanan, Jan. 18, 1964 (div. Dec. 1996; children—April Lynn, Verna Lea; m. Maude Harrison, Aug. 23, 1997. Student, Rutgers U., 1954-59, Columbia, 1960-62, George Washington U., 1967-69, Wesley Theol. Sem., 1991-95. Ordained chaplain United Ch. of Christ, 1995. Pers. mgmt. specialist U.S. Civil Service Commn., N.Y.C., 1962-65; tng. officer personnel div. Washington, 1966, tng. officer Bur. Tng., 1967, coordinator Project 250 Bur. Tng., 1968-70, dir. personnel, 1970-74; dir. fed. EEO, 1974-77; staff dir. personnel Def. Logistics Agy., 1977-92; assoc. minister People's Congregational Ch., 1995—; chaplain Springvale Terrace, 1995—; chmn. personnel adminstrn. faculty U.S. Dept. Agr. Grad. Sch. Contbr. to: Ency. of Edn. 1971. Trustee Govt. Svcs., Inc., Washington; chmn. merit pers. bd. Md.-D.C. Park and Planning Commn., Silver Spring, 1974-86; mem. Fed. Pers. Mgmt. Career Bd.; pres. bd. dirs. Worldwide Assurance for Employees of Pub. Agys.; chmn. Montgomery County Merit Sys. Protection Bd., 1989-95. 1st lt. arty. U.S. Army, 1959-60. Recipient Spl. citation U.S. Civil Service Commn., 1969, William A. Jump Meml. award, 1970. Meritorious Svc. award Def. Logistics Agy., 1980, Exceptional Svc. award, 1986; inducted into Def. Logistics Agy. Hall of Fame, 1998. Mem. ASTD (exec. bd., chmn. cmty. svcs. 1966-68), D.C. Sociol. Soc., Am. Personnel and Guidance Assn., Soc. Personnel Adminstrn. (exec. com. 1971-74), Internat. Personnel Mgmt. Assn. (exec. coun. 1977). Am. Sociol. Assn. (employment com. 1971-74), Am. Fgn. Svc. Assn., NAACP, Am. Soc. on Aging, Coll. of Chaplains, Phi Sigma Delta. Home: 7309 Pinehurst Pkwy Chevy Chase MD 20815-3140

HUDSON, AUDREY, journalist. Student, Western Ky. U., 1981-85. News dir. WQHY-FM/WDOC-AM, Prestonsburg, Ky., 1985-87; rsch. dir., scheduler Office of Gov. John Y. Brown, Louisville, 1987; mktg. dir. The Bank Josephine, Prestonsburg, 1988; press sec. Judge Will T. Scott Congl. Campaign, Pikeville, Ky., 1988; news editor, reporter Homewood Ind. Newspaper, Birmingham, Ala., 1988-89, Vail (Colo.) Daily Newspaper, 1989-93; press sec. Office of U.S. Congressman Scott McInnis, Washington, 1993-97; editor publs. Rep. Nat. Conv., San Diego, 1996; press sec. Office of U.S. Senator Ben Nighthorse Campbell, Washington, 1997-99; Capitol Hill corr. Washington Times, 1999—. Recipient First Pl. Regional award for Ky./Tenn. best feature in radio United Press Internat., 1986, Pub. Svc. award Colo. Assn. Pubs., Editors, Reporters, 1990. Mem. U.S. Senate Press Secs. Assn., Rep. Comm. Assn. (v.p. and acting pres. 1996), Soc. Profl. Journalists. Office: Washington Times 3600 New York Ave NE Washington DC 20002

HUDSON, CELESTE NUTTING, education educator, reading clinic administrator, consultant; b. Nashville, Sept. 18, 1927; d. Joan Winthrop Chandler and Hilda Bass (Alexander) Nutting; m. Frank Alden Hudson III, Dec. 30, 1948 (dec.); children: Frank Alden Hudson IV (dec.), Jo Ann Hudson Algermisen, Celeste Jame Hudson; m. Robert Daniel Quartell, June 3, 1989. BS, Oreg. Coll. Edn., 1952; MS, So. Ill. U., 1963, PhD, 1973. Cert. tchr., Tenn., Oreg., Mo. Iowa. Tchr. pub. schs., Crossville, Tenn., 1949-51, Salem, Oreg., 1952-53, West Walnut Manor, Mo., 1953-54; tchr. Normandy Sch. Dist., St. Louis County, Mo., 1954-66; reading coord. Sikestown (Mo.) Pub. Schs., 1966-71; traveling cons. Ednl. Devel. Labs., Huntington, N.Y., 1970-71; mem. clin. staff So. Ill. U. Reading Ctr., 1972; asst. prof. edn. St. Ambrose Coll., 1972-75, U. Tenn., Chattanooga, 1975-76; project dir. Learning Skills Ctr. St. Ambrose U. (formerly St. Ambrose Coll.), 1976-80, asst. prof. edn., 1976-78, assoc. prof., 1979-86, prof., 1986-94, prof. emeritus, 1995—; dir. elem. edn. St. Ambrose U., 1972-75, 76-94, chmn. dept. edn., 1980-84, divsn. chmn., 1984-87, faculty vice chair, 1989-90, faculty chair, 1990-91; cons. in field. Author: Handbook for Remedial Reading, 1967, Cognitive Listening and the Reading of Second Grade Children, 1973, The Effect of Visual Fatigue on Readong, 1990, Longitudinal Study of Children in Clinical Reading, 1994. Mem. Kimberly Village Bd., Davenport, Iowa, 1979-83; chmn. worship com., Asbury Meth. Ch., 1985-90, choir, 1978—, mem. bell choir, 1995-97; co-chmn. Sarah Ctr., 1996—. Mem. AAUP, ASCD, AAUW (Lit. club), DAR, UDC, UDC Real Granddaughter Club, BettendorfLionels Asn. Tchr. Educators (treas. 1998—), Iowa Assn. Colls. Tchr. Edn. (exec. bd. 1989-92, Intenat. Reading Assn. (Scott County coun.), Am. Assn. Colls. Tchr. Edn., Muss. Bend Coun., Assn. Tchrs. Educators, New Eng. Women (pres.-elect 1994-95, pres. 1996-98), Original Music Students Club (corr. sec. 1995-96), Orgn. Tchr. Educators Reading, Internat. Platform Assn., Women in Ednl. Adminstrn., Quad City Women's Investment Club, Renaissance-Ferpsichorean Dance Club (24 Dance Club Group, 1996—), Women of the Moose, Alpha Delta Kappa (past pres.), Kappa Delta Pi (sponsor 1974-96), Phi Delta Kappa. Address: St Ambrose U Box E 140 518 W Locust St Davenport IA 52803-2829

HUDSON, CHARLES DAUGHERTY, insurance executive; b. La Grange, Ga., Mar. 17, 1927; s. J.D. and Janie (Hill) H.; m. Ida Cason Callaway, May 1, 1955; children: Jane Alice Hudson Craig, Ellen Pinson Hudson Harris, Charles Daugherty, Ida Hudson Hughes. Student, Auburn U., 1945-48, LHD (hon.), 1992; LLD, La Grange Coll.; LHD (hon.), Mercer U., 1987. Ptnr. Hudson Hardware Co., La Grange, 1950-57; ptnr. Hammond-Hudson Ins. Agy., La Grange, 1957-58, owner, 1958-78; pres. Hammond, Hudson & Holder INc., 1978-94, chmn. bd., 1994—; bd. dirs., mem. exec. com. Citizens & So. Nat. Bank, La Grange, 1964-90; bd. dirs. Citizens & So. Ga. Corp., Citizens & So. Nat. Bank, Atlanta, C&S Investment Advisors, Inc., Atlanta, C&S Ga. Corp.; acting pres. La Grange Coll., 1979-80; v.p., bd. dirs. la Grange Industries, 1956—, Hudson Maddox Enterprises, 1965-95; ptnr. PCH Properties, 1981—; chmn. bd. dirs. First Annuity Corp., La Grange; bd. dirs., chmn. trust com. NationsBank of Ga. Recipient Pres.'s award Colonial Life Ins. Co., 1966, 69-70, 75-80, Disting. Alumni award Ga. Mil. Acad.-Woodward Acad., 1971, Disting. Svc. award Ga. Hosp. Assn., 1980, Respect Law award Optimists Assn., 1977, Van Landingham Commitment to Edn. award, 1996, Pub. Svc. award Ga. Assn. AIA, 1977, Leading Producer award Aetna Life and Casualty, 1979; Paul Harris fellow, 1984. Mem. Am. Legion, Ga. Assn. Ind. Ins. Agts., Ga. Sch. Bd. Assn. (area dir.), SAR, Amicale de Group LaFayette (hon.). Chattahoochee Valley Art Assn., La Grange C. of C. (bd. dirs.), Newcomen Soc. N.Am., Ga. Hosp. Assn. (trustee 1980—), U. Ga. Gridiron Secret Soc., Highland Country Club (chmn. bd. 1999—), Lafayette Club, Commerce Club Atlanta, Aetna Life and Casualty Presidents, Masons, Shriners, Elks, Rotary (pres. 1964-65), Sigma Alpha Epsilon, Beta Gamma Sigma. Home: 407 Country Club Rd Lagrange GA 30240-2031 Office: Hammond Hudson & Holder Inc 206 W Haralson St Lagrange GA 30240-2722

HUDSON, CHRISTOPHER JOHN, publisher; b. Watford, Eng., June 8, 1948; s. Joseph Edward and Gladys Jenny Patricia (Madgwick); m. Lois Jeanne Lyons, June 16, 1979; children: Thomas, Ellen, Ronald, Timothy. BA with honors, Cambridge U., Eng., 1969, MA with honors, 1972. Promotion mgr. Prentice-Hall Internat., Eng., 1969-70; area mgr. Prentice-Hall Internat., Eng., France, 1970-71; mktg. mgr. Prentice-Hall Internat., Englewood Cliffs, N.J., 1971-74, dir. mktg., 1974-76, asst. v.p., 1976; group internat. dir. I.T.T. Pub., N.Y.C., 1976-77; pres. Focal Press, Inc., N.Y.C., 1977-82; v.p., pub. Aperture Found. Inc., N.Y.C., 1983-86; head publs. J. Paul Getty Trust, L.A., 1986—. Author: Guide to International Book Fairs, 1976; pub. Aperture, 1983-86, J. Paul Getty Mus. Jour., 1986—. Mem. adv. coun. Nat. Heritage Village, Kioni, Greece; mem. trade with eastern Europe com. Assn. Am. Pubs., N.Y., 1976-79, internat. fairs com., 1986-88. Mem. Internat. Assn. Mus. Publs. (Frankfurt, Fed. Republic Germany, chmn. 1992-95), U.S. Mus. Publ. Group (chmn. 1989—), Internat. Pubs. Assn., Hellenic Soc. (London), Oxford & Cambridge Club (London), Internat. Assn. Scholarly Pubs. (sec.-gen. 1994-97, chmn. internat. contracts com.). Avocation: rural preservation projects in England, Greece and California. Office: J Paul Getty Mus 1200 Getty Ctr Dr Ste 1000 Los Angeles CA 90049-1687

HUDSON, DAVID M., minister; b. Charleston, W.Va., Sept. 24, 1948; s. Charles R. and Margaret M. (Coleman) H.; m. Brenda J. Roach, Sept. 22, 1967; children: Nathaniel, Derek. Student, W.Va. State Coll., 1966, Apostolic Bible Inst., 1966-67, Tex. Bible Coll., 1968; DTh (hon.), Ind. Bible Coll., 1988. Ordained minister United Pentecostal Ch., 1973. Youth pres. United Pentecostal Ch., Indpls., 1980-85; sr. pastor Riverside Apostoic Ch., 1985—; exec. presbyter United Pentecostal Ch., St. Louis, 1994-96, harvestime radio commr., 1990—, gen. bd. presbyters, 1994-96; adj. prof. Ind. Bible Coll., Indpls., 1995—; bd. govs. Apostolic Coalition, Washington, 1987-91; mem. adv. bd. Passion-Fire Internat., 1998—; sec. treas. W.Va. dist. United Pentecostal Ch., Charleston, 1994—; internat. spkr. in field. Editor Apostolic Voice, 1987-89. Bd. dirs. Citizens Concerned for Cmty. Values, Morgantown, W.Va., 1990—; co-chmn. Israel prayer breakfast Religious Roundtable, Memphis, 1991. Named Nat. Pres. of Yr. United Pentecostal Ch., 1984, Internat. Pres. of Yr., 1985. Avocations: travel, reading, fitness. Home: PO Box 2069 Morgantown WV 26502-2069

HUDSON, DENNIS LEE, lawyer, retired government official, arbitrator, educator; b. St. Louis, Jan. 5, 1936; s. Lewis Jefferson and Helen Mabel (Buchanan) H.; children: Karen Marie, Karla Sue, Mary Ashley. BA, U. Ill., 1958; JD, John Marshall Law Sch., 1972. Bar: Ill. 1972, U.S Dist. Ct. (so. dist.) Ill. 1972, U.S. Dist. Ct. (no. dist.) Ill. 1972. Insp., IRS, Chgo., 1962-72; spl. agt. GSA, Chgo., 1972-78, spl. agt.-in-charge, 1978-83, regional insp. gen., 1983-87; supervisory spl. agt., Dept Justice-GSA Task Force, Washington, 1978; arbitrator Cir. Ct. Cook County, Ill.; prof. of criminal justice Coll. Dupage. Bd. govs. Theatre Western Springs, Ill., 1978-81, 91-92; deacon Grace Lutheran Ch., LaGrange, Ill., 1977-81. Served with U.S. Army, 1959-61. John N. Jewett scholar, 1972. Mem. ABA, Ill. Bar Assn. Home: 109 51st Pl Western Springs IL 60558-2002 Office: Coll Dupage Bus & Svcs Div 22D Saint Lambert Rd Glen Ellyn IL 60137

HUDSON, DONALD J., retired stock exchange executive; b. Vancouver, B.C., Can., Sept. 26, 1930. BA in Econs. and Math., U. B.C., 1952; LLD (hon.), Simon Fraser U., 1993. With Shell Oil Co. of Can. Ltd., 1952-53; dir. sales devel. Can. Pacific Airlines, Vancouver, 1953-64; sr. v.p. Pacific div. T. Eaton Co., Ltd., Vancouver, 1964-81; pres. Vancouver Stock Exch., 1982-95; bd. dirs. Brit. Pacific Properties Ltd., Norwich Union Life Ins. (Can. bd.). Bd. dirs. Infowest Svcs., Inc., Internat. Fin. Ctr., Vancouver; mem. Vancouver Econ. Devel. Commn. Mem. Vancouver Lawn Tennis Club, Vancouver Club.

HUDSON, EDWARD RANDALL, JR., gas, oil industry executive; b. Ft. Worth, Tex., July 24, 1934; s. Edward Randall and Josphine Terrell (Smith) H.; m. Ann Frasher, Sept. 19, 1959; children: Edward Randall III, Frasher Hudson Pergande. BA, U. Tex., 1955; JD, Harvard U., 1958. Owner, oil prodr. Hudson Oil, Ft. Worth. Vice-chmn. cultural property com. U.S. Info. Agy.; bd. dirs. Kimbell Art Found., Aspen Ctr. Physics; sec. bd. dirs. Burnett Found.; chmn. bd. dirs. Modern Art Mus. Ft. Worth; nat. com., founding co-chmn. bd. dirs. Aspen Art Mus. Mem. Ft. Worth Club, River Crest Country Club, Argyle, Knickerbocker, Steeplechase, Order of the Alamo, Phi Beta Kappa. Avocations: art collector contemporary U.S. and folk art. E-mail: eh34@compuserve.com. Home: 55 Westover Ter Fort Worth TX 76107 also: 750 Castle Creek Dr Aspen CO 81611 Office: Hudson Oil 616 Texas St Fort Worth TX 76102

HUDSON, EDWARD VOYLE, linen supply company executive; b. Seymour, Mo., Apr. 3, 1915; s. Marion A. and Alma (Von Gonten) H.; m. Margaret Carolyn Greely, Dec. 24, 1939; children: Edward G., Carolyn K. Student, Bellingham Normal Coll., 1933-36, U. Wash. Asst. to mgr. Natural Hard Metal Co., Bellingham, 1935-37; ptnr. Met. Laundry Co., Tacoma, 1938-39; propr., mgr. Peerless Laundry & Linen Supply Co., Tacoma, 1939—; propr. Ind. Laundry & Everett Linden Supply Co., 1946-74, 99 Cleaners and Launderers Co., Tacoma, 1957-59; chmn. Tacoma Pub. Utilities, 1959-60; trustee United Mut. Savs. Bank; bd. dirs. Tacoma Better Bus. Bur., 1977—. Pres. Wash. Conf. on Unemployment Compensation, 1975-76; pres. Tacoma Boys' Club, 1970; v.p. Puget Sound USO, 1972-91; elder Emmanuel Presbyn. Ch., 1974—; past campaign mgr., pres. Tacoma-Pierce County United Good Neighbors. Recipient Disting. Citizen's cert. USAF Mil. Airlift Com., 1977; U.S. Dept. Def. medal for outstanding pub. svc., 1978. Mem. Tacoma Sales and Mktg. Execs. (pres. 1957-58), Pacific NW Laundry, Dry Clearning and Linen Supply Assn. (pres. 1959, treas. 1965-75), Internat. Fabricare Inst. (dir. dist. 7, treas. 1979, pres. 1982), Am. Security Coun. Bd., Tacoma C. of C. (pres. 1965), Air Force Assn. (pres. Tacoma chpt. 1976-77, v.p. Wash. state 1983-84, pres. 1985-86), Navy League, Puget Sound Indsl. Devel. Coun. (chmn. 1967), Tacoma-Ft. Lewis Olympia Army Assn. (past pres.), Elks Club (vice chmn. bd. trustees 1984, chmn. 1985-86), Shriners (potentate 1979), Masons, Scottish Rite, Tacoma Club, Tacoma Country and Golf Club, Jesters Club, Rotary (pres. Tacoma chpt. 1967-68), Tacoma Knife and Fork Club (pres. 1964). Republican. Home: 3901 N 37th St Tacoma WA 98407-5636 Office: Peerless Laundry & Linen Supply Co 2902 S 12th St Tacoma WA 98405-2598

HUDSON, ERNIE, actor; b. Benton Harbor, Mich., Dec. 17, 1945. Movies include Joy of Sex, 1984, Ghostbusters, 1984, Love on the Run, 1985, The Dirty Dozen: The Fatal Mission, 1988, Ghostbusters II, 1989, The Hand That Rocks the Cradle, 1992, Wild Palms, 1993, Heart and Souls, 1993, Sugar Hill, 1994, No Escape, 1994, The Crow, 1994, The Cowboy Way, 1994, Airheads, 1994, Speechless, 1994, The Basketball Diaries, 1995, Congo, 1995, The Substitute, 1996, Operation Delta Force, 1997, Mr. Magoo, 1997, Stranger in the Kingdom, 1998, October 22, 1998, Butter, 1998, Best of the Best 4: Without Warning, 1998, Shark Attack, 1999, Lillie, 1999, Everything's Jake, 1999; tv movies inlcude Tornado!, 1996, The Cherokee Kid, 1996, Clover, 1997; guest appearences include Taxi, Little House on the Prairie, The White Shadow, Baa Baa Black Sheep, Bosom Buddies, The Dukes of Hazzard, Gimme a Break!, Super Mario Bros. Super Show, Tales from the Crypt, Superman, Arlis$, others. *

HUDSON, FRANKLIN DONALD, diversified company executive, consultant; b. Asheville, N.C., July 21, 1933; s. Halbert Austin and Lillian Naomi (Cook) H.; m. Rosemary Wheatley, Dec. 1, 1956; children: Lawrence Jamison, Lauren Jean. B.E.E., Yale U., 1955; M.B.A., NYU, 1962; postgrad., Pace U., 1972-75. Sales rep. RCA, N.Y.C., 1959-62; Latin Am. gen. mgr. Fed. Pacific Electric Co., P.R., 1962-68; dir. mktg. GTE Sylvania, 1968-71; dir. Home Equipment div. Singer Co., N.Y.C., 1971-75; v.p. internat. Corometrics Med. Systems, Inc., Wallingford, Conn., 1975-78; v.p. planning and devel. Norlin Corp., White Plains, N.Y., 1978-81; founder, exec. v.p. Integrated Genetics, Inc., 1981-85; founder, bd. dirs. Organogenesis Inc., 1985-89; founder, pres. TSI Corp., 1987-90, Neuromedica, Inc., 1990-93; biotech. cons., 1995—; pres., dir. VIMRX Pharms., Inc., Stamford, Conn., 1994-95; chmn. Bio-Brite, Inc., 1990—; bd. dirs. Cel-Sci. Corp.; adj. prof. NYU, Boston U. Mem. Conn. Rep. Fin. Com., 1968-74; asst. dir. Campaign for Yale, 1978; bd. trustees Quinsigamond Coll., 1989-92. Capt. USAF, 1956-58. Mem. Russell Trust Assn., Assn. Yale U. Alumni (bd. dirs.), Longwood Cricket Club, Sippican Tennis Club, Kittansett Club, Mory's Club, Tau Beta Pi. Episcopalian.

HUDSON, GARY MICHAEL, corporate executive; b. Lander, Wyo., July 28, 1946; s. Frank L. and Sarah Elizabeth (Jones) H.; m. Linda Ann Shaw, July 5, 1985; 1 child, Zachary Michael. BA, U. Wyo., 1968; MA, Western Ky. U., 1970. Tchr. Hopkinsville (Ky.) Pub. Schs., 1968-69; tchr., counselor Warren County Sch., Hadly, Ky., 1969-70; counselor, social worker Wyo. State Tng. Sch., Lander, 1970-72; counselor, adminstr. Ctrl. Wyo. Coll., Riverton, 1972-75; CEO Cmty. Entry Svcs., Riverton, 1975-98, founder, CEO emeritus, 1998—. Contbr. articles and revs. to profl. jours.; mem. editorial adv. bd. Sta. KTRZ-TV, Riverton, 1989-90. Mem. adv. bd. Cen. Wyo. Coll. Trades and Industry, Riverton, 1989-91, Human Devel. Svcs. Program, 1990-94, Wyo. Dept. Health, 1991-93, Pineridge Hosp., Lander, 1986-88; chair employer com. Rocky Mountain Regional Head Injury Ctr., 1991-92; chair Regional Svcs. Providers Wyo., 1990-92; bd. dirs. Riverton Bicentennial Com., 1976, Wyo. Assn. Retarded Citizens, Cheyenne, 1983-86, Nat. Assn. Devel. Disability Couns., Washington, 1980-81, Rocky Mountain Brain Injury Ctr., 1991-97; bd. dirs. CES Found., Inc., 1997—, sec.; pres. Nat. Assn. Persons in Supported Employment Found., 1998; membership chair Wind River coun. Boy Scouts Am. Recipient Regional Dir.'s award Region 8 HEW, 1977; CES named Bus. of Yr., Riverton C. of C., 1998. Mem. Wyo. Assn. Rehab. Facilities (chmn. 1984-85, sec. 1985-87), Fremont County Assn. Retarded Citizens, Lions, Masons (master 1984-85), Hugh de Payne Commandry (comdr. 1985-86), Rotary of Lander (pres.-elect, bd. dirs., Paul Harris fellow). Episcopalian. Avocations: backpacking, fishing, golf, reading, llamas. E-mail: ghudson@tcine.net. Home: 2980 Sinks Canyon Rd Lander WY 82520-9714 Office: Community Entry Svcs 2441 Peck St Riverton WY 82501-2272

HUDSON, HAROLD DON, veterinarian; b. Audrain County, Mo., Nov. 22, 1943; s. Harold F. and Greta Arlene (Boyd) H.; A.A., Hannibal (Mo.) La Grange Coll., 1963; B.S., U. Mo., 1967, D.V.M., 1970; m. Carole Jacqueline Spence, Aug. 30, 1964; children—Dale Brent, Kim Marie. Asso. Clarinda (Iowa) Vet. Clinic, 1970-71, Bethany (Mo.) Vet. Clinic, 1971-72, Vet. Clinic, Mexico, Mo., 1972—. Mem. AVMA, Mo. Vet. Med. Assn., Am. Assn. Bovine Practitioners, Am. Assn. Swine Practitioners. Baptist. Home: 933 Emmons St Mexico MO 65265 Office: 1624 Us Highway 54 E Mexico MO 65265-3536

HUDSON, HAROLD JORDON, JR., retired insurance executive; b. Kansas City, Mo., Mar. 10, 1924; s. Harold Jordan and Fannie (Jenkins) H.; m. Patricia Louise Orr, Oct. 1, 1949. B.S., U. Mo., 1945, LL.B., 1948; grad., Advanced Mgmt. Program, Harvard U., 1968. Bar: Mo. 1948. Practiced in Kansas City, until 1952; atty. Comml. Union Co., Kansas City, 1952-53, Cleve., 1953-56; with Gen. Reins. Corp., N.Y.C., 1956-83; asst. sec. Gen. Reins. Corp., 1958-61, sec., 1961-62, v.p., 1963-68, sr. v.p., 1968-70, pres., 1970-71, 1971-72, chief exec. officer, 1971-83, chmn., 1973-83, also dir.; chmn. Reins. Assn. Am., 1975-76. Mem. Mo. Bar, Phi Delta Phi, Kappa Alpha. Clubs: Brook (N.Y.C.); Indian Harbor Yacht, Greenwich Country (Greenwich, Conn.); Cat Cay Yacht (Bahamas); Card Sound Golf. Office: PO Box 10350 Stamford CT 06904-2350

HUDSON, JACQUELINE, artist; b. Cambridge, Mass.; d. Eric and Gertrude (Dunton) H. Student, Columbia U., Art Students League, Sch. of the Nat. Acad. One-woman shows include Burr Gallery, N.Y.C., Rockport (Mass.) Art Assn., Present Day Club, Princeton, N.J., Maine Art Gallery, Wiscasset, Moulton Union, Bowdoin Coll., 1979; exhibited in group shows at NAD, Pa. Acad. Fine Arts, Libr. of Congress, Cin. Mus., Riverside Mus., Portland (Maine) Mus. Art, Dayton Art Inst., Bixler Mus., Colby Coll., Maine Art Gallery, Wiscasset, Bowdoin Coll., Farnsworth Mus., Rockland, Maine, Vallombreuse Gallery, Palm Beach, Fla., Galerie Salammbo, Paris, others; represented in permanent collection Libr. of Congress, Farnsworth Mus.; pvt. collections. Recipient Pennell Purchase prize Libr. of Congress, 1951; Allen Kander Found. award Rockport Art Assn., 1957, Thelma Karr Graphic prize, 1986; Edith Wengenroth Meml. prize, 1971, 75; Alice Standish Buell Meml. prize Nat. Assn. Women Artists, 1968, Helen Turner Graphic prize, 1974, Donna Miller Meml. prize, 1980, Edith Erlanger Meml. award, 1996, 3rd Graphic prize Butler Inst. Am. Art, 1983. Mem. Art Students League, Nat. Assn. Women Artists (Elizabeth Erlanger Meml. award 1996), Rockport Art Assn. (medal of honor 1989, excellence in graphics prize 1992, Stow Wengenroth Meml. prize excellence in graphics 1999), Monhegan (Maine) Assn. (chmn. mus. com. 1963-67).

HUDSON, JANE DUCLOS, management consultant, writer; b. Great Barrington, Mass., Sept. 23, 1949; d. Edward Warren and Elaine Duclos (Connelly) H.; m. Donald Borod, Nov. 11, 1978; children: James Hudson, Catherine Duclos. BA magna cum laude, Newton Coll. Sacred Heart, 1971; postgrad., Syracuse U., 1971-72; MA, George Washington U., 1975; MALS, Wesleyan U., 1995. Cert. mgmt. cons., 1984. Social sci. analyst Fed. Hwy. Adminstrn., Washington, 1972-73; mgmt. instern GSA, Washington, 1973-74, mgmt. analyst, 1974-75; mgmt. analyst Nat. Archives and Records Svc., Washington, 1976-78; program analyst Nat. Archives and Records Svc., N.Y.C., 1978-80; mgmt. cons. Booz-Allen & Hamilton, N.Y.C., 1980-82, Price Waterhouse, Hartford, Conn., 1984—; ind. mgmt. cons., writer, 1984—; adj. faculty Teikyo Post U., 1998—; ind. mgmt. cons., writer, 1984—. Maxwell fellow Syracuse U., 1971-72, Herbert H. Lehman Fellow, 1971-72. Office: Moving Woods PO Box 270360 Hartford CT 06127-0360

HUDSON, JEFFREY REID, lawyer; b. Santa Monica, Calif., Mar. 15, 1952; s. Caswell Hadden and Donna Rita (Mazzulla) H.; children: Joan Louise, Reid Adams. BA, Claremont McKenna Coll., 1974; JD, Harvard U., 1978. Bar: Calif. 1978. Assoc. Gibson, Dunn & Crutcher, L.A., 1978-85, ptnr., 1986—. Office: Gibson Dunn & Crutcher 333 S Grand Ave Ste 4400 Los Angeles CA 90071-3197*

HUDSON, JERRY CHARLES, communications educator; b. Carthage, Tex., July 1, 1941; s. Thomas Newton and Sybil (Barton) H.; B.S., W. Tex. State U., 1971, M.A., 1972; Ph.D., N. Tex. State U., 1980; m. Sue Carol Fowler, Aug. 30, 1968; children: Aleshia Lin, Jerry Charles II. With various radio and television stas. in Tex. and N.Mex., 1960-72; prof. mass comms. Tex. Tech. U., 1978—; dir. Sch. Mass Comms., 1987-92; dir. grad. studies Sch. Mass Comms., 1993—; media dir. U.S. Dept. Labor, Jecor Votrakon, Riyadh, Saudi Arabia, 1984-85; dir. mass communications Lamar U., Beaumont, Tex., 1972-78; pres. Southwest Edn. Coun. for Journalism and Mass Comms., 1993-94; pres. Tex. Assn. Ednl. Broadcasters, 1975-76. Recipient AMOCO Teaching Excellence award, 1981, Pres's. Excellence Acad. Achievement award, 1995, 10th Dist. Am. Advtg. Educator of the Yr., 1996. Mem. Am. Advtg. Assn., Internat. Academy of Bus., Direct Mktg. Assn., Lubbock Advtg. Fedn. (bd. dirs.), Kappa Tau Alpha (Disting. Faculty award 1980). Republican. Methodist.*

HUDSON, JERRY E., foundation administrator; b. Chattanooga, Mar. 3, 1938; s. Clarence E. and Laura (Campbell) H.; m. Myra Ann Jared, June 11, 1957; children: Judith, Laura, Janet, Angela. B.A., David Lipscomb Coll., 1959; M.A., Tulane U., 1961, Ph.D., 1965; LL.D. (hon.), Pepperdine U., 1983; D of Comm. (hon.), Tokyo Internat. U., 1997; LHD (hon.), U. Portland, 1997, Willamette U., 1997. Systems engr. IBM, Atlanta, 1961; prof. Coll. Arts and Scis., Pepperdine U., 1962-75; provost, dean Coll. Arts and Scis., Malibu Campus, Pepperdine U., 1971-75; pres. Hamline U., St. Paul, 1975-80, Willamette U., Salem, Oreg., 1980-97; exec. v.p. Collins Found., Portland, Oreg., 1997—; dir. Portland Gen. Co., E.I.I.A. Mem. Nat. Assn. Ind. Colls. (bd. dirs.), Phi Alpha Theta. Office: Collins Found 1618 SW 1st Ave Portland OR 97201-5752

HUDSON, JESSE TUCKER, JR., financial executive; b. Roanoke, Va., Sept. 25, 1920; s. Jesse Tucker and Bernice Mable (Ragland) H.; m. Bert Wood, June 10, 1944; children: Greg, David, Amy. BA, U. Va., 1945, postgrad., 1945-46. Staff analyst T. Coleman Andrews & Co., Richmond, Va., 1947-50; sr. staff A.M. Pullen & Co., Richmond, 1950-54; asst. contr. Miller & Rhoads, Inc., Richmond, 1954-60; vice chancellor fin. U. Pitts., 1960-64; v.p. fin. Colonial Stores, Inc., Atlanta, 1964-70; sr. v.p. fin. Mgmt. Sci. Am., Atlanta, 1970-71; sr. v.p., chief fin. officer Southeast Banking Corp., Miami, Fla., 1970-78; fin. v.p. Reynolds Metals Co., Richmond, 1978-83; dir. exec. MBA program U. Richmond, 1983-85; pres., chief exec. officer

Hudson & Hudson, Hudson-Richmond Assocs., 1985—; adj. prof. fin. U. Richmond, 1983-88, Va. Commonwealth U., Richmond, 1990—; bd. dirs. Va. Panel Corp., Waynesboro, Va., Acme Markets of Va., Inc., Tazewell; adv. bd. Ctr. for Advance Studies U. Va., Charlottesville, 1982-88; chmn. profl. devel. Fin. Execs. Inst., N.Y.C., 1981-85. Pres. Young Republican Group, Richmond, 1952-58; alt. del. Rep. Nat. Conv., Phila., 1954. Maj. USAR; ret. Mem. Fin. Execs. Inst., Union League Club (N.Y.C.), Commonwealth Club (Richmond), Rotary (Richmond chpt.). Episcopalian. Avocations: golf, reading. Home: PO Box 716 Urbanna VA 23175-0716

HUDSON, JOEL B., civilian military employee; b. Kenansville, N.C., Sept. 29, 1939; m. Latrelle Rackley; children: Gregg, Cyndi, Christopher. AA, Campbell Coll.; BS, E. Carolina Coll., 1961; M in Personnel Adminstrn., George Washington U., 1969. Tchr. Roseboro (N.C.)-Salemburg H.S., Warwick H.S., Newport News, Va.; mgmt. analyst Office Asst. Chief Staff, Comptroller, Ft. Eustis, Va., 1962, Office Dep. Chief Staff, Comptroller, Ft. Monroe, Va., 1966; chief mgmt. improvement br. Office Dep. Chief Staff, Resource Mgmt., 1973-75; dep. dir. studies and analyses staff Office Adminstrv. Asst. Sec. Army, 1975-78; dir. plans and projects Office Adminstrv. Asst. Sec. Army, Washington, 1978-89, dir. policy and plans/safety, security and support svcs., 1989-95, dep. adminstrv. asst., 1995-96, adminstv. asst., 1996—. With USAR, 1963-69. Office: 105 Army Pentagon Washington DC 20310-0105

HUDSON, JOHN IRVIN, retired career officer; b. Louisville, Oct. 12, 1932; s. Irvin Hudson and Elizabeth (Reid) Hudson Hornbeck; m. Zetta Ann Yates, June 27, 1954; children: Reid Irvin, Lori Ann, John Yates, Clark Ray. BS in Bus. Mgmt., Murray State U., 1971. Commd. 2nd lt. USMC, 1954, advanced through grades to lt. gen., 1987; comdg. officer Marine Fighter Attack Squadron 115, Vietnam, 1968, Marine Corps Air Sta., Yuma, Ariz., 1977-80; asst. wing comdr. 2nd Marine Air Wing, Cherry Point, N.C., 1980-81; comdg. gen. Landing Force Tng. Command/At.4th Marine Amphibious Brigade, Norfolk, Va., 1981-83, 3rd Marine Aircraft Wing, El Toro, Calif., 1985-87, First Marine Amphibious Force, Campen, Calif., 1986-87; dep. chief staff for manpower Hdqrs. USMC, Washington, 1987-89; dir. U.S. Marine Corps Edn. Ctr., Quantico, Va., 1983-85; ret. active duty Hdqrs. USMC, Washington, 1989. Apptd. to Ariz. State Transp. Bd., 1994—, chmn. 1999. Decorated DFC, DSM, Bronze Star, Air medals, Silver Hawk; flew 308 combat missions in Vietnam in F-4 Phantom; inductee Early and Pioneer Naval Aviators' Assn., 1998. Mem. VFW, Golden Eagles, Marine Corps Aviation Assn. (life), Marine Corps Assn., Marine Corps Hist. Soc., Order of Daedalians (life). Avocations: sports; sailing; hunting; fishing. Home: 12439 E Del Rico Yuma AZ 85367-7366

HUDSON, JOHN LESTER, chemical engineering educator; b. Chgo., 1937; s. John Jones and Linda Madeline (Panozzo) H.; m. Janette Glenore Caton, June 29, 1963; children: Ann, Barbara, Sarah. BS, U. Ill., 1959; MS in Engring., Princeton U., 1960; PhD, Northwestern U., 1962. Registered profl. engr., Ill. Asst. prof. chm. engring. U. Ill.-Urbana, 1963-69, assoc. prof., 1969-75; prof., chmn. dept. chem. engring. U. Va., Charlottesville, 1975-85; mem. Ctr Advanced Studies U. Va., 1985-86, prof., 1986-88, Wills Johnson prof., 1988—; mgr. Ill. Div. Air Pollution Control, Springfield, 1974-75; cons. to various industires and govt. agys., 1966—. Contbr. articles to profl. jours. Recipient Humboldt award, 1989; NSF fellow, 1962, Fulbright fellow, 1961-63, 82-83. Mem. AIChE (Wilhelm award 1991), Am. Chem. Soc. Home: 1920 Thomson Rd Charlottesville VA 22903-2419 Office: U Va Dept Chem Engring Thornton Hall Charlottesville VA 22903-2442

HUDSON, JON BARLOW, sculptor; b. Billings, Mont., Dec. 17, 1945; s. Benjamin Rexford and Jean Elizabeth (Barlow) H.; m. Deborah Gay Brush Henderson. BFA, Calif. Inst. Arts, Valencia, 1971, MFA, 1972; BFA, Dayton Art Inst., 1975. Field supr. Ralph M. Parsons-USAID, Dakar, Senegal, 1968-69; grad. tchg. asst. Calif. Inst. Arts, Valencia, 1971-72; supr. equipment fabric Royal Drift Gold Mine, Magalia, Calif., 1972-74; adj. instr. Wright State U., Dayton, 1975, 76-77; asst. prof. Stephens Coll., Columbia, Mo., 1975-76, Antioch U., Yellow Springs, Ohio, 1980; instr., vis. artist Carving Studio, Proctor, Vt., 1987, 88. Sculpture commns. and projects include Boone Nat. Bank, 1976, Pub. Libr. Metro Dade County, Homestead, Fla., 1979, Nat. Radio Astronomy Obs., 1980, Eastern Pacific Corp., Santa Ana, Calif., 1981, Health Care and Retirement Corp., Lima, Ohio, 1981, U. Nebr. Temple Theater, Lincoln, 1982, Case Western Res. U. Putnam Collection, Cleve., 1982, Warner/Lamber Corp., Morris Plains, N.J., 1984, Taylor & Martin Corp., Atlanta, 1984, Mead Corp., Dayton, 1985, Guarantee Trust Corp., Chgo., 1985, Quantum Chem. Corp., Cin., 1986, Ohio Co., Columbus, Ohio, 1986, Fed. Mogul Corp., Lititz, Pa., 1987, World Expo 88, Brisbane, Australia, 1988, Amarillo (Tex.) Internat. Airport, 1988, S & L Data Corp., Cin., 1989, Wittenberg U. Chackers Theater, Springfield, Ohio, 1989, Heart House Clinic, Springfield, Ohio, 1991, Mulia Tower, Jakarta, Indonesia, 1991, Royal Abjar Hotel, Dubai, UAE, 1992, Green County Pub. Libr., Yellow Springs, Ohio, 1992, St. Antonio da Platina, Parana, Brazil, 1992, Dunaferr Sculpture Park, Dunaujvaros, Hungary, 1993, Europos Parkas, Vilniaus, Lithuania, 1994, Benburb Heritage Park, County Armagh, No. Ireland, 1995, Lion & Lamb Peace Arts Ctr., Bluffton (Ohio) Coll., 1997, Lapidea Naturstein, Mayen, Germany, 1997, Med. Coll. Ohio, Toledo, 1998. Recipient Profl. Devel. award Ohio Arts Coun., Lithuania, 1994; Ludwig Vogelstein Fund grantee, 1996; Lusk Meml. fellow Inst. Internat. Edn., 1982-83. Mem. Nat. Sculpture Factory (Cork, Ireland), Sculptor's Soc. Ireland, Internat. Sculptor Ctr., Royal Soc. Brit. Sculptors (internat. assoc.). Office: Hudson Sculpture Ltd PO Box 710 Yellow Springs OH 45387-0710

HUDSON, JULIE DANIELLE, newspaper editor; b. Evergreen Park, Ill., July 10, 1971; d. Ronald Carl Hudson and Barbara Jean (Drakulich) Stell. BA in English, DePaul U., 1993. Asst. publicist Dearborn Fin. Publ., 1993; intern Chgo. Mag., 1993; publicity asst. Dearborn Fin. Publ., 1993-94; editl. asst. Chgo. Tribune, 1994—. Avocations: flamenco dancing, yoga.

HUDSON, KATHERINE MARY, manufacturing company executive; b. Rochester, N.Y., Jan. 19, 1947; d. Edward Klock and Helen Mary (Rubacha) Nellis; m. Robert Orneal Hudson, Sept. 13, 1980; 1 child, Robert Klock. Student, Oberlin coll., 1964-66; BS in Mgmt., Ind. U., 1968; postgrad., Cornell U., 1968-69. Various postitions in fin., investor rels., communications, gen. mgr. instant photography Eastman Kodak Co., Rochester, 1970-87, chief info. officer, 1988-91, v.p., gen. mgr. printing and pub. imaging, 1991-93; pres., CEO W.H. Brady, Milw., 1994—, Brady Corp., Milw., 1999—; bd. dirs. Honeywell and Case Corp. Mem. adv. coun. Ind. U. Sch. Bus., 1994—; trustee Alverno Coll., 1994—; bd. dirs. Med. Coll. Wis., 1995—. Recipient Chief of the Yr. award Info. Week Mag., 1990, Athena award Rochester C. of C., 1992, WESG Breaking Glass Ceiling award, 1993, Sacajewea award, 1995; Lehman fellow N.Y. State, 1968; named Wis. Bus. Leader of Yr., 1995. Republican. Avocations: golf, fishing, creative writing. Office: Brady Corp 6555 W Good Hope Rd PO Box 571 Milwaukee WI 53201-0571*

HUDSON, LAURA LYN WHITAKER, scientific researcher; b. Reno, May 24, 1960; d. Ernest Leo and Carol Suzanne (Kettering) Whitaker; m. Bradley Joe Hudson, Nov. 29, 1996; children from previous marriage: Jackie Kalinowski, Justin Stender, Jason Stender. AA, Scottsdale Community Coll., 1982; HPhD, London Inst. Applied Rsch., 1994. Habilitation technician Gomper's Rehab. Ctr. and Ariz. Tng. Program, Phoenix, 1979-82; sec., bookkeeper CEW Sound Recordings, Phoenix, 1979-82; sec. Electronic Test Ctr., Groton, Mass., 1984; exec. v.p., dir. sci. rsch., devel. and investment Children United to Save the Planet, Phoenix, 1991-94; exec. v.p. Arachne's Web, Phoenix, 1994—. Mem. Mentally Ill Kids In Distress, Phoenix, 1990, Lithium Alliance, Phoenix, 1992, Nat. Alliance for Mentally Ill, Phoenix, 1992, Smithsonian Inst., 1992. Named Internat. Woman of Yr., Internat. Biog. Ctr., England, 1991-92, Woman of Yr., Am. Biog. Inst., 1992; recipient Silver Shield of Honor, 1992. Mem. NAFE (assoc.), World Found. Successful Women (assoc.), Women's Inner Circle of Achievement, Lifetime Achievement Acad., Am. Biog. Inst. Rsch. Assn. (assoc. and advisor). Avocations: writing on uses and limitations of herbal medicines, animal dissection, North Am. Indian art and craft work. Home: PO Box 30931 Phoenix AZ 85046-0931

HUDSON, LEONARD DEAN, physician; b. Everett, Wash., May 7, 1938; s. Marshall W. and Blanche V. (Morgan) H.; children: Sean Marshall, Sherry Elizabeth, Kevin Arthur. BS, Wash. State U., Pullman, 1960; MD, U. Wash., Seattle, 1964. Diplomate: Am. Bd. Internal Medicine (pulmonary disease). Intern Bellevue Hosp. Ctr., N.Y.C., 1964-65; resident in internal medicine N.Y. Hosp., 1965-66, U. Wash. Hosps., 1968-69; chief resident Harborview Med. Ctr., Seattle; also instr. U. Wash. Med. Sch., 1967-70; Am. Thoracic Soc. fellow in pulmonary diseases U. Colo. Med. Ctr., 1970-71, instr., then asst. prof. medicine, 1971-73; mem. faculty U. Wash. Med. Ctr., 1973—, assoc. prof. medicine, 1976-82, prof., 1982—, head pulmonary critical care medicine divsn., 1985—; chief pulmonary critical care medicine divsn., med. dir. MICU, Harborview Med. Ctr., 1976-86; chmn. Tb adv. com. Wash. Dept. Social and Health Svcs. Author papers, revs. in field. With USPHS, 1966-68. Named Outstanding Resident, Harborview Med. Ctr. Fellow ACP, Am. Coll. Chest Physicians (state gov. 1980-87); mem. Am. Fedn. Clin. Rsch., Am. Thoracic Soc. (sec.-treas. 1983-84, v.p. 1993-94, pres.-elect 1994-95, pres. 1995-96), Western Soc. Clin. Rsch., Assn. Am. Physicians, Wash. Lung. Assn. (dir., Vol. Hall of Fame 1977), Wash. Thoracic Soc., Seattle Flounders Soc., Phi Beta Kappa. Democrat. Office: Harborview Med Ctr Mailbox 359762 325 9th Ave Seattle WA 98104-2420

HUDSON, LINDA, health care executive; b. Tuscaloosa, Ala., Feb. 12, 1950; d. Elvin and Clara (Duke) Hudson; m. Charles Garrett Kimbrough, May 26, 1984. BS in Edn., U. Ala., 1971; MS in Psychology, U. So. Miss., 1984. Lic. profl. counselor. Recreational therapist West Ala. Rehab. Ctr., Tuscaloosa, 1971-72; flight attendant Delta Air Lines, Miami and New Orleans, 1972-80; pvt. practice psychotherapist Hattiesburg (Miss.) and Atlanta, 1984—; program dir. Eating Disorders Adventist Health System/Wedst, Atlanta, 1985-88, regional dir./cons., 1986-87, exec. dir. mental health svcs., 1988-89; owner Hudson Cons. Assocs., 1989—, nat. cons., 1986—. Contbr. articles to profl. jours. Mem. Covington Jr. Svc. League, La., 1981-83; co-chmn. St. Tammany Rep. Polit. Action Com., 1980-81; coord. United Way of St. Tammany Parish, 1979-80. Mem. Am. Assn. Mental Health Counselors, Ga. Mental Health Counselors Assn., Nat. Coun. Sexual Addiction and Compulsivity (bd. dirs., pres.). Democrat. Avocations: interior design, antiques, swimming. Office: Ste 238 1090 Northchase Pkwy Marietta GA 30067-6402

HUDSON, MANLEY O., JR., lawyer; b. Boston, June 25, 1932; s. Manley O. and Janet (Aldrich) H.; m. Olivia d'Ormesson, July 1, 1971; children: Nicholas Aldrich, Antonia Maria. A.B., Harvard U., 1953, LL.B., 1956. Bar: N.Y. 1964. Law clk. Justice Stanley Reed, U.S. Supreme Ct., Washington, 1956-57; assoc. Cleary, Gottlieb, Steen & Hamilton, 1958-68; ptnr. Cleary, Gottlieb, Steen & Hamilton, N.Y.C., London, Paris, 1968-83, London, 1983—. Contbr. articles to profl. jours. Mem. ABA, Assn. of Bar of City of N.Y., Am. Soc. Internat. Law, Coun. Fgn. Rels., Century Assn. Office: City Place House, 55 Basinghall St, London EC2V 5EH, England

HUDSON, MARK WOODBRIDGE, lawyer; b. Pasadena, Calif., May 14, 1940; s. Victor Stuart and Mary Charlotte (Woodbridge) H.; m. Marsha Fae Alderson, Dec. 20, 1969; children: Peter, Ashley, Holly. BA, U. Calif., Berkeley, 1961; JD, U. Calif., San Francisco, 1967. Bar: Calif., 1968, U.S. Dist. Ct. 1968, U.S. Ct. Appeals (9th cir.) 1968. Atty. Dunn, Hart & McDonald, San Francisco, 1968-73; assoc. Sedgwick, Detert, Moran & Arnold, San Francisco, 1973-78, of counsel, 1979—. 1st lt. U.S. Army, 1961-63. Mem. Calif. Bar Assn., Assn. Def. Counsel, San Francisco Bar Assn. Democrat. Home: 15 Robertson Ter Mill Valley CA 94941-3358 Office: Sedgwick Detert Moran & Arnold 1 Embarcadero Ctr Ste 1600 San Francisco CA 94111-3716*

HUDSON, MCKINLEY, retired army officer, zoo deputy director; b. Cin., May 13, 1941. BS, Ctrl. State U., Wilberforce, Ohio, 1963; MS, So. Ill. U., 1974; MA, Naval War Coll., Newport, R.I., 1986. Commd. 2d lt. U.S. Army, 1963, advanced through grades to col., 1985, retired, 1993, commdr. 548th composite support battalion, 1983-85; commdr. 80th area support group U.S. Army, Chevres, Belgium, 1986-88; chief of staff mil. traffic mgmt. command U.S. Army, Oakland, Calif., 1988-93; dep. dir. Nat. Zoological Park Smithsonian Instn., Washington, 1994—. Decorated Legion of Merit, Bronze Star with Oak Leaf cluster. Mem. Assn. U.S. Army, Assn. Am. Zoos and Aquariums, U.S. Army Transp. Corps. Regiment (Disting. Mem. Regiment 1993), Nat. Defense Transp. Assn. (Nat. award for disting. svc. 1992), Kappa Alpha Psi. Office: Nat Zoological Park 3001 Connecticut Ave NW Washington DC 20008-2537

HUDSON, MICHAEL CRAIG, political science educator; b. New Haven, Conn., June 2, 1938; s. Robert Bowman and Joan (Loram) H.; m. Vera George Wahbe, June 16, 1963; children: Leila Olga, Aida Joan. BA with honors, Swarthmore Coll., 1959; MA, Yale U., 1960, PhD, 1964; Cert. in Arabic, Princeton U., 1961. History tchr. Am. Community Sch., Beirut, Lebanon, 1962-63; instr. Swarthmore (Pa.) Coll., 1963-64; asst. prof. Bklyn. Coll., CUNY, N.Y.C., 1964-70; assoc. prof. Johns Hopkins U., Sch. Advanced Internat. Studies, Washington, 1970-75; assoc. to prof. Georgetown U., Washington, 1975—; dir. Georgetown U. Ctr. for Contemporary Arab Studies, Washington, 1976-89; Seif Ghobash prof. of Arab studies Georgetown U., Washington, 1980—; bd. dirs. Nat. Council on U.S./Arab Rels., Washington; cons., lectr. U.S. State Dept., U.S. Info. Agy.; commentator on Middle Ea. affairs to U.S. and internat. news media; lectr. at univs. in Mid. East, Europe, Japan, China, Australia. Mem. editorial bd. Internat. Jour. of Middle East Studies, 1980-86, Cambridge U. Press Mid. East Studies, 1989-98; author: The Precarious Republic (Lebanon), 1968, Arab Politics: The Search for Legitimacy, 1977; co-author: World Handbook of Political and Social Indicators, 1972; editor: The Palestinians: New Directions, 1990, Middle East Dilemma: The Politics and Economics of Arab Integration, 1999; contbr. numerous articles to jours. in field. Trustee René Moawad Found., Lebanon. Robert R. McCormick fellow Yale U., 1959-63, fellow Ford Found., 1970-71, Guggenheim fellow, 1975-76, Fulbright fellow, 1994; grantee Am. Philos. Soc., 1965, 68. Fellow Middle East Studies Assn. of N.Am. (pres. 1987); mem. The Middle East Inst., Am. Polit. Sci. Assn., Internat. Studies Assn., Coun. on Fgn. Rels., Am. Inst. Yemeni Studies. Avocations: drawing, painting, book collecting, swimming, running. Office: Georgetown U Ctr for Contemporary Arab Studies 251 Intercultural Ctr Washington DC 20057-1020

HUDSON, MILES, special education educator; b. Brewer, Maine, Aug. 22, 1940; s. Fredrick and Elsie (Bailey) H. BS, U. Maine, Farmington, 1963. Cert. spl. edn. tchr., Maine. Head tchr. for autistic and psychotic children Devereaux Found., Rutland, Mass.; vocat. instr. Bangor (Maine) Mental Health Inst.; program dir. Agape House, Ellsworth, Maine.; spl. edn. tchr. Town of Jonesport (Maine) Schs.; ret., 1992; mem. Countywide Regional Tchr. Support Com. Author: Survey of Special Education Classes in Maine, 1963. Home: PO Box 101 Lubec ME 04652-0101

HUDSON, PAUL STEPHEN, lawyer, realty company executive, consultant; b. N.Y.C., June 25, 1947; s. William Birchill and Maybelle (Schleicher) H.; m. Eleanor J. Rossi, June 6, 1970; children: Stephen, Melina (dec.), Paul, David. BS, U. Mich., 1968; JD, Cleve. State U., 1974. Bar: Ohio 1974, N.Y. 1976. Systems analyst Chase Brass & Copper Co., Cleve., 1969-71; investigator Ohio Civil Rights Commn., Cleve., 1971-73; legal intern Cleve. Legal Aid Soc., 1973; staff atty. N.Y. Pub. Interest Rsch. Group, Inc., Albany, 1974-77; legis. counsel Pub. Utility Law Project, Albany, 1977; counsel N.Y. State Crime Victims Bd., Albany and N.Y.C., 1977-87; cons. ABA, Washington, 1982-83, Nat. Inst. Justice, Hindelans Criminal Justice Ctr., 1987; pres. Kent & Haroldsen Assocs., Inc., 1981-95; pvt. practice, Albany, N.Y. and N.Y.C., 1992—, cons.; spl. to dep. min. leader N.Y. State Senate, 1994; exec. dir. Aviation Consumer Action Project, Washington, 1997—. Contbr. articles to profl. jours. Co-chmn., co-founder Ohio Pub. Interest Rsch. Group, Cleve., 1974; exec. dir. N.Y. Student Voter Registration Drive, Albany and N.Y.C., 1976; pres. Citizens Protecting the Environment, Schenectady, 1979-80; chmn. Victims of Pan Am Flight 103, 1989; pres. Families of Pan Am 103-Lockerbie, 1989-92; mem. FAA Aviation Adv. Rule Making and Security Com., 1991—, adv. com., 1997—. Mem. ABA (crime victims com. 1984-94), Nat. Orgn. of Victims Assistance (chmn. litigation com. 1983-84). Democrat. Presbyterian. also: 90 State St Albany NY 12207 also: PO Box 202 Glen Echo MD 20812

HUDSON, RALPH P., physicist; b. Wellingborough, Eng., Oct. 14, 1924; came to U.S., 1949, naturalized, 1960.; s. Harold and Ada (Jenkinson) H.; m. Nancy Brisby, July 9, 1947; children: Geoffrey R., Wendy E. BA, Merton Coll., Oxford U., 1944; MA, Oxford U., 1949, PhD, 1949. Sci. officer U.K. Ministry Supply, Birmingham, Eng., Montreal, Que. and Chalk River, Ont., Can., 1944-46; vis. lectr. Purdue U., 1949-50, asst. prof., 1950-51; with Nat. Bur. Standards, Washington, 1951-80; chief cryogenic physics sect. Nat. Bur. Standards, 1954-61, chief heat div., 1961-78; dep. dir. Center for Absolute Phys. Quantities, 1978-80; dir. publs. Internat. Bur. Weights and Measures, Sèvres, France, 1980-89; program dir. low temperature physics NSF, Washington, 1989-92; cons. in field, 1993—; guest worker fundamental constants data ctr. Nat. Inst. Stds. & Tech., 1998—. Editor: Metrologia, 1980-89, editl. cons., 1995—. Mem. U.K. Home Guard, 1941-43, U.K. Atomic Energy Program, 1944-46. Recipient Silver and Gold medals Dept. Commerce, 1957; Samuel Wesley Stratton award Nat. Bur. Standards, 1964; Edward U. Condon award, 1976; Guggenheim fellow, 1960-61. Fellow Am. Phys. Soc., Franklin Inst. (John Price Wetherill medal 1962); mem. Philos. Soc. Washington (pres. 1974-75). Club: Cosmos (Washington). Spl. rsch. on behavior of matter near absolute zero temperature. Home: 5500 Uppingham St Chevy Chase MD 20815-5508

HUDSON, RICHARD LLOYD, retired educator, clergyman; b. Watertown, N.Y., Dec. 1, 1920; s. Milo Alfred and Marion (Davidson) H.; m. Beatrice Evalin Olson, Apr. 23, 1955; children: Margery Elise, Pamela Kristine. AB, Syracuse U., 1944, PhD, 1970; BD, Yale U., 1947, STM, 1950. Ordained to ministry United Meth. Ch., 1947;. Asst. minister Rome (N.Y.) Meth. Ch., 1946-48, Meth. Ch., Parish, N.Y., 1950-54; commentator Religion Makes News, Sta. WSYR, Syracuse, N.Y.; dir. pub. rels. Syracuse Area United Meth. Ch., 1954-56; minister Meth. Ch., Carthage, N.Y., 1956-58; Cokesbury fellow, grad. asst. Syracuse U., 1958-61; mem. faculty Wyoming Sem., Kingston, Pa., 1961-64; mem. faculty New Eng. Coll., Henniker, N.H., 1964-83, prof., 1971-83, prof. emeritus, 1983—; adj. prof. history Post Coll., Waterbury, Conn., 1985-91, Quinnipiac Coll., Hamden, Conn., 1987-97. Author: A Burden for Souls, 1950, A Student's Guide to the New Testament, 1963, The Challenge of Dissent, 1970; editor: The Only Henniker on Earth, 1980. Chmn. Henniker Hist. Dist. Commn., 1976-83; docent Canterbury Shaker Village, 1975-83, New Haven Colony Hist. Soc., 1984-93, bd. dirs. 1988-90. Mem. North Haven Mayflower Soc. (hon. mem.), Theta Chi Beta, Tau Theta Upsilon, Tabard. Home and Office: 44 Cloudland Rd North Haven CT 06473-4006

HUDSON, RICHARD MCLAIN, JR., journalist, researcher; b. L.A., June 18, 1925; s. Richard McLain Hudson and Helen Theodora Grant; m. Helen Aurora Lundstrom, Dec. 6, 1958; children: Lucinda, Anne. BS, U. Minn., 1946. Teaching asst. econs. U. So. Calif., L.A., 1946-47; editor Monrovia (Calif.) Daily News-Post, 1948-50, Pasadena (Calif.) Star-News, 1950-52, Stars & Stripes, Darmstadt, Germany, 1953-54, Picture News, N.Y.C., 1955-57; mng. editor Caracas (Venezuela) Daily Jour., 1958-60; founding editor War/Peace Report, N.Y.C., 1960-77, Global Report, N.Y.C., 1977—; exec. dir. Ctr. for War/Peace Studies, N.Y.C., 1960—; host weekly TV series Global Forum, Peace Through the UN, 1986-87; prin. arch. Binding Triad Sys. Global Decision-Making. Author: (with Ben Shahn) Kuboyama and the Saga of the Lucky Dragon, 1965. Mem. Dem. County Com., N.Y., 1980-92. Ensign, USN, 1944-46. Mem. UN Corrs. Assn., World Federalist Assn. (bd. dirs. 1980—). Avocations: fishing, photography, tennis, biking. E-mail: hudson@cwps.org. Home: 150 W 80th St New York NY 10024-6310 Office: Ctr for War/Peace Studies 180 W 80th St # 211 New York NY 10024-6301

HUDSON, ROBERT FRANKLIN, JR., lawyer; b. Miami, Fla., Sept. 20, 1946; s. Robert Franklin and Jane Ann (Reed) H.; m. Edith Mueller, June 19, 1971; children: Daniel Warren, Patrick Alexander. BSBA in Econs., U. Fla., 1968, JD, 1971; summer cert., U. London, 1970; LLM in Taxation, NYU, 1972. Bar: Fla. 1971, N.Y. 1975. Law clk. to judge Don N. Laramore U.S. Ct. Claims, Washington, 1972-73; assoc. Wender, Murase & White, N.Y.C., 1973-77; ptnr. Arky, Freed, Stearns et al, Miami, 1977-86; ptnr. Baker & McKenzie, Miami, 1986—, mem. policy com., 1990-93, mem. client credit com., 1992—, mng. ptnr. Miami office, 1996-98; mem. adv. bd. Tax Mgmt., Inc., Washington, 1986—, Fgn. Investment N.Am., London, 1990-96; legal counsel to her majesty's Britanic Counsel, Miami. Author: Federal Taxation of Foreign Investment in U.S. Real Estate, 1986; contbr. articles to legal publs. Bd. dirs. Fla. Philharmonic, 1996-97, Performing Arts Ctr. Found., 1994—, Concert Assn. Fla., 1992—, exec. com., 1993-98, vice chmn., 1994-98. Mem. ABA, Fla. Bar Assn. (chmn. tax sect. 1989-90, Outstanding Spkr. 1995), Internat. Fiscal Assn. (v.p. S.E. region U.S. br. 1985-92, exec. coun. 1987—), Inter-Am. Bar Assn., Internat. Bar Assn., Internat. Tax Planning Assn., Coll. Tax Lawyers, World Trade Ctr. (bd. dirs. 1992-94), S.E./U.S. Japan Assn., Japan Soc. South Fla. (chmn. pub. affairs com. 1991-93, bd. dirs. 1993—, treas. 1995-96, pres. 1996-99. Democrat. Methodist. Avocations: skiing, boating, photography, travel, hiking. Office: Baker & McKenzie 1200 Brickell Ave Ste 1900 Miami FL 33131-3257

HUDSON, ROBERT PAUL, medical educator; b. Kansas City, Kans., Feb. 23, 1926; s. Chester Lloyd and Jean (Emerson) H.; m. Olive Jean Grimes, Aug. 1, 1948 (div. 1963); children: Robert E., Donald K., Timothy M.; m. Martha Isabelle Holter, July 10, 1965; children: Stephen, Laura. BA, U. Kans., 1949, MD, 1952; MA, Johns Hopkins U., 1966. Instr. U. Kans., Kansas City, 1958-59, assoc. in medicine, 1959-63, asst. prof., 1964-69, assoc. prof., 1969—, prof., chmn. history of medicine, 1969-95, ret. Author: Disease and Its Control, 1983; mem. editl. bd. Bull. History of Meidcine, Balt., 1981-94; contbr. articles to profl. jours. 1st lt. U.S. Army, 1953-55. Master ACP; mem. Am. Assn. for History of Medicine (pres. 1984-86), Am. Osler Soc. (bd. govs., pres. 1987-88). Home: 12925 S Frontier Rd Olathe KS 66061-9676 Office: Kans U Med Ctr 39th and Rainbow Blvd Kansas City KS 66160

HUDSON, RONALD MORGAN, aviation planner; b. Anniston, Ala., May 7, 1954; s. James Alphus and Mildred Christine (Morgan) H.; m. Marsha Carol Smith, Dec. 27, 1974 (div. Aug. 1989); children: Jereme Brandon, Sara Elizabeth; m. Connie M. Luckey, Nov. 13, 1993. BS in Aviation Mgmt., Auburn U., 1976. Aviation planner Wainwright Engring. Co., Montgomery, Ala., 1978-81, Ralph Burke Assocs., Park Ridge, Ill., 1981-85; sr. assoc. mgr. aviation Knight Architects, Engrs., Planners, Inc., Chgo., 1985-96; sr. assoc. and aviation mgr. Hanson Engrs. Inc., Oak Brook, Ill., 1996—. Mem. Am. Planning Assn., Am. Inst. Cert. Planners, Am. Assn. Airport Execs., Ill. Pub. Airports Assn. Avocations: biking, travel. Home: 1710 E Oakton St Arlington Heights IL 60004-5000

HUDSON, ROY DAVAGE, retired pharmaceutical company executive; b. Chattanooga, June 30, 1930; s. Roy and Everence (Wilkerson) H.; m. Constance Joan Taylor, Aug. 31, 1956; children: Hollye Lynne, David Kendall. BS, Livingstone Coll., 1955; MS, U. Mich., 1957, PhD, 1962; MA, Brown U., 1968; LL.D., Lehigh U., 1974, Princeton, 1975. Prof. pharmacology U. Mich. Sch. Medicine, 1961-66; prof. med. sci. Brown U. Sch. Medicine, 1966-70, assoc. dean grad. sch., 1966-69; pres. Hampton U., 1970-76; dir. rsch. planning and coordination Parke, Davis Pharm. Co., Ann Arbor, Mich., 1976; v.p. rsch. planning Warner Lambert/Parke-Davis Pharm. Rsch. Divsn., Ann Arbor, 1977-79; mgr. sci. liaison Upjohn Co., Kalamazoo, Mich., 1979-81; mgr. CNS diseases rsch. Upjohn Co., 1981, dir. CNS diseases rsch., 1985-87; v.p. pharm. rsch. divsn. Europe Upjohn Co., Brussels, 1987-90; corp. v.p. pub. rels. Upjohn Co., Kalamazoo, 1990-92, ret., 1992; adj. prof. Black Americana studies Western Mich. U., Kalamazoo, 1993; interim exec. dir., CEO Guidance Clinic, Kalamazoo, 1993; interim pres. Livingstone Coll., Salisbury, N.C., 1995-96; dir. Parke-Davis & Co., United Va. Bank-Citizens and Marine, United Va. Bankshares, Comerica Bank-Mich., Chesapeake and Potomac Telephone Co. of Va. Contbr. articles to profl. jours., chpts. to books. Mem. screening com. Danforth Grad. Fellowships, 1962—; mem. adv. council Danforth Grad. Fellows program Danforth Found., 1972—; chmn. Va. Com. on Selection Rhodes Scholars, 1973; mem. Commn. on Fed. Relations, Am. Council on Edn., 1972—, bd. dirs., 1973—; mem. adv. council to dir. NIH, 1974—; Mem. R.I. Commn. Econ. Devel., 1967-69, R.I. Urban League scholarship com., 1966-70; mem. inst. policy commn. So. Regional Edn. Bd.; bd. dirs. Afro-Am. Soc. Conn. Coll., Kalamazoo Area Math and Sci. Ctr., Kalamazoo Area Academic Achievement Program, ARC; bd. dirs., v.p. Nat. Assn. Equal Opportunity in Higher Edn.; trustee Brown U., Livingstone Coll., Peninsula United Community Services, Spelman Coll. Served with USAF, 1948-52. Recipient Disting. Alumni award Livingstone Coll.; Outstanding Civilian Service award U.S. Army.; Danforth Grad. fellow, 1955-61. Mem. Am. Soc.

Pharmacology and Exptl. Therapeutics, Peninsula C. of C., NAACP (life, 1st v.p., Golden Heritage), AAAS, N.Y. Acad. Scis., Sigma Xi, Phi Kappa Phi, Phi Sigma, Beta Kappa Chi, Kappa Delta Pi, Omega Psi Phi, Gamma Alpha, Alpha Kappa Mu. Home: 7057 Oak Highlands Dr Kalamazoo MI 49009-7508

HUDSON, SAMUEL CAMPBELL, JR., art educator, artist, sculptor; b. Richmond, Va., Aug. 25, 1939; s. Samuel Campbell Sr. and Kizzie Moss (Barker) H.; m. Susan Holley Hudson (dec. 1966); children: Samuel Campbell III, Kimberly Ann; m. Sara Caroline Magers, Aug. 16, 1973. AA, Richmond Profl. Inst., 1963; BFA, Va. Commonwealth U., 1973; MFA, U. N.C., 1975. Art instr. U. N.C., Greensboro, 1973-74, Guilford Tech. C.C., Jamestown, N.C., 1974-76; asst. prof. art Nazareth Coll. Rochester (N.Y.), 1978-83; prof. art, dean student affairs Studio Sch. Visual Rsch., Rochester, 1983-87; asst. prof. art, dir. O'Connor Gallery Rosary Coll., River Forest, Ill., 1988-98; vis. artist Davidson C.C., Lexington, N.C., summer 1976; vis. prof. design U. Miss., University, 1976-77; dir. A.W. Mitchell & Co., Inc., Fredericksburg, Va., 1990-99; editl. adviser Collegiate Press, Alta Loma, Calif., 1991-93; cons. Greensboro Artists' League, 1985-87; art dir. Capital Ideas, Inc., Richmond, Va., 1963-66; judge 14th Annual Keuka Lake Art Show, Hanndsport, N.Y., 1980, 1st Annual Poster Competition N.Y. Assn. Retarded Children, Rochester, 1980, The Oak Park (Ill.) Art League Fall Festival '89 Exhibit; juror Annual Nazareth Coll. Art Student Competition and Exhbn., Rochester, N.Y., 1979, 80, 81, 82, 83; judge, juror Greensboro (N.C.) Artists' League's 13th Annual Nat. Painting, Drawing, and Sculpture Competition, 1982, Annual Rosary Coll. Fine Arts Club Competition and Exhbn., River Forest, Ill., 1991, 92, 93; cons. visual studies Cons. Assocs., Chgo., 1997—. One man exhbns. include Little Gallery, Rochester, 1982, Studio Gallery Ctr. Creative Arts, Greenboro, N.C., 1986, O'Connor Gallery, River Forest, Ill., 1989, others; group exhbns. include The 21st Nat. Art on Paper, 1984 (award 1985), The Marietta 11th Nat., 1977 (award 1978), Nat. On-Paper Show '82, 1982 (award 1982), Salmagundi Annual Summer Show, N.Y.C., 1982, 83, 84, 85, The 50th Anniversary of U. N.C.-Greensboro, 1986, Wehterholt Galleries, Washington, 1991, 92, 93, River Forest (Ill.) Pub. Lib. Gallery, 1993, others. Gallery asst. Civic Arts Coun. Kid Art, Oak Park, Ill., 1993; curator, judge Fra Angelico Art Found., River Forest, 1992; judge, juror Midwest Assn. Religious Talent, Milw., 1992. Grantee W.T.D. Pumphery Found., 1983-85. Mem. Coll. Art Assn. Am., Nat. Trust for Hist. Preservation, Kappa Pi. Democrat. Avocations: in-line skating, weight-training, furniture design. Home: 149 W Park Dr Lombard IL 60148-3320

HUDSON, STANTON HAROLD, JR., public relations executive, educator; b. Syracuse, N.Y., Jan. 28, 1951; s. Stanton Harold Sr. and Lucille (Shea) H. *Mother, Lucille, the first in her family to receive a college degree (B.S., Syracuse University), instilled in her children a deep appreciation for a college education. Sister, Cynthia Staten, is a vice principal of the Inverness Middle School, in Inverness, Florida. Brother-in-law, Edward Staten, is principal of Citrus High School. Sister, Deborah Hudson, is a teacher of the developmentally disabled and a curriculum specialist. Niece, Mary Elizabeth Staten, is a sophomore at Florida State University. Niece, Jennifer, is a sophomore at Citrus High School and nephew, Charles Edward, is in the 8th grade at Inverness Middle School. Stanton and his two sisters attended Canisius College in Buffalo, New York.* Cert. lang. and history, L'Univ. de Caen, France, 1970; BA in History/Polit. Sci., Canisius Coll., 1972; postgrad., SUNY Sch. of Law, Buffalo, 1974-76, Syracuse U., 1995-98. Legis. asst., asst. pub. rels. dir. Erie County Rep. Com., Buffalo, 1971-73; dir. pub. rels. and fin. Greater Niagara Frontier Coun. Boy Scouts Am., Buffalo, 1977-79; dir. pub. rels. Ellis Singer & Webb Advt., Buffalo, 1979-80; asst. v.p., mgr. mktg. communications M&T Bank, Buffalo, 1980-85; exec. dir. Shea's Ctr. for the Performing Arts, Buffalo, 1986; pres. Hudson Mktg. Communications, Buffalo, 1987-88; sr. dir. advt. and pub. rels. Blue Cross of Western N.Y., Inc., Buffalo, 1988-91; prin. Fredrickson & Hudson Assocs., Buffalo, 1991-92, Hudson & Assocs. Pub. Rels., Buffalo, 1992—; adj. prof. SUNY, Buffalo, 1987-93; asst. prof. Canisius Coll., 1993—, dir. grad. program Orgnl. Comm. & Devel., 1995—. *Mr. Hudson has nearly 25 years of progressively responsible experience in the public relations field. He has been recognized as a strategic, innovative thinker, attaching a high priority to measurable results. He has a broad range of experience as a liaison between organizations and their publics and deals effectively with the complexities of organizational relationships, both internally and externally. As a volunteer, he donates his time and talent to demonstrate the value, role and scope of public relations to numerous civic organizations and cultural institutions. Always willing to roll up his shirt sleeves to work as well as to advise, he brings passion, insight and creativity to his many volunteer efforts.* Editor employee newsletter M&T Bank Observer, 1981, 82 (Project PICA Grand award United Way of Buffalo and Erie County); mng. editor employee newsletter Blue Cross Ink, 1991 (Excalibur award Pub. Rels. Soc. Am. 1990, 91, 94, 95, 97). Bd. mem. and mem. mktg. com. Am. Lung Assn., Western N.Y., Buffalo, 1983—; bd. dirs. Am. Lung Assn., N.Y. State, Albany, 1987—, exec. com. 1992—, v.p., 1995, 96-97, pres., 1998—, chmn. ann. meeting com., 1994, chair N.Y. state coalition on smoking and health, 1995-96, vice chair mktg. and comms. com., tobacco control steering com., task force on mktg., 1996—, mem. revenue generation com., 1998-99, nat. customer svc. team mem., 1998-99, mem. coun., 1999—; chmn. pub. rels. and mktg. coms. Greater Buffalo chpt. ARC, 1989-92, bd. dirs., 1991-92; bd. dirs. ARC Blood Svcs., N.Y.-Pa. Region, 1993—; bd. dirs., exec. com. Greater Buffalo Opera Co., 1991-93; trustee, mem. mktg. com. Theodore Roosevelt Inaugural Nat. Hist. Site Found., 1994—, chair 2001 centennial celebration com.; bd. dirs., co-chair mktg. com. Buffalo Coun. on World Affairs, 1994—; mem. Success By 6 awareness com. Buffalo and Erie County United Way, 1997—, mem. Leadership Coun., 1997—; mem. County Cultural Resources Adv. Bd., Erie County, 1999—. Recipient Francis V. Hanavan Meml. award for volunteer svc. Am. Lung Assn. W. N.Y., 1997, Gold Quill award Internat. Assn. of Bus. Communicators, 1984. Mem. Pub. Rels. Soc. Am. (accredited pub. rels. practitioner, counselors acad. educators sect., pres. Buffalo/Niagara chpt. 1990-91, treas. 1994-96, nat. assembly del. 1997—, treas. N.E. dist. 1992, chair-elect N.E. dist. 1993, chair 1994, nat. continuing edn. bd., 1993-95, nat. nominating com. 1995, nat. profl. advisor Pub. Rels. Student Soc. Am. 1996—, nat. women in pub. rels. com. 1996-98, nat. commn. pub. rels. edn. 1997—, Practitioner of the Yr. Buffalo/Niagara chpt. 1993, Excalibur award 1993, 94, 95, 97, universal accreditation bd. 1998—, Nat. Paul M. Lund Pub. Svc. award 1997, Nat. Conf. for Cmty. and Justice Brotherhood/Sisterhood award 1999), Am. Mktg. Assn. (v.p. comms. Buffalo/Niagara chpt. 1991-92), Western N.Y. Comms. Steering Com. (chair 1991-92), Coordinated Care Mgmt. Corp. (mktg. com. 1994-98), Rotary (past dir.). Avocations: theater, jazz, reading, cross-country skiing, travel. Home: 839 Auburn Ave Buffalo NY 14222-1418 Office: Hudson & Assocs Pub Rels One Franklin Pk N Buffalo NY 14202-1111

HUDSON, TAJQUAH JAYE, managed health care executive; b. Paris, Tex., Oct. 16, 1959; d. Bob and Ramona (Pollan) Dennison. BS, E. Cen. Okla. State U., 1981; MS in Health, Wichita State U., 1987; cert. managed care exec. program, U. Mo., 1997. Diplomate Am. Coll. Health Care Execs. Program coord. Valley View Hosp., Ada, Okla., 1982-85; mgr. regional mktg., communications EQUICOR-Equitable HCA Corp., Wichita, Kans., 1986-89; regional adminstr. Aetna Health Plans, Overland Park, Kans., 1989-92; chief bus. and strategic devel. officer U. Kans. Med. Ctr., Kansas City, 1992—; speaker in field. Home: 10550 Noland Rd Overland Park KS 66215-4311

HUDSON, W. GAIL, social worker; b. Waxahachie, Tex., Apr. 15, 1953; d. Billy M. and Sarah W. (Bowen) H.; m. Garry H. Gillan, Sept. 7, 1991; 1 child, Logan Thomas Gillan. BS, S.W. Tex. State U., 1975, MA, 1976; PhD, So. Ill. U., 1979; MSW, U. Tex., Arlington, 1989. Lic. master social worker, advanced clin. practitioner. Asst., assoc. prof. Millikin U., Decatur, Ill., 1978-87; dept. chair communications Millikin U., Decatur, 1984-87; adj. faculty U. Tex., Arlington, 1987-89; social work fellow M.D. Anderson Hosp., Houston, 1988; social work intern U. Houston Counseling, 1989; social worker U. Houston Counseling & Testing, 1989-92, dir. employee assistance program, 1992—; rep. AIDS Consortium of Tex., 1991; tng. cons. Caterpillar Tractor Co., Decatur, 1979-81; planning com. Nat. Conf. Against Sexual Assault, 1994; cons. Profl. Devel. Program, Decatur, 1979-81; adj. grad. faculty dept. counseling psychology U. Houston, 1991—. Cons. Houston Area Planning Commn. for Substance Abuse Program, 1990-91; treas. ERA Decatur, 1978-82; vol. Coalition Against Domestic Violence, Decatur, 1979-81. Cons. Houston Area Planning Commn. for Substance Abuse Program, 1990-91; prin. investigator/dir. prevention of substance abuse. U. Houston and Higher Edn. Consortium, Houston/Galveston, 1991-94. Grantee U.S. Dept. Edn. Mem. NASW, NOW, Am. Coll. Personnel Assn. (bd. dirs. 1991, 94), Am. Assn. Counseling and Devel.. Avocations: dancing, reading, writing, music, going to auctions and flea markets. Home: 1123 Burning Tree Rd Humble TX 77339-3933 Office: U Houston Counseling 4800 Calhoun Rd Houston TX 77004-2610

HUDSON, WALTER TIREE, artist; b. Lynchburg, Va., Apr. 10, 1943; s. Randolph Ward Hudson and Frances Anderson Tyree; m. Patricia Fay Dearing, Aug. 23, 1963 (div. Sept. 1972); children: Walter Preston Tyree, William Alfred Dearing. Grad. h.s., Campbell County, Va.; student, Ctrl. Va. C.C., 1997. Reader Lynchburg Pub. Libr., 1976—. Exhibited at The Framery, 1985—, Seven Hills Art Club, 1985-88, Amelia Pride, 1988, Lynchburg (Va.) Pub. Libr., 1987—, Lynchburg Recreation Dept., 1988—, Daily Bread, 1989—, Adult Daycare Ctr.-Va. Bapt. Hosp., 1989-94, Va. Episcopal Sch., 1993-97, Lynchburg Art Festival, 1991, Elks Nat. Home, 1992, Ehrich's Optitions, 1992—, U. Tex., Houston, 1993, Lynchburg Fine Arts Ctr., Lynchburg PO, 1994, Lynchburg Voter Registration Office, 1995, Free Clinic of Va., 1995, Irby L. Hudson Collection, 1995, Lynchburg Social Svcs., 1987—, Lynchburg Pub. Housing Authority, 1986—, 101 Quinlan St., 1996, Doggiewood Collection, 1996, Linchbird and Linchberg "1997", De Z Night Jump, 1997, 707 Mansfield Street, 1998, Ah Holloween Spring, 1998, Spring Fling 98, Blue Berg, 1998, Community Market, 1999, Linchbird, Red, White and Blue, 1999, Spring Fling, 1999; holder 50 copyrights. Active Aaronic and Melchizedek Priesthood, LDS Ch. With U.S. Army, Airborne, 1960-63. Mem. Lynchburg Stamp Club, Blue Ridge All Airborne Club. Republican. Mormon. Avocations: stamp collecting, reading, walking. Home: 3475 Fort Ave Apt 326 Lynchburg VA 24501-3834

HUDSON, WENDY JOY, software manager; b. New Brunswick, N.J., May 27, 1955; d. Herbert Roy and Dorothy Louise (Kaepernik) Hansen; m. William Howard Hudson, June 12, 1982. BA in Computer Sci., Rutgers U., 1977, MS in Computer Sci., 1979. Computer cons. Bell Labs., Holmdel, N.J., 1977-79; sr. mem. tech. staff Concurrent Computer, Tinton Falls, N.J., 1979-81; mgr. Concurrent Computer, Tinton Falls, 1981-83, sr. mgr., 1983-89, prin. mgr., 1989-91; mgr. Transarc, Pitts., 1991-92; group mgr. Ilex Sys., Shrewsbury, N.J., 1992-95; mgr. IBM, Dayton, N.J., 1995-97, Lucent Techs., Bell Labs., Holmdel, N.J., 1997—. Contbr. articles to profl. jours. Mem. Assn. Computing Machinery. Republican. Episcopalian. Avocations: genealogy, skiing, bicycling, traveling. Home: 619 High Bridge Rd Colts Neck NJ 07722-1320 Office: Lucent Techs Bell Labs 943 Holmdel Rd Holmdel NJ 07733-2611

HUDSON, WILLIAM JEFFREY, JR., manufacturing company executive; b. Ill., May 20, 1934; s. William J. Sr. and Olga Georgevna (de Tarnowsky) H.; m. Margaret Royal, June 11, 1957; children: William J. III, Scott D., Robert C. BS in Elec. Engring., Cornell U., 1957, M. Cert. Elec. Engring., 1957; postgrad., Drexel U., 1959-61. With AMP Inc., Harrisburg, Pa., 1961—, market rschr., 1961-65, mgr. product planning Syscom, 1965, product mgr. Selective Signal, 1965-67, new product mgr. Capitron, 1967-73, new product mgr. Electron Devices Divsn., 1973-76, mgr. Devel. Engring. Circuit Components Divsn., 1976-77, mgr. Signal Components Divsn., 1977-81, group dir. connector and electronic products group, 1981-82, divisional v.p. connector and electronic products group, 1982-83; divisional v.p. Far East ops. Tokyo, 1983-89, corp. v.p. Asia/Pacific, 1989-91; exec. v.p. internat. Harrisburg, 1991-92, pres., CEO, 1993-98, vice chmn., 1998—, also bd. dirs.; bd. dirs. Goodyear Tire and Rubber Co.; bd. dirs. carpenter Tech. Corp., Cornell U. Coun. Engring. Adv. Coun. Contbr. articles to profl. jours.; 12 patents in field. Bd. dirs. Pinnacle Health Found., 1994—; mem. bd. advisors Hershey Med. Ctr., 1994—. Lt. (j.g.) USN, 1957-61. Mem. Nat. Elec. Mfrs. Assn. (exec. com., bd. govs. 1994-99), Nat. Assn. Mfrs. (exec. com., bd. dirs. 1993-98, vice chmn. 1997-98), Elec. Mfrs. Club (bd. dirs. 1993-98), Mgmt. Execs. Soc., Bus. Roundtable, U.S. Coun. Internat. Bus., exec. com., Conf. Bd., Am. C. of C. (Pres. Clinton apptd. adv. commn. trade policy, chmn. Pacific Basin Econ. Coun. 1997-99). Office: AMP Inc 470 Friendship Rd Harrisburg PA 17111-1203

HUDSON, WILLIAM MARK, insurance company executive, owner; b. Parkesburg, W.Va., Oct. 30, 1932; s. Morton Arden and Dorthy (Medealf) H.; m. Margie Webb, Oct. 3, 1953; children: William Mark II, Jay Lynn, Janet. Student, Fla. U., 1964-65, Fla. LaSalle U., 1971. Sgt. USMC, Albany, Ga., 1951-54; mgr. W.T. Grant Co., several cities, 1954-65; owner, agent Bill Hudson Ins. and State Farm Ins. Co., Orange Pk., Fla., 1965—; pres. BILMARJA, Inc., Orange Pk., 1987—; owner Atlantic Travel, 1998—. Chmn. Clay County (Fla.) Transp. Authority, 1988-90, 95-96; owner Get a Way Travel, Orange Park, 1994-98—, Atlantic Travel Deltona, 1998—; elder, chmn. fin. com. St. Giles Presbyn. Ch., Orange Prk, 1990—; treas. Clay County C. of C., 1987-88; mem. stewardship com. St. Augustine Presbyn. Ch., chmn. planned giving com., 1996-98; bd. dirs. Clay County Gator Club, 1998—. Mem. Rotary (Paul Harris fellow 1983, Morocco Patrol (capt. 1989-90), Shriners (pres. Motor Corp. 1974-75, pres. Patrol Assn. 1989-90, sec. southeastern Motor Corps 1972-74), Masons (vice chmn. 1996-97, pilgramage com. 1993-94, chmn. membership com. 1990-93), Order of Demolay, Knights Comdr. of Ct. of Honour, Legion of Honor (dean 1996-97). Republican. Presbyterian. Avocations: helping burned and crippled children, boating. Office: Bill Hudson Ins Co 793 Blanding Blvd Ste A Orange Park FL 32065-5792

HUDSON, YEAGER, philosophy educator, minister; b. Meridian, Miss., Aug. 14, 1931; s. William Ernest and Effie (Yeager) H.; m. Margaret Louise Hight, Dec. 20, 1953; children: Paul Brinton, Gareth Yeager. A.B., Millsaps Coll., 1954; S.T.B., Boston U., 1958, Ph.D., 1965; M.A. (hon.), Colby Coll., 1977. Ordained to ministry United Methodist Ch., 1963. Instr. philosophy Colby Coll., Waterville, Maine, 1959-65, asst. prof., 1965-70, assoc. prof., 1970-77, prof., chmn. dept., 1977-89, Charles A. Dana prof. philosophy, 1994—; Fulbright lectr. Ahnednager Coll., (India), 1967-68. Author: Emerson and Tagore: The Poet as Philosopher, 1988, Philosophy of Religion, 1990; editor: Profile of a College, 1972, Philosophy of Religion: Selected Readings, 1991; co-editor: Revolution, Violence and Equality, 1990, Philosophical Essays on the Ideas of a Good Society, 1988, Terrorism, Justice and Social Values, 1991, Communitarianism, Liberalism and Social Responsibility, 1991, The Bill of Rights: Bicentennial Reflections, 1993, Freedom, Dharma and Rights, 1993, The Social Power of Ideas, 1995, Editor: Rending and Renewing the Social Order, 1996, Technology, Morality and Social Policy, 1998, Globalism and the Obsolescence of the State, 1999. Mem. Am. Philos. Assn., N.Am. Soc. for Social Philosophy (bd. officers), Am. Inst. Indian Studies (trustee 1980—), Assn. Asian Studies. Office: Colby Coll Dept Philosophy Waterville ME 04901 *There is widespread agreement among the thinkers and seers of nearly every society concerning the highest ideals according to which humans should live. The tragedy is that we still lack the moral will to put our ideals into effect in practical international affairs.*

HUDSON, YVONNE MORTON, elementary education educator; b. Cin., July 25, 1943; d. Eugene Benjamin and Eura Selenora (Williams) Morton; m. McKinley Hudson, Aug. 27, 1966; children: Shawna, McKinley Jr. BS in Primary Edn., U. Cin., 1965; MEd, Boston U., Mons, Belgium, 1988. Cert. tchr., Calif.; advanced profl. cert., Md. Tchr. Cin. Bd. Edn., 1965-66, 67-68, 71-73; tchr. Anne Arundel County Pub. Schs., Annapolis, Md., 1968-69, 73-76, Dept. Def. Dependents Schs., Kaiserslautern, Fed. Republic Germany, 1980-83, San Francisco Unified Sch. Dist., 1989-94, Montgomery County Pub. Schs., Rockville, Md., 1994—; mem. Sch. Adv. Bd., Kaiserslautern, 1981-83. Vice pres. PTO, Kaiserslautern, 1981-82, San Francisco, 1991, pres., Ft. McClellan, Ala., 1984-85; mem. Ft. McClellan Elem. Sch. Bd., 1984-85; troop leader Girl Scouts U.S.A., East Point, Ga., 1977-80, bd. dirs. North Atlantic coun., 1987-88. Recipient Patriotic Civilian Svc. award Dept. Army, 1988; named Parent of Yr. George Washington H.S., San Francisco, 1994. Mem. NEA, ASCD, AAUW, Internat. Reading Assn., Calif. Tchrs. Assn., United Educators San Francisco (rep. 1989-94, negotiating team 1989-94, ethnic leadership awareness com. 1989-94, exec. bd. dirs. 1992-94, tchr. ctr. policy bd. 1992), Montgomery County Edn. Assn. (bd. dirs., minority affairs com. 1998—), Nat. Coun. Negro Women, Presidio Officers Wives Club, Alpha Kappa Alpha. Avocations: reading, travel, shopping, collecting. Home: 13 Cabin Creek Ct Burtonsville MD 20866-1841 Office: Rock View Elem Sch 3901 Denfeld Ave Kensington MD 20895-1510

HUDSON-YOUNG, JANE SMITHER, real estate investor; b. Altavista, Va., July 5, 1937; d. Victor Nelson and Elois Reynolds Smither; A.A.S. summa cum laude in Mgmt., Central Va. Community Coll., 1978; m. J. Lee Hudson, May 15, 1954; 1 child, Michael Edward; m. Gordon M. Young, July 9, 1989. Adminstrv. asst. Altavista (Va.) High Sch., 1954-55; with Lane Co., Inc., Altavista, 1956-89, exec. sec. to chmn. bd., 1976-81, exec. sec. to chmn. exec. com., 1981-84, spl. asst. for pub. rels. communications, 1984-86, acct. exec. nat. accts, 1986, asst. sales mgr. contract div., 1986-87, mktg. adminstr., 1988-89; realtor R. B. Carr & Co., Altavista, 1980-87, assoc. broker, 1985-87; mem. adv. bd. Am. Fed. Savs. and Loan, 1985-89. Corr. Lynchburg (Va.) News., 1966-72. Mem. town coun. Town of Altavista, 1980-86; sec. Altavista Community Improvement Coun., 1981-82; mem. bd. deacons First Bapt. Ch., Altavista, 1980-83. Home and Office: 1100 Heritage Plantation Dr Pawleys Island SC 29585

HUDSPETH, ALBERT JAMES, biomedical researcher, educator; b. Houston, Nov. 9, 1945; s. Chalmers Mac and Demaris (DeLange) H.; m. Ann Maurine Packard, Feb. 12, 1977; children: James Chalmers, Ann Maurine Demaris. BA, Harvard U., 1967, MA, 1968; PhD, 1973, MD, 1974. Mem. biology faculty Calif. Inst. Tech., Pasadena, 1975-83; prof. physiology U. Calif., San Francisco, 1983-89; former prof. cell biology and neurosci. U. Tex. Southwestern Med. Ctr., Dallas, 1989-95; now F.M. Kriby prof. Rockefeller U., 1995—; investigator Howard Hughes Med. Inst., 1993—. Recipient W. Alden Spencer award N.Y. Acad. Scis., 1985, Javits Neurosci. Investigator award NIH, 1985-91, Cole award Biophys. Soc., 1991, Dana award Charles A. Dana Found., 1994, L.S. Rosenstiel award Brandeis U., 1997. Mem. NAS, Phi Beta Kappa, Alpha Omega Alpha. Office: Rockefeller Univ Campus Box 314 1230 York Ave New York NY 10021-6399

HUDSPETH, CHALMERS MAC, lawyer, educator; b. Denton, Tex., Oct. 18, 1919; s. Junia Evans and Ethel (Burns) H.; m. Demaris Eleanor De Lange, Jan. 30, 1945; children: Albert James, Thomas Richard, Helen Demaris. B.A., Rice U., Houston, 1940; J.D., U. Tex., 1946. Bar: Tex. 1946. Pvt. practice Houston, 1947—; of counsel De Lange Hudspeth McConnell and Tibbets LLP, 1988—; asst. prof. law U. Tex. at Austin, 1946-47; lectr. govt. Rice U., 1947—, bd. govs., 1980-89, trustee, 1982-89, trustee emeritus, 1989—; bd. dirs. Stewart Info. Services Corp., Stewart Title Guaranty Co. Contbr. articles to profl. jours. Mem. bi-racial com. Houston Ind. Sch. Dist., 1955-56; trustee, v.p. Brown Found., 1983-89. Served to lt. USNR, 1942-45. Fellow Am. Bar Found., Tex. Bar Found., Am. Coll. Trust and Estate Counsel; mem. ABA, Tex. Bar Assn., State Bar Tex. (dir. 1966-68, v.p. 1968-69), Houston Philos. Soc. (pres. 1964-65), Houston Com. on Fgn. Relations (chmn. 1973-74), Petroleum Club of Houston, Chancellors, Order of Coif, Phi Delta Phi. Office: De Lange Hudspeth McConnell & Tibbets LLP Eight Greenway Plz Ste 1300 Houston TX 77046

HUDSPETH, EMMETT LEROY, physicist, educator; b. Denton, Tex., Dec. 3, 1916; s. Junia Evans and Ethel Leonice (Burns) H.; m. Mary Alice Barnes, Dec. 2, 1944; children: John, Philip, Anne, Paul. A.B., Rice Inst., 1937, M.A., 1938, Ph.D., 1940. Fellow physics Rice Inst., 1937-40; fellow Bartol Research Found., 1940-41, asst. dir., 1946-50; staff mem. radiation lab. Mass. Inst. Tech., 1941-45; prof. physics U. Tex., Austin, 1950-87, prof. emeritus, 1987—; dir. Nuclear Physics Lab. (U. Tex.), 1950-72; cons. USN, 1943-45; adviser Sec. War, 1942; com. on Undersea Warfare, 1947-49; sci. adv. com. Radiobiol. Lab., U. Tex. and USAF, 1954-58. Contbr. articles to profl. jours. Republican nominee from Tex. 10th Dist. for U.S. Ho. of Reps., 1978. Fellow Am. Phys. Soc., A.A.A.S.; mem. Phi Beta Kappa, Sigma Xi. Rsch. nuclear physics, disintegration of light elements, energy levels of nuclei and others. Home: 4100 Jackson Ave Apt 279 Austin TX 78731-6004

HUDSPETH, GREGG WILLIAM, landscape architect; b. Canyon, Tex., Nov. 14, 1959; s. Elmer and Winnie H. B of Landscape Arch., Tex. Tech. U., 1982. Registered landscape architect, Tex., Ala., Fla., Ga., S.C. Landscape architect Richardson Verdoorn, Inc., Austin, Tex., 1983-87, Niles Bolton Landscape Group, Atlanta, 1987—. 1st lt. USAF, 1982-83. Mem. Am. Soc. Landscape Architects (pres. Ga. chpt. 1992-93), Am. Planning Assn., Congress for the New Urbanism. Avocation: golf. Office: Niles Bolton Landscape Group 3060 Peachtree Rd NW Ste 600 Atlanta GA 30305-2236

HUDSPETH, HARRY LEE, federal judge; b. Dallas, Dec. 28, 1935; s. Harry Ellis and Hattilee (Dudney) H.; m. Vicki Kathryn Round, Nov. 27, 1971; children: Melinda, Mary Kathryn. BA, U. Tex., Austin, 1955, JD, 1958. Bar: Tex. 1958. Trial atty. Dept. Justice, Washington, 1959-62; asst. U.S. atty. Western Dist. Tex., El Paso, 1962-69; assoc. Peticolas, Luscombe & Stephens, El Paso, 1969-77; U.S. magistrate El Paso, 1977-79; judge U.S. Dist. Ct. (we. dist.) Tex., El Paso, 1979—; chief judge U.S. Dist. Ct. (we. dist) Tex., El Paso, 1992—. Bd. dirs. Sun Carnival Assn., 1976, Met. YMCA El Paso, 1980-88. Mem. ABA, El Paso Bar Assn., U. Tex. Ex-students Assn. (exec. coun. 1980-86), Chancellors, Order of Coif, Phi Beta Kappa. Democrat. Mem. Christian Ch. (Disciples of Christ). Office: US Dist Ct We Dist Tex 433 US Courthouse 511 E San Antonio St El Paso TX 79901-2401*

HUDSPETH, STEPHEN MASON, lawyer; b. Pitts., Jan. 22, 1947; s. Harold Mason and Edna Mary (Lawrenson) H.; m. Rebecca Anne Ellis, Apr. 3, 1971; children: David, Catherine. BA, MA magna cum laude, Yale U., 1968, JD, 1971. Bar: N.Y. 1973, Pa. 1973, U.S. Dist. Ct. (so. and ea. dists.) N.Y. 1973, Mass. 1974, U.S. Dist. Ct. (ea. dist.) Pa. 1975, U.S. Ct. Appeals (1st cir.) 1976, U.S. Ct. Appeals (2d cir.) 1973, U.S. Ct. Appeals (3d cir.) 1977, U.S. Supreme Ct. 1980, Maine 1987. Assoc., Lord, Day & Lord, N.Y.C., until 1979, ptnr., 1979-86, ptnr., Coudert Bros., 1986—, N.Y.C., mem. exec. com., 1990-93, also head litigation dept., 1994—; adj. asst. prof. bus. law Wagner Coll., 1973-83. Co-author: (book) Transfer Pricing Under U.S. Law, 1995; contbr. articles to books and profl. jours. Vestryman St. Alban's Episcopal Ch., S.I., N.Y., 1979-85, warden, 1985-87; chmn. Stewardship Commn. Diocese of N.Y., 1987-95; vestryman St. Matthew's Episcopal Ch., Wilton, Conn., 1989-92, warden, 1992-95. Served from 2d lt. to capt. C.E., USA', 1968-73. Mem. ABA, N.Y. State Bar Assn., Assn. Bar City N.Y., Phi Beta Kappa. Episcopalian. Office: Coudert Bros 1114 Avenue Of The Americas New York NY 10036-7703

HUDZINSKI, LEONARD GERARD, social worker; b. Aug. 14, 1946. BA in Psychology and Sociology, Findlay (Ohio) Coll., 1968; MSW, U. Mich., 1971; PhD, U. Pitts., 1975. Diplomate Clin. Social Work Examiners. Tchg. asst. dept. sociology Findlay Coll., 1966-68; psychology specialist Lyster Army Hosp., Ft. Rucker, Ala., 1969-70; psychiat. social worker Toledo (Ohio) Mental Health Ctr., 1972; instr. in applied social rsch. and social work Med. Coll. Ohio, 1974-77; head divsn. clin. social work Ochsner Med. Instns., New Orleans, 1977—; dir. Ochsner Ctr. for Elimination of Smoking; asst. clin. prof. psychiatry La. State U. Med. Ctr.; asst. clin. prof. Tulane Med. Ctr.; program dir., adminstr. State of Ohio Epilepsy Deinstitutionalization Assistance Program, 1976-77. Contbr. articles to profl. jours.; mem. editorial bd.: Headache Quar., 1989—. Bd. dirs. Biofeedback Certification Inst. Am., Wheat Ridge, Colo., 1995. Served with U.S. Army, 1968-70. Fellow Am. Assn. for Study of Headache; mem. Assn. for Advancement of Behavior Therapy, Assn. Applied Psychophysiology and Biofeedback, La. Assn. Applied Psychophysiology and Biofeedback (past pres.), Am. Assn. for Study of Headache, NASW, La. Assn. for Clin. Social Work Vendorship (bd. dirs., treas., pres.), ACSW, Am. Fedn. for Clin. Rsch. Home: 274 Garden Rd River Ridge LA 70123-1953 Office: Ochsner Med Instns 1514 Jefferson Hwy New Orleans LA 70121-2429

HUEBL, HUBERT C., surgeon; b. Glendive, Mont., Sept. 12, 1932; s. Hubert Carl Huebl and Ida Mae Myers; m. Helen Katherine Sugrue, Feb. 23, 1963; children: John, Michael, Katherine Doyle, Carolyn. BA, U. Chgo., 1952; MD, Washington U., 1956. Bd. cert. gen. and thoracic surgery. Intern gen. and thoracic surgery Bellevue Hosp., N.Y.C., 1959-62, Wayne State U., Detroit, 1962-67; thoracic surgeon Cardiothoracic Assocs., Malden, Mass., 1968-77; gen. surgeon Dearborn (Mich.) Surg. Assocs., 1977—. Lt. USNR, 1957-59. Mem. ACS, AMA, Soc. Thoracic Surgeons, Mich. State Med. Soc., Wayne County Med. Soc. Roman Catholic. Office: Dearborn Surg Assocs Ste 209 18181 Oakwood Dearborn MI 48123

HUEBNER, EMILY ANN, home healthcare administrator, consultant; b. Woodstock, Ill., Oct. 27, 1951; d. John Craft and Mary Ann (Freund) Draper; m. Dennis E. Huebner, May 8, 1982; children: John Dennis, Laura Marie. BSN, St. Xavier Coll., Chgo., 1973; MS, U. Ill., Chgo., 1979. Dir. profl. svcs. 5-Hosp. Homebound Elderly program, Chgo.; adminstr. In-Home Healthcare Chgo./North Chgo.; mem. faculty Hosp. Learning Ctrs., L.A.; v.p. clin. svc. Health Mgmt. Assocs., Hinsdale, Ill., 1990-99; pvt. practice health care cons. Northbrook, Ill., 1999—; presenter mgmt. seminars U. So. Calif., Ind. U., St. Xavier Coll. Author: The Home Care and Documentation Guide: An Orientation and Resource Manual for Home Health Practitioners. Mem. Ill. Coun. Home Health Agys., Sigma Theta Tau. E-mail: eahueb@aol.com. Home and Office: 3905 Radcliffe Dr Northbrook IL 60062-4219

HUEBNER, JOHN STEPHEN, geologist; b. Bryn Mawr, Pa., Sept. 9, 1940; s. John Mudie and Elizabeth (Converse) H.; m. Emily Mayer Zug, June 16, 1962; children: Christopher Converse, Jeffrey Worrell. A.B. magna cum laude, Princeton U., 1962; Ph.D., Johns Hopkins U., 1967. Rsch. geologist U.S. Geol. Survey, 1967-97; cons. NASA, 1976-78; lectr. George Washington U., 1971; sec.-treas. Am. Geol. Inst., 1974-75. Assoc. editor Jour. Geophys. Rsch., 1977-79; Contbr. articles profl. jours. Pres. Wood Acres Citizens Assn., 1977-78; sec. Cosmos Club Found., 1998-99. Recipient Meritorious Svc. award U.S. Dept. Interior, 1995. Fellow Mineral. Soc. Am. (bd. dirs. 1985-88, recipient MSA award 1978); mem. AAAS, Geochem. Soc. (treas. 1972-75), Am. Geophys. Union, Geol. Soc. Washington (v.p. 1991, pres. 1992), Cosmos Club (Washington), Sigma Xi. Home: 6102 Cromwell Dr Bethesda MD 20816-3410

HUEBNER, SUZANNE MARIE, insurance company executive; b. Wausau, Wis., Mar. 31, 1958; d. Marvin J. and Janet S. (Reinhold) H. BBA in Risk Mgmt. and Ins., U. Wis., 1980. CLU, CPCU. Individual life product analyst Wausau (Wis.) Ins. Cos., 1981-82, individual life product coord., 1982-85, dir. individual life products, 1985-87, casualty mktg. specialist, 1987-91, market devel. coord., 1991-94, dir. market R&D, 1994-97, dir. mktg., prodr. svcs., 1997—; instr. Wausau Ins. Cos. and North Cen. Tech. Coll., Wausau, 1989—. Loaned exec. United Way, 1997. Mem. Am. Soc. CLUs, CPCU Soc., U. Wis. Bus. Alumni, Wausau Country Club (ladies golf chmn. 1992, treas. 1997). Office: Wausau Ins Cos 2000 Westwood Dr Wausau WI 54401-7802

HUELS, STEVEN MARK, laboratory analyst; b. Dunkirk, N.Y., Oct. 12, 1960; s. Robert Paul and Agnes Eve (Grzeskowiak) H. BS in Physics and Math. with honors, SUNY, Fredonia, 1982; MS in Astronomy, Pa. State U., 1984. Rsch. asst. Lord Corp., Erie, Pa., 1980-81, SUNY Rsch. Found., Fredonia, 1981-82; grad. asst. N.Mex. State U., Las Cruces, 1982-83, Pa. State U., University Park, 1983-84; quality control lab. mgr. Chem. Process and Supply Corp., Dunkirk, N.Y., 1985-89; sci. writer Am. Coll. Testing Program, Iowa City, 1990-92; sr. lab. analyst Dunkirk Water Pollution Control Facility, 1992—. Recipient scholarship N.Y. State Bd. Regents, 1978, Anne Walker Meml. scholarship, 1978, Bausch and Lomb Hon. Sci. medal, 1978, Ruth Tice Callahan award for Acad. Excellence, 1979, Fredonia Alumni Assn. Freshman award, 1979. Mem. Am. Phys. Soc. (astrophysics and chem. physics divsns.), N.Y. Acad. Scis., Soc. Photo-Optical Instrumentation Engrs., The Planetary Soc., Nat. Weather Svc. Coop. Observer, Pa. State U. Alumni Assn. (life), Marshall Martz Meml. Astron. Assn., Phi Eta Sigma, Pi Mu Epsilon (mem. N.Y. Pi chpt.), Theta Psi Omicron. Republican. Roman Catholic. Home: 843 Central Ave Dunkirk NY 14048-3346 Office: Wright Park Dr Dunkirk NY 14048

HUENEFELD, THOMAS ERNST, financial consultant, retired banker; b. Cin., July 7, 1937; s. Carl Ernst and Catherine Louise (Messer) H.; m. Catherine Ann Cogburn, Feb. 5, 1960; children: Richard Ernst, Amy Cogburn. BS in Bus. Adminstrn., U. Fla., 1961; grad. Nat. Comml. Lending Grad. Sch., U. Okla., 1975. Cert. comml. lender Am. Bankers Assn.; cert. lender-bus. banking Inst. Cert. Bankers. Mgmt. trainee Huenefeld Co., Cin., 1961-62, asst. sec., buyer, 1963-65; credit analyst First Nat. Bank Cin. (now Star Bank, N.A.), 1966-68, asst. cashier, 1968-69, asst. v.p., 1969-75, v.p., 1975-83, sr. v.p., 1983-96; ret., 1996; cons. Star Banc Corp., Cin., 1997-98; dir. Wolf Machine Co., S. Eastern Materials Corp., Archiable Electric Co., Eastern Machinery Co., Ninth St. Garage, Inc., Logan & Kanawha Coal Co., Inc., Safeguard Corp. Bd. mgrs. Emanuel Cmty. Ctr., Cin., 1965-70, pres., 1968-70; trustee Huenefeld Meml., Inc., Cin., 1965-72, treas., 1965-69; trustee Funds for Self Enterprise, Cin., 1972-76, pres., 1973-76; trustee Cin. Musical Festival Assn., 1976-82, mem. exec. com., 1977-79; trustee Cmty. Ltd. Care Dialysis Ctr., Cin., 1978-85, Merc. Libr., 1979—, v.p., chmn. fin. com., 19983-88; trustee MagnaCare Health Plan, 1988-91, v.p., chmn. fin. com., 1990-91; adv. bd. Riemenschneider Bach Inst. Baldwin-Wallace Coll., 1988—; mem. history adv. bd. Cin. Mus. Ctr., 1997—; adv. bd. Scarlet Oaks Retirement Comm., 1998—; trustee Betts Ho. Rsch. Ctr., 1999—. Mem. Am. Fin. Assn. (life), Fin. Mgmt. Assn. (life), Robert Morris Assocs. (life), Cin. Assn. Credit and Fin. Mgmt. (dir. 1972-76), Am. Inst. Banking, Newcomen Soc. N.Am., Ohio Hist. Soc. (life), Cin. Hist. Soc. (life, trustee 1979-87, mem. exec. com. 1983-85, v.p. 1985-89), Cin. Preservation Assn. (trustee 1989-95, adv. bd. 1995—), Cincinnatus Assn. (exec. com. 1983-84), Cin. Country Club, Queen City Club, Bankers Club, The Assemblies (chmn. 1972-73), Univ. Club (bd. govs. 1982-89), Univ. Club Cin. Found. (trustee 1989-96), Fanfare (pres. 1979-80), Friends William Howard Taft Birthplace (trustee 1997—), Sigma Chi. Republican. Methodist. Home and Office: 3440 Principio Ave Cincinnati OH 45208-4240

HUENEMANN, RODNEY KARL, state administrator, executive; b. Mason City, Iowa, Dec. 8, 1954; s. Karl Gerhardt and Cecilia Elfrieda (Mettler) H.; m. Karen Lynn Fisher, Sept. 22, 1979; 1 child, Brandon. BA in Sociology and Social Work, U. No. Iowa, 1977. Devel. dept. dir. Upper Des Moines Opportunity, Emmetsburg, Iowa, 1977-84; program planner Iowa Office for Planning and Programming, Des Moines, 1984-85, program adminstr., 1985-86; chief Iowa Bur. Cmty. Svcs., Iowa Dept. Human Rights, Des Moines, 1986-98; adminstr., cmty. svcs. adminstrn. Ariz. Dept. Econ. Security, Phoenix, 1998—; part-time county corr. Des Moines Register, 1982-84; part-time property mgr. Edward Wordrip, Westport, Conn., 1985-88; spkr. in field. Mem. Palo Alto County Rep. Party Ctrl. Com., Emmetsburg, 1979-83; initiator, co-chair Iowa State Homeless Assistance Coordinating Com., Des Moines, 1990-94; mem. staff/parish rels. com. 1st United Meth. Ch., Des Moines, 1995-97. Recipient Pub. Policy award Mid Iowa Cmty. Action, Marshalltown, 1995. Mem. Nat. Assn. Cmty. Action Agys. (cert. cmty. action profl., mem. edn. com. 1990-94, mem. cert. adv. group 1990-94), nat. Assn. for State Cmty. Svcx. Programs (bd. dirs. 1987-93, mem. mgmt. info. syss. 1989-92, ways and means com. 1995—).

HUENING, WALTER CARL, JR., retired consulting application engineer; b. Boston, Feb. 10, 1923; s. Walter Carl and Gladys (Whittemore) H.; m. Margaret Laurence McGeary, Aug. 5, 1944 (dec. 1986); children: Peter Carl, Susan Laurence Huening Locke; m. Elizabeth Ann Young Wright, Apr. 9, 1988. BSEE magna cum laude, Tufts U., 1944. Registered profl. engr., N.Y., Ohio. Instr. elec. engring. Tufts U., Medford, Mass., 1946-48; distbn. engr. plant engring. dept. GE, Lynn, Mass., 1948-50; application engr. indsl. power engring. GE, Schenectady, N.Y., 1952-56; product planner protective devices dept. GE, Plainville, Conn., 1956-58; design engr. vacuum cleaner dept. GE, Cleve., 1958-59; application engr. comml. and mcpl. dept. GE, Schenectady, 1960-62, application engr. steel mill, 1962-68, cons. application engr. indsl. power engring., 1968-89; mem. U.S. nat. com. Internat. Electrotech. Commn., tech. advisor on Tech. Com. 73 matters, 1972-89. Contbr. tech. papers to jours. and chpts. to books; patentee vacuum cleaner latch. Lt. comdr. USNR, 1944-46, 50-52, ret. Fellow IEEE (life, R. H. Kaufmann award 1988, Indsl. and Comml. Power Systems Dept. Achievement award 1989, prizes for papers 1970, 82); mem. Tau Beta Pi. Independent. Avocations: photography, collecting recorded traditional jazz music. Address: 1229 Godfrey Ln Niskayuna NY 12309-1241

HUESTIS, CHARLES BENJAMIN, former academic administrator; b. Seattle, Jan. 27, 1920; s. Claude Erwin and Eloise Marie (Pettit) H.; m. Kathryn Alice Porter, Mar. 1, 1942; children: Stephen Porter, Jeffrey Charles, Robin Rebecca. Student, Griffin Murphy Coll., Seattle, 1938-39, U. Calif. Berkeley, 1946. With Seattle First Nat. Bank, 1941; acct. Rheem Mfg. Co., Richmond, Calif., 1946-51; chief acct. aircraft div. Rheem Mfg. Co., Downey, Calif., 1951-54; corp. comptroller Rheem Mfg. Co., 1954-56; v.p., treas. Hall-Scott Inc., Berkeley, Calif., 1956, exec. v.p., dir., treas., 1956-57; adminstrv. cons. Overseas Nat. Airways, Oakland, Calif., 1957-58; controller El Segundo div. Hughes Aircraft Co., 1958-59, controller Tucson div., 1959, treas., chmn. finance com., 1960-66, v.p., 1962-66; v.p., treas., dir. Am. Mt. Everest Expdn., 1963; v.p. bus. and finance Duke U., Durham, N.C., 1966-83, sr. v.p., 1983-85, sr. v.p. emeritus, 1985—; dir. Technomics, Inc., Falls Church, Va., 1966-76; chmn. bd. Sta. WDBS, 1970-76; dir. Seren Tech. Corp., San Francisco. Bd. dirs. Santa Barbara (Calif.) Research Ctr., 1959-66; bd. dirs., mem. exec. com. Research Triangle Found., Research Triangle Park, N.C., 1969-85; trustee Research Triangle Inst., Research Triangle Park, 1967-70, Sierra Club Found., 1969-79; commr. N.C. Marine Fisheries, 1985-87; trustee N.C. Nature Conservancy., 1977-86, 87-96, chmn., 1979-83; bd. dirs. Univ. Tech. Corp., 1987-89, N.C. Ednl. Facilities Fin. Agy., 1987-91—; climbing leader Duke-Gettysburg Expdn. to Kurdistan, 1982. Mem. Explorers Club (v.p. research and edn. 1987-88), Am. Alpine Club. Home: 1803 Woodburn Rd Durham NC 27705-5724 Office: Duke U Durham NC 27706

HUETER, DIANA T., health facility executive; married; 2 children. BBA, Lamar U., 1973, MBA, 1974. Fin. specialist, bus. office mgr., materials mgmt. buyer Humana Beaumont (Tex.) Med.- Surg. Hosp., 1975-78; CFO Carrollton (Tex.) Med. Ctr., 1978-79; sr. v.p., v.p., asst. v.p./ops. interim exec. dir. Baylor Inst. Rehab., asst. v.p./fin., ins. mgr., discharged patient accounts mgr. Baylor Health Care Sys., Baylor U. Med. Ctr., Dallas, 1979-94; exec. v.p./COO St. Vincent Infirmary Med. Ctr., Little Rock, 1994-95; pres., CEO St. Vincent Health System, Little Rock, 1995—; adj. prof. health adminstrn. Grad. Program U. Ark., Little Rock, 1996—; bd. dirs. Ctrl. Ark. Radiation Therapy Inst., 1996—. Chair healthcare svcs. divsn. Pulaski County United Way Campaign, 1995; mem. Ark. Women's Leadership Forum; bd. dirs. Nat. Family Partnership of Ark., 1994-95; vol. St. Vincent Aux., Ctrs. Youths & Families. Named one of Outstanding Young Women of Am., 1986, Top 100 Women in Ark., 1995, 96. Mem. Am. Hosp. Assn., Am. Coll. Healthcare Execs. (del.), Tex. Hosp. Assn. (bd. dirs. edn. com. 1982-88, chair edn. com. 1986-87, bd. dirs. 1989-93, v.p. 1992, pres. 1993, bd. dirs. com. affiliated socs. 1993, state bd. coun. policy devel. 1993), Healthcare Fin. Mgmt. Assn. (nat. com. patient accounting 1988, nat. matrix bd. coun. profl. excellence 1988). Office: St Vincent Health System 2 Saint Vincent Cir Little Rock AR 72205-5402*

HUETHER, CARL A., biology educator; b. Aug. 22, 1937. BS, Ohio State U., 1959; MS, N.C. State Coll., 1963; PhD, U. Calif., Davis, 1966. From asst. prof. to assoc. prof. U. Cin., 1966-83, prof. biology, 1983—; rsch. fellow human genetics Johns Hopkins U. Sch. Medicine, Balt., 1977-78. E-mail: carl.huether@uc.edu. Office: U Cin Dept Biol Scis Cincinnati OH 45221-0006

HUETTNER, RICHARD ALFRED, lawyer; b. N.Y.C., Mar. 25, 1927; s. Alfred F. and Mary (Reilly) H.; children—Jennifer Mary, Barbara Bryan; m. 2d, Eunice Bizzell Dowd, Aug. 22, 1971. Marine Engrs. License, N.Y. State Maritime Acad., 1947; B.S., Yale U. Sch. Engring., 1949; J.D., U. Pa., 1952. Bar: D.C. 1952, N.Y. 1954, U.S. Ct. Mil. Appeals 1953, U.S. Ct. Claims 1961, U.S. Supreme Ct. 1969, U.S. Ct. Appeals (fed. cir.) 1982, also other fed. cts, registered to practice U.S. Patent and Trademark Office 1957, Canadian Patent Office 1968. Engr. Jones & Laughlin Steel Corp., 1954-55; assoc. atty. firm Kenyon & Kenyon, N.Y.C. 1955-61; mem. firm Kenyon & Kenyon, 1961-96, of counsel, 1996-98; specialist patent, trademark and copyright law. Trustee N.J. Shakespeare Festival, 1972-79, sec., 1977-79; trustee Overlook Hosp., Summit, N.J., 1978-84, 86-89, vice chmn. bd. trustees, 1980-82, chmn. bd. trustees, 1982-84; trustee Overlook Found., 1981-89, chmn. bd. trustees, 1986-89, emeritus trustee, 1991; trustee Colonial Symphony Orch., Madison, N.J., 1972-82, v.p. bd. trustees 1974-76. pres. 1976-79; chmn. bd. overseers N.J. Consortium for Performing Arts, 1972-74; mem. Yale U. Council, 1978-81; bd. dirs. Yale Communications Bd., 1978-80; chmn. bd. trustees Center for Addictive Illnesses, Morristown, N.J., 1979-82; rep. Assn. Yale Alumni, 1975-80, chmn. com. undergrad. admissions, 1976-78, bd. govs., 1976-80, chmn. bd. govs., 1978-80; chmn. Yale Alumni Schs. Com. N.Y., 1972-78; assoc. fellow Silliman Coll., Yale U., 1976—; bd. dirs., exec. com. Yale U. Alumni Fund, 1978-81; mem. Yale Class of 1949 Council, 1980—; bd. dirs. Overlook Health Systems, 1984—. Served from midshipman to lt. USNR, 1945-47, 52-54; cert. JAGC 1953; Res. ret. Recipient Yale medal, 1983, Disting. Svc. to Yale Class of 1949 award, 1989, Yale Sci. and Engring. Meritorious Svc. award, 1992. Fellow N.Y. Bar Found.; mem. ABA, N.Y. State Bar Assn., Assn. Bar City N.Y., N.Y. Patent Trademark Copyright Law Assn. (chmn. com. mtgs. 1961-64, chmn. com. econ. matters 1966-69, 72-74), AAAS, N.Y. Acad. Scis., N.Y. County Lawyers Assn., Am. Intellectual Property Law Assn., Internat. Patent and Trademark Assn., Am. Judicature Soc., Yale Sci. and Engring. Assn. (v.p. 1973-75, pres. 1975-78, exec. bd. 1972-79), Fed. Bar Coun. Clubs: Yale (N.Y.C.); Yale of Central N.J. (Summit) (trustee 1973-88, pres. 1975-77), Morris County Golf (Convent, N.J.); The Graduates (New Haven). Home: 150 Green Ave Madison NJ 07940-2513

HUEY, CONSTANCE ANNE BERNER, mental health counselor; b. Tacoma, Wash., Jan. 20, 1938; d. Julian Boyd Berner and Beatta Kathryn (Day-Berner) Schoel; m. Donn R. Huey, July 26, 1961 (dec. June 1990); 1 child, Jennifer Anne. BA, U. Wash., 1959, MEd, 1976; cert. alcohol studies, Seattle U., 1980. Cert. mental health counselor, Wash. Speech, Eng. tchr. Pub. H.S., Seattle, 1959-68; tchr., supr., adminstr. U. Wash., Seattle, 1968-82; instr. in addiction studies program Seattle U., Seattle, 1980-86; pvt. practice, 1980—; cons. in field; guest speaker Bastyr U.; presenter and trainer in numerous workshops and seminars. Contbg. author: We Did the Best We Could, 1993; guest on radio talk shows. Mem. Am. Counseling Assn., Seattle Counseling Assn., Women's Mental Health Assn., Nat. Assn. Alcoholism and Drug Abuse Counselors, Washington Assn. Alcoholism and Drug Abuse Counselors. Avocations: gardening, walking, reading, embroidery, traveling. Home: 1800 Taylor Ave N Apt 10 Seattle WA 98109-2656

HUEY, F. B., JR., minister, theology educator; b. Denton, Tex., Jan. 12, 1925; s. F.B. and Alma Gwendolyn (Chambers) H.; m. Nonna Lee Turner, Dec. 22, 1950; children: Mary Anne Huey Lisbona, Linda Kaye Huey Miller, William David. BBA, U. Tex., 1945; MDiv, Southwestern Bapt. Theol. Sem., 1958, PhD, 1961. Ordained to ministry So. Bapt. Conv., 1956. Pastor Bolivar Bapt. Ch., Sanger, Tex., 1956-59, Univ. Bapt. Ch., Denton, 1959-61; prof. Old Testament So. Brazil Bapt. Theol. Sem., Rio de Janeiro, 1961-65; prof. Old Testament Southwestern Bapt. Theol. Sem., Ft. Worth, 1965-95, chmn. D in Ministry program, 1978-79, assoc. dean for PhD program, 1984-90; ret., 1995; pastor Rush Creek Bapt. Ch., Arlington, 1989-93; guest prof. Bapt. Theol. Sem., Ruschlikon, Switzerland, 1971-72; guest prof. Canadian So. Bapt. Sem., Cochrane, Can., 1996. Author: Exodus: Bible Study Commentary, 1977, Chinese edit., 1983, Yesterday's Prophets for Todays' World, 1980, Chinese edit., 1991, Jeremiah: Bible Study Commentary, 1981, Chinese edit., 1982, Numbers: Bible Study Commentary, 1981, Chinese edit., 1988, Ezekiel-Daniel, 1983, (with others) Student's Dictionary for Biblical and Theological Studies, 1983, Helps for Beginning Hebrew Students, 1981, Jeremiah-Lamentations: New American Commentary, 1993; translator: (with others) New American Standard Bible, 1971, New International Version Bible, 1978, International Children's Version Bible, 1983; editor Southwestern Jour. Theology, 1975-78; contbr. articles to profl. jours. Mem. Soc. Bibl. Lit., Nat. Assn. Profs. Hebrew, Nat. Assn. Bapt. Profs. Religion, Delta Sigma Pi, Beta Gamma Sigma, Theta Xi. Home: 6128 Whitman Ave Fort Worth TX 76133-3547

HUEY, J(OSEPH) WISTAR, III, import/export executive; b. Balt., Dec. 8, 1938; s. J. Wistar, Jr. and Louisa Thompson (Macgill) H.; m. Rebecca MacRae Wilson, Feb. 2, 1963 (div. 1975); children: Cameron MacRae, Elizabeth Stewart, Rebecca Macgill, Joseph Wistar IV; m. Lucia Coy Humes, Dec. 6, 1975 (div. 1980); m. Mary Joyce Noell, Sept. 8, 1998. BA, Johns Hopkins U., 1962. Underwriter emeritus Firemans Fund Ins. Co., Balt., 1962-70; v.p. comml. ins. Stump, Harvey & Cook, Inc., Balt., 1970-77; sr. account exec. Tongue Brooks & Co., Inc., Balt., 1977-85; v.p. comml. ins. Wye Ins., Inc., Balt., 1985-89; v.p. mktg. Ins., Inc., Balt., 1989-91; founder, CEO Chesapeake Antique & Classic Motorcars, Ltd., Balt., 1991—, mktg. dir., cons.; cons., dir. Mortons Gourmet and Wine Importers Internat., Ltd., Balt.; bd. dirs. Gaumer Enterprises, Balt., C.J. Dugan Real Estate, Balt., Talbott and Talbott Lingual Rsch. Labs., Inc., Balt.; chmn. bd. dirs. H.E.D. Telecons., Inc.; mktg. dir., cons. Gross Coate 1658, Easton, Md. Mem. Internat. Platform Assn., Md. Hist. Soc., Bentley Driver's Club. Avocations: Highland Bagpipes, banjo, guitar, chess, bridge. Fax: (410) 465-2769. Home: Greystone Ste 303 3700 College Ave Ellicott City MD 21043-4663

HUEY, WARD L(IGON), JR., media executive; b. Dallas, Apr. 26, 1938; s. Ward Ligon and Irene Helen (Freeman) H.; m. Marian Kennedy Powell, Oct. 28, 1961; children: Ward L. III, David Powell. BA, So. Meth. U., 1960. Successively with dept. prodn., sales svc. mgr. local sales, regional sales mgr., gen. sales mgr. Sta. WFAA-TV, Dallas, 1960-67, sta. mgr., 1972-75; v.p., gen. mgr. Belo Broadcasting Corp., Dallas, from 1975; vice chmn. bd. dirs., pres. broadcast div. A. H. Belo Corp., Dallas, 1987—; chmn. affiliate bd. govs. ABC-TV, 1981-82; chmn. bd. TV Operators Caucus, 1989. Mem. exec. com. So. Meth. U. Meadows Sch. Arts, 1986—, Goodwill Industries Dallas, 1978-79, State Fair Tex., 1992—; bd. dirs. Children's Med. Found. Tex., Dallas, 1985-94, Dallas Found., 1993—; trustee So. Meth. U., 1996—. Mem. Maximum Svc. TV Assn. (vice chmn. 1988-94), TV Bur. Advt. (past bd. dirs., exec. com. 1984-88), Assn. Broadcast Execs. Tex. (bd. dirs. 1977-78), Dallas Advt. League (bd. dirs. 1975-76), Salesmanship Club Dallas (pres. 1992-93), Dallas Country Club. Methodist. Avocations: skiing, boating, swimming, golf, music. Office: A H Belo Corp 400 S Record St Dallas TX 75202-4841*

HUF, CAROL ELINOR, tax service company executive; b. Milw., Apr. 21, 1940; d. William Weiss and Florence H. (Melcher) Weiss Lange; m. Walter Franklin Huf, Sept. 9, 1961; children: Mardell Leslie, Walter Albert III. Student, Valparaiso U., 1958-60, Waukesha County Tech. Inst., 1968-69. Tax preparer H&R Block, Milw., 1967-84, instr. tax sch., 1969-83; job svc. interviewer State of Wis., Waukesha, 1984; pres. Personalized Tax Svc., Inc., West Allis, Wis., 1984—; divsn. mgr. Primerica (formerly A.L. Williams), 1986. Vol. worker Girl Scouts US, Waukesha, 1970-80, Boy Scouts Am., Waukesha, 1975-92; swimming referee Wis. Interscholastic Athletic Assn., Milw., 1972-84. Recipient award Boy Scouts Am. Mem. Nat. Soc. Pub. Accts., Wis. Womens Pub. Links Golf Assn. (past pres., 2d v.p. 1988—, state tournament chairperson 1987, 90, 94), U.S. Golf Assn. (regional affairs com. 1991—), Nat. Assn. Tax Practitioners (Wis. bd. dirs. 1989-96), Wis. Assn. Accts., Met. Swimming Ofcls., Edgewood Golf Club (pres. Big Bend, Wis. 1984-86). Lutheran. Home: 5508 Bauers Dr West Bend WI 53095-8782 Office: Personalized Tax Service Inc 10533 W National Ave Milwaukee WI 53227-2041 also: PTS 111 N Main St West Bend WI 53095

HUFBAUER, GARY CLYDE, economist, lawyer, educator; b. San Diego, Apr. 3, 1939; s. Clarence Clyde and Arabelle Maxwell (McKee) H.; children: Randall Clyde Revelle (dec.), Ellen Arabelle Scripps; m. Valerie Parra, 1996. AB, Harvard U., 1960; PhD, King's Coll., Cambridge U., Eng., 1963; JD, Georgetown U., 1980. Bar: D.C. 1980, Md. 1980. Mem. faculty dept. econs. U. N.Mex., Albuquerque, 1963-74, prof., 1970-74; dir. internat. tax staff U.S. Dept. Treasury, Washington, 1974-77; dep. asst. Sec. Treasury, Internat. Trade and Investment Policy, 1977-80; mem. firm Rose, Schmidt, Chapman, Duff & Hasley, Washington, 1980-85; dep. dir. Internat. Law Inst., Georgetown Law Ctr., Washington, 1980-85; Wallenberg prof. fin. Georgetown U., Washington, 1985-92; dir. studies Coun. on Fgn. Rels., N.Y.C., 1997-98; sr. fellow Inst. Internat. Econs., Washington, 1982-85, 92-97, 98—; mem. Harvard Devel. Adv. Svc., Pakistan, 1967-69; vis. prof. Stockholm Sch. Econs., 1974, Cambridge U., 1973, Georgetown U., 1975. Author: Economic Sanctions Reconsidered, 1990, Western Hemisphere Economic Integration, 1995. Ford Found. fellow, 1966-67; Fulbright rsch. scholar, 1973. Mem. Am. Econ. Assn., Nat. Economists Club. Episcopalian. Office: Inst for Internat Econs 11 Dupont Cir NW Ste 600 Washington DC 20036-1207

HUFBAUER, KARL GEORGE, historian of science; b. San Diego, July 7, 1937; s. Clarence Clyde and Arabelle Maxwell (McKee) H.; m. Sarah Grant Brannon, Aug. 6, 1960; children: Sarah Beth, Benjamin Grant, Ruth Arabelle. BS in Engring. Sci., Stanford U., 1959; diploma in history and philos. sci., Oxford (Eng.) U., 1961; PhD in History of Sci., U. Calif., Berkeley, 1970. From asst. prof. to prof. dept. history U. Calif., Irvine, 1966—; contract historian NASA, Washington, 1984-90; chair dept. history U. Calif., Irvine, 1992-96; dir. UC Scandinavian Study Ctr., Luad, Sweden, 1997-99. Author: Formation of German Chemical Community, 1982, Exploring the Sun, 1991 (Emme prize 1993). Co-presiding officer Stop Polluting Our Newport, Newport Beach, Calif., 1987-92. Mem. Green Party. Avocations: scuba diving, hiking, cooking. Home: 8750 Chestnut Cir Apt 2 Kansas City MO 64131-2855 Office: Dept History U Calif Irvine CA 92697

HUFF, C(LARENCE) RONALD, public policy and criminology educator; b. Covington, Ky., Nov. 10, 1945; s. Nathaniel Warren G. and Irene Opal (Mills) H.; m. Patricia Ann Plankenhorn, June 15, 1968; children: Tamara Lynn, Tiffany Dawn. BA, Capital U., 1968; MSW, U. Mich., 1970; PhD, Ohio State U., 1974. Social worker Franklin County Children's Svcs., Columbus, Ohio, 1968; social work intern Pontiac (Mich.) State Hosp. and Family Svc. Met. Detroit, 1969-70; dir. psychiat. social work Lima (Ohio) State Hosp., 1970-71; chief psychiat. social worker N.W. Cmty. Mental Health Ctr., Lima, 1971-72; grad. tchg. assoc. sociology Ohio State U., 1972-74; asst. prof. social ecology U. Calif., Irvine, 1974-76; asst. prof. sociology Purdue U., 1976-79; assoc. prof. pub. policy/mgmt., dir. Criminal Justice Rsch. Ohio State U., Columbus, 1979-99, prof., 1987-99, dir. Sch. Pub. Policy and Mgmt., 1994-99; dean Sch. Social Ecology U. Calif., Irvine, 1999—, prof. criminology, law and society, 1999—; vis. prof. U. Hawaii, 1995; cons. Bur. Justice Stats., Nat. Inst. Justice, Nat. Inst. Corrections, Nat. Inst. Juvenile Justice and Delinquency Prevention, U.S. Senate Jud. Com., NSF, FBI, others; expert witness fed. cts. Author: Youth Violence: Prevention, Intervention, and Social Policy, 1999, Convicted But Innocent: Wrongful Conviction and Public Policy, 1996, (Outstanding Acad. Book award Choice Mag., 1996), The Gang Intervention Handbook, 1993, Gangs in America, 1990, 2d edit., 1996, House Arrest and Correctional Policy: Doing Time at Home, 1988, The Mad, The Bad, and The Different: Essays in Honor of Simon Dinitz, 1981, Attorneys as Activists: Evaluating the American Bar Association's BASICS Program, 1979, Contemporary Corrections: Social Control and Conflict, 1977, Planning Correctional Reform, 1975, and others; contbr. articles to profl. jours., chpts. to books. Recipient Nat. Security award Mershon Found., 1980, prize New Eng. Sch. Law, 1981, Outstanding Tchg. award, 1985, Donald R. Cressey award Nat. Coun. on Crime and Delinquency, 1992, Paul Tappan award Western Soc. Criminology, 1993, Herbert Bloch award Am. Soc. Criminology, 1994; grantee ABA, 1974-77, Purdue U., 1978, Dept. Justice, 1978-79, 85-88, 91-95, Ohio Dept. Mental Health, 1982-83, 84-85, 85-87, Gov.'s Office Criminal Justice, 1985-88, 92-95, 98, Ohio Dept. Youth Svcs., 1989-90, Ohio State U./Ohio Bd. Regents, 1990-92. Fellow Western Soc. Criminology; mem. ABA, Acad. Criminal Justice Scis., Am. Soc. Pub. Adminstrn., Am. Soc. Criminology (exec. bd., Herbert Bloch award 1994),Nat. Coun. on Crime and Delinquency, Phi Kappa Phi, Phi Beta Delta. Office: U Calif Irvine Sch Social Ecology 300 Social Ecology I Irvine CA 92697-7065

HUFF, CYNTHIA OWEN, nursing educator, nurse practitioner; b. Danville, Va., Sept. 29, 1948; d. McCoy and Virgie (Griffin) Owen; m. William R. Huff, May 17, 1969; children: Michael, Tonya. BSN, U. Tenn., 1985, MSN, 1986, EdD, 1995. Cert. family nurse practitioner. Staff nurse, charge nurse Knox County Health Dept., Knoxville, Tenn., 1979-82; staff nurse Bapt. Hosp. East Tenn., Knoxville, Tenn., 1982-86; asst. chair grad. studies Carson-Newman Coll., Jefferson City, Tenn., 1986—, mem. C.C. coun., grad. coun., edn. coun.; advisor Carson Newman Coll., 1995-98. Contbr. articles to profl. jours. Vol. ARC, 1990-97, Runaway Shelter, 1994-98. Mem. ANA, Tenn. Nurses Assn., Sigma Theta Tau (grantee 1994). Office: Carson Newman Coll Russell St Jefferson City TN 37760

HUFF, DALE DUANE, hydrologist, educator; b. Portland, Oreg., Mar. 22, 1939; s. Dale and Gudrun (Jacobson) H.; m. Janis K. Watkins, Sept. 29, 1962; children: Lisa, Dean. BS in Chemistry, Stanford U., 1961, MS in Hydrology, 1964, PhD in Hydrology, 1968. Radiochemist Hazelton Nuc. Sci., Palo Alto, Calif., 1961-63; asst. prof., assoc. prof. civil and environ. engring. U. Wis., Madison, 1968-74; mem. rsch. staff environ. scis. div. Oak Ridge (Tenn.) Nat. Lab., 1974-90, mgr. hydrologic support program Groundwater Program Office, 1990—; adj. prof. geol. scis. geology dept. U. Tenn., Knoxville, 1988-91; co-founder, treas. Tenn. Hydrology Symposium; mem. steering com. Tenn. Water Resources Symposium. Contbr. over 50 articles on hydrology, hydrologic modeling and simulaton, waste mgmt. and corrective actions to profl. jours. Recipient Outstanding Instr. award ASCE student chpt. U. Wis. Coll. Engring., 1970, Environ. Protection award Oak Ridge Nat. Lab., 1982. Mem. Am. Inst. Hydrology (cert. profl. hydrologist, pres. Tenn. sect. 1990—), Assn. Groundwater Scientists and Engrs., Am. Water Resources Assn. (organizing com. Tenn., treas. 1993-94, svc. award 1994), Am. Geophys. Union. Achievements include first computer simulation model for transport of radionuclides in a natural watershed; research on hydrologic transport of contaminants, design of hydrologic and water quality monitoring systems, application of hydrologic sciences to environmental restoration. Avocation: square dancing. Office: Oak Ridge Nat Lab Groundwater Program Office PO Box 2008 Oak Ridge TN 37831-2008*

HUFF, DAVID L., geography educator. BS, U. Oreg., 1955; MBA, U. Wash., 1957, PhD, 1960. Now Century Club prof. depts. geography and mktg. adminstrn. U. Tex., Austin. Office: Univ Tex Dept Of Geography Austin TX 78712

HUFF, DAVID RICHARD, funeral home executive; b. St. Joseph, Mo., Aug. 24, 1948; s. Harry Francis and Frances Emily (Knopinski) H.; m. Catherine Ann Chitwood, Aug. 7, 1976. BA, Rockhurst U., 1970; PA, U.S. Med. Ctr., 1975; postgrad., Fla. State U., 1975-76, Loyola U., New Orleans, 1989-90; grad. Cath. ministry, Ctr. for Pastoral Life/Ministr, 1997. Lic. funeral dir., Mo.; lic. educator, Mo.; lic. med. records specialist; lic. pharmacy specialist. Tchr. St. Francis Sch., St. Joseph, 1970; med. records clk. Fed. Prison Health Systems, Leavenworth, Kans., 1971; hosp. adminstrv. asst. Fed. Prison Health Systems, Leavenworth, 1971-73, physician asst., 1974-84; asst. hosp. adminstr. Fed. Prison Health Systems, El Reno, Okla., 1977-79; health systems adminstr. Fed. Prison Health Systems, Big Spring, Tex., 1979-84; bus. mgr. Heaton-Bowman-Smith Funeral Home, Inc., St. Joseph, Mo., 1984—; corp. treas. Heaton-Bowman-Smith FH Inc., St. Joseph, 1991—. Coord. comty. health screenings City of Big Spring, 1980-84; bd. suprs. Citizens Fed. Credit Union, Big Spring, Tex., 1981-84, sec., 1983-84; Roman Cath. Eucharistic Min., 1970— (Diocese Kansas City-St. Joseph, Mo., 1970-73, 84—, Springfield-Cape Girardeau, Mo., 1973-74, Pensacola-Tallahassee, Fla., 1974-77, Oklahoma City, 1977-79, San Angelo, Tex., 1979-84); lay min. Our Lady of Guadalupe Parish, St. Joseph, 1986—; vol. lay Cath. chaplain Mo. Dept. Corrections, 1995—; bd. dirs. Am. Heart Assn., Big Spring, 1982-83, Country Sq. Home Assn., St. Joseph, 1987-92, pres., chmn. bd. dirs., 1988-89, v.p., 1989-90; hon. bd. dirs. Rockhurst Univ., Kansas City, 1983-91, 99—; Dem. committeeman Buchanan County, Mo., 1988-94, treas., 1990-92; vice-chair Mo. 28th Legis. Dist. (formerly 9th) Dem. Com., 1990-92, chmn., 1992-94; host/sponsor students EFL Internat., 1986-96. Mem. St. Joseph C. of C. (Diplomat's Club 1985-92), OLG 3-M (treas. 1989-92), KC (4th degree), Alpha Sigma Nu. Democrat. Roman Catholic. Avocations: gardening, philatelic collection, international travel. Home: 4211 Buckingham Ct Saint Joseph MO 64506-2427 Office: Heaton-Bowman-Smith Funeral Home 3609 Frederick Blvd Saint Joseph MO 64506-3033

HUFF, GARY D., lawyer; b. Seattle, May 9, 1950. BA cum laude, U. Wash., 1972, JD, 1975. Bar: Wash. 1975. Lawyer Karr Tuttle Campbell, Seattle, 1986—. Mem. ABA, Wash. State Bar Assn., Seattle-King County Bar Assn., Phi Beta Kappa. Office: Karr Tuttle & Campbell 1201 3rd Ave Ste 2900 Seattle WA 98101-3028

HUFF, GAYLE COMPTON, advertising/marketing executive; b. Washington, Nov. 28, 1956; d. Walter Dale and Jeanne (Parker) C.; m. Lanny Ross Huff, May 22, 1982. B in Gen. Studies, U. Mich., 1978. Mgr. br. merchandising CBS Records, Chgo., 1978; local promotion, mktg. mgr. CBS Records, Indpls., Boston, N.Y.C., 1978-81; spl. projects supr. Pickwick Internat. Musicland Group, Mpls., 1981-82; account exec. Campbell-Mithun Advt., Mpls., 1982-85; mktg. mgr., communications Universal Foods Corp., Milw., 1985-86; nat. advt. mgr. Thorobred Advt. Agy. (Jockey Internat., Inc.), Wis., 1986-88; dir. consumer and trade advt. Thorobred Advt. Agy. (Jockey Internat., Inc.), 1988-89, v.p. advt., 1990-92; dir. mktg./advt. Allen-Edmonds Shoe Co., Port Washington, Wis., 1993-95; v.p., dir. Fin. Mktg. Plus Direct Mktg. Group, Libertyville, Ill., 1995-97; dir. mktg. & merchandising AR Accessories Group Inc., Milw., Wis., 1997-98; v.p. creative svcs. Tucker-Knapp Integrated Mktg. Comms., Schaumburg, Ill., 1998—; v.p., sec. Java Masters, Inc., 1992—. Mem. Traffic Audit Bur. for Media Measurement (bd. dirs. 1988-93), Assn. Nat. Advertisers (print adv. com., out of home advt. com. 1989-92). Avocations: dance, gymnastics, golf. Office: Tucker-Knapp Integrated Mktg Comms Ste 520 1100 E Woodfield Rd Schaumburg IL 60173

HUFF, JANE VAN DYKE, secondary education educator; b. Marshall, Mo., Aug. 7, 1948; d. Leonard Scott and Bertha Mae (Carmean) Van Dyke; m. George Sweat Huff, June 27, 1970; children: Ethan Van Dyke, Katherine Van Dyke. BA cum laude, So. Meth. U., 1970. Cert. tchr. K-8, Mo. Tchr. 2d grade Marshall Pub. Schs., 1970-73, substitute tchr. K-12, 1985-93, tchr. 6th grade social studies, 1993—. Organist Marshall 1st United Meth. Ch., 1971—; bd. dirs. Marshall Pub. Edn. Found., 1993—, Marhsall Pub. Schs. Citizens' Adv. Bd., 1988—, Marshall Philharm. Orch., 1980—, pres., 1990—; bd. dirs. Marshall Mcpl. Bd., 1985—, Marshall C.C., 1989—. Mem. Mo. State Tchrs. Assn., Phi Beta Kappa, Alpha Kappa Delta. Avocations: music, musical accompaniment, tennis. Home: 331 E North St Marshall MO 65340-2225

HUFF, JANET HOUSE, special education educator; b. Kansas City, Mo., Sept. 5, 1947; d. Arthur William and Juanita Joan (Cook) House; m. William Earl Huff, Dec. 20, 1975; children: Ryan, Anesi. BS in Edn., Emporia State U., 1970; postgrad., Calif. State U., Bakersfield, 1986-89; MA in Edn., U. Phoenix, 1998. Cert. psychology, educationally handicapped and spl. tchr. I, Colo. Tchr. spl. edn. Kansas City (Kans.) Unified Sch. Dist., 1970-73, S.W. Bd. Coop. Svcs., Cortez, Colo., 1973-74, Mesa County Valley Sch. Dist. 51, Grand Junction, Colo., 1974-86, Bakersfield (Calif.) City Schs., 1986-89, Fresno (Calif.) Unified Sch. Dist., 1989-90, Cherry Creek Sch. Dist. 5, Aurora, Colo., 1990-92, Jefferson County Sch. Dist. 1, 1992—. Lutheran.

HUFF, JOHN DAVID, church administrator; b. Muskegon, Mich., Nov. 20, 1952; s. Lucius Barthol and Marian (Brainard) H.; m. Diane Lynn Church, May 17, 1975; children: Joshua, Jason, Jessica. B in Religious Edn., Reformed Bible Coll., 1977; MA in Sch. Adminstrn., Calvin Coll., 1983; postgrad., Western Mich. U. Cert. ch. educator. Dir. edn. 1st Christian Reformed Ch., Visalia, Calif., 1977-79, Bethany Reformed Ch., Grand Rapids, Mich., 1979-83; dir. edn. Haven Reformed Ch., Kalamazoo, 1983-90, exec. dir. ops., 1990-93; exec. dir. Manitoqua Ministries, Frankfort, Ill., 1993—; cons. David C. Cook Pubs., 1988-90, Office Evangelism Reformed Ch. in Am., 1987-91; tchr. trainer, mem. renewal forum Synod of Mich. Reformed Ch. in Am., 1987-90; regional evangelism trainer Synod of Mid-Am., 1995—; bd. dirs. Chgo. Christian Counseling Ctr., 1995—, bd. officer, 1996—; v.p. Illiana Classis Reformed Ch. in Am., 1999, pres., 2000. Author: Effective Decision Making for Church Leaders, 1988, Leader's Guide for Out of the Saltshaker and into the World, 1988. Vice chmn. Youth Com. Bill Glass Crusade, Visalia, 1978, chmn. Cen. Valley Ch. Workers Conf., Visalia, 1978; mem. Youth Com. City-Wide Easter Svcs., Visalia, 1979; trustee Reformed Bible Coll., Grand Rapids, 1984-91, mem. exec. com., 1985-91, asst. sec. bd. dirs., 1986-87, sec. bd. dirs., 1987-90; chmn. S.W. Mich. Christian Discipleship Com., 1984-85. Recipient DeVos award Reformed Bible Coll., 1977; Mich. State scholar, 1970. Mem. Bibl. Archeol. Soc., Christian Educators-Reformed ch. Am., Inst. for Am. Ch. Growth (cons. 1986-93), Christian Mgmt. Assn. Cen. Valley Youth Ministers (sec. 1978-79), Alban Inst., Am. Camping Assn. (bd. dirs. Ill. chpt. 1995-98), Christian Camping Internat., Delta Epsilon Chi. Republican. Avocations: reading, racquetball, golf, civil war info. Home and Office: 8122 W Sauk Trl Frankfort IL 60423-9785 *Half of being smart is knowing what you're dumb at!.*

HUFF, LULA ELEANOR, controller, accounting educator; b. Columbus, Ga., July 5, 1949; d. Walter Theophilus and Sally Lunsford; m. Charles Efferidge Huff Jr., June 11, 1972; 1 child, Tamara Nicole. BA, Howard U., 1971; MBA, Atlanta U., 1973. CPA, Ga. Acct. Ernst and Young, Columbus, 1973-76; internal auditor First Consol. Gov., Columbus, 1976-84; instr., chair dept. acctg., dir. pers. mgmt. Troy State U., Phenix City, Ala., 1979-89; sr. fin./cost analyst Pratt and Whitney, Columbus, 1984-89; controller Pratt and Whitney, Southington, Conn., 1989-92, Columbus, 1992-95; contr. for Precision Components Internat. Pratt and Whitney Joint Venture, Columbus, 1995-96; tax commn. Columbus Consolidated Govt., Columbus, Ga., 1997—; tchr. Troy State U., Phenix City. Mem. fin. bd. Diocese of Savannah; mem. Liberty Theater Hist. Preservation Bd., Columbus Housing Authority Bd., Columbus Hist. Found. Bd., Columbus Literate Cmty. Program Inc. Bd., Columbus Beyond 2000, 1989-90; active Concharty coun. Girl Scouts, Inc., Women of Achievement, 1995; active Chattahoochee Valley Cmty. Found., Inc. Recipient Disting. Black Citizen award Sta. WOKS, 1978, Black Excellence award Nat. Assn. Negro Bus. and Profl. Women's Clubs, Inc., 1977, Outstanding Svc. award St. Benedict Cath. Ch., 1971-76, cert. of merit Congressman Jack Brinkley, 1976, Achievement award Links Inc., 1976, Outstanding Achievement and Svcs. award 1st African Bapt. Ch., 1975, Ga. Jaycees Outstanding Young Woman award, 1989, Leadership Columbus award C. of C., 1983-84, Women on the Move award Spencer Owlettes, 1992; named Outstanding Woman of Yr., Ledger Enquirer Newspaper, 1976, Profl. Woman of Yr., Iota Phi Lambda, 1977, Bus. Woman of Yr., 1979, Columbus Ga. Outstanding Young Woman, Jaycees, 1980, Columbus Young Woman, 1980. Mem. NAACP, Am. Mgmt. Assn., Ga. Soc. CPAs, Howard U. Alumnae Assn., Urban League, Push, Toastmasters Am., Links, Inc. (Achievement award 1976), Columbus C. of C., Delta Sigma Theta (auditor 1991). Roman Catholic. Avocation: swimming. Home: PO Box 1742 Columbus GA 31902-1742

HUFF, MARILYN L., federal judge; b. 1951. BA, Calvin Coll., Grand Rapids, Mich., 1972; JD, U. Mich., 1976. Assoc. Gray, Cary, Ames & Frye, 1976-83, ptnr., 1983-91; judge U.S. Dist. Ct. (so. dist.) Calif., San Diego, 1991-98, chief judge, 1998—. Contbr. articles to profl. jours. Mem. adv. coun. Calif. LWV, 1987—, Am. Lung Assn.; bd. dirs. San Diego and Imperial Counties, 1989—; mem. LaJolla Presbyn. Ch. Named Legal Profl. of Yr. San Diego City Club and Jr. C. of C., 1990; recipient Superior Ct. Valuable Svc. award, 1982. Mem. ABA, San Diego Bar Found., San Diego Bar Assn. (bd. dirs. 1986-88, v.p. 1988, chmn. profl. edn. com. 1990, Svc. award to legal profession, 1989, Lawyer of Yr. 1990), Calif. State Bar Assn., Calif. Women Lawyers, Am. Bd. Trial Advs., Libel Def. Resource Ctr., Am. Inns of Ct. (master 1987—, exec. com. 1989—), Lawyers' Club San Diego (adv. bd. 1989-90, Belva Lockwood Svc. award 1987), Univ. Club, Aardvarks Lt. Office: US Dist Ct Courtroom 1 940 Front St San Diego CA 92101-8994

HUFF, MARSHA ELKINS, lawyer; b. Tulsa, Apr. 11, 1946. BA with honors, U. Tulsa, 1968, MA, 1970; JD cum laude, Loyola U. of Chgo., 1974. Bar: Wis. Ptnr. Foley & Lardner, Milw. mem. editorial bd. Loyola U. Law Jour., 1973-74. Mem. ABA (mem. sect. taxation). Office: Foley & Lardner Firstar Ctr 777 E Wisconsin Ave Ste 3800 Milwaukee WI 53202-5367

HUFF, RICKY WAYNE, sales executive; b. Willits, Calif., Sept. 30, 1953; s. Walter Richard and Janine Norma (Iles) H.; m. Donna Elizabeth Todd, Sept. 17, 1977; children: Brianne Ashley, Kendra Danielle. AA, Santa Rosa (Calif.) Jr. Coll., 1973; BA, Chico (Calif.) State U., 1975. Swim instr., lifeguard Chico YMCA, 1973; mall maintenance Chico Plz., 1973-74; warehouseman Stihl. Co., Chico, 1974-75; delivery driver Downey (Calif.) Unified Sch. Dist., 1975-76; regional mgmt. trainee Montgomery Ward, Norwalk, Calif., 1976-78; sr. sales rep. Fisher-Price Toys, East Aurora, N.Y., 1978-86; key account rep. Rubbermaid, Wooster, Ohio, 1986-87; dir. of sales Century Products Co., Macedonia, Ohio, 1987-96; owner, pres. RH Sales & Mktg., Downey, Calif., 1996—; nat. sales mgr. Relax-R Corp., St. Albans, Vt., 1998—. Author: (handbook) Contract Services, Retail Service Program, 1986, Independent Sales Force Sales Manual, 1989. Vol. YMCA, Downey, 1977—, campaigner, 1986, 93—, fin. com., 1995—, bd. mgrs., 1996—, mem. exec. com., 1998—; chief of Chonook tribe and wampon bearer YMCA Indian Princesses, Downey, 1992—, Nation Chief, 1997—; bd. dirs. 1st Presbyn. Ch., Downey, 1987-89, Downey Family YMCA, 1996—; coach Lakers Jr. League Girls Basketball, YMCA, 1996—. Mem. Western Toy and Hobby Reps Assn., Downey DeMolay (adv. 1976-78), Willits DeMolay (master councilor 1970-71). Republican. Presbyterian. Avocations: basketball, biking, racketball, running, remodeling houses. Home: 8120 Pageant St Downey CA 90240-2744

HUFF, ROBERT WHITLEY, obstetrician, gynecologist, educator; b. San Antonio, 1937. MD, Baylor U., 1966. Diplomate Am. Bd. Med. Genetics, Am. Bd. Ob-Gyn., Am. Bd. Maternal and Fetal Medicine. Intern Ben Taub Gen. Hosp., Houston, 1966-67; resident in ob-gyn. Bexar County Hosp., San Antonio, 1969-72; now prof. U. Tex., San Antonio; mem. staff Med. Ctr. Hosp., San Antonio. Office: U Tex Health Sci Ctr ObGyn 7703 Floyd Curl Dr San Antonio TX 78284-6200*

HUFF, RONALD GARLAND, mechanical engineer; b. Toledo, Ohio, Dec. 29, 1930; s. Blenn Chalmer and Helen Ester (Schling) H.; m. Nancy Carroll Warns, June 29, 1957; children: Dennis Lee, Deborah Lynn. BSME, U. Toledo, 1953. Aero. engr. Nat. Adv. Com. for Aeronautics, Cleve., 1955-58; aerospace tech. NASA, Cleve., 1958-87; cons./proprietor Ronald G. Huff & Assocs., Cleve., 1986—. Contbr. articles to profl. jours. Photographer North Olmsted Band Boosters, Ohio, 1974-80; active PTA, North Olmsted, 1969-72. 1st lt. U.S. Army, 1953-55. Mem. ASME (chmn. winter ann.meeting 1986), AIAA. Congregationalist. Achievements include patent on supersonic jet noise suppressor; method for measuring internal hot gas side wall temperatures in thin wall generatively cooled rocket engines. Home and Office: Huff & Assocs 3741 Cinnamon Way Westlake OH 44145-5717

HUFF, RUSSELL JOSEPH, public relations and publishing executive; b. Chgo., Feb. 24, 1936; s. Russell Winfield and Virgilist Marie (McMahon) H.; m. Beverly Diane Staschke, 1968; 1 child, Michelle Lynn. BA in Philosophy cum laude, U. Notre Dame, 1958; BS in Theology, Cath. U. Santiago (Chile), 1960; MA in Comm. Arts, U. Notre Dame, 1968. Ordained priest Roman Cath. Ch., 1962. Exec. editor Cath. Boy and Miss., Notre Dame, Ind., 1963-68; mng. editor Nation's Schs., McGraw Hill, Chgo., 1968-70; v.p. pub. affairs Homart Devel. Co., Chgo., 1971-76; dir. pub. rels. Sears, Roebuck Co. Internat. Ops., Chgo., 1976-82; dir. pub. affairs Sears Roebuck Found. Internat. Projects, Chgo., 1981-82; sr. v.p., sales and mktg. dir. Mineca Internat., Inc., Chgo., 1982-84; v.p., pub. rels. Lofino Poppa Devel. Corp., Sarasota, Fla., 1984-85; pres., co-owner R.J. Huff & Assocs., Inc., Sarasota, 1985—; real estate broker Sarasota, 1985—. Author: Come Build My Church, 1966, One Wings of Adventure, 1967, Wings of WWII, 1985, Companion to Wings of World War II, 1987, Winging It, Vols. I and II, 1992; editor, pub. (quar. jour.) Wings and Things of the World, 1987-93, Wings and Things of the World for Sale, 1993-95; cons., editl. contbr. Aviation Treasures, 1995—; sr. editor The Nobody's Fool Fin. Market Analyst Pub., 1996-98. Care min. leader Ch. Incarnation Parish Coun., mem. future planning and rev. com. Recipient Outstanding Mag. award Cath. Press Assn., 1965, 67; named for Best Cover, Nation's Schs., 1968; cert. Gemol. Inst. Am.; cert. jr. coll. tchr., Calif. Mem. Pub. Rels. Soc. Am. (accredited 1976—), Chicagoland Mil. Collectors Soc. (dir. quar. expositions 1981-82), Am. Soc. Mil. Insignia Collectors, Orders and Medals Soc. Am., Nat. Fgn. Trade Coun., Pub. Affairs Coun., Conf. Bd., Internat. Bus. Coun., Internat. Vis. Ctr. Chgo., Ptnrs. of the Ams. (cert. for advancement L.Am. rels. 1980), Säa Paulo Ptnrs. (cert. for advancement Brazil-U.S. rels. 1979, dir. Ill.), Chgo. Assn. of Commerce and Industry, U.S.-Spanish C. of C. of Middle West (dir.), War Memorabilia Collectors Soc. (exec. dir.). Roman Catholic. Office: RJ Huff & Assocs Inc 4062 Kingston Ter Sarasota FL 34238-2632

HUFF, SHEILA LINDSEY, secondary education educator, coach; b. Rockport, Ind., Oct. 29, 1951; d. William Nathaniel and Thelma Cordelia (Crawley) Lindsey; m. Aug. 7, 1976 (div. 1984); children: Aaron Drake, Andrew Christopher. BS, Ind. State U., 1973, MS, 1975. Cert. health and phys. edn. tchr., Ind., lic. secondary administrn. and supervision. Asst. dir. residence hall Ind. State U., Terre Haute, 1973-74, dir. residence hall, 1974-76; coach boys tennis Evansville (Ind.) Vanderburgh Sch. Corp., 1976-78, girls track coach, 1976—, girls volleyball coach, 1985-89, tchr. phys. edn. and recreation, summer 1985-90; asst. prin. Glenwood Middle Sch.; assoc. prof. U. So. Ind.; instr. in CPR, ARC, Evansville, 1980-90; advisor Health Profls. Adv. Bd., Evansville, 1989-90; interim prof. U. So. Ind., Evansville, 1989—, assoc. prof., 1990—; asst. athletic dir. Bosse H.S., 1995—. Community instr. ARC, Evansville, 1986-90. Mem. AAHPERD, NEA, Nat. Assn. Secondary Sch. Prins., Ind. Assn. Secondary Sch. Prins., Ind. Tchrs. Assn., Ind. Health, Phys. Edn. and Recreation Assn. Evansville Tchrs. and Coaches Assn. Baptist. Avocations: reading, crafts, sports, cooking. Home: 1706 N Thomas Ave Evansville IN 47711-4452

HUFF, STANLEY EUGENE, dermatologist; b. Bremen, Ind., June 5, 1918; s. Otho H. and Gertrude M. (Nufer) H.; m. Helen Leonard, Oct. 30, 1946; children: John, Margaret, Thomas, Stephen, Katherine, Mary. B.S., U. Notre Dame, 1940; M.D., Northwestern U., 1944; M.S. in Dermatology, U. Minn., 1949. Intern Wesley Meml. Hosp., Chgo., 1944; pvt. practice Evanston, Ill., 1950—; mem. staff Evanston Hosp.; prof. clin. dermatology Northwestern U. Med. Sch. Vice pres. Evanston United Fund, 1960-62. Served with M.C. AUS, 1944-46. Mem. Am. Acad. Dermatology (pres. 1968), Am. Dermatol. Assn. (v.p. 1979-80), Soc. Investigative Dermatology, AMA, Evanston C. of C. Club: Kiwanis. Address: 75 Balmoral Ave Winnetka IL 60093-3101

HUFF, WILLIAM BRAID, publication company executive; b. Lynn, Mass., Apr. 18, 1950; s. Harold Butler and Mary Stewart (Braid) H.; m. Karen Murphy, May 4, 1985; children: Thomas Murphy, Kathryn Braid. BS, Bowdoin Coll., 1972; MBA, Dartmouth Coll., 1974. CPA, Mass. Staff acct. Arthur Andersen, Boston, 1974-76; controller Affiliated Broadcasting, Boston, 1976-82, treas., 1982-86, sr. v.p., 1984-86; controller Affiliated Publs., Boston, 1982-86, v.p., 1986-89, chief fin. officer, 1989-91, exec. v.p., CFO, 1991-97; sr. v.p., CFO Boston Globe Newspaper Co., 1992-97, pres., CFO, 1997—. Active Literacy Vols. of Mass. Mem. AICPAs, Mass. Soc. CPA's. Republican. Episcopalian. Club: Weston Golf. Avocations: golf, skiing, soccer. Home: 5 Sherman Bridge Rd Wayland MA 01778-1213 Office: Boston Globe PO Box 2378 135 Morrissey Blvd Boston MA 02107-2378*

HUFFAKER, E. WAYNE, artist; b. Flin Flon, Man., Can., June 14, 1933; s. Marvin F. and Janice (Barton) H.; m. Shirley K. Huffaker, Apr. 3, 1951 (dec. 1968); children: Tony, Gary, Laura, Renee; m. Linda S. Huffaker, May 21, 1984; 1 child, Brandon. AA, Ventura (Calif.) Coll., 1968. Info. svcs. supr. Conoco, Inc., Houston, 1956-95. Automobilia artist done for commn., mag., books and box-lid art, as well as speculation pieces to offer as originals or ltd. edit. prints. With USNR, 1950-62. Mem. Colored Pencil Soc. Avocations: sports, custom and classic cars. Home: 19606 Spring Sage Ct Houston TX 77094-2627 Office: PMB 168 925 S Mason Rd Katy TX 77450-3874

HUFFAKER, JOHN BOSTON, lawyer; b. Nashville, Nov. 1, 1925; s. William Bruce and Pauline (Watson) H.; m. Grace Murray Logan, Jan. 14, 1954 (dec. June 15, 1989); children: Margaret, Christiana H. Logansmith; m. Judith Hudson Webster, Oct. 24, 1992. B.S., Yale U., 1946; LL.B., U. Va., 1948. Bar: Va., Pa., D.C., U.S. Supreme Ct. Assoc. Cummings, Stanley, Truitt & Cross, Washington, 1949-51; legis. atty. Joint Com. on Taxation, Washington, 1953-56; assoc. Duane, Morris & Heckscher, Phila., 1956-61; ptnr. Rawle & Henderson, Phila., 1961-66, Pepper Hamilton LLP, Berwyn, Pa., Phila. and Washington, 1966—; spl. advisor Tax Mgmt., 1960—; pres. Consular Corps of Phila., 1990-91. Departmental editor Jour. Taxation, 1976—; contbr. articles to profl. jours. Named hon. consul Republic of Madagascar, 1982—; bd. dirs. Welcome House, Doylestown, Pa., 1970—, v.p., 1976-80, pres., 1980—, chmn. overseas ops. com., 1984—, chmn., 1988—, bd. dirs. Pearl S. Buck Found., 1984—, vice chmn. internat. ops., 1994-96, chmn. 1990-94, chmn. fin. com., 1998—; chmn. Wharton Sch. Tax Conf., 1981-83, Phila. Tax Conf., 1996-97, planned giving coun. U. Va. Lt. USN, 1951-53. Bldg. in The Philippines named in recognition of work (with wife) in behalf of neglected and abandoned children in The Philippines. Fellow Am. Coll. Tax Counsel; mem. ABA (chmn. com. income of estates and trusts, sect. taxation 1981-83, spl. adviser 1983-85, chmn. QSST subcom. 1984—), Phila. Bar Assn. (tax sect. coun. 1976-81), Consular Corps Phila. (pres. 1989-91), Merion Cricket Club, Phila. Skating Club & Humane Soc., Univ. Club Washington, Sons of Confederate Vets. Republican. Presbyterian. Home: 229 Pennswood Rd Bryn Mawr PA 19010-3615 Office: Pepper Hamilton & Scheetz 1235 Westlakes Dr Ste 400 Berwyn PA 19312-2416 also: 3000 N 2nd St Philadelphia PA 19133-3610*

HUFFEY, VINTON EARL, clergyman; b. Luana, Iowa, July 7, 1915; s. Walter Angus and Tilda Boleta (Olson) H.; m. Lillian Bertha Crouse, June 22, 1942; children: Naomi, Rhoda, Stephen, Deborah. Student, Ctrl. Bible Coll., Springfield, Mo., 1936-38, North Ctrl. Bible Coll., Mpls., 1938-40. Ordained to ministry Assemblies of God, 1942. Pastor Assemblies of God, Oelwein, Iowa, 1940-43, LeMars, Iowa, 1943-47; evangelist Assemblies of God, Iowa and Mo., 1947-48; pres. youth Assemblies of God, Iowa and North Mo., 1948-52, editor News of West Ctrl., 1948-52; pastor Assemblies of God, Ames, Iowa, 1952-58, Monrovia, Calif., 1958-78; crusader inner-city evangelism Assemblies of God, 1978-93; pastor Assemblies of God, South Pasadena, Calif., 1993-96; motivation lectr. Assemblies of God, 1980-92; originator inner-city revolving loan fund, mem. urban task force So. Calif. Dist. Assemblies of God, Irvine, Calif., Springfield, Mo., Gen. Counsel of the Assemblies of God, 1982. Author: (pamphlet) The Church and America's Inner-cities, 1981; author of poems. Mem. Think Am. Com. City Coun., Duarte, Calif., 1962, lit. rev. com., 1965; chmn. What About Duarte? L.A. County Dept. Human Rels. City of Hope, Duarte, 1963. Recipient Decade of Harvest award So. Calif. Dist. Coun. Assemblies of God, Irvine, Calif., 1994. Republican. Avocations: travel, deep sea fishing. Home and Office: 161 N Mayflower Ave Monrovia CA 91016-2000

HUFFINE, COY LEE, retired chemical engineer, consultant; b. Knoxville, Tenn., Apr. 2, 1924; s. Coy Mann and Inez Belle (Story) H.; m. Virginia Elizabeth Browne, Mar. 31, 1951; children: Jeremy Bennett, Lucinda Jane. B.S., U. Tenn., 1945, M.S., 1947; Ph.D., Columbia U., 1953. Prin. engr. aircraft nuclear propulsion program Gen. Electric Co., Oak Ridge and Cin., 1951-59; research ceramist Gen. Electric Research Lab., Schenectady, 1959-60; project mgr. devel. and mfg. Apollo spacecraft Heat Shield, space sys. div. Avco Corp., Lowell, Mass., 1960-67; with IBM, Rochester, Minn., 1968-87, mgr. component tech., info. systems div., 1980-87; cons. and lectr. in field; lay-lectr. on history and philosophy of sci. Unitarian-Universalist Ch. Served with USN, 1945-46. Mem. Am. Inst. Chem. Engrs., AIME, Nat. Inst. Ceramic Engrs., Am. Ceramic Soc., N.Y. Acad. Scis., Sigma Xi. Home: 2247 5th Ave NE Rochester MN 55906-4017

HUFFINGTON, ANITA, sculptor; b. Balt., Dec. 25, 1934; d. Norris Jackson and Agnes (Hook) H.; m. Manuel Rubin Duque, Sept. 17, 1957 (div. Nov. 1964); 1 child, Lisa Huffington Duque; m. Henry Sutter, Dec. 4, 1964. BA, CCNY, 1973, MFA, 1975. Resident La Napoule (France) Art Found., 1996. One- woman exhbns. include U. Ark., Fayetteville, 1982, Valley House Gallery, Dallas, 1986, Benton Gallery, Southampton, N.Y., 1989, Ark. Art Ctr., Little Rock, 1990, O'Hara Gallery, N.Y.C., 1994, 96, 99, U. Ctrl. Ark., Conway, 1997, Triangle Gallery, San Francisco, 1998; 2-person show Lisa Kurts Gallery, Memphis, 1995; 3-person shows Louis Stern Gallery, West Hollywood, Calif., 1996, Triangle Gallery, San Francisco, 1996; group exhbns. include Internat. Women's Art Festival, N.Y.C., 1976, U. Ark., Fayetteville, 1978, 92, Ark. Arts Ctr., Little Rock, 1979-81, Territorial Restoration Gallery, Little Rock, 1981, Harris Gallery, Houston, Tex., 1981-93, Sculptural Arts Mus., Altanta, 1982, Benton Gallery, Southampton, N.Y., 1988, Kornbluth Gallery, Fair Lawn, N.J., 1989, 7th Regiment Armory Art Show, N.Y.C., 1989-99, Ft. Smith (Ark.) Art Ctr., 1990, Salon de Mars, Paris, 1992, U. Pa., Phila. U.S. Artists Art Fair, Pa. Acad., 1992-97, ARTexas, Dallas, 1993-94, Art Fair Seattle, 1995-96, Art Miami (Fla.), 1996, 98, Triangle Gallery, San Francisco, 1996, Am. Acad. Arts and Letters, N.Y.C., 1997, Columbus (Ga.) Mus. and Miss. Mus. Art, Jackson, 1997, Am. Acad. Arts and Letters, 1997, Two Sculptors, Inc., N.Y.C., 1998, Valley House Gallery, Dallas, 1998, Palm Beach Invitational, 1998, 99, others; featured in various profl. publs., mags., newspapers and videos. Recipient Jimmy Ernst award Am. Acad. Arts and Letters, 1997, others; Visual arts fellow Ark. Arts Coun.

HUFFINGTON, ARIANNA, writer; b. Athens, Greece, July 15, 1950; came to U.S., 1980; d. Constantine and Helen; m. Michael Huffington, Apr. 12, 1986 (div. 1997); children: Christina, Isabella. MA in Econ., Cambridge U., Eng., 1971. Author: The Female Woman, 1973, After Reason, 1978, Maria Callas: The Woman Behind the Legend, 1981, Picasso: Creator and Destroyer, 1988, The Gods of Greece, 1993, The Fourth Instinct, 1994, Greetings From the Lincoln Bedroom, 1998.

HUFFINGTON, ROY MICHAEL, business executive, former ambassador; b. Tomball, Tex., Oct. 4, 1917; s. Roy Mackey and Bertha (Michel) H.; m. Phyllis Gough, Oct. 26, 1945; children: R. Michael, Terry Huffington Dittman. BS, So. Meth. U., 1938; MA, Harvard U., 1941, PhD, 1942, grad. advanced mgmt. program, 1976; LHD, So. Meth. U., 1990. Tchg. fellow Harvard U., Cambridge, Mass., 1939-42, instr. geology, 1942; sr. geologist, divn. exploration geologist Humble Oil and Refining Co., Houston, 1946-56; pres. Roy M. Huffington, Inc., Houston, 1956-83, chmn. bd., 1956-90; chmn., pres. Roy M. Huffington, Inc., 1993—; U.S. amb. to Austria, Vienna, 1990-93; bd. dirs. Huffco Group, Inc., Houston; bd. dirs. Am. Petroleum Inst., Washington, 1983-90, 93—; bd. dirs. Brookings Inst., Washington, 1984-88, mem. exec. com., 1993—, hon. life trustee, 1988-90, 93—; chmn. Salzburg Seminar, 1994—, bd. dirs., 1992-94. Contbr. articles to profl. jours. Bd. dirs. Tex. Med. Ctr., 1989-90, 93—, Houston Mus. Natural Sci., 1981-86, Kid Care, Inc., Houston, 1993—; trustee Huffington Found., 1987—, Baylor Coll. Medicine, 1986-90, 93—, Webster U., Vienna, 1992—, George Bush Libr. Found., Tex. A&M U., 1993—; bd. visitors M.D. Anderson Cancer Ctr., 1980-90, 93—, Sheltering Arms Found. for Elderly, 1994-97, Sch. Politics and Econs., Claremont (Calif.) Grad. U., 1995—; bd. govs. Mid. East Inst., 1982-88; life mem. devel. bd. U. Tex. Health Sci. Ctr.; life mem. The Rothko Chapel, 1996—, dir., 1981-90, 93—; mem. leadership com. James A. Baker III Inst. for Pub. Policy, Rice U., 1993—. Lt. comdr. USNR, 1942-45, USNR, 1942-54. Decorated Bronze Star with combat V; recipient Alumni Achievement award Harvard U. Bus. Sch., 1982, Oil Drop award petroleum divsn. ASME, 1985, Gold Medallion Oil Pioneer award Indonesian Govt., 1985, John Rogers award Southwestern Legal Found., 1987, Disting. Alumni award So. Meth. U., 1988, Internat. Businessman of Yr. award Houston World Trade Assn., 1988, Amb. of Yr. award Diplomatic Club, Vienna, 1992, Disting. Svc. award Permian Basin sect. Soc. Econ. Paleontologists and Mineralogists, 1996, Grosse Goldene Ehrenzeichen award for svcs. to the Rep. of Austria, 1997; named to Tex. Bus. Hall of Fame, 1992. Fellow AAAS (life), Geol. Soc. Am. (trustee 1988-90, hon. found. trustee 1991—); mem. Am. Assn. Petroleum Geologists (Michel T. Halbouty Human Needs award 1991, trustee assoc. found. 1980-90, 93—), Ind. Petroleum Assn. Am. (dir. 1979-80), Mid-Continent Oil and Gas Assn., Tex. Ind. Prodrs. and Royalty Owners Assn., Tex. Mid-Continent Oil and Gas Assn. (dir. 1972-84, Disting. Svc. award 1988), Houston Geol. Soc., Am. Inst. Profl. Geologists, 25-Yr. Club of the Petroleum Industry, Internat. Assn. for Energy Econs. Washington (pres.'s adv. coun. 1997—), All-Am. Wildcatters (chmn. 1986-87), Asia Soc. N.Y. (chmn. 1982-89, trustee 1978-82, hon. life trustee 1989-90, 93—), Am. Austrian Found. N.Y. (trustee 1993—), The U.S. Indonesia Soc. (Washington, dir. 1994—), Pacific Coun. on Internat. Policy (L.A.), Coun. on Fgn. Rels., World Econ. Forum, Coun. Am. Ambs., Interferon Found. (vice chmn., co-founder, 1979-90), U.S. Navy League, Nat. Petroleum Coun., SAR, The Doctors Club of Houston, The Houston Club (bd. dirs. 1967-70, v.p. 1969-70), The Houston Country Club (mem. ho. com. 1979-81), Met. Club N.Y.C. (mem. govs. adv. bd. 1974-77), Met. Club of Washington, Petroleum Club of Houston (mem. food com. 1966-67, mem. fin. com. 1969-70, bd. dirs. 1978-80, 1st v.p. 1980-81), Ramada-Tejas Club, Alpha Tau Omega (bd. govs. Found. 1993—, Disting. Alumni award 1987). Republican. Presbyterian. Office: PO Box 4337 Houston TX 77210-4337

HUFFMAN, CAROL KOSTER, retired middle school educator; b. L.I., N.Y., Nov. 4, 1933; d. Harry C. Jr. and Mary M. (Wilchin) Koster; m. William Leslie Huffman. BS, Hofstra U., 1954, MS, 1967. Cert. elem., art, nursery and spl. edn. tchr., N.Y.; cert. advanced Irlen screener I and area coord. Dir. Child's World Sch., New Orleans; in-svc. instr. Half Hollow Hills Schs., Dix Hills, N.Y.; instr. in spl. edn. Hofstra U., Hempstead, N.Y.; resource, self-contained program, art and learning strategies tchr. Half Hollow Hills Schs., Dix Hills, N.Y.; cons. for curriculum, spl. edn. and reading; rschr. identification and ednl. accomodations for students with visual disabilities affecting schoolwork. Former editor: The Communicator; editor The Phoenix. Former del. N.Y. State Retirement Sys. Mem. AFT (former del.), N.Y. State United Tchrs. (former del.), Half Hollow Hills Tchr. Assn. (exec. bd.), Kappa Pi, Kappa Delta Pi. Rschr. ednl. accomodations for autistic individuals through the use of visual aids (Irlen lens and filters).

HUFFMAN, DAVID CURTIS, minister; b. Burlington, N.C., Mar. 28, 1950; s. Donald Tyson and Merle (Walker) H.; m. Elaine Janine Wolf, June 25, 1988; children: Katherine Elizabeth Wolf, Anna Elaine Huffman. BA, U. N.C., 1972; MDiv, Princeton Theol. Sem., 1976. Ordained to ministry Presbyn. Ch. (U.S.A.), 1976. Student asst. min. Franklin Lakes (N.J.) Presbyn. Ch., 1973-76; asst. min. Old South Ch., Boston, 1976-79, assoc. min., 1979-81; pastor Trinity Presbyn. Ch., Raleigh, N.C., 1981—; chmn. profl. devel. com. Orange Presbytery, Durham, N.C., 1982-84, chmn. peacemaking com., 1982-85, mem. com. on ministry, 1983-87; chmn. com. on ministry New Hope Presbytery, Rocky Mount, N.C., 1988-90, 93, examinations com., 1995—; pres. Presbyn. Urban Coun., Raleigh, 1988; commr. to gen. assembly Presbyn. Ch., U.S.A., 1995. Merrill fellow Harvard Div. Sch., 1986. Mem. Raleigh Ministerial Assn., Soc. Bibl. Lit., Phi Beta Kappa, Beta Theta Pi. Democrat. Home: 8705 Mansfield Dr Raleigh NC 27613-1337 Office: Trinity Presbyn Ch 3120 New Hope Rd Raleigh NC 27604-4948

HUFFMAN, DAVID GEORGE, electrical engineer; b. Fresno, Calif., Apr. 13, 1965; s. Fred Norman and Sharon (Richardson) H.; m. Johnnie Ann Valtierra, Sept. 21, 1991; children: Matthew Christopher Kenerly, Makenna Francisca-Elise. BSEE, Fresno State U., 1988. Field engr. Power Systems Testing Co., Fresno, Calif., 1988-93, dir. engring., 1993—, mgr., 1994—, gen. mgr., CEO, 1999—. Mem. Internat. Electronic and Electrical Engrs. Assn., Eta Kappa Nu. Avocations: golf, model building, reading, traveling, skydiving. Office: Power Systems Testing Co 4688 W Jennifer Ave Ste 108 Fresno CA 93722-6418

HUFFMAN, DONNA LOU, interior designer; b. Uvalde, Tex., Sept. 25, 1948; d. Herbert Quarrells Jr. and Wanna Lou (Ray) Haile; children: Laura Anne, Christopher J. BS, U. Houston, 1969, MEd, 1973. Owner Rainbow Design LLC, Littleton, Colo., 1975—; owner Health By Design, distbr. Rexall Showcase Internat.; spkr. in field. Designer Parade of Homes, 1989, Jr. Symphony Guild Showhome, 1996; designs featured in Colorado Homes and Lifestyles, Denver Post. Founder, pres. Priime Tiime Today, Littleton, Colo., 1993—. Republican. Baptist. Avocations: water fitness, fly fishing, white water rafting. Office: Rainbow Design LLC PO Box 2829 Littleton CO 80161-2829

HUFFMAN, DOUGLAS SCOTT, educator and administrator college level; b. Mpls., Jan. 1, 1961; s. David I. and Barbara Jean H.; m. Deborah Lynn Nelson, June 16, 1985. BA in Ministries, Northwestern Coll., St. Paul, Minn., 1983; MA in Biblical Studies New Testament, Wheaton (Ill.) Coll., 1985; MA in Christian Thought, Trinity Evangel. Divinity Sch., Deerfield, Ill., 1989, PhD in New Testament Exegesis & Theology, 1994. Asst. prof. Bible Northwestern Coll., St. Paul, Minn., 1994-97; dean admissions, asst. prof. Bible Northwestern Coll., St. Paul, 1997-99, dean admissions and records, assoc. prof. Bible, 1999—; travel tour leader mission trips and study tours to Mex., Israel, Europe, China. Speaker: camps and chs. nationwide. Recipient Trinity Faculty scholarship, Trinity Evangelical Divinity Sch., Deerfield, Ill., 1989. Fellow Inst. for Biblical Rsch.; mem. Evangelical Theolog. Soc., Soc. Biblical Lit. E-mail: dsh@nwc.edu. Avocations: film, books. Home: 890 Patton Rd New Brighton MN 55112 Office: Northwestern Coll 3003 Snelling Ave N Saint Paul MN 55113

HUFFMAN, DURWARD ROY, academic administrator, electrical engineer; b. Little Mountain, S.C., Jan. 22, 1939; s. Roy Otho and Mabel Amanda (Huffstettler) H.; m. Lillian Hope Farrell, Apr. 18, 1959; children: Donald Durward, Heatherlyn. BSEE, Heald Engring. Coll., 1963; MSEE, U. Colo., 1966; EdD in Higher Edn., U. Sarasota, 1980. Registered profl. engr., Pa. Asst. design engr. Westinghouse Elec. Corp., Sunnyvale, Calif., 1963-64; instr. elec. engring. U. Colo., Boulder, 1965-67; elec. engr. Corning (N.Y.) Glass Works, 1967-68; sr. process control engr. Corning Glass Works, Wellsboro, Pa., 1968; assoc. prof. elec.-electronic engring. tech. Luzerne County C.C., Wilkes-Barre, Pa., 1968-73, chmn. dept., 1971-73; faculty Midlands Tech. Coll., Columbia, S.C., 1973-75; assoc. dean Nashville State Tech. Inst., 1976-87, acting dean instrn., 1985-86; pres. No. Maine Tech. Coll., Presque Isle, 1987—; presenter in field; chair tech. accreditation commn. Accreditation Bd. Engring. and Tech., 1989-90; acad. officer Me. Tech. Coll. Sys., Augusta, 1994—. Editor-in-chief, Jour. Engring. Tech., 1990-92, pub. editor, 1987-89. Mem. steering com. Ctrl. Aroostook County (Maine) Job Opportunity Zone, 1988-91; bd. dirs. Leaders Encouraging Aroostook Devel., 1988—, sec., 1988-93; bd. dirs. Maine Rsch. and Productivity Coun., 1988-92. Fellow Accreditation Bd. Engring. and Tech.; mem. IEEE (sr.), Am. Soc. Engring. Edn. (divsn. engring. tech. exec. bd. 1981-82, sec. 1982-84), Am. Tech. Edn. Assn., Am. Assn. C.C. (commn. on cmty. and workforce devel. 1995-97, com. on academic, student, cmty. devel. 1998—), Engring. Tech. Leadership Inst. (mem. exec. com. 1978-79, 86-87), New Eng. Assn. Schs. and Colls. (chairperson accreditation team 1990, 95, 97, 98, team mem. 1994-96), Rotary (chairperson com. on vocat. svc. 1988-89, dist. 7810 scholarships subcom. 1996—), Presque Isle Club, Eta Kappa Nu. Republican. Avocation: vol. work accreditation postsecondary ednl. instns. and programs. Office: No Maine Tech Coll 33 Edgemont Dr Presque Isle ME 04769-2016

HUFFMAN, EDGAR JOSEPH, oil company executive; b. Hartford City, Ind., Aug. 24, 1939; s. Floyd Edgar and Elizabeth Jean (Rawlings) H.; m. Margaret Mary Brenet, May 3, 1980; children: Donovan L. Walker, Maryanne Ramirez. BBA, Ind. Cen. U., 1961; MA, NYU, 1968. V.p. corp. profitability Valley Nat. Bank, Phoenix, 1978-82, v.p. corp. planning, 1982-85; v.p., chief exec. officer Visa Industries Ariz., Phoenix, 1985—; chmn. bd. dirs. Montessori Day Schs., Inc., Phoenix, 1981; bd. dirs. Basic Earth Scis., Calpeco III, Denver. Office: Visa Industries Ariz 9201 N 7th Ave Phoenix AZ 85021-3518

HUFFMAN, GREGORY SCOTT COMBEST, lawyer; b. Austin, Tex., Dec. 19, 1946; s. Calvin Combest and Olive Agnes (Weaver) H.; m. Mary L. Murphy, Feb. 1, 1986. Student, Stanford U., France, 1966-67; BA in History with distinction, Stanford U., 1969; postgrad., London Sch. of Econs., 1971-72; JD, Harvard U., 1973. Bar: Tex. 1973, U.S. Dist. Ct. Tex. 1974, U.S. Ct. Appeals (5th cir.) 1975, U.S. Supreme Ct. 1976. From assoc. to sr. ptnr. Thompson & Knight, Dallas, 1973—, also dir. Chief editor (monographs) Texas Free Enterprise and Antitrust Act, 1984-90, Texas Antitrust and Related Statutes, 1991—. Pres. Northern Hills Neighborhood Assn., 1980; bd. dirs. Common Cause of Tex., 1979-81, Love Field Citizens Action Commn., 1980-83, Appleseed Found., 1996—; adminstrv. chmn., bd. dirs. Tex. Appleseed; active Tex. Supreme Ct. Adv. Com. on Professionalism. Fellow Tex. Bar Found., Dallas Bar Found.; mem. ABA (antitrust and litigation sect.), Tex. Bar Assn. (antitrust and litigation sect., chmn. unlawful practice law com. 1981-83, chmn. lawyer referral svc. com. 1982-83, bd. legal specialization 1974-77, chmn. antitrust and bus. litigation sect. 1991-92, bd. dirs. 1983—, task force on unauthorized practice of law), Dallas Bar Assn. (antitrust sect., sec.-treas. 1981, chmn. unauthorized practice law com. 1979, chmn. lawyer referral svc. com. 198-81, chmn. profl. svcs. com. 1986-87, bd. dirs. antitrust sect. 1981, 89—, bd. dirs. litigation sect. 1988), Harvard Law Sch. Assn. Tex. (pres. 1987-88), Tower Club Dallas, Phi Beta Kappa, Sigma Alpha Epsilon. Methodist. Home: 8234 Garland Rd Dallas TX 75218-4417 Office: Thompson & Knight 1700 Pacific Ave Ste 3300 Dallas TX 75201-4693

HUFFMAN, JAMES THOMAS WILLIAM, oil exploration company executive; b. Norman, Okla., Mar. 27, 1947; s. Thomas William and Dorlese M. (Hicks) H.; m. Donna L. Haile, Aug. 27, 1969; children—Laura Anne, Christopher James. B.B.A., Baylor U., 1970. C.P.A. Mgr. Arthur Andersen & Co., Houston, 1970-76; sr. mgr. Price, Waterhouse & Co., Denver, 1976-79; v.p. Credo Petroleum Corp., 1978-80, pres., 1980-81, chmn., chief exec. officer, 1981—, also dir.; dir. Huffman Heat Exchangers Inc.; dir. XF&R, Inc.; pres., dir. SECO Energy Corp.; pres., dir. United Oil Corp. Mem. Am. Inst. C.P.A.s, Tex., Colo. socs. C.P.A.s, Petroleum Landman, Ind. Petroleum Assn. Am., Ind. Petroleum Assn. Mountain State, Petroleum Accts. Soc.

HUFFMAN, JOAN BREWER, history educator; b. Springfield, Ohio, Aug. 18, 1937; d. James Clarence and Berniece (Notter) Brewer; m. James Russell Huffman, Aug. 21, 1959; children: Jill Elizabeth, Jean Elaine. AB, Ohio U., 1959; MA, Ga. State U., 1968, PhD, 1980. Adj. prof. Wesleyan Coll., Macon, Ga., 1981-82; instr. history Macon Coll., 1968-72, asst. prof., 1972-81, assoc. prof., 1981-86, prof., 1986—; owner The Printed Page, Macon, Ga., 1993-97, Picture Perfect, 1995—; chmn. History adv. com. U. System Ga., 1986-87. Contbr. articles to profl. jours. Mem., bd. dirs. Oklahatche Pk., Perry, Ga., 1966-68, Macon Coll. Found., 1985-90, Ga. Humanities Coun., Atlanta, 1983-87. Katharine C. Bleckley scholar English-Speaking Union, 1977; recipient Gov.'s award in the humanities, 1998. Mem. N.Am. Conf. on Brit. Studies, Am. Hist. Assn., Southern Hist. Assn. (membership com. 1988-89), Ga. Assn. Historians (pres. 1982-83), Phi Beta Kappa, Phi Alpha Theta (award 1978). Home: 135 Covington Pl Macon GA 31210-4445

HUFFMAN, JOHN ABRAM, JR., minister; b. Boston, May 24, 1940; s. John A. and Dorothy (Bricker) H.; m. Anne Mortenson, June 19, 1964; children: Suzanne Marie (dec.), Carla Lynne, Janet Leigh. BA, Wheaton (Ill.) Coll., 1962; MDiv, Princeton Theol. Sem., 1965, DMin, 1983; MA, U. Tulsa, 1969. Ordained to ministry Presbyn. Ch. (U.S.A.), 1965. Sr. pastor Key Biscayne (Fla.) Presbyn. Ch., 1968-73, 1st Presbyn. Ch., Pitts., 1973-78, St. Andrew's Presbyn. Ch., Newport Beach, Calif., 1978—; moderator Everglades Presbytery, Presbyn. Ch., Fla., 1972, Presbytery of Los Ranchos, 1988; bd. dirs. Gordon-Conwell Theol. Sem., S. Hamilton, Mass., 1969—, Christianity Today, Inc., Carol Stream, Ill., 1976—, World Vision Internat., Inc., Monrovia, Calif., 1986—; chmn. World Vision U.S. Federal Way, Washington. Author: "Joshua" vol. of The Communicator's Commentary, 1986. Named Man of the Yr. in Religion, Jr. C. of C., 1977. Office: St Andrew's Presbyn Ch 600 St Andrews Rd Newport Beach CA 92663-5325

HUFFMAN, LOUISE TOLLE, elementary education educator; b. Tallahassee, Fla., July 24, 1951; d. Donald James and Mary Alice (McNeill) Tolle; m. Terry Lee Huffman, July 17, 1976; children: Cody McNeill, Hunter Tolle. BSEd in Spl. Edn./Elem. Edn., So. Ill. U., 1973; MSEd, No. Ill. U., 1979. Cert. elem. tchr., spl. edn. tchr., Ill. Title I reading tchr. Tonica, Ill., 1973-74; learning disabilities tchr. St. Charles, Ill., 1974-78; spl. edn. tchr. McWayne Elem. Sch., Batavia, Ill., 1978-80; tchr. grades 1, 3, 4, and 5 Stepple Run Elem. Sch., Naperville, Ill., 1980—; facilitator of tchr. workshops Jurica Sci. Mus./Benedictine U., Lisle, Ill., 1992-97; facilitator sci. workshops Mus. Sci. and Industry, Chgo., 1991-96; Saturday Morning TV Sci. tchr. Dist. 203, Naperville, 1994; author Earth Rhythms Saturday Sch. program Benedictine U., 1996. Author: Antarctica: A Living Classroom, 1991; contbr. articles to Cobblestone Mag., Good Apple Newspaper, Children's Digest. Bd. dirs. Cmty. United Meth. Ch. Sunday Sch., Naperville, 1995-98, Cub Scout Pack 503, Naperville, 1994-97; vol. PADS Homeless Shelter, Naperville, 1997. Recipient award of excellence Ill. Sci. Tchrs. Assn., 1992, 96, mini-grant Naperville Found., 1994. Methodist. Home: 964 Sylvan Cir Naperville IL 60540-5532 Office: Steeple Run Elem Sch 65151 Steeple Run Dr Naperville IL 60540

HUFFMAN, MERVIN NICKY, educator; b. Gastonia, N.C., Dec. 11, 1944; s. Mervin Franklin and Frances Elizabeth (Wiggins) H.; m. Paula Denise Byrum, July 29, 1973; children: Mark Adrian, Matthew Christopher. BS in English, Appalachian State U., 1967; MA in English, U. N.C., Chapel Hill, 1972. Tchr. English Gastonia (N.C.) County Schs., 1967-70; reporter The Gastonia Gazette, 1970-71; tchr. English York (S.C.) Sch. Dist. #1, 1972—; supr. Paramounts Carowinds, Charlotte, N.C., 1983—. Mem. NEA, Gideons Internat. Democrat. Mem. Ch. of God. Home: 720 Ralphs Blvd Gastonia NC 28052-7726 Office: York Comprehensive High Sch 1010 Devinney Rd York SC 29745-2127

HUFFMAN, PATRICIA JOAN, retired accounting coordinator; b. Elmira, N.Y., Mar. 29, 1941; d. F. John and Alice E. (Patterson) Garbay; m. Edward L. Huffman, May 28, 1960; children: Debra L. Palmer, Thomas E., Matthew M. AA in Bus. Adminstrn., Corning C.C., 1984, AA in Data Processing, 1984; BS in Acctg., Elmira Coll., 1991. Clk. typist Hardinge's Bros., Elmira, N.Y., 1959-62, Gen. Precision Labs., Pleasantville, N.Y., 1965-66; data entry clk. Reader's Digest, Pleasantville, 1966-68, Elmira Data Processing, 1968-69; acctg. clk. Am. LaFrance, Elmira, 1969-73, GE, Elmira, 1973-75, Elmira Star-Gazette, 1975-77; various temporary positions Manpower, Elmira, Corning, N.Y., 1980, 84-85; part-time clk. Atlantic & Pacific Tea Co., Horseheads, N.Y., 1980-82; from sales tax clk. to acctg. coord. Corning, Inc., 1985-96; ret. Corning, Inc., Corning, N.Y., 1996—, 1996. Author: (poem) Those Black Nights/Where Dreams Begin, 1993 (Editor's Choice award 1993), In Sorrow/Outstanding Poets of 1994 (Editor's Choice award 1994), Remember the Good Times My Love/Dance on the Horizon, 1994 (Editor's Choice award 1994), Lissa/Best Poems of 1995 (Editor's Choice award 1995), Prairie Rattler/Best Poems of 1996, (Editor's Choice award 1996), The Night My Cat Died/Best Poems of the '90s (Editor's Choice award 1996), Pray the Rosary/Best Poems of 1998. Sec. Ladies of Charity, Elmira, 1984-86, v.p., 1992-96, pres., 1996-98, regional v.p., 1999—; bd. dirs., N.E. reg. v.p. Ladies of Charity U.S.A., 1999—; lector St. Mary Our Mother Ch., Horseheads, N.Y., 1986-90. Mem. Internat. Soc. Poets (mem. adv. panel mem. 1993—, Internat. Poet of Merit award 1993-95). Avocations: poetry writing, charity work. Home: 31 Wolcott Dr Horseheads NY 14845-1183

HUFFMAN, ROBERT ALLEN, JR., lawyer; b. Tucson, Dec. 30, 1950; s. Robert Allen and Ruth Jane (Hicks) H.; m. Marjorie Kavanagh Rooney, Dec. 30, 1976; children: Katharine Kavanagh, Elizabeth Rooney, Robert Allen III, Simeon Ross. BBA, U. Okla., 1973, JD, 1976. Bar: Okla. 1977, U.S. Dist. Ct. (no. dist.) Okla. 1977, U.S. Ct. Appeals (10th cir.) 1978, U.S. Supreme Ct. 1982. Assoc. Huffman, Arrington, Kihle, Gaberino & Dunn, Tulsa, 1977-81, ptnr. 1981-97, ptnr. Edwards & Huffmann LLP, 1997—. Mem. ABA, Tulsa County Bar Assn., Fed. Energy Bar Assn. Republican. Roman Catholic. Clubs: Southern Hills Country (Tulsa), Summit Club. Home: 4136 S Wheeling Ave Tulsa OK 74105-4232 Office: Edwards & Huffman LLP South Yale Ste 1470 Two Warren Pl 6120 Tulsa OK 74136

HUFFMAN, ROBERT MERLE, insurance company executive; b. Libertyville, Iowa, Nov. 8, 1931; s. Hollis Hiram and Jessie Ila (Harrison) H.; m. Carolyn A. Stowell, Dec. 10, 1955; children: Cheryl E. Hawkins, John D., Debra L. Otte. Student, Drake U., 1967. Various positions Grinnell (Iowa) Mut. Reins. Co., 1955-71; sec.-treas., CEO Clark Mut. Ins. Co., Kahoka, Mo., 1971—. Treas., mgr. Kahoka Housing Corp. (retirement facility), 1973-82; pres. Kahoka C. of C., 1973-74. Mem. Nat. Assn. Mut. Ins. Cos. (bd. dirs. Merit Soc. 1990-93, Svc. award 1993), Mo. Assn. Mut. Ins. Cos. (chmn. bd. 1989-90, bd. dirs. 1983-86, past vice-chmn., past chmn.-elect, chmn. 1989-90, former mem. legis. com.), Kiwanis (v.p.). Baptist. Office: Clark Mut Ins Co 108 N Washington St Kahoka MO 63445-1458

HUFFMAN, ROSEMARY ADAMS, lawyer, corporate executive; b. Orlando, Fla., Oct. 18, 1939; d. Elmer Victor and Esther (Weber) Adams; divorced; 1 child, Justin Adams Fruth. A.B. in Econs., Ind. U., 1959, J.D., 1962; LL.M., U. Chgo., 1967. Bar: Ind. 1962, Fla. 1963. Dep. prosecutor Marion County, Ind., 1963; ct. administr. Ind. Supreme Ct., 1967-68; pro-tem judge Marion County Mcpl. Ct., 1969-70; jud. coordinator Ind. Criminal Justice Planning Agy., 1969-70; dir. ctr. for Jud. Edn., Inc., 1970-73; pub. Jud. Xchange, 1972-73; instr. bus. law Purdue U., Indpls., 1962-63, Ind. U., Indpls., 1963-64; asst. Ind. Jud. Council, 1965; legis. intern Ford Found., 1965; sole practice, Indpls., 1962—; pres., owner Abacus, Inc., Indpls., 1980—. Mem. Ind. Bar Assn., Fla. Bar Assn. Home and Office: 6630 E 56th St Indianapolis IN 46226-1781

HUFFMAN, SARILEE SHESOL, elementary school educator; b. Peoria, Ill., July 24, 1949; d. Mitchell Shesol and Jacqueline C. (Szold) Temkin; m. Kent Dwight Huffman, Aug. 8, 1971; children: Miriam Ilise, Joel David. BA, Ill. State U., 1971; MEd, Nat. Louis U., Evanston, Ill., 1992. Jr. high sch. tchr. math. El Paso (Ill.) Dist. 375, 1971-72; payroll supr. U. Chgo., 1972-78; water billing clk. Village of Villa Park, Ill., 1978-79; payroll supr. Ill. Auto Electric Co., Elmhurst, 1979-80; jr. high sch. tchr. math. Woodridge (Ill.) Sch. Dist. 68, 1980—. Pres. Women's Am. Orgn. for Rehab. through Tng., 1997-98. Mem. NEA, Nat. Coun. Tchrs. Math., Ill. Edn. Assn., Ill. Coun. Tchrs. Math., Woodridge Edn. Assn., Nat. Middle Sch. Assn., Assn. Ill. Middle Schs. Home: 626 Bunker Hill Ct Naperville IL 60540-7128 Office: Jefferson Jr High Sch 7200 Janes Ave Woodridge IL 60517-2318

HUFFMAN, THOMAS PATRICK, secondary education educator; b. Salem, Ind., Aug. 22, 1963; s. Patrick Henry and Patricia (Stewart) H.; m. Cynthia Densford, June 27, 1987; children: Mackenzie Lucille, Christopher Scot. BA in Biosci., DePauw U., 1985; MA in Edn., U. Phoenix, 1997. Quality control mgr., asst. ops. mgr. Wayne Dairy Products, Richmond, Ind., 1985-86; acct. mgr. Klenzade Divsn. Ecolab Inc., St. Paul, 1986-88; realtor West USA Realty, Phoenix, 1988-94; secondary sci. educator, sci. dept. chair, asst. prin. Westview H.S., Avondale, Ariz., 1994—; athletic trainer Tolleson (Ariz.) H.S., 1994—. Named to Pres.'s Roundtable, Phoenix Assn. Realtors, 1993. Mem. Am. Mensa, Sigma Alpha Epsilon. Avocations: golf, skiing. Home: 19001 N 67th Dr Glendale AZ 85308-5718 Office: Westview High Sch 10850 W Garden Lakes Pkwy Avondale AZ 85323

HUFFMAN, WALTER B., army officer; b. Keesler AFB, Miss., Oct. 8, 1944; m. Anne Robison; children: Burl, Becky, Ross. BS, Tex. Tech U., 1967, MEd, 1968, JD with highest honors, 1977. Commd. 2d lt. U.S. Army, 1968, advanced through grades to maj. gen.; judge adv. in various assignments including Desert Shield/Desert Storm, 1977-97; judge advocate gen. U.S. Army, 1997—. Editor-in-chief Tex. Tech Law Rev. Decorated Legion of Merit with one oak leaf cluster, Bronze Star medal with 2 oak leaf clusters. Office: US Army 220 Army Pentagon Washington DC 20310-2200

HUFFMAN, WILLIAM RAYMOND, emergency physician; b. Nashville, Dec. 9, 1946; s. Raymond W. and Elizabeth (Charlton) H.; m. Janet Richards Bailey, Aug. 19, 1972; children: Alan Drew, Mandie Elaine. BS in Biology, Tenn. Tech. U., 1969; MD, U. Tenn., 1972. Diplomate Am. Bd. Emergency Medicine. Intern, resident US Naval Hosp., San Diego, 1972-74; dir. emergency medicine Miller Hosp., Nashville, 1976-77; emergency physician Bapt. Hosp., Nashville, 1977—, chmn. emergency dept., 1981-83; pres. emergency dept. Mid Tenn. Emergency Phys. PC, Nashville, 1980-86; dir. emergency med. svcs. Rutherford County, Murfreesboro, Tenn., 1984-88. Fellow Am. Acad. Emergency Physicians, Am. Coll. Emergency Physicians. Home: 2500 N Berrys Ch Rd Brentwood TN 32027 Office: Mid Tenn Emergency Phys PC 1900 Church St Ste 511 Nashville TN 37203-2227

HUFFMAN-HINE, RUTH CARSON, adult education administrator, educator; b. Spencer, Ind., Sept. 13, 1925; d. Joseph Charles Carson and Bess Ann Taylor; m. Joe Buren Hine; children: Paulette Walker, Larry K., Annette M. AA in Fine Arts, Ind. Cen. Coll., 1967; BS in Edn., Butler U., 1971; MS in Adult Edn., Ind. U., 1976; PhD in Ednl. Adminstrn., Greenwich U., 1995. Cert. elem. edn. Subs. tchr. Met. Sch. Dist. Wayne Twnshp., Indpls., 1956-60; tchr. of homebound Met. Sch. Dist. Decatur Twnshp., Indpls., 1964-66; adult edn. tchr. Met. Sch. Dist. Wayne Twnshp., Indpls., 1971-75, adminstr. adult edn., 1975—; cons. Ind. Adoption System, Indpls., 1985—; regional rep. Ind. Assn. Adult Adminstrs., 1984—; program rep. Ind. Literacy Coordinators, Indpls., 1985—; speaker, mem. literacy research and evaluation com. Ind. Adult Literacy Coalition, Indpls., 1980-86. Author: Driving Regulations and Courtesies, It Happened at the Pond, 1997, We Build Walls, 1999; co-author Learning for Everyday Living, 1978, Table Approach to Education, 1984, Developing Educational Competencies for Individuals Determined to Excel, 6 vols., 1980 (ERIC System award 1980), (ERIC System award 1985), Collection, Evaluation, Dissemination of Special Research Projects, 1984, Automobile Driving Rules and Regulations, 1988. Vice com. person Rep. Orgn., Indpls., 1968-72; charter mem., sec. Project READ, LITERACY, 1988. Recipient Extra Mile award Met. Sch. Dist. Wayne Twp., 1990. Mem. Internat. Reading Assn. (Celebrate Literacy award 1984), Ind. Assn. for Adult & Continuing Edn. (treas. 1984—, pres. 1990-93, Outstanding Adult Educator 1979), Beta Phi Delta (pres. 1986—), Beta Phi, Delta Kappa Gamma (v.p. 1985-86, fellowship chmn. 1982-84), Phi Delta Kappa. Republican. Mem. Christian Ch. Avocations: reading, music, bicycling. Home: 138 Abner Creek Pky Danville IN 46122-9602 Office: Adult Basic Edn Ctr 5248 W Raymond St Indianapolis IN 46241-4700

HUFFSTETLER, PALMER EUGENE, lawyer; b. Shelby, N.C., Dec. 21, 1937; s. Daniel S. and Ethel (Turner) H.; m. Mary Ann Beam, Aug. 9, 1958; children: Palmer Eugene, Ben Beam, Brian Tad. BA, Wake Forest U., 1959, JD, 1961. Bar: N.C. 1961. Practiced in Kings Mountain, N.C., 1961-62, Raleigh, N.C., 1962-64; with State Farm Ins. Co., Orlando, Fla., 1962; gen. legal counsel Carolina Freight Corp., Cherryville, N.C., 1964-93, sec., 1969-90, sr. v.p., 1969-89, also dir., 1971-94, exec. v.p., 1985-93, pres., 1993-95;

ret., 1995; pres., CEO Blue Chip Inc., 1997—. Author, composer: Senior Man on Carolina Line, Fifty Years Ago. Chmn. Cherryville Zoning Bd. Adjustment, 1967-70; mem. N.C. Gasoline and Oil Insp. Bd., 1974-76; class chmn. Wake Forest Coll. Fund, 1971-79, decade chmn., 1981-82; mem. governing body, chmn. adminstrv. com. So. Piedmont Health Systems Agy., 1975-77; mem. Cherryville Econ. Devel. Commn., 1982-87, Cherryville Econ. Devel. Com., 1995-97; pres. Cherryville Devel. Corp., 1986—; bd. dirs. C. Grier Beam Truck Mus., 1982—, pres. 1982-96; bd. dirs. Schiele Mus., Gastonia, N.C., 1985-88, Gaston Meml. Hosp., 1990-93, vice-chmn. bd.; mem. N.C. Gov.'s Hwy. Safety Commn., 1985-88; mem. v.p. Ctrl. and So. Rate Bur., 1984-89; trustee Brevard Coll., 1987-93. Mem. N.C. State Bar, N.C. Bar Assn. Methodist (mem. adminstrv. bd. 1965-69, 71-72, chmn. adminstrv. bd., trustee 1970-73, fin. com. 1994—, fin. com. 1994—). Home: 2141 Fairways Dr Cherryville NC 28021-2115

HUFNAGEL, GLENDA ANN LEWIN, human relations educator and administrator; b. Ronake, Ala., Apr. 13, 1948; d. Clifford Herbert and Gladys (Halsey) Lewin; children: Lisa, Jessica. MA, U. Okla., 1979, M of Human Rels., 1990, PhD, 1999. Asst. prof. Ctrl. State U., Edmond, Okla., 1984-85, Oklahoma City C.C., 1976-84, Rose State Coll., Midwest City, Okla., 1984-90; asst. prof. U. Okla., Norman, 1991—, asst. dir. human rels. advanced program, 1997—; v.p. People Energy, Oklahoma City, 1984-85; pres. Comm. Cons., Norman, Okla., 1982—; adj. asst. prof. Russel Sage Coll., Albany, N.Y., 1989—. Contbr. articles to profl. jours. Bd. dirs. Women's Resource Ctr., Norman, Okla., 1980-85, advisor, 1985—; advisor Norman's Battered Women's Shelter, 1985—. Mem. Nat. Women's Studies Assn., NOW, South Ctrl. Women's Studies Assn. (pres. 1995—), Phi Kappa Phi (charter). Democrat. Avocations: camping, reading, travel, sewing, photography. Home: 1704 Homeland Ave Norman OK 73072-5743 Office: U Okla Dept Human Rels 601 Elm Ave Rm 728 Norman OK 73012

HUFNAGEL, HENRY BERNHARDT, financial advisor; b. Evanston, Ill., May 17, 1942; s. Henry and Olga (Bernhardt) H.; 1 child, Jennifer Babette. BS in Bus., Ariz. State U., 1964; MS in Fin., U. Colo., 1969. CPA, Ill. Commd. USAF, 1964; advanced through ranks to col.; served as auditor, budget and pub. affairs officer USAF, various cities, 1964-73; trust adminstr. Continental Bank, Chgo., 1973-77; sales rep. Boeing Co., Chgo., 1977-87; account mgr. British Telecom, Rosemont, Ill., 1987-93; sr. account mgr. GE Info. Svcs., Inc., Chgo., 1994-95; nat. sales exec. SPS Payment Sys., Inc., Chgo., 1995-98; fin. advisor Morgan Stanley Dean Witter, Riverwood, Ill., 1999—. Mem. AICPA, Air Force Assn. (state treas.). Republican. Presbyterian. Avocations: skiing, travel, bowling, golf. Home: 214 Charles Pl Wilmette IL 60091-3008

HUFSCHMIDT, MAYNARD MICHAEL, resources planning educator; b. Catawba, Wis., Sept. 28, 1912; s. John Jacob and Emma Lena (Von Arx) H.; m. Elizabeth Louise Leake, July 5, 1941; children: Emily Ann, Mark Andrew. BS, U. Ill., 1939; MPA, Harvard U., 1955, DPA, 1964. Planner Ill. State Planning Commn., Chgo., 1939-41; engr. U.S. Nat. Resources Planning Bd., Washington, 1941-43; budget examiner U.S. Bur. Budget, Washington, 1943-49; program staff mem. Office of Sec., Dept. Interior, Washington, 1949-55; research asso. Grad. Sch. Public Adminstrn., Harvard U., 1955-65; prof. depts. city and regional planning, environ. scis. and engring. U. N.C., Chapel Hill, 1965—; fellow Environ. and Policy Inst., East-West Center, Honolulu, 1979-85, acting dir., 1985-86, sr. cons., 1986-89, sr. fellow, 1990-94; cons. U.S. Bur. Budget, 1961, Council Econ. Advisers, 1965-67, Nat. Acad. Scis., 1967, 69-70, Pan-Am. Health Orgn., 1967, 70, WHO, 1970, 71, 76, 77, Resources for Future, 1955, 56, 72-74. Author: (with Arthur Maass and others) Design of Water-Resource Systems, 1962, (with Myron B. Fiering) Simulation Techniques for Design of Water-Resource Systems, 1966; Editor: Regional Planning—Challenge and Prospects, 1969; editor: (with Eric L. Hyman) Economic Approaches to Natural Resource and Environmental Quality Analysis, 1982, (with David E. James and others) Environment, Natural Systems and Development: An Economic Valuation Guide, 1983, (with John A. Dixon) Economic Valuation Techniques for the Environment, 1986, (with K. William Easter and John A. Dixon) Watershed Resources Management, 1986, (with Janusz Kindler) Approaches to Integrated Water Resources Management in Humid Tropical and Arid and Semiarid Zones in Developing Countries, 1991, (with Michael Bonell and John S. Gladwell) Hydrology and Water Management in the Humid Tropics, 1993. Recipient Clemens Herschel award Boston Soc. Civil Engrs., 1958, Pub. Svc. award U.S. Dept. Interior, 1994; named Friend of Univs. Coun. on Water Resources, 1990; sr. postdoctoral rsch. fellow NSF, 1971.

HUFSTEDLER, SETH MARTIN, lawyer; b. Dewar, Okla., Sept. 20, 1922; s. Seth Martin and Myrtle (Younts) H.; m. Shirley Ann Mount, Aug. 16, 1949; 1 child, Steven. B.A. magna cum laude, U. So. Calif., 1944; LL.B., Stanford U., 1949. Bar: Calif. 1950. Pvt. practice L.A.; assoc. Lillick, Geary & McHose, 1950-51; with Charles E. Beardsley, 1951-53; ptnr. Beardsley, Hufstedler & Kemble, 1953-81, Hufstedler, Miller, Carlson & Beardsley, 1981-88, Hufstedler, Kaus & Ettinger, L.A., 1988-94; Hufstedler & Kaus, 1994-95; sr. of counsel Morrison & Foerster LLP, 1995—; mem. Calif. Jud. Coun., 1977-78. Legis. editor Stanford U. Law Rev., 1948-49. Sec. regional planning coun. United Way, 1971-75; co-chmn. Pub. Commn. County Govt., L.A., 1975-76, 89-92; trustee AEFC Pension Fund, 1978-82; mem. Calif Citizens Commn. on Tort Reform, 1976-77; bd. visitors Stanford Law Sch., chmn., 1972-73. Lt. (j.g.) USNR, 1943-46. Mem. ABA (chmn. action commn. to reduce ct costs and delay 1979-81, mem. coun. sr. bar div. 1986-89, chmn. 1987-88), Los Angeles County Bar Assn. (trustee 1963-65, 66-70, pres. 1969-70, Shattuck Price award 1976), State Bar Calif. (bd. govs. 1971-74, pres. 1973-74), Am. Judicature Soc., Am. Law Inst., Am. Coll. Trial Lawyers, Am. Bar Found. (bd. govs. 1975-86, pres. 1982-84), Chancery Club (pres. 1974-75), Order of Coif, Phi Beta Kappa, Phi Kappa Phi, Delta Tau Delta. Democrat. Office: Morrison & Foerster 555 W 5th St Ste 3500 Los Angeles CA 90013-1024

HUFSTEDLER, SHIRLEY MOUNT (MRS. SETH M. HUFSTEDLER), lawyer, former federal judge; b. Denver, Aug. 24, 1925; d. Earl Stanley and Eva (Von Behren) Mount; m. Seth Martin Hufstedler, Aug. 16, 1949; 1 son, Steven Mark. BBA, U. N.Mex., 1945, LLD (hon.), 1972; LLB, Stanford U., 1949; LLD (hon.), U. Wyo., 1970, Gonzaga U., 1970, Occidental Coll., 1971, Tufts U., 1974, U. So. Calif., 1976, Georgetown U., 1976, U. Pa., 1976, Columbia U., 1977, U. Mich., 1979, Yale U., 1981, Rutgers U., 1981, Claremont U. Ctr., 1981, Smith Coll., 1982, Syracuse U., 1983, Mt. Holyoke Coll., 1985; PHH (hon.), Hood Coll., 1981, Hebrew Union Coll., 1986, Tulane U., 1988. Bar: Calif. 1950. Mem. firm Beardsley, Hufstedler & Kemble, L.A., 1951-61; practiced in L.A., 1961; judge Superior Ct., County L.A., 1961-66; justice Ct. Appeals 2d dist., 1966-68; circuit judge U.S. Ct. Appeals 9th cir., 1968-79; sec. U.S. Dept. Edn., 1979-81; ptnr. Hufstedler & Kaus, L.A., 1981-95; sr. of counsel Morrison & Foerster LLP, L.A., 1995—; emeritus dir. Hewlett Packard Co., US West, Inc.; bd. dirs. Harman Internat. Industries. Mem. staff Stanford Law Rev, 1947-49; articles and book rev. editor, 1948-49. Trustee Calif. Inst. Tech., Occidental Coll., 1972-89, Aspen Inst., Colonial Williamsburg Found., 1976-93, Constl. Rights Found., 1978-80, Nat. Resources Def. Coun., 1983-85, Carnegie Endowment for Internat. Peace, 1983-94; bd. dirs. John T. and Catherine MacArthur Found., 1983—; chair U.S. Commn. on Immigration Reform, 1996-97. Named Woman of Yr. Ladies Home Jour., 1976; recipient UCLA medal, 1981. Fellow Am. Acad. Arts and Scis.; mem. ABA (medal 1995), L.A. Bar Assn., Town Hall, Am. Law Inst. (coun. 1974-84), Am. Bar Found., Women Lawyers Assn. (pres. 1957-58), Am. Judicature Soc., Assn. of the Bar of City of N.Y., Coun. on Fgn. Rels., Order of Coif. Office: Morrison & Foerster LLP 555 W 5th St Ste 3500 Los Angeles CA 90013-1024

HUFTALEN, LISA FREEMAN, corporate executive, graphic designer; b. New Kensington, Pa., Feb. 24, 1953; d. Paul Eugene and Phyliss Maureen (Gravengaard) Freeman; m. Howard Benjamin Huftalen Jr., Sept. 13, 1987. Student, Iowa State U., 1971-75; BA in Graphics and Mktg., R.I. Coll., 1986. Visual merchandiser Army & Air Force Exch. Svc., Ft. Devens, Mass., 1978-81; art dir. Gro Com Group Pub., Barrington, R.I., 1981-82; mgr. advt. and mktg. svcs. Alumiline Corp., Lincoln, R.I., 1982-85; v.p., art dir. Gerald A. Schwarz & Assocs., Guilford, Conn., 1985-87; pres. L.E. Designers, Inc., Old Saybrook, Conn., 1987—, 1978—; graphic designer, vol. Save the Bay, Providence, 1982-87. Pres. River Colony Assn., Guilford, 1987-89. Mem. Old Saybrook C. of C. Republican. Congregationalist. Avocations: producing stained glass windows and signs, drawing, painting. E-mail: lisa@ledesigners.com. Office: LE Designers Inc 900 Boston Post Rd Old Saybrook CT 06475-2136

HUG, CARL CASIMIR, JR., pharmacology and anesthesiology educator; b. Canton, Ohio, Dec. 20, 1936; s. Carl Casimir and Aimee Cecelia (McArdle) H.; m. Marilyn Ann France, May 12, 1956; children: Patricia Ann DeStephano, Michael Stephen, Joan Marie Daniel, Mary Lynn Higgins, Lori Renee Mauldin. BS in Pharmacy summa cum laude, Duquesne U., 1958; PhD in Pharmacology, U. Mich., 1963, MD with distinction, 1967. Diplomate Am. Bd. Anesthesiology (bd. dirs. 1984-96, v.p. 1990-92, pres. 1992-93). From instr. to assoc. prof. pharmacology U. Mich., Ann Arbor, 1963-71; from assoc. prof. anesthesiology and pharmacology to prof. Emory U. Sch. Medicine, Atlanta, 1972—, dep. chmn. for rsch., 1987-95, dep. chmn. for acad. affairs, 1995—; vis. rsch. prof. U. Leiden, The Netherlands, 1982. Author: Alfentanil: Pharmacology and Uses in Anesthesia, 1984; editor Pharmacokinetics of Anaesthesia, 1984; editor Anesthesiology, 1979-88. Chmn. St. Francis Sch. Bd., Ann Arbor, 1967-71; coach Little League, Ann Arbor, 1967-71; various lay positions Corpus Christi Cath. Ch., Stone Mountain, Ga., 1972-96, St. John Neumann Cath. Ch., Lilburn, Ga., 1997—; pres. Assn. Univ. Anesthetists, 1983-87; bd. dirs. Found. for Anesthesiology Edn. and Rsch., 1993—, v.p., 1995—98, pres., 1998—. Named Tchr. of Yr. Emory U. Anesthesiology, 1989, hon. lectr. at multiple Univs. Fellow Royal Coll. Anaesthetists (Eng.) (hon.), Australian and New Zealand Coll. Anaesthetists (hon.); mem. Belgian Soc. Anesthesia and Reanimation (hon.), Am. Soc. Anesthesiologists (mem., chmn. various coms. 1976—, Rovenstine lectr. 1999). Office: Emory Univ Hosp Dept Anesthesiology 1364 Clifton Rd NE Atlanta GA 30322-1061

HUG, JAMES EDWARD, religious organization administrator; b. Omaha, May 10, 1941; s. Edwin Joseph and Dorothy Ann (Spellecy) H. AB in Philosophy, Spring Hill Coll., 1965, MA in Philosophy, 1966; MA in Christian Spirituality, St. Louis U., 1973; PhD in Christian Ethics, U. Chgo., 1981. Ordained Jesuit priest, 1972. Instr. in philosophy Creighton U., Omaha, 1966-69; mem. editorial staff Theology Digest, 1969-73; lectr. in Christian spirituality St. Louis U., 1972-73; instr. in Christian ethics Jesuit Sch. Theology, Chgo., 1978-80; sr. fellow Woodstock Theol. Ctr., Washington, 1981-85; rsch. dir. Ctr. of Concern, Washington, 1986-88, exec. dir., 1989—; bd. dirs. Internat. Devel. Conf., Washington; cons. The Cath. Healthcare Assn. Author: Scripture Sharing on Bishops' Pastoral, 1987; co-author: Social Revelation: Profound Challenge for Christian Spirituality, 1987; editor, contbr.: Dimensions of the Healing Ministry, 1989; editor: Tracing the Spirit: Communities, Social Action..., 1983. Bd. dirs. Cen. Am. Refugee Ctr., Washington, 1983-85, Religious Task Force on Cen. Am., Washington, 1988—, U.S. Cath. Mission Assn., Washington, 1988—. Mem. Soc. Chirstian Ethics, Cath. Theol. Soc. Am. Office: Ctr of Concern 1225 Otis St NE Washington DC 20017-2519

HUG, PROCTER RALPH, JR., federal judge; b. Reno, Mar. 11, 1931; s. Procter Ralph and Margaret (Beverly) H.; m. Barbara Van Meter, Apr. 4, 1954; children: Cheryl Ann, Procter James, Elyse Marie. B.S., U. Nev., 1953; LL.B., J.D., Stanford U., 1958. Bar: Nev. 1958. With firm Springer, McKissick & Hug, 1958-63, Woodburn, Wedge, Blakey, Folsom & Hug, Reno, 1963-77; U.S. judge 9th Circuit Ct. Appeals, Reno, 1977—; U.S. chief judge 9th Circuit Ct. Appeals, 1996—; dep. atty. gen. State of Nev.; v.p. dir. Nev. Tel. & Tel. Co., 1958-77. Mem. bd. regents U. Nev., 1962-71, chmn., 1969-71; bd. visitors Stanford Law Sch.; mem. Nev. Humanities Commn., 1988-94; vol. civilian aid sect. U.S. Army, 1977. Lt. USNR, 1953-55. Recipient Outstanding Alumnus award U. Nev., 1967, Disting. Nevadan citation, 1982; named Alumnus of Yr. U. Nev., 1988. Mem. ABA (bd. govs. 1976-78), Am. Judicare Soc. (bd. dirs. 1975-77), Nat. Judicial Coll. (bd. dirs. 1977-78), Nat. Assn. Coll. and Univ. Attys. (past mem. exec. bd.), U. Nev. Alumni Assn. (past pres.), Stanford Law Soc. Nev. (pres.). Office: US Ct Appeals 9th Cir US Courthouse Fed Bldg 400 S Virginia St Ste 708 Reno NV 89501-2181

HUG, RICHARD ERNEST, environmental company executive; b. Paterson, N.J., Jan. 11, 1935; s. Gustave T. and Nelly (Rutishauser) H.; m. Lois-Ann Schack, Sept. 1, 1956; children: Donald R., Cynthia A. BS, Duke U., 1956, M in Forestry, 1957. Engr. forest products div. Koppers Co., Inc., Pitts., 1957-62, tech. rep., 1962-66, tech. sales rep., 1966-68, area sales mgr., 1968-70, mgr. product devel., 1970-72, gen. mgr. laminated products, 1972-73, v.p., gen. mgr. environ. systems div., 1973-74, corp. v.p., 1973-83; pres., chief exec. officer, owner Environ. Elements Corp., Balt., 1983-88, from chmn., CEO to chmn. bd., 1988-95, chmn. emeritus, 1995—; owner, chmn. Deco-Sign Products, Inc., 1991—; owner, CEO, chmn. Hug Enterprises, Inc., 1991—; owner, chmn. The Great Am. Car Wash, etc., Inc., 1992—. Bd. dirs. Blue Cross-Blue Shield Md., 1973-94, Greater Balt. Com., 1978, 84-88, Ind. Coll. Fund Md., 1978-88, Loyola Coll. Md., 1982—, U. Md. Med. System, 1985-95, Jr. Achievement Ctrl. Md., 1985-95, Duke U. Sch. Environ., 1986—, chair, 1988-95, Am. Auto Assn., Md., 1988—, Mid Atlantic Am. Auto Assn., 1990—, Balt. Symphony Orch., 1989—, Md. Internat. Ctr., 1989-95, Downtown Balt. Ctr., 1991-94, Environ. Forum, 1993-95, Hospice Chesapeake, 1993-98, Diehl Graphsoft, 1996—, Marco Group, 1985—. Mem. Chesapeake Pres. Orgn. (chmn. 1994-95), Chief Exec. Officers Orgn., Water and Wastewater Equipment Mfrs. Assn. (bd. dirs. 1983-88), Inst. Clear Air Cos. (bd. dirs. 1980-94, pres. 1990-94), Nat. Assn. Mfrs. (bd. dirs. 1983-94), Md. Ctr. Bus. Mgmt. (bd. dirs. 1984-95, chmn. 1987-92), Md. Bus. Responsibility Govt. (bd. dirs. 1995—), Md. C. of C. (bd. dirs. 1981-95, v.p. 1981-84, chmn. 1985-87), Ctr. Club (bd. govs. 1993—, membership chmn. 1994—v.p. 1997—). Republican. Presbyterian. Home: 992 Stonington Dr Arnold MD 21012-1654 Office: Environ Elements Corp 3700 Koppers St Baltimore MD 21227-1020

HUGEE, ELTON BERNARD, university official, retired military enlisted man; b. West Palm Beach, Fla., July 5, 1955; s. Arthur and Dorothy Jean (Walden) Jenkins; m. Nan Kyong Shin, Mar. 17, 1978 (div. Nov. 1988); children: Celina Latrice, Michael Bernard; m. Maria Zenaida Hugee, Oct. 11, 1990; 1 child, Zenaida Maia. AAS in Human Rsch. Tech., Air U., Maxwell AFB, Ala., 1985; BS in Bus., Coll. of St. Mary, Omaha, 1985; MBA, U. S.D., 1993. Enlisted USAF, 1973, advanced through grades to master sgt., 1991; base INTRO mgr. USAF, Osan Air Base, Korea, 1981-82, noncommissioned officer in charge evaluation unit, 1982; chief officer command records br. USAF, Offutt AFB, Nebr., 1982-86; supt. pers. utilization USAF, Yokota Air Base, Japan, 1986-90, supt. promotion and testing, 1986-90; base career advisor USAF, Ellsworth AFB, S.D., 1990-92, total quality mgmt. officer, 1992; supt. pers. assistance, 1992-93, ret., 1993; asst. prof. Johnson C. Smith U., Charlotte, N.C., 1995-97; acct. Clark Atlanta U., 1997-98, dir. Title III programs, 1998—. Avocations: teaching karate, reading, chess, enjoying time with family. Home: 626 Beckwith St SW Atlanta GA 30314 Office: Clark Atlanta U 223 James P Brawley Dr SW Atlanta GA 30314

HUGESSEN, JAMES K., judge; b. July 26, 1933; m. Mary R. Stavert, Sept. 12, 1958; five children. BA, Oxford U., 1954, MA, 1958; BCL with honors, McGill U., 1957. Bar: Que. 1958. With McCarthy, Tétreault, 1958-72; dir. Can. Inst. for the Adminstrn. Justice, 1974-79, v.p., 1979-80; judge Ct. Martial Appeal Ct. of Can., 1975—; dep. justice Supreme Ct. of the N.W. Territories, 1977-92; lectr. law McGill U.; apptd. Puisne judge Superior Ct., Montréal, 1972, apptd. assoc. chief justice, 1973, apptd. judge of the ct. of appeal Fed. Ct. Can., Ottawa, 1983; chmn. Task Force on Release of Inmates, 1972; mem., pres. Com. du droit de la preuve de l'Office de révision du Code civil de la province de Québec, 1968-75; D.B. Goodman Vis. fellow Faculty of Law, U. Toronto, 1977; chmn. seminar com. Can. Jud. Coun., 1980-83; chmn. stds. and accreditation devel. com., 1981-83. Dir. Touring Club, Montreal; vice-chancellor Diocese of Montréal; sec. Can. Club Montréal. Mem. Royal St. Lawrence Yacht Club, Rideau Club, Red Birds' Ski Club. Avocations: skiing, yachting, riding. Home: 81 Queen St, Almonte, ON Canada KOA 1AO Office: Fed Ct of Canada, Kent & Wellington Sts, Ottawa, ON Canada K1A 0H9*

HUGET, CHARLENE DOROTHY, library director; b. Detroit, Feb. 16, 1939; d. John and Genevieve Makara; m. John Charles Huget, Sept. 10, 1960 (div. Jan. 1990); children: John Michael, Jennifer Anne, Melissa Beth. BS in Psychology, Oakland U., 1982; MLS, U. Mich., 1990. Libr. Davis, Culpepper & Saroki, PC, Detroit, 1990-92; reference libr. Muskingum County Libr. Sys., Zanesville, Ohio, 1992-94; dir. Brighton (Mich.) Dist. Libr., 1994—. Mem. ALA, Pub. Libr. Assn., Mich. Libr. Assn., Detroit Suburban Libr. Roundtable, Friends of the Brighton Libr., Rotary Internat. Avocations: skiing, jogging, reading. E-mail: chuget@tln.lib.mi.us. Office: Brighton Dist Libr 200 Charles H Orndorf Dr Brighton MI 48116

HUGG, GERALDINE BERTHA, retired gerontology specialist, journalist; b. N.Y.C., Oct. 15, 1913; d. Jerry Joseph and Bertha Ann (Strnad) Novotny; m. Alan Eddy Hugg, Mar. 10, 1982 (dec. Feb. 1997). BA in Journalism, U. Wis., 1949; MS in Pub. Rels., Boston U., 1953. lic. profl. gerontology U. Mich., Drake U. Departmental sec. U. Conn., Storrs, 1933-41, departmental asst., 1941-43; asst. editor, publs. editor divsn. comm. U. Conn., 1950-60; specialist Inst. Gerontology, U. Conn., 1960-67; dir. Windham Area Sr. Ctr., Willimantic, Conn., 1967; cons. and field rep. Conn. State Dept. Aging, Hartford, 1967-76; ret., 1976; advisor Conn. Coun. Sr. Citizens, 1960—. Contbg. editor Sr. Age Newspaper 1976—; contbr. columns various newspapers. Vol. social action and edn. Conn. Soc. Gerontology, 1961-99; participant Am. People Amb. Program, People to People Program, China, 1994, South Africa, 1995, Russia and Estonia, 1996. Sgt. USMCR, 1943-45. Recipient David C. King award Conn. Soc. Gerontology, Hartford, 1985, award 100 Years of Women, 1993. Mem. Czechoslovak Am. Club (pres. 1939), Zonta Internat. West Hartford (bd. dirs. 1970—), Womens Internat. League Peace and Freedom, Ch. Women United (bd. dirs., adv.). Democrat. Universalist. Avocations: swimming, oil painting, hiking. Home: 275 Steele Rd Apt 422 Hartford CT 06117-2716

HUGGARD, JOHN PARKER, lawyer; b. Midland, Tex., Dec. 7, 1945; s. Peter John and Dorothy (Sampson) H. BA, U. N.C., 1971, JD, 1975; MA, Duke U., 1989. Bar: N.C. 1975, U.S. Dist. Ct. (ea. dist.) N.C. 1975, U.S. Ct. Appeals (4th cir.) 1975, U.S. Tax Ct. 1976, U.S. Ct. Claims 1976, U.S. Ct. Customs 1977, U.S. Ct. Mil. Appeals 1977, U.S. Dist. Ct. D.C. 1979, U.S. Supreme Ct. 1979, U.S. Ct. Internat. Trade 1981, U.S. Ct. Customs and Patent Appeals 1982; cert. fin. planner. Sr. ptnr. Hensley & Overby, Raleigh, N.C., 1975-88, Huggard, Obiol & Blake, PLLC, Raleigh, 1988—; alumni disting. prof. Law and Econs. N.C. State U., Raleigh, 1975—. Author: The Adminstration of Decedents' Estates in North Carolina, 1985, North Carolina Estate Settlement Guidebook, 1995, Living Trust/Living Hell-Why You Should Avoid Living Trusts, 1998; contbr. articles to profl. publs. With USMC, 1964-68, capt. USNR. Mem. ABA, Am. Bus. Law Assn., Assn. Trial Lawyers Am., N.C. Bar Assn., N.C. Acad. Trial Lawyers, N.C. Coll. Advocacy, Acad. Outstanding Tchrs., Wake County Bar Assn., Phi Beta Kappa. Democrat. Roman Catholic. Avocation: flying. Home: 8621 Kings Arms Way Raleigh NC 27615-2029 Office: Huggard Obiol & Blake PLLC 124 Saint Marys St Raleigh NC 27605-1809

HUGGETT, MONICA, performing company executive. Artistic dir. Portland Baroque Orch., Oreg. Office: Portland Baroque Orch 1425 SW 20th Ave Ste 105 Portland OR 97201

HUGGINS, BOB, college basketball coach; b. Morgantown, W.Va., Sept. 21, 1953; m. June Ann Fillman; children: Jenna Leigh, Jacqueline. BS magna cum laude, U. W.Va., 1977, MA in Health Adminstrn., 1978. Grad. asst. basketball coach U. W.Va., Morgantown, 1977-78; asst. basketball coach Ohio State U., Columbus, 1978-90; head coach Walsh Coll., Canton, Ohio, 1980-83; asst. basketball coach U. Ctrl. Fla., Orlando, 1983-84; head basketball coach U. Akron, Ohio, 1984-89, U. Cin., 1989—; mem. basketball coaching staff U.S. World Univ. Games team, 1993. Founder Bob Huggins Found., 1997-98. Named Coach of the Yr. dist. 22 NAIA, 1981-82, 1982-83, area 6, 1982-83, , Mid-Ohio Conf., 1981-82, 1982-83, Ohio Valley, 1984-85, Metro Conf., 1989-90, Dapper Dan Man of Yr., 1986-87, dist. 4 USBWA, 1991-92, Mideast Coach of Yr. Basketball Times, 1991-92, 95-96, Co-Nat. Coach of Yr., 1991-92 Hoop Scoop mag., finalist for AP Coach of Yr., 1991-92, Ohio Coll. Coach of Yr. Columbus Dispatch, 1991-92, 1995-96, Nat. Coll. Coach of Yr., Playboy Mag., 1992-93, Midseason Coach of Yr. USA Today, 1991-92 season; recipient Ray Meyer award Gt. Midwest conf., 1991-92, 92-93. Office: Univ Cincinnati Men's Basketball 340 Shoemaker Ctr Cincinnati OH 45221-0021

HUGGINS, CANNIE MAE COX HUNTER, retired elementary school educator; b. Belton, Tex., July 16, 1916; d. Jesse Daniel and Mary Alice (Hamilton) Cox; m. William Dudley Hunter, June 5, 1938 (div. 1967); children: Darline, Bob Roy; m. Bertrand Huggins, Aug. 4, 1979 (dec. July 19, 1980). BS, Mary Hardin Baylor Coll., 1940; MS, San Marcos Tchrs. Coll., 1942; postgrad., U. Tex., 1946-47, Tex. Tech. U., 1956-70, U. San Diego, 1975, St. Mary's U., 1976. Cert. educator, Tex. Tchr. pub. schs. Belton, 1935-38, Galveston, Tex., 1938-42; mem. staff testing dept. U. Ariz., 1942-43; reading cons. Phoenix Pub. Schs., 1943-45; tchr.-counselor pub. schs. Killeen, Tex., 1946-54; classroom tchr. Lubbock, Tex., 1954-74; tchr. first grade bilingual lang. devel. Posey Elem. Sch., Lubbock, Tex., 1974-96; pres. CM Corp. First aid chmn. ARC, Lubbock County, 1960-63, first aid instr., 1956—; area dir. March of Dimes, 1958-63; tchr. high sch. dept. First Bapt. Ch., Lubbock, 1960—; state advisor U.S. Congl. Adv. Bd., 1985—; mem. Lubbock Hospice Vol. Program. Recipient Outstanding Svc. award ARC, 1966; Bronze award CONTACT Lubbock. Mem. Assn. Childhood Edn. Internat., NEA, Tex. Tchrs. Assn., Tex. Classroom Tchrs. Assn., Nat. PTA, Tex. Edn. Assn., Lubbock Educators Assn., Lubbock Classroom Tchrs. Assn., AAUW, Am. Bus. Women's Assn., South Plains Writers Guild, YWCA, Lubbock C. of C., Killeen C. of C., Univ. City Club (Lubbock). Baptist. Home: 4626 30th St Lubbock TX 79410-2423

HUGGINS, CHARLES EDWARD, obstetrician-gynecologist, educator; b. Hartsville, S.C., Nov. 16, 1944; s. Charles Witherspoon Huggins and Frances Sue (Fountain) Evans; m. Mary Ellen Esto, May 29, 1966; children: Chadwick Edward, Laura Ruth, Mary Elizabeth. BS, Wofford Coll., 1965; MD, Med. U. S.C., 1969. Diplomate Am. Bd. Ob-Gyn. Intern Strong Meml. Hosp., Rochester, 1969-70; resident in ob-gyn. Med. U. S.C. Hosp., Charleston, 1970-74; chief of ob-gyn. Roper Hosp., Charleston; vice chmn. ob-gyn. dept. Bon Secours St. Francis Hosp., Charleston, 1999—; clin. assoc. prof. Med. U. S.C.; mem. exec. bd. Roper Hosp., Charleston,1992-95, perinatal adv. bd., Charleston, 1992-95; vice-chmn. dept. ob-gyn Bon Secours St. Francis Hosp., 1999. Leader Boy Scouts of Am., Mt. Pleasant, S.C., 1978-88; coach Hungry Neck Internat. Soccer, Mt. Pleasant, 1978-88. Lt. Cmdr. USN, 1974-76. Fellow ACOG, South Atlantic Assn. Ob-Gyn. (chair state com. 1995-98); mem. AMA, Am. Fertility Soc., NYAS, S.C. Med. Assn., Charleston County Med. Soc., Pi Kappa Phi (archon 1962—), Phi Rho Sigma. Presbyterian.

HUGGINS, CHARLOTTE SUSAN HARRISON, secondary school educator, author, travel speciali; b. Rockford, Ill., May 13, 1933; d. Lyle Lux and Alta May (Bowers) H.; m. Rollin Charles Huggins, Apr. 26, 1952; children: Cynthia Charlotte Peters, Shirley Ann Cooper, John Charles. *On father's side, a direct descendant of Sir Antoine Trabue, a French Huguenot who came to Maniken-Town, Virginia, in 1692, and of Joseph Sallee, also of Maniken-Town, who gave money and supplies to the Revolutionary cause during the American Revolution. On mother's side, direct descendant of Thomas Newbold, who arrived in America in 1678, settling in Lewes, Delaware. Great-great grandfather Francis Marion Newbold married Comfort Rodney, niece of Delaware's best-known patriot, Caesar Augustus Rodney. Francis Marion Newbold moved West in 1820. His son became a large landowner in Moultrie County, Illinois.* Student, Knox Coll., 1951-52; AB magna cum laude, Harvard U., 1958; MA, Northwestern U., 1960, postgrad., 1971-73; cert. in conversation French, Berlitz Lang. Sch. Asst. editor Hollister Publs., Inc., Wilmette, Ill., 1959-65; tchr. advanced placement English New Trier H.S., Winnetka, Ill., 1965—, master tchr., 1979, lead tchr., 1988; with Task Force Commn. on Grading, 1973-74; Sabbatical project 1 yr. world travel History-Lit. Prospectus; cons. Asian Studies New Trier, 1987-88; mem. New Trier Supts. Commn. on Censorship, 1991; critic tchr. Northwestern U.; cons. McDougall-Littel's Young Writer's Manual, 1985-88; asst. sponsor Echoes, 1981—, Trevia, 1982, 83; sponsor New Trier News, 1988—; pres. Harrison Farms, Inc., Lovington, Ill, 1976—; spkr. North Suburban Geneal. Soc., 1990; presenter Asian lit. Ill. Humanities Coun., 1992, Nat. Scholastic Press Assn., No. Ill. Sch. Press Assn., 1992, 93, 94; instr., travel expert New Trier Adult Edn. Keys to the World's Last Mysteries, 1986—. *Currently engaged in a writing project about a friend and prominent Cambodian who was killed in 1979 during the Khmer Rouge revolution in Cambodia. The book will include a personal correspondence, interviews with family and friends, and extensive research based on travel to France and Southeast Asia. A second work-in-progress is a history of Ms.*

Huggins' family, the Newbolds, describing their immigration from England in 1678, their life in Delaware in the 1700's, and their journey west to settle in Indiana and Illinois. Author: A sequential Course in Composition Grades 9-12, 1979, A History of New Trier High School, 1982, Passage to Anaheim: An Historical Biography of Pioneer Families, 1984, Cambodia: A Place in Time, 1987; (video tapes) The Glory That Was, 1987. Mem. women's bd. St. Leonard's House, Chgo., 1965-75; Ctrl. Sch. PTA Bd., Wilmette, 1960-64; mem. jr. bd. Northwestern U. Settlement, Chgo., 1965-75, 98, pres. 1999—. Recipient DAR citizenship award, 1953, Phi Beta Kappa award, 1957, Am. Legion award, 1959; cert. of merit Graphic Arts Competition Printing Industries of Am., 1983, 1st place award Am. Scholastic Press Assn., 1990, cert. of merit Am. Newspaper Pubs. Assn., 1990. Mem. MLA, NEA, ASCD, Ill. Edn. Assn., New Trier Edn. Assn. (sec. 1992, pres.-elect 1994, pres. 1995-96), Nat. Coun. Tchrs. English, Ill. Assn. Tchrs. English, Women Comm., Inc., Northwestern U. Alumni Assn., Jr. Aux. U. Chgo. Cancer Rsch. Bd., Mary Crane League, Nat. Huguenot Soc., Ill. Huguenot Soc., Nat. Soc. DAR, Columbia Scholastic Press Assn. (del 1990, newspaper judge, medalist award), Ill. Journalism Edn. Assn. (awards chmn., bd. dirs. 1992—, sec. 1994-97), Quill and Scroll (George Gallup award 1990, bd. dirs. 1992-93), Nat. Scholastic Press Assn. (spring convention rep. 1991-92, 92-93, 93-94, 94-95, 95-96, newspaper judge, conv. del. 1991, All-Am. Newspaper award 1990-91, 91-92, Fall and Spring conv. presenter 1993-94, 94-95, 95-96, 96—), Art Inst. Chgo. (life), Terra Mus. Chgo. (charter), Lyric Opera (assoc.), Women's Club Wilmette, Mich. Shores Club, Univ. Club Chgo., Knox Coll. Alumni Assn., Radcliffe Coll. Alumnae Assn., Harvard U. Alumni Assn. (admissions candidate interviewer), Pi Beta Phi (North Shore Chgo. alumnae bd., publicity chair). Home: 700 Greenwood Ave Wilmette IL 60091-1748 Office: 385 Winnetka Ave Winnetka IL 60093-4238

HUGGINS, DELMA BUSTAMANTE, community nurse, family nurse practitioner; b. Tucson, July 19, 1947; d. Jose R. and Beatrice (Garcia) Bustamante; divorced; 1 child, Damian J. ADN, Pima Community Coll., Tucson, 1972; BSN, U. Phoenix, Tucson, 1984; MSN, U. Ariz., 1996. RN, Ariz.; cert. orthopedic nurse, family nurse practitioner. Staff nurse, profl. nurse mgr. St. Mary's Hosp. Health Ctr., Tucson, 1972-86; profl nurse case mgr. Carondelet Cmty. Nursing Svcs., Tucson, 1986-96; FNP, Carondelet Health Network Cmty. Nursing Svcs., Tucson, 1996—, Cmty. Outreach Office, Tucson. Mem. ANA, Am. Acad. Nurse Practitioners, Nat. Assn. Hispanic Nurses, Tucson Assn. Hispanic Nurses, Catholic Nurses Assn., Ariz. Nurses Assn., Nat. Assn. Orthopaedic Nurses, Old Pueblo Orthopaedic Nurses Assn., Sigma Theta Tau. Office: Cmty Outreach Office 1701 W St Marys Rd Tucson AZ 85745

HUGGINS, M. WAYNE, protective services agency administrator; m. Wanda S. Huggins; children: Sarah, Wayne Jr., Jacob. Grad., George Mason U., 1978, FBI Nat. Acad., 1982, Princeton U. Mem. U.S. Secret Svc. Exec. Protection Svc.; trooper Va. State Police, 1971-78; chief dep. sheriff Fairfax County, Va.; sheriff Fairfax County, 1980-90; apptd. dir. U.S. Dept. of Justice's Nat. Inst. of Corrections; exec. dir. Commn. on Accreditation for Law Enforcement Agys. Inc.; supt. Va. State Police, 1994—. Mem. Nat. Sheriffs' Assn. (chair detention and corrections com.), Am. Correctional Assn. (bd. commrs., chmn. bd. 1986-90). Office: VA Dept State Police PO Box 27472 Richmond VA 23261

HUGGINS, RICHARD LEONARD, development director; b. Wheeling, W.Va.; s. Gerald and Josephine Huggins. BA, Davis and Elkins Coll., Elkins, W.Va., 1960; MDiv, Union Theol. Sem., Richmond, Va., 1963; postgrad., Princeton Sem., Pitts. Sem. Ordained to ministry Presbyn. Ch. Sr. pastor Presbyn. chs., Pa., N.J., 1963-76, Internat. Ch., Aruba, 1976; pastor First Presbyn. Ch., New Cumberland, W.Va., 1976-86; regional rep. for Fla. Presbyn. Ch. Found., Inc., 1986-89, regional mgr. for 13 states and P.R., 1989-91; pres., CEO HRT Assocs., 1991-92; cons. for funds devel., mktg. and strategic planning Altamonte Springs, Fla., 1992-94; dir. Fla. Presbyn. Homes, Lakeland, 1994-98; resource devel. officer Thornwell Home and Sch., 1999; bd. chmn. Multicultural Ctr., Inc. Charter mem. Ctrl. Fla. Planned Giving Coun.; past pres. Duvall Home Found.; del. Pa. Constl. Conv., 1967-67; chmn. City Planning Commn. Named Disting. West Virginian, State of W.Va., 1980, God and Svc. medal Boy Scouts Am., 1984; named to Outstanding Young Men of Am., 1969. Mem. Am. Mgmt. Assn., Am. Planning Assn., Nat. Soc. Fund Raising Execs., Nat. Coun. for Non-Profit Bds., Health, Human Svcs. Bd. (exec. bd., chair). Home: 1601 Archers Path Lakeland FL 33809-5063

HUGGINS, ROBERT BRIAN, nonprofit organization official; b. Schenectady, N.Y., Apr. 11, 1953; s. Lawrence P. and Mary A. (Flynn) H. BS, Villanova U., 1975; MBA, Temple U., 1980; grad. mgmt. skills program, Nat. Acad. for Voluntarism, Alexandria, Va., 1994. Mktg. analyst Phila. Saving Fund Soc., 1976-77, advt. mgr., 1978-80, dir. advt., 1981-84, dir. spl. projects, 1985-86; account exec. United Way Southeastern Pa., Phila., 1987-89, sr. account exec., 1990-95, asst. v.p., 1996—.

HUGH, GREGORY JOSEPH, finance company executive; b. Chgo., Sept. 23, 1942; s. Dong Loy and Shee (Moy) H.; m. Linda Lim, Mar. 10, 1963; children: Dianne Elizabeth, Brian Gregory. BA, St. Ambrose U., Davenport, Iowa, 1964. Cert. Real Estate Brokerage Mgr., Grad. Realtor Inst. V.p. Lava-Simplex Internat., Chgo., 1967-69; advt./sales promotion mgr. Baker Rhodes Mktg. Corp., Bloomington, Minn., 1969-73; dir. advt. Mail Mktg. & Sys., Inc., Bloomington, 1973-74; mfrs. rep. Mutual Bus. Assocs., Hopkins, Minn., 1974-76; sales mgr. Realty World-Hessburg Realtors, Shorewood, Minn., 1976-79; reg. rep. Waddell & Reed, Inc., Bloomington, 1979-86; owner/broker Good Earth Realty, Inc., Minnetonka, Minn., 1979-86; br. mgr. Realty World - TCF Realty, Inc., Minnetonka, 1986-87; reg. mgr. TCF Fin., Inc., Excelsior, Minn., 1987-89; v.p. Cityside Fin., Minnetonka, Minn., 1989; account mgr. Mut. Bus. Assocs., Minnetonka, 1990—; pres. Hugh Enterprises, Inc., Minnetrista, Minn., 1995—; instr. Inst. Fin. Edn., Chgo., 1987-88. Author: Personal Financial Planning...The Sensible Approach to Investing, 1982; contbr. articles to fin. jours. Res. officer St. Bonificus-Minnetrista Dept. Pub. Safety, 1987-90. Mem. Greater Mpls. Area Bd. Realtors (cert. real estate brokerage mgr. and GRI designations). Home: 6520 S Bay Dr Excelsior MN 55331-9684

HUGHART, THOMAS ARTHUR, minister; b. Morgantown, W.Va., Feb. 21, 1932; s. Joseph Marvin and Helen Hood (Williams) H.; m. Gloria Joyce Wiley, Feb. 1, 1958; children: Andrew William, Heidi Ellen, Bradford David. BA, Coll. of Wooster, 1953; MDiv, Union Theol. Sem., N.Y.C., 1956; STD, San Francisco Theol. Sem., San Anselmo, Calif., 1982. Ordained to ministry Presbyn. Ch. (U.S.A.), 1956. Assoc. min. Watchung Presbyn. Ch., Bloomfield, N.J., 1956-59; pastor Bedford (N.Y.) Presbyn. Ch., 1959-89, co-pastor, 1989-95; interim sr. pastor First Presbyn. Ch., Greenwich, Conn., 1995-97, Ctrl. Presbyn. Ch., N.Y.C., 1997—; mem. Presbyn. Conf. Assn., N.Y.C., 1985—; moderator Presbytery of Hudson River, 1975. Democrat. Home: 459 Old Post Rd PO Box 447 Bedford NY 10506-0447 Office: Ctrl Presbyn Ch 593 Park Ave New York NY 10021-7309

HUGHES, ALFRED CLIFTON, bishop; b. Boston, Dec. 2, 1932; s. Alfred Clifton and Ellen Cecelia (Hennessey) H. A.B., St. John's Sem. Coll., 1954; S.T.L., Gregorian U., Rome, 1958, S.T.D., 1961. Ordained priest Roman Cath. Ch., 1957, ordained bishop, 1981. Asst. pastor St. Stephen's Parish, Framingham, Mass., 1958-59, Our Lady Help of Christians, Newton, Mass., 1961-62; lectr. St. John's Sem., Brighton, 1962-65, spiritual dir., 1965-81, rector, 1981-86; aux. bishop Archdiocese of Boston, 1981-93; regional bishop of Merrimack Region, 1986-90; vicar for adminstrn. Archdiocese of Boston, 1990-93; bishop of Baton Rouge, 1993—; chmn. NCCB Com. on Doctrine, 1991-94. Author: Preparing for Church Ministry, 1979; contbr. articles to profl. jours. Mellon and Davis Founds. grantee, 1976. Mem. Catholic Theol. Soc. Am. Office: Cath Life Ctr PO Box 2028 1800 S Acadian Thruway Baton Rouge LA 70821-2028*

HUGHES, ALLEN, music critic; b. Brownsburg, Ind., Dec. 28, 1921; s. Maurice McKinley and Bess (Collyer) H.; m. Marian Nina Berklich, Mar. 28, 1964. Student, George Washington U., 1940-42; B.A., U. Mich., 1946, B.Mus., 1947; postgrad., N.Y. U., 1948-50. Lectr. music Toledo Mus. Art, 1946-47; asst. editor, critic Mus. Am., 1950-53; free-lance writer Paris, France, 1953-55; music critic N.Y. Herald Tribune, 1955-60; mem. music faculty Bklyn. Coll., 1958-60; music critic N.Y. Times, 1960-61, asst. dance critic, 1961-62, dance critic, 1962-65, music critic, 1965-86. Served to lt. (j.g.) USNR, 1943-46. Office: 80 E 11th St New York NY 10003-6000

HUGHES, ANN HIGHTOWER, retired economist, international trade consultant; b. Birmingham, Ala., Nov. 24, 1938; d. Brady Alexander and Juanita (Pope) H. BA, George Washington U., 1963, MA, 1969. Asst. U.S. trade rep. Exec. Office of Pres., Washington, 1978-81; dep. asst. sec. trade agreements Dept. Commerce, Washington, 1981-82, dep. asst. sec. Western Hemisphere, 1982-95; dir. C & M Internat., Washington, 1995-97; ret. Recipient meritorious exec. award Pres. of U.S., 1982, 88, disting. exec. award, 1993.

HUGHES, ANN NOLEN, psychotherapist; b. Ft. Meade, Md.; d. George M. and Georgie T. Nolen; m. Edwin L. Hughes, Oct. 21, 1961; 1 child, Andrew G. BS in Psychology, Rollins Coll., 1985, MA in Counseling, 1986; student in pub. speaking and human rels., Dale Carnegie Inst., 1981; student, Duke U., 1950-52. Lic. mental health counselor; nat. cert. counselor; nat. cert. gerontol. counselor. Supr. top secret control, audio/visual small parts supply U.S. Army, Continental U.S. and Tokyo; adminstrv. sec. Sys. Devel. Corp., Rand Corp., Santa Monica, Calif.; adminstrv. asst., editor, exec. sec., adminstrv. sec. Aerospace Corp., El Segundo, Calif.; staff therapist Circles of Care, Melbourne, Fla.; developer program for leading divorce support groups for Brevard Women's Ctr. Various leadership positions PTA, Pittsford, N.Y., Brookfield, Wis., 1968-81; mem. Brevard Cmty. Chorus, 1991—, adv. bd., 1997; docent Space Coast Sci. Ctr., 1991-92; vol. ref. desk Suntree-Viera Libr., 1997-98; mem. Citizen's Emergency Response Team (CERT). Mem. ACA, DAR, Am. Soc. Aging, Assn. for Adult Devel. and Aging, Space Coast PC User's Group, Nat. Geneal. Soc., Geneal. Soc. South Brevard, Suntree Country Club, Suntree Master Homeowners Assn. (Twin Lakes rep. 1997—), Brevard County Alumnae Assn. of Kappa Kappa Gamma, Kappa Kappa Gamma. Presbyterian. Avocations: photoimaging, fitness, genealogy, voice, choral singing. Office: PO Box 410162 Melbourne FL 32941-0162

HUGHES, ARTHUR HYDE, accountant, consultant; b. Lansing, Mich., May 15, 1952; s. Francis Aloysius and Alice Catherine (Hyde) H.; m. Ellen Marie Krempa, Feb. 13, 1982; children: Bradley Allan, Allison Marie. BS magna cum laude, Fla. State U., 1974; postgrad., U. Tex., Dallas, 1978. CPA, Tex. Treas. Excella Trading Corp., Ft. Worth, 1977-79; with ARCO, Dallas, 1975—; revenue analyst Gas Revenue Acctg., Dallas, 1975-82; sr. acct. Oil Revenue Acctg., Dallas, 1982-85; client rep. Revenue Projects Group, Dallas, 1985-87; supr. Gas Data Svcs., Dallas, 1987-88, Gas Systems Redevel., Dallas, 1988-89; production acctg. cons. ARCO, Dallas, 1989-90, sr. revenue compliance auditor, 1990-96; internat. acct. ARCO Algeria, 1996; pvt. practice petroleum auditing, cons., 1996-97; mgr. exploration prodn. and fin. software Allegro Devel., Inc., 1997-98; prin. cons. Oracle Energy Co., 1998—; mem. Petroleum Data Exch. Steering Com., Denver, 1985-87, chmn. Gas Revenue Acctg., Data Exch. Com. (subs Petroleum Data Exch.) Dallas, 1986-87, spl. com. electronic data exch. of Coun. of Petroleum Acctg. Socs., Dallas, 1986—. Contbr. articles to profl. jours.; developer petroleum industry Gas Revenue Acctg. Data Exchange system with Gen. Elec., 1985. Alternate del. Tex. Rep. Conv., 1982; active Nat. Right to Life, Washington. Mem. AICPA, Tex. Soc. CPAs, Petroleum Acctg. Soc., NRA (life), Tex. Rifle Assn., Ducks Unltd., Toastmasters, Gun Owner, Am., Mensa, Intertel, Phi Eta Sigma, Phi Kappa Phi, Beta Gamma Sigma. Roman Catholic. Avocations: target shooting, reading, chess. Home and Office: 6405 Limerick Ln Garland TX 75044-3435

HUGHES, BARBARA BRADFORD, nurse, real estate manager; b. Bragg City, Mo., Jan. 21, 1941; d. Lawrence Hurl Bradford and Opal Jewel (Prater) Puttin; m. Robert Howard Hughes, Dec. 9, 1961; children: Kimberly Ann Hayden, Robert Howard II. ASN, St. Louis Community Coll., 1978; student, Webster U., 1980. RN, Mo. Med. surg. nurse Alexian Bros. Hosp., St. Louis, 1979-80; staff nurse Midwest Allergy Cons., St. Louis, 1980; nurse high altitude Aviation Nurse, Ltd., St. Louis, 1980-81; cardiac telemetry staff nurse Jefferson Meml. Hosp., Crystal City, Mo., 1992-94; vol. nurse Med. Ministry Internat., Plano, Tex., 1998—; pvt. practice real estate mgmt., 1962—. Vol. Luth. Hosp., St. Louis, 1967-70; mem. Mo. Bot. Garden, St. Louis, 1976—, Mo. Hist. Soc., 1993—, St. Louis Zoo Friends Assn., 1986-87, Nat. Trust for Hist. Preservation, 1990—; Channel 9-Ednl. TV, St. Louis; vol. blood drive ARC, St. Louis, 1980; vol. health tchr. Spartan Aluminum Products, Sparta, Ill., 1984. U. Mo. scholar, 1959. Mem. Mo. Pilots Assn., Women in Aviation Internat. (charter), U.S. Pilots Assn., Tyospaye Club, Aircraft Owners and Pilots Assn., Med. Ministries Internat. Republican. Avocations: flying, gardening, reading. Home and Office: 736 Windsor Harbor Rd Imperial MO 63052-2503 also office: Med Ministry Internat Plano TX

HUGHES, BARNARD, actor; b. Bedford Hills, N.Y., July 16, 1915; s. Owen and Madge (Kiernan) H.; m. Helen Stenborg, Apr. 19, 1950; 2 children. Student, Manhattan Coll., DHL (hon.), 1989. Stage debut with Shakespeare Fellowship Co. in The Taming of the Shrew, N.Y.C., 1934; actor (plays) including Please, Mrs. Garibaldi, 1939, Herself, Mrs. Patrick Crowley, 1939, The Ivy Green, 1949, Dinosaur Wharf, 1951, The Teahouse of the August Moon, 1956, A Bell for Adano, 1957, Home of the Brave, 1957, The Will and The Way, 1957, Enrico IV, 1958, A Majority of One, 1959, Advise and Consent, 1960, Rosmersholm, 1962, A Doll's House, 1963, The Advocate, 1963, Nobody Loves and Albatross, 1963, Hamlet, 1964, I Was Dancing, 1964, Generation, 1965, Hogan's Goat, 1965, How Now Dow Jones, 1967, The Wrong-Way Light Bulb, 1969, Sheep on the Runway, 1970, Line, 1971, Abelard and Heloise, 1971, Older People, 1972, Hamlet, 1972, Much Ado About Nothing, 1972 (Tony nomination 1973), Uncle Vanya, 1973, The Good Doctor, 1973, The Merry Wives of Windsor, 1974, Pericles, Prince of Tyre, 1974, All Over Town, 1974, The Three Sisters, 1977, The Devil's Disciple, 1977, 78, Da, 1978 (Tony award Best Actor 1978, Outer Critics Circle award 1978), Homeward Bound, 1980, Iceman Cometh, 1981, 85, Translations, 1981, Tartuffe, 1982, Angels Fall, 1982, 83, End of the World, 1984, The Sky is No Limit, 1984, You Can't Take It With You (Abbey Theatre, Dublin, Ireland), 1989, Prelude to A Kiss, 1990, Da, 1993, (films) including The Young Doctors, 1961, Hamlet, 1964, Midnight Cowboy, 1969, Where's Poppa?, 1970, Deadhead Miles, 1970, The Pursuit of Happiness, 1971, The Hospital, 1971, Cold Turkey, 1971, Rage, 1972, Sisters, 1973, Oh God!, 1977, First Monday in October, 1981, Tron, 1982, Best Friends, 1982, Maxie, 1985, Where are the Children?, 1986, The Lost Boys, 1987, Da (Olymoia Theatre, Dublin, Ireland), 1988, Doc Hollywood, 1991, Sister Act II: Back in the Habit, 1993, Odd Couple II, 1997, The Cradle Will Rock, 1998, (TV movies) including Guilty or Innocent: The Sam Sheppard Murder Case, 1975, 1975, Tell Me My Name, 1977, See How She Runs, 1978, Homeward Bound, 1980, The Sky's No Limit, 1984, Agatha Cristie's A Carribean Mystery, 1983, Night of Courage, 1986, A Hobo's Christmas, 1987, Day One, 1989, Home Fires Burning, 1989, Guts and Glory: The Rise and Fall of Oliver North, 1989, The Incident, 1990, Miracle Child, 1993; star: (TV series) Doc, 1975-76, Mr. Merlin, 1981-82, The Cavanaughs, 1986-87, Blossom, 1991-93. With U.S. Army. Recipient St. Clair Bayfield award, 1973; elected to Theatre Hall of Fame, 1991. Office: Howard Aronson Withum Smith Brown 328 Newman Springs Rd Red Bank NJ 07701-5654

HUGHES, BLAKE, retired architectural institute administrator, publisher; b. N.Y.C., June 24, 1914; s. Ferdinand Holme and Ines (de Cordova) H.; m. Betty Jean Wolf, Aug. 26, 1951; children: Diane Elizabeth, Brian Blake. Degre de civilisation, Sorbonne U., Paris, 1935; AB summa cum laude, Dartmouth Coll., 1936; postgrad., Columbia U., 1936-37. Salesman Edward B. Smith & Co., Smith, Barney & Co., investment bankers, N.Y.C., 1936-38, N.Y. Life Ins. Co., 1939-40; promotion mgr. Engring. News Record, Constrn. Methods, McGraw-Hill Inc., N.Y.C., 1947-50; promotion mgr., dir. mktg. Archtl. Record F.W. Dodge Corp., N.Y.C., 1951-61; assoc. pub. Archtl. Record McGraw-Hill Inc., N.Y.C., 1961-68, pub. Archtl. Record, 1968-80, pub. House & Home, 1976-77; pres. Internat. Inst. for Architecture, Washington, 1978-81. Trustee Unity (Maine) Coll., 1965-75; pres. Internat. Archtl. Found., 1973-78; bd. dirs. Nat. Home Improvement Coun., 1976-77. Lt. USNR, 1940-45. Decorated Order of Fatherland War (Russia). Mem. Union Internat. Architects (archtl. critics com. 1978-80), Appalachian Housing Inst. (bd. dirs.), Charleston Art Guild (pres. 1990-91), English Speaking Union (pres. Charleston chpt. 1995-96), Carolina Yacht Club, Phi Beta Kappa, Delta Sigma Rho. Home: 109 E Bay St Apt 2C Charleston SC 29401-2549

HUGHES, BRENDA BETHEA, state legislator; b. High Point, N.C.; married. BS, N.C. Ctrl. State U.; postgrad., Ctrl. Mich. U. Mem. Md. Ho. of Dels., Annapolis, 1993-98, mem. ways and means com., 1993-98; adminstr. The Port of Balt., 1998—. Mem. Prince Georges County Bd. Edn., 1988-93, Gov.'s Commn. on Disruptive Youth, 1993—. Mem. Delta Sigma Theta. Office: The Port of Balt E Pratt St World Trade Ctr/19th Flr Baltimore MD 21202*

HUGHES, BYRON WILLIAM, lawyer, oil exploration company executive; b. Clarksdale, Miss., Nov. 8, 1945; s. Byron B. and Francis C. (Turner) H.; m. Sarah Eileen Goodwin, June 23, 1973 (div.); children: Jennifer Eileen, Stephanie Ann. BA, U. Miss., 1968; JD, Jackson Sch. Law (now Miss. Coll. Law), 1971. Bar: Miss. 1971, U.S. Supreme Ct. 1975; cert. real estate appraiser. Atty., abstractor Miss. Hwy. Dept., 1971-76; atty., ind. landman Byron Hughes Oil Exploration Co., Jackson, Miss., 1976-92; prosecutor, child support enforcement atty., Miss. Dept. Human Svcs., 1992—; tchr. high sch.; real estate broker. Mem. ABA, Miss. Bar Assn., Hinds County Bar Assn., Bolivar County Bar Assn., Am. Judicature Soc., Nat. Assn. Real Estate Appraisers, Miss. Child Support Assn., Miss. Assn. Petroleum Landmen, Ala. Landmen Assn., Black Warrior Basin Petroleum Landmen Assn., Am. Assn. Petroleum Landmen (cert. profl. landman 1991), Ole Miss. Law Alumni Assn., Miss. Coll. Alumni Assn., Miss. Art Assn., Sigma Delta Kappa. Methodist. Home: PO Box 1485 Jackson MS 39215-1485 Office: PO Box 1485 Jackson MS 39215-1485

HUGHES, CARL ANDREW, municipal construction executive; b. Lexington, Ky., Dec. 14, 1948; s. Carl Hampton and Edna Victoria (Douglas) H.; m. Lynn Russo-Hughes; 1 child, Sadie. BA, Fugazzi Bus. Coll., 1969. Pres. Hughes Constrn. Corp., Lexington, 1972-80; pres., CEO Bluegrass Painting Co., Inc., 1980—. Avocations: fishing, reading. Home: 112 Desha Rd Lexington KY 40502

HUGHES, CHARLES MARTIN, retired educator; b. Telford, Pa., Nov. 8, 1921; s. Asa Malcolm and Mabel (Colson) H.; m. Evelyn Wilson, Nov. 22, 1952; children: Ray, Gale, Melissa. BS, Haverford Coll., 1950; MEd, Temple U., 1952. Math tchr. Souderton (Pa.) H.S., 1952-59; math tchr., registrar, dir. DP Essex C.C., Baltimore County, Md., 1959-82; programmer Pen Engring. & Mfg., Danboro, Pa., 1982-94. Author: Basic Math for College Freshman, 1966, My Hands, 1990. Tournament chmn. Md. Tennis Assn. and Mid Atlantic Tennis Assn., Balt., 1966-75. Staff sgt. U.S. Army Air Corps, 1942-45. Avocations: tennis, writing. Home: 593 Geigle Hill Rd Ottsville PA 18942-9798

HUGHES, CHARLES R., JR., health facility administrator; b. Montgomery, Ala., June 13, 1964; s. Charles R. Sr. and Dolly (Boatfield) H.; m. Angela Hagan, Mar. 18, 1988. AS in Nursing, Troy State U, 1987, B. in Liberal Arts, 1987. RN, Ala. Staff nurse emergency room Elmore County Hosp., Wetumpka, Ala.; charge nurse critical care unit Bapt. Med. Ctr., Montgomery, Ala.; nursing supr. Community Hosp., Tallassee, Ala., critical care dir. Active ARC. Mem. Ala. Nurses Assn., Am. Heart Assn.

HUGHES, CLYDE MATTHEW, religious denomination executive; b. Huntington, W.Va., Dec. 7, 1948; s. Donald Lee and Audrey Arlene (Stevens) H.; m. Linda May Daniels, June 10, 1972; children: Crystal, Dustin, Tina, Wesley, Timothy, Penny, Heidi, Robin. Diploma, Amb. Bible Inst., London, Ohio, 1972; BA, Cedarville (Ohio) Coll., 1974; MA, Meth. Theol. Sch. in Ohio, 1980; DD, Heritage Bible Coll., Dunn, N.C., 1994. Ordained to ministry Internat. Pentecostal Ch. of Christ, 1974. Pastor Internat. Pentecostal Ch. of Christ, Hillsboro, Ohio, 1981-82; nat. dir. Sunday sch. Internat. Pentecostal Ch. of Christ, London, 1976-82, dir. ch. ministries, 1982-84, asst. gen. overseer, 1984-90, gen. overseer, chmn. gen. bd., 1990—; bd. dirs. Beulah Heights Bible Coll., Atlanta, 1982—, chmn. bd. 1990-96. Editor-in-chief The Pentecostal Leader; contbr. articles to religious pubs. Chmn. bd. dirs. Locust Grove Rest Home, 1990-98. Mem. Nat. Assn. Evangs. (bd. dirs. 1990—), Madison County Evang. Assn. (bd. dirs. 1990—), Pentecostal/Charismatic Chs. N.Am. (bd. dirs. 1994—). Home: 7040 Danville Rd London OH 43140-9766

HUGHES, CYNTHIA L., festival director, writer, editor; b. Lincoln, Nebr., Jan. 20, 1958; d. Harry Alfred and Dona Carrie Hughes. BS, U. Kans., 1981. Copy editor Austin (Tex.) Am.-Statesman, 1981-82, copy chief—lifestyle, 1983-84; copy editor Tex. Monthly, Austin, 1985, copy chief, 1985-89, dep. exec. editor, 1989-92; owner In Other Words, Austin, 1992—; dir. Tex. Book Festival, Austin, 1996—; bd. dirs. Red Wheelbarrow Press, Austin. Tchr. Sunday sch. Unity Ctr. of Positive Prayer, Austin, 1995—; asst. youth edn. dir. Unity Ch. of Austin, 1992-94. Avocations: creative writing, cooking, sports viewing, music, travel. Office: Tex Book Festival 610 Brazos Ste 110 Austin TX 78701

HUGHES, DAVID MICHAEL, oil service company executive, rancher; b. Knoxville, Tenn., Mar. 20, 1939; s. Cleo L. and Lucille (Farmer) H.; m. Louise Love, Mar. 17, 1960 (div. 1971); children: David Michael Jr., Sheryl Lynn; m. Elizabeth Grove, Mar. 16, 1974; children: Christopher Grove, Andrew Carter. BCE, U. Tenn., 1962. Founder, owner World Wide Divers, Inc., Morgan City, La., 1962-69; founder, past chmn. bd. Oceaneering Internat., Inc., Houston, 1969-90; founder, owner Broken Arrow Ranch, Ingram, Tex., 1975—; founder, pres. Tex. Wild Game Coop., Ingram, 1981—, Game Ranching, Inc., Ingram, 1986—; bd. dirs. Oceaneering Internat., Inc., 1969—. Author: Broken Arrow Ranch Cookbook, 1984; patentee underwater corrosion meter and underwater camera, device for identifying a characteristic of an object or the contents of a container. Mem. Hist. Preservation Com., Ingram, 1986-87; mem. Adv. Coun. Tex. Marine Sci. Inst., 1980-91; hon. chmn. Hunters for the Hungry, 1991—, nat. chmn. Named "Who's Who in Tex. Food and Wine", Dallas Morning News Poll, 1992. Mem. Assn. Diving Contractors (pres. 1967-71, Galletti award 1981), Exotic Wildlife Assn. (pres. 1987-89), Chi Epsilon (nat. conv. del. 1961). Republican. Avocations: woodworking, hunting, cooking. Home: Broken Arrow Ranch PO Box 530 Ingram TX 78025-0530 Office: Tex Wild Game Coop 104 Hwy 27 W PO Box 530 Ingram TX 78025-0530

HUGHES, DEBORAH ENOCH, circuit court clerk; b. Lynchburg, Va., Mar. 24, 1953; d. George Alexander Enoch and Inez (Hailey) Enoch Green; m. Frank Plunkett Hughes, Apr. 24, 1971; children: Frank P. II, Neal Thomas. Grad. in Data Processing, Ctrl. Va. C.C., 1974. Cert. circuit ct. clk., Va. Dep. real estate office Divsn. Commr. of Revenue, Rustburg, Va., 1971-75; data processing chief entry clk. Campbell County Sch. Bd., Rustburg, Va., 1975-79; dep. clk. Circuit Ct. Clk.'s Office, Campbell County, 1979-91, clk., 1992—. Mem. Va. Circuit Ct. Clk.'s Assn., Va. Assn. Elected Constnl. Officers (sec.). Office: Campbell County Circuit Ct Clks Office PO Box 7 Rustburg VA 24588-0007

HUGHES, DONNA JEAN, librarian; b. Alexandria, Va., Mar. 24, 1959; d. John William and Wilma Connie (Beavers) H. BS cum laude, Longwood Coll., Farmville, Va., 1981; MS in Libr. Sci., U. N.C., Chapel Hill, 1985. Lic. tchr., Va. Children's libr. Thomas Hackney Braswell Meml. Libr., Rocky Mount, N.C., 1983-88; Wake County Pub. Librs., Raleigh, N.C., 1988-90; children's svcs. and outreach svcs. libr. Handley Regional Libr., Winchester, Va., 1990—. Mem. youth svcs. adv. com. Libr. of Va., Richmond, 1991-96; music dir. Broadway (Va.) Bapt. Ch., 1990—, Sunday sch. dir., 1991-98; co-founder singles ministry Sunset Avenue Bapt. Ch., Rocky Mount, 1984-90; singer Shenandoah Valley Chorus, 1990-95, Evangelism Missions Panama, 1996-99. Named Employee of Yr., City of Winchester, 1992. Mem. ALA, Va. Libr. Assn. (Jefferson Cup award com. 1995-96), Children and Young Adult Roundtable (chair 1994-95), Lord Fairfax Assn. of Educators of Young Children, Nat. Assn. Educators of Young Children, Nat. Storytelling Assn., Quota Internat. (com. chair, bd. dirs. 1994-96), New Market Garden Club (com. chair 1992—), Phi Kappa Phi. Baptist. Avocations: storytelling, barbershop singing, gardening, swimming, hymn singing. Office: Handley Regional Library 100 W Piccadilly St Winchester VA 22601-3916

HUGHES, EDWARD F. X., physician, educator; b. Boston, Jan. 10, 1942; s. Joseph Daniel and Edith (Dempsey) H.; m. Susan Lane Mooney, Feb. 11, 1967; children: Edward, John, Dempsey. BA in Philosophy, Amherst Coll., 1962; MD, Harvard U., 1966; MPH, Columbia U., 1969. Intern, resident surg. Columbia-Presbyn. Med. Ctr., N.Y.C., 1966-68; instr. to assoc. prof. Mt. Sinai Sch. Medicine, N.Y.C., 1969-77; rsch. assoc. Nat. Bur. Economic Research, N.Y.C., 1970-77; founder, dir. ctr. health svc. policy rsch. Northwestern U. Med. Sch., Chgo., 1977-94; prof. preventitive medicine J. L. Kellogg Grad. Sch. Mgmt., Northwestern U., Evanston, 1977—; dir. health svcs. mgmt. program J. L. Kellogg Grad. Sch. Mgmt., Northwestern U., Evanston, Ill., 1977—; cons. Nat. Ctr. Health Services Research, Rockville, Md., 1975-82, AMA, Chgo., 1981-83, Midwest Bus. Group on Health, Chgo., 1983-85. Editor: Hospital Cost Containment: A Policy Analysis, 1979, A Perspective on Quality in American health Care, 1988 (Bradley award 1962, Health Career Scientist award 1973-75); mem. editl. bd. Managed Care, Jour. Clin. Outcomes, Group Health News, Counseline; contbr. articles to profl. jours. Health Care Financing Adminstrn. grantee, Washington, 1978-84, Ford Found., 1983-86, Robert Wood Johnson Found, 1978-82, NIH, 1983-95, Pew Charitable Trusts, 1990-92, Baxter Found., 1991-96. Fellow N.Y. Acad. Medicine, Am. Coll. Physician Execs.; mem. APHA, Assn. Health Svcs. Rsch. (co-founder, v.p. 1981-83, bd. dirs. 1981-84), Assn. Tchrs. Preventive Medicine (bd. dirs. 1973-76), Med. Adminstrs. Conf., Nat. Assn. Managed Care Physicians (med. adv. bd.), Boston Latin Sch. Chgo. Club (bd. dirs. 1983-86), Chapoquoit Yacht Club (West Famouth, Mass.), Beta Gamma Sigma. Home: 810 Lincoln St Evanston IL 60201-2405 Office: JL Kellogg Sch Mgmt 2001 Sheridan Rd Evanston IL 60208-0814

HUGHES, EDWARD JOHN, artist; b. North Vancouver, B.C., Feb. 17, 1913; s. Edward Samuel Daniell and Katherine Mary (McLean) H.; m. Fern Rosabell Irvine Smith, Feb. 10, 1940 (dec. 1974). Grad., Vancouver Sch. Art, 1933; D Fine Art (hon.), U. Victoria, 1995; DLL (hon.), Emily Carr Inst. Art & Design, Vancouver, B.C., 1997. Exhbns. include retrospective, Vancouver Art Gallery, 1967, Surrey Art Gallery, Art Gallery of Greater Victoria, Edmonton Art Gallery, Calgary Glenbow Gallery, 1983-85, Nat. Gallery Can., Beaverbrook Gallery, Fredericton, 1983-85; represented in permanent collections, Nat. Gallery Can., Ottawa, Art Gallery Ont., Toronto, Vancouver Art Gallery, Montreal Mus. Fine Art, Greater Victoria Art Gallery; ofcl. Army war artist, 1942-46. Served with Can. Army, 1939-46. Recipient Can. Council grants, 1958, 63, 67, 70. Mem. Royal Can. Acad. Arts. Presbyterian. Address: 2449 Heather St, Duncan, BC Canada V9L 2Z6

HUGHES, EDWARD T., retired bishop; b. Lansdowne, Pa., Nov. 13, 1920. Student, St. Charles Sem., U. Pa. Ordained priest Roman Catholic Ch. 1947. Ordained titular bishop Segia and aux. bishop Phila., 1976-86; 2d bishop Diocese of Metuchen, N.J., 1986-97; ret. Diocese of Metuchen, 1997. *

HUGHES, EDWIN LAWSON, retired information systems company executive; b. Pittsburg, Kans., Aug. 11, 1924; s. Edwin Byron and Vera (Lawson) H.; m. Ann Turner Nolen, Oct. 21, 1961; 1 child, Andrew George; children from previous marriage: John Lawson, James Prescott. BSEE, Mo. Sch. Mines, 1949; MSEE, U. Ill., 1950. Registered profl. engr. Fla. Rsch. assoc. digital computer lab. U. Ill., 1949-53; rsch. assoc. Internat. Telemeter Corp., L.A., 1953-54; with Lockheed Missile Sys. Divsn., L.A., 1954-56; group leader Systems Devel. Corp., Santa Monica, Calif., 1957-60; tech. dir. Gen. Motors, Oak Creek, Wis., 1960-71; v.p. engrng. Xerox Corp., Webster, N.Y., 1971-81, Santec Corp., Amherst, N.H., 1981-82; chmn., pres., chief exec. officer Fla. Data Corp., Melbourne, 1982-83; pvt. practice cons. Melbourne, 1984-88; ret. Contbr. articles and papers to profl jours.; inventor computers, copiers; patentee in field. Com. mem. Boy Scouts Am., Pittsford, N.Y., 1974-76; mem. Brevard Cmty. Chorus. With U.S. Army, 1943-46, ETO. Mem. IEEE (sr.), Space Coast PC Users Group (pres. 1991-95, 97-99, sec. 1988-91, treas. 1995-97), Suntree Country Club. Republican. Avocations: skiing, choral singing, tennis, home computers. Home and Office: 447 Pauma Valley Way Melbourne FL 32940-1918

HUGHES, EDWIN STRODE, public relations executive; b. Austin, Tex., Oct. 6, 1936; s. Frank Miller and Lorine (Mitchell) H.; m. Linda Lee Bennett, June 24, 1961; children: Frank Mitchell, Lee Gordon. B of Journalism, U. Tex., Austin, 1960. Writer, photographer Dallas Morning News, 1958-65; info. supr. Southwestern Bell Telephone, Dallas, 1965-68; gen. info. mgr. Southwestern Bell Telephone, St. Louis, 1968-72; divsn. mgr. external rels. Southwestern Bell Telephone, San Antonio, 1974-86; divsn. mgr. advt. and pub. rels. Southwestern Bell Telephone, Dallas, 1986-90; head employee com. Bell Telephone Labs., Murray Hill, N.J., 1972-74; owner Ed Hughes & Assocs., Tijeras, N.Mex., 1991-95, Laramie, Wyo., 1996-98; pub. rels. counsel Loveland, Colo., 1999—. Pres. East Mountain C. of C., 1994; bd. dirs. Alamo area coun. Boy Scouts Am., San Antonio, 1985-86; pres. San Antonio Bus. Com. for the Arts, 1985. Master sgt. U.S. Army NG, 1954-66. Recipient Award of Excellence Internat. Conf. of Indsl. Editors, 1966. Mem. Pub. Rels. Soc. of Am. (accredited), N.Mex. Pub. Rels. Soc. Am. (pres. 1995, 1st place award of excellence 1995), Tex. Pub. Rels. Assn. (pres. 1983, Best of Tex. award 1980), No. Plains Pub. Rels. Soc. Am. (pres. 1997-98). Republican. Methodist. Home and Office: 2195 Kennington Ct Loveland CO 80538

HUGHES, FRANCIS P., medical researcher. Exec. v.p. Am. Bd. of Anesthesiology, Raleigh, N.C. Office: Am Bd Anesthesiology 4101 Lake Boone Trl Ste 510 Raleigh NC 27607-7506

HUGHES, GARY L., artist, sculptor; b. Apr. 6, 1930. BFA, Md. Inst. Coll. Art, Balt. Animation prodr. Gary Hughes, Inc., Bethesda, Md., 1963-84. E-mail: hugheseg@erols.com. Home: 5314 Tuscarawas Rd Bethesda MD 20816

HUGHES, GEORGE FARANT, JR., retired safety engineer; b. Roanoke, Va., June 22, 1923; s. George Farant and Pattie (Shafer) H.; m. Frances Miriam Perdue, July 1, 1950. BS, Va. Mil. Inst., 1948. Registered profl. engr., Va., Calif.; cert. safety profl. With roadway maintenance dept. N. & W. Ry. Co., Roanoke, 1948, with Liberty Mut. Ins. Co., Roanoke, Balt., 1949-61, asst. div. mgr., Pitts., 1962-63; safety supr. Westinghouse Electric Corp., Balt., 1963-64; supr. safety and accident prevention, Buffalo, 1965-67; safety dir. U.S. Naval Weapons Sta., Yorktown, Va., 1967-73; head occupational safety U.S. Naval Safety Center, Norfolk, Va., 1973-83, dep. dir. shore safety programs, 1984-88, ret., 1988. Served with AUS, 1943-46, 50-52. Decorated Bronze Star with oak leaf cluster, Purple Heart. Mem. Am. Soc. Safety Engrs. (profl. mem.), Western N.Y. Safety Conf. (dir. 1966-67), Nat. Soc. Profl. Engr., Va. Safety Assn. (bd. dirs. 1979-88), Nat. Eagle Scout Assn., SAR, Assn. Presevation Va. Antiquities (bd. dirs. 1984-87), Vets. Safety. Home: 520 Randolph St Williamsburg VA 23185-3518

HUGHES, GRACE-FLORES, former federal agency administrator, consultant; b. Taft, Tex., June 11, 1946; d. Adan Flores and Catalina San Miguel; m. Harley Arnold Hughes, May 25, 1980. BA, U. D.C., 1977; MPA, Harvard U., 1980. Sec. Dept. Air Force Kelly AFB, San Antonio, 1967-70, Pentagon-Office Sec. of Def., Washington, 1970-72; program asst., social sci. analyst HEW, Washington, 1972-78; social sci. analyst, acting dir. Office Hispanic Ams. HHS, Washington, 1978-81; vis. prof. Nebr. Wesleyan U., Lincoln, 1982-83, U. Nebr., Omaha, 1984; spl. asst. SBA, Washington, 1985-88, assoc. adminstr. for minority small bus., 1988; dir. community rels. Dept. Justice, Washington, 1988-92; pres. Grace, Inc., Alexandria, Va.; now ptnr. TFS & Assocs., Inc.; spl. asst. Reagan/Bush '84 Campaign, Nebr. and Washington, 1984, 50th Presdl. Inaugural, Washington, 1984-85, Office Pub. Liaison, The White House, 1985. Author: The Bureaucrat, Categorized Workforce, 1992; co-author: New Book of Knowledge, 1980; chair adv. bd. Harvard Jour. Hispanic Policy, 1989—; The Use and Abuse of Diversity Mag., 1994, Hispanic Mag., 1996. Adv. mem. U.S. Senate Rep. Task Force, Washington, 1988-91; alumni exec. bd. J.F. Kennedy Sch. Govt., Harvard U., Cambridge, Mass., 1989-93; mem. Rep. Hispanic Assembly, 1984—; appointed by Gov. Allen of Va. to Bd. for Profl. and Occupational Regulations, 1994—, Bd. for Agr. and Consumer Svcs., 1997—. Recipient Excellence award Nev. Econ. Devel. Corp., 1988, Leadership award Am. GI Forum, Omaha, 1989; named one of 100 Most Influential Hispanics in U.S. Hispanic Bus. Mag., 1988. Mem. Assn. Pub. Adminstrs. (Outstanding Pub. Svc. award 1990), Hispanic Bus. Roundtable, Coun. in Excellence in Govt. (prin.), Fedn. Rep. Women, Mex.-Am. Women's Nat. Assn., Univ. Club (Washington). Roman Catholic. Avocations: tennis, jogging, aerobics, equestrian. Home and Office: 5208 Bedlington Ter Alexandria VA 22304-3551

HUGHES, J. DEBORAH, quality management consultant; b. Pitts., Mar. 24, 1948; d. James Francis and Margaret V. (Wuillmier) H. Diploma, Columbia Sch. Nursing, Pitts., 1969; BSN, La Roche Coll., Pitts., 1987; M in Pub. Mgmt./Healthcare, Carnegie Mellon U., 1988. RN, Pa.; cert. med. staff coord.; cert. profl. in healthcare quality. Clin. asst. to exec. v.p. Forbes Health System, Pitts., 1983-88; dir. med. staff svcs. Monongahela Valley Hosp., Pitts., 1988-90; quality tracking mgr. Humana, Louisville, 1990-91, regional quality mgmt. dir., 1991-92; sr. cons. MetriCor, Inc., Louisville, 1992-94, mgr. accreditation svcs., 1994-95; mgr. accreditation svcs. HCIA, Inc., Louisville, 1995-96, sr. quality mgmt. cons., JCAHO liaison, 1996-98; mgr. accreditation svcs. Performance Improvement, 1998—. Author study guide and publ. newsletter. Mem. Nat. Assn. Med. Staff Svcs., Nat. Assn. for Health Care Quality (study guide task force 1996—), Ky. Assn. for Healthcare Quality (treas. 1996—), Am. Hosp. Assn., Ky. Assn. for Risk Mgmt. Avocations: exercising, biking, reading, music. Office: HCIA 3033 Ledge Brook Ct Louisville KY 40241

HUGHES, JAMES BAKER, JR., retail executive, consultant; b. Englewood, Calif., Nov. 15, 1938; s. James Baker Hughes Sr. and Mary Alma (Nettleton) Gaston; m. Jeanette Ann Martin, July 20, 1968; children: Heather, Hollis Ann. BS, U. Houston, 1961. CPA, Tex. V.p. Deep River Armory, Inc., Houston, 1958-65, pres., 1965-88; sales mgr. Tex-Products Machinery & Supply, Houston, 1989-92, acct., 1992-97; mng. dir. Transportes Pesados Ams. S.A., Guatemala City, Guatemala, 1997-98; dir. internat. projects INTECCSA, Guatemala City, 1997-98; dir. fgn. projects Sarco, Inc., Sterling, N.J., 1998—; dir. Interactive Sys., Inc., Houston, 1999—; instr. continuing edn. U. Houston, 1976-77; assoc. prodr. Chisos Film Prodns., Houston, 1969-70; cons. State of Mex. Police Dept., 1976-78, Smithsonian Instn., 1988; CFO French Prodn. Inc., Houston, Arena Power Co., Houston, Electro-Peten S.A., Guatemala City, Guatemala, La Rucia Aviation, Inc., Saxet Foods, LLC, Houston, Bald Eagle Mining Co., Expedite Oyster, Inc.; treas. Bald Eagle Mining Co., Inteccsa, Guatemala City. Author: Confederate Gunmakers, 1961, Mexican Military Arms, 1968; contbr. articles to profl. jours.; inventor range finding sight. Rep. campaign worker Harris County, Tex.; various pos. St. Martin's Episcopal Ch., Houston, 1954-95; bd. dirs. Young Reps. Harris County, 1968; dir. fin. Inst. for Rsch. on Small Arms in Internat. Security, Alexandria, Va., 1993—; treas. Sean Ashley House, Houston, 1993-97, adv. dir., 1997—. Recipient Bronze Benefactor Medal Royal Life Saving Soc., 1978. Mem. Nat. Rifle Assn. (life), Houston Gun Collectors Assn. (life, pres. 1960-61), Inst. Internac. De Historia Mil. in Mexico City (hon.), Soc. du Vignoble LeGodet (Paris, bd. dirs. 1985-95). Republican. Clubs: Meml. Drive Country (pres. 1978-79), Racquet (Houston). Avocations: hunting, fishing, white-water rafting. Office: PO Box 571716 Houston TX 77257-1716

HUGHES, JAMES M., protective services official; m. Paula Hughes; children: Jamie, Kelly, Katie. BS, Mary Coll., 1973; postgrad., Northwestern U. Traffic Inst., 1979-80; MS in Pub. Adminstrn., U. N.D., 1984. Cert. instr. hwy patrol accident investigation. With N.D. Hwy Patrol, 1974—, trooper, 1974-80; sgt., dist. sgt. N.D. Hwy Patrol, Grand Forks and Bismarck, 1980-88; lt., dept. safety and pub. rels. officer N.D. Hwy Patrol, 1988, capt., dept. tng. dept., 1989-91, dist. comdr. Williston dist., 1992-93, supt., 1993—. Office: ND Hwy Patrol 600 E Boulevard Ave Bismarck ND 58505-0240

HUGHES, JAMES MITCHELL, epidemiologist; b. Pitts., Aug. 11, 1945; s. James Paul and Adelaide (Mitchell) H.; m. Pamela Mary Parsons, June 12, 1971; children: Andrew Saban, Mitchell Parsons. BA, Stanford U., 1966, MD, 1971. Diplomate Am. Bd. Preventive Medicine, Am. Bd. Internal Medicine, Am. Bd. Infectious Diseases. Intern U. Wash., Seattle, 1971-72; epidemic intelligence svc. officer Ctr. for Disease Control, Atlanta, 1973-75; resident internal medicine U. Wash., Seattle, 1972-73, 75-76; fellow infectious diseases U. Va., Charlottesville, 1976-78; chief water-related diseases activity, asst. chief enteric diseases br. Bur. Epidemiology, Ctr. for Disease Control, Atlanta, 1978-81; chief surveillance and prevention br., asst. dir. med. sci. hosp. infections program Ctr. for Infectious Diseases, Ctrs. for Disease Control, Atlanta, 1981-83, dir. hosp. infections program, 1983-88; dep. dir. Nat. Ctr. for Infectious Diseases, Ctr. for Disease Control, Atlanta, 1988-92; dir. Nat. Ctr. for Infectious Diseases, Ctrs. for Disease Control and Prevention, 1992—; clin. assoc. prof. Emory U., Atlanta; clin. asst. prof. dir. geographic medicine, dept. medicine, U. Va., Charlottesville, 1979-82; clin. asst. prof. div. infectious dieases, dept. medicine Emory U., Atlanta, 1981-93; staff physician Atlanta VA Hosp., 1989—. Contbr. articles to profl. jours., chpts. to books. Baseball coach North Decatur (Ga.) Youth Assn., 1981-90; pres. Westchester Sch. PTA, Decatur, 1986-87. Asst. surgeon gen. USPHS, 1973-75, 76—. Recipient Meritorious Svc. medal USPHS, Atlanta, 1986, Outstanding Svc. medal, 1989, Disting. Svc. medal, 1997. Fellow ACP, Infectious Diseases Soc.; mem. AAAS, APHA, Am. Soc. Microbiology, Am. Soc. Tropical Medicine and Hygiene, Am. Epidemiol. Soc., Royal Soc. Tropical Medicine and Hygiene, Soc. Epidemiol. Rsch., U. So. Calif. Alumni Assn. (bd. govs. 1995-97), Stanford U. Alumni Club Ga. (pres. 1980-82). Avocations: youth sports, tennis, travel. Office: Nat Ctr Infectious Disease Mail Stop C12 CDC 1600 Clifton Rd NE Atlanta GA 30329-4018

HUGHES, JAMES PAUL, physician; b. Wilkinsburg, Pa., Apr. 9, 1920; s. Paul S. and Sara C. (Coleman) H.; m. Adelaide C. Mitchell, June 21, 1944; 1 son, James Mitchell. BS, U. Pitts., 1944, MD, 1945; D in Indsl. Medicine, U. Cin., 1952. Diplomate: Am. Bd. Preventive Medicine. Intern St. Francis Hosp., Pitts., 1945-46; resident in pathology Univ. Hosps., Cleve., 1948-49; fellow in indsl. medicine Kettering Lab. U. Cin., 1949-51; physician The Tex. Co., 1951-52, The Ethyl Corp., Cin., 1952-57; chief Bur. Indsl. Health Dept. Health City of Cin., 1952-55; med. dir. Kaiser Aluminum & Chem. Corp., Oakland, Calif., 1957-82; sr. ptnr. Hughes-Lewis Assocs., Oakland, Calif., 1982-88; asst. prof. indsl. medicine U. Cin., 1952-55; asso. prof. preventive medicine Ohio State U., 1955-57; exec. v.p., dir. Kaiser Found. Internat., 1967-76; project dir. U.S. Peace Corps Health projects, W. Africa, 1966-68, USAID med. relief project, Port Harcourt, Nigeria, 1970-72, Health Services on Bandama River project, Kossou, Ivory Coast, 1970-72; v.p. health servs. Kaiser Industries Corp., 1972-74; clin. assoc. prof. occupational medicine U. Calif., San Francisco, 1979-96; med. dir. occupational health services Merritt Peralta Med. Ctr., Oakland, Calif., 1982-86; mem. hearing bd. Bay Area Air Quality Mgmt. Dist., Calif., 1989-98; mem. U. Calif. Pres.'s Coun. on Nat. Labs., Lawrence Berkeley, Lawrence Livermore, Los Alamos, mem. panel on environment, safety, and health, 1993-98. Author: (with N.H. Proctor) Chemical Hazards of the Workplace, 1978, 4th edit., 1996; editor-in-chief Health Hazards of the Workplace Report, 1989-91. Chmn. com. for Industry Council Tropical Health Harvard U. Sch. Public Health, 1969-76. Served to capt. U.S. Army, 1946-48. Decorated Officier de l'Ordre Nat. Ivoirien Abidjan, 1972. Fellow ACP, Am. Coll. Occupational and Environ. Medicine (past pres., Health Achievement award 1972, Kehoe award 1982, Knudsen award 1996); mem. Inst. Medicine/NAS. Home: 124 Guilford Rd Piedmont CA 94611-3805

HUGHES, JEROME MICHAEL, education foundation executive; b. St. Paul, Oct. 1, 1929; s. Michael Joseph and Mary (Malloy) H.; m. Audrey M. Lackner, Aug. 11, 1951; children—Bernadine, Timothy, Kathleen, Rosemarie, Margaret, John. BA, Coll. of St. Thomas, St. Paul, 1951; MA, U. Minn., 1958; EdD, Wayne State U., 1970; postdoctoral fellow, U. Minn., 1985. Tchr. Shakopee Sch. Dist., Minn., 1951-53; tchr. St. Paul Sch. Dist., 1953-61, counselor, 1963-66, rsch. asst., 1966-67, edn. cons., 1968-87; mem. Minn. Senate, St. Paul, 1966-93, chmn. edn. com., 1973-83, chmn. elections and ethics com., 1983-93, pres., 1983-93; mem. faculty U. Minn., 1986-95; pres. Minn. Edn. Found., Roseville, 1992—; mem. Edn. Commn. of States, Denver, 1973-93; mem. Nat. Cmty. Edn. Adv. Coun., Washington, 1980-83; mem. Nat. Conf. State Legislature Stafe/Fed. Assembly, 1983-93; adj. faculty U. Minn., 1986-95. Chair Goodwill/Easter Seals, 1993-95; bd. dirs. Nat. Parenting Assn. Minn., 1994-97, State Legis. Leaders Found., 1985-93. Mott fellow, 1967-68, Ford Found. fellow George Washington U., 1974-75, Bush Summer fellow, U. Calif., 1975; Disting. Policy fellow George Washington U., 1977-78; postdoctoral fellow U. Minn., 1980-81; recipient Pennell award Minn. Fedn. Tchrs., 1974; Disting. Svc. award Minn. Elem. Sch. Prins. Assn., 1982; named Community Educator of Yr. Minn. Community Edn. Assn., recipient other awards. Mem. Phi Delta Kappa. Democrat. Avocations: travel, reading, discussion, exercise. Office: Minn Edn Found PO Box 13643 Roseville MN 55113-0643

HUGHES, JOAN MOTTOLA, education association representative; b. July 3, 1953. BA, Gordon Coll., Wenham, Mass., 1974; MEd, Lesley Coll., 1979, Columbia U., 1996; postgrad., Harvard U., 1985. Tchr. English, Georgetown (Mass.) Pub. Schs., 1974-86; field rep. Conn. Edn. Assn., Wilton, 1986—; field rep. Mass. Tchrs. Assn., Boston, part-time 1983-86. Mem. Indsl. Rels. Rsch. Assn., Phi Delta Kappa, Kappa Delta Pi. E-mail: joanh@cea.org. Office: 7 Hollyhock Rd Wilton CT 06897-4414

HUGHES, JOHN, chemical company executive; b. St. David's, Wales, Apr. 10, 1943; came to U.S., 1964; s. Essex James and Mary Ann (Harris) H.; m. Linda Kay Petersen; children: Stacey Ann, Bradford James. BS in Chemistry, U. Wales, 1964; MBA, U. Chgo., 1968. With AMCOL Internat., Arlington Heights, Ill., 1965—; now chmn., CEO AMCOL Internat, Arlington Heights, Ill. Office: AMCOL Internat 1500 W Shure Dr Arlington Heights IL 60004-1443

HUGHES, JOHN J., federal judge, educator; b. 1946. BS, Villanova U., 1968, JD, 1971. Bar: N.J. 1971. Law clk. N.J. Dept. Law and Pub. Safety, Trenton, 1971; assoc. Sterns & Greenberg, Trenton, 1972; asst. N.J. pub. defdneer for Essex and Hunterdon regions Office Pub. Defender, Trenton, 1972-75; asst.-in-charge Trenton-Camden offices Office Fed. Pub. Defender for N.J. Dist., 1976-91; magistrate judge for N.J., U.S. Magistrate Ct., Trenton, 1991—; lectr. Widener U. Sch. Law; mem. Jud. Conf. Com. on Defender Svcs. Bd. dirs. Mobile Meals Trenton; trustee Georgian Court Coll. Fellow Am. Bar Found.; mem. ABA, Fed. Magistrate Judges Assn., N.J. Bar Assn., Assn. Criminal Def. Lawyers N.J. (Chief Judge Lawrence A. Whipple Meml. award), Brehon Law Soc., Seton Hall Law Sch. Inn Ct. (master). Office: 6000 US Courthouse 402 E State St Trenton NJ 08608-1507

HUGHES, JOHN RUSSELL, physician, educator; b. DuBois, Pa., Dec. 19, 1928; s. John Henry and Alice (Cooper) H.; m. Mary Ann Dick, June 14, 1958; children: John Russell Jr. (dec.), Christopher Alan, Thomas Gregory, Cheryl Ann. AB summa cum laude, Franklin and Marshall Coll., 1950; BA with honors, Oxford (Eng.) U., 1952, MA with honors, 1955, DM (hon.), 1976; PhD, Harvard U., 1954; MD, Northwestern U., 1975. Neurophysiologist NIH, 1954-56; dir. electroencephalography dept. Meyer Hosp., SUNY, 1956-63; dir. div. lab. scis., including electroencephalography Northwestern U. Med. Center, 1963-77, prof. neurology, 1968—; dir. EEG and Epilepsy Clinic, U. Ill. Med. Center, 1977—; staff U. Ill. Hosp., Community Hosp., Geneva, Delnor Hosp., St. Charles; dir.neurophysiology Humana-Michael-Reese Med. Ctr., 1992—; cons. Chgo. VA Westside Hosp., Mercyville and Copley Meml. Hosp., Aurora, Ill., others; participant debate on brain death BBC-TV; bd. dirs. Am. Bd. EEG and Neurophysiology; participant Am. Med. EEG Assn.; rep. Internat. Fedn. EEG and Clin. Neurophysiology lectr. tour of Africa, 1989; keynote speaker Internat. Course of Neurophusiology, Oxford U., 1993, invited speaker, 1996; invited spkr. Damascus Med. Sch., Syria, 1998. Author: Functional Organization of the Diencephalon, 1957, Atlas on Cerebral Death and Coma, 1976, Chinese Translation, 1997, Japanese Translation, 1998, EEG in Clinical Practice, 1982, 2d edit., 1994, EEG Evoked Potentials in Psychiatry and Behavioral Neurology, 1983; contbr. articles to profl. jours. Command Surgeon, USAR, 1986-90, with Army Med. R & D Command, 1990—, mobilization replacement for maj. gen., comdr. Recipient Alumni award Franklin and Marshall Coll., 1978. Mem. Am. Electroencephalography Soc. (treas. 1965-68), Eastern Electroencephalography Soc. (sec.-treas. 1961-64), Central Electroencephalography Soc., Am. Med. EEG Assn. (bd. dirs.), Am. Bd. EEG and Neurophysiology (bd. dirs.), Internat. EEG and Clin. Neurophysiology (bd. dirs.), Am. Acad. EEG (bd. dirs.), Brit. Soc. of neurophysiology (hon.), Chgo. Acad. Medicine, Am. Epilepsy Soc., Am. Physiol. Soc., Soc. Neuroscis., Am. Acad. Neurology, Phi Beta Kappa, Sigma Xi (lectr. 1960—). Rsch. on coding in central nervous system, new theory on neural mechanisms in olfaction, electro-clin. correlations in different types of epilepsy, organic aspects in juvenile delinquency. Home: 720 Roslyn Ter Evanston IL 60201-1722 Office: U Ill Consultation Clinic Epilepsy 912 S Wood St Chicago IL 60612-7325 *Always be ahead of your colleagues in every endeavor by having done it before they do. Do what you must do now to leave time for innovation later.*

HUGHES, JOHN W., film producer, screenwriter, film director; b. Mich., Feb. 18, 1950; m. Nancy Ludwig; children: John III, James. With Needham Harper & Steers, Chgo.; copywriter, creative dir. Leo Burnett Co.; editor National Lampoon; founder, pres. Hughes Entertainment, 1985—. Screenwriter: National Lampoon's Class Reunion, 1982, National Lampoon's Vacation, 1983, Mr. Mom, 1983, Nate and Hayes, 1983, National Lampoon's European Vacation, 1985, (as Edmond Dantes) Beethoven, 1992, 101 Dalmations, 1996; screenwriter, prodr.: Pretty in Pink, 1986, Some Kind of Wonderful, 1987, The Great Outdoors, 1988, National Lampoon's Christmas Vacation, 1989, Home Alone, 1990, Career Opportunities, 1990, Dutch, 1991, Home Alone 2: Lost in New York, 1992, Dennis the Menace, 1993, Baby's Day Out, 1994, Miracle on 34th Street, 1994, 101 Dalmations, 1996, Flubber, 1997, Home Alone 3, 1997, Reach the Rock, 1998; screenwriter, dir.: Sixteen Candles, 1984, Weird Science, 1985; screenwriter, dir., prodr.: The Breakfast Club, 1985, Ferris Bueller's Day Off, 1986, Planes, Trains and Automobiles, 1987, She's Having a Baby, 1988, Uncle Buck, 1989, Curly Sue, 1991; prodr.: Only the Lonely, 1991. Recipient Commitment to Chgo. award, 1990; named NATO/ShoWest Prodr. of Yr., 1990. Office: care Jacob Bloom Bloom & Dekom 150 S Rodeo Dr Beverly Hills CA 90212-2408 also: Hughes Entertainment 10201 W Pico Blvd Los Angeles CA 90064-2606 also: care Jack Rapke CAA 9830 Wilshire Blvd Beverly Hills CA 90212-1804*

HUGHES, J(OHNSON) DONALD, history educator, editor; b. Santa Monica, Calif., June 5, 1932; s. Johnson and Vannelia Anna (Blanchfield) H.; m. Pamela Louise Peters, June 8, 1964; children: Peter, Melissa, Joy. A.B., UCLA, 1954; S.T.B., Boston U., 1957, Ph.D., 1960; postgrad., Am. Sch. Classical Studies, Greece, 1966-67. Asst. prof. history U. Denver, 1967-72, assoc. prof. history, 1972-77, prof. history, 1977—, Evans prof., 1994—. Author: Ecology in Ancient Civilizations, 1975; In The House of Stone And Light, 1978 (Nat. Pk. Service award 1977-78); American Indian Ecology, 1983, Pan's Travail: Environmental Problems of the Ancient Greeks and Romans, 1994; editor: Ecological Consciousness, 1981, The Face of the Earth: Environment and World History, 1999; editor Environ. Rev., 1983-85, mem. editl. bd., 1986-95; mem. editorial bd. Environ. Ethics, 1981-89, The Trumpeter: Jour. Ecosophy, 1987-98, Environ. History, 1995—. Boston U. fellow, 1957; Danforth Found. assoc., 1965—; Lindbergh grantee, 1987. Mem. Am. Inst. Archaeology, Am. Soc. Environ. History (exec. bd. 1983-85), Forest History Soc., Am. Hist. Assn., Phi Beta Kappa. Home: Apt 1001 2580 S University Blvd Denver CO 80210-6105 Office: U Denver Dept History Denver CO 80208

HUGHES, KAREN SUE, geriatrics nurse; b. Wooster, Ohio, Oct. 16, 1955; d. Alvin S. and Pauline Katheryn (Troyer) Yutzy; m. Christopher Charles Marek, Sept. 3, 1977 (div. 1993); m. Raymond H. Hughes, July 20, 1993. LPN, Wayne County Vocat. Sch., 1974; BSN, Akron U., 1994. LPN, RN, Ohio. Nurse, nurse aide Wooster Community Hosp., 1974-76; nurse Apple Creek (Ohio) Devel. Ctr., 1976-77, Smithville Western Care Ctr., Wooster, 1977-78, 78-80; supervisory nurse Gruter Found., Wooster, 1980-87; light indsl. worker Victor Temporary Svcs., Mansfield, Ohio, 1988-89; plant mgr. asst. Detroit Detroit Inc., Wayne, Mich., 1988-89; LPN charge nurse West View Manor, Wooster, 1989, Doylestown (Ohio) Health Care Ctr., 1989-93; charge nurse Manor Care Barberton, Ohio, 1993-94; RN supr., asst. dir. nursing Manor Care of Barberton, Ohio, 1994-95; nurse Healthaven Nursing Home, Akron, Ohio, 1995-96, Austin Health Care Ctr., Wooster, Ohio, 1996—. Avocations: reading, flower gardening, crafts, cooking, sewing. Home: 9500 Mennonite Rd Wadsworth OH 44281-9309

HUGHES, KEITH WILLIAM, banking and finance company executive; b. Cleve., July 1, 1946; s. Delmar Vern and Margaret Virginia Hughes; m. Cheryl Foster, Aug. 30, 1969; 1 child, Amy. BS, Miami U., Oxford, Ohio, 1968, MBA, 1969. Mktg. mgr. Continental Bank, Chgo., 1970-73; exec. v.p. broker/dealer subs. Assos. Corp., 1973-74; v.p. mktg. Northwestern Nat. Bank, 1974-76; sr. v.p. Crocker Bank, San Francisco, 1976-81; exec. v.p., dir. Assos. Corp., Dallas, 1981-85; sr. exec. v.p. Assos. Corp., 1985-88, vice-chmn., 1988-91; pres., chmn, CEO Assocs. Corp., 1995-96; chmn., CEO Assocs. First Capital Corp., 1996—. Active United Way (chmn. Dallas campaign), Cancer Found., Dallas Mus. of Art. Mem. Am. Bankers Assn., Bank Mktg. Assn., Consumers Bankers Assn., Nat. Consumer Fin. Assn., Olympic Club (San Francisco), Los Colinas Country Club (Tex.), Crescent Club (Dallas), Ocean Reef Club (Key Largo). Office: Assocs First Capital Corp. PO Box 660237 250 Carpenter Freeway Dallas TX 75266-0237*

HUGHES, KENNETH G., elementary school educator; b. Colorado Springs, Colo., Feb. 12, 1952; s. George V. and Martha (Stark) H. BS in Elem. Edn., U. Pitts., 1983; MEd in Edn. Leadership, U. Ctrl. Fla., 1993. Cert tchr., Fla., Pa., Ohio; cert. Level 1 adminstrv., Fla. Head tchr. Learning Tree, Inc., Pitts., 1983-85; tchr. 1st grade, 3d grade, 4th grade Dr. Phillips Elem. Sch., Orlando, Fla., 1985-89; tchr. 1st grade, 4th grade McCoy Elem. Sch., Orlando, 1989-91; tchr. curriculum resource Dr. Phillips Elem. Sch., Orlando, 1991-95; 1st grade tchr. Windsor Elem. Sch., Elyria, Ohio, 1998—; adult edn. ESOL, Mid-Fla. Tech. Inst., Orlando, 1990-91. Recipient Innovative Classroom Practices award-Orange County, Walt Disney World, 1991,92. Mem. Phi Delta Kappa. Home: 77 Starling Ct Elyria OH 44035-7311

HUGHES, KENT HIGGON, economist; b. Portland, Oreg., Feb. 23, 1941; s. John Kenneth and Gwladys (Higgon) H.; m. Virginia Carrington Sammon; children: John Kenneth, Jeff, Krista. BA, Yale U., 1962; LLB, Harvard U., 1965; PhD, Washington U., 1976. Bar: D.C. 1971. Fellow Internat. Legal Ctr., Sao Paulo, Brazil, 1967-69; atty. Urban Law Inst., Washington, 1970-71; legis. counsel Office of Sen. Vance Hartke, Washington, 1971-72; analyst Congl. Rsch. Svc., Washington, 1973-76; sr. economist Joint Econ. Com., Washington, 1977-82; legis. dir. Office Sen. Gary Hart, Washington, 1983-84; staff dir. trade subcom. Ho. Reps. Fgn. Affairs Com., Washington, 1985-87; chief economist Dem. policy com. U.S. Senate, Washington, 1987-90; pres. Coun. on Competitiveness, 1990-93; assoc. dep. sec. of commerce U.S. Dept. of Commerce, Washington, 1993-99; pub. policy scholar Woodrow Wilson Internat. Ctr., Washington, 1999—. Author: Trade, Taxes, Transnationals, 1979; contbr. articles to profl. jours. Mem. ABA, Am. Econ. Assn., D.C. Bar Assn. Avocations: languages, rugby, collecting political memorabilia. Home: 4961 Allan Rd Bethesda MD 20816-2721 Office: Woodrow Wilson Internat Ctr One Woodrow Wilson Plaza 1300 Pennsylvania Ave NW Washington DC 20004-3027

HUGHES, KEVIN PETER, lawyer; b. N.Y.C., Sept. 8, 1943; s. George and Mae (Kilduff) H.; m. Margaret Ellen Comiskey, Nov. 18, 1967; children: Erin, Cara, Deirdre. BA, Manhattan Coll., 1965; JD, St. John's U., 1968. Bar: N.Y. 1968, U.S. Dist. Ct. (so. dist., ea. dist.) N.Y. 1971, U.S. Ct. Appeals (2d cir.) 1975, U.S. Supreme Ct. 1980. Law clerk to justice N.Y. Ct. Appeals, Albany, 1968-70; assoc. Weil, Gotshal & Manges, N.Y.C., 1970-77, ptnr., 1977—; arbitrator Am. Arbitration Assn., N.Y.C., 1984—. Mem. ABA (litigation sect.), N.Y. State Bar Assn., Plandome Country Club (Manhasset, N.Y.). Republican. Roman Catholic. Avocations: skiing, golf. Home: 27 Chapel Rd Manhasset NY 11030-3601 Office: Weil Gotshal & Manges 767 5th Ave Fl Concl New York NY 10153-0119

HUGHES, LIBBY, author; b. Pitts., Aug. 11, 1932; d. Lloyd Alfred and Vera Abby (Walker) Pockman; m. R. John Hughes, Aug. 20, 1955 (div. 1988); children: Wendy E., Mark E. BA, U. Ala., 1954; MFA, Boston U., 1955. Profl. actress Kenya, S. Africa, 1955-59; drama critic and feature writer Cape Cod Newspapers, 1977-86, assoc. pubr., 1977-81, pubr., 1981-85; pres. Desert Starfield Prodns., 1994. Author: Bali, 1969, Margaret Thatcher, 1989, Benazir Bhutto, 1990, Nelson Mandela, 1992, Good Manners for Children, 1992, H. Norman Schwarzkopf, 1992, West Point, 1992, Valley Forge, 1992, Colin Powell, 1996, School Manners Workbook, 1998, Christopher Reeve, 1997, Tiger Woods, 1999, Yitzhak Rabin, 1999; editor: Ginger Rogers Autobiography, 1989, 91; author 20 plays. Bd. dirs. Wisdom Inst., 1984-86, Cape Cod Mus., 1984-86. Mem. Dramatists Guild, Authors Guild, Ala. Wildlife Rescue Svc. (pres. 1988-89), Nat. Soc. Arts and Letters (chpt. pres. 1984-86, protocol officer 1984-86), Nat. League Am. Pen Women. Avocations: theatre, news, wildlife, breeding Rhodesian Ridgebacks. Home: PO Box 1000 Orleans MA 02653-1000

HUGHES, LINDA J., newspaper publisher; b. Princeton, B.C., Can., Sept. 27, 1950; d. Edward Rees and Madge Preston (Bryan) H.; m. George Fredrick Ward, Dec. 16, 1978; children: Sean Ward, Kate Ward. BA, U. Victoria (B.C.), 1972; LittD (hon.), Athabasca U., 1997. With Edmonton Jour., Alta., Can., 1976—, from reporter to asst. mng. editor, 1984-87, editor, 1987-92, pub., 1992—. Southam fellow U. Toronto, Ont., Can., 1977-78. Office: Edmonton Journal, 10006 101st St PO Box 2421, Edmonton, AB Canada T5J 2S6

HUGHES, LYNN NETTLETON, federal judge; b. Houston, Sept. 9, 1941; m. Olive Allen. BA, U. Ala., 1963; JD, U. Tex., 1966; LLM, U. Va., 1992. Bar: Tex., 1966. Pvt. practice, Houston, 1966-79; judge Dist. Ct. Tex., Houston, 1979-85; U.S. dist. judge So. Dist. Tex., Houston, 1985—; adj. prof. South Tex. Coll. Law, 1973—, U. Tex., 1990-91; Tex. del. Nat. Conf. State Trial Judges, 1983-85; cons. Tex. Jud. Budget Bd., 1984; lectr. Tex. Coll. Judiciary, 1983; mem. task force on revision rules of civil procedure Supreme Ct. Tex., 1993-94; cons. on constn. Republic of Moldova, 1993, European Community, 1989, Ukraine, 1995, Romania, 1996, Albania, 1997. Mem. adv. bd. Houston Jour. Internat. Law, 1981—, chmn., 1989-99; mem. adv. dirs. Internat. Law Inst., U. Houston, 1995—. Trustee Rift Valley Rsch. Mission, 1978—; mem. St. Martin's Episcopal Ch.; dir. Houston World Affairs Coun., 1997—. Fellow Tex. Bar Found.; mem. ABA, Fed. Bar Assn. (bd. dirs. Houston chpt. 1986-89), Am. Law Inst., Maritime Law Assn., Houston Bar Assn., Tex. Bar Assn. (nominations com. jud. sect. 1983, court cost, delay and efficiency com. 1981-90, vice chmn. 1984-86, selection, compensation and tenure state judges com. 1981-85, vice chmn. 1982-83, liaison with law schs. com. 1987-92, plain lang. com. 1989-96), Am. Judicature Soc., Am. Soc. Legal History, Am. Anthrop Assn., Houston Philos. Soc., Am. Inns of Ct. XV (pres. 1986-92), Phi Delta Phi. Office: US Court House 11122 515 Rusk Ave Houston TX 77002-2605

HUGHES, MARCIA MARIE, lawyer, mediator, trainer; b. Montrose, Colo., Oct. 12, 1949; d. John Atkinson and Catherine Marie (Buskirk) H.; m. James Terrell, Dec. 26, 1990; 1 child, Julia. BA, U. Colo., 1972; JD with honors, George Washington U., 1976; MA in Psychology, U. Colo. Bar: Colo. 1976, U.S. Dist. Ct. Colo. 1976, U.S. Ct. Appeals (10th cir.) 1976. Adminstrv. aide Bur. Accounts Treasury Dept., Washington, 1972-73; legis. aide to Congresswoman Patricia Schroeder Washington, 1973-74; legal intern Consumer Product Info. Ctr., Washington, 1974-75, Media Access Project, Washington, 1975-76; law clk. to Hon. William E. Doyle U.S. Ct. Appeals (10th cir.), Denver, 1976-77; asst. atty. gen. Colo. Atty. Gen.'s Office, Denver, 1977-79; spl. asst. to dir. Colo. Dept. Health, Denver, 1979-81; assoc. Rothgerber, Appel, Powers & Johnson, Denver, 1982-85; ptnr. Cockrel, Quinn & Creighton, Denver, 1985-87; pres. Hughes, Duncan & Dingess, Denver, 1987-90, Marcia M. Hughes, P.C., Denver, 1990-99, Collaborative Growth, L.L.C., 1993—; exec. dir. Salt Creek Sch., 1998—; exec. dir. Salt Creek Sch. Youth Edn. Corp., 1999—; pub. speaker on conflict resolution, mediation, environ. issues and child abuse awareness and prevention. Bd. dirs. Jefferson County chpt. ARC, 1999—, Influence Denver X, Capitol Hill United Neighborhoods, 1977-86; v.p. Nat. Assn. Neighborhoods, 1980-81; bd. dirs. Ecumenical Housing Corp., 1982-85; participant Leadership Denver, 1984-85; active Big Sisters Colo., Denver, 1987-93; vice chmn. Kempe Children's Found., bd. dirs., 1991-95, chair pub. affairs Com.; bd. dirs. Colo. Found. Children and Families, 1993-96, pres., 1995-96; apptd. mem. family issues task force Colo. Legislature, Influence X Denver. Named one of Outstanding Young Women in Colo., 1980, Big Sister of Yr., 1991. Mem. Colo. Profl. Soc. on Abuse of Children (bd. dirs.), Colo. Bar Assn. (chmn. environ. sect., officer 1982-86), Colo. Hazardous Waste Com. (chmn. 1982-85). Avocations: writing, hiking, gardening, reading. Home: PO Box 10758 Golden CO 80401 Office: PO Box 10758 Golden CO 80401-0610

HUGHES, MARGARET EILEEN, law educator, former dean; b. Saskatoon, Sask., Can., Jan. 22, 1943; d. E. Duncan and Eileen (Shaver) Farmer; m. James Roscoe Hughes, May 21, 1966; children: Shannon Margaret, Krista Lynn. BA, U. Sask., 1965, LLB, 1966; LLM, U. Mich., 1968, MSW, 1968. Asst. prof. law U. Windsor, Ont., Can., 1968-71, assoc. prof. law, 1971-75; exec. interchange Dept. Justice, Ottawa, 1975-77, counsel, 1977-78; prof. law U. Sask., 1978-84; dean law U. Calgary, Alta., Can., 1984-89, prof., 1989—; faculty sr. univ. adminstrs.'s course Centre Higher Edn., R & D, Banff, Can., 1990—; bd. dirs. Indsl. Rels. Rsch. Group, 1990—; co-chair Annual Labour Arbitration Conf., 1990—. Contbr. articles to profl. jours. and chpts. to books. William Cooke fellow U. Mich. Faculty Law, 1966-68. Mem. Law Soc. Alta., Law Soc. Sask., Legal Edn. Soc. Alta. (bd. dirs. 1984-89), Law Soc. Alta. (legal edn. com. 1984-89), Can. Assn. Law Tchrs., Council Can. Law Deans (sec. 1986-87, chmn. 1987-88), Can. Inst. Resources Law (exec. com. 1984-89, bd. dirs. 1984-89), Can. Research Inst. for Law and Family (exec. com. 1986-88, bd. dirs. 1986-89, 97—). Avocations: swimming, skiing. Office: U Calgary Faculty Law, 2500 University Dr NW, Calgary, AB Canada T2N 1N4

HUGHES, MARGARET JANE, nurse; b. L.A., Sept. 13, 1950; d. John Lawarence and Etta May (Kenny) H. BSN, U. St. Thomas, Houston, 1984; ADN, Saddleback Coll., Mission Viejo, Calif.,, 1980; cert. in perfusion, Tex. Heart Inst., Houston, 1976. RN, Calif., Tex., Hawaii; CCRN; cert. BLS, ACLS, perfusionist. Nurse ICU Saddleback Hosp., Laguna Hills, Calif., 1974-76, 79-81; perfusionist Baylor Coll. Medicine, Houston, 1973-79, 81-86; nurse ICU VA Hosp., L.A., 1986-90; nurse, perfusionist Kay Med. Group, L.A., 1987-90; nurce ICU Hilo (Hawaii) Hosp., 1990-91; nurse recovery room King Khaled Eye Hosp., Riyadh, Saudi Arabia, 1992; clin. nurse specialist Kay Med. Group, L.A., 1992; nurse ICU and recovery room Kona (Hawaii) Hosp., 1992-94; clin. nurse specialist Sciemed Ltd., Cairo, 1994; nurse UCLA Dental Sch., 1994-95; nurse ICU, Whittier (Calif.) Hosp., 1995-96; resource nurse Glendale (Calif.) Meml. Hosp., 1996—. Vol. Am. Heart Assn., Kona, 1993, Diabetic Assn., Kona, 1993. Mem. AACN. Democrat. Roman Catholic. Avocations: traveling, reading. Home: 17011 Pinehurst Ln Apt A Huntington Beach CA 92647-5541 Office: Glendale Mem Hosp Glendale CA 91204-2594

HUGHES, MARIJA MATICH, law librarian; b. Belgrade, Yugoslavia; came to U.S., 1960, naturalized, 1971; d. Zarija and Antonija (Hudowsky) Matich. BA in Music, Mokranjac, Belgrade; BA in English, U. Belgrade and Calif. State U.; MLS, U. Md.; student, McGeorge Sch. Law; MHA in Health Care Adminstrn., George Washington U., 1985, M. in Adminstrv. Scis., 1989. Counselor, gen. mgr. Career Counseling Service, Sacramento, Calif., 1962-64; sec. to mgr. Sacramento State Coll., 1965-66; student librarian High John program U. Md., Fairmont Heights, 1967; reference librarian Calif. State Law Library, Sacramento, 1968; head reference library-faculty liasion librarian Hastings Coll. Law U. Calif., San Francisco, 1969-72; head law librarian AT&T, Washington, 1972-73; chief law librarian Nat. Clearinghouse Library, U.S. Commn. on Civil Rights, Washington, 1973-86; tech. info. specialist U.S. Dept. Labor, OSHA, Tech. Date Ctr., 1988—; owner, pub. Hughes Press. Author, compiler: The Sexual Barrier, Legal and Econ. Aspects of Employment, 1970-73, The Sexual Barriers: Legal, Medical, Economic and Social Aspects of Sex Discrimination, 1977, Computer Health Hazards, 1990, 93, 96 (English translation), Sick from Computers, 1994, Computers, Antennas, Cellular Telephones and Power Lines Health Hazards, 1996; contbr. articles to profl. jours. Mem. Cellular Phone Task Force, Ad Hoc Assn. Parties Concerned About FCC's Radio Frequency Health Safety Rules. Mem. Am. Assn. Law Librs., Bioelectromagnetics Soc., Consumer Utilities Bd., Am. Acad. Environ. Medicine. Home: 2400 Virginia Ave NW Apt C501 Washington DC 20037-2612

HUGHES, MARVALENE, academic administrator. Student, Tuskegee U., NYU, Columbia U.; PhD in Counseling and Adminstrn., Fla. State U.; postgrad., Harvard U., U. Calif., San Diego. Dir. counseling and career devel. Eckerd Coll., Fla.; dir. counseling svcs. and placement, prof. San Diego State U.; assoc. v.p. student affairs Ariz. State U.; v.p. student affairs, prof. counseling and human svcs. U. Toledo; v.p. student affairs, vice provost, prof. ednl. psychology U. Minn.; pres. Calif. State U., Stanislaus, 1994—; nat., internat. keynote spkr.;. Contbr. chpts. to books and articles to profl. jours. Bd. dirs. United Way (chair 1996-99), Leadership Calif. for Exec. Women;s co-chair Pacific Telesis Consumer Adv. Bd.; mem. Am. Coun. on Edn.'s Commn. on Govtl. Rels.; elected to NCAA's Pres.'s Coun.; mem. NCAA budget and fin. com.; presdl. appointee NCAA student interest com.; chair Calif. State U. statewide remedial redn. com. Mem. Am. Coll. Pers. Assn. (nat. pres.), Nat. Assn. for Counseling Svcs., Nat. Assn. Land Grant Univs. and Colls. (student affairs divsn.), Am. Assn. State Colls. and Univs. Office: 801 W Monte Vista Ave Turlock CA 95382-0256*

HUGHES, MARY ELIZABETH, interior designer; b. Charleston, W.Va., Sept. 7, 1940; d. Denver Lewis and Ida Frances (Fink) Morgan; children: George Charles IV, Justin Morgan, Mary Frederick. Student, Randolph-Macon Woman's Coll., 1958-60; BS, W.Va. U., 1963; AAS, Art Inst. Pitts., 1981. Cert. secondary edn., interior design. French tchr. Kanawha County Schs., Charleston, W.Va., 1963-64, Marshall County Schs., Moundsville, W.Va., 1964-70; sr. designer Boury, Inc. Contract Design, Wheeling, W.Va., 1985-87; head designer Stone and Thomas Design Studio, Wheeling, 1987-88; dir. archtl. design Boury, Inc. Contract Design, Wheeling, 1980-92; owner Hughes Design Gallery, Glen Dale, W.Va., 1981-92, Wheeling, W.Va., 1993—; pres., CEO Hughes Design Gallery, Inc., Wheeling, 1993—; guest lectr. history of furniture Art Inst. Pitts., 1990. Designer Jonathan Seafood Restaurant, Rochester, N.Y., 1986-87, Sheraton Inn South, Pitts., 1986-87, Elby's Restaurants, Ohio, Pa., W.Va., 1985-88. Shoney's Restaurants, Columbus, Ohio, 1989-92, TJ's Sports Garden, Wheeling, 1991, Rosa's Spaghetti House (prototype), Parkersburg, W.Va., 1992-93, Bank One, Wheeling, 1993-98, Holiday Inn South, Pitts., 1994-95, Weirton Health Care, 1993-97, One Valley Bank, Wheeling, Moundsville, 1995-99, Wheeling Nisshin, 1996-97, Ohio County WV Courthouse, 1997-99, Oglebay Park, 1999—, Reynolds Hosp. Birthing Ctr., 1999—. Mem. Hist. Landmarks Commn., Marshall County, W.Va., 1986-90, adv. com. W.Va. Dept. Culture and History, 1992; mem. interior furnishings com. W.Va. Gov.'s Mansion, Charleston, 1986—, chmn., 1998—; bd. dirs. W.Va. Mansion Preservation Found., Charleston, 1989—; bd. dirs., past pres. No. Panhandle Behavioral Health Ctr., W.Va., 1981-91, Northwood Found., 1994—; mem. stewardship commn. Episcopal Diocese of W.Va., Charleston, 1988-90; pres. Jr. League Wheeling, 1976-78; mem. Episcopal Endowment Fund Com., W.Va., 1990-92; vacancy cons. Episcopal Diocese W.Va., 1993-98; mem. foundation bd. dirs. W.Va. No. C.C., 1991—. v.p., 1993—; bd. dirs. Wheeling Symphony, 1995—. Named Interior Design Alumni of Yr. Art Inst. Pitts., 1990. Mem. Am. Soc. Interior Designers (profl., pres. Pa. West chpt. 1998-99), Internat. Interior Design Assn., Sandcrest Found. (bd. dirs.), Rotary, Chi Omega, Kappa Delta Pi, Alpha Delta Kappa. Democrat. Avocations: swimming, gardening, reading. Home: 509 Wheeling Ave Glen Dale WV 26038-1639 Office: Hughes Design Gallery 600 National Rd Wheeling WV 26003-6598

HUGHES, MARY KATHERINE, lawyer; b. July 16, 1949; d. John Chamberlain and Marjorie (Anstey) H.; m. Andrew H. Eker, July 7, 1982. BBA cum laude, U. Alaska, 1971; JD, Willamette U., 1974; postgrad., Heriot-Watt U., Edinburgh, Scotland, 1971. Bar: Alaska 1975. Ptnr. Hughes, Thorsness, Gantz, Powell & Brundin, Anchorage, 1974-95, mem. mgmt. com., 1991-92; mcpl. atty. Municipality of Anchorage, 1995—. Trustee Willamette U., 1997—; bd. dirs. Alaska Repertory Theatre, 1986-88, pres., 1987-88; commr. Alaska Code Revision Commn., 1987-94; mem. U. alaska found., 1985—, trustee, 1990—; bd. visitors U. Alaska Fairbanks, 1994; bd. dirs. Anchorage Econ. Devel. Corp., 1989—, chmn., 1994; mem. com. bd. Providence Alaska Found., 1998—; lawyer rep. 9th Cir. Jud. Conf., 1995—. Fellow Am. Bar Found.; mem. AAUW, Alaska Bar Assn. (bd. govs. 1981-84, pres. 1983-84), Anchorage Assn. Women Lawyers (pres. 1976-77), Internat. Lawyers Assn. (state chair 1995-96, regional v.p. 1997—), Soroptimists (v.p. 1986-87, pres. 1986-87), Delta Theta Phi. Republican. Roman Catholic. Home: 1592 Coffey Ln Anchorage AK 99501-4977 Office: Municipality Anchorage PO Box 196650 Anchorage AK 99519-6650

HUGHES, MARY SORROWS, artist; b. Washington, Oct. 28, 1945; d. Howard Earl and Martha Jane (Summerville) Sorrows; m. Frank Brook Hughes, May 22, 1967; 1 child, Broox Bradley. BA in Art, Centenary Coll., 1967, BA in Edn., 1978. Draftsman for civil engring. dept. Texaco, New Orleans, 1967-70; owner, freelance artist Shreveport, La., 1979—. Illustrator Total Tales, 1984; included in The Best of Watercolor, 1995, Best of Watercolor: Painting Color, 1997, Floral Inspirations, 1998; represented in permanent collections Southwestern Electric Power Co., Shreveport, Burgess Moving Inc. Collection, Calif. Bd. dirs. Child Care Svcs., Inc. of N.W. La., Shreveport, 1987-91, pres., 1991; Artport Airport Exhibit and Fundraiser for AIDS, Shreveport, 1991-97; worker Habitat for Humanity, Shreveport, 1992, 94; trustee St. Luke's Meth. Ch., Shreveport, 1993-95, chairperson for bldg. com., 1986. Recipient Gary, Field, Landry & Bradford award Seventh Exhbn. of La. Women Artists, Baton Rouge, 1994. Mem. Hoover Watercolor Soc. (pres. 1986, treas., publicity chair, others), Southwestern Watercolor Soc. (Signature Mem. award 1991, Edgar A. Whitney award 1992), Watercolor West (Yarka St. Petersberg Merchandise award 1995, Signature Mem. award 1996, Watercolor W. Burgess Purchase Prize award 1998), La. Artists (pres. 1994, 98), Med. Aux. Wive's Club, Shreveport Art Guild. Democrat. Avocations: exercise, gardening, traveling, reading, playing the flute. Home: 530 Atkins Ave Shreveport LA 71104-4448 Studio: 1700 Creswell Ave Shreveport LA 71101-4726

HUGHES, MICHAEL, civil engineer. BS in Civil Engring., Okla. State U., 1969, MS in Civil Engring., 1970, PhD in Civil Engring., 1991. Registered profl. engr., Okla., Ark. Grad. rsch. asst. sch. civil engring. Okla. State U., Stillwater, 1969-70; mgr. environ. affairs Okla. Gas and Electric Co., Stillwater, 1970-94; dir. ctr. for local govt. tech. Okla. State U., Stillwater, 1994—; apptd. mem. air quality control coun. Okla. Dept. Environ. Quality, 1993. Contbr. articles to profl. jours. Lt. col. USAR, 1967—. Mem. ASCE (past pres.), Soc. of Am. Mil. Engrs. (past pres.), Engring. Club of Oklahoma City (past pres.), Internat. Facility Mgmt. Assn. (past pres.), Okla. Soc. Environ. Profls., Environ. Fedn. Okla. (chmn. bd. dirs.), Chi Epsilon. Office: OK State Univ Ctr Local Govt Tech 308 Ctd Stillwater OK 74078-8086*

HUGHES, MICHAEL RANDOLPH, evangelist; b. Newport News, Va.; s. Luke Jr. and Patsy Ruth (Jewell) H.; m. Carolyn Delight Williamson, Mar. 20, 1981; children: Amanda, Patsy. Diploma, Memphis Sch. Preaching, 1976; cert. in theology, Ala. Christian Sch. Religion, 1982, BA, 1984; MS, Troy State U., 1987; postgrad., So. Christian U., 1992—. Min. Newport News Ch. of Christ, 1977-80, 81-83, Ch. of Christ of Clyattville, Ga., 1980-81, 83-85, City Boulevard Ch. of Christ, Waycross, Ga., 1985-87, Hampton (Va.) Ch. of Christ, 1988-92; instr. Bible Ga. Christian Sch., Dasher, 1985-87; min. Green's Lake Road Ch. of Christ, East Ridge, Tenn., 1992-97, Marion (Ark.) Ch. of Christ, 1997—; dir., instr. Bible, Idlewild Christian Camp, Surry, Va., 1977-80; youth worker Ga. Christian Children's Home, Dasher, 1985-87; missionary Mil. Outreach, Germany, 1988-90, Chs. of Christ, India, Malaysia, Taiwan, 1992—; program analyst HB Software, 1996—; co-founder, co-owner HB Software, 1997—. Author: Tax Record System, 1980; contbr. articles to relgious publs. Community organizer North End Huntington Heights Preservation Assn., Newport News, 1977-80; tax preparer VITA, Valdosta, Ga., 1986-87. Recipient award of merit Memphis Sch. Preaching, 1977. Mem. Givens Orgn., Memphis Sch. Preaching Alumni Assn. (bd. dirs. 1991-95, 98—). Avocations: coin collecting, tennis, bowling. Home: 72 Military Rd Marion AR 72364-1832 Office: Marion Ch Christ PO Box 209 Marion AR 72364-0209

HUGHES, MICHAELA KELLY, actress, dancer; b. Morristown, N.J., Mar. 31; d. Joseph Francis and Mary Elizabeth (Coughlin) H. Scholarship student, Houston Ballet Acad., 1970-73; part-time scholarship student, Sch. Am. Ballet, 1971. Founder, owner Classic Stocking Co., 1992—. Child actress with Alley Theatre, Houston, 1969, 71, mem. Houston Ballet, 1974, Eliot Feld Ballet, N.Y.C., 1975—, prin. dancer, 1974-79, mem. Am. Ballet Theatre, 1979-81; Broadway appearances include On Your Toes, 1982, as Gloria Upson in Mame, 1983, Raggedy Ann, 1986, as Cassie in A Chorus Line, 1987, Anything Goes, 1988, (films) Hellfighters, A Chorus Line, Alice, The Human Quality; appeared as Fiona in Another World (serial), Loving, Saturday Night Live, Veronica's Closet (sitcom), numerous television comls. Mem. AFTRA, SAG, AEA, Am. Guild Mus. Artists.

HUGHES, MIKE, advertising executive; b. Washington, May 27, 1948; s. James Richard and Ann Marie (Lucas) H.; m. Ginny Lee Ferguson, Apr. 12, 1975; children—Preston Ferguson, Jason Christopher. B.A., Washington & Lee U., 1970. Reporter, Richmond News Leader (Va.), 1965-70, Richmond Times Dispatch, 1967-70; copy editor and reporter Richmond News Leader, 1970; copywriter Clinton E. Frank Advt., 1971-72; Martin & Woltz Advt., Richmond, 1973; creative dir. Lawler & Ballard, Richmond, 1974; founder, ptnr. Hughes Wynne, Richmond, 1975-78; exec. v.p., creative dir., Martin Agy., Richmond, 1978—, dir., 1983—, vice chmn., 1986—; pres., creative dir. Martin Agy.; bd. dirs. Mktg. Arts Corp.; mem. exec. com., 1978—; dir. Alan Newman Research, Richmond, 1982—. Contbr. articles to Richmond mag. Mem. adv. bd. Va. Commonwealth U. Sch. Mass Communications. Recipient Clio awards, 1979—, N.Y. Art Dirs. awards, 1978—; CA mag. awards, 1978—. Mem. One Club for Copy and Art (One Show awards 1978—), Advt. Club of Richmond (bd. dirs., v.p. scholarship chmn., Addy awards chmn., program chmn., pub. service chmn., Addy awards). Home: 7501 Riverside Dr Richmond VA 23225-1244 Office: Martin Agy One Shockoe Plz Richmond VA 23219-4132*

HUGHES, MONICA, author; b. Liverpool, Eng., Nov. 3, 1925; arrived in Can., 1952; d. Edward Lindsay and Phyllis Ince; m. Glendon Earl Hughes, Apr. 22, 1957; children: Liz, Adrienne, Russell, Tom. With NRC, Ottawa, Can., 1952-57; writer's resident Toronto Librs., Windsor Libr., Medicine Hat, U. Alta., 1984-85, Edmonton Pub. Libr., 1988-89, Henry Kreisel Lecture, 1987, Writers and Pub. Adv. Coun., 1985-88. Author 28 novels including The Keeper of the Isis Light, 1980, Hunter in the Dark, 1982, Space Trap, 1983, My Name is Paula Popowich!, 1983, Devil on my Back, 1984, Sandwriter, 1985, The Dream Catcher, 1986, Blaine's Way, 1988, Log Jam, 1987, The Promise, 1989, The Refuge, 1989, Little Fingerling, 1989, Invitation to the Game, 1990, The Crystal Drop, 1992, A Handful of Seeds, 1993, The Gold Aquarians, 1994, Castle Tourmandyne, 1995, Where Have You Been Billy Boy?, 1995, The Seven Magpies, 1996, The Faces of Fear, 1997, The Story Box, 1998, What if. . .?, 1998, 2 picture books and numerous short stories pub. in anthologies and collections. With Women's Royal Naval Svc., WWII. Recipient the Beaver award, 1980, Vicky Metcalf award, 1981, 83, Alta. Culture Juvenile Novel award, 1981, Can. Coun. Prize for Children's Lit., 1981, 82, IBBY Cert. of honor, 1982, Young Adult Novel award Libr. Assn., 1983, Silver Feather award, Germany, 1986, Alta. Achievement award, 1988, Boeken Leeuw, Book Lion, Belgium, 1987, City of Edmonton Cultural Creative Arts award, 1988, Sr. Writing grant Alta. Found. for Lit. Arts, 1989. Mem. Writers' Union of Can., Writers' Guild of Alta., Can. Soc. Authors, Illustrators and Performers, PEN Internat., SF Can., Internat. Bd. on Book for Young People, Writers' Guild Alta. (sec. 1988-89, R. Ross Annett award 1983, 84, 87, 92). Home: 13816 110A Ave, Edmonton, AB Canada T5M 2M9

HUGHES, MORRIS NELSON, JR., foreign service officer; b. Humboldt, Nebr., Sept. 2, 1945; s. Morris Nelson and Calista (Cooper) H.; m. Betty de Jong, Mar. 5, 1998; children: Guy C., Catherine A. AB, U. Nebr., 1967. Consular officer Consulate Gen., Merida, Mex., 1970-72; polit. officer Am. Embassy, Mexico City, 1972-73; polit. officer Am. Embassy, Moscow, 1976-78, adminstrv. officer, 1983-85; adminstrv. officer Am. Embassy, Paris, 1988-92; dep. chief of mission Am. Embassy, Yaounde, Cameroon, 1993-96; amb. Am. Embassy, Bujumbura, 1996—; polit./mil. officer Sup Hdqrs. Allied Powers Europe, Mons, Belgium, 1978-79; adminstrv. officer U.S. Dept. of State, Washington, 1979-83, pers. officer, 1985-88; mem. Sr. Seminar, Washington, 1992-93. Mem. monitoring bd. State Dept. Fed. Credit Union, Washington, 1987-88; bd. dirs. Am. Fgn. Svc. Protection Assn., Washington, 1981-83. 1st lt. USMC, 1967-69, Vietnam. Decorated Purple Heart, Bronze Star. Mem. Am. Fgn. Svc. Assn., Am. Legion. Avocations: tennis, computer science, reading, music, movies. Office: Am Embassy Bujumbura Dept State Washington DC 20521-2100

HUGHES, NORAH ANN O'BRIEN, bank securities executive; b. Taftville, Conn., Aug. 17, 1948; d. William James and Mabel (Gouin) O'Brien; m. Gary Lee Hughes, Sept. 27, 1975. BA, Cushing Coll., Brookline, Mass., 1970; MA, NYU, 1972. V.p. instnl. sales trading Pitfield, Mackay & Co., Inc., N.Y.C., 1972-83; v.p. U.S. Treasury Bond trading Carroll, McEntee & McGinley, N.Y.C., 1983-84; v.p., mgr. U.S. Treasury trading Swiss Bank Corp. Internat. Securities, N.Y.C., 1984-89; 1st v.p., mgr. U.S. Treasury trading and sales Swiss Bank Corp. Govt. Securities Inc., N.Y.C., 1989-91; pres. Sumitomo Bank Securities, Inc., N.Y.C., 1991-97, 1997—. Mem. Women's Fin. Assn., Women's Econ. Round Table, Corp. Bond Club N.Y., Women's Bond Club N.Y. Avocations: skiing, golf. Home: 1 Hickory

Tree Ln Far Hills NJ 07931-2300 Office: Sumitomo Bank Securities Inc 277 Park Ave New York NY 10172

HUGHES, OWEN WILLARD, artist; b. Fremont, Ohio, Mar. 31, 1919; s. George Alfred and Maude Alice (Wilson) H.; m. L. Virginia Pedicord, Apr. 5, 1942; 1 child, Sue Ellen. Grad., Famous Artists Sch., Westport, Conn., 1964; degree, Rochester Inst. Tech., 1970; grad., Sch. Modern Photography, 1984. Artist, sign painter Consolidated Outdoor Display Co., Fremont, 1938-40; cartoonist, artist Ohio Power Co., Tiffin, 1940-41; artist, sign. painter, airplane nose artist 8th and 9th air forces USAF, 1941-45; supr. art and sign work 9th Troop Carrier Command Display at USAF Exhibit, Eiffel Tower, Paris, 1945; artist, sign painter Consolite Outdoor Display Co., Fremont, 1945-48, Hughes-Park Art & Signs, Fostoria, Ohio, 1948-52, Rogers Indsl. Display Co., Cleve., 1952-53; artist, silk screener Murray-Ohio Bicycle Co., Cleve., 1953-54; artist, carton designer Victor Wagner & Son Folding Cartons, Cleve., Buffalo, 1954-59, Bloomer Bros., Riegel, Rexham, Fibreboard, Foldpak, Newark, 1959-81; owner Hughes Art & Signs, Newark, 1981—; artist, sign painter Nat. War Plane Mus., Elmira, N.Y., 1986—. Commd. to paint nose art on P-38 that was forced down on a glacier in Greenland, 1942, was recovered from 268 feet deep in ice, 1992, being reconstructed in Middlesboro, Ky. (will be one of 6 P-38's currently flying). Staff sgt. USAAF, 1942-45, ETO. Mem. Lions. Republican. Methodist. Avocations: coin collecting, stamp collecting, model railroading, photography, camping. Home and Office: 320 E Miller St Newark NY 14513

HUGHES, PATRICIA E., secondary education educator; b. Duluth, Minn., Jan. 11, 1940; d. Earl H. and Bernice Ione (Fuhrman) Dahlgren; m. Warren G. Hughes, June 1, 1958; children: Sherri, David, Michael. BS, Bemidji State U., 1967, MS, 1982. English tchr. Blackduck (Minn.) Pub. Sch., 1967-68; English tchr., German I, II mid. level Kelliher (Minn.) Sch., 1969—. Contbr. articles to profl. jours. Recipient Tchr. Achievement award Ashland Oil Co.; named to Minn. Honor Roll of Tchrs., 1993, Bemidji State U. Tchr. of Yr. Hall of Fame, 1998. Mem. NEA, Nat. Coun. Tchrs. English, Minn. Coun. Tchrs. English, Minn. Edn. Assn., Minn. Coun. Tchrs. Fgn. Lang., Kelliher Edn. Assn. Home: PO Box 59 Kelliher MN 56650-0059

HUGHES, PATRICIA NEWMAN, academic administrator; b. Vicksburg, Miss., Apr. 16, 1964; d. Horace Wilbur Sr. and Florence (Hearn) Newman; m. Tommy Wade Hughes, Dec. 29, 1990; children: Newman Price, Dylan Wade; stepchildren: Amber Brooke, Kala Marie. BA, Miss. State U., 1986. Coord. prospect rsch. Office of Devel. Miss. State U., 1989-93, coord. prospect mgmt. Office of Devel., 1993-96, coord. prospect and donor rels. Office of Devel., 1997-98, asst. dir. devel., 1998—. Mem. Assn. Profl. Rschrs. for Advancement, Coun. Advancement and Support of Edn. Democrat. Baptist. Avocations: reading, boating, camping. Office: Miss State U PO Drawer 6149 200 Walker Rd Mississippi State MS 39762

HUGHES, PATRICK M., career officer; b. Sept. 19, 1942. Commd. officer U.S. Army, advanced through grades to lt. gen., 1996—. Office: DIA 7400 Defense Pentagon Washington DC 20301-7400

HUGHES, PAUL ANTHONY, minister, musician, songwriter, author, publisher; b. Tulsa, Sept. 14, 1957; s. James Barrie and Naomi Ruth (Kinard) H. BS in Indsl. Distbn., Tex. A&M U., College Station, 1980; MDiv in Christian Edn., Assemblies of God Theol. Sem., Springfield, Mo., 1986; postgrad., Baylor U., 1987. Ordained to ministry Assemblies of God, 1989. Pastoral asst., adult tchr., asst. supt. Magnolia Hill Assembly of God, Livingston, Tex., 1988-90; tchr. Bible, musician, religious writer, songwriter, 1990—; asst. pastor First Assembly of God, Liberty, Tex., 1992-94; adult Bible tchr. Evangel Assembly of God, Houston, 1994-96. Editor, pub.: Insight on Religion, History and Society, 1995—; contbr. articles, book revs.; owner, pub. Pneumatikos website. Singles dir., prayer emphasis dir. Grace Assembly of God, Houston, 1996-98; founding pastor West Loop Ch., Houston, 1999—. Mem. Soc. Bibl. Lit., Soc. Pentecostal Studies. Home: 1111 Woods Dr Liberty TX 77575-3609 *"Truth is just truth; you can't have opinions about truth." - Peter Schickele.*

HUGHES, ROBERT DAVIS, III, theological educator; b. Boston, Feb. 16, 1943; s. Robert Davis and Nancy (Wolfe) H.; m. Barbara Brunn, June 12, 1965; children: Robert David, Thomas Dunstan. BA, Yale U., 1966; MDiv, Episcopal Divinity Sch., 1969; MA, St. Michael's Coll., U. Toronto, Ont., Can., 1973, PhD, 1980. Ordained deacon Episcopal Ch., 1969, priest, 1970. Assoc. rector Good Shepherd Ch., Athens, Ohio, 1969-72; vicar Epiphany Ch., Nelsonville, Ohio, 1969-72; asst. curate St. Anne's Ch., Toronto, 1972-75; instr. Sch. of Theology, U. of the South, Sewanee, Tenn., 1977—, assoc. prof. systemic theology, 1984-92; prof. systematic theology U. of the South, Sewanee, Tenn., 1992—; bd. dirs. Anglican Ctr. Christian Family Life, Sewanee, 1981—; mem. Dept. Christian Edn. Ecumenical Commn. Alcohol and Drug Commn., Diocese Tenn., 1981-88. Contbr. articles to various publs. Soloist Toronto Chamber Soc., 1975-77; pres., soloist Sewanee Chorale, 1977—; vol. Community Chest, Boy Scouts Am., Sewanee, 1979-84; pres. Sewanee Chem. Dependency Assn., 1982; bd. trustees St. Andrew's Sewanee Sch., 1997—. Episcopal Ch. Found. fellow, 1972—, Kent fellow Danforth Found., 1975-77; Sabbatical grantee Mercer and Conant funds., 1984, 91, 98; vis. scholar Divinity Sch. U. Cambridge, 1998. Mem. AAUP (v.p. chpt. 1982-83, pres. 1985-87, v.p. state conf. 1990-94, pres. 1994-96, nat. coun. 1997—), Soc. of Anglican and Lutheran Theologians (sec.-treas. 1986-95, v.p. 1995-96, pres. 1996-97), E.Q.B. Club (bd. dirs. 1981-83), Crystal Lake Yacht Club (Frankfort, Mich.). Office: Sch of Theology 335 Tennessee Ave Sewanee TN 37383-0001

HUGHES, ROBERT EDWARD, elementary education educator; b. Lynn, Mass., Apr. 24, 1944; s. Frederick Ambrose and Frances Josephine (Martin) H.; m. Susan Martha Strang, Sept. 9, 1967; children: Lisa, Jayme, Shawna. BA in Elem. Edn., Ariz. State U., 1970, MA in Elem. Edn., 1974. Cert. tchr., Ariz. Tchr. Madison Sch. Dist., Phoenix, 1970—; mem. Sch. Site Base Mgmt. Team, Phoenix, 1992-94, Sch. Profl. Coun., Phoenix, 1990—, Dist. Math. and Social Studies Com., Phoenix, 1974-90, coach boys and girls athletic teams, Phoenix, 1970-90. With USAF, 1962-66. Mem. Madison Fedn. Tchrs. (v.p. 1975-78, pres. 1978-79). Avocations: coaching, camping, travel. Office: Madison # 1 Sch 5525 N 16th St Phoenix AZ 85016-2901

HUGHES, ROBERT HARRISON, former agricultural products executive; b. Puunene, Hawaii, Mar. 23, 1917; s. Robert Edwin and Alice Thayer (Walker) H.; m. Nadine Jeannette Hegler, Aug. 24, 1940 (div. 1983); children: Robert Lawrence, Linton Alice, Carole Nadine.; m. Judith R. Gething, Jan. 28, 1983. B.Sc. in Sugar Tech, U. Hawaii, 1938. With Hawaiian Comml. & Sugar Co., 1939-65, sugar mill supt., 1951-63, prodn. mgr., 1963-65; v.p. tech. services C. Brewer & Co., Ltd., Honolulu, 1965-69, sr. v.p. Hawaiian ops., 1969-77, exec. v.p., 1977-80, dir. subs., 1966-80; pres. Hawaiian Sugar Planters Assn., Aiea, 1981-85; dir. Mauna Loa Resources Inc., 1986-95. Mem. bd. regents U. Hawaii, 1961-66; trustee Hawaii Conf. Found., 1966-85, Hawaii Loa Coll., 1980-89, Moloka'i Mus. and Cultural Ctr., 1984-91, Hawaiian Hist. Soc., 1990-94, U. Hawaii Found., 1963-65, 73-78, pres., 1967-68; bd. dirs. Hawaii Multi-Cultural Ctr., 1979-81, Samaritan Counseling Ctr. Hawaii, 1985-91; chmn. adv. bd. Cancer Rsch. Ctr., Hawaii, 1979-81; pres. Hawaii conf. United Ch. of Christ, 1962-63. Mem. Hawaiian Sugar Planters Assn. (dir. 1972-80), Hawaiian Hist. Soc. Home: 7148 Kukii St Honolulu HI 96825-1602

HUGHES, ROBERT LACHLAN, newspaper executive; b. Regina, Saskatchewan, Can., June 1, 1944; s. Robert Wesley and Helen Elizabeth (MacLachlan) H.; m. Barbara Elaine Barootes, June 28, 1980; children: Geoffrey Robert, Ryan Stewart Gordon. Office boy, gen. reporter, police reporter, sports reporter Regina (Sask.) Leader-Post, 1962-69; sports columnist Saskatoon (Sask.) Star-Phoenix, 1969-70, Calgary Albertan, Can., 1970-72; sports editor, columnist Regina Leader-Post, 1972-88, mng. editor, news columnist, 1988-94, pub., 1994-96, editor-in-chief, 1996—. founding dir. Gord Currie Youth Devel. Fund, Brad Hornung Found.; dir. leader Post Carrier Found. Recipient Can. 125 medal Govt. of Can., 1992; named to Hall of Fame Can. Football Football Reporters of Can., 1990. Mem. Can. Mng. Editors Assn. (bd. dirs. 1989-94), Can. Daily Newspapers Assn., Royal United Svcs. Inst., Royal Regina Golf Club, Wascana C.C., Assiniboia Club. Avocations: golf, reading, writing, cycling, public speaking. Office: The Leader-Post, 1964 Park St, Regina, SK Canada S4P 3G4

HUGHES, ROBERT MERRILL, control system engineer; b. Glendale, Calif., Sept. 11, 1936; s. Fred P. and Gertrude G. (Merrill) H.; AA, Pasadena City Coll., 1957; 1 child, Tammie Lynn Cobble. Engr. Aerojet Gen. Corp., Azusa, Calif., 1957-64, 66-74; pres. Automatic Electronics Corp., Sacramento, 1964-66; specialist Perkin Elmer Corp., Pomona, Calif., 1974-75; gen. mgr. Hughes Mining Inc., Covina, Calif., 1975-76; project mgr. L&A Water Treatment, City of Industry, Calif., 1976-79; dir. Hughes Industries Inc., Alta Loma, Calif., 1979—; pres. Hughes Devel. Corp., Carson City, Nev.; chmn. bd. Hughes Mining Inc., Hughes Video Corp. Registered profl. engr., Calif., Nev.; lic. gen. bld. contractor. Mem. AIME, Nat. Soc. Profl. Engrs., Instrument Soc. Am., Am. Inst. Plant Engrs. Republican. Patentee in field. Office: PO Box 915 Carson City NV 89702-0915

HUGHES, SANDRA MICHELLE, education administrator, educator; b. Port Arthur, Tex., Oct. 18, 1944; d. Romain Joseph and Bessie Irene (Jones) Prejean; m. Donald Atley Hughes, Sept. 5, 1964; children: Heather Patrice, Matthew Donald. Student, Stephen F. Austin U., 1963-64, Lamar U., 1964-65. Area pres. Womens Aglow Internat., Houston, 1977-80; Ptnrs. in Edn. asst. Alief Ind. Sch. Dist., Houston, 1990-92; Ptnrs. in Edn. specialist Katy (Tex.) Ind. Sch. Dist., 1992—; cons. Strategic Planning Svcs., Houston, 1997—. Author/editor Partners in Education Ann. Report, 1992-97 (Tex. Sch. Pub. Rels. award 1997); co-author, editor: (workbook) Strategic Planning for Partnerships, 1997. Young adult Sunday sch. tchr. First Bapt. Ch., Katy, 1990—; mktg. com./bd. Jr. Achievement, West Houston, Tex., 1992—. Recipient Exemplary Program award Nat. Assn. Ptnrs. in Edn., 1995, Sci. Edn. Workgroup award Exxon Chem. Ams., 1996. Mem. Nat. Assn. Facilitators, Tex. Sch. Pub. Rels. Assn., Tex. Assn. Ptnrs. in Edn.(area coord. 1995-97), Houston West C. of C. (edn. com. 1995—), Delta Kappa Gamma (hon.). Republican. Baptist. Avocations: gourmet cooking, walking. Home: 1707 Stone Meadows Ln Houston TX 77094-3409 Office: Katy Ind Sch Dist PO Box 159 Katy TX 77492-0159

HUGHES, STANLEY JOHN, mycologist; b. Llanelli, S. Wales, Sept. 17, 1918; emigrated to Can., 1952, naturalized, 1967; s. John Thomas and Gertrude (Roberts) H.; m. Lyndell Anne Rutherford, Oct. 11, 1958; children—Robert Conway, Glenys Anne, David Stanley. B.Sc. with honors, U. Wales, Aberystwyth, 1941, M.Sc., 1943, D.Sc., 1954. Asst. to advr. mycologist Nat. Agrl. Advisory Ser. U. Wales, 1941-45; asst. mycologist Commonwealth Mycological Inst., Kew, Eng., 1945-52; mycologist Research br. Agr. Can. Central Exptl. Farm, Ottawa, Ont., 1952-58; sr. mycologist Research br. Agr. Can. Central Exptl. Farm, 1958-62; prin. mycologist Rsch. br. Agr. Can. Central Exptl. Farm (Ctr. for Land and Biol. Resources Rsch., 1962-83; hon. rsch. assoc., 1983—; Sr. research fellow New Zealand Dept. Sci. and Indsl. Research, 1963; Exchange scientist Nat. Research Councils of Can. and Brazil, 1974. Contbr. articles in field to profl. jours. Recipient Jakob Eriksson Gold medal, 1969; George Lawson medal, 1981. Fellow Royal Soc. Can., Linnean Soc. London (fgn. mem.); mem. Mycological Soc. Am. (pres. 1975; Disting. mycologist award 1985); British Mycological Soc. (fgn. v.p. and honorary mem. 1987), Internat. Mycological Assn. (v.p. 1977-83, hon. v.p. XVI internat. botanical congress 1999). Mem. United Ch. of Can. Home: 360 Hamilton Ave, Ottawa, ON Canada K1Y 1C5 Office: Ea Cereal/Oilseed Rsch Ctr, Agrl and Agri-Food Can, Ctrl Exptl Farm, Ottawa, ON Canada K1A 0C6

HUGHES, STEVEN BRYAN, gas measurement company executive; b. Holdenville, Okla., Feb. 15, 1956; s. Harvey and Rosella Mae (Storts) H.; m. Ronda Lynn Coker, May 18, 1974; children: Stephen, Rachel, Caleb. BS in Mgmt. Info. System, LaSalle U., 1998. Measurement technician Transok Pipeline Co., Wetumka, 1977-80; supr. gas measurement Transok Pipeline Co., Tulsa, 1980; owner, cons. Hughes Gas Measurement, Wetumka, 1980-93, pres., 1993—; ptnr. Data Resource Systems, Wetumka, 1991—; gas measurement cons. Illini Carrier, L.P., Granite City, Ill., 1990-92; contract measurement mgr. Oxley Petroleum, Tulsa, 1988—. Author, developer: (computer software) Wellhead Data Collection Program, 1991-98; editor, developer: (computer software) Total Flow/Chart Conversion Program, 1992-94. Teen Sunday sch. tchr. Pentecostal Holiness Ch., Wetumka, 1984-98, Sunday sch. supt., 1984-99, deacon bd. mem., 1990-99; cub master troop 483 Boy Scouts Am., Wetumka, 1985-86. Recipient Leadership award Pentecostal Holiness Ch., Wetumka, 1985. Mem. Soc. Petroleum Engrs. (assoc.). Democrat. Avocations: genealogy, musician. Home: 2917 Hwy 75 Wetumka OK 74883-9714 Office: Hughes Gas Measurement Inc 2919 Hwy 75 Wetumka OK 74883-9714

HUGHES, THOMAS LOWE, foundation executive; b. Mankato, Minn., Dec. 11, 1925; s. Evan Raymond and Alice (Lowe) H.; m. Jean Hurlburt Reiman, May 7, 1955 (dec. Dec. 1993); children: Thomas Evan, Allan Cameron; m. Jane Dudley Casey Kuczynski, Nov. 25, 1995. BA summa cum laude, Carleton Coll., 1947, LHD (hon.), 1974; BPhil and MA in Politics (Rhodes scholar), Balliol Coll., Oxford (Eng.) U., 1949; LLB, JD, Yale U., 1952; LLD (hon.), Washington Coll., 1973, Denison U., 1980, Fla. Internat. U., 1986; HHD (hon.), Washington and Jefferson Coll., 1979. Bar: Minn. 1952, U.S. Supreme Ct. 1960, U.S. Dist. Ct. D.C. 1968. Profl. staff mem. U.S. Senate Subcom. on Labor and Labor-Mgmt. Relations, Com. on Labor and Pub. Welfare, 1951-52; assoc. prof. polit. sci. and internat. rels. U. So. Calif., 1953; asso. prof. polit. sci. and internat. relations Trinity Coll., Tex., 1954, George Washington U., 1957-58; exec. sec. to gov. of Conn., 1954-55; legis. counsel Sen. Hubert Humphrey, 1955-58; adminstrv. asst. U.S. Rep. Chester Bowles, 1959-60; spl. asst. to under sec. state Dept. State, 1961, dep. dir. intelligence and research, 1961-63, dir. intelligence and research with rank of asst. sec. state, 1963-69; minister, dep. chief mission Am. embassy, London, 1969-70; planning and coordination staff Dept. State, 1970-71; pres., trustee Carnegie Endowment for Internat. Peace, 1971-91, pres. emeritus, hon. trustee, 1991—; former chmn. nuclear proliferation and safeguards adv. panel Office Tech. Assessment, Congress U.S.; co-chmn. Coun. P.R.-U.S. Affairs; internat. adv. bd. Battelle, Pacific Northwest Nat. Lab. Author: The Hohenzollerns; editor: Indian Chiefs of Southern Minnesota; mem. editorial bd. Fgn. Policy Mag., 1971—, chmn., 1971-91; contbr. articles to nat. periodicals. Vol. Kibbutz Ein Hashofet, Israel, 1950; trustee, sec. German Marshall Fund U.S., 1972-82; trustee Am. Inst. Contemporary German Studies; trustee Am. Acad. in Berlin; bd. dirs. Arms Control Assn.; mem. Trilateral Commn., 1973-83; former bd. govs. Ditchley Found., Eng.; vis. com. Ctr. for Internat. Studies, Harvard U., 1971-76; bd. visitors Sch. Fgn. Svc., Georgetown U.; mem. adv. coun. Woodrow Wilson Sch., Princeton U.; mem. adv. bd. Fundacion Luis Munoz Marin, San Juan, P.R.; chmn. U.S.-U.K. Bicentennial Fellowships Com. on Arts, 1975-78; trustee Social Sci. Found., U. Denver; mem. adv. com. Hubert H. Humphrey Inst. Pub. Affairs U. Minn.; staff dir. platform com. Dem. Nat. Conv., 1960. Served to maj. JAGC, USAF, 1952-54. Recipient Arthur S. Fleming Outstanding Pub. Svc. award, 1964. Mem. Institut Internat. de Geopolitique Paris, N.Y. Coun. Fgn. Rels., Inst. Current World Affairs (trustee), Internat. Inst. Strategic Studies London (trustee Am. com.), Am. Acad. Diplomacy, Am. Assn. Rhodes Scholars, Washington Inst. Fgn. Affairs (v.p., mem. exec. com.), Atlantic Coun. U.S. (bd. dirs., mem. exec. com.), Oxford-Cambridge Assn. Washington (former chmn.), Women's Fgn. Policy Group (mem. adv. coun.), New England Hist. Geneal. Soc., Scottish Genealogy Soc., Soc. Mayflower Descs., Mid-Atlantic Club (chmn.), Cosmos Club (chmn. adv. bd. jour.), Century Assn. (N.Y.C.), Oxford (Eng.) Union, Knight of St. John (Johanniterorden, Bailey Brandenburg), Phi Beta Kappa, Phi Delta Phi. Episcopalian. Office: German Hist Inst 1607 New Hampshire Ave NW Washington DC 20009-2562

HUGHES, THOMAS PARKE, history educator; b. Richmond, Va., Sept. 13, 1923; s. Hunter Russell and Mary Bronaugh (Quisenberry) H.; m. Agatha Chipley, Aug. 7, 1948; children: Thomas P. (dec.), Agatha H., Lucian P. B.M.E., U. Va., 1947, Ph.D., 1953. Instr. U. Va., Charlottesville, 1951-54; asst. prof. history Sweet Briar (Va.) Coll., 1954-56; assoc. prof. history Washington and Lee U., Lexington, Va., 1956-63, M.I.T., Cambridge, 1963-66; prof. history Inst. Tech., So. Meth. U., Dallas, 1969-73; mem. faculty U. Pa., Phila., 1973-94, prof. history and sociology of sci., 1973-94, Andrew W. Mellon prof., 1987-94, prof. emeritus, 1994—; vis. assoc. prof. history Johns Hopkins U., Balt., 1966-69; Torsten Althin prof. Royal Inst. Tech., Stockholm, 1985-90; founding rsch. prof. Tech. Univ., Darmstadt, Fed. Republic Germany, 1986-87; vis. rsch. prof. Wissenschaftszentrum Berlin, 1988-94; vis. prof. MIT, 1991, 93, 94—, E.T.H. Zürich, 1997, Stanford U., 1999. Author: Elmer Sperry: Inventor and Engineer, 1971 (Dexter prize), Networks of Power: Electrification in Western Society 1880-1930, 1983 (Dexter prize), American Genesis: A Century of Invention and Technological Enthusiasm 1870-1970, 1989 (Pulitzer Prize finalist); editor: (with Agatha C. Hughes) Lewis Mumford: Public Intellectual, 1990, Rescuing Prometheus, 1998. Mem. adv. coun. Smithsonian Inst., 1984-90; com. mem. Alfred P. Sloan Tech. Svcs., 1994—; chmn. Nat. Rsch. Coun. com., 1996-99. Served to lt. (j.g.) USN, 1943-46. Fulbright postdoctoral fellow Germany, 1958-59; NSF fellow, 1975; Rockefeller Found. fellow, 1975; Council Learned Socs.-Smithsonian fellow, 1969; Social Sci. Research Council fellow, 1972; Inst. Advanced Study fellow, Berlin, 1983; Guggenheim fellow, 1986. Mem. Soc. History of Tech. (pres. 1978-80, Leonardo da Vinci medal 1984), Soc. Social Studies Sci. (Bernal prize 1990), History of Sci. Soc. (coun. 1976-79), Am. Acad. Arts and Scis., Johns Hopkins U. Soc. of Scholars, Swedish Royal Acad. of Engring. Scis., Phi Beta Kappa.

HUGHES, VERNON WILLARD, physics educator, researcher; b. Kankakee, Ill., May 28, 1921. AB, Columbia U., 1941, PhD in Physics, 1950; MS, Calif. Inst. Tech., 1942; PhD (hon.), U. Heidelberg, Germany, 1977. Rsch. assoc. radiation lab. MIT, Cambridge, Mass., 1942-46; instr., lectr. in physics Columbia U., N.Y.C., 1949-52, assoc. prof. physics, 1958-59; asst. prof. U. Pa., Phila., 1952-54; from asst. prof. to prof. Yale U., New Haven, 1960-69, assoc. chmn. dept., 1960-61, chmn. dept., 1961-66, Donner prof., 1969-78, Sterling prof., 1978-91, Sterling prof. physics emeritus, 1991—; vis. I I Rabi prof. Columbia U., 1984, adj. prof., 1984—; trustee Assn. Univs. Inc., 1962-92, hon. trustee, 1992—; mem. Naval Rsch. Adv. Com., 1968-74; vis. prof. Japan Soc. Promotion Soc. Sci., 1974, 96; vis. prof. Slac Stanford (Calif.), 1978-79, Col France, 1981, Scuola Normale Superiore, Pisa, Italy, 1982; cons. Los Alamos Sci. Lab., Oak Ridge Nat. Lab., NSF, NRC, Dept. Energy, many others. Fellow AAAS, Am. Acad. Arts and Scis., Am. Phys. Soc.; mem. NAS. Office: Yale U Dept Physics PO Box 208121 260 Whitney Ave New Haven CT 06520-8121

HUGHES, VESTER THOMAS, JR., lawyer; b. San Angelo, Tex., May 24, 1928; s. Vester Thomas and Mary Ellen (Tisdale) H. Student, Baylor U., 1945-46; B.A. with distinction, Rice U., 1949; LLB cum laude, Harvard U., 1952. Bar: Tex. 1955. Law clk. U.S. Supreme Ct., 1952; assoc. Robertson, Jackson, Payne, Lancaster & Walker, Dallas, 1955-58; ptnr. Jackson, Walker, Winstead, Cantwell & Miller, Dallas, 1958-76, Hughes, Luce, Hennessy, Smith & Castle, Dallas, 1976—, Hughes & Hill, Dallas, 1979-85, Hughes & Luce, Dallas, 1985—; bd. dirs. Exell Cattle Co., Amarillo, Tex., LX Cattle Co., Amarillo, Murphy Oil Corp., El Dorado, Ark., Austin Industries, Dallas; adv. dir. First Nat. Bank Mertzon; tax counsel Communities Found. of Tex., Inc.; mem. adv. com. Tex. Supreme Ct., 1985-93. Contbr. articles on fed. taxation to profl. jours. Bd. dirs. Juvenile Diabetes Found. Inc., Dallas, 1982—; trustee Dallas Bapt. Coll., 1967-77; v.p., trustee, exec. com. Tex. Scottish Rite Hosp. for Children, 1967—; bd. overseers vis. com. Harvard Law Sch., 1969-75. 1st lt. JAGC U.S. Army, 1952-55. Mem. ABA (coun. sect. taxation 1969-73), Tex. Bar Assn., Dallas Bar Assn., Am. Law Inst. (coun. 1958—), Am. Coll. Tax Counsel, Southwestern Legal Found., Am. Coll. of Trust and Estate Counsel, Met. Club (Washington), Harvard Club (N.Y.C.), Masons, Order Ea. Star, Phi Beta Kappa, Sigma Xi. Democrat. Baptist. Avocations: traveling, community and church activities, reading. Office: Hughes & Luce 1717 Main St Ste 2800 Dallas TX 75201-4685

HUGHES, WALTER THOMPSON, physician, pediatrics educator; b. Cleve., May 16, 1930; s. Walter Thompson and Millie Hasentine (Collette) H.; m. Frances J. Skinner, Nov. 24, 1957; children: Carla, Gregory, Christopher. MD, U. Tenn., 1954. Diplomate Am. Bd. Pediatrics. Resident in pediatrics U. Tenn. Coll. Medicine, Memphis, 1955-57, prof. pediatrics and microbiology, 1969-77, prof. pediatrics, 1981—; mem. St. Jude Children's Rsch. Hosp., Memphis, 1969-77, mem., chair dept. infectious diseases, 1981-95; mem. staff Walter Reed Army Med. Ctr., Ft. Dietrich, Md., 1957-59; pvt. practice pediatrics Cleve., 1959-61; instr. to prof. U. Louisville Sch. Medicine, 1961-69; Eudowood prof. pediatrics, dir. div. infectious diseases Johns Hopkins U. Sch. Medicine, Balt., 1977-81; Arthur Ashe chair in pediat. AIDS rsch. St. Jude Children's Rsch. Hosp., Memphis, 1993-98, emeritus mem., 1998—. Capt. U.S. Army, 1957-59. Fellow Am. Acad. Pediatrics; mem. Am. Pediatric Soc., Infectious Diseases Soc. Am., Soc. Pediatric Rsch., Pediatric Infectious Diseases Soc. (pres. 1983-85). Republican. Methodist. Home: 854 River Park Dr Memphis TN 38103-0804 Office: St Jude Children's Rsch Hosp 332 N Lauderdale St Memphis TN 38105-2729

HUGHES, WAUNELL MCDONALD (MRS. DELBERT E. HUGHES), retired psychiatrist; b. Tyler, Tex., Feb. 6, 1928; d. Conrad Claiborne and Bernice Oletha (Smith) McDonald; B.A., U. Tex. at Austin, 1946; M.D., Baylor U., 1951; m. Delbert Eugene Hughes, Aug. 14, 1948; children—Lark, Mark, Lynn, Michael. Intern VA Hosp., Houston, 1951-52; resident Parkland Hosp., Dallas, 1964-67; practiced gen. medicine in Tyler, Tex., 1952-64; acting chief psychiatry service VA Hosp., Dallas, 1967-68, asst. chief, 1968-73, chief Mental Hygiene Clinic and Day Treatment Center, 1973-82, unit chief acute inpatient psychiatry Med. Center, 1982-88; clin. instr. psychiatry Southwestern Med. Sch., U. Tex. Health Sci. Center, Dallas, 1968-88; psychiat. cons. Dallas Family Guidance Clinics, 1990. Chmn. pre-sch. vision and hearing program Pilot Club, Tyler, 1960-64. Mem. Am. Med. Women's Assn. (pres. Dallas 1980-81, archivist 1997—), Am. Psychiat. Assn., Am. Group Psychotherapy Assn., (pres. Dallas chpt. 1984-86), North Tex. Soc. Psychiat. Physicians (co-chair Mental Health Mental Retardation pro bono clinic com. Dallas chpt. 1989-91, mem. patient advocacy com. 1992—), Dallas Area Women Psychiatrists (archivist 1985—, pres. 1997-99), Alpha Epsilon Iota (pres. 1950-51). Home: 3428 University Blvd Dallas TX 75205-1834

HUGHES, WILLIAM ANTHONY, bishop; b. Youngstown, Ohio, Sept. 23, 1921; s. James Francis and Anna Marie (Philbin) H. Degree, St. Charles Sem., Balt., St. Mary's Sem., Cleve.; M.A. in Edn, Notre Dame U., 1956. Ordained priest Roman Catholic Ch., 1946; pastor chs. in Boardman and Massillon, Ohio, 1946-55; prin. Cardinal Mooney High Sch., Youngstown, 1956-65; supt. schs. Diocese of Youngstown, 1965-72, episcopal vicar of edn., 1972-73, vicar gen., 1973-74; aux. bishop, 1974-79; bishop of Covington, Covington, Ky., 1979—; ret. bishop Covington, KY. Office: Cathedral of Assemption 1140 Madison Ave Covington KY 41011-3116*

HUGHES, WILLIAM FOSTER, career officer, surgeon, obstetrician, gynecologist; b. Lexington, Va., July 1, 1944; s. John Anderson Jr. and Mary Elizabeth (Shaner) H.; m. Susan Lee Aplegate, July 12, 1969; children: Carolyn Michelle, John Robert, Jennifer Marie. BS, U.S. Mil. Acad., 1966; MD, Med. Coll. Va., 1978; postgrad., U.S. Army War Coll., 1989. Diplomate Nat. Bd. Med. Examiners, Am. Bd. Ob-Gyn. Commd. 2nd lt. U.S. Army, 1966, advanced through the grades to col., 1990; combat infantryman-platoon leader, co. comdr. U.S. Army, Vietnam, 1967-68, attack helicopter pilot, 1970-71; airfield comdr. Tipton Army Airfield, Ft. Meade, Md., 1973-74; intern in ob-gyn. Tripler Army Med. Ctr., Honolulu, Hawaii, 1978-79, resident in ob-gyn., 1979-82; staff physician Martin Army Cmty. Hosp., Ft. Benning, Ga., 1982-86; divsn. surgeon 101st Airborne Divsn., Ft. Campbell, Ky., 1986-88; command surgeon U.S. Special Ops. Command, MacDill Air Force Base, Fla., 1989-93; hosp. comdr. Darnall Army Cmty. Hosp., Ft. Hood, Tex., 1993-95; v.p. prodn. Info. Co., 1997—; cons. Med Nat., Inc., 1999—; asst. prof. dept. ob-gyn. Tex. A&M U., College Station, 1994—; cons. Army Surgeon Gen., 1995-96. Decorated Silver Star, DFC, Purple Heart. Fellow ACOG, ACS; mem. Am. Coll. Physician Execs. Avocations: golf, fishing, running. E-mail: bhughes578@aol.com. Home: 712 Coyote Cir Harker Hts TX 76548-2170

HUGHES, WILLIAM FRANKLIN, JR., ophthalmologist, emeritus educator; b. Indpls., Apr. 18, 1913; s. William F. and Alta (Rentschler) H.; m. Wanema Dickey, June 28, 1941 (dec. 1969); children: William Franklin III, Jacqueline Alter, Sarah Lee; m. Jane M. Stockdale, 1970. A.B., Amherst Coll., 1934; M.D., Johns Hopkins, 1938. Diplomate Am. Bd. Ophthalmology (mem. 1968-80). Intern, asst. resident and resident in ophthalmology Johns Hopkins, 1938-44, asst. prof. ophthalmology, 1944-46, research work, 1941-46; pvt. practice in ophthalmology Ind. U. Sch. of Medicine, 1946-47; prof. ophthalmology U. Ill., 1947—, head dept., 1947-58; ophthalmologist-in-chief Research and Ednl. Hosps. and Ill. Eye and Ear Infirmary, 1947-58; chmn. dept. ophthalmology Presbyn.-St. Luke's Hosp., Chgo., 1956-79; prof. ophthalmology Rush Med. Coll., 1971-81, prof. emeritus, 1981—; past mem. ophthalmology com. NRC. Author: Office Management of Ocular Diseases, 1953; mem. editorial bds. Archives of

Ophthalmology, 1951-62, 81-84; editor Year Book Ophthalmology, 1959-81; contbr. articles on chem. burns of eyes, cataract extraction, beta irradiation, retinal detachment, corneal diseases and corneal transplantation. Mem. AMA, Assn. Research in Ophthalmology (trustee 1949-55), Am. Ophthal. Soc. (council 1971-76, pres. 1981), Chgo. Ophthal. Soc. (past pres.), Inst. of Med. Chgo., Billings Med. Club of Chgo. (pres. 1965), Sigma Xi, Alpha Kappa Kappa, Phi Kappa Psi. Home: 4 Court Of Mohawk Vly Lincolnshire IL 60069-3211

HUGHES, WILLIAM JOHN, former congressman, diplomat; b. Salem, N.J., Oct. 17, 1932; s. William W. and Pauline H.; m. Nancy L. Gibson; children: Nancy Lynne, Barbara Ann, Tama Beth, William John. AB, Rutgers U., 1955, JD, 1958, LLD (hon.), 1995; LHD (hon.), Mt. Vernon Coll., 1984; LLD (hon.), Richard Stockton State Coll., 1994, Glassboro State Coll., 1992; AA (hon.), Cumberland County Coll., 1994. Bar: N.J. 1959. Ptnr. Loveland, Hughes & Garrett, Ocean City, N.J., 1968-78; 1st asst. pros. atty. Cape May County, N.J., 1960-70; mem. 94th-103rd Congresses from 2d N.J. dist., Washington, D.C., 1974—; amb. to Panama U.S. Dept. State, 1995-98; Clifford P. Case prof. of pub. affairs Rutgers U., 1997. Bd. govs. Shore Meml. Hosp., Sommers Point, N.J., 1972-76. Recipient Ann. Planning award Am. Planning Assn., 1979, Disting. Citizen award Atlantic Area coun. Boy Scouts Am., 1982, Legislator of Yr. award VFW, 1982, Pres.'s award Nat. Dist. Attys. Assn., 1982, Legis. Leadership award Nat. Assn. Chain Drug Stores, 1984, Humanitarian citiation Food Mktg. Chain Drug Stores and N.J. Food Council, 1984, Legis. award Nat. Assn. Police Orgns., 1984, Legis. Achievement award Fed. Law Enforcement Officers Assn., 1984, Man of Yr. award Girl Scouts Am., 1986, Legis. award N.J. Foster Parents Assn., 1986, Leo Fraser Super Achiever award Juvenile Diabetes Found., 1987, Arthur E. Armitage Sr. Disting. Alumni award Rutgers U., 1987, Disting. Info. Processing Pub. Service award Data Processing Mgmt. Assn., 1987, Rutgers U. medal, 1992, Distinction in Pub. Svc. award Am. Rivers, 1993, Congressional Advocacy award, 1994, Spirit of South Jersey award South Jersey Devel. Coun., 1994, Career Achievement award in pub. svc. N.J. Edn. Assn., 1995; named Congressman of Yr., Nat. Assn. Police Orgns., 1986, Hall of Disting. Alumni award Rutgers U., 1997, Jefferson medal award N.J. Intellectual Property Law Assn., 1995. Mem. ABA, N.J. Bar Assn., Ocean City Hist. Soc. (bd. dir. 1972-76), Ocean City C. of C. (bd. dir. 1960—), Exch. of Ocean City Club (pres. 1965-66, Nat. Big E. award 1965), Masons (master lodge, Worshipful Master 1969). Democrat. Episcopalian. Home: 1019 Wesley Rd Ocean City NJ 08226-4754

HUGHES, WILLIAM JOSEPH, management consultant; b. Kansas City, Mo., Oct. 11, 1953; s. Joseph Rowland and Ann (Hemingway) H.; m. Mary Alice Knight, Apr. 25, 1981; children: Charles, Allison, Kirstin. BSME, U. Va., 1975. Various positions Brown & Root, Inc., Houston, 1975-79; sr. cons. Arthur Andersen & Co., S.C., Houston, 1979-81, mgr., 1981-87; ptnr. Andersen Cons., Houston, 1987—. Editor, contbg. author: Natural Gas Trends, 1988. Mem. ASME, Houston Club. Episcopalian. Avocations: sailing, skiing, golf, tennis. Office: Andersen Cons 711 Louisiana St Ste 1200 Houston TX 77002-2716

HUGHES, WILLIAM LEWIS, former university official, electrical engineer; b. Rapid City, S.D., Dec. 2, 1926; s. Clarence William and Newell (Chase) H.; m. Stella Marie Platt, June 9, 1950; children: Elizabeth Helen, James Edward, Judith Lee, Michael George. B.S. in Elec. Engring, S.D. Sch. Mines and Tech., 1949; M.S., Iowa State U., 1950, Ph.D., 1952. Broadcast and TV engr., 1946-49; mem. faculty Iowa State U., 1949-60; prof. elec. engring., 1959-60; prof. elec. engring., head Sch. Elec. Engring., Okla. State U., Stillwater, 1960-76; Clark A. Dunn prof. engring. Sch. Elec. Engring., Okla. State U., 1976-86, dir. Engring. Energy Lab., 1976-86; pres. InEn Corp, 1972-88; v.p. S.D. Sch. Mines and Tech., Rapid City, 1988-93; pres. Dakota Alpha Inc., 1994—; chmn. ad hoc com. NAS, 1976, 79, mem. bd. sci. and tech. in devel., 1983; chmn. NAS/Philippine Govt. del. to Philippines, 1978, Indonesia, 1979, India, 1979, 85, 89, Thailand, 1990, 93; cons. industry and govt.; mem. indsl. com. TV frequency allocation studies FCC, 1957-59. Author: Nonlinear electrical Networks, 1960; also articles; co-author: Lines, Waves and Antennas, 1961, 2d edit., 1973; contbr. sects. to 6 engring. handbooks. Served with USNR, World War II. Named S.D. Profl. Engr. of Yr., S.D. Engring. Soc., 1995. Fellow IEEE; mem. NSPE (life, Disting. Svc. award 1997), Sigma Xi, Sigma Tau, Tau Beta pi, Eta Kappa Nu, Pi Mu Epsilon. Patentee nonlinear systems, color TV systems, direct energy conversions systems. Home: 6118 Greenleaf Ct Rapid City SD 57702-8845

HUGHES, WINIFRED SHIRLEY, writer, illustrator; b. West Kirby, Cheshire, Eng., July 16, 1927; d. Thomas James and Kathleen (Dowling) H.; m. John Sebastian Papendiek Vulliamy, Apr. 26, 1952; children: Edward, Tom, Clara. Diploma in fine arts, Ruskin Sch. Drawing and Fine Art, Oxford, Eng., 1949. Free-lance writer, illustrator London, 1950—; lectr. invs., colls.; overseas lectrs. include tours to Australia, U.S.l mem. Pub. Lending Right Registrar's Adv. Com., 1984-88, Libr. and Info. Svc. Coun., 1989-92. Author: (children's books) Lucy and Tom series, 6 vols., 1960-87, The Trouble with Jack, 1970, Sally's Secret, 1973, Helpers, 1975, It's Too Frightening for Me, 1977, Dogger, 1977, Moving Molly, 1978, Up and Up, 1979, Here Comes Charlie Moon, 1980, Alfie Gets in First, 1981, Alfie's Feet, 1982, Charlie Moon and the Big Bonanza Bust Up, 1982, Alfie Gives a Hand, 1983, An Evening at Alfie's, 1984, The Nursery Collection, 6 vols., 1985-86, Another Helping of Chips, 1986, Out and About, 1988, The Big Alfie and Annie Rose Story Book, 1988, Angel Mae, 1989, The Big Concrete Lorry, 1989, The Snow Lady, 1990, Wheels, 1991, The Big Alfie Out-of-Doors Story Book, 1992, Bouncing, Giving, 1993, Stories by Firelight, 1993, Chatting, 1994, Hiding, 1994, Rhymes for Annie Rose, 1995, "Enchantment in the Garden", 1996, Alfie and the Birthday Surprise, 1997, The Lion and the Unicorn, 1998, Abel's Moon, 1999. Recipient Other award Children's Rights, 1976, Kate Greenaway award Lib. Sv. Gt. Britian, 1978, silver Pencil award Dutch Children's Book Coun., 1980, Eleanor Farjeon award Children's Book Circle, 1984. Mem. Children's Writers and Illustrators Group of Soc. of Authors, (chmn. 1994-96), Libr. Assn. (hon. fellow), O.B.E. for svcs. to Chldns. Lit., 1999. Avocations: looking at paintings, sewing, sketching. Office: Random House/Bodley Head, 20 Vauxhall Bridge Rd, London SW1V 2SA, England

HUGHS, MARY GERALDINE, accountant, social service specialist; b. Marshalltown, Iowa, Nov. 28, 1929; d. Don Harold, Sr., and Alice Dorothy (Keister) Shaw; A.A., Highline Community Coll., 1970; B.A., U. Wash., 1972; m. Charles G. Hughs, Jan. 31, 1949; children: Mark George, Deborah Kay, Juli Ann, Grant Wesley. Asst. controller Moduline Internat., Inc., Chehalis, Wash., 1972-73; controller Data Recall Corp., El Segundo, Calif., 1973-74; fin. adminstr., acct. Saturn Mfg. Corp., Torrance, Calif., 1974-77; sr. acct., adminstrv. asst. Van Camp Ins., San Pedro, Calif., 1977-78; asst. adminstr. Harbor Regional Ctr., Torrance, Calif., 1979-87; active bookkeeping svc., 1978—; instr. math. and acctg. South Bay Bus. Coll., 1976-77. Sec. Pacific N.W. Mycol. Soc., 1966-67; treas., bd. dirs. Harbor Employees Fed. Credit Union; mem. YMCA Club. Recipient award Am. Mgmt. Assn., 1979. Mem. Beta Alpha Psi. Republican. United Ch. of Christ. Author: Iowa Auto Dealers Assn. Title System, 1955; Harbor Regional Center Affirmative Action Plan, 1980; Harbor Regional Center - Financial Format, 1978—; Provider Audit System, 1979; Handling Client Funds, 1983. Home and Office: 32724 Coastsite Dr Unit 107 Palos Verdes Estates CA 90275-5860

HUGLER, EDWARD C., lawyer, federal and state government; b. Phila., Feb. 7, 1950; s. Edward Tarman and Lavina Rita (Kelchner) H.; m. Anna Louise Wolgast, June 13, 1987; children: Samuel Rives, Sarah Elizabeth. BA, U. Md., 1973; JD, Sch. of Law, Pepperdine U., 1976. Bar: D.C., Calif. Atty. advisor to adminstrv. law judge, Office of Hearing and Appeals U.S. Dept. of the Interior, 1977-78; atty., advisor, Office of the Solicitor U.S. Dept. of Labor, 1978-81, counsel for Standards and Legal Advice, Office of the Solicitor, 1981-88, dep. assoc. solicitor, Office of the Solicitor, 1988-89, dep. adminstr. for Coal Mine Safety and Health, Mine Safety and Health Adminstrn., 1989-91, dep. asst. sec. for Mine Safety and Health, 1991—, acting asst. sec. for Mine Safety and Health, 1993-94; acting adminstr. for metal and nonmetal safety and health U.S. Dept. of Labor/Mine Safety and Health Adminstrn., 1998-99; acting dep. asst., sec. for adminstrn. and mgmt. OASAM, Washington, 1999—. Office: OASAM Mine Safety & Health Admin 200 Constitution Dr NW Washington DC 20210*

HUGO, MIRIAM JEANNE, educator, counselor; b. Pitts., Feb. 28, 1926; d. James Elmer and Gladys Marguerite (Bartlett) Hugo. BS, Miami U., Oxford, Ohio, 1948; MA, Ohio State U., 1953; PhD, Ohio U., 1969. Cert. counselor, Fla. Tchr. Lemon-Monroe Twp., Hamilton County, Ohio, 1948-49; head tchr. Ohio State Juvenile Diagnostic Ctr., Columbus, 1950-54, Columbus Children's Psychiat. Hosp., Columbus, 1954-59; tchr. Exptl. Class for Emotionally Disturbed Children, Miami, Fla., 1959-60; elem. sch. counselor Dade County (Fla.) Schs., Miami, 1960-66, sch. psychologist, 1969-70; counseling psychologist U. Wis., Eau Claire, 1970-76, assoc. dir. counseling svcs., 1976-84, assoc. dean of students, 1984-90, ret., 1990; mem. adv. bd. County Coun. on Drug and Alcohol Abuse Prevention, Eau Claire, 1983, Planned Parenthood of Eau Claire, 1976-77. Mem. exec. bd. Friends of L.E. Phillips Meml. Pub. Libr., Eau Claire, 1993-96, v.p., 1993-94, pres., 1994-95. Mem. AAUW, Kiwanis Internat. (bd. dirs. Clear Water Club 1997-98), Phi Delta Kappa. Democrat. Episcopalian. Avocations: reading, travel, art and painting, volunteering. Home: 1450 Cummings Ave Eau Claire WI 54701-6569

HUGO, NANCY, county official, alcohol and drug addiction professional; b. Cedar Rapids, Iowa, May 4, 1944; d. Roger S. and Phyllis Anita (Wenger) Conrad; m. Marshall G. Hugo (div.), Apr. 5, 1968; 1 child, Andrea. BS, Drake U., 1966; MS, Pepperdine U., 1987; adminstrn. credential, U. Calif., Irvine, 1989. Cert. adminstr., middle sch. educator, Calif. Tchr., asst. prin. Ocean View Sch. Dist., Huntington Beach, Calif., 1966-90; coord. alcohol and drug prevention edn., tobacco use prevention edn., sch. crisis response, program mgr. juvenile ct. schs. drug and alcohol programs Orange County Dept. Edn., Costa Mesa, Calif., 1990—, coord. phys. edn., 1991-93, coord. bus. edn. partnership, 1993-95. Author: No Butts...About Quitting Tobacco Use, A Tobacco Cessation Program; co-author: Snuff Out Teen Tobacco and Nix Spit. Mem. ASCD, NEA, Assn. Calif. Sch. Adminstrs., Calif. Edn. Assn., Calif. Assn. Health Phys. Edn. Recreation and Dance, Calif. Tchrs. Assn. Home: 25 Cerrito Irvine CA 92612-2603 Office: Orange County Dept Edn 200 Kalmus Dr Costa Mesa CA 92626-5922

HUGO, NORMAN ELIOT, plastic surgeon, medical educator; b. Beverly, Mass., Sept. 23, 1933; s. Victor Joseph and Helen Bernadette (Box) H.; m. Geraldine P. Tonry, Oct. 10, 1959; children: Helen, William, Geraldine, Norman, Catherine. BA, Williams Coll., 1955, DSc (hon.), 1989; MD, Cornell U. Med. Coll., 1959. Intern, resident Cornell U. Surg. Svc., Bellevue Hosp., N.Y.C., 1959-63, resident N.Y. Hosp.-Cornell Med. Ctr., 1963-65, univ. instr. surgery, 1965-66; asst. prof. Ind. U.; asst. chief plastic surgeon Walter Reed Army Med. Ctr., 1967-69, assoc. prof. U. Chgo., 1969-71; chief plastic and reconstructive surgery Michael Reese Hosp., Chgo., 1969-71, Passavant Hosp., Chgo., 1971-79; assoc. prof. Northwestern U., Chgo., 1971-82; dir. plastic surgery Lakeside VA Hosp., 1971-77; chief plastic and reconstructive surgery Columbia U.-Presbyn. Med. Ctr., N.Y.C., 1982-95; prof. Columbia U. Coll. Physicians & Surgeons, 1982-98, prof. emeritus, 1998—. Maj. M.C., AUS, 1967-69. Diplomate Am. Bd. Plastic Surgery, dir., 1982-88, vice chmn., 1987-88, residency review com., accreditation coun. grad. med. edn., 1994-98. Mem. ACS, Am. Soc. Plastic & Reconstructive Surgeons (trustee 1981-84, historian 1982-84, v.p. 1985-86, pres. elect 1986-87, pres. 1987-88, bd. dirs. Ednl. Found.), Am. Assn. Plastic and Reconstructive Surgery (trustee 1982-84), Am. Soc. Aesthetic Plastic Surgery (sec. 1979-82), Chgo. Soc. Plastic Surgery (sec. 1979-81, v.p. 1981-82), Plastic Surgery Research Council, Am. Cleft Palate Soc., Assn. Acad. Surgery, Soc. Head and Neck Surgeons, N.Y. Acad. Sci., AMA (del. 1983-88), Am. Burn Soc. Clubs: Williams, Union (N.Y.C.); University (Chgo.). Home: 37 Carriage Ln New Canaan CT 06840-4401 Office: Columbia U Coll Physicians and Surgeons 161 Fort Washington Ave New York NY 10032-3713

HUGOSON, GENE, state legislator, farmer; b. Sept. 1945; m. Patricia Hugoson; one child. BA, Augsburg Coll.; postgrad., Mankato State U. Farmer; Dist. 26A rep. Minn. Ho. of Reps., St. Paul, 1986-95; commr. Agr. Dept., 1995—; former mem. econ. devel., internat. trade and redistricting coms., Minn. Ho. of Reps.; mem. Agr., rules and legis. adminstrn., transp. and transit, and taxes coms.; asst. minority leader. Home: RR 2 Box 218 Granada MN 56039-9530 Office: State of Minn Dept of Agr 90 Plato Blvd W Saint Paul MN 55107-2004

HUH, JAE YOUNG, finance company executive; b. Feb. 14, 1969. MS, George Washington U., 1994, MBA, 1995. Bus. analyst Freddie Mac, McLean, Va., 1995-96; investment officer Internat. Fin. Corp., Washington, 1996—. E-mail: jhuh@ifc.org. Home: 3001 Park Center Dr Apt 909 Alexandria VA 22302

HUHEEY, MARILYN JANE, ophthalmologist; b. Cin., Aug. 31, 1935; d. George Mercer and Mary Jane (Weaver) H.; B.S. in Math., Ohio U., Athens, 1958; M.S. in Physiology, U. Okla., 1966; M.D., U. Ky., 1970. Tchr. math. James Ford Rhodes High Sch., Cleve., 1956-58; biostatistician Nat. Jewish Hosp., Denver, 1958-60; life sci. engr. Stanley Aviation Corp., Denver, 1960-63, N.Am. Aviation Co., Los Angeles, 1963-67; intern U. Ky. Hosp., 1970-71; emergency room physician Jewish Hosp., Mercy Hosp., Bethesda Hosp. (all Cin.), 1971-72; ship's doctor, 1972; resident in ophthalmology Ohio State U. Hosp., Columbus, 1972-75; practice medicine specializing in ophthalmology, Columbus, 1975—; mem. staff Univ. Hosp., Grant Hosp., St. Anthony Hosp., 1975-79; clin. asst. prof. Ohio State U. Med. Sch., 1976-84, clin. assoc. prof., 1985—, dir. course ophthalmologic receptionist/aides, 1976; mem. Peer Rev. Systems Bd., 1986-92, exec. com., 1988-92; mem. Ohio Optical Dispensers Bd., 1986-91; bd. dirs. Ctrl. Ohio Radio Reading Svc., 1997—. Dem. candidate for Ohio Senate, 1982. Diplomate Am. Bd. Ophthalmology. Fellow Am. Acad. Ophthalmology; mem. AAUP, Am. Assn. Ophthalmologists, Ohio Ophthalmol. Soc. (bd. govs. 1984-89, del. to Ohio State Med. Assn. 1984-88), Franklin County Acad. Medicine (profl. rels. com. 1979-82, legis. com. 1981-89, edn. and program com. 1981-88, chmn. 1982-85, chmn. cmty. rels. com. 1987-90, chmn. resolution com. 1987-92, mem. fin. com. 1988-92), Ohio Soc. Prevent Blindness (chmn. med. adv. bd. 1978-80), Ohio State Med. Assn. (dr.-nurse liaison com. 1983-87), Columbus EENT Soc., Am. Coun. of the Blind (bd. dirs. 1995-96), Life Care Alliance (pres. sustaining bd. 1987-88), United Way (planning com. 1992-93), LWV, Columbus Council World Affairs, Columbus Bus. and Profl. Women's Club, Columbus C. of C., Grandview Area Bus. Assn., Federated Dem. Women of Ohio, Columbus Area Women's Polit. Caucus, Phi Mu. Clubs: Columbus Met. (forum com. 1982-85, fundraising com. 1983-84, chmn. 10th anniversary com. 1986), Mercedes Benz (dir. 1981-83), Zonta, (program com. 1984-86, chmn. internat. com. 1983), Herb Soc. Home: 2396 Northwest Blvd Columbus OH 43221-3829 Office: 1335 Dublin Rd Ste 25A Columbus OH 43215-1000

HUHN, DARLENE MARIE, county official, poet; b. Kearny, N.J., Feb. 13, 1967; d. Charles Joseph and Theresa Catherine (Foertsch) H. AAS, Essex County C.C., Newark, 1990. Sec. Hudson County Vo-Tech., North Bergen, N.J., 1983-84; law clk. Skoloff & Wolfe, Livingston, N.J., 1984-87; data entry clk. Robith, Lyndhurst, N.J., 1987-94; income maint. technician Hudson County Welfare, Jersey City, 1994—. Author: (poetry) Decisions, 1995, Have Faith, 1995 (Internat. Soc. Poetry Poet of Merit 1995, 96). Vice pres. Rosary Soc., East Newark, N.J., 1994-97; mem. pastoral coun. Deanery 14 Archdiocese of Newark, 1990-96. Recipient Golden Poet award World of Poetry, 1987-90, Achievement award Cath. Youth Orgn., 1991, Editor's Choice award Nat. Libr. Poetry, 1996; named Best Poet of 1988, Am. Poetry Assn., 1988, Famous Poet, Famous Poetry Soc., 1996, 98, Diamond Homer Trophy, 1998; inducted Internat. Poetry Hall of Fame, 1996. Mem. Phi Theta Kappa. Democrat. Avocations: poetry, science fiction book writing, classical music. Home: 330 N 2nd St East Newark NJ 07029-2721

HUHS, JOHN I., international lawyer; b. Galveston, Tex., Sept. 18, 1944; s. Roy E. and Martha Mae (Hansen) H.; m. Vivian C. Swindley, 1970 (div. 1978). BA, U. Wash., 1966; MBA, Stanford U., 1970, JD, 1970. Bar: N.Y. 1971, D.C. 1981. Internat. cons. Satra Cons. Corp., N.Y.C., 1970-73; sr. staff White House Office Mgmt. & Budget Nat. Security, Internat. Affairs, Washington, 1974-75; ptnr. Pisar & Huhs, N.Y.C., 1976-84; sr. v.p., gen. counsel Tendler, Beretz Assocs., Ltd., N.Y.C., 1985-87; pvt. practice N.Y.C., 1987-88; ptnr., chmn. internat. dept. LeBoeuf, Lamb, Greene & MacRae, N.Y.C., 1989—; prin. Ctr. Excellence in Govt., 1984—. Contbr. articles on internat. law, bus. and fin. to profl. jours.; comment editor Stanford Law Rev. Mem. bd. visitors Stanford Law Sch., 1996-98. Mem. ABA (coun. sect. internat. law and practice 1988-92, chmn. com. internat. comml. trans. 1985-90, com. on Soviet and Ea. European law 1982-85, rep. to Union Internat. Avocats 1991-94), N.Y. State Bar Assn. (chmn. internat. investment devel. com. 1987-91), Assn. Bar City N.Y. (internat. trade com. 1987-89, com. Newly Ind. States of Former Soviet Union 1989—), D.C. Bar Assn., Univ. Club N.Y.C., 175 E. 74th Corp. (pres.). Home: 175 E 74th St New York NY 10021-3218 Office: LeBoeuf Lamb Greene MacRae 125 W 55th St New York NY 10019-5369

HUI, WILLIAM MAN WAI, chiropractor; b. Hong Kong, Mar. 21, 1959; came to the U.S., 1966; s. Wing Hong and Lai Kwan (Lee) H.; m. Bing Yee Wong, Oct. 12, 1985; 1 child, Ranan Nathanial. D in Chiropractic, N.Y. Chiropractic Coll., 1985. Dir., sole proprietor, doctor Flushing (N.Y.) Chiropractice & Health Office, 1985—. Conf. com. mem. Covenant Ch. Presbyn. Ch. Am., 1990-97, 99; bd. mem. Main St. Plaza Condominium, 1991-99, pres., 1995-97, 98—; team physician Lion's Club, 1996. Mem. Am. Chiropractic Assn. (mem. sports coun.). Republican. Presbyterian. Avocations: tennis, basketball, skiing, vocal performance, karate. Office: Flushing Chiropractic & Health Office 13338 41st Rd Ste 2N Flushing NY 11355-3662

HUIBREGTSE, JAYNE LYNNOR, medical surgical nurse; b. Pipestone, Minn., Jan. 27, 1952; d. Vern Ray and Alvera Augusta (Wittfoth) H. Diploma, Sioux Valley Hosp. Sch. Nursing, 1973. RN, Minn., S.D. Psychiat. staff nurse McKennan Hosp., Sioux Falls, S.D.; dir. nursing svc. Palisade Manor Nursing Home, Garretson, S.D.; staff nurse operating rm. Sioux Valley Hosp., Sioux Falls; staff and charge nurse Pipestone County Med. Ctr. Mem. Minn. Nurses Assn.

HUITT, JIMMIE L., rancher, oil, gas, real estate investor; b. Gurdon, Ark., Aug. 21, 1923; s. John Wesley and Almedia (Hatten) H.; m. Janis C. Mann, Oct. 30, 1945; children—Jimmie L., Jr., Allan Jerome. B.S. in Chem. Engring., La. Tech. U., 1944; M.S. in Chem. Engring., U. Okla., 1948, Ph.D., 1951. Registered profl. engr., La. Research engr. Mobil Oil Corp., Dallas, 1951-56, Gulf Research Co., Pitts., 1956-67; ops. coordinator Kuwait Oil Co., London, 1967-71; gen. mgr. Gulf Oil-Zaire, Kinshasa, 1971-74; mng. dir. Gulf Oil-Nigeria, Lagos, 1974-76; sr. v.p., exec. v.p. Gulf Oil Exploration and Prodn. Co., Houston, 1976-81, pres., 1981-85; rancher Four Jays Ranch, Industry, Tex., 1986—. Contbr. articles to profl. jours.; patentee in field. Served to 1st lt. U.S. Army, 1944-47. Mem. Soc. Petroleum Engrs. (chmn. various coms. 1956—). Republican. Lodges: Masons, Shriners. Office: Four Jays Ranch PO Box 236 Industry TX 78944-0236

HUIZENGA, EDWARD RICHARD, mortgage banker; b. Monterey, Calif., Dec. 2, 1931; s. Jake Dick and Brenda (Schofield) H.; m. Ida Theresa Yeme, Nov. 18, 1954; 1 child, Cindy Ann Huizenga. Student, Monterey (Calif.) Peninsula, 1951, Calif. Poly., 1954-55. Office mgr. Dept. HUD, Fresno, Calif., 1970-85; builder account mgr. All Valley Mortgage, Fresno, 1986-88, Commonweath United Mortgage, Fresno, 1989-92, N.Am. Mortgage, Fresno, 1992—. Named to Calif. Builders Hall Fame, 1997. Mem. Builders Industry Assn. (dir. SJV chpt., life dir. ctrl. coast chpt., Oscar Spano award 1994, Pres.'s award 1988, 94, Assoc. of Yr. award 1989), Nat. Assn. Home builders (housing fin. com.), CBIA (dir.). Republican. Roman Catholic. Avocations: duck hunting, snow skiing, golf. Home: 5023 W Spruce Ave Fresno CA 93722-3443 Office: North American Mortgage Co 1320 E Shaw Ave Fresno CA 93710-7919

HUIZENGA, GEORGIANA R., public library director, storyteller; b. Painesville, Ohio, Aug. 11, 1945; d. George Blair and Mildred Louise (Cone) Sheers; m. Keith Garrett Huizenga Jr., Aug. 12, 1967; children: Jennifer Lynn, Andrew Blair. BA, Bowling Green State U., 1967. Libr. assoc. Bowling Green (Ohio) State U., 1967-68; ref. libr. Wood County Pub. Libr., Northwood, Ohio, 1970-80, br. libr., 1980-93; libr. dir. Harris-Elmore (Ohio) Pub. Libr., 1993—. Columnist: (book rev.) Suburban Press newspaper, 1981-84; author numerous poems. Sec., charter mem. Woodmore Acad. Boosters, Elmore, 1994-97; pres. Ch. Coun., Elmore, 1985, 98; mem. Prin. Comm. Team, Elmore, 1993-98, Cmty. Woodmore H.S., Elmore, 1994, 95. Mem. ALA, Ohio Libr. Coun. (membership com. 1995-98), Ohio Pub. Libr. Info. Network (libr. issues task force 1994-96), Elmore Study Club (pres. 1997-98), Pride n' Joy Mother's Club (pres. 1979-80, 94-95). Democrat. United Ch. of Christ. Avocations: reading, storytelling, public speaking, writing, volunteering. E-mail: Huizenge@oplin.lib.oh.us. Home: 16020 W Portage River S Elmore OH 43416 Office: Harris-Elmore Pub Libr PO Box 45 328 Toledo St Elmore OH 43416

HUIZENGA, HARRY WAYNE, entrepreneur, entertainment corporation executive, professional sports team executive; b. Evergreen Park, Ill., Dec. 29, 1939; s. G. Harry and Jean (Riddering) H.; m. Martha Jean Pike, Apr. 17, 1972; children: H. Wayne Jr., H. Scott, Ray Goldsby, Pamela Ann. Student, Calvin Coll., 1957-58. Vice chmn., pres., chief operating officer Waste Mgmt. Inc., Oak Brook, Ill., 1968-84; chmn. Huizenga Holdings, Inc., Ft. Lauderdale, Fla., 1984—; chmn., chief exec. officer Blockbuster Entertainment Corp., Ft. Lauderdale, 1987-94; owner Florida Marlins, Miami, 1992—; co-owner Miami Dolphins, Joe Robbie Stadium; owner Florida Panthers, Miami Arena. Mem. Fla. Victory Com., 1988-89, Team Repub. Nat. Com., Washington, 1988-90; organizer Broward Victory 90 PAC, Ft. Lauderdale, 1989-90. Recipient Entrepreneur of Yr. award Wharton Sch. U. Pa., 1989, Excalibur Award Bus. Leader of Yr. News/Sun Sentinel, 1990, Silver Medallion Brotherhood award Broward Region Nat. Conf. Christians and Jews, 1990, Laureates award Jr. Achievement Broward and Palm Beach Counties, 1990, Jim Murphy Humanitarian Award The Emerald Soc., 1990, Entrepreneur of Yr. award Disting. Panel Judges Fla., 1990, Man of Yr. Billboard/Time Mag., 1990, Man of Yr. Juvenile Diabetes Found., 1990, Fla. Free Enterpriser of Yr. award Fla. Coun. on Econ. Edn., 1990, commendation for youth restricted video State of Fla. Office of Gov., 1989, Hon. Mem. Appreciation award Bond Club Ft. Lauderdale, 1989; honored with endowed teaching chair Broward Community Coll., 1990. Mem. Lauderdale Yacht Club, Tournament Players Club, Fisher Island Club, Ocean Reef Club, Cat Cay Yacht Club, Coral ridge Country Club, Linville Ridge Country Club. Avocations: golf, collecting antique cars. Office: Huizenga Holdings 450 E Las Olas Blvd Ste 1500 Fort Lauderdale FL 33301-2291 Office: Huizenga Holdings Inc 200 S Andrews Ave Fort Lauderdale FL 33301-1864*

HUIZENGA, JOHN ROBERT, nuclear chemist, educator; b. Fulton, Ill., Apr. 21, 1921; s. Harry M. and Josie B. (Brands) H.; m. Dorothy J. Koeze, Feb. 1, 1946; children—Linda J., Jann H., Robert J., Joel T. A.B., Calvin Coll., 1944; PhD., U. Ill., 1949. Lab. supr. Manhattan Wartime Project, Oak Ridge, 1944-46; instr. Calvin Coll., Grand Rapids, Mich., 1946-47; assoc. scientist Argonne Nat. Lab., Chgo., 1949-57; sr. scientist Argonne Nat. Lab., 1958-67; professorial lectr. chemistry U. Chgo., 1963-67; prof. chemistry and physics U. Rochester, 1967-78, Tracy H. Harris prof. chemistry and physics, 1978-91, Tracy H. Harris prof. emeritus chemistry and physics, 1991—, chmn. dept. chemistry, 1983-88; vis. prof. Joliot-Curie Lab., U. Paris, 1964-65, Japan Soc. for Promotion of Sci., 1968; chmn. Nat. Acad. Sci.-NRC Com. on Nuclear Sci., 1974-77; mem. energy rsch. adv. bd. Dept. Energy, 1984-90; numerous adv., vis. coms. to univs., govt. and nat. labs. Author: (with R. Vandenbosch) Nuclear Fission, 1973; (with W.U. Schröder) Damped Nuclear Reactions, 1984; Cold Fusion: The Scientific Fiasco of the Century, 1992; contbr. articles to profl. jours. Fulbright fellow Netherlands, 1954-55; Guggenheim fellow Paris, 1964-65; Guggenheim fellow Berkeley, Calif., 1973; Guggenheim fellow Munich, W.Ger., 1974; Guggenheim fellow Copenhagen, 1974; recipient E.O. Lawrence award AEC, 1966, Leroy Rundle Grumman medal, 1991; named Disting. Alumnus Calvin Coll., 1975. Fellow AAAS, Am. Phys. Soc., Am. Acad. Arts and Scis.; mem. NAS (chmn. NAS-NRC com. on nuclear and radiochemistry 1988-91), Am. Chem. Soc. (award for nuclear applications in chemistry 1975), Phi Beta Kappa, Sigma Xi, Phi Kappa Phi. Home: 43 McMichael Dr Pinehurst NC 28374-6702

HUKINS-RODRIGUE, DANA ANN, community health nurse; b. Raceland, La., Nov. 1, 1964; d. Herman Cecil and Diana Ann (Chiasson) H. BSN, Nicholls State U., Thibodaux, La., 1986. RN, La.; sexually transmitted disease nurse clinician. Nurse II, staff pediatrics nurse South La. Med. Ctr., Houma, 1986-88; nurse, pub. health nurse III Lafourche Parish

Health Unit, Thibodaux, 1988—. Mem. Nicholls State U. Nursing Honor Soc., Sigma Theta Tau.

HULBERT, DANIEL JOYCE, theater critic, entertainment writer; b. Mpls., Apr. 8, 1954; s. Dan R. and Elaine (Perry) H.; m. Shelly McCook, Aug. 13, 1989 (div. Jan. 1995); 1 child, George McCook Hulbert; m. Cathleen Dolman, Nov. 2, 1996. BA in English, Yale U., 1976; MA, Columbia U., 1977. News asst. The N.Y. Times, N.Y.C., 1978-81; theater critic Dallas Times Herald, 1981-87, Atlanta Jour./Constn., 1987—. Recipient 3d place citation for criticism, Am. Assn. Sunday and Feature Editors, 1997. Presbyterian. Avocations: reading, golf, hiking, whitewater rafting, tennis. Office: Atlanta Jour/Constn 72 Marietta St NW Atlanta GA 30303-2804

HULBERT, JAMES RICHARD, health care educator, researcher; b. Detroit, July 11, 1944; s. Frank L. and Margaret (Rentenbach) H.; m. Sue Ellen Bell, Aug. 12, 1978. Cert., Georg August U., Göttingen, Germany, 1964-65; BA, U. Iowa, 1967, MA, 1975; MS, Iowa State U., 1982, PhD, 1985. Vol. vocat. agr. tchr. and sch. farm project U.S. Peace Corps, Sarawak, Malaysia, 1967-69; camp dir. Childrens' Home, Cedar Rapids, Iowa, 1969-72; psychiat. asst. Psychiat. Hosp., U. Iowa, Iowa City, 1972-75, coord. biostatis. cons. Coll. Medicine, 1986-90; sch. counselor Marion (Iowa) Schs., 1975-79; rsch. asst. Iowa State U., Ames, 1979-85; sr. rsch. assoc. Wilder Rsch. Found., St. Paul, 1990-93; prof. rsch. dept. Northwestern Coll. Chiropractic, Bloomington, Minn., 1994—; cons. Bell Hulbert Assocs., St. Paul, 1993—. Contbr. articles to profl. jour. Block leader Fairmount Block Club, St. Paul, 1994—. Mem. Am. Statis. Assn., Cairn Terrier Club Am., Twin Cities Cairn Terrier Club. Avocations: all-breed conformation dog shows, fly tying and fishing, homebrewing.. Home: 2133 Fairmount Ave Saint Paul MN 55105-1149 Office: Northwestern Coll Chiropractic 2501 W 84th St Bloomington MN 55431-1602

HULBERT, LINDA ANN, health sciences librarian; b. Racine, Wis., Nov. 10, 1947; d. David and Ruth (Alk) H.; m. A. Kent Rissman, Dec. 1, 1991; m. Shelley B. Plattner, Aug. 24, 1969 (div. 1976). BA, Washington U., St. Louis, 1969; MLS, U. Iowa, Iowa City, 1973; MA in Pub. Adminstrn., St. Louis U., 1993. Sch. librarian Parkway Sch. Dist., St. Louis, 1969-70, Mehlville Sch. Dist., St. Louis, 1970-71; adj. lectr. in libr. science Syracuse U., 1985; med. ref. libr. U. Iowa Health Scis. Ctr., Iowa City, 1973-77; collection devel. librarian SUNY, Health Scis. Ctr., Syracuse, 1977-87; asst. dir. tech. svcs. St. Louis U., 1988; tech. and access svcs. libr. So. Ill. U., Edwardsville, 1998—; cons. in field. Mem. ALA, Med. Libr. Assn. (membership com. 1980-83), St. Louis Med. Libraries (chair 1984-97). Avocations: downhill skiing, biking, walking, reading. Office: So Ill U at Edwardsville Box 1063 Edwardsville IL 62026

HULBERT, PAUL WILLIAM, JR., paper, lumber company executive; b. Washington, June 21, 1944; s. Paul William and Charlotte Mary (Johnson) H.; m. Katharine Bren, Aug. 10, 1985; children: Paul William III, Jennifer Linda, Brian. BA in History, Denison U., 1966; MBA, U. Mich., 1971. Contr. Wickes Land Devel., Saginaw, Mich., 1969-71; mng. dir. Wickes Europe, The Hague, The Netherlands, 1971-75; v.p. corp. devel. Wickes Corp., San Diego, 1975-77; sr. v.p., gen. mgr. Wickes Lumber, Saginaw, 1978-80; sr. v.p., group officer Wickes Cos., Inc., San Diego, 1980-82, Santa Monica, Calif., 1982-85; pres. Sequoia Supply Divsn. Wickes Corp., Irvine, Calif., 1985-86; pres. Sequoia Supply, Inc., Irvine, 1987-89, Prime Source, Inc., Dallas, 1990—. Avocations: sports, coaching youth sports, golf. Office: Prime Source Inc 1800 John Connally Dr Carrollton TX 75006-5403*

HULBERT, RICHARD WOODWARD, lawyer; b. Cambridge, Mass., Sept. 24, 1929; s. Woodward Dennis and Clifford (Halliday) H.; m. Dorothy Marie Hanni, Apr. 21,1954; children: Jonathan, Ann, Laura, Mary. AB, Harvard U., 1951, LLB, 1955. Bar: N.Y. 1956. Assoc. Cleary, Gottlieb, Steen & Hamilton, N.Y.C., 1955-65, ptnr., 1966-83, 89-96; ptnr. Cleary, Gottlieb, Steen & Hamilton, Paris, 1983-89; mng. ptnr. Cleary, Gottlieb, Steen & Hamilton, N.Y.C., 1979-84, of counsel, 1996—; lectr. in law U. Calif., Berkeley, 1988; adj. prof. NYU Law Sch., 1990—; vice chmn. internat. ct. arbitration Internat. C. of C., 1994—. Trustee Bklyn. Mus., 1992—. Sheldon fellow in history Harvard U., 1951-52. Mem. ABA, N.Y. Bar Assn., Assn. of Bar of City of N.Y., Bklyn. Bar Assn., N.Y. County Lawyers Assn., Am. Law Inst., Century Assn., India House, Heights Casino. Democrat. Home: 141 Henry St Brooklyn NY 11201-2501 Office: Cleary Gottlieb et al 1 Liberty Plz Fl 38 New York NY 10006-1470

HULBERT, SAMUEL FOSTER, college president; b. Adams Center, N.Y., Apr. 12, 1936; s. Foster David and Wilma May (Speakman) H.; m. Joy Elinor Husband, Sept. 3, 1960; children: Gregory, Samantha, Jeffrey. B.S. in Ceramic Engring., Alfred U., 1958, Ph.D., 1964. Registered profl. engr., La, S.C. Asst. varsity and freshman football coach Alfred U. (N.Y.), 1959-61; lab. instr. N.Y. State Coll. Ceramics, Alfred, 1958-59; instr. math and physics Alfred U., 1960-64; asst. prof. ceramic and metall. engring. Clemson U. (S.C.), 1964-68, head div. interdisciplinary studies, assoc. prof. materials and bioengring., 1968-71; assoc. dean engring research and interdisciplinary studies, prof. materials engring. and bioengring., dir. materials engring. and bioengring., 1970-73; prof. bioengring., dean Sch. Engring. Tulane U., New Orleans, 1973-76; pres.-designate spl. asst. to pres. Rose-Hulman Inst. Tech., Terre Haute, Ind., 1976, pres., 1976—; bd. dirs. Ind. Bus. Modernization & Tech. Corp., Integral Tech., Inc., Thomas & Skinner, Inc., Civitas Bank. Mem. editorial bd. Annals of Biomed. Engring., 1974, Jour. Biomed. Materials Rsch., 1970—; contbr. articles in field of biomaterials and artificial organ design to profl. jours. Mem. exec. com. Wabash Valley chpt. Boy Scouts Am.; mem. Ind. Humanities Coun., 1991—. Recipient medal Italian Soc. Orthopaedics, 1973, Delitala medal Instituto Ortopedico Rizzoli, 1973, Clemson award for outstanding contbns. to biomaterials, 1973, George Winters award European Soc. Biomaterials, 1982, Lifetime Achievement award Ind. Health Industry Forum, 1996; Ernst & Young Supporter of Indiana Entrepreneurship award, 1998. Fellow Am. Inst. for Med. and Biol. Engring., Bionatal Scis. and Engring., Internat. Acad. Ceramics; mem. Am. Soc. Artificial Internal Organs, Biomed. Engring. Soc., Soc. Biomaterials (dir. 1974—, pres. 1975-76), Am. Ceramic Soc., Nat. Inst. Ceramics Engrs., Am. Soc. Engring. Edn., Ind. Colls. and Univs. Assn., Ind. Colls. of Ind., Ind. Conf. Higher Edn., Assn. Ind. Tech. Univs. (sec., treas. 1977-78, pres. 1987-90), Presidents of Ind. Colls. and Univs., Vigo County Hist. Soc. (dir. 1979—, pres. 1995—), Keramos, Blue Key, Ind. Acad., Internat. Acad. Ceramics, Rotary, Sigma Xi. Republican. Office: Rose Hulman Inst Tech Office of Pres 5500 Wabash Ave Terre Haute IN 47803-3999

HULBERT, STEPHEN, state agency administrator. BS in Edn., Worcester (Mass.) State Coll., 1966; MEd, U. Mass., 1968; DEd, SUNY, Albany, 1972. Dir. student activities and residence life Western New England Coll., Springfield, Mass., 1968-70; cons. Univ. Assocs. Inc., Washington, 1971-72; exec. asst. to the pres. Mansfield (Pa.) U., 1972-77; v.p. for fin. and adminstrn. Slippery Rock (Pa.) U., 1977-88; v.p. adminstrv. svcs., treas. bd. trustees U. Northern Colo., Greeley, 1988-91; interim pres. U. Northern Colo., 1991, sr. v.p., 1992-94, provost, v.p. for acad. affairs, 1994-96; commr. higher edn., CEO R.I. Bd. of Govs. for Higher Edn., Providence, 1996—; govs. cabinet State of R.I. and Providence Plantations; mem. R.I. Juvenile Justice Oversight Commn. Mcpl. coun. Grove City, Pa., 1986-88; adv. bd. Franklin Regional Hosp., Franklin, Pa., 1985-88; exec. bd. Longs Peak Coun. of Boy Scouts Am., 1991-96, disting. citizen com. chair, 1992, others; mayor's adv. task force City of Greeley, 1992-96, Lincoln Park planning com., 1989-92, privatization com., 1989; bd. dirs. The Greeley Dream Team, Inc., 1991, U. No. Colo. Found., Inc., 1991-96, R.I. Children's Crusade for Higher Edn., U. of No. Colo. Rsch. Corp., Inc., 1988-96, chair 1994-96, vice chair 1992-94, corp. treas. 1988-92; bd. advisors Edn. Comms. Consortia, Inc., 1988—; legis. liaison com. Colo. Commn. on Higher Edn., 1989-92; bd. govs. Colo. Alliance for Sci., 1995-96. Mem. Am. Assn. for Higher Edn., State Higher Edn. Exec. Officers, Nat. Assn. of System Heads, Phi Delta Kappa. Fax: 401-222-2545. E-mail: shulbert@etal.uri.edu. Home: 59 Tilden Ave Newport RI 02840 Office: Office of Higher Edn 301 Promenade St Providence RI 02908-5748

HULBURT, LUCILLE HALL, artist, educator; b. Portland, Oreg., Oct. 31, 1924; d. Allen Bergen and Agnes Edna (Davis) Hall; m. Frank Theodore Hulburt, Nov. 28, 1943; children: Robert, Carol Davalos, Clarke. Grad. h.s., Whitefish, Mont. Asst. milliner, illustrator Hat Co., N.Y.C., 1944; cafe owner, operator San Diego, 1950-52; profl. artist Vancouver, Wash., 1978—; resident artist Artist's Gallery 21, Vancouver, 1988—; tchr. children and adult art clases, schs. and home studio, Vancouver, 1978—; artist in residence Wash. State Arts Commn., 1987-88; co-founder, coop. Artists Gallery 21, Vancouver, 1988—; cons. nat. Western Art Show and Auction, Trails West, Vancouver; organizer, com. mem. ann. Summer Art at the Ctr., Vancouver, 1986; judge/jurist art exhibits at county fairs, western art shows various locations in Wash. and Oreg., 1980—. Founder, pres. Boundary Assn. Retarded Children, Bonners Ferry, Idaho, 1964-65; com. mem. 1st Bldg. Com., Columbia Arts Ctr., Vancouver, 1980-81; bd. mem. Local Arts Promotion, Vancouver, 1992, 93. Recipient Best of Show award Western Art Show and Auction, Chinook, Mont., 1983, 84, Community Svc. award Arts Coun., Clark County, Wash., 1988, Windsor-Newton award Watercolor 91, 1991. Mem. S.W. Wash. Watercolor Soc. (co-founder, pres. 1979, 80, 84), Soc. Washington Artists (Grumbacher Silver medal 1990), Am. Artists Profl. League, Order Ea. Star (life), N.W. Watercolor Soc. Avocations: gardening, sewing, swimming. Office: Hulburt Studio 5515 NE 58th St Vancouver WA 98661-2146

HULCE, DURWARD PHILIP, theatrical lighting designer; b. Baton Rouge, Apr. 30, 1948; s. Durward Clare and Kathryn Venita (Lee) H. BA, La. State U., 1974; cert. completion, Patrice Lumumba U., Moscow, 1975. Head stage electrician Miller Outdoor Theater, Houston, 1984-90; tour leader Ariel Birding Tours, 1986—; theatrical lighting designer Nightlights of Houston, 1988—; head stage electrician Houston Ballet, 1991—. Editor: Texas Gulf Coast Birding And Naturalist Web. Houston Audubon Soc. (pres. 1997-99, bd. dirs. 1995—). Sgt. USAF, 1968-72. Mem. Am. Ornithol. Union, Cooper Ornithol. Soc., Wilson Ornithol. Soc., Orgn. for Tropical Studies, Internat. Coun. for Bird Preservation, Tex. Ornithol. Soc. (life), Houston Outdoor Nature Club, compiler Houston, Old River & Trinity River xmas birds counts. Avocations: birding, ornithology, tropical ecology, Christmas bird counts. Home and Office: Ariel Birding Tours 339 W 23rd St Houston TX 77008-2030

HULCE, RANDY C., hotel executive. BS in Sociology/Bus., Western Mich. U.; MBA, Northwestern U. With Holiday Inn World Wide, divisional v.p., sr. asset mgr.; with Sunstone Hotel Properities; pres. Sunstone Hotel Properties, San Clemente. Office: Sunstone Hotel Mgmt Inc PO Box 4240 San Clemente CA 92672-4240

HULCE, TOM, actor; b. Detroit, Dec. 6, 1953. Student, N.C. Sch. Arts. Broadway theater debut in Equus, 1975; off-Broadway appearances include A Memory of Two Mondays, 1976, Candida, 1977, Innocent Thoughts and Harmless Intentions, 1977, Julius Caesar, 1978, SummerFolk, 1979, The Seagull, 1980, Romeo and Juliet, 1981, Twelve Dreams, 1981-82, The Rise and Fall of Daniel Rocket, 1982, The Glass Menagerie, 1985, The Normal Heart, 1986, Haddock's Eyes, 1987, Eastern Standard, 1988, Nothing Sacred, 1988, A Few Good Men, 1990; films include September 30, 1955, 1978, Nat. Lampoon's Animal House, 1978, Those Lips, Those Eyes, 1980, Amadeus, 1984 (Acad. Award Best Actor nomination Acad. Motion Picture Arts and Scis.), Echo Park, 1986, Slam Dance, 1987, Shadow Man, 1988, Dominick and Eugene, 1988, Parenthood, 1989, Black Rainbow, 1989, The Inner Circle, 1992, Fearless, 1993, Mary Shelley's Frankenstein, 1994, Wings of Courage, 1995, Hunchback of Notre Dame (voice), 1996; appeared in TV films John Henry, 1987, Murder in Mississippi, 1990 (Golden Globe award nomination), The Heidi Chronicles, 1995, TV series The Adams Chronicles, 1976. Office: Creative Artists Agy 9830 Wilshire Blvd Beverly Hills CA 90212-1825*

HULIN, FRANCES C., prosecutor. AB, Northwestern U., 1957; JD, U. Ill., Urbana, 1971. Bar: Ill. 1973. Asst. states atty. Champaign County, IL, 1973-76, Macon County, Ill., 1977-78; prosecutor U.S. Attys. Office, Ctrl. Dist. Ill., 1978-93; U.S. atty. Dept. Justice, Springfield, Ill., 1993—. Office: US Attys Office 600 E Monroe St Ste 312 Springfield IL 62701-1626

HULING, MORRIS, fire chief; b. Albuquerque, N.M., June 2, 1955. Fire fighter City of Albuquerque, 1978-97, fire chief, 1997—. Office: Fire Dept PO Box 2086 Albuquerque NM 87103-2086*

HULINGS, NORMAN MCDERMOTT, JR., energy consultant, former company executive; b. Tulsa, Aug. 25, 1923; s. Norman McDermott and Mildred Lillian (Marr) H.; children—Sharon Lee, Lisa Marr. B.S. in Petroleum Prodn. Engring, U. Tulsa, 1949. Registered profl. engr., Okla. With Okla. Natural Gas Co., 1949-80; v.p. gas supply Okla. Natural Gas Co., Tulsa, 1960-73; sr. v.p. Okla. Natural Gas Co., 1973-80; pres. ONEOK Energy Cos., Tulsa, 1980-86; pvt. practice cons. in oil and gas, 1986—; adv. com. engring. dept. Tulsa U. Bd. dirs. Tulsa chpt. ARC, Tulsa Philharmonic Orchestra; naval aviator. Lt. comdr. USNR, 1942-65. Named to Hall of Fame U. Tulsa, 1979. Mem. AIME, Am. Gas Assn. (award merit 1963), Ind. Petroleum Assn. Am., Interstate Natural Gas Assn., Interstate Oil Compact Commn. Home and Office: 7430 S Winston Ave Tulsa OK 74136-6118*

HULKA, BARBARA SORENSON, epidemiology educator; b. Mpls., Mar. 1, 1931; d. Herbert Fritchof and Mable (Alquist) Sorenson; m. Jaroslav Fabian Hulka, Nov. 13, 1954; children: Carol Ann, Gregory Fabian, Bryan Herbert. BS, Radcliffe Coll., 1952; MS, Juilliard Sch. Music, 1954; MD, Columbia U., 1959, MPH, 1961. Diplomate: Am. Bd. Preventive Medicine; Lic. physician, Pa., N.C. Research asst. prof. U. Pitts., 1966-67; asst. prof. U. N.C., Chapel Hill, 1967-71, assoc. prof., 1972-76, prof., 1977—, chmn. dept. epidemiology, 1983-93, Kenan prof., 1987—; adj. prof. medicine Duke U. Med. Ctr., Durham, N.C., 1982—; chmn. epidemiology and disease study sect. NIH, 1979-83, mem. Endpoint Rev. Safety Monitoring and Adv. Com., Breast Cancer Prevention Trial, Nat. Surg. Adjuvant Breast and Bowel Project, 1992—; bd. sci. counselors Nat. Cancer Inst., 1980—; mem. Inst. of Medicine com. toxic shock syndrome Nat. Acad. Sci., 1981-82; mem. Sci. Rev. and Evaluation Bd. subcom. VA, 1983—; mem. subcom. on long-term effects of short-term exposure to chem. agts. Nat. Acad. Scis., 1985—; mem. preventive medicine and pub. health test com. Nat. Bd. Med. Examiners, 1985—; mem. consensus conf. on smokeless tobacco Nat. Cancer Inst. Panel, 1986; chair WHO steering com. of Task Force on Safety and Efficacy of Fertility Regulating Methods, 1990—; counsellor Internat. Soc. for Environ. Epidemiology, 1990—; mem. Pres.' Cancer Panel Spl. Commn. on Breast Cancer, Nat. Cancer Inst., 1992-93; mem. bd. scientific counselors divsn. cancer etiology, Nat. Cancer Inst., NIH, 1992—; chair WHO steering com. of task force Epidemiologic rsch. in reproductive health, WHO, 1990—. Mem. editorial bd. Postgrad. Medicine, 1985—; assoc. editor Cancer Epidemiology, Biomarkers and Prevention, 1995; contbr. articles to profl. jours., chpts. to books. Bd. dirs. Am. Cancer Soc., 1993—. Recipient Disting. Achievement award Am. Soc. Preventive Oncology, 1991; Health Resources Adminstrn. grantee, 1975-77; tng. grantee in cancer epidemiology Nat. Cancer Inst., 1980—; prostate cancer grantee Nat. Cancer Inst., 1983-85; travel study fellow WHO, 1978. Fellow Royal Soc. Medicine; mem. APHA (governing coun. 1976-78, chmn. epidemiol. sect. 1976-77), NAS (Inst. Medicine 1988, mem. com. crossroads nuclear test 1994, mem. comm. antiprogestins 1992-93, mem. com. passive smoking 1985—), Am. Coll. Epidemiology (Abraham Lilienfield award 1994), Soc. Epidemiol. Rsch. (pres. 1975-76, exec. com. 1973-77), Am. Epidemiol. Soc., N.C. Pub. Health Assn. (award for excellence, stats. and epidemiology sect. 1975), Am. Coll. Preventive Medicine (bd. regents 1986), Delta Omega. Home: 2317 Honeysuckle Dr Chapel Hill NC 27514 Office: U NC Sch Pub Health Dept Epidemiol CB 7400 2104 E McGavran-Grnbrg Hall Chapel Hill NC 27599*

HULKA, JAROSLAV FABIAN, obstetrician, gynecologist; b. N.Y.C., Sept. 29, 1930; s. Jaroslav Hugo and Milada (Touskova) H.; m. Barbara E. Sorenson, Nov. 13, 1954; children—Carol Ann, Gregory Fabian, Bryan Herbert. B.A., Harvard U., 1952; M.D., Columbia U., 1956. Diplomate: Am. Bd. Ob-Gyn. Intern Roosevelt Hosp., N.Y.C., 1956-57; resident Sloane Hosp. for Women, Columbia-Presbyn. Med. Center, N.Y.C., 1957-60; Josiah Macy, Jr. fellow Columbia-Presbyn. Med. Center, 1960-61; practice medicine specializing in Ob-Gyn, 1961—; asst. prof. Ob-Gyn U. Pitts. Sch. Medicine, 1961-66, asso. mem. grad. faculty, 1962-66, acting chmn. dept. Ob-Gyn, 1963-64; asso. prof. dept. Ob-Gyn Sch. Medicine, U. N.C., Chapel Hill, 1967-76; prof. dept. Ob-Gyn and dept. maternal and child health Sch. Medicine, U. N.C., 1976-96. Author: Textbook of Laparoscopy, 1985, 3d edit., 1997; patentee in field. Assoc. dir. Carolina Population Center, 1967-74. Recipient Excel award Soc. of Laparoendoscopic Surgeons, 1994. Fellow ACOG; mem. Soc. for Gynecol. Investigation, Am. Assn. Gynecol. Laparoscopists (pres. 1980), Am. Fertility Soc., Soc. Reproductive Surgeons (founding), N.C. State Bar (legal specialization 1990-96), Planned Parenthood Fed. Am. (chair nat. med. com. 1991-94), Soc. Physicians for Reproductive Choice and Health (founding). Home: 2317 Honeysuckle Rd Chapel Hill NC 27514-1716 Office: U NC Hosp Dept Ob-Gyn Chapel Hill NC 27514

HULKO, ROBERT LEE, recording studio executive; b. Port Arthur, Ont., Can., June 28, 1941; s. Leo Birger and Anne Freda (Smedberg) H. Student, Ryerson Poly., Toronto, Ont., 1960. Rec. engr. Toronto (Ontario) Bd. of Edn., 1961-64; tech. dir. Univ. N.Y., Buffalo, N.Y., 1964-66; free lance engr. N.Y.C., 1966-68; pres. Sterling Sound Inc., N.Y.C., 1968-98, Katmandu Corp., 1999—. Mem. Soc. Motion Picture and TV Engrs., Audio Engring. Soc., NARAS. Office: PO Box 219 Solebury PA 18963

HULL, BRETT A., professional hockey player; b. Belleville, Ont., Can., Aug. 9, 1964; s. Bobby Hull. Student, U. Minn., Duluth, 1984-86. Profl. hockey player Calgary Flames, 1986-88; with St. Louis Blues, 1988-96; forward Dallas Stars, Dallas, 1997-; player NHL All-Star team, 1989-94, AHL All-Star first team, 1986-87, NHL All-Star first team, 1989-90, 91-92. Recipient Lady Byng Meml. Trophy 1989, 90, Hart Meml. trophy, 1990-91, WCHA Freshman of the Year award, 1984-85, Dudley Garrett Meml. trophy, 1986-87, Dodge Ram Tough award, 1989-90, 90-91, Lester B. Pearson award, 1990-91, Pro Set NHL Player of the Year award, 1990-91; named Sporting News NHL Player of Yr., 1990-91, Sporting News All-Star first team, 1989-90, 91-92, All-Star game Most Valuable Player, 1992; Stanley Cup Champions, Dallas Stars, 1999. Led NHL in Goals Scored, 1989-92. Office: Dallas Stars 211 Cowboys Pkwy Irving TX 75063*

HULL, CATHY, artist, illustrator; b. N.Y.C., Nov. 4, 1946; d. Max H. and Magda M. (Stern) H.; m. Neil S. Janovic; 1 child, Julie. B.A., Conn. Coll., 1968; cert., Sch. Visual Arts, N.Y.C., 1970. Instr. illustration and portfolio Sch. Visual Arts, N.Y.C., 1983-94, Parsons Sch. Design, N.Y.C., 1994—; juror The 6th World Cartoon Gallery, Skopje, 1974, Soc. Pub. Designers, N.Y.C., 1982, Soc. Illustrators, N.Y.C., 1983, The Biennale of Humor, Fredrikstad, Norway, 1987, The 6th Internat. Simavi Cartoon Competition, Istanbul, Turkey, 1988. Contbr. to anthologies, books, mags. and newspapers including Time, Penthouse, Newsweek, Esquire, Sports Illustrated, N.Y. Times, Bus. Week, Travel & Leisure, Money, others; group shows include The 17th Nat. Print Exhbn., Bklyn., 1970, AIGA Show, N.Y.C., 1970-71, 74, Printing Industries Am., 1971, Soc. Illustrators, 1973, 80, 85, 94, World Cartoon Gallery, Skopje, 1972-75, Art Dir.'s Club, 1974, 82, Internat. Cartoon Exhbn., Istanbul, Turkey, 1974, Switzerland, 1974, 78, 80, 82, 90, Athens, Greece, 1975, Soc. Publ. Designers, 1974, 82, Musée de Beaubourg, Paris, 1977, Pacific Design Ctr., L.A., 1980, The Md. Inst., 1981, Scottsdale (Ariz.) Ctr. for Arts, 1981, Soc. Newspaper Design, 1984-85, Butler Inst. Am. Art, Youngstown, Ohio, 1983, Am. Peace Poster Exhibit, 1985, Quebec City Exhbn.; represented in permanent collections including Mus. Caricatures and Cartoons, Basel, Switzerland, 1980, 90, Soc. Illustrators Advt. Ann. show, 1993, Smithtown Twp. Arts Coun., 1995; designer playing cards sold at Cooper Hewitt Mus., N.Y., N.Y. Pub. Libr., L.A. County Mus. Art, St. Louis Art Mus., Chgo. Mus. Art, Nat. Mus. Scotland, Seibu, Japan, Contemporary Mus. of Honolulu, Contemporary Mus. San Diego, High Mus. Atlanta, others. Office: 180 E 79th St New York NY 10021-0437

HULL, CHARLES, performing company executive; b. Vienna, Austria; m. Ann Hull; children: Alizon, Hilary. BSBA, Lehigh U. Mng. dir. Theatreworks/USA, N.Y.C., 1969—; pres. Prodr. League Theatre for Young Audiences.; creator subscription series for Off-Broadway theatre; developer Field Trip program; mgr. touring program. former actor commls., Off Broadway prodns. With USAF. Mem. Prodrs. Assn. Children's Theatre (pres.). Office: Theatreworks/USA 151 W 26th St New York NY 10001-6810*

HULL, CHARLES WILLIAM, special education educator; b. East St. Louis, Ill., Feb. 23, 1936; s. William Semple Hull and Jessie Marie (Brennan) Poole; m. Beverly Kay Julian, Aug. 19, 1967; 1 child, William Kenneth. BA in Econs., Cen. Meth. Coll., 1964; MEd, Olivet Nazarene Coll., 1974; AA (hon.), Joliet Jr. Coll., 1987. Tchr. elem. grades Taft Sch., Lockport, Ill., 1965-67; tchr. spl. edn. S.W. Cook County Coop. Assn. for Spl. Edn., Oak Forest, Ill., 1967—. Permanent exhibits include Tchr's Ret. Office Bldg., Springfield, Ill. Past bd. dirs., v.p., chmn. fund raising Easter Seals Will and Grundy Counties; dist. leader Am. Cancer Soc., 1984, residential campaign chmn., 1985; vol., mem. adv. bd. Big Bros.-Big Sisters Will County; Cub Scouts com. chmn. Boy Scouts Am., 1980-81, commr. Rainbow coun., bd. dirs. troop 6l; mem. choir, past trustee Faith United Meth. Ch.; Will County walkathon chmn. March of Dimes, 1979; chmn. Canal Days events Will County Hist. Soc., 1987; active numerous other orgns. Cpl. USMC, 1955-58. Recipient Congl. Medal of Merit, 1985, Frederick Bartleson Meml. award Will County Hist. Soc., 1985, Citizen of Week award Sta. WBBM, Chgo., 1985, Leadership award Am. Cancer Soc., 1985, Outstanding Svc. award Big Bros.-Big Sisters Will County, letter of commendation Pres. of U.S., 1986, 89, Disting. Svc. award Joliet Jr. Coll., 1987, Citizen of Month award Southtown Economist, plaque KC. Mem. 1st Marine Div. Assn., Coun. for Exceptional Children, Internat. Platform Assn., Will County Old-Timers Baseball Assn., Am. Legion, Masons (32 degree), Shriners (pres. Joliet club 1983, Shriner of Yr. 1989), KC, Moose, Medina Temple, Lions (pres. Manhattan club 1984, chmn. youth and fgn. exch. dist. 1986-87, bd. dirs. Lockport chpt.), Will County Hist. Soc. (pres. 1989), Royal Order Scotland, Masons, Phi Delta Kappa. Republican. Methodist. Home: 403 N Farrell Rd Lockport IL 60441-2363 Office: SW Cook County Coop Assn Spl Edn 6020 151st St Oak Forest IL 60452-1841

HULL, CORDELL WILLIAM, business executive; b. Dayton, Ohio, Sept. 12, 1933; s. Murel George and Julia (Barto) H.; m. Susan G. Ruder, May 10, 1958; children: Bradford W., Pamela H., Andrew R. B.E., U. Dayton, 1956; M.S., MIT, 1957; J.D., Harvard U., 1962. Bar: Ohio 1962; Registered profl. engr., Mass. Atty. Taft, Stettinius & Hollister, Cin., 1962-64, C & I Girdler, Cin., 1964-66; gen. counsel, treas., pres. C&I Girdler, Internat., Brussels, 1966-70; v.p. Bechtel Overseas Corp., San Francisco, 1970-73; pres., dir. Am. Express Mcht. Bank, London, 1973-75; v.p., treas. Bechtel Corp. and Bechtel Power, San Francisco, 1975-80; pres. Bechtel Fin. Services, San Francisco, 1975-82; v.p., chief fin. officer Bechtel Group Inc., 1980-85; pres. Bechtel Power Corp., 1987-89, dir.; chmn. Bechtel Enterprises, 1990-95; bd. dirs., mem. exec. com. Sequoia Ventures, Inc., Fremont Group, Inc., Bechtel Group, Inc.; chmn. C. Hull Enterprises; bd. dirs. Darby Overseas Ltd. Trustee U. Dayton. Mem. Bankers Club, Knickerbocker Club, Pacific Union Club, Links, Menlo Country Club, Am. Soc. Macro Engrs. Office: Bechtel Group Inc 50 Beale St San Francisco CA 94105-1813 also: C Hull Enterprise 5800 El Camino Real Ste 240 Menlo Park CA 94025-4875

HULL, DAVID GEORGE, aerospace engineering educator, researcher; b. Oak Park, Ill., Mar. 27, 1937; s. John Lawrence Hull and Elizabeth Christine (Carstensen) Meyer; m. Meredith Lynn Kiesel, June 2, 1962 (div. July 1980); children: David, Andrew, Matthew; m. Vicki Jan Poole, June 30, 1983; children: Katherine, Emily. BS, Purdue U., 1959; MS, U. Wash., 1962; PhD, Rice U., 1967. Staff assoc. Boeing Sci. Research Labs., Seattle, 1959-64; research assoc. Rice U., Houston, 1964-66; asst. prof. U. Tex., Austin, 1966-71, assoc. prof., 1971-77, prof., 1977-85, M.J. Thompson Regents prof., 1985—; cons. several aerospace cos. Assoc. editor 2 jours.; reviewer several engring. jours.; contbr. more than 50 articles to profl. jours. Recipient/corecipient more than 50 grants and contracts; recipient award Best paper, AAS/AIAA Space Flt. Mechanics Conf., Albuquerque, 1995. Fellow AIAA (assoc., atmospheric flight mechanics tech. com. 1974-77, guidance and control tech. com. 1984-87); mem. AAS (sr. mem.), Delta Tau Delta (treas. Purdue U. 1958-59). Office: U Tex ASE/EM C0600 Austin TX 78712

HULL, DAVID STEWART, literary agency executive; b. Oshkosh, Wis., Mar. 21, 1938; s. Erastus Hewitt and Charlotte Anne (v. Kussowitz) H.; B.A. (gen. fellow 1960), Dartmouth Coll., 1960; postgrad. U. London, 1960-61. Story editor Universal Pictures-MCA, East Coast office, 1966-69; editor Coward McCann, Inc. N.Y.C., 1970-71; v.p. James Brown Assocs., Inc., N.Y.C., 1971-81; lit. agt. Peter Lampack Agy., N.Y.C., 1981-87; pres. Hull

House Lit. Agy., Inc., 1987—. Vestryman, Episc. Ch. of the Resurrection, N.Y.C.; guest curator New-York Hist. Soc., 1986. Served to 2nd lt., USAR, 1961-62. Clubs: Coffee House, St. George's Soc. Author: Film in the Third Reich, 1969, 2nd edit., 1973; James Henry Cafferty, N.A., 1986. Hon. friend of Am. wing Met. Mus. Art, 1987—. Home and Office: 240 E 82nd St New York NY 10028-2703

HULL, DENNIS JACQUES, counselor; b. Orange, N.J., June 8, 1945; s. Jacques Lionel and Ora May (Holdman) H.; m. Elizabeth Ann Martin, Sept. 7, 1969; 1 child, Jonathan. BA in Psychology, Calif. State Univ., Hayward, 1968, MS in Counseling, 1975. Cert. counselor Nat. Bd. Cert. Counselors, Inc. Counselor L.A. Harbor Coll., Wilmington, Calif., 1979-84; counselor Western Nev. C.C., Carson City, 1984-86, coord. counseling svcs., 1987-94, dir. counseling svcs., 1994—. With USAF, 1968-72. Mem. Am. Counseling Assn., Nat. Acad. Advising Assn., Calif. Assn. Counseling Devel., Calif. C.C. Counselors Assn. (bd. dirs., so. conf. chair 1983-84), Nev. Counselors Assn., Nev. Coll. Counselors Assn. Office: Western Nev Cmty Coll 2201 W College Pkwy Carson City NV 89703-7316

HULL, ELAINE MANGELSDORF, psychology educator; b. Houston, Aug. 15, 1940; d. Paul August and Mary Eleanor (Stephens) Mangelsdorf; m. Richard Thompson Hull, May 30, 1962; 1 child, Geoffrey Alaric (dec.). BA, Austin Coll., Sherman, Tex., 1963; PhD, Ind. U., 1967. Asst. prof. psychology SUNY, Buffalo, 1967-73, assoc. prof., 1973-86, prof., 1986—, dir. biopsychology grad. program, 1986—. Author: Study Guide to Accompany Kalat's Biological Psychology, 1988; contbr. articles to sci. jours. Recipient Chancellor's award for excellence in teaching SUNY, Buffalo, 1975, award for teaching SUNY Students Assn., 1986, N.Y. State Union of Univ. Profls. Excellence award 1990. Mem. AAAS, Soc. for Neurosci., Internat. Soc. for Psychoneuroendocrinology, Ea. Psychol. Assn., N.Y. Acad. Sci. Democrat. Avocations: jogging, classical music. Office: SUNY Park Hall Buffalo NY 14260

HULL, FRANK MAYS, federal judge; b. Augusta, Ga., Dec. 9, 1948; d. James M. Hull Jr. and Frank (Mays) Pride; m. Antonin Aeck, Apr. 16, 1977; children: Richard Hull Aeck, Molly Hull Aeck. AB, Randolph-Macon Women's Coll., 1970; JD cum laude, Emory U., 1973. Bar: Ga. 1973, U.S. Ct. Appeals (5th cir.) 1973, U.S. Dist. Ct. (no. dist.) Ga. 1974, U.S. Ct. Appeals (11th cir.) 1982. Law clk. to Hon. Elbert P. Tuttle U.S. Ct. Appeals (5th cir.), Atlanta, 1973-74; assoc. Powell, Goldstein, Frazer & Murphy, Atlanta, 1974-80, ptnr., 1980-84; judge State Ct. Fulton County, Atlanta, 1984-90, Superior Ct. Fulton County, Atlanta, 1990-94, U.S. Dist. Ct. (no. dist.) Ga., 1994-97, U.S. Ct. Appeals (11th cir.), 1997—; mem. commn. on family violence State of Ga., 1992-94, commn. on gender bias in jud. sys., 1988-90. Bd. dirs. Met. Atlanta Mediation Ctr., Inc., 1976-79, Atlanta Vol. Lawyers Assn., 1988-91; mem. Leadership Atlanta, 1986—, program co-chair criminal justice com., 1988-89; Sunday sch. tchr. Cathedral St. Philip, Atlanta, 1983-88, childrens com., 1981-82, outreach com., 1989-91. Fellow AAUW, 1973—. Mem. ABA (fin. sec. long range planning com. tort and ins. practice sect. 1979-82, chmn. contract documents divsn., forum com. on constrn. industry 1983-85, editl. staff jour. 1981-85, vice chmn. fidelity and surety law com. 1978-85), Ga. Bar Assn., Am. Judicature Soc. (bd. dirs. 1990-96), Atlanta Bar Assn., Ga. Assn. Women Lawyers, Nat. Assn. Women Judges, Order of Coif. Office: US Ct of Appeals 56 Forsyth St NW Atlanta GA 30303-2289

HULL, GRAFTON HAZARD, JR., social work educator; b. Great Bend, Kans., Nov. 24, 1943; s. Grafton H. and Mary Kathryn (Hagerty) H.; m. Jannah Mather; children: Michael, Patrick, Robert Hurn, Jacob Hurn. BS, U. Wis., Madison, 1967; MSW, Fla. State U., 1969; EdD, U. S.D., 1979. Social worker Cen. State Hosp., Milledgeville, Ga., 1969; chief social work sect. Mental Hygiene Cons. Svc., Ft. Knox, Ky., 1969-71; social worker, then social work supr. Manitowoc County Dept. Social Svc., Manitowoc, Ky., 1971-74; asst. prof., chair dept. sociology Morningside Coll., Sioux City, Iowa, 1974-79; assoc. prof., chair dept. social welfare U. Wis., Whitewater, 1979-82, prof., chair dept., 1982-88; prof., chair dept. social work U. Wis., Eau Claire, 1988-93; dir. Sch. Social Work S.W. Mo. State U., Springfield, 1993-96; dir. divsn social work Ind. Univ. NW, Gary, 1996—; site visitor Coun. Social Work Edn., Washington, 1981—; cons. in field. Co-author: Understanding Generalist Practice, Building the Undergraduate Social Work Library, Case Studies in Generalist Practice, Generalist Practice with Organizations and Communities, The Macro Skills Workbook; cons. editor Jour. Social Work Edn., 1989-95, Aretê, 1993—; mem. editl. bd. Advances in Social Work; contbr. articles to profl. jours. Bd. dirs. Gary Neighborhood Svcs., Lake United Visitation Ctr.; chmn. Landmarks Commn., Whitewater, 1982-88; city councilman, mem. Planning and Architecture Rev. Commn., City of Whitewater, 1987-88. Capt. U.S. Army, 1969-71. Recipient Wis. Social Work Educator of Yr., 1991, City of Whitewater Hist. Preservation award, 1988, Outstanding Svc. award U. Wis.-Eau Claire, 1993, Outstanding Social Worker award Ind. House of Reps., 1999. Mem. NASW (chair west ctrl. Wis. br. 1989-91), Baccalaureate Program Dirs. Assn. (pres. 1991-93), Coun. Social Work Edn. (commn. on accreditation 1987-93, bd. dirs. 1993-96), Wis. Coun. Social Work Edn. (pres. 1984-91), Inst. Advancement Social Work Rsch. (sec.-treas. 1993-95), Mo. Consortium of Social Work Edn. Programs (pres. 1995-96), Ind. Assn. for Social Work Edn. Democrat. Avocations: travel. Home: 802 W 66th Pl Merrillville IN 46410-3221 Office: Ind Univ NW Gary IN 46408

HULL, GRETCHEN GAEBELEIN, lay worker, writer, lecturer; b. Bklyn., Feb. 5, 1930; d. Frank Ely and Dorothy Laura (Medd) Gaebelein; m. Philip Glasgow Hull, Oct. 24, 1952; children: Jeffrey R., Sanford D., Meredyth Hull Smith. BA magna cum laude, Bryn Mawr Coll., 1950; postgrad., Columbia U., 1950-52; DLitt (hon.), Houghton Coll., 1995. Major presenter Internat. Coun. on Bibl. Inerrancy, Chgo., 1986; guest lectr. London Inst. on Contemporary Christianity, 1988; lectr. at large Christians for Bibl. Equality, St. Paul, 1988—; major presenter Presbyn. Ch. (U.S.A.) Nat. Abortion Dialogue, Kansas City, Mo., 1989; disting. scholar lectr. Thomas F. Staley Found., Stony Brook, N.Y., 1991; elder Presbyn. Ch. (U.S.A.); mem. Madison Ave. Presbyn. Ch., N.Y.C.; vis. prof. Regent Coll., Vancouver, B.C., 1992. Author: Equal to Serve, 1987; (with others) Women, Authority and the Bible, 1986, Applying the Scriptures, 1987, Study Bible for Women (New Testament), 1996, The Global God, 1998; editor Priscilla Papers, 1989—; contbg. editor Perspectives, 1992—; mem. editl. bd. Prism, 1994—; contbr. articles to religious mags. Trustee Cold Spring Harbor Village Improvement Soc., 1966-69, Soc. of St. Johnland, Kings Park, N.Y., 1972-75. Mem. Woman's Union Missionary Soc. Am. (bd. dirs. 1954-71), Presbyns. United for Bibl. Concerns (bd. dirs. 1973-75), L.I. Presbytery (gen. coun. 1981-83), Christians for Bibl. Equality (bd. dirs. 1987-94), Latin Am. Mission (trustee 1989-95), Evangelicals for Social Action (bd. dirs. 1991-99), Network Presbyn. Women in Leadership (steering com. 1994-98), Presbyterians for Renewal (bd. dirs. 1994—). Home and Office: Oyster Bay Cove 1120 Cove Edge Rd Syosset NY 11791-9602

HULL, HERBERT MITCHELL, plant physiologist, researcher; b. La Jolla, Calif., Aug. 19, 1919; s. Daniel Ray and Emma (Kammeyer) H.; m. Mary Randall Mattison, Mar. 4, 1950; children: Laurinda Lee, Daniel James. A.A., Pasadena City Coll., 1939; B.S., U. Calif., Berkeley, 1946; Ph.D., Calif. Inst. Tech., 1951. Research fellow Calif. Inst. Tech., 1949-52; plant physiologist U.S. Dept. Agr., Tucson, 1952-78; prof. renewable natural resources U. Ariz., 1966-85, prof. emeritus, 1985—. Served with USAAF, 1941-46. Fellow AAAS, Ariz.-Nev. Acad. Sci.; mem. Am. Soc. Plant Physiologists, Bot. Soc. Am., Sigma Xi, Alpha Zeta, Delta Kappa Omicron. Presbyterian. Home: 4040 W Sweetwater Dr Tucson AZ 85745-9757

HULL, JAMES ERNEST, religion and philosophy educator; b. Laurel, Miss., June 30, 1928; s. Tillette Reyphord and Gladys Evelyn (Reeves) H.; m. Jo Welch, July 7, 1956; children: Alan Walter, Timothy Olen, Richard James. AB, So. Meth. U., 1950, MDiv cum laude, 1952; PhD, U. Edinburgh (Scotland), 1959; postgrad., Yale U., 1968, U. Oxford, U. Cambridge, Eng. Ordained to ministry Meth. Ch., 1953. Preacher Ch. of Scotland and Meth. chs., Scotland, 1956; assoc. pastor St. Mary's Parish Kirk, Haddington, Scotland, 1957-58; minister Scarsdale (N.Y.) Congregational Ch., 1958-60; prof., chmn. dept. religion and philosophy Lambuth Coll., Jackson, Tenn., 1960-66; prof., chmn. dept. religion and philosophy Greensboro (N.C.) Coll., 1966—, Jefferson-Pilot prof. religion and philosophy, 1976-97; arts cons. various denominations throughout the South, 1966—, various sems., 1966—, S.E. jurisdiction United Meth. Chrs., 1968-78; cons., tchr. chs., Miami, Fla., 1972-80; mem. World Theol. Conf., Oxford U., Eng., 1969, Archaeol. Dig., Beersheba, Israel, 1973. Author: Beyond the Dream, Live Justice-Love Peace, Symphony of Spirit and Stone, On the Way, 1976, Ecumenical Celebrations—Interfaith Resource Leader, 1991; contbr. a rticles to profl. jours. Assoc. minister Grace United Meth. Ch., Greensboro, 1978-79; gen. coun. U. Edinburgh, del., 1976—; min. United Meth. WNC Conf., 1948-97, ret., 1997. Lt. USN, 1953-56. Recipient commendation 11th Workshop Christian-Jewish Rels., Charleston, S.C., 1989, 1st Nat. award for exemplary teaching Gen. Bd. Higher Edn. and Ministry, United Meth. Ch.; named one of 10 Most Outstanding Citizens, Greensboro News and Record, 1985; Lilly scholar Duke U., 1976; Bryan Found. grantee, 1991, 96. Mem. AAUP, N.C. Assn. Profs. of Religion, Piedmont Interfaith Coun. (co-founder), Civitan Club (chaplain). Avocations: gardening, music, travel. Home: 5409 Southwind Rd Greensboro NC 27455-1152

HULL, J(AMES) RICHARD, retired lawyer, business executive; b. Keokuk, Iowa, Dec. 5, 1933; s. James Robert and Alberta Margaret (Bouseman) H.; m. Patricia M. Kiesner, June 14, 1958; children—Elizabeth Ann Hull Whims, James Robert, David Glen. B.A., Ill. Wesleyan U., 1955; J.D., Northwestern U., 1958. Bar: Ill. 1958, Fla. 1978. V.p., sec., gen. counsel Honeggers & Co., Inc., Fairbury, Ill., 1959-65, also bd. dirs.; staff atty. Am. Hosp. Supply Corp., Evanston, Ill., 1965-68, chief atty., asst. sec., 1968-70, corp. sec., 1970-71, corp. sec., corp. gen. counsel, 1971-79, gen. counsel, 1979-84; sr. v.p., sec., gen. counsel Household Internat. Inc., Northbrook, Ill., 1984-93, sr. v.p., of counsel, 1993-94; ret.; ret.; mem. planning com. Northwestern U. Corp. Counsel Inst., 1992-93, chmn. Northwestern Corp. Counsel Ctr., 1993. Bd. trustees, bd. visitors Ill. Wesleyan U.; pres. Prestancia Cmty. Assn. Fellow Am. Bar Found., Am. Law Inst.; mem. ABA, Ill. Bar Assn., Fla. Bar Assn., Chgo. Bar Assn. (chmn. corp. law dept.), North Shore Gen. Counsels, Northwestern U. Sch. Law Alumni Assn. (pres.), Sigma Chi, Legal Club (Chgo.), Law Club (Chgo.), Skokie Country Club (Glencoe, Ill.), Gator Creek Golf Club (Sarasota, Fla.), T.P.C. Club (Prestancia, Fla.), Prestancia Cmty. Assn. (pres. 1995-96), Champion Hills Golf Club (Hendersonville, N.C.). Home: 4634 Mirada Way Unit 24 Sarasota FL 34238-4547 Summer Home: 4634 Mirada Way Unit 24 Sarasota FL 34238-4547 *Success will come to those who plan and rehearse. Set your goals, define your strategies and implement your tactics. Your goals must always determine and never justify the means toward achievement.*

HULL, JANE DEE, governor, former state legislator; b. Kansas City, Mo., Aug. 8, 1935; d. Justin D. and Mildred (Swenson) Bowersock; m. Terrance Ward Hull, Feb. 12, 1954; children: Jeannette Shipley, Robin Hillebrand, Jeff, Mike. BS, U. Kans., 1957; postgrad., U. Ariz., 1972-78. Spkr. pro tem Ariz. Ho. of Reps., Phoenix, 1993, chmn. ethics com., chmn. econ. devel., 1993, mem. legis. coun., 1993, mem. gov.'s internat. trade and tourism adv. bd., 1993, mem. gov.'s strategic partnership for econ. devel., 1993, mem. gov.'s office of employement implementation task force, 1993, spkr. of house, 1989-93, house majority whip, 1987-88; secretary of state State of Arizona, Phoenix; gov. State of Ariz., Phoenix, 1997—. Bd. dirs. Morrison Inst. for Pub. Policy, Beatitudes D.O.A.R., 1992, Ariz. Town Hall, Ariz. Econs. Coun.; mem. dean's coun. Ariz. State U., 1989-92; assoc. mem. Heard Mus. Guild, Cactus Wren Rep. Women, ; mem. Maricopa Med. Aux., Ariz. State Med. Aux., Freedom Found., Valley Citizens League, Charter 100, North Phoenix Rep. Women, 1970, Trunk 'N Tusk Legis. Liaison Ariz. Rep. Party, 1993; Rep. candidate sec. of state, 1994. Recipient Econ. Devel. award Ariz. Innovation Network, 1993. Mem. Nat. Orgn. of Women Legislators, Am. Legis. Exch. Coun., Nat. Rep. Legislators Assn. (Nat. Legislator of Yr. award 1989), Soroptimists (hon.). Republican. Roman Catholic. Address: Office of Gov State Capitol 1700 W Washington Ave Phoenix AZ 85007-2812

HULL, JANE LAUREL LEEK, retired nurse, administrator; b. Ontario, Calif., July 4, 1923; d. William Abram and Susan Bianca (Pethick) Leek; R.N., Columbia Presbyn. Sch. Nursing, 1944; B.A., Redlands U., 1977; ; m. James B. Hull, Oct. 10, 1944 (dec.); children—James W., William P., Kenneth D. Supr. obstetrics Mid-Valley Hosp., Peckville, Pa., 1945-46; sch. and surg. nurse acute nursing Scranton (Pa.) State Hosp., 1947-52; nurse San Antonio Community Hosp., Upland, Calif., 1953-55; office nurse H.L. Archibald, Upland, 1965; vis. nurse Pomona West End Inc., continuity of care coordinator, Claremont, Calif., 1968-73, exec. dir., 1973-92 (named pres. 1991); tchr. ARC nursing course to high sch. students; cons. Livingston Meml. Vis. Nurse Assn. Ventura, Calif. Recipient Woman Achiever award, Pomona Valley, 1983, Excellence in Edn. award Nat. Assn. Home Care, 1988. Treas. PTA, Pomona, Calif.; vol. exec. dir. Inland Hospice Assn., 1979-80, accreditation commn., 1988-89. Nat. Found. for Hospice/Home Care, 1988. Mem. Am. Assn. Retired Persons (local coord.), Calif. Nurses Assn. (pres. dist. 53 1958), Calif. Assn. for Health Services at Home (dir.), Calif. League Nursing, Nat. Homecaring Council (dir.). Home Care Aide Assn. Am. (chmn.), bd. mem. Nat. Assn. of Home Care. Republican. Club: Zonta (Ontario, Upland, pres., 1976). Organizer Homemaker Dept. in Vis. Nurse Assn., 1972, pres., 1991; developer (with Don Baxter Corp.) plugs for in-dwelling Foley catheters, 1963. Home: 543 W F St Ontario CA 91762-3117

HULL, JOHN DANIEL, IV, lawyer; b. Washington, Feb. 27, 1953; s. John Daniel III and Arlene (Reemer) H. BA cum laude, Duke U., 1975; JD, U. Cin., 1978. Bar: D.C. 1978, U.S. Dist. Ct. D.C. 1983, U.S. Ct. Appeals (D.C. cir.) 1984, Md. 1989, Pa. 1989, U.S. Dist. Ct. (we. dist.) Pa. 1989, U.S. Ct. Appeals (3d cir.) 1989, U.S. Supreme Ct. 1989. Legis. asst. 93d & 96th U.S. Congresses, Washington, 1974, 78-81; assoc. Rose, Schmidt & Dixon, Washington, 1981-87, ptnr., 1988-92; founding ptnr. Hull McGuire PC, Pitts., Washington, and San Diego, 1992—. Mem. U. Cin. Law Rev., 1976-77, editor student articles, 1977-78. Mem. ABA (sect. natural resources, energy and environ. law and litigation, intellectual property), Bar Assn. D.C., Md. Bar Assn., Pa. Bar Assn., Calif. Bar Assn., Duke Club, Tara Club. Office: Hull McGuire PC 32d Fl USX Tower 600 Grant St Pittsburgh PA 15219-2702 also: Hull McGuire PC 1155 Connecticut Ave NW Ste 300 Washington DC 20036-4327 also: Hull McGuire PC 15644 Via Calanova San Diego CA 92128-4462

HULL, JOHN DOSTER, retired insurance company executive; b. White Plains, N.Y., Oct. 24, 1924; s. Robert Franklin and Mary Catharine (Doster) H.; m. Joyce Elizabeth Holroyd, June 12, 1948 (div. Oct. 1966); children: Thomas Scott, Amy Louise Hull Campbell, James Burgess, Bonnie Jo Hull Hart; m. Alice Ida Moore, Dec. 11, 1970. BA, Hiram Coll., 1951; MS in Fin. Svcs., Am. Coll., 1983; postgrad. in law, U. Md., 1949. CLU, Chartered fin. cons. Personnel placement officer U.S. VA, Washington, 1951-55; adminstrv. asst. U.S. Navy Dept., Washington/Orlando, Fla., 1955-60; agt. Mut. Life of N.Y., Orlando, 1960-67; dist. mgr. Jefferson Standard Life, Orlando, 1967-69; assoc. mgr. Acacia Mut. Life, Orlando, 1969-71; account mgr. The Acacia Group, Orlando, 1971-94, ret., 1994; instr. Orange County Adult Edn. and Rollins Coll., Orlando and Winter Park, Fla., 1973-77; lectr. Stetson U., Rollins Coll. and U. Cen. Fla., Orlando, 1975-78. Mem. Alcohol, Drug Abuse and Mental Health Planning Coun., Dist. 7, 1985-91, chair forensics subcom.; bd. dirs. Safety Coun. fo Ctrl. Fla., 1985-93; mem. state com. Seminole County Dem. Party, 1988-91; treas. Unitarian Ch. Endowment Fund, 1988-94, others. Recipient scholarship Cen. Fla. CLU Soc., Orlando, 1978. Mem. Am. Soc. CLUs and Chartered Fin. Cons. (pres. 1976-77), South Orlando Sertoma (pres. 1966-68, 87, Outstanding Mem. 1969), Mental Health Assn. Fla. (v.p. 1982-83), Mental Health Assn. Ctrl. Fla. (pres. 1993-94, Golden Bell award), Mental Health Assn. Oragne County Pres. 1983-84), U. Club Winter Park (bd. dirs., chair philos. discussion group, v.p. programs 1997, v.p. fin. 1998), DAV and EX-POWs in Romania, Nat. Assn. Life Underwriters (Nat. Quality award, Nat. Sales Achievement award), Million Dollar Round Table. Unitarian. Avocations: gardening, music, reading, carpentry. Home: 546 Lake Ave Altamonte Springs FL 32701-3639

HULL, LEWIS WOODRUFF, manufacturing company executive; b. Scranton, Pa., Oct. 16, 1916; s. Robert Alonzo and Clara Lucelia (Woodruff) H.; m. Margaret (Burns) Carson, June 7, 1947; children: Arthur, Martha, Stephen, Rebecca. BS in Chem. Engring., MIT, 1938. Div. mgr. F. J. Stokes Co., Phila., 1938-52; chmn. Hull Corp., Hatboro, Pa., 1952—; bd. dirs. Hull Internat. Ltd., Girvan, Scotland, Hull-Japan Ltd., Tokyo, Penn Engring. and Mfg. Inc., Danboro, Pa., Advanced System Design, Evergreen, Colo., Willow Grove Bank, Maple Glen, Pa., Pa. Free Enterprise Foun., Erie, Pa., Horizon Resources, Inc., Golden, Colo., Performance Controls Inc., Willow Grove, Pa., Finmac Inc., Hatboro, Pa., Avantext Inc., Reading, Pa., Tree Growers Inc., Wayland, Mass. Contbr. articles to profl. jours.; patentee in field. Bd. dirs. Heritage Conservancy, Doylestown, Pa. Mem. Mid-Atlantic Employers Assn. (bd. dirs.), Plastics Pioneers Assn. (pres.), Rotary. Republican. Avocations: sailplaning, tennis. Home: 277 W Bristol Rd Southampton PA 18966-1070 Office: Hull Corp Davisville Rd Hatboro PA 19040-4202

HULL, LINDA WEAVER, outreach coordinator; b. Woodstock, Va., Jan. 16, 1956; d. Garland and Francis (Rice) Weaver; m. Randy Dale Hull, July 27, 1970; children: Cynthia, Laura, Randa, Jessica. Student, Lord Fairfax C.C., 1997—. Co-dir. Pioneer Outreach, Woodstock, 1986—. Vol. Ctrl. H.S., Woodstock, co-coord. Central H.S. after prom party. Home and Office: Pioneer Outreach 422 Walton Farm Rd Woodstock VA 22664-4004

HULL, LOUISE KNOX, retired elementary educator, administrator; b. Springfield, Mo., May 24, 1912; d. William E. and Ruby Joe (Bradshaw) K.; m. Berrien J. Hull, Jan. 1, 1953. BS in Edn., S.W. Mo. State U., 1933; postgrad. Colo. U., 1939, Northwestern U., 1945; MA, NYU, 1952. Cert. elem. and secondary tchr., Mo. Elem. tchr. R12 Sch. Dist., Springfield, 1936-70, supr. tchr., 1956-70, mem. adv. com. to supt., 1955-57. Chmn. Christian edn. com. Westminster Presbyn. Ch., 1953-66, trustee, 1983-86, chmn. bd. trustees, 1986, circle chair, 1986-89, mem. women's adv. bd., 1987-89, rep. witness and fin. com., 1990; pres. Women of Ch., 1970-73, 90-92, pres. bd. trustees, 1983-86; life mem. Wilson Creek Found., Springfield, 1954-67; sec. Greene County Hist. Soc., Springfield, 1960-96, life mem.; mem. Springfield Little Theater Guild, 1970—, Hist. Preservation Soc., Springfield, 1980—; docent Mus. Ozarks, Springfield, 1976-85; chmn. dist. Ill, John Calvin Presbytery, 1974-76, sec., 1977-80; vol. St. John's Regional Med. Ctr., 1970-78. Mem. Springfield Ret. Tchrs. Assn. (life), Mo. Ret. Tchrs. Assn. (life), Ozarks Genealogy Soc (sec. 1985-87, pub. info. rep. 1987-89), DAR (Rachel Donelson chpt.), Mo. Fedn. Women's Clubs (chmn. home life com. 1986-89), Springfield City Fedn. Women's Clubs (pres. 1990-92), Parlimentarian Sorosis Club (pres. Springfield 1980-82, chmn. hobby dept. 1986-88, 94-96, chmn. fine arts dept. 1988-90, mem. perpetual endowment com. 1992-96, chmn. 1994, parliamentarian 1998—), Alpha Delta Pi (treas. house corp. 1932-60), Alpha Delta Kappa (sec. 1965-67, corr. sec. Psi chpt. 1990-92).

HULL, MAGDALEN ELEANOR, reproductive medicine physician, educator; b. N.Y.C., Sept. 22, 1953; m. John Leo; children: John Francis, Genevieve, Stephanie. BS, Fordham U., 1975; MD, N.Y. Med. Coll., 1979; MPH in Health Policy Mgmt., Columbia U., 1995. Bd. cert. Nat. Bd. Examiners, Part I, II, III; bd. cert. in ob-gyn and reproductive endocrinology and infertility, recert.; lic. N.Y., Mich. Intern, resident Albert Einstein Coll. Medicine, 1979-83; fellow in reproductive endocrinology and infertility Wayne State U. Sch. Medicine, 1983-85; clin. instr. dept. ob-gyn. Wayne State U. Sch. Medicine, Hutzel Hosp., Detroit, 1983-85; asst. prof. ob-gyn. SUNY, Stony Brook, 1995—, asst. prof. dept. ob-gyn. divsn. reproductive endocrinology, 1985-94; chief reproductive medicine dept. ob-gyn. Winthrop-Univ. Hosp., Mineola, N.Y., 1995—; cons. staff Winthrop-Univ. Hosp., Mineola, 1985-94; assoc. med. dir. IVF Am. at L.I., Mineola, 1991-93; med. bd. Planned Parenthood, N.Y.C., 1995-96; lectr. in field. Contbr. articles to profl. jours. Mem. ACOG, Am. Med. Women's Assn. (pres. Suffolk County br. 1990-95), Am. Soc. Reproductive Medicine, Assn. Profs. of Ob-Gynecology, Endocrine Soc., N.Am. Menopause Soc., Soc. for Study of Reproduction, Soc. Reproductive Endocrinologists, Soc. Reproductive Surgeons, Am. Assn. Gynecologic Laparascopists, Am. Inst. Ultrasound in Medicine, N.Y. Obstet. Soc., Nassau County Ob-Gyn. Soc., Suffolk County Ob-Gyn. Soc. Office: Winthrop-Univ Hosp 259 1st St Mineola NY 11501-3987

HULL, MARGARET RUTH, artist, educator, consultant; b. Dallas, Mar. 27, 1921; d. William Hynes and Ora Carroll (Adams) Leatherwood; m. LeRos Ennis Hull, Mar. 29, 1941; children: LeRos Ennis, Jr., James Daniel. BA, So. Meth. U., Dallas, 1952; postgrad., So. Meth. U., 1960-61; MA, North Tex. State U., 1957; postgrad., R.I. Sch. Design, 1982. Art instr. W.W. Bushman Sch., Dallas Ind. Sch. Dist., 1952-57, Benjamin Franklin Jr. High Sch., Dallas, 1957-58; art instr. Hillcrest H.S., Dallas, 1958-61, dean, pupil personnel counselor, 1961-70; designer, coord. visual art careers cluster Skyline H.S., Dallas, 1970-71; developer curriculum devel./writing art Booker T. Washington Arts Magnet H.S., Dallas, 1971-82, coord. visual arts careers cluster, 1976-82, artist, ednl. cons., 1982-96; tchr. children's painting Dallas Mus. Fine Art, 1956-70; mus. reprodns. asst. Dallas Mus. Art, 1984-93. Group shows include Dallas Mus. Fine Arts, 1958, Arts Magnet Faculty Shows, 1978-82, Arts Magnet H.S., Dallas Art Edn. Assn. Show, 1981, D'Art Membership Show, Dallas, 1982-83; represented in pvt. collections. Trustee Dallas Mus. Art, 1978-84; vol. League Dallas Mus. Art, 1982-99. Mem. Tex. Designer/Craftsmen, Craft Guild Dallas, Fiber Artists Dallas, Dallas Art Edn. Assn., Tex. Art Edn. Assn., Nat. Art Edn. Assn., Dallas Counselors Assn. (pres. 1968), Delta Delta Delta.

HULL, MARION HAYES, communications educator, researcher; b. Bronx, N.Y., Feb. 23, 1940; d. David Vernon and Jessie C. (Summerville) Hayes; m. Bernard Samuel Hull, Aug. 24, 1974; children: Karla Williams, Bernard S. II. BJ, L.I. U., 1961; MA in TV Writing, NYU, 1967; PhD in Polit. Sci., Am. U., 1996. Instr. Norfolk (Va.) State U., 1967-70; asst. prof. Shaw U., Raleigh, N.C., 1970-72; comm. specialist U.S. Dept. Justice, Washington, 1972-73; dir. telecom. programs Booker T. Washington Found., Washington, 1973-82; asst. prof. comm. Howard U., Washington, 1982—; newscaster Sta. WAVY-TV, Portsmouth, Va., 1969-70; U.S. del. The World Adminstn. Radio Conf., (plan. com.) Washington, 1978-79; vis. scholar Rand Afrikaanse U., 1998. Author: (chpt.) Public-Cable Handbook, 1975-76; mem. editl. adv. bd. The Montgomery Times, 1990—; contbr. articles to profl. periodicals. Cmty. amb. City of Raleigh (N.C.), Sweden, 1971; exch. amb. Expt. Internat. Living, 1972—; com. Maryland Pub. Broadcasting Commn., 1998—; mem. The White House Conf. Minority Ownership, Washington, 1973; mem. cable comm. adv. com. Montgomery County (Md.) Govt., 1982-86, chmn. consumer adv. bd., 1989-95; chair clubs and orgns. United Negro Coll. Fund, Washington, 1989—; spkr. Montgomery County Pub. Schs., 1992—; bd. dirs., v.p. program com. Leadership Montgomery, 1996—. Recipient Excellence in Svc. award United Negro Coll. Fund, 1994, grad. Leadership Montgomery, 1995; Ford Found. grantee, 1968. Mem. Assn. Edn. Journalism and Mass Comm. (accreditation chair 1994—, sec. commn. on minorities), Women's Inst. Freedom of the Press, Capital Press Club (pres., Leadership award 1977), Alpha Kappa Alpha (pres. local chpt. 1980-85, advisor to undergraduates 1990—, Leadership award 1984). Democrat. Baptist. Office: Howard U Sch Comm 525 Bryant St NW Washington DC 20059-2326

HULL, MCALLISTER HOBART, JR., retired university administrator; b. Birmingham, Ala., Sept. 1, 1923; s. McAllister Hobart and Grace (Johnson) H.; m. Mary Muska, Mar. 23, 1946; children: John McAllister, Wendy Ann. B.S. with highest honors, Yale, 1948, Ph.D. in Physics, 1951. Tech. asst. Los Alamos Lab., 1944-46; From instr. to asso. prof. physics Yale U., 1951-66; prof. physics, chmn. dept. Oreg. State U., 1966-69; prof. physics, chmn. dept. State U. N.Y. at Buffalo, 1969-72, dean Grad. Sch., 1972-74, dean. grad. and profl. edn., 1974-77; provost U. N.Mex., 1977-85, counselor to pres., 1985-88, prof. emeritus physics, 1988—; adviser to supt. schs., Hamden, Conn., 1958-65. Author papers, books, chpts. in books, articles in encys. Bd. dirs. Western N.Y. Reactor Facility, 1970-72; trustee N.E. Radio Obs. Corp., 1971-77; pres. Western Regional Sci. Labs., 1977; chmn. tech. adv. com. N.Mex. Energy Research Inst., 1981-83, mem., 1983-88; co-chmn. Nat. Task Force on Ednl. Tech., 1984-86. Served with AUS, 1943-46. Faculty fellow Yale U., 1964-65. Fellow Am. Phys. Soc.; mem. Am. Assn. Physics Tchrs. (chmn. Oreg. sect. 1967-68). Office: U NMex Dept Physics and Astronomy Albuquerque NM 87131 *Experience says that every man is sometimes wise, no man is always wise. One mustdevelop the willingness to listen for wisdom from whatever source, the judgmentto identify it, the skill to use it: only in this way can one's talents, however modest or extensive, be optimally enhanced and the number of wasted efforts minimized.*

HULL, PATRICIA ANN, nursing administrator; b. Johnstown, Pa., May 26, 1942; d. Willard Earl and Florence Lucy (Grove) Merritt; m. Bruce Edward Dunn, July 31, 1965 (div. Aug. 1975); children: Rachel Dunn

Bayush, Kelly Dunn Thomas, Heather Dunn Wyant; m. Harry Edwin Hull, May 21, 1988. Diploma in nursing, Conemaugh Hosp. Sch. Nursing, Johnstown, 1963. Cert. gerontol. nurse. Staff nurse Conemaugh Hosp., 1963-64; head nurse, supr. 1710 USAF Hosp., Savannah, Ga., 1964-66; part-time staff nurse Rochester (N.Y.) Gen. Hosp., 1966; part-time supr., clinic emergency rm. U. Miami (Fla.), 1967-68; staff supr. Arbutus Park Manor, Johnstown, 1979-92, dir. nursing, 1992—. Dist. rep., sec. Western Pa. Conf. United Meth. Bd. Health and Welfare, 1987-92; mem. Christ United Meth. Ch., Johnstown, health and welfare chmn., 1986-91, Stephens min., 1994—, trustee, adminstrv. bd., 1980-92; vol. ARC, Johnstown flood, 1977, blood drives; former Brownie, Girl Scout leader, Talus Rock Girl Scout Coun. 1st lt. USAF Nurse Corps, 1964-66. Recipient State of Pa. Gerontol. Nursing Study grant Indiana U. Pa., 1992. Mem. Pa. Assn. Dirs. Nursing Adminstrn/Long Term Care, Am. Soc. Long Term Care Nurses. Avocations: profl. artist, ecology. Home: 1128 Boyd Ave Johnstown PA 15905-4413 Office: Arbutus Park Manor 207 Ottawa St Johnstown PA 15904-2399

HULL, PHILIP GLASGOW, lawyer; b. St. Albans, Vt., Feb. 17, 1925; s. Charles Herman and Gladys Gertrude (Glasgow) H.; AB, Middlebury Coll., 1949; LLB (Ellis fellow, Kent scholar, Stone scholar), Columbia U., 1952; m. Gretchen Elizabeth Gaebelein, Oct. 24, 1952; children: Jeffrey R., Sanford D., Meredyth Hull Smith. Bar: N.Y. 1952, Fla. 1977. Staff mem. sub-com. on adminstrn. internal revenue laws, com. on ways and means U.S. Ho. of Reps., Washington, 1951; assoc. Winthrop, Stimson, Putnam & Roberts, N.Y.C., 1952-63, ptnr., 1964-97, sr. counsel, 1998—. Mem. Sch. Revenue Com., Cold Spring Harbor, N.Y., 1963-65; bd. dirs. Eagle Dock Found., Cold Spring Harbor, 1971-74, People's Symphony Concerts, N.Y.C., 1977—. L.I. Philharm, 1979-81; trustee Latin Am. Mission, Miami, Fl., 1969-79; elder Ctrl. Presbyn. Ch., Huntington, N.Y., 1958-78; mem. nat. missions bd. United Presbyn. Ch. U.S.A., 1967-73; trustee Madison Ave. Presbyn. Ch., N.Y.C., 1989-94, pres., 1993-94; mem. Lloyd Harbor Conservation Adv. Coun., 1973-77. With U.S. Army, 1943-46. Mem. N.Y. State Bar Assn., Fla. Bar Assn., Am. Coll. Trust and Estate Counsel, Christian Legal Soc. (dir. 1984-97), Fellowship Christians in Univs. and Schs. (trustee 1983-90), Univ. Club N.Y.C. (bd. dirs. 1986-90), Cold Spring Harbor Beach, Blue Key, Phi Beta Kappa. Office: Winthrop Stimson Putnam & Roberts One Battery Park Pla New York NY 10004-1490

HULL, RAYMOND WHITFORD, public relations executive; b. Cohoes, N.Y., Oct. 13, 1946; s. Raymond W. and J. Ruth (Barber) H. BS, Syracuse U., 1971. Spl. asst. to Gov. Nelson A. Rockefeller, Albany, N.Y., 1971; conf. asst. to commr. N.Y. State Dept. Environ. Conservation, Albany, 1971-74; exec. dir. Spl. Joint Legis. Commn. on Petroleum Distbn., Albany, 1974-75; asst. headmaster Hoosac Sch., Hoosick, N.Y., 1975-77; area coordinator N.Y. State Assembly, Albany, 1977-79; staff dir. N.Y. State Senate Com. on Energy, Albany, 1979-85; dir. pub. affairs Niagara Mohawk Power Corp., Albany, 1985-89; pub. affairs cons. Albany, 1990-96; assoc. commr. N.Y. State Dept. Motor Vehicles, Albany, 1996—. V.p. Rensselaer City Sch. Bd., N.Y., 1981-86; treas. bd. trustees Hoosac Sch., 1974-81, Rennsselaer City Hist. Soc., 1980—, pres., 1994; trustee Rennselaer county hist. Soc., 1986-94. Republican. Episcopalian. Clubs: Ft. Orange (Albany); SAR (N.Y.C.). Avocations: hist. architecture, art. Home: The Patroon Agts House 15 Forbes Ave Rensselaer NY 12144-1622

HULL, RICHARD THOMPSON, retired philosophy educator, non-profit executive; b. Oklahoma City, Dec. 29, 1939. Student, Park Coll., 1959-60; BA in Philosophy, Austin Coll., 1963; PhD in Philosophy, Ind. U., 1971. Lectr. dept. philosophy SUNY, Buffalo, 1967-71, from asst. to full prof. dept. philosophy, 1971-97, prof. emeritus dept. philosophy, 1997—; headmaster Calasanctius Preparatory Sch., Buffalo, N.Y., 1983-86; pers. cons. M. David Lowe Pers. Svcs., Houston, 1989-90; exec. dir. Tex. Coun. for the Humanities, Austin, 1997—. Editor: W.H. Werkmeister's Martin Heidegger on the Way, 1996, Ethical Issues in the New Reproductive Technologies, 1990, A Quarter Century of Value Inquiry, 1994, Presidential Addresses of the American Philosophical Association 1901-2000, vols. 1 and 2, 1999. Scholar-in-residence Buffalo Gen. Hosp., 1994-95. Mem. Am. Philos. Assn., Am. Soc. for Value Inquiry (pres.). E-mail: rthull@public-humanities.org. Office: Tex Coun for the Humanities Bldg A 3809 S 2nd St Austin TX 78704

HULL, RITA PRIZLER, accounting educator; b. Lone Tree, Iowa, Mar. 29, 1936; d. Ernest Ralph and Mildred Lennis (Huskins) Prizler; m. J.W. Hull, May 29, 1954 (div. 1963); children: Mark, Marshall; m. John O. Everett, Sept. 1, 1976. BA in Acctg., Augustana Coll., Rock Island, Ill., 1967; MA in Acctg., Western Ill. U., 1973; PhD in Bus. Adminstrn., Okla. State U., 1978. CPA, Ill.; cert. internal auditor, Ill. Auditor Price Waterhouse & Co., Chgo., 1967-70; asst. prof. acctg. Bowling Green (Ohio) State U., 1976-78; assoc. prof. No. Ill. U., DeKalb, 1978-82; prof. Va. Commonwealth U., Richmond, 1982—. Contbr. articles, papers to profl. publs. Recipient Outstanding Women award Greater Richmond area, YWCA, 1995. Mem. AICPA, NOW (treas. Richmond chpt. 1987-88), Am. Soc. Women Accts. (treas. Richmond chpt. 1986-87, sec. 1987-88, pres. 1988-90, nat. bd. dirs. 1990-93, nat. sec. 1991-92, nat. v.p. 1992-93, Nat. Woman of Achievement award, 1994), Am. Acctg. Assn. (Trueblood seminars com. 1987-88, acctg. educator awards com. 1988-90, awards evaluation com. 1990-91, chmn.-elect gender issues in acctg. sect. 1991-92, chmn. 1992-93, coun. 1992-93), Inst. Internat. Auditors, Acad. Acctg. Historians. Democrat. Avocations: travel, reading, gardening. Home: 810 Keats Rd Richmond VA 23229-6520 Office: Va Commonwealth U 1015 Floyd Ave Richmond VA 23284-9000

HULL, ROBERT GLENN, retired financial administrator; b. Ottumwa, Iowa, Sept. 14, 1929; s. C. Glenn and DeElda L. (Davidson) H.; m. Donna Marie Hastriter, Jan. 26, 1951; children: Cynthia Ann Hull Williams, Steven Kent. B.A., Friends U., 1956; M.S., Emporia Kans. State U., 1966. With Nat. Coop. Refinery Assn., McPherson, Kans., 1957-91; treas., comptroller Nat. Coop. Refinery Assn., 1968-76, v.p. finance, 1976-91; dir. Jayhawk Pipeline Corp., Clear Creek Cos. Bd. dirs. Central Coll., McPherson. Served with USAF, 1951-55. Mem. Fin. Execs. Inst., Nat. Assn. Accountants for Coops., Am. Petroleum Inst., Delta Pi Epsilon. Republican. Methodist. Clubs: Petroleum, McPherson Country. Home: 417 S Grand St Mcpherson KS 67460-4912

HULL, ROGER HAROLD, college president; b. N.Y.C., June 18, 1942; s. Max Harold and Magda Mary (Stern) H.; children: Roberto Franklin, Lincoln Macgregor. A.B. cum laude, Dartmouth Coll., 1964; LL.B., Yale U., 1967; LL.M., U. Va., 1972, S.J.D., 1974; LHD, Rockford Coll., 1988; LLD, Beloit Coll., 1992. Bar: N.Y. 1968. Assoc. firm White & Case, N.Y.C., 1967-71; spl. counsel to gov., Va., 1971-74; spl. asst. to chmn., dep. staff dir. Interagy. Task Force Law of Sea, NSC, 1974-76; v.p. devel. Syracuse U., N.Y., 1976-79, v.p. devel. and planning, 1979-81; pres. Beloit (Wis.) Coll., 1981-90, Union Coll., Schenectady, N.Y., 1990—; chancellor Union U., 1990—; mem. U.S. del. Law of Sea Conf., 1974-76; adj. prof. Syracuse Univ. Law Sch., 1976-81; bd. visitors Coll. William and Mary, Williamsburg, Va., 1970-74; mem. pub. instns. task force Assn. Gov. Bds., 1975. Author: The Irish Triangle, 1976; co-author: Law and Vietnam, 1968. Vice chair Schenectady 2000; adv. com. mem. Schenectady County Econ. Devel. Corp. Named Schenectady Co-Person of Yr., 1998. Mem. Am. Soc. Internat. Law, Univ. Club, Millbrook Golf and Tennis Club. Office: Union Coll Pres Office Schenectady NY 12308

HULL, SUZANNE WHITE, retired administrator, author; b. Orange, N.J., Aug. 24, 1921; d. Gordon Stowe and Lillian (Siegling) White; m. George I. Hull, Feb. 20, 1943 (dec. Mar. 1990); children: George Gordon, James Rutledge, Anne Elizabeth Hull Sheldon. BA with honors, Swarthmore Coll., 1943; MSLS, U. So. Calif., 1967. Mem. staff Huntington Libr., Art Gallery and Bot. Gardens, San Marino, Calif., 1969-86, dir. adminstrn. and pub. svcs., 1972-86, also prin. officer; cons. Women Writers Project, Brown U., 1989—. Author: Chaste, Silent and Obedient, English Books for Women, 1475-1640, 1982, 88, Women According to Men: The World of Tudor-Stuart Women, 1996; editor: State of the Art in Women's Studies, 1986. Charter pres. Portola Jr. H.S. PTA, L.A., 1960-62; pres. Children's Svc. League, 1963-64, YWCA, L.A., 1967-69; mem. alumni coun. Swarthmore Coll., 1959-62, 83-86, mem.-at-large, 1986-89; mem. adv. bd. Hagley Mus. and Libr., Wilmington, Del., 1983-86, Betty Friedan Think Tank, U. So. Calif., 1985-93; hon. life mem. Calif. Congress Parents and Tchrs.; bd. dirs. Pasadena Planned Parenthood Assn., 1978-83, mem. adv. com., 1983—; founder-chmn. Swarthmore-L.A. Connection, 1984-85, bd. dirs., 1985-92; founder Huntington Women's Studies Seminar, 1984, mem. steering com., 1984-91, mem. adv. bd., 1991-96; mem. organizing com. Soc. for Study of Early Modern Women, 1993-94; adv. bd. the Early Modern Englishwoman: A Facsimile Libr. of Essential Works, 1995—. Mem. Monumental Brass Soc. (U.K.), Renaissance Soc., Brit. Studies Conf., Western Assn. Women Historians, Soc. Study of Early Modern Women, Authors Guild, Beta Phi Mu (chpt. dir. 1981-84). Home: 1465 El Mirador Dr Pasadena CA 91103-2727 Office: 1151 Oxford Rd San Marino CA 91108-1218

HULL, THOMAS GRAY, federal judge; b. 1926; m. Joan Brandon; children: Leslie, Brandon, Amy. Student, Tusculum Coll.; JD, U. Tenn., 1951. Atty. Easterly and Hull, Greeneville, Tenn., 1951-63; mem. Tenn. Ho. of Reps., 1955-65; atty., prin. Thomas G. Hull, 1951-72; chief clk. Tenn. Ho. of Reps., 1969-70; judge 20th Jud. Cir., Greeneville, Morristown and Rogersville, Tenn., 1972-79; legal counsel to Tenn. Gov. Lamar Alexander, 1979-81; judge U.S. Dist. Ct. (ea. dist.) Tenn., 1983—. Served as cpl. U.S. Army, 1944-46. Mem. Tenn. Bar Assn. (chmn. East dist. com. 1969), Greenville Bar Assn. (pres. 1969-71), Tenn. Jud. Conf. (del. 1972-79, vice chmn. 1974-75, com. to draft uniform charges for trial judges). Republican. Office: Office of US Dist Judge 211 US Courthouse 101 W Summer St Greeneville TN 37743-4944*

HULL, TOM ALLAN, mechanics educator; b. Centralia, Wash., Feb. 3, 1956; s. Royce Keith and Barbara (Peyton) H. BS in Indsl. Arts, Western Wash. U., Bellingham, 1984; MEd, Oreg. State U., 1987. Cert. Autmotive Svc. Excellence master mechanic; indsl. mechanics vocat. tchg. cert.; lic. tchr., Oreg. Mailroom clk. Daily Chronicle, Centralia, 1970-74; cmty. antennae technician McCaw Comms., Wash., 1974-84; classroom tchr. South Umpqua H.S., Myrtle Creek, Oreg., 1984—; chmn. site coun. South Umpqua H.S., Myrtle Creek, 1994-96, mem. work exp. adv. bd., 1996—; past chmn., mem. South Umpqua Sch. Imp. Team, Myrtle Creek, 1992—; field worker Plastics Industry/Diesel Mech., Myrtle Creek, 1984-95. Editor, author: (newsletter) Quarter Inch Dr., 1993—; contbr. book revs. and tech. articles to profl. jours. Team teach plastics class PMC, Glendale, Oreg., 1995. Named Douglas County Educator of Yr., Masons, 1995, Oreg. Tech. Tchr. of Yr., Tech. Educators Oreg., 1996. Mem. Soc. Automotive Engrs., Soc. for History of Tech., Am. Truck Hist. Soc., Coun. Tech. Tchr. Edn., Soc. Indsl. Archaeology, Josephine County Pistol Club (pres., sec., treas. 1993—). Avocations: running, reading, handgun competition. Home: 319 Taylor St Myrtle Creek OR 97457-9733 Office: South Umpqua H S 501 Chadwick Ln Myrtle Creek OR 97457-9765

HULL, WILLIAM EDWARD, theology educator; b. Birmingham, Ala., May 28, 1930; s. William Edward and Margaret (King) H.; m. Julia Wylodine Hester, July 26, 1952; children: David William, Susan Virginia. BA, Samford U., 1951; MDiv, So. Bapt. Theol. Sem., Louisville, 1954, PhD, 1960; postgrad., U. Gottingen, Germany, 1962-63, Harvard U., 1971. Ordained to ministry Bapt. Ch., 1950. Pastor Beulah Bapt. Ch., Wetumpka, Ala., 1950-51, Cedar Hill Bapt. Ch., Owenton, Ky., 1952-53, 1st Bapt. Ch., New Castle, Ky., 1953-58; from instr. to assoc. prof. So. Bapt. Theol. Sem., Louisville, 1954-67, prof., 1967-75, dean theology and provost, 1969-75; pastor 1st Bapt. Ch., Shreveport, La., 1975-87; provost Samford U., Birmingham, Ala., 1987-96, univ. prof., 1996—. Author: Gospel of John, 1964, Broadman Bible Commentary, 1970, Beyond the Barriers, 1981, Love in Four Dimensions, 1982, The Christian Experience of Salvation, 1987, (with others): Professor in the Pulpit, 1963, The Truth That Makes Men Free, 1966, Salvation in Our Time, 1978, Set Apart for Service, 1980, Celebrating Christ's Presence Through the Spirit, 1981, The Twentieth Century Pulpit, Vol. II, 1981, Minister's Manual, 1983-87, Biblical Preaching: An Expositor's Treasury, 1983, Preaching in Today's World, 1984, Heralds to a New Age, 1985, Getting Ready for Sunday: A Practical Guide for Worship Planning, 1989, Best Sermons 2, 1989; contbr. articles to profl. publs. Mem. Futureshape Shreveport (La.) Commn., 1985-87. Recipient Denominational Svc. award Samford U., 1974, Liberty Bell award Shreveport Bar Assn., 1984, Brotherhood and Humanitarian award NCCJ, 1987. Mem. Nat. Assn. Bapt. Profs. Religion (pres. 1967-68), Am. Acad. Religion, Soc. Biblical Lit., The Club (Birmingham), Vestavia Country Club (Birmingham), Rotary, Phi Kappa Phi, Phi Eta Sigma, Omicron Delta Kappa. Home: 435 Vesclub Way Birmingham AL 35216-1357

HULL, WILLIAM FLOYD, JR., former museum director, ceramic consultant; b. Pomeroy, Wash., June 27, 1920; s. William Floyd and Margherita Sophia (Bose) H.; m. Carolyn Elizabeth Wose, July 19, 1947 (dec. 1977); children: Alfred Frederick (dec.), Margherita Ely. B.A. in Romance Langs, Wash. State U., 1946. Mng. dir. G.R. Crocker & Co., Syracuse, N.Y., 1948-57; dir. Everson Mus. Art, Syracuse, 1957-61; asso. dir. N.Y. State Council Arts, 1961-66; exec. dir. Ky. Arts Commn., 1966-71; dir. Palmer Mus. Art, Pa. State U., 1971-83, emeritus dir., 1983—; mem. state-fed. panel Nat. Endowment Arts, 1973-77. Author: Danish Ceramic Design, 1981. Served with AUS, 1942-45. Home and Office: 40 Portland Pier Apt 3 Portland ME 04101-4720

HULL, WILLIAM MARTIN, JR., ophthalmologist; b. Rock Hill, S.C., June 23, 1937; s. William Martin and Elizabeth (McDowell) H.; m. Anna Transou, Dec. 14, 1963; children: William Martin III, Alice Howard. BS, Davidson Coll., 1959; MD, Duke U., 1963. Diplomate Am. Bd. Ophthalmology. Intern in medicine Duke Hosp., Durham, N.C., 1963-64, resident in ophthalmology, 1964-67; practice medicine specializing in ophthalmology, Rock Hill, S.C., 1969—; pres. Rock Hill Eye Clinic; mem. staff Piedmont Med. Ctr., 1969—, chief of staff, 1980; bd. dirs. First Union of S.C., People First of Rock Hill. Chmn. S.C. Med PAC, 1975—; bd. dirs. Rock Hill ARC, 1976-80, Catawba Sch., Rock Hill, 1976-81; bd. dirs. S.C. Bd. Health and Environ. Control, 1994—, vice-chmn. Maj. M.C., U.S. Army, 1967-69, Vietnam. Fellow Am. Acad. Ophthalmology; mem. S.C. Med. Assn. (trustee 1978—, vice chmn. bd. trustees 1983-84), S.C. Ophthalmology Assn., (exec. com. 1976-81), York County Med. Soc. (v.p., then pres. 1976-80), Rock Hill C. of C. (bd. dirs. 1978-81), Rock Hill Country Club, Rock Hill Cotillian Club (pres. 1976-81). Episcopalian. Avocations: tennis, skiing, reading, traveling, golfing. Home: 550 Meadowbrook Ln Rock Hill SC 29730-3729 Office: Rock Hill Eye Clinic DEHEC Bd 1565 Ebenezer Rd Rock Hill SC 29732-1806

HULME, DARLYS MAE, banker; b. Buckingham, Iowa, Apr. 2, 1937; d. Leland James and Dorothy Mae (Nation) Philp; m. Harlan Dale Hulme, Dec. 4, 1955 (div. Nov. 1971); children: Debra Jean Hulme Hanneman, Richard Dale. Student Iowa Sch. Banking, 1974, Sch. Bank Adminstrn. U. Wis.-Madison, 1982. Bookkeeper, Farmers Savs. Bank, Traer, Iowa, 1954-55, asst. cashier, 1962-72, v.p., 1973-83, sr. v.p., 1983-93, exec. v.p., 1993—, also bd. dirs.; acct. North Tama Housing, Inc., Traer, 1974-94; sec. to bd. Talen, Inc., Talen Aviation, Ltd., Traer; dir., vice chmn., exec. v.p., 1996—, cashier, 1988-96; sec. bd. dirs. Farmers Savs. Bank Trust, Vinton, Iowa, 1988—; dir., sec. to bd. Traer Nursing Care Ctr., Inc.; mem. Iowa State Banking Bd., 1985-97. Mem. Nat. Assn. Bank Women (group treas. 1980-81, group v.p. 1981-82, group pres. 1982-83, state membership chair 1983-84, regional membership chair 1984-85), Iowa Bankers Assn. (mem. edn. com. 1985-86), Iowa Disting. Woman in Banking. Republican. Methodist. Club: PEO (Traer) (corr. sec. 1988, v.p. 1991). Avocations: gardening, traveling. Home: 108 Riverview Dr Vinton IA 52349-2358 Office: Farmers Savs Bank 611 2nd St Traer IA 50675-1230

HULME, MARY ANN K., women's health nurse, administrator; b. Galion, Ohio, July 25, 1952; d. Walter Herman and Mary Elizabeth (Prim) Kumm; m. Roy Allan Hulme, Jan. 8, 1977; children: Eric A., Ann E. BSN, Capital U., 1974; MSN, Case Western Res. U., 1993. RN, Ohio; cert. in ob-gyn., neonatal nursing ANCC. Staff and charge nurse, labor and delivery St. Ann's Hosp., Columbus, Ohio, 1974-76, head nurse, dir. ob-gyn. outpatient clinic, 1976-77; clin. nurse, sr. clin. nurse, head nurse mgr. labor/delivery Univ. Hosps., Cleve., 1977-94; head nurse mgr. labor/delivery antepartum U. Hosps. Cleve., Cleve., 1994-98, head nurse mgr. labor and delivery, 1998—; clin. instr. maternity and gynecology nursing Case Western Res. U., Cleve., 1986—, Kent State U., 1995—. Contbr. articles to profl. jours. With United Way Svcs., 1998. Recipient Silver medals U.S. Figure Skating Assn. Mem. ANA, Assn. Womens Health, Obstet. and Neonatal Nursing, Assn. Oper. Room Nurses, Ohio Nurses Assn., Lake Erie Coun. Nurse Execs., Cleve. Skating Club, Greater Cleve. Nurses Assn. (bd. dirs.), Cleve. Skating Club, Sigma Theta Tau. Lutheran. Avocations: ice dancing, curling, running. Home: 16070 S Park Blvd Cleveland OH 44120-1673

HULSE, DEXTER CURTIS, manufacturing executive; b. Woodland, Calif., Oct. 6, 1952; s. Dexter Curtis Hulse and Geraldine Ezabell (Ratliff) Curtis; children: Sandra Marie, Jennifer Lynn; m. Diane F. Schultz, Feb. 24, 1995. B.Indsl. Engring., Shawnee State U., Portsmouth, Ohio, 1973; Deg. in Computer Aided Design, Shawnee State U., 1992. Numerical control operator Lodge & Shippley, Cin., 1973-76; journeyman machinist Nat. Mine Svc. Co., Ashland, Ky., 1976-86; regional mgr. A.L. Williams Mktg., Minford, Ohio, 1982-87; pres. D & D Emergency, Wheelersburg, Ohio, 1987-88; gen. gmr. Dexter Mfg., Wheelersburg, Ohio, 1988—; instr. Shawnee State U., 1988—; sr. insp. Piketon Uranium Enrichment Facility Lockheed Martin Utility Svc., 1995-98; mem. computer-aided design adv. bd. Shawnee State U., 1990-94; CAD/CAM instr. Buckeye Hills Career Ctr., Rio Grande, Ohio, 1998—; cons. Scioto Bus. Cons., Wheelersburg, 1986—. Vol. fireman Porter Twp. Fire Dept., Wheelersburg, 1984-87. Mem. Ch. Nazarene. Avocations: canoeing, ATV's, computers. Office: 8088 Bell St Wheelersburg OH 45694-1613

HULSE, GEORGE ALTHOUSE, retired steel company executive; b. Norristown, Pa., July 7, 1934; s. Malcolm Carter and Kathareen Alice (Althouse) H.; m. Sara Lyle, Aug. 19, 1962; children: Jenna A., Geoffrey L., S. Allison. B.S., Carnegie Inst. Tech., 1956. Metallurgist Crucible Steel Co., Pitts., 1956-60; asst. chief metallurgist Green River Steel Corp., Owensboro, Ky., 1960-64, supr. melting, 1964-70, v.p. ops., 1970-72, pres., 1972-87; pres., owner Carousel Nut Products, Ic., Owensboro, 1987-93; pres. Green River Steel Corp., Owensboro, 1993-97; ret., 1997. Active Jr. Achievement Owensboro, 1981—, Ky. Gov.'s Econ. Devel. Com., 1975. Served to 1st lt. C.E., U.S. Army, 1957-59. Mem. Am. Iron and Steel Inst. Republican. Methodist. Avocations: golf; tennis; sailing. Home: 4117 Masonwoods Ln Owensboro KY 42303-7590

HULSE, JAMES WARREN, history educator, writer; b. Pioche, Nev., June 4, 1930; s. James Gordon and Berene (Cutler) H.; m. Betty Kay Wynkoop, June 20, 1962; children: Jane Hulse Dixon, James C. BA, U. Nev., 1952, MA, 1958; PhD, Stanford U., 1962. Reporter Nev. State Jour., Reno, 1954-58; asst. prof. Ctrl. Wash. Coll., Ellensburg, 1961-62; from asst. prof. to prof. U. Nev., Reno, 1962-97; ret., 1997. Author: Forming of Communist International, 1964, Revolutionists in London, 1970, The Silver State, 1991, 2nd edit., 1998, Reputations of Socrates, 1995. Pres., bd. dirs. Common Cause, Nev., 1985—. Unitarian Universalist. Home: 940 Grandview Ave Reno NV 89503-2643 Office: U Nev Reno NV 89557

HULSE, ROBERT DOUGLAS, high technology executive; b. Niagara Falls, N.Y., Aug. 16, 1943; s. Robert Edwin and Helen Louise (Kenny) H.; m. Nancy Louise Musser, Aug. 20, 1966 (div. 1986); children: Anne Warren, Robert Alexander; m. Karen Alice Karlberg, Dec. 31, 1987. AB, Princeton U., 1965; SMChemE, MIT, 1966, SM in Mgmt., 1968. Mgr. bus. analysis Halcon Internat. Inc., N.Y.C., 1968-73, dir. bus. planning, 1973-76; v.p., gen. mgr. Halcon Catalyst Industries, Little Ferry, N.J., 1976-82; v.p. planning & devel. Engelhard Industries, Iselin, N.J., 1982-84; pres., chief exec. officer i-STAT Corp., Princeton, N.J., 1984-86, Sunstone Inc., Dayton, N.J., 1986-87; vice chmn. Princeton Entrepreneurial Resources, 1988-90; pres., chief exec. officer SDTX Technologies, Inc., Princeton, 1989—; v.p. bus. devel. Enzon, Inc., Piscataway, N.J., 1991-94; exec. dir. The Sage Group, Bridgewater, N.J., 1995—, also bd. dirs.; COO, Hemispherx Biopharma, Inc., Phila., 1996-97; gen. ptnr. SAE Ventures, New Canaan, Conn., 1997—; cons. in field; dir. SDTX Technologies, Inc., Princeton, 1989—; pres., dir. Captiva Technologies, Princeton, 1989—; dir. Carnegie Venture Resources, Inc., Princeton, The Sage Group, Bridgewater. Dir. Gotham Light Opera Soc., N.Y.C., 1969-73; treas. Bloomingdale House of Music, N.Y.C., 1979-84. Named Univ. scholar Princeton U., 1961. Mem. The Licensing Execs. Soc., The Union League Club, Doubles, Sigma Xi, Phi Beta Kappa. Republican. Episcopalian. Avocations: chess, tennis. Home: 706 Sayre Dr Princeton NJ 08540-5835 Office: The Sage Group Inc 245 Rte 22 W Ste 304 Bridgewater NJ 08807-2560

HULSE, RUSSELL ALAN, physicist; b. N.Y.C., Nov. 28, 1950; s. Alan Earle and Betty Joan (Wedemeyer) H. BS, Cooper Union, 1970; MS, U. Mass., 1972, PhD, 1975. Rsch. assoc. Nat. Radio Astronomy Observatory, Charlottesville, Va., 1975-77; mem. tech. staff Princeton (N.J.) U. Plasma Physics Lab., 1977-80, staff rsch. physicist, 1980-84, rsch. physicist, 1984-92, prin. rsch. physicist, 1992—, head advanced modeling scis. lab., 1994—. Contbr. articles to profl. jours. Recipient Nobel prize in physics, 1993. Fellow Am. Phys. Soc.; mem. Am. Astron. Soc. Avocations: nature photography, bird watching, cross-country skiing, canoeing, hiking. Office: Princeton U Plasma Physics Lab James Forrestal Rsch Campus PO Box 451 Princeton NJ 08543-0451*

HULSEBERG, PAUL DAVID, financial executive, educator; b. Elmhurst, Ill., Mar. 13, 1950; s. Arnold Henry and Viola (Kliewer) H.; m. Mary Kate Tessman, 1970 (div. 1977); children: Amy, Mandy; m. Gwen Ann Preston, May 17, 1980 (div. 1994); children: Christian, Nicole; m. Peggy Joyce Jones, 1997; children: Todd, Scott. BS in Mgmt., Oklahoma City, 1985; MBA in Info. Systems, Oklahoma City U., 1989. Cert. data processor. Database adminstr. Locke Supply Co., Oklahoma City, 1975-78; programming mgr. CMI, Inc., Oklahoma City, 1978-81; CFO NAPA Okla., Oklahoma City, 1981—; assoc. prof. info. systems, mgmt. and econs. Oklahoma City U., 1985—; CEO Mirrorstone Mfg., mfrs. bd. game Tao, Oklahoma City, 1986—; regional exec. Okla. region Sports Car Clubs Am. Author boardgame Tao, 1986. Treas., trustee Edgemere Park Preservation, Inc., Oklahoma City, 1984-93. Mem. Alpha Chi, Beta Gamma. Methodist. Avocations: skiing, aikido, auto racing. Home: PO Box 24046 Oklahoma City OK 73124-0046 Office: Oklahoma City U PO Box 24046 Oklahoma City OK 73124-0046

HULSEBOSCH, CHARLES JOSEPH, truck manufacturing company executive; b. N.Y.C., Dec. 14, 1933; s. Albert J. and Marie (Gough) H.; m. Elizabeth Ferguson, July 6, 1957; children: Albert, Daniel, Joseph, Kristine, Thomas, Howard, John. A.B., Dartmouth, 1955; M.B.A., Amos Tuck Sch., 1956. Fin. analyst Ford Motor Co., 1956-60; from budget mgr. to controller Renault, Inc., N.Y.C., 1960-63; with United Fruit Co., 1963-69, treas., 1967-69; v.p., treas. Libby, McNeill & Libby, 1969-74, v.p. fin., bd. dirs., 1974-77; v.p. fin., treas., dir. Oshkosh Truck Corp., Wis., 1978-91, ret., 1991; part owner Wis. Flyers, Continental Basketball Assn., 1985-87. Mem. Oshkosh City Coun., 1981-85; treas. Lourdes Acad. Found., Oshkosh, 1986-89, Lourdes Acad.; bd. dirs., 1980-86, chmn. bd., 1986. Mem. Fin. Execs. Inst., Newcomen Soc., Oshkosh Country Club, Zeta Psi. Republican. Roman Catholic. Home: 5059 Valley Heights Rd Oshkosh WI 54904-9354

HULSEY, RACHEL MARTINEZ, secondary education educator; b. Laredo, Tex., Jan. 30, 1950; d. Manuel Conrado and Julia (Solis) Martinez; m. Joe A. Hulsey, Jan. 13, 1973 (div. Feb. 1992); children: John Travis, Marisa Andrea, Joseph Robert; m. Joe A. Hulsey, Jan. 13, 1994. BA, Our Lady of the Lake U., 1971; MA, U. Tex., 1977. Tchr. Harlandale Mid. Sch., San Antonio, 1971-77; reading supervisor Harlandale I.S.D., San Antonio, 1977-83; English tchr. Judson Ind. Sch. Tchr., San Antonio, 1983—; writing trainer N.J. Writing Project in Tex., San Antonio, 1992—, reading trainer, 1995—; cons. in field. Mem. NEA, Tex. State Edn. Assn., San Antonio Romance Authors, Alamo Writers Assn. Roman Catholic. Avocations: writing, reading, collecting books, dancing, exercising. Office: Judson HS Converse TX 78104

HULSHOF, KENNY, congressman; b. Sikeston, Mo., May 22, 1958; m. Renee Lynn Howell. BS, U. Mo., 1980; JD, U. Miss., 1983. Mem. 105th-106th Congress from Missouri 9th Dist., 1997—; mem. Congressional Way & Means Com., 1997—. Rep. candidate for Boone County Prosecutor, 1992, U.S. House, 1994, 96. Roman Catholic. Office: Ho of Representatives 412 Cannon Washington DC 20515-2509

HULSLANDER, MARJORIE DIANE, auditor; b. Towanda, Pa., Mar. 8, 1938; d. Robert Alfred and Catharine Agnes (Brennan) Neiley; m. John

Edgar Hulslander, June 14. 1958; children: Thomas Alfred, Cindy Lou Hulslander Loss, Timothy John. Bookkeeper G.L.F. Petroleum, Inc., Towanda, Pa., 1956-59; sec., treas. West Burlington Milk Producers, Troy, Pa., 1961-67; clk. Valley Stockyards, Inc., Athens, Pa., 1967-80; tax collector West Burlington Twp., Troy, Pa., 1968-87; auditor, chmn. Bradford County, Towanda, Pa., 1988-98. Committeewoman Bradford County Rep. Party, West Burlington Twp., 1980-98; Pres., founder Troy Fire Dept. Ladies Auxiliary Sta. 11, West Burlington Twp., 1988-90, treas., 1990-92, pres., 1996-97; exec. Pa. State Auditors Assn., 1992-95; treas. Bradford County Rep. Women, Towanda, Pa., 1994-95, pres., 1996-98; auditor State Rep. Women Fin. Records, 1994-95. Mem. Union Grange (#155 treas.). Republican. Episcopalian. Avocations: walking, dancing, traveling. Home: RR 3 Box 318 Troy PA 16947-9439 Office: Court House Towanda PA 18848

HULSTON, JOHN KENTON, lawyer; b. Dade County, Mo., Mar. 29, 1915; s. John Fred and Myrtle Rosa (King) H.; m. Ruth Amis Luster, Dec. 18, 1944; 1 son, John Luster. AB, Drury Coll., Springfield, Mo., 1936; JD, Mo. U., Columbia, 1941, D (hon.), 1997. Bar: Mo. 1941, U.S. Supreme Ct. 1949. Tchr., coach Ash Grove (Mo.) High Sch., 1936-38; pvt. practice law Springfield, 1946—; co-founder, dir., v.p., sec. Reed Oil Co., Big Spring, Tex., 1951-68, Pioneer Oil Co., Ft. Worth, 1954-79; operator, chmn. Copperhead Hill farms (beef production), 1955—; chmn. Bank of Ash Grove, 1959—, Citizens Home Bank, Greenfield, Mo., 1966—; pres. Bank of Springfield, 1968-69, Bank of Billings, 1987—; vice chmn., dir., mem. exec. com. Centerre Bank of Springfield (now NationsBank), 1969-89; sec., dir., v.p., mem. exec. com. Ozark Air Lines Inc. (now TWA), St. Louis, 1971-86; sec., dir., v.p. Ozark Holdings Inc. (now TWA), St. Louis, 1984-88; nominal ptnr. Hulston, Jones, Gammon & Marsh, 1984—; instr. real estate law Drury Coll., 1948-64; vis. lectr. corp. law E.R. Breech Sch. Bus., 1953. Author: An Ozarks Boy's Story, 1971, An Ozarks Lawyer's Story, 1976, History of Bank of Ash Grove, 1883-1983, 1983, A Look at Dade County, Missouri, 1905-85, 1985, Panhandle Profiles, 1889-1989, 1989, Lester E. Cox, 1895-1968, 1992, Daniel Boone's Sons in Missouri, 1947, West Point and Wilson's Creek--1861, 1955, Harry S. Truman v. J. William Chilton, 197 S.W. 346, (with Paul W. Barrett) and Duty of Mental Health Care Provider to Restrain Their Patients or Warn Third Parties (with Timothy E. Gammon), Vol. 56, 1991 Missouri Law Review, Vol. 60, 1995; contbr. articles to profl. jours. Chmn. Wilson's Creek Nat. Battlefield Commn., 1969-79; vice chmn. Springfield Home Rule Charter Commn., 1953; chmn. Springfield City Charter Commn., 1977; pres. Greene County Estate Planning Council, 1952; trustee Springfield Pub. Library, 1957-63, Drury Coll., 1966-95, State Hist. Soc. Mo., 1974—, life trustee, 1996—; trustee Cox Health Sys., 1959—, pres., 1966, vice chmn., 1967—; chmn. Greene County Dems., 1947-48; introduced Pres. Harry S. Truman at 1st Whistle Stop Speech, Springfield, July 5, 1948; presdl. elector, 1948; mem. Mo. Civil War Centennial Commn., 1961-65; life trustee Drury Coll., 1966—; trustee Mo. U. Law Sch. Found., Columbia, pres., 1985-87; co-founder Civil War Round Table of the Ozarks, 1948, Wilson's Creek Battlefield Found., 1952, Greene County Hist. Soc., 1962, The Hist. Mus. Springfield-Greene County, 1974; mem. devel. fund bd. Mo. U., Columbia, 1986-90. Maj. U.S. Army, WWII, 1941-46. Recipient Springfield Young Man of Year award, 1950, Disting. Alumni award Drury Coll., 1974, Springfieldian of Year award, 1978, The Missourian award, 1998, Spl. commendation U.S. Dept. Interior, Nat. Park Service, 1981, Faculty-Alumni Gold medal award Mo. U., Columbia, 1988, Citation of Merit Mo. U. Law Sch., Disting. Svc. award Mo. U. Alumni Assn., 1993; inductee into Writers Hall of Fame, 1995. Fellow Am. Bar Found. (life); mem. ABA (real property, probate/trust reporter Mo. 1974-96), Am. Judicature Soc., Am. Acad. Hosp. Attys., Am. Soc. Law, Ethics and Medicine, Mo. Bar Assn. (1st chmn. legal aid 1952), Springfield Met. Bar Assn. (pres. 1973), Springfield C. of C. (pres. 1950, 51, 54), Supreme Ct. of Mo. Hist. Soc. (co-founder, trustee 1984-90), SAR, Order of Coif, Phi Delta Phi, Kappa Alpha Order. Democrat. Presbyterian. Clubs: Hickory Hills Country (Springfield); University of Mo. Jefferson (trustee 1976-82). Lodges: Masons (32 deg.), Shriners (potentate 1963), Jester. Home: 1300 E Catalpa St Springfield MO 65804-0134 Office: 2060 E Sunshine St Springfield MO 65804-1815 *Awareness of one's limitations sometimes is the spur to sustained effort creating worthwhile achievements.*

HULSTRAND, GEORGE EUGENE, lawyer; b. Cannon Falls, Minn., Aug. 3, 1918; s. John George and Alice Elizabeth (Holm) H.; m. Mabel Elizabeth Ericson, Sept. 7, 1946; children: George E. Jr., Brian Douglas, Darlene Lucette, Jeanne Louise. BA, Gustavus Adolphus Coll., 1943; JD, Yale U., 1946. Bar: Minn. 1947, U.S. Dist. Ct. Minn. 1951, U.S. Supreme Ct. 1977, U.S. Ct. Claims 1990. Assoc. Roy A. Hendrickson, Willmar, Minn., 1947-53; ptnr. Hulstrand, Anderson, Larson, Hanson & Saunders, Willmar, 1953-97; pvt. practice Willmar, 1997—; asst. county atty. Kandiyohi County, Willmar, 1947-50. Contbr. articles to mags. Mem. Willmar City Coun., 1953-56; chmn. Willmar Planning Commn., 1956-57, 74-80, Kandiyohi County Dem.-Farmer-Labor Party, Willmar, 1957-72; bd. dirs. Willmar Cmty. Coll. Found., 1965-94. Mem. ABA, Minn. Bar Assn. (bd. govs. 1977-83, cert. sr. counselor 1997), 12th Dist. Bar Assn., Am. Judicature Soc., Willmar Jaycees (Disting. Service award 1952, Outstanding Citizen award 1979). Lutheran. Lodges: Lions, Elks. Avocations: music, writing, golf, travel. Home: 325 N 7th St Willmar MN 56201 Office: Wilmar Bldg 201 4th St SW PO Box 1860 Willmar MN 56201-1860

HULT, GERT TOMAS MIKAEL, international business executive, educator; b. Uppsala, Sweden, June 11, 1967; came to U.S., 1987; s. Gert G. and L. Margareta (Söderkvist) H.; m. Laurie W., June 6, 1993. Mech. Engring. Degree, Fyrisskolan, Uppsala, Sweden, 1987; BSB, MBA, Murray State U., 1990, 91; PhD, U. Memphis, 1995. Cert. mech. engr. Founding mem. Inmark Consulting Group LLC, Memphis, 1994-96; asst. prof. internat. bus. U. Ark., Little Rock, 1994-96; dir. internat. bus. Fla. State U., Tallahassee, 1996—; cons. Fed. Express Corp., Memphis, 1993—. Editor: (book) Enhancing Knowledge Development in Marketing, 1997; contbr. articles to profl. jours. Mem. Acad. Internat. Bus., Am. Mktg. Assn. (program chair 1997, 98), Acad. of Mktg. Sci., Acad. of Mgmt., Decision Scis. Inst., So. Mktg. Assn. Lutheran. Avocations: golf, tennis, travel. Office: Fla State U Coll of Bus Tallahassee FL 32306

HULT, SUSAN FREDA, history educator; b. Roslyn, N.Y., Jan. 29, 1956; d. Thomas Joseph and Rosemary (Arthur) Freda; m. Allan Richard Hult, Nov. 18, 1978 (div. 1982). BA in Polit. Sci., Fla. So. Coll., 1977; MA in History, Clemson U., 1985; postgrad., Rice U., 1985-89, U. Houston, 1989—. Read-a-Thon coord. Multiple Sclerosis Soc., Tampa, Fla., 1977-78; divsnl. sales mgr., asst. buyer Ivey's Fla., Winter Park, 1978-81; pers. dir. Tampa Hilton Hotel, 1981-82; grad. asst. Clemson (S.C.) U., 1984-85; prof. history Ctrl. Coll., Houston, 1986—, dept. chair history/philosophy/geography, 1995—; vis. asst. prof. history U. Alaska Southeast, Sitka, 1993-94; adj. instr. Sheldon Jackson Coll., Sitka, 1994; archivist Liberty Life Ins. Co., Greenville, S.C., 1985; pres. faculty assn. coun. Houston C.C. Sys., 1995-96, pres.-elect, 1994-95, sec., 1992-93, treas., 1991-92, chair, 1992-93, chair salary com., 1992-94, chair fundraising com., 1991-92, chair governance com., 1990-91; presenter in field. Editl. asst. Papers of Jefferson Davis, Rice U., 1987-88, Jour. So. History, 1985-87. Mem., vol. Houston Grand Opera Guild, 1994—, Houston Ballet Guild, 1994—; mem. Houston Fedn. Profl. Women, 1995—; campaign worker various Dem. candidates, Houston, 1987— vol. Project Nicaragua, 1994, 95, 98, 99. NEH grantee, 1994-95, 98, Houston C.C. Sys. grantee, 1991-95, Fulbright-Hays grantee, 1994, 99, East-West Ctr. grantee, 1998; Illabelle Shanahan Morrisin fellow Alpha Chi Omega Found., 1985. Mem. Am. Assn. Women C.C.s, Orgn. Am. Historians, Tex. C.C. Tchrs. Assn., Tex. Assn. Women C.C.s, Assn. Women Adminstrs., Houston Fedn. Profl. Women, C.C. Humanities Assn., Phi Alpha Theta, Omicron Delta Kappa, Kappa Delta Pi, Phi Theta Kappa (Tex./N.Mex. adv. bd. 1996—, Horizon award 1996, seminar leader 1995-96). Avocations: reading, singing, the arts, photography, tennis. Home: 4006 Julian St Houston TX 77009-5243 Office: Ctrl Coll/Houston CC Sys 1300 Holman St # 1229 Houston TX 77004-3834

HULTBERG, JOHN, artist; b. Berkeley, Calif., Feb. 8, 1922; s. John Waldemar and Mabel Olive (Hammer) H.; m. Hilary Editha Blesh, June 9, 1948 (div. 1956); children: Carl Rudolph, Stephanie Maria; m. Lynne Drexler, Sept. 1985. AB, Fresno State Coll., 1943; student, Calif. Sch. Fine Arts, 1947-49, Art Students League, N.Y.C., 1949-51. Exhibited San Francisco Mus. Art, 1947-49, Los Angeles Mus., 1949, New Talent show, Mus. Modern Art, 1952, one man shows Korman Gallery, N.Y.C., 1953, Martha Jackson Gallery, N.Y.C., 1955, Corcoran Gallery, Washington, 1955, Butler Art Inst., Ohio, 1955, UN Exhibit, San Francisco, 1955, Galerie Rive Droit, Paris, 1954-55, Galerie Nina Dausset, Paris, 1954, Galeria Spazio, Rome, 1955, Mus. Modern Art, Rome, 1955, Guild Hall, East Hampton, N.Y., 1955, I.C.A., London, 1956, others; rep. in collections Met. Mus. Art, Whitney Mus., Roy R. Neuburger, Edward Root, Michel Tapie.; author 5 books. Served as lt. (j.g.) USNR, 1943-46. Recipient prize San Francisco Mus. watercolor ann., 1948; prize San Francisco oil ann., 1941; hon. mention Los Angeles Centennial painting exhibit, 1949; 1st prize Corcoran Biennial Exhibit, Washington, 1955; prize Congress for Cultural Freedom Exhbn. for painters under 35, Europe, 1955; hon. mention Carnegie Internat. Ex-hon., 1955; Norman Harris medal at 65th ann. exhbn. Art Inst. Chgo.; Altman prize NAD, 1972, 85, Shatlov award, 1983, also another award; Albert Bender fellow San Francisco, 1949; Guggenheim fellow, 1956; Nat. Endowment Arts grantee, 1981. Mem. NAD. Home: 141 W 73rd St New York NY 10023

HULTGREN, DENNIS EUGENE, farmer, management consultant; b. Union County, S.D., Mar. 19, 1929; s. John Alfred and Esther Marie (Johnson) H.; grad. high sch.; m. Nelda Ethelyn Olson, Aug. 3, 1957; children: Nancy Hultgren Klemme, Jean Hultgren Doty, Jahn Dennis, Ruth Dorothy Hultgren Henneman. Farmer, Union County, 1953—; commr., chmn. Union County Planning and Zoning Bd., 1972-83; mem. bd. bylaw revision Union County Electric Co., 1983-85. Pres. bd. Union Creek Cemetery, 1958—; pres. bd. mgrs. Union-Sayles Watershed Dist., 1965-70; exec. bd. S.D. Farm Bur., Union County, 1996—, pres., 1998—. Treas., Sioux Valley Twp., Union County, 1980—; treas., bd. dirs. W. Union Sch., 1957-67; chmn. Union County Sch. Bd., 1961-68; pres. Alcester (S.D.) Sch. Bd., 1970-77; chmn. Alcester PTA, 1967-68; mem. tech. bd. rev. Southeastern Council Govts., Sioux Falls, S.D., 1976-77; bd. dirs. Siouxland Interstate Met. Planning Council, Sioux City, Iowa, 1977-83, sec. council ofcls., 1978-83; bd. dirs. Old Opera House Community Theater, Akron, Iowa, Akron Area Action Assn., 1983-85, 1983-84, Akron Devel. Corp., 1985-90; Rep. precinct committeeman, 1970—, Union County Rep. Cen. Com., 1970—; chmn. S.D. State Bd. Equalization, 1987-95; mem. synod stewardship bd. Western Iowa Synod Luth. Ch., 1987-90, elected synod assembly bus. and coun. com., 1991-93, synod bus. and coun com., 1997—, synod coun. Western Iowa Synod, 1997—; S.D. del. Rep. Nat. Conv., New Orleans, 1988. Served with AUS, 1951-53, Korea. Recipient outstanding dedication and service award Old Opera House Community Theatre, 1984, Sioux City Siouxland Disting. Citizen award Siouxland Interstate Met. Planning Council, 1983, Jefferson award Sta. KELO-TV, 1985, Outstanding Community Service award Lions Internat., 1985. Mem. Farm Bur., Farmers Union (exec. bd. Union County 1987-90), S.D. Livestock Feeders Assn., Nat. Cattlemen's Assn., Associated Sch. Bds. S.D. (Merit award 1976), Am. Legion (exec. bd. Akron 1978-92, comdr. Akron 1980-81, 85-86, historian 1981-96, trustee 1983-90, 96—, vice comdr. 9th dist. 1989, chaplain 9th dist. 1990, comdr. 9th dist. 1991, chmn. athletics and contest com., 1991-92, 97—, judge advocate 9th dist., Iowa, 1993—), VFW (Alcester, S.D. vice-comdr. 1995-97). Lutheran (mem. bd. 1967-70, 82-84, 90-93, lay chmn. 1970, 82-93, chmn. centennial com. 1974). Address: Hulteboda Farm 47953 309th St Akron IA 51001-7575

HULTMAN, CHARLES WILLIAM, economics educator; b. Oelwein, Iowa, Apr. 6, 1930; s. John William and Alma (Loeb) H.; m. Irene Oliver, June 7, 1957; children: Susan, Gregory. BA, Upper Iowa U., 1952; MA, Drake U., 1957; PhD, U. Iowa, 1960. Asst. prof. U. Ky., Lexington, 1960-64, prof. econs., 1967—, chmn. dept., 1969-71, CSX prof. bus. and pub. policy, 1988—, assoc. dir. Ctr. for Devel. Change, 1971-73, assoc. dean for rsch., 1976-85; vis. assoc. prof. U. Calif., 1964-65, prof. of banking and fin. Univ. Coll., Dublin, Ireland, 1990; fall sememster Ford Found. prof. Fudan U., Shanghai, China, 1989. Author: International Finance, 1963, American Business and the Common Market, 1964, Problems of Economic Development, 1967, Ireland in the World Economy, 1969, (with M. Wasserman, R. Ware) International Economics, 1969, Comparison of Projected Unemployment Insurance Costs, 1973, The Environment of International Ban King, 1990; book rev. editor: Internat. Devel. Rev.; mem. editorial adv. bd. Sage Papers in Internat. Studies; assoc. editor internat. econs. Wall Street Rev. Books; acting editor: Jour. Growth and Change, 1979-86. Chmn. Ky. Coun.Econ. Advisors, 1976-85; mem. So. Growth Policies Bd., 1976-90. With U.S. Army, 1952-55. Fulbright lectr. Ireland, 1967-68. Mem. Am. Econ. Assn., So. Econ. Assn., Midwest Econ. Assn., Eastern Econ. Assn. (exec. bd. 1980-84). Lutheran. Home: 3341 Crown Crest Rd Lexington KY 40517-2809

HULTQUIST, PAUL FREDRICK, electrical engineer, educator; b. Holdrege, Nebr., Mar. 24, 1920; s. Fred Oscar and Lalan Ragnhild (Swanberg) H.; m. Juanita Marie Tokheim, Apr. 7, 1946; children: Fredrick James, Ann Marie. Student, Bethany Coll., Lindsborg, Kans., 1940-41, Hastings Coll., 1943-44; B.A. cum laude, U. Colo., 1945, Ph.D. (AEC predoctoral fellow) Physics, 1954. Instr. applied math. U. Colo., Boulder, 1945-48, 52-55; asst. prof. U. Colo., 1955-59, assoc. prof., 1959-63; prof., asst. dean engring. U. Colo., Colorado Springs, 1965-71; prof. elec. engring., assoc. dean U. Colo., Denver, 1971; prof. elec. and computer engring. U. Colo., 1971-88, prof. computer sci., 1982-88, prof. emeritus, 1988—; lectr. math. and computer sci. U. Nebr., Omaha, 1989-95; sr. scientist Tech. Support, Inc., Omaha, 1993—; assoc. dir. Univ. Computer Center U. Colo., 1973-76; assoc. rsch. scientist Lockheed Missiles and Space Co., Palo Alto, Calif., 1956-57; sr. staff scientist Ball Aerospace & Techs., Boulder, 1963-65; cons. in field. Author: Numerical Methods for Engineers and Computer Scientists, 1988; contbr. numerous articles, revs. to profl. publs. Trustee Bethphage Mission, Inc., Omaha, 1966-76, 78-84, 85-90, chmn., 1980-84, 86-90, mem. human resources com., 1997—; trustee Bethphage Residential Ctrs., 1983-88, Bethphage Mission South, Austin, Tex., 1990-97; trustee Bethphage Mission East, Hartford, Conn., 1989-95, chmn., 1991-93; trustee Bethphage Mission Pacific, Portland, Oreg., 1995-97, chmn., 1995-97; chmn. bd. Advent Svcs., Inc., Omaha, 1998—; mem. bd. parish edn. United Luth. Ch. Am., 1958-62, Luth. Ch. in Am., 1963-66, 68-72, mem. mgmt. com. divsn. parish svcs., 1972-78, 80-87, chmn., 1982-87; bd. dirs. Luth. Sch. Theology at Chgo., 1967-69, 72-78, chmn., 1975-78; bd. dirs. Pacific Luth. Theol. Sem., Berkeley, 1981-88; adv. mem. The Bethphage Found., 1992—. Mem. Assn. Computing Machinery, Soc. Indsl. and Applied Math., IEEE (sr.), Math. Assn. Am., Soc. Computer Simulation, Phi Beta Kappa, Sigma Xi, Tau Beta Pi. Democrat. Home: 6803 N 68th Plz Omaha NE 68152-2177

HULTSTRAND, CHARLES JOHN, architect; b. Mt. Vernon, Ohio, Dec. 26, 1951; s. Donald M. and Marjorie R. (Richter) H.; m. Kathi, Brooke, Andrew, Caroline, Clay, Kristi, Scott. BSE, Princeton U., 1974; MArch, Rice U., 1977. Registered architect, S.C. Assoc., project designer Golemon & Rolfe Architects, Houston, 1977-83; prin., exec. v.p., dir. of design Boudreaux, Hultstrand & Co., Ltd., Columbia, S.C., 1983—; guest lectr. Clemson (S.C.) U. Coll. Architecture, 1993-97; mem. steering com. Onions & Orchids Award Program, Columbia, 1988, jury mem., 1989; mem. steering com. Columbia R/UDAT Commn., 1987. Pres. parent tchr. fellowship Ben Lippen Sch., Columbia, 1991-94, mem. bd. mgrs., 1991-99, v.p. bd., 1995-99; mem. fundraising com., 1993-94; deacon Cornerstone Presbyn. Ch., Columbia, 1988-91, First Presbyn. Ch., Columbia, 1997-99; pres. Yokemen Svc. Orgn., 1982-83; vol. ARC Hurricane Hugo Relief, 1990, SCETV Fundraising, Columbia, 1991. Mem. AIA (pres. S.C. chpt. 1996, v.p./pres.-elect S.C. chpt. 1995, sec.-treas. S.C. chpt. 1993-94, chmn. spkrs. bur. 1988-90, dir. Columbia sect. 1988-90, chmn. govt. affairs commn. S.C. chpt. 1990-93, bd. dirs., advisor intern devel. program 1990-94), S.C. Archtl. Soc. (bd. dirs./sec. 1997—), Columbia Design League (bd. dirs. 1997-98), Columbia Coun. Archs. (pres. 1986-87, bd. dirs. 1984-87), Princeton Alumni Assn. S.C. (treas. 1990-94), Greater Columbia C. of C. Avocations: reading, walking, tennis, golf. Office: Boudreaux Hultstrand & Co PO Box 5695 Columbia SC 29250-5695

HULTSTRAND, DONALD MAYNARD, bishop; b. Parkers Prairie, Minn., Apr. 16, 1927; s. Aaron Emmanuel H. and Selma Avendla (Liljegren) H.; m. Marjorie Richter, June 11, 1948; children—Katherine Ann, Charles John. B.A. summa cum laude, Macalester Coll., 1950; B.D. summa cum laude, Kenyon Coll., 1953; M.Div. summa cum laude, Colgate-Rochester Theol. Sem., 1974; D.D. honoris causa, Nashotah Divinity Sch., 1986. Ordained priest Episcopal Ch., 1953, consecrated bishop, 1982. Vicar St. John's Episcopal Ch., Worthington, Minn., 1953-57; rector Grace Meml. Ch., Wabasha, Minn., 1957-62, St. Mark's Episcopal Ch., Canton, Ohio, 1962-68, St. Paul's Episcopal Ch., Duluth, Minn., 1969-75; assoc. rector St. Andrew's Episcopal Ch., Kansas City, Mo., 1968-69; exec. dir. Anglican Fellowship of Prayer, 1975-79; rector Trinity Episcopal Ch., Greeley, Colo., 1979-82; bishop Episcopal Diocese of Springfield, Ill., 1982-91; exec. bd. Episcopal Radio (TV Found.), Atlanta, 1982-87, Anglican Fellowship of Prayer, 1968-93; adv. bd. Episcopal Boys' Homes, Salinas, Kans., 1983-91; com. of execs. Ill. Conf. Chs., 1982-91; mem. House of Bishops, 1982—, Minn. Standing Com., 1970-73; chmn. Minn. Examining Chaplains, 1954-61; chaplain Pewsaction Fellowships U.S.A., 1983-92; pres. Living Ch. Found., 1992—; advisor Diocesan Youth of Minn., 1956-60. Author: The Praying Church, 1978, And God Shall Wipe Away All Tears, 1968, Intercessory Prayer, 1972, Upper Room Dialogues, 1980, Revelations of Effective Prayer, 1995; co-author: The Parish as a Center of Prayer, 1996. Bd. dirs. Sr. Citizens Housing, Duluth, 1972-75, St. Luke's Hosp., Duluth, 1969-75; pres. Low-Rent Housing Project, Greeley, 1979-82. Served with USNR, 1945-46. Recipient Disting. Service award Young Life Minn., 1974; named hon. canon Diocese of Ohio, Cleve., 1967. Mem. Pi Phi Epsilon. Address: 1701 S Le Homme Dieu Dr NE Alexandria MN 56308-8504

HULY, JAN C., career officer; b. Phila., Mar. 29, 1948; m. Patricia; children: Allison, Nicholas, Lauren. BSBA, U. Calif., Berkeley, 1969; grad., Basic Sch., Amphibious Warfare Sch., 1976; MA in Personnel Mgmt., Ctrl. Mich. U.; grad., Marine Corps Command and Staff, Quantico, Va., 1985, U.S. Army War Coll., 1990. Commd. 2d lt. USMC, 1969, advanced through grades to brig. gen., 1995; with 1st Bn. 3rd Marines 1st Marine Brigade, 3rd Bn. 4th Marines 3d Marine Divsn.; series comdr., bn. adjutant, recruit co. comdr., dir. recrui Marine Corps Recruit Depot, San Diego, 1972-76; bn. staff officer, rifle co. comdr., asst. ops. officer 5th 1st Marine Divsn., Camp Pendleton, Calif., 1976-79; comdr. Marine Detachment USS Ranger, 1979-80; with Joint Chiefs of Staff, Washington, 1980-82; with personnel mgmt. divsn. Hdqs. Marine Corps, 1982-84; exec. officer 2nd Marine Divsn., Camp Lejeune, N.C., 1985, comdg. officer for bn. landing team 1/8 SOC; exec. officer 2nd Surveillance, Reconnaissance and Intellige 2nd Marine Expeditionary Force; asst. and head of the enlisted assignment br. Hdqs. Marine Corps, 1990-92; dep. asst. chief of staff for ops. 2nd Marine Divsn., Saudi Arabia and Kuwait; comdg. officer 22nd Marine Expeditionary Unit, 1992-94; asst. dep. chief of staff plans, policy and ops., 1998—. Decorated Legion of Merit with Gold star. Office: Marine Forces Reserve New Orleans LA 70146 also: Hdqs Marine Corps 2 Navy Annex Rm 2210 Divsn Pub Affairs Washington DC 20380-1775*

HUM, VANCE YORK, technology consulting executive; b. San Francisco, Apr. 19, 1948; s. Bing Wai and Jean Bik-Tsun (Pong) H.; m. Carolyn Hwa Cheung, July 2, 1972; children: Matthew Ta, Christina Lee, Jonathan Derek-Lee. *Father Bing Wai emigrated to America at the age of fourteen to join his Minneapolis merchant father. He received his B.S. Radio Engineering degree (precursor to electronics engineering) in 1943 from Tri-State College in Indiana and joined the U.S. Army-Air Force during World War II. After marrying Jean Bik-Tsun, they raised Vance, Sharon (Conroy), Warren, and Vern. He spent the balance of his professional career as a senior electronics engineer at the Department of the Navy. His grandson is currently a third generation electronics engineering student at Worcester Polytechnic Institute.* Bsee, u. mD., 1971; postgrad., George Washington U., 1977-83, U. Md., 1983—. Engr. Singer-Link Divsn., Silver Spring, Md., 1970; engr., field engr. Bendix Field Engring., Columbia, Md., 1971-72; primary examiner U.S. Patent & Trademark Bd., Arlington, Va., 1972-83; v.p. ops. Cheung Labs., Inc., Lanham-Seabrook, Md., 1983-86; v.p. fin. Cheung Labs. Inc., Lanham-Seabrook, Md., 1985-86; v.p. ops. Century Techs., Inc., Silver Spring, 1988-89; CEO, bd. dirs. Marc's Distbg., Inc., Jessup, Md., 1987-88; CEO, pres. I.M. Systems Group, Inc., Kensington, Md., 1986-87, 89—; chmn. bd. dirs. I.M. Systems Group, Inc., Md., 1989—; chmn. audit/supervisory com. Lee Fed. Credit Union, Washington, 1977-83; mem. adv. bd. Pacific Savs. and Loan Assn., McLean, Va., 1979-80; chmn. strategic planning com. Nat. Assn. Corp. Dirs., Balt.-Washington, 1989. Troop treas. Boy Scouts Am., Bethesda/Chevy Chase, Md., 1993—. Mem. Herndon (Va.) C. of C. (chief exec. bd. 1999). Avocations: tennis, golf, karate, skiing, gardening. Office: IM Sys Group Inc 3401 Bexhill Pl Kensington MD 20895-3105

HUMBERT, CHERYL ANN, field nurse; b. Cin., Dec. 9, 1962; d. Thomas Anthony and Marilyn Rita Humbert. BSN, U. Cin., 1990. RN, Ohio; cert. ACLS, TNCC. Staff nurse med. ICU Univ. Hosp., Cin., 1990-92, staff nurse emergency, 1992-97; after hours triage nurse coord. Alliance Primary Care, Cin., 1995-98; home health nurse Option Care, Cin., 1997—. Author: (poetry) On the Threshold of A Dream, 1989, The Witness, 1988. Mem. AACN, Ohio Nurses Assn. (media com. 1995-98). Roman Catholic. Office: Option Care Ste 114 25 Whitney Dr Milford OH 45150

HUMBLE, MONTY GARFIELD, lawyer; b. Cameron, Tex., Dec. 20, 1951; s. Don Garfield Humble and Betty Sue (Maedgen) French; m. Donell Lou Moss, Mar. 12, 1976 (div. June 1981); m. Macy A. Melton, Oct. 23, 1993; children: Megan Elizabeth, John Marshall, Nicole Marie, Crawford Melton. BA, U. Tex., 1974, JD, 1976. Assoc. Clark, Thomas, Winters and Shapiro, Austin, Tex., 1972-82, Vinson & Elkins, Houston, 1982-86; ptnr. Vinson & Elkins, Dallas, 1986—. Bd. dirs. Ft. Worth Ballet, 1990-94, Dallas Opera, 1987-92; gen. counsel Superconducting Super Collider Devel. Authority, 1987-94; mem. Leadership Dallas, 1988; mem. legal advisors Dallas City Charter Revision Com., 1990; mem. Greater Dallas Planning Coun. Fellow Dallas Bar Found.; mem. ABA, State Bar Tex., Nat. Assn. Bond Lawyers (steering com. 1985-87, 94-96), Health Care Fin. Mgrs. Assn. (bd. dirs. 1990-92), Crescent Club, Bent Tree Country Club. Republican. Office: Vinson & Elkins LLP 2001 Ross Ave Ste 3700 Dallas TX 75201-2975

HUME, BEVERLY ANN, English and linguistics educator; b. Red Bluff, Calif., July 21, 1950; d. Lloyd Cooley and Ruth A. Reeve Hume; m. Craig Robert Thorne, Aug. 12, 1988. BA in English, Calif. State U., Sacramento, 1973, MA, 1975; PhD in English, U. Calif., Davis, 1983. Vis. lectr. U. Calif., Davis, 1983-85; vis. asst. prof. Emory U., Atlanta, 1985-86, Ga. Tech., Atlanta, 1986-87; assoc. prof. English Ind. U.-Purdue U., Fort Wayne, Ind., 1987—; regional cons. Ind. Humanities Endowment Grant, Indpls., 1993; presenter in field. Contbr. articles to profl. jours. Summer rsch. grantee Ind. U., 1988, 94. Mem. MLA, Nature Conservancy. Avocations: creative environmental writing. E-mail: Hume@ipfw.indiana.edu.

HUME, BRIT (ALEXANDER BRITTON HUME), journalist; b. Washington, June 22, 1943; s. George and Virginia Powell (Minnigerode) H.; m. Clare Stoner, Feb. 10, 1965 (div. 1992); children: Louis, Virginia, Alexander Jr.; m. Kim Schiller, June 1, 1993. BA, U. Va., 1965. Reporter Hartford (Conn.) Times, 1965-67, UPI, Hartford, Conn., 1967, Balt. Evening Sun, 1968; fellow Washington Journalism Ctr., 1969; reporter Jack Anderson Column, Washington, 1970-72; freelance journalist Washington, 1973; cons. ABC News, Washington, 1973-76, corr., 1976-97; columnist Washington Post Writers Group, 1987—; chief Washington corr., mng. editor Fox News, Washington, 1997—. Author: Death and the Mines, 1971, Inside Story, 1974. Recipient Emmy award, 1992; named Best in Bus. by Am. Journalism Rev., 1992, 94. Mem. Met. Club, Chevy Chase Club, St. Andrews Soc. Episcopal. Office: FOX News 400 N Capitol St NW Ste 550 Washington DC 20001-1502

HUME, ELLEN HUNSBERGER, media analyst, journalist; b. Chevy Chase, Md., Apr. 24, 1947; d. Warren Seabury and Ruth (Pedersen) H.; m. John Shattuck, Feb. 14, 1991; 1 child, Susannah; stepchildren: Jessica, Rebecca, Peter. BA, Harvard U., 1968; PhD (hon.), Daniel Webster Coll., 1990. Reporter Somerville (Mass.) Jour., 1968-69; feature writer Santa Barbara (Calif.) News Press, 1969-70; pub. service dir., copy writer KTMS Radio, Santa Barbara, 1970-72; edn. reporter Ypsilanti (Mich.) Press, 1972-73; bus. reporter Detroit Free Press, 1973-75; met. reporter L.A. Times, 1975-77; congl. reporter L.A. Times, Washington, 1977-83; White House corr., polit. writer Wall St. Jour., Washington, 1983-88; exec. dir. Shorenstein Ctr. on Press and Politics Harvard U., Cambridge, Mass., 1988-93; moderator The Editors TV program, Montreal, Que., 1990-93; adj. lectr. Kennedy Sch. Govt., 1991-93, Medill Sch. Journalism, 1993-94; commentator Washington Week in Rev. PBS-TV, 1973-88, CNN, 1993-97; exec. dir. The Democracy Project, PBS, 1996-98. Kennedy Inst. Politics fellow Harvard U., 1981, Annenberg Washington Program fellow, 1993-95. Mem. Coun. of Fgn. Rels., Fund for Free Expression, Nat. Press Club. Methodist. Address: Am Embassy Prague US Dept of State Washington DC 20521-5630

HUME, JAMES BORDEN, corporate professional, foundation executive; b. Halifax, N.S., Can., Nov. 6, 1950; s. Thomas White and Elizabeth Mae (Spears) H.; m. Penelope Ann Morris, June 3, 1972; children: Kathryn Ann, David Stuart. BA, U. Calgary, 1972. Chartered acct. V.p. TIW Industries Ltd., Ottawa, Ont., 1978-80; pres. Hume Mgmt. Cons. Ltd., Calgary, Alta., 1980-85, Kanesco Holdings Ltd., Calgary, 1985—; pres. The Kahanoff Found., Calgary, 1984—, also bd. dirs., 1984—. V.p. CH/PH Community Assn., Calgary; bd. dirs. YMCA, Calgary, Southern Alberta Inst. Tech., United Way of Calgary. Mem. Can. Inst. Chartered Accts. Office: Kahanoff Foundation, 400 Third Ave Ste #4206, Calgary, AB Canada T2P 4H2*

HUMES, CHARLES WARREN, counselor, educator; b. Cambridge, Mass.; s. Charles W. and Alice E. Humes; m. Marilyn A. Harper, Aug. 7, 1965; children: Rebecca Ellyn Gelber, Malinda Maye. MA, NYU, 1952; EdM, Springfield Coll., 1956; EdD, U. Mass., 1968. Lic. profl. counselor, Va.; cert. profl. counselor, Ariz. Sch. psychologist Westfield Pub. Schs. (Mass.), 1955-62; dir. guidance Westfield Pub. Schs. (Mass.), 1962-70; assoc. prof. Springfield Coll. (Mass.), 1968-70; dir. pupil svc. and spl. edn. Greenwich Pub. Schs. (Conn.), 1970-80; assoc. prof. No. Va. Grad. Ctr., Va. Tech. U., Falls Church, 1980-88, prof. 1988-93, prof. emeritus, 1993—; pvt. practice, Vienna, Va. and Phoenix, 1985—. V.p. Westfield Area Child Guidance Clinic, 1963-65, pres., 1965-66; mem. Greenwich Hosp. Nursing Coun., 1970-75. Mem. APA, ACA (cons.), SAR (registrar, genealogist Palo Verde chpt. 1997—), Conn. Assn. Counselor Edn. & Supervision (pres. 1979-80), Ariz. Counselors Assn., Nat. Geneal. Soc., Phi Delta Kappa (v.p. Va. Tech. 1982-83), Phi Kappa Phi. Author: Pupil Services: Development, Coordination, Administration, 1984; Contemporary Counseling: Services, Applications, Issues, 1987. Book rev. editor Sch. Counselor, 1984-93. Contbr. over 60 articles on counseling to profl. jours. Home and Office: 15038 E Palomino Blvd Fountain Hills AZ 85268-4813

HUMES, DAVID WALKER, accountant; b. Flint, Mich., Apr. 19, 1954; s. Daniel Baker and Mary Nell (Walker) H.; divorced; children: Baker Maxwell, Madison Campbell; m. Judith Lea Humes; stepchildren: Adam Miller, Justin Miller. BA, Centre Coll., 1976. CPA, Ky.; lic. real estate agt., lic. ins. agt., Ky.; cert. personal trainer/fitness counselor Aerobics and Fitness Assn. Am. CPA Coopers & Lybrand, Louisville, 1976-80; internal auditor Brown & Williamson Tobacco Co., Louisville, 1980-81; controller Ashford Stud, Versailles, Ky., 1981-83; treas. James Motor Co., Lexington, Ky., 1983-84; pvt. practice David W. Humes CPA PSC, Versailles, 1984—; controller Payson Stud, Inc., 1996—; pres. Number One Sun, Inc. dba Versailles Athletic Club, 1991—. Bd. dirs. BGT for Hist. Preservation, Lexington, 1987-92, v.p., 1989, pres., 1990-91; rep. for Midway to Archtl. Rev. Bd. of Woodford County, Versailles, 1988-90; chmn. BGT Revolving Fund, Lexington, 1988-89; campaign treas. Barrows for Ky. Ho. of Reps., Trapp for Urban County Govt. 10th Dist. Councilman, Trapp for Ky. Ho. of Reps.; mem. Midway City Coun., 1990-93; appointee Versailles-Woodford County Planning and Zoning Bd., Versailles-Woodford County Tech. Rev. Com., 1990-92. Mem. AICPA, Ky. Soc. CPAs, Woodford County Fair Saddle Horse Show (advisor 1988-93), ISSAC Shelby Soc. of Centre Coll., Nat. Trust for Hist. Preservation, Lions Club Internat. Democrat. Roman Catholic. Avocations: volleyball, horseback riding, hist. renovation. Home: 110 Maple St Versailles KY 40383-1419 Office: PO Box 999 Versailles KY 40383-0999

HUMES, GRAHAM, investment banker; b. Williamsport, Pa., Oct. 8, 1932; s. Samuel and Elenor (Graham) H.; m. Elizabeth Schwartz Hershey, June 17, 1978; children: Margaret, Kathryn, Malcolm, Elizabeth, John Hershey, Lisa Hershey. BA, Williams Coll., 1954; MBA, Harvard U., 1958. Mng. ptnr. Butcher & Singer, Inc., Phila., 1958-74; sr. v.p. Girard Bank-Mellon Bank, Phila., 1974-87; mng. dir. Legg Mason Wood Walker, Inc., Phila., 1987-93; founder, gen. dir. CARESBAC, St. Petersburg, Russia, 1993-95; prin. Compass Capital Ptnrs., Ltd., Radnor, Pa., 1995—; chmn. Cherry Valley (N.Y.) Spring Water Co.; bd. dirs. Brunschwig & Fils, Inc., N. White Plains, N.Y., Technitrol Inc., Trevose, Pa., Baltic Cranberry Corp., St. Petersburg, Russia; trustee Fgn. Policy Rsch. Inst., Phila. Mem. Merion Cricket Club, Phila. Club, Harvard Bus. Sch. Club. Republican. Home: 262 Radnor Chester Rd Radnor PA 19087-5113 also: PO Box 368 Cherry Valley NY 13320-0368 Office: Compass Capital Ptnrs 259 N Radnor Chester Rd Ste 220 Radnor PA 19087-5259

HUMES, H(ARVEY) DAVID, nephrologist, educator; b. Honolulu, Nov. 20, 1947; s. William and Nancy Humes; m. Dolores Humes; 1 child, Michael David. BA, U. Calif., Berkeley, 1969; MD, U. Calif., San Francisco, 1973. Diplomate Am. Bd. Internal Medicine. Intern Moffit Hosp. and U. Calif. Hosps., San Francisco, Calif., 1973-74; resident U. Calif. Hosps., San Francisco, 1974-75; clin. fellow nephrology U. Pa. Hosp., Phila., 1975-76; rsch. fellow lab. kidney & electrolyte physiology Peter Bent Brigham Hosp., Boston, Mass., 1976-77; from instr. to asst. prof. medicine Harvard U., Boston, Mass., 1977-79; from asst. prof. to assoc. prof. internal medicine U. Mich., Ann Arbor, 1979-86, prof. internal medicine, 1986—, John G. Searle prof., 1996—; founder, gen. ptnr., mgr. EpiGenesis, LLC; founder, dir., pres. Nephros Therapeutics, Inc.; dir., v.p. Acad. Network for Clin. Rsch. Inc.; mem. Scientific Adv. Bd., NephRx; cons. Sandoz Pharm., Bristol-Meyers-Squibb, Sterling-Winthrop, AmGen.; instr., asst. prof. Peter Bent Brigham Hosp., Harvard Med. Sch., Boston, 1977-79; dir., chief Nephrology Rsch. Labs., U. Mich., Ann Arbor, 1980-81, chmn. internal medicine, 1996—; chief med. svc. VA Med. Ctr., Ann Arbor, 1983-96. Mem. editl. bd. Am. Jour. Medicine, Seminars in Nephrology, Internat. Yearbook of Nephrology; contbr. articles to profl. jours. Grantee Nat. Kidney Found., 1981-85, 87-88, PHS, 1987—, VA, 1982—, Am. Heart Assn., 1982-87, 94-95. Fellow ACP, AAAS; mem. Am. Physiol. Soc., Assn. Prof. Medicine, Assn. Am. Physicians, Am. Soc. Clin. Investigation, Am. Heart Assn., Am. Soc. Nephrology, Am. Fedn. Clin. Rsch., Internat. Soc. Nephrology, Nat. Kidney Found. (Pres. award), Nat. Kidney Found. Mich., Cen. Soc. Clin. Rsch. (v.p.), Alpha Omega Alpha, Phi Beta Kappa. Achievements include development of bioartificial kidney; research in cellular basis of acute renal failure, biochemical basis of aminoglycoside-induced acute renal failure, cyclosporine nephrotoxicity, lipid alterations in ischemic acute renal failure, free radical induced mitochondrial injury, molecular basis of renal repair in acute renal failure, molecular basis of kidney tubulogenesis. Office: U Mich Med Ctr 1500 E Medical Center Dr Ann Arbor MI 48109-0005 also: U Mich Med Ctr PO Box 368 Ann Arbor MI 48106-0368

HUMES, JAMES CALHOUN, lawyer, communications consultant, author, professor; b. Williamsport, Pa., Oct. 31, 1934; s. Samuel Hamilton and Elenor Kathryn (Graham) H.; m. Dianne Stuart, July 25, 1957; children: Mary Stuart Quillen, Rachel Bailey. Student, Hill Sch., Stowe Sch., Eng., Williams Coll., 1953-55; A.B., George Washington U., 1959, J.D., 1962. Bar: Pa. 1963. Mem. Pa. Ho. of Reps., Harrisburg, 1962-65; exec. dir. Phila. Bar Assn., 1967-69; presdl. asst. policy planning sect. White House, Washington, 1969-70; dir. Office Policy and Plans, U.S. Dept. State, Washington, 1970-72; presdl. asst. White House Staff, Washington; White House cons. to Pres. Ford, Washington, 1976-77; Woodrow Wilson fellow Smithsonian Instn., Washington, 1982-83; adj. prof. Williams Coll., 1986—; Chmn. Ryals leadership and lang. U. So. Colo., Pueblo; mem. U.S. Commn. for UNESCO; adj. prof. U. Pa., 1985-96; editl. advisor Pres. Ford's memoirs A Time To Heal. Author: Sweet Dream, 1966, Instant Eloquence, 1973, Podium Humor, 1975, Roles Speakers Play, 1976, How to Get Invited to the White House, 1977, Speaker's Treasury of Anecdotes, 1977, Winston Churchill: Speaker of the Century, 1980, Talk Your Way to the Top, 1980, Standing Ovation, 1988, Sir Winston Method, 1991, The Benjamin Franklin Factor, 1992, My Fellow Americans, 1992, Citizen Shakespeare, 1993, More Podium Humor, 1993, Wit and Wisdom of Churchill, 1994, Wit and Wisdom of Benjamin Franklin, 1995, Wit and Wisdom of Abraham Lincoln, 1996, (ghost writer) Confessions of a White House Ghost, 1997, Nixon's Ten Commandments of Statecraft, 1997. Decorated Order of Brit. Empire. Fellow Royal Soc. of Art; mem. S.R., St. Nicholas Soc. N.Y., Pilgrims, St. Andrew's Soc. Phila., Soc. of Cin., Order of Magna Charta, Athenaeum Club, Union League Club, Phila. Cricket Club, Brook Club (N.Y.). Republican. Presbyterian. Home: 4404 Turnberry Crescent Pueblo CO 81001

HUMICK, THOMAS CHARLES CAMPBELL, lawyer; b. N.Y.C., Aug. 7, 1947; s. Anthony and Elizabeth Campbell (Meredith) H.; m. Nancy June Young, June 7, 1969; 1 child, Nicole Elizabeth Campbell. BA, Rutgers U., 1969; JD, Suffolk U., 1972; postgrad. London Sch. Econs. and Polit. Sci., 1977-78. Bar: N.J. 1972, U.S. Ct. Appeals (3d cir.) 1976, U.S. Supreme Ct. 1977, N.Y. 1981. Law clk. Superior Ct. N.J., 1972-73; assoc. Riker, Danzig, Scherer & Debevoise, Newark and Morristown, N.J., 1973-77; ptnr. Francis & Berry, Morristown, 1978-84, Dillon, Bitar & Luther, Morristown, 1985-92, Schenck, Price, Smith & King, Morristown, 1992—; arbitrator U.S. Dist. Ct. N.J., 1985—; del. to Jud. Conf. for Third Jud. Cir. U.S., 1975-79; mem. dist. X ethics com. N.J. Supreme Ct., 1983-87; judicial selection com. Morris County, 1995-99. Contbr. author: Valuation for Eminent Domain, 1973; mem. editl. bd. Suffolk U. Law Rev., 1970-71, New Jersey Lawyer, 1993-94. Trustee The Peck Sch., 1993-98, Richmond Fellowship of N.J., 1982-89, pres., 1984. Mem. ABA, N.J. Bar Assn., Fed. Bar Assn., Morris County Bar Assn. (trustee 1995—), Bay Head Yacht Club. Republican. Presbyterian. Home: PO Box 191 Oldwick NJ 08858-0191 Office: Schenck Price Smith & King 10 Washington St Morristown NJ 07960-7117

HUMKE, RAMON LYLE, utility executive; b. Quincy, Ill., Nov. 19, 1932; s. E.G. and Florence K. (Koch) H.; m. Carolyn Jacobs Humke, Nov. 20, 1955; 1 child, Steven K. Ed., Quincy Coll., 1952-53, Springfield (Ill.) Coll., Ill., 1956-58, Carleton Coll., 1968; LLD, U. Indpls., 1988. Various mgmt. positions Ill. Bell Telephone Co., 1951-73; dir. forecasting and productivity AT&T, N.Y.C., 1974-75; v.p. pers. Ill. Bell Tel. Co., Chgo., 1978-82; v.p. corp. affairs Ameritech, Chgo., 1982-83; pres., CEO Ind. Bell Telephone Co. Inc., Indpls., 1983-89, Ameritech Svcs., Chgo., 1989-90; pres., COO Indpls. Power & Light Co., 1990—, also bd. dirs.; vice chmn. Ipalco Enterprises, Inc. Indpls., Indpls., 1991—; also bd. dirs. Ipalco Enterprises, Inc., Indpls.; chmn. bd. Meridian Ins. Group, Meridian Mut. Ins. Co.; bd. dirs. LDI Mgmt. Chmn. Infrastructure Commn., 1990, Indpls.; bd. dirs. Indpls. Downtown, Inc., 1992—; adv. bd. Crossroads of Am. chpt. Boy Scouts Am. With U.S. Army, 1953-56, ETO. Named Ky. Col., 1983, Ark. Traveler, 1985, Sagamore of the Wabash, 1987, 89; recipient medal of merit U.S. Treasury Dept., 1984, 85, Charles Whistler award, 1989, Benjamin Harrison medallion award, 1990, Americanism award, 1991, Good Scout award Boy Scouts Am., 1993, Hoosier Heritage award, 1993, Ind. Acad., 1996. Mem. Indpls. C. of C. (chmn. 1997-98, dir.), Columbia Club, Crooked Stick Golf Club, Indpls. Athletic Club, Meridian Hills Country Club, Skyline Club (bd. govs.), Twin Lakes Golf Club. Avocations: golf, wilderness hiking, U.S. history.

HUML, DONALD SCOTT, manufacturing company executive; b. Lake Geneva, Wis., May 8, 1946; s. Robert Francis and Shirley (Roberts) H.; m. Joyce Cora Featherstone, Oct. 2, 1965; children: Tiffany Lynn, Alison Michelle, Andrew Scott. BBA, Marquette U., 1969; MBA, Temple U., 1980. Mgr. treasury ops. Allis-Chalmers Corp., West Allis, Wis., 1970-73; dir. fin. services CertainTeed Corp., Valley Forge, Pa., 1973-75, asst. treas., 1975-78, v.p., treas., 1978-81, v.p., comptroller, 1981-83, v.p., div. pres., 1983-86, v.p., group pres., 1986-89, v.p., chief fin. officer, 1989-90; v.p., CFO Saint-Gobain Corp., Valley Forge, Pa., 1990-94; sr. v.p., CFO Snap-on Inc., Kenosha, Wis., 1994—; bd. dirs. Cameron Ashley Inc.; mem. adv. bd. Marquette U. Sch. Bus. Adminstrn. Mem. Am. Mgmt. Assn., Fin. Execs. Inst., Conf. Bd. CFO Coun., Leading CFOs, Beta Gamma Sigma. Republican. Roman Catholic. Avocations: tennis, running, reading. Home: 1126 Royal Birkdale Ct Lake Geneva WI 53147-5013 Office: Snap-on Inc 2801 80th St Kenosha WI 53143-5699

HUMMEL, CHARLES FREDERICK, museum official; b. Bklyn., Sept. 16, 1932; s. Charles Frederick and Helen (Yost) H.; m. Marlene Simons, Aug. 16, 1952; children: Mark, Jonathan, Laura, Jeffrey. B.A. magna cum laude, CCNY, 1953; M.A., U. Del., 1955. Curatorial asst. Henry Francis du Pont Winterthur Museum, Winterthur, Del., 1955-58; asst. curator Henry Francis du Pont Winterthur Museum, 1958-60, assoc. curator, 1960-67, curator, 1967-79, dep. dir. collections, 1979-89, dep. dir. mus. and library dept., 1989-91, ret., 1991; adj. assoc. prof. art history U. Del., Newark, 1964-93, prof., 1993—; v.p. Early Am. Industries Assn., 1981-86, chmn. grants-in-aid com., 1978-95, chmn. publs. com., 1995—, also bd. dirs. Author: With Hammer in Hand, 1968, 4th printing, 1982, Winterthur Guide to American Chippendale Furniture, 1976; co-author: exhbn. catalogue The Pennsylvania Germans: A Celebration of their Arts, 1683-1850, 1982; contbr. to: Brit. Ency. Am. Art, 1973. Pres. Northridge Civic Assn., Claymont, Del., 1961-63; pres. Greenville (Del.) PTA, 1972-74; mem. adv. com. J. Paul Getty Trust/Am. Fedn. Arts, Mus. Mgmt. Inst., 1986-92; mem. Nat. Inst. Conservation, Washington, 1973-91, v.p., 1979-83; sec. Am. Assn. Mus., 1988-91; trustee Chipstone Found., Milw., 1991—, Landmarks Soc. Phila., 1992-98, Wood Turning Ctr., Phila., 1993—; apptd. by Pres. Clinton nat. mus. svcs. bd. Inst. Mus. and Libr. Svcs., 1995—; mem. com. overseers Strawbery Banke Museum, 1994—; trustee adv. com. The Concord Museum, 1983-91; mem. adv. coun. Md. Hist. Soc., 1995—. Fellow Winterthur Program in Early Am. Culture, 1953-55; recipient Katherine Coffey award Mid-Atlantic Assn. Mus., 1989. Mem. Am. Assn. Museums, Hajji Baba Soc. N.Y., Phi Beta Kappa, Phi Alpha Theta. Unitarian (v.p., trustee 1963-66). Office: Winterthur Mus Winterthur DE 19735

HUMMEL, DANA D. MALLETT, librarian; BA in Art History, Smith Coll., 1957; MA in Libr. and Info. Sci., Denver U., 1968; postgrad. Def. Lang. Inst., 1961, Instituto Mexicano-Norteamericano de Relationes Culturales, 1962, John F. Kennedy Ctr. for Spl. Warfare, 1974, Nat. War Coll., 1976, No. Va. Bus. Sch., 1978, Cath. U. Am., 1981; diploma U. Italiana per Stranieri, Perugia, Italy, 1997. Head libr., administrn., Howard AFB Libr., C.Z., 1969-70; asst. libr. Holmes Intermediate Sch., 1970-71; tchr. Spanish and substitute tchr. J.E.B. Stuart High Sch., 1972-77; sec. Office of exec. dir.-Africa The World Bank, 1978-79; personal sec. to rector Falls Ch. (Va.), 1979-81; mgr. Info. Svcs. Ctr., BDM Internat. subs. Ford Aerospace Co., McLean, Va., 1981-88. Mem. vestry Falls Ch. Episcopal Ch., 1982; del. Republican State Conv., 1981, 86; pres. Ravenwood Civic Assn., 1979-80, 80-81, 81-82; rep. Mason Dist., Fedn. Civic Assns.; mem. ann. plan rev. task force Mason Dist., 1981-82; gov. trustee Fairfax County Pub. Libr. Bd., 1982-88; chmn. bd. trustees Fairfax County. Named Outstanding Woman of Yr., Fairfax County Bd. Suprs. and Com. of Women, 1982. Mem. AAUP, ALA, Am. Soc. for Info. Sci., Spl. Libr. Assn., Va. Libr. Assn., D.C. Libr. Assn., Women in Def., Villa D'Este Assn. (bd. dirs. 1995—, pres. 1997-98), Jr. League Sarasota, Fla. Home: 7355 Villa D Este Dr Sarasota FL 34238-5649

HUMMEL, GENE MAYWOOD, retired bishop; b. Lancaster, Ohio, Nov. 12, 1926; s. Ivan Maywood and Anna Mildred (Black) H.; m. R. Jeannine Lane, June 17, 1950; children: Gregory L., G. Michael. Student, Miami U., Oxford, Ohio, 1944, Dartmouth Coll., 1944-45; BS in Agr, Ohio State U., 1949, BS in Agrl. Engring, 1950. Supr. North Am. Aviation Inc., Columbus, Ohio, 1951-57; prodn. control chief Martin Co., Orlando, Fla., 1957-61; ordained to ministry Reorganized Ch. of Jesus Christ of Latter Day Saints, 1961; ministerial asst. to Center Stake bishop, Independence, Mo., 1961-63; bishop San Francisco Bay Stake, 1964-70, Hawaii, 1968-70; bishop Center Stake, 1970-72; bishop, mem. Presiding Bishopric Internat. Ch., 1972-88, presiding bishop, 1988-92; ret., 1992; dir. Health Care Systems, Inc., 1983-92, Ctr. Place Improvement Inc., Independence, Cen. Profl. Bldg., Inc., Independence, E.A. Smith Retirement Ctr., Inc., Cen. Devel. Assn., Inc., Boatmans Bank of Kansas City, Mo.; dir., v.p. Systems Communication, Inc., Independence, 1975-92. Mem. corp. body Independence Sanitarium and Hosp., 1972-92; bd. dirs. Mid-Am. Health Network, Kansas City, 1983-92. With USNR, 1944-45.

HUMMEL, GREGORY WILLIAM, lawyer; b. Sterling, Ill., Feb. 25, 1949; s. Osborne William and Vivian LaVera (Guess) H.; m. Teresa Lynn Beveroth, June 20, 1970; children: Andrea Lynn, Brandon Gregory. BA, MacMurray Coll., 1971; JD, Northwestern U., 1974. Bar: Ill. 1974, U.S. Dist. Ct. (no. dist.) Ill. 1974. Assoc. Rusnak, Deutsch & Gilbert, Chgo., 1974-78; ptnr. Rudnick & Wolfe, Chgo., 1978-97, Bell, Boyd & Lloyd, Chgo., 1997—. Editor Jour. Criminal Law & Criminology Northwestern U., 1973-74; co-author: Illinois Real Estate Forms, 1989; contbr. articles to law jours. Mem. gov. coun. Luth. Gen. Hosp. Advocate Health Care Sys.; trustee Mac Murray Coll., Jacksonville, Ill., 1986—, Homes for Children Found; bd. dirs. Chgo. area coun. Boy Scouts Am., ChildServ. Mem. Nat. Inst. Constrn. Law and Practice, Internat. Bar Assn. (co-chmn. com. internat. constrn. projects), Am. Coll. Constrn. Lawyers (past pres.), Urban Land Inst. (chmn. pub.-pvt. partnership coun.), Chgo. Dist. Coun. (chmn.), Lambda Alpha Internat. (Ely chpt. past pres.). Office: Bell Boyd & Lloyd Three First Nat Plaza 70 W Madison St Ste 3300 Chicago IL 60602-4207

HUMMEL, JOSEPH WILLIAM, hospital administrator; b. Vinton, Iowa, Dec. 7, 1940; married. BA, Calif. State U., 1965; M Health Adminstrn., U Calif., 1966. Adminstrv. instr. Merrithew Meml. Hosp., Martinez, Calif., 1965; adminstrv. res. Mt. Zion Hosp. and Med. Ctr., San Francisco, 1966-67, adminstrv. pat. care, 1967-68, adminstrv. asst., 1968-70; assoc. adminstr. Valley Med. Ctr., Fresno, Calif., 1970-74; CEO Kern Med. Ctr., Bakersfield, Calif., 1974-86; adminstr. Kaiser Found. Hosp., L.A., 1987—, sr. v.p. area mng. Mem. Calif. Hosp. Assn. (bd. dirs. 1983-89). Home: 2050 Maginn St Glendale CA 91202-1128 Office: Kaiser Found Hosp 4747 W Sunset Blvd Los Angeles CA 90027-6021*

HUMMEL, KAY JEAN, physical therapist; b. Cleve., Apr. 24, 1943; d. Lloyd Elmer and Olive Agnes (Latou) Hetherington; m. Charles William Hummel (div. Feb. 1984); children: Patrick H., Robin E. BA, Miami U., Oxford, Ohio, 1965; cert. in phys. therapy, Columbia U., N.Y., 1966. Lic. phys. therapist, La.; cert. ofcl. Games Uniting Mind and Body. Staff phys. therapist St. Joseph's Hosp., Chgo., 1966-68, Wrightwood Extended Care Facility, Chgo., 1967-68, Suburban Hosp., Bethesda, Md., 1969, Holy Cross Hosp., Silver Spring, Md., 1969-70; asst. chief phys. therapist Community Gen. Hosp., Syracuse, N.Y., 1970-76; itinerant phys. therapist Caddo Parish Schs., Shreveport, La., 1976—; pvt. practice Shreveport, 1985—; bd. dirs. Games Uniting Mind & Body, Inc. Mem. U.S. Cerebral Palsy Athletic Assn. (regional classifier), Presbyn. Women: Presbytery of the Pines Coord. Team, North La. Scottish Soc., Kappa Delta Alumni Assn. Office: 3004 Knight St Shreveport LA 71106

HUMMER-SHARPE, ELIZABETH ANASTASIA, genealogist, writer; b. Morristown, N.J., Dec. 15, 1931; d. Harold Arlington and Sophia Anastasia (Dombrowski) Hummer; divorced; children: Dean T., Dana E., Robert K., Jean F., Christopher K. Student, Santa Monica Coll., 1968-69. Cashier L. Bamberger Co., Morristown, 1949; telephone sales, asst. office mgr. L.A. Times, Santa Monica, 1968-69; unit sec. St. Johns Hosp., Santa Monica, 1969-75; telephone sales L.A. Times, Culver City, 1976-79; mktg. dir. Ramsgate Films, Santa Monica, 1976-78; sr. file clk. Crown Wholesale Co., L.A., 1979-80; telephone sales L.A. Times, Santa Monica, 1988-91. Bd. dirs. Desert Opera Theatre, Palmdale, Calif., 1994-99; vol. on call ARC, Palmdale. Mem. Internat. Platform Soc., Antelope Valley Geneal. Soc., Nat. Audubon Soc., Arbor Day Found., Planetary Soc. (charter mem.), UFO Soc., Bibl. Archaeology Soc., Smithsonian Inst. Roman Catholic. Avocations: traveling, walking, jewelry making, art, gardens. Address: 3203 E Avenue S3 Palmdale CA 93550-6620

HUMPHREVILLE, JOHN DAVID, lawyer; b. Harrisburg, Pa., Feb. 4, 1953; s. Robert E. and Winifred (MacNulty) H.; m. Laurie Wettstone, Mar. 6, 1976; children: Caroline Elizabeth, John Evin. BS, Pa. State U., 1977; MA in Govt. Adminstrn., U. Pa., 1984; JD, Cath. U. Am., 1986. Bar: Fla. 1986, U.S. Dist. Ct. (mid. dist.) Fla. 1987, D.C. 1988. Dir. bur. real estate Pa. Dept. Gen. Svcs., Harrisburg, 1979-80; dep. adminstrv. asst. to gov. State of Pa., Harrisburg, 1980-83; assoc. Shackleford, Farrior, Stallings & Evans, P.A., Tampa, Fla., 1986-90; ptnr. Icard, Merrill, Cullis, Timm, Furren & Ginsburg, P.A., Tampa, 1990; asst. to atty. gen. U.S. Dept. Justice, Washington, 1990-91, spl. counsel Asst. Atty. Gen. environ. divsn., 1991; ptnr. Quarles & Brady, Naples, Fla., 1991—; mem. Fed. Jud. Adv. Commn., 1989-91. Avocations: surfing, swimming, triathlons. Office: Quarles & Brady 4501 Tamiami Trl N Ste 300 Naples FL 34103-3023

HUMPHREY, ARTHUR EARL, university administrator, retired; b. Moscow, Idaho, Nov. 9, 1927; s. Samuel Earl and Iris May (Rowe) H.; m. Sheila Claire Darwin, June 13, 1951; children: Andrea Lynn, Allyson Dawn. BS in Chem. Engring., U. Idaho, 1948, MS, 1950, DSc (hon.), 1974; PhD, Columbia U., 1953; MS in Food Tech, Mass. Inst. Tech., 1959; DSc (hon.), Lehigh U., 1993. Mem. faculty U. Pa., Phila., 1953-80; prof. chem. engring. U. Pa., 1961-80, dir. Sch. Chem. Engring., 1962-72, dean Coll. Engring. and Applied Sci., 1972-80; provost, acad. v.p. Lehigh U., Bethlehem, Pa., 1980-86; T.L. Diamond prof. biochem. engring. Lehigh U., 1986-92, dir. Ctr. Molecular Biosci. and Biotech., 1986-92, T.L. Diamond prof. and provost emeritus, 1992—; dir. Biotech Inst. Pa. State U., University Park, 1992-95, prof. chem. engring., 1992-97; bd. dirs. United Engr. Trust, 1991-92, carpenter 1980-97, New Brunswick Scienfitic, 1972-74; NSF sci. tchr. fellow MIT, 1958-59; Fulbright lectr. U. Tokyo, Japan, 1963, U. NSW, Australia, 1970; guest lectr. Inst. Biology, Czechoslovakian Acad. Sci., 1964, Tech. Inst., Budapest, 1966; I.I.T. Delhi, New Delhi, India, 1970, Tungai U., Taichung, Taiwan, 1968; cons. Merck Sharp & Dohme, 1957-63, Merck Chem. Co., 1963-64, 80-84, 92-97, Sun Oil Co., 1961-68, Bioferm, 1964-67, Cryotherm, 1966-67, Fermentation Design, 1967-74, E.R. Squibb, 1967-73, Air Products, 1971-89, Hoffmann La Roche, 1989-97. Author: ann. Fermentation Rev., 1960-64; author textbooks on biochem. engring.; contbr. over 275 articles to profl. jours. Pres. Phila. Trail Club, 1960-61; councilor Appalachian Trail Conf., 1961-67; co-chmn. 3d Internat. Fermentation Symposium; mem. engring. adv. bd. NSF, 1972-73; mem. single cell protein working group, protein adv. group WHO-FAO-UN; chmn. group on prodn. substances by microbial means U.S.-USSR Cooperation in Sci. and Tech.; chmn. OSTP briefing com. on chem. and process engring. for biotech. Recipient Disting. Svc. medal U. Pa., 1993, John Fritz medal United Engrs. Trust, 1996. Fellow Am. Inst. Med. Biol. Engrs. (founding); mem. NAE (membership com. 1978-79, 85-87), Internat. Assn. Microbiol. Socs. (sec.-gen. econ. and applied microbiology), Am. Chem. Soc. (chmn. divsn. microbiology chem. and tech. 1967, divsn. disting. svc. award 1979, M. Johnson award 1996), AIChE (pres. 1991, chmn. food and bioengring. divsn. 1972, prof. progress award 1972, food and bioengring. award 1973, inst. lectr. 1975, founders award 1989, v.p. 1990, Van Antrewpen svc. award 1995), Japanese Soc. Fermentation Tech., Am. Soc. Microbiology, Trail Club (Phila.), Appalachian Mountain Club (Boston), Horse-Shoe Trail Club (Phila.), Sigma Xi, Sigma Tau. *

HUMPHREY, CHESTER BOWDEN, cardio-thoracic surgeon; b. Marblehead, Mass., July 29, 1939; s. Leonard Graves and Mary Louise (Bowden) H.; m. Joyce Claire Jazwinski, Mar. 20, 1971; 1 child, Andrew Bowden. BS, Dickinson Coll., 1961; MD, Temple U., 1965. Diplomate Am. Bd. Thoracic Surgery, Am. Bd. Surgery. Intern Hartford Hosp., 1965-66, resident in gen. surgery, 1966-71; resident in thoracic and cardiovascular surgery Naval Regional Med. Ctr., San Diego, 1973-75; cardio-thoracic surgeon Hartford (Conn.) Thoracic & Cardiovascular Group, 1976—. Adv. com. Town of West Hartford (Conn.) Paramedics, 1989—. Comdr. USN, 1970-76. Fellow Am. Coll. Surgeons, Am. Coll. Cardiology, Am. Coll. Chest Physicians; mem. Soc. for Thoracic Surgeons, Denton Cooley Surg. Soc., New England Soc. for Vascular Surgery. Office: Hartford Thoracic & Cardiovascular Group 85 Seymour St Ste 325 Hartford CT 06106-5522

HUMPHREY, DIANA YOUNG, fund raiser, travel consultant; b. Balt., Feb. 7, 1938; d. Edwin Parson and Elizabeth Miller (Hoskins) Young; m. David Henry Carls, July 27, 1963 (div. Dec. 17, 1997); children: Peter Van Patten Carls, Elizabeth Roy Carls, Susan Montanye Carls; m. George Lee Humphrey, May 22, 1999. AB, Smith Coll., Northampton, Mass., 1960. Lic. real estate broker, Mass., 1978. Fgn. rights sales Little, Brown & Co., Inc., Boston, 1960-63; speech writer DNA Rsch., N.Y.C., 1963-64; vol. fund raiser John V. Lindsay, N.Y.C., 1964-65, Smith Coll., Northampton, Mass., 1970-75, 90-95, Smith Coll. Club, Concord, Mass., 1976-89, Jr. League of Boston, 1967—; bd. mem. devel. Ctr. House, Inc., Boston, 1981-94; fund raiser events Boston Symphony Orch., 1975—; fund raising, events Mass. Soc. for Prevention of Cruelty to Children, Boston, 1997—. Editor: Huntington Hartford Gallery Modern Art, N.Y.C., 1963. Speechwriter, Nelson A. Rockefeller Presdl. campaign, N.Y.C., 1963-64; active John V. Lindsay for Mayor, N.Y.C., 1964-65; mem., chmn. Wayland (Mass.) Planning Bd., 1976-81, Wayland Housing Partnership, 1987—; mem. Patriots' Trail coun. Girl Scouts U.S. Mem. Jr. League of Boston, Weston Golf Club. Episcopalian. Avocations: golf, travel, gardening, singing, politics. Home: 42 Cutting Cross Way Wayland MA 01778-3845

HUMPHREY, DORIS DAVENPORT, publishing company executive, consultant, educator; b. Woodbury, Tenn., June 3, 1943; d. Luther and Gladys (Alexander) Davenport; m. John Sparkman Humphrey, Sept. 15, 1941 (dec.); children: Heather, Holly. BS, Middle Tenn. State U., 1965; MBE, Ga. State U., 1972, EdS, 1977, PhD, 1983; postgrad., Bryn Mawr Coll., 1989. Sec., coord. creative svcs., asst. to pres. Noble-Dury & Assocs., Nashville, 1965-69; asst. account exec. McCann-Erickson & Assocs., Atlanta,

1969-70; adj. and full-time instr. DeKalb C.C., 1970-79; coord. internship program Raymond Walters Coll., U. Cin., 1980-83, chmn. dept. ofice adminstrn., 1981-86; asst. dean bus. and office mgmt. Delaware County C.C., Media, Pa., 1987-90; pres. Career Solutions Tng. Group, Paoli, Pa., 1990; lectr. in field; curriculum cons. Author: The Medical Office: A Reference Manual, 1986, 2d edit., 1997, Pediatric Associates, P.C., 3d edit., 1996, Contemporary Medical Office Procedures, 2d edit., 1996, The Medical Manager, 2d edit., 1995, School to Work Series, 1994, 2d edit., 1996; pub. Real Life, Career Launcher, 1998, Reality, 1999. Mem. Nat. Bus. Edn. Assn., Am. Vocat. Assn., Friend Bus. Edn. State Pa., Delta Pi Epsilon. Presbyterian.

HUMPHREY, EDWARD WILLIAM, surgeon, medical educator; b. Fargo, N.D., Dec. 6, 1926; s. Edward W. and Minnie (Ramstad) H.; m. Noreen Sander, Sept. 23, 1950; children: Katherine Lisa, Joan Karen. B.A., U. Minn., 1948, M.D., 1951, Ph.D. in Physiology, 1959. Mem. faculty U. Minn. Med. Sch., Mpls., 1958-94, prof. surgery, 1965-94; prof. emeritus, 1994—; interim chair U. Minn. Med. Sch., Mpls., 1993-94; mem. staff VA Hosp., Mpls., 1958-94; chief surg. svc. VA Hosp., 1962-93. Author: Manual of Pulmonary Surgery, 1982, (with D. McQuarrie) Reoperative General Surgery, 1992, 2d edit., 1996; contbr. articles to profl. jours. Mem. A.C.S., Minn. Surg. Soc., Am., Central surg. assns., Soc. Univ. Surgeons, Am. Physiol. Soc., Am. Soc. Cell Biology, Am. Assn. Thoracic Surgery, Soc. Internat. De Chirurgie, Soc. Exptl. Biology and Medicine, Sigma Xi, Alpha Omega Alpha. Rsch. in fields of cancer, pulmonary physiology, biological transport, thoracic surgery. Home: 95 Harbour Passage Hilton Head Island SC 29926-1264

HUMPHREY, GEORGE MAGOFFIN, II, plastic molding company executive; b. Cleve., Mar. 19, 1942; s. Gilbert Watts and Louise (Ireland) H.; m. Marguerite Burton, June 19, 1964 (div. 1989); children: Mary O., Sandra; m. Patience Ryan, June 22, 1991. B.A., Yale U., 1964; J.D., U. Mich., 1967. Bar: Ohio 1967. Sales rep. Hanna Mining Co., Cleve., 1970-72, European rep., 1972-77, sales rep., 1977-78, mgr. sales, 1978, v.p. sales, 1978-80, sr. v.p. fin., 1980-81, sr. v.p. sales, dir., 1981-84; mng. dir. Russell Reynolds Assocs., Cleve., 1984-87; gen. ptnr. Philips Industries, Ltd., Cleve., 1987-94; pres. Extrudex, Cleve., 1990—. Trustee Case Western Res. U., Cleve. Mus. Art, Cleve. Mus. Natural History, Cleve. Scholarship Programs, Inc., Univ. Hosps. Cleve. Served to capt. USMC, 1967-70. Mem. Union Club (Cleve.). Republican. Episcopalian. Home: 18 W Mather Ln Bratenahl OH 44108-1158 Office: Extrudex 310 Figgie Dr Painesville OH 44077-3028

HUMPHREY, HUBERT HORATIO, III, state attorney general; b. Mpls., June 26, 1942; s. Hubert Horatio and Muriel (Buck) H.; m. Nancy Lee Humphrey, Aug. 14, 1963; children: Lorie, Pam, Hubert Horatio IV. B.A. in Polit. Sci., Am. U., Washington, 1965; J.D., U. Minn., 1969. Bar: Minn. Sole practice law, 1970-82; mem. Minn. State Senate, 1972-82; atty. gen. State of Minn., St. Paul, 1983-98. Bd. mgmt. Northwest br. YMCA. Named Trial Lawyer of Yr., Trial Lawyers for Pub. Justice, 1998. Mem. ABA, Minn. Bar Assn., Hennepin County Bar Assn., Nat. Assn. Atty.'s Gen. (pres. 1993-94). Mem. Democratic-Farmer-Labor Party. Office: 2722 University Ave SE Minneapolis MN 55414*

HUMPHREY, KAREN A., college director; d. Martin and Eleanor (Schwartau) Annexstad; married Charles W. Humphrey; children: Karna, Kirk. BA in Am. Studies, U. Minn. Cmty. affairs editor KRBI Radio, St. Peter, Minn., 1976-77; assoc. editor Dassel Cokato Enterprise and Dispatch, Dassel, Minn., 1979-89; legis. asst. to U.S. Sen. Dave Durenberger, 1989-95; comms. cons. Karen Humphrey and Co., Watertown, Minn., 1995-98; cmty. rels. mgr. Barnes & Noble, Minnetonka, Minn.; pres. Minn. Hist. Soc., St. Paul, 1996-98; dir. planned giving Bethany Coll., Lindsborg, Kans., 1998—. Mem. U. Minn. Alumni Assn., Norwegian-Am. Hist. Assn., Minn. Pub. Radio, Dassel Leikarring, Oral History Assn., Kans. State Hist. Soc. (bd. dirs.). Office: Bethany Coll 421 N 1st St Lindsborg KS 67456

HUMPHREY, LOIS M., English educator; b. Denver, Mar. 31, 1956; d. Wallace J. and Alma R. (Olson) LeClaire; m. David L. Humphrey, June 15, 1979 (div. July 1985); children: Sarabeth Humphrey, Andrew Humphrey. BA, Brescia Coll., 1995; postgrad., U. So. Ind., 1999—. Cert. secondary education tchr. Sales ops. mgr. ProTech Pub. and Comms., Santa Claus, Ind., 1987-91; tchr. Cloverport (Ky.) Ind. Schs., 1996-98; tech. writer Whirlpool Corp. Keller Crescent Co., Evansville, Ind., 1998—; cluster leader KERA, Frederick Fraize H.S., Cloverport, 1997-98; cons. in field, Tell City, Ind., 1995—; coord./tchr. Extended Sch. Svcs., Cloverport, 1996-98. Assoc. editor: Open 24 Hours mag. 1994-95; editor: (booklet) Flood of '97. Tchr./vol. Perry County Literacy Coun., Tell City, 1991—, Adult Basic Edn., 1992-95; vol. Coats for Kids, Tell City, 1990-92. Recipient Lucinda Clements award Brescia Coll., Owensboro, 1995. Mem. Nat. Coun. Tchrs. of English, Ky. H.S. Journalism Assn. Avocations: reading, photography, music. E-mail: lhumphrey@kellercrescent.com. Home: PO Box 56 Tell City IN 47586-0056 Office: Keller Crescent Co Cloverport Ind Schs 1100 E Louisiana St Evansville IN 47711 also: Keller Crescent Co PO Box 3 Evansville IN 47701

HUMPHREY, LOUISE IRELAND, civic worker, equestrienne; b. Morehead City, N.C., Nov. 1, 1918; d. R. Livingston and Margaret (Allen) Ireland; m. Gilbert W. Humphrey, Dec. 27, 1939; children:Margaret (Mrs. K. Bindhart), George M. II, Gilbert Watts; ed. pvt. schs. Nurse's aide ARC, 1944-64; past. dir. Nat. City Bank, Cleve., Nat. City Corp., Cleve., 1981-86; trustee, Mus. Arts Assn.; hon. trustee, past pres. Vis. Nurse Assn.; hon. trustee Lake Erie Coll., life trustee United Way Cleve., trustee Archbold Med. Ctr. and Hosp., Thomasville, Ga.; hon. trustee Case Western Res. U., Bus. Coun. Interntat. Understanding, Inc.; bd. dirs. Monticello (Fla.) Opera House; mem., past trustee, 2d v.p. Jr. League Cleve.; past pres., hon. chmn. bd. dirs. Met. Opera Assn., N.Y.; bd. mem. Lincoln Ctr., N.Y.; bd. dirs. Thomas County Entertainment Found.; past pres. No. Ohio Opera Assn.; mem. adv. bd. Coll. of Veterinary Medicine Bd. U. Fla., gainseville; past mem. Ohio Arts Council, 1975-85; treas., trustee Wildlife Conservation Fund Am.; former master foxhounds Chagrin Valley Hunt, Gates Mills, Ohio; past dir., zone v.p. U.S. Equestrian Team, Inc., now hon. life dir.; mem. Garden Club Cleve.; bd. dirs., past pres. Nat. Homecaring Council; treas., bd. mem. Wildlife Legis. Fund Am. Conservation Fund; past pres. bd. dirs. Thomasville Cultural Ctr. Home: Box 91102 Woodfield Springs Plantation Miccosukee Cpo FL 32309

HUMPHREY, MATTHEW CAMERON, computer scientist, consultant; b. Alexandria, Va., May 1, 1963; s. Elbert Ray and Doris Bernadine Humphrey; m. Audrey Buck Li Kuek, Aug. 24, 1991; children: Leanna Mei, Erin Fei, Nathan Ray. BS in Computer Sci., Va. Tech., 1985, MS in Computer Sci., 1988; PhD, U. Waikato, Hamilton, New Zealand, 1996. Software designer Dialog Mgmt. Sys., Blacksburg, Va., 1985-87; cons., software engr. Software Productivity Consortium, Blacksburg, 1987-88; from lectr. to assoc. prof. U. Waikato, Hamilton, 1991-97; cons., software arch. Ave. Techs., Inc., Alexandria, Va., 1997; rsch. software engr. Pacific-Sierra Rsch. Corp., Arlington, Va., 1997—. Contbr. articles to profl. jours. and confs. Scout leader New Zealand Scouting Assn., Hamilton, 1989-91. E-mail: matth@fl-s.infi.net. Office: Intellisure 11 Wild Plum Ct Stafford VA 22554

HUMPHREY, NEIL DARWIN, university president, retired; b. Idaho Falls, Idaho, May 20, 1928; s. Clair Pierce and Freda (Hatfield) H.; m. Mary Pat Smith, Aug. 21, 1950; children: Ann Humphrey Melcher, Therese Humphrey Hymer. BA in Polit. Sci., Idaho State U., 1950; MS in Govt. Mgmt., U. Denver, 1951; EdD, Brigham Young U., 1974; LHD (hon.), U. of Akron, 1991; LLD (hon.), U. Nev., 1995. Exec. sec. Nev. Taxpayers Assn., 1955-59; budget dir. Nev., 1959-61; bus. mgr. U. Nev., 1961-64, v.p. fin., 1964-67, acting pres., 1967-68; chancellor U. Nev. System, 1968-77; pres. U. Alaska, 1977-78; v.p. for fin. affairs Youngstown (Ohio) State U., 1978-79, exec. v.p., 1979-84, pres., 1984-92; bd. dirs. Comml. Intertech Corp. Home: 3290 Lapwing Ln Reno NV 89509-3987

HUMPHREY, OWEN EVERETT, retired education administrator; b. Wautoma, Wis., Oct. 25, 1920; s. Marion A. and Flora A. (Helms) H.; m. Billye A. Cox, Apr. 6, 1946 (dec. Dec. 1974); children: Reba, Ivye. BS, U. Wis., Whitewater, 1947; MS, U. Ark., 1949; advanced cert., U. Ill., 1954. Life gen. supervisory cert. grades K-14. Elem. classroom tchr. Four Corners Sch., Plainfield, Wis., 1941-42; jr. high art and sci. tchr. Jefferson Sch., Sheboygan, Wis., 1947-48; elem. classroom tchr. and prin. Holcomb, Mo., 1949-50, Lincoln Sch., Mattoon, Ill., 1950-55; supervising prin. various elem. schs., Peotone, Ill., 1955-57; elem. tchr. Nameoki Sch., Granite City, Ill., 1957-59; elem. prin. Maryville Sch., Granite City, 1959-67; curriculum coord. Sch. Dist. #9, Granite City, 1967-79; adminstrv. asst. Regional Supt. of Schs., Madison County, Ill., 1979-81, 85-87; ret., 1987; leader parent study groups Ea. Ill. U., Mattoon, 1950-54; PTA field unit organizer Ill. Congress of Parents and Tchrs., Mattoon, 1952-54; coord. local dist. planning Sch. Dist. #9, Granite City, 1973-79; rep. Ill. State Curriculum Coun., Springfield, 1980-81. Co-author: The Greening of Gateway East, 1984; contbr. poetry to Nat. Libr. of Poetry anthologies; contbr. articles to profl. jours. Dir. chorus Area Coun. PTA, Mattoon, 1950-54, Granite City Area Coun. PTA, 1957-59; dir. Granite City Steel Mixed Chorus, 1958-60; actor Area Theatrical Soc., Collinsville, Ill., 1994. Sgt. U.S. Army Infantry, 1942-45, ETO. Recipient Area Coun. PTA award Granite City, Ill., 1979. Mem. NEA (life), ASCD (life), Ill. ASCD (life, bd. dirs.), Internat. Poets Soc. (life), Collinsville Area Theatrical Soc., Phi Delta Kappa (Gateway East chpt. sec., historian, v.p., pres., Svc. Key award 1984, George H. Reavis Assoc. award 1991). Avocation: composing music and lyrics. Home: 18 Wilson Park Dr Granite City IL 62040-3550

HUMPHREY, PAUL, commercial writer; b. N.Y.C., Jan. 4, 1915; s. Joseph Lee and Winifred (Bell) H.; m. Eleanor Nicholson, June 22, 1945; children: Paula, Paul, Joel. BA, U. Rochester, 1940, MA, 1940. Vice prin. Penfield (N.Y.) High Sch., 1946-47; instr. U. Rochester (N.Y.), 1947-48; dir. FE Compton & Co., Chgo., 1949-61; ind. writer Spencerport, N.Y., 1962—. Contbr. articles to profl. jours. Mem. Rochester Poets Soc. (pres. 1957), Poets & Writers N.Y.C., Authors Guild N.Y.C., Writers and Books. Avocations: antique automobiles, opera, travel. E-mail: rlwalsh@frontiernet.net. Home and office: 2329 S Union St Spencerport NY 14559-2229

HUMPHREY, PHYLLIS A., writer; b. Oak Park, Ill., July 22, 1929; d. Richard William and Antoinette (Chalupa) Ashworth; m. Herbert A. Pihl, Sept. 13, 1946 (div. 1957); children: Christine Pihl Gibson, Gary Fraizer Pihl; m. Curtis H. Humphrey, June 21, 1965; 1 child, Marc. AA, Coll. San Mateo, Calif., 1972; postgrad., Northwestern U., 1945-47. Ptnr. Criterion House, Oceanside, Calif., 1972—. Author: Wall Street on $20 a Month, 1986, Golden Fire, 1986, Sweet Folly, 1990, Flying High, 1995, Once More With Feeling, 1998; author radio scripts Am. Radio Theatre, 1983-84; contbr. short stories and articles to popular mags. Mem. Mensa. Republican. Christian Sci. Ch. Avocations: reading, travel. Office: Criterion House PO Box 586295 Oceanside CA 92058-6295

HUMPHREY, STEPHEN, college dean; b. 1945; married; 3 children. BA in Biology, Earlham Coll., 1966; postgrad. in zoology, So. Ill. U.; PhD, Okla. State U., 1971. Asst. curator in mammalogy Fla. State Mus., Gainesville, 1971-76, assoc. curator in mammalogy, 1976-80; curator in ecology Fla. Mus. Natural History U. Fla., Gainesville, 1980—, interim dean coll. natural resources and environment, 1993-98, dean of coll., 1998—; affiliate prof. zoology U. Fla., 1972-78, affiliate prof. wildlife ecology, 1981—, provost's task force on natural resources and the environment, 1991-92, v.p. faculty coord. com. for new coll. of natural resources and the environment, 1992-93; commr., vice-chair environmental regulation commn. Fla. Dept. Environ. Protection, 1991—; interim chair dept. wildlife ecology and conservation U. Fla., 1996-97. Co-author: Endangered Animals of Thailand, 1990; editor: Rare and Endangered Biota of Florida, vol. 1 Mammals, 1992; author: (book chpts.) Biology of Bats of the New World Family Phyllostomatidae, 1979, Wild Mammals of North America: Biology, Management, and Economics, 1982, Animal Extinctions, 1985, Tropical Rain Forest: The Leeds Symposium, 1985; author numerous monographs; contbr. over 50 articles to profl. jours. CFO Soc. for Conservation Biology, 1990—; co-chair com. Save The Manatee, 1993-95. Recipient Bill Sadowski Meml. Pub. Svc. award Fla. Bar Assn., 1995; grantee Fla. Game and Fresh Water Fish Commn., 1994—. Mem. Am. Soc. Mammalogists, British Ecol. Soc., Ecol. Soc. Am., Internat. Soc. Ecol. Econs., Soc. for Conservation Biology, The Wildlife Soc. Office: U Fla Coll Natur Resources/ Environment 330 Little Hall PO Box 118100 Gainesville FL 32611-8100*

HUMPHREY, WATTS SHERMAN, technical executive, author; b. Battle Creek, Mich., July 4, 1927; s. Watts Sherman Humphrey and Katharine (Strong) Osborne; m. Barbara Falon, May 22, 1954; children: Katharine, Lisa, Sarah, Watts Jr., Peter, Erica, Christopher. BS in Physics, U. Chgo., 1949, MBA, 1951; MS in Physics, Ill. Inst. Tech., 1950; PhD in Software Engrng. (hon.), Embry Riddle Aero. U., 1998. Electronics engr. Fermi Inst. U. Chgo., 1949-51, dir. sci. pers. Chgo. Midway Lab., 1951-53; mgr. computing devel. Sylvania Electric Products, Natick, Mass., 1953-59; instr. computer design Northeastern U., Boston, 1956-59; with IBM, White Plains, N.Y., 1959-86, mgr. teleprocessing systems devel., 1959-64, dir. systems application engrng., Armonk, N.Y., 1964-65, dir. time sharing systems, White Plains, 1965-66, dir. programming, 1966-68, v.p. tech. devel., Armonk, 1968-70, dir. Endicott (N.Y.) Labs., 1970-72, dir. policy devel., Armonk, 1972-79, dir. tech. assessment, White Plains, 1979-83, dir. programming quality and process, Poughkeepsie, N.Y., 1983-86; dir. software process program Software Engrng. Inst. Carnegie Mellon U., Pitts., 1986-91, fellow, 1991—; chmn. adv. bd. IBM Systems Rsch. Inst., N.Y.C., 1973-82. Author: Switching Circuits with Computer Applications, 1958, Managing for Innovation, Leading Technical People, 1987, Managing the Software Process, 1989, A Discipline for Software Engineering, 1995, Managing Technical People, Innovation, Teamwork and the Software Process, 1997, Introduction to the Personal Software Process, 1997, Introduction to the Team Software Process, 1999; contbr. numerous articles to profl. jours.; patentee in field; mem. editl. bd. Jour. Systems and Software, 1988-96, Software Process, Improvement and Practice, 1996—, Empirical Software Engrng., 1996—. bd. examiners Malcolm Baldridge Nat. Quality Award, 1991; sci. adv. com. Std. System Ctr. USAF, 1989-92. With USN, 1944-46. Recipient Aerospace Software Engineering award Am. Inst. of Aeronautics and Astronautics, 1993. Fellow IEEE (editorial bds. Spectrum 1982-83, The Institute 1982-83, reviewer Software 1984, Computer 1984, IBM System Jour. 1989); mem. Assn. for Computing Machinery, Inst. for Radio Engrs. (chmn. computer sect. 1959). Republican. Avocations: running, skiing, duplicate bridge. Office: Carnegie Mellon U Software Engring Inst 4500 5th Ave Pittsburgh PA 15213-2612

HUMPHREYS, CHARLES RAYMOND, JR., retired research chemist; b. Wilmington, N.C., Aug. 14, 1911; s. Charles Raymond and Lilian Miller (Kenly) H.; m. Mary Lillian Knotts, June 22, 1940; 1 child, Howard Joshua. BS in Chemistry, Duke U., 1934. Analytical chemist duPont Ctrl. Chem. Dept., Wilmington, 1934-38; rsch. chemist original nylon rsch. sect. duPont, Wilmington, 1939-43, supr. field rsch. textile fibers dept., 1943-48; asst. mgr. tech. svd. Ducilo, Buenos Aires, Argentina, 1948-50, mgr. tech. svc. and market analysis, 1951-53; asst. mgr. export sales, textile fibers duPont, Wilmington, 1954-56, sr. rsch. chemist textile rsch. end use devel., 1956-72. Author: The Devil's Left Ear, 1989, Panthers of the Coastal Plain, 1994; patentee in field. Lectr. to civic groups, Wilmington, N.C., 1973-96. Mem. Lower Cape Fear Bird Club, Hobby Greenhouse. Republican. Avocations: nature, wildlife photography, travel, fishing, wildlife research. Home: 1132 Princeton Dr Wilmington NC 28403-2529

HUMPHREYS, DAVID JOHN, lawyer, trade association executive; b. Scranton, Pa., Jan. 30, 1936; s. David Evan and Josephine Mary (Tarrant) H.; m. Laura Margaret Baker, Aug. 11, 1973; children—Cecelia, Katie, Mary Claire, Theresa, Monica, Douglas, Justin, Brian, Casey, Molly. B.A., St. Mary's U., 1959; J.D., Cath. U., 1963. Bar: Va., D.C., U.S. Supreme Ct. 1972. Salesman Kraft Foods Co., 1959-63; pvt. practice law Washington; mem. firm Sorrell, Jones & Paulson, 1964-69, Paulson & Humphreys, 1969-79, Humphreys & Loftus, 1979-91; Washington counsel Recreational Vehicle Inst., 1969-74; gen. counsel, exec. sec. Recreation Vehicle Industry Assn., 1974-79, pres., 1979—, gen. counsel, 1979-85, 91-94; chmn. bd. Am. Recreation Coalition, 1979—; mem. adv. bd. U.S. Congl. Travel and Tourism Caucus, 1980-94; bd. dirs., mem. exec. com. Govt. Affairs Coun. of Travel Industry, 1985—; trustee Travel Data Ctr., 1985-91. Served with Air N.G., 1959-63. Recipient Paul Abel award, 1977. Mem. Va. State Bar, Bar Assn. D.C., Hwy. Users Fedn. (bd. dirs. 1981—), Travel Industry Assn. (bd. dirs. 1985—, exec. com. 1986-99, chmn. bd. 1990-91, inducted Hall of Leaders 1994). Office: PO Box 2999 Reston VA 20195-0999

HUMPHREYS, GEORGE H., II, surgery educator; b. N.Y.C., Nov. 22, 1903; s. John Sanford and Maria Mitchell (Champney) H.; m. Edith Sturgis, Oct. 4, 1930 (dec. 1980); children: John Sanford, Cornelia H. Rea, Edith H. Mas. AB, Harvard U., 1925, MD, 1929; DMS, Columbia U., 1935. Intern in surgery Presbyn. Hosp., N.Y.C., 1930-32, jr. surg. fellow, 1932-33, sr. surg. fellow, 1934-35, asst. attending surgeon, 1942-46, attending surgeon, dir. surg. svc., 1946-69; asst. in surgery Coll. Physicians & Surgeons, Columbia U., N.Y.C., 1932-34, instr. surgery, 1934-40, asst. prof. clin. surgery, 1940-46, Valentine Mott prof. of surgery, chmn., 1946-69, prof. emeritus, 1969—; asst. vis. surgeon City Hosp., N.Y.C., 1936-40; vis. surgeon, dir. surgery 1st Surg. Svc. Welfare Hosp., N.Y.C., 1939-42; vis. surgeon, dir. Francis Delafield Hosp., N.Y.C., 1949-69; vis. prof. surgery Nat. Univ., Taipei, Taiwan, 1960, 69-70. Author chpts. to books; contbr. articles to profl. jours. Trustee Mary Imogene Bassett Hosp., Cooperstown, N.Y., 1955-87; chief Unitarian svc. com. Med. Mission, Colombia, 1948; pres. Am. Bur. Med. Advancement, N.Y. and Taipei, Taiwan, 1975-80. Recipient Republic of China medal, 1977, 83. Fellow ACS; mem. Am. Assn. Thoracic Surgery, Am. Surg. Soc., Soc. Univ. Surgeons, Century Assn., others. Avocations: carving, gardening. Home: 209 Handle Rd Handle Rd West Dover VT 05356

HUMPHREYS, HOMER ALEXANDER, former principal; b. nr. Waynesboro, Va., Feb. 7, 1902; s. Lewis Greenberry and Annie (Sampson) H.; B.A., Bridgewater Coll., 1928; M.A., U. Va., 1941, research fellow, 1943-44; m. Ruth Elizabeth Gilbert, Sept. 1, 1926; children—Faye (Mrs. Hezekiah Sadler), Joye (Mrs. James Malcolm Hart Harris, Jr.), Anne (Mrs. Richard Edward Talman), Homer Alexander, Jane (dec.), Kaye. Instr. Moyock (N.C.) High Sch., 1928-29; prin. Darlington Heights (Va.) High Sch., 1929-33, Green Bay (Va.) High Sch., 1934-44; supervising prin. West Point (Va.) High Sch., 1944-65; gen. supr. instrn. Williamsburg-James City County Schools, 1965-67; instr. Bridgewater Coll., summer 1944; dir. aviation edn. Mont. State U., Missoula, also Eastern Coll. Edn., Billings, Mont., summers 1954, 55, U. Va., Charlottesville, summers 1956-71; instr. Coll. William and Mary Extension, 1963-68. Coordinator, Civil Def., King William County and Town of West Point, 1950-61. Served from 2d lt. to lt. col. USAF, CAP, 1945—; dir. aviation edn. Va. Wing, Civil Air Patrol, 1956-65. Mem. NEA (past 2d zone v.p. dept. audio-visual instrn.), Va. High Sch. League (chmn. 1955-57), King William-King and Queen Edn. Assn. (pres. 1956-58), Phi Delta Kappa. Kiwanian (pres. West Point 1949, lt. gov. capital dist. div. four 1956). Author: A History of Education in Prince Edward County, Va., 1941; column Wings Over Va., 1956-62; also numerous articles, reports and surveys. Home: PO Box Hu Williamsburg VA 23187-3624

HUMPHREYS, JOSEPHINE, novelist; b. Charleston, S.C., Feb. 2, 1945; d. William Wirt and Martha (Lynch) Humphreys; m. Thomas A. Hutcheson, Nov. 30, 1968; children: Allen, William. AB, Duke U., 1967; MA, Yale U., 1968. Author: Dreams of Sleep, 1984 (Ernest Hemingway Found. award 1985), Rich in Love, 1987, The Fireman's Fair, 1991. Recipient Lyndhurst Found. prize, 1985, Hillsdale prize, 1993; Guggenheim fellow, 1984. Home and Office: 2663 Bayonne St Sullivans Island SC 29482-9669 also: care Harriet Wasserman Agy 137 E 36th St Ste 190 New York NY 10016-3528*

HUMPHREYS, KAREN M., judge; b. Ashland, Kans., Feb. 18, 1948; d. Frederick Mitchell and Carrie (Arnold) H. BA in History and Am. Studies, Univ. of Kans., 1970, JD, 1973. Bar: Kans. 1973, U.S. Dist. Ct. Kans. 1978, U.S. Supreme Ct. 1980. Estate and gift tax atty. IRS, Dept. of Treasury, 1973-75; staff atty. Legal Aid, 1975-76; founder, mng. atty. Senior Citizen Law Project, 1976-78; asst. U.S. atty. Topeka, Kans., 1978-83, Wichita, Kans., 1983-86; assoc. Redmond, Redmond & Nazar, 1986-87; staff atty. FDIC, 1987; dist. judge State of Kans., 18th Judicial Dist., 1987-93; magistrate judge U.S. Dist. Ct. Kans., Wichita, 1993—; bd. dirs. Women's Studies at Wichita State Univ., Kans. Health Inst. and Prairie View Inc.; advisory bd. Jr. League. Recipient Matrix award Women in Comm., 1989. Mem. Am. Bar Assn., Kans. Bar Assn., Wichita Bar Assn. (President's award for outstanding svc. 1988), Nat. Assn. of Women Judges, Wichita Women Attys. Assn. (Louise Mattox award 1994). Protestant. Avocations: traveling, reading. Office: US Courthouse 401 N Market St Rm 322 Wichita KS 67202-2000

HUMPHREYS, KENNETH KING, engineer, educator, association executive; b. Pitts., Jan. 19, 1938; s. Meredith Harold and Olga (Adamitis) H.; m. Harriet Elizabeth Moss, May 6, 1961; children: Kenneth King, Keith Alan, Kevin James, Karen Elizabeth. B.S., Carnegie Inst. Tech., 1959, postgrad., 1961-62; postgrad., U. Pitts., 1965; M.S., W. Va. U., 1967; PhD, Kennedy Western U., 1990. Registered profl. engr., Pa., N.C., W.Va.; cert. cost engr. U.S., Mex., Internat. Tech. asst. Applied Research Lab.-U.S. Steel Corp., 1959-60; tech. assoc. Applied Research Lab.-U.S. Steel Corp., Monroeville, Pa., 1960-62; asst. technologist Applied Research Lab.-U.S. Steel Corp., Universal, Pa., 1962-63, assoc. research engr., 1963-65; cost engr. W. Va. U. Coal Research Bur., Morgantown, 1965-67, sr. staff and cost engr., 1967-71, asst. dir., 1971-81; asst. prof. Coll. Mineral and Energy Resources-W. Va., Morgantown, 1970-73; assoc. prof. Coll. Mineral and Energy Resources-W. Va. U., Morgantown, 1973-76, prof., 1976-82, adj. prof., 1982-92, asst. to dean, 1971-77, chmn. minerals program, 1978-81, asst. dean acad. affairs, 1979-82; exec. dir. Am. Assn. Cost Engrs., 1971-92; engrng. cons. metallurgy and fuel tech., 1963-82; engrng. cons. cost engrng. and project mgmt., 1993—. Author: Basic Cost Engineering, 1981, 2d edit., 1986, 3d edit., 1996, What Every Engineer Should Know About Ethics, 2000; editor: Control and Management of Capital Projects, 2d edit., 1992, reprint edit., 1998; co-author, co-editor: Basic Mathematics and Computer Applications for Coal Preparation and Mining, 1983; co-author, assoc. editor: Coal Preparation, 4th edit., 1979; co-author, editor: Project and Cost Engineers' Handbook, 2d edit., 1984, 3d edit., 1993; co-author, co-editor: Mechanical Estimating Guidebook, 5th edit., 1987, 6th edit., 1995; co-author, editor: Jelen's Cost and Optimization Engineering, 3d edit., 1991; editor: Effective Project Management Through Applied Cost and Schedule Control, 1996; What Every Engineer Should Know About Ethics, 1999; contbr. articles to prof. jours.; patentee in field. Leader Allegheny Trails, Piedmont and Mountaineer area couns. Boy Scouts Am., 1961—, dist. commr. Mountaineer area coun., 1969-72, dist. tng. chmn., 1972-74, 90, chmn. coun. tng., 1975-77, exec. bd., 1987-89, leadership devel. com., area 6 East Cen. region, 1977-79, dist. commr. Piedmont coun., 1996-97, rechartering com., 1997—; deacon 1st Presbyn. Ch., Morgantown, W.Va., 1968-70, ruling elder, 1972-75, 90-92, pres. congregation, 1975-77; deacon Waldensian Presbyn. Ch., Valdese, N.C., 1995-97, treas., 1995-96. Recipient Silver Beaver award Mountaineer Area Coun. Boy Scouts Am., 1973, Disting. Silver Beaver award Boy Scouts Am., 1990; recipient award of merit Mountaineer Area Coun. Boy Scouts Am., 1969, Woodbadge award Mountaineer Area Coun. Boy Scouts Am., 1971, 50-Year Vets. award Boy Scouts Am., 1998, Het Schaap mit vijf Poten award Royal Netherlands Industries Fair, 1977; named Hon. West Virginian Gov. West Virginia, 1974. Fellow Assn. Cost Engrs. (U.K.), Am. Assn. Cost Engrs. (nat. chmn. 1969-71, Mem. of Moment, nat. bd. dirs. 1971, exec. dir. 1971-92, award of merit 1993, award recognition 1979, pub. Cost Engrng. mag. 1981-92, co-editor trans. 1982-92, pres. No. W.Va. sect. 1989-91, pres. Catawba Valley, Charlotte, N.C. sect. 1994-96); mem. NSPE, Soc. Mexicana de Ingenieria Economica Financiera y de Costos (Mex.), Cost Engrng. Assn. So. Africa, Internat. Cost Engrng. Coun. (sec.-treas. 1976—), Profl. Engrs., N.C. (ethics steering com. 1995—), W.Va. Soc. Profl. Engrs. (bd. dirs. 1971-76, 83-92, v.p. 1980-81, pres. 1982-83, W.Va. Engr. of Yr. 1986), Morgantown Soc. Profl. Engrs. (pres. 1969-70, bd. dirs. 1970-76), Am. Assn. Engrng. Socs. (bd. govs. 1979-83), Coun. Engrng. Splty. Bds. (pres.-elect 1990-92, pres. 1992-93), Sigma Xi, Beta Theta Pi (asst. gen. sec. 1987-91), Alpha Phi Omega. Democrat. Home and Office: 1168 Hidden Lake Dr Granite Falls NC 28630-8592

HUMPHREYS, KIRK, mayor; b. 1950. BA, U. Okla., 1972. Pres. Century Investments, Inc., Oklahoma City, 1989—; mayor Oklahoma City, 1998—. Office: Office of the Mayor City Hall 200 N Walker Ave Ste 302 Oklahoma City OK 73102-2232

HUMPHREYS, LLOYD GIRTON, research psychologist, educator; b. Lorane, Oreg., Dec. 12, 1913; s. John Pryor H. and Gertrude (Stephenson) H.; m. Dorothy Jane Windes, Dec. 27, 1937 (dec. July 12, 1995); children: John Daniel, Michael Stephenson, Margaret Anne, Susan Jeanne. BS, U. Oreg., 1935; MA, Ind. U., 1936; PhD, Stanford U., 1938. Instr. Northwestern U., 1939-42, asst. prof., 1945-46; assoc. prof. U. Wash., 1946-48,

Stanford U., Calif., 1948-51; rsch. psychologist U.S. Air Force, San Antonio, 1951-57; prof. psychology U. Ill., Champaign-Urbana, 1957—, chmn. dept. psychology, 1959-69, acting dean Coll. Liberal Arts and Scis., 1979-80; asst. dir. sci. edn. NSF, 1970-71; mem. bd. human resource data and analyses NRC, 1974-77, Commn. on Human Resources, 1978-82; mem. Ill. Gov.'s Blue Ribbon Commn. on Occupational Licensing, 1977-78; bd. dirs. Am. Insts. for Rsch., 1978-94; mem. expert com. on pediatric neurobehavioral evaluations EPA, 1983, cons. clean air sci. adv. com., mem. sci. adv. bd., 1983. Editor Psychol. Bull., 1964-68, Am. Jour. Psychology, 1968-80. Mem. com. on techniques for the enhancement of human performance NRC, 1985-88; mem. sci. adv. group for Project A and Bldg. the Career Force of Army Rsch. Inst., 1982-93; cons. RGI, Inc. Served from 2d lt. to capt. USAAF, 1942-45. Recipient Rsch. award Am. Ednl. Rsch. Assn., 1995, Ednl. Testing Svc. in Psychometrics award, 1995, Career Rsch. award APA Divsn. 5, 1997. Mem. AAAS (chmn. sect. I 1962-63, v.p. 1963, council 1974-77, chmn. sect. J 1979-80), Psychometric Soc. (pres. 1959-60), Psychonomic Soc. (chmn. governing bd. 1962-63), Soc. Exptl. Psychologists, Am. Psychol. Soc., Chmns. Grad. Tng. Depts. Psychology (chmn. 1962-66), Phi Beta Kappa, Sigma Xi, Beta Gamma Sigma, Phi Delta Kappa, Delta Upsilon. Home: 1434 E 2370 North Rd White Heath IL 61884-9323 Office: U Ill Dept Psychology 603 E Daniel St Champaign IL 61820-6232

HUMPHREYS, PAUL WILLIAM, philosophy educator, consultant; b. London, Jan. 17, 1950; came to U.S., 1971; s. William Edward and Florence C. (Didcock) H.; m. Diane Gail Snustad, July 14, 1984; children: Emily Victoria, Alexandra Elizabeth. BSc, U. Sussex, U.K., 1971; MA, MS, Stanford U., 1974, PhD, 1976. From asst. to assoc. prof. philosophy U. Va., Charlottesville, 1978-91, prof., 1991—, chmn., 1996-97, 99—; v.p. Assn. for Founds. Sci., 1995-99; seminar dir. NEH, Va., 1991, 95. Author: Chances of Explanation, 1989; editor: Synthese, 1991-98, Founds. of Sci., 1993-98, Oxford Studies in the Philosophy of Sci., 1999—. Recipient Travel award Fulbright, 1971, Scholars award NSF, 1984. Mem. Am. Philos. Assn., Philosophy Sci. Assn. (mem. gov. bd. 1997—). Home: 323 Kent Rd Charlottesville VA 22903-2409 Office: U Va Dept Philosophy Charlottesville VA 22903

HUMPHREYS, ROBERT LEE, advertising agency executive; b. Burbank, Calif., Dec. 30, 1924; s. Robert E. and Nancy Lucille (Gum) H.; m. Marie Dorthea Wilkinson, May 10, 1951; children: Dina Lizette, Gia Monique Thompson. BS in Mktg., UCLA, 1947. Merchandising rep. Life mag., L.A., 1947-48; promotion mgr. Fortune mag., N.Y.C., 1948-49; copywriter BBDO, L.A., 1950-51; account exec. KNBC-TV, L.A., 1951-52; v.p., account group mgr. Foote, Cone & Belding, L.A., 1952-62; CEO, chmn. emeritus Western divsn. Grey Advt., Inc., L.A., 1962—, dir., 1963-92; dir. William O'Neil Fund, Beverly Hills, Calif. Featured guest on Corp. Viewpoint, PBS, 1978. Founding pres. UCLA Chancellor's Assocs., 1967—; founding chmn. Motorcycle Safety Coun., 1966; founding vice chmn. UCLA Found., 1967—; mem. president's circle Los Angeles County Mus. Art, 1983—; bd. dirs. Advt. Industry Emergency Fund, Banning Park Mus., 1991-96. Mem. Am. Advt. Fedn. (bd. dirs. 1982-92), World Affairs Coun., Hollywood Radio and TV Soc. (bd. dirs. 1976-82), L.A. Advt. Club (bd. dirs. 1974-76), Sierra Club (life), Bel Air Bay Club, Phi Gamma Delta. Home: 12830 Parkyns St Los Angeles CA 90049-2630 Office: Grey Advt Inc 6100 Wilshire Blvd Los Angeles CA 90048-5107

HUMPHREYS, ROBERT RUSSELL, lawyer, consultant, arbitrator; b. Eugene, Oreg., May 7, 1938; s. Russell Wallace and Roberta Lois (Bennett) H.; m. Natalia Dimitrievna Lucenko; children: Tatyana Roberta, Grigori Robert. BA, U. Wash., 1959; LLB, George Washington U., 1965. Bar: Va. 1965, D.C. 1966, U.S. Dist. Ct. (D.C.), U.S. Ct. Appeals (D.C. cir.). Law clk. Barco, Cook & Patton, Washington, 1963-64, Keller & Heckman, Washington, 1964; mgr. pub. affairs services Air Transport Assn. Am., Washington, 1965-66; asst. to v.p. fed. affairs, 1966-71; spl. counsel com. on labor and human resources U.S. Senate, Washington, 1971-77; commr. Rehab. Services Adminstrn., HEW, Washington, 1977-80; ptnr. Hoffheimer & Johnson, Washington, 1980-83, Humphreys & Mitchell, Washington, 1983-88; cons. MARC Assocs., Inc., Washington, 1988-94; pvt. practice law, Washington, 1988—; pres. The Humphreys Group, Washington, 1991—; pres., ceo Jennings Randolph Inst., Washington, 1998—; spkr. nat., internat. confs. Author: Compliance Manual on Americans with Disabilities Act; contbr. articles to profl. jours. Incorporator, bd. dirs., treas., counsel Nat. Ctr. for Barrier-Free Environ., 1975-77, 81-84; bd. dirs. Va. Spl. Olympics, 1982-84. Mem. D.C. Bar Assn., George Washington U. Law Alumni Assn., Va. State Bar, Phi Delta Phi. Prin. Senate draftsman for Black Lung Benefits Act, 1972, Rehab. Act, 1973, Randolph-Sheppard Act Amendments, 1974, Black Lung Benefits Reform Act, 1977.

HUMPHREYS-HECKLER, MAUREEN KELLY, nursing home administrator; b. N.Y.C., Aug. 5, 1961; d. Henry James and Eileen Frances (Kelly) Humphreys; m. Robert P. Heckler, Sept. 12, 1992. BA, Villanova U., 1983; M in Mgmt., Pa. State U., 1998. Lic. nursing home adminstr., personal care adminstr., Pa.; cert. nursing home adminstr.; registered housing profl. Asst. adminstr. Pennsburg (Pa.) Manor, 1983-84, adminstr., 1984-85; adminstr. Roslyn (Pa.) Nursing and Rehab. Ctr., 1985-88; exec. adminstr. Gracecare, Inc., Blue Bell, Pa., 1988-92; adminstr. St. Mary Manor, Lansdale, Pa., 1992-98; dir. resident svcs. The Fairfax, Ft. Bervoir, Va., 1998—. Fellow Am. Coll. Health Care Adminstrs.; mem. Cath. Health Care Assn., Villanova U. Alumni Assn., Am. Assn. Sovereign Mil. Order of Knights of Malta (Dame). Republican. Roman Catholic. Avocations: golf, travel, reading, wine collecting. Home: 222 Lower Country Dr Gaithersburg MD 20877 Office: The Fairfax 9140 Belvoir Woods Pky Fort Belvoir VA 22060

HUMPHRIES, FREDERICK S., university president; b. Apalachicola, Fla., Dec. 26, 1935; m. Antoinette Humphries; children: Frederick S., Robin Tanya, Laurence Anthony. B.S. magna cum laude, Fla. A&M U., 1957; Ph.D. in Phys. Chemistry (fellow), U. Pitts., 1964. Pvt. tutor sci. and math., 1959-64; asst. prof. chemistry U. Minn., Mpls., 1966-67; asso. prof. chemistry Fla. A&M U., 1964-67, prof. chemistry, 1964-67, dir. 13 coll. curriculum program, 1967-68; dir. summer confs. Inst. for Services to Edn., 1968-74, dir. interdisciplinary program, 1973-74, dir. two-univs. grad. program in sci., 1973-74, v.p., 1970-74; pres. Tenn. State U., Nashville, 1974-85, Fla. A&M U., Tallahassee, 1985—; cons. to various colls. and univs.; mem. bd. grad. advocates Meharry Med. Coll. 1976, co-chmn. Reston's Black Focus, 1973; bd. dirs. So. Growth, Nat. Merit Scholarship Corp. Bd.; bd. regents 5-Yr. Working Group for Agriculture, chmn. State Univ. System of Fla.; adv. coun. Panhandle Regional Ctr. Excellence in Math., Sci., Computers, Tech.-FAMU & U., West Fla.; Nat. Assn. Ednl. Opportunities sci. and tech. adv. com., vice chmn. bd. dirs.; mem. Nissan adv. com. HBCUs. Contbr. articles on higher edn. to profl. publs. Chmn. Fairfax county Anti-Poverty Commn., 1972-74, White House Sci. and Tech. Adv. Com., on Edn. Blacks in Fla.; bd. dirs. YMCA, 1975—, Walmart Corp., Brinker Internat., Barnett Bank Tallahassee; bd. ann. minority bus. Youth Ednl. Svc. Embarkment; commn. Future of South, 1986, com. tech. and innovation commn.; steering com. Apalachicola Bay Area Resource Planning and Mgmt.; subcom. Fed. Student Fin. Assistance-Office for the Advancement of Pub. Black Colls., chmn. adv. com. Recipient Disting. Svc. to Advancement of Edn. for Black Americans award Inst. for Svcs. to Edn., Disting. Edn. and Adminstr.; Meritorious award Fla. A&M U., Human Rels. award Met. Human Rels. Commn., Nashville, 1978, Thurgood Marshall Ednl. Achievement award Johnson Publ. Co., 1990; named an Outstanding Alumnus of Pitts. U., 1986. Mem. NIH (nat. adv. com. neurol. and communicative disorders and stroke coun.), AAUP, AAAS, NAACP, Am. Chem. Soc., Am. Assn. Higher Edn., Nat. Assn. State Univs. and Land-Grant Colls. (chmn.), Nat. Assn. Equal Opportunity Bd. Dirs. (chmn.), Assn. Minority Rsch. Univ., Alpha Kappa Mu (pres., award), Alpha Phi Alpha (Meritorious Svc. award). Office: Fla A&M U Office of President Tallahassee FL 32307*

HUMPHRIES, J. BOB, lawyer; b. Birmingham, Ala., Nov. 18, 1946. BS, Fla. State U., 1968, MBA, 1972, JD cum laude, 1971. Bar: Fla. 1972, Ga. 1974. Atty. Fowler, White, Gillen, Boggs, Villareal and Banker P.A., Tampa, Fla. Bus. editor Fla. State U. Law Rev., 1971. Chmn. bd. Tampa-Hillsborough County Pub. Libr., 1986-87; bd. trustees Cmty. Found. Tampa Bay; bd. dirs., exec. mem. Tampa Bay Performing Arts Ctr.; trustee Cmty. Found. Tampa Bay; bd. dirs. Tampa Bay Downtown Partnership. Mem. ABA, State Bar Ga., Fla. Bar (chmn. tax sect., mem. environ. and land use law sect., corp., banking and bus. law sect., and real property, probate and trust law sect.), Phi Delta Phi. E-mail: bhtaxlaw@fowlerwhite.com. Office: Fowler White Gillen Boggs Villareal and Banker 501 E Kennedy Blvd Ste 1700 Tampa FL 33602-5200

HUMPHRIES, JOAN ROPES, psychologist, educator; b. Bklyn., Oct. 17, 1928; d. Lawrence Gardner and Adele Lydia (Zimmermann) Ropes; m. Charles C. Humphries, Apr. 4, 1957; children: Peggy Ann, Charlene Adele. *Grandmother, Gertrude Moody Zimmerman was Dwight L. Moody's niece. Although his ministry was awesome, his heart was with the schools he founded in Northfield, Massachusetts. During these days, it was very difficult for a girl to get a goodeducation. Uncle Dwight would ride his carriage through the hills of New England, despairing and wondering what would happen to the young country girls unable to get an education. Would they be destined to make apple pies as house-wives forever? So he founded a school for girls (Northfield Seminary) so they could have careers and happy families. To him this was of the upmost importance.* BA, U. Miami, 1950; MS, Fla. State U., 1955; PhD, La. State U., 1963. Registered lobbyist State of Fla. Part-time instr. psychology dept. U. Miami, Coral Gables, Fla., 1964-66; prof. behavioral studies dept. Miami-Dade C.C., 1966—; Presenter, lectr. in field. Prodr., prin host (videos) Strategies in Global Modern Academia: Issues and Answers in Higher Education, 1993-94; prodr., host (video) Strategies in Global Modern Academia: Issues and Answers in Higher Education II, Strategies in Global Modern Acadmia, 1995, III, 1996-97, lect., Fostering, Enhancing and Improving Knowledge of American View of Constitutional Law from Psychological Perspective, given abroad cruise ship Costa Romantica; editl. staff, maj. author: The Application of Scientific Behaviorism to Humanistic Phenomena, 1975, rev. edit., 1979. Mem. Biofeedback Delegation to the People's Republic of China and Hong Kong, 1995, Citizen Amb. Program, Psychic Arts Delegation to Russia, 1997, Citizen Amb. Program. Mem. AAUP (past v.p. and sec., pres. Miami-Dade C.C. chpt. 1986—, past v.p. Fla. conf., 1986-88, mem. exec. bd. Fla. conf. 1989-90, mem. nat.), AAUW (life, former v.p. Tamiami br. 1983-88, Appreciation award 1977), Biofeedback Soc. of Am. (pres. 1989—), Biofeedback Assn. Fla. (pres. 1990—), Internat. Platform Assn. (gov. 1979—, Silver Bowl award 1993), APA, Am. Psychol. Soc. (charter), Fla. Psychol. Assn., Mexico Beach C. of C. (bus. 1991—), North Campus Speaker's Bur. (award for cmty. lecture series), Physicians for Social Responsibility, Internat. Soc. for Study Subtle Energies and Energy Medicine (charter), Inst. Evaluation, Diagnosis and Treatment (past v.p. 1975-87, pres. 1987—, former bd. dirs.), Dade-Monroe Psychol. Assn., Assn. Applied Psychophysiology and Biofeedback, Noetic Scis., Colonial Dames 17th Century, N.Y. Acad. Scis. (life), Regines in Miami, Soc. Mayflower Descs. (elder William Brewster colony), Hereditary Order of Descendants of Colonial Govs., Country of Coral Gables Club (life), Jockey Club (life), Phi Lambda (founder's plaque 1976, Appreciation award 1987), Phi Lambda Pi. Democrat. Achievements include research in biofeedback and human consciousness. Home: 1311 Alhambra Cir Coral Gables FL 33134-3521 Office: Miami Dade CC North Campus 11380 NW 27th Ave Miami FL 33167-3418

HUMPHRIES, JOHN O'NEAL, physician, educator, university dean; b. Columbia, S.C., Oct. 22, 1931; s. Arthur Lee and Helen Elliott (O'Neal) H.; m. Mary Ellen Cregan, Mar. 13, 1954; children: Arthur Thomas, Ellen Cregan, John Elliott. BS, Duke U., 1952; MD, Johns Hopkins U., 1956. Diplomate Am. Bd. Internal Medicine (mem. bd. subsplty. cardiovascular disease 1974-79). Intern Johns Hopkins Hosp., 1957; asst. resident Osler Med. Service, Osler Med. Svc., 1958-60; resident physician pvt. med. svc. Osler Med. Service, 1962-64, staff physician, 1962-79; rsch. fellow in cardiology U. London, St. George's Hosp., 1960-61; rsch. fellow in cardiology Johns Hopkins U. Med. Sch., 1956-57, 61-62, mem. faculty, 1964-79, Robert L. Levy prof. cardiology, 1975-79, prof. medicine, 1976-79; O.B. Mayer Sr. and Jr. prof. medicine U. S.C., Columbia, 1979-86, prof. medicine, 1979-96; disting. prof. medicine, dean emeritus, 1997—; chmn. dept. medicine U. S.C., Columbia, 1979-87, dean Sch. Medicine, 1983-94. Contbr. articles to med. publs.; mem. editl. bd. various jours. Bd. dirs. Md. Ballet, Balt., 1975-78. Fellow ACP (bd. govs. for S.C. chpt. 1986-90), Am. Coll. Cardiology (bd. govs. for Md. chpt. 1973-76); mem. Am. Fedn. Clin. Rsch., Am. Heart Assn. (fellow coun . clin. cardiology, chmn. postgrad. edn. com., exec. com. 1972-75), Cen. Md. Heart Assn. (pres. 1972-73), Md. Heart Assn. (pres. 1976-77), Assn. Univ. Cardiologists, Am. Clin. and Climatol. Assn., Alpha Omega Alpha. Office: U SC Sch Medicine Columbia SC 29208

HUMPHRIES, PAMELA JEAN, women's health nurse; b. Lincoln, Nebr., Feb. 21, 1959; m. Craig S. Humphries, July 18, 1980; children: Jason Michael, Melissa Lynne. Diploma, Deaconess Hosp. Sch. Nursing, St. Louis, 1980. Cert. electronic fetal monitoring; registered diagnostic med. sonographer. Gynecology staff nurse St. Mary's Health Ctr., Richmond Heights, Mo., 1980-84, high risk labor and delivery staff nurse, 1984-89, fetal evaluation and treatment unit staff nurse, 1989-94; nurse mgr. home uterine activity monitoring divsn. Biomed. Sys., St. Louis, 1994-95, reimbursement coord. home uterine activity monitoring divsn., 1995; obstetric staff nurse Barnes Jewish St. Peter's, 1995—; sonographer physician's office, 1997—. Home: 26 Williamsburg Ct Saint Charles MO 63303-5036

HUMPHRIES, SANDRA LEE FORGER, artist, teacher; b. Norwalk, Conn., Dec. 1, 1946; d. Edmund Ernest and Grace Muriel (Seale) Forger; m. Stanley Humphries Jr., Aug. 10, 1968 (div. July 1992); children: Colin, Courtney; m. Corby Knight, June 2, 1998. BFA, R.I. Sch. Design, 1968; MA, U. N.Mex., 1994. Studio artist Albuquerque, 1980—; instr. watercolor Sandra Humphries Fine Art, Albuquerque, 1992—; dir. Shows Gallery, Albuquerque, 1994-96, Sandra Humphries Gallery, Albuquerque, 1997—. Exhibited in group shows at Rocky Mountain Watermedia Exhbn., 1983, 86, 89, 90, 91, Western Fedn. Watercolor Socs., 1984, 86, 87, 90, Am. Watercolor Soc. Exhbn., 1985, Nat. Watercolor Soc. Exhbn., 1989, Artists of the West Invitational, 1993, 94, 95, 96. Mem. Nat. Watercolor Soc. (signature), Rocky Mountain Watermedia Soc. (signature), N.Mex. Watercolor Soc. (signature). Home: 3503 Berkeley Pl NE Albuquerque NM 87106-1349

HUMPHRY, DEREK, association executive, writer; b. Bath, Somerset, Eng., Apr. 29, 1930; came to U.S., 1978; s. Royston Martin and Bettine (Duggan) H.; m. Jean Edna Crane, May 5, 1953 (dec. Mar. 1975); children: Edgar, Clive, Stephen; m. Ann Wickett Kooman, Feb. 16, 1976 (div. 1990); m. Gretchen Crocker, 1991. Student pub. schs. Reporter, Evening News, Manchester, Eng., 1951-55, Daily Mail, London, 1955-63; editor Havering Recorder, Essex, Eng., 1963-67; sr. reporter Sunday Times, London, 1967-78; spl. writer L.A. Times, 1978-79; founder, exec. dir. Hemlock Soc. N.Am., L.A., 1980-92, pres. 1988-90. Author: Because They're Black, 1971 (M.L. King award 1972), Police Power and Black People, 1972; Jean's Way, 1978, Let Me Die Before I Wake, 1982, The Right to Die, 1986, Final Exit, 1991, Dying With Dignity, 1992, Lawful Exit, 1993, Freedom to Die, 1998. With Brit. Army, 1948-50. Recipient Socrates award for right-to-die activism, 1997. Mem. World Fedn. Right-to-Die Socs. (newsletter editor 1979-84, 1992-94, sec.-treas. 1983-84, pres. 1988-90), Ams. Death with Dignity (v.p. 1993), Hemlock Soc. No. Calif. (v.p. 1994), Euthanasia Rsch. and Guidance Orgn. (pres. 1993—). Home and Office: 24829 Norris Ln Junction City OR 97448-9559

HUMPHRY, JAMES, III, librarian, publishing executive; b. Springfield, Mass., July 21, 1916; s. James and Elizabeth Lucy (Ames) H.; m. Priscilla Eaton, Dec. 26, 1942; children: Susan H. Fitch, Elizabeth Ames Schnabel. AB, Harvard U., 1939; MS, Columbia U., 1941. Reference asst. N.Y. Pub. Library, 1939-41, 46, chief map divsn., 1946; librarian, prof. bibliography Colby Coll.; bus. mgr. Colby Coll. Press, 1947-57; chief librarian Met. Mus. Art, 1957-68; v.p. H.W. Wilson Co., Bronx, 1968-82, pres., dir. found., 1995—, also bd. dirs., 1965—; prof. Pratt Inst., Bklyn., 1982—; lectr. Columbia Sch. Libr. Svc., 1967-68; vis. assoc. prof. Grad. Sch. Libr. Studies, U. Hawaii, 1983; libr. cons. Am. Heritage, 1965-68, John Wiley & Sons, 1966-69, Coun. Advancement Small Colls., 1956, Gossage Regan Assocs., N.Y.C., 1988-96; coord. Maine Libr. Assn. for ALA sponsored Library Services bill, 1948-49, 55-57; nat. bd. Libr. Presdl. Papers, 1967-69; adminstr. grants-in-aid program N.Y. State Council Arts, 1967-68. Compiler, Library of Edwin Arlington Robinson, 1950; Editor: (with Carl J. Weber) Fitzgerald's Rubaiyat, 1959; Contbr. articles to mags. and jours. Trustee, chmn. adv. com. Archives Am. Art, 1967-88; mem. fine arts vis. com. Harvard U., 1967-73; mem. adv. council St. John's U. Congress for Librarians, 1963-67; bd. dirs. Huguenot YMCA; trustee N.Y. Met. Reference and Research Library Agy., 1967-77, Westchester Library System, 1974-83, New Rochelle Pub. Libr., 1977-87, Thomas Paine Nat. Hist. Assn., 1980-96; pres. Westchester Libr. System. 1980-82, New Rochelle Pub. Library 1979-80, 82, New Rochelle Pub. Libr. Found., 1994-96. With AUS, 1942-46, maj. U.S. Army, 1951-54; lt. col. USAR. Mem. ALA (councilor 1959-63, 67-69, chmn. com. on Wilson index reference services div. 1959-65, mem. subscription books com. 1963-66), Met. Mus. Art Employees Assn. (pres. 1961-63, gov. 1958-66), Maine Library Assn. (pres. 1955-56), Am. Assn. Museums (chmn. library group), Archons of Colophon (convener 1963-65), N.Y. Library Assn. (cons.), Spl. Libraries Assn. (chpt. vice chmn., chmn. mus. group 1962-64, N.Y. conf. chmn. 1967), Assn. Coll. and Research Libraries (pres., dir. 1966-69), Internat. Council Museums (corr.). Clubs: Grolier, N.Y. Library (council 1959-67, pres. 1965-66), Harvard (N.Y.C.). Home: 10 Ridge Rd New Rochelle NY 10804-4711 also: 1600 Ala Moana Blvd Honolulu HI 96815-1427 Office: 950 University Ave Bronx NY 10452-4224

HUMWAY, RONALD JIMMIE, state agency administrator; b. Little Rock, Aug. 1, 1945; s. James Joseph and Rosalie (Ferguson) H.; m. Deborah Ann Northcutt, June 26, 1970; children: James Russell, Zachary Paul. AA, Southwestern Coll., Oklahoma City, 1967; BS in Econs., Oklahoma City U., 1969; BS in Acctg., U. Ark., Little Rock, 1978. CPA, Ark.; cert. fraud examiner. Field auditor Holiday Inns, Inc., Memphis, 1969-70; field auditor, supr. Ark. Div. Legis. Audit, Little Rock, 1970—; regional mgr. Ark. Div. Legis. Audit, Jonesboro, 1985—. Served with USAR, 1963-71. Mem. AICPA, Assn. Govt. Accts. (sec.-treas. Ctrl. ARk. chpt. 1976-77), SCV, Assn. Cert. Fraud Examiners. Baptist. Avocations: coin collecting, photography, golf. Home: 2709 White Cir Jonesboro AR 72404-6961 Office: Ark Div Legis Audit 2920 Mcclellan Dr Ste 1110 Jonesboro AR 72401-7207

HUNANE, KEVIN, talent agent. Talent agt. Creative Artists Agy., Beverly Hills, Calif. Office: Creative Artists Agy 9830 Wilshire Blvd Beverly Hills CA 90212*

HUNDELT, CRAIG THOMAS, engineering executive, realtor; b. St. Louis, Oct. 23, 1947; s. Lester William and Lydia Pearl Hundelt; m. Norma E. Colon-Munoz, Feb. 14, 1976 (div. Dec. 1995); children: Miguel, Elizabeth. BSBA, U. Denver, 1975. Cert. energy mgr. Agrl. commodity sales rep. James McLain, St. Louis, 1975-76; v.p. mech. divsn. Consol. Mech. and Elec. Inc., St. Louis, 1976-82; mgr. of plant ops. Normandy Osteo. Hosps., St. Louis, 1982-86; facility mgr. VA Med. Ctr., St. Louis, 1987-95, engring. tech., 1995—; owner real estate properties. With U.S. Army, 1968-71. Mem. Sheet Metal A/C Contractors Nat. Assn., Hosp. Engrs. and Maintenance Assn. of St. Louis (pres. 1986-87), Am. Soc. of Hosp. Engring., Assn. Energy Engrs. Avocations: music, history. Office: VAMC 1 Jefferson Barracks Rd Saint Louis MO 63125-4181

HUNDER, GENE GERALD, physician, educator; b. Lake City, Minn., Feb. 7, 1932; s. Tilman James and Melita Henrietta (Bremer) H.; m. Ingeborg Anne Hanson, May 6, 1990; children: Heidi, Jennifer, Gregory, Grant, Naomi, Stephanie. Student, St. Olaf Coll., 1950-52; BA, U. Minn. (Mpls.), 1954, MD, 1958, MS, 1963. Diplomate Am. Bd. Inteeeeeernal Medicine. Intern. Strong Meml. Hosp., Rochester, N.Y., 1958-59, resident, 1959-61; resident Mayo Clinic, Rochester, Minn., 1961-64; instr. internal medicine Mayo Grad. Sch., Rochester, Minn., 1966-67, asst. prof. internal medicine, 1968-73, assoc. prof., 1973-78, prof., 1978—, full mem. internal medicine, 1981—, cons. internal medicine and rheumatology; prof. internal medicine Mayo Clinic Mayo found., Rochester, Minn., 1978—; head sect. rheumatology Mayo Clinic, 1976-81; chmn. rheumatology rsch. com., 1976-81, 87, clin. investigator tng. program Mayo Grad. Sch., 1981-84, div. rheumatology 1987-96; mem; editorial bd. Jour. Arthritis and Rheumatism, 1973-83, 87-92; Philip Showalter Hench lect. Ariz. Med. Soc., Phoenix, 1965; Charles W. Thomas lectr. Med. Coll. Va., Charlottesville, 1979; Carl Pearson lectr. Los Angeles County Med. Assn., 1983; Henry J. Lehrhoff lectr. Clarkson Hosp., Omaha, 1989, Nana Swartz lectr. Swedish Med. Soc., 1994, gilbert Galens Meml. lectr. William Beaumont Hosp., Detroit, 1995. Co-author: Physical Exmaination of the Joints, 1978; Editor: Rheumatology, 1978, Atlas of Rheumatology, 1998, Mayo Clinic on Arthritis, 1999; assoc. editor: Jour. Lab and Clin. Medicine, 1979-81; editor Jour. Current Opinion in Rheumatology, 1992—' contbr. numerous sci. articles to med. jours. Fellow ACP; Nu Sigma Nu scholar, 1995; Minn. Med. Found. acad. scholar, 1995. Mem. Jour. Rheumatology, 1982—, Jours. Musculoskeletal Medicine, 1983—, Ann Intern. Med., 1998—, ho, dels. Arthritis Found., Atlanta, 1980-83, trustee, 1985; mem. exec. com. Minn. Arthritis Found., Mpls., 1984-90; mem. AMA, Am. Assn. Immunologists, Am. Fedn. Clin. Research, Am. Bd. Internal Medicine, AAAS. Cen.Clin. Research Club, Cen. Soc. Clin. Research (mem. program com.), Am.Soc. Clin. Rheumatology (pres.), Am.Coll.Rheumatology (mem. exec. com. 1976-77), v.. cen. region 1987, pres. cen. region, 1989, bd. dirs. 1988-92, Master award 1997), Phi Beta Kappa, Alpha Omega Alpha. Republican. Lutheran. Home: RR 1 Box 132B Zumbro Falls MN 55991-9725 Office: Mayo Clinic 200 1st St SW Rochester MN 55902-3008

HUNDLEY, JAMES W., III, business executive; b. Balt., June 19, 1950; s. James W. Jr. and Virginia (Baird) H. BA, Princeton U., 1972; MBA, Loyola Coll., Balt., 1985. Exec. dir. Balt. Zoo, 1978-86; dir. corp. rels. World Wilflife Fund, Washington, 1986-88; devel. dir. Nat. Geog. Soc., Washington, 1988-94; sr. cons. The Conservation Co., Washington, 1992-94; prin. Hundley Assocs., Washington, 1994-96; dir. N.Y. office Rand Corp., N.Y.C., 1996—. Home: 280 Park Ave S Apt 26E New York NY 10010-6135 Office: Rand Corp Ste 1532 342 Madison Ave Rm 1532 New York NY 10173-1599

HUNDLEY, NORRIS CECIL, JR., history educator; b. Houston, Oct. 26, 1935; s. Norris Cecil and Helen Marie (Mundine) H.; m. Carol Marie Beckquist, June 8, 1957; children: Wendy Michelle Hundley Harris, Jacqueline Marie Hundley Reid. A.A., Mt. San Antonio Coll., 1956; A.B., Whittier Coll., 1958; Ph.D. (Univ. fellow), UCLA, 1963. Instr. U. Houston, 1963-64; asst. prof. Am. history UCLA, 1964-69, assoc. prof., 1969-73, prof., 1973—, chmn. exec. com. Inst. Am. Cultures, 1976-93, chmn. univ. program on Mex., 1981-94, acting dir. Latin Am. Ctr., 1989-90, dir. Latin Am. Ctr., 1990-94; mem. exec. com. U. Calif. Consortium on Mex. and the U.S., 1981-86; mem. adv. com. Calif. water atlas project Calif. Office Planning and Research, 1977-79. Author: Dividing the Waters: A Century of Controversy Between the United States and Mexico, 1966, Water and the West: The Colorado River Compact and the Politics of Water in the American West, 1975, The Great Thirst: Californians and Water 1770s-1990s, 1992; co-author: The Calif. Water Atlas, 1979, California: History of a Remarkable State, 1982; editor: The American Indian, 1974, The Chicano, 1975, The Asian American, 1976; co-editor: The American West: Frontier and Region, 1969, Golden State Series, 1978—; mng. editor Pacific Hist. Rev., 1968-97; mem. bd. editors Jour. San Diego History, 1970—; mem. editorial bd. cons. Calif. Hist. Soc., 1980-89; contbr. articles to profl. jours. Bd. dirs. John and LaRee Caughey Found., 1983—, Henry J. Bruman Ednl. Found., 1983—, Forest History Soc., 1987-93. Recipient award of merit Calif. Hist. Soc., 1979; Am. Philos. Soc. grantee, 1964, 71, Ford Found. grantee, 1968-69, U. Calif. Water Resources Ctr. grantee, 1969-72, 91, Sourisseau Acad. grantee, 1972, NEH grantee, 1983-89, Hewlett Found. grantee, 1986-89, U. Calif. Regents faculty fellow in humanities, 1975, Guggenheim fellow, 1978-79, Hist. Soc. So. Calif. fellow, 1996—. Mem. Am. Hist. Assn. (exec. coun. Pacific Coast br. 1968-97, v.p. 1993-94, pres. 1994-95), Western History Assn. (coun. 1985-88, 93-97, pres. 1994-95, Winther award 1973, 79), Orgn. Am. Historians. Office: UCLA Dept History Los Angeles CA 90095

HUNDLEY, RONNIE, academic administrator; b. Columbus, Ga., July 18, 1950; s. Jack and Gwendolyn B. (Sasser) Hawthorne; m. Kathy A. Marcure, Apr. 28, 1972; children: Noel, Rhonda, Maria. BSME in Engring., U. Wash., 1974; MSME, Navy Postgrad., 1982, Degree of Engr., 1984. Registered profl. engr., Wash. Dir. engring. tech. Henry Cogswell Coll., Everett, Wash., 1989-91, acad. dean, 1991-93, pres., 1993—. Comdr. USN, 1968-89. Mem. ASME, Am. Assn. Higher Edn., Rotary. Avocations: hiking, watercolor. Office: Henry Cogswell Coll 2808 Wetmore Ave Ste 100 Everett WA 98201-3518

HUNDLEY, TODD RANDOLPH, professional baseball player; b. Martinsville, Va., May 27, 1969; s. Randy Hundley. Student, William Rainey Harper Coll., Ill. Selected 2d round free-agt. draft N.Y. Mets, 1987, catcher,

1991-98; catcher L.A. Dodgers, 1998—; selected to Nat. League All-Star Team, 1996. Office: LA Dodgers Shea Stadium 1000 Elysian Park Ave Los Angeles CA 90012*

HUNDT, PAUL ANTHONY, financial planner; b. La Crosse, Wis., June 9, 1942; s. Bernard and Catherine (Schams) H.; m. Patricia Arnold, Oct. 26, 1974; children: Peter A., Mary Elizabeth. BS in Am. History, St. Mary's U. Minn., 1964; postgrad., U. San Francisco, 1967-68. CFP, 1978. Lawn equipment sales mgr. Internat. Harvestor Co., Madison, Wis., 1968-69; account exec. Merrill Lynch Pierce Fenner & Smith, Milw., 1969-73; fin. planner Hundt Fin. Svcs., Inc., Milw., 1973—; real estate developer Hundt Properties Co., La Crosse County, Wis., 1976—; bd. dirs. Internat. Assn. Fin. Planners, Milw. chpt., 1994—. Author: The Economic and Political History of the Township of Washington, LaCrosse County Wisconsin, 1853-1900, 1964, Investing-Why You Should Seek A Business Owner's Double Digit Rate of Return, Why You Should Consider the Paul Hundt Personal Investment Strategy, 1998; contbr. articles to periodicals. Mem., del. Rep. Party Wis., Waukesha County, 1975—; founder, CEO, bd. chmn. Aquinas Academy, Menomonee Falls, Wis., 1989—; mem. Regnum Christi. Lt. USNR, 1965-68. Mem. Bd. Adv. ITS Asset Mgmt, L.P., Rotary Club Brookfield, Wis. (sec. 1986-87, Paul Harris fellow 1982). Roman Catholic. Avocations: model railroading, gardening, golf, skiing, tennis, baseball. Office: Hundt Fin Svcs Inc 165 Bishops Way Ste 128 Brookfield WI 53005-6215

HUNDT, REED ERIC, federal agency administrator, lawyer; b. Ann Arbor, Mich., Mar. 3, 1948; s. Neal H. and Viola (Pullan) H.; m. Elizabeth Ann Katz, Oct. 26, 1980; children: Adam Elias, Nathaniel Pullan, Sara. BA, Yale U., 1969, JD, 1974. Bar: U.S. Dist. Ct. Md. 1974, U.S. Ct. Appeals (4th cir.) 1975, U.S. Dist. Ct. (cen. and no. dists.) Calif. 1976, U.S. Ct. Appeals (9th cir.) 1976, U.S. Supreme Ct. 1977, U.S. Tax Ct. 1978, U.S. Ct. Appeals (3d cir.) 1979, U.S. Dist. Ct. D.C. 1980, U.S. Ct. Appeals (D.C. cir.) 1980. Law clk. to presiding justice U.S. Ct. Appeals (4th cir.), Balt., 1974-75; assoc. Latham & Watkins, Washington, 1975-81, ptnr., 1982-94; now chmn. FCC, Washington, 1994-97; prin. Charles Ross Ptnrs., LLC, Bethesda, Md., 1997—. Book rev. editor Yale U. Law Rev., 1974-75; author: (chpt. 9) Antitrust Adviser '85; contbr. articles to profl. jours. Mem. Environ. Task Force of Dem. Policy Com., Washington, 1986. Mem. ABA. Home: 6416 Brookside Dr Bethesda MD 20815-6649 Office: Charles Ross Ptnrs LLC 7316 Wisconsin Ave Ste 400 Bethesda MD 20814-2978

HUNEKE, JOHN GEORGE, minister; b. Bklyn., Aug. 6, 1931; s. John Jacob and Adelaide (Peper) H. BA, Columbia U., 1953; MDiv, Luth. Theol. Sem., Phila., 1956; ThM, Harvard U., 1958. Ordained to ministry Luth. Ch., 1958. Asst. pastor Holy Trinity Luth. Ch., Bklyn., 1957-59; asst. to the pastor Trinity Luth. Ch., Middle Village, Queens, N.Y., 1959-60; pastor St. John's Luth. Ch., Greenpoint, Bklyn., 1960-73, Luth. Ch. of the Reformation, Bklyn., 1973—; instr. religion Wagner Coll., S.I., 1957-58; stewardship com. Met. N.Y. Synod Luth. Ch. Am., 1966-73. Author: Our Church 1867-1967, 1967, Our Church, February 13, 1898-1998, 100 Years, 1998. Bd. govs. Greenpoint Br. YMCA, Bklyn., 1963-73. Mem. Ordained Clergy Evang. Luth. Ch. Am. (Timotheans). Avocation: fishing. Home: Ridgewood 6016 Palmetto St Flushing NY 11385-3241 Office: Luth Ch Reformation 105 Barbey St Brooklyn NY 11207-2201 *As a Pastor for more than forty years, I have found satisfaction in my endeavor to be compassionate, to be present (to be there) where people hurt, and to have vision of the mission and message of justification by God's grace through faith. As the years go by, life becomes more meaningful to see other people realize that God loves all of us.*

HUNG, JAMES CHEN, engineer, educator, consultant; b. Foochow, Republic of China, Dec. 18, 1929; s. David Shen and Pearl C. (Chao) H.; m. Sufenne Huang, Apr. 3, 1958; children: John Y., Samuel M., Stephen T. BEE, Nat. Taiwan U., 1953; MEE, NYU, 1956, DEng, 1961. Registered profl. engr., Tenn. Instr. NYU, 1956-61; asst. prof. U. Tenn., Knoxville, 1961-62, assoc. prof., 1962-65, prof., 1965-84, disting. service prof., 1984—; v.p. Poly-Analytics, Inc., Knoxville; hon. prof. Nanjing U. of Aerospace & Astrophysics, 1989, South China U. of Tech., 1994, Peoples Republic of China; cons. prof. Northwestern Poly. U., Chongging U., S.W. China Tchrs. U., 1984—. Contbr. numerous articles to profl. jours. Recipient Technology award NASA, 1969, Cert. NASA, 1970, Brooks Disting. Engring. Prof. award, U. Tenn., 1973. Fellow IEEE (editor IEEE Trans. on Indsl. Electronics, gen. chmn. internat. symposium on indsl. electronics Xian, China 1992, gen. chmn. internat. conf. indsl. tech. 1994, 96, Anthony J. Hornfeck Svc. award 1995), Indsl. Electronics Soc. (v.p. 1996, pres.-elect 1997, pres. 1998-99); mem. Sigma Xi, Tau Beta Pi, Eta Kappa Nu, Phi Kappa Phi. Methodist. Office: U Tenn Knoxville TN 37996

HUNG, MEI-JONG CHOW, social worker; b. Taipei, Taiwan, Republic China, Oct. 7, 1937; s. Wen-tung Yeh Chow; m. Chao-huang Hung, Mar. 24, 1964; children: Jennifer Ching-yi, John Ching-tsung. BS, Nat. Taiwan U., 1960; MSW, Simmons Sch. Social Work, 1963. Cert. social worker, hypnotherapist. Mental health counselor Taipei Pub. Health Teaching Demonstration, 1963-66; asst. prof. Taiwan U., 1964-66; social work supr. Johns Hopkins Hosp., Balt., 1969-71; pvt. practice social work Columbia, Md., 1972—. Vol. community recreational social work, 1988—. WHO fellow. Mem. NASW, Acad. Cert. Social Workers. Home and Office: 7255 Meadow Wood Way Clarksville MD 21029-1714 Address: PO Box 140 Fulton MD 20759

HUNG, TIN-KAN, engineering educator, researcher; b. Nanking, Republic of China, June 12, 1936; came to U.S., 1961; s. Mao-Hsiang and Yu-Hwa (Cheng) H.; m. Shu-Nan Cho, Feb. 14, 1971; children: Chee-Hahn, Chee-Ming, Chee-Yuen. BS, Nat. Cheng-Kung U., Taiwan, 1959; MS, U. Ill., 1962; PhD, U. Iowa, 1966. Research assoc. Inst. Hydraulic Rsch. U. Iowa, Iowa City, 1963-66, research engr., 1966-67; vis. assoc. prof. U. Ill.-Chgo., 1972; asst. prof., assoc. prof. Carnegie-Mellon U., Pitts., 1967-75; research prof. U. Pitts., 1975-89, prof., 1989—; cons. NRC, Republic of China, 1978-82. Mem. editorial bd.: Jour. Engring. Mechanics, 1974-80, 82, Jour. Hydraulic Research, 1980—; mem. publ. bd.: Internat. Jour. Sci. and Engring., 1983-90; contbr. articles to profl. jours. Recipient award NRC, 1979, Disting. Alumnus award of hydraulic and ocean engring. Nat. Cheng-Kung U.; Rsch. grantee NSF, 1971-74, 78-80, 85-89, 94-99, Rsch. grantee NIH, 1976-90. Fellow AIMBE (founder), ASME (biomechanics com. 1974-76, 84-94, honors com. 1985-90); mem. ASCE (chmn. fluids com. 1976-78, bioengring. com. 1978-80, others, W.L. Huber civil engring. rsch. prize 1978), Internat. Assn. Hydraulic Rsch., Sigma Xi, Chi Epsilon. Home: 3918 Hickory Hill Rd Murrysville PA 15668-9513 Office: U Pitts 949 Benedum Engring Hall Pittsburgh PA 15261*

HUNGATE, CAROLYN WOLF, health and public services administrator; b. Canton, Ill., Dec. 15, 1940; d. Roy Elton and Ada Adella (Lehmbeck) Wolf; m. James Herbert Jones, May 8, 1959 (dec. Aug. 1971); children: Adella Sue Jones-Beyer, Kevin Elton; m. Timothy Scott Hungate, June 2, 1984. BSN, Bradley U., Peoria, Ill., 1965, MA in Counseling, 1967, MSN, 1991; EdD in Ednl. Adminstrn., Ill. State U., 1977. RN, Ill. Staff nurse Peoria State Hosp., Bartonville, Ill., 1961-63, instr., 1965-68; faculty nursing Ill. Ctrl. Coll., East Peoria, 1968-84, chair dept. nursing, 1984—; parish nurse Bethel Lutheran Ch., Morton. Bd. dirs. Am. Heart Assn., Peoria, 1971—, Alzheimer's Assn., Peoria, 1990—, Mental Health Assn., Peoria, 1990—, Women in Mgmt., Peoria, 1989—; panel mem. United Way, Peoria, 1993—; mem. sch. bd. Bethel Luth. Sch., 1994-96. Recipient Mildred Pfleiderer award Bradley U. Alumni Assn., 1993, Heart of Yr. award Ill. affiliate Am. Heart Assn., 1995; named Charlotte Danstrom Woman of Achievement, Women in Mgmt., 1989. Mem. Ill. Nurses Assn. (7th dist. treas. 1976-80), Delta Kappa Gamma, Kappa Delta Pi, Sigma Theta Tau. Lutheran. Avocations: walking, ballroom dancing, growing roses, raising pygmy goats. Home: 2447 California Rd Pekin IL 61554-8467 Office: Ill Ctrl Coll 201 SW Adams St Peoria IL 61635-0001

HUNGATE, JOSEPH IRVIN, III, computer scientist; b. San Antonio, Nov. 17, 1956; s. Joseph Irvin Jr. and Betty Lou (Hatzenbuehler) H.; m. Santa Michelle Haines, May 15, 1993; children: Brittany Nicole, Annabel Sue, Charlotte Elizabeth. BS in Computer Sci., U. S.C., 1979, MS in Computer Sci., 1981; postgrad., U. Va., 1982-83. Tchg. asst. U. S.C., Columbia, 1979-81; sr. systems analyst GE, Charlottesville, Va., 1981-85; mgr. software devel. TRW, Fairfax, Va., 1985-88, prin. investigator, 1996-97; mgr. field engring. TRW, London, 1988-93; supervisory computer scientist Nat. Inst. Stds. and Tech. U. S. Dept. Commerce, Gaithersburg, Md., 1993-96; supervisory computer scientist Office of Insp. Gen., U.S. Dept. Commerce, 1997-99; assoc. dir. info. resource mgmt. office Ctrs. for Disease Control, Atlanta, 1999—; mem. EIA Working Group RS-511, Detroit, 1983-85; recruitment coord. Affirmative Action, Fairfax, 1986-88; spl. liaison European Workshop on Open Sys., Brussels, 1993-96; chmn. Open Sys. Implementator's Workshop, Gaithersburg, 1993-97. Mem. Va. Student Aid Found., Charlottesville, 1985—; vol. coord. blood svcs. ARC, Fairfax, 1985-88; vol. Arlington County (Va.) Dem. Com., 1985—; bd. dirs. Hungate Family Hist. Soc., Inc., Chevy Chase, Md., 1989—. Recipient commendation USN, London, 1990; scholar S.C. Ednl. Found., 1975. Mem. IEEE Computer Soc., Assn. for Computing Machinery, Am. Mgmt. Assn., Sigma Phi Epsilon. Methodist. Avocations: collecting wine, golf, sailing, skeet, travel. Home: 967 N Rochester St Arlington VA 22205-1524 Office: US Dept Commerce Rm 7876 14th & Constitution Ave NW Washington DC 20230

HUNGER, JENNY RUTH, geographer; b. Cleve., Jan. 13, 1969; d. William Adolph and Jane Marie (Walker) H. BA in Geography, Valparaiso U., 1991; MS in Geography, Okla. State U., 1993. Cmty. planner No. Okla. Devel. Assn., Enid, 1992-93; GIS devel. specialist City of Kansas City, Mo., 1994; asst. mgr. rsch. svcs. Mid-Am. Regional Coun., Kansas City, 1994-97; project mgr. database mktg. UMB Bank NA, Kansas City, 1997-98; cons. Thompson Assocs., Ann Arbor, 1999—; guest instr. U. Mo., Kansas City, 1997-98; phys. geography instr./geographic info. system instr. Johnson County C.C., Overland Park, Kans., 1997-98. Mem. Assn. Am. Geographers, Valparaiso Univ. Guild (pres. 1997-98). Lutheran. Avocations: volleyball, aerobics, travel, bartending. Office: Thompson Assocs 2929 Plymouth Rd Ste 200 Ann Arbor MI 48105

HUNGERFORD, DAVID SAMUEL, orthopedic surgeon, educator; b. Rochester, N.Y., May 4, 1938; s. Francis Samuel and Marjorie Ellen (Wilson) H.; m. Uta-Heide Jung, July 20, 1962; children: Marc Wilson, Kyle Sasha, Lars Daniel. BA, Colgate U., 1960; MD, U. Rochester, 1964. Diplomate Am. Bd. Orthopaedic Surgery. Asst. prof. orthopaedic surgery Johns Hopkins U., Balt., 1972-78; chief orthopaedic surgery VA Hosp., Balt., 1975-80; chief orthopaedic surgery Good Samaritan Hosp., Balt., 1972—, chief div. arthritis surgery, 1979—; assoc. prof. orthopaedic surgery Johns Hopkins U. Sch. Medicine, Balt., 1978-86, prof. orthopaedic surgery, 1987—; cons. Balt. City Hosp., 1972-85, Children's Hosp., 1972-80, East Balt. Med. Ctr., 1972-78; co-dir. Johns Hopkins U. Ctr. for Osteonecrosis Rsch. and Edn., 1995—; bd. dirs. Nat. Osteonecrosis Found., 1996—. Author: Progress in Orthopaedics, 1977, Ischemia and Necroses of Bone, 1980, Total Knee Arthroplasty: A Comprehensive Approach, 1984, Total Hip Arthroplasty: A New Approach, 1984, Bone Circulation, 1984, Disorders of the Patello Femoral Joint, 1990, Videobook of Total Knee Arthroplasty, 1994; editor Jour. Arthroplasty, 1985-93. Elder Cen. Presbyn. Ch., Balt., 1974—; dir. Crippled Children's United Rehab. Effort, 1997—, Christian Orthopaedic Ptrs., 1997—; chmn. bd. MAP, Internat., 1998—. Maj. U.S. Army, 1969. Recipient George Hoyt Whipple award, 1965; Colgate U. scholar, 1956-59, GM scholar, 1956-59, U. Rochester scholar, 1959-61, Girdlestone Meml. scholar Oxford U., Eng., 1969-70; fellow USPHS fellow, Paris, 1961-62, Carl Berg traveling fellow, 1973. Mem. Johns Hopkins Med. and Surg. Soc., Md. Orthopaedic Soc., Arthritis Found., Md. Soc. Rheumatic Diseases, Am. Rheumatism Assn., Orthopaedic Rsch. Soc., Hip Soc., Am. Assn. Orthopaedic Surgeons, Am. Assn. Hip Knee Surgeons, Soc. Internat. de Chirurgie Orthopedique et de Traumatologie, Knee Soc. (pres. 1994). Republican. Home: 10715 Pot Spring Rd Cockeysville Hunt Valley MD 21030-3019 Office: Good Samaritan Hosp Profl Office Bldg G-1 5601 Loch Raven Blvd Baltimore MD 21239-2991 also: Johns Hopkins U Sch Medicine Dept Orthopaedic Surgery Baltimore MD 21205

HUNGERFORD, EDWARD ARTHUR, humanities professional educator; b. Bremerton, Wash., Sept. 24, 1921; s. Arthur and Mamie (Fredlund) H.; m. Sheila J. Lamar, June 3, 1950; children: Emily, Nancy. BA, U. Puget Sound, 1947; MA, Cornell U., 1948; PhD, NYU, 1960. Instr. English U. Puget Sound, Tacoma, 1949-50, U. Del., Newark, 1952-56; rep. textbook Houghton Mifflin Co., Boston, 1956-59; asst. prof. English Ctrl. Wash. U., Ellensburg, 1959-66; prof. English So. Oreg. U., Ashland, 1966-88; ret., 1988. Contbr. articles to profl. jours. Mem. Modern Lang. Assn., Virginia Woolf Soc. (founding). Avocations: book collecting, skiing.

HUNGERFORD, GARY A., insurance executive, columnist, author, editor; b. Bklyn., Apr. 20, 1948; s. Jean and Ann (Czarnikiewicz) H.; m. Eleanor Haragsim, Oct. 4, 1969. BBA cum laude, The Coll. of Ins., N.Y.C., 1974; MBA, The Coll. of Ins., 1978; grad., U.S. Army Svc. and Rifle Small Arms Firing Sch., 1992. CPCU. With Guardian Life Ins. Co., 1965-67, Providence Washington Ins. Co., 1967-68, The Atlantic Cos., 1968-74, Midland Ins. Co., 1974-76, Drake Ins. Co. of N.Y., 1976-78, Mead Reinsurance Corp., 1978-80, Yorktown Indemnity Co., 1980-82, Tri-County Facilities, Ltd./Tri-County Facilities N.J., Inc., 1982-85; pres., CEO Spl. Risk Facilities, Ltd., Lindenhurst, N.Y., 1985—; chmn., CEO CompuPub. Svcs., Ltd., Lindenhurst, 1987—; chmn. Hungerford Arms Co., Ltd., Lindenhurst, 1988—; v.p., dir. Protective Ins. Agy., Ridgewood, N.Y., 1983—; Past editor, pub. Lindenhurst's Chamber News, 1990-95; columnist The South Bays' News, Lindenhurst's Chamber News, the Suffolk Alliance of Sportsmen's Newsletter, The Bullet. Author: History of New York State Rifle and Pistol Associations, 1997. Sponsor U.S. Olympic Shooting Team; life mem. The N.Y. State Conservation Coun.; mem. Glock Sport Shooting Found.; mem. N.Y. Senate Small Bus. Adv. Com. With U.S. Army, 1968-70. Mem. Soc. CPCU, Soc. for Ins. Rsch., Ind. Ins. Agts. Assn., Casualty and Surety Soc. N.Y., Profl. Ins. Agts. N.Y., Profl. Ins. Wholesalers Assn., Coll. Ins. Alumni Assn., Ind. Ins. Agts. N.Y., Coll. Ins. MBA Soc., Gun Owners of Am. (life), Lindenhurst C. of C. (past chmn.), Nat. Assn. Desktop Publishers, M-1 Carbine Collectors Assn., Inc., Garand Collectors' Assn., L.I. Computer Assn., NRA (life, mem. field support team, polit. preference com. 1992, Inst. for Legis. Action, Polit. Victory Fund, Golden Eagles), Citizens' Com. for Right To Keep and Bear Arms (life, Citizen of Yr. 1990), N.Y. State Rifle and Pistol Assn. (life, past bd. dirs., chmn. fin. com., range com., mem. printing com., hist. com., omnibus com.), Northeastern Arms Collectors Assn., N.Am. Fishing Club (charter), N.Am. Hunting Club (life), Nassau County Fish and Game Assn., Suffolk Alliance of Sportmen (del., past firearms chmn., past v.p., dir.), Disting. Knights Shooting Club (v.p.), Whitetails Unltd., Lindenhurst Lions Club, Old Bethpage Rifle and Pistol Club (trustee), Nat. Assn. Federally Lic. Firearms Dealers, Second Amendment Found. (life), United Gamefish Anglers, Inc. (life), Law Enforcement Alliance of Am. (life), L.I. Beach Buggy Assn., Shooters' Com. on Polit. Edn. (life), Wildlife Forever, Izaak Walton Soc., N.Y. State Sportfishing Fedn., Varmint Hunters Assn. Republican. Avocations: chess, fishing, hunting, shooting sports, computers, photography. Office: Spl Risk Facilities Ltd 101 N Wellwood Ave Lindenhurst NY 11757-4001

HUNGERFORD, LUGENE GREEN, physicist; b. Birmingham, Ala., Sept. 1, 1924; d. Wesley Corinth and Anna Mae (Majors) Green; m. Herbert Eugene Hungerford, Nov. 4, 1949. BS in Physics, Birmingham-So. Coll., 1946; MS in Physics, U. Ala., 1950; postgrad., U. Tenn., 1952-54, Wayne State U., 1957-61, Purdue U., 1967-69. Gen. mgr., engr. Iron Fireman Stoker Co., Birmingham, Ala., 1947-48; instr. math. Snead Jr. Coll., Boaz, Ala., 1948; teaching asst. U. Ala., Tuscaloosa, 1949-50; substitute tchr. Knoxville City Schs., 1951-55; tchr. math. Knox County Schs., Knoxville, 1953-54; asst. prof. physics Wayne State U., Detroit, 1955-56, 59-60; adminstrv. asst., v.p., treas., dir. Calif. Nuclear, Inc., Lafayette, Ind., 1963-68; dir. Nuclear Engring. Co., Walnut Creek, Calif., 1969-72; v.p., treas., cons. engr. Nuclear Mgmt., Inc., West Lafayette, Ind., 1968-82; sec.-treas., bd. dirs. Bio Svcs., Inc., Lafayette, 1972-79; treas., bd. dirs. Media Tech, Inc., Lafayette, 1971-79, Chemtree Corp., Central Valley, N.Y., 1971-79; pres., treas., bd. dirs. Hungerford Nuclear Inc, Vero Beach, Fla., 1984-95, nuclear cons., 1996—. Mem. AAUW, Am. Nuclear Soc., Health Physics Soc., Sigma Xi. Republican. Episcopalian. Home and Office: 159 Salem Glen Way SE Conyers GA 30013-5326

HUNGNESS, LISA SUE, English language educator, consultant; b. Chgo., May 12, 1971; d. Stanley Torlife and RoVena Sue (Knetsch) H. BA in English, Ind. U., 1994; postgrad., Harvard U., 1999—. Lic. secondary tchr., Ohio. Grad. student tchr. Matravers Sch., Westbury, Eng., 1994; English educator Lebanon (Ohio) H.S., 1995—; devel. cons. Southwestern Ednl. Pub., Cin., 1996—; h.s. advisor Jr. Coun. World Affairs, Lebanon, Ohio, 1996—; class advisor student coun. Lebanon H.S., 1996—; curriculum devel. writer Lebanon City Schs., 1997—, instrnl. coun., 1998—. Author: Teacher's Test Bank: American Literature for Life and Work, 1997, C2000 Assessment Portfolio and Test Bank, 1999. Vol. at-risk student mentor Lebanon H.S., 1995—; vol. h.s. program coord. Otterbein Retirement Cmty., Lebanon, 1996—; mem. League of Women Voters, Cin., 1997—; vol. Advocating Control for Our Tchrs., Warren County, 1998—. Recipient Golden Apple Achiever award Ashland Inc., 1996, 97, Tchg. Excellence award Jiffy Lube and Channel 12 WTCW, Cin., 1997, Excellence in Tchg. award Area Progress Coun. Inc., Warren County, Ohio, 1997, Excellence in Tchg. award Ashland Inc./Ohio Edn. Assn., 1998, Fulbright-Hays Seminars Abroad award, 1999; grantee Nat. Coun. Tchrs. English, 1998. Mem. Lebanon Edn. Assn., NEA, Nat. Coun. Tchrs. English, Ohio Coun. Tchrs. English and Lang. Arts, Friends of Academics (h.s. rep. 1997—), Phi Delta Kappa Ednl. Fraternity. Avocations: scuba diving, travelling, dance, piano, artwork. Home: Apt 208 1600 Massachusetts Ave Cambridge MA 02138

HUNHOFF, SISTER PHYLLIS, foundation administrator; b. Yankton, S.D., Aug. 22, 1932; d. Herman and Mary (Huber) H. RN, Sacred Heart Hosp., Yankton, S.D.; BA in Sociology, Mount Marty Coll., 1970; M in Rehab. Adminstrn., U. San Francisco, 1978; cert. in theology, St. Louis U., 1990; LHD (hon.), Nebr. Wesleyan U., 1996. Nursing supr. St. Thomas More Hosp., Canon City, Colo., 1955-59, St. Mary's Hosp., Pierre, S.D., 1959-60; DON Sacred Heart Hosp., Yankton, S.D., 1962-63; nursing supr. Sacred Heart Monastery Infirmary, Yankton, 1965; pres., CEO Madonna Rehab. Hosp., Lincoln, Nebr., 1965-89, Madonna Found., Lincoln, 1990—; treas. S.E. Nebr. Health Planning Coun., Lincoln, 1974-76; pres. Statewide Health Coordinating Coun., Lincoln, 1981-82. Chair Lincoln Cmty. Devel./Support Svcs. Coun., Lincoln, 1993-94; bd. dirs. Better Lincoln Com., 1970-73; chairperson Nebr. Assn. Homes for Agy. Legis. Com., 1982-83; mem. U.S. Civil Rights Commn., Nebr. chpt. 1993-98. Recipient Svc. to Mankind award Sertoma, 1991; named Woman of Yr. Nebr. chpt. Arthritis Found., 1994, Ct. of Honor, Askarben, Omaha, 1994. Mem. Benedictine Sisters of Sacred Heart Monastery (dir.), Benedictine Oblates of Lincoln, Am. Assn. Healthcare Philanthropy. Roman Catholic. Avocations: tennis, reading, cooking. Home: 5441 Glade St Lincoln NE 68506-2121 Office: The Madonna Found 5401 South St Lincoln NE 68506-2150

HUNIA, EDWARD MARK, foundation executive; b. Sharon, Pa., Jan. 8, 1946; s. Edward and Estelle (Maleski) H.; m. Mary Sue Marburger, Sept. 25, 1976; children: Stephen, Adam. BSME, Carnegie Mellon U., 1967, MSME, 1968; MBA, U. Pitts., 1971. CFA. Sr. systems analyst Pitts. Plate Glass Industries, 1968-73; asst. to treas. Carnegie Mellon U., Pitts., 1973-76, dir. internal audit, 1976-78, asst. controller, dir. fin. systems, 1978-81, treas., 1981-90; v.p. for finance, treas. U. Pitts., 1990-92; sr. v.p., treas. The Kresge Found., Troy, Mich., 1992—. Mem. Assn. for Investment Mgmt. and Rsch., Fin. Analysts Soc. Detroit. Avocations: tennis, golf, running, books. Home: 4393 Barchester Dr Bloomfield Hills MI 48302-2116 Office: The Kresge Found PO Box 3151 Troy MI 48007-3151

HUNING, DEVON GRAY, actress, dancer, audiologist, photographer, video producer and editor; b. Evanston, Ill., Aug. 23, 1950; d. Hans Karl Otto and Angenette Dudley (Willard) H.; divorced; 1 child, Bree Alyeska. BS, No. Ill. U., 1981, MA, 1983. Actress, soloist, dancer, dir. various univ. and community theater depts., Bklyn., Chgo. and Cranbrook, B.C., Can., 1967—; ski instr. Winter Park (Colo.) Recreation Assn., 1975-79; house photographer C Lazy U Ranch, Granby, Colo., 1979; audiologist, ednl. programming cons. East Kootenay Ministry of Health, Cranbrook, 1985-89; ind. video prodn./asst., 1991—; owner Maxaroma Espresso and Incredible Edibles, 1993-95; pres. Sound Comms., 1989—; writer, prodr., editor Sta. KTVZ, Bend, Oreg., 1996-97; master of ceremonies East Kootenay Talent Showcase, EXPO '86, Vancouver B.C., Can., 1986; creator, workshop leader: A Hearing Impaired Child in the Classroom, 1986. Producer, writer, dir., editor (video) Down With Decibels, 1992; author: Living Well With Hearing Loss: A Guide for the Hearing-Impaired and Their Families, 1992. Sec., treas. Women for Wildlife, Cranbrook, 1985-86; assoc. mem. adv. bd. Grand County Community Coll., Winter Park, Colo., 1975-77; assoc. mem. bd. dirs. Boys and Girls Club of Can., Cranbrook, 1985. Mem. Internat. Marine Animal Trainers Assn. Avocations: snow and water skiing, scuba diving, dancing, marine animals, studying animal behavior.

HUNKELE, LESTER MARTIN, III, retired federal agency administrator; b. Bklyn., Aug. 16, 1947; s. Lester Martin Jr. and Agnes Veronica (Tarpey) H.; m. Diane Kathryn Sotiridy, Mar. 30, 1974. BS, U.S. Mil. Acad., 1969; MS in Constrn. Engring., Purdue U., 1975; diploma, Indsl. Coll. Armed Forces, 1988. Registered profl. engr., Va.; cert. plant engr. Commd. 2d lt. U.S. Army, 1969, advanced through grades to capt., 1979; lt. col. USAR, 1990; ret., 1995; logistics officer 809 Engring. Batallion, 1970-71; engr. officer 809 Engring. Bn., Thailand, 1970-71; engr. officer army engring. sch. U.S. Army, Ft. Belvoir, Va., 1971-74; asst. area engr. Balt. dist. C.E. U.S. Army, 1975-79; resigned U.S. Army, Washington, 1979; civil engr. office chief engrs. Dept. Army, Washington, 1979-81, asst. chief constrn. mgmt. office chief army res., 1981-83; asst. head facilities HQs USMC, Washington, 1983-85; dir. facilities office asst. sec. def. res. affairs Dept. Def., Washington, 1985-88, prin. dir. materiel and facilities, 1988-89; dep. asst. sec. for facilities Dept. Vets. Affairs, Washington, 1989-92, dep. asst. sec. facilities oversight, 1992-93; exec. dir. Pa. Ave. Devel. Corp., Washington, 1993-96; exec. project mgr. Gen. Svcs. Adminstrn., Washington, 1996; project exec. Clark Constrn. Group, 1996-99; assoc. v.p. Daniel Mann Johnson and Mendenhall, Arlington, Va., 1999—; project exec. Clark Constrn. Group, 1996—. Mem. NSPE (mem. govt. adv. group), Am. Inst. Plant Engrs., Soc. Am. Mil. Engrs. (dir. Washington chpt. 1984-88), Fed. Exec. Inst. Alumni Assn. (membership chmn. 1987), West Point Soc. (co-founder Annapolis chpt. 1986—), Urban Land Inst., Lambda Alpha. Avocations: sailing, skiing, scuba diving. Home: 3259 Chrisland Dr Annapolis MD 21403-4352 Office: DMJM 100 Boundary Channel Dr Arlington VA 22202-3712

HUNKELER, JOHN DOUGLAS, ophthalmologist; b. Kansas City, Mo., Oct. 11, 1941; s. Walter F. and Ruth (Tenny) H.; m. Mary Reiff, Jan. 14, 1968; 1 child, Amy. BA, Harvard U., 1963; MD, U. Kans., 1967. Physician, pres. Hunkeler Eye Ctrs., Kansas City, Mo., 1973—; prof., chmn. dept. U. Kans. Med. Ctr., Kansas City; bd. dirs. NovaMed EyeCare Mgmt., Chgo. Elder, Second Presbyn. Ch., Kansas City, Mo.; mem. adv. bd. Harvard/Radcliffe Club, Kansas City; chmn. State Ballet of Mo., Kansas City. Capt. USAF, 1968-70. Mem. AMA, Am. Soc. Cataract and Refractive Surgeons, Kansas City Soc. Ophthalmology and Otolaryngology. Avocations: golf, support for the performing arts. Home: 5326 Mission Woods Rd Shawnee Mission KS 66205-2008 Office: Hunkeler Eye Ctrs 4321 Washington St Ste 6000 Kansas City MO 64111-5911

HUNKER, FRED DOMINIC, internist, medical educator; b. Montgomery, Ala., Nov. 13, 1947; s. Joseph Frederick and Frances Cecelia (Armbruster) H.; m. Edith Margaret McCulloch, Sept. 25, 1976; children: Marie Elizabeth, Emily Kathleen, Jacob Dominic. BA in English, Creighton U., 1969; MD, U. Nebr., 1974. Diplomate Nat. Bd. Med. Examiners, Am. Bd. Internal Medicine, subspeciality pulmonary medicine (mem. self-evaluation process com. for pulmonary disease 1992-96); lic. physician Ala. Intern U. Ala. Sch. Medicine, Birmingham, 1974-75, resident, chief resident and instr. medicine, 1975-77, 78-79, fellow in pulmonary medicine, 1977-78, clin. asst. prof., 1979-93, clin. assoc. prof., 1993—; founder Montgomery Pulmonary Cons., P.A., 1979; pres. med. staff St. Margaret's Hosp., 1986-88; regional adv. bd. Mut. Assurance Inc., Birmingham, 1990-95; chmn. dept. medicine Bapt. Med. Ctr., 1982-84, chmn. ICU com. 1987-91, exec. com., 1982-84, 97—; exec. com. St. Margaret's Hosp./Humana Montgomery, 1988-97. Contbr. articles to profl. jours. Bd. dirs. Am. Lung Assn. Ala., 1984—, exec. com. 1990—, v.p., 1996-97, pres., 1997—; Montgomery adv. bd. S.E. Health Plan, 1985-88; physician vol. Project Hope, Maceio, brazil, 1973; bd. dirs. Queen of Mercy Elem. Sch., 1986-91, Combined Montgomery Cath. Schs., 1992—; founding mem., bd. dirs. Endowment Found. for Queen of Mercy Sch.; chmn. Physician's divsn. United Way Campaign, 1987-88; charter mem., bd. dirs. Physicians and Dentists Charities, Montgomery, 1988-91, Leadership Montgomery Class X, 1993-94. Knight Comdr. of the Equestrian Order of the Holy Sepulchre, 1990—. Fellow Am. Coll. Chest Physicians; mem. AMA, ACP (assoc.), Am. Thoracic Soc. (coun. of chpt. reps., state rep. 1988-94, tng. and continuing med. edn. com. 1992-94), Ala. Thoracic Soc. (pres. 1986-87), Nat. Assn. Med. Dirs. of Respiratory Care, Med. Assn. State of Ala., Med. Soc. Montgomery County (pres. 1988-89, bd. censors 1989-96), Montgomery C. of C., KC (3d degree), Capital City Club. Roman Catholic. Avocations: saltwater fishing, wing shooting, hunting. Home: 1595 Gilmer Ave Montgomery AL 36104-5619 Office: Montgomery Pulmonary Cons 1440 Narrow Lane Pky Montgomery AL 36111-2654

HUNKINS, RAYMOND BREEDLOVE, lawyer, rancher; b. Culver City, Calif., Mar. 19, 1939; s. Charles F. and Louise (Breedlove) H.; m. Mary Deborah McBride, Dec. 12, 1968; children: Amanda, Blake, Ashley. BA, U. Wyo., 1966, JD, 1968. Ptnr. Jones, Jones, Vines & Hunkins, Wheatland, Wyo., 1968—; mem. local rules com. U.S. Dist. Ct., 1990—; spl. counsel U. Wyo., Laramie, State of Wyo., Cheyenne; mem. faculty Western Trial Adv. Inst., 1993—, Wyo. Supreme Ct. Commn. Jud. Salary and Benefits, 1996—; owner Thunderhead Ranches, Albany and Platte Counties, Wyo.; gen. ptnr. Split Rock Land & Cattle Co.; spl. asst. atty. gen., Wyo. Chmn. Platte County Reps., Wheatland, 1972-74, chmn. adv. coun. Coll. of Commerce and Industry, U. Wyo., 1978-79; bd. dirs. U. Wyo. Found., 1996—, Am. Heritage Ctr., 1995—; mem. Gov.'s Crime Commn., 1970-78; pres. Wyo. U. Alumni Assn., 1973-74, commr. Wyo. Aeronautics Commn., 1987—; moderator United Ch. Christ. With USMC, 1955-57. Fellow Am. Coll. Trial Lawyers (Wyo. state chmn.), Internat. Soc. Barristers, Am. Bd. Trial Advs.; mem. ABA (aviation com. 1980-86, forum com. on constrn. industry litigation sect.), Wyo. Bar Assn. (chmn. grievance com. 1980-86, mem. com. on civil pattern jury instrns.), Wyo. Trial Lawyers Assn. (past pres.), Lions, Elks. Office: Jones Jones Vines & Hunkins PO Drawer 189 9th and Maple Wheatland WY 82201

HUNNICUTT, CHARLES ALVIN, lawyer; b. LaGrange, Ga., Dec. 7, 1950; s. William Oliver and Mary Olivia (Leggett) H. BS, Am. U., 1972; JD, U. Ga., 1975; LLM, U. Brussels, Belgium, 1976. Bar: Ga. 1975, D.C. 1978, U.S. Dist. Ct. D.C. 1978, U.S. Ct. Appeals (D.C. cir.) 1978, U.S. Ct. Internat. Trade 1980, U.S. Ct. Appeals (fed. cir.) 1981, U.S. Supreme Ct. 1981. Dep. dir. State of Ga. Office, Brussels, Belgium, 1975-76; ops. mgr. Presdl. Pers. The White House, Washington, 1976-77; exec. asst. to under sec. internat. trade U.S. Dept. Commerce, Washington, 1977-80; legal advisor to chmn. Internat. Trade Commn., Washington, 1980-87; ptnr. Robins, Kaplan, Miller & Ciresi, Washington, 1987-96, mng. ptnr., 1989-91; advisor to Govt. of Ukraine on accession to Gen. Agreement on Tariffs and Trade World Trade Orgn., Kiev, 1994-95; asst. sec. for aviation and internat. affairs U.S. Dept. Transp., Washington, 1996-99; ptnr. Robins, Kaplan, Miller & Ciresi, Washington, 1999—; adj. prof. Am. U. Coll. Law, Washington, 1988-91. Mem. ABA (internat. trade steering com.), Bar Assn. D.C., Ga. State Bar, Washington Fgn. Law Soc. (pres. 1987-88), Am. Soc. Internat. Law (exec. coun. 1999—), Fed. Bar Assn., Internat. Bar Assn. Democrat. Presbyterian. E-mail: cahunnicutt@robins.com. Office: Robins Kaplan Miller & Ciresi 1801 K St NW Ste 1200 Washington DC 20006

HUNNICUTT, RICHARD PEARCE, metallurgical engineer; b. Asheville, N.C., June 15, 1926; s. James Ballard and Ida (Black) H.; BS in Metall. Engring., Stanford, 1951, MS, 1952; m. Susan Haight, Apr. 9, 1954; children: Barbara, Beverly, Geoffrey, Anne. Rsch. metallurgist Gen. Motors Rsch. Labs., 1952-55; sr. metallurgist Aerojet-Gen. Corp., 1955-57; head materials and processes Firestone Engring. Lab., 1957-58; head phys. scis. group Dalmo Victor Co., Monterey, 1958-61, head materials lab., 1961-62; v.p. Anamet Labs., Inc., 1962-82, exec. v.p., 1982—; partner Pyrco Co. Author: Pershing, A History of the American Medium Tank T20 Series, 1971, Sherman, A History of the American Medium Tank, 1978, Patton, A History of the American Main Battle Tank, vol. 1, 1984, Firepower, A History of the American Heavy Tank, 1988, Abrams, A History of the American Main Battle Tank, vol. 2, 1990, Stuart, A History of the American Light Tank, Vol. 1, 1992, Sheridan, A History of the American Light Tank Vol. 2, 1995, Bradley: A History of American Fighting and Support Vechicle, 1999. Served with AUS, 1943-46. Mem. Electrochem. Soc., AIME, Am. Soc. Metals, ASTM, Am. Welding Soc., Am. Soc. Lubrication Engrs. Research on frictional behavior of materials, development of armored fighting vehicles. Home: 9432 Swan Lake Dr Granite Bay CA 95746-7205 Office: 3400 Investment Blvd Hayward CA 94545-3811

HUNNICUTT, ROBERT WILLIAM, engineer; b. Pauls Valley, Okla., Aug. 12, 1954; s. James Warren Hunnicutt. BS, N.Mex. State U., 1980; postgrad., U. Ariz., 1996—. Sr. assoc. engr. IBM, Tucson, 1980-94. Mem. Nat. Assn. of Deaf, Ariz. Assn. of Deaf. Avocations: photography, astronomy, skiing, reading, philately. Home: 8383 S Pistol Hill Rd Vail AZ 85641-6146

HUNNICUTT, VICTORIA ANNE WILSON, retired school system administrator, educator; b. Tyler, Tex., July 23, 1944; d. Leroy G. and N. Joseline (Bobo) Wilson; m. John Walter Hubble, July 29, 1967 (div. Oct. 1972); m. Buford D. Hunnicutt, Aug. 1, 1982. BA, Emory and Henry Coll., 1966; MEd, Mercer U., 1970; Ed Specialist, U. Ga., 1993; EdD, Ga. So. U., 1998. Tchr. Spanish/English Marion (Va.) Sr. H.S., 1966-67; tchr. Spanish Ballard Hudson Middle Sch., Macon, 1967-68; reading specialist Robins AFB Sch. System, Warner Robins, Ga., 1973-74, Spanish tchr., 1968-70, classroom tchr., 1970-86, computer/sci. specialist, 1986-90, prin. Robins Elem. Sch., 1991, curriculum coord., 1990—; adj. prof. Tift Coll., Forsyth, Ga., 1985-88, Ft. Valley State Coll., 1993—. Treas. Bibb County Dem. Women, Macon, Ga., 1986-88, membership chair 1989-93. Mem. AAUW, ASCD, NSTA, NAFE, Nat. Coun. Tchrs. of English, Ga. Coun. of Internat. Reading Assn., Internat. Reading Assn., HOPE Coun. (pres., 1994-95), Ga. coun. of Internat. Reading Assn., Nat. Audubon Soc., Ocmulgee Audubon Soc. (edn. chair 1986-93, v.p. 1991-92), Air Force Assn. (treas. chpt. 296 1989-91, v.p. for aerospace edn. chpt. 296 1991-97, 1998—, v.p. chpt. 296 1993-94, v.p. for aerospace edn. Ga. State AFA, 1992-97, 1998—, regional v.p. for aerospace edn. 1997—, Air Force Assn., Natl. Bd. of Trustees, Aerospace Edn. Found., 1998—, Tchr. of Yr. 1995, Jane Shirley McGee award 1990, Medal of Merit 1990, Exceptional Svc. award 1997). Democrat. Methodist. Avocations: reading, gardening. Office: Robins AFB Sch System 1050 Education Way Robins AFB GA 31098-1043

HUNSAKER, FLOYD B., accountant; b. Collinston, Utah, Sept. 6, 1915; s. Allen G. and Mary Ann (Bowcutt) H.; grad. high sch.; m. Zella D. Hepworth, Mar. 3, 1943; children: Marcia (Mrs. Marvin Bahr), Charlene (Mrs. Abelino Ancira), Sonia (Mrs. Val Fisher), Rhonda (Mrs. Kim Veigel), Tamara (Mrs. Randy Beardall), Shelia (dec. 1945). Lic. ins. salesman, security dealer, notary pub., Lincoln County, Wyo. Owner, operator dairy farm, Bedford, Wyo., 1946-70; acct., Afton, Wyo., 1959—; owner Credit Bur. Star Valley, Afton, 1967-87; mcpl. judge Town of Afton, 1967-77; local office claimstaker Wyo. Unemployment Compensation Dept., 1975-85. Pres., Holdaway Sch. PTA, 1960; active Boy Scouts Am., 1946-49, 58-67; chmn. Cub Scouts com., 1987-95; bd. dirs. Star Valley Sr. Citizens, 1981-83, 84-88; pres. Lower Valley 4-H council, 1961-62, leader, 1959-63; chmn. Star Valley chpt. Am. Revolution Bicentennial Adminstrn., 1975-76, Star Valley chpt. ARC, 1976-96; hon. bd. dirs. Lincoln County Chpt. ARC; ward pres. Sunday Sch., 1985-87; mem. Wyo. Centennial Com., 1990; subdivider Fertile Acres 1981-88; archtl. designer Star Valley Vets. Meml. Monument, 1990; mem. Lincoln County Selective Svc. Bd., 1984-96. Pub. Star Valley Bus. Directory, 1990—. Recipient 50 Yr. Vol. award ARC, 1992, First Place award Farm Bur. Talent Contest; Floyd B. Hunsaker Day named in his honor, 1995. Served with Devils Brigade, 1941-45; ETO. Mem. Farm Bur. (exec. sec. Lincoln County 1961-66), Internat. Platform Assn., Afton C. of C. (dir. 1973-74), Star Valley C. of C. (dir. 1988—, exec. sec. 1989-90, treas. 1991—, Outstanding Cmty. Svc. award 1994), VFW (post svc. officer 1949—, post quartermaster 1959—, dist. comdr. Wyo. 1974-75, 77-78, state dept. jr. vice comdr. 1978-79, sr. vice comdr. 1979-80, state comdr. 1980-81, dist. comdr. 1982-83, 86-88, chmn. state audit com. 1985-94), Am. Legion (post svc. officer, adj. treas. 1975—). Mem. Ch. of Jesus Christ of Latter-day Saints. Home: PO Box 516 323 Adams St Afton WY 83110 Office: 498 Washington St Afton WY 83110

HUNSAKER, RICHARD KENDALL, lawyer; b. L.A., June 2, 1960; s. Richard Allan and Patricia Kendall (Cook) H.; m. Laura Constance Haile, Oct. 8, 1988; children, Charles Nicholas, Laura Caroline. BA, U. Ill., 1982, MA, 1983; JD, Washington U., St. Louis, 1986. Bar: Ill. 1986, U.S. Dist. Ct. (cen. and no. dists.) Ill. 1987, U.S. Ct. Appeals (7th cir.) 1990, Wis. 1992. Speech coach Champaign (Ill.) Central High Sch., 1979-81; instr. speech communications, asst. debate coach U. Ill., Urbana, 1982-83; assoc. Heyl, Royster, Voelker & Allen, Springfield, Ill., 1986-87; assoc. Heyl, Royster, Voelker & Allen, Rockford, Ill., 1987-93, ptnr., 1994—. Author: Advanced Real Estate Law in Illinois - Environmental Liabilities, 1992, (with others) Advanced Real Estate Law in Illinois: Environmental Liability, 1992. Mem. ABA (tort and ins. practice, litigation and natural resources, energy and environ. law sects.), Ill. Bar Assn. (assoc., ins. law sect. 1990-92, civil practice and procedure, workers compensation, tort law and environ. control law sects.), Ill. Assn. Def. Trial Counsel, Winnebago County Bar Assn. (editl. bd. lawyer, legal-med., trial practice and continuing legal edn. coms.), Seventh Cir. Bar Assn., Def. Rsch. Inst. Methodist. Avocations: golf, biking, backpacking. Home: 1418 National Ave Rockford IL 61103-7144 Office: Heyl Royster Voelker & Allen 321 W State St Rockford IL 61101-1137

HUNSAKER, SCOTT LESLIE, gifted and talented education educator; b. Provo, Utah, Oct. 22, 1953; s. Melvin J and Ruth Lofthouse (Pulsipher) H.; m. Rebecca Naser, June 2, 1982; children: Adam Scott, Jacob Christian, Rachel Noelle. BA cum laude, Brigham Young U., 1977, MEd, 1982; PhD, U. Va., 1991. Classroom tchr. Alpine Sch. Dist., Orem, Utah, 1977-85; gifted coord. Alpine Sch. Dist., American Fork, Utah, 1986-87; rsch. asst. U. Va., Charlottesville, 1987-91; asst. prof. U. Ga., Athens, 1991-95, Utah State U., Logan, 1995—; presenter workshops and papers to internat., nat., state, and local confs. Co-author: Suggestions for Program Development in Gifted Education; contbr. articles to profl. jours. Mem. Mormon Tabernacle Choir. Governor's fellow U. Va., 1989. Mem. Am. Edn. Rsch. Assn., Nat. Assn. Gifted Children (bd. dirs. 1992-98, edn. commn. 1999—, creativity div. chair 1989-90, John C. Gowan Grad. Student award 1989, Early Leader award 1991), Coun. Exceptional Children/The Assn. for Gifted, Utah Assn. for Gifted Children (3rd v.p. of publs. 1999—). LDS. Avocation: presidential trivia. Office: Dept Elem Edn Utah State Univ Logan UT 84322-2805

HUNSBERGER, ALICE CHANDLER, religion educator, human rights activist; b. Washington, June 25, 1952; d. George Shepherd and Ruth Margaret (Stillman) H.; m. Angelo Gelpi, Aug. 12, 1977 (div. Aug. 1994); 1 child, Adriane. BA cum laude, NYU, 1974; MA, Columbia U., 1977, MPhil, 1979, PhD, 1992. Rsch. asst. Middle East langs. Columbia U., N.Y.C., 1974-77; instr. Queens Coll./CUNY, N.Y.C., 1977, Aryamehr U. Tech., Isfahan, Iran, 1977-78, U. P.R., Rio Piedras, 1978; devel. assoc. Seamen's Ch. Inst., N.Y.C., 1984-88; assoc. dir. devel. Amnesty Internat., N.Y.C., 1988-99; adj. asst. prof. program in religion Hunter Coll./CUNY, N.Y.C., 1992-95; dir. corp. and found. rels. NYU Stern Sch. Bus., N.Y.C., 1999—; lectr. in internat. human rights and Islamic philosophy; cons. various orgns., 1993—; seminar lectr. Cambridge (Eng.) U., 1994, Inst. for Ismaili Studies, London, 1997. Tech. editor Soc. for Islamic Philosophy and Sci., N.Y.C., 1980-91. Recipient 2d prize for Best Dissertation in Iranian Studies, Found. for Iranian Studies, 1992. mem. Middle East Studies Assn., Soc. for Iranian Studies (treas. 1992-94), Columbia U. Seminar in Iranian Studies, Am. Acad. Religion, Am. Philos. Soc. Democrat. Avocation: learning languages. Office: NYU Stern Sch Bus Tisch Hall 40 W 4th St Ste 531 New York NY 10012

HUNSBERGER, ROBERT EARL, mechanical engineer, manufacturing executive; b. San Diego, Nov. 9, 1947; s. Arnold and Edith Mae (Miller) H.; m. Charlotte Louise Herr, Mar. 30, 1968; children: David Arnold, Allen Robert. BSME, San Diego State Coll., 1969, MBA, 1975. Project engr. Gen. Atomic Co., San Diego, 1970-75; pvt. practice commodity mktg. specialist San Diego, 1975-77; from devel. engr. to sourcing mgr. Solar Turbines, Inc., San Diego, 1977-95, product engr., 1995—, 1995—. Contbr. articles to profl. jours. Leader local Webelos, 1981-82; com. chmn. Boy Scouts Am., Ramona, Calif., 1982-83, cub master, 1983-84, com. mem., 1982—, com. chmn., 1985-86. Recipient Spirit of Courage award San Diego Inst. Burn Medicine, 1979, Cert. Commendation Calif. Hwy. Patrol, 1979. Mem. Ramona Hist. Soc., Cessna 120/140 Club, Z Club San Diego, Model A. Restorers Club. Republican. Avocations: experimental aircraft construction, antique auto restoration, aviation history, classic aircraft restoration.

HUNSBERGER, RUBY MOORE, electronics manufacturing corporation executive, religious organization representative; b. Nappanee, Ind., Feb. 28, 1913; d. Clinton Clarence and Irene Mae (Moyer) Clyde; m. Clarence Cecil Moore, Dec. 21, 1933 (dec. Jan. 1979); children: Clyde W., Edwin C., Kay E. Moore Branch; m. Lowell Harold Hunsberger, Feb. 1, 1982 (dec. Aug. 1988). Student, Presbyn. Hosp., Chgo., 1932. Missionary Sta. HCJB, Quito, Ecuador, 1939-45, spl. rep., 1945—; v.p. Crown Internat., Inc., Elkhart, Ind., 1950-79, chmn. bd., 1979-92; pres. Sta. WFRN AM&FM, Elkhart, 1979-94; bd. dirs. Sta. WFRN, Crown Internat. Del. Missionary Ch., Nappanee, 1980, 82, 89-90, 93—; bd. dirs. Hubbard Hill Estates, 1992—. Mem. Elkhart C. of C. Republican. Home: 28070 County Rd 24 Elkhart IN 46517-9774 Office: Crown Internat Inc 1718 W Mishawaka Rd Elkhart IN 46517-9439

HUNSICKER, GERRY, professional sports executive; b. Collegeville, Pa.; m. Irene Hunsicker; 1 dau., Kelly. BS, St. Joseph's U., Pa., 1972. Pitching coach, asst. athletic dir. Fla. Internat. U., Miami, 1973-78; staff Houston Astros, 1978-81; v.p. Paine Webber, Houston, 1984-88; dir. minor league ops. N.Y. Mets, 1988-90, dir. baseball ops., 1990-95; gen. mgr. Houston Astros, 1995—. Office: Houston Astros PO Box 288 Houston TX 77001-0288*

HUNSINGER, DOYLE J., electronics executive; b. Hazelton, Pa., Nov. 12, 1947; s. Doyle J. and Doris Adele (Price) H.; m. Diane Barbara Trivigno, Oct. 12, 1968; children: Doyle III, Dana. BS in Mktg., Fairleigh Dickinson U., 1974. Various positions Sears, Roebuck & Co., Watchung, N.J., 1966-79; mdse. asst. Sears New York Group, Wayne, N.J., 1979-81; v.p., treas. CMF Key Services, Kenilworth, N.J., 1983-85; pres. CMF Bus. Supplies, South Plainfield, N.J., 1985—, DSI Delivery Sys., Inc., South Plainfield, N.J., 1987—, CMF Design Sys. Inc., South Plainfield, 1987-96; CFO, bd. dirs. McCook Tech., Huntington Beach, Calif., 1997-98; mem. distbr. council Memorex Corp., Santa Clara, Calif., 1983-86, also 3M; chmn. Media Recycling, South Plainfield, N.J. Committeeman Somerset County Rep. Orgn., Watchung, 1974—, mcpl. chmn. 1980—, fin. chmn. 1996—, exec. com. 1996—; treas. Watchung Candidates Com., 1983-92; cons. Union County (N.J.) Dist. 1 Adv. Bd., 1985-92; capt. Watchung Fire Dept., 1980-83, trustee, 1988-92; v.p., coach Watchung Little League baseball, 1982-83; scoring chmn. N.J. Synchronized Swimming, 1982-84; bd. dirs. Wilson Meml. Ch., Watchung, 1977-79, 83—, fin. chmn. 1984—. Served with USNG, 1967-74. Mem. N.J. Exempt Firemans Assn., Nat. Bus. Forms Assn., Union County C. of C., Cen. Jersey C. of C. (3M distributor coun. 1993-94). Club: Watchung Fire (pres. 1979). Lodge: Optimists (sec. Watchung club 1975-76). Avocations: swimming, fishing, golf. Home: 701 Valley Rd Plainfield NJ 07060-6148 Office: CMF Bus Supplies Inc PO Box 339 South Plainfield NJ 07080-0339

HUNSPERGER, ELIZABETH JANE, art and design consultant, educator; b. Phila., Aug. 30, 1938; d. Francis Charles and Elizabeth Julia (Rudolph) Thorpe; m. Robert George Hunsperger, Sept. 13, 1958; 1 child, Lisa Marie. AA in Design, Santa Monica Coll., 1974; student, UCLA, 1975-76; BA in Art History, U. Del., 1978; postgrad., Rutgers U., 1978-81; MA in Edn., Del. State Coll., 1993. Designer Huntingdon Mills, Phila., 1960-63, Rothschild's, Ithaca, N.Y., 1963-65, Cornell U., Ithaca, 1965-67; freelance designer Malibu, Calif., 1967-76; art and design cons., lectr. Art & Sci. Assocs., Newark, Del., 1980—; art tchr. Cath. Diocese of Wilmington, 1988-95; art and spl. edn. tchr. Red Clay Consolidated Sch. Dist. A.I. duPont H.S., Greenville, Del., 1995-97, Shorehaven Sch., Chesapeake City, Md., 1997-99, A.I. duPont Inst., Wilmington, Del., 1999—; with Leech Sch., 1994; bd. dirs. Gallery 20, Newark, Del., 1982-86. Exhbns. include Malibu Art Assn. Show, 1973, 74, Newark Art Show, 1987, 88. Founding mem. bd. dirs., v.p. Newark Housing Ministry, Inc., 1983-94, pres., 1989-91; mem. social concerns com. and drug and alcohol task force Del.; active Coun. Exceptional Children. Recipient Outstanding Svc. award YWCA, Santa Monica, Calif., 1972, award of recognition Missionhurst, 1982, Gov.'s Vol. of the Yr. award State of Del., 1990. Mem. Nat. Art Edn. Assn., Am. Craft Coun., Art Educators of Del. (bd. dirs., pres.), Debutante Assemlby Club (N.Y.C.). Episcopal. Home: 1014 New London Rd Newark DE 19711-2116

HUNSTEIN, CAROL, state supreme court justice; b. Miami, Fla., Aug. 16, 1944. AA, Miami-Dade Jr. Coll., 1970; BS, Fla. Atlantic U., 1972; JD, Stetson U., 1976, LLD (hon.), 1993. Bar: Ga. 1976; U.S. Dist. Ct. 1978; U.S. Ct. Appeals 1978; U.S. Supreme Ct. 1989. Legal practice Atlanta, 1976-84; judge Superior Ct. of Ga. (Stone Mt. cir.), 1984-92; justice Supreme Ct. of Ga., Atlanta, 1992—; chair Ga. Commn. on Gender Bias in the Judicial System 1989—; pres. Coun. of Superior Ct. Judges of Ga., 1990-91; adj. prof. Sch. Law Emory U., 1991—. Bd. dirs. Ga. Campaign Adolescent Pregnancy Prevention, 1992—. Recipient Clint Green Trial Advocacy award 1976, Women Who Made A Difference award Dekalb Women's Network 1986, Outstanding Svc. commendation Ga. Legislature, 1993, Cmty. Svc. award Emory U. Legal Assn. for Women Students., 1993. Mem. Ga. Assn. of Women Lawyers, Nat. Assn. of Women Judges (dir. 1988-90), Bleckley Inn of Ct., State Bar Ga. Office: Supreme Ct Ga 523 State Judicial Bldg Atlanta GA 30334-9007*

HUNSUCKER, ROBERT DUDLEY, physicist, electrical engineer, educator, researcher; b. Portland, Oreg., Mar. 15, 1930; s. Robert Deets and Johnnie Morris (Kuykendal) H.; m. Judith Mary Cotter, Apr. 28, 1956 (dec. Nov. 1980); children: Edith Louise, Jeanne Marie, Cynthia Lee; m. Phyllis Marie Hoover, July 25, 1981. BS in Physics, Oreg. State U., 1954, MS in Physics, 1958; PhDEE, U. Colo., 1969. Asst. prof. Geophysics Inst. U. Alaska, Fairbanks, 1958-64, assoc. prof. Geophysics Inst., 1971-78, prof. Geophysics Inst., 1978-87; physicist Nat. Bur. Standards, Boulder, Colo., 1964-67; sr. project leader ITS Office of Telecommunications Sci., Boulder, 1967-71; prof. emeritus physics and elec. engring., sr. cons. U. Alaska, Fairbanks, 1988—; radio propagation cons.; adj. prof. Pa. State U., Oreg. Inst. Technology. Author two tech. books; editor-in-chief Radio Sci., 1995—; assoc. editor Radioscientist/URSI Bull.; contbr. articles to profl. jours. Served to lt. USNR, 1954-67. Fellow AAAS, IEEE (Alaska Engr. of Yr. Alaska sect. 1988, recipient outstanding achievement award IEEE region 6, 1988); mem. Am. Geophys. Union, U.S. Commission Internat. Union of Radio Sci., Sigma Xi, Sigma Pi Sigma, Eta Kappa Nu. Republican. Avocations: private pilot, fishing, hunting, amateur radio operation, writing. Office: Oreg Inst Technology Rm PV-282 EET Dept 3201 Campus Dr Klamath Falls OR 97601

HUNSUCKER, (CARL) WAYNE, architectural firm executive, educator; b. Morganton, N.C., Feb. 16, 1945; s. Earnest Howard and Reba (Laughridge) H.; m. Edith Mabel Whittaker Guisto, May 23, 1990; children: Wendy Edith Guisto, Bret Thomas Guisto. Student, Old Dominion Coll.; BFA, Coll. William and Mary, 1968; BArch with Distinction, U. Ariz., 1975. Lic. architect, Calif., Nev., Idaho, Oreg., Wash., Ariz.; cert. Nat. Coun. Archtl. Registration Bds. Archtl. draftsman Woodmoor Corp., Colorado Springs, Colo., 1971-72; architect-in-training James Gresham & Assocs., Tuscon, 1975-76; prin., pres. Hummel Hunsucker Archs., Boise, Idaho, 1976—; prin.-in-charge office ops. Hummel Hunsucker Archs., Spokane, Wash., 1998—; part-time draftsperson Forrest Coile & Assocs., Newport News, Va., 1959-63; asst. instr. U. Ariz. Prin. works include U.S. Courthouse and Fed. Office Bldg., Boise, Idaho, Earl F. Chandler Bldg., Boise, Orchard Pl. Office Complex, Boise, 1st Security Bank addition and remodel, Nampa Main Br., Blue Cross Idaho, Idaho N.G. Armory Annex, Boise, various bldgs. Mt. Home AFB (Citation and Design awards Dept. Air Force), Mountain Home Town Jr. High Sch. addition; co-author: (text books) Architectural Drafting, 1976, Neighborhood Planning - Case Study of the Sam Hughes Neighborhood. Bd. dirs. Ada County Hist. Soc., 1989-90, Boise; mem. Lincoln Day Banquet Com., Boise, 1984-86; mem. licensing bd. Idaho Outfitters and Guides, 1996—; bd. mem. Bldg. Owners and Mgrs. Assn., Boise chpt., 1998. 1st lt. U.S. Army, 1969-71, Vietnam. Recipient Citation award USAF, Best Stand Alone Bldg. award TAC Air Force, 1984, Henry Adams Fund for Excellence award. Mem. AIA (state pres. 1990, pres. ctrl. sect. Idaho chpt. 1988, Silver medal 1976), Nat. Coun. Archtl. Registration Bds. Avocations: bird hunting, fishing, boating. Office: Hummel Hunsucker Archs PA 802 W Bannock St Ste 700 Boise ID 83702-5844

HUNT, ALBERT R., newspaper executive; b. Charlottesville, Va., Dec. 4, 1942; s. Albert R. and Ann G. (Lillard) H.; m. Judy C. Woodruff, Apr. 5, 1980; children: Jeffrey Woodruff, Benjamin Woodruff, Lauren Ann Lee. BA in Polit. Sci., Wake Forest U., 1965. Reporter Wall St. Jour., N.Y.C., 1965-67, Boston, 1967-69; reporter Wall St. Jour., Washington, 1969-71, polit. reporter, 1972-83, bur. chief, 1983-93, exec. editor, 1993—. Author: (with others) American Elections of 1980, American Elections of 1982, American Elections of 1984, Elections American Style, 1987; participant in TV program CNN Capital Gang. Bd. visitors Wake Forest U., Winston-Salem, N.C., 1979-85, trustee, 1987; bd. dirs. Ottaway Newspapers, Inc.; sr. adv. bd. Shorenstein Barone Ctr. for Press, Politics and Pub. Policy, Harvard U., Cambridge, Mass.; pres. Dow Jones Newspaper Fund, 1993. Mem. Am. Polit. Sci. Assn. (congl. fellowship adv. com. 1981—). Office: Wall St Jour 1025 Connecticut Ave NW Ste 800 Washington DC 20036-5419*

HUNT, BILL, artist, educator; b. Lynn, Mass.. BFA, Mass. Coll. Art; MFA, U. Ill. Substitute drawing tchr. Mass. Coll. Art, Boston, 1960; instr. art U. Ill., Urbana, 1960-62; head dept. art Putney Sch., 1964-84; instr. U. Syracuse, N.Y., 1967; asst. prof. art U. Fla., Pensacola, 1972-73, artist-in-residence, 1983, vis. lectr., 1997; instr. Inst. Allende, San Miguel, Mex., 1993-97, 1997; instr. San Miguel Allende, 1994-96. One-man shows include Ward-Nasse Gallery, Boston, 1967, 69, 70, N.Y.C., 1971, 75, 77, River Gallery, Brattleboro, Vt., 1979, Hansen Gallery, U. Fla., Pensacola, 1983, Ava Gallery, Hanover, N.H., 1984, Tyler Gallery, Marlboro (Vt.) Coll., 1987, River Valley Art Ctr., Windham Coll., Putney, Vt., 1989, Gerard Gallery, Windsor, Vt., 1990, Beside-Myself-Gallery, Arlington, Vt., 1990, 95, Concord (Mass.) Art Ctr., 1991, Inst. Allende, San Miguel, 1994, 98; exhibited in group shows at Art Inst. Chgo., 1964, U.S. Info. Agy., 1965, Mus. Fine Arts, Boston, 1967-68, Avery Fisher Hall, Lincoln Ctr., N.Y.C., 1972, Ringling Mus., Sarasota, Fla., 1973, Curry Mus., Manchester, N.H., 1973, Portland (Maine) Mus. Art, 1973, Boston Ctr. Arts, 1975, Stratton (Vt.) Arts Festival, 1987-98, Goldsmith Gallery, Boothbay Harbor, Maine, 1990, Klingerman Gallery, San Miguel, 1991, 97, Inst. Allende, San Miguel, 1993-98, Cigarts, 1997-98, Windham Coll., 1997. E-mail: hkstudio@sover.net. Office: 338 Hickory Ridge Rd South Putney VT 05346

HUNT, BOBBY RAY, electrical engineering educator, consultant; b. McAlester, Okla., Aug. 24, 1941; s. George Clifford and Shirley Mason (Core) H.; m. Susan Elizabeth Caldwell, Aug. 21, 1965; children: Vicki Lynn, Lori Jean. B.Sc. in Aero. Engring., Wichita State U., 1964; M.S. in Elec. Engring., Okla State U., Stillwater, 1965; Ph.D. in Systems Engring., U. Ariz., Tucson, 1967. Mem. tech. staff Sandia Lab., Albuquerque, 1967-68; staff mem. group leader Los Alamos Nat. Lab., 1968-75; prof. elec. engring. U. Ariz., Tucson, 1975—; v.p., group chief scientist Sci. Applications Internat. Corp., Tucson, 1981—; cons. in field, 1981-89; dir. Internat. Imaging Systems, Milpitas, Calif., 1981—. Author: (with H.C. Andrews) Digital Image Restoration, 1976. NDEA fellow, 1964; NASA fellow, 1966. Fellow IEEE, Optical Soc. Am. Home and Office: 6747 N Los Leones Dr Tucson AZ 85718-1809 *In college I saw and bought a stick-on decal which has been, since that time, my motto and philosophy of life. The slogan on the sticker was a definition of luck that includes the Capriciousness of Dame Fortune, but also the responsibility of the individual in taking care of his own life. I've tried to live by that slogan, imperfectly of course, and have found that to the extent I have lived by it, I've been lucky. To the extent I've not lived by it, I've found no reason to curse my Bad Luck. The slogan on the decal said "Luck--when preparation meets opportunity."*

HUNT, BRIAN L., program manager. MA, Cambridge U.; ScM, PhD, Brown U. Acting program mgr. Northrop Grumman Corp., Hawthorne, Calif., England, 1967-79; tech. mgr. Northrop Corp., 1979-90, 92-97; chmn. aerospace engring. U. Md., 1990-92; program mgr. F/A 18A/B/C/D Northrop Grumman Corp., 1997-98; v.p. engring. and tech. air combat sys. Northrop Grumman Corp., El Segundo, Calif. Recipient AIAA Aircraft Design award, 1996. Office: Northrop Grumman Corp FCOO/W5 1 Northrop Ave Hawthorne CA 90250*

HUNT, COLLEEN A., educational consultant; b. Atlantic, Iowa, Feb. 24, 1950; d. Paul W. and Arvis A. (Saxton) McKeane; m. William D. Hunt, Apr. 11, 1981; children: Sarah N., Emily B. BS, N.W. Mo. State U., 1976; MS, Iowa State U., 1983. Coord., instr. Iowa Western C.C., Council Bluffs, 1978-89, asst. dir. vocat.-tech. edn., 1989-92, assoc. dean Sch. Applied Sci.

and Tech., 1993-99; cons. Dept. Edn., 1999—; exec. bd. State Coun. Vocat. Edn., Des Moines, 1988-95; mem. Council Bluffs Adv. Bd., 1989—. Mem. Assn. for Career and Tech. Edn. (region III rep.), Iowa Vocat. Assn. (pres. 1995), Iowa Bus. Edn. Assn. (area rep. 1986-92, Outstanding Postsecondary Bus. Educator 1988), S.W. Iowa Vocat. Assn. (pres. 1994), Phi Delta Kappa. Methodist. Avocations: reading, needlework, antiquing. Home: 12528 525th St Elliott IA 51532-4031

HUNT, DAVID CLAUDE, sales and marketing executive; b. Chippewa Falls, Wis., June 16, 1957; s. Claude Martin and Lucille Johanna (Gehl) H.; m. Cheryl Elizabeth Martens, Mar. 21, 1980; children: Elizabeth Anne, Rebecca Jeanne. B in Music Edn., U. Wis., Eau Claire, 1980. Bookkeeper Claude Hunt Dry Wall Service, Chippewa Falls, 1971-79; band dir. Glenwood City (Wis.) Middle Sch., 1980; band dir., computer instr. Toulon-Lafayette (Ill.) Schs., 1980-84; band dir. Cathedral High Sch., St. Cloud, Minn., 1984-86; with computer sales dept. Team Electronics, St. Cloud, 1986; dir. edn. sales and mktg. Computers of St. Cloud, 1987-91, dir. support svcs., 1992; devel. dir. Ed Tech, St. Cloud, 1993; pres. Hunt Enterprises, 1994—; mktg. comm. mgr. JDL Techs., Mpls., 1995—; instr. in computers Dist. 742 Schs. Community Edn., St. Cloud, 1985-90; cons. Computer Tutor Svcs., St. Cloud, 1985-88; presenter at profl. confs. Contbr. articles to profl. jours.; editor: (newsletter) Education Solutions, 1987-93, (newsletters) VolksNews, 1991-96, Nat. Ednl. Networking News Svc., 1997—; pub. 3 Web sites, 1997—. Mem. nat. adv. bd. Achievement Acad., 1984; founder, dir. Stark County Cmty. Band, 1981-83; mem. com. Ctrl. Luth. Ch., Chippewa Falls, 1979; mem. coun. Salem Luth. Ch., St. Cloud, 1989-91, Discovery Elem. Sch. Site Coun., 1993-96; bd. dirs. Lutheran Bible Inst. Mpls., 1999—. Recipient Computing Family of Yr. 5th pl. award, 1986, Apple Computer Ednl. Newsletter award, 1988-89, Apple Edn. Visionary award, 1992. Mem. Nat. Assn. Desktop Pubs., Internat. Soc. for Tech. in Edn., Ctrl. Minn. Volkssport Assn. (co-founder, v.p. 1991, treas. 1993), Am. Volkssport Assn. (program devel. com. 1991-93, publicity com. 1993-95, recipient Meritorious Svc. award 1993, com. state orgn. procedures 1995-97), Minn. Volkssport Assn. (treas. 1989, pres. 1990-93), Assn. Internet Profls., North Star Trail Travelers (bd. dirs. 1997—), Phi Mu Alpha Sinfonia. Republican. Avocations: volkssports, walking, electronics, radio, music. Office: JDL Techs Inc 5555 W 78th St Edina MN 55439-2702

HUNT, DAVID FORD, lawyer; b. Ft. Worth, Apr. 7, 1931; s. John Greffrey and Bernice (Ford) H. BS, North Tex. State U., 1954; JD, Vanderbilt U., 1960. Bar: Tex. 1961, U.S. Dist. Ct. (no. dist.) Tex., U.S. Dist. Ct. (we. dist.) Tex., U.S. Dist. Ct. (ea. dist.) Tex.U.S. Ct. Appeals (5th and 11th cir.), U.S. Supreme Ct. Law clk. to U.S. dist. judge No. Dist. Tex., 1960-62; pvt. practice, Dallas, 1962-94; prtnr. Jenkens & Gilchrist, P.C., Dallas, 1980-92, of counsel, 1993-94; atty. pvt. practice, Denton County, Tex., 1995—; chmn. com. on admissions Dist. 6 Tex. State Bd. Law Examiners, 1978-87. Contbr. articles to legal jours. Co-chmn. pollwatchers com. Dallas County Republican Com., 1964; Sec. Bootstrap Ranch, 1972-74; pres. So. Methodist U. Lambda Chi Edn. Found., 1972-76, dir. Internat. Lambda Chi Edn. Found., 1966-68. Served with AUS, 1954-56. Mem. Tex. Bar Assn., Tex. Bar Found., Dallas Bar Assn., Vanderbilt U. Law Sch. Alumni Assn. (pres. Dallas chpt. 1972-75), Lambda Chi (chancellor 1966-68). Home and Office: 1849 Bridle Bit Rd Flower Mound TX 75022-6571

HUNT, DENNIS, public relations executive. BA in English, Notre Dame U.; MA in Edn. Adv. mgr., contbg. editor San Francisco Bus. Mag.; exec. v.p., gen. mgr. Deaver & Hannaford; mng. ptnr. Hunt/Marmillion Assocs., 1983-88; exec. v.p., gen. mgr. Ogilvy Adams &Rinehart, 1988-92; pres. Stoorza, Ziegaus, Metzger & Hunt, Sacramento, 1992-99, sr. cons., 1999—; adj. instr. Santa Monica (Calif.) Coll. Office: Stoorza Ziegaus Metzger & Hunt 555 Capitol Mall Ste 600 Sacramento CA 95814-4502*

HUNT, DIANA DILGER, university administrator, educator; b. Ridgewood, N.J., Feb. 25, 1953; d. Daniel G. Dilger and Ruth M. Wheeler; m. Douglas Gordon Hunt, Nov. 1, 1987; children: Daniel Gordon, Kevin Douglas. BS, Quinnipiac Coll., 1975; MPA, L.I. U., 1997. Staff therapist Bergen Pines Hosp., Paramus, N.J., 1976-81; sr. occupational therapist Rockland Childrens Psychiatric Ctr., Orangeburg, N.Y., 1981-82; program dir. psychiatry Bergen Pines Hosp., Paramus, N.J., 1985-87, dir. occupational therapy, 1982-91; dir. rehab. svcs. Ramapo Ridge Hosp. of the Christian Health Care Ctr., Wyckoff, N.J., 1991-96; program dir., adolescent day treatment program Ramapo Ridge Hosp. of the Christian Health Care Ctr., 1993-96; assoc. dir. clinical edn. Mercy Coll., Dobbs Ferry, N.Y., 1997—; adj. instr. Dominican Coll., Orangeburg, N.Y., 1995-98. Mem. Am. Occupl. Therapy Assn. (N.J. rep. 1998—, Achievement award for leadership and program devel. 1998), N.J. Occupl. Therapy Assn. (award of merit adminstrn. 1987, award of merit for practice 1995, pres. 1992-94), Profl. Health Adminstrn. Assn., Am. Coll. Healthcare Execs., Pi Alpha Alpha. Home: 8 Windsor Ter Mahwah NJ 07430-2815

HUNT, DONALD EDWARD, planning and engineering executive; b. St. Paul, May 31, 1951; s. Edward Laymond and Alice Lorraine (Jones) H.; m. Diane Marie Legatt, July 27, 1973; children: Alicia, Kevin. B of Environ. Design, U. Minn., 1973, B of Landscape Architecture, 1975; M of City and Regional Planning, Harvard U., 1978. Project planner BRW, Inc., Mpls., 1974-75; project mgr. BRW, Inc., 1978-82; prin. BRW, Inc., Denver, 1982-89; pres. BRW, Inc., 1990—. Mem. affirmative action goals com. City of Denver, 1989-95; bd. dirs. Cherry Creek Vista Park Dist., Englewood, Colo., 1985-89, Cherry Creek Arts Found., Denver, 1989-92, Children's Mus. of Denver, 1993—, Denver Civic Ventures, 1994—. Mem. Am. Planning Assn., Am. Soc. Landscape Architects, Urban Land Inst. Avocations: skiing, golfing. *

HUNT, DONALD FREDERICK, chemistry educator; b. Hyannis, Mass., Apr. 25, 1941; s. Sheldon Leslie and Vena Elizabeth (Knowles) H.; m. Linda Lee Carson, June 12, 1965; children: Amanda Montgomery, Caroline Moore. BS in Chemistry, U. Mass., 1962, PhD in Chemistry, 1967. Asst. prof. chemistry U. Va., Charlottesville, 1967-73, assoc. prof., 1973-78, prof., 1978-93, Univ. prof. chemistry and pathology, 1993—. Recipient Charles H. Stone award ACS-Piedmont Sect., 1990, Va.'s Outstanding Scientist award Va. Sci. Mus., 1992, Pehr Edman award Methods in Protein Sequence Analysis Conf., 1992, Disting. Contbn. award Am. Soc. for Mass Spectrometry, 1994, The Christian B. Anfinsen award Protein Soc., 1996. Mem. Am. Chem. Soc. (Chem. Instrumentation award 1997). Home: 970 Old Ballard Rd Charlottesville VA 22901-9457 Office: U Va Chemistry Dept McCormick Rd Charlottesville VA 22901

HUNT, DONNELL RAY, retired agricultural engineering educator; b. Danville, Ind., Aug. 11, 1926; s. Ray Hadley and Sarah Leona (Booty) H.; m. Dorothea Marie May, Sept. 2, 1951; children: David Carter, DeAnne Elizabeth. BS, Purdue U., 1951; MS, Iowa State U., 1954; PhD, Iowa State, 1958. Registered profl. engr., Ill. Instr. to assoc. prof. agrl. engring. Iowa State U., Ames, 1951-60; assoc. prof. U. Ill., Urbana, 1960-68, prof., 1968-96; asst. dean, dir. coop. edn. program Coll. Engring. U. Ill., 1986-96; cons. in field. Author: Farm Power and Machinery Management, 9th edit., 1995, Farm Machinery Mechanisms, 1972, Engineering Models for Agricultural Production, 1986. Served with U.S. Army, 1945-46. Fulbright awardee Ireland, 1968-69. Fellow Am. Soc. Agrl. Engrs.; mem. Am. Soc. Engring. Edn. Republican. Presbyterian. *

HUNT, EFFIE NEVA, former college dean, former English educator; b. Waverly, Ill., June 19, 1922; d. Abraham Luther and Fannie Ethel (Ritter) H. A.B., MacMurray Coll. for Women, 1944; M.A., U. Ill., 1945, Ph.D., 1950; postgrad., Columbia U., 1953, Univ. Coll., U. London, 1949-50. Keypunch operator U.S. Treasury, 1945; spl. librarian Harvard U., 1947, U. Pa., 1948; Instr. English U. Ill., 1950-51; librarian Library of Congress, Washington, 1951-52; asst. prof. English Mankato State Coll., 1952-59; prof. Radford Coll., 1959-63, chmn. dept. English, 1961-63; prof. Ind. State U., 1963-86; dean Ind. State U. (Coll. Arts and Scis.), 1974-86, dean and prof. emerita, 1987—. Author articles in field. Fulbright grantee, 1949-50. Mem. AAUP, MLA, Nat. Council Tchrs. English, Am. Assn. Higher Edn., Audubon Soc. Home: 3365 Wabash Ave Apt 4 Terre Haute IN 47803-1655 Office: Ind State U Root Hall Eng Dept Terre Haute IN 47809

HUNT, FRANCIS HOWARD, retired navy laboratory official; b. Emporia, Kans., Apr. 12, 1919; s. Frederick Raymond and Mabel (Holmes) H.; BA, Wesleyan U., 1941; m. Kathleen McLean, June 4, 1945 (dec. Sept. 1992); children: Deborah Mary, Laurie Jane, Peter Raymond; m. Mary Alice Fish, July 16, 1993. Supr. records Columbia U. div. War Research, New London, Conn., 1941-43, tech. editor, writer, 1943-44; with U.S. Navy Underwater Sound Lab., Fort Trumbull, New London, Conn., 1945-70, successively asst. to asst. tech. dir., 1945-47, staff asst. to tech. dir., head tech. info. div., 1947-60; assoc. tech. dir. for administrn., 1960-70; asso. dir. center operations Naval Underwater Systems Center, Newport, R.I., 1970-76. Mem. East Lyme Zoning Bd. of Appeals, 1956—; sec., 1960-78, chmn., 1978-97; past mem. East Lyme Flood and Erosion Control Bd., Niantic (Conn.) Boy Scout Com., East Lyme Jr. High Sch. Planning Com.; mem. Conn. Fedn. Planning and Zoning Agencies. Bd. dirs. Niantic Public Library, 1962-83; bd. dirs. Child Guidance Clinic Southeastern Conn., 1959-62, East Lyme Nursing Assn., 1964-66; mem. East Lyme Republican Town Com., 1981-90; justice of peace, East Lyme, 1985—. Served with AUS, 1944-45. Decorated Purple Heart, Bronze Star Medal; recipient Outstanding mem. Town Commn. East Lyme C. of C., 1972, 81, named "Melvin Jones Fellow for Dedicated Humanitarian Services" by Lions Clubs International Foundation, 1997. Mem. IEEE, Conn., Lebanon, Columbia hist. socs., Nat. Assn. Ret. Fed. Employees, Conn. Soc. Genealogists, R.I. Geneal. Soc., Conn. Huguenot Soc. (pres. 1990-96), Soc. Colonial Wars in Conn., Conn. Soc. SAR (mem. bd. mgrs. 1980-87, registrar 1984-87, Patriot medal 1987, Silver good citizenship medal 1992), Soc. of Cin., Nat. Huguenot Soc. (chaplain gen. 1993-95), Soc. Mayflower Descendents in Conn., Gov. William Bradford Compact, New Eng. Historic Geneal. Soc. Congregationalist. Club: Lions (past pres.). Home: 2 Strawberry Ln Niantic CT 06357-1936

HUNT, FRANKLIN GRIGGS, lawyer; b. Jenks, Okla., Dec. 21, 1930; s. John Wesley and Alta (Johnson) H.; m. Marilyn Glenn Maxfield, July 12, 1958; children—Laura Suzanne, Molly Frances. A.B., Harvard U., 1952, LL.B., 1959. Bar: N.Y., 1960. Assoc. Lord, Day and Lord, N.Y.C., 1959-64, ptnr., 1965-93, of counsel, 1993-94; sr. advisor Morgan, Lewis & Bockius, N.Y.C., 1994—. Assoc. editor Am. Maritime Cases, 1982-92; contbr. articles to profl. jours. Mem. adv. bd. Inst. Intercultural Studies, N.Y.C., 1985—. Lt. (j.g.) USN, 1952-55. Mem. ABA, N.Y.C. Bar Assn., Maritime Law Assn. U.S., AAAS, Am. Phys. Soc. Avocations: ballet; archaeology. Home: 43 W 61st St Apt 22M New York NY 10023-7618 Office: Morgan Lewis & Bockius 101 Park Ave Fl 33 New York NY 10178-0060

HUNT, FREDERICK TALLEY DRUM, JR., association executive; b. Martinque, French West Indies, Sept. 19, 1947; s. Frederick Talley Drum and Eleanor Conly H.; BA, Vanderbilt U., 1970; m. Acacia Lynn Graham, Dec. 4, 1976. Dir. program devel. Manufactured Housing Inst., Washington, 1973-74; pres. Hunt Assocs., Washington, 1974-75, asst. dir. field svcs., Nat. Assn. Life Underwriters, 1975-77; dir. comm., govt. liaison Am. Acad. Actuaries, Washington, 1977-80; pres. Soc. Profl. Benefit Adminstrs., 1980—; pres., owner Hunt Mgmt. Systems, 1982—; advisor White House, Congress and various govt. agys.; speaker on human resources and employee benefits. Contbr. articles to profl. jours. Mem. govt. liaison com. Internat. Found. Employment Benefit Plans. Mem. Can. Hist. Soc., Soc. of Cincinnati, Mil. Order Loyal Legion, Aztec Club of 1847, Met. Club. Home: Westmoreland Hills 5308 Blackstone Rd Bethesda MD 20816-1803 also Home: 228 Riverside Rd Edgewater MD 21037 Office: Hunt Mgmt Systems 2 Wisconsin Cir Ste 670 Chevy Chase MD 20815-7043

HUNT, GEORGE ANDREW, lawyer; b. Salina, Utah, Mar. 5, 1949; s. Loyd G. and Inez Hunt; m. Elizabeth Jean Brandise, July 28, 1973 (div.); children: Rachael, Rinaldo, Andrew, Geoffrey. BS in Internat. Relations cum laude, U. Utah, 1971, JD, 1974. Bar: Utah 1974, U.S. Dist. Ct. Utah 1974, U.S. Ct. Appeals (10th cir.) 1976, U.S. Supreme Ct. 1978, U.S. Ct. Appeals (9th cir.) 1984. Assoc. Snow, Christensen & Martineau, Salt Lake City, 1974-78, ptnr., 1978-90; founding ptnr. Williams & Hunt, Salt Lake City, 1991—. Pres. U. Utah Coll. of Law, Salt Lake City, 1974. Mem. Utah Bar Assn. (bar examiner 1976-80, chmn. constrn. law sect. 1985-88), Salt Lake County Bar Assn. (mem. exec. com. 1979-90, treas. 1984, sec. 1985, v.p. 1986-87, pres. 1987-88), U. Coll. of Law (bd. trustees 1993-96), Alta Club. Republican. Roman Catholic. Avocations: flying, reading, music, gardening. Office: Williams & Hunt PO Box 45678 Salt Lake City UT 84145-0678

HUNT, GEORGE NELSON, bishop; b. Louisville, Dec. 6, 1931; s. George N. and Jessie Mae (Alter) H.; m. Barbara Noel Plamp, June 18, 1955; children: Susan, Paul, David. BA, U. South, Sewanee, Tenn., 1953; MDiv, Va. Theol. Sem., Alexandria, 1956; DD, Yale U., 1980; LHD, U. R.I., 1996. Ordained to ministry Episcopal Ch., 1956; vicar Holy Trinity Ch., Gillette, Wyo., 1956-60; priest in charge St. John's Ch., Upton, Wyo., 1957-60, St. Francis Ch., Reno Junction, Wyo., 1959-60; asst. St. Paul's Ch., Oakland, Calif., 1960-62; rector St. Alban's Ch., Worland, Wyo., 1962-65, St. Anselm's Ch., Lafayette, Calif., 1965-70, St. Paul's Ch., Salinas, Calif., 1970-75; exec. officer Episcopal Diocese Calif., 1975-80; bishop Episcopal Diocese R.I., Providence, 1980-94; interim bishop Episcopal Diocese Hawaii, 1995-96; ret., 1996; cons. to bishop of N.J., 1997-98. Episcopalian.

HUNT, GEORGE WILLIAM, priest, magazine editor; b. N.Y.C., Jan. 22, 1937; s. George Aloysius and Grace Winifred (Jordan) H. AB, Fordham U., 1961, MA, 1963; PhL, Woodstock Coll., 1961, STL, 1967; STM, Yale U., 1968; PhD, Syracuse U., 1974; DHL (hon.), Spring Hill Coll., 1991, Loyola Coll., Balt., 1993, Fairfield U., 1996. Joined S.J., 1954; ordained priest Roman Cath. Ch., 1967. Asst. prof. St. Peter's Coll., Jersey City, 1968-70; assoc. prof. Le Moyne Coll., Syracuse, N.Y., 1973-81; vis. prof. Georgetown U., Washington, 1983-84; pres., editor in chief Am. mag., N.Y.C., 1984-98; dir. Ctr. of Religion and Culture Fordham U., Bronx, N.Y., 1999—. Author: (literary criticism) John Updike and the Three Great Secret Things, 1980 (Christianity lit. award 1981), John Cheever: The Hobgoblin Company of Love, 1983.Y. Trustee Boston Coll., 1985—, Carnegie Coun. on Ethics and Internat. Affairs, 1986—, Holy Cross Coll., Worcester, Mass., 1990—, Loyola Coll., Balt., 1994—, Le Moyne Coll., Syracuse, 1995—; trustee emeritus U. Detroit, 1984—. Home and Office: Fordham Univ Ctr of Religion and Culture 441 E Fordham Rd Bronx NY 10458

HUNT, GORDON, lawyer; b. L.A., Oct. 26, 1934; s. Howard Wilson and Esther Nita (Dempsey) H. BA in Polit. Sci, UCLA, 1956; JD, U. So. Calif., 1959. Bar: Calif. 1960. Law clk. Appellate Dept., Superior Ct. L.A. County, 1959-60; mem. firm Behymer & Hoffman, Los Angeles, 1960-65; partner firm Behymer, Hoffman & Hunt, Los Angeles, 1965-68; ptnr. firm Munns, Kofford, Hoffman, Hunt & Throckmorton, Pasadena, 1969-90, Hunt, Ortman, Blasco, Palffy & Rossell, Pasadena, 1990-95; mem. Hunt, Ortman, Blasco, Palffy & Rossell Inc., 1995—; lectr. UCLA, various yrs.; chmn. legal adv. com. Assoc. Gen. Contractors Calif., 1985; arbitrator L.A. Superior Ct., State of Calif. Author: Construction Surety and Bonding Handbook; co-author: California Construction Law, 15th edit.; contbr. numerous articles to legal jours. Mem. ABA, Calif. Bar Assn. (del. Conv. 1964-69), L.A. County Bar Assn. (real property com. 1965-66, exec. com. 1970-72, sec. 1972-73, vice chmn. 1972-75, chmn. real property sect. 1975-76, co-chmn. continuing edn. bar com. 1969-71), Am. Arbitration Assn. (arbitrator, mediator). Office: 301 N Lake Ave Fl 7 Pasadena CA 91101-4108

HUNT, H(AROLD) KEITH, business management educator, marketing consultant; b. Apr. 16, 1938; married; 8 children. BS in Mktg. and Mgmt., U. Utah, 1961, MBA, 1962; PhD in Mktg., Northwestern U., 1972. Instr. Imperial Valley Coll., El Centro, Calif., 1962-64; teaching asst. Northwestern U., 1964-66, instr., 1966-67; asst. prof. bus. adminstrn. and journalism U. Iowa, 1967-73; cons., staff mem. Office Policy Planning and Evaluation, FTC, Washington, 1973-74; assoc. prof. bus. adminstrn. U. Wyo., Laramie, 1974-75; assoc. prof. bus. mgmt. Brigham Young U., Provo, Utah, 1975-78; prof. Brigham Young U., Provo, 1978—; participant, chmn. various workshops, seminars, meetings; research expert, cons., expert witness on consumer research FTC, 1974-81; cons., expert witness div. drug advt. FDA, 1975-82; cons., adv. on consumer research Consumer and Corp. Affairs Can., 1978-82. Editor: Advances in Consumer Research, vol. 5, 1977; co-editor conf. proc. (with Francees Magrabi) Interdisciplinary Consumer Research, 1980, (with Ralph Day) Consumer Satisfaction/Dissatisfaction and Complaining Behavior, 8 vols., 1975-85, Jour. 1988—. Elected to Orem City Coun., Utah, 1986-93. Recipient Maeser Research award Brigham Young U., 1981; scholar-in-residence adv. dept. U. Ill., 1979; vis. research scholar Coll. Home Econs., U. Ala., 1980; vis. research scholar dept. mktg. and transp. U. Tenn., 1981; NSF grantee, 1975-77. Mem. Assn. Consumer Research (pres. 1979, exec. sec. 1983—, 1st Disting. Svc. award 1989), Am. Acad. Advt. (pres. 1982-83, exec. sec. 1983-86, elected fellow 1987), Am. Mktg. Assn., Soc. Consumer Psychology, Am. Council on Consumer Interests, Beta Gamma Sigma, Kappa Tau Alpha, Omicron Delta Epsilon, Phi Kappa Phi. Home: 835 High Country Dr Orem UT 84097-2370 Office: Brigham Young U Grad Sch Mgmt 632 TNRB Provo UT 84602-1133

HUNT, HELEN, actress; b. L.A., June 15, 1963; d. Gordon and Jane H. TV appearances include Amy Prentiss, The Swiss Family Robinson, The Fitzpatricks, It Takes Two, Having Babies, Land of Little Rain, Weekend, Mary Tyler Moore Show, Family, St. Elsewhere; TV movies include Pioneer Woman, All Together Now, Death Scream, The Spell, Transplant, Angel Dusted, Child Bride of Short Creek, The Miracle of Cathy Miller, Desperate Lives, Quarterback Princess, Bill: On His Own, Choices of the Heart, Sweet Revenge, Why Are You Here?, Murder In New Hampshire: The Pamela Smart Story, 1991, In the Comfort of Darkness, 1992; TV series Mad About You, 1992-99 (Emmy nomination, Lead Actress - Comedy, 1993, 94, Golden Globe award for Best Actress, musical or comedy, 1994, 95, Emmy award for Best Leading Actress in a Comedy series, 1996); films include Rollercoaster, 1977, Girls Just Want To Have Fun, 1985, Trancers, 1985, Empire, 1985, Peggy Sue Got Married, 1986, Project X, 1987, Miles From Home, 1988, Next Of Kin, 1989, The Waterdance, 1992, Only You, 1992, Bob Roberts, 1992, Mr. Saturday Night, 1992, Kiss of Death, 1995, Twister, 1996, As Good As It Gets, 1997 (Acad. award Best Actress in a Leading Role 1997), Twister: Ride It Out, 1998, Twelfth Night, 1998. *

HUNT, HOWARD F(RANCIS), psychologist, educator; b. Morgantown, W.Va., May 29, 1918; s. Harrison R. and Jane (Fisher) H.; m. Ida Altman, Aug. 16, 1941; children: Carol Ann Hunt Stark, William H., Steven C., John H. AB, Mich. State Coll., 1940; PhD, U. Minn., 1943. Diplomate clin. psychology Am. Bd. Examiners Profl. Psychology. Instr. psychology U. Minn., 1943-44; asst. prof. psychology Stanford U., 1946-48; assoc. prof. U. Chgo., 1948-54, prof., 1954, chmn. dept. psychology, 1955-62; chief psychiat. research (psychology) N.Y. State Psychiat. Inst., N.Y.C., 1962-77; prof. med. psychology Coll. Physicians and Surgeons, Columbia U., 1962-77; prof. psychology Columbia U., 1962-77; prof. psychology in psychiatry Cornell U. Med. Coll., N.Y.C., 1977-84; clin. prof. psychology in psychiatry Cornell U. Med. Coll., 1984—; attending psychologist N.Y. Hosp.-Cornell Med. Center, 1978-89; fellow (Center for Advanced Study in Behavioral Sci.), 1959-60; chmn. psychopharmacology rev. com. NIMH, 1958-61, mem., 1971-74, mem. bd. sci. counselors, 1961-65; mem. brain scis. com. Nat. Acad. Sci.-NRC, 1974-78; mem. N.Y. State Health Adv. Council, 1975-78. Contbr. articles to profl. publs.; editorial bd.: Jour. Psychiatry and the Law; editl. adviser on psychology: Ency. Brit., 1957-98; editor: Dorsey Press Psychology Series, 1959-75, Jour. Abnormal Psychology, 1964-70. Bd. dirs. Founds. Fund for Rsch. in Psychiatry, 1963-66; bd. dirs. Children's Village, Dobbs Ferry, N.Y., v.p., 1964-89. Lt. (j.g.) USNR, 1944-46. Recipient Salmon medal in psychiatry, 1978. Fellow AAAS, APA, Ea. Psychol. Assn.; mem. Sigma Xi, Phi Kappa Phi, Kappa Sigma. Mem. Religious Soc. of Friends. Home and Office: 19 Northwood Dr Vineland NJ 08360-4107

HUNT, J. B., transportation executive. Chmn. J.B. Hunt Group, Lowell, Ark., sr. chmn. Office: JB Hunt Transport Services Inc 615 JB Hunt Corporate Dr Lowell AR 72745*

HUNT, JAMES BAXTER, JR., governor, lawyer; b. Guilford County, N.C., May 16, 1937; s. James Baxter and Elsie (Brame) H.; m. Carolyn Joyce Leonard, Aug. 20, 1958; children: Rebecca Hunt Hawley, James Baxter Hunt III, Rachel Nilender, Elizabeth Amigh. BS in Agrl. Edn., N.C. State U., 1959, MS in Agrl. Econs., 1962; JD, U. N.C., 1964. Bar: N.C. 1964. Econ. advisor H.M. Govt. of Nepal for Ford Found., 1964-66; ptnr. Kirby, Webb and Hunt, 1966-72; lt. gov. State of N.C., 1973-77, gov., 1977-85, 93—; ptnr. Poyner and Spruill, Raleigh, N.C., 1985-93; originator, bd. dirs. Triangle East; chmn. N.C. State U. Emerging Issues Forum; bd. visitors Wake Forest U.; founding chmn. Nat. Bd. for Profl. Tchg. Stds., 1987, Nat. Ctr. for Pub. Policy and Higher Edn., 1998. Author: Rally Around the Precinct, 1968. Trustee Atlantic Christian Coll.; state pres. Young Dems., 1968; del. Dem. Nat. Conv., 1968; mem. Carnegie Forum on Edn. and Econ. Task Force on Teaching as a Profl., 1986; chmn. Nat. Bd. for Profl. Teaching Standards, 1987—, Nat. Commn. on Teaching and Am.'s Future, 1994. Recipient 1st Harry S. Truman award Nat. Young Dems., 1975, James Bryant Conant award Edn. Commn. States, 1984, Nat. 4-H Outstanding Alumnus award, 1984, Soil Conservation Honors award, 1986, Child Health Advocate award Am. Acad. Pediatrics, 1994, Friend of Edn. award, 1999; named Outstanding Young Man of Yr., Wilson Jr. C. of C., 1969, Outstanding Govt. Ofcl. in Cmty. Edn., Nat. Assn. Cmty. Edn., 1977. Mem. Nat. Govs. Assn. (chmn. task force on technol. innovation mem. exec. com., chmn. edn. com. of the states and nat. task force on edn. for econ. growth 1982-83, leadership team on controlling crime and violence 1994, chmn. nat. edn. goals panel 1997—). Presbyterian. Office: Office of the Governor 116 W Jones St Raleigh NC 27603-8001

HUNT, JAMES CALVIN, academic administrator, physician; b. Lexington, N.C., Sept. 11, 1925; s. James Lee and Sarah Della (Frank) H.; m. Irene Kivett, Sept. 17, 1949; children—James Calvin, Michael S., Cynthia Irene. A.B., Catawba Coll., 1949; M.D., Bowman Gray Sch. Medicine, 1953; M.S., U. Minn., 1958; ScD, Wake Forest U., 1992. Intern N.C. Bapt. Hosp., Winston-Salem, 1953-54; resident, fellow Mayo Grad Sch. Medicine, Rochester, Minn., 1954-58; practice medicine, specializing in internal medicine (cardiovascular-renal diseases) Rochester, 1958-78; cons., instr. to asst. prof. dept. medicine Mayo Clinic and Mayo Med. Sch., 1958-63, assoc. prof., chmn. div. nephrology, 1963-72, prof., chmn. dept. medicine, 1973-78; prof., assoc. dean clin. ednl. programs Mayo Med. Sch., 1972-74; prof. medicine U. Tenn., Memphis, 1978—, dean Coll. Medicine, 1978-81, v.p. health affairs, chancellor Univ. Health Scis. Ctr., 1981-93, univ. disting. prof., dir. clin. scholars program, 1993—; mem. adv. coun. Nat. Heart, Lung and Blood Inst., NIH, 1976-81. Contbr. articles to med. jours. Pres. Nat. Kidney Found., 1973-76; trustee Le Bonheur Children's Med. Ctr., 1981-93, Christian Bros. Coll., 1983-95; mem. cmty. adv. bd. Bapt. Meml. Hosp., 1986—; mem. Congl. Tech. Adv. Coun., 1987-96, chair, 1995-96; mem. bd. dirs. Memphis Downtown Neighbors Assn., 1995—, pres., 1997—; mem. adv. bd. Goals for Memphis, 1987-95; bd. dirs. Memphis YMCA, Bapt. Meml. Coll. of Health Scis.; mem. adv. bd. Rhodes Coll. With USAAF, 1943-46, ETO. Recipient Disting. Svc. award Bowman Gray Sch. Medicine, Wake Forest U., 1975, Disting. Alumnus award Catawba Coll., 1974, Educator of Yr. award Memphis State U., 1986, Outstanding Alumnus award Mayo Found., 1991, Gift of Life award Nat. Kidney Found., 1991. Fellow A.C.P., Am. Coll. Cardiology, Am. Heart Assn. (council on circulation); mem. Internat., Am. socs. nephrology, Internat. Soc. Hypertension, Soc. Nuclear Medicine, Council for High Blood Pressure Research, Am. Soc. Internal Medicine, AMA, Am. Soc. Clin. Pharmacology and Therapeutics, Sigma Xi, Alpha Omega Alpha, Phi Rho Sigma. Home: 150 Harbor Isle Cir S Memphis TN 38103-0886 Office: U Tenn Memphis Health Scis Ctr 62 S Dunlap St Memphis TN 38103-4903

HUNT, JAMES CHRISTOPHER, physics and astronomy educator, history of science researcher; b. Dawson Springs, Ky., Nov. 26, 1965; s. Jimmy and Patricia Ann (Thorpe) H.; m. Manish K. Mishra, June 12, 1999. BS in Physics, Murray State U., 1987; MS in Physics, U. Md., 1990, MA in History, 1996. Instr. Prince George's C.C., Largo, Md., 1990-93; asst. prof. Prince George's C.C., Largo, Md., 1993-96; assoc. prof. Prince George's C.C., Largo, Md., 1996—; honors program coord. Prince George's Cmty. Coll., Largo, Md., 1997-99. Mem. Nat. Ctr. Sci. Edn., History of Sci. Soc., Astron. Soc. Pacific, Com. Scientific Investigation of Claims of Paranormal (assoc.), Delta Lambda Phi. (chpt. pres. 1991-93, nat. extension chair 1994-96). Office: Prince Georges CC Dept Sci 301 Largo Rd Upper Marlboro MD 20774-2109

HUNT, JAMES L., lawyer; b. Chgo., Oct. 20, 1942. BA magna cum laude, DePauw U., 1964; JD, Northwestern U., 1967. Bar: Calif. 1967. Atty. McCuthen, Doyle, Brown & Enersen, San Francisco; atty. rep. 9th Cir. Jud. Conf., 1991-94; bd. dirs. The Lurie Co.; trustee The Lurie Found. Assoc. editor: Northwestern U. Law Rev., 1966-67. Bd. dirs. San Francisco Giants; bd. visitors Northwestern U. Law Sch., 1989—. Mem. Am. Coll. Trial

Lawyers, Phi Beta Kappa, Order of the Coif. Office: McCutchen Doyle Brown & Enersen 3 Embarcadero Ctr San Francisco CA 94111-4003*

HUNT, JEFFREY BRIAN, lawyer; b. Huntington, W.Va., Sept. 23, 1958; s. Bernard Ray and Nadine Dora (Meadows) H.; m. Krista Moorman, May 14, 1983. BA magna cum laude, Marshall U., 1980; JD summa cum laude, U. Ky., 1983. Bar: Mo. 1983, Ill. 1984, U.S. Ct. Appeals (8th cir.) 1984. Assoc. Lewis & Rice, 1983-93; mem. Lewis, Rice & Fingersh, L.C., St. Louis, 1993—; adj. instr. Washington U., St. Louis, 1983-89, 96—. Mem. ABA (vice chair tort and ins. practice sect. pretrial practice and procedure, 1996—, vice chair TIPS sect. civil procedure and evidence 1996—), Bar Assn. Met. St. Louis, Order of Coif, Omicron Delta Kappa. Democrat. Methodist. Avocations: tennis, softball, baseball, basketball, golf. Home: 2220 Stonegate Manor Ct Chesterfield MO 63017-7126 Office: Lewis Rice and Fingersh LC 500 N Broadway Ste 2000 Saint Louis MO 63102-2147

HUNT, JOHN DAVID, retired banker; b. Worcester, Mass., May 2, 1925; s. John J. and Honorea B. (Tully) H.; m. Claire A. Sullivan, June 25, 1949; children: Barbara A., Kathryn R. AB, Brown U., 1949; postgrad. Advanced Mgmt. Program, Harvard U., 1973; DBA (hon.), Anna Maria Coll., 1982. Accountant Harry W. Wallis & Co., Worcester, 1949-50; with Worcester County Nat. Bank (now Fleet Bank), 1952—; asst. v.p. Worcester County Nat. Bank (now Shawmut Worcester County Bank N.A.), 1959-61, v.p., 1961-69, sr. v.p., 1969-73, exec. v.p., 1973-77, pres., 1977-87, chmn. bd., 1983, chmn. exec. com., 1987-90, ret., 1990; bd. dirs. Worcester Bus. Devel. Corp., pres., 1981-82, chmn., 1987-99; trustee Allmerica Investment Trust, 1977-95, Allmerica Securities Inc., 1977-95, Mass. Biotech Rsch. Inst., 1985-98; instr. Am. Inst. Banking, 1957-60. Chmn. fund drive Greater Worcester United Appeal, 1972; Bd. dirs. United Cerebral Palsy Assn. Worcester County, 1957-67, bd. dirs. U. Mass. Medical Ctr. Found.; Worcester Better Bus. Bur., 1964-69, Catholic Charities Worcester, 1971-75, United Way Worcester, NCCJ, 1979-86; trustee Hahnemann Hosp., 1966-78, Assumption Coll., 1975-80; corporator St. Vincent Hosp.; mem. Worcester Redevel. Authority, 1983-85; adv. bd. dept. mgmt. Worcester Poly. Inst.; chmn. Civic Ctr. Commn., 1985-90; trustee Fund Edn. in Econs., 1980-85, chmn., 1984-85; bd. dirs. Worcester Mcpl. Research Bur., Inc., 1985-89. Served to lt. USNR, 1943-47, 50-52. Recipient Outstanding Young Man award Worcester County, 1961, Isaiah Thomas award Advt. Club Worcester, 1987, Peace medal State of Israel, 1987. Mem. Am. Inst. Banking, Robert Morris Assocs. (bd. govs. 1966-71, pres. New Eng. chpt. 1969-70), Am. Bankers Assn. (governing council), Mass. Bankers Assn., bd. govs. (1974-79, chmn. 1977), Worcester Area C. of C. (chmn. 1984, bd. dirs. 1980—), Alpha Delta Phi. Republican. Roman Catholic. Clubs: Worcester County Brown, Worcester, Worcester Country, Oyster Harbors. Home: 770 Salisbury St Worcester MA 01609-1155 Office: 1 Innovation Dr Worcester MA 01605-4307

HUNT, JOHN EDWIN, insurance company executive, consultant; b. Ozark, Ala., Jan. 13, 1918; s. Tim Atticus and Ada (Arnold) H.; m. Winnifred Prichard; children: Jacqueline, John Edwin Jr., Geoffery, Scott, Richard; md. 2d Leona Snowden. Student, Columbus U., Washington, 1938-40, Pace U., 1940-41; diploma in banking, Am. Inst. Banking, 1942; diploma in ins., Travelers Ins. Co., 1944. Aide to regional adminstr., chief auditor Fed. Housing Adminstrn., Washington, 1938-40; with trust dept. Riggs Nat. Bank, Washington, 1940-42; asst. trust officer Fla. Nat. Bank, Jacksonville, 1942-44; asst. mgr. Travelers Ins. Co., Jacksonville, 1944-45, gen. agt. regional br., 1945-58; pres. John E. Hunt & Assocs., Tallahassee, 1972-84; chmn. bd. dirs. Hunt Ins. Group-Spl. Law Enforcement Agy. and Self-Ins. Fund Adminstrn., Tallahassee, 1984-97; pres. John Hunt & Assocs., Miami, Fla., 1958-72; chmn. emeritus Hunt Ins. Group, Tallahassee, 1997—; pres. Ins. Cons. and Analysts, Tallahassee, 1972-95; bd. dirs. Renex Corp. Past chmn. pvt. industry coun. Pres. Reagan's Job Tng. Partnership Act; past mem. Gov's Adv. Coun. for Ins.; bd. dirs. Great Smoky Mountains Railway; founder Fla. Police Chiefs Edn. & Rsch. Found., Inc.; trustee, mem. pres.'s coun. Fla. So. Coll., Lakeland, 1986-97. trustee emeritus, 1997—. Mem. Fla. Assn. Surplus Lines, Fla. Assn. Ins. Agts., Com. of 99 (past pres., bd. dirs., law enforcement com. 1984-85), Greater Miami Mortgage Brokers Assn. (pres. 1964-65), Fla. Jr. C. of C. (nat. dir., state v.p. 1950-52), Fla. Police Chiefs Assn. (hon., life), Fla. Sheriffs Assn. (hon., life), Killearn Golf and Country Club, Fla. Econ. Club, Tiger Bay Club, Govs. Club, Masons, Shriners, Elks (life). Republican. Avocation: yachting. Home: PO Box 14015 Tallahassee FL 32317-4015 Office: Hunt Ins Group Inc 2324 Centerville Rd Tallahassee FL 32308-4318*

HUNT, JOHN MORTIMER, JR., classical studies educator; b. Bryn Mawr, Pa., Sept. 21, 1943; s. John Mortimer and Ruth Pierson (Ott) H. AB, Lafayette Coll., 1965; postgrad. fellow, Cornell U., 1965-66; MA, Bryn Mawr Coll., 1968, PhD, 1970. From asst. prof. to assoc. prof. classical studies Villanova (Pa.) U., 1970-91, prof., 1991—, chmn. of dept. of classical studies, 1993—; Latin instr. Lafayette Coll., Easton, Pa., 1970; vis. assoc. prof. U. Calif., Santa Barbara, 1978. Mem. editorial bd. Classical Philology, 1976—; contbr. articles to profl. publs. Mem. Soc. Mayflower Desc. in Pa. (state historian enealogist , co-editor The Pa. Mayflower), Pa. Soc. S.R., Soc. Colonial Wars in Pa., Colonial Soc. Pa., Ancient and Honorable Artillery Co. of Mass., The Franklin Inn Club. Episcopalian. Avocations: genealogy, early Am. history, opera. Office: Villanova U Dept Classical Studies Villanova PA 19085

HUNT, JOHN WESLEY, English language educator; b. Tulsa, Jan. 19, 1927; s. John Wesley and Alta (Johnson) H.; m. Marjorie Louise Bowen, Aug. 8, 1951; children: Stuart Griggs, Susan Scott, Emily Johnson. B.A., U. Okla., 1949; student, U. Minn., 1947; Ph.D., U. Chgo., 1961. Asst. prof. English Earlham Coll., Richmond, Ind., 1956-62, assoc. prof., 1962-66, prof., 1966-72, chmn. English dept., Bain-Swiggett prof. English lang. and lit., 1968-71, assoc. acad. dean, 1971-72; dean Coll. Arts and Sci. Lehigh U., Bethlehem, Pa., 1972-87, prof., 1972-87, Univ. Svc. prof., 1987-91, prof. emeritus, dean emeritus Coll. Arts and Sci., 1992—. Author: William Faulkner: Art in Theological Tension, 1965; Asst. editor, Bull. Ill. Soc. Med. Research, 1954-56; mem. editorial bd.: Quest, 1952-56, Earlham Rev, 1966-72; co-editor: Perspectives on a Cuckoo's Nest, 1977; Contbr. chpts. to books, articles to profl. jours. Served with USNR, 1944-46. Recipient Danforth Tchr. Study grant, 1960-61, E. Harris Harbison award for distinguished teaching Danforth Found., 1965, Carnegie Humanities Program grant, 1967-68; Ira Doan Distinguished Tchr. Travel award Earlham Coll., 1970; Ford Found. Humanities Devel. Fund grant, summers 1970, 71; U. Chgo. fellow, 1952-54; Kent fellow, 1952—; Lilly postdoctoral fellow Lilly Endowment, Inc., 1964-65. Fellow Soc. for Values in Higher Edn. (chmn. postdoctoral selection com. 1968-70); mem. Nat. Coun. Tchrs. English, MLA, Ann. Conf. Modern Lit., Soc. for Study So. Lit., Gt. Lakes Colls. Assn. (acad. coun. 1967-72, exec. com. 1968-72, sec. 1968-71, dir. 1971-72), Lawrence Henry Gipson Inst. for 18th Century Studies (coun. 1972-89), Phi Beta Kappa. Home: PO Box 432 Springtown PA 18081-0432

HUNT, LAMAR, professional football team executive; b. 1932; s. H.L. and Lyda (Bunker) H.; m. Norma Hunt; children: Lamar, Sharron, Clark, Daniel. Grad., So. Meth. U. Founder, owner Kansas City Chiefs, NFL, 1959—, pres., 1959-76, chmn., 1977-78; founder, pres. AFL, 1959; (became Am. Football Conf.-NFL 1970) pres. Am. Football Conf., 1970—. Bd. dirs. Profl. Football Hall of Fame, Canton, Ohio. Named Salesman of Yr., Kansas City Advt. and Sales Execs. Club, 1963, Southwesterner of Yr., Tex. Sportswriters Assn., 1959. Office: Kans City Chiefs 1 Arrowhead Dr Kansas City MO 64129-1651*

HUNT, LAWRENCE HALLEY, JR., lawyer; b. July 15, 1943; s. Lawrence Halley Sr. and Mary Hamilton (Johnson) H.; children: Caroline Smith, Laura Hamilton, Darwin Halley. AB, Dartmouth Coll., 1965; cert., l'Inst. de'Etudes Politiques, Paris, 1966; JD, U. Chgo., 1969. Bar: N.Y. 1970, Ill. 1971, U.s. Ct. Appeals (9th cir.) 1980, U.S. Ct. Appeals (2d cir.) 1981, U.S. Supreme Ct. 1981. Assoc. Davis Polk & Wardwell, N.Y.C., 1969-70; assoc. Sidley & Austin, Chgo., 1970-75, ptnr., 1975—; advisor securities adv. com. Ill. Sec. of State, Springfield, 1977-87; prof. grad. program fin. svcs. law Ill. Inst. Tech.-Chgo.-Kent Coll. Law, 1987—. James D. Reynolds scholar Dartmouth Coll., 1965-66. Mem. ABA (com. on commodity regulation, past chmn. subcom. on futures commn. merchants, mem. exec. coun.), Mid-Day Club, Chgo. Club, Indian Hill Club. Office: Sidley & Austin One First Nat Plz Chicago IL 60603

HUNT, LINDA, actress; b. Morristown, N.J., Apr. 2, 1945. Student, Interlochen Arts Acad., Mich., Goodman Theatre and Sch. of Drama, Chgo. Stage appearances include Hamlet, 1972, 74, The Soldier's Tale, 1974, The Knight of the Burning Pestle, 1974, Down by the River Where Waterlilies are disfigured Every Day (off-Broadway debut) 1975, Ah, Wilderness (Broadway debut) 1975, The Rose Tattoo, 1977, Five Finger Excuse, 1975, The Recruiting Officer, 1978, Elizabeth Dead, 1980, A Metamorphis in Miniature (Obie award), 1983, Mother Courage and Her Children 1983, Top Girls (Obie award) 1983, Little Victories, 1983, End of the World, 1983, (Tony nomination 1984), Aunt Dan and Lemon, 1985, The Cherry Orchard, 1988; films include Popeye, 1980, The Year of Living Dangerously, 1982 (Acad. award Best supporting actress 1983), Dune, 1984, The Bostonians, 1984, Eleni, 1985, Silverado, 1985, Waiting for the Moon, 1987, She-Devil, 1989, Kindergarten Cop, 1990, If Looks Could Kill, 1991, Rain Without Thunder, 1993, Twenty Bucks, 1993, Younger and Younger, 1993, Ready to Wear (Prét-a-Portér), 1994, Pocahontas, 1995 (voice only), Eat Your Heart Out, 1997, Amazon (voice), 1997, The Relic, 1997, Out of the Past, 1998, Pocahontas II: Journey to a New World (voice, 1998; TV appearance in Ah, Wilderness, 1976, Fame (series) 1978, The Room, 1987, Chico Mendes: Voice of the Amazon, 1989, The Room Upstairs (T.V. movies) 1987, Distant Lives (host) 1989, Space Rangers (series), 1993. Office: care William Morris Agy 151 S El Camino Dr Beverly Hills CA 90212-2704*

HUNT, LORRAINE T., state official; m. Charles Hunt; 3 children. Former pres., CEO Perri Inc.; founder, also bd. dirs. Continental Nat. Bank; lt. gov. State of Nev., 1999—; bd. dirs. First Security Bank Nev.; chmn. bd. trustees Las Vegas Convention and Visitors Authority; former commr. and vice chair Nev. Commn. on Tourism; dir. Nev. Hotel/Motel Assn.; vice chmn. Nev. Motion Picture Found., Nev. Motion Picture Commn. Commr. Clark county Commn., 1995-99. Office: 101 N Carson St Ste 2 Carson City NV 89701 also: 555 E Washington Ave Ste 5500 Las Vegas NV 89101*

HUNT, MARK ALAN, museum director; b. Topeka, May 21, 1949; s. Ira B. and Marjorie May (McConnell) H.; m. Cynthia E. Rush, Feb. 21, 1976; children: Alexander Rush, Alice Claire. BA magna cum laude, Washburn U., 1971; MA, Cooperstown Grad. Programs, N.Y. State U. Coll., Oneonta, 1982; grad., Mus. Mgmt. Inst. U. Calif., Berkeley, 1983. Dir. Plymouth (Mich.) Hist. Mus., 1976; curator exhibits Kans. Hist. Soc., Topeka, 1976, asst. dir. mus., 1976-79, dir. mus., 1979-88, dir. mus. and hist. sites, 1988-90; dir. Nat. Scouting Mus., Murray (Ky.) State U., 1990-96, Ronald Reagan Presdl. Libr. and Mus., Simi Valley, Calif., 1996—; cons. Menninger Found., 1980, Nat. Endowment Humanities, 1974, 75, 77, 1978, Mus. Assessment Program; instr. mus. adminstrn., U. Kans., 1987-89; mem. adv. coun. Ea. Ill. U. Hist. Adminstrn. Program, 1992-96. Contbr. articles to profl. jours. Bd. dirs. Mulvane Art Ctr., Washburn U., 1988-89, Land Between the Lakes Assn., 1994-96; mem. master planning com. Ward-Meade Hist. Park, 1986-89; mem. Bus. Coun. for Arts, 1990-96; grad. Leadership Murray, 1994, Murray Tourism Commn., 1995-96; mem. Ventura County (Calif.) Cultural Tourism Collaborative, Moorpark (Calif.) Coll. Found. Bd., 1999. Recipient award for excellence Kans. Mus. Assn., 1991; Wiseman scholar, 1967-68, Washburn scholar, 1968-71; Clark fellow, 1973-74, Alumni fellow Washburn U., 1998. Mem. Am. Assn. State and Local History (chmn. state membership com. 1976-85, cons., mem. program com. ann. meeting 1988, 92, mem. edn. com. 1981-84, mem. local arrangements com. ann. meeting 1985, mem. membership task force 1993-97, mem. nat. governing coun. 1991-95), Mountain Plains Mus. Assn. (mem. bd. 1977, Kans. rep.), Calif. Assn. Mus. (dist. rep. on CAM bd. 1998—), Kans. Mus. Assn. (pres. 1978-80, Excellence award 1991), Ky. Assn. Mus. (bd. dirs. 1994-96), Am. Assn. Mus. (mem. accreditation vis. com., mem. mus. studies task force 1988-89), Southea. Mus. Assn. (bd. dirs. 1995-96), Murray-Calloway County C. of C., Rotary (Simi Valley noon chpt.), Kappa Sigma, Phi Kappa Phi. Methodist. Home: 12497 Mountain Trail St Moorpark CA 93021-2775 Office: Ronald Reagan Pres Libr/Mus 40 Presidential Dr Simi Valley CA 93065-0600

HUNT, MARTHA, sales executive, researcher; b. N.Y.C., May 17, 1924; d. Paul Andrew and Monika (Dobberstein) Pankau; children: Philip Brian Hunt, Susan Monica Hunt. Student, Syracuse U., 1943-47. Asst. controller Commonwealth Fund, N.Y.C., 1947-50; sales tech. Caldwell & Bloor, Mansfield, Ohio, 1958-64; sales promotion mgr. Vita Craft Corp., Shawnee, Kans., 1964-91, cons., 1964—; mem. Meeting Planners Internat., Kans. City, 1982—. Author and editor: cookbooks, 1965-91. Pres. League Women Voters, Akron, Ohio, 1951-53; gov. Soroptimist Internat. of Am., 1978-80 (bd. dirs., Phila. 1978-80); pres. Soroptimist Internat. Kans. City, 1973-74; bd. dirs. Kans. City, Mo. cpt. Shepherd's Ctr., 1972—; nat. bd. dirs. Shepher's Ctrs. Am., 1990—; bd. dirs. Rose Brooks Ctr., 1979-86, v.p., 1984-85; bd. dirs., founder Safehome, Inc., 1979—; pres. Metro Citizens Crusade Against Crime, Kans. City., 1983. Recipient Meritorious Svc. award, Kans. City Police Dept., 1975, Disting. Govs. award, Soroptimist Internat. Am., Phila., 1978-79, 79-80, Woman of Distinction award Santa Fe Trl. Girl Scouts, 1993, Soroptimist Internat. Am., 1995, Milan Hulbert Humanitarian awrd Sales Profls. Internat., 1996. Mem. Kappa Kappa Gamma (pres. 1948-49), Alumnae Assn. (N.Y.C.). Republican. Presbyterian. Avocations: traveling, volunteering.

HUNT, MARY ALICE, library science educator; b. Lima, Ohio, Apr. 14, 1928; d. Blair T. and Grace (Henry) H. BA, Fla. State U., Tallahassee, 1950, MA, 1953; PhD, Ind. U., Bloomington, 1973. Instr., librarian Fla. State U., Tallahassee, 1955-61, asst. prof., 1961-74, assoc. prof., 1974-82, prof., 1982-95, assoc. dean, 1986-95, prof. emerita, 1995—. Author: Transitions: An Informal History of a School Celebrating its 50th Anniversary, 1997; co-author: (book) Multimedia Indexes, Lists, etc., 1975; editor: (book) Multimedia Approach To Children's Literature, 1983, (periodical) FSU/SLIS Alumni Newsletter, 1966-95, Florida Libraries, 1961-67; assoc. editor: (book) Folders of Ideas for Library Excellence, 1991. Mem. ALA (councilor at large 1986-94, 96—), Southeastern Library Assn., Fla. Assn. Media in Edn., Delta Kappa Gamma, Pi Lambda Theta (life), Pi Kappa Phi, Beta Phi Mu. Avocations: gardening, reading, photography. Home: 1603 Kolopakin Nene Tallahassee FL 32301-4733

HUNT, MARY ELIZABETH, association executive; b. June 1, 1951. BA magna cum laude, Marquette U., Milw., 1972; M.Theol. Studies, Harvard Div. Sch., 1974; MDiv, Jesuit Sch. Theology, Berkeley, Calif., 1979; PhD, Grad. Theol. Union, Berkeley, Calif., 1980. Vis. prof. theology ISEDET, Frontier Internship in Mission, Buenos Aires, 1980-82; co-dir., co-founder Women's Alliance for Theology, Ethics and Ritual, Silver Spring, Md., 1983—; vis. asst. prof. religion Colgate U., Hamilton, N.Y., 1986-87; lectr., condr. workshops in field; adj. asst. prof. women's studies program Georgetown U., 1995—; mem. women's adv. com. Concilium. Author: Fierce Tenderness: A Feminist Theology of Friendship, 1990; contbr. numerous articles to profl. jours.; mem. editl. bd. Jour. Feminist Studies in Religion, Jour. Religion and Abuse, Theology and Sexuality Jour. Scholar, Marquette U., Harvard Div. U.; recipient Isaac Hecker award Paulist Ctr., Boston, Prophetic Figure award Women's Ordination Conf., prize Crossroad Women's Studies, 1990. Mem. Am. Acad. Religion, Phi Sigma Tau, Alpha Sigma Nu. Fax: 301-589-3150. E-mail: mhunt@hers.com. Office: Women's Alliance Theology 8035 13th St Ste 5 Silver Spring MD 20910-4870

HUNT, MARY REILLY, organization executive; b. N.Y.C., Apr. 17, 1921; d. Philip R. and Mary C. (Harten) Reilly; m. Robert R. Hunt, Apr. 10, 1943,; children: Marianne Schram, Philip R., Robert R., Elise Paul. Student, CCNY, 1939. Tax investigator Ind. Dept. Revenue, 1970-80; pres. Ind. Right to Life, 1973-77; treas. Nat. Right to Life, 1973-77, Washington, 1974, 77, 78, mem. exec. com., 1974, 76-81, vice chmn., 1976, exec. dir., 1978, dir. devel., 1979-94, v.p. devel., 1994-97, hon. bd. mem., 1983—; v.p. devel. Nat. Life Ctr., Woodbury, 1997—; pres. Mary Reilly Hunt & Assoc., Inc., South Bend, Ind., 1985—. Bd. dirs., v.p. YWCA, 1968-73, bd. dirs. Mental Health Assn. St. Joseph Co., 1972-78; candidate for state legis., 1988; mem. St. Joseph County Rep. Women precinct com., South Bend, 1964-79, alt. del. to Nat. Rep. Conv., 1976, 84, 88, 92; mem. Souht Bend Symphony Women's Assn. Recipient St. Patrick's medal St. Patrick's Coll. and Sem. (Ireland), 1996. Mem. NAFE, Women Bus. Owners, Am. Soc. Sovereign Mil. Order of Malta. Republican. Roman Catholic. Avocations: gardening, antique collecting. Office: Nat Life Ctr 1102 N Lafayette Blvd South Bend IN 46617-1136

HUNT, MAURICE ARTHUR, English educator, researcher; b. Lansing, Mich., Oct. 30, 1942; s. Elmore Clare and Irene Elizabeth H.; m. Pamela Helene Coyle, June 24, 1978; children: Alison, Jeffrey, Andrew, Thomas. BA, U. Mich., 1964; MA, U. Calif., Berkeley, 1966, PhD, 1970. Instr. English Coll. Marin, Kentfield, Calif., 1970-73; lectr. English Dominican Coll., San Rafael, Calif., 1974-75; vis. asst. prof. English Ariz. State U., Tempe, 1980-81; from asst. to assoc. prof. English Baylor U., Waco, Tex., 1981-93, prof. English, 1993—, chair dept. English, 1996—; mem. adv. bd. writing ctr. Tex. A&M U., College Station, Tex., 1985—; dir. Baylor Advanced Placement Inst., Waco, 1994-95, Baylor Freshman Composition Program, Waco, 1982-98; mem. exec. com. S. Ctrl. Renaissance Conf., College Station, 1988-90. Author: Shakespeare's Romance of the Word, 1990, Shakespeare's Labored Art, 1995; editor: Approaches to Teaching "The Tempest" and Other Late Romances, 1992, "The Winter's Tale": Critical Essays, 1995; assoc. editor Papers on Lang. and Lit., 1996—, The Upstart Crow: A Shakespeare Jour., 1990—; mem. editl. bd. Shakespeare and the Classroom, 1993—; contbr. articles to profl. jours. Fundraiser United Way Bay Area, San Francisco, 1976-80; bd. dirs. Alameda County Tng. and Employment Bd., Oakland, Calif., 1977-78. Rsch. grantee Baylor U., 1986—. Mem. MLA, Fulbright Grants (mem. so. region, mem. nat. screening com.), Shakespeare Assn. Am., S. Ctrl. Renaissance Conf. (mem. exec. com. 1984—), Phi Beta Kappa. Democrat. Episcopalian. Avocations: jogging, sports. E-mail: MauriceúHunt@Baylor.edu. Home: 321 Oakwood Ln Hewitt TX 76643 Office: Baylor U 500 Speight Ave Waco TX 76798-7404

HUNT, MICHAEL O'LEARY, wood science and engineering educator; b. Louisville, Dec. 9, 1935; s. George Henry and Tressie (Truax) H.; children: Elizabeth H. Schwartz, Lynne T. Lattimer, Michael O. Jr. BS, U. Ky., 1957; M.Forestry, Duke U., 1958; PhD, N.C. State U., 1970. Product engr. Wood Products div. Singer Co., Pickens, S.C., 1959-60; asst. prof. wood sci. Purdue U., West Lafayette, Ind., 1960-70, assoc. prof., 1970-79, prof. and dir. Wood Rsch. Lab., 1979—. Contbr. articles to over 70 scientific and technical publs. V.p. Wabash Valley Trust for Historic Preservation, Lafayette, 1991-98. Recipient Servaas Meml. award Hist. Landmarks Found. of Ind., 1994, H. Fannon award Lafayette Neighborhood Housing Svcs., 1998. Mem. ASTM, Forest Products Soc. (pres. 1990-91, Fred Gottschalk Meml. award 1984), Soc. of Wood Sci. and Tech., Rotary. Achievements include patent for lightweight, high-performance structural particleboard. Office: Purdue Univ Wood Rsch Lab West Lafayette IN 47907-1200

HUNT, PETER HULS, theatrical director, theatrical lighting designer; b. Pasadena, Calif., Dec. 16, 1938; s. George Smith and Gertrude (Ophuls) H.; m. Virginia Osborn, Jan. 19, 1965 (div. Jan. 1972); m. Barbette Tweed, Feb. 6, 1972; children: Max, Daisy, Amy. BA, Yale U., 1961, MFA in Drama, 1963. Free-lance lighting designer N.Y.C., 1959-69, free-lance theatre dir., 1969—; free-lance motion picture dir. Los Angeles, 1972—; artistic dir. Williamstown Theatre Festival, 1989-96. Dir.: (plays) "1776," 1969 (Tony award 1970), Give 'Em Hell Harry, 1975; (TV movie) Skeezer, 1981 (Peabody award 1982); (cable TV play) Bus Stop, 1982 (ACE award 1983), The Scarlet Pimpernel B'way, 1997. Recipient Christopher award, 1972, Edgar award, 1982. Office: Elkins & Elkins 16830 Ventura Blvd Ste 300 Encino CA 91436-1709

HUNT, PETER ROGER, film director, writer, editor; b. London, Mar. 11, 1925; came to U.S., 1975; s. Arthur George and Elizabeth H.; widowed; 1 child, Nicholas Constantine. Student, London Sch. Music. Actor English Repertory Theater, London. Camera asst., asst. editor various documentaries; asst. editor various feature films. London Film Co.; scriptor various films Hill in Korea, Admirable Crichton, Next to No Time, Paradise Lagoon, Cry From the Streets, Greengage Summer (Am. title: Loss of Innocence), Ferry to Hong Kong, H.M.S. Defiant (Am. title: Damn the Defiant), Sink the Bismarck, Operation Snaffu; supervising editor, 2d unit dir.: Dr. No, Call Me Bwana, From Russia with Love, Goldfinger, Ibcress File, Thunderball, You Only Live Twice, Jigsaw Man, Desperate Hours; assoc. producer: Chitty Chitty Bang Bang; dir.: On Her Majesty's Secret Service, Gullivers Travels (film and animated), Gold, Shout at the Devil, Death Hunt, Wild Geese II, Assassination, Hyper Sapien, Marlowe, Shirley's World, Persuaders, (NBC-TV movie) Beasts in the Streets, (ABC-TV miniseries) Last Days of Pompeii, (CBS-TV spl.) Eyes of a Witness. Mem. Assn. Cinematic Technicians Great Britain, Broadcasting Entertainment Cinematograph Theatre Union, Dirs. Guild of Am., Motion Picture Acad. Arts, Acad. TV, Broadcasting, Entertainment, Cinematograph, Theatre Union. Office: 2337 Roscomare Rd Ste 2-145 Los Angeles CA 90077-1851

HUNT, RAY L., petroleum company executive; b. 1943; s. H.L. and Ruth (Ray) H.; m. Nancy Ann Hunt; 5 children. BBA, So. Meth. U., 1965. With Hunt Oil Co., Dallas, 1958—; chmn., pres., CEO Hunt Consolidated Inc., Dallas, 1994—. Mem. Am. Petroleum Inst. (exec., pub. policy com.). Office: Hunt Consolidated Inc Fountain Pl 1445 Ross At Field Dallas TX 75202-2785*

HUNT, ROBERT BRIDGER, gynecologist; b. Columbia, S.C., Jan. 23, 1940; s. James Wesley and Marie Edwards Hunt; m. Katherine, Apr. 5, 1971; 1 child. MD, Med. U. S.C., 1964. Diplomate Am. Bd. Ob-Gyn. Pvt. practice specializing in gynecology Boston, 1973—. Editor: Atlas of Female Infertility Surgery, Hysterosalpingography: Techniques and Interpretations. Lt. USNR, 1965-67. Mem. AOA, Am. Assn. Gynecol. Laparoscopists (editor-in-chief jour. 1993—), Boston Obstetrical Soc. (sec.-treas. 1991-94). Home: 129 Dedham St Dover MA 02030-2223 Office: 319 Longwood Ave Boston MA 02115-5728

HUNT, ROBERT CHESTER, construction company executive; b. Dayton, Ohio, 1923. Grad., Case Inst. Tech., 1942. With Huber Hunt & Nichols Inc., Indpls., 1947—, sec., 1950-51, gen. mgr., 1951-52, v.p., 1952-56, vice chmn., CEO, 1956—, vice chmn.; dir. Bank One Indpls., N.A., formerly Am. Fletcher Nat. Bank. Office: Hubber Hunt & Nichols Inc 2450 S Tibbs Ave Indianapolis IN 46241-4837*

HUNT, ROBERT GARY, medical consultant, oral and maxillofacial surgeon; b. San Diego, July 10, 1945; s. Harvey E. and Pauline A. (Nazarovic) H.; m. Diane G. Hunt, Apr. 26, 1975; 1 child, Christine G. AA, Mesa Coll., San Diego, 1971; BS in Medicine, U. nebr., 1979, MD, 1979; DDS, U. So. Calif., 1976. Diplomate Am. Bd. Oral and Maxillofacial Surgery, Nat. Bd. Med. Examiners; lic. physician, Calif., Nebr.; lic. dentist, Calif., Nebr. Oral and maxillofacial surgeon in pvt. practice San Diego, 1981—. With USAF, 1965-70. Fellow Am. Assn. Oral and Maxillofacial Surgeons, Am. Coll. Oral and Maxillofacial Surgeons, Internat. Coll. Surgeons, Internat. Soc. Plastic, Aesthetic and Reconstructive Surgery, Am. Coll. Oral Implantology; mem. AMA, ADA, So. Calif. Acad. Oral Pathology, Mensa, Omicron Kappa Upsilon, Phi Kappa Phi, Alpha Tau Epsilon, Delta Sigma Delta, others. Home: 2240 Sunset Blvd San Diego CA 92103-1120

HUNT, ROBERT GAYLE, former government official; b. Greeley, Colo., Aug. 2, 1933; s. Ray and Myrtle Marie (Dunham) H.; m. Harriet Gertrude McNeel, June 10, 1955 (div. 1978); children: Leslie Lynn Hunt King, Linda Jean, Julia Gail Hunt Walsh, Gregg Bryan, Robert John. BA, U. No. Colo., 1955; MPA, Syracuse U., 1957; student, Fed. Exec. Inst., Charlottesville, Va., 1973, Western Exec. Sem. Ctr., (fed. govt.), 1991. Various positions housing and cmty. devel. programs HUD, Washington, 1957-79; spl. asst. to dep. asst. sec. FHA, 1979-89; dir. mgmt. svcs. divsn., 1989-97; Pres. Kings Park Civic Assn., Springfield, Va., 1966-67; elder Providence Presbyterian Ch., Fairfax, Va., 1968-71, 79-82, 1986-89; pres. Fairfax County Fedn. Citizens Assn., 1970-71; chmn. Citizens for Sch. Bonds, 1973; mem. Fairfax County Sch. Bd., 1973-77; pres. Social Ctr. for Psychiat. Rehab., Inc., Merrifield, Va., 1983-85; treas., 1990-96; pres. Fairfax Com. of 100, 1986-88; bd. dirs. No. Va. Mental Health Assn., Annandale, 1988-94, v.p., 1992-93, vice-chmn.; Fairfax County Adv. Task Force on Cultural Facility, 1988-89; spokesperson Clean Water Coalition, 1970; supt. Fairfax County Pub. Sch., cmty. adv. com., 1997-99; mem. pres.'s cir. Psychiat. Rehab. Svcs., Inc., Fairfax, 1994—, mem. planned giving com., 1996-97; mem. exec. com., bd. dirs. Cmty. Ministry No. Va., Oakton, Va., 1996—, chmn., 1997—. Pres. Kings Park Civic Assn., Springfield, Va., 1966-67; elder Providence Presbyterian Ch., Fairfax, Va., 1968-71, 79-82, 86-89; pres. Fairfax County Fedn. Citizens Assn., 1970-71; chmn. Citizens for Sch. Bonds, 1973; mem.

Fairfax County Sch. Bd., 1973-77; pres. Social Ctr. for Psychiat. Rehab., Inc., Merrifield, Va., 1983-85; chmn. Fairfax Cmty. Ministry, 1983-85, treas., 1990-96; pres. Fairfax Com. of 100, 1986-88; bd. dirs. No. Va. Mental Health Assn., Annandale, 1988-94, v.p., 1992-93, vice-chmn.; Fairfax County Adv. Task Force on Cultural Facility, 1988-89; spokesperson Clean Water Coalition, 1970; supt. Fairfax County Pub. Sch., cmty. adv. com., 1997-99; mem. pres.'s cir. Psychiat. Rehab. Svcs., Inc., Fairfax, 1994—, mem. planned giving. com., 1996-97; mem. exec. com., bd. dirs. Cmty. Ministry No. Va., Oakton, Va., 1996—, chmn., 1997—. Named Outstanding Citizen, Kings Park Civic Assn., 1975; recipient citations Fairfax County Sch. Bd., 1973, Disting. Svc. award, 1977. Mem. Chesapeake Harbobur Yacht Club. Avocations: sailing, fishing. Home: 8910 Cromwell Dr Springfield VA 22151-1120

HUNT, ROBERT WILLIAM, theatrical producer, data processing consultant; b. Seattle, June 8, 1947; s. William Roland and Margaret Anderson (Crowe) H.; m. Marcie Loomis, Aug. 24, 1968 (div. Dec. 1975); 1 child, Megan; m. Susan Moyer, June 17, 1989 (div. Oct. 1997); children: Donovan, Jillian. BA, U. Wash., 1969. CPA, Wash. Data processing cons Arthur Andersen & Co., Seattle, 1968-78; owner, cons. Robert W. Hunt & Assocs., Seattle, 1978—; exec. producer Village Theatre, Issaquah, Wash., 1979—; developer Francis J. Gaudette Theatre, Issaquah, Wash., 1994; cons. San Francisco Mus. Modern Art, 1981-90, Mus. of Flight, Seattle, 1983-90, Met. Mus. N.Y.C., 1984-85; contracted for acquired mgmt. Everett (Wash.) Performing Arts Ctr., 1998—. Creator arts computer software; prodr. (mus.) Eleanor, 1987, Heidi, 1989, Charlie and the Chocolate Factory, 1989, Book of James, 1990, Funny Pages, 1991, Jungle Queen Debutante, 1991, Glimmerglass, 1995, City Kid, 1995, Bootlegger, 1996, 4:00 AM Boogie Blues, 1998, Crossing Over, 1999; creator, writer (pop group music and video) The Shrimps, 1984. Chmn. com. Seattle Arts Commn., 1975-78; treas. Arts Resource Svcs., Seattle, 1976-78; gen. mgr. Musicomedy Northwest, Seattle, 1977-79; bd. dirs. Theatre Puget Sound. Grantee Seattle Arts Commn., 1978-79, Wash. State Arts Commn., 1980—, King County Arts Commn., 1980—, Nat. Endowment for the Arts, 1992—. Mem. Wash. Soc. CPAs., Nat. Alliance of Mus. Theatre Producers (treas., bd. dirs.), Seattle Rotary. Office: Village Theatre 303 Front St N Issaquah WA 98027-2917

HUNT, ROGER LEE, judge; b. Overton, Nev., Apr. 29, 1942; s. Ferlin Hansen and Verda (Peterson) H.; m. Mauna Sue Hawkes, July 20, 1965; children: Roger Todd (dec.), Rachelle, Kristina, Tyler, Melanee, Ryan. Student, Coll. So. Utah; BA, Brigham Young U., 1966; JD, George Washington U., 1970. Bar: Nev. 1970, U.S. Dist. Ct. Nev. 1970, U.S. Supreme Ct. 1977, U.S. Ct. Appeals 1980. Dep. dist. atty. Clark County Dist. Atty.'s Office, Las Vegas, Nev., 1971; assoc. Rose & Norwood, Las Vegas, 1971-73; sr. ptnr. Edwards, Hunt, Hale & Hansen, Las Vegas, 1973-92; U.S. magistrate judge U.S. Dist. Ct. Nev., Las Vegas, 1992—. Office: US Dist Ct Foley Fed Bldg #2300 300 Las Vegas Blvd Ste 2300 Las Vegas NV 89101-5883

HUNT, ROGER SCHERMERHORN, healthcare administrator; b. White Plains, N.Y., Mar. 7, 1943; s. Charles Howland and Mildred Russell (Schermerhorn) H.; m. Mary Adams Libby, June 19, 1965; children: Christina Markle, David. BA, DePauw U., 1965; MBA, George Washington U., 1968. Adminstrv. resident Lankenau Hosp., Phila., 1966-68; asst. adminstr. Hahnemann Med. Coll. and Hosp., Phila., 1968-71, hosp. dir., 1971-74, assoc. v.p., hosp. adminstr., 1974-77; dir. Ind. U. Hosps., Indpls., 1977-84; pres. Luth. Gen. Hosp., Park Ridge, Ill., 1984-90; pres., CEO Fontbonne Health System, Toronto, 1990-92; sr. v.p. Northwestern Healthcare Network, Chgo., 1993-96; pres., CEO ViaHealth, Rochester, 1996—; bd. dirs. Phila. Blood Center, 1972-74; chmn. Alliance of Indpls. Hosps., 1981; pres. United Hosp. Services, 1979-81; assoc. prof. hosp. adminstrn. Ind. U. Sch. Medicine, 1977-84; vice chmn. Pa. Emergency Health Services Council, 1975-77; pres. Chester County Emergency Med. Service Council, 1971-77. Pres. Wayne Area Jr. C. of C., 1970-71, state dir., 1971-72; bd. dirs. Rochester Philharm. Orch., 1998—. Fellow Am. Coll. Healthcare Execs. (regent for Ind. 1984, Ill. 1988-90, Postgrad. tng. award 1968); mem. Am. Hosp. Assn., Hosp. Assn. of N.Y. State, Ind. Hosp. Assn. (bd. dirs. 1982-84), Met. Chgo. Healthcare Coun. (bd. dirs. 1986-95), DePauw U. Alumni Assn. (bd. dirs. 1988-94), Greater Rochester Metro C. of C. (bd. dirs. 1998—). Office: ViaHealth 150 N Chestnut St Rochester NY 14604-1437

HUNT, RONALD DUNCAN, veterinarian, educator, pathologist; b. L.A., Oct. 9, 1935; s. Charles H. and Margaret (Duncan) H. B.S., U. Calif.-Davis, 1957, D.V.M. with highest honors, 1959; student, UCLA, 1954-55. Research fellow pathology Harvard Med. Sch., 1963-64, research assoc. pathology, 1964-69, prin. assoc. pathology, 1969-72, assoc. prof. comparative pathology, 1972-77, prof. comparative pathology, 1977-99, prof. comparative pathology emeritus, 1999—; dir. Animal Resources Center Harvard Med. Sch., 1979-89; dir. New Eng. Regional Primate Research Center, Southborough, Mass., 1976-98. Author: (with T.C. Jones) Veterinary Pathology, 1972, 5th edit., 1983, (with T.C. Jones and U. Mohr) Endocrine System, Respiratory System, Digestive System, Urinary System, Genital System; contbr. numerous articles on research on vet. pathology to profl. jours.; editorial bd.: Lab Animal Medicine, 1969—, Jour. Med. Primatology, 1977—, Internat. Life Scis. Inst, 1981—, Am. Jour. Vet. Research, 1978-80. Trustee Charles Louis Davis DVM Found., 1979—; exec. com. Tufts U. Sch. Vet. Medicine, 1979-82. Served with Vet. Corps U.S. Army, 1959-63. Mem. Am. Coll. Vet. Pathologists, AVMA, U.S. and Can. Acad. Pathology, Am. Soc. Exptl. Pathology, Am. Soc. Clin. Pathologists, Am. Assn. Lab. Animal Sci., Am. Soc. Primatology, Internat. Primatological Soc., Am. Assn. Accreditation of Lab. Animal Care (exec. com. 1989), Internat. Soc. Primatology. *Aside from more customary reasons for advancement, I believe the factor of most importance to my career has been the ability to work as a member of a team, yet simultaneously remain independent and maintain broad vision, to pursue observations not necessarily related to primary objectives.*

HUNT, RONALD FORREST, lawyer; b. Shelby, N.C., Apr. 18, 1943; s. Forrest Elmer and Bruna Mignolia (Brackett) H.; m. Judy Elaine Shultz, May 19, 1965; 1 child, Mary. A.B., U. N.C., 1966, J.D., 1968. Bar: N.C. 1968, D.C. 1973. Mem. staff SEC, Washington, 1968-69, legal asst. to chmn., 1970-71, sec. of commn., 1972-73; dep. gen. counsel, sec. Student Loan Mktg. Assn., Washington, 1973-78, sr. v.p., gen. counsel, sec., 1979-83, exec. v.p., gen. counsel, 1983-90; pvt. practice New Bern, N.C., 1991—; vice chmn. First Capital Corp., Southern Pines, N.C., 1984-90; bd. dirs. Student Loan Mktg. Assn., Washington, SLM Holding Corp., Reston, Va.; chmn. bd. dirs. Nat. Student Loan Clearinghouse, Reston, 1993-95, 97—. Mem. Montgomery County Comm. Landlord and Tenant Affairs, Md., 1976-81, chmn., 1979-81; bd. dirs. D.C. chpt. ARC, 1976-83; trustee Arena Stage, Washington, 1984-89, Washington Theatre Awards Soc., 1988-90. Republican. Presbyterian. Avocations: sailing; gardening.

HUNT, SAMUEL PANCOAST, III, lawyer, corporate executive; b. Farragut, Idaho, Apr. 7, 1943; s. Samuel Pancoast and Caroline Hart (Crum) H.; m. Cynthia Knight Boice, May 20, 1978; 1 child, Christine Boice. AB, U. N.C., 1965; JD cum laude, Columbia U., 1970. Bar: Mass. 1970, U.S. Dist. Ct. Mass. 1970. Assoc. Hale & Dorr, Boston, 1970-73; asst. gen. counsel SCA Svcs. Inc., Boston, 1973-84; v.p., gen. counsel, sec. GSX Corp., Boston, 1984-87; v.p., gen. counsel, sec., clk. H.P. Hood Inc., Boston, 1987-89; v.p., gen. counsel Residuals Mgmt. Group Air and Water Techs. Corp., Boston, 1989-91; v.p., gen. counsel, sec. Metcalf & Eddy Cos., Inc., Wakefield, Mass., 1991-95, PerSeptive Biosystems, Inc., Framingham, Mass., 1996—; speaker Urban Land Inst., New Eng. Corp. Counsel Assn.; legal counsel FIRST Inc., Boston, 1975-82, bd. dirs., 1971-82, pres. 1980-82; panel chmn., speaker New Eng. Corp. Counsel Assn.. Town coord. Gov. Dukakis' Campaigns, 1974, 78. Democrat. Episcopalian. Avocations: tennis, golf, skiing. Home: 31 Brookfield Rd Wellesley MA 02481-2420 Office: Perseptive Biosystems 500 Old Connecticut Path Framingham MA 01701-4574

HUNT, SWANEE G., public policy educator, former ambassador; b. Dallas, May 1, 1950; m. Charles Alexander Ansbacher; 3 children. BA, Tex. Christian U., 1972; MA, Ball State U., 1976, Iliff Sch. of Theology, 1977; PhD, Iliff Sch. of Theology, 1986; PhD (hon.), Webster U., 1994. Founder, chmn. Hunt Alternatives Fund, 1981—; co-founder, co-dir. Karis Community, 1980-83; min. pastoral care Capital Heights Presbyn. Ch., 1983; commr., vice chair Denver Community Mental Health Commn., 1983-87; with Gov. Policy Acad. on Families and Children at Risk, 1989-90; chair Colo. Coord. Coun. Housing and the Homeless, 1989-92; U.S. amb. to Austria, 1993-97; dir. women and pub. policy program Kennedy Sch. Govt. Composer The Witness Cantata, 1985. Bd. dirs. Ctr. Reproductive Law and Policy, Charter Fund, Am. Mental Health Fund Nat. Adv. Bd., Colo. Children's Campaign, Denver Civic Ventures, Inc., The Missing Half, Pub. Edn. Coalition, U. Colo. Ctr. Health Ethics and Policy Rev. Bd., 1987-89, Women and Founds./Corp. Philanthropy; co-founder, trustee Women's Found. Colo.; chair Mayor's Human Capital Agenda Coun., 1992-93; co-chair Denver Initiative Children and Families. Recipient Martin Luther King Humanitarian award U. Colo., 1992, NCCJ, 1992, Denver Urban Ministries, 1991, United Meth. Ch., 1989, Internat. Women's Forum, 1989, Sta. KUSA-TV, 1989, Caring Connection, 1989, Nat. Mental Health Assn., 1985, Mental Health Assn. Colo., 1984, 94, Mile High award United Way, 1993, Am. Heritage award Anti-Defamation League, 1995, Cordon Bleu du Saint Esprit Peace award, 1996, Humanitarian Lifetime Svc. award Denver Holocaust Awareness, 1997. Office: 168 Brattle St Cambridge MA 02138-3309 also: Kennedy Sch Govt Nine JF Kennedy St Rm T1 Cambridge MA 02138*

HUNT, T(HOMAS) W(EBB), retired religion educator; b. Mammoth Spring, Ark., Sept. 28, 1929; s. Thomas Hubert and Ethel Clara (Webb) H.; m. M. Laverne Hill, July 22, 1951; children: Melana Claire Hunt Monroe. MusB, Ouachita Bapt. U., 1950; MusM, N. Tex. State U., 1957, PhD, 1967. Faculty Southwestern Bapt. Theol. Sem., Ft. Worth, 1963-87; life cons. for prayer Bapt. Sunday Sch. Bd., Nashville, 1987-94, ret., 1994; lectr. in field. Author: The Doctrine of Prayer, 1986, Music in Missions, 1986, The Disciple's Prayer Life, 1988, Church Ministry Prayer Manual, 1994, The Mind of Christ, 1995, In God's Presence, 1995; contbr. The Disciple's Study Bible, 1987. Mem. Assn. Mins. and Coords. Discipleship. Home: 3915 Cypress Hill Dr Spring TX 77388-5798 *In a rapidly changing world, we rely on a God who does not change.*

HUNT, WALTER, county government official; b. Nashville, Sept. 24, 1938. BS, Tenn. State U., Nashville, 1978. Liaison U.S. Congress, Nashville, 1976-86; spl. asst. Mayor's Office, Nashville, 1986-87; exec. dir. Metro Action Commn., Met. Govt. of Nashville and Davidson County, Nashville, 1987—. Founding mem. Nashville office 100 Black Men, 1992—; chmn. bd. Northwest YMCA, 1985—; mem. Tenn. Assn. Action Agys., 1987—. Served with U.S. Army, 1970-76. Head Start Wraparound program grantee HUD, 1996; Cmty. Svcs. Block grantee U.S. Dept. HHS. Office: Metro Action Commn Metro Govt of Nashville 1624 5th Ave N Nashville TN 37208-2295

HUNT, WAYNE ROBERT, SR., state government official; b. Mt. Holly, N.J., Feb. 23, 1948; s. Edward Middleton Sr. and Sarah Isabel (Pope) H.; m. Elizabeth Evans Caputi, Oct. 23, 1982; children: Brandi Leigh, Wayne Robert Jr., Joshua David, Jacob Cody. BSBA, William Jewell Coll., 1970; MPA, Rutgers U., 1993; student, Command and Gen. Staff Coll., 1995; postgrad., Trinity Coll. and Theol. Sem., 1997—. Cert. pub. mgr., facilitator. Mgr. Edward M. Hunt & Son Inc., Mt. Holly, N.J., 1970-79; spl. staff officer mech. sect., engrng. divsn. N.J. Dept. Def., Trenton, 1979-82, asst. bur. chief facilities mgmt. bur., 1982-88; contracting officer/bur. chief installations divsn. ops. bur N.J. Dept. Mil. and Vets. Affairs, Lawrenceville, 1986-94; dir. installations divs. N.J. Dept. Mil and Vets Affairs, Lawrenceville, 1994-99, chief info. officer, 1999—; field assoc. orgnl. leadership development sc. Nat. Guard Bur., 1986-92. Deacon New Life Christian Ch.; past pres. Union Fire Co. #2. Lt. col. N.J. Army Nat. Guard, 1970—. Recipient Proclamation for Svc. to State, Gov. James J. Florio, 1993, Cert. of Recognition, Drumthwacket Found., 1992, Letter of Appreciation, N.J. Statue of Liberty Svc., N.J. Dept. Mil. and Vets. Affairs Group award, 1995, NGANJ Pres.'s award, 1997, Rancocas Valley Regional H.S. VIP Hall of Fame, 1997. Mem. ASPA, Internat. Facilities Mgmt. Assn., Internat. Who's Who of Profls., Am. Mgmt. Assn., Constrn. Specifications Inst., Pub. Sector Mgrs. Assn., N.J. Soc. Cert. Pub. Mgrs., Am. Acad. Cert. Pub. Mgrs., N.G. Exec. Dirs. Assn. (nominations com., chmn. by-laws com.), N.G. Assn. of U.S., N.G. Assn. of N.J. (sec. 1987—, Pres.'s award 1997), 114th Regimental Assn., Trenton Artillery Officers Assn., Enlisted Assn. N.J., Trinity Ctr. Conflict Mgmt., Masons (32 deg.), Elks, Pi Alpha Alpha. Avocations: golf, camping, jogging, weight training. Home: 247 N Pennsylvania Ave Morrisville PA 19067-1103 Office: NJ Dept Mil and Vet Affairs 101 Eggerts Crossing Rd Lawrenceville NJ 08648-2805

HUNT, WILLIAM B., cardiopulmonary physician; b. Lexington, N.C., Sept. 27, 1927; s. William B. and Maxine (Cox) H.; married; children: William B., III, Anne, Alex, Sarah. BS, Wake Forest U., 1948; MD, Bowman Gray Sch. Medicine, Winston Salem, N.C., 1953. Diplomate Am. Bd. Internal Medicine, Am. Bd. Allergy and Immunology. Intern, resident U. Va., Charlottesville, 1953-55, resident, fellow, 1957-59, assoc. prof., 1960-75, asst. dean Sch. Medicine, 1972-75; fellow gastroenterology Bowman Gray Sch. Medicine, Winston Salem, 1959-60; instr. internal medicine N.Y. Med. Coll., N.Y.C., 1959-60; from clin. assoc. prof. medicine to clin. prof. medicine East Carolina Sch. Medicine, Greenville, N.C., 1975—; staff physician Craven Regional Med. Ctr., New Bern, N.C., 1975—, med. dir. cardiopulmonary svcs., 1975-95; cons. N.C. Health Dept., TB Control Br., 1997—. Pres. Ea. Area Health Edn. Ctr., 1990-95. Recipient Douglas Southhall Freeman award Va. Lung Assn., 1973, Disting. Alumnus award Bowman Gray Sch. Medicine, 1973, Robert Bageant award Va. Soc. Respiratory Care, 1987. Fellow Am. Coll. Chest Physicians, Am. Thoracic Soc., Am. Coll. Physicians; mem. N.C. Med. Soc. (councillor 1978, exec. com. 1981), Va. Thoracic Soc. (pres. 1974), N.C. Thoracic Soc. (pres. 1984), N.C. Lung Assn. (pres. 1986), Craven Pamlico Jones Med. Soc. (pres. 1984). Democrat. Episcopalian. Avocations: skiing, golf, flying, sailing, tennis. Home: 19 Batts Hill Rd New Bern NC 28562-7365 Office: Craven Regional Med Ctr 2000 Neuse Blvd New Bern NC 28560-3499

HUNT, WILLIAM E., SR., state supreme court justice; b. 1923. BA, LLB, U. Mont., JD, 1955. Bar: 1955. Judge State Workers' Compensation Ct., 1975-81; justice Mont. Supreme Ct., Helena, 1984—. Office: Mont Supreme Ct Justice Bldg Rm 315 215 N Sanders St Helena MT 59620-4522

HUNT, WILLIAM EDWARD, neurosurgeon, educator; b. Columbus, Ohio, Nov. 26, 1921; s. William Willard and Marian Almina (Lerch) H.; m. Virginia A. Reimold, Mar. 17, 1945 (div. 1972); children: William W., C. David, Virginia R.; m. Charlotte M. Curtis, June 15, 1972 (dec. Apr. 1987); m. Carole A. Miller, Sept. 17, 1988. B.A. cum laude, Ohio State U., 1943, M.D. with honors, 1945. Rotating intern Phila. Gen. Hosp., 1945-46; asst. resident in gen. surgery White Cross Hosp., Columbus, 1948-49; asst. resident in neurosurgery Barnes Hosp., St. Louis, 1949-50; resident Barnes Hosp., 1951-52; fellow neurosurgery Washington U. Med. Sch., St. Louis, 1950-51; instr. neurosurgery Washington U. Med. Sch., 1952-53; asst. anatomy Ohio State U. Med. Sch., 1945, mem. faculty, 1953-90, prof. surgery, dir. div. neurol. surgery, 1964-89, prof. surgery emeritus, 1991. author: Tolosa-Hunt Syndrome; contbr. articles to profl. jours. Served to capt. M.C., AUS, 1946-48. Grantee USPHS, Spinal Cord Injury Research Center, Bremner Fund, others. Mem. Royal Soc. Medicine, Soc. Internat. Chirurgie, Am. Surg. Assn., Congress Neurol. Surgeons (v.p. 1967), Neurosurg. Soc. Am. (pres. 1979), Am. Assn. Neurol. Surgeons (chmn. coms., v.p. 1983), The Soc. Neurol. Surgeons (pres. 1979-80), Am. Acad. Neurol. Surgeons, ACS, AMA, Soc. Neurosci., Ohio State Neurosurg. Soc. (pres. 1961, 78), Ohio State Med. Assn. (del. 1968-69), Acad. Medicine Columbus and Franklin County (chmn. public relations com. 1975), Phi Beta Kappa, Alpha Omega Alpha, Sigma Xi. Episcopalian.

HUNT, WILLIS B., JR., federal judge. Former judge Houston, Superior Ct. Ga.; justice Ga. Supreme Ct., Atlanta, 1986-95, chief justice, 1994-95; judge U.S. Dist. Ct. (no. dist.) Ga., Atlanta, 1995—. Office: US Dist Ct (no dist) Ga 75 Spring St SW Atlanta GA 30306*

HUNT-CLERICI, CAROL ELIZABETH, academic administrator; b. N.Y.C., Mar. 14, 1938; d. William Laubach and Mary Alice (Grace) Hunt; m. Francis Anthony Clerici, May 17, 1958; children: Francis Anthony Jr., David William, Paul Camelio. AB, Boston Coll., 1987, MA, 1990. Faculty pers. asst. academic v.p. office Boston Coll., Chestnut Hill, Mass., 1984—; psychol. counselor Summerhill House, Norwood, Mass., 1989—; rep. staff adv. senate Boston Coll., Chestnut Hill, Mass., 1981-98, vice-chair, 1985-86, 90-91, chair, 1986-88; sec. Martin Luther King Jr. Com., 1989-98. Rep. Walpole (Mass.) Town Meeting, 1977-82. Mem. APA (assoc.), AAUW. Avocations: theater, reading, music, travel.

HUNTE, BERYL ELEANOR, mathematics educator, consultant; b. N.Y.C.. BA, CUNY-Hunter Coll., 1947; MA, Columbia U., 1948; PhD, NYU, 1965. Instr. math. So. U., Baton Rouge, 1948-51; tchr. math. Bloomfield (N.J.) H.S., 1951-57; tchr. maths. Friends Sem., N.Y.C., 1957-62; asst. prof. maths. Rockland C.C., Suffern, N.Y., 1962-63; instr. maths., supr. tchr. trainees NYU, N.Y.C., 1964; chmn. dept. math. Borough of Manhattan C.C., N.Y.C., 1964-67, 70-73, prof. maths., 1970-95, prof. maths. emerita, 1996, acting dean students, 1985-87, acting dean acad. affairs, 1987-88; dean for spl. projects CUNY, 1988-89; assoc. U. Seminar on Higher Edn., Columbia U., N.Y.C., 1989-95. Author: (with others) (textbook) Mathematics Through Statistics, 1973. Mem. YWCA Greater N.Y. NSF fellow, summer 1960, 1963-64, Chancellor's Faculty fellow CUNY, 1980. Mem. N.Y. Acad. Scis., Am. Math. Soc., CUNY Acad. for Humanities and Scis. (bd. dirs. 1991—, first v.p. 1994—), UN Assn. N.Y.C. (bd. dirs., sec. 1980-86). Avocations: opera, concerts, ballet, bridge.

HUNTEN, DONALD MOUNT, planetary scientist, educator; b. Montreal, Mar. 1, 1925; came to U.S., 1963, naturalized, 1979; s. Kenneth William and Winnifred Binnmore (Mount) H.; m. Isobel Ann Rubenstein, Dec. 28, 1949 (div. Apr. 1995); children: Keith Atherton, Mark Ross; m. Ann Louise Sprague, May 21, 1995. B.Sc., U. Western Ont., 1946; Ph.D., McGill U., 1950. From research asso. to prof. physics U. Sask. (Can.), Saskatoon, 1950-63; physicist Kitt Peak Nat. Obs., Tucson, 1963-77; sci. adv. to assoc. adminstr. for space sci. NASA, Washington, 1976-77; prof. planetary scis. U. Ariz., Tucson, 1977-88, Regents prof., 1988—; cons. NASA, 1964—. Author: Introduction to Electronics, 1964; (with J.W. Chamberlain) Theory of Planetary Atmospheres, 1987; contbr. articles to profl. jours. Recipient Pub. Svc. medal NASA, 1977, 85,96, medal for exceptional sci. achievement, 1980. Mem. Am. Phys. Soc., Can. Assn. Physicists (editor 1961-63), Am. Geophys. Union (John Adam Fleming medal 1998), Am. Astron. Soc. (chmn. div. planetary scis. 1977), Internat. Astron. Union, Internat. Union Geodesy and Geophysics, Internat. Assn. Geomagnetism and Aeronomy, AAAS, Nat. Acad. Scis., Explorers Club. Club: Cosmos (Washington). Home: 3445 W Foxes Den Dr Tucson AZ 85745-5102 Office: U Ariz Dept Planetary Scis Tucson AZ 85721

HUNTER, BARBARA WAY, public relations executive; b. Westport, N.Y., July 14, 1927; d. Walter Denslow and Hilda (Greenawalt) Way; m. Austin F. Hunter, Jan. 24, 1953; children: Kimberley, Victoria. BA, Cornell U., 1949. Assoc. editor Topics Pub. Co., N.Y.C., 1949-51; publicist Nat. Dairy Product Corp., N.Y.C., 1951-53; account exec. Sally Dickson Assn., 1953-56; assoc. D-A-Y Pub. Relations (div. Ogilvy & Mather Co.), N.Y.C., 1964-70, exec. v.p., 1970-84, pres., 1984-89; pres. Hunter & Assocs., Inc., 1989-97, chmn., 1997—; bd. dirs. Mr. Steak Inc., Denver. Trustee Cornell U., Ithaca, N.Y., 1980-85; lifetime mem. Cornell U. Coun.; bd. dirs. Point O'Woods Assn., Fire Island, N.Y., 1980-87. Recipient Sparkplug award Internat. Foodservice Mfrs. Assn., 1970, Matrix award N.Y. Women in Communications Inc., 1980, Entreprenurial Woman award Women Bus. Owners, 1981, Nat. Headliner award Women in Communications Inc., 1984. Fellow Pub. Rels. Soc. Am. (pres. 1984, pres.-elect 1983, treas. 1982, pres. N.Y. chpt. 1986, Nat. Gold Anvil award 1993); mem. Internat. Pub. Rels. Assn., Found. Pub. Rels. Rsch. and Edn. (trustee 1982, 84), Women's Forum, Cornell Club of N.Y., The Club at Point O'Woods. Home: 137 E 38th St New York NY 10016-2650 Office: Hunter & Assocs 41 Madison Ave New York NY 10010-2202

HUNTER, BERNICE THURMAN, writer; b. Toronto, Nov. 3, 1922; d. William Henry and Francelina (Coe) Thurman; m. Lloyd Hunter, Nov. 16, 1942; children: Anita Louise, Heather Anne. Comml. diploma, Runnymede Coll., 1939. Bookkeeper T. Eaton Co., Toronto, 1940-45, office worker, 1967-72; speaker Toronto Sch. Bd., 1982—. Author: (children's books) That Scatterbrain Booky, 1981 (IODE award 1982), The Railroader, 1988 (Vicky Metcalf award 1990), A Place for Margaret, 1989 (Can. Authors award 1990), The Firefighter, 1992 (Silver Birch award 1993, Red Cedar Book award 1997-98). Mem. Writers Union of Can., Canscaip. Home: 3333 Finch Ave E, Scarborough, ON Canada M1W 2R9

HUNTER, BROTHER EAGAN, education educator; b. Cedar Rapids, Iowa, June 9, 1922; s. John William and Nellie (Connors) H. BA, U. Iowa, 1944; MEd, U. Tex., 1971. Tchr. Churchill Jr. H.S., Galesburg, Ill., 1944-45, Ctrl. Cath. H.S., South Bend, Ind., 1946-47, Msgr. Coyle H.S., Taunton, Mass., 1947-50; tchr., vice prin., dir. studies Notre Dame H.S., Sherman Oaks, Calif., 1950-61, prin., 1978-80; tchr., vice prin., dir. studies St. Francis H.S., Mountain View, Calif., 1961-64, prin., 1964-70; prin. Notre Dame H.S., Biloxi, Miss., 1971-77; faculty St. Edward's U., Austin, 1977-78, prof. edn., 1980—; pres. Archdiocese of L.A. English Com., 1951-53, Guidance Coun., 1955-60; cons. So. Assn. Colls. and Schs., 1974-77, State of Miss., Dept. Edn., 1974-77; reg. advisor Nat. Cath. Edn. Assn., Secondary Sch. Dept., 1974-77, reg. cons., 1977-80; del. Gov.'s Conf. on Edn., Miss., 1975; bd. trustees St. Edward's U., Austin, 1978-80; mem. liturgical commn. Diocese of Austin, 1980-88, coun. of religious, 1983, adminstrv. coun. mem., 1986-88; liaison rep. Intercollegiate Studies Inst., Inc., 1983-98, Tex. Elem. Prins. and Suprs. Assn., 1984-93; mem. sch. bd. St. Michael's Cath. Acad., Austin, 1984-85; mem. state selection com. U.S. Senate Youth Program, 1986; del. Study Mission to People's Rep. of China, 1987; liaison rep. Tex. Acad. Skills Project, 1988-89; del. Nat. Cath. Edn. Assn.'s Reg. Congress for Tex., Ark., Okla., N.Mex. from Diocese of austin, 1991, numerous others. Contbr. numerous articles to profl. jours. Recipient Disting. Profl. Svc. award Nat. Assn. Sec. Sch. Prins., 1978, Ednl. Leadership-Austin award St. Michael's Acad., 1992, Selective Service citations Pres. U.S., 1975. Mem. ASCD. Home and Office: Saint Edward's Univ 3001 S Congress Ave Austin TX 78704-6425

HUNTER, BYNUM MERRITT, lawyer; b. Greensboro, N.C., June 13, 1925; s. Hill McIver and Annie (Merritt) H.; m. Ann Fulenwider, June 22, 1957 (div. 1968); children: Ann Shirley, Mary Parker; m. Mary Lane Yancey, Aug. 7, 1969 (div. 1978); m. Mary Bonneau McElveen, June 13, 1980; 1 son, Bynum Jr. AB, U. N.C., 1945, JD, 1949. Bar: N.C. 1949. Ptnr. Smith, Helms, Mullis & Moore. Served with USNR, 1943-46, 51-53. Fellow Am. Coll. Trial Lawyers, Am. Bar Found. (life mem.); mem. ABA, Internat. Assn. Def. Counsel, Am. Judicature Soc., Greensboro Bar Assn. (pres. 1965-66), N.C. Bar Assn., Zeta Psi, Phi Delta Phi. Club: Rotary. Home: 710 Country Club Dr Greensboro NC 27408-5714 Office: Smith Helms Mulliss & Moore Ste 1400 PO Box 21927 300 N Green St Greensboro NC 27420-1927

HUNTER, DAVID WITTMER, security brokerage executive; b. Pitts., Aug. 11, 1928; s. Frank H. and Josephine (Wittmer) H.; m. Mary Louise Clark, July 26, 1952; children: Peter C., Susan E., David Wittmer. BA cum laude, Amherst Coll., 1950; MBA, Harvard U., 1952. Ptnr., McKelvy & Co., 1954-69; exec. v.p., CEO Parker/Hunter, Inc., 1969-71, pres., CEO, 1971-78, chmn., chief exec. officer, 1978-83, chmn. bd., 1983-90; chmn. bd. Hunter Assocs., Inc., 1992—; bd. dirs. Lockhart Iron & Steel, Pitts., Fidelity Guard Svcs., Inc., Pitts., Kiene Diesel Accessories, Addison, Ill., Mestek, Inc., Justifacts, U.S. Tool and Die. Pres. Richland Youth Found., 1968-782; bd. dirs. Better Bus. Bur., 1967-74, Pitts. Pub. Theater, pres., 1984-85, Pitts.-Allegheny County chpt. ARC chmn. 1973-76, 89-92, chmn. nat. conv., 1985, Algor, Inc., 1993, Minority Capital Found., West Penn AAA, also chmn.; trustee, vice chmn. Shady Side Acad., 1965-75, 87-90; pres. Enterprise & Edn. Found., 1987—, former dir. and vice chmn.; corp. bd. dirs. North Hills Passavant Hosp. With AUS, 1952-54. Recipient Yale Aurelian award, 1946. Mem. Investment Bankers Assn. (pres. Western Pa. group 1970, chmn. Mid-Atlantic group 1972), Securities Industry Assn. (gov. 1973-78, chmn. bd. dirs. 1977, chmn. governing coun. 1978, trustee econ. edn. 1978—, mem. SIA Econ. Edn. Found), Nat. Assn. Securities Dealers Inc. (bd. govs. 1984-87, chmn. bd. govs. 1986-87), Fin. Analysts Fedn., Chi Psi, Securities Industry Assn., Duquesne Club. Republican. Presbyn. Clubs: Bond (Pitts.), Harvard-Yale-Princeton (Pitts.), Harvard Business School (Pitts.); University, Butler Country, Rolling Rock. Home: Lookout Farm Hardt Rd Gibsonia PA 15044 Office: Hunter Assocs Inc Koppers Bldg 436 7th Ave Fl 5 Pittsburgh PA 15219-1818

HUNTER, DIANNE M., English educator. BA, Alfred U., 1966; PhD, SUNY, Buffalo, 1972. From asst. prof. to prof. English Trinity Coll., Hartford, Conn., 1972-89; prof. Trinity Coll., Hartford, 1989—; tchg. asst. SUNY, Buffalo, 1968-71. E-mail: dhunter@mail.trincoll.edu. Office: 115 Vernon St Hartford CT 06106

HUNTER, DONALD FORREST, lawyer; b. Mpls., Jan. 30, 1934; s. Earl Harvey and Ruby Cecilia (Lagerson) H.; m. Marlys Ann Zilge; Jeffrey, Cheri, Kathryn. BA, U. Minn., 1961, JD, 1963. Bar: Minn. 1963, U.S. Dist. Ct. Minn. 1965, U.S. Ct. Appeals (8th cir.) 1965, Ill. 1977, U.S. Dist. Ct. (no. dist.) Ill. 1991, U.S. Supreme Ct. 1986. Assoc., then ptnr. Gislason, Dosland, Hunter & Malecki, New Ulm, Minn., 1963-76; exec. v.p., sec., gen. counsel Wirtz Prodn. Ltd. Ice Follies/Holiday on Ice, Chgo., 1976-79; ptnr. Gislason, Dosland, Hunter & Malecki, Mpls., 1979-99; of counsel Gislason & Hunter, 1999—; chmn. bd. dirs. Chgo. Milw. Corp., 1977-81; pres. Chgo. Milw. R.R., 1977-81; bd. dirs. First Security Bank, Chgo.; bd. dirs., officer First Security Bancorp, Inc., Chgo., 1993—; bd. dirs., sec. Wirtz Corp., Chgo. Blackhawk Hockey Team and related cos. Fellow Am. Coll. Trial Lawyers; mem. ABA, Am. Judicature Soc., Minn. Bar Assn. (bd. of govs. 1973-76), 5th Dist. Bar Assn. (pres. 1971-72), Hennepin County Bar Assn., Minn. Def. Lawyers Assn. (bd. dirs. 1976), Internat. Assn. Ins. Counsel, U.S. Supreme Ct. Hist. Assn. Office: Gislason & Hunter PO Box 5297 9900 Bren Rd E Ste 215E Hopkins MN 55343-9666

HUNTER, DOUGLAS LEE, media executive, former elevator company executive; b. Greeley, Colo., May 3, 1948; s. Delmer Eural and Helen Converse (Haines) H.; m. Janet Lee Snook, May 26, 1970; children: Darin Douglas, Joel Christopher, Eric Andrew, Jennifer Lee. Student, Phillips U., Enid, Okla., 1979; postgrad., N.Am. Bapt. Sem., Sioux Falls, S.D., 1977-79. Elevator constructor Carter Elevator Co., Inc., Sioux Falls, 1971-72, rep., 1972-74, contr., 1974-78, sec.-treas., 1978-82, v.p., 1982-87, pres., 1987-93; ptnr. Lifters Ltd., Sioux Falls, 1984-90, CEO, 1987-96; bd. dirs. Home Fed. Savs. Bank, HF Fin. Corp.; U.S. del. Forum Bus. in Vietnam, Ho Chi Minh City, 1993; guest lectr. Nat. Econs. U., Hanoi, Vietnam, 1995. Mem. gen. bd. Christian Ch., Indpls., 1984-88; mem. regional bd. Christian Ch. in the Upper Midwest, Des Moines, 1985-87; bd. dirs. Glory House, Sioux Falls, 1983-86; leader Bible Study Fellowship, Sioux Falls, 1981-92; vice chmn. Greater Sioux Empire Billy Graham Crusade, 1986-87; mem. internat. bd. dirs. Fellowship of Cos. for Christ Internat., 1993-95, v.p., 1994-97; pres. Media Asia, Inc., Atlanta, 1998—; bd. dirs. Am. Mongolia Found., 1992-99; active S.D. Trade Del. to Mongolia, 1993-99; trustee N.Am. Bapt. Sem., 1989—; bd. dirs. Providence Christian Acad., 1998—, chmn., 1999—. Named Outstanding Young Religious Leader Sioux Falls Jaycees, 1974. Mem. S.D. Family Bus. Coun., Sen. Larry Pressler's Small Bus. Adv. Com., Nat. Assn. Elevator Contrs., Nat. Assn. Elevator Safety Authorities, Constrn. Specifications Inst., Christian Businessmen's Com. U.S., Sioux Falls C. of C. Republican. Avocations: golf, tennis, reading, music. Home: 695 Wyndham Place Cir Lawrenceville GA 30044-3629 Office: Media Asia Inc Atlanta GA 30044

HUNTER, DUNCAN LEE, congressman; b. Riverside, Calif., May 31, 1948; m. Lynne Layh, 1973; children: Robert Samuel, Duncan Duane. J.D., Western State U., 1976. Bar: Calif. 1976. Practiced in San Diego; mem. 97th Congress from 42d Dist. Calif., 98th-106th Congresses from 45th Dist. Calif., 1980—, 103d-105th Congress from 52d Calif. dist.; mem. nat. security com., subcom. mil. installations and facilities, chmn. subcom. on mil. procurement, subcom. on mil. pers. Served with U.S. Army, 1969-71, Vietnam. Decorated Air medal, Bronze Star. Mem. Navy League. Republican. Baptist. *

HUNTER, DURANT ADAMS, executive search company executive; b. North Adams, Mass., Nov. 25, 1948; s. Richard Andrew and Lucy (Adams) H.; m. Sara Hoagland, June 10, 1978; children: John, Abigail. AB, U. N.C., 1971; MPA, George Washington U., 1973. Staff asst. to Congressman Silvio O. Conte U.S. Ho. of Reps., Washington, 1971-72; program dir. Internat. Mgmt. and Devel. Inst., Washington, 1973-74; asst. v.p. J.P. Morgan Co., N.Y.C., 1974-81; v.p., COO James Hunter Machine Co., North Adams, 1981-83; exec. v.p. HM Internat., Wellesley, Mass., 1983-85; mng. dir. Boyden Internat., Boston, 1985-89; ptnr. Gardiner Stone Hunter Internat., Boston, 1989-92; pres., CEO Pendleton James Assocs. Inc., Boston, 1992—. Mem. Wellesley Planning Bd., 1983-86; bd. dirs., vice chmn. Boys and Girls Clubs, Boston, 1988—, Wide Horizons Children's Svcs., Waltham, Mass., 1989—, Mass. Cultural Coun.; trustee The Wang Ctr. for the Performing Arts, Boston, 1995—; bd. dirs. Mass. Cultural Coun. Mem. Bus. Assocs. Club (pres. 1989), Univ. Club, The Country Club, The Economic Club N.Y. Home: 153 Ridgeway Rd Weston MA 02493-2724 Office: 1 International Pl Boston MA 02110-2602

HUNTER, EARLE LESLIE, III, professional association executive; b. Juneau, Alaska, Nov. 23, 1929; s. Earle and Mary Uinta (Kirk) H.; m. Helen Doreen Dawson, Jan. 19, 1954; children: Barbara, James, Robert. BS, Ill. Coll. Optometry, Chgo., 1956, O.D., 1957, D.O.S., 1988, D.O.S., New England Coll. of Optometry, 1995. Practice optometry, Juneau, 1957-59, McMinnville, Oreg., 1959-71; dir. clinics Pacific U., Forest Grove, Oreg., 1971-74; dir. primary care Am. Optometric Assn., St. Louis, 1974-78, asst. exec. dir., 1978-84, interim exec. dir., 1984-85, dep. exec. dir., 1985-87, exec. dir., 1987-95; sec. Z.80 com. Am. Nat. Standards Inst., 1974-95. Contbr. articles to profl. jours. County chmn. various gubernatorial campaigns; vice chmn. Oreg. Health Commn., 1971-74. Named Optometrist of Yr., Oreg. Optometric Assn., 1971, Jr. Citizen of Yr., Jaycees, McMinnville, Oreg., 1961. Fellow Am. Acad. Optometry, Am. Pub. Health Assn.; mem. Optical Soc. Am., St. Louis Soc. Assn. Execs. (pres. 1983-84), Am. Soc. Assn. Execs. (com. 1981-93), U.S. C. of C. (assn. com.), Tomb and Key, Beta Sigma Kappa. Republican. Episcopalian. Clubs: University (St. Louis). Lodges: Masons, Elks. Avocations: sailing, golf. Home: 213 Orchard Ave Saint Louis MO 63119-2523

HUNTER, EDWIN FORD, JR., federal judge; b. Alexandria, La., Feb. 18, 1911; s. Edwin Ford and Amelia (French) H.; m. Shirley Kidd, Nov. 9, 1941; children—Edwin Kidd, Janin, Kelley. Student, La. State U., 1930-33; LL.B., George Washington U., 1938. Bar: La. bar 1938. Mem. firm Smith, Hunter, Risinger & Shuey, Shreveport, 1940-53; mem. La. Legislature, 1948-52; exec. counsel Gov. La., 1952-53; mem. La. State Mineral Bd., 1952; judge, now sr. judge U.S. Dist. Ct., Western Dist. La., 1953—, also mem. adv. com. on civil rules., 1971-76. Served as lt. USNR, 1942-45. Mem. Am. Bar Assn. (La. state chmn. jr. bar sect. 1945), Am. Legion (post comdr. 1945, judge adv. Dept. La. 1948), Sigma Chi. Roman Catholic. Home: 1000 Bayou Oak Ln Lake Charles LA 70605-2634 Office: US Dist Ct 611 Broad St Ste 243 Lake Charles LA 70601-4380

HUNTER, ELMO BOLTON, federal judge; b. St. Louis, Oct. 23, 1915; s. David Riley and Della (Bolton) H.; m. Shirley Arnold, Apr. 5, 1952; 1 child, Nancy Ann (Mrs. Ray Lee Hunt). AB, U. Mo., 1936, LLB, 1938; Cook Grad. fellow, U. Mich., 1941; PhD (hon.), Coll. of Ozarks, 1988. Bar: Mo. 1938. Pvt. practice Kansas City, 1938-45; sr. asst. city counselor, 1939-40; ptnr. Sebree, Shook, Hardy and Hunter, 1945-51; state circuit judge Mo., 1951-57; Mo. appellate judge, 1957-65; judge U.S. Dist. Ct., Kansas City, Mo., 1965—, now sr. judge; instr. law U. Mo., 1952-62; mem. jud. selection Elmo B. Hunter Citizens Ctr., Am. Judicature Soc. Contbr. articles to profl. jours. Mem. Bd. Police Commrs., 1949-51; Trustee Kansas City U., Coll. of Ozarks; fellow William Rockhill Nelson Gallery Art. 1st lt. M.I., AUS, 1943-46. Recipient 1st Ann. Law Day award U. Mo., 1964, Charles E. Whittaker award, 1994, SAR Law Enforcement Commendation medal, 1994, citation of Merit Mo. Law Sch., 1996. Fellow ABA; mem. Fed., Mo. bar assns., Jud. Conf. U.S. (mem. long range planning com., chmn. ct. adminstrn. com.), Am. Judicature Soc. (bd. govs., mem. exec. com., pres., chmn. bd., Devitt Disting. Svc. to Justice award 1987), Acad. Mo. Squires, Order of Coif, Phi Beta Kappa, Phi Delta Phi. Presbyterian (elder). Office: US Dist Ct 659 US Courthouse 811 Grand Blvd Ste 201 Kansas City MO 64106-1904

HUNTER, FORREST WALKER, lawyer; b. Arlington, Va., Jan. 25, 1950; s. Dallas Walker and Ann Arsell (Wheat) H.; m. Susan Gladys Zsamer, June 8, 1974; children: Andrew Chastain, Alison Christian. BA, U. Va., 1972; JD, Emory U., 1975. Bar: Ga. 1975, U.S. Dist. Ct. (no. dist.) Ga. 1978, U.S. Ct. Appeals (5th cir.) 1978, U.S. Ct. Appeals (11th cir.) 1981, U.S. Dist. Ct. (mid. dist.) Ga. 1982, U.S. Dist. Ct. (so. dist.) Ga. 1983, U.S. Ct. Appeals (6th cir.) 1988, U.S. Dist. Ct. (we. dist.) Mich. 1994, U.S. Ct. Appeals (7th cir.) 1996. Atty. Office Chief Counsel IRS, Dept. Treasurey, Washington, 1975-77; sr. atty. Office. Regional Counsel IRS, Dept. Treasurey, Atlanta, 1977-81; assoc. Jones, Bird & Howell and Alston & Bird, Atlanta, 1981-85; ptnr. Alston & Bird, Atlanta, 1985—. Bd. dirs. Boys and Girls Clubs of Metro Atlanta, 1984. Mem. Am. Acad. Hosp. Attys., Ga. Acad. Hosp. Attys., Lawyers Club Atlanta, Atlanta Bar Assn., U. Va. Alumni Assn., Emory U. Alumni Assn. Office: Alston & Bird 1 Atlantic Ctr 1201 W Peachtree St NW Ste 4200 Atlanta GA 30309-3424

HUNTER, FRANK A., secondary education educator; b. Torrington, Wyo., May 9, 1936; s. Raymond S. and Lois B. (Sawyer) H. BA, Hastings (Nebr.) Coll., 1958; MA, U. Nebr., Lincoln, 1962. Cert. secondary tchr., Colo. Tchr. English, speech and theatre Gering (Nebr.) H.S., 1958-61; with scenery shop U. Nebr., Lincoln, 1961-62; tchr. speech and theatre Sterling (Colo.) H.S., 1965—, chair creative arts dept., 1966-89. Served with U.S. Army, 1962-65, Europe. Named Star Tchr., C. of C., 1980. Mem. NEA, Masons, Elks, Lions Internat. (sec. 1972-76), Am. Legion. Office: 400 W Broadway St Sterling CO 80751-3052

HUNTER, GARRETT BELL, investment banker; b. N.Y.C., Apr. 11, 1937; s. John W. and Helene (Bond Lipe) H.; m. Lynn M. Cowell, Oct. 6, 1962; children: Lee, Andrew, Sarah. AB in Philosphy, Brown U., 1960; MBA in Fin., NYU, 1965; postgrad., Stonier Grad. Sch. Banking, 1973. V.p. Midlantic Nat. Bank, Newark, 1960-73, Nat. State Bank, Elizabeth, N.J., 1973-77; sr. v.p. R.I. Hosp. Trust Nat. Bank, Providence, 1977-89; pres. Bus. Devel. Co. of R.I., 1989—; bd. dirs. Lab-Volt, Farmingdale, N.J., Bus. Devel. Co. of R.I., Providence, R.I., Atlantek, Inc., Wakefield, R.I. Home: 150 Tamarack Dr East Greenwich RI 02818-2204

HUNTER, HARLEN CHARLES, orthopedic surgeon; b. Estherville, Iowa, Sept. 23, 1940; s. Roy Harold and Helen Iola (King) H.; m. JoAnn Wilson, June 30, 1962; children: Harlen Todd, Juliann Kristin. BA, Drake U., 1962; DO, Coll. Osteo. Med. and Surgery, Des Moines, 1967. Diplomate Am. Osteo. Bd. Orthop. Surgery, Am. Osteo. Acad. Sports Medicine. Intern Normandy Osteo. Hosp., St. Louis, 1967-68, resident in orthops., 1968-72, chmn. dept. orthops., 1976-77; founder, orthop. surgeon Mid-States Orthop. Sports Medicine Clinics of Am., Ltd. SPORTS Med. Ctrs., Chesterfield, Mo., Fairview Heights, Ill., Jerseyville, Ill., Herman, Mo., 1977—, Hunter Trauma Team, 1988-92; founder, pres. Life Style Health Systems, 1992; assoc. prof. orthop. Kansas City Coll. Osteopathy, 1993; adj. prof. Lake Erie Coll. Osteo. Medicine, 1995—; mem. staff Outpatient Surgery Ctr., St. Louis, Luth. Med. Ctr., St. Joe's of Kirkwood; clin. instr. Kirksville Coll. Osteo. Medicine; orthop. cons., team physician to high schs.; pres. Health Specialists, Inc.; program dir. sports medicine Family Physicians, 1993, 94; sponsor, lectr. sports and occupl. emergency medicine, 1997—; host weekly TV program Raceology Weekly Spl. on Motorsports; mem. med. adv. bd. Mo. Athletic Activities Assn.; cons. sports medicine Sports St. Louis newspaper; founder Ann. Sports Medicine Clinic for Trainers and Coaches, 1 yr. fellowship in sports medicine; nat. lectr. various social, profl. orgns.; adj. clin. assoc. prof. Coll. Osteo. Surgery, Des Moines; orthop. surgeon Iowa State Boys Basketball Tournament, 1966-85; founder Mobile Sports Medicine Semi Truck, 1988, Hunter Sports Medicine Clinic, Belleville, Ill.; sponsor U.S. Biathalon Assn., 1989; staff photographer Internat. Speedway, 1973—, Daytona Internat. Speedway, 1979-96; adv. bd. Motorsport Rsch. Group Human Performance Internat., Daytona Beach, Fla., 1990—. Co-author: Motorsports Medicine, 1992; contbr. articles to profl. jours. Recipient Clinic Spkr. award Iowa H.S. Baseball Coaches Assn., 1982, 83, Hall of Fame award Mo. Athletic Trainers Assn., 1987, Sibley Medallion award for outstanding svc. Lindenwood U., Ann. Outstanding Soccer Player of Yr. award Mo. Athletic Club, Hunter 100 Stock Car Race, Peveley, Mo.; Harlen C. Hunter Sports Complex named in his honor Lindenwood U., St. Charles, Mo., 1988. Fellow Am. Coll. Osteo. Surgeons, Am. Osteo Acad. Orthops. (past chmn. com. on athletic injuries), Am. Osteo. Acad. Sports Medicine; mem. Am. Osteo. Assn., Mo. Assn. Osteo. Physicians and Surgeons (medallion award 1990), Am. Coll. Sports Medicine, Am. Orthop. Soc. Sports Medicine (del. sports medicine exch. program to China 1985), AMA, Am. Coll. Occupational Medicine, St. Louis Met. Med. Assn., Sports Car Club Am. (med. dir. pro racing 1989-91), World Congree Motorsport Scis., St. Louis Auto Racing Club (Amb. award 1989, 91), 500 Old Timers Club, The Butler Soc., Masons, Shriners. Republican. Methodist. Home: 1230 Walnut Hill Farm Dr Chesterfield MO 63005-4524 Office: Hunter SPORTS Med Ctr 13355 Olive Blvd Chesterfield MO 63017-3108

HUNTER, HENLEY A., federal judge; b. 1944. BA, U. Ark., 1966; JD, La. State U., 1969. Law clk. La. Ct. Appeals (2d cir.), 1969; ptnr. Eatman & Hunter, 1970-87; chief bankruptcy judge U.S. Dist. Ct. (we. dist.) La., Alexandria, 1987—. Mem. ABA, La. State Bar Assn., Alexandria Bar Assn., Am. Judicature Soc., Nat. Conf. Bankruptcy Judges. Fax: (318) 443-8195. Office: US Dist Ct (we dist) La 300 Jackson St Alexandria VA 71301

HUNTER, HERBERT ERWIN, aerospace engineer; b. Washington, June 11, 1934; s. Herbert C. and A. Paula (Dieterich) H.; m. Helen Louise Shelhorse, June 11, 1956 (div. 1978); children: Erwin, David, Shirley Black, Patricia Copeland, Linda Markiewicz; m. Jeanne Theresa Parent, Nov. 25, 1978; stepchildren: Richard Kinsella, William Kinsella, Katey McMahon, Philip Kinsella. BS in Aerospace Engring., U. Md., 1956; MS in Aerospace Engring., Calif. Inst. Tech., Pasadena, 1957, PhD in Aerospace Engring., 1960. Dept. mgr. AVCO Corp., Wilmington, Mass., 1963-73; pres., founder, chmn. bd. dirs. Adapt Svc. Corp., Reading, Mass., 1973-83; assoc. fellow Nichols Rsch. Corp., Huntsville, Ala., 1983-94; pres., co-founder Applied Data Trends, Inc., Huntsville, 1994—, dir., 1994—. Contbr. articles to Jour. Aerospace Scis., Jour. Math Physics, Jour. Climate Applied Meteorology, Jour. Atmospheric Ocean Tech. With USAF, 1960-63. Mem. AAAS, AIAA, Am. Meteorol. Soc., Soc. of Photo-Optical Instrumentation Engrs. Baptist. Home: 8912 Hogan Dr SE Huntsville AL 35802-3436 Office: Applied Data Trends Inc PO Box 4445 Huntsville AL 35815-4445

HUNTER, JACK DUVAL, lawyer; b. Elkhart, Ind., Jan. 14, 1937; s. William Stanley and Marjorie Irene (Upson) H.; m. Marsha Ann Goodsell, Nov. 14, 1958; children: Jack, Jon, Justin. BBA, U. Mich., 1959, LLB, 1961. Bar: Mich. 1961, Ind. 1962. Atty. Lincoln Nat. Life Ins. Co., Ft. Wayne, Ind., 1961-64, asst. counsel, 1964-68, v.p., gen. counsel, 1975-79, sr. v.p., gen. counsel, 1979-86, exec. v.p., gen. counsel, 1986—; asst. gen. counsel, asst. sec. Lincoln Nat. Corp., Ft. Wayne and Phila., 1968-71, gen. counsel, 1971—, v.p., 1972-79, sr. v.p., 1979-86, exec. v.p., 1986—,. Life trustee Ind. Nature Conservancy, chmn. bd. trustees, 1993-95. Recipient Oak Leaf award Nature Conservancy, 1997. Mem. ABA, Ind. State Bar Assn., Allen County Bar Assn., Assn. Life Ins. Counsel (pres. 1995-96), Am. Coun. Life Ins. (chmn. legal sect. 1991). Office: Lincoln Nat Corp 1500 Market St Ste 3900 Philadelphia PA 19102-2112

HUNTER, JACK DUVAL, II, lawyer; b. Ann Arbor, Mich., July 15, 1959; s. Jack Duval and Marsha Ann (Goodsell) H.; m. Denise Marie Hodge, June 27, 1981; children: Adam Duval, Benjamin Robert. BSCE, Purdue U., 1982, MSCE, 1984; JD, St. Mary's U., 1986. Bar: Tex. 1986, U.S. Dist. Ct. (so. dist.) Tex. 1987, U.S. Ct. Appeals (5th cir.) 1987, U.S. Supreme Ct. 1990; engr. in tng., Ind., Tex. Assoc. Johnson & Davis, Harlingen, Tex., 1986-88; asst. dist. atty. Hidalgo County Courthouse, Edinburg, Tex., 1989-91; gen. atty. Immigration and Naturalization Svc., 1991-93; pvt. practice lawyer Harlingen, Tex., 1993—, Edinburg, 1996—; adj. prof. Reynaldo G. Garza Sch. of Law, 1989-91. Assoc. editor St. Mary's Law Jour., 1984-86. Bd. dirs. Harlingen Boys' and Girls' Club, 1987-88. Mem. NRA (life), Coll. State Bar Tex., State Bar Tex. (adminstrn. of rules and evidence com.), Cameron County Bar Assn., Hidalgo County Bar Assn., Juvenile Ct. Conf. Com. (lectr. 1990), Tex. State Rifle Assn. (life), Buckmasters (life), Valley Sportsmen Club of the Lower Rio Grande Valley (life), Order of Barristers, Whittington Ctr. (life), Phi Delta Phi. Democrat. Baptist. Fax: 956-383-3736. Office: 204 E Cano St Edinburg TX 78539-4510

HUNTER, JAIRY C., JR., academic administrator; b. Feb. 27, 1942; married; two children. Student, U. S.C., Lancaster, 1965-66; AA in Acctg. magna cum laude, Wingate (N.C.) Coll., 1967; BS cum laude, Appalachian State U., Boone, N.C., 1969, MA, 1970, MA in Bus. Adminstrn., 1971; PhD, Duke U., Durham, N.C., 1977. Pres. Charleston Southern U., Charleston, S.C., 1984—; lectr. in field. Mem. Assn. S.C. Coll. & Univ. Pres's. (pres.), Assn. Colls. & Univs. South (pres.), Alpha Chi, Kappa Delta Pi. Home: 103 Hutchinson Ln Summerville SC 29483-3774 Office: Charleston So U Office of Pres PO Box 118087 Charleston SC 29423-8087*

HUNTER, JAMES AUSTEN, JR., lawyer; b. Phoenix, June 19, 1941; s. James Austen and Elizabeth Aileen (Holt) H.; m. Donna Gabriele, Aug. 24, 1973; 1 child, James A. A.B., Cath. U. Am., 1963, LL.B., 1966. Bar: N.Y. 1967, Pa. 1975, U.S. Supreme Ct. 1974. Assoc. firm Sullivan & Cromwell, N.Y.C., 1967-74; assoc. firm Morgan, Lewis & Bockius, Phila., 1974-77; ptnr. Morgan, Lewis & Bockius, 1977—. Home: 1001 Red Rose Ln Villanova PA 19085-2118 Office: Morgan Lewis & Bockius 1701 Market St Philadelphia PA 19103

HUNTER, JAMES D. (JIM), brigadier general Canadian Air Force; b. Manitoba, Can., June 9, 1949. BA in History with hons., U. Manitoba, 1971; MA in Mil. History, U. Ala., 1984. Enrolled officer cadet Canadian Forces, 1968, advanced through grades to brigadier gen., 1998, helicopter pilot, flying instr. various stas., 1971-80; career mgr. Helicopter Comty., 1980-83; posted to U.S. Air Force Command and Staff Coll. Maxwell AFB, Ala., 1983-84; flight comdr., dep. commanding officer 408th Tactical Heliocopter Sqdn., Canadian Forces, Edmonton, Alberta, Can., 1984-85; comdr. 408th Tactical Heliocopter Sqdn., Canadian Forces, Edmonton, 1985-86; attaché Can. Forces Czech, Slovak and Hungarian Republics,, various cities, 1990-93; dep. chief staff tng. Air Command Hdqtrs., Winnipeg, Manitoba, Can., 1993-95; dep. chief of staff pers. Air Command Hdqtrs., Winnipeg, 1995-96; wing comdr. 15th Win, Moose Jaw, Sasktchwn., Can., 1996-98; dep. comdr. Continental N.Am. Aerospace Defense Command Region, Tyndall AFB, Fla., 1998—; dep. Canadian contingent comdr. and commanding officer Rotary Wing Aviation Unit Multinat. Force and Observers in Sinai Peninsula, Egypt, 1986. Decorated Multi-nat. Forces and Observers medal, Can. Forces Decoration with Clasp. Office: Cont US NORAD Office Pub Affairs 501 Illinois Ave Ste 1 Tyndall AFB FL 32403-5549

HUNTER, JAMES GALBRAITH, JR., lawyer; b. Phila., Jan. 6, 1942; s. James Galbraith and Emma Margaret (Jehl) H.; m. Pamela Ann Trott, July 18, 1969 (div.); children: James Nicholas, Catherine Selene; m. Nancy Grace Scheurwater, June 21, 1992. B.S. in Engring. Sci., Case Inst. Tech., 1965; J.D., U. Chgo., 1967. Bar: Ill. 1967, U.S. Dist. Ct. (no. dist.) Ill. 1967, U.S. Ct. Appeals (7th cir.) 1967, U.S. Ct. Claims, 1976, U.S. Ct. Appeals (4th and 9th cirs.) 1978, U.S. Supreme Ct. 1979, U.S. Dist. Ct. (cen. dist.) Ill. 1980, Calif. 1980, U.S. Dist. Ct. (cen. and so. dists.) Calif. 1980, U.S. Ct. Appeals (5th cir.) 1982, U.S. Ct. Appeals (fed. cir.) 1982. Assoc. Kirkland & Ellis, Chgo., 1967-68, 70-73, ptnr., 1973-76; ptnr. Hedlund, Hunter & Lynch, Chgo., 1976-82, Los Angeles, 1979-82; ptnr. Latham & Watkins, Hedlund, Hunter & Lynch, Chgo. and Los Angeles, 1982—. Served to lt. JAGC, USN, 1968-70. Mem. ABA, State Bar Calif., Los Angeles County Bar Assn., Chgo. Bar Assn. Clubs: Metropolitan (Chgo.), Chgo. Athletic Assn., Los Angeles Athletic. Exec. editor U. Chgo. Law Rev., 1966-67. Office: Latham & Watkins Sears Tower Ste 5800 Chicago IL 60606-6306 also: 633 W 5th St Los Angeles CA 90071-2005

HUNTER, J(AMES) PAUL, English language educator, literary critic, historian; b. Jamestown, N.Y., June 29, 1934; s. Paul W. and Florence I. (Walmer) H.; m. Kathryn Montgomery, July 1, 1971; children: Debra, Lisa, Paul III, Anne, Ellen Harris. A.B., Ind. Central Coll., 1955; M.A., Miami U., Oxford, Ohio, 1957; Ph.D., Rice U., 1963. Instr. U. Fla., Gainesville, 1957-59; instr. Williams Coll., Williamstown, Mass., 1962-64; asst. prof. U. Calif., Riverside, 1964-66; assoc. prof. English Emory U., Atlanta, 1966-68, prof., 1968-80, chmn. dept., 1973-79; prof. English, dean Coll. Arts and Sci., U. Rochester, N.Y., 1981-86; prof. English U. Chgo., 1987—, Chester D. Tripp prof. humanities, 1990-96, Barbara E. and Richard J. Franke prof. humanities, 1996—; dir. Chgo. Humanities Inst., 1996—; gen. editor Bedford Cultural Edits., 1994—. Author: The Reluctant Pilgrim, 1966, Occasional Form, 1975, Norton Introduction to Poetry, 7th edit., 1998, Norton Introduction to Literature, 7th edit., 1999, New Worlds of Literature, 2d edit., 1994, Before Novels, 1990; co-editor: Rhetorics of Order/Ordering Rhetorics, 1989; editor: Norton Critical Edition of Mary Shelley's Frankenstein, 1996. Guggenheim fellow, 1976-77, NEH fellow, 1985-86, Nat. Humanities Ctr. fellow, 1986, 95-96. Mem. MLA, Am. Soc. 18th Century Studies (Louis Gottschalk prize 1991, 2d v.p. 1994-95, 1st v.p. 1995-96, pres. 1996-97), Southeastern Am. Soc. 18th Century Studies (pres. 1977-78), So. Atlantic MLA (pres. 1992-93), N.E. Am. Soc. 18th Century Studies (pres. 1982-83). Office: U Chgo Dept English 404 Wieboldt Hall Chicago IL 60637

HUNTER, JOEL CARL, clergyman, educator; b. Shelby, Ohio, Apr. 18, 1948; s. Wilbur Westerman and Jean Ellen (Bashore) H.; m. Becky Gaylene Beeson, July 2, 1972; children: Joshua, Isaac, Joel. BS in Edn., Ohio U., 1970; MDiv, Christian Theol. Sem., Indpls., 1973, D Ministry, 1974. Ordained to ministry United Meth. Ch., 1975. Assoc. min. Bradley United Meth. Ch., Greenfield, Ind., 1970-71, Southport (Ind.) United Meth. Ch., 1971-74; sr. min. Faith United Meth. Ch., Princeton, Ind., 1974-78, Mt. Auburn United Meth. Ch., Greenwood, Ind., 1978-85, Northland Cmty. Ch., Longwood, Fla., 1985—; chmn. Min.'s Forum, Orlando, Fla., 1993—; adj. prof. practical theology Ref. Theol. Sem., Orlando; bd. dirs. Gospel to the Unreached Millions. Author: Prayer, Politics, and Power, 1988, The Challenging Road, 1995, Finding Your Purpose, 1995, Overcoming Adversity, 1996, Learning to Love, 1997, Transforming Faith, 1998; also articles; radio broadcast Fit for the Journey, 1996—. Bd. dirs. Liberty Coun., Orlando, 1994-97; cons. Cmty. Issues Forum, Orlando, 1993—, Interfaith Alliance, Orlando, 1995; tchr. Worldview Seminar, Orlando, 1995; chmn. Northland Found. for Arts and Edn., Longwood, 1995—; paradigm Pioneer Leadership Network, Tyler, Tex., 1995—. Avocations: mentoring, art student, weightlifting, running. Office: Northland Cmty Ch 530 Dog Track Rd Longwood FL 32750-6546*

HUNTER, JOHN GERARD, plastic surgeon; b. N.Y.C., Oct. 6, 1955; s. Vincent Ambrose and Ann Theresa (Milligan) H.; m. Ann Mary DiMaio, Sept. 18, 1982 (div. 1991). BS, Fordham U., 1977; MD magna cum laude, SUNY, Bklyn., 1983. Diplomate Nat. Bd. Med. Examiners, Am. Bd. Plastic Surgery. Intern, resident in surgery Mt. Sinai Med. Ctr., N.Y.C., 1983-86; resident, chief resident in plastic surgery SUNY Health Sci. Ctr., Bklyn., 1986-88, clin. instr. plastic surgery, 1988-91, clin. asst. prof. plastic surgery, 1991-96; asst. attending surgeon St. Luke's-Roosevelt Hosp. Ctr., N.Y.C., 1990—, Cabrini Med. Ctr., N.Y.C., 1988-92, Beekman Downtown Hosp., N.Y.C., 1988-93, 1988-94, assoc. attending surgeon, 1994-96; attending and chief plastic surgery N.Y. Meth. Hosp.; clin. asst. prof. plastic surgery Cornell U., 1996—; plastic surgery cons. N.Y.-N.J. Knights, 1991-93. Contbr. articles to profl. jours. Mosby scholar Mosby Pub. Co., 1983. Fellow ACS, Am. Acad. Pediatrics, N.Y. Acad. Medicine; mem. AMA, Am. Soc. Plastic and Reconstructive Surgeons, N.Y. Regional Soc. Plastic and Reconstructive Surgery (treas. 1997-99), N.Y. Surg. Soc., Am. Soc. Aesthetic Plastic Surgery, Alpha Omega Alpha. Home: 400 E 52nd St Apt 17D New York NY 10022-6411

HUNTER, J(OHN) ROBERT, insurance consumer advocate; b. New Orleans, Nov. 20, 1936; s. J. Robert and Alberta M. (Cox) H.; m. Carole A. Means, Mar. 6, 1976; children: Laura Jeanne, James Douglas, John Robert, III. BS, Clarkson Coll. Tech., 1958; grad. Program for Sr. Mgrs., Harvard U., 1976. Dir. of ins. Atlantic Mut. Ins. Co., 1960-61; supervisory actuary Ins. Svcs. Office, N.Y.C., 1961-67; asst. actuary Mut. Ins. Rating Bur., N.Y.C., 1967-71; chief actuary Fed. Ins. Adminstrn., HUD, Washington, 1971-74; acting adminstr. Fed. Ins. Adminstrn., HUD, 1974-76, adminstr., 1976-77, dep. fed. ins. adminstr., 1977-80; founder, pres. Nat. Ins. Consumer Orgn., 1980-93; ins. commr. State of Tex., 1993-94; dir. ins. Consumer Fedn. Am., Arlington, Va., 1994—. Author: Taking the Bite Out of Insurance, 1980, Profitability and Investment Income in Property Casualty Insurance, 1983, Insurance in California, 1986, Pay at the Pump Private No Fault Auto Insurance, 1992, Proposition 103 Revisited: A Consumer Triumph, 1993, Auto Insurance, Progress but More to Be Done, 1995, America's Distrous Disaster Insurance System, 1998. Pres. Freeport (N.Y.) Cmty. Chorale, 1970-71; pres., founder Rockville (Md.) Musical Theatre, 1974-75; vestryman Christ Ch., Alexandria, 1982-84, 91-93. Recipient award for excellence Sec.

HUD, 1977. Fellow Casualty Actuarial Soc.; mem. Am. Acad. Actuaries, Internat. Actuarial Assn. Home: 2202 N 24th St Arlington VA 22207

HUNTER, JUANITA K., nurse, educator; b. Buffalo, Feb. 12; d. Albert and Mamie (Lang) Kirkland; widowed; children: Jeffery Alan, Wayne Bernard, Gail Deneen. Diploma, Edward J. Meyer Meml. Hosp., 1950; BS, SUNY, Buffalo, 1971, MSN, 1974, EdD, 1983. Staff nurse Erie County Dept. Health, Buffalo, asst. clin. dir.; pub. health nurse coord. Buffalo VA Med. Ctr.; clin. assoc. prof. SUNY, Buffalo; project dir. Nursing Ctr. for Homeless. Contbr. articles to profl. publs. Grantee HHS, 1987-93. Mem. Fellow Am. Acad. Nursing; mem. ANA (chair cabinet on human rights 1983-87), N.Y. State Nurses Assn. (pres. 1987-89), Sigma Theta Tau (disting. lectr. 1989-99). Home: 114 Century Rd Buffalo NY 14215-1357

HUNTER, KERMIT, writer, former university dean; b. Hallsville, W.Va., Oct. 3, 1910; s. Otis John and Lillian Elizabeth Robinson (Farley) H. B.A., Ohio State U., 1931; M.A. in Theatre, U. N.C., 1949, Ph.D. in English Lit, 1956; D.Litt., Emory and Henry Coll., 1958; L.H.D., Okla. Christian Coll., 1971. Successively newspaper reporter C. of C. sec.; choir dir., organist, and piano study Juilliard Inst., 1931-40; bus. mgr. N.C. Symphony Orch., 1946; prof. drama Hollins Coll., Va., 1956-64; first dean Meadows Sch. Arts, So. Methodist U., Dallas, 1964-76; writer in residence So. Methodist U., 1976-78; sr. lectr. U. Tex., Arlington, 1978-93. Author, producer more than 40 hist. dramas, especially Unto These Hills, 1950, with total audience over 14 million. Served to lt. col. AUS, 1940-45. Decorated Legion of Merit. Home: 10412 Stone Canyon Rd #101N Dallas TX 75230-4834 *"A thing of beauty is a joy forever; its loveliness increases; it wll never pass into nothingness; but still will keep a bower quiet for us, and a sleep full of sweet dreams, and health, and quiet breathing." John Keats.*

HUNTER, KIM (JANET COLE), actress; b. Detroit, Nov. 12, 1922; d. Donald and Grace Mabel (Lind) Cole; m. William A. Baldwin, Feb. 11, 1944 (div. 1946); 1 dau., Kathryn Emmett; m. Robert Emmett, Dec. 20, 1951; 1 son, Sean Emmett. Ed. pub. schs.; student acting with, Charmine Lantaff Camine, 1938-40, Actors Studio. First stage appearance, 1939; played in stock, 1940-42; Broadway debut in A Streetcar Named Desire, 1947; appeared in (tour) Two Blind Mice, 1950, Darkness at Noon, N.Y.C., 1951, The Chase, 1952, N.Y.C., They Knew What They Wanted, N.Y.C., 1952, The Children's Hour, N.Y.C., 1952, The Tender Trap, N.Y.C., 1954, Write Me a Murder, N.Y.C., 1961, Weekend, N.Y.C., 1968, The Penny Wars, N.Y.C., 1969, (tour) And Miss Reardon Drinks a Little, 1971-72, The Glass Menagerie, Atlanta, 1973, The Women, N.Y.C., 1973, (tour) In Praise of Love, 1975, The Lion in Winter, N.J., 1975, The Cherry Orchard, N.Y.C., 1976, The Chalk Garden, Pa., 1976, Elizabeth the Queen, Buffalo, 1977, Semmelweiss, Buffalo, 1977, The Belle of Amherst, N.J., 1978, N.H., 1986, The Little Foxes, Mass., 1980, To Grandmother's House We Go, N.Y.C, 1980, Another Part of the Forest, Seattle, 1981, Ghosts, 1982, Territorial Rites, 1983, Death of a Salesman, 1983, Cat on a Hot Tin Roof, 1984, Life with Father, 1984, Sabrina Fair, 1984, Faulkner's Bicycle, 1985, Antique Pink, 1985, A Delicate Balance, 1986, Painting Churches, 1986, Jokers, 1986, Remembrance, 1987, Man and Superman, 1987-88, N.Y.C., The Gin Game, Lancaster, Pa., 1988, A Murder of Crows, N.Y.C., 1988, Watch on the Rhine, 1989, Suddenly Last Summer, 1991, A Smaller Place, 1991, Open Window, Houston, 1992, The Cocktail Hour, Pitts., 1992, The Belle of Amherst, Vero Beach., Fla., Palm Beach, Fla., Chester, Mass., 1992, Conn., 1993, The Eye of the Beholder, N.Y.C., 1993, Love Letters, Springfield, Mass., 1993, Worcester, Mass., 1993, Northhampton, Mass., 1994, Do Not Go Gentle, Bristol, Pa., 1994, The Gin Game, Chester, Mass., 1994—, tour, 1994-95, All the Way Home, Williamstown, Mass., 1995, The Children's Hour, Conn. Repertory Theatre, 1995, Middlesex Canal, N.Y.C., 1996, In Troubled Waters, Tampa Fla., 1996, The Visit, N.Y.C., 1996, Driving Miss Daisy, Chester, Mass., and Queens, N.Y., 1996, An Ideal Husband, Broadway, 1996-97, Greytop in Love, Phila, 1998, Love Letters, Mass., 1999, Love From Shakespeare to Coward, N.Y.C., 1999; frequent appearances summer stock and repertory theater, 1940—; appeared Am. Shakespeare Festival, Stratford, Conn., 1961; film debut The Seventh Victim, 1943, films include Tender Comrade, 1943, When Strangers Marry (re-released as Betrayed), 1944, You Came Along, 1945, A Canterbury Tale, 1949, Stairway to Heaven, 1946 (re-released with original title A Matter of Life and Death, 1995), A Streetcar Named Desire (Oscar award best supporting actress), Anything Can Happen, 1952, Deadline U.S.A., 1952, Storm Center, 1956, Bermuda Affair, 1957, The Young Stranger, 1957, Money, Women, and Guns, 1958, Lilith, 1964, Planet of the Apes, 1968, The Swimmer, 1968, Beneath the Planet of the Apes, 1970, Escape from the Planet of the Apes, 1971, Dark August, 1975, The Kindred, 1987, Two Evil Eyes, 1991, A Price Below Rubies, 1997, Midnight in the Garden of Good and Evil, 1997, The Hiding Place, 1999, Abilene, 1999, The Virtuoso, 1999; TV debut Actors' Studio program, 1948; TV appearences include Requiem for a Heavyweight, 1956, The Comedian, 1957, Give Us Barabbas, 1961, 63, 68, 69, Love, American Style, Colombo, Cannon, Night Gallery, Mission Impossible, The Magician, 1972-73, Marcus Welby, Hec Ramsey, Griff, Police Story, Ironside, Medical Center, Bad Ronald, Born Innocent, 1974, Ellery Queen, 1975, Lucas Tanner, This Side of Innocence, Once an Eagle, Baretta, Gibbsville, Hunter, 1976, The Oregon Trail, 1977, Project UFO, Stubby Pringle's Christmas, 1978, Backstairs at the White House, 1979, Specter on the Bridge, 1979, Edge of Night, 1979-80, FDR's Last Year, 1980, Skokie, 1981, Scene of the Crime, 1984, Three Sovereigns for Sarah, 1985, Hot Pursuit, 1985, Private Sessions, 1985, Martin Luther King, Jr., The Dream and the Drum, 1986, Drop Out Mother, 1987, (mini-series) Cross of Fire, 1989, Murder, She Wrote, 1990, Vivien Leigh: Scarlett and Beyond, 1990, Bloodlines: Murder in the Family, 1993, Class of '96, 1993, All My Children, 1993, Hurricane Andrew, 1993, L.A. Law, 1994, Mad About You, 1994, As The World Turns, 1997, Blue Moon, 1999; recordings include From Morning 'Til Night (and a Bag Full of Poems), 1961, Come, Woo Me, 1964, The Velveteen Rabbit, 1989; author Kim Hunter: Loose in the Kitchen, 1975. Recipient Donaldson award for best supporting actress in A Streetcar Named Desire, 1948, also on Variety N.Y. Critics Poll 1948, for film version 1952; winner AMPAS's Oscar, Look award, Hollywood Fgn. Corrs. Golden Globe award, Emmy nominations for Baretta, 1977, Edge of Night, 1980, Fla. Carbonell (for Big Mama in Cat on a Hot Tin Roof) award, 1984, Edwin Forrest award, 1999. Mem. Acad. Motion Picture Arts and Scis., ANTA, Actors Equity Assn. (council 1953-59), Screen Actors Guild, AFTRA. *Enjoy. If I don't like what I'm doing, it never works. That doesn't mean the pangs of creation don't exist—it only means I avoid like the plague anything I can't believe in, or might be ashamed of afterwards. It's also helped me to keep in mind a hand-me-down from my father— "It is first of all to be, then to know and to do, and only incidentally to have." All this doesn't necessarily add up to monetary "success"—but it does much for a personal satisfaction in work and in living.*

HUNTER, LARRY DEAN, lawyer; b. Leon, Iowa, Apr. 10, 1950; s. Doyle J. and Dorothy B. (Grey) H.; m. Rita K. Barker, Jan. 24, 1971; children: Nathan (dec.), Allison. BS with high distinction, U. Iowa, 1971; AM, U. Mich., 1974, JD magna cum laude, 1974, CPhil in Econs., 1975. Bar: Va. 1975, Mich. 1978, Calif. 1992. Assoc. McGuire Woods & Battle, Richmond, Va., 1975-77; asst. counsel, internat. counsel Clark Equipment Co., Buchanan, Mich., 1977-80; ptnr. Honigman, Miller, Schwartz and Cohn, Detroit, 1980-93; asst. gen. counsel Hughes Electronics Corp., L.A., 1993-98, corp. v.p., 1998—; sr. v.p., gen. counsel DIRECTV, Inc., El Segundo, Calif., 1996—; chmn. pres. DIRECTV Japan Mgmt., Inc., Tokyo, 1998—; mem. faculty Wayne State U. Law Sch., Detroit, 1987-89. Mem. Order of Coif. Home: 306014 Shiroganedai, Minato-ku, Tokyo 108-0071, Japan Office: DIRECTV Japan Mgmt Inc, 4-20-3 Ebisu, Shibuya-ku, Tokyo 150-6023, Japan

HUNTER, LARRY LEE, electrical engineer; b. Versailles, Mo., Mar. 5, 1938; s. Donnan Kleber and Molly Opal (Roe) H.; m. Marcella Ann Avey, Feb. 1, 1959; children: Cynthia Lynn Hunter Hulen, Stuart Roe. BSEE, U. Mo., 1963; MBA, Fla. Inst. Tech., 1984. System test engr. McDonnell Aircraft Corp., St. Louis, 1963-65; design engr. Magnavox Co., Urbana, Ill., 1965-66, R&D engr., 1966-67; project engr. LTV Electrosystems, Garland, Tex., 1967-68, systems engr., 1968-70; program mgr. Dorsett Electronics, Tulsa, 1970-73; program mgr. Harris Corp., Melbourne, Fla., 1973-75, bus. area mgr., 1975-85; v.p. mktg., engring., program mgmt. Teledyne Lewisburg, Tenn., 1985-88; pres. L.H. Assocs., Columbia, Tenn., 1988-90; gen. mgr. Precision Cable div. AMP Inc., Greensboro, N.C., 1990-96, dir. global cable sys. bus. group, 1996-97; pres. L. Hunter Assocs., Inc., Tampa, Fla., 1997—. Inventor thermometer; contbr. articles to profl. jours. Mem. IEEE, Eta Kappa Nu. Republican. Methodist. Avocations: hunting, fishing, golf. Home: 16309 E Course Dr Tampa FL 33624-1127

HUNTER, LORIE ANN, women's health nurse; b. Royal Oak, Mich., Aug. 8, 1969; d. Ronald and Rose Katherine (Thurman) L. BSN, Mercy Coll. Detroit, 1991. clinical nurse. Nurse extern Detroit Med. Ctr.- Sinai Hosp., Detroit, 1989-91, RN, 1991—. Mem. NAACOG, NLN, Student Nurse's Assn. Mich., Mich. Coll. Nursing. Home: 3367 Kilmer Dr Troy MI 48083-5082

HUNTER, MARIE HOPE, library media generalist; b. Troy, N.Y., Nov. 21, 1950; d. Roger Walter Joseph and Cecilia Yvonne (Daudelin) Miller; m. Robert Hutchinson Hunter, June 3, 1972 (div. Sept. 1978); 1 child, Teal Miller. BA, Johnson (Vt.) State Coll., 1972; MS in Edn., Ind. U., 1978. Elem. tchr. Lo Nisky Elem. Sch., U.S. V.I., 1972-74; libr. Lockhart Elem. Sch., U.S. V.I., 1974-77; evening libr. Johnson State Coll., 1978-79; libr. Ticonderoga (N.Y.) Mid. Sch., 1980-85; libr. media generalist Richmond Mid. Sch., Hanover, N.H., 1985—; Author: (student workbooks) The Topic Paper Workbook: A Guided Process, 1993, The Thesis Paper Workbook: A Guided Process, 1994. Trustee Lebanon (N.H.) Pub. Libr. Named Tchr. of Yr., Richmond Mid. Sch./U. Vt., 1992. Mem. Vt. Ednl. Media Assn., N.H. Edn. Media Assn. Avocations: travel, golf, racquetball, fishing. Office: Richmond Mid Sch 39 Lebanon St Hanover NH 03755-2147

HUNTER, MATTIE SUE (MOORE), health facility administrator; b. Brownwood, Tex., Apr. 7, 1944; d. Robert and Florence Irene (Shaw) Moore; divorced; children: Roberta Sharlene, Hank William, Charlie Ervin. Student, Howard Payne Coll., 1963-64. Unit mgr., supr. Girling Health Care, Inc., Austin, Tex., 1976—. Mem. Tex. Assn. Home Care, Brownwood Garden Culture Club (pres. 1996-97), Hist. Soc., Blvd. Beautification. Democrat. Mem. Church of Christ. Avocations: greenhouse, gardening, craft making, bowling, cooking.

HUNTER, MICHAEL, publishing executive; b. Atlanta, Dec. 11, 1941; s. Joel H. and Eleanor Johnson; m. Katherine Garlick, Aug. 2, 1975. BA cum laude, Harvard U., 1964; postgrad., Columbia U., 1965-67. Dir. Spectrum Books, Prentice-Hall Inc., Englewood Cliffs., N.J., 1974-80; pres. Gen. Pub. div. Prentice-Hall Inc., Englewood Cliffs., N.J., 1980-85; pres. Hunter Pub. Co., N.Y., 1985—. Mem. Am. Assn. Pubs. (exec. council Gen. Pub. div.). Club: University (N.Y.C.). Home: 239 S Beach Rd Hobe Sound FL 33455-2511 Office: Hunter Pub Co 130 Campus Plz Edison NJ 08837-3936

HUNTER, MICHAEL JAMES, state government official, lawyer, educator; b. Enid, Okla., July 2, 1956; s. James Chester Hunter and Phyllis Merle Brinker; m. Cheryl Lynn Plaxico, Dec. 26, 1981; children: Barret Michael, Hayden Brock. BA in History, Okla. State U., 1978; JD, U. Okla., 1982. Bar: Okla. Ptnr. Crabtree & Miller, Okla. City, 1981-85, George, Moore, Hammons & Hunter, Okla. City, 1985-87; of counsel Musser & Bunch, Okla. City, 1987-93; gen. counsel Okla. Corp. Commn., 1993-94; chief of staff Congressman J.C. Watts, Jr., 1995-99; sec. of state State of Okla., 1999—. Del. Rep. Nat. Conv., Detroit, 1980, New Orleans, 1988; chmn. Rep. Caucus, 1988-90; state rep. Okla. Ho. of Reps., Okla. City, 1984-90, mem. Constitution Revision Study Commn. Named One of Okla.'s Best Legislators, The Daily Oklahoman, Okla. City, 1987; recipient Legis. Appreciation award, Okla. Dist. Atty.'s Assn., Okla. City, 1988. Mem. Okla. Bar Assn., Okla. County Bar Assn. Presbyterian. Avocations: baseball, books, movies. Office: Sec of State 2300 N Lincoln Blvd Rm 101 Oklahoma City OK 73105*

HUNTER, MILTON, army officer; b. Houston, May 1, 1943; m. Karina Bechtle; children: Alexander, Patrick. BS in Archtl. Engring., Wash. State U., 1967; M in Engring., U. Wash.; grad. Exec. Devel. Program, U. Va.; postgrad., Tex. A&M U., Harvard U.; DSc (hon.), N.J. Inst. Tech., 1997. Registered profl. engr. Commd. 2d lt. U.S. Army, 1967, advanced through grades to maj. gen.; instr. Tactical Bridging br., dept. applied engring. U.S. Army Engr. Sch., Ft. Belvoir, Va.; with U.S. Army Corps of Engrs., comdr. and dist. engr. Seattle Dist.; comdg. gen., divs. engr. South Pacific, chief of staff U.S. Army Corps of Engrs., Washington; comdg. gen., divsn. engr. North Atlantic divsn. U.S. Army Corps of Engrs., to 1997, Washington, 1997—. Decorated Legion of Merit (2), Bronze Star medal, others; recipient Disting. Alumni award Wash. State U., 1991; named to Outstanding Young of Am., 1979. Fellow Soc. Am. Mil. Engrs.; mem. Army Engr. Regtl. Assn., Assn. U.S. Army, Tau Beta Pi. Office: US Army Corps of Engrs 20 Massachusetts Ave NW Washington DC 20314-1000

HUNTER, NANCY DONEHOO, education educator; b. Atlanta, July 11, 1956; d. Joseph Andrew and Sophia (Sellers) Donehoo; m. Charles James Hunter IV, Dec. 1, 1979; children: Katherine Elizabeth, Charles James V. BA, Asbury Coll., 1981; MA, Morehead (Ky.) State U., 1984; EdS, U. Ky., 1998. Dir. Christian edn. 1st United Meth. Ch., Clewiston, Fla., 1981-82; assoc. prof. Maysville (Ky.) C.C., 1983—; mem. partnership coordination coun. Destination Graduation, Frankfort, Ky., 1989-91; tutor trainer Ky. Literacy Coun., Frankfort, 1990—. Author: Peer Tutor Trainer Manual, 1989. Bd. dirs. Community Literacy Coun., Mason County, Ky., 1988—; choir dir. Trinity Meth. Ch., Maysville, 1990—. Recipient Vol. Svc. award Mason County Schs., 1987, 91; grantee U.S. Dept. Edn., 1989-91. Mem. ASCD, Internat. Reading Assn., Nat. Assn. Devel. Educators, Coll. Reading and Learning Assn., Ky. Assn. Devel. Educators (treas. 1989-90, conf. dir. 1989—, pres. 1999). Avocations: needlework, gardening, travel, music. Home: PO Box 203 Washington KY 41096-0203 Office: Maysville Community Coll US 68 Maysville KY 41056

HUNTER, OREGON K., JR., physiatrist; b. L.A., Apr. 7, 1949. BA in Biol. Scis., Calif. State U., 1971, MA in Secondary Edn., 1972, MD, 1976. Diplomate: Am. Bd. Electrodiagnostic Medicine, Am. Bd. Phys. Medicine and Rehab., Am. Acad. Disability Evaluating Physicians, Am. Acad. Pain Mgmt., Nat. Bd. Med. Examiners, Am. Coll. Occupational & Environmental Medicine, Basic Curriculum in Occupatinal Medicine. Flexible intern San Joaquin Gen. Hosp., 1976-77; resident in Phys. Medicine and Rehab., Davis Med. Ctr. U. Calif., 1981-84; med. officer student health svc. Calif. State U., 1977-80; from staff physician to med. dir. Aquarian Effort Medical Clinic, 1979-84; med. officer student health svc. Humboldt State U., Arcata, Calif., 1980-81; with Kaiser Permanente Med. Group, 1984, Readicare Urgent Care Centers of Am., Inc., 1984; pvt. practice phys. medicine and rehab., 1984; staff physiatrist med. dir. Rehab. Hosp. of the Pacific, 1985-87; staff VA Med. Ctr., 1987; pvt. practice med. rehab., occupational neuromuscular medicine, electrodiagnostic medicine Rehab. Medicine Assocs., 1987—; clin. faculty phys. medicine anf rehab. U. Calif., 1984-85; clin. instr. phys. medicine and rehab. U. Hawaii, 1986-88; clin. asst. prof. phys. medicine and rehab. Dept. Community Health and Family Medicine, Coll. Medicine U. Fla., 1988—; cons. Office of Treas., Dept. Ins., State of Fla. on Fla. Impairment Guide, 1994, Healthcare Performance Occupational Injury Reserve Protocol Determination, 1993; organizer/moderator Med. Provider Breakout Session, Fla. Worker's Compensation Inst. 48th Annual Ednl. Conf., 1993; mem. med. oversight com. NFRMC Ctr. Psychol. Svcs., 1993; mem. phys. adv. com. divsn. workers comp. Dept. Labor and Employment Security State of Fla., 1993, numerous others. Contbr. numerous articles to med. jours. vol. sports med. exams Pig Bowl, Sacramento, 1983; team mem. Spina Bifida Bicycle Race, 1982. Recipient Physician of the Yr. award Nat. Assn. Rehab. Providers in Pvt. Sector, honors Family Practice Clerkship UCD, 1975-76, Dermatology Clerkship, 1975, Pres.'s Scholarship, 1973. Fellow Am. Acad. Disability Evaluating Physicians, Am. Acad. Phys. Medicine and Rehab.; mem. Am. Assn. Electrodiagnostic Medicine, Am. Coll. Legal Medicine (assoc. in medicine), Am. Coll. Occupational & Environmental Medicine, Am. Congress Rehab. Medicine, Am. Acad. Pain Mgmt., N.Am. Spine Soc., Internat. Assn. for the Study of Pain, Internat. Rehab. Medicine Assn., So. Soc. Phys. Medicine and Rehab., Fla. Med. Assn., Fla. Soc. Phys. Medicine and Rehab., Marion County Med. Soc., Phi Kappa Phi. Office: Ste 1100 2300 SE 17th St Ste 1100 Ocala FL 34471-4414

HUNTER, PATRICIA PHELPS, physician assistant; b. Nyack, N.Y., Oct. 11, 1952; d. Everett Edward and Evelyn Phelps; m. George Patton Hunter, June 26, 1982; children: Eric I., Kurt A. BA in Psychology & Spanish magna cum, Oneonta State U., 1974; BS in Physician Asst., Hahnemann Med. U., 1981; MS in Pub. Health, West Chester U., 1984. Rsch. asst. Oneonta (N.Y.) State U., 1973-74, Dartmouth Med. Sch., Hanover, N.H., 1974-76; paramedic San Francisco Ambulance, 1977-79; physician asst. Montgomery Hosp., Norristown, Pa., 1981—. Fellow Am. Acad. Physician Assts. (cert.); mem. Assn. for Retarded Citizens, Nat. Orgn. Rare Disorders, Nat. Orgn. Apraxia and Dyspraxia, MCIU Parents Group (recording sec. 1998—). Avocations: skiing, scuba diving. Home: 331 Collegeville Rd Collegeville PA 19426-3030 Office: Montgomery Hosp Clinic 15 W Wood St Norristown PA 19401-3300

HUNTER, R. HAZE, former state legislator; b. Cedar City, Utah, Oct. 5, 1924; m. Betty B. Hunter. Student, U. Utah. Chmn. bd. North East Furniture; pres. NEFCO Fin.; owner B&H Family Ptnr.; mem. Utah State Legislature, 1980-92, Utah State Bldg. Bd., 1996—; mem. State and Local Affairs standing com., 1981-82, 85-86, 87-88; chmn. Bus. and Consumer Consumer Concerns standing com., 1983-84, mem. 1981-82, 85-86; chmn. Gen. Govt. and Capitol Facilities appropriations com., 1988-89, mem. 1983-84; mem. Bus. Labor and Agriculture appropriations com., 1981-82, 85-86, Bus. Labor and Econ. Devel. standing com., 1987-88, constl. revision com., law and justice adv. com.; apptd. to Utah State Bldg. Bd., 1995. Bishop, high councilman Ch. of Latter Day Saints; chmn. Vally View Hosp. Found. Bd., 1999. Mem. Iron Mission Park C. of C. (past pres., mem. Southern Utah devel. com.), Lions (past pres. Cedar City chpt., past dist. gov.). Office: 295 S Ridge Rd Cedar City UT 84720-2905

HUNTER, REBECCA KATHLEEN, accountant, personnel administrator; b. Phila.; d. Charles George and Margaret Ann H.; m. Carl Frederick Thomas, June 3, 1994. AA in Acctg., Frederick (Md.) C.C., 1991; BBA in Acctg., Hood Coll., 1995. Staff acct., office mgr. Kent Briddell Constrn. Co., Mt. Airy, Md., 1986-93; payroll staff acct. Program Resources Inc., Ft. Detrick, Md., 1993-94; sr. acct., pers. adminstr. Digital Systems Corp., Walkersville, Md., 1994—. Beneficial Hodson scholar Hood Coll./Hodson Trust, Frederick, 1992-95; recipient award for acad. excellence in bus. career curriculum C. of C. Frederick County, 1991. Mem. ASPCA, Humane Soc. of U.S., Phi Kappa Phi, Phi Theta Kappa, Sigma Beta Delta. Avocations: raising Golden Retriever dogs, sewing, embroidery.

HUNTER, RICHARD EDWARD, physician; b. Worcester, Mass., May 30, 1919; s. William and Catherine (Powers) H.; m. M. Minta Shaw, Jan. 30, 1993; children: Todd Wayne, Elayne Cheryl, Jill Elizabeth, Amy Louise. A.B., Clark U., 1941; M.D., Boston U., 1944. Diplomate Am. Bd. Ob-Gyn. Intern Worcester City Hosp., 1944-45; resident in gen. surgery Framingham (Mass.) Union Hosp., 1947; resident in ob-gyn Mercy Hosp., Balt., 1947-49; practice medicine specializing in ob-gyn Worcester, 1949—; prof. dept. ob-gyn U. Mass., Worcester, 1976—, chmn. dept. ob-gyn, 1976-89, emeritus prof., 1989—. Contbr. articles to med. jours. Served with U.S. Army, 1945-47. Mem. ACS, ACOG, New Eng. Assn. Gynecologic Oncologists, Soc. Gynecologic Oncology, Boston Obstetric Soc., New Eng. Cancer Soc., Am. Soc. Clin. Oncology, Soc. Gynecologic Surgeons, Royal Soc. Medicine. Republican. Home: 406 Browning Ln Worcester MA 01609-1163 Office: 55 Lake Ave N Worcester MA 01655-0002

HUNTER, RICHARD SAMFORD, JR., lawyer; b. Montgomery, Ala., May 8, 1954; s. Richard Samford and Anne (Arendell) H.; m. Jane Messer, June 28, 1981; children: Richard Samford III, Benjamin Arendell. Student, Berklee Coll. of Music, 1974-75; BA, U. N.C., 1977; JD, Cumberland Sch Law of Samford U., 1980. Bar: N.C. 1980, U.S. Dist. Ct. (ea. and mid. dists.) N.C. 1981; cert. Am. Bd. Trial Advs. Assoc. Green & Mann, Raleigh, N.C., 1980-82, Smith, Debnam, Hibbert & Pahl, Raleigh, 1982-85; ptnr. Futrell, Hunter & Bingham, Raleigh, 1985-97; Pres., North Carolina Acad. of Trial Lawyers, 1993-94; pres. elect, 1992-93; exec. comm., 1987-94; bd., 1984-87; chair, Auto Torts Sect., 1998—, program chmn. media law U. N.C., Chapel Hill, 1983-84; mem. faculty NCATL Nat. Inst. Trial Advocacy, 1987; lectr. in field. Author: Insurance Law for the General Practitioner, 1992, North Carolina Bar Assn. Desk Book, 1992, Traumatic Medicine, 1995; composer, performer (TV musical) The Tomorrow Show, 1975; contbr. articles to profl. jours. Corp. fund raiser United Way, Wake County, N.C., 1984-85; mem. clergy's sermon evaluation com. Christ Episc. Ch., Raleigh; bd. dirs. Raleigh Chamber Music Guild, 1986-88; bd. dirs. Food Bank of N.C., 1990—. Fellow So. Trial Lawyers Assn., Roscoe Pound Found.; mem. ABA (mem. litigation sect.), ATLA, Am. Bd. Trial Advocates (cert.), N.C. Bar Assn., Wake County Bar Assn. (bd. dirs. 1987-88, chmn. 1988), Assn. Trial Lawyers Am. (Stalwart fellow Roscoe Pound Found.), N.C. Acad. Trial Lawyers (speaker various seminars, chmn. speakers bur. 1984-85, bd. govs. 1986—, v.p. pub. svc. and info. com. 1988-90, v.p. membership 1990-91, v.p. legis. 1991—, pres. 1993-94, exec. com. 1987-94, chmn. auto torts sect. 1998—, mem. edn. com. 1985-88), Kiwanis, Sphinx, Phi Alpha Delta. Democrat. Avocations: sports, music, hunting, fishing. Fax: 919-831-8734. E-mail: hunteratty@aol.com. Home: 813 Graham St Raleigh NC 27605-1124 Office: 1st Union Capitol Ctr 1700 150 Fayetteville St Mall Raleigh NC 27601-2919

HUNTER, ROBERT DEAN (BOB HUNTER), state legislator, retired university official; b. Dodge City, Kans., June 25, 1928; s. Grover Cleveland and Grace Mae (Grubb) H.; m. Shirley Margaret Long, May 27, 1954; children: Kent Wayne, Carole Hunter Phillips, Leslie Dean. BS, Abilene Christian U., 1952, MBA, 1976; LLD (hon.), Pepperdine U., 1974; LHD (hon.), Tex. Wesleyan U., 1979; LittD (hon.), U. St. Thomas, 1983; LLD (hon.), Abilene Christian U., 1993, Hardin-Simmons U., 1997. Dir. spl. events Abilene (Tex.) Christian U., 1956-57, dir. alumni rels., 1957-61, asst. to pres., 1961-69, v.p. pub. rels. and devel., 1969-74, v.p., 1974-85, sr. v.p., 1985-93, v.p. emeritus, lectr. sch. bus., 1993—; mem. dist. 79 Tex. Ho. Reps., 1986-92, mem. dist. 71, 1992—; exec. v.p. Ind. Colls. and Univs. Tex., 1970-80, acting pres. 1980-81; co-chair spl. ho. select com. on NAFTA and GATT; com. chmn. State, Fed. and Internat. Rels.; mem. intergovernmental affairs com. So. Legis. Conf.; mem. arts and tourism com. Nat. Conf. State Legislatures; mem. task force on trade and transp. Am. Legis. Exch. Coun.; mem. internat. com. Coun. State Govts. Deacon Univ. Ch. Christ, Abilene, 1956—; bd. dirs. Tex. Mcpl. League, 1970-73, Tex. Bus. Hall of Fame Found., 1986—, chmn. scholarships and awards, West Tex. Rehab. Ctr., Meals on Wheels Plus, Day Nursery Abilene, Abilene Opera Assn., Boys and Girls Clubs Abilene, Vol. Coun. Abilene, Atty. Gen.'s Child Support Vol. Svc. Bd., Community Justice Coun., Restitution Ctr. Taylor, Callahan, Coleman Counties, Chisholm Trail Coun. Boy Scouts Am., Abilene Philharmonic Orch., Abilene YMCA, Abilene Bus. Aid, founding coord., Abilene United Way, Abilene Bicentennial Commn.; mem. Abilene City Coun., 1970-73; apptd. by Gov. Briscoe Tex. Adv. Coun. for Tech. and Vocat. Edn., 1977-83, chmn., 1980-83; apptd. by Gov. Clements mem. Tex. Hist. Commn., 1983-86; adv. bd. dirs. Abilene Mental Health Assn., Mus. Abilene, Salvation Army, Kenley Sch., Tex. Coalition Prevention Child Abuse. Lt. (j.g.) USNR, 1953-56, Korea. Recipient Leadership award Jr. League, 1965, Outstanding Svc. award Abilene Ind. Sch. Dist., 1990, Boss of Yr. We. Horizons chpt. Am. Bus. Women's Assn., 1994, Friend of Bus. award Tex. C. of C., 1994. Mem. VFW (Clayton M. Leach Post 2012), Tex. Conservative Coalition, Rotary (pres. 1983-84, Paul Harris fellow 1984, elected dist. gov. elect 1985), Tex. Lyceum Assn., Abilene C. of C. (various coms.), Abilene Black C. of C., Abilene Hispanic C. of C., Abilene Zool. Soc., Abilene Jaycees (named One of Ten Outstanding Young Men in Abilene 1968, 69), Am. Legion. Republican. Office: Abilene Christian U PO Box 29003 Abilene TX 79699

HUNTER, ROBERT GRAMS, retired English language educator; b. Milbank, S.D., Nov. 12, 1927; s. Donald Raymond and Esther (Grams) H.; m. Anne Ziesmer, Aug. 25, 1956; children: Timothy, Catherine. B.A., Harvard, 1949; M.A., Columbia, 1957, Ph.D., 1962. Instr. Robert Coll., Istanbul, Turkey, 1949-52; successively instr., asst. prof., asso. prof. Dartmouth, 1959-70; Kenan prof. English Vanderbilt U., Nashville, 1970-82; Frensley prof. English So. Meth. U., Dallas, 1982-97; ret., 1997. Author: Shakespeare and the Comedy of Forgiveness, 1965, Shakespeare and the Mystery of God's Judgments, 1976. Served with AUS, 1952-54. Home: 5923 Hillcrest Ave Dallas TX 75205-2262

HUNTER, SALLY IRENE, interior designer; b. East Liverpool, Ohio, Oct. 8, 1936; Charles E. and Thelma E. (Rice) H. BA, Kalamazoo Coll., 1958. Certified Am. Soc. Interior Designers. Interior designer The Higbee Co., Cleve., 1958-70; interior designer, v.p., dir. of design Harrisons Fine Furniture and Interiors, Lakewood, Ohio, 1970—. Mem. Nat. Trust Hist.

Preservation. Mem. Am. Soc. Interior Designers (profl.), Cleve. Mus. Art, Cleve. Zool. Soc. Home: 22535 Detroit Rd Cleveland OH 44116-2056 Office: Harrisons Fine Furniture & Interiors 14518 Detroit Ave Cleveland OH 44107-4317

HUNTER, SARAH ANN, community health nurse; b. Clarksdale, Miss.; d. Albert Wiliam and Allean Hunter. Cert. in practical nursing, Miss. Delta Jr. Coll., Clarksdale, 1973; ADN, Alcorn State U., Natchez, Miss., 1979, BSN, 1986. Staff nurse N.W. Miss. Regional Med. Ctr., Clarksdale, 1974; head nurse Jefferson County Hosp., Fayette, Miss., 1979; supervising nurse Medgar Evers Home Health, Fayette, 1986; discharge planning nurse Quitman County Hosp., Marks, Miss., 1991; asst. DON DON Ruleville Health Care Ctr., 1992-93; oper. rm. circulator Bolivar County Hosp., Cleveland, Miss., 1993—; orientation inservice coord. Delta Cmty. Home Health, 1995.

HUNTER, SUE PERSONS, former state official; b. Hico, Tex., Aug. 21, 1921; d. David Henry and Beulah (Boatwright) Persons m. Charles Force Hunter; children: Shelley Hunter Richardson, Kathy Hunter McCullough, Margaret Hunter Brown. BA, U. Tex., 1942. Air traffic controller CAA (now FAA), San Antonio and Houston, 1942-52; writer Bissonet Plaza News, 1969-72; coordinator Goals for La., 1971-74; adminstrv. dir. Jeff Publs. Inc., 1974; press sec. Jefferson Parish Dist. Atty., 1972-75, communications cons., 1975-78; adminstr. Child Support Enforcement Div., 1979-85; contbg. editor The Jeffersonian, 1975-76. Pres. United Ch. Women East Jefferson (La.), 1958-59; mem. LWV Jefferson Parish, La., 1961—, pres., 1961-63, bd. dirs., 1993-96; bd. dirs. LWV of Louisiana, 1962-67, pres., 1967-71; mem. probation services com. Cmty. Svcs. Coun., Jefferson, 1966-73, v.p., 1970-72; mem. Library Devel. Com. La., 1967-71, Nat. Com. for Support of Pub. Schs., 1967-72; mem. Goals Found. Council Met. New Orleans, 1969-75, sec. 1970, 72; mem. Goals La. Task Force State and Local Govt., 1969-70; pres. MMM Investment Club, 1969-72; bd. dirs. New Orleans Area Health Planning Council, 1969-75, Friends of Westminster Tower, 1986, Coun. for Internat. Visitors, 1990—, pres. 1991-93, programmer, 1994—; bd. dirs. Jefferson Twenty Five, 1991—, v.p., 1995-96, pres. 1997-98; mem. adv. coun. La. State Health Planning, 1971-76; title I adv. council La. State Dept. Edn., 1970-72; vice chmn. Jefferson Women's Polit. Caucus, 1977-78, chmn., 1979, treas., 1980; Nat. Women's Political Caucus, 1997—; bd. dirs. New Orleans Area/Bayou-River Health Systems Agy., 1978-82, pres., 1980, 81; mem. Task force for La. Talent Bank of Women, 1980; exec. bd. La. Child Support Enforcement Assn., 1980-86, pres., 1982-84; bd. dirs., legis. chmn. Nat. Child Support Enforcement Assn., 1983-86; mem. Gov.'s Commn. on Child Support Enforcement, 1984-88; mem. La. Statewide Health Coordinating Coun., 1980-83, mgmt. com. edn. fund League of Women Voters La., 1988-89; clk. of session Parkway Presbyn. Ch., 1998—. Recipient Outstanding Citizens award Rotary Club, Metairie, La., 1962, River Ridge award, 1976. Mem. Am. Assn. Individual Investors (pres. New Orleans chpt. 1986-88), New Orleans Panhellenic (pres. 1956-57), Fgn. Rels. Assn. (bd. dirs. New Orleans chpt. 1992—, sec. 1996—), Les Pelicaneers (pres. 1988-90), Earn and Learn Investment Club (pres. 1992-94), Alpha Xi Delta. Home: 210 Stewart Ave New Orleans LA 70123-1457

HUNTER, TANYA ANTOINETTE, insurance biller; b. Aug. 10, 1972. BS, Troy State U., 1994; MPA, Ind. State U., 1996. Grad. asst. Ind. State U., Terre Haute, 1995-96; ins. biller Bapt. Health, Montgomery, Ala., 1998—. E-mail: w.hunter@cwix.com.

HUNTER, VICTOR LEE, marketing executive, consultant; b. Garrett, Ind., Mar. 1, 1947; s. John Joseph and Martha May (Brown) H.; m. Linda Ann Loudermilk, Dec. 19, 1969; children: Jed, Andrew, Matthew, Holly. BS, Purdue U., 1969; MBA, Harvard U., 1971. Dir. mktg. Kreuger, Inc., Green Bay, Wis., 1971-75; pres. B&I Furniture, Milw., 1975-81, Hunter Bus. Direct, Milw., 1981—; bd. dirs. Koss Corp., Milw. Author: Business-to-Business Marketing: Creating a Community of Customers, 1997. Lay leader United Meth. Ch., Whitefish Bay, Wis., 1985. Mem. Direct Mktg. Assn., Direct Mktg. Club, Bus. to Bus. Direct Mktg. Coun. Office: Hunter Business Direct PO Box 12970 4650 N Port Washington Rd Fl 1 Milwaukee WI 53212-1024

HUNTER, WILLIAM DENNIS, lawyer; b. Boise, Idaho, June 26, 1943; s. William Gregory and Lorene (Persilla) H.; m. Jane Emily Porter, Apr. 30, 1966; children: Keith Alan, Elise Aubrey. BA, Stanford U., 1965; JD, U. Calif., San Francisco, 1973. Bar: Calif. 1973, U.S. Dist. Ct. (no. dist.) Calif. 1974, U.S. Ct. Appeals (9th cir.) 1974, U.S. Supreme Ct. 1996. Assoc. Pettit & Martin, San Francisco, 1973-79, ptnr., 1980-92, counsel, 1993-95; counsel Collette & Erickson LLP, San Francisco, 1995—. Bd. dirs. City Celebration, Inc., San Francisco, 1984-91, pres., 1989-91. Recipient Service award Calif. Nature Conservancy, 1987. Mem. ABA, Calif. State Bar Assn., San Francisco Bar Assn., Nat. Assn. Installation Devel. (regional dir. 1993—), Order of Coif. Democrat. Office: Collette & Erickson LLP 555 California St Ste 4350 San Francisco CA 94104-1708

HUNTER, WILLIAM JAY, JR., lawyer; b. Champaign, Ill., Sept. 19, 1944; s. William Jay and Joan Edna (Werstler) H.; m. Jennifer Diane Newcomer, Jan. 3, 1970; children: Matthew Jay, Amy Elizabeth, Nathan Andrew. BA in Econs., Northwestern U., 1965; JD, George Washington U., 1974. Bar: D.C. 1975, U.S. Dist. Ct. D.C. 1975, U.S. Ct. Appeals (D.C. and 5th cirs.) 1978, U.S. Supreme Ct. 1978, U.S. Ct. Appeals (9th cir.) 1980, U.S. Ct. Appeals (7th dir.) 1986, Ky. 1988, U.S. Ct. Appeals (6th cir.) 1992. From assoc. to ptnr. Howrey & Simon, Washington, 1974-86; v.p., gen. counsel, sec. Capital Holding Corp. (now Providian Corp.), Louisville, 1987-88; dep. gen. counsel I.C.H. Corp. (now Southwestern Life Corp., Dallas), Louisville, 1989-92; ptnr. Middleton & Reutlinger, Louisville, 1992—. Designer of pension products; litigator; contbr. numerous articles to profl. jours. Mem. Jefferson County AIDS Task Force, Louisville, 1988. 1st lt. U.S. Army, 1968-70, Korea. Democrat. Presbyterian. Avocations: skiing, gardening. Home: 2540 Ransdell Ave Louisville KY 40204-2115 Office: 2500 Brown Williamson Tower Louisville KY 40202*

HUNTER BLAIR, PAULINE CLARKE, author; b. Kirkby-in-Ashfield, Eng., May 19, 1921; d. Charles Leopold and Dorothy Kathleen (Milum) Clarke; m. Peter Hunter Blair, Feb., 1969. B.A. with honors, Somerville Coll., Oxford U., Eng. Free-lance writer, 1948—; lectr. Contbr., Eastern Daily Press, book reviewer, Times Lit. Supplement.; works include: under name Pauline Clarke: The Pekinese Princess, 1948, The Great Can, 1952, The White Elephant, 1952, Smith's Hoard, 1955, The Boy with the Erpingham Hood, 1956, Sandy the Sailor, 1956, James, the Policeman, 1957, James and the Robbers, 1959, Torolv the Fatherless, 1959, 2d edit., 1973, re-issued, 1991, The Lord of the Castle, 1960, The Robin Hooders, 1960, James and the Smugglers, 1961, Keep the Pot Boiling, 1961, The Twelve and the Genii, 1962 (pub. in U.S. as The Return of the Twelves, 1963) (Library Assn. Carnegie medal 1962, Lewis Carroll Shelf Award, 1963, Deutsche Jugend Buchpreis 1968), Silver Bells and Cockle Shells, 1962, James and the Black Van, 1963, Crowds of Creatures, 1964, The Bonfire Party, 1966, The Two Faces of Silenus, 1972; under pseudonym Helen Clare: Five Dolls in a House, 1953, Merlin's Magic, 1953, Bel, The Giant and Other Stories, 1956, Five Dolls and the Monkey, 1956, Five Dolls in the Snow, 1957, Five Dolls and Their Friends, 1959, Seven White Pebbles, 1960, Five Dolls and the Duke, 1963, The Cat and the Fiddle; and Other Stories from Bel, the Giant, 1968; also author short stories and plays for adults. Mem. Brit. Soc. Authors, Nat. Book League. Home: Church Farm House, Bottisham, Cambridge CB5 9BA, England Office: care Curtis Brown Ltd, Haymarket House 28/29 Haymarket, London SW1Y 4SP, England also: care John Cushman Assocs Inc 24 E 38th St New York NY 10016-2564

HUNTER-BONE, MAUREEN CLAIRE, magazine editor; b. Teaneck, N.J., Aug. 18, 1946; d. Eugene Francis and Audrey Dolores (Connellan) Hunter; m. Stanley Bone, Nov. 2, 1974; children: John Hunter Bone, Caroline Vandervoort Bone. BA in English lit., St. Mary's Coll., Notre Dame, Ind., 1968. Writer Scholastic Mags., N.Y.C., 1968-69, from asst. editor to editor, 1969-79; freelance writer N.Y.C., 1979-87; sr. editor 3-2-1 Contact Mag., N.Y.C., 1987; editor Kid City Mag., N.Y.C., 1988-90, editor-in-chief, 1990-91; editor-in-chief Kid City and Ghostwriter mags. Ghostwriter Books, Ghostwriter Newspaper Feature, N.Y.C., 1991-94; v.p., editor-in-chief juvenile periodicals Children's TV Workshop, N.Y.C., 1994—. Author: First Follow Nature, 1970, Adventures with a 3-Spined Stickleback, 1972. Mem. nat. ednl. adv. com. U.S. Bicentennial Com., Washington, 1988-91; bd. advisors Epiphany Community Nursery Sch., N.Y.C., 1987-92. Mem. Am. Soc. Mag. Editors (screening judge for nat. mag. awards 1993-96), Ednl. Press Assn. (bd. dirs. 1991-93, Disting. Achievement award 1988-95). Avocations: painting, music. Office: Childrens TV Workshop One Lincoln Plz New York NY 10023*

HUNTER-MCLEAN, ELANA M., critical care and trauma nurse; b. Reedsburg, Wis., Mar. 30, 1957; d. Vernon A. Hunter; m. Roger D. McLean, June 4, 1983. BSN, Coll. of St. Teresa, Rochester, Minn., 1979. RN, Tex., Wyo., Ariz.; cert. in acls, advanced trauma life support, aeromed. care. Med.-surg. nurse Seton Med. Ctr., Austin, Tex.; nurse ICU, Sheridan County Meml. Hosp., Sheridan, Wyo.; nurse ICU Tempe (Ariz.) St. Luke's Hosp.; critical care nurse John C. Lincoln Hosp., Phoenix, Scottsdale (Ariz.) Meml. North Hosp.; flight nurse Life Flight, Scottsdale, Ariz.

HUNTER-STIEBEL, PENELOPE, art historian, art dealer; b. Washington; d. Burton Leath and Beulah (Wooten) H.; m. Gerald G. Stiebel; 1 child, Hunter. BA, Barnard Coll., 1968; MA, NYU, 1971. With Met. Mus. of Art, N.Y.C., 1969-83, asst. curator, 1975-79, assoc. curator, 1979-83; curatorial cons. N.Y.C., 1983-86; prin. Rosenberg & Stiebel, Inc., N.Y.C., 1986—; exhbn. curator Met. Mus. Art, Rochester (N.Y.) Meml. Art Gallery, Detroit Inst. Art, Philbrook Mus., Portland (Oreg.) Mus. Art. Office: Rosenberg & Stiebel Inc 32 E 57th St New York NY 10022-2513

HUNTHAUSEN, RAYMOND GERHARDT, archbishop; b. Anaconda, Mont., Aug. 21, 1921; s. Anthony Gerhardt and Edna (Tuchacherer) H. A.B., Carroll Coll., 1943, St. Edward's Sem., 1946; M.S., Notre Dame U., 1953; LL.D., DePaul U., 1960; postgrad. summers, St. Louis U., Cath. U., Fordham U. Ordained priest Roman Cath. Ch., 1946. Instr. chemistry Carroll Coll., 1946-57, football, basketball coach, 1953-57, pres., 1957-62; bishop Helena Diocese, Mont., 1962-75; archbishop of Seattle, 1975-91. Recipient Martin Luther King Jr. award Fellowship of Reconciliation, 1987. Mem. Am. Chem. Soc. Office: Chancery Office 910 Marion St Seattle WA 98104-1274*

HUNTINGTON, CURTIS EDWARD, actuary; b. Worcester, Mass., July 30, 1942; s. Everett Curtis and Margaret (Schwenzfeger) H. B.A., U. Mich., 1964, M.Actuarial Sci., 1965; J.D., Suffolk U., 1976. With New Eng. Mut. Life Ins. Co., Boston, 1965-93; v.p., auditor New Eng. Mut. Life Ins. Co., 1980-84, corp. actuary, 1984-93; prof. math., dir. actuarial program U. Mich., Ann Arbor, 1993—; treas. Actuarial Edn. and Rsch. Fund, 1986-89, chmn., 1989-92, dir. 1985—, exec. dir., 1994—. Trustee The Actuarial Found., 1998—. Served with USPHS, 1965-67. Mem. Soc. Actuaries (gen. chmn. edn. and exam. com. 1985-87, bd. govs. 1986-89, v.p. 1989-91), Am. Acad. Actuaries (bd. dirs. 1997—), Am. Soc. Pension Actuaries (dir. 1996—), Am. Coll. Life Underwriters, Internat. Actuarial Assn. (sec., nat. corr. U.S.), New Zealand Soc. Actuaries. Office: U Mich Dept of Math 2864 East Hall Ann Arbor MI 48109-1109

HUNTINGTON, EARL LLOYD, lawyer, retired natural resources company executive; b. Orangeville, Utah, Sept. 2, 1929; s. Lloyd S. and Hannah Annette (Cox) H.; m. Phyllis Ann Reed; children: Jane, Ann, Stephen. BS, U. Utah, 1951, JD, 1956; LL.M., Georgetown U., 1959. Bar: Utah 1956, D.C. 1959, N.Y. 1966, Conn. 1988. Trial atty. Dept. Justice, Washington, 1956-63; counsel Texasgulf Inc., N.Y.C., 1963-74, v.p., gen. counsel, 1974-81, sr. v.p., gen. counsel, 1981-90, also bd. dirs., 1981-94; sr. v.p., gen. counsel, dir. Elf Aquitaine Inc., 1982-90, ret., 1990. Case note editor U. Utah Law Rev., 55-56. Served with U.S. Army, 1951-53. Mem. Monarch Country Club, Country Club Darien, Order of Coif, Phi Delta Phi, Beta Gamma Sigma. Home: 2269 SW Manor Hill Dr Palm City FL 34990-5713

HUNTINGTON, HILLARD GRISWOLD, economist; b. Boston, Apr. 10, 1944; s. Hillard Bell and Ruth Smedley (Wheeler) H.; m. Honor Mary Griffin, Sept. 30, 1972; children: Honora Redmond, Emma Anne Hillard. BS, Cornell U., 1967; MA, SUNY, Binghamton, 1972, PhD, 1974. Staff economist Fed. Energy Adminstrn., Washington, 1974-77; dir., sr. economist Data Resources, Inc., Washington, 1977-80; exec. dir. Energy Modeling Forum Stanford (Calif.) U., 1980—; vol. U.S. Peace Corps., Pub. Utilities Authority, Monrovia, Liberia, 1967-69; vis. rsch. assoc. Inst. Devel. Studies, U. Nairobi, Kenya, 1972-73; mem. joint U.S.-U.S.S.R. Nat. Acad. Sci. Panel on Energy Conservation, 1986-90; mem. peer rev. panel Nat. Acid Precipitation Assessment Program Task Force, Ctrs. for Excellence Govt. Can.; consultant to Argonne Nat. Lab., Electric Power Rsch. Inst., numerous others. Editor Macroeconomic Impacts of Energy Shocks, 1987, N. Am. Natural Gas Markets: selected tech. studies, 1989, Designing Competitive Electricity Markets, 1998. Named Life Fellow, Clare Hall, U. Cambridge, Eng. Mem. Internat. Assn. Energy Econs. (v.p. publs. 1990-92, program chmn. N.Am. conf., program chmn. internat. conf.), Am. Statis. Assn. (com. on energy stats. 1992-94), Am. Econ. Assn., U.S. Assn. Energy Econs. (pres. 1997). Home: 305 Hermosa Way Menlo Park CA 94025-5821 Office: Stanford U 406 Terman Ctr Stanford CA 94305

HUNTINGTON, IRENE ELIZABETH, special education educator; b. Whitman AFB, Mo., Mar. 9, 1965; d. James Bartholomew Palacio and Martina Marlene (Vasquez) Brown, stepfather Gilbert Arthur Brown. BA, Oreg. State U., 1987; MS, Western Oreg. State Coll., 1989. Cert. tchr., Colo., Nev. Tchr. spl. edn. Kapa'a (Kauai, Hawaii) Elem. Sch., 1989-90, Kapa'a High Sch., 1990-91, Louisville (Colo.) Mid. Sch., 1991-96, Pau-Wa-Lu Mid Sch, Gardnerville, Nev., 1996—. Rural Cross cultural grantee for spl. edn. Western Oreg. State Coll., 1988-89. Mem. NEA, Alpha Omicron Pi. Avocations: travel, learning, outdoor activities, reading.

HUNTINGTON, JAMES CANTINE, JR., equipment manufacturing company executive; b. Detroit, Mar. 21, 1928; s. James Cantine and Joanna (Donlon) H.; m. Bettyanne Hopkins, Sept. 21, 1973; children: James, Ann, Patricia, Carol, Judith, Amy. B.E.E., Cornell U., 1950. Mktg. exec. Harnischfeger Corp., Milw., 1953-62; cons. Milw., 1962-64; mgr. Colt Industries, Beloit, Wis., 1964-67; v.p., dir. Clark Equipment Co., Buchanan, Mich., 1967-76; sr. v.p. Am. Standard, Inc., 1976-88; ret., 1988; bd. dirs. Westinghouse Air Brake Co. Served with AUS, 1945-47, 50-53. Mem. Constrn. Industry Mfrs. Assn., Delta Kappa Epsilon, Tau Beta Pi, Eta Kappa Nu. Home: 613 Twin Pine Rd Pittsburgh PA 15215-1568

HUNTINGTON, LAWRENCE SMITH, investment banker; b. N.Y.C., June 13, 1935; s. Prescott B. and Sarah H. (Powell) H.; m. Olivia Hallowell (div.); children—Christopher Bowditch, Charles Stewart Butler, Matthew Hallowell; m. Caroline Ballard. B.A., Harvard U., 1957; LL.B., New York Law Sch., 1964, LLD (hon.), 1998. With Fiduciary Trust Co. Internat., N.Y.C., 1961—, pres., 1970-83, chief exec. officer, 1973—, chmn. bd., 1983—; dir. Bus. Execs. for Nat. Security, 1993—, Woods Hole Rsch. Ctr., 1994—, chmn., 1997—. Bd. dirs. St. Luke's-Roosevelt Hosp., N.Y.C., 1974, chmn., 1975-81, 96—; bd. dirs. World Wildlife Fund, Washington, 1977—, chmn., 1984-86, mem. nat. coun., 1996—; bd. dirs. Trinity Ch., N.Y.C., Citizens Budget Com., N.Y.C., 1970—, trustee, 1970—, chmn. 1978-84, The Commonwealth Fund, 1989—, N.Y. Law Sch., 1984—, chmn., 1992-97, Opsail, 1992—; mem. adv. bd. N.Y. State Common Retirement Fund Investment Com., 1981-87; dir. Josiah Macy, Jr. Found., 1981—; trustee Santa Fe Inst., 1988—, South Street Seaport, 1988—; mem. adv. bd. NASD Internat. Mkts., 1994-99. Lt. USCG, 1959-61. Clubs: N.Y. Yacht (trustee), Century Assn., Am. Alpine. Home: 12 Henderson Pl New York NY 10028-7557 Office: Fiduciary Trust Co Internat Two World Trade Ctr 94th Floor New York NY 10048-0772

HUNTINGTON, ROBERT GRAHAM, environmental business consultant; b. Mt. Holly, N.J., Mar. 12, 1934; s. Harold Graham and Mary Helen (Curtis) H.; m. Patricia Ann Pearsall, Jan. 28, 1956; children: Gracia Curtis, Anne Wolcott Huntington Fielden. BSME, Union Coll., 1956; MS in Engrng., Harvard U., 1959, postgrad., 1968. Prin. devel. engr. Carrier R&D Corp., Syracuse, N.Y., 1959-60; corp. v.p. Am. Air Filter Corp., Louisville, 1960-85; v.p. Allis Chalmers Corp., Milw., 1979-85; sr. v.p. Rsch. Cottrell Corp., Branchburg, N.J., 1985-86; sr. v.p., subs. dir. Environtl. Elements Corp., Balt., 1986-96; owner, prin. Huntington Cons., Cooperstown, N.Y., 1994—; pres. Indsl. Gas Cleaning Inst., Alexandria, 1982-84, dir., 1965-85; chmn. Environtl. Industry Coun., Washington, 1985-94; adv. bd. Power Industry Coun., Detroit, 1989-94;. Patentee in field. Trustee bd. advisors Union Coll., Schenectady, 1989—, past chmn., mem. dean's engrng. coun., 1989—; past dir. Pro Musica Rara, Balt.; dir. Glimmer Glass Opera Co., Cooperstown, N.Y., 1996—; pres. Glimmerglass Opera Guild, 1996—. With U.S. Army, 1956-59. Mem. Susquehanna Soc. for Prevention Cruelty to Animals (bd. dirs. 1995—), Cooperstown Country Club, Ctr. Club (Balt.), Assn. of Iron and Steel Engrs., Hon. Order of Ky. Cols., Samuel Huntington Hist. Preservation Trust. Presbyterian. Avocations: performing arts, educational leadership, historic preservation, technology, civic contribution. Home: 13 Main St Cooperstown NY 13326-1329

HUNTINGTON, SAMUEL PHILLIPS, political science educator; b. N.Y.C., Apr. 18, 1927; s. Richard T. and Dorothy S. (Phillips) H.; m. Nancy Alice Arkelyan, Sept. 8, 1957; children: Timothy Mayo, Nicholas Phillips. BA, Yale U., 1946; MA, U. Chgo., 1948; PhD, Harvard U., 1951. Instr. govt. Harvard U., Cambridge, Mass., 1950-53, asst. prof. govt., 1953-58, prof., 1962—, Thomson prof. govt., 1967-81, Clarence Dillon prof. internat. affairs, 1981-82, Eaton prof. sci. of govt., 1982—, chmn. dept., 1982-95; Albert J. Weatherhead univ. prof., 1995—; research assoc. def. policy Brookings Instn., Washington, 1952-53; faculty research fellow Social Sci. Research Council, N.Y.C., 1954-57; asst. dir. Inst. War and Peace Studies, Columbia U., 1958-59, research assoc., 1958-63, assoc. dir., 1959-62, assoc. prof. govt., 1959-62, Ford research prof., 1960-61; research assoc. Ctr. for Internat. Affairs, Harvard U., 1963-64, mem. faculty, 1964—, exec. com., 1966—, assoc. dir., 1973-78, acting dir., 1975-76, dir., 1978-89; dir. John M. Olin Inst. for Strategic Studies, 1989—; vis. fellow All Souls Coll., Oxford (Eng.) U., 1973; coordinator security planning Nat. Security Council, 1977-78; trustee Inst. Def. Analysis, 1985-98; cons. numerous govt. agys.; chmn. Harvard Acad. Internat. & Area Studies, 1996—. Author: The Soldier and the State, 1957, The Common Defense, 1961, Political Order in Changing Societies, 1968, American Politics: The Promise of Disharmony, 1981, The Third Wave: Democratization in the Late Twentieth Century, 1991, The Clash of Civilizations and the Remaking of the World Order, 1996; co-author: Political Power: USA-USSR, 1964, The Crisis of Democracy, 1975, No Easy Choice: Political Participation in Developing Countries, 1976; editor: Changing Patterns of Military Politics, 1962, The Strategic Imperative, 1982; co-editor: Foreign Policy (quar.), 1970-77, Authoritarian Politics in Modern Society, The Dynamics of Established One-Party Systems, 1970, Global Dilemmas, 1985, Reorganizing America's Defense, 1985, Understanding Political Development, 1986; also articles. Chmn. coun. on Vietnamese studies S.E. Asia Devel. Adv. Group, 1966-69; mem. Presdl. Task Force on Internat. Devel., 1969-70, Commn. on U.S.-Latin Am. Rels., 1974-76, Commn. on Integrated Long-Term Strategy, 1986-88, Commn. on Protecting and Reducing Govt. Secrecy, 1995-97; trustee Internat. Devel. Found., 1969-76. Served with AUS, 1946-47. Recipient Silver Pen award Jour. Fund, 1960, Grawemayer World Order award, 1992; fellow Ctr. for Advanced Study in Behavioral Scis., Stanford, 1969-70. Fellow Am. Acad. Arts and Scis.; mem. Internat. Polit. Sci. Assn. (coun. 1973-75), Coun. on Fgn. Rels., Internat. Inst. Strategic Studies, Am. Polit. Sci. Assn. (coun. 1969-71, v.p. 1984-85, pres.-elect 1985-86, pres. 1986-87). Office: Harvard U John M Olin Inst Ctr for Internat Affairs 1737 Cambridge St Cambridge MA 02138-3016

HUNTINGTON, THOMAS MANSFIELD, editor; b. Augusta, Maine, July 15, 1960; s. Milton Francis and Lillian Rose (Munn) H.; m. Beth Ann Smith, Mar. 23, 1991; children: Katherine Smith, Samuel Murphy. BA, U. So. Calif., 1982. Mng. editor Saturday Rev., Washington, 1985-86, Air & Space/Smithsonian, Washington, 1988-96; editor Historic Traveler, Harrisburg, Pa., 1996-99, Am. History, 1998—. Office: Am History 6405 Flank Dr Harrisburg PA 17112-2750

HUNTLEY, JAMES ROBERT, government official, international affairs scholar and consultant; b. Tacoma, Wash., July 27, 1923; s. Wells and Laura H.; m. Colleen Grounds Smith, May 27, 1967; children by previous marriage: Mark, David, Virginia, Jean. BA magna cum laude in Econs., Sociology, U. Wash., 1948, postgrad. sociology and internat. relations (Carnegie fellow), 1951; MA in Internat. Relations, Harvard U., 1956. Cons. Wash. Parks Recreation Commn., Olympia, 1949-51; exchange of persons officer U.S. Fgn. Service, Frankfurt, Nuremberg, Germany, 1952-54; dir. cultural center USIA, Hof/Saale, Germany, 1954-55; USIA postgrad. scholar Harvard U., 1955-56; asst. to Pres.'s coordinator for Hungarian relief Washington, 1956; European regional affairs officer USIA, Washington, 1956-58; dep. pub. affairs officer U.S. Mission to European Communities, Brussels, 1958-60; mem. U.S. Delegation to Atlantic Congress, London, 1959; sec. organizing com. Atlantic Inst., Brussels and Milan, 1960; exec. officer and co-founder Atlantic Inst., Paris, 1960-63; dir. Atlantic Inst. (N.Am. Office), Washington, 1963-65; founder, sec. Com. Atlantic Studies, 1963-65; sec. edn. com. NATO Parliamentarians Conf., Brussels, 1960-64; program asso., internat. affairs div. Ford Found., N.Y.C., 1965-67; sec. gen. Council Atlantic Colls., London, 1967-68; ind. writer, cons., lectr., internat. affairs Guildford, Eng., 1968-74; founder, sec. Assn. Mid-Atlantic Clubs, 1970-74; founder, sec. gen. Standing Conf. Atlantic Orgns., 1972-74; rsch. fellow, sr. advisor to pres. on internat. affairs Battelle Meml. Inst., Seattle, 1974-83; pres., chief exec. officer Atlantic Council of U.S., Washington, 1983-85; ind. cons., author internat. affairs, 1985—; European corr., environ. affairs Saturday Rev./World, 1972-74; Corrs. World Wide, London, 1970-74; European corr. Non-Profit Report, 1970-74. Author: The NATO Story, 1965, (with W.R. Burgess) Europe and America - The Next Ten Years, 1970, Man's Environment and the Atlantic Alliance, 1972, Uniting the Democracies, 1980, Pax Democratica—A Strategy for the 21st Century, 1998; contbr. articles to profl. jours. Bd. dirs. Internat. Standing Conf. Phlanthropy, 1969-74, Assn. to Unite Democracies, 1976-94, Seattle Com. Fgn. Rels., 1975-78, World Affairs Coun. Seattle, 1975-83, adv. bd. 1986—, Bainbridge Island Land Trust, 1994-97; founding chmn. Coms. for a Cmty. of Democracies, 1979-92; co-founder 21st Century Found., 1987—; mem. adv. bd. 21st Century Trust, London, 1988—; co-founder Next Century Initiative, 1992-95, New Century Initiative, 1996—, pres. 1996-98. Recipient Disting. Eagle Scout award 1995. Mem. Rainier Club (Seattle), DACOR (Washington). Home and Office: 1811 Eagle Harbor Ln NE Bainbridge Island WA 98110-2142 *For a full life, embrace a worthy cause. Mine is the unity of the democracies. America's most precious asset is its free political system. It can be successfully defended only if we merge our force, our hearts and our fortune with like-minded peoples. Like-mindedness is not simply a gift of history; it must be cultivated. My life's aim has been to forge consensus among the democracies as a prelude to the creation of a free, just, and durable world order.*

HUNTLEY, ROBERT ROSS, physician, educator; b. Wadesboro, N.C., Sept. 6, 1926; s. George W. and Louise (Ross) H.; m. Joan Cornoni, Apr. 10, 1976; children: Katherine, Robert, Julia, Elizabeth, Jeffress. B.S. in Chemistry, Davidson Coll., 1947; M.D., Bowman-Gray Sch. Medicine, 1951. Diplomate: Am. Bd. Preventive Medicine (trustee 1974-78), Am. Bd. Family Practice. Intern U. Mich. Hosp., Ann Arbor, 1951-53; resident, fellow N.C. Meml. Hosp., Chapel Hill, 1959-62; pvt. practice medicine Warrenton, N.C., 1953-58; from instr. to assoc. prof. medicine and preventive medicine U. N.C., Chapel Hill, 1959-68, adj. prof. health policy and adminstrn. Sch Pub. Health, 1989—; asso. dir. Nat. Center for Health Services Research, HEW, 1968-70; prof., chmn. dept. community and family medicine Georgetown U., 1970-89, prof. emeritus, 1989—; pres. Georgetown U. Community Health Plan, Inc., 1972-80; chmn. health care tech. study sect. HEW, 1978-82; adj. prof. dept family medicine U. N.C. Sch. Medicine, 1994—. Editor various profl. books; contbr. articles to profl. jours. Served with USN, 1945-46. Mem. APHA, Assn. Tchrs. Preventive Medicine, D.C. Med. Soc., N.C. Med. Soc., Acad. Medicine Washington (emeritus). Democrat. Methodist.

HUNTLEY, ROBERT STEPHEN, newspaper editor; b. Winston-Salem, N.C., Mar. 6, 1943; m. Linda Fabry; children: Kristine Elizabeth, Katherine Vallie. BA in Journalism, U. N.C., 1965. Reporter UPI, various locations, 1965-69; writer, editor broadcast and gen. news depts. UPI, Chgo., 1969-77, exec. editor nat. broadcast dept., 1977-78; bur. chief Commodity News Svc., Chgo., 1978-79, U.S. News & World Report, Chgo., 1979-82; assoc. editor U.S. News & World Report, Washington, 1982-85, sr. editor, 1985-86; reporter, rewrite specialist Chgo. Sun Times, 1986-90, met. editor, 1990-91, asst. mng. editor/metro, 1991-97, editl. page editor, 1997—; bd. dirs. City News Bur., Chgo, 1993-97, pres., 1996. Recipient Stick-O-Type award for feature writing Chgo. Newspaper Guild, 1987, Appreciation cert. for outstanding contbns. to freedom of info. Nat. Ctr. Freedom of Info. Studies at Loyola U.-Chgo., 1993. Mem. Ill. Freedom of Info. Coun. (v.p. 1994). Office: Chgo Sun-Times 401 N Wabash Ave Chicago IL 60611-5642

HUNTLEY-SPEARE, ANNE, language educator; b. Gettysburg, Pa., Apr. 10, 1952; d. James Benjamin and Dorothy Uadah (Ely) Huntley; m. Redfield LeBaron Speare, June 28, 1975 (div. 1989); 1 child, Johanna Pocahontas. BA in German, Roanoke Coll., 1974; MA in German, U. Va., 1989; postgrad., Pa. State U., 1989—. Cert. tchr., Pa. Tchr. Campbell County Schs., Va., 1974-76, Inlingua Sprachschule, Dortmund, Germany, 1981-83, Ecolingua Sprachakademie, Nuernberg, Germany, 1986-87, Juniata Coll., 1990; instr. foreign language Pa. State U., 1990-93; tchr. Northern Tioga Sch. Dist., Pa., 1993-94; substitute tchr. Hollidaysburg, 1996—, Altoona (Pa.) Area Sch. Dist., 1996—; grading asst. U. Va., 1989. Contbr. articles to profl. jours. Mem. adult choir Zion Luth. Ch., Hollidaysburg, Pa., 1994—, co-leader Ruth Cir., 1997-98; counselor Caroline Furnace Luth. Youth Camp, St. David's Ch., Va., 1972-73; jr. choir dir. Trinity Luth. Ch., Kalamazoo, 1977-79, St. Mark Luth. Ch., Charlottesville, Pa., 1989. Dupont fellow U. Va., 1987-88, 88-89, Commonwealth fellow U. Va., 1987-88; Randall-MacIver scholar U. Va., 1987-88, Keller scholar Pa. State U., 1991-92. Mem. MLA. Lutheran. Avocations: singing, child rearing, doing handicrafts. Home: 227 Willowbrook Vlg Duncansville PA 16635-7116

HUNTOON, ABBY ELIZABETH, artist, teacher; b. Providence, R.I., Sept. 8, 1951; d. William Huntoon and Marjorie (Aldrich) Bradshaw; m. Phil Kaelin, Sept. 25, 1993. BS, Trinity Coll., 1973; MFA from program in Artisanry, Boston U., 1985. Instr. Boston U., 1983-84; co-owner, adminstr., tchr. Sawyer St. Studios, South Portland, Maine, 1989—; project coord. Main Coll. of Art, 1988, mem. Maine Arts Commn., Visual Arts Panel, 1988-92; summer instr. Maine Coll. of Art, 1989, 90; workshop conductor Maine Coll. of Art, 1989, 95, U. Southern Maine, 1991. Artist: works exhibited at Makers 86, Bowdoin Mus. of Art, Brunswick, Maine, 1986, Ceramics Now, 27th Ceramic Nat. Exhibition (traveling U.S. for 2 years), 1987, Maine Coast Artists, Portland, Maine, 1988, 46th Ceramics Annual, Lang Art Gallery, Scripps Coll., Claremont, Calif., 1990; Northeastern Splendor (chosen ceramics rep. from Maine) Boston, 1991, Makers 93, Portland Mus. of Art, 1993; one person shows Architectural Ceramics, Frick Gallery, Belfast, Maine, 1990, 93; two person show Lakes Gallery, South Casco, Maine, 1995, Old York Hist. Soc., 1997, Round Top Ctr. for the Arts, 1997, Robert Clements Gallery, Portland, 1997; corp. collections include Putnam Hayes and Bartlett Inc., Cambridge, Mass., Standish Ayer and Wood, Boston, The Index Group Inc., Cambridge. Recipient Merit award Maine Crafts Assn., 1986; grantee: NEA, 1988. Avocations: sailing, skiing, political activities. Office: Sawyer Street Studios 131 Sawyer St South Portland ME 04106

HUNTOON, CAROLYN LEACH, physiologist; b. Leesville, La., Aug. 25, 1940; m. Harrison H. Huntoon; 1 child, Sally Ann. BS in Biology, Northwestern State Coll., Natchitoches, La., 1962; degree in med. technol., Ochsner Found. Hosp., New Orleans, 1962; MS in Physiology, Baylor U., 1966, PhD, 1968; D (hon.), Northwestern State U., 1994. Head endocrinology lab. NASA Johnson Space Ctr., Houston, 1968-74, head endocrine and biochemistry labs., 1974-76, spl. asst. to dir., 1976-77, chief space metabolism and biochemistry br., 1976-77, chief biomed. labs. br., 1977-84, assoc. dir., 1984-87, dir. space and life scis., 1987-94, dir., 1994-96, spl. asst. to NASA adminstr., office sci. and technol. policy, exec. office pres., 1996—; mem. astronaut selection bd. NASA-Johnson Space Ctr., dep. chief for personnel devel. astronaut office; mem. sci. adv. bd. USAF. Contbr. articles to profl. jours. With USAF, 1985—. Recipient Arthus S. Fleming award, Career Achievement award Nat. Civil Svc. League, Paul Bert award, Hubertus Strughold award, Yuri Gagarin medal USSR Fedn. Cosmonautics, 1987, Presdl. Rank Meritorious Exec. award, 1991, Disting. Rank award, 1993; named Outstanding Alumna Northwestern State U., 1977, Outstanding Woman in Sci., Am. Women in Sci., Disting. profl. Woman of Yr., U. Tex. Health Sci. Ctr., 1985, Outstanding Scientist, State of Tex., 1991. Fellow AIAA, Am. Astronautical Soc. (Lovelace award 1991, Space Flight award 1994), Aerospace Med. Assn. (Louis H. Bauer Founder's award); mem. Assn. Bus. and Profl. Women, Am. Physiol. Soc., Endocrine Soc., Internat. Acad. Astronautics. Office: OSTP EOP Old Exec Office Bld 17th St and Penn Ave Washington DC 20502*

HUNTOON, ROBERT BRIAN, chemist, food industry consultant; b. Braintree, Mass., Mar. 1, 1927; s. Benjamin Harrison and Helen Edna (Worden) H.; m. Joan Fairman Graham, Mar. 1, 1952; children: Brian Graham, Benjamin Robert, Elisabeth Ellen, Janet Lynne, Joelle. BS in Chemistry, Northeastern U., 1949, MS, 1961. Analytical chemist Mass. Dept. Public Health; microbiologist Met. Dist. Commn. Mass. Dept. Public Health, Boston, 1950-53; rsch. and devel. chemist Heveatex Corp., Melrose, Mass., 1953-56; with Gen. Foods Corp., 1956-70; acting quality control mgr. Gen. Foods Corp., Woburn, Mass., 1965-67; head group rsch. and devel. Gen. Foods Corp., Tarrytown, N.Y., 1967-70; dir. quality control U.S. Flavor div. Internat. Flavors & Fragrances, Teterboro, N.J., 1970-83, mgr. tech. svcs., 1983-87, mgr. product devel., 1987-89, cons., 1989-92; ind. cons. product devel., 1989—. Contbr. articles on flavor and food quality control to profl. and co. publs.; patentee gelatin compositions and mfg. processes. Served with USCG, 1945-46. Mem. Essential Oils Assn. (com. mem.), Flavor and Extracts Mfg. Assn. (com. mem.), Am. Chem. Soc., Inst. Food Technologists, Internat. Platform Assn., Indsl. Mgmt. Club (v.p. 1967) (Woburn), Croton Yacht Club, Saugus River Yacht Club (treas. 1967-68). Republican. Presbyterian. Office: 7 Scotland Hill Park Chestnut Ridge NY 10977-5908

HUNTRESS, BETTY ANN, former music store proprietor, educator; b. Poughkeepsie, N.Y., Apr. 29, 1932; d. Emmett Slater and Catherine V. (Kihlmire) Brundage; m. Arnold Ray Huntress, June 26, 1954; children: Catherine, Michael, Carol, Alan. BA, Cornell U., 1954. Tchr. high sch., Bordentown, N.J., 1954-55; part-time asst. to prof. Delta Coll., Northwood Inst., Midland, Mich., 1958-71; part-time tchr. Midland Pub. Schs., 1968—; owner, mgr. The Music Stand, Midland, 1979-82. Bd. dirs. Midland Center for Arts, 1978-86 ; v.p. MCFTA (Arts Center), 1980-84, Friends of the Ctr., 1985— ; mem. charter bd. mgrs. Matrix Midland Ann. Arts and Sci. Festival, 1977-80; cons. Girl Scouts U.S., 1964-76; mem. Mich. Internat. Council, 1975-76; bd. dirs. Literary Council Midland County, 1986-94, sec., 1987-91; mem. Midland Hist. Soc., 1990—, mem. Dow centennial com., 1996-98. Named Midland Musician of Yr., 1977. Mem. Music Soc. Midland Center for Arts (dir. 1971-86, chmn. 1976-79), AAUW (dir. 1962-73, pres. 1971-73, mem. mich. state div. bd. 1973-75, 1st v.p. Mich. state div. 1983-85 , bd. dirs. 1993-95, outstanding woman as agt. of change award 1977, fellowship grant named in her honor 1976), Midland Symphony League Soc. (2d v.p.), LWV (bd. dirs. 1986-90, com. charter schs. 1995—), Community Concert Soc., Women's Study Club of Midland (pres. 1995-96), Friends of Libr.,Kappa Delta Epsilon, Pi Lambda Theta, Alpha Xi Delta. Presbyterian. Home: 5316 Sunset Dr Midland MI 48640-2536

HUNTRESS, WESLEY THEODORE, JR., scientist; b. Washington, Apr. 11, 1942; s. Wesley Theodore and Elizabeth Agnes (Moran) H.; m. Roseann Albano, June 22, 1973; 1 child, Garret. BS, Brown U., 1964; PhD, Stanford U., 1968. Scientist Jet Propulsion Lab., Pasadena, Calif., 1968-88; dep. dir earth sci. NASA, Washington, 1988-90, dir. solar system exploration, 1990-93, assoc. adminstr. space sci., 1993-98; dir. geophys. lab. Carnegie Instn. Washington, 1998—. Office: Geophys Lab Carnegie Instn Washington 5251 Broad Branch Rd NW Washington DC 20015-1305

HUNTSMAN, JON MEADE, chemical company executive; b. 1937. BS, U. Pa., 1959; MBA, U. So. Calif., 1970. With Olson Bros, Inc., North Hollywood, Calif., from 1961; assoc. adminstr. HEW, spl. asst. to the pres., 1971-72; with Huntsman Container Corp., Salt Lake City, 1972-83, Huntsman Chem. Corp, Salt Lake City, 1982—; chmn. bd. dirs., CEO Huntsman Corp., Salt Lake City, 1996—. Pres. mission LDS Ch., Washington, 1980-83. Office: Huntsman Corp 500 Huntsman Way Salt Lake City UT 84108-1235

HUNTSMAN, LAWRENCE DARROW, lawyer; b. Salt Lake City, Jan. 21, 1934; s. Orson Lawrence and Vera Maude (Day) H.; BS, Pa. State U., 1956; LLB, George Washington U., 1959; m. Lynn Maroe; children by previous marriage: Laura, Kathleen, Marguerite, Holbrook. Admitted to Va. bar, 1959, D.C. bar, 1961; clk. D.C. Superior Ct., 1959-60; asst. corp. counsel, D.C., 1960-61; assoc. Welch, Mott & Morgan, 1961-64, Miller, Brown, Gildenhorn, 1964-69; ptnr. Brown, Gildenhorn & Statland, Washington, 1969-75; pres. Pan Mediterranean Shipping Corp., 1975-82, Assorted Techs., Inc., 1994-97; dir. Ashley Corp.; gen. counsel KeyByte Techs., Inc., 1993-97. Mem. D.C. Bar Assn., Va. Bar Assn. E-mail: ldhuntsman@earthlink.net. Home: 11645 Chapel Rd Clifton VA 20124-1907 Office: 1101 17th St NW Washington DC 20036-4704 also: 10374 Democracy Ln Fairfax VA 22030-2522

HUNTSMAN, LEE, university provost, academic administrator. Provost, v.p. acad. affairs U. Wash., Seattle. Office: U Wash PO Box 351237 Seattle WA 98195-1237

HUNTTING, CYNTHIA COX, artist; b. San Francisco, Sept. 2, 1936; d. E. Morris and Margaret (Storke) Cox; m. Edward Tyler Huntting Jr., Mar. 8, 1969 (div. 1974). *Cynthia Cox Huntting is a ninth generation Californian. José Francisco Ortega, a direct ancestor of her's, was discoverer of the San Francisco Bay.* BA, Smith Coll., 1958; San Francisco Art Inst., 1959. Artist Emporium White House, San Francisco, 1958-61; artist, staff Pace Program Stanford U., 1962-64; artist World Affairs Council No. Calif., San Francisco, 1964-67; artist pvt. practice San Francisco, 1968—; mem. Modern Art Council Bd. San Francisco Mus. Modern Art, 1970-78. Active Jr. League San Francisco, Inc. Mem. Birnam Wood Golf Club (Montecito, Calif.), Town and Country, Calif. Tennis. Republican. Episcopalian. Avocations: tennis, fly fishing. Home and Office: 2720 Lyon St San Francisco CA 94123-3815

HUNTWORK, JAMES RODEN, lawyer; b. Milw., May 6, 1948; s. Daniel Lawrence and Gladys (Roden) H.; m. Patience Tipton Huntwork, July 7, 1972; children: Andrew Stuart, Sarah Noel. BA with distinction, Shimer Coll., 1968; JD, Yale U., 1972, MA Econs., 1973. Bar: Ariz. 1977. Atty. Sullivan & Worcester, Boston, 1972-77, Jennings, Strouss & Salmon, Phoenix, 1977-91, Fennemore Craig, Phoenix, 1992-98, Salmon, Lewis & Weldon, Phoenix, Ariz., 1998—. Dir. exec. com. Phoenix Econ. Growth Corp., 1987-91; state ballot security chmn. Ariz. Rep. Party, Phoenix, 1992—; originator The Comml. Law Project for Ukraine, 1991—. Co-recipient Judge Learned Hand Human Rels. award Am. Jewish Com., 1992. Mem. ABA, Ariz. Bar Assn., Maricopa County Bar Assn., Phoenix C. of C. (N.Am. Free Trade Task Force 1991-95). Republican. Office: Salmon Lewis & Weldon 4444 N 32nd St Ste 200 Phoenix AZ 85018-3956

HUNTZICKER, WILLIAM EDWARD, journalism educator; b. St. Paul, Aug. 18, 1946; s. Kenneth Verndale and Edith Hale (Bennion) H.; m. Linda DeLaurenti, 1974; children: James William, Rachel Lyn. BA in History, Mont. State U., 1968; MA in Am. Studies, U. Minn., 1973, PhD, 1978, cert. social studies, 1989. Ranch hand various family ranches, Miles City, Mont., 1964; electronic tech. Teledyne, Inc., Miles City, 1965; reporter, photographer Miles City Daily Star, 1966-67; reporter, editor Associated Press, Mpls., 1968-69; writer U. Minn. News Svc., Mpls., 1970-79; asst. prof. journalism U. Wis., River Falls, 1979-86; media writer Minn. Ho. of Reps., St. Paul, 1987; lectr. sch. of journalism and mass communication U. Minn., Mpls., 1988-97; asst. prof. mass comm. Bemidji (Minn.) State U., 1997-99; writer/editor Minn. Hist. Soc., St. Paul, 1999—; freelance Wis. corr. St. Paul Pioneer Press, 1984-86; editl. advisor The Minn. Daily, U. Minn., 1989-90, 92-97. Author: The Popular Press: 1833-65, 1999; contbr. articles to profl. jours. Chair parks com. Marcy Holmes Neighborhood Assn., Mpls., 1977-86, pres., 1981-82, sec., 1982-83; co-pres. S.E. Mpls. Planning and Coord. Com., 1982-83, sec., 1978-79. Congregationalist. Home: 415 8th St SE Minneapolis MN 55414-1223 Office: Minn Hist Soc 345 Kellogg Blvd W Saint Paul MN 55102

HUNZICKER, WARREN JOHN, research consultant, physician, cardiologist; b. Lawrence, Kans., Sept. 26, 1920; s. Carl John and Edith (Glenn) H.; m. Marjorie Jean Owen, Apr. 16, 1946; children—Karen Hunzicker Putnam, Kathleen Ann. A.B., U. Kans., 1942, M.D., 1944; postgrad. in medicine, Harvard U. Hosps., Peter Bent Brigham and Boston City Hosps., 1946-48. Intern St. Luke's Hosp., 1944-45; practice medicine specializing in cardiology Spokane, Wash., 1948-51, 54-58; med. dir. Nat. Life & Accident Co., Nashville, 1958-60; v.p., med. dir. Kansas City Life, Mo., 1960-80; sr. v.p. med. N.Am. Reassurance, N.Y.C., 1980-86; assoc. clin. prof. medicine U. Mo., Kansas City, 1961-82; dir. M.I.B. Inc., Boston; med. cons. Life Ins. Med. Research Fund, Washington, 1983-97; bd. dirs. Kansa City Life Ins. Co. Contbr. articles to profl. jours. Served to lt. M.C., USNR, 1941-46, 52-53, Korea. Levine fellow in cardiology Harvard U. (Peter Bent Brigham Hosp.), 1951-52. Fellow Am. Coll. Cardiology; mem. AMA, Council Life Ins. (chmn. med. sect. 1971-72), Assn. Ins. Med. Dirs. (exec. council 1971-73), Mo. Med. Assn., Union League of N.Y.C. Republican. Methodist. Avocations: fishing; hiking. Home: 1248 Stratford Rd Kansas City MO 64113-1326

HUPALO, MEREDITH TOPLIFF, artist, illustrator; b. Tarpon Springs, Fla., Apr. 28, 1917; d. Walter and Maurine (Martin) Topliff; cert. in design Pratt Inst., 1938; m. Nicholas Hupalo, July 13, 1940 (dec. Sept. 1977); children: Walter Topliff, John Nicholas. One-woman shows: Tarpon Springs Public Libr., 1945, Valley Stream (N.Y.) Mus., 1962, Contemporary Arts, Inc., N.Y.C., 1966, Jet Clubs Internat., N.Y.C., Henry Waldinger Libr., Valley Stream, N.Y., 1977, East River Savs. Bank, Valley Stream, 1978; two-person show: Art League of Daytona Beach, 1986; represented in permanent collection Valley Stream Pub. Libr., Tarpon Springs (Fla.) Pub. Libr., Eastern Airlines Exec. Offices, N.Y.C.; tchr. printmaking Nassau County (N.Y.) Home Extension Svc.; art adviser Valley Stream Mus., 1962-64; illustrator Eastern Airlines, 1964-68; artist Shell Oil Co., 1968-70; designer Continental Can Co., N.Y.C., 1970-73; art tchr. Astor (Fla.) Community Ctr., 1980-82. Active Mt. Dora Ctr. for the Arts of Lake County, 1991. Recipient spl. award oil painting 34th Nat. Spring Exhbn. Nat. Art League L.I., 1964, gold medal in oil painting 35th Membership Show, 1965; 1st pl. fine art Fla. Silver Springs Arts & Crafts Festival, 1980; 1st place award Umatilla Fall Festival (Fla.), 1983 merit award, 1985; merit award Tampa Realistic Artists, 1984; Best in Show award Nat. League Am. Pen Women, 1984; 1st pl. Fla. Extension Homemakers Cultural Arts; Award of Distinction, Pioneer Art Settlement, 1987, Honorable Mention Pioneer Art Settlement, 1991, 1st Pl. award Ann. Lake County Juried Art Show Mt. Dora Ctr. for Arts, 1992, Best in Show and 1st in Graphics awards Umatilla Fall Festival, 1993. Mem. Fla. Watercolor Soc. (assoc., participating artist I), Nat. Art League L.I. (treas. 1959-60), Art League of Daytona Beach (Lillian Gittner Meml. award 1988, 64th membership show Grumbacher gold award 1996), Nat. League Am. Pen Women (Fla. br. 1987, v.p. 1991, Grumacher silver medal 1995), Mus. Arts and Scis., DeLand Mus., Astor Area C. of C. (dir. 1981-82). Methodist. Works include Paintings With Markers, 1972. Home: 400 E Howry Apt 801 Deland FL 32724-5437

HUPCHICK, DENNIS PAUL, history educator, writer; b. Monongahela, Pa., Sept. 3, 1948; s. Louis Paul and Ethel Joan Hupchick; m. Anne-Marie Jaszenski, June 4, 1976; stepchildren: Beatrice Girard, Isabelle Girard. BA, U. Pitts., 1970, MA, 1972, PhD, 1983. Libr. hist. collections cons. Tamburitzan Nat. Folk Arts Ctr., Inc., Pitts., 1983-84, 88; rsch. cons. Graphic Arts Tech. Found., 1984-85; assoc. prof. history Wilkes U., Wilkes-Barre, Pa., 1990—; dir. East European and Russian studies minor degree program Wilkes U., Wilkes-Barre, 1991—. Author: The Bulgarians in the Seventeenth Century: Slavic Orthodox Society under Ottoman Rule, 1993, Culture and History in Eastern Europe, 1994, Conflict and Chaos in Eastern Europe, 1995; co-author: (with Harold E. Cox) A Concise Historical Atlas of Eastern Europe, 1996 (Outstanding Acad. Bk. of 1997, 1998). Lang. fellow Nat. Def. Fgn. Lang. Fellowship, 1974-75, 75-76, 77-78; Exch. Rsch. fellow to Bulgaria, Internat. Rsch. and Exchs. Bd., 1976-77; Rsch. scholar Fulbright Program, 1989. Mem. Am. Assn. Advancement of Slavic Studies, Bulgarian Studies Assn. (pres. 1992-95). Avocations: photography, military miniatures, book collecting, carpentry. E-mail: dhupchi@wilkes1.wilkes.edu. FAX: 570-408-1005. Office: Wilkes Univ Dept History 170 S Franklin St Wilkes-Barre PA 18766

HUPKE, DAVID R., photographer; b. Streator, Ill., Mar. 31, 1963; s. Horst and Waltraud (Ollmann) H. AAS in Photography, Colo. Inst. Art, Denver, 1997. Trail photographer Charles Sommers Canoe Base/Boy Scouts Am., Ely, Minn., 1983; counselor, photographer Vision Quest, Erie, Pa., 1985-87; instr., photographer Outward Bound, Fla., 1987-91; counselor, photographer Moose Internat., Mooseheart, Ill., 1991-95; photographer Hupke Imaging, Pekin, Ill., 1995—. Photo-documentary 50cc scooter journey traveling across Am., 1993, photo-documentary 50cc scooter journey Mt. Evans Observatory, 1997; contbr. to Pekin Mag., 1993; group exhibitions include Erie (Pa.) Summer Festival Arts, 1995; represented in permanent collections Dorothy Molter Mus., Ely, Minn., 1995, 96. Scoutmaster, Boy Scouts Am., Mooseheart, 1992-95. Exhibited at Denver ZIP 802. Home: 708 Arlan Dr Pekin IL 61554-5202

HUPP, HARRY L., federal judge; b. L.A., Apr. 5, 1929; s. Earl L. and Dorothy (Goodspeed) H.; m. Patricia Hupp, Sept. 13, 1953; children: Virginia, Karen, Keith, Brian. AB, Stanford U., 1953, LLB, 1955. Bar: Calif. 1956, U.S. Dist. Ct. (cen. dist.) Calif. 1956, U.S. Supreme Ct. Pvt. practice law Beardsley, Hufstedler and Kemble, L.A., 1955-72; judge Superior Ct. of Los Angeles, 1972-84; appointed fed. dist. judge U.S. Dist. Ct. (cen. dist.) Calif., L.A., 1984-97, sr. judge, 1997—. Served with U.S. Army, 1950-52. Mem. Calif. Bar Assn., Los Angeles County Bar Assn. (Trial Judge of Yr. 1983), Order of Coif, Phi Alpha Delta. Office: US Dist Ct 312 N Spring St Ste 218P Los Angeles CA 90012-4704

HUPP, ROBERT MARTIN, artistic director, educator; b. Laurel, Del., July 20, 1959; s. Robert William and Martha Angeline (Martin) H.; m. Laura Ann Hood, Mar. 26, 1988; children: Dillon Robert, William Lloyd, Spencer Martin. Cert. acting, Nat. Shakespeare Co. Conservatory, 1983; BA in Dramatic Arts and Theatre Lit. magna cum laude, Dickinson Coll., 1981; MA, NYU, 1999. Mgr. box office Cubiculo Theatre, N.Y.C., 1981-82; actor Octagon Repertory Co., Worchester, N.Y., 1982; actor Nat. Shakespeare Co., N.Y.C., 1983-84, assoc. tour dir., 1984, asst. dir., 1985; mng. dir. Jean Cocteau Repertory, N.Y.C., 1984-88; assoc. artistic dir. jean Cocteau Repertory, N.Y.C., 1988-89, artistic dir., 1989—; assoc. prof. Dickinson Coll., Carlisle, Pa., 1993—; chair dept. theatre and dance Dickinson Coll., Carlisle, 1995-97; panelist theatre programs N.J. State Coun. Arts, 1985-98, panelist major impact pro panelist tech. assistance fund N.Y.C. Dept. Cultural Affairs 1988-89; panelist cultural grants Westchester (N.Y.) County Arts Coun., 1989; guest dir. GeVa Theatre, Rochester, N.Y., 1990-91; guest lectr. Baruch Coll., N.Y.C., 1992—; vis. instr. Dickinson Coll., Carlisle, 1991-93; guest instr. Nat. Shakespeare Conservatory, N.Y.C., 1991—; lectr. in field. Appeared in plays Misalliance, Much Ado About Nothing, Hamlet, A Funny Thing Happened..., Arsenic and Old Lace, Man of La Mancha, Twelfth Night, Spoon River Anthology; asst. dir. Macbeth, 1985, Othello, 1985, 87, Three Sisters, 1988, Break of Noon, 1988; dir. Cabaret, 1981, Good, 1989, On the Verge, 1989, Travesties, 1989, Leonce and Lena, 1990, The Infernal Machine, 1990, A Man's A Man, 1991, The Skin of Our Teeth, 1991, Barbeque in 29 Palms, 1991, Lysistrata, 1992, Orchards, 1992, Under Milk Wood, 1992, Much Ado About Nothing, 1993, Anything Goes, 1993, The First Lulu, 1993, Romance Language, 1993, Three Sisters, 1994, Napoli Milionaria, 1995, Our Town, 1995, Major Barbara, 1996, The Winter's Tale, 1996, Mother Courage and Her Children, 1997, Balm in Gilead, 1997, The Cure at Troy, 1997, Twelfth Night, 1998, Misalliance, 1998, Caesar & Cleopatra, 1999; prodr. The Prince of Homburg, 1989-90, A Man's Man, 1989-90, Life is a Dream, 1989-90, Travesties, 1989-90, The Importance of Being Earnest, 1989-90, Julius Caesar, 1990-91, Wozeck/Leonce and Lena, 1990-91, When We Dead Awaken, 1990-91, The Infernal Machine, 1990-91, Misalliance, 1990-91, Endgame, 1991-92, Mary Stuart, 1991-92, Galileo, 1991-92, The Skin of Our Teeth, 1991-92, The Cenci, 1992-93, Much Ado About Nothing, 1992-93, The Idiot, 1992-93, An Old Actress in the Role of Dostoevsky's Wife, 1992-93, Under Milk Wood, 1992-93, The Brothers Karamozov, 1993-94, Iphigenia at Aulis, 1993-94, Heartbreak House, 1993-94, Enrico IV, 1993-94, The First Lulu, 1993-94, The Keepers, 1994-95, The Country Wife, 1994-95, The Cherry Orchard, 1994-95, Hamlet, 1994-95, Waiting for Godot, 1995-96, Nathan The Wise, 1995-96, The Lady From the Sea, 1995-96, What the Butler Saw, 1996-97, Six Characters in Search of an Author, 1996-97, The Lucky Chance, 1996-97; contbr. articles to profl. jours. Recipient Manhattan Borough Pres.' Citation for Excellence in the Arts, 1989, Off Off Broadway Rev. award for Sustained Excellence, 1997, Piradello Soc. Am. award for Contributions to Theatre, 1998; rsch. grantee Mellon Found., 1993. Mem. Alliance Resident Theatres N.Y. (bd. dirs. 1987-93), Internat. Theatre Inst., Theatre Comm. Group. Home: 257 Walnut St Carlisle PA 17013-3735 Office: Jean Cocteau Repertory Bouwerie Lane Theatre 330 Bowery New York NY 10012-2462

HUPPAUF, BERND R., educator; b. Waldenburg, Germany, Oct. 19, 1942; came to U.S., 1994; s. Walter and Hertha H.; m. Barbara Arnscheid; children: Anna, Fabian, Markus. DPhil, Tubingen U., Germany, 1970. Asst. prof. Tubingen U., Germany, 1970-73, Regensburg U., Germany, 1973-78; prof. U. New South Wales, Australia, 1976-93, NYU, N.Y.C., 1994—. Author: Von Sozialer Utopie, 1971; co-author: Methodendiskission, 1972, 95; editor: Ansichten vom Krieg, 1984, War, Violence and Modernity, 1997. Home: 119 Bergen St Brooklyn NY 11201 Office: 19 University Pl New York NY 10003

HUPPER, JOHN ROSCOE, lawyer; b. N.Y.C., June 16, 1925; s. Roscoe Henderson and Dorothy Wallace (Healy) H.; m. Joyce Shirley McCoy, June 14, 1952; children: John R. Jr., Gail J., Craig W. AB, Bowdoin Coll., 1949; LLB, Harvard U., 1952. Bar: N.Y. 1954, U.S. Supreme Ct. 1960. Assoc. Cravath, Swaine & Moore, N.Y.C., 1952-60, ptnr., 1961-95. Overseer Bowdoin Coll., 1970-82, trustee, 1982-95; trustee Allen-Stevenson Sch., 1968-96; bd. dirs. Legal Aid Soc., N.Y.C., 1971-76, Travelers Aid Soc., N.Y., 1962-79. Served with U.S. Army, 1943-46. Fellow Am. Coll. Trial Lawyers; mem. ABA, N.Y. State Bar Assn., N.Y. County Lawyers Assn., Assn. of Bar of City of N.Y., N.Y. Supreme Ct. (com. character and fitness appellate divsn. 1st dept. 1992—, spl. master appellate divsn. 1st dept. 1982—), Apawamis Club, Down Town Assn., Univ. Club, Union Club. Republican. Home: 105 E 67th St New York NY 10021-5901 Office: Cravath Swaine & Moore 825 8th Ave New York NY 10019-7475

HUR, SU-RYONG, physician, anesthesiologist; b. Korea, Feb. 8, 1942; s. Hyung Keun and JaeKyung (Kim) H.; m. Myung Ja; children: Jennifer, Steven, Michelle. MD, Seoul Nat. U., 1966. Diplomate Am. Bd. Anesthesiology. Intern Union Hosp., Fall River, Mass., 1966-67; resident St. Vincent's Hosp, Worcester, Mass., 1967-68, Mass. Gen. Hosp., Boston, 1968-71; staff anesthesiologist St. Michael's Hosp., 1975—; asst. prof. anesthesiology Med. Coll. Wis., 1971-75, mem. clin. faculty anesthesiology, 1976—. *Dr. Su-Ryong Hur is an Anesthesiologist particularly interested in Blood Conservation during Surgery. He has been using combined techniques of Hemodilation and Hypotensive Anesthesia in Spinal Fusion Surgery since 1986. With this technique, only a handful of patients needed Homologous Transfusion out of more than 1,000 patients who underwent Spinal Fusion Surgery. A number of his articles are published in professional journals.* Contbr. articles to profl. jours. Fellow Am. Coll. Anesthesiologists; mem. AMA, Internat. Anesthesia Rsch. Soc., Am. Soc. Anesthesiologists, Korean Am. Med. Assn., Wis. Soc. Anesthesiologists, State Med. Soc. of Wis., Med. Soc. of Milw. County, Milw. Soc. of Anesthesiologists. Fax (home): 414-241-3415; fax (office): 414-527-5145. Office: St Michael Hosp Dept Anesthesiology 2400 W Villard Ave Milwaukee WI 53209

HURABIELL, JOHN PHILIP, SR., lawyer; b. San Francisco, June 2, 1947; s. Emile John and Anna Beatrice (Blumenauer) H.; m. Judith Marie Hurabiell, June 7, 1969; children; Marie Louise, Michele, Heather, John Philip Jr. JD, San Francisco U., 1976. Bar: Calif. 1977. Atty. pvt. practice, San Francisco, 1977-86; ptnr. Huppert & Hurabiell, San Francisco, 1985—; pres. San Francisco S.A.F.E., Inc., 1983-88, pres. emeritus, 1988—. Editor, primary author: C.A.L.U. Business Practices Guidelines, rev. edit., 1980. Treas. Rep. election coms.; 1st v.p. Bling Babies Found., 1989-91, bd. dirs., sec., 1995-97, 98—; bd. dirs. Calif. State Mining and Mineral Mus., 1990-93. With USN, Vietnam. Decorated Navy Commendation medal. Mem. Calif. Bar Assn., Assn. Trial Lawyers Am., San Francisco Trial Lawyers Assn., Lawyers Club San Francisco, St. Thomas More Soc., St. Francis Hook & Ladder Soc. (trustee), The Family Club, Ferrari Club Am. (pres., chmn. Pacific region 1997-98, regional dir. 1998—), Golden Gate Breakfast Club, KC, Alhambra Lodge (organizing regional dir. 1983-85). Roman Catholic. Avocation: racing vintage automobiles. Office: Huppert & Hurabiell 1390 Market St Ste 1201 San Francisco CA 94102-5306

HURAS, WILLIAM DAVID, bishop; b. Kitchener, Ont., Can., Sept. 22, 1932; s. William Adam and Frieda Dorothea (Rose) H.; m. Barbara Elizabeth Lotz, Oct. 5, 1957; children—David, Matthew, Andrea. BA, Waterloo Coll., Ont., 1954; BD, Waterloo Sem., Ont., 1963; MTh, Knox Coll., Toronto, Ont., 1968; MDiv, Waterloo Luth. U., 1973; DD (hon.), Wilfred Laurier U., Waterloo, 1980, Huron Coll., London, Ont., 1989. Ordained to ministry Luth. Ch. in Am., 1957. Pastor St. James Luth. Ch., Refrew, Ont., 1957-62, Advent Luth. Ch., North York, 1962-78; bishop Eastern Can. Synod Luth. Ch. in Am., Kitchener, 1978-85, Eastern Synod Evangel. Luth. Ch. in Can., 1986-98; mem. exec. com. Can. sect. of Luth. Ch. in Am., 1969-79; mem. exec. com. Luth. Merger Commn., Can., 1978-85; pres. Luth. Council Can., 1985-88. Bd. govs. Waterloo Luth. U., 1966-75, Waterloo Luth. Sem., 1973-75, 78—. Mem. Order of St. Lazarus of Jerusalem (Ecclesiastical Grand cross 1985). Office: Eastern Synod Evang Luth Ch in Can, 50 Queen St N 3d Fl, Kitchener, ON Canada N2H 6P4 *We are called by God and God covets an affirmative response. To say "yes" to God is to say "yes" to all of life and to all of God's people.*

HURCOMB, LAURA GRACE, visual artist; b. Glendale, Calif., Aug. 13, 1963; d. Doris Irene (Gleason) H.; m. Richard Halverson, Feb. 26, 1984; children: Jordan, Logan Hurcombhalvorsen. Student, Johnson County Cmty. Coll., 1993-95; BFA, Kansas City (Mo.) Art Inst., 1998. Art tchr. Midland Acad., Shawnee, Kans., 1993-95; visual artist H Studios, Overland Park, Kans., 1996—, HUR Studio, Kansas City, 1998—. Prin. works include sculpture Toy and Miniature Mus., Kans. City, Mo.; executed Murals Pleasentill, Mo., 1997; exhibited in group shows at City of Hanstholm Denmark, 1997, Unitarian Ch., 1997. Art tchr. Boys & Girls Club Kans. City, 1995-96; muralist Bartel Hall Storytellers, Kans. City, 1997; exhibition Famous Foot Wear, A Benefit to Stamp Out AIDS Kans. City Art Inst., 1997. Merit scholar Kans. City Art Inst., 1995. Mem. Surface Design Assn., Sons of Norway. Adventist. Avocations: surfing the www, music, animals, gardening. E-mail: hurgrace@juno.com. Home: 7929 Newton St Overland Park KS 66204-3463

HURD, BYRON THOMAS, newspaper executive, retired; b. Roseville, Mich., 1933; s. Clark Frank and Evelyn (Sybelden) H.; m. Barbara Jean Ekeroth; children: Thomas E., Roger A., J. Douglas, James B. BSBA in Advt. and Mktg., Wayne State U., 1954. Sales mgr. Detroit Free Press, 1954-55, Milne & Jones, Royal Oak, Mich., 1955-56, Detroit Times, 1956-59; account mgr. Milne Circulation Sales, Inc., Bloomfield Hills, Mich., 1959-65; agt. Bankers Life Co., Des Moines, Iowa, 1965-66; promotion mgr. Chgo. Today, Chgo. Tribune, 1966-74; owner, cons. Circulation Specialists, Homewood, Ill., 1974-77; exec. dir. circulation The Star Newspapers, Chicago Heights, Ill., 1977-95; ret., 1995; panelist, discussion leader, session master, com. mem. No. Ill. Newspapers Assn., DeKalb. Contbr. Publishers handbook, 1988. Elder, pres. governing bd. Flossmoor (Ill.) Community Ch., 1988. Mem. Cen. States Circulation Mgrs. Assn., Suburban Newspapers Am. (conf., sem. com. mem.), Audit Bur. Circulation (voting rep.), Circulation Mgmt. Ill., Rotary (dir. community svc. 1978-79, dir. internat. svc. 1979-80, sec. 1981-82, v.p. 1982-83, pres. 1983-84, dist. dir. pub. rels. 1984-86, dist. govs. aide 1986-87, dist. dir. vocat. svc. 1987-88, host Soviet Emerging Leaders 1988, Finnish 1989, dist. dir. group study exchange with India 1990, dist. conf. com. master ceremonies 1987-88, dist. conf. com. chmn. 1989-90), Flossmoor Country Club (sports and pastimes com. mem. 1988). Avocations: golf, skiing, racquetball, drawing , painting.

HURD, DAVID N., federal judge; b. 1937. BS, Cornell U., 1959; JD with honors, Syracuse U., 1963. Bar: N.Y. Ptnr. O'Shea, Griffin, McDonald, Hurd and Stevens, Utica, 1970-91; magistrate judge for no. dist. N.Y., U.S. Magistrate Ct., Utica, 1991—. Mem. Am. Coll. Trial Lawyers, N.Y. State Bar Assn., Oneida County Bar Assn. Office: 300 Federal Bldg 10 Broad St Utica NY 13501-1233

HURD, ERIC RAY, rheumatologist, internist, educator; b. Columbus, Kans., July 5, 1936; s. Myron Alexander and Isobel (Moore) H.; m. Beverly Jean Button, June 14, 1962; children: Sherryl Lynn, Susan Rae, Brent Eric. BS, U. Tulsa, 1958; MD, U. Okla., 1962. Intern St. John's Hosp., Tulsa, 1962-63, resident in internal medicine, 1963-65; research fellow U. Tex., Dallas, 1965-67, instr. internal medicine, 1967-68, asst. prof., 1968-73, assoc. prof., 1973-80, prof., 1980—; cons. rheumatologist, attending physician Parkland, VA Hosps.; dir. John Peter Smith Hosp. Arthritis Clinic, Ft. Worth; chief rheumatology VA Hosp., 1982—, mem. immunology research merit rev. bd.; assoc. Baylor Arthritis Ctr., 1981—; mem. med. and sci. com. North Tex. Arthritis Found., bd. med. dirs., 1988—, chmn. profl. edn. com.; traveling guest lectr. Tex. Med. Assn., Belgium and Fed. Republic Germany, 1990. Contbr. articles to profl. jours. Served to maj. U.S. Army, 1963-74. Recipient Clin. Scholar award Arthritis Found., 1975-77; named Outstanding Cons. Faculty Mem. John Peter Smith Hosp., 1983-84, Outstanding Part-time Clin. Prof. John Peter Smith Hosp., 1989-90. Mem. ACP, Am. Assn. Immunologists, Am. Fedn. Clin. Research, Am. Rheumatism Assn. (cooperating clinics com. 1968-74, Founding Fellow 1986), Tex. Rheumatism Assn. (sec.-treas. 1976-79, 2d v.p. 1979-80), Tex. Med. Soc., Dallas County Med. Soc., Phi Eta Sigma. Democrat. Methodist. Office: Arthritis Ctrs of Tex 712 N Washington Ave Ste 200 Dallas TX 75246-1632

HURD, GALE ANNE, film producer; b. L.A., Oct. 25, 1955; d. Frank E. and Lolita (Espiau) H. Degree in econs. and communications, Stanford U., 1977. Dir. mktg. and publicity, co-producer New World Pictures, L.A., 1977-82; pres., producer Pacific Western Prodns., L.A., 1982—. Producer: (films) The Terminator, 1984 (Grand Prix Avoiriaz Film Festival award), Aliens 1986 (nominated for 7 Acad. awards, recipient Best Sound Effects Editing award, Best Visual Effects award Acad. Picture Arts & Scis.), Alien Nation (Saturn award for best sci. fiction film), The Abyss, 1989 (nominated for 4 Acad. awards, Best Visual Effects award), The Waterdance, 1991 (2 IFP Spirit awards, 2 Sundance Film Festival awards), Cast a Deadly Spell, 1991 (Emmy award), Raising Cain, 1992, No Escape, 1994, Safe Passage (Beatrice Wood award for Creative Achievement), 1994, The Ghost and the Darkness, 1996, The Relic, 1996, Going West in America, 1996, Dante's Peak, 1997, Virus, 1997, Dead Man on Campus, 1997, Armageddon, 1998, Dick, 1998; exec. producer: (films) Switchback, 1997, Tremors, 1990, Downtown, 1990, Terminator 2, 1991 (winner 3 Acad. awards), Witch Hunt, 1994, Sugartime, 1995; creative cons. (TV program) Alien Nation, 1989-90. Juror Focus Student Film Awards, 1989, 90, Nicholl Fellowship Acad. Motion Picture Arts & Scis., 1989—; mem. Show Coalition, 1988—; mem. Hollywood (Calif.) Women's Polit. Com., 1987—; mem. U.S. Film Festival Juror; bd. dirs. IFP/West, Artists Rights Found.; trustee Am. Film Inst.; bd. dirs. L.A. Internat. Film Festival, Coral Reef Rsch. Found., Ams. for a Safe Future; mentor Peter Stark Motion Picture Producing Program, Sch. of Cinema-TV, U. of So. Calif., Women in Film Mentor Program. Recipient Spl. Merit award Nat. Assn. Theater Owners, 1986, Stanford-La Entrepreneur of Yr. award Bus. Sch. Alumni L.A., 1990, Fla. Film Festival award, 1994. Mem. AMPAS (producer's br. exec. com. 1990—), Am. Film Inst. (trustee 1989—), Americans for a Safe Future (bd. dirs. 1993—), Women in Film (bd. dirs. 1989-90). Inst. for Rsch. on Women and Gender (nat. adv. panel 1997—), Feminist Majority, Phi Beta Kappa. Avocations: scuba diving, Paso Fino horses. Office: Pacific Western Prodns 270 N Canon Dr Ste 103 Beverly Hills CA 90210-5323*

HURD, J. NICHOLAS, executive recruiting consultant, former banker; b. Boston, Dec. 10, 1942; m. Joan Hinton; children: Jennifer H. Auber, Marshall H., P. MacKenzie. B.A. in Econs., Hobart Coll., 1965; postgrad., Stanford U. Bus. Sch., Grad. Sch. Credit and Fin. Mgmt., summers 1971-73; grad. Advanced Mgmt. Program, Harvard U., 1979. Dist. mgr. Mfrs. Hanover Trust, N.Y.C., 1965, 74-77; sr. v.p. Hartford (Conn.) Nat. Bank, 1977-82; exec. v.p. Old Stone Bank, Old Stone Corp., Providence, 1982-84; mng. dir. Russell Reynolds Assocs., Inc., Boston, 1984—; corporate Ptnrs. Healthcare Sys., Boston. Bd. overseers The Huntington Theatre Co., Boston. Mem. R.I. Country Club (Barrington), Southport Yacht Club (West Southport, Maine), Harvard Club (Boston). Office: Russell Reynolds Assocs Inc Old City Hall 45 School St Ste 3D Boston MA 02108-3296

HURD, JAMES A., JR., prosecutor. BA, Howard U., 1968; JD, U. Md., 1975. Dep. dist. atty. Dept. Justice, Denver, chief counsel for Met. Consumer Fraud Office, chief dep. dist. atty., until 1980; asst. U.S. atty. for V.I. Dept. Justice, St. Croix, 1980-81; with dist. atty. office Dept. Justice, St. Thomas, 1984-92, 1st asst. U.S. atty., 1992-94; dir. Office Legal Edn. Dept. Justice, Washington, 1994-95; U.S. atty. for dist. V.I. Dept. Justice, St. Thomas, 1995—. Office: Fed Bldg & US Courthouse Ste 260 5500 Veterans Dr Charlotte Amalie VI 00802-6214*

HURD, JERRIE, writer; b. Idaho Falls, Idaho, Apr. 3, 1949; d. Jared Wirkus and Colleen Nielsen; m. Jon Hurd, June 30, 1967; children: Devin Jared, Ethan Jon. BA, U. Colo., 1969; MFA, U. Oreg., 1981. Author: Miss Ellie'sPurple Sage Saloon, 1995, Kate Burke Shoots the Old West, 1997, The Lady Pinkerton Gets Her Man, 1997. Mem. Women Writing the West (pres., founder 1996-98), Weste Writers Am. (bd. dirs. 1998—), Women of West Mus. (bd. dirs., treas. 1996—). Democrat. Office: PO Box 12 Boulder CO 80306

HURD, PAUL GEMMILL, lawyer; b. Salt Lake City, Nov. 23, 1946; s. Melvin and Marjorie Hurd. BS, Portland State U., 1968; JD, Lewis and Clark Coll., 1976. Bar: Oreg. 1976, Wash. 1984, U.S. Dist. Ct. Oreg. 1980, U.S. Ct. Appeals (9th cir.) 1981, U.S. Supreme Ct. 1988. Sr. dep. dist. atty. Multnomah County Dist. Atty., Portland, Oreg., 1976-80; trial counsel Burlington No. R.R., Portland, 1980-84; asst. gen. counsel Freightliner Corp., Portland, 1984-89, assoc. gen. counsel, 1989—. Trustee Leukemia Assn. of Oreg., Portland, 1984-90. Mem. ABA, Oreg. Bar Assn., Wash. Bar Assn., Multnomah Bar Assn., Am. Corp. Counsel Assn. (bd. dirs. N.W. chpt.), Nat. Inst. for Trial Adv. (diplomate 1982). Republican. Presbyterian. Avocations: cross country skiing, reading history, bicycling. Office: Freightliner Corp Legal Dept PO Box 3849 Portland OR 97208-3849

HURD, PAULA, state official; b. Coffeeville, Kans., Feb. 11, 1943. MS, U. No. State, 1969. Dir. divsn. field mgmt. S.D. Dept. Social Svcs., Pierre, 1979—. Office: Dept Social Svcs Field Mgmt 700 Governors Dr Pierre SD 57501

HURD, RICHARD NELSON, pharmaceutical company executive; b. Evanston, Ill., Feb. 25, 1926; s. Charles DeWitt and Mary Ormsby (Nelson) H.; m. Jocelyn Fillmore Martin, Dec. 22, 1950; children: Melanie Gray, Suzanne Dewitt. BS, U. Mich., 1946; PhD U. Minn., 1956. Chemist Gen. Electric Co., Schenectady, N.Y., 1948-49; R&D group leader Koppers Co., Pitts., $D, 1956-57; rsch. chemist Mallinckrodt Chem. Works, St. Louis, 1956-63, group leader, 1963-66; group leader Comml. Solvents Corp., Terre Haute, Ind., 1966-68; sect. head Comml. Solvents Corp., Terre Haute, 1968-71; mgr. sci. affairs G. D. Searle Internat. Co., Skokie, Ill., 1972-73, dir. mfg. and tech. affairs, 1973-77; rep. to internat. tech com. Pharm. Mfrs. Assn., Skokie, Ill., 1973-77; v.p. tech. affairs Elder Pharms., Bryan, Ohio, 1977-81; v.p. rsch. & devel. U.S. Proprietary Drugs & Toiletries div. Schering-Plough Corp., Memphis, 1981-83; v.p. sci affairs Moleculon, Inc., Cambridge, Mass., 1984-88; v.p. regulaatory affairs Pharmaco-LSR, Inc., Austin, Tex., 1989-94; prin. Hurd & Assocs., Inc., Evanston, ILL., 1994—. Contbr. articles to profl. jours. Mem. Ferguson-Florissant (Mo.) Sch. Bd., 1964-66; bd. dirs. United Fund of Wabash Valley (Ind.), 1969-71. With USN, 1943-46, 53-55. E.I. DuPont de Nemours & Co., Inc. fellow, 1956. Fellow AAAS; mem. Am. Acad. Dermatology, Am. Soc. Photobiology, Am. Chem. Soc., N.Y. Acad. Sci., Am. Pharm. Assn., Am. Assn. Pharm. Scientists, Food and Drug Law Inst., Drug Info. Assn., Sigma XI, Mich. Shores Club (Wilmette, Ill.). Presbyterian. Patentee in field; co devel. of Ralgro and Oxsoralen; rsch on thioamides as a class of organic compounds, devel. of macrocyclic synthetic routes for natural producs, devel. of psoralens for photochemotherapy of dermatologic disorders. E-mail: hurdreg@earthlink.net.

HURD, SUZANNE SHELDON, federal agency health science director; b. Elmira, N.Y., Dec. 17, 1939; d. Victor Sheldon H. BS, Bates Coll., 1961; MS, U. Wash., 1963, PhD, 1967. Post-doctoral fellow U. Calif., Berkeley, 1967-69; grants assoc. NIH, Bethesda, Md., 1969-70; health sci. adminstr. Nat. Heart, Lung and Blood Inst., Bethesda, 1970-78, dep. dir. div. lung diseases, 1979-84, dir. divsn. lung diseases, 1984—; acting dir. Nat. Inst. Nursing Rsch., Bethesda, 1994-95; acting dir. Women's Health Initiative Nat. Heart, Lung and Blood Inst., Bethesda, 1997—. Mem. Am. Thoracic Soc.

HURD, VERONICA TEREZ, career soldier; b. Lincoln Park, Mich., Aug. 11, 1962; d. James Julius Nelson and Julia Marie Shipp; m. Henry Hurd; children: Henry, Charles. AA, U. Md., 1989; BS, Upper Iowa U., 1995; MS, Ctrl. Mich. U., 1997; postgrad., The Union Inst., 1997—. Enlisted U.S. Army, 1980, advanced through grades to sgt. first class, 1983, equal opportunity advisor, 1993-97. Mem. AAUW, NAFE, Profl. Secs. Internat., Nat. Black MBA Assn., Am. Mgmt. Assn., OD Network. Avocations: quilting, sewing, cross stitching, cooking, reading.

HURET, MARILYNN JOYCE, editor, puzzle constructor; b. N.Y.C., Dec. 5; d. Hyman and Clara (Weinberg) Moskowitz; m. Barry Saul Huret, Feb. 11, 1961; children: Abbey Beth, Eric Alan. BA in Math., Adelphi U., 1961. Tchr. math. Dist. 281, Robbinsdale, Minn., 1974-77; puzzle constructor Marvel Comics, N.Y.C., 1982-88, Great Puzzle Catalog, N.Y.C., 1982-83; editor, online sysop Crossword Am. LYRIQ Internat., 1995—; editor, Crossword America, puzzle mag. on-line LYRIQ Internat., Divsn. Enteractive, Inc., 1996-98; editor Crossroads Media Group, Inc., Newtown, Conn., 1998—; mem. Bucks County Courier Times Readers Adv. Group, 1995—; presenter in field; editor, developer, constructor Crossroads Media Group, Inc.; computer sci. tchr., coord. Politz Acad., Phila., 1999. puzzle constructor Soft Disk Electronic Pub., N.Y. Times, Bucks County Courier, Yardley News; writer biog. articles for crossword mag.; contbr. Crosswúrd Mag., 1995—, Crosswords Diagramless Acrostics, Cryptograms For IDG Puzzle Series, Vols. I, II, III, IV, V, 101 Crossword Puzzles for Dummies, IDG Series; editor: Crossword Am. puzzle mag. on-line; crossword puzzle constructor N.Y. Times; writer, presenter More Bytes For the Buck (A Guide to Purchase of Computing Hardware & Components. Coop. weather observer Sta. WOR, N.Y.C., 1965-71; severe storm weather spotter NOAA, 1972-77, Mpls., 1977-79, Racine, Wis., 1980—, Phila., Mt. Holly, N.J.; commr. pub. safety City of Golden Valley, Minn., 1972-77; judge Delaware Valley Sci. Fairs, Phila., 1984—; adminstr. David Libr. of Am. Revolution, Washington Crossing, Pa., 1988-95.; dep. coord. emergency mgmt. Lower Makefield Twp., Pa., 1989—; bd. dirs. Delaware Valley Philharmonic Orch., mem. season planning com.; guild mem. Newtown (Pa.) Symphony; mem. MACA, 1997—. Recipient Svc. Appreciation award Golden Valley City Coun., 1977. Mem. LWV, AAUW (editor Makefield Area Connections 1993-96, Named Gift award 1994, Outstanding Woman of Yr. Makefield area 1995, organizer puzzle tournaments), Spl. Libr. Assn. (assoc.), Am. Cryptogram Assn., Am. Women in Computing, Nat. Puzzlers League, Bucks County Librs. Assn., Lower Bucks Computer Users Group, Adelphi U. Alumni Assn., Toastmasters, Spiffy's Gang. Home: 484 Kings Rd Yardley PA 19067-4652 Office: Crossroads Media Group Inc divsn Enteractive Inc 3 Dinglebrook Ln Newtown CT 06470-1125

HUREWITZ, MIRIAM F., copyeditor; b. Albany, N.Y., Oct. 18, 1921; d. E. Martin and Rose (Boochever) Freund; m. Jacob C. Hurewitz, Mar. 29, 1946; children: Barbara Aronson, Anne Rosenbloom. BA, Cornell U., 1943. With Office of Strategic Svcs., Washington, 1943-45; editl. asst. Am. Mgmt. Assn., N.Y.C., 1945-46; rschr. Fortune Mag., N.Y.C., 1946-48; self-employed editor N.Y.C., 1948-61; copyeditor Crowell-Collier, N.Y.C., 1961; self-employed editor N.Y.C., Palo Alto, Calif., 1961-64; copyeditor, copy chief Crowell-Collier and Macmillan, N.Y.C., 1964-67; sr. editor Columbia U. Press, N.Y.C., 1967-68; copyediting dept. supr. Harcourt Brace Jovanovich, N.Y.C., 1968-70; copyediting mgr. Macmillan, Inc., N.Y.C., 1970-75; purveyor of editl. svcs. N.Y.C., 1975—; instr., copyediting/proofreading Parsons/New Sch., N.Y.C., 1985-87; adj. asst. prof. NYU, 1990-93. Mem. Women's Nat. Book Assn. (job referral chair, hospitality chair, awards chair), Editl. Freelancers Assn., Phi Beta Kappa. Democrat. Jewish. Avocations: reading, gardening, swimming, travel. Home: 3 Hyatt Ln Westport CT 06880-3012 Office: 445 Riverside Dr # 42 New York NY 10027-6801

HURLBERT, ROBERT P., lawyer; b. Detroit, Aug. 30, 1944; s. James F. and Mildred K. (Fleischer) H.; m. Sharon Ann Van Tornhout, July 1, 1967; children: Elizabeth A., Janet L. BA, U. Detroit, 1965; JD, U. Mich., 1968. Bar: Mich. 1968, U.S. Dist. Ct. (ea. dist.) Mich. 1968, U.S. Ct. Appeals (6th cir.) 1971, U.S. Supreme Ct. 1979, U.S. Dist. Ct. (we. dist.) Mich. 1990, Ill. 1993, U.S. Dist. Ct. (no. dist.) 1993, U.S. Ct. Appeals (7th cir.) 1994. Asst. U.S. atty. U.S. Dept. Justice, Detroit, 1971-73, spec. asst. U.S. atty., 1973-74; assoc. Dickinson, Wright et al, Bloomfield Hills, Mich., 1968-71, 73-76, ptnr., 1976-92; ptnr. Dickinson, Wright et al, Chgo., 1993-96; mem. Dickinson, Wright, P.L.L.C., Bloomfield Hills, 1998—; assoc. Dickinson, Wright-Ill., 1998—. Mem. Fed. bar Assn. (pres. 1985-86), Mich. Bar Assn., Oakland County Bar Assn.; fellow Am. Coll. Trial Lawyers. Office: Dickinson Wright Moon Et Al 525 N Woodward Ave Ste 1000 Bloomfield Hills MI 48304-2969

HURLBERT, ROGER WILLIAM, information service industry executive; b. San Francisco, Feb. 18, 1941; s. William G. and Mary (Greene) H.; m. Karen C. Haslag, Nov. 6, 1982; children: Sage, Mica, Chula, Monk, Morris. BS in Community Devel., So. Ill. U., 1965. Newspaper editor and reporter various, San Francisco Bay Area, 1958-62; pvt. practice investigation Ill., 1963-65; advisor San Francisco Planning Urban Rsch. Assn., 1969-87; pres. Sage Info. Svcs., San Francisco, 1988—. Compiler Western States Land Data Base, 1972—. Pres. Haight-Ashbury Neighborhood Coun., San Francisco, 1959-61. With U.S. Army, 1966-68, Vietnam. Recipient Cert. of Merit San Francisco Coun. Dist. Merchants Assn., 1972. Mem. Real Estate Info. Providers Assn. (sec. 1998—), Direct Mktg. Assn., Mail Advt. Svc. Assn. Internat., League of Men Voters (v.p. 1959—). Democrat. Office: Sage Info Svcs 13606 Arnold Dr PO Box 1832 Glen Ellen CA 95442

HURLBURT, HARLEY ERNEST, oceanographer; b. Bennington, Vt., Apr. 12, 1943; s. Paul Rhodes and Evelyn Arlene (Lockhart) H.; m. Cheryl Elaine Finch, Jan. 10, 1998. BS in Physics (scholar), Union Coll., Schenectady, 1965; MS, Fla. State U., 1971, PhD in Meteorology, 1974. NASA trainee Fla. State U., 1970-72; postdoctoral fellow advanced studies program Nat. Center Atmospheric Research, Boulder, Colo., 1974-75; staff scientist JAYCOR, Alexandria, Va., 1975-77; oceanographer Naval Oceanographic and Atmospheric Rsch. Lab. (merged with Naval Rsch. Lab., 1992), Stennis Space Center, Miss., 1977—, br. head, 1983-85; adj. faculty Marine Sci. U. So. Miss., Stennis Space Ctr,, 1993—, Meteorology Fla. State U., Tallahassee, 1995—; mem. nat. adv. panels NASA satellite surface stress working group, 1981-84, minerals mgmt. service interagy. adv. group, 1982-89, world ocean circulation experiment working group on numerical modeling, 1984-96, USN space oceanography working group, 1986-89; co-chmn. working group on global prediction systems, ocean prediction workshop, 1986; internat. working group on acoustic monitoring of world ocean Sci. Com. Oceanic Rsch., 1991—; internat. working group on modelling subarctic North Pacific circulation North Pacific Marine Sci. Orgn., 1994-95; mem. sci. steering team Global Ocean Data Assimilation Experiment, 1998—; project leader to develop the world's first eddy-resolving global ocean prediction model for the USN, 1987—. Contbr. numerous articles to profl. jours. V.p. Burgundy Citizens Assn., 1976-77. Weather officer USAF, 1965-69. Recipient Disting. Scientist medal 13th Internat. Colloquium, Liege, Belgium, 1981, Publ. award for best basic research paper Naval Ocean Research and Devel. Activity, 1980, 90; Office Naval Research grantee, 1975-77, 84—, Dept. Energy grantee, 1975-78, Tex. A&M U. grantee, 1976, Office of Naval Technology grantee, 1987-93, Space Warfare Systems grantee, 1989-94, Advanced Rsch. Projects Agy. grantee, 1993-95, Strategic Environ. Rsch. and Devel. Program grantee, 1994-95, Def. Dept. High Performance Computing Challenge grantee, 1997—, Nat. Ocean Partnership Program grantee, 1997—. Mem. Am. Meteorol. Soc., Am. Geophysical Union, Oceanography Soc., Phi Sigma Kappa, Sigma Xi (Kaminski Publ. award 1991), Sigma Tau, Chi Epsilon Pi. Methodist. Home: 507 Hermitage Ct Pearl River LA 70452-3903 Office: Naval Rsch Lab Code # 7323 Stennis Space Center MS 39529

HURLBUT, ROBERT HAROLD, health care services executive; b. Rochester, N.Y., Mar. 9, 1935; s. Harold Leroy and Martha Irene (Fincher) H.; m. Barbara Cox, June 14, 1958; children: Robert W., Christine A. Student, Coll. Hotel Adminstrn., Cornell U., 1953-56. Adminstr., dir. Pillars Nursing Home, Rochester, 1956—, Elmcrest Nursing Home, Churchville, N.Y., 1960—, Elm Manor Nursing Home, Canandaigua, N.Y., 1960—, Penfield Nursing Home, Rochester, 1963—, Avon (N.Y.) Nursing Home, 1964—, Newark (N.Y.) Nursing Home, 1965—, Lakeshore Nursing Home, Rochester, 1972—; bd. dirs. Marine Midland Bank, Blue Cross/Blue Shield Rochester, Living Ctrs. of Am.; organizer, adminstrv. dir. hdqrs. Rohm Svcs. Corp., Rochester, 1964—; organizer, pres. hdqrs. Vari-Care Inc., Rochester, 1969-93; commr. N.Y. State Ins. Fund; mem. Cornell U. Hotel Sch. Adv. Coun. Mem. bd. trustees St. John Fisher Coll., Eastman Dental Ctr.; pres. Hurlbut Trust, 1994; mem. bd. govs. Strong Meml. Hosp. Fellow Am. Coll. Health Care Adminstrs.; mem. Greater Met. C. of C. (past chmn. bd. dirs.), Genesee Valley Club, Oak Hill Club, Cornell Club, Lambda Chi Alpha. Home: 200 Sheldon Rd Honeoye Falls NY 14472-9316 Office: Hurlbut Trust 740 East Ave Rochester NY 14607-2107

HURLBUT, TERRY ALLISON, pathologist; b. Richmond, Va., Nov. 24, 1957; s. Terry A. and Evelyn I. (Randlette) H.; m. Sharon L. Clouston, Oct. 24, 1998. BS, Yale Coll., 1980; MD, Baylor Coll. Medicine, 1985. Pathology residency Vanderbilt Univ., 1986-89; fellowship pathology Dartmouth Medical Sch., 1989-91; pathology residency Monmouth Medical Ctr., Long Branch, N.J., 1991-93; clinical pathologist Kimball Medical Ctr, Lakewood, N.J., 1993-95; dir. informatics Lakewood Pathology Assn., Lakewood, N.J., 1993—; clinical pathologist Meml. Hosp. Burlington County, Mt. Holly, N.J., 1996—. Co-author: The Laboratory Consultant, 1992; contbr. article to profl. jours. Fellow Coll. Am. Pathologists. Baptist. Office: Lakewood Pathology Assocs 175 Madison Ave Mount Holly NJ 08060

HURLEY, ALFRED FRANCIS, academic administrator, historian, retired military officer; b. Bklyn., Oct. 16, 1928; s. Patrick Francis and Margaret Teresa (Coakley) H.; m. Joanna Helen Leahy, Jan. 24, 1953; children: Alfred F., Thomas J., Mark P., Claire T., John K. BA summa cum laude, St. John's U., 1950; MA, Princeton U., 1958, PhD, 1961. Enlisted USAF, 1950, commd. lt., 1952, prof.. head dept. History, 1966-80; mem USAF Acad., 1976-80; advanced through grades to brig. gen. USAF, ret., 1980; v.p. adminstrv. affairs U. North Tex. (formerly North Tex. State U.), Denton, 1980-82, pres., 1982—; chancellor U. North Tex. and U. North Tex. Health Sci. Ctr., Ft. Worth, 1982—; mem. adv. com. USAF hist. program sect. USAF, Washington, 1982-86, chmn., 1984-86; mem. bd. visitors Air U., 1993-97. Author: Billy Mitchell, Crusader for Air Power, 1964, (rev. edit.), 1975; co-editor: Air Power and Warfare, 1979. Mem. Dallas Citizens Coun., 1998—. Decorated Legion of Merit (2); Guggenheim fellow, 1971-72, Eisenhower Inst., Smithsonian fellow, 1976-77; recipient Pres.'s medal St. John's U., 1990. Mem. Soc. for Mil. History (trustee 1973-78, 81-85), Air Force Hist. Found. (trustee 1980—), Am. Assn. State Colls. and Univs. (coun. state reps. 1989-92), Am. Coun. Edn. (commn. leadership 1993-96), Am. Hist. Assn. (chmn. NASA fellowship com. 1993), Coalition Urban and Met. Univs. (co-chair 1993—), Tex. Coun. Pub. Univ. Prsidents and Chancellors (chmn. 1987-89), Alliance for Higher Edn. of North Tex. (trustee 1983-89, chmn. coun. of pres. 1989-90), North Tex. Commn. (bd. dirs. 1986—, chmn. 1995-97). Roman Catholic. Home: 828 Skylark Dr Denton TX 76205-8012 Office: U North Tex Office Pres & Chancellor Denton TX 76203-3737

HURLEY, CHERYL JOYCE, book publishing executive; b. Pitts., Oct. 30, 1947; d. John and Violet Dernorsek; m. Kevin Hurley, July 27, 1974. Lang. and lit. cert., Université de Lyon, France, 1968; AB, Ohio U., 1969; MA, U. Mich., 1971. Research assoc. MLA, N.Y.C., 1972-74, dir. spl. programs, 1974-79; pub. The Library of America, N.Y.C., 1979—, pres., 1988—; cons. in field. Contbr. articles to profl. jours. Trustee French Inst./Alliance Francaise, 1992—, v.p., exec. com., 1994—; mem. libr. com. Hort. Alliance of Hamptons, 1989—, adv. com. N.Y. 100 Centennial, 1997—; mem. humanities adv. coun. N.Y. Pub. Libr., 1996—; trustee Samuel H. Kress Found., 1999—. Rackham fellow, 1969-70. Mem. Grolier Club, Century Assn., Am. Antiquarian Soc. (bd. overseers 1996-98, councillor, 1999—), Bridgehampton Club, Phi Beta Kappa. Home: 1172 Park Ave New York NY 10128-1213 Office: Libr of Am 14 E 60th St New York NY 10022-1006

HURLEY, DANIEL T. K., judge; b. Fitchburg, Mass., Feb. 24, 1943; A.B. cum laude, St. Anselm's Coll., 1964; J.D., George Washington U., 1968. Bar: Fla. 1969, Calif. 1979, D.C. 1969. Asst. county solicitor Palm Beach County (Fla.), 1970-73; exec. asst. state atty. 15th Jud. Circuit Fla., West Palm Beach, 1973-75, judge, 1977-79, 86-94, chief judge, 1988-93; judge Palm Beach County Ct., 1975-77, 4th Dist. Ct. Appeals, Fla., West Palm Beach,

1979-86; U.S. Dist. judge So. Dist. Fla., West Palm Beach, 1994—. Office: US Courthouse 701 Clematis St Rm 352 West Palm Beach FL 33401-5111*

HURLEY, DENIS R., federal judge; b. 1937. BS, U. Pa., 1959; MBA, Columbia U., 1962; LLB, Fordham U., 1966. Assoc. Bond, Schoenck and King, Syracuse, N.Y., 1966-68; prin. asst. dist. atty. Dist. Attys. Office, Suffolk County, N.Y., 1968-70; assoc., then ptnr. Pike, Behringer & Hurley (and successor firms), Riverhead, N.Y., 1970-82; judge N.Y. State Family Ct., 1983-87; acting justice N.Y. Supreme Ct., Suffolk County, 1987-88; judge N.Y. State County Ct., Suffolk County, 1988-91; fed. judge U.S. Dist. Ct. (ea. dist.) N.Y., Bklyn., 1991—. Office: US Dist Ct 225 Cadman Plz E Brooklyn NY 11201*

HURLEY, FRANCIS T., archbishop; b. San Francisco, Jan. 12, 1927. Ed., St. Patrick Sem., Menlo Park, Calif., Catholic U. Am. Ordained priest Roman Cath. Ch., 1951; with Nat. Cath. Welfare Conf., Washington, asst. sec., 1958-68; assoc. sec. Nat. Cath. Welfare Conf., now U.S. Cath. Conf., 1968-70; consecrated bishop, 1970; titular bishop Daimlaig and aux. bishop Diocese of Juneau, Alaska, 1970-71; bishop of Juneau, 1971-76, archbishop of Anchorage, 1976—. Office: Archdiocese of Anchorage Chancery Office 225 Cordova St Anchorage AK 99501-2409

HURLEY, FRANK THOMAS, JR., realtor; b. Washington, Oct. 18, 1924; s. Frank Thomas and Lucille (Trent) H.; m. Betty Guisinger, Aug. 9, 1997; A.A., St. Petersburg Jr. Coll., 1948; B.A., U. Fla., 1950. Reporter St. Petersburg (Fla.) Evening Independent, 1948-53; editor Arcadia (Calif.) Tribune, 1956-57; reporter Los Angeles Herald Express, 1957; v.p. Frank T. Hurley Assos., Inc. realtors, 1958-64, pres., 1964—; sec., dir. Beau Monde, Inc., 1977-79. Elected St. Petersburg Beach Bd. Commrs., 1965-69; chmn. Pinellas County Traffic Safety Council, 1968-69; apptd. mem. Pinellas County Hist. Commn., 1993—; apptd. Pinellas County Sesquicentennial Coord. Com., 1995; pres. Pass-A-Grille Community Assn., 1963, Gulf Beach Bd. Realtors, 1969; mem. St. Petersburg Mus. Fine Arts, St. Petersburg Beach Aesthetic and Hist. Rev. Bd., chmn. 1994-96; bd. govs. Palms of Pasadena Hosp., 1979-86. Served with USAAF, 1943-46. Mem. Fla. Assn. Realtors (dir., dist. v.p. 1971), St. Petersburg Suncoast Assn. Realtors (life, Ambassadors award, 1994), St. Petersburg Beach C. of C. (dir., pres. 1975-76, Citizen of Yr. award 1983), Fla. Hist. Soc., Am. Legion, Pass-a-Grille Yacht Club, Sigma Delta Chi, Sigma Tau Delta. Author: Surf, Sand and Post Card Sunsets, 1977. Home: 2808 Sunset Way Saint Pete Beach FL 33706 Office: 2506 Pass A Grille Way Saint Petersburg Beach FL 33706-4160

HURLEY, HARRY JAMES, JR., dermatologist; b. Phila., Oct. 10, 1926; s. Harry James and Margaret (McHenry) H.; m. Jeanne Florence Geiger, July 15, 1950; children: Susan, Harry James III, Jeffrey, Marilyn, Nancy. Student, St. Joseph's Coll., Phila., 1943-45; MD, Jefferson Med. Coll., Phila., 1949; DSc in Medicine, U. Pa., 1958. Diplomate Am. Bd. Dermatology (bd. dirs., examiner 1974-83, exec. com. 1978-79, chmn. edn. com. 1979-84, v.p. 1982-83, pres. 1983-84, asst. exec. dir. 1985-92, exec. dir. 1993—, Disting. Svc. award 1984). Rotating intern Fitzgerald-Mercy Hosp., Darby, Pa., 1949-50, resident in ob-gyn., 1950-51; resident in dermatology and syphilogy U. Pa. Hosp., 1951-53; rsch. fellow USPHS, 1955-56; mem. faculty U. Pa. Sch. Medicine, 1956-59, 62—, assoc. prof. dept. dermatology, 1962-68, prof. clin. dermatology, 1978—; prof. dermatology, chief sect., chief dermatol. sect. coll. hosp. Hahnemann Med. Coll., Phila., 1959-62; chief dermatology Phila. Gen. Hosp., 1962-73; attending dermatologist Fitzgerald-Mercy Hosp., 1956-80, Bryn Mawr Hosp., 1956-75, Am. Oncologic Hosp., Phila., 1960-62, U. Pa. Hosp., 1962-80; chmn. adv. bd. Nat. Program Dermatology, 1974-75; pres. Dermatology Found., 1975-76; cons., advisor in field. Contbr. numerous articles to profl. jours.; editor: Jour. Geriatric Dermatology, 1993—; bd. editors Modern Dermatology, 1968, Dermatology Forum, 1984; editorial cons. Annals Internal Medicine, 1982-84. Capt. M.C., USAR, 1953-55. Recipient Rsch. Recognition award Phila. chpt. Nat. Cystic Fibrosis Found., 1959, Clarence E. Shaffrey medal and award St. Joseph's U., 1980, Finnerud award Dermatol. Found., 1991, Everett Fox lectr. and award Am. Acad. Dermatology, 1994. Fellow ACP (chmn. self-assessment program sect. dermatology 1976); mem. Am. Acad. Dermatology (bd. dirs. 1972-75, chmn. coun. govtl. liaison 1974-75, mem. nominating com. 1977-80, chmn. audit com. 1988-89), AMA (chmn. residency rev. com. 1979-82), Am. Dermatol. Assn. (bd. dirs. 1977-82, pres. 1983-84, chmn. nominating com. 1987), Soc. Investigative Dermatology, Pa. Acad. Dermatology (pres. 1969-70, Disting. SVc. commendation 1973), Pa. Med. Soc., Delaware County Med. Soc., Coll. Physicians Phila., Phila. Dermatol. Soc. (pres. 1970-71, editor. proc. 1968-69), Overbrook Golf Club (Bryn Mawr, Pa.; bd. dirs. 1988—, v.p. 1993), Alpha Epsilon Delta. Home: 4119 Echo Valley Ln Newtown Square PA 19073-1623 Office: 39 Copley Rd Upper Darby PA 19082-2511*

HURLEY, JEFFREY SCOTT, fabric company administrator; b. Pitts., Feb. 19, 1963; s. William Stephen and Mary Agnes (Wholey) H. BS in Chemistry, Gannon U., Erie, Pa., 1985; MS in Chemistry, Ga. Inst. Tech., Atlanta, 1990, PhD in Chemistry, 1992. Sr. rsch. chemist Hoechst Celanese Corp, Charlotte, N.C., 1992-95, bicomponent staple product devel. mgr., 1995-96, applications and devel. mgr. specialty staple products, 1996-97, mgr. bus. analysis and tech. assessment, 1997-98; mgr. absorbent products Buckeye Techs., Memphis, 1998—; cons., Atlanta, 1989-92; mem. adv. bd. Nonwovens Coop. Rsch. Ctr., 1997—; mem. tech. adv. bd. Assn. Nonwovens Fabvric Industry, 1997—. Author: Emerging Technologies in Hazardous Waste Management IV, 1994; contbr.: Phase Transfer Catalysis, 1994. Mem. Am. Chem. Soc. (organic, polymer material sci. and engrng. and polymer divsn., Carolina Piedmont sect.). Achievements include development and support of a chemical mechanism modeling the generation of gaseous byproducts during the thermal decomposition of radioactive waste slurries stored at the Hanford (Wash.) Reservation, a new mechanism and kinetics concerning hydroxide promoted liquid-liquid phase transfer catalysis of simple organic reactions which contracts the current interfacial and exatraction mechanisms; research and development of novel monomers and polymers from lab through production scale and investigation of novel polymerization techniques and polymerization process design and application. Office: Buckeye Techs PO Box 80407 Memphis TN 38108-0407

HURLEY, JOHN ARTHUR, government official; b. N.Y.C., Aug. 22, 1935; s. John Herbert and Alice Carolyn (Lubeck) H.; m. Margaret Allen Boocock, Nov. 25, 1961 (div. 1980); children: John A. (Jack) III, Sarah Brett Hurley Dewing; m. Eileen Bridget Hayes, Feb. 14, 1987. BA in Econs., Rutgers U., 1957; MA in Internat. Rels., Am. U., 1966; MS in Mgmt., Nat.-Louis U., 1995. Rsch. analyst Dept. State, Washington, 1962-65; budget examiner Bur. Budget, Washington, 1965-70; asst. divsn. chief Office Mgmt. and Budget, Washington, 1970-73; asst. commr. U.S. Customs Svc., Washington, 1973-78; regional commr. U.S. Customs Svc., Balt., 1978-82; dep. asst. commr. U.S. Customs Svc., Washington, 1984-86; customs attaché U.S. Customs Svc., London, 1986-92, area dir., 1992—. 1st lt. USAF, 1959-62, brig. gen. (ret.) USAFR. Decorated Legion of Merit. Mem. Internat. Assn. Chiefs of Police (internat. policy com.), Fed. Law Enforcement Officers, Sr. Execs. Assn., Inst. Mgmt. Cons., Phi Beta Kappa. Avocations: reading, tennis, horseback riding, trains, teaching. Home: 9001 Cherrytree Dr Alexandria VA 22309-2902 Office: US Customs Svc HQ 1300 Pennsylvania Ave NW Washington DC 20229

HURLEY, LAURENCE HAROLD, medicinal chemistry educator; b. Birmingham, U.K., Jan. 29, 1944; s. Harold Harcourt and May (Cottrell) H.; children: Bridget, Nicole. BPharm, U. Bath, U.K., 1967, DSc, 1996; PhD, Purdue U., 1970. Apprentice pharmacist Boots the Chemist, Birmingham, 1963-64; hosp. pharmacist Birmingham Gen. Hosp., 1967; postdoctoral fellow U. B.C., Vancouver, 1970-71; asst. prof. U. Md., Balt., 1971-73; from asst. to assoc. to full prof. U. Ky., Lexington, 1973-80; prof. U. Tex., Austin, 1981—, Henry Burlage prof., 1983-86, James Bauerle prof., 1986-88, George Hitchings prof. drug design, 1988-91, George Hitchings regents chmn. drug design, 1992—; cons. Upjohn Co., Kalamazoo, 1979-95, Smith Kline French, Phila., 1984-87, Abbott Labs., 1992-94; mem. sci. adv. bd. Sun Pharm. Corp.; chmn. bioorganic and natural products study sect. NIH, 1986-88; dir. Chemistry Inst. Drug Devel., San Antonio; founder, scientific dir. "Cytenex". Sr. editor Jour. Medicinal Chemistry; contbr. numerous articles to profl. jours. Recipient George Hitchings award in innovative drug design, 1988, Volwiler Rsch. Achievement award, 1989, Rsch. Achievement award in medicinal chemistry Am. Pharm. Assn., 1992; named Outstanding Investigator Nat. Cancer Inst., 1989, 94. Fellow AAAS; mem. Am. Chem. Soc. (Medicinal Chemistry award 1994). Democrat. Home: 5811 Mesa Dr Apt 1316 Austin TX 78731-3762 Office: U Tex Coll Pharmacy Austin TX 78712

HURLEY, LAWRENCE JOSEPH, lawyer; b. Plainfield, N.J., Nov. 17, 1946; s. Luke Michael and Gertrude Marie (Bremer) H.; m. Allyson J. Kingsley, May 28, 1977; children: Michael William, Kathryn Elizabeth. BS, U. Dayton, 1969; JD, Cath. U. Am., 1974. Bar: N.J. 1974, U.S. Dist. Ct. N.J., 1974, D.C. 1976, N.Y. 1980, U.S. Ct. Appeals (3rd cir.) 1980, U.S. Dist. Ct. (ea. and so. dists.) N.Y. 1981, U.S. Ct. Appeals (2nd cir.) 1981, U.S. Ct. Appeals (D.C. cir.) 1982. Law clk. Superior Ct. N.J., New Brunswick, 1974-75; assoc. Lynch, Mannion, Lutz & Lewandowski, New Brunswick, 1975-76, Stryker, Tams & Dill, Newark, 1976-79; atty. AT&T Comm., Basking Ridge, N.J., 1979-85; asst. prosecutor in charge of econ. crimes and ofcl. corruption Morris County Prosecutor's Office, Morristown, N.J., 1985-89; ptnr. Voorhees & Acciavatti, Morristown, 1989-91; sr. atty. AT&T, 1991-96; mng. corp. labor and employment counsel Lucent Techs., 1996—. With U.S. Army, 1969-71. Decorated Bronze Star. Mem. ABA (litigation sect. 1976—, labor law sect. 1981-86, criminal law sect. 1985-91, labor law sect. 1991—), N.J. State Bar Assn. (labor law sect. 1981—). Office: Lucent Techs Rm B2D10 283 King George Rd Warren NJ 07059-5134

HURLEY, LINDA KAY, psychologist; b. Kansas City, Mo., June 4, 1951; d. James O. and Phyllis L. (Steil) H. BS, U. Mo., 1973; BA, Am. U., 1978, MA, 1983, PhD, 1986. Lic. psychologist, Tex. Assoc. psychologist Tarrant County Mental Health/Mental Retardation, Ft. Worth, 1983-84; intern in med. psychology Oreg. Health Scis. U., Portland, 1984-85; instr. in pediatrics and psychology U. Tex. Southwestern Med. Ctr., Dallas, 1985-88, asst. prof., 1988-96; psychologist, dir. tng. Child Study Ctr., Ft. Worth, 1990-91; pediatric psychologist Ft. Worth Pediatrics, 1991—; trustee Ronald McDonald House (Friends of Children, Inc.), 1986-89. Co-author: (with Michael C. Roberts) Managing Managed Care, 1997. With USAF, 1974-77. Mem. APA (clin. psychology divsn., clin. child psychology sect.), Ft. Worth Area Psychol. Assn. (treas. 1994, pres.-elect 1996, pres. 1997, past-pres. 1998), Soc. Pediat. Psychology (bd. dirs.), Assn. Advancement of Behavior Therapy, Soc. Rsch. in Child Devel., Tex. Psychol. Assn., Ft. Worth Camera Club (bd. dirs. 1997-99), Phi Kapppa Phi. Avocations: cooking, music, photography. Office: 851 W Terrell Ave Fort Worth TX 76104-3161

HURLEY, MARK JOSEPH, bishop; b. San Francisco, Dec. 13, 1919; s. Mark J. and Josephine (Keohane) H. Student, St. Joseph's Coll., Mountain VIew, Calif., 1939, St. Patrick's Sem., Menlo Park, Calif., 1944; postgrad., U. Calif., Berkeley, 1943-45; PhD, Cath. U. Am., 1947; JCB, Lateran U., Rome, 1963; LLD, U. Portland, 1971. Ordained to priest Roman Cath. Ch., 1944. Asst. supt. schs. Archdiocese, San Francisco, 1944-51; tchr. Serra High Sch., San Mateo, Calif., 1944; prin. Bishop O'Dowd High Sch., Oakland, Calif., 1951-58, Marin Cath. High Sch., Marin County, Calif., 1959-61; supt. schs. Diocese, Stockton, Calif., 1962-65; chancellor, diocesan counsultor Diocese, 1962-65; asst. chancellor Arcdiocese, San Francisco, 1965-67; vicar gen. Arcdiocese, 1967-69; titular bishop Thunusuda; aux. bishop Thunusuda, San Francisco, 1967-69; bishop Santa Rosa, Cal., 1969—; pastor St. Francis Assisi Ch., San Francisco, 1967—; prof. grad. schs. Loyola U., Balt., 1946, U. San Francisco, 1948, San Francisco Coll. Women, 1949, Dominican Coll., San Rafael, Calif., 1949, Cath. U. Am., 1954; prof. theology Beda Coll. Rome, 1987—, Angelicum U., Rome, 1989—; Del. Conf. Psychiatry and Religion, San Francisco, 1957; mem. bd. Calif. Com. on Study Edn., 1955-60; cons. Congregation for Cath. Edn., 1986—; del.-at-large Cal., White House Conf. on Youth, 1960; Cath. del., observer Nat. Council Chs., Columbus, Ohio, 1964; del. edn. conf. German and Am. educators, Nat. Cath. Edn. Assn., Munich, Germany, 1960; mem. commns. sems., univs. and schs. II Vatican Council, Rome, 1962-65; mem. commn. Christian formation U.S. Cath. Conf. Bishops, 1968; asst. archdiocesan coordinator Campaign on Taxation Schs. Calif., 1958, Rosary Crusade, 1961; adminstr. Cath. Sch. Purchasing Div., 1948-51, St. Eugene's Ch., Santa Rosa, Calif., 1959, St. John's Ch., San Francisco, 1961; mem. U.S. Bishops' Press Panel, Vatican Council, 1964-65, U.S. Bishops' Com. on Laity, 1964, U.S. Bishops' Com. Cath.-Jewish Relationships, 1965—, U.S. Bishops' Com. on Ecumenical and Interreligious Affairs, 1970, Conf. Maj. Superiors of Men, 1970; chmn. citizens Com. for San Francisco State Coll., 1968—; mem. adminstrn. bd. Nat. Council Cath. Bishops, 1970, mem. nominating com., 1971; mem. Internat. Secretariat for Non-Believers, Vatican, 1973; chmn. Secretariat for Human Values, Nat. Conf. Cath. Bishops, Washington, 1975; mem. Secretariat for Non-Believers, Vatican, 1986—; Vatican del. World Intellectual Properties Orgn., Washington, 1990; adj. prof. philosophy Grad. Theol. Union, Berkeley, Calif., 1994; prof. theology U. San Francisco, 1994-97; radio commentator AM 1400, San Francisco, 1994-99, Sta. KPL SAM, Orange, Calif. Syndicated columnist San Francisco Monitor, Sacramento Herald, Oakland Voice, Yakima (Wash.) Our Times, Guam Diocesan Press, 1949-66, TV speaker and panelist, 1956-67; author: Church State Relationships in Education in California, 1948, Commentary on Declaration on Christian Education in Vatican II, 1966, Report on Education in Peru, 1965, The Church and Science, 1982, Blood on the Shamrock, 1989, The Unholy Ghost, 1992, Vatican Star, Star of David, 1996. Trustee N.Am. Coll., Rome, 1970, Cath. U. Am., 1978—, Cath. Relief Services, 1979; cons. Congregation for Edn.; mem. Secretariat for Non-Belief, Vatican City; bd. dirs. Overseas Blind Found., Ctr. for Theology and Natural Sci., Berkeley, FlaxTrust Corp., Belfast, Christians and Israel, Berkeley. Address: 273 Ulloa St San Francisco CA 94127-1226

HURLEY, MIKE, English language educator; b. St. Paul, Aug. 21, 1939. BS, N.D. State U., 1962; MA, Ind. U., 1972; MA in Tchg., Bridgewater State Coll., 1982. Enlisted USN, 1962, commd. ensign, 1964, advanced through grades to lt. comdr., 1971; resigned, 1986; seaman, journalist USS Independence, 1963-64; press escort officer UN Command, Seoul, 1964-65; asst. public affairs officer Sixth Naval Dist., Charleston, 1965-67; asst. head orientation Chief of Navy Info., The Pentagon, 1968; instr. Def. Info. Sch., Fort Harrison, Ind., 1969-71; force public affairs officer U.S. Naval Forces, Vietnam, 1971-72; resigned USN, 1972; exec. dir. Cmty. Svc. Officers, Fall River, Mass., 1973-75; assoc. dir. Citizens for Citizens, Fall River, 1975-83; assoc. prof. Bridgewater (Mass.) State Coll., 1984—; pub. Segregansett Press, Bridgewater, 1990—. Contbr. short fiction to profl. publs. With USNR, 1983-86. Avocation: philatelist. Office: Segregansett Press PO Box 545 Bridgewater MA 02324-0545

HURLEY, MORRIS ELMER, JR., management consultant; b. Berkeley, Calif., Mar. 26, 1920; s. Morris Elmer Sr. and Alice Grace (Johnson) H.; m. Jeanne Marie Bassett, Jan. 31, 1943; children: Morris Elmer III, James, Richard, Steven, Robert. A.B., Harvard, 1941, M.B.A., 1943; Ph.D., Syracuse U., 1956. Asst. dean Coll. Bus. Adminstrn., Syracuse (N.Y.) U., 1946-53, acting dean, 1953-54, dean, 1954-58, instr. mgmt., 1946-48, asst. prof., 1948-53, assoc. prof., 1953-57, prof., 1957-60; prof. Istituto Direzionale ENI, San Donato Milanese, Italy, 1958, IPSOA Istituto Post-Universitairo Torino, Italy, 1959-61; dir. mgmt. edn. programs U. Berkeley, Berkley, 1961—; assoc. economist N.Y. Dept. Commerce, 1948; rsch. aide Study for Ford Found., 1949; cons. prof. IBM Exec. Sch. Blaricum, Holland, 1960-61; mem. San Francisco C.C. Faculty, 1974-91, pres. acad. senate, 1979-81; bd. dirs. WIZ Corp., Empire Casting Co. Author: Elements of Business Administration, 1953, Economic Development Regionalism, 1956, Business Administration, 2d edit., 1960, Managing Human Endeavor, 1975, Supervision and Management, 1980, Business Management, 1991, Supervision, 1992, Presentation of Reports, 1993, Sexual Harassment, 1993, Training the Trainer, 1994. Mem. Syracuse city planning commn., 1957-58; bd. dirs. Portsmouth (Va.) Community Chest, 1944-46, Frank S. Hiscock Legal Aid Soc., Syracuse, 1951-54; mem. Piedmont Charter Rev. Commn., 1981-82. Served from ensign to lt. USNR, 1943-46; mem. Res. Mem. ASTD, Am. Econ. Assn., Acad. Mgmt., Acad. Polit. and Social Sci., George F. Baker Scholars, Phi Beta Kappa, Beta Gamma Sigma, Pi Eta, Sigma Iota Epsilon, Alpha Kappa Psi. Home and Office: 36 Greenbank Ave Piedmont CA 94611-4334

HURLEY, SAMUEL CLAY, III, investment management company executive; b. Peoria, Ill., Jan. 25, 1936; s. Samuel Clay Jr. and Wilmina Marie (Loveless) H.; m. Dorothy Jane Atkinson, Aug. 19, 1967; children: Samuel C. IV, Bruce Hilliard. AB in Econs., Brown U., 1958; MBA in Fin., Northwestern U., 1960; postgrad., Harvard U., 1984—. Portfolio mgr. Continental Ill. Nat. Bank, Chgo., 1960-62; mgr. bank rels. Internat. Harvester Co. (later Navistar), Chgo., 1962-71; asst. treas. Internat. Harvester Credit Corp., Chgo., 1962-71, Anchor Hocking Corp. (now owned by Newell Corp.), Lancaster, Ohio, 1971-74; treas. Anchor Hocking Corp. (now owned by Newell Corp.), Lancaster, 1975—, v.p., 1983-87; gen. ptnr. Steele and Co. Ltd., Columbus, Ohio, 1988-90; pres. Hurley Investment Counsel Ltd., Lancaster, 1990—. Trustee Lancaster-Fairfield Cmty. Hosp., 1984-91, Fairfield County Hospice, Fairfield County Found.; mem. Fairfield County Bd. Mental Retardation and Devel. Disabilities, Lancaster, 1981-95. Mem. Lancaster Country Club, Rotary, Capitol Club (Columbus). Republican. Episcopalian. Home: 148 E Wheeling St Lancaster OH 43130-3705 Office: 109 N Broad St Ste 350 Lancaster OH 43130-3785

HURLEY, THOMAS P., city clerk. MS, Okla. City U., 1963. Asst. city clk. Oklahoma City, Okla., 1973-78; city clk. Oklahoma City, 1978—. Mem. Internat. Inst. of Mcpl. Clks. Office: Office of City Clk City Hall 200 N Walker Ave Oklahoma City OK 73102-2232

HURLEY, WILLIAM JOSEPH, chemical company executive; b. Phila., July 26, 1940; s. Thomas Patrick and Louise Catherine (Culhane) H.; m. Rosemary Anne Gorman, Aug. 17, 1963; children: William J. Jr., Sharon A., Sean T., Megan M. BS in Chemistry, Villanova U., 1962; PhD in Chemistry, Princeton U., 1967. Rsch. chemist DuPont Co., Wilmington, Del., 1967-71, Parlin, N.J., 1971-73; rsch. supr. DuPont Co., Parlin, 1973-74, Rochester, N.Y., 1974-80; tech. mgr. DuPont Co., Wilmington, 1983-86, venture mgr., 1986-88, tech. mgr., 1988-89; lab. dir. DuPont Co., Circleville, Ohio, 1989-93; mgr. tech. pers. DuPont Co., Wilmington, 1993-94, mgr. corp. bus. devel., 1994—; devel. mgr. P.O. Magnetics, B.V., Eindhoven, The Netherlands, 1981-83; adj. prof. Villanova U., 1998—, Pa. State U., 1999—. NSF fellow, 1966. Mem. Am. Chem. Soc. (Outstanding Student award 1962). Avocations: boating, hiking, tennis. Office: DuPont Co Chestnut Run Plz Wilmington DE 19880

HURLOCK, JAMES BICKFORD, lawyer; b. Chgo., Aug. 7, 1933; s. James Bickford and Elizabeth (Charls) H.; m. Margaret Lyn Holding, July 1, 1961; children: James Bickford III, Burton Charls, Matthew Hunter. AB, Princeton U., 1955; BA, Oxford U., 1957, MA, 1960; JD, Harvard U., 1959. Bar: N.Y. 1960, U.S. Supreme Ct. 1967. Assoc. White & Case, N.Y.C., 1959-66, ptnr., 1967—. Trustee N.Y. Presbyn. Hosp., Parker Sch. Fgn. and Comparative Law, Internat. Devel. Law Inst., Mystic Seaport Mus., Woods Hole Oceanog. Inst. Rhodes scholar, 1955. Mem. ABA, N.Y. State Bar Inst., Am. Law Inst., Am. Assn. Internat. Law. Republican. Episcopalian. Clubs: Links, River, N.Y. Yacht. Home: 46 Byram Dr Greenwich CT 06830-7008 Office: White & Case Bldg Ll 1155 Avenue Of The Americas New York NY 10036-2787

HURN, RAYMOND WALTER, minister, religious order administrator; b. Ontario, Oreg., June 27, 1921; s. Walter H. and Bertha Sultana (Gray) H.; m. Madelyn Lenore Kirkpatrick, Dec. 30, 1941; children: Constance Isbell, Jacqueline Oliver. BA, Bethany (Okla.) Nazarene Coll., 1963, DD (hon.), 1967; postgrad., U. Tulsa, 1946-47, Fuller Sem., Pasadena, Calif., 1978-81. Ordained to ministry Ch. of Nazarene, 1943. Pastor Ch. of Nazarene chs., Kans., Okla., Ga., Oreg., 1943-59; dist. supt. Ch. of Nazarene, Tex., 1959-68; dir. home missions and ch. extension Internat. Hdqrs. Ch. of Nazarene, Kansas City, Mo., 1968-85, gen. supt., 1985-93. Author: Mission Possible, 1973, Black Evangelism, Which Way from Here, 1973, Spiritual Gifts Workshop, 1977, Finding Your Ministry, 1980, Mission Action Sourcebook, 1980, Unleashing the Lay Potential in the Sunday School, 1986, The Rising Tide: New Churches for the New Millenium, 1997. Recipient Exec. award Am. Inst. Ch. Growth, 1980, B award Bethany Nazarene Coll., 1982, Heritage award So. Nazarene U., 1993, Lifetime Achievement award Assn. of Nazarene Bldg. Prof., 1993, Multicultural Fellowship award, 1993; named Gen. Supt. Emeritus, 23rd Gen. Assembly of the Ch. of the Nazarene, 1993.

HURON, RODERICK EUGENE, small business owner; b. Chesapeake, Ohio, Dec. 5, 1934; s. Raymond Clarence and Minnie Opal (Williams) H.; m. Autumn June Hostetter, July 24, 1956; children: Lila Kay Huron Albinger, Eric Scott, Sara Lynn Huron Myers. BA, Ky. Christian Coll., 1956; MEd, U. Pitts., 1967; postgrad., U. Akron, 1968-70. Ordained to ministry Christian Chs. and Chs. of Christ, 1958; cert. meeting profl. Min. Highlawn Ch. of Christ, Huntington, W.Va., 1956-57; youth min. 1st Christian Ch., Canton, Ohio, 1957-62; min. LaBelle View Ch. of Christ, Steubenville, Ohio, 1962-67, West Akron (Ohio) Ch. of Christ, 1968-71; missionary Toronto (Can.) Christian Mission, 1971-75; sr. min. North Industry Christian Ch., Canton, 1976-84; dir.-elect N.Am. Christian Conv., Cin., 1984-86, conv. dir., 1986-97; pres. Meeting Excellence, Cin., 1997—; min. of membership devel. Lakeside Christian Ch., Ft. Mitchell, Ky., 1997—; min. involvement Lakeside Christian Ch., Lakeside Park, Ky., 1997—; guest on various TV and radio programs. Author: Do You Know Who You Are, 1976, Checkpoint, 1979 (Sherwood E. Wirt award Billy Graham Evangelistic Assn.), Christian Minister's Manual, 1984 (Gold Medallion award Evang. Christian Pub. Assn.), Say Hello to Life, 1984, Bible Stories for Children, 1995; contbr. numerous articles to religious jours. Republican.

HURST, DEBORAH, pediatric hematologist; b. Washington, May 9, 1946; d. Willard and Frances (Wilson) H.; m. Stephen Mershon Senter, June 14, 1970; children: Carlin, Daniel. BA, Harvard U., 1968; MD, Med. Coll. Pa., 1974. Diplomate Nat. Bd. Med. Examiners, Am. Bd. Pediatrics, Am. Bd. Pediatric Hematology-Oncology. Intern Bellevue Hosp., NYU Hosp., N.Y.C., 1974-75, resident in pediatrics, 1975-76; ambulatory pediatric fellow Bellevue Hosp., N.Y.C., 1976-77; hematology, oncology fellow Bellevue Hosp., Columbia U., N.Y.C., 1977-80; assoc. hematologist Childrens Hosp. Oakland, Calif., 1980-92; asst. clin. prof. U. Calif. San Francisco Med. Ctr., 1992—; med. dir. Bayer Corp., Berkeley, Calif., 1992-98; dir. clin. devel. Chiron Corp., Emeryville, Calif., 1998—; hematology cons. Assn. Asian/Pacific Community Health Orgns., Oakland; dir. Satellite Hematology Clinic/Valley Childrens Hosp., Fresno, Calif., 1984-92; cons. state dept. epidemiology Calif. State Dept. Health, Berkeley, 1992; chelation cons. lead poisoning program Childrens Hosp., Oakland, 1986-92. Contbr. articles to profl. jours. Vol. cons. lead poisoning State Dept. Epidemiology and Toxicology, Berkeley, 1986-92. Fellow Am. Acad. Pediatrics; mem. Am. Soc. Hematology, Am. Soc. Gene Therapy, Hemophilia Rsch. Soc., N.Y. Acad. Sci., Nat. Hemophilia Found., Internat. Soc. Thrombosis and Hemostasis. Office: Chiron Corp 4560 Horton St Emeryville CA 94608-2900

HURST, GREGORY SQUIRE, artistic director, director, producer; b. Oak Park, Ill., Dec. 1, 1947; s. Claude Squire Hurst and Marcia (Tooker) Allen; m. Joyce Barbara Baum, Apr. 4, 1981; children: Alexander Squire, Adam Spencer. BS, Miami U., Oxford, Ohio, 1969; MA, U. Wis., 1973; MFA, U. N.C., 1975. Dir. theater Wayland Acad., Beaver Dam, Wis., 1969-73; instr. acting U. N.C., Chapel Hill, 1973-75; chmn. theater dept. Tarkio (Mo.) Coll., 1975-77; producing artistic dir. Pa. Stage Co., Allentown, 1979-88, George St. Playhouse, New Brunswick, N.J., 1988-97; artistic dir. Mule Barn Theatre, Tarkio, 1975-77; mem. theater panel Mo. Arts Coun., St. Louis, 1975-77, Pa. Coun. Arts, Harrisburg, 1982-85; cons. Found. Devel. Am. Profl. theatre, N.Y.C., 1983; on-site evaluator Nat. Endowment Arts, Washington, 1984-97; mem. mus. theater task force Rockefeller Found., Phila., 1985; founding mem. Playmakers Reperatory Theatre, 1975. Librettist (mus. play) Song of Myself, 1981; stage dir. (world premieres) Feathertop, Great Expectations, (with Hinton Battle) Shim Sham, (with Estelle Parsons) Forgiving Typhoid Mary (named One of Best 5 Plays in Am., Time mag. 1991), Greetings, Copperhead, (with John Cullum) Jekyll and Hyde, (with Michael Murphy) Near the End of the Century, (with Joel Higgins, Christine Andreas) Fields of Ambrosia, West End London Aldwych Theatre, 1996, (with Michael Rupert) Relativity, Sing a Christmas Song (Peter Udell), 1997; nat. tour The Acting Co. The Glass Menagerie; dir. TV shows General Hospital, One Life to Live, Another World, The Guiding Light. Area leader Allentown and Cen. Jersey United Way, 1981-92; exec. v.p., bd. dirs. Stage Dirs. and Choreographers Found., 1989-92, pres., 1992-98. Recipient Downtown Improvement award City of Allentown, 1987, Outstanding Contbn. award Theatre Assn. Pa., 1988, Vision, dedication, leadership award SDC Found., 1998; Tony nomination for best musical Swinging On A Star; named Best Dir. in N.J. Belmont Avenue Social Club, 1994, Les Liaisons Dangereuse, 1989. Mem. Dirs. Guild of Am., Soc. Stage Dirs., Dramatist Guild, Actors Equity Assn., Phi Kappa Tau. Democrat. Avocations: golf, antiques, travel, swimming, gourmet cooking. Home: 3 Fernwood Ct East Brunswick NJ 08816-3333

HURST, JOHN EMORY, JR., retired airline executive; b. Phoenix, Feb. 9, 1928; s. John Emory and Kathryne Ann (Prechtel) H.; m. Sara Waugh; children—Craig K., Susan M., John J. BS, U.S. Mil. Acad., 1950; MS, U. Ill., 1956; MA, Columbia U., 1960; grad., U.S. Army Command and Gen. Staff Coll., 1964, Naval War Coll., 1968. Registered profl. engr., N.Y., Fla. Commd. 2d lt. U.S. Army, 1950, advanced through grades to col., 1970; served in U.S. Army, Korea, 1950-51, Vietnem, 1964-65; mem. Dept. of Army Staff, 1969-71; ret. U.S. Army, 1971; from v.p. to sr. v.p. Eastern Airlines, Miami, Fla., 1971-86. Mem. ASCE. Republican. Episcopalian. Avocations: horseback riding; running. Address: RR 1 Box 451 Independence VA 24348-9732*

HURST, KENNETH THURSTON, publisher; b. London, Apr. 3, 1923; came to U.S., 1947, naturalized, 1953; s. Ralph Thurston and Karen (Tottrup) H. Student pvt. schs. Account exec. Hutzler Advt. Agy., Dayton, Ohio, 1948-53; advt. and promotion mgr. McGraw-Hill Book Co., N.Y.C., 1953-58; advt. and publicity mgr. Hawthorn Books, Inc., N.Y.C., 1958-61; gen. mgr. Prentice-Hall of India Pvt. Ltd., New Delhi, 1961-63; v.p., gen. mgr. Prentice-Hall Internat., Inc., Englewood Cliffs, N.J., 1963-70; exec. v.p. Prentice-Hall Internat., Inc., 1970, now pres.; dir. Internat. Book Distbr., Ltd., Prentice-Hall S.E. Asia Ltd., Prentice-Hall India Ltd.; State Dept. adviser to Brazil and Burma; adviser AID Mission to Turkey, 1964, Morocco, 1965; cons. U.S. Info. Agy., U. N.C., U. Scranton, SUNY, MIT, Faculty Folio mag.; lectr. State Dept. Program Bur., NYU, Rockland Community Coll., U. Scranton, Drew U., Wagner Coll., Lake Forest (Ill.) Coll., Olivet (Mich.) Coll., Rosemont Coll., Pa., Oberlin Coll., Ohio, Corning Coll., N.Y., U. Cen. Fla., U. So. Fla., Edison C.C., Pepperdine Coll., Calif., Chestnut Hill (Pa.) Coll., Spearfish Coll., S.D., Rockpoint Colony, Cornell U., Stanford U., Russell Sage Coll., Fla. State U.; faculty ann. pubs. seminar; co-chmn. Internat. Sports Awards, 1982, Pub. Hall of Fame, 1984; mem. policy bd. Ctr. for the Book; chmn. Books Across the Sea. Co-author: Books for National Growth, 1965, Indian Publishing Since Independence, 1980, American Books Abroad, 1986, Spiritual Insights for Daily Living, 1986; author: Live Life First Class, 1985, Paul Brunton: A Personal View, 1988, Living the Good Life, 1989; contbr. articles to profl. jours. Mem. Spiritual Adv. Coun., Elizabeth Kubler-Ross Ctr.; mem. com. to balance budget Ctr. Applied Rsch. in Edn., Internat. Inst. Integral Scis.; trustee Valley Cottage Free Libr.; chmn., mem. nat. exec. coun. Spiritual Frontiers Fellowship; chmn. N.Y. Easter Seal dr., 1983, Paul Brunton Philosophic Found.; bd. dirs. Ctr. for Positive Living; pres., bd. dirs. Collier County Friends of Libr. Assn.; mem. Lee County Libr. Adv. Bd.; v.p. Las Vistas Assn. With Fleet Air Arm Royal Navy, 1942-47. Recipient Presdl. E award and E Star, Pub. Hall of Fame. Mem. Asia Soc., St. John's Old Boys' Assn., Assn. Am. Pubs. (chmn. internat. div., chmn. del. to India 1979, 84, to Thailand 1981), Am. Mgmt. Assn., Inst. Bus. Planning, Mensa, Acad. Religion (trustee), Inst. Near-Death Studies (bd. dirs.), Circumnavigators Club, Forum Club (bd. dirs.), Eng. Speaking Union (bd. dirs.), Internat. Club Fla., Overseas Press Club, Fla. Coun. Humanities, Neapolitan Club, Boston Athletic Club, Publishers Club, Englewood Club (gov.), Rotary (bd. dirs.). Republican. Episcopalian.

HURST, LELAND LYLE, natural gas company executive; b. Mooreland, Okla., Oct. 16, 1930; s. Lewis Walter and Ellen Sarah (Riggs) H.; m. Karen Lee Lamkin, Jan. 24, 1969; children: Courtney Anne, Caroline Leigh. B.S. in Indsl. Engring., Okla. State U., 1952; M.S. in Petroleum Engring., U. Tulsa, 1958. Registered profl. engr., Okla. With Amoco Prodn. Co., 1958-80; engr. Amoco Prodn. Co. (various locations), 1958-68; staff engr. Amoco Prodn. Co., Calgary, Alta., Can., 1968-70; div. engr. supr. Amoco Prodn. Co., Denver, 1970-73; area supt. Amoco Prodn. Co., Liberal, Kans., 1973-74; asst. div. engr. Amoco Prodn. Co., Denver, 1974-75, gas sales mgr., 1975-80; v.p. Amoco Gas Co., Houston, 1980-81, pres., dir., 1981-86; v.p. mktg. KN Energy Inc., Gasco Inc., 1986-87; v.p. interstate ops., exec. v.p. Gasco Inc., 1987-88, sr. v.p. ops., 1988-95, also bd. dirs., 1992-95; exec. v.p., dir. Indsl. Mechanics Inc., 1987-95, Sunflower Pipeline Co., 1988-95, Rocky Mountain Gas Co., 1992-95, 1992-95; exec. v.p., dir. No. Gas Co. Wyo., 1992-95, 1992-95; bd. dirs., v.p. KN Front Range Oper. Co., KN Wattenberg Co., KN Wattenberg Ltd. Liability Co.; bd. dirs. RMNG Gathering Co., TCP Gathering Co.; v.p. Panola/Rusk Gatherers, Am. Energy Holdings, Inc., Am. Gas Storage, L.P., Am. Gathering, L.P., Am. Processing, L.P., Am. Oil and Gas Corp., Am. Pipeline Co., Am. Webb, Inc., AOG Holdings, Inc., AOG Mgmt., Inc., Caprock Pipeline Co., Red River Gas Pipeline Corp., Red River Pipeline, L.P., RRP Fin. Corp., Webb/Duval Gatherers, Westar Transmission Co., 1995. With Chem. Corps U.S. Army, 1953-55. Served with Chem. Corps U.S. Army, 1953-55. Mem. Rocky Mountain Gas Men's Assn. (bd. dirs. 1977), Soc. Petroleum Engrs. (editl. com. 1953-55), Rocky Mountain Oil and Gas Assn. Colo. (pres. 1995-97, indsl. mechanic chmn. 1995—), Natural Gas Men of Houston-New Orleans (v.p.), Houston Club, Denver Petroleum Club. Republican. *

HURST, MARY JANE, English language educator; b. Hamilton, Ohio, Sept. 21, 1952; d. Nimrod and Leckie Gaines; m. Daniel L. Hurst, June 5, 1974; 1 child, Katherine Jane. BA summa cum laude, Miami U., 1974; MA, U. Md., 1980, PhD, 1986. Tchr. Groveport (Ohio) High Sch., 1974-77; tchg. asst. U. Md., College Park, 1978-79, master tchr., 1979-82; asst. prof. English, Tex. Tech U., Lubbock, 1986-92, assoc. prof., 1992-99, prof., 1999—; vis. scholar Stanford U., summer 1987; steering com. Nat. Cowboy Symposium, Lubbock, 1988-89. Author: The Voice of the Child in American Literature, 1990; tech. editor: HTLV-I and the Nervous System, 1989; book rev. editor S.W. Jour. Linguistics, 1995-98; contbr. articles to profl. jours. Mem. Lubbock Cultural Affairs Coun., 1986-92, Lubbock Symphony Guild, 1992—; vol. Meals on Wheel, Lubbock, 1986—, Habitat for Humanity, Lubbock, 1986—. Mem. AAUW (alt. fellowships panel in linguistics 1988-90), AAUP (regional v.p. 1990-94), MLA, Linguistic Soc. Am., Linguistic Assn. S.W. (pres. 1996-97, exec. dir. 1998—), Coll. Tchrs. English Tex., South Ctrl. Modern Lang. Assn., Phi Beta Kappa, Phi Kappa Phi, Sigma Tau Delta, Alpha Lambda Delta. Avocations: geneaology, traveling, West Highland White Terriers. Office: Tex Tech U Dept English Lubbock TX 79409

HURST, MICHAEL WILLIAM, psychologist; b. Medford, Oreg., Dec. 9, 1947; s. William George and Betty Muriel (Stevens) H.; m. Patricia C. Scully, Aug. 22, 1970 (div. 1981); 1 child, Michelle P.; m. Renee Catherine Sancoff, Aug. 20, 1988; children: Rachel C., James M., Elizabeth R. BS, MIT, 1970; MEd, Boston U., 1972, EdD, 1974. Lic. psychologist, Mass., N.H.; cert. employee assistance profl. Rsch. assoc. Powell Assocs., Inc., Cambridge, Mass., 1970-72; rsch. and teaching fellow dept. counselor edn. Boston U., 1972-73, post-doctoral fellow and instr. dept. psychosomatic medicine, 1973-74, asst. prof. psychiatry, 1974-80, assoc. prof. psychiatry, 1980-98; attending psychologist Univ. Hosp., Boston, 1978—; pres. Hurst Assocs., Inc., Boston, 1978-91; cons. to numerous orgns., 1978—; v.p. Am. PsychMgmt./Hurst Assocs., Inc., 1991-92; managed behavioral health care cons., 1992-93; pres. InStream Corp., 1993-98, Nat. Leadership Coun., Inst. Behavioral Healthcare, 1994—, Informatics Consulting Group LLC, 1999—. Cons. editor: Behavioral Medicine, 1982-91; patentee in field; contbr. articles to profl. jours. Bd. dirs., treas. Mass. Spl. Needs Assn., Inc., Groton, 1973-76; bd. dirs., steering com. Mass. Psychol. Health Plan Inc., Groton, 1979-82; pres., v.p. Pine Acre Park Assn., Hampstead, N.H., 1982-85. Fellow Mass. Psychol. Assn.; mem. APA, Am. Psychopathological Assn. (Morton Prince prize 1978), N.Y. Acad. Scis., Phi Delta Kappa, Delta Upsilon Alumni Assn. (bd. dirs. 1979-82). Republican. Episcopalian. Avocations: flying, shooting, boating. Home: 3 Eastwood Dr Windham NH 03087-1638

HURST, ROBERT JAY, securities company executive; b. N.Y.C., Nov. 5, 1945; s. Kurt and Jeanette (Sachs) H.; children: Alexander, Amanda. BA, Clark U., 1966; M in Govt. Adminstrn., U. Pa., 1968, Pub. Fin. fellow, 1969. With investment banking divsn. Merrill Lynch, Pierce, Fenner & Smith, Inc., N.Y.C., 1969-74, v.p., 1974; v.p. Goldman, Sachs & Co., N.Y.C., 1974-80, gen. ptnr., 1980—; mem. mgmt. com. Goldman Sachs & Co., 1990, cohead investment banking divsn., 1996, head investment banking divsn., 1996—, mem. exec. com., 1995, vice chmn., 1997; bd. dirs. IDB Holding Corp., VF Corp., Goldman Sachs Group, Inc., 1997. Mem. bd. overseers Wharton Sch. U. Pa., mem. coun. fgn. rels.; trustee Com. Econ. Devel.; v.p., bd. trustees Whitney Mus. Am. Art; chmn. Jewish Mus., 1991. Mem. Univ. Club., Atlantic Golf Club (Bridgehampton), Sunningdale (N.Y.), Maroon Creek Club (Aspen). Office: Goldman Sachs & Co 85 Broad St New York NY 10004-2456

HURT, CHARLIE DEUEL, III, dean, educator; b. Charlottesville, Va., Sept. 20, 1950; s. Charlie Deuel Jr. and Timie Oletta (Young) H.; m. Susan Edith Scudamore, May 15, 1981. BA, U. Va., 1971; MLS, U. Ky., 1975; PhD, U. Wis., 1981. Engring. librarian U. Va., Charlottesville, 1975-78, automation librarian, 1977-78; asst. prof. McGill U., Montreal, Que., Can., 1981-84, assoc. prof., 1984; assoc. prof. Simmons Coll., Boston, 1984-86; dir., prof. lib. sch. U. Ariz., Tucson, 1986-98, assoc. dean social and behavioral sci., 1998—; prin. Info. Prime, Montreal, 1984—; cons. Scudamore & Assocs. Montreal, 1984-85. Author: Information Sources in Science and Technology, 1998; co-author: Scientific and Technical Literature, 1990; contbr. articles to profl. jours. Hollowell grantee Simmons Coll., 1984. Mem. IEEE, Am. Soc. Info. Sci., Am. Mgmt. Assn., N.Y. Acad. Sci. Avocations: statistics, computing. Home: 1820 W Wimbledon Way Tucson AZ 85737-9070 Office: U Ariz Coll Social & Behavioral Sci 200 W Douglass Tucson AZ 85721

HURT, DAVINA THERESA, educator; b. Yonkers, N.Y., May 11, 1972; d. David Wallace and Sadie Theresa (Jeffries) H. BS, Hampton U., 1995; bus. edn. cert., Nazareth Coll., 1997. Student intern IBM, Rochester, 1991; factory worker ITT, Rochester, 1994; contractor Man Power, Rochester, 1992-95; acctg. First Federal S&L, Rochester, N.Y., 1995-97; substitute tchr. Rochester City Sch. Dist., 1998; computer tchr. Josh Lofton H.S. Bd. dirs. Ctr. for Youth Svcs., 1988-90. Mem. AAUW. Home: 22 Dejonge St Rochester NY 14621-4606

HURT, FRANK, labor union administrator. Bus. agt. Local 57 Bakery, Confectionery and Tobacco Workers Internat. Union, 1972, mem. internat. union staff, 1979; pres. Bakery, Confectionary and Tobacco Workers International Union, Kensington, Md., 1992—; mem. exec. coun. AFL-CIO, 1993—, v.p.; pres. Internat. Union Food Workers, 1997—; v.p., mem. exec. com. Indsl. Union Dept.; trustee Joint Labor Mgmt. Com. Retail Food Industry; bd. dirs. Free Trade Union Inst., Union Labor Life Ins. Co., Am. Income Life Ins. Co., Asian-Am. Free Labor Inst., Food Allied and Svc. Trades Dept. Office: Bakery Confectionary and Tobacco Worker's Internat Union 10401 Connecticut Ave Kensington MD 20895-3951*

HURT, JAMES RIGGINS, English language educator; b. Ashland, Ky., May 22, 1934; s. Joe and Martha Clay (Riggins) H.; m. Phyllis Tilton, June 5, 1958; children: Christopher, Ross, Matthew. AB, U. Ky., 1956, MA, 1957; PhD, Ind. U., 1965. Asst. prof. Ind. U., Kokomo, 1963-66; asst. prof. U. Ill., Urbana-Champaign, 1966-69; asso. prof. U. Ill., 1969-73, prof. English, 1973—. Author: Aelfric, 1972, Catiline's Dream, 1972, Film and Theatre, 1974, Writing Illinois, 1992, (play) Abraham Lincoln Walks at Midnight, 1980; co-editor: Literature of the Western World, 1984. Served with U.S. Army, 1957-59. Fellow Ill. Ctr. Advanced Study, 1979-80, 86-87. Mem. MLA, Ill. State Hist. Soc. Home: 1001 W William St Champaign IL 61821-4508 Office: 325 English Bldg 608 S Wright St Urbana IL 61801-3613

HURT, NATHAN HAMPTON, JR., mechanical engineer; b. Clifton, Mo., June 7, 1921; s. Nathan Hampton Sr. and Mary Lillian (Mayo) H.; m. LuCretia Ann Cutler, Feb. 16, 1946 (dec. 1980); children: Steven Eugene, Mark Lindsay; m. Karin Elisabeth Tuttle, Aug. 30, 1980; 1 stepchild, Christine Yvonne Reed; adopted children: Audrey Barbara, Nikki Alexandra. Student in mech. engring. Mont. Sch. Mines, 1944, U. So. Calif., 1944-46; B.S. in Mech. Engring., U. Colo., 1947. Engr. Goodyear Tire and Rubber Co., Akron, Ohio, 1947-87, program mgr., Rio de Janeiro, Brazil, 1959-62, plant mgr. Akron Rubber Chems. Plant, 1962-63, plant mgr., Logan, Ohio, 1963-68; supt. plant engring. Goodyear Atomic Corp., Piketon, Ohio, 1952-56, mgr. plant engring., 1968-72, dep. gen. mgr., 1972-77, gen. mgr., 1977-85, pres., 1985-87; ret., 1987; mgr. bus. devel. Los Alamos Tech. Assocs., 1987-94; v.p. IDM Environ. Corp., Oak Ridge, 1994-98; dir. Sharp and Assocs., 1998—. Mem. Chief Logan council Boy Scouts Am., 1970-80; bd. dirs. Ross County Med. Ctr., Chillicothe, Ohio, 1974. Mem. Chillicothe C. of C., Waverly C. of C., Jackson C. of C., Portsmouth C. of C., ASME (pres. 1991-92), Am. Inst. Chem. Engrs., Am. Soc. Engring. Mgmt., Atomic Indsl. Forum, Rotary. Avocations: golf, racquetball, snow skiing. Fax: 423-483-0552. E-mail: nhhurt@sharpenv.com. Home: 424 Mariner Point Dr Clinton TN 37716-5993 Office: Sharp and Assocs Inc 601-D Scarboro Rd Oak Ridge TN 37830-7371

HURT, ROBERT HOWARD, chemical engineering educator; b. Dover, N.J., June 27, 1960; s. William Clark and Patricia June (Bergstrom) H.; m. Beth Ann (Marothy) H., Feb. 24, 1980; children: Emily, Lucille. BS, Mich. Technol. U., 1982; PhD, MIT, 1987. Sr. rsch. engr. Bayer AG, Leverkusen, West Germany, 1987-90; sr. mem. tech. staff Sandia Nat. Labs, Livermore, Calif., 1990-94; assoc. prof. Brown U., Providence, R.I., 1994—. Contbr. articles to profl. jours. Rsch. grantee U.S. DOE, 1995; rsch. contract Elect Power Rsch. Inst., 1995. Mem. AIChE, The Combustion Inst., Am. Carbon Soc. Home: 8 Bay Rd Barrington RI 02806-4304 Office: Brown Univ Divsn Engring Box D 182 Hope St Providence RI 02912-9037

HURT, WILLIAM, actor; b. Washington, Mar. 20, 1950; m. Mary Beth Hurt (div. 1982); m. Heidi Henderson, Mar. 5, 1989; children: Alexander, Sam. Grad., Tufts U., 1972; student, Juilliard Sch. Appeared with Oreg. Shakespeare Festival prodn. A Long Days Journey into Night, 1975, N.Y.C.; actor: (stage) debut in Henry V, 1977, also My Life, 1977, Ulysses in Traction, Lulu, 1978, Fifth of July, 1978, Hamlet, 1979, Mary Stuart, 1979, Childe Byron, 1981, The Diviners, 1981, The Great Grandson of Jedediah kohler, 1982, Richard II, 1982, A Midsummer Night's Dream, 1982, Hurlyburly, 1984, Joan of Arc at the Stake, 1985, Love Letters, 1989, Beside Herself, 1989, Ivanov, 1991, (films) including Altered States, 1980, Eyewitness, 1981, Body Heat, 1981, The Big Chill, 1983, Gorky Park, 1983, Kiss of the Spider Woman 1984 (Best Actor award Cannes Film Festival 1985, Acad. award for best actor 1985), Children of a Lesser God (nominated Acad. award for best actor 1986), 1986, Broadcast News, 1987 (nominated Acad. award for best actor), A Time of Destiny, 1988, The Accidental Tourist, 1988, I Love You To Death, 1990, Alice, 1990, The Doctor, 1991, Untilthe End of the World, 1991, Mr. Wonderful, 1993, The Plague, 1993, Trial by Jury, 1994, Second Best, 1994, Smoke, 1995, Michael, 1996, Jane Eyre, 1996, Un divan à New York, 1996, Shakespeare's Sister, 1997, Loved, 1997, Dark City, 1997, Lost in Space, 1998, One True Thing, 1998; mem. Circle Repertory Co., N.Y.C; appeared in Chekhov's Ivanov at Yale Repertory Theatre, New Haven, Conn., 1990; T.V. appearances, Verna: USO Girl, 1980, All The Way Home, 1981, Best of Families. Recipient 1st Spencer Tracy Award, 1988, for outstanding screen performances and profl. achievement, Theatre World award Work with Circle Repatory Theatre, 1978. Office: c/o Hilda Quille/William Morris 151 S El Camino Dr Beverly Hills CA 90212-2704*

HURT, WILLIAM HOLMAN, investment management company executive; b. L.A., Mar. 29, 1927; s. Holman G. and Mary E. (Ortloff) H.; m. Sheridan Ann Stephens, Aug. 10, 1950 (div. May. 1970); children: Kelley Anne Hurt Purnell, Kathleen Constance, Courtney Diana Hurt MacMillan; m. Sarah Sherman, May 28, 1970. BS magna cum laude, U. So. Calif., 1949; MBA, Harvard U., 1951. With Dean Witter & Co., Los Angeles, 1951-71; ptnr. Dean Witter & Co., 1959, sr. v.p., 1968-70, exec. v.p., dir., mem. exec. com., dir. mktg. and rsch., 1969-71; vice chmn. bd., chmn. exec. com. Capital Rsch. Co., 1972-77; chief exec. officer Capital Group, Inc., L.A., 1978-82; chmn. Capital Strategy Rsch., Inc., 1982—; mem. adv. com. Coldwell Banker Funds, 1978—. Mem. bd. councilors Grad. Sch. Bus., U. So. Calif., L.A., 1978-88, vis. com., 1990—; bd. dirs. L.A. Children's Hosp., 1985—. Served with USNR, 1945-46. Mem. Calif. Club, L.A. Athletic Club, N.Y. Athletic Club, Phi Kappa Phi, Beta Gamma Sigma, Kappa Alpha. Republican. Office: 333 S Hope St Los Angeles CA 90071-1406

HURTADO, EDUARDO, soccer player; b. Esmeraldas, Ecuador, Jan. 12, 1969. Past mem. Centro Juvenil Deportivo, Ecuador, Correcaminos, Mex., Saint Gallen, Switzerland, Colo Colo, Chile; mem. L.A. Galaxy, 1996-97, N.Y. Metrostars, 1997—; mem. Nat. Team of Ecuador. *

HURTADO, RODRIGO CLAUDIO, allergist, immunologist; b. Chile, 1939. MD, U. Chile, Santiago, 1964. Diplomate Am. Bd. Allergy and Immunology, , Am. Bd. Pediatrics. Intern U. Chile, 1964, resident, 1968-71; fellow allergy and infectious diseases Georgetown U., Washington, 1972-74; pvt. practice Washington, 1974—; clin. asst. prof. Georgetown U. Med. Sch., Washington. Mem. Am. Acad. Pediatrics and Immunology, Am. Acad. Allergy Asthma and Immunology, Am. Acad. Pediatrics, Am. Coll. Allergy. Office: 3450 N Beauregard St Alexandria VA 22302-1200*

HURTEAU, GILLES DAVID, retired obstetrician, gynecologist, educator, dean; b. Cornwall, Ont., Can., Nov. 28, 1928; s. Joseph A. and Antoinette (St-Laurent) H.; m. Janine Anita Carriere, June 16, 1956; children: Michele, Jean, Louise, Pierre, Gilles Andre. BA, U. Ottawa, 1951; MD, CM, McGill U., 1955. Licentiate, Med. Council Can., 1956; cert. in ob-gyn, 1961. Instr. and clin. asst. Yale U. Med. Sch., New Haven, 1961-62; asst. prof. U. Ottawa Med. Sch., Ont., 1963-66, assoc. prof., 1966, prof. and chmn. dept. ob-gyn, 1967-76, dean Sch. Medicine, 1976-89, dean faculty health scis., 1978-89; exec. dir./registrar Royal Coll. Physicians and Surgeons Can., Ottawa, 1990-95; bd. govs., mem. exec. com. U. Ottawa, 1995—; bd. dirs. Ont. Cancer Treatment and Rsch. Found., 1983-92, Physicians Svcs. Inc. Found. Ont., 1984-86, 95—, Assoc. Med. Svcs. Inc., Ont., 1998—. Mem. editorial bd. European Jour. Ob-Gyn and Reproductive Biology, 1970-78; contbr. articles to profl. jours., chpts to books. Mem. council Ottawa-Carleton Dist. Health Council, 1978-84; mem. Joint Research Rev. Task Force, Ont. Council Health, 1977-81. Fellow Royal Coll. Physicians and Surgeons Can. (coun. 1970-78, v.p. 1976-78), Royal Coll. Physicians Ireland; mem. Coun. Ont. Faculty of Medicine (1976-89), Assn. Can. Med. Colls. (pres. 1981-82). Home: 31 Durham (Priv)-Unit 203, Ottawa, ON Canada K1M 2J1 *Ce que nous connaissons est peu de chose; ce que nous ignorons est immense.*

HURTER, ARTHUR PATRICK, economist, educator; b. Chgo., Jan. 29; s. Arthur P. and Lillian T. (Thums) H.; m. Florence Evalyn Kays; children—Patricia Lyn, Arthur Earl. BSChemE, Northwestern U., MSChemE, MA in Econs., PhD in Econs. Chem. engr. Zonlite Rsch. Lab., Evanston, Ill., 1957-58; assoc. dir. Rsch. Transp. Ctr., Northwestern U., Evanston, 1963-65; asst. prof. dept. Indsl. Engring. and Mgmt. Scis. Tech. Inst., Northwestern U., 1962-66, prof., 1970—; prof. of transp., 1992—; chmn. dept. Northwestern U., 1969-89, assoc. prof. fin. Grad. Sch. Mgmt., 1969-70, prof., 1970—; faculty mem. Newspaper Mgmt. Ctr., Transp. Ctr., 1989—; cons. U. Chgo., ESCOR, Sears Roebuck & Co., Standard Oil of Ind., Ill.; bd. dirs. Ill. Environ. Health Rsch. Ctr., 1972-77; mem. com. Sci. Tech. Adv., Ill. Inst. Natural Resources, 1980-84. Author: The Economics of Private Truck Transportation, 1965, Facility Location and the Theory of Production, 1989; contbr. articles to profl. jours. Pres. Coun. St. Scholastical H.S., 1972-80; elder Granville Ave. Presbyn. Ch., 1976-89; deacon 1st Presbyn. Ch., Evanston. Grantee Resources for the Future, 1964, Office of Naval Research, 1965, NSF, Social Sci. Research Council dissertation fellow. Mem. Am. Econ. Assn., Regional Sci. Assn., Ops. Research Soc. Am., Inst. Mgmt. Scis., Inst. Indsl. Engrs., Sigma Xi, Phi Lambda Upsilon, Tau Beta Pi, Alpha Pi Mu (Disting. Engr. award). Home: 1505 W Norwood St Chicago IL 60660-2414 Office: Dept Indsl Engring Mgmt Sci Technological Inst Northwestern U Evanston IL 60208

HURWICZ, LEONID, economist, educator; b. Moscow, 1917; came to U.S., 1940; LLM, U. Warsaw, Poland, 1938; DSc (hon.), Northwestern U., 1980; D honoris causa, U. Autónoma de Barcelona, Spain, 1989; D of Econs. honoris causa, Keio U., Tokyo, 1993; LLD (hon.), U. Chgo., 1993; D honoris causa, Warsaw Sch. Econs., Poland, 1994. Rsch. assoc. Cowles Commn. U. Chgo., 1944-46; from assoc. prof. to prof. Iowa State U., Ames, 1946-49; prof. econ., math. and stats. U. Ill., 1949-51; prof. econ., math. and stats. U. Minn., Mpls., 1951-99, Regents' prof., 1969-88, Regent's prof. emeritus, 1988—, Carlson prof. econs., 1989-92, prof. econs., 1992—; vis. prof. econs. Stanford (Calif.) U., 1955-56, 58-59, Harvard U., Cambridge, Mass., 1969-71, U. Calif., Berkeley, 1976-77, Northwestern U., Evanston, Ill., 1988-89, U. Calif., Santa Barbara, 1998, Calif. Inst. Tech., 1999; Fisher lectr. U. Copenhagen, 1963; hon. prof. Cen. China U. Sci. and Tech., Wuhan, 1984; vis. lectr. People's Univ., Beijing, People's Republic of China, 1986, Tokyo U., 1982, Australian Econometric Mtgs., Melbourne, 1997; vis. Fulbright lectr. Bangalore U., India, 1965-66. Author and editor: (with K.J. Arrow) Studies in Resource Allocation Processes, 1977; (with K.J. Arrow and H. Uzawa) Studies in Linear and Non-Linear Programming, 1958; (with J.S. Chipman et al) Prefences, Utility and Demand, 1971, (with D. Schmeidler and H. Sonnenschein) Social Goals and Social Organization, 1985; hon. editor: Econ. Design, 1993; contbr. articles to profl. jours. Sherman Fairchild Disting. scholar Calif. Inst. Tech., 1984-85; recipient Nat. Medal Sci., 1990; fellow Ctr. Advanced Studies in Behavioral Scis., 1955-56. Fellow Econometric Soc. (pres. 1969), Am. Econ. Assn. (disting.; Ely lectr. 1972); mem. NAS, Am. Acad. Arts and Scis. Office: Univ Minn Dept Econs 271 19th Ave S Minneapolis MN 55455-0430

HURWITZ, CHARLES EDWIN, manufacturing company executive; b. Kilgore, Tex., May 3, 1940; s. Hyman and Eva (Engler) H.; m. Barbara Raye Gollub, Feb. 24, 1963; children: Shawn Michael, David Alan. BA, U. Okla., Norman, 1962. Chmn. bd., pres. Investam. Group, Inc., Houston, 1965-67, Summitt Mgmt. & Research Corp., Houston, 1967-70; chmn. bd. Summit Ins. Co. of N.Y., Houston, 1970-75; with MCO Holdings, Inc. (and predecessor), Los Angeles, from 1978, chmn. bd., chief exec. officer, from 1980, dir., from 1978; chmn., pres., CEO Maxxam Inc., Houston, also dir. Jewish. Office: Maxxam Inc 5847 San Felipe St Houston TX 77057-3005

HURWITZ, DAVID, entreprenuer, consultant; b. N.Y.C., June 29, 1948; s. George and Belle (Weiner) H.; m. Ilene Michele Jaffe, June 14, 1970; children: Joshua Richard, Jonathan Benjamin, Deborah Anne. B of Chem. Engring., CCNY, 1970; MBA, Fairleigh Dickinson U., 1974. Corp. planning mgr. Allied Corp., Morristown, N.J., 1981-84; v.p. planning and bus. devel., gen. mgr. biotech. divsn. Fisher Sci. Co., Pitts., 1984-88, v.p., gen. mgr. internat. divsn., 1988-89; pres., CEO Lab. Data Systems, Pitts., 1989-91; gen. mgr. Allied Signal Corp., Morristown, N.J., 1991-95; pres., cons. Randolph (N.J.) Mgmt. Group, 1995—; pres., CEO Allerton Enterprises LLC, Rockaway, N.J., 1996—. Mem. Comml. Devel. Assn. Avocations: collecting historical items, sports. Office: Allerton Enterprises LLC 2 Mount Prospect Ave Dover NJ 07801-3748

HURWITZ, JOHANNA (FRANK), author, librarian; b. N.Y.C., Oct. 9, 1937; d. Nelson and Tillie (Miller) Frank; m. Uri Hurwitz, Feb. 19, 1962; children: Nomi, Beni. BA, Queens Coll., 1958; MLS, Columbia U., 1959. Libr. children's sect. N.Y. Pub. Libr., 1959-64; lectr. in children's lit. Queen's Coll., N.Y.C., 1965-69; libr. Calhoun Sch., N.Y.C., 1968-75, New Hyde Park (N.Y.) Sch. Dist., 1975-77; libr. children's sect. Great Neck (N.Y.) Pub. Libr., 1978-92. Author: Busybody Nora, 1976, Nora and Mrs. Mind-Your-Own-Business, 1977, The Law of Gravity, 1978, Much Ado About Aldo, 1978, Aldo Applesauce, 1979, New Neighbours for Nora, 1979, Once I Was a Plum Tree, 1980, Superduper Teddy, 1980, Aldo Ice Cream, 1981, Baseball Fever, 1981, The Rabbi's Girls, 1982, Tough-Luck Karen, 1982, Rip-Roaring Russell, 1983, DeDe Takes Charge!, 1984, The Hot and Cold Summer, 1984, The Adventures of Ali Baba Bernstein, 1985, Russell Rides Again, 1985, Hurricane Elaine, 1986, Yellow Blue Jay, 1986, Class Clown, 1987, Russell Sprouts, 1987, The Cold and Hot Winter, 1988, Teacher's Pet, 1988, Anne Frank: Life in Hiding, 1988, Hurray for Ali Baba Bernstein, 1989, Russell and Elisa, 1989, Astrid Lindgren: Storyteller to the World, 1989, Class President, 1990, Aldo Peanut Butter, 1990, School's Out, 1991, E Is for Elisa, 1991, Roz and Ozzie, 1992, Ali Baba Bernstein, Lost and Found, 1992, The Up and Down Spring, 1993, Make Room for Elisa, 1993, Leonard Bernstein: A Passion for Music, 1993, New Shoes for Silvia, 1993, A Word to the Wise, 1994, School Spirit, 1994, A Llama in the Family, 1994, Ozzie on His Own, 1995, Birthday Surprises, 1995, Elisa in the Middle, 1995. Even Stephen, Down and Up Fall, 1996—, Spring Break, 1997, Ever-Clever Elisa, 1997, Helen Keller: Courage in the Dark, 1997, Faraway Summer, 1998, Starting School, 1998, A Dream Come True, 1998, Llama in the Library, 1999, Just Desserts Club, 1999. Recipient Bluebonnet award Tex. Libr. Assn., 1987, Wyoming Indian Paintbrush award 1987, W.Va. Children's Book award 1989, Sunshine State award Fla. Libr. Assn., 1990, Miss. Children's Book award Miss. Libr. Assn., 1990, S.C. Children's Book award, 1990, Garden State award N.J. Sch. Libr. Assn., 1991, 94, Weekly Reader Book Club award, 1993. Mem. PEN, Author's Guild, Soc. Children's Book

Writers, Amnesty Internat. Address: 10 Spruce Pl Great Neck NY 11021-1904

HURWITZ, JOSHUA JACOB, physician; b. Boston, Nov. 24, 1921; s. Albert Hurwitz and Ada Godinski; m. Rose Kosofsky, Mar. 24, 1946; children: Joel, Deborah, Ruth, Charles. Grad., Harvard Coll., 1943; MD, Harvard Med. Sch., 1946. Bd. cert. urology. Surg. intern Beth Israel Hosp., Boston, 1946-47; urology resident New Eng. Med. Ctr., 1990-93; physician New Eng. Med. Ctr., Boston, 1951-65, Mass. Gen. Hosp., Boston, 1954-61, Waltham (Mass.) Hosp., 1951-95, Edith N. Rogers VA Hosp., Bedford, Mass. Capt. U.S. Army, 1943-46, 47-49, 49-50. Office: Edith N Rogers VA Hosp Springs Rd Bedford MA 01730

HURWITZ, LAWRENCE NEAL, investment banking company executive; b. Austin, Tex., Mar. 21, 1939; s. John and Sarah Ruth (Blumenthal) H.; m. Kathleen O'Day, Feb., 1977 (div. Dec. 1985); 1 child, Kimberlee Colleen; m. Mynette Lee, Nov., 1989 (div. Jan. 1996); 1 child, Jonathan Lee. Student, U. Tex., 1957-59; MBA with distinction, Harvard U., 1961. With rsch. dept. Harvard U., 1961-62; asst. to v.p. Atlantic Rsch. Corp., 1962-65; comptr. TelAutograph Corp., 1965; dir. Gen. Artists Corp., 1965-69; pres. Sprayregen & Co., N.Y.C., 1969-83; chmn. Country Junction, Inc., 1969-82; mktg. dir. Beneflex, Inc., 1985-86; v.p. Tech. Liberation Capital, Inc., Houston, 1986-89, Amex Systems, Houston, 1986-89; v.p., chief fin. officer Intile Designs, Inc., Houston, 1989-94; pres. Lawrence Fin. Ptnrs., L.A., 1990—; dir. Kings Rd Entertain Pacific Coast Apparel Max Studios; vice chmn., mem. exec. com. Empire Life Ins. Co. Am.; dir., mem. exec. com. Old Town Corp., Stratton Group Ltd., Sayre & Fisher Co., Tech. Tape, Inc., DFI Communications Inc., Columbia Gen. Corp., Cal. Data Systems Corp.; bd. dirs. Leon Max Inc., Pacific Coast Apparel, Air Motive Holdings Inc., Indsl. Electronic Hardware Corp., Bloomfield Bldg. Industries, Inc., Apollo Industries, Inc., Aberdeen Petroleum Corp., Investors Book Club, Inc., Ling Fund, Am. Land Co., Terrific Nutrient & Chem. Corp., N. Lake Corp., Datatronics, Inc., Merada Industries, Inc., AK Electric Corp., Aerocon, Inc., Hallmark Communications, Inc., Detroit Gray Iron & Steel Foundries, Inc., Fin. Tech., Inc., Wid's Films & Film Folks, Investors Preferred Life Ins. Co., Langdon Group, Inc., Essex Systems Corp., Chelsea Nat. Bank, Newport Chem. Industries, Inc. Editor: How to Invest in Letter Stock, 1970, Spin-Offs and Shells, 1970. Mem. Harvard Bus. Sch. Club, Comml. Fin. Assn., Am. Cash Flow Assn. (pres. L.A. chpt.), Harvard Club (v.p. Orange County). Jewish. Home: 701 Teakwood Rd Los Angeles CA 90049-1327 Office: 11661 San Vicente Blvd Ste 408 Los Angeles CA 90049-5112

HURWITZ, MARK FRANCIS, filtration company executive, research engineer; b. Kileen, Tex., Dec. 4, 1953; s. Martin and Theodora Francis Hurwitz; m. Ingrid Kay McWilliams, April 13, 1975; children: Christopher David, Amber Marie. BSME, Northwestern U., Evanston, Ill., 1975; MS, U. of Rochester, 1980; PhD, Cornell U., 1996. Registered profl. engr., N.Y. Design engr. Xerox Corp., Rochester, N.Y., 1975-80; project engr. Pall Corp., Cortland, N.Y., 1980-88, mgr. computational and applied math, 1988-98, tech. dir. design and process analysis, 1998—. Patentee in field. Mem. ASME, NSPE, N.Y. Soc. of Profl. Engrs. Office: Pall Corp 3669 St Rte 281 Cortland NY 13045-8857

HURWITZ, MARK HENRY, sales executive; b. Newark, Dec. 2, 1951; s. Murry L. and Elaine (Goldsmith) H.; m. Patricia B. Zeitler, Oct. 21, 1984; 1 child, Sarah Elizabeth. BA in Fine Arts Edn. cum laude, Kean Coll. N.J., 1974, MA in Fine Arts Edn. magna cum laude, 1982. Cert. tchr., N.J. Art tchr. Montgomery High Sch., Skillman, N.J., 1974-82; sales coord. Burger's Motorcycles, Three Bridges, N.J., 1982-85; acct. exec. Roger Wade Prodns., N.Y.C., 1985-88; v.p. sales Slide Systems, Inc., N.Y.C., 1988—; cons. documentary Liberty, for PBS, 1997. Editor monthly newsletter The Brigade Courier, 1987, quarterly The Express, 1988; freelance photographer The N.Y. Times Mag., 1979; cons. (TV documentary) Liberty! The American Revolution, 1997. Mem. Nat. Eagle Scout Assn., Brigade of the Am. Revolution (pres., comdr. 1993-97, past pres., comdr. 1997-99, nat. bd. mem.-at-large 1979-82, 87-90, dir. pub. rels. 1976-87), 3d N.J. Regiment (pres., comdr. 1990-92, paymaster 1977-78), B'nai B'rith. Democrat. Jewish. Avocations: revolutionary war living history, motorcycling, photography. Home: 396 Meisel Ave Springfield NJ 07081-2316 Office: Slide Sys Inc 19 W 36th St Fl 3D New York NY 10018-7909

HURWITZ, SOL, writer, consultant; b. Washington, Aug. 31, 1932; s. Morris Aaron and Rose (Honig) H.; m. Nina Deutch, May 3, 1959; children: Linda, Mark Aaron, Laura. BA, Harvard U., 1953, postgrad., 1955-56, advanced mgmt. program, 1977. Various communication and broadcasting positions Washington, 1956-60, N.Y.C., 1960-66; assoc. dir. info. Com. for Econ. Devel., N.Y.C., 1966-67, dir. info., 1967-72, v.p., 1972-80, sr. v.p., 1980-90, pres., 1990-97, trustee, 1990—; bd. dirs. Albert Shanker Inst., Washington, Families and Work Inst., N.Y.C. Contbr. articles to N.Y. Times, Washington Post, Christian Sci. Monitor, Barron's, Harvard Mag., others. Trustee Rye (N.Y.) Bd. Edn., 1970-76; overseer Colby Coll., Waterville, Maine, 1980—. With USN, 1953-55. Mem. Coun. on Fgn. Rels., Harvard Club N.Y.C., Manursing Island Club (Rye). Avocations: single sculling, hiking, tennis, music, theater. Home and Office: 800 Forest Ave Rye NY 10580-3202

HURWITZ, TED H., sports conference administrator; b. Bronx, N.Y., Aug. 5, 1938; s. Solomon David and Betty (Fine) H.; m. Norma Figueroa, May 31, 1970; children: David, Lina, Amy. BS in Math., CCNY, 1961; MS in Phys. Edn., Lehman Coll., 1971. Sr. programmer System Devel. Corp., Paramus, N.J., 1961-64; sr. systems analyst Am. Airlines, Briarcliff Manor, N.Y., 1964-67; freshman basketball coach CCNY, 1968-69; athletic dir., basketball coach, tennis coach Lehman Coll., Bronx, 1969-91; exec. dir. CUNY Athletic Conf., 1991—; player, coach Maccabi Tel Aviv, 1968; cons. summer camps Town of Greenburgh, N.Y., 1989—. Named to CCNY Athletic Hall of Fame, 1996, Lehman Coll. Athletic Hall of Fame, 199. Avocations: basketball, tennis. Home: Apt 3A2 101 Old Mamaroneck Rd White Plains NY 10605 Office: CUNY Athletic Conf Lehman Coll Bronx NY 10468

HUSA, KAREL JAROSLAV, composer, conductor, educator; b. Prague, Czechoslovakia, Aug. 7, 1921; came to U.S., 1954, naturalized, 1959; s. Karel and Bozena (Dongresova) H.; m. Simone Perault, Feb. 2, 1952; children: Catherine, Anne-Marie, Elizabeth, Caroline. M summa cum laude, Conservatory and Acad. Music, Prague, 1945, 47; grad., Conservatoire de Paris, France, 1948; license for conducting, Ecole Normale de Paris, 1947; MusD (hon.), Coe Coll., 1976, Cleve. Inst., 1985, Ithaca Coll., 1986, Baldwin-Wallace Conservatory, 1991, Hartwick Coll., 1997, New Eng. Conservatory, 1998; DHL (hon.), Coll. St. Vincent, 1996. Guest condr. Czechoslovak Radio, Prague, 1945-46; guest condr. orchs. in Hamburg, Brussels, Paris, Zurich, Suisse Romande, London, Manchester, Prague, Stockholm, Hong Kong; guest condr. orchs. in Singapore, Japan; guest condr. orchs. in Cin., Buffalo, N.Y.C., Boston, Rochester, N.Y., Balt., San Diego, Syracuse, N.Y.; faculty Cornell U., Ithaca, N.Y., 1954—; prof. music Cornell U., 1954—, dir. univ. symphony and chamber orchs., 1972-92, Kappa Alpha prof. music emeritus. Composer: Symphony, 1953, Fantasies for Orchestra, 1957, Divertimento for Brass, 1959, Poem for Viola and Orchestra, 1959, Elegy and Rondeau for Saxophone and Orchestra, 1961, Divertimento for String Orchestra, 1948, String Quartet No. 2, 1952, Portrait for String Orch., 1953, Mosaiques for Orchestra, 1961, Fresque for Orchestra, rev. 1964, Sonatina for Piano, 1943, Sonatina Violin and Piano, 1945, Sonata for Piano, 1949, Evocations of Slovakia for Clarinet, Viola and Cello, 1951, Eight Duets for Piano, 1955, Twelve Moravian Songs, 1956, Poem for Viola and Orchestra, 1962, Serenade for Woodwind Quintet and Orchestra, 1963, Concerto for Brass Quintet and Orch., 1965, Two Preludes; flute, clarinet, bassoon, 1966, Music for Percussion, 1966, Concerto for alto saxophone, concert band, 1967, String Quartet No. 3, 1968 (Pulitzer prize 1969), Music for Prague; for Band, 1968, for Orch., 1969, Apotheosis of this Earth for Winds, 1970, Concerto for Percussion and Winds, 1971, Two Sonnets from Michelangelo for Orch, 1971, Concerto for Trumpet and Wind Orch., 1973, Apotheosis of this Earth for Chorus and Orch, 1973, Sonata for Violin and Piano, 1972-73, The Steadfast Tin Soldier; for narrator and orch., 1974, Sonata for Piano, No. 2, 1975, Monodrama, ballet for orch, 1975, An American Te Deum; for mixed chorus, baritone solo, band and organ, 1976, for orch., 1978, Landscapes for Brass Quintet, 1977, Fanfare for Brass Ensemble, 1980, Pastoral for Strings, 1980, Three Moravian Songs, 1981, The Trojan Women, ballet for orch., 1981, Sonata a Tre, 1982, Concerto for Wind Ensemble, 1982 (Sudler award 1983), Cantata, 1983, Smetana Fanfare for Wind Ensemble, 1984, Variations for Violin, Viola, Cello and Piano, 1984, Symphonic Suite for Orch., 1984, Intrada for Brass Quintet, 1984, Concerto for Orchestra, 1986, Concerto for Organ and Orch., 1987, Frammenti for Organ solo, 1987, Concerto for Trumpet and Orch., 1987, Concerto for Violoncello and Orch., 1988 (Grawemeyer award 1993), String Quartet No. 4, 1990, Youth Overture, 1991, Cayuga Lake (Memories), 1992, Concerto for Violin and Orch., 1993, Five Poems for Wood-Wind Quintet, 1994, Les Couleurs Fauves, 1995, Midwest Celebration Fanfare, 1996, Celebration for Orchestra, 1997, Postcard from Home, 1997, others; commns. from, UNESCO, Koussevitsky Found., Nat. Endowment for Arts, Friends of Music at Cornell, Fine Arts Found. Chgo., Chgo. Symphony Orchestra, Butler U., Washington Music Soc., Coe Coll., N.Y. Philharmonic, U. So. Calif., Kerze Found., also others.; editor: French Baroque Music: Reconstructions of Old French Baroque works by Lully and Delalande, 1961-68. Recipient prize Prague Acad. Arts, 1948, French Govt. award, 1946-47, L. Boulanger award, 1952, Pulitzer prize in music, 1969, Acad. Inst. Arts and Letters award, 1989, Grawemeyer award U. Louisville, 1993, Serge Koussevitzky Music Found. award, 1993, Czech Republic's medal of merit of 1st degree Pres. V. Havel, 1995, medal of Honor, City of Prague, 1998; Guggenheim fellow, 1964-65. Mem. Internat. Inst. Arts and Letters (life), Am. Acad. Arts and Letters, Belgian Royal Acad. Arts and Scis., Am. Music Ctr., Am. Acad. Arts and Letters, Internat. Soc. Contemporary Music, French Soc. Composers, Am. Fedn. Musicians, Kappa Gamma Psi (hon.), Kappa Kappa Psi (hon.), Delta Omicron (hon.), Phi Mu Alpha (hon.). Avocations: painting, sports. Home: 4535 S Atlantic Ave Apt 2106 Daytona Beach FL 32127-7047 Office: Cornell U Dept Music Ithaca NY 14853 *As long as there will be museums, concerts, orchestras, libraries, our works will be measured against the masterpieces of the past. For this reason, the search for technical perfection must continue even today, in addition to new ideas and contents. One cannot exist without the other.*

HUSAIN, AATIF MAIRAJ, neurologist; b. Rawalpindi, Punjab, India, Sept. 3, 1967; s. Mairaj and Suraiya Mairaj Husain; m. Sarwat Mohsin, Apr. 12, 1998. BS, Punjab U., 1986, MBBS, 1989. Diplomate Am. Bd. Psychiatry and Neurology, Am. Bd. Clin. Neurophysiology, Am. Bd. Sleep Medicine, Am. Bd. Electrodiagnostic Medicine; lic. physician, N.C. Intern in family practice Henry Ford Hosp., Detroit, 1990-91; resident in neurology Med. Coll. of Pa., Phila., 1991-95; fellow in neurophysiology Duke U., Durham, N.C., 1995-97, assoc. in medicine, 1997—; clin. dir. Durham VA Med. Ctr., 1998—; dir. EP lab. Duke U. Med. Ctr., Durham, 1998—; mem. profl. adv. bd. Epilepsy Found. N.C., 1997-99; dir. evoked potentials lab., Duke U. Med. Ctr., 1998-99, Neurodiagnostic Ctr., VA Med. Ctr., Durham, 1998-99. Contbr. articlesl to profl. jours. Fellow Am. Assn. Electrodiagnostic Medicine, Am. Sleep Disorders Assn.; mem. Am. Acad. Neurology, Am. Epilepsy Soc., Am. Clin. Neurophysiologyo Soc. Moslem. Office: Duke U Med Ctr 202 Bell Bldg Box 3678 Durham NC 27710

HUSAIN, TAQDIR, mathematics educator; b. Matiamau, India, July 16, 1929; emigrated to Can., 1961, naturalized, 1966; s. Abdul Razzaq and Mashooqa (Beg) Ali; m. Martha Tempelhof, Mar. 30, 1959; children: Asra, Ahmad, Masud. B.A., Muslim U., Aligarh, India, 1950, M.A., 1952; Ph.D., Syracuse U., 1960. Lectr. Muslim U., 1952-53, Forman Christian Coll., Lahore, Pakistan, 1955-57; instr. Syracuse (N.Y.) U., 1957-61; asst. prof. Ottawa (Ont., Can.) U., 1961-64; assoc. prof. McMaster U., Hamilton, Ont., 1964-67, prof., 1967-94; prof. emeritus McMaster U., Hamilton, 1995—; chmn. dept. math. scis. McMaster U., 1967-73, 79-82. Author: Open Mapping and Closed Graph Theorems in Topological Vector Spaces, 1965, Introduction to Topological Groups, 1966, Topology and Maps, 1977, Barrelledness in Topological and Ordered Vector Spaces, 1978, Multiplicative Functionals on Topological Algebras, 1983, Orthogonal Schauder Bases, 1991; assoc. editor: Can. Jour. Math, 1979-86; contbr. articles to profl. jours. Recipient Internat. prize Friedric Vieweg und Sohn Pub. House, Braunschweig, West Germany, 1963; Tata research fellow Tata Inst., Bombay, India, 1953-55. Mem. Am. Math. Assn., Am. Math. Soc., Canadian Math. Soc. (council 1969-75).

HUSAR, JOHN PAUL, newspaper columnist, television panelist, broadcaster; b. Chgo., Jan. 29, 1937; s. John Z. and Kathryn (Kanupke) H.; AA, Dodge City Coll., 1958; BS in Journalism, U. Kans., 1962; m. Louise Kay Lewis, Dec. 28, 1963; children: Kathryn Coyle, Laura. Reporter, Clovis (N.Mex.) News-Jour., 1960; night wire editor Okinawa Morning Star, 1961; city editor Pasadena (Tex.) Daily Citizen, 1962; bus. editor Topeka Capital-Jour., 1963; regional news editor Wichita (Kans.) Beacon, 1963-65; sports columnist and writer Chgo. Tribune, 1966—; co-host Great Outdoors Sta. WGN Radio, Chgo, 1998—; panelist ESPN-TV. Chmn., Village of Willow Springs (Ill.) Zoning Commn., 1975-77; mem. Ill. Forestry Adv. Com., 1981-82; mem. adv. com. Ill.-Mich. Canal Nat. Heritage Corridor, 1982; profl.-in-residence U. Kans. Sch. Journalism, 1985; trustee William Allen White Found., 1996—. Served with U.S. Army, 1960-62. Recipient 1st pl. award in sportswriting Ill. UPI, 1977, Ill. AP, 1984, 1st pl. award in feature writing Bowling mag., 1979, environ. reporting award Chgo. Audubon Soc., 1979, Disting. Alumnus award Dodge City Coll., 1983, 2d pl. award for pub. svc. reporting Ill. AP, 1980, 2d pl. award for sports column writing, 1981, spl. writing award Chgo. Tribune, 1980, Jacob A. Riis award Friends of Parks, 1981, Peter Lisagor award Chgo. chpt. Sigma Delta Chi, 1985, DuPont Stren Edit. Excellence award, 1986, Founders award Ill.-Mich. Canal Nat. Heritage Corridor Civic Ctr. Authority, 1987, Ryobi Am. Conservation Writing award 1987, Stren-Plano-Remington Lifetime Conservation Achievement award, 1996, Ill. Outdoor Writer of Yr. award, 1996, Ill. Dept. Natural Resources Fisheries award, 1997, Conservation Leadership award Chgo.'s Openlands Project, 1998, Native Sons & Daughters award Ill. Conservation Found., 1999. Mem. Round Table Profl. Daily Newspaper Outdoor Writers (nat. chmn. 1990-92), Assn. of Great Lakes Outdoor Writers (past dir.), Golf Writers Assn. Am. (past dir.), Baseball Writers Assn. Am., Outdoor Writers Assn. Am., Green River Sportsmen's Club (bd. dirs.), Phi Kappa Theta. Office: Chgo Tribune Co 435 N Michigan Ave Chicago IL 60611-4066

HUSAR, WALTER GENE, neurologist, neuroscientist, educator; b. Jersey City, Sept. 24, 1956; s. Walter and Ksenia H. (Dawybida) H. BS in Biology summa cum laude, St. Peter's Coll., Jersey City, 1978; MS in Microbiology, Rutgers U., 1982; MD, UMDNJ-N.J. Med. Sch., 1988. Diplomate Nat. Bd. Med. Examiners; lic. physician, N.J., N.Y. Adj. instr., then adj. lectr. microbiology St. Peter's Coll., 1979-84; intern in neurology and internal medicine U. Medicine and Dentistry N.J., Newark, 1988-89, resident, then adminstrv. chief resident in neurology, 1989-92; instr. dept. neuroscis. to asst. prof. neuroscis. U. Medicine and Dentistry N.J., 1992-99, 99—; attending physician dept. neuroscis. U. Hosp. U. Medicine and Dentistry N.J., Newark, 1992—; staff attending physician VA Med. Ctr., East Orange, N.J., 1992—; cons. physician dept. medicine divsn. neurology Holy Name Hosp., Teaneck, N.J., 1992—, 1992—; attending physician St. Clare's Hosp. (formerly N.W. Covenant Med. Ctr.), Denville, N.J., 1997—; pvt. practice Denville, 1997—. Mem. bd. health Twp. of East Hanover, N.J., 1993—, v.p., 1996-97, pres., 1998—; mem. stroke coun. Am. Heart Assn., 1992-96. Fellow Acad. Medicine N.J.; mem. AMA, Med. Soc. N.J., Morris County Med. Soc., Am. Acad. Neurology (assoc.), Am. Assn. Electrodiagnostic Medicine (assoc.). Home: 10 Christine Dr East Hanover NJ 07936-3039 Office: Ctrl Morris Neurology 145 Diamond Spring Rd Denville NJ 07834-2744

HUSARIK, ERNEST ALFRED, educational administrator; b. Gary, Ind., July 2, 1941; married, 2 children. BA in History, Olivet Nazarene U., Kankakee, Ill., 1963; MS in Ednl. Adminstrn., No. Ill. U., DeKalb, 1966; PhD in Ednl. Adminstrn. and Curriculum Devel., Ohio State U., Columbus, 1973; m. Elizabeth Ann Bonnette; children: Jennifer, Amy. Supt., Ontario (Ohio) Pub. Schs., 1973-75; supt. Euclid (Ohio) Pub. Schs., 1975-86, Westerville (Ohio) Pub. Schs., 1986—. Past pres. Sch. Study Coun. Ohio; bd. govs. Westerville Fund; mem. adv. and distbn. com. Martha Holden Jennings Found. Named one of top 100 Edn. Adminstrs. North Am., Exec. Educator, 1993; Ohio Supr. of the Year, 1994, Exec. Educator, 1993. Pres. Westerville chpt. Am. Heart Assn.; past chair, Franklin County Ednl. Coun. Mem. Am. Assn. Sch. Adminstrs., Buckeye Assn. Sch. Adminstrs. (dir., pres.), Ohio Math. and Sci. Coal. (exec. bd.), Sci. and Math. Achievement Required for Tomorrow, Ohio State U. Edliners (pres.), Nat. ASCD, Ohio Assn. Supervision and Curriculum Devel., Franklin County Area Supt's. Assn. (exec. com.), Westerville Area C. of C. (bd. dirs.), Olivet Nazarene U. Alumni Assn. (past mem. alumni bd. dirs.), Rotary (pres. Westerville, Rotarian of Yr.), Phi Delta Kappa (past chpt. pres.), Sigma Tau Delta. Contbr. articles in field to profl. jours. Home: 1029 Wood Glen Rd Westerville OH 43081-3240 Office: 336 S Otterbein Ave Westerville OH 43081-2334

HUSARIK, STEPHEN, music educator; b. Chgo., May 23, 1944; s. Stephen Husarik Sr. and Inez Medley. MusB with honors, U. Ill., 1970, MusM, 1972, postgrad., 1972-77; PhD, U. Iowa, 1983. Tchg. asst. U. Ill., Urbana, 1972-74; lectr. Sampson C.C., Clinton, N.C., 1976; tchg. asst. U. Iowa, Iowa City, 1977, 79; instr. Lewis U., Lockport, Ill., 1978, Trinity Coll., Palos Hills, Ill., 1980; instr. music and humanities Moraine Valley Coll., Palos Hills, Ill., 1984-89; head carillonneur Westark Coll., Ft. Smith, Ark., 1995—, instr. music and humanities, 1992—. Sr. editor Am. Keyboard Artists, 1987-92; co-author: A History of Westark Coll., 1999; editor Who's Who in the Humanities, 1990-92; contbr. numerous articles to Piano Quar., Am. Music, Clavier mag., Nat. Assn. Humanities Edn. Jour., Classical Mag.; rec. artist: (piano solos) Pictures at an Exhbn. by Mussorgsky, Scott Joplin and the Ragtime Classics. Field reader Council for Post-Secondary Edn., Washington, 1987. Recipient Nat. Edpress Assn. award, 1987; grantee NEH, 1984, 89, 94, Ark. Humanities Coun., 1997. Mem. Am. Musicol. Soc., Am. Liszt Soc., Guild of Carillonneurs of N. Am., Coll. Music Soc., Nat. Assn. Humanities Edn. (newsletter editor 1993-94), Westark Coll. Faculty Senate (chair 1998). Office: Westark Coll Humanities Divsn Box 3649 Fort Smith AR 72913-3649

HUSBAND, JOHN MICHAEL, lawyer; b. Elyria, Ohio, Apr. 7, 1952; s. Clint F. and Emma H.; m. Jan Lee Umbenhour, Sept. 15, 1975; children: Heather, John. BS, Ohio State U., 1974; JD, U. Toledo, 1977. Law clk. U.S. Ct. Appeals (10th cir.), Denver, 1977-78; ptnr. Holland & Hart, Denver, 1978—, chair labor and employment law dept., 1991—; counsel Western Gov.'s Office, Denver, 1984, Vols. of Am., Denver, 1984. Editor, The Colorado Lawyer, Employment and Labor Rev., 1984—; co-editor Colo. Employment Law Letter; contbr. articles to profl. jours. Bd. dirs. Colo. Safety Assn., 1984—, Denver Four Mile House, Town of Bow Mar, 1987-90, 1984; mem. Denver Leadership Assn.; sec., treas. Colo. Safety Assn., 1988—; bd. govs. U. Toledo Coll. Law. Inductee Elyria Sports Hall of Fame, 1997. Mem. ABA (labor law sect., individual rights and responsibilities com., co-chair pub. subcom. individual rights and responsibilities com.), Assn. Trial Lawyers Am., Nat. Inst. Trial Advocate, Ohio Bar Assn., Colo. Bar Assn. (labor sect.), Denver Bar Assn., Colo. Safety Assn. (exec. com. sec. treas. 1987—). Republican. Lutheran. Home: 5280 Ridge Trl Littleton CO 80123-1410 Office: Holland & Hart LLP PO Box 8749 555 17th St Ste 2900 Denver CO 80202-3979

HUSBAND, WILLIAM SWIRE, computer industry executive; b. Hinsdale, Ill., Dec. 18, 1939; s. William Thompson and Arlene Martha (Frey) H.; m. Janet Goatley, Nov. 26, 1965; children: Scott, Andrea. BS, Iowa State U., 1962. Mktg. rep. IBM, San Francisco, 1966-70; dist. mktg. mgr. DPF, Des Plaines, Ill., 1971-78; v.p. Celtic Computer Investment Co., Palatine, Ill., 1978; pres. 20th Century Sys., Inc., Palatine, Ill., 1978-96; dir. tech. AT&T Capital, Bloomfield Hills, Mich., 1996—, v.p. tech., 1997—; v.p. tech. Newcourt Credit, 1998; presenter symposium for U. Calif.-Berkeley Systems Technology Inst., Milan, 1987, 88, 89; speaker World Congress of Computing, Chgo., 1988. Author, pub.: Computer Acquisition and Disposition Planning, 7th edit., 1987; editor: COMPUTALK mag., 1987—, IBM Technology and Product Strategies in the 80's, 1986; contbg. editor: Computer Econs. mag., 1986—. Active Buehler YMCA, Palatine Boys' Baseball, 1978-85. Served to lt (j.g.) USN, 1962-66. Office: Newcourt Fin 2285 Franklin 2nd Fl Bloomfield Hills MI 48302-2017

HUSBY, DONALD EVANS, engineering company executive; b. Mpls., Nov. 30, 1927; s. Olaf and Elsie Louise (Hagen) H.; m. Beverly June Tilbury, Sept. 24, 1949. B.S., S.D. State U., 1952. Student engr., jr. asst., sr. engr., mgr. new products Westinghouse Electric Corp., Cleve., 1952-72; engring. mgr., v.p. engring. lighting div. Harvey Hubbell, Inc., Christiansburg, Va., 1972-76; pres. Elliptipar Inc., West Haven, Conn., 1976-78; fellow engr., mgr. engring. sect. Westinghouse Electric Corp., Vicksburg, Miss., 1978-82; engring. mgr. new products devel. Cooper Industries Crouse-Hinds LTG Products div., 1982-84; utility sales mgr. central region Cooper Lighting, Mpls., 1985-89; chief exec. officer Husby & Husby Inc., Madison, Minn., 1990—; mem. indsl. adv. counsel Underwriters Labs.; provider ednl. seminars in lighting, tech. expert for NVLAP, NIST, U.S. Dept. Commerce. Contbr. articles to profl. jours. Served with USNR, 1945-47. Fellow Illuminating Engrs. Soc. (chmn., sec., dir., Disting. Service award 1989); mem. Internat. Municipal Signal Assn., Soc. Plastics Engrs., Nat. Elec. Mfrs. Assn., Am. Nat. Standards Inst., Am. Soc. Quality Control, Miss. Engring. Soc., D.C. Soc. Profl. Engrs., Designers Lighting Forum., Mensa Internat., Toastmasters Internat. Mem. Christian Ch. Patentee in field. Home and Office: 705 5th Ave PO Box 66 Madison MN 56256-0066

HUSE, JAMES G., federal agency administrator; b. Medford, Mass.. Grad., Boston Coll., 1965. From spl. agt. to asst. dir. U.S. Secret Svc.; asst. inspector gen. for investigations Office Inspector Gen., Social Security Adminstrn., dep. inspector gen., acting inspector gen. With U.S. Army, Vietnam. Office: Social Security Adminstrn Office Inspector Gen 6401 Security Blvd Baltimore MD 21235

HUSE, JOHNA KATHLEEN, secondary school educator; b. Longview, Tex., Jan. 5, 1973; d. John Edward and Janis Kay (Williams) Underwood; m. Douglas Aaron Huse, Mar. 16, 1996; 1 child, Meredith. AA, Kilgore (Tex.) Coll., 1991; BA, U. North Tex., 1993. Cert. tchr., Tex. Tchr. English W.T. White H.S., Dallas, 1994-95, Chapel Hill Middle Sch., Tyler, Tex., 1995—. Mem. adv. Site-Based Decision Com., Tyler, Tex., 1996—; chmn. Incentive Com., Tyler, 1997-98. Mem. Tex. State Tchr. Assn. (assoc. rep.). Republican. Methodist. Avocations: reading, cooking, writing children's books.

HUSEBOE, ARTHUR ROBERT, American literature educator; b. Sioux Falls, S.D., Oct. 6, 1931; s. Carl and Lillian Ruth (Auby) H.; m. Doris Louise Eggers, May 27, 1953. BA, Augustana Coll., 1953; MA, U. S.D., 1956; PhD, Ind. U., 1963; LHD (hon.), Dana Coll., 1984. Teaching assoc. Ind. U., Bloomington, 1959-60; instr. U. S.D., Vermillion, 1960-61; prof. Augustana Coll., Sioux Falls, S.D., 1961—; pres. S.D. Humanities Found., Sioux Falls, 1994-96, Fedn. of State Humanities Couns., Washington, 1988-91; exec. dir. Nordland Heritage Found., Sioux Falls, 1980—, Ctr. Western Studies, Augustana, 1989—. Author: An Illustrated History of the Arts in South Dakota, 1989, Sir George Etherege, 1987, Herbert Krause, 1985, Sir John Vanbrugh, 1976. Bd. dirs. S.D. Symphony, Sioux Falls, 1966—; mem. Nordland Fest Assn., Sioux Falls, 1975—. With U.S. Army, 1953-55. Grantee NEH, 1975-77, 79-83, 92-94; recipient Gov.'s award in the Arts State of S.D., 1989. Mem. MLA, We. Lit. Assn. (pres. 1976-77), Norwegian-Am. Hist. Assn. (bd. dirs.), S.D. Hist. Soc. Lutheran. Avocations: travel, theater, classical music. Home: 813 E 38th St Sioux Falls SD 57105-5939 Office: Ctr for Western Studies Augustana Coll Box Sioux Falls SD 57197

HUSHEN, JOHN WALLACE, manufacturing company executive; b. Detroit, July 28, 1935; s. J. Wallace and Hilda Carol (Jean) H.; m. Margaret Corinne Aho, Apr. 25, 1959 (div. May 1978); children: Susan Lisa, Jane Louise, Peter Matthew; m. Lane Gay Johnston, Feb. 8, 1985; 1 child, John Case. BA, Wayne State U., 1958. Reporter The Detroit News, 1959-66; campaign press sec. Griffin for Senate, Mich., 1966; press sec. U.S. Senator Robert P. Griffin, Washington, 1967-70; dir. pub. info. U.S. Dept. Justice, Washington, 1970-74; dep. press sec. Pres. Gerald R. Ford, Washington, 1974-76; dir. govt. relations Eaton Corp., Washington, 1976-79; dir. pub. affairs Eaton Corp., Cleve., 1979-81; v.p. govt. rels. Eaton Corp., Washington, 1981-91; v.p. corp. affairs Eaton Corp., Cleve., 1991—. Trustee Citizens League Rsch. Inst., Cleve., pres., 1998—; trustee YMCA, Cleve.; mem. Pub. Affairs Coun. Mfrs. Alliance. Mem. Bus.-Govt. Rels. Coun., Assn. Former Senate Aides, Senate Press Secs. Assn. (pres. 1969-70), Union Club, Capitol Hill Club. Avocations: skiing, golf. Office: Eaton Corp 1111 Superior Ave E Cleveland OH 44114-2584

HUSHING, WILLIAM COLLINS, retired corporate executive; b. St. Louis, Jan. 22, 1918; s. Sumner Kinney and Anne (Sandner) H.; m. Mary Hardy, Jan. 10, 1946 (dec. 1986); children: Druscilla (dec.), Rebecca Ann. BS in Elec. Engring, U.S. Naval Acad., 1939; MS in Naval Constrn.

and Engring, MIT, 1944; student, Harvard Bus. Sch., 1962; DSc (hon.), U. N.H., 1968. Commd. ensign U.S. Navy, 1939, advanced through grades to rear adm., 1967; aide, spl. asst. to chief (Bur. Ships), 1955-57; indsl. engr., comptroller U.S. Naval Shipyard, Mare Island, Calif., 1957-60; supr. shipbldg. U.S. Navy, Electric Boat div. Gen. Dynamics Corp., Groton, Conn., 1960-64; comdr. Naval Shipyard, Portsmouth, N.H., 1964-69; retired, 1969; exec. v.p. Bath Iron Works, 1969-70; pres. Forster Mfg. Co., Inc., 1970-72; mgmt. cons. Kensington Mgmt. Cons., Inc., Stamford, Conn., 1972-78; pres. Maine Multi-Power, Inc., Bath, 1979-91. Decorated Navy Commendation medal, Legion of Merit with Star. Mem. Am. Soc. Naval Engrs. Lutheran. Home: 1640 Twelve Oaks Way Apt 103 No Palm Beach FL 33408-3265

HUSKEY, HARRY DOUGLAS, information and computer science educator; b. Whittier, N.C., Jan. 19, 1916; s. Cornelius and Myrtle (Cunningham) H.; m. Velma Elizabeth Roeth, Jan. 2, 1939 (dec. Jan. 1991); children: Carolyn, Roxanne, Harry Douglas, Linda; m. Nancy Grindstaff, Sept. 10, 1994. BS, U. Idaho, 1937; student, Ohio U., 1937-38; MA, Ohio State U., 1940, PhD, 1943. Temp. prin. sci. officer Nat. Phys. Labs., Eng., 1947; head machine devel. lab. Nat. Bur. Standards, 1948; asst. dir. Inst. Numerical Analysis, 1948-54; asso. dir. computation lab. Wayne U., Detroit, 1952-53; asso. prof. U. Calif., Berkeley, 1954-58, prof., 1958-68, vice chmn. elec. engring., 1965-66; prof. info. and computer sci. U. Calif., Santa Cruz, 1968-85, prof. emeritus, 1985—; dir. Computer Center, 1968-77, chmn. bd. info. sci., 1976-79, 82-83; vis. prof. Indian Inst. Tech., Kanpur; (Indo-Am. program), 1963-64, 71, Delhi U., 1971; cons. computer div. Bendix, 1954-63; vis. prof. M.I.T., 1966; mem. computer sci. panel NSF, Naval Research Adv. Com.; cons. on computers for developing countries UN, 1969-71; chmn. com. to advise Brazil on computer sci. edn. NAS, 1970-72; project coord. UNESCO/Burma contract, 1973-79; mem. adv. com. on use microcomputers in developing countries NRC, 1983-85. Co-editor: Computer Handbook, 1962. Recipient Disting. Alumni award Idaho State U., 1978, Pioneer award Nat. Computer Conf., 1978, IEEE Computer Soc., 1982; U.S. sr.scientist awardee Fulbright-Alexander von Humboldt Found., Mathematisches Institut der Tech. U. Munich, 1974-75, 25th Ann. medal ENIAC; inducted into U. Idaho Alumni Hall of Fame, 1989. Fellow AAAS, ACM, IEEE (edit. bd., editor-in-chief computer group 1965-71, Centennial award 1984), Brit. Computer Soc.; mem. Am. Math. Soc., Math. Assn. Am., Assn. Computing Machinery (pres. 1960-62), Am. Fedn. Info. Processing Socs. (governing bd. 1961-63), Sigma Xi. Designed SWAC computer, Bendix G-15 and G-20 computers. Home: 10 Devant Ln Bluffton SC 29910-4534 Office: U Calif Computer & Info Sci Santa Cruz CA 95064

HUSKINS, DENNIS G., internist; b. Queens, Sept. 19, 1946; s. Louis J. and Florence (Niece) H.; m. Joan Goldstein, Feb. 22, 1981 (div. Dec. 1989); children: Sage, Chelsea, Chantal; m. Cathy Coloschmidt, Sept. 23, 1991. BA, Wesleyan U., 1968; postgrad., Columbia U., 1969-73, St. Luke's Hosp. Ctr., N.Y.C., 1973-77. Bd. cert. internist. Internist Norwalk (Conn.) Med. Group P.C., 1977—; sr. attending physician Norwalk Hosp., 1988—; assoc. clin. prof. medicine Yale U., 1988—; chmn. of bd. Fairfield County Med. Assn., 1990, 91; bd. dirs. Conn. Med. Ins. Co., chmn. claims com., 1992—; pres. Norwalk Med. Group P.C., 1994-96. Appeared on cable TV shows. Fellow ACP. Avocations: skiing, sports-performance cars, American motorcycles. Office: Norwalk Med Group 40 Cross St Norwalk CT 06851-4647

HUSMAN, CATHERINE BIGOT, insurance company executive, actuary; b. Des Moines, Feb. 10, 1943; d. Edward George and Ruth Margaret (Cumming) Bigot; m. Charles Erwin Husman, Aug. 5, 1967; 1 child, Matthew Edward. BA with highest distinction, U. Iowa, 1965; MA, Ball State U., 1970. Actuarial asst. Am. United Life Ins. Co., Indpls., 1965-68, assoc. actuary, 1971-74, group actuary, 1974-84, v.p., corp. actuary, 1984-97, v.p., chief actuary, 1997—; mem. group tech. com. Mut. Life Ins. Co.; mem. profitability studies com. Life Office Mgmt. Assn. Inc. Mem. women's adv. com. United Way Cen. Ind., 1991-93; bd. dirs., mem. fin. com., St. Elizabeth's Home, 1991—, sec., 1994, mem. exec. com., treas., 1995; bd. dirs., mem. adminstrv. svcs., mem. exec. com. Heritage Place, 1993—, treas., 1995—. Fellow Soc. Actuaries; mem. Am. Acad. Actuaries, Actuaries Club Ind., Ky. and Ohio, Actuarial Club Indpls. (pres. 1979-80), Kiwanis (bd. dirs.), Phi Beta Kappa. Republican. Roman Catholic. Avocations: reading, tennis. Home: 1411 N Claridge Way Carmel IN 46032-8333 Office: Am United Life Ins Co 1 American Sq Indianapolis IN 46282-0001

HUSS, WILLIAM LEE, computer consultant; b. Freedom, Wis., May 18, 1956; s. Donald John and Elaine Mary (Vandenberg) H.; m. Beth Ellen Braun, Oct. 4, 1980 (div. Sept. 1984); m. Carol Ann Lindemann, Dec. 26, 1987. BBA, U. Wis., Oshkosh, 1978. CPA, Wis. Staff acct. Clifton, Gunderson & Co., Neenah, Wis., 1979-80; contr., sec.-treas. Chief Equipment, Inc., Oshkosh, 1980-83; tax and systems mgr. Exptl. Aircraft Assn., Oshkosh, 1983-89; acctg. prof. Marian Coll., Fond du Lac, Wis., 1986-89; v.p. fin., sec., treas. Weaver's Bus. Interiors, Inc., Milw., 1989-92; acctg. mgr. The Tribute Co., Inc., Delafield, Wis., 1993-96; contr. Saelens Corp., Johnson Creek, Wis., 1996-97; info. systems cons. Omni Resources, Inc., Brookfield, Wis., 1998; analyst Ameritech, Brookfield, 1998—; acctg. instr. Fox Valley Tech. Inst., Oshkosh, 1980-92. Adv. editor book revs. McGraw Hill Book Co., 1983. Vol. Big Brother, 1976-89; pres., bd. dirs. Big Bros. of Oshkosh, 1985-88. Fellow Wis. Inst. CPA's; mem. Am. Inst. CPA's. Roman Catholic. Avocations: astronomy, reading, bicycling, racquetball, coin and book collecting. Home: N68 W27126 Oakdale Ln Sussex WI 53089-2340 Office: Ameritech 200 S Executive Dr Brookfield WI 53005

HUSSAIN, M. MAHMOOD, medical educator. BSc, Osmania U., Hyderabad, India, 1976, MSc in Biochemistry, 1978; MPhil in Enzymology, U. Hyderabad, India, 1979; PhD in Biochemistry, Okla. State U., 1984; Lic. Med. in Biochemistry, U. Copenhagen, 1986. Danida fellow Panum Inst., U. Copenhagen, 1980-81; grad. rsch. asst. dept. biochemistry Okla. State U., 1981-84; rsch. assoc. sect. molecular genetics Boston U. Med. Ctr., 1984-87; postdoctoral fellow Gladstone Found. Labs. for Cardiovascualr Disease, U. Calif., San Francisco, 1987-88, staff rsch. investigator, 1988-91; asst. prof. depts. pathology and biochemistry Med. Coll. Pa., Phila., 1991-95; assoc. prof. Allegheny U. of the Health Scis., Phila., 1995—; reviewer grants for extramural funding by Am. Heart Assn., Southeastern Pa. affiliate, 1995—. Reviewer Jour. Biol. Chemistry, European Jour. Clin. Investigation, Jour. Lipid Rsch., Arteriosclerosis and Thrombosis, Biochim. Biophys. Acta, Lipids; contbr. articles to profl. jours., chpts. to books. Recipient Nat. Merit scholarship Govt. India, 1976-78, Rsch. award Boston U. Sch. Medicine, 1986; Danish Internat. Devel. fellow, 1980-81; grantee Am. Heart Assn., Southeastern Pa. affiliate, 1993—, NIH, 1995—. Mem. AAAS, Am. Heart Assn. (Coun. on Arteriosclerosis), N.Y. Acad. Scis., Phi Lambda Upsilon. Home: 2245 E County Line Rd Ardmore PA 19003-2731 Office: Allegheny-M C P 2900 W Queen Ln Philadelphia PA 19129-1033

HUSSAIN, SYED TASEER, biomedical educator, researcher; b. Lahore, Pakistan, Sept. 18, 1943; came to U.S., 1970; s. S. Fayyaz and Riaz (Fatima) H. BS, Punjab U., Pakistan, 1963, BS with honors, 1964, MS, 1965; PhD, U. Utrecht, The Netherlands, 1969. Instr. Howard U. Coll. Medicine, Washington, 1972-73, asst. prof., 1973-76, assoc. prof., 1977-85, prof. anatomy, 1985—; dir. gen. Pakistan Mus. of Natural History, Pakistan Sci. Found., Islamabad, 1985-87; grants reveiwer NSF, 1980—, NATO, 1987—, Nat. Geog. Soc., 1985—; frequent invited spkr. on evolutionary processes, biological changes, climate change and human health. Contbr. articles to profl. jours. Grantee Smithsonian Instn., 1974-94, NSF, 1977—, Nat. Inst. Environ. Health Scis., 1994. Fellow Pakistan Acad. Geol. Scis.; mem. AAAS, Am. Assn. Anatomy, Soc. Vertebrate Paleontology. Achievements include research in evolution in locomotion and hearing mechanism in mammals; human health and forced climate change; influence of increased temperatures on diseases. Avocations: horseback riding, tennis. Office: Howard Univ Coll Medicine 520 W St NW Washington DC 20001-2337

HUSSAR, DANIEL ALEXANDER, pharmacy educator; b. Phila., Feb. 12, 1941; s. Alexander and Anna (Nagel) H.; m. Suzanne Rose Fix, Aug. 26, 1967; children—Eric Fix, Christopher Nagel, Timothy Daniel. B.S. in Pharmacy, Phila. Coll. Pharmacy and Sci., 1962, M.S., 1964, Ph.D., 1967. Mem. faculty Phila. Coll. Pharmacy and Sci., 1966—, prof. pharmacy, 1971—, dir. dept., 1971-75, Remington prof., 1975—, dean faculty, 1975-84; Fellow Am. Found. Pharm. Edn., 1962-64, NSF, 1964-66. Author articles, chpts. in books. Mem. Am. Pharm. Assn. (trustee 1977-80), Pa. Pharm. Assn. (pres. 1975-76), Am. Soc. Hosp. Pharmacists, Pa. Soc. Hosp. Pharmacists, Drug Info. Assn. (pres. 1977-78). Home: 1 Boulder Creek Ln Newtown Square PA 19073-1703 Office: U Scis Phila 600 S 43rd St Philadelphia PA 19104-4418

HUSSEIN, AHMED DIA, investment banker; b. Cairo, Egypt, May 28, 1941; came to U.S. 1966.; s. Ali Mohamed and Yemen Mostafa (El-Emawy) H.; m. Marjorie Battersby, May 20, 1977 (div. 1981); 1 child, Ali; m. Maha Anwar Nowailaty, Dec. 7, 1990; children: Youmn, Omar, Yasmine. BEE, Cairo U., 1963; MSc, Am. U. Cairo, 1965; postgrad. diploma in stats., Cairo U., 1965; MSC in Math., Poly. Inst. N.Y., Bklyn., 1969; PhD in Elec. Engring., Poly. Inst. N.Y., 1969. Research assoc. Nat. Research Inst., Cairo, 1963-66; lectr. CUNY, 1966-70; sr. engr. IBM, East Fishkill, N.Y., 1969-70; asst. to assoc. prof. Am. U. Cairo, 1970-77; cons. engr. N.Y.C., 1977-79; account exec. Moseley Hallgarten, N.Y.C., 1979-80; v.p. L.F. Rothschild, N.Y.C., 1980-81; sr. v.p. Prudential Bache Securities, N.Y.C., 1981-86, Oppenheimer & Co., N.Y.C., 1986-87; v.p. Smith Barney, N.Y.C., 1987-89; sr. v.p. Shearson Lehman Hutton, Inc., N.Y.C., 1989-92, Dean Witter Reynolds, Inc., 1992-96; chmn., CEO Nat. Investment Co., N.Y.C., Cairo, Egypt, 1996—. Contbr. articles to profl. jours. Received Gold medal for social svcs. Cairo U., 1958; Fulbright scholar, 1965. Moslem. Avocation: bridge. Office: Nat Investment Co 30 Rockefeller Plz Ste 1936 New York NY 10112-1999 also: Nat Investment Co, 6 Dar El Shafa St 6th Fl, Garden City Cairo Egypt

HUSSELMAN, GRACE, retired innkeeper, educator; b. Paterson, N.J., July 24, 1923; d. Edward and Lydia (Kliphouse) Van Allen; m. Samuel Husselman, June 3, 1944; children: Samuel Glenn, Howard Lloyd. BA, William Paterson Coll., 1981. With pers. office Wright Aero Corp., Fairlawn, N.J., 1942-45; libr. asst. Wyckoff (N.J.) Pub. Libr., 1964-66; libr. dir. Allendale (N.J.) Pub. Libr., 1967-81; elem. sch. tchr., assoc. ednl. media splst. Coolidge Elem. Sch., Wychoff, N.Y., 1981-84, Shrewsbury (Vt.) Mountain Sch.; owner Ye Olde Buckmaster Inn, 1984-98; ret., 1998. Reading merit badge counselor Boys Scouts Am.; pioneer guide Pioneer Girls, nat. youth v.p., sec. friendship cir.; sec. bookstore com. Christian Growth Ministries; mem. bd. deacons Shrewsbury Cmty. Ch.; bd. dirs. Shrewsbury Libr., Vt.; mem. Cmty. Reformed Ch. Mem. N.J. Bergen-Passaic Libr. Assn., Hist. Soc. Shrewsbury (pres., sec.), Kappa Delta Pi. Home: Crestwood Village 140 Constitution Blvd Apt B Whiting NJ 08759-1904

HUSSEY, JOHN FRANCIS, physician, geriatrician; b. Richmond Hill, N.Y., Jan. 6, 1951; s. John F. Sr. and Jean (Peczyinski) H.; m. Ann Pelley, Sept. 10, 1979; children: Leo, Nicholas. BS in Biology, St. Johns U., 1972; MD, Creighton U., 1976. Intern, resident St. Joseph's Hosp., Omaha; pvt. practice, Augusta, Maine, 1982-90; med. cons. Augusta Mental Health Inst., 1990-95; geriatrician, psychiatry cons. Togus (Maine) VA Hosp., 1995—. Capt. USPHS, 1979-82. Fellow Am. Acad. Family Physicians; mem. Am. Geriat. Soc., Kennebec County Med. Assn. (treas. 1995-96, pres. 1996-97). Office: VA Hosp 1 VA Ctr Sta 1705 Togus ME 04330-6795

HUSSEY, WARD MACLEAN, lawyer, former government official; b. Providence, Mar. 13, 1920; s. Charles Ward and Agnes (Shaw) H.; children—Thomas Ward, Carolyn Anne Hussey Bourdow, Wendy Ellen Hussey Addison. AB, Harvard U., 1940, LLB, 1946; MA, Columbia U., 1944. Bar: D.C. 1946. With Office of Legis. Counsel, U.S. Ho. of Reps., 79th to 100th Congresses, Washington, 1946-89, dep. legis. counsel, 1970-72, legis. counsel, 1972-89; adviser to fgn. govts. on tax reform, 1989—. Co-author: Basic World Tax Code, 1992, rev. edit., 1996. With USNR, 1942-46. Fellow Harvard Internat. Tax Program (sr.). Home: 312 Princeton Blvd Alexandria VA 22314-4719

HUSSEY, WILLIAM BERTRAND, retired foreign service officer; b. Bellingham, Wash., Oct. 23, 1915; s. Bertrand Brokaw and Ruth (Axtell) H.; m. Fredricka Boone, Dec. 31, 1940 (div. 1957); children: Christina, Pamela, Eva, William Bertrand, Peter; m. Piyachart Bunnag, May 20, 1959. B.S., Boston U., 1938; postgrad., UCLA, 1939-40, Naval War Coll., 1953-54. Asst. housing mgmt. supr. U.S. Housing Authority, 1941-42; chmn. London (Eng.) Liaison Group, also State Dept. rep., 1948-52; spl. State Dept. rep., Rome, 1949, Paris, 1950; chmn. regional conf., Dhahran, Saudi Arabia, 1949, chief civil-mil. relations sect., Munich, Germany, 1952-53, adminstrv. officer, Frankfurt, Germany, 1953-55, attache, Rangoon, Burma, 1955-56, consul, Chiengmai, Thailand, 1957-59; acting dep. chief plans and devel. staff Bur. Ednl. and Cultural Affairs, Dept. State, 1959-60, dep. chief cultural presentations div., 1960-61; mem. del. regional confs. in, Beirut, Lebanon and Kampala, Uganda, 1960; group leader Nat. Strategy Seminar, Asilomar, Calif., 1960; counselor of embassy, Lome, Republic of Togo, 1961-65, Blantyre, Malawi, 1965-66; chargé d'affaires Am. embassys, Maseru, Lesotho, and Tananarive, Madgascar, 1966-67, Port Louis, Mauritius, 1967-68; UN rep., Western Pacific, Apia, Western Samoa, 1969-74, fgn. affairs cons., 1974—; del. UN Law of Sea Conf., 1975-80; assoc. v.p. Los Angeles Olympic Organizing Com., 1982-84; dir. govt. relations Statue of Liberty Centennial, Liberty Weekend, 1986. Served with U.S. Mcht. Marine, 1930-33; served to lt. comdr. USN, 1942-48, ETO; PTO; capt. Res. Recipient Superior Service award Sec. of State, 1968. Address: 5563B Via Portora Laguna Hills CA 92653-6902 *We must learn from mistakes. The measure is less the occasional stumble than how quickly and sharply the common cadence of our heritage is restored.*

HUSSMAN, LAWRENCE EUGENE, writer, retired educator; b. Mar. 20, 1932. MA, U. Mich., 1957, EdD, 1964. Prof. Wright State U., Dayton, Ohio, 1965-93; Fulbright prof. U. Warsaw, 1993-94; vis. prof. Univ. Aberta, Lisbon, 1995-96.

HUSSMANN, WILLIAM G., JR., federal judge; b. 1950. BA, Valparaiso U., 1972, JD, 1975. Bar: Ind. Pvt. law practice, 1976-81; dep. atty. gen. State of Ind., 1981-83; staff atty., disciplinary com. Ind. Supreme Ct., 1983-86; magistrate judge U.S. Dist. Ct. (so. dist.) Ind., Evansville, 1988—. Office: Federal Bldg Rm 328 101 NW Martin L King Blvd Evansville IN 47708

HUSSUNG, ALLEEN MOSETTE, literary agent; b. Sheridan, Mont., July 19, 1934; d. Carl Stanley and Alleen (White) Aune; divorced; children: Carleen Simone, Bill Hussung. Diploma in Voice, Juilliard Sch. Music, 1955. Singer various tours, clubs, TV, film, radio and Broadway prodns., 1955-69; producer Windmill Dinner Theatres, Tex., 1969-70, Candlewood Theatre, New Fairfield, Conn., 1973; agent Samuel French, Inc., N.Y.C., 1974—; lit. agt., head profl. dept. Samuel French, Inc., Country Home, Swan Lake, N.Y. Mem. Am. Theatre Actors (bd. dirs. 1977—). Avocations: gardening, boating on private lake, horseback riding. Home: 60 W 68th St New York NY 10023-6020

HUST, BRUCE KEVIN, lawyer; b. Cin., Aug. 16, 1957; s. George Julius and Shirley Mae (Glaser) H. BA, U. Cin., 1979; JD, No. Ky. U., 1985. Bar: Ohio 1986, U.S. Dist. Ct. (so. dist.) Ohio 1987. Pvt. practice Cin., 1986-99; trial counsel Hamilton County Pub. Defender's Office, Cin., 1988—; assoc. Wm. Eric Minamyer Esq. Co., LPA, Cin., 1999—. Vol. Lawyers for Poor, Cin., 1986-87, 90—; precinct exec. mem. Hamilton County Rep. Ctrl. Com., 1988—. With Ohio Naval Militia, 1988-94; journalist USNR, 1994—. Mem. Ohio State Bar Assn., Cin. Bar Assn., Ohio Assn. Criminal Def. Lawyers, Masons, Odd Fellows. Mem. United Ch. of Christ. Avocations: reading, current events, politics, writing and performing comedy. Home: 4247 Delridge Dr Cincinnati OH 45205-2025 Office: Pub Defender's Office Wm Howard Taft Law Ctr 230 E 9th St Fl 2D Cincinnati OH 45202-2174

HUSTAD, THOMAS PEGG, marketing educator; b. Mpls., June 15, 1945; s. Thomas Earl Pegg and John Charles and Dorothy Helen (Anderson) H.; m. Sherry Ann Thomas, Jan. 30, 1971; children: Kathleen, John. BS in Elec. Engring., Purdue U., 1967, MS in Indsl. Mgmt., 1969, PhD in Mktg., 1973. Vis. asst. prof. Purdue U., West Lafayette, Ind., 1971-72; asst. prof. Faculty of Adminstrv. Studies York U., Toronto, Ont., Can., 1972-74; assoc. prof. York U., Toronto, 1974-76, assoc. prof., mktg. area coord., 1976-77; assoc. prof. mktg. Sch. Bus. Ind. U., Bloomington-Indpls., 1977-82, prof., 1982—; chmn. MBA program, 1983-85, program chmn. Ind. U. Ann. Bus. Conf., 1983, 84, co-founder Exec. Forum; adj. prof. philanthropic studies, 1992-96; vis. prof. City U. Hong Kong, 1997, Ljubljana U., Slovenia, 1998; exec. dir. Ind. U. Internat. Bus. Forum, 1981-85; cons. N.Am. corps., Can. Govt.; condr. seminars for U.S., Singapore, Can., European, Asian and Venezuelan industry; mem. selection com. for Outstanding Corp. Innovator award, 1978—. Author: Approaches to the Teaching of Product Development and Management, 1977, (with others) PDMA Handbook of New Product Development, 1996; editor-in-chief: International Competition: The American Challenge, 1986, Managing the Product Development Process, 1989, Product Development: Prospering in a Rapidly Changing World, 1990; founder, editor-in-chief Jour. Product Innovation Mgmt., 1986—; contbr. articles to books and profl. jours. Fulbright fellow, 1987; recipient Eli Lilly MBA Tchg. Excellence award, 1990; named Best Bet Tchr., Bus. Week Mag.; fellow Ind. Univ. Ctr. for Entrepreneurship and Innovation, John and Marilyn Kosin Faculty fellow, 1993—; Crawford fellow of Product Innovation, 1993, 98; recipient Elsevier Sci. Pub. Co. Editorship award, 1993; Thomas P. Hustad Best Paper award named in his honor, 1998. Mem. Am. Mktg. Assn. (award 1973), Product Devel. and Mgmt. Assn. (program chmn. 3d ann. conf., v.p. confs. 1979, pres.-elect 1980, pres. 1981, dir. 1982-83, chmn. publ. com. 1982-84, sec./treas. 1984-96, mgr. assn. office 1984-96, bd. dirs. 1984—, Presdl. award 1987), Ancient and Hon. Arty. Co. Mass., Internat. Assn. Jazz Record Collectors, Brown U. Alumni Assn. (Associated Alumni award 1963), Phi Eta Sigma, Tau Beta Pi, Beta Gamma Sigma. Home: 3101 Daniel St Bloomington IN 47401-2421 Office: Ind U Kelley Sch Bus 1309 E 10th St Bloomington IN 47405-1701

HUSTED, RALPH WALDO, former utility executive; b. Martinsville, Ill., Apr. 2, 1911; s. Seth and Mary (Church) H.; m. Margaret Walden, Mar. 18, 1937; children: Catherine (Mrs. William R. Burleigh), David W. LL.B., Benjamin Harrison Law Sch., 1936. Bar: Ind. 1935. With Indpls. Power & Light Co., 1929—, sec., counsel, 1957-64, v.p. legal, sec., 1964-73, exec. v.p. adminstrn., 1973-74, pres., chief exec. officer, 1974-75, chmn. bd., chief exec. officer, 1975-76. Hon. trustee Intercollegiate Studies Inst., Inc., Wilmington, Dela.; bd. dirs. Liberty Fund, Indpls. Mem. Ind., Indpls., Am. bar assns. Home: 6230 Breamore Rd Indianapolis IN 46220-4922 Office: 25 Monument Cir Indianapolis IN 46204-2936

HUSTED, RUSSELL FOREST, research scientist; b. Lafayette, Ind., Apr. 4, 1950; s. Robert Forest and Miriam Ruth (Jackson) H.; m. Nancy Lee Driscoll, Oct. 25, 1969 (div. Feb. 1986); children: Jacqueline Marie, Randall Forest; m. Ruth Elaine Hurlburt, Nov. 12, 1988. BS in Chemistry with highest distinction, Colo. State U., 1972; PhD in Pharmacology, U. Utah, 1976. Post-doctoral fellow dept. medicine U. Iowa, Iowa City, 1976-79, rsch. scientist dept. medicine, 1979-81, 1982—; asst. prof. U. Conn. Sch. Medicine, Farmington, 1981-82. Contbr. articles to profl. jours. Mallinckrodt scholar Colo. State U., 1968. Mem. AAAS, Am. Soc. Nephrology, Am. Physiol. Soc., Soc. Gen. Physiology, N.Y. Acad. Sci., Sigma Xi. Democrat. Methodist. Office: Univ Iowa 3180 Medical Labs Iowa City IA 52242

HUSTING, PETER MARDEN, advertising consultant; b. Bronxville, N.Y., Mar. 28, 1935; s. Charles Ottomar and Jane Alice (Marden) H.; m. Carolyn Riddle, Mar. 26, 1960; children: Jennifer, Gretchen, Charles Ottomar; m. Myrna Diaz, May 11, 1996. B.S., U. Wis., 1957; grad., Advanced Mgmt. Program, Harvard U., 1974. Sales rep. Crown Zellerbach Corp., San Francisco, 1958-59; media analyst Leo Burnett Co., Chgo., 1959-61, time buyer, 1961-62, asst. account exec., 1962-63, account exec., 1963-68, v.p., account supr., 1968-72, sr. v.p., account dir., 1972-79, group exec., 1979-86, exec. v.p., 1979-92, dir. human relations internat., 1986-92, also bd. dirs., ret., 1992; pres. Husting Enterprises, Chgo., 1993—; dir. Bernina of Am., Inc., Columbian Mutual Life Ins. Co., Efficient Mktg. Svcs., Inc., 1996-97. Trustee Shedd Aquarium Soc., Chgo., 1980—, life hon. trustee, 1995—; bd. dirs. Chgo. Better Govt. Assn., 1976-92, Leadership Coun. Met. Open Cmtys., Chgo., 1980-86, Lyric Opera Guild, 1971-78, Chgo. Forum, 1969-76. Served with AUS, 1958. Republican. Clubs: Indian Hill (Winnetka) (bd. govs. 1975-79), The Valley Club (Montecito, Calif.), Coral Casino Club (Santa Barbara). Avocations: flying, swimming, hunting, trekking, golf. Office: Husting Enterprises 150 S Wacker Dr Ste 3100 Chicago IL 60606-4202

HUSTOLES, MARY JO, elementary education educator; b. Detroit, May 5, 1952; d. Robert Nelson Henderson and Mary Josephine (Henderson) Thornton; m. Paul John Hustoles; children: Elizabeth Anne, Brian Edward. BS in Spl. Edn., Wayne State U., 1973; MS in Learning Disabilities, NW Mo. State U., 1980; EdS in Elem. Edn., Mankato (Minn.) State U., 1991. Tchr. learning disabilities Claremont (Mo.) Elem. Sch., 1977-78, Shenandoah (Iowa) Elem. Sch., 1978-83, Smylie Wilson Jr. High Sch., Lubbock, Tex., 1983-84, Lafayette High Sch., Oxford, Miss., 1984-85; tchr. Jefferson Elem. Sch., Mankato, 1985-86, Hoover Elem. Sch., North Mankato, 1986—; grade level leader tchr. Dist. 77, Mankato, 1991-93; presenter nat. and internat. workshop reading, writing, "Chicago Math." Mem. Internat. Reading Assn., Nat. Coun. Tchrs. Math., ASCD. Avocations: walking, reading. Home: 120 Center St Mankato MN 56001-3862

HUSTOLES, PAUL JOHN, theater educator; b. Chgo., Mar. 4, 1952; s. Edward J. and Mary Catherine (Syoen) H.; m. Mary Jo Henderson, June 23, 1973; children: Elizabeth A., Brian E. BFA, Wayne State U., 1973; MA, U. Mich., 1974; PhD, Tex. Tech U., 1984. Teaching asst. U. Mich., Ann Arbor, 1974-77; artistic dir. MM Prodns., Ann Arbor, 1976-77; dir. theatre, assoc. prof. Tarkio (Mo.)Coll., 1977-83; artistic dir. The Mule Barn Theatre, Tarkio, 1977-83; instr. Tex. Tech U., Lubbock, 1983-84; assoc. prof., mng. dir. dept. theatre U. Miss., Oxford, 1984-85; producer Highland Summer Theatre, Mankato, Minn., 1985—; chmn., prof. dept. theatre and dance Minn. State U., Mankato, 1985—; acting v.p. for univ. advancement Mankato State U., 1993-94. Prodr. more than 350 theatrical prodns.; artistic dir. over 135 theatrical prodns. Mem. Kennedy Ctr./Am. Coll. Theatre Festival (vice chmn. region V 1992-94, chmn. region V 1994-97), Mid-Am. Theatre Conf., Assn. Theatre in Higher Edn., Minn. Citizens for Arts, Minn. Alliance for Arts in Edn., Assn. for Comm. Adminstrs., Nat. Assn. Schs. Theatre. Office: Mankato State U Dept Theatre Arts Mankato MN 56002

HUSTON, ANJELICA, actress; b. L.A., July 8, 1951; d. John and Enrica Huston; m. Robert Graham, 1992. Student, Loft Studio. Actress appearing in Hamlet, Roundhouse Theatre, London, Tamara, Il Vittorale Theatre, L.A.; appeared in films including A Walk with Love and Death, 1969, Hamlet, 1969, Sinful Davey, 1969, Swashbuckler, 1976, The Last Tycoon, 1976, The Postman Always Rings Twice, 1981, This is Spinal Tap, 1984, The Ice Pirates, 1984, Prizzi's Honor, 1985 (Academy award for best supporting actress 1985, N.Y.Film Critics award 1985, L.A. Film Critics award 1985), Captain Eo, 1986, Gardens of Stone, 1987, The Dead, 1987 (Best Actress award Ind. Filmakers 1987), Mr. North, 1988, A Handful of Dust, 1988, Witches, 1989, Crimes and Misdemeanors, 1989, Enemies, A Love Story, 1989 (Acad. award nomination 1990), The Grifters, 1990 (Acad. award nomination 1991), The Addams Family, 1991, The Player, 1992, Addams Family Values, 1993, Manhattan Murder Mystery, 1993, The Crossing Guard, 1995, The Perez Family, 1995, Buffalo '66, 1997, Phoenix, 1998, Ever After, 1998, Breakers, 1999, Agnes Browne, 1999; TV films include the Cowboy and the Ballerina, 1984, Faerie Tale Theatre, A Rose for Miss Emily, Lonesome Dove, 1989, Family Pictures, 1993, And The Band Played On, 1993, Buffalo Girls, 1995; dir. Bastard Out of Carolina, 1996, Agnes Browne, 1999; TV guest appearances Laverne & Shirley, 1976, Inside the Actors Studio, 1994. Office: Internat Creative Mgmt 8942 Wilshire Blvd Beverly Hills CA 90211-1934*

HUSTON, BEATRICE LOUISE, retired banker; b. Grantsburg, Wis., Dec. 26, 1932; d. Elvin and Fay Cynthia (Sybrant) H.; m. Gerald W. Huston, June 30, 1951 (dec.); 1 child, Linda Sandell. BA, Met. State U., Minn., 1992. With Northwest Bus. Service, Mpls., 1950-51, Progressive Machine Co., Huntington Park, Calif., 1951-52; v.p. and corp. sec. Apache Corp., Mpls., 1954-87; v.p. stock transfer Norwest Bank, Minn., 1987-98. Mem. Am. Soc. Corp. Secs. Lutheran. Home: 8264 Xerxes Ave S Minneapolis MN 55431-1003

HUSTON, DEVERILLE ANNE, lawyer; b. Great Falls, Mont., Mar. 2, 1947; d. Orion Joseph and Beverly Rosemary (Mower) H. BA, U. Minn., 1969; JD, William Mitchell Coll. Law, 1975. Bar: Minn. 1975, Ill. 1976, U.S. Dist. Ct. (no. dist.) Ill. 1976). Assoc. Sidley & Austin, Chgo., 1977-83, ptnr., 1983—. Fellow Am. Bar Found.; mem. ABA, Chgo. Bar Assn., Chgo. Fin. Exch., Law Club. Office: Sidley & Austin 1 First Natl Plz Chicago IL 60603-2003*

HUSTON, FRED JOHN, retired automotive engineer; b. Muskegon, Mich., June 12, 1929; s. Fred and Sadie (Borgman) Huston; m. Jacqueline Terry, Apr. 28, 1957; children: Sandra, William. BSME, Mich. Tech. U., 1952. Engr. trainee IHC (Navistar), Ft. Wayne, Ind., 1952, test engr., 1953; mech. engr. asst. Aberdeen (Md.) Proving Ground, 1953-55; test engr. IHC (Navistar), Ft. Wayne, 1956, project engr., 1956-82; supr., chassis engr. M.A.N. Truck & Bus Corp., Cleveland, N.C., 1983-86; design engr. Thomas Built Buses, Inc., High Point, N.C., 1987-88, supr. body design, 1988-89, supr. chassis design, 1989-91, sr. staff engr., 1992-94; ret., 1994. With U.S. Army, 1953-55. Mem. Soc. Automotive Engrs. Methodist. Avocations: automobile restoration, swimming. Home: 603 Westchester Dr High Point NC 27262-7426

HUSTON, HARRIETTE IRENE OTWELL (REE HUSTON), retired county official; d. Harry C. Otwell and Fannie (Mitchell) Otwell Geffert; m. Dan E. Huston, Jan. 21, 1951; children: Terry Dane, Dale Curtis, Ronald William, Randall Philip. BS, Kans. State Coll., 1951. Cert. life & health ins. agt., Wash.; cert. wastewater operator in tng., Wash. Tchr. Kans., Ill., 1955-68; assoc. home economist McCall's Patterns Co., N.Y.C., 1959-62; counselor, owner Dunhill of Seattle Personnel, 1968-75; enrollment officer, trainer, adminstrv. sec. Teller Tng. Insts., Seattle, 1975-76; life and health ins. agt. Lincoln Nat. Sales, Seattle, 1976-77; office mgr., adminstrv. sec. ARA Transp. Group, Seattle, 1977-78; asst. to the pres. Pryde Corp., Bellevue, Wash., 1978-80; sr. sec. Municipality of Met. Seattle, 1980-92, project asst., 1992-93; adminstrv. specialist II King County Dept. Met. Svcs. (formerly Municipality of Met. Seattle, 1993-95; primary and secondary substitute tchr. Sequim (Wash.) Pub. Schs., 1996—. Co-author: Homemaking textbook, 1956; contbr. articles to profl. jours.. Sec. exec., mem. gen. bd. Bellevue Christian Ch., Disciples of Christ, 1976-77, 86-87, chmn. flowers com., 1978-83, elder, 1978, deacon, 1987; bd. dirs., sec. Surrey Downs Cmty. Club, Bellevue, 1983-85; mem. choir Sequim Presbyn. Ch., 1994-98, elder, 1996-99, chair congl. life com., 1996-99, mem. Presbyn. Women, 1994—; vol. leader, coord. Linking Home and Sch. Through the Workplace, 1992-93; vol. Sequim-Dungeness Hosp. Guild Thrift Shop, 1999—. Recipient Clothing award check McCall's Patterns Co., N.Y.C., 1962, Certs. of Merit Metro Hdqrs., Seattle, 1981, 82, 83, 86, 89. Mem. Bellevue Bridge Club. Avocations: flower gardening and arranging, interior decorating, home remodeling. Home: 1783 E Sequim Bay Rd Sequim WA 98382-7657

HUSTON, HEIDI LYNN, medical/surgical nurse; b. Johnstown, Pa., Dec. 15, 1966; d. Thomas and Karol Anne (Kirchner) Zwiener. Diploma, Conemaugh Valley Meml. Hosp., Johnstown, 1987; RN, BSN, U. Pitts., Johnstown, 1993. Cert. in trauma nursing, peritoneal dialysis, CPR, med./surg. nurse, cardiac monitoring. Nurse Conemaugh Valley Meml. Hosp., 1987—; admissions coord. Conemaugh Rehab. Unit, Crichton Ctr. Advanced Rehab., 1996—. Mem. Conemaugh Valley Meml. Alumni (sec. peer rev. com.), Alumni of U. Pitts. at Johnstown. Home: RD 5 Box 678 Coonridge Rd Johnstown PA 15905

HUSTON, JOHN, professional golfer; b. Mt. Vernon, Ill., June 1, 1961; m. Sjuzanne Huston; children: Jessica, Travis. Grad., Auburn U. Profl. golfer, 1983—; winner Honda Classic, 1990, Walt Disney World/Oldsmobile Classic, 1992, Doral-Ryder Open, 1994, Hawaii Open, 1998. Medalist 1987 Qualifying Tournament; won Honda Classic, 1990, JC Penney Classic with Amy Benz, 1988, Walt Disney/Oldsmobile Classic, 1992, Doral-Ryder Open, 1994, Motorola Western Open, 1995, United Airlines Hawaiian Open, 1995, Buick Invitational Calif., 1995, Buick Challenge, 1995, Mercedes Championship, 1995. Office: PGA Am Box 109601 100 Avenue Of Champions Palm Beach Gardens FL 33410*

HUSTON, JOHN CHARLES, law educator; b. Chgo., Mar. 21, 1927; s. Albert Allison and Lillian Helen (Sullivan) H.; m. Joan Frances Mooney, Aug. 1, 1954; children: Mark Allison, Philip John, Paul Francis James; m. Inger Margareta Westerman, May 4, 1979. AB, U. Wash., Seattle, 1950; JD, U. Wash., 1952; LLM, NYU, 1955. Bar: Wash. 1952, N.Y. 1964, U.S. Dist. Ct. (we. dist.) Wash. 1953, U.S. Ct. Appeals (9th cir.) 1953, U.S. Tax Ct. 1977, U.S. Supreme Ct. 1993. Assoc. Kahin, Carmody & Horswill, Seattle, 1952-53; teaching fellow NYU Law Sch., 1953-54; asst. co-dir. U. Ankara Legal Research Inst., Turkey, 1954-55; asst. prof. NYU, 1953-57; asst. prof. Syracuse U., N.Y., 1957-60, assoc. prof., 1960-65, prof., 1960-67; prof., assoc. dean U. Wash., Seattle, 1967-73, prof. law, 1973-96, prof. emeritus, 1996—; adj. prof. Asia-Pacific Law Inst., Bond Univ., Australia; of counsel Carney, Badley, Smith & Spellman, Seattle; vis. prof. U. Stockholm, 1986, U. Bergen, 1989, Bond U., Australia, 1991. Author: (with Redden) The Mining Law of Turkey, 1956, The Petroleum Law of Turkey, 1956, (with Muckleston and Cross) Community Property: General Considerations, 1971, (with Price and Treacy) 4th edit., 1994, (with Sullivan and others) Administration of Criminal Justice, 166, 2d edit., 1969, (with Miyatake and Way) Japanese International Taxation, 1983, supplements through 1997, (with Cross and Shields) Community Property Desk Book, 1989, supplement, 1997, (with Williams) Permanent Establishment, 1993. With USNR, 1945-46; capt. USAFR. Mem. ABA, Am. Coll. Trust and Estate Coun., Wash. State Bar Assn. (chmn. tax sect. 1984-85), King County bar Assn., Japanese Am. Soc. Legal Studies, Internat. Fiscal Assn. (past regional v.p., mem. coun.). Fax: (206) 525-1758. E-mail: huston@u.washington.edu. Office: U Wash Sch Law 1100 NE Campus Pkwy Seattle WA 98105-6605

HUSTON, JOHN DENNIS, English educator; b. N.Y.C., Sept. 21, 1939; s. A. Arthur H. and Jacquelin (Buchenau) Hawkins; m. Priscilla Jane, June 13, 1964 (div. July 1985); children: Katherine, Penn; m. Lisa B. Bryan, Aug. 8, 1988; stepchildren: Rudy Bryan, Kirby Bryan. BA, Wesleyan U., 1961; MA, Yale U., 1964, PhD, 1966. Instr., English Yale U., New Haven, Conn., 1966-67, asst. prof., 1967-69; assoc. prof. Rice U., Houston, 1969-80, prof., English, 1980—; dir. freshman humanities Rice U., 1988-94, master Hanszen Coll., 1978-82, 92—. Author: Shakespeare's Comedies of Play, 1981; co-editor: Classics of the Renaissance Theater, 1969. Named CASE Prof. of Yr., 1989-90, Disting. Alumnus Wesleyan U., 1991; recipient Wilbur Cross medal Yale Grad. Sch., 1992. Mem. Coll. English Assn. (bd. dirs. 1989-92), Phi Beta Kappa. Democrat. Avocations: running, racquetball, squash, skiing, fishing. Home: Hanszen House Rice U 2476 Bolsorer PMB 486 Houston TX 77005 Office: Rice U Dept English PO Box 1892 Houston TX 77251-1892

HUSTON, JOHN LEWIS, chemistry educator; b. Lancaster, Ohio, Aug. 19, 1919; s. John Allen and Olive Blanche (Wilson) H.; m. Mary Margaret Lally, Sept. 12, 1964. A.B., Oberlin Coll., 1942; Ph.D., U. Calif. at Berkeley, 1946. Instr. chemistry Oreg. State U., Corvallis, 1946-49; asst. prof. Oreg. State U., 1949-52; mem. faculty Loyola U. at Chgo., 1952—, assoc. prof., 1954-68, prof., 1968-84, prof. emeritus, 1984—; cons. Argonne (Ill.) Nat. Lab., 1964—. Contbr. articles to profl. jours. AEC grantee, 1947-52, NSF grantee, 1953-58. Mem. Am. Chem. Soc., Phi Beta Kappa, Sigma Xi. Home: 4401 Keeney St Skokie IL 60076-3203 Office: Loyola U Dept Chemistry Chicago IL 60626

HUSTON, JOHN WILSON, air force officer, historian; b. Pitts., Mar. 6, 1925; s. James Leslie and Kathryn Rachel (Ray) H.; m. Dorothy Winters Bampton, Aug. 27, 1960; children: Ann, John. BA, Monmouth Coll., 1948; MA, U. Pitts., 1950, PhD, 1957. Served as 1st lt. USAAF, 1943-45; advanced through grades to maj. gen. USAF Res., 1976; recalled to active duty as chief Office of Air Force History, Dept. Air Force, Washington, 1976—; lectr. history U. Pitts., 1949-56; prof. U.S. Naval Acad., Annapolis, 1956-76; chmn. dept. history U.S. Naval Acad., 1971-76; vis. prof. U. Rochester, 1964, Ball State U., 1965, 67, U. Md., 1969; Disting. vis. prof. USAF Acad., 1994-95. Decorated D.S.M., D.F.C. with oak leaf cluster, Air medal with 3 oak leaf clusters, Joint Service Commendation medal, Air Force Commendation medal. Home: 115 E Lake Dr Annapolis MD 21403-4444 Office: Hdqrs USAF AF/CVAH Bolling AFB Washington DC 20332-0001

HUSTON, KATHLEEN MARIE, library administrator; b. Sparta, Wis., Jan. 7, 1944. BA, Edgewood Coll., 1966; MLS, U. Wis., Madison, 1969. Libr. Milw. Pub. Libr., 1969-90; city libr. Milw. Pub. Libr. System, 1991—. Office: Milwaukee Pub Libr 814 W Wisconsin Ave Milwaukee WI 53233-2309

HUSTON, MARGO, journalist; b. Waukesha, Wis., Feb. 12, 1943; d. James and Cecile (Timlin) Bremner; student U. Wis., 1961-63; AB in Journalism, Marquette U., 1965; m. James Huston, Dec. 9, 1967 (div.); 1 son, Sean Patrick. Editorial asst. Marquette U., Milw., 1965-66; feature editor, reporter Waukesha Freeman, 1966-67; feature reporter Milw. Jour., 1967-70; reporter Spectrum, women's and food sections, 1972-79, editl. writer, 1979-84, polit. reporter, 1984—, asst. picture editor, 1985-91, copy editor, 1992-95; reporter Milw. Jour. Sentinel (merger Milw. Jour. and The Sentinel), 1995—; instr. mass comm. U. Wis., Milw. Recipient Penney-Mo. award for consumer abortion series, 1977, Pulitzer Prize for investigation into plight of elderly, 1977, Clarion award, 1977, Knight of Golden Quill award, Milw. Press Club, 1977, Wis. AP writing award, 1977, special award Milw. Soc. Profl. Journalists, 1977, Penney-Mo. Paul Myhre award for excellence, 1978; By-Line award Marquette U. Coll. of Journalism, 1980; Wis. UPI best editorial award, 1982; Wis. Women's Network award for journalist achievement for women's issues, 1983, Dick Goldensohn Fund award, 1991, 1st place award for investigative reporting Inland Press Assn., 1997, 98, 2d award Enterprise interpretive reporting Wis. Newspaper Assn., 1998; Wis. Arts Bd. Literary Arts grantee, 1992. Mem. Milw. Press Club. Office: Milwaukee Journal Sentinel 333 W State St Milwaukee WI 53203-1309

HUSTON, MICHAEL JOE, lawyer; b. Logansport, Ind., Dec. 21, 1942; s. Harry Hobart and Dorothie Ann (Chew) H.; m. Joan Frances Jernigan, June 12, 1965; children: Scott Howard, Todd Michael, Julie Ann. BS, U.S. Military Acad., 1965; JD, Ind. U., 1972. Bar: Ind. 1972, U.S. Dist. Ct. (so. dist.) Ind. 1972, U.S. Dist. Ct. (no. dist.) Ind. 1975, U.S. Ct. Appeals (D.C. cir.) 1980. Commd. 2nd lt. U.S. Army, 1965, advanced through grades to capt., 1967, resigned, 1970; assoc. Baker & Daniels, Indpls., 1972-78, ptnr., 1979—. Contbr. articles to profl. jours. Bd. dirs., pres. Woodland Springs Homeowners Assn., Carmel, Ind., 1976-82; trustee Carmel United Meth. Ch., 1982-84. Fellow Ind. Bar Found. (master fellow 1991); mem. ABA, Ind. State Bar Assn., Indpls. Bar Assn., West Point Soc. Ind. (pres. 1996-98), Geist Sertoma Club (pres. 1996-97). Office: Baker & Daniels 300 N Meridian St Ste 2700 Indianapolis IN 46204-1782

HUSTON, NANCY LOUISE, writer, educator; b. Calgary, Alta., Can., Sept. 16, 1953; arrived in France, 1973; d. James Palmer Huston and Mary-Louise (Kester) Engels; m. Tzvetan Todorov, May 18, 1981; children: Léa, Alexandre. BA, Sarah Lawrence Coll., 1975; diploma in semiology, Ecole de Hautes Etudes, Paris, 1977. writer-in-residence Am. U. Paris, 1989; instr. women's studies Columbia U., Paris, 1982-88; vis. prof. French Lit. U. Mass., Amherst, 1990; vis. prof. French Lit. Harvard U., Cambridge, 1994. Author: Les Variations Goldberg, 1981 (prix Contrepoint), Plainsong, 1993, Cantique des Plaines, 1993 (prix du Gouverneur-Gènèral, prix Lucioles, prix Suisse-Can.), La Virevolte (prix L de Limoges, prix Louis-Hèmon de l'Acadèmie Languedoc), The Goldberg Variations, 1996, Slow Emergencies, 1996, Instruments des tènèbres, 1996 (Prix Goncourt des Lycèens, Prix Elle-Quebec, Prix du Livre Inter), Instruments of Darkness, 1997, L'Empreinte de l'ange, 1998 (prix des Libr., Quèbec, Grand prix des Lectrices de Elle), Prodige, 1999, The Mark of the Angel, 1999; (nonfiction) Dire et Interdire, 1980 (prix Binet-Sangle de l'Acadèmie Français). Recipient several exploration grants, Can. Coun., several writing grants Centre Nat. des Lettres. Avocations: harpsichord, piano, yoga.

HUSTON, SAMUEL RICHARD, health facility executive; b. Newton, Iowa, Apr. 21, 1940; s. Marshall Dwight and Miriam Evelyn (Peake) H.; m. Ann M. Huston; children: Carmen Colleen, Christopher Dwight. BA, U. No. Iowa, 1962; MA, State U. Iowa, 1964. Asst. adminstr. med. ctr. Hosp. of Vt., Burlington, 1964-66; assoc. dir. No. New Eng. Regional Med. Program, Burlington, 1966-68; asst. adminstr. Univ. Hosp. Cleve., 1968-70, assoc. adminstr., 1974-78, sr. v.p., 1978-83, exec. v.p., chief oper. officer, 1983-86; assoc. dir. Duke Hosp., Durham, N.C., 1970-72; pres., chief exec. officer Lehigh Valley Hosp. Ctr., Allentown, Pa., 1986-87, Allentown Hosp.-Lehigh Valley Hosp. Ctr., 1987-90; chief exec. officer Lehigh Valley Health Network, Lehigh Valley Hosp., Allentown, 1990-93; pres., CEO St. Luke's Med. Ctr., Cleve., 1994-97, St. Luke's Found. of Cleve., 1997—. Avocations: reading, music, hunting, golf. Home: 2770 Chesterton Rd Shaker Heights OH 44122-1805 Office: St Lukes Found 11000 Euclid Ave Ste 312 Cleveland OH 44106-1714

HUSTON, STEVEN CRAIG, lawyer; b. Morris, Ill., June 3, 1954; s. Raymond P. and Evelyn M. (Bass) H. BA, Ill. Coll., 1977; JD, John Marshall Law Sch., 1980; MBA, Northwestern U., 1989. Bar: Ill. 1980, U.S. Dist. Ct. (no. dist.) Ill. 1980, U.S. Ct. Appeals (7th cir.) 1980. Assoc. Siegel, Denberg et al, Chgo., 1980-83; staff atty. Wm. Wrigley Jr. Co., Chgo., 1983-84; asst. sec. legal William Wrigley Jr. Co., Chgo., 1984-94, asst. v.p. legal, 1994-96, counsel North Am., 1996—. Mem. ABA, Chgo. Bar Assn. Office: Wm Wrigley Jr Co 410 N Michigan Ave Chicago IL 60611-4213

HUSTON, TED LAIRD, psychology educator; b. Glendale, Calif., Aug. 3, 1943; s. Robert Sanford Huston and Robley Elizabeth (Theinhardt) Geis; m. Linda Christine Welshofer, Dec. 31, 1946; children: Megan, Kelly. Student, Pasadena City Coll., 1961-63; BS, Lewis and Clark Coll., Portland, Oreg., 1965; postgrad., San Diego State Coll., 1965-67; PhD, SUNY, Albany, 1972. Instr. SUNY, Albany, 1969-71; asst. prof., assoc. prof. then prof. Pa. State U., State University, 1972-84; Amy McLaughlin Centennial Prof. of Human ecology and Psychology U. Tex., Austin, 1984—. Author: Close Relationships, 1983; editor: Social Exchange in Developing Relationships, 1979, Foundations of Interpersonal Attraction, 1974; mem. editorial adv. bd. Jour. Social Issues, 1982-88, Jour. Social and Personal Relationships, 1983, 87, 89-92, Jour. Family Psychology; bd. cons. editors Jour. Personality and Social Psychology, 1979-83. NIMH grantee crime and delinquency sect., 1975-77, life course com., 1980-83, NSF grantee social psychology, 1993-96. Fellow APA; mem. Soc. Exptl. Social Psychologists, Nat. Coun. on Family Rels., Soc. for Psychol. Study Social Issues, Soc. Southwestern Social Psychologists, Internat. Soc. for Study Personal Relationships (pres. 1992-94), Phi Beta Kappa (charter). Democrat. Avocations: walking, travel, book collecting, vernacular architecture, photography. Office: U Tex Depts Human Ecology & Psychology Austin TX 78712*

HUSZAGH, FREDRICK WICKETT, lawyer, educator, information management company executive; b. Evanston, Ill., July 20, 1937; s. Rudolph LeRoy and Dorothea (Wickett) H.; m. Sandra McRae, Apr. 4, 1959; children: Floyd McRae, Fredrick Wickett II, Theodore Wickett II. B.A., Northwestern U., 1958; J.D., U. Chgo., 1962, LL.M., 1963, J.S.D., 1964. Bar: Ill. 1962, U.S. Dist. Ct. D.C. 1965, U.S. Supreme Ct. 1966. Market researcher Leo Burnett Co. Chgo., 1958-59; internat. atty. COMSAT, Washington, 1964-67; assoc. Debevoise & Liberman, Washington, 1967-68; asst. prof. law Am. U., Washington, 1968-71; program dir. NSF, Washington, 1971-73; assoc. prof. U. Mont., Missoula, 1973-76, U. Wis.-Madison, 1976-77; exec. dir. Dean Rusk Ctr., U. Ga., Athens, 1977-82; prof. U. Ga., 1982—; chmn. TWH Corp., Athens, 1982—; chmn. Profession Mgmt. Techs., Inc., Athens, 1993-96; cons. TWH Scv. Corp.; cons. Pres. Johnson's Telcommunications Task Force, Washington, 1967-68; co-chmn. Nat. Gov.'s Internat. Trade Staff Commn., Washington, 1979- 81. Author: International Decision-Making Process, 1964; Comparative Facts on Canada, Mexico and U.S., 1979; also articles. Editor Rusk Ctr. Briefings, 1981-82. Mem. Econ. Policy Council, N.Y.C., 1981-89. NSF grantee, 1974-78. Republican. Presbyterian. Home: 151 E Clayton St Athens GA 30601-2702 Office: U Ga Law Sch Athens GA 30602

HUSZAR, ARLENE CELIA, lawyer, mediator; b. N.Y.C., May 1, 1952; d. Charles and Dora (Toffoli) H.; m. Victor M. Yellen, May 6, 1978; 1 child: Mariette Huszar Yellen. BA, Fla. Atlantic U., 1973; JD, U. Fla., 1976. Bar: Fla. 1977, U.S. Dist. Ct. (mid. and no. dists.) Fla. 1978, U.S. Ct. Appeals (5th and 11th cirs.) 1978, D.C. 1979, U.S. Supreme Ct. 1982; cert. fed. and cir. ct. mediator, arbitrator. Pvt. practice Gainesville, Fla., 1977-80; mng. atty. Fla. Instl. Legal Svcs., Gainesville, 1980—. Author: (with others) Adoption, 1992, Termination of Parental Rights, 1997. Mem. City of Gainesville Citizens Adv. Com. for Cmty. Devel., 1976-79, Fla. Bar Com. on the Legal Needs of Children, 1984-85; mem. steering com. juvenile law sect. Nat. Legal Aid and Defender Assn., 1986-87; vice chmn. Alachua County Citizens Adv. Com., Dept. Criminal Justice Svcs., 1986-95; precinct committeewoman Alachua County Dem. Exec. Com., 1986-96; Queen of Peach parish coun. (sec. 1995-97, pres. 1998). Named one of Outstanding Young Women of Am., 1975. Mem. ATLA, Nat. Assn. Counsel for Children, Eighth Jud. Cir. Bar Assn. (bd. dirs. 1994—), Fla. Acad. Profl. Mediators, North Ctrl. Fla. Mediation Coun. Roman Catholic. Office: Fla Instl Legal Svcs 1110 NW 8th Ave Ste C Gainesville FL 32601-4969

HUT, PIET, astrophysics educator; b. Utrecht, Holland, Sept. 26, 1952; came to U.S., 1981; s. Jan Lambertus Hut and Jenneke Johanna Hut-Broekroelofs; m. Eiko Ikegami, July 26, 1991. MS, U. Utrecht, 1977; PhD, U. Amsterdam, Holland, 1981. Asst. prof. astronomy dept. U. Calif., Berkeley, 1984-85; mem. Inst. for Advanced Study, Princeton, N.J., 1981-84, prof., 1985—; Contbr. articles to prof. jours. Mem. Am. Astron. Soc., Dutch Astron. Club, Astron. Soc. Japan. Office: Inst for Advanced Study Olden Ln Princeton NJ 08540

HUTCHENS, EUGENE GARLINGTON, college administrator; b. Birmingham, Ala., Nov. 26, 1929; s. Wallace Luther and Reydonia (Corry) H.; m. Betty Frances Goode, Aug. 26, 1951; children: Dale Eugene, Wayne Goode, Dennis Wade. BA, Samford U., 1952; ThM, New Orleans Bapt. Theol. Sem., 1970; MS in Econs., U. Mo.-Columbia, 1972. Ordained to ministry, 1952. Min. North Brewton (Ala.) Bapt. Ch., 1952-56, 1st Bapt. Ch., Ashland, Ala., 1956-63, Highlands Bapt. Ch., Huntsville, Ala., 1963-67; tchr. pub. schs. Huntsville, 1967-71; instr. econs. N.W. Ala. State Jr. Coll., 1972-77, acting pres., 1981, dir. Tuscumbia campus, 1977-89; adminstrv. asst. Shoals C.C., 1989-93, asst. to dean, 1993-95; pastor emeritus Weeden Heights Bapt. Ch., Florence, 1995; owner radio stas., WKNI AM, Lexington, Ala., WFIX, Rogersville, Ala., 1991-96, mem. Ala. Bapt. State Exec. Bd., 1961-63; v.p. Ala. Bapt. State Pastors Conf., 1966, Ala. Bapt. Historical Commission, 1992—. NSF grantee, 1971-72. Mem. NEA, Ala. Edn. Assn., Ala. Jr. and C.C. Assn. (exec. com. 1981-84). Home: 801 E 2nd St Tuscumbia AL 35674-2206

HUTCHENS, TYRA THORNTON, physician, educator; b. Newberg, Oreg., Nov. 29, 1921; s. Fred George and Bessie (Adams) H.; m. Betty Lou Gardner, June 7, 1942; children: Tyra Richard, Robert Jay, Rebecca (Mrs. Mark Pearsall). BS, U. Oreg., 1943, MD, 1945. Diplomate: Am. Bd. Pathology, Am. Bd. Nuclear Medicine. Intern Minn. Gen. Hosp., Mpls., 1945-46; AEC postdoctoral research fellow Reed Coll., Med. Sch. U. Oreg., 1948-50; NIH postdoctoral research fellow Med. Sch. U. Oreg., 1951-53; mem. faculty Oreg. Health Scis. U., 1953—, prof., chmn. dept. clin. pathology, 1962-87, prof. emeritus, 1987—, prof. radiotherapy, 1963-71, allied health edn. coordinator, 1969-77; vis. lectr. radiobiology Reed Coll., 1955, 56. Mem. adv. bd. Oreg. Regional Med. Program, 1968-75; mem. statuatory radiation adv. com. Oreg. Bd. Health, 1957-69, chmn., 1967-69; founding trustee Am. Bd. Nuclear Medicine, 1971-77, 82-84, sec., 1973-75, 84-85 ; voting rep. Am. Bd. Med. Specialties, 1973-78, chmn. com. long range planning, 1976-78; mem. sci. adv. bd. Armed Forces Inst. Pathology, 1978-83; chmn. Portland Com. on Fgn. Affairs, 1990-91. Lt. (j.g.) M.C., USNR, 1946-48. Charter mem. Acad. Clin. Lab. Physicians and Scientists, Soc. Nuclear Medicine (de Hevesey Nuclear Medicine Pioneer award 1995), Am. Coll. Nuclear Physicians; mem. Oreg. Pathologists Assn. (pres. 1968), Pacific N.W. Soc. Nuclear Medicine (pres. 1958), AMA, Coll. Am. Pathologists (bd. govs. 1967-74, pres. 1977-79, chmn. commn. on internat. affairs 1979-83, chmn. planning com. 1987 World Congress Pathology), Am. Soc. Clin. Pathologists (bd. registry med. technologists 1967-71), World Assn. of Socs. of Pathology (bur. of pathology 1981-87, 89-93, v.p. 1985-87, pres. 1989-91, chmn. commn. on world stds. 1981-86, Gold Headed Cane award 1995), World Pathology Found. (pres. 1987-89, trustee 1989-91), Assn. Clin. Pathologists (hon.), Italian Soc. Lab. Medicine (hon.), Phi Beta Kappa, Sigma Xi, Alpha Omega Alpha. Rsch., publs. radioactive carbon tracer studies of lipid metabolism, clin. radioisotope techniques. Home: 15385 SW Petrel Ln Beaverton OR 97007-8182 Office: Oreg Health Scis U 3181 SW Sam Jackson Park Rd Portland OR 97201-3011

HUTCHEON, LINDA ANN, English language educator; b. Toronto, Aug. 24, 1947; d. Vincent Roy and Elisa (Rossi) Bulfon Bortolotti; m. Michael Alexander Hutcheon, May 30, 1970. BA, U. Toronto, 1969, PhD, 1975; MA, Cornell U., 1971. Prof. McMaster U., Hamilton, Ont., Can., 1976-88, U. Toronto, 1988—; vis. prof. U. Toronto, 1980-81, 81-82, 84-85; U. Wis., Madison, 1995, U. Ga., 1998. Author: Narcissistic Narrative, 1980 (choice award 1980-81), Formalism and the Freudian Aesthetic, 1984, A Theory of Parody, 1985, A Poetics of Postmodernism, 1988, The Canadian Postmodern, 1988, The Politics of Postmodernism, 1989, Splitting Images, 1991, Irony's Edge, 1995, (with H. Hutcheon) Opera: Desire, Disease, Death, 1996; assoc. editor RS/SI, Toronto, 1982-84, U. Toronto Quar., 1993—; mem. editl. bd. Texte, Toronto, 1983—, English Studies in Can., 1984-94, Italian Canadiana, 1984—, Textual Practice, 1987—, Can. Rev. Comparative Lit., 1987—, Can. Poetry, 1987-93, PMLA, 1990-92, essays on Can. Writing, 1992—, Contemporary Lit., 1992— Modern Fiction Studies, 1993—, CLIO, 1994—, Parallax (U.K.), 1994—. Woodrow Wilson Found. fellow, 1969, Social Scis. and Humanities Rsch. Coun. Can. fellow, 1983, 93-95, 96-99, co-fellow maj. collaborative rsch. initiatives, 1996—; Can. Coun. fellow, 1972-75, Killam Found. fellow, 1978-80, 86-88, Connaught fellow, 1991-92, Guggenheim fellow, 1992-93. Mem. MLA (del. assembly 1985-88, exec. coun. 1992-96, 2d v.p. 1998, 1st v.p. 1999), Assn. Can. Coll. and Univ. Tchrs. English (exec. mem. 1978-81), Can. Comparative Lit. Assn. (sec.-treas. 1981-83), Internat. Comparative Lit. Assn. (coord. com. lit. history 1992-97).

HUTCHEON, WILDA VILENE BURTCHELL, artist; b. Ft. Fairfield, Maine, Sept. 9; d. Harvey George and Alanda Gallope (Hersey) Burtchell; m. Philip S. Hutcheon, Mar. 26, 1955 (dec. July 1992). Grad., Fed. design Sch., 1944; student seascape, Art Students League, 1963, student landscape painting, 1965, student portraiture, 1969; DFA (hon.), London Inst. Applied Rsch., 1990. Color cons., studio receptionist, 1954-56, art instr./lectr., 1960s; supr. art dept. Maine State Art Exhbn., Presque Isle, 1959-62; curator fine arts Nylander Mus., Caribou, Maine, 1958-63; art instr./judge Aroostook County, Maine, 1958-94; lectr./cons. in field. One woman shows include Woodfords Congregational Ch., Portland, Maine, 1967, Talent Tree Gallery, Augusta, Maine 1974, Maine State, Poland Springs, Restigouche Mus., New Brunswick, Can., 1978, Madison Ave., N.Y.C., 1978, Ogunquit Art Ctr., 1978, 16th Internat. Congress of Arts Group, Washington, 1989, Woods Edge Gallery, Perham, Maine, 1994; group shows include Talent Tree Gallery, Augusta, 1974, Laguna Beach, Calif., 1986-87; exhibited in permanent collections at Cary Meml. Hosp., Caribou, Maine, others, also in pvt. collections. Exec. coord. Beautification Arts and CRafts, Ft. Fairfield, 1986; art chmn. Maine Potato Blossom Festival, Ft. Fairfield, 1963; chmn. Aroostook County Cultural Ctr. Project, 1971. Recipient Internat. Art Gold medal Best of Show, IPA, Washington, Internat. Creative Achievement award New Orleans, Internat. Best of Show, New Eng., Internat. Disting. award for outstanding achievement and svc. in creative art with induction into Disting. Leadership Hall of Fame; commd. Ky. Col., Nat. Award for Svc., Provl. Photographers of A., 1962, Hastings Cup for Continued Excellence, P.P.A.N.E., 1964, Pres.'s Club for Outstanding Merit, M.P.P.A., 1969, numerous awards at art shows; named Woman of Yr. Caribou Bus. & Profl. Women, 1997; recipient achievement award AAUW, 1997. Mem. Caribou C. of C., Cambridge World Found. of Successful Women, Nat. Mus. of Women in the Arts (charter), Caribou Garden Club (pres. 1968), Art Soc. Caribou (pres. 1964), Am. Portrait Soc., Nat. Trust for Hist. Preservation, The Portrait Inst., Profl. Photographers of Am., Beaverbrook Art Gallery (Can.), Maine Assn. of Women in Fine and Performing Arts, Farnsworth Mus., Bus. and Profl. Women's Club, Internat. Platform Assn. Republican. Ch. of Christ. Avocations: geology, archaeology, gardening, travel sketching, philosophy. Home and Studio: 26 Home Farm Rd Caribou ME 04736-2473

HUTCHERSON, CHRISTOPHER ALFRED, marketing, recruiting and educational fundraising executive; b. Memphis, June 13, 1950; s. Alfred Wayne Hutcherson and Loretta (Morris) Kindsfather; m. Glenda Ann Champ, May 22, 1971 (dec. 1995); m. Barbara A. Haralson, Sept. 27, 1998. *Mr. Hutcherson credits his success to a combination of traits he learned from several extraordinary people. Loretta Kindsfather, mother/business professional (tunnelvision, persistence, fearlessness). Glenda Hutcherson, deceased first wife (how to love and never give up). Barbara Hutcherson, 2nd wife (how to appreciate love, happiness, and life). Vince Ray, marine/executive (dedication/loyalty). Dan Hillard and Mark Elstad, executives (teamwork and commitment), Wayne Hutcherson, father/farmer (work ethic). Brunetta*

Morris, grandmother/elementary school principal (love of education). Clarence Morris, grandfather/cotton gin manager (serve others with unselfishness). Henry Kindsfather, stepfather/cowboy (consistency/respect for others). Ben Gollehon, band teacher (competitiveness). BS, U. Houston, 1972, MA in Adminstrn., 1977, postgrad., 1977-79. Cert. tchr. and adminstr., Tex. Pvt. music instr. Spring Br. and Pasadena Ind. Sch. Dists., Tex., 1968-75; jr. high and high sch. band dir. Deer Park (Tex.) Ind. Schs., 1972-80; recruiter M. David Lowe Personnel, Houston, 1981; sales dir. Instl. Financing Svcs., Benicia, Calif., 1982-85; sales mgr. Instl. Financing Svcs., Benicia, 1985-87; nat. tng. dir. Champion Products and Svcs., San Diego, 1987-88, west coast and midwest sales mgr., 1988-89; pres. Camelot, Inc., Auburn, Calif., 1989-91; pres., CEO Camelot Telephone Assistance Program, Inc., Folsom, Calif., 1991-92; nat. dir. sales and mktg. edn. and devel. Nat. Scrip Ctr., Inc., Santa Rosa, Calif., 1992-95; exec. v.p. Scrip Plus Inc., Fresno, Calif., 1995-96; chmn., pres., CEO Children's Heros, Inc., Auburn, 1996—; fund raising cons. non-profit orgns., 1982—; speaker in field. *Mr. Hutcherson is one of the nation's preeminent cause related marketing experts. His career achievements have placed him in "Who's Who" sixteen times in six categories. He is acknowledged as a leader who can bring vision to reality. As a speaker, he delivers an address reflective of commitment to improve children's educational opportunities. He has written an entire methodology and curriculum for national voluntarism. He is dedicated to children with an enthusiasm that motivates people to action. He has raised over 178 million dollars for schools. His life is devoted to developing a permanent source of funding for this nation's schools.* Judge Tex. jr. high and high sch. bands, 1974-81, regional band chmn., 1973-77; choir dir. St. Hyacinth Ch., Deer Park, 1979-81; vice chmn. Ch. Coun. St. Hyacinth Ch., 1980; founder Tex. Region XIX Jr. High Band Competition, 1973 (Spl. Achievement award 1979); 1st chair clarinet Tex. All-State Band, 1968; founder, pres. Glenda Hutcherson Heros Found., 1996—; creator Heroes Reward Card Program, 1996—; founder, pres. Childrens Heros Fund. Mem. Kappa Kappa Psi (v.p. Outstanding Mem. award 1970). Republican. Roman Catholic. Avocations: golf, reading, movies. Home: 14105 Lodestar Dr Grass Valley CA 95949-8362

HUTCHERSON, DONNA DEAN, retired music educator; b. Dallas, July 10, 1937; d. Lamar Shaffer and Lenora Fay (Newbern) Clark; m. George Henry Hutcherson, Jan. 31, 1959; children: Lamar, Michael, Mark Lee, Holly (dec.), Shela. B. Music Edn., Sam Houston State U., Huntsville, Tex., 1959; MA in Music, Stephen F. Austin State U., Nacogdoches, Tex., 1974; postgrad., Memphis State U., 1986-89. Cert. tchr. music K-12, Orff levels 1, 2, 3, Master, cert. computer literacy, Tex. Tchr. music 4th and 5th grades Carthage (Tex.) Ind. Sch. Dist., 1958-59; tchr. music grades 1-5 and H.S. choir Hallsville (Tex.) Ind. Sch. Dist., 1969-75, tchr. music K-4, 1975-78, tchr. music grades 3-4, 1978-86, tchr. music 4th grade, 1986-97; ret., 1997; contbr. Jour. of Music Edn. Delegation to Vietnam Citizen Ambassador Program, 1993; chmn. Tex. Ann. Conf. United Meth. Ch. Commn. on Archives/History. Contbr. articles to profl. jours. Fellow United Meth. Musicians in Worship and Other Arts; mem. Music Educators Nat. Conf. (registered music educator), Tex. Music Educators Conf. (state Tri-M chmn. 1993-98), Tex. Music Educators Assn. (region IV chmn. 1975-93), Am. Orff Schulewerk Assn., Tri M Internat. Music Honor Soc. (local chpt. sponsor 1992—, hon. mem.). Methodist. Avocations: square dancing, clogging, sewing, travel, church work. E-mail: ddhutch@juno.com. Home: 119 Mcpherson Rd Hallsville TX 75650-7707

HUTCHERSON, KAREN FULGHUM, healthcare executive; b. Winston-Salem, N.C., Oct. 1, 1951; d. John Fulghum and Viola Sprinkle Shaw; m. Victor J. Hutcherson, Dec. 18, 1970; children: Shannon Renae, Ashley Michelle. Diploma, N.C. Bapt. Hosp. Sch. Nursing, 1972; BSN, N.C. A&T State U., 1981; MBA, Wake Forest U., 1990. RN. Staff nurse N.C. Bapt. Hosp., Winston-Salem, 1972; oncology nurse clinician Cancer Ctr., Wake Forest U., Winston-Salem, 1972-81; oncology nurse educator Bowman Gray Sch. of Med., Wake Forest U., Winston-Salem, 1981-87, dir. nursing cancer ctr., 1982-87; asst. dir. clin. support svcs. Bowman Gray Sch. Medicine, Winston-Salem, 1987-96; cons. healthcare and orgnl. devel. Hayes Consulting and Tng. Group, Inc., Winston-Salem, 1996; dir. consulting svcs. Mgmt. Directions of N.C., Winston-Salem, 1996-97, regional v.p., 1997—; curriculum coord., primary inst. Cancer Ctr., 1980-87; mem. spkrs. bur. A.H. Robbins Pharms. Co., 1983-88; cons. S.E. Cancer Control Consortium, Winston-Salem, 1987-90. Author: Patient Education in Understanding Cancer: An Introductory Handbook, 1986; co-author: Understanding Cancer Treatment: A Guide for You and Your Family, 1988, Cancer Chemotherapy Guidelines, 5th edit., 1985. Chmn. western div. nursing com. N.C. Am. Cancer Soc., 1981-82, speakers' bur., 1982, bd. dirs. 1988-92.; mem. spl. rev. com. clin. community oncology program Nat. Cancer Inst., Bethesda, Md., 1987. Recipient Leadership award Babcock Grad. Sch. Mgmt., Wake Forest U., 1992. Mem. ANA, Am. Acad. Ambulatory Nursing Adminstrn., Med. Ctr. Nursing Assn., Piedmont Oncology Assn. (numerous coms.), Oncology Nursing Soc. (mem. com.), Nat. League for Nursing, Am. Orgn. Nursing Execs., Med. Group Mgmt. Assn. (chair NC govt. rels. com. 1998), S.E. Cancer Control Consortium, N.C. Nurses Assn. (legis. com. 1989, vice chmn. commun. health coun., del. conv. 1987, 88, 89, 90, 91), Sigma Theta Tau. Home: 754 Lacock Ave Rural Hall NC 27045-9742 Office: Mgmt Directions of N C Ste 300 2000 Frontis Plz Blvd Winston Salem NC 27103-5616

HUTCHESON, J. STERLING, allergist, immunologist, physician; b. Richmond, Va., Apr. 17, 1936; s. James P. and Daisy-Clarke (Lorentz) H.; m. Nancy Montgomery Sanders, May 20, 1961; children: Anne Farrar, Betsy Dulaney. Student, Roanoke Coll., Va., 1953-55; BA, U. Va., 1955-57; MD, The Johns Hopkins U., 1957-61. Diplomate Am. Bd. Allergy and Clin. Immunology. Intern in medicine U. Va., Charlottesville, Va., 1961-62; resident in medicine Med. Coll. Va., Richmond, Va., 1962-64; fellow in allergy and immunology U. Va., Charlottesville, Va., 1964-65; asst. prof. medicine Med. Coll. Va., 1967-68; staff Nalle Clinic, Charlotte, 1968-89; pvt. practice Carolina Asthma and Allergy Ctr., 1990—; founder Allergy Clinic USAF Acad. Hosp., Colo., 1965-67; cons. Blue Cross/Blue Shield of N.C.; adj. assoc. prof. pediats. U. N.C. Sch. Medicine, Carolinas Med. Ctr., Charlotte. Bd. trustees Charlotte County Day Sch., 1974-85; bd. dirs. Friends of Music Queens Coll., 1994-96. Capt. USAF M.C. Fellow Am. Acad. Allergy, Asthma and Immunology, Am. Coll. Allergy, Asthma and Immunology; mem. Southeastern Allergy Assn., N.C. Soc. Allergy and Clin. Immunology (former pres.). Episcopalian. Avocations: gardening, hiking, classical music, reading, painting. Home: 4200 Arbor Way Charlotte NC 28211-3812 Office: Carolina Asthma & Allergy Bldg 400 2711 Randolph Rd Charlotte NC 28207-2027

HUTCHESON, JACK ROBERT, hematologist, medical oncologist; b. Rock Hill, S.C., Dec. 26, 1946; s. Jack Robert and Lillian Massey (Dunlap) H.; m. Charlene Marie Dixon, Sept. 14, 1974; children: Gregory Allen, Julia Lynn. BS in Biology, Wake Forest U., 1969; MD, Med. U. S.C., 1973. Diplomate in internal medicine, hematology, oncology Am. Bd. Internal Medicine. Straight med. intern U. Md. Hosp., Balt., 1973-74, resident in medicine, 1974-76; fellow in hematology Med. U. S.C., Charleston, 1976-78; fellow in oncology Emory U., Atlanta, 1978-79; oncologist, hematologist Oncology and Hematology Assocs. of S.W. Va. Inc., Roanoke, 1979—; med. dir. Carilion Health Sys. Oncology Svc. Line, Roanoke, 1996—; instr., assoc. investigator in hematology Med. U. S.C./VA Hosp., Charleston, 1977-78; assoc. prof. medicine U. Va., Roanoke. Contbr. articles to med. jours. Pres. Scottish Soc. Va. Highlands, Roanoke, 1996; chair com. on smoking cessation Va. br. Am. Cancer Soc., Roanoke, 1980. Recipient Berson Yalow award Soc. Nuclear Medicine, 1977; VA Career Devel. grantee for hematology, 1977-78; decorated Knight of Grace, Mil. Hospitalier, Order of St. Lazarus, Order Don Carlos I (Portugal), knight comdr. Order Crown of Thorns, Order of St. Catherine of Sinai. Fellow ACP; mem. Am. Soc. Clzn. Oncology, Am. Soc. Hematology. Presbyterian. Avocations: Jaguar auto restoration, genealogy, Scottish/Celtic activities. Home: 2860 S Jefferson St Roanoke VA 24014-3320 Office: Oncol and Hematol Assocs 2013 S Jefferson St Roanoke VA 24014-2419

HUTCHESON, J(AMES) STERLING, lawyer; b. Nanking, China, Oct. 17, 1919; s. Allen Carrington and Strausie (McCaslin) H.; m. Marilyn Brown, Dec. 26, 1944; children—James Sterling, Holly Hutcheson Jasperson, Joanne Hutcheson Denton, Scott Brown, Allen McCaslin. B.A., Princeton U., 1941; LL.B., Stanford U., 1949. Bar: Calif. 1949, U.S. Dist. Ct. (no. dist.) Calif. 1949, U.S. Ct. Apls. (9th cir.) 1949, U.S. Dist. Ct. (so. dist.) Calif. 1950, U.S. Ct. Mil. Appeals 1955, Clk. jud. com. Calif. State Assembly, 1949; assoc., then ptnr. Gray, Cary, Ames & Frye, San Diego, 1950-93; ptnr. emeritus Gray, Cary Ware & Freidenrich, 1994—. Mem. San Diego City Traffic Commn.; bd. dirs. San Diego County Hosp. and Health Facility Planning Commn.; trustee Francis Parker Sch., San Diego, 1956-59, pres. bd., 1957-58; trustee La Jolla (Calif.) Country Day Sch., 1956-59. Served to comdr. USNR, 1941-45. Mem. Internat. Assn. Def. Counsel (state editor 1958, 61-63, 66-67, chmn. legal malpractice subcom. 1962, exec. com. 1976-79), State Bar Calif. (lectr. continuing edn. bar 1960, 63, mem. disciplinary bd. 1973-77, referee rev. bd. 1979-83, client security fund 1977-78), San Diego County Barristers, San Diego County Bar Assn. (sec. 1963-64, v.p. 1964-65, chmn. med. legal com. 1961-62), Am. Bd. Trial Advs., Assn. So. Calif. Def. Counsel (dir. 1974-76), Southwestern Legal Found. (lectr. 1963), Am. Coll. Trial Lawyers, Def. Research Inst. (regional v.p. Pacific 1971-74), Navy League, Phi Alpha Delta. Republican. Presbyterian. Club: Princeton of San Diego (pres. 1955-71). Home: 7784 Hillside Dr La Jolla CA 92037-3944 Office: Gray Cary Ware & Freidenrich 401 B St Ste 1700 San Diego CA 92101-4240

HUTCHESON, JERRY DEE, manufacturing company executive; b. Hammon, Okla., Oct. 31, 1932; s. Radford Andrew and Ethel Mae (Boulware) H.; B.S. in Physics, Eastern N. Mex. U., 1959; postgrad. Temple U., 1961-62, U. N.Mex., 1964-65; m. Lynda Lou Weber, Mar. 6, 1953; children—Gerald Dan, Lisa Marie, Vicki Lynn. Research engr. RCA, 1959-62; sect. head Motorola, 1962-63; research physicist Dikewood Corp., 1963-66; sr. mem. tech. staff Signetics Corp., 1966-69; engrng. mgr. Litton Systems, Sunnyvale, Calif., 1969-70; engrng. mgr. Fairchild Semiconductor, Mountain View, Calif., 1971; equipment engr., group mgr. Teledyne Semiconductor, Mountain View, 1971-74; dir. engrng. DCA Reliability Labs., Sunnyvale, 1974-75; founder, prin. Tech. Ventures, San Jose, Calif., 1975—; chief exec. officer VLSI Research, Inc., 1981—. Democratic precinct committeeman, Albuquerque, 1964-66. Served with USAF, 1951-55. Registered profl. engr., Calif. Mem. Nat. Soc. Profl. Engrs., Profl. Engrs. Pvt. Practice, Calif. Soc. Profl. Engrs., Semiconductor Equipment and Materials Inst., Soc. Photo-Optical Instrumentation Engrs., Am. Soc. Test Engrs., Presbyterian. Club: Masons. Contbr. articles to profl. jours. Home: 5950 Vista Loop San Jose CA 95124-6562 Office: VSLI Rsch 1754 Technology Dr Ste 117 San Jose CA 95110-1308

HUTCHESON, JOHN AMBROSE, JR., history educator; b. Winston-Salem, N.C., July 18, 1944; s. John Ambrose and Virginia Lee (Tillotson) H.; m. Marilyn Louise Beaver, July 15, 1967; children: Virginia Louise, Catherine Leigh. AB, U. N.C., 1966, MA, 1968, PhD, 1973. Asst. prof. history Dalton (Ga.) State Coll., 1974-90, assoc. prof. history, 1990-97, prof. history, 1997—, chair divsn. bus. adminstrn. and social sci., 1997-99, chmn. divsn. soc. sci., 1999—. Author: Leopold Maxse and the National Review, 1989; contbr. articles to profl. jours. Bd. dirs., sec. Creative Arts Guild, Dalton, 1994—. Mem. Am. Hist. Assn., So. Hist. Assn., So. Conf. Brit. Studies (exec. coun. 1995-98, pres. 1999—), Carolinas Symposium on Brit. Studies (pres. 1995), Ga. Assn. Historians, World History Assn., Phi Alpha Theta. Democrat. Episcopalian. Home: 2204 Mathis Ln Dalton GA 30720-2942 Office: Dalton State Coll 213 College Dr Dalton GA 30720-3745

HUTCHESON, MARK ANDREW, lawyer; b. Phila., Mar. 29, 1942; s. John R. and Mary Helen (Willis) H.; m. Julie A. Olander, June 13, 1964; children: Kirsten Elizabeth, Mark Andrew II, Megan Ann. BA, U. Puget Sound, 1964; LLB, U. Wash., 1967. Bar: Wash. 1967, U.S. Dist. Ct. (we. and ea. dists.) Wash., U.S. Ct. Appeals (9th cir.), U.S. Supreme Ct. Staff counsel Com. on Commerce U.S. Senate, Washington, 1967-68; assoc. Davis Wright Tremaine, Seattle, 1968-72; ptnr. Davis, Wright Tremaine, Seattle, 1973—; mng. ptnr., chief exec. officer Davis Wright Tremaine, Seattle, 1989-94; chmn. Davis, Wright Tremaine, Seattle, 1994—; mem., co-founder labor law com. Nat. Banking Industry, 1984—. Co-author: Employer's Guide to Strike Planning and Prevention, 1986; contbr. articles to profl. jours. Pres., trustee Virginia Mason Hosp., Seattle, 1980—, Overlake Sch., Redmond, Wash., 1984-89, Epiphany Sch., Seattle, 1982-84, Legal Aid for Wash. Fund, 1991—; bd. dirs. Vis. Nurse Svcs., Seattle-King County, 1985-88; trustee Pacific N.W. Ballet, 1991—, Pacific N.W. Assn. Ind. Schs., 1996-98. Nelson T. Hartson scholar U. Wash., 1966; Deerfield fellow Heritage Found., Deerfield, Mass., 1963. Mem. ABA (health care forum, employment law sect.), Seattle-King County Bar Assn. (employment law sect.), Am. Acad. Hosp. Attys., Am. Hosp. Assn. (labor rels. adv. com. 1978—), Coll. Labor and Employment Lawyers, Greater Seattle C. of C. (bd. dirs. 1991-94), Rainier Club, Seattle Tennis Club, Univ. Club, Order of Coif. Episcopalian. Avocations: sailing, tennis, skiing, reading, travel. Office: Davis Wright Tremaine 2600 Century Sq 1501 4th Ave Ste 2600 Seattle WA 98101-1688

HUTCHESON, THAD THOMSON, JR., international executive; b. Houston, Mar. 2, 1941; s. Thad T. and Caroline (Brownlee) H.; m. Rebecca Trueheart Brown, Dec. 3, 1991; children: Genevieve (Mrs. Keen Butcher), Curtis Thomson. BA, Princeton U., 1963; SPIA in Asian Studies, Woodrow Wilson Sch. Pub. and Internat. Affairs, 1963; JD with honors, U. Tex., 1966. Sr. ptnr. Baker & Botts, Houston, 1966-95; sr. v.p. Enron Internat., 1995—; dir. Am. Oil and Gas Corp., 1984-93; chmn. Internat. Ctrs. for Arbitration, 1992-97. Editor: Tex. Law Rev., 1964-66. Mem. bd. visitors U. Tex. Law Sch., 1976-92, past chmn.; vis. prof. Tex. Law Sch., 1983-86; past bd. dirs. Houston Mus. Fine Arts, Contemporary Arts Mus., DePelchin Children's Ctr.; mem. bd. visitors, exec. com. Tex. U. Cancer Found., M.D. Anderson Cancer and Tumor Inst., 1978-92; statewide chmn. Tex. Attys. for Reagan/Bush, 1980, co-chmn., 1984; participant Rep. convs., 1960—; mem. V.P.'s Policy Com. Internat. Trade and Debt, 1987-88. Fellow Am. Bar Found.; mem. ABA (com. corp. laws 1975-81, com. fed. regulation of securities 1980-94), Am. Law Inst. (ife), Tex. State Bar Assn., Boothbay Yacht Club, Eagle Lake Rod & Gun Club, Houston Country Club. Office: Enron Corp 333 Clay St Houston TX 77002-4000

HUTCHESON, THOMAS WORTHINGTON, educational administrator; b. Lake Forest, Ill., July 1, 1958; s. Harold Randolph and Minna Margaret (Adams) H. BA, U. Mass., 1980, MEd, 1987, EdD, 1993. Music tchr., 1975—; instr. edn. U. Mass., Amherst, 1987-89, v.p. Grad. Student Senate, 1988-89, rsch. asst. dept. econs., 1989-91; rsch. cons. Nat. Priorities Project, Northampton, Mass., 1991-92; estate cons. Sandwich, Mass., 1996-99; music critic The Recorder, Greenfield, Mass., 1996—; project coord. Bonnyvale Environ. Edn. Ctr., Brattleboro, Vt., 1996—, cons., 1992; Contbr. articles to profl. jours.; musician, 1974—; arranger choral works: Welcome, Yule!, 1994—; dir. Shapeshifters vocal quartet, 1997—. Chmn. Pub. Transp. Com., Amherst, 1989-90; mem. Franklin County Planning Bd., Greenfield, Mass., 1993—, Overall Econ. Devel. Program Policy Com., Greenfield, 1996—; chmn. Com. on Elec. Industry Deregulation, Greenfield, 1996-99. Mem. Am. Planning Assn., Internat. Soc. for Ecol. Econs. Democrat. Soc. of Friends. Avocations: vexillology, heraldry, Scottish country dance, family archives, traditional music. Home: 11 Bridge St # 2 Millers Falls MA 01349-1339

HUTCHIN, NANCY LEE, process engineering and change management consultant; b. Ft. Belvoir, Va., June 16, 1949; d. Walter James and Iyllis Elizabeth (Lee) H.; m. Stephen Lawrence Guiland Nov. 27, 1970 (div. 1983); children: Kai-Long Stephen Guiland, Petra Lee Guiland; m. John Edward Money, Jun. 7, 1986 (div. 1994). BA summa cum laude, U. Md., 1973, MA, 1976. Prin. sci. B-K Dynamics, Rockville, Md., 1978-86; sr. cons. James Martin Assoc., Reston, Va., 1986-88; cons. San Diego, 1989-95; cons. employee SAIC, San Diego, 1993-95; staff cons. Intergraph, Reston, 1995-99; practice mgr. Keane Fed. Sys., Inc., Rockville, Md., 1999—; contbr. editor Enterprise Reengineering, 1994-96; assoc. pub. Black Riders, 1994-96; program com. Tools & Methods for Bus. Engrng. Conf., 1995; mem. program com. Nat. Bus. Process Reengrng. Conf., 1996, 98, SDPS Integrated Design and Process Tech. Conf., 1996, 98; bd. dirs. Strategic Info. Mgmt. & Tech. Solutions, Inc., Ogden, Utah; track chair changing human behavior Europe 98 Process and Knowledge Mgmt. Conf., London, 1998; presenter in field. Contbr. articles to profl. jours. Mem. Women in Tech. DC chap., Soc. of Info. Mgmt., Soc. Design and Process Sci. Avocations: walking, travel, blues music. Office: Keane Fed Sys Inc 1375 Piccard Dr # 200 Rockville MD 20850

HUTCHINGS, GEORGE HENRY, food company executive; b. Fort Worth, June 23, 1922; s. George H. and Emma (Harder) H.; m. Edith Van Gils, Mar. 23, 1946 (dec.); children: Mark Dennism Lisa Ellen; m. Elizabeth T. Storey, Apr. 10, 1968 (dec.). Student, Tex. A&M, 1940-42. Analyst mktg. research Frito Food Mfg., Dallas, 1946; mgr. mktg. research Frito Food Mfg., Los Angeles, 1946-57; div. sales mgr. Frito Food Mfg., San Mateo, Calif., 1958-60, div. gen. mgr., 1961, v.p., 1961-62; v.p. for ops. Western zone, 1962—; pres. Nalley's, Inc., Tacoma, 1964, Nalley's div. W.R. Grace & Co., 1966—; ret. Nalley's div. W.R. Grace & Co., Tacoma, 1972-81; pres. Wash. Beverages, Inc., Tacoma, 1972-81; dir., mem. exec. com. Puget Sound Nat. Bank, Tacoma; cons. 1964-83; dir. mem. examining com. Key Bank of Wash., Tacoma, 1993-94, ret., 1994. Served to capt. USAAF, 1942-46. Decorated D.F.C., Air medal with 7 clusters. Mem. Tacoma Country and Golf Club, Masons. Lutheran. Home: 7419 North St SW Tacoma WA 98498-5213 *A man must know what he stands for before he can logically take a stand against anything.*

HUTCHINGS, JOHN BARRIE, astronomer, researcher; b. Johannesburg, Republic of South Africa, July 18, 1941; arrived in Can., 1967; BSc, Witwatersrand U., Johannesburg, 1962; MSc, Witwatersrand U., 1964; PhD, U. Cambridge, Eng., 1967. Rsch. scientist Dominion Astrophys. Obs., Nat. Rsch. Coun. Can., Victoria, B.C., 1967—. Author numerous rsch. papers and revs., 1964—. Recipient Gold medal Sci. Coun. B.C., 1983. Fellow Royal Soc. Can.; mem. Internat. Astron. Union, Am. Astron. Soc., Can. Astron. Soc. (Beals award 1982). Office: Dominion Astrophys Obs, 5071 W Saanich Rd, Victoria, BC Canada V8X 4M6

HUTCHINGS, PETER LOUNSBERY, insurance company executive; b. N.Y.C., Nov. 1, 1943; s. Robert Spaulding and Kathryn Eleanor (Lounsbery) H.; m. Marsha Kayser, May 27, 1966 (div. 1980); children: Michael, Daniel; m. Martha Deborah Wolfgang, Jan. 16, 1983. BA, Yale U., 1964. CLU, ChFC. Mem. actuarial program MONY, N.Y.C., 1964-68, dir. group systems, 1969, asst. v.p., 1970-73; v.p., actuary Blue Cross and Blue Shield of Greater N.Y., N.Y.C., 1973-77, sr. v.p., 1977-83; ptnr. Kwasha Lipton, Fort Lee, N.J., 1983-87; exec. v.p., CFO Guardian Life Ins. Co. Am., N.Y.C., 1987—; bd. dirs. Guardian Investors Svcs. Corp., N.Y. Guardian Ins. & Annuity Co.; pres. bd dirs. 300 CPW Corp., 1995-98; pres. bd. dirs., Fam. Svcs. Life Ins. Co. (Guardian sub.), 1998—; pres., bd. dirs. Park Ave. Life (Guardian sub.), Vis. Nurse Svc. of N.Y. Bd. dirs. 14th St. Bus. Improvement Dist., N.Y.C., 1992-99, pres., 1995-99; bd. dirs. 14th St.-Union Sq. Local Devel. Corp., 1993-99, Partnership for the Homeless, 1999—, Children's Orch. Soc., 1999—. With U.S. Army N.G., 1965-70. Fellow Soc. Actuaries; mem. Am. Acad. Actuaries, Actuarial Soc. Greater N.Y. (pres. 1992-93). Democrat. Protestant. Avocations: photography, music, travel. Home: 300 Central Park W Apt 14B New York NY 10024-1513 Office: The Guardian 7 Hanover Square New York NY 10004

HUTCHINS, CARLEEN MALEY, acoustical engineer, violin maker, consultant; b. Sprinfield, Mass., May 24, 1911; d. Thomas W. and Grace (Fletcher) Maley; m. Morton A. Hutchins, June 6, 1943; children: William Aldrich, Caroline. AB, Cornell U., 1933; MA, NYU, 1942; DEng (hon.), Stevens Inst. Tech., 1977; DFA (hon.), Hamilton Coll., 1984; DSc (hon.), St. Andrews Presbyn. Coll., 1988; LLD (hon.), Concordia U., Montreal, Que., Can., 1992. Tchr. sci. Woodward Sch., Bklyn., 1934-38, Brearley Sch., N.Y.C., 1938-49; asst. dir., asst. prin. All Day Neighborhood Schs., N.Y.C., 1943-45; sci. cons. Coward McCann, Inc., 1956-65, Girl Scouts Am., 1967-65, Nat. REcreation Assn., 1957-65; permanent sec. Catgut Acoustical Soc., Montclair, N.J., 1962—. Author: Life's Key, DNA, 1961, Moon Moth, 1965, Who Will Drown the Sound, 1972; author (with others): Science Through Recreation, 1964; contbr. violin acoustics sect. Grove's Dictionary of Music and Musicians, 1964, 96; editor: (2 vols.) Musical Acoustics, Pat I, Violin Family Components, 1975, Musical Acoustics, Part II, Violin Family Functions, 1976, The Physics of Music, 1978, Research Papers in Violin Acoustics, 1973-94, 96; contbr. articles to profl. jours. in Sci. Am. Jour. of the Acoustical Soc. Am., Jour. Audio Engrng. Soc., Physics Today, Am. Viola Soc., Catgut Acoustical Soc. Martha Baird Rockefeller Fund for Music grantee, 1966, 68, 74; Guggenheim fellow, 1959, 61; recipient several spl. citations in music, Carleen Maley Hutchins medal (1st recipient) Catgut Acoustical Soc.; grantee Nat. Sci. Found., 1971, 74, Hon. Fellowship award Acoustical Soc. Am., 1988. Fellow AAAS (electorate nominating com. 1974-76, Outstanding Performance in the Scis. award 1994), Audio Engrng. Soc. (life), Acoustical Soc. Am. (emeritus, membership com. 1980-86, exec. coun. 1984-87, medal and awards com. 1987-89, nominating com. 1987-88, Silver Acoustics Medal 1981, tech. com. music acoustics 1964—, chmn. pres.'s ad hoc com. 1987-88, archives com. 1988—, mem. com. on women 1989-97); mem. So. Calif. Violin Makers Assn. (hon.), Viola da Gambda Soc. Am. (hon.), Scandinavian Violin Makers Assn. (hon.), N.Y. Viola Soc., Guild Am. Luthiers, Am. Viola Soc., Violoncello Soc., Amateur Chamber Music Players Assn., Am. Philos. Soc. (award violin acoustics 1968, 81), Mich. Violin Makers Assn., Materials Rsch. Soc., Three O'Clock Club, Dot and Cirle, others, Sigma Xi, Pi Lambda Theta, Alpha Xi Delta. Home and Office: Catgut Acoustical Soc Inc 112 Essex Ave Montclair NJ 07042-4121

HUTCHINS, CYNTHIA BARNES, special education educator; b. Macon, Ga., Apr. 29, 1954; d. Robert O. and Emily Ann (Coody) Barnes; m. Joe Thrash Hutchins, June 15, 1975; children: Joey, Jason. BS in Edn., U. Ga., 1976, MEd, 1981; EdS, Brenau U., 1996. Cert. tchr., Ga. Tchr. Bethlehem (Ga.) Elem. Sch., 1976-78, Winder (Ga.) Elem. Sch., 1983-85, Auburn (Ga.) Elem. Sch., 1985-92; tchr., staffing coord. Bramlett Elem. Sch., Auburn, 1992—; mem. spl. edn. adv. com., mem. inclusion task force, mentor tchr., tchr. support specialist Barrow County, 1990—. Sunday sch. tchr. Midway Meth. Ch., Carl, Ga., 1975-80, 90-93; leader Boy Scouts Am., Barrow County, 1986-90; active PTO. Named Tchr. of Yr., Auburn Elem. Sch., 1986, Tchr. of Yr. Bramlett Elem., 1998, Barrow Co. Tchr. of Yr., 1998. Mem. ASCD, Coun. for Exceptional Children, Alpha Delta Kappa, Phi Delta Kappa. Avocations: crafts, reading, white water rafting, traveling. Home: 1165 Bankhead Hwy Winder GA 30680-3431

HUTCHINS, EDITH ELIZABETH, payroll administrator; b. Prince Frederick, Md., July 14, 1966; d. Aaron Ray and Alma Marie (Phillips) H.; 1 child, Jonathan Alexander Sawyer. BS in Acctg. summa cum laude, Hampton (Va.) U., 1988; postgrad., Am. U., 1997—. CPA, Md. Staff acct. Deloitte & Touche, Morristown, N.J., 1988-89; account exec. KEZB Radio, El Paso, Tex., 1990; cost acct. Helen of Troy, El Paso, 1990; fin. cons., Prince Frederick, 1993—; tax preparer, Lexington Pk., Md., 1993—; writer, prodr. radio commls., 1990. Vol. NAACP, Calvert County, 1996. Mem. AICPA, Md. Assn. CPAs, Alpha Kappa Alpha. Democrat. Avocations: missionary work, acting, promotional modeling, tennis, travel. Home: 650 Gunsmoke Cir Lusby MD 20657-3148

HUTCHINS, FRANK MCALLISTER, advertising executive; b. Rochester, N.Y., July 7, 1922; s. Francis Irving and Barbara Woodward (Arnold) H.; m. Jeanne Mathilda Bahn, Aug. 24, 1945; children: Katharine Arnold, Virginia Ann, Patricia Arms, Constance Anne. A.B., Dartmouth Coll., 1947, M.B.A., 1948. Editor-in-chief Dartmouth Yearbook, 1943; bus. mgr. Dartmouth Daily Newspaper, 1947-48; account exec. Hutchins Advt. Co., Inc., Rochester, 1948-50; v.p., gen. mgr. Hutchins Advt. Co., Inc., 1950, pres., treas., from 1951, chmn. bd., chief exec. officer, until 1971; chmn. exec. com. Hutchins/Darcy, Inc., 1971-75, chmn. bd., chief exec. officer, 1976-77; chmn., chief exec. officer Hutchins/Young & Rubicam Inc., Rochester, 1978-82, chmn., 1983-89; trustee Vista Family of Funds, N.Y.C., 1982-94. Bd. dirs. United Way, Rochester, pres., 1974-75; bd. dirs. YMCA, Rochester, pres., 1969-71; trustee, mem. exec. com. Rochester Inst. Tech., 1968—, chmn. bd., 1981-84; trustee, mem. exec. com. Internat. Mus. Photography, 1975—; trustee, mem. exec. com., chmn. devel. com. Paul Smith's Coll. Arts & Scis., 1989—, vice chmn. of bd., 1995—; trustee Adirondack Pk. Inst., 1989—, pres., 1989-93, v.p. devel., 1993—; mem. alumni coun. Dartmouth Coll., 1969-72. With OSS, AUS, 1943-45; as 2d lt. inf., 1945-46. Mem. Rochester C. of C. (trustee 1970—, pres. 1978), Rochester Advt. Coun. (chmn. bd. 1957, bd. dirs.), Greater Rochester Visitors Assn. (chmn. bd. 1989-91, exec. com., bd. dirs. 1965—), Rochester Jr. C. of C. (pres. 1952-53), Am. Assn. Advt. Agys. (sec.-treas. 1972-73), Dartmouth Club (pres. Rochester chpt. 1951-52), Country Club of Rochester (pres. 1960-61, bd. stewards 1973-76), Genesee Valley Club, Theta Delta Chi. Episcopalian (vestryman, sr. warden St. Paul's Episcopal Ch., Rochester). Home: 75 Indian Spring Ln Rochester NY 14618-2527 Office: Hutchins/DAC 400 Midtown Tower Rochester NY 14604-2001

HUTCHINS, GEORGIA CAMERON, critical care nurse, nursing educator; b. Detroit, Jan. 21, 1957; d. Jessie Cameron and Letha A. (Minor) Taylor; m. Joseph Hutchins, Aug. 28, 1976; children: Justin C., Jason E., Jarron E. BSN, Alcorn State U., 1990; MSN, Univ. Med. Ctr., Jackson, Miss., 1996; student, Alcorn State U., 1999—. CPR instr.; cert. electronic fetal monitoring. Asst. prof. nursing Alcorn State U., 1997—. Mem. NSNA, Eliza Pillars State RNs Assn. Home: 10 Upper Kingston Rd Natchez MS 39120-9704

HUTCHINS, J. MARK, university administrator; b. Monticello, Ark., Jan. 19, 1966; s. Albert Curtis and Judith Jan (Halbert) H.; m. Elizabeth McCabe Lipscomb, Nov. 24, 1990; children: Jan Kathryn, Claudia. BGS, La. Tech. U., 1989, MA, 1990. Cert. fund-raising exec. Acad. fund coord. La. Tech. Devel. Office, Ruston, 1989-90; phonathon coord. U. Tex., Austin, 1990-91; asst. to the dean for devel. U. Tex. Coll. of Bus., Austin, 1991-93; dir. annual giving Miss. State U., 1993-98; v.p. instnl. advancement Wood Coll., Mathiston, Miss., 1998—. Vol. Starkville (Miss.) Pub. Schs. bond issue, 1996. Named Outstanding Young Man in Am., 1996. Mem. Nat. Soc. of Fund Raising Execs., Coun. for Advancement and Support of Edn., Pub. Rels. Assn. of Miss. (v.p. 1994-98), So. Pub. Rels. Fedn. Methodist. Home: 503 Spruce Ln Starkville MS 39759-2743 Office: Wood Coll Instnl Advancement PO Box 289 Mathiston MS 39752-0289

HUTCHINS, JAMES LEIGH, quality assurance professional; b. Bangor, Maine, Aug. 11, 1950; s. Elbridge Leland and Harret Alice (Johnson) H.; m. Dolores Jean Sweezey; children: Sandra Kay, Alice Elizabeth. BS in Electronics Tech., Chapman Coll., Orange, Calif., 1981. Quality assurance engr. McDonnell Douglas Astronautics, Monrovia, Calif., 1983-84; sr. quality assurance engr. Comarco Weapons Sys. Divsn., Ridgecrest, Calif., 1985-86, Endevco, San Juan Capistrano, Calif., 1986; sr. reliability engr. Los Alamos Tech. Assocs., Albuquerque, 1986-88; software product assurance specialist Northrop-Grumman, Palmdale, Calif., 1988-97; cons. Northrop-Grumman, Palmdale, 1997-98; mem. tech. staff, S/W quality Boeing, Anaheim, Calif., 1998—. Vice chair L.A. Dem. Ctrl. Com., Region 1, 1994-95; 36th Assembly Dist. coord., Calif. Dem. Party, 1993. Sgt. USMC, 1969-78. Named Man of Yr. 36th Assembly Dist. L.A. County Dem. Ctrl. Com., 1993. Mem. Am. Soc. Quality Control, Elks, Masons, Shriners. Democrat. Avocations: writing poetry, politics. Home: 25605 River Bank Dr # E Yorba Linda CA 92887

HUTCHINS, JOAN MORTHLAND, manufacturing executive, farmer; b. Pasadena, Calif., Aug. 8, 1940; d. Andrew and Constance Amelia (Gordon-Grant) Morthland; children: Andrew Bush, Georgia Bush, Alan Hutchins, Paul Hutchins. AB, Radcliffe Coll., 1961; hon. degree, Royal Coll. Music, London, 1979; AAS, SUNY, Farmingdale, 1985. Jr. mathematician Shell Devel. Co. (Shell Oil), Emeryville, Calif., 1961-63; mathematician Corp. for Econ. and Indsl. Rsch., London, 1964-65; mgmt. cons. McKinsey & Co., N.Y.C., 1965-67; v.p. devel. Compotite Corp., L.A., 1985-87, pres., 1987-89, pres., CEO, 1989—; pres., CEO MBH Farms, Inc., Elizaville, N.Y., 1986—. Editor McKinsey & Co. Mgmt. Scis. News Bull., 1965-67; contbr. articles to profl. jours. Mem. bd. overseers Harvard U., Cambridge, Mass., 1994—, pres., 1999—, mem. overseers vis. com. Harvard athletic dept., 1986-91, mem. overseers vis. com. Arnold Arboretum, 1995—, chmn., 1997—, mem. overseers vis. com. Harvard Grad. Sch. Edn., 1995—; bd. dirs., v.p. Royal Music Found., N.Y.C., 1978-90; trustee Bowdoin Coll. Summer Music Festival, Brunswick, Maine, 1978-88, L.I. Biol. Assn., Cold Spring Harbor, N.Y., 1986-88. Mem. Am. Nat. Stds. Inst. (nat. waterproofing stds. com. 1988—), Harvard U. Alumni Assn. (bd. dirs. 1990-93), Harvard-Radcliffe Club L.I. (pres. 1988-90). Avocations: skiing, music, sports, ice hockey, travel. Home: 8 Seawanhaka Pl Oyster Bay NY 11771-1629 Office: Compotite Corp 355 Glendale Blvd Los Angeles CA 90026-5032

HUTCHINS, MARY LOUISE, library director; b. Saginaw, Mich., Feb. 8, 1936; d. Herman Martin and Margaret May Janssen; m. Richard Gilbert Hutchins, July 6, 1963; children: Linda Leeanne Hutchins-Knowles, Sharon Suzanne. BA, U. Mich., 1958, MA in Libr. Sci., 1961. Cmty. libr. Willard Libr., Battle Creek, Mich., 1961-63; readers' adv. libr. Flint (Mich.) Pub. Libr., 1964-66; vis. instr. Sch. Libr. Sci. U. Iowa, Iowa City, 1974-75; adminstrv. asst. to libr. dir. U. Miami Sch. Law, Coral Gables, Fla., 1976-80; head reference dept. Verona (N.J.) Pub. Libr., 1981-86; cons. for inter-libr. loan and reference No. Ill. Libr. Sys., Rockford, 1986-88; dir. Bement Pub. Libr., St. Johns, Mich., 1988-94, Branch Dist. Libr., Coldwater, Mich., 1994—; chair Libr. Adv. Coun., Albion, Mich., 1996—. Active Branch County Econ. Growth Alliance, Coldwater, 1995, 96, Work Group on Teen Suicide, Coldwater, 1998. Recipient Celebrating Literacy award Clinton Reading Coun., Clinton County, Mich., 1990. Mem. ALA, Mich. Libr. Assn. (sec. pub. policy com. 1990-94, Leadership Acad. grad. 1993), Coldwater/Branch County C. of C. Quaker. Avocations: peace and civil rights activities, classical music, swimming. E-mail: hutchinsmj@cbpu.com. Fax: 517-279-7134. Home: 601 River Rd Coldwater MI 49036 Office: Branch Dist Libr 10 E Chicago Coldwater MI 49036

HUTCHINS, ROBERT AYER, architectural consultant; b. N.Y.C., Oct. 19, 1940; s. Robert Senger and Evelyn Reed (Brooks) H.; m. Saran Niel Morgan, Jan. 4, 1964; children: Amey, Elisabeth, Margaret. BA, Harvard U., 1962, MArch., 1965; MDiv, McCormick Theol. Sem., 1992. Registered architect. Skidmore, Owings & Merrill, Chgo., 1966-89, ptnr., 1980-89. Pres., Chgo. Architecture Found., 1983-86, v.p., 1986-89; v.p., bd. dirs. Lincoln Park Zool. Soc., Chgo., 1976-91; bd. govs. Met. Planning Coun., Chgo., 1977—; bd. trustees McCormick Theological Sem., 1990-91. Mem. AIA (corp.), Chgo. Cultural Affairs Adv. Bd. (vice chmn. 1984-90), Chgo. Presbytery Svc. Corps., 1995—.

HUTCHINS, WILLIAM BRUCE, III, utility company executive; b. Tuscaloosa, Ala., Jan. 28, 1943; s. William B. Jr. and Mildred Louise (Lemley) H.; m. Priscilla Nichols, Oct. 30, 1965; children: Frances, Christopher. BS in Acctg., U. Ala., 1966, MBA, 1978; postgrad., Harvard U., 1987. Cert. mgmt. acct. Jr. acct. Ala. Power Co., Birmingham, 1966-67, So. Co. Services, Inc., Atlanta, 1971-72; sr. acct. Ala. Power Co., Birmingham, 1972-74, asst. to comptroller, 1974-75, asst. to exec. v.p., 1975-76, mgr. fin. and rev. planning, 1976-80, gen. mgr. fin. planning, 1980-81, asst. treas., 1981-83, v.p., treas., 1983-91, sr. v.p., chief fin. officer, 1991-94, exec. v.p., CFO, 1994—. Served to capt. USAF, 1967-71. Mem. Fin. Execs. Inst., Nat. Assn. Accts., Nat. Mgmt. Assn., Beta Gamma Sigma, Beta Alpha Psi, Omicron Delta Epsilon. Office: Ala Power Co PO Box 2641 Birmingham AL 35291-0001

HUTCHINSON, ANN, development director; b. East Stroudsburg, Pa., May 15, 1950; d. David Ellis and Susie (Ingalls) H.; m. Paul Harrison McAllister, Jan. 2, 1986. BS in Vocat. Edn., Fla. Internat. U., 1985; MBA, Pepperdine U., 1990. Cert. advanced vocat. tchr., Fla.; cert. cmty. coll. educator, Ariz.; cert. pub. mgr. Motorcycle technician Ft. Lauderdale, Fla., 1973-78; machinist Ft. Lauderdale, 1978-79; instr., motorcycle tech. Sheridan Vocat. Tech. Sch., Hollywood, Fla., 1979-85; adminstr., tng. program Am. Honda Motorcycle Divsn., Torrance, Calif., 1985-86, curriculum developer motorcycles svc. tech., 1986-90, coll. program coord., 1990-94; edni. devel. dir. Clinton Tech. Inst., Phoenix, 1994-96; dep. mgr. tng. unit Ariz. State Dept. Econ. Security, Phoenix, 1996—; chmn. high tech. acad. steering coms. Pasadena (Calif.) United Sch. Dist., 1991-94; ednl. cons. Ctr. for Occupation R & D Sch.-to-Work Awards, 1994-97. Examiner for Gov.'s Award for Excellence, 1997-98; mem. Ams. with disabilities act com. Ariz. Dept. Econ. Security, 1995—; mem. Desert Hill Improvement Assn., 1996—, bd. dirs., 1998—; examiner Ariz. State Quality awards, 1997-98. Recipient State of Ky. Colonel award, 1990. Mem. Cert. Pub. Mgr. Assn. (cert.), Am. Motorcycle Assn., Am. Vocat. Assn., ASTD, Vocat. Indsl. Clubs Am. (co-chmn. motorcycle tech. com. 1988-90, 94—, automotive nat. tech. com. 1990-94, adv. Hollywood, Fla. 1979-85), Toastmasters Internat. (Zenger Miller cert. 1996—). Avocations: hiking, camping, st. motorcycle riding. Office: Ariz Dept Econ Security Office Orgn and Mgmt Devel 1140 E Washington St Rm 206 Phoenix AZ 85034-1051

HUTCHINSON, ASA, congressman; b. Benton County, Ark., Dec. 3, 1950; m. Susan Burrell; children: Asa III, Sarah, John, Seth. BS in Acctg., Bob Jones U.; JD, U. Ark. Atty. U.S. Dist. Ct. (we. dist.) Ark., 1982-85; ptnr. Karr & Hutchinson, Fort Smith, Ark., 1986-96; rep. Ark. 3rd dist. U.S. House of Reps., 1996—; mem. judiciary com. U.S. Congress, subcom. crime, subcom. constitution, transp. and infrastructure com., subcom. Water Resources and Environment, subcom. aviation, Govt. Reform, subcom. Criminial Justice, Drug Policy and Human Resources; co-chair Freshmen Bipartisan Campaign Finance Reform Task Force; apptd. to Speakers Task Force for Drug-Free Am.; co-chmn., chmn. Rep. Ctrl. Com. of Ark., 1990-95; past mem. Ark. Jud. Ethics Commn., Ark. Election Commn., Ark. Election Law Revision Commn.; condr. democracy workshops in Russia, 1994; del. White House Conf. on Aging, 1995; past bd. mem. Western Ark. chpt. Alzheimer's Assn. Named One of Ten Outstanding Young Leaders in Ark., Ark. Jaycees, 1986. E-mail: Asa.Hutchinson@mail.house.gov. Office: 1535 Longworth House Office Bldg Washington DC 20515

HUTCHINSON, BARBARA WINTER, middle school educator; b. Pitts., Dec. 20, 1952; d. Raymond Francis and Dorothy (Kunkel) Winter; m. Matthew Hutchinson, June 8, 1973; children: Matthew Martin, Jennifer Elizabeth. BA, Westminster Coll., 1974. Cert. tchr., Pa. Tchr. Shaler Area Sch. Dist., Glenshaw, Pa., 1975-84; tchr. North Allegheny Sch. Dist., Pitts., 1984—, staff devel. leader, 1991—; mem. dist. adv. coun., profl. issues com. North Allegheny Sch. Dist., Pitts., 1993—, mem. instrnl. responsibility com., 1996—, total quality in edn. process com., 1996—, quality improvement team, 1996-97; presenter coop. learning workshops. Author: Primary Assistance, 1979, History of the Avonworth School District, 1990; co-author curriculum materials. Mem. Cmty. Presbyn. Ch. Ben Avon, Pa., 1976—; pres., program dir. Ben Avon Area Hist. Assn., 1988—; bd. dirs., sec., program chair Avon Club Found., 1990-93; mem. Ben Avon Centennial Com., 1990-93; co-leader local troop Girl Scouts U.S., 1991-92; bd. dirs. Sacred Heart Sch., Pitts., 1991-92. Recipient Found. Excellence award, 1996, Citation for Tchg. Excellence, Pa. Ho. of Reps. Mem. Am. Fedn. Tchrs., North Allegheny Fedn. Tchrs. (mem. exec. coun. 1992-96, treas. 1996-98, secondary v.p. 1998-99, 1st v.p. 1999—), Pa. Fedn. Tchrs., Kappa Delta Pi. Avocations: sewing, wood refinishing, reading, writing, home decorating. Home: PO Box 93 105 Dogwood Ln Connoquenessing PA 16027 Office: Marshall Middle Sch 5145 Wexford Run Rd Wexford PA 15090-7458

HUTCHINSON, BERNARD THOMAS, ophthalmologist; b. Flatwoods, W.Va., Jan. 13, 1934; s. Bernard Mearns and Helen Louise (Buseman) H.; m. B. June Greene, Aug. 17, 1956; 1 child, Daniel. AB, W.Va. U., 1955, BS, 1956; MD, Harvard U., 1958. Diplomate Am. Bd. Ophthalmology (bd. dirs. 1988—, chmn. 1995), Nat. Bd. Med. Examiners. Intern Pa. Hosp., Phila., 1958-59; ophthalmic fellow Howe Lab. of Ophthalmology Harvard Med. Sch., Boston, 1961-63; resident in ophthalmology Mass. Eye and Ear Infirmary, Boston, 1963-65, fellow in glaucoma, 1965-66; from asst. to assoc. prof. ophthalmology Harvard Med. Sch., Boston, 1965—; asst. clin. prof. Boston U., 1965-67; surgeon in ophthalmology Mass. Eye and Ear Infirmary, 1978—, assoc. chief of ophthalmology, 1985-90; cons. staff Mass. Gen. Hosp., 1965—; vis. prof. Pa. State Med. Ctr., 1977, U. Mich., 1977, W.Va. U., 1978, Med. Coll. Wis., 1978, Duke U., 1979, Wills Eye Hosp., 1979, 87, Med. Coll. Wis., 1980, U. Oreg., 1988, U. So. Calif., 1991, U. South Fla., 1989—, U. Fla., 1990, Emory U., 1991, W.Va. Sch. Medicine, 1992, Cleve. Clinic, 1993, Wills Eye Hosp., 1994, Govt. Ophthalmic Coll. in Madras, India, 1981, U. Fla., 1982, W.Va. U. Sch. Medicine, 1982, Pacific Presbyn. Med. Ctr., 1987; mem. Ea. Mass. PSRO; bd. dirs. Opthalmic Mutual Ins. Co.. Mem. editorial bd. AMA Archives of Ophthalmology, 1966-76, The Harvard Med. Sch. Health Letter, 1976—, Ophthalmology Alert, 1981-84; contbr. articles to profl. jours. Recipient Appleton Croft award W.Va. U. Sch. Medicine, 1956, Man of Vision award Nat. Soc. to Present Blindness, 1984, Lucien Howe medal, 1991. Fellow ACS; mem. AMA, Am. Acad. Ophthalmology (sec. for ophthalmic practice 1988—, pres.- elect 1992, pres., 1993, past pres. 1994, chmn. nat. eye care project 1981-91, 94, v.p. pub. svc. Fedn. 1994, hon. award 1982, sr. honor award 1992, Lucien Howe medal 1991, honor guest 1996), Suffolk County Med. Soc., Mass. Med. Soc. (chmn. ophthalmology sect. 1977-78), New Eng. Ophthalmol. Soc. (profl. svc. rev. com. 1973-77, chmn. program com. 1981-83, v.p. 1993, pres. 1996-97), Mass. Soc. Eye Physicians and Surgeons (exec. com. 1969—, treas. 1969-74, pres. 1978-79, councillor 1981-84), Assn. for Rsch. in Ophthalmology), Eye Study Club. Home: 59 Chestnut St Boston MA 02108-3508 Office: Ophthalmic Cons Boston 50 Staniford St Ste 600 Boston MA 02114-2587

HUTCHINSON, CHARLES EDGAR, engineering educator; b. Parkersburg, W.Va., Dec. 18, 1935; s. Charles Edgar and Elizabeth Hana (Eggleton) H.; m. Elva Anneta Butland, Aug. 20, 1960; children: Charles Edgar IV, John Mathew. BEE, Ill. Inst. Tech., 1957; MEE, Stanford U., 1961, PhD, 1963. Instr. USN ROTC, 1959-60; tchg. asst. Stanford (Calif.) U., 1960-63; lectr. UCLA, 1963-65; assoc. prof. U. Mass., Amherst, 1965-69, prof., 1969-84, acting assoc. dean acad. affairs, 1977, acting assoc. dean research affairs, 1977-78, head dept. electrical and computer engring., 1978-82; prof., dean Thayer Sch. Engring. Dartmouth Coll., Hanover, N.H., 1984-94, 97-98, John H. Krehbiel Sr. prof. for emerging technologies, 1994—; lectr. Sch. Medicine, Boston U., 1971-72; cons. The Analytic Scis. Corp., Reading, Mass., 1967-98, MacLean Fogg Co., 1988—, Molex, Inc., 1988—, Baxter Health, 1992—, Tally Sys., Inc., 1997—; bd. dirs. Markem Corp., Keene, N.H., Speciality Equipment Cos., Belvidere, Ill., Hypertherm, Inc., Hanover, N.H., Med. Media Techs., Inc., Lebanon, N.H. Lt. USN, 1957-60. Mem. IEEE (chmn. edn. com. 1983-86, bd. govs. profl. group on aerospace and electronic systems 1983-86, profl. groups on automatic control and on computers), Am. Soc. Engring. Edn. (chmn. computers in edn. div. 1975-77, New Eng. sect. 1965—), Assn. for Media-Based Edn. for Engrs. (vice chmn. 1983, bd. dirs. 1980-84), Sigma Xi, Eta Kappa Nu (nat. bd. dirs. 1966-69, chmn. nat. publicity com. 1968-73, faculty advisor 1966-68, 74-76), Tau Beta Pi (profl. 1967). Republican. Avocations: horse showing, horse breeding. Home: Apple Blossom Ln Canaan NH 03741 Office: Dartmouth Coll Thayer Sch Engring Hanover NH 03755

HUTCHINSON, CHARLES SMITH, JR., book publisher; b. Topeka, Oct. 17, 1930; s. Charles S. and Cecil Marguerite (Weidenhamer) H.; m. Elizabeth Dunbar Hall, June 16, 1956; children: Amy Elizabeth, Todd Charles. BA, Principia Coll., 1952. Editor-in-chief, sec., dir. Burgess Pub. Co., Mpls., 1955-65; editor-in-chief coll. and profl. books, dir. Reinhold Book Corp., N.Y.C., 1965-68; editor-in-chief profl. and reference books Van Nostrand Reinhold Co., N.Y.C., 1968-70; pres., chmn. bd. dirs. Dowden, Hutchinson and Ross, Inc., Stroudsburg, Pa., 1970-78, v.p., sec., 1978-80; v.p. Hutchinson Ross Pub. Co., Stroudsburg, 1980-83; sci. pub. Van Nostrand Reinhold Co., N.Y.C., 1984-86; mng. dir. Hutchinson Assocs., Prescott, Ariz., 1987-91; pres. Geosci. Press, Inc., Tucson, 1989—, Harbinger House, Inc., Tucson, 1992-94; mng. ptnr. Picacho Peak Press, L.L.C., Tucson, 1994—. Bd. dirs. Hist. Farms Assn., Stroudsburg, 1980-86, pres., 1985-86; treas. Stroudsburg chpt. Kiwanis, 1977-78, v.p., 1978-80, pres., 1980-81. Recipient NuJay award Mpls. Jaycees, 1957, Disting. Pres. award Kiwanis, 1981. Fellow Geol. Soc. Am.; mem. Rocky Mountain Books Pubs. Assn. Home: 5520 N Camino Arenosa Tucson AZ 85718-5416

HUTCHINSON, DAVID MICHAEL, economist; b. Washington, Feb. 11, 1944; s. Edmond Carlton Hutchinson; m. Helen Kwok-Wai Ho, Jan. 30, 1988; children: Michael Breton, Elena Michelle. BA in Econ., Southwestern U., 1964; postgrad, Fgn Svc. Sch. Econ., 1974-75; MA in Econ., George Washington U., 1979. Sys. analyst Brown Engring. Co., Huntsville, Ala., 1964-65; internat. economist Office East West Trade U.S. Dept. State, Washington, 1967-69, program officer Office Export Adminstrn., 1970-77; dep. dir. Market Expansion Divsn. Office Textiles & Apparel U.S. Dept. Commerce, Washington, 1980-88, spl. asst. to dep. asst. sec. extiles Apparel Consumer Goods, 1988-95, acting dep. asst. sec. Textiles Apparel Consumer Goods, 1995, dir. Office Textiles Apparel, 1995—. With USAR, 1966-72. Avocations: computers, piano, guitar, squash, reading. Home: 9100 Town Gate Lane Bethesda MD 20817

HUTCHINSON, DONALD WILSON, state commissioner of financial institutions; b. Seattle, Dec. 29, 1936. BS in Bus. and Edn., Mont. State U., 1960; Grad. Degree in Banking, Pacific Coast Banking Sch., Seattle, 1979. With First Nat. Bank, Bozeman, Mont., 1963-69, Owatonna, Minn., 1969-71; with First Security Bank, Livingston, Mont., 1971-82; v.p. Bank of Sheridan, Mont., 1983-84; gen. mgr., cons. Pryor Creek Devel. Co., Billings, Mont., 1984-85; chief lending officer Valley Bank of Belgrade, Mont., 1986-90; commr. State of Mont. Divsn. Banking and Fin. Instns., Helena, 1990—. Dir. Livingston (Mont.) Meml. Hosp., Livingston Alcohol & Drug Abuse Ctr., Gallatin County (Mont.) Big Bros. and Big Sisters; mem. Belgrade City/County Planning Bd.; treas., bd. trustees, Paul Clark Home/ McDonald's Family Place, Butte, Mont. Mem. Livingston Rotary Club (past pres.). Office: Divsn Banking & Fin Instns PO Box 200546 Helena MT 59620-0546*

HUTCHINSON, JANET LOIS, historical society administrator; b. Washington, May 2, 1917; d. Lewis Orrin and Gertrude Elizabeth Hutchinson; divorced; 1 child, Jefferson Troy Siebert. Grad., So. Sem. and Jr. Coll., Buena Vista, Va., 1936; student, N.Y. Sch. Expression, 1923-30, Christine Dobbins Sch. Dance; studied with, Maude Adams, Clare Tree Major, 1934-35. Owner Broadlawn Inn Art Gallery, Camden, Maine, 1955-64; dir. Old Merchants House Mus., N.Y.C., 1962-63, Hist. Soc. Martin County, Stuart, Fla., 1965-91, Elliott Mus., Stuart, 1965-91; dir. House of Refuge Mus., Stuart, 1965-91, dir. emeritus, 1991—; pres., editl. cons. Hutchinson/Paige, Stuart, 1991—. Author: Tiny Timid's Christmas Wish, 1953, The History of Martin County, 1975; host: (TV interview show) Chronicle. Active Nat. Hist. Preservation Soc., Nat. History Soc., Fla. History Soc.; bd. dirs. Pioneer Occupationa Ctr. for Handicapped, St. Michael's Pvt. Sch.; adv. bd. St. Joseph's Coll. and Fla. Inst. of Tech. Named Woman of Yr., AAUW, 1975. Mem. DAR (Halpatiokee chpt.), Antique Car Assn., Smithsonian Instn., Nat. Soc. Lit. and Arts, Nat. Pen Women (hon. mem.), Salmaqundi Club, Nat. Arts Club. Home: 1023 NW Spruce Ridge Dr Stuart FL 34994-9513

HUTCHINSON, JOHN WOODSIDE, applied mechanics educator, consultant; b. Hartford, Conn., Apr. 10, 1939; s. John Woodside and Evelyn (Eastburn) H.; m. Lizzi Spanggaard; children: Leif, David, Robert. B.S., Lehigh U., 1960; M.S., Harvard U., 1961, Ph.D., 1963; D.Sc. (hon.), Royal Inst. Tech., Stockholm, 1985, Tech. U. Denmark, Lyngby, 1992. Asst. prof. Harvard U., Cambridge, Mass., 1964-69, Gordon McKay prof. applied mechanics, 1969—. Contbr. articles to profl. jours. Guggenheim Found. fellow, 1974. Fellow ASME (Arpard L. Nadai award 1991); mem. AAAS, ASTM (Irwin medal 1982), NAE,, NAS.

HUTCHINSON, JOSEPH CANDLER, retired foreign language educator; b. Hazelhurst, Ga., Jan. 10, 1920; s. George Washington and Lillie Arizona (Rowan) H.; m. June Cruce O'Shields, Aug. 12, 1950 (div. 1980); children: Junie O'Shields, Joseph Candler. *Education was a priority in his family. Father, Reverend George W. Hutchinson (Emory, BA 1908, MA 1925), was a pioneer in religious education for the Florida Methodist Conference. Mother, Lillie Rowan H. (Wesleyan, BA 1909, Emory, MA 1925), was also a pioneer in religious education. They were the first couple to receive an MA together at Emory. Sister, Novelle Lane (Florida Southern College, BA 1932, Wesleyan Conservatory, BM 1933, graduate work at Scaritt and Julliard), was an accomplished concert pianist. Brother, J. Glenn Hutchinson (Emory, BA 1939, UNC, MA 1939, U. Chicago, PhD 1973) was a professor of Sociology and a pacifist and civil rights advocate.* BA, Emory U., 1940, MA, 1941; PhD, U. N.C., 1950; postgrad., U. Paris, 1951,53. Tchr. Tech. High Sch., Atlanta, 1941-42; instr. French, German, Italian Emory U., Atlanta, 1946-47; instr. U. N.C., Chapel Hill, 1947-50, asst. prof., 1954, assoc. prof., 1954-57; asst. prof. Sweet Briar (Va.) Coll., 1950-51; assoc. prof. Tulane U., New Orleans, 1957-59; fgn. lang. splst. U.S. Office Edn., Washington, 1959-64; acad. adv. hqrs. Def. Lang. Inst., Washington, 1964-74; acad. adv. hqrs. Def. Lang. Inst., Monterey, Calif., 1974-77, dir. tng. devel. Fgn. Lang. Ctr., 1977-82; asst. acad. dean Def. Lang. Inst., Monterey, 1982-85, dean of policy, 1985-88; vis. prof. U. Va., Charlottesville, 1966, Arlington, 1970, Georgetown U., 1968, Am. U., 1971; cons. Coun. Chief State Sch. Officers, 1960, U. Del., 1966, U. Colo., 1968, U. Ill., 1968; U.S. del. Bur. Internat. Lang. Coordination NATO, 1964-79, 81-82, 86-87. *Director of the Language Laboratory (U.S. Army CIC School, 1951-53, UNC, 1955-57, Tulane U. 1957-59). Authored a book, Modern Foreign Languages in High School: The Language Laboratory (1961), for U.S. Government as official teaching resource for the National Defense Education Act. Played a leading role in the development of educational technology, including professional liason and consultation with state education agencies and speaking at professional conferences. He was the principal academic policy advisor and developer for the Department of Defense's worldwide Defense Foreign Language Program. He was a guest speaker at the First International Conference on Foreign Language Education and Technology (Tokyo, 1981).* Author: Using the Language Laboratory Effectively: School Executive's Guide, 1964, The Language Laboratory: Equipment and Utilization in Trends in Language Teaching, 1966, others; editor: Dialogue on Language Instruction, 1986-88; contbr. articles to profl. jours. Served with U.S. Army spl. agent counter intelligence corps, 1942-46, 51-53. Decorated Bronze Star, 5 Battle Stars-Europe, battlefield commn. Mem. Am. Coun. Edn. (task force on internat. edn. 1973), NEA (sec. dept. fgn. langs. 1961-64), AARP/VOTE (17th congl. dist. team), Higher Edn. Assn., Monterey Peninsula, Am. Coun. Tchg. Fgn. Lang., MLA, Am. Mgmt. Assn., Am. Soc. Tng. and Devel., Nat. Assn. Ret. Fed. Employees (v.p. Monterey chpt. 1990, pres. 1991-92), Monterey Choral Soc., Camerata Singers, Washington Linguistics Club (v.p. 1970-72). Episcopalian.

HUTCHINSON, OLIN FULMER, JR., transportation executive, data processing consultant; b. Batesburg, S.C, Nov. 28, 1943; s. Olin Fulmer Sr. and Alma Marie (Rogers) H.; m. Mary Susan Edge, Mar. 18. 1972; children: Jason Fulmer, Crystal Marie. B in Commerce, U. Richmond, 1970; postgrad. in computers, Charlotte, N.C., 1975—. Corp. traffic mgr. Lea Industries, Inc., Richmond, Va., 1964-71; branch mgr. C&B Fork Lift, Inc., Lynchburg, Va., 1971-74; v.p. Fuller Transp., Inc., Columbia, S.C., 1977-78; traffic mgr. Seabrook Blanching, Sylvester, Ga., 1978-80; mgr. domestic transp. Belk Stores Svcs., Inc., Charlotte, 1980—; owner Computer Svcs., Charlotte, 1981—; speaker on hist. topics; owner, driver Hutchinson Racing Team, Richmond, 1969-72. Author various hist. books and poems; editor, compiler: My Dear Mother & Sisters (Alfred B. Mulligan), 1992. Active community affairs, Charlotte, 1980—. Mem. S.C. Hist. Soc., Dutch Fork Geneal. and Hist. Soc., Old Newberry Dist. Geneal. Soc., West Atando Bus. Assn. (v.p., treas. 1980—), SAR, SCV (1st lt. comdr. 1985-86), Mil. Order Stars and Bars, Ye Olde Mecklenburg Geneal. Soc., Sertoma (various offices). Avocations: sports, mechanics, guns. Home: 4706 Cheviot Rd Charlotte NC 28269-4559 Office: Belk Stores Svcs Inc 2801 W Tyvola Rd Charlotte NC 28217-4525

HUTCHINSON, PARK WILLIAM, JR., theatre educator; b. Lancaster, Pa., Apr. 14, 1935; s. Park William and Thelma Mae (Beam) H.; m. Patsy Ann Flory, Aug. 15, 1955 (div. May 1981); 1 child, Suzanne Flory Hutchinson; m. Jeri Ann McElroy, Sept. 18, 1982. BA, Franklin Marshall Coll., 1957; BD, Princeton Theol. Sem., 1960; MA, Columbia U., 1962; PhD, Northwestern U., 1968. Instr. Tougaloo (Miss.) Coll., 1962-64, asst. prof., 1964-65, dir. speech & theater, 1962-65; asst. prof. theatre R.I. Coll., Providence, 1968-71, assoc. prof., 1971-74, prof., 1974—, chair dept. theater and dance, 1996-98, chair dept. music theater and dance, 1998—; dir. dance & drama Mathewson St. United Meth. Ch., Providence, 1969-75; dir. R.I. Gov.'s Sch. for Youth in the Arts, Providence, 1970-72; art. dir. NewGate Theatre, Providence, 1991-92. Dir. over 75 plays and readings, 1957—. Mem. exec. bd. R.I. Festival Theatre, Providence, 1971, Coll. of Fellows, New Eng. Theatre Conf., Boston, 1987—; theatre coord. R.I. Arts in Edn. Project, Providence, 1970-72. Danforth Found. fellow, 1965-66, 67-68; grantee R.I. Com. for Humanities, 1975—, R.I. Coun. Arts, 1978—. Mem. Assn. Theatre in Higher Edn., Phi Beta Kappa. Avocations: hist. portrayals: Jefferson, Thoreau, Wilde, Poe, Darrow, etc. Home: 7 Wadsworth Ave Smithfield RI 02917-4109 Office: RI Coll 600 Mount Pleasant Ave Providence RI 02908-1924

HUTCHINSON, PETER ARTHUR, artist; b. London, Mar. 4, 1930; s. Arthur William Woodhams and Linda Mary (West) Hutchinson. BFA, U. Ill., 1960. Author art books; contbr. articles, short stories to profl. publs.; one-man shows include Galerje Isy Brachot, Brussels, 1989, John Gibson Gallery, N.Y.C., 1990, Galerie Hadrien Thomas, Paris, 1990, James Mayor Gallery, London, 1996, Galerie Damasquine, Brussels, 1997, Galerie Bugdahn und Kaimer, Düsseldorf, Germany, 1998, Kunstverein, Ulm, Germany, 1998, Holly Solomon Gallery, 1998; exhibited in group shows including Mus. Modern Art, N.Y.C., 1969, Acad. Art, Berlin, 1988, Herter Gallery, U. Mass. Traveling Exhbn., 1989, ZOE Gallery, Boston, 1990. Mem. visual arts com. Fine Arts Work Ctr., Provincetown, Mass., 1979-85, 88—. Fellow Aspen Ctr. for Arts, 1970-71, NEA, 1974, D.A.A.D., Berlin, 1988; grantee Adolph and Esther Gottlieb Found., 1987, Krasner-Pollack

Found., 1989. Mem. Am. Rock Garden Club. Avocations: botany, history, biology, horticulture. Home and Studio: 10 Holway Ave Provincetown MA 02657-1327

HUTCHINSON, RICHARD WILLIAM, geology educator, consultant; b. London, Ontario, Can., Nov. 17, 1928; s. William Henry and Ada Georgina (Armitage) H.; m. Beryl Marie Rafuse: children: Susan Janet, Leslie Ann Hutchinson Cox, Cynthia Joan Hutchinson Bennett, Carla Jean Hutchinson Ida. BS in Geology, U. Western Ont., 1950; MS in Geology, U. Wis., Madison, 1951, PhD in Geology, 1954. Project geologist Am. Metal Climax, Toronto, Can., 1954-60; staff geologist Am. Metal Climax, N.Y.C., 1960-64; assoc. prof. U. Western Ont., London, 1964-69, prof., 1969-83; Charles F. Fogarty prof. econ., geology Colo. Sch. of Mines, Golden, 1983-94, prof. emeritus, 1994—; cons. geologist Chevron Resources Co., San Francisco, 1976-85, UN Revolving Fund, N.Y.C., 1978-85, UN Devel. Program, N.Y.C., 1976-81, BHP-Utah Internat., Inc., San Francisco, 1984-90, Placer Dome Inc., 1992—, others. Fellow Geol. Assn. Can. (Duncan R. Derry Gold medal 1983), Soc. Econ. Geologists (pres. 1983, Silver medal 1985), Geol. Soc. Am. (councillor 1987-90); mem. Can. Inst. Mining and Metallurgy (Barlow Gold medal 1971, 79), Soc. Geologie Applique aux Gites Mineraux, Prospectors and Developers Assn. Can., Colo. Sci. Soc., Denver Region Exploration Geologists Soc., Geol. Soc. Republic South Africa (Jubilee medal 1990). Avocations: skiing, racquet sports, sailing. E-mail: 105532.1563@compuserve.com. Office: Colo Sch Mines Dept of Geology and Geol Engring Golden CO 80401

HUTCHINSON, THOMAS CUTHBERT, ecology and environmental educator; b. Sunderland, Eng., Feb. 18, 1939; emigrated to Can., 1967; s. Walter and Margaret Amelia (Bell) H.; s. Vivien Coyne, Sept. 8, 1961 (div. 1981); 1 dau., Sally Louise; m. Magda Havas, 1982. B.S. with honors in Botany, Manchester (Eng.) U., 1960; Ph.D. in Ecology, Sheffield (Eng.) U., 1966. Sir James Knott fellow Newcastle (Eng.) U., 1964-67; asst. prof. dept. botany Toronto U., 1967-71, assoc. prof., 1971-74, prof., 1974-90, chmn. dept., 1976-82; assoc. dir. Inst. Environ. Scis., U. Toronto, 1974-76; prof. faculty of forestry U. Toronto, 1978-90; prof., chair environ. and resource study Trent U., Petersborough, Ont., 1991-94; prof. environ. resource studies program Trent U., Petersburg, 1994—; chmn. com. environ. quality criteria NRC Can. Co-author: Environmental Consequences of Nuclear War, 1986; editor: Heavy Metals in Environment, 1977, Acid Rain Effects on Forests, Crops and Wetlands, 1987; co-editor: Acid Rain Effects on Vegetation, 1980; editor Environ. Revs., 1993—; assoc. editor Jour. Applied Ecology, Ecotoxicology, Environ. Pollution, Environ. Health; contbr. articles to profl. jours. Mem. Royal Agrl. Winter Fair Ont. Com., 1992—. Recipient Faculty Alumni award U. Toronto, 1984, Civic medal City of Toronto, 1991. Fellow Royal Soc. Can., Explorers Club (Miroslaw Romanowski medal 1998); mem. Am. Agronomy Soc., Coun. of Nat. Scis. and Engring. Rsch. (pres. 1994—), Can. Bot. Assn. (George Lawson medal 1982, Trent faculty rsch. award 1998), Am. Ecol. Soc., Brit. Ecol. Soc., Arctic Inst. N.Am., Rare Breeds Can. (bd. dirs. 1992—), Can. Cotswold Longwool Assn. (sec.-treas. 1993—). Home: RR # 2, Indian River, ON Canada K0L 7B8 Office: Trent U, Trent U Environ Resource, 1600 W Bank Dr, Peterborough, ON Canada K9J 7B8*

HUTCHINSON, TIM, senator; b. Bentonville, Ark., 1949; m. Donna King; children: Jeremy, Tim, Joshua. MA in Polit. Sci., U. Ark. Co-owner, mgr. Sta. KBCV-FM, 1982-89; mem. 94th-98th Congresses from Ark., 1984-88, 103rd Congress from 3rd Ark. dist., 1993-96; senator from Ark. U.S. Senate, 1996—; instr. history John Brown U., Siloam Springs, Ark.; mem. labor and human resource com., environment and pub. works com., vets. affairs com., rules and adminstrn. com.; mem. U.S. Senate armed svcs. com., health, edn., labor and pensions, com., vets.' affairs com., spl. subcom. on aging. Active Northwest Ark. C.C. Found. Named rep. of Yr. Ark. Fraternal Order Police, 1988, 90, Ark. Assn. of Chiefs of Police, 1990, 91. Mem. Bentonville Bella Vista C. of C., Bentonville Kiwanis Club. Republican. Baptist. Home: 309 Razorback Dr Bentonville AR 72712-6242 Office: US Senate 245 Dirksen Senate Ofc Bldg Washington DC 20510*

HUTCHISON, ANDREW SANDFORD, bishop. LTh, Trinity Coll., 1969; DD (hon.), Monteal Diocesan Theol. Coll., 1993, Trinity Coll., 1994. Ordained deacon, priest, bishop. Asst. curate Christ Ch., Toronto, 1969; rector Parish of Minden, Haliburten Highland, Ont., Can., 1970-74, St. Francis Ch., Toronto, 1974-81, St. Luke Ch. East York, Toronto, 1981-84; rector, dean Christ Ch. Cathedral, Montreal, 1984-90; bishop Diocese of Montreal, 1990-98; bishop ordinary Can. Forces, Ottawa, 1997—; pres. Montreal Diocesan Theol. Coll.; vis. Bishop's U., Lennoxville; bd. govs. Lakefield Coll., Ontario, 1994-97. Office: Montreal Diocese, 1444 Union Ave, Montreal, PQ Canada H3A 2B8

HUTCHISON, BARBARA BAILEY, singer, songwriter. Recipient Grammy award for Best Musical Album for Children "Sleepy Time Lullabyes", 1996. Office: care Dakota Records Box 33514 Nashville TN 37202*

HUTCHISON, CLYDE ALLEN, JR., chemistry educator; b. Alliance, Ohio, May 5, 1913; s. Clyde Allen and Bessie Gertrude (Bicksler) H.; m. Sarah Jane West, Dec. 29, 1937; children: Clyde Allen Hutchison III, Sarah Jane, Robert West. BA, Cedarville Coll., 1933, DSc (hon.), 1953; PhD, Ohio State U., 1937. NRC postdoctoral fellow Columbia U., N.Y.C., 1937-38, research assoc., 1938-39; research assoc. SAM Labs., N.Y.C., 1943-45; asst. prof. U. Buffalo, 1939-45; research assoc. Manhattan project U.Va., Charlottesville, 1942-43; mem. faculty U. Chgo., 1945—, asst. prof. chemistry Enrico Fermi Inst., 1945-48, asst. prof. dept. chemistry and Enrico Fermi Inst., 1948-50, assoc. prof., 1950-54, prof., 1954-63, chmn. dept. chemistry, 1959-62, Carl William Eisendrath prof., 1963-69, Carl William Eisendrath Disting. Service prof., 1969-83, Carl William Eisendrath Disting. Service prof. emeritus, 1983—; mem. adv. panel in chemistry NSF, 1960-63; bd. dirs. Ohio State U. Research Found., Columbus, 1963-68; mem. chemistry research evaluation panel USAF Office Sci. Research, 1966-70; mem. adv. panel for inorganic materials div. Inst. Materials Research, Nat. Bur. Standards, 1968-70; mem. corp. vis. com. dept. chemistry MIT, Cambridge, 1971-72; mem. NRC Evaluation Panel for Phys. Chemistry, 1977-80; lectr. various orgns., 1959-82; cons. Los Alamos Sci. Lab., 1953-62, Argonne Nat. Lab., Ill., 1946-83; mem. adv. panel Brookhaven Nat. Lab., Brookhaven, N.Y., 1960-63, Oak Ridge Nat. Lab., 1963-66; vis. lectr. Japan Soc. for the Promotion Sci., 1975, Chinese Acad. Scis., 1986. Contbr. articles to various publs. Recipient Centennial Achievement award Ohio State U., 1970; recipient Peter Debye award in phys. chemistry Am. Chem. Soc., 1972; Guggenheim fellow Oxford U., 1955-56, 72-73; Eastman Prof. U. Oxford, 1981-82. Fellow Am. Acad. Scis., Am. Phys. Soc. (council 1967, div. chmn. 1965); mem. Nat. Acad. Scis., AAAS, Sigma Xi. Office: Montgomery Pl 5550 S South Shore Dr Apt 1015 Chicago IL 60637-5058

HUTCHISON, DEBORAH L., critical care nurse; b. Manhattan, Kans., Jan. 8, 1953; d. Patrick J. Sr. and Charlene S. (Baughman) Donnellan; m. James C. Hutchison III, Aug. 7, 1981; children: Todd, Jason, Tommy, Cynthia, Susan, Melissa. Diploma, St. John's Sch. Nursing, 1989; BS in Psychology cum laude, S.W. Mo. State U., 1983, MS in Biology, 1986. RN; cert. critical care. Grad. teaching asst. S.W. Mo. State U., Springfield; burn technician St. John's Hosp., Springfield, nurse, surg. intensive care unit. Mem. Am. Assn. Critical Care Nurses.

HUTCHISON, DONNA MCANULTY, humanities educator; b. Eglin AFB, Fla., Sept. 8, 1951; d. Donal Hawley and Shirley Annette (Wise) McAnulty; m. Roy L. Hutchison, July 12, 1970; 1 child, R. Aaron. BS in Edn., Henderson State U., Arkadelphia, Ark., 1972, MS in Edn., 1978. Cert. master tchr., Ark. Tchr., chair art dept. Magnet Cove (Ark.) H.S., 1972-74; instr. art dept. Ouachita Bapt. U., Arkadelphia, 1978-85; chmn. art dept. Arkadelphia H.S., 1985-87; tchr. honors English Corning (Ark.) H.S., 1987-93; instr. humanities dept. Ark. Sch. Math. and Sci., Hot Springs, 1993—, chair humanities dept., 1997—. Exhibited in group shows at Herr-Chambliss Gallery, Hot Springs, 1983-85, Joint Ednl. Consortium Show, 1983, 85, West Tex. Watercolor Soc. Show, 1984. Paul and Virginia Henry grantee Ouachita Bapt. U., 1983, AEGIS grantee Ark. Dept. Edn., 1996, 97, 99, Eisenhower grantee, 1997, Goals 2000 grantee Fed. Dept. Edn., 1997. Mem. NEA, Nat. Coun. Tchrs. of English, Ark. Edn. Assn., Arkadelphia Country Club (v.p. bd. dirs. 1986). Avocation: watercolor painting. Home: 107 Overlook Ct Hot Springs National Park AR 71913-2237 Office: Ark Sch Math & Scis 200 Whittington Ave Hot Springs National Park AR 71901-3408

HUTCHISON, DORRIS JEANNETTE, retired microbiologist, educator; b. Carrsville, Ky., Oct. 31, 1918; d. John W. and Maud (Short) H. B.S., Western Ky. State Coll., 1940; M.S., U. Ky., 1943; Ph.D., Rutgers U., 1949. Instr. Russell Sage Coll., 1942-44, Vassar Coll., 1944-46; research asst. Rutgers U., 1946-48, research assoc., 1948-49; instr. Wellesley Coll., 1949-51; asst. Sloan-Kettering Inst., N.Y.C., 1951-56; assoc. Sloan-Kettering Inst., 1956-60, assoc. mem., 1960-69, mem., 1969-90, mem. emeritus, 1990—, sect. head, 1956-90, acting chief div. exptl. chemotherapy, 1965-66, div. chief drug resistance, 1967-72, co-head lab. exptl. tumor therapy, 1973-74, lab. head drug resistance and cyto-regulation, 1973-84, coordinator field edn., 1975-81; instr. Sloan-Kettering div. Cornell U. Grad. Sch. Med. Sci., N.Y.C., 1952-53, rsch. assoc., 1953-54, asst. prof., 1954-58, assoc. prof., 1958-70, prof. microbiology, 1970-90, prof. emeritus, 1990—, chmn. biology unit, 1968-74, assoc. dir., 1974-87; assoc. dean Cornell U. Grad. Sch. Med. Sci., 1978-87, asst. dean Cornell U., Ithaca, 1978-87; mem. Meml. Sloan-Kettering Cancer Ctr., 1984-90, mem. emeritus, 1990—; del. dir. Am. Cancer Soc., Inc., 1986-90. Bd. dirs. Westchester div. Am. Cancer Soc., 1976-90, exec. com., 1976-91; project chmn. Target 5, 1977-80, v.p., 1979-81, pres., 1981-83, sec., 1983-87, charter mem. So. Westchester Unit, 1984, pres., 1984-86. Faculty fellow Vassar Coll., 1946; USPHS fellow, 1951-53; Philippe Found. fellow Paris, 1959; named to Ky. Cols., 1988. Fellow N.Y. Acad. Sci., Am. Acad. Microbiology (charter), N.Y. Acad. Medicine (assoc.); mem. AAAS, Am. Assn. for Cancer Edn., Am. Assn. Cancer Research (emeritus), Harvey Soc., Genetics Soc. Am., Am. Inst. Nutrition, Am. Soc. for Microbiology (hon., councilor N.Y.C. br. 1954-58, pres. N.Y.C. br. 1958-60, nat. councilor 1961-63, chmn. nat. meeting 1967, mem. pres.'s fellowship com. 1973-76, chmn. 1975-76), Soc. for Cryobiology (hon. mem.), Am. Genetic Assn., Internat. Soc. Biochem. Pharmacology, N.Y. Soc. Ky. Women (pres. 1988—), N.Y. Found. Ky. Women (pres. 1990—), Bronxville Field Club. Numerous publs. antibiotics and chems. effective in treatment of Tb and leukemia, reports on mechanisms explaining how leukemic cells become resistant to treatment; searches for more effective antileukemia drugs. Home: Southgate Bronxville NY 10708 *Achieving goals and providing support and guidance to others, who also wished to become contributors to the well-being of mankind, have been prime concerns to me. The slings and arrows during this time have been totally offset by the personal satisfaction felt as a result of our intangible and tangible achievements.*

HUTCHISON, JAMES ARTHUR, JR., architectural and engineering company executive; b. Gainesville, Mo., Oct. 25, 1917; s. James Arthur and Dora Ethel (James) H.; m. Imogene Cox, Dec. 5, 1946; children: Judith Lynn, Janet Gayle, James Arthur III. BS in Mech. Engring., Okla. State U., 1940; BS in Aero. Engring., Spartan Sch. Aeronautics, 1942; BS in Acctg., Okla. Sch. Accountancy, 1963. Registered profl. engr. Del., N.J., Md., V.I. Asst. chief engr. Spartan Aircraft Co., Tulsa, Okla., 1943-51; owner H&H Engring. & Constrn. Co., Tulsa, 1951-68; sr. liaison engr. ILC Industries Inc. Appollo Astronaut Program, Dover, Del., 1968-72; v.p. Diamond State Engring., Inc., Dover, 1972-78; founder, chmn. bd. dirs. The JAED Corp., Smyrna, Del., 1978—. Chmn. bd. trustees, chmn. bldg. com. 1st Bapt. Ch., Dover, 1979-90. Mem. Am. Inst. Steel Constrn., Am. Concrete Inst., Ctrl. Del. Pilots Assn. (pres. 1977-78). Republican. Avocation: aircraft flight instruction. Office: The JAED Corp 6 Village Sq Smyrna DE 19977-1852

HUTCHISON, JANE CAMPBELL, art history educator, researcher; b. Washington (D.C.), July 20, 1932; d. James Paul and Leone Bailey (Warrick) H. BA fine arts, Western Maryland Coll., 1954; MA art history, Oberlin Coll., 1958; PhD art history, U. Wis., 1964. Tech. illustrator/ Dept. Model Basin U.S. Navy, Washington (D.C.), 1954-56; rsch libr. Toledo Mus. of Art, 1957-59; teaching asst. U. Wis., Madison, 1959-60,61-63; vis. asst. prof. Temple U., Phila., summer 1968; from instr. to assoc. prof. U. Wis., Madison, 1964—, prof., 1975—, dept. chmn., 1977-80, 92-93; cons. NEH, Washington (D.C.), 1972-77, Inst. Internat. Edn., N.Y.C., 1977,82,89, Nat. Gallery of Art, Washington, 1982-83, Rijksmuseum, Amsterdam, 1984, Cin. Art Mus., 1990—. Author: Master of the Housebook, 1972, Early German Artists, vol. I, 1980, vol. II, 1981, vol. III, 1991, vol. IV, 1996, Albrecht Dürer: A Biography, 1990 (German edit., 1994). Pres. Madison chpt. AAUP, 1979-81, Midwest Art History Soc., 1983-85; sec.-treas. Historians of Netherlandish Art, 1995—; pres. St. Andrew's Soc. Madison, 1995—. Grad. fellow Oberlin Coll., 1955-57, fellow U. Wis., 1959-60, 61-63, Fulbright fellow Rijksuniversiteit Utrecht, Netherlands, 1960-61, rsch. grantee NEH, Germany, 1982, German Acad. Exch. Svc., Germany, summer 1989; Grant in aid Am. Coun. Learned Soc., Amsterdam, 1984; recipient Alumni award Western Md. Coll. Trustees, 1987. Mem. AAUP (pres. Madison chpt. 1979-81), Internat. Coun. Mus., Am. Assn. Mus., Medieval Acad. Am., Coll. Art Assn., Univ. Club U. Wis. (bd. dirs. 1976-80, pres. 1980), Wis. Assn. Scholars (v.p. Madison chpt. 1990—), Midwest Art History Soc. (pres. 1983-85), Historians of Netherlandish Art (sec.-treas. 1995-99), Print Coun. Am. E-mail: jchutchi@facstaff.wisc.edu. Home: 2261 Regent St Madison WI 53705-5321 Office: U Wis Dept Art History 800 University Ave Madison WI 53706-1414

HUTCHISON, KAY BAILEY, senator; b. Galveston, TX, July 22, 1943; d. Allan and Kathryn Bailey; m. Ray Hutchison. BA, U. Tex., 1992, LLB, 1967. Bar: Tex. 1967. TV news reporter Houston, 1969-71, pvt. practice law, 1969-74; press sec. to Anne Armstrong Rep. Nat. Com., 1971; vice-chair Nat. Transp. Safety Bd., 1976-78; asst. prof. U. Tex., Dallas, 1978-79; sr. v.p., gen. counsel Republic Bank Corp., Dallas, 1979-81; pntr. Boyd-Levinson, Ltd., Houston and Dallas, 1981-91; mem. Tex. Ho. of Reps., 1972-76; elected treas. State of Tex., 1990; U.S. senator from Tex. Washington, 1993—; mem. appropriations com., commerce, sci. and transp. com., environment and pub. works com., rules and adminstrn. com.; chmn., bd. visitors, US Military Acad. at West Point, US Delegate to Commn. on Security and Cooperation in Europe (The Helsinki Commn.), co-chair, Congressional Oil and Gas Caucus; owner McCraw Candies; co-founder Fidelity Nat. Bank. Recipient Eagle award valued commitment to our nation's Hispanic Cmty., 1993; named Rep. Woman of Yr. Nat. Fedn. Rep. Women, 1995, Outstanding U. Tex. Alumnus, 1995, Texan of Yr. Tex. Legis. Conf., 1997; named to Tex. Women's Hall of Fame, 1997. Fellow, U. Tex. Law Alumni Assn. (pres. 1985-86). Republican.

HUTCHISON, PAT, nurse, administrator; b. Omaha, Mar. 4, 1943; d. Earl Edward and Sylvia Lorraine (Kronen) Moore; m. James M. Hutchison, June 23, 1963; children—Michael, Danny. Diploma in nursing, St. Joseph's Sch. Nursing, 1968; student Central Ariz. Coll., 1976-82; BS in Health Service Adminstrn., U. Phoenix, 1983; BS in Nursing, U. Phoenix, 1988. R.N.; cert. in advanced cardiac life support, Ariz. Nurse Armish Maag Hosp., Teheran, Iran, 1969-71; supr. Hoemako Hosp., Casa Grande, Ariz., 1973-84; asst. dir. nursing Casa Grande Regional Med. Ctr., 1984-86, nursing supr., 1986—. Nursing chmn. ARC, Casa Grande, 1986—, also bd. dirs., instr. disaster tng., 1982—; instr. cardiopulmonary resuscitation Am. Heart Assn., Casa Grande, 1978—. Recipient Care award Ariz. Hosp. Assn., 1984, Service and Appreciation award Bus. and Profl. Women's Assn., 1984. Mem. Ariz. Nurses in Mgmt., Emergency Nurses Assn. Democrat. Roman Catholic. Avocations: traveling; camping; boating; reading. Home: 1308 N Center Ave Casa Grande AZ 85222-3408 Office: Casa Grande Regional Med Ctr 1800 E Florence Blvd Casa Grande AZ 85222-5303

HUTCHISON, STANLEY PHILIP, lawyer, retired; b. Joliet, Ill., Nov. 22, 1923; s. Stuart Philip and Verna (Kinzer) H.; m. Helen Jane Rush, July 25, 1945; children: Norman, Elizabeth. BS, Northwestern U., 1947; LLB, Ill. Inst. Tech., 1951. Bar: Ill. 1951. Legal asst. Washington Nat. Ins. Co., Evanston, 1947-51; asst. counsel Washington Nat. Ins. Co., 1951-55, asst. gen. counsel, 1955-58, asso. gen. counsel, 1958-60, gen. counsel, 1960-63, v.p., gen. counsel, dir., 1963-66, exec. v.p., gen. counsel, dir., 1966-67, exec. v.p., gen. counsel, sec., dir., 1967-70, chmn. exec. com., 1970-73, vice chmn. bd., 1974-75, chmn. bd., chief exec. officer, 1976-88; pres. Wash. Nat. Corp., 1970-83, chief exec. officer, 1978-88, chmn. bd., 1983-88; ret., 1988—; bd. dirs. Washington Nat. Corp. Mem. pres.'s coun. Nat. Coll. Edn., 1977-88, adv. coun. Kellogg Grad. Sch. Mgmt. Northwestern U., 1981-88; bd. dirs. Evanston Hosp. Corp., 1983-88. Lt. (j.g.) USNR, 1942-46. Mem. Assn. Life Ins. Counsel, Am. Coun. Life Ins. (bd. dir. 1977-81), Ill. Life Ins. Coun. (bd. dir. 1978-86, pres. 1983-85), Inc. Econs. Soc. Am. (bd. dir. 1977-85, chmn. 1981-82), Health Ins. Assn. Am. (bd. dirs. 1982-88, chmn. 1987-88). Home: PO Box 2339 Carefree AZ 85377-2339

HUTCHISON, VICTOR HOBBS, biologist, educator; b. Blakely, Ga., June 15, 1931; s. Joseph Victor and Veva (Hobbs) H.; m. Theresa Dokos, Dec. 14, 1952; children—Victoria Ann, John Christopher, David Michael, Kenneth Hobbs. B.S., N. Ga. Coll., 1952; M.A., Duke, 1956, Ph.D., 1959. Instr. Duke, 1957-58, faculty fellow, So. Fellowship Fund fellow, 1958-59; mem. faculty U. R.I., 1959-70, prof. biology, 1968-70; dir. Inst. Environ. Biology; 1966-70; prof., chmn. dept. zoology U. Okla., Norman, 1970-80; George Lynn Cross research prof. zoology U. Okla., 1979—; research prof. Universidad de Los Andes, Bogotá, Colombia, 1965-66; prin. investigator Nat. Geog. Soc.-U. R.I. herpetological expdn. to Colombia, 1964-65, Nat. Geog. Soc.-U. Okla. expdns. to Lake Titicaca, 1975, to Cameroon, 1981. Editor Animal Natural History series, 1991—; rsch. and articles on heat tolerances of lower vertebrates, effects of day-length on metabolism and temperature tolerance of lower vertebrates, physiology of lower vertebrates, physiol. ecology of amphibians and reptiles, respiration in amphibians, behavioral thermoregulation. Guggenheim fellow, 1965-66. Fellow AAAS; mem. Am. Inst. Biol. Sci., Am. Soc. Ichthyologists and Herpetologists (pres. 1988), Am. Physiol. Soc., Ecol. Soc. Am., Herpetologists League (exe. com. 1968-71), Soc. Study Amphibians and Reptiles (bd. govs. 1986-88, pres. 1998-99), Explorers Club, Sigma Xi, Phi Sigma, Phi Kappa Phi. Achievements include demonstration of facultative endothermy in brooding pythons; research on role of skin in amphibian respiration; development of standardized method for determination of critical thermal maximum in animals. Home: 2010 Crestmont Ave Norman OK 73069-6414 Office: U Okla Dept Zoology Norman OK 73019

HUTENSTINE, MARIAN LOUISE, journalism educator; b. Bloomsburg, Pa., Jan. 26, 1940; d. Ralph Benjamin and Marian Louise (Engler) H. BS, Bloomsburg State U., 1961, MEd, 1966; postgrad., Rutgers U., 1962-63; PhD, U. N.C., 1985. Tchr. h.s. English and journalism, chmn. dept., 1961-66, asst. prof. Lock Haven (Pa.) U., 1966-73, assoc. prof. English, 1973-74; tchg. asst., lectr. Sch. Journalism, U. N.C., Chapel Hill, 1974-76; cons., dir. Diener & Assocs., Research Triangle Park, N.C., 1974-86; asst. prof. journalism Coll. Comm. U. Ala., Tuscaloosa, 1977-93; assoc. prof. comm. Coll. Comm. and Fine Arts Jacksonville State U., 1993-95; assoc. prof. Radford (Va.) U., 1995-97; prof., head dept. comm. Miss. State U., 1997—; cons. various publs., Ala., 1977—. Contbr. papers to profl. lit. Adult leader, vol. worker Episc. Ch., 1994—. NDEA fellow, Newspaper Fund fellow Rutgers U., 1962-63. Mem. ACLU, NAFE, Assn. Edn. in Journalism and Mass Comm., Nat. Fedn. Press Women, Ala. Media Profls. (Communicator of Yr. 1994), Ala. SPJ Club, Kappa Tau Alpha. Home: 494 Fombys Ferry Rd Ohatchee AL 36271-5146 Office: Miss State U Dept Comm PO Box Pf Mississippi State MS 39762-6006

HUTH, EDWARD JANAVEL, physician, editor; b. Phila., May 15, 1923; s. Edward Gaston and Suzanne Madeleine (Janavel) H.; m. Carol Elizabeth Monnik, Apr. 6, 1957; children: John Edward, James Janavel. BA, Wesleyan U., Middletown, Conn., 1945; MD, U. Pa., 1947. Diplomate Am. Bd. Internal Medicine, Nat. Bd. Med. Examiners. Intern Hosp. of U. Pa., 1947-48, resident medicine, 1949-51, ward physician, 1951-61; mem. Diagnostic Clinic, 1959-61; postdoctoral fellow Life Ins. Med. Research Fund, 1952-53; spl. research fellow USPHS, Univ. Coll. Hosp., London, Eng., 1957-58; asst. instr. pharmacology Sch. Medicine, U. Pa., Phila., 1948-49, assoc. in medicine, 1951-58, asst. prof. medicine, 1958-61; assoc. prof. comparative medicine Sch. Vet. Medicine, 1963-68; adj. asst. prof. medicine Sch. Medicine, U. Pa., 1966-71, assoc. prof. clin. medicine, 1971-74, adj. clin. prof. medicine, 1974-78, adj. prof. medicine dept. medicine Assoc. Faculty, 1978—; asst. prof. medicine Woman's Med. Coll., Phila., 1961-62, assoc. prof., 1962-65; chmn. com. on 4th edit. CBE Style Manual Coun. Biology Editors, 1971-78, chmn. com. on 6th edit., 1990-95; mem. biomed. comms. study sect. NIH, 1972-76; chmn. subcom. 10 of Com. Z39 Am. Nat. Stds. Inst., 1974-77; mem. UNISIST Working Group on Primary Sources of Info., UNESCO, Paris, 1973-74; bd. regents Nat. Libr. Medicine, 1979-83. Author: Medical Style and Format, 1987, How to Write and Publish Papers in the Medical Sciences, 1990, Writing and Publishing in Medicine, 1998, SI Units for Clinical Medicine, 1998; asst. editor Annals of Internal Medicine, 1960-63, assoc. editor, 1963-71, editor, 1971-90, editor emeritus, 1990-93, 95—, book rev. editor, 1990-93, 95-96, interim editor, 1994-95; editor Online Jour. Current Clin. Trials, 1991-94, also articles. Served with AUS, 1943-46, PTO. Fellow ACP, AAAS (coun. 1968, editor Online Jour. Current Clin. Trials 1991-94), Royal Coll. Physicians (London), Am. Med. Writers Assn. (pres. 1967-68); mem. Coun. Biology Editors (dir. 1970-75, chmn. 1973-74), European Assn. Sci. Editors, Coll. Physicians Phila., Soc. for Scholarly Pub. (dir. 1988-92), Phi Beta Kappa, Sigma Xi, Alpha Omega Alpha, Zeta Phi. Home and Office: 1124 Morris Ave Bryn Mawr PA 19010-1712

HUTH, PAUL CURTIS, ecosystem scientist, botanist; b. Kingston, N.Y., Feb. 18, 1947; s. Berthold Carl and Ruth Doris (Persons) H.; m. Ann Louise Friess, May 22, 1983. BS, SUNY, New Paltz, 1972, MA, 1979. Lab. technician N.Y. State Agrl. Experiment Sta., Highland, 1967-76; quality control inspector N.Y. State Dept. Agr. and Markets, Albany, 1980; regional enumerator N.Y. State Crop Reporting Svc., Albany, 1980-81; field supr. Fed. Crop Ins. Corp. USDA, Harrisburg, Pa., 1981-82; ecosystem rsch. scientist Mohonk Preserve, Inc., New Paltz, 1983-88, dir. rsch., 1989—; cons. Hudsonia, Ltd., Bard Coll., Annendale, N.Y., 1984-95; chair rsch. and records com. John Burroughs Natural History Soc., High Falls, N.Y., 1986—; coop. weather observer Nat. Oceanic and Atmospheric Adminstrn., Mohonk Lake, N.Y., 1990—. Editorial bd. Up River/Down River mag., 1990-92; contbr. articles to Environ. Entomology, Northeastern Geology. Bd. dirs. Ea. N.Y. chpt. Nature Conservancy, Albany, 1988-94, Klyne Esopus Hist. Soc. Mus., Ulster Park, N.Y., 1989-91; mem.-at-large Ulster County Environ. Adv. Bd., Kingston, 1990-95, John Burroughs Assn., N.Y.C., 1992-93, 1st v.p. Mem. Am. Soc. Ichthyologists and Herpetologists, Ecol. Soc. Am., Am. Assn. Applied Sci., Am. Soc. Environ. History, Am. Ornithologists' Union, Am. Soc. Mammalogists, Am. Inst. Biol. Sci., Linnaean Soc. N.Y., Torrey Botan. Club, N.Y. Flora Assn., Royal Horticultural Soc. Achievements include specialized, long-term research on Shawangunk Mountain ecosystem in southeastern N.Y. Home: PO Box 45 Esopus NY 12429-0045 Office: Mohonk Preserve Inc 1000 Mountain Rest Rd New Paltz NY 12561-2825

HUTNER, SEYMOUR HERBERT, microbiologist, protozoologist; b. Bklyn., Oct. 28, 1911; s. Julius and Fannie (Zuckerman) H.; m. Reina Albagli, 1938 (dec. 1955); 1 child, Reed Albagli; m. Margarita Silva, Aug. 18, 1956. B.S., CCNY, 1932; Ph.D., Cornell U., 1937; Sc.D. (hon.), St. Francis Coll., Bklyn., 1984. Rsch. assoc. dept. physics MIT, 1935-36; technician Labs. and Rsch. Div., N.Y. State Health Dept., 1938-41; staff Haskins Labs., N.Y.C., 1941—; Haskins adj. prof. biology Pace U., N.Y.C., 1970-77, prof. emeritus in residence, 1977—; vis. prof. Inst. Microbiology, U. Brazil, Rio de Janeiro, 1963-64, U. Ill., Urbana, 1967, U. Brazilia, 1970; adj. prof. Fordham U., N.Y.C., 1964-69; bus. mgr. Jour. Phycology, 1963-67; mem. botany com. N.Y. Bot. Garden, 1974-77; cons. rsch. unit vector pathology U. Nfld.; mem. bd. reviewers J. Protozoology, 1993—. Editor: (with A. Lwoff) Biochemistry and Physiology of Protozoa, vol. 2, vol. 3, 1964; co-editor: (with M. Levandowsky) Biochemical Physiological Protozoology, 4 vols., 2d edit.; co-editor Illustrated Guide to the Protozoa, 1985; mem. editorial bd. Jour. Protozoology, 1953-85, 90—; editor publs. 5th Internat. Congress Protozoology, 1977; adv. editor Environ. Rsch., 1961-62; co-founder Jour. Protozoology, Jour. Phycology. Mem. Central Park Conservancy, Common Cause, People for Am. Way. Fellow N.Y. Acad. Scis., Am. Acad. Microbiology; mem. Soc. Protozoologists (hon., pres. 1961-62, chmn. com. spl. publs. 1963-84), Soc. Gen. Microbiology, Am. Soc. Microbiology, Am. Assn. Cancer Rsch., Biochem. Soc., Am. Chem. Soc., Acad. Scis. Brazil (corr.), Royal Soc. Tropical Medicine and Hygiene. Achievements include introduction of EDTA and similar potent chelators into biology by use of high yield, precipitate-free pure cultures of freshwater and marine algae and protozoa; development (with others) of widely used Euglena and chrysomonad assays for vitamin B12; of the Crithidia assay for biopterin which cofactors synthesis of catecholamines; of the drug eflornithine, clinically successful against West African human trypanosomiasis (sleeping sickness). Home: 142 W End Ave Apt 7U New York NY 10023-6124 Office: Pace U Haskins Labs 1 Pace Plz New York NY 10038-1502

HUTSALIUK, YAREMA, public relations executive, military officer; b. N.Y.C., Aug. 5, 1960; s. Liuboslav and Renata (Kozicka) H. BA, Columbia U., 1982, M. Internat. Affairs, 1985. Media analyst Fleishman Hillard Pub. Rels., N.Y.C., 1987; account mgr. The Alexander Co. Pub. Rels., N.Y.C., 1988; account exec. Schlesinger Assocs. Pub. Rels., N.Y.C., 1988-90; pvt. practice N.Y.C., 1990—; pub. affairs officer NYG, 1990-93; internat. pub. rels. counsel Boreal Capital Group, N.Y.C., 1992—; pub. rels. counsel Thirteen/WNET Miles Ednl. Film Prodns., 1992-93; press liaison officer U.S. Agy. Internat. Devel./Internews, Kiev, Ukraine, 1995; account exec. A. B. Isaacson, Inc., 1996—; freelance, Ea. Europe, 1997-98. Contbr. The Encyclopedia of New York City, 1995; contbr. numerous articles on N.Y. N.G. in Desert Shield and Desert Storm and on African-Americans in the U.S. mil. Decorated Mil. commendation medal, 1991, 98, Order of Lafayette, 1995, Mil. and Naval Order of U.S., 1996; recipient award Black Officers Assn., 1993, Dean's Pin award Columbia Coll. Alumni Assn., 1997. Mem. Bklyn. Soc. for Ethical Culture, Soc. of Friends Mus. of Legion of Honor (Paris). Roman Catholic. Avocations: collecting ikons and antiques, opera, military history. Home: 260 Riverside Dr New York NY 10025-5254

HUTSON, DON, lawyer; b. Kansas City, Mo., Nov. 4, 1931; s. Alpha Henry and Lola (Walmer) H.; m. Betty Jane Switzer, Sept. 7, 1952; children: Eric, Sheila, Robin, Heather. A.B. with honors, Central Coll., Fayette, Mo., 1953; postgrad., U. Mo., 1954; J.D. with honors, George Washington U., 1958. Ordained to ministry Internat. Conv. Christian Chs., 1949; bar: Mo. 1958. Min. Oak Grove Christian Ch., Mo., 1949-53; tchr., coach various schs., Mo., 1952-54; staff asst. to Senator Stuart Symington, 1955-59; mem. firm Hutson, Schmidt, Hammett & Yates, P.C., Kansas City, Mo., 1958-83, Miller & Hutson, Lebanon, Mo., 1983-91, Hutson, Hutson & Grimes, Lebanon, 1991-94; Hutson, Hutson & Hutson, Lebanon, 1995—; asst. pros. atty. Jackson County, 1959-63. Mem. ABA, Fed. Bar Assn., Kansas City Bar Assn., Am. Judicature Soc., Am. Trial Lawyers Assn., Mo. Trial Lawyers Assn., Lebanon (Mo.) C. of C., Sigma Epsilon Pi, Phi Alpha Delta (internat. justice 1974-76), Pi Kappa Delta. Democrat. Home: 22941 Primrose Dr Lebanon MO 65536-5309 Office: Hutson Hutson & Hutson 211 E Commercial St Lebanon MO 65536-3213

HUTSON, JEFFREY WOODWARD, lawyer; b. New London, Conn., July 19, 1941; s. John Jenkins and Kathryn Barbara (Himberg) H.; m. Susan Office, Nov. 25, 1967; children: Elizabeth Kathryn, Anne Louise. AB, U. Mich., 1963, LLB, 1966. Bar: Ohio 1966, Hawaii 1970. Assoc. Lane, Alton & Horst, Columbus, Ohio, 1966-74, ptnr., 1974—. Trustee, vice-chmn. Six Pence Sch., 1983-88; mem. com. creeds and professionalism Ohio Supreme Ct., 1989-90; chair, bd. dirs. Northwest Counseling Svcs., 1990-92; regional v.p. Def. Rsch. Inst, 1991-93. Lt. comdr. USNR, 1967-71. Fellow Am. Coll. Trial Lawyers; mem. ABA, Ohio Bar Assn. (past chmn. litigation sect.), Ohio Assn. Civil Trial Attys. (past pres.), Columbus Bar Assn., Internat. Assn. Def. Counsel, Faculty Def. Coun. Trial Acad., Scioto Country Club, Athletic Club. Avocations: cycling, reading, music. Office: Lane Alton & Horst 175 S 3rd St Ste 700 Columbus OH 43215-5100

HUTT, PETER BARTON, lawyer; b. Buffalo, Nov. 16, 1934; s. Lester Ralph and Louise Rich (Fraser) H.; m. Eleanor Jane Zurn, Aug. 29, 1959; children: Katherine Zurn, Peter Barton, Sarah Henderson, Everett Fraser. BA magna cum laude, Yale U., 1956; LLB, Harvard U., 1959; LLM, NYU, 1960. Bar: N.Y. 1959, D.C. 1961, U.S. Supreme Ct. 1967. Assoc. firm Covington & Burling, Washington, 1960-68, partner, 1968-71, 75—; chief counsel FDA, Washington, 1971-75; bd. dirs. Cogetix, Inc., Salt Lake City, Circe Biomed., Inc., Lexington, Mass., Emisphere Tech., Inc., Hawthorne, N.Y., Interneuron Pharms, Inc., Waltham; mem. adv. com. to dir. NIH, 1976-81; mem. com. on rsch. tng. NAS, 1976-80; bd. dirs. Calif. Health Care Inst., San Diego, 1996—; counsel to Alcoholic Beverage Med. Rsch. Found., 1984-85, chmn. bd. dirs., 1986-92; mem. Nat. Com. to Review Current Procedure for Approval of New Drugs for Cancer and AIDS, Nat. Cancer Inst., 1988-90; mem. nat. bd. Scripps Clinic and Rsch. Found., La Jolla, 1977-85, 90-95; mem. internat. bd. Scripps Instns. of Med. and Sci., 1995—, Ctr. for Study Drug Devel., Tufts U. Ctr., 1976-99, Calif. Healthcare Inst., San Diego, 1996—, Ctr. for Advanced Studies, U. Va., 1982—, Inst. for Health Policy Analysis, Georgetown U., 1982-89, Am. Pharm. Inst., Washington, 1988-92; mem. Com. on Food Laws and Regulations, Inst. Food Tech.; mem. adv. com. Progress and Freedom Found., 1994-97; mem. adv. bd. Frazier Healthcare Investments, Seattle, 1993—, Sprout Group, N.Y. and Menlo Park, 1993—, Polaris Venture Ptnrs., Waltham, Mass., 1995—, Vanguard Medica Ltd., Guildford, Eng., 1993-99; mem. various panels U.S. Congl. Office Tech. Assessment NAS; lectr. on food and drug law Harvard U., 1994—, Stanford U., 1998; mem. adv. bd. Columbia U. Sch. Pub. Health, 1997—. Author: (with Patricia Wald) Dealing with Drug Abuse, 1972, (with Richard Merrill) Food and Drug Law, 1991, (with Bruce Kuhlik) Understanding Export Law, 1998; editor-in-chief U.S. Food Labeling Law, 1991; contbg. editor: Legal Times of Washington, 1978-86; mem. editorial bd. various jours.; editor: Food and Drug Law: An Electronic Book of Student Papers. Bd. dirs. Sidwell Friends Sch., Washington, 1976-84; bd. dirs. Legal Action Ctr., N.Y.C., 1976—, vice-chmn., 1984-98; bd. dirs. Found. for Biomed. Rsch., 1976—, vice chmn., 1989—; trustee Washington Lawyers Com. for Civil Rights & Urban Affairs, 1976—; bd. dirs. Soc. Risk Analysis, 1985-88, 89-92, counsel, 1992—; mem. vis. com. Harvard Sch. Pub. Health, 1980-86. Recipient award of merit FDA, 1972, 75, Disting. Svc. award HEW, 1974, Underwood-Prescott award MIT, 1977. Fellow Soc. Risk Analysis; mem. ABA (former chmn. life scis. com., sect. on sci. and tech.), Inst. Medicine of NAS (mem. Devel. of Drugs and Vaccines Against AIDS roundtable 1988-94, bd. on health care svcs. 1998—). Episcopalian. Club: Metropolitan (Washington). Home: 402 Prince St Alexandria VA 22314 Office: Covington & Burling 1201 Pennsylvania Ave NW Washington DC 20004-2401

HUTTENBACK, ROBERT ARTHUR, academic administrator, educator; b. Frankfurt, Germany, Mar. 8, 1928; s. Otto Henry and Dorothy (Marcuse) H.; m. Freda Braginsky, July 12, 1954; 1 dau., Madeleine Alexandra. B.A., U. Calif. at Los Angeles, 1951, Ph.D., 1959; postgrad., Sch. Oriental and African Studies, U. London, Eng., 1956-57. Mem. faculty Calif. Inst. Tech., Pasadena, 1958-78; asst. prof. Calif. Inst. Tech., 1960-63, assoc. prof., 1963-66, prof. history, 1966-78, master student houses, 1958-69, dean students, 1969-72, chmn. div. humanities and social scis., 1971-77; chancellor U. Calif., Santa Barbara, 1977-86; cons. Jet Propulsion Lab., Pasadena, 1966-68. Author: British Relations with Sind, 1799-1843, An Anatomy of Imperialism, 1962, (with Leo Rose and Margaret Fisher) Himalayan Battleground-Sino-Indian Rivalry in Ladakh, 1963, The British Imperial Experience, 1966, Gandhi in South Africa, 1971, Racism and Empire, 1976; (with Lance Davis) Mammon and the Pursuit of Empire, 1986. Served to 1st lt. U.S. Army, 1951-53.

HUTTER, ADOLPH MATTHEW, JR., cardiologist, educator; b. Fond du Lac, Wis., Feb. 22, 1937; s. Adolph Matthew and Janet (Kay) H.; m. Sylvia H. Murray, June 18, 1960; children: Janice Marie, Adolph Joseph, Elizabeth Kay, Matthew Murray, Jonathan James. BS summa cum laude, Georgetown U., 1959; MD, U. Wis., 1963. Diplomate Am. Bd. Internal Medicine, Am. Bd. Cardiovascular Diseases; lic. physician, Mass. Med. intern Strong Meml. Hosp., Rochester, N.Y., 1963-64; clin. assoc. Nat. Cancer Inst., Bethesda, Md., 1964-66; asst. resident Strong Meml. Hosp., 1966-67, assoc. resident, 1967-68; fellow in medicine (oncology) Georgetown U. Sch. Medicine, Washington, 1965-66; clin. and rsch. fellow in cardiology Mass. Gen. Hosp., Boston, 1968-70; instr. medicine Harvard U. Med. Sch., Boston, 1970-72, asst. prof., 1972-76, assoc. prof., 1976—; vis. prof. 70 univs. and med. ctrs., 1979-96; asst. in medicine Mass. Gen. Hosp., 1970-72, asst. physician, 1972-76, assoc., 1976-84, physician, 1984—, assoc. dir. CCU, 1970-81, dir., 1981-86, chmn. med. intensive care coord. com., 1986—; cardiologist Boston Bruins hockey team, 1972—, New Eng. Patriots football team, 1982—. Contbr. over 100 articles to med. jours. Recipient Howard H. Blakeslee award Am. Heart Assn., 1974. Fellow ACP, Coun. on Clin. Cardiology of Am. Heart Assn. (mem. com. on postgrad. edn. 1972-75, mem. com. on sci. sessions program 1973-75, mem. sci. sessions com. 1979-81, vice chmn. com. on cardiovasc. disease of elderly 1987-89), Am. Coll. Cardiology (chmn. 1987-90, v.p. 1990-91, pres. 1992-93, past pres. 1993-94, mem. program com. on sci. sessions 1975-76, mem. credentials com. 1976-83, chmn. 1981-83, asst. sec. 1981-82, sec. 1984-85, mem. long-range planning com. 1981-83, mem. ACCEL com. 1982-90, mem. ACCEL edn. bd. 1987-90, 93—, mem. strategic planning com. 1988-92, mem. exec. com. 1990-94, trustee 1981-85, 87-95, chmn. govt. rels. com. 1984-90, chmn. chpt. rels. com. 1993—, mem. chmn. award com. 1993-95, mem. tech. and practice exec. com. 1994—), European Soc. Cardiology, AAAS; mem. Am. Clin. and Climatol. Assn., U. Wis. Med. Alumni Assn., Mass. Med. Soc., Alpha Omega Alpha. Roman Catholic. Avocations: tree work, tennis. Office: Mass Gen Hosp Ambulatory Care Ctr 15 Parkman St Ste 467 Boston MA 02114-3117*

HUTTER, GARY MICHAEL, environmental engineer; b. Harvey, Ill., May 10, 1948; s. Samuel and Ann H.; m. Shelley Hamilton, June 16, 1973; 1 child, Emily. BSME, U. Ill., 1970, MS in Environ. Engring., 1977; PhD in Environ. and Occupational Health, U. Ill., Chgo., 1991. Registered profl. engr., Ill.; cert. safety profl. R&D engr. Universal Oil Products Co., Des Plaines, Ill., 1970-73; test engr. Ford Motor Co., Dearborn, Mich., 1973-75; compliance engr. Ford Motor Co., Dearborn, 1977-81; environ. engr. Ill. EPA, Ottawa, 1975-76; sr. engr. Euclid (Ohio) Inc., 1981-84, Triodyne Inc., Niles, Ill., 1984-98; pres. Triodyne Environ. Engring. Inc., Niles, 1990-98; engr. Meridian One-Consulting Engrs., Inc., Des Plaines, Ill., 1998—. Contbr. articles to profl. jours. Recipient Grad. Student award, Am. Chem. Soc., 1989; U.S. EPA fellow, Washingt, 1976. Mem. Am. Nat. Stds. Inst., Nat. Safety Coun., Soc. Automotive Engrs., Water Pollution Control Assn., Air and Waste Mgmt. Assn., Phi Kappa Phi. Achievements include research into industrial hygiene problems in machine tool industry. Home: 3802 Michael Dr Glenview IL 60025-1007

HUTTNER, RICHARD M., publishing executive; b. N.Y.C., Oct. 13, 1947; s. Matthew and Helen (Fried) H.; m. Marcia P. Bernstein, Oct. 12, 1980; children: Elizabeth, Matthew. BA, Yale U., 1969; MBA, Stanford U., 1971. Editor in chief Fawcett Gold Medal Books, N.Y.C., 1975-77; pres. Richard Huttner Agy., Inc., N.Y.C., 1977-81; v.p., pub. Rodale Press, Inc., Emmaus, Pa., 1981-85; v.p. mktg. Daytimers, Inc., Allentown, Pa., 1985-86; chief exec. officer Parenting Unltd., Inc., N.Y.C., 1987-93; v.p. books and info. svcs. Am. Express Pubs., N.Y.C., 1993-94; pres. Sr. Golfer Mag., Boston, 1995-96; mng. dir. Replica Books, Boston, 1997-98; COO Levenson Inst., Inc., Boston, 1998-99; pres., CEO Humanities Inc., Valhalla, N.Y., 1999—. Author: Superbowl, 1981; contbr. articles to popular mags. Capt. USAR, 1971-75. Avocations: running, tennis.

HUTTNER, SIDNEY FREDERICK, librarian; b. Portal, N.D., Feb. 18, 1941; s. Frederick W. and Fern May (Nolting) H.; m. Elizabeth Ann Stege, Oct. 24, 1981; 1 child, Erica Marie. BA in Tutorial Studies, U. Chgo., 1963, MA in Philosophy, 1969. Asst. head spl. collections U. Chgo. Libr., 1970-80; head George Arents Rsch. Libr. Syracuse (N.Y.) Libr., 1980-84; curator spl. collections U. Tulsa Libr., 1984-98; head spl. collections U. Iowa Librs., 1999—. Author: A Register of Artists, Engravers, Booksellers, Bookbinders, Printers and Publishers in New York City, 1821-1842, 1993. Fellow Woodrow Wilson Found., 1963-64. Avocation: bookbinding. Home: 5 Glendale Cir Iowa City IA 52245-3208 Office: Spl Collections U Iowa Librs Iowa City IA 52240-1420

HUTTO, EARL, retired congressman; b. Midland City, Ala., May 12, 1926; s. Lemmie and Ellie Hutto; m. Nancy Myers, July 8, 1967; children: Lori, Amelia Ann. BS, Troy State U., 1949; postgrad., Northwestern U., 1951. Tchr. Cottonwood (Ala.) High Sch., 1949-51; sports and program dir. Sta. WDIG, Dothan, Ala., 1951-54; sports dir. Sta. WEAR-TV, Pensacola, Fla., 1954-60; pres. Sta. WPEX-FM, Pensacola, 1960-65; sports dir. Sta. WSFA-TV, Montgomery, Ala., 1961-63; sports dir., state news editor Sta. WJHG-TV, Panama City, Fla., 1963-74; mem. Fla. Ho. of Reps., 1972-78, 96th-103rd Congresses from 1st Fla. dist., 1978-94; mem. Armed Svcs. com., Merchant Marine Fisheries com.; chmn. subcom. Coast Guard Navigation, 1987-88, readiness subcom, 1989-94; chmn. tech. transfer panel, 1983, spl. ops. panel, 1984-89. Chmn. state govt. divsn. United Way, 1976, 77; mem. exec. bd. Gulf Coast coun. Boy Scouts Am.; deacon 1st Bapt. Ch., Pensacola, Fla.; bd. dirs. Bapt. Hosp., Hospice of N.W. Fla., Pensacola Hist. Soc. With USN, 1944-46. Recipient State Leadership award Sunshine State Assn. for the Blind, 1973; Legislator of Yr. award Fla. Assn. Retarded Children, 1974; Woodmen of the World Conservation award, 1974; Conservationist of Yr. award Bay County Audubon Soc., 1975; Legis. award Fla. Assn. Community Colls., 1978; Watchdog of Treasury award Nat. Associated Businessmen, 1979-80, 86, 88, 90; Alumnus of Yr. award Troy State U., 1980; Christian Statesman award, 1981; Leadership award Am. Security Council, 1982-87; Guardian of Small Bus. award Nat. Fedn. Ind. Businesses, 1986, 88, 90, Disting. Svc. award U.S. Navy League, 1988, Leg award Nat. Assn. Boating Law Adminstrs., 1988, Am. Sec. Co. Eagle of Freedom award, 1990-91, Legislator of Yr. award Am. Sec. Co., 1992, Peace In Strength award, 1991, Disting. Svc. award Am. Logistics Assn., 1994, Lynn Rylander award Am. Def. Preparedness Assn., 1994, Charles Dick medal of merit USNG Assn., 1994. Mem. Am. Def. Preparedness Assn. (Rylanda award 1994), Am. Logistics Assn. (Dist. Svc. award 1994), U.S. Nat. Guard Assn. (Charles Dick medal of merit 1994), Troy State U. Alumni Assn., Rotary. Club: Civitan (dep. gov. Ala.-West Fla. dist. 1967-71). Home: 3459 River Gardens Cir Pensacola FL 32514-8162

HUTTO, JAMES CALHOUN, retired financial executive; b. Florence, S.C., Jan. 7, 1931; s. James Samuel and Miriam Haynes (Calhoun) H.; m. Sarah Doylene Renfroe, Aug. 22, 1953 (div. 1975); children—Martha Haynes, James Calhoun; m. Eleanor Christine Bradshaw, Feb. 13, 1976. B.S. in Commerce, Citadel Mil. Coll. of S.C., 1953; M.A. in Auditing, Sch. Bank Adminstrn., U. Wis., 1970. Certified internal auditor. Asst. br. mgr. C.I.T. Corp., N.Y.C., 1955-58; part owner Quality Tire Service, Inc., Orangeburg, S.C., 1958-61; auditor Am. Bank & Trust Co., Orangeburg, 1961-71; gen. auditor Br. Banking & Trust Co., Wilson, N.C., 1971-73; gen. auditor, v.p. Bank of N.C., Jacksonville, 1973-78; comptroller Humphrey Heating & Roofing Inc., Jacksonville, 1979-81; fin. dir. City of Jacksonville, 1981-85; comptroller Jacobs Builders, Inc., Jacksonville, 1985-93; ret., 1993; instr. Am. Inst. Banking. Served to 1st lt., arty. AUS, 1953-55. Mem. Bank Adminstrn. Inst. (dir. Columbia, S.C. chpt.), Am. Inst. Banking, Inst. Internal Auditors, Bank Adminstrn. Inst. Sch. Alumni Assn. Home: 4 Laran Rd Jacksonville NC 28540-5724

HUTTON, ANNE MOORE, museum consultant; b. Jan. 6, 1946; d. William Clifton and Frances Woods Moore; m. Michael P. Mezzatesta, Mar. 14, 1970 (div. 1987); children: Philip Moore, Alexander Woods, Marya Frances; m. Ernest Watson Hutton Jr., Apr. 20, 1996; stepchildren: Elizabeth, Elinor Hutton. BA in Art History, Columbia U., 1969, MA, 1971, MA in Edn., 1971, MA in Art History, 1982. Tchr. Manassas (Va.) High Sch., 1971-72, Poly. Prep. Country Day Sch., Bklyn., 1972-74; edn. instr. Kimbell Art Mus., Ft. Worth, 1980-83, rsch. assoc., lectr., 1983; assoc. mus. educator, outreach dir. Dallas Mus. Art, 1986-88; curator of edn., lectr. dept. art Oberlin (Ohio) Coll., 1988-90, curator acad. programs, lectr. dept. art, 1991-92; dir., lectr. dept. art The Allen Meml. Art Mus. at Oberlin Coll., 1991-96. Bd. trustees Intermus. Conservation Assn. Mem. Assn. Art Mus. Dirs. Office: 15 W 36th St New York NY 10018

HUTTON, DAVID GLENN, environmental scientist, consultant, chemical engineer; b. Tarentum, Pa., Jan. 23, 1936; s. D. Ray and Z. Alberta (Rieger) H.; m. Judith Ann Gaumer, Dec. 27, 1965; children: Steven L, Michael W. BSChemE, Pa. State U., 1957, MSChemE, 1960. Rsch. engr. DuPont Co., Deepwater, N.J., 1960-68, sr. rsch. engr., 1968-71, sr. process engr., 1971-78, process assoc., 1978-81; tech. specialist DuPont Co., Wilmington, Del., 1981-82; environ. cons. DuPont Co., Newark, Del., 1982-92, D.G. Hutton, Inc., Newark, 1992-97; ret., 1997. Author chpt.: Carbon Adsorption Handbook, 1978, Environmental Chemistry of Dyes and Pigments, 1996; contbr. articles to profl. jours.; patentee in field. Chmn. Citizens Adv. Coun., Newark High, 1985-89, Secondary Citizens Adv. Coun., Christina Sch. Dist., 1985-90. Mem. Del. Camera Club (treas. 1996—). Methodist. Home and Office: 18 Scotch Pine Rd Newark DE 19711-7047

HUTTON, EDWARD LUKE, diversified public corporation executive; b. Bedford, Ind., May 5, 1919; s. Fred and Margaret (Drehobl) H.; m. Kathryn Jane Alexander; children—Edward Alexander, Thomas Charles, Jane Clarke. B.S. with distinction, Ind. U., 1940, M.S. with distinction, 1941; LLD (hon.), Ind. U., Cumberland Coll., 1992. Dep. dir. Joint Export Import Agy. (USUK), Berlin, 1946-48; v.p. World Commerce Corp., 1948-51; asst. v.p. W.R. Grace & Co., 1951-53, cons., 1960-65, exec. v.p., gen. mgr. Dubois Chems. div., 1965-66, group exec. Specialty Products Group and v.p., 1966-68, exec. v.p., 1968-71; cons. internat. trade and fin., 1953-58; fin. v.p., exec. v.p. Ward Industries, 1958-59; pres., chief exec. officer Chemed Corp., Cin., 1971-93; chmn., CEO, 1993—; dir. Chemed Corp., Cin.; chmn. Omnicare, Inc., Cin., 1981—; dir. Omnicare, Inc.; chmn., dir. Roto-Rooter, Inc., 1984-96; chmn. bd. dirs. Nat. San. Supply Co., 1983-97. Co-chmn. Pres.'s Pvt. Sector Survey on Cost Control, exec. com., subcom.; former trustee Millikin U., 1973-84. 1st lt., U.S. Army. Recipient Disting. Alumni Svc. award Ind. U., 1987. Mem. AAUP (governing bd. dirs. 1958—), Econ. Club, Princeton Club, Univ. Club, Queen City Club, Bankers Club. Home: 6680 Miralake Ln Cincinnati OH 45243-2722 Office: Chemed Corp 255 E 5th St Ste 2600 Cincinnati OH 45202-4700

HUTTON, ERNEST WATSON, JR., urban designer, city planner; b. Ft. Myers, Fla., Oct. 25, 1944; s. Ernest Watson and Vera (Bowling) H.; m. Gretchen Bachrach, June 20, 1970 (div.); children: Elizabeth, Elinor; m. Anne Moore, Apr. 20, 1996; stepchildren: Philip, Alexander, Marya Mezzatesta. BA, Princeton U., 1966; BArch., U. Pa., 1968, MArch., M in City Planning, 1970. Sr. urban designer Jonathan Devel. Corp., Mpls., 1970-73, New Community Enterprises, Mpls., 1972-73, Arlen Realty & Devel. Corp., N.Y.C., 1973-74; sr. assoc. Llewelyn-Davies Internat., N.Y.C./Toronto/London, 1974-80; ptnr. Buckhurst Fish Hutton Katz Inc., N.Y.C., 1980-92; prin. Hutton Assocs., Inc., N.Y.C., 1993—; mem. Union Square Alliance, 1995—; bd. dirs. Ky.-W.Va. Coal Co., 1996—. Author: (with others) Cultural Facilities in Mixed Use Development, 1986; prin. works include Pitts. Cultural Dist./CNG Tower/Benedum Ctr., 1980-87 (HUD Nat. Merit award), Roanoke Vision Plan/Neighborhood Partnership, 1980-94 (Am. Planning Assn. Nat award), Hartford Riverfront Recapture Plan, 1981-85, 96-97 (Nat. Waterfront award 1997), Knoxville Downtown/Riverfront Plan, 1987-92, Rutland (Vt.) Downtown Plan, 1988-89, 95, Charlotte Dist., 1986-87, 91, Akron Downtown Plan, 1993-94, Conn. Scenic Byway Plan, 1994-98, Bridgeport Cultural Plan, 1995-98, Buffalo Waterfront, 1997-98. Fellow Inst. Urban Design; mem. Mayors Inst. City Design, Am. Inst. Cert. Planners, Am. Planning Assn., Urban Land Inst., Am. Vaudeville Inc. (pres., bd. dirs. 1989-92), Lucille Ball Comedy Festival (mng. prodr. 1991), Cap and Gown Club (Princeton, N.J.). Home: 172 Pacific St Brooklyn NY 11201-6214 Office: Hutton Assocs Inc 13th Fl 15 W 36th St New York NY 10018

HUTTON, HERBERT J., federal judge; b. 1937. AB, Lincoln U., 1959; JD, Temple U., 1962. With Housing and Home Fin. Agy., 1962-64; mem. firm Norris Brown & Hall, 1964-69, Norris, Wells & Neal, 1969-72, Norris & Wells, 1972-76, Simpkins & Tucker, 1977-88; hearing officer Bd. Revision Taxes, Phila., 1982-88; judge U.S. Dist. Ct. (ea. dist.) Pa., Phila., 1988—. Recipient Bd. Dirs. City Trusts' award, 1988. Mem. Phila Bar Assn. (Medal of Svc. 1982), Phila. Bar Found. (trustee), Fed. Judges Assn. Office: US Dist Ct 9614 US Courthouse 601 Market St Philadelphia PA 19106-1713 *Notable cases include: Antinoph, et al vs. Laverall Reynolds Securities, Inc., et al., U.S. Dist.Ct., ea. dist. Pa., C.A. No. 88-3664, 703 F.Supp. 1185, which involved securities, fraud and breach of contract; Johnson vs. Phila. Electric Co., U.S. Dist.Ct., ea. dist. Pa., C.A. No. 88-0085, which involved civil rights, Title VII Civil Rights Act of 1964 and 42 U.S.C. 1981.**

HUTTON, JOHN EVANS, JR., surgery educator, retired military officer; b. N.Y.C., Sept. 9, 1931; s. John Evans and Antoinette (Abbott) H.; m. Barbara Seward Joyce, Apr. 15, 1961; children: John III, Wendy, James, Elizabeth. BA, Wesleyan U., 1953; MD, George Washington U., 1963. Diplomate: Am. Bd. Surgery, Am. Bd. Med. Examiners. Commd. 2d lt. USMC, 1953, advanced through grades to capt., 1962; discharged USMCR; commd. capt. U.S. Army, 1963, advanced through grades to brig. gen., 1989; intern, resident in gen. surgery Walter Reed Army Med. Ctr. U.S. Army, Washington, 1963-68, fellow vascular surgery, 1969-70, asst. chief vascular surgery, 1970-71, mem. staff gen. surgery svcs., 1969-71, chief dept. surgery, 1981-84, White House physician, 1984-86, physician to the Pres., 1987-88; chief surgeon 91st Evacuation Hosp. U.S. Army, Vietnam, 1968-69, chief vascular surgery, asst. chief gen. surgery, 1971-74; chief gen. and vascular surgery, program dir., gen. surgery residency Letterman Army Med. Ctr. U.S. Army, San Francisco, 1975-81; comdr. 47th Field Hosp., Honduras, 1984; commanding gen. Madigan Army Med. Ctr. U.S. Army, Tacoma, Wash., 1989-92; ret., 1992; prof. clin. surgery, chief div. gen. surgery, dept. surg. Uniformed Svcs. U. Health Scis., Bethesda, Md., 1992—, mem. faculty senate, 1996—; mem. students promotion com., 1993-96, mem. instl. rev. bd., 1993-96, mem. com. appointments, promotion and tenure, 1998—, pres. elect faculty senate, 1997, pres. faculty senate, 1998; assoc. clin. prof. surgery U. Calif., San Francisco, 1978-81; assoc. prof. surgery, vice chmn. dept. surgery Uniformed Svcs. U. Health Scis., Bethesda, 1981-84, prof. surgery, 1985—; clin. prof. surgery Tulane U. Sch. Medicine, 1988—, George Washington Sch. Medicine, Washington, 1985—. Contbr. articles, photographs to profl. publs. Mem. men and boys choir Grace Cathedral, San Francisco, 1971-75. Decorated D.S.M., Bronze Star, Meritorious Svcs. medal with oak leaf cluster, Army commendation medal, Navy Commendation medal, Joint Svc. Commendation medal, Vietnam Svc. Medal with Four Bronze Svc. Stars, Natl. Defense Svc. Medal with Two Bronze Svc. Stars, Naval Occupation Medal, WWII, Vietnam Honor medal 1st class, Vietnam Cross of Gallantry; recipient Barron Dominique Larrey award for excellence in surgery; named to Mil. Order of Med. Merit, 1982; named Prominent Alumnus, George Washington U., 1990. Fellow ACS (Met. Washington chpt.); mem. Internat. Cardiovasc. Soc., Soc. Clin. Vascular Surgery, Am. Assn. for the Surgery of Trauma, Soc. Mil. Vascular Surgery, Chesapeake Vascular Soc., Bay Surg. Soc. (hon.), U.S. Naval Acad. Sailing Squadron, Metropolitan Washington Chapt., Amer. Coll. of Surgs., The Acad. of Med., St. Francis Yacht Club (membership com. 1978-81), Soc. for Mil. Consultants to the Armed Forces (counsilor). Republican. Episcopalian. Avocations: music, photography, competitive sailing, coaching. Home: 1707 Priscilla Dr Silver Spring MD 20904-1610 Office: Uniformed Svcs U Health Scis Dept Surgery 4301 Jones Bridge Rd Bethesda MD 20814-4712

HUTTON, MARY J., guidance counselor; b. Kansas City, Mo., Nov. 21, 1951; d. Bill H. and Vera M. (Needels) Harmon; m. Douglas L. Hutton, June 1, 1974; children: Dylan M., Marissa S. Cert. in Elem. Edn., Northwest Mo. State U., 1973; M in Counseling, U. Iowa, 1985. Tchr. Mid-Buchanan Community Sch., St. Joseph, Mo., 1973-74; co-dir. Adolescent Ctr. FAMCO, Cedar Rapids, Iowa, 1974-76; employment specialist State of Iowa, Iowa City, 1976-80; employment mgr. Mercy Hosp., Iowa City, 1980-85; guidance counselor Linn Mar Community Sch., Cedar Rapids, 1985—. Mem. St. Paul's United Meth. Ch. Mem. NEA, Linn Mar Edn. Assn., Iowa Assn. for Counselors. Avocations: needle work, reading, children, Tae Kwon Do (black belt). Home: 2366 Towne House Dr NE Cedar Rapids IA 52402-2228 Office: Bowman Woods 151 Boyson Rd NE Cedar Rapids IA 52402-1415

HUTTON, PAUL ANDREW, history educator, writer; b. Frankfurt, Germany, Oct. 23, 1949; naturalized citizen; s. Paul Andrew and Louise Katherine (Johnson) H.; m. Vicki Lynne Bauer, 1972 (div. 1985); 1 child, Laura; m. Lynn Terri Brittner, Dec. 31, 1988 (div. 1996); children: Lorena, Paul. BA, Ind. U., 1972, MA, 1974, PhD, 1981. Editorial asst. Jour. Am. History, Bloomington, Ind., 1973-77; instr. history Utah State U., Logan, 1977-80, asst. prof., 1980-84; asst. prof. U. N.Mex., Albuquerque, 1984-86, assoc. prof., 1986-96; prof. U. N.Mex., Albuquerque, 1996—. Author: Phil Sheridan and His Army, 1985; editor: Ten Days on the Plains, 1985, Soldiers West, 1987, The Custer Reader, 1992, (series) Eyewitness to the Civil War, 1991-93, Frontier and Region, 1997; assoc. editor Western Hist. Quar., 1977-84; editor N.Mex. Hist. Rev., 1985-91. Mem. Little Bighorn Battlefield Indian Meml. Adv. Com., Nat. Park Svc., 1994—. Recipient Evans Biography award Brigham Young U., 1986, Paladin award Mont. Hist. Soc., 1991, Western Heritage award Nat. Cowboy Hall of Fame, 1996, 99; named Mead Disting. Rsch. fellow Huntington Libr., 1988. Mem. Orgn. Am. Historians (Ray A. Billington award 1986), Western Hist. Assn. (exec. dir. 1990—), Soc. for Mil. History, Western Writers Am. (exec. bd. 1997-99, Spur award 1985, Pres. award 1998), Writers Guild Am. West. Office: Dept History Univ NMex Albuquerque NM 87131-1181

HUTTON, TIMOTHY, actor; b. Malibu, Calif., Aug. 16, 1960; s. Jim and Maryline H.; m. Debra Winger, March 16, 1986 (div.); 1 child, Emmanuel Noah. Appeared in TV movies Zuma Beach, 1978, Best Place to Be, 1979, Baby Makes Six, 1979, Friendly Fire, 1979, Young Love, First Love, 1979, Father Figure, 1980, The Oldest Living Graduate, 1980, Sultan and the Rock Star, 1980, A Long Way Home, 1981, We're Family Again, 1981, Zelda, 1993; films include Ordinary People, 1980 (Best Supporting Actor Acad. award 1981), Taps, 1981, Daniel, 1983, Iceman, 1984, Turk 182, 1985, The

Falcon and the Snowman, 1985, Made in Heaven, 1987, A Time of Destiny, 1988, Everybody's All-American, 1988, Betrayed, 1988, Torrents of Spring, 1990, Q & A, 1990, The Temp, 1993, The Dark Half, 1993, French Kiss, 1995, Scenes from Everyday Life, 1995, The Substance of Fire, 1996, Mr. and Mrs. Loving, 1996, Beautiful Girls, 1996, City of Industry, 1997, Playing God, 1997, Deterrence, 1998, The General's Daughter, 1999; Broadway includes Prelude to a Kiss, 1990, Babylon Gardens, 1991; dir. video Drive, 1984 (The Cars song); dir. episode Amazing Stories, 1985 (Grandpa's Ghost). Recipient Oscar for best supporting actor, Ordinary People, 1980. Office: CAA 9830 Wilshire Blvd Beverly Hills CA 90212-1804*

HUTTON, WILLIAM MICHAEL, manufacturing company owner; b. Herrin, Ill., June 15, 1948; s. William T. and Violet (Childress) H.; m. Lois A. Piontkowski, Sept. 7, 1968; children: Cynthia L., Pamela. BS in Mgmt. Scis., So. Ill. U., 1972; MA in Ops. Mgmt., Norwich U., 1991. Cert. foodservice profl., SME mfg. engr. Mgr. machining ops. Ingersoll-Rand, Phillipsburg, N.J., 1973-83; mgr. of mfr. Bendix Aerospace Corp., Eatontown, N.J., 1983-84; v.p. ops. Follett Corp., Easton, Pa., 1984-87, pres., COO, 1988-95; CEO Wilkra Co., Inc., Portland, Pa., 1995, also bd. dirs.; ptnr. Filtration Mfg. Co.; cons. to small mfg. co.; exec. in residence So. Ill. U., 1991—, also guest lectr. MBA classes Coll. Bus., S.S. U.; guest lectr. MBA classes Moravian Coll.; bd. dirs. Bustin Industries. Author: Competitve Strategy, A Heuristic Model for Linking Manufacturing and Marketing, 1992. Chmn. adv. bd. Coll. Bus. and Adminstrn., So. Ill. U., 1989—, Ben Franklin Inst., 1991—; bd. dirs. Forum Lehigh Valley. Recipient Alumni Achievement award So.Ill. U., 1992, named to Hall of Fame Coll. Bus., 1994. Mem. So. Ill. U. Alumni Assn., Young Pres.'s Orgn., Grouse Soc., Soc. Manufacturing Engrs., Ducks Unlimited. Republican. Roman Catholic. Avocations: computer-aided design, springer spaniel training, fly fishing, upland hunting. E-mail: hutton@wilkra.com. Home: 4640 Hillview Dr Nazareth PA 18064-8525 Office: Wilkra Co Rt 611 and Church St Portland PA 18351

HUTZELMAN, MARTHA LOUISE, lawyer; b. Hamilton, Ohio, Jan. 2, 1958; d. Donald Evert and Jeanne Louise (Thompson) H.; 1 child, Isolda Marie Meade. BA, Ohio No. U., 1979; JD, U. Ariz., 1982. Bar: Okla. 1983, Va. 1995, U.S. Tax Ct. 1991. Tax staff acct. Arthur Andersen & Co., Oklahoma City, 1982-83; benefits tax counsel Kerr-McGee Corp., Oklahoma City, 1983-91; sr. trial atty. IRS, Washington, 1991-95; shareholder Bosley & Hutzelman P.C., Alexandria, Va., 1995—. Mem. ABA (mem. employee benefits com. tax sect. 1996—). Home: 9025 Andromeda Dr Burke VA 22015-3504 Office: Bosley & Hutzelman PC 801 N Fairfax St Ste 209 Alexandria VA 22314-1757

HUTZLER, LISA ANN, mental health nurse, adult clinical psychologist; b. Marietta, Ohio, Oct. 8, 1955; d. Donald Hayes and Winifred Maxine (Clark) Hutzler; m. Ernest Edwin Miller Jr., May 24, 1980; children: Nathan Andrew Miller, Daniel Seth Miller. BA in Psychology, Marietta Coll., 1977; AAS, Parkersburg Community Coll., W.Va., 1980; MA in Psychology, W. Va. Grad. Coll., 1995. RN, W.Va. RN adult psychiat. unit Cuyahoga Falls (Ohio) Gen. Hosp., 1982-83; staff nurse adult mental health St. Joseph's Hosp., Parkersburg, 1980-82, 85-91; personal care nurse Braley and Thompson, Vienna, W. Va., 1992-93. Vol. Boy Scouts Am./standard first aid instr., ARC. Mem. ANA, W.Va. Nurses Assn.

HUVAERE, RICHARD FLOYD, auto dealer; b. Detroit, Dec. 2, 1944; s. Jerome and Kathryn Huvaere; m. Joan F. Nimmo, May 23, 1970 (div. 1989); children: Jason J.D., Sara E.L.; m. Stephanie Marie Roscia, May 27, 1995; stepchildren: Ronald, Ryan. A in Auto Mktg., Northwood U., Midland, Mich., 1966, BA in Bus., 1968. Pres., CEO Richmond (Mich.) Chrysler-Plymouth Dodge, 1968—; vice chmn. Mich. Auto Dealers Self-Insured Fund, Ypsilanti, 1988; chmn. Auto Dealers Ins. Co. Ltd., Bermuda; pres. Richmond Travel, Richmond Marine, Dick Huvaere Land, Inc.; sec.-treas. Startec Security, Inc., Diversified Data Svcs., Inc., Huvaere Group Co. Chmn. Centennial Bldg. Fund, Richmond, 1990-95; mem. St. Clair County Airport Adv. Bd., Port Huron, Mich., 1988-94; capt. U.S. Merchant Marine, 1990. Recipient Outstanding Alumni award Northwood U., 1989. Mem. Nat. Auto Dealers Assn., Mich. Auto Dealers Assn. (bd. dirs.), Detroit Auto Dealers Assn., Greater Detroit Chrysler-Plymouth Dealers Assn., Greater Detroit Dodge Dealers Assn., Richmond C. of C., Rotary, Grosse Pointe Power Squadron, Detroit Yacht Club, The Old Club, Ocean Reef Club. Republican. Lutheran. Avocation: boating. Home: Roseburn Pl 36035 Washington St Richmond MI 48062-1039 Office: Richmond Chrysler-Plymouth 67567 S Main St Richmond MI 48062-1925

HUVOS, ANDREW, internist, cardiologist, educator; b. Budapest, Hungary, Apr. 23, 1930; came to U.S., 1950; s. Julian Gyula and Magdolna (Matyas) H.; m. Monique Chatriot, June 8, 1959; children: Christine, Anne, Philip. Student, Free U. Brussels, 1948-50, Harvard U., 1951; MD, Boston U., 1955. Diplomate Am. Bd. Internal Medicine, Am. Bd. Cardiovascular Disease. Resident in medicine Yale-New Haven Med. Ctr., 1955-59; fellow in cardiology Mass. Gen. Hosp., Boston, 1961-63; physician-in-charge cardiac catheterization lab. Univ. Hosp., Boston, 1963-70; chief cardiology Faulkner Hosp., Boston, 1970-74, chief medicine, 1974-95; lectr. medicine Harvard Med. Sch., Boston, 1974-86; lectr. medicine and physiology Boston U. Sch. Medicine, 1976—; prof. medicine Tufts U. Sch. Medicine, Boston, 1985-97, prof. emeritus, 1997—; dir. Tufts Assoc. Health Plan, 1979-81. Contbr. articles to med. jours., chpts. to books. Chmn. bd. trustees Ecole Bilingue, Inc., Arlington, Mass., 1970-74; trustee Boston Med. Libr., 1981-85. Capt. M.C., U.S. Army, 1959-61. Recipient Excellence in Teaching award Boston U. Sch. Medicine, 1974; USPHS grantee, 1977-83. Fellow ACP, Am. Coll. Cardiology, Am. Coll. Chest Physicians (pres. New Eng. States chpt. 1981-83); mem. Am. Heart Assn. (fellow couns. clin. cardiology and circulation), Dorchester Med. Club, Roxbury Clin. Record Club, Alpha Omega Alpha. Presbyterian. Avocations: opera, classical music. Office: Faulkner Hosp Boston MA 02130

HUVOS, CHRISTOPHER L., psychologist; b. Budapest, Hungary, June 18, 1946; came to U.S., 1956; s. Kornel and Anna Maria (Ledniczky) H.; m. Sally Brewster Moulton, Aug. 7, 1982; 1 child, Emma Brewster Moulton Huvos. AB, Harvard U., 1968, MAT, 1972; PsyD, Mass. Sch. Profl. Psychology, 1983. Lic. psychologist. Mental health assoc. VA, Boston, 1979-80; psychologist Milton (Mass.) Acad., 1981-85; prin. psychologist Met. State Hosp., Waltham, Mass., 1985-88, chief psychologist, 1988-92; pvt. practice Arlington, Mass., 1983—; clin. instr. dept. psychiatry Harvard Med. Sch., Boston and Cambridge, 1986—; psychologist Westborough State Hosp., 1992-95; psychologist Tewksbury Hosp., 1995—, dir. psychology tng., 1996—; trustee Mass. Sch. Profl. Psychology, Dedham, 1986—. Editor: Mass. Psychol. Assn. Newsletter, 1984-89. Fellow Mass. Psychol. Assn. (bd. dirs. 1987-89); mem. Am. Psychol. Assn. Office: Tewksbury Hosp Dept Psychology 365 East St Tewksbury MA 01876-1998

HUWILER, JOAN P., public relations executive, consultant; b. New Haven, Conn., June 15, 1963; d. Paul F. and Joan E. (Tickey) H. BA in Comm., Southern Conn. State Univ., 1985; MS in Journalism, Boston Univ., 1990. Account coord. Coates Pub. Rels. subs. Mason & Madison Advertising, Bethany, Conn., 1985-86; devel. fund raiser Atty. Gen. Joe Lieberman, Hartford, Conn., 1986; dep. press sec. Office Atty. Gen., State of Conn., Hartford, Conn., 1986-89; media dir. NOW Legal Def. and Edn. Fund, N.Y., 1990-92; cons., 1992-96; exec. dir. Schooner Inc., New Haven, Conn., 1992-93; comms. officer Cmty. Found. for Greater New Haven, New Haven, Conn., 1996-99; mktg. and comm. mgr. S. Ctrl. Regional Water Auth., New Haven, 1999—; teaching asst. Boston Univ., 1989-90; pub. info. officer Hamden Bd. of Edn., 1984-85; writer, cons. Bank Mart, Bridgeport, Conn., 1985-86. Recipient Vanguard spl. merit award Women in Comm., 1991. Mem. Comm. Network in Philanthropy, Pub. Rels. Soc. Am. Democrat. Avocations: reading, cooking, gardening. Office: S Ctrl Conn Regional Water Auth 90 Sargent Dr New Haven CT 06511

HUXFORD, J. DAVID, retired sales representative; b. Syracuse, N.Y., Jan. 2, 1925; s. James H. and Marion Louise (McNally) H.; m. Theodora Annette Weeks, Oct. 31, 1946; four children. BA in Econs., Notre Dame U., 1951. Supply & cost mgr. L.A.B. Corp., Skaneateles, N.Y., 1953-58; contract sales Pitts. Plate Glass Co., Syracuse, 1958-62; archl. rep. PPG Industries, Inc., Skaneateles, 1962-75; contract sales B.R. Johnson & Son, Inc., Syracuse, 1975-77; mfr.'s rep. Roberts-Gordon Inc., Buffalo, Syracuse, 1978-92. Pres. Prodrs. Coun., Syracuse chpt., 1968-69; first industry mem. pres. Constrn. Specifications Inst., Syracuse chpt., 1974-75; trustee Village Bd., Skaneateles, 1963-64, N.Y. State Hunter Instr., 1953-86, chmn. planning bd., 1990—, Nat. Rifle Assn. (life Mem.). Ret. Capt. USMC Reserve, 1942-63. Home: 52 Fennell St Skaneateles NY 13152-1122

HUXLEY, SIR ANDREW (FIELDING), physiologist, educator; b. London, Nov. 22, 1917; s. Leonard and Rosalind (Bruce) H.; m. Jocelyn Richenda Gammell Pease, July 5, 1947; children: Janet Rachel, Stewart Leonard, Camilla Rosalind, Eleanor Bruce, Henrietta Catherine, Clare Marjory Pease. BA, Cambridge (Eng.) U., 1938, MA, 1941, ScD (hon.), 1978; MD (hon.), U. Saar, 1964, Marseille U., 1979, Humboldt U., Berlin, 1985, Ulm U., 1993, Charles U., Prague, 1998; DSc (hon.), U. Sheffield, Eng., 1964, U. Leicester, Eng., 1967, London U., 1973, U. St. Andrews, Scotland, 1974, U. Aston, Birmingham, Eng., 1977, U. Western Australia, 1982, Oxford U., 1983, U. Pa., 1984, Harvard U., 1984, U. Keele, 1985, East Anglia U., 1985, U. Md., 1987, Brunel U., 1988, U. Hyderabad, 1991, Glasgow U., 1993, Witwatersrand U., 1998; LLD (hon.), U. Birmingham, 1979, Dundee U., 1984; Dr (hon.), York U., 1981, Toyama Med. and Pharm. U., 1995; DHL (hon.), NYU, 1982. Mem. rsch. staff Anti-Aircraft Command, 1940-42, Admiralty, 1942-45; fellow Trinity Coll., Cambridge, 1941-60, 90—, hon. fellow, 1967-90, master, 1984-90, dir. studies, 1952-60; demonstrator Cambridge U., 1946-50, asst. dir. rsch., 1951-59, reader exptl. biophysics, 1959-60; Jodrell prof. physiology U. Coll. London, 1960-69, Royal Soc. rsch. prof., 1969-83, hon. fellow, 1980; emeritus prof. physiology U. London, 1983—; Herter lectr. Johns Hopkins U., 1959; Jesup lectr. Columbia U., 1964; Forbes lectr., 1966; Croonian lectr. Royal Soc., 1967, Florey lectr., 1982, Blackett Meml. lectr., 1984; Fullerian prof. Royal Inst., London, 1967-73; Hans Hecht lectr., Chgo., 1975; Sherrington lectr. Liverpool U., 1976-77; Centenary Colloquium lectr. Berlin Inst. Physiology, 1977; Cecil H. and Ida Green vis. prof. U. B.C., 1980; 6th ann. Darwin Lecture, 1982, Romanes Lecture, Oxford U., 1983; Tarner lectrs. Trinity Coll., Cambridge, 1988; Maulana Abul Kalam Azad Meml. Lecture, New Delhi, 1991; C.G. Bernhard lecture, Stockholm, 1993. Author: Reflections on Muscle, 1980; editor Jour. Physiology, 1950-57, chmn. bd. Publs. on analysis of nerve conduction (with Hodgkin), physiology of striated muscle, devel. of interference microscope and ultramicrotome. Trustee Brit. Mus. (Natural History), 1981-90, Sci. Mus., 1984-88. Created knight bachelor, 1974; decorated Order of Merit, 1983, Grand Cordon of Sacred Treasure (Japan), 1995; recipient (with A.L. Hodgkin and J.C. Eccles) Nobel prize for physiology or medicine, 1963, Swammerdam medal Soc. for Advancement of Natural Scis., Medicine and Surgery, Amsterdam, 1997; Imperial Coll. Sci. and Tech. hon. fellow, 1980; Queen Mary and Westfield Coll. fellow, 1987. Fellow Royal Soc. (Copley medal 1973, council 1960-62, 77-79, 80-85, pres. 1980-85), Royal Acad. Engring. (hon.), Inst. Biology (hon.), Royal Soc. Can. (hon.), Royal Soc. Edinburgh (hon.), Indian Nat. Sci. Acad. (fgn.); mem. Physiol. Soc. (hon., rev. lectr. on muscular contraction 1973), Internat. Union Physiol. Scis. (pres. 1986-93), Brit. Biophys. Soc., Royal Acad. Scis., Letters and Fine Arts Belgium (assoc.), Muscular Dystrophy Group Gt. Britain and No. Ireland (chmn. med. research com. 1974-81, v.p., 1981—), Royal Instn. Gt. Britain (hon.), Anat. Soc. Gt. Britain and Ireland (hon.), Am. Philos. Soc., Brit. Assn. Advancement Sci. (pres. 1976-77), NAS (U.S.) (fgn. assoc.), Royal Acad. Medicine Belgium (assoc.), Dutch Soc. Scis. (fgn.), Am. Soc. Zoologists (hon.), Royal Irish Acad. (hon.), Japan Acad. (hon.), Nature Conservancy (coun. 1985-88). Home and Office: Manor Field, 1 Vicarage Dr Grantchester, Cambridge CB3 9NG, England

HUXLEY, HUGH ESMOR, molecular biologist, educator; b. Birkenhead, Eng., Feb. 25, 1924; s. Thomeas Hugh and Olwen (Roberst) H. BA, Cambridge (Eng.) U., 1948, MA, 1950, PhD, 1952, ScD, 1964; DSc (hon.), Harvard U., 1969, U. Chgo., 1974, U. Pa., 1975, U. Leicester, 1989. Rschr. molecular biology unit Med. Rsch. Coun., Cavendish Lab., Cambridge, 1948-52, sci. staff, 1954-55; external staff dept. biophysics Med. Rsch. Coun., U. Coll., London, 1956-61; external staff dept. biophysics Med. Rsch. Coun. Lab. Molecular Biology, London, 1962-87, dep. dir., 1977-87; prof. biology rosenteil Basic Med. Scis. Rsch. Ctr., Brandeis U., Waltham, Mass., 1987-97; dir. Basic Med. Scis. Rsch. Ctr., Brandeis U., Waltham, 1988-94, prof. emeritus, 1997—. Editor: Progress in Biophysics and Molecular Biology, 1960-66; mem. editl. bd. Jour. Cell Biology, 1959-63, Jour. Molecular Biology, 1962-70, 79-86, 90-93, Jour. Cell Sci., 1966-70; contbr. articles to profl. jours. Officer RAF, 1943-47. Decorated Order Brit. Empire; recipient Feldberg prize, 1963, Hardy prize, 1965, Louisa Gross Hurwitz prize, 1971, Internat. Feltrinelli prize, 1974, Gairdner aard, 1975, Baly medal Royal Coll. Physicians, 1975, E.B. Wilson medal Am. Soc. Cell Biology, 1983, Albert Einstein award World Cultural Coun., 1987, Franklin medal, 1990, Disting. Scientist award Electron Microscopy Soc. Am., 1991; Commonwealth Fund fellow Mass. Inst. Tech., 1952-54, Christ's Coll. fellow Cambridge U., 1954-56, hon. fellow, 1981, King's Coll. fellow, 1961-67, Churchill Coll. fellow, 1967-87. Fellow Royal Soc. (Royal medal 1977, Copley medal 1997), Am. Biophysical Soc.; mem. NAS (hon. fgn. assoc.), Physiol. Soc., Brit. Biophys. Soc., European Molecular Biology Orgn., Am. Acad. Arts and Scis. (hon. fgn.), Danish Acad. Scis., Leopoldina Acad. Home: 349 Nashawtuc Rd Concord MA 01742-1616

HUXLEY, MARY ATSUKO, artist; b. Stockton, Calif., Mar. 5, 1930; d. Henry K. and Kiku H. (Kisanuki) Taniguchi; m. Harold Daniels Huxley, 1957. Student, Armstrong Coll., Berkeley, Calif., 1950, San Francisco Art Inst., 1968; pvt. studies with, Thomas C. Leighton, 1970-75. art show judge regional art clubs, corps., pvt. orgns., and county fairs, 1972-99. Solo shows include Artists' Coop., San Francisco, 1973, 75, 76, The Univ. Club, San Francisco, 1976, I. Magnin, San Mateo, 1976, Palo Alto Med. Found., 1992, Galerie Genese, San Mateo, 1993; exhibited in group shows at Catharine Lorillard Wolf Art Club, N.Y.C., 1979, Knickerbocker Artists of Am., N.Y.C., 1979, Salmagundi Club Ann., N.Y.C., 1981, Butler Inst. Am. Art, Youngstown, Ohio, 1982, Am. Artists Profl. League, N.Y.C., 1982, 83, 86, 87, 88, Oil Painters of Am. Ann. Nat. Juried Shows, Gallery at Long Grove, Ill., 1993, 94, Taos, N.Mex., 1997, Oil Painters of Am. Ann. Pacific Coast Regional Juried Show, Jones & Terwilliger Gallery, Carmel, Calif., 1997, San Francisco Ann. Art Festival, 1970-74, Renaissance Gallery, Santa Rosa, Calif., 1973, Paramount Theater, Oakland, Calif., 1974, Met. Club Invitational, San Francisco, Marin Soc. Artists Ann., Ross, Calif., 1976, 79, Soc. Western Artists Ann., San Francisco, 1976, 78, 80, Peninsula Art Assn. Ann., Belmont, Calif., 1980, Fresno (Calif.) Fashion Fair Ann., 1981, 84, De Saisset Gallery, U. Santa Clara, Calif., 1979, Lodi (Calif.) Ann. Grape and Art Festival, 1970, 71, 72, 73, 74, 75, 76, 77, 78, 79, 81, San Mateo County Ann. Floral Fiesta, 1975, 76, 77, 78, 79, 81, Charles & Emma Frye Mus. Gallery, Seattle, 1975, Redwood City Women's Club Ann. Flower Show, 1978, Fremont Art Assn. Anns., 1987, 88, 89, numerous others; represented in numerous pvt. and corp. collections in U.S., Europe and the Far East. Recipient Marjorie Walter Spl. award San Mateo County Exhbn., 1975, Gold medallion and 1st award San Mateo County Fair Fine Arts Exhbn., 1976, Best of Show award Cultural Arts of Palo Alto and Palo Alto Art Club, 1979, Best of Show and 1st award U. Art Ctr. and Palo Alto Art Club Ann., 1981, Spl. Merit award Oakland Art Assn., John Muir Med. Ctr. Ann., 1989, 1st award Burlingame Art Soc. Anns., 1976, 77, 1st award Redwood City Women's Club Ann. Flower Show, 1978, 1st award Soc. Western Artists Palo Alto Med. Ctr. Ann., 1983, 1st award Soc. Soc. Western Artists John Muir Med. Ctr. Ann., 1986, 1st award Fremont Art Assn. Ann., 1989, numerous others. Fellow Am. Artists Profl. League; mem. Soc. Western Artists (signature, trustee 1986-97, bd. dirs. 1972-75, 98, chmn. juried exhbns. 1972-81), Am. Soc. Classical Realism, Oil Painters Am. (signature), Allied Artists Am., Marin Soc. Artists (signature), Palo Alto Cultural Ctr. Studio: PO Box 5467 San Mateo CA 94402-0467

HUXTABLE, ADA LOUISE, architecture critic; b. N.Y.C.; d. Michael Louis and Leah (Rosenthal) Landman; m. L. Garth Huxtable. AB magna cum laude, Hunter Coll.; postgrad., Inst. Fine Arts, NYU; hon. degrees, Harvard U., Yale U., NYU, Washington U., U. Mass., Oberlin Coll., Miami U., R.I. Sch. Design, U. Pa., Radcliffe Coll., Oberlin Coll., Smith Coll., Skidmore Coll., Md. Inst., Mt. Holyoke Coll., Trinity Coll., LaSalle U., Pace Coll., Pratt Inst., Colgate U., Hamilton U., Williams Coll., Rutgers U., Finch Coll., Emerson Coll., C.W. Post Coll. at L.I. U., Cleve. State U., Bard Coll., Fordham U., Parsons Sch. Design, Mass. Coll. Art. Asst. curator architecture and design The Museum of Modern Art, N.Y.C., 1946-50; Fulbright fellow for advanced study in architecture and design Italy, 1950, 52; free-lance writer, contbg. editor to Progressive Architecture and Art in America, 1950-63; architecture critic N.Y. Times, N.Y.C., 1963-82; mem. editorial bd. N.Y. Times, 1973-82; Cook lectr. in Am. instns. U. Mich., 1977; Hitchcock lect. U. Calif.-Berkeley, 1982; corp. vis. com. Harvard U. Grad. Sch. Design, Sch. Visual and Environ. Arts; bd. dirs. N.Y. Landmarks Conservancy; mem. adv. bd. Am. Trust Brit. Libr.; archtl. cons. Nat. Gallery, London, J. Paul Getty Trust, L.A., San Francisco Pub. Libr., Mus. Contemporary Art, Chgo., archtl. critic The Wall Street Jour., 1996—. Author: Pier Luigi Nervi, 1960, Classic New York, 1964, Will They Ever Finish Bruckner Boulevard?, 1970, Kicked a Building Lately?, 1976, The Tall Building Artistically Reconsidered: The Search for a Skyscraper Style, 1985, Goodbye History, Hello Hamburger 1986, Architecture Anyone? 1986, The Unreal America: Architecture and Illusion, 1997. Recipient 1st Pulitzer prize for disting. criticism, 1970, Spl. award Nat. Trust for Historic Preservation, 1971, Archtl. Criticism medal AIA, 1969, medal for lit. Nat. Arts Club, 1971, Diamond Jubilee medallion City N.Y., 1973, Mayor's Cultural award, 1984, Woman of Yr. award AAUW, 1974, Sec.'s award for conservation U.S. Dept. Interior, 1976, Thomas Jefferson medal U. Va., 1977, Archtl. Criticism medal Acad. d' Architecture Française, 1988; Guggenheim fellow for studies in Am. architecture, 1958, MacArthur fellow, 1981-86, Henry Allen Moe prize Humanities Am. Philosophical Soc., 1992. Fellow Am. Acad. Arts and Scis., Royal Inst. Brit. Architects (hon.), AAAL; mem. AIA (hon.), Am. Acad. Arts and Letters, Soc. Archtl. Historians. Home: 969 Park Ave New York NY 10028-0322

HUYCK, MARGARET HELLIE, psychology educator; b. Waterloo, Iowa, Apr. 14, 1939; d. Ole Ingeman and Mary Elizabeth (larsen) Hellie; m. William Thomas Huyck, June 24, 1961; children: Elizabeth, Karin. BA, Vassar Coll., 1961; MA, U. Chgo., 1963, PhD, 1970. Lic. psychologist, Ill. Asst. prof. Ill. Inst. Tech., Chgo., 1969-75, assoc. prof., 1975-89, prof. dept. psychology, 1990—; prof. dept. psychology; vis. lectr. U. Oslo, 1977-78; lectr. Provident Hosp. Sch. Nursing, Chgo., 1964-66, Am. Soc. Aging, 1989-91; cons. Northwestern U., Evanston, Ill., 1973-79, Elgin (Ill.) Mental Health Ctr., 1975-77, No. Trust Bank, Chgo., 1981-85, Evanston Hosp., 1992-93. Author: Growing Older, 1974; co-author: Adult Development, 1982. Bd. mem. S.E. Chgo. Commn. Recipient Rsch. award NIMH, 1982-86. Fellow Gertontol. Assn. Am., Gerontol. Soc. Am. (sec. 1991-94); mem. APA (sci. policy fellow Office Behavioral and Social Sci. Rsch./NIH 1997-98), Older Women's League Ill. (pres. 1994-97). Unitarian-Universalist. Office: Ill Inst Tech Inst Psychology Chicago IL 60616-3732

HUYER, ADRIANA, oceanographer, educator; b. Giessendam, The Netherlands, May 19, 1945; arrived in Can., 1950; came to U.S., 1975; d. Jacob Catharinus and Sophia (Van Loon) H.; m. Robert Lloyd Smith. BS, U. Toronto, 1967; MS, Oreg. State U., 1971, PhD, 1974. Scientific officer Marine Scis. Branch, Ottawa, Can., 1967-73; rsch. scientist Marine Environ. Data Svc., Ottawa, Can., 1974-75; rsch. assoc. Oreg. State U., Corvallis, 1975-76, rsch. asst. prof., 1976-79, asst. prof., 1979-80, assoc. prof., 1980-85, prof., 1985—; vis. scientist Csiro Marine Labs, Hobart, Australia, 1988. Contbr. articles to profl. jours. Mem. AAAS, Am. Meterol. Soc., Am. Geophys. Union, Can. Meterol. and Oceanographic Soc., Am. Soc. Limnology and Oceanography. Office: Oreg State U Coll Oceanic/Atmospher Scis 104 Ocean Adminstrn Bldg Corvallis OR 97331

HUYETT, DEBRA KATHLEEN, elementary education educator; b. Massillon, Ohio, Oct. 10, 1955; d. William Wilbur and Vivian Delores (Anderson) H. BA, Stetson U., 1978. Cert. elem. and early childhood edn. tchr., Fla. Dir. assistance and long distance operator Gen. Telephone, Myrtle Beach, S.C., summer 1974-76; desk clk. Bon Villa Motel, Myrtle Beach, summer 1976-79; tchr. Lake Orienta Elem. Sch., Altamonte Springs, Fla., 1978-88, Bear Lake Elem. Sch., Apopka, Fla., 1988—; curriculum rep. Lake Orienta Elem. Sch., 1980-88, v.p. PTA, 1984-85; mem. Sch. Adv. Bd., 1995-97. Campaign vol. City Coun. Rep., Massillon, 1973; counselor Orange County Jail Ministry, Orlando, Fla., 1988-91; cmty. counselor EurAuPair, 1996-98. Named to Most Admired Men and Women of the Yr., 1995. Mem. Fla. Reading Conv. (chairperson Orlando chpt. 1983-84, chairperson for transp. and tours 1985-86), Seminole Edn. Assn. (faculty rep. Sanford, Fla. chpt. 1980-81), Seminde County Reading Coun., Delta Kappa Gamma. Republican. Baptist. Avocations: travel, reading, beach. Home: 893 Little Bend Rd Altamonte Springs FL 32714-7514

HUYGENS, REMMERT WILLIAM, architect; b. Haarlem, The Netherlands, Apr. 19, 1932; came to U.S., 1956, naturalized, 1963; s. Willem and Antoinette (Bruynzeel) H. Diploma dept. architecture, Amsterdam HTS, 1955. With Marcel Breuer, N.Y.C., 1956; pvt. practice architecture Boston, 1960—. Prin. works include: Campus Rivers Country Day Sch., Weston, Mass., 1960, Longy Concert Hall, Cambridge, Mass., 1966, Interfaith Religious Ctr. Columbia, Md., 1967, campus N.H. Coll., Manchester, 1969-81, The Village of Loon Mountain, Lincoln, N.H., 1973—, Cath. Med. Ctr. Manchester, N.H., 1974, Milford (Conn.) Pub. Library, 1976, Framingham (Mass.) Pub. Library, 1977, Village Green at Stowe, Vt., 1980—, rsch. bldgs. for Biogen Inc., Cambridge, Mass. and Geneva, 1980, Indian Head Nat. Bank, Nashua, N.H., 1981, Pub. Lib., Framingham, 1982, Teradyne Circuits Inc., Nashua, 1983, Riverview office tower, Cambridge, 1985, Cochituate Place office bldg., Framingham, 1986 One Memorial Drive office tower, Cambridge, 1986, Constitution Office Complex, 1987, Water's Edge Resort, Westbrook, Conn., 1987, Franklin Park Zoo, Boston, 1989, Ipswich (Mass.) Country Club, 1989; office parks, residential communities and pvt. residences in U.S., Holland, France, Switzerland, Malaysia, numerous corporate headquarters and rsch. facilities for Genzyme Corp., Enzytech Inc., BioSurface Technology Inc., ImmunoGen Inc., Digital Equipment Corp., urban planning Guangzhou, China, 100-story office tower, Guangzhou, China, 1990, work exhibited at N.Y. Archtl. League, N.Y. Mus. Modern Art, Brockton Art Ctr., Boston Arch. Ctr.; works pub. in numerous books and jours., U.S., Eng., Holland, Italy, Japan, France, Belgium, including: Arch. Record, Archtl. Forum, AIA Jour., Am. Home, House and Garden, Progressive Arch., House Beautiful, N.Y. Times, Boston Globe. Recipient Abu-Dhabi Conf. Ctr. award, First award Internat. Masonry Inst., numerous others. Fellow AIA (Progressive Architecture Design awards, honor awards New England regional coun., award of merit R.I. chpt., Conn. Soc. Architects./AIA Design award). Office: R W Huygens Arch Inc 125 Old Connecticut Path Wayland MA 01778-3201

HUYGHE, PATRICK ANTOINE, science writer; b. Newport News, Va., Aug. 28, 1952; s. Alain Emile and Gladys (Louka) H.; m. Carolyn Ann Schoemer, Oct. 23, 1988; 1 child, Alexandra. BA in Psychology, U. Va., 1974; MS in Pub. Comm., Syracuse U., 1976. Staff editor US Mag. The N.Y. Times, N.Y.C., 1977-78; staff writer Newsweek Focus Newsweek, Inc., N.Y.C., 1980; contbg. editor Sci. Digest, Hearst Mags., N.Y.C., 1981-84; sci. writer-in-residence Va. Poly. and State U., Blacksburg, 1986; ind. prodr. Innovation Sta. WNET, N.Y.C., 1987-90; freelance writer N.Y., 1979—; contbg. editor Omni, Gen. Media Internat., 1995-98; cons. Liberty Sci. Ctr., Jersey City, N.J., 1992, Petrosains Discovery Ctr., Malaysia, 1996-97, Small Comets Website, U. Iowa, 1997—. Author: Glowing Birds, 1985, Columbus Was Last, 1992, The Field Guide to Extraterrestrials, 1996; co-author: The Big Splash, 1990, The Field Guide to Bigfoot, Yeti, and other Mystery Primates Worldwide, 1999. Fellow Josiah Macy Found., 1985, Hopkins Found., 1996. Mem. Authors Guild, Nat. Assn. Sci. Writers, Soc. for Sci. Exploration. Address: PO Box 577 Jefferson Valley NY 10535

HUYLER, JEAN WILEY, media and interpersonal communications consultant, hypnotherapist; b. Seattle, Mar. 30, 1935; d. Othello Phillip and Agnes Olivia (Snarr) Dickert; m. Richard Wiley, Apr. 1955 (div. 1963); children: Richard Kenneth Jr., Cynthia Jean; m. Garey Heath Huyler, Mar. 2, 1968 (div. 1972). BA, Marylhurst Coll., 1978; MA in Social Scis., Pacific Luth. U., Parkland, Wash., 1979; DLitt, Fairfax U., New Orleans, 1989; Degree in Hypnotherapy, Tacoma Coll., 1990. Ordained to ministry ReCreationists Assembly, 1991. Bur. mgr., reporter Lynnwood (Wash.) Enterprise, 1961-63; city editor, reporter/photographer Everett (Wash.) Daily Herald, 1963-71; spl. sects. editor Seattle Post-Intelligencer, 1971; sr. econ. editor Rainier Bancorp., Seattle, 1971-72; assoc. editor, women's editor Valley Newspapers, Kent, Wash., 1973-75; CEO Jean Wiley Huyler Comm., Gig Harbor, Wash., 1975—, EdCom-UpCom-One Step Beyond-TravCom, Gig Harbor, Wash., 1981—; environ. editor-writer Bonneville Power Adminstrn.-U.S. Dept. Interior, Portland, Oreg., 1976-77; communications service dir. Wash. State Sch. Dirs. Assn., Olympia, 1977-81. Author: Communications is a People Process, 2d edit., 1981, Crisis Communications, 2d edit., 1981, De-mystifying the Media, 2d edit., 1981; editor, designer: For the

Record: Tacoma Schools, 1984 (Nat. Sch. Pub. Rels. Assn. award 1985), Lifespan Learning on Centerstage of the Future, 1988, Learning to Learn: New Techniques for Corporate Education, 1989. Recipient Superior Performance award Wash. Press Assn., 1964, Communicator of Achievement, 1987, Pres.'s award, 1994, Nat. Excellence in Edn. Comms. award Nat. Assn. State Edn. Dept. Info. Officers, 1979, numerous other nat. and regional cmty. svc. and comm. awards. Mem. Nat. Fedn. Press Women (exec. bd. 1971-91, v.p. 1973-75, pres. 1975-77, Communicator of Achievement award 1988), Wash. Press Assn. (pres. 1971-73), Nat. Guild Hypnotists. Avocations: travel writing and photojournalism, adventuring.

HUYSMAN, JAMES DAVID, healthcare executive, consultant; b. N.Y.C., Jan. 27, 1955; s. Michel and Arlene Muriel (Weiss) H.; m. Betsy Catherine Bergner, May 29, 1988. BA in Cmty. Psychology with high honors, U. Fla., 1977; M in Clin. Social Work, Barry U., Miami Shores, Fla., 1987. Diplomate NASW; lic. clin. social worker; cert. addictions profl.; registered lic. real estate broker. Dir. vocat. program Fellowship House, South Miami, Fla., 1984-86; therapist Ctrs. for Psychol. Growth, Miami, Fla., 1986-88; v.p. outreach The Bradford Group, Birmingham, Ala., 1988-92; dir. aftercare The Geraldo Rivera Show, N.Y.C., 1991—; v.p. devel. CareNet Psychol. Mgmt., Nashville, 1993-96; chmn., CEO Ptnrs. in Health Mgmt., Ft. Lauderdale, Fla., 1996—; dir. Aftercare Leeza Show, 1996—; cons. to Rev. Jesse Jackson, Rainbow Coalition, Washington, 1990-91, largest pub./pvt. treatment grant, Washington, 1989-90, Howell Heflin D.C. Treatment Grant, Bradford Group, Washington, 1989-90, Bennett/Klehr Drug Policy Office, Washington, 1989-90, Geraldo Rivera, Montel Williams, Les Brown, Leeza, other talk shows; founder, dir. 1st Healthcare Network and Aftercare Program for Talk TV; creator nat. talk show; CEO At the End of the Day Prodns. Contbr. over 300 articles to nat. newspapers; appeared on over 70 nat. syndicated talk shows. Bus. devel. OrNoA Healthcorp. Tenet Health Sys. Recipient Friends Day Founder recognition Cmty. Mental Health Agys., Miami, 1986. Mem. ACLU, Nat. Wildlife Fedn., Nature Conservancy, World Wildlife Fund, Habitat for Humanity, Fla. Alcohol and Drug Abuse Assn. Democrat. Jewish. Avocations: motorcycling, travel, Miami ballet, theater, collecting animation and memorabilia. Home: 900 Bay Dr Apt 1002 Miami Beach FL 33141-5634 Office: Ptnrs in Health Mgmt 1700 E Las Olas Blvd Ste 102 Fort Lauderdale FL 33301-2466 also: Ptnrs in Health Mgmt 3050 Biscayne Blvd Ste 908 Miami FL 33137-4143

HUZAR, ELEANOR GOLTZ, history educator; b. St. Paul, June 15, 1922; d. Edward Victor and Clare (O'Neill) Goltz; m. Elias Huzar, June 21, 1950 (dec. Dec. 1950); m. Bruce I. Granger, Oct. 11, 1991. BA, U. Minn., 1943; MA, Cornell U., 1945, PhD, 1948. Instr. history Stanford U., Palo Alto, Calif., 1948-50; asst. prof. classics U. Ill., Urbana, 1951-55; assoc. prof. history S.E. Mo. Coll., Cape Girardeau, 1955-59; assoc. prof. classics Carleton Coll., Northfield, Minn., 1959-60; prof. history Mich. State U., East Lansing, 1960-90, chmn. program in classical studies, 1965-90; mem. selection com. Nat. Endowment for Humanities, Washington, 1979-84, Coun. for Internat. Exchg. Scholars, Washington, 1979-81, Mich. Rhodes Scholars, Ann Arbor, 1981-84, Prix de Rome, Am. Acad., N.Y.C., 1978-80. Author: Mark Antony: A Biography, 1978; contbr. articles and revs. to profl. jours. George Boldt fellow Cornell U., 1947-48. Mem. Classical Assn. of Mid. West and South (pres. 1984-85), Am. Hist. Assn., Am. Philol. Assn., Archael. Inst. Am. (local pres. 1979-80), Mich. Classical Conf. (pres. 1984-85), Am. Acad. in Rome (adv. coun. 1963-92, exec. com. 1970-73, 88-92), Am. Sch. in Athens (mng. com. 1964-92), Phi Beta Kappa, Phi Kappa Phi. Democrat. Roman Catholic. Avocations: hiking, skiing, traveling. Home: 1375 Burcham Dr East Lansing MI 48823-3671

HVASS, SHERYL RAMSTAD, lawyer. BA, U. Minn., 1972; JD with honors, U. N.D., 1975. Bar: Minn. 1975, N.D. 1975, U.S. Dist. Ct. Minn. 1975, U.S. Dist. Ct. N.D. 1975, D.C. 1978, U.S. Ct. Appeals (8th cir.), U.S. Supreme Ct. 1978. Asst. Hennepin County Pub. Defender, 1975-78; asst. U.S. atty. U.S. Dist. Ct. Minn., 1978-81; assoc. Henson & Efron, PA, 1981-82; adj. prof. law sch. law Hamline U., 1983-86; judge Hennepin County Ct., Mpls., 1982-86; ptnr. Rider, Bennett, Egan & Arundel, Mpls., 1986—; co-chair Fed. Practice Com. for Dist. Minn., 1980-82; mem. faculty Nat. Inst. for Trail Advocacy, 1983—. Active Greater Mpls. Girl Scouts Am. Coun., 1992—, nominations com. 1993; bd. dirs. Mpls. Children's Med. Ctr., 1992, ethics com., 1993; mem. adv. coun. Women's Intercollegiate Athletics, U. Minn., 1987—, vice chair, 1988-89, chair, 1989-91; bd. dirs. YMCA Met. Mpls., 1986—, co-chair program svcs. com. 1987-88, chair pub. rels./pub. affairs com. 1988-92, vice-chmn. 1992—; bd. mgmt. Downtown YMCA, 1984-87; bd. dirs. Search Inst., 1984-88; active Minn. Women's Econ. Roundtable, 1985—; bd. visitors U. N.D. Law Sch., 1982—, U. Minn. Law Sch., 1997—. Recipient Women to Watch award, 1983, Karen Gibbs Women of Achievement award Twin West C. of C., 1985, Civil Justice award Am. Bd. Trial Advocates, 1992. Fellow ABA (life, mem. exec. coun. nat. conf. bar pres. 1992-93, standing com. on assn. comm. 1992-95); mem. Fed. Bar Assn. (sec. Minn. chpt. 1981-83), Nat. Assn. Women Judges (chair site selection com. 1984-86, co-chair judicial selection com. 1985-86), Internat. Soc. Barristers, Minn. State Bar Assn. (chair young lawyers sect. 1981-81, chair legal edn. and admissions com. 1982-84, task force on minority hiring 1986-87, exec. com. 1990—, pres. 1997), Minn. Judges Assn. (chair jury instrn. com. 1984-86, exec. com. 1984-86), Minn. Women Lawyers (exec. com. 1978-83, chair speakers bur. 1978-79, pres. 1981-82), Hennepin County Bar Assn. (vice chair young lawyers com. 1977, sec. 1988-89, treas. 1989-90, pres. 1991-92). Office: Commissioner/Department Corrections 1450 Energy Park Drive Suite 200 Saint Paul MN 55108-5212*

HWANG, CORDELIA JONG, chemist; b. N.Y.C., July 14, 1942; d. Goddard and Lily (Fung) Jong; m. Warren C. Hwang, Mar. 29, 1969; 1 child, Kevin. Student Alfred U., 1960-62; BA, Barnard Coll., 1964; M.S., SUNY-Stony Brook, 1969. Rsch. asst. Columbia U., N.Y.C., 1964-66; analytical chemist Veritron West Inc., Chatsworth, Calif., 1969-70; asst. lab. dir., chief chemist Pomeroy, Johnston & Bailey Environ. Engrs., Pasadena, Calif., 1970-76; chemist Met. Water Dist. So. Calif., Los Angeles, 1976-79, rsch. chemist 1980-91, sr. chemist 1992—; mem. Joint Task Group on Instrumental Identification of Taste and Odor Compounds, 1983-85, instr. Citrus Coll., 1974-76; chair Joint Task Group on Disinfection by-products: chlorine, 1990. Mem. Am. Chem. Soc., Am. Water Works Assn. (cert. water quality analyst level 3, Calif.-Nev.), Am. Soc. for Mass Spectometry. Office: Met Water Dist So Calif 700 Moreno Ave La Verne CA 91750-3303

HWANG, DAVID HENRY, playwright, screenwriter; b. L.A., Aug. 11, 1957; s. Henry Yuan and Dorothy Yu (Huang) H.; m. Kathryn A. Layng, Dec. 17, 1993; 1 child, Noah. BA in English, Stanford U., 1979; postgrad., Yale Drama Sch., 1980-81. Playwright: FOB, 1980 (Obie award 1981), The Dance and the Railroad, 1981 (CINE Golden Eagle award 1982), Family Devotions, 1981, Sound and Beauty, 1983, The Sound of a Voice, 1984, As the Crow Flies, 1986, Rich Relations, 1986, M. Butterfly, 1988 (Tony award for best play 1988, Outer Critics Circle award for best Broadway play 1988, Pulitzer prize for drama nomination 1988), (musical) 1000 Airplanes on the Roof, 1988, Bondage, 1992, Face Value, 1993, Trying to Find Chinatown, 1996-98 (Obie award 1997, Tony nomination Best Play 1998), (musical) Golden Child, 1996, The River, 1997, (adaptation) Peer Gynt, 1998; librettist: The Voyage, 1992; screenwriter: (films) M. Butterfly, 1993, Golden Gate, 1993, (television) Forbidden Nights, 1990. Mem. Pres.'s Com. Arts and Humanities, 1994—. Fellow Rockefeller Found., 1983, Guggenheim Found., 1984, Nat. Endowment Arts, 1987; recipient Drama-Logue award 1980, 86, 98, John Gassner award, 1988. Mem. Dramatists Guild (bd. dirs. 1988—). Democrat. Office: Writers & Artists Agy care William Craver 19 W 44th St Ste 1000 New York NY 10036-6095 also: CAA 9830 Wilshire Blvd Beverly Hills CA 90212-1804

HWANG, JOHN DZEN, municipal official; b. Shanghai, China, Sept. 8, 1941; came to U.S., 1956; s. John Ding and Sylvia H.; m. Gloria Hoi-Hoon Lum, June 17, 1967; children: John Dar, Andrew Cherng, Audrey Ming. BSEE, U. Calif., Berkeley, 1964; MA, Oreg. State U., 1966, PhD, 1968. Ops. rschr. Army Weapons Command, Rock Island, Ill., 1970-71; program mgr. Army Air Mobility R&D Lab., Moffett Field, Calif., 1971-75; divsn. chief Def. Comm. Agy., Arlington, Va., 1975-82; assoc. dir. Fed. Emergency Mgmt. Agy., Washington, 1982-96; gen. mgr. Info. Tech. Agy. City of L.A., 1996—. Editor: Analytical Concepts of Command and Control, 1976. Capt. U.S. Army, 1968-70. Univ. fellow Dept. Def., Harvard Bus. Sch., Boston, 1981. Home: 2157 Moreno Dr Los Angeles CA 90039-3061

HWANG, TZU-YANG, minister; b. Kaohsiung, Taiwan, Republic of China, Sept. 21, 1953; came to U.S., 1985; d. Chi-Chou and Iu-Chih (Tsai) Huang; m. Wei-Chih Shih Hwang, Sept. 6, 1980. MDiv, Tainan Theol. Sem., 1980; ThM, Princeton (N.J.) Theol. Sem., 1986; PhD, Chinese for Christ Theol. Sem., Rosemead, Calif., 1990. Ordained to ministry Presbyn. Ch. Chairperson, min. Presbytery's Zrhlin Dists. Ch., Champhua, Taiwan, 1981-83; min., lectr., sr. editor Tainan Theol. Sem., 1983-85; founder, min. The Youth Fellowship of Kingston Presbyn. Ch., Princeton, 1985-86; head of religion edn., lectr. Good Shepherd Formosan Presbyn. Ch., Monterey Park, Calif., 1987-88; head of religion edn., lectr. Chinese for Christ Theol. Sem., 1987-88, dir. theology and philosophy, dean students, sr. editor, 1990-94; founder., pres., prof., CEO Am. Chi Chou Theo-Philosophical Inst., 1995—; Vis. Scholar, Harvard U. Div. Sch., Duke U. Div. Sch., 1991-92; sr. pastor, pres. Light Christ Ch.; chmn., pres., incorporator, bd. dirs., Light Christ Found. Contbr. articles to profl. jours. With Chinese Def., 1972-74. mem. Am. Acad. Religion, Soc. Biblical Literature, ABIRA (internat. and continental gov., internat. Order of Ambassadors), Internat. Biog. Ctr. (dir. gen. honors list), Assn. IBC, Internat. Order of Merit (bd. mem.), Leading Intellectuals of World (founding charter mem., noble mem.), others. Home: 11768 E Roseglen St El Monte CA 91732-1446 Office: Am Chi Chou Theo-Phil Inst PO Box 4163 11804 Hemlock St El Monte CA 91732-1413

HYAMS, HAROLD, lawyer; b. Bklyn., May 19, 1943; s. Frank Charles and Celia (Silverstein) H.; m. Simone Elkeharrat, Nov. 18, 1973; children: Gabriel, Galite, Emilie, Jonathan. BA, U. Vt., 1965; MA in Latin Am. Studies, Georgetown U., 1966; JD, Syracuse U., 1970. Bar: N.Y. 1971, Ariz. 1974, U.S. Dist. Ct. Ariz. 1974, U.S. Ct. Appeals (9th cir.) 1974. Asst. to the gen. counsel Am. Express Co., N.Y.C., 1970-72; atty. Legal Aid Soc., Bklyn., 1973; ptnr. Harold Hyams and Assocs., Tucson, 1974—; mem. panel of arbitrators Am. Arbitration Assn., N.Y.C., 1971-73. Mem. Commn. on Ariz. Environ., 1988. Mem. Am. Bd. Trial Advs., Ariz. Trial Lawyers Assn., Pima County Bar Assn., Assn. Trial Lawyers Am. (adv. bd. trial advocates 1990, cert. specialist in personal injury and wrongful death 1991). Avocation: travel. Home: 3175 N Elena Maria Tucson AZ 85750-2915 Office: 680 S Craycroft Rd Tucson AZ 85711-7108

HYAMS, PETER, film director, producer, cinematographer; b. July 26, 1943. Motion picture dir., prodr., cinematographer. Films include 2010, 1984, Running Scared, 1986, The Monster Squad, 1987; cinematographer, dir. The Presidio, 1988, Narrow Margin, 1990, Stay Tuned, 1992, Timecop, 1994, Sudden Death, 1995, The Relic, 1997; dir. films Capricorn One, 1978, End of Days, 1999, also T.V. films; writer The Hunter, 1980, Outland, 1981, The Star Chamber, 1983. Office: c/o DGA 7920 Sunset Blvd Los Angeles CA 90046*

HYATT, DOROTHY ANN, volunteer; b. N.Y.C., July 14, 1931; d. Gustav Henry and Irene Virginia (Bernad) Stiehl; m. James William Hyatt, Nov. 25, 1950 (div. 1980); children: James W., Kenneth Henry, Catherine Ann Hyatt Costanzo. Grad. H.S., Bronx, N.Y. Author of poetry. Nat. bd. sec. Resources Unltd., New Canaan, Conn., 1984-94, pres. RU Clay Calss, Norwalk, Conn., 1985-95, sec. RU Creative Writing, Stamford, Conn., 1985-92; corp. sect. WCKORP Human Svc. Wickett Inc., Norwalk, 1986—; adminstrv. asst. Abram Heisler, Esq. Atty. at Law, Norwalk, 1992—. Recipient Silver Poet award World of Poetry, Sacramento, 1989. Republican. Roman Catholic. Avocation: creative writing. Office: Wckorp Human Svcs PO Box 2087 Norwalk CT 06852-2087

HYATT, RAYMOND RUSSELL, JR., educator; b. Pawtucket, R.I., June 8, 1950; s. Raymond R. and Bernice Kenyon (Dawson) H.; m. Siobhan E. Gallagher, Nov. 19, 1994; children: Jessica Lynn, Emily Rae. BS in Applied Math., Brown U., 1980; MS in Math., MIT, 1982. Rsch. asst. dept. math., methologist MIT, Cambridge, Mass., 1980-82; instr. dept. math. Northeastern U., Boston, 1982, sr. rsch. methodologist, 1982-87, asst. prof. computer sci., 1987-88, Daniel Webster Coll., 1984-86; lectr. in computer sci. div. grad. studies Rivier Coll, Hashua N.H., 1988—; project dir. Harvard Med. Sch., 1996—; dir. acad. computing Daniel Webster Coll., Nashua, N.H., 1982-87, chmn. computer systems, 1983—; research Brown U., Providence, 1977-78. Contbr. articles to profl. jours. Program coordinator for R.I. Muscular Dystrophy Assn., Cranston, 1979-80. Mem. Am. Math. Soc., AAAS, Assn. Computing Machinery, N.Y. Acad. Scis., Sigma Xi (assoc.). Club: MIT of N.H. Home: PO Box 493 Belmont MA 02478-0004 Office: Dept Health Care Policy Harvard Med Sch Boston MA 02115

HYATT-SMITH, ANN ROSE, non-profit organization executive, consultant; b. Portchester, N.Y., Sept. 25, 1953; d. David M. and Lenore (Moerschelle) Hyatt; m. Geoffrey D. Smith, June 24, 1984; children: Rachel Elana, Joshua Richard Lev. BA in Lit., State U. Coll., Oneonta, N.Y., 1975; M in Profl. Studies, New Sch. for Social Research, 1986. Asst. to sec.-gen. Israel Interfaith Com., Jerusalem, 1977-79; field rep. United Jewish Appeal/Fedn. Jewish Philanthropies, N.Y.C., 1979-81; asst. v.p. United Way of N.Y.C., 1981-83; dir. devel. Hebrew Arts Sch., Merkin Concert Hall, N.Y.C., 1983-84; asst. dir. devel. St. Vincent's Hosp. and Med. Ctr. N.Y., N.Y.C., 1984-86; program mgr. Bernd Brecher and Assocs., Inc., N.Y.C., 1986-88; pres. Hyatt Smith Assocs., White Plains, N.Y., 1988-91; dir. devel. The Shield Inst., N.Y.C., 1991-95; dir. devel. and alumni rels. Sch. Law, Pace U., White Plains, N.Y., 1995—; adj. faculty New Sch. for Social Research and Learning Alliance. V.p., treas. Village Ind. Dems., N.Y.C., 1985-86. Mem. Nat. Soc. Fund Raising Execs. (advanced cert. fund raising exec.), Assn. Devel. Officers, Planned Giving Group of Greater N.Y., Women in Fin. Devel., Coun. Advancement and Support Of Edn. Jewish.

HYBL, WILLIAM JOSEPH, lawyer, foundation executive; b. Des Moines, July 16, 1942; s. Joseph A. and Geraldine (Evans) H.; m. Kathleen Horrigan, June 6, 1967; children: William J. Jr., Kyle Horrigan; BA, Colo. Coll., 1964; JD, U. Colo., 1967. Bar: Colo. 1967. Asst. dist. atty. 4th Jud. Dist., El Paso and Teller Counties, 1970-72; pres., dir. Garden City Co., 1973—; dir. Broadmoor Hotel, Inc., 1973—, also vice-chmn., 1987—; chmn., CEO, trustee El Pomar Found, Colorado Springs, Colo., 1973—; pres. U.S. Olympic Com. 1991-92, 96—; vice chair USAA, San Antonio; dir. KN Energy Inc., Lakewood, Colo., FirstBank Holding Co. of Colo., Lakewood; mem. Colo. Ho. Reps., 1972-73; spl. counsel The White House, Washington, 1981. Pres., trustee Air Force Acad. Found.; sec., dir. Nat. Jr. Achievement; vice chmn. bd. U.S. Adv. Commn. on Pub. Diplomacy, 1990-97; civilian aide to sec. of army, 1986—. Capt. U.S. Army, 1967-69. Republican.

HYDE, CATHERINE RYAN, novelist, short story writer; b. Buffalo, N.Y., Apr. 17, 1955. instr. writer's conf. Cuesta Coll., San Luis Obispo, Calif.; adminstrv. asst. Santa Barbara (Calif.) Writer's Conf. Author: (novel) Funerals for Horses, 1997, Pay it Forward, 1999, (short story collection) Earthquake Weather, 1998. Recipient Raymond Carver Short Story contest Humboldt State U., 1994, 96, Tobias Wolff award for fiction The Bellingham Rev., 1997. E-mail: hardy@best.com. Office: The Hardy Agy 3020 Bridgeway # 204 Sausalito CA 94965

HYDE, CLARENCE BRODIE, II, oil company executive; b. Ft. Worth, Oct. 22, 1937; s. Clarence Edgar and Frances McCain (Williams) H.; m. Sylvia Flower, June 5, 1960; children: C. Brodie III, Brooke Allison, Brett Kinlock, Blair Elizabeth. BS, Tex. Wesleyan Coll., 1961, LLD (hon.), 1968; MBA, U. Tex., 1963; grad., So. Meth. U., 1973. V.p., asst. mgt. lending group, chmn. loan com. Ft. Worth Nat. Bank, 1964-76; ind. oil prodr. Ft. Worth, 1976-78; pres., chmn. bd. Hyde Oil & Gas Corp., Ft. Worth, 1978—; pres. Hyde Resources Corp., 1997—, Hyde Energy Corp., 1993—; mem. exec. com., dir. River Plz. Nat. Bank, Ft. Worth, 1983-86; trustee, v.p., treas. The Hyde Found., Ft. Worth, 1981—. Bd. dirs. Tarrant County chpt. Salvation Army, 1969-79, chmn. bd., 1972-74; trustee Trinity Valley Sch., Ft. Worth, 1970; mgmt. com. Camp Amon Cartr, Ft. Worth, 1970-76, adv. mem., 1976—; trustee Tex. Wesleyan Coll., 1971-96, chmn. bd., chmn. exec. com., 1990-94; bd. dirs. Big Bros. Tarrant County, 1971; trustee W.A. Moncrief Radiation Ctr., Ft. Worth, 1971—, v.p., 1986—; bd. dirs., mem. exec. Harris Hosp., Ft. Worth, 1971-88, Harris Meth. Health Systems, 1983-87; bd. dirs., treas. Tarrant County chpt. ARC, 1971-73, bd. dirs., 1989-91; bd. dirs., exec. com. Ft. Worth Opera Assn., 1971-99, v.p., treas., 1972-74; bd. dirs., exec. com. Hurst-Euless (Tex.)-Bedford Hosp., 1973-80; bd. dirs. Ft. Worth Arts Coun., 1972-95, pres., 1973-75; chmn. Cmty. Pride Campaign, 1972; bd. dirs. Ann Waggoner Scholarship Fund, 1984—; fin. com. Ft. Worth Country Day Sch., 1985-89; pres. MCR-Trans Co. (subs. Moncried Radiation Ctr.), 1987-94; bd. dirs. Cancer Care Svcs., 1994-95, adv. bd. dirs., 1995—. Named Alumnus of Yr., Tex. Wesleyan Coll., 1985. Mem. Ind. Petroleum Assn. Am., Tex. Ind. Prodrs. & Roualgy Owners Assn., Tex. & Southwestern Cattle Raisers Assn., Tex. Hosp. Assn., Rivercrest Country Club, Shady Oaks Country Club (Ft. Worth), Steelechase Club (Ridotto), Ft. Worth Petroleum Club, Crescent Club (Dallas). Republican. Methodist. Avocations: hunting, fishing, travel. Home: 8 Westover Rd Fort Worth TX 76107-3103 Office: Hyde Oil & Gas Corp 6300 Ridglea Pl Ste 1018 Fort Worth TX 76116-5778

HYDE, DAVID ROWLEY, lawyer; b. Norwalk, Conn., Aug. 21, 1929; s. Thomas Arthur and Mary Julia (Sass) H.; m. Valerie Rosemary Worrall, Dec. 30, 1961; children: Meredith Ellen, Timothy Worrall. A.B., Yale U., 1951, LL.B., 1954. Bar: Conn. 1954, N.Y. 1956, U.S. Supreme Ct. 1969. Assoc. Cahill Gordon & Reindel, N.Y.C., 1954-59, 64-65, ptnr., 1966-90, sr. counsel, 1991—; chief civil div. U.S. Atty.'s Office, 1961-63. Home: 35 W 12th St New York NY 10011-8501 Office: Cahill Gordon & Reindel 80 Pine St Fl 17 New York NY 10005-1790

HYDE, GEOFFREY, satellite communications research executive; b. Toronto, Apr. 10, 1930; came to U.S., 1959; s. Harry Gregory and Eleanor Lillian (Orloff) H.; m. Rhoda Phillips, June 7, 1953; children: Philip Ralph, Thomas Michael, Carol Deborah. BASc in Engring. Physics, U. Toronto, 1953, MASc, 1959; PhDEE, U. Pa., 1967. Engr. Can. GE, Peterborough, Ont., 1953-55, Sinclair Radio Labs., Toronto, 1955-57, AVRO Aircraft Co., Malton, Ont., 1958-59, RCA, Moorestown, N.J., 1959-68; asst. to dir. RF Transmission Lab. COMSAT Labs., Clarksburg, Md., 1968-74; mgr. propagation studies dept. COMSAT Labs., Clarksburg, 1974-80, sr. staff scientist, 1980-83, asst. to dir., 1984-89, cons., 1989-99, chief satellite com., 1999—. Sarnoff fellow. Fellow IEEE; mem. AIAA, IEEE Antennas and Propagation Soc. (co-recipient Best Paper award 1968), Internat. Union Radio Sci. (U.S. nat. com., commns. B, F), Assn. Profl. Engrs. Province Ont. (lic.). Home: 15116 Red Clover Dr Rockville MD 20853-1642*

HYDE, HENRY JOHN, congressman; b. Chgo., Apr. 18, 1924; s. Henry Clay and Monica (Kelly) H.; m. Jeanne Simpson, Nov. 8, 1947; children: Henry J., Robert, Laura, Anthony. Student, Duke U., 1943-44; BS, Georgetown U., 1946; JD, Loyola U., Chgo., 1949. Bar: Ill. 1950. Mem. Ill. Gen. Assembly, 1967-74, 94th-106th Congresses from 6th Ill. dist., 1975—; mem. internat. rels. com., chmn. jud. com. Served with USN, 1944-46. Mem. Chgo. Bar Assn. Republican. Roman Catholic. Office: US Ho of Reps 2110 Rayburn Washington DC 20515-1306*

HYDE, HERBERT LEE, lawyer; b. Bryson City, N.C., Dec. 12, 1925; s. Ervin M. and Alice (Medlin) H.; m. Kathryn Long, Dec. 25, 1949; children: Deborah, Lynn, Karen, Benjamin, Jane, William. AB, W. Carolina U., 1951; JD, NYU, 1954. Bar: N.C. 1954, U.S. Dist. Ct. (we. dist.) N.C. 1954, U.S. Ct. Appeals (4th cir.) 1957, U.S. Supreme Ct. 1962, U.S. Dist. Ct. (mid. dist.) N.C. 1975, U.S. Dist. Ct. (ea. dist.) N.C. 1980. Ptnr. Van Winkle, Buck, Wall, Starnes & Hyde, Asheville, N.C., 1954-79; sole practice Asheville, 1979—; sec. N.C. Dept. Crime Control and Pub. Safety, Raleigh, 1979. Author: Genuine Hyde, 1976. Senator N.C. Senate, Raleigh, 1964-66, 1990—; mem. N.C. Ho. of Reps., Raleigh, 1972-76; chmn. Dem. Exec. Com. of Buncombe County, Asheville, 1988—; chmn. Dem. Congl. Dist. 11, 1988-90, N.C. Senate, Raleigh, 1990—, N.C. State Dems., 1990—. Democrat. Home: 93 Eastview Cir Asheville NC 28806-1150 Office: PO Box 7266 Asheville NC 28802-7266

HYDE, HOWARD LAURENCE, lawyer; b. Boston, Sept. 4, 1957; s. Morris Morton and Evelyn Lee (Weinstein) H.; m. Nancy J. Paulu, May 18, 1985; children: Emma Catherine, Benjamin Tuttle. AB, Dartmouth Coll., 1979; JD, Harvard U., 1982. Bar: Mass. 1983, D.C. 1987, U.S. Dist. Ct. Mass. 1984, U.S. Ct. Appeals (1st. cir.) 1984. Jud. clk. Minn. Supreme Ct., St. Paul, 1982-83; assoc. Gaston Snow & Ely Bartlett, Boston, 1983-86; assoc. Arnold & Porter, Washington, 1986-91, spl. counsel, 1992—. Mem. ABA (Bus. law sect.). Avocations: fly fishing, canoeing. Office: Arnold & Porter 555 12th St NW Washington DC 20004-1206

HYDE, JAMES A., service executive; b. Oklahoma City, Nov. 16, 1945; s. Charles D. and Margret W. (Dray) Hyde; divorced; children: James A. Jr., Laurie. BBA in Acctg., U. Okla., 1969; JD, Oklahoma City U., 1972. CPA, Okla. Tax acct. Kerr McGee Corp., Oklahoma City, 1969-70; controller Bone & Joint Hosp., Oklahoma City, 1970-74, hosp. adminstr., 1974—; clinic adminstr., pres. McBride Clinic, Inc., Oklahoma City, 1974—; bd. dirs. Park Ave. N.A., Oklahoma City, Okla. Hosp. Assn., MPSI, Dewey, Okla.; sec.-treas. Bone and Joint Hosp. Bldg. Corp., Oshco, Inc.; sec., mng. ptnr. Merth Leasing Co. Chmn. Arthritis Bowl, 1980-81, Downtown Oklahoma City City Spring Arts Festival, 1979—, allocation com. United Way, 1986; Co-chmn. Oklahoma City Fall Arts Festival, 1983; pres., bd. dirs. Arthritis Found. 1981—; pres. Oklahoma City Area Hosp. Council, 1981-82; mem. Okla. Estate Planning Council, adv. and informational group Businessmen's Forum for Sen. Don Nichols, goals com. Oklahoma City C. of C. Mem. Am. Acad. Med. Adminstrs., Am. Soc. Hosp. Attys., Healthcare Fin. Mgmt. Assn., Am. Inst. CPA's, Okla. Soc. CPA's, Okla. State Bd. Pub. Accountancy, ABA, Okla. County Bar Assn., Okla. State Bar Assn., Young Pres. Orgns., Phi Gamma Delta, Phi Delta Phi. Democrat. Methodist. Clubs: Dinner, Golf and Country (Oklahoma City). Avocations: golf, tennis, cooking, travel. *

HYDE, JAMES FRANKLIN, chemist, consultant; b. Solvay, N.Y., Mar. 11, 1903; s. Burton DeForest and Amelia (Bennett) H.; m. Hildegard Erna Lesche, June 25, 1928; children: Ann Hildegard, James F. Jr., Sylvia Hyde Schuster. AB, Syracuse U., 1923, MA, 1925; PhD, U. Ill., 1928; DSc (hon.), Syracuse U., 1957, Mich. State U., 1975. Postdoctoral fellow Harvard U., 1928-30; chemist Corning Glass Works, 1930-51; sr. scientist, chem. researcher Dow Corning Corp., 1951-75; indsl. chem. rsch. cons. Marco Island, Fla., 1975—; abstractor Glasstechnische Berichte Chem. Abstracts, Ceramic Abstracts. Contbr. articles to profl. jours. Recipient Mich. Patent Law Assn. award, 1963, Perkin medal Am. sect. Soc. Chem. Industry, 1971, Midgley award Detroit sect. Am. Chem. Soc., 1974, Fire of Genious award Saginaw Valley Patent Law Assn., 1982, Midland Matrix Festival award for exellent in sci., 1978; named Whitehead Meml. Lectr. engring. sect. NRC, 1971; elected to Plastics Hall of Fame, 1975. Mem. Am. Chem. Soc., Am. Inst. Chemists, AAAS, N.Y. Acad. Scis., Alpha Chi Sigma, Sigma Xi, Phi Beta Kappa. Achievements include approximately 120 patents and publications for silicone and glass related technology; invention of vapor flame process for forming vitreous silica used in making astronomical telescope mirror blanks and optical fibers; pioneering research in organo-silicon chemistry which initiated the silicone industry. Home: 544 Yellowbird St Marco Island FL 34145-2846

HYDE, LAWRENCE HENRY, JR., industrial company executive; b. Cambridge, Mass., July 10, 1924; s. Lawrence Henry and Catherine I. (McMahon) H.; m. Lois A. Crehan, May 31, 1947; children—Abigail Ellen, Stephen Lawrence, Lawrence Henry III. AB, Harvard U., 1946, MBA, 1947. With Ford Motor Co., 1947-65, dir. internat. purchasing office, 1960-62; v.p. Philco, 1962-64; with Harris Corp., Cleve., 1965-73; from dir. internat. ops. to group v.p. internat. Am. Motors Corp., Detroit, 1974-83, v.p. internat., 1974-77; group v.p., pres. AM Gen. Corp., 1977-81, exec. v.p., 1982-83; with LTV Corp., 1983-85; divsn. pres. AM Gen., 1983-85; with Harris Graphics Corp., 1985-86, also chmn. bd. dirs.; with Sonex Rsch., Inc., 1986—, also chmn. bd. dirs., 1986-93, pres., 1997—; bd. dirs. Whatman plc., Karnak Investments, Ltd., Bermuda; chmn. U. Investment Fund Cairo. Trustee Am. U., Cairo. Office: Sonex Rsch Inc 23 Hudson St Annapolis MD 21401-3100

HYDE, RICHARD LEE, investigator. B in Interdisciplinary Studies, Ga. State U., 1989. Police officer City of Atlanta, 1980-89; assignment mgr. WAGA-TV, Atlanta, 1989-90, 91-95; dir. pub. affairs Ga. State Bd. Pardons and Paroles, Atlanta, 1990-91; chief investigator Office of Atty. Gen., State of Ga., Atlanta, 1995—. Recipient Meritorious Heroism award Atlanta Dept. Pub. Safety, 1983, Excellence in Investigative Jour. award AP, 1989, First Place award Soc. Profl. Journalists, Emmy, 1989, 90, 93, 94, Excellence in Legal Journalism award Am. Bd. Trial Advocates, 1993. Office: 40 Capital Square 141 Judicial Bldg Atlanta GA 30334

HYDE, THOMAS D., lawyer. Sr. v.p., sec., gen. counsel Raytheon Co., Lexington, Mass. Office: Raytheon Co 141 Spring St Lexington MA 02173

HYDER, BETTY JEAN, art educator; b. Elizabethton, Tenn., Oct. 19, 1940; d. Earl Bennick and Bonnie Thelma (Humphrey) Buck; m. Billy Joe Hyder, 1962 (div. 1990); 1 child, Billie Jean Hyder Wallace. BS, East Tenn. State U., 1962, MA, 1970, BA, 1971; postgrad. Tenn. Arts Acad., Belmont U., 1985-94. Visual art specialist grades K-5 Andrew Johnson Sch., Kingsport, Tenn., 1962—; visual art specialist Palmer Ctr. for Handicapped Students, Kingsport, 1976-80. Author: (art textbook) What's Cooking in Art?, 1987; works exhibited in one-woman show East Tenn. State U., 1979; interviewed and taught class for CNN Revolution in Edn., 1989; exhibited work at Renaissance Ctr., Kingsport, 1992, Arts and Crafts festival, Roan Mt., Tenn., 1990, Arts Acad. Capital Bldg., Nashville, 1991, Earth Day at Bays Mt., Kingsport, 1991-92; student art exhibited widely in Kingsport. Artist (booth art) Fun Fest, Kingsport, 1990; chairperson PTA cultural art com., Kingsport, 1989-94; chairperson Christian Fellowship for Singles, Kingsport, 1991-93; singer Christian Single Ensemble, Kingsport, 1991-94; presenter Tenn. Arts Acad., Nashville, 1993; host Pentel's Internat. Children's Exhibit from Japan, 1993; coord. Christine LaGuardia Phillips Cancer Ctr. exhibit, Kingsport, 1984-94; presenter East Tenn. Edn. Assn. art workshop, Knoxville, 1987, 90, 93; hospitality chair. Christian Fellowship for Singles; chair Kingsport Arts Assn., 1994; mem. Crackerjack Singers. Named Kingsport City Schs. Outstanding Educator of Yr., 1987. Mem. NEA, PTA, Tenn. Edn. Assn., Kingsport Edn. Assn. (publicity, pub. rels. chmn. 1962, chairperson edn. profl. stds. com. 1986-88), East Tenn. Art Edn. Assn., Nat. Art Edn. Assn., Delta Kappa Gamma (chairperson legis. com.), Madrigal Drama Players. Republican. Mem. Avoca Christian Ch. Avocations: floral design, water colors, ceramics, Christian choir & ensemble. Office: Andrew Johnson Sch 1001 Ormond Dr Kingsport TN 37664-3283

HYDER, FRANK J., artist, educator; b. Camden, N.J., Oct. 29, 1951; s. Charles and Frances (Roach) H.; m. Helen May Meyrick, July 14, 1974; children: Ethan, Ian, Eric, Ellena, Elissa, Andrew. BFA, Md. Inst. Coll. Art, Balt., 1972; MFA, U. Pa., 1975. Adj. faculty Camden County Coll., Blackwood, N.J., 1976-83; vis. critic U. Pa., Phla., 1995-97; prof. painting Moore Coll. Art and Design, Phila., 1983—. Exhibited in one-man shows at Mus. Am. Art, 1989, Carnegie Mus., 1996, Museo de Arte Contemporaneo, Caracas, 1996, Museo Contemporaneo Coro Venezuela, 1996, Museo del Nat., Lima, Peru, 1996, Mus. of Anthropology, Medellin, Colombia, 1995, Am. Renaissance Expo, Atlanta, 1996; represented in permanent collections at Phila. Mus. Art, Mus. Am. Art, Museo Contemporaneo Caracas, Libr. of Congress, Dept. of State. Recipient Pa. State Coun. on Arts award for painting, 1988, 93, Artist Internation Program Network award, 1995, 96; MidAtlantic NEA grantee, 1993. Address: 631 N 2nd St Philadelphia PA 19123-3001

HYDRISKO, STANLEY JOSEPH, financial company executive; b. Windsor, Vt., Sept. 4, 1927; children: Rosemary, Robert. BS, U. Vt., 1951, postgrad., 1951-52. Cert. internal auditor, fraud examiner; chartered bank auditor. Bank examiner Fed. Reserve Bank, Boston, 1952-57; auditor Harvard Trust Co. (now Bank of Boston), Cambridge, Mass., 1957-70; asst. v.p. Baybanks Inc. (now Bank of Boston), Boston, 1970-80; sr. auditor 1st Am. Bank, Lake Worth, Fla., 1981-82; v.p. Cen. Fin. Corp., Randolph, Vt., 1982-94; ret., 1994. With U.S. Infantry, 1945-47. Avocations: fishing, photography. Home: 2156 US Rte 5 N Windsor VT 05089-9708

HYERS, THOMAS MORGAN, physician, biomedical researcher; b. Jacksonville, Fla., June 16, 1943; s. John and Joan (Clemens) H.; m. Elizabeth Mclean, June 12, 1965; children: Justin, Adam. BS, Duke U., 1964, MD, 1968. Diplomate Am. Bd. Internal Medicine, Am. Bd. Pulmonary Diseases. Intern in medicine Cleve. Met. Gen. Hosp., 1968-69; asst. chief Nat. Blood Resource Br., Nat. Heart, Lung and Blood Inst., NIH, 1971-72, pulmonary disease adv. com., 1983-86; resident in medicine U. Wash., Seattle, 1972-74; chief resident, instr. medicine, 1974-75; fellow in pulmonary diseases U. Colo. Health Scis. Ctr., Denver, 1975-76, research fellow Cardiovascular Pulmonary Research Lab., 1976-77, asst. prof. medicine, staff physician respiratory care, assoc. investigator, 1977-82; research assoc. Denver VA Med. Ctr., 1979-82; assoc. prof. medicine, dir. div. pulmonary diseases St. Louis U. Med. Ctr., 1982-85, prof. medicine, divsn. dir., 1985-98; dir. NIH Specialized Ctr. Research in Adult Respiratory Failure, 1983-93. Contbr. articles to profl. jours. Served to comdr. USPHS, 1969-71. Named hon. Ky. col. grantee NIH, Nat. Heart, Lung and Blood Inst. Fellow ACP, Am. Coll. Chest Physicians; mem. Am. Heart Assn. (mem. councils on thrombosis and cardiopulmonary disease), Internat. Soc. Thrombosis and Haemostasis, Am. Lung Assn. (Eastern Mo. chpt.), Am. Fedn. Clin. Research, Am. Physiol. Soc., Western Soc. Clin. Investigation, Am. Thoracic Soc., Phi Beta Kappa. Office: CARE Clin Rsch 533 Couch Ave Ste 140 Saint Louis MO 63122-5561

HYLAND, BARBARA CLAIRE, state legislator; b. Sept. 17, 1943; m. George Hyland, 1966; children: Kevin, Dana. BA, Regis Coll., 1965. Svc. adv. N.J. Bell, Clifton, 1965-66, New England Telephone, Arlington, Mass., 1966-67; receptionist, adminstrv. asst. Maple Grove Manor Convalescent Home, Norwood, Mass., 1967-68; sec. Codex Corp., Mansfield, Mass., 1985-86; legal sec. John H. Michelmore & Robert E. Cutler, Jr., Foxboro, Mass., 1986-91; mem. Mass. Ho. of Reps., 1992—, mem. health care, housing, urban devel. coms., mem. house ways and means com., pers. and adminstrn. com.; mem. house ways & means com., pers. & adminstrn. com. Mass. Ho. of Reps. Pres. PTA, 1975-77; chmn. playing fields subcom., Foxboro, 1977-86, Foxboro Rep. Town Com., 1989—; mem. sch. com., Foxboro, 1977-86, chief negotiator, 1982-86; coord. WeLD/Cellucci Gubernatorial Campaign, Foxboro, 1989-90. Mem. Pi Gamma Mu. Office: State House Rm 541 Boston MA 02133*

HYLAND, DOUGLAS K. S., museum administrator, educator; b. Salem, Mass., Oct. 7, 1949; s. Samuel F. and Patricia E. Hyland; m. Stephanie duP. Bredin, May 24, 1969 (div. 1976); children: Samuel Irenee, Octavia duP.; m. Alice R. Merrill, Nov. 28, 1981; 1 child, Cassandra A. Grad. cum laude, Brooks Sch., 1967; B.A., U. Pa., 1971; M.A., U. Del., 1975, Ph.D., 1980. Asst. prof. Kress dept. art history U. Kans., 1979-82; curator European and Am. Painting Spencer Mus., 1979-82; vis. prof. Southwestern U., Memphis, 1983-84; dir. Memphis Brooks Mus., 1982-84, Birmingham Mus. Art, Ala., 1984-91, San Antonio Mus. Art, 1992-98, Fuller Mus. Art, Brockton, Mass., 1998—. Author: Marius Dezayas: Conjurer of Souls, 1982, Lorenzo Bartolini and Italian Influence on American Sculpture, 1985, Anders Zorn, 1986, Marie Laurencin: Artist and Muse, 1989, Birmingham Photography, 1989, Harriet and Harmon Kelley Collection of African American Art, 1993, 500 Years of French Art, 1995. Mem. overview panel Nat. Endowment for the Arts, 1988-90. Named Samuel H. Kress fellow, 1977, Attingham fellow, 1981; recipient Chevalier des Arts et Lettres, Republic of France, 1991. Mem. Assn. Art Mus. Dirs. (chmn. mus. ops. com. 1985-89), Am. Assn. Mus. Coll. Art Assn., S.E. Mus. Coun. Home: 7 Daniel Dr North Easton MA 02356 Office: Fuller Mus Art 455 Oak St Brockton MA 02301-1399

HYLAND, GEOFFREY FYFE, energy service company executive; b. Montreal. B in Engring., McGill U., Montreal, 1966; MBA, York U., Toronto, Ont., Can., 1972. Pres., COO Shaw Industries Ltd, Rexdale, Ont., 1987, pres., CEO, 1994—; bd. dir. Shaw Industries Ltd, Tecsyn Internat., Inc., Enerflex Sys., Ltd. Mem. Allendale Ins. Adv. Bd., 1992. Office: Shaw Industries Ltd, 25 Bethridge Rd, Etobicoke, ON Canada M9W 1M7

HYLAND, PATRICIA ANN (PAT HYLAND), writer; b. Buffalo, N.Y., Jan. 3, 1938; d. William Edward and Genevieve Martha (Warner) Pfister; m. William Lloyd Hyland, Aug. 30, 1958; children: Jennifer, Jeffrey, Todd, Timothy, Brian. BS in Bus. Adminstrn., St. Joseph's Coll., N. Windham, Maine, 1984; BSN, Mercy Coll. Nursing, San Diego, 1958. Author: Presidential Libraries and Museums: An Illustrated Guide, 1995; contbr. articles to profl. publs. Spkr. presdl. libraries, nat. archives and hist. groups. Mem. Washington Ind. Writers. Home: 6505 Kalmia St Springfield VA 22150-1138

HYLAND, WILLIAM FRANCIS, lawyer; b. Burlington, N.J., July 30, 1923; s. Theodore J. and Margaret M. (Gallagher) H.; m. Joan E. Sharp, Apr. 20, 1946; children: William Francis, Nancy E. Hyland Wiley, Stephen J., Emma L. Hyland McCormack, Margaret M. Hyland Frank, Thomas M. B.S. in Econs, U. Pa., 1944, LL.B., 1949; D.H.L., Hahnemann Med. Sch. and Hosp., 1976. Bar: N.J. 1949, U.S. Supreme Ct. 1960. Of counsel Riker, Danzig, Scherer, Hyland & Perretti, Morristown, N.J.; atty. gen. N.J., 1974-78; bd. dirs. Pa.-Am. Water Co., N.J.-Am. Water Co. Mem. N.J. Gen. Assembly from Camden County, 1954-61, speaker of house, 1958, acting gov., N.J., 1958; chmn. N.J. Sports and Expn. Authority, 1978-82, commr., 1974-84; pres. N.J. Bd. Pub. Utility Commrs., also mem. cabinet govs. Meyner, Hughes, Byrne, N.J., 1961-68, 74-78; chmn. N.J. Atomic Energy Council, 1968-69, N.J. Commn. Investigation, 1969-71; co-chmn. Reapportionment Commn.; chmn. Brazilian Mission Com., 1962-65; permanent del. Fed. Jud. Conf. 3d Circuit.; del.-at-large Dem. Nat. Conv., 1964, del., 1968; assoc. trustee U. Pa., 1960-74. Served as officer USNR, 1943-46, ETO, PTO. Decorated knight Order of St. Gregory (Pope Paul VI), 1964; recipient Distinguished Service award Camden County Jaycees, 1954, Outstanding Young Man in Govt. N.J. award N.J. Jaycees, 1958, Myrtle Wreath award Camden County So. N.J. region Hadassah, 1977, Pub. Service award Anti-Defamation League of B'nai B'rith, 1982; named Outstanding Citizen of N.J. Advt. Club. N.J., 1979. Mem. ABA (fellow N.J. chpt.), Camden County Bar Assn. (pres. 1959), Nat. Assn. R.R. and Utilities Commrs. (exec. com. 1965-68), Nat. Assn. Attys. Gen. (exec. com. 1975-78, v.p. 1976, pres. elect 1977-78), Phi Kappa Psi. Home: 1 Polo Club Rd Far Hills NJ 07931-2474 Office: Riker Danzig Scherer Hyland & Perretti Headquarters Plz 1 Speedwell Ave Ste 2 Morristown NJ 07960-6823

HYLE, CHARLES THOMAS, marketing specialist; b. Atlanta, Feb. 7, 1961; s. Howard Hopkins and Mary C. (McQuaid) H.; m. Sarah Jane Snyder. BS, BS cum laude, 1984. Syss. cons. MSA, Atlanta, 1984-88; mktg. svcs. mgr. worldwide UNISYS Corp., Atlanta, 1988-92; mktg. rep. Marcam Corp., 1992-96; product engr. SAP America, Inc., Atlanta, 1996—. Scoutmaster Boy Scouts Am. Mem. Am. Prodn. Inventory Control Soc. Avocations: fishing, diving. Office: SAP America Inc Ste 2900 5555 Glenridge Connector NE # 9th-fl Atlanta GA 30342-4739

HYLE, JACK OTTO, orthomolecular psychologist; b. Allentown, Pa., Oct. 19, 1929; s. Lewis Calvin Hyle and Martha Elizabeth (Werft) Hart; m. Anna Louise LeCompte, July 29, 1950; children: Marsha, Jay, Bruce, Susan, Beth. BS in Edn., Bob Jones U., 1959; M in Edn., Temple U., 1961; PhD, Manahath Edn. Ctr., 1967; PMD, Fla. Inst. Tech., 1981. Toll switchman Bell Telephone Co., Harrisburg, Pa., 1950-56; tchr. math. Cen. Dauphin High Sch., Harrisburg, 1959-64; psychologist Narramore Found., Harrisburg, 1964-69; pvt. practice Harrisburg, 1969-89; instr. Pa. State U., 1963-64; prof. of behavioral medicine Fla. Inst. Tech., Melbourne, 1982-85. Contbr. to book, Out of Mighty Waters, 1982; pioneer Orthomolecular Procedure. Scoutmaster Boy Scouts Am., Altoona, Pa., 1947-55; commr., Harrisburg, Pa., 1960-61; Sunday sch. tchr. Grace Brethren Ch., Harrisburg, 1960-70, 89-98. Sgt. USMC, 1947-50. Recipient Hon. Trophy Boy Scouts Am., 1954; named Eagle Scout, 1946. Mem. NEA (life), Internat. Acad. Preventive Medicine, Am. Acad. Anti-Aging Medicine, Occidental Inst. Rsch. Found., Inst. for the Study of Optimal Nutrition. Republican. Avocations: hunting, travel, reading. Home: 5840 Longview Rd Harrisburg PA 17112-3130

HYLKO, JAMES MARK, health physicist, certified quality auditor; b. Detroit, Sept. 11, 1961; s. James John and Frances Rose (Gorski) H. BS in Biochemistry, Ea. Mich. U., 1984; MPH in Health Physics, U. Mich., 1986. Lab. tech. dept. chemistry Ea. Mich. U., Ypsilanti, 1980-84; environ. radiochemist Argonne (Ill.) Nat. Lab., 1984; radiochemist U. Mich., Ann Arbor, 1984-86; health physics tech. Monticello (Minn.) Nuclear Sta., 1985; rsch. scientist/grad. asst. U. Va., Charlottesville, 1986-88; health physicist Fluor Daniel Inc., Chgo., 1988-92, Roy F. Weston, Inc., Albuquerque, 1992—; instr. dept. chem. and nuclear engring. U. N.Mex., 1993-98; guest lectr. Purdue U., 1991; invited spkr. Inst. Atomic Energy, Swierk-Otwock, Poland, 1991. Contbr. over 90 articles to various jours.; tech. reviewer, contbg. editor Jour. Radiation Protection Mgmt., RSO Mag., Power Mag.; book reviewer Jour. Health Physics, and Sci. Books and Films; tech. reviewer Jour. Nuc. Tech. Judge N.Mex. Regional and State Sci. and Engring. Fair, 1993-97. Fellow Inst. Nuclear Power Ops., 1986. Mem. Health Physics Soc. (history com., Rio Grande chpt. exec. bd., treas., co-chair 1999 Midyear Symposium, pres. 1998-99), Am. Nuc. Soc., Am. Soc. Quality Control (cert.), Toastmasters (pres. Fluor Daniel chpt. 1990). Home: 10800 Lowe St NE Albuquerque NM 87111-1837 Office: Roy F Weston Inc 6501 Americas Pkwy NE Ste 800 Albuquerque NM 87110-8146

HYLTON, HANNELORE MENKE, retired manufacturing executive; b. Duesseldorf, Germany, June 10, 1936; came to U.S., 1959, naturalized, 1977; d. Heinz and Margot (Frank) Menke; m. Richard E. Hylton, Aug. 23, 1974. Diploma, Bus. Coll., Duesseldorf, 1956, Alliance Française, Paris, 1956. Exec. sec. G.S. May Internat., Duesseldorf, 1957-59, Embassy of Pakistan, Washington, 1960, Nat. Indsl. Council, Washington, 1961-63; with Pubco Corp., McLean, Va., 1963-83, v.p., 1970-79, exec. v.p., chief adminstrv. officer, 1979-83, dir., 1971-83; v.p., treas., sec., dir. Brookwood Enterprises, Inc., Quinton, Va., 1984-89; bd. dirs. Brookwood Enterprises. Mem. Windermere Country Club. Home: 12524 Butler Bay Ct Windermere FL 34786-6100

HYLTON, JOHN BAKER, music educator, university administrator; b. Connersville, Ind., Mar. 9, 1950; s. Joe Lewis and Betty (Baker) H.; m. Doris Ella Berkemeyer, Mar. 12, 1982; children: Mark, Jerry, Susan. BS in Music Edn., Gettysburg Coll., 1972; MEd, Pa. State U., 1976, EdD, 1980. Cert. tchr. music, Pa. Choral dir., tchr. music York (Pa.) City Sch. Dist., 1972-77; tchg. asst. Pa. State U., Univ. Park, 1977-80; asst. prof. music U. Mo., St. Louis, 1980-86, assoc. prof., 1986-95, prof., 1995—, chmn. dept. music, dir. fine arts outreach program, 1995—. Author: Comprehensive Choral Music Education, 1995; mem. editl. bd. Mo. Jour. Rsch. in Music Edn. (editor 1994-96), Update: Applications of Music Education Rsch., 1990-96; advisory reviewer Handbook on Rsch. in Music Edn., 1992; contbr. articles to profl. jours. Recipient Alumni Achievement award Pa. State U., 1999. Mem. Am. Choral Dirs. Assn. (life, newsletter editor 1988-96), Music Educators Nat. Conf., Soc. for Rsch. in Music Edn., Soc. for Music Tchr. Edn., Phi Mu Alpha Sinfonia, Phi Delta Kappa. Avocations: battlefield guide Gettysburg Nat. Mil. Park, church musician, Hiking, civil war history. E-mail: john-hylton@umsl.edu. Office: U Mo at St Louis Dept Music 8001 Natural Bridge Rd Saint Louis MO 63121

HYLTON, THOMAS JAMES, author; b. Reading, Pa., Dec. 20, 1948; s. William Harold and Mary Harriet (Kitzmiller) H.; m. Frances Wismer, Aug. 31, 1970. BA, Kutztown U. of Pa., 1970. Reporter, then copy editor The Mercury, Pottstown, Pa., 1970-86, editl. writer, 1986-94. Author: Save Our Land, Save our Towns: A Plan for Pennsylvania, 1995. Co-founder, sec. Trees Inc., Pottstown, 1983; co-founder Preservation Pottstown, 1984, 10,000 Friends of Pa., 1998. Recipient Am. Planning Assn. award, 1988, 90, 94, Honor award Nat. Trust for Hist. Preservation, 1997, Pulitzer prize for editl. writing, 1990; Pulliam fellow, 1993. Republican. Presbyterian. Home: 222 Chestnut St Pottstown PA 19464-5508

HYMAN, ABRAHAM, electrical engineer; b. Bklyn., Mar. 8, 1934; s. Rubin and Regina (Holzman) H.; m. Marianne Daniel, June 19, 1955; children: Debra Hyman Rathauser, Lori, Karen. BEE, Poly. Inst. Bklyn., 1954; MS, Newark Coll. Engring., 1954. Registered profl. engr., N.Y. Chief elec. engr. Med. Equipment Research and Devel. Lab., Fort Totten, N.Y., 1955-64; head lab. Office Naval Research, Port Washington, N.Y., 1964-66; tech. adminstr. AEC, Upton, N.Y., 1966-71; supr. indsl. hygienist U.S. Dept. Labor, Westbury, N.Y., 1971-80, regional indsl. hygienist, N.Y.C., 1980-84; mgr. health and safety Unisys Corp., Great Neck, N.Y., 1984-95; safety and health cons., New Hyde Park, N.Y., 1995—; cons. Poison Control Ctr., East Meadow, N.Y., 1981—; adj. assoc. prof. Staten Island Coll., N.Y., 1983-95; lectr. Queensborough C.C., Queens, N.Y., 1994-96. Patentee in field. Bd. dirs. Am. Lung Assn., East Meadow, 1974—. Mem. IEEE, Am. Acad. Environ. Engrs. (diplomate), Nat. Soc. Profl. Engrs., Am. Conf. Indsl. Hygienists, Sci. Research Soc. Am., Sigma Xi. Avocations: photography, swimming, bicycling. Home and Office: 142 Claudy Ln New Hyde Park NY 11040-1635

HYMAN, ALBERT LEWIS, cardiologist; b. New Orleans, Nov. 10, 1923; s. David and Mary (Newstadt) H.; m. Neil Steiner, Mar. 27, 1964; 1 son, Albert Arthur. BS, La. State U., 1943; MD, 1945; postgrad., U. Cin., U. Paris, U. London, Eng. Diplomate: Am. Bd. Internal Medicine. Intern Charity Hosp., 1945-46, resident, 1947-49, sr. vis. physician, 1959-63; resident Cin. Gen. Hosp., 1946-47; instr. medicine La. State U., 1950-56, asst. prof. medicine, 1956-57; asst. prof. Tulane U., 1957-59, assoc. prof., 1959-63, assoc. prof. surgery, 1963-70, prof. research surgery in cardiology, 1970—, prof. clin. medicine Med. Sch., 1983—, adj. prof. pharmacology Med. Sch., 1974—; dir. Cardiac Catheterization Lab., 1957—; sr. vis. physician Touro Hosp., Touro Infirmary, Hotel Dieu; chief cardiology Sara Mayo Hosp.; cons. in cardiology USPHS, New Orleans Crippled Children's Hosp., St. Tammany Parish Hosp., Covington La. area VA, Hotel Dieu Hosp., Mercy Hosp., East Jefferson Gen. Hosp., St. Charles Gen. Hosp.; electrocardiographer Metairie Hosp., 1959-64, Sara Mayo Hosp., Touro Infirmary, St. Tammany Hosp.; cons. cardiovascular disease New Orleans VA Hosp.; cons. cardiology Baton Rouge Gen. Hosp., U.S. Dept. Justice, Fed. Social Security Agy.; Barlow lectr. in medicine U. So. Calif., 1977; mem. internat. sci. com. IV Internat. Symposium on Pulmonary Circulation, Charles U., Prague. Mem. editorial bd. Jour. Applied Physiology; contbr. over 250 articles to profl. jours. Recipient award for rsch. of the Hadassah, 1980, Vis. Scientist award Wellcome Found., Univ. Coll., London, 1991, Disting. Achievement award Am. Heart Assn., 1992, 93, Dickinson-Richards lectr., 1990, Albert Hyman award for excellence in cardiology Tulane U. Med. Sch., 1997; Tulane Med. Sch. Sect. on Cardiology fellow, 1997; Hymen Mayerson Meml. Lctr. in cardiovascular physiology Tulane U. Med. Sch., 1999. Fellow ACP, Am. Coll. Chest Physicians, Am. Coll. Cardiology, Am. Fedn. Clin. Rsch.; mem. AAUP, Am. Heart Assn. (fellow coun. on circulation, fellow coun. on clin. cardiology, mem. coun. on cardiopulmonary medicine, regional rep. coun. clin. cardiology, chmn. sci. com. cardiopulmonary coun. 1981, chmn. cardiopulmonary coun., rsch. com. bd. dirs., editl. bd. mem. Circulation Rsch., edit. bd. mem. Am. Jour. Physiology, Heart Disease and Stroke, Jour. Applied Physiology, Dickinson Richards Meml. Lectr. 1986, 92, Disting. Sci. Achievement award 1990, 93), La. Heart Assn. (v.p. 1974, Albert L. Hyman Ann. Rsch. award, Wellcome Rsch. Found. Vis. Scientist award Univ. Coll. London 1992, Disting. Achievement award outstanding sci. contbns. to cardiopulmonary medicine), Am. Soc. Pharmacology and Exptl. Therapeutics, So. Soc. Clin. Investigation (chmn. membership com.), So. Med. Soc. (Seale-Harris award 1988), Am. Physiol. Soc., N.Am. Soc. Pacing and Electrophysiology, Orleans Surg. Soc. (hon.), New Orleans Surg. Soc. (hon.), N.Y. Acad. Scis., Nat. Am. Heart Assn. (vice-chmn. rsch. com.), Alpha Omega Alpha. Achievements include research in cardiopulmonary circulation. Home: 5467 Marcia Ave New Orleans LA 70124-1052 Office: 3601 Prytania St New Orleans LA 70115-3610

HYMAN, ANDREW M., lawyer; b. Bklyn., Dec. 4, 1955; s. Jack and Dorothy (Harrison) H.; m. Corbey René Low, Oct. 14, 1990; children: Doriana Michelle, Ezra Harrison, Mikayla Sarah. Student, Hobart Coll., Geneva, N.Y., 1973-75; BA, Vassar Coll., 1977; JD, Union U., Albany, N.Y., 1980. Bar: N.Y. 1981, U.S. Dist. Ct. (so. and ea. dists.) N.Y. 1984, U.S. Dist. Ct. (mid. dist.) Pa. 1992. Counsel comml. real estate dept. LeFrek Orgn., Rego Park, N.Y., 1980-84; sr. atty. divsn. housing and cmty. renewal State of N.Y., N.Y.C., 1984-86; sr. counsel N.Y. State Urban Devel. Corp., N.Y.C., 1986-95; pvt. practice Port Washington, N.Y., 1995-96; gen. counsel Banana Kelly Cmty. Improvement Assn., Bronx, 1996-98; dep. dir., spl. counsel Bronx Overall Econ. Devel. Corp., 1997—, gen. counsel, 1998—. Zone leader Port Washington West, Nassau Dem. County Com., 1995—; treas. Ind. Dem. Club, Inc., Flushing, N.Y., 1982-88. Mem. N.Y. State Bar Assn., Assn. Bar City of N.Y., N.Y. County Lawyers Assn. Jewish. Home: 38 Amherst Rd Port Washington NY 11050-4102 Office: Bronx Overall Economic Devel Corp 198 E 161st St Bronx NY 10451

HYMAN, ARTHUR, philosopher, educator, dean; b. Schwaebisch Hall, Germany, Apr. 10, 1921; came to U.S., 1935; s. Isaac and Rosa (Weil) H.; m. Ruth Link-Salinger, Feb. 25, 1951; children: Jeremy Saul, Michael Samuel, Joseph Isaiah. BA, St. John's Coll., 1944; MA, Harvard U., 1947, PhD, 1953; MHL, Jewish Theol. Sem., 1955, DHL (hon.), 1987; DHL (hon.), Hebrew Union Coll., 1994. Prof. Yeshiva U., N.Y.C., 1961-91, dean, prof., 1992—; vis. prof. Columbia U., N.Y.C., 1971-91, Hebrew U., Jerusalem, 1988, 1969-70, U. Calif., San Diego, 1977, Yale U., 1981, Cath. U. Am., Washington, 1991-92; coun. mem. World Union Jewish Studies, Jerusalem, 1993—. Co-editor: (with J.J. Walsh) Philosophy in the Middle Ages, 1967; editor, translator: Averroes' De Substantia Orbis, 1986; editor (ann.) Maimonidean Studies, 1991—. Fellow Nat. Endowment Humanities, 1980-81, Ford Found., 1951-52, Acad. Jewish Philosophy, 1982—; recipient scholarship achievement award Nat. Found. Jewish Culture, 1999. Fellow Am. Acad. Jewish Rsch. (pres. 1992-94), Soc. Medieval and Renaissance Philosophy (pres. 1978-80), Soc. Internat. pour l'Etude de la Philosophie Médiévale. Democrat. Jewish. Home: 845 W End Ave Apt 2A New York NY 10025-8436 Office: Yeshiva Univ BRGS 500 W 185th St New York NY 10033-3201

HYMAN, EDWARD SIDNEY, physician, consultant; b. New Orleans, Jan. 22, 1925; s. David and Mary (Newstadt) H.; m. Jean Simons, Sept. 29, 1956; children: Judith, Sydney, Edward David, Anne. BS, La. State U., 1944; MD, Johns Hopkins U., 1946. Diplomate: Am. Bd. Internal Medicine, Intern Barnes Hosp., Washington U., St. Louis, 1946-47; fellow in medicine Stanford U., San Francisco, 1949-51, asst. resident in medicine, 1950-51, Peter Bent Brigham Hosp., Boston, 1951-53; teaching fellow in medicine Harvard U., Boston, 1952-53; practice medicine specializing in internal medicine, New Orleans, 1953—; dir. kidney unit Charity Hosp., New Orleans, 1953-55; investigator Touro Research Inst., New Orleans, 1959; dir. Hyman Corp.; mem. staff Sara Mayo Hosp., 1954-79, chief of staff, 1968-70, trustee, 1970-78; mem. staff Touro Infirmary, New Orleans, St. Charles Hosp.; panelist Pres.'s Commn. on Health Needs of Nation, 1952; cons. water quality New Orleans Sewerage and Water Bd., 1978; mem. research adv. com. Cancer Assn. New Orleans, 1976-81, La. Bd. Regents, 1983. Contbr. articles to profl. jours. NIH grantee, 1960-81; Am. Heart Assn. grantee, 1962-65. Fellow ACP; mem. Am. Fedn. Clin. Rsch., Am. Soc. Artificial Internal Organs, Am. Physiol. Soc. Biophys. Soc. (chmn. local arrangements 1971, 77, 81, 87), Am. Soc. Microbiology, AAAS, Pvt. Drs. Am. (co-founder 1968, v.p. 1968-84, Dist. Svc. award 1981), Orleans Parish Med. Soc. (gov. 1972-80), La. State Med. Soc. (ho. of dels. 1970-81), Surfaces in Biomaterial Found. Jewish. Subspecialties: Internal medicine; Biophysics. Current work: Clincial internal medicine, biochemistry, biophysics, nephrology, artificial organs, water quality, government in medicine, cause of death in renal failure, significance of bacteria in urine. Isolated aldosterone, 1949; patentee sheet plastic oxygenator (artificial heart), oil detection device; inventor telephone transmission of electrocardiogram, early data transmission; inventor hydrogen platinum detection of heart shunts, Method for detection of bacteria in urine, Systemic Coccal Disease (SCD), Desert Storm Syndrome (following the Persian Gulf War) as a bacterial disease (SCD), grantee treatment of Gulf War Syndrome as a form of SCD, Silicone Implant Disease as a bacterial disease, as a manifestation of Systemic Coccal Disease. Office: 3525 Prytania St Ste 220 New Orleans LA 70115-3586

HYMAN, HAROLD M., history educator, consultant; b. Bklyn., July 24, 1924; s. Abraham and Rebecca (Hermann) H.; m. Ferne Beverly Handelsman, Mar. 11, 1946; children: Lee Rosenthal, Ann Root, William Hyman. BA with honors, U. Calif. L.A., 1948; MA, Columbia U., 1950, PhD, 1952; LHD (hon.), Lincoln Coll., 1984. summer instr. Columbia U., 1953, U. Wash., 1960, Bklyn. Coll., 1962, U. Chgo., 1965; vis. asst. prof. UCLA, 1955-56; sr. Fulbright lectr. in Am. History and Law, grad. faculty polit. sci. U. Tokyo, 1973; faculty of law Keio U., 1973; adj. prof. legal history Bates Coll. Law U. Houston, 1977, of Am. legal history U. Tex. Law Sch., 1986; Meyer vis. disting. prof. legal history NYU Sch. Law, 1982-83; cons. and spkr. in field. Asst. prof. Earlham Coll., 1952-55; assoc. prof. Ariz. State U., 1956-57; prof. UCLA, 1957-63, U. Ill., 1963-68; William P. Hobby prof. History Rice U., 1968-96, William P. Hobby prof. history emeritus, 1997—; speaker in field. Author: Era of the Oath: Northern Loyalty Tests During the Civil War and Reconstruction (Albert J. Beveridge award Am. Hist. Assn. 1981), 1954, To Try Men's Souls: Loyalty Tests in American History (Sidney Hillman Found. prize 1960), 1981, Stanton: The Life and Times of Lincoln's Secretary of War, 1962, Soldiers and Spruce: Origins of the Loyal Legion of Loggers and Lumbermen: The Army's Labor Union of World War I, 1963, A More Perfect Union: The Impact of the Civil War and Reconstruction on the Constitution, 1973, Union and Confidence:

The 1860s, 1976, (with William Wiecek) Equal Justice Under Law: Constitutional History, 1833-1880, 1982, paperback, 1983, Quiet Past and Stormy Present? War Powers in American History, 1986, American Singularity: The 1787 Northwest Ordinance, the 1862 Homestead-Morrill Acts, and the 1944 GI Bill, 1986, Oleander Odyssey: The Kempners of Galveston, 1870-1980, (Coral H. Tullis Meml. prize Tex. A&M U. Press 1990, T. R. Fehrenbach Book award Tex. Hist. Comsn. 1990, Ottis Lock Endowment award E. Tex. Hist. Assn. 1991), 1990, The Reconstruction Justice of Salmon P. Chase: In re Turner and Texas v. White, 1997, Character and Craftsmanship: A History of Houston's Vinson & Elkins Law Firm, 1917-1990s, 1998; editor (with Ferne B. Hyman) The Circuit Court Opinions of Salmon Portland Chase, 1972; contbr. numerous articles to profl. jours. Elected lay mem. Houston Bar Assn. Grievance Com., 1985-88; mem. numerous U. coms. The Constitution, Law, and Am. Life in the Nineteenth Century: A conf. named in his honor, Rice U. and NYU Sch. Law, 1989; named U.S. Presdl. appointee to permanent com. Oliver Wendell Holmes Trust, 1993-2001. Mem. Am. Hist. Assn. (numerous coms. and offices), Am. Soc. Legal History (pres . 1993-95), Orgn. Am. Historians (various coms. and offices), So. Hist. Assn. Avocation: fishing. Office: Rice University Dept History-MS 42 PO Box 1892 Houston TX 77251-1892

HYMAN, JEROME ELLIOT, lawyer; b. Rosedale, Miss., Dec. 26, 1923; s. Mose and Mary Ann (Sprecher) H.; m. Isabelle Miller, July 1, 1960. A.B., Coll. William and Mary, 1944; LL.B. magna cum laude (Fay diploma), Harvard U., 1947. Bar: N.Y. 1949, D.C. 1960. Mem. fgn. funds control staff Dept. Treasury, U.S. Mil. Govt., Frankfurt and Berlin, Germany, 1945-46; law clk. to judge U.S. Ct. Appeals, Boston, 1947-48; assoc. firm Cleary, Gottlieb, Steen & Hamilton, N.Y.C., 1948-58, ptnr., 1959-93, counsel, 1994—; trustee, mem. exec. com. Practising Law Inst., N.Y.C., 1972-97, v.p., 1979-86, pres., 1986-96, chmn. bd. trustees, 1996-97, chmn. emeritus, 1997—; sr. v.p., gen. counsel Pan Am World Airways, Inc., 1982-84. Bd. editors: Harvard Law Rev., 1945-47. Pres. Lexington Dem. Club, N.Y.C., 1956-58; counsel N.Y. Com. for Stevenson, 1956; del. various Dem. state and jud. convs.; alumni mem. Harvard Law Sch. Placement Com., 1976-79; nat. chmn. maj. gifts com. Harvard Law Sch. Fund, 1978-80; mem. overseers com. to visit Harvard Law Sch., 1986-92; trustee Lawyers' Com. for Civil Rights Under Law, 1981—; trustee Citizens Budget Commn., N.Y.C., 1991-94, trustee emeritus, 1994—; trustee Endowment Assn. of the Coll. of William and Mary, 1997—. Fellow Am. Bar Found.; mem. ABA, Assn. Bar City N.Y. (chmn. com. corp. law 1984-87), Am. Law Inst., Am. Judicature Soc., N.Y. County Lawyers Assn., Tribar Opinion Commn., Harvard Law Sch. Assn. N.Y.C. (trustee 1980-83, v.p. 1984-85, pres. 1985-86), Nat. Harvard Law Sch. Assn. (mem. coun. 1990-93, mem. exec. com. 1991-93), Sky Club, Phi Beta Kappa Assocs. Home: 1125 Park Ave Apt 10B New York NY 10128-1243 Office: Cleary Gottlieb Steen & Hamilton One Liberty Plaza New York NY 10006-1470

HYMAN, JOHN ALLEN, securities executive; b. New Haven, Mar. 4, 1961; s. Herbert Gordon and Vivian Leigh (Miller) H.; m. Merri Robin Brenner, Oct. 17, 1987. BA, Franklin & Marshall Coll., 1983; MBA, Coll. William and Mary, 1985. V.p. Drexel Burnham Lambert, N.Y.C., 1985-89; 1st v.p. Smith Barney Harris Upham & Co., N.Y.C., 1989—. Republican. Jewish. Avocations: photography, sailing, cross-country skiing. Home: 1235 Park Ave Apt 5A New York NY 10128-1759 Office: Smith Barney Harris Upham 1345 Avenue Of The Americas New York NY 10105

HYMAN, LESTER SAMUEL, lawyer; b. Providence, July 14, 1931; s. Carl and Alice (Adelman) H.; m. Helen Reeder Sidman, Sept. 19, 1959 (div. 1982); children: David, Andrew, Elizabeth. AB, Brown U., 1952; LLB, Columbia U., 1955. Bar: D.C. 1955, Mass. 1955, U.S. Supreme Ct. 1957. Atty. SEC, Washington, 1955-57; chief asst. to Gov. State of Mass., Boston, 1962-64, sec. commerce, 1964-65; sr. cons. HUD, Washington, 1966-67; ptnr. Leva, Hawes & Symington, Washington, 1969-82; founding ptnr. Swidler & Berlin, Washington, 1982—; lectr. John F. Kennedy Sch. Govt. Harvard U., 1968-69; bd. dirs. CDS Internat., 1988-94. mem. Internat. Obever Team for nat. election in Haiti, 1990. Bd. dirs. Ctr. Nat. Policy, Washington, 1980—; bd. advisors Close-Up Found.; bd. govs. Am. Jewish Commn., 1980-84; Dem. chmn., Mass., 1967-69, del. Dem. Nat. Conv., 1968, mem. Dem. Charter Reform Commn., 1970, D.C. Cmty. Humanities, 1988-90; bd. dirs. Cmty. Coll. of Brit. V.I., 1989—, Young Artists, 1989-94; mem. adv. bd. Internat. legal Studies Program, Washington Coll. Law, Am. U., 1990—; apptd. by Pres. Clinton to Franklin Delano Roosevelt Meml. Commn., 1994; trustee Norton Simon Mus. of Art, Pasadena, Calif., 1995-97; mem. U.S. Presdl. Del. to Guatamalan Peace Accord Singing, 1996; chmn. Liberia Internat. Ship and Corp. Registry, 1998. Named Outstanding Young Man of Yr., Greater Boston Jr. C. of C., 1964. Mem. Performing Artists Soc. of Am. (mng. dir. 1997). Home: 3826 Van Ness St NW Washington DC 20016-2228 Office: Swidler Shereff Friedman 3000 K St NW Ste 300 Washington DC 20007-5109

HYMAN, LEWIS NEIL, investment company executive, investment advisor; b. Johnstown, Pa., Aug. 5, 1949; s. Albert and Helene (Rose) H.; 1 child, Hannah Rose. BA magna cum laude, U. Pitts., 1971, JD, 1974. Bar: Pa. 1974, U.S. Dist. Ct. 1974, U.S. Supreme Ct. 1974; registered investment advisor. Asst. dist. atty. Allegheny County Dist. Atty.'s Office, Pitts., 1974-79; pvt. practice lawyer Pitts., 1979-82, 89-91; investment banker Smith Barney, N.Y.C., Phila., 1982-86; v.p. investment banking and market devel. FGIC, Inc., N.Y.C., 1987-89; pres. The Hartwood Group, Pitts., 1991—, Hartwood Advisors, Inc., Pitts., 1991—; officer Strategic Benefits Group, Inc., Pitts., 1991-95; lectr. U. Pitts., 1989-91, Allegheny C.C., Pitts., 1989-91, Pa. State U., Pitts., 19890-91, Joseph M. Katz Grad. Sch. Bus./U. Pitts., 1995. Univ. scholar U. Pitts., 1971. Mem. Pa. Bar Assn., Internat. Assn. Fin. Planners (participant cmty. pub. awareness TV program 1994—), Pitts. Assn. Fin. Planners, Phi Beta Kappa. Avocations: tennis, golf, swimming, photography, sculpture, skiing. Office: The Hartwood Group 5401 Walnut St Pittsburgh PA 15232-2276

HYMAN, MARY BLOOM, science education programs coordinator; m. Sigmund M. Hyman, 1947; children: Carol Ann Hyman Williams, Nancy Louise. BS, Goucher Coll., 1971; MS, Johns Hopkins U., 1977. Asst. dir. Edn. Md. Sci. Ctr., Balt., 1976-81, dir. edn., 1981-90; coord. sci. edn. programs Loyola Coll., Balt., 1990—, coord. Inst. for Child Care Edn., 1992—. Trustee Goucher Coll.; mem. Baltimore County Pub. Schs. Com. for Sch.-Based and Sch.-Linked Child Care; bd. dirs. Balt. Sch.-Age Child Care Alliance; mem. Gov.'s Task Force on Compensation of Child Care Providers, 1995-96; bd. dirs. Johns Hopkins U. Ctr. Talented Youth. Recipient Disting. Women award Gov.'s Office, Annapolis, Md., 1981; Meritorious Svc. award Johns Hopkins U., 1983; Outstanding Svc. to Sci. Edn. award. Assn. Sci. Dept. Chairmen of Balt. County Pub. Schs., 1989. Mem. Md. Assn. Sci. Tchrs. (bd. dirs.), Phi Beta Kappa, Phi Delta Kappa. Home: 10815 Longacre Ln Stevenson MD 21153-0665

HYMAN, MICHAEL BRUCE, lawyer; b. Elgin, Ill., July 26, 1952; s. Robert I. and Ruth (Cohen) H.; m. Leslie Bland, Aug. 14, 1977; children: Rachel Joy, David Adam. BSJ with honors, Northwestern U., 1974, JD, 1977. Bar: Ill. 1977, U.S. Supreme Ct. 1989. Asst. atty. gen. Antitrust div. State of Ill., Chgo., 1977-79; atty. Much Shelist Freed Denenberg Ament & Rubenstein, Chgo., 1979-85, ptnr., 1985—; chmn. panelist various continuing legal edn. seminars. Columnist Editor's Briefcase, CBA Record, 1988-90, 93—, The Red Pencil, 1986-89; contbr. chpt. to book, articles to profl. jours. Trustee North Shore Congregation Israel, Glencoe, 1980-89, 95—, v.p., 1987-89. Mem. ABA (mem. sect. litigation, chmn. antitrust litigation com. 1987-90, editor-in-chief Litigation News 1990-92, mng. editor 1989-90, assoc. editor 1985-89, chmn. monographs and unpub. papers com. 1992-95, task force on civil justice reform 1991-93, editor-in-chief Litigation Docket, 1995—, mem. jud. divsn., lawyers conf., membership com. chair 1999—), Chgo. Bar Assn. (editor-in-chief CBA Record 1988-90, 93—, CBA News 1994-98, bd. mgrs. 1992-94), Ill. Bar Assn. (rep. on assembly 1986-92, 94-99, antitrust coun. 1981-87, chmn. coun. 1985-86, vice chair, sec., co-editor newsletter 1982-85, chmn. bench and bar sect. coun. 1990-91, professionalism com. 1992-95, chair 1993-94, vice chair ARDC com. 1995-96, chair ARDC com. 1996-97, mem. cable tv com. 1995—, chairman 1997-99), Am. Soc. Writers on Legal Subjects (mem., chair book award com. 1997—), others. Jewish. Avocations: books, writing, Abraham Lincoln. Office: Much Shelist Freed Denenberg Ament & Rubenstein 200 N La Salle St Ste 2100 Chicago IL 60601-1026

HYMAN, MILTON BERNARD, lawyer; b. L.A., Nov. 19, 1941; s. Herbert and Lillian (Rakowitz) Hyman; m. Sheila Goldman, July 4, 1965; children: Lauren Davida, Micah Howard. BA in Econs. with highest honors, UCLA, 1963; JD magna cum laude, Harvard U., 1966. Bar: Calif. 1967. Assoc. Irell & Manella, LLP, L.A., 1970-73, ptnr., 1973—. Co-author: Partnerships and Associations: A Policy Critique of the Morrisey Regulations, 1976, Consolidated Returns: Summary of Tax Considerations in Acquisition of Common Parent of Subsidiary Member of Affiliated Group, 1980, Tax Aspects of Corporate Debt Exchanges, Recapitalization and Discharges, 1982, Tax Strategies for Leveraged Buyouts and Other Corporate Acquisitions, 1986, Preservation and Use of Net Operating Losses and Other Tax Attributes in a Consolidated Return Context, rev. edit., 1992, Collier on Bankruptcy Taxation, 1992, Real Estate Workouts and Bankruptcies, 1993, Current Corporate Bankruptcy Tax Issues, 1993, Tax Strategies for Corporate Acquisitions, Dispositions, Financing, Joint Ventures, Reorganizations, and Restructurings, 1995; author: A Transactional Encounter with the Partnership Rules of Subchapter K: The Effects of the Tax Reform Act of 1984, 1984, Net Operating Losses and Other Tax Attribute of Corporate Clients, 1987. Past pres., bd. dirs. Sinai Temple, West Los Angeles, Calif. Capt. JAGC, U.S. Army, 1967-70. Sheldon traveling fellow Harvard U., 1966-67. Mem. ABA (chmn. com. affiliated and related corps. 1981-83), Calif. State Bar Assn., Am. Law Inst. (fed. income tax project tax adv. group 1976—), Masons, Camp Ramah Club (bd. dirs. Calif.), Phi Beta Kappa. Jewish. Office: Irell & Manella Ste 900 1800 Avenue Of The Stars Los Angeles CA 90067-4276*

HYMAN, MONTAGUE ALLAN, lawyer; b. N.Y.C., Apr. 19, 1941; s. Allan Richard and Lilyan P. (Pollock) H.; m. Susann Podell, Jan. 25, 1965; children—Jeffrie-Anne, Erik. B.A., Syracuse U., 1962; J.D., St. Johns U., 1965. Bar: N.Y. 1965, U.S. Dist. Ct. (so. and ea. dists.) N.Y. 1967, U.S. Supreme Ct. 1973, U.S. Ct. Appeals (2d cir.) 1982. Assoc. Warburton, Hyman, Deeley & Connelly, Mineola, N.Y., 1965-67; ptnr. Hyman & Deeley, Mineola, 1967-69, Koeppel, Hyman, Sommer, Lesnick & Ross, Mineola, 1969-72, Hyman & Hyman, P.C., Garden City, N.Y., 1972-80, Costigan, Hyman, Hyman & Herman, P.C., Mineola, 1980-87, Certilman Haft Balin Buckley Kremer & Hyman, 1987-88, Certilman Balin Adler & Hyman, 1988—; lectr. Hofstra U., Adelphi U., Columbia Appraisal Soc., Practicing Law Inst. Trustee L.I. Jewish Med. Ctr.; chmn. The Rehabilitation Inst.; bd. trustees North Shore L.I. Jewish Health System. Mem. Nassau County Bar Assn., N.Y. State Bar Assn., Inst. Property Taxation. Contbr. articles to profl. jours. Office: Certilman Balin Adler & Hyman LLP 90 Merrick Ave East Meadow NY 11554-1571

HYMAN, MORTON PETER, shipping company executive; b. N.Y.C., Jan. 9, 1936; s. Irving S. and Dora (Pfeffer) H.; m. Chris Oliphant Stern, Mar. 18, 1979; children: Sarah Anne, David Jacob. BA, Cornell U., 1956, LLD with distinction, 1959; DHL (hon.), N.Y. Med. Coll. Bar: N.Y. 1960. Assoc. Proskauer Rose Goetz & Mendelsohn, N.Y.C., 1959-63; officer, dir. Overseas Discount Corp., N.Y.C., 1963—, pres., 1983—; officer, dir. Overseas Shipholding Group, Inc., N.Y.C., 1969—, pres., 1971—; bd. dirs. Discount Bank and Trust Co. Bd. editors Cornell Law Rev. Vice-chmn. N.Y. State Health Planning Commn., 1977-78; mem. Pub. Health Coun. N.Y., 1971—, vice chmn., 1975-85, chmn., 1985-95; co-chmn. N.Y. State Health Issues Forum; chmn. N.Y. State Health Care Capital Policy Adv. Com., 1982-94; chmn. bd. trustees Beth Israel Med. Ctr., Continuum Health Ptnrs, Inc.; vice chmn. bd. trustees St. Luke's-Roosevelt Hosp. Ctr.; vice-chmn. bd. Regents Long Island Coll Hosp.; chmn. N.Y. State Joint Exec. and Legis. Task Force on Delivery of Health Care, 1977-80; chmn. N.Y. State Joint Exec. and Legis. Com. on Residential Health Care Facilities, 1977-80; trustee The Brearley Sch., 1993-97; mem. pres. coun. United Hosp. Fund; bd. dirs. United Jewish Appeal Fedn., 1986-91; mem. bd. overseers Albert Einstein Coll. Medicine of Yeshiva U. 2d lt. AUS, 1956-57. Fellow N.Y. Acad. Medicine; mem. N.Y. Bar Assn., Harmonie Club, Order of Coif, Phi Kappa Phi. Republican. Home: 998 5th Ave New York NY 10028-0102 Office: Overseas Shipholding Group Inc 511 Fifth Ave New York NY 10017-4903

HYMAN, PAULA E(LLEN), history educator; b. Boston; d. Sydney Max and Ida Frances (Tatelman) H.; m. Stanley Harvey Rosenbaum, June 7, 1969; children: Judith Hyman Rosenbaum, Adina Hyman Rosenbaum. B.J.Ed., Hebrew Coll., Brookline, Mass., 1966; B.A., Radcliffe Coll., 1968; M.A., Columbia U., 1970, Ph.D., 1975. Asst. prof. Columbia U., N.Y.C., 1974-81; assoc. prof. history Jewish Theol. Sem., N.Y.C., 1981-86, dean Sem., Coll. Jewish Studies, 1981-86; Lady Davis. vis. assoc. prof. Hebrew U. of Jerusalem, 1986; Lucy Moses prof. history Yale U., New Haven, 1986—. Series editor Ind. U. Press. Bloomington, 1982—; contbg. editor Sh'ma Mag., N.Y.C., 1977—; author: From Dreyfus to Vichy, 1979, The Emancipation of the Jews of Alsace, 1991, Gender and Assimilation in Modern Jewish History, 1995; co-author: The Jewish Woman in America, 1976; co-editor: The Jewish Family; Myths and Reality, 1986, Jewish Women in America: An Historical Encyclopedia, 2 vols., 1997; contbr. articles to publs. Vice chmn. Zionist Acad. Coun., N.Y.C., 1982-83. NEH summer grantee, 1977;Am. Coun. Learned Socs. fellow, 1978; grantee N.Y. Council for Humanities, 1980, NEH fellow, 1986-87. Fellow Am. Acad. Jewish Rsch. (treas. 1995—); mem. Am. Hist. Assn. (com. 1983), Assn. for Jewish Studies (bd. dirs. 1978-81, 83-85, 86—, v.p. for mem., 1995-97), Nat. Found. Jewish Culture (chairperson acad. adv. com. 1996—), Leo Baeck Inst. (bd. dirs. 1979—), Yivo Inst. for Jewish Rsch., Phi Beta Kappa. Jewish. Office: Yale U Dept History New Haven CT 06520*

HYMAN, ROGER DAVID, lawyer; b. Oak Ridge, Tenn., Apr. 23, 1957; s. Marshall Leonard and Vera Lorraine (McKinney) H.; m. Elsa Laurencio; 1 child, Cristina Alicia. BA, Vanderbilt U., 1979; JD, U. Tenn., 1984. Clk. Oak Ridge Nat. Lab., 1977-78, 81; air personality, news reporter Stas. WKDA, WKDF, Nashville, 1979; program dir. Sta. WBIR-FM, Knoxville, Tenn., 1979-80; assoc. atty. Hindman & Holt, Attys., Knoxville, Tenn., 1984-85; asst. atty. gen. State of Tenn., Knoxville, 1986-95; with Law Offices of Roger D. Hyman Powell, Tenn., 1995-97; ptnr. Hyman & Carter, Attys., Powell, Tenn., 1997—. Bd. dirs. Knoxville Christian Sch., 1991-93. Democrat. Mem. Ch. of Christ. Home: 2713 Windemere Ln Powell TN 37849-3782 Office: Hyman & Carter PO Box 1304 Powell TN 37849-1304

HYMAN, SEYMOUR, capital and product development company executive; b. N.Y.C., June 19, 1927; s. Morris and Fannie (Baumwall) H.; m. Sandra Kammerman, Feb. 25, 1973. B.S., N.Y. State Maritime Coll., 1948; student, Bklyn. Poly. Inst., 1944-45, Columbia, 1949-51; M.S., N.Y. U., 1949. Chief mfg. engring. U.S. Naval Clothing Factory, Bklyn., 1950-51; chief indsl. engr. Peter Pan Mfg. Co., E. Newark, N.J., 1951-53; chief prodn. engr. Seampruf Inc., N.Y.C., 1953-54; founder, pres., chmn. bd. Herculite Protective Fabrics, Inc., N.Y.C., 1954-76; vice chmn. bd. Eckmar Corp., N.Y.C., 1969-75; co-founder pres., chmn. bd. Health-Chem. Corp., N.Y.C., 1971-76; pres. Delta Ventures Corp., N.Y.C., 1977—. Served with USNR, 1945-48. Mem. Soc. Plastic Engrs. Club: Mason (Shriner). Home: 425 E 58th St New York NY 10022-2300

HYMAN, SEYMOUR C(HARLES), arbitrator; b. N.Y.C., June 3, 1919; s. Jack and Rose (Bernhardt) H.; m. Charlotte Bank, June 26, 1943; children—Carol Joan, Judith Fay. B.Ch.E., CCNY, 1939; M.Sc., Va. Poly. Inst., 1940; Ph.D., Columbia U., 1950. Registered profl. engr., N.Y., N.J. Engr. Ashland Oil and Refining Co., Ky., 1940-42; prin. engr. Signal Corps Labs., Ft. Monmouth, N.J., 1942-47; dep. chancellor City U. N.Y., 1947-77; pres. William Paterson Coll. N.J., Wayne, 1977-85; arbitrator, 1985—; cons. Atomic Power Reactors, 1950-66. Mem. River Edge Regional Sch. Bd., 1960-61. *I have two guidelines. I have individual and final responsibility for everything I do or not do. I am proud to be identified with my work product.*

HYMAN, SIGMUND M., benefits consultant; b. Balt., Aug. 4, 1921; m. Mary Bloom, Nov. 28, 1947; children: Carol A. Hyman Williams, Nancy L. BS in Econs., Franklin and Marshall Coll., 1947. CLU. Chmn. S.M. Hyman Co., Balt., 1956-77, S.M. Hyman Co. Ltd., London, 1971-77, Bus. Data Services, Balt., 1963-77; gen. agt. New Eng. Life Ins. Co., Boston, 1960-79; v.p. William M. Mercer, Inc., Balt., 1977-80; benefits cons. Balt., 1980—; assoc. Coun. Profit-Sharing Industries, 1960-82, Am. Pension and Profit-Sharing Inst. Purdue U., 1961-82, Balt. Mayor's Pension Study Com., 1966-90, Mayor's Bus. Adv. Coun., 1977-86; mem. Gov.'s Commn. on Competitive Forces Facing Md.'s Horse Racing Industry, 1994—. Mem. exec. com. Greater Balt. Com., 1960-80; vice chmn. Md. Acad. Scis., 1970-90; bd. dirs. Balt. Mus. Art, 1973-79, Goodwill Industries Balt., 1981—; trustee emeritus Franklin and Marshall Coll., Lancaster, Pa., 1973—; chmn. internat. affairs com. Johns Hopkins U., Balt., 1979-80. 1st lt. AUS, 1941-46, ETO, 1951-53, Korea. Decorated Purple Heart; named Disting. Citizen of Balt., 1976, Outstanding Alumnus, Franklin and Marshall Coll., 1981. Mem. Balt. C. of C. (v.p. 1970-78), Balt. Center Club, Suburban Balt. Country Club. Avocations: ham radio, golf, art collecting. Office: PO Box 248 Stevenson MD 21153-0248

HYMAN, STEVEN EDWARD, federal agency administrator, psychiatrist, educator. BA summa cum laude, Yale U., 1974; BA with honors, MA in History and Philosophy of Sci., U. Cambridge, Eng., 1976; MD cum laude, Harvard U., 1980. Diplomate Am. Bd. Psychiatry and Neurology. Intern in medicine Mass. Gen. Hosp., Boston, 1980-81, clin. and rsch. fellow in endocrinology and neurology, 1983-84, rsch. fellow in molecular biology, 1984-88, dir. rsch. dept. psychiatry, 1990-96, dir. divsn. addictions, 1992-95, supr. psychiatric residents, 1984—, dir. neurosci. and biolo. psychiatry curriculum for residents, lectr., 1986—; clin. fellow in medicine Harvard U., Boston, 1980-81, clin. fellow in psychiatry, 1981-84, rsch. fellow in genetics, 1984-87; from instr. in psychiatry to asst. prof. psychiatry Harvard Med. Sch., Boston, 1987-92, assoc. prof. psychiatry, 1993-98, prof. psychiatry, 1998—; dir. NIMH, Rockville, Md., 1996—; mem. sci. coun. NARSAD, 1996—; mem. adv. com. Howard Hughes Med. Inst., 1998—, Riken Brain Scis. Inst., Tokyo. Author: (with G.W. Arana) Handbook of Psychiatric Drug Therapy, 1987, 2d edit., 1991, 3d edit. (with G.W. Arana, J.R. Rosenbaum), 1995, (with E. Nestler) The Molecular Foundations of Psychiatry, 1993; editor numerous textbooks; mem. editl. bd. Jour. Geriat. Psychiatry and Neurology, 1987-96, Psychosomatics, 1988-96, Harvard Rev. Psychiatry, 1992—, Am. Jour. Med. Genetics, 1992—, Jour. Neurochemistry, 1994—, Archives Gen. Psychiatry, 1996—, Molecular Psychiatry, 1996—, Neurobiology of Disease, 1996—. Mellon fellow, 1974-76, Dupont-Warren fellow, 1983-84, Langhlin fellow Am. Coll. Psychiatry, 1983; recipient Laughlin award Nat. Psychiatric Endowment Fund, 1984, Physician Scientist award NIDDK, 1985-90, Philip Isenberg award for best tchr. selected by graduating residents McLean Hosp., 1985, Rsch. Scientist Devel. award level 2, 1995-96. Mem. APA, Am. Coll. Neuropsychopharmacology, Soc. Neurosci., Soc. Biolo. Psychiatry. Fax: 301-443-2578. E-mail: shyman@nih.gov. Office: NIMH 6001 Exec Blvd Rm 8235 Bethesda MD 20892-9669*

HYMANN, PAUL G., JR., federal judge; b. 1952. BA, Vanderbilt U., 1974; JD, U. Miami, 1977. Bar: Fla. Atty. Britton, Cohen, Kaufman & Schantz, Miami, Fla., 1977-79, 81-83; asst. U.S. atty. So. Dist. Fla., Miami, 1979-81; atty. Holme, Roberts & Owen, Denver, 1983-93; bankruptcy judge U.S. Bankruptcy Ct. (so. dist.) Fla., Ft. Lauderdale, 1993—. Mem. Dade County Bar Assn. Office: 403 US Courthouse 299 E Broward Blvd Fort Lauderdale FL 33301-1944

HYMEL, L(EZIN) J(OSEPH), prosecutor; b. Baton Rouge, July 2, 1944; s. Lezin Joseph Sr. and Alma K. Hymel; m. Linda N., Oct. 6, 1973; children: Traci Lyn, Shea Roach Bonaventure, Kimberly Kaye. BS in Geology, La. State U., 1966, JD, 1969. Bar: La., U.S. Dist. Ct. (ea. dist.) La., U.S. Dist. Ct. (mid. dist.) La., U.S. Dist. Ct. (we. dist.) La., U.S. Ct. Appeals (5th cir.). Pvt. practice Baton Rouge, 1969-70; staff atty. Office State Atty. Gen., Baton Rouge, 1970-71, asst. atty. gen., 1972-78, dir. criminal divsn., 1992-93; asst. dist. atty. Office 19 Jud. Dist. Atty., Baton Rouge, 1978-79; city judge Baton Rouge City Ct., 1980-83; state dist. ct. judge criminal divsn. 19th Jud. Dist. Ct, Baton Rouge, 1983-90, state dist. ct. judge civil divsn., 1991-92; U.S. atty. Office U.S. Atty., Dept. Justice, Baton Rouge, 1994—. Office: US Atty Mid Dist La Russell B Long Fed Bldg 777 Florida St Baton Rouge LA 70801-1717*

HYMER, MARTHA NELL, elementary education educator; b. Magnolia, Ark., Apr. 2, 1956; d. Elton N. and Nell Merle (Hill) Amburn; m. Gerald Lee Hymer, Nov. 21, 1980; children: Angela Colleen, Melissa Nicole. BS in Edn., Lubbock Christian Coll., 1978. Tchr. R.L. Wright Elem. Sch., Sedgwick, Kans., 1979—; evaluator for Kans. literature, 1993; site based coun. mem. Unified Sch. Dist. 439, 1993, chairperson, 1996-97. Pres. Families with a Difference, Newton, Kans., 1985-87; sec. Cooper Parent Tchr. Orgn., 1991-97. Mem. Ch. of Christ. Avocations: family, cooking, sewing. Home: 334 E 8th St Newton KS 67114-2708

HYMERS, ROBERT LESLIE, JR., pastor; b. Glendale, Calif., Apr. 12, 1941; s. Robert Leslie Hymers Sr. and Cecelia Juanita (Flowers) McDonell; m. Ileana Patricia Cuellar, Sept. 27, 1982; children: Robert Leslie Hymers III, John Wesley Hymers (twins). BA, Calif. State U., L.A., 1970; MDiv, Golden Gate Bapt. Theol. Sem., 1973; DMin, San Francisco Theol. Sem., 1981; ThD, La. Bapt. Theol. Sem., 1989. Ordained to ministry Bapt. Ch., 1972. Pastor Ch. of the Open Door, San Rafael, Calif., 1973-75, Fundamentalist Bapt. Tabernacle, L.A., 1975—; guest TV programs. Author: Holocaust II, 1978, The Ruckman Conspiracy, 1989, Inside the Southern Baptist Convention, 1990, Dicisionism and the Death of America, 1999; contbr. articles to profl. jours. Republican. Office: Fundamentalist Bapt PO Box 15308 Los Angeles CA 90015-0308

HYMES, DELL HATHAWAY, anthropologist, educator; b. Portland, Oreg., June 7, 1927; s. Howard Hathaway and Dorothy (Bowman) H.; m. Virginia Margaret Dosch, Apr. 10, 1954; 1 adopted child, Robert Paul; children: Alison Bowman, Kenneth Dell; 1 stepchild, Vicki (Mrs. David Unruh). BA, Reed Coll., 1950; MA, Ind. U., 1953, PhD, 1955; postgrad., UCLA, 1954-55. From instr. to asst. prof. Harvard U., 1955-60; from assoc. prof. to prof. U. Calif., Berkeley, 1960-65; prof. anthropology U. Pa., 1965-72, prof. folklore and linguistics, 1972-88, prof. sociology, 1974-88, prof. edn., 1975-88, dean Grad. Sch. Edn., 1975-87; prof. anthropology and English U. Va., 1987-90, Commonwealth prof. anthropology, 1990-98, Commonwealth prof. English, 1990-98, emeritus, 1998—; bd. dirs. Social Sci. Rsch. Coun., 1965-67, 69-70, 71-72. Author: Language in Culture and Society, 1964, The Use of Computers in Anthropology, 1965, Studies in Southwestern Ethnolinguistics, 1967, Pidginization and Creolization of Languages, 1971, Reinventing Anthropology, 1972, Foundations in Sociolinguistics, 1974, Soziolinguistik, 1980, Language in Education, 1980, In Vain I Tried to Tell You, 1981, (with John Fought) American Structuralism, 1981, Essays in the History of Linguistic Anthropology, 1983, Vers la Competence de Communication, 1984, Ethnography, Linguistics, Narrative Inequality, 1996; assoc. editor: Jour. History Behavioral Scis., 1966-93, Am. Jour. Sociology, 1977-80, Jour. Pragmatics, 1977—; contbg. editor: Alcheringa, 1973-80, Theory and Society, 1976-96; editor: Language in Society, 1972-92. Trustee Ctr. for Applied Linguistics, 1973-78. With AUS, 1945-47. Fellow Ctr. Advanced Study Behavioral Scis., 1957-58, Fellow Clare Hall, Cambridge, Eng., Guggenheim fellow, 1969-70, Nat. Endowment for Humanities sr. fellow, 1972-73. Fellow Am. Acad. Arts & Scis., Am. Folklore Soc. (pres. 1973-74), Brit. Acad.; mem. AAAS (coun. 1979-80), Am. Anthrop. Assn. (exec. bd. 1968-70, pres. 1983), Am. Assn. Applied Linguistics (pres. 1986), Linguistic Soc. Am. (exec. bd. 1967-69, pres. 1982), Coun. on Anthropology and Edn. (pres. 1978), Consortium Social Sci. Assns. (pres. 1984-85), Folklore Fellows Finland. Home: 205 Montvue Dr Charlottesville VA 22901-2022

HYMES, NORMA, internist; b. N.Y.C., July 20, 1949; d. Richard and Ellen (Posner) H.; m. Vincent M. Esposito, Nov. 1978 (div.); l child, Richard Hymes-Esposito. BS, Oberlin Coll., 1971; MD, Mt. Sinai, 1975. Diplomate Bd. of Internal Medicine. Intern, resident Maimonides Med. Ctr., Bklyn., 1975-78; internist Manhattan Health Plan, N.Y.C., 1978-81, Manhattan Med Group, P.C., N.Y.C., 1981-92, N.Y. Med. Group, P.C., 1992—. Mgr. The Colonnade Condominium, N.Y.C., 1982-85; trustee N.Y. Soc. For Ethical Culture, N.Y.C., 1989-93, 96—. Mem. ACP, Am. Med. Women's Assn. Office: NY Med Group 172 Amsterdam Ave New York NY 10023-5034

HYMOWITZ, THEODORE, plant geneticist, educator; b. N.Y.C., Feb. 16, 1934; s. Bernard and Ethel (Rose) H.; m. Ann Einhorn, Dec. 25, 1960 (div. 1985); children: Madeleine, Sara, Jessica; m. Barbara E. Bohen, June 11, 1989 (div. 1998). BS, Cornell U., 1955; MS, U. Ariz., 1957; PhD, Okla. State U., 1963. Agronomist IRI Rsch. Inst., Campinas, Brazil, 1964-66; from asst. to assoc. prof. U. Ill., Urbana, 1967-75, prof., 1975—. With U.S. Army, 1957-59. Recipient Rsch. award Land of Lincoln Soybean Assn.,

1990, Funk award, 1991; scholar Loeb Found., Stillwater, Okla., 1961-62, Fulbright scholar, 1962-63. Fellow AAAS, Linnean Soc. London, Am. Soc. Agronomy, Crop Sci. Soc. Am. (Frank N. Meyer medal 1988). Achievements include research in the establishment of chromosomal map of the soybean, inheritance of the absence of seed lectin in soybeans, elucidation of genomic relationships among species in the genus Glycine, development of soybean cultivar lacking the Kunitz trypsin inhibitor, history of the introduction of the soybean to N.Am. Office: U Ill Dept Crop Sci 1102 S Goodwin Ave Urbana IL 61801-4730

HYNDMAN, DAVID WILLIAM, geological sciences educator; s Donald William and Shirley Ann Hyndman. BS, U. Ariz., 1989; MS, Stanford U., 1993, PhD, 1995. Hydrologist intern Oak Ridge Nat. Lab., 1987; hydrologist U.S. Geol. Survey, Tucson, 1988-90; asst. prof. dept. geol. scis. Mich. State U., East Lansing, 1995—. Assoc. editor Ground Water, 1998—; contbr. chpt. to book, articles to profl. jours. Recipient Superior Performance award U.S. Geol. Survey, 1989, Spl. Achievement award, 1988; Lilly Tchg. fellow, 1997-98. Mem. Am. Geophys. Union, Geol. Soc. Am. Avocations: golf, downhill skiing, hiking. Office: Mich State U Dept Geol Scis 206 Natural Science East Lansing MI 48824-1115

HYNDS, ERNEST, journalism educator. Head dept. journalism Univ. Ga., Athens. Office: University of Georgia Coll of Journalism & Communications Dept of Journalism Athens GA 30602-3018

HYNE, JAMES BISSETT, chemistry educator, industrial scientist, consultant; b. Dundee, Scotland, Nov. 23, 1929; emigrated to Can., 1954, naturalized, 1969; s. William Simpson and Winifred Moore (Bissett) H.; m. Ada Leah Jacobson, Sept. 3, 1958. B.Sc., St. Andrews U., Scotland, 1951, Ph.D., 1954. Instr. Yale U., 1956-59; asst. prof. Dartmouth U., 1959-60; prof., head dept. chemistry U. Alta., Calgary, 1960-90, prof. emeritus, 1990—; dean grad. studies, prof. chemistry U. Calgary, 1966-89; pres. Hyjay R & D Ltd., Calgary, 1978—; dir. rsch. Alta. Sulphur Rsch., Ltd., 1964-94; cons. oil, gas and sulphur/sulphur fertilizer industries in Can., U.S. and Gt. Britain; pres. Can. Assn. Grad. Schs., 1969-70. contbr. articles on sulphur chemistry and tech. to profl. jours. Served with Can. Cameron Highlanders of Ottawa, 1954-58. Recipient Can. Centennial medal, 1967, R.S. Jane Meml. award for exceptional achievement in chem. engring. and indsl. chemistry, 1977, Queen Elizabeth II Jubilee medal, 1977, Alta. Achievement Excellence award, 1980, Bell Forum award for corp.-univ. cooperation in rsch., 1990; NRC fellow, 1954-56; Arthur B. Purvis Meml. lectr. Soc. Chem. Industry, 1991. Mem. Am. Chem. Soc., Chem. Soc., Chem. Inst. Can., Assn. Chem. Profession of Alta. (founding). Fax: (403) 229-2760. Office: 312 Superior Ave SW, Calgary, AB Canada T3C 2J2

HYNES, GARRY, theatre director; b. Ballaghaderreen, Ireland. Grad., U. Coll. Galway; DLL (hon.), Nat. U. Ireland, 1997. Founder Druid Theatre Co., Galway, 1975—, artistic dir., 1975-91, 95—; artistic dir. The Abbey Theatre, 1991-94. Prodns. include: The Playboy of the Western World, Bailegangaire, Conversations on a Homecoming, Wood of the Whispering, 'Tis a Pity She's a Whore, Lovers' Meeting, The Loves of Cass McGuire, The Beauty Queen of Leenane, The Leenane Trilogy, A Whistle in the Dark, King of the Castle, The Plough and the Stars, The Power of Darkness, Famine, Portia Coughlan, The Man of Mode, The Love of the Nightingale, The Colleen Bawn, The Lonesome West, A Skull in Connemara, Mr. Peter's Connections. Winner Tony award for best director (The Beauty Queen of Leenane), 1998; DLL (hon.) Nat. Coun. of Ednl. Awards, 1988. Office: The druid Theatre Co, Chapel Ln, Galway Ireland*

HYNES, HUGH BERNARD NOEL, biology educator; b. Devizes, Eng., Dec. 20, 1917; s. Harry George Claude and Anne Minnie Lucy (Meyer) H.; m. Mary Elizabeth Hinks, Oct. 24, 1942; children—Richard Olding, Elisabeth Anne, Andrew John, Julian David. BSc, U. London, 1938, PhD, 1941, DSc, 1958. With Brit. Ministry Agr., 1941, Brit. Colonial Agrl. Ser., 1942-46; faculty U. Liverpool, Eng., 1947-64; prof. biology U. Waterloo, Ont., Can., 1964-83, Disting. prof. emeritus, 1983—; cons. in field. Author: The Ecology of Running Water; contbr. numerous articles to profl. jours. Decorated Can. Centennial medal; recipient Naumann/Thienemann medal, Internat. Limnological Assn. Fellow Royal Soc. Can.; mem. Freshwater Biol. Assn., Internat. Assn. Theoretical and Applied Limnology, N.Am. Benthol. Soc. Home: 127 Iroquois Pl, Waterloo, ON Canada N2L 2S6 Office: U Waterloo, Dept Biology, Waterloo, ON Canada N2L 3G1

HYNES, RICHARD OLDING, biology researcher and educator; b. Nairobi, Kenya, Africa, Nov. 29, 1944; s. Hugh Bernard Noel and Mary Elizabeth (Hinks) H.; m. Fleur Marshall, July 29, 1966; children: Hugh Jonathan, Colin Anthony. BA with honors, U. Cambridge, Eng., 1966, MA, 1970; PhD, MIT, 1971. Asst. prof. biology MIT, Cambridge, 1975-78, assoc. prof., 1978-83, prof. Dept. Biology, 1983—, assoc. head Dept. Biology, 1985-89, head, 1989-91, dir. Ctr. for Cancer Rsch., 1991—; investigator Howard Hughes Med. Inst., Chevy Chase, Md., 1988—. Author: Fibronectins, 1990; editor Tumor Cell Surfaces and Malignancy, 1979, Surfaces of Normal and Malignant Cells, 1979; contbr. articles to profl. jours. Guggenheim Found. fellow, 1982; recipient internat. award Gairdner Found., 1997. Fellow AAAS, Am. Acad. Arts and Scis., Royal Soc. London; mem. Inst. Medicine NAS,, Nat. Acad. Scis. Office: MIT Ctr Cancer Rsch E17-227 77 Massachusetts Ave Cambridge MA 02139-4307*

HYNES, SAMUEL, English language educator, author; b. Chgo., Aug. 29, 1924; s. Samuel Lynn and Margaret (Turner) H.; m. Elizabeth Igleheart, July 28, 1944; children: Miranda, Joanna. BA, U. Minn., 1947; MA, Columbia U., 1948, PhD, 1956. Mem. faculty Swarthmore Coll., 1949-68, prof. English lit., 1965-68; prof. English Northwestern U., Evanston, Ill., 1968-76; prof. English Princeton U., 1976-90, Woodrow Wilson prof. lit., 1978-90, Woodrow Wilson prof. lit. emeritus, 1990—. Author: The Pattern of Hardy's Poetry, 1961, (Explicator award 1962), William Golding, 1964, The Edwardian Turn of Mind, 1968, Edwardian Occasions, 1972, The Auden Generation, 1976, Flights of Passage: Reflections of a World War Two Aviator, 1988, A War Imagined: The First World War and English Culture, 1990, The Soldiers' Tale, 1997 (Robert F. Kennedy Book award 1998); editor: Further Speculations by T.E. Hulme, 1955, The Author's Craft and Other Critical Writings of Arnold Bennett, 1968, Romance and Realism, 1970, Complete Poetical Works Thomas Hardy, Vol. I, 1982, Vol. II, 1984, Vol. III, 1985, Vols. IV & V, 1995, Thomas Hardy, 1984, Complete Short Fiction of Joseph Conrad, vols. I-III, 1992, Vol. IV, 1993. Served to maj. USMCR, 1943-46, 52-53. Decorated Air medal, DFC; Fulbright fellow, 1953-54, Guggenheim fellow, 1959-60, 81-82, Bollingen fellow, 1964-65, Am. Coun. Learned Socs. fellow, 1969, 85-86; NEH sr. fellow, 1973-74, 77-78, 89-91. Fellow Royal Soc. Lit.; mem. Phi Beta Kappa. Home: 130 Moore St Princeton NJ 08540-3359

HYNES, TERENCE MICHAEL, lawyer; b. Jersey City, Mar. 26, 1954; s. Robert Francis and Eleanor (McGuirk) H.; m. Kathryn Wilson, Jan. 25, 1986; children: Shaylyn Michelle, Meaghan Elizabeth, Patrick Francis. BA in Politic. Sci. with highest distinction, Rutgers Coll., 1976; JD, Duke U., 1979. Bar: D.C. 1979, Interstate Commerce Commn. 1979, U.S. Dist. Ct. (D.C. dist.) 1979, U.S. Ct. Appeals (D.C. cir.) 1979, U.S. Ct. Appeals (7th cir.) 1981, U.S. Ct. Appeals (1st and 2d cirs.) 1997. Assoc. Sidley & Austin, Washington, 1979-86, ptnr., 1986—. With comml. practice clinic Duke U. Law Sch., 1983-89; mem. nat. coun. law sch. fund Duke U., 1986-91; mem. Duke Law Sch. Alumni Coun., 1997—. Mem. ABA (pub. utility law sect. 1979—, antitrust law sect. 1979—), Assn. Transp. Law, Logistics and Policy, Duke U. Gen. Alumni Assn. (bd. dirs. 1984-86). Roman Catholic. E-mail: thynes@sidley.com. Office: Sidley & Austin 1722 I St NW Ste 600 Washington DC 20006-3795

HYNES-LASEK, NANCY ELLEN, secondary education educator; b. Jersey City, N.J., June 13, 1956; d. Timothy Joseph and Alice Mae (Menig) H. BA, Jersey City State Coll., 1978, MA, 1979. Cert. nursery tchr., N.J., elem. tchr., N.J., prin., supr., N.J., reading tchr., N.J. Tchr. St. Bridget's Sch., North Bergen, N.J., 1978; tchr. reading, writing Bd. Edn. East Orange (N.J.), 1979-86; unit coord. HSPT program Bd. Edn. City of East Orange (N.J.), 1985; dir. Nancy's Sch. Dance, West N.Y., 1981-85; tchr. computer Bd. Edn. City of Elizabeth (N.J.), 1986-95; tchr. Huntington Learning Ctr., Woodbridge, N.J., 1987—; reading tchr. Bd. Edn. City of Elizabeth (N.J.), 1992-95, Plainfield (N.J.) Bd. Edn., 1995—, 1995-96; reading tchr. Passaic (N.J.) Bd. Edn., 1997-98; prof. reading Middlesex County Coll., Edison, N.J., 1998—; tchr. elem. sch. City of Linden (N.J.) Bd. Edn., 1999; mem. com. Computer Curriculum Guide, 1989, Language Arts Curriculum Guide, 1989; tchr. dance N.J. Workshop Arts, Westfield, 1990; prof. reading Middlesex C.C., Edison, N.J., 1996—. Chmn. Dance for Heart, 1985; mem. com. Jingle Bells Run for Arthritis, 1994-95; capt. Profl. Dance and Exercise Group, 1993—. Grantee Bd. Edn. City of Elizabeth, 1989. Mem. ASCD, Phi Delta Kappa (historian 1989-91), Secondary Sch. Women's Club (Elizabeth). Roman Catholic. Avocations: skiing, dancing, reading, tennis. E-mail: adnancmattewebtv.net. Home: 1702 Forest View Dr Avenel NJ 07001-2172 Office: Middlesex County College Dept Reading Edison NJ 08818

HYODO, HARUO, radiologist, educator; b. Honai-chyo, Nishiuwa-gun, Ehime, Japan, Mar. 3, 1928. B of Medicine, Tokushuma U., 1959, MD, 1966. Chief clinic of radiology Nat. Kochi Hosp., 1963-65; chief divsn. of radiology Ehime Prefectural Ctrl. Hosp., 1970-77; prof. dept. radiology Dokkyo U. Sch. Medicine, Mibu, Tochigi, Japan, 1977-90; dir. emeritus Ikeda Meml. Hosp., Sukagawa, Fukushima, Japan, 1990—; asst. dir. Fukuda Meml. Hosp., Mooka, Tochigi, 1993—; guest prof. Dokkyo U. Sch. Medicine, 1994—, Tenjin (China) 2d Med. Coll., 1986—. *Dr. Haruo Hyodo is a radiologist. In 1982, he dedicated a panel of early gastric cancer to the German Roentgen Museum at Remscheid-Lennep in Germany. The panel is displayed at the exhibition hall. The panel contains double contrast X-ray images, freshly resected specimen, cross section of the specimen and histological pictures.* Patentee in field. With Japanese Navy, 1944-45. Mem. German Radiol. Soc., Japanese Radiol. Soc. (cert. radiologist), Japanese Soc. Med. Imaging Tech. (pres. ann. gen. mtg. 1989-90), Japan Biliary Assn. (pres. ann. congress 1987-88), Japanese Med. Imaging Tech. Assn. (councilor 1980-95). Avocations: photography, motoring, playing ball, fishing. Home: 1-9-3 Saiwai-chiyo, Mib-machi, Shimotsuga-gun Tochigi 321-0203, Japan Office: Fukuda Meml Hosp, 3-10 Namiki-chiyo, Mooka Tochigi 321-43, Japan

HYON, WON SOP, certified public accountant, auditor; b. Seoul, Korea, May 1, 1968; came to the U.S., 1979; s. Chong Chul and Dong Pok (Yi) H.; m. Anita Hiromi Mukai, June 6, 1993; 1 child, Alexander. BS in Bus. Adminstrn., Drake U., 1990, MBA., 1998. CPA, Iowa. Sr. auditor Ernst & Young, LLP, DesMoines, Iowa, 1990-94; sr. internal audit mgr. Pioneer Hi-Bred Internat., Inc., DesMoines, 1994—. Mem. AICPA, Am. Coll. Forensic Examiners (diplomate Am. Bd. Forensic Acctg.), Info. Sys. Audit and Control Assn. (cert. info. sys. auditor, v.p. Iowa chpt. 1995-96), Inst. Cert. Internal Auditors (cert. internal auditor), Inst. Mgmt. Accts., Fin. Mgmt. Assn. Internat., Iowa Soc. CPAs. Avocations: reading, sports, martial arts, movies. Office: Pioneer Hi-Bred Internat Inc 800 Locust St Ste 400 Des Moines IA 50309-3622

HYSLOP, GARY LEE, librarian; b. Oakland City, Ind., June 8, 1944; s. H. Boyd and Berniece (McKinney) H. BA, Oakland City U., 1966; MS, Ind. State U., 1974; MLS, Ind. U., 1987. Tchr. Dubois (Ind.) High Sch., 1966-67, Admiral King High Sch., Lorain, Ohio, 1967-71, Washington (Ind.) Community Schs., 1973-77; mgr., officer F & M Fed. Savs. & Loan, Bloomington, Ind., 1977-81; broker, realtor Properties Unltd., Bloomington, 1981-82; tchr. Howe (Ind.) Mil. Sch., 1982-84, Madison (Ind.) Schs., 1984-86; asst. libr. Calif. State U., Bakersfield, 1988-91; dir. admissions and placement Sch. Libr. and Info. Sci. Ind. U., Bloomington, 1991-93; dir. Curriculum Materials Ctr. U. Cen. Fla., 1993—. Vol. Kern County Beethoven Festival, Bakersfield, 1988; bd. dirs. Bakersfield Community Theatre, 1989-91, nominating com., 1990-91; bd. regents/united faculty of Fla. task force on libr. issues Fla. State U. System, 1997-98. Recipient Meritorious Performance and Profl. Promise award Calif. State U., 1989, Excellence in Librarianship award U. Ctrl. Fla., 1999. Mem. ALA, SELA, Fla. Faculty Assn., UCF Librs. (personnel adv. com.), Fla. Assn. Coll. Rsch. Librs. (bd. dirs. 1994-97), 15th Ann. Task Force of the Libr. Instrn. Round Table, United Faculty of Fla. (senator 1997—, chpt. sec.), NEA Rep. Assembly (del. to Fla. tchg. profession 1998-99). Avocation: keyboard instruments. Office: U Cen Fla Curriculum Materials Ctr 1025 Neely St Oviedo FL 32816-2666

HYTIER, ADRIENNE DORIS, French language educator; d. Jean and Katharine Hytier Matson. BA summa cum laude, Barnard Coll., 1952; MA, Columbia U., 1953, PhD, 1958. Instr. French Vassar Coll., 1959-61, asst. prof., 1961-66, assoc. prof., 1966-70; prof. French Vassar Coll., Poughkeepsie, N.Y., 1970-96, Lichtenstein Dale prof. French, 1974-96; vis. assoc. prof. Columbia U., 1966, U. Calif., 1968-69. Editor for French lit.: The 18th Century: A Current Bibliography Since 1970, 21 vols., Two Years of French Foreign Policy: Vichy 1940-42, 1958, 2d edit., 1974, Les Dépêches diplomatiques du Comte de Gobineau en Perse, 1959, La Guerre, 1975, 4th edit., 1991; author revs. and articles. Decorated chevalier des Palmes Académiques, 1974; fellow Guggenheim Found., 1967-68. Mem. MLA, Am. Soc. 18th Century Studies, NE Soc. for 18th Century Studies, Internat. Soc. 18th Century Studies, Phi Beta Kappa. Home: 71 Raymond Ave Poughkeepsie NY 12601-6106 Office: Vassar Coll Box 372 Poughkeepsie NY 12604-0372

IACHETTI, ROSE MARIA ANNE, retired elementary education educator; b. Watervliet, N.Y., Sept. 22, 1931; d. Augustus and Rose Elizabeth Archer (Orciuolo) Iachetti; BS, Coll. St. Rose, 1961; MEd, U. Ariz., 1969. Joined Sisters of Mercy, Albany, N.Y., 1949-66; tchr. various parochial schs. Albany (N.Y.) Diocese, 1952-66; tchr. Headstart Program, Troy, N.Y., 1966; tchr. fine arts Watervliet Jr. and Sr. High Sch., 1966-67; tchr. W.J. Meyer Sch., Tombstone, Ariz., 1968-71, Colonel Johnston Sch., Ft. Huachuca, Ariz., 1971-78; tchr. Myer Sch., Ft. Huachuca, 1978-89, coord. program for gifted and talented, 1981-85. Author (monograph) Tombstone's Gracious Lady-Madeline Giacoma Wyatt, 1997. Ann. chmn. Ariz. Children's Home Assn., Tombstone, 1 73-74; trustee Tombstone Sch. Dist. #1, 1972-80; active Dem. Club; mem. Bicentennial Commn. for Ariz., 1972-76, Tombstone Centennial Commn., 1979-80, chmn. Centennial Ball, 1980; pres. Tombstone Community Health Svcs., 1978-80; mem. Tombstone City Coun., 1982-84, finance commn., 1994, Inner Senatorial Cir., 1989-91; governing bd. Southeast Ariz. Area Health Edn. Coun., 1985-98, bd. dirs., 1984-98, pres., 1990-91, 94-96; patron Our Lady of Santa Rita Abbey, Met. Opera Guild; v.p. Sacred Heart Parish Bd., 1991-92; councilperson Tombstone City, 1982-84, 94-96; Mem. Ariz. Edn. Assn. (so. regional dir. 1971-73), Ft. Huachuca Edn. Assn., Tombstone Dist. 1 Edn. Assn. (mem. bd. 1971-80), Ariz. Sch. Bd. Assn., NEA (del. 1971-73), Ariz. Classroom Tchrs. Assn. (del. 1969-71), Ariz. Rural Health Assn. (1997-98), Internat. Platform Assn., Tombstone Bus. and Profl. Women's Club, Am. Legion Aux., Tombstone Assn. Arts, Inner Senatorial Circle, Pi Lambda Theta, Delta Kappa Gamma, (pres. 1982-84), Phi Delta Kappa (historian 1979-82, 2d v.p. 1982-83). Home: 990 Bayley Place Dr Cincinnati OH 45233-1664

IACOBELLI, MARK ANTHONY, dentist; b. Cleve., Aug. 27, 1957; s. Anthony Peter and Irene Margaret (Pordash) I. BS, Case Western Res., 1979, DDS, 1982. Dentist, co-owner Iacobelli & Iffland, Canton, Ohio, 1982-85; gen. practice dentistry North Royalton, Ohio, 1985—; co-lectr. Jamison Cons. and Midwest Implant Inst. Named one of Outstanding Young Men Am., 1982. Fellow Acad. Gen. Dentistry; mem. ADA, Ohio Dental Assn., Cleve. Dental Assn., Am. Assn. Functional Orthodontics (Achievement award 1982), Padua Franciscan Alumni Assn. (chmn. devel. drive 1986, chmn. 1989, 90). Republican. Roman Catholic. Avocations: running, biking, skiing, golf. Office: 8030 Corporate Cir North Royalton OH 44133

IACOBELLIS, SAM FRANK, retired aerospace company executive; b. Fresno, Calif., Aug. 17, 1929; s. Frank and Mary (Ceppaglia) I.; m. Helene Myers, June 11, 1954; children: Sam F. II, Lee Ann. B MechE, Calif. State U., Fresno, 1952; M in Engring., UCLA, 1963. Registered profl. mech. and nuclear engr., Calif. Design engr. N.Am. Aircraft div. Rockwell Internat., Los Angeles, 1952-53, engring. supr., 1953-57; v.p. Rocketdyne div. Rockwell Internat., Canoga Park, Calif., 1957-73; pres. Atomics Internat. div. Rockwell Internat., Canoga Park, Calif., 1973-78, Energy Systems Group div. Rockwell Internat., Canoga Park, Calif., 1978-81; exec. v.p., B-1B program mgr. N.Am. Aircraft Ops. div. Rockwell Internat., El Segundo, Calif., 1981-84, pres., B-1B program mgr., corp. v.p., 1984-88; pres. Aerospace Ops. Rockwell Internat., El Segundo, Calif., 1988-89, exec. v.p., chief oper. officer, 1989-93; exec. v.p., dep. chmn. major programs Rockwell Internat., Seal Beach, Calif., 1993-95; co-founder, chmn. bd. Warner Ctr. Bank, 1981-90; bd. dirs. U.S. Space Found., Calif. Bus. Roundtable. Patentee turbomolecular vacuum pump, rocket engine design. Mem. engrs. council Calif. State U., Fresno, 1983, UCLA Sch. Engring., 1983; trustee UCLA Found., 1985; bd. dirs. Calif. State U. Found., 1988. Named Engring. Alumnus of Yr., UCLA, 1980, Alumnus of Yr., Calif. State U., Fresno, 1982, Engr. of Yr., San Fernando Valley Engrs. Coun., L.A.; recipient Indsl. Tech. Mgmt. award Region II, Soc. Mfg. Engrs. Fellow AIAA (hon. 1996, pres.-elect 1997, pres. 1998—). Club: Bel Air (Calif.) Country. Avocations: golf, tennis, fishing, hunting. Home: 5585 Wellesley Dr Calabasas CA 91302-3112

IACOBUCCI, FRANK, lawyer, educator, jurist; b. Vancouver, B.C., Can., June 29, 1937; s. Gabriel and Rosina (Pirillo) I.; m. Nancy Elizabeth Eastham, Oct. 31, 1964; children—Andrew Eastham, Edward Michael, Catherine Elizabeth. B of Commerce, U. B.C., Vancouver, 1959, LLB, 1962; LLM, Cambridge U., Eng., 1964, Diploma in Internat. Law, 1966; LLD (hon.), U. B.C., 1989, U. Toronto, 1989, U. Ottawa, 1995, U. Victoria, 1996. Bar: Ont. 1970, Queen's Counsel, 1986. Assoc. Dewey Ballantine et al, N.Y.C., 1964-67; assoc. prof. law U. Toronto, 1967-71, prof. law, 1971-85, assoc. dean faculty of law, 1973-75, v.p. internal affairs, 1975-78, dean faculty of law, 1979-83, v.p., provost, 1983-85; vis. fellow Wolfson Coll., Cambridge, Eng., 1978; dep. min. of justice and dep. atty. gen. Govt. of Can., Ottawa, Ont., 1985-88; chief justice Fed. Ct. of Can., Ottawa, 1988-90; justice Supreme Ct. Can., Ottawa, 1991—; mem. Permanent Ct. of Arbitration, 1997—; former cons. Ont., Alta., Can. govts.; mem. Ont. Securities Commn., Toronto, 1982-85; dir. Cambridge Can. Trust, 1984-91; mem. Can. Jud. Coun., 1988-91, exec. com., edn. com.; gov. Can. Jud. Centre, 1989-91; gov. Nat. Jud. Inst., 1992—; mem. adv. coun. Internat. Centre Criminal Law Reform and Criminal Justice Policy, 1991-93, dir. 1993—. Co-author: Canadian Business Corporations, 1977, Cases and Materials on Partnerships and Canadian Business Corporations, 1983; co-editor: Materials on Canadian Income Tax, 6th edit., 1985; contbr. chpts. to books, articles to profl. jours. Mem. Islington Residents and Ratepayers Assn., 1971-85; v.p. Nat. Congress Italian Cans., 1980-83, dir. Toronto dist., 1979-83; v.p. Can. Inst. Advanced legal Studies, 1981-85, bd. govs., 1981-85, 91-98; dir. U. Toronto Found., 1997—; mem. adv. bd. Inst. Can. Studies, U. Ottawa, 1998—. Newton Rowell fellow Can. Inst. Internat. Affairs, 1962, McKenzie-King traveling fellow U. B.C., 1963; recipient Law Soc. medal Law Soc. Upper Can., 1987, Ordine al merito Nat. Congress Italian Canadians, Toronto Dist., 1989, 125th Anniversary of Confedn. Can. medal, 1992, Lion d'Or award, Ordre des Fils d'Italie au Canada (Montreal), 1995, Cosentino dell'Anno award, Fedn. of Clubs Cosentini of Ont., 1995, Man of the Yr. award Can. Italian Bus. and Profl. Assn. Toronto, 1985, Italo-Can. of the Yr. award Confratellanza Italo-Canadese, Vancouver, 1985, Commendatore dell'Ordine Al Merito della Repubblica Italiana, 1993, Man of Yr. award Brotherhood Interfaith Soc., Vancouver, Can., 1999; named hon. citizen Mangone, Italy, 1996. Mem. Multicultural History Soc. Ont. (bd. dirs. 1976-88), Le Club de Golf Rivermead (Aylmer, Quebec), Sigma Tau Chi, Phi Gamma Delta (Disting. Fiji award 1987). Avocations: tennis, golf, other sports. Office: Supreme Ct Can, Wellington St, Ottawa, ON Canada K1A 0J1

IACOBUCCI, GUILLERMO ARTURO, chemist; b. Buenos Aires, May 11, 1927; s. Guillermo Cesar and Blanca Nieves (Brana) I.; m. Constantina Maria Gullich, Mar. 28, 1952; children: Eduardo Ernesto, William George. MSc, U. Buenos Aires, 1949, PhD in Organic Chemistry, 1952. Came to U.S., 1962, naturalized, 1972. Research chemist E.R. Squibb Research Labs., Buenos Aires, 1952-57; research fellow in chemistry Harvard U., Cambridge, Mass., 1958-59, prof. phytochemistry U. Buenos Aires, 1960-61; sr. research chemist Squibb Inst. Med. Research, New Brunswick, N.J., 1962-66; head bio-organic chemistry labs. Coca-Cola Co., Atlanta, 1967-74, asst. dir. corp. research and devel., 1974-87, mgr. biochemistry and basic organic chemistry group, 1988-93, ret. 1993; adj. prof. chemistry Emory U., 1975—. John Simon Guggenheim Meml. Found. fellow, 1958. Fellow Am. Inst. Chemists; mem. AAAS, Assn. Harvard Chemists, Am. Chem. Soc., N.Y. Acad. Scis., Am. Soc. Pharmacognosy, Phytochemical Soc. N.Am., Smithsonian Instn., Planetary Soc., Sigma Xi. Achievements include structure/activity correlations and molecular design of sweeteners; use of enzymes in asymmetric organic synthesis; natural products chemistry; contbr. articles on organic chemistry to sci. jours. Patentee in field. Home: 160 N Mill Rd NW Atlanta GA 30328-1837 Office: Emory U Dept of Chemistry 1515 Pierce Dr NE Atlanta GA 30322-1003

IACONO, JAMES MICHAEL, research center administrator, nutrition educator; b. Chgo., Dec. 11, 1925; s. Joseph and Angelina (Cutaia) I.; children: Lynn, Joseph, Michael, Rosemary. BS, Loyola U., Chgo., 1950; MS, U. Ill., 1952, PhD, 1954. Chief Lipid Nutrition Lab. Nutrition Inst. Agrl. Rsch. Svc. USDA, Beltsville, Md., 1970-75; dep. asst. adminstrv. nat. program Agrl. Rsch. Svc. USDA, Washington, 1975-77, assoc. adminstr. office human nutrition, 1978-82; dir. Western Human Nutrition Rsch. Ctr. Agrl. Rsch. Svc. USDA, San Francisco, 1982-94; adj. prof. nutrition Sch. Pub. Health UCLA, 1987—. Author over 100 rsch./tech. publs. and chpts. in books relating to nutrition and biochemistry and lipids. With U.S. Army, 1944-46. Recipient Rsch. Career Devel. award NIH, 1964-70. Fellow Am Heart Assn. (coun. on arteriosclerosis and thrombosis), Am. Inst. Chemists; mem. Am. Inst. Nutrition, Am. Soc. Clin. Nutrition, Am. Oil Chemists Soc. Office: USDA ARS Western Human Nutrition Rsch Ctr PO Box 29997 San Francisco CA 94129-0997

IACOVO, MICHAEL JAMAAL, medical consultant, small business owner; b. Brockton, Mass., Dec. 7, 1955. BS, Northeastern U., 1981; MD, U. Mich., 1985. Cert. residential builder, Mich. Tchr., cons. Adolescent Rehab. Program, Boston, 1979-80; med. cons. United Med. Techs., Detroit, 1987—; pres., owner Stonehouse Constrn., Inc., Detroit, 1986—; clin. toxicologist Metpath Inc., 1989-94; dir. Boston U. Med. Ctr.; v.p., founder Minority Residential Builders Assn., Detroit, 1986-87. Mem. Com. to Re-elect Gov. Blanchand, Detroit, 1986. Mem. Black Med. Students Assn. (treas. 1984-85), Constrn. Assn. of Mich., Phi Chi Med. Frat. Democrat. Avocations: skiing, dancing, cabinetry, travel, gardening. Home: 65 Greentree Ln Apt 48 Weymouth MA 02190-2017 Office: Stonehouse Constrn Inc 65 Greentree Ln Apt 48 Weymouth MA 02190-2017

IADAVAIA, ELIZABETH ANN, marketing professional; b. N.Y.C., June 28, 1960; d. Vincent Anthony and Sally (D'Angelo) I. BA in Econs., Georgetown U., 1982; postgrad., CUNY, 1996. Rsch. asst. Montefiore Hosp. Neurophysiology Labs., N.Y.C., 1979-80; in mktg. rsch. Sch. Bus. Adminstrn. Georgetown U., Washington, 1981-82; adminstrv. asst. Kolter Devel. Corp., N.Y.C., 1983-85; dir. ops. Merrill Lynch Realty, Stamford, Conn., 1985-88, Crown Group Real Estate Devel. & Fin., White Plains, N.Y., 1988-92; dir. mktg. Equitable, New Hyde Park, N.Y., 1992-94, N.Y.C., 1995-96; dir. mktg. Ingrao, Inc., N.Y.C., 1996—. Mem. St. Catherines Parish Coun., Bronxville. Winner 13th and 14th ann. Agy. Newsletter contest Life Ins. Mktg. and Rsch. Assn. Mem. N.Y. State MBA Assn., Sch. of the Holy Child Alumni Assn. (bd. dirs., chmn. Rye, N.Y. chpt. 1983—), Georgetown U. Alumni Assn. (class chmn. 1986—), Women in Sales Assn. (v.p. 1988-97), Nat. Second Mortgage Assn., VIP Young Adult Club (pres. 1985-87). Home: 17 Archer Dr Bronxville NY 10708-4601 Office: Ingrao Inc 150 E 65th St New York NY 10021-6608

IADIPAOLO, DONNA MARIE, educator, writer, director, artist, performer; b. Ventura, Calif., June 4, 1967; d. Rene and Sandra (Ciccarelli) I. BA in English with honors, U. Mich., 1990; MA Theatre Arts and Comm. with hons., Ea. Mich. U., 1997. Cert. secondary English, social studies, journalism, drama, and math. tchr., Mich. Freelance writer Metro Times, Ann Arbor, Mich., 1989-90, Village Voice, N.Y.C., summer 1990; mng. editor Ear Mag. of New Music, N.Y.C., 1991; assoc. editor Ins. and Tech. Mag., N.Y.C., 1991; tchr. High Scope Ednl. Found., Ypsilanti, Mich., 1993; tchr. Wylie E. Groves H.S. & Covington Mid. Sch. Birmingham (Mich.) Pub. Schs., 1993-95, h.s. and mid. sch. forensic coach, 1993-95; tchr. Dexter (Mich.) H.S., 1995-98; tchr. adolescent summer sch. U. Mich.-Housing and Children Svcs., Ann Arbor, 1993; budget dir., mem. adv. bd. WCBN-FM Campus Radio Sta., 1993-94. Mem. Mich. Interscholastic Forensic Assn. (award 1994, 97, 98), Mich. Speech Coaches Assn., Mich. Interscholastic Press Assn., Nat. Assn. Student Activity Advisors, Nat.

Coun. Tchrs. English, Edn. TheatreAssn., Theatre Comm. Avocations: reading, music, nature, painting, theatre, creative writing.

IAFRATE, GERALD CARL, motion picture company executive, lawyer; b. Denver, Aug. 17, 1951; s. Vincenzo and Anita M. (Iacobelli) I.; m. Linda S. Hartzell, June 26, 1980 (div. Jan. 1983); 1 child, Mario J.; m. Jennine Saltzman, Dec. 10, 1992 (dec. May 1994). BS in Anthropology, NYU, 1971; DC, Cleve. Chiropractic Coll., Kansas City, Mo., 1975; JD, U. San Francisco, 1988. Bar: Calif., 1988, N.Y., 1988; diplomate Nat. Bd. Chiropractic Examiners, 1975; lic. chiropractor Mo., 1975. Pvt. practice, ptnr. Midwest Chiropractic Clinics, Inc., Cameron, Mo., 1976-83; legal affairs commnr. USPHS, Washington, 1989-94; dep. insp. gen., Atlantic Maritime Adminstrn., Washington and London, 1991-92; admiralty law counsel U.S. Naval Inst., Annapolis, Md., 1992-98; pres. Ilex-Ryder Entertainment, Inc., L.A., 1995—; of counsel for admiralty and maritime affairs Mass. Heavy Industries, Inc., Quincy, Mass., 1998—. Contbr. treatise Columbia Internat. Law Rev., 1988. Mem. Emissary Assembly World Jewish Congress, N.Y.C., 1991—. Rear admiral USPHS, 1989-94. Diplomate Command Staff Coll., Ft. Leavenworth, Kans., 1990. Mem. ABA, Res. Officers Assn., Am. Legion (Honor award 1996), Brit. Royal Anthropol. Soc., Beverly Hills Rotary Club. Republican. Jewish. Avocations: building computers, fly fishing, camping. Office: Ilex-Ryder Entertainment 1901 Ave Of The Stars Los Angeles CA 90067-6004 also: Ilex-Ryder Prodns Kaufman Astoria Studios 34-12 36th St Astoria NY 11106

IAKOVOS (DEMETRIOS A. COUCOUZIS), retired archbishop; b. Imvros, Turkey, July 29, 1911; s. Athanasios and Maria Coucouzis. Grad., Theol. Sch. of Halki, Ecumenical Patriarchate, 1934; STM, Harvard, 1945; DD, Boston U., 1960, Bates Coll., 1970, Dubuque U., 1973, Assumption Coll., 1980; LHD, Franklin and Marshall Coll., 1961, Southeastern Mass. Tech. Inst., 1967, Am. Internat. Coll., 1972, Cath. U., 1974, Loyola Marymount U., 1979, Queen's Coll., 1982; LLD, Brown U., 1964, Seton Hall U., 1968, Coll. Holy Cross, 1966, Fordham U., 1966, Notre Dame U., 1979, N.Y. Law Sch., 1982, St. John's U., 1982; HHD, Suffolk U., 1967, Stonehill Coll., 1980; DST, Berkeley Div. Sch., 1962, Gen. Theol. Sem., 1967, Thessalonica U., 1975; DLitt, PMC Colls., 1971; others. Ordained deacon Greek Orthodox Ch., 1934; archdeacon Greek Orthodox Ch., Met. Derkon, 1934-39; prof. Archdiocese Theol. Sch., Pomfret, Conn., 1939; ordained priest, 1940; parish priest Hartford, Conn., 1940-41; preacher Holy Trinity Cathedral, N.Y.C., 1941-42; parish priest St. Louis, 1942; dean Cathedral of Annunciation, Boston, 1942-54; dean Holy Cross Orthodox Theol. Sch., Brookline, Mass., 1954, now pres.; bishop of Holy Cross Orthodox Theol. Sch., Melita, Malta, 1954-56; rep. Ecumenical Patriarchate, World Council Chs., Geneva, 1955-59; then co-pres. coun. Ecumenical Patriarchate, World Council Chs., 1959-68; elevated to Metropolitan, 1956; archbishop, N. and S. Am., Holy Synod of Ecumenical Patriarchate, 1959-96; ret., 1996; chmn. Standing Conf. Canonical Bishops in the Americas; mem. adv. bd., v.p. Religion in American Life. Author works in Greek, French, English, German. Pres. St. Basil's Acad., Garrison, N.Y.; chmn. trustees Hellenic Coll., Brookline; trustee Anatolia Coll., Salonika, Greece. Recipient Man of Yr. award B'nai B'rith, 1962; recipient Nat. award NCCJ, 1962, Clergyman of the Yr. award Religious Heritage Am., 1970, Presdl. Citation as Disting. Am. in Voluntary Service, 1970, Man of Conscience award Appeal of Conscience Found., 1971, Presdl. Medal of Freedom, 1980, Interreligious award Religion in Am. Life, 1980, Clergyman of Yr. award N.Y.C. Council Churches, 1981, others. Mem. Am. Bible Soc. (bd. mgrs.). Address: 31 S Park Ave Rye NY 10580*

IAMELE, RICHARD THOMAS, law librarian; b. Newark, Jan. 29, 1942; s. Armando Anthony and Evelyn Iamele; m. Marilyn Ann Berutto, Aug. 21, 1965; children: Thomas, Ann Marie. BA, Loyola U., L.A., 1963; MSLS, U. So. Calif., 1967; JD, Southwestern U., L.A., 1976. Bar: Calif. 1977. Cataloger U. So. Calif., L.A., 1967-71; asst. cataloger L.A. County Law Libr., 1971-77, asst. ref. libr., 1977-78, asst. libr., 1978-80, libr. dir., 1980—. Mem. ABA, Am. Assn. Law Librs., Calif. Libr. Assn., So. Calif. Assn. Law Librs., Coun. Calif. County Law Librs. (pres. 1981-82, 88-90). Office: LA County Law Libr 301 W 1st St Los Angeles CA 90012-3140

IAMMARINO, RICHARD MICHAEL, pathologist, student support services director; b. Cleve., Aug. 17, 1926; s. Salvatore M. and Corinne Marie I.; m. Therese Margaret Dolan, Aug. 9, 1952. BS in Natural Sci., John Carroll U., 1949; MD, Stritch Sch. Medicine, Chgo., 1953; MS in Counseling Psychology, West Va. U., 1990. Diplomate Am. Bd. Pathology, subsplties. in anatomic and clin. pathology; lic. M.D. Ohio, Pa., W.Va. Intern St. Vincent Charity Hosp., Cleve., 1953-54; resident in internal medicine Crile VA Hosp., Cleve., 1954-55, resident in pathology, 1955-56; resident-fellow in pathology U. Kans. Med. Ctr., Kansas City, 1956-58; rsch. fellow in pathology Cleve. Met. Gen. Hosp., 1958-59; assoc. in pathology to assoc. prof. pathology U. Pitts. Sch. Medicine, 1962-79; prof. pathology W.Va. U., Morgantown, 1979-88, emeritus prof. pathology, 1989—, dir. Health Profl. Support Svc., 1989—; dir. program in med. tech., U. Pitts., 1966-69, pathologist cons. to dept. med. tech., 1969-79; med. dir. program in med. tech., W.Va. U., 1979-88, adj. prof. pathology, 1988-89, acting med. dir. blood bank, 1988-89. Contbr. numerous articles to profl. jours., chpts. to books. Mem. adv. com. to Med. Lab. Tech. Dept., Allegheny Cmty. Coll., 1967-79; founding mem., past chmn. bd. dirs., Western Pa. Montessori Sch., Inc., 1964-79; mem. blood svcs. com. Morgantown chpt. ARC, 1980-84; mem. parish coun. St. Johns U. Parish, 1980-82; bd. mem. Morgantown Hospice, Inc., 1982-88, acting pres., 1981-82, pres., 1982-83, profl. adv. coun., 1983-86, hon. life bd. mem., 1989, recipient appreciation award 1993. Recipient various rsch. grants; fellow in pathology Western Reserve U. Fellow Coll. Am. Pathologists; mem. Acad. Clin. Lab. Physicians and Scientists, W.Va. Med. Soc., Monongalia County Med. Soc., Toastmasters Internat. (CTM award 1998, pres. mountaineer chpt. 1998-99). Office: WV Univ Med Ctr PO Box 9122 Morgantown WV 26506-9122

IAMMARTINO, NICHOLAS R., corporate communications executive. B in Chem. Engring., Cooper Union; M in Chem. Engring., NYU; MBA in Fin., Adelphi U. Process engr. Esso Rsch. and Engring. Co., 1969-71; bus. and tech. news writer Chem. Engring. mag. McGraw-Hill, 1971-76; chem. industry securities analyst Merrill Lynch, 1976-78; from sr. writer to bus. pubs. mgr. dept. corp. comm. Celanese Corp., 1979-85; corp. mgr. fin. comm. and adminstrn. Philip Morris, Inc., 1985; dir. fin. comm. Borden, Inc., N.Y., 1986-89, dir. external comm., 1989, dir. pub. affairs, 1994-95; v.p. pub. affairs Borden, Inc., Columbus, Ohio, 1995—. Bd. dirs. Borden Found., Inc.; mem. assn. bd. Columbus Zool. Pk. Assn. Office: Borden Inc 180 E Broad St Columbus OH 43215-3799

IANNACCONE, ALESSANDRO, ophthalmologist, clinical scientist; b. Rome, Oct. 15, 1965; s. Guido and Maria Laura (Ciccarelli) I.; m. Monica Mary Jablonski, Dec. 29, 1996; 1 child, Andrew. MD, U. La Sapienza, Rome, 1989, diploma in ophthalmology, 1993. Rsch. assoc. Scheie Eye Inst., U. Pa., Phila., 1995-96; rsch. assoc. dept. ophthalmology U. Tenn., Memphis, 1996-97, asst. prof. dept. ophthalmology, 1998—; dir. visual electrophysiology lab. and retinal degeneration rsch. ctr. Lebonheur Children's Med. Ctr., U. Tenn., Memphis, 1997—. Contbr. articles to profl. jours. Recipient 1st prize for clin. study Italian Assn. Retinitis Pigmentosa and Low-Vision, 1991; grantee Shaimberg Neurosci. Rsch. Program, 1998, 99, Internat. Soc. Eye Rsch., 1998. Mem. Internat. Soc. Eye Rsch., Am. Acad. Ophthalmology, Assn. Rsch. in Vision and Ophthalmology, Internat. Soc. Clin. Electrophysiology of Vision (travel grant 1999), Italian Soc. Ophthalmology (Young Investigator award 1997). Avocations: photography, travel, sports, music. Home: 2453 Carrol Ridge Ln Cordova TN 38018-2434 Office: U Tenn Dept Ophthalmology 956 Court Ave Ste D-228 Memphis TN 38103-2814

IANNI, FRANCIS ALPHONSE, state official, former army officer; b. New Castle, Del., Aug. 2, 1931; s. Francisco and Mary (Marcozzi) I.; m. Ann Louise Wiggin, Apr. 16, 1955 (div.); children: Steven, Christina, Marisa, Jeanne, Marjorie; m. Carmela Jane Marsilii Carroll, Aug. 8, 1994. B.S., U.S. Mil. Acad., 1954; M.M.A. & S., U.S. Command and Gen. Staff Coll., 1963; M.A., U. Va., 1966. Served with Del. N.G., 1945-50; commd. 2d lt., inf. U.S. Army, 1954, advanced through grades to maj. gen., 1977; ret., 1977; adj. gen. State of Del., Wilmington, 1977-81; dir. Hwy. Safety, 1981-88; adj. prof. Goldey-Beacom Coll., Wilmington, 1988—. Author: World War One Remembered, 1993. Decorated Silver Star, Def. Superior Service medal, Legion of Merit with oak leaf cluster, Bronze Star, D.F.C., Air medal. Mem. Assn. U.S. Army, N.G. Assn., VFW, Am. Legion. Roman Catholic. Home: 807 Seville Ave Wilmington DE 19809-2130 Office: 4701 Limestone Rd Wilmington DE 19808-1927

IANNI, FRANCIS ANTHONY JAMES, anthropologist, psychoanalyst, educator; b. Wilmington, Del., Mar. 29, 1929; s. Innocenzo and Rosa C. (Novellino) I.; m. Ursula Elizabeth Reuss, July 17, 1971; children: Juan, Anthony, Andrea. BS in Psychology, Pa. State U., 1949, MA in Anthropology, 1950, PhD, 1952; grad., N.Y. Psychoanalytic Inst., 1981. Cert. psychologist, N.Y. State, cert. psychoanalysis Bd. Profl. Standards. Instr. psychology, anthropology Russell Sage Coll., Troy, N.Y., 1952-53, asst. prof., 1954-55, assoc. prof., 1955-56; asst. prof. Yale U., New Haven, 1956-57; prof. U. Coll., Addis Ababa, Ethiopia, 1958-61; assoc. commr. rsch. HEW, Washington, 1961-65; prof. psychology dept. U. Florence, Italy, 1965; prof., dir. Horace Mann-Lincoln Inst., Columbia U., N.Y.C., 1965-80, prof., curator, Klingenstein fellow, 1965—; cons. med. psychology St. Luke's-Roosevelt Psychiat. Ctr., N.Y.C., 1977—; cons. U.S. Dept. Edn., 1966—, U.S. Dept. Justice, 1974—. Author: American Social Legislation, 1955, Culture, System and Behavior, 1965, A Family Business, 1972, Black Mafia, 1974, Conflict and Change in Education, 1976, Cultural Relevance, 1973, The Crime Society, 1977, The Search for Structure: A Report on American Youth Today, 1990, The Acculturation of the Italo-Americans of Norristown, Pennsylvania: 1900-1950, 1991. Mem. Mayor's Task Force on Organized Crime, N.Y.C., 1974-79, Nat. Commn. on Criminal Justice Standards and Goals, 1974-75. With USN, 1943-46. Ford Found. fellow, 1951; Fulbright grantee, 1971, 74. Fellow Am. Sociol. Assn., Am. Anthrop. Assn.; mem. Am. Psychoanalytic Assn. (cert. in psychoanalysis), Am. Psychol. Assn., N.Y. Psychoanalytic Soc. Home: 91 Portland Rd Highlands NJ 07732 Office: Teachers Coll Columbia U PO Box 7 New York NY 10027-0007

IANNICELLI, JOSEPH, chemical company executive, consultant; b. N.Y.C., Aug. 5, 1929; s. Peter and Catherine (Gugliotti) I.; m. Betty Peterson, June 28, 1978; children: Mark, Rex, Gina. SB, MIT, 1951, PhD, 1955. Rsch. chemist Textile Fibers, E.I. DuPont, Wilmington, Del., 1955-60; tech. dir. Clay Div. J.M. Huber, Macon, Ga., 1960-70; founder, chief exec. officer Aquafine Corp., Brunswick, Ga., 1970—, Aero-Instant Corp., Brunswick, Ga., 1988—; co-founder IMPEX Corp., Brunswick, Ga., 1988—; cons. Consol. Goldfields Australia, Sydney, 1976-78, Rio Tinto, Madrid, 1980-82, Hoganes, Malmo, Sweden, 1984. Author: Evaluation and Comparison of Crossfield and Solenoid Field Magnetic Filters, 1981; co-author: A Survey-Benneficiation of Industrial Minerals, 1980; contbr. over 30 articles to profl. jours. Pres. Ga. Tidewater Conservation Assn., Brunswick, 1991-92; bd. dirs. Jekyll Island (Ga.) Citizens Assn., 1992-96, pres., 1993-95; govt. appointment as mem. Jekyll Island (Ga.) Citizens Resource Coun., 1995-97; foreman Glynn County Grand Jury, Brunswick, 1989.; chmn. Glynn Union of Taxpayers, 1996—; mem. Glynn County Bd. Edn., 1998—. Recipient Rsch. grant NSF, 1980, 84, Elec. Power Rsch. Inst., 1980, Resolution of Commendation, Ga. Ho. of Reps., 1995. Fellow Am. Inst. Chemists; mem. Tech. Assn. of Pulp and Paper Industry (chmn. pigments com. 1971-72). Achievements include over 100 patents including paramagnetic separator and process, silane modified organo clays, mercaptan scrubber; performed first high temperature superconducting magnetic separation of minerals as part of a team consisting of Aquafine, DuPont and Sumitomo, 1996. Home: 28 Saint Andrews Dr Jekyll Island GA 31527-0901 Office: Aquafine Corp 3963 Darien Hwy Brunswick GA 31525-2423

IANNITELLI, SUSAN B., state legislator; b. Pawtucket, R.I., June 12, 1953; m. Ralph E. Iannitelli; 1 child, Ralph E. BA, Wheaton Coll., 1974; JD, Mercer U., 1977. Atty. Iannitelli Law Offices; rep. dist. 57 R.I. Ho. of Reps., Providence, 1998; mem. judiciary com., joint com. on vet. affairs, R.I. Ho. of Reps. Mem. Rep. State Ctrl. Com., Rep. Town Com. Office: RI House of Reps State House Providence RI 02903*

IANNO, TONY, member of Canadian parliament; b. Trinity-Spadina, Can., 1957; m. Christine Innes; 3 children. BS, U. Toronto, Ont., Can. M.P. from Trinity-Spadina dist. Ho. of Commons, Can., 1993—; mem. standing com. on industry, nat. liberal caucus com. on econ. devel., vice chair Can. heritage com.; apptd. P.M.'s Task Force on Aging, 1996—; chair Can.-Portugal Parliamentary Friendship Group. Active in cmty. affairs, including ratepayers assns., charities, and working with emotionally challenged children. Office: House of Commons, Rm 477 West Block, Ottawa, ON Canada*

IANNOLI, JOSEPH JOHN, JR., university development executive; b. Worcester, Mass., Oct. 28, 1939; s. Joseph John and Alice Bernadette (Moore) I.; A.B., Franklin and Marshall Coll., 1962; M.A., Syracuse U., 1967; m. Gail V. Cummings, Oct. 21, 1972; children—Juliet, Christopher. Devel. officer Franklin & Marshall Coll., Lancaster, Pa., 1965-68; asso. dir. med. devel. U. Miami, 1968-70; adminstr. Children's Hearing and Speech Ctr., 1970-73; asst. dir., cons. Am. Bankers Assn., Washington, 1973-74, Marts & Lundy, Inc., N.Y.C., 1974-78; dir. capital support and planned giving U. Hartford, Conn., 1978-82; v.p. devel. Ripon (Wis.) Coll., 1982-90; chief devel. officer Am. Inst. Physics, Washington, 1990-92; pres., CEO M&I Advancement Group, Annapolis, Md., 1992-96; v.p. Mid-Atlantic region First Counsel, Inc., Annapolis, 1996—; sr. cons. J.M. Lord & Assos.; lectr. in field. Bd. dirs. Wau-Bun council Girl Scouts U.S.A. Cert. fund raising exec. Mem. Nat. Soc. Fund Raising Execs., Coun. for Advancement and Support of Edn., Fund Raising Inst., Bushnell Meml. Steering Com., 1980-82, Ripon area C. of C. (bd. dirs. 1985-89). Office: First Counsel Inc 3134 Catrina Ln Annapolis MD 21403-4339

IANNOTTI, JOSEPH PATRICK, orthopedic surgeon; b. N.Y.C., Dec. 16, 1954; s. Frank Thomas and Victoria (Artuso) I.; m. Cindy Baskind, July 12, 1975; 1 child, Matthew. BS, Fordham U., 1975; MD, Northwestern U., 1979; PhD in Cell Biology, U. Pa., 1987. Diplomate Am. Bd. Orthopaedic Surgery. Resident in orthopedic surgery U. Pa., Phila., 1979-83, chief resident, 1983-84, asst. prof. orthopedic surgery, 1984-93, assoc. prof., 1993-97, prof., 1997—, interim chmn. dept. orthopedic surgery; chief of shoulder svc. Hosp. of U. Pa., Phila., 1988—. Author, editor: Rotator Cuff Disorders, 1992; editor: Orthopaedic Knowledge Update, 1992, Basic Science Orthopaedics, 1994; contbr. over 100 articles to profl. publs. NIH postdoctoral fellow U. Pa., 1980-81; recipient career devel. award NIH, 1984-89, DeForest Willard award U. Pa., 1984; N.Am. travel fellow Am. Orthopaedic Assn., 1985, Am. Brit. Can. fellow, 1993. Fellow Am. Acad. Orthopaedic Surgeons; mem. Orthopaedic Rsch. Soc., Am. Shoulder and Elbow Surgeons, Acad. Orthopaedic Soc., Pa. Orthopaedic Soc. Office: Presbyn Med Ctr 1 Cupp Pavillion 39th and Market St Philadelphia PA 19104*

IANNUZZI, JOHN NICHOLAS, lawyer, author, educator; b. N.Y.C., May 31, 1935; s. Nicholas Peter and Grace Margaret (Russo) I.; m. Carmen Marina Barrios, Aug. 1979; children: Dana Alejandra, Christina Maria, Nicholas Peter II, Alessandro Luke; children from previous marriage: Andrea Marguerite, Maria Teresa. BS, Fordham U., 1956; JD, N.Y. Law Sch., 1962. Bar: N.Y., U.S. Dist. Ct. (so. and ea. dists.) N.Y. 1964, U.S. Dist. Ct. (no. and we. dists.) N.Y. 1965, U.S. Ct. Appeals (2d cir.) 1965, U.S. Supreme Ct. 1971, U.S. Dist. Ct. Conn. 1978, U.S. Tax Ct. 1978, U.S. Ct. Appeals (5th and 11th cirs.) 1982, U.S. Ct. Appeals (4th cir.) 1988, Wyo. 1994. Assoc. Law Offices of H.H. Lipsig, N.Y.C., 1962, Law Offices of Aaron J. Broder, N.Y.C., 1963; ptnr. Iannuzzi & Iannuzzi, N.Y.C., 1963—; adj. prof. trial advocacy Fordham U. Law Sch. Author: (fiction) What's Happening, 1963, Part 35, 1970, Sicilian Defense, 1974, Courthouse, 1977, J.T., 1984, (non-fiction) Cross-Examination: The Mosaic Art, 1984, Trial Strategy and Psychology, 1992. Mem. ABA, N.Y. County Bar Assn., N.Y. Criminal Bar Assn., Columbian Lawyers Assn., Lipizzan Internat. Fedn. (v.p.). Roman Catholic. Home: 118 Via Settembre, 9 Rome Italy Office: Iannuzzi & Iannuzzi 233 Broadway New York NY 10279-0001 also: 775 Park Ave Huntington NY 11743-3976 also: Front St Millbrook NY 12545 also: 345 Franklin St San Francisco CA 94102-4427 also: Advokatunburo Schumacher, Bunishoferstrasse 51, 8706 Zurich Switzerland also: 1592 Pine Ave W, Montreal, PQ Canada also: 120 Adelaide St W, Toronto, ON Canada H3B 3G3

IANZITI, ADELBERT JOHN, industrial designer; b. Napa, Calif., Oct. 10, 1927; s. John and Mary Lucy (Lecair) I.; student Napa Jr. Coll., 1947, 48-49; m. Doris Moore, Aug. 31, 1952; children: Barbara Ann Ream, Susan Therese Shifflett, Joanne Lynn Lely, Jonathan Peter, Janet Carolyn Kroyer. AA, Fullerton Jr. Coll., 1950; student UCLA, 1950, Santa Monica Community Coll., 1950-51. Design draftsman Basalt Rock Co. Inc. div. Dillingham Heavy Constrn., Napa, 1951-66, chief draftsman plant engring., 1966-68, process designer, 1968-82, pres. employees assn., 1967; now self-employed indsl. design cons. V.p., Justin-Siena Parent-Tchr. Group, 1967. Mem. Aggregates and Concrete Assn. No. Calif. (vice-chmn. environ. subcom. 1976-77), Constrn. Specifications Inst., Native Sons of the Golden West, Nat. Italian Am. Found., World Affairs Coun. No. Calif., Internat. Platform Assn., Commonwealth of Calif. Club. Republican. Roman Catholic. Home and Office: 2650 Dorset St Napa CA 94558-6110

IAQUINTO, JOSEPH FRANCIS, electrical engineer; b. Phila., Nov. 9, 1946; s. Francis Edward Iaquinto and Maria Carmina (Mancini) Feldman; m. Jo-Carol Maniscalco, Nov. 21, 1977; children: Joseph Michael, Jonathan Franklin. BSEE, Drexel U., 1969; MSEE, Stanford U., 1971. Registered professional engineer, Pa., Va. Teaching asst. Stanford (Calif.) U., 1969-71; sr. project engr. GM Corp., 1971-75; regional system engring. mgr. Memorex Corp., King of Prussia, Pa., 1975-77; sr. prin. engr. Computer Sci. Corp., Falls Church, Va., 1977-80; dir. devel. Tesdata Systems Corp., Tyson's Corner, Va., 1980-82; staff engr. HRB-Singer Co., Lantham, Md., 1982-84; sr. staff engr. Lockheed Electronics Co., Vienna, Va., 1984-86; mem. tech. staff MRJ div. Perkin Elmer, Oakton, Va., 1986-89; system engr. Ford Motor Co., Dearborn, Mich., 1989-93; engring. mgr. A.C. Nielsen, Dunedin, Fla., 1993-94; mgr. sys. engring. E'On Corp., Reston, Va., 1994-95; mem. tech. staff TASC, Reston, Va., 1995—. Author: Memorex 1380 Internal and Lesson Plan, 1977, Simulation of Microwave Propagation in the Atmosphere, 1987; co-author: (with H. Brandt) Control Engineering Application to Automobiles, 1973; author: (with others) Secure Internetwork Data Communications, 1979, Mission Planning System Specification, 1985; contbr. articles to tech. publs. Instr. ARC, Mich. and Pa., 1971-77; treas. Macomb County Young Reps., Sterling Heights, Mich., 1975; councilman Longacre PTA, Farmington, Mich., 1990-92. Recipient acad. scholarship Phila. Sch. System. Mem. IEEE, Nat. Soc.Profl. Engrs., Inst. Soc. Am. Roman Catholic. Achievements include development of first microprocessor based direct digital engine fuel control algorithm at GM, of first microcomputer based direct digital wheel lock control algorithm at GM; co-invention of a classified secure network inter network communications protocol; co-conversion of classical signal processing algorithms to massively parallel computer algorithms; modification of system engineering technology to suit automotive electronics applications; invented methodology to use FMEAs and reliability engineering processes to create robust Network Management & Control system for wireless/wireline data communications network.

IASEMIDIS, LEONIDAS D., neuroscience educator; b. Athens, Jan. 21, 1959; came to U.S., 1982; s. Dimitrios Leonidas and Fani (Castia) I.; m. Vassiliki Roulia, July 6, 1986; 1 child, Thalia. BS in Elec. Engring., Nat. U. Athens, 1982; MS in Biomed. Engring., U. Mich., 1985, MS in Physics, 1986, PhD in Biomed. Engring., 1991. Rsch. assoc. Biomed Engring. program U. Mich., Ann Arbor, 1987-91, postdoctoral rsch. fellow Biomed. Engring. program, 1991-93; rsch. ast. prof. neurology U. Fla., Gainesville, 1994-97; tech. dir. clin. neurophysiol. lab. Gainesville VA Med. Ctr., 1993-97; rsch. asst. prof. elec. engring. U. Fla., Gainesville, 1994—, rsch. asst. prof. dept. neurosci., 1998—. Recipient Fellowship for Excellence award State Scholarship Found. Greece, 1977-82; Horace H. Rackham fellow U. Mich., 1989-90. Avocations: soccer, music, tennis, cinematic arts (directing). Office: Rsch Svc (151) VA Med Ctr 1601 SW Archer Rd Gainesville FL 32608-1135

IATESTA, JOHN MICHAEL, lawyer; b. Orange, N.J., Dec. 29, 1944; s. Thomas Anthony and Marie Monica I.; m. Paulina Clare Pascuzzi, July 11, 1971. BS magna cum laude, Seton Hall U., 1967, JD cum laude, 1976; MS, Fordham U., 1968; LLM in Corp. Law, NYU, 1986. Bar: N.J. 1976, U.S. Dist. Ct. N.J. 1976, U.S. Ct. Appeals (3d cir.) 1981, N.Y. 1982, U.S. Supreme Ct. 1985. Law sec. to presiding judge appellate div. Superior Ct. N.J., Trenton, 1976-77; assoc. Wilentz, Goldman & Spitzer, Woodbridge, N.J., 1977-81, D'Alessandro, Sussman & Jacovino, Florham Park, N.J., 1981-83; corp. counsel, 1983—, Rhodia Inc., Cranbury, N.J. Recipient Book prize Tchrs. Coll. Columbia U., 1967. Mem. ABA, N.J. Bar Assn., Am. Corp. Counsel Assn., Order of the Cross & Crescent, Delta Epsilon Sigma, Kappa Delta Pi. Office: Rhodia Inc 259 Prospect Plains Rd Cranbury NJ 08512-3712

IATRIDIS, PANAYOTIS GEORGE, medical educator; b. Alexandria, Egypt, Dec. 10, 1926; naturalied citizen, 1975; m. Catherine Iatridis; children: Yanna, Mary. MD, U. Athens, Greece, 1951, DSc with honors in Physiology, 1968. Lic. physician Greece, Egypt, N.C., Ind., Ill. Resident Univ. Med. Clinic, Athens, 1951-53; resident Greek Hosp., Alexandria, Egypt, 1953-55, asst. dir. dept. medicine, 1959-62; rsch. assoc. dept. physiology U. N.C., Chapel Hill, 1963-66, asst. prof. physiology, 1969-72, faculty grad. sch., 1969-72; vis. rsch. scientist Protein Found./Harvard Sch. Pub. Health, Boston, 1966; rsch. scientist dept. physiology U. Athens, 1967-69; faculty Ind. U.; prof. physiology, biophysics and medicine, asst. dean Ind. U., Gary, dir. N.W. Ctr. for Med. Edn.; mem. search and screen com. Exec. Dir. of Lake County Med. Ctr. Devel. Agy., 1984; pres., CEO N.W. Ctr. Med. Svcs. Corp., 1985—; bd. dirs. Lake Shore Health Sys. of Ancilla Sys. Corp., 1986—, mem. quality assurance com., 1986—; lectr. in field; lectr. in field. Contbr. numerous articles and abstracts to profl. jours.; editl. bd. Ind. Medicine, 1992—. Mem. coun. St. Iakovos Greek Orthodox Ch., 1985; bd. dirs. World Affairs Coun. of N.W. Ind., 1985—; mem. ad hoc com. on AIDS Gary Cmty. Sch. Corp., 1985; bd. visitors Modern Greek Studies, Ind. U., Bloomington, 1985; mem. N.W. Ind. Forum Found., 1987—; chmn. Porter Starke Infection Control Com., 1988—; bd. dirs. N.W. Ind. Symphony, 1988-89; mem. N.W. Ind. Forum legis. Subcom., 1988, edn. com., 1992—; bd. dirs. N.W. Ind. chpt. Am. Lung Assn., 1977-84, exec. com., 1979-84; bd. dirs. Am. Cancer Soc., 1978-83, mem. med. edn. com., 1978-83; mem. coun. SS Constantine and Helen, Greek Orthodox Cathedral, Merrillville, Ind., 1979-81; vice chmn. Cmty. Health Assn., Lake County, 1979-81, chmn. med. adv. com., 1979-81, chmn. editl. bd., 1980-81; mem. rsch. com. Ind. affiliate Am. Heart Assn., 1982-84, vice chmn., 1983-84; mem. City of Gary Econ. Devel. Commn., 1984; group leader People to People Med. Edn. Delegation to People's Republic of China, 1984; founder, 1st pres. Greek Orthodox Ch. of Porter County, 1980-81. Recipient medal of St. Paul Greek Orthodox Archdiocese of North and South Am.; grantee Dept. HEW/NIH/USPHS, 1973-76, Lake County Med. Ctr. Devel. Agy., 1975-82, 82-85, 85, 85-86, 86-87, 86, 87, 88, 89, 90, 91, 92, Ind. State Bd. Health, Divsn. Maternal and Child Health, 1985, 858-86, 86-87, 87-89, Innkeepers Tax for Med. Edn., 1993, 94. Fellow ACP; mem. Acad. Athens (corr.), Ind. State Med. Soc. (commn. on med. edn. 1986—, vice chmn. commn. on conv. arrangements 1988), Porter County Med. Soc. (care of indigent com. 1986), Lake County Med. Soc. (care of indigent com. 1986), Rotary (chmn. membership devel. com. 1987-88). Office: Ind U NW Ctr for Med Edn 3400 Broadway Gary IN 46408-1101*

IAVICOLI, MARIO ANTHONY, lawyer; b. Camden, N.J., Aug. 11, 1939; s. Vito Anthony and Angelina Jessie (Marchionese) I.; m. Arlene V. LeDonne, July 6, 1963; children—Michelle, Denise, Laura. B.M.E., Drexel U., 1962; J.D., U. Pa., 1965. Bar: N.J. bar 1965. Asso. law firm Samuel P. Orlando, Camden, 1965-66, Ballen & Batoff, Camden, 1966-68; partner law firm Maressa, Console & Iavicoli, Berlin, N.J., 1968-72; first asst. prosecutor Camden County, 1972-74; pvt. practice law Pennsauken, N.J., 1974—; Counsel to speaker N.J. Gen. Assembly, 1970-72, N.J. Automobile Ins. Study Commn., 1970-74, Camden County Charter Study Commn., 1974, Camden County Republican party, 1974-76, N.J. Rep. party, 1976—; solicitor Haddenfield Borough, 1980—. Author: No Fault and Comparative Negligence in New Jersey, 1973; Drafter: N.J.'s No Fault Law and other companion legislation, 1970-73. Chmn. Camden County Rep. Com., 1978—; Rep. state committeeman, 1976—; mem. Electoral Coll. from, N.J., 1976; solicitor Pennsauken Twp., 1975—; Vice pres. Haddonfield Home Sch. Assn., 1972-73; Bd. dirs. Drexel U. Class Endowment Fund; trustee Haddonfield Civic Assn. Named One of N.J.'s 5 Outstanding Young Men, 1974; recipient Ocean County Bar Assn. award, 1975. Mem. Camden County Jr. C. of C. (counsel 1967-68), Am., N.J., Camden County bar assns., Sons of Italy, Drexel U. Alumni Assn. (v.p. 1991—). Roman Catholic. Club: Rotarian. Home: 340 Marquis Rd Haddonfield NJ 08033-4011 Office: 43 Kings Hwy W Haddonfield NJ 08033-2114

IBACH, DOUGLAS THEODORE, minister; b. Pottstown, Pa., July 23, 1925; s. Hiram Christian and Esther (Fry) I.; BS in Edn., Temple U., 1950, postgrad. Sch. Theology, 1950-52; MDiv, Louisville Presbyn. Theol. Sem., 1954; m. Marion Elizabeth Torok, Sept. 2, 1950; children—Susan Kay, Marilyn Lee, Douglas Theodore, Grace Louise. Ordained to ministry Presbyn. Ch., 1953; pastor, Pewee Valley, Ky., 1952-55, West Nottingham Presbyn. Ch., Colora, Md., 1955-61, Irwin, Pa., 1961-67, Knox Presbyn. Ch., Falls Church, Va., 1967-72, United Christian Parish Reston (Va.), 1972-87; exec. dir. Camping Assn. of the Presbyteries of Northwestern Pa., Mercer, Pa., 1986-90; pastor Pulaski (Pa.) Presbyn. Ch., 1990-94; parish assoc. Presbyn. Parish of the Valleys, Middletown, Va., 1994-98; pastor Nineveh Presbyn. Ch., Front Royal, Va., 1999—. Youth ministry cons. Nat. Capital Union Presbytery, 1967-86; ecumenical officer Nat. Capital Presbytery, chmn. stewardship com., 1986—; mem. ecumenical rels. com. Synod of Virginias, also mem. Interfaith Conf. of Metro Washington; bd. dirs. Reston Inter-Faith, Inc.; dir. Presbyn. Internat. Affairs Seminars. adv. bd. Christmas Internat. House; mem. ch. devel. and redevel. com., Christian edn. com. Lake Erie Presbytery, stated supply Pulaski (Pa.) Presbyterian Ch.; pres. New Wilmington Ministerium; exec. dir. Camping Assn. of Presbyteries of No. Pa., 1986-90; chair ecumenical task force Shenandoah Presbytery; bd. dirs. E.A.R.S., Beaver Castle Girl Scout Coun.; sec. Winchester-Frederick County Ministerium, 1995—. With USNR, 1943-44. Mem. Council Chs. Greater Washington (pres., chmn. instl. ministry commn.), Piedmont Synod U.P. Ch. (dir. youth, camping), Acad. Parish Clergy Assn. Presbyn. Christian Educators, Fairfax County Council Chs. (pres.), Com. 100 Fairfax County, Mercer Fun Club (bd. dirs.), Rotary (v.p., sec. Stephens City chpt. 1995—). Home: 110 Suffolk Cir Stephens City VA 22655-3417 Office: Presbyn Parish of the Valley 7152 Middle Rd Middletown VA 22645-2119

IBACH, ROBERT DANIEL, JR., library director; b. Lynch, Nebr., Dec. 31, 1940; s. Robert Daniel Sr. and Mabel Bertine (Selstad) I.; m. Paula Joanne Hubbling, June 11, 1977. B.R.E., Detroit Bible Coll., 1963; BD, Grace Theol. Sem., Winona Lake, Ind., 1966, ThM, 1969; MLS, Ind. U., 1975. Ordained minister, 1989. Libr. Grace Coll. and Sem., Winona Lake, 1969-86; library dir. Dallas Theol. Sem., 1986—; archaeologist Heshbon (Jordan) Expedition, 1971-76; library cons. Inst. of Holy Land Studies, Jerusalem, 1989. Author: Archaeological Survey of the Hesban Region, 1987; contbg. author: Hesban After 25 Years, 1994, Dictionary of Biblical Imagery, 1998; periodical revs. editor: Bibliotheca Sacra, 1988—; cons. editor Jour. Religious & Theol. Info., 1991—; contbr. articles to profl. jours., 1972—. Mem. Soc. Bibl. Lit., Am. Theol. Libr. Assn., Am. Libr. Assn., Tex. Libr. Assn. Home: 3229 Colby Cir Mesquite TX 75149-1875 Office: Dallas Theol Sem 3909 Swiss Ave Dallas TX 75204-6411

IBAÑEZ, ALVARO, patent design company executive, artist; b. Bucaramanga, Santander, Colombia, Jan. 18, 1951; came to U.S., 1981; s. Epimenio and Maria Delia (Muñoz) I.; m. Marta Cecilia Arias, Dec. 30, 1971 (div. Dec. 1991); children: Carlos Humberto, Alvaro Antonio, Diana Saray, Sandra; m. Denise DeVries, Sept. 6, 1997; children: Elena, Austin, Paul, Delia Denise. Fine arts, David Manzur Acad., Bogotá, Colombia, 1972; structural draftman, ACADITEC, Bogotá, Colombia, 1974. Elem. tchr. German Pena Sch., Bogotá, Colombia, 1971; with sales dept. Grolier Internat., Bogotá, Colombia, 1973-74; civil engring. draftsman Adminstrv. Dept. Cmty. Action, Bogotá, Colombia, 1974-76; gen. ins. mgr. Gilabert & CIA, Santa Marta, Colombia, 1976-77; farmer El Roble Ranch, Santa Marta, Colombia, 1976-77; sales mgr. Onix Ltda., Bucaramanga, Colombia, 1977-78; owner, mgr. Distrisiba Ltda., Bucaramanga, Colombia, 1977-80; sales mgr. Coramex Andina Ltda., Bogotá, Colombia, 1980-81; with Radian, Inc., Alexandria, Va., 1984—, Birch, Stewart, Kolasch & Birch, Falls Church, Va., 1985—, Diversified Technologies, Alexandria, Va., 1986—; pres., founder A-Ibañez Art Design, Inc., Falls Church, Va., 1985—; founder Sunrise Studio Gallery, Kilmar, Va., 1996—, Pennie & Edmonds, L.L.P., Washington, 1998—; freelance Pub. Health Ctr., Bogotá, Colombia, 1971-74, Guillermo Victorino SA, Bogotá, 1973-74, Felix A, Clavijo Co., Bogotá, 1973-75, Metron Publicity, Bucaramanga, Colombia, 1977-80, Tulio Ramirez, 1980-81, Fabio Hernandez Salazar, Bogotá, 1980-81; with Lascaris Design Group Internat., Washington, 1984. One-man shows include Georgetown Streets, Washington, 1981, Sovran Bank CC, Springfield, Va., 1985; exhibited in group shows at David Manzur Acad., Bogotá, Colombia, 1974, Dicas Fine Arts Ctr., Bogotá, Colombia, 1979, Santander Indsl. U., Bucaramanga, Colombia, 1979, Arlington Ctr., Va., 1982, Falls Church Recreation Park, Va., 1982, Latin Am. Art League, Alexandria, Va., 1991, Desfile de las Americas, Washington, 1993, Martin Luther King Meml. Libr., Washington, 1994, 96, Art Mus. Ams.-Orgn. Am. States, Washington, 1994, Strathmore Hall Arts Ctr., North Bethesda, Md., 1994, AT&T, Oakton, Va., 1994, Washington, 1994, Cultural Mexican Inst., Washington, 1994, Montgomery County Exec. Office Bldg., Rockville, Md., 1994, Bell Atlantic, Arlington, Va., 1994, Silver Spring, Md., 1994, Torpedo Factory Art League, Alexandria, Va., 1994, Moscoso Gallery, Washington, 1995, Fla. Mus. Hispanic and Latin Am. Art, Miami, 1995, Montgomery County Exec. Office Bldg., Rockville, Md., 1995, NASA Hdqs., Washington, 1995, Pan Am. Health Orgn., Washington, 1995, SED Ctr., Washington, 1996, (retrospective) Falls Church (Va.) Recreation Ctr., 1997, Bell Atlantic Hdqrs., Arlington, Va., 1997, D.C. Arts in the Alley/Georgetown U., Washington, 1998, Moca Gallery, Washington, 1998, Del Ray Artisans, Alexandria, 1998, Barnes & Noble Seven Corners, Falls Church, 1998. Sponsor World Vision, Tacoma, Wash., 1987—, Child Devel. Ctr., Falls Church, Va., 1989—, Crystal Cathedral, Glandale, Calif., 1992—, Beverley Hills United Meth. Ch., Alexandria, Va., 1997, Arts in the Alley Georgetown, D.C., 1998. Recipient 1st prize drawing Prismacolor Contest, 1958. Mem. Worldwide Fine Art Promotions, Hispanic Museo Art, Art League, Torpedo Factory. Republican. Avocations: paint, gardening, music, travel. E-mail: aiad@erols.com. Office: A Ibañez Art Design Inc 1744 Kalorama Rd NW B Washington DC 20009-2632

IBANEZ, MANUEL LUIS, university official, biological sciences educator; b. Worcester, Mass., Sept. 23, 1935; s. Ovidio Pedro and Esperanza Fe (Perez) I.; m. Jane Marie Bourquard, Oct. 16, 1970; children: Juana Lia Cristina, Vincent Ovidio, William Dayan, Marc Albert. B.S. cum laude, Wilmington Coll., 1957; M.S., Pa. State U., 1959, Ph.D., 1961. Asst. prof. Bucknell U., Lewisburg, Pa., 1961-62; postdoctoral fellow UCLA, 1962; sr. biochemist IICA de la OEA, Turrialba, Costa Rica, 1962-65; assoc. prof., chmn. dept. U. New Orleans, 1965-70, prof., 1977-90, assoc. dean grad. sch., 1978-82, assoc. vice chancellor acad. affairs, 1982-83, acting vice chancellor, 1983-85, vice chancellor acad. affairs, provost, 1985-89, prof. emeritus, 1990—; pres. Tex. A&M U., Kingsville, 1989-98, Disting. prof. biology, 1998—. Author: Basic Biology of Microorganisms, 1972; contbr. articles to profl. jours. Regent Smithsonian Inst., 1994—; mem. Alliance for Good Govt., New Orleans, 1980. NSF coop. fellow, 1958-61. Mem. Am. Assn. State Colls. and Univs., Kingsville C. of C. (pres. 1991), Rotary, KC, Sigma Xi. Democrat. Roman Catholic. Avocations: chess; tennis; cycling; collections. Office: Tex A&M Univ-Kingsville Office of Pres PO Box 101 Kingsville TX 78364-0101

IBARGUEN, ALBERTO, newspaper executive; b. Rio Piedras, P.R., Feb. 29, 1944; s. Albert E. and Angelica (Bigas) I.; m. Susana E. Lopez, Jan. 8, 1969; 1 child, Diego. BA in History, Wesleyan U., Middletown, Ct., 1966; JD, U. Pa., 1974. Bar: Conn. 1974. Atty. Legal Aid Soc., Hartford, Conn., 1974-76; dir., counsel Conn. Election Commn., Hartford, 1976-77; ptnr. Cloud & Ibarguen, Hartford, 1977-78; atty. Updike, Kelly & Spellacy, Hartford, 1978-79; dep. gen. coun., v.p. public affairs, v.p. pvt banking Conn. Nat. Bank, Hartford, 1979-84; sr. v.p. Hartford Courant, 1984-86; exec. v.p. ops. Newsday/N.Y. Newsday, N.Y.C., 1986-95; pub. El Nuevo Herald, Miami, Fla., 1995-98; v.p. The Miami Herald, 1995-98, pub., 1998—; chmn. Miami Publishing Co., 1998—. Bd. dirs. Lincoln Ctr. for Performing Arts, N.Y.C., 1990-96, Dade County Found., Com. to Protect Journalists, Fla. Philharm., Pub. Broadcasting Sys., 1997—; trustee Wesleyan U., 1992-95, Smith Coll., 1995-97; mem. bus. commn. Met. Mus. Art, 1990-95. Mem. N.Y. Athletic Club. Office: The Miami Herald One Herald Plaza Miami FL 33132-1693

IBARRA, JOSE, city council. BA in Mexican-Am. studies, U. Ariz., 1994. Campaign mgr. Mayor George Miller, 1991; with Border Vol. Corps., 1991-94; aide County Supv. Raul Grijalva, 1994; city coun. Tucson, 1995—, vice-mayor. Office: 940 W Alameda St Tucson AZ 85745-2932

IBEN, ICKO, JR., astrophysicist, educator; b. Champaign, Ill., June 27, 1931; s. Icko and Kathryn (Tomlin) I.; m. Miriam Genevieve Fett, Jan. 28, 1956; children: Christine, Timothy, Benjamin, Thomas. BA, Harvard U., 1953; MS, U. Ill., 1954, PhD, 1958. Asst. prof. physics Williams Coll., 1958-61; sr. research fellow in physics Calif. Inst. Tech., Pasadena, 1961-64; assoc. prof. physics MIT, Cambridge, 1964-68, prof., 1968-72; prof. astronomy and physics, head dept. astronomy U. Ill., Champaign-Urbana, 1972-84, prof. astronomy and physics, 1972-89; holder of Eberly family chair in astronomy Pa. State U., 1989-90; disting. prof. astronomy and physics U. Ill., Urbana, 1989—; vis. prof. astronomy Harvard U., 1966, 68, 70; vis. fellow Joint Inst. for Lab. Astrophysics U. Colo., 1971-72; vis. prof. astronomy and astrophysics U. Calif. at Santa Cruz, 1972; vis. prof. physics and astronomy Inst. for Astronomy U. Hawaii, 1977; mem. adv. panel, astronomy sect. NSF, 1972-75; mem. vis. com. Aura Observatories, 1979-82; vis. scientist astronomical council Union Soviet Socialist Rep. Acad. of Sci., 1985; sr. vis. fellow Australian Nat. U., 1986; vis. prof. U. of Bologna, Italy, 1986; sr. research fellow U. of Sussex, Eng., 1986; George Darwin lectr. Royal Astronomical Soc., London, 1984; McMillin lectr. Ohio State U., 1987; vis. eminent scholar Univ. Ctr. Ga., 1988; guest prof. Christian Albrechts Universität zu Kiel, 1990. Contbr. articles to profl. jours. John Simon Guggenheim Meml. fellow, 1985-86; recipient Eddington medal Royal Astron. Soc., 1990. Fellow Japan Soc. for Promotion of Sci.; mem. Am. Astron. Soc. (councilor 1974-77, Henry Norris Russell lectr. 1989), U.S. Nat. Acad. of Scis., Internat. Astronom. Union. Home: 3910 Clubhouse Dr Champaign IL 61822-9280 Office: U Ill Dept of Astronomy 1002 W Green St Urbana IL 61801-3074

IBERALL, ARTHUR SAUL, physicist, publisher; b. N.Y.C., June 12, 1918; s. Benjamin and Anna (Katz) I.; m. Helene Rubenstein, Jan. 28, 1940; children: Eleanora Iberall Robbins, Pamela Iberall Rubin, Althea, Valerie Iberall O'Connor. B.S., CCNY, 1940, postgrad., 1940-41; postgrad., George Washington U., 1942-45; hon. degree, Ohio State U., 1976. Gen. physicist Nat. Bur. Standards, Washington, 1941-53; research dir. ARO Equipment Corp., Cleve., 1953-54; chief physicist Rand Devel. Corp., Cleve., 1954-65; chief scientist, pres. Gen. Tech. Services, Inc., Upper Darby, Pa., 1965-81; editor, pub. CP2: Commentaries-Physical and Philosophical, 1990—; vis. scholar UCLA, 1981-92; grad. teaching U. Calif., Irvine, 1993. Author: Toward a General Science of Viable Systems, 1972, On Pulsatile and Steady Arterial Flow, 1973, Physics of Membrane Transport, 1973, Bridges in Science: From Physics to Social Science, 1974, On Nature, Life, Mind and Society, 1976, What's Wrong with Evolution, 1989, How to Run a Society, 1991, Foundations for Social and Biological Evolution, 1993, (with H. Soodak) Primer for HomeoKinetics: A Physical Foundation for Complex Systems, 1998; editor: (with J. Reswick) Technical and Biological Problems of Control; A Cybernetic View, 1970, (with A. Guyton) Regulation and Control in Physiological Systems, 1973; assoc. editor: Am. Jour. Physiology, Integrative and Comparative Physiology, 1976-90; contbr. tech. articles to profl. jours. Festschift in his honor U. Conn., Storrs, 1998. Fellow ASME (chmn. auto. control div. 1973); mem. Am. Phys. Soc., N.Y. Acad. Scis., Biomed. Engrng. Soc. (Alza Disting. lectr. 1975), Am. Cybernetic Soc., Microcirculation Soc., Instrument Soc. Am., Biophys. Soc., Sigma Xi. Democrat. Jewish. Club: Cosmos. Achievements include 35 yrs. of continuing rsch. in study of phys. complexity; integration of interdisciplinary study based on phys. principles as unique new discipline. Home: 5070 Avenida Del Sol Laguna Hills CA 92653-1876 *Three things stand out—developing the integrity of self as a human being, learning how to participate in a good family life, and integrating, in a singular fashion, the thrust of a general physical science with all aspects of reality both personal and societal. The first two themes require no special note here. Many have mastered the rules. The third is worth an added comment. Consider the Enlightenment's claim of a unified science capable of dealing with nature, life, humankind, mind, and society. Would it not be worthy of a man's life pursuit. It is.*

IBERS, JAMES ARTHUR, chemist, educator; b. Los Angeles, June 9, 1930; s. Max Charles and Esther (Imerman) I.; m. Joyce Audrey Henderson, June 10, 1951; children—Jill Tina, Arthur Alan. B.S., Calif. Inst. Tech., 1951, Ph.D., 1954. NSF post-doctoral fellow Melbourne, Australia, 1954-55; chemist Shell Devel. Co., 1955-61, Brookhaven Nat. Lab., 1961-64; mem. faculty Northwestern U., 1964—, prof. chemistry, 1964-85, Charles E. and Emma H. Morrison prof. chemistry, 1986—. Recipient Disting. alumni award Calif. Inst. Tech., 1997. Mem. NAS, Am. Acad. Arts and Sci., Am. Chem. Soc. (inorganic chemistry award 1979, Disting. Svc. in the Advancement of Inorganic Chemistry award 1992, Linus Pauling award 1994), Am. Crystallographic Assn. Home: 2657 Orrington Ave Evanston IL 60201-1760 Office: Northwestern U Dept Chemistry Evanston IL 60208-3113

IBI, KEIKO, film director; b. Tokyo; came to U.S., 1991; m. Greg Pak. Student in lit., Japan Women's U.; student, Syracuse (N.Y.) U.; degree, NYU, 1996, MFA in Film, 1998. Motion picture dir., writer, 1999—. Films include The Personals: Improvisations on Romance in the Golden Years, 1998 (Oscar award for documentary 1999). Office: c/o DGA 110 W 57th St New York NY 10019*

IBISH, YUSUF HUSSEIN, retired educator; b. Damascus, Syria, Mar. 29, 1926; came to U.S., 1984; s. Hussein Ahmad Ibish and Wajiha Abd al-Rahman El-Youssef; children: Suna, Hussein, Karim. BA, Am. U., Beirut, 1951, MA, 1951; PhD, Harvard U., 1961. Prof. Am. U., Beirut, 1961-85, Washington, 1985-87; prof. Amherst (Mass.) Coll., 1982-84, Cambridge U., Eng., 1990-91; lectr. in field. Author numerous books. Ford fellow Ford Found., 1956-58; Harvard fellow Harvard U., 1958-59; Rockefeller fellow Rockefeller Found., 1950-60; Rockefeller Rsch. grantee Rockefeller Found., 1963-66. Mem. al-Furgan Found. (advisor 1993—). Muslim. Avocation: Arabic calligraphy. Home: 950 25th St NW # 210 Washington DC 20037

IBRAHIM, IBRAHIM N., bishop; b. Telkaif, Mosul, Iraq, Oct. 1, 1940; came to U.S., 1978; s. Namo Ibrahim and Rammo Yono. Grad., Mosul Sem., Iraq, 1951, St. Sulpice Sem., Paris, 1962; D.S.T., Rome, 1975. Dir. sem. Baghdad, Iraq, 1964-68; assoc. pastor St. Joseph Ch., Baghdad, 1975-78; pastor Chaldean Ch., Los Angeles, 1979-82; bishop Chaldean Church of U.S.A., Southfield, Mich., 1982—; first Bishop Eparch Eparchy of St. Thomas the Apostle/Chaldean Cath. Diocese Am., Detroit, 1985—. Home: Chaldean Diocese USA 25603 Berg Rd Southfield MI 48034-2561*

IBRAHIM, MOUNIR LABIB, physician, psychiatrist; b. Cairo, July 26, 1948; s. Labib and Olga (Bassili) I. Diploma, Cairo U., 1967, Diploma Sch. of Medicine, 1972. Diplomate Am. Bd. Psychiatry and Neurology, also with added qualifications in geriatric psychiatry. Psychiat. resident Behman Psychiat. Hosp., Cairo, 1974-76; intern, resident Rass-El-Tin Hosp., Alexandria, Egypt, 1972-74; postdoctoral tng. St. Barnabas Med. Ctr., N.J., 1979; house officer, resident in psychiatry/behavioral medicine Bowman Gray Sch. Medicine, Winston-Salem, N.C., 1980-84; med. dir. psychiatry and dir. psychiat. edn. Forsyth Meml. Hosp., Winston-Salem, 1987-95; pvt. practice in gen. psychiatry Winston-Salem, 1987—; clin. assoc. prof. Bowman Gray Sch. of Medicine, Winston-Salem, 1992—; med. dir., partial psychiat. hospitalization program No. Hosp. of Surry County, Mt. Airy, N.C., 1996, Caldwell meml. Hosp., Lenoir, N.C., 1996-98, Alexander Cmty. Hosp., Taylorsville, N.C., 1997-98; presenter in field. Contbr. articles to profl. jours. Recipient 6th Ann. Nancy C.A. Roeske M.D. Cert. of Recognition for Excellence in Med. Student Edn., 1996. Mem. Am. Psychiat. Assn., Am. Assn. Geriatric Psychiatry, N.C. Psychiat. Assn., Christian Med./Dental Soc. Avocations: travel, reading, music, spiritual growth. Office: 1400 Millgate Dr Ste A Winston Salem NC 27103-1338

ICE, BILLIE OBERTA, retail executive; b. Grantsville, W.Va., July 17, 1962; d. Clovis Drexell and Sherron Lea (Fowler) I. BA, Glenville (W.Va.) State Coll., 1984. Asst. mgr. Hecks Discount Stores, Nitro, W.Va., 1985-87; softlines mgr. Hills Dept. Stores, Canton, Mass., 1991-92, gen. mgr., 1992—, hardlines mgr., 1991; gen. mgr. plan Hills Dept. Stores, 1991-92, gen. mgr., 1992-93; store mgr. Revco Drug Stores, Twinsburg, Ohio, 1993-97, CVS Pharmacy, Woonsocket, R.I., 1997—. With U.S. Army, 1981-82. Mem. Nat. Assn. Female Execs., VFW Ladies Aux., Am. Legion. Democrat. Baptist. Avocations: stamp and coin collecting. Home: PO Box 1401 Johnson City TN 37605-1401 Office: Revco Drug Store 305 W Sullivan St Kingsport TN 37660-3621

ICE, MARIE, education educator; b. Wiley, Colo., Jan. 18, 1938; d. Irvan Oliver and Jennie Elizabeth (Parrish) I. BA, U. No. Colo., 1967, MA, 1971; PhD, U. Mo., 1983. Cert. tchr., Colo., Mo. Instr., supervisory tchr. Cen. Mo. State U., Warrensburg; asst. prof., dir. elem. edn. Marymount Coll., Salina, Kans.; prof. Calif. State U., Bakersfield, 1986—, reading program coord., 1986-91, dir. elem. edn. program, 1995-97; postdoctoral trainee child lang. program U. Kans. Mem. Internat. Reading Assn., Nat. Reading Conf., Nat. Coun. Tchrs. of English. Home: 3508 Sweetbriar Way Bakersfield CA 93311-2756

ICE, ORVA LEE, JR., history educator, retired; b. Elkhart, Ind., Mar. 10, 1920; s. Orva Lee Sr. and Frances Marian (Grimes) I.; m. Jean Ellen Ice, July 31, 1944. AB, U. Pitts., 1942; MA, U. Chgo., 1948; EdM, Wayne State U., 1959; PhD, Mich. State U., 1970. Cert. social worker, Mich. Export mgr. J.C. Jensen Co., Chgo., 1949-52; counselor Gary (Ind.)-Lake County Schs.; tchr. East Detroit (Mich.) Pub. Schs.; registrar Macomb Community Coll., Warren, Mich., 1961-68, prof. history, 1971—, prof. spl. studies in Asia and Latin Am., 1984-98, ret., 1998. With U.S. Army, 1942-46. Fulbright fellow. Mem. ASCD, Latin Am. Studies Assn., Asian Studies Assn, Phi Delta Kappa. Home: 11926 15 Mile Rd Sterling Heights MI 48312-5108

ICEMAN, SHARON LORRAINE, elementary education educator; b. Canton, Ohio, Nov. 2, 1953; d. Robert H. and Jean (Cyphert) Young; m. Rodney Alan Iceman, Aug. 5, 1978; children: Lisa Lorraine, Julie Alane. BS, Malone Coll., Canton, 1975; MS, U. Akron, 1980. Cert. elem. tchr., Ohio. Tchr. 1st grade Plain Local Schs., Canton, tchr. 2d grade. Jennings scholar, 1978-79. Mem. NEA, Ohio Edn. Assn., Plain Local Tchr. Assn.

ICENHOWER, DELLA MAUDE, retired school librarian; b. Dalby Springs, Tex., July 18, 1929; d. Clarence Winston and Sarah Della (Young) Dalby; m. James Robert Icenhower, June 3, 1951; 1 child, John Dalby. BS, U. North Tex., 1950; MEd, Tex. A&M U., Commerce, 1955. Tchr. Pewitt Ind. Sch. Dist., Naples, Tex., 1950, Lufkin (Tex.) Ind. Sch. Dist., 1951, Falls County Schs., Rosebud, Tex., 1952-56, Borger (Tex.) Ind. Sch. Dist., 1956-64, Fritch (Tex.) Ind. Sch. Dist., 1964-68; sch. libr. Childress (Tex.) Ind. Sch. Dist., 1967-70, Mansfield (Tex.) Ind. Sch. Dist., 1970-90; steering com. Mansfield Ind. Sch. Dist., 1994—, technology com., 1997—, supt. search com., 1980-81, election ofcl., 1991—, vol., 1990—; mem. adv. bd. Mansfield Pub. Libr., 1976—. Mem. Delta Kappa Gamma, Phi Delta Kappa, Alpha Delta Kappa, Model A Ford Club. Democrat. Baptist. Home: 1 Circle Park Ct Mansfield TX 76063-3210

ICENHOWER, ROSALIE B., retired elementary school principal; b. Dallas, Wis., Nov. 15, 1929; d. Theodore M. and Zella (Burch) Hughes; m. Paul L. Icenhower, Mar. 14, 1958; children: Deborah, Jonathan, David, Rebecca. BA cum laude, Calif. State U., Turlock, 1971; MEd, U. Wash., 1975; PhD, Columbia Pacific U., 1986; postgrad., Seattle Pacific U., 1990. Cert. secondary and continuing elem. tchr., prin., Wash., secondary tchr., Calif. Former mem. adj. faculty Seattle Pacific U.; tchr. English Modesto (Calif.) City Schs.; elem. sch. tchr., curriculum dir. Heritage Christian Sch., Bothell, Wash., prin.; freelance writer, seminar spkr.; rschr. in field. Contbr. articles, poems, book revs. to profl. jours., newspapers, mags. Fellow Nat. Prins. Acad. Mem. Northwest Christian Writers Assn. Republican. Baptist. Home: 12617 NE Hollyhills Dr Bothell WA 98011-2512 *The greatest achievement in the world is of little value if one fails to love God and care for the needs of those who cannot help themselves.*

ICHAPORIA, PALLAN R., pharmaceutical marketing executive; b. Bombay, India, Aug. 15, 1952; came to U.S., 1976; s. Rustomji E. and Navajbai Rustomji (Umrigar) I.; m. Hutoxi Ichaporia, May 27, 1952; children: Burjor, Rashna, Farida. MBA, Phillips U., 1981; DBA, Okla. U., 1988. Mktg. & sales profl. Lamb Svcs., Okla., 1976-86, Bristol Myers Squibb, Evansville, Ind., 1986—. Author: The Gathas of Asho Zarathushtra, 1993; co-author: (with Helmut Humbach) The Heritage of Zarathushtra: A New Translation of His Gathas, 1994, Translation of Zamyad Yasht with Commentary and Glossary, 1997; contbr. articles to profl. jours.

ICHEL, DAVID W., lawyer; b. Newark, May 14, 1953; s. Albert L. and Sylvia (Dreskin) I. BA, Duke U., 1975, JD, 1978. Bar: N.Y. 1979, N.J. 1978, U.S. Supreme Ct. 1983, U.S. Ct. Appeals (2nd cir.) 1984, U.S. Ct. Appeals (9th cir.) 1985, U.S. Dist. Ct. (so. dist.) N.Y. 1979, U.S. Dist. Ct. (ea. dist.) N.Y. 1980, U.S. Dist. Ct. N.J. 1978. Assoc. Simpson, Thacher & Bartlett, N.Y.C., 1978-84, ptnr., 1985—; bd. dirs. MFY Legal Svcs., Inc. Author, co-editor: Introduction to Business Insurance, 1986; author, editor: Professional Liability Insurance, 1984/85; contbr. articles on ins. law to profl. jours. Mem. exec. com. divsn. lawyers United Jewish Appeal. Mem. Am. Law Inst., Am. Arbitration Assn. (arbitrator), Phi Beta Kappa. Office: Simpson Thacher & Bartlett 425 Lexington Ave Fl 15 New York NY 10017-3954*

ICHIISHI, TATSURO, economics and mathematics educator; b. Seoul, Dec. 16, 1943; came to U.S., 1970; s. Jitsuro and Tomiko (Tanaka) I.; m. Barbara Ann Franklin, Sept. 7, 1973. BA in Econs., Keio U., Tokyo, 1966, MA in Econs., 1968; MA in Math., U. Calif., Berkeley, 1975, PhD in Econs., 1974. Rsch. assoc. Keio U., Tokyo, 1968-73; vis. rsch. fellow Cath. U. Louvain, Heverlee, Belgium, 1974-75; lectr., rsch. assoc. Northwestern U., Evanston, Ill., 1975-76; asst. prof. Carnegie-Mellon U., Pitts., 1976-80; assoc. prof. U. Iowa, Iowa City, 1980-83, prof., 1983-86; prof. Ohio State U., Columbus, 1987—. Author: Game Theory for Economic Analysis, 1983, The Cooperative Nature of the Firm, 1993, Microeconomic Theory, 1997; editor: (with Abraham Neyman and Yair Tauman) Game Theory and Applications, 1990; assoc. editor Rev. of Econ. Design, 1997—; editl. bd. Internat. Jour. of Game Theory, 1997—, Advances in Mathematical Economics, 1998—, Games and Economic Behavior, 1998—; contbr. articles to profl. jours. Recipient Nikkei-Tosho Bunka Sho award Nihon Keizai Shinbun and Japan Ctr. for Econ. Rsch., 1994; CORE fellow, 1974-75; NSF grantee, 1978-82, 82-85, 92-96. Mem. Rsch. Ctr. Math. Econs. (Japan), Soc. for Advancement of Econ. Theory, Econometric Soc., Game Theory Soc. Office: Ohio State U Dept Econs 1945 N High St Columbus OH 43210-1120

ICHINO, YOKO, ballet dancer; b. Los Angeles, Cali.. Studied with Mia Slavenska, L.A. Mem. Joffrey II, N.Y.C., Joffrey Ballet, N.Y.C., Stuttgart Ballet, Fed. Republic Germany; tchr. ballet, 1976; soloist Am. Ballet Theatre, 1977-81; guest appearances, 1981-82; prin. Nat. Ballet Can., Toronto, Ont., 1982-90; various guest appearances including World Ballet Festival, Tokyo, 1979, 85, Tokyo Ballet, 1980, with Alexander Godunov and Stars, summer, 1982, Sydney Ballet, Australia, N.Z. Ballet, summer 1984, Ballet de Marseille, 1985-87, Deutsche Opera Ballet Berlin, 1985-90, Munich Opera Ballet, 1987-90, Australian Ballet, 1987, 89, Staatsoper Berlin, 1989, 90, Komische Opera, Berlin, 1991-93, David Nixon's Dance Theater, Berlin, 1990, 91, Birmingham Royal Ballet, 1990-93, Deutsche Opera Ballet, Berlin, 1994-95; tchr. Australian Ballet, 1989, Birmingham Royal Ballet, 1991, 93, Nat. Ballet of Ca., 1993, Cullberg Ballet, Sweden, 1994, Nat. Ballet Sch., 1994, 95, Ballet de Monte-Carlo, 1994, Geneva Ballet, 1995—, Nederlands Dance Theater, 1995, Rambert Dance, 1995 ; tchr. numerous ballet workshops; dir. profl. program Ballet Met, 1995. First Am. women recipient medal Third Internat. Ballet Competition, Moscow, 1977.

ICHIYAMA, DENNIS YOSHIHIDE, design educator, consultant, administrator; b. Aiea, Hawaii, May 28, 1944; s. Edwin Kiyotada and Florence Fusae (Inoshita) I. BFA, U. Hawaii, 1966; MFA, Yale U., 1968; postgrad., Allgemeine Gewerbeschule, Basel, Switzerland, 1975-77. Instr. U. Bridgeport, Conn., 1968-70; sr. graphic designer Graphic Communications Ltd., Hong Kong, 1970-71; instr. Carnegie-Mellon U., Pitts., 1971-74; asst. prof. Cornell U., Ithaca, N.Y., 1974-75; assoc. prof. Ind. U., Bloomington, 1977-78; asst. prof. U. Ill., Chgo., 1978-79; assoc. prof. Wichita (Kans.) State U., 1979-81; prof., chmn. divsn. art and design Purdue U., West Lafayette, Ind., 1985-92, head dept. visual and performing arts, 1993—; design cons. U.S. Postal Svc., Washington, 1986, Purdue U. Press, West Lafayette, 1989—, Interior Design Educators Coun., Ithaca, 1985-87; vis. scholar U. Iowa Ctr. for the Book, 1990; fellow to Ctr. for Artistic endeavor Purdue U. Sch. Liberal Arts, 1992. Design work exhbns. in Can., U.S., Germany, Finland, France, Czechoslovakia; exhibited in shows at Centre Georges Pompidou, 1985, Poster Biennale, Warsaw, 1982, Biennale of Graphic

Design, Brno, Czechoslovakia, 1982, 92; represented in collection of the Plakatsammlung of the Kunstgewerbemuseum, Zurich, Rochester Inst. of Tech. Libr., N.Y., Lahti Art Mus., Finland; author essays in Contemporary Designers, 1985, T Y P O G R A M S, book revs.; book reviewer Choice (ALA, Assn. Coll./Rsch. Librs.). Grantee Nat. Endowment for Humanities, 1984; IAC master fellow Ind. Arts Commn., 1985, Nat. Endowment for Arts, 1989. Mem. Am. Ctr. for Design, Am. Inst. Graphic Arts, Graphic Design Educators Assn., Alliance Typographique Internat., Nat. Coun. Art Adminstrs. (nat. bd. dirs. 1998—), Internat. Coun. Fine Arts Deans, Coll. Art Assn. Am., Arts Ind. (state coun. 1993-99), Hui na opio o Hawaii (advisor 1986-93), Greater Lafayette Music Art Bd. Buddhist. Avocations: Swiss posters, artists books, Chinese and Japanese seals, printing history, hand bookbinding and letterpress printing. Office: Purdue U Dept Visual/Performing Arts CA # 1 West Lafayette IN 47907-1352

IDA, SHOICHI, artist; b. Kyoto, Japan, Sept. 13, 1941; came to U.S., 1970; s. Ida Kikuji and Ida Yukie. BA, Kyoto Mcpl. U. Art, MFA, BA (hon.). Cert. mus. curator. lectr. dept. sculpture, printmaking Kyoto Mcpl. U. Art, 1965-68, 70-72, Ohio State U., Columbus, 1974, Columbus Inst. Printmaking, 1974, SUNY, New Paltz, 1974, Kala Art Inst., Berkeley, Calif. 1979, San Francisco Art Inst., 1979, Art Inst. Chgo., 1980, U. Alta., 1981, Calif. Coll. Art and Craft, 1986, Whitman Coll., Walla Walla, Wash., 1989, Art Mus. Cin., 1989, others; panelist in field. Solo exhbns. include Gallery Azuchi, Osaka, Japan, 1966, Dragon, Inc., Paris, 1970, Gallery Crews, N.Y.C., 1970, Himezi Gallery, Tokyo, 1974, 75, 76, Gallery Coco, Kyoto, Japan, 1976, Tokyo Gallery, 1977, 79, 82, 86, 92, Suzuki Gallery, N.Y.C., 1979, San Francisco Art Inst., 1979, Yoh Art Gallery, Osaka, 1979, 80, 82, 83, 84, 87, 88, 90, 92, Mary Baskett Gallery, Cin., 1981, 90, Gallery Ueda, Tokyo, 1983, 85, 87, 88, 89, 90, 92, Gallery 24, Osaka, 1983, 86, Chgo. Art Fair, 1993, Suzuki Gallery, N.Y., 1993, Life Gallery TEN, Fukuoka, Japan, 1994, Gallery Ueda, Tokyo, 1994, Perimeter Gallery, Chgo., 1994, Gallery Mori, Tokyo, 1994, many others; innumerable group exhbns. Japan, Europe, U.S, 1966—, include Kyoto Mcpl. Mus. Art, Mcpl. Mus. Mod. Art, Paris, Nat. Mus. Modern Art, Tokyo, Kyoto, San Jose (Calif.) Mus. Art, Mus. Modern Art, Chgo.; exhbns. Internat. Biennale Prints and Drawings; represented in collections Nat. Libr., Paris, Victoria and Albert Mus., London, MOMA, N.Y.C., Swedish Art Assn., Osaka (Japan) Contemporary Art Ctr., Museo de Arte Contemporaneo, Ibiza, Spain, Mus. Modern Art, Krakow, Poland, L.A. County Mus. Art, Art Acad. Cin., Smithsonian Internat.-Arthur M. Sackler Gallery, Deutsch Bank AG, Frankfurt, Ger., Hara Mus. Contemporary Art, Tokyo, numerous others. Recipient Peter Millard prize 7th Brit. Internat. Print Biennale, Bradford, Eng., 1982, (with Robert Rauschenberg) Award for Excellence Internat. Cultural Exchange NEA, Washington, 1986, Grand Priz Suntory Prize Suntory Found., 1989, Aequo Prize 12th Internat. Print Biennale, Krakow, Poland, 1988, The Suntry Grand prize, 1989, others; French Govt. grantee, 1968, Japan Soc. N.Y.C. grantee, 1974, Asian Cultural Coun. grantee, N.Y.C., 1986, Hitachi Found. grantee, Washington, 1986, Centrum Found. grantee, Commn. Centennial Wash. State, 1989. Office: care Perimeter Gallery 210 W Superior St Chicago IL 60610-3508 also: 2924 Russell St Berkeley CA 94705-2334*

IDASZAK, JEROME JOSEPH, economic journalist; b. Chgo., Dec. 28, 1945; s. Joseph Edward and Estelle Charlotte (Grelecki) I.; m. Geraldine Rae Fehst, Sept. 4, 1976; children: Alexander Jerome, Joshua Adam. B.Journalism, Northwestern U., Evanston, Ill., 1967, M.Journalism, 1968. Reporter Rockford Morning Star, Ill., 1968-70; reporter Chgo. Tribune, Deerfield, Ill., 1974-76; fin. reporter Chgo. Sun Times, 1976-82, fin. columnist, 1982-90, Washington corr., 1985-90; freelance writer and editor, 1991; assoc. editor Kiplinger Washington Editors, 1992—; fin. commentator Sta. WBBM-AM, Chgo., 1984-85; contbr. Sta. WBEZ-FM, Chgo., 1987-93; grad. journalism instr. Northwestern U., 1984. Author: (newspaper series) Farm problems, 1983 (Peter Lisagor award 1984); Asian economy & growth, 1979 (Peter Lisagor award 1980). Vol., U.S. Peace Corps, 1970-72. Brookings Instn. fellow, 1979. Mem. Soc. Profl. Journalists, Nat. Returned Peace Corps. Vols., Chgo. Headline Club (bd. dirs. 1980-85, pres. 1984-85).

IDEMAN, JAMES M., federal judge; b. Rockford, Ill., Apr. 2, 1931; s. Joseph and Natalie Ideman; m. Gertraud Erika Ideman, June 1, 1971. BA, The Citadel, 1953; JD, U. So. Calif., 1963. Bar: Calif. 1964, U.S. Dist. Ct. (cen. dist.) Calif. 1964, U.S. Ct. Mil. Appeals 1967, U.S. Supreme Ct. 1967. Dep. dist. atty. Los Angeles County, 1964-79; judge Los Angeles County Superior Ct., 1979-84; appointed judge U.S. Dist. Ct. (cen. dist.) Calif., L.A., 1984-98, sr. judge, 1998. Served to 1st lt. U.S. Army, 1953-56, col. AUS Ret. Republican. Office: US Dist Ct 312 N Spring St Los Angeles CA 90012-4704*

IDING, ALLAN EARL, lawyer; b. Milw., Apr. 29, 1939; s. Earl Herman and Erna Adeline (Albrecht) I.; m. Anne Louise Chaconas, July 9, 1961; children: Kent Earl, Krista Anne Templeman, Bradford A., Andrea Beth Brozynski. BS, Marquette U., 1961, LLB, 1963; DHL (hon.), Nashotah (Wis.) House, 1990. Bar: Wis. 1963, U.S. Dist. Ct. (ea. dist.) Wis. 1963, U.S. Ct. Appeals (7th cir.) 1963. Law clk. U.S. Ct. Appeals (7th cir.), Chgo., 1963-64; assoc. Whyte Hirschboeck Dudek, S.C., Milw., 1964-71, mem., 1971—; bd. dirs. Elicar Corp. Trustee Nashotah House, 1976—; pres., bd. dirs. Wis. DeMolay Found., Milw., 1985—, Wis. Health and Ednl. Facilities Authority, 1978-85, Todd Wehr Found., Inc., Wis. Masonic Home, Inc.; mem. Wauwatosa (Wis.) Police and Fire Commn., 1978-83. Mem. Blue Mound Golf and Country Club (bd. dirs.), Milw. Athletic Club, Masons (grand master Wis. 1981-82). Republican. Episcopalian. Avocation: golf. Home: 9212 Wilson Blvd Milwaukee WI 53226-1729 Office: Whyte & Hirschboeck Dudek SC Ste 2100 111 W Wisconsin Ave Milwaukee WI 53203-2501

IDLE, ERIC, actor, screenwriter, producer, songwriter; b. South Shields, Eng., Mar. 29, 1943. Pres. The Cambridge Footlights, 1964-65. TV shows include The Frost Report, Monty Python's Flying Circus, 1969-74, Rutland Weekend TV, 1975; films include And Now For Something Completely Different, 1971, Monty Python and the Holy Grail, 1975, The Rutles, 1978, Monty Python's Life of Brian, 1979, Monty Python Live at the Hollywood Bowl, 1982, Monty Python's The Meaning of Life, 1983, Yellowbeard, 1983, National Lampoon's European Vacation, 1985, Transformers: The Movie, 1986, The Adventures of Baron Munchausen, 1988, Nuns on the Run, 1990, Too Much Sun, 1991, Mom and Dad Save the World, 1993, Splitting Heirs, 1993, Casper, 1995, The Wind in the Willows, 1996, Burn Hollywood Burn, 1998, Dudley Do-Right, 1999. also: William Morris 151 S El Camino Dr Beverly Hills CA 90212-2704 Office: Grant & Tani Inc 9100 Wilshire Blvd Ste 1000 Beverly Hills CA 90212-3415

IDOL, JOHN LANE, JR., English language educator, writer, editor; b. Deep Gap, N.C., Oct. 28, 1932; s. John Lane and Annie Lulu (Watson) I.; m. Marjorie Anne South, Nov. 24, 1955. BS, Appalachian State U., 1958; MA, U. Ark., 1961, PhD, 1964. English tchr. Blowing Rock (N.C.) Union Sch., 1958-59; English tchr., writer Clemson (S.C.) U., 1965-95; dir. grad. studies in English Clemson U., 1969-74; table leader Ednl. Testing Svc., Princeton, N.J., 1990—. Author: Thomas Wolfe Companion, 1987; co-author: Hawthorne and the Visual Arts, 1991; editor: The Hound of Darkness (Thomas Wolfe), 1986; co-editor: Mannerhouse (Thomas Wolfe), 1985, Nathaniel Hawthorne, The Contemporary Reviews, 1994, The Party at Jack's (Thomas Wolfe), 1995, Hawthorne and Women, 1999; contbr. articles and poems to lit. jours. Treas. Clemson Area Arts Coun. 1984-85; chmn. Adv. Com. on Accomodation Taxes, 1985-90; pres. Friends of Clemson Community Libr., 1989-90; sec. Chapel Hill-Carrboro Cmty. Chorus, 1997-98. With U.S. Air Force, 1951-55. Recipient Award of Merit, AAUP, S.C. chpt., 1986; NDEA fellow U. Ark., 1959; named Alumni Disting. Prof., Clemson U., 1993. Mem. MLA, Nathaniel Hawthorne Soc. (pres. 1984-86, editor Nathaniel Hawthorne rev. 1983-92), Herman Melville Soc., Thomas Wolfe Soc. (pres. 1981-83), Southeastern Name Soc. (pres. 1988-90), Philol. Assn. of the Carolinas (pres. 1984, Honored Tchr. 1986), Soc. for Study of So. Lit. (v.p. 1992-94, pres. 1994-96), Mark Twain Circle, Phi Beta Kappa (Piedmont Area pres. 1981-83, 89-91), Phi Kappa Phi. Avocations: choral singing, softball, birding, photography, book collecting. Home: PO Box 413 Hillsborough NC 27278-0413

IDZIK, DANIEL RONALD, lawyer; b. Depew, N.Y., Jan. 20, 1935; s. Daniel Henry and Ann Mary (Kolakowski) I.; m. Kathleen Osborne, Oct. 6 1989; children by previous marriage: Christopher, Rebecca, Laura, Susan. BS, SUNY, Buffalo, 1956; LLB, Harvard U., 1963. Bar: N.Y. 1964. Exec. v.p. U.S. Nat. Student Assn., Phila., 1956-57; assoc. sec. World Univ. Svc., Geneva, 1957-60; chief counsel N.Y. State Senate Commn. on Labor and Industry, Albany, 1965; from assoc. counsel to gen. counsel Booz, Allen & Hamilton, Inc., N.Y.C., 1967-98; ret., 1998. Chmn. Philharmonia Virtuosi, Westchester County, N.Y., 1988-90, pres. 1987-88, bd. dirs. 1985-91; pres. Coun. for Arts in Westchester, 1983-85, bd. dirs., 1980-85; chmn., Friends of Neuberger Mus., Purchase, N.Y., 1991-93, pres., 1990, bd. dirs., 1987-97; bd. dirs. Buffalo State Coll. Found., 1985—, Jacob's Pillow, 1996—. Recipient Disting. Alumni award SUNY Buffalo, 1986, Arts award Coun. for the Arts in Westchester, 1990. Mem. ABA, Assn. of Bar of City of N.Y, Harvard Club of N.Y. (mem. bd. mgrs. 1997—). Democrat. Home: PO Box 158 30 Pond Blvd Otis MA 01253 also: Booz Allen & Hamilton Inc 8283 Greensboro Dr Mc Lean VA 22102-3802

IDZIK, MARTIN FRANCIS, lawyer; b. Depew, N.Y., Apr. 2, 1942; s. Daniel Henry and Ann Mary (Kolakowski) I.; m. Patricia Ann O'Brien, Aug. 7, 1965; children: Andrew, Amy. BS, Canisius Coll., 1963; JD, U. Notre Dame, 1966. Bar: N.Y. 1966. Assoc. Phillips, Lytle et al., Buffalo, 1971-76, ptnr., 1977-78; ptnr. Phillips, Lytle et al., Jamestown, N.Y., 1979—; bd. trustees Randolph Children's Home, 1993—. Acting village justice, East Aurora, N.Y.,1972-79; bd. dirs. Chautauqua County Humane Soc., 1989-93, Downtown Jamestown Devel. Task Force, 1988-92, Jamestown YMCA, 1985-87, N.Y. State affiliate of Am. Heart Assn., 1983-85, Southwestern chpt. Am. Heart Assn., 1981-85, United Way South Chautauqua County, 1997—, Jamestown Cmty. Learning Coun., 1995—; chmn. fund for the Arts in Chautauqua County, 1984-88; pres. Arts Coun. Chautauqua County, 1982-84; mem. Jamestown Civic Ctr. Task Force, 1982-86, N.Y. State Mgmt. Atty.'s Conf., 1978—. Capt. JACG, U.S. Army, 1967-71. Mem. ABA, N.Y. State Bar Assn., Erie County Bar Assn., Jamestown Bar Assn. (pres. 1991-92), No. Chautauqua County Bar Assn., Sportsmen's Club (Stow, N.Y.). Office: Phillips Lytle Hitchcock 307 Chase Bank Bldg PO Box 1279 Jamestown NY 14702-1279*

IENNER, DON, music company executive. Chmn. Columbia Records Group, N.Y.C. Office: Columbia Records 550 Madison Ave New York NY 10022-3211*

IERARDI, ERIC JOSEPH, school system administrator; b. Bklyn., May 11, 1950; s. Joseph and Angelina (Vitale) I. BA, St. Francis Coll., 1973; MEd, Fordham U., 1987. Asst. dir. James A. Kelly Local Hist. Studies Inst., 1973; St. Francis Coll. tchr. St. Bartholomew's Sch., 1974-78; tchr. Our Lady of Grace Sch., Bklyn., 1978-86; tchr. St. Mary Star of Sea Sch., 1986-87, asst. on edn. to Bklyn. borough pres., 1979; dist. rep., mgr. Congressman Stephen J. Solarz, 1981-82; prin. St. Francis Xavier Sch., Vicksburg, Miss., 1987-89, St. Francis Paola Sch., Bklyn., 1989-91, St. Pius V, Jamaica, Queens, N.Y., 1991-96; adminstr. David A. Boody Intermediate Sch. 228, Bklyn.; instr. prof. Hinds C.C., Miss. Author: Gravesend: The Home of Coney Island, 1975, Gravesend: Brooklyn, Coney Island & Sheepshead Bay, 1996, Brooklyn in the 1920s, 1998; contbg. editor Bklyn. Mag., 1978-79. Past mem. Cmty. Planning Bd. 11, Bklyn.; past pres. Gravesend Dem. Club; commr. deeds City N.Y. Named Hon. Mayor, Gravesend, Eng., 1977; recipient Calabrian of Yr. award Brutium Cultural Club, 1979; knighted, named to Order of Merit of Savoy, His Royal Highness Prince Victor Emmanuel IV of Savoy. Mem. Assn. Tchrs. Social Studies, Columbia Tchrs. Assn., Gravesend Hist. Soc. (pres.), Circolo Culturale Club, U. S. Fla. Club, Order Sons of Italy. Democrat. Roman Catholic.

IERARDI, STEPHEN JOHN, physician; b. Honolulu, July 5, 1960; s. Ernest John and Robert Ann (Hackett) I.; m. Erica Ewing, May 28, 1989; children: Daphne Alexandra, Weston Eric. BA in Biology, Williams Coll., 1982; MD, U. Rochester, 1986. Diplomate Am. Bd. Family Physicians. Intern U. Calif. at Irvine Med. Ctr., Orange, 1986-87, resident, 1987-89, chief resident, 1988-89; physician Laguna Hills, Calif., 1989—; med. dir. Lake Forest Nursing Ctr., 1993-96; chief of medicine Saddleback Meml. Med. Ctr., Laguna Hills, 1996, chmn. family practice, 1994-96. Recipient UCI Care awards Univ. Calif. at Irvine Med. Ctr., 1986-89. Fellow Am. Acad. Family Physicians, AMA (Physician Recognition award 1996); mem. Am. Acad. Family Physicians, Calif. Acad. Family Physicians. Avocations: surfing, sailing, windsurfing, skiing, travel. Home: 13 Pacifico Laguna Niguel CA 92677-4242 Office: Saddleback Family Medicine 24411 Health Center Dr Laguna Hills CA 92653-3633

IEYOUB, RICHARD PHILLIP, state attorney general; b. Lake Charles, La., Aug. 11, 1944; s. Phillip Assad and Virginia Khoury I.; m. Caprice Brown, Feb. 3, 1995; 1, child, Khoury Myhand. BA in history, McNeese State U., 1968; JD, La. State U., 1972. Bar: La. 1972, U.S. Supreme Ct. Spl. prosecutor to atty. gen. State of La., Baton Rouge, 1972-74; assoc. Camp, Carmouche, Lake Charles, 1974-76; mem. Stockwell, Sievert, Lake Charles, 1976-78, Baggett, McCall, Singleton, Ranier, Ieyoub, Lake Charles, from 1978; sole practice Lake Charles; dist. atty. Calcasieu Parish, 1985-92; atty. gen. State of La., 1992—; instr. criminal law McNeese State U.; chmn. La. Drug Policy Bd., New Orleans Met. Crime Task Force; mem. La. Commn. on Law Enforcement, President's Commn. on Model State Drug Laws, 1992—; mem. bd. dirs. La. State U. Alumni Assn. Bd. dirs. S.W. La. Health Counseling Svcs., Crime Stoppers of Lake Charles; mem. Parish coun. Immaculate Conception Cathedral Parish, Lake Charles; vice chmn. La. coord. coun. on the prevention of drug abuse and treatment of drug use; mem. La. commn. on law enforcement; apptd. by gov. to adv. bd. La. D.A.R.E.; chmn. New Orleans Metropolitan Crime Task Force, Gov's. Military Adv. Commn. Named Outstanding Pub. Ofcl. for Diocese Lake Charles, 1990; recipient Disting. Alumnus award McNeese State U., 1994. Mem. ABA (vice chmn. prosecution function com.), Assn. Trial Lawyers Am., Nat. Assn. Criminal Def. Lawyers, La. Bar Assn. (lectr. criminal law), Nat. Dist. Attys. Assn. (pres., bd. dirs. 1990-91), Nat. Assn. Attys. Gen. (exec. working group on prosecutorial rels.), La. Dist. Attys. Assn. (pres., bd. dirs. 1989-90), Nat. Coll. Dist. Attys. (bd. regents 1991), S.W. La. Bar Assn. (exec. com. 1979), So. Attys. Gen. Assn. (elected chmn.), Sierra Club. Democrat. Roman Catholic. Office: Justice Dept PO Box 94005 Baton Rouge LA 70804-9005*

IFEDIORA, OKECHUKWU CHIGOZIE, nephrologist, educator; b. Onitsha, Nigeria, Mar. 1, 1955; came to U.S., 1986; s. Jeremiah Chukwudebe and Victoria Nonye (Menyua) I.; m. Efeti Osagie Udaze, Mar. 20, 1993; children: Amala Chukwu Tochukwu, Nwamaka Chidima. BSc with hons., U. Ife, Nigeria, 1978; MBChB, U. Ife, 1981. Diplomate Am. Bd. Internal Medicine, Am. Bd. Nephrology. Intern Gen. Hosp., Onitsha, 1981-82; med. officer Apex Med. Ctr., Igbo-Ukwu, Nigeria, 1982-86; resident Harlem Hosp., N.Y.C., 1987-90; fellow in nephrology Lankenau Hosp., Phila., 1990-92; cons. Nephrology Cons., Monroe, La., 1992-97; cons., v.p. Renal Assocs., Monroe, 1997—; asst. clin. prof. La. State U., Conway Hosp., Monroe, 1994—. Contbr. articles to profl. jours. Fellow ACP; mem. AMA, Am. Soc. Nephrology, Internat. Soc. Nephrology, Ouachita Med. Soc., Nat. Kidney Found., Monroe C. of C., Monroe Atheletic Club. Avocations: tennis, photography, swimming, travelling. Home: 3102 Claiborne Cir Monroe LA 71201-2006

IFERT, DANETTE EILEEN, communication educator; b. Olney, Md., Oct. 3, 1968; d. Norman Daniel and Anna Eileen (Norwood) I. BA, W.Va. Wesleyan Coll., Buckhannon, 1990; MA, Northwestern U., Evanston, Ill., 1992, PhD, 1994. Vis. instr. W.Va. Wesleyan Coll., Buckhannon, 1993-94, asst. prof. comm., 1995—, dir. forensics, 1995-98; asst. prof. comm. Tex. Tech U., Lubbock, 1994-95. Contbr. articles to profl. jours.; mem. editl. rev. bd. Comm. Rsch. Reports, 1996—. Mem. choir 1st United Meth. Ch., Buckhannon, 1995—. Travel grantee Appalachian Coll. Assn., 1995-98; Salzburg Seminar fellow, 1998; recipient Top Paper award in interpersonal comm. Ea. Comm. Assn., 1995, 97. Mem. AAUW (v.p. programs 1997-98), Nat. Comm. Assn., United Meth. Women, Ea. Comm. Assn. (life, chair interest group 1997-98, advt. mgr. 1998), Internat. Comm. Assn., Phi Kappa Phi (pres. 1996-98). Office: WVa Wesleyan Coll 59 College Ave Buckhannon WV 26201-2600

IFFT, LEWIS GEORGE, III, company administrator; b. Uniontown, Pa., July 21, 1951; s. Lewis George Jr. and Miriam Katherine Wilson; m. Kathleen Marie Andersen, Mar. 26, 1983; children: Christopher Andrew Ifft, Jonathan Lewis Ifft. BS in Bus. Adminstrn., Bowling Green (Ohio) State U., 1973; MBA, Rensselaer Polytechnic Inst., Troy, N.Y., 1979. Ops. mgr. Battery Products Divsn. Union Carbide Corp., 1973-80; asst. reg. mgr. Eastern Region TransAmerica Corp., Elizabeth, NJ, 1980-82, reg. mgr. Eastern Region, 1982; regional mgr. Central Region TransAmerica Corp., Chgo., 1982-89; v.p. The Fred Barbara Co., Chgo., 1989-90; v.p., gen. mgr. Global Internat. Systems, 1990—; mem. bd. dirs. Global Internat. Systems, Inc., Oakland, Calif. Presbyn. Office: Global Intermodal Systems 11700 Wallisville Rd Houston TX 77013-3498

IFFY, LESLIE, medical educator; b. Budapest, Hungary, May 17, 1925; came to U.S., 1969; s. Zoltan and Rozsa (Lantos) I.; m. Maureen B. Deeney. MD, U. Budapest, Hungary, 1949; MD (hon.), Semmelweis U., Budapest, 1993. Diplomate Am. Bd. Ob-Gyn. Resident, fellow Országos Testnevelési és Sportegészségügyi Intézet Hosp. Ministry of Health, Budapest, 1951-56; fellow U. Wash., Seattle, 1964; asst. prof. Temple U., Phila., 1969-70; assoc. prof. U. Ill., Chgo., 1971-72, Jefferson Med. Coll., Phila., 1972-73; prof. U. Medicine and Dentistry of N.J., Newark, 1974—; dir. obstetrics U. Hosp., Newark, 1974—. Contbr. over 170 articles to profl. jours. and chpts. to books; editor: Perinatology Case Studies, 1978, 85, Obstetrics and Perinatology, 1981 (in English and Spanish), Operative Perinatology, 1984 (in English, Spanish and Japanese), Operative Obstetrics, 2d edit., 1992. Recipient Dr. Robert Jardine Rsch. prize U. Glasgow, 1963, Ford Found. rsch. fellowship, Seattle, 1964, hon. fellowship Hungarian Obstet. Soc., 1986. Fellow Royal Coll. Surgeons (Can.); mem. Cen. Assn. Ob-Gyn. (life), Chgo. Gynecol. Soc., Am. Coll. Legal Medicine (bd. dirs. 1989-95), Royal Coll. Physicians (Edinburgh, Scotland, licentiate), Royal Faculty Physicians and Surgeons (Glasgow, Scotland, licentiate), Romanian Soc. Obstetricians and Gynecolodists (hon.). Avocations: music, chess, literature. Home: 5 Robin Hood Rd Summit NJ 07901-3718 Office: NJ Med Sch UMDNJ 150 Bergen St Newark NJ 07103-2406

IGARASHI, PETER, nephrologist, educator, researcher; b. L.A., Dec. 31, 1956; married; 2 children. BS in Biomed. Scis. with highest honors, U. Calif., Riverside, 1978; MD, UCLA, 1981. Diplomate Am. Bd. Internal Medicine. Intern & resident dept. internal medicine Davis Med. Ctr. U. Calif., Sacramento, 1981-84; postdoctoral fellow nephrology dept. internal medicine Sch. Medicine Yale U., New Haven, 1984-87, asst. prof. medicine dept. internal medicine, 1987-92, assoc. prof. medicine, 1992—; attending physician Yale-New Haven Hosp., 1987—, Vets. Affairs Conn. Health Care Systems, West Haven, 1987—; dir. nephrology fellowship recruitment/selection Yale U., 1992—; chmn. renal physiology-molecular biology physiol. processes abstractr review com. Am. Soc. Nephrology, 1990; ad hoc mem. NIH Gen. Medicine B study sect., 1996; spkr. in field. Editl. bd. Am. Jour. Physiology: Renal, Fluid and Electrolyte Physiology, 1996—; contbr. articles to profl. jours. Recipient Merck Med. Book award, 1981, Lange Med. Book award, 1981, Physician-Scientist award NIH, 1985-90; grantee NIH; Carl Fuglie Meml. scholar, 1978. Mem. AAAS, Am. Heart Assn. (kidney coun., New Eng. regional peer review com. 1991-94, rsch. com. Conn. affiliate 1994—, New Investigator award 1990-93, Established Investigator award 1995—, grantee), Am. Soc. Nephrology, Nat. Kidney Found. (fellowship review com. 1988-91), Am. Soc. Biochemistry & Molecular Biology, Am. Physiology Soc., Salt and Water Club, Phi Beta Kappa, Alpha Omega Alpha. Office: Yale U Sch Medicine Dept Nephrology 2073 LMP PO Box 208029 New Haven CT 06520-8029*

IGASAKI, PAUL M., federal agency administrator. BA, Northwestern U.; JD, U. Calif., Davis. Rep. Japanese Am. Citizens League, Washington; exec. dir. Asian Law Caucus, San Francisco; vice chmn. EEOC, Washington, 1994-97, 98—, chmn., 1997-98; leadership of EEOC task force resulted of overhaul of case processing and creation of a Nat. Enforcement Plan; as cmty. liaison with City of Chgo.'s Human Rels. Commn., provided mgmt. and legal counsel, served as Mayor Harold Washington's liaison to Asian Am. communities; served on Mayor Washington's Affirmative Action Coun. and as 1st dir. of Chgo. Commn. on Asian Am. Affairs; worked for ABA as dir. of Pvt. Bar Involvement Project and as pro bono coord.; Reginald Heber Smith fellow in cmty. law, working as staff atty. with Legal Svcs. of Northern Calif.; legal asst. to chmn. Calif. Agrl. Labor Rels. Bd.; while a student was intern to U.S. Rep. Abner J. Mikva (D-Ill.). Served as pres. Chgo. Japanese Am. Citizens League; v.p. founder Chgo. Asian Bar Assn.; bd. dirs. Nat. Legal Aid and Defender Assn.; exec. com. Leadership Conf. on Civil Rights. Mem. ABA, State Bar of Calif. (exec. com. legal svcs. sect.). Office: US EEOC Office of the Chmn 1801 L St NW Washington DC 20507-0001*

IGBINEWEKA, ANDREW OSABUOHIEN, public administration/political science educator; b. Benin City, Edo State, Nigeria, Nov. 30, 1947; came to U.S., 1973, naturalized; s. Igbineweka Moses Iditua and Victoria Ilekhue (Idahor) Igbineweka; m. Pauline Omono Airen, June 24, 1980; children: Ofumwegbe, Oyemwen, Osagie, Osasu, Osaruyi. BA, U. Mary Hardin-Baylor, 1976; MA, U. North Tex., 1979, PhD, 1982. Libr. Immaculate Conception Coll., Benin City, 1968-69; clerical officer High Ct. of Justice Jud. Dept., Benin City, 1969-73; tchg. asst. U. North Tex., Denton, 1976-79; lectr. II, asst. prof. U. Benin, Benin City, 1983-85, lectr. I, 1985-89, sr. lectr., 1989-92, head dept., 1990-91; Disting. vis. prof. U. Calgary, Alta., Can., 1992; vis. prof. Indiana U. Pa., 1992-94; ind. rsch. cons. Pitts., 1994—; mem., cons. U. Benin Consulting Svcs., 1984-92; therapist Suzanne and Assocs. and Western Bell, Pitts., 1997—; casemanager Shuman Juvenile Detention Ctr., Pitts., 1998—; therapeutic staff support, therapist Sharp Visions Inc., Pitts., 1999—, therapeutic staff support and mobile therapist, Pressly Ridge Schs, Pitts., 1999—. Contbr. chpts. to books and articles to profl. jours. Chmn. Getty's Dormitory, U. Mary Hardin-Baylor, Belton, Tex., 1974-75, v.p. Internat. Club, 1974-75, chmn. Bapt. Students Union Internat., 1974-76, pres., founder chess club, 1975-76; chmn. constn. revision com. Nigerian Students Assn., U. North Tex., 1977, pres., 1981-82; senate mem. U. Benin, 1990-91; chmn. Aduwa Club constn. revision com., Benin City, 1992; vol. Lay Reader's Assn., St. Albert's Cath. Ch., U. Benin, 1984-92, Parish Laity Coun., 1984-92, Group Svcs. to Aged Patients of Beacon Manor, Inc., spring 1994; active St. Paul Cathedral, 1999—. Recipient Internat. Student Scholarship award Southwestern U., Georgetown, Tex., 1973-74, U. Mary Hardin-Baylor, Belton, 1974-76, 75-76, Hon. Scholarship award, 1975-76; grantee U. Benin, Benin City, 1984-85, 87-88, Indiana U. Pa., 1992-93, 93-94. Mem. ASPA, Am. Polit. Sci. Assn., Policy Studies Orgn., Internat. Polit. Sci. Assn. (rsch. com.), Nigerian Inst. Mgmt. Cons. (pub. rels. officer 1986-97), U.S. Chess Fedn. (U. Pitts. chess club chpt.), Pitts. Chess Club, Pi Sigma Alpha, Phi Alpha Theta. Avocations: chess, billiards, soccer coaching, religious activities, cruising the Internet.

IGER, ROBERT A., broadcast executive; b. N.Y.C., 1951; m. Willow Bay, Oct. 1995; children: Kate, Amanda, Max. Grad. magna cum laude, Ithaca Coll. Studio supr. ABC-TV, 1974-76; various pos. ABC-TV Sports, 1976-85; former v.p. program planning, development ABC Sports, 1985-87, v.p. program planning and acquisition, 1987-88; exec. v.p. ABC TV Network Group, 1988-89, pres., 1992-94; pres. ABC Entertainment, 1989-92; exec. v.p. Capital Cities/ABC Inc., N.Y.C., 1993-94, pres., COO, 1994-96; pres. ABC, Inc., N.Y.C., 1996—. Trustee Ithaca Coll. Office: ABC Inc 77 W 66th St Rm 100 New York NY 10023-6298

IGGERS, GEORG GERSON, history educator; b. Hamburg, Germany, Dec. 7, 1926; came to U.S., 1938, naturalized, 1949; s. Alfred G. and Lizzie (Minden) I.; m. Wilma Abeles, Dec. 23, 1948; children: Jeremy, Daniel, Karl Jonathan. BA, U. Richmond, 1944; AM, U. Chgo., 1945, PhD, 1951; post-grad., New Sch. Social Rsch., 1945-46. Instr. U. Akron, Ohio, 1948-50; assoc. prof. Philander Smith Coll., Little Rock, 1950-57; from assoc. prof. to prof. Dillard U., New Orleans, 1957-63; assoc. prof. Roosevelt U., Chgo., 1963-65; prof. history SUNY, Buffalo, 1965—, disting. prof., 1978-97, chmn., 1981-84, prof. emeritus, 1997—; mem. Conf. Group Ctrl. European History, vice chmn., 1989-90, chmn., 1990-91; vis. prof. U. Ark., Fayetteville, 1956-57, 64, U. Rochester, 1970-71, U. Leipzig, Germany, 1992; vis. assoc. prof. Tulane U., New Orleans, 1958-60, 63; vis. scholar Technische Hochschule Darmstadt, Germany, 1991, Forschungsschwerpunkt zeithistorische Studien, Potsdam, Germany, 1993; fellow Woodrow Wilson Ctr. Internat. Scholars, Washington, 1993-94; vis. prof. Aarhus (Denmark) U., 1998, Zentrum für Zeithistorische Forschung Potsdam, Germany, 1998, U. New Eng. (Australia), 1999. Author: The Cult of Authority, 1958, The German Conception of History, 1968, New Directions in European Historiography, 1975, Geschichtswissenschaft im 20 Jahrhundert, 1993, Historiography in the Twentieth Century, 1997; editor: with Harold T. Parker) International Handbook of Historical Studies, 1979, The Social History of Politics, 1986, (with James Powell) Leopold von Ranke and the Shaping of the Historical Discipline, 1990, Ein anderer historischer Blick Beispiele ostdeutscher Sozialgeschichte, 1991, Marxist Historiography in Transformation, 1991; co-editor Storia della Storiografia jour., Geschichtswissenschaft der DDR as Forschungsproblem, Historische Zeitschrift, Sonderbaud 27, 1998; mem. editl. bd. Zeitschrift für Geschichtswissenschaft, History and Theory. Bd. dirs., counselor Draft and Mil. Counseling Ctr., Buffalo, 1967-89; bd. dirs.Citizens Coun. Human Rels., Buffalo, 1965—; chmn. edn., exec. coms. NAACP, Little Rock, 1951-56, chmn. edn. com., New Orleans, 1957-63, bd. dirs, Buffalo, 1965—, chmn. edn. com., 1965-75, co-chmn. health com., 1979-85. Fellow Guggenheim Found., 1960-61, Rockefeller Found., 1961-62, NEH, 1971-72, 78-79, 85-86, Ctr. Interdisciplinary Rsch., Bielefeld, Fed. Republic Germany, 1986-87; hon. fellow Fulbright Commn. 1978-79, 85-86, 87; recipient Kittler award Technische Hochschule Darmstadt, 1988, Alexander von Humboldt Rsch. prize 1993. Mem. Internat. Commn. Historiography (v.p. 1980-95, pres. 1995—), Am. Hist. Assn., German Studies Assn., Acad. Scis. of German Dem. Republic (fgn. mem. 1990-92). Home: 100 Ivyhurst Rd Amherst NY 14226-3441 Office: Dept History Park Hall SUNY Buffalo NY 14260-4130

IGLEHART, PATRICIA ANN, strategy and market planning executive; b. Waco, Tex., Jan. 2, 1944; d. Stephen Austin and Susie Odell (White) I.; m. Lance Dunn Shaw, June 11, 1965 (div. Dec. 1970). Student, Tex. A&M U., 1962-65; BS, N.Mex. State U., 1966; M in Natural Scis., Ariz. State U., 1971; MS in Applied Math. & Statistics, SUNY, Stony Brook, 1975; MS in Math., NYU, 1978; PhD in Math., Stevens Inst. Tech., 1996. Math. tchr. Gadsden H.S., Anthony, N.Mex., 1966-67, Glendale (Ariz.) Union H.S. Dist., 1968-69; math. dept. chmn. Phoenix H.S. Dist., 1969-73; sys. engr. IBM U.S. Eastern Area, Springfield, N.J., 1977-79, Piscataway, N.J., 1979-84; product adminstr. IBM ISG U.S., White Plains, N.Y., 1984-86; sys. engring. mgr. IBM NA Eastern Area, Harrison, N.Y., 1986-89; sr. program mgr. market rsch. studies and IT opportunity analysis IBM NA S&D Market Analyses, White Plains, N.Y., 1989-98; with e-bus. market intelligence Internet divsn. IBM, 1999—; mem. IBM NA Sr. Fin. Mgmt. Group, 1998; CEO, owner Dry-Glo Mktg., Carmel, N.Y., 1987-90. Sec. bd. Mt. Carmel Assembly of God, Carmel N.Y.; bd. dirs. Carmel Civic Assn.; bd. mgrs. Woodland Trail. Mem. Am. Math. Soc., Math. Assn. Am., Phi Kappa Phi. Democrat. Avocation: playing piano. Home: S-75 Woodland Tr Carmel NY 10512

IGLEHART, T. D., bishop. Bishop Ch. of God in Christ, San Antonio, Tex.; pastor Childress Meml. Ch. of God in Christ, San Antonio. Office: Ch of God in Christ 901 N Pine San Antonio TX 78202*

IGLEWICZ, BORIS, statistician, educator; b. Omsk, USSR, Oct. 11, 1939; came to U.S., 1952, naturalized, 1959; s. Solomon and Faiga (Brucker) I.; m. Raja Brody, May 24, 1973; children—David, Alana. B.S., Wayne State U., 1962; M.A., 1963; Ph.D., Va. Poly. Inst., 1967. Instr. math. Mich. Tech. U., 1963-64; asst. prof. stats. Case Western Res. U., 1967-69; asso. prof. stats. Temple U., 1969-74, prof., 1974—, dir. Ph.D. program in stats., 1970-76, chmn. dept., 1978-82, dir. biostats. group, 1992-93, dir. biostats. rsch. ctr., 1993—; v.p., dir. Meco Metals Corp., 1974; vis. prof. Harvard U., 1984-85. Author: (with J. Stoyle) An Introduction to Mathematical Reasoning, 1973, (with D.C. Hoaglin) How to Detect and Handle Outliers, 1993; contbr. articles to profl. jours., chpts. to books. NIH fellow, 1964-67; advanced rsch. fellow Harvard U., 1978. Fellow Royal Statis. Soc., Am. Statis Assn. (pres. Phila. chpt. 1981-83); mem. Biometric Soc., Inst. Math. Stats., Internat. Stats. Inst., Am. Soc. Quality Control (sr. mem.), Sigma Xi, Pi Mu Epsilon, Beta Gamma Sigma. Home: 1912 Rolling Ln Cherry Hill NJ 08003-3328 Office: Temple U Dept Stats Philadelphia PA 19122

IGNARRO, LOUIS J., pharmacology educator; b. Bklyn., May 31, 1941. BA in Pharmacy, Columbia U., 1962; PhD in Pharmacology, U. Minn., 1966. Prof. dept. molecular and med. pharmacology UCLA Sch. Medicine. Contbr. articles to profl. jours. Postdoctoral fellow NIH, 1966-68; recipient Rsch. Career Devel. award USPHS, 1975-80, Nobel prize in Medicine, 1998. Mem. NAS, Alpha Omega Alpha (hon.). Achievements include research in the biochemical, physiological, and pathophysioilogical roles of nitric oxide and cyclic GMP in mammalian cell function; the transcriptional, translational and catalytic regulation of constitutive and inducible nitric oxide synthases; the role of other biochemical pathways in the regulation of biosynthesis and metabolism of nitric oxide; the biochemical and chemical mechanisms by which nitric oxide elicits cytotoxic effects on invading target cells and microorganisms; the role of nitric oxide as a neurotransmitter in non-adrenergic non-cholinergic neurons innervating various issues. Office: UCLA Sch Medicine Dept Molecular & Med Pharmacology 23-315 CHS 10833 LeConte Ave Los Angeles CA 90095-1735*

IGNATAVICIUS, DONNA DENNIS, geriatrics and case management consultant; b. Salisbury, Md., Dec. 20, 1949; d. Barney J. and Mary P. (McCann) Dennis; m. Charles Ignatavicius, Nov. 22, 1978; children: Paul W. Elliott Jr., Stephanie M. Diploma, Peninsula Gen. Hosp., Salisbury, Md., 1969; BSN, U. Md., Balt., 1976, MS, 1981. RN, Md.; cert. gerontol. nurse and nursing case mgmt. Instr. Union Meml. Sch. of Nursing, Balt., 1978-81, U. Md. Sch. of Nursing, Balt., 1982-87; dir. nursing William Hill Manor, Easton, Md., 1988-91; owner DI Assocs., 1987—; clin. nurse specialist Meml. Hosp., Prince Frederick, Md., 1998—; lectr., seminar leader on gerontology and orthopedic topics, 1981—. Author: Medical-Surgical Nursing: across the Health Care Continuim (3d edit.), 1999, Pocket Companion for Medical-Surgical Nursing, (3d. edit.), 1999; contbr. articles in rsch. to profl. jours. Recipient Rsch. grant Md. Found. for Nursing; named Outstanding Grad. Student in Nursing Edn., U. Md., 1981. Mem. ANA, Md. Nurses Assn., Case Mgmt. Soc. of Am., Sigma Theta Tau. Home: 14660 Burnt Store Rd Hughesville MD 20637-2628

IGNATIEV, ALEX, physics researcher; b. Wehingen, Germany, Feb. 14, 1945; U.S. citizen; married; two children. BS, U. Wis., 1966; PhD in Material Sci., Cornell U., 1972. Postdoctoral fellow material sci. SUNY, Stony Brook, 1971-73; from asst. prof. to assoc. prof. physics and chemistry U. Houston, 1974-83, prof. physics and chemistry, 1983—; assoc. dir. Magnetic Info Rsch. Lab., 1984-89; mem. energy lab. U. Houston, 1975—; lectr. physics Aarhus U., Denmark, 1977-78; Fulbright sr. scholar, 1983; assoc. dir. Space Vacuum Epitaxy Ctr., 1986-88, dir. 1988—; task leader Tex. Ctr. for Superconductivity, 1987—. Assoc. editor Vacuum, Space Forum, Research Trends; contbr. numerous articles to profl. jours. Mem. AIAA, AAAS, Am. Phys. Soc., Am. Vacuum Soc., Am. Chem. Soc., Internat. Solar Energy Soc, The Materials Rsch. Soc., Sigma Xi. Office: U Houston-Space Vacuum Epitaxy Ctr Sci & Rsch Bldg 4800 Calhoun Rd Houston TX 77004-2610*

IGNATIUS, ALAN (ADI), magazine editor; b. Burbank, Calif., Sept. 10, 1958; s. Paul Robert and Nancy Sharpless (Weiser) I.; m. Dorinda Elliott, May 12, 1989; children: Oliver, Linus, Isaac. Student, Nankai U., Tianjin, China, 1980; BA, Haverford Coll., 1981; postgrad., Columbia U., 1991. News editor Petroleum News, Hong Kong, 1981-82; editor Asia 2000, Hong Kong, 1982-83; copy editor Asian Wall Street Jour., Hong Kong, 1983-84, editor Page One, 1984-85, reporter, 1985-87; bur. chief Wall Street Jour., Beijing, 1987-90, Moscow, 1992-94; mng. editor Ctrl. European Econ. Rev., Brussels, 1994-95; bus. editor Far Eastern Econ. Rev., Hong Kong, 1995-96; dep. editor Time Asia, Hong Kong, 1996—. Zuckerman fellow Columbia U., 1990-91. Office: 18 Whitfield Rd 34/F, Causeway Bay Hong Kong

IGNATONIS, SANDRA CAROLE AUTRY, special education educator; b. Dixon Mills, Ala., June 6, 1942; d. Charles Franklin Autry; m. Algis Jerome Ignatonis, June 15, 1968; children: Audra Carole, David Jerome. BA, Samford U., 1964; cert. in Gifted Edn., Kennesaw State U., 1989. Cert. tchr., Ga. Tchr. Jefferson County Bd. Edn., Birmingham, Ala., 1964, Huntsville (Ala.) Bd. Edn., 1964-71, Epiphany Cath. Sch., Miami, Fla., 1981, Cobb County Bd. Edn., Marietta, Ga., 1982, Bartow County Bd. Edn., Cartersville, Ga., 1990-92, Sequoria Group, Inc., Roswell, Ga., 1996; with Atlanta real estate divsn. Regions Bank, Atlanta, 1997—; mem. Sch. Self-Governance Com., Emerson, Ga., 1990-91, Soccer Adv. Bd., Marietta, 1985-89; judge, mem. Social Sci. Fair Competitions, Huntsville, 1964-71. Team mom Metro N. Youth Soccer Assn., Marietta, 1991-92; block parent Somerset Subdivision, Marietta, 1982-86; polit. chmn. Student Nat. Edn. Assn., Samford U., Birmingham, Ala., 1963-64. Recipient grant Samford U. Faculty, 1963. Mem. Ga. Supporters of Gifted, Profl. Assn. Ga. Educators, bd. dirs., Somerset Homeowners, 1997-99. Republican. Roman Catholic. Avocations: tennis, bowling, gardening, needle work, reading. Office: Regions Bank 400 Embassy Row 6600 Peachtree Dunwoody Rd NE Atlanta GA 30328-1649

IGNOFFO, CARLO MICHAEL, insect pathologist-virologist; b. Chicago Heights, Ill., Aug. 24, 1928; s. Joseph and Lucy (Sardo) I.; m. Florence F. Mielcarek, Sept. 3, 1949. B.S., No. Ill. U., 1950; M.S., U. Minn., 1954, Ph.D., 1957. Asst. prof. Iowa Wesleyan Coll., Mt. Pleasant, 1957-59; insect pathologist U.S. Dept. Agr., Brownsville, Tex., 1959-65; dir. entomology Internat. Minerals & Chems. Corp., Wasco, Calif. and Libertyville, Ill., 1965-71; lab. dir. U.S. Dept. Agr., Columbia, Mo., 1971-91; prof. dept. entomology U. Mo., 1974—. Served with Chem. Corps U.S. Army, 1954-56. Mem. AAAS, Internat. Orgn. Biol. Control (pres. 1974), Am. Inst. Biol. Scis., Soc. Invertebrate Pathology (editorial bd. 1965-68, assoc. editor 1992—, treas. 1968-70), Entomol. Soc. Am. Isolated, commercialized 1st viral pesticide; patentee in field. Office: Research Park 1503 S Providence Rd Columbia MO 65203-3535

IGNOFFO, MATTHEW FREDERICK, English language educator, writer, counselor; b. Chgo., July 22, 1945; s. Matthew Frederick and Virginia (Fenelon) I. BS, Loyola U., Chgo., 1967, PhD, 1972; MA, Northwestern U., 1968; reading specialist, Monmouth U., West Long Branch, N.J., 1981. Assoc. prof. English, U.S. Mil. Acad. Prep. Sch., Ft. Monmouth, N.J., 1972—; lectr. Monmouth U., 1996—. Author: What the War Did to Whitman, 1975, One Perfect Lover, 1988, Coping With Your Inner Critic, 1989 (Book Report Recommended 1990), Everything You Need to Know About Self-Confidence, 1996 (N.Y. Pub. Libr. Recommended 1996), 2nd edit., 1999. Capt. U.S. Army, 1972-77. Mem. MLA. Home: 19 Park Ave Eatontown NJ 07724-1610 Office: USMA Prep Sch Dept English Fort Monmouth NJ 07703

IGNOZZI, BRYAN K., management consultant; b. Pitts., Feb. 3, 1971; s. Gus Kenneth and Edith Jan (Andring) I. BS, Allegheny Coll., 1993; MBA, Rollins Coll., 1997. Real estate assoc. J&K Realty, Lower Burrell, Pa., 1991-94; cons. PNC Bank Corp., Pitts., 1994-96; prof. So. Coll., Orlando, 1998—; mgmt. cons. Dreifus Assocs. Ltd., Orlando, 1997-99; sr. cons. KPMG, LLP, Charlotte, N.C., 1998—. Vol. Habitat for Humanity. Mem. Nat. Assn. Campus Card Users, Smart Card Industry Assn., Am. Mktg. Assn. Roman Catholic. Home: 807 Odell Ct Matthews NC 28105 Office: KPMG LLP 2800 Two First Union Ctr Charlotte NC 28282

IGO, GEORGE JEROME, physics educator; b. Greeley, Colo., Sept. 2, 1925; s. Henry J. and Ida J. (Danielsen) I.; m. Nancy Tebow, May 12, 1953; children: Saffron, Peter Alexander. AB, Harvard Coll., 1949; MS, U. Calif., Berkeley, 1951, Phd, 1953. Postdoctoral Yale Univ., 1954, Brook Haven Nat. Lab., Upton, N.Y., 1955-57; instr. Stanford Univ., Palo Alto, Calif., 1957-59; guest prof. Univ. Heidelberg, Germany, 1960; staff mem. Lawrence Berkeley (Calif.) Lab., 1961-66, Los Alamos (N.Mex.) Nat. Lab., 1966-68; prof. UCLA, 1969—. With U.S. Army, 1944-46. Recipient Fulbright Travel award, 1960, Saclay, France, 1970, Sr. Scientist award Alexander von Humboldt Found., 1991, 95. Fellow Am. Phys. Soc. Office: UCLA Dept Physics 405 Hilgard Ave Los Angeles CA 90095-9000

IGOE, TERENCE B., airport terminal executive; b. Phila., Nov. 9, 1941; s. Thomas B. and Elizabeth R. (Graham) I.; m. Patricia Diane Voss, Sept. 14, 1974; children: Michael, Suzanne. BS in Aviation Mgmt., Met. State Coll. Denver, 1974. Accredited airline exec. Adminstrv. asst. Stapleton Internat. Airport, Denver, 1975-80; airport mgr. Cheyenne (Wyo.) Airport Bd., 1980, Natrona County Internat. Airport, Casper, Wyo., 1980-84; pres. Met. Knoxville Airport Authority, 1984—; bd. dirs. Airports Coun. Internat. N.Am.; examiner Am. Assn. Airport Execs., 1991-93. Bd. dirs. Jr. Achievement of East Tenn., Nat. Kidney Found. East Tenn. Capt. U.S. Army, 1966-71, Vietnam. Mem. Skal Club, Rotary. Avocation: pvt. pilot. Home: 10550 Lakecove Way Knoxville TN 37922-5529 Office: Knoxville Airport Authority PO Box 15600 Knoxville TN 37901-5600*

IGUSA, JUN-ICHI, mathematician, educator; b. Japan, Jan. 30, 1924; came to U.S., 1953; s. Shiro and Rui (Fukushima) I.; m. Yoshie Yamamoto, Oct. 7, 1948; children—Kiyoshi, Takeru, Mitsuru. MA, Tokyo Imperial U., 1945; PhD, Kyoto (Japan) U., 1953. Assoc. prof. Kyoto (Japan) U., 1949-53; research assoc. Harvard U., 1953-55; mem. faculty Johns Hopkins, 1955—, prof. math., 1961-93, prof. emeritus, 1993—, J.J. Sylvester chair, 1986-93; chmn. bd. dirs. Japan-U.S. Math. Inst. Johns Hopkins U., 1987-93. Author: Theta Functions, 1972, Forms of Higher Degree, 1978; editor-in-chief: Am. Jour. Math., 1978-93. Mem. Math. Soc. Japan, Am. Math. Soc., Phi Beta Kappa. Home: 14209 Greencroft Ln Hunt Valley MD 21030-1111 Office: Johns Hopkins Univ Baltimore MD 21218

IGWE, GODWIN JOSEPH, chemical engineer; b. Omoku, Nigeria, Jan. 1, 1952; came to U.S., 1988, naturalized citizen, 1998; s. Christianah (Ellah) I.; m. Rose C. Okoroego, Jan. 7, 1971; children: Maureen, Chukwudi, Chukwuemeka. BSChemE, U. Kiel, 1977; MPhil, U. Leeds, U.K., 1981; PhD, U. Bradford, Eng., 1983. Registered profl. engr., Tex. Dir. Flopetrol (Schlumberger) Nigeria Ltd., Lagos, Nigeria, 1985-87; dir./mem. governing coun. Rivers State Govt. Sch. of Basic Studies, Port Harcourt, Nigeria, 1987-88; prof. chem. engring. Prairie View (Tex.) A & M U., Prairie View, 1989-91; sr. staff engr. Conoco Inc., Ponca City, Okla., 1992-93; sr. rsch. engr. DuPont Ctrl. R&D, Wilmington, Del., 1993—; cons. Core Labs. Integrated Environ. Svcs., Western Atlas Corp., Houston, 1991; prof. chem. engring. U. Benin, Nigeria, 1990; vis. prof. chem. engring. Tex. A&M Dept. Chem. Engring., College Station, Tex., 1988-89; sr. lectr. Dept. of Chem. and Petrochem. Engring., Rivers State U. of Sci. and Tech., Port Harcourt, 1984-88; chem. engr. Schleicher & Schull, GmbH Filter Mfrs., Dassel, Germany, 1976; world bank cons., 1989—. Author: Needle Felts in Gas and Dust Filtration, Surface Structure of Needle-felted Gas Filters: Microscopical Examination Techniques, Powder Technology and Multiphase Systems; contbr. articles to profl. jours. including Jour. of Magyar Textiltechnika, Jour. of Indsl. Engring. Chemistry Rsch., Jour. of Chem. Engring. and Tech., Jour. of the Textile Inst., Indian Jour. of Tech., others. Robert S. McNamara fellowship World Bank, 1988, Alexander von Humboldt fellowship, 1992. Mem. AIChE (bd. dirs. environ. divsn. 1997—), Soc. of Petroleum Engrs., Water Environ. Fedn., The Metal Soc., Am. Filt. and Sep. Soc. (editl. bd.). Achievements include patent on organic destruction of contaminants in soil and polyamide, polyurethane micro blend and process; research on surface area measurement and gas permeametry at sub-atmospheric pressures, influence of some production parameters on the characteristics of needle felts for air filtration. Avocations: table tennis, world affairs, travelling. Home: 16 Anderson Ln Newark DE 19711-3064 Office: EI DuPont de Nemours BMP 14/2288 Barley Mill Plz Wilmington DE 19880

IHARA, MICHIO, sculptor; b. Paris, France, Nov. 17, 1928; s. Usaburo and Shigeko (Shinkai) I.; m. Doreen Joyce Kaplan, July 7, 1966; 1 child, Akeo. BFA, Tokyo U. Fine Arts, 1953. Fulbright fellow MIT, 1961-62, rsch. assoc., 1962-64; instr. Musashino U. Fine Arts, Tokyo, 1966-69. One-man shows Kanegis Gallery, Boston, 1964, Tokyo Gallery, 1970, Staempfli Gallery, N.Y.C., 1977, 80, 84; numerous group shows in Japan and U.S., 1957-74; important works include marble mural Chuo-koron Pub. Co, Tokyo, 1957; copper relief 275 Wyman St. Office Bldg, Waltham, Mass., 1963; altar canopy Josenji Temple, Tokyo, 1965; metal screen Imperial Theatre, Tokyo, 1966; relief Internat. Christian U, Tokyo, 1967, Fuji Film Co. Bldg, Tokyo, 1969; sculpture Internat. Sculptors Symposium, Osaka, 1970, Wellesley (Mass.) Office Park, 1973, Fitchburg (Mass.) Pub. Library; civic sculpture, Auckland, N.Z., 1977, Constellation Place, Balt., 1978; metal screen Rockefeller Center, N.Y.C., 1978, Neiman-Marcus, Beverly Hills, Calif., New World Hotel, Hong Kong, Pavilion Hotel, Singapore; wall sculpture S.E. Bank, Miami, 1983; suspended sculptures Marriott Marquis Hotel, N.Y.C., 1985, wall sculpture Harvard U., 1985, 89, wind sculpture, Tallahassee City Hall, 1989, tower sculpture Tokyo City Hall, 1991, suspended sculptures AT&T Plaza, Chgo., 1991, Colorado Springs Airport, 1994, Wall Sculpture Ikenoue Ch., Tokyo, 1995, suspended sculpture Lorillard Headquarters, N.C., 1997, interactive sculpture Cyclelight, Boston 1st Night, 1993. Trustee The Artists Found. Mass. JDR 3d Fund grantee, 1970-71; recipient award Mass. Council Arts and Humanities, 1974, Nat. Inst. Arts and Letters/Am. Acad. Arts and Letters award in art, 1973; Graham Found. fellow, 1963-64; MIT Center for Advanced Visual Studies fellow, 1970-73. Mem. Japan Artists Assn. Address: 63 Wood St Concord MA 01742-2225

IHDE, AARON JOHN, history of science educator emeritus; b. Neenah, Wis., Dec. 31, 1909; s. John Lewis and Ella (Haase) I.; m. Olive Jane Tipler, June 14, 1933 (dec. Mar. 28, 1988); children: Gretchen (Mrs. Hendrick Serrie), John. BS, U. Wis., 1931, MS, 1939, PhD, 1941. Chemist Blue Valley Creamery Co., Chgo., 1931-38; instr. chemistry Butler U., Indpls., 1941-42; mem. faculty U. Wis.-Madison, 1942—, prof. chemistry, integrated liberal studies and history of sci., 1958-80, emeritus prof., 1980—, chmn. dept. integrated liberal studies, 1963-70; Carnegie intern in gen. edn. Harvard, 1951-52; Mem. Wis. Food Standards Adv. Com., 1955-68, chmn., 1964-65. Author: The Physical Universe, 1963, Development of Modern Chemistry, 1964, 2d edit., 1984, Selected Readings in the History of Chemistry, 1965, (with others) Joseph Priestley, Scientist, Theologian, and Metaphysician, 1980, Chemistry: As Viewed from Bascom's Hill, 1990. Recipient Dexter award history of chemistry divsn. Am. Chem. Soc., 1968, U. Wis. Chancellors award for disting. teaching, 1978. Mem. AAAS, History of Sci. Soc., Am. Chem. Soc. (Dexter award history of chemistry div. 1968), Soc. History of Tech., Wis. Acad. Scis., Arts and Letters (pres. 1963-64), Sigma Xi, Phi Lambda Upsilon. Unitarian. Home: 636 Mecca Dr Sarasota FL 34234-2713

IHDE, DANIEL CARLYLE, health science executive; b. Parsons, Kans., July 10, 1943; m. Mary Katherine Nanninga, 1968; children: Steven C., Douglas H. BS summa cum laude, Ea. N.Mex. U., 1964; MD, Stanford U., 1969. Diplomate Nat. Bd. Med. Examiners, Am. Bd. Internal Medicine. Intern, then resident The N.Y. Hosp., N.Y.C., 1969-71; fellow in med. oncology Meml. Hosp., N.Y.C., 1971-73; clin. assoc. medicine br. Nat. Cancer Inst., Bethesda, Md., 1973-75, sr. investigator VA Med. Ctr., 1975-81, dep. chief, head clin. investigations sect. Nat. Naval Med. Ctr., 1981-91, dep. dir., 1991-94; asst. prof. medicine Georgetown U., Washington, 1978-82, clin. asst. prof, 1982-83; assoc. prof. medicine Uniformed Svcs. U. Health Scis., Bethesda, 1981-85; prof. medicine U. Health Scis., Bethesda, 1985-91, dir. divsn. hematology/oncology, dept. medicine, 1987-90; chief med. oncology, prof. medicine Washington U., St. Louis, 1994-98; dir. Cancer Ctr. Planning Grant, 1995-98; prof. medicine U. South Fla., Tampa, 1998-99; cons. in med. oncology VA Med. Ctr., Washington, 1982-83; cons., mem. oncology drugs adv. com. FDA, 1991-95; mem. splty. bd. med. oncology Am. Bd. Internal Medicine, 1991-96; mem. clin. rsch. subpanel Nat. Cancer Inst., 1978-80, mem. drug decision network com., 1979-83, mem. promotion/tenure rev. panel, 1983-85. Editor-in-chief Jour. Nat. Cancer Inst., 1989-94; assoc. editor Cancer Treatment Reports, 1979-84, Cancer Investigation, 1988-93, Cancer Rsch., 1989-90, Clin. Cancer Rsch., 1994—; mem. editorial bd. Jour. Clin. Oncology, 1992-94; guest editorial bd. Japanese Jour. Clin. Oncology, 1992—; assoc. editor European Jour. Cancer, 1995-96, mem. editl. bd., 1996—; contbr. articles to profl. jours. With USPHS, 1973-85. Recipient Med. Alumni Rsch. award Stanford U., 1969, Outstanding Alumni award Ea. N.Mex. U., 1980, USPHS Commendation medal, 1984, Merit award NIH, 1992. Fellow ACP; mem. Am. Soc. Clin. Oncology (ad hoc com. FDA liaison 1988-89, chairperson ann. meeting 1989, chair nominating com. 1990-91, chair lung/head and neck/CNS sect. program com. 1991-92), Am. Assn. Cancer Rsch. (program com. 1985-86, 91-92, chair ann. meeting 1985, 96, 92), Internat. Assn. Study Lung Cancer (chair worldwide conf. 1980, 85, 88, 91, 94).

IHDE, DON, philosophy educator, university administrator; b. Hope, Kans., Jan. 14, 1934; s. Melvin Millard and Nell Pearl (Reikeman) I.; m. Carolyn W. Ihde (div.); children: Leslie Ann, Lisa Ihde-Costa, Eric Martin; m. Linda Einhorn, Apr. 4, 1985; 1 child, Mark Hillel. BA, U. Kans., 1956; MDiv, Andover Newton Theol. Sem., 1959; PhD, Boston U., 1964; prof. honoraria, El Rosario U., Bogota, Columbia, 1982. Asst. prof. So. Ill. U., Carbondale, 1964-67, assoc. prof., 1968-69; assoc. prof. SUNY, Stony Brook, 1969-70, prof., 1971-86, dean humanities and fine arts, 1985-90, leading prof., 1986—, disting. prof., 1997—. Author: Hermeneutic Phenomenology, 1971, Sense and Significance, 1973, Listening and Voice, 1976, Experimental Phenomenology, 1977, Technics and Praxis: A Philosophy of Technology, 1979, Existential Technics, 1983, Conequences of Phenomenology, 1986, Technology and the Life World, 1990, Instrumental Realism, 1991, Philosophy of Technology, 1993, Postphenomenology, 1993, Expanding Hermeneutics, 1998; editor: The Conflict of Interpretations (Paul Ricouer); (with Richard M. Zaner) Phenomenology and Existentialism, 1973, Selected Studies in Phenomenology and Existential Philosophy, vol. IV, 1974, Interdisciplinary Phenomenology, vol. VI, 1977; (with Hugh J. Silverman) Selected Studies in Phenomenology and Existential Philosophy, vols. IX, XI, 1985; mem. editorial bd. Ind. U. Press, Northwestern U. Press. Recipient Jr. award So. Soc. for Philosophy and Psychology, 1966; summer rsch. fellow So. Ill. U., 1966, 67, 68, 69; Fulbright rsch. fellow U. Paris, 1967-68, sr. fellow NEH, 1972, vis. rsch. fellow Australian Nat. U., 1985, vis. scholar U. Sydney, 1991; grantee SUNY, Stony Brook, 1970, NSF, 1981. Mem. AAAS, Am. Philos. Assn. (mem. program com. 1976, 88, nominating com. 1981-83), Am. Psychol. Assn. (mem. sect. D), Heidegger Conf., Husserl Circle, Merleau-Ponty Circle, Nat. Assn. Sci., Tech. and Soc., Soc. Phenomenology and Existential Philosophy (exec. co-dir. 1972-75, 81-84), Soc. Philosophy and Tech. (bd. dirs. 1983-86, editor Ind. series), Phi Beta Kappa. Office: SUNY Dept Philosophy Stony Brook NY 11794-3391

IHDE, MARY KATHERINE, mathematics educator; b. St. Louis, Jan. 19, 1942; d. Harold Orville and Katharine Marie (Bartsch) Nanninga; m. Daniel Carlyle Ihde, Dec. 22, 1968; children: Steven Carlyle, Douglas Harold. BA in Math., Northwestern U., 1964; MS in Math. Edn., Stanford U., 1968. Cert. tchr., N.Y., Calif., Md. Tchr. math. Shawnee Mission (Kans.) H.S. Dist., 1964-67; math. specialist Columbia Grammar and Prep. Sch., N.Y.C., 1969-72; tchr. math. Georgetown Visitation Prep. Sch., Washington, 1981-84; lectr. math. Mt. Vernon Coll., Washington, 1984-85; tchr. math. Nat. Cathedral Sch. for Girls, Washington, 1985-93, chmn. dept., 1989-92; instr. math. Maryville U., St. Louis, 1994-95, Webster U., St. Louis, 1994-95; tchr. math., curriculum coord. Whitfield Sch., St. Louis, 1995-96; math. curriculum cons., 1996—. Recipient 2nd place state level competition award Mathcounts, 1992, 4th place, 1993; fellow Shell Oil Corp., 1967-68. Mem. Nat. Coun. Tchrs. Math., Math. Assn. Am., Pi Lambda Theta. Address: 8505 Kings Rail Way Tampa FL 33647

IHLANFELDT, WILLIAM, investment company executive, consultant; b. Belleville, Ill., Dec. 12, 1936; s. Raymond William and Olivia Anna (Boycourt) I.; m. D. Jeannine Huguelet, May 7, 1978; children: Troy, Kimberly, Holly. B.S., Ill. Wesleyan U., 1959, LL.D., 1980; M.A., Northwestern U., 1963, Ph.D., 1970. Adminstr., Monticello Coll., Godfrey, Ill., 1959-60; tchr., coach Rich Twp. High Sch., Park Forest, Olympia Fields, Ill., 1960-64; dir. fin. aid Northwestern U., Evanston, Ill., 1964-67, dean admission and fin. aid, 1973-78, v.p. instnl. relations, 1978-96; mng. dir. Hartline Investment Corp., Chgo., 1997—; chmn. pub. policy Consortium Financing Higher Edn., Cambridge, Mass., 1979-83; chmn. Fedn. Ill. Ind. Colls. and Univs., Springfield, 1981-83; chmn. Fedn. Com. on State Funding, 1993-95; Student Loan Mktg. Assn., Washington, 1975-95, CyberMark, 1995-96, Constrn. Loan Assn., 1995-98; cons. in field. Author: Achieving Optimal Enrollments and Tuition Revenues, 1980; contbr. chpts. to books, articles to profl. publs. Founder, Northwestern U. Chgo. Action Project, Evanston, 1966; Northwestern U./Evanston Research Park, 1984, pres., CEO, 1986-96; co-founder Ill. Ind. Higher Edn. Loan Authority, Northbrook, Ill., 1981; founder Ill. Rsch. Park Authority, 1996. Wieboldt Found. grantee, 1966, 67, 68. Mem. Indian Hill Club (Winnetka, Ill.), Univ. Club (Chgo.), Phi Delta Kappa. Avocations: tennis, golf, skiing.

IHNE, EDWARD ALAN, railroad official, city official; b. Seaford, N.Y., Nov. 9, 1951; s. Edward J. and Monica Ann (Selfridge) I.; m. Judith Palmer, June 9, 1973; children: Lisa, Shaun. BS in Mgmt., SUNY, Empire State, 1994. Transp. mgr. L.I. R.R.; dep. mayor Village of Patchogue, N.Y., commr. pub. safety, 1996-99. Vice chmn. Brookhaven Town Conservative Com., 1990-99; mem. exec. com. Suffolk County Conservative Party, 1992-99; N.Y. State Conservative del., 1992-99. Recipient Am. Eagle award Brookhaven Town Conservative Com., 1991. Mem. NRA, Suffolk County Dep. Sheriff Benevolent Assn. (assoc.), Patchogue Fire Dept. Benevolent and Exempt Assn., Elks. Roman Catholic. Home: 26 E 4th St Patchogue NY 11772-2312 Office: 14 Baker St Patchogue NY 11772-3815

IHRIE, JOHN RICHARD, III, art educator; b. Washington; s. John R. Jr. and Mary Frances (Collins) I.; m. Irma Wolf, Sept. 7, 1946 (div. June 1969); m. Mary Haddad, July 18, 1969. Student, Corcoran Sch. Art, 1935; LLB, Columbus U., 1942. Creator art tchg. srs. programs OASIS, Washington, 1994—, IONA, Washington, 1996—. Pastelist, watercolorist mediums used in painting series German Village, 1970's, Arlington House, Lee Mansion, 1970's, Nova Scotia, 1957, Bicentennial Sketch Book, Washington Mall, 1973-76, England, Scotland, Ireland, 1991, Jerusalem and Palestine of 19th Century, 1991-96. Mem. Corcoran Art Gallery, Smithsonian. With USCG. Presbyterian. Avocation: singing Irish songs. Home: Pastellery 3924 Livingston St NW Washington DC 20015

IHRIE, ROBERT, oil, gas and real estate company executive; b. Phila., Jan. 4, 1925; s. Theodore Richard and Ella Martha (Anderson) I.; m. Dorothy Myrtle Waltz, July 8, 1944 (div. 1983); children: Robert Jr., Richard William, David Wayne, Nancy Ellen; m. Nancy Jean Joseph, June 8, 1984. BS, valedictorian, Ursinus Coll., 1943; MBA with high distinction, Harvard U., 1947. From process engr., econ. analyst, foreman, head tng. dept. to head bus. analysis dept. Esso Standard Oil Co., Baton Rouge, 1947-59; head demand and supply coord. and planning dept. Exxon Corp., N.Y.C., 1959-62; asst. dep. adminstr. AID, asst. sec. of state Dept. State, Washington, 1962-64; v.p. Lippincott and Margulies, Inc., N.Y.C., 1965-68; sr. v.p. Am. Trading and Prodn. Corp., Balt., 1968—, also bd. dirs.; bd. dirs. Am. Trading Real Estate Properties, Balt. With U.S. Army, 1943-46. Baker scholar Harvard Grad. Sch. Bus., 1947; recipient Presdl. Citation. Mem. Am. Contract Bridge League (life master 1977). Presbyterian. Avocations: roller dance skating, coaching softball, theater, travel. Home: 212 E Ridgely Rd Timonium MD 21093-5239 Office: Am Trading & Prodn Corp PO Box 238 Baltimore MD 21203-0238

IHRIG, EDWIN CHARLES, JR., mathematics educator; b. Washington, June 26, 1947; s. Edwin Charles and Lenore (Kokas) I.; m. Laurie Heather McColgan, July 6, 1974; 1 child, Karen Ann. BS, U. Md., 1969, MA, 1970; PhD, U. Toronto (Can.), 1974. Postdoctoral fellow math. dept. U. New Brunswick, Fredericton, Can., 1974-75; asst. prof. math. dept. Dalhousie U., Halifax, N.S., Can., 1975-76, McMaster U., Hamilton, Ont., Can., 1976-79; assoc. prof. math. dept. Ariz. State U., Tempe, 1979-85, prof. math. dept., 1985—. Contbr. articles to Gen. Relativity, Nuclear Physics, Combinatorics, Differential Geometry, Group Theory. Home: 1032 E Riviera Dr Tempe AZ 85282-5533 Office: Ariz State U Dept Math Tempe AZ 85287

IHRIG, JUDSON LA MOURE, chemist; b. Santa Maria, Calif., Nov. 5, 1925; s. Harry Karl and Luella (LaMoure) I.; m. Gwendolyn Adele Montz, July 22, 1950; children—Kristin, Neil Marshall. B.S., Haverford Coll., 1949; M.A., Princeton U., 1951, Ph.D., 1952. Asst. prof. chemistry U. Hawaii, 1952-58, assoc. prof., 1958-72, prof., 1972-94, dir. honors program, 1958-64, 87-95, dir. liberal studies program, 1973-79, chmn. chemistry dept., 1981-86; prof. emeritus, 1994—; cons. chemistry local firms. Author publs. in field. Served with AUS, 1945-46. Mem. Am. Chem. Soc., Phi Beta Kappa, Sigma Xi. Home: 386 Wailupe Cir Honolulu HI 96821-1525 Office: U Hawaii 2545 The Mall Honolulu HI 96822-2233

II, JACK MORITO, aerospace engineer; b. Tokyo, Mar. 20, 1926; came to U.S., 1954, naturalized, 1966; s. Iwao and Kiku Ii.; children: Keiko, Yoshiko, Mutsuya. BS, Tohoku U., 1949; MS, U. Wash., 1956, PhD in Aero. and Astronautics, 1964; M in Aero. Engring., Cornell U., 1959; PhD in Engring., U. Tokyo, 1979. Reporter Asahi Newspaper Press, Tokyo, 1951-54; aircraft designer Fuji Heavy Industries Ltd. Co., Tokyo, 1956-58; mem. staff structures rsch. Boeing Co., Seattle, 1962—. Contbr. numerous articles on aerodyns. to sci. jours. Mem. AIAA, Japan Shumy and Culture Soc. (pres. 1976-96), Sigma Xi. Congregationalist. Office: The Boeing Co MS 67-HC Seattle WA 98124

IIDA, SHUICHI, physicist, educator; b. Kobe, Hyogo-Ken, Japan, Jan. 30, 1926; s. Shunzoh and Sono (Ueda) I.; m. Kyoko Matsuoka, Apr. 29, 1955; children: Mariko Takahara, Junko Kose. BS in Physics, U. Tokyo, 1947, PhD in Physics, 1958. Asst. prof. physics U. Tokyo, 1952-58, assoc. prof., 1958-68, prof., 1968-86, prof. emeritus, 1986; prof. Teikyo U., Sagamiko, Kanagawa, Japan, 1988-89, Utsunomiya, 1989-96; vis. prof. AT&T Bell Labs., Murray Hill., N.J., 1961-63. Contbr. articles to profl. jours. Mem. Am. Physics Soc., Magnetics Soc. IEEE, Japan Soc. Powder and Powder Metallurgy, N.Y. Acad. Sci., Magnetics Soc. Japan, Japan Inst. Metals, Physics Soc. Japan. Achievements include patents for ferrites; founder of unifying frame for physics; introduction of essential q-number theory in biophysics; solution of EPR problem; solution of wave-particle dualism; proposal of frontier notion principle; proposal of filamentary current loops for c-number structure of lepton and hadron particles; proposal of parasiton state pion in nuclei, existence of contra-particle for neutrinos and pions, Iida diagram for parity violation problems, completely electromagnetic origin of particle masses; completely electromagnetic origin of weak and strong interactions. Home and Office: 4-23-11 Funabashi, Setagaya-ku Tokyo 156-0055, Japan

IJIRI, YUJI, accounting and economics educator; b. Kobe, Japan, Feb. 24, 1935; came to U.S., 1959; s. Takejiro and Hiroko (Hanno) I.; m. Tomoko Nishimura, June 17, 1962; children: Lisa, Yumi. LLB, Ritsumeikan U., Kyoto, Japan, 1956; MS, U. Minn., 1960; PhD, Carnegie Mellon U., 1963; LLD (hon.), DePaul U., 1990; DSc in Bus. Adminstrn. (hon.), Bryant Coll., 1991. CPA, Japan. Staff mem. Price Waterhouse & Co., Tokyo, 1957-59; asst. prof. grad. sch. bus. Stanford (Calif.) U., 1963-65, assoc. prof. grad. sch. bus., 1965-67; prof. grad. sch. indsl. adminstrn. Carnegie Mellon U., Pitts., 1967-75, Robert M. Trueblood prof. acctg. and econs., 1975-87, Robert M. Trueblood univ. prof. acctg. and econs., 1987—; cons. Gulf Oil Corp., Pitts., 1968-85. Co-author: Skew Distributions and the Sizes of Business Firms, 1977, Kohlers Dictionary for Accountants, 6th edit., 1983, New Directions in Creative and Innovative Management, 1988; author: Momentum Accounting and Triple-Entry Bookkeeping, 1989; editor: Creative and Innovative Approaches to the Science of Management, 1993. Named inductee Acctg. Hall of Fame, Ohio State U., 1989. Fellow Acctg. Researchers Internat. Assn. (pres. 1979-81); mem. Am. Acctg. Assn. (pres. 1982-83, Outstanding Educator 1987), Fin. Execs. Inst. (chpt. bd. dirs. 1977-81), Beta Alpha Psi. Home: 5 Bayard Rd Apt 118 Pittsburgh PA 15213-1904 Office: Grad Sch Indsl Adminstrn Carnegie Mellon U Pittsburgh PA 15213

IKARD, FRANK NEVILLE, JR., lawyer; b. Wichita Falls, Tex., June 26, 1942; s. Frank Neville and Jean (Hunter) I.; children: Frank III, Jean, Charles; m. Kathleen P. Ikard, Feb. 14, 1998. BA, U. Tex., 1965, JD, 1968. Bar: Tex. 1968; cert. Tex. Estate Planning and Probate Law Bd. of Legal Specialization. Assoc. then ptnr. Clark, Thomas, Winters, & Shapiro, Austin, Tex., 1968-84; mng. ptnr. Jenkens & Gilchrist, Austin, 1985-88; ptnr. Johnson & Gibbs, Austin, 1988-92, Ikard & Golden, Austin, 1992—. Pres. probate and trust law coun. Tex. Acad. Real Estate, Austin, 1988-89; bd. dirs. Paramount Theatre, Austin, 1988-89, pres. bd. dirs., 1991-92; mem. fiduciary litigation com. Am. Coll. Trust and Estate Coun., 1991-92. Fellow Am. Coll. Probate Counsel, Tex. Bar Found.; mem. State Bar Tex. (chmn., sec.-treas. legis. com. real estate, probate trust law sect. 1983-84, coun. chmn.), Travis County Bar Assn., Tarry House, Headliners, Austin Club. Avocations: fly fishing, photography. Home: 1107 Gaston Ave Austin TX 78703-2507 Office: Ikard & Golden Ste 500 106 E Sixth St Austin TX 78701-2429

IKAWA-SMITH, FUMIKO, anthropologist, educator; b. Kobe, Japan, Sept. 10, 1930; arrived in Canada, 1960; d. Jokei and Sachi (Nakano) Ikawa; m. Takao Sofue, Jan. 1955 (div. 1958); m. Philip Edward Lake Smith, Nov. 1959; 1 child, Douglas Philip Edward. BA, Tsuda Coll., Tokyo, 1953; student Tokyo Met. U., 1954-55; AM in Anthropology, Radcliffe Coll., 1959; PhD in Anthropology, Harvard U., 1974. Asst. prof. McGill U., Montreal, Can., 1968-74, assoc. prof., 1974-79, chmn. dept. anthropology, 1975-80, prof., 1979—, dir. Ctr. East Asian Studies, 1983-88, chmn. dept. East Asian langs. and lits., 1983-88, assoc. acad. vice prin., 1991-96; vis. prof. Canadian studies Kwansei Gakuin U., Japan, 1996-97. Editor: Early Palaeolithic in South and East Asia, 1978, Proceedings of the First Meeting of The Social Sciences Association of Canada, 1989; mem. editl. bd. Anthrop. Sci., 1998—. Fellow Am. Anthrop. Assn. (exec. mem.-at-large archeology divsn. 1988-90), Current Anthropology (assoc.); mem. Pacific Sci. Assn. (life), Soc. Am. Archeology, Japan Studies Assn. Can. (acting pres. 1988-90, pres. elect 1999—), Indo-Pacific Prehistory Assn. (exec. com. 1990-98), Can. Asian Studies Assn. (chair Japan com. 1991-94), Quebec-Japan Bus. Forum, Internat. Amb.'s Club (dir. 1998—). Sigma Xi. Avocations: horticulture, piano. Home: 3955 Ramezay Ave, Montreal, PQ Canada H3Y 3K3 Office: McGill U Dept Anthropology, 855 Sherbrooke St W, Montreal, PQ Canada H3A 2T7

IKEDA, KAZUYOSI, physicist, poet; b. Fukuoka, Japan, July 15, 1928; s. Yosikatu and Misao (Misumi) I.; m. Mieko Akiyama, Nov. 20, 1956; children: Hiroko Ikeda Yamaguti, Yosihumi. *Father, Yosikatu Ikeda (deceased), as director of a gas company in Fukuoka, Japan, devoted his life to the development of the gas industry and the popularization of gas utilization in the city. Mother, Misao Ikeda, aged 95, has helped her husband for many years, taking care of all household matters. Wife, Mieko Ikeda, studied English literature at Fukuoka Women's University and, as a young girl, was trained to play the piano, which continues to be her hobby. Wife's father, Rokurobee Akiyama (deceased), was a university professor of German literature and published many literary books. Daughter, Hiroko Yamaguti, married, has a Master of Arts degree and is teaching linguistics in a university. Son, Yosihumi Ikeda, studied in the Faculty of Literature of Kyushu University and is highly interested in translating English.* 1st degree Rigakusi, Kyushu U., Fukuoka, Japan, 1951, DSc, 1957; D Environ. Sci. (hon.), Internat. Earth Environment U., 1993; DLitt (hon.), London Inst. Applied Rsch., 1995; diploma of honor, Inst. Affaires Internat., 1995. Asst. dept. physics Kyushu U. Faculty Sci., Fukuoka, 1956-60, assoc. prof. dept. physics, 1960-65; assoc. prof. dept. applied physics Osaka (Japan) U. Faculty Engring., 1965-68, prof. theoretical physics dept. applied physics, 1968-89, prof. theoretical and math. physics dept. math. scis., 1989-92, prof. emeritus, 1992—; pres. Internat. Earth Environment U., Japan, 1995—, prof. theoretical physics, 1992—. *Kazuyosi Ikeda, Doctor of Science, Honorary Doctor of Literature, is a scientist and poet. He has made outstanding contributions to science as a professor of theoretical physics and mathematical physics at Osaka University, publishing more than 100 papers and numerous books. His sphere of achievement is wide, ranging from statistical mechanics of an assembly of molecules to mechanical theory of a comet. In particular, his unique, rigorous mathematical theory of phase transitions and singularities has been widely noticed and very highly evaluated in the international academic world. He is also an eminent poet who has published numerous poems, in beautiful seven and five syllable meter, in Japanese and English. His unique poems on myriad subjects, based on his sincere love of creation, have gained many enthusiastic, admiring readers throughout the world.* Author: Statistical Thermodynamics, 1975, Mechanics Without Use of Mathematical Formulae--From a Moving Stone to Halley's Comet, 1980, Invitation to Mechanics--From the Fundamentals of Calculus to the Motion of a Comet, with Appendix on a comet in ancient times, 1985, (collection of poems) Bansyoo Hyakusi, 1986, Basic Mechanics, 1987, Basic Thermodynamics--From Entropy to Osmotic Pressure, 1991, The World of God, Creation and Poetry, 1991, Poems on the Hearts of Creation, 1993, Mountains, 1995, North South East and West, 1996, Graphical Theory of Relativity, 1998, Hearts of Myriad Things in the Universe, 1998, Kazuyosi's Poetry on the Animate and the Inanimate, 1998, Poems on Love and Peace, 1998; editor Modern Poetry, 1996—; contbr. more than 100 articles to profl. jours.; author serialized poems, essays on poetry. Hon. founder Olympoetry Movement, 1992—. Recipient Yukawa Commemorative Scholarship award Yukawa Found., 1954, World Biographical Hall of Fame award Hist. Preservations Am., 1990, prize Catania e il suo Vulcano Accademia Ferdinandea, 1994, Albert Einstein Acad. Cert. award for outstanding achievement Albert Einstein Internat. Acad. Found., 1998, Internat. Artistic-Literary prize of Primavera Catanase Accademia Ferdinandea, 1997, Pandit prize Indian Coun. Natural Medicine Rsch., 1999; named Knight of Yr., Internat. Writers and Artists Assn., 1995, Knight Templar Order, Lofsensic Ursinius Order, Holy Grail Order, Universal Knights Order, San Ciriaco Order, 1995, Order of Pegasus Highest Degree, Olympoetry Movement Fund, 1996. Fellow United Writers' Assn. (life), World Lit. Acad., Internat. Poets Acad. (life, Internat. Eminent Poet award 1993); mem. N.Y. Acad. Scis., Am. Biog. Inst. Rsch. Assn. (dep. gov. 1989—, continental gov. 1998—), World Inst. Achievement, Lifetime Achievement Acad. (Golden Acad. award 1991), Phys. Soc. Japan (com. mem. 1970—, chmn. Osaka br. 1976-77, 83-84, editor jour. 1976-78), Internat. Biog. Assn. (life patron 1990—), Internat. Biog. Ctr. (dep. dir. gen. 1989—), World Acad. Arts and Culture, World Congress of Poets, Confedn. Chivalry (mem. grand coun. 1991—, Chevalier Grand Cross 1991), Accademia Ferdinandea Scienze Lettere Arti (academician of honor 1994—), Order Internat. Fellowship (charter 1994—), World Parnassians Guild Internat. (hon. dir. 1995—), Acad. M.I.D.I. (senator 1995—), Coun. of States for Protection of Life (senator 1995—), Academia Argentina (academician 1995—), Internat. Parliament for Safety and Peace (Medalla al Merito 1995), Modern Poets Soc. (bd. dirs. 1996—), Accademia Internazionale Trinacria Lettere-Arte-Scienze (academician of merit 1997—), Leading Intellectuals of the World (founding charter mem. 1998—). Home: Nisi-7-7-11 Aomadani, Minoo-si Osaka 562-0023, Japan Office: Osaka U Fac Engring, Dept, Math Scis, 2-1 Yamadaoka, Suita-si Osaka 565-0871, Japan

IKEDA, MOSS MARCUS MASANOBU, retired state education official, lecturer, consultant; b. L.A., Sept. 11, 1931; s. Masao Eugene and Masako (Yamashina) I.; m. Shirley Yaeko Okimoto; children: Cynthia Cecile Ikeda Tamashiro, Mark Eugene, Matthew Albert. BE, U. Hawaii, 1960, MEd, 1962; postgrad. Stanford U., 1961-62; M in Mil. Art and Sci., U.S. Army Command and Gen. Staff Coll., 1975; grad. U.S. Army War Coll., 1976; EdD, U. Hawaii, 1986. Tchr., Farrington H.S., Honolulu, 1962-64; vice-prin. Kailua Intermediate Sch. 1964-65; adminstrv. intern Central Intermediate Sch., Honolulu, 1965-66; vice-prin. Kaimuki H.S., Honolulu, 1966-67; prin. Kawananakoa Intermediate Sch., Honolulu, 1967-68, Kailua H.S., 1969-71, Kalaheo H.S., Kailua, 1972-77; ednl. specialist Hawaii Dept. Edn., Honolulu, 1977-79, ednl. adminstr., 1979-95, ret., 1995; frequent spkr. on edn.; lectr. U. Hawaii, 1987—. Served with AUS, 1951-57, 68-69, col. U.S. Army ret. Decorated Legion of Merit, Army Commendation medal. Mem. Nat. Assn. Secondary Sch. Prins., Western Assn. Schs. and Colls. (past bd. dirs., pres., chair), Accrediting Commn. for Schs. (chair, commr. 1992-94), Network for Outcome-Based Schs., Commonwealth Coun. for Ednl. Adminstrn., Assn. U.S. Army, Res. Officers Assn., Go For Broke Assn., Army War Coll. Alumni Assn., Hawaii Govt. Employees Assn., Hawaii Assn. Ind. Schs. (bd. dirs. emeritus), Phi Delta Kappa, Phi Kappa Phi. Home and Office: 47-494 Apoalewa Pl Kaneohe HI 96744-4565

IKEDA, SATOSHI, thoracic and cardiovascular surgeon; b. Tokyo, Sept. 15, 1940; came to U.S., 1967; s. Kazuhiko and Aiko (Igarashi) I.; m. Nancy L. Beaty (div.); 1 child, Charles Formosa; m. Maureen Frances Kerwin, June 3, 1976 (div.); children: Morna, Leah, Daniel. MD, Keio U., Tokyo, 1965. Diplomate Am. Bd. Surgery, Am. Bd. Thoracic Surgery. Intern U. Wis., Madison, 1966-67, resident, 1967-71; surg. resident Michael Reese Hosp., Chgo., 1971-73; resident in thoracic surgery Thomas Jefferson U. Hosp., Phila., 1974-76; pvt. practice surgeon Wilmongton, Del., 1976—. Fellow ACS. Zen Buddhist. Avocations: fishing, skiing, tennis. Home: Brandywine Park #502 1704 N Park Dr Wilmington DE 19806-2144 Office: 2300 Pennsylvania Ave Wilmington DE 19806-1392

IKEDA, TSUGUO (IKE IKEDA), social services center administrator, consultant; b. Portland, Oreg., Aug. 15, 1924; s. Tom Minoru and Tomoe Ikeda; m. Sumiko Hara, Sept. 2, 1951; children: Wanda Amy, Helen Mari, Julie Ann, Patricia Kiyo. BA, Lewis & Clark Coll., 1949; MSW, U. Wash., 1951. Social group worker Neighborhood House, Seattle, 1951-53; exec. dir. Atlantic St. Ctr., Seattle, 1953-86; pres. Urban Partnerships, Seattle, 1986-88, Tsuguo "Ike" Ikeda and Assoc., Seattle, 1988—; cons. Seattle, 1988—; cons. Commn. on Religion and Race, Washington, 1973, North Northeast Mental Health Ctr., Portland, 1985; affirmative action cons. NASW, Washington, 1977; cons./trainer various other orgns.; conf. coord. Beyond the Mask of Denial Wash. State Conf. on Drug/Alcohol/Substance Abuse in the Asian/Pacific Islander Cmtys., 1993; coord. Minority Mental Health Colloquium in Wash., 1994-95; coord. Asian Pacific Islander Coming Home Together Summit-95, Tacoma, Asian Pacific Bi-Ann. Leadership Conf., 1995-96, craftsmanship trainer, 1996, 97, 98; Tsuguo "Ike" Ikeda, Pub. Svc. ann. award established in 1987; trainer region II Dept. Children and Family Svcs., Yakima, Wash., 1997, API Cons. and Tng. Project, 1998. Mem. Nat. Task Force to develop standards and goals for juv. delinquency, 1976; mem. Gov.'s Select Panel for social and health svcs., Olympia, Wash., 1977; chmn. Asian Am. Task Force, Community Coll., Seattle dist., 1982, King County Coordinated Health Care Initiative Client Edn., Mktg. Subcom., 1993; div. chmn. social agys. Seattle United Way campaign, 1985; vice-chmn. Wash. State Com. on Vocat. Edn., Olympia, 1985-86, chmn. 1986-87; chmn. regional adv. com. Dept. Social and Health Svcs., 1990-91; mem. Gov. Mike Lawry's Commn. on Ethics Govt., Campaign Practices, 1993—; mem. exec. task force King County Dept. Youth Svcs., 1996-97. With Mil. Intelligence Lang. Sch., 1945-46. Recipient cert. appreciation U.S. Dept. Justice, Washington, 1975-76, Am. Dream award Cmty. Coll. Dist., Seattle, 1984, Asian Counseling & Referral Svc., 1991, 95, Wing Lake Mus., 1991-92, Atlantic St. Ctr., 1992, Seattle Chinese Post, 1992, Bishop's award PNW Conf., U. Meth. Ch., Tacoma, Wash., 1984, cmty. svc. award Seattle Rotary Club, 1985, Outstanding Citizen award Mcpl. League, Seattle and King County, 1986, Outstanding Leadership award Dept. Social and Health Svcs., 1993, cmty. award South Pacific Islander Program Seattle Pub. Schs., 1993, Pasasalmat award Filipino Youth Activities, 1993, Brass Ring award Asian Am. Polit. Alliance, 1993, Cmty. award South Pacific Islander, 1993, Comm. Svc. award Asian Counseling and Referral Svc., 1994, Disting. Alumnus award Multicultural Alumni Partnership U. Wash. Alumni Assn., 1996, award Gen. Bd. Global Ministies, United Meth. Ch., 1995, Alvirita Little Svc. award Therapeutic Health Svc., 1999; recognized as Community Treasure, United Way of King County, 1996. Mem. NASW (chpt. pres., Social Worker of Yr. 1971, Social Work Pioneer 1995), Vol. Agy. Exec. Coalition (pres., Outstanding Cmty. Svc. award 1979), Ethnic Minority Mental Health Consortium (chmn., Outstanding Leader 1992, David E. "Ned" Skinner Cmty. Svc. award 1990), Minority Exec. Dirs. Coalition (organizer, mem. chmn. 1980-86). Democrat. Methodist. Avocations: collecting mint Am. stamps and memorabilia about Japanese Am. incarceration during World War II.

IKENBERRY, HENRY CEPHAS, JR., lawyer; b. Cloverdale, Va., Mar. 23, 1920; s. Henry Cephas and Bessie (Peters) I.; m. Margaret Sangster Henry, July 3, 1943; children: Anna Catherine Ikenberry Fawell, Mary Margaret Ikenberry Rauck. B.A., Bridgewater Coll., 1947; J.D., U. Va., 1947. Bar: Va. 1947, W.Va. 1948, D.C. 1948, U.S. Supreme Ct. 1954, U.S. Ct. Claims 1972, U.S. Ct. Appeals (fed. cir.) 1982. Asso. firm Steptoe & Johnson, Washington, 1947-49, 50-53; partner, former chmn. exec. com. Steptoe & Johnson, 1953-85, of counsel, 1986-92; asst. counsel Gen. Aniline & Film Co., N.Y.C., 1949-50; mem. com. on unauthorized practice D.C. Ct. Appeals, 1972-76. Ruling elder Chevy Chase Presbyn. Ch., Washington, 1970-72; trustee Mary Baldwin Coll., Staunton, Va., 1979-92, mem. exec. com., 1987-92. Lt. comdr. USNR, 1941-46, ETO, PTO, Okinawa, The Philippines. Recipient Alumni citation Bridgewater Coll., 1960; named Ky. col., 1973. Mem. Bar Assn. D.C. (chmn. com. on corp. law 1960-61, com. comml. bus. law 1969-72), Raven Soc., Am. Legion, Metropolitan Club, Chesapeake Bay Yacht Club, Chevy Chase Club, Talbot Country Club (Easton, Md.), Order of Coif, Phi Delta Phi, Tau Kappa Alpha. Home: Pine Lodge 26783 Miles River Rd Easton MD 21601-5013 also: 8101 Connecticut Ave Apt N308 Chevy Chase MD 20815-2824 also: Pine Lodge 26783 Miles River Rd Easton MD 21601-5013

IKENBERRY, STANLEY OLIVER, education educator, former university president; b. Lamar, Colo., Mar. 3, 1935; s. Oliver Samuel and Margaret (Moulton) I.; m. Judith Ellen Life, Aug. 24, 1958; children: David Lawrence, Steven Oliver, John Paul. BA, Shepherd Coll., 1956; MA, Mich. State U., 1957, PhD, 1960, LHD (hon.); LLD (hon.), Millikin U.; LHD (hon.), Ill. Coll., Rush U., W.Va. U., Towson State U., Bridgewater (Va.) Coll., Bradley U. Instr. office Mich. State U., 1958-60, instr. instl. rsch. office, 1960-62; asst. to provost for instl. rsch., asst. prof. edn. W.Va. U., 1962-65, dean coll. human resources and edn., assoc. prof. edn., 1965-69; prof., assoc. dir. ctr. study higher edn. Pa. State U., 1969-71, sr. v.p., 1971-79; pres. U. Ill., Urbana, 1979-95, pres. emeritus, Regent prof., 1995—; pres. Am. Coun. on Edn., Washington, 1997—; bd. dirs. Pfizer, Inc., N.Y.C., UtiliCorp United Inc., Kansas City, Mus. Natural History; bd. overseers TIAA/CREF. Contbr. articles to profl. jours. Past chmn. Carnegie Found. for Advancement Tchg.; bd. dirs. Nat. Mus. Natural History. Named hon. alumnus Pa. State U. Mem. Am. Coun. Edn. (past chmn., pres. 1996—), Assn. Am. Univs. (past chmn.), Comml. Club Chgo., Mid-Am. Club, Tavern Club (Chgo.), Cosmos Club (Washington). Office: Am Coun on Edn One Dupont Cir Washington DC 20007

IKINS, RACHAEL ZACOV, writer, illustrator, photographer; b. Auburn, N.Y., July 5, 1954; d. Samuel Theodore and Phyllis Sylvia (Zacovitch) Killian; m. Phillip M. Ikins, Jan. 23, 1987. BS in Child and Family Studies, Syracuse (N.Y.) U., 1982. Pvt. practice sign lang. interpreter for the deaf Syracuse, 1980-81, Bd. of Coop. Ednl. Svcs., Syracuse, 1980-83; photographer, author greeting cards, Syracuse and Skaneateles, N.Y., 1985—, advertisements, West Columbia, S.C., 1985—. Columnist (poetry) Devon Rex Newsletter, 1995-96, Jour. Pot Bellied Pigs, 1994-96; author poetry. Recipient Honorable Mention, World of Poetry, 1991, New Eng. Writer's Conf., 1991. Jewish. Avocations: horticulture, natural history, sculpture, woodworking, animal husbandry. Home and Office: 2636 E Genesee St Syracuse NY 13224-1521

IKLE, DORIS MARGRET, energy efficiency company executive; b. Frankfurt, Germany, May 28, 1928; came to U.S., 1937; d. Richard and Sonia (Pappenheimer) Eisemann; m. Fred Charles Ikle, Dec. 23, 1959; children—Judith, Miriam. B.A., NYU, 1949, M.A., 1953; postgrad. Columbia U., 1957. Economist, Nat. Bur. Econ. Research, N.Y.C., 1949-54, Am. Bankers Assn., 1954-56, Rand Corp., Santa Monica, Calif., 1957-60; Inst. Energy Analysis, Washington, 1976-77; cons. U.S. Dept. Commerce, Washington, 1975-76; founder, chmn., CEO CMC Energy Svcs., Bethesda, Md., 1977—; adv. council Am. for Energy Independence, 1985—. Author: The Complete Energy Audit Book, 1980, (software) Energy Audit Systems, 1984; contbr. articles to profl. jours. Home: 7010 Glenbrook Rd Bethesda MD 20814-1223 Office: CMC Energy Svcs 7300 Pearl St Bethesda MD 20814-3321

IKLÉ, RICHARD ADOLPH, lawyer; b. Mineola, N.Y., Mar. 25, 1930; s. Adolph M. Ikle and Ruth Clark; children: Roger Scott, Lisa Kristina, Richard Keith. BA, Amherst Coll., 1953; JD, Columbia U., 1960. Bar: N.Y. 1961, Fla. 1975. Ptnr. Thacher, Proffitt & Wood, N.Y.C., 1960-90; sr. atty. FDIC, N.Y.C., N.J., 1990—. Deacon Community Ref. Ch., Manhasset, N.Y., 1975-80, elder, 1980-82. Lt. USNR, 1953-56. Mem. ABA, N.Y. State Bar Assn., Fla. Bar Assn., Manhasset Bay Yacht Club (Port Washington, N.Y.). Avocations: sailing, mountain climbing.

ILANIT, TAMAR, psychologist; b. Tel Aviv, May 5, 1929; d. Aharon and Ada (Berman) Pougatch; came to U.S., 1950, naturalized, 1970; grad. Levinski Tchr. Sem., 1949; Ph.D., U. So. Calif., 1959; m. Apr. 15, 1948; children—Rona, Gill. Research dir. United Cerebral Palsy Assn., Los Angeles, 1959-61; instr. Pepperdine U., Los Angeles, 1962-64; spl. cons. White Meml. Med. Center, Los Angeles; pvt. practice clin. psychology, Los Angeles, 1963—; mem. disability evaluation panel Social Security Adminstrn., 1961-85. Mem. Am. Psychol. Assn., Los Angeles County Psychol. Assn., Sigma Xi, Phi Beta Kappa, Phi Kappa Phi. Jewish. Contbr. articles to profl. jours. Office: 1964 Westwood Blvd Ste 430 Los Angeles CA 90025-4651

ILAR, CRAIG SCOTT, audio engineer; b. Charleston, W.Va., Jan. 30, 1966; s. George D. Ilar and Norma Jean (James) Witt. Cert., Full Sail, Orlando, Fla., 1989. Asst. program dir., on-air personality WSCW-WJYP Radio, South Charleston, W.Va., 1986-87; intern W.Va. Pub. Radio, Charleston, 1989; instr. U. Charleston, 1990; image and sound cons. to various local artists Charleston, 1989—; on air personality, asst. program dir., asst. music dir. WXRC, Charlotte, N.C., 1995-96; live sound engr., prodr., mgr. Scarlett Threshold, 1996-99. Home: 713 Garvin Ave Charleston WV 25302

ILCHMAN, ALICE STONE, foundation administrator, former college president, former government official; b. Cin., Apr. 18, 1935; d. Donald Crawford and Alice Kathryn (Biermann) Stone; m. Warren Frederick Ilchman, June 11, 1960; children: Frederick Andrew Crawford, Alice Sarah. BA, Mt. Holyoke Coll., 1957; MPA, Maxwell Sch. Citizenship, Syracuse U., 1958; PhD, London Sch. Econs., 1965; LHD, Mt. Holyoke Coll., 1982, Franklin and Marshall Coll., 1983. Asst. to pres., mem. faculty Berkshire C.C., 1961-64; lectr. Ctr. for South and S.E. Asia Studies U. Calif., Berkeley, 1965-73; prof. econs. and edn., dean Wellesley (Mass.) Coll., 1973-78; asst. sec. ednl. and cultural affairs Dept. State, 1978; asso. dir. ednl. and cultural affairs Internat. Communication Agy., 1978-81; advisor to sec. Smithsonian Instn., 1981; pres. Sarah Lawrence Coll., Bronxville, N.Y., 1981-98; chmn. bd. Rockefeller Found., N.Y.C., 1998—; intern, asst. to Sen. John F. Kennedy, 1957; dir. Peace Corps Tng. Program for India, 1965-66; chmn. com. on women's employment NAS. Author: The New Men of Knowledge and the New States, 1968, (with W.F. Ilchman) Education and Employment in India, The Policy Nexus, 1976; Hon. fellow Wadham Coll., Oxford. Trustee Mt. Holyoke Coll., 1970-80, Mass. Found. for Humanities and Pub. Policy, 1974-77, East-West Ctr., Honolulu, 1978-81, Expt. in Internat. Living, The Markle Found., The Rockefeller Found., chmn. bd. dirs., acting pres., 1998; trustee The U. of Cape Town, South Africa, Corp. Adv. Bd., Hotchkiss Sch.; mem. Smithsonian Coun., Yonkers Emergency Fin. Control Bd., 1982-88, Am. Ditchley Found. Program Com., Internat. Rsch. and Exch. Bd., Com. for Econ. Devel., The Masters Sch., Save The Children, Chamber Music Soc. Lincoln Ctr.; bd. dirs. NYNEX, Seligman Group of Investment Cos.; hon. fellow Wadham Coll. Oxford U. Hon. fellow Wadham Coll., Oxford U. Mem. Nat. Acad. Pub. Adminstrn., NOW Legal Def. Edn. Fund, Coun. Fgn. Rels., Century Assn. (N.Y.C.), Bronxville Field Club. Home: 18 Highland Cir Bronxville NY 10708-5908 Office: The Rockefeller Found 420 5th Ave New York NY 10018-2729

ILCHMAN, WARREN FREDERICK, university administrator, political science educator; b. Denver, Sept. 6, 1933; s. Frederick Warren and Imogene (Trovinger) I.; m. Alice Crawford Stone, June 11, 1960; children: Frederick Andrew Crawford, Alice Sarah Crawford. BA, Brown U., 1955; PhD, Cambridge (Eng.) U., Eng., 1959. Asst. prof. Ctr. Devel. Econs. Williams Coll., Williamstown, Mass., 1960-64; from asst. prof. to prof. polit. sci. U. Calif., Berkeley, 1965-73, dir. Ctr. South and Southeast Asian Studies, 1970-73; vis. prof., research assoc. Ctr. Population Studies, Harvard U., Cambridge, Mass., 1973-74; prof. polit. sci. and econs., dean arts and scis. Grad. Sch., Boston U., 1974-76; program adviser internat. div. Ford Found., N.Y.C., 1976-80; v.p. for research and grad. studies SUNY, Albany, 1980-83, provost Nelson A. Rockefeller Coll. Pub. Affairs and Policy, 1983-87, dir. Rockefeller Inst. Govt., 1983-87, exec. v.p., 1987-90; pres. Pratt Inst., Bklyn., 1990-93; exec. dir. ctr. Philanthropy Ind. Univ., Indpls., 1993-97; dir. Paul and Daisy Soros Found., N.Y.C., 1998—. Author: Professional Diplomacy in the U.S, 1961, New Men of Knowledge and the Developing Nations, 1966, Professionals as Agents of Change, 1968, The Political Economy of Change, 1969, rev. edit., 1998 (translated into French, Spanish, Japanese, Hindi and Arabic), Political Economy of Development, 1972, Comparative Public Administration and The Conventional Wisdom, 1973, Policy Sciences and Population, 1975, Education and Employment: The Policy Nexus, 1976, New York in the Year 2000, 1986, Caring and Coping, 1986, Capacity to Change, 1997, Philanthropy on the World's Tradition, 1998. Bd. dirs. The Masters Sch., The Gen. Theol. Sem. Marshall scholar U.K.; recipient Harbison prize Danforth Found., 1969. Mem. Am. Soc. Pub. Adminstrn. (Burchfield award 1965), Asia Soc., Am. Polit. Sci. Assn., N.Y. Acad. Pub. Adminstrn. (Al Smith award), Assn. Asian Studies, Nat. Acad. Pub. Adminstrn., Univ. Club, Bronxville Field Club, Phi Beta Kappa. Episcopalian. Home: 18 Highland Cir Bronxville NY 10708-5908 Office: Paul and Daisy Soros Fellowship Program 400 W 59th St New York NY 10019

ILES, LAWRENCE IRVINE, liberal arts educator; b. Epsom, U.K., June 8, 1954; s. Irvine Edmund Douglas and Bridget Margaret (Dobson) I.; m. Betty Louise McLane. BA, U. Newcastle Upon Tyne, 1975; MA, U. London, 1978, U. Ill., 1982. Hon. vis. fellow Grad. Sch. Internat. Studies, Birmingham U., Edgaston, U.K., 1987; adj. instr. Johnson County C.C., Overland Park, Kans., 1991-92; vis. tchr. Roedean Internat. Coll., Brighton, U.K., 1992-93; lectr. Oakland Coll., St. Albans, 1993—; tutor Bartholomew's Coll., Brighton, U.K., 1992-93, 96; ind. lectr. polit. sci. and global perspectives Kirksville, Mo., 1996—. Author: Modern History Course Planner, 1988; contbr. numerous articles to profl. jours. State organizer Socialist Party USAS, N.Y.C., 1994—; dep. chair Hove Co-Resistency Labor Party, 1996. Mem. History Book Guild of Am. Home: 503 S Stanford St Kirksville MO 63501-3878

ILES, ROGER DEAN, accountant; b. Detroit, June 11, 1950; s. Virgil Llewellyn and Mary Elizabeth (Lynn) I.; m. Gail Ann Swatzell, Jan. 10, 1971; 1 child, Gwendolyn Christine. *Maternal great-grandfather John Fletcher "Fletch" Huckaba, originally from Alabama, was a disabled Union army veteran of the Civil War. He later settled in Lawrenceburg, Tennessee. Maternal Grandfather John Levi Lynn was a Baptist preacher, serving in Tennessee, Arkansas, and Missouri. Roger Iles' mother (1913-1989) has nursing scholarships named in her honor at Middle Tennessee State University and at Crichton College in Memphis, Tennessee. His father (1914-1999) was a World War II Army Air Force veteran and a mechanical engineer with Ford Motor Company. His daughter was born in Altnagelvin, Northern Ireland, in 1972; she graduated Crichton College 1996.* AA, Regents Coll., 1990; BS magna cum laude, Crichton Coll., 1992; MBA, U. Memphis, 1997. Enlisted USN, 1969, advanced through grades to chief electronics technician, 1969-89; ret., 1989; switchman Mich. Bell Telephone Co., Dearborn, 1968-69; acct., cashier, alumni advisor Crichton Coll., Memphis, 1989—; adj. faculty Crichton Coll., Memphis, 1998—, U. Memphis, 1998—; chmn., mgr. Shade Tree Engring., Inc., Munford, Tenn., 1992—. Mem. Gideons Internat. (zone leader, pres. Tipton County South Camp), Assn. Bus. Adminstrs. of Christian Colls., So. Assn. Coll. and Univ. Bus. Officers (profl. devel. com.). Republican. Baptist. Avocations: auto racing, target shooting. Fax: 901 367-3866. E-mail: iles@crichton.edu. Home: 59 Jennifer Cv Brighton TN 38011-6056 Office: Crichton Coll 6655 Winchester Rd Memphis TN 38115-4335

ILETT, FRANK, JR., trucking company executive, educator; b. Ontario, Oreg., June 21, 1940; s. Frank Kent and Lela Alice (Siver) I.; m. Donna L. Andlovec, Apr. 3, 1971; children: James Frank, Jordan Lee. BA, U. Wash., 1962; MBA, U. Chgo., 1969. CPA, Idaho, Ill., Wash. Acct. Ernst & Young, Boise, Cleve., Spokane, 1962-69; mgr. Ernst & Young, Boise, 1970-72; regional mgr. Ernst & Young, San Francisco, 1972-73; treas. Interstate Mack, Inc., Boise, 1973-81, pres., CEO, 1981-82; pres. Interstate NationLease, Inc., Boise, 1975-81, Contract Carriers, Inc., Boise, 1983-89, Ilett Transp. Co., Boise, 1985-90; chmn. Carriers/West, Inc., Salem, Oreg., 1986-89; CFO, White GMC Trucks, 1988-92; v.p., CFO, May Trucking Co., Payette, Idaho, 1992-94; acct., mng. ptnr. Frank Ilett, Jr., CPA, Boise, 1994—; spl. lectr. Boise State U., 1964-67, 94—, St. Mary's Grad. Sch., Moraga, Calif., 1989-92 ; v.p. I.D.E.A.L., Inc., Nampa, Idaho, 1997—; cons. Calif. Hosp. Commn., 1973, Idaho Hosp. Assn., 1974; chmn. Mack Truck Western Region Distbr. Coun., 1979-82; mem. nat. distbr. adv. com. Mack Trucks, Inc., 1980-82; dir. stds. enforcement Idaho State Bd. Accountancy, 1983-84. Contbr. articles to profl. jours. Named Arthur Andersen Outstanding Acctg. Prof., 1996. Mem. AICPA, Gen. Soc. Mayflower Descs., SAR, Crane Creek Country Club, Masons, Shriners, Alpha Kappa Psi (Outstanding Bus. Prof. award 1997). Episcopalian. Home and Office: 1701 Harrison Blvd Boise ID 83702-1015

ILGEN, DANIEL RICHARD, psychology educator; b. Freeport, Ill., Mar. 16, 1943; s. Paul Maurice and Marjorie V. (Glasser) I.; m. Barbara Geiser, Dec. 26, 1965; children—Elizabeth Ann, Mark Andrew. BS in Psychology, Iowa State U., 1965; MA, U. Ill., 1968, PhD in Indsl.-Orgnl. Psychology, 1969. Asst. prof. dept. psychology U. Ill., Urbana, 1969-70; instr. Dutchess County C.C., Poughkeepsie, NY, 1971-72; from asst. prof. to prof. dept. psychol. scis. Purdue U., West Lafayette, Ind., 1972-83; area head indsl.-orgnl. psychology Purdue U., 1978-83; Hannah prof. organizational behavior depts. mgmt. and psychology Mich. State U., East Lansing, 1983—; vis. assoc. prof. dept. mgmt. and orgn. U. Wash., Seattle, 1978-79; vis. prof. dept. mgmt. U. Western Australia, 1991. Co-author: (with J.C. Naylor and R.D. Pritchard) A Theory of Behavior in Organizations, 1980; (with E.J. McCormick) Industrial Psychology, 1985; contbr. chpts. to books and articles to profl. jours.; editor Organizational Behavior and Human Decision Processes. Capt. M.I., U.S. Army, 1970-72. Grantee Purdue U. Found., 1973-77, 81-82, U.S. Army Rsch. Inst., 1974-82, Office Naval Rsch., 1982-86, 90—. Fellow Am. Psychol. Assn. (edn. tng. com., coun. reps. 1985-87), Soc. Indsl. and Organizational Psychology of Am. Psychol. Assn. (pres. 1987-88), Am. Psychol. Soc.; mem. Acad. Mgmt., Soc. Organizational Behavior, Sigma Xi. Office: Mich State U Depts Mgmt And Psychol East Lansing MI 48824-1117

ILIEV, MILKO NIKOLOV, physicist, researcher; b. Dobritch, Bulgaria, Sept. 30, 1941; came to U.S., 1996; s. Nikola Markov and Gergana (Popova) I.; m. Maria Slavcheva Toumanguelova-Ilieva, Nov. 5, 1969; children: Gergana, Nina. MS, U. Kiev, Ukraine, 1966; PhD, U. Sofia, Bulgaria, 1973, DSc, 1990. Asst. prof. U. Sofia, 1970-80, assoc. prof., 1980-90, prof., 1990-95, head dept. gen. physics, 1985-91, dean Faculty Physics, 1989-91; rsch. prof. U. Houston, 1996—; mem. nat. adv. bd. condensed matter physics, Bulgaria, 1986-96; task leader Tex. Ctr. Superconductivity U. Houston, 1996—. Author: (textbook) Optics, 1998; contbr. articles to profl. jours. Alexander Von Humboldt Found. fellow, Bonn, Germany, 1976-78. Mem. AAAS, Am. Phys. Soc., European Phys. Soc. Office: Tex Ctr Suprconductivity U Houston Houston TX 77204-5932

ILIN, ANDREW V., software engineer; b. Obinsk, Russia, Apr. 4, 1961; came to U.S., 1991; s. Valery P. and Svetlana I. (Gimpel) I.; m. Elena Y. Matros, June 3, 1982; 1 child, Katya Andrea. MS in Applied Math., Leningrad State U., 1983, PhD in Applied Math., 1986. Rsch. assoc. Leningrad State U., 1981-86, Laser Ctr., Moscow, 1987-91; rsch. assoc. U. Houston, 1991-93, rsch. asst. prof., 1993-96; sr. engring. sys. analyst Lockheed Martin, Houston, 1996—; cons. Cogni Seis Devel., Houston, 1992-94, Matros technologies, St. Louis, 1993—; organizer Tex. Finite Element Rodeo, Houston, 1996. Organizer, editor Internat. Conf. on Special and High Order Methods, 1995; contbr. more than 40 articles to profl. jours. Achievements include development and implementation of the advanced computational techniques in fluid mechanics, biochemistry and physics. Avocations: tennis, game of Go, Russian stamps. Home: 1208 Harbor Town Sugar Land TX 77478 Office: ASPL JSC/NASA 13000 Space Center Blvd Houston TX 77059

ILITCH, MARIAN, professional hockey team executive, food service executive; m. Michael Ilitch; children: Denise Ilitch Lites, Ron, Mike Jr., Lisa Ilitch Murray, Atanas, Christopher, Carole. Owner, sec.-treas. Detroit Red Wings; owner, sec.-treas. Detroit Tigers Baseball Team, 1993—, also bd. dirs.; sec.-treas., vice chair Little Caesar Internat.; sec.-treas. Olympia Arenas, Inc., Fox Theatre. Recipient Pacesetter award, 1988, Michiganian of Yr. award, 1988, Nat. Preservation award Nat. Trust Hist. Preservation, 1990. Office: Little Ceasars Enterprises 2211 Woodward Ave Detroit MI 48201-3400 also: Detroit Tigers Tiger Stadium 2121 Trumbull St Detroit MI 48216-1343*

ILITCH, MICHAEL, professional hockey team executive; m. Marian Ilitch; children: Denise Ilitch Lites, Ron, Mike Jr., Lisa, Atanas, Christopher, Carole. Founder, owner Little Caesars Restaurant, 1959—; owner, pres. Detroit Red Wings Hockey Team, 1982—; founder Blue Line Distributing, Am.'s Pizza Cafe; owner Olympia Arenas, Inc. (formerly Olympia Stadium Corp.), 1983—, Adirondack Red Wings Hockey Team, Detroit Drive of Arena Football League; owner, chmn., former pres. Detroit Tigers Baseball Team; with Detroit Tigers' farm system, 3 yrs. Founder Little Caesars Love Kitchen program, 1985—. With USMC, 4 yrs. Recipient a Lester Patrick trophy, 1991, Bus. Statesman award Harvard Bus. Sch. Club Detroit, 1990, Joe Louis award Sports Illustrated Mag. and Detroit Inst. Arts, Humanitarian of Yr. award March of Dimes, Nat. Preservation award Nat. Trust for Hist. Preservation, Pvt. Sector Initiative Presdl. citation Reagan Administrn., Volunteerism Presdl. citation Bush Adminstrn. Office: Detroit Red Wings 600 Civic Center Dr Detroit MI 48226-4419 also: Detroit Tigers Tiger Stadium 2121 Trumball Ave Detroit MI 48216 also: Little Caesars Enterprizes 2211 Woodward Ave Detroit MI 48201-3467*

ILLE, BERNARD GLENN, insurance company executive; b. Ponca City, Okla., Feb. 8, 1927; s. Frank Louis and Marie (Cornwell) I.; m. Mary Lou Allen, Aug. 23, 1952; children—Meredith, Les, Frank. B.B.A. in Fin., U. Okla., 1950. CLU. Agt. Phoenix Mutual Life, Hartford, Conn., 1950-54; gen. agt. Farmers and Bankers Life, Wichita, Kans., 1954-56; asst. v.p. agy. United Founders Life, Oklahoma City, 1956-58, agt. v.p., 1958-60, exec. v.p., dir. agy., 1960-66, pres., 1966-88, pres., chief exec. officer, 1988-94; pres., CEO First Life Assurance Co., Oklahoma City, 1994—; pres. BML Cons., Oklahoma City, 1994—; apptd. reciever Mid-Continental Life Ins. Co., 1999—; bd. dirs., chmn. audit com., LSB Industries, (NYSE); bd. dirs. Oklahoma City, Quail Creek Bank, Oklahoma City. Organizer Big Brothers, Oklahoma City, 1960; past pres., organizer Nat. Football Found., Oklahoma City, 1969. Recipient Young Pres. Orgn. award, 1966, U. Okla. Kappa Alpha Man of Half Century award. Mem. Okla. Life. Ins. Guaranty Assn. (chmn. 1984-94), Okla. Assn. Life Ins. Cos. (past pres. 2 terms), Exec. Svc. Corps. Okla. (chmn.), Quail Creek Golf and Country Club (organizer), Oak Tree Golf and Country Club, Petroleum Club, PGA West Country Club (Palm Springs, Calif.), La Quinta Golf and Country Club (Palm Springs), Carmel (Calif.) Valley Golf and Country Club, Palm Beach Golf and Polo Club (West Palm Beach), Kiawah Country Club (Kiawah Island, S.C.), Order Knights of Holy Sepulchre. Democrat. Roman Catholic. Home: 11004 Magnolia Park Oklahoma City OK 73120-5210 Office: BML Cons PO Box 21080 Oklahoma City OK 73156-1080

ILLICH, IVAN, educator, researcher; b. Vienna, Austria, Sept. 4, 1926; s. Peter and Ellen (Regenstreif) I. Lic.U. Philos., Gregorian U., Rome, 1945, Lic.U. Theology, 1950; PhD, U. Salzburg, 1951. Ordained priest Roman Cath. Ch., 1951. Priest in Puerto Rican cmty. N.Y.C., 1951-56; v.p. U. Santa Maria, Ponce, P.R., 1956-60; staff lectr. dept. polit. sci. Fordham U., N.Y.C., 1960-76; rschr. Ctr. Intercultural Documentation, Cuernavaca, Mexico, 1961-76; pres. bd. Ctr. Intercultural Documentation, 1963-68, mem., 1968-76; mem. Coun. Higher Edn., Commonwealth of P.R., 1959-61; guest prof. U. Kassel, W.Ger., 1979-81; mem. Berlin Inst. Advanced Study, 1981-82; Disting. guest prof. U. Calif., Berkeley, 1982; guest prof. U. Marburg, W.Ger., 1983-84; prof. humanities and scis. grad. dept. philosophy Pa. State U., 1986-97; Karl Jaspers prof. U. Oldenburg, W.Ger., 1990-91; guest prof. U. Bremen, W.Ger., 1991—; guest prof. doctoral program in architecture U. Pa., 1990-95. Author: Celebration of Awareness, Deschooling Society, Tools for Conviviality, Energy and Equity, Medical Nemesis, Towards a History of Needs, The Right to Useful Unemployment, Shadow Work, Gender, H2O and the Waters of Forgetfulness, ABC: The Alphabetization of the Popular Mind , In the Mirror of the Past: Lectures and Addresses 1978-90, In the Vineyard of the Text: A Commentary to Hugh's Didascalicon. Mem. Authors Guild. Home and Office: Apdo Postal 479-1, 62000 Cuernavaca Morelos, Mexico

ILLSTON, SUSAN Y., judge; b. 1948. BA, Duke U., 1970; JD, Stanford U., 1973. Ptnr. Cotchett, Illston & Pitre, San Francisco, 1973-95; judge U.S. Dist. Ct. (no. dist.) Calif., San Francisco, 1995—. Author: Insurance Coverage in a Toxic Tort Case, A Guide to Toxic Torts, 1987, California Complex Litigation Manual, 1990. Active Legal Aid Soc. San Mateo County, Svc. League San Mateo County. Recipient Appreciation for Vol. Svcs. cert. No. Dist. Calif. Fed. Practice Program, 1989, Svc. and Appreciation cert. 1992. Mem. ABA, ATLA, Assn. Bus. Trial Lawyers, San Mateo County Bar Assn. (Eleanor Falvey award 1994), State Bar Calif. (mem. jud. coun., mem. ethics com. 1975-79, mem. com. on women in law 1985-87, mem. jud. nominees evaluation commn. 1988, mem. exec. com. on litigation 1990-93), Calif. Women Lawyers, Calif. Trial Lawyers Assn., Trial Lawyers for Pub. Justice. Office: US Dist Ct No Dist Calif PO Box 36060 450 Golden Gate Ave San Francisco CA 94102-3661*

ILOGU, EDMUND CHRISTOPHER ONYEDUM, priest; b. Ihiala, Anambra, Nigeria, Apr. 25, 1920; came to U.S., 1986; s. Nwaku and Agnes Ugboego (Asuzu) I.; m. Elizabeth Chineze Obiago, Apr. 25, 1946; children: Ikechukwu, Chidi, Gordon, Dennis, Noel, Comfort, Rosemary, Ezinne. Assoc. degree, London Coll. Div., 1953; STM, Union Theol. Sem., N.Y.C., 1958; MA, Columbia U., 1959; PhD, State U. Leiden, The Netherlands, 1974. Ordained priest Anglican (Episcopal) Ch., 1950. Prof. religion, head dept. U. Nigeria, Nsukka, 1967-76; commr. pub. complaints Anambra State Nigeria, Enugu, 1980-86; Episcopal chaplain Howard U., Washington, 1988-90; priest-in-charge Calvary Episcopal Ch., Washington, 1990-92, St. John's Mount Rainier, Md., 1994-96; apptd. Archdeacon emeritus Enugu Diocese, 1998—; hon. canon St. Bartholomew's Cathedral, Enugu, 1972—; mem. Washington Diocesan Conv., 1988—; adj. prof. ch. history and mission Wesley Theol. Sem., Washington, 1987-91; adj. prof. African philosophy U. D.C., 1991-96. Author: West Meets East, 1956, Social Philosophy for the New Nigerian Nation, 1962, Christianity and Ibo Culture, 1974, Igbo Life and Thought, 1988. Founder, priest in charge Nigerian Lang. Anglican Ch., Washington, 1988—. Mem. Internat. Assn. for Sociology of Religion, Rotary Internat. (news editor Enugu 1980-81, Paul Harris fellow). Home: 8025 New Riggs Rd Hyattsville MD 20783-2229 *Best things of life are nearly always shared, at least between two persons, signifying the communality of life. We share stories, we share joys, laughter, love, sorrow, success and failure. Attainment of the most important aspects of life, I think, is in the community human beings share with the Spiritual Plurality of Being that Creates, Saves and Inspires. How much we miss in life when we neglect the fellowship our essential nature of communality demands of us! To live in this fellowship is, in a nutshell, what love of God and of neighbors means to me.*

ILOGU, NOEL OBIAJULU, internist; b. Ibadan, Oyo, Nigeria, Dec. 15, 1961; came to U.S., 1994; s. Edmund Christopher and Elizabeth Chineze (Obiago) I.; m. Sandra Nneka Ike, July 15, 1995; 1 child, Chudi. MD, U. Benin, Nigeria, 1985. Diplomate Am. Bd. Internal Medicine. Career registrar Burnley (Eng.) Gen. Hosp., 1992-94; resident St. Peter's Med. Ctr., New Brunswick, N.J., 1994-97; pvt. practice, Somerset, N.J., 1997—; cons. on tobacco issues in Agrica, Lagos, Nigeria, 1997—. Mem. AMA, ACP, APHA, Am. Soc. Addiction Medicine, Royal Coll. Physicians (Edinburgh), NAACP. Avocations: squash, swimming, listening to jazz. Home: 35 Stratford Dr Somerset NJ 08873-4825 Office: Pinnacle Med Group 1 Worlds Fair Dr Somerset NJ 08873-1362

ILSON, BERNARD, public relations executive; b. N.Y.C.; s. Abraham and Goldie Itzkowitz; m. Carol Ruth Geller; children: David, James. BA, Bklyn. Coll.; MA, Columbia U.; PhD, NYU, 1998. Writer NBC TV, N.Y.C., 1955-57; acct. exec. David Alber Assocs., N.Y.C., 1957-58; v.p. Rogers, Cowan and Brenner, N.Y.C., 1958-63; pres. Bernie Ilson, Inc., N.Y.C., 1963—; founder Hall of Fame of Am. Humor; past/present clients include The Ed Sullivan Show, The Beatles at Shea Stadium, All in the Family, The Monkeys, The Patridge Family, Grammy Awards, Entertainer of Yr. Awards, Motown Records, Tony Bennett, Liberty Mut. Ins. Co., Control Data Corp., Am. Soc. for Hypertension, Missoula Children's Theater, Grand Ole Opry, Hee Haw, The Negotiation Inst., Liberty Mut. Legends of Golf, NBC TV Network, Simon and Schuster. Watercolor artist: Bklyn. Mus. Biennial Watercolor Show, 1954; one-man shows: Keulik Gallery, N.Y.C., Nemisis Galley, N.Y.C.; pub., founder Ilson's Inside Information, 1991—. Mem. Writers Guild Am., Acad. TV Arts and Scis., Country Music Assn., Kappa Delta Pi. Club: Explorers. Avocations: painting, fishing. Office: 65 W 55th St New York NY 10019-4913

ILTIS, HUGH HELLMUT, plant taxonomist-evolutionist, educator; b. Brno, Czechoslovakia, Apr. 7, 1925; came to U.S., 1939, naturalized, 1944; s. Hugo and Anne (Liebscher) I.; m. Grace Schaffel, Dec. 20, 1951 (div. Mar. 1958); children: Frank S., Michael George; m. Carolyn Merchant, Aug. 4, 1961 (div. June 1970); children: David Hugh, John Paul. B.A., U. Tenn., 1948; M.A., Washington U., St. Louis and Mo. Bot. Garden, 1950, Ph.D., 1952. Rsch. asst. Mo. Bot. Garden, 1948-52; asst. prof. botany U. Ark., 1952-55; mem. faculty U. Wis.-Madison, 1955—, curator herbarium, 1955-69, prof., 1967-93, prof. emeritus, 1993—, curator, 1955-69, dir. univ. herbarium, 1969-93, dir. emeritus, 1993—; vis. prof. U. Va., Biol. Sta., 1959; world-wide lectr. in field; expdns. to Costa Rica, 1949, 89, Peru, 1962-63, Mex., 1960, 71, 77, 78, 79, 81, 82, 84, 87, 88, 90, 93, 94, 95, 96, Guatemala, 1976, Ecuador, 1977, St. Eustatius, P.R., 1989, USSR, 1975, 79, Nicaragua-Honduras, 1991, Venezuela, 1991, Hawaii, 1967; mem. adv. bd. Flora N.Am., 1970-73, Gov. Wis. Commn. State Forests, 1972-73; rsch. assoc. Mo. Bot. Gardens, Bot. Rsch. Inst. of Tex. Author articles flora of Wis., Capparidaceae, biogeography, evolution of maize, human ecology, especially innate responses to, and needs for, natural beauty and diversity, nature and cultiv. plant germ plasm preservation, especially Latin Am.; co-author: Flora de Manantlán, 1995. Co-instigator Reserva Biosfera Sierra de Manantlán, Jalisco, Mex. (co-discoverer Zea diploperennis). With U.S. Army, 1944-46. Recipient Biologia award U. Tenn., 1948, Feinstone Environ. award SUNY, Syracuse, N.Y., 1990, Conservation award Conservation Coun. Hawaii, 1990, Nat. Wildlife Fedn. Spl. Achievement award, 1992, Puga medal U. de Guadalajara, Mex., 1994. Fellow AAAS, Linnean Soc. (London); mem. Am. Inst. Biol. Scis., Bot. Soc. Am. (Merit award 1996), Soc. Econ. Botany (Econ. Botanist of Yr. award 1998), Am. Soc. Plant Taxonomists (Asa Gray award 1994), Internat. Assn. Plant Taxonomy, Soc. Bot. Mex., Soc. Study Evolution, Ecol. Soc. Am., Wis. Acad. Arts, Sci. and Letters, Forum for Corr.-Internat. Ctr. Integrative Studies, Nature Conservancy (trustee Wis. chpt., Nat. Oakleaf award 1963), Wilderness Soc., Sierra Club, Nat. Parks Assn., Citizens Natural Resources Assn. Wis., Natural Resource Def. Coun., Environ. Def. Fund, Friends of Earth, Cenozoic Soc., Zero Population Growth, Soc. Conservation Biology (Disting. Achievement award 1994), Sigma Xi, Phi Kappa Phi. Home: 2784 Marshall Pky Madison WI 53713-1023 Office: U Wis Dept Botany 430 Lincoln Dr Madison WI 53706-1313 *If we are to remain healthy and sane, we must concern ourselves with the concept of an Optimum Human Environment, one which must include large portions of the wild and natural environment that shaped our bodies and souls through natural selection over the past millions of years. Hence, only in the preservation of nature, of the world's ecosystems and their species, and in a clear comprehension of evolution, can we find the foundations for a meaningful new ethic that will insure a livable world for our children. We have to become good ancestors.*

IMAM, M. ASHRAF, materials scientist, educator; b. Patna, Bihar, India, Sept. 7, 1945; came to U.S. 1970; s. Naimuddin Ahmad and Zakia (Begum) Ahmad; m. Shamim Akhtar, June 22, 1979; children: Nabil S., Rahil U., Mariam S. BS, Ranchi U., India, 1966; MS, Carnegie-Mellon U., 1972; DSc, George Washington U., 1976. Rsch. assoc. George Washington U., Washington, 1976-78, rsch. scientist, 1978-81, adj. prof., 1981—; guest scientist Nat. Inst. Standard, Gaithersburg, Md., 1974—; sr. rsch. scientist Geo-Centers Inc., Newton, Mass., 1981-84; metallurgist Naval Rsch. Lab., Washington, 1984—. Contbr. articles to profl. jours.; editor: Structure and Deformation of Boundaries, 1986, Advances in Low-Carbon High Strength Ferrous Alloys, 1993, Advanced Materials and Processing, 1998. MRL fellow Carnegie Mellon U., 1971-72, CSIR fellow, 1966-68, others. Fellow Am. Soc. of Metals Internat.; mem. ASM, The Minerals, Metals, Materials Soc. (titanium com. 1980—, phys. metallurgy com. 1980—, mech. metallurgy com. 1980—), Sigma Xi. Achievements include 8 patents. Home: 1159 Mill Garden Ct Great Falls VA 22066-1845 Office: Naval Rsch Lab Code 6320 4555 Overlook Ave SW Washington DC 20375-0001

IMBAULT, JAMES JOSEPH, manufacturing executive; b. Muskegon, Mich., Oct. 31, 1944; s. Joseph Lionel and Ruth Pauline (Schutter) I.; m. Vallery Ann Rumisek, Dec. 29, 1967; children—Michelle, Allan. A.S., Muskegon Community Coll., 1965; B.S. Mech. Engring. with honors, Mich. Tech. U., 1967; postgrad. UCLA, 1972-73. Sr. mem. tech. staff RCA, E.A.S.D., Van Nuys, Calif., 1968-74; mech. engring. mgr. Litton Italia SPA, Rome, Italy, 1974-78; electromech. engring. mgr. Incosym, Inc., Westlake Village, Calif., 1978-82, v.p., 1982-88, also dir.; dir. ops. Precision Products Plant Northrop, Norwood, Mass., 1988-97; v.p., gen. mgr. Electroswitch, Weymouth, Mass., 1997—. Patentee in field. Recipient Meritorious Performance award Muskegon Community Coll., 1965; Mich. Tech. U. scholar, 1965-67. Mem. Nat. Soc. Profl. Engrs., ASME, AIAA, Mich. Tech. U. Alumni Assn., Pi Tau Sigma, Tau Beta Pi, Phi Kappa Phi. Republican. Home: 12 Hayden Dr Foxboro MA 02035-1127 Office: Electroswitch 180 King Ave Weymouth MA 02188-2927

IMBEAU, STEPHEN ALAN, allergist; b. Portland, Oreg., Nov. 25, 1947; s. David A. and Marjory Anne (Jacobsen) I.; m. Shirley Ruth Burke, Aug. 18, 1979; children: Stephanie Frances, Andrew Paul, Charles Burke. BA, U. Calif., Berkeley, 1969; MD, U. Calif., San Francisco, 1973. Diplomate Am. Bd. Internal Medicine, Am. Bd. Allergy. Intern U. Wis., Madison, S.C., 1973-74; resident in internal medicine U. Wis., Madison, 1974-75, resident in allergy, 1976-78, resident in infectious diseases, 1978-79; pvt. practice, Florence, S.C., 1980—; mem. S.C. budget and control bd. S.C. Data Oversight Coun., 1993-98. Contbr. articles to profl. jours. Chmn. Florence Symphony Orch., 1985-91; bd. dirs. Big Bros., 1989-92, Am. Lung Assn., 1982-86, Florence County Progress, chmn. 1993-95. Fellow ACP; mem. AMA (S.C. alt. del. 1992-98), Am. Acad. Allergists, S.C. Med. Soc. (trustee 1988-90, sec. bd. 1990-94, treas. 1995-97, S.C. Ambassador of the Yr. 1995, pres.-elect 1997, pres. 1998-99), Am. Acad. Allergy, Asthma and Immunology (alt. del. to AMA 1999—), Florence County Med. Soc. (pres. 1984-

85), Lions (pres. 1987-88). Avocations: reading, hunting, stamp collecting. Home: 950 Park Ave Florence SC 29501-5734 Office: 8W E Cheves St Ste 420 Florence SC 29506-2769

IMBER, GERALD, plastic surgeon; b. N.Y.C., Jan. 9, 1941; s. George Howard and Rose (Weiss) I.; children: Peter, Jason, Gregory. MD, SUNY, 1966. Diplomate Am. Bd. Plastic Surgery. Intern L.I. Jewish Med. Ctr., 1966-67; resident Kaiser Hosp., L.A., 1970-72, N.Y. Hosp., 1972-74, USAF Griffiss AFB Hosp., Rome, N.Y., 1970-72; attending surgeon N.Y. Hospital, N.Y.C., 1974—; dir. Imber Clinic, N.Y.C., 1982—; asst. clin. prof. of surgery N.Y. Presbyn. Hosp.-Cornell U. Med. Coll., N.Y.C. Author: Youth Corridor, 1997, For Men Only, 1998, Body Temperature, 1999. Trustee Inwood House, N.Y.C., 1998—. Capt. USAF, 1968-70. Mem. Am. Soc. Plastic Surgeons, N.E. Soc. Plastic Surgeons, N.Y. State Med. Soc., N.Y. County Med. Soc. Avocations: polo, sailing. E-Mail: drimber@aol.com. Office: Imber Clinic 1009 5th Ave New York NY 10028

IMBER, RICHARD JOSEPH, physician, dermatologist; b. Darby, Pa., Apr. 9, 1944; s. Joseph and Geraldine (Frances) I.; m. Helen Lee Stick, Nov. 18, 1971. BS, U. Dayton, 1966; MD, Temple U., 1970. Diplomate Am. Bd. Dermatology. Intern Denver Presbyn. Med. Ctr., 1970-71; resident dept. dermatology U. Colo. Health Sci. Ctr., 1971-74; chief of dermatology USAF Acad., Colorado Springs, 1974-76; sr. staff dermatologist Colo. Permanente Med. Group, Denver, 1976-83; dermatologist Denver Skin Clinic, 1983—; asst. clin. prof. dermatology U. Colo. Med. Sch., Denver, 1974—. Contbr. articles to profl. jours. Maj. USAF, 1974-76. Fellow Am. Acad. Dermatology; mem. Pacific Dermatologic Assn., Colo. Med. Soc., Denver Med. Soc., Colo. Dermatologic Soc. (sec.-treas. 1980, v.p. 1981, pres. 1982). Avocation: scuba diving. Home: 4020 S Bellaire St Englewood CO 80110-5028 Office: Denver Skin Clinic 2200 E 18th Ave Denver CO 80206-1205

IMBODEN, JOHN BASKERVILLE, psychiatry educator; b. Morrilton, Ark., Sept. 17, 1925. MD, Johns Hopkins U., Balt., 1950. Diplomate Am. Bd. Neurology and Psychiatry; lic. physician, Md. Intern Cin. Gen. Hosp., 1950-51; resident Johns Hopkin's Hosp., 1951-52, 54-56; pvt. practice psychiatry Balt., 1963—; chief dept. psychiatry Sinai Hosp. of Balt., 1969-90; assoc. prof. psychiatry Johns Hopkins U., Balt., 1963—. Co-author: Practical Psychiatry in Medicine; contbr. articles to profl. jours, chpts. to books. With U.S. Army, 1952-54. Fellow Am. Psychiat. Assn.; mem. Am. Psychoanalytic Assn. Office: 600 Wyndhurst Ave Baltimore MD 21210-2489

IMBRIE, ANDREW WELSH, composer, educator; b. N.Y.C., Apr. 6, 1921; s. Andrew C. and Dorothy (Welsh) I.; m. Barbara Cushing, Jan. 31, 1953; children: Andrew, John (dec.). A.B., Princeton U., 1942; M.A., U. Calif.-Berkeley, 1947. Instr. music U. Calif., Berkeley, 1947, 49-51, asst. prof., 1951, assoc. prof., 1957-60, prof., 1960-91, Jerry and Evelyn Hemmings Chambers chair dept. music, 1989-92; composer-in-residence Tanglewood Music Ctr., Lenox, Mass., summer 1991; guest prof. Brandeis U., 1982, U. Ala., 1992, U. Chgo., 1994, 96-97, Northwestern U., 1994, NYU, 1995, Fromm prof., Harvard U., fall, 1997. Compositions include 3 symphonies, 5 string quartets, trios, sonatas, songs, orchestral and choral works, Angle of Repose (opera), 3 piano concerti, concerti for violin, cello and flute, Dance-cantata Prometheus Bound, Requiem in memoriam John Imbrie, Adam (cantata). Bd. dirs. Koussevitzky Found.; bd. govs. San Francisco Symphony, 1982-91. Recipient Circle award N.Y. Music Critics, 1943-44; Alice M. Ditson fellow Columbia U., 1946-47; fellow Am. Acad. in Rome, 1947-49; grantee Nat. Inst. Arts and Letters, 1950; Guggenheim fellow, 1953-54, 60-61; merit award Boston Symphony Orch., 1955; creative arts award Brandeis U., 1958; Naumburg award, 1960; grantee Nat. Found. on Arts and Humanities; composer in residence Am. Acad. Rome, 1967-68; recipient Walter Hinrichsen award Columbia U., 1971. Mem. Am. Acad. Arts and Letters, Am. Acad. Arts and Scis., Phi Beta Kappa. Club: Bohemian (San Francisco). Home: 2625 Rose St Berkeley CA 94708-1920

IMBRIE, JOHN, oceanography educator. Prof. dept. geol. scis. Brown U., Providence, now prof. emeritus. Recipient G. Unger Vetlesen prize Columbia U., 1995. Home: 55 Pamden Ln Seekonk MA 02771-5114 Office: Brown U Dept Geol Sci Providence RI 02912*

IMBROGNO, CYNTHIA, magistrate judge; b. 1948. BA, Indiana U. Pa., 1970; JD cum laude, Gonzaga U., 1979. Law clk. to Hon. Justin L. Quackenbush U.S. Dist. Ct. (Wash. ea. dist.), 9th circuit, 1980-83; law clk. Wash. State Ct. of Appeals, 1984; civil rights staff atty. Ea. Dist. of Wash., 1984-85, complex litigation staff atty., 1986-88; with Preston, Thorgrimson, Shidler, Gates & Ellis, 1988-90, Perkins Coie, 1990-91; magistrate judge U.S. Dist. Ct. (Wash. ea. dist.), 9th circuit, Spokane, 1991—. Office: 856 US Courthouse 920 W Riverside Ave Spokane WA 99201-1010

IMEL, JOHN MICHAEL, lawyer; b. Cushing, Okla., Aug. 4, 1932; s. Arthur Blaine and Hazel Monnet (Kelly) I.; m. Patricia Ann Carney, July 31, 1954; children: Blythe Michele, Kathryn Ann, Dixie Lynn, Sally Louise. BS, U. Okla., 1954, JD, 1959. Bar: Okla. 1959, U.S. Dist. Ct. (no. dist.) Okla. 1961, U.S. Ct. Appeals (10th cir.) 1961, U.S. Supreme Ct. 1962, U.S. Dist. Ct. (we. dist.) Okla. 1967, U.S. Dist. Ct. (ea. dist.) Okla. 1971. Asst. atty. County of Tulsa, 1959-60; mcpl. judge City of Tulsa, 1960-61; U.S. atty. U.S. Dept. Justice, Tulsa, 1961-67; ptnr. Moyers, Martin, Santee Imel & Tetrick, Tulsa, 1967—. Regent U. Okla., Norman, 1981-88, chmn., 1987-88; trustee Children's Med. Ctr., Tulsa, 1979-84. Capt. USNR, 1954-56. Fellow Am. Bar Found., Am. Coll. Trial Lawyers (state chmn. 1987-88); mem. Am. Inns of Ct. (program chmn. 1989-90, Exemplary Leadership award 1996), So. Hills Country Club (bd. govs. 1993-99), Tulsa Club (pres. 1990), Rotary (pres. 1968-69). Democrat. Methodist. Avocations: golf, swimming, tennis, reading. Home: 3920 E 58th Pl Tulsa OK 74135-7823 Office: Moyers Martin Santee Imel & Tetrick 320 S Boston Ave Ste 920 Tulsa OK 74103-3722

IMESCH, JOSEPH LEOPOLD, bishop; b. Grosse Pointe Farms, Mich., June 21, 1931; s. Dionys and Margaret (Margelisch) I. B.S., Sacred Heart Sem., 1953; student, N.Am. Coll., Rome, 1953-57; S.T.L., Gregorian U., Rome, 1957. Ordained priest Roman Cath. Ch., 1956; sec. to Cardinal Dearden, 1959-71; pastor Our Lady of Sorrows Ch., Farmington, Mich., 1971-77; titular bishop of Pomaria and aux. bishop of Detroit, 1973-79; asst. bishop N.W. Region, 1977-79; bishop of Joliet Ill., 1979—. Office: Chancery Office 425 Summit St Joliet IL 60435-7155*

IMHOF, SUSAN ANNE, Poet; b. Alexandria, Va., May 22, 1967; d. William Anthony and Nancy Louise (Davis) I.; 1 child, Evan Davis Wollerton. BA in English, U. Va., 1989; MFA in Poetry, Warren Wilson Coll., 1994. Editor Blue Penny Quarterly, Charlottesville, Va., 1997-98; freelance poet, writer, editor, 1994—, writing tchr., 1998—. Author: (periodicals) Va. Quarterly Rev., Seneca Rev., New Va. Rev., Iris, Willow, Poetry Motel, others. Bd. mem. Westminister Child Care Ctr., Charlottesville, 1998—; reader Va. Festival of the Book, Chartlottesville, 1996-99. Recipient Wagenheim Prize for Fiction, 1989. Mem. Apple Mountain Poets. E-mail: wollertn@cstonc.net.

IMHOFF, PAMELA M., marketing educator; b. Lone Pine, Calif., Jan. 12, 1955; d. Buel Franklin Avery and Barbara Ann (Cohen) Wallace; m. Dennis Wayne Wallace,Mar. 28, 1972 (dec. Feb. 1973); 1 child, Jennifer Michelle; m. John Allen Imhoff, July 15, 1989; 1 child, Joshua Avery. AS, Tulsa Jr. Coll., 1975; BS, N.E. Okla. State U., 1978; MS, Okla. State U., 1981. Mktg. tchr., coord. Charles C. Mason H.S., Tulsa, Okla., 1978-79, Meml. H.S., Tulsa, Okla., 1979-80, Union H.S., Tulsa, Okla., 1980-91; mktg. tchr., coord. mktg. edn. Tulsa Tech. Ctr., Okla., 1991—; salesmanship instr. Tulsa Jr. Coll., Okla., 1980; sales rep. Advertising Everything, Tulsa, Okla., 1984-86. Contbr. articles to profl. jours.; presenter in field. Mem. Gracemont Bapt. Ch., 1973—, Sunday sch. tchr., 1973-78; vol. Nat. Govs. Assn. Conf., Okla., 1993; mem. Tulsa Fire Fighter's Women's Aux., 1989—; coord., sponsor Turkey Challenge for Tulsa Area Schs., 1991—; vol., fundraiser United Way, 1982-90, Muscular Dystrophy Assn., 1980-90, Salvation Army, 1980-90; sponsor Sr. Citizen Day Target Stores, 1980-90. Recipient Tchr. of Yr. award AVA, 1994. Mem. NEA, Am. Vocat. Assn. (nat. conf. 1989, 90, 92, 93, mem. resolutions com. 1993—, nat. policy leadership seminar 1993, 94, chmn. Am. Vocat. Assn. conf. mktg. edn. divsn. 1993, tchr. of yr. Am. Vocat. Assn. regional IV 1994, nat. tchr. of yr. 1995), Nat. Bus. Edn. Assn., Okla. Edn. Assn., Okla. Vocat. Assn. (strategic planning com. 1994, chmn., mem. awards com. 1992—, mem. polit. action com. 1989—, rep. regional and nat. confs., 1988—, mem. awards banquet planning com. 1993, mem. adv. com. and exec. com. 1988-92, mem. membership svcs. com. 1991-92. tchr. of yr. 1993), Okla. Mktg. Edn. Tchrs. (chmn. awards com. 1992—, chmn. consititution com. 1984-92, pres. 1990-91, 1991-92, pres.-elect 1989-90, sec., treas. 1988-89, reporter 1987-88, mktg. tchr. of yr. 1993), Mktg. Edn. Assn., DECA (sec. state activities and awards com. 1982-86, mem. state exec. coun. 1982, 84, 85, 87, 93, 94, adv. state officers 1982, 84, 85, 87, 93, 94, adv., presenter, participant state fall leadership devel. conf., CSU mini-conf., OSU DECAthalon 1978—, event mgr. nat. conf. 1986, 90, 93, series dir. nat. conf. 1993, adult asst. nat. conf. 1980-92, 94, adv. nat. and state winners 1978—), Tulsa Area Vo-Tech Assn. Classroom Tchrs. Avocations: aerobics, reading. Office: Tulsa Tech Ctr 3420 S Memorial Dr Tulsa OK 74145-1390*

IMHOFF, REED, retired city manager; b. Millport, Pa., Dec. 20, 1934; s. Raymond Kreiner and Hannah Elizabeth (Reider) I.; m. Joyce Elaine Sweigart, July 2, 1954; children: Randolph Scott, Timothy Lee. AS, Internat. Corr. Schs. Laborer Borough of Ephrata, Pa., 1951-55, equipment operator, 1962-69, pub. works dir., 1969-90; cook Schrafft's Restaurant, Denver, 1957-62; city mgr. Borough of Akron, from 1990. Capt. fire police Akron Fire Dept., 1993-97. With U.S. Army, 1957-59. Mem. Lions Club. Avocations: woodworking and painting, motorcycling, working at home. Home: 63 Heritage Rd Akron PA 17501-1148

IMHOFF, WALTER FRANCIS, investment banker; b. Denver, Aug. 7, 1931; s. Walter Peter and Frances Marie (Barkhausen) I.; m. Georgia Ruth Stewart, June 16, 1973; children: Stacy, Randy, Theresa, Michael, Robert. BSBA, Regis U., Denver, 1955; D Pub. Svc. (hon.), Regis U., 1991. Asst. v.p. Coughlin & Co., Denver, 1955-60; pres., chief exec. officer Hanifen, Imhoff Inc., Denver, 1960—; guest lectr. U. Colo., 1976. Trustee Regis Coll., 1975-95, treas., 1976-79, vice chmn., 1981, chmn., 1982-89, life trustee, 1998—; bd. dirs. NCCJ, 1980-89, chmn. 1986-89, life trustee 1998—; bd. dirs. Arapahoe Libr. Found., 1990-94, Channel 6 Ednl. TV, treas. 1996-97, vice chmn., 1997-98, chmn., 1998—; bd. dirs. Highland Hills Found., 1993—; bd. dirs. Denver Area coun. Boy Scouts Am., 1986—, v.p., 1989—; bd. dirs. St. Joseph's Hosp., mem. exec. com., 1991, vice chmn., 1994, chmn., 1995-98; bd. dirs. Kempe Children's Found., 1992, chmn., 1994-97; chmn. Colo. Concern, 1988—. Named Outstanding Alumnus Regis Coll., 1970. Mem. Bond Club Denver (pres. 1965), Colo. Mcpl. Bond Dealers Assn. (pres. 1973), Mid-Continent Securities Industry Assn. (dir. 1972-75), Securities Industry Assn. (chmn. S.W. region 1991-95, dir. 1993-96), Nat. Assn. Security Dealers, Pub. Securities Assn. (dir. 1972-75), Denver C. of C. (bd. dirs. 1986-91, treas. 1989-91), Rose Hosp. Found., Centennial C. of C. (vice chmn.), NAACP, Alpha Kappa Psi, Alpha Sigma Nu. Republican. Roman Catholic. Club: Denver (pres. 1981-82). Home: 10432 E Ida Pl Englewood CO 80111-3753 Office: 1125 17th St Ste 1600 Denver CO 80202-2024

IMIG, JOHN DAVID, medical educator; b. Bloomington, Ill., Nov. 20, 1962; m. Melinda L. Peel, June 9, 1984; children: Allyson E., Emily R. BA in Biology magna cum laude, Blackburn Coll., Carlinville, Ill., 1985; PhD in Physiology, U. Louisville, 1990. Postdoctoral fellow Med. Coll. Wis., Milw., 1990-93; instr. rsch. physiology Tulane U. Sch. Medicine, New Orleans, 1993-95, rsch. asst. prof. physiology, 1995-98, asst. prof. physiology, 1998—. Various editorial positions with profl. jours.; contbr. articles to profl. jours. LeRoy Edn. Assn. scholar, 1981, faculty Blackburn Coll. scholar, 1982, 84; Merck Sharp & Dohme fellow, 1992, NIH fellow, 1992-95. Fellow Am. Heart Assn. (coun. kidney in cardiovascular disease, high blood pressure rsch.); mem. Am. Physiol. Soc., Micorcirculatory Soc., Golden Key. Home: 3702 E Grandlake Blvd Kenner LA 70065-2441 Office: Tulane U Med Ctr Dept Physiology 1430 Tulane Ave New Orleans LA 70112-2699

IMIG, WILLIAM GRAFF, lawyer, lobbyist; b. Omaha, Aug. 13, 1941; s. Jacob H. and Gretchen (Kirk) I.; m. Joyce Stevens, Dec. 18, 1976; children: Scott, Kari, Steven. BA, Cornell U., 1963, LLB, 1965. Bar: Colo. 1965, U.S. Ct. Appeals (10th cir.) 1965, U.S. Supreme Ct. 1969. Assoc. Sherman & Howard, Denver, 1965-66; v.p., shareholder Ireland, Stapleton, Pryor & Pascoe, Denver, 1970-92; pvt. practice, Denver, 1992—; Colo. counsel Nat. Assn. Ind. Insurers, Des Plaines, Ill., 1971—; Colo. legis. counsel Allstate Ins. Cos., 1982—. Bd. editors Cornell Law rev., 1964-65. Vice chmn., chmn. Colo. Gov.'s Adv. Com. on Ins. and Econ. Devel., 1987-90; trustee Colo. chpt. Nat. Multiple Sclerosis Soc., 1995—; exec. bd. Colo. Assn. of Continue Entities, 1994-96; mem. Working Com. on Risk Based Solvency, Denver, 1991-93, Colo. Bicycle Adv. Bd., Denver, 1992-97, counsel Save the Pavilion, 1989-94. Capt. JAGC, U.S. Army, 1966-70. Mem. Colo. Bar Assn. (bd. govs. 1974-77, pro bono award 1985), Federalist Soc., Am. Arbitration Assn. (arbitrator), City Club of Denver, Denver Law Club, Phi Kappa Phi. Republican. Episcopalian. Home and Office: 1795 Monaco Pky Denver CO 80220-1644

IMLAH, MARYPAT, sales, advertising and marketing executive; b. Bklyn., Oct. 25, 1957; d. Kenneth William Joseph and Ann Marie (Beckley) Olivarius; m. Craig Alexander Olivarius-Imlah, Sept. 18, 1982; children: Christopher Edward, Jamison Robert, Meghan Patricia. BS in Mktg. and Communications, Ramapo State Coll. N.J., 1979; MBA in Mktg. and Mgmt., Fairleigh Dickinson U., 1985. Researcher, pub. rels. MacNeil/Lehrer Report, WNET-TV, N.Y.C., 1977; salesperson Terrace Realty, Montvale, N.J., 1977-79; direct mail advt. copywriter Prentice-Hall, Inc., Englewood Cliffs, N.J., 1979-81; editor, promotional designer Beauty & Barber Supply Inst., Englewood, N.J., 1981-83; nat. dir. advt. and pub. rels. Emerson Radio Corp., North Bergen, N.J., Vermont, Va., 1983—; founder, pres. Imagery Print & Advt., Print Brokerage Design Agy., Promotional Items.

IMMELT, STEPHEN J., lawyer; b. Columbus, Ohio, Dec. 27, 1951; s. Joseph Francis and Donna (Wallace) I.; m. Susann Randolph Carroll, June 7, 1976; children: Catherine Carroll, Molly Maccubbin. BA, Yale U., 1974; JD, U. Md., 1977. Bar: Md. 1977, D.C. 1995, U.S. Dist. Ct. Md. 1978, U.S. Dist. Ct. D.C. 1988, U.S. Ct. Appeals (4th cir.) 1978, U.S. Ct. Appeals (D.C. Cir.) 1988, U.S. Ct. Appeals (6th and 9th cirs.) 1992. Law clk. to Hon. Harrison L. Winter U.S. Ct. Appeals (4th cir.), Balt., 1977-78; assoc. Piper & Marbury, Balt., 1978-79, 85-86, ptnr., 1986-89; ptnr. Hogan & Hartson, Balt., 1989—; asst. U.S. atty. U.S. Dept. Justice, Balt., 1979-83; mem. adv. bd. Johns Hopkins U. Sch. Nursing, Balt., 1990-98. Bd. dirs. Md. chpt. The Nature Conservancy, Chevy Chase, 1985-96, Valleys Planning Coun., Towson, Md., 1991-97, Balt. Zoo, 1994—, Balt. Choral Arts Soc., 1994—. Democrat. Avocations: golf, skiing, gardening, outdoors. E-mail: SJImmelt@HHLAW.com. Office: Hogan & Hartson 111 S Calvert St Ste 1600 Baltimore MD 21202-6191

IMMERMAN, MIA FENDLER, artist; b. Antwerp, Belgium, 1935; arrived in U.S., 1948; d. Bernard and Berthe (Gangel) Fendler; m. Benjamin Joseph Immerman, Dec. 23, 1951 (div. Mar. 1967); children: Bruce, Bernard. 3-yr. cert., Pratt Inst., 1954; 1-yr. cert., Art Student's League, 1955; art student, Best Studios, New Sch. Social Rsch., Art Students League, G. Grosz, Leo Manso, Charles Seide, Antonio Frasconi. Illustrator mags., colorist, stylist Cohn-Hall, Marx, N.Y.C., 1955-56; textile designer Studio-Art, Inc., N.Y.C., 1955-57; freelance designer N.Y. and N.J.; art collection in Heckscher Mus., Huntington, N.Y., 1977, also pvt. collections, L.I., N.Y., Europe, 1980-96; lectr. on chess and art at museums and librs. One person shows Gallery 84, 1982 (Medal 1982), Va. Tech., 1992 (medal 1992); exhibited in group shows Brussels, Paris, Queens, North Shore, L.I., Antwerp, N.Y., N.J.; When Memory Speaks, four paintings reproduced in scholarly book by Nellie Toll, 1998. Orgn. ADL/Hidden Children spkr. about the holocaust to schs., 1991-98. Recipient numerous awards for art, 1967-96; Art League scholar Pratt Inst., 1951-54. Mem. Queens Chess Club (trophies). Jewish. Avocations: chess (Top 50 Women in U.S. Chess, 1990), writing short stories and editorials, acting from scripts. Home: 75-40 Austin St Forest Hills NY 11375

IMMKE, KEITH HENRY, lawyer; b. Peoria, Ill., Jan. 18, 1953; s. Francis William and Pearl Lenora (Kime) I. BA, U. Ill., 1975; JD, So. Ill. U., 1978. Bar: Ill. 1978, U.S. Dist. Ct. (so. and ea. dist.) Ill. 1979. Assoc. Lawrence E. Johnson & Assocs., P.C., Champaign, Ill., 1979-87; staff atty. Dept. Ins. State Ill., Springfield, 1987-88; legal counsel Underground Storage Tank program (now Divsn. Petroleum and Chem. Safety), 1988-98; asst. legal counsel Office Fire Marshal State Ill., 1988—; legal counsel Underground Storage Tank Program (now Div. Petroleum and Chem. Safety 1988-98), asst. legal counsel; Office Fire Marshal State Ill., 1998—. Mem. ABA, Ill. State Bar Assn., U. Ill. Alumni Assn., Phi Kappa Phi, Pi Sigma Alpha, Phi Alpha Delta. Office: State Ill Office Fire Marshal Div Petroleum and Chem Safety 1035 Stevenson Dr Springfield IL 62703-4259

IMPARATO, ANTHONY MICHAEL, vascular surgeon, medical educator, researcher; b. N.Y.C., July 29, 1922; s. Silverio and Olga (Santilli) I.; m. Agatha Maria Petriccione, Dec. 19, 1943; children: Maria April Imparato Phillips, Karen Elsa Imparato Cotton. AB, Columbia U., 1943; MD, NYU, 1946. Diplomate Am. Bd. Surgery; cert. spl. qualifications in gen. vascular surgery. Intern U.S. Naval Hosp., Bklyn., 1946-47; fellow in anatomy NYU Med. Sch., 1949-50; successively intern, asst. resident in surgery, resident, chief resident in surgery NYU Med. Center Bellevue Hosp., 1950-56; mem. faculty NYU Med. Center, 1956—, dir. div. vascular surgery, 1975-92, prof. surgery, 1975—; cons. Norwalk (Conn.) Hosp.; leader People-to-People delegation in vascular surgery: western Europe 1982, Soviet Union, 1985; ops. com. "Cooperative VA Study on Asymptomatic Carotid Stenosis", 1983-87 and Nascet, 1987-92; hon. pres. Societa Italiana Prevenzione Ictus Cerebrale, 1997, 98. Author articles in field, chpts. in textbooks. Served as officer M.C. USNR, 46-49, 50. Grantee NIH, 1976-81. Fellow ACS, Am. Coll. Cardiology; mem. Am. Heart Assn. (fellow Stroke Coun.), Am. Surg. Assn., Soc. for Vascular Surgery (pres. 1984-85), Internat. Cardiovascular Soc., Soc. Clin. Vascular Surgery, Soc. Angiologia Uruguay, Royal Australasian Coll. Surgeons (hon.), Soc. Internat. Chirurgie, N.Y. Regional Vascular Soc. (co-founder, pres. 1982-84), N.Am. Soc. Pacing and Electrophysiology (founding mem.), James IV Assn. Surgeons (dir., treas.), Lithuanian Vascular Soc. (hon.), Alpha Omega Alpha. Office: NYU Faculty Practice Area 530 1st Ave Ste 6-f New York NY 10016-6481

IMPARATO, EDWARD THOMAS, writer; b. Flushing, N.Y., Jan. 6, 1917; s. Charles and Romilda (Delli Bovi) I.; m. JEan Catherine De Garmo, Aug. 1, 1947. BS, U. Tampa, 1963. V.p. Merrill Lynch, Clearwater, Fla., 1963-74; fin. cons. J.C.I., Inc., Belleair, Fla., 1974-92; free-lance author Belleair, Fla., 1992—; CEO, chmn. (INSAT) Internat. Systems, Clearwater, 1987-92. Author: How to Manage Your Money, 1964, Into Darkness, 1994, MacARthur-Melbourne to Tokyo, 1996, Rescue from Shangri-La, 1997, History of the 374th Troop Carrier, 1997. Col. USAF, 1938-61. Recipient, Legion of Merit, Dist. Flying Cross, Air medal with Bronze Oak Leaf Cluster, Amer. Def. Svc. Medal, WWII Victory Medal, Natl. Def. Svc. Medal, Amer. Campaign Awd., Medal for Humane Action. Mem. Order Daedalians, Retired Officers Assn. Independent. Home and office: 155 Bayview Dr Belleair FL 33756

IMPELLIZERI, MONICA, pension fund administrator, consultant; b. N.Y.C., June 7, 1920; d. Benjamin and Elizabeth (Priolo) LoPinto; m. Mario E. Impellizeri, June 8, 1941; children: MaryLou, LilaMonica. Student, NYU, 1952-55, 55-57. Asst. advt. mgr. Lily Tulip Cups, Inc., N.Y.C., 1940-45; asst. pub. sch. adminstr. N.Y.C. Bd. of Edn., 1950-68; cons. Imperllizeri Assocs., Inc., Ft. Lee, N.J., 1972—, v.p., 1985—. Author: Yesterday's Tomorrow, 1982; one woman shows include East End Arts Coun., Riverhead, N.Y., 1991; exhibited in Parrish Art Mus., Southampton, N.Y., 1974; artist in oils and water colors. Volunteer art instr. Westchester (N.Y.) Nursing Homes, 1965-71; bd. trustees Friends of Westhampton Free Libr., Westhampton Beach, N.Y., 1985—, Westhampton Free Libr., Westhampton Beach, 1990—. Recipient St. Gaudens medal, N.Y.C., 1936. Mem. Am. Contract Bridge League, Bus. and Profl. Lodge (bd. trustees Queens, N.Y. chpt. 1970—), Southampton Artists, Westhampton Artists. Avocations: golf, gardening, volunteer work, politics.

IMPELLIZZERI, ANNE ELMENDORF, insurance company executive, non-profit executive; b. Chgo., Jan. 26, 1933; d. Armin and Laura (Gundlach) Elmendorf; m. Julius Simon Impellizzeri, Oct. 12, 1961 (dec.); children: Laura, Theodore (dec.). BA, Smith Coll., 1955; MA, Yale U., 1957. CLU; ChFC. Tchr. Amity Regional H.S., Woodbridge, Conn., 1957-58; adminstrv. and editl. asst. East Europe Inst., N.Y.C., 1958-59; health educator Met. Life Ins. Co., N.Y.C., 1959-62, 71-76, adminstrv. asst. pub. affairs, 1976-78, asst. v.p., corp. social responsibility, 1978-80, v.p., 1980-85, v.p. group ins., 1985-88; v.p. N.Y.C. Partnership, 1988-90; pres., CEO Blanton-Peale Inst., N.Y.C., 1990-98; exec. dir. Russel Wright's Manitoga, Garrison, N.Y., 1998—; dir. Nuveen Mcpl. Funds, 1994—; trustee Smith Coll., 1991-96, Support Ctr. for Nonprofit Mgmt., 1995—, Scenic Hudson, 1997—; mem. Bus. Urban Issues Coun. of the Conf. Bd., 1981-85, chair, 1983-85. Trustee Lakeland Bd. Edn., Westchester County, N.Y., 1967-71, pres., 1970-71; bd. dirs. Nat. Safety Coun., 1974-80; pres. Am. Assn. Gifted Children, 1975-85, chair, 1985-90. Named to Acad. of Women Achievers, YWCA N.Y., 1978; Fulbright grantee, 1955-56. Mem. Assn. Yale Alumni (bd. govs. 1985-88), Phi Beta Kappa. Office: Manitoga PO Box 249 Garrison NY 10524

IMPERATO, JOSEPH JOHN, lawyer, composer; b. Jersey City, N.J., Mar. 14, 1956; s. Joseph Francis Imperato and Edith Roslyn (Dubin) Schwimmer. Student, Oberlin Coll., 1974-76; BA, Fla. State U., 1978, JD, 1981. Bar: Fla. 1983. Trial atty., tng. instr. Office of Pub. Defender, Miami, Fla., 1982—; lectr., mock trial coach Dade County sec. schs. and univs., Miami, 1993—. Composer musical scores Fox TV Network, 1992-94; composer comml. jingles, 1975— (Addy award 1976), original songs, 1974— (Billboard Mag. Songwriting award 1995); composer, producer original childrens' musicals, 1997—. Mem. ASCAP. Office: Office of Pub Defender 1320 NW 14th St Miami FL 33125-1609

IMPERATO, PASCAL JAMES, physician, health administrator, author, editor, medical educator; b. N.Y.C., Jan. 13, 1937; s. James Anthony and Madalynne Marguerite (Insante) I.; m. Eleanor Anne Maiella, June 4, 1977; children: Alison Madalynne, Gavin Humbert, Austin Clement. BS, St. John's U., 1958, DSc (hon.), 1977; MD, SUNY, Downstate Med. Ctr., 1962; M in Pub. Health and Tropical Medicine, Tulane U., 1966, DSc (hon.), 1996. Diplomate Am. Bd. Preventive Medicine, Nat. Bd. Med. Examiners. Fgn. fellow Assn. Am. Med. Colls., Kenya, Tanzania, Uganda, 1961; intern dept. internal medicine L.I. Coll. Hosp., 1962-63, resident dept. medicine, 1963-65; fgn. rsch. fellow Tulane Univ.-U. del Valle, Cali, Colombia, 1965; N.Y. Acad. Medicine/Glorney Raisebeck fellow Tulane U., New Orleans, 1965-66; med. epidemiologist smallpox eradication-measles control program Ctrs. Disease Control/USPHS, Mali, 1966-72; dir. Bur. Infectious Disease Control, N.Y.C. Dept. Health, 1972-74, prin. epidemiologist, dir. immunization program, 1972-74, 1st dep. commr., 1974-77, dir. pub. health residency tng. program, 1974-77; chmn. N.Y.C. Swine Influenza Immunization Task Force, 1976-77; med. cons. Africa Bur., U.S. AID, 1974; commr. health N.Y.C., 1977-78; chmn. N.Y.C. Bd. Health, 1977-78; chmn. bd. N.Y.C. Health and Hosps. Corp., 1977-78; chmn. exec. com. N.Y.C. Health Systems Agy., 1977-78; acting health services adminstr. N.Y.C., 1977-78; clin. instr. dept. medicine Cornell U. Med. Coll., N.Y.C., 1972-74, asst. clin. prof., 1974-78, asst. clin. prof. dept. pub. health, 1974-77, assoc. clin. prof., 1977-78, adj. prof., 1979—; clin. assoc. prof. dept. preventive medicine, cmty. health SUNY Health Sci. Ctr. at Bklyn., 1974-77, lectr., 1977-78, prof. and chmn., 1978-94; disting. svc. prof. and chmn., 1994—; mem. staff N.Y. Hosp. 1972-78, L.I. Coll. Hosp., 1973—, State U. Hosp., 1978—, Kings County Hosp., 1978—; lectr. dept. cmty. medicine Mt. Sinai Sch. Medicine, CUNY, 1974-90; lectr. dept. health adminstrn. Sch. Pub. Health, Columbia U., 1982-89; cons. N.Y. State Dept. Edn., 1982-87, NAS, 1985, dept. cmty. health svcs. and ambulatory care Brookdale Hosp. Med. Ctr., 1987-96; cons. program for appropriate tech. in health U.S. AID, 1985-89; med. dir. R&D and Epidemiology Island Peer Rev. Orgn., 1991—. Author: Doctor in The Land of the Lion, 1964, (with Osa Johnson) Last Adventure, 1966, Bwana Doctor, 1967, The Treatment and Control of Infectious Diseases in Man, 1974, The Cultural Heritage of Africa, 1974, A Wind in Africa: A Story of Modern Medicine in Mali, 1975, What To Do About the Flu, 1976, African Folk Medicine, 1977, Historical Dictionary of Mali, 1977, 3rd edit., 1996, Dogon Cliff Dwellers: The Art of Mali's Mountain People, 1978, Medical Detective, 1979, (with Eleanor Imperato) Mali: A Handbook of Historical Statistics, 1982, The Administration of a Public Health Agency: A Case Study of the New York City Department of Health, 1983, Buffoons, Queens and Wooden Horsemen, 1983, (with Greg Mitchell) Acceptable Risks, 1985, (with Robert I. Goler) Early American Medicine, 1987, Arthur Donaldson

Smith and the Exploration of Lake Rudolf, 1987, Mali: A Search for Direction, 1989, (with Eleanor Imperato) They Married Adventure: The Wandering Lives of Martin and Osa Johnson, 1992, Quest for the Jade Sea: Colonial Competition Around an East African Lake, 1998; editor: Acquired Immunodeficiency Syndrome: Current Issues and Scientific Studies, 1989; Historical and Contemporary Aspects of Communicable Disease Control, 1996; contbr. articles to profl. jours.; cons. editor N.Y. State Jour. Medicine, 1983, dep. editor, 1983-86, editor, 1986-93; editor Jour. Cmty. Health, 1985—; mem. editl. bd. Explorers Jour., 1979-88, Am. Jour. Chinese Medicine, 1985—, The Pharos, 1995—; mem. med. adv. bd. Med. Herald, 1992—; chairperson publs. com. Annals of Epidemiology, 1996—. Bd. dirs. Pub. Health Rsch. Inst., 1977-78, Cmty. Coun. Greater N.Y., 1977-78, Med. Health and Rsch. Assn., 1977-78, Greater N.Y. Hosp. Assn., 1977-78, N.Y. Heart Assn., 1983-84, Primary Care Devel. Corp., 1995—; bd. trustees Milton Helpern Libr. Legal Medicine, 1977-89, hon. trustee, 1989—; hon. trustee Martin and Osa Johnson Safari Mus., 1964—; mem. adv. bd. Physicians for Social Responsibility, 1983—; mem. N.Y. State Bd. Medicine, 1985-95, vice chmn., 1990-93, chmn., 1993-95; mem. bd. zoning and appeals Village of Plandome Heights, N.Y., 1986-90, trustee, 1990-92; mem. sci. adv. bd. Explorers Club, 1988-93; chmn. N.Y.C. Met. Area Task Force on Syphilis, 1990-91; mem. bd. regents L.I. Coll. Hosp., 1992—; mem. N.Y.C. Mayor-Elect Giuliani's Health Care Adv. Group, 1993; mem. N.Y. State Coun. on Grad. Med. Edn., 1994-98; co-chmn. adv. commn. on pub. health N.Y.C. Coun., 1994—; mem. N.Y. State Bd. for Profl. Med. Conduct, 1994—. Lt. comdr. USPHS, 1966-69. Recipient Meritorious Honor award and medal Dept. State, 1971, US AID Meritorious Honor award and medal, 1970, Outstanding Alumnus award Tulane U., 1978, Delta Omega Nat. Merit award, 1978, Frank Babbot award SUNY, 1980, Disting. Alumni Achievement award, and medal SUNY, 1987, Spl. Service award for smallpox eradication USPHS, 1987; Fulbright scholar, North Yemen, 1985. Fellow ACP, Royal Soc. Tropical Medicine and Hygiene, Royal African Soc., Am. Coll. Epidemiology, Am. Coll. Preventive Medicine; mem. Am. Soc. Tropical Medicine and Hygiene, N.Y. Soc. Tropical Medicine (v.p. 1976-77, pres. 1989-90), East African Wildlife Soc., African Studies Assn., Author's Guild, Explorers Club, Delta Omega, Alpha Omega Alpha. Roman Catholic. Office: Box 43 450 Clarkson Ave Brooklyn NY 11203

IMPERATO-MCGINLEY, JULIANNE LEONORE, endocrinologist, educator; b. N.Y.C., Sept. 22; d. Thomas and Marian (Crispinelli) Imperato; m. Patrick W. McGinley, Aug. 27, 1966; children: Alexandra Claire, Ian Patrick McGinley. BS in Chemistry cum laude, Coll. Mt. St. Vincent, 1961; MD in Pub. Health with honors, SUNY, 1965. Intern in internal medicine St. Vincent's Hosp. and Med. Ctr., N.Y.C., 1965-66, resident in internal medicine, 1966-68; fellow in reproductive endocrinology NYU and Lenox Hill Hosps., N.Y.C., 1968-69; NIH fellow in endocrinology Cornell U. Med. Coll., N.Y.C., 1969-72; asst. physician The N.Y. Hosp., N.Y.C., 1969-72, physician to out-patient dept., 1972-75, asst. attending, 1975-81; from instr. in medicine to asst. prof. medicine Cornell U. Med. Ctr., N.Y.C., 1972-81; assoc. attending physician The N.Y. Hosp., N.Y.C., 1982—; assoc. prof. medicine Cornell U. Med. Coll., N.Y.C., 1982-93, assoc. dir. Gen. Clin. Rsch. Ctr., 1991-93, chief sect. androgen physiology divsn. endocrinology, 1992—, dir. Gen. Clin. Rsch. Ctr., 1993—, chief divsn. endocrinology, 1993—, prof. medicine, 1993-98, Rochelle Belfer prof. medicine, 1998—; cons. prof. Nat. U. Pedro Henriquez Urena, Santo Domingo, Dominican Republic, 1987, St. Vincent's Hosp. and Med. Ctr., N.Y.C., 1978—; mem. internat. adv. bd. 3rd Internat. Conf. on Geriat. Nephrology and Urology, 1991-92; expert ad hoc grant reviewer behavioral medicine study sect. NIH, 1984, ad hoc mem. biopsychology study sect., 1982, ad hoc mem. site visit team biophysiology study sect., 1981; organizing com. Serono Symposium on Sexual Differentiation, 1982; plenary lectr. Merck Med. Adv. Coun. Meeting, St. Andrews, Scotland, 1991, European Soc. for Pediat. Endocrinology, Vienna, Austria, 1990; mem. Gordon Rsch. Conf., Plymouth, N.H., 1986; Macomber lectr. in human sexuality Harvard Med. Sch., Dept. Ob-Gyn., Boston, 1980. Assoc. editor Jour. Clin. Endocrinology and Metabolism, 1993—, mem. editl. bd., 1993—; reviewer: Acta Endocrinologica, Archives of Internal Medicine, Clin. Endocrinology, Endocrine Revs., Endocrinology, Jour. Andrology, Jour. Clin. Endocrinology and Metabolism, Jour. Urology, New England Jour. Medicine; contbr. over 100 articles to profl. jours. NIH fund rschr.; active fundraising and drug donations The Robert Reid Cabral Children's Hosp., Santo Domingo, 1988—. Recipient award for outstanding clin. rsch. Dominican Pediat. Endocrine Soc., 1988, Rsch. award 1st prize Am. Acad. Pediats., sect. urology, 1984, Nicholas Pichardo award and lectr. for outstanding rsch. contbns. to advancement of medicine in Dominican Republic, Santo Domingo, 1980, also numerous rsch. grants; acad. scholar Coll. Mt. St. Vincent, 1961. Mem. AAAS, Am. Fedn. for Clin. Rsch., Endocrine Soc. (chair, lectr. symposium on steroid 5a-reductase ann. meeting San Antonio 1992, membership com. 1989-91, chair membership com. 1991-92, chair meetings 1984-88), N.Y. Acad. Scis., Soc. for Study of Reprodn., Harvey Soc., Women in Endocrinology, Kappa Gamma Pi. Roman Catholic. Office: NY Hosp-Cornell U/Weill Med Coll Divsn Endocrin/Gen Clin Rsc 525 E 68th St New York NY 10021-4885*

IMRAY, THOMAS JOHN, radiologist, educator; b. Milw., Nov. 11, 1939; s. George William and Genevieve (Bresnehan) I.; m. Carla Marie Rake, Aug. 17, 1963; children: John Scott, Jean Ann, Jeff William. BA, Marquette U., 1961, MD, 1965. Diplomate Nat. Bd. Med. Examiners, Am. Bd. Radiology (guest examiner 1975-76, 79, 85-93). Intern St. Mary's Hosp., San Francisco, 1965-66; resident in radiology U. Minn., Mpls., 1966-70, instr., 1969-70; asst. prof. Med. Coll. of Wis., Milw., 1973-77, assoc. prof., 1977-80; assoc. prof. U. Calif., Irvine, 1980-82; prof. and chmn. dept. radiology U. Nebr. Med. Ctr., Omaha, 1982-96, prof. dept. radiology, 1996—; vis. prof. Vanderbilt U., Nashville, 1976, 82, U. Wis., Madison, 1978, SUNY Downstate Med. Ctr., Bklyn., 1978, Harvard Med. Sch., Boston, 1980, Loyola U. Sch. Medicine, Maywood, Ill., 1980, UCLA-Wadsworth VA Hosp., 1981, UCLA, 1982 Northwestern U. Sch. Medicine, Chgo., 1984, Meth. Hosp., Indpls., 1984, U. Mo., Kans. City, 1985, U. Iowa, Iowa City, 1986, U. Ark., Little Rock, 1987, Keio U. Sch. Medicine, Tokyo, 1989, Mich. State U., 1993. Contbr. articles to profl. jours. Mem. Tech. Task Force on Diagnostic Radiology Nebr. Dept. Health, 1983-84; Major U.S. Army M.C., 1970-73. Co-recipient Magna Cum Laude in Sci. Exhibits award Am. Soc. Neuroradiology, 1987; GE grantee, 1985-87. Fellow Am. Coll. Radiology; mem. AMA (rep. to radiology residency rev. com., 1987), Radiol. Soc. N. Am. (award 1981, 82), Am. Coll. Radiology (com. on satellite communications 1981-83), Am. Roentgen Ray Soc. (award 1986), Assn. Univ. Radiologists, Soc. Chmn. Acad. Radiology Depts., Am. Soc. Uroradiology, Nebr. State Radiol. Soc., Nebr. State Med. Assn., Omaha Metro Med. Soc., Omaha Mid-West Clin. Soc. (hosp. and svc. exhibits com. 1984, award 1986), Omaha C. of C. (task force on edn. 1983-85, edn. coun. steering com. 1984, edn. coun. 1985), Rotary Internat. (program com. 1986), Marquette U. Club (bd. dirs. Omaha chpt., 1987), Alpha Omega Alpha (alumni and faculty mems. com., 1986). Roman Catholic. Avocation: swimming. Office: Nebr Health Sys Dept Radiology 981045 Nebr Med Ctr Omaha NE 68198-1045

IMTIAZ, KAUSER SYED, aerospace engineer; b. Karachi, Pakistan, Jan. 26, 1952; came to U.S., 1973; s. Syed Imtiaz Ahmad and Rehana Imtiaz; m. Lubna Kauser, July 25, 1982; children: Hina Kauser, Yusra Kauser. BS in Aerospace Maintenance Engring., St. Louis U., 1977; MS in Aerospace Engring., Wichita State U., 1979. Lic. pvt. pilot, airframe and powerplant mechanic. Sr. engr. Beech Aircraft Corp., Wichita, Kans., 1978-82, 84-89; aircraft engr. Saudia Airlines Royal Fleet, Jeddah, Saudi Arabia, 1982-84; tech. specialist McDonnell Douglas Helicopter Co., Mesa, Ariz., 1989-91; prin. engr. Boeing Aerospace Co., Huntsville, Ala., 1991-98, assoc. tech. fellow, 1998—. Author: (computer codes) Fatigue Life Calculation & Fracture Control, 1980, co-author: Lunar and Planetary Landers for Human Exploration Missions, 1992, Alternative Configurations and Subsystem Analysis for the First Lunar Outpost, 1993. Mem. AIAA (sr. mem.), Pi Mu Epsilon, Alpha Sigma Nu. Muslim. Achievements include development of methodology and computer codes for crack propagation and aircraft fatigue life prediction; research in manned and unmanned missions to the Moon and Mars; structural analysis of state of the art aerospace programs such as Internat. Space Station, Beech Aircraft Starship, V22 Osprey, McDonnell Douglas Apache AH-64, NOTAR, LHX and C-17, Airforce TTTS project; development of guidelines for Saudia Royal B747 maintenance program. *

IMUS, DON, radio host; m. Deirdre Imus. Radio host WNBC, 1971-88, WFAN, 1988—; TV host MS/NBC, 1996—. Author: God's Other Son; co-author: (with Fred Imus) Two Guy's Four Corners, 1997; appeared on Prime Time Live, Larry King, David Lettermen, 60 Minutes, The Today Show. Host radiothon CJ Found. for Sids and the Tomorrow's Children's Fund, 1990—. Recipient three Marconi awards; named Major Market Personality of the Year, Syndicated Personality of the Year; Named Emerson Radio Hall Fame, Nat. Assn. Broadcasters Broadcasting Hall of Fame, Time Mags. Most Influential Ams., 1997. Office: Westwood One Entertainment 1675 Broadway New York NY 10019-5820 also: care WFAN-AM 34-12 36th St Astoria NY 11106*

IMWINKELRIED, EDWARD JOHN, law educator; b. San Francisco, Sept. 19, 1946; s. John Joseph and Enes Rose (Giannelli) I.; m. Cynthia Marie Clark, Dec. 30, 1978; children—Marie Elise, Kenneth West. B.A., U. San Francisco, 1967, J.D., 1969. Bar: Calif. 1970, Mo. 1984, U.S. Supreme Ct. 1974. Prof. law U. San Diego, 1974-79; prof. law Washington U., St. Louis, 1979-85, U. Calif.-Davis, 1985—; disting. faculty mem. Nat. Coll. Dist. Attys., Houston, 1978—. Author: Evidentiary Foundations, 1980, 4th rev. edit., 1998, Uncharged Misconduct Evidence, 1984, rev. edit., 1999; co-author: Materials for Study of Evidence, 1983, 4th edit., 1997, Scientific Evidence, 1986, 2d rev. edit. 1993, Pretrial Discovery: Strategy and Tactics, 1986, Courtroom Criminal Evidence, 1987, 2d edit., 1993, California Evidentiary Foundations, 1988, 2d edit., 1994, Dynamics of Trial Practice, 1989, 2d edit., 1995, Exculpatory Evidence, 1990, 2d edit., 1996, Florida Evidentiary Foundations, 1991, 2d edit., 1997, Illinois Evidentiary Foundations, 1991, 2d edit., 1997, Texas Evidentiary Foundations, 1992, 2d edit., 1998, New York Evidentiary Foundations, 1993, 2d edit., 1997, Evidentiary Distinctions, 1993, Colorado Evidentiary Foundations, 1997; contbg. editor Champion pub. Assn. Criminal Def. Lawyers, 1983, Courtroom Law Bull. Mem. Am. Acad. Forensic Sci., ABA (continuing edn. com. 1983-84), Am. Assn. Law Schs. (chmn. evidence sect. 1983). Democrat. Roman Catholic. Avocation: jogging. Home: 2204 Shenandoah Pl Davis CA 95616-6603 Office: U Calif Law Sch Davis CA 95616

INABA, LAWRENCE AKIO, educational director; b. Honolulu, May 19, 1932; m. Violet C. Oki, Mar. 19, 1955; 1 child, Lori. BEd, U. Hawaii, 1960, MEd, 1963; PhD, Ohio State U., 1970; EdD, Ashiya U., Japan, 1980. Cert. tchr., Hawaii. Electronics instr. Roosevelt High Sch., Honolulu, 1959-68; rsch., teaching assoc. Ohio State U., Columbus, 1968-70; program specialist vocat. edn. Dept. Edn., Honolulu, 1970-75, adminstr. vocat. edn., 1975-76, edn. dir., 1976-85; state dir. vocat. edn. U. Hawaii, Honolulu, 1985-90; dir. Ashiya U. Rsch. Ctr., Honolulu, 1991—; cons. in field. Author: Analysis of Job Tasks, 1973, Effective Use of Advisory Committee, 1975, Content Identification and Validation, 1974, Trends and Developments in Vocational Education, 1984. NDEA fellow, 1967. Mem. Hawaii Vocat. Assn., Am. Vocat. Assn. (Guidance Divsn. Svc. award 1991), Hawaii Electronics Assn., Am. Tech. Educators Assn., Epsilon Pi Tau (Disting. Svc. award 1988, Laureate citation 1978), Phi Delta Kappa. Avocation: electronics. Home: 3791 Pukalani Pl Honolulu HI 96816-3813 Office: 1117 Kapahulu Ave Honolulu HI 96816-5811

INABINET, LAWRENCE ELLIOTT, retired pharmacist; b. Orangeburg, S.C., June 15, 1933; s. Boysie Benjamin and Alrona Minerva (Robinson) I.; m. Velma Vincent Ferguson (div.); children: Rhett Elliott, Bonny Susan Murphy. BS in Pharmacy, U. S.C., 1963. Registered pharmacist, S.C. Retail pharmacist chain and ind. drug stores, 1963-69; staff hosp. pharmacist S.C. State Hosp., Columbia, S.C., 1969-71; staff pharmacist Hawthorne Pharmacy, Columbia, S.C., 1971-72, Hemingway (S.C.) Pharmacy, 1990-93, Revco Drug Stores, Marion, S.C., 1993-95; pharmacy supr. S.C. Dept. Corrections, Columbia, 1972-79; retail pharmacist Ind. Drug Stores, 1979-84; hosp. pharmacist Baker Hosp., North Charleston, S.C., 1984-86; asst. dir. pharmacy Marion (S.C.) Meml. Hosp., 1986-90. Author: (text) Civilian-Military Time Converter; patentee medicating device for animals, timepiece for converting mil. to civilian time and vice versa, 1997; contbr. poems to pubs. Deacon Bapt. ch. With USN, 1954-58. Mem. Am. Legion, Masons (past master, masonic knight templar), Kappa Psi. Avocations: guitar, song writing, sports cards, music. Home: 1-B Greenwood Park Marion SC 29571-9406

INBODY, DALE DEWAYNE, farmer; b. New Paris, Ind., Dec. 27, 1925; s. John Paul and Laura (Haberstich) I.; m. Doris Ilene Burkey, Mar. 23, 1957; children: Randal, Thomas, Carla. Pres. Elkhart Co. Farm Bur. Coop., Goshen, Ind. 1st lt. Elkhart County Fire Dept., Goshen, 1951-71; v.p. Elkhart County Planning Commn.; pres. Elkhart County Bd. Zoning Appeals. Sgt. U.S. Army, 1954-56. Mem. Gideons Internat., Ind. Farm Bur. Co-op. Assn. (bd. dirs. 1983-91, pres. Gideons-Elkhart South Camp), Countrymark Co-op (bd. dirs. 1991-92), Goshen Kiwanis Club. Democrat. Methodist.

INCANDELA, GERALD JEAN-MARIE, artist; b. Tunis, Tunisia, Feb. 19, 1952; came to U.S., 1977; s. Laurent and Gilda (Solina) I. BA, Janson De Sailly, Paris, 1970; postgrad., U. of Nanterre, Paris, 1971-73. One man shows include Felicity Samuel Gallery, London, 1978, Gallery Jean Chauvelin, Paris, 1978, Charles Cowles Gallery, N.Y., 1981, Robert Fraser Gallery, London, 1984, Mus. Modern Art, Oxford, Eng., 1986, Paul Kasmin, N.Y., 1988, SEBU, Japan, 1990; exhbns. in group shows at Hal Bromm Gallery, 1975, Grey Art Gallery, 1977, Corcoran Gallery, 1978, Jacksonville (Fla.) Mus., 1981, The Drawing Ctr., N.Y.C., 1982, Met. Mus. of N.Y.C., 1982, Mus. of Modern Art, 1983, Walker Art Ctr., 1986, J. Paul Getty Mus., Santa Monica, 1998. Home and Office: 88 Lexington Ave New York NY 10016-8943

INCAPRERA, FRANK PHILIP, internist; b. New Orleans, Aug. 24, 1928; s. Charles and Mamie (Bellipanni) I.; m. Ruth Mary Duhon, Sept. 13, 1952; children: Charles, Cynthia, James, Christopher, Catherine. BS, Loyola U. of South, 1946; MD, La. State U. Med. Sch., 1950. Diplomate Am. Bd. Internal Medicine. Intern Charity Hosp., New Orleans, 1950-51, resident, 1951-52; resident VA Hosp., New Orleans, 1952-54; practice medicine specializing in internal medicine New Orleans, 1957-97; med. dir. Internal Medicine Group, 1973-97, chief med. officer, 1997-99; med. dir. Owens-Ill. Glass Co., New Orleans, 1961-85, Kaiser Aluminum Co., Chalmette, La., 1975-84, Tenneco Oil Co., Chalmette, 1978-84, Luth. Nursing Home, 1990-99; assoc. med. dir. Cigna Health Plan of La., 1991-99; co-founder Med. Ctr. E. New Orleans, 1975; clin. assoc. prof. medicine Tulane U. Sch. Medicine, 1971-87, clin. prof. medicine, 1987—, clin. prof. medicine La. State U., 1994—; adv. bd. Healthcare New Orleans, 1991-96; mem. New Orleans Bd. Health, 1966-70. Bd. dirs. Meth. Hosp., 1971-97, sec. 1992-96, Chateau de Notre Dame, 1977-92, New Orleans Opera Assn., 1975—; mem. New Orleans Human Rels. Com., 1968-70; bd. dirs. Emergency Med. Svcs. Coun., 1977-86, pres. La. southeastern region, 1979-81; bd. dirs. New Orleans East Bus. Assn., 1980-85, v.p. 1981-83; bd. dirs. Luth. Towers, 1988-89, Peace Lake Towers, 1988-89, La. State U. Med. Ctr. Found. Bd., 1989-91, Cristo Sana, 1997—; mem. pastoral care adv. com. So. Bapt. Hosp., 1982-83; mem. pres.'s adv. bd. coun. Loyola U. of South, 1989-96. Capt. USAF, 1955-57. Lifetime award Outstanding Svc. Cefalutana Soc., La., 1998. Fellow ACP (gov. 1995-99, Laureate award 1993), Am. Geriatrics Soc.; mem. AMA, Am. Coll. Physicians Execs., La. Med. Soc. (v.p. 1975-76), Orleans Parish Med. Soc. (sec. 1972-74), New Orleans Acad. Internal Medicine (pres. 1969), La. Occupl. Medicine Assn. (pres. 1971-72), La. State Med. Soc. (v.p. 1975-76), La. Soc. Internal Medicine (exec. com. 1975-98, pres. 1983-85), New Orleans East C. of C. (dir. 1979-85), La. State U. Med. Sch. Alumni Assn. (pres. 1989-90, Alumnus of Yr. 1996), Order of St. Louis, Blue Key, Optimists Club (bd. dirs. 1964-69, New Orleans), Delta Epsilon Sigma, Alpha Omega Alpha (Beta chpt.). Home: 2218 Lake Oaks Pky New Orleans LA 70122-4345 Office: 10001 Lake Forest Blvd New Orleans LA 70127-5240

INCAUDO, JOSEPH AUGUST, engineering company executive; b. 1940. MA, UCLA, 1961; MBA, Harvard U., 1964. CPA, Calif. Cons., auditor Touche Ross & Co., L.A., 1964-68; contr. Bullocks, L.A., 1969-76; v.p. ops. May Co., L.A., 1976-78; v.p. fin. Tobias Kotzin Corp., L.A., 1978-80; v.p., CFO Vinnell Corp., Alhambra, Calif., 1980-83; sr. v.p., CFO/CAO Aecom Tech. Corp., L.A., 1983—; bd. dirs. Resource Scis. of Arabia Ltd., Inst. of Social and Econ. Policy in the Middle East, John F. Kennedy Sch. Govt., Harvard U. Office: Aecom Tech Corp 3250 Wilshire Blvd # 5 Los Angeles CA 90010-1577

INCROPERA, FRANK PAUL, mechanical engineering educator; b. Lawrence, Mass., May 12, 1939; s. James Frank and Ann Laura (Leone) I.; m. Andrea Jeanne Eastman, Sept. 2, 1960; children: Terri Ann, Donna Renee, Shaunna Jeanne. BSME, MIT, 1961; MS, Stanford U., 1962, PhD, 1966. Jr. engr. Barry Controls Corp., Watertown, Mass., 1959; thermodynamics engr. Aerojet Gen. Corp., Azusa, Calif., 1961; heat transfer specialist Lockheed Missiles and Space Co., Sunnyvale, Calif., 1962-64; mem. faculty Purdue U., 1966-98, prof. mech. engring., 1973-98, head dept., 1989-98; dean of engring. Notre Dame (Ind.) U., 1998—; cons. in field. Author: Introduction to Molecular Structure and Thermodynamics, 1974, Fundamentals of Heat Transfer, 1985, 90, 96; Fundamentals of Heat and Mass Transfer, 1981, 85, 90, 96, Liquid Cooling of Electronic Devices by Single-Phase Convection, 1999; also articles. Recipient Solberg Teaching award Purdue U., 1973, 77, 86, Potter Teaching award, 1973, Von Humboldt sr. scientist award Fed. Republic Germany, 1988. Fellow ASME (Melville medal 1988, Heat Transfer Meml. award 1988, Worcester Reed Warner award 1995); mem. Am. Soc. Engring. Edn. (Ralph C. Roe award 1982, George Westinghouse award 1983), Nat. Acad. Engring. Achievements include invention of bloodless surg. scalpel. Office: Notre Dame U Coll Engring 257 Fitzpatrick Hall Notre Dame IN 46556

INCULET, ION I., electrical engineering educator, research director, consultant; b. Iasi, Moldova, Romania, Feb. 11, 1921; arrived in Can., 1948; s. Ion C. and Ruxanda (Basota) I.; m. Marion Elsie Smith, Aug. 25, 1951; children: Richard, Catherine, Diana. Diploma in engring., Politechnica, Bucuresti, Romania, 1944; M in Engring. Sci., Laval U., Que., 1962; DTechSc (hon.), Bucharest U., Romania, 1993; DSc (hon.), We. Ont. Can. U., 1996. Advance devel. engr. Can. GE, Peterborough, Ont., 1948-56; mgr. engring., Que. Can. GE, 1956-64; prof. elec. engring. U. Western Ont., London, 1964—, dir. environ. engring., 1966-68, dir. Applied Electrostatics Rsch. Ctr., 1986—; pres. Elstat, Ltd., London, 1972—; cons. in field. Author: 1 book; contbr. over 110 articles to profl. jours., book chpts.; holder 27 patents. Recipient T.C. Keefer medal Can. Soc. Civil Engring., 1994-95. Fellow IEEE (Centennial medal 1984), Can. Acad. Engring., Inst. Electrostatics of Japan; mem. NSPE (engring. medal 1984), Industry Applications Soc. IEEE (Outstanding Achievement award 1983), Romanian Acad. (hon.). Avocation: skiing. Home: 81 Lloyd Manor Crescent, London, ON Canada N6H 3Z4 Office: U Western Ont Engring Bldg, Electrostatics Rsch Ctr, London, ON Canada N6A 5B9

INDICK, JANET, sculptor, educational administrator; b. Bklyn., Mar. 3, 1932; d. Charles and Sarah (Goldsmith) Suslak; m. Benjamin Philip Indick, Aug. 23, 1953; children: Michael Korie, Karen Leigh Indick Maizel. BS in Art, Hunter Coll., 1953, postgrad., 1953; postgrad., New Sch., 1961-62. Tchr. kindergarten pub. schs. Elizabeth, N.J., 1953-54; dir. nursery sch. Teaneck Jewish Ctr., N.J., 1964-92; mem. Teaneck Arts Adv. Bd., 1982-88. Commns. include sculpture for Netzach Yisrael, Teaneck Jewish Ctr., 1974, Etz Chaim 1981, Sanctuary Wall Menorah 1983, Temple Beth Rishon, Wyckoff, N.J., 1981, 83, Menorah, Franklin Lakes Pub. Sch., 1983, North Shore Synagogue, Syosset, N.Y., 1993, Temple Sharey Telfilo Israel, South Orange, N.J., 1993; one-woman shows include Discovery Art Gallery, Clifton, N.Y., 1976, Mari Art Gallery, Westchester, N.Y., 1983, Hebrew Tabernacle, N.Y.C., 1984, Chubb Corp., Basking Ridge, N.J., 1985, Edward Williams Gallery, Fairleigh Dickinson U., Hackensack, N.J., 1986, Vineyard Gallery, N.Y.C., 1986, Maurice M. Pine Gallery, Fairlawn (N.J.) Pub. Libr., 1990, Quietude Garden Gallery, East Brunswick, N.J., 1991-92, Bergen Mus. Art. & Sci., Paramus, N.J., 1994, N.Y.C. Boathouse Cafe, 1998, Interchurch Ctr., N.Y., 1999; juried exhbns. include Morris Mus., N.J., 1979, 84, Newark Mus., N.J., 1982, Jersey City Mus., N.J., 1983, Hebrew Tabernacle, N.Y.C. 1984, Parsons Gallery, N.Y.C., 1984, Lillian Heidenberg Gallery, N.Y.C., 1984-96, Shering-Plough Corp., Madison, N.J., 1987, Kerygma Gallery, Ridgewood, N.J., 1989-96, Marabella Gallery, N.Y.C., 1989, So. Vt. Art Ctr., Manchester, 1990, Nat. Assn. Women Artists Traveling Exhbns., 1989-90, 96, Traveling Exhbns., 1998-99, Fgn. Traveling Exhbns., India, 1989-90, Columbus (Ohio) Mus. Fine Art, 1989-90, Balt. Mus. Art, 1989-90, Marunouchi Gallery, N.Y.C., 1994, Waterside Gallery, W. Stockbridge, Mass., 1995, L'Atelier Gallery, Piermont, N.Y., 1994-96, Polo Gallery, Edgewater, N.J., 1994-99; represented in collections Jane Voorhees Zimmerli Art Mus. Rutgers U., New Brunswick, N.J., Corp. Towers Perrin, N.Y.C., AMP Corp., Harrisburg, Pa., Myron Mfg. Corp., Maywood, N.J., Chiropractic Health Care, Bergenfield, N.J., Bergen Mus., Paramus, N.J., Weingroup Equities Corp., N.Y.C., Hubbards Cupboard Corp., Edison, N.J., Rosenthal Art Equities, N.Y.C., Franklin Lakes (N.J.) Pub. Schs., Temple Beth Rishon, Wykoff, N.J., North Shore Synagogue, Syosset, N.Y., Temple Sharey Tefilo, South Orange, N.J., Teaneck (N.J.) Jewish Ctr. Recipient Sculpture awards Nat. Assn. Painters and Sculptors, 1978, 80, Sculpture award Art in the Park, Paterson, N.J., 1977, Merit award IFFRA/AIA Forum on Religion, Art and Architecture, 1984, H.W. Frismuth Bronze Sculpture award, 1992, Corp. award, 1995, Pauline Law Sculpture prize, 1974, Clara Shainess Meml. award, 1994, Jeffrey Childs Willis Meml. award, 1997; N.J. State Coun. Arts fellow, 1981. Mem. Nat. Assn. Women Artists (pres. 1997-99), N.Y. Soc. Women Artists (sculpture chair 1990-99), Artists Equity, Catherine Lorrilard Wolfe Art Club (bd. dirs. 1994-96, 1st award for sculpture 1999). Democrat. Jewish. Home: 428 Sagamore Ave Teaneck NJ 07666-2626

INDIEK, VICTOR HENRY, finance corporation executive; b. Spearville, Kans., Nov. 15, 1937; s. Ben W. and Helen Ann (Schreck) I.; m. Marlene Gould, June 2, 1962; children: Kathy, Kevin. Student, U. Nebr., 1955-57; BS in Bus., U. Kans., 1959; postgrad., U. Nebr., 1955-57. CPA, Kans. Audit mgr. Arthur Andersen & Co., Kansas City, Mo., 1961-70; pres., chief exec. officer Fed. Home Loan Mortgage Corp., Washington, 1970-77; pres., dir. Builders Capital Corp., Los Angeles, 1977-84; chief fin. officer, exec. v.p. Fin. Corp. of Am., Irvine, Calif., 1984-88; pres., chief exec. officer FarWest Savs. and Loan Assn., Newport Beach, Calif., 1988—; with Kennedy Wilson, 1989-98; pvt. practice in real estate, 1998—; v.p. and pres. regional Assn. Small Businesses Investment Cos., 1979-81, bd. govs. nat. assn., 1982. Mem. Selective Service Bd., Santa Monica, Calif., 1978; capt. United Fund, Kansas City, 1968. Served with USN, 1959-61. Republican. Roman Catholic. Avocations: boating, skiing. Office: Kennedy Wilson 50 Hillsdale Dr Newport Beach CA 92660

INDIVIGLIA, SALVATORE JOSEPH, artist, retired naval officer; b. N.Y.C., Nov. 16, 1919; s. Joseph and Alfonsina Barbara (Gaeta) I.; widower Jan. 1986; children: Barbara Ann (dec.), Joseph, Lawrence, Dianne. BA, Pratt Inst., 1948; AS, U.S. Naval Acad., 1976. Mural painter asst. Crimi Studio, N.Y.C., 1939-42; art dir. Advt. Printin Co., N.Y.C., 1946-63; art tchr. Mechanics Inst., N.Y.C., 1962-66; v.p. Vogue Wright Studios, N.Y.C., 1963-80; dir. art Electrographic Corp., N.Y.C., Chgo., 1968-70; artist, account exec. Chelsea Photo/Graphics, Inc., N.Y.C., 1981-84; official USN combat artist, Washington, 1960-89. Exhibited in group show Smithsonian Inst., Operations Palette, 1965, Joe & Emily Lowe Found., 1955, 1963 (Liquitex award 1997); painter Am. Artist Mag., 1971; painter watercolors USN Combat Art Collection. N.Y. State Naval Militia, 1962, 91, 94, 96, 97. Comdr. USNR, 1962-79. Decorated Navy Commendation medal, Croce Al Merito Di Guerra Italian Govt., 1945, Vietnamese Cross Gallantry with Palm Vietnamese Govt., 1964-67. Republican. Roman Catholic. Avocations: playing guitar, singing country & western music. Home: 974 Lorraine Dr Franklin Square NY 11010-1813

INDYK, MARTIN S., diplomat; b. London, July 1, 1951. BE, Sydney U.; PhD in Internat. Rel., Australian Natl. U. Spec. asst. to the pres. & sr. dir. for Near East & So. Asian affairs Natl. Sec. Council; deputy dir. current intelligence for the Mid-East Australia, 1978; exec. dir Washington Inst. for Near East Policy, 1985; U.S. amb. to Israel U.S. Dept. of State, 1995-97; asst. sec. Near Ea. affairs, 1997—; sr. mem. Sec. Christopher's Mid-East peace team; White House Rep. U.S.-Israel Sci. & Tech. Commission; adj. prof. Johns Hopkins Sch. Adv. Internat. Studies. Office: US Dept State Near Ea Affairs 2201 C St NW Washington DC 20520-6243*

INFANTE, EDWARD A., federal judge; b. 1940. AB, Boston Coll., 1962; JD, Boston U., 1965. Law clk. to Hon. Edward McEntree 1st cir. U.S. Ct. Appeals; fed. pub. defender so. dist. U.S. Dist. Ct. Calif., 1970; bus. litigation and white collar criminal def. Pedersen, Flowers & Infante, San Diego, 1971-72; ptnr. bus. litigation Schall, Boudreau & Gore, San Diego, 1986-88; apptd. magistrate judge no. dist. U.S. Dist. Ct. Calif., 1990; adj. prof. Santa Clara U. Sch. Law, 1990—. With USN, 1966-69, USNR, 1980-90. Mem. Nat. Magistrate Judges Assn. (treas. 1979, v.p. 1980, pres. 1981). Fax: (408) 535-5376. Office: 4198 US Courthouse 280 S 1st St San Jose CA 95113-3002

INFANTE, ETTORE FERRARI, mathematician, educator, university administrator; b. Modena, Italy, Aug. 20, 1938; came to U.S., 1954; s. Ferdinando Bassani and Cecilia (Ferrari) I.; m. Trudi C. Miller; children: Cecilia Ann, Michael Gregory. BA, U. Tex., 1958, BS, 1959, PhD, 1962; MA (hon.), Brown U., 1968. Asst. prof. U. Tex., Austin, 1962-65; asst. prof. Brown U., Providence, 1964-68, assoc. prof., 1968-72, prof., 1972-84; div. dir. math. and computer sci. NSF, Washington, 1981-84; prof. math., dean Inst. Tech. U. Minn., Mpls., 1984-91, sr. v.p. for acad. affairs, provost, 1991-96; prof. math., dean Coll. Arts and Scis. Vanderbilt U., Nashville, 1997—; cons. Humble Oil & Refining Co., Houston, 1962-64, NSF, 1980-81, various research organizations and univs., 1964—. Contbr. numerous articles to profl. jours.; patentee in field. Grantee NSF, 1967-84, Office Naval Rsch., 1968-79, Army Rsch. Office, 1967-82, Ctr. Nat. Recherche Scientifique, France, 1972-73; Ford Found. fellow, 1964-65. Fellow Am. Acad. Mechanics; mem. IEEE (sr.), ASME, Soc. for Indsl. and Applied Math. (coun. 1980-82, trustee 1985-91, disting. speaker 1966-68), Am. Math. Soc. Roman Catholic. Office: Vanderbilt U 301 Kirkland Hall Nashville TN 37240

INFANTE-OGBAC, DAISY INOCENTES, sales and real estate executive, marketing executive; b. Marbel, The Philippines, Aug. 3, 1946; came to U.S., 1968; d. Jesus and Josefina (Inocentes) I.; children: Desiree Josephine, Dante Fernancio, Darrell Enerico; m. Rosben Reyes Ogbac, Jan. 30, 1987. AA with highest honors, Notre Dame of Marbel, Philippines, 1963; AB in English magna cum laude, U. Santo Tomas, Manila, 1965, BS in Psychology, 1966; MA in Communications, Fairfield U., 1971. Columnist, writer Pinoy News mag., Chgo., 1975-76, Philippine News, Chgo., 1977-80; cons. EDP Cemco Systems, Inc., Oak Brook, Ill., 1980-81; pres. Daisener, Inc., Downers Grove, Ill., 1980-82; cons. EDP Robert J. Irmen Assocs., Hinsdale, Ill., 1981-82; pres. Data Info. Systems Corp., Downers Grove, Ill., 1982-84; broker, co. mgr. Gen. Devel. Corp., Chgo., 1984-86; columnist, writer Via Times, Chgo., 1984-86; owner, pres. Marbel Realty, Chgo., 1984-88; exec. v.p. Dior Enterprises, Inc., Chgo., 1986-88; real estate sales mgr. M.J. Cumber Co., Grand Cayman, Cayman Islands, 1988-89, Vet. Real Estate, Orlando, Fla., 1989-90; sales mgr. All Star Real Estate, Inc., Orlando, 1990-92; ruby network mktg. exec. Melaleuca, Inc., 1991—; pres. Dior Enterprises, Inc., Orlando, 1992—; bd. dirs. Network Mktg. Alliance, 1996—. Author: Songs of Love, Prayer, and Worship to the Lord, 1998, Poems of My Youth, 1982; (lyrics and music) My First Twenty Songs, 1981; featured contbr. poems; American Poetry Anthology, vol. VIII, no. 4, Best New Poets of 1987; inventor fryer-steamer. Sec. Movement for a Free Philippines, 1984. Mem. NAFE, Am. Soc. Profl. Exec. Women, Philippine C. of C. (sec. Chgo. chpt. 1985), Bayanihan Internat. Ladies Assn., Lions (twister Fil-Am. club 1978-79). Roman Catholic. Avocations: bowling, swimming, racquetball, tennis.

INFINGER, GLORIA ALTMAN, nursing administrator; b. Charleston, S.C., Feb. 16, 1941; d. Norman B. and Gladys V. Risher; m. Norman M. Infinger, May 21, 1961; children: Robert M., Michael S. Diploma, Med. U.S.C., 1962. RN, S.C.; cert. nurse adminstr., register cen. svc. technician. Nurse Med. U. S.C. Med. Ctr., Charleston, 1962-68, nursing supr., asst. dir. evening shift, 1974-86, mgr. sterile processing, 1986-94, sterile processing cons., 1994; office nurse John Aycock, M.D., Mt. Pleasant, S.C., 1968-69; asst. head nurse Charleston Meml. Hosp., 1969-73; part-time RN Med. U. S.C., 1995-98; part-time salesperson Margiotta's Inc., 1998—. Mem. AHA, Am. Soc. for Hosp. Ctrl. Svc. Pers., S.C. Assn. for Hosp. Ctrl. Svc. Pers. (founder 1992), N.C. Assn. for Hosp. Ctrl. Svc. Pers., Internat. Assn. Hosp. Ctrl. Svc. Material Mgmt., S.C. State Employees Assn. Office: Margiotta's Sewing Machine Inc 874 Orleans Rd Ste #5 Charleston SC 29407

INFUSINO, ACHILLE FRANCIS, construction company executive; b. Kenosha, Wis., Feb. 8, 1953; s. Frank and Irene (Rende) I.; m. Joyce Marie, Nov. 22, 1975; children: Daniel, Nicholas, Jaclyn, Timothy. BA, Carthage Coll., 1982; MBA, Marquette U., 1987. Pres. Infusino Bros. Constrn. Co., Inc., Kenosha, 1987—, Cellular City Communications, Kenosha, 1987—; founder, sr. project mgr. Project Mgmt. Cons., Kenosha, 1994—; instr. Carthage Coll., 1990. Bd. dirs. Kenosha Area Devel. Corp., 1981-87, Salvation Army Adv. Bd., Kenosha, 1983-85; pres. St. Joseph's Interparish Jr. High Sch., Kenosha, 1986-91; chmn. Bd. Building Appeals, City of Kenosha, 1986-88. Mem. Italian Am. Soc., MBA Execs., Assn. Constrn. Insps., Environ. Assessment Assn. Avocations: youth athletic programs, little league baseball. Office: Project Mgmt Cons 3614 16th Pl Kenosha WI 53144-3376

ING, CLARENCE SINN FOOK, preventive medicine physician, ophthalmic surgeon; b. Stockton, Calif., Oct. 1, 1938; s. Clarence S. and Isabel L. (Low) I.; m. May Chan, July 9, 1961; children: Michael, Stephen, Jeffrey, Daniel, Michelle. BA, La Sierra U., 1959; MD, Loma Linda U., 1963, MPH, 1990. Diplomate Am. Bd. Ophthalmology, Am. Bd. Preventive Medicine. Intern San Joaquin Gen. Hosp., Stockton, Calif., 1963-64; dir. emergency med. svc. St. Francis Hosp., Lynwood, Calif., 1966, Cmty. Hosp. San Gabriel, Calif., 1967; resident ophthalmology Hollywood Presbyn. Hosp., L.A., 1967-70; med. missionary Bella Vista Hosp., Mayaguez, P.R., 1970-78; staff physician Wildwood (Ga.) Sanitarium & Hosp., 1978-81; med. missionary, chief staff Armer Ishoda Meml. Hosp., Majuro, Marshall Islands, 1981-82; med. missionary Youngberg Adventist Hosp., Singapore, 1982-89; resident preventive medicine Loma Linda U. Med. Ctr., 1990-91; med. missionary, dir. Wellness Ctr. Youngberg Adventist Hosp., Singapore, 1992-97; med. dir. Weimar Inst., 1997—. Capt. U.S. Army, 1964-66. Fellow Am. Acad. Ophthalmology; mem. Am. Coll. Preventive Medicine. Avocations: alpine skiing, scuba diving, golf, jogging, tennis. Fax: 530-637-4443. E-mail: csfing1@juno.com. Office: Weimar Inst PO Box 486 20601 W Paoli Ln Weimar CA 95736-0486

INGAGLIO, DIEGO AUGUSTUS, dentist; b. Phila., Dec. 4, 1922; s. Salvatore and Maria Concetta (Giordano) I.; D.D.S., U. Pa., 1947; m. Geraldine Jean Capizzi, July 11, 1948; children: Marie, Francene. With Phila. Mouth Hygiene Dept., 1947-50; asst. clin. dir. Emerson R. Sausser Med. Dental Clinic, Jefferson Hosp., Phila., 1950-51; pvt. practice dentistry, Drexel Hill, Pa., 1953—; staff Suburban Gen. Hosp., Norristown. Mem. Congressional Adv Bd. Editor-in-chief U. Pa. Dental Jour., 1945-47. Integenerational com. Upper Twp. Elem. Sch. With AUS, 1943-45, 51-53. Past pres. mature adults Resurrection Ch., Marmora, N.J., lector for mass readings, mem. Friends for Life com.; mem. Upper Twp. Elem. Sch. Intergenerational Coun.; mem. Resurrection Ch. Liturgy Group. Fellow Acad. Gen. Dentistry, Acad. Dentistry Internat., Royal Soc. Health; mem. ADA, AAAS, Pa. Dental Assn., Chester-Delaware County Dental Assn., Am. Internat., Philadelphia County Socs. Clin. Hypnosis, Nat. Space Inst., Phila. Physhodontontic Soc. (past pres.), Royal Soc. Hygiene, Nat. Assn. Fed. Lic. Firearms Dealers, NRA, Cape May County Serra Group (pres.), Heritage Found., Omicron Kappa Upsilon, Psi Omega. Address: 670 Breckley Rd Marmora NJ 08223-1158

INGALLS, MARIE CECELIE, former state legislator, retail executive; b. Faith, S.D., Mar. 31, 1936; d. Jens P. and Ida B. (Hegre) Jensen; m. Dale D. Ingalls, June 20, 1955; children: Duane, Delane. BS, Black Hills State Coll., 1973, MS, 1978. Elem. tchr. Meade County Schs., Sturgis, S.D., 1957-72, Faith Sch. Dist. 46-2, 1973-76; elem. prin. Meade Sch. Dist. 46-1, Sturgis, 1976-81; owner, operator Ingalls, Sturgis, 1978—; mem., asst. majority whip S.D. House Reps., Pierre, 1986-92; lobbyist S.D. Legislature. Former sec. S.D. Rep. Orgn; Rep. nominee S.D. Commr. Sch. and Pub. Lands, 1998. Recipient Woman of Achievement award City of Sturgis, 1986, Retail Bus. of Yr. 1998. Mem. S.D. Cattlewomen, S.D. Stockgrowers (edn. chair), S.D. Farm Bur. (bd. dirs. dist. V), Faith C. of C. (pres. 1989), Sturgis C. of C. (past bd. dirs.). Republican. Lutheran. Avocations: knitting, crocheting, piano, reading. Home: PO Box Pox # 31 Mud Butte SD 57758 Office: Ingalls 1032 Main St Sturgis SD 57785-1587

INGALLS, RICK LEE, fundraising consulting executive; b. Petoskey, Mich., May 19, 1946; s. Frank and LaVera Mae (Trumpoer) I.; m. Linda Sue Berry, Oct. 21, 1967 (div. May 1980); children: Robert Michael, Angela Lynn; m. Donna Marie DeWitt, June 8, 1985. AA, Ark. State U., 1976; BA, Park Coll., 1980. Exec. dir. Ark. chpt. March of Dimes, Little Rock, 1978-81; sr. dir. Cmty. Svc. Bur., Inc., Dallas, 1981-87; pres. Am. Fund Raising Svcs., Tampa, Fla., 1987—; cons. firm devel. Rietdorf, Tombras & Cox, Knoxville, Tenn., 1989-91; instr. Miss. Ctr. for Non-Profits, Jackson, 1996-97. Contbr. chpt. to: Fund Raising Ideas for Non-profits, 1995; author, editor (brochures) A Heritage to Preserve—YMCA, 1989 (Addy award 1990), Homes for Kids—Hope For the Future, 1995; author brochure Phi Theta Kappa's Key Opportunity, 1992 (Best of Category award 1993). With USAF, 1966-70. Recipient Outstanding Young Man award Ctrl. Ark. C. of C., Little Rock, 1979, 94. Mem. Nat. Soc. Fund Raising Execs. (cert.). Avocation: golf. Home: 1641 W Snow Cir Tampa FL 33606-2558 Office: Am Fund Raising Svcs 1641 W Snow Cir Tampa FL 33606-2558

INGALLS, ROBERT LYNN, physicist, educator; b. Spokane, Wash., June 15, 1934; s. Keith Irving and Ruth Louise (Strauss) I.; m. Liisa Vasama, Jan. 28, 1961 (div. Apr. 1993); children: Karen Liisa, Johanna Louise, David Robert. B.S., U. Wash., 1956; M.S., Carnegie Inst. Tech., 1960, Ph.D., 1962. Instr. physics Carnegie Inst. Tech., 1961-63; research asso. U. Ill., 1963-65, research asso. prof., 1965-66; asst. prof. U. Wash., Seattle, 1966-69; asso. prof. U. Wash., 1969-74, prof. physics, 1974—; vis. scholar State U. Groningen, Netherlands, 1972-73. Bassoonist, Seattle Symphony Orch., 1952-57; contbr. articles on solid state and high pressure physics, Mossbauer effect X-ray absorption and quasicrystal tilings to profl. jours., books and encys.; pioneer in electric quadruple splitting theory in ferrous compounds, X-ray absorption fine structure studies of materials at high pressure. AEC contract, 1967-77; NSF grantee, 1976-83; Dept. Energy grantee, 1983—. Mem. AAAS, Am. Phys. Soc., Fedn. Am. Scientists, Sigma Xi, Sigma Phi Epsilon, Zeta Mu Tau. Office: U Wash Dept Physics Seattle WA 98195

INGARD, KARL UNO, physics educator; b. Gothenburg, Sweden, Feb. 24, 1921; married, 1948; 4 children. EE, Chalmers U. Tech., Sweden, 1944; tech. lic., Chalmers U. Tech., 1948; PhD in Physics, Mass. Inst. Tech., 1950; D, Chambers Inst. Tech., Sweden, 1979. Rsch. engr. nat. lab. Def., Stockholm, 1945-46; dir. acoustics lab. Chalmers U. Tech., Sweden, 1946-52; from asst. prof. to assoc. prof. Mass. Inst. Tech., 1952-66, prof. physics, 1966-91, prof. aeronautics and astronautics, 1971-91, prof. emeritus physics, aeronautics and astronautics, 1991—. Armstrong Cork fellow Mass. Inst. Tech., 1950, Guggenheim fellow, 1959; recipient Gustaf Dalen medal, Sweden, 1970, John Ericsson medal Am. Soc. Swedish Engrs., 1972, Rayleigh medal Inst. Acoustics, Eng., 1981, Per Bruel Gold medal Am. Soc. Mech. Engrs., 1989. Fellow Acoustical Soc. Am. (Biennial award 1954, Gold medal 1997), Am. Physics Soc.; mem. NAE, Inst. Noise Control Engrs., Sigma Xi. Achievements include research in plasma physics and acoustics. Address: Bldg #6-108 77 Massachusetts Ave Cambridge MA 02139*

INGARI, FRANK A., communications executive. Pres., CEO, dir. Shiva Corp., Bedford, Mass., 1993-98; CEO Growth Ally, Winchester, Mass., 1998—; bd. dirs. Sybase, Inc.; bd. govs. Mass. Telecomm. Coun., chmn. programs com. Office: Growth Ally 10 Mount Vernon St Ste 230 Winchester MA 01890-2704*

INGBER, DONALD ELLIOT, pathology and cell biology educator, bioengineer; b. Oceanside, N.Y., May 1, 1956; s. David and Helen Edith (Horowitz) I. BA, MA, Yale U., 1977, MPhil, 1981, MD, PhD, 1984. Fellow Harvard Med. Sch., Children's Hosp., Boston, 1984-86; instr. pathology Harvard Med. Sch., Brigham and Women's Hosp., Boston, 1986-88, asst. prof. pathology, 1988-92, assoc. prof. pathology, 1992-99; prof. pathology Harvard Med. Sch., Children's Hosp., Boston, 1999—; cons. in biotechnology Neomorphics, Boston, 1988-92, Biosyn R, Balt., 1987-88, Digene Diagnostics, Balt., 1990, Collaborative Rsch., Bedford, 1991-96, Advanced Tissue Sciences, La Jolla, Calif., 1992-96, Merck Corp.; founder Molecular Geodesics, Inc., 1996—. Contbr. articles to profl. jours., chpts. to books; writer TV scripts; artist cartoons for postcards; assoc. producer TV spl. R.C. Bates Travelling fellow, 1976; recipient Johnson & Johnson Rsch. Fund award, 1990, Whitaker Health Scis. Fund award, 1990, Am. Cancer Soc. Faculty Rsch. award, 1991. Mem. Am. Soc. Cell Biology, Tissue Culture Soc., Am. Soc. for Space and Gravitational Biology, Am. Assn. Cancer Rsch., Materials Rsch. Soc. Achievements include patents for angiogenesis inhibitors, biomimetic materials, medical devices, filtration systems, and tissue engineering applications; development of concept of a "Tensegrity Model" for cell and tissue architecture; discovery of a new class of anticancer drugs which inhibit blood vessel growth (angiogenesis), including TNP-470; demonstration of importance of extracellular matrix and mechanical stresses as regulators in tissue development. E-mail: ingber@a1.tch.harvard.edu. Office: Children's Hosp 300 Longwood Ave Boston MA 02115-5737

INGE, MILTON THOMAS, American literature and culture educator, author; b. Newport News, Va., Mar. 18, 1936; s. Clyde Elmo and Bernice Lucille (Jackson) I.; m. Betty Jean Meredith, 1958 (div. 1976); 1 child, Scott Thomas; m. Tonette Long Bond, 1982 (div. 1990); 1 stepchild, Michael Gordon Bond; m. Donaria Romeiro Carvalho, 1998. B.A., Randolph-Macon Coll., 1959; M.A., Vanderbilt U., 1960, Ph.D., 1964. Instr. English Vanderbilt U., 1962-64; asst. prof. Am. thought and lang. Mich. State U., 1964-68, assoc. prof., 1968-69; assoc. prof. English Va. Commonwealth U., Richmond, 1969-73, prof., 1973-80, chmn. dept. English, 1974-80; prof., chmn. dept. English, Clemson U., S.C., 1980-84; resident scholar in Am. studies USIA, Washington, 1982-84; Blackwell prof. humanities Randolph-Macon Coll., Ashland, Va., 1984—; reader English Composition Test Coll. Entrance Exam Bd., 1967, 69, 77, 80; Va. Cultural Laureate, 1992; dir. USIA Summer Inst. in Am. Studies, 1993, 94, 95. Author: Donald Davidson: Essay and Bibliography, 1965, (with T.D. Young) Donald Davidson, 1971, The American Comic Book, 1985, Comics in the Classroom, 1989, Great American Comics: 100 Years of Cartoon Art, 1990, Comics as Culture, 1990, Faulkner, Sut, and Other Southerners, 1992, Perspectives on American Culture: Essays on Humor, Literature, and the Popular Arts, 1994, Anything Can Happen in a Comic Strip: Centennial Reflections on an American Art Form, 1995; editor: (books) Sut Lovingood's Yarns, 1966, 2d edit. 1987, High Times and Hard Times, 1967, Agrarianism in American Literature, 1969, A.B. Longstreet, 1969, Faulkner: A Rose for Emily, 1970, Wm. Byrd of Westover, 1970, Studies in Light in August, 1971, Frontier Humorists: Critical Views, 1975, Ellen Glasgow: Centennial Essays, 1976,(with J. Bryer and M. Duke), Black American Writers: Bibliographic Essays, 2 vols., 1978, Handbook of American Popular Culture, Vol. I, 1978, Vol. II, 1980, Vol. III, 1981, 3 vols. rev. and expanded edits., 1989, Concise Histories of American Popular Culture, 1982, (with E.E. MacDonald), James Branch Cabell: Centennial Essays, 1983, (with J. Bryer and M. Duke), American Women Writers: Bibliographical Essays, 1983, Huck Finn Among the Critics: A Centennial Selection, 1984, rev. edit., 1985, Truman Capote: Conversations, 1987, Naming the Rose: Essays on Umberto Eco's "The Name of the Rose", 1988, Handbook of American Popular Literature, 1988, A Nineteenth Century American Reader, 1988, The Comics, 1991, (with Sergei Chakovsky) Russian Eyes on American Literature, 1992, Dark Laughter: The Satiric Art of Oliver W. Harrington, 1993, Why I Left America and Other Essays of Oliver W. Harrington, 1993, William Faulkner: The Contemporary Reviews, 1994, (with James E. Caron) Sut Lovingood's Nat'ral Born Yarnspinner: Essays on George Washington Harris, 1996, Mark Twain's A Connecticut Yankee in King Arthur's Court, 1997, The Achievement of William Faulkner: A Centennial Tribute, 1998; Conversations with William Faulkner, 1999, "Co. Aytch," or a Side Show and Other Sketches by Samuel R. Watkins, 1999, editor jours. Resources for American Literary Study, 1971-79, American Humor: An Interdisciplinary Newsletter, 1974-79; gen. editor Greenwood Press Bio-Bibliographies and Reference Guides in Popular Culture, Cambridge U. Press Am. Critical Archives, U. Press Miss. Studies in Popular Culture; book reviewer: Nashville Tenneseean, Richmond Times-Dispatch. Bd. dirs. Friends of Richmond Pub. Libary; bd. dirs. San Francisco Acad. Comic Art. Fellow So. Fellowship Fund, 1959-62, Newberry Libr., 1987, Va. Found. for Humanities, 1987, 93; grantee Fulbright-Hays, 1967-68, 71, 79, 88, 94, Mich. State U., 1965, 66, 68, Am. Philos. Soc., 1970, Clemson U., 1981, NEH, 1986, 91, 92; recipient Disting. Alumnus award Randolph-Macon Coll., 1995. Mem. MLA (del. assembly 1976-78, chmn. elections com. 1980), South Atlantic MLA (program com. 1982-85, chmn. 1986, v.p. 1987, pres. 1988-89), Am. Studies Assn., Popular Culture Assn., Am. Humor Studies Assn. (pres. 1978, 88, Charlie award 1996), Soc. Study So. Lit. (exec. coun. 1971-73, 78-80, 86-88), Melville Soc., Ellen Glasgow Soc. (exec. coun. 1974-84, pres. 1987-88), Mus. Cartoon Art (nominating com. Hall of Fame 1975-95), Brit. Assn. for Am. Studies, European Assn. for Am. Studies, So. Studies Forum (founder, exec. coun. 1988—), Popular Culture Assn. in South (v.p. 1987-88, pres. 1988-89), Mark Twain Cir. (chmn. nominating com. 1987-88), Mark Twain Cir. Am. (hon.), Cosmos Club, Phi Beta Kappa, Omicron Delta Kappa, Pi Delta Epsilon, Lambda Chi Alpha. Home: PO Box 129 Ashland VA 23005-0129 Office: Randolph-Macon Coll Ashland VA 23005

INGELHART, LOUIS EDWARD, journalism educator, retired; b. Minco, Okla., Jan. 19, 1920; s. Louis C. and Estella Lorinda (Burns) I.; m. Margaret Jeanette Wade, Nov. 24, 1948 (dec.); children: Sharon Margaret, James Louis. AA, Mesa Coll., 1940; BA, Colo. No. U., 1942, MA, 1947; PhD, Mo. U., 1953. Tchr. English Fruita (Colo.) Union H.S., 1946; instr. English Colo. No. U., Greeley, 1946-47; instr. journalism, dir. pub. rels. Wayne (Nebr.) State U., 1947-50; instr. journalism Stephens Coll., Columbus, Mo., 1952-53; dir. pub. info., prof. journalism Ball State U., Muncie, Ind., 1953-83, dir. student publs., chmn. dept. journalism, 1953-83, ret., 1983; mem. exec. bd. Student Press Law Ctr., 1990-97, bd. dirs. Author: Freedom For the College Student Press, 1985, Press Law and Press Freedoms for High School Publications, 1986, Press Freedoms, 1987, What Americans Have Said About Freedom of Expression, 1993, Student Publications, 1993, Press and Speech Freedoms in America 1619-1995, 1997, Press and Speech Freedoms in the World From Antiquity Until 1998, 1998; co-author: Public Relations Problems, 1951, Journey Toward Freedom, 1994; contbr. numerous articles to profl. jours. Staff sgt. USAF, 1942-46. Recipient Pioneer award Nat. Scholastic Press Assn., 1970, Journalism Achievement award Dow Jones Newspaper Fund, 1983, Silver Medal award Muncie Am. Advt. Fedn., 1986, Hugh Hefner First Amendment award Playboy Mag., 1989, Disting. Svc. award C.C. Journalism Assn., 1996; named Outstanding Alumnus Mesa State Coll., 1985. Mem. AAUP, Soc. Profl. Journalists (First Amendment award 1990, named to Hall of Fame Ind. chpt.), Coll. Media Advisers (Noel Ross Streader award 1981, named Outstanding Adviser Student Newspaper 1969, Louis E. Ingelhart First Amendment award 1984, named to Hall of Fame 1994), Ind. Assoc. Press Mng. Editors Assn. (life), Assn. for Edn. in Journalism, Am. Fedn. Tchrs., Assn. for Edn. in Journalism and Mass Communations (spl. citations secondary edn. divsn. 1984), Ind. H.S. Press Assn. (life, Louis Ingelhart Svc. award 1985), Columbia Scholastic Press Advisers Assn. (life, Golden Crown award 1975, Gold Key award 1972), Quill and Scroll (hon.), Ball State U. Alumni Assn. (life), First Amendment Congress (v.p. 1980-97, exec. bd. dirs.), Journalism Edn. Assn. (Carl Towley award 1972), U. No. Colo. Alumni Assn. (Trail Blazer award 1983), Phi Delta Kappa (Hardy Disting. Svc. award 1991). Mem. Ch. Disciples of Christ. Avocation: writing. Home: 615 N Tyrone Dr Muncie IN 47304-3141

INGELS, JACK EDWARD, horticulture educator; b. Indpls., Mar. 28, 1942; s. Carl Eugene and Mary Louise (Fultz) I. BS, Purdue U., 1964; MS, Rutgers U., 1966; postgrad., Ball State U., 1968-70. Rsch. asst. Rutgers U., New Brunswick, N.J., 1964-66; prof. SUNY, Cobleskill, 1966-89, disting. teaching prof., 1990—; hort. cons. J.C. Penney Corp., N.Y.C., 1966-69; landscape designer, 1966—; hort. and/or landscape cons. numerous small cos., 1970—; pres. J. Ingels Assoc., 1991—. Author: Landscaping: Principles and Practices, 5th edit., 1997, Ornamental Horticulture: Science, Operations, and Management, 2d edit., 1995. Chmn. Cobleskill Restoration and Devel., Inc., 1991—, bd. dirs., 1988—; pres. Timothy Murphy Gourmet Soc., 1989—; mem. Schoharie County Coun. on Arts, Cobleskill, Albany Inst. of History and Art; bd. dirs. Cobleskill Partnership, 1996—. Mem. Associated Landscape Contractors Am., Northeastern N.Y. Nursery Assn., Genesee-Finger Lakes Nursery Assn., Univ. Club (Albany, N.Y.), Moose, Elks. Avocations: gourmet cooking, landscape garden history, travel. Home: Jay Ridge Apts Cobleskill NY 12043 Office: SUNY Horticulture Dept Cobleskill NY 12043 *To teach is a privilege that permits me to touch lives. To teach well is my obligation.*

INGELS, MARTY, theatrical agent, television and motion picture production executive; b. Bklyn., Mar. 9, 1936; s. Jacob and Minnie (Crown) Ingerman; m. Jean Maire Frassinelli, Aug. 3, 1960 (div. 1969); m. Shirley Jones, 1977. Ed., Erasmus High Sch., 1951-53, Forest Hills High Sch., 1953-55. Founder Ingels Inc., 1975—; formed Stoneypoint Prodns., 1981; TV and motion picture producer U.S. and abroad. Star: Dickens and Fenster series, ABC-TV, 1964; co-star: Pruitts of Southampton, 1968-69; films include Armored Command, 1962, Horizontal Lieutenant, 1965, Busy Body, 1967, Ladies Man, 1966, If It's Tuesday This Must Be Belgium, 1970, Wild and Wonderful, 1965, Guide for a Married Man, 1968; numerous TV appearances. Active various charity drives. Owner world's largest celebrity brokerage service, 1974; widely noted as the Henry Kissinger of Madison Avenue. Office: 701 N Oakhurst Dr Ste 1 Beverly Hills CA 90210*

INGEMAN, JERRY ANDREW, artist; b. Hallock, Minn., Nov. 3, 1950; s. Lavern Norman and Helaine Ann (Carlson) I.; m. Karen Kay Koll, June 25, 1983; 1 child, Maja Chalong. AA with distinction, Willmar (Minn.) State Jr. Coll., 1971; BA magna cum laude, St. Cloud State U., Minn., 1988. Purchasing agt. Nat. Bushing and Parts, St. Cloud, 1971-79; graphic artist St. Cloud State U., 1979-80; supr. Perkins Restaurant, St. Cloud, 1980-82; owner Jaiman Arts, 1985—; editl. asst. Payne Studios, Mpls., 1996—; cons. artifact restoration Evelyn Payne Hatcher Mus. of Anthropology, St. Cloud, 1984—. Exhibited in group shows throughout U.S.; contbr. booklets to profl. jours. Winner Best of Show Celebration of the Arts, Cedar Rapids, Marion, Iowa, award of Excelence Art in the Park, Appleton, Wis., Founder's award Arts in the Park, Brainerd, Minn., 1st prize craft competition Art Horizon, N.Y.C., Best in Jewelry Oconomowoc Festival of Arts. Mem. Am. Craft Coun., Minn. Artists Assn. Lake Country Pastel Soc. (charter), Internat. Sculpture Ctr., Soc. N.Am. Goldsmiths. Avocations: hiking, writing and illustrating, swimming, cooking, landscape gardening and design. Office: Jaiman Arts PO Box 236 Monticello MN 55362-0236

INGER, GEORGE ROE, aerospace engineering educator; b. Detroit, Jan. 27, 1933; m. Janet Inger (dec. 1987); 2 children. BS in Aerospace Engring., Wayne State U., Detroit, 1954; MS in Aerospace Engring., Wayne State U., 1956; PhD in Aerospace Engring., U. Mich., 1960. Research asst. U. Mich., Ann Arbor, 1960; gas dynamics specialist Douglas Missiles & Space Sys., Santa Monica, Calif., 1960-61; mem. tech. staff Aerospace Corp., El Segundo, Calif., 1961-66; instr. UCLA, 1966-67; br. chief McDonnell-Douglas Aircraft, West Huntington Beach, Calif., 1967-70; vis. prof. Von Karman Inst. Fluid Dynamics, Brussels, Belgium, 1970-71; prof. aerospace engring. Va. Poly. Inst. and State U., Blacksburg, 1971-81; prof., chmn. dept. aerospace engring. sci. U. Colo., Boulder, 1981-83; Glenn Murphy Disting. prof. aerospace engring. Iowa State U., Ames, 1983—. Contbr. numerous articles to profl. jours. Named Tau Beta Pi Eminent Engr., 1987' Von Humboldt awardee, 1977, 86, others. Mem. ASME, AIAA, Am. Astron. Soc., Am. Soc. Engring. Edn., Am. Aviation Hist. Soc. Office: Iowa State U 324 Town Engineering Ames IA 50010

INGERMAN, PETER ZILAHY, infosystems consultant; b. N.Y.C., Dec. 9, 1934; s. Charles Stryker and Ernestine (Leigh) I.; m. Carol Mary Pasquale, Dec. 19, 1970 (div. May 1980); m. Colleen Frances McGaffey, Sept. 13, 1996. AB, U. Pa., 1958, MSEE, 1963; PhD, Greenwich U., 1991. CLU; cert. data processor, computer programmer, sys. profl., emergency med. technician. Rsch. investigator U. Pa., Phila., 1958-63; tech. dir. programming rsch. Westinghouse, Balt., 1963-65; mgr. RCA, Cherry Hill, N.J., 1965-71; mem. staff RCA, Cherry Hill, 1971-72; sr. staff cons. Equitable Life Assurance Soc. of U.S., N.Y.C., 1972-77; pvt. practice Equiable Life Assurance Soc. of U.S., Willingboro, N.J., 1977—; adj. prof. computer sci. Pratt Inst. Tech., 1968-73; mem. working groups Internat. Fedn. Info. Processing, 1962—; rep. Conf. Data Systems Langs., 1967-71, Am. Nat. Standards Inst., 1960-69. Bd. dirs. Phila. Health Plan, Inc., 1975-77, Crossroads Runaway Program, Inc., 1981-82, Willingboro Emergency Squad, 1986-89, Compliance, Inc., 1989—, Providence House, 1991-94, vice chair, 1991-94. Author: A Syntax-Oriented Translator, 1966, Russian transl., 1969; contbr. articles to profl. jours.; patentee electronic circuits. Bd. dirs. Phila. Health Plan, Inc.1975-77, Crossroads Runaway Program, Inc., 1981-82, Willingboro Emergency Squad, 1986-89, Compliance, Inc., 1989—, Providence House, 1991-94, vice chair 1991-94. Fellow Brit. Computer Soc.; mem. IEEE (life sr.), AAAS, Assn. Computing Machinery, Data Processing Mgmt. Assn., Am. Cryptogram Assn., Brit. Engring. Coun. (chartered info. sys. practioner, chartered info. sys. engr., chartered engr.), Independent Computer Cons. Assn. (treas. 1999—), Am. Guild Organists (co-dean S.W. Jersey chpt. 1997-98, dean 1998-99), N.J. Acad. Scis., Mensa, Triple Nine Soc., Sigma Xi (life), Epsilon Pi Epsilon. Office: 40 Needlepoint Ln Willingboro NJ 08046-1997

INGERSOLL, ANDREW PERRY, planetary science educator; b. Chgo., Jan. 2, 1940; s. Jeremiah Crary and Minneola (Perry) I.; m. Sarah Morin, Aug. 27, 1961; children: Jeremiah, Ruth Ingersoll Wood, Marion, Minneola, George. BA, Amherst Coll., 1960; PhD, Harvard U., 1965. Rsch. fellow Harvard U., Cambridge, Mass., 1965-66; asst. prof. planetary sci. Calif. Inst. Tech., Pasadena, 1966-71, assoc. prof., 1971-76, prof., 1976—; mem. staff summer study program Woods Hole (Mass.) Oceanopgraphic Inst., 1965, 70-73, 76, 80, 92; prin. investigator Pioneer Saturn Infrared Radiometer Team, NASA; mem. Voyager Imaging Team, NASA, Cassini Imaging Team; interdisciplinary scientist, Mars Global Surveyor Project, Galileo Project, NASA. Bd. trustees Poly. Sch., Pasadena. Fellow AAAS, Am. Geophys. Union, Am. Acad. Arts and Scis.; mem. Am. Astron. Soc. (vice-chmn. div. planetary sci. 1988-89, chmn. 1989-90). Office: Calif Inst Tech Dept Planetary Sci 150-21 Pasadena CA 91125

INGERSOLL, PAUL MILLS, banker; b. Phila., Apr. 13, 1928; s. John H.W. and Frances Paul (Mills) I.; m. Eleanor S. Koehler, Oct. 6, 1951; children: Eleanor Ingersoll Sylvestro, Rita W., Frances M. B.A., Princeton U., 1950. With Provident Nat. Bank, Phila., 1963-78; v.p. adminstrn. and exec. mgmt. Provident Nat. Bank, 1969, sr. v.p. retail banking div., 1969-73, pres., chief adminstrv. officer, 1973-78; pres., bd. dirs. Beaver Mgmt. Corp.; bd. dirs. Rittenhouse Trust Co.; cons. Christie, Manson & Woods Internat., Inc. Trustee Emeritus Drexel U., Bryn Mawr (Pa.) Hosp. 1st lt. AUS, 1950-52. Recipient Human Relations award Am. Jewish Com., 1973. Republican. Episcopalian. Club: Merion Cricket.

INGERSOLL, ROBERT STEPHEN, former diplomat, federal agency administrator; b. Galesburg, Ill., Jan. 28, 1914; s. Roy Claire and Lulu May (Hinchliff) I.; m. Coralyn Eleanor Reid, Sept. 17, 1938; children: Coralyn Eleanor, Nancy, Joan (dec.), Gail, Elizabeth. Grad., Phillips Acad., 1933; BS, Yale U., 1937. With Armco Steel Corp., 1937-39, Ingersoll Steel & Disc div. (later Ingersoll Products div.), 1939-41, 42-54; pres. Ingersoll Products div., 1950-54; adminstrv. v.p. Borg-Warner Corp., 1953-56, pres., 1956-61, chmn., 1961-72, CEO, 1958-72, also dir.; with Cen. Rsch. Lab., 1941-42; U.S. amb. to Japan, 1972-73; asst. sec. state for East Asian Affairs U.S. Dept. State, Washington, 1974, dep. sec. state, 1974-76; ptnr., bd. dirs. First Chgo. Capital Mkts. Asia Ltd.; chmn. Panasonic Found.; mem. Bus. Coun. Pres. Winnetka (Ill.) Sch. Bd., 1957-63; dep. chmn., life bd. trustees U. Chgo.; trustee Smith Coll., 1966-71, Aspen Inst. Humanistic Studies, Calif. Inst. Tech.; past bd. dirs. Johnson Found., Trilateral Commn. N.Am.; past mem. coun. Yale U.; past mem. adv. coun. Caterpillar Asia Pacific; past vice-chmn. Pacific adv. coun. United Techs. Nat. Park Found. Mem. Japan Soc. (chmn. N.Y.C. chpt. 1978-85), Chgo. Coun. Fgn. Rels., Coun. Fgn. Rels. N.Y.C., Indian Hill Club, Chgo. Club, Econ. Club (Chgo., Phoenix), Comml. Club, Yale Club (N.Y.C.), Bohemian Club, Desert Forest Golf Club, Desert Mountain Club, Old Elm Club. Home and Office: One Arbor Ln Apt 202 Evanston IL 60201

INGHAM, CHARLES ANDREW, literature and English language educator; b. Manchester, Eng., Aug. 6, 1952; came to U.S., 1982; s. Alan Roy and Jean (Fox) I.; m. Elaine Elizabeth Jones, Sept. 28, 1974; 1 child, Lewis Alexander. BA in Lit. with Honors, U. Essex, U.K., 1976; MPhil in Lit., U. Essex, 1985. Lectr. San Diego State U., 1982-91, U. San Diego, 1983-85; assoc. prof. English Palomar Coll., San Marcos, Calif., 1991—. Co-editor Ochre Mag., 1976-80; author short stories and poems. Recipient Gavel award Alpha Gamma Sigma, 1994, Nat. Inst. Staff and Orgnl. Devel. Excellence award U. Tex. at Austin, 1995; grantee Dept. Edn. and Sci., 1976, travel grantee, 1978.

INGHAM, EDWARD A., career officer; b. Seattle, June 30, 1962; s. Edward Alfred and Norma Marie (Arnegaard) I.; m. Renee Franceschi, Apr. 13, 1985; children: Connan Edward, Dillon James. BS in Engring. Scis., USAF Acad., 1984; MS in Syss. Engring., Air Force Inst. Tech., 1993, PhD, 1996. Cert. sr. pilot USAF. Commd. USAF, advanced through grades to maj., 1980; T-37 instr. pilot USAF, Phoenix, Ariz., 1984-89, F-16 pilot, 1996—; F-16 instr. pilot USAF, Misawa AFB, Japan, 1989-92; T-37 flight examiner USAF, Phoenix, 1988-89, mission comdr., Misawa AFB, 1992. Mem. Order Daedalians, Assn. Grads. USAF Acad., Tau Beta Pi, Eta Kappa Nu. Roman Catholic. Avocations: fitness, sports. Home: 21186 N 62 Ave Glendale AZ 85308

INGHAM, NORMAN WILLIAM, Russian literature educator, genealogist; b. Holyoke, Mass., Dec. 31, 1934; s. Earl Morris and Gladys May (Rust) I. AB, Middlebury Coll. in German and Russian cum laude, 1957; postgrad. Slavic philology, Free U. Berlin, 1957-58; MA in Russian lang. and lit., U. Mich., 1959; postgrad. in Russian lang. and lit., Leningrad (USSR) State U., 1961-62; PhD in Slavic langs. and lit., Harvard U., 1963. Cert. genealogist. Postdoctoral researcher Czechoslovak Acad. Scis., Prague, Czechoslovakia, 1963-64; asst. prof. dept Slavic langs. and lits. Ind. U., Bloomington, 1964-65; asst. prof. Harvard U., Cambridge, Mass., 1965-70, lectr., 1970-71; assoc. prof. U. Chgo., 1971-82, prof., 1982—, chmn. dept., 1977-83, dir. Eastern Europe and USSR lang. and area ctr., 1978-91; mem. Am. Com. Slavists, 1977-83; mem. com. Slavic and Ea. European studies U. Chgo., 1979-91, chmn., 1982-91, also other coms.; dir. Ctr. for East European and Russian/Eurasian Studies, 1991-96; rep. internat. Rsch. and Exch. Bd.; cert. genealogist, 1994—. Author: E.T.A. Hoffman's Reception in Russia, 1974; editor: Church and Culture in Old Russia, 1991; co-editor: (with Joachim T. Baer) Mnemozina: Studia litteraria russica in honorem Vsevolod Setchkarev; mem. editorial bd. Slavic and East European Jour., 1978-87, adv. bd., 1987-89; assoc. editor Byzantine Studies, 1973-81; contbg. editor The Am. Genealogist, 1995—; contbr. and translator articles and book revs. Fulbright fellow, 1957-58, vis. fellow Dumbarton Oaks Ctr. for Byzantine Studies, 1972-73. Mem. Am. Assn. Advancement Slavic Studies (rep. coun. on mem. instns. 1985-96, area rep. nat. adv. com. for Ea. European lang. programs 1985-96), Am. Assn. Tchrs. Slavic and East European Langs., Early Slavic Studies Assn. (v.p. 1993-95, pres. 1995-97), Chgo. Consortium for Slavic and East European Studies (v.p. 1982-84, 98—, pres. 1984-86, 98—, exec. coun. 1992-94), Phi Beta Kappa. Avocation: golf. Office: U Chgo Slavic Dept 1130 E 59th St Chicago IL 60637-1539

INGHAM, ROBERT FRANCIS, marketing professional; b. New Orleans, June 24, 1946; s. Robert Francis and Jeanne (Spahos) I.; 1 child, Bobby II. AAS, DeKalb Community Coll., 1980. Office mgr., owner H&RB Lock, Waynesboro, Ga., 1974-76, HFL Tax Svc. Household Fin., Augusta, Ga., 1986, Tax Ctrs. Am. Montgomery Ward, Augusta, 1988; cons. Concept Energy Systems Inc., Augusta, 1991-93. Sgt. U.S. Army. Mem. Assn. Energy Engrs., Vietnam Vets. Am. (treas. 1990). Democrat. Baptist. Achievements include invention of functional design of automatic pinsetting machine. Office: Bignell Ins Agy Ingham's Income Tax Svc 3178 Deans Bridge Rd Augusta GA 30906-3378

INGHRAM, MARK GORDON, physicist, educator; b. Livingston, Mont., Nov. 13, 1919; s. Mark Gordon and Luella Gallagher (McNay) I.; m. Evelyn Mae Dyckman, May 12, 1946; children: Cheryl Ann, Mark Gordon III. BA, Olivet Coll., 1939; PhD, U. Chgo., 1947. Physicist Manhattan Project, 1942-45; sr. physicist Argonne Nat. Lab., 1945-47; mem. faculty U. Chgo., 1947—, successively instr., asst. prof., assoc. prof., prof., Samuel K. Allison Disting. Service prof. physics, 1969-85, emeritus, 1985—, chmn. dept. physics, 1959-70, acting dir. Inst. for Study of Metals, 1960-61, asso. dean div. of phys. scis., 1964-71, master Phys. Sci. Coll. div., 1981-85, assoc. dean div. phys. sci., 1981-85, assoc. dean Coll., 1981-85; mem. com. nuclear geophysics Nat. Acad. Sci., 1953-60, mem. com. sci. and pub. policy, 1966-69, mem. com. on exploration of moon and planets, 1958-61. Asso. editor: Jour. Chem. Physics, 1957-60; editorial bd.: Rev. Sci. Instruments, 1958-61; author articles in sci. jours. Fellow Am. Phys. Soc., Am. Acad. Arts and Scis.; mem. Nat. Acad. Scis. (J. Lawrence Smith medal 1957), AAAS. Home: 3077 N Lakeshore Dr Holland MI 49424-6022

INGIS, GAIL, interior designer, educator, writer, photographer, artist; b. U.S., Nov. 1, 1935; d. Bernard and Claire Gerber; m. Thomas H. Claus; children: Linda, Richard, Paul. Student in bus. Bklyn. Coll., 1953; grad. in interior architecture and design N.Y. Sch. Interior Design, 1973, BFA, 1980; postgrad. Pratt Inst., N.J. Inst. Tech., Parsons Sch. of Design. Prin. Ingis Design Assoc., Woodcliff Lake, N.J./Madison, Conn., 1970—; interior designer The Design Store, locations in Washington, Md., N.J., 1977-78; prof. Kean Coll., Union, N.J., 1977-80, The King's Coll., Briarcliff Manor, N.Y., 1980-82, N.Y. Sch. Interior Design, 1980-82; mem. design staff Bloomingdale's, N.Y.C., 1981-82; founder, prin. Interior Design Inst. (merged with Berkeley Coll. Bus.), Woodcliff Lake, N.J., 1982-91, chmn. interior design dept., 1988-91; head interior designer Africa Inland Mission, Pearl River, N.Y., 1991-95; founder D'Image Inc., Saddle River, N.J., 1986; chmn. design team Refurbishing Renovation Conn. Hospice, 1996-98. Troop leader Girl Scouts U.S., N.Y.C. and Woodcliff Lake, 1964-69. Recipient Wall St. Gallery award for Watercolor Painting, 1997. Mem. Am. Soc. Interior Designers (admissions com. N.J. chpt. 1978, edn. chmn. 1978-86, 94-95, co-chmn. pro-licensing com. 1984-86, com. legis. for interior designers 1988-90, bd. dirs. 1985-87, 94-95; bd. dirs. Conn. chpt. 1996-97, editor newsletter Conn. chpt. 1996-97, 98, svc. awards 1978, 83-87), AIA profl. affiliate, Inst. Bus. Designers, U.S. Profl. Tennis Assn. (cert. tennis instr.), Illuminating Engring. Soc. N.Am., Interior Design Educators Coun., Madison Art Soc., Guilford Art League, Shoreline Alliance Arts, New Haven Arts Coun., Lyme Art Assn. Home and Office: PO Box 688 Madison CT 06443-0688

INGLE, GRANT M., organizational psychologist, consultant; b. Springfield, Mass., June 28, 1947; s. George W. and Jeannette (Donaldson) I.; m. Carla F. Brennan, Oct. 29, 1994. BA in Psychology, Amherst Coll., 1969; MS in Social Psychology, U. Amherst, 1974, PhD in Orgnl. Psychology, 1980. Program asst. Training Corp. of Am., Washington, 1969-70; owner/operator Meriwether Herbs, Belchertown, Mass., 1972-76; process cons. Resource Network U. Mass., Amherst, 1976-82; cons., ptnr. and founding mem. Conway Cons., Conway, Mass., 1977-82; process cons. Office Human rels. U. Mass., Amherst, 1982-87, project mgr., 1986, dir. Office Human Rels., 1989—; pvt. practice orgnl. psychology Amherst, 1982—; mem. grad. faculty Labor Rels. and Rsch. Ctr., U. Mass., Amherst, 1984—; lectr. in field. Contbr. articles to profl. jours. Charter mem. The Meta Network; chmn. Conway Planning Adv. Com.; chmn. workplace edn. project adv. bd. U. Mass., Amherst; bd. dirs. Men's Resource Ctr., Amherst; mem. civil rights adv. bd. Northwestern Dist. Atty.'s Office; mem. affirmative action adv. bd. U. Mass. Mem. Orgnl. Devel. Network. Avocations: cross country skiing, sailing, gardening, cycling. E-mail: ingle@admin.umass.edu. Office: Office of Human Relations University of Mass 202 Middlesex House Amherst MA 01003

INGLE, JAMES CHESNEY, JR., geology educator; b. Los Angeles, Nov. 6, 1935; s. James Chesney and Florence Adelaide (Geldart) I.; m. Fredricka Ann Bornholdt, June 14, 1958; 1 child, Douglas James. B.S. in Geology, U. So. Calif., 1959, M.S. in Geology, 1962, Ph.D. in Geology, 1966. Registered geologist, Calif. Research assoc. Univ. So. Calif., 1961-65; vis. scholar Tohoku U., Sendai, Japan, 1966-67; asst., assoc. to full prof. Stanford U., Calif., 1968—; W.M. Keck prof. earth scis. Stanford U., 1984—, chmn. dept. geology, 1982-86; co-chief scientist Leg 31 Deep Sea Drilling Project, 1973, co-chief scientist Leg 128 Ocean Drilling Program, 1989; geologist U.S. Geol. Survey W.A.E. 1978-81. Author: Movement of Beach Sand, 1966; contbr. articles to profl. jours. Recipient W.A. Tarr award Sigma Gamma Epsilon, 1958; named Disting. lectr. Am. Assn. Petroleum Geologists, 1986-87, Joint Oceanographic Institutions, 1991; A.I. Leverson award Am. Assn. Petroleum Geologists, 1988. Fellow Geol. Soc. Am., Calif. Acad. Scis.; mem. Cushman Found. (bd. dirs. 1984-91), Soc. Profl. Paleontologists and Mineralogists (Pacific sect. 1958—, pres. 1993-94), Am. Geophys. Union.

INGLE, JOAN MARIE, nurse practitioner; b. Balt., Nov. 2, 1943; d. Edgar Allen and Mary Virginia (Reese) Peppler; m. Elbert L. Fisher, Nov. 12, 1966 (div. Mar. 1976); children: Heather Marie, Todd Perry; m. William Kenneth Ingle, Dec. 25, 1979. RN, Bon Secours Sch. Nursing, Balt., 1964; student, U. N.C., 1979-82, BSN, Towson State U., 1993; cert. FNP Mountain Area Health Edn. Ctr./U. N.C., Chapel Hill. Staff nurse Doctors Hosp., Coral Gables, Fla., 1965-68, charge nurse CCU, 1976-78; staff nurse CCU, South Miami Hosp., Miami, Fla., 1978-79; home care supr. Med. Pers. Pool, Asheville, N.C., 1980-81, dir. nurses, 1981-82, dir. home health, 1982-84, 86; nurse practitioner, York Hosp. Trauma/Emergency Ctr., 1987-90, Walter P. Carter Ctr., U. Md., 1990-98, Johns Hopkins Hosp., Balt., 1998—. Mem. ANA, Pa. Nurses Assn., Nurse Practitioners Assn. Md., Am. Coll. Nurse Practitioners, Am. Acad. Nurse Practitioners, Sigma Theta Tau. Republican. Baptist. Home: Sheffield Dr Dallastown PA 17313 Office: Johns Hopkins Hosp 600 N Wolfe St Baltimore MD 21205

INGLE, RICHARD MAURICE, research scientist; b. Carrollton, Ga., July 2, 1946; s. Maurice Dale and Marietta (Swanagon) I.; m. Susan Reeve, (Oct. 27, 1948); children: Kimberly, Deborah, Elizabeth, Reeve. BA, West Ga. Coll., 1967; MS, Ga. Inst. Tech., 1969; meteorology cert., Tex. A&M U., 1970; PhD, Ga. Inst. Tech., 1980. Programmer West Ga. Coll., Carrollton, 1965-67; grad. teaching asst. Ga. Inst. Tech., Atlanta, 1967-68; analog/hybrid applications engr. Lockheed Co., Marietta, Ga., 1968-69; grad. teaching asst. Ga. Inst. Tech., Atlanta, 1973-75; asst. prof. West Ga. Coll., Carrollton, 1975-79; sr. computer scientist Computer Scis. Corp./NASA, Kennedy Space Center, Fla., 1979-81; assoc. prof., coord. computer sci. degree program West Ga. Coll., Carrollton, 1981-85; prin. rsch. scientist, head systems tech. br. Ga. Tech. Rsch. Inst., 1985—; cons. NASA, Kennedy Space Center, 1981—. Author: Selective Display Model, 1972, Modeling Fluid Networks, 1984; contbr. articles to profl. jours. Bd. dirs. Kiwanis Club, Carrollton, 1982-85, Carrollton High Sch. Band Boosters, 1986-88; elder First Christian Ch., Carrollton, 1983—; bd. dirs. Ga. Tech. Christian Campus Fellowship, Atlanta, 1987-96; vol. missionary to India, 1994—. Capt. USAF, 1969-73. Scholar Boykin Found. Mem. IEEE, Math. Assn. Am., Am. Math. Soc., Assn. Computing Machinery, Phi Kappa Phi (pres. 1983-84), Chi Epsilon Pi. Avocations: hiking, travel, music, physical conditioning. Home: 305 Dixie St Carrollton GA 30117-3310

INGLE, ROBERT D., newspaper editor, newspaper executive; b. Sioux City, Iowa, Apr. 29, 1939; s. Walter J. and Thelma L (McCoy) I.; m. Martha N. Nelson, Sept. 12, 1964 (div. 1984); 1 child, Julia L.; m. Sandra R. Reed, Mar. 2, 1985. B.A. in Journalism and Polit. Sci., U. Iowa, 1962. Various positions Miami Herald, 1962-75, asst. mng. editor, 1975-77, mng. editor, 1977-81; exec. editor San Jose (Calif.) Mercury News, 1981-93, pres., exec. editor, 1993-95; v.p. Knight-Ridder Inc., San Jose, Calif., 1995-99; pres. Knight-Ridder Ventures New Media, San Jose, Calif., 1999—. Pres. Calif. First Amendment Coalition, 1990-92. Mem. AP Mng. Editors Assn., Am. Soc. Newspaper Editors. Office: Knight Ridder New Media 50 W San Fernando St Ste 700 San Jose CA 95113-2413

INGLEFIELD, JOSEPH T., JR., allergist, immunologist, pediatrician; b. Duquesne, Pa., Apr. 29, 1930. MD, U. Rochester, 1957. Diplomate Am. Bd. Allergy & Immunology, Am. Bd. Pediatrics. Intern William Beaumont Army Hosp., El Paso, Tex., 1957-58; resident Tripler Army Hosp., Honolulu, 1958-60; fellow in pediatrics and allergies Children's Hosp., Washington, 1969-72; with Fairfax Hosp., Falls Church, Va. Mem. AMA, MSV, Am. Acad. Pediatrics, Assn. Am. Physicians, North Va. Pediatric Soc. Office: 107 N Virginia Ave Falls Church VA 22046-3324 also: 6329 Linway Ter Mc Lean VA 22101-4108*

INGLEHART, RONALD FRANKLIN, political science educator; b. Milw., Sept. 5, 1934; s. Gerald Almon and Helen Clara (Krippene) I.; m. Babette Feinberg, Aug. 16, 1963 (div. Sept. 1968); children: Elizabeth Lynn, Rachel Jennifer; m. Marita Rohr Rosch, May 5, 1986; children: Ronald Charles, Marita Helen. BA, Northwestern U., 1956; MA, U. Chgo., 1962, PhD, 1967. Asst. prof. U. Mich., Ann Arbor, 1967-71, assoc. prof., 1971-76, prof. polit. sci., 1977—, program dir. Inst. for Social Rsch., 1984—; vis. prof. U. Mannheim, Germany, U. Geneva, U. Kyoto, Japan, U. Kobe, Japan, Free U., Berlin, Leiden U., U. Rome, U. Belo Horizonte; mem. adv. coun. Berlin Sci. Ctr., 1992—, Ctr. for Polit. Studies, Ann Arbor, 1995—. Author: The Silent Revolution, 1977, Culture Shift, 1990, Modernization and Postmodernization, 1997, Human Values and Beliefs, 1998; mem. editl. bd. seven scholarly jours. Co-founder Euro-Barometer Surveys, Brussels, 1974—; chair World Values Surveys Hdqrs., Ann Arbor, 1988—, Global Environ. Survey, 1996—. Mem. Internat. Soc. for Polit. Psychology, Internat. Polit. Sci. Assn., Am. Polit. Sci. Assn., Midwest Polit. Sci. Assn. Avocation: writing childrens stories. Home: 2626 Geddes Ave Ann Arbor MI 48104-2715 Office: Inst for Social Rsch 326 Thompson St Ann Arbor MI 48104-2214

INGLES, JAMES H., community college dean; b. May 3, 1944. BS Broadcasting, U. Fla., 1967, MEd Media, 1970; post-grad, Simmons Coll. TV prodn. asst. Sta. WUFT-TV, Gainesville, Fla., 1968-71; coord. audio visual TV svcs. Learning Resources Ctr., Bristol C.C., Fall River, Mass., 1971-77, asst. dir. adminstrv., prodn. svcs. Learning Resources Ctr., 1977-91, dir. Learning Resources Ctr., 1992-96, asst. dean learning resources, 1997—. Office: Bristol CC 777 Elsbree St Fall River MA 02720-7307

INGLES, JOSEPH LEGRAND, social services administrator, political science educator; b. June 15, 1939; s. Vernal Willard and Helen Josephine (Graziano) I.; m. Hazel Jeanette Palmer, Aug. 18, 1962; children: Sally Van Dyke, Christine Walker, Joette Smith, Robert, Michael. *Wife Jeanette runs business in home and is dedicated and talented homemaker. Daughter Sally and husband LeGrand VanDyke have four sons and own a cabinet business, Richfield, Utah. Daughter Christine and husband Gary Walker have three children (one son, two daughters). Christine teaches math at Utah Valley Community College, Gary is in carpet business, Lindon, Utah. Daughter Joette and husband Kevin Smith have one daughter. Joette in cosmetology and Kevin practices physical therapy at the Hanover (Pa.) Rehab Center. Sons Michael and Robert are serving Mormon church missions: Michael in Washington, D.C. South and Robert in Dallas* BS, Brigham Young U., 1964; PhD, U. Mo., 1968. Rsch. asst. U. Mo., Columbia, 1967-68; grant policy specialist HEW, Washington, 1970-71; asst. prof. govt. and politics U. Md., College Park, 1968-75; dir. human resources Wasatch Front Regional Coun., Bountiful, Utah, 1975-77; utility consumer adv. Com. on Consumer Svc. Utah, 1977-93; medicaid mgr., third party liability and health, Utah Dept. Human Services, Salt Lake City, 1993-94, child support mgr. Intake, Locate, and Orders Office of Recovery Svcs., 1994-96, computer software trainer, 1996—; spl. faculty mem. family and consumer studies U. Utah, 1995; cons. Ellingson Kilpack Assocs., Salt Lake City, 1972, Bonneville Rsch. Corp., Santa Monica, Calif., 1971, U.S. Dept. Commerce, 1970; spl. faculty mem. Salt Lake Ctr. Brigham Young U., 1988—. Mem. West Bountiful City Coun., 1982-88; fellow NDEA, 1964-67; U. Md. grantee, 1969. Fellow Am. Soc. Pub. Adminstrn. (fellowship 1970-71); mem. Nat. Assn. Regulatory Utility Commrs. staff subcom. on consumer affairs, 1982-93; mem. gas com. Nat. Assn. State Utility Consumer Advs., 1983-93. Mormon. Lodge: Snowbird Iron Blosam (chmn., budget and fin. com. 1987—). Home: 1485 N 1100 W Woods Cross UT 84087-1828

INGLESE, CATHY, university head women's basketball coach. BS magna cum laude, So. Conn. State U., 1980. Asst. coach U. N.H., 1983-86; head coach U. Vt., 1986-93, Boston Coll., 1993—. Named Outstanding Female Athlete at So. Conn., 1980; named to So. Conn. Athletic Hall of Fame, Conn. Softball Hall of Fame, Conn. Women's Basketball Hall of Fame, Sheehan H.S. Hall of Fame, Off Club of Greater New Haven Hall of Fame. Office: Boston Coll Athletic Assn Silvio O Conte Forum Chestnut Hill MA 02167*

INGLETT, BETTY LEE, retired media services administrator; b. Augusta, Ga., Oct. 6, 1930; d. Wilfred Lee and Elizabeth Arelia (Crouch) I. BS in Edn., Ga. State Coll. for Women, 1953; MA in Library, Media and Edn. Adminstrn., Ga. So. U., 1980; EdD in Edn. Adminstrn., Nova U., 1988. Tchr. James L. Fleming Elem. Sch., Augusta, Ga., 1953-63, Murphey Jr. High Sch., Augusta, 1963-64, Sego Jr. High Sch., Augusta, 1964-68, Glenn Hills High Sch., Augusta, 1968-75; media specialist Nat. Hills Elem. Sch., Augusta, 1975-80; prin. Lake Forest Elem. Sch., Augusta, 1980-84, Joseph R. Lamar Elem. Sch., Augusta, 1984-86; dir. edni. media services Richmond County Bd. Edn., Augusta, 1986-92; ret., 1992; owner, operator Betty Inglett Enterprises, Augusta. Contbr. articles to profl. jours. Bd. dirs. Am. Heart Fund, 1975-80, Am. Cancer Fund, 1986—; del. Dem. State Conv., 1982; council mem. PTA. (life), 1985. Named Adminstr. of Yr., 1988-89. Mem. Richmond County Edn. Assn. (sec. v.p. 1961-63, Adminstr. of Yr. 1989-90), AAUW (v.p. 1957-59), NEA, Ga. Assn. Edn., Ga. Assn. Ednl. Leaders, Ga. Library Media Dept., Ga. Library Assn., Ga. Assn. Instructional Tech., Ga. Assn. Curriculum Instructional Supr., Profl. Leadership Assn., Cen. Savannah River Area Library Assn., Alpha Delta Kappa, Phi Delta Pi, Phi Delta Kappa. Baptist.

INGLIS, JAMES, telecommunications company executive; b. Cleve.; s. Richard and Anne Bowen (Edwards) I.; m. Carolyn Jane Corcoran, June 17, 1967; children: James Jeffrey, Katherine Akins. BA, Amherst Coll., 1967; MS, Stanford U., 1968, PhD, 1973. Asst. prof. dept. stats. U. Rochester, N.Y., 1972-78; tech. staff mem. AT&T Bell Labs., Holmdel, N.J., 1978-81, tech. supr., 1981-87, dept. head., 1987-1996; divsn. mgr. AT&T Labs., Holmdel, 1996—. Contbr. articles to profl. jours. Pres. Fair Haven Cmty. Appeal, 1991-98—, Fair Haven Libr. Bd., 1991-94. Mem. Am. Statis. Assn.

INGLIS, PATRICIA MARCUS, lawyer; b. Pitts., July 29, 1952; d. E. Robert and Betty (Rosenfield) Marcus; m. David S. Inglis, Nov. 10, 1989; children: Jaclyn Ivy, Kathryn Sara. BA in History and Polit. Sci., U. Rochester, 1974; JD, Case Western Res. U., 1977. Summer assoc. Jones, Day, Reavis & Pogue, Cleve., 1976; assoc. Schiff, Hardin & Waite, Chgo., 1977-82; assoc. Benesch, Friedlander, Coplan & Aronoff, Cleve., 1982-84, ptnr., 1984—, mem. mgmt. com., 1987-91, chair profl. pers. com., 1988-95. Trustee, v.p. Montefiore; trustee Jewish Cmty. Fedn. of Cleve. Mem. ABA, Cleve. Bar Assn., Case Western Res. U. Law Alumni Assn., Order of the Coif. Office: Benesch Friedlander Coplan & Aronoff 2300 BP America Bldg 200 Public Sq Cleveland OH 44114-2301

INGLIS, ROBERT D. (BOB INGLIS), former congressman, lawyer; b. Oct. 11, 1959; m. Mary Anne Williams, Aug. 7, 1982; children: Robert D. Jr., Mary Ashton, Anne McCullough, Mabel Andrews, Sara Meade. AB summa cum laude in Polit. Sci., Duke U., 1981; JD, U. Va. Sch. Law, 1984. Atty. Leatherwood, Walker, Todd & Mann P.C., Greenville, S.C.; mem. 103rd-105th Congresses from 4th S.C. dist., Washington, D.C., 1993-98; mem. Budget/Judiciary com. Chmn. 4th Congl. Dist. South Carolinians to Limit Congl. Terms; mem. Leadership Greenville Class XVI; loaned exec. Greenville County United Way, 1987; mem. exec. com. Greenville County Rep. Party; mem. exec. com. First Monday in Greenville. Mem. Ga. Bar Assn., S.C. Bar Assn., Greenville County Bar Assn., Phi Beta Kappa. Office: PO Box 87 Greenville SC 29602*

INGLIS, WILLIAM DARLING, internist, health facility administrator; b. Columbus, Ohio, Aug. 12, 1931; s. John Cockins and Helen (Morgan) I.; m. Laura Hammer, June 5, 1955 (dec. Jan. 1974); children: Ruth Anne Inglis, William Darling Inglis IV; m. Suzanne Smith, May 7, 1977; 1 child, Andrew Scott Inglis. BA, Washington & Jefferson Coll., 1953; MD, Jefferson Med. Coll., 1957. Diplomate Am. Bd. Internal Medicine, Am. Bd. Pulmonary Medicine, Am. Bd. Palliative Medicine. Intern Meth. Episcopal Hosp., Phila., 1957-58; resident in internal medicine Jefferson Med. Coll., Phila., 1958-59, Walter Reed Army Hosp., Washington, 1962-65; commd. U.S. Army, 1959, advanced through grades to lt. col., 1966, ret., 1968; instr., fellow in pulmonary disease U. Louisville, 1968-69; ptnr. W. F. Milliton Med. Clinic, Columbus, Ohio, 1969-74; med. dir. hospice Riverside Meth. Hosp., Columbus, Ohio, 1994—, med. dir. home care, 1996—; med. dir. Mind/Body Inst., Columbus, Ohio, 1994-96; clin. assoc. prof. Ohio State U., Columbus, 1969—; chmn. pulmonary sect., Riverside Meth. Hosps., Columbus, 1969-83, chmn. dept. medicine, 1983-86, pres. med. staff, 1988-89. Chmn. health svcs. United Cmty. Coun., Columbus, 1970-72; vol. physician Columbus Med. Assn. Free Clinic, 1974-99, Columbus Hospice, 1978-85; trustee Washington and Jefferson Coll., Washington, Pa., 1985-89. Decorated U.S. Army Commendation medal. Fellow ACP (laureate), Am. Coll. Chest Physicians; mem. AMA, Nat. Hospice Orgn. (ethics com. 1997—), Am. Acad. Hospice & Palliative Medicine, Med. Forum (pres. 1983). Presbyterian. Avocation: running. Home: 8531 Pitlochry Ct Dublin OH 43017-9770 Office: Hospice at Riverside/Grant 3595 Olentangy River Rd Columbus OH 43214-3440

INGOLD, CATHERINE WHITE, academic administrator; b. Columbia, S.C., Mar. 15, 1949; d. Hiram Hutchison and Annelle (Stover) White; m. Wesley Thomas Ingold, June 13, 1970; 1 child, Thomas Bradford Hutchison. Student, U. Paris-Sorbonne, 1969; BS in French with honors, Hollins Coll., 1970; MA in Romance Langs., U. Va., 1972, PhD in French, 1979; DHum honoris causa, Francis Marion U., Florence, S.C., 1992. Assoc. prof. romance langs. Gallaudet U., Washington, 1973-88, dir. hons. program, 1980-85, dean arts and scis., 1985-86, provost, v.p. acad. affairs, 1986-88;

pres. Am. U. of Paris, 1988-92, Curry Coll., Milton, Mass., 1992-96; dep. dir. Nat. Fgn. Lang. Ctr. John Hopkins U., 1996—. Recipient Prix Morot-Sir de Langue et Littérature françaises (Hollins). Mem. MLA, Nat. Collegiate Honors Coun., Lychnos Soc. (U.Va.), Phi Beta Kappa. Episcopalian. Home: 2015 N Brandywine St Arlington VA 22207-2200 Office: Nat Fgn Lang Ctr 1617 Massachusetts Ave NW Washington DC 20036-2209

INGOLD, KEITH USHERWOOD, chemist, educator; b. Leeds, Eng., May 31, 1929; s. Christopher Kelk and Edith (Usherwood) I.; m. Carmen Cairine Hodgkin, Apr. 7, 1956; children: Christopher Frank (dec.), John Hilary, Diana Hilda. BSc with honors in Chemistry, Univ. Coll., London, 1949; DPhil, Oxford (Eng.) U., 1951; DSc (hon.), U. Guelph, 1985; LLD (hon.), Mt. Allison U., 1987; DSc (hon.), St. Andrews U., Scotland, 1989, Carleton U., 1992, McMaster U., 1995; LLD (hon.), Dalhousie U., 1996. Postdoctoral fellow NRC Can., Ottawa, 1951-53, rsch. officer, 1955-77, assoc. dir. chemistry, 1977-90, disting. rsch. scientist, 1990—; adj. prof. U. Guelph, Ont., Can., 1985-87, Brunel U., U.K., 1983-94, Carleton U. Ottawa, Can., 1991—, St. Andrews U., U.K., 1997—; postdoctoral fellow U. B.C., 1953-55; vis. scientist Chevron Rsch. Co., Richmond, Calif., 1966, Univ. Coll., London, 1969, 72, Ford Motor Co., 1971, Esso Rsch. and Engring. Co., Linden, N.J., 1973, U. Western Ont., 1975, 1993, Iowa State U., 1975, U. Bologna, Italy, 1975, 93, U. Adelaide, Australia, 1979, U. Grenoble, France, 1983, Australian Nat. U., 1987, U. Freiburg, Germany, 1990, 91, U. Essen, Germany, 1990, U. Dusseldorf, Germany, 1991, U. Leiden, The Netherlands, 1992, 93, U. St. Andrews, Scotland, 1998. Decorated Order of Can., 1995; recipient Can. Silver Jubilee medal, 1977, Humboldt Sr. Rsch. Fellowship award, Germany, 1989, Veris award, 1989, Lansdown Visitor award U. Victoria, B.C., 1990, Mangini prize U. Bologna, 1990, Davy medal, 1990, Izaak Walton Killam Meml. prize Can. Coun., 1992, Mangini gold medal Italian Chem. Soc., 1997, Gold medal for sci. and engring. Natural Scis. and Engring. Coun. Can., 1998; Carnegie fellow U. St. Andrews, Scotland, 1977; vis. fellow Japan Soc. for Promotion of Sci., 1982, Italian Nat. Rsch. Coun., 1983; Nat. Sci. Coun. Republic China lectr., 1992. Fellow Royal Soc. Can. (treas. 1979-81, Centennial medal 1982, Henry Marshall Tory medal 1985), Royal Soc. (London, Davy medal 1990), Chem. Inst. Can. (medal 1981, Syntex award for phys. organic chemistry 1983), Univ. Coll. (London); mem. Am. Chem. Soc. (award petroleum chemistry 1968, Pauling award 1988, Arthur C. Cope scholar 1992, James Flack Norris award phys. organic chemistry 1993), Chem. Soc. (award kinetics and mechanism 1978), Can. Soc. Chem. (v.p. 1985-87, pres. 1987-88, Alfred Bader award in organic chemistry 1989), Royal Soc. Chemistry (Ingold lectr. 1990). Achievements include research papers on free radical chemistry. Home: 72 Ryeburn Dr, Gloucester, ON Canada K1V 1H5 Office: Nat Rsch Coun of Can, Steacie Inst for Molecular Scis, Ottawa, ON Canada K1A 0R6

INGRAHAM, EDWARD CLARKE, JR., foreign service officer; b. Mineola, N.Y., Feb. 2, 1922; s. Edward Clarke and Dorothy Hathaway (Sutton) I.; m. Susan Hartman, Jan. 25, 1947; children: John Edward, James William, Elizabeth Ann Ingraham Reed. B.A., Dartmouth Coll., 1943; postgrad., Cornell U., 1957-58. Editorial asst. Moody's Investors Service, N.Y.C., 1946-47; joined U.S. Fgn. Service, 1947; vice consul Cochabamba, Bolivia, 1947-48; 3d sec. embassy La Paz, Bolivia, 1948-50; vice consul Hong Kong, 1950-51, Perth, Australia, 1951-54; consul Madras, India, 1954-56; 2d sec. embassy Djakarta, Indonesia, 1958-60; officer charge Australia-New Zealand affairs State Dept., 1961-62, officer charge Indonesian affairs, 1962-65; assigned Nat. War Coll., 1965-66; chief of embassy polit. sect. Rangoon, Burma, 1966-69; dep. dir. research and analysis for East Asia, State Dept., 1969-71; polit. counselor embassy Islamabad, Pakistan, 1971-74; dir. Office of Indonesian, Malaysian and Singapore Affairs, State Dept., Washington, 1974-77; dep. chief mission Am. embassy, Singapore, 1977-79; diplomat in residence Lake Forest (Ill.) Coll., 1979-80; freedom of info. advisor U.S. Dept. State, 1980—; mem. U.S. del. ANZUS council meeting, Canberra, Australia, 1962, Intergovtl. Group on Indonesia, Amsterdam, Netherlands, 1975, 77. Served with USAAF, 1943-45, ETO. Mem. Am. Fgn. Service Assn. Address: 7700 Sebago Rd Bethesda MD 20817-4844

INGRAHAM, JEANNE, pediatric nurse practitioner; b. Newport News, Va., Aug. 21, 1961; d. Talcott Leroy and Lucy Rebecca (Lathrop) I. BSN, Med. U. S.C., 1983; MSN in pediatrics, U. Va., 1985, cert. PNP, 1986. RN, Ga., Va.; cert. instr. pediatric life support and pediatric advanced life support. Staff nurse pediatrics U. Va. Hosp., Charlottesville, 1983-86; staff nurse pediatric ICU Egleston Children's Hosp., Atlanta, 1987-89, clin. nurse specialist critical care medicine, liver transplantation, 1989-96, coord. pediatric liver transplant program, 1990-96; pediatric nurse practitioner Egleston Pediatric Group, Decatur, Ga., 1996—. Mem. AACN, Nat. Assn Pediatric Nurse Assocs. and Practitioners, Sigma Theta Tau.

INGRAHAM, JOHN WRIGHT, banker; b. Evanston, Ill., Nov. 10, 1930; s. Harold Gillette and Mildred (Wright) I.; m. Barbara Gaye Barker, Nov. 8, 1967; children—Kimberly, Elizabeth, Scott. A.B., Harvard U., 1952, M.B.A., 1957; postgrad., NYU Grad. Sch. Bus., 1963-68. Jr. lending positions Citicorp, N.Y.C., 1957-66, sr. lending positions, 1966-70, head instl. recovery mgmt., 1970-78, dep. chmn., credit policy com., 1979-92, sr. v.p. oversight N.Am lending, 1979-84, sr. v.p. oversight Latin Am. lending, 1985-88, sr. v.p. oversight global pvt. bank lending and investing, 1988-92; dir. Dynamo M Fund, Nassau, Bahamas, 1995-98; global risk mgr. Citibank, N.Y.C., 1993—; bd. dirs. Dynamo M Fund, Nassau, Bahamas; past bd. dirs. Ark. Best Corp., Ft. Smith, Sprague Techs., Inc. Greenwich, Conn.; chmn. audit com. Presto Industries, Houston, 1986-88; vice chmn. bd. Penn Cen. Corp., Cin., 1978-84, chmn. fin. com., 1982-91, past bd. dirs.; rep. banking industry before coms. and hearings U.S. Ho. Reps., U.S. Senate, 1976-78; mem. N.Y. Crime Stoppers, N.Y.C. Police Found., 1993—. Trustee Noble and Greenough Sch., Dedham, Mass., 1987-94; mem. bus. adv. coun. to dean Grad. Sch. Bus., U. Ark, Fayetteville, 1985-95; mem. com. for Asia rsch. HArvard U. John King Fairbanks Ctr., Cambridge, Mass., 1993—. Lt. USN, 1952-55, Korea. Mem. Fin. Acctg. Standards Bd. (task force 1974-81), Robert Morris Assocs. (bd. dirs. 1972-75, Disting. Svc. award 1978), Union Club, Piping Rock (Locust Valley, L.I.), Gulfstream Bath and Tennis Club (Fla.), Ocean Club (Fla.), Harvard Club Boston, St. Andrews Soc. State of N.Y. Republican. Christian Scientist. Home: 950 Park Ave New York NY 10028-0320 Office: Citicorp 399 Park Ave New York NY 10022-4614 also: 6880 N Ocean Blvd Boynton Beach FL 33435-3317

INGRAHAM, JOSEPH EDWIN, financial officer; b. New Orleans, Oct. 29, 1946; s. Joseph Francis and Dorothy Margaret (Treiber) I.; m. Jeanne Arlene Galouye, July 18, 1970; children: Barbara Jeanne, Ashley Elizabeth, Joseph Francis II. BBA, Loyola U., New Orleans, 1969. CPA, La. Acct. Shell Oil Co., New Orleans and Houston, 1969-73; sr. acct. Peat, Marwick, New Orleans, 1973-76, Bourgeois, Bennett, Thokey & Hickey, New Orleans, 1976-77, Alexander Grant, New Orleans, 1977-79; treas. Bergeron Industries, New Orleans, 1979-83; exec. dir. fin. svcs. Archdiocese of New Orleans, 1983—. Staff sgt. USMCR, 1963-71. Republican. Roman Catholic. Office: Archdiocese of New Orleans 7887 Walmsley Ave New Orleans LA 70125-3496

INGRAM, ALVIN JOHN, surgeon; b. Jackson, Tenn., Mar. 31, 1914; s. Alvin Hill and Margaret (Gallagher) I.; m. Catherine Davis, Feb. 7, 1943; children: Mildred Ingram Dyer, Catherine Ingram Doyle, Peggy Ingram Tagg. BS, U. Tenn., 1939, MD, 1939, MS in Orthopaedic Surgery, 1947. Diplomate Am. Bd. Orthopaedic Surgery (dir. 1972-78, v.p. 1976, pres. 1976-78; mem. residency rev. commn. orthopedic surgery 1972-76, chmn. 1975-76). Intern Univ. Hosp., Ann Arbor, Mich., 1939-40; asst. resident surgery Univ. Hosp., 1940-41; fellow orthopaedic surgery Campbell Clinic, Memphis, 1941-42, 46-47; mem. staff Campbell Clinic, 1947-90; ret., dep. chief of staff, 1967-69, chief of staff, 1970-78, chief of staff emeritus, 1979—; pvt. practice orthopaedic surgery Memphis, 1947-83; med. dir. Crippled Children's Hosp., 1948-61, chief staff, 1961-70; orthopaedic cons. Smith and Nephew Richards, 1984-92; med. dir. Les Passes Cerebral Palsy Treatment Center, 1953-56; med. adv. com. Memphis and W. Tenn. chpt. Nat. Found. Infantile Paralysis, 1947-57, chmn., 1947-55; med. adv. com. Shrine Sch. Crippled Children, 1947-56; med. adv. bd. Variety Club Convalescent Hosp., 1952-56; assoc. prof. orthopaedic surgery U. Tenn. Coll. Medicine, 1960-71, prof., chmn. dept., 1971-79, prof. emeritus, 1979—; mem. staff Bapt. Meml. Hosp., exec. com. med. staff, 1969-70, chmn. orthopaedic dept., 1970-74, pres. med. staff, 1973; mem. staff St. Joseph Hosp.; mem. staff LeBonheur Children's Hosp. (trustee 1968-71); cons. staff Meth. Hosp. Program; chmn. 2d Tenn. Conf. Handicapped Children, 1958; chmn. med. div. United Fund Shelby County, 1961, mem. budget com., 1963-65; dir. at large Nat. Assn. Blue Shield Plans, 1965-70; mem. Gov. Tenn. Adv. Bd. Crippled Children's Service, 1961-77, chmn., 1967-77; mem. exec. com. Am. Bd. Med. Specialties, 1980-83; mem. Tenn. Bd. Med. Examiners, 1981-86, adv. council on Orthopaedic Resident Edn., 1982-86. Contbr. to books. Mem. ofcl. bd. St. John's Meth. Ch., 1952—, vice chmn. ofcl. bd., 1965, 66, 69, 70, chmn., 1971-72, gen. chmn. every mem. canvass, 1955-57, 63, pres. men's club, 1958, sec. stewardship, 1964-65; bd. dirs. Front St. Theatre, Memphis, 1963-64; mem. adminstrv. bd. Christ Meth. Ch., 1982-85, 88-91, trustee, 1984-85. Maj. M.C., AUS, 1942-46. Recipient U. Tenn. Coll. Medicine Disting. Alumnus award, 1997. Mem. Am. Acad. Orthopaedic Surgeons (chmn. program com. 1954, 71, mem. manpower com. 1974-81), Am. Orthopaedic Assn. (chmn. program com., pres. 1973), Central Orthopaedic Club (charter), Tenn. Orthopaedic Soc. (pres. 1963-64), Willis C. Campbell Club (pres. 1967), Internat. Soc. Orthopaedics and Traumatology, So. Orthopaedic Assn. (Disting. So. Orthopaedic Surgeon award 1989), Am. Acad. Cerebral Palsy (chmn. program com. 1955, publs. com. 1957, exec. com. 1958, pres. 1958-59), Pediatric Orthopedic Soc. (pres. 1973), Pediatric Orthopedic Soc. N.Am. (Disting. Pioneer award 1990), ACS (mem. grad. edn. com. 1974-76), AMA (ho. of dels. 1961-64, trustee 1964-70, sec. treas. 1968-70, sec. bd. trustees 1968-70), So. Med. Assn., Tenn. Med. Assn., Memphis and Shelby County Med. Soc. (pres. 1962, bd. censors 1963-65, ho. of dels. 1965), Nat. Acad. Sci. Inst. Medicine (council 1972-75), Memphis Ind. Practice Assn. (med. dir. 1983-84), U.S. C. of C. Home: 585 S Greer St Apt 1101 Memphis TN 38111-3232

INGRAM, ARTONYON S., psychology educator; b. Fremont, N.C., Dec. 2, 1962; s. Gliffie and Doris Ingram. BS, Atlantic Christian Coll., 1985; cert. in drugs and alcohol abuse, Pierce Coll., Steilacoom, Wash., 1993, AA, 1993; MEd, City U., Bellevue, Wash., 1995; cert. parent educator, Clover Pk. Tech. Coll., 1995. Teaching parent Onslow Mental Health Ctr., Jacksonville, N.C., 1987-89; social svcs. asst. Rainer Vista Health Care, Puyallup, Wash., 1990-91, Lakewood Health Care, Tacoma, Wash., 1990-91; group life counselor Jessie Dyslin Boys Ranch, Tacoma, Wash., 1991-92; case mgr. Puget Sound Ctr., Tacoma, Wash., 1991; counselor intern Dotters Counseling Ctr., Puyallup, Wash., 1992-93, Cross Rd. Treatment Ctr., Tacoma, 1993; instr. Clover Pk. Tech. Coll., Tacoma, 1993—. Counselor First Bapt. Ch., Jacksonville, N.C. With USNG, 1981-88. Army Nat. Guard scholar, 1978-81, L.N. Forbes scholar, Boeing Engring. scholar, 1993. Mem. Nat. Assn. Alcoholism and Drug Abuse Counselors, Chem. Dependency Profls. Home: 3202 S Mason Ave Apt L106 Tacoma WA 98409-8506 Office: Tacoma Washington Clover Pk Tech Coll Psych Tacoma WA 98498

INGRAM, CHARLES CLARK, JR., energy company executive; b. Dec. 10, 1916; s. Charles Clark and Winnie (Edwards) I.; m. Maxine Waterbury, Jan. 29, 1939; children: James C., Jack R. BS, U. Okla., 1940; LLD, Oral Roberts U., 1983. Registered profl. engr., Okla. With Oneok Inc., Tulsa, 1940—, pres., 1966-71, CEO, 1966-81, chmn., 1966-87, chmn. emeritus, 1987—; former chmn. bd. trustees Frontiers of Sci. Found. of Okla., Inc., 1973-74; former adv. bd. Downtown Tulsa Unlimited; former bd. govs. Am. Citizenship Ctr., Oklahoma City; mem. pres.'s bd. visitors, chmn. Tulsa Engring. Coun., U. Okla. Maj. AUS, WWII, 1941-46. Named to Okla. Hall of fame, 1982. Mem. AIME, Am. Assn. Petroleum Geologists, Am. Gas Assn. (chmn. 1979-80), So. Gas Assn. (past pres.), Engrs. Soc. Tulsa, Okla. State C. of C. (pres. 1981), Oklahoma City C. of C., Tulsa C. of C., Nat. Alliance Businessmen (chmn. Ea. Okla. and Tulsa 1973-74), Propeller Club U.S., Summit Club, So. Hills Country Club (gov., past pres.), Cedar Ridge Country Club (Tulsa), Masons, Sigma Tau, Sigma Gamma Epsilon. Baptist. Office: Oneok Inc 100 W 5th St PO Box 871 Tulsa OK 74102-0871

INGRAM, DALE, consumer products company executive. Dir. pub. rels. internat. Wal-Mart Stores Inc., Bentonville, Ark. Office: Wal-Mart Stores Inc 702 SW 8th St Bentonville AR 72716*

INGRAM, DAVID, entertainment company executive; b. Dec. 13, 1962; m. Sarah LeBrun; 1 child, Henry LeBrun. BA in History cum laude, Duke U., 1985; MBA in Mktg., Vanderbilt U., 1989. Dir. rsch. Duke U. Capital Campaign Office, Durham, N.C., 1985-87, dir., found. Young Alumni for The Capital Campaign, 1986-87; asst. to treas. Ingram Industries, Inc., Nashville, 1989-91; dir. sales Ingram Entertainment Inc., La Vergne, Tenn., 1991-92, asst. v.p. sales, 1992-93, v.p. major accounts, 1993-94, pres., COO, 1994—; chmn. bd. visitors The Duke Primate Ctr., 1987—; bd. dirs. Montgomery Bell Acad. Mem. Video Software Dealers Assn. (nat. bd. dirs.), Belle Meade Country Club, Golf Club Tenn., Caves Valley Golf Club, Green Spring Valley Hunt Club, Delta Tau Delta. Avocations: golf, cycling, running, tennis, hunting, reading, investments. Office: Ingram Entertainment Inc Two Ingram Blvd La Vergne TN 37089 also: Ingram Industries Inc One Belle Meade Pl 4400 Harding Rd Nashville TN 37205-2250*

INGRAM, DONALD, insurance company executive. Acct. Nations Bank of Ga.; CEO Godwins Inc. (now called Aon Cons.), Chgo. Office: Aon Cons 123 N Wacker Dr Ste 1000 Chicago IL 60606-1700*

INGRAM, DOUGLAS HOWARD, psychoanalyst; b. N.Y.C., Feb. 8, 1943; s. Sidney David and Sylvia (Wilensky) I.; m. Nancy Sue Reiner, Dec. 26, 1976; children: Alexander Isaac, Benjamin Zachary. AB, Columbia Coll., 1964; MD, NYU, 1968. Diplomate Am. Bd. Psychiatry and Neurology. Pvt. practice N.Y.C., 1972—; med. dir. Karen Horney Clinic, N.Y.C., 1979-83; clin. prof. psychiatry N.Y. Med. Coll., Valhalla, N.Y., 1998—. Editor-in-chief Am. Jour. Psychoanalysts, 1991—. Fellow Am. Acad. Psychoanalysts (pres. 1997-98); mem. Assn. for Advancement of Psychoanalysis (pres. 1981-82), Am. Inst. Psychoanalysts (dean 1997—). Office: 4 E 89th St New York NY 10128-0636

INGRAM, GEORGE, business executive; b. Montclair, N.J., Dec. 10, 1920; s. George and Frances Elizabeth (Watts) I.; m. Olive May Holtz, Feb. 15, 1947; children: Patricia (Mrs. S. K. Bone), George III (dec.), Sara, John. B.S., Yale U., 1942; M.S., Stevens Inst. Tech., 1948. Registered profl. indsl. engr., Pa. Indsl. engr. RCA, 1942-45; cons. mgmt. engr. Stevenson, Jordan & Harrison, Inc., N.Y.C., 1945-51; controller Riegel Paper Corp., 1951-57, Raytheon Co., Lexington, Mass., 1957-60; v.p. Raytheon Co., 1960-61, v.p. fin., 1961-63, sr. v.p., dir., 1963-68; sr. v.p. Champion Internat., Inc., N.Y.C., 1968-69; exec. v.p. Champion Internat., Inc., 1969-72, dir., 1968-72; pres., chief exec. officer, dir. Reed-Ingram Corp., N.Y.C., 1972-77; cons. Reed-Ingram Corp., 1977-83; pres. Dionis Corp., Nantucket, Mass., 1977-87; chmn. bd., dir. Deerfield Splty. Papers, Inc., 1973-77, Oneida Packaging Products, Inc., 1973-77, Canadian Glassine Co., Ltd., 1973-77; chmn., sec., dir. Arctos Corp., Quaker Hill, Conn., 1980-86; pres., treas., dir. Fitchburg Engring. Corp., Mass., 1980-86; dir. M/A Com, Inc., Burlington, Mass., 1968-91. Trustee Coll. of Wooster, Ohio, 1970-88. Mem. Fin. Execs. Inst. (past pres. Boston; past chmn. nat. com. securities and exchanges regulation), ASME, Phi Gamma Delta. Republican. Episcopalian. Club: Nantucket Yacht. Home and Office: PO Box 1138 Nantucket MA 02554-1138

INGRAM, GEORGE CONLEY, judge; b. Dublin, Ga., Sept. 27, 1930; s. George Conley and Nancy Averett (Whitehurst) I.; m. Sylvia Williams, July 26, 1952; children: Sylvia Lark, Nancy Randolph, George Conley. A.B., Emory U., 1949, LL.B., 1951. Bar: Ga. 1952. City atty. City of Smyrna, Ga., 1958-64, City of Kennesaw, Ga., 1964; judge Cobb County Juvenile Ct., 1960-64, Superior Ct., Cobb Jud. Cir., 1964-68; justice Supreme Ct. Ga., 1973-77; spl. asst. atty. gen. State of Ga., 1979-86; ptnr. Alston & Bird, Atlanta, 1977-98; sr. judge State of Ga., 1998—; staff, faculty Judge Advocate Gen. Sch. U.S. Army U. Va., 1952-54. Trustee Cobb Cmty. Found., The Eleventh Cirs. Hist. Soc. Inc., Tommy Nobbis Ctr. Found., Inc.; emeritus mem. Emory Law Sch. Coun. 1st lt. JAGC, USAR, 1952-54. Recipient Disting. Svc. award Kennesaw Mountain Jaycees, 1961, Ga. Jaycees, 1961, Emory Law Sch. Alumni Assn., 1985; Disting. Citizen award City of Marietta, Ga., 1973; Len Gilbert Leadership award Cobb County C. of C., 1985; Cobb County Citizen of Yr. award, 1990; hon. life mem. Ga. PTA. Fellow Am. Bar Assn. Found., Am. Coll. Trial Lawyers, Internat. Soc. Barristers, Am. Acad. Appellate Lawyers, Marietta-Cobb Mus. Art; mem. ABA, Am. Law Inst., State Bar Ga. (Tradition of Excellence award 1987), Cobb and Atlanta Bar Assn., Lawyers Club of Atlanta, Old War Horse Lawyers Club, Cobb County C. of C. (Pub. Svc. award, 1970) Georgian Club (bd. mem.), Rotary, Order of Coif (hon.), Phi Delta Phi, Omicron Delta Kappa. Methodist. Home: 540 Hickory Dr Marietta GA 30064-3602

INGRAM, GEORGE HERSCHEL, university administrator, writer; b. Woodbury, N.J., Dec. 15, 1939; s. George Herschel and Ruth Chambers (Powell) I.; children: Pamela Anne (Ingram) Walsh, George Herschel III. BS in Comm., Temple U., 1962. Reporter The Press, Atlantic City, N.J., 1962-64, Trenton (N.J.) Times, 1964-66, The Phila. Inquirer, 1966-69; asst. to v.p. univ. rels. Temple U., Phila., 1969-80, spl. asst. to pres., 1980-82, dir. Univ. News Bur.,, 1982-93, assoc. v.p. univ. rels., 1993—; Co-author: Fishing the Delaware Valley, 1997 (paperback 1998). Recipient Scales of Justice award Phila. Bar Assn., 1968. Mem. Outdoor Writers Assn. Am., Phila. Pub. Rels. Assn., Am. Littorial Soc. Avocations: freelance writing, fishing, hunting, travel. E-mail: odysseus@astro.ocis.temple.edu. FAX: 215-204-8563. Home: 505 Bank Ave Riverton NJ 08077 Office: Temple Univ Broad and Oxford St Philadelphia PA 19122

INGRAM, GREGORY LAMONT, artist; b. Greensboro, N.C., Apr. 10, 1961. Student, Pratt Inst., 1979, N.Y.C. Tech. Coll., 1979-82. Artist's cert. N.Y.C. Dept. Cultural Affairs, 1985. Messenger, apprentice Ted Bates Worldwide-Backer Speilvogel Bates, N.Y.C., 1976-83; dispatcher ArtSpeaks, N.Y.C., 1983-90; gallery asst. Gallery Henoch, N.Y.C., 1984-90; messenger, apprentice Cosmic Sound Delight, N.Y.C., 1986; audience coord. Motion Promotions, N.Y.C., 1993-94; art cons. N.Y.C. Housing Authority, 1994-95; dir. G.L.I. Graphics, 1995-97; cmty. vol. Americorps (Black Ch. Edn. Nat. Ministries Unit), Jamaica, N.Y., 1997—; cons. in art and design N.Y.C. Housing Authority, 1994-95, East N.Y. Urban Youth Corps, 1996-98. One-man shows Spring Creek Br. Libr., Bklyn., 1986, New Lots Br. Libr., Bklyn., 1986; group exhibits include Bklyn. Terminal Show, N.Y.C., 1983, Fun Gallery, N.y.C., 1983, Profile Gallery, N.Y.C., 19984, Storefront Gallery, N.Y.C., 1985, 86, Anthax Gallery, Stamford, Conn., 1985, O K Harris Gallery, N.Y.C., 1985, Pub. Image Gallery, N.Y.C., 1986; represented in permanent collections at June Kelly Gallery, N.Y.C., Rush Fine Arts, N.Y.C., Jack Tilton Gallery, N.Y.C., O.K. Harris Gallery, N.Y.C., Gallery Henoch, N.Y.C. Mem. Mcpl. Art Soc., Bklyn. Botanic Garden, Rush Fine Arts, Operation Greenthumb, Citizen's Com. Avocations: collecting, reading, writing, athletics, exploring. Office: June Kelly Gallery Broadway New York NY 10012 Address: 359 Wortman Ave Brooklyn NY 11207

INGRAM, JAMES, popular musician; b. Akron, Ohio, Feb. 16. Co-performer (songs) One Hundred Ways, 1981 (Grammy Award, best rhythm and blues vocal performance, 1981), Just Once, 1981, Baby Come to Me, 1982, How Do You Keep the Music Playing, 1983, (with Michael MacDonald) Yah Mo B There, 1983 (Grammy Award, best rhythm and blues duo, 1984), What About Me, 1984; songwriter (album) It's Your Night, 1983, It's Real, 1989, The Power of Great Music, 1991, Always You, 1993. Academy award nominee, Best Original Song, 1993 (for "The Day I Fall in Love" from Beethoven's 2nd). Address: care Warner Bros Records PO Box 6868 Burbank CA 91510-6868

INGRAM, JAMES, state agency administrator. With FBI; dep. asst. dir. FBI, Washington; agt. in charge N.Y. office FBI; appt. to command Miss. Dept. of Pub. Safety. Office: Dept of Pub Safety PO Box 958 Jackson MS 39205

INGRAM, KENNETH FRANK, retired state supreme court justice; b. Ashland, Ala., July 7, 1929; s. Earnest Frank and Alta Mary (Allen) I.; m. Judith Louise Brown, Sept. 3, 1954; children: Jennifer Lynn Ingram Malone, Kenneth Frank Jr. BS, Auburn U., 1951; LLB, Jones Law Sch., 1963. Bar: Ala. 1963, U.S. Dist. Ct. (no. dist.) Ala. 1965, U.S. Dist. Ct. (mid. dist.) Ala. 1966. City councilman City of Ashland, Ala., 1956-58; mem. Ho. of Reps., Ala., 1958-66; presiding judge 18th Jud. Cir. Ct., Ala., 1968-87; judge Ala. Ct. Civil Appeals, Montgomery, 1987-89, presiding judge, 1989-91; assoc. justice Ala. Supreme Ct., Montgomery, 1991-97; mem., chmn. Ala. Jud. Inquiry Commn., 1979-87. Contbr. articles on jud. ethics to profl. pubs. With USMC, 1952-54. Mem. Ala. Bar Assn., Masons. Democrat. Methodist. Avocations: woodworking, metalcrafting, tennis, swimming. Home: 264 1st St N PO Box 729 Ashland AL 36251-0729

INGRAM, MARGI, real estate broker; b. Central, Ala.; d. Jack and Dru (Graham) I. BS, U. Ala., 1969, postgrad., 1971-72. Tchr. pub. schs. Birmingham, Ala., 1970-78; broker Gilliland & Co., Birmingham, 1978-79; broker, pres. Ingram & Assocs., Birmingham, 1979—; mktg. cons. Collateral Mktg., Birmingham, 1982-84, Royal Homes, Inc., 1982—, Gibson-Anderson-Evins, 1983—, City Fed. Savs. & Loan Assn., 1983-85, Thornton Constrn., Harbert Constrn. Bd. dirs. Humane Soc. Birmingham, 1980—; bd. dirs. United Cerebral Palsy, pres., 1999; trustee Hew Hours Mktg. Group Am. Named Bus. Exec. of Yr. Birmingham Bus. Jour., 1985. Mem. Nat. Assn. Realtors, Ala. Assn. Realtors, Birmingham Bd. Realtors (sec. 1999, Realtor of Yr. award 1998), Fed. Land Inst., Sales Mktg. Execs. Internat., Greater Birmingham Homebuilders Assn. (bd. dirs. 1999—), Birmingham C. of C. (trustee). Democrat. Episcopalian. Avocations: golf, travel, reading. Office: Ingram Hayes & Assocs 2336 20th Ave S Birmingham AL 35223-1006

INGRAM, MARTHA RIVERS, company executive; b. Charleston, S.C.; m. Bronson Ingram (dec. 1995); children: Orrin H. II, John R., David B., Robin I. Grad., Vassar Coll. Chmn. bd. dirs. Ingram Industries Inc., Nashville; CEO, chair Ingram Industries Inc., 1996—; bd. dirs. Baxter Internat., Weyerhaeuser Co., First Am. Corp., Ashley Hall, Vassar Coll., Harpeth Hall Sch., Ingram Micro Inc.; mem. adv. bd. Kennedy Ctr. for Performing Arts, Washington. Chmn. Tenn. Bicentennial Commn., 1996; bd. dirs. Tenn. Performing Arts Ctr., Nashville Ballet, Nashville Opera, Nashville Inst. for Arts, Nashville Symphony, Nashville Cmty. Found.; past chmn. United Way's Alexis de Tocqueville Soc.; founder, bd. dirs. Tenn. Repertory Theater; bd. trustees Vanderbilt U. Mem. Nashville Area C. of C. Office: Ingram Industries Inc One Belle Mead Pl 4400 Harding Rd Nashville TN 37205-2250*

INGRAM, ORRIN HENRY, II, transportation executive. Grad., Vanderbilt U., 1982. With Ingram Industries Inc., Nashville, Tenn., 1982—, co-pres.; chmn., CEO Ingram Barge Co., Nashville, Tenn. Bd. dirs. Boys and Girls Club Mid. Tenn., Cumberland Mus., Friends of Warner Pks., Vanderbilt Cancer Ctr., Bapt. Hosp. Corp. Mem. U.S. Polo Assn. (bd. govs., pres.). Office: Ingram Industries Inc 4400 Harding Rd Nashville TN 37205

INGRAM, OSMOND CARRAWAY, JR., minister; b. Birmingham, Ala., Sept. 5, 1952; s. Osmond Carraway and Frances Elizabeth (McReynolds) I.; m. Ann Lochamy, Dec. 21, 1973; children: Joshua Carraway, Jared Scott. BS, U. Ala., Birmingham, 1973; M in Religious Edn., Southwestern Sem., Ft. Worth, 1977. Ordained to ministry Bapt. Ch., 1978; cert. youth Sunday sch. cons. Bapt. Sunday Sch. Bd. Min. music and youth First Bapt. Ch., Elkhart, Tex., 1976-78; assoc. pastor youth and outreach Bethel Bapt. Ch., Houston, 1978-80; min. edn. and youth Vinesville Bapt. Ch., Birmingham, 1980-81; min. youth Calvary Bapt. Ch., Scottsboro, Ala., 1981-85, First Bapt. Ch., Minden, La., 1985-89; assoc. pastor youth Immanuel Bapt. Ch., Lexington, Ky., 1989-91; minister edn. and youth 1st Bapt. Ch., Elizabethton, Tenn., 1993-98; dean weekend coll. Dallas Bapt. U., 1998-99, dean adult edn., 1999—; mem. Pregnancy Aid Ctr., Minden, bd. dirs. 1986-89, sec. and treas., 1988-89. Author: Youth in Discovery, 1991-99, What Would Jesus Do: Youth Interactive Edition, 1998; contbr. articles to profl. jours. Mem. La. Bapt. Youth Mins. Assn. (sec. and treas. 1987-88, v.p. 1988-89), Ky. Bapt. Religious Edn. Assn., Ky. Bapt. Youth Mins. Assn. Home: 407 Phillips Ct Arlington TX 76010-4463 Office: 3000 Mountain Creek Pkwy Dallas TX 75211-9209 *In a society that is on the brink of moral decay, and filled with hopelessness and uncertainty, I find that it is possible to have peace, joy, and hope. Thankfully, the Savior in whom I trust, provides peace and joy for today, and hope for tomorrow.*

INGRAM, RICHARD THOMAS, educational association executive; b. McKeesport, Pa., Sept. 29, 1941; s. Henry Stephen and Jean Catherine (Lis) I.; m. Mollie Mangan Brown, Apr. 6, 1968; children: Kirsten Collins, David Thomas. BS, Indiana U. Pa., 1963; MEd, U. Pitts., 1964; EdD, U. Md., 1969. High sch. tchr. Monroeville (Pa.) Sch. Dist., 1963-64; dir.

psychometric svcs. U. Md., College Park, 1965-69; adj. instr. U. So. Calif., 1976, U. Va., 1971-79; program assoc. Assn. Governing Bds. of Univs. and Colls., Washington, 1971-74, exec. dir., 1974-78, exec. v.p., 1978-92, pres., 1992—; dir. United Educators Ins. Risk Retention Group, Inc., Washington, 1988—, Am. Coun. on Edn., 1995-96; adv. commr. Edn. Commn. of States, Denver, 1985-95; trustee Dickinson Coll., Pa., 1995—. Editor, author: Governing Public Colleges and Universities, 1993, Governing Independent Colleges and Universities, 1993. Trustee U. Charleston, W.Va., 1980-89, Connelly Sch. of Holy Child, Potomac, Md., 1987-93. Capt. U.S. Army, 1969-71, Vietnam. Recipient Disting. Alumni award Ind. U. Pa., 1992, Outstanding Alumnus Citation, Pa. Coll. Alumni Assn., 1994, Coll. Edn. Alumni Assn. award U. Md., 1996. Mem. Am. Assn. Higher Edn., Lakewood Country Club, Cosmos Club, Phi Delta Kappa. Democrat. Avocations: skiing, camping, fly fishing. Home: 12017 Gregerscroft Rd Potomac MD 20854-2148 Office: Assn Governing Bds Univ and Colls 1 Dupont Cir NW Ste 400 Washington DC 20036-1136

INGRAM, ROBERT M., communications company executive; b. Hattiesburg, Miss., Nov. 23, 1950; s. Harold V. and Mattie Louise I.; m. Betty L. DeVolpi, June 7, 1975. BA in Comm., U. So. Miss., 1972; MA in Linguistics, Brown U., 1985. Dir. cmty. svcs. Detroit Hearing & Speech ctr., 1972-74; instr., curriculum specialist Madonna U., Livonia, Mich., 1979-80; pres., CEO Am. Sign Lang. Assocs., Hayward, Calif., 1975-85; mgr. intercultural tng. Applied Materials Japan, Tokyo, 1985-87; diversity program mgr. Hewlett-Packard Co., Palo Alto, Calif., 1987-94; mgr. ops. and adminstrn. Air Touch Internat., Seoul, Korea, 1994-95; pres., CEO Ingram Comms., Union City, Calif., 1994-99; program mgr. Calif. Relay Svc., MCI WorldCom, Riverbank, Calif., 1999—. Author/pub.: (booklet) Mind Over Matter: The Americans With Disabilities Act and Reasonable Job Accommdations for People with Psychiatric Disabilities, 1995; author: Principles and Procedures of Teaching Sign Languages, 1977. Adv. bd. Archimedes Project, Ctr. for Study of Lang. and Info., Stanford U., 1983—; spl. advisor Pres.'s Com. on Employment of People with Disabilities, Washington, 1987-94; mem. Ariz. Coun. for the Deaf, Phoenix, 1978-79; founder Silicon Valley Diversity Roundtable, 1988—. Named Toastmaster of the Yr., Toastmasters Internat., 1989; George C. Marshall fellow Marshall Found., Copenhagen, 1976-77. Fellow Linguistic Soc. Am.; mem. ASTD, Nat. Spkrs. Assn., Internat. Soc. of Sign Lang. Interpreters (chmn. 1976-83). Democrat. Avocations: creative writing, graphic arts. Office: Calif Relay Svc tions MCI WorldCom 6436 Oakdale Rd Riverbank CA 95367

INGRAM, ROLAND HARRISON, JR., physician, educator; b. Birmingham, Ala., Mar. 10, 1935; s. Roland Harrison and Florence (Emerson) I.; m. Marguerite Lewis Colville, June 25, 1961; 1 child, Mary Elizabeth. BS, U. Ala., 1957; MD cum laude, Yale U., 1960; MA (hon.), Harvard U., 1980. Intern Peter Bent Brigham Hosp., Boston, 1960-61; resident Barnes Hosp., St. Louis, 1963, 64, Yale U. Med. Center, 1964-65; from asst. prof. to assoc. prof. medicine Emory U. Sch. Medicine, 1968-70, prof. medicine, 1970-73, 92—; asso. prof. medicine Harvard Med. Sch., 1973-79; dir. respiratory divsn. Brigham and Women's Hosp., Boston, 1973-89; dir. respiratory div. Beth Israel Hosp., Boston, 1980-85; Parker B. Francis prof. medicine Harvard Med. Sch., 1979-89; vice chmn. dept. medicine U. Minn., 1989-92; chief internal medicine Hennepin County Med. Ctr., Mpls., 1989-92; chief internal medicine Emory Crawford Long Hosp., 1992—, chief pulmonary critical care divsn., 1992-98; M. West Looney prof. medicine Emory U. Sch. Medicine, 1992—. Assoc. editor Jour. Clin. Investigation, 1983-85; mem. editorial bds.: New England Jour. of Medicine, 1974-77, Jour. of Applied Physiology, 1978-84, Am. Rev. of Respiratory Diseases, 1980-87; contbr. numerous articles to profl. jours. Served with USPHS, 1961-63. Recipient Rsch. Career Devel. award Nat. Heart and Lung Inst., 1968-73, Edward Livingston Trudeau medal Am. Lung Assn., 1996. Mem. ACP, Am. Soc. Clin. Investigation, Assn. Am. Physicians, Am. Physiol. Soc., Am. Thoracic Soc. (pres. 1983-84), Am. Clin. Climatol. Assn., Phi Beta Kappa, Alpha Omega Alpha. Office: Emory Crawford Long Hosp 550 Peachtree St NE Atlanta GA 30365-3900

INGRAM, SAMUEL WILLIAM, JR., lawyer; b. Utica, N.Y., Mar. 20, 1933; s. Samuel William and Mary Elizabeth (Rosen) I.; m. Jane Austin Stokes, Sept. 30, 1961; children: Victoria, William. BS, Vanderbilt U., 1954; LLB, Columbia U., 1960. Bar: N.Y. 1960. Assoc. Sullivan & Cromwell, N.Y.C., 1960-67; assoc. Shea Gallop Climenko & Gould, N.Y.C., 1967-68; ptnr. Shea & Gould and predecessors, N.Y.C., 1968-89, Hutton, Ingram, Yuzek, Gainen, Carroll & Bertolotti LLP, N.Y.C., 1989—. Bd. dirs. Legal Aid Soc., N.Y.C., 1974-86, sec., 1978-86; trustee Green Mountain Valley Sch., Waitsfield, Vt., 1984-87. Served to 1st lt. USMC, 1954-57. Mem. ABA, N.Y. State Bar Assn., Assn. of Bar of City of N.Y. Avocations: athletic and outdoor activities. Home: 332 Long Ridge Rd Pound Ridge NY 10576-2005 Office: Hutton Ingram Yuzek Gainen Carroll & Bertolotti LLP 250 Park Ave New York NY 10177

INGRAM, SHIRLEY JEAN, social worker; b. Louisville, Oct. 22, 1946. BA in Social Sci., U. Hawaii, Pearl City, 1979; MSW, Fla. State U., 1982. Lic. clin. social worker, Fla.; bd. cert. diplomate social worker, qualified clin. social worker, Md.; cert. family mediator Fla. Supreme Ct., 1991; registered play therapist/supr. Case mgr. Geriatric Residential Treatment Ctr., Crestview, Fla., 1982-84; case mgmt. supr. Okaloosa Guidance Ctr., Fort Walton Beach, Fla., 1984-86; family counselor Harbor Oaks Hosp., Fort Walton Beach, 1986-87; pvt. practice Fort Walton Beach, 1987-95; social worker USAF Family Advocacy Office, Hurlburt Field, Fla., 1995—. Mem. Mental Health Assn. Okaloosa County (sec. bd. dirs. 1988—, mem. adv. bd. dirs. Area Agy. on Aging, chmn. adv. bd. dirs., Okaloosa County Area Agy. on Aging, pres.), NASW, Long Term Care Ombudsman Coun., AAUW, Sertoma. Home: 3 Palm Dr Shalimar FL 32579-2123 Office: USAF Family Advocacy Office Hurlburt Field FL 32579

INGRAM, WILLIAM AUSTIN, federal judge; b. Jeffersonville, Ind., July 6, 1924; s. William Austin and Marion (Lane) I.; m. Barbara Brown Lender, Sept. 18, 1947; children: Mary Ingram Mac Calla, Claudia, Betsy Ingram Friebel. Student, Stanford U., 1947; LL.B., U. Louisville, 1950; LLD honoris causas, Santa Clara U., 1994. Assoc., Littler, Coakley, Lauritzen & Ferdon, San Francisco, 1951-55; dep. dist. atty. Santa Clara (Calif.) County, 1955-57; mem. firm Rankin, O'Neal, Luckhardt & Center, San Jose, Calif., 1955-69; judge Mcpl. Ct., Palo Alto-Mountain View, Calif., 1969-71, Calif. Superior Ct., 1971-76; judge U.S. Dist. Ct. (no. dist.) Calif., San Jose, 1976-88, chief judge, 1988-90; sr. judge, 1990—. Served with USMCR, 1943-46. Fellow Am. Coll. Trial Lawyers. Republican. Episcopalian. Office: US Dist Ct 280 S 1st St Rm 5198 San Jose CA 95113-3002

INGRASSIA, ANTHONY FRANK, human resource specialist; b. Middletown, N.Y., Sept. 22, 1926; s. Joseph and Mary (Dina) I.; m. Eleanor Mae Birkholz, Aug. 9, 1952; children: Michael, Mary, Steve, Laura, Anne, Jane, Lisa, Timothy. BA, U.Wis., 1948. Sports writer Milw. Sentinel, 1948-62; exec. v.p. Milw. Newspaper Guild, 1952-62; asst. dir. Dist. Coun. 48 Am. Fedn. State, County, Mcpl. Employees, AFL-CIO, Milw., 1962-64; labor rels. specialist, labor rels. dir. U.S. P.O. Dept., Washington, 1964-69; dir. office labor-mgmt. rels. U.S. CSC, Washington, 1970-78; asst. dir. labor-mgmt. rels. U.S. Office Pers. Mgmt., Washington, 1979-82, asst. dir. agy. compliance and evaluation, 1982-86, dep. assoc. dir. pers. sys. and oversight, 1986-90, chmn. fed. prevailing rate adv. com., 1990-96; vice-chmn., acting chmn. Fed. Salary Coun., Washington, 1992-95, vice-chmn., 1995—; U.S. del. Internat. Labor Orgn., Pub. Employee Conf., Geneva, 1975-77, 86; spkr. seminar on collective bargaining U. Tel Aviv, Israel, 1979; cons. civil svc. reform Govt. Hungary and Poland, Budapest and Warsaw, 1991; cons. civil svc. Govt. of Saudi Arabia, Riyahd, 1986. Vol. Arlington (Va.) Food Assistance Ctr., 1992-97, Hospice, 1996—. Recipient presdl. rank awards Disting. Govt. Exec., 1980, Meritorious Govt. Exec., 1988. Mem. Soc. Fed. Labor Rels. Profls. (outstanding contbn. to fed. labor rels. award 1983-87), KC. Roman Catholic. Avocations: gardening, church choir, golfing. Home: 3306 18th St N Arlington VA 22207-3702

INGRASSIA, PAUL JOSEPH, publishing executive; b. Laurel, Miss., Aug. 18, 1950; s. Angelo Paul and Regina M. (Iacono) I.; m. Susan Marie Rougeau, Sept 29, 1973; children—Adam, Charles, Daniel. BS, U. Ill., 1972; MA, U. Wis., 1973. Editorial writer Lindsay-Schaub Newspapers, Decatur, Ill., 1973-76; staff reporter Wall St. Jour., Chgo., 1977-80; news editor Wall St. Jour., 1980-81; bur. chief Wall St. Jour., Cleve., 1981-85; bur. chief Wall St. Jour., Detroit, 1985-93, sr. editor, 1993-94; asst. v.p. Dow Jones Telerate, 1994-95; v.p. news svcs., exec. editor Dow Jones & Co., 1995-98; exec. editor, COO Dow Jones Newswires, 1996-98, pres., 1998—. Author: (with Joseph B. White) Comeback: The Fall and Rise of the American Automobile Industry, 1994. Recipient Pulitzer prize for beat reporting, 1993, Gerald Loeb award, 1993, Disting. Svc. to Journalism award U. Wis., 1995. Mem. U. Ill. Alumni Assn. (bd. dirs. 1980-87). Roman Catholic. Home: 111 Division Ave Summit NJ 07901-3050 Office: Harborside Fin Ctr 600 Plaza Two Ste 1950 Jersey City NJ 07311-1103*

INGSTRUP, OLE MICHAELSEN, Canadian government agency official; b. Denmark, 1941; children: Ditte, Anne, Emmanuel, Melissa. BA in Philosophy, Aarhus U., Denmark, 1961, M in Law, 1966, PhD in Law, 1970. Assoc. prof. law Aarhus U., 1966-69; dep. warden, then warden and chief exec. officer various Danish prisons, 1969-73; chmn. planning com. Danish Ministry Justice, 1973-83; rep. European Com. on Crime Problems, 1977-83, chmn. select com. Prison Regimes and Prison Leave; spl. advisor to commr. Correctional Svc. of Can., Ottawa, 1983-86, commr., 1988-92, 96—; chmn. Nat. Parole Bd., Ottawa, 1986-88; prin. Can. Ctr. for Mgmt. Devel., Ottawa, 1992-95; sr. advisor to privy council office, Skelton-Clark fellow Queen's U., 1995-96. Author: Suspended Sentences, Prisoners' Legal Rights, (with others) Structural Change in Prison Management, Use and Abuse of Prison Leave, Criminal Responsibility, Essays in Criminal Law, Crime Control in Denmark; contbr. articles to profl. jours; reviewer law books. Office: Correctional Svc of Can, Correctional Svc of Can, 340 Laurier Ave W, Ottawa, ON Canada K1A OP9*

INGWERSEN, MARTIN LEWIS, shipyard executive; b. Sandusky, Ohio, Nov. 5, 1919; s. John Christian and Irene Catherine (Hinkey) I.; m. Blanche Robinson, Apr. 26, 1947; children: Brenda, Richard Charles, Martin Lewis. BS, U. Notre Dame, 1941; postgrad., Western Res. U., 1941, Princeton U., 1943. Asst. to hull supt. Gt. Lakes Engring. Works, Ashtabula, Ohio, 1941-43, asst. supt., 1946-49; supt. plant Am. Ship Bldg. Co., Buffalo, 1948-50; mgr. plant Toledo, 1950-52; mgr. plant Lorain, Ohio, 1952-53, v.p. ops., 1954-58; v.p., works mgr. Ingalls Shipbldg. Corp., Pascagoula, Miss., 1958-65, v.p. ops., 1965-67; pres. Md. Shipbldg. and Drydock Co., Balt., 1967-68; exec. v.p. Lockheed Shipbldg. Co., Seattle, 1968-73; pres. Lockheed Shipbldg. and Constrn. Co., Seattle, 1973-76, exec. v.p. office of pres., 1976-86, trustee, 1973-86; cons. shipbldg. and ship repair, 1986—; bd. dirs. Puget Sound Bridge and Dry Dock Co., Seattle, Colby Crane & Mfg. Inc., Seattle. Served to lt. USNR, 1943-46. Mem. Am. Bur. Shipping, Soc. Naval Architects and Marine Engrs., Am. Soc. Naval Engrs., Navy League, Propeller Club U.S., Notre Dame Club of Boca Raton. Roman Catholic. Home and Office: 17652 Charnwood Dr Boca Raton FL 33498-6426

INHOFE, JAMES M., senator; b. Des Moines, Nov. 17, 1934; m. Kay Kirkpatrik; children: Jim, Perry, Molly, Katy. BA, U. Tulsa, 1973. Pres. Quaker Life Ins. Co.; mem. Okla. Ho. Reps., 1966-69, Okla. State Senate, 1969-77; mayor City of Tulsa, 1978-84; mem. 1st Dist. Okla. Ho. of Reps., 1987-94; U.S. senator from Okla., 1995—, mem. armed svcs. com., intelligence com., mem. environment and pub. works com. Served with U.S. Army, 1955-56. Republican. Office: 453 Russell Senate Bldg Washington DC 20510-3601

INIGO, RAFAEL MADRIGAL, retired electrical engineering educator; b. Madrid, June 18, 1932; came to U.S., 1963; s. Rafael G. and Francisca V. (Madrigal) I.; m. Eliana Soto, Apr. 29, 1961; children: C. Paulina, Alvaro A. Ing. El., U.T.F. Santa Maria, Val Chile, 1957; MSEE, U. Va., 1965, DSc in EE, 1966. Registered profl. engr., Va. Elec. engr. Branden Coppe Co., Coya, Chile, 1957-61; asst. prof. elec. engring. U.T.F. Santa Maria, Valparaiso, Chile, 1961-66; prof. elec. engring. UT Santa Maria, Valparaiso, 1966-68; assoc. prof. elec. engring. Va. Mil. Inst., Lexington, 1968-74, prof. elec. engring., 1974-78; assoc. prof. elec. engring U. Va., Charlottesville, 1978-85, prof. elec. engring., 1986-97, prof. emeritus, 1997—. Author: Teoria de Circuitos, 1977, Vision por Computador, 1986; contbr. articles to profl. jours. Helen Wessel fellow U. Va., 1959, AID fellow U.S. Govt., 1963; Fulbright scholar Univ. Tech. Nat. Faculty Cordoba, Argentina, 1997. Avocations: photography, canoeing. Office: U Va Thornton Hall Dept Elec Engring Charlottesville VA 22903-6073

INK, DWIGHT A., government agency administrator; b. Des Moines, Sept. 9, 1922; s. Dwight P. and Edna (Craun) I.; m. Margaret Child, Aug. 31, 1948; children: Stephen, Bruce, Lawrence, Barbara, Lauri; m. Dona A. Wolf, Feb. 14, 1981. BS, Iowa State U., 1947; MA, U. Minn., 1951. Budget and personnel officer City of Fargo (N.D.), 1948-50; chief mcpl. water sect. Bur. Reclamation Dept. Interior, Bismark, N.D., 1950-51; chief reports and statistics br. Savannah River Ops. Office AEC, Oak Ridge, 1952-55; exec. asst. to chmn. AEC, Washington, 1958-59, asst. gen. mgr., 1959-66; 1st asst. sec. for adminstrn. HUD, Washington, 1966-69; asst. dir. for exec. mgmt. Office of Mgmt. and Budget, Washington, 1969-73; dep. adminstr., acting adminstr. GSA, Washington, 1973-76, acting adminstr., Mar.-July 1985; exec. dir., pres. personnel project mgmt. CSC, Washington, May-Nov. 1977; v.p. Nat. Consumer Coop. Bank, Washington, 1980-81, U.S. Synthetic Fuels Corp., Washington, 1982-84; ind. cons. McManis and Assocs., Washington, 1984-85; asst. adminstr. AID, Washington, 1985-88; pres. Inst. of Pub. Adminstrn., N.Y.C., 1988-93, pres. emeritus, 1994—; exec. dir. Alaska Reconstrn. Commn.; pres. Am. Consortium Internat. Pub. Adminstrn., 1980-83; adminstr. Cmty. Svcs. Adminstrn., 1981; chmn. White House Task Force on Edn., 1965; bd. dirs. N.Am. Mgmt. Coun., 1989-93; vice chair nat. adv. bd. Ctr. Study of Presidency. Chmn. Charter Commn. S.C., 1955; mem. exec. com. Ga.- Carolina Council Boy Scouts Am., 1954-55. Served to capt. USAR, 1942-58. Recipient Arthur Fleming award as one of the 10 Outstanding Young Men in Govt. U.S. C. of C., 1961, Disting. Svc. award AEC, 1966, Outstanding Achievement awards U. Minn., 1969, Iowa State U., 1986, Disting. Svc. award GSA, 1975, Outstanding Leadership award Assn. Govt. Accts., 1976, Commrs. award for Disting. Svc., CSC, Pub. Adminstr. of Yr. award Brigham Young U., 1978. Mem. Am. Pub. Works Assn. (bd. dirs.), Am. Soc. Pub. Adminstrn. (pres. 1978-79), Nat. Civil Service League (bd. dirs., career service award 1966), Pub. Adminstrn. Service (bd. dirs.), Nat. Acad. Pub. Adminstrn. (trustee), Internat. Inst. Adminstrv. Sci. (v.p. 1980-86), Coun. on Fgn. Rels., Delta Sigma Rho, Phi Kappa Phi. Home: 16 Anchorage Pt Hilton Head Island SC 29928-3059

INKELES, ALEX, sociology educator; b. Bklyn., Mar. 4, 1920; s. Meyer and Ray (Gewer) K.; m. Bernadette Mary Kane, Jan. 31, 1942; 1 child, Ann Elizabeth. BA, Cornell U., 1941, MA, 1946; postgrad., Washington Sch. Psychiatry, 1943-46; PhD, Columbia U., 1949; student, Boston Psychoanalytic Inst., 1957-59; A.M. (hon.), Harvard U., 1957; prof. honoris causa, Faculdade Candido Mendez, Rio de Janerio, 1969. Social sci. research analyst Dept. State and OSS, 1942-46; cons. program evaluation br., internat. broadcasting div. Dept. State, 1949-51; instr. social relations Harvard U., Cambridge, Mass., 1948, lectr., 1948-57, prof. sociology, 1957-71, dir. studies social relations Russian Research Ctr., dir. studies social aspects econ. devel. Ctr. Internat. Affairs, 1963-71, research assoc., 1971-79; Margaret Jacks prof. edn., prof. sociology Stanford U., Calif., 1971-78, prof. sociology, 1978-90; sr. fellow Hoover Inst., 1978—; prof. emeritus, 1990—; mem. exec. com. behavioral sci. div. NRC, 1968-75; lectr. Nihon U., Japan, 1985. Author: Public Opinion in Soviet Russia, 1950 (Kappa Tau Alpha award 1950, Grant Squires prize Columbia 1955); with R. Bauer, C. Kluckhohn) How the Soviet System Works, 1956, (with R. Bauer) The Soviet Citizen, 1959, Soviet Society (edited with H.K. Geiger), 1961, What is Sociology?, 1964, Readings on Modern Sociology, 1965, Social Change in Soviet Russia, 1968, (with D.H. Smith) Becoming Modern, 1974 (Hadley Cantril award 1974), Exploring Individual Modernity, 1983; editor: (with Masamichi Sasaki) Comparing Nations and Cultures, 1996, National Character: A Psychosocial Perspective, 1997, One World Emerging? Convergence and Divergence in Industrial Societies, 1978; editor-in-chief Ann. Rev. Sociology, 1971-79; editl. cons. Internat. Rev. Cross Cultural Studies; editl. bd. Ethos, Jour. Soc. Psychol. Anthropology, 1978; editor Founds. Modern Sociology Series; adv. editor in sociology to Little, Brown & Co.; contbr. articles to profl. jours. Recipient Cooley Mead award for Disting. Contbn. in Social Psychology, 1982; fellow Ctr. Advanced Study Behavioral Sci., 1955, Founds. Fund Research Psychiatry, 1957-60, Social Scis. Research Council, 1959, Russell Sage Found., 1966, 85, Fulbright Found., 1977, Guggenheim Found., 1978, Bernard van Leer Jerusalem Found., 1979, Rockefeller Found., 1982, Eisenhower Assn., Taiwan, 1984; NAS Disting. Scholar Exchange, China, 1983; grantee Internat. Rsch. and Exchs. Bd., 1989, NSF, 1989. Fellow AAAS (co-chmn. western ctr. 1984-87, chmn. Talcott Parsons award com. 1988-93), Am. Philos. Soc., APA; mem. NIMH, Nat. Inst. Aging (monitoring com. health retirement survey 1990—), Nat. Acad. Scis. (corr. human rights com. 1986-88, mem. com. on scholarly comms. with People's Republic of China, chmn. panel on social sci. and humanities, NRC panel on issues in democratization 1991-92), Am. Sociol. Soc. (coun. 1961-664, v.p. 1975-76), Ea. Sociol. Soc. (pres. 1961-62), World Assn. Pub. Opinion Rsch., Am. Assn. Pub. Opinion Rsch., Inter-Am. Soc. Psychology, Sociol. Rsch. Assn. (exec. com. 1975-79, pres. 1979), Soc. for Study Social Problems. Home: 1001 Hamilton Ave Palo Alto CA 94301-2215 Office: Stanford U Hoover Instn Stanford CA 94305

INKLEY, JOHN JAMES, JR., lawyer; b. St. Louis, Nov. 7, 1945; s. John James Sr. and Morjorie Jane (Kenna) I.; m. Catherine Ann Mattingly, Apr. 13, 1971; children: Caroline Marie, John James III. BSIE, St. Louis U., 1967, JD, 1970; LLM in Taxation, Washington U., St. Louis, 1976. Bar: Mo. 1970, U.S. Dist. Ct. (we. dist.) Mo. 1970, U.S. Dist. Ct. (ea. dist.) Mo. 1975, U.S. Tax Ct. 1975, U.S. Supreme Ct. 1975. Assoc. Padberg, Raack, McSweeney & Slater, St. Louis, 1970-73; ptnr. Summer, Hanlon, Summer, MacDonald & Nouss, St. Louis, 1973-81; city atty. City of Town and Country, Mo., 1979-84, spl. counsel, 1984-88; ptnr. Hanlon, Nouss, Inkley & Coughlin, St. Louis, 1981-83; ptnr., chmn. banking and real estate dept. Suelthaus & Kaplan, St. Louis, 1983-91; ptnr. Armstrong Teasdale LLP (and predecessor firm), St. Louis, 1991—; co-chmn. bus. svcs. group, 1993—; exec. com. St. Louis, 1994—. Mem. ABA, Mo. Bar Assn., Bar Assn. Met. St. Louis. Roman Catholic. Home: 35 Muirfield Ln Saint Louis MO 63141-7382 Office: Armstrong Teasdale LLP 1 Metropolitan Sq Ste 2600 Saint Louis MO 63102-2740

INKLEY, SCOTT RUSSELL, JR., state agency administrator; b. Cleve., Mar. 22, 1952; s. Scott Russell Sr. and Josephine (Newcomer) I.; m. Roxanne Munn, Aug. 21, 1982; children: Scott Russell III, Jonathan Welsh, Katherine Chisholm. Certificat d'assiduete, U. Grenoble, France, 1969; BA, Coll. of Wooster, 1974; cert. completion drug studies inst., Ohio State U., 1975; MA, George Washington U., 1979; postgrad., U. S.C., 1979. Specialist edn. Solon (Ohio) Mental Health Ctr., 1974-76; analyst research S.C. Ho. of Reps., Columbia, 1979-82, analyst research and dir. research, Joint Bond Rev. Com., 1981-91, dir. research Ways and Means Com., 1982-91, dir. Policy Devel. and Evaluation Com., 1992, dep. dir. state budget and control bd., 1992-95; dir. S.C. Bus. Gateway, 1995—; mem. higher edn. funding adv. com., Columbia, 1984-91; advisor State Exec. Mgmt. Tng., Columbia, 1986-91. Lectr., facilitator S.C. Youth Leadership, 1984-91. Named one of Outstanding Young Men Am., 1985. Mem. Nat. Assn. State Budget Officers (exec. com. 1983-91), Fiscal Affairs and Govt. Ops. Assn., So. Legis. Conf., Nat. Conf. State Legislators, Internat. Platform Assn., Order of Palmetto. Home: 1025 Lawhorn Rd Blythewood SC 29016-8982 Office: 1201 Main St Ste 420 Columbia SC 29201-3200

INKSTER, JULI, professional golfer; b. Santa Cruz, Calif., June 24, 1960; m. Brian Inkster, July, 1980. Student, San Jose State U. Professional golfer, 1983—; winner Nabisco/Dinah Shore Invitational, 1984, 89, DuMaurier Classic, 1984, Lady Keystone Open, 1985, 86, McDonald's Classic, 1986, Atlantic City Classic, 1986, 88, Crestar Classic, 1988, 89, Safeco Classic, 1988, Bay State Classic, 1991, JAL Big Apple, 1992, U.S. Women's Open, 1999, Longs Drugs Challenge, 1999, Welch's/Circle K Championships, 1999. Office: care LPGA 100 International Golf Dr Daytona Beach FL 32124-1082*

INLOW, RUSH OSBORNE, chemist; b. Seattle, July 10, 1944; s. Edgar Burke and Marigale (Osborne) I.; BS, U. Wash., 1966; PhD, Vanderbilt U., 1975; m. Gloria Elisa Duran, June 7, 1980. Chemist, sect. chief U.S. Dept. Energy, New Brunswick Lab., Argonne, Ill., 1975-78, chief nuclear safeguards br. Albuquerque ops., 1978-82, sr. program engr. Cruise missile systems, 1983-84, program mgr. Navy Strategic Systems, 1984-85, dir. weapon programs div., 1985-88, dir. prodn. ops. div., 1988-90, asst. mgr. safeguards and security, 1990-94, asst. mgr. nat. def. programs, 1994-96, deputy mgr. 1996—; apptd. Fed. Sr. Exec. Svc., 1985. Served with USN, 1966-71. Tenn. Eastman fellow, 1974-75; recipient Pres. Meritorious Exec. award The White House, Pres. Clinton, 1994. Mem. Am. Chem. Soc., Sigma Xi. Republican. Episcopalian. Contbr. articles to profl. jours.

INMAN, BILLIE JO (ANDREW), writer, retired English educator; b. May 16, 1929. BA, Midwestern State U., 1950; MA, Tulane U., 1951; PhD, U. Tex., 1961. Prof. English U. Ariz., Tucson, 1962-94; ret., 1994; writer Tucson, 1994; ret. E-mail: bjainman@aol.com. Home: 5531 E North Wilshire Dr Tucson AZ 85711-4569

INMAN, BOBBY RAY, investor, former electronics executive; b. Rhonesboro, Tex., Apr. 4, 1931; s. Herman H. and Mertie F. (Hinson) I.; m. Nancy Carolyn Russo, June 14, 1958; children: Thomas, William. B.A., U. Tex., 1950; grad., Nat. War Coll., 1972. Commd. ensign U.S. Navy, 1952, advanced through grades to adm., 1981; asst. naval attache Stockholm, 1965-67; exec. asst., sr. aide to vice chief naval ops. Washington, 1972-73; asst. chief staff intelligence on staff comdr. in chief U.S. Pacific Fleet, 1973-74; dir. Naval intelligence Dept. Navy, Washington, 1974-76; vice dir. Def. Intelligence Agy., 1976-77; dir. Nat. Security Agy., Ft. Meade, Md., 1977-81; dep. dir. CIA, 1981-82; chmn., pres., chief exec. officer Microelectronics and Computer Tech. Corp., Austin, Tex., 1983-86; chmn. bd., chief exec. officer Westmark Systems, Inc., Austin, 1986-89; pvt. investor Austin, 1990—. Decorated Def. D.S.M., Navy D.S.M., Legion of Merit, Def. Superior Service medal, Meritorious Service medal, Nat. Security medal, Joint Services Commendation medal. Office: 701 Brazos St Ste 500 Austin TX 78701-3232

INMAN, DENNIS H., federal judge; b. 1947. BS, U. Tenn., JD. Chanellor Tenn. Ct. Chancery 3d Dist., 1984-95; magistrate judge U.S. Dist. Ct. (ea. dist.) Tenn., Greenville, 1995—. Fax: (423) 638-1293. Office: US Courthouse 101 Summer St W Greenville TN 37743

INMAN, JAMES RUSSELL, claims consultant; b. Tucson, May 24, 1936; s. Claude Colbert and Myra Eugenia (Langdon) I.; m. Charleen M. Bowman, Feb. 22, 1964 (div. 1977); m. Margaret Williams Kendrick, Apr. 26, 1996. Student, Pomona Coll., Claremont, Calif., 1954-60. Supr. res. dept. Honnold Libr. Claremont Coll., 1959-60; supr. casualty claims CNA Ins., L.A., 1961-70; asst. mgr., asbestos specialist, head entertainment claims Firemen's Fund, L.A., Beverly Hills, 1970-83; pres. Wilnor Corp., L.A., 1982—; claims auditor dirs. and officers claims Harbor/Continental Ins., L.A., 1984-86; claims mgr. Advent Mgmt., L.A., 1987, Completion Bond Co., Century City, Calif., 1988; asst. to pres., claims specialist Am. Multiline Corp., L.A., 1988-92; sr. claims specialist Reliance Ins. Co., Glendale, Calif., 1992-94; expert witness in field. Mem. First Century Families: Calif.; mem. com. Baldwin Hills Dam Disaster, 1968-72; pres. Alcohol Info. Ctr., L.A., 1983-85. Mem. L.A. Athletic Club, Wilshire Country Club. Republican. Avocations: classic cars, American and English silver. Home: 623 S Arden Blvd Los Angeles CA 90005-3814

INMAN, JEAN A., political party official. Chmn. Mass. Rep. Party, Boston. Office: Mass Republican Party 21 Milk St Fl 4 Boston MA 02109-5408

INMAN, LARRY JOE, coach; b. Summer County, Tenn., Jan. 3, 1948; m. Bobby Gene Follis; children: Jody, Latrice, Tiffany. BS, Austin Peay State U., Clarksville, Tenn., 1970; M, Tenn. State U., 1977. Head coach basketball Gallatin (Tenn.) H.S., 1970-73, Mt. Juliet (Tenn.) H.S., 1973-78; head coach women's basketball Mid. Tenn. State U., Murfreesboro, 1978-86, Ea. Ky. U., Richmond, 1987—. Named Coach of Yr., Ohio Valley Conf., 1979-80, 82-83, 84-85, 90-91, 94-95, 96-97. Mem. Womans Basketball Coaches Assn. Office: Eastern Ky U Womens Athletic Dept Lancaster Ave Richmond KY 40475

INMAN, MARIANNE ELIZABETH, college administrator; b. Berwyn, Ill., Jan. 9, 1943; d. Miles V. and Bessee M. (Hejtmanek), Pizak; m. David P. Inman; Aug 1, 1964. BA, Purdue U., 1964; AM, Ind. U., 1967; PhD, U. Tex., 1978. Dir. Comml. Div. World Instruction and Translation, Inc., Arlington, Va., 1969-71; program staff mem. Ctr. for Applied Linguistics, Arlington, 1972-73; lectr. in French No. Va. Community Coll., Bailey's

Crossroads, 1973; faculty mem., linguistic researcher Tehran (Iran) U., 1973-75; intern mgmt. edn. rsch. & devel. S.W Ednl. Devel. Lab., Austin, Tex., 1977-78; asst. prof., program dir. Southwestern U., Georgetown, Tex., 1978; dir. English lang. inst. Alaska Pacific U., Anchorage, 1980-87, chairperson all-U. requirements, 1984-88, assoc. dean acad. affairs, 1988-90; v.p. dean of coll. Northland Coll., Ashland, Wis., 1990-95; pres. Ctrl. Meth. Coll., Fayette, Mo., 1995—; contbr. Pres. Commn. Foreign Lang. and Internat. Studies, Washington, 1978-79; manuscript evaluator The Modern Lang. Jour., Columbus, Ohio, 1979-84; cons. Anchorage Sch. Dist., 1984-90; cons., evaluator N. Cen. Assn. Colls. and Schs., Chgo., 1990—; mem. dean's task force Coun. on Ind. Colls., 1993-95; pres. Ind. Colls. and Univs. Mo., 1996—. Co-author: English for Medical Students, 1976; co-author and editor: English for Science and Engineering Students, 1977; contbr. articles to profl. jours. Treas. Alaska Humanities Forum, Anchorage, 1982-87; mem. Anchorage Matanuska-Susitna Borough Pvt. Industry Coun., 1983-86; mem. Sister Cities Commn., Anchorage, 1984-90; mem. Multicultural Edn. Adv. Bd., Anchorage, 1987-90; active speakers bur. Wis. Humanities Com., 1992-95, Mcpl. Libr. Bd., 1993-95; active Mo. Humanities Coun., 1997—; mem. bd. Great Rivers Coun. Boy Scouts Am., 1996—. Named Fellow of Grad. Sch., U. Tex. Austin, 1977-78, Nat. Teaching Fellow, Alaska Pacific U., Anchorage, 1980-81; recipient Pub. Svc. award Sister Cities Commn., Anchorage, 1987, Kellogg Found. Nat. fellowship, Battle Creek, Mich., 1988-91. Mem. League of Women Voters, Nat. Assn. Women in Edn., Am. Assn. for Higher Edn., Am. Coun on Teaching of Foreign Langs., Tchrs. of English to Speakers of Other Langs., Nat. Coun. Tchrs. of English, Alpha Chi, Alpha Lambda Delta, Delta Rho Kappa, Gold Peppers, Kappa Delta Pi, Mortar Bd., Omicron Delta Kappa, Phi Kappa Phi, Pi Delta Phi, Pi Lambda Theta, Sigma Delta Pi, Sigma Kappa. Avocations: community theater, hiking, camping, fishing. Office: Ctrl Meth Coll 411 CMC Sq Fayette MO 65248-1198

INMAN, MITCHELL LEE, JR., accountant; b. North Platte, Nebr., Nov. 9, 1969; s. Mitchell Lee Sr. and Karen Joan (Hazelrigg) I.; m. Janet Marie Leisy, Oct. 6, 1995. BS in Bus. Adminstrn., Midland Luth. Coll., 1992. CPA, Nebr. Staff acct. Brune & Oelkers, CPA's, Dodge, Nebr., 1992, 93, 98—, McChesney Martin Sagehorn, P.C., North Platte, 1994-98; sec.-treas., dir. KJ's Boots and Western Wear, Inc., Hershey, Nebr., 1995—, KJ's Korner, Inc., Hershey, 1995—. Sec. Maria Luth. Ch., Hershey, 1995, 96, treas., 1997. Recipient Most Wanted award Am. Heart Assn., Lincoln County, Nebr., 1995. Mem. AICPA, Nebr. Soc. CPA's. Democrat. Lutheran. Avocations: agriculture, bowling. Office: Brune & Oelkers CPAs PO Box 126 Dodge NE 68633

INMAN, WILLIAM PETER, lawyer; b. Cleve., June 29, 1936; s. James B. and Lillian (Frances) I.; m. Judith A. Clay, Feb. 5, 1994; children: William Peter, Elizabeth, David. Student, Miami U., 1954-55; B.A., Ohio State U., 1958; J.D., Case Western Res. U., 1960, M.B.A., 1966. Bar: Ohio 1960, Tex. 1985. Tax accountant U.S. Steel Corp., Cleve., 1960-63; asso. trust counsel Central Nat. Bank of Cleve., 1963-66; atty. Sherwin-Williams Co., Cleve., 1966-67; tax counsel Sherwin-Williams Co., 1967, mgr. tax dept., 1967-68, corporate dir. taxes, 1968-69, asst. sec., dir. taxes, 1969-71, sec., dir. taxes, 1971-75, v.p., sec., asst. treas., 1975-78, v.p., treas., chief fin. officer, 1978-80; v.p. fin., chief fin. officer RTE Corp., Waukesha, Wis., 1980-83; fin. cons. Houston, 1983-85; corp. sec., gen. counsel Mera Bank, Phoenix, 1985-88; gen. counsel CADTEL Sys. Inc., Phoenix, 1988-95, Ariz. Bus. Assocs., L.L.C., Phoenix, 1995—. Mem. Greater Cleve. Growth Assn., 1969-80; Trustee Ohio Pub. Expenditure Council, 1969-80, v.p., 1970-73, pres., 1973-75, chmn. bd., 1975-77. Mem. Am. Soc. Corp. Secs., Fin. Execs. Inst., Cleve. Treasurers Club, N.A.M., Ohio Mfrs. Assn., Am., Ohio, Greater Cleve., Tex., Maricopa County, Ariz. bar assns., Estate Planning Council of Cleve., Phi Delta Phi, Beta Gamma Sigma, Beta Alpha Psi. Home: 5364 E Juniper Ave Scottsdale AZ 85254-1152 Office: 5364 E Juniper Ave # 175 Scottsdale AZ 85254-1152

INNANEN, LARRY JOHN, lawyer, food products executive; b. Tillsonburg, Ont., Can., Nov. 28, 1950; s. Leo and Aili Aune (Heino) I.; m. Patricia Anne Nagy, July 9, 1971; children: Michael, Meridith, David. LLB, U. We. Ont., 1973. Bar: Ont. 1975. Lawyer Gibson, Linton & Toth, Tillsonburg, Ont., Can., 1975-76; pvt. practice Tillsonburg, 1976-82; corp. solicitor John Labatt Ltd., London, Ont., Can., 1982-87, corp. sec., 1987-90; dir. legal svcs.-Can. ops. John Labatt Ltd., London, Ont., 1990-92; exec. v.p., gen. counsel Labatt Breweries of Can., 1992—. Mem. Law Soc. Upper Can., Can. Corp. Counsel Assn., Can. Bar Assn., Coun. Sr. Legal Execs. Home: 2192 Winding Woods Dr, Oakville, ON Canada L6H 5T9 Office: Labatt Breweries of Can, Labatt Brewing Co Ltd, 181 Bay St Ste 200, Toronto, ON Canada M5J 2T3*

INNERST, CAROL JEAN, journalist; b. York, Pa., June 7, 1937; d. Gene Carlyton and Delilah Helen (Spangler) McCleary; m. Preston Eugene Innerst, Sept. 25, 1966; children: Preston Eugene Jr., Christine Carol. AA, York Jr. Coll., 1957; BA, U. Md., 1959. Reporter, photographer The Gazette and Daily, York, 1957-65; reporter, editor The Call-Chronicle, Allentown, Pa., 1965-66; religion/edn. writer The Phila. Bull., 1966-82; edn. writer The Washington Times, 1982-98; freelance writer, 1999—; adj. fellow Hudson Inst., Indpls., 1995, 96; vis. fellow Alexis de Tocqueville Instn., Arlington, Va., 1999—. Editor: (jour.) News & Views, 1995, 96. Mem. Edn. Writers Assn.

INNERST, PRESTON EUGENE, newspaper editor, journalist; b. York, Pa., Apr. 1, 1927; s. Morgan C. and Edna L. I.; m. Carol Jean McCleary, Sept. 25, 1966; children: Robert, Carol, Preston Eugene, Christine. Ed., Gettysburg (Pa.) Coll. With Gazette and Daily, York, 1943-64; city editor Gazette and Daily, 1956, 60-64; with Phila. Inquirer, 1964-70, night city editor, 1968-70; with Phila. Bull., 1970-82, asst. mng. editor, 1977-78, mng. editor/night, 1978-82; with Washington Times, 1982—, dep. mng. editor, 1993-97, sr. dep. mng. editor, 1997—. Served with USMC, 1945-46. Mem. AP Mng. Editors Assn., So. Newspaper Pubs. Assn. Office: Washington Times 3600 New York Ave NE Washington DC 20002-1947

INNES, DAVID GEORGE, environmental and safety engineer; b. Batavia, N.Y., Nov. 2, 1949; s. John Fredrick and Madonna Betraice (Lapp) I.; m. Janet Marian Taub, Dec. 26, 1971; 1 child, Steven. AAS in Chem. Tech., Monroe C.C.; BS in Edn., SUNY, Geneseo. Cert. safety profl. Prodn. worker Stuart Olvar Holtz Inc., Rochester, N.Y., 1971-77, lab. supr., 1981-87; lab. shift supr. Stromburg Carlson, Rochester, 1977-81; group leader Taylor Instrument, Rochester, 1987-89; environ. health and safety engr. AMTX, Canandaigua, N.Y., 1989-93; environ. engr. Xerox Corp., Canandaigua, 1993-95, environ. health and safety coord., 1995—; mem. chem. tech. adv. com. Monroe C.C., Rochester, 1985—. Author (manual) Protype Title III Instructions, 1986. Co-chmn. WXXI Auction steering com., Rochester, 1997. Mem. Am. Electroplates and Surface Finishers, Semiconductor Safety Assn., Am. Soc. Safety Engrs. Avocations: hiking, golf, volleyball, volunteering. Office: Xerox Corp 5450 Campus Dr Canandaigua NY 14424-8200

INNES, DAVID LYN, university official, educator; b. Cleve., Dec. 19, 1941; s. Harry Donald and Mildred Marie (Svozil) I.; m. Janet Lynn Koons, Sept. 5, 1964; children: Debra Lynn, Jonathan Lyn. BS, Ohio Wesleyan U., 1964; MS, U. Cin., 1966; PhD, Ohio State U., 1969. Instr. Ohio State U., Columbus, 1969-70; asst. to assoc. prof. Temple U., Phila., 1970-80; prof. Sch. Medicine, Mercer U., Macon, Ga., 1980—; assoc. v.p. grants and founds. Mercer U., Macon, 1982-84, asst. to the provost for med. affairs, 1985-88, asst. provost for med. affairs, 1988-93, asst. v.p. for health and biosafety, 1993-96, assoc. v.p. for univ. rsch. and biosafety, 1996—. Contbr. articles and abstracts to profl. jours. Mem. bd. Edn., Willow Grove, Pa., 1973-79, Mental Health Adv. Com., Abington, Pa., 1979-80. Grantee NIH, 1978, constrn. grantee NIH, 1987. Mem. Am. Assn. for Lab. Sci., Am. Gastroenterology Assn., Am. Physiol. Soc., Fedn. Am. Socs. for Exptl. Biology, Ga. Assn. for Biomed. Rsch. (treas., bd. dirs. 1988-98), Ga. Higher Edn. Network Environ. Health and Safety (v.p. 1994-96, pres. 1996-97), Sigma Xi (rsch. grantee), Phi Kappa Phi. Republican. Methodist. Avocations: swimming, biking. Office: Mercer U Sch Medicine 1550 College St Macon GA 31207-1500

INNES, GEORGE MICHAEL, emergency medicine physician; b. N.Y.C., Jan. 16, 1961; s. George Michael and Marie Innes; m. Jeanmarie Innes, June 8, 1985; children: George Michael, Colleen Elizabeth, Shawn Emidio, Erin Marie, Kathleen Ann. BS in Biomed. Sci., CUNY, 1983; MD, Mt. Sinai Med. Sch., 1985; M Med. Mgmt., Tulane U., 1998. Diplomate Am. Bd. Emergency Medicine, Am. Bd. Forensic Examiners, Am. Bd. Forensic Medicine (adv. bd. 1995-97), , Am. Bd. Med. Mgmt., Nat. Bd. Med. Examiners; cert. nat. emergency med. svcs. dir., EMT and paramedic, N.Y.; cert. ACLS instr., advanced trauma life support instr. Intern in internal medicine Booth Meml. Med. Ctr., Flushing, N.Y., 1985-86; resident in emergency medicine Univ. Hosp. at Jacksonville, Fla., 1986-88; dir. emergency med. svcs. St. Peter's Hosp., Albany, N.Y., 1988-90; assoc. dir. emergency and outpatient svcs. Albany Meml. Hosp., 1990-96, dir. emergency med. svcs., 1990-96; dir. dept. emergency medicine Samaritan Med. Ctr., Watertown, N.Y., 1996—, mem. trauma task force, 1997—, vice chief staff, 1999—; mem. med. control bd. Regional Emergency Med. Orgn., 1988-86, asst. acad. dir., 1990-95; ; dep. med. dir. Hson-Mohawk Valley Region, 1986-88; med. dir. advanced EMT-paramedic program Hudson Valley C.C., Troy N.Y., 1989-94; cruise ship physician various ship lines, 1991-95; clin. instr. emergency medicine Albany Med. Coll., 1988-96; v.p., sec. Capital Region Emergency Medicine, PC, 1990-96; med. reporter Sta. WTEN-TV, Albany, 1991-92, Sta. WWNY-TV, Watertown, 1996; bd. dirs., ptnr. Case Assessment Rev. & Evaluation, LLC, 1998—; pres., CEO, Emergency Medicine Cons., P.C., 1996—; chmn. N.Y. Emergency Medicine Polit. Action Com., 1988—, vice chmn., 1995-98; mem. N.Y. State Emergency Med. Svcs. Coun., 1990-94; mem. quality assurance com. Capital Dist. Physicians Health Plan, 1992-96; chmn. credentials com. Blue Shield Northeastern N.Y., 1995-96. Contbr. articles to med. jours. Med. dir. Town of Watertown, 1996—; coach Pop Warner Football, Adams, N.Y., 1997—; med. dir. Jefferson County Emergency Med. Svcs., Watertown, 1997—; bd. dirs. Med. Ednl. and Sci. Found. N.Y., 1994-97. Recipient CARE award Univ. Hosp. Jacksonville, 1987, Physician of Yr. award Hudson Mohawk Valley Regional Emergency Med. Svcs. Coun., 1992, leadership award Glaxo Wellcome-AMA, 1998. Fellow Am. Coll. Emergency Physicians (coun. 1991—, bd. dirs. N.Y. chpt. 1992-98), Am. Coll. Forensic Examiners, Am. Coll. Phys. Execs. (cert. in med. mgmt., chmn. group on new physician execs. 1993-94), Am. Coll. Med. Examiners; mem. AMA (governing coun. young physicians sect. 1995—, chmn. 1997-98, physician's recognition award 1988—), Am. Acad. Emergency Medicine (bd. dirs. 1995-96), AMAP (fedn. adv. com. 1996—, vice chmn. 1998—), Med. Soc. State N.Y. (membership com. 1993-94, ho. of dels. 1990—, emergency med. svcs. com. 1992—, publ. and comm. com. 1994—, exec. com. young physicians sect. 1994—, fin. com. 1996—, physicians discipline com. 1998—, councilor 1994—, exec. coun. 1992—), Jefferson County Med. Soc. (v.p. 1997-98, pres. 1998—), Jefferson Ind. Practice Assn. (steering com. 1997—, contracts com. 1997—), Jefferson Physicians Orgn. (HMO blue com. 1997—). Republican. Roman Catholic. Avocations: scuba diving, fishing, camping. Fax: 315 785-4314. E-mail: ginnes!interserv.com. Home: 15581 Pheasant Run Rd Watertown NY 13601 Office: Samaritan Med Ctr 830 Washington St Watertown NY 13601

INNES, LAURA, actress; b. Pontiac, Mich., Aug. 16, 1960. BA in Theater, Northwestern U. Appeared in local and nat. plays, including A Streetcar Named Desire, Edmund, Two Shakespearean Actors, Our Town, Three Sisters; appeared in TV series, including Wings, ER, My So-Called Life, Party of Five, Brooklyn Bridge, Louis; appeared in feature film Deep Impact, 1998. Office: Warner Bros TV Prodns c/o ER 4000 Warner Blvd Burbank CA 91522*

INNESA, LEVKOVA-LAMM, art critic, writer, curator; b. Moscow, Aug. 21, 1939; came to U.S., 1982; d. Efim Levkov and Irine Nikitina; m. Leonid Lamm, Jan. 9, 1969; 1 child, Olga. Degree in film engring., Leningrad Inst. Film Engrs., 1965; postgrad., Moscow Inst. Fgn. Langs., 1966-68. Freelance writer, art critic Lit. Rev., Moscow, 1967-82, Books' World, Literary Russia, Moscow, 1977-81, Novoe Russkoe Slovo, N.Y.C., 1983-95, Voice of Am., Liberty radio, N.Y.C., 1983-90, Panorama, L.A., 1984—, Contemporania Internat., Flash Art, N.Y. and Milan, 1988-90; chief curator Eduard Nakhamkin Fine Art, N.Y.C., 1989-91; freelance writer, art critic AP, N.Y.C., 1992—; ind. curator Baruch Coll. Gallery, N.Y.C., 1987, The Russian State Mus., Leningrad, 1990, The Artis House, Moscow, 1990, Berman Gallery, N.Y.C., 1991. Author: Back to Square One, 1991; co-author: Transit: Russian Art Between East and West, 1989, Kulturim Stalinism, 1994. Mem. Nat. Writers Union, Internat. Assn. Art Critics. Avocation: travel. Home and Office: 310 East 23rd St 3A New York NY 10010

INNES-BROWN, GEORGETTE MEYER, real estate and insurance broker; b. Wilmington, Del., Mar. 20, 1918; d. George and Flora Sue (Saunders) Meyer; m. Andrew T. Innes, Jr., Nov. 26, 1947 (dec.); m. Roy Glen Brown, Jr., Mar. 6, 1991. Grad. Real Estate Law, theory, Conveyancing and Practice, Phila. Bd. Realtors Sch., 1945; grad. Fire, Marine, Casualty Ins., North Phila. Realty Bd. Sch., 1946; cert. appraiser, Villanova Coll., 1974. Lic. realtor, Pa., ins. broker and appraiser, Phila. Ins. broker, realtor Phila., 1945—, ins. broker, 1946—, also appraiser; residential and single family home builder, Bucks County, Pa., Princeton, N.J., 1955-61. *Ms. Innes-Brown was inducted into the International society of Poetry in 1997 and has received the Golden Poetry award several times. The Society is publishing a book of her poems at the end of this year with her photograph and personal biography.* Mem., spkr. Juniata Pk. Civic Assn., Phila., 1984. Recipient Knights Legion award Italian-Am. Press, 1971. Mem. Nat. Assn. Realtors (sec.-treas. and v.p. chpt. 1975-80), Am. Bus. Women's Assn. (chpt. v.p. 1971, Businesswoman of Yr. 1971), Phila. Women's Realty Assn. (pres. bd. govs. 1949-85, pres. 1949-51, Woman of Yr. 1972-73), Phila. Bd. Realtors (v.p. residential divsn. 1975), North Phila. Realty Bd. (v.p. 1975, 76, pres. 1977, Gustav A. Wick award 1979), Del. Coun. Realty Bds. (sec. 1974), Real Estate Multiple Listing Burs. (treas. 1972-76), Sigma Lambda Soc. (chpt. pres. 1948). Avocations: golf, dancing, gardening, cooking, embroidery. Home: 1162 Walnut Ter Boca Raton FL 33486-5565

INNIS, ROY EMILE ALFREDO, organization executive; b. St. Croix, V.I., June 6, 1934; s. Alexander and Georgianna (Thomas) I.; m. Doris Valdena Funnye, Feb. 13, 1965; children: Roy Jr. (dec.), Alexander (dec.), Cedric, Patricia, Corinne, Kwame, Niger, Kimathi Mugabe. Student, CCNY, 1953-58. Chem. technician Vick Chem. Co., 1961-63; research asst. cardiovascular research labs. Montefiore Hosp., 1963-67; mem. CORE, 1963—, edn. chmn. Harlem group, 1964-68, chmn., 1965-68, 2d nat. vice chmn., 1967-68, asso. nat. dir., 1968, nat. dir., 1968-70, nat. chmn., nat. dir., 1970-82, nat. chmn., 1982—; founder and chmn. CORE Cmty. Sch., Bronx, N.Y., 1977; exec. dir. Harlem Commonwealth Council, 1967-68; 1st ofcl. N.Am. del. Orgn. African Unity, Ethiopia, 1973, Uganda, 1975. Contbr.: chpt. to The Endless Crisis, 1973, Black Economic Development, 1970; pub.: chpt. to Profiles in Black, 1976. Served with AUS, 1950-52. Research fellow Met. Applied Research Center, 1967. Office: 817 Broadway New York NY 10003-4709*

INNMON, (TARA) ARLENE KATHERINE, artist, dancer, writer, storyteller, healer; b. Mpls., Oct. 28, 1950; d. Morris Jentof and Hulda Cecilia (Levine) Bangsund; children: Carl David, Erica Arlene. BS in Occupl. Therapy, U. Minn., 1973. Activities dir. Mother of Perpetual Health Home, Brownsville, Tex., 1973-74; occupl. therapist Corpus Christi (Tex.) Med. Ctr., 1975-76, Mpls. Soc. for Blind, 1976-81, Grand Ave. Rest Home, Mpls., 1985-87. One-woman shows include Gus Lucky's Gallery, Mpls., 1987, Paul Whitney Larsen Gallery, St. Paul, 1998; group exhbns. include Art of Eye I, 1985—, II (multi-yr. traveling exhibits), 1998—, Katherine Nash Gallery, Mpls., 1994, Art and Soul Festival, San Francisco, 1999; represented in permanent collections Bloomington, Minn. Mem. Minn. Chpt. Abortion Rights, Mpls., 1981; bd. mem. Candle in the Window, Mpls., 1998. Recipient first place award drawing Sister Kenny Internat. Show, Mpls., 1988, People's Choice award bronze Sister Kenny Internat. Show, Mpls., 1990, Artist Appreciation award Very Spl. Arts, Mpls., 1997, Jaehny award, 1998, first place award Artists Beyond Disabilities, Long Beach, Calif., 1997. Mem. SASE, Minn. Dance Alliance, The Loft. Avocations: dancing, reading. Home: 2016 27th Ave S Minneapolis MN 55406-1108

INNS, HARRY DOUGLAS ELLIS, optometrist; b. Tryconnel, Ont., Can., June 4, 1922; s. Thomas Henry and Eleanor (Ellis) I.; children from previous marriage: Susan Elizabeth, Douglas Michael; m. Helen Lynne Mitchell. Student, U. Toronto, 1946-48; grad., Ont. Coll. Optometry, 1950, OD, 1958. Practice optometry specializing in contact lenses, Brantford, Ont., 1963—. Contbr. articles to profl. jours.; patentee Inns extension disc to facilitate corneal measurements. Served to lt. with RCAF, 1941-45. Fellow Assn. Contact Lens Practitioners Eng., Am. Acad. Optometry, Royal Soc. Health, Heraldry Soc. Can. (bd. dirs.); mem. Internat. Soc. Contact Lens Specialists (congress chmn.), Ont. Optometrical Assn., Can. Assn. Optometrists, Internat. Optometric and Optical League, Ont. Assn. Optometrists (Edn. Program award 1976, Contact Lens Program award 1978, Internat. Lecture award 1979, Appreciation award 1980, Disting. Service award 1981), Better Vision Inst., Nat. Eye Research Found., Can. Public Health Assn., Am. Optometric Assn., Brantford C. of C., Am. Soc. Contact Lens Specialists (sec.), Waterloo Alumni Assn., Monarchist League Can., 78th Fraser Highlanders (maj.), Royal Can. Mil. Inst., Royal Can. Air Force Assn., Beta Sigma Kappa. Clubs: Anglican Men's, Kiwanis (Brantford, Ont.). Home: 67 Tutela Heights, Brantford, ON Canada N3T 1A4 Office: 36 King George Rd, Brantford, ON Canada N3R 5K1

INOCENCIO, E. BING, college president; came to U.S., 1979; Grad. journalism, Ateneo De Manila U.; MS in Mktg. and Advt., U. Ill.; MA in Bus. and Applied Econs., U. Pa., PhD in Econs. and Comm. Assoc. dean bus., math. and tech. C.C. of Balt.; instructional dean humanities and social scis. Inst. at Montgomery Coll., Takoma Park, Md.; dean instrn. and acad. svcs. Cumberland County Coll., Vineland, N.J.; assoc. provost acad. adminstrn. N.Y.C. Tech. Coll. CUNY; pres. L.A. Pierce Coll., 1996—. Fulbright scholar U. Ill.; fellowship Ford Found. Wharton Sch., Harvard Bus. Sch, Kellogg fellow, 1991; named One of Rising Stars in cmty. leadership League for Innovation in the C.C., 1993. Office: 6201 Winnetka Ave Woodland Hills CA 91371

INOUE, AKIRA, law educator; b. Japan, 1938. LLB, Hitotsubashi U., Tokyo, 1962, LLM, 1967. Cert. full prof. grad. sch. of law, coun. for establishment of univs., Minister of Edn., Japan. Asst. prof. Seijo U. Faculty Law, Tokyo, 1977-79, prof., 1980—, prof. Grad. Sch. Law, 1987—; vis. scholar Inst. Comparative Law, U. Jean Moulin (Lyon III), Lyon, France, 1976-77, 89, Inst. Comparative Law Paris, U. Law, Econs. and Social Scis. (Paris 2), 1989. Co-author: (with others) (books) Important Problems of Modern Commercial Law, 1983, Grand Dictionary on Law of Corporations, 1984, Present Problems of Commercial Law, 1985, Powers and Liablilites of Directors, 1994. Mem. Japan Assn. Private Law, Assn. Econ. Jurisprudence, Japanese Maritime Law Assn., The Air Law Inst. of Japan. Office: Seijo U Faculty of Law, 6-1-20 Seijo Setagaya-ku, Tokyo 157, Japan

INOUÉ, SHINYA, microscopy and cell biology scientist, educator; b. London, Eng., Jan. 5, 1921; came to U.S, 1948, naturalized, 1989; s. Kojiro and Hideko (Yano) I.; m. Sylvia McCandless, July 18, 1952; children: Heather C., Jonathan H., Christopher W., Stephen K., Theodore D. Rigakushi, Tokyo U., 1941; MA, Princeton U., 1950, PhD, 1951; MA (hon.), Dartmouth Coll., 1959, U. Pa., 1966. Instr. U. Wash. Med. Sch., Seattle, 1951-53; asst. prof. Tokyo Met. U., 1953-54; rsch. assoc., assoc. prof. U. Rochester, N.Y., 1954-59; instr. Marine Biol. Lab., Woods Hole, Mass., 1961—, NATO Summer Schs., Cannes, Stressa, Szeged, 1967, 70, 75; prof., chmn. Dartmouth Med. Sch., Hanover, N.H., 1959-66; prof. U. Pa., Phila., 1966-89; Disting. Scientist Marine Biol. Lab., Woods Hole, 1980—; cons. Am. Optical Co., 1954-60, NSF, 1962-65, NIH, 1965-70, Hamamatsu Photonics K.K., Hamamatsu City, Japan, 1988—, Nikon Corp., Tokyo, 1994—; pres. Universal Imaging Corp., Falmouth, Mass., West Chester, Pa., 1984-87, chmn. bd. dirs., 1987-93. Author: Video Microscopy, 1986; co-author: Video Microscopy, 2d edit., 1997; co-editor: Molecules and Cell Movement, 1975; contbr. articles to profl. jours.; mem. editorial bd. several sci. jours., 1964—; ad hoc reviewer, advisor on sci. and tech. NSF, NIH, many univs., founds.; patentee in optics. Trustee Marine Biol. Lab., 1970-77, 81-85, 92, mem. sci. coun., 1993—. Recipient Rosenstiel award Brandeis U., 1988, Brown-Hazen award State of N.Y., 1988; Guggenheim Found. fellow, 1971-72; cancer rsch. scholar Am. Cancer Soc., N.Y.C., 1955-58. Fellow AAAS, Am. Acad. Arts Scis., Royal Microscopial Soc. (hon.); mem. NAS, Biophys. Soc. (coun. 1968-71), Soc. Gen. Physiologists (coun., pres. 1962-065, 69-70), Am. Soc. Cell Biology (coun. 1970-73, E.B. Wilson award 1992), Optical Soc. Am., Microscopy Soc. Am. (Disting. Scientist award 1995), N.Y. Microscopical Soc. (Ernst Abbe award 1997). Avocations: reading, photography. Home: 40 Shore St Falmouth MA 02540-3146 Office: Marine Biol Lab 7 M B L St Woods Hole MA 02543-1015

INOUYE, DANIEL KEN, senator; b. Honolulu, Sept. 7, 1924; s. Hyotaro I. and Kame Imanaga; m. Margaret Shinobu Awamura, June 12, 1949; 1 child, Daniel Ken. A.B., U. Hawaii, 1950; J.D., George Washington U., 1952. Bar: Hawaii 1953. Asst. pub. prosecutor Honolulu, 1953-54, pvt. practice, 1954—; majority leader Territorial Ho. of Reps., 1954-58, Senate, 1958-59; mem. 86th-87th U.S. Congresses from Hawaii, U.S. Senate from Hawaii (now 106th Congress), 1962—; sec. Senate Dem. Conf., 1978-88; chmn. Dem. Steering Com., Senate Com. on Appropriations; chmn. subcom. def., mem. Commerce Com.; chmn. subcom. on communications Select Com. on Intelligence, 1976-77, ranking mem. subcom. budget authorizations, 1979-84; former chmn. Select Com. Indian Affairs; mem. Select Com. on Presdl. Campaign Activities, 1973-74; chmn. Sen. select com. Secret Mil. Assistance to Iran and Nicaraguan Opposition, 1987; ranking minority mem. Appropriations subcom. on defense, Commerce, Sci., & Transp. subcom on surface transp. & merchant marine; mem. Indian Affairs Com., Rules & Adminstrn. Com. Joint Com. on the Libr. & Congl. Intern Program, Dem. Steering & Coordination Com., Joint Com. on Printing. Author: Journey to Washington. Active YMCA, Boy Scouts Am. Keynoter; temporary chmn. Dem. Nat. Conv., 1968, rules com. chmn., 1980, co-chmn. conv., 1984. Pvt. to capt. AUS, 1943-47. Decorated D.S.C., Bronze Star, Purple Heart with cluster; named 1 of 10 Outstanding Young Men of Yr. U.S. Jr. C. of C., 1960; recipient Splendid Am. award Thomas A. Dooley Found., 1967 Golden Plate award Am. Acad. Achievement, 1968. Mem. DAV (past comdr. Hawaii), Honolulu C. of C., Am. Legion (Nat. Comdr.'s award 1973). Methodist. Clubs: Lion. (Hawaii), 442d Veterans (Hawaii). Home: 469 Ena Rd Honolulu HI 96815-1749 Office: US Senate 722 Hart Senate Bldg Washington DC 20510-1102

INSEL, MICHAEL S., lawyer; b. N.Y.C., Apr. 19, 1947; s. Ralph David and Lillian Ruth (Solomon) I.; married; 1 child, Louis Leo. BA, Duke U., 1969; JD, NYU, 1973. Bar: N.Y. 1974, Fla. 1984. Assoc. Kelley Drye & Warren, N.Y.C., 1973-82, ptnr., 1982—; pres. French Am. Vintners LLC; bd. dirs. Kobrand Corp., N.Y.C., Maison Louis Jadot, S.A., Beaune, France, L & L, S.A., Boe, France, Western Wine Svcs., Inc., North Bergen, N.J., Kobrand Found., N.Y.C., E.C. Kopf Found., N.Y.C., Goodwill Industries, Astoria, N.Y.; trustee Elsie del Fierro Charitable Trust, N.Y.C., 1985—, Barbara Bell Cumming Found., N.Y.C., 1991—. Bd. dirs. St. Francis Vineyards, Sonoma, Calif.; bd. dirs. Domaine Carneros, Napa, Calif. Mem. ABA, N.Y. State Bar Assn., Fla. Bar, Assn. Bar of City of N.Y. Avocations: sailing, golf, opera. Office: Kelley Drye & Warren 101 Park Ave New York NY 10178-0002

INSELMAN, LAURA SUE, pediatrician; b. Bklyn., Nov. 2, 1944; d. Alexander M. and Rae (Bloom) Inselman. BA, Barnard Coll., 1966; MD, Med. Coll. Pa., 1970. Diplomate Am. Bd. Pediatrics, Am. Bd. Pediatric Pulmonology. Intern and resident St. Lukes Hosp. Ctr., N.Y.C., 1970-73; fellow in pediatric pulmonary disease Babies Hosp., N.Y.C., 1973-76; chief pediatric pulmonary div. Interfaith Med. Ctr., Bklyn., 1976-81; chief pediatric pulmonary div. North Shore Univ. Hosp., Manhasset, N.Y., 1981-86; clin. dir. pediatric pulmonary div. Newington Con. Children's Hosp., 1987-92; pulmunologist, med. dir. dept. respiratory care duPont Hosp. for Children., Wilmington, Del., 1992—; asst. prof. pediatrics Cornell U. Med. Coll., N.Y.C., 1981-86; asst. clin. prof. pediatrics, Yale U. Sch. Medicine, New Haven, 1987-92; asst. prof. pediatrics, U. Conn. Health Ctr., Farmington, 1987-92; assoc. prof. pediatrics, Jefferson Med. Coll. Thomas Jefferson U. Hosp., Phila., 1992—; mem. staff Good Samaritan Hosp., West Islip, N.Y., 1982-87. Bd. dirs. Am. Lung Assn. Nassau-Suffolk, East Meadow, N.Y., 1983-86, Del., 1992—. Fellow Am. Acad. Pediatrics, Am. Coll. Chest Physicians; mem. Am. Thoracic Soc., Am. Fedn. Med. Rsch., N.Y. Acad. Medicine, Harvey Soc., Soc. Pediatric Rsch. Office: DuPont Hospital for Children 1600 Rockland Rd Wilmington DE 19803-3607

INSERRA, LAWRENCE R., retail executive; b. 1927. Pres., CEO Inserra Supermarkets, Inc., Hasbrouck Heights, N.J., 1947—. Office: Inserra Supermarkets 20 Ridge Rd Mahwah NJ 07430-2328*

INSKEEP, JAMES R., process control engineer; b. Tarrytown, N.Y., May 29, 1971; s. Ronald G. and Judith L. (Leeds) I. AS in Engring. Sci., Westchester C.C., Valhalla, N.Y., 1992; BSEE, Clarkson U., 1994. Application engr. II Foxboro (Mass.) Co., 1994—. Recipient Arthur James Hackett scholarship The Found., Westchester C.C., 1992, Clarkson Merit scholarship, 1992, 93. Mem. Tau Beta Pi, Phi Theta Kappa. Avocations: camping and backpacking, ecology, wilderness preservation, conservation. Home: 9 Jackson St Apt 1 North Attleboro MA 02763-1007

INSKEEP, RICHARD GLENN, publishing executive; b. Aug. 25, 1924. BS, Ind. U., 1950. Pub. Fort Wayne (Ind.) Jour. Gazette, 1973-97; pres. Jour. Gazette Co., Fort Wayne, 1973—. Pres. Jour. Gazette Found., 1987—. Recipient Sagamore of Wabash award, 1962, 69, Ind. U. Disting. Alumni award, 1992, Hoosier Press Freedom Found. award 1996; inducted into Ind. Journalism Hall of Fame, 1991, Greater Fort Wayne Bus. Hall of Fame, 1998. Home: 11023 Carnoustie Ln Fort Wayne IN 46804 Office: 701 S Clinton St Fort Wayne IN 46802

INSLEE, JAY R., congressman, lawyer; b. Feb. 9, 1951; s. Frank and Adele Inslee; m. Trudi Anne Inslee; children: Jack, Connor, Joe. BA in Econs., U. Wash., 1973; JD magna cum laude, Willamette U., 1976. Atty. Peters, Fowler & Inslee, Selah, Wash., 1976-92; city prosecutor City of Selah, 1976-82; mem. from 14th dist. Wash. State Ho. of Reps., 1988-92; mem. 100th-103d Congresses from 4th Dist. State of Wash., 1992-95; atty. Gordon, Thomas, Honeywell, et al., Seattle, WA, 1995-96; Regional dir., region 10 US dept. Health & human svcs., Seattle, 1997-98; mem. U.S. Congress from 1st Wash. dist., 1999—; mem. resources com., 1999—, mem. banking and fin. svcs. com., 1999—. Chair Selah Sch. Bond Com., 1980; bd. dirs. New Valley Osteopathic Hosp., 1978-86. Mem. Wash. State Trial Lawyers Assn. (bd. dirs. 1984-88). Democrat. Office: US Ho of Reps 308 Cannon HOB Washington DC 20515*

INSLER, STANLEY, philologist, educator; b. N.Y.C., June 23, 1937. A.B., Columbia Coll., 1957; postgrad., U. Tubingen, 1960-62; Ph.D., Yale U., 1963. Mem. faculty Grad. Sch., Yale U., 1963—, now prof. Sanskrit and comparative philology; cons. NEH. Contbr. numerous articles on ancient langs. and lits. of India and Iran to profl. publs; translator Songs of Zarathustra. Recipient fellowships Ford Found., fellowships Woodrow Wilson Found., fellowships Yale U. Mem. Am. Oriental Soc. (pres., fin. dir.), Deutsche Morgenlandische Gesellschaft, Philological Soc., Cambridge, Eng. Royal Asiatic Soc. Gt. Brit. and Ireland, Assn. Française des Sanskritists, Societe Asiatique. Office: Yale U Dept Linguistics Box 208236 New Haven CT 06520-8236

INSPRUCKER, NANCY RHOADES, air force officer; b. Fort Campbell, Ky., June 16, 1959; d. Glen Lee and Mary Josephine (Lasell) Rhoades; m. John L. Insprucker III, July 20, 1991. BS in Astro Engring., U.S. Air Force Acad., 1981; MS in Aero. and Astronaut. Engring., Stanford U., 1985. Commd. 2d lt. U.S. Air Force, 1981, advanced through grades to lt. col., 1998; satellite test engr. space div. Los Angeles, 1981-84; instr. dept. astronautics USAF Acad., Colorado Springs, Colo., 1985-88; chief payload devel. and integration divsn. Office Sec. Air Force, L.A. AFB, 1988-90, chief mission processing divsn., 1990-92; chief sys. engr. Office Def. Landsat, Pentagon, Washington, 1992-94, chief sys. engr. divsn. Office of Space Sys. Office Asst. Sec. Air Force, 1994-95, dir. advanced spacecraft acquisition Office Space & Tech. Office Asst. Sec. Air Force, 1995-97; Gen. Moorman space chair Joint Mil. Intelligence Coll., 1997—. Recipient Medal of Merit, Nat. Air Force Assn., 1985; named Colorado Springs Mil. Woman of Yr., Gazettte Telegraph newspaper, 1987. Mem. Air Force Assn., Am. Astronautical Soc., Soc. Women Engrs. Avocations: aerobics, long distance running, reading. Home: 2202 Central Ave Vienna VA 22182-5193 Office: The Pentagon Washington DC 20050

INSTONE, JOHN CLIFFORD, manufacturing company executive; b. Phila., Mar. 5, 1924; s. John Leonard and Anna Lena Instone; m. Mary Elizabeth Ketchell, Feb. 12, 1949; children: Linda Jane, John Clifford, Jr. B.S. in Mech. Engring., Drexel U., Phila., 1947. Engr., Proctor Electric Co., Phila., 1947-49; mfg. engr. IRC, Phila., 1949-51; div. gen. mgr. Proctor-Silex Corp. (div. SCM Corp.), Phila. and Mount Airy, N.C., 1951-60; with SL Industries Inc., Marlton, N.J., 1960—; pres., chief exec. officer SL Industries Inc., 1979—; also dir., chmn. bd. New Rochelle Mfg. Co., Inc., N.Y.C., 1984—; dir., chmn. bd. Montevideo Tech., Inc., Minn., 1985—; chmn. bd. SL Auburn, Inc., N.Y.C., SL Internat., Inc. Patentee electro-mech. mounting device, elec. outlet strip. Served to 1st lt. AUS, 1943-45. Mem. Am. Mgmt. Assn. Clubs: Rotary, Elks. Home: 465 Pelham Rd Cherry Hill NJ 08034-2748 Office: SL Industries Inc 520 Fellowship Rd # A-114 Mount Laurel NJ 08054-3407

INTEMANN, ROBERT LOUIS, physics educator, researcher; b. North Bergen, N.J., Feb. 23, 1938; s. Joseph Louis and Mildred Henrietta (Wood) I.; m. Marguerite Carmela DiNonno, Aug. 22, 1964; 1 child, Peter Michael. BE, Stevens Inst. Tech., 1959, MS, 1961, PhD, 1964. Asst. prof. physics Temple U., Phila., 1964-73, assoc. prof. physics, 1973-84, prof., 1984—, chmn. dept., 1985-90, asst. dean of coll. Arts and Scis., 1971-81; vis. scientist Atomic Energy Research Establishment, Harwell, Eng., 1970. Contbr. numerous research articles on theoretical atomic physics. Mem. AAUP, Am. Phys. Soc., Am. Assn. Physics Tchrs., AAAS, Sigma Xi. Avocations: skiing, tennis, photography, travel. Home: 209 Revere Ave Glenside PA 19038-4108 Office: Temple U Dept Physics Philadelphia PA 19122

INTIHAR-HOGUE, CYNTHIA ANN, nursing administrator; b. Johnstown, Pa., Dec. 17, 1962; d. Paul and Ann H. (Pfister) Orris. Diploma, Conemaugh Valley Meml. Hosp., Johnstown, 1983; BSN, U. Pitts., 1994. Cert. case mgr.; advanced cert. continuity of care. Med.-surg. nurse Conemaugh Valley Meml. Hosp., 1983-84, nurse, dept. emergency medicine, 1984-86, nurse, flight svc., 1986-89, nurse, home health agy., 1989-95, ICU-CCU nurse, 1989-90; individual case mgr. Blue Cross of Western Pa., Johnstown, 1992-95, nurse mgr., 1994-95; mgr. health svcs. operations Blue Cross of Western Pa., 1995-97, mgr. network case mgmt., 1997-99; mgr. comml. care and case mgmt., healthcare mgmt. svcs. Highmark Blue Cross Blue Shield, Pitts., 1999—; case mgmt. cons., Individual Case Mgmt. Health Related Svcs., Inc. Mem. Belmont Fire and Ambulance Co., 1988-91.

INTRATER, CHERYL WATSON WAYLOR, career marketing consultant; b. Montreal, Que., Can., Sept. 8, 1943; naturalized, 1978; d. Alan Douglas and Jean Mary (Hughes) Watson; m. Donald L. Intrater, Nov. 11, 1990. BBA, Ga. State U., 1980. CPCU. Supr. divsn. Liberty Mut., Atlanta, 1969-76; instr. ins. DeKalb Coll., Clarkston, Ga., 1978-79; mgr. divsn. Kemper Group, 1979-85; owner Ins. Support Svcs., Inc., Overland Park, Kans., 1986-91; v.p. Fortune and Co. Risk Mgrs., Inc., Overland Park, 1987—; owner Career Trend, Overland Park, 1994-97; v.p., ptnr., prin., career mktg. cons. Alexander, Hoyt & Assocs., Overland Park, 1997—; adv. coun. Johnson County C.C. Ins. Inst., Overland Park, 1990—; interim dir. profl. continuing edn. Johnson County C.C., 1994; lectr. in field. Vol. Girl Scouts U.S.A. Leadership Devel., 1987-95. Mem. Nat. Assn. Ins. Women (named Region V Ins. Profl. of Yr. 1992, cert. profl. ins. woman, Outstanding Mem. of Yr. 1992), Greater Kansas City Ins. Assn. (pres. 1989-90), Ins. Women of Greater Kansas City, CPCU Soc. (Kansas City chpt.), Mission (Kans.) Area C. of C. (chmn. budget and fin. com. 1994, 95), Toastmasters Internat. (past dist. officer, parliamentarian 1991-96, Able Toastmaster), Overland Park C. of C., Greater Kansas City C. of C. Republican. Avocations: sky diving, fencing, fitness training, reading, traveling. Office: 9200 Indian Creek Pkwy Ste 203 Overland Park KS 66210-2008

INTRIERE, ANTHONY DONALD, physician; b. Greenwich, Conn., May 9, 1920; s. Rocco and Angelina (Belcastro) I.; m. Carol A. Yarmey, Aug. 1, 1945; children: Sherry Shoemaker, Michael, Nancy M., Lisa A. MD, U. Mich., 1944. Intern, New Rochelle (N.Y.) Hosp., 1944-45; pvt. practice, Greenwich, Conn., 1947-53, Olney, Ill., 1956-61, Granite City, Ill., 1961-74, San Diego, 1975—; fellow in internal medicine Cleve. Clinic, 1953-55; fellow in gastroenterology Lahey Clinic, Boston, 1955-56. Capt. M.C., AUS, 1945-47. Fellow Am. Coll. Gastroenterology (assoc.); mem. AMA, ACP (assoc.), Am. Soc. Internal Medicine, Fifty Yr. Club Ill. State Med. Soc. Home: 9981 Caminito Chirimolla San Diego CA 92131-2001

INTRILIGATOR, DEVRIE SHAPIRO, physicist; b. N.Y.C.; d. Carl and Lillian Shapiro; m. Michael Intriligator; children: Kenneth, James, William, Robert. BS in Physics, MIT, 1962, MS, 1964; PhD in Planetary and Space Physics, UCLA, 1967. NRC-NASA rsch. assoc. NASA, Ames, Calif., 1967-69; rsch. fellow in physics Calif. Inst. Tech., Pasadena, 1969-72, vis. assoc., 1972-73; asst. prof. U. So. Calif., 1972-80; mem. Space Scis. Ctr., 1978-83; sr. rsch. physicist Carmel Rsch. Ctr., Santa Monica, Calif., 1979—; dir. Space Plasma Lab., 1980—; cons. NASA, NOAA, Jet Propulsion Lab.; chmn. NAS-NRC com. on solar-terrestrial rsch., 1983-86, exec. com. bd. atmospheric sci. and climate, 1983-86, geophysics study com., 1983-86; U.S. nat. rep. Sci. Com. on Solar-Terrestrial Physics, 1983-86; mem. adv. com. NSF Divsn. Atmospheric Sci. Co-editor: Exploration of the Outer Solar System, 1976; contbr. articles to profl. jours. Recipient 3 Achievement awards NASA, Calif. Resolution of Commendation, 1982. Mem. AAAS, Am. Phys. Soc., Am. Geophys. Union, Cosmos Club. Achievements include being a participant Pioneer 10/11 missions to outer planets; Pioneer Venus Orbiter, Pioneers 6, 7, 8 and 9 heliocentric missions. Home: 140 Foxtail Dr Santa Monica CA 90402-2048 Office: Carmel Rsch Ctr PO Box 1732 Santa Monica CA 90406-1732

INTRILIGATOR, MARC STEVEN, lawyer; b. Oceanside, N.Y., July 14, 1952; s. Alan and Sally (Jacobs) I.; m. Roxann Kathleen Hoff, Aug. 28, 1977; children: Seth Adam, Joshua Ross, Daniel Benjamin. BA, SUNY, Binghamton, 1974; JD, Boston U., 1977. Bar: N.Y. 1978. Assoc. Dreyer and Traub, N.Y.C., 1977-83, assoc. ptnr., 1984-85, sr. ptnr., 1985-96; of counsel Fischbein Badillo Wagner Harding, N.Y.C., 1996—. Projects editor: Boston U. law rev., 1976-77. Trustee, past pres. Croton Jewish Ctr. Mem. ABA, Assn. of Bar of City of N.Y., Highlands Country Club (pres., trustee), Tau Epsilon Phi. Office: Fischbein Badillo Wagner Harding 909 3rd Ave New York NY 10022-4731

INTRILIGATOR, MICHAEL DAVID, economist, educator; b. N.Y.C., Feb. 5, 1938; s. Allan and Sally Intriligator; m. Devrie Shapiro; children: Kenneth, James, William, Robert. SB in Econs., MIT, 1959; MA, Yale U., 1960; PhD, MIT, 1963. Asst. prof. econs. UCLA, 1963-66, assoc. prof., 1966-72, prof., 1972—, prof. dept. polit. sci., 1981—, prof. dept. policy studies, 1994—, dir. Ctr. Internat. and Strategic Affairs, 1982-92; dir. Jacob Marschak Interdisciplinary Coll. 1977—; cons. Inst. Def. Analysis, 1974-77, ACDA, 1968, Rand Corp., 1962-65. Author: Mathematical Optimization and Economic Theory, 1971, also Taiwanese, Spanish and Russian edits., Econometric Models, Techniques and Applications, 1978, also Greek and Spanish edits., 2d edit. (with Ronald Bodkin and Cheng Hsiao), 1996, (with others) A Forecasting and Policy Simulation Model of the Health Care Sector, 1979; mem. adv. editorial bd. Math. Social Scis., 1983—; assoc. editor Jour. Optimization Theory and Applications, 1979-91, Conflict Mgmt. and Peace Sci., 1980—; co-editor: (series) Handbooks in Economics, 1980—, Advanced Textbooks in Economics, 1972—; editor: (with Kenneth J. Arrow) Handbook of Mathematical Economics, 3 vols., 1981-85; (with Zvi Griliches) Handbook of Econometrics, 3 vols., 1983-86, (with B. Brodie and R. Kolkowicz) National Security and International Stability, 1983, (with H.A. Jacobsen) East-West Conflict: Elite Perceptions and Political Options, 1988, numerous others; contbr. articles to profl. jours. Woodrow Wilson fellow, 1959-60; MIT fellow, 1960-61; recipient Disting. Teaching award UCLA, 1966; Ford fellow, 1967-68; Warren C. Scoville disting. teaching award UCLA, 1976, 79, 82, 84. Fellow Econometric Soc.; mem. Internat. Inst. Strategic Studies, Council Fgn. Relations, others. Office: UCLA Dept Econs Los Angeles CA 90095-1477

INUI, THOMAS SPENCER, physician, educator; b. Balt., July 10, 1943; s. Frank Kazuo and Beulah Mae (Sheetz) I.; m. Nancy Stowe, June 14, 1969; 1 child, Tazo Stowe. BA, Haverford Coll., 1965; MD, Johns Hopkins U., 1969, ScM, 1973. Diplomate Am. Bd. Internal Medicine. Intern Johns Hopkins Hosp., Balt., 1969-70, resident in internal medicine, 1970-73; clin. scholar Johns Hopkins U., Balt., 1971-73, chief resident, instr., 1973-74; chief of medicine USPHS Indian Hosp., Albuquerque, 1974-76; chief gen. medicine, dir. health svc. rsch. Seattle VA Med. Ctr., 1976-86; dir. Robert Wood Johnson clin. scholars program U. Wash., Seattle, 1977-92, prof. dept. medicine and health svcs., 1985-92, head div. gen. internal medicine, 1986-92; prof., chmn. of dept. ambulatory care and prevention Harvard Med. Sch. and Harvard Pilgrim Health Care, Boston, 1992—. Contbr. articles to profl. publs. Surgeon USPHS, 1974-76. Fellow ACP; mem. APHA (mem. coun. 1988-90), Soc. Gen. Internal Medicine (pres. 1988-89, mem. coun. 1983-89), Am. Fedn. Clin. Rsch., Assn. Health Svcs. Rsch., Soc. Tchrs. of Family Medicine, Inst. Medicine, Phi Beta Kappa, Alpha Omega Alpha.

INVERARITY, ROBERT BRUCE, artist. Instr. Cornish Sch., Seattle, 1927-28, YWCA, San Francisco, 1929-30; dir. Sch. Creative Art, Vancouver, Can., 1931-33, U. Wash., Seattle, 1933-37; state dir. Fed. Art Project, Wash. State, 1937-39, Wash. State Art and Craft Project, WPA, Seattle, 1939-41; art dir. Boeing Aircraft Co., Seattle, 1946-47; asst. dir. F. Archer Sch. Photography, L.A., 1947-49; dir. Mus. Internat. Folk Art, Santa Fe, 1949-54, Adirondack Mus., Blue Mountain Lake, N.Y., 1954-65, Adirondack Hist. Assn., Blue Mountain Lake, 1954-65; designer art books and classical series U. Calif. Press, Berkeley, 1967-69; dir. Phila. Maritime Mus., 1969-76; assoc. Sch. Am. Rsch., Santa Fe, 1949-54; mem. UNESCO Internat. Congress of Mus. Conf. on Mus. and Race, Paris, 1951; rsch. asst. Yale U., New Haven, 1951-52; cons. Human Rels. Area Files, Inc., New Haven, 1951-52; trustee Mus. Navajo Ceremonial Art, Sante Fe, N. Mex., 1950-54, Eskimo Art Inc., Ann Arbor, Mich., 1953-55; mem. adv. bd. Heard Mus., Phoenix, 1952-54, N.Y. State Coun. on the Arts, 1961-65, Nat. Art Mus. of Sport, N.Y.C., 1962-63; mus. cons. Ariz. Pioneers Hist. Soc., Tucson, Ariz., 1954, Adirondack Hist. Assn., 1954, N.Y. State Bd. Regents, Albany, 1963. One-man shows include Seattle (Wash.) Fine Arts Soc., 1928, Blanding Sloan Workshop Gallery, San Francisco, 1929, 722 Montgomery, San Francisco, 1930, Lowman & Handford, Seattle, 1930, Hudson's Bay Co., Vancouver, 1931, Vancouver (Can.) Art Gallery, 1932, Gump Gallery, San Francisco, 1935, Mary Dale Studios, Tacoma, 1935; exhibited in groups shows at 13th Annual Exhbn. N.W. Artists Seattle Arts Soc., 1927, 28, Curtis Galleries, San Francisco, 1929, Studio on Wheels, Santa Barbara, 1930, El Paseo Gallery, Palm Springs, 1930, Studio on Wheels, Ventura, Calif., 1930, Henry Gallery-Univ. Wash., 1930, Bklyn. Soc. of Etchers-Bklyn. Mus., 1931, Chgo. World's Fair, 1933, Seattle Art Mus., 1935, N.Y. World's Fair, 1939, Oakland Art Gallery, 1941, Calif. Watercolor Soc.-L.A. County Mus., 1942, 43, L.A. Art Assn., 1948, others; art columnist Seattle (Wash.) Daily Times, 1930-31; syndicate columnist for sixteen major West Coast newspapers, 1931; contbr. articles to profl. jours. With USN 1941-45. Mem. Calif. Watercolor Soc., Academie Latine (Paris), Phi Beta Kappa. Home: 800 Prospect St Apt 1F La Jolla CA 92037-4203*

INVERSO, MARLENE JOY, optometrist; b. Los Angeles, May 10, 1942; d. Elmer Encel Wood and Sally Marie (Sample) Hirons; m. John S. Inverso, Dec. 16, 1962; 1 child, Christopher Edward. BA, Calif. State U., Northridge, 1964; MS, SUNY, Potsdam, 1975; OD, Pacific U., 1981. Cert. doctor optometry, Wash., Oreg. English tchr. Chatsworth (Calif.) High Sch., 1964-68, Nelson A. Boylen Second Sch., Toronto, Ont., Can., 1968-70, Gouverneur (N.Y.) Jr.-Sr. High Sch., 1970-74, 76-77; reading resource room tchr. Parishville (N.Y.) Hopkinton Sch., 1974-75; optometrist and vision therapist Am. Family Vision Clinics, Olympia, Wash., 1982—; coord. Lng. Disability Clin. SUNY, summers, 1975-77; mem. adv. com. Sunshine House St. Peter Hosp., Olympia, 1984-86, Pacific U. Coll. Optometry, Forest Grove, Oreg. 1986. Contbr. articles to profl. jours. Mem. Altrusa Svc. Club, Olympia, 1982-86; tchr. Ch. Living Water, Olympia, 1983-88, Olympia-Lacey Ch. of God, 1989—, sec. women's bd., 1990; bd. advisors Crisis Pregnancy Ctr., Olympia, 1987-89; den mother Cub Scouts Am. Pack 202, Lacey, Wash., 1987-88; vol. World Vision Countertop ptnr., 1986-97. Fellow Coll. Optometrists in Optometric Devel.; mem. Am. Optometric Assn. (sec. 1983-84), Assn. Children and Adults with Learning Disabilities, Optometric Extension Program, Sigma Xi, Beta Sigma Kappa. Avocations: bible study, professional speaking, training, and teaching. Home: 4336 Libby Rd NE Olympia WA 98506-2555

INVERSO, PETER A., state legislator; b. Trenton, N.J., Dec. 24, 1938; m. Geraldine Gonos, 1962; children: Donna Maria, Marylyn, Susan, Anthony, Diana. BS, Rider U., 1960. CPA, CEFM. Freeholder Mercer County, N.J., 1981-83, 87-89; senator dist. 14 N.J. State Senator, 1991—; ptnr. Druker, Raul and Fein. Address: Druker, Rahl & Fein 3691A Nottingham Way Hamilton NJ 08690-2611*

INZETTA, MARK STEPHEN, lawyer; b. N.Y.C., Apr. 14, 1956; s. James William and Rose Delores (Cirnigliaro) I.; children: Michelle, Margot, Mallory. BBA summa cum laude, U. Cin., 1977; JD, U. Akron, 1980. Bar: Ohio 1980, U.S. Dist. Ct. (no. dist.) Ohio 1980. Legal intern City of Canton, Ohio, 1979-80; assoc. W.J. Ross Co., LPA, Canton, 1980-84; asst. gen. counsel Wendy's Internat. Inc., Columbus, Ohio, 1984—; instr. real estate law Stark Tech. Coll., Canton, 1983. Case and comment editor: Akron Law Rev., 1979-80. Instr. religious edn. St. Peter's Cath. Ch.; bd. dirs. Brookside Village Civic Assn., 1985-87, treas., 1986-87; chmn. campaign Earle Wise Appellate Judge, North Canton, Ohio, 1982; legis. dir. Children's and Parents' Rights assn., 1996-97, chmn., 1997—, State of Ohio Child Support Guidelines Commn., 1995-97, 99—; State of Ohio Task Force on Family Law and Children, 1998-99. Recipient Am. Jurisprudence award Lawyers Coop. Pub. Co., 1978, Dir. of Yr. award North Canton Jaycees, 1982, Presdl. award of honor, 1984, Dist. Dir. award of honor Ohio Jaycees, 1984. Mem. ABA, Ohio Bar Assn., North Canton Jaycees (bd. dirs. 1981-82, v.p. 1982-83, pres. 1983-84), North Canton C. of C. (bd. dirs. 1983-84). Democrat. Roman Catholic. Home: 775 Suntree Dr Westerville OH 43081-5086 Office: Wendy's Internat Inc 4288 W Dublin Granville Rd Dublin OH 43017-1442

IODICE, ARTHUR ALFONSO, biochemist; b. Rome, N.Y., Nov. 7, 1928; s. Gaetano and Loretta (Pace) Iodice. AB, Columbia U., 1950; PhD, SUNY, Syracuse, 1958. Postdoctoral fellow U. Calif., Berkeley, 1958-60, rsch. assoc., 1960-62; rsch. assoc. Inst. Muscle Disease, N.Y.C., 1962-65, asst. mem., 1965-69, assoc. mem., 1969-74; rsch. scientist Masonic Med. Rsch. Lab., Utica, N.Y., 1975—. Contbr. articles to profl. jours. Jane Coffin Childs Meml. Fund med. rsch., postdoctoral fellow U. Calif., 1958-60. Mem. AAAS, Electrophysiol. Soc., Am. Heart Assn., N.Y. Acad. Scis. Home: PO Box 663 Rome NY 13442-0663 Office: Masonic Med Rsch Lab 2150 Bleecker St Utica NY 13501-1738

IONA, MARIO, retired physics educator; b. Berlin, June 17, 1917; came to U.S., 1941, naturalized, 1948; s. Mario G.V. and Dorothee (Berendes) I.; m. Nancy Mossman, Aug. 31, 1949; children: Steven, Ann. PhD, U. Vienna, Austria, 1939; postgrad., U. Uppsala, Sweden, 1939-41. Research asst., instr. U. Chgo., 1941-46; from asst. prof. to prof. physics U. Denver, 1946-85, prof. emeritus, 1985—; coord. High Altitude Labs., Mt. Evans and Echo Lake, Colo., 1946-82; cons. pvt. practice Denver, 1985—; cons. Denver Schs., 1962-65, 84, Jefferson County Schs., Golden, Colo., 1973, Adams County Sch. Dist. 12, Northglenn, Colo., 1985; vis. prof. U. No. Colo., summer 1971; specialist U. Saugar, India, summer, 1966; cons. various manuscript revs., 1975—. Assoc. editor: Physics Tchr., 1962-65, column editor, 1970—. Treas., sec., pres. Group Health Assn., Denver, 1952-66. Fellow AAAS; mem. Am. Phys. Soc., Am. Assn. Physics Tchrs. (chmn. com. on SI units and metric edn. 1987-91, Disting. Svc. citation 1971, Millikan Lecture award 1986), Colo.-Wyo. Acad. Sci. (pres. 1974-75), Nat. Sci. Tchrs. Assn., AAUP. Home: 2333 S Columbine St Denver CO 80210-5421 Office: Dept Physics & Astronomy Univ Denver Denver CO 80208-2238

IONE, CAROLE, psychotherapist, writer, playwright, director; b. Washington, D.C., May 28, 1937; d. Hylan Garnet Lewis and Leighla (Whipper) Ford; m. Salvatore Bovoso (div.); children: Alessandro, Santiago, Antonio. Student, Bennington (Vt.) Coll., 1959, NYU, New Sch. for Social Rsch.; practitioner, Helix Inst. for Psychotherapy and Healing, 1986-87, Chinese Healing Arts Ctr., 1995. Cert. qi gong therapist, hypnotherapist. Artistic dir. Renaissance House, N.Y.C., 1961, 62; founder, artistic dir., editor Letters (now Live Letters), N.Y.C., 1974—; editor of poetry choices Village Voice, N.Y.C., 1980-84; contbg. editor Essence, N.Y.C., 1981-83; co-artistic dir., v.p. Pauline Oliveros Found., Kingston, N.Y., 1985—; dir. Writers in Performance Manhattan Theatre Club, N.Y.C., 1985-86; psychotherapist Kingston and N.Y.C., 1986—; poetry curator Unison Lng. Ctr., New Paltz, N.Y., 1990-91; past v.p., curator Deep Listening Space; bd. dirs. Ministry MAAT, Inc. Author: Pride of Family: Four Generations of American Women of Color, 1991; playwright, dir. Njinga the Queen King, 1991—. Mem. mayor's task force, Kingston, N.Y., 1996. Recipient S.C. Commn. for the Humanities award, 1983, Rockefeller Found. award, 1992, NEA award, 1992, N.Y. State Coun. for the Arts award, 1992, Charitable Trust award PEW, 1993, Dance Theater Workshop Suitcase Fund award, 1993. Fellow The Mac Dowell Colony, YADDO, Edward Albee Found., The Writer's Room; mem. Nat. Writers Union, Internat. Women's Writing Guild, The Author's Guild, Poets and Writers. Avocations: painting, visual arts, poetry. Office: Pauline Oliveros Found PO Box 1956 Kingston NY 12402-1956

IONESCU TULCEA, CASSIUS, research mathematician, educator; b. Bucharest, Rumania, Oct. 14, 1923; naturalized, 1967; s. Ioan and Ana (Caselli) Ionescu Tulcea. M.S., U. Bucarest, 1946; Ph.D., Yale, 1959. Mem. faculty U. Bucarest, 1946-57, assoc. prof., 1952-57; research assoc. Yale U., 1957-59, vis. lectr., 1959-61; assoc. prof. U. Pa., 1961-64; prof. U. Ill., Urbana, 1964-66; prof. Northwestern U., Evanston, Ill., 1966-90, prof. emeritus, 1990—. Author: Hilbert Spaces (in Rumanian), 1956, A Book on Casino Craps, 1980, A Book on Casino Blackjack, 1982; co-author: Probability Calculus (in Rumanian), 1956, Calculus, 1968, An Introduction to Calculus, 1969, Honors Calculus, 1970, Topics in the Theory of Liftings, 1969, Sets, 1971, Topology, 1971, A Book on Casino Gambling, 1976; contbr. articles to profl. jours. Recipient Asachi prize Rumanian Acad., 1957. Office: Northwestern U Math Dept Lunt Bldg 2033 Sheridan Rd Evanston IL 60208

IONTA, ROBERT W., federal judge, lawyer. Part-time magistrate judge for N.Mex., U.S. Magistrate Ct., Gallup, 1985—. Office: 300 W Hill Ave Gallup NM 87301-6311

IORIO, JOHN EMIL, retired education educator; b. Bklyn., Dec. 20, 1932; s. Frederick and Helen (Grandillo) I.; m. Helen Capobianco, Dec. 20, 1958; children: Frederick Joseph, John Richard. BS in Polit Sci., Manhattan Coll., 1954; MS in Elem. Edn., Bklyn. Coll., 1967; profl. diploma Adminstrn./Supervision, Fordham U., 1984. Cert. elem. tchr., adminstr., prin. supt. N.Y.S., N.Y.C. Elem. tchr. N.Y.C., 1965-72; adminstrv. asst. P.S. 214K, Dist. 19, N.Y.C., 1972-74, asst. prin., 1974-75; adminstr. Office of Fed. and State Reimbursable Programs, N.Y.C., 1975-76; asst. prin. Ps. 153Q, Dist. 24, N.Y.C., 1976; asst. prin., head of sch. PS 128Q Dist. 24, Queens, N.Y., 1976-79; prin. PS 128Q Dist. 24, Queens, 1979-87; community supt. Dist. 24, Queens, 1987-90; adj. prof. Fordham U., 1991; presenter at many ednl. confs. and workshops. 1983-90. Contbr. articles to profl. jours. Recipient Builder of Brotherhood award, Nat. Conf. Christians and Jews, 1981, Arts in Edn. Programs award, Young Audiences of N.Y., 1989, Project Innovation Spl. Merit award, Education mag., 1990, others; named Educator of Yr. Assn. Tchrs. of N.Y., 1988; grantee Nat. Endowment for Humanities, 1981. Home: 155-57 Bridgeton St Howard Beach NY 11414-2809

IOVENKO, MICHAEL, lawyer; b. N.Y.C., Jan. 19, 1930; s. Michael James and Ludmila (Tenchova) I.; m. Sarah Montague Bingham, Dec. 3, 1965 (div. Nov. 1976); children: Christopher, William; 1 stepchild, Barry B. Ellsworth; m. Nancy R. Newhouse, Mar. 6, 1983. BA, Dartmouth Coll., 1951; JD, Columbia U., 1954. Asst. gen. sec. World Univ. Service, Geneva, 1955-58; assoc., then ptnr. Putney, Twombly, Hall & Hirson, N.Y.C., 1959-70; U.S. del. Gen. Assembly UN, N.Y.C., 1967; dep. supt., gen. counsel N.Y. State Banking Dept., N.Y.C., 1971-72; ptnr. LeBoeuf, Lamb, Leiby & MacRae, N.Y.C., 1972-85, Hughes Hubbard & Reed, N.Y.C., 1986-89, Breed, Abbott & Morgan, N.Y.C., 1989-93, Hughes Hubbard & Reed, N.Y.C., 1993—. Contbr. articles to profl. jours. Pres., bd. dirs. N.Y. State Council Family Child Care Agys., 1981-85; bd. dirs., v.p. Berkshire Farm Ctr. for Youth, Canaan, N.Y.; pres. Legal Aid, N.Y.C., French-Am. Found., 1995—. Mem. ABA, N.Y. State Bar Assn. (chair banking law com. 1986-90, bus. law sect. 1995-96), Assn. of Bar of City of N.Y. (exec. com. 1988-92, treas. 1998—), Century Club, Downtown Assn. Democrat. Avocations: piano, gardening. Home: 154 W 88th St New York NY 10024-2402 Office: Hughes Hubbard & Reed One Battery Park Plz New York NY 10004

IOVINE, JIMMY, recording industry executive; b. Brooklyn, NY, 1953; s. Jimmy Iovine Sr.; Former engineer The Record Plant, New York, N.Y.; ind. prodr., co-head of Interscope Records, 1991—. Office: care Interscope

Communications 10900 Wilshire Blvd Ste 1230 Los Angeles CA 90024-6532*

IOZZI, ALESSANDRA, mathematician, educator; b. Rome, Italy, Jan. 25, 1959. Grad., U. Rome, 1982; MS, U. Chgo., 1985, PhD, 1989. Lectr. U. Chgo., 1986-89, U. Pa., Phila., 1989-91; fellow Math. Scis. Rsch. Inst., Berkeley, Calif., 1991-92; mem. Inst. for Advanced Study, Princeton, N.J., 1992-93; asst. prof. U. Md., College Park, 1993—. Contbr. articles to profl. jours. Fellow Consiglio Nazionale delle Richerche (Italy), 1981-82, Fulbright fellow, 1984-89; grantee NSF, 1989-92, Am. Math. Soc., 1990. Mem. Am. Math. Soc., Assn. Women in Math., Unione Matematica Italiana. E-mail: iozzi@math.umd.edu. Office: U Md Dept Math Rm 1301 College Park MD 20742-4015

IPPEN, ERICH PETER, electrical engineering educator; b. Fountain Hill, Pa., Mar. 29, 1940; s. Arthur Thomas and Elisabeth Anne (Wagenplatz) I.; m. Dorothea Ellen Swansen, Sept. 24, 1966; children: Erich Peter, Jason Timothy. S.B., MIT, 1962; M.S., U. Calif.-Berkeley, 1965, Ph.D., 1968. Mem. tech. staff Bell Labs., Holmdel, N.J., 1968-80; vis. prof. MIT, Cambridge, 1977-78, prof. elec. engring., 1980—, Elihu Thomson prof. elec. engring., 1987—, prof. physics, 1996—; cons. Bell Labs., 1981—, Allied Corp., Mt. Bethel, N.J., 1982-90. Contbr. articles to profl. jours.; patentee in field. Recipient Edward Longstreth medal Franklin Inst., 1982, Harold E. Edgerton award Soc. Photo-Optical Instrumentation Engrs., 1989, John Scott award City of Phila., 1991. Fellow Am. Acad. Arts and Scis., Optical Soc. Am. (R.W. Wood prize 1981), IEEE (Morris E. Leeds award 1983, Wuantum Elecs. award 1997), Am. Phys. Soc. (Arthur L. Schawlow prize 1997); mem. NAS, NAE, Sigma Xi. Home: 156 School St Belmont MA 02478-3516 Office: MIT 77 Massachusetts Ave Cambridge MA 02139-4307

IQBAL, ZAFAR, biochemist, neurochemist; b. Lucknow, India, July 12, 1946; came to U.S., 1972, naturalized, 1979; s. Shujaat Ali and Saleha (Begum) Siddiqui. Cert. proficiency in French, Lucknow U., 1965; Ph.D., All India Inst. Med. Scis., New Delhi, 1971. Jr. research fellow Council Sci. and Indsl. Research, India, 1963-66, research fellow, 1967-68; research scholar Directorate Gen. Health Services, India, 1966-67; asst. research officer Indian Council Med. Research, 1968-71; research assoc. in physiology, investigator Ind. U. Sch. Medicine, Indpls., 1972-82, asst. prof. med. biophysics, 1977-82, asst. prof. biochemistry, 1979-82; asst. prof. neurology and neurosci. Northwestern U. Sch. Medicine, Chgo., 1982-85; assoc. prof. pharmacology Chgo. Med. Sch., 1985-88; assoc. prof. neurology Northwestern U. Inst. for Neuroscience, Chgo., 1989-95; adj. prof. neurology and neurosci. Northwestern U. Med. Sch., 1995—; mem. Northwestern U. Ctr. Devel. Biology, Chgo., 1989—; health sci. specialist VA Cen. Office Med. Rsch. Svc., Washington, 1995—. Contbg. author: Macromolecules in Storage and Transfer of Biological Information, 1969, Macromolecules and Behavior, 1972, Growth and Development of the Brain, 1975, Mechanism, Regulation and Special Function of Protein Synthesis in the Brain, 1977, Peripheral Neuropathies, 1978, Neurochemistry and Clinical Neurology, 1980, Calcium-Binding Proteins, 1980, Axoplasmic Transport, 1981, Calcium and Cell Function, 1982; editor: Axoplasmic Transport, 1986, Recent Progress in Polyamine Research, 1986, The Physiology of Polyamines, 1987; mem. editorial bd. Neurochem. Rsch.; contbr. articles to profl. jours. Rsch. grantee NIH, 1973-77, Muscular Dystrophy Assn. Am., 1975-77, 94-97, Am. Cancer Soc., 1979-80, NSF, 1981, 84, Juvenile Diabetes Found., 1981, Am. Diabetes Assn., 1980; recipient internat. travel award NSF, 1984, Fidia Rsch. Found. award, 1987, UN Devel. Program Internat. Expert award, 1987, 93, award Am. Soc. for Biochemistry and Molecular Biology, 1994. Mem. AAAS, Am. Physiol. Soc., Indian Acad. Neurosci., Soc. Biol. Chemists (India), Internat. Brain Rsch. Orgn., Internat. Soc. Neurochemistry (award 1994), Soc. Neurosci., Am. Soc. Neurochemistry, Ind. Acad. Sci. (chmn. cell biology 1982-83), N.Y. Acad. Scis., Biophys. Soc., Soc. Exptl. Biology and Medicine, Assn. Scientists of Indian Origin Am. (counselor 1986—), Ameer Khusro Soc. Am. (v.p.), Sigma Xi. E-mail: iqbzaf@mail.va.gov. Home: 1300 507 S Arlington Ridge Arlington VA 22202

IQBAL, ZAFAR MOHD, cancer researcher, biochemist, pharmacologist, toxicologist, consultant, molecular biologist; b. Hyderabad, India, Dec. 12, 1938; came to U.S., 1965, naturalized, 1973; s. M.A. and Haleemunissa (Begum) Rahim. BSc, Osmania U., 1958, MSc, 1962; PhD, U. Md., 1970. Diplomate Am. Bd. Forensic Medicine, Am. Bd. Forensic Examiners. Fellow in molecular pharmacology Nat. Cancer Inst./NIH, Bethesda, Md., 1971-74; asst. prof. pharmacology Case Western Res. U., Cleve., 1974-76; assoc. dir. ERC programs in occupational toxicology U. Ill. Med. Ctr., Chgo., 1980-81, assoc. prof. microbiology, 1977-80, assoc. prof. occupational medicine and environ. health, 1976-93, assoc. prof. preventive medicine, 1982-93; faculty grad. coll. U. Ill., Chgo., 1977-93, dir. Carcinogenesis Labs., 1983-93, chair recombinant DNA instnl. com., 1982-93; staff HIV hazards in rsch. com. U. Ill. Grad. Coll. Faculty, Chgo., 1976-93; dir. Toxicology-Cancer, Chgo., 1987—; affiliate Lurie Cancer Ctr. Northwestern U., Chgo., 1996—; cons. in field to OSHA, 1980-81, Clements Assocs., 1976-79, Expert Resources, 1982—, Ill. Cancer Coun., 1981-82, Toxicology Cancer, 1987—; lectr. continuing edn.; grant reviewer study sects. NIH; merit grant reviewer VA, 1981-82; mem. tech. bd. panel Gt. Lakes Protection Fund, 1989—; participant profl. confs.; NSF-Coun. Sci. and Indsl. Rsch. exch. scientist, 1981; sponsor, trainer India-U.S. exch. scientists NSF, 1985-86; peer reviewer: (jours.) Sci., Cancer Rsch., Jour. Biochem., Toxicology, Carcinogenesis, others; also books and films; spl. advisor RRL (India) Dirs., 1980-86; mem. U.S. AID's-Asia Environ. Partnership and Environ Tech. Network Asia, 1994—, Environ. and Tech. Network Asia-Latin Am. Program, 1996—; chair recombinant DNA com. U. Ill., Chgo., 1983-93; contbr. WHO Internat. Agy. for Rsch. Cancer, Tallinn, 1975, Budapest, 1979, Tokyo, 1981, Banff, 1983; mem. exec. bd. sci. and tech. advs. Am. Bd. Forensic Exams., 1997—. Author, editor: Molecular Mechanisms of Toxic Response; Pancreatic Carcinogenesis Mechanisms; editor Jour. Molecular Toxicology and Carcinogenesis; mem. editorial adv. bd. Forensic Examiner, 1995—; exec. bd. sci. and tech. advisors Am. Bd. Forensic Examiners, 1996—; contbr. more than 60 articles to profl. jours. NSF-CSIR exch. scientist, 1981; sponsor, trainer India-U.S. Exch. Scientists, NSF, 1985-86; spl. advisor RRL (India) Dirs., 1980—; pres. Rahim Meml. Found., 1995—. Fellow Coun. Sci. and Indsl. Rsch., India, 1963-65; Fogarty Internat. fellow Nat. Cancer Inst., NIH, 1970-71, staff fellow, 1971-74; grantee Nat. Cancer Inst./NIH, Nat. Inst. Occupational Safety and Health, EPA, State of Ill., 1974-93. Fellow Am. Coll. Forensic Examiners (life, diplomate, bd. cert. forensic medicine, editl. bd. advisors 1995—); mem. AAAS, Am. Assn. Cancer Rsch., Am. Pancreatic Assn., N.Y. Acad. Scis., Am. Chem. Soc., Soc. Toxicology, Am. Coll. Toxicology, Nat. Registry of Forensic Examiners, B.E.S.T. N.Am., Registry Global World Leaders, Soc. Toxicology (molecular biology, carcinogenesis and mechanism splty. sects.), NIHAA, Sigma Xi. Office: Toxicology-Cancer PO Box 60267 Chicago IL 60660-0267

IRANI, RAY R., oil and gas and chemical company executive; b. Beirut, Lebanon, Jan. 15, 1935; came to U.S., 1953, naturalized, 1956; s. Rida and Naz I.; children: Glenn R., Lillian M., Martin R. BS in Chemistry, Am. U. Beirut, 1953; PhD in Phys. Chemistry, U. So. Calif., 1957. Rsch. scientist, then sr. rsch. scientist Monsanto Co., 1957-67; assoc. dir. new products, then dir. research Diamond Shamrock Corp., 1967-73; with Olin Corp., 1973-83, pres. chems. group, 1978-80; corp. pres., dir. Olin Corp., Stamford, Conn., 1980-83, COO, 1981-83; chmn. Occidental Petroleum Corp. subs. Occidental Chem. Corp., Dallas, 1983-94; CEO Occidental Petroleum Corp. subs. Occidental Chem. Corp., Dallas, 1983-91; chmn. Can. Occidental Petroleum Corp. Ltd., Calgary, 1987—; exec. v.p. Occidental Petroleum Corp., L.A., 1983-84, pres., COO, 1984-91, pres., 1991-96, chmn., CEO, 1991—, also bd. dirs.; bd. dirs. Am. Petroleum Inst., Oxy Oil and Gas USA Inc., Occidental Oil and Gas Corp., Occidental Petroleum Investment Corp., Cedars Bank, Kaufman and Broad Home Corp., Jonsson Cancer Ctr. Found./UCLA. Author: Particle Size; also author papers in field; numerous patents in field. Vice chmn. Am. U. Beirut; trustee U. So. Calif., St. John's Hosp. and Health Ctr. Found., Natural History Mus. Los Angeles County; bd. govs. Los Angeles Town Hall, Los Angeles World Affairs Coun. Mem. Nat. Petroleum Coun., Am. Inst. Chemists, Am. Chem. Soc., Sci. Rsch. Soc. Am., Indsl. Rsch. Inst., The Conf. Bd., The CEO Roundtable, Nat. Assn. Mfrs. (bd. dirs.), Am. Petroleum Inst. (bd. dirs.), U.S.-Russia Bus. Coun. Office: 10889 Wilshire Blvd Los Angeles CA 90024-4201*

IRBY, HOLT, lawyer; b. Dodge City, Kans., July 4, 1937; s. Jerry M. and Virgie (Lorean) I.; m. LaVerne Smith, May 27, 1956; children: Joseph, Kathy, Kay, Karon, James. BA, Tex. Tech. U., 1959; JD, U. Tex., 1962. Bar: Tex. 1962, U.S. Dist. Ct. (no. dist.) Tex. 1963. Asst. city atty. City of Lubbock, Tex., 1962-63; assoc. Hugh Anderson, Lubbock, 1963-66; gen. counsel, sec. Mercantile Fin. Corp., Dallas, 1966-69; gen. counsel, v.p. Ward Food Restaurants, inc., Dallas, 1969-71; pvt. practice Garland, Tex., 1971—; mem. lawyer referal com. State Bar Tex., 1977, 78. Mem. bd. deacons First Bapt. Ch., Garland, 1979-84, chmn., 1976-77; bd. dirs. Garland Assistance Program, 1980, Habitat for Humanity of Greater Garland, Inc., 1997—, Dallas Life Found., 1980-90, Toler Children's Cmty., 1983-85; bd. dirs. Garland Civic Theatre, 1986—, pres., 1990-91, 92-93, v.p., 1991-92; mem. Garland Drug Task Force, 1990; deacon South Garland Bapt. Ch., 1992—, chmn., 1993-94, 98-99. Mem. Tex. Trial Lawyers Assn., Tex. Assn. Bank Counsel, Tex. Bar Assn., Garland Bar Assn. (bd. dirs. 1986-96, sec. 1992-93, v.p. 1993-94, pres. 1995-96), Dallas Bar Assn., Praetor Legal Frat. (named outstanding mem. 1962), Lubbock Jaycees (dir. 1963-65), Kiwanis (dir. 1973-74). Office: Bank of Am Tower 705 W Avenue B Ste 404 Garland TX 75040-6241

IRBY, STUART CHARLES, JR., construction company executive; b. Jackson, Miss., Oct. 20, 1923; s. Stuart C. and Elizabeth (McIlwaine) I.; m. Margaret Morris Lyons, Nov. 14, 1950; children: Margaret Morris, Stuart McIlwaine, Charles Lyons, Joseph Anderson, Richard Whiting. Student, Ala. Poly. Inst., U. Miss.; BS, La. State U., 1948; postgrad., Grad. Inst. Internat. Studies, Geneva, Switzerland. V.p. Irby Constrn. Co., Jackson, 1948-55, pres., 1955-89, chmn. bd., 1975-98; pres. Stuart C. Irby Co., Jackson, 1970-87, chmn. bd., 1975-98; pres. Power and Communication Contractors Assn., 1964. Chmn. bd. French Camp (Miss.) Acad., 1980-94; former bd. dirs. Jackson C. of C., U.S. Bus. and Indsl. Coun. Cpl. U.S. Army, 1942-45, ETO. Presbyterian. Avocations: tennis, swimming, sailing, dancing. Home: 3922 Stuart Pl Jackson MS 39211-6752 Office: Stuart C Irby Co 815 S State St PO Box 1819 Jackson MS 39215-1819

IRELAN, ROBERT WITHERS, retired metal products executive; b. Takoma Park, Md., Mar. 10, 1937; s. Charles Morris and Julia Mae (McKenzie) I.; m. Barbara Lucille Mitchell, Mar. 21, 1959; children: Robert Withers Jr., Jonathan M. BS, U. Md., 1960. Copy reader, copy editor Wall St. Jour., Washington, 1960-66; assoc. editor Nation's Bus. Mag., Washington, 1966-68; pub. rels. rep. Kaiser Industries Corp., Oakland, Calif., 1968-70; exec. asst. to chmn. Kaiser Affiliated Cos., Oakland, 1970-79; mgr. corp. rels. Kaiser Aluminum & Chem. Corp., Oakland, 1979-82; midwest regional v.p. pub. affairs Kaiser Aluminum & Chem. Corp., Ravenswood, W.Va., 1982-85; corp. v.p. pub. rels. Kaiser Aluminum & Chem. Corp., Oakland, 1985-97, ret., 1997; corp. v.p. pub. rels. Maxxam Inc., Houston, 1990-99; ret., 1999. Co-author, co-editor: Lessons of Leadership, 1967. Mem. Pub. Rels. Soc. Am. (pres. Oakland-East Bay chpt. 1990, Eddy 1987), U. Md. Alumni Assn., Rancho Murieta Country Club. Democrat. Lutheran. Avocations: golf, travel, theatre, sports, reading. Home: 6798 Terreno Dr Rancho Murieta CA 95683

IRELAND, FAITH, judge; b. Seattle, 1942; d. Carl and Janice Enyeart; m. Chuck Norem. BA, U. Wash.; JD, Willamette U., 1969; M in Taxation with honors, Golden Gate U. Past assoc. McCune, Godfrey and Emerick, Seattle; pvt. practice Pioneer Square, Wash., 1974; judge King County Superior Ct., 1984-98, 1998; past dean Washington Jud. Coll., past mem. Bd. Ct. Edn. Served on numerous civic and charitable bds.; past pro-bono atty. Georgetown Dental Clin.; past bd. dirs. Puget Sound Big Sisters, Inc.; founding mem. Wing Luke Asian Mus., 1967—, past pres., past bd. dirs.; bd. dirs. Youth and Fitness Found., 1998. Recipient Disting. Svc. award Nat. Leadership Inst. Jud. Edn., 1998; named Judge of Yr. Washington State Trial Lawyer's Assn., Man of Yr. for efforts in founding Wing Luke Asian Mus. Mem. Washington Women Lawyer's (founding mem., Pres.'s award, Vanguard award), Wash. State Trial Lawyer's Assn. (past chair bd. dirs), Superior Ct. Judges Assn. (past bd. dirs., pres. 1996-97, vice chair bd. dirs. jud. adminstrn. 1996-98), Rainer Valley Hist. Soc. (founding mem., life), Rotary (bd. dirs. Seattle No. 4 1998). Office: Washington Supreme Ct Temple Justice PO Box 40929 Olympia WA 98504-0929*

IRELAND, GENE E., surgeon; b. Kansas City, Mo., Aug. 12, 1943; m. Patricia Ireland; children: Drew, Ginger, Trish, Alissa. DDS with distinctions, U. Mo., 1969; MD, U. Conn., 1975. Asst. prof., acting chief oral & maxillofacial surgery U. Conn., Farmington, 1972-74; instr. plastic surgery U. Va. Med. Ctr., Charlottesville, 1979-80; tchr., preceptor student svcs. & edn. resources U. Cin. Med. Ctr., 1985-86; dir. dept. plastic surgery Good Samaritan Hosp., Cin., 1986-89; dir. dept. plastic surgery Christ Hosp., Cin., 1990—, pres. elect med. staff, 1997-99, pres. med. staff, 1999—. Fellow Am. Coll. Surgeons; mem. Am. Assn. Oral & Maxillofacial Surgeons, Am. Soc. Plastic Reconstructive Surgeons. Avocations: golf, diving. Office: Plastic Surgery Group Inc 7840 Montgomery Rd Cincinnati OH 45236

IRELAND, HERBERT ORIN, engineering educator; b. Buckley, Ill., June 12, 1919; s. Harvey Glenn and Anna Estella (Perkinson) I.; m. Mary Leota Austin, Mar. 1, 1941; children: Orin Lee, Marin Fae, Jeanne Lu. B.S., U. Ill., 1941, M.S., 1947, Ph.D., 1955. From research asst. to prof. civil engring. U. Ill., Urbana, 1946-79, emeritus, 1979—; cons. soil mechanics and found. engring., 1946—. Contbr.: sect. to Structural Engineering Handbook, 1968; also articles profl. jours. Served from 2d lt. to maj., C.E. AUS, 1941-46. Fellow Am. Soc. C.E., Geol. Soc. Am.; mem. Am. Ry. Engring. Assn., Sigma Xi, Tau Beta Pi, Chi Epsilon. Methodist. Home: 1132 E Township Road 209 Gilman IL 60938-6114

IRELAND, KATHY, actress; b. Glendale, Calif., 1962; d. John and Barbara Ireland; m. Greg Olsen, 1988; 1 child, Erik. Appearances in Sports Illustrated's Ann. Swimsuit Issues, 25th Anniversary Show Swimsuit Edit.; films include: Alien from L.A., 1988, Necessary Roughness, 1991, Mom and Dad Save the World, 1992, National Lampoon's Loaded Weapon I, 1993, The Player, Mr. Destiny, "Amore," "Backfire"; TV films include Beauty and the Bandit, 1994, Danger Island, 1994, Miami Hustle, 1995, Gridlock, 1996; TV appearances include: Down the Shore, The Edge, Tales from the Crypt, Without a Clue, Grand, Charles in Charge, Perry Mason, Boy Meets World, Melrose Place, The Watcher, Deadly Games, Sabrina the Teenage Witch, Suddenly Susan, Gun, Cosby. Office: 16th Fl 1900 Avenue of the Stars Los Angeles CA 90067-4301

IRELAND, PATRICIA, association executive; b. Oak Park, Ill., Oct. 19, 1945; d. James Ireland and Joan Filipek; m. James Humble, 1968. Grad., U. Miami Law Sch., 1975. Flight attendant Pan Am. World Airlines, 1967-75; ptnr. Stearns, Weaver, Miller, Weissler, Alhadeff and Sitterson, Miami; legal counsel Dade County and Fla. NOW; dir. Project Stand Up for Women NOW, initiator Global Feminist Conf.; NOW rep. European Parliament, Nat. Congress Brazilian Women, German-Am. Women's Confs., Cuban Women's Fedn., European Women's Solidarity Conf., England's Nat. Abortion Campaign; exec. v.p. NOW, from 1987, pres., 1991—. Contbr. law rev. Univ. Miami Law Sch. Office: NOW 1000 16th St NW Ste 700 Washington DC 20036-5799*

IRELAND, PATRICK, artist; b. Ireland, 1935; came to U.S., 1957; One-man shows in U.S., 1966—, include Betty Parsons Gallery, 1970, 74, Charles Cowles Gallery, N.Y., 1980, 82, 84, 86, 90, 98, Corcoran Gallery Art, Washington, 1974, Los Angeles County Mus. Art, 1975, Seattle Art Mus., 1977, Fogg Art Mus., 1981, Bklyn. Mus., 1982, Drawings, 1965-85, Nat. Mus. Am. Art, Washington, 1985, The Clocktower, N.Y., 1986, Kent State U., 1986, Everson Mus., 1987, Artspace, San Francisco, 1987, Orpheus Gallery, Belfast, 1989, Galerie Hoffman, Frankfurt, Germany, 1990; retrospective exhbn. Elvehjem Mus., Madison, Wis., 1992, Inst. Contemporary Art P.S.I., N.Y., 1993, Butler Inst. Am. Art, 1994, Mus. Art Brigham Young U., 1995, Crawford Mcpl. Gallery Art, Cork, Ireland, 1995, The Ogham Cycle, Cobh, Ireland, 1996, Language performed/matters of identity, Orchard Gallery, Derry, N. Ireland, 1998; exhibited in group shows Inst. of Contemporary Art, London, 1967, The Golden Door, Hirshhorn Mus., 1976, Documenta, Kassel, 1977, Bienale, Venice, 1980, Leo Castelli Gallery, N.Y., 1982, Bklyn. Mus., 1983, Yale U. Art Gallery, 1982, Detroit Inst. of Arts, 1987, Mus. Tamayo, Mexico City, 1991, Langage et Pouvoir, Paris, 1996; art and the amer. exp., mus. of art, Kalamazoo, 1998; represented in permanent collections Centre Georges Pompidou, Paris, Irish Mus. Modern Art, Dublin, Met. Mus. Art, N.Y.C., Nat. Gallery Australia, Hirshhorn Mus. and Sculpture Garden, Hugh Lane Gall. of mod. art, Dublin; Detroit Inst. Art, Nat. Mus. Am. Art, D.C. Studio: 15 W 67th St New York NY 10023-6226

IRENAS, JOSEPH ERON, judge; b. Newark, July 13, 1940; s. Zachary and Bessie (Shain) I.; m. Nancy Harriet Jacknow, 1962; children: Amy Ruth, Edward Eron. A.B., Princeton U., 1962; J.D. cum laude, Harvard U., 1965; postgrad. NYU Sch. Law, 1967-70. Bar: N.J. 1965, N.Y. 1982. Law sec. to justice N.J. Supreme Ct., 1965-66; assoc. McCarter & English, Newark, 1966-71, ptnr., 1972-92, judge U.S. Dist. Ct. N.J., 1992—; trustee Hamilton Investment Trust, Elizabeth, N.J., 1980-83; mem. N.J. Supreme Ct. Dist. Ethics Com., 1984-86, vice chmn., 1986; adj. prof. law Rutgers Sch. Law, Camden, 1985-86, 88-97, N.J. Bd. Bar Examiners, 1986-88. Contbr. articles to legal jours. Chmn. bd. trustees United Hosps. of Newark, 1982-83; trustee United Hosps. Found., 1985-92, United Way Essex County, 1988-92, treas., 1990-92. Fellow Royal Chartered Inst. Arbitrators (London), Am. Bar Found.; mem. ABA, Am. Law Inst., N.J. Bar Assn., Camden County Bar Assn., Nassau Club, Harbor League Club. Republican. Jewish. Office: Mitchell H Cohen US Courthouse One John F Gerry Plaza PO Box 2097 Camden NJ 08101-2097

IREY, CHARLOTTE YORK, dance educator; b. Oklahoma City, Apr. 29, 1918; d. Charles William and Annie Charlotte (Upsher) York; m. Eugene Floyd Irey, June 10, 1942; 1 child, Susan Gail. B.S. with honors, U. Wis., 1940; M.A., U. Colo., 1965 Instr. dance Stephens Coll., Columbia, Mo., 1940-43; prof. dance U. Colo., Boulder, 1945-88, chmn. dance div., dept. theatre and dance, 1973-88. Author: (with Frances Bascom) Costume Cues, 1952. Recipient Robert L. Steans award U. Colo., Boulder, 1973, Thomas Jefferson award, 1980; Charlotte York Irey Studio/Theatre at U. Colo., Boulder named in her honor, 1984. Mem. Nat. Dance Assn. (pres. 1975-76, Scholar of Yr. 1982-83, Heritage honoree 1990), AAHPERD, Am. Coll. Dance Festival, Coun. Dance Adminstrs., Congress Dance Rsch., Am. Dance Guild. Episcopalian.

IRION, ARTHUR LLOYD, psychologist, educator; b. Springfield, Mo., May 14, 1918; s. Theophil William Henry and Edith Grace (Ham) I.; m. Isabelle Virginia Cox, 1944; children: John, Millard, Janet. B.A., U. Mo., 1939; M.A., State U. Iowa, 1941, Ph.D., 1947. From instr. to assoc. prof. U. Ill., 1947-51; prof., chmn. dept. psychology Tulane U., 1951-68; prof. U. Mo.-St. Louis, 1968-80, prof. emeritus, 1980—; vis. prof. U. Colo., summer 1953, U. Mich., summers 1966, 67, U. Richmond, 1978; mem. Bd. La. Examiners of Psychologists, 1967-68. Author: (with John McGeoch) The Psychology of Human Learning, 1952; also numerous tech. articles and chpts.; Cons. editor: Jour. Exptl. Psychology, 1954-67, Perceptual and Motor Skills, 1952-80, Jour. Motor Behavior, 1969-80. Served with AUS, 1942-46. Fellow Am. Psychol. Assn., AAAS; mem. Psychonomic Soc., Mo. Psychol. Assn., So. Soc. Philosophy and Psychology (pres. 1981-82), Phi Beta Kappa, Sigma Xi. Home: 1016 W 12th St Rolla MO 65401-2156

IRIS (SILVERSTEIN), BONNIE, artist, writer, educator; b. N.Y.C., Aug. 15, 1941; d. Bernard and Hannah Kramer; m. Richard Harold Silverstein, May 27, 1967 (div. Oct. 1987). BA, Queens Coll., 1962; MA, NYU, 1963; postgrad., Art Students League N.Y., 1970-92, Sch. Visual Arts, 1979-85, New Sch. for Social Rsch., 1979-87, Cooper Union, 1986. Asst. editor IEEE, N.Y.C., 1963-68; prodn. mgr. AIAA, N.Y.C., 1973-75; assoc. editor Watson-Guptill Publs., N.Y.C., 1975-79, devel. editor, 1979-82, sr. editor, 1982-88; acquisitions editor North Light Books, Cin., 1988-90; contbg. writer Watercolor mag. and Am. Artist, N.Y.C., 1977—, Step-by-Step Graphics, Peoria, Ill., 1995-96; art workshop tchr. Rocky Mountain Nat. Park, 1994—, Foothills Art Ctr., Golden, Colo., 1995—; worshops in Placerville, Calif., Saratoga Springs, N.Y., Albuquerque, 1999, Buena Vista, Calif.; represented by David Haslam Gallery, Boulder, Colo., Arts of Georgetown and Arts of Silver Plume, Colo., Niwot Gallery, Colo., Foothills Art Ctr., Golden, Printed Page Boulder; juror art shows Longmont Art Club, 1996, Depot Art Group, Littleton, Colo., 1996, Tri-City Art Show, 1995; painting demonstrations, critiques for art assns., Boulder, Denver area, 1994—. One woman show at Delectable Egg Restaurant, Denver, 1995, NCAR Gallery, 1996; group shows include Art Students League of N.Y. Gallery, 1970-92, Nat. Arts Club, N.Y.C, 1990, 91, Salmagundi Club, N.Y.C., 1992, Creede Repertory Theatre, 1993-95, Genre Gallery, Inaugural Colo. Sr. Art Show, 1994, Boulder Art Assn., 1993-98, Foothills Art Ctr., 1994, Hildebrandt Gallery, Littleton, Colo., 1994, Faces of Women Show, Las Vegas, N.Mex., 1995, No. Colo. Annual Art Exhbn., Ft. Collins, 1996, Thompson Valley Art League, Loveland, Colo., This is Colo. Exhbn., Littleton, 1995, 97, Longmont Artists Guild, 1995, Louisville Arts Festival, 1995, 96, Glenwood Springs Ann. Fall Festival, 1994-97, Eight Plein Air Painters Invitational, Boulder, 1998, others; featured in Artists mag., 1991, Best of Oil Painting, 1997, Painting and Drawing Animals, 1998—; slide lecture Monet and Me, Dairy Ctr. for Arts, 1998. Mem. Art Students League N.Y. (life), Foothills Art Ctr., Boulder Art Assn. (program dir. 1994-97), Louisville Art Assn., Allied Artists (assoc.), Knickerbocker Artists (assoc.), others. Avocations: reading, theater, movies, hiking, travel. Home and Studio: 4500 19th St Lot 124 Boulder CO 80304-0615

IRISH, DIANA MARIA, wildlife rehabilitation agent; b. Grand Rapids, Mich., May 24, 1950; d. Robert Leroy and June Lorraine (Centilli) Newman; m. Harvey Alan Irish, Nov. 22, 1968; children: Timothy, Jamy, Corey, Windy, Robert, Wayne, Shellie. Grad. h.s., Grand Rapids, Mich. Author: My Talking Heart, 1992, Pictures of My Mind, 1994, Wings of Thought; recordings include A Rose for My Daddy and Forest Lane in (tape) Hilltop Country, 1998, Hight Country, Light of the World, Roll Gordon Roll, 1999, Freedom in the Meadow and Prayer of Our Ancesters in (CD) High Country, 1998, Rainbows End, Little Windy and Please Don't Worry in (CD) Light of the World, 1998. Bd. dirs. Coalition Rep. for Govt., Grand Rapids, 1997-99. Recipient Golden Poet award World of Poetry, 1988-97, Homer Honor Soc., 1990, Poet of Merit Internat. Soc. of Poets; named to Internat. Poets Hall of Fame, 1997-99. Mem. Weaving Ethnisity (sec. 1995-99), C.R.G. (bd. dirs. 1998-99), Grand Valley Am. Indian Lodge (bd. dirs., sec. 1992-99), Inter Tribal (mem.-at-large). Avocations: writing, fishing, hunting, Native American dancing, doll designer. Home: 1670 123rd Ave Hopkins MI 49328-9629

IRISH, LEON EUGENE, lawyer, educator, non-profit executive; b. Superior, Wis., June 19, 1938; s. Edward Eugene and Phyllis Ione (Johnson) I.; m. Karla W. Simon; children: Stephen T., Jessica L., Thomas A., Emily A. B.A. in History, Stanford U., 1960; J.D., U. Mich., 1964; D.Phil in Law, Oxford (Eng.) U., 1973. Law clk. to Asso. Justice U.S. Supreme Ct. Byron R. White, 1967; cons. Office Fgn. Direct Investments, Dept. Commerce, 1967-68; spl. rep. sec. def. 7th session 3d UN Conf. Law of Sea; mem. Caplin & Drysdale, chartered, Washington, 1968-85; prof. law U. Mich. Law Sch., Ann Arbor, 1985-88; ptnr. Jones, Day, Reavis & Pogue, Washington, 1988-93; v.p., sr. counsel Aetna Life and Casualty Co., Hartford, Conn., 1993-95; pres. Internat. Ctr. Not-for-Profit Law, Washington, 1994—; pres., CEO United Way Internat., Alexandria, Va., 1996; sr. legal cons. World Bank NGO Law, 1997—; adj. prof. Georgetown U. Law Ctr., 1975-85; regent Am. Coll. Tax Counsel, 1986-89; mem. IRS Commr.'s Adv. Group, 1987; bd. dirs. Vols. Tech. Assistance, Found. for Devel. of Polish Agr.; vis. fellow World Bank, 1995-96. Contbr. articles to legal jours. Bd. dirs., sec. Ctr. Comm., Health and Environ. Mem. ABA, D.C. Bar Assn., Am. Law Inst., Am. Coll. Tax Counsel, Coun. on Fgn. Rels. Democrat. Episcopalian. Home: 1410 Hopkins St NW Washington DC 20036-5904

IRIYE, AKIRA, historian, educator; b. Tokyo, Japan, Oct. 20, 1934; s. Keishiro and Naoko (Tsukamoto) I.; m. Mitsuko Maeda, May 14, 1960; children: Keiko, Masumi. B.A., Haverford Coll., 1957; Ph.D., Harvard U., 1961. Instr. in history Harvard U., Cambridge, Mass., 1961-64, lectr. in history, 1964-66; asst. prof. history U. Calif., Santa Cruz, 1966-68; assoc. prof. U. Rochester, 1968-69; assoc. prof. U. Chgo., 1969-71, prof., 1971-89, disting. service prof., 1983-89, chmn. dept. history, 1979-85; prof. history Harvard U., 1989-91, Charles Warren prof. history, 1991—; vis. prof. Ecole des Hautes Etudes en Sciences Sociales, Paris, 1986-87, London Sch. Econs., 1992. Author: books, including After Imperialism, 1965, Across the Pacific, 1967, Pacific Estrangement, 1972, The Cold War in Asia, 1974, Power and Culture, 1981, The Origins of the Second World War in Asia and the Pacific, 1987, China and Japan, 1992, The Globalizing of America, 1993, Cultural Internationalism and World Order, 1997, Japan and the Wider World, 1997;

editor: The Chinese and the Japanese, 1980, other books. John Simon Guggenheim fellow, 1974-75. Mem. Am. Hist. Assn. (pres. 1988), Am. Acad. Arts and Scis., Orgn. Am. Historians, Soc. Historians Am. Fgn. Relations (pres. 1978). Office: Harvard U Dept History Cambridge MA 02138

IRIZARRY, ESTELLE DIANE, foreign language educator, author, editor; b. Paterson, N.J., Nov. 13, 1937; d. Morris Jerome and Ceil Pearl (Schwartz) Roses; m. Manuel Antonio, Dec. 14, 1963; children: Michael Carl, Steven Edward, Nelson Paul. BA, Montclair State Coll., 1959; MA, Rutgers U., 1963; PhD in Philosophy, The George Washington U., 1970. Tchr. Glen Rock (N.J.) H.S., 1958-60, Ramapo (N.J.) Regional H.S., 1960-63; instr. U. P.R., Rio Piedras, 1963-66, Howard U., Washington, 1966-68, George Washington U., Washington, 1968-70; prof. Georgetown U., Washington, 1970—; editor Spanish sect. Humanities Computing Yearbook, Oxford, U.K., 1988, Hispania, 1993—. Author: Escritores-pintores espanoles, 1990, Estudios Sobre Rafael Dieste, 1992, Informática y Lieteratura, 1997. Recipient Tomas Barros Essay Prize, U. La Coruna, Spain, 1990; grantee Quincentennial Grant, P.R. Comm. for the Quincentenary, 1989; lecturer Humanities, P.R. Found. for the Humanities, San Juan, P.R., 1987. Mem. Am. Assn. Tchrs. Spanish and Portuguese, N.Am. Acad. of the Spanish Lang., Royal Spanish Acad. (corr.), Sigma Delta Pi. Avocations: writing, painting, literary computing. Home: 1600 N Oak St Apt 1615 Arlington VA 22209-2758 Office: Georgetown U ICC 407 Washington DC 20057

IRIZARRY, MICHAEL CARL, neurologist, neuroscientist, educator; b. Hato Rey, PR, Dec. 12, 1965; s. Manuel Antonio and Estelle Diana (Roses) I. BS in Math., minor in chem., Georgetown U., 1986, MD, 1990. Diplomate Am. Bd. Neurology and Psychology. Clin. fellow in medicine Harvard U., Boston, 1990-91; med. intern Mass. Gen. Hosp., Boston, 1990-91; clin. fellow in neurology Harvard U., 1991-96, instr. in neurology, 1996—; grad. asst. in neurology Mass. Gen. Hosp., 1996—; rschr. in Alzheimer's Disease Mass. Gen. Hosp., Alzheimer's Disease Rsch. Unit, 1994—. Co-editor, co-author: (textbook) Neurologic Disorders in Women, 1997; contbr. articles to profl. jours. Recipient Will Solimene award of excellence, New England chap. Am. Med. Writers Assn., 1998, rsch. grantee NIH; 1997. Mem. Am. Acad. Neurology, Soc. Neurosci. Jewish.

IRIZARRY-YUNQUE, CARLOS JUAN, lawyer, educator; b. Sabana Grande, P.R., June 24, 1922; s. Luis Manuel and Isabel (Yunque) Irizarry-Y.; m. Georgina Ortiz, Nov. 23, 1996; 1 dau., Lida Isis Irizarry Egele. B.A., U. P.R., 1943, LL.B., 1949. Bar: P.R. Supreme Ct 1949, U.S. Circuit Ct 1952, U.S. Supreme Ct 1962. Legal advisor Dept. of Agr. and Commerce of P.R., San Juan, 1949-50, P.R. Police Dept., San Juan, 1950-53; asst. dist. atty. Ponce, P.R., 1953-56; prof. law Cath. U. of P.R., Ponce, 1966-73; assoc. justice of Supreme Ct. of P.R., San Juan, 1973-86; prof. law Interam. U. P.R., San Juan, 1986—. Author: Responsabilidad Civil Extracontractual, 1996, 3rd edit., 1998. Served with U.S. Army, 1943-46, 50-52. Mem. ABA, Inter Am. Bar Assn., P.R. Bar Assn., Am. Legion, Phi Alpha Delta. Roman Catholic. Club: Lions. Office: InterAm U Sch of Law 85 Federico Costa San Juan PR 00918

IRONS, GEORGE VERNON, SR., history educator; b. Demopolis, Ala., Aug. 7, 1902; s. Andrew George and Belle (Allen) I.; m. Irma Velma Wright, June 16, 1926; children—George Vernon, William Lee. A.B., U. Ala., 1924, M.A., 1925; postgrad., Emory U., 1929, U. N.C., 1928; Ph.D., Duke U., 1936; postgrad., Ohio State U., 1952, Columbia U., 1957. Asst. prin. Perry County High Sch., Marion, Ala., 1925-27; master Darlington Sch. for Boys, Rome, Ga., 1927-31; asst. dept. history Duke U., 1931-33; prof. history and polit. sci. Samford U., Birmingham, Ala., 1933-45; chmn. dept. Samford U., 1945-67, chmn. div. social scis., 1962-67, prof. history, 1945-76; participant Danforth Found. Seminar on Higher Edn., Bronxville, N.Y., 1957, Ford Found. Seminar in Polit. Sci., Berea, Ky., 1960. Contbr. articles to profl. jours., programs to Ala. Ednl. TV Network. Mem. Jefferson County Jud. Commn., 1950-52; mem. Civil War Centennial Commn. Ala., 1961-65, Home Service Council, ARC, 1947-50; asso. dir. Freedoms Found. Seminar, Valley Forge, Pa., 1968, 70, 72, trustee Birmingham area chpt.; bd. dirs. Birmingham Council Parents and Tchrs. Served from capt. to lt. col., A.A.A. AUS., 1941-45. Recipient George Washington Honor medal Freedoms Found., 1962, Honor Cert. of award, 1963; Disting. prof. award Samford Bd. Trustees, 1968; univ. grand marshall, 1969—; dedication univ. yearbook, 1941, 60, 69, 74; honoree George V. Irons Day, 1974; named to Ala. Sports Hall of Fame, 1978; nominee Rhodes Scholarship, 1924. Mem. So. Hist. Assn., Ala. Hist. Assn. (past mem. exec. com., past mem. editorial bd.), Baptist Hist. Assn., Birmingham-Jefferson Hist. Assn. (treas. 1980—, Ann. award in Local History 1981), John H. Forney Hist. Soc., Ala. Writers Conclave (treas., past v.p.), Ala. Guidance Assn., Ala. Acad. Sci. (past v.p.), Res. Officers Assn., United Daus. of the Confederacy (Jefferson Davis medal 1991), Phi Beta Kappa, Phi Alpha Theta, Omicron Delta Kappa, Pi Gamma Mu, Kappa Phi Kappa, Phi Sigma Kappa, Phi Kappa Phi (past pres.). Home: 316 Gran Ave Birmingham AL 35209-4120 *I have found that when encountering obstacles in the achievement of certain popular and well-publicized goals, I have been able to realize substantial attainment in other fields of action—areas less traversed and dramatized, yet offering rich opportunities for service and usefulness. Fundamental to my happiness and peace of mind is an assurance of God's love for me, and God's vital presence in all human affairs. Fear God and keep His commandments.*

IRONS, ISIE IONA, retired nursing administrator; b. Rixford, Pa., Oct. 26, 1934; d. William Ellis and Catherine (Fitzgerald) Irons. Grad. RN, Buffalo Gen. Hosp., 1955; BSN, U. Buffalo, 1959; MPH, U. N.C., 1962. OPD clin. dir. Buffalo Gen. Hosp.; nursing supr. N.Y. Telephone, Buffalo; asst. staff mgr., nursing mgr. So. Bell, Atlanta, asst. staff mgr. Recipient Best Bedside Nursing award, 1955. Home: 6435 Windsor Trace Dr Norcross GA 30092-2376

IRONS, JEREMY JOHN, actor; b. Cowes, Eng., Sept. 19, 1948; s. Paul Dugan and Barbara Anne (Sharpe) I.; m. Sinead Moira Cusack, Mar. 28, 1978; children: Samuel James, Maximilian Paul. Actor: (stage appearances) including John the Baptist in Godspell, 1973, Mick in The Caretaker, 1974, Petruchio in The Taming of the Shrew, 1975, Harry Thunder in Wild Oats, Royal Shakespeare Co., 1976-77, 86, James Jameson in Rear Column, 1978, The Real Thing, 1984 (Tony award 1984); title role in Richard II, Leontes in Winter's Tale, The Rover, Royal Shakespeare Theater, Stratford-Upon-Avon, Eng., 1986-87; (films) Nijinsky, 1979, The French Lieutenant's Woman, 1981, Betrayal, 1982, Moonlighting, 1982, The Wild Duck, 1983, Swann in Love, 1983, The Mission, 1985, Chorus of Disapproval, 1988, Australia, 1988, Dead Ringers, 1988 (named Best Actor N.Y. Film Critics' Circle, 1988), Danny, the Champion of the World, 1989, Reversal of Fortune, 1990 (Acad. award, best actor, 1991), Kafka, 1991, Waterland, 1992, Damage, 1992, M. Butterfly, 1993, The House of the Spirits, 1994, The Lion King, 1994 (voice), Die Hard with a Vengeance, 1995, Stealing Beauty, 1996, Lolita, 1997, The Chinese Box, 1997, Man in the Iron Mask, 1998; (TV appearances) Alex Hepburn in The Captain's Doll, 1982, Charles Ryder in Brideshead Revisited, 1980-81, Tales from Hollywood, 1992. Address: Hutton Mgmt, 4 Old Manor Close, Askett Bucks HP27 9NA, England*

IRONS, WILLIAM GEORGE, anthropology educator; b. Garrett, Ind., Dec. 25, 1933; s. George Randall and Eva Aileen (Veazey) I.; m. Marjorie Sue Rogasner, Nov. 4, 1972; children—Julia Rogasner, Marybeth Rogasner. B.A., U. Mich., 1960, M.A., 1963, Ph.D., 1969; postgrad., London Sch. Econs., 1964-65. With Army C.E., 1956-58; asst. prof. social relations Johns Hopkins U., 1969-74; asst. prof. anthropology Pa. State U., 1974-78; assoc. prof. anthropology Northwestern U., Evanston, Ill., 1978-83, prof., 1983—; cons. Nat. Geog. Soc., NSF, AAAS, Social Sci. Research Council, Time-Life Books, U. Wash. Press, Random House, Worth Pubs., Rutgers U. Press, U. Tex. Press, Pelenum Press, Oxford U. Press, Cornell U. Press. Author: Perspectives on Nomadism, 1972, The Yomut Turkmen, 1975, Evolutionary Biology and Human Social Behavior, 1979; mem. bd. editors Ethology and Sociobiology. Mem. coun. Human Behavior and Evolution Soc. Served with AUS, 1954-56. Grantee NSF, 1973, 76, 83, 85, 86, Ford Found., 1974, Harry Frank Guggenheim Found., 1976. Fellow AAAS, Am. Anthrop. Assn.; mem. Assocs. in Current Anthropology, Human Behavior and Evolution Soc. (coun.), Internat. Soc. Human Ethology, Internat. Soc. for Behavioral Ecology, Ctr. for Advanced Studies in Religion and Sci., Inst. for Religion in an Age of Sci., Phi Kappa Phi. Achievements include research on Turkmen of Iran, human behavioral ecology, evolutionary ethics. Home: 2604 Payne St Evanston IL 60201-2133 Office: Northwestern U Dept Anthropology 1810 Hinman Ave Evanston IL 60208-0809

IRONS, WILLIAM LEE, lawyer; b. Birmingham, Ala., June 9, 1941; s. George Vernon and Velma (Wright) I. BA, U.Va., 1963; JD, Samford U., 1966. Bar: Ala. 1966, U.S. Dist Ct. (no. dist.) Ala. 1966, U.S. Ct. Appeals (5th cir.) 1966. Dir. mil. justice Maxwell AFB, Ala., 1963-69; law clk. Speir, Robertson & Jackson, Birmingham, 1964-66; asst. judge adv. Whiteman AFB, Mo., 1966-67, Gunter AFB, 1967-68; ptnr. Speir, Robertson, Jackson & Irons, 1970-71, Speir & Irons, 1971-72, William L. Irons & Assocs., 1972—; U.S. trustee, 1964-86; instr. sr. officers Judge Adv. Gen.'s Sch. Air War coll., Air Univ., Maxwell AFB. Candidate Ala. Ho. Reps. 1966. Deacon, Sunday sch. supt. Mountain Brook Bapt. Ch. Served to capt. USAF Strategic Air Command. Decorated Commendation medal and citation USAF, Cong. medal of honor; named Outstanding Jr. Officer Vietnam War, USAF, 1969; DuPont Regional scholar U.Va. Mem. ABA, Birmingham Bar Assn., Assn. Trial Lawyers Am., Nat. Assn. Cert. Judge Advs., Fed. Bar Assn., Nat. Res. Officer Assn., Newcomen Soc., St. Andrews Soc., SAR (pres. Ala. chpt., writer numerous cover stories on Am. Revolution era, Taylor award 1990, U.S. Senate Commendation for Authorship of Colonial Navy 1992, senate commendation state of N.Y. for Chronicles of the Am. Revolutionary War 1995), Descendants of Washington's Army at Valley Forge (capt. of the guard, com. admiral state of Md. 1995), Nat. Lawyers Club, Birmingham Exec. Club (pres. 1978-79), Sigma Delta Kappa. Democrat. Baptist. Home: 3855 Cove Dr Birmingham AL 35213-3801 Office: 1227 City Federal Bldg Birmingham AL 35203

IRONS, WILLIAM V., state legislator; b. Providence, May 11, 1943; s. Milton H. and Harriet Viall I.; m. Mary Durand, 1968; children: Joan, Sarah, Katherine. BS, U. N.H., 1966. CLU. Civil engr. Green Engring., Boston, 1967-68, BIF Industries, Providence, 1968-72; ins. agt. Jack Awde, CLU Ins. Agy., Providence, 1972-81; owner Irons & Assocs. Ins. Agy., Warwick, R.I., 1981—; mem. R.I. State Senate, Providence, 1983—; labor com., chmn. corp. com.; farmer Gov. Energy Coordinating Coun. Sponsor Rumford Little League; former chmn. Newman YMCA, 1980-81; mem. Am. Cancer Soc., R.I. State Dem. Com., 1976-80, East Providence Dem. City Com., 1980—, Dem. Ward Com., 1980—. Sgt. R.I. Army Nat. Guard, 1966-72. Mem. Am. Soc. CLU, R.I. Life Underwriters Assn. (past pres.), Rumford Lions Club. Roman Catholic. Address: PO Box 16210 Rumford RI 02916-0696*

IRSAY, JAMES STEVEN, professional football team owner; b. Lincolnwood, Ill., June 13, 1959; s. Robert Irsay and Harriet Pogerzelski; m. Margaret Mary Coyle, Aug. 2, 1980; children: Carlie Margaret, Casey Coyle, Kalen. B in Broadcast Journalism, So. Meth. U., 1982. With Balt. Colts., from early 1970's; owner, CEO Indpls. Colts; bd. dirs. Noble Ind. Composer, performer single Hoosier Heartland, 1985, single and video Go Colts, 1985, Colors, 1990. Bd. dirs. United Way Ctrl. Ind.; dir. Greater Indpls. Progress Com. Avocations: weight lifting, guitar, songwriting. Office: Indpls Colts 7001 W 56th St Indianapolis IN 46254

IRVAN, ERNIE (SWERVIN' IRVAN), professional race car driver; b. Salinas, Calif., Jan. 13, 1959. Winner Daytona 500, 1991. Address: Robert Yates Racing Inc 115 S Dwelle St Charlotte NC 28208-2929*

IRVIN, JAMES SAMUEL, company executive; b. Roanoke Rapids, N.C., May 19, 1944; s. Samuel James Irvin and Vivian Little Crane; m. Michelle McMullan Irvin, Nov. 7, 1981 (div. 1988); children: Deborah Graves, Jean Irvin, Jennifer McMahon, Aynsley Irvin. Cert. acoutical engr. Pres. Ototex, Inc., Richmond, Va., 1972-81, Wilson Dist. Co., Richmond, 1981-87, Irvin & Assoc. Inc., Virginia Beach, Va., 1987-95; gen. mgr. Oakwood Homes, Rocky Mount, N.C., 1996-98, Clayton Homes, Elizabeth City, N.C., 1998—. Active Civitan, Richmond, 1982-85. Mem. Masons. Republican. Baptist. Avocations: golf, travel. Office: Clayton Homes d/b/A Luv # 207 1560 N Road St Elizabeth City NC 27909

IRVIN, MARK CHRISTOPHER, real estate consultant, broker and developer; b. San Antonio, Oct. 29, 1955; s. Eugene Jr. and Patricia Alice (Blomfield) I.; m. Linda S. Irvin, Nov. 27, 1976; 1 child, Christopher Ross. AS in Bus. and Transp., Eastfield Coll., 1979; BBA, So. Meth. U., 1986. Cert. comml. investment mem.; cert. specialist in indsl. and office real estate. Ptnr. PICOR Comml. Real Estate Svcs., Tucson, 1987-94; prin. Mark Irvin Comml. Real Estate Svcs., Tucson, 1994—; arbitrator State Bar Ariz.; Tucson rep. Office Finders Network. Bd. dirs., past pres. Boys and Girls Clubs Tucson; mem. Greater Tucson Econ. Devel. Coun. Mem. Soc. Indsl. and Office Realtors, Nat. Assn. Realtors, Tucson Assn. Realtors, Tucson Office Brokers Roundtable Assn. (founder, past pres.), Tucson Met. C. of C., Rotary, Phi Theta Kappa. Republican. Avocations: cycling, racquetball, fly fishing, white water rafting. Fax: 520-620-1830. E-mail: mcirvin@rtd.clm. Office: Mark Irvin Comml Real Estate Svcs 33 N Stone Ave Ste 1650 Tucson AZ 85701-1415

IRVIN, MARY ELEANOR YTURRIA, artist; b. Aug. 31, 1948. Student, Mt. Vernon Coll., Washington; BFA, U. Tex.; M Art Edn., U. Houston. Tchr. art Luth. H.S., Houston; owner, mgr., tchr. Eleanor Y. Irvin Art Sch., Houston and Tulsa. Active fund raisers for Am. Cancer Soc., 1991—, Susan G. Komen Found. for Breast Cancer, 1997—; founder We Care, support group for breast cancer survivors, 1991. Home and Studio: 1114 E 25th St Tulsa OK 74114

IRVIN, MICHAEL JEROME, professional football player; b. Ft. Lauderdale, Fla., Mar. 5, 1966. BA in Bus. Mgmt., U. Miami, 1988. Wide receiver Dallas Cowboys, 1988—. Played in Pro Bowl, 1991-95; named wide receiver The Sporting News NFL All-Pro team, 1991; named outstanding Player of Pro Bowl, 1991. Led league in receiving yards, 1991; played in Super Bowl XXVII, 1992, XXVIII, 1993, XXX, 1995. Office: Dallas Cowboys One Cowboys Pky Irving TX 75063*

IRVIN, MONTE, retired baseball player; b. Columbia, Ala., Feb. 25, 1919. Baseball player N.Y. Giants, 1949-55, Chgo. Cubs, 1956; scout N.Y. Mets, 1967-68. Named to Baseball Hall of Fame, 1973; mem. World Series Champions, 1954. Office: care Nat Baseball Hall Fame PO Box 590 Cooperstown NY 13326-0590

IRVIN, THOMAS T., state commissioner of agriculture; b. Hall County, Ga., July 14, 1929; s. C.T. and Gladys Lee (Hogan) I.; m. Edna Bernice Frady, June 1, 1947; children: James, Johnny, David, Londa Irvin Wilson, Lisa Irvin Collier. Owner lumber bus. Clarkesville, Ga., 1944-67; exec. sec. to Gov. State of Ga., Atlanta, 1967-69, commr. agriculture, 1969—; pres. So. U.S. Trade Assn., New Orleans, 1982-83, 91-92, So. Assn. State Depts. Agriculture, Atlanta, 1972-73, Nat. Assn. State Depts. Agriculture, Washington, 1986-87. Contbr. articles to profl. jours. Chmn. bd. trustees Hazel Grove Elem. Sch., Habersham County, Ga., 1952-56; state rep. Ga. Gen. Assembly, 1956-67; mem., chmn. Habersham County Bd. Edn., 1956-76; dir. Ga. Sch. Bds. Assn., 1959-69, pres., 1968-69; mem. Stone Mountain Meml. Assn., 1969-78, chmn., 1969-74; chmn. bd. trustees Truett-McConnell Coll., 1990-96, chmn., 1996-97; chmn. Ga. Devel. Authority; deacon Antioch Bapt. Ch.; mem. Ga. Finance and Investment Com., Ga. Bldg. Authority, Ga. Agrirama Authority, Ga. State Employees Benefit Coun., Ga. Pay-for-Performance Task Force. Recipient Disting. Svc. award Ga. Sch. Bds. Assn., 1976, Outstanding Svc. award Stone Mountain Meml. Assn., 1978, Nat. award for Agrl. Excellence, 1988, Workhorse of Yr. award Southeastern Poultry and Egg Assn., 1989, Richard B. Russell Pub. Svc. award Ga. Assn. Dem. County Chairmen, 1990, Environ. Friend Industry award Ga. Green Industry Assn., 1993, Disting. Svc. award U. Ga. Coll. Vet. Medicine, 1994, award of merit Ga. Med. Assn., 1992; named to Hall of Fame, Ga. Agrirama, 1990, Vidalia Onion Hall of Fame, 1990; named Dem. of Yr., Ga. Young Dems., 1990. Mem. AGHON Soc., Gridiron Soc., Masons (grand master of Ga., 33 degree scottish rite, Disting. Svc. award for Ga.), Shriners. Democrat. Baptist. Office: Ga Dept Agriculture Capitol Sq Atlanta GA 30334

IRVINE, EDWARD D., police chief; b. Glenn Jean, W.Va., Mar. 30, 1936. AS, U. Akron, 1972, BS, 1980; postgrad., U. Va.; diploma, FBI Nat. Acad., 1983. Detective Police Dept., Akron, Ohio, 1963, detective cmty. rels. dept., 1967, sgt., 1971, lt., 1980, capt., 1988, dep. chief, 1991. Recipient Leadership award Toastmasters, 1996. Mem. Masons (32d degree), Alpha Phi. Office: 217 S High St Akron OH 44308

IRVINE, JOHN ALEXANDER, lawyer; b. Sault Ste. Marie, Ont., Can., Mar. 10, 1947; s. Alexander and Ruth Catherine (Woolrich) I.; children from previous marriage: John Alexander, Allison Brooks; m. Lynda Kaye Myska Jenkins, May 24, 1981; children: James Woolrich, William Myska. BS, Auburn U., 1969; JD, Memphis State U., 1972. Bar: Tenn. 1972, Ohio 1982, Tex. 1985. Law clk. U.S. Dist. Ct. (we. dist.) Tenn., 1972-73; asst. dist. atty. gen. 15th Jud. Cir. Tenn., 1973-78; assoc. Glankler, Brown, Gilliland, Chase, Robinson and Raines, Memphis, 1978-81; asst. gen. counsel Mead Corp., Dayton, Ohio, 1981-84; ptnr. Porter & Clements, Houston, 1984-87; prin. Boyer, Norton & Blair, 1987-89; ptnr. Thelen, Marrin, Johnson & Bridges, 1989-94, mng. ptnr. Houston office, mem. mgmt. com., 1991-94; ptnr. Porter & Hodges, L.L.P., 1995—. Bd. dirs. Make-A-Wish Found. Tex. Gulf Coast, 1985-86. Fellow Tex. Bar Found., Houston Bar Found.; mem. ABA (vice chmn. com. corp. counsel litig. sect. 1989-91, co-chmn. intellectual properties litig. com. 1996—), Internat. Assn. Def. Counsel, Am. Arbitration Assn. (bd. arbitrators), Nat. Assn. Securities Dealers (bd. arbitrators), Tex. Bar Assn., Tenn. Bar Assn., Fed. Bar Assn. (v.p. 1998—, treas. 1997-98), Memphis Bar Assn. (YLS, bd. dirs. 1976, treas. 1977), Ohio Bar Assn., Houston Bar Assn., Coll. State Bar Tex., Memphis State U. Law Sch. Alumnae Assn. (pres. 1975-76, 77-78), 5th Cir. Ct. Appeals Bar Assn., U.S.C. of C. (coun. on antitrust policy 1983—), Phoenix Club of Memphis (bd. dirs. 1977-79), Champions Golf Club, Houston Met. Racquet Club, Briar Club. Republican. Presbyterian. Avocations: sports, travel, reading.

IRVINE, PHYLLIS ELEANOR, nursing educator, administrator; b. Germantown, Ohio, July 14, 1940; m. Richard James Irvine, Feb. 15, 1964; children: Mark, Rick. BSN, Ohio State U., 1962, MSN, 1979, PhD, 1981; MS, Miami U., Oxford, Ohio, 1966. Staff nurse VA Ctr., Dayton, Ohio, 1962-66; mem. nursing faculty Miami Valley Hosp. Sch. Nursing, Dayton, 1968-78; teaching asst., lectr. Ohio State U., Columbus, 1979-82; assoc. prof. Ohio U., Athens, 1982-83; prof., dir. N.E. La. U., Monroe, 1984-88; prof., dir. sch. nursing Ball State U., Muncie, Ind., 1988—. Reviewer Health Edn. Jour., Reston, Va., 1987; contbr. articles to profl. jours. Mem. Mayor's Commn. on Needs of Women, La., 1984-88; 1st v.p., bd. dirs. United Way of Ouachita, La., 1986-88. Mem. ANA, Ind. Nurses Assn., Ind. Coun. Deans and Dirs. of Nursing Edn. (pres. 1992-98), Internat. Coun. Women's Health Issues (bd. dirs. 1986-92, 98-2000), Assn. for the Advancement Health Edn., Sigma Theta Tau. Office: Ball State U Cn418 Nursing Muncie IN 47306

IRVINE, REED JOHN, media critic, corporation executive; b. Salt Lake City, Sept. 29, 1922; s. William John and Edna (May) I.; m. Kay Araki, Aug. 14, 1948; 1 son, Donald. A.B., U. Utah, 1942; postgrad., U. Colo., 1943-44, U. Wash., 1949; M.Litt., Oxford U., Eng., 1951. With Gen. Hdqrs. of Allied Occupation of Japan, Tokyo, 1946-48; economist bd. govs. Fed. Res. System, Washington, 1951-63, adviser internat. fin., 1963-77; chmn. bd. Accuracy in Media, Inc., Washington, 1971—; editor AIM Report; syndicated columnist, radio commentator; chmn. Accuracy in Academia, 1985—. Author: Media Mischief and Misdeeds, 1984; co-author: (with Cliff Kincaid) Profiles of Deception, 1990, (with Joseph C. Goulden and Cliff Kincaid) The News Manipulators, 1993. Dir. Council Def. of Freedom, Washington, 1970—. Served with USNR, 1942-43, USMC, 1943-46, PTO; to capt. USMCR, 1944-46. Recipient George Washington medal Freedom Found., 1980, Ethics in Journalism award World Media Assn., 1987. Mem. Phi Beta Kappa. Mem. LDS Ch. Office: Accuracy in Media Inc 4455 Connecticut Ave NW # 330 Washington DC 20008-2328

IRVINE, ROSE LORETTA ABERNETHY, retired communications educator, consultant; b. Kingston, N.Y., Nov. 14, 1924; d. William Francis and Julia A.; m. Robert Tate Irvine Jr., Dec. 18, 1965 (dec. June 1968). BA, Coll. St. Rose, 1945; MA, Columbia U., 1946; PhD, Northwestern U., 1964. Tchr. English Kingston High Sch., 1946-47; tchr. English and speech Croton-Harmon High Sch., Croton-on-Hudson, N.Y., 1947-49; instr. speech SUNY, New Paltz, 1949-53; asst. prof. SUNY, New Platz, 1953-57, assoc. prof., 1957-64, prof. speech communication, 1964-85, prof. emeritus, 1985—; guest prof. Yousoi U., Seoul, Republic Korea, 1970; U.S. del. U.S. Bi-Nat. Conf., Manila, 1976; adv. bd. Rondout Nat. Bank Norstar (now Fleet Bank), 1973-85; U. Chancellor's adv. bd. SUNY Senate, Albany, 1974-80; guest prof. Celtic lore Princess Grace Libr., Monaco, 1987; cons., rschr., writer, 1985—; presenter in field. Contbr. articles to Speech Teacher, Educational Forum, Readers Theatre, others. Mem. Nat. Jr. League, Kingston, 1958-90; dir. Puppet Theater for Srs., N.Y., 1982-83; bd. trustees Friends of the Senate House State Hist. Site, Kingston, 1996—, pres. 1999—; bd. Ulster County adv. coun. to Office of Aging, 1998—; mem. allocations com. United Way Ulster County, 1998—. Honor Tuition scholar Coll. St. Rose, Albany, N.Y., 1941; named Outstanding Educator of Am., 1971. Mem. AAUW (liaison SUNY New Paltz 1966-85), Speech Comm. Assn. (mem. legis assembly 1967-68, emeritus), N.Y. State Speech Assn. (emeritus), Zeta Phi Eta, Delta Kappa Gamma, Kappa Delta Pi, Pi Lambda Theta. Roman Catholic. Avocations: historic preservation, golf, swimming, travel, local history. Home: 105 Lounsbury Pl Kingston NY 12401-5231 Office: Comm Dept SUNY New Paltz NY 12561

IRVINE, VERNON BRUCE, accounting educator, administrator; b. Regina, Sask., Can., May 31, 1943; s. Joseph Vern and Anna Francis (Phillip) I.; m. Marilyn Ann Craik, Apr. 29, 1967; children: Lee-Ann, Cameron, Sandra. B. Commerce, U. Sask., 1965; MBA, U. Chgo., 1967; PhD, U. Minn., 1977. Cert. mgmt. acct. Researcher, Sask. Royal Commn. on Taxation, Regina, 1964; lectr. acctg. Coll. Commerce, U. Sask., Saskatoon, 1967-69, asst. prof., 1969-74, assoc. prof., 1974-79, prof., 1979—, head dept. acctg., 1981-84; profl. program lectr. Inst. Chartered Accts., Regina, 1982-84, Soc. Mgmt. Accts., Saskatoon, 1982-84, 94-95. Co-author: A Practical Approach to the Appraisal of Capital Expenditures, 1981; Intermediate Accounting: Canadian Edition, 1982, 5th edit., 1998; contbr. articles to acctg. jours. Grantee John Wiley & Sons, Ltd., 1981, 85, 87, 88, 92, 93, 96, Soc. Mgmt. Accts. Can., 1979, Pres.'s Fund, U. Sask., 1978, Nelson Can. grantee, 1990. Bd. dirs. Big Sisters of Sask., 1987-90. Fellow Soc. Mgmt. Accts. Can. (bd. dirs. 1979-82, 85-87, 89-92, chmn. Nat. Edn. Svcs. com.); mem. Can. Acad. Acctg. Assn. (pres. 1994-95, pres.- elect 1993-94, sec. 1992-93, exec. com., chmn. mem. com. 1989-91), Internat. Acctg. Stds. Com. (Can. rep. 1984-87, 96-97), Internat. Fedn. Accts. Coun. (tech. advisor 1988-90), Soc. of Mgmt. Accts. of Sask. (pres. 1980-81), Sutherland Curling Club (treas. 1979-83), Saskatoon Golf and Country Club (bd. dirs. 1988-90). Home: 45 Canton Crescent, Saskatoon, SK Canada S7J 2T2 Office: U Sask, Commerce Bldg 25 Campus Dr, Saskatoon, SK Canada S7N 5A7

IRVINE, WILLIAM BURRISS, management consultant; b. Wheeling, W.Va., July 20, 1925; s. Russell Drake and Elizabeth (Carney) I.; m. Allen Claywell; children: William, Mary, Edward. BA in Econs., Cornell U., 1949. V.p. Basil L. Smith Sys., Phila., 1949-66; pres. Pa. Graphic Arts, Inc., Phila., 1966-78, Classified Devel. Corp., Bryn Mawr, Pa., 1978—; pres. Victor O'Neil Studios divsn. Herff Jones, Inc., N.Y.C., 1972-75; trustee Cornell Delta Phi Ednl. Found., N.Y., 1985—; bd. dirs. Main Lng Sch. Night, 1998—. Author: Treasury of College Humor, 1947. Mem. St. Elmo Club of Phila., St. Elmo Club of N.Y., Delta Phi (sec. 1960-62). Republican. Roman Catholic.

IRVING, A. MARSHALL, marine engineer; b. Waterbury, Md., Apr. 10, 1929; s. Walter Reid and Gertrude Elizabeth (Bennett) I.; m. Arline Doris Timmermann, July 19, 1952; children: Marshall Reid, William Anderson, Laurie Anne, Pamela Leigh. BS in Marine Engring., U.S. Merchant Marine Acad., Kings Point, N.Y., 1951; MS in Mgmt. Engring., L.I. U., 1969. Registered profl. engr. N.Y. Marine engr. U.S. Lines Co., N.Y.C., 1951-52; design engr. Sikorsky Aircraft, Bridgeport, Conn., 1953; project engr. to quality control engr. Dayton T. Brown Inc., Bohemia, N.Y., 1953-72; main engines officer USS Intrepid, N.Y.C., 1954-56; gen. mgr. Cougar Inc., Chgo., 1972-73; adminstrv. law judge N.Y. State Dept. Environ. Conservation, Stony Brook, 1973-89; litigation cons. Mineola, N.Y., 1983—; environ. assoc. Town of Huntington, Long Island, 1992-94; retired, 1994; subcom. chmn. and sec. Am. Nat. Stds. Inst. Z90, N.Y.C., 1968—; dir., sec. Snell Meml. Found., St. James, N.Y., 1983-92. Designer prototype weapons delivery system for naval aircraft, 1968. Trustee, dir. Setauket Neighborhood

House, 1975—. Mem. ASTM, NSPE, Am. Soc. Safety Engrs. Republican. Episcopalian. Avocations: boating, scuba diving, skiing, target shooting, antiquarian horology. Home: 48 Mud Rd Setauket NY 11733-2233

IRVING, CLARENCE L., JR. (LARRY IRVING), federal official; b. Bklyn., July 7, 1955; m. Leslie Annett Wiley, Nov. 7, 1987. BA, Northwestern U., Evanston, Ill., 1976; JD, Stanford U., 1979. Bar: D.C. 1980. Assoc. Hogan & Hartson, Washington, 1979-83; legis. dir., counsel Rep. Mickey Leland, 1983-87; staff chmn. Ho. Fair Employment Practices Com., 1985-87; sr. counsel mass media Subcom. Telecomm. and Fin., Ho. Com. Energy and Commerce, 1987-92; asst. sec. comm. and info. policy Dept. of Commerce, Washington, 1993—; presidentially appointed mem. commn. to reform IRS. Bd. visitors Stanford Law Sch., 1989-92; bd. dirs. Ho. of Rep. Child Care Ctr., Inc. Named one of 50 Most Influential People in the Year of the Internet, Newsweek Mag., 1995. Mem. ABA, D.C. Bar Assn., Nat. Conf. Black Lawyers. Office: US Dept of Commerce Nat Telecomm & Info Adminstrn 14th St & Constitution Ave NW Washington DC 20230*

IRVING, DONALD C., English educator; b. Watseka, Ill., Mar. 11, 1938; s. Carl Richard and Magdalene Louise (Martin) I.; m. Janet Kay O'Neal, June 27, 1962 (div. Nov. 1993); children: Kathleen, Michael. BA, U. Ill., 1960; MA, So. Ill. U., 1962; PhD, Ind. U., 1969. Instr. English Ctrl. Mo. State U., Warrensburg, 1962-64; from instr. to prof. English Grinnell (Iowa) Coll., 1968-96, assoc. dean faculty, 1983-88, chmn. Am. studies, 1974-76, 84-86, chmn. English dept., 1972-74, 90-92, dir. off-campus studies, 1983-88. Mem. initial planning com. DARE, Grinnell, 1980-82. Office: Grinnell Coll Dept English/Am Studies PO Box 805 Grinnell IA 50112-0805

IRVING, GEORGE STEVEN, actor; b. Springfield, Mass., Nov. 1, 1922; s. Abraham and Rebecca (Sack) Shelasky; m. Maria Karnilova, Oct. 17, 1948; children: Alexander, Katherine. Student, Leland Powers Sch. of Theatre, Boston, 1941. Actor (on Broadway) play, Oklahoma, 1943, Lady in the Dark, 1943, Call Me Mister, 1946, Along Fifth Avenue, 1949, Gentlemen Prefer Blondes, 1949, Two's Company, 1952, Me and Juliet, 1953, Can-Can, 1954, Bells Are Ringing, 1957, The Beggar's Opera, 1957, The Good Soup, 1957, Irma La Douce, 1960, Romulus, 1962, Bravo Giovanni, 1962, Seidman and Son, 1962, Tovarich, 1963, A Murderer Among Us, 1964, Alfie, 1964, Anya, 1965, Galileo, 1967, The Happy Time, 1968, Promenade, 1969, An Evening With Richard Nixon, 1972 (Drama Desk award), Irene, 1973 (Tony award for best supporting actor 1973), On Your Toes, 1983, Me and My Girl, 1986, Cinderella, The Merry Widow, N.Y. City Opera, 1994; stock and touring prodns.

IRVING, GEORGE WASHINGTON, III, veterinarian, research director, consultant; b. N.Y.C., Apr. 25, 1940; s. George Washington Jr. and Frances (Connell) I.; m. Alice Marie Graves, Dec. 21, 1968; 1 child, George Washington IV. BS, U. Md., 1962; DVM, Purdue U., 1965; MS, Tex. A&M U., 1970. Diplomate Am. Coll. Lab. Animal Medicine, Am. Coll. Vet. Preventive Medicine. Commd. 1st lt. USAF, 1966, advanced through ranks to col., 1984; base veterinarian Niagara Falls Internat. Airport, N.Y., 1966, 388th Tactical Fighter Wing, Korat, Thailand, 1966-67; base veterinarian Wilford Hall USAF Med. Ctr., Lackland AFB, Tex., 1968; asst. chief vet. edn. br. USAF Sch. Aerospace Medicine, San Antonio, 1970-75; chief div. lab. animal medicine Armed Forces Inst. Pathology, Washington, 1976-79; grad. Armed Forces Staff Coll., 1975-76, Air War Coll., 1977; program mgr. Air Force Office Sci. Rsch., Bolling AFB, D.C., 1979-82, dir. life sci., 1982-83; USAF liaison U.S. Army Med. R & D Command, Ft. Detrick, Md., 1983-84, dir. med. chem. def. rsch. program, 1984-87; cons. to surgeon gen. USAF, Washington, 1983-95; dir. Armed Forces Radiobiology Rsch. Inst., Bethesda, Md., 1987-91; staff dir. Human Systems Ctr., Brooks AFB, Tex., 1991-94, vice comdr., 1994-95, dir. re-engring., 1995-96; ret. USAF, 1996; v.p. Conceptual MindWorks, Inc., 1996—, v.p. sci. and tech. support svcs.; instr. grad. rsch. program NIH, Bethesda, 1976-85; merit rev. VA, Washington, 1978-84; cons. Stunkard, Miller Assocs., Bowie, Md., 1976-79. Editor: Selected Topics in Laboratory Animal Medicine, 15 vols., 1971-75; contbr. articles to jours. and chpts. to books; editor: Contemporary Topics in Laboratory Animal Sciences, 1995-97. Vice-minister Secular Franciscan Order, Holy Name Province, 1989-91; min. Tex. Dist., Sacred Heart Province, 1992-94, Los Tres Compañeros/The 3 Companions Region, 1994-98. Decorated Legion of Merit, Def. Superior Svc. medal. Fellow Aerospace Med. Assn.; mem. AVMA, Assn. Mil. Surgeons of U.S. (McCallam award 1988), D.C. Vet. Med. Assn. (pres. 1982), Am. Assn. for Lab. Animal Sci. (pres. nat. capital area br. 1981-82, v.p. 1998, pres. 1999), San Antonio Life Scis. Assn., Brooks Aerospace Found., Brooks Heritage Found., Brooks AFB Rod and Gun Club (pres. 1973-74). Republican. Roman Catholic. Office: Conceptual MindWorks Inc 4318 Woodcock Dr Ste 210 San Antonio TX 78228-1316

IRVING, JACK, advertising executive. Exec. v.p., media dir. Saatchi & Saatchi Advt., N.Y.C. Office: Saatchi & Saatchi Advt 375 Hudson St New York NY 10014-3658*

IRVING, JACK HOWARD, technical consultant; b. Cleve., Dec. 31, 1920; s. William M. and Lottie (Green) I.; m. Florence Friedman, Feb. 1, 1948; children: Paul Howard, Karen Joy, Michael William. BS, Calif. Inst. Tech., 1942; MA, Princeton U., 1948; Ph.D. in Physics, Princeton, 1965. Mem. staff radiation lab. MIT, Cambridge, 1942-45; asst. physics Princeton (N.J.) U., 1946-48; fellow chemistry Calif. Inst. Tech., 1948-49; head systems planning and analysis dept. research and devel. labs. Hughes Aircraft Co., 1949-54; head spl. devices dept. Ramo-Wooldridge Corp., 1954-55, head intelligence systems dept., 1955-56, spl. asst. to exec. v.p., 1956-57, spl. asst. to pres. space tech. labs., 1957-58; corp. staff sci. Thompson Ramo-Wooldridge, Inc., 1958-60; asst. dir. Advanced Systems Planning div. Space Tech. Labs., Inc., 1960; v.p., gen. mgr. systems research and planning div. Aerospace Corp., El Segundo, Calif., 1960-63, v.p. corp. planning, 1965-72, v.p., gen. mgr. environment and urban div., 1972-75; tech. cons. and product devel. Jack H. Irving Assocs., Los Angeles, 1976—; vice chmn. Cabintaxi Corp., 1983-99; mgr. Applied Rsch. & Tech., 1994—; aerospace vis. fellow Princeton, 1963-65; mem. com. on interplay of engring. with biology and medicine Nat. Acad. Engring., 1967-73; chmn., dir. Med. Systems Tech. Services, Inc., 1968-80; dir. Commuter Transp. Services Inc., 1974-87, mem. exec. com., 1974-79, treas., 1975-78, mem. audit com., 1979-90, chmn., 1979-84. Prin. author: Fundamentals of Personal Rapid Transit, 1978; Contbr. articles to tech. publs. Asso. fellow Am. Inst. Aeros. and Astronautics; mem. Advanced Transit Assn., Am. Phys. Soc., Sigma Xi. Directed study fire control systems, ligical design and programming first airborne digital computer, Minuteman ballistic missile, comm. satellites, personal rapid transit; inventor rotary positive displacement pumps, compressors and expanders and their application to engines, including power generation and automobile engines. Home: 13202 Jonesboro Pl Los Angeles CA 90049-3643

IRVING, JOHN WINSLOW, writer; b. Exeter, N.H., Mar. 2, 1942; s. Colin F.N. and Frances (Winslow) I.; m. Shyla Leary, Aug. 20, 1964 (div. 1981); children: Colin, Brendan; m. Janet Turnbull, June 6, 1987; 1 child, Everett. Student, U. Pitts., 1961-62, U. Vienna, 1963-64; B.A., U. N.H., 1965; M.F.A., U. Iowa, 1967. Asst. wrestling coach Phillips Exeter Acad., 1964-65; asst. prof. English Windham Coll., 1967-69, 70-72, Mt. Holyoke Coll., 1975-78; writer-in-residence U. Iowa, 1972-75; with Bread Loaf Writer's Conf., 1976, Brandeis U., 1978-79; asst. wrestling coach Northfield Mt. Hermon Sch., 1981-83, Fessenden Sch., 1984-86; head wrestling coach Vermont Acad., 1987-89. Author: (novels) Setting Free the Bears, 1969, The Water-Method Man, 1972, The 158-Pound Marriage, 1974, The World According to Garp, 1978, The Hotel New Hampshire, 1981, The Cider House Rules, 1985, A Prayer for Owen Meany, 1989, A Son of the Circus, 1994, A Widow for One Year, 1998, others, (collection of short stories and essays) Trying to Save Piggy Sneed, 1996; contbr. short stories and revs. to other publs. Rockefeller Found. grantee, 1971-72; Nat. Endowment for Arts fellow, 1974-75, Guggenheim fellow, 1976-77. Address: care Random House Inc 201 E 50th St New York NY 10022*

IRVING, MICHAEL HENRY, architect; b. N.Y.C., Aug. 2, 1923; s. E. duPont and Carolyn (Mann) I.; m. Flora Miller, June 7, 1947 (div. 1981); children: Michelle Mann, Duncan Duer, Macculloch Miller, Fiona; m. Patricia Luces, July 1981. B.A., Harvard U., 1945; M.Arch., Columbia U., 1953. With archtl. firms Harrison & Abramovitz, N.Y.C., 1953-54, Sherwood, Mills & Smith, Stamford, Conn., 1954-60; pvt. practice Westport, Conn., 1961-63, N.Y.C., 1964-69, New Canaan, Conn., 1969-91; ptnr. Irving & Jacob, Norwalk, Conn., 1991—. Trustee Whitney Mus. Am. Art; past trustee Norwalk Hosp., New Canaan Country Sch.; bd. dirs. Stamford (Conn.) Museum and Nature Center; mem. Norwalk Bldg. Bd. Appeals. Served with USNR, 1943-46. Mem. AIA, Archtl. League N.Y., Am. Arbitration Assn. Home: Old Saugatuck Rd Norwalk CT 06855-2025 Office: 60 Old Saugatuck Rd Norwalk CT 06855-2823

IRVING, THOMAS BALLANTINE, retired Spanish language educator, consultant; b. Preston, Ont., Can., July 20, 1914; s. William John and Jessie Christina (MacIntyre) I.; m. Amanda Antillón, Aug. 17, 1950 (div. 1955); children: Diana, Lillian, Nicholas; m. Evelyn Esther Uhrhan, June 30, 1961. BA, Toronto U., 1937; Maîtrise ès Lettres, Montreal U., 1938; PhD, Princeton U., 1940. Instr. Spanish U. Calif., Berkeley, 1940-42, Carleton U., Ottawa, Can., 1942-44; dir. Colegio Nueva Granada, Bogotá, Colombia, 1944-45; asst. prof. Wells Coll., Aurora, N.Y., 1945-46; catedrático U. de San Carlos, Guatemala, 1946-48; from assoc. prof. to prof. U. Minn., Mpls., 1948-65; prof. North Ctrl. Coll., Naperville, Ill., 1965-67, U. Guelph, Ont., Can., 1967-69; prof. U. Tenn., Knoxville, 1969-80, ret., 1980; dir. summer sch. U. San Carlos, Guatemala City, 1946-48; trustee, dean Am. Islamic Coll., Chgo., 1981-86; vis. prof. U. Americas, Puebla, Mex., 1984. Author: Darío y la patria, 1958, Falcon of Spain, 1954, Islam Resurgent, 1979, Kalilah and Dimnah, 1980, The Maya's Own Words, 1986, The Qur'an: First American Version, 1985, Selections from the Noble Reading, 1968, rev. edit., 1980. Lt. Royal Can. Naval Svc., 1942-44. Fulbright fellow, Iraq, 1956-57; recipient Star Imtiaz, Govt. Pakistan, 1983. Mem. Lions Club. Muslim. Avocations: transculturation, Islamic world, Central America. Home: 3721 Mercier Dr Pascagoula MS 39581

IRWIN, ANNA MAE, English language educator; b. Petrolia, Kans., Aug. 19; d. Clarence Newton and Elsie Mildred (Stump) Williams; m. Everett Irwin, Sept. 1, 1938; children: Stanley, Pamela, Steven. BS, Northeastern State U., Tahlequah, Okla., 1940; postgrad., Denver U. and Colo. U., 1960-80. Bookkeeper, typist Fed. Bur. Pub. Rds., Denver, 1942-45; tchr. Denver Pub. Schs., 1945-46; typist State Dept. Employment, Denver, 1958-60; tchr. Aurora (Colo.) Pub. Schs., 1960-84; tutor ESL for refugees State Dept. Edn., Denver, 1988-91. Mem. adv. bd., bd. dirs. Unity Ch., Denver, 1986—; mem. and pres. aux. Goodwill Industries, Denver, 1996—, 2d v.p., 1st v.p. 1992-96, pres. 1993-96; state del., county del., congl. del., precinct com. woman Rep. Party, Denver, 1970-84. Recipient Mary Venable Svc. award for vol. work Goodwill Industries, 1996. Mem. Book Review Club (v.p., program chmn. 1990-93), Cherry Creek Womens Club. Avocations: bridge, travel, book review, ceramics.

IRWIN, BYRON, management executive; b. Pottstown, Pa., June 25, 1941; s. Ronald and Gertrude (Gilbert) I.; divorced; children: Bart, Mark, Mila, Erik. BA, Drew U., 1966; MBA, George Washington U., 1968. Assoc. dir. Thomas Jefferson U. Hosp., Phila., 1971-78; pres., CEO, United Health Svcs., Binghamton, N.Y., 1978-83, Alta BAtes Corp., Berkeley, Calif., 1983-84; dir. APM, N.Y.C., 1984-94; v.p. IBM, Hawthorne, N.Y., 1994-97; ptnr. Ernst & Young, LLP, N.Y.C., 1997—; mem. adv. bd Liberty Mut. Ins. Co., 1978-83, Binghamton SUNY Grad. Mgmt. Coun., 1978-83; speaker in field, 1980—. Contbr. numerous articles to profl. jours. Chmn. code com. N.Y. State Hosp. Rev and Planning Coun., Albany, N.Y., 1978-83; mem. adv. coun. Bd. Coop. Edn. Svc., Binghamton, 1978-83. Rsch. grantee Hartford Found., 1981-82. Mem. Am. Coll. Healthcare Execs., Am. Hosp. Assn., Am. Mgmt. Assn., Hosp. Assn. N.Y. (bd. dirs.). Avocations: skiing, hiking, tennis, racquetball.

IRWIN, DEBORAH JO, secondary education educator, flutist; b. Ellensburg, Wash., Aug. 3, 1952; m. Brent Willard Irwin, June 15, 1974; children: Tony, Nick. BA in Music Edn., Cen. Wash. U., 1974, MA in Music, 1978. Tchr. Federal Way (Wash.) Schs., 1974-75, Auburn (Wash.) Schs., 1975—; prin. flutist Tacoma Concert Band, 1982—, Renton (Wash.) Pks. Band, 1978-82; tchr. The Flute Studio, Federal Way, 1983-84; piccolo player, flutist Fed. Way Philharm., 1997—; mem., historian Fireside Concert Series, Auburn, 1983-84. Mem. mus. groups Windsong, Scirrocco. Mem. NEA, Seattle Musicians Union, Seattle Flute Soc. Home: 28012 188th Ave SE Kent WA 98042-5439

IRWIN, GEORGE RANKIN, physicist, mechanical engineering educator; b. El Paso, Tex., Feb. 26, 1907; s. William Rankin and Mary (Ross) I.; m. Georgia Shearer, June 10, 1933; children: Joseph Ross, Mary Susan Irwin Gillett, Sarah Belle Irwin Lofgren, John Shearer. A.B., Knox Coll., 1930; M.S., U. Ill., 1933, Ph.D., 1937; D.Eng. (hon.), Lehigh U., 1977. Asso. prof. physics Knox Coll., 1935-36; fellow physics U. Ill., 1936-37; physicist U.S. Naval Research Lab., 1937-67; prof. mechanics Lehigh U., 1967-72; prof. mech. engring. U. Md., 1972—; vis. prof. U. Ill., 1961, 70; hon. lectr. Internat. Congress on Fracture, 1981. Contbr. articles to profl. jours. Recipient Navy Disting. Civilian Service award, 1947; Knox Coll. Alumni Assn. Achievement award, 1949; Navy Conrad award, 1969; Grand medal French Metall. Soc., 1976; Clamer award Franklin Inst., 1978; Md. Gov.'s citation, 1982; Tetmajer-medal Techn., U. Vienna, 1985. Fellow ASTM (Dudley medal 1960, hon. mem. 1974), Washington Acad. Sci.; mem. Royal Soc. London (fgn.), Soc. Exptl. Mech. (Murray lectr. 1973, Lazan award 1977, fellow 1985), ASME (Thurston lectr. 1966, Nadai award 1977, Timoshenko medal 1986), Am. Soc. Metals (Sauver award 1974, Gold medal 1988), Nat. Acad. Engring. Pioneer devel. fracture mechanics. Home: 7306 Edmonston Rd College Park MD 20740-3018 Office: U Md Dept Mech Engring College Park MD 20742*

IRWIN, GERALD PORT, physician; b. Muncie, Ind., July 11, 1945; s. Francis Inlow and Helen Marcella (Morgan) I.; m. Martha Sue Vincent, Mar. 10, 1946; 1 child, Tamara Suzette. AB in Biol. Sci., Ind. U., 1968; MD, Ind. U., Indpls., 1972. Diplomate Am. Bd. Family Physicians. Intern and resident Ball Meml. Hosp., Muncie, Ind., 1972-73; pvt. practice Alexandria, Ind., 1973—. Med. dir. Richland Twp. Fire Dept., Anderson. Mem. AMA (physician recognition award 1992-95, 98-2001), Am. Acad. Family Physicians,Ind. State Med. Assn., Ind. Assn. Family Physicians, Lions, Elks. Methodist. Avocations: computers, backpacking. Office: PO Box 124 Alexandria IN 46001-0124

IRWIN, GLENN WARD, JR., medical educator, physician, university official; b. Roachdale, Ind., July 18, 1920; s. Glenn Ward and Elsie (Browning) I.; m. Marianna Ashby; children: Ann Graybill Irwin Warden, William Browning, Elizabeth Ashby Irwin Schiffli. BS, Ind. U., Bloomington, 1942; MD, Ind. U., Indpls., 1944; LLD (hon.), Ind. U., 1986, Marian Coll., 1987. Diplomate: Am. Bd. Internal Medicine. Intern Meth. Hosp., Indpls., 1944-45; resident in internal medicine Ind. U. Med. Ctr., Indpls., 1945-46, 48-50; mem. faculty Ind. U., Indpls., 1950—, instr. , asst. prof. then assoc. prof., 1950-61, prof. medicine, 1961-86, prof. emeritus, 1986, dean Sch. Medicine, 1965-73, dean emeritus, 1986, v.p., 1974-86; chancellor Ind. U.-Purdue U., Indpls., 1973-74, chancellor emeritus, 1989; sr. assoc. Ind. U. Found. Bd. dirs. Goodwill Industries of Ctrl. Ind., Indpls., Greater Indpls. Progress Com., Greater Indpls. YMCA, Walther Med. Rsch. Inst., Walther Oncology Ctr., Indpls. Health Inst., Eiteljorg Mus. Western Art and the Am. Indian; elder 2d Presbyn. Ch. Served to capt. M.C. U.S. Army, 1946-48. Recipient Disting. Alumnus award Ind. U. Sch. Medicine, 1972, Otis R. Bowen Physician County Service award, Benjamin Harrison award, Ind. Acad. award; named Sagamore of the Wabash, Gov. of Ind., 1961, 79, 86. Fellow ACP (gov. for Ind. 1964-70); mem. AMA, Ind. State Med. Assn., Marion County Med. Soc., Ind. Soc. of Chgo., 500 Festival Assn., James Whitcomb Riley Meml. Assn. (bd. govs. 1986—), Newcomen Soc., Sigma Xi, Alpha Omega Alpha, Beta Gamma Sigma, Sigma Theta Tau. Clubs: Columbia (Indpls.), Contemporary (Indpls.), Meridian Hills Country, Skyline (bd. dirs.). Lodge: Masons (33 degree), Rotary. Home: 8025 N Illinois St Indianapolis IN 46260-2938 Office: Ind U-Purdue U at Indpls 1120 South Dr Indianapolis IN 46202-5135

IRWIN, HALE S., professional golfer; b. Joplin, Mo., June 3, 1945; s. Hale S. and Mabel M. (Philipps) I.; m. Sally Jean Stahlhuth, Sept. 14, 1968; children: Becky, Steven. B.S. in Marketing, U. Colo., 1968. Profl. golfer, 1968—; tour dir. PGA Am., 1978-79, v.p., 1979; joined Sr. PGA, 1995—. State chmn. Mo. Easter Seal campaign, 1977. Winner Heritage Classic, 1971, 73, 94, Piccadilly World Match Play, 1974-75, U.S. Open Championship, 1974, 79, 90, Western Open, 1975, Atlanta Golf Classic, 1975, 77, Glen Campbell-L.A., 1976, Fla. Citrus, 1976, Hall of Fame Classic, 1977, Australian PGA, 1978, South African PGA, 1979, World Cup, 1979, Hawaiian Open, 1981, Buick Open, 1981, 90, Bridgestone Classic Japan, 1981, Brazilian Open, 1982, Inverrary Classic, 1982, Bing Crosby Pro-Am., 1984, Meml. Tournament, 1983, 85, Bahamas Classic, 1986, Fila Classic, 1987, MCI Heritage Golf Classic, 1994, Ameritech Sr. Open, 1995, 98, Vantage Championship 1995, 97, Am. Express Invitational 1996, PGA Srs.' Championship, 1996, 97, 98, Mastercard Championship, 1997, LG Championship, 1997, Las Vegas Sr. Classic, 1997, 98, Burnet Sr. Classic, 1997, BankBoston Classic, 1997, 98, Boone Valley Classic, 1997, 99, Hyatt Regency Maui Kaanapali Classic, 1997, Toshiba Sr. Classic, 1998, U.S. Sr. Open, 1998, Energizer Sr. Tour Championship, 1998, Nationwide Championship, 1999. Mem. Phi Gamma Delta. Republican. Presbyn. Tour victories include Heritage Classic, 1971, 73, 94, U.S. Open, 1974, 79, Western Open, 1975, Atlanta Golf Classic, 1975, 77, Glen Campbell-Los Angeles, 1976, Fla. Citrus, 1976, Hall of Fame Classic, 1977, Hawaiian Open, 1981, Buick Open, 1981, Inverrary Classic, 1982, Bing Crosby Pro-Am, 1984, Meml. Tournament, 1983, 85, Bahamas Classic, 1986. Office: Golf Svcs Inc 9909 Clayton Rd Ste 209A Saint Louis MO 63124-1120 also: Sr PGA Tour 112 TPC Blvd Ponte Vedra Beach FL 32082-3046*

IRWIN, JAMES RICHARD, JR., writer, editor; b. Norristown, Pa., Nov. 6, 1955; s. J. Richard and Sara Jane (Hunsicker) I.; m. Angela Marie Brillante, May 27, 1994; children: David, Neil, Nicholas. BFA, NYU, 1977; MFA, San Francisco Art Inst., 1982. Prin. ptnr. Falling Spring Films, Chambersburg, Pa., 1978-80; journalist, comms. cons. Irwin Comms., San Francisco, 1980-86; prin. ptnr. Ellis-Irwin Assocs., San Francisco, 1986-90; assoc. dir. Marian Locks Gallery, Phila., 1990-91; editor TV Guide, Radnor, Pa., 1991-92; asst. prof. William Paterson U., Wayne, N.J., 1992-94; prin. Irwin & Assocs., Wayne, 1994-97; mng. editor Comcast Online, Union, N.J., 1997—. Editl. bd. N.J. Jour. of Comm., 1993—; media artist many films, performances and shows; creator, organizer over 36 fine art, media and history exhbns.; contbr. articles to profl. publs. Interdisciplinary project grant Rockefeller Found./Nat. Endowment for the Arts, 1986, Youth grant Nat. Endowment for the Humanities, 1980; recipient Art award San Francisco Mus. of Modern Art, 1984. Mem. N.J. Comm. Assn. (exec. bd. 1996—), Self Employed Artists and Writers Network. Avocations: tennis, basketball. Office: Comcast Online in the Garden State 800 Rahway Ave Union NJ 07083-6652

IRWIN, JAY R., federal judge. Apptd. part-time magistrate judge U.S. Dist. Ct. Ariz. Office: 325 W 19th St Yuma AZ 85364-5624

IRWIN, JOHN DAVID, electrical engineering educator; b. Mpls., Aug. 9, 1939; s. Arthur Fowle and Virginia (Farnham) I.; m. Patricia Edith Watson, Aug. 26, 1961; children: Geri Marie, John David, Laura Lynne. BEE, Auburn U., Ala., 1961; MS, U. Tenn., 1962, PhD, 1967. Mem. tech. staff Bell Labs., Holmdel, N.J., 1967-68; supr. Bell Labs, Holmdel, N.J., 1968-69; asst. prof. elec. engring. Auburn U., 1969-72, assoc. prof., 1972-73, assoc. prof., head dept., 1973-76, prof., head dept., 1976—, Earle C. Williams Eminent Scholar and dept. head, 1993—; pres. Southeastern Ctr. for Elec. Engring. Edn., Orlando, Fla., 1983-84. Author: (with Nelson and Carroll) Introduction to Computer Logic, 1975, Industrial Noise and Vibration Control, 1979, (with E.R. Graf) Basic Engineering Circuit Analysis, 1984, 5th edit., 1996, (with V.P. Nelson, H.T. Nagle, B.D. Carroll, J.D. Irwin) Digital Logic Circuit Analysis and Design, 1995, (with D.V. Kerns) Introduction to Electrical Engineering, 1995, On Becoming An Engineer, 1997; editor-in-chief The Industrial Electronics Handbook, 1997, Emerging Multimedia Computer Communication Technologies. Fellow IEEE (editor jour. Indsl. Electronics 1982-83, Centennial medal 1984, IEEE-Indsl. Electronics Soc. A.H. Hornfeck Svc. award 1986, IEEE Region III Outstanding Educator award 1989); mem. IEEE Edn. Soc. (pres. 1989-90, IEEE-Indsl. Electronics Soc. Achievement award 1991, IEEE Edn. Soc. award 1991, IEEE Edn. Soc. Soc. McGraw HIll/Jacob Millman award 1993, Undergrad. Tchg. award 1998). Roman Catholic. Home: PO Box 2740 Auburn AL 36831-2740 Office: Auburn U Auburn AL 36849

IRWIN, JOHN ROBERT, oil and gas drilling executive; b. Melbourne, Australia, July 24, 1945; came to U.S., 1969; s. Robert L. and Daisy O. I.; m. Margo E. Mayon, 1979; children: Joshua R., Elizabeth. J. BE with honors, Melbourne U., M Engring. Sci., 1969; MS in Indsl. Adminstrn., Purdue U., 1970; AMP, Harvard Bus. Sch., 1990. Registered profl. engr., Australia. Various fin. positions Kerr-McGee Corp., Okla, Wis., Tex., La., 1970-72; ops. engring positions Kerr-McGee Corp., Wales, Scotland, Denmark, Singapore and Myanmar, 1972-75; mgr. ops. Transworld Drilling Co. (subs. Kerr-McGee Corp.) Sharjah, Nigeria and La., 1975-79; mgr. ops. Atwood Oceanics, Inc., Houston, 1979-80, gen. mgr., 1980, v.p., 1980-88, exec. v.p., 1988-92; pres., CEO, 1992—; bd. dirs. Atwood Oceanics, Inc. Mem. Internat. Assn. Drilling Contractors (vice chmn.), Inst. Engrs. Australia, Govs. Club (Houston). Avocations: reading, history, Australian football. Office: Atwood Oceanics Inc PO Box 218350 Houston TX 77218-8350

IRWIN, JOHN THOMAS, humanities educator; b. Houston, Apr. 24, 1940; s. William Henry and Marguerite Harriet (Hunsaker) I.; m. Laura Elizabeth Scott, Sept. 23, 1978 (div. 1991); m. Meme Amosso, May 29, 1993. BA, U. St. Thomas, 1962; MA, Rice U., PhD, 1970. Supr. public affairs library NASA Manned Spacecraft Center, Houston, 1966-7; asst. prof. English, Johns Hopkins U., 1970-74, prof. writing seminars, 1977—, Decker prof. in humanities, 1984—, chmn., 1977-96; editor Ga. Rev., U. Ga., 1974-77. Author: Doubling and Incest/Repetition and Revenge, 1975, expanded edit., 1995, The Heisenberg Variations, 1976, American Hieroglyphics, 1980, The Mystery to a Solution, 1994, Just Let Me Say This About That, 1998; editor: Johns Hopkins Press Fiction and Poetry series, 1978—; mem. editl. bd. Poe Studies, Ariz. Quar.; contbr. articles to profl. jours. Served with USNR, 1963-66. Recipient John Gardner medal Rice U., 1970, Christian Gauss prize, 1994, Scaglione prize for comparative lit., 1994; Danforth fellow, 1962, Guggenheim fellow, 1991. Mem. MLA, Assn. Lit. Scholars and Critics, Poe Studies Assn. (v.p. 1995-97), Faulkner Soc., F. Scott Fitzgerald Soc., Tudor and Stuart Club. Home: 5313 Springlake Way Baltimore MD 21212-3413 Office: Johns Hopkins U Writing Seminars Gilman 135 Baltimore MD 21218

IRWIN, JOHN THOMAS, retired counselor; b. Kewanee, Ill., July 31, 1939; s. Edward William and Rosemary (Zeglis) I. BA, U. Notre Dame, 1961; MS in Edn., No. Ill. U., 1964. Tchr. Salt Creek Sch., Villa Park, Ill., 1961-63; H.S. counselor Ctrl. Schs., Burlington, Ill., 1963-77; H.S. counselor, prevention coord. Kaneland Schs., Maple Park, Ill., 1977-93; prevention coord. Batavia (Ill.) Schs., 1993-95; prevention specialist Country of Lithuania, 1993—. Recipient Williams Prevention award Ill. State Police, 1989. Roman Catholic. Home: 729 Forest View Dr Geneva IL 60134-3237

IRWIN, JOHN WESLEY, publisher; b. Toronto, Ont., Can., July 11, 1937; s. John Coverdale Watson and Annie Elizabeth (Hiltz) I.; m. Marjorie Eleanor Gray, Dec. 16, 1961; children—John Joseph, Marjorie Elizabeth, Peter David Gordon, Andrew James Gray. B.A. with honours, U. Toronto, 1959. Tchr., 1959-60; pres. Book Soc. Can. Ltd. (ednl. books), Agincourt, Ont., 1960-83, Irwin Pub. Inc., 1983-89, Ednl. Project Resources Can. Ltd., Willowdale, Ont., 1994-96; exec. dir. Scripture Union-Can., 1997—. Chmn. bd. trustees McMaster Div. Coll., Hamilton, Ont., 1988-99. Recipient Canadian Confedn. medal, 1967. Mem. Assn. Canadian Pubs. (treas. 1977), Canadian Edn. Assn., Can. Copyright Inst. (gov. 1970-77, 81—), Inter-Varsity Christian Fellowship Can. (dir. 1973—, chmn. 1979-91), Canadian Feed the Children (chmn. 1992-95). Baptist. Clubs: Peiromai (Toronto), Empire. Home: 81 Bayview Ridge, Willowdale, ON Canada M2L 1E3 Office: 1885 Clements Rd Unit 226, Pickering, ON Canada L1W 3U4

IRWIN, KENNY, professional race car driver; b. Indianapolis, Aug. 5, 1969. 7 wins USAC Stoops Freightliner Sprint Car Series, 1993, finished 2d in points USAC Silver Crown Series, 1996; 5 full seasons USAC Skoal Nat. Midget Series, including 8 wins, 20 2d-place, 59 top-5, 87 top-10, 1996 championship; NASCAR Craftsman Truck Series, 1997—, including 2 wins Metro Dade-Homestead Motorsports Complex, Tex. Motor Speedway, 10th-place finish in series point standings. Recipient Raybestos Rookie of Yr. award, 1998, NASCAR Craftsman Truck Series Rookie of Yr. 1996, USAC

Stoops Freightliner Sprint Car Series Rookie of Yr. 1993. Avocations: golf, pool. *

IRWIN, LAMOUR MITCH, real estate developer; b. Sault Sainte Marie, Mich., July 8, 1952; s. Frank Lamour and Mildred (Holt) I.; m. Cynthia Williams, June 21, 1975; children: Jeffrey Mitchel, Andrew Ryan. BA, Lake Superior State U., 1974. State sen. State of Mich., 1979-90; pres. Irwin Group, Ltd., East Lansing, Mich., 1991—. Trustee Mich. 4-H Found., 1993—. Recipient Outstanding Alumnus award Lake Superior State U., 1989. Avocations: horseback riding, private pilot.

IRWIN, LINDA BELMORE, marketing consultant; b. Portland, Oreg., Apr. 29, 1950; d. Calvin C. and Dorothy B. (Belmore) Harper; m. Michael Hugh Irwin, June 24, 1989. Student, Portland State U., 1968-72. With Hyatt Regency, New Orleans, 1975-78; catering Hyatt Regency-Capitol Hill, Washington, 1978-80; dir. catering Hyatt, Anaheim, Calif., 1978-80; mgr. Dockside Yacht Sales, Annapolis, Md., 1981-85; dir. sales and mktg. Loew's Hotel, 1985-86; dir. mktg. Annapolis Marriot, 1986-88; ind. mktg. cons. Washington, Dallas, Cin., 1988—. Amb. State of Md., Annapolis, 1986-88; mktg. chair Tourism Coun. Annapolis and Anne Arundel County; curricula advisor Anne Arundel C.C.; mem. fund raising com. Ch. Circle Beautification Trust. Mem. Nat. Banquet mgrs. Guild (founder L.A. chpt.), Nat. Assn. Female Execs. (area dir. 1985—), Annapolis C. of C. (ambassador 1985-88), Greater Washington Soc. of Assn. Execs., Anne Arundel Trade Coun., Md. Tourism Coun. (adv. bd.), Internat. Platform Assn. Republican. Episcopalian. Avocations: calligraphy, sailing, traveling, literature, ballet.

IRWIN, MARK, writer, educator; b. Faribault, Minn., Apr. 9, 1953; s. William Thomas and Mary Lou Irwin. BA, Case Western Res. U., 1974, PhD, 1982; MFA, U. Iowa, 1980. Assoc. prof. Cleve. Inst. Art, 1985-90; asst. prof. Ft. Lewis Coll., Durango, Colo., 1990-92; vis. poet U. Denver, 1992-93, Ohio U., Athens, 1993-94, U. Colo., Boulder, 1997-98. Translator: Ardis Anthology of Eastern European Poetry, 1982, New Directions, 46, 1982, Notebook of Shadows (Philippe Denis), 1982, Ask the Circle to Forgive You (Nichita Staescu), 1983; author: (poems) The Halo of Desire, 1987, Against the Meanwhile, 1989, Quick, Now, Always, 1996, White City, 1999; editor: Museum Pieces; contbr. poems to periodicals. Recipient Nation/Discovery award, 1984, Pushcart prize, 1994-95, 97-98, Colo. Recognition Lit. award, 1996; Traveling fellow Wright-Plaisance, 1977; Fulbright Traveling fellow, 1981; Individual fellow Ohio Arts Coun., 1985-86; fellow Helene Wurlitzer Found., 1988; grantee Lilly Found., 1989, NEA fellowship, 1993. Avocations: hiking, wildlife preservation, animal protection. Home: 3875 S Cherokee St Englewood CO 80110

IRWIN, MARTIN, psychiatrist; b. N.Y.C., Oct. 15, 1949. BA, Cornell U., 1967; MD, U. Pa., 1971. Resident in psychiatry U. Chgo., 1975-79, fellow in child psychiatry, 1977-79; dir. psychiat. in-patient unit Children's Meml. Hosp., Chgo., 1979-82; dir. child neuropsychiatry in-patient unit, dir. tng. Tulane U. Med. Ctr., New Orleans, 1982-84; chief children's in-patient unit, dir. med. student edn. Badley Hosp./Brown U., Providence, 1984-88; dir. div. child and adolescent psychiatry SUNY Health Sci. Ctr., Syracuse, 1988—, assoc. prof., 1988-98, prof., 1998—; vis. prof. Ben Gurion U., Beersheva, Israel, 1994-95. Author: Psychiatric Hospitalization of Children, 1982, ADHD: A No-Nonsense Guide for Primary Care Physicians, 1996; contbr. articles to profl. jours. Mem. Am. Psychiat. Assn., Am. Acad. Child Psychiatry, Soc. for Biol. Psychiatry, Profs. Child Psychiatry. Office: SUNY Health Sci Ctr 750 E Adams St Syracuse NY 13210-2399

IRWIN, MELINDA KAY, physical education educator; b. Bellefonte, Pa., Feb. 3, 1953; d. David and Barbara (Bigelow) Adams; m. James Richard Irwin, June 22, 1997; children: Alison, James Jr. BS, U. Pitts., 1975. Gymnastic coach Ellis Sch., Shadyside, Pa., 1974-75; tchr., coach Churchill Schs., Pitts., 1975-79; aquatic dir., coach Meadville (Pa.) YMCA, 1980-83; tchr. Crawford Ctrl. Schs., Meadville, 1988—, first aid trainer, basketball cheerleading coach, 1998—; instr. Growing Health, Health for I.U., 1995-98. Cheerleading coach (football and basketball) Meadville area schs., 1998—; sec. Meadville Football Boosters, 1998; first aider Meadville Med. Ctr., Crawford Ctrl. Schs., 1998. Mem. U.S. Figure Skating Assn., Meadville Figure Skating Club (pres. 1991-95), Figure Skating Club Erie (sec. 1996-97). Home: 259 Jefferson St Meadville PA 16335-1425

IRWIN, MIRIAM DIANNE OWEN, book publisher, writer; b. Columbus, Ohio, June 14, 1930; d. John Milton and Miriam Faith (Studebaker) Owen; m. Kenneth John Irwin, June 5, 1960; 1 child, Christopher Owen Irwin. BS in Home Econs., Ohio State U., 1952, postgrad. in bus. adminstrn., 1961-62. Editorial asst. Am. Home Mag., N.Y.C., 1953-56; salesman Owen Realty, Dayton, Ohio, 1957-58, Clevenger Realty, Phoenix, 1958-59; home economist Columbus and So. Ohio Electric Co., 1959-60; pub. Mosaic Press, Cin., 1977—; pub. distbr. D'Bridge Email Systems N.Am. (a Mosaic Press div.), 1991—; owner Bibelot Bindery, 1987—. Author: Lute and Lyre, 1977, Forty is Fine, 1977, Miriam Mouse's Survival Manual, 1977, Miriam Mouse's Costume Collection, 1977, Miriam Mouse's Marriage Contract, 1977, Miriam Mouse, Rock Hound, 1977, Silver Bindings, 1983; editor: Tribute to the Arts, 1984, Chunging, 1996; contbg. author Publisher's Favorite, 1988; illustrator: Corals of Pennekamp, 1979. Daytime crew chief Wyoming Life Squad, Ohio, 1966-71. Mem. Miniature Book Soc. (past bd. dirs., chairperson 1987-89). Presbyterian. Avocation: book collecting. E-mail: mirwin@one.net. Home and Office: 358 Oliver Rd Cincinnati OH 45215-2615

IRWIN, PAT, federal magistrate judge; b. Leedey, Okla., June 12, 1921; s. Marvin J. and Ollie D. (Newton) I.; m. Margaret Boggs, Aug. 18, 1950; children: William, Margaret. Student, Southwestern State Coll., 1939-41, U. Okla., 1941-42, 46-49; LLB, U. Okla., 1949, JD, 1961. Bar: Okla. 1949. County atty. Dewey County, 1949-50; sec. to commrs. land office Okla. Sch. Land Commn., 1955-58; justice Okla. Supreme Ct., 1959-83, chief justice, 1969-70, 81-82; U.S. magistrate judge western dist. Okla., 1983—; presiding judge appellate div. Okla. Ct. on Judiciary, 1971-74; mem. exec. council Conf. Chief Justices, 1971-72. Mem. Okla. Senate, 1951-54. U.S. Naval aviation cadet, 1942-43, capt. USMCR, 1943-46, PTO. Decorated DFC (2), Air medal (8). Mem. Am. Legion, Masons, Delta Theta Phi. Office: US Courthouse 200 NW 4th St Oklahoma City OK 73102-3026

IRWIN, PAUL GARFIELD, former minister, humane society executive; b. Brantford, Ont., Can., Apr. 3, 1937; came to U.S., 1956; s. Wesley G. and Evelyn (Shelby) I.; m. Jean Rose Hathaway, Sept. 5, 1960; children—Christopher, Jonathan, Craig. B.A., Roberts Wesleyan U., N.Y., 1960; M.Div., Colgate Rochester Theol. Sem., 1964; S.T.M., Boston U., 1967; LL.D. (hon.), Rio Grande Coll., Ohio, 1981. Ordained to ministry United Meth. Ch., 1962. Pastor chs. in Boston, 1962—; v.p. Humane Soc. of U.S., Washington, 1976-92, pres., CEO 1992—; v.p. Nat. Assn. Advancement of Humane and Environ. Edn., 1980—; dir. World Soc. Protection of Animals, London, 1984—. Mem. Asia Soc. (bd. dirs.), Am. Bible Soc. (bd. dirs. 1985—). Office: Humane Soc US 2100 L St NW Washington DC 20037-1525*

IRWIN, PETER JOHN, orthopaedic surgeon; b. East St. Louis, Ill., July 7, 1934; s. Peter and Anne (Sokalski) Iwasyszyn; m. Kathryn Swanson, June 15, 1960; children: Kathryn Linda, Mary Elizabeth, Amy Marie, Kenneth John, James Patrick. BS in Biology, St. Louis U., 1955, MD, 1959. Diplomate Am. Bd. Orthopaedic Surgery, Am. Bd. Forensic Medicine. Intern Creighton Meml. St. Joseph Hosp., Omaha, 1959-60; resident in orthopaedic surgery U. Ark. Med. Ctr., Little Rock, 1961-65, tchg. staff, 1965-97; pvt. practice Fort Smith, Ark., 1965-97; mem. staff Sparks Regional Med. Ctr., 1965-97, St. Edward Mercy Med. Ctr., 1965-97; retired, 1997; mem. staff St. Edward Mercy Med. Ctr., 1965-97—; mem. staff Sparks Regional Med. Ctr., 1965-97, chief of staff, 1979, bd. dirs., 1980-87; ret. 1998. Lt. comdr. M.C., USN, 1966-68. Fellow ACS, Am. Acad. Orthopaedic Surgeons (councillor 1983-89); mem. AMA, So. Med. Assn., Sebastian County Med. Soc. (pres. 1997), Ark. Orthopaedic Assn. (pres. 1976-77), Mid-Am. Orthopaedic Assn. (founding mem., pres. 1993-94), Clin. Orthopaedic Soc., Inc., Mid-Ctrl. States Orthopaedic Soc. (pres. 1979-80), So. Orthopaedic Assn., Am. Orthopaedic Soc. for Sports Medicine, Am. Soc. Sports Medicine, Ark. Hand Club.

IRWIN, PHILIP DONNAN, lawyer; b. Madison, Wis., Sept. 6, 1933; s. Constant Louis and Isabel Dorothy (Elfving) I.; divorced; m. Sandra L. McMahan, Sept. 14, 1985; children: Jane Donnan, James Haycraft, Victoria Wisnom, Philip Donnan Jr. BA, U. Wyo., 1954; LLB, Stanford U., 1957. Bar: Wyo. 1957, Calif. 1958. Assoc. O'Melveny & Myers, Los Angeles, 1957-65, ptnr., 1965—; mem. planning com. Inst. Fed. Taxation of U. So. Calif. Law Ctr., 1976—, chairperson, 1995-98; spkr. legal seminars. Contbr. articles legal jours. Trustee Mackenzie Found., Los Angeles, 1969—. Republican. Episcopalian. Club: California (Los Angeles). Office: O'Melveny & Myers 400 S Hope St Rm 1861 Los Angeles CA 90071-2899

IRWIN, R. ROBERT, lawyer; b. Denver, July 27, 1933; s. Royal Robert and Mildred Mary (Wilson) I.; m. Sue Ann Scott, Dec. 16, 1956; children—Lori, Stacy, Kristi, Amy. Student U. Colo., 1951-54, B.S.L., U. Denver, 1955, LL.B., 1957. Bar: Colo. 1957, Wyo. 1967. Asst. atty. gen. State of Colo., 1958-66; asst. div. atty. Mobil Oil Corp., Casper, Wyo. 1966-70; prin. atty. No. Natural Gas Co., Omaha 1970-72; sr. atty. Coastal Oil & Gas Corp., Denver 1972-83, asst. sec. 1972-83; ptnr. Baker & Hostetler, 1983-87; pvt. practice 1987—. Mem. Colo. Bar Assn., Arapahoe County Bar Assn., Rocky Mountain Oil and Gas Assn. Republican. Clubs: Los Verdes Golf, Petroleum, Denver Law (Denver). Office: 650 S Alton Way Apt 4D Denver CO 80231-1669

IRWIN, ROBERT HUGH CRAWFORD, manufacturing company executive; b. Chadds Ford, Pa., Mar. 26, 1928; s. Andrew Polluck and Helen Baker (Chalfant) I.; m. Elizabeth Symonds; children: Lauren, Lisa. BSME, U. Del., 1951. Various engring. positions Chrysler Corp., Detroit, 1951-60; exec. mfg. positions Chrysler Australia Ltd., Adelaide, 1960-67, Chrysler St. Louis Truck Plant, 1967-68; dir. mfg. Chrysler U.K., London, 1968-77; dir. internat. mfg. Chrysler Corp., Detroit, 1977-80; v.p. ops. Batesville (Ind.) Casket Co., 1980-84, pres., 1984-89; vice chmn., CEO LeRoy Industries, 1991-94; bd. dirs. Exide Corp., Leroy Industries, Die Moulding Co. Avocations: golf, swimming, boating, farming. Home: 831 Newhall Rd Unionville PA 19375

IRWIN, ROBERT JAMES ARMSTRONG, investment company executive; b. Buffalo, June 27, 1927; s. Robert J.A. and Dorothy (McLean) I.; m. Donna Henwood, Sept. 10, 1966; children: William Baird, Helen Mitchell, Elizabeth Flora, Robert J.A. IV, Ronald Henwood, Derrick Millet. B.A., Colgate U., 1949; postgrad., U. Buffalo, 1949-50, Babson Inst. Finance, Wellesley, Mass., 1952-53. With Marine Trust Co. Western N.Y., Buffalo, 1958-66; v.p. Marine Midland Banks, Inc., N.Y.C., 1966-69; sr. v.p. Marine Midland Banks, Inc., 1969-71; exec. v.p. Dreyfus-Marine Midland Mgmt. Corp., 1970-72; sr. exec. v.p. Niagara Share Corp., Buffalo, 1972-74, pres., 1974-92, chief exec. officer, 1988-92, also bd. dirs.; chmn. bd. ASA Ltd., 1993—; mem. adv. bd. Mfrs. and Traders, M&T Bank Corp. Bd. dirs. Boys Club of Western N.Y., 1953, U. Cape Town Fund, Inc., Hauptman Woodward Med. Rsch. Inst., 1975—; trustee Baird Found., 1965—, Old Ft. Niagara Assn., 1986—, Ridley Coll. Scholarship Fund, Inc., James H. Cummings Found., 1978—, Libr. Found. Buffalo & Erie County; trustee, treas. St. Barnabas Coll. Fund Inc. Mem. Saturn Club, Mid Day, Buffalo Canoe, Royal Canadian Yacht (Toronto), Univ. Club (N.Y.C.). Home: 6 Saint Andrews Walk Buffalo NY 14222-2010 Office: Ellicott Sta PO Box 1210 Buffalo NY 14205-1210

IRWIN, SAMUEL MACDONALD, toy company executive; b. Toronto, Ont., Can., June 11, 1927; s. Samuel Beatty and Beatrice Isobel (Whiteside) I.; m. Elinor Jane Somerville, June 4, 1949; children—George Macdonald, David Samuel, Peter Matthews, Patti-Ann. Student, Ridley Coll., 1944-46, U. Toronto, 1946-49. Salesman Irwin Toy Ltd., Toronto, 1949-59, exec. v.p., 1954, pres., 1984-89, chmn. bd. dirs., 1989—. Co-chmn. bd. dirs. Ridley Coll., St. Catharines, 1977, bd. govs., 1967—; past chmn. Children's Broadcast Inst., Toronto. Mem. Can. Toy Mfrs. Assn. (chmn. bd. dirs. 1983), Lambton Golf Club, Badminton Racquet Club Toronto, St. Andrews Country Club (Delray Beach, Fla.), Peterborough Golf and Country Club, Toronto Golf Club, Country Club of Fla. (Village of Golf). Conservative. Anglican. Avocations: golf; tennis; squash. Office: Irwin Toy Ltd, 43 Hanna Ave, Toronto, ON Canada M6K 1X6

IRWIN, STANLEY ROY, music educator, singer, conductor; b. Henderson, Tex., Jan. 23, 1941; s. Forrest Herbert and Hazel Marie (Gray) Irwin; m. Jane Parker, June 14, 1969; 1 child, Mark Alexander. BA, Baylor U., 1963; B Ch. Music, Southwestern Bapt. Theol. Sem., 1966; MusM, Southern Meth. U., 1969; MusD, Ind. U., 1988; diploma, Internat. Opera Ctr., 1974. Instr. music, choir dir. Simpson Coll., Indianola, Iowa, 1971-73; profl. singer Zurich Opera, Switzerland, 1973-75; prof. voice, dir. choirs Sch. Music DePauw U., Greencastle, Ind., 1975—. Profl. singer Indpls. Symphony Orch., 1978-79, 83, 85, Manhattan Philharmonic, N.Y., 1988, Philharmonia of London, 1988, Martinuu Philharmonic, 1995, Indpls. Chamber Orch., 1996-97, PBS, 1982, 91, NPR 1983, 85, Ill. Pub. Radio, 1982, 87, 91, WQXR, N.Y., 1988, Carnegie Hall, 1987, 96, Avery Fisher Hall, Lincoln Ctr., 1988, Barbican Hall, London, 1988, Dvorak Hall, Prague, 1995, Konzerthaus, Vienna, 1995, Indpls. Festival Orch., 1993, rec. (CD Gothic), 1993; condr. various concerts Kennedy Ctr., 1979, Lincoln Ctr., 1984, Music Ctr., L.A., 1986, Carnegie Hall, 1990, 94, 98, White House, 1990, Acad. of the Arts, Honolulu, 1996—, New Eng. Symphonic Ensemble, 1998; contbr. articles to profl. jours. Bd. dirs. DePauw Choir, Greencastle, 1977—. Grantee DePauw U., 1983, 1987, John W. and Janice B. Fisher Fund, 1990. Mem. Nat. Assn. Tchrs. Singing, Am. Choral Dirs. Assn., AAUP, Pi Kappa Lambda (pres. Omicron chpt. 1986—). Avocations: golf, biking, gardening. Home: 522 E Washington St Greencastle IN 46135-1723 Office: DePauw Univ Sch Music Performing Arts Ctr 121E Greencastle IN 46135

IRWIN, WILLIAM RANKIN, lawyer; b. Springfield, Ill., Feb. 26, 1940; s. William Ross and Helen Katherine (O'Brien) I.; m. Alyce-Kaye Moffett, Oct. 1969 (div.); children: Elizabeth, Stephanie; m. Brenda L. Reinertson, Oct. 1, 1983; children: Matthew, Cydney. BA with honors, U. Ill., 1962; LLB with honors, U. Calif., Berkeley, 1965. Bar: Calif. 1966. Asst. Adminstrv. Office of the Cts., San Francisco, 1965-66; assoc. atty., ptnr. Brobeck, Phleger & Harrison, San Francisco, 1966—. Mem. ABA (litigation sect., com. on ins. coverage), Calif. Bar Assn., Bar Assn. of San Francisco, Order of Coif, Phi Delta Phi. Avocations: sailing, travel, reading. Office: Brobeck Phleger & Harrison Spear St Tower 1 Market St San Francisco CA 94105-1420*

ISA, SALIMAN ALHAJI, electrical engineering educator; b. Okene, Kogi, Nigeria, Aug. 13, 1955; came to U.S., 1983; s. Isa Onusagba and Mariyamoh (Anawureyi) I. MSEE, Syracuse U., 1984, PhD, 1989. Elec. engr. Radio Oyo (NYSC), Ibadan, Nigeria, 1979-80, Aladja Steel Plant, Warri, Nigeria, 1980-82; grad. tchg. asst. Syracuse (N.Y.) U., 1985-89; assoc. prof. S.C. State U., Orangeburg, 1989—. Contbr. articles to profl. jours. Bd. dirs. Rev. Ravanel Scholarship Fund, Charleston, S.C., 1990—; pres. Nigerian Student Union, Syracuse U., 1986-89. Mem. IEEE, Material Rsch. Soc., Am. Vacuum Soc., Phi Beta Delta Honor Soc. Office: SC State Univ PO Box 7355 300 College St NE Orangeburg SC 29117-0001

ISAAC, STEVEN RICHARD, communications executive; b. Utica, N.Y., Dec. 19, 1947; s. Anthony Richard and Camille Cecilia (Potaro) I.; m. Martha Cash, Oct. 9, 1982; children: Charles Wesley, Spencer Anthony. BA in English, U. Buffalo, 1969; MS in Comm., Syracuse U., 1973; postgrad. in bus. adminstrn. program, Fordham U., 1978. Prin. Media Design Assocs., N.Y.C., 1973-75; dir. multimedia products The Am. Mgmt. Assn., N.Y.C., 1975-78; ptnr. Tng. by Design, Inc., N.Y.C., 1978-79; founder, chmn. and chief exec. officer Martin Direct, Inc. (formerly The Stenrich Group Inc.), N.Y.C., 1979-96; founder, CEO Martin Interactive, 1995-96; bd. dirs., exec. v.p., COO, The Martin Agy., 1996; pres. mktg. group Cadmus Comm. Corp., Richmond, Va., 1996-97, exec. v.p., 1997—. Author: Words for Phone: Writing Winning Telephone Scripts; contbr. articles to profl. jours. Mem. cmty. adv. bd. 1st Capital Bank. Mem. Am. Mktg. Assn., Direct Mktg. Assn., Richmond Ad Club, Kiwanis (past pres. Ashland Club). Methodist.

ISAAC, WALTER LON, psychology educator; b. Seattle, May 31, 1956; s. Walter and Dorothy Jane (Emerson) I.; m. Susan Victoria Wells. BS, U. Ga., 1978; MA, U. Ky., 1983; postgrad. U. Ga., 1988-89; PhD, U. Ky., 1989. Advanced EMT Athens (Ga.) Gen. Hosp., 1977-79; teaching asst., rsch. asst. U. Ky., Lexington, 1979-87, instr. gifted student program, 1985, 87; instr. evening classes U. Ga., Athens, 1988, temp. asst. prof., 1989; asst. prof. psychology, mem. grad. faculty East Tenn. State U., Johnson City, 1989-98; asst. prof. psychology Ga. Coll. & State U., Milledgeville, 1998—; councilor for Coun. on Undergrad. Rsch, 1999—; reviewer McGraw-Hill Pub. Co., Cambridge, Mass., 1990—. Contbg. author: Aging and Recovery of Function, 1984; contbr. articles to profl. jours. Bd. dirs. Upper East Tenn. Sci. Fair, Inc., 1992-98; advisor to Gamma Beta Phi Honor Soc., 1994-97. Mem. Am. Psychol. Soc., Southeastern Psychol. Assn., Soc. for Neurosci., Sigma Xi (grantee 1987). Avocations: stained glass, photography, canoeing. Home: 3739 Sussex Way Milledgeville GA 31061-4314 Office: Ga Coll & State U Dept Psychology CBX 90 Milledgeville GA 31061

ISAAC, WILLIAM MICHAEL, investment firm executive, former government official; b. Bryan, Ohio, Dec. 21, 1943; s. Charles R. and Ruth L. (Hallberg) I.; m. Carma Sue Dunbar, Aug. 15, 1965 (div. 1993); m. Christine Verney, Nov. 16, 1998; children: David M., Stephanie A. B.S., Miami U. Oxford, Ohio, 1966; LL.D. (hon.), Miami U. Oxford, 1984; J.D. summa cum laude, Ohio State U., 1969. Bar: Wis. 1969, Ky. 1974, D.C. 1986. Mem. firm. Foley & Lardner, Milw., 1969-74; v.p., gen. counsel, sec. First Ky. Nat. Corp., Louisville, 1974-78; chmn. FDIC, Washington, 1978-85; ptnr. Arnold & Porter, Washington, 1985-93; chmn. The Secura Group, Washington, 1985—, Secura Burnett Co. LLC, San Fransisco, 1992; mem. Depository Instns. Deregulation Com., 1981-85, Bush Task Group, 1982-85; chmn. Fed. Fin. Instns. Exam. Council, 1983-85; bd. dirs. Kistler Aerospace Corp. 1998—, The Assocs. Fin. Corp., Dallas, 1998—. Co-author: Bank Holding Companies: A Practical Guide to Bank Acquisitions and Mergers, 1972; contbr. articles on banking to profl. jours. Mem. nat. coun. Coll. Law, Ohio State U., Columbus, 1980—; mem. bus. adv. coun. Miami U., Oxford, Ohio, 1982—; trustee Miami U. Found., 1988-96; bd. dirs. Ohio State U. Found., Goodwill Found. Sarasota. Mem. ABA, Wis. Bar Assn., Ky. Bar Assn., Fed. Nat. Mortgage Assn. (adv. bd. 1989-90), Ctr. Positive Living. Republican. Presbyterian. Office: The Secura Group 7799 Leesburg Pike Ste 800N Falls Church VA 22043-2413

ISAACS, AMY FAY, political organization executive; b. Phoenix, Nov. 11, 1946; d. Richard and Bessie (Wagner) Hamburger; m. John David Isaacs, Oct. 6, 1974; children: Rachel Elizabeth, Stanley Richard. Student, U. Cologne, Germany, 1967-68; BA, Am. U., 1969; MA, Sch. for Internat. Tng., Brattleboro, Vt., 1970. With AID, Washington, 1965-66; tchr. English, Turkish Am. Univs. Assn., Istanbul, 1969; direct mail and fundraising cons., Washington, 1986-87; sr. coord. communications Planned Parenthood Fedn. Am., Washington, 1987-89; various positions Ams. for Dem. Action, Washington, 1969-86, nat. dir., 1989—. Observer del. Liberal Internat., Stockholm, 1984; del. Am. Coun. on Germany, Berlin, Dallas, 1985-87; mem. fin. com. Dukasis for Pres., Washington, 1987-88; mem. quality of care com. Group Health Assn., Washington, 1987-93. Democrat. Jewish. Home: 2018 Pierce Mill Rd NW Washington DC 20010-1023 Office: Ams for Dem Action 1625 K St NW Ste 210 Washington DC 20006-1611*

ISAACS, ANNE ELIZABETH, writer; b. Mar. 2, 1949. BA in English magna cum laude, U. Mich., 1971, MS in Behavior and Environment, 1975. Program dir. Schuylkill Environ. Edn. Ctr., Phila., 1975-76; ednl. programs coord. Alberta Parks Visitor Svcs. Branch, Edmonton, Can., 1977-80; ednl. cons. various, 1981-89. Author: Swamp Angel, 1994 (recipient Caldecott honor and numerous other awards), Treehouse Tales, 1997, Cat Up a Tree, 1998.

ISAACS, DIANE S., English educator; b. Washington, Nov. 11, 1939; d. Arthur William Scharfeld and Lucille Speer Smith; m. Stephen D. Isaacs, June 8, 1963 (div. 1999); children: Deborah, David, Sharon. BA with honors, Smith Coll., 1961; MA, Stanford U., 1972; EdD, Columbia U., 1981. Cert. tchr. English K-12, Social Studies, 7-12, prin., N.Y., N.J. English tchr. George Mason H.S., Falls Church, Va., 1963-65, Woodrow Wilson H.S., Washington, 1966-71; English/Social Studies tchr. Fieldston Sch., Riverdale, N.Y., 1971-74; English tchr. Sidwell Friends Sch., Washington, 1974-78; asst. prof. Afro-Am. studies U. Minn., Mpls., 1978-83; vice prin. humanities Tenafly, N.J., 1985-87; assoc. prof. Fordham U., Bronx, 1983—; English dept. chair Wayne Hills, N.J., 1997—. Sec., treas. adminstrv. unit dist. dept. chairs, 1998—, class meml. chair Smith Coll., 1991—; class sec. Nat. Cathedral Sch., 1957—. Recipient Yauncer award N.Y. State Bd. of Regents, 1991. Mem. NCTE (exec. com. conf. on English 1992-98), CEL, ASA, MLA, AAUW. Avocations: theatre, black memorabilia, travel, folk art. E-mail: dsipst@aol.com. Home: 100 Winston Dr Cliffside Park NJ 07010-3240 Office: Coll of Liberal Studies Fordham U 118 Keating Hall Bronx NY 10458

ISAACS, GERALD WILLIAM, retired agricultural engineering educator, consultant; b. Crawfordsville, Ind., Sept. 3, 1927; s. William Paul and Verna Ethel (Johnson) I.; m. Phyllis Joyce Seaton, Aug. 22, 1948; children: Joyce Irene (dec.), David Gerald, Donald Phillip, Joseph Lee (dec.), Susan Verna, Linda Kay. BSEE, Purdue U., 1947, MSEE, 1949; PhD in Agrl. Engring., Mich. State U., 1954. Registered profl. engr., Fla. Grad. asst. agrl. engring. dept. agrl. engring. Mich. State U., E. Lansing, 1952-54; instr. agrl. engring. Dept. Agrl. Engring, Purdue U., W. Lafayette, Ind., 1948-52, from asst. prof. agrl. engring to prof. agrl. engring., 1954-1964, prof., head dept. agrl. engring., 1964-81; prof., chmn. dept. agrl. engring. U. Fla., Gainesville, 1981-91, prof. emeritus, 1991—; cons. engr. various mfg. and legal firms, 1958—. Contbr. articles to profl. jours. Recipient Massey Ferguson Gold medal Am. Soc. Agrl. Engrs., 1991, Silver medal Max Eyth Gesselschaft, Germany, 1979. Mem. Polish Acad. Sci., Rotary Internat. (dir. 1976-78, Paul Harris fellow 1993). Lutheran. Avocations: photography, travel, music. Office: U Fla Dept Agrl Engring Frazier Rogers Hall Gainesville FL 32611

ISAACS, HAROLD, history educator; b. Newark, Dec. 19, 1936; s. Albert Lewis and Bertha (Wohl) I.; m. Doris Carol Mack, Apr. 25, 1974. BS in History, U. Ala., University, 1958, MA in History, 1960, PhD in History, 1968. Grad. tchg. fellow in history U. Ala., University, 1959-62; instr. in history Memphis State U., 1962-65; asst. prof. history Ga. Southwestern State U., Americus, 1965-70, assoc. prof. history, 1970-79, prof. history, 1979—; bd. dirs. Ga. Consortium, Inc., World Communities Theater. Author: Jimmy Carter's Peanut Brigade, 1977; founder, editor Jour. of Third World Studies, 1984—. Advisor Young Dems., Ga. Southwestern State U., 1965-80; founder, coord. Third World in Perspective Program Seminar Series, 1981—; coord. Black Leaders Lecture Series, 1981. Recipient Tchr. of Yr. award Alpha Phi Alpha, 1982, Outstanding Svc. award Americus Early Bird Civitan Club, 1983, Outstanding Historian and Humanitarian award SABU, 1994, Presdl. Citation for Disting. Svc., 1995, Outstanding Svc. to African Am. and Third World Studies SABU 1996-97, 1997. Mem. Assn. Third World Studies, Inc. (founder, pres., exec. dir., 1983-91, treas. 1983-97, Presdl. award 1992), Latin Am. Studies Assn., World History Orgn., Am. Hist. Assn. Democrat. Jewish. Home: 180 Lakeshore Dr Americus GA 31709-8233 Office: Ga Southwestern State U Dept History and Polit Sci 800 Wheatley St Americus GA 31709-4376

ISAACS, ROBERT CHARLES, retired lawyer; b. N.Y.C., July 16, 1919; s. David and Elsie (Weiss) I.; m. Doris Frances Shapiro, Nov. 20, 1943 (dec. 1982); 1 child, Leigh Richard; m. Mary Lou Anderson, Dec. 12, 1986. BA cum laude, NYU, 1941, JD (Maurice Goodman Meml. prize), 1943. Bar: N.Y. 1943. Asst. dep. atty. gen. N.Y. State Dept. Law, Albany, 1943, spl. asst. atty. gen., 1946; ptnr. Nordlinger Riegelman Benetar, N.Y.C., 1946-71, Aranow Brodsky Bohlinger Benetar & Einhorn, N.Y.C., 1972-79; ptnr. Benetar Isaacs Bernstein & Schair, N.Y.C., 1979-88; vice chmn. Lebanon (N.H.) Zoning Bd. Adjustment, 1988—; adj. prof. law St. John's U. Sch. Law, N.Y.C., 1961-72. Served to capt. U.S. Army, 1943-45, 51. Mem. ABA, N.Y.C. Bar Assn., N.Y.U. Alumni Club. Contbr. articles to profl. publs. Home: 5 Village Grn West Lebanon NH 03784-1506

ISAACS, ROGER DAVID, public relations executive; b. Boston, Oct. 23, 1925; s. Raphael and Agnes (Wolfstein) I.; m. Joyce R. Wexler, Oct. 23, 1949; children: Gillian, Jan. Student, U. Wis., 1943; AB, Bard Coll., 1949. With Pub. Rels. Bd., Inc., Chgo., 1948—, account supr., 1948-51, ptnr., 1951-60, exec. v.p., 1960-66, pres., 1966-75, chmn., pres., 1975-86; chmn. PRB, a Needham Porter Novelli Co., Chgo.; exec. v.p., gen. mgr. Doremus Porter Novelli, Chgo., 1986-89; sr. counselor Porter/Novelli, Chgo., 1989-91, The Fin. Rels. Bd., Inc., Chgo., 1991—; bd. dirs. North Bank, Chgo. Past bd. dirs. Anti-Defamation League Chgo., Jewish Family and Community

Svc., Sr. ctrs. Met. Chgo., Highland Park Hosp., Met. Crusade of Mercy, Suburban Fine Arts Ctr., Asthma and Allergy Found., Spertus Coll. Judaica; community adv. bd. Sta. WBEZ; bd. dirs. v. chmn. Chgo. Crime Commn.; libr. visiting com. Spertus Inst. With AUS, 1943-45. Decorated Purple Heart. Mem. Pub. Rels. Soc. Am. (accredited), Birchwood Club, Monroe Club, Publicity Club Chgo. Home: 1045 Hillcrest Rd Glencoe IL 60022-1215 Office: The Fin Rels Bd Inc 875 N Michigan Ave Chicago IL 60611-1803

ISAACS, SUSAN, novelist, screenwriter; b. Bklyn., Dec. 7, 1943; d. Morton and Helen (Asher) I.; m. Elkan Abramowitz, Aug. 11, 1968; children: Andrew, Elizabeth. Student, Queens Coll., 1965, DHL (hon.), 1996; LittD (hon.), Dowling Coll., 1988. From editorial asst. to sr. editor Seventeen mag., N.Y.C., 1965-70; freelance writer, 1970-76. Author: Compromising Positions, 1978, Close Relations, 1980, Almost Paradise, 1984, Shining Through, 1988, Magic Hour, 1991, After All These Years, 1993, Lily White, 1996, Red, White and Blue, 1998, Brave Dames and Wimpettes: What Women Are Really Doing on Page and Screen, 1999; screenwriter Compromising Positions, 1985; screenwriter, co-producer Hello Again, 1987. Trustee Queens Coll. Found.; bd. dirs. North Shore Child and Family Guidance Assn; adv. bd. Nassau County Coalition Against Domestic Violence; bd. trustees Walt Whitman Birthplace Assn. Recipient Poets and Writers for Writers award, 1996, The John Steinbeck award, 1999. Mem. PEN, Mystery Writers Am., Nat. Book Critic Circle, Poets and Writers (bd. dirs. 1994—, chmn. 1998—), Authors Guild, Internat. Assn. Crime Writers, Feminists for Free Expression, Creative Coalition. Jewish.

ISAACSON, ALLEN IRA, lawyer; b. N.Y.C., Nov. 10, 1938; s. Bernard and Sylvia Isaacson; m. Dena Mishkoff, Mar. 8, 1970; 1 child, David Andrew. AB, Princeton U., 1960; LLB, Yale U., 1963; postgrad., U. Melbourne, Australia, 1963-64; LLM in Taxation, NYU, 1973. Bar: N.Y. 1966. Assoc. Fried, Frank, Harris, Shriver & Jacobson, N.Y.C., 1966-70, ptnr., 1970—; bd. dirs. FR Holdings, Inc., Trebol Internat. Corp., N.V. Fulbright fellow, 1963-64. Mem. ABA, N.Y. State Bar Assn., Assn. of Bar of City of N.Y. Home: 15 W 81st St New York NY 10024-6022 Office: Fried Frank Harris Shriver & Jacobson 1 New York Plz Fl 22 New York NY 10004-1980

ISAACSON, ARLINE LEVINE, association executive; b. Bklyn., Jan. 28, 1946; d. Harry and Sally (Fogelman) Levine; m. Leslie Robert Isaacson, Oct. 31, 1964 (div. July 1970); 1 child, Eric Michael. AAS in Hotel and Restaurant Mgmt., N.Y.C. Tech. Coll., 1983. Restaurant and lounge mgr. Holiday Inn, N.Y.C., 1982-83; mgr. Astors, St. Regis Hotel, N.Y.C., 1983-84; banquet and conf. mgr. Mariner 15 Conf. Ctr., N.Y.C., 1984-85; dir. banquets, confs. and sales Sardi's Restaurant Corp., N.Y.C., 1985-87; dir. catering sales Days Inn Hotel, N.Y.C., 1987-91; catering sales mgr. St. Moritz on the Park Hotel, N.Y.C., 1991-92; dir. catering Roosevelt Hotel, N.Y.C., 1992-93; catering sales mgr. Sheraton Park Ave., N.Y.C., 1993-97; exec. dir. Wharton Bus. Sch. Alumni Assn., N.Y.C., 1997—. Dem. vol. Koch Relection Campaign, N.Y.C., 1985. Mem. Food and Beverage Mgrs. Assn. (sec. 1984-88, 91, exec. dir. 1995—), Roundtable for Women in Food Svc. (treas. 1986-87), Meeting Planners Internat., Soc. Incentive Travel, Hotel Sales and Mktg. Assn., Internat. Food Svc. Execs., N.Y.C. Tech. Coll. Alumni Assn. (bd. dirs. 1986—, v.p. 1986-87). Jewish. Avocations: dancing, travel, theatre, gourmet cooking. Home: 1836 E 18th St Brooklyn NY 11229-2965 Office: Wharton Club of NY PO Box 297-006 Brooklyn NY 11229-7006

ISAACSON, EDITH L., civic leader; b. N.Y.C., Jan. 18, 1920; d. I.A. and Bertha (Evans) Lipsig; m. Selian Hebald; children: Anne Mandelbaum, Selian Jr.; m. William J. Isaacson. Student, Radcliffe Coll., 1936-39, 41; LLB, St. Lawrence U., 1943. Pres. Forest Knolls Corp., N.Y.C., 1960-95, Norman Homes Corp., N.Y.C., 1968-95; bd. govs. Medford Leas Residents Assn., 1990-92, v.p., 1991-92. Author biographies Am. artists; writer club handbooks. Fellow Pierpont Morgan Libr., N.Y.C.; mem. Carnegie Coun. Ethics Internat. Affairs, founders com. Am. Symphony Orch., N.Y., 1962; nat. sec. Women's Am. Orgn. Rehab. through Tng., 1950; trustee Allergy Found. Am.; bd. govs. Medford Leas Residents Assn., 1991; mem. Res. Fund Com., 1992—. Mem. Radcliffe Coll. Alumnae Assn. (chmn. clubs 1966), Harvard Clyb (N.Y.C.), Cosmopolitan Club (N.Y.C.) (bd. govs. 1987—), Radcliffe Club (pres. Washington 1969, N.Y.C. 1959, 63, bd. sponsors 1974).

ISAACSON, MELVIN STUART, library director; b. N.Y.C., Apr. 12, 1949; s. Max and Ida (Savitsky) I.; m. Shelley Allyn Thielle, Apr. 3, 1976; 1 child, Scott Brandon. BA in English, Bklyn. Coll., 1972; MLS, Pratt Inst., 1973. Cataloger Yeshiva Univ., N.Y.C., 1973-76, John Jay Coll. of Criminal Justice, N.Y.C., 1976-77; head cataloger Pace Univ., N.Y.C., 1977-81; head of original monographs cataloging Columbia Univ., N.Y.C., 1982-87; head of cataloging Columbia Univ., Health Sci. Libr., N.Y.C., 1987; libr. dir. Pace Univ., N.Y.C., 1988-94; assoc. dir. librs. N.Y.C. Pace U., 1994—, assoc. univ. libr., 1998—. Mem. ALA, Archons of Collophon, N.Y. Tech. Svcs. Librs. (sec., treas. 1983-84, membership/social chair 1984-85), Assn. Coll. and Rsch. Librs. N.Y., Westchester Acad. Libr. Dirs. Orgn., Beta Phi Mu. Avocations: theater, travel, swimming, physical fitness, reading. Home: 1415 Milford Ter Teaneck NJ 07666-2248 Office: Pace U Henry Birnbaum Libr Pace Plz New York NY 10038

ISAACSON, MILTON STANLEY, research and development company executive, engineer; b. Dayton, Ohio, Apr. 23, 1932; s. Max and Sylvia Mariam (Kirsin) I.; m. Joan Sue Koor, Sept. 4, 1955; children: Julie Fay, Jill Ellen, Jan Lynn. BSEE, Ohio State U., 1955. Registered profl. engr., Ohio. Successively design engr., mgr. quality control, div. mgr., dir. R & D Globe Industries, Dayton, 1957-70; pres. Nu-Tech Industries, Inc., Trotwood, Ohio, 1970—; officer, bd. dirs. Food Svcs., Dayton, 1970-95. Patentee brushless DC motors and medical devices. Bd. dirs. Grace House Sexual Abuse Resource Ctr., Dayton, 1985—, pres., 1985-89; bd. dirs. Temple Israel Found., 1987-90, pres., 1990; v.p. Jewish Fedn. Greater Dayton, 1984—; bd. dirs. Big Bros./Big Sisters of Greater Dayton, 1965-95, pres., 1978-79; bd. dirs. Old Time Newsies, 1969—, pres., 1991-92. 1st lt. USAF, 1955-57. Recipient Dr. Alan F. Wasserman Leadership award Jewish Fedn. Dayton, 1972, Boss of the Yr. award Nat. Trail chpt. Am. Bus. Womens Assn., 1975, Outstanding Pub. Svc. award Sta. WKEF, Dayton, 1979, Outstanding Svc. award Big Bros./Big Sisters of Greater Dayton, 1977, 88, Hon. Judge Carl D. Kessler Meml. award The Grace House, 1991. Mem. IEEE, Rotary (pres. Trotwood club 1989, sec. 1993—), Eta Kappa Nu. Avocations: fishing, traveling. Office: Nu-Tech Industries Inc 5905 Wolf Creek Pike Dayton OH 45426-2439

ISAACSON, RICHARD EVAN, microbiologist; b. Chgo., Oct. 25, 1947; s. Edward Kenneth and June Lorraine (Rosenfeld) I.; m. Barbara Lee Southon, Dec. 26, 1970; children: William Jonathan, Amanda Joan, Daniel Edward. BS, U. Ill., 1969, PhD, 1974. Microbiologist Nat. Animal Disease Ctr., Ames, Iowa, 1974-78; asst. prof. U. Mich., Ann Arbor, 1978-83; mgr. Pfizer, Inc., Groton, Conn., 1983-89; assoc. prof. U. Ill., Urbana, 1989-95, prof., asst. dept. head, head divsn. microbiology/immunology, 1995—; scientific dir. Ctr. for Zoonosis Rsch. and Infectious Diseases, 1996—, acting dept. head, 1997; mgr. panel on animal health and well-being Nat. Rsch. Initiative Competitive Grants Program USDA, 1994-95, panel on ensuring food safety, 1999. Editor: Recombinant DNA Vaccines, Rationale and Strategies, 1992, Gastrointestinal Microbiology, 1997; mem. editl. bd. Infection and Immunity, Washington, 1983-86, Animal Biotech., N.Y.C., 1991—, Am. Jour. Vet. Rsch., 1995—; contbr. over 90 articles to profl. jours. NIH grantee, 1979, USDA competitive grantee, 1982, 90, 93, 95, 97, 98; recipient Rsch. Excellence award Pfizer, 1998. Mem. AAAS, Am. Soc. Microbiology, Am. Acad. Microbiology, Sigma Xi, Phi Zeta. Achievements include discovery and development of first federally licensed recombinant DNA vaccine, EcoBac TM. Office: Univ Ill Vet Pathobiology 2001 S Lincoln Ave Urbana IL 61802-6178

ISAACSON, ROBERT LEE, psychology educator, researcher; b. Detroit, Sept. 26, 1928; s. Emil Alfred and Evelyn (Johnson) I.; m. Susan Doherty, Dec. 16, 1956 (div. 1972); children—Gunnar, Lars, Mary Ingrid, Mary Christina; m. Ann W. Braden, Dec. 31, 1974; stepchildren—Richard, Milly Braden. A.B. in Psychology, U. Mich., 1950, M.S. in Psychology, 1954, Ph.D. in Psychology, 1958. Co-dir. U. Fla. Ctr. for Neurobiol. Sci., Gainesville, 1970-78; grad. research prof. U. Fla., Gainesville, 1977-78; disting. prof. psychology SUNY, Binghamton, 1978—; dir. SUNY Ctr. for Neurobehavioral Sci., Binghamton, 1978-88. Author: Limbic System, 2d edit., 1982; editor: (with others) Expression of Knowledge, 1982, The Hippocampus, vols. 3-4, 1986, The Vulnerable Brain and Environmental Risks, vols. 1-2, 1992, vol. 3, 1994. Pres. Alachua County Assn. for Retarded Children, Gainesville, 1973-75; chmn. dist. III Human Rights Advocacy Com., Gainesville, 1975-77. Served with USN, 1950-53, Korea. Holloway fellow U.S. Navy, 1946-50; grantee NSF, NIH, U.S. Army Surgeon Gen. Fellow APA, AAAS; mem. Internat. Behavioral Neurosci. Soc. (councilor 1991-95, pres.-elect 1998, pres. 1999), Soc. for Neurosci. (pres. cen. N.Y. chpt. 1982-84), Assn. Neurosci. Depts. Programs, Am. Physiol. Soc., Sec. Health Rehab. Svcs. State of Fla. (mem. Blue Ribbon com. 1976). Office: SUNY Dept Psychology Binghamton NY 13902-6000

ISAACSON, ROBERT LOUIS, investment company executive; b. Chgo., Apr. 21, 1944; s. Abe B. and Laverne (Skolka) I. BS, Mich. State U., 1966. Mktg. mgr. Florasynth, Inc., San Francisco, 1966-69; br. mgr. Florasynth, Inc., Lincolnwood and Palo Alto, Calif., 1969-72; br. office mgr. Geldermann, Palo Alto, 1972-76; founder, pres. Commodity Investment Cons., Los Altos, Calif., 1976—, Future Funding Cons., Menlo Park, Calif., 1976—; co-founder, co-chmn. Nat. Assn. Futures Trading Advisors; bd. dirs. Futures Industry Assn. Edn. and Tng., Williams & Clarissa, Inc.; bd. dirs., exec. com., membership com. Nat. Futures Assn.; membership Nat. Futures Assn. Regional Bus. Conduct Com.; v.p. Lind-Waldock Co., Chgo.; pres. Interalliance U.S.A. Contbr. articles to mags and profl. jours. Founder Fun for Lunch Bunch. With U.S. Mil., 1966-72. Recipient Doncheon award Managed Accounts Report, 1984. Mem. San Francisco Futures Soc., Managed Futures Assn. (past co-chmn., bd. dirs.), Asian Pacific Managed Futures Assn. (bd. dirs., founding mem.), World Trading Day CARE (exec. com.), Peninsula Commodities Club, Elks, Kiwanis. Avocations: jogging, biking, horseback riding, flying, sailing. Home: 380 La Questa Way Woodside CA 94062-2428 Office: Commodity Investment Cons Future Funding Cons 380 La Questa Way Woodside CA 94062-2428

ISAACSON, WALTER SEFF, editor; b. New Orleans, May 20, 1952; s. Irwin and Betsy (Seff) I.; m. Cathy Wright, Sept. 15, 1984; 1 child, Elizabeth Carter. BA, Harvard U., 1974; MA, Oxford U., Eng., 1976. Reporter Sunday Times London, 1976-77; reporter, columnist States-Item, New Orleans, 1977-78; staff writer Time mag., N.Y.C., 1978-79; polit. corr. Time mag., Washington, 1979-81; assoc. editor Time mag., N.Y.C., 1981-84, sr. editor, 1985-91, asst. mng. editor, 1991-93; editor New Media Time Inc., N.Y.C., 1993-96; mng. editor Time mag., 1996—. Author: Pro and Con, 1983, Kissinger: A Biography, 1992; co-author: The Wise Men, 1986 (Harry Truman Book prize 1987). Rhodes scholar, 1974; recipient Overseas Press Club award, N.Y.C., 1981, 84, 87. Mem. Coun. Fgn. Rels., Century Assn. Office: Time Mag Time-Life Rockefeller Ctr New York NY 10020

ISAAK, LARRY A., state agency administrator; m. Ruth Isaak; children: David, Corey. BSBA in Acctg., U. N.D., 1973, MBA, 1996. CPA. Asst. legis. budget analyst and auditor N.D. Legis. Coun., 1974-81; with Office of Mgmt. and Budget, 1981-84, state's exec. budget analyst; asst. commr. for adminstr. N.D. Univ. System, 1984-92, vice chancellor for adminstrv. affairs, 1984-94, chancellor, 1994—; student affairs and liaison Student Affairs Coun., N.D. Student Assn.; dir. higher edn. computer network. Mem. AICPA, State Higher Edn. Exec. Officers Assn., N.W. Acad. Computing Consortium (past v.p., bd. dirs.), Nat. Assn. of State Higher Edn. Fin. Officers (chair 1994), State Soc. of Cert. Pub. Accts. (chair, mem. govtl. acctg. com.). Office: Higher Edn Bd 600 E Blvd Bismarck ND 58501-3961*

ISABELLA, MARK DOUGLAS, communication consultant; b. Phillipi, W.Va., Apr. 5, 1962; s. Thomas and Delores (Stockett) I.; m. Elizabeth Ann Bennett, Oct. 8, 1988. AA, Fairmont State Coll., 1982, BS, 1984; MA, Marshall U., 1993. From info. rep. to adminstrv. asst. W.Va. Dept. Human Svcs., Charleston, 1985-89; from sr. personnel specialist to devel. cons. W.Va. Divsn. Personnel, Charleston, 1989—; owner Isabella & Assocs., Charleston, 1996—. Mem. ASTD, Internat. Personnel Mgmt. Assn. Roman Catholic. Office: WVa Divsn Personnel 1900 Kanawha Blvd E Bldg 6 Charleston WV 25305-0009

ISABELLA, MARY MARGARET, lawyer; b. Pitts., Oct. 16, 1947; d. Sebastian C. and Joanna C. (dec.) (Ferris) I. BS in Biology, Duquesne U., 1969; cert. med. technologist, Mercy Hosp., Pitts., 1970; JD, Duquesne U., 1975. Bar: Pa. 1976, U.S. Dist Ct. (we. dist.) Pa. 1976, U.S. Supreme Ct., 1982. Sole practice Pitts., 1977—; instr. Wheeling (W.Va.) Coll., 1978-80. mem. coun. Brentwood Whitehall Assn., Pitts., 1984-90; bd. dirs. Dukes Ct., Duquesne U.; bd. govs. Law Alumni Assn., treas., 1993, sec., 1994-95. Mem. ABA (vice chair sole practice sect., 1994—), Pa. Bar Assn., Allegheny County Bar Assn., Delta Theta Phi (past asst. dist. chancellor). Republican. Roman Catholic. Lodge: Italian Sons and Daughters of Am. (trustee local chpt.). Office: 4101 Brownsville Rd Bldg 200 Pittsburgh PA 15227-3336

ISAF, FRED THOMAS, lawyer; b. Jacksonville, N.C., Nov. 18, 1950; s. Thomas Fred and Rowanda (Maloof) I.; m. June J. Jeffcoat, Aug. 18, 1973; children: Julie, Thomas, Christa. BA, Duke U., 1972; JD, Emory U., 1975, LLM in Taxation, 1978. Bar: Ga. 1975. Ptnr. Peterson, Young, Self & Asselin, Atlanta, 1980-86; shareholder Roberts and Isaf, PC, Atlanta, 1986-94, Roberts, Isaf & Summers, PC, Atlanta, 1994—. Contbr. article to profl. jour. Dir. Pinecrest Acad., 1995—. Mem. State Bar Ga., Cherokee Town and Country Club (dir. 1994-96, 99, sec. 1993, v.p. 1997, pres. 1998), Order of the Coif, Order of Barristers. Office: Roberts Isaf & Summers PC 1100 Abernathy Rd NE Ste 1100 Atlanta GA 30328-5629

ISAKI, LUCY POWER SLYNGSTAD, lawyer; b. Jersey City, Oct. 21, 1945; d. Charles Edward and Ann Mary (Power) Slyngstad; m. Paul S. Isaki, Aug. 26, 1967. BA summa cum laude, Seattle U., 1977; JD cum laude, U. Puget Sound, 1977. Bar: Wash. 1977. Case worker San Joaquin County Welfare, Stockton, Calif., 1968-70, Alameda County Welfare, Oakland, Calif., 1971-73; legal intern King County Prosecutor's Office, 1976-77; law clk. to hon. Justice Hamilton Wash. Supreme Ct., 1977-78; ptnr. Bogle & Gates, Seattle, 1978-99, mem. exec. com., 1990-94; sr. asst. atty. gen. State of Wash., 1999—; cons. Region X, HHS, 1975; chair Atty. Gen. Gregoire's Task Force on Alternative Dispute Resolution, 1993-94. Bd. dirs. King County Family Svcs., Seattle, 1982-84, Wash. State Coun. Crime and Delinquency, 1981; treas. Mother's Against Violence in America, 1994; trustee U. Puget Sound, 1985—, Seattle Youth Symphony, 1995, Ea. Wash. U., 1998—; chmn. law sch. bd. visitors Seattle U., 1984-96; trustee Legal Found., Wash., 1992-95, sec. bd. dirs. 1993, v.p. bd. dirs. 1994, pres. 1995. Dean's scholar U. Puget Sound, 1976-77; recipient Disting. Law Grad. award U. Puget Sound, 1984, Majis award Seattle U., 1997. Mem. Wash. Women Lawyers (pres. Seattle-King County chpt. 1982), ABA (del. ABA Ho. Delegates, 1995-97), Wash. State Bar Assn., King County Bar Assn. (sec. 1986-87, trustee 1987-90, treas. 1995-97, 1st v.p. 1998, pres. 1999—), Wash. Women Lawyers (v.p. 1984), King County Bar Found. (trustee 1987-90), U. Puget Sound Law Alumni Soc. (pres. 1979). Democrat. Home: 2018 Federal Ave E Seattle WA 98102-4142 Office: Atty Gen's Office 601 Union St 900 4th Ave Ste 2000 Seattle WA 98164

ISAKOFF, SHELDON ERWIN, chemical engineer; b. Bklyn., May 25, 1925; s. Harry and Rebecca I.; m. Anita Ginsburg, Aug. 18, 1946; 1 son, Peter D. B.S., Columbia U., 1945, M.S., 1947, Ph.D., 1952. Guest fellow Brookhaven Nat. Lab., Upton, N.Y., 1949-50; with E.I. duPont de Nemours & Co., Inc., Wilmington, Del., 1951-90; dir. engring. research and devel. E.I. duPont de Nemours & Co., Inc., 1975-90, ret., 1990; mem. Nat. Materials Adv. Bd., 1980-82; adj. prof. Columbia U., 1990—; trustee, United Engring. Trust, 1992-98, pres., 1995-97. Vice chair bd. Chem. Heritage Found., 1992-94, chair, 1995-98. With USNR, 1943-46. Recipient Engleston medal Columbia U., 1994, Alumni medal, 1996. Fellow AIChE (past dir., Founders award 1980, Inst. lectr. 1984, materials divsn. award 1986, v.p., pres.-elect 1989, pres. 1990, Thomas H. Chilton award, Wilmington sect. 1994, Mgmt. Divsn. award 1997, Van Antwerpen award 1997), AAAS; mem. NAE, Am. Chem. Soc., Sigma Xi, Tau Beta Phi, Phi Lambda Upsilon. Home: 102 Center Mill Rd Chadds Ford PA 19317-9212

ISAKSEN, ROBERT L., bishop; b. Bklyn.; m. Beverly Sievertsen; children: Elisabeth, Lois. BA, Concordia Coll., Moorhead, Minn., 1957; MDiv, Luther Sem., St. Paul, 1961; STM, N.Y. Theol. Sem., 1971; DD (hon.), Upsala Coll., 1990. Ordained to ministry Am. Luth. Ch., 1961. Vicar St. Timothy Luth. Ch., Chgo., 1960; pastor Bethlehem, Bronx, N.Y., 1961-62, St. Peters, Bronx, 1962-68, Bethlehem, Baldwin, N.Y., 1972-81; Bronx Luth. coord. Planning Assn. of Bronx Luth. Chs., 1968-72; mission dir. Am. Luth. Ch., 1981-87; bishop New Eng. Synod Evang. Luth. Ch. in Am., Worcester, Mass., 1987—; adv. bishop to Bd. for Outreach, Evang. Luth. Ch. in Am., 1988-91, adv. bishop to Ch. Coun., 1992-97; chair Boston Ch. Leaders Covenant, 1995-96; pres. New Eng. Conf. Ch. Leaders, 1993. Bd. dirs. Luth. Immigration and Refugee Svcs., N.Y.C., 1983-87. Address: New Eng Synod Evang Luth Ch in Am 20 Upland St Worcester MA 01607-1624

ISAKSON, JOHNNY, congressman; b. Atlanta; m. Dianne Isakson; 3 children. BBA, U. Ga., 1966. Businessman Atlanta; mem. U.S. Congress from 6th Ga. dist., 1999—; mem. Edn. and the Workforce, Transp. and Infrastructure coms. Winner in a February, 1999, spl. election to succeed Rep. Newt Gingrich, who resigned. Represented Cobb County in the Ga. legislature 17 yrs. Unsuccessful Rep. candidate for gov. of Ga. in 1990. Unsuccessful Rep. primary candidate for U.S. Senate in 1996. Sunday sch. tchr. Mt. Zion Meth. Ch., 1978—. Office: 2428 Rayburn HOB Washington DC 20515*

ISARD, PHILLIP ISAAC, medical nutritionist; b. L.A., May 18, 1949; s. Henry and Claris (Kaufman) I. D Holistic Health, Washington U., St. Louis, 1995; ScD, Washington U., 1996, PhD, 1998. Disc jockey WRTF, WCAU, KRTH, Pa. and Calif., 1967-74; sr. investigator dept. exptl. surgery Hahneman Hosp., Phila., 1968-74, sr. fellow dept. surg. rsch., 1969-72; chief small animal surgery biokinetics rsch. lab. Temple U., Phila., 1968-72; pub. HJ4F Press./Psychic Assembly Books, Bethayres, Pa., 1972—; pvt. practice med. nutritionist Bethayres, 1990—; cons. in nutrition, Northumberland Med. Ctr., Huntington County, Pa., 1992—, Charing-Cross Hosp., Abington, Pa., 1994—. Author: None Dare Call It Cure, 1996; contbr. articles to profl. jours. Vol. various Montgomery County (Pa.) orgns., 1970—. Fellow Am. Coll. Nutrition; mem. Am. Holistic Med. Assn., Am. Inst. Holistic Health (diplomate), Amateur Radio Clubs (various achievement awards 1990—). Uniterian-Universalist. Avocations: aviation, equitation, amateur radio, astronomy, scuba diving. Home and Office: 567 Hoyt Rd Huntingdon Valley PA 19006-8101

ISARD, WALTER, economics educator; b. Phila., Apr. 19, 1919; m. Caroline Berliner, July, 1943; children: Peter, Susan, Toni, Michael, Scott A., Roberta J., Anni K., Arthur. AB, Temple U., 1939; MA, Harvard U., 1941, PhD, 1943; postgrad., U. Chgo., 1941-42; hon. degrees, Poznan Acad. Econs., 1976, Erasmus U., 1978, U. Karlsruhe, 1979, Umea U., 1980, U. Ill., 1982, Binghamton U., 1997. Lectr., rsch. assoc. Harvard U., 1949-53, vis. prof., 1965-70; assoc. prof. regional econs. MIT, 1953-56, assoc. dir. sect. urban and regional studies, 1953-55, dir., 1955-56; prof. econs. U. Pa., Phila., 1956-79; past chmn. dept. regional sci., chmn. dept. peace sci.; prof. Cornell U., 1979—; vis. prof. regional sci. Yale U., 1960-61; exec. sec. Peace Rsch. Soc. (Internat.), 1955; cons. Resources for Future; hon. prof. U. Peking, 1993—, Northwestern U., China, 1993—; co-chair ECAAR, 1996. Author: Atomic Power, An Economic and Social Analysis, 1952, Location and Space-Economy, 1956, Municipal Costs and Revenues, 1957, Methods of Regional Analysis, 1960, General Theory, 1969, Spatial Dynamics and Optimal Space-Time Development, 1979, Conflict Analysis and Practical Conflict Management, 1983, Arms Races, Arms Control and Conflict Analysis, 1988, Understanding Conflict and Science of Peace, 1992, Commonalities in Art, Science and Religion, 1997, Methods of Interregional and Regional Analysis, 1998; editor: Regional Sci. Studies series, Peace Econs., Peace Sci. and Pub. Policy. Fellow AAAS, World Acad. Art and Sci. (pres. 1977-81), Am. Acad. Art and Sci., Am. Geog. Soc.; mem. NAS, Regional Sci. Assn. (pres., Founders medal 1978), Am. Econ. Assn., Econometric Soc., Assn. Am. Geographers, Peace Sci. Soc., August Lösch Ring, Phi Beta Kappa. Home: 3218 Garrett Rd Drexel Hill PA 19026-2912 Office: Cornell U Uris Hall Bldg 436 Ithaca NY 14853-7601

ISAY, DAVID AVRAM, writer, radio producer; b. New Haven, Conn., Dec. 5, 1965; s. Richard Alexander and Jane (Franzblau) I. BA, NYU, 1987. Pub. radio producer Sound Portrait Prodns., N.Y.C., 1988—. Author: (book) Holding On, 1996; co-author: (book) Our America, 1997; producer numerous radio documentaries, 1988—. Recipient Peabody award, U. Ga., 1992, 96, Guggenheim fellowship, N.Y.C., 1994, Robert F. Kennedy Journalism award, RFK Found., Washington, 1995, 96. Office: Sound Portraits Prodns Inc 230 E 12th St # 9H New York NY 10003-9101

ISAY, RICHARD ALEXANDER, psychiatrist; b. Pitts.; s. Milton and Jeanette (Myers) I.; children: David, Joshua. AB, Haverford Coll., 1952-56; MD, U. Rochester, 1957-61; postgrad. psychoanalysis, Western New England Inst., New Haven, 1968-73. Cert. in psychiatry, 1969, psychoanalysis, 1974. Resident in psychiatry Yale U., New Haven, 1962-65; asst. clin. prof. psychiatry Yale U. Sch. Medicine, New Haven, 1967-75; pvt. practice psychiatry and psychoanalysis, 1967—; assoc. clin. prof. psychiatry Yale Child Study Ctr., New Haven, 1975-81, Cornell U. Med. Coll., N.Y.C., 1981—; mem. faculty Ctr. for Psychoanalytic Tng. and Rsch., Columbia U., N.Y.C., 1981—; assoc. clin. prof. psychiatry Cornell U. Med. Coll., N.Y.C., 1981-88, clin. prof. psychiatry, 1989—; pres. Western New England Psychoanalytic Soc., New Haven, 1979-81. Assoc. editor: Models of the Mind, Their Relationship to Clinical Work, 1985; author: Being Homosexual, Gay Men and Their Development, 1989, Becoming Gay: The Journey to Self-Acceptance, 1996; contbr. articles to profl. jours. Bd. dirs. Nat. Lesbian and Gay Health Assn., 1987-97, v.p., 1992-97; bd. dirs. Hetrick Martin Inst., 1992-95. Lt. comdr. USN, 1965-67. Fellow Am. Psychiat. Assn. (gay, lesbian and bisexual issues com. 1987-93, chmn. 1991-93); mem. Am. Psychoanalytic Assn. (cert., chmn. program com. 1981-84), Internat. Psycho-Analytical Assn. (chmn. Am. program com. 1979-81), Phi Beta Kappa. Office: 55 East End Ave New York NY 10028-7928

ISAYEV, AVRAAM ISAYEVICH, polymer engineer, educator; b. Privolnoe, Azerbaijan, Russia, Oct. 17, 1942; s. Isai S. and Basia (Rabayeva) I.; m. Lubov M. Dadasheva, July 26, 1969; 1 child, Daniela. MSChemE, Azerbaijan Inst. Oil & Chem., Baku, 1964; PhD in Polymer Engring., USSR Acad. Scis., Moscow, 1970; MS in Applied Maths., Inst. Electronic Machine Bldg., Moscow, 1975. Rsch. assoc. State Rsch. Inst. Nitrogen Industries, Severodonetsk, Russia, 1965-66; predoctoral Inst. of Petrochem. Synthesis Russia Acad. Sci., Moscow, 1967-69, rsch. assoc., 1970-76; sr. rsch. fellow Israel Inst. Tech., Haifa, 1977-78; sr. rsch. assoc. Cornell U., Ithaca, N.Y., 1979-83; assoc. prof. Inst. Polymer Engring., U. Akron, Ohio, 1983-87, prof., dir. mold tech., 1987—; guest prof. U. Aachen, Germany, 1986, U. Linz, Austria, 1993, Kyoto Inst. Technology, Japan, 1996, Inst. Polymer Rsch., Dresden, Germany, 1997, U Sao Carlos, Brazil, 1997; expert on plastics processing technologies, Malaysia, 1995. Editor: Injection Compression Molding Fund, 1987, Modelling of Polymer Processing, 1991, Liquid Crystalline Polymer Systems Technological Advances, 1996; mem. editorial bd. Advances in Polymer Tech., 1989-90, Jour. Elastomers and Plastics, 1992—, Progress in Polymer Processing Series, 1993—, Jour. Applied Polymer Sci., 1995—, Jour. Polymer Engring., 1997—; contbr. articles to Internat. Ency. of Composites, Ency. of Polymer Sci. and Engring., others. Expert witness U.S. Ho. of Reps., Washington, 1988; expert U.S. Army Rsch. Office, 1991; mem. rev. panel NSF, Washington, 1991, 94. NASA fellow, 1985; recipient Laureate of Young Scientists USSR Acad. Scis., 1970, Cert. of Appreciation, U. Akron Bd. Trustees, 1988, 93, Outstanding Rschr. award U. Akron Alumni Assn., 1996, Silver medal The Inst. Materials, London, 1997; named Disting. Corp. Inventor, Am. Soc. Patent Holders, 1995. Mem. Am. Chem. Soc. (Melvin Mooney Disting. Tech. award rubber divsn. 1999), N.Y. Acad. Scis., Soc. Plastics Engrs. (Cert. of Recognition 1994), Polymer Processing Soc. (treas. 1989-91), Soc. Rheology. Jewish. Achievements include (20) patents for Self-Reinforced Composites, Devulcanization of Rubbers and Decrosslinking of Crosslinked Plastics; fundamental research in polymer and composite processing. Office: U Akron Inst Polymer Engring 260 S Forge St Akron OH 44325-0301

ISBELL, ALAN GREGORY, editor, writer, publisher; b. Denver, June 7, 1951; s. Morris Leroy Isbell and Ida Belle (Lanyon) Whittemore; m. Wendy Sadako; children: Zane Michael, Evan Kele, Reyn Sadao. AA with honors, Coll. Alameda, 1975; BS, U. Colo., 1978. Reporter Douglas County News Press, Castle Rock, Colo., 1978-80; bur. chief Glenwood Post, Glenwood

Springs, Colo., 1980-83; news editor Sun Press, Kaneohe, Hawaii, 1984-86; editor Mauian mag., Lahaina, Hawaii, 1986-87, Haleakala Times, Makawao, Hawaii, 1994, Maui Inc. Mag., Makawao, 1994, Today Mag., Kihei, Hawaii, 1994; pub., editor Maui Tribune, Wailuku, Hawaii, 1994-95; editor South Maui Times, Kihei, Hawaii, 1988-93, 96; gen. assignment reporter Maui News, 1998; owner, operator Write Now! Desktop Pub. and Web Page Svcs., 1995-99; contbg. editor Colorado River Jour., 1981-83; regional corr. AP, 1981-83; Hawaii corr. World News, N.Y.C., 1986-88; freelance writer, Maui, 1987-88; Maui news corr. Sta. KGMB-TV, Honolulu, 1987-88, Honolulu Star Bulletin, 1989-90; editor and gen. mgr. South Maui Weekly, 1999—. Recipient award Colo. Press Assn., 1983. Mem. Hawaii Pubs. Assn. (awards 1990, 92-93, 95), Soc. Profl. Journalists, Maui Assn. Reporters and Editors. Home: 1465 Kilinoe Pl Wailuku HI 96793-9334

ISBELL, DAVID BRADFORD, lawyer, legal educator; b. New Haven, Feb. 18, 1929; s. Percy Ernest and Dorothy Mae (Crabb) I.; m. Florence Bachrach, July 21, 1971; children: Christopher Pascal, Virginia Anne, Nicholas Bradford. BA, Yale U., 1949, LLB, 1956. Bar: Conn., 1956, D.C. 1957. Assoc. Covington & Burling, Washington, 1957-59, 61-65, ptnr., 1965-98, sr. counsel, 1998—; asst. staff dir. U.S. Commn. on Civil Rights, Washington, 1959-61; lectr. Sch. Law U. Va., 1962—, Georgetown U. Law Ctr., 1996—. Bd. dirs. ACLU, 1965-92. 2nd lt. U.S. Army, 1951-53. Mem. ABA (mem. ho. dels. 1986-96, chairperson com. on ethics and profl. responsibility 1991-94), D.C. Bar (gov. 1978-82, pres. 1983-84), Cosmos Club. Home: 3709 Bradley Ln Bethesda MD 20815-4256 Office: Covington & Burling 1201 Pennsylvania Ave NW PO Box 7566 Washington DC 20044-7566

ISBELL, HAROLD M(AX), writer, investor; b. Maquoketa, Iowa, Sept. 20, 1936; s. H. Max and Marcella E. Isbell; m. Mary Carolyn Cosgriff, June 15, 1963; children: Walter Harold, Susan Elizabeth, David Harold, Alice Kathleen. BA cum laude, Loras Coll., 1959; MA, U. Notre Dame, 1962; grad., U. Mich., 1982. Instr. U. Notre Dame, South Bend, Ind., 1963-64; asst. prof. San Francisco Coll. for Women, 1964-69; assoc. prof. St. Mary's Coll., 1969-72; with Continental Bank & Trust Co., Salt Lake City, 1972-83, v.p., 1977-83, comml. credit officer, 1978-83, also bd. dirs. Editor, translator: The Last Poets of Imperial Rome, 1971, Ovid: Heroides, 1990; contbr. to publs. in field of classical Latin lit. and contemporary Am. lit. Trustee Judge Meml. Cath. H.S., Salt Lake City, 1977-84; mem. Utah Coun. for Handicapped and Developmentally Disabled Persons, 1980-81; bd. dirs. Ballet West, 1983-90, emeritus, 1990—, Story Line Press, 1994—, Smuin Ballets, San Francisco, 1994-97; founder Cath. Found. Utah, pres., 1984-86, trustee, 1984-89. Mem. AAAS, MLA, Medieval Acad. Am., Alta Club. Democrat. Roman Catholic.

ISBELL, ROBERT, writer; b. Anderson, S.C., Nov. 26, 1923; s. Henry Pope and Aileen Annette (Dixon) I.; m. Frances Griffin, Apr. 19, 1953; children: Lyn, Andrea, Eden. AB in Journalism, U. S.C., 1948. Mng. editor Florence (S.C.) Morning News, 1950-53; v.p. Bankers Trust of S.C., Columbia, 1963-68, sr. v.p., 1972-76, exec. v.p., 1976-86; pres. Robert Isbell & Co. Inc., Banner Elk, N.C., 1986-93; sr. v.p. S.C. Nat. bank, Columbia, 1969-71; mem. faculty Sch. Banking of South, La. State U., summers, 1971-72. Author: Atlanta: A City of Neighborhoods, 1993, The Last Chivaree, 1996, The Keepers, 1999. Served with AUS, 1943-46, PTO. Recipient Silver medal Am. Advt. Fedn., 1966, Thomas Wolfe Lit. award, 1996, Willie Parker Peace History Book award, 1997; inducted into Lambda Chi Alpha Hall of Fame, 1997. Episcopalian. Home: 1003 Belle Isle Villas Georgetown SC 29440-8532

ISBERG, REUBEN ALBERT, radio communications engineer; b. Chugwater, Wyo., Dec. 11, 1913; s. Albert Gust and Laura Carolina (Thun) I.; m. Dorothe Louise Hall, Feb. 23, 1936; children: Jon Lewis, Barbara Louise Isberg Johnson, Edward Russel. AB in Phys. Sci., U. No. Colo., 1935. Registered profl. engr., Calif. Radio and TV engr. W2XBS/WNBT-NBC, N.Y.C., 1939-42; electronic devel. engr. div. war rsch. Columbia U., Mineola, N.Y., 1942-46; chief engr. KRON-TV, San Francisco, 1946-52; ind. cons. TV engr. various locations, 1952-54; sr. engr. Ampex Corp., Redwood City, Calif., 1954-60; statewide communications engr. U. Calif., Berkeley, 1960-67; ind. cons. radio communications engr. Berkley, 1967—; chair sub-com. for FM radio stereo standards NSRC, Washington,1 960-61; mem. com. for establishing 2500 MHz instrnl. TV svc., FCC, 1965-67. Contbr. to profl. publs. Named Honored Alumnus, U. No. Colo., 1993. Fellow IEEE (chair awards com. vehicular tech. soc. 1984-90, Avant Garde medal and cert. 1991), Audio Engring. Soc., Soc. Motion Picture and TV Engrs., Radio Club Am.; mem. Acoustical Soc. Am., Soc. Cable TV Engrs., Inst. Radio Engrs. (chair San Francisco sect. 1951). Republican. Congregationalist. Achievements include work on guided radio communications in subways, mines, ships and buildings, U.S. and Can. patents for tunnel distributed antenna system with signal taps coupling approximately the same amount of energy. Home: Apt B127 32200 SW French Prairie Dr Wilsonville OR 97070-5454

ISBISTER, JAMES DAVID, pharmaceutical business executive; b. Mt. Clemens, Mich., Mar. 31, 1937; s. Russell Lowell and Clara (Wild) I.; m. Jenefir Diane Wilkinson, July 23, 1960; children: Wendy Jill Kalavritinos, Kirstin Ann Hammond. BA cum laude, U. Mich., 1958; postgrad., Princeton; postgrad. (Woodrow Wilson fellow), 1958-59; MA (scholar), George Washington U., 1966. Asst. to asst. sec. adminstrn. HEW, Washington, 1963-65; exec. officer Nat. Library Medicine, Bethesda, 1965-67, NIMH, Rockville, Md., 1967-70; dep. dir. NIMH, 1970-73; vis. academic London Sch. Econs., 1973-74; dir. U.S. Alcohol, Drug Abuse and Mental Health Adminstrn., 1974-77; v.p. Orkand Corp., 1977-78; assoc. dir. Internat. Comm. Agy., 1978-80; exec. Washington rep. Blue Cross/Blue Shield Assn., 1980-82, sr. v.p., 1982-86; sr. v.p. Consol. Healthcare, Inc., 1986-89; pres. Combined Technologies, Inc., 1987-89; pres., CEO Pharmavene Inc., 1990-97, chmn., 1995-97; vice-chmn. Shire Labs., 1997-98; bd. dirs. Delsys Pharm. Corp., Flagstar Bancorp., Tackson Ltd., chmn.; chmn. Nat. Adv. Mental Health Council, 1974-75, Nat. Adv. Coun. on Alcohol Abuse and Alcoholism, 1974-75, Internat. Conf. on Prevention, 1976; v.p. U.S. Com. Study Internat. Health Care, 1972-74; com. on substance abuse Inst. Medicine, NAS, 1987-90, com. on clin. practice guidelines, 1990-92, com. on dental edn., 1992-97. Editorial adv. bd.: Mental Health Digest, 1970-72, Adminstrn. in Mental Health, 1972-75. Mem. budget com. Washington Met. Health and Welfare Council, 1965-70; bd. dirs. Bedford Springs Festival for the Performing Arts, 1983-87 . Served with USAF, 1959-60, 61-62. Episcopalian. Home: 9521 Accord Dr Rockville MD 20854-4302 Office: Pharmavene Inc 1550 E Gude Dr Rockville MD 20850-5308

ISBISTER, JENEFIR DIANE WILKINSON, microbiologist, researcher, educator, consultant; b. Rahway, N.J., June 4, 1936; d. Edwin Guy and Alvira Marie (Andrews) Wilkinson; m. James David Isbister, July 23, 1960; children: Wendy Jill Isbister Kalavritinos, Kirstin Ann Isbister Hammond. BS, Newberry (S.C.) Coll., 1957; MS in Med. Tech., Jefferson Med. Sch., Phila., 1958; PhD in Microbiology, U. Md., 1977. Med. technologist Princeton (N.J.) Hosp., 1958-60; instr. med. tech. sch. George Washington U., Washington, 1960-62, rsch. asst., 1976-77; rsch. microbiologist Environ. Biospherics, Inc., Rockville, 1978-80; group leader environ. microbiology dept. Atlantic Rsch. Corp., Alexandria, Va., 1980-89; pvt. practice cons. microbiologist Potomac, Md., 1989—; sr. tech. advisor ARCTECH, Inc., Chantilly, Va., 1989-92; adj. prof. George Mason U., 1988-92, rsch. prof., 1992—; cons. Orkand Corp., Silver Spring, Md., 1979-80, U.S. DOE, Pitts., 1988-89. Contbr. to book, articles to profl. jours. Sci. fair judge Montgomery and Fairfax County Schs., Md. and Va., 1975—; bd. dirs. Bedford (Pa.) Springs Music Festival, 1984-89. Va.-Carolina Chem. Corp. scholar, 1953; recipient Congl. High Tech. award Congl. Caucus for Sci. and Tech., 1985. Mem. ASTM (vice chair 1983-92, 99—), Am. Soc. for Microbiology, Am. Soc. for Clin. Pathologists, Cosmos Club, Phi Kappa Phi, Phi Sigma, Chi Beta Phi. Episcopalian. Avocations: reading, music, tennis, restoring old houses and furniture. Home: 9521 Accord Dr Rockville MD 20854-4302 Office: George Mason U SRIF Dept Fairfax VA 22303

ISCOE, IRA, psychology educator; b. N.Y.C., Feb. 1, 1921; s. Samuel and Anna (Leff) I.; m. Louise Koches, July 29, 1951; children: Craig, Neil, Ellen. BA, Sir George William's Coll., 1940; attended, McGill U., 1941; MA, UCLA, 1949, PhD, 1951. From asst. prof. psychology to assoc. prof. psychology U. Tex., Austin, 1951-61, prof. psychology, 1961—, dir. Inst. Human Devel., 1978-96, Ashbel Smith prof. psychology, 1986-96, Ashbel Smith prof. emeritus, 1996—; dir. counseling ctr. U. Tex., Austin, 1968-78, Plan II Honors Program, 1981-86; disting. vis. scientist NIMH, Rockville, Md., 1978-79; cons. VA Hosp., Dallas, San Antonio, Temple, Tex., 1958—, NIMH, Washington, 1961—. Author: Coping, Adaptation, & Lifestyle, 1975; editor: Community Psychology in Transition, 1977, Social & Psychological Problems of Women, 1984. Pres. Human Opportunities Corp., Austin, 1964-67; chair Child Care Commn., Austin, 1986-92; mem. Com. Mental Health of Children, Tex., 1989-92; chair Com. Cmty. Care of Severly Mentally Ill, Austin, 1987-90; vol. psychol. svcs. Staff sgt. US Army, 1942-46, PTO. Decorated Bronze Medal; Gerontology Rsch. grantee Hogg Found. Mental Health, 1983-88, Child Abuse and Neglect Rsch. grantee Children's Bur., 1984-87. Fellow APA (bd. profl. affairs 1978-82, Disting. Svc. award 1980, rep. coun. 1964-67, 82-85, pres. divsn. cmty. psychology); mem. Tex. Psychol. Assn. (pres. 1967) SW Psychol. Assn. (pres. 1968). Democrat. Jewish. Avocations: hiking, cooking. Home: 3300 Greenlee Dr Austin TX 78703-1528 Office: U Tex Austin Psychology Dept Mezes Hall 330 Austin TX 78712

ISDALE, CHARLES EDWIN, chemical engineer; b. DeQuincy, La., Mar. 10, 1942; s. Vester Edwin and Katherine Gwendolyn (Wincey) I.; m. Lucille Brown, Aug. 26, 1962; children: Charles Edwin Jr., Jennifer Denise Hunt, Amberly Lauren. BSChemE, La. State U., 1965; MBA, So. Ill. U., 1978. Registered profl. engr., Ill., La. Chem. engr. Firestone Synthetic Rubber, Lake Charles, La., 1965-69, A.E. Staley Mfg. Co., Decatur, Ill., 1969-72; dir. engring. and maintenance VIOBIN Corp., Monticello, Ill., 1972-80; pres. Control Enterprises, Inc., Savoy, Ill., 1980-95; Control Enterprises, Inc., College Station, Tex., 1995-97; sr. lectr. dept. chem. engring. Tex. A&M U., College Station, 1998—; cons. Nabisco Brands, East Hanover, N.J., 1984—, Clorox, Jackson, Miss., 1987—, Alpharma, Chicago Heights, Ill., 1987—, Chinook Group, Sombra, Ont., Can., 1987—. Active Brazos Valley Cmty. Ch., Bryan, Tex. Mem. AIChE (sect. chmn. 1972-73), Instrument Soc. of Am. (Man of Yr. 1986). Achievements include design of a configurable multivariate control method, a method for removal of solvent to low ppm levels from enzymes, design of a batch wheat germ oil extraction plant, design of an animal gland extraction plant; patents on processing beef lung for production of heparin. Home: 715 Canterbury Dr College Station TX 77845-7903 Office: PO Box 10297 College Station TX 77842-0297

ISDANER, LAWRENCE ARTHUR, accountant; b. Phila., June 6, 1934; s. Irving and Frances (Ford) I.; m. Audrey Goldstein, Apr. 4, 1957; children: Scott Alan, Bart Matthew. BS, U. Pa., 1956. CPA, Pa. Mng. mem. Isdaner & Co. LLC, CPAs, Bala Cynwyd, Pa., 1967—; bd. dirs. EMC Tech. Inc.; founding dir., chmn. bd. Allegiance Bank of N.Am., 1998—. Author: Army Industrial Fund and Cost Accounting Manual, 1958. Bd. dirs. Golden Slipper Club, Phila., 1974—; pres., 1977, Inst. for Arts in Edn., 1991—; internat. bd. dirs. Pop Warner Little Scholars, Phila., 1992—. With U.S. Army, 1957-59. Mem. AICPA, Pa. Inst. CPAs, Germantown Cricket Club, Desert Mountain Club, Kiwanis. Avocation: tennis. Home: 1720 Balsam Ln Villanova PA 19085-1802 Office: Three Bala Plz Ste 501 West Bala Cynwyd PA 19004-3484

ISELIN, DONALD GROTE, civil engineering and management consultant; b. Racine, Wis., Sept. 5, 1922; s. Harry Paul and Rose Ellen (Grote) I.; m. Jacqueline Myers, June 9, 1945; children—Donna Iselin Broom, Michael D., Madeline M. B.S., U.S. Naval Acad., Annapolis, 1945; M.C.E., Rensselaer Poly. Inst., 1948; cert. in advanced mgmt. program, Harvard U., 1971. Registered profl. engr., D.C. Commd. ensign U.S. Navy, 1945, advanced through grades to rear adm., 1971; dep. chief civil engrs. U.S. Navy, Washington, 1973-76, chief civil engrs., 1977-81; ret., 1981; group v.p. Kaiser Engrs., Oakland, Calif., 1981-85. Decorated Legion of Merit (4); recipient Stephen Decatur award NAvy League, 1968, Alumnus Engr. award Marquette U., 1980, Disting. Svc. medal Pres. U.S , 1981. Fellow Soc. Am. Mil. Engrs. (pres. 1978-79); mem. NAE, ASCE, NSPE, AIA (hon.). Republican. Roman Catholic. Home: 2695 Sycamore Canyon Rd Santa Barbara CA 93108-1913

ISELIN, JOHN JAY, university president; b. Greenville, S.C., Dec. 8, 1933; s. William Jay and Fannie Harrington (Humphreys) I.; m. Josephine Lea Barnes, Sept. 8, 1956; children: William Jay II, Benjamin Barnes, Josephine Lea, Fannie U. Minot, Alison Jay, Russell. AB, Harvard U., 1956, PhD, 1965; B.A., Corpus Christi Coll., U. Cambridge, Eng., 1958, M.A., 1963; hon. degree, Adelphi U., L.I. U., Lander Coll. Rsch. fellow Brookings Inst., Washington, 1960-61; sr. writer Congl. Quar., Washington, 1961; corr.-editor Newsweek mag., 1962-65, sr. editor nat. affairs, 1965-69; v.p., pub. Harper & Row Publs. Inc., N.Y.C., 1969-71; pres., trustee Ednl. Broadcasting Corp., Channel 13, sta. WNET, N.Y.C., 1971-87; pres. The Cooper Union for the Advancement of Sci. and Art, N.Y.C., 1988—. Mem. bd. overseers Harvard U., 1970-76; mem. Acad. Polit. Sci., Am. Friends of U. Cambridge; mem. Nat. Geog. Soc., Josiah Macy Jr. Found., Ventures in Edn., Waterford Inst. Recipient Disting. Citizen award trustees SUNY. Mem. Coun. on Fgn. Rels., Metropolitan Club (Washington), Century Club, Harvard Club of N.Y.C. Home: 153 W 12th St New York NY 10011-8201 Office: The Cooper Union 30 Cooper Sq Fl 3 New York NY 10003-7125

ISELY, HENRY PHILIP, association executive, integrative engineer, writer, educator; b. Montezuma, Kans., Oct. 16, 1915; s. James Walter and Jessie M. (Owen) I; m. Margaret Ann Sheesley, June 12, 1948; children: Zephyr, LaRock, Lark, Rodin, Kemper, Heather Capri. Student, South Oreg. Jr. Coll., Ashland, 1934-35, Antioch Coll., 1935-37. Organizer Action for World Fedn., 1946-50, N.Am. Coun. for People's World Conv., 1954-58; Organizer World Com. for World Constl. Conv., 1958, sec. gen., 1959-66; sec. gen. World Constn. and Parliment Assn., Lakewood, Colo., 1966—; organizer worldwide prep. confs. World Constn. and Parliment Assn., 1963, 66, 67, 1st session People's World Parliament and World Constl. Conv., Switzerland, 1968; editor assn, jour. Across Frontiers, 1959—; co-organizer Emergency Coun. World Trustees, 1971; co-organizer World Constituent Assembly, Innsbruck, Austria, 1977, Columbo, Sri Lanka, 1978-79, Troia, Portugal, 1991; organizer Provisional World Parliament 1st session, Brighton, Eng., 1982, 2nd Session, New Delhi, India, 1985, 3d Session, Miami Beach, Fla., 1987; mem. parliament, 1982—; sec. Working Commn. to Draft World Constn., 1971-77, pres. World Svc. Trust, 1972-78, ptnr. Builder Found., Vitamin Cottages, 1955—, (chmn. bd. dirs., 1985—), pres. Earth Rescue Corps., 1984-90, sec.-treas. Grad. Sch. World Problems, 1984— (prof. world problems, 1990—), cabinet mem. Provisional World Govt., 1987—, pres. World Govt. Funding Corp., 1986—, Emergency Earth Rescue Adminstrn., 1995—, co-organizer Global Ratification and Elections Network, 1991— (sec. 1992—), prin. organizer 4th session Provisional World Parliament, Barcelona, 1996, organizer first More Oxygen for the World conf., San Antonio, 1998, now organizing 5th session of Provisional World Parliament, Baghdad, Irag. Author: The People Must Write the Peace, 1950, A Call to All Peoples and All National Governments of the Earth, 1961, Outline for the Debate and Drafting of a World Constitution, 1967, Strategy for Reclaiming Earth for Humanity, 1969, Call to a World Constituent Assembly, 1974, Proposal for Immediate Action by an Emergency Council of World Trustees, 1971, Call to A Provisional World Parliament, 1981, People Who Want Peace Must Take Charge of World Affairs, 1982, Plan for Emergency Earth Rescue Administration, 1985, Plan for Earth Finance Credit Corporation, 1987, Climate Crisis, 1989, Technological Breakthroughs for A Global Energy Network, 1991, Bill of Particulars: Why the U.N. Must Be Replaced, 1994, Manifesto for the Inauguration of World Government, 1994, Call to the Fourth Session of the Provisional World Parliament, 1995, Fifth Session, 1997, Critique of the Report of the Commission on Global Governance, 1995, Using Credit Cards and Electronic Accounting to Initiate New Global Finance System, 1996, Double Jeopardy and the Phytoplankton Project, 1997, The Fallacy of Treating Labor as a Commodity, 1998; co-author, editor: A Constitution for the Federation of Earth, 1974, rev. edit., 1991, also author several other world legis. measures adopted at Provisional World Parliament, 1968-96; co-author: Plan for Collaboration in World Constituent Assembly, 1991, Creator treatment for screen drama History Hangs by a Thread, 1993; designer: prefab modular panel system of constrn., master plan for Guacamaya project in Costa Rica. Candidate for U.S. Congress, 1958, organizer first conv. More Oxygen for the World, San Antonio, 1998. Recipient hon. rsch. doctorate in edn., 1989, Honor award Internat Assn. Educators for World Peace, 1975, Ghandi medal, 1977, Honor award Internat Soc. Universalism, 1993. Mem. ACLU, Am. Acad. Polit. Sci., Fellowship of Reconciliation, World Union, World Federalist Assn., World Future Soc., Earth Island Inst., Populatin Reference Bur., Earth Action, People's Congress, Life Ext. Found., Interfaith Alliance, Internat. Assn. for Hydrogen Energy, Friends of Earth, Wilderness Soc., Solar Energy Soc., Sierra Club, Amnesty Internat., World Resources Inst., Human Rights Watch, Nat. Nutritional Foods Assn., Environ. Def. Fund, Greenpeace, Ctr. for Study of Democratic Instns., War Resistors League, Audubon Soc., Worldwatch Inst., Internat. Assn. Constl. Law, Earth Regeneration Soc., Zero Population Growth, Caner Control Soc., Mt. Vernon Country Club. Socialist. Fax: 303-237-7685. E-mail: wcpagren@aol.com. Home: Lookout Mountain 241 Zephyr Ave Golden CO 80401-9589 Office: 8800 W 14th Ave Lakewood CO 80215-4817

ISEMAN, JOSEPH SEEMAN, lawyer; b. N.Y.C., May 29, 1916; s. Percy Reginald and Edith Helene (Seeman) I.; m. June Lorraine Bang, Dec. 10, 1966; children: Peter A., Frederick J., Ellen M.; stepchildren: Anne Hamilton, Susan E. Hamilton, William C. Hamilton. *Both sets of great-grandparents migrated in the 1840s from German small towns to small towns ranging from Pennsylvania to South Carolina. Wife's grandfather left family dairy farm in Norway and became a butcher in Minnesota. The first American generation included salesmen, wholesalers and dentists. Wife is a designer. Our children's occupations include computer specialists, writers, social workers and money managers.* BA magna cum laude, Harvard U., 1937; LLB, Yale U., 1941; LHD (hon.), Am. U. of Paris, 1997. Bar: N.Y. State 1941, D.C. 1970, France, 1986. Investigator, clk. Comml. Factors Corp., 1937-38; atty. WPB, 1941-42; mng. dir. Iranian Airways Corp., 1946; asso. Chadbourne, Wallace, Parke & Whiteside, N.Y.C., 1946-50, Paul, Weiss, Rifkind, Wharton & Garrison, N.Y.C., 1950-53; ptnr. Paul, Weiss, Rifkind, Wharton & Garrison, 1954-86, counsel, 1987—; counsel Charles F. Kettering Found., 1965-84. *When I die, various taxing authorities will take most of what I've been able to accumulate. Therefore, as I have aged, I have found it painless to give as generously as I can to the persons I love and the causes I respect, and have tried to develop, regardless of cost, a stimulating, far-flung and useful retirement existence. In addition to being a lawyer, Mr. Iseman has had a number of secondary careers, including: serving as managing director of the Iranian Airways Corporation in 1946, contributing to the introduction of public television in the New York area, and serving as acting president of Bennington College in Vermont.* Author: A Perfect Sympathy, 1937; contbr. articles to profl. jours. Sec., bd. dirs. Acad. for Ednl. Devel.; bd. dirs. Victim Svcs., 1980—, also chmn.; bd. dirs. Am. U. Paris, 1987—, also vice chmn.; trustee Bennington Coll., 1969-81, acting pres., 1976. Capt. USAAF, 1942-46. Woodrow Wilson vis. fellow Coll. William and Mary, 1977, Ripon Coll., 1979, Rollins Coll., 1980, De Pauw U., 1980, Fisk U., 1981, Albright Coll., 1982, Hood Coll., 1983, Southwestern U., 1984. Mem. ABA, N.Y. State Bar Assn., Assn. of Bar of City of N.Y., Century Assn., Coveleigh Club, Cercle de L'Union Interalliée Club of Paris, Am. Club of Paris , Phi Beta Kappa. Democrat. Office: 1285 6th Ave Rm 2917 New York NY 10019-6028 also: 62 Rue Du Faubourg, St. Honoré 75008 Paris France

ISEMINGER, GARY HUDSON, philosophy educator; b. Middleboro, Mass., Mar. 3, 1937; s. Boyd Austin and Harriet Herring (Hudson); m. Andrea Louise Grove, Dec. 18, 1965; children: Andrew, Ellen. BA, Wesleyan U., 1958; MA, Yale U., 1960, PhD, 1961. Instr. Philosophy Yale U., 1961-62; instr. Philosophy Carleton Coll., Northfield, Minn., 1962-63, asst. prof., 1963-68, assoc. prof., 1968-73; prof., 1973-94; William H. Laird prof. philosophy and liberal arts Carleton Coll., Northfield, Minn., 1994—; vis. fellow Kings Coll., London, 1966, U. Lancaster, 1991; chair student-faculty adminstrn. com. Carleton Coll., 1970-71, dept. philosophy, 1972-75, 86-89, 98—, ednl. policy com., 1973-74, English dept. rev. com., 1973-74, com. Lucas Lectrs. in Arts, 1977-81, presdl. inauguration, 1987, edn. dept. rev. task force, 1988, Am. studies program rev. com., 1992, mem. tenure and devel. rev. com., 1985-87, Coll. Coun., 1987; acad. vis. London Sch. Econs., 1971; vis. prof. philosophy U. Minn., 1979, Mayo Med. Sch., 1986, 87, U. Lancaster, 1994, Trinity Coll. Dublin, 2000; Belgum meml. lectr. St. Olaf Coll., 1997; panelist divsn. fellowships NEH, 1980, 91; commentator Minn. Pub. Radio, 1981; dir. London arts program Associated Colls. Midwest, 1982; cons. Harvard U. Press, Univ. Calif. Press, Prentice-Hall, Cornell U. Press, Holt, Rinehart and Winston, Vanderbilt U. Press, Jour. Aesthetics and Art Criticism, Dialogue, Notre Dame Jour. Formal Logic, Jour. of Philosophy and Phenomenological Rsch.; external reviewer, evaluator various philosophy depts.; presenter in field. Author: An Introduction to Deductive Logic, 1968, Logic and Philosophy: Selected Readings, 1968, 2d edit., 1980, Knowledge and Argument, 1984, Intention and Interpretation, 1992; mem. editl. bd. Am. Philos. Quar., 1989-92, Jour. of Aesthetics and Art Criticism, 1993—; contbr. articles, revs. to profl. jours. Active Minn. Humanities Commn., 1984-90, chair 1988-89;. Grantee NSF Coun. Philos. Studies, 1968, Bush Found., 1983, Sloan Found. 1984, Faculty Devel. Endowment, 1989, 94, 2000, NEH, 1990, 91; recipient summer stipend NEH, 1971, 78, Disting. Alumnus award Wesleyan U., 1993; Woodrow Wilson fellow, 1958, fellow Univ. Coll., London, 1975, 78, Inst. Adv. Studies in the Humanities, U. Edinburgh, 1985; vis. scholar Cambridge U., 1996. Mem. AAUP (pres. Carleton chpt. 1967-68), Am. Philos. Assn. (program com. western divsn. 1982, task force on the philosophy major 1989-90, program com. ctrl. divsn. 1991, chmn. com. on tchg. philosophy 1993-96, com. to award Matchette prize in philosophy 1993-95, bd. officers 1993-96), Am. Soc. Aesthetics (trustee 1996-99), Minn. Philos. Soc. (pres. 1978-79), Phi Beta Kappa (pres. Carleton chpt. 1968-69). Avocations: classical percussion, jazz vibraphone, choral singing, composition, conducting. Office: Carleton College One North College St Northfield MN 55057-4007

ISENBERG, ABRAHAM CHARLES, shoe manufacturing company executive; b. Lynn, Mass., Feb. 24, 1914; s. Louis and Alice (Lown) I.; m. Thelma F. Sisenwine, Oct. 30, 1938; children: Gerald, Lee Carol, Edward. B.S., Wharton Sch., U. Pa., 1935. Cert. paralegal vol., county ct. mediator, lic. mediator, Fla. With Consol. Nat. Shoe Corp., Norwood, Mass., 1935—; exec. v.p. Consol. Nat. Shoe Corp., 1967-68, pres., CEO, 1968-72, chmn. bd., treas., 1972-74; Vice chmn. shoe divsn. Greater Boston area Combined Jewish Philanthropies, 1968—. Bd. dirs. New Eng. Anti-Defamation League of B'nai B'rith. Mem. Two Ten Assocs. (bd. dirs. 1956—, v.p. 1969—), Am. Footwear Assn. (bd. dirs. 1968, regional v.p. 1970—), Am. Footwear Inst. (trustee 1970-74), Boston Boot and Shoe Club (exec. com. 1967—, v.p. 1969, pres. 1973), Brandeis U. Men's Assocs. (bd. dirs. 1966—), Beta Sigma Rho. Clubs: Hebrew Rehab. Ctr. Men's (bd. dirs. 1970-72), B'nai B'rith (bd. dirs. 1979—). Home: 3450 S Ocean Blvd Palm Beach FL 33480-5999 *I have found that being honest and ethical with those I associated with in business or community affairs was the most rewarding behavior I could follow. I realize that some who act entirely contrary to these principles appear to be very successful, but I would not want success on those terms.*

ISENBERG, HENRY DAVID, microbiology educator; b. Giessen, Germany, Mar. 9, 1922; came to U.S., 1937, naturalized, 1943; s. Gerson and Flora (Gruenebaum) I.; m. Lila S. Grossman, Feb. 15, 1948; children—Ina Pepi Isenberg Stein, Gerald Alan. BS, CCNY, 1947; MA, Bklyn. Coll., 1951; PhD, St. Johns U., 1959. Diplomate Am. Bd. Microbiology (chmn. 1976-79, Disting. Svc. award 1994). Asst. dir. Angrist Labs., 1947-54; chief microbiology L.I. Jewish Med. Ctr., New Hyde Park, N.Y., 1954-97, chief emeritus, cons., 1997—; cons. clin. microbiology Mt. Sinai Med. Ctr., 1997—; cons. Univs. Space Rsch. Assn., 1998—; asst. clin. prof. orthopedic surgery SUNY Downstate Med. Ctr., Bklyn., 1963-68, assoc. clin. prof. orthopedic surgery, 1968-71, professorial lectr. orthopedic surgery, 1971-89; prof. clin. pathology SUNY Health Sci. Ctr., Stony Brook, 1970-89; clin. prof. microbiology and immunology U. South Fla. Sch. Medicine, 1982-87; prof. lab. medicine Albert Einstein Coll. Medicine, 1989-96, prof. pathology, 1996—; cons. in microbiology NASA, 1990—; professorial lectr. pathology Mt. Sinai Sch. Medicine, 1998—. Editor Jour. Clin. Microbiology, 1974-79, editor in chief, 1979-89; editor: CRC Critical Revs. in Microbiology, 1978-81; editor in chief: CRC Forum in Bacteriology; sect. editor Manual of Clin. Microbiology, 4th edit.; editor: Manual of Clinical Microbiology, 5th edit.; editor in chief Clinical Microbiology Procedures Handbook, 1991—, Essential Procedures in Clinical Microbiology, 1997—; mem. editorial bd. Applied Microbiology, 1969-74; contbr. numerous articles to profl. jours. and books; patentee in field. Served with U.S. Army, 1943-45. Named Microbiologist of Yr. Lab World Mag., 1978; recipient Kimble awrd, 1980; Profl. Recognition award Am. Bd. Microbiology/Am. Acad. Microbiology, 1994. Fellow Am. Acad. Microbiology (bd. govs.), N.Y. Acad. Scis., Am. Inst. Chemists, Infectious Disease Soc. Am., N.Y. Acad.

Medicine; mem AAAS, Am. Soc. Microbiology (Becton-Dickinson award 1979, Alexander C. Sonnenwirth Meml. Lectr. award 1989, Disting. Svc. award N.Y. br. 1991, nat. 1996, hon. mem. 1999), Harvey Soc., Sigma Xi. Jewish. Home: 26922D Grand Central Pkwy Floral Park NY 11005-1010 Office: L I Jewish Med Ctr New Hyde Park NY 11042

ISENBERG, HOWARD LEE, manufacturing company executive; b. Chgo., Dec. 21, 1936; children: Suzanne, Marc, Alan. BS, U. Pa., 1958. CPA, Ill. V.p. Conley Electronics, Chgo., 1960-63; v.p. Barr Co. div. Pittway Corp., Niles, Ill., 1963-68, pres. Barr Co. div., 1969-92; v.p. Pittway Corp., Niles, Ill., 1970-92, CCL Custom Mfg. (acquired Barr Co. in 1992), 1992—. Bd. dirs., mem. exec. com. Options for People, Chgo., 1982—; vice chmn., trustee Lake Forest (Ill.) Acad., 1986—; trustee Providence-St. Mel H.S., Chgo., 1985-95; chmn. The Barr Fund, 1993—. Home: 325 Oak Creek Dr Wheeling IL 60090-6741 Office: CCL Custom Mfg 6133 N River Rd Ste 800 Rosemont IL 60018-5175

ISENBERG, STEVEN LAWRENCE, publishing executive, retired; b. Detroit, Oct. 19, 1940; s. A.G. Jerry and Lucille (Potaschnik) I.; m. Barbara Lee Levy, Nov. 26, 1967; 1 child, Christopher Michael. BA in English, U. Calif., Berkeley, 1962; BA in English Lang. and Lit., Oxford (Eng.) U., 1964, MA, 1966; JD, Yale U., 1976. Bar: N.Y. 1976. Asst. to dir. Bur. Budget, N.Y.C., 1967-68; chief staff, asst. to mayor Office of Mayor, N.Y.C., 1969-73; litigator Breed, Abbott and Morgan, N.Y.C., 1976-82; asst. to pub. Newsday, L.I., N.Y., 1982-83; pub., CEO So. Conn. Newspapers, Stamford, 1983-86; assoc. pub. Newsday, N.Y. Newsday, N.Y.C., 1986-90; pub. Sports, inc., N.Y.C., 1987-88; exec. v.p. mktg. L.A. Times, 1991-92; deputy pub. Newsday/N.Y. Newsday, Melville, 1992-95; pub. N.Y. Newsday, 1994-95; Reuters fellow Green Coll., Oxford, 1997; vis. prof. U. Calif., Berkeley, 1996; chmn. bd. trustees Adelphi U., Garden City, N.Y.; lectr. Yale Coll., 1999; vis. scholar, lectr. The New Sch., 1999. Mem. presdl. campaign staff Robert F. Kennedy, 1968, John V. Lindsay, 1972; pres. adv. bd. U. Call. Coll. Letters and Scis., Berkeley; bd. overseers CARE; bd. dirs. Mcpl. Arts Soc.; chmn. bd. trustees Adelphi U., L.I., N.Y. Mem. Coun. Fgn. Affairs, Yale Club, Century Assn. Democrat. Jewish. Home: 151 Central Park W Apt 3N New York NY 10023-1514

ISENBERG, WALTER L., recreational facility executive. Grad., Cornell U. Exec. v.p. ops., founder Sage Hospitality Resources, L.P., Denver. Office: Sage Hospitality Resources LP 1512 Larimer St Ste 800 Denver CO 80202-1623*

ISENBERGH, MAX, lawyer, musician, educator; b. Albany, N.Y., Aug. 28, 1913; s. David William and Tess (Solomon) I.; m. Pearl Evans, Aug. 10, 1939; children: Tess, David William, Joseph. AB, Cornell U., 1934; JD, Harvard U., 1938, LLM, 1939, AM, 1942. Bar: N.Y. 1938, U.S. Supreme Ct. 1945, D.C. 1950. Grad. fellow Harvard U. Law Sch., 1938-39; tutor U. Chgo. Law Sch., 1939-40; various govt. postitions, 1940-48; law clk. to U.S. Supreme Ct. Justice Hugo Black, 1941-42; with office of gen. counsel War Shipping Adminstrn., 1942-43; spl. asst. to atty. gen. U.S., 1944-48; counsel European ops. Am. Jewish Com., 1948-50; legal adviser Point Four Program, State Dept., 1950-51; gen. counsel Pres.'s Materials Policy Commn., 1951-52; dep. gen. counsel AEC; sr. cons. internat. affairs AEC, prin. draftsman charter Internat. Atomic Energy Agy., 1952-56; advisor to Jean Monnet on establishment of Euratom, 1954-55; spl. attaché for atomic energy Am. Embassy, Paris, 1956-61; dep. asst. sec. of state for edn. and cultural affairs, 1961-62; chmn. U.S. del. to UNESCO Conf. on Protection Cultural Property, 1962; counsel to bd. dirs. Communications Satellite Corp., 1962-63; trustee Stern Family Fund, 1963-64; prof. George Washington U. Sch. Law, 1963-65, U. Md. Law Sch., 1970-84; vis. prof. U. Va. Law Sch., 1965-66, 68, 69, Yale U. Law Sch., 1966-67, 1984-85, Am. U. Law Sch., 1969-70, 72, 73-82; cons. Peace Corps, 1966-67; prof. law Salzburg Seminar Am. Studies, Austria, summer 1965; cons. IAEA, Vienna, Austria, European Nuclear Energy Agy., Paris; participated as del., adviser, ofcl. observer numerous internat. confs.; exec. com. 3d Inter-Am. Music Festival; lectr., TV panelist on arts, law, atomic energy, 1956—. Editor: Harvard Law Rev., 1937-38; author articles, book revs., music and art criticism; clarinetist concerts, in U.S. and Europe. Mem. D.C. Mayor's Task Force Arts and Humanities, 1978. Recipient Rockefeller Pub. Service award, 1954. Mem. Am. Law Inst., Am. Fedn. Musicians, Phi Beta Kappa, Pi Lambda Phi (past pres. chpt.). Club: Cosmos (Washington). Office: 2216 Massachusetts Ave NW Washington DC 20008-2812

ISENSTEIN, LAURA, library director; b. Toledo. BA in History, U. Mich., 1971, MA in Libr. Sci., 1972. Libr. Baltimore County Pub. Libr., 1972-81, area branch mgr., 1981-85, coord. info. svcs., 1985-94; founder, prin. LIA Assocs., Tng. Consultancy, 1988—; dir. Pub. Libr. Des Moines, 1995—; mem. OCLC Adv. Coun. for Pub. Librs.; spkr. in field. Mem. editl. bd. Jewish Press; contbr. articles to profl. jours. Mem. cmty. edn. advt. coun. Des Moines Pub. Schs.; mem. Mayors' Select Com. Shared Svcs. Focus Group. Mem. ALA, Pub. Libr. Assn. (chmn., mem. various coms.), Urban Librs. Couns., Iowa Libr. Assn., Rotary Internat., Greater Des Moines Leadership Inst. Avocations: gourmet cooking, travel, reading mysteries. Office: Pub Libr Des Moines 100 Locust St Des Moines IA 50309-1791

ISETT, DEBORAH MICHELE GUNTHER, elementary education educator; b. Allentown, Pa., Nov. 26, 1949; d. William Harrison and Virginia (Quigley) Gunther; m. James Douglas Isett, Aug. 10, 1973; children: David Joseph, Chadley James. BS in Elem. Edn., Kutztown U., 1972, MEd, 1975, postgrad., 1992—; postgrad., Pa. State U., 1992—, Millersville U., East Stroudsburg U., U. Alaska, Pa. State U., Kutztown U. Educator Boyertown (Pa.) Area Sch. Dist., 1972—; elem. edn. educator Kutztown U.; mem. math. guide com. Boyertown Area Sch. Dist., 1992-93, mem. math. curriculum writing, 1997—, mentor for new tchrs.; mem. instrnl. support team (WIST), Washington Elem. Sch., Barto, Pa., 1989-96. Com. mem. Boy Scouts Am., 1973-76; com. chmn. Colebrookdale Twp. Anniversary, 1991; coun. v.p. Huff's Luth. Ch., Barto, 1987, coun. mem., 1984-87. Mem. NEA, Pa. State Edn. Assn., Boyertown Edn. Assn. (mem.-at-large 1982), Berks Talkline. Lutheran. Avocations: travel, reading, fitness walking, swimming, basket weaving. Home: 290 N Funk Rd Boyertown PA 19512-8616 Office: Washington Elem Sch 1406 Route 100 Barto PA 19504-8704

ISGETT, DONNA CARMICHAEL, critical care nurse, administrator; b. Ga., July 12, 1963; d. William Eugene and Sara Lois (Brazier) Carmichael; m. Carroll Eugene Clark Jr.(div.); m. John Thomas Isgett. AD, Floyd Coll., 1984; BS, Ga. State U., 1989; MSN, Med. U. S.C., 1990. RN, Ga., S.C. Emergency nurse Redmond Pk. Hosp., Rome, Ga., 1984-86; charge nurse emergency Piedmont Hosp., Atlanta, 1986-89; flight nurse Med. U. S.C., Charleston, 1989-92; dept. dir. mobile ICU Roper Lifelink Emergency Transport Svc., Charleston, S.C., 1992-97; asst. v.p. mgmt. McLeod Regional Med. Ctr., Florence, S.C., 1997—. Mem. ANA, AACN (CCRN), Nat. Flight Nurse Assn., Emergency Nurses Assn., Phi Kappa Phi. Home: 103 Nez Perce St Darlington SC 29532-4237 Office: McLeod Regional Med Ctr Nursing Adminstrn 555 E Chevis St Florence SC 29501

ISGUR, NATHAN GERALD, physicist, educator; b. Houston, May 25, 1947; s. Moses Abraham and Betty (Winograd) I.; m. Karin Signe Bergsagel, Sept. 1, 1984; children: Abraham Daniel, Benjamin Isaac. BS, Calif. Inst. Tech., 1968; PhD, U. Toronto, 1974. Prof. U. Toronto, 1975-92, William and Mary Coll., Williamsburg, Va., 1990—; leader theory group Thomas Jefferson Nat. Accelerator Facility, Newport News, Va., 1990—. Contbr. over 100 articles to profl. jours. Recipient Steacie prize Nat. Scis. and Engring. Rsch. Coun., Can., 1986. Fellow Royal Soc. Can. (Rutherford prize 1989), Am. Phys. Soc.; mem. Can. Assn. Physicists (Herzberg medal 1984). Office: Jefferson Lab 12000 Jefferson Ave Newport News VA 23606-4323

ISH, DANIEL RUSSELL, law educator, academic adminstrator; b. Loon Lake, Sask., Can., Aug. 28, 1946; s. Leme Jay and Obeline Delia (Sicotte) I.; m. Diane Maureen Cote, Sept. 2, 1967 (div. 1970); m. Bonnie Jeanne Bolger, Dec. 22, 1970; children: Jason Bolger, Rachel Bolger. LLB, BA, U. Sask., 1970; LLM, Osgoode Hall Law Sch., Toronto, Ont., Can., 1974. Bar: Alta. 1971, Sask. 1979; called to Queen's Counsel, 1991. Lawyer H. Lloyd MacKay, Banff, Alta., 1970-71; asst. prof. law McGill U., Montreal, Que., Can., 1972-75; assoc. prof. U. Sask., Saskatoon, 1975-80, prof. law, 1980—, asst. dean law, 1977-78, dean, 1982-88, 96-97; dir. Ctr. for Study of Cooperatives, 1989-95; Fulbright fellow Stanford U., 1995-96. Author: The Taxation of Canadian Co-operatives, 1975, The Law of Canadian Co-operatives, 1981, Co-operatives in Principle and Practice, 1992, Legal Responsibilities of Directors and Officers in Canadian Cooperation, 1996. Pres. Univ. Credit Union, Saskatoon, 1979-80. Mem. Law Found. Sask. (bencher 1982-88), Law Soc. Sask. (trustee 1982-88). Avocations: skiing, running. Office: U Sask, Coll Law, Saskatoon, SK Canada S7N 0W0

ISHAQ, MOUSA HANNA, materials engineer; b. Aboud, Jordan, Dec. 30, 1951; came to U.S., 1977; s. Hanna Yacoub and Salma Azar Ishaq; m. Kristin M. Peterson, Jan. 14, 1978; 1 child, John P. BS in Engring., Am. U., Cairo, 1977. Jr. engr. IBM, Essex Junction, Vt., 1978, assoc. engr., 1978-82, sr. assoc. engr., scientist, 1982-85, staff engr., scientist, 1985-87, adv. engr., scientist devel., 1987-97, sr. engr., scientist devel., 1997—; tech. transfer rev. bd. IBM, 1998—. Inventor in field. Pres. Burlington-Bethlehem-Arad Sister City Project, Burlington, Vt., 1995—, task force, 1991; adv. bd. U.S./Arab Children's Artwork Exch., Burlington, 1991-94; mem. Vermounters for Peace in the Middle East, Vergennes, Vt., 1985—, Resettlement Coordinating Cambodian Refugees, Burlington, 1983-85. Democrat. Lutheran. Avocations: travel, gardening, reading, swimming, fishing. Home: PO Box 341 Essex Junction VT 05453 Office: IBM 1000 River Rd Essex Junction VT 05452

ISHERWOOD, JON, sculptor; b. Eng., May 7, 1960; came to U.S., 1984; s. John and Stella (Stelfox) I.; m. Helen Isherwood, Apr. 2, 1964. BA with honors, Canterbury (Eng.) Coll. Art, 1983; MA, Syracuse U., 1987. vis. artist Cyprus Coll. Art, 1981-83, 91, Canterbury Coll. of Art, 1988, Bennington (Vt.) Coll., 1991, 95, U. Alta., Edmonton, Can., 1991, 92, 96, Franconia Sculpture Park, Shafer, Minn., 1996, Buffalo State Coll., 1996, The Krasl Art Ctr., St. Joseph, Mich., 1997; studio mgr., asst. to Sir Anthony Caro, Eng., U.S., 1982-93; sculpture tech. asst. Triangle Artist Workshop, Pine Plains, N.Y., 1984-86; fellow sculpture dept. Syracuse U., 1985-87, organizer, coord. show, 1986, tchg. asst., 1987; participant Triangle Artists Workshop, Pine Plains, 1988-93, Hardingham Sculpture Workshop, Norfolk, Eng., 1990, Triangle Marseille, France, 1995, Africa '95, Yorkshire Sculpture Park, Wakefield, Eng., 1995; guest spkr. Internat. Sculpture Conf., San Francisco, 1994; disting. vis. prof. SUNY, Plattsburgh, 1994; dir. Triangle Artists Workshop, Pine Plains, 1989-97. Commns. include SUNY, Plattsburgh, 1995, Evening Star Bldg., Washington, 1996; one-man exhbns. include U. Kent, Eng., 1982, Artisera Prints, Syracuse, N.Y., 1985, Comart Gallery, Syracuse, 1985, Arts Ctr., Old Forge, N.Y., 1987, Chapman Gallery, Cazenovia, N.Y., 1987, Schweinfurth Mus., Auburn, N.Y., 1987, Five Points Gallery, East Chatham, N.Y., 1992, Kathleen Laverty Gallery, Edmonton, Can., 1992, David Beitzel Gallery, N.Y.C., 1993, Usdan, Bennington Coll., 1995, C. Grimaldis Gallery, Balt., 1996, Sculpture Ct., South Hampton, L.I., 1997, C. Grimaldis Gall., Baltimore, Weatherspoon Art Gall., North Carolina, 1998, Pyramid Hill Sculpture Park, Ohio, 1999; group exhbns. include Kylos Gallery, Pathos, Cyprus, 1981, St. Augustines Gardens, Eng., 1982, Cyprus Coll. of Art, Lemba, 1983, Great Lingford Art Ctr., Milton Keynes, Eng., 1983, Drew Gallery, Canterbury, Eng., 1983, Comart Gallery, Syracuse, 1984, 86, Wood House Gallery, Leeds, Yorkshire, Eng., 1985, 14 Sculptors Gallery, N.Y.C., 1985, Lowe Art Gallery, Syracuse U., 1986, SUNY, New Paltz, 1986, Hamilton Coll., Elmira, N.Y., 1986, Balt. Inst. of Art, 1986, Arts Ctr., Old Forge, N.Y., 1987, Cornell U., Ithaca, N.Y., 1987, Artists of Ctrl. N.Y., 1987, Schweinfurth Mus., Auburn, N.Y., 1988, Chesterwood, Stockbridge, Mass., 1988, Triangle Artist Workshop Exhbn., Pine Plains, 1988-93, Five Points Gallery, East Chatham, N.Y., 1990, 91, Usdan Gallery, Bennington Coll., 1991, Andre Enunerich Gallery, Top Gallant Farm, Pawling, N.Y., 1991, Lorraine Kessler Gallery, Poughkeepsie, N.Y., 1992, Kouros Sculpture Ctr., Ridgefield, Conn., 1992, Erector Sq. Gallery, New Haven, Conn., 1993, Philip Berman Sculpture Exhbn., Allentown, Pa., 1993, City Poughkeepsie Sculpture Park, N.Y., 1993, Sculptors Drawings, Schenectady, N.Y., 1993, Outdoor Sculpture, Stanford, Conn., 1994, Outdoor Sculpture, Sage Jr. Coll. and Russell Sage Coll., Albany, N.Y., Philip & Muriel Berman Mus., Ursinus Coll., Collegeville, Pa., 1994, Art Omi-Invitational Sculpture Exhbn., Omi, N.Y., 1994, Lorraine Kessler Gallery, Poughkeepsie, 1994, Am. Sculpture, Naumkeag, Stockbridge, Mass., 1994, C. Grimaldis Gallery, Balt., 1995, 96, 97, Yorkshire Sculpture Park, Wakefield, Yorkshire, Eng., 1995, Grounds for Sculpture, Hamilton, N.J., 1995, Triangle Marseille, Ecole d'Art de Marseille, France, 1995, Hardingham Sculpture, Christ Ch. Mansion Lawns, Ipswich, Eng., 1995, Kouros Sculpture Park, Ridgefield, Conn., 1995, 97, Gallery One Ten Green Street, N.Y.C., 1995, Chgo. Navy Pier Art Fair, 1995, SUNY Plattsburgh Art Mus., 1996, 97, Ledgic House, Omi, 1996, Socrates Sculpture Park, Long Island City, N.Y., 1996, Franconia Sculpture Park Benefit Exhbn., Shafer, Minn., 1996, Hualien County Cultural Ctr. Internat. Stone Exhbn., Taiwan, 1997, Chgo. Navy Pier, 1997, Aids Benefit Auction, Hopewell, N.Y., 1997, Pier Walk, Chicago, 1998, Sculpture at Goodwood, Goodwood, Eng., Sculpture, C. Grimaldi's Gall., Baltimore, 1999, Wood St. Gall., Chicago, Verdania Gall., Chicago, Outdoor Sculpture in Wash. D.C.; pub. collections include Grounds for Sculpture, Hamilton, N.J., Evening Star, Washington, Bennington Coll., Vt., Krasl Art Ctr. Saint Joseph, Mich., SUNY Plattsburgh, U. Staten Island, N.Y., Everson Mus., Syracuse, N.Y., Munson-Williams-Proctor Inst., Utica, N.Y., Schweinfurth Mus., Auburn, N.Y., Schine Ctr., Syracuse U., NYU, Phillip & Muriel Berman Mus., Ursinus Coll., Collegeville, LeHigh Hosp., Allentown, Pa.; pvt. collections located in France, United Kingdom, U.S.A., Can., Cyprus. Recipient award Pollock Krasner Found., 1993. Home: 2639 Rt 9 Hudson NY 12534

ISHIBASHI, EIICHI, engineering researcher and educator; b. Fukuoka, Japan, Mar. 7, 1929; s. Hajime and Miyako (Inoue) I.; m. Shizuko Ushijima, Mar. 1957; 1 child, Masahiro. B of Engring., Kyushu U., Fukuoka, 1952, DEng, 1968. Engr. Hitachi (Japan) Co., 1952-62; sr. rschr. Hitachi Rsch. Lab., 1962-69; rsch. mgr. Power Reactor and Nuclear Fuel Devel. Corp., Oarai, Japan, 1969-76; prof. Oita (Japan) U., 1976-92, designated prof., 1991-92; prof. Nippon Bunri U., Oita, 1992—; adviser Kyushu Elec. Co., Fukuoka, 1979-80; dir. Solar Energy Rsch. Lab., Oita U., 1981-83, mem. coun., 1987-89; chmn. Rsch. Commn. on The Energy Problem, Ecol. Fedn., Kyushu-Yamaguchi, 1994—. Contbr. articles to profl. jours. Recipient Tech. Devel. award Atomic Energy Soc. Japan, 1977. Mem. Japan Soc. Mech. Engrs. (prize 1969). Avocations: fishing, classical music. Home: 1-1-35 Miyazaki-dai, Oita 870-1137, Japan Office: Nippon Bunri Univ, Ichigi 1727, Oita 870-0397, Japan

ISHIHARA, OSAMU, electrical engineer, physicist, educator; b. Osaka, Japan, Nov. 15, 1948; came to U.S., 1974; s. Mamoru and Tomoe (Maeda) I.; m. Yohko Miyake, May 5, 1974; children: Reiko, Takeki, Yuko, Sachiko. BS, Yokohama (Japan) Nat. U., 1972, MS, 1974; PhD, U. Tenn., 1977. Postdoctoral fellow U. Saskatchewan, Saskatoon, Can., 1977-80, profl. rsch. assoc., 1980-84; assoc. prof. dept. elec. engring. Tex. Tech. U., Lubbock, 1985-87, assoc. prof. dept. elec. engring. and physics, 1987-89, prof. dept. elec. engring. and physics, 1989—; vis. prof. dept. energy engring. Yokohama (Japan) Nat. U., 1992; vis. prof. dept. elec. engring. and computer sci. Kumamoto (Japan) U., 1993; grad. advisor Dept. Elec. Engring., Tex. Tech. U., Lubbock, 1986-94, faculty advisor Eta Kappa Nu, 1987-94; faculty advisor Assn. Japanese Students, 1990—; bd. dirs. South Plains Regional Sci. and Engring. Fair, Lubbock, 1990—. Contbr. rsch. articles to profl. jours. Japan Soc. Promotion of Sci. fellow, 1974-77. Fellow IEEE Nuclear and Plasma Sci. Soc.; mem. Am. Phys. Soc. (Plasma Physics divsn.), Phys. Soc. Japan, Sigma Xi, Phi Kappa Phi, Phi Beta Delta. Avocations: tennis, astronomy. Office: Texas Tech Univ Dept Of Elec Engring Lubbock TX 79409

ISHII, AKIRA, medical parasitologist, malariologist, allergologist; b. Kochi, Japan, July 11, 1937; s. Katsuhiko and Fusae Ishii; m. Fuyuko Ishii, Mar. 20, 1968; children: Ken, Shin, Taku. MD, U. Tokyo, 1964, D Med. Sci., 1969; MSc, U. London, 1970. Cert. malaria advanced epidemiology. Rsch. assoc. Inst. Infectious Disease, U. Tokyo, 1969-74; asst. prof. Toyko Med. and Dental U., 1974-78, Inst. Med. Sci., U. Tokyo, 1978-79; prof. Miyazaki (Japan) Med. Coll., 1979-84, Okayama (Japan) U. Med. Sch., 1984-90; dir. dept. parasitology NIH, Tokyo, 1990-95; prof. Jichi Med. Sch., 1995—; com. mem. Japanese Internat. Coop. Agy., Tokyo, 1978-89; panel mem. U.S.-Japan Coop. Med. Program Parasitic Diseases, 1991-95, China-Japan Parasitology Seminar. Mem. editl. bd. Japanese Jour. Pub. Health, Med. Entomology and Zoology, Protozool. Rsch. Fellow Am. Soc. Tropical Medicine and Hygiene, Royal Soc. Tropical Medicine and Hygiene; mem. Japanese Soc. Parasitology (councilor, Koizumi prize), Japanese Soc. Tropical Medicine, Japanese Soc. Med. Ent. Zoology (councilor, Soc. prize), Japanese Soc. Allergologists (councilor), Japanese Soc. Infectious Disease (councilor), Japanese Soc. Internat. Health (councilor, mem. exec. bd.), German-Japan Assn. for Protozoan Diseases (coun. mem.), Japan Soc. Med. Entomology and Zoology. Avocations: mountain trips, tennis, golf. Home: 1-14-11 Matsubara, Setagayaku Tokyo 156, Japan

ISHII, ANTHONY W., judge. PharmD, U. of the Pacific, 1970; JD, U. Calif., Berkeley, 1973. Judge U.S. Dist. Ct. (ea. dist.) Calif., 1997—. Office: 1130 O St Fresno CA 93721

ISHII, YOSHINORI, geophysics educator; b. Tokyo, Mar. 14, 1933; s. Kichijiro and Kei Ishii; m. Hiroko Hisamune, Nov. 24, 1963; children: Yutaka, Makoto, Akira. BS, U. Tokyo, 1955, ED, 1977. Exploration geophysicist Teikoku Oil Co., Tokyo, 1955; rsch. geophysicist Japan Petroleum Exploration Co., Tokyo, 1955-67, sr. geophysicist, 1970-71; sr. geophysicist Japan Nat. Oil Corp., Tokyo, 1967-70; assoc. prof. geophysics U. Tokyo, 1971-78, prof. geophysics, 1978-93, prof. emeritus, 1993—; dep. dir. gen. Nat. Inst. Environ. Studies, Ibaraki, Japan, 1994-96, dir. gen., 1996-98; pres. Inst. Environtl. Tech. Promotion in Asia, 1998—; mem. Sci. Coun. of Japan, Tokyo, 1988-91. Author: Introduction to Remote Sensing, 1981, Geophysical Engineering, 1988, Energy and Global Environmental Problems, 1995; co-author several books; contbr. numerous articles to profl. jours. Mem. Engring. Acad. Japan, Soc. Exploration Geophysicists of Japan (pres. 1984-85, 1988-89, Best Paper award, Tokyo, 1976), Remote Sensing Soc. Japan, (v.p. 1981-88, pres. 1990-92), Japanese Assn. for Petroleum Tech. (v.p. 1982-86). Avocations: golf, computer. Home: 8-2-14 Hisagi, Zushi, Kanagawa 249-0001, Japan Office: No 2 Takano 204, Minamiaoyama, Minato-ku, Tokyo 107-0062, Japan

ISHIKAWA-FULLMER, JANET SATOMI, psychologist, educator; b. Hilo, Hawaii, Oct. 17, 1925; d. Shinichi and Onao (Kurisu) Saito; m. Calvin Y. Ishikawa, Aug. 15, 1950; 1 child, James A.; m. Daniel W. Fullmer, June 11, 1980. B of Edn., U. Hawaii, 1950, MEd, 1967; MEd, U. Hawaii, 1969, PhD, 1976. Diplomate Am. Acad. Pain Mgmt. Prof. Honolulu Bus. Coll., 1953-59; prof., counselor Kapiolani Community Coll., Honolulu, 1959-73; prof., dir. counseling Honolulu Community Coll., 1973-74, dean of students, 1974-77; psychologist, pres., treas. Human Resources Devel. Ctr., Inc., Honolulu, 1977—; cons. United Specialties Co., Tokyo, 1979, Grambling (La.) State U., 1980, 81, Filipino Immigrants in Kalihi, Honolulu, 1979-84, Legis. Ref. Bur., Honolulu, 1984-85, Honolulu Police Dept., 1985; cofounder Waianae (Hawaii) Child and Family Ctr., 1979-92. Co-author: Family Therapy Dictionary, 1991, Manabu: The Diagnosis and Treatment of a Japanese Boy with a Visual Anomaly, 1991; contbr. articles to profl. jours. Commr. Bd. Psychology, Honolulu, 1979-85; co-founder Kilohana United Meth. Ch. and Family Ctr., 1993—. Mem. APA, ACA, Hawaii Psychol. Assn., Pi Lambda Theta (sec. 1967-68, v.p. 1968-69, pres. 1969-70, 96—), Delta Kappa Gamma (sec., v.p. scholarship 1975, Outstanding Educator award 1975, Thomas Jefferson award 1993, Francis E. Clark award 1993). Avocations: jogging, tennis, dancing. Home: 154 Maono Pl Honolulu HI 96821-2529 Office: Human Resources Devel Ctr 1750 Kalakaua Ave Apt 809 Honolulu HI 96826-3725

ISHIMARU, AKIRA, electrical engineering educator; b. Fukuoka, Japan, Mar. 16, 1928; came to U.S., 1952; s. Shigezo and Yumi I.; m. Yuko Kaneda, Nov. 21, 1956; children: John, Jane, James, Joyce. BSEE, U. Tokyo, 1951; PhDEE, U. Wash., 1958. Registered profl. engr., Wash. Engr. Electro-Tech. Lab, Tokyo, 1951-52; tech. staff Bell Telephone Lab, Holmdel, N.J., 1956; asst. prof. U. Wash., Seattle, 1958-61, assoc. prof., 1961-65, prof. elec. engring., 1965-98, prof. emeritus, 1998—; vis. assoc. prof. U. Calif., Berkeley, 1963-64; cons. Jet Propulsion Lab., Pasadena, Calif., 1964—, The Boeing Co., Seattle, 1984—. Author: Wave Propagation & Scattering in Random Media, 1978, Electromagnetic Wave Propagation, Radiation and Scattering, 1991; editor: Radio Science, 1982; founding editor Waves in Random Media, U.K., 1990. Recipient Faculty Achievement award Burlington Resources, 1990; Boeing Martin professorship, 1993. Fellow IEEE (editl. bd., Region VI Achievement award 1968, Centennial medal 1984, Antennas and Propagation Disting. Achievement award 1995, Heinrich Hertz medal 1999), IEEE Geosci. and Remote Sensing (Disting. Achievement award 1998), Acoustical Soc. Am., Optical Soc. Am. (assoc. editor jour. 1983); mem. NAE, Internat. Union Radio Sci. (chmn. commn. B, John Howard Dellinger Gold medal 1999). Home: 2913 165th Pl NE Bellevue WA 98008-2137 Office: U Wash Dept Elec Engring PO Box 352500 Seattle WA 98195-2500

ISHLER, MARGARET FISHER, education educator; b. Bellefonte, Pa., Oct. 19, 1934; d. Fred Raymond Fisher and Margaret (Hoffmeister) Fisher Hess; m. Richard Eves Ishler, Dec. 27, 1956 (div. June 1978); children: Frederick, Theodore. BA in English Edn., Pa. State U., 1956, MA in English, 1960; EdD, U. Toledo, 1972. English tchr. Bald Eagle (Pa.) H.S., 1956-57, Marion (N.Y.) Ctrl. Sch., 1957-59, York (Pa.) Suburban H.S., 1959-60; adj. instr. English Pa. State U., York, 1962-64; instr. York Coll., 1964-65; adj. inst. English U. Toledo, 1966-68, grad. asst., 1968-71; from asst. prof. to prof. Bowling Green (Ohio) State U., 1972-90, dir. field experiences and stds. compliance, 1985-90; head dept. curriculum and instrn. U. No. Iowa, Cedar Falls, 1990-96, prof. curriculum and devel., 1997—, acting dir, teacher edn., 1998—; mem. Nat. Coun. for Accreditation of Tchr. Edn. Bd. Examiners, 1998—. Co-author: Creating the Open Classroom, 1974, Teaching in a Competency-Based Program, 1977, Dynamics of Effective Teaching, 4th edit., 1999; contbr. articles to profl. jours. Bd. dirs. Wittenberg (Ohio) U., 1984-86, Luth. Student Chapel, Bowling Green, 1988-91, Ohio Luth. Campus Ministry, Columbus, 1986-87, Christian Cmty. Devel. Bd., Waterloo, Iowa, 1992-96. Recipient Christa McAuliff Showcase for Excellence award, 1990. Mem. Am. Assn. Colls. Tchrs. Edn. (rep. 1985—), Ohio Assn. Techr. Educators (exec. sec. 1980-87, Disting. Educator 1982, pres. 1982), Iowa Assn. Tchr. Educators (pres. 1992-94), Assn. Tchrs. Educators (pres. 1996-97), Phi Kappa Phi, Pi Lambda Theta, Phi Gamma Mu. Avocations: travel, golf, poetry. Office: U No Iowa 618 Schindler Edn Ctr Cedar Falls IA 50614

ISHMAEL, WILLIAM EARL, land use planner, civil engineer; b. Mt. Sterling, Ky., Mar. 11, 1946; s. Charles William and Alice Clay (Trimble) I. BSCE, Duke U., 1968; MA in Urban Planning, U. Mich., 1975. Registered civil engr., Calif., Ky.; registered planner Am. Inst. Cert. Planners. Petroleum engr. Humble Oil (now Exxon), New Orleans, 1968-69; dep. dir. Richmond (Va.) Regional Planning Commn., 1975-78; sr. planner Nolte and Assocs., Sacramento, 1978—, assoc. of the corp., 1984-90, v.p., mng. prin., 1990—; bd. dirs. Nolte de Mexico, SA de C.V./Mexico City. Mem. City Planning Commn., Sacramento, 1983-89, vice chmn., 1985, chmn., 1986; mem. steering com. state of cmty. luncheon League of Women Voters, 1999; mem. exec. com. Sacramento Dist. Coun. of Urban Land Inst., 1996-99; bd. dirs. Sacramento Heritage, 1983-88, chmn., 1985-86; chmn. Urban Design Task Force for Downtown Sacramento, 1986; active Big Bros., 1978-83. Lt. USN, 1969-72. Named Mover and Shaper Heir Apparent, Exec. Pl. Mag., 1986. Mem. Am. Planning Assn. (dir. pro tem 1981-83, Disting. Svc. award 1983), Sacramento Hispanic C. of C. (mem. trade mission to Mex. 1998), Sacramento Met. C. of C. (del. cap-to-cap trip 1986, 87, 88, 97, 98), Chi Epsilon. Office: Nolte & Assocs 1750 Creekside Oaks Dr Ste 200 Sacramento CA 95833-3640

ISIDORO, EDITH ANNETTE, horticulturist; b. Albuquerque, Oct. 14, 1957; d. Robert Joseph and Marion Elizabeth (Miller) I. BS in Horticulture, N.Mex. State U., 1981, MS in Horticulture, 1984; postgrad., U. Nev., Reno, 1992—. Range conservationist Soil Conservation Service, Estancia, Grants, N.Mex., 1980-82; lab. aide N.Mex. State U. Dept. Horticulture, Las Cruces, 1982, 83-84; technician N.Mex. State U. Coop. Extension Service, Las Cruces, 1983-84, county agrl. extension agt., 1985; area extension agt. U. Nev., Reno, Fallon, 1985—; hay tester Nev. Agrl. Services, Fallon, 1988-92; owner wholesale greenhouse Garden of Edith, 1996—. Mem. AAUW, Am. Soc. Hort. Sci., Am. Horticulture Soc., Am. Botany Soc., Am. Horticulture Therapy Assn., Alpha Zeta, Pi Alpha Psi. Avocations: flute, ch. choir, hiking, gardening, macrame. Home: 3900 Sheckler Rd Fallon NV 89406-8202 Office: Churchill County Coop Extension 1450 Mclean Rd Fallon NV 89406-8880

ISLEIB, DONALD R., retired agricultural researcher; b. Paterson, N.J., June 2, 1927; married; three children. BS, Rutgers U., 1951, MS, 1952;

PhD, Iowa State U., 1954. Asst. chem. weed control and plant physiologist Rutgers U., 1951-52, Iowa State U., 1952-54; assoc. prof. farm crops Mich. State U., 1954-61; agr. rsch. mgr. Frito-Lay, Inc., 1961-65, Internat. Minerals and Chem. Corp., 1965-71; from sci. advisor to dir. Mich. Dept. Agr., 1971-74, chief dep. dir., 1974-79; exec. sec. Mich. Toxic Substance Conrol Commn., 1980; dir. bean/cowpea collaborative rsch. support program Mich. State U., East Lansing, 1981-83, assoc. dean, dir. Inst. Internat. Agr., 1983-98; ret., 1998. Mem. Potato Assn. Am. (pres. 1966), Am. Soc. Agr., Crop Sci Soc. Office: Mich States Univ Inst of Internationl Agriculture 324 Agriculture Hall East Lansing MI 48824-1039

ISLEY, ALEXANDER MAX, graphic designer, lecturer; b. Durham, N.C., Nov. 16, 1961; Max and Jane (Skinner) I. BED, N.C. State U., 1983; BFA, Cooper Union, 1984. Designer M & Co., N.Y.C., 1984-87; art dir. Spy Mag., N.Y.C., 1987-88; pres. Alexander Isley Inc., N.Y.C., 1988-93; art dir. Archaeology mag., N.Y.C., 1988—, Forbes FYI Mag., N.Y.C., 1990—; design dir. Nickelodeon Mag., N.Y.C., 1993—; lectr. various graphic design orgns., 1984—. Recipient Herb Lubalin Meml. award Art Dirs. Club N.Y., 1984, more than 200 awards for design and art direction; work is in permanent design collection Smithsonian Instn.; Nat. Endowment for Arts fellow, 1984. Mem. Am. Ctr. Design, Am. Inst. Graphic Arts, Soc. Pub. Designers, Soc. Environ. Graphic Designers. Office: Alexander Isley Inc 4 Old Mill Rd Redding CT 06896-3204

ISMACH, ARNOLD HARVEY, retired journalism educator; b. N.Y.C., Dec. 28, 1930; s. Louis and Augusta (Lacher) I.; m. Judy Daniels, June 20, 1959 (div. 1975); children: Richard, Theresa. BA, U. Okla., 1951; MA, UCLA, 1970; PhD, U. Wash., 1975. News editor Union-Bulletin, Walla Walla, Wash., 1954-56; reporter, editor Sun-Telegram, San Bernardino, Calif., 1956-69; prof. journalism U. Minn., Mpls., 1973-85; dean journalism U. Oreg., Eugene, 1985-94, prof. journalism, 1994-97; cons. Pub. Rels. Ctr., L.A., 1970-75; pres. Comm. Rsch. Ctr., Mpls., 1973-85. Co-author: New Strategies, 1976, Enduring Issues, 1978, Reporting Processes, 1981. Pres. Planned Parenthood S.W. Oreg., 1998-99; dir. ACLU Oreg., 1994—. Sgt. U.S. Army, 1951-54. Mem. Soc. Profl. Journalists, Assn. for Edn. in Journalism, Am. Assn. Pub. Opinion Rsch. Democrat. Avocation: photography.

ISMAIL, RAGHIB (ROCKET ISMAIL), professional football player; b. Newark, Nov. 18, 1969. Student, U. Notre Dame. With Toronto Argonauts, 1991-93, L.A. Raiders, 1993-97; wide receiver Carolina Panthers, 1999, Dallas Cowboys, 1999—. NCAA Indoor Sprinting Champ. Office: Dallas Cowboys One Cowboys Pky Irving TX 75063*

ISMAIL, YAHIA HASSAN, dentist, educator; b. Egypt, Jan. 20, 1938; came to U.S., 1961; s. Hassan Kareem and Horia (Soloman) I.; m. Launa Lutz, Sept. 5, 1968; children: Alan Kareem, Zane Ziad. DDS, Cairo U., 1959; MS, U. Pitts., 1965, DMD, 1973, PhD, 1973. Instr. Dental Sch. Cairo U., 1959-62; asst. prof. prosthodontics U. Pitts., 1962-68, assoc. prof., 1968-70, prof., 1970—, dir. prosthodontic grad. program, 1970—, chmn. dept. prosthodontics, 1973-95; prof., chmn. dept. prosthodontics, dir. acad. affairs Dental Medicine, U. Pitts., 1995—; vis. prof., Paris and Marseille, France, Cairo and Alexandria, Egypt; prof. of implantology and prosthodontics, European U., Brussels; mem. staff VA Hosp., Montefiore Hosp., Univ. Med. Center Hosp., St. Margaret's Hosp. Contbr. articles to profl. jours., textbooks. Bd. dirs. Ridgewood Civic Assn., 1969-73; cubmaster Allegheny Trails council Boy Scouts Am.; coach Youth Soccer League Allegheny County. Fellow Internat. Coll. Dentists, Am. Coll. Dentists, Royal Soc. Medicine, Am. Coll. Oral Implantologists, Internat. Congress Oral Implantologists, Am. Acad. Implant Prosthodontics (pres. elect 1989-90, pres. 1990-92); mem. ADA, Internat. Assn. Dentofacial Abnormalities (bd. dirs., sec., treas. 1973-77), Internat. Congress Oral Implantologists (v.p. 1985-86, pres. 1988-89), Am. Prosthodontic Soc. (internat. circuite courses humanities citation), Pa. Prosthodontic Assn. (past pres.), Prosthodontic Soc. Western Pa. (past pres.), Dental Soc. Western Pa. (bd. dirs.), Am. Coll. Oral Implantologists (pres. 1984-86), Am. Coll. Prosthodontists, Am. Assn. Dental Schs., Internat. Assn. Dental Rsch., Royal Coll. Physicians, Omicron Kappa Upsilon. Republican. Club: Univ. Office: U Pittsburgh Sch Dental Med Pittsburgh PA 15261 *Talk about ideas and philosophies rather than other people.*

ISNARD, ARNAUD, venture capitalist; b. Paris, Dec. 8, 1956; s. Louis and Jacqueline (Rongieras) I.; m. Monica Campos, Oct. 24, 1998. Student, U. Arts and Metiers, Paris, 1978, C. of C. and Industry, Paris, 1979. Co-founding ptnr. Barracuda SARL, Paris, 1978-80; bus. development exec. Thomson CSF, Los Angeles, 1980-83; internat. fin. exec. Thomson CSF, Paris, 1983-84; co-owner, mng. dir. Venture Capital Fund Am., Inc., N.Y., 1984—; co-founder, mng. dir. Coller Isnard Ltd., London, 1990—; founder, mng. ptnr., CEO Arcis Group, Paris, London and N.Y.C., 1993—. Served with French Navy, 1977-78. Mem. Nat. Venture Capital Assn., European Venture Capital Assn., N.Y. Venture Capital Forum, French-Am. C. of C. Avocations: flying, sailing, golfing. Office: Venture Capital Fund Am Inc 509 Madison Ave New York NY 10022-5501

ISOGAI, MASAHARU, women's apparel executive; b. 1939. AMP, Harvard U., 1985. With Ogiya, 1958-76, Jusco Co. Ltd., 1976-88; exec. v.p., gen. mgr. Jusco USA, Inc., 1988-96, sr. advisor, 1996—; dir. Talbots, 1993—; chmn. Revman, 1994—. Mem. Japanese Youth Goodwill Mission to U.S., 1964. Mem. Japanese C. of C. & Industry N.Y. (bd. dirs.), Japanese Am. Assn. N.Y. (bd. dirs.), Assn. for Better N.Y. (mem. exec. com.). Office: Jusco USA Inc 520 Madison Ave 24th Fl New York NY 10022-4213

ISOM, CHARLES L., legislative staff member; b. North Platte, Nebr., Aug. 20, 1974. BJ, U. Nebr., 1997. Dep. press sec. Senator Chuck Hagel, Washington, 1997-98; press sec. Rep. Bill Barrett, Washington, 1998—. Mem. U. Nebr. Alumni Assn. Office: Office US Rep Bill Barrett 2458 Rayburn House Office Washington DC 20515-2703*

ISOM, HARRIET WINSAR, ambassador; b. Heppner, Oreg., Nov. 4, 1936; d. Blaine Eugene and Evelyn (Struve) I. BA, Mills Coll., 1958; MALD in Law and Diplomacy, Tufts U., 1960. Joined Fgn. Svc., U.S. Dept. State, Washington, 1961; various positions in Africa and Asia; dep. chief mission Am. Embassy, Bujumbura, Burundi, 1974-77; consul Am. Consulate, Medan, Sumatra, Indonesia, 1977-78; polit. counselor Am. Embassy, Jakarta, Indonesia, 1978-81; chargé d'affaires Am. Embassy, Vientiane, Laos, 1986-89; sr. assignments officer Bur. Pers. Dept. State, Washington, 1982-84, dir. Korean affairs Bur. East Asian and Pacific Affairs, 1984-86; amb. to Republic of Benin, Cotonou, 1989-92, Republic of Cameroon, Yaounde, 1993-96; ret., 1996.

ISOM, LLOYD WARREN, management consultant; b. Arkansas City, Kans., Feb. 9, 1928; s. Loyd Denver and Cora Louvina (Messner) I.; m. Marjorie Louise Ghramm, Aug. 30, 1950 (dec. Mar. 1984); m. Rita McClain, June 9, 1989; children: Cynthia Louise, John Warren. BS, Drake U., 1952. CLU. Pres., dir. First Security Group, Milw., 1965-68; v.p. mktg. Liberty Life, Greenville, S.C., 1968-71; pres., dir. Am. Health & Life, Balt., 1971-75, Pierce Nat. Life, L.A., 1975-77, Continental Life & Acc. Ins. Co., Boise, 1978-80; pres., owner Ins. Mgmt., Inc., Boise, 1980-82; v.p. Am. Gen. Corp., Houston, 1982-88; pres., dir. Sierra Health and Life Ins. Co., Las Vegas, 1988-90; mgmt. cons., ins. mgmt. and mktg. Las Vegas, 1990—; bd. dirs. Sierra Health & Life, Las Vegas; chmn. adv. bd. for risk and ins. mgmt. U. Nev., Las Vegas, 1995-96. Chmn. project 90 Coll. of Idaho, 1980—. With USN, 1946-48. Mem. Am. Coll. Life Underwriters. Republican. Presbyterian. Avocations: golf, swimming, spectator sports.

ISOM, REBECCA JAYNE, newspaper editor, newspaper columnist; b. Hinton, W.Va., Oct. 25, 1964; d. Richard Thomas and Lee Anna (Williams) Harvey; m. John Wilson Isom, Dec. 22, 1986. BA magna cum laude, Ferrum Coll., 1987. Graphic artist Swift Creek Press, Hopewell, Va., 1987-88; TV ops. mgr. Channel 2 TV, Prince George, Va., 1988-90; radio announcer WHAP Radio, Hopewell, 1990-91; news reporter The Hopewell News, 1991-94, features editor, 1994-96, mng. editor, 1996-98; copy editor The Press-Index, Petersburg, Va., 1998—; mem. quality control com. The Hopewell News, 1993-98. Author (play) Puss in Boots, 1985; editor Spotlight, 1994-95, The Hopewell News, 1996—, The Fort Lee Trumpeter, 1996—. Judge Hopewell Jaycees Christmas Parade, 1992, Allied Signal Calendar Contest, Hopewell, 1992, 96. Mem. Va. Press Assn. (1st place spot news writing 1992, 2nd place column writing 1992, 3rd place lifestyles page design 1994, 3rd place column writing 1996), So. Newspaper Pubs. Assn. Avocations: sculpture, creative writing. Office: The Progress Index 15 Franklin St Petersburg VA 23803

ISOM, VIRGINIA ANNETTE VEAZEY, nursing educator; b. Tallapoosa County, Ala., Nov. 19, 1936; d. Jimmy L. and Bessie (Pearson) Veazey; m. William G. Isom, May 1959; children: William Gary, Marleah, James Leland. BSN, Tuskegee Inst., 1959; MSN, Syracuse U., 1974; PhD, Howard U., 1997. Cert. in nursing adminstrn. Am. Nurses' Credentialing Ctr.; cert. med.-surg. nursing. Asst. prof. med. surg. nursing Howard U. Coll. Nursing, Washington, 1975-86; edn. and tng. quality assurance coord. Howard U., Washington, 1986-87; patient care coord. Howard U. Hosp., Washington, 1987-88, coord. for spl. projects, 1988-90; prof. nursing Prince George's C.C., Largo, Md., 1992—. Contbr. articles to profl. jours. Mem. ANA (cert. clin. specialist med. surg. nursing), Md. Nurses' Assn., Sigma Theta Tau. Home: 534 Round Table Dr Fort Washington MD 20744-5638 Office: Prince George's C C Dept Nursing Largo MD 20772

ISON, CHRISTOPHER JOHN, investigative reporter; b. Crandon, Wis., Aug. 20, 1957; s. Luther Arnold Jr. and Penny (Koyn) I.; m. Nancy Cassutt, Aug. 1, 1988. BA, U. Minn., 1983. Editor in chief Minn. Daily, Mpls., 1982-83; reporter News-Tribune & Herald, Duluth, Minn., 1983-86, Star Tribune, Mpls., 1986—. Recipient Pulitzer prize for investigative reporting, 1990. Mem. Investigative Reporters and Editors. Office: Star Tribune 425 Portland Ave Minneapolis MN 55488-0002*

ISPASS, ALAN BENJAMIN, utilities executive; b. N.Y.C., July 18, 1953; s. Murray and Judy (Spielvogel) I.; m. Adele R. Rochlin, June 8, 1975; children: Marc Stephen, Laura Beth. BCE, The Cooper Union, 1974; M in Environ. Engring., Manhattan Coll., 1975. Registered profl. engr., Fla., Va. Asst. engr. Riddick Assocs., N.Y.C., 1970-74, engr., 1974-77; engr. Planning Rsch. Corp., Cocoa Beach, Fla., 1977-79; sr. engr. Planning Rsch. Corp., Cocoa Beach, 1979-80; process engr. Orange County Utilities, Orlando, Fla., 1980-82, chief engr., 1982-83, engr. mgr., 1983-84, dep. dir., 1984-85, dir., 1985-99; prin. Hagler Bailly, 1999—; Judge Pollution Engring. Awards, 1979, Internat. Sci. and Engring. Fair, 1991, Fed. Engring. of Yr. Award, 1992, Fla. Inst. Cons. Engrs. Excellence Awards, 1993. Co-author papers and presentation on utility mgmt. and competitiveness. Dep. dir. Civil Def. Civil Emergency, 1985-95; mem. Orange County Vol. Adv. Coun., 1991-95, Teach-in 2000, Orange County Sch. Bd., 1992-93, Seminole County Water Resources Task Force, 1992-94, civil and environ. dept. acad. adv. com. U. Ctrl. Fla., 1992—, environ. tech. adv. com. Seminole C.C., 1993—, instl. rev. bd. Orlando Regional Med. Ctr., 1993—. Recipient award Civil Engring. Dept., Cooper Union, 1971; named one of Top 10 Pub. Works Leaders of Yr. Am. Pub. Works Assn., 1992. Fellow Fla. Engring. Soc. (mem. various coms., bd. dirs. 1985-86, 91-94, mem. exec. com. 1985-86, 91-94, v.p. 1991-94, Fla. Young Engr. of Yr. 1988, Engr. of Yr. 1992); mem. NSPE (mem. various coms., gov. 1985-87, exec. bd. 1987-93, vice chmn. 1987-89, chmn.-elect 1989-90, chmn. 1990-91, govt. practice divsn. v.p. 1990-91, chmn. exec. appt. subcom. 1991, chmn. legis. net subcom. 1991-93), Commn. Legis. and Govt. Rels., Am. Acad. Environ. Engrs. (diplomate, admissions com. 1993—, dep. chair admissions com. 1994—), Am. Water Works Assn. (mem. Fla. edn. com. 1986-87), Water Environment Fedn. (instr. for short sch. 1981, 83, chmn. privatization subcom. 1996—), Assn. Met. Water Agys. (mem. regulatory oversight com. 1986-87, mem. legis. com. 1987-96, mem. source water protection com. 1996—), Assn. Met. Sewerage Agys. (mem. resolutions com. 1986-92, chair competitive mgmt. com. 1996-99, pres.'s award 1998), Solid Waste Assn. N. Am., Am. Pub. Works Assn., Humane Soc. Seminole County, Wekiva Hunt Club Cmty. Assn. (crimewatch coord. 1982-83), Order of the Engr., Tau Beta Pi, Chi Epsilon. Home: PO Box 915411 Longwood FL 32791-5411 Office: Hagler Bailly 1800 Pembrook Dr Ste 300 Orlando FL 32810

ISQUITH, FRED TAYLOR, lawyer; b. N.Y.C., June 6, 1947; s. Stanley and Rita (Hoskwith) I.; m. Susan Nora Goldberg, May 23, 1976; children: Fred, Rebecca. BA, Brooklyn Coll. of CUNY, 1968; JD, Columbia U., 1971. Bar: N.Y. 1972, D.C. 1976, U.S. Dist. Ct. (so. and ea. dists.) N.Y. 1975, U.S. Dist. Ct. (no. dist.) N.Y. 1988, U.S. Dist. Ct. (we. dist.) Mich. 1992, U.S. Dist. Ct. Ariz. 1994, U.S. Dist. Ct. (ctrl. dist.) Ill. 1996, U.S. Ct. Appeals (2d cir.) 1975, U.S. Ct. Appeals (8th cir.) 1985, U.S. Ct. Appeals (3d cir.) 1986, U.S. Ct. Appeals (4th cir.) 1990, U.S. Supreme Ct. 1983. Assoc. Fulbright & Jaworski, N.Y.C., 1971-75, Kaye Scholer et al, N.Y.C., 1975-80; ptnr. Wolf Haldenstein Adler Freeman & Herz, N.Y.C., 1980—; bd. trustees St. Chad's Coll. Found.; bd. dirs. 103 East 84th St. Corp., N.Y.C., Sheinkopf Communications, Ltd.; lectr. Am. Conf. Inst., N.Y. State Bar Assn.; mediator Supreme Ct. State N.Y. County N.Y. Comml. Divsn.; arbitrator Am. Arbitration Assn. Author: An Introduction to Securities Arbitration, 1994, Real Estate Exit Strategies, 1994; editor, weekly columnist The Class Act. Mem. ABA, N.Y. State Bar Assn. (coms. on securities and legis.), N.Y. County Lawyers Assn. (chair bus. torts), D.C. Bar Assn., Assn. of Bar of City of N.Y., Bklyn. Bar Assn. (civil practice law and rules com., legis. com. and fed. ct. coms.), Columbia Club. Office: Wolf Haldenstein Adler Freeman & Herz 270 Madison Ave New York NY 10016-0601

ISRAEL, ALLEN D., lawyer; b. Seattle, Nov. 28, 1946; m. Nettie Israel. BSME, U. Wash., 1968, MBA, 1971, JD, 1978. Bar: Wash. 1978. Ptnr. Foster Pepper & Shefelman, PLLC, Seattle, 1978—. Office: Foster Pepper & Shefelman PLLC 1111 3rd Ave Ste 3400 Seattle WA 98101-3299

ISRAEL, BARRY JOHN, lawyer; b. Rockford, Ill., Mar. 14, 1946; s. Robert John and Bettie Jane (Erickson) I.; m. Lynne Charlene Thomsen; children: Alison, Ashley, Brenna. BA, U. So. Calif., L.A., 1968; JD, George Washington U., 1974. Bar: Calif. 1975, D.C. 1976, U.S. Supreme Ct. 1978, U.S. Dist. Ct. Mariana Islands 1985. Assoc. Clifford & Warnke, Washington, 1975-83; ptnr. Stovall, Spradlin, Armstrong & Israel, Washington, 1983-86, Dorsey & Whitney, Washington, 1988-92, Stroock, Stroock & Lavan, Washington, 1992-95; spl. counsel, pres. Federated States of Micronesia, 1982-84; spl. asst. atty. gen. Territory Guam, 1990-95; bd. dirs. Bank of the Federated States of Micronesia. Author: (guides) Investment Guides to the Federated States of Micronesia and the Republic of the Marshall Islands, 1989. 1st lt. U.S. Army, 1969-72. Democrat. Avocations: travel, tennis. Home: 1310 Shoreline Dr Santa Barbara CA 93109-2124

ISRAEL, DAVID, journalist, screenwriter, producer; b. N.Y.C., Mar. 17, 1951; s. Hyman and Edith Oringer I.; m. Lindy De Koven, Aug. 8, 1987. B.S. in Journalism, Northwestern U., 1973. Reporter Chgo. Daily News, 1973-75; columnist Washington Star, 1975-78, Chgo. Tribune, 1978-81, Los Angeles Herald Examiner, 1981-84; chmn., pres. Big Prodns., Inc., Los Angeles; producer, writer OCC Prodns., Los Angeles, 1985-88; exec. prodr., writer Lorimar Television, L.A., 1988-92, Paramount Pictures, Hollywood, 1992-93; writer, exec. prodr. Stephen J. Cannell Prodns., Inc., Hollywood, 1993-95; dir. office of Pres., Los Angeles Olympic Organizing Com., 1984; exec. prodr. House of Frankenstein, NBC, Universal, 1997, exec. prodr. Mutiny, NBC, 1999. supervising prodr., writer: A Comedy Salute to Baseball, NBC, 1985; supervising prodr., writer: Fast Copy, NBC, 1985-86; co-creator, supervising prodr.: Crimes of the Century, 1987-88; co-exec. prodr., writer: Midnight Caller, NBC, Lorimar TV, 1988-91, The Untouchables, Paramount TV, 1992-93; exec. prodr., writer: Jake Lassiter: Justice on the Bayou, NBC, Stephen J. Cannell Prodns., 1995; exec. prodr., writer: Pandora's Clock, NBC, Citadel Entertainment, 1996; consulting prodr., writer, Turks, CBS Studios, U.S.A., 1998—. Mem. AFTRA, Writers Guild Am., Chgo. Athletic Assn. Office: c/o Jared Levine, Nelson Guggenheim Felker & Levine 10880 WilshireBlvd Ste 2070 Los Angeles CA 90024

ISRAEL, JEROLD HARVEY, law educator; b. Cleveland, Ohio, June 14, 1934; s. Harry and Florence S. (Schoenfeld) I.; m. Tanya M. Boyarsky, Sept. 28, 1959; children—Lewis, Laurie, Daniel. BBA, Western Res. U., 1956; LLB, Yale U., 1959. Bar: Ohio 1959, Mich. 1967. Law clk. to Justice Potter Stewart U.S. Supreme Ct., Washington, 1959-61; asst. prof. Law Sch. U. Mich., Ann Arbor, 1961-64, assoc. prof., 1964-67, prof., 1967-96, Alene and Allan F. Smith prof., 1983-96, prof. emeritus, 1996—; Ed Rood Eminent Scholar in trial advocacy and procedure U. Fla. Coll. Law, Gainesville, 1993—; exec. sec. Mich. Law Revision Commn., 1972-92; co-reporter Uniform Rules of Criminal Procedure, Nat. Conf. Commrs. Uniform State Laws; Alene and Allen F. Smith prof. emeritus U. Mich., Ann Arbor, 1996—. Co-author: Criminal Procedure Treatise, 1984, Criminal Procedure Hornbook, 1992, Modern Criminal Procedure, 1994, Criminal Procedure and the Constitution, 1998, White Collar Crime, 1996. Office: U Fla Law Sch Gainesville FL 32611-2038

ISRAEL, LESLEY LOWE, political consultant; b. Phila., July 21, 1938; d. Herman Albert and Florence (Segal) Lowe; m. Fred Israel, Dec. 18, 1960; children: Herman Allen, Sanford Lawrence. BA, Smith Coll., 1959. Dir. media advance Humphrey for Pres., Washington, 1967-68, dir. politic. intelligence, 1972; dir. scheduling Bayh for Pres., Washington, 1971; spl. asst. Jackson for Pres., Washington, 1975-76; coord. nat. labor Kennedy for Pres., Washington, 1979-80; sr. v.p. The Kamber Group, Washington, 1981-87; pres., CEO Politics, Inc., Washington, 1987-95; bd. dirs. The Kamber Group, Washington, Internat. Found. for Election Sys. Pres. Jewish Cmty. Ctr. of Greater Washington, Rockville, Md., 1981-83, internat. election monitor and coord., 1995—; bd. mgrs. Adas Israel Synagogue, 1981-83; mem. Dem. Charter Commn., 1982-83, Dem. Del. Selection Commn., 1983-84, Dem. Site Selection Com., 1989-90, 90—; mem. Nat. Dem. Club, 1986—; chmn. Washington regional bd. ADL, 1991-94, mem. nat. commn., 1991-94, mem. nat. exec. commn., 1994—, chmn. Washington affairs com.; fmr. chmn. Washington Bd. Friends of Tel Aviv U.; sr. election officer Orgn. Security and Coop. in Europe, Bosnia, 1996. Recipient Spl. Svc. award Jewish Cmty. Ctr., 1984; named one of 100 Most Powerful Women, Washingtonian mag., 1990. Jewish. Home: PO Box 69 Royal Oak MD 21662-0069

ISRAEL, MARGIE OLANOFF, psychotherapist; b. Atlantic City, Apr. 30, 1927; d. Herman and Mary (Salter) Olanoff; m. Allan Edward Israel, Sept. 20, 1953; 1 child, Janet. Student U. Miami, 1945-46, 50, Am. Acad. Dramatic Arts, 1946-47; BA in Psychology cum laude, Hunter Coll., 1970; MSW with honors in fieldwork, Hunter Sch. Social Work, 1972; psychoanalytic tng. N.Y. Soc. Freudian Psychologists, 1965-70, Manhattan Ctr. for Advanced Psychoanalytic Studies, 1972-74, 76. Bd. cert. diplomate in clin. social work Am. Bd. Examiners of Clin. Social Workers. Celebrity interviewer Lunchin' with Marge radio show Sta. WFPG, Atlantic City, 1947-48; co-host Steel Pier Midnight radio show, 1949; publicity writer Hy Gardner Astor Hotel, N.Y.C., 1948; writer theatrical interviews Miami (Fla.) Daily News, 1950-51; sec. to exec. dir. Hebrew Old Age Ctr., Atlantic City, 1951-55; sec. to dir. TV-films and radio Nat. Office, Am. Cancer Soc., N.Y.C., 1959-66, asst. to dir. TV-films and radio,1966-70; social worker Bellevue Hosp., N.Y.C., 1972-76; field instr. socialworkN.Y. U., 1975-76; pvt. practice psychotherapy, N.Y.C., 1973—, Providence, 1991—, Wilmington, N.C., 1996—. Fellow N.Y. State Soc. Clin. Social Work, Am. Orthopsychiat. Assn.; mem. NASW (diplomate), Nat. Fedn. Socs. Clin. Social Work (com. on psychoanalysis), Acad. Cert. Social Workers, N.Y. Acad. Scis. AAAS, Psi Chi. Home and Office: 5711 Andover Rd Wilmington NC 28403-3409

ISRAEL, MARTIN HENRY, astrophysicist, educator, academic administrator; b. Chgo., Jan. 12, 1941; s. Herman and Anna Catherine (Herczeg) I.; m. Margaret Ellen Mitouer, June 20, 1965; children: Elisa, Samuel. SB, U. Chgo., 1962; PhD, Calif. Inst. Tech., 1969. Asst. prof. physics Washington U., St. Louis, 1968-72, assoc. prof., 1972-75, prof., 1975—, assoc. dir. McDonnell Ctr. for Space Scis., 1982-87, acting dean faculty arts and scis., 1987-88, dean faculty, 1988-94, vice chancellor, 1994-95, vice chancellor acad. planning, 1995-97; mem. com. on space astronomy and astrophysics NRC, 1976-79; mem. High Energy Astrophysics Mgmt. Ops. Working Group NASA, 1976-84, co-chair Cosmic Ray Program Working Group, 1980-87, mem. space and earth scis. adv. com., 1985-88, chair Particle Astrophysics Magnet Facility Definition Team, 1985-87, mem. astrophysics coun., 1986-87, prin. investigator Heavy Nuclei Expt. High Energy Astronomy Obs., 1971-89, mem. structure and evolution of the universe subcom., 1996-99, chair ACCESS steering com., 1998—, chair Space Sta. Utilization adv. subcom., 1998—; chair Space Sci. Working Group, Assn. Am. Univs., 1983-85; chair nat. organizing com. 19th Internat. Cosmic Ray Conf., 1985, 1982-85. Contbr. articles on cosmic ray astrophysics and observation of elemental and isotopic composition of cosmic rays to profl. jours. Recipient Exceptional Sci. Achievement award NASA, 1980; Sloan Found. fellow, 1970. Fellow Am. Phys. Soc. (chair astrophysics divsn. 1980-81); mem. Am. Astron. Soc. (mem. exec. com. high energy astrophysics divsn. 1982-84), AAUP, AAAS. Home: 2 Valley View Pl Saint Louis MO 63124-1810 Office: Washington U Campus Box 1105 1 Brookings Dr Saint Louis MO 63130-4899

ISRAEL, MICHAEL DAVID, healthcare executive; b. N.Y.C., June 18, 1953; s. Milton and Martha (Greenberg) I.; m. Therase Marie Yienger, May 3, 1981; children: Danny, Jeff, Laura Eleanor. AB in Econs. and Bus. Adminstrn., Rutgers U., 1975; MPH, Yale U., 1977. Staff assoc. Delaware Valley Hosp., Phila., 1977-78; asst. dir., then assoc. dir. Intercare Health Svcs., Princeton, N.J., 1978-83; v.p. Bayshore Cmty. Health Svc., Holmdel, N.J., 1983-84; v.p. devel. and ops. Shadyside Health, Edn. & Rsch. Corp., Pitts., 1984-87; sr. v.p., exec. v.p. St. Luke's Episcopal Hosp., Houston, 1987-93; COO Duke U. Hosp., Durham, N.C., 1993-96, CEO, v.p., chief hosp. and clin. facility, 1996—. USPHS fellow. Office: Duke U Hosp Trent Dr Box 3708 Durham NC 27710*

ISRAEL, PAUL NEAL, computer design engineer, author; b. Balt., Apr. 22, 1959; s. Sheldon Leonard and Sheila Lee (Goldmacher) I. BS in EECS, U. Calif., Berkeley, 1981. Project mgr. computer sci. dept. U. Calif., Berkeley, 1981-82; design engr. Electronic Signature Lock Corp., Berkeley, 1983; staff engr. Qantel Bus. Systems, Hayward, Calif., 1983-89; sr. hardware design engr. SBE, Inc., Concord, Calif., 1989-90; engring. contractor Renegade Systems, Sunnyvale, Calif., 1990-92; prin. engr. Unisys Corp., San Jose, Calif., 1992-95; sr. design engr. Network Virtual Systems, Inc., San Jose, 1995—. Awarded U.S. patent June, 1997, for Avoiding Instability in Computer Logic, awarded U.S. patent Oct., 1998, for method for cycle request with quick termination without waiting for the cycle to reach the destination by storing information in queue. Mem. IEEE, Assn. Computing Machinery, Bay Area Sci. Fiction Assn. Avocations: model railroading, writing, sports, science fiction. Office: Network Virtual Systems Inc 2077 Gateway Pl Ste 220 San Jose CA 95110-1016

ISRAEL, RICHARD STANLEY, investment banker; b. Oakland, Calif., Sept. 27, 1931; s. Sybil Noble, July 29, 1962; children: Richard Lee, Lynne, Lawrence. BA, U. Calif., Berkeley, 1953, MA, 1953. Copy editor San Francisco Chronicle, 1953-59; publicist CBS TV Network, L.A., 1959-62; sr. v.p. Rogers & Cowan, Beverly Hills, Calif., 1962-69; v.p. Cantor, Fitzgerald, Beverly Hills, 1969-73; pres. Sponsored Cons. Svcs., L.A., 1973—; bd. dirs. Hurst Labeling Systems. Pres. North Beverly Dr. Homeowners Assn., Beverly Hills, 1986-88; v.p. Temple Emanuel, Beverly Hills, 1988-93, L.A. chpt. Juvenile Diabetes Found. Internat, 1987—. With U.S. Army, 1956-58. Recipient Alumni citation U. Calif. Alumni Assn., Berkeley, 1984. Mem. L.A. Venture Assn. (pres. 1987), Assn. for Corp. Growth (pres. bd. dirs. L.A. chpt.). Democrat. Avocations: volleyball, travel. Office: Sponsored Cons Svcs 8929 Wilshire Blvd Ste 214 Beverly Hills CA 90211-1951

ISRAEL, ROBERT ALLAN, statistician; b. N.Y.C., Mar. 30, 1933; s. John J. and Ray (Sladkus) I.; m. Barbara Diane Johnston, Jan. 26, 1953; children: John, Richard, Deborah, Pamela, James, Michael. BA, Hofstra Coll., 1954; MS, Columbia U., 1957. Med. analyst Md. State Health Dept., Balt., 1959-63, chief div. statis. rsch., 1963-66; chief mortality stats. br. Nat. Ctr. for Health Stats., Washington, 1966-68, dir. div. vital stats., 1968-72, assoc. dir. for ops., 1972-75, dep. dir., 1975-92, assoc. dir. for internat. stats., 1992-95, ret., 1995; head WHO collaborating ctr. for disease classification for North Am., 1975-95, ret., 1995; dep. exec. dir. Internat. Inst. for Vital Registration and Statistics, 1997—. Co-author: The Methods and Materials of Demography, 1973; co-editor: Encyclopedia of Biostatistics, 1997. Recipient Superior Svc. award U.S. Pub. Health Svc., 1972, 79, scholarship N.Y. State Bd. Regents, 1950-54, fellowship U.S. Public Health Svc., 1956-58, Special Recognition award Asst. Sec. for Health. Fellow APHA (stats. sect. award 1986), Am. Statis. Assn.; mem. Internat. Statis. Inst., Internat. Assn. Ofcl. Stats.

ISRAEL, STANLEY C., chemistry educator; b. Bklyn., Dec. 30, 1942; s. Henry I. and Lillian I.; m. Sonja F., 1966; 1 child, Aaron M. BS, Parsons

Coll., 1965; PhD, Lowell Tech. Inst., 1970. Instr. chemistry Lowell (Mass.) Tech. Inst., 1968-72; asst. prof. chemistry U. Lowell, 1972-77; dir. chem. rsch. Flammability Rsch. Ctr., U. Utah, Salt Lake City, 1975-77; assoc. prof. chemistry U. Lowell, 1977-80, prof. chemistry, 1980—, head polymer sci. program, 1980-82, head dept. chemistry, 1982—; cons. in field. Mem. editorial bd. Polymers for Advanced Technologies, N.Y.C. Recipient Div. Officer award Am. Chem. Soc., 1989, 85, 83, Phoenix award, 1989, A.L. Lipschitz award, 1987, Kyoto U. medal, 1986, Student Affiliate Advisor award Am. Chem. Soc., 1978. Mem. AAAS, AAUP, Am. Chem. Soc., Am. Soc. for Mass Spectrometry, N.Y. Acad. Sci., Sigma Xi. Jewish. Achievements include patents in chemistry and polymer science; pioneering research on Direct Pyrolysis-Chemical Ionization Mass Spectrometry for the study of the reactions and mechanisms of thermal decomposition of polymeric materials. Office: U Mass Lowell One University Ave Lowell MA 01854

ISRAEL, STEVE, town councilman; b. Brooklyn, N.Y., May 30, 1958; s. Howard and Madeline Israel; m. Randi Elkins, June 5, 1983; children: Carly, Elana. BA, George Washington U., 1982. Congl. aide U.S. Congress, Washington, 1979-83; consultant Steve Israel Assoc., Huntington, N.Y., 1985--; asst. county exec. County of Suffolk, Hauppauge, N.Y., 1988-92; town councilman Town of Huntington, 1993--; exec. dir. Inst. on the Holocaust and Law, Huntington, 1998--. Author/editor: Great Jewish Speeches, 1994. Founder Ctr. for Prejudice Reduction, Great Neck, N.Y., 1990; dir. Pederson-Krag Ctr., Huntington, 1996; founder, dir. L.I. Fgn. Affairs Forum, Mingola, N.Y., 1998. Life mem. NAACP; assoc. mem. Sons of Italy. Democrat. Jewish. Avocations: writing, historical rsch. E-mail: israel@li.net. Office: Steve Israel Assocs 18 W Carver St Huntington NY 11743-3322

ISRAEL, WERNER, physics educator; b. Berlin, Oct. 4, 1931; s. Arthur and Marie (Kappauf) I.; m. Inge Margulies, Jan. 26, 1958; children—Mark Abraham, Pia Lee. B.Sc., U. Cape Town, 1951, M.Sc., 1954; Ph.D., Trinity Coll., Dublin, 1960; D.Sc. (hon.), Queen's U., Kingston, Ont., 1987; Docteur honoris causa, U. Francois Rabelais, France, 1994; DSc (hon.), U. Victoria, B.C., Can., 1999. Asst. prof. physics U. Alta., 1958-68, prof., 1968-85, Univ. prof., 1985-96; adj. prof. dept. physics and astronomy U. Victoria, BC, Can., 1996—; hon. prof. dept. physics and astronomy U. B.C., B.C., Can.; Sherman Fairchild disting. scholar Calif. Inst. Tech., 1974-75; vis. prof. Dublin Inst. Advanced Studies, 1966-68, U. Cambridge, 1975-76, Institut Henri Poincare, 1976-77, U. Berne, 1980, Kyoto U., 1986, 98; vis. fellow Gonville and Caius Coll., Cambridge, 1985; fellow Can. Inst. for Advanced Rsch., 1986—. Editor: Relativity, Astrophysics and Cosmology, 1973; co-editor: General Relativity, An Einstein Centenary Survey, 1979, 300 Years of Gravitation, 1987. Decorated officer Order of Can.; recipient Izaak Walton Killam meml. prize, 1984, Joint medal in math. physics Ctr. de Recherche Math./Can. Assn. Physicists, 1995, Tomalla Found. for Gravitational Rsch. prize, 1996. Fellow Royal Soc. Can., Royal Soc. (London); mem. Can. Assn. Physicists (medal of Achievement in Physics 1981), Internat. Soc. Gen. Relativity and Gravitation (pres. 1997—). Jewish. Office: U Victoria, Dept Physics and Astronomy, Victoria, BC Canada V8W 3P6

ISRAELACHVILI, JACOB NISSIM, chemical engineer; b. Tel Aviv, Israel, Aug. 19, 1944; came to U.S., 1986; s. Haim Israelachvili and Hela (Noma) Galili; m. Karina Haglund, Sept. 14, 1971; children: Josefin, Daniela. BA, U. Cambridge, 1968, MA & PhD, 1972. Prof. U. Calif., Santa Barbara, 1986—; v.p. Internat. Assn. Colloid & Interface Scientists, 1986-89. Author: Intermolecular and Surface Forces, 1985, 2d edit., 1991; contbr. rsch. articles to profl. pubs. Fellow Australian Nat. U., Canberra, 1974-86, Rsch. fellow U. Stockholm, Sweden, 1972-74; recipient Matthew Flinders medal, 1986. Fellow Royal Soc. London, Australian Acad. Sci.; mem. Nat. Acad. of Engring. (fgn. assoc. 1996), Alpha Chi Sigma. Office: Santa Barbara CA 93106

ISRAELIEVITCH, JACQUES H., violinist, conductor; b. Cannes, France, May 6, 1948; came to U.S., 1965, naturalized, 1976; s. Isidore and Simone (David) I.; m. Gail Ivy Bass, Aug. 27, 1972 (div. 1985); children: David James, Michael Benjamin, Joshua Alexander; m. Gabrielle Rubin, Dec. 22, 1985. Performer's cert., Ind. U., 1968. mem. faculty Am. Conservatory Music, Chgo., 1974-78; co-founder Camerata Soc. Chgo., 1974; artist in residence Webster U., 1978-88. Asst. concertmaster Chgo. Symphony Orch., 1972-78; concertmaster St. Louis Symphony Orch., 1978-88, Toronto Symphony Orch., 1988—; solo appearances with orchs. and in recital, France, Spain, Portugal, Italy, Germany, Japan, U.S., Can.; founder Chgo. Pops Orch., 1975; performed world premiere The Darkly Splendid Earth, The Lonely Traveller, 1991; recorder 7 solo CDs, including Suite Hebraique, 1995, Suite Française, 1997, The Romance and Rhapsody of Max Bruch, 1997. Decorated chevalier Order of Arts and Letters (France); recipient 1st prize Paris Conservatory Music, 1964; named winner Paganini Internat. Competition, Italy, 1965, Alumnus of Yr. Ind. U., 1973. Mem. Am. Fedn. Musicians, Soc. Am. Musicians. Club: Arts of Chgo. Office: Toronto Symphony Orch, 212 King St W Ste 550, Toronto, ON Canada MH5 1K5

ISRAELOV, RHODA, financial planner, writer, entrepreneur; b. Pitts., May 20, 1940; d. Joseph and Fannie (Friedman) Kreinen; divorced; children: Jerome, Arthur, Russ. BS in Hebrew Edn., Herzlia Hebrew Tchrs. Coll., N.Y.C., 1961; BA in English Lang. and Lit., U. Mo., Kansas City, 1965; MS, Coll. Fin. Planning, 1991. CFP, CLU. Hebrew tchr. various schs., 1961-79; ins. agt. Conn. Mut. Life, Indpls., 1979-81; fin. planner Smith Barney, Inc., Indpls., 1981—, 1st v.p., 1986—; instr. for mut. fund licensing exams. Pathfinder Securities Sch., Indpls., 1983-87; cons. channel 6 News, 1984-85. *Ms. Israelov serves as Senior Beacon columnist and appears on the weekly radio program, "A Moment for Your Money." She also serves as director for The International Association for Financial Planning, and for The Society for Cultural Experience in Schools. Ms. Israelov is First Vice-President of Investments for Salomon Smith Barney. She also served as Director for the Society for Cultural Experience in Schools.* Weekly fin. columnist Indpls. Bus. Jour., 1982—; bi-weekly fin. columnist Jewish Post & Opinion, 1982-86; regular guest WTUX Radio, 1990-94; monthly columnist, sr. Beacon, 1985—. Recipient Gold Medal award Personal Selling Power, 1987; named Bus. Woman of Yr., Network of Women in Bus., 1986. Mem. Inst. Cert. Fin. Planners, Nat. Assn. Life Underwriters, Women's Life Underwriters' Conf. (treas. Ind. chpt. 1982, v.p. chpt. 1983), Internat. Assn. Fin. Planners (v.p. Ind. chpt. 1983-84, bd. dirs., sec.), Am. Soc. CLU, Women's Life Underwriters Conf., Nat. Coun. Jewish Women, Nat. Assn. Profl. Saleswomen, Nat. Spkrs. Assn. (pres. Ind. chpt. 1986-87, treas. 1984), Registry Fin. Planning Practitioners, Toastmasters (chpt. ednl. v.p. 1985-86), Soroptimists (bd. dirs.), Ctrl. Ind. Mensa. Avocations: pinao, folk, square and ballroom dancing, theatre. Office: Smith Barney Bank One Center Tower 111 Monument Cir Ste 3100 Indianapolis IN 46204-5193

ISRAELS, LYONEL GARRY, hematologist, medical educator; b. Regina, Sask., Can., July 31, 1926; s. Simon and Sarah (Girtle) I.; m. Esther Hornstein, June 3, 1950; children: Sara, Jared. BA, U. Sask., 1946; MD, U. Man., 1949, MScawd, 1950. Intern Winnipeg Gen. Hosp., 1948-49; resident internal medicine and hematology Salt Lake County Hosp., 1950-52; fellow in hematology Kantonsspital, Zurich, 1952-53; dept. biochemistry U. Man., 1953-55, asst. prof. biochemistry, 1955-59, asst. prof. medicine, 1959-62, assoc. prof. medicine, 1962-66, prof. medicine, 1966—, Disting. prof., 1983—, acting head dept. medicine, 1977-79; dir. Manitoba Inst. Cell Biology, 1970-73, sr. scientist, 1992—; exec. dir. Manitoba Cancer Treatment and Rsch. Found., 1973-92; attending physician Health Sci. Centre; cons. in hematology Children's Centre, Winnipeg; mem. Med. Rsch. Coun. Can., 1973-75; chmn. Manitoba Health Rsch. Coun., 1980-87, mem. sci. coun. Internat. Agy. Cancer Rsch., 1989-93, chmn. sci. coun., 1992-93; sen. sci. Manitoba Can. Treatment and Rsch. Found., 1993—. Contbr. articles on biochem. and immunol. aspects of blood, blood forming organs and cancer to sci. jours. Fellow RCPC; mem. Am. Soc. Clin. Investigation, Can. Soc. Clin. Investigation (pres. 1968), Royal Coll. Physicians and Surgeons Can., Can. Hematol. Soc. (pres. 1972-74), Nat. Cancer Inst. Can. (pres. 1976-78). Decorated Order of Can.; L.G. Israels chair in hematology at Ben Gurion U. in his honor, 1996. Home: 502 South Dr, Winnipeg, MB Canada R3T 0B1 Office: 100 Olivia St, Winnipeg, MB Canada R3E 0V9

ISRAELSKY, ROBERTA SCHWARTZ, speech pathologist, audiologist; b. N.Y.C., July 19, 1954; d. Julian H. and Sylvia (Fenster) Schwartz; m. Brad Richard Israelsky, June 24, 1984; children: Erica, Evan. BA, Temple U., 1976; MA, Hahnemann Med. Coll., 1977, Trenton State, 1978. Speech/language pathologist W Deptford Twp Sch., W. Deptford, N.J., 1978-81, Sunny Day Autistic Sch., Cherry Hill, N.J., 1981-83; adj. prof. sign lang., voice and articulation Glassboro St. Coll., Glassboro, N.J., 1982-89; speech, sign lang. pathologist and diagnostician Camden Co. Educ. Serv. Comm., Stratford, N.J., 1983-88; pvt. practice Voorhees, N.J., 1983—; prof. speech Camden County Coll., Blackwood, N.J., 1989—; speech/lang. pathologist Gloucester City Schs., 1990-94; speech/lang. specialist Mt. Holly Schs., Mt. Holly, N.J., 1994—; adult supr. B'nai B'rith Girls, Cherry Hill, 1975-77; cons. Sign Lang. Assn. N.J., 1983. Author, Hearing and Publication, Consumer Guide to Hearing Aids, 1978. v.p. ORT, Cherry Hill, 1986-89, Women Tech. Soc., 1988-89, Hadassah, 1985-89. Mem. Am. Speech, Lang., Hearing Assn. (cert. clin. competence), N.J. Speech, Lang. Hearing Assn., TripCounty Speech, Lang., Hearing Assn. Democrat. Jewish. Avocation: singing, acting. Home and Office: 425 Hialeah Dr Cherry Hill NJ 08002-2037

ISRAILI, ZAFAR HASAN, scientist, clinical pharmacologist, educator; b. Moradabad, India, July 2, 1934; came to U.S., 1961, naturalized, 1977; s. Siddiq Hasan and Zahida Khatun I.; m. Sally Jean Smith, Oct. 24, 1970; children: Shahnaz Joy, Taj Hasan, Rana Shereen. BSc, Aligarh M. U., 1951, MSc (Merit scholar), 1953; PhD, U. Kans., 1968. Lectr. chemistry Aligarh M. U., 1953-54, sr. rsch. scholar, 1954-57; rsch. asst., jr. sci. officer AEC India, 1957-61; rsch. assoc. U. Kans., 1968-69; sr. rsch. chemist Alza Corp., Lawrence, Kans., 1969-70; asst. prof. medicine and chemistry Emory U., Atlanta, 1970-75, assoc. prof. chemistry, 1975-78, assoc. prof. medicine, 1975—, prof. chemistry, 1978—; rsch. pharmacologist Atlanta VA Med. Ctr., Decatur, 1979-87; mem. sci. staff Grady Hosp., Atlanta, 1974—. Editor Ethnicity and Disease, 1997—; assoc. editor Drug Metabolism Revs., 1974—; mem. editl. bd. Drug Devel. Rsch., 1979—; mem. editl. com. Archives Venezuelan Pharm. Ter., 1983—; contbr. numerous articles to profl. jours., chpts. to books. Recipient Asia Found. award, 1962; Merck Sharpe & Dohm grantee, 1977, 85, 87, NIH grantee, 1978-83, VA grantee, 1979-87, Am. Heart Assn. grantee, 1989-91. Mem. Am. Soc. Clin. Pharmacology and Therapeutics, Am. Soc. Pharmacology and Exptl. Therapeutics, Soc. Exptl. Biology and Medicine, Am. Assn. Cancer Rsch., Am. Aging Assn., Am. Chem. Soc., Am. Soc. Hypertension, Chem. Soc. London, Internat. Soc. for Study Xenobiotics, Interam. Soc. Clin. Pharm. Therapeutics (pres.-elect 1997—), Internat. Soc. on Hypertension in Blacks, Am. Heart Assn., Sigma Xi, Rho Chi, Phi Lambda Upsilon. Moslem. Home: 3567 Cloudland Dr Stone Mountain GA 30083-4005 Office: Emory Univ Sch Medicine Dept Medicine 69 Butler St NE Atlanta GA 30303-2607

ISRANI, KIM, civil engineer; b. Dadu, Pakistan, Dec. 24, 1930; s. Watumal and Vani I.; m. Yashi Israni, May 26, 1964; children: Vijay, Mamta, Sanjay. BS in Engring., Poona U., 1960; MS in Engring., Memphis State U., 1972. Asst. dir. Ctrl. Water and Power Commn., New Delhi, Ind., 1960-70; civil engr. Pollard Cons., Memphis, 1971-73; design engr. Talbot & Assoc., Orlando, Fla., 1974-75; facilities engr. Dept. Nat. Resources, Des Moines, 1976-91; environ. specialist Dept. Agr., Des Moines, 1992—. Author: India: A Superpower, 1989; contbr. articles to profl. jours. Chmn. Indian sect. Internat. Food Fair, Des Moines, 1977—; dir. Indian dance group Iowa State Fair, Des Moines, 1982—. Mem. Iowa Assn. Profl., Managerial and Sci. State Employees (bd. dirs. 1986—), Iowa Engring. Soc., Toastmasters Internat. Republican. Hindu. Avocations: reading, writing, boating, swimming, foreign travel. Home: 3510 81st St Des Moines IA 50322-2307 Office: Dept Agr Wallace Bldg Des Moines IA 50319

ISSAWI, CHARLES PHILIP, economist, educator; b. Cairo, Egypt, Mar. 15, 1916; came to U.S., 1947, naturalized, 1957; s. Elias and Alexandra (Abouchar) I.; m. Janina M. Haftke, July 20, 1946. BA, Magdalen Coll., Oxford (Eng.) U., 1937, MA, 1944; LLD (hon.), Am. U., Cairo, 1987. With Egyptian Ministry Fin., 1937-38; chief research Nat. Bank Egypt, 1938-43; adj. prof. Am. U., Beirut, Lebanon, 1943-47; mem. Middle East unit, econ. dept. UN Secretariat, 1948-55; faculty Columbia U., 1955-75, prof. econs., 1961-75; dir. Columbia U. (Near and Middle East Inst.), 1962-64; Bayard Dodge prof. Near Eastern studies Princeton U., 1975-86; adj. prof. econs. NYU, 1987-91; cons. FAO, 1955, UN, 1956, 70. Author: Egypt: An Economic and Social Analysis, 1947, An Arab Philosophy of History, 1950, Mushkilat Qaumiyya, 1959, Egypt in Revolution, 1963; co-author: The Economics of Middle Eastern Oil, 1962, The Economic History of Iran, 1971, Oil, the Middle East and the World, 1972, Issawi's Laws of Social Motion, 1973, enlarged edit., 1991, The Economic History of Turkey, 1980, The Arab World's Legacy, 1981, The Economic History of the Middle East and North Africa, 1982, The Fertile Crescent, 1988; editor: The Economic History of the Middle East, 1800-1914, 1966, Modern Arab Thought, 1983; co-author Rebirth Europe Since World War II, 1992, The Middle East Economy: Decline and Recovery, 1995, Cross-cultural Encounters and Conflicts, 1998, Growing Up Different, 1999. Guggenheim fellow, 1961, 68; Social Sci. Research Council fellow, 1962, 75. Fellow Middle East Inst. (bd. editors jour. 1958—); mem. Council Fgn. Relations, Middle East Studies Assn. (v.p. 1968, pres. 1973, bd. editors jour. 1970-78, 90—), Econ. History Assn., Middle East Econ. Assn. (pres. 1978), Am. Geog. Soc. (councillor 1981-85). Home: Pennswood Village Newton PA 18940-2401 Office: Princeton U Dept Near Eastern Studies Princeton NJ 08544

ISSEL, DANIEL PAUL, sports team executive, former professional basketball coach; b. Batavia, IL, Oct. 25, 1948; m. Cheri Issel; children: Sheridan, Scott. Student, U. Ky. Basketball player Ky. Cols., 1970-75, Denver Nuggets, 1975-85; broadcast analyst U. Ky., 1987-88; color analyst, mgr. player edn. and career enhancement programs Denver Nuggets, 1988-92, head coach, 1992-94; prin. Courtland Farms Horse Racing. •

ISSELBACHER, KURT JULIUS, physician, educator; b. Wirges, Germany, Sept. 12, 1925; came to U.S., 1936, naturalized, 1945; s. Albert and Flori (Strauss) I.; m. Rhoda Solin, June 22, 1955; children: Lisa, Karen, Jody, Eric. AB, Harvard U., 1946, MD cum laude, 1950. Intern, then resident Mass. Gen. Hosp., Boston, 1950-53; investigator NIH, 1953-56; chief gastrointestinal unit Mass. Gen. Hosp., 1957-89, chmn. com. rsch., 1967, dir. Cancer Ctr., 1987—; prof. medicine Harvard Med. Sch., 1966—, chmn. exec. com. depts. medicine, 1968-97, Mallinckrodt prof. medicine, 1972-97, disting. Mallinckrodt prof. medicine, 1998—, chmn. univ. cancer com., 1972-87; mem. governing bd. NRC, 1987-90; mem. sci. bd. FDA, 1993. Editor-in-chief: (Harrison) Principles of Internal Medicine, 1976, 91-99. Recipient Award for Disting. Achievement in Nutrition Bristol-Myers Squibb, 1991, Sci. Bd. FDA, 1993-97. Fellow ACP (John Phillips award for Disting. Achievement in Clin. Medicine 1989), Am. Acad. Arts and Scis.; mem. NAS (chmn. food and nutrition bd. 1983-88, mem. exec. com., mem. coun. 1987-90, chmn. com. on risk assessment of hazardous air pollutants 1991-94), Am. Gastroenterology Assn. (pres. 1974-75, Julius Friedenwald medal for outstanding achievement in gastroenterology 1985), Assn. Am. Physicians Pres. 1977-78). Achievements include research in molecular and genetic changes in malignant cells metastasis and colon cancer. Home: 20 Nobscot Rd Newton MA 02459-1323 Office: Cancer Ctr Mass Gen Hosp 139 13th St Charlestown MA 02129-2023

ISSLER, HARRY, lawyer; b. Cologne, Germany, Nov. 14, 1935; came to U.S., 1937; s. Max and Fanny (Grunbaum) I.; m. Doris Helen Lukow, June 1, 1958; children: Adriane P. Schorr, M. Valerie Priestley, Stephanie L. Beck. BS, U. Wis., 1955; JD, Cornell U., 1958. Bar: N.Y. 1958, U.S. Supreme Ct. 1962, U.S. Ct. Mil. Appeals 1967, U.S. Dist. Ct. (so. and ea. dists.) N.Y. 1960, U.S. Customs Ct. 1964, U.S. Tax Ct. 1964; cert. specialist in civil trial advocacy Nat. Bo. Trial Advocacy. Assoc. Wing & Wing, N.Y.C., 1958-60, Fuchsberg & Fuchsberg, N.Y.C., 1960-62; ptnr. Issler & Fein, N.Y.C., 1963-68, Shaw, Issler & Rosenberg, N.Y.C., 1968-70; pvt. practice N.Y.C., 1970-79; sr. ptnr. Issler & Schrage, PC, N.Y.C., 1979—; arbitrator Civil Ct., N.Y. County, 1979-91; hearing officer N.Y. State Tax Appeals, 1975-77, Supreme Ct. of N.Y., N.Y. County Med. Malpractice Panel, 1980-91; judge advocate N.Y. State; mem. neutral evaluator mediation panel Supreme Ct., N.Y. County, 1997—. Trustee N.Y. State Mil. Ednl. Found., 1997—. With U.S. Army, 1958-59, N.Y. Army N.G., 1963-88, ret. brig. gen., 1988. Ford Found. scholar, 1951-55. Mem. N.Y. State Bar Assn., Assn. of Bar of City N.Y., Am. Trial Lawyers Assn., N.Y. State Trial Lawyers Assn., 42d Infantry Div. Officers Club (N.Y.C., pres. 1979-80), Officers Club (U.S. Mcht. Marine Acad.), 42d Infantry Rainbow Div. Assn. (pres. 1989), Phi Alpha Delta, Pi Lambda Phi (Omega chpt. pres. 1953-54). Home: 50 Sutton Pl S New York NY 10022 Office: The Law Firm of Harry Issler PLC 65 E 55th St New York NY 10022-3219

ISTEL, JACQUES ANDRE, mayor; b. Paris, Jan. 28, 1929; came to U.S., 1940, naturalized, 1951; s. Andre and Yvonne Mathilde Cremieux I.; m. Felicia Juliana Lee, June 14, 1973; 1 dau. by previous marriage, Claudia Yvonne. A.B., Princeton, 1949. Stock analyst Andre Istel & Co., N.Y.C., 1950, 55; pres. Parachutes Inc., Orange, Mass., 1957-87, Intramgmt. Inc., N.Y.C., 1962-80; chmn. Pilot Knob Corp., 1982—; mayor Town of Felicity, Calif., 1986—; curator Ctrl. Point for Memories, Calif., 1992—; pres. VI World Parachuting Championships, 1962; capt. U.S. Parachuting team, 1956, capt., team leader, 1958; chmn. Mass. Parachuting Commn., 1961-62; lifetime hon. pres. Internat. Parachuting Commn., Fedn. Aero. Internat., 1965—; chmn. Hall of Fame of Parachuting, 1973—; chmn. Imp. Co. water commn. 1997—; founder Nat. Collegiate Parachuting League, 1957; founder World Commemorative Ctr., 1993. Author: Coe the Good Dragon at the Center of the World, 1985, Coe le Bon Dragon au Centre du Monde, 1985. Contbr. articles to encys., profl. publs. Trustee Inst. for Man and Sci., 1975-82; bd. dirs. Marine Corps Scholarship Found., 1975-85. Served with USMC, 1952-54; lt. col. Res. Recipient Leo Stevens award, 1958, Diplome Paul Tissandier, 1969. Mem. Nat. Aero. Assn. (bd. dirs. 1965-68), Fedn. Internat. des Centres (pres. 1990—), Cercle de l'Union Interalliée (Paris), Marine Corps Res. Officers Assn., DAV (life), Racquet and Tennis Club (N.Y.C.), Princeton Club (N.Y.C.). Holder world record, parachuting, 1961; patentee in field; co-leader Nat. Geog. Soc. Vilcabamba Expdn., 1964. Home: Northview Felicity CA 92283 also: 10 rue Galilée, 75116 Paris France Office: 1 Center Of The World Plz Felicity CA 92283-7777

ISTOCK, VERNE GEORGE, banker; b. Sept. 20, 1940. BA in Econs., U. Mich., 1962, MBA in Fin., 1963. Credit analyst trainee NBD Bancorp, Inc., Detroit, 1963-71, group head, 1971-77, head U.S. divsn., 1977-82, sr. v.p., 1979-82, exec. v.p., 1982-85, vice chmn., dir., 1985-93, chmn., CEO, 1994-95, also bd. dirs.; chmn. NBD Bank; pres., CEO First Chgo. NBD Corp., Chgo., 1995—, chmn., 1996—; bd. dirs. Kelly Svcs. Inc.; dir. Internat. Monetary Conf., Masco Corp., Detroit Renaissance, Fed. Res. Bd. Chgo. Dir., treas. United Way Cmty. Svcs. of Southeastern Mich.; bd. trustees Citizens Rsch. Coun.; mem. U. Mich. Corp. Adv. Coun.; dir. Chgo. Coun. on Fgn. Rels. Mem. U. Mich. Alumni Assn. (past pres., lifetime dir.), Bankers Roundtable (dir.), Econ. Club Chgo., Mich. Bus. Roundtable, Civic Com., Comml. Club of Chgo., Econ. Club Detroit (bd. dirs.), Ill. Bankers Roundtable (bd. dirs.). Office: First Chicago NBD Corp One First National Plz Chicago IL 60670

ISTOOK, ERNEST JAMES, JR. (JIM ISTOOK), congressman, lawyer; b. Foxworth, Tex., Feb. 11, 1950; s. Ernest James and Dessie Cordelia Lyne I.; m. Judy Lee Bills, 1973; children: Amy, Butch, Chad, Diana, Emily. BA, Baylor U., 1971; JD, Oklahoma City U. Sch. Law, 1977. Reporter, State Capitol Stas. KOMA-TV, WKY-Radio, Oklahoma City, 1972-77; dir. Okla. Alcoholic Beverage Control Bd., 1977-78; legal counsel Okla. Gov. David Boren, 1978; dir. Warr Acres/Putnati City C. of C., 1982-86; councilman City of Warr Acres, Okla., 1982-86; atty. Istook & Assocs., 1983-93; mem. Okla. Ho. of Reps., 1986-93, 103rd-106th Congress from 5th Okla. dist., Washington, D.C., 1993—; bd. dirs. Met. Libr. System, 1982-86, chmn., 1985-86; mem. appropriations com. Named Taxpayer Friend of Yr., 1991, One of Ten best Legislators, 1992. Mem. Kappa Nu. Republican. Mormon. Office: US Ho Reps 119 Cannon Office House Members Washington DC 20515-3605*

ITA, JOHN BRADLEY, history educator; b. Burlington, Iowa, Aug. 1, 1960. BS in History, No. Mont. Coll., 1982; BS in Social Scis., Western Mont. Coll., 1985; M in Ednl. Counseling, Mont. State U., Havre, 1997. Tchr. Flintridge Prep. Sch., LaConoda, Calif., 1986-90, Havre Pub. Sch., 1990—; educator, coach Turner (Mont.) Pub. Sch., 1982-84; dir. housing student svcs. Western Mont. Coll., Dillon, 1984-86. Bd. dirs. Bear Paw Youth Guidance Ctr., Havre, 1997—.

ITABASHI, HIDEO HENRY, neuropathologist, neurologist; b. Los Angeles, July 7, 1926; s. Masakichi and Mitsuko (Kobayashi) I.; m. Yoko Osawa, Feb. 3, 1952; children: Mark Masa, Helen Yoko. A.B., Boston U., 1949; postgrad., Yale U., 1949-50; M.D., Boston U., 1954. Diplomate: in neuropathology Am. Bd. Pathology. Intern U. Mich. Hosp., Ann Arbor, 1954-55; resident in neurology U. Mich. Hosp., 1955-58; assoc. rsch. neurologist U. Calif., San Francisco, 1958-60; asst. clin. prof. U. Calif., 1964-65; asst. neuropathologist Langley Porter Neuropsychiat. Inst., San Francisco, 1960-65; cons. Neuropathologist San Francisco Gen. Hosp., 1964-65; cons. neuropathology dept., chief med. examiner-coroner Los Angeles County, 1977—; assoc. prof. neurology, pathology U. Mich. Med. Sch., Ann Arbor, 1968-71; prof.-in-residence pathology and neurology UCLA, 1975-93, prof. emeritus, 1993—, acting vice chair dept. pathology Sch. Medicine; acting chair pathology Harbor-UCLA Med. Ctr., 1990-91; cons. VA Hosp., Sepulveda, Calif., 1977-92; spl. fellow in neuropathology Nat. Inst. Neurol. Diseases and Blindness, 1958-60. Contbr. numerous articles on neurol. disorders to med jours. Mem. Am. Assn. Neuropathologists, Am. Acad. Forensic Scis., Nat. Assn. Med. Examiners, Am. Acad. Neurology. Office: Harbor-UCLA Med Ctr Dept Pathology 1000 W Carson St Torrance CA 90502-2004

ITANO, HARVEY AKIO, biochemistry educator; b. Sacramento, Nov. 3, 1920; s. Masao and Sumako (Nakahara) I.; m. Rose Nakako Sakemi, Nov. 5, 1949; children: Wayne Masao, Glenn Harvey, David George. BS, U. Calif., Berkeley, 1942; MD, St. Louis U., 1945; PhD, Calif. Inst. Tech., 1950; DSc (hon.), St. Louis U., 1987. Intern City of Detroit Receiving Hosp., 1945-46; commd. officer USPHS, Bethesda, Md., 1950-70; advanced through grades to chief, sect. on chem. genetics, Nat. Inst. Arthritis and Metabolic Diseases, NIH, USPHS, Bethesda, 1962-70, mem. hematology study sect., NIH, 1959-63; research fellow then sr. research fellow, Calif. Inst. Tech. USPHS, Pasadena, 1950-54; prof. Dept. Pathology U. Calif. San Diego, La Jolla, 1970-88, prof. emeritus, 1988—; vis. prof. Osaka (Japan) U., 1961-62, U. Chgo., 1965, U. Calif., San Francsico, 1967; cons. sickle cell anemia, mem. hematology study sect. 1953-63, various sickle cell anemia rev. coms., 1970-81, NIH, Bethesda. Editor: (with Linus Pauling) Molecular Structure and Biological Specificity, 1957; contbr. articles to profl. jours. George Minot lectr., AMA, 1955; Japan Soc. for Promotion of Sci. fellow, Okayama U., 1983-84. Mem. AAAS, NAS, Am. Acad. Arts and Scis., Am. Chem. Soc. (Eli Lilly award in Biol. Chemistry 1954), Am. Soc. Biochemistry and Molecular Biology, Am. Soc. Hematology, Internat. Soc. Hematology, Phi Beta Kappa, Sigma Xi, Alpha Omega Alpha. Office: U Calif Dept Pathology La Jolla CA 92093-0506

ITKIN, DAVID, music director, conductor. MusB, Eastman Sch. Music, MusM; Mus D, Ind. U. Music dir. Kingsport Symphony Orch., Birmingham Opera Theater; assoc. condr. Ala. Symphony Orch., 1988-93; music dir., condr. Ark. Symphony Orch., Little Rock, 1993—; music dir., cond. Lake Forest Symphony Orch., 1997—; guest condr. San Diego Symphony, Seoul Philharm., Colo. Symphony, Huntsville Symphony, State of Ala. Ballet, Waterloo-Cedar Falls Symphony, Charleston (S.C.) Symphony; artistic dir., condr. Lucius Woods Festival Concerts, Shanghai Broadcast Symphony, Delaware Symphony, New Hampshire Symphony, Indpls. Chamber Orch., Balt. Chamber Orch. Office: Ark Symphony Orch PO Box 7328 Little Rock AR 72217

ITKIN, IVAN, state legislator; b. N.Y.C., Mar. 29, 1936; s. Abraham Aaron and Eda (Kreger) I.; m. Judith Ann Weiss, Aug. 19, 1962 (div. 1975); children: Marc Eric, Laurie Rachel; m. Joyce Lee Hudak, July 12, 1975; 1 child, Max Eugene. BSChemE, Poly. Inst., Bklyn., 1956; M in Nuclear Engring., NYU, 1957; PhD in Math., U. Pitts., 1964; D of Pub. Svc. (hon.), Chatham Coll., 1994. Assoc. scientist Bettis Atomic Power Lab. Westinghouse Electric Corp., Pitts., 1957-59, scientist, 1959-64, sr. scientist, 1964-71, fellow scientist, 1971-73; mem. Pa. Ho. of Reps., Harrisburg, 1973—; majority caucus chmn. Pa. Ho. of Reps., 1982-90, majority whip, 1990-92, majority leader, 1993-94, Democratic whip, 1995—; Dem. candidate for Pa. gov., 1998; chmn. sci., tech., and resource planning com. Nat. Conf. State Legislators, Denver, 1988; del. Dem. Nat. Conv., 1984, 96; U.S. presdl. elector, 1992, 96. Election judge 19th Dist., 14th Ward, Pa., 1966-68; chmn. 14th Ward Dem. Com., Pitts., 1970-72. Recipient Keystone award Alcoholism and Addiction Assn., 1983, Award of Appreciation, Nat. Fedn. Blind, 1983, Disting. Svc. award Pa. Coll. Optometry, 1986; named House

Mem. of Yr., Pa. Jewish Coalition, 1983. Mem. ACLU, Am. Nuclear Soc., Am. Jewish Congress, Nat. Assn. Jewish Legislators, B'nai B'rith. Fax: (717) 787-9014. Home: 6954 Reynolds St Pittsburgh PA 15208-2612 Office: Pa Ho of Reps 428 Main Capitol Building Harrisburg PA 17120-0022*

ITKIN, ROBERT JEFFREY, lawyer; b. Newark, Feb. 20, 1956. BSBA, Boston U., 1978; JD, Am. U., 1985. Bar: N.Y. 1986, Ariz. 1986 (cert. real estate specialist), U.S. Dist. Ct. Ariz. 1986. Assoc. Evans, Kitchel & Jenckes, Phoenix, 1986-89; ptnr. Morrison & Hecker, Phoenix, 1989-90; v.p., assoc. gen. counsel Finova Capital Corp., 1990—. Mem. ABA, Maricopa County Bar Assn. (pres. corp. counsel divsn. 1995-96, bd. dirs. 1995-97). Office: FINOVA Capital Corp 7272 E Indian School Rd Scottsdale AZ 85251-3921

ITNYRE, JACQUELINE HARRIET, systems analyst; b. Camden, N.J., May 13, 1941; d. John Harold and Harriet Geraldine (Rankine) Bruynell; m. Thomas James Itnyre, Oct. 13, 1968 (dec. 1978); children: Beth Thierry, John. AS in Engring., Mercer County Coll., 1961; BA in Liberal Studies, San Jose State U., 1980, MLS, 1981. Media ctr. mgr. Milpitas (Calif.) Unified Sch. Dist., 1975-81; tech. libr. Lockheed Missiles and Space Co., Sunnyvale, Calif., 1981, programmer, 1982-83; with ground support Challenger-Space Lab 2 Lockheed Missiles and Space Co., Palo Alto, Calif., 1984-85; systems mgr. gen. clin. rsch. ctr. Stanford (Calif.) U. Med. Sch., 1985-87, computing systems specialist divsn. epidemiology, 1988-96, local network adminstr. cancer biology rsch. labs., 1996—; local network adminstr. cancer biology rsch. labs., 1996—. Edna B. Anthony scholar San Jose State U., 1981. Mem. Assn. for Computing Machinery, ALA, Nature Conservancy, Sierra Club. Avocations: cycling, travel, sewing, drawing, genealogy. Home: 310 Santa Clara Ave Redwood City CA 94061-3409

ITO, NOBORU, electric power industry executive; b. Qindao, Santon, China, Dec. 17, 1921; s. Eisho and Raiko (Watanabe) I.; m. Sachiko Tsuchiya (dec. Nov. 1978); children: Junko, Kyoko. B degree, Tohoku U., Sendai, 1946, D degree, 1973. Engr. Toyo Comm. Co., Kawasaki, 1946-50, Oi Electric Co., Tokyo, 1950-57; chief rschr. Oi Electric Co., Yokohama, 1964-69, dir., 1970-83, cons., 1984-91; pres. Leo-B Corp., Yokohama, 1992—; scientist Tokyo U., 1960-63, 89-91; lectr. Yamagata U., 1982-83; scientist U. So. Calif., L.A., 1985-86. *Up to 1960, slow and noisy mechanical calculators had been used in offices. In 1961, he designed the world's first electronic calculator named "Aleph-Zero" (pat. s43-19065 Japan) of which calculation speed was 30 times quicker than that of a mechanical one. Since then the size, weight, speed, power consumption and cost have drastically improved, and various kinds of calculators from many manufacturers have spread all over the world. In 1960, he started to develop pocket-bell systems; nearly ten years later several manufacturers and organizations have consecutively participated in these markets. Since then, pocket-bell systems have been used for the nation-wide communications networks. The names of "Pocket-bell" and "Poke-bell" were given by him and his colleague, and now they are common names in Japan. He has accepted more than 30 patents by Japan Patent Agency.* Recipient invention prize Japan Inst. Invention, 1982, dir. prize Sci. and Tech. Agy. of Japan, 1982, yellow ribbon prize Japan Govt., 1984. Mem. IEEE (sr.), N.Y. Acad. Scis., Japan Phys. Soc., Japan Merits Club. Avocations: learning foreign languages, car trips. Office: Leo-B Corp, R1012 6-13-53 Kikuna, Kohokuku Yokohama 222, Japan

ITOH, TATSUO, engineering educator; b. Tokyo, May 5, 1940; s. Yohnosuke and Kimi (Okamoto) I.; m. Seiko Fukumori, June 16, 1969; children: Akihiro, Eiko. B.S., Yokohama Nat. U., Japan, 1964, M.S., 1966; Ph.D., U. Ill., 1969. Registered prof. engr., Tex. Research assoc. U. Ill., Urbana, 1969-71, research asst. prof., 1971-76; sr. research engr. Stanford Research Inst., Menlo Park, Calif., 1976-77; assoc. prof. U. Ky., Lexington, 1977-78; assoc. prof. U. Tex., Austin, 1978-81, prof., 1981-90, Hayden Head prof., 1983-90; prof.and TRW endowed chair UCLA, 1991—; guest rschr. AEG-Telefunken, Ulm, Fed. Republic of Germany, 1979; vis. prof. Def. Acad. Japan, 1991, U. Leeds, Eng., 1994—; hon. vis. prof. Nanjing Inst. Tech., China; hon. prof. Beijing Aeronautical and Astron. U., China, 1995—; adj. rsch. officer Comms. Rsch. Lab., Ministry of Post and Telecom., Japan, 1994; cons. Tex. Instruments, Dallas, 1979, Hughes Aircraft. Guest editor: Transactions, 1981; inventor millimeter-wave line, 1975, quasi-optical mixer, 1982, non-contact TD, 1995, high-power photo detector, 1995. Recipient Engring. Found. faculty awards, 1980-81, Billy and Claude Hocott Disting. Rsch. award, 1988, Disting. Alumnus award U. Ill., 1990, Shida award Min. of Post and Telecom., Japan, 1998, Japan Microwave prize Asia-Pacific Microwave Conf., 1998. Fellow IEEE; mem. Microwave Theory and Techniques Soc. (hon. life; editor 1983-85, pres. 1990, jour. editor Microwave and Guided Wave Letters 1991-94), Internat. Sci. Radio Union (chmn. USNC commn. D 1988-90, chmn. commn. D 1993-96, long range planning com. 1996—), Inst. Electronics and Comm. Engrs. Home: 919 Levering Ave Apt 405 Los Angeles CA 90024-6617 Office: UCLA Dept Elec Engring Los Angeles CA 90095-1594

ITOH, WILLIAM H., former ambassador; b. Tokyo, Japan, May 30, 1943; m. Melinda White; children: Charlotte, Caroline. BA in Social Science, MA in History, Anthropology, U. N.Mex., 1971. Sec. tchr. Albuquerque Pub. Schs., 1967-68; asst. prof. history Calif. State U., Humboldt, 1972-73; U.S. Dept. State staff asst. and exec. officer Bur. Congressional Rels., 1975-76, congressional rels. office, 1980-83; country officer for Japan Bur. East Asian and Pacific Affairs, 1978-80, spl. asst., 1983-84; spl. asst. Office of Under Sec. for Pol. Affairs, 1984-86; consular and pol. officer U.S. Embassy, London, 1976-78; U.S. consul gen. Western Australia, Perth, 1986-90; dep. exec. sec. and acting exec. sec. Dept. State, 1991-93; exec. sec. Nat. Security Council White House, Washington, 1993-95; amb. to Kingdom of Thailand U.S. Dept. of State, 1995-98. Logistics officer USAF, 1967-69. Address: 2782 N Wakefield St Arlington VA 22207*

ITTLESON, H(ENRY) ANTHONY, foundation executive; b. June 23, 1937; s. Henry and Nancy (Strauss) I.; m. Marianne Sundby, Feb. 6, 1961; children: Henry Philip, Christina Bee, Stephanie. B.A., Brown U., 1960. Credit adminstr. The CIT Group Inc., N.Y.C., 1961-68, v.p. Equipment Financing subs., 1968-70, asst. to pres., 1970-71, v.p. mktg., 1971-78, v.p. financing div., 1978-81, exec. v.p., 1981-92, exec. spl. projects, 1988-92; chmn. Travent Ltd., 1987-97; chmn., pres. Ittleson Found., 1973—; chmn., pres. Travent Ltd., 1987-97, Ittleson Found., 1973—. Bd. fellows emeritus Brown U.; trustee Brooks Sch., Brown U. Mem. Brown U. Club, Regency Whist Club, Deepdale Golf Club, Meadow Club, Nat. Golf. Links of Am., L.I. Wyandanch Club (Eastport, N.Y.), Shinnecock Hills Golf Club, Brays Island (S.C.), Cordillera Golf Club (Colo.), Loch Lomond Golf Club, Phi Gamma Delta. Home: Poco Sabo Plantation 1185 Poco Sabo Ln Green Pond SC 29446

ITTNER, H. CURTIS, architect; b. St. Louis, Dec. 7, 1925; s. William Butts and Mignon (Morrow) I.; m. Doris Wilhelmina Dahlen, June 14, 1950; children: Gail Malin (dec), Cynthia Sherwood, H. Curtis Jr. BArch, Washington U., 1951. Registered architect, Mo. Exec. v.p. William B. Ittner, Inc., St. Louis, 1951-72; chmn., CEO Ittner & Bowersox, Inc., St. Louis, 1972-88. Pres. Thomas Dunn Memls., St. Louis, 1986-92; alderman City of Frontenac, Mo., 1965-69; chmn. Alumni Fund of Washington U., 1990-91. Decorated Bronze Star. Fellow AIA (pres. St. Louis chpt. 1985, chmn. scholarship fund 1973—, host chmn. AIA Nat. Conv. 1986-89); mem. Mo. Coun. Architects (bd. dirs. 1984, Disting. Svc. award 1988), Rotary Club St. Louis, Bellerive Country Club. Republican. Episcopalian. Avocations: tennis, golf, greenhouse gardening. Home: 124 Frontenac Frst Saint Louis MO 63131-3220

ITTNER, HELEN LOUISE, entrepreneur; b. Saginaw, Mich., June 12, 1935; d. David Harvey and Helen (Austin) Jones; m. Frederick E. Ittner; children: David (dec.), Philip. BA, St. Mary's Coll., 1981. Pres. H.L.I. Enterprises, Inc., Moraga, Calif., 1988—. Mem. Moraga Sch. Bd., 1981-85, pres., 1984-85; bd. dirs. Hospice of Contra Costa, 1990-94, Hearst Castle Preservation Found. , 1992—; directress Altar Guild, St. Stephen's Episcopal Ch., 1993-95; breast cancer adv. U. Calif. San Francisco Spl. Projects of Rsch. Excellence, 1997—. Mem. AAUW (Disting. Woman award 1991). Republican. Episcopalian. Home: 1858 School St Moraga CA 94556-1729

ITTS, ELIZABETH ANN DUNHAM, psychotherapist, consultant, designer; b. Columbus, Ohio, May 11, 1928; d. Dalton Dee and Elizabeth Farrell (Beck) Dunham; m. Frank Joseph Itts, June 23, 1951; children: Cynthia Ann Robbins, Mark Dunham, Deirdre Elizabeth Jones, Andrea Lee Schoenfeld. Student, St. Mary of the Springs, Columbus, Ohio, 1946-47; BFA in Archtl. Design, Ohio State U., 1950; MS in Edn. Guidance, Youngstown (Ohio) State U., 1979. Lic., cert. counselor Nat. Bd. Cert. Counselors. Dir. activity ctr. pilot program Mahoning County Health Dept., Youngstown, 1974-76; dir. Career Devel. Ctr. for Women, Youngstown, 1978-79; asst. to dir. Youngstown State U. Alumni Assn., 1979-81; pvt. practice psychotherapist, cons., 1981-85, 87-92; dir. career planning, placement and spl. programs Kent State U., Salem, Ohio, 1985-87; writer grants funding for workshops, 1980-81; established career planning and placement office Kent State U., Salem, 1985, initiated and developed human svcs. tech. degree, 1986-87; writer acad. challenge grants; chmn. curriculum devel. Inst. Learning Retirement Youngstown State U., 1994—. Mem. Planning and Zoning Commn., Canfield, Ohio, 1980-90, Ohio Speakers Forum, 1990, Friends of Art (Butler Art Gallery), Youngstown, 1965—, Ohio Hist. Soc., Columbus, 1984—; chmn. nominating com. United Way Scholarship Commn., Youngstown, 1978-82. Mem. Am. Assn. Counseling and Devel., Ea. Ohio Counselor's Assn., Jr. Women's League. Roman Catholic. Avocations: painting, sculpture, poetry. Home and Office: 820 Blueberry Hill Dr Canfield OH 44406-1038

ITURBIDE, GRACIELA, photographer; b. Mexico City, May 16; m. 1962; children: Manuel, Claudia, Mauricio. Student, U. Nat. Autanoma Mexico, 1969-72. Asst. Manuel Breva. Exhibited works at Galeria JoséClemente Orosco, Mexico City, 1975, Midtown Y Gallery, N.Y.C., 1976, Centre Georges Pompldeu, Paris, 1982,. Recipient prize UN Internat. Labor Orgn., 1986, W. Eugene Smith award, 1987; grantee Consejo Mexicano de Fotografia, 1983, Guggenheim Found., 1987. Mem. Mexican Coun. Photography (founding mem.). Home: c/o Cityscape Assocs 32 E Colorado Blvd Pasadena CA 91105*

ITZKOFF, NORMAN JAY, lawyer; b. N.Y.C., Oct. 9, 1940; s. Louis and Rose Itzkoff; divorced; 1 child, Francesca Sandra. BS with honors, U. Buffalo, 1961; LLB cum laude, Columbia U., 1965. Bar: N.Y. 1965, U.S. Dist. Ct. (so. and ea. dists.) N.Y. 1967, U.S. Ct. Appeals (2d cir.) 1967, U.S. Supreme Ct. 1971. Law clk. to judge U.S. Dist. Ct. (so. dist.) N.Y., N.Y.C., 1965-66; assoc. Cravath, Swaine & Moore, N.Y.C., 1966-74; assoc. Rosenman & Colin, N.Y.C., 1974-76, ptnr., 1976-86; litigation counsel Siemens Corp., N.Y.C., 1988-93; cons., arbitrator and mediator, 1994—; gen. counsel Assn. Internat. Photography Art Dealers Inc., N.Y.C., 1981-91. Editor: Dealing with Damages, 1983, Columbia U. Law Rev., 1963-65. Mem. adv. bd. Catskill Ctr. for Photography, Woodstock, N.Y., 1982-87; chmn. adv. bd. Ctr. for Photography at Woodstock, 1987-88. Harlan Fiske Stone scholar. Mem. ABA (jud. adminstrn. div. lawyers conf., com. on jud. qualification and selection, com. jud.compensation, sect. of litigation, com. corp. counsel), Fed. Bar Coun., N.Y. State Bar Assn. (antitrust law sect., mem. coms. on court adminstrn. and practice and procedure, comml. and fed. litigation sect., com. on corp. counsel, entertainment arts and sports law sect., com. on fine arts , internat. law and practice sect. coms. internat. dispute resolution and subcom. arbitration, mcpl. law sect., trial lawyers sect., com. on fed. cts., com. on litigation mgmt. and econs.), Assn. of Bar of City of N.Y. (adv. bd. demonstration observation com., com. on nuclear tech. and law, com. on art law, liaison art law com., chmn. subcom. on state legislation 1983-84, Am. Arbitration Assn. (panel), Ctr. Pub. Resources (com. on disputes with distbrs., dealers and franchisees), Beta Gamma Sigma. Clubs: Columbia, Westchester Rugby (N.Y.C.). Avocations: fine art photography, running. Home and Office: 2600 Netherland Ave Riverdale NY 10463-4801

ITZKOWITZ, NORMAN, history educator; b. N.Y.C., May 6, 1931; s. Jack and Gussie (Schmier) I.; m. Leonore Krauss, June 13, 1954; children: Jay Noah, Karen Lisa. BA magna cum laude, CCNY, 1953; MA, Princeton U., 1956, PhD, 1959. Instr. depts. history and Oriental studies Princeton U., 1958-61, asst. prof. Oriental studies, 1961-66, assoc. prof. Near Eastern studies, 1966-73, prof., 1973—, master Wilson Coll., 1975-89; vis. prof. CCNY, summer 1959, Tchrs. Coll., Columbia U., 1964, N.Y. U., 1969, 72, 74, Hebrew U., Jerusalem, 1970, U. B.C., summer 1971. Author: (with V. Volkan and A. Dod) Richard Nixon: A Psychobiography, 1997, Ottoman Empire and Islamic Tradition, 1980, (with V. Volkan) The Immortal Atatürk, 1984. Ford Found. fellow, 1954-59; HEW, SSRC, Littauer Found. fellow, 1970, 74. Mem. Am. Hist. Assn., Am. Oriental Soc. Jewish. Office: Princeton U 108 Jones Dr Princeton NJ 08540 *The goal of life is to be a mensch, a decent human being.*

IVANCEVIC, WALTER CHARLES, former gas distribution company executive; b. Midland, Pa., Nov. 4, 1920; s. Pasko Rudolph and Mary (Santic) I.; m. Kirsten M.; 1 child, Mary Elizabeth Ivancevic Nichols. BSc in Acctg., U. Notre Dame, 1943, LLB, 1944. Pres., The Equity Corp., N.Y.C., 1962-65; v.p. Assocs. Investment Co., South Bend, Ind., 1967-70; pres. No. Utilities, 1975-89; dir. Bay State Gas Co., Westborough, Mass., 1979-89. Mem. Cumberland Bar Assn., Pine Tree Conservation Soc. (pres. Portland, Ma ine 1972-89). Republican. Roman Catholic. Home: Chiltington Court 15230 Cedarwood Ln Naples FL 34110-7607

IVANICK, CAROL W. TRENCHER, lawyer; b. Springfield, Mass., Mar. 6, 1939; d. Joseph George and Daisy Wolf; m. Michael Ira Trencher, July 30, 1960 (div. Feb. 1984); children: Christopher, Daniel, Deborah; m. Peter Alan Ivanick. BA, Wellesley Coll., 1959; JD, Yale U., 1962. Bar: N.Y. 1963. Assoc. Cleary, Gottlieb et al, N.Y.C., 1962-67; ptnr. Dewey, Ballantine, Bushby, Palmer & Wood, N.Y.C., 1976—; chmn. adv. com. Pension Benefit Guaranty Corp., Washington, 1978-80; visiting lectr. Yale Law Sch., New Haven, Conn., 1978-79, 82-83. Avocations: ceramics, bowling, tennis. Home: 110 Riverside Dr New York NY 10024-3715 Office: Dewey Ballantine 1301 Avenue Of The Americas New York NY 10019-6022

IVANIER, PAUL, steel products manufacturing company executive; b. Cernauti, Romania, Oct. 12, 1932; s. Isin and Fancia Ivanier; m. Lily Neilinger, June 13, 1954; children: Shirley Retter, Janet Neuman, Philip. McGill U., 1957; PhD (hon.), Ben-Gurion U. Chartered acct. With Ivaco Inc. (formerly Sivaco Wire and Nail Co.), Montreal, v.p. ops., exec. v.p., 1969-76, pres., chief exec. officer, dir., 1976—; bd. dirs. Ivacan Inc. (formerly Canron Inc.), Docap (1985) Corp., Bakermet Inc. Grand patron Montreal Mus. Fine Arts; mem. bd. govs. U. Montreal, Concordia U., Royal Victoria Hosp. Corp.; internat. bd. govs. Ben-Gurion U.; bd. dirs. Weizmann Inst. Scis., Med. Rsch. Found. Jewish Gen. Hosp. Mem. Can. Steel Producers Assn. (bd. dirs. past vice chmn.), Can. Steel Trade and Employment Congress (bd. dirs., founder), Order of Can., Club des Entrepreneurs/Conseil du Patronat du Quebec (Laureate 1989), Elmridge Golf and Country Club, Mt. Royal Club. Office: Ivaco Inc, 770 rue Sherbrooke St W, Montreal, PQ Canada H3A 1G1

IVANOV, VLADIMIR GENNADIEVICH, biomedical engineer; b. Ivano-Frankovsk, USSR, May 26, 1960; s. Gennadii Borisovich and Elena Grigorievna (Evdokimova) I.; m. Tatiana Dmitrievna Baranova, Oct. 23, 1980; children: Anna, Alexander. MSc in Engring., Moscow Inst. of Electronics, 1983; PhD, Russian Acad. of Sci., 1988. Rsch. staff Acoustical Inst., Moscow, 1983-89, head of lab., 1989-92; gen. mgr. Brain Functions Lab., Kawasaki, Japan, 1992-95; chief scientist Telefactor Corp., West Conshohocken, Pa., 1995—; asst. prof. Moscow Inst. of Electronics, Moscow, 1986-89. Contbr. articles to profl. jours. including Methods of Info. in Medicine, Proc. on Non-Invasive Approach to Func. Localization, Acoustical Physics, Statistical Hydroacoustics. Small Bus. Innovation Rsch. grantee NIH, 1996, 97. Mem. IEEE, Engring. in Medicine and Biology Soc. Office: Telefactor Corp 1094 New Dehaven St West Cnshohocken PA 19428-2713

IVANOVITCH, MICHAEL STEVE, economist; b. Cetinje, Yugoslavia, Sept. 9, 1939; children: Alexandra, Nicholas, Alexander. Diploma in Law, U. Belgrade, Yugoslavia, 1961; MBA, Columbia U., 1972, M of Philosophy, 1976, PhD, 1977. Rsch. assoc. Columbia U. Inst. on Western Europe, N.Y.C., 1977-78; prof. Columbia U. Grad. Sch. Bus., N.Y.C., 1978-88; internat. economist Fed. Res. Bank of N.Y., N.Y.C., 1978-79; prin. adminstr., sr. economist Orgn. for Econ. Cooperation and Devel., Paris, 1979-89; pres. MSI Global, Inc., N.Y.C. and Paris, 1989—; adj. prof. Columbia U.; advisor Credit Agricole, Paris, 1989—, The Yasuda Life Ins. Co., London and Tokyo, 1990—, The Meiji Life Ins. Co., Tokyo, 1991—, Merrill Lynch, 1996—, Salomon Smith Barney, 1996—, ANZ Bank, 1997—, Sumitomo Trust & Banking Corp., 1997—. Democrat. Russian Orthodox. Avocation: music. Home and Office: MSI Global Inc 340 W 57th St New York NY 10019-3706

IVANS, WILLIAM STANLEY, electronics company executive; b. New Rochelle, N.Y., June 17, 1920; s. William S. and Marion (Schultz) I.; m. Rebecca Peck Llewellyn, May 18, 1962; children: Dennis Llewellyn, Denise Ivans Laurent; stepchildren: Virginia Liebner Yates, Joan Renee Liebner de Savigliano. B.S. in Elec. Engring, Pa. State U., 1942. With Convair div. Gen. Dynamics Corp., San Diego, 1946-57; chief electronics engr., 1954-57; v.p. engring. Cohu Electronics, Inc. (name changed to Cohu, Inc. 1972), San Diego, 1957-65, pres., 1965-83, chief exec. officer, 1968-83, dir., chmn. bd.; bd. dirs. T-Systems Internat.; U.S. rep. gliding com. Fedn. Aero Internat., 1960-65, 66—, v.p., 1974-76, pres., 1976—. Chmn. San Diego Dist. Export Council, 1985, 86, San Diego Internat. Trade Commn., 1987—; bd. dirs. San Diego Opera, 1995—. Served as officer USAAF, 1942-46, ETO. Recipient Lilienthal medal, 1950. Mem. Soaring Soc. Am. (pres. 1963-64), Nat. Aero. Assn. (bd. dirs. 1963-64, 90—, Elder Statesman of Aviation 1994). Home: 807 La Jolla Rancho Rd La Jolla CA 92037-7409 Office: 5755 Kearny Villa Rd San Diego CA 92123-1111

IVANY, ROBERT RUDOLPH, military officer, historian; b. Wels, Austria, Feb. 4, 1947; came to U.S., 1950; s. George Robert and Eva (Baranyai) I.; m. Marianne O'Donnell, July 29, 1973; children: Christopher, Mark, Julianne, Brian. BS, U.S. Mil. Acad., 1969; MA, U. Wis., 1976, PhD, 1980; postgrad., Army War Coll., 1989. Commd. 2d lt. U.S. Army, 1969, advanced through grades to lt. col., 1986; assoc. prof. dept. history U.S. Mil. Acad., West Point, N.Y., 1976-79; ops. officer 2d Squadron, 2d Armored Cav., Fed. Republic Germany, 1979-81; staff officer War Plans div. Pentagon, Washington, 1983; mil. aide to Pres. White House, Washington, 1984-86; comdr. 1st Squadron, 3d Armored Cav., Ft. Bliss, Tex., 1986-88; Student Army War Coll., 1989—. Decorated Superior Svc. medal, Legion of Merit, Bronze Star, Meritorious Svc. medal. Mem. U.S. Armor Assn. Avocations: reading; writing. Home: 5120 E Jefferson Detroit MI 48214

IVEN, CHRIS, journalist; b. Kansas City, Mo., July 3, 1972; s. Henry Joseph and Patricia Ann (Samson) I. BA in Polit. Sci., Denison U., 1994; MS in Journalism, Syracuse U., 1996. Journalist Syracuse (N.Y.) Herald-Jour., 1996, Providence Jour.-Bull., 1997—. Active Big Bros. of R.I., Pawtucket, 1997. Avocations: triathlons, gardening, sailing. Home: 105 Taber Ave Providence RI 02906 Office: Providence Jour Bull 650 Washington Hwy Providence RI 02865

IVENS, MARY SUE, microbiologist, mycologist; b. Maryville, Tenn., Aug. 23, 1929; d. McPherson Joseph and Sarah Lillie (Hensley) I.; B.S., E. Tenn. State U., 1949; M.S. (NIH research trainee), Tulane U. Sch. Medicine, 1963; Ph.D., La. State U. Sch. Medicine, 1966; postgrad. Oak Ridge Inst. Nuclear Studies, Emory U. Sch. Medicine. Dir. microbiol. and mycol. labs. Lewis-Gale Hosp., Roanoke, Va., 1953-56; rsch. mycologist Ctrs. Disease Control, Atlanta, 1957-60; rsch. assoc. La. State U. Sch. Med., 1963-66, instr. medicine, 1966-72, instr. Microbiology, 1966-72, clin. prof., 1972—; dir. mycology lab, La. State U. Sch. Med., 1963-72; lectr. Sch. Dentistry, La. State U. Med. Ctr., 1968-70; assoc. prof. natural scis. Dillard U., New Orleans, 1972—; assoc. Marine Biol. Lab., Woods Hole, Mass., 1978— ; cons. in field. Commr. WHO conf. on ctr. for Mycotic sera 1969; chmn. Gold Medal Award Com. Sigma Xi, 1978; mem. La. assn. def. counsel expert witness bank, 1985—; bd. dirs. La. coun. Girl Scouts U.S., Community Relationships Greater New Orleans, Zoning Bd. River Ridge (La.); mem. exec. bd. River Ridge Civic Assn., 1982—, sec., 1982-84; chmn. pers. bd. Riverside Bapt. Ch., River Ridge; dir. Outreach First Baptist Ch., New Orleans, 1989—. Recipient Rosicrucian Humanitarian award, 1981; Macy fellow, MBL, Woods Hole, 1978-79; grantee NSF, NIH; diplomate Am. Bd. Microbiology. Mem. Internat. Soc. Human and Animal Mycology, Med. Mycological Soc. Am., Am. Soc. Microbiology (nat. com. on membership 1983-87), AAAS, Nat. Inst. Sci., Sigma Xi. Author articles in field. Home: 408 Berclair Ave New Orleans LA 70123-1504 Office: Dillard U Div Natural Sci New Orleans LA 70122

IVER, ROBERT DREW, dentist; b. Miami, Fla., Feb. 6, 1947; s. William Henry and Jeanette (Minden) I.; m. Lisa Marie Stettner-Iver, May 5, 1974. Student, Ohio State U., 1965-66, U. Miami, 1966-68; DDS, Georgetown U., 1972. Pvt. practice dentistry Miami Beach, Fla., 1974—. Lt. USNR, 1968-81. Fellow ADA; mem. Fla. Dental Assn., East Coast Dist. Dental Soc., Acad. Gen. Dentistry, Miami Beach Dental Soc., Gold Coast Acad. Gen. Dentistry, Am. Radio Relay League, N.Am. Fishing Club, Dade Radio Club Miami, Everglades Amateur Radio Club. Avocations: sports fishing, ham radio operating. Office: 1205 Lincoln Rd Ste 203 Miami FL 33139-2365

IVERIUS, PER-HENRIK, physician, biochemist, educator; b. Stockholm, Sept. 26, 1942; s. Karl Gösta and Märta Kristina (Engelbert) I. B in Med. Sci., U. Uppsala, Sweden, 1963, PhD in Med. Biochemistry, 1971, MD, 1975. Diplomate Am. Bd. Internal Medicine, Am. Bd. Endocrinology and Metabolism. Intern, resident Emmanuel Hosp., Portland, 1978-80; asst. prof. med. biochemistry U. Uppsala, 1972-74; sr. research fellow U. Wash., Seattle, 1980-82, acting instr. medicine, 1982-85; mem. staff VA Med. Ctr. and U. Utah Hosp., Salt Lake City, 1985—; asst. prof. medicine U. Utah, Salt Lake City, 1985-92, assoc. prof. medicine, 1992—. Contbr. articles to profl. jours. Recipient Research Career Devel. award Swedish Med. Research Council, 1971-74; fellow Arthritis Found., 1975-78. Mem. AAAS, ACP, Am. Fedn. Med. Rsch. (sr.), Am. Heart Assn., Am. Diabetes Assn., N.Y. Acad. Scis., The Endocrine Soc. Office: VA Med Ctr 500 Foothill Dr Salt Lake City UT 84148-0001

IVERS, DONALD LOUIS, judge; b. San Diego, May 6, 1941; s. Grant Perrin and Margaret (Ware) I. BA, U. N.Mex., 1963; JD, Am. U., 1971. Bar: U.S. Dist. Ct. (D.C. 1972, U.S. Ct. Appeals (D.C. cir.) 1972, U.S. Ct. Mil. Appeals 1972, U.S. Supreme Ct. 1975. Assoc., Brault, Graham, Scott, Brault, Washington, 1972-78; chief counsel Republican Nat Com., Washington, 1978-81, gen. counsel 1980 Rep. Nat. Conv. Site Selection Com., 1979-80; chief counsel Fed. Hwy. Adminstrn., U.S. Dept. Transp., Washington, 1981-85; counselor to sec., chmn. sec.'s safety rev. task force U.S. Dept. Transp., Washington, 1984-85; gen. counsel VA, 1985-89; acting gen. counsel U.S. Dept. Vet. Affairs, 1989-90, asst. to the sec., 1990; assoc. judge U.S. Ct. Appeals Vet. Claims, 1990—. Capt. U.S. Army, 1963-68, Vietnam, lt. col. Res., ret. Decorated Bronze Star, Air medal, Parachute badge. Mem. D.C. Bar Assn., Delta Theta Phi. Office: US Ct Appeals Vet. Claims 625 Indiana Ave NW Washington DC 20004-2901

IVERSEN, DAVID STEWART, librarian; b. Ames, Iowa, Sept. 5, 1963; s. James Delano and Margery Lynne (Peters) Iversen. BA in English, Dana Coll., 1986; MA in Libr. Sci., U. Iowa, 1987; MA in Scandinavian Studies, U. Wis., 1990. Multisvc. libr. Concordia Coll., Moorhead, Minn., 1990-91; libr. catalogue serials Rider U., Lawrenceville, N.J., 1991-95; head of cataloging Cowles Libr., Drake U., Des Moines, 1995-96; cataloging libr. Olson Libr., Minot (N.D.) State U., 1996—. Translator: (book chpt.) 1986: A Danish-American Family Saga, 1986, (short story) Old Hans Nielsen's Last Christmas, 1987; compiler (bibliography) Danish Utopias in America, 1988; reviewer: (by Niels Peter Stilling and Anne Lisbeth Olsen) A New Life: Danish Emigration to North America as Described by the Emigrants Themselves in Letters, 1842-1946, 1997; translations of article and short stories by Carl Hansen from Danish to English. Travel grantee U. Wis., 1989. Mem. ALA, Assn. Libr. Collections and Tech. Svcs., Assn. Coll. and Rsch. Librs., Soc. for Advancement of Scandinavian Studies, Danish Am. Heritage Soc., Danish Immigrant Mus., Red River Danes, Alpha Mu Gamma. Lutheran. Avocations: reading, singing, walking. Office: Minot State U Gordon B Olson Libr 500 University Ave W Minot ND 58707-0002

IVERSON, ALLEN, basketball player; b. Hampton, Va., June 7, 1975. Grad., Georgetown U., 1996. Basketball player Phila. 76ers, 1996—. Named AP First Team All-Am., 1994, Big East Conf. Defensive Player of Yr. 1995-96, NBA Rookie of Month, Apr., Nov., 1997, MVP Schick Rookie game, 1997; recipient Schick Rookie of Yr., 1997. Avocations: drawing, reading. Office: Philadelphia 76ers First Union Ctr 3601 S Broad St Philadelphia PA 19148-5287*

IVERSON, CAROL JEAN, retired library media specialist; b. Villisca, Iowa, July 2, 1937; d. Paul Gerald and Garnet Blanche (Dunn) Smith; m. Merlin Gerald Iverson, June 11, 1961; children: Robert Mark, Jean Marie Iverson Howe. BA, U. No. Iowa, 1960. Elem. tchr. Manning (Iowa) Community Schs., 1957-58, Mason City (Iowa) Sch. Dist., 1960-61, Manson (Iowa) Community Schs., 1961-63, Blooming Prairie (Minn.) Community Schs., 1963-64, 65-66; elem. tchr., K-12 librarian Rockwell (Iowa) Swaledale Community Schs., 1973-80; libr. media specialist Mason City Sch. Dist., 1980-96. County co-chair Cerro Gordo County Reps., Howard Baker campaign, 1979; campaign worker Dukakis for Pres., 1987. Mem. AAUW (v.p. 1989-91, pres. 1993-95), NEA (del. rep. assembly), Iowa State Edn. Assn. (del., resolutions com. 1975-78), Iowa Ednl. Media Assn. (legis. chair 1987-89), Delta Kappa Gamma (pres. Internat. chpt. 1986-88, Upsilon state pres. 1999-2001), Phi Delta Kappa. Democrat. Lutheran. Avocations: travel, gardening, reading, children's literature. Home: 1505 Limestone Ct Mason City IA 50401-6976

IVERSON, FRANCIS KENNETH, metals company executive; b. Downers Grove, Ill., Sept. 18, 1925; s. Norris Byron and Pearl Irene (Kelsey) I.; m. Martha Virginia Miller, Oct. 24, 1945; children: Claudia (Mrs. Wesley Watts Sturges), Marc Miller. Student, Northwestern U., 1943-44; B.S., Cornell U., 1946; M.S., Purdue U., 1947, Dr. (hon.); Dr. (hon.), U. Nebr. Research physicist Internat. Harvester, Chgo., 1947-52; tech. dir. Illium Corp., Freeport, Ill., 1952-54; dir. mktg. Cannon-Muskegon Corp., Mich., 1954-61; exec. v.p. Coast Metals, Little Ferry, N.J., 1961-62; v.p. Nucor Corp. (formerly Nuclear Corp. Am.), Charlotte, N.C., 1962-65, pres., chief exec. officer, dir., 1965-85, chmn., chief exec. officer, 1985-96, also bd. dirs., chmn.; bd. dirs. Wachovia Corp., Wal-Mart Stores Inc., Wikoff Color Corp. Contbr. articles to profl. jours. Served to lt. (j.g.) USNR, 1943-46. Named Best Chief Exec. Officer in Steel Industry, Wall St. Transcript, 1995; recipient Nat. Metal of Tech., 1991. Mem. AIME, NAM, Am. Soc. Metals, Quail Hollow Country Club. Office: Nucor Corp 2100 Rexford Rd Charlotte NC 28211-3484

IVERSON, PAUL, government agency administrator. BS in edn., So. Utah State Coll., 1970; MS in Ednl. Adminstrn., U. Nev., Las Vegas, 1976. Tchr. 5th grade Clark County Sch. Dist., 1970-75, sci. curriculum coord., 1975-80; adminstr. conservation and planning Nev. Dept. Energy, 1980-83; dep. dir. Nev. Dept. Minerals, 1983-95; adminstr. Nev. Divsn. Agr., 1995—; spkr. in field. Office: Nev Divsn Agr 350 Capitol Hill Ave Reno NV 89502

IVERSON, PETER JAMES, historian, educator; b. Whittier, Calif., Apr. 4, 1944; s. William James and Adelaide Veronica (Schmitt) I.; m. Kaaren Teresa Gonsoulin, Mar. 7, 1983; children: Erika, Jens, Tim, Scott. BA in History, Carleton Coll., 1967; MA in History, U. Wis., 1969, PhD in History, 1975. Vis. asst. prof. Ariz. State U., Tempe, 1975-76; from asst. prof to prof. U. Wyo., Laramie, 1976-86; coordinator div. social and behavioral scis. Ariz. State U., Phoenix, 1986-88; prof. history Ariz. State U., Tempe, 1988—; vis. prof. Carleton Coll., 1991; Panelist, reviewer Nat. Endowment Humanities, Washington, 1986—. Author: The Navajos: A Critical Bibliography, 1976, The Navajo Nation, 1981, Carlos Montezuma, 1982, The Navajos, 1990, When Indians Became Cowboys: Native Peoples and Cattle Ranching in the American West, 1994, Barry Goldwater: Native Arizonan, 1997, We Are Still Here: American Indians in the 20th Century, 1998, Riders of the West: Portraits From Indian Rodeo, 1999; co-editor: Indians in American History, 1998; editor: The Plains Indians of the 20th Century, 1985; co-editor: Major Problems in American Indian History, 1994; assoc. editor The Historian, 1990-95; editl. bd. Pacific Hist. Rev., 1986-88, Jour. Ariz. History, 1987-89, Social Sci. Jour., 1988-96, Montana: The Magazine of Western History, 1993—. Acting dir. McNickle Ctr. for History of Am. Indian, Newberry Libr., 1994-95, mem. adv. bd., 1993—; bd. dirs. Ariz. Humanities Coun., 1993-99; chmn. Wyo. Coun. Humanities, 1981-82; mem. Heard Mus., Phoenix, 1986—, Desert Bot. Garden, Phoenix, 1986—. Recipient Chief Manuelito Appreciation award Navajo Nation, 1984; Newberry Libr. fellow, Chgo., 1973-74, Nat. Endowment Humanities fellow, 1982-83, Leadership fellow Kellogg Found., Battle Creek, Mich., 1982-85, Disting. Achievement award Carleton Coll. Alumni Assn., 1992; NEH fellow, 1999-2000; Guggenheim Found. fellow, 1999-2000. Mem. Am. Soc. Ethnohistory (coun. 1991-93, chmn. program com. 1994, chmn. prize com. 1987), Western Social Sci. Assn. (pres. 1988-89), Orgn. Am. Historians, Western History Assn. (chmn. prize com. 1991, co-chmn. program com. 1995—, coun. 1995-98). Office: Ariz State U Dept History Tempe AZ 85287-2501

IVERSON, WAYNE DAHL, landscape architect, consultant; b. Mt. Horeb, Wis., Oct. 27, 1931; s. Inman Oliver and Anna Mathilda (Dahl) I.; m. Barbara Ruth Lusk, May 17, 1958; children: David, Ann, Caroline. BS, U. Wis., 1955, MS, 1956. Landscape architect Nat. Pk. Svc., San Francisco, 1956-58, Inyo Nat. Forest, Bishop, Calif., 1958-66; regional landscape architect, So. region U.S. Forest Svc., Atlanta, 1966-67, Calif. region, 1967-86; prin. Scenic Resource Mgmt., Sedona, Ariz., 1987—. Author: (handbook) National Forest Landscape Management, (with others) Landscape Assessment, 1975, (with others) American Landscape Architecture, 1989. co-founder No. Ariz. Trust Lands, Sedona, 1988 mem. bd. adjustment City of Sedona, 1989; mem. pks. and recreation com. Coconino County, Flagstaff, Ariz., 1989-97; bd. dirs. Keep Sedona Beautiful, Inc., 1988-97. Cpl. U.S. Army, 1952-54, Korea. Recipient 1st Alumni award Landscape Architecture dept., U. Wis., Madison, 1981, Award of Excellence, Nat. Soc. for Pk. Resources, 1982, Presdl. Design award Nat. Endowment for Arts, 1984, 1st Arthur Hawthorne Carhart award U.S. Forest Svc., 1992. Fellow Am. Soc. Landscape Architects. Avocations: hiking, travel, photography, nature study. Office: Scenic Resources Mgmt 115 Highland Rd Sedona AZ 86336-6152

IVES, ADRIENE DIANE, real estate executive; b. Washington, Oct. 6, 1951; d. Edwin Forrest and Carolyn Elizabeth (Wray) Warner; m. Perry Nelson Ives, May 12, 1972; children: Jesse Warner, James Robert. BS, U. Md., 1973. Residential broker. Tchr. Charles County (Md.) Bd. Edn., 1973-83, Broad Creek Day Sch., Ft. Washington, Md., 1983-85; sales counselor L.K. Farrall, Ltd., Camp Springs, Md., 1985-90; tchr. real estate Farrall Inst., Waldorf, Md., 1990—; assoc. broker Century 21, Donald & Assocs. Inc., Ft. Washington, 1990-96, Century 21, AAA Realty, Ltd., Clinton, Md., 1996—; tchr. Christian Children's Ministry, Washington, 1982-83; v.p. The Warner Corp., Washington, 1982-83; bd. dirs. Nat. Plumbing Supply, Inc., Washington; devel. agt. Burgundy Farm Country Day Sch., Alexandria, Va., 1986-91; isntr. real estate edn. Farrall Inst., 1990. Author: Nat. City Christ Church, 1988, 89; contbr. articles to jours. Bd. dirs. Broad Creek Country Day Sch., 1982-83; bd. deaconesses Nat. City Christian Ch., Washington, 1989-91. Recipient Citizenship award Prince Georges County Police, Forestville, Md., 1986. Mem. Prince Georges Assn. Realtors (Disting. Sales Assoc. of the Yr. 1995), Women's Coun. Realtors (pres. local chpt. 1994-95), Resdl. Sales Coun. (CRS designation), Brokers and Mgrs. Coun. (CRB cert.). Republican. Mem. Christian Ch. (Disciples of Christ). Avocations: jogging, swimming. Office: Century 21 AAA Realty Ltd 9000 Old Branch Ave Clinton MD 20735-2566

IVES, COLTA FELLER, museum curator, educator; b. San Diego, Apr. 5, 1943; m. E. Garrison Ives, June 14, 1966; 1 child, Lucy Barrett. BA, Mills Coll., 1964; MA, Columbia U., 1966. Staff Met. Mus. Art, N.Y.C., 1966—, curator in charge prints and photographs, 1975-93, curator dept. drawings and prints, 1993—; adj. prof. Columbia U., 1970-85. Author: The Great Wave, 1974, Art Libraries Assn. award, 1975, The Flight Into Egypt, 1972, R. Rauschenberg Photos In and Out City Limits: New York, 1981, French Prints in the Era of Impressionism and Symbolism, 1988, Toulouse-Lautrec in the Metropolitan Museum of Art, 1996; co-author: The Painterly Print, 1980, Pierre Bonnard: The Graphic Art, 1989, Daumier Drawings, 1992, Goya in the Metropolitan Museum of Art, 1995, The Private Collection of Edgar Degas, 1997 (Best Show of 1997-98 N.Y.C. Mus. Internat. Assn. Art Critics). Chmn. grants com. Met. Mus. Art, 1986-87. Mem. Print Council Am. (exec. bd. 1975-77, 84-87, v.p. 1989-93). Office: Met Mus Art Fifth Ave New York NY 10028-0198

IVES, EDWARD DAWSON, folklore educator; b. White Plains, N.Y., Sept. 4, 1925; s. Warren Livingston and Millicent Clarissa (Dawson) I.; m. Barbara Ann Herrel, Sept. 8, 1951; children—Stephen John, Nathaniel Edward, Sarah Ruth. A.B., Hamilton Coll., 1948; M.A., Columbia U., 1950; Ph.D., Ind. U., 1962; LL.D., U. P.E.I., 1986; DLitt, Meml. U., Newfoundland, 1996. Instr. English Ill. Coll., Jacksonville, 1950-53; lectr. CCNY, 1953-54; instr. English U. Maine, Orono, 1955-62, asst. prof., 1962-64, assoc. prof., 1964-69, prof. folklore, 1969—, chmn. anthropology dept., 1983-89; dir. Northeast Archives Folklore and Oral History, 1971—, Maine Folklife Ctr., 1992—. Author: Larry Gorman: The Man Who Made the Songs, 1964, reprinted 1993, Lawrence Doyle: The Farmer-Poet of Prince Edward Island, 1971, Joe Scott: The Woodsman-Songmaker, 1978, The Tape Recorded Interview, 1980, reprinted 1995, George Magoon and the Down East Game War, 1988, reprinted 1993, Folksongs of New Brunswick, 1989; (with Bruce Jackson) The World Observed, 1996, The Bonny Earl of Murray, 1997, Drive Dull Care Away, 1999. Served with USMC, 1943-46. Guggenheim fellow, 1965-66. Fellow Am. Folklore Soc.; mem. Oral History Assn. Home: RR 1 Box 535 Bucksport ME 04416-9708

IVES, J. ATWOOD, financial executive; b. Atlanta, May 1, 1936; s. Stephen Bradshaw and Ellen (Atwood) I.; m. Elizabeth Saalfield; children: Ian, Anna, Benjamin. BA in Econs., Yale U., 1959; MBA, Stanford U., 1961; AMP, Harvard U., 1975. CPA, Calif. Acct. Price, Waterhouse & Co., San Francisco, 1961-64; fin. analyst Textron, Inc., Providence, 1964-66; ptnr., v.p. Paine Webber Jackson & Curtis, 1966-74; dir. Gen. Cinema Corp., Chestnut Hill, Mass., 1970-92, sr. v.p. fin., CFO, 1974-83, exec. v.p., CFO, 1983-84, vice-chmn., CFO, 1985-91, mem. office of chmn., 1983-91; vice-chmn., CFO The Neiman Marcus Group, Inc., 1987-91, also bd. dirs.; chmn., CEO Eastern Enterprises, 1991—; trustee Ea. Enterprises, Weston, Mass., 1989—; dir. or trustee of several mut. funds advised by Mass. Fin. Svcs. Co.; corp. adv. bd. Stanford U. Grad. Sch. of Bus., Carroll Sch. of Mgmt., Boston Coll. Trustee Mus. Fine Arts, Boston; bd. dirs. United Way of Mass. Bay, Mass. Bus. Roundtable. With U.S. Army, 1961-62. Recipient award Haskins and Sells Found., 1961. Home: 17 W Cedar St Boston MA 02108-1211 Office: Eastern Enterprises 9 Riverside Rd Weston MA 02493-2281

IVES, JOHN DAVID (JACK IVES), geography and environmental sciences educator; b. Grimsby, Eng., Oct. 15, 1931; came to U.S., 1967; s. Harry and Ellen May (Mackay) I.; m. Pauline Angela H. Cordingley, Sept. 11, 1954; children: Nadine Elizabeth, Anthony Ragnar, Colin Harry, Peter Robert. BA in Gen. Geography/Geology, U. Nottingham, 1952, BA in Geography, 1953; PhD, McGill U., Montreal, Que., Can., 1956. Postdoctoral rsch. asst. Arctic Inst. N.Am., 1956-57, dir. McGill Subarctic Rsch. Lab.; asst. prof. geography dept. McGill U., 1957-60; asst. dir. geog. br. Canadian Fed. Dept. Mines and Tech. Surveys, chief div. phys. geography, 1960-64; dir. geog. br. Canadian Fed. Dept. Energy, Mines and Resources, Ottawa, Ont., 1964-67; dir. Inst. Arctic and Alpine Rsch.; prof. geography U. Colo., Boulder, 1967-79, prof. mountain geography, 1980-89; prof., chmn. dept. geography U. Calif., Davis, 1989-93, prof. mountain geoecology divsn. environ. studies, 1994-97; rsch. prof. Carleton U., Ottawa, Can., 1997—; guest prof. U. Bern, Switzerland, 1976-77; chmn. internat. working group UNESCO Man and the Biosphere Project 6; chmn. IGU Commn. on Mountain Geoecology and Sustainable Devel., 1972-80, 88-96; mem. adv. com. program natural resources UN U., 1978-85, coord. project on mountain ecology and sustainable devel., 1979—, official univ. del. to Rio de Janeiro Earth Summit, UN Conf. on Environment and Devel., 1992; chmn. Canadian Nat. Adv. Com. on Geog. Research, 1964-67; mem. subcom. snow and ice NRC of Can., 1964-67; mem. commn. on ecology Internat. Union for Conservation Nature and Natural Resources. Co-author: The Himalayan Dilemma: Reconciling Development and Conservation, 1989; co-editor: Arctic and Alpine Environments, 1974; founder, chmn. editorial bd.; Arctic and Alpine Research, 1967-81; contbr. articles to profl. jours. U. Colo. Coun. on Rsch. and Creative Work grantee for Nunatak study in Arctic Norway, 1973; rsch. grantee NASA, 1971-82; rsch. grantee NSF, 1969-79; Guggenheim Meml. fellow, 1976-77; hon. academician Yunnan Acad. of Social Sci., China, 1994—. Fellow Royal Geog. Soc., Geol. Soc. Am., Arctic Inst. N.Am. (bd. govs.); mem. Glaciological Soc., Internat. Mountain Soc. (founding pres. 1980, editor Mountain R & D quar. 1981—), Am. Assn. Geographers, Chinese Glaciological Soc., Ctrl. Himalayan Environ. Assn., World Mountain Network Newsletter, 1990. Home: 412 Thessaly Cir, Ottawa Ontario, CANADA K1H 5W5 Office: Carleton Univer Dept of Geography, 1125 Colonel By Drive, Ottawa, ON Canada K1S 5B6 *I find comfort in adhering to a personal optimism; even if we can only envisage a partial solution, or a tiny step forward, we must try. The world is worth trying for and we can best do this through working with our fellow men and women.*

IVES, SAMUEL CLIFTON, minister; b. Farmington, Maine, Nov. 13, 1937; s. Alfred H. and Alice (Smith) I.; m. Jane Petherbridge, June 6, 1959; children: Bonnie, Stephen, Jonathan. BA, U. Maine, 1960; STB, Boston U., 1963, D of Ministry, 1983. Pastor Cape Elizabeth (Maine) United Meth. Ch., 1962-68, First United Meth. Ch., Bangor, Maine, 1968-73; dir. Maine Conf. Coun. on Ministries, Winthrop, Maine, 1973-77; sr. pastor Waterville (Maine) United Meth. Ch., 1977-86; dist. supt. So. Dist. United Meth. Ch., Portland, Maine, 1986-92; elected bishop United Meth. Ch., assigned to W.Va., Charleston, 1992—; del. Gen. Conf. United Meth. Ch., 1972, 74, 80, 84, 88, 92; mem. exec. com. Maine Coun. Chs., 1981-92; pres. Appalachian Devel. com., 1996—; v.p. W.Va. Coun. of Chs. Mem. Gen. Bd. Discipleship United Meth. Ch., 1984-92, pres. Gen. Commn. on Religion and Race, 1996—. Mem. Assn. Couples for Marriage Enrichment (cert. leader and trainer 1979—). Home: 1804 Shadybrook Rd Charleston WV 25314-2268

IVESTER, (RICHARD) GAVIN, industrial designer; b. San Jose, Calif., May 28, 1963. BS in Indsl. Design, San Jose State U., 1987; postgrad., Domus Acad., Milan, 1989. Materials clk., project coord., product designer Apple Computer, Cupertino, Calif., 1981-87, indsl. designer, 1987-92; prin. Tonic Indsl. Design, Palo Alto, Calif., 1992-97; dir. footwear design Nike, Inc., Beaverton, Oreg., 1997—; guest lectr. Stanford (Calif.) U., 1991—; indsl. designer for Apple Computer, Silicon Graphics, Sun Microsys., Bell Sports, Sony Microsys., Hewlett-Packard, Samsung, Digidesign, Nike. Co-inventor PowerBook; patentee in field. Recipient Ann. Design Rev. awards ID, 1988, 90, 91, 92, Industrie Forum Hannover Top Ten Design award for Macintosh Power Books, Germany, 1992, 93, Top Ten Design award for Newton, 1994, Gold award for Macintosh PowerBooks, Indsl. Designers Soc. Am., 1992, 93. Avocations: playing bass in a rock band, painting, bicycling. Office: Nike Inc One Bowerman Dr MJ-4 Beaverton OR 97005-6453*

IVESTER, MELVIN DOUGLAS, beverage company executive; b. New Holland, Ga., Mar. 26, 1947; s. Howard Edward and Ada Mae (Pass) I.; m. Victoria Kay Grindle, Mar. 20, 1969. BBA cum laude, U. Ga., 1969. Acct., Ernst & Ernst, Atlanta, 1969-75; mgr. Ernst & Whinney, Atlanta, 1975-79; asst. contr., dir. corp. auditing The Coca-Cola Co., Atlanta, 1979-81, v.p., contr., 1981-83, sr. v.p. fin., 1983-84; sr. v.p., CFO, 1985-89, pres. European Cmty. Group, 1989-90, pres., Coca-Cola USA, 1990-91, pres. Coca-Cola N.Am. Group, 1991-93, prin. oper. officer, 1993-94; pres., COO The Coca-Cola Co., 1994-97, also bd. dirs.; chmn., CEO The Coca-Cola Co., 1997—; bd. dirs. Georgia Pacific Corp., Sun Trust, Inc., trustee Morehouse Coll., Am. Enterprise Inst. Pub. Policy Rsch.; former trustee, dir. U. Ga. Found. With USAR, 1970-76. Club: Capital City, Peachtree Golf Club. Home: 411 Peachtree Battle Ave NW Atlanta GA 30305-4032 Office: The Coca-Cola Co 1 Coca Cola Plz NW Atlanta GA 30313-2499

IVEY, DONALD GLENN, physics educator; b. Clanwilliam, Man., Can., Feb. 6, 1922; s. Carle and Sheila (Reid) I.; m. Marjorie Eileen Frisby, June 28, 1944; children: Donna Marleen, Sharon Eileen, David Donald Glenn. BA, U. B.C., Vancouver, Can., 1944, MA, 1946; PhD, U. Notre Dame, 1949. Instr. U. B.C., 1944-46; rsch. assoc. U. Notre Dame, South Bend, Ind., 1946-49; asst. prof. physics U. Toronto, Ont., Can., 1949-57, assoc. prof., 1957-63, prof., 1963-87, prin. New Coll., 1963-74, v.p., 1980-84, prof. emeritus, 1987—. Author: (high sch. textbook) Physics, 1955, (univ. textbook) Physics, 1974; writer, performer TV series Two for Physics, also others, 1958-65, ednl. films Frames of Reference, also others, 1960-63. Recipient award for best sci. edn. film Edison Found., 1962; libr. named in his honor U. Toronto, 1975. Mem. Can. Assn. Physicists, Am. Assn. Physics Tchrs. (Disting. Svc. citation 1979, Millikan award 1987), Am. Phys. Soc., Sigma Xi. Avocation: tennis. Home: 34 Yewfield Cres, Don Mills, ON Canada M3B 2Y6 Office: U Toronto, U Toronto Dept Physics, 60 St George St, Toronto, ON Canada M5S 1A7*

IVEY, ELIZABETH S., acoustician, physicist; b. Schenectady, N.Y., Apr. 21, 1935; married, 1957 (div.), remarried, 1982; 5 children. BS in Physics, Simmons Coll., 1957; MA in Teaching, Harvard U., 1959; PhD in Mech. Engrng. Acoustics, U. Mass., 1976. Prof. physics Simmons Coll., 1958-59, Bucknell U., 1960-63; prof. physics Colo. State U., Ft. Collins, 1964-68, assoc. dean faculty, 1982-85, Louise Wolff Kahn prof., from 1985; prof. physics Smith Coll., 1969-90, chmn. dept. physics, 1983-90; provost Macalester Coll., St. Paul, 1990-95, U. Hartford, West Hartford, Conn., 1995—; vis. prof. Yale U., 1982. Bd. dirs. Minn. Inst. Talented Youth, 1990-95, World Press Inst., 1990-93, St. Paul Area United Way, 1990-95. Recipient Woman Engr. award Soc. Women Engrs., 1988. Mem. AAAS, Acoustical Soc. Am., Am. Assn. Physics Tchrs. Office: U Hartford Office of the Provost 200 Bloomfield Ave West Hartford CT 06117-0395

IVEY, JUDITH, actress; b. El Paso, Tex., Sept. 4, 1951; d. Nathan Aldean and Dorothy Lee (Lewis) I.; m. Tim Braine, 1989; children: Maggie, Thomas Carter. BS, Ill. State U., 1973. Actress in stage plays: The Sea, 1974, The Philanthropist, Hay Fever, Romeo and Juliet, Two Gentlemen of Verona, Mourning Becomes Electra, 1975, Don Juan, Cactus Flower, As You Like It, Design for Living, 1976, The Goodbye People, The Moundbuilders, Oh, Coward, Much Ado About Nothing, 1977-78, Bedroom Farce, 1979, Dusa, Fish, Stas and VI, 1980, Piaf, 1980-81, The Dumping Ground, 1981, The Rimers of Eldritch, 1981, Pastorale, 1982, Two Small Bodies, 1982, Steaming, 1982-83 (Tony award 1983, Drama Desk award 1983), Second Lady, 1983, Hurlyburly, 1984 (Tony award 1985, Drama Desk award 1985), Precious Sons, 1986, Blithe Spirit, 1987, Mrs. Dally Has a Lover, 1988, Park Your Car in Harvard Yard, 1991, The Moonshot Tape, 1994 (Obie award 1994), A Fair Country, 1996, A Madhouse in Goa, 1997; films include: Harry and Son, 1984, The Lonely Guy, 1984, The Woman in Red, 1984, Compromising Positions, 1985, Brighton Beach Memoirs, 1986, Hello Again, 1987, Sister Sister, 1988, Miles from Home, 1988, Love Hurts, 1989, In Country, 1989, Alice, 1990, Everybody Wins, 1990, There Goes the Neighborhood, 1992, Washington Square, 1996, Pre, 1996, A Life Less Ordinary, 1996, Devil's Advocate, 1997, Without Limits, 1998; TV films include: The Shady Hill Kidnapping, 1980, Dixie Changing Habits, 1982, We Are The Children, 1986, The Long, Hot Summer, 1985, Jesse and the Bandit Queen, 1986, Decoration Day, 1990, The Betty Broderick Story, 1992, On Promised Land, 1994, Almost Golden, 1995, What the Deaf Man Heard, 1997; TV series: Down Home, 1990-91, Designing Women, 1992-93, The Five Mrs. Buchanans, 1994, Buddies, 1995. Address: 419 Larchmont Dr # Ste 17 Los Angeles CA 90004*

IVEY, MICHAEL WAYNE, mortgage broker; b. Albany, Ga., Nov. 27, 1964; s. Samuel Warlick and Barbara Ann (Norton) I. BBA, U. Ga., 1986. Cert. mortgage broker. Mortgage broker First So. Mortgage, Atlanta, 1986-87, Fed. Savs. Bank, Atlanta, 1987-88, Paragon Mortgage Corp., Atlanta, 1988-94; br. mgr. Globe Mortgage, Atlanta, 1994-95; regional v.p. 1st Mortgage Network, Atlanta, 1995-97; CEO, pres., cert. mortgage broker Capital City Mortgage Corp., Atlanta, 1997—; hon. comdr. Dobbins Air Res. Base, NAS Atlanta, 1998; bd. dirs. Powers Ridge Office Park, Cobb County Children's Ctr. Exec. coun. mem. Realtors Polit. Action Com., Cobb County, Atlanta, 1987-95; mem. Leadership Cobb, 1996-97. Mem. Mortgage Broker Assn., Cobb County Bd. Realtors (affiliate), Cobb Insiders (pres. 1989-90), Cobb C. of C. (Leadership Cobb Class 1996-97, Hon. Comdrs. 1998), Marietta Kiwanis, Vinings Rotary. Republican. Methodist. Home: 4682 Dudley Ln NW Atlanta GA 30327-3331 Office: Capital City Mortgage Corp Bldg 7 Ste 2100 1827 Powers Ferry Rd NW Atlanta GA 30339-1827

IVEY, WILLIAM JAMES, foundation executive, writer, producer; b. Detroit, Sept. 6, 1944; s. William James and Grace Christine (Hammes) I.; m. Saundra Keyes, June 19, 1969 (div. 1976); m. Patricia A. Hall, Mar. 5, 1977 (div. 1982). B.A. in History, U. Mich., 1966; M.A. in Folklore and Ethnomuscicology, Ind. U., 1969. Dir. Country Music Found., 1971—; chmn. Nat. Endowment for the Arts, 1998—; assoc. prof. music Bklyn. Coll., 1979-80; adj. prof. music Blair Sch. Vanderbilt U., 1983-84; chmn. folk music panel Nat. Endowment Arts, 1976-78, chmn. folk arts panel, 1985-86; bd. dirs. Nashville Songwriters Assn., 1974-75. Prin. writer 1987 Grammy Lifetime Achievement Awards, CBS-TV, 1988 Grammy Awards, CBS-TV; writer, producer In The Hank Williams Tradition, PBS-TV, 1990; co-producer Marlboro Music Festival, 1989-91; writer, producer Country Music Hall of Fame, CBS TV, 1992; contbr. articles to profl. jours., chpts. to books. Recipient Billboard Country Liner Notes of Year award, 1974; Grammy award nominations, 1975, 83, Best Album Notes; sr. research fellow Inst. Studies Am. Music, 1979-80. Mem. Writer's Guild Am., Nat. Acad. Rec. Arts and Scis. (trustee 1976-80, 88-89, 91-95, v.p. 1980-81, 83-84, nat. pres. 1981-83, nat. chmn. 1989-91), Am. Folklore Soc. (exec. bd. 1982-85), Soaring Soc. Am., Nashville Area C. of C. (chmn. conv. and visitors com. 1984-88), Nashville Tourism Commn., Nat. Acad. TV Arts and Scis. (bd. govs. Nashville chpt. 1984-88), Acad. TV Arts and Scis., Copyright Soc. of the South, Pres. Com. on the Arts and the Humanities. Office: NEA 1100 Pennsylvania Ave NW Washington DC 20506*

IVINS, MARSHA S., aerospace engineer, astronaut; b. Balt., Apr. 15, 1951; d. Joseph L. Ivins. BS in Aerospace Engring., U. Colo., 1973. Lic. pilot. Engr. NASA-Lyndon B. Johnson Space Ctr., 1974—, with crew sta. design br., 1974-80, engr. flight simulation, 1980—, astronaut, 1985—, mission specialist shuttle flight STS-32, 1990, mission specialist shuttle Atlantis Flight, 1992. Mem. Exptl. Aircraft Assn., 99's, Internat. Aerobatic Club. Achievements: flying, reading, baking. Address: NASA Johnson Space Ctr CB Astronaut Office 2101 Nasa Rd 1 Houston TX 77058-3607*

IVINS, MOLLY, columnist, writer; b. Texas, 1944; d. Jim and Margo I. BA, Smith Coll., 1966; postgrad., Inst. Polit. Sci., 1966; MA in Journalism, Columbia U., Paris, 1967. Former reporter The Houston Chronicle, The Mpls. Star Tribune, 1964-1976; reporter The Texas Observer, Austin, 1970-76, The New York Times, 1976-82; Rocky Mountain bur. chief The New York Times, Denver, Colo., 1976-82; former columnist The Dallas Times Herald, 1982-91; columnist Fort Worth Star-Telegram, 1992—. Author: Molly Ivins Can't Say That, Can She?, 1991, Nothin' But Good Times Ahead, 1993; contbr. to periodicals including The Nation, N.Y. Times Book Rev., Mother Jones, Ms., Progressive, others. Office: Fort Worth Star-Telegram 1005 Congress Ave Ste 920 Austin TX 78701-2415

IVINS, STEVEN DAVID, editor; b. Phila., Feb. 17, 1937; s. Charles Max and Edith Ann (Levy) I.; m. Nancy Sanger, Oct. 11, 1974 (div. 1991); children: Mark, Carol, Julie. BS in Econs., U. Pa., 1959, LLB, 1962; LLM, George Washington U., 1969. Bar: Pa. 1962, D.C. 1974. Staff atty. Machinery & Allied Products Inst., Washington, 1964-66, IRS, Washington, 1967-70; atty., adviser Commerce Dept., Washington, 1970-72; assoc. editor Kiplinger Tax Letter, Washington, 1972-75, editor, 1975—. Author: Office of International Operations, 1964, Accumulated Earnings Tax, 1967. Mem. Arlington (Va.) Sch. Bd., 1989-93; mem. Six-Yr. Planning Coms., Arlington Schs., 1985-86; pres. County Coun. of PTA, Arlington, 1988-89, Sycamore Hts. Homeowners Assn., 1994—, Big Bros. of No. Va., 1967-69, Arlington County Planning Commn., 1998—; trustee Arlington County Retirement Sys., 1997—, pres., 1998—. Recipient Outstanding Citizen award, Arlington Sch. Bd., 1988; named Big Brother of Yr., No. Va. Big Bros., 1966. Mem. ABA, D.C. Bar Assn., Fed. Bar Assn., Arlington C. of C. Hebrew. Avocations: bridge. Office: Kiplinger Washington Editors 1729 H St NW Washington DC 20006-3904

IVLEV, BORIS IVANOVICH, physicist; b. Elets, Russia, Apr. 1, 1947; s. Ivan Georgievich and Natalia Borisovna (Pisarevskaia) I.; m. Irina Anatolievna Pavlova; 1 child, Vera. MRS, Phys. Tech. Inst., Moscow, 1970; PhD, Landau Inst., Moscow, 1973, Doctoral Degree, 1980; Diploma of Sr. Researcher, 1982. Rschr. Landau Inst., Moscow, 1970-90, head of superconductivity dept., 1990; researcher U. So. Calif., 1991; rschr. ETH, Zurich, 1992-94; prof. U. San Luis Potosi, Mexico, 1994-96; cons. Oak Ridge Nat. Lab., 1995—; cons. Los Alamos Nat. Lab., 1991—. Mem. Am. Phys. Soc., AAAS. Office: 2616 W Mission Rd Apt 106 Tallahassee FL 32304-2552

IVORY, BENNIE, editor; b. Hot Springs, Ark., June 19, 1951. Exec. editor, v.p. news group The Courier-Journal, Louisville, Ky., 1997—. Office: The Courier Journal 525 W Broadway Louisville KY 40202-2137*

IVORY, JAMES FRANCIS, film director; b. Berkeley, Calif., June 7, 1928; s. Edward Patrick and Hallie Millicent (DeLoney) I. BFA, U. Oreg., 1951; MA in Cinema, U. So. Calif., 1957. Ptnr. Merchant-Ivory Prodns., N.Y.C., 1963—. Dir. films: Venice: Theme and Variations, 1957, The Sword and the Flute, 1959, The Householder, 1963, The Delhi Way, 1964, Shakespeare Wallah, 1965, The Guru, 1969, Bombay Talkie, 1970, Adventures of a Brown Man in Search of Civilization, 1971, Savages, 1972, Autobiography of a Princess, 1975, The Wild Party, 1975, Roseland, 1977, Hullabaloo over Georgie and Bonnie's Pictures, 1978, The Europeans, 1979, The Five Forty Eight, 1979, Jane Austen in Manhattan, 1980, Quartet, 1981, Heat and Dust, 1983, The Bostonians, 1984, A Room with a View, 1986 (Acad. Award nominee for best dir.), Maurice, 1987 (Silver Lion shared award with Ermanno Olmi for best dir. Venice Film Festival 1987), Slaves of New York, 1989, Mr. and Mrs. Bridge, 1990, Howards End, 1992 (Acad. Award nominee for best dir., Cannes Internat. Film Festival 45th Anniversary Prize), The Remains of the Day, 1993 (Academy award nominee, Best dir. 1993), Jefferson in Paris, 1995, Surviving Picasso, 1996, A Soldier's Daughter Never Cries, 1998, (sets and costumes) Handel's Apollo e Dafne Maggio Musicale, Florence, 1997; articles to profl. jours. Served to cpl. U.S. Army, 1953-55. Comdr. des Arts et Lettres (France), 1996; Guggenheim fellow, 1973. Mem. Dirs. Guild Am. (D.W. Griffith award 1995). Democrat. Roman Catholic. Office: Merchant-Ivory Prodns 250 W 57th St New York NY 10107

IVORY, MING MARIE, political scientist; b. Tokyo, Aug. 28, 1949; d. T. Austin and E. Virginia (Christine) I. BS, Tufts U., 1971; MA, U. Pa., 1973; PhD, MIT, 1986. Rsch. asst. Smithsonian Inst., Washington, summer 1970, 71; faculty assoc. Hampshire Coll., Amherst, Mass., 1973-75; profl. asst. NSF, Washington, 1975; sci. reporter Sta. WVHY-FM, Phila., 1976; profl. asst. Office of Sci. Advisor World Bank, Washington, 1977; cons. Internat. Sci. & Tech. Inst., Washington, 1978-79; sci. policy specialist U.S. Agy. for Internat. Devel., Washington, 1979-80, environ. protection specialist, 1980-85; asst. prof. Creighton U., Omaha, 1986-92; vis. asst. prof. Madison Inst. James Madison U., Harrisonburg, Va., 1992-95; assoc. prof. Coll. Integrated Sci. and Tech., 1995—; cons. Bd. on Sci. and Tech. for Internat. Devel. NRC, 1992, Carnegie Corp., 1996. Del. Mass. Govs. Conf. on Librs. and Info. Svcs., 1978; elected del. White House Conf. on Librs. and Info. Svcs., 1979. Mem. Am. Polit. Sci. Assn., Soc. for Internat. Devel., Soc. for Social Studies of Sci. Democrat. Unitarian. Avocations: graphic arts, hiking. Home: 3155 Flint Ave Harrisonburg VA 22801-9036 Office: James Madison U Coll Integrated Sci & Tech Harrisonburg VA 22807

IVORY, PETER B. C. B., medical administrator; b. St. Germans, Eng., Jan. 15, 1927; s. Charles A. and Kathleen H. (Bishop) I.; m. Eleanor Nelson, June 29, 1957 (dec.); children—Mark, Anne; m. Eve Ervin, Dec. 6, 1974; 1 dau., Celeste. M.D., U. London, Eng., 1954. Diplomate: Am. Bd. Psychiatry and Neurology. With Fla. Div. Mental Health, 1961—; clin. dir. Fla. State Hosp., Chattahoochee. Life mem. Am. Psychiat. Assn. Home: PO Box 3193 Tallahassee FL 32315-3193 Office: Fla State Hosp Chattahoochee FL 32324-1000

IVRY, ALFRED LYON, history of, Jewish and Islamic philosophy educator; b. Bklyn., Jan. 14, 1935; s. Morris and Belle (Malamud) I.; m. Joann Saltzman, June 15, 1958; children: Rebecca, Jonathan, Sara Beth, Jessica. B.A., Bklyn. Coll., 1957; M.A., Brandeis U., 1958, Ph.D., 1963; D.Phil., Oxford (Eng.) U., 1971. From asst. prof. to assoc. prof. Cornell U., Ithaca, N.Y., 1967-74; prof. Ohio State U., Columbus, 1974-76; prof. Sch. Near Eastern and Judaic Studies Brandeis U., Waltham, Mass., 1976-89, Walter S. Hilborn prof. Mid. Eastern Studies, 1977-89; Skirball prof. Hebrew and Judaic studies NYU, N.Y.C., 1989—, prof. Mid. East studies, 1989—; co-chmn. Colloquium in Medieval Philosophy, Boston, 1977-81, 84-89 ; chmn. Colloquium in Medieval Philosophy NYU, 1990—. Mem. editl. bd.: Univ. Press of New Eng., 1982, 84, 86; editor: (translator) Al-Kindi's Metaphysics, 1974, Moses of Narbonne: Perfection of the Soul, 1977, Alexander Altmann: The Meaning of Jewish Existence, 1991, Averroes' Middle Commentary on Aristotles De anima, 1993. Trustee Boston Hebrew Coll., 1981-87, adj. prof., 1983-90. Fulbright fellow, 1963-65, 72, 1982-83; grantee NEH, 1978-79, 80-81. Fellow Am. Oriental Soc., Am. Philos. Assn., Assn. for Jewish Studies (bd. dirs. 1971-74), Medieval Acad. Am., Soc. Medieval and Renaissance Philosophy (bd. dirs. 1985-90, v.p. 1993-94, pres. 1995-96), Am. Acad. for Jewish Rsch. (bd. dirs. 1989—). Jewish.

IVY, BERRYNELL BAKER, critical care nurse; b. Shreveport, La., June 24, 1954; d. Berry William and Zilphia Margaret (Nix) Baker; m. Kenneth James Ivy, Sr.,Apr. 17, 1988. ADN, Northwestern State U., 1981. RN, La., Tex.; cert. BLS, ACLS; cert. neurosci. RN; cert. CCRN. Charge nurse Doctors Hosp., Shreveport, La., 1982-85; staff nurse ICU Schumpert Med. Ctr., Shreveport, La., 1985-88; staff nurse ICU Bayshore Med. Ctr., Pasadena, Tex., 1988-89, asst. head nurse ICU, 1989-92; staff nurse/charge nurse ICU Bossier Med. Ctr., Bossier City, La., 1993—; co-chmn. profl. practice com., approved designated requester La. Organ Procurement Agy., Bossier City, 1988—. Mem. AACN, Nat. League Nurses, Am. Assn. Neurosci. Nurses, Soc. Critical Care Medicine. Avocations: raising boxers, sports, travel. Home: PO Box 52 Haughton LA 71037-0052

IVY, EDWARD JOSEPH, plastic surgeon; b. Jan. 23, 1958. MD, Georgetown U., 1985. Resident in surgery Mayo Clinic, Rochester, Minn., 1985-90, fellow in plastic surgery, 1990-92; fellow in aesthetic surgery Manhattan (N.Y.) Eye, Ear and Throat Hosp., 1993-98; pvt. practice plastic surgery San Francisco. Home: 22 Hunting Hill Dr Dix Hills NY 11746-6567

IVY, JOHN L., medical educator, researcher; b. Portsmouth, Va., Dec. 26, 1946. BS in Phys. Edn., Old Dominion U., 1970; MA in Exercise Physiology, U. Md., 1974, PhD in Exercise Physiology, 1976. Tchr. phys. edn. and sci. Thomas Eaton Jr. H.S., Hampton, Va., 1970; biology and physiology tchr., asst. football coach, head golf coach Kecoughtan H.S., Hampton, Va., 1971-73; asst. prof. biokinetics rsch. lab. dept. phys. edn. Temple U., Phila., 1976-77; rsch. assoc. Human Performance Lab., Ball State U., Muncie, Ind., 1976-77; postdoctoral fellow dept. preventive medicine Washington U. Sch. Medicine, St. Louis, 1978-80; asst. prof. dept. phys. edn. Coll. Health and Sch. Medicine dept. pharmacology U. S.C., Columbia, 1980-82; asst. prof. dept. kinesiology and health edn. Coll. Edn. U. Tex., Austin, 1982-84, assoc. prof. dept. kinesiology and health edn. Coll. Edn., 1984-89, prof., dir. exercise scis. labs. dept. kinesiology and health edn. Coll. Edn. and divsn. pharmacology Coll. Pharmacy, 1989—, Margie Gurley Seay Centennial prof., 1998—, chmn. dept. kinesiology and health edn., 1999—; cons. clin. diabetes and nutrition sect. NIH, Phoenix, 1985-87; cons. com. mil. nutrition rsch. U.S. Army, 1987-88; mem. adv. bd. performance team Women's Athletic Dept. U. Tex., 1988—; cons. Sports and Cardiovasc. Nutritionists, 1989-92, outside mem. long range planning com., 1989-90; cons. Shaklee U.S., Inc., 1988—; mem. adv. bd. Q Health Club, 1994-96; cons. U.S. Olympic Com. Sports Medicine com. nutrition, 1992-94; mem. com. mil. nutrition and rsch. rev. panel NAS, 1995—. Contbr. articles to profl. jours., chpts. to books; jour. reviewer: Am. Jour. Physiology, Endocrinology and Metabolism, 1993—, Jour. Optimal Nutrition, 1993—, Diabetes, 1987-88, Internat. Jour. Sports Nutrition, 1995—; sect. editor physiology Rsch. Quar. for Exercise and Sport, 1988-91; mem. editl. bd. Medicine and Sci. in Sports and Exercise, 1987—; reviewer: Jour. Applied Physiology, Am. Jour. Physiology, Medicine and Sci. in Sports and Exercise, Internat. Jour. of Sports Medicine, Rsch. Quar., Am. Jour. Clin. Nutrition, Diabetes, Jour. Clin. Investiagation, Internat. Jour. Sports Nutrition; presenter in field. Recipient Nat. Rsch. Svc. award NIH, 1978-80; grantee NIH, Tex. Heart Assn., Ross Products, Pfizer, Inc., Shaklee U.S., Inc., U.S Olympic Rsch. Com. Fellow Am. Coll. Sports Medicine (midwest chpt. 1977-79, southeast chpt. 1980-82, Tex. chpt. bd. trustees 1985-86, 92-95, Tex. chpt. exec. dir. 1986-91, bd. trustees rep. for basic and applied sci. 1986-89, ambassador 1986—, mem. rsch. rev. com. 1991-95, organizer, chair symposium diabetes and exercise I regulation of muscle glucose metabolism acute and chronic effects of exercise 1988), Am. Acad. Kinesiology Phys. Edn.; mem. Am. Physiol. Soc., Am. Diabetes Assn. (mem. nutrition scis. and metabolism coun., mem. exercise coun., sec. exercise coun. 1991-93, program chair exercise coun. 1993, organizer, chair symposium role of exercise and phys. activity in the prevention of type II diabetes 1992, organizer, chair symposium exercise through the ages, 1994, grantee, rsch. award 1996), Am. Inst. Nutrition, Am. Soc. Clin. Nutrition, Inc., Phi Epsilon Kappa, Sigma Xi. Office: U Tex Dept Kinesiology Austin TX 78712*

IVY, ROBERT ADAMS, JR., architect, editor-in-chief; b. Columbus, Miss.; m. Holly Ivy; children: Virginia Edmunds, Robert Adams, Benjamin Ledyard. BA cum laude, U. South, 1969; BArch, Tulane U., 1976. Consulting arch. Columbus, 1981-96; editor-in-chief Archtl. Record Mag., N.Y.C., 1996—. Author: Fay Jones: Architect, 1991; editor Architecture South mag., 1993-96; prodr., screenwriter (documentary film) 1,000 Homes. Pres. Greater Columbus, 1987-89; co-founder Greater Columbus Learning Ctr., Inc.; trustee Columbus-Lowndes Libr., 1984—, also chmn., 1987, 91; vestry mem. St. Paul's Episcopal Ch., Columbus, 1985-87; mem. adv. bd. The Dwelling Pl., Ctr. for So. Culture, 1993—. Lt. USNR, 1970-73. Fellow AIA (bd. dirs. 1993-96); mem. Am. Architecture Found. (bd. regents 1993-96), Miss. Inst. of Arts and Letters (bd. dirs. 1993—), Rembrandt Club. Office: Archtl Record 2 Penn Plz New York NY 10121

IWAMOTO, RALPH SHIGETO, artist; b. Honolulu, Sept. 13, 1927; s. Shigeo and Hatsu (Hibi) I.; m. Kathleen M. Zimmerman, Nov. 23, 1963. Student, Bklyn. C.C., 1949-51, Art Students League, 1948-49, 51-53. One-man shows at Regina Gallery, N.Y.C., 1955, Gima Gallery, Honolulu, 1956, Columbia (S.C.) Mus. Art, 1959, Watson Gallery, Elmira (N.Y.) Coll., 1968, Westbeth Gallery, N.Y.C., 1973, 74, SCAF Gallery, Sharon, Conn., 1986, St. Mary's Coll., St. Mary's City, Md., 1989; exhibited in group shows at Bergen County Cmty. Mus., Paramus, N.J., 1983, Newark Mus., 1983, Bloomingdale Gallery, Stamford, Conn., 1984, Haragiku Mus., Tokyo, 1984, Isetan Gallery, Tokyo, 1985, Kenkeleba Gallery, N.Y.C., 1985, Nassau C.C., Garden City, N.Y., 1986, Contemporary Artists Guild, GSA Gallery, N.Y.C., 1986, Contemporary Mus., Honolulu, 1990, Wadsworth Atheneum, Hartford, Conn., 1991, Zimmerli Art Mus., Rutgers U., New Brunswick, N.J., 1997, Taipei Gallery, N.Y.C., 1997, Chgo. Cultural Ctr., 1997, Japanese Am. Nat. Mus., L.A., 1997, Bedford Gallery, Walnut Creek, Calif., 1998, Taipei Fine Arts Mus., Taiwan, 1998, Kaohsiung Mus., Taipei, 1998, Mokuma Mus. Contemporary Art, Kochi, Japan, 1999, Fukuoka Art Mus., Kyushu, 1999, Senshu Mus. Art, Akita, Japan, 1999; represented in permanent collections at Butler Inst. Am. Art, Youngstown, Ohio, Sheldon Swope Art Gallery, Terre Haute, Ind., Herbert Johnson Mus./Cornell U., Ithaca, N.Y., State Found. on Culture and Arts, Honolulu, Thurston Twigg-Smith Collection/Contemporary Arts Mus., Honolulu, Honolulu Advertiser Publ. Collection, Honolulu, St. Mary's Coll. Gallery, St. Mary's City, Md., Wadsworth Atheneum, Hartford, Conn., Zimmerli Mus./Rutgers U., New Brunswick, N.J., Japanese Cultural Ctr. of Hawaii, Honolulu, others, also pvt. collections. With U.S. Army, 1946-48. Recipient Purchase prize Butler Inst. Am. Art, 1957; John Hay Whitney Found. fellow, 1958; Adolph and Esther Gottlieb Found. grantee, 1987. Mem. N.Y. Artists Equity. Home: 463 West St Apt A1110 New York NY 10014-2040

IWEKA, VANESSA ANN, nurse midwife, educator; b. Jackson, Ala., Feb. 27, 1957; d. Willie James and Addie Mae (Moore) Hightower; m. Kingsley Eloka Iweka, June 10, 1981; children: Evette, Emmanuel, Phillip. Cert., S.W. State Tech. Coll., Mobile, Ala., 1975; BSN, U. South Ala., 1983; nurse-midwife cert., U. So. Calif., 1988. LPN, RN; cert. nurse-midwife; cert. ARC instr. Staff nurse Springhill Meml. Hosp., Mobile, 1975-81; staff nurse, midwife King/Drew Med. Ctr., L.A., 1983-86; staff nurse U. So. Calif. Med. Ctr., L.A., 1986-87; nurse, midwifery instr. Charles Drew Univ. of Medicine and Sci., L.A., 1991—; staff nurse, midwife King/Drew Med. Ctr., L.A.; nurse, midwife King/Drew Med. Ctr., 1989—; rev. instr. RONA Ednl. Inst., L.A. Mem. Calif. Nurses Assn., Phi Theta Kappa. Address: PO Box 1424 Moreno Valley CA 92556-1424

IX, ROBERT EDWARD, food company executive; b. Woodcliffe, N.J., Oct. 15, 1929; s. William Edward and Helen Elizabeth (Gorman) I.; m. Mildred Gilmore, June 27, 1959; children: Helen Adele, Alesia Gilmore, Robert Owens Gilmore, Julia Ryan, Christopher Prouty. A.B., Princeton U., 1951; M.B.A., Wharton Grad. Sch., U. Pa., 1956; LL.D. (hon.), Marymount Coll., 1978, Sacred Heart U., Conn., 1984. Mgmt. cons. Arthur D. Little Inc., Cambridge, Mass., 1956-64; mktg. dir. Browne-Vintners Co., Distillers Corp.-Seagrams Ltd., N.Y.C., 1964-66; v.p. mktg. Schweppes (USA) Ltd., N.Y.C., 1966-68; pres. Schweppes (USA) Ltd., 1968; pres., chief exec. officer Cadbury Schweppes Inc., Stamford, Conn., 1970-78; chmn., chief exec. officer Am. region Cadbury Schweppes P.L.C., 1976-86; bd. dirs. Cadbury Schweppes P.L.C., London, N.E. Bancorp Inc., Union Trust Co., New Eng. Frozen Foods, Inc., Am. Thread Co., Binney & Smith Inc., Royal Doulton Co. Inc., Loctite Corp., Health Waters Inc., O'Shaughnessy Funds, Inc. Trustee Marymount Coll., also chmn.; trustee Greenwich (Conn.) Acad., Trinity Pawling Sch. (N.Y.); mem. adv. council N.Y. Med. Coll., Valhalla, N.Y. Served to lt. comdr. USNR, 1951-55. Decorated Knight Sovereign Mil. Order Malta. Mem. Young President's Orgn., World Bus. Council, Chief Execs. Forum, Southwestern Area Commerce and Industry Assn. Conn. (dir. 1970-80 , chmn. bd. 1976-77), Def. Orientation Conf. Assn. (dir.), Grocery Mfrs. Am. (dir. 1981-85), U.S. Navy League (dir. Conn.). Roman Catholic. Clubs: Univ. (N.Y.C.); Belle Haven (Greenwich); Greenwich Country; Landmark (Stamford) (chmn. bd. govs.). Office: 60 Arch St Greenwich CT 06830-2507

IZANT, ROBERT JAMES, JR., pediatric surgeon; b. Cleve., Feb. 4, 1921; s. Robert James and Grace (Goulder) I.; m. Virginia Lincoln Root, Sept. 27, 1947; children: Jonathan G. II, Mary Root, Timothy Holman. AB cum laude, Amherst Coll., 1943; MD, Western Res. U., 1946. Diplomate: Am. Bd. Surgery, Am. Bd. Pediatric Surgery. Resident in surgery U. Hosp., Cleve., 1946-52; resident in pediatric surgery Boston Children's Med. Center, 1952-55; asst. prof. pediatric surgery Ohio State U., 1955-58; prof., dir. pediatric surgery and pediatrics Case Western Res.U., 1958-90, prof. emeritus pediatric surgery and pediatrics, 1990—; dir. div. pediatric surgery Univ. Hosps. Cleve., Rainbow Babies and Children's Hosp.; also MetroHealth Ctr. Hosp., 1958-86; mem. adv. bd. Ohio State Services for Children with Med. Handicaps, 1957—. Co-author: The Surgical Neonate; contbr. articles to profl. jours. Served to lt. (j.g.) M.C. USNR, 1947-49. Fellow A.C.S., Am. Acad. Pediatrics; mem. Central Surg. Assn., Am. Assn. Surgery of Trauma, AMA, Cleve. Surg. Soc. (pres. 1971-72), Cleve. Acad. Medcine (dir. 1971-74), Am. Trauma Soc. (founding mem.), Teratology Soc., Lilliputian Surg. Soc., No. Ohio Pediatric Soc., Brit. Assn. Pediatric Surgery, Pediatric Surgery Biology Club, Am. Pediatric Surg. Assn. (founding mem., pres. 1987-88), Western Res. U. Sch. Medicine Alumni Assn. (pres. 1961-62), Am. Burn Assn., Sigma Xi, Alpha Omega Alpha, Nu Sigma Nu, Delta Kappa Epsilon. Fax: (216) 791-2747. E-mail: rizant@aol.com. Home: 2275 Harcourt Dr Cleveland Heights OH 44106-4614 Office: Rainbow Babies and Childrens Hosp University Cir Cleveland OH 44106

IZARD, C. DOUGLASS, tax specialist; b. Hazelhurst, Miss., May 19, 1948; s. William Cilburn and Hilda Jand (Douglass) I.; m. Deborah Kay Higginbotham, July 14, 1968 (div. Jan. 1992); 1 child, Gregory D.; m. Ellen Reinhart Kidd, May 20, 1995. BS in Acctg., Delta State U., 1970; MBA, Miss. Coll., 1978; PhD in Acctg., U. Miss., 1981. Staff Peat Marwick Mitchell & Co., New Orelans, 1970; acct. Miazza, DeMiller & Word, Jackson, Miss., 1970-73, pvt. practice, Jackson, Miss., 1973-78; teaching asst. U. Miss., Oxford, 1978-80; assoc. prof. U. Tenn., Knoxville, 1980-95; dean sch. taxation IRS, Washington, 1995-97; nat. dir., tax knowledge mgmt. KPMG, Washington, 1997—. Contbr. articles to profl. jours. Lt. col. U.S. Army, 1994-95. Avocations: boating, diving, fishing, hiking,. Office: KPMG LLP 2001 M St NW Washington DC 20036

IZARD, JOHN, lawyer; b. Hartford, Conn., Mar. 4, 1923; s. John and Elizabeth (Andrews) I.; m. Mary Bailey, apr. 16, 1955; children: Sarah Izard Pariseau, John Jr., David Bailey. BS, Yale U., 1945; LLB, U. Va., 1949. Bar: Ga. 1950. Assoc. King & Spalding, Atlanta, 1949-52, ptnr., 1952-90; mem. Adminstrv. Conf. U.S., Washington, 1978-82. Editor-in-chief Va. Law Rev., 1948; contbr. articles to legal periodicals. Mem. Nat. Com. To Study Antitrust Laws and Procedures, Washington, 1978; trustee Episcopal Media Ctr., Atlanta, 1988—, chmn., 1992-96; trustee U. Va. Law Sch. Found., Charlottesville, 1974-97. Lt. (j.g.) USNR, 1944-46, PTO. Mem. ABA (chmn. antitrust sect. 1974-75), Ga. Bar Assn. (chmn. antitrust sect. 1969-71), Atlanta Legal Aid Soc. (pres. 1960), Lawyers Club Atlanta, Capital City Club (bd. dirs. 1976-79), Peachtree Golf Club, Piedmont Driving Club. Democrat. Episcopalian. Home: 4061 Glen Devon Dr NW Atlanta GA 30327-3613 Office: King & Spalding 191 Peachtree St NE Atlanta GA 30303-1740

IZENOUR, STEVEN, architect; b. New Haven, July 16, 1940; s. George Charles and Hildegard (Hilt) I.; m. Elisabeth Margit Gemmill, July 2, 1964; children: Ann, Tessa, John. BA, Swarthmore Coll., 1962; BArch, U. Pa., 1965; MEd, Yale U., 1969. Cert. architect, Pa. Draftsman George C. Izenour & Assocs., New Haven, 1958-65; prin. Venturi, Scott-Brown & Assocs., Phila., 1969—; prin. of mktg. Venturi, Scott-Brown, Phila., 1992—; design critic Sch. Architecture, Drexel U., Phila., 1969-72, 91—, U. Pa., Phila., 1972-91. Co-author: Learning from Las Vegas, 1972, White Towers, 1979. Bd. dirs. Phila. Zool. Gardens, 1989—. Recipient Silver medal Pa. Soc. Architects, 1986. Mem. AIA (Silver medal Phila. chpt. 1985, Nat. Honor award 1987). Avocation: cycling. Office: Venturi Scott Brown & Assocs 4236 Main St Philadelphia PA 19127-1603*

IZENSTARK, JOSEPH LOUIS, radiologist, physician, educator; b. Chgo., Mar. 29, 1919; s. Paul and Flora (Berger) I.; m. Elizabeth Kaplan, June 25, 1944; 1 child, Susan Rebecca. BA, U. Calif., Berkeley, 1948; MD, U. Calif., San Francisco, 1951. Diplomate: Am. Bd. Radiology, Am. Bd. Nuc. Medicine. Intern USPHS, Chgo., 1951-52; resident Kern Gen. Hosp., Bakersfield, Calif., 1952-53; resident in radiology Cedars of Lebanon Hosp., L.A., 1955-56; chief radiology resident Los Angeles County Harbor Gen. Hosp., Torrance, Calif., 1957-58; practice medicine Inglewood, Calif., 1953-55; practice radiology Bakersfield, 1971—; dir. radiology Imperial Hosp., Inglewood, 1959-60; asst. prof. radiology Tulane U., 1960-62, assoc. prof., 1963; assoc. prof. radiology Emory U., 1963-67, dir. nuc. medicine, 1963-67; prof. radiology U. So. Calif., 1969-72; prof. health scis. Bakersfield State Coll., 1973-83; chief nuc. medicine Cedars of Lebanon Hosp., 1968-71; med. dir. edn. Bakersfield Meml. Hosp., 1983-87; spl. cons. radiol. health USPHS, Calif. Bur. Radiol. Health, U.S. Army; mem. La. Atomic Energy Adv. Coun.; dir. nuc. medicine Crawford W. Long Meml. Hosp.; mem. USPHS Commn. on Radiation Exposure Evaluation, Med. Bd. Calif., 1982-91. Author: Anatomy and Physiology for X-ray Technicians, 1961; contbr. articles to profl. jours. With AUS, 1941-45. Recipient Cert. of Merit, City of New Orleans, 1962, Physician of Yr. award Bakersfield Meml. Hosp., 1988, Outstanding Physician Contbns. to Medicine award Calif. State Assembly, 1992. Fellow Am. Cancer Soc., Am. Coll. Radiology; mem. Soc. Nuclear Medicine (pres. So. Calif. chpt. 1976), So. Valley Radiol. Soc. (pres. 1975), Kern County Med. Soc. (pres. 1978). *Set your goal in a definite clear outline taking each step one at a time, as if climbing a ladder. Think about your goals; don't talk about them. Concentrate your abilities, your studies, your friends while denying yourself luxuries. Make your own decisions; stick by them. Don't have regrets. Be honest, sincere, and dedicated without regard to time. Finally, don't give up the fight—stick to your goal.*

IZUCHUKWU, JOHN IFEANYICHUKWU, industrial and mechanical engineer; b. Uke, Nigeria, May 6, 1955; came to U.S., 1976; s. Michael Chike and Cecilia Obiageli (Ikeakor) I.; m. Michele Anthea Palmer, July 22, 1989; children: Michael, John, Joseph. BS in Indsl. Engring., U. Portland, Oreg., 1980, MS in Mech. Engring., 1984; PhD in Indsl. Engring., Northeastern U., 1994. Base mgr. OEM Mfg., Digital Equipment Corp., Portland, Oreg., 1980-85; computer-aided software engring. mgr. Digital Equipment Corp., Marlboro, Mass., 1985-87, mgr. mech. design automation, 1987; mgr. concurrent engring. and application ctr. for tech. Digital Equipment Corp., Rochester, N.Y., 1989-91; group mgr. aerospace product strategy Digital Equipment Corp., Marlboro, 1991-93, worldwide strategy mgr., integrated product devel., 1993-95; team leader, R & D Ethicon Endo-Surgery, Inc., Cin., 1995—; sr. dir. global rsch., devel. and engring. Mallinckrodt, Inc., St. Charles, Mo., 1998—; adj. prof. decision scis. Babson Coll., Wellesley, Mass., 1994-95. Contbr. articles to engring. jours., including Jour. Mfg. Sci. and Engring. Mem. ASME, Inst. Indsl. Engring. (sr. mem.). Home: 18002 Pine Canyon Ct Wildwood MO 63005-4938 Office: Mallinckrodt Inc 3 Missouri Research Park Dr Saint Charles MO 63304-5685

IZZI, JOHN, educator, author; b. Providence, Dec. 31, 1931; s. Joseph and Elizabeth (Kinney) I.; B.A., Providence Coll., 1953; M.Ed., R.I. Coll., 1965; postgrad. (NSF grantee), U. Vt., 1959, 60, 63, Seton Hall U., 1961, Yale U., 1966, Boston U., 1968-70; m. Patricia Margaret Crowley, Aug. 27, 1979; children: John, Matthew, Jessica; children by previous marriage: Kathleen, Donna, James. Tchr. various schs., R.I., 1955-62; head math. dept. Seekonk (Mass.) High Sch., 1966-67; state supr. math. Mass. Dept. Edn., 1967-68; tchr. Pilgrim High Sch., Warwick, R.I., 1962-66, head math. dept., 1968-72; head math. dept. Toll Gate H.S., Warwick, 1972-88; coord. secondary sch. R.I. Hosp., 1988-89; tchr. math. and sci. Westport (Mass.) H.S., 1989-91, math adviser, biology/sci. tchr.; adj. faculty Bristol C.C., Mass., 1992-94; pres. Smallstate Co., Warwick, 1975—; prin. Warwick Adult Edn., 1987-88; extension lectr. U. R.I., 1976—; math. coach Toll Gate Acad. Decathlon State Champions, 1985, New Eng. Math League Divsn. Champions, 1989-90; dir. Prep Inst., Warwick, Math. Edn. Service, Providence, 1965-66, Toll Gate Metrication Project, Warwick, 1972-73; creator 1st federally funded sch. metrication project in U.S. 1972, Izzi Metric Slide Chart, 1974, Izzi Decimal Notation, 1974; dir. Smallstate Math. Inst., Warwick, 1989-90, Smallstate Scholarship Svc., Warwick, 1991-93; pres. Smallstate Pub., 1994-96; advisor Am. Security Com., 1973-79; pres. P & J Izzi Assocs., Warwick, 1995-97, Sand Pond Assocs., Warwick, 1997-99; metrication cons. Nat. Coun. Tchrs. Math., 1973—, computer software reviewer, textbook reviewer 1981-88; adj. faculty C.C. R.I., 1981-85, Bristol C.C., Mass., 1992-94. Mem. Mass. Gov.'s Hwy. Safety Act Com., 1967-68. Served with U.S. Army, 1953-55. Recipient Distinguished Achievement award Ednl. Press Assn. Am., 1974; named Best Math. Tchr. in Am. Ky. Ednl. TV, 1990. Mem. NEA, Am. Fedn. Tchrs., Nat. Council Tchrs. Math., Assn. Supervision and Curriculum Devel., Am. Assn. Sch. Adminstrs. Metric Assn., Assn. Tchrs. Math. in New Eng., New Eng. Regional Metric Assn. (edn. commr. 1976-80), Mass. Dept. Edn. Assn. (v.p. 1967-68). Textbook reviewer AAAS, 1968-74; book reviewer Phi Delta Kappan, 1974-76. Author: Metrication, American Style, 1974, Looking at the Metric System, 1977, Adult Metric Guide, 1977, Basic Metric Competency Test, 1977, My Irish, Voices of America, 1991; editorial adviser New Eng. Math. Jour., 1982-85; contbr. articles to various publs. Home: 243 Greenwood Ave Warwick RI 02886-2015 Office: 1212 Post Rd Warwick RI 02888-3259

IZZO, HERBERT JOHN, language and linguistics educator, researcher; b. Saginaw, Mich., July 17, 1928; s. Joseph Anthony and Eleanor Bertha (Karau) I.; m. Barbara Suzanne McLaughlin, Sept. 22, 1958 (div); children: Victoria Sue, Alexander John, Sylvia Rachel, Daniel Stanley; m. Olga Frances Koutna, Dec. 30, 1989. *The family's teaching tradition began in 1913 when 19-year-old Eleanor, daughter of German immigrant farmers, taught her first class in a one-room school in Elkton, Michigan. Her son became a teacher and so did two of his children: Alex is a professor of mathematics and Vicky an elementary teacher like her grandmother. When Professor Olga Koutna became Mrs. Izzo, the Izzo teaching tradition was merged with a still older one; for Olga's grandfather was a science teacher in Moravia when Eleanor was barely a child, and Olga's late father Otakar was a professor of chemistry at the University of Brno.* BA in Spanish, U. Mich., 1950, MA in Spanish and Italian, 1951, BS in Chemistry, 1953, PhD in Linguistics, 1965. Asst. prof. fgn. langs. Mansfield (Pa.) State Coll., 1957; chargé de cours Huê (Vietnam) U., 1958-59; instr. Spanish U. Ariz., Tucson, 1960-61; instr. Spanish and linguistics Stanford (Calif.) U., 1961-64; asst. prof. Spanish San Jose (Calif.) State U., 1964-68; from assoc. to prof. linguistics U. Calgary, Alberta, Can., 1968—, prof. emeritus, 1988—; vis. prof. Romance linguistics U. Mich., Ann Arbor, 1977-78, 93-94; vis. prof. linguistics U. Bucharest, Romania, 1975-76; vis. prof. Italian, Stanford U., 1990-91; vis. scholar U. Mich., 1997—; mem. adv. bd. Quaderni d'Italianistica, Can., 1979—. Author: Tuscan and Etruscan, 1972; editor: The Sixth LACUS Forum, 1980, Italic and Romance, 1985; editor for linguistics Can. Jour. of Italian Studies, 1988—; translator Lost Papers of Ludwig von Mises, 1998—. Bd. dirs. Fathers Alberta, Calgary, 1986-87. Recipient grad. fellowship U. N.Mex., 1953, Award for Advanced Study, Am. Coun. Learned Socs., 1963, Fulbright-Hays award U.S. Dept. State, 1966, 75. Mem. Am. Assn. Italian Studies, Linguistic Assn. Can. of U.S. (conf. organizer 1978), N.Am. Assn. for History of Lang. Scis. (v.p. 1977-80), Am. Assn. Tchrs. of Italian (life), Linguistic Soc. Am. (life), Am. Assn. Tchrs. of Spanish and Portuguese (life), Can. Soc. Italian Studies (nominating com. 1977-78, adv. bd. 1974-80), Phi Beta Kappa. Libertarian. Avocations: music, history, running. Home: 2515 Deake Ave Ann Arbor MI 48108-1330 Office: Dept Linguistics U Calgary, University Dr, Calgary, AB Canada T2N 1N4

IZZO, LUCILLE ANNE, sales representative; b. Rochester, N.Y., Apr. 1, 1954; d. Peter George and Dorothy June (Cusimano) I. B of Gen. Studies, U. Conn., 1995. Regional sales mgr. T.R. Miller Co., Inc., New Milford, Conn., 1986-87; program mgr. Jr. Achievement SW Conn., Stamford, 1987-88, adviser, cons., 1986-93; sec. Eastman Kodak Co., Rochester, 1972-84; consumer products sales rep. Eastman Kodak Co., Oklahoma City, 1984-86; copy products sales rep. Eastman Kodak Co., Stamford, 1988-91; office imaging sales rep. Eastman Kodak Co., Hartford, Conn., 1992—, major account rep., 1994-96; acct. exec. Lexis-Nexis, Danbury, Conn., 1996-98; maj. account mgr. Gartner Group, Stamford, Conn., 1998—; grad. asst. Dale Carnegie Human Rels. Course, 1987, 88, 96. Bus. cons. Region One Jr. Achievement Conf., 1988, 90; guest speaker West Conn. Jr. Achievement Conf., 1990; adviser, recruiter Greater Rochester Jr. Achievement, 1980-83, Small Bus. Owner, Accessorize, 1994—. Mem. NAFE, Am. Mgmt. Assn. Avocations: travel, reading, music, dance. Home: 166 Old Brookfield Rd Unit 2-5 Danbury CT 06811-4030

IZZO, MARY ALICE, real estate broker; b. Mesa, Ariz., Aug. 5, 1953; d. Edward Lee and Evangeline Lauda (Gorraiz) Meeker; m. Michael David Izzo, Dec. 26, 1971 (div. 1999); children: Michael Wade, Clinton Jarred, Antoinette Marie. Student, Pioneer Coll., 1977, Yavapai Coll., 1984-93, 98—. Cert. broker, realtor, Ariz. Sales agt. Babbit Bros., Flagstaff, Ariz., 1970-76; owner Cottonwood (Ariz.) Tees, 1978-84; realtor Weston Realty, Cottonwood, 1985-86, Coldwell Banker Mabery Real Estate, Cottonwood, 1986-89; sales agent, assoc. broker The Glenarm Land Co., Cottonwood, 1989-97; office mgr., sec. Izzo & Sons Contracting, 1985-97, Wilhoit Water Co., 1991-93; sales assoc. Walmart, 1995-96, asst. regional commr. AYSO, 1996-97; broker, owner ISO Realty, 1997—; office mgr., sec. Gonzales & Sons Electric, 1996-97; para educator Mingus Union H.S., Cottonwood, 1997-99. Author: Current Customer Cook Book, 1984. Bd. dirs. cub scouts Boy Scouts Am., 1984, 87; bd. dirs. AYSO Soccer, Verde Valley, Ariz., 1984-87, 92—, soccer coach tournament all girls' traveling team, 1993-95, 97, 98, also pub. dir., asst. regional commn., purchaser, 1996—; leader youth group, Cottonwood; sec. Journey-Yauapai County Bd. of Suprs. Dist. 3, 1999—. Democrat. Roman Catholic. Avocations: soccer, horseback riding, hiking, sewing, swimming. E-mail: maizzo@cybertrails.com. and mary.izzo@co.yauapai.az.us. Home: 649 E Elm St Cottonwood AZ 86326-4456

IZZO, THOMAS, college basketball coach; b. Iron Mountain, Mich., Jan. 30, 1955; m. Lupe Izzo; 1 child, Raquel. Grad., No. Mich. U., 1977. Head coach Ishpeming (Mich.) H.S., 1977-79; asst. coach No. Mich. U., 1979-83; with Mich. State U., East Lansing, 1983—, head coach Spartans, 1995—. Named to No. Mich. U. Hall of Fame, 1990, Upper Peninsula Hall of Fame, 1998. Office: Mich State U Athletic Dept 222 Breslin Ctr Jensen Fieldhouse East Lansing MI 48824*

JABARA, MICHAEL DEAN, investment banker, entrepreneur; b. Sioux Falls, S.D., Oct. 26, 1952; s. James M. and Jean Marie (Swiden) J.; m. Gundula Beate Dietz, Aug. 26, 1984; children: James Michael, Jenna Mariel. Student, Mich. Tech. U., 1970-72; BSBA, U. Calif., Berkeley, 1974; MBA, Pepperdine U., 1979. Mgr. original Sprint project team So. Pacific Communications Corp., 1976-78; network product mgr. ROLM Corp., 1978-81; cons. McGraw Hill Co., Hamburg (Fed. Republic of Germany) and London, 1982-83; founder, chief exec. officer Friend Techs. Inc. (merger VoiceCom Systems, Inc., acquired by Premiere Techs., Inc. 1997), San Francisco, 1984-88; pres. VoiceCom Ventures, San Francisco, 1988-93; mng. dir. Telecom, EMS Group Ltd., London, 1993-95; owner Jabara & Co. LLC, Glenbrook, Nev., 1993—, TOIR LLC, Glenbrook, 1998—; chmn. bd., COO Bingo Card Minder Corp., Stateline, Nev., 1996. Patentee in field. Bd. dirs. Tahoe-Douglas C. of C.; chmn. Tahoe Citizens Com., 1995—. Mem. Infor. Industry Assn. (conf. program chair 1995), Assn. for Corp. Growth, Caribbean Cable TV Assn., Satellite Broadcasters & Comms. Assn., Pepperdine Bus. Alumni, U. Calif. Berkeley Bus. Alumni, Mich. Tech Alumni Assn., The Classic Cars of the Candy Store, Reno Jaguar Club, Tahoe-Douglas Rotary, Lighting W Ranch Golf Club. Avocations: classic cars, private pilot, golf. Fax: 702-749-5002. E-mail: jabaraco@sierra.net. Office: Jabara & Co PO Box 568 Glenbrook NV 89413-0568

JABBARI, AHMAD, publishing executive; b. Tehran, Iran, Feb. 28, 1945. BA, Pa. State U., 1967, MA, 1969; MA, Washington U., St. Louis, 1974; PhD, Washington U., 1978. Assoc. prof. econs. and mgmt. Centre Coll. of Ky., 1976-78; editor, chief Mazda Publishers, Costa Mesa, Calif., 1978—. Office: Mazda Publishers Box 2603 3100 Airway Ave Ste 137 Costa Mesa CA 92626-4614*

JABBARI, BAHMAN, neurologist, educator; b. ZanJan, Iran, Jan. 22, 1942; came to U.S., 1968; s. Taghi Jabbari and Fatemeh Golzar-Jabbari; m. Fattaneh Tavassoli, Dec. 30, 1949. Undergrad. MD programs, Tehran (Iran) Med. Sch., MD, 1966. Diplomate Am. Bd. Psychiatry and Neurology with added qualification in clin. neurophysiology; licensed MD in Md., D.C. Intern Walter Reed Army Med. Ctr., Newark, 1968-69; resident in neurology Albany (N.Y.) Med. Ctr., 1969-72; fellow Tulan Med. Sch., New Orleans, 1972-73, asst. prof., 1974-76; from assoc. prof. neurology to prof., chair Uniformed Svcs. U., Bethesda, Md., 1978-98, prof., chair neurology, 1998—; adj. prof. George Washington U., Washington, 1985—, Georgetown U., Washington, 1986—; dir. clin. neurophysiology Walter Reed Army Med. Ctr., Washington, 1977—; cons. NIH epilepsy branch, Bethesda, 1998—. Col. U.S. Army, 1976—. Recipient VA Superior Performance award. Mem. Internat. Movement Disorder Soc., Am. Epilepsy Soc., Am. Acad. Neurology, Am. Neurological Assn., Am. Soc. Clin. Neurophysiology. E-mail: bjabbari@mxa.usuhs.mil. Office: Dept Neurology USUHS 4301 Jones Bridge Rd Bethesda MD 20814

JABERG, EUGENE CARL, theology educator, administrator; b. Linton, Ind., Mar. 27, 1927; s. Elmer Charles and Hilda Carolyn (Stuckmann) J.; m. Miriam Marie Priebe; children: Scott Christian, Beth Amy, David Edward. BA, Lakeland Coll., 1948; BD, Mission House Theol. Sem., 1954; MA, U. Wis., 1959, PhD, 1968. Ordained to ministry, United Ch. of Christ, 1959. Staff announcer WKOW-TV, Madison, Wis., 1955-58, 67-68; minister Pilgrim Congl. Ch., Madison, 1956-57; assoc. prof. speech Mission House Theol. Sem., Plymouth, Wis., 1958-62; asst. prof. communications United Theol. Sem., New Brighton, Minn., 1962-76; prof. communications United Theol. Sem., New Brighton, 1976-91, dir. admissions, 1984-87, dir. MDiv program, 1988-90, prof. emeritus, 1991—, acting dir. Masters programs, 1997-99; bus. ptnr. Dimension 3 Media Svcs., Mpls., 1988-90; coord. spl. projects CTV North Suburbs Cable Access, 1992—; vis. scholar Cambridge U., England. Author, editor: A History of Lakeland-Mission House, 1962; author: The Video Pencil, 1980; contbr. articles, revs. to various publs.; producer films, videotapes. Artistic dir. Interfaith Players, Mpls., 1965-73; TV producer, moderator Town Meeting of Twin Cities, Mpls., 1967-70; producer, writer, host various radio and TV series, Mpls., 1970—; mem. Ctr. Urban Encounter, Mpls., 1972-74, New Brighton Human Rights Commn., 1975-77; bd. mem. office communications United Ch. Christ, N.Y.C., 1975-81; mem. North Suburban System Cable Access Commn., 1986-91. Corr. U.S. Army, 1949-50. Kaltenborn Radio scholar, 1957; grantee Assn. Theol. Sems., 1983; recipient Minn. Community TV award, 1993, Judges Choice award Alliance of Cmty. Media, 1999. Mem. Religious Speech Communication Assn. (co-chmn. 1972-74), World Assn. Christian Communication. Democrat. Avocations: travel, hiking, spectator sports, film. Home: 1601 Innsbruck Dr Minneapolis MN 55432-6046 Office: United Theol Sem 3000 5th St NW Saint Paul MN 55112-2507

JABLON, ELAINE, education consultant; b. N.Y.C., Dec. 8, 1950; d. James and Frances (Augone) Georgallas; m. Steven Ira Jablon, June 23, 1976. AA in Early Childhood Edn., Marjorie Webster Jr. Coll., Washington, 1971; BEd in Elem. Edn., U. Miami, 1973, MEd in Learning Disabilities, 1974. Tchr. Broward County Pub. Schs., Ft. Lauderdale, Fla., 1974-76; tchr. Orange County Pub. Schs., Orlando, Fla., 1976-77, substitute tchr., 1977-82; substitute tchr. Osceola County (Fla.) Pub. Schs., 1977-82; cons. edn. cen. Fla., 1977—; counselor youth diversion program, Orlando, 1978-80. Vol. Jack Eckerd for Fla. Gov., Kissimmee, 1977-78; info. rep. Epilepsy Found. of Am., Osceola, 1980-87. Mem. AAUW (chairwoman), ASCD, Am. Bus. Women's Assn. (edn. chairwoman 1980-82), Fla. Network for Family and Parent Edn. (founding mem.), Assn. Early Childhood Edn. Internat., The Fla. Ctr. for Children and Youth, Council Exceptional Children -- Early Childhood Divsn. and Learning Disabilities Divsn., Learning Disabilities Assn., Fla. Fedn. Council for Learning Disabilities (writing com.), Fla. Assn. for Children and Adults with Learning Disabilities, U. Miami Alumni Assn. Cen. Fla., Kissimmee Bus. and Profl. Women's Club (pres. 1985-86., v.p. 1986—, recipient citation). Lodge: Sons of Italy of Orlando (trustee 1978-80), Sons of Italy of Osceola County (trustee 1988). Avocations: walking, swimming, reading. Office: 808 Hastings Dr Kissimmee FL 34744-5804

JABLONSKI, CAROL JEAN, communication professional, educator; b. Milw., July 12, 1951; d. George G. and Eleanor Virginia (Schmidt) J.; m. John Tyler Jones, Mar. 14, 1987. BA, Allegheny Coll., 1973; MA, Purdue U., 1975, PhD, 1979. Asst. prof. U. Va., Charlottesville, 1978-81, Ind. U., Bloomington, 1981-86; assoc. prof. comm. U. South Fla., Tampa, 1986—; cons. Tampa Electric Power Corp. Spkrs. Bur., 1986, 91-92, Fla. Power Corp. Spkrs. Bur., St. Petersburg, 1987-90; vis. assoc. prof. Wake Forest U., Winston-Salem, N.C., 1990-91; chair, coord. gen. edn. coun. U. South Fla., Tampa, 1993-96. Contbr. articles to profl. jours. United Way coord. U. South Fla., Tampa, 1988-89; workshop leader for women in transition Women's Ctr., Alpha House, Tampa, 1994. Grantee Fla. Humanities Coun., 1993-94, U. South Fla., 1997. Mem. Nat. Comm. Assn. (chair pub. address divsn. 1991-92; Karl Wallace award 1982), So. States Comm. Assn. Office: U South Fla CIS 1040 4202 E Fowler Ave Tampa FL 33620-9951

JABLONSKI, JAMES ARTHUR, lawyer; b. Sheboygan, Wis., Nov. 12, 1942; s. John Alfred and Dena (Kaat) J. BBA, U. Wis., 1965, JD, 1968. Bar: Wis. 1968, Calif. 1969, U.S. Ct. Appeals (7th cir) 1969, U.S. Supreme Ct. 1974, Colo. 1976, U.S. Ct. Appeals (8th and 10th cirs.) 1976. Assoc. Pillsbury, Madison & Sutro, San Francisco, 1969-72; asst. prof. law Washington U., St. Louis, 1972-76; ptnr. Gorsuch Kirgis L.L.C., Denver, 1976—. Mem. Colo. Bar Assn., Wis. Bar Assn. (bd. govs. 1990-92), Denver Bar Assn. Democrat. Club: Pinehurst Country (Denver). Office: Gorsuch Kirgis Tower 1 1515 Arapahoe St Ste 1000 Denver CO 80202-2120

JABLONSKI, ROBERT LEO, architect; b. Chgo., Mar. 28, 1926; s. Leo Frank and Rose (Domian) J. BS, U. Ill., 1950. Lic. architect Nat. Coun. Archtl. Registration Bd., 1965. Chief planner Nat. Council YMCA, Chgo., 1957-64; assoc. univ. architect U. Ill., Chgo., 1964-69; coordinator architect U. Chgo., 1969-70; dir. bldg. program City of Chgo., 1970-88; prin. Robert Jablonski Mgmt. Svcs., architect, Chgo., 1988—. Served with U.S. Army, 1940-46, ETO. Roman Catholic. Avocations: tennis, swimming.

JABRE, EDDY-MARCO, architect; b. Beirut, July 10, 1948; came to U.S., 1986; s. Farid and Lody (Abourizk) J.; m. Ifrandate Alame, Oct. 12, 1974; children: Moune, Joe, Marc. Architect DPLG, Ecole Nationale Superieure Des Beaux Arts, Paris, 1975; urban planner, Universite Paris XII, Vincennes, 1976. Ptnr. Atelier D'Etudes Raspail, Paris, 1975-78; dir. F.S.K., Riyadh, Saudi Arabia, 1978-80; sr. ptrn., pres. Copreco, Riyadh, Saudi Arabia, 1980-86; pres. Nedcorp, Winchester, Mass., 1986—, Maine Nedcorp, Winchester, 1987—, Atrium Custom Homes, Winchester, 1989—. Avocations: swimming, reading. Office: Atrium Custom Homes PO Box 368 Winchester MA 01890-0468

JABS, ARTHUR DEAN, plastic surgeon; b. Monterey Park, Calif., Dec. 21, 1953; s. Arthur Dean and Janet Louise Jabs; m. Leslie Bowman, May 31, 1975 (div. June 1999); children: Hilary, Connor. BA, U. So. Calif., 1975; PhD, U. Ill., Chgo., 1980, MD, 1984. Diplomate Am. Bd. Plastic Surgery, Nat. Bd. Med. Examiners. Resident in gen. surgery St. Vincent's Hosp., N.Y.C., 1984-87; fellow in plastic surgery Columbia Presbyn. Med. Ctr., N.Y.C., 1987-89; staff surgeon Walter Reed Army Med. Ctr., Washington, 1989-92; pvt. practice specializing in plastic surgery Bethesda, Md., 1992—; clin. assoc. prof. surgery Uniformed Svcs. U. Health Scis., Bethesda, 1992—, U. Conn., 1993-96; attending surgeon Suburban Hosp., Bethesda, Shady Grove Adventist Hosp., Rockville, Md., Holy Cross Hosp., Silver Springs, Md., Fairfax Hosp., Falls Church, Va., Arlington (Va.) Hosp., Fair Oaks Hosp., Columbia-Reston (Va.) Hosp., Charlotte Hungerford Hosp., Torrington, Conn., 1992-97, Winsted (Conn.) Meml. Hosp., 1992-96; attending surgeon dept. plastic surgery Walter Reed Army Med. Ctr., Washington, 1989-92; cons. plastic surgery NIH, Bethesda, 1991-92; presenter. Contbr. articles to profl. jours. Maj. U.S. Army Med. Corp., 1989-92. Fellow Am. Soc. Plastic and Reconstructive Surgeons, Am. Soc. Aesthetic Plastic Surg., Northeastern Soc. Plastic and Reconstructive Surgeons; mem. Nat. Capital Soc. Plastic Surgeons. Avocations: tennis, wing shooting. Office: Cosmetic Surgery Assocs 10215 Fernwood Rd Ste 280 Bethesda MD 20817

JABS, CAROLYN R., writer; b. Cleve., Nov. 3, 1950; d. Gerhardt A. and Esther R. (Poggemeier) J.; m. David L. Zamichow, June 30, 1982; children: Bert, Jessie, Zachary. BA, Wittenberg U. Freelance writer, 1977—. Author: Re/Uses, 1982, The Heirloom Gardener, 1983; former contbg. editor Family PC Mag.; contbr. articles to consumer publs. Mem. AAUW, Women in Comm., Am. Soc. Journalists, Auditory Verbal Assn. N.W. Ohio (co-founder). Avocations: book clubs, bicycle touring, gardening.

JACCARD, JERRY-LOUIS, music educator, translator; b. Pasadena, Calif., Feb. 19, 1944; s. F.L. Jack and Dolly R. Jaccard; m. Alta A. Jaccard. B in Music Edn., U. Ariz., 1965; M in Music Edn., Holy Names Coll., 1976; EdD, U. Mass., 1995. Music specialist Kayenta (Ariz.) Pub. Schs., 1969-73, Show Low (Ariz.) Pub. Schs., 1973-80; dir. Kodaly Musical Tng. Inst., Inc. Hartt Sch. Music, U. Hartford, West Hartford, Conn., 1980-83; music specialist West Hartford Pub. Schs., 1982-83; assoc. prof. music Brigham Young U., Provo, Utah, 1993—; cons. Waterford Sch., Granite Sch. Dist., Provo City Schs., Salt Lake City, 1995—; presenter in field. Revision editor: Joy Through the Magic of Music, 1999; contbr. chpt. to book. Vol. music and curriculum specialist Provo City Schs., 1994—. Mem. ASCD, Internat. Kodaly Soc., Orgn. Am. Kodaly Educators (western divsn. pres., nat. chair rsch. and publs.), Fondation de la Famille Jaccard (life). Mem. LDS Ch. Avocations: travel, culture, family history, languages, gardening. E-mail: jljaccard@byugate.byu.edu. Fax: 801-378-4236. Office: Brigham Young Univ C-582 HFAC Sch Music Provo UT 84601

JACHE, ALBERT WILLIAM, retired chemistry educator, scientist; b. Manchester, N.H., Nov. 5, 1924; s. William Frederick and Esther (Ruemely) J.; m. Lucy Ellen Hauslein, June 14, 1948; children: Ann Gail, Ellen Ruth, Philip William, Heidi Verena. BS, U. N.H., 1948, MS, 1950; PhD, U. Wash., 1952. Sr. chemist Air Reduction Co., Murray Hill, N.J., 1952-53; rsch. assoc. dept. physics Duke U., 1953-55; asst. prof. dept. chemistry Tex. A&M U., College Station, 1955-58, assoc. prof., 1958-61; cons. Ozark Mahoning Co., Tulsa, 1960-61, assoc. rsch. dir., 1961-64; sr. rsch. assoc. Olin Mathieson Chem. Corp. (now Olin Corp.), New Haven, 1964-67, sect. mgr., 1965-67, cons., 1967-75; prof. chemistry Marquette U., Milw., 1967-90, prof. emeritus, 1990—, chmn. chem. dept., 1967-72, dean Grad. Sch., 1972-77, assoc. acad. v.p. for health scis., 1974-77, assoc. v.p.-acad. affairs, 1977-85; scientist-in-residence Argonne (Ill.) Nat. Lab., 1985-86, scientist, 1991-96, temporary appointment, 1991-96; program coordination com. Med. Center S.E. Wis.; lectr. U. Tulsa, 1963-64, New Haven Coll., 1967; cons. Allied Chem. Corp., 1977-78; salt panel com. remediation buried and tank wastes NAS/NRC, 1996-97. Trustee Milw. Sci. Ednl. Found.; pres. Milw. Sci. Ednl. Trust, 1973—; trustee Argonne Univs. Assn., 1977-80; chmn. Assn. Grad. Schs. in Cath. Univs., 1973-75; mem. AUA nuclear engring. edn. com. U. Chgo, 1977-89, chmn., 1984, sec., 1989; double bass player River Cities Symphony Orch., Evergreen Comty. Orch., Evergreen String Ensemble. With AUS, 1943-46. Fellow AAAS, Am. Inst. Chemists; mem. Am. Chem. Soc. (chmn.-elect, program chmn. div. fluorine chemistry 1981, chmn. div. fluorine chemistry 1982), Sigma Xi, Omicron Kappa Upsilon. Achievements include research and numerous patents in the area of inorganic fluorine chemistry with emphasis on anhydrous hydrogen fluoride as a solvent or reaction medium and Hypofluorite chemistry. Home: 301 Ohio St Marietta OH 45750-3139 Office: Marquette U Dept Chemistry Milwaukee WI 53233

JACHNA, JOSEPH DAVID, photographer, educator; b. Chgo., Sept. 12, 1935; m. Virginia Kemper, 1962; children: Timothy, Heidi, Jody. BS in Art Edn., Inst. Design, Ill. Inst. Tech., 1958, MS in Photography, 1961. Part-time photographic asst. Derwin Studio Darkroom, Chgo., 1953-54; photo-technician Eastman Kodak Labs., Chgo., 1954; photographer's asst. DeSort Studio, Chgo., 1956-58; free-lance photographer Chgo., 1961—; instr. photography Inst. Design, Ill. Inst. Tech., Chgo., from 1961; instr. photography U. Ill., Chgo., from 1969, now prof. One-man shows include Art Inst. Chgo., 1961, St. Mary's Coll., Notre Dame, Ind., 1963, U. Ill., Chgo., 1965, 77, Lightfall Gallery Art Ctr., Evanston, Ill., 1970, U. Wis., Milw., 1970, Ctr. for Photog. Studies, Louisville, 1974, Nikon Photog. Salon, Tokyo, 1974, Afterimage Gallery, Dallas, 1975, Visual Studies Workshop Gallery, Rochester, N.Y., 1979, Chgo. Ctr. for Contemporary Photography, 1980, Focus Gallery, San Francisco, 1981, Photogenesis, Albuquerque, 1983, Andover (Mass.) Gallery, 1984, Chgo. State U., 1985, Tweed Mus. Art, Duluth, Minn., 1986, Gallery 954, Chgo., 1993, State of Ill. Galleries, Chgo., Lockport and Springfield, 1994, Fermilab, Batavia, Ill., 1995; exhibited in group shows at Art Inst. Chgo, 1963, 83, MIT, Cambridge, 1968, Walker Art Ctr., Mpls., 1973, 89, Renaissance Soc. Gallery U. Chgo., 1975, Mus. Contemporary Art, Chgo., 1977, 96—, Mus. Art RISD, Providence, 1978, Carpenter Ctr. Visual Arts, Harvard U., Cambridge, 1981, Nexus, Atlanta, 1983, Nat. Mus. Art., Washington, 1984, San Francisco Mus. Modern Art, 1985, Internat. Ctr. Photography, Tucson, 1992, Gallery 312, Chgo., 1996, Stockholm Subway, Sweden, 1999; represented in permanent collections, Mus. Modern Art, N.Y.C., Internat. Mus. Photography, George Eastman House, Rochester, N.Y., MIT, San Francisco Mus. Modern Art, Mpls. Inst. Arts, Art Inst. Chgo., Ctr. Photog. Studies, Louisville, Ctr. for Creative Photography, U. Ariz., Tucson. Ferguson Found. grantee, 1973; Nat. Endowment for Arts grantee, 1976; Ill. Arts Council, 1979; Guggenheim fellow, 1980. Office: U Ill Sch Art and Design 106 Jefferson Hall M/C036 929 W Harrison St Chicago IL 60607-7038

JACK, DIXIE LYNN, software consultant, social worker; b. Orlando, Fla., Apr. 7, 1943; d. Alex and Dorothy Ellen (Dixon) J. BA, U. Wash., 1965; AA, Highline C.C., Des Moines, 1971. Tchr. Archdioses, Burien, Wash., 1968-70, Tukwila (Wash.) Sch. Dist., 1970-75; fin. svcs. technician Dept. Welfare, Seattle, 1982-84; social worker, supr. Dept. Children and Family Svcs., Everett, Wash., 1984-94; user support/tng. mgr. Lockheed Martin, Hartford, Conn., 1995-97; computer based tng. mgr. Am. Mgmt. Sys., Manchester, Conn., 1997; implementation, bus. process cons. Ctr. for Support of Families, Chevy Chase, Md., 1998; cons. Juvenile Justice, Supreme Ct., Seattle, 1988-95. Mem. Assn. Univ. Women, Hartford Club. Home: 13116 E 41st Dr Yuma AZ 85367-6146

JACK, JANIS GRAHAM, judge; b. 1946. RN, St. Thomas Sch. Nursing, 1969; BA, U. Balt., 1974; JD summa cum laude, South Tex. Coll., 1981. Pvt. practice Corpus Christi, Tex., 1981-94; judge U.S. Dist. Ct. (so. dist.) Tex., Corpus Christi, 1994—; jud. mem. The Maritime Law Assn. U.S.; bd. dirs. South Tex. Coll. Law. Mem. ABA, Fed. Judges Assn., Fifth Cir. Dist. Judges Assn., Nat. Assn. Women Judges, Tex. Bar Found., State Bar Tex., The Philos. Soc. Tex., Order of Lytae, Phi Alpha Delta. Office: US Dist Ct 521 Starr St Corpus Christi TX 78401-2349

JACK, MINTA SUE, hospital department head; b. Huntsville, Tex., Aug. 24, 1935; d. Clinton Orrin and Dorris Eugenia (Pierce) Bunn; m. Samuel Garred Jack, Jr., June 8, 1957 (div. 1984); children: Samuel Garred III, Paul Alan. BA with distinction, U. N.Mex., 1957. Cert. secondary educator. High sch. tchr. Albuquerque Pub. Schs., 1957-58; bd. dirs. Delta Delta Delta, Reno, 1962-63; com. chmn. Tustin (Calif.) Sch. Dist. PTO, 1965-70, Red Hill Luth. Sch., Tustin, 1970-74; bd. dirs. Assistance League of Tustin, 1972-83, Performing Arts Ctr. Guilds, Orange County, Calif., 1983-88; bd.d irs. Delta Delta Delta, Orange County, Calif., 1987-91; dir., vol. Western Med. Ctr., Santa Ana, Calif., 1986—. Vol. leader Boy Scouts/Little League, Tustin, 1966-72; vol. Olympic Organizing Com., L.A., 1984; assoc. Mexican Am. Nat. Women, Santa Ana, 1988-90; mem. Freedom Found./Valley Forge, Santa Ana, 1988-90. Recipient Writing award, 1989, Newsletter award, 1991, Community Svc. award Disneyland, 1981, Amelia Earhart award U. Calif., 1989, Ernestine Grigsby award Delta Delta Delta, 1989; named Woman of Yr. nominee Panhellenic Assn., 1989. Mem. AAUW, So. Calif. Assn. Dirs. of Vol. Svcs. (bd. dirs. 1987-91), Am. Soc. Dirs. Vol. Svcs. (membership com. 1989), Assistance League of Tustin (pres. 1980-81), Westmed Gold Club (membership com. 1986-92), Chapman Univ. Music Assocs. (bd. dirs. 1987-92), Mortar Bd., Delta Delta Delta (pres. 1988-89, bd. dirs. 1988-91), Dirs. Vols. in Agencies, Phi Kappa Phi, Phi Alpha Theta, Pi Lambda Theta. Episcopalian. Avocations: music, gardening, travel. Home: 7634 E Appaloosa Trl Orange CA 92869-2406 Office: Western Med Ctr 1001 N Tustin Ave Santa Ana CA 92705-3502

JACK, NANCY RAYFORD, supplemental resource company executive, consultant; b. Hughes Springs, Tex., June 23, 1939; d. Vernon Lacy and Virginia Ernestine (Turner) Rayford; m. Kermit E. Hundley, Dec. 19, 1979; 1 child by previous marriage, James Bradford Jack, III. Cert. in bus. adminstrn., Keller Grad. Sch. Mgmt., 1980; cert. in acctg., Harper Coll., 1972, cert. in corp. law and tax law, paralegal, 1973. Sr. sec. Gould, Inc., Rolling Meadows, Ill., 1971-73; staff asst. Gould, Inc., 1973-74, asst. sec., 1974-77, corp. sec., 1977-89, v.p., 1985-89; pres. The Corp. Ofcl. Sec., Wheaton, Ill., 1989-92, Corp. Minutes and More, Wheaton, 1992-99. Recipient cert. of leadership YWCA Met. Chgo., 1975. Mem. Fair Oaks Ranch Golf and Country Club, Beta Sigma Phi. Home and Office: 8929 Fair Oaks Pkwy Fair Oaks TX 78015-4647

JACKEL, LAWRENCE, publishing company executive; b. N.Y.C., July 25; s. Solomon and Sylvia (Fisher) J.; m. Ellen Jane Koons, Sept. 29, 1985; children: Kenneth Isaac, Molly Laurie, Sarah Kate. BBA, CCNY, 1961, MBA, 1966. Acct. Aviquipo, Inc., N.Y.C., 1961-62; fin. exec. Litton Industries, N.Y.C., 1962-68; group controller Alloys Unltd., Inc., N.Y.C., 1968-69; v.p. fin. Litton Ednl. Pub., Inc., N.Y.C., 1969-72, 1969-72; pres. Delmar Pubs. div. Litton Ednl. Pub., Inc., Albany, N.Y., 1973-80, 1973-80; exec. v.p., pres. Litton Ednl. Pub., Inc., N.Y.C., 1976-80; owner, pres. Tab Books Inc., 1980-90, 1980-90; group v.p. McGraw Hill, Blue Ridge Summit, Pa., 1990-92; pres. Jackel Group Inc.-Cons. and Pubs., Venice, Fla., 1992-93; vice chmn., CEO, owner Lectorum Publs., Inc., N.Y.C., 1993-96; chmn. Promotional Sales Books LLC, N.Y.C., 1996—. Mem. Univ. Club. Democrat. Jewish. Home: 6961 N La Tierra Tucson AZ 85750-1034

JACKEL, SIMON SAMUEL, food products company executive; b. N.Y.C., Nov. 11, 1917; s. Victor and Sadie (Unger) J.; m. Betty Carlson, Jan. 22, 1954; children: Phyliss Marcia (dec.), Glenn Edward. BS, CCNY, 1938; postgrad. studies, U. Ill., 1941-42; AM, Columbia U., 1947, PhD, 1950. Head fermentation divsn. Fleischmann Lab., Stamford, Conn., 1944-59; v.p. R&D Vico Products Co., Chgo., 1959-61; lab. dir. Quality Bakers of Am. Coop. Inc. divsn. Sunbeam Baked Foods, Greenwich, Conn., 1961-74; v.p. rsch. dir. Sunbeam Baked Foods, Greenwich, 1974-84; dir. R&D, mem. operating com. Bakers R&D Svc., Greenwich, 1969-84; pres. Plymouth Tech. Svcs., Tarpon Springs, Fla., 1951—; internat. cons., 1984—; mem. sci. adv. com. Am. Inst. Baking, 1970-91, sanitation edn. adv. com., 1978-81. Tech. editor Bakery Prodn. and Mktg. Mag., 1968-85; contbr. articles to tech. jours.; patentee in field. Dir. hearing aid audiology Jewish Home and Hosp. for Aged, N.Y.C., 1951-76; mem. industry adv. com. N.D. State U., 1977-85; chmn. investment com., bd. dirs. Clearwater Unitarian Universalist Ch. Found., 1994—; treas., mem. bd. Unitarian Universalist Ch. of Clearwater, 1997-98. Recipient USAAF Exceptional Civilian Svc. award 1943, Wisdom Hall of Fame award, 1978, USPHS rsch. grantee 1947-50. Fellow AAAS, Am. Inst. Chemists, Am. Assn. Cereal Chemists (chmn. milling and baking divsn. 1973-74, Charles N. Frey award 1981, bakery columnist Cereal Foods World 1984-95, hon. fellow 1993); mem. Am. Chem. Soc. (50 yr. membership award 1995), Am. Soc. Bakery Engrs. (chmn. tech. info. svc. com. 1979-95), Am. Bakers Assn. (nutrition com. 1971-77, chmn. tech. liason com. to U.S. Dept. Agr. 1975-87, food tech. regulatory affairs com. 1977-91; alt. gov. 1978-87, assoc. gov. 1988-95), Ind. Bakers Assn. (cons. food safety com. 1977-80, labeling com. 1978-84, tech. affairs com. 1978-84, co-chmn. labeling and good mfg. practices com. 1984-94), Inst. Food Technologists, N.Y. Acad. Sci., N.Y.C. Chemists Club, Sigma Xi, Phi Lambda Upsilon. Home and Office: 684 Hidden Lake Dr Tarpon Springs FL 34689-2600

JACKENDOFF, RAY SAUL, linguistics educator; b. Chgo., Jan. 23, 1945; s. Nathaniel and Elaine Muriel (Flanders) J.; children: Amy Sarah, Beth Liana. BA, Swarthmore Coll., 1965; PhD, MIT, 1969. Instr. UCLA, 1969-70; asst. prof. linguistics Brandeis U., Waltham, Mass., 1971-73, assoc. prof., 1973-79; prof., 1979—; chmn. linguistics and cognitive sci. Brandeis U., Waltham, Mass., 1979-92; Guggenheim fellowship, 1993-94. Author: Semantic Interpretation in Generative Grammar, 1972 (Arts Humanities award Coun. Grad. Schs. in U.S. 1974), X-Bar Suntax: A Study of Phrase Structure, 1977, Semantics and Cognition, 1983, (with F. Lerdahl) A Generative Theory of Tonal Music, 1983, Consciousness and the Computational Mind, 1987, Semantic Structures, 1990, Languages of the Mind, 1992, Patterns in the Mind, 1993, The Architecture of the Language Faculty, 1997; mem. editl. bd. Music Perception, Cognitive Sci., Studia Linguistica, Natural Lang. and Linguistic Theory, Trends in Cognitive Scis. Soloist Boston Pops Orch., 1980. Mem. Linguistic Soc. Am. (exec. com. 1996-99), Soc. for Philosophy and Psychology (pres. 1990-91). Jewish. Home: 79 Goden St Belmont MA 02478-2934 Office: Brandeis U Program Linguistics & Cognitive Waltham MA 02454

JACKER, CORINNE LITVIN, playwright; b. Chgo., June 29, 1933; d. Thomas Henry and Theresa (Bellak) Litvin. Student, Stanford U., 1950-52; BS, Northwestern U., 1954, MA, 1955, postgrad., 1955-56. Editor Liberal Arts Press, 1959-60, Macmillan Co., 1960-63, Scribner's, 1963-65; story editor Sta. WNET-TV, N.Y.C., 1969-71, CBS-TV, N.Y.C., 1972-74; instr. playwrighting NYU, 1976-78; vis. prof. playwriting Yale U., 1979-81; adj. prof. Princeton U., 1986, 88, Columbia U., 1988—, Breadloaf Sch. of English, 1988, NYU, 1990-91; sci. cons. Benton Project for Broadcasting, U. Chgo., 1988-90. Exec. story editor, head writer (TV series) Best of Families, PBS, N.Y.C., 1975-77; head writer (TV series) Another World, 1981-82; author: Man, Memory, and Machines, 1964 (N.Y. Pub. Library 50 Best Books of Yr. 1964), Window on the Unknown, 1966 (AAAS 50 Best Books of Yr. 1966), A Little History of Cocoa, 1966, The Black Flag of Anarchy, 1968 (Pubs. Weekly 25 Best Books of Yr. 1968), The Biological Revolution, 1971, The Chocolate Bar Bust, 1994; playwright: The Scientific Method, 1970, Seditious Acts, 1970, Travellers, 1973, Breakfast, Lunch, & Dinner, 1975, Bits and Pieces, 1975 (Obie award 1975), Harry Outside, 1975 (Obie award 1975), Night Thoughts & Terminal, 1976, Other People's Tables, 1976, My Life, 1977, After the Season, 1978, Later, 1979, Domestic Issues, 1981, In Place, 1982, Songs from Distant Lands, 1985, (adaptation) Hedda Gabbler, 1989, The Island, 1991, (adaptation) The Three Sisters, 1992, In The Dark, 1993, Light, 1993, Getting Home, 1994, A New Life, 1995, The Promised Land, 1995, The Machine Age, 1996; TV writer, including: 3 episodes Actors' Choice, NET, 1970 (Emmy citation 1970); Virginia Woolf: The Moment Whole, NET, 1972 (CINE Golden Eagle award 1972); story editor: 4 episode series Benjamin Franklin, CBS, 1974 (Emmy citation 1974); The Adams Chronicles, 1975 (Peabody award 1975); Bicentennial Minutes, 1975, Loose Change, 1978, 3 episode series, NBC, 1978; 3 episodes of Best of Families, NET, 1978; The Jilting of Granny Weatherall, NET, 1980; Night Thoughts and Terminal BBC, 1978; Overdrawn at the Memory Bank, NET, 1983 (Rotterdam Film Festival, Am. Film Inst. Video Feature Film Festival). Rockefeller Found. grantee, 1979-80; residency Villa Serbelloni, Bellagio, Italy, 1987. Mem. Dramatists Guild, Writers Guild Am. East, PEN. Home and Office: 110 W 86th St New York NY 10024-4049

JACKIW, ROMAN, physicist, educator; b. Lublinec, Poland, Nov. 8, 1939; came to U.S., 1949; s. Nicholas and Zenobia (Kostyk) J.; m. So-Young Pi, Sept. 4, 1981; children: Simone Ahlborn, Nicholas, Stefan Pi. BA, Swarthmore Coll., 1961; PhD, Cornell U., 1966. Jr. fellow Harvard Soc. of Fellows, Cambridge, Mass., 1966-69; from asst. prof. to Jerrold Zacharias prof. physics MIT, Cambridge, 1969—; vis. prof. Rockefeller U., N.Y.C., 1977-78, U. Calif., L.A., Santa Barbara, 1980, Columbia U., N.Y.C., 1989-90. Contbr. over 150 articles to profl. jours. Alfred P. Sloan fellow Sloan Found., 1969-71, J.S. Guggenheim fellow Guggenheim Found., 1977-78; recipient Dannie Heineman prize in math. physics Am. Phys. Soc., 1995, Dirac medal and prize Internat. Ctr. for Theoretical Physics, Trieste, Italy, 1998. Fellow Am. Acad. of Arts and Scis., Am. Phys. Soc.; mem. NAS. Achievements include research on fundamental processes in nature. Office: MIT 6-320 77 Massachusetts Ave Cambridge MA 02139-4307

JACKLE, KAREN DEE, real estate executive; b. Santa Ana, Calif., June 26, 1945; d. Franklin Suits and Dorothy (Miller) Todd; m. Paul Herman Jackle, Oct. 12, 1968; children: Lara Irene, Julie Maureen. BA in History, Calif. State U., Long Beach, 1967. Elem. tchr. L.A. City Schs., 1967-68; social worker Los Angeles Dept. Pub. Social Svcs., 1968-70; with Seablue Pools, Salisbury, Rhodesia, 1970; co-owner, property mgr., appraiser Paul Jackle & Assocs., Inc., Huntington Beach, Calif., 1971—; property mgr., appraiser Paul Jackle & Assocs., Huntington Beach, Calif., 1973-86; property developer, mgr. Paul Jackle & Assocs., Huntington Beach, 1986—; pres. June Coast Corp., 1993—. Mem. Sister City Club, Huntington Beach, 1986-92; vice chmn. Huntington Beach Human Rels. Taskforce, 1997-98, chmn. events, 1997; block rep. H. Seacliff Homeowners Assn.; mem. Huntington Beach Intrastructure Com., 1998. Recipient achievement award Orange County Human Rels. Task Force, 1998. Mem. AAUW (Huntington Beach chpt., chmn. edn. found. 1991-92, chmn. membership 1992-94, mem. mentoring program 1990-94, pres. 1995-97, pub. policy com. 1997-99, Mentor award 1991). Avocations: aerobics, walking, theater, reading, travel. Office: 18652 Florida St Ste 300 Huntington Beach CA 92648-6069

JACKMAN, JAY M., psychiatrist; b. Bklyn., June 4, 1939; s. James Jeremiah and Dora (Emmer) J.; m. Judith Gail Meisels, Nov. 23, 1963 (div. Sept. 1987); children: Tenaya, Rashi, Jason Scott; m. Myra Hoffenberg Strober, Oct. 21, 1990. BA, Columbia U., 1960; MD, Harvard U., 1964; JD, U. Calif., San Francisco, 1999. Diplomate Am. Bd. Psychiatry and Neurology; subsplty. cert. forensic psychiatry . Rotating intern San Francisco County Gen. Hosp., 1965; psychiat. resident Stanford U., 1969; asst. dir. community psychiatry Mt. Zion Hosp., San Francisco, 1969-70; dir. drug treatment programs Westside Community Mental Health Ctr., San Francisco, 1970-74; pvt. practice San Francisco, 1969-74; dir. Lanakila Clinic Kalihi-Palama Community Mental Health Ctr., Honolulu, 1974-75; pvt. practice specializing in forensic psychiatry, Honolulu, 1975-90, Stanford, Calif., 1990—; cons. Salvation Army Addiction Treatment Facility, Honolulu, 1974-81; chmn. Task Force on Drugs, Nat. Coun. Community Mental Health Ctrs., 1971-75; chmn. no. sect. Calif. Assn. Methodone Programs, 1973-74. Contbr. articles on substance abuse to profl. jours. Trustee Foothill-DeAnza C.C. Bd., 1993-98; active Mayor's Adv. Com. on Drug Abuse, Honolulu, 1975-77. Mem. Am. Psychiat. Assn. (commn. on drugs 1973-77), Am. Acad. Psychiatry and Law, Am. Coll. Forensic Psychiatrists, Ctrl. N.Y. Psychiat. Soc., Calif. Attys. for Criminal Justice. Democrat. Jewish. Avocations: backpacking, hiking, dancing, scuba diving, beach walking.

JACKMAN, LLOYD MILES, chemistry educator; b. Goolwa, Australia, Apr. 1, 1926; came to U.S., 1967; s. Charles Stuart and Florence Olive (Green) J.; m. Marie Alma Sandow, 1950; children—Richard Miles, Donald Charles, Andrew Thorpe. BSc, U. Adelaide, Australia, 1945, BSc with honors, 1946, MSc, 1948, PhD, 1951. Asst. lectr. organic chemistry Imperial Coll., London, Eng., 1952; lectr. Imperial Coll., 1953; reader U. London, 1961-62; prof., head dept. organic chemistry U. Melbourne, Australia, 1962-67; prof. chemistry Pa. State U., 1967-91, prof. emeritus, 1992—. Author: Applications of NMR in Organic Chemistry. Beit fellow U. London, 1951-52; NSF sr. fgn. fellow, 1965; Guggenheim fellow, 1973-74; Wilsmore fellow chemistry, Melbourne, Australia; recipient Humboldt award, Fed. Republic Germany, 1977, 89. Fellow AAAS, Chem. Soc. London, Am. Chem. Soc., Royal Australian Chem. Inst. Home: 710 Glenn Rd State College PA 16803-3414 Office: 152 Davey Lab University Park PA 16802-6300

JACKMAN, ROBERT ALAN, retail executive; b. N.Y.C., Mar. 22, 1939; s. Joseph and Kate Queenie (Silverman) J.; m. Lois Wiederschall, June 10, 1962; children: Jennifer Sharon, Deborah Lynn. BS, U. Bridgeport, 1961. Dir. sales Mattel Inc., Hawthorne, Calif., 1963-75; sr. v.p. mktg. and sales Tyco Industries Inc., Moorestown, N.J., 1975-78; gen. mgr. Aurora Products Inc., Stamford, Conn., 1978-80; ptnr. Scott Lancaster Jackman Mills Atha, Westport, Conn., 1980-83; pres., chief exec. officer Leisure Dynamics Inc. div. Coleco Industries, Westport, 1983-86; with Oak Tree Publs., San Diego, 1983-87; exec. v.p. Coleco Industries Inc., West Hartford, Conn., 1986-88; gen. mgr. Tomy Am., Inc., Southport, Conn., 1988-90, also bd. dirs.; owner Yes I Can, 1990—; cons. Harvard U. Bus. Sch. Club, N.Y.C., 1984. Patentee in field. With USAR, 1961-62. Recipient Disting. Alumni award U. Bridgeport (Conn.), 1986. Mem. U. Bridgeport Mktg. Coun., Mission Hills Country Club (Rancho Mirage, Calif.). Avocations: tennis, music, reading. Home: 348 Forest Hills Dr Rancho Mirage CA 92270-1455 Office: 35-325 Date Palm Dr Ste 131 Cathedral City CA 92234-7031

JACKMAN, THOMAS M., newspaper reporter, columnist; b. Alexandria, Va., Jan. 9, 1961; s. William Edward and Sigrid (Stanley) J. AB in English/Am. Studies, U Notre Dame, 1982. News asst. The New York Times, N.Y.C., 1982-84; reporter/columnist The Kansas City (Mo.) Star, 1984-98; reporter The Washington Post, Fairfax, Va., 1998—. Author: Rites of Burial, 1992. Recipient 1st place best info. graphic Mo. Press Assn., 1997, best sports story, 1994. Mem. Investigative Reporters & Editors. Avocations: sports, music, politics, tavern research. Home: 3205 Arrowhead Cir Apt J Fairfax VA 22030-7318 Office: The Washington Post Ste 220 4020 University Dr Fairfax VA 22030

JACKOBOICE, SANDRA KAY, artist; b. Detroit, July 22, 1936; d. Virgil Ellsworth and Lucile Elizabeth (Dillemuth) LeSeur; m. Edward James Jackoboice, Jan. 11, 1958; children: E. Michael, Timothy Jon. BA, Aquinas Coll., Grand Rapids, Mich., 1989. Co-owner The Fashion Plate, Grand Rapids, 1975-79; wardrobe cons. Steketees, Grand Rapids, 1980-82; owner Color Plus, Grand Rapids, 1983—; profl. image cons. to various businesses and tng. groups, Grand Rapids, 1983-90; art program dir. Franciscan Life Process Ctr., Lowell, Mich., 1990—. Exhibited in solo shows at FMB, Lowell, 1993, 95, City Hall, Bielsko-Biala, Poland, 1995, Terryberry Gallery, Grand Rapids, 1997, Frederik Meijer Gardens, Grand Rapids, 1998; group shows include LaRive Gallery, South Haven, Mich., Bot. Images Exhbn., Lansing, Mich., Artists Alliance Group Shows; permanent collections include Bergama Gallery, Grand Rapids, Tripp Gallery, Las Vegas, Sculpture Showcase, New Hope, Pa., Linda Lundeen Gallery, Las Cruces, N.Mex. Mem. Arts Coun. Greater Grand Rapids, 1997; mem. Downtown Mgmt. Bd., Grand Rapids, 1993-96; mem. Grant Rapids Parking Commn., 1993-96; mem. Jr. League, Grand Rapids, 1962—. Recipient awards for art work. Mem. Women's City Club (past bd. dirs.), Great Lakes Pastel Soc. (pres. 1997—), Artists Alliance, Grand Valley Artists, Am. Soc. Bot. Artists, Midwest Pastel Soc., Rivertown Artists Guild, others. Republican. Christian. Avocations: travel, art, tennis, golf. Office: Color Plus PO Box 6775 Grand Rapids MI 49516-6775

JACKOBS, MIRIAM ANN, dietitian; b. Sioux City, Iowa, Apr. 8, 1940; d. Abraham and Mary (Wadedo) Kaled; m. John Joseph Jackobs, Aug. 28, 1965; children: Mark James, Daniel Michael, Thomas Vincent. Student, St. Louis U., 1963; BS, Briar Cliff Coll., 1963; MS, Iowa State U., 1965; MA in Religion, Athenaeum of Ohio, Cin., 1995. Lic. in dietetics, Ohio. Instr. nutrition Ariz. State U., Tempe, 1965-67, Willoughby (Ohio) Eastlake Sch., 1967-69; clinical dietitian Migrant Clinic of Seneca County, Tiffin, Ohio, 1969-75; nutrition instr. Heidelberg Coll., Tiffin, 1969-75; founder, cons. dietitian Nutrition Cons. Svcs., 1974-94; oncology dietitian Hall Radiation Ctr., Cedar Rapids, 1983-87; nutrition instr. Mt. Mercy & Coe Colls., Cedar Rapids, 1976-87; clinical dietitian The Brethren's Home, Greenville, Ohio, 1987-89; dir. dietary dept. Washington Manor Retirement Ctr., Centerville, Ohio, 1989-90; instr. Kettering (Ohio) Adult Sch., 1988-90, Mt. St. Joseph Coll., 1989—; adj. asst. prof. Wilmington Coll., 1990—; owner, cons. Spectrum Consulting, 1994—. Author: (book) Food Prep Manual, 1968, Diet Manual, 1988, rev. edit., 1992, 97; contbr. articles on nutrition to prof. jours. Com. chmn. LWV, Ohio and Iowa, 1970-82; fund raising chmn. PTA, Cedar Rapids, 1984-86; unit leader dist. coun. Boy Scouts Am., 1973-88; organizer Greenville Summer Symphony, Ohio, 1988. Recipient Silver Beaver award Boy Scouts Am., Alumni Svc. award Briarcliff Coll., 1971 St. George award Archdiocese Dubuque, 1985, Ohio Dietetic Assn. Mem. Merit award, 1998; Gen. Foods Found. fellow Iowa State U., 1965; Dole Leadership grantee, 1992. Mem. Am. Dietetic Assn., Ohio Dietetic Assn., Ohio Cons. Dietitions (newsletter editor 1988-95, chairperson 1995-96), Greater Cin. Dietetic Assn. (coun. on practice chair elect 1997-98, chair 1998—, grantee 1997), Greater Cin. Cons. Dietitians (newsletter editor 1991, health care facilities sec./chair-elect 1997-98, chair 1998—), Gerontology Practice Group, Hunger Malnutrition Dietetics Practice Group (newsletter editor 1996-98, treas. 1998—), Cedar Rapids Youth Orch., Coe Woman (pres. 1977-78). Roman Catholic. Avocations: music, hiking, race walking, traveling, art. Home and Office: Spectrum Cons 7733 Westwind Dr Cincinnati OH 45242-5027

JACKOWIAK, PATRICIA, lawyer; b. Chgo., Feb. 3, 1959; d. Leonard John and Margaret Mary (Iozzi) J. BA, Loyola U., Chgo., 1981; JD, John Marshall Law Sch., 1984. Bar: Ill. 1985. Asst. state's atty. Cook County, Chgo., 1987-89, supr. trial atty. bur. child support enforcement, legal advisor law student's spl. and perjury projects, chmn. employee rels. com., 1988-89, com. mem. domestic rels. div. Pro-se task force, 1989; dep. commr. Consumer Protection div. Dept. Consumer Svcs. City of Chgo., 1989-96; dep. dir. Dept. Adminstrv. Hearings City of Chgo., 1996—; summer atty. Ct. Claims and Antitrust divsn. Office of Ill. Atty. Gen., 1985, 86; com. mem. domestic rels. divsn. Cook County The Pro-Se Task Force Com.; mem. Chgo. divsn. Ford Consumer Appeals Bd., 1989-92, chair, 1991-92. Pres. Santa Lucia Sch. Bd., Chgo., 1987—; chairperson Santa Lucia Parish Carnival Com., 1987—; chairperson employee rels. com. Child Support divsn., 1988-89; dir. religious edn. Santa Lucia Parish, 1985—; mem. freshman recruiting and fundraising coms. Parents Assocs. Loyola U., Chgo., 1987-90; mem. elder care task force Dept. Health, Aging and Disability, Dept. Consumer Svcs. City of Chgo., 1989-96; commencement speaker St. Barbara High Sch., Chgo., 1993, 97, adv. bd., 1994—, co-chair 1998—. Recipient Local Parish award Cath. Youth Orgn./Archdiocese of Chgo., 1991; disting. elem. grad. award Nat. Cath. Ednl. Assn., Santa Lucia Sch., 1994, Superior Pub. Svc. award, 1998. Mem. ABA, Nat. Assn. Adminstrv. Law Judges, Nat. Indsl. Scale Assn., Nat. Conf. Weights and Measures, Blue Key, Pi Sigma Alpha. Democratic. Roman Catholic. Office: Dept Adminstrv. Hearings Ste 600 740 N Sedgewick 6th Fl Chicago IL 60610

JACKS, ROGER LARRY, secondary education educator; b. Oskaloosa, Iowa, May 24, 1942; s. Roger Melvin and Sue May (Howard) J.; m. Joan R. Cates, June 20, 1992. BA in Social Studies, U. No. Colo., 1966; MA in Sociology, Pepperdine U., 1977; MS in Ednl. Leadership, Nova U., 1996. Cert. social studies secondary edn., Nev.; cert. adminstrn. secondary edn., Nev. Commd. 2d lt. USAF, 1966, advanced through grades to col., 1986; B-52 aircrew USAF, Loring AFB, Maine, 1968-72; SR-71 aircrew USAF, Beale AFB, Calif., 1972-77; air staff USAF, Norton AFB, Calif., 1977-81; flight test staff USAF, Edwards AFB, Calif., 1981-85; Base comdr. USAF, Arnold AFB, Tenn., 1985-88, Beale AFB, 1988-90; aerospace prof. USAF-U. Ariz., 1990-92; N.W. Region comdr. USAF, Peterson AFB, Colo., 1992-93; tchr. student activities Rancho H.S., Las Vegas, Nev., 1993-95; magnet sch. coord. Rancho H.S., Las Vegas, 1995—; appointed dean of students Ranch High School, 1999—. Contbr. articles to profl. jours. Mem. mil. com. Marysville (Calif.) C. of C., 1988-90; mem. exec. coun. Boy Scouts Am., Sutter Butte, Marysville, 1988-90; mem. Youth in Aviation, Las Vegas, 1995—. Mem. NEA, ASCD, Air Force Assn. (Thunderbird chpt., medal of merit 1996), Nellis Officers Club, Ret. Officers Assn. Avocations: computers, golf, reading, fitness. Office: Rancho High Sch 1900 E Owens Ave North Las Vegas NV 89030-7099

JACKSON, ALISA SIMMONS, geriatrics nurse, administrator; b. Ozark, Ala., Nov. 10, 1960; d. Edwin Horace and Helen J. (Hagler) Simmons; m. Bobby F. Jackson, Nov. 14, 1998. BSN, Auburn U., 1983. Charge nurse ICU, house supr. Dale County Hosp., Ozark; charge nurse PICU East Ala. Med. Ctr., Opelika; dir. med. testing Eye Ctr. South/Eye Network Assocs., Dothan, Ala.; DON Oakview Manor Nursing Facility, Ozark; regional adminstr. Flowers Hosp. Home Care Svcs. div. Enterprise (Ala.) Agy., asst. dir. clin. svcs. Flowers Hosp. Home Care Svcs. Eastern div.; regional adminstr. Home Care Svcs. Author policy and procedure manual. Mem. AACCN, Alpha Epsilon Delta, Sigma Theta Tau. Home: 106 Country Ln Dothan AL 36301

JACKSON, ALLEN KEITH, museum administrator; b. Rocky Ford, Colo., July 22, 1932; s. Monford L. and Leliah Jean (Hipp) J.; m. Barbara May Hollard, June 13, 1954; children: Cary Vincent, Deborah Kay and Edward Keith (twins), Fredrick James. B.A., U. Denver, 1954; postgrad., Cambridge (Eng.) U., 1955; Th.M. (Elizabeth Iliff Warren fellow), Iliff Sch. Theology, 1958; Ph.D., Emory U., 1960. Meth. student minister Erie, Colo., 1955-58; ordained elder Meth. Ch., 1958; instr. sociology Emory U., 1958-60; chaplain, asst. prof. religion and sociology Morningside Coll., Sioux City, Iowa, 1960-62; dean coll. Morningside Coll., 1962-67; pres. Huntingdon Coll., Montgomery, Ala., 1968-93; exec. dir. natural heritage Idaho Mus. Natural History, Idaho State U., Pocatello, 1993—. Contbr. articles to profl. jours. Past pres. Montgomery Area United Appeal. Fulbright scholar Cambridge U., 1955; honor fellow Emory U., 1960. Mem. Ala. Assn. Ind. Colls. and Univs. (pres. 1969-71), Ala. Council Advancement Pvt. Colls. (pres. 1975-81), Phi Beta Kappa, Omicron Delta Kappa, Beta Theta Pi. Club: Rotarian. Home: 633 W McNabb Rd Inkolm ID 83245 Office: Idaho State Univ Box 8040 Pocatello ID 83209 *A worthy aim it seems to me, is to seek the Truth and to share the truths you find.*

JACKSON, ALPHONSO, utility company executive; b. Marshall, Tex., Sept. 9, 1946; s. Arthur and Henriette (Green) J.; m. Marcia A. Clark-Jackson, June 18, 1988; children: Annette Watkins, Lesley Jackson. BS, Truman State U., 1968, MA, 1969; JD, Washington U., St. Louis, 1973. Dir., cons. svcs. Laventhol & Horwath, St. Louis, 1982-87; CEO Dept. of Pub. and Assisted Housing, Washington, 1987-89; pres. and CEO Housing Authority/City of Dallas, 1989-96. Bd. dirs. Zale-Lipshy Hosp., Dallas, 1992, Truman State U., 1995, Tex. So. U., 1998, Children's Med. Ctr., Dallas, 1994; chmn. Gen. Svcs. Commn. State of Tex., Austin, 1998. Recipient Chmn.'s award Nat. Boys and Girls Clubs of Am., 1997. Fellow The Aspen Inst. Avocations: jogging, tennis, reading. Office: Ctrl and SW Corp-Tex 1616 Woodall Rodgers Fwy Dallas TX 75202-1234

JACKSON, ANDREW PRESTON, library director; b. Bklyn., Jan. 28, 1947; s. Walter Luther Sr. and Bessie (Lindsey) J. BS, CUNY, 1990, MLS, 1996; pub. librs. profl. cert., SUNY. Asst. supr. pers. processing unit Human Resources Adminstrn. Agy. Child Devel. Pers. Dept., N.Y.C., 1968-70, coord. pers. svcs., 1970-76; customer rels. mgr., contracts mgr. Robinson Chevrolet, Novato, Calif., 1976-79; office mgr. Sesame Press, Inc., N.Y.C., 1979-80; exec. dir. Langston Hughes Cmty. Libr. and Cultural Ctr., Corona, N.Y., 1980—; lectr. Black history, N.Y.C., 1986—. Contbr. articles to profl. jours. Bd. mem. Cmty. Adv. Bd. Elmhurst (N.Y.) Hosp. Ctr., 1983-97, Queens Pub. TV, Flushing, N.Y., 1989—, York Coll. Alumni, Inc., Jamaica, N.Y., 1990-93, 96—; vice-chair cmty. adv. bd. Otis Bantum Correctional Ctr. N.Y.C. Dept. Corrections, Rikers Island, N.Y., 1990-95; convener Churchman's Fellowship Corona Congl. Ch., 1987-89; chmn. Gen. Social Svcs. Adv. Coun., Cmty. Planning Bd., Area 3 and 5, 1984-87; treas. No. Blvd. Mcht.'s Assn. Corona, 1985—; mem. York Coll. Cmty. adv. Coun., 1997—; mem. N.Y. State Freedom Trails Commn., Queens Underground R.R. com. Staff sgt. USAF, 1964-68, Vietnam. Decorated Bronze Star; named Man of Yr. Nat. Assn. Negro Bus. & Profl. Women's Club, Inc., 1991, Ombudsman award, 1982, East Elmhurst Alumni Inc. Hall of Fame, 1998; recipient Cmty. Svc. award East Elmhurst Track Club, 1986, Tabernacle Cmty. C.M.E. Ch., Nat. Assn. Univ. Women (north shore br.), Cmty. award East Elmhurst-Corona Civic Assn., 1989, Outstanding Leadership in Queens award Queens Fedn. of Churches, 1988, Cert. of Appreciation Kiwanis, 1991, Cmty. Svc. award Minority Mgmt. Assn., N.Y.C., 1992, Cert. of Recognition August Martin H.S., 1992, Gov.'s award African-Americans of Distinction, N.Y. State Gov., 1994, Disting. Grad. award Nat. Assn. Equal Opportunity in Higher Edn., 1994, Cert. of Honor, Queens Borough Pres., 1994, Giving It Back, award W.C. Bryant H.S., 1995, Youth Devel. award 115th Police Precinct Coun., 1994; Disting. Alumni award York Coll. Alumni Assn., Inc., 1996, Fufilling The Dream award CBS-TV, 1996, Scroll of Honor, 4W Circle of Arts and Enterprise, 1996, Cmty. Svc. award Nat. Coun. Negro Women, 1997, Cmty. Svc. award Elmcor Alumni Assn., 1998, Comty. Svc. award Concerned African-Am. of Flushing, 1998. Mem. NAACP, ALA, ALA Black Libr. Caucus, Pub. Librs. Assn., Libr. Adminstrn. and Mgmt. Assn., N.Y. Black Librs. Caucus, N.Y. Libr. Assn. Avocations: bike riding, basketball, speaking with youth, reading. Home: 25-14 97th St East Elmhurst NY 11369-1923 Office: Queens Borough Pub Libr Langston Hughes Comm Libr 10209 Northern Blvd Corona NY 11368-1138

JACKSON, ANN WILLIAMS, publisher; b. Holland, Mich., Jan. 22, 1952; d. Byron Allen and Rozanne (Simon) Williams; m. Charles Miller Jackson, Oct. 18, 1980; children: Sam, Nicholas, Lucy. BA magna cum laude, Middlebury Coll., 1974; MBA, Columbia U., 1980. Fin. analyst Time Inc., N.Y.C., 1980-82; direct mail mgr. Time Life Books, London, 1982-85; bus. mgr. Money mag. Time Inc., N.Y.C., 1985-87, bus. mgr. Sports Illustrated mag., 1987-89, gen. mgr. Sports Illustrated mag., 1989-92, gen. mgr. People mag., 1992-94, pub. In Style mag., 1994—, group pub. Style mag., 1999—; bd. dirs. Nat. Parenting Assn., N.Y.C., Fashion Group Internat., N.Y.C., Cancer Rsch. Inst., N.Y.C. Mem. Advt. Women of N.Y., Women in Comms., Bronxville Field Club, Phi Beta Kappa. Avocations: skiing, hiking, tennis, sailing, gardening. Office: In Style Time Inc 1271 6th Ave New York NY 10020-1300*

JACKSON, ANNE (ANNE JACKSON WALLACH), actress; b. Allegheny, Penn., Sept. 3, 1926; d. John Ivan and Stella Germaine (Murray) J.; m. Eli Wallach, Mar. 5, 1948; children: Peter, Roberta, Katherine. Studied with Sanford Meisner and Herbert Berghof at Neighborhood Playhouse, with Lee Strassberg at Actor's Studio. Profl. debut: Cherry Orchard; mem. Am. Repertory Co.; Broadway plays include: Summer and Smoke, Oh, Men! Oh, Women!, Middle of the Night, Major Barbara, Rhinoceros, Luv, Waltz of the Toreadors, Diary of Anne Frank, 1978, Twice Around the Park, 1982-83, Nest of the Woodgrouse, 1984, Café Crown, 1989, Love Letters, 1991-92, Lost in Yonkers, 1992, In Person, 1993, The Flowering Peach, 1994, off-Broadway plays: Tennessee Williams Remembered, 1999, Mr. Peter's Connection, 1998, The Typists, The Tigers; film appearances include: So Young, So Bad, 1950, Secret Life of an American Wife, 1968, Dirty Dingus McGee, 1970, Lovers andOther Strangers, 1970, The Shining, 1980, Sam's Son, 1985, Funny About Love, 1992, Folks, 1992, Johnnie Twennies, 1998; TV appearances include: 84 Charing Cross Road, Private Battle, Everything's Relative, 1987, Law & Order, 1997; TV films: Family Man, Golda I and II, Out on a Limb, Baby M, 1988, The Rescuers: The Lady on the Bicycle, 1997; author: (autobiography) Early Stages, 1979. Recipient Obie award. Office: care Paradigm 200 W 57th St Ste 900 New York NY 10019-3211*

JACKSON, BARBARA PATRICIA, city manager; b. Englewood, N.J., Feb. 2, 1952; d. Howard Webster and Ruth Agatha (Fields) Allen; m. James Allen Jackson, Jan. 7, 1978; children: A. Denise Watson, Demenica, James A. II. BA in Bus. Adminstrn., Antioch Coll., Yellow Springs, Ohio, 1974; MBA, U. Nev., Las Vegas, 1985; postgrad., U. Laverne, 1994—. Bus. ofc. supr. Ctrl. Tel. & Utilities Corp., Las Vegas, 1975-78; mgmt. analyst Clark County Sanitation Dist., Las Vegas, 1984-88, Clark County Regional Flood Control Dist., Las Vegas, 1988-89; sr. mgmt. analyst City of Las Vegas City Mgrs. Office, 1989-90, mgmt. svcs. coord., 1990-91, spl. asst. to city mgr., 1991-92; dep. dir. City of Las Vegas Parks and Leisure Activities, 1992—; dep. dir. of Hum. Res. City of Las Vegas Human Resources, Las Vegas, NV, 1998—; pres., owner JFA & Assocs., Las Vegas, 1995—; adj. prof. U. Phoenix, Las Vegas, 1995—; instr. United Way So. Nev./U. Nev., Las Vegas, 1995—; affiliated ptnr. Williams Group, Oakland, Calif., 1996. Bd. dirs. United Way So. Nev., Las Vegas, 1986-92, Neighborhood Justice Adv. Bd., Las Vegas, 1993-94. Recipient Rose award Profl. Black Women's Alliance, Las Vegas, 1990, commendations Nat. League Cities, Washington, 1991, Nat. Black Caucus of Local and Elected Ofcls., Washington, 1991, Nev. League Cities, 1990; named Disting. Woman of South Nev., 1998. Mem. ASPA, Nev. Recreation and Pk. Assn., Nat. Forum for Black Pub. Adminstrs. (past chpt. pres. 1990-92), Nat. Recreation and Pk. Assn., Non-profit Mgmt. Assn., Las Vegas C. of C. (charter mem. Leadership Las Vegas 1987—), Delta Sigma Theta (past chpt. v.p. 1992-94). Democrat. Baptist. Avocations: reading, computers, crafts, movies, travel. Office: City of Las Vegas Dept Human Resources 400 E Stewart Ave Las Vegas NV 89101

JACKSON, BART, educator, game developer; b. Jersey City, Feb. 29, 1944; married; 3 children. MS, Rutgers U., 1963, EdD, 1965, PhD, 1968. Author, developer: (games) Pentaminoes, 1968, Role Playing, 1972-88, Magic, 1993. Mem. Raritan (N.J.) City Coun., 1976-86. Recipient outstanding toy award Parents Mag., 1995.

JACKSON, BENJAMIN TAYLOR, retired surgeon, educator, medical facility administrator; b. Jacksonville, Fla., Apr. 28, 1929; s. Julian Harold and Helen Louise (Blasingame) J.; m. Alda Jean Davis, June 18, 1953; children: Benjamin Taylor Jr., Jean Leigh, Kimberly Louise, Jillian Davis. MD, Duke U., 1954; MS, Brown U., 1982. Diplomate Am. Bd. Surgery. Instr. Med. Coll. of Va., Richmond, 1963-64; asst. prof. Sch. of Medicine Boston U., 1964-67, assoc. prof. Sch. of Medicine, 1967-75, prof. Sch. of Medicine, 1975-80; vis. surgeon U. Hosp., Boston, 1975-80; prof.

Brown U. Sch. Medicine, Providence, 1980-97; prof. in surgery emeritus, 1997—; prof. surgery rsch., chief surg. svc. VA Med. Ctr., Providence, 1980-97, cons. in surgery, 1997—; prof. surgery (rsch.), 1999—. Contbr. articles to profl. jours. Capt. U.S. Army, 1955-57. Mem. ACS, Soc. Univ. Surgeons, Soc. for Gynecologic Investigation. Methodist. Home: 11 October Ln Weston MA 02493-1724 Office: VA Med Ctr Davis Pk Providence RI 02908

JACKSON, BETTY L. DEASON, real estate developer; b. Wichita, Kans., Mar. 31, 1927; d. Orville John and Ida Mabel (Wolfe) Deason; m. James L. Jackson, July 2, 1966 (dec. Feb. 1983); children: Rebecca Lou, Jennifer Mae. AA, SW Baptist U., Bolivar, Mo., 1946; BA, Cen. Mo. State U., 1963; MA, U. Mo., 1964. Lic. realtor, Kans. Salesperson Sears, Kansas City, Mo., 1943-44; bookkeeping clk. Hallmark Cards, Kansas City, Mo., 1945-46; civil service Camp Pendleton, Oceanside, Calif., 1947; sec. Ford Motor Co., Kansas City, Mo., Jim Taylor Olds Co., Independence, Mo., 1952-54; tchr. Consol. Sch. Dist. #2, Mo., 1954-55; tchr. adminstr. Consol. Sch. Dist. #2, Raytown, Mo., 1963-78; owner mgr. B.J.'s Florist Car Wash Laundramat, Stockton, Mo., 1979-82; owner, ptnr. J and S Realty, Stockton, Mo., 1983—; officer J-S Corp., Stockton, 1986-94. Mem. Nat. Assn. Realtors, Mo. C. of C., AARP, Greater Ozark Bd. Realtors. Democrat. Baptist. Avocations: play organ, piano, church clubs. Home: 1316 Lakeview Cir Stockton MO 65785-9394 Office: Coldwell Banker J-S Realty 203 South St PO Box 159 Stockton MO 65785

JACKSON, BILLY MORROW, artist, retired art educator; b. Kansas City, Mo., Feb. 23, 1926; s. Alonzo David and Opal May (Morrow) J.; m. Blanche Mary Trice, June 12, 1949 (div. Jan. 1988); children: Lon Allan, Robin Jackson Todd, Aron Drew, Sylvia Marie; m. Siti Mariah, Feb. 1988. BFA, Washington U., St. Louis, 1949; MFA, U. Ill., 1954. Prof. art U. Ill., Champaign, 1954-87; ret. U. Ill., 1987. One man show Jane Haslem Gallery, Washington, 1990; represented in permanent collections at Smithsonian Inst., Washington, Nat. Gallery of Art, Washington, NASA Archives, Washington, Union League Club Chgo., Boston Pub. Libr., Met. Mus. Art, N.Y.C., Mus. of Legion of Honor, San Francisco, Libr. of Congress, Washington, Springfield (Mo.) Art Mus., Conn. Acad. of Fine Arts, Hartford, Artist's Guild, St. Louis, Phila., Free Libr., Evansville (Ind.) Mus. of Arts & Scis., Joslyn Art Mus., Omaha, Norfolk Mus., Omaha, Reading (Pa.) Pub. Libr. and Art Gallery, Lakeview Ctr. of Art, Peoria, Ill., Butler Inst. Am. Art, Youngstown, Ohio, Civic Ctr. Art Collection, Springfield, Ill., N.Y. Hilton, N.Y.C., Ill. State Mus., Springfield, World Book Ency., Chgo., Rockefeller Ctr., Dulin Gallery of Art, Knoxville, Tenn., Swope Mus., Terre Haute, Ind., Bur. of Peclamation, Washington, EPA, Washington, Krannert Art Mus., U. Ill., Champaign, Wichita (Kans.) Art Mus., Gov.'s State Coll., Park Forest South, Ill., Champaign Nat. Bank, Parkland Coll., Champaign, Sheldon Meml. Gallery of Art, U. Nebr., Lincoln, Busey First Nat. Bank, Champaign, 1st Nat. Bank, Champaign, Swanlund Bldg., Bechmann Inst., U. Ill., Champaign, Keday (Malaysia) State Mus.; commd. mural state Capitol Bldg., Springfield, Ill., Mara Inst. of Tech., Malaysia, Ill. Sch. for Deaf, Jacksonville, Quincy (Ill.) Vet. Hosp. and Home; subject of book Billy Morrow Jackson: Interpretations ot Time and Light (Howard E. Wooden), 1990, In Our Time, 1997, Krannert Art Mus., Champaign, Ill. Served to pvt. USMC, 1944-46, Okinawa. Democrat. Home: 706 W White St Champaign IL 61820-4706 Office: U Ill Art and Design Peabody at 4th St Champaign IL 61820

JACKSON, BLYDEN, English language educator; b. Paducah, Ky., Oct. 12, 1910; s. George Washington and Julia Estelle (Reid) J.; m. Roberta Bowles, Aug. 2, 1958. AB, Wilberforce U., 1930; AM, U. Mich., 1938, PhD (Rosenwald fellow 1947-49), 1952; LHD (hon.), U. Louisville, 1977; LittD (hon.), Wilberforce U., 1978, U.N.C.-Chapel Hill, 1985, U. Ky., 1990. Tchr. English, pub. schs. Louisville, 1934-45; asst., then assoc. prof. English Fisk U., 1945-54; prof. English, head dept. Southern U., 1954-62, dean Grad. Sch., 1962-69; prof. English U. N.C., 1969-81; assoc. dean U. N.C. (Grad. Sch.), 1973-76, spl. asst. to dean, 1976-81; disting. vis. prof. U. Miss., U. Del., Wayne State U.; spl. rsch. criticism Negro lit. Author: Black Poetry in America, 1974, The Waiting Years, 1976, A History of Afro-American Literature, Vol. 1, 1985; co-author: Black Poetry in America; adv. editor So. Lit. Jour.; contbr. articles to profl. jours. Established Historic Jackson Home Found., 1999. Established Blyden and Roberta Jackson Grad. fellowship in English, U. N.C., Chapel Hill., 1989, Historic Jackson Home Found., 1999; Jackson Hall U. N.C. admissions bldg. named in his owner, 1991. Mem. MLA (chmn. 20th century lit. div. 1976), Nat. Coun. Tchrs. English (Disting. lectr. 1970-71, chmn. coll. sect. 1971-73, trustee rsch. found. 1975-79), Coll. Lang. Assn. (v.p. 1954-56, pres. 1956-58, assoc. editor bull. and jour.), Speech Assn. Am., N.C. Tchrs. English, Alpha Phi Alpha. Home: 102 Laurel Hill Rd Chapel Hill NC 27514-4323

JACKSON, BOBBY RAND, minister; b. Wilson, N.C., Dec. 14, 1931; s. Joel John and Bessie Francis (Mayo) J.; m. Martha Jane Ketteman, May 30, 1953; children: Stephen Rand, Philip Wayne. B.A., Free Will Baptist Bible Coll., Nashville, 1954; M.A., Bob Jones U., Greenville, S.C., 1955. Ordained to ministry Free Will Baptists Ch., 1951; evangelist Free Will Baptists Ch., Nashville, 1955—; asst. moderator Nat. Assn. Free Will Baptists, Nashville, 1972-77; moderator Nat. Assn. Free Will Baptists, 1978-87, mem. exec. com., 1972-87, chmn. exec. com., 1978-87; presiding officer of gen. bd. Nat. Assn. Free Will Baptists, Nashville, 1978-87. Author: Messages That Matter, 1960, Six Steps to Successful Living, 1962, Awakening in the Wilderness, 1965, Beyond the Stars, 1966; soloist: record albums Softly and Tenderly, 1968, Then Sings My Soul, 1969, Fill My Cup, Lord, 1970, My God and I, 1978, Songs from Two Generations, 1985. Mem. Free Will Baptist Bible Coll. Alumni Assn., Bob Jones U. Alumni Assn. Home: 1412 E 14th St Greenville NC 27858-4734

JACKSON, BRENDA S., nursing educator; b. Richmond, Va., Jan. 24, 1948; d. Jobe Vernon and Alma Louise (Sanderson) Smith; m. Charles H. Jackson, III, Aug. 28, 1976; children: Charles H. IV, Jobe Sanderson. BSN, Med. Coll. Va., Richmond, 1970; MSN, U. Tex. Health Sci. Ctr., San Antonio, 1976; PhD, U. Tex., Austin, 1984. Evening charge nurse SICU San Antonio Community Hosp.; care corps Santa Rosa Med. Ctr., San Antonio; asst. prof. U. Tex. Health Sci. Ctr., San Antonio; prof., dir. nursing programs U. of Incarnate Word, San Antonio; assoc. prof. U. Tex. Health Sci. Ctr., San Antonio. Contbr. articles to profl. jours. 1st lt. USAF, 1971-74. Named Mildred McIntyre Nurse Vol. of the Yr., Tex. affiliate of Am. Heart Assn., 1987. Mem. Am. Assn. Critical Care Nurses, Am. Nursing Assn., Tex. Nursing Assn., Nat. League Nursing, Tex. League for Nursing, Am. Heart Assn. (bd. dirs., pres. affiliate), Sigma Theta Tau (chpt. past pres., immediate past pres.), Phi Kappa Phi, Sigma Zeta, Alpha Sigma Chi, Delta Alpha. Home: 307 Zornia Dr San Antonio TX 78213-2115

JACKSON, CARMAULT BENJAMIN, JR., physician; b. Newton, Mass., Apr. 19, 1924; s. Carmault Benjamin and Mabel (Robbins) J.; m. Lynda D. Shaneman; children—Carmault Benjamin, III, Thomas J., Molly Ann. M.D., U. Pa., 1952. Intern Hosp. of U. Pa., 1952-53, resident, 1953-56; internal medicine specialist U.S. Air Force, NASA Space Task Group, 1958-61; practice medicine specializing in internal medicine San Antonio, 1961-76; assoc. dir., asso. prof. medicine M.D. Anderson Hosp. and Tumor Inst., Houston, 1977-79; adminstr. Met. Gen Hosp., San Antonio; med. adv. H. B. Zachry Co., San Antonio, Tower Life Ins. Co.; vice chmn. Tex. Health Coordinating Council. Served with U.S. Army, 1942-45; Served with USAF, 1956-61. Decorated Purple Heart with 2 oak leaf clusters, U.S.A.F. Commendation medal. Mem. AMA, So. Med. Assn., Tex. Med. Assn., Tex. Soc. Internal Medicine, Am. Soc. Internal Medicine, Tex. Acad. Internal Medicine, Am. Occupational Medicine Assn., Bexar County (Tex.) Med. Soc., Inst. Medicine, Nat. Acad. Scis.

JACKSON, CAROL E., federal judge. BA, Wellesley Coll., 1973; JD, U. Mich., 1976. With Thompson & Mitchell, St. Louis, 1976-83; counsel Mallinckrodt, Inc., St. Louis, 1983-85; magistrate U.S. Dist. Ct., Ea. Dist. Mo., 1986-92, dist. judge, 1992—; adj. prof. law Washington U., St. Louis, 1989-92. Trustee St. Louis Art Mus., 1987-91; dir. bi-state chpt. ARC, 1989-91, Mo. Bot. Garden. Mem. Nat. Assn. Women Judges, Fed. Magistrate Judges Assn., Mo. Bar, St. Louis County Bar Assn., Bar Assn. Metro. St. Louis, Mound City Bar Assn., Lawyers Assn. St. Louis. Office: US Courthouse 1114 Market St Rm 812 Saint Louis MO 63101-2034*

JACKSON, CEDRIC DOUGLAS TYRONE, SR., minister; b. Amarillo, Tex., Feb. 8, 1962; s. Collis Wayne Jackson and Claudine (Brown) Chatman; m. Linda Jeannine Parker, July 1, 1989; children: Jeanniece LeeAnna Lynn, Cedric Douglas Tyrone, Jr., Carlin David Theodore. BA in Pastoral Ministries, ThB in Bibliology, Am. Bapt. Theol. Sem., 1991. Ordained to ministry Bapt. Ch., 1986; nat. cert. recovery specialist; cert. chem. dependency counselor. Assoc. min. Union Bapt. Ch., Atlanta, 1980-81; presiding min. Cosmopolitan Gospel Ministries, Cleve., 1981—; assoc. min. Olivet Instl. Bapt. Ch., Cleve., 1982-92, St. James Missionary Bapt. Ch., Nashville, 1987-89, Mt. Olivet Missionary Bapt. Ch., Hendersonville, Tenn., 1989-91; linkage coord. Alcohol and Drug Addiction Svcs. Bd. of Cuyahoga County, 1995—; proprietor Cosmopolitan Enterprises, 1990—; pres. Clark Atlanta U. Christian Fellowship, 1981-82. Counselor Nashville Union Rescue Mission, 1987-88; deputy registrar Cuyahoga County Bd. Elections, Cleve., 1986-89; active Operation PUSH. L.H. Woolfolk Mem. scholar Am. Bapt. Theol. Sem., Nashville, 1988-89; recipient Meritorious Svc. award Clark Atlanta U. Campus Ministries, 1981-82. Mem. NAACP, Progressive Nat. Bapt. Conv., Inc., Nat. Bapt. Conv., USA, Inc., Am. Bapt. Chs., USA, Bapt. Ministers Conf. Cleve. and Vicinity, Inc. Home and Office: Cosmopolitan Gospel Ministries 3314 Hyde Park Ave Cleveland Heights OH 44118 *Attempting to reform the soul of society without regenerating the souls of individuals, is like composing a musical symphony with no concept of rhythm, harmony or melody. One will make a catastrophic mess long before one makes a masterpiece.*

JACKSON, CHARLES IAN, writer, consultant; b. Keighley, Yorkshire, Eng., Feb. 11, 1935; s. Harry Sydney and Nellie (Crabtree) J.; m. Margaret Cochrane Storrie, July 10, 1963 (div. 1987); 1 child, Janet Clare Louise. B.A., London U., 1956; M.S., McGill U., 1959, Ph.D., 1961. Lectr. in geography London Sch. Econ., 1959-69; head econ. geography sect. Can. Dept. Energy, Mines and Resources, Ottawa, Ont., 1969-71; dir. planning and priorities Ministry of State for Urban Affairs, Ottawa, Ont., Can., 1972-78; sr. econ. affairs officer UN Econ. Commn. Europe, Geneva, Switzerland, 1978-81; exec. dir. Sigma Xi, New Haven, Ct., 1981-87; cons. water resources UN Econ. Commn. Europe, 1966-67; cons. German Marshall Fund U.S., 1975-77, Ford Found., 1977, Environment Can., 1994-95; rsch. dir. Can. Ho. of Commons Standing Com. on Environment, 1991-92; dir. Chreod Ltd., 1993-97; assoc. fellow Timothy Dwight Coll., Yale U. Translator tech. lit. from French; editor City Futures in Britain and Canada, 1991 and other books in field; author articles on history, resource mgmt. and geography; co-author Great Lakes: Great Legacy?, 1990; columnist (monthly mag.) Notes from Ptolemy, 1969-99. Dir., sec. Found. Preservation of Capt. Cook's Ships., 1999—. Recipient Darton prize Royal Meteorol. Soc., 1962; recipient Evan Durbin prize Inst. Econ. Affairs, 1964. Mem. Hakluyt Soc. (council 1967-69), Champlain Soc., Soc. for History of Discoveries, Quinnipiack Club (New Haven),.

JACKSON, CHARLES WAYNE, food products executive, former telecommunications industry executive; b. Louisville, June 3, 1930; s. Wayne O. and Geneva Drake J.; m. Sallie I. Lambert, June 21, 1952 (div. Feb. 1980); m. Elizabeth J. Soptic, June 1, 1979; children: Thomas, Carol E., Charles N. BEE, Ga. Inst. Tech., 1952. Student engr. AT&T, Cin., 1954-55; dist. plant engr. AT&T, Jacksonville, Fla., 1955-56; comml. rep to acctg. asst. AT&T, Atlanta, 1956-59; transmission systems engr. to plant design engr. AT&T, Kansas City, 1963-66; project mgr. to dir. major project Western Elec. Co., N.Y.C., 1966-69; engr. dir. TWX coord. to bus. relations dir. AT&T, N.Y.C., 1969-75; dir. pvt. lines rates Long Lines Co., Somerset, N.J., 1975; dir. pvt. lines rates to dir. planning Long Lines Co., Bedminster, N.J., 1975-81; dir. data prog. svcs. to dir. svc. devel. mktg. dept. AT&T, Bedminster, 1981-87; cons. pvt. practice Brandenburg, Ky., 1987-90; v.p. H&R Block Franchise, 1990-92; owner Squire Taber Apple Orchard, 1992—; v.p. Echo Enterprises, Inc., 1991—. 1st. lt. U.S. Army, 1952-54. Mem. Ky. State Horticulture Soc. (v.p., dir.), Elks. Methodist. Avocations: photography, horticulture. Home and Office: 1194 Adkins Rd Rineyville KY 40162-9722

JACKSON, CHERYL K., English educator; b. Shreveport, La., Feb. 19, 1945; d. Elmer Nelse and Virginia Mae (DeVore) Kellerman; m. Donald T. Jackson, Aug. 7, 1971; 1 child, Brian Christopher. BA in English, Westminster Coll., New Wilmington, Pa., 1967; MEd in Sec. Edn./English, Pa. State U., 1976. Cert. tchr. sec. English, reading, Pa. Tchr. English Gateway Sr. H.S., Monroeville, Pa., 1967-71, I.C. Norcom H.S., Portsmouth, Va., 1972-73; adj. instr. English Tidewater C.C.-Portsmouth Campus, Portsmouth, 1981-92; instr. Tidewater C.C. Portsmouth Campus, 1992-95, asst. prof., 1995—; dir. Ethelyn Hardesty Morgan scholarship Tidewater C.C.-Portsmouth Campus, Portsmouth, 1996—; seminar instr. effective bus. comm., stress mgmt., others. Lector Ch. of the Resurrection, Portsmouth, 1980-88. Frick scholar for tchrs. The Frick Found., Pitts., 1970. Mem. Nat. Coun. Tchrs. English. Avocations: reading, crochet, travel, bicycling. Office: Tidewater Cmty Coll 7000 College Dr Portsmouth VA 23703-6158

JACKSON, CLAUDREEN, special education educator; b. Detroit, June 21, 1939; d. Herbert and Grace (Gilmore) Gilbert; m. Pervis A. Jackson; children: Cindy, Stephanie, Shawn, Pervis A. Jr. B in Spl. Edn., U. Detroit, 1989; M of Learning Disabilities, 1993. Parent trainer Genesee Sch. Dist., Flint, Mich., 1986-89; tchr. Detroit Pub. Schs., 1989—; presenter and planning com. Spl. Connection Conf., Detroit, 1984-90. Author: (poetry) Let There Be Light, 1995; contbr. articles to profl. jours. Mem. Detroit Spl. Edn. Parents Adv. Com., 1981—; mem. community adv. com. Wayne State U., Detroit, 1984-90; mem. adv. coun. apptd. by Gov. Blanchard, 1984—; speaker United Way Speakers Bur., 1984-90; pres. Wayne County Soc. for Autistic Citizens, Detroit, 1984-85; bd. dirs. Mich. Soc. for Autistic Citizens, Lansing, 1984-90. Recipient Exceptional Parent award Coun. for Exceptional Citizens, 1989, Booker T. Washington Educator's Achievement award, 1996; finalist Mich. Tchr. of Yr., 1998. Democrat. Baptist. Home: 3464 Oakman Blvd Detroit MI 48204-1213

JACKSON, CYNTHIA MARIE, elementary school educator; b. Phila., Dec. 18, 1941; d. Clarence and Dorothy (Booker) Cook; m. Howard C. Jackson, Nov. 14, 1964 (div. May 1983); 1 child, Michelle Yvette. BS in Edn., Cheyney (Pa.) U., 1964. Cert. tchr. elem. edn., Pa. Elem. tchr. Phila. Sch. Dist., 1964-67, Chester-Upland Sch. Dist., Chester, Pa., 1967—. Mem. ASCD, Nat. Coun. Tchrs. English. Democrat. Baptist. Avocations: classical music, opera, museums, shopping. Home: 1927 Elston St Philadelphia PA 19138-2702 Office: Smedley Middle School 1701 Upland St Chester PA 19013-5734

JACKSON, CYNTHIA WILLIFORD, special education educator; b. Mobile, Ala., Oct. 30, 1949; d. Gerald Dee and Mary Evelyn (Johnson) W.; m. Alan P. Jackson, Aug. 18, 1973; 1 child, Julie Lynette. BS in Elem. Edn., John Brown U., 1971; MS in Spl. Edn., U. Ctrl. Ark., 1972; EdD, U. Ala., 1998. Cert. tchr., Ala. Resource tchr. Decatur (Ark.) Elem. Sch., 1972-73, Montgomery (Ala.) County Sch. System, 1973-75, Birmingham (Ala.) City Schs., 1976-80; instr. Horizons Program-UAB, Birmingham, 1992-94; rsch. asst., adj. U. Ala., Tuscaloosa, 1995-98, asst. prof., 1998-99; asst. prof. State U. West Ga., Carrollton, 1999—; pvt. cons. Auburn (Ala.) City Schs., 1989-91; psychometrist, Montgomery, 1975-76. Author: (with others) Profile of Commitment, 1995; contbr. chpt. to Mental Retardation, 5th edit.; contbr. articles to profl. jours. Mem. Coun. for Exceptional Children, Kappa Delta Pi, Phi Delta Kappa. Baptist. Avocations: reading, needlepoint, walking. Home: 2521 Altadena Forest Cir Birmingham AL 35243-4618 Office: U Ala Coll Edn PO Box 870231 Tuscaloosa AL 35487-0154

JACKSON, DANIEL WYER, electrical engineer; b. Louisville, June 28, 1929; s. Dugald Caleb Jr. and Elisabeth Uhl (Wyer) J.; m. Doris C. Maier, Oct. 1, 1955; children: Daniel B., Barbara E., Gordon S. BSEE, Lehigh U., 1950. Registered profl. engr., Va. Test engr. GE Co., Lynn, Mass., and Schenectady, N.Y., 1950-51; test engr. gen. engring. lab. GE Co., Schenectady, 1953; sr. evaluation engr. industry control dept. GE Co., Schenectady and Salem, Va., 1954-62; product prodn. engr. industry control dept. GE Co., Salem, 1962-68, design engr., 1968, product engr., 1968-69, sr. product engr., 1969-81, sr. product engr. drive systems dept., 1981-91; freelance engr. Roanoke, Va., 1991-98; ret., 1998; bd. dirs. Southcon, Inc., L.A., 1991-95, conv. dir., 1994, chmn. bd., 1994-95. Adult leader Boy Scouts Am., Schenectady & Roanoke, 1954-80; officer of election Roanoke County, Va., 1962-87, 98; deacon Covenant Presbyn. Ch., Roanoke, 1969-72, elder, 1974-76, 92-94, 97-99. 1st lt. U.S. Army, 1951-53, Korea. Recipient Silver Beaver award Blue Ridge coun. Boy Scouts Am., 1979. Mem. IEEE (life, sr., bd. dirs. 1990-91, region 3 dir. 1990-91, chmn. admissions and advancement com. 1999, chmn. nat. engrs. week com. 1991-92, chmn. prof. activities coun. engrs. info. com. 1993, vice chmn. region 3 1988-89, chmn. Va. coun. 1985-86, chmn. Va. mountains sect. 1981-82, chmn. EAB profl. devel. com. 1994-96, chmn. EAB continuing edn. com. 1992-93, chmn. USAB awards and recognition com. 1994-96, outstanding svc. awards 1983, 86, 93, 98, centennial medal 1984, meritorious svc. to ednl. activities bd. award 1991), NSPE (pres. Roanoke chpt. 1974-75), Va. Soc. Profl. Engrs. (outstanding svc. award 1976). Republican. Home: 5704 Castle Rock Rd Roanoke VA 24018-6106

JACKSON, DAVID GORDON, religious organization administrator; b. Derby, N.Y., Nov. 5, 1936; s. Peter Thomas and Sarah (Staubitz) J. BS, SUNY, Buffalo, 1960; MDiv, Huntington Coll. Theol. Sem., 1964. Ordained elder Ch. of the United Brethren in Christ, 1969. Dir. youth work Ch. United Brethren in Christ, Huntington, Ind., 1966-73, adminstrv. asst., treas., 1973-79; exec. sec., treas. Internat. Soc. Christian Endeavor, Columbus, Ohio, 1979-84, exec. dir., 1981—; exec. dir. World's Christian Endeavor Union, Columbus, 1984—; adj. lectr. U. Calif. San Francisco, 1980—, asst. clin. prof., 1986—. Office: CEI PO Box 2106 1221 E Broad St Columbus OH 43205-1404*

JACKSON, DAVID LEE, real estate executive; b. Youngstown, Ohio, Dec. 3, 1946; s. Harold Truman and Helene Irene (DeVoe) J.; m. Lauren Janine Hite, May 27, 1977. BA, Malone Coll., 1968; MA, Kent State U., 1975. Br. mgr. Boebinger Realtors, Alliance, Ohio, 1975-80; real estate broker, pres. D.L. Jackson Agy., Inc., Alliance and Canton, Ohio, 1980-92; agt. Nationwide Ins., Alliance, Ohio, 1993—. Mem. Alliance Area Bd. Realtors (pres. 1982), Canton-Massillon Bd. Realtors, Rotary. Republican. Avocation: golf. Home and Office: 5337 Cherokee Ave NW North Canton OH 44720-6841

JACKSON, DAVID ROBERT, school system administrator; b. Long Beach, Calif., Jan. 15, 1945; s. Harlan Leroy and Helen Louise (Worthen) J.; m. Stacey Ann Bryan, Nov. 13, 1971; children: David, Daniel, Chad, Loren, Darcy. Student, Fullerton Coll., 1963-64, Brigham Young U., 1965-67, Santa Ana Coll., 1977, Orange Coast Coll., 1977-78. Mgr. trainee Carl Karcher Enterprizes, Fullerton, Calif., 1964; asst. mgr. Household Fin. Co., Santa Ana., Calif., 1964-65; mgr. Chateau Apres Lodge, Park City, Utah, 1965-69; pres. Aero Wash Co., Santa Ana., Calif., 1970-79; pres., exec. dir. Fairmont Schs. Inc., Anaheim, Calif., 1979—. Former leader Boy Scouts Am.; bishop LDS Ch., Corona, 1990-96; chmn. Orange County 2000, Calif., 1991-93, also bd. dirs. Mem. Nat. Ind. Pvt. Sch. Assn. (bd. dirs. 1981—, founding mem., pres. 1993-98), Calif. Assn. Nationally Recognized Schs. (founder, pres. 1992-93), Orange County Pvt. Sch. Assn. (pres. 1990-93, founder). Republican. Avocations: snow skiing, geneology, private pilot. Office: Fairmont Sch 100 S Anaheim Blvd Anaheim CA 92805-3848

JACKSON, DEMPSTER MCKEE, retired naval officer; b. San Diego, Nov. 17, 1930; s. Riley Richmond and Ruth (Remington) J.; m. Mary-Lin Moore, June 27, 1955; children: David, Dennis, Riley, Demarie. BSEE, U.S. Naval Acad., 1952; postgrad., U.S. Naval Postgrad. Sch., 1963. Commd. ensign USN, 1952, advanced through grades to rear adm., 1978, comdr. USS King, 1970-71, head undersea surveillance div., 1972-74, mgr. undersea surveillance project, 1974-78, mgr. anti-submarine systems project, 1978-79, asst. dep. comdr. undersea warfare, Naval Sea Systems Command, 1979-81, dep. comdr. Combat Systems, Naval Sea Systems Command, Navy Dept., 1981-83, ret., 1983. Decorated Legion of Merit, Bronze Star, others. Mem. SAR, Soc. Mayflower Descs. Home: 1422 Carrington Ln Vienna VA 22182-1422

JACKSON, DENISE SUZANNE See SUTHERLAND, DENISE JACKSON

JACKSON, DENNIS K., military career officer; b. Cheyenne, Wyo., Nov. 16, 1946. Grad., U. Wyo.; MBA, Fla. Inst. Tech.; grad., Command and Gen. Staff Coll., Def. Sys. Mgmt. Coll., Indsl. Coll. Armed Forces. Commd. officer U.S. Army, advanced through grades to maj. gen.; with 1st Bn., 37th Armor, 1st Armored Divsn. U.S. Army, Germany, 1969-72; comdr. 707th Maintenance Bn., 7th Inf. Divsn., Divsn. G4 U.S. Army, spl. asst. to Chief of Staff of Army, Dept. Army Hdqrs., comdr. 25th Inf. Divsn. Support Command, 1992-94, exec. officer to commdg. gen. U.S. Army Material Command; dir. logistics, engring. and security assistance (J4) U.S. Pacific Command; comdr. 19th Theater Army Area Command U.S. Army, Taegu, Korea; comdr. Ordnance Ctrs. and Schs., 30th Chief of Ordnance U.S. Army, 1998—. Decorated Army Achievement medal with oak leaf cluster, Army Commendation medal with two oak leaf clusters, Meritorious Svc. medal with four oak leaf clusters, Bronze Star, Legion of Merit with two oak leaf clusters, Def. Superior Svc. medal, Disting. Svc. medal. Office: US Ordnance Ctr and Sch Aberdeen Proving Ground MD 21005

JACKSON, DILLON EDWARD, lawyer; b. Washington, Apr. 18, 1945; s. Paul David and Virginia (Dillon) J.; children: David I., Anne E.; m. Misha Halvarsson, Aug. 19, 1989. BA, Middlebury (Vt.) Coll., 1967; JD, U. Wash., 1970. Bar: Wash. 1970, U.S. Dist. Ct. (we. and ea. dists.) Wash. 1970, U.S. Ct. Appeals (9th cir.) 1970, U.S. Dist. Ct. Ariz. 1991. Assoc. Kleist & Helmick, Seattle, 1971-73, Powell Livengood & Silvernale, Kirkland, Wash., 1973-75; ptnr. Keller Jacobsen Jackson & Snodgrass, Bellevue, Wash., 1975-85, Hatch & Leslie, Seattle, 1985-91, Foster Pepper & Shefelman, Seattle, 1991—; chairperson creditor rights and bankruptcy dept. Am. Bankruptcy Bd. Cert.; mem. adv. bd. Applied Environ. Tech., Seattle, 1992—; bd. mem. Consumer Credit Counseling, Seattle, 1975-79; chmn. publs. com. Am. Bankruptcy Inst. Co-author: Commercial Law Desk Book, 1995; contbg. author: Advance Chapter 11 Bankruptcy Practice, 1989-95. Pres. Dox Coop., Seattle, 1989-91. Fellow Am. Coll. Bankruptcy, 1990. Mem. ABA, Wash. State Trial Lawyers Assn., Wash. State Bar Assn. (creditor-debtor sect., chairperson 1984-88), Continuing Legal Edn. Bd. (chairperson 1991-92). Office: Foster Pepper & Shefelman PLLC 1111 3rd Ave Ste 3400 Seattle WA 98101-3299

JACKSON, EARL, JR., medical technologist, retired; b. Paris, Ky., Sept. 4, 1938; s. Earl Sr. and Margaret Elizabeth (Cummins) J. BA, Ky. State U., 1960; postgrad., U. Paris, 1978. Clin. rsch. coord. Harvard U., Boston, 1962-64; chem. devel. specialist Electro-Power Pacs, Corp., Cambridge, Mass., 1964-67; sr. rsch. tech. Mass. Gen. Hosp., Boston, 1967-81, med. tech. specialist, 1991-95; ret., 1995. Contbr. articles to profl. jours. Mem. AAAS, NY. Acad. Scis., Am. Assn. Clin. Chemistry, Am. Soc. Clin. Microbiology, N.E. Assn. for Microbiology and Infectious Disease. Democrat. Home: 501 Fenwick Dr San Antonio TX 78239-2532

JACKSON, EDGAR B., JR., medical educator; b. Rison, Ark., May 30, 1935; m. Thelma Jackson, 1957; children: Gary, David, Michael, Laura. BA, Case Western Res. U., 1962, MD, 1966. Intern Cleve. Met. Gen. Hosps., 1966-67, chief resident medicine, 1969-70; from sr. instr. medicine to asst. prof. to asst. clin. prof. Case Western Res. U., 1970-83, assoc. clin. prof., 1983-86, clin. prof. medicine, 1986—; chief of staff, sr. v.p. for clin. affairs Univ. Hosps. of Cleve.; asst. dean Case Western Res. U., 1971-74, asst. prof. comty. medicine, 1974-79, comty. health, 1977-88. Contbr. numerous articles to profl. jours. With U.S. Army, 1959-61. Carnegie Common Wealth Clin. scholar, 1970-72. Mem. APHA, Am. Sickle Cell Anemia Assn. Inc. Office: Univ Hosp 11100 Euclid Ave Cleveland OH 44106-1736*

JACKSON, ELIJAH, JR., communication executive. AA in Gen. Studies and Broadcasting, Ricks Coll., Rexburg, Idaho, 1982; AA in Theatre, Brigham Young U., Hawaii, 1984, AA in Speech Comm., 1984; BA in Comm., U. Hawaii at Manoa, 1987; postgrad., U. Southwestern La., Lafayette, Polk C.C., Winter Haven, Fla., Kapiolani C.C., Honolulu, HI. Tng. Prog. by Federal Mogul Corp., 1998; entrepreneurship tng., Hawaii C. of C., Honolulu, 1987; Bus. Etiquette and Protocol, U. of Hawaii Manoa, 1986; Fin. Mgmt. for Closely held Bus., Bank of Hawaii, 1985; Eng. Tech., Tampa Tech. Inst., 1981. Editor Oceanic Cablevision, Am. TV Corp., Time Warner Inc.; pvt. practice radio and TV project budget mgr., prodr., dir, videographer; legis. aide Com. on Consumer Protection and Commerce State of Hawaii Legislature; CEO Jackson Program, 10 years, Jackson Pacific Joint Venture, 10 years, Jackson Instructional TV Sys., 10 years; trustee, fiduciary, promoter JBS Inc. Parent Corp., Hawaii, Fla.; CEO, pres., promoter Jackson Family Limited Partnership, Ltd., 13 years, Jackson Family Limited Trust, 13 years, JBS Inc. Parent Corp., 13 years, Elijah Jackson, Jr., Inc., 13 years, Delesia Renee Jackson Inc., 13 years; legal rschr., legislative aide State of Hawaii, 13th Legislature Com. on Consumer Protection and Commerce, Hawaii, 1 year; intern field prod., videographer, ABC affiliate, KITV channel 4, 1 year; graphic design, photography, cons. video system design Sony and CMX videos, 2 years; trustee, pres. Jackson Internatl. Mgmt. Limited, Nassau, Bahamas. Radio/TV project budget mgr., prod., dir., videographer; editor for Oceanic Cablevision a/k/a Amer. TV Corp. a/k/a Time Warner Inc. d/b/a Honolulu TV Comm. Corp. Mem. ABA, Amer. Payroll Assn. Address: PO Box 92895 Lakeland FL 33804-2895

JACKSON, ELIZABETH RIDDLE, writer, translator, educator; b. Boston, May 13, 1926; m. Matthew Casey and Katharine (Kerr) Riddle; m. Gabriel Jackson, Dec. 1949 (div. Sept. 1969); children: Katharine, Rachel. BA, Reed Coll., 1947; MA, Wellesley Coll., 1959; Doctorat de l'Université, Sorbonne U., Paris, 1963. Statistician Nat. Bur. Econ. Rsch., N.Y.C., 1947-48; tchr. math. Putney (Vt.) Sch., 1948-49; tutor French Goddard Coll., Plainsfield, Vt., 1953-55; lectr. in French Knox Coll., Galesburg, Ill., 1963-65; assoc. humanities U. Calif. San Diego, La Jolla, 1965-66; prof. French San Diego State U., 1969-87; cons. Toronto (Can.) U. Press, PMLA; mem. rev. panel NEH, Washington, 1977; mem. screening com. Fulbright Study Abroad, 1981-92. Author: L'Evolution de la Mémoire Involontaire dans l'oeuvre de Marcel Proust, 1966, Worlds Apart: Structural Parallels in the Poetry of Paul Valéry, Saint-John Perse, Benjamin Péret and René Char, 1976, Secrets Observateurs...: la Poésie d'André Chénier, 1993; translator: A Marvelous World: Poems by Benjamin Péret, 1985, Meidosems (by Henry Michaux), 1993. Grantee French Govt., 1960-61, Fulbright Found., 1960-61, Ctr. Nat. Rsch. Sci., France, 1965. Mem. Amnesty Internat., So. Oreg. Learning in Retirement (chair curriculum com.). Avocations: music, hiking. Home: 1122 Tolman Creek Rd Ashland OR 97520-3651

JACKSON, ELMER JOSEPH, lawyer, oil and gas company executive; b. Fairmont, Nebr., Sept. 16, 1920; s. Elmer Ellsworth and Kathleen Johanna (Sullivan) J.; m. Mary Elinor Booth, Sept. 1, 1943; children: Mary K., Teresa G., Cecilia A., Jean A., Joseph E., James O., Elizabeth J. LL.B. cum laude, U. Nebr., 1947. Bar: Nebr. 1947, Colo. 1980. With Stanolind Oil & Gas Co., Tulsa, 1948-52, K N Energy, Inc., 1952-84; exec. v.p., gen. counsel, sec., dir. Midlands Energy Co., 1984-85; chief exec. officer, 1985-89; chmn. bd. Plains Petroleum Co., 1988-91; pvt. practice, 1991—. Trustee Legal Aid Found. Colo., 1990-91; Served with U.S. Army, 1942-46. Decorated Bronze Star, Air medal; knight St. Gregory; recipient Alumni Achievement award U. Nebr., 1991. Mem. Colo. Bar Assn., Nebr. Bar Assn., Am. Assn. Corp. Counsel, Colo. Assn. Corp. Counsel (pres. 1989-90), Am. Judicature Soc. Republican. Roman Catholic. Club: K.C.

JACKSON, ERIC ALLEN, philatelist; b. Long Beach, Calif., Jan. 3, 1955; s. Allen Joseph and Janice Meredith (Lyen) J.; m. Theresa Kathleen Strauss Jackson, Mar. 21, 1975 (div. Jan. 1997); children: Amy Marie, Jared Brady, Luke Allen. Student, Chapman Coll., Orange, Calif., 1973-75. Owner pvt. practice, Anaheim, Calif., 1973-81; cons. William C. Tatham Stamp Co., Whittier, Calif., 1979-81; owner Whittier (Calif.) Philatelic Svcs., 1981-87; pvt. practice Herndon, Va., 1987-88, Leesport, Pa., 1988—; expert com. The Philatelic Found., N.Y.C., 1979—, Am. Philatelic Soc., State College, Pa., 1979—, Profl. Stamp Expertising, Miami, 1987—; bd. dirs., v.p. Am. Revenue Assn., Rockford, Iowa, 1980—; cons. Scott Pub. Co., Sidney, Ohio, 1980—. Contbr. articles to profl. jours. Mem. Am. Stamp Dealers Assn. (bd. dirs. 1998—), Am. Philatelic Soc., Am. Revenue Assn., Collectors Club of N.Y., Revenue Soc. Great Britain, Berks County C. of C., Berks County Hist. Soc., Nat. Trust for Historic Preservation. Republican. Avocations: antiques, baseball, fishing. Home: RR 2 Box 2810 Reading PA 19605-9763 Office: Eric Jackson Co PO Box 728 Schoolside Pla Ste A-1 Leesport PA 19533-0728

JACKSON, ERIN DENISE, speech therapist; b. Norfolk, VA., Mar. 1, 1960; d. Jerry Eugene and Willie Delores (Jones) J. BA, Norfolk State U., 1982; MA, Hampton U., 1985. Lic. speech pathologist, Va. Cashier K-Mart, Norfolk, 1983; speech therapist Essex County Pub. Schs., Tappahannock, Va., 1986, Virginia Beach (Va.) City Pub. Schs., 1986—; Vol. Manning Convalescent Home, Portsmouth, Va., 1985—. Mem. Speech-Hearing Assn. Va., Coun. for Exceptional Children, Virginia Beach Reading Coun., Norfolk State Alumni Assn., Zeta Phi Beta (sec. 1989-90). Avocations: swimming, cake decorating, sewing, classical piano, collecting dolls.

JACKSON, ERNEST, JR., broadcasting executive; m. Willda Jackson; 1 child, Matthew. Student, Corning (N.Y.) C.C., 1968; BS in Radio and TV, Ithaca (N.Y.) Coll., 1978. Sr. account exec. WGCL-FM, Cleve., 1977-78; gen. mgr. WDWQ-FM/WQIZ-AM, St. George/Charleston, S.C., 1978-82; gen. sales mgr. WDIA-AM, 1982-83; v.p., gen. mgr. WHRK-FM/WDIA-AM Radio, divsn. Ragan Henry Comm. Group, Memphis, 1985-89, WOWI/WBSK Radio, divsn. US Radio, LP, Norfolk, Va., 1989-93, KMJQ/KYOK Radio, divsn. Noble Broadcast Group, Inc., Houston, 1993-94, KMJQ RAdio, divsn. Clear Channel Radio Inc., Houston, 1992—. Office: KMJQ (FM) 24 E Greenway Plz Ste 1508 Houston TX 77046-2467*

JACKSON, EUGENE BERNARD, librarian; b. Frankfort, Ind., June 18, 1915; s. John Herman and Goldie Belle (Michael) J.; m. Ruth Lillian Whitlock, Aug. 6, 1941. BS with distinction, Purdue U., 1937; BS in Libr. Sci. with honors, U. Ill., 1938, MA, 1942; LHD (hon.), Purdue U., 1994. Asst. engring. library U. Ill., 1938-40; asst. charge newspaper div. U. Ill. Library, 1940-41; documents librarian U. Ala., 1941-42; with tech. dept. Detroit Pub. Library, 1942-46; chief reference library Wright Field, Ohio; chief library sect. Central Air Documents Office, Dayton, Ohio, 1946-49; chief research information sect. Research and Devel. Command, Q.M.C., Washington, 1949-50; chief div. aero. intelligence NACA, 1950-52, chief div. research information, 1952-56; head library dept. research labs. Gen. Motors Corp., Warren, Mich., 1956-65; chmn. corp. com. tech. lit. Gen. Motors Corp., 1959-65; dir. information retrieval and library services IBM Corp., Armonk, New York, 1965-71; library cons. in automation, Grad. Sch. Library Sci. U. Tex., Austin, 1971-72; prof. library sci. U. Tex., 1971-85, prof. emeritus, 1985—; mem. chancellors coun. The U. Tex. Sys., 1996—; v.p. Engring. Index, Inc., 1967-68, pres., 1968-73; also dir. Attendee Gordon Research Confs. on Sci. Information, N.H., 1964—; vis. summer lectr. U. Mich., 1965, U. Ill., 1968; mem. task force United Engring. Info. System, 1966; cons.; U.S. mem. documentation com., adv. group aero. research and devel. NATO, Paris, France, 1953-61, chmn., 1955-56, dep. chmn., chmn. elect., 1960-61; McBee lectr. Simmons Coll., Boston, 1956; ofcl. U.S. del. gen. assemblies Fedn. International de Documentation, Tokyo, 1967, The Hague, 1968, Buenos Aires, 1970, Budapest, 1972, chmn. U.S. nat. com., 1970-72. Author: (with Ruth L. Jackson) Industrial Information Systems, 1978; editor: Special Librarianship, a New Reader, 1980; contbr. articles to profl. jours., chpts. to books. Mem. tech. adv. com. Macomb County (Mich.) Planning Commn. Served with AUS, 1943-46. Named Pioneer in Info. Sci., Chem. Heritage Found., 1998. Mem. Spl. Libraries Assn. (pres. 1962-63), A.L.A., Am. Soc. Info. Scis., AIAA (sec. Mich. 1964-65), Assn. Records Mgrs. and Adminstrs. Protestant Episcopalian (vestryman, lic. lay reader). Home: 8512 Silver Ridge Dr Austin TX 78759-8143

JACKSON, FRANCIS CHARLES, physician, surgeon; b. Rutherford, N.J., Sept. 2, 1917; s. Frank Emil and Margaret Charlotte (Kuhn) J.; m. Joan Gloria Mortenson, Sept. 1, 1949; children: Geoffrey P., Bradford M., Gregory C., Donna E. B.A., Yale U., 1939; M.D., U. Va., 1943. Diplomate Am. Bd. Surgery, Nat. Bd. Med. Examiners. Intern N.Y. Hosp.-Cornell Med. Center, 1944, asst. resident surgery, 1945, from asst. resident surgery to 1st asst. chief resident surgeon, 1947-49, chief resident surgeon, 1950; practice medicine specializing in gen. and vascular surgery Pitts., 1952-70; cons., chief surgeon Arabian Am. Oil Co., Dhahran, Saudi Arabia, 1951; asst. chief surg. service VA Center, Togus, Maine, 1952; chief surg. service, dir. Gen. Surg. Residency Program, VA Hosp., Pitts., 1952-70; dir. surg. service VA Central Office, Washington, 1970-72; spl. asst. to chief med. dir. for emergency and disaster med. services VA Central Office, 1972-73, dir. emergency and disaster med. services staff, 1973-75; mem. cons. staff Presbyn.-Univ. Hosp., Pitts., 1959-70; asst. in surgery Sch. Medicine Cornell U., 1946-49, asst. in anatomy, 1946, instr. surgery, 1950; asst. prof. surgery Sch. Medicine U. Pitts., 1953-60, assoc. prof. surgery, 1961-65, prof. surgery, 1965-70, sec. exec. com. dept. surgery, 1964-70, MEND coordinator, 1967-68; clin. prof. surgery Georgetown U. Sch. Medicine, George Washington U. Sch. Medicine, Washington, 1970-75; chmn. dept. surgery Sch. Medicine Tex. Tech U., Lubbock, 1975-80; prof. surgery Sch. Medicine Tex. Tech U., 1975—, assoc. dean clin. edn., 1980-82; med. dir. S. Plains Emergency Med. Services, 1978-92; prof., chmn. emeritus dept. of surgery Tex. Tech. Med. Sch. Medicine, 1996; cons. Carnegie-Mellon Inst., 1969-71, Westinghouse Electric Corp. (Health Systems), AVCO Corp.; chmn. local com. VA Adj. Cancer Chemotherapy Study, 1957-70; chmn. exec. com. Operation Prep. Pitts. Annual Med.-CD Disaster Drill, 1958-60; mem. ad hoc com. disaster med. surveys, div. med., vice chmn. com. emergency med. services Nat. Acad. Scis.-NRC, 1964-74; mem. surg. drugs adv. com. FDA, 1971-75; mem. panel on physicians asst. CSC, 1971-73; cons. on emergency and disaster services USPHS, 1965-72; VA rep., alternate observer, nat. health resources adv. com. Office Preparedness, 1972-75; VA rep., mem. interdepartmental com. on emergency med. services HEW, 1974-75; mem. ad hoc com. on emergency med. services communications, interdepartmental adv. com. on radio communications Office Telecommunications Policy, 1973-75. Author: Role of Medicine in Emergency Preparedness, 1968; contbr. articles to surg. jours.; creator surg. exhibits. Trustee Peddie Sch., 1972-74. Served as lt. (j.g.) USNR, 1945-46, to lt. comdr., M.C. 1953-55. Recipient Pfizer award of merit U.S. CD Council, Mpls., 1960, Key to City Louisville, 1964, Billings Gold Medal award AMA, 1966. Fellow A.C.S. (past chmn. residents program com. Southwestern Pa. chpt.; chmn. subcom. disaster, surgery and communications of trauma com., trauma com. 1966-78, exec. com. 1976-78, pres. Southwestern Pa. chpt. 1970, gov. 1970-74); mem. AMA (chmn. com. disaster med. care, Council Nat. Security 1958-67), Pa. Med Soc. (chmn. commn. on emergency med. services), Allegheny County Med. Soc., Soc. Biol. Research U. Pitts. Sch. Medicine, Pitts. Surg. Soc., Am. Assn. Surgery of Trauma, So. Surg. Assn., Assn. VA Surgeons (founding), Central Surg. Assn., Soc. Surgery Alimentary Tract, Assn. Mil. Surgeons U.S. (Stitt award 1968), Pitts. Acad. Medicine (Man of Year award 1969), D.C. Med. Soc., Am. Surg. Assn., Société Internat. de Chirurgie, Tex. Surg. Soc., Tex. Med. Assn. (chmn. surg. sect. program com. 1981-82, subcom. on accreditation of continuing med. edn. programs 1983-92, com. on continuing edn. 1959-92, cons.), Lubbock Surg. Soc., Lubbock-Crosby-Garza County Med. Soc., Alpha Omega Alpha. Lodge: Rotary. Office: Dept of Surgery Sch Medicine Tex Tech U Lubbock TX 79430

JACKSON, FRANCIS JOSEPH, research and development company executive; b. Providence, May 23, 1932; s. Francis Joseph and Mary Elizabeth (Ryan) J.; m. Mary Veronica Brennan, Sept. 1, 1956 (div. Mar. 1983); children: Mary Cecilia, Paul Francis, Thomas Edward.; m. Nancy M. McMahon, May 21, 1983. B.S. magna cum laude, Providence Coll., 1954; Sc.M., Brown U., 1957, Ph.D., 1960. Rsch. assoc. Brown U., 1959-60; sr. scientist Bolt Beranek & Newman Inc., Cambridge, Mass., 1960-68; divsn. v.p. Bolt Beranek & Newman Inc., 1968-77, v.p., 1977-79, sr. v.p. (emeritus), 1979—; cons., 1999—; adj. prof. Cath. U., 1973-77. Contbr. articles to profl. jours. Recipient Personal Achievement award Providence Coll., 1989, 75th Diamond Jubilee award Providence Coll., 1992. Fellow Acoustical Soc. Am.; mem. IEEE (sr.), Am. Inst. Physics, Cosmos, Winchester Country Club (bd. dirs. 1992-94), Delta Epsilon Sigma. Home and Office: 14A Plato Ter Winchester MA 01890-2229

JACKSON, G. JAMES, protective services official; b. Columbus, Ohio. Student, Harvard U., Ohio State U., Northwestern U., FBI Acad. Patrolman Columbus Divsn. Police, 1958-67, sgt., 1967-71, lt., 1971-74, capt., 1974-77, dep. chief, 1977-90, chief, 1990—. With USMC. Office: Office Chief Police 120 Marconi Blvd Columbus OH 43215-2376*

JACKSON, GAYLE PENDLETON WHITE, venture capitalist, international energy specialist; b. Orange, N.J., June 22, 1946; d. Harold Dee and Marion Marvin (Harris) W.; m. Lothrop Brewster Jackson II, June 8, 1968 (div. 1986); m. Frederick T. Kraus, June 11, 1995; stepchildren: Grant, Madeleine, Caroline. BA cum laude, Smith Coll., 1967; MA in Polit. Sci., Washington U., 1969, PhD in Polit. Sci., 1972. Asst. prof. polit. sci. Washington U., St. Louis, 1972-73; market analyst Ralston Purina Co., St. Louis, 1973-74, adminstr. corp. energy dept., 1974-76; regional rep. to Sec. of Commerce U.S. Dept. of Commerce, Kansas City, Mo., 1976-78; dir. corp. planning Peabody Coal Co., St. Louis, 1978-81; v.p. bus. devel. Gateway Terminals, Peabody Holding Co., St. Louis, 1981-82; v.p. Premier Coal Sales Co., Peabody Holding Co., St. Louis, 1982-85; prs. Gayle P.W. Jackson, Inc., St. Louis, 1985—; chief of staff coal industry adv. bd. Internat. Energy Agy., Paris, 1985-95. Chmn., pres. St. Louis County Local Devel. Co., 1979-84, adv. Ctr. New Inst. Econ., Washinton U., St. Louis, 1998—, bd. dirs. Smith Coll., Northampton, Mass., 1997—, Webster U., St. Louis, 1983-95, Ctr. for Internat. Pvt. Enterprise, 1993—, SSM Health Care, 1995—, United Nations Assn., 1998—, bd. adjustment City of Clayton, St. Louis, 1985-91; editl. adv. bd. Econ. Reform Today, 1996—. Recipient Spl. Leadership award St. Louis YWCA, 1984; fellow Woodrow Wilson, 1971-72, Fulbright-Hays, 1971-72. Mem. Mo. Women's Forum (pres. 1992), Internat. Women's Forum (bd. dirs. 1986-94, treas. 1991-93, v.p. 1993-95, leadership found. 1993-97). Avocations: tennis, alpine and cross-country skiing, wilderness hiking, running, piano. Office: Gayle P W Jackson Inc 6445 Cecil Ave Saint Louis MO 63105-2224

JACKSON, GEORGE LYMAN, nuclear medicine physician; b. Arlington, Mass., Dec. 17, 1923; s. William and Alice (Tenney) J.; m. Alyce Verne Yeager, Sept. 7, 1946; children: Scott Douglas, Carole Elizabeth, Diane Priscilla, Richard Lee. B.S. cum laude, Franklin and Marshall Coll., 1944; M.D., U. Pa., 1948. Diplomate: Am. Bd. Internal Medicine, Am. Bd. Nuclear Medicine. Intern Hosp. U. Pa., 1948-49, resident, 1949-52; practice medicine specializing in internal medicine Harrisburg, Pa., 1952-63; dir. med. edn., acting med. dir. Harrisburg Hosp., 1963-68, dir. undergrad. fellowships, 1968-69, head sect. nuclear medicine, 1965-75, med. dir. dept. nuclear medicine, 1975-89; asst. prof. medicine Hahnemann Med. Coll., 1963-68, assoc. prof., 1968-70; clin. assoc. prof. M.S. Hershey Med. Centre, Pa. State U., 1970-76, clin. prof., 1976-90; dir. Harrisburg Hosp. Sch. Nuclear Medicine Tech.; adj. faculty Harrisburg Area Community Coll., Millersville State Coll.; cons., chmn. med. adv. com. Lebanon (Pa.) VA Hosp., 1968-75; nuclear medicine adv. Pa. Dept. Edn., Pa. Med. Soc., Pa. Blue Shield. Author, pub.: Of Thee I Sing, 1993, The Eclectic Club of Harrisburg, 1997; contbr. articles to profl. jours. Mem. Cen. Dauphin Sch. Bd., 1971-73; bd. dirs. Bethesda Mission, Harrisburg Hosp. Med. Edn. and Rsch. Found.; bd. dirs. New Hope Ministries, 1987-93, pres. 1988-93; chmn. archives and collections com. No. York County Hist. and Preservation Soc., 1998—. With USNR, 1942-45. Fellow ACP (govs. com. for coll. affairs 1969-76, gov. 1976-80, laureate 1985), Soc. Nuclear Medicine, Am. Coll. Nuclear Physicians (bd. regents), Am. Coll. Nuclear Medicine; mem. Am. Thyroid Assn., Pa. Soc. Internal Medicine (past pres.; chmn. liaison com.), Pa. Coll. Nuclear Medicine (pres.), Joint Rev. Com. Nuclear Medicine Tech., Phi Beta Kappa, Alpha Omega Alpha. Presbyterian. Home: 22 N Baltimore St Dillsburg PA 17019-1210 *The efforts of my adult life have been directed primarily at three priorities—family, profession, church. Success in achieving any of these is a consequence of a combination of providence, help from others and personal attributes. Help from others involves, principally, my family (in its largest sense) and of these my wife is most important. She is a source of understanding, wise counsel, inspiration, support and balance. My associates help significantly by their dedication, industry and responsibility. Personal attributes are hard work, absolute honesty, religious belief, and a conviction that the only justification for my professional life is to help the sick patients whom I am privileged to serve.*

JACKSON, GEORGE MARK, writer, photographer; b. Atlanta, Aug. 27, 1952; s. George Marshall and Kathleen (Keating) J. BA, U. Ala., 1976; MA, U. Ctrl. Fla., 1988. Film critic Metro Mag., Bham, Ala., 1978-79, S. Side News, Orlando, Fla., 1979; lit. critic Sentinel Star (Orlando Sentinel), 1979-81; freelance writer, hist. rschr., 1981—. Author: (novel) (under pseudonym Kano Shinichi) Ninja-Men of IGA, 1989; contbr. articles and photography to mags. Mem. Friendship Force Treasure Coast (editor newsletter 1991). Home and Office: 2043 SE Isabell Rd Port Saint Lucie FL 34952-8865

JACKSON, GERALDINE, entrepreneur; b. Barnesville, Ga., Oct. 30, 1934; d. Charles Brown and Christine (Maddox) J.; 1 child, Prentiss Andrew. Nurses aide Grady Hosp., Atlanta; mail handler U.S. Post Office, Cicero, Ill.; sec., tour guide Walgreens Lab., Chgo.; credit clk. Sterling Jewelers, Atlanta. Mem. Nat. Law Enforcement Officer Meml. Fund; assoc. mem. presdl. task force Rep. Nat. Com.; active Sacred Heart League. Mem. AARP, DAV, NAACP, Nat. Assn. Police Orgn., Internat. Assn. Chief Police, Ga. Sheriff's Assn., Nat. Right to Life. Democrat. Home: 1890 Myrtle Dr SW Apt 422 Atlanta GA 30311-4954

JACKSON, GILCHRIST L., surgeon; b. Dayton, Ohio, Sept. 30, 1948; s. William Hughes Jr. and Margaret Langhorne (Alexander) J.; m. Katina Ballantyne, Nov. 28, 1970; children: Marina, Alex, Scott, George. BA, Vanderbilt U., 1970; MD, U. Louisville, 1974. Fellow U. Tex. M.D. Anderson Cancer Ctr., Houston, 1979-80, faculty, 1980-81; active staff Kelsey-Seybold Clinic, Houston, 1981—; active staff St. Luke's Episc. Hosp., Houston, 1981—, Meth. Hosp., Houston, 1981—, VA Hosp., Houston, 1981-83, Ben Taub Hosp., Houston, 1981—; courtesy staff Tex. Children's Hosp., Houston, 1981—; mem. dir. Crump Cancer Ctr., Houston, 1984-95, Kelsey-Seybold Cancer Program, 1994—; prin. investigator Tex. Cmty. Oncology Network, Nat. Surg. Adjuvant Breast and Bowel Project, 1986-95. Contbr. articles to profl. jours. Active student recruitment com. Vanderbilt U., 1991, Mus. Fine Arts, Houston, 1995, Mus. Natural Sci., Houston, 1995; bd. dirs. West Univ. Little League, Houston, 1990, 91. Mem. Am. Cancer Soc. (pres. 1987-89, v.p. 1985-87), Thyroid Soc. Am., Am. Coll. Surgeons. Republican. Presbyterian. Avocations: golf, tennis, fishing, travel, bicycling. Office: Kelsey Seybold Clinic Dept Surgery 2727 W Holcombe Blvd Houston TX 77025

JACKSON, GREGORY WAYNE, orthodontist; b. Chgo., Sept. 4, 1950; s. Wayne Eldon and Marilyn Frances (Anderson) J.; m. Nora Ann Echtner, Mar. 17, 1973; children: Eric, David. Student, U. Ill., 1968-70; DDS with honors, U. Ill., Chgo., 1974; MSD, U. Wash., 1978. Practice dentistry specializing in orthodontics Chgo., 1978—; instr. orthodontic dept. U. Ill. Coll. Dentistry, Chgo., 1978-81. Coach Little League Baseball, Oak Brook, Ill., 1986-89. Served to lt. USN, 1974-76. Mem. ADA, Ill. State Dental Soc., Chgo. Dental Soc., Am. Assn. Orthodontists, Midwestern Soc. Orthodontists, Ill. Soc. Orthodontists, Omicron Kappa Upsilon. Evangelical. Avocations: golf, tennis, skiing. Office: 6435 S Pulaski Rd Chicago IL 60629-5148

JACKSON, HAROLD, journalist; b. Birmingham, AL, Aug. 14, 1953; s. Lewis and Janye (Wilson) J.; m. Denice Estell Pledger, Apr. 30, 1977; children: Annette Michelle, Dennis Jerome. BS in Journalism and Polit. Sci., Baker U., 1975. Reporter Birmingham Post-Herald, Ala., 1975-80, UPI, Birmingham, Ala., 1980-83; state news editor UPI, 1983-85; asst. nat. editor Phila. Inquirer, 1985-86; asst. city editor Birmingham News, Ala., 1986-87; editorial writer Birmingham News, 1987-94; editl. page writer The Balt. Sun, 1994—; journalist-in-residence Loyola Coll., Balt., 1997-98. Trustee Baker U., 1997—. Recipient Pulitzer Prize for editorial writing, 1991. Mem. Nat. Assn. Black Journalists (Journalist of Yr. award 1991), Birmingham Assn. Black Journalists (pres. 1987-90), Soc. Profl. Journalists (Green Eyeshade award 1989). Presbyterian. Avocations: reading, aerobic exercise. Office: Balt Sun 501 N Calvert St Baltimore MD 21202-3604

JACKSON, HERB, artist, educator; b. Raleigh, N.C., Aug. 16, 1945; s. Walter H. and Virginia (Rogers) J.; m. Laura Dudley Grosch, June 9, 1967; children: Leif, Ulysses. B.A., Davidson Coll., 1967; postgrad., Philips Universität; M.F.A., U. N.C., 1970. William H. Williamson Prof. Art Davidson (N.C.) Coll., 1969—, chmn. dept. art, 1977-94; dir. Art Gallery, 1974—; mem. artist adv. bd. Mint Mus. Art, Charlotte, N.C., 1979—. One-man shows include: Mint Mus. Art, Charlotte, 1973, U. Nev., Reno, 1973, Rahr Mus., Manitowoc, Wis., 1973, Jane Haslem Gallery, Washington, 1974, Nielsen Gallery, Boston, 1974, Impressions Gallery, Boston, 1975, 81, Hahn Gallery, Phila., 1976, Dryden Gallery, Charlotte, 1976, Van Straaten Gallery, Chgo., 1977, Frances Aronson Gallery, Atlanta, 1978, N.C. Mus. Art, Raleigh, 1979, Rowe Gallery, U. N.C., Charlotte, 1979, Southeastern Center for Contemporary Art, Winston-Salem, N.C., 1981, Phyllis Weil Gallery, N.Y.C., 1981, 83, 85, 87, 88, 90, Princeton Gallery Fine Art, 1982, 83, Oxford Gallery (Eng.), 1982, DBR Gallery, Cleve., 1983, 84, Mint Mus. Art, Charlotte, N.C., 1983, Springfield Mus. Art (Mo.), 1983, Asheville Mus. Art (N.C.), 1983, Nat. Acad. Scis., Washington, 1983, Cheekwood Art Ctr., Nashville, 1983, Reading Art Mus. (Pa.), 1984, Gulbenkian Found., Lisbon, Portugal, 1984, Huntsville Mus. Art (Ala.), 1984, Jerald Melberg Gallery, Charlotte, N.C., 1984, 85, 87, 88, 90, 92, 93, 94, 96, 97, 98, 99, Fay Gold Gallery, Atlanta, 1986, 88, 92, Cumberland Gallery, Nashville, 1987, 96, Judy Youens Gallery, Houston, 1988, Peden Gallery, Raleigh, N.C., 1988, 92, 93, Asheville (N.C.) Mus. Art, 1988, Allene Lapides Gallery, Santa Fe, 1989-90, Maurine Littleton Gallery, Washington, 1990, Hickory (N.C.) Mus. Art, 1993, St. Johns Mus. Art, Wilmington, N.C., 1993, Bi-Nat. Cultural Ctr., Arequipa, Peru, 1994, parchman Stremmel Gallery, San Antonio, Tex., 1995, Somerhill Gallery, Chapel Hill, N.C., 1996, 98, Christa Faut Gallery, Davidson, N.C., 1996, 97; numerous group shows, 1962—, latest being Internat. Print Biennale, Bradford, Eng., 1979, Mint Mus., Charlotte, 1979, 81, Southeastern Center Contemporary Art, Winston-Salem, 1979, Internat. São Paulo (Brazil) Bienal, 1979, Spring Mills Ann. Competition, Lancaster, S.C., 1980, Weatherspoon Gallery, Greensboro, N.C., 1980, Impressions Gallery, Boston, 1980, Associated Am. Artists, Phila., 1980, Am. Acad. and Inst. Arts and Letters, N.Y.C., 1981, 1987, Bklyn. Mus. Art, 1981, World's Fair, Knoxville, Tenn., 1982, Davos, Switzerland, 1983, Palazzo Venezia, Rome, 1984, Miss. Mus. Art, 1984, U. Denver, 1984, Albuequerque Mus. Art, 1985, Fla. State U., 1985, St. John's Mus. Art, Wilmington, N.C., 1986, U. Tex., San Antonio, 1987, Contemporary Arts Ctr. New Orleans, 1988, Kunstsammlungen der Veste Coburg, Fed. Republic Germany, 1988, Lorenzelli Fine Art, Milan, 1989, Exhbn. Hall of Union of Moscow Artists, Moscow, 1989, Samuel P. Harn Mus., Gainesville, Fla., 1990, New Orleans Mus. Art, 1995; represented in permanent collections: Balt. Mus. Art, Phila. Mus. Art, Victoria and Albert Mus., London, Whitney Mus. Art, N.Y.C., Mpls. Inst. Arts, Nat. Acad. Sci., Washington, Indpls. Mus. Art, Bklyn. Mus., USIA, Japan, U. Wis., Sheboygan, Yale U., New Haven, Mus. Fine Arts, Boston, N.Y. Public Library, Library of Congress, Washington, Mint Mus., Charlotte, So. Ill. U., Edwardsville, Kalamazoo Inst. Arts, Mus. Fine Arts, Springfield, Mass., Utah Mus., Salt Lake City, U. Nebr., Lincoln, U. Calif., Riverside, Minn. Mus. Art, St. Paul, Brit. Mus., London, others. Fellow Southeastern Ctr. for Contemporary Art Southeastern Seven, 1981, N.C. Visual Arts, 1984, Nat. Endowment for Arts and So. Arts Fedn., 1986. Mem. Coll. Art Assn., So. Graphics Council, Charlotte Artists Coalition (dir. 1980-81), Mecklenberg-Charlotte Arts and Sci. Council (dir. 1977-79), Southeastern Coll. Art Conf. Home: PO Box 10 Davidson NC 28036-0010 Office: Davidson Coll Dept Art PO Box 1720 Davidson NC 28036-1720 *The artist's integrity is all he truly has, after all the trends, fads, and movements have faded into history. I try to make art which will stand as a personal statement.*

JACKSON, ISAIAH, conductor; b. Richmond, Va., Jan. 22, 1945; s. Isaiah Allen and Alma Alverta (Norris) J.; m. Helen Tuntland, Aug. 6, 1977; children: Benjamin, Katharine, Caroline. BA cum laude, Harvard U., 1966; MA, Stanford U., 1967; MS, Juilliard Sch. Music, 1969, DMA, 1973. Founder, condr. Juilliard String Ensemble, N.Y.C., 1970-71; asst. condr. Am. Symphony Orch., N.Y.C., 1970-71, Balt. Symphony Orch., 1971-73; assoc. condr. Rochester (N.Y.) Philharmonic Orch., 1973-87; music dir. Dayton (Ohio) Philharm. Orch., 1987-95, 1987-95; prin. condr. Royal Ballet, Covent Garden, London, 1986, music dir., 1987-90; prin. guest condr. Queensland (Australia) Symphony Orch., 1993-96; music dir. Youngstown (Ohio) Symphony, 1996—; prin. guest condr. Canberra (Australia) Symphony Orch., 1996-98; guest condr. N.Y. Philharm. Orch., 1978, Boston Pops Orch., 1983, 90-94, Detroit Symphony Orch., 1983, 85, San Francisco Symphony, 1984, Toronto Symphony, 1984, 90, Orch. de la Suisse Romande, 1985, 88, BBC Concert Orch., 1987, Berlin Symp hony, 1989-95, Dallas Symphony, 1993, Royal Liverpool Philharm., 1995, Houston Symphony, 1995; numerous recordings for Koch, Australian Broadcasting Corp. Recipient First Gov.'s award for arts in Va., Commonwealth Va., 1979, Signet Soc. medal for the arts Harvard U., 1991. Office: Thea Dispeker Inc 59 E 54th St New York NY 10022

JACKSON, JACQUELINE DOUGAN, educator, author; b. Beloit, Wis., May 3, 1928; d. Ronald Arthur and Vera Arlouine (Wardner) Dougan; m. Robert Sumner Jackson, June 17, 1950 (div. 1973); children—Damaris Lee, Megan Trever, Gillian Patricia, Jacqueline Elspeth. B.A., Beloit Coll., 1950, H.H.D., 1977; M.A., U. Mich., 1951; D.Litt., MacMurray Coll., 1976. Instr. English Kent (Ohio) State U., 1964-68; prof. lit. U. Ill. (formerly Sangamon State U.), Springfield, 1970—. Writer, presenter: radio shows The Author is You, U. Wis. WHA Sch. of Air, 1969-78, Reading and Writing and Radio, WSSU, Springfield, Ill., 1975-94; author: Julie's Secret Sloth, 1953, The Taste of Spruce Gum (Notable Book award 1966), 1966 (Dorothy Canfield Fisher award 1967), Missing Melinda, 1967, Chicken Ten Thousand, 1968, Spring Song, 1969, The Orchestra Mice, 1970, The Endless Pavement, (with William Perlmutter), 1973, Turn Not Pale, Beloved Snail, 1974, Stories from the Round Barn, 1997; author-illustrator: The Paleface Redskins, 1958, The Ghost Boat, 1969; illustrator: (Chad Walsh) Knock and Enter, 1953. Mem. Phi Beta Kappa. Episcopalian. Home: 816 N 5th St Springfield IL 62702-5215

JACKSON, JAMES F., nuclear engineer; b. Ogden, Utah, Aug. 15, 1939; s. Allyn Boyd and Virginia (Dixon) J.; m. Joan Borger, Aug. 25, 1960; children: James D., Bret A., Tracy L., Wendy L. BS, U. Utah, 1961; MS, MIT, 1962; PhD, UCLA, 1969. Rsch. engr. Atomics Internat., L.A., 1962066; nuclear engr. Argonne Nat. Lab., Idaho Falls, Idaho, 1969-72; group leader Argonne Nat. Lab., Argonne, Ill., 1972-74; assoc. prof. Brigham Young U., Provo, Utah, 1974-76; cons. Los Alamos (N.Mex.) Nat. Lab., 1974-76, group/div. leader, 1976-82, dep. assoc. dir., 1979-81, div. leader, 1983-84, assoc. dir., 1984-86, dep. dir., 1986-98, staff mem., 1998—. Contbr. articles to jours. in field. Mem. exec. bd. Community Devel. Com., Los Alamos, 1989-93; bd. dirs. Los Alamos Citizens Against Substance Abuse, 1989-93. Recipient E.O. Lawrence award Dept. Energy, Washington, 1983. Mem. NAE, Am. Nuclear Soc. (safety div. 1967—, exec. com. 1977-80), Tau Beta Pi. Republican. Mem. LDS Ch. Avocations: history, motorsports, photography. Home: 536 Sheffield Dr Provo UT 84604-5666 Office: Los Alamos Nat Lab Ofc of Deputy Dir Los Alamos NM 87545

JACKSON, JAMES LEWIS PERDUE, II, entertainment company executive; b. Chattanooga, May 29, 1946; s. James Oliver and Nellie Mae (Perdue) J.; 1 foster child, Abner Isaias Quinones. AA, Long Beach (Calif.) City Coll., 1972, Riverside (Calif.) City Coll., 1974; CC, Am. Bus. Inst., 1989. Cert. tax audit rep. IRS. Head designer, owner Jai et' Cie Haute Couture, L.A., 1983—; head artist and image devel. Platinum Gold Prodns., L.A., 1990-94; CEO, owner TOJA Entertainment Group, N.Y.C., L.A., 1990—; exec. v.p. Leg Records, L.A., 1995-96; food and beverage mgr. Gershwin Hotel, N.Y.C., 1997-98; ptnr. The LeBlanc Group, N.Y.C., 1997-98. West Coast mng. editor Twin Cities Exec. Mag., L.A., 1991-93; prodr. Three Points of Light Prodns., N.Y.C., 1996-99; costume designer Zipper Films, N.Y.C., 1997; author (screenplay) The Mary Wells Story, 1998; exec. prodr. The Tennis Shoe Cowboy, 1999, The Pink Triangle, 1999. Sustaining mem. Rep. Nat. Com., L.A., 1983; active N.Y. Black Rep. Coun., N.Y.C., 1999. With USN, 1964-69. Republican. Buddhist. Avocations: horse back riding, snow skiing, modern dance, opera, ballet. E-mail: Jai@cool@aol.com and TOJAEntGrp@aol.com. Fax: 212-368-5907. Office: TOJA Entertainment Group PO Box 1075 New York NY 10037

JACKSON, JAMES SIDNEY, psychology educator; b. Detroit, July 30, 1944; s. Pete James and Johnnie Mae (Wilson) J. BS, Mich. State U., 1966; MA, U. Toledo, 1970; PhD, Wayne State U., 1972. Probation counselor Lucas County Juvenile Ct., Toledo, Ohio, 1967-68; tchg. and rsch. asst. Wayne State U., Detroit, 1968-71; from asst. prof. to prof. psychology U. Mich., Ann Arbor, 1971—, faculty assoc. Rsch. Ctr. Group Dynamics, 1971—, dir. Rsch. Ctr. Group Dynamics, 1996—, rsch. scientist, 1986—, faculty assoc. Inst. Gerontology, 1976—, faculty assoc. Ctr. Afro-Am. and African Studies, 1982—, interim dir. Ctr. Afro-Am. and African Studies, 1998—, assoc. dean Rackham Sch. Grad. Studies, 1987-92, prof. pub. health, 1990—, dir. program for rsch. on Black Ams., 1976—, Daniel Katz Disting. Univ. prof. psychology, 1995—, Daniel Katz Collegiate prof., 1994-95; Hill Disting. vis. prof. U. Minn., 1995; chair social psychology tng. program U. Mich., 1980-86, 93-96; cons. Emergency Sch. Aid Project, 1973-74, Commn. on Equal Opportunity in Psychology, 1970, Project to Provide Psychol. Svcs. to Head Start Programs, 1973-74, European Econ. Commn. Project on Racism, Xenophobia and Immigration, 1989—; mem. com. on aging and com. on status of Black Ams., NAS; mem. com. on African Am. Population Year 2000 U.S. Census Bur.; mem. nat. adv. com. Boston Mus. Sci., 1998—; mem. Nat. Adv. Coun. on Aging, NIH, 1996-99; mem. Nat. Adv. Coun. on Aging Nat. Inst. Aging; invited rschr. Ecole des Hautes Etudes en Scis. Sociales, Paris, 1992—; disting. lectr. gerontology UCLA, 1992; mem. steering com. Nat. Acad. Aging Soc., 1995—. Author: The Black American Elderly: Research on Physical and Psychosocial Health, 1988, African American Elderly, 2d edit., 1997, (with Gurin P., Hatchett S.) Hope and Independence: Blacks Response to Electoral and Party Politics, 1989, Life in Black America, 1991, (with Chatters L., Taylor R.) Aging in Black America, 1993, (with H. Neighbors) Mental Health in Black America, 1996, (with R. Taylor and L. Clatters) Family Life in Black America, 1997, (with R. Gibson) Health in Black America, 1998; editl. cons. Jour. Behavioral and Social Scientists; editl. bd. Jour. Gerontology, Applied Social Psychology Ann., Psychol. Bull., Jour. Social Issues; cons. editor Psychology and Aging; contbr. articles to profl. jours. Bd. dirs. Pub. Commn. on Mental Health, Ronald McDonald House, Ann Arbor, 1993—; bd. trustees Greenhills Sch., Ann Arbor, 1997—. Recipient Disting. Faculty Svc. award U. Mich., 1976; Urban Studies fellow Wayne State U., 1969-70; NSF fellow, 1969; Sr. Postdoctoral fellow Groupe d'Études et de Recherches sur la Science, École des Hautes Études en Sciences Sociales, 1986-87; Sr. Ford Found. Minority Postdoctoral fellow, 1986-87; Fogarty Sr. Internat. fellow, 1993-94; Robert W. Kleemeier award for rsch., Gerontol. Soc. Am. Fellow Am. Psychol. Assn. (divs. 9-20, policy and planning bd., fin. com. 1984-86, award for early contbns. 1983), Am. Psychol. Soc., Gerontol. Soc. Am. (task force on minority issues in gerontology, chmn. 1988-92, ann. sci. conv. program com.); mem. Assn. Advancement of Psychology (trustee 1973-89, chmn. 1978-80), Black Students Psychol. Assn. (nat. chmn. 1970-71), Assn. Black Psychologists (nat. chmn. 1972-73), Soc. Psychol. Study of Social Issues, World Future Soc., Assn. Behavioral and Social Scientists, Gerontol. Soc. Am. (chair behavioral and social scis. sect. 1997-98), Internat. Platform Assn., NIMH (nat. mental health coun. 1989-93, panel on equal access com. on instl. cooperation 1989-92), Psi Chi, Alpha Phi Alpha. Home: 517 Fairview Cir Ypsilanti MI 48197-2112 Office: U Mich 5110 Inst Social Rsch 426 Thompson St Ann Arbor MI 48104-2321

JACKSON, JANET DAMITA, singer, dancer; b. Gary, Ind., June 16, 1966; d. Joseph and Katherine J.; m. James DeBarge, 1984 (div. 1985). Albums include Janet Jackson, Dream Street, 1984, Control, 1986, Rhythm Nation 1814, 1991, janet, 1993; actress (TV series) Good Times, 1977, A New Kind of Family, Diff'rent Strokes, Fame; (films) Poetic Justice, 1993 (Academy award nomination Best Original Song 1993). Recipient 6 Am. Music awards, 1987, 1988, 1991, 5 Grammy nominations, MTV Video Vanguard award, 1990, Grammy award, Best R&B song 1994 for "That's the Way Love Goes" with Terry Lewis and James Harris III; MTV Best Female Video for "If". Office: A & M Records Inc 1416 N La Brea Ave Los Angeles CA 90028-7596

JACKSON, JANET ELIZABETH, city attorney, association executive; b. Randolph, Va.; d. Robert and Joan (Morton) J.; 1 child, Harrison Michael Sewell. BA, Wittenberg U., 1975; JD, George Washington U., 1978. Bar: Ohio 1978, U.S. Dist. Ct. (so. dist.) Ohio 1979, U.S. Dist. Ct. (no. dist.) Ohio 1983. Asst. atty. gen. Office Ohio Atty. Gen., Columbus, 1978-80, chief crime victims compensation sect., 1980-82, chief workers compensation and civil rights sects., 1983-87; with Sindell, Sindell & Rubenstein, Cleve., 1982-83; judge Franklin County Mcpl. Ct., Columbus, 1987-97; city atty. City of Columbus, 1997—; atty. gen.'s ethics and profl. responsibility adv. coun.; joint task force gender bias Ohio Supreme Ct. and Ohio State Bar Assn.; mem. com. to study impact of substance abuse on cts., Supreme Ct., 1989-90. Chair bd. trustees YWCA, 1988-95; vice-chair bd. trustees, mem. exec. com. United Way Franklin County; chair Right from the Start Community Forum; bd. dirs. Met. Women's Ctr., 1980-86, S.E. Community Mental Health Ctr., 1987, Columbus Urban League, 1987-90, Maryhaven, 1987-89, Riverside Meth. Hosp.; trustee Wittenberg U.; chair task force child care City of Columbus; vol. Columbus Pub. Schs.; past mem., chairperson Minority Task force on AIDS; mem. AIDS community adv. coalition, 1987-90, task force domestic violence, 1988; mem. svc. team Explorer Divsn. Boy Scouts Am.; trustee Franklin U. Recipient Sharon Wilkin award Met. Women's Ctr., Dr. Martin Luther King Jr. Humanitarian award Love Acad., 1987, Polit. Leadership award 29th Dist. Citizens' Caucus, 1987, Citizenship award Omega Psi Phi, 1987, Outstanding Accomplishments award Franklin County Dem. Women, 1988, Community Svc. award Met. Dem. Women's Club, 1989, Warren Jennings award Franklin County Mental Health Bd., 1989, Martin Luther King Jr. Humanitarian award Columbus Edn. Assn., 1991, Women of Achievement award YWCA, 1992, Citizen's award Columbus Assn. Edn. Young Children, 1993, Citations award Pi Lambda Theta, 1993, Blue Chip award Social Svcs., 1994, Peacemaker award Choices, David D. White award Black Alumni Assn. Capitol Law Sch., Cmty. Svc. award Columbus-Franklin County AFL-CIO. Mem. Internat. Mcpl. Lawyers Assn. (state chmn., mem. steering com. legislation and pub. policy and mgmt.), Nat. Conf. Black Lawyers (Disting. Barrister award 1988, John Mercer Langston award 1994), Ohio State Bar Assn. (coun. dels. 1993—, commn. racial and ethnic fairness, bd. govs. women in the profession sect.), Columbus Bar Assn., Women Lawyers Franklin County, The Links, Inc. (pres. Twin Rivers chpt. 1992-94), Columbus Mortar Bd. Alumni Club, Golden Key Nat. Honor Soc. (hon.). Office: Columbus City Atty City Hall 90 W Broad St Rm 200 Columbus OH 43215-9013

JACKSON, JEANNE PELLEGREN, apparel executive; b. Denver, Aug. 10, 1951; d. John James and Barbara (Grove) Pellegren; m. Douglas Emmett Jackson, Nov. 23, 1984; children: Lindsay, Craig. BS in Fin., U. Colo., 1974; MBA, Harvard Bus. Sch., 1978. Buyer, mgr. Bullocks Dept. Stores, L.A., 1978-85; v.p. merchandise mgr. to sr. v.p. direct mail pvt. brands Saks Fifth Ave., N.Y.C., 1985-89; sr. v.p. merchandising Walt Disney Attractions, Orlando, 1989-92; exec. v.p. merchandising Victoria's Secret, Columbus, Ohio, 1992—; instr. mktg. U. So. Calif., L.A., 1979-81; adv. bd. Navy Exch., Norfolk, Va., 1991—. Bd. dirs. Orlando Mus. Art, 1990-92. Republican. Avocations: skiing, tennis.

JACKSON, JESSE, JR., congressman; b. Greenville, S.C., Mar. 11, 1965; m. Sandra Jackson. BS, N.C A&T U., 1987; MA, Chgo. Theol. Sem.; JD, U. Ill., 1993. Mem. 105th-106th Congress from 2nd La. dist., Washington, 1997—, mem. banking and fin. svcs., small bus. coms., 1997—. Mem. U.S. House of Reps., 2nd Dist., Ill., 1995—. Baptist. Office: US Ho of Reps 313 Cannon Washington DC 20515-1302*

JACKSON, JESSE LOUIS, civic and political leader, clergyman; b. Greenville, S.C., Oct. 8, 1941; s. Charles Henry and Helen Jackson; m. Jacqueline Lavinia Brown, 1964; children: Santita, Jesse Louis, Jonathan Luther, Yusef DuBois, Jacqueline Lavinia. Student, U. Ill., 1959-60; B.A. in Sociology and Economics, N.C. A&T State U., 1964; postgrad., Chgo. Theol. Sem., D.D. (hon.); hon. degrees, N.C. A&T State U., Pepperdine U., Oberlin U., Oral Roberts U., U. R.I., Howard U., Georgetown U. Ordained to ministry Baptist Ch., 1968; founder (with others) Operation Breadbasket joint project So. Christian Leadership Conf., Chgo., 1966; nat. dir. Operation Breadbasket joint project So. Christian Leadership Conf., 1967-71; founder, exec. dir. Operation PUSH (People United to Serve Humanity), Chgo., 1971—; candidate for Democratic nomination for Pres. U.S., 1983-84, 87-88; nat. pres. Nat. Rainbow Coalition Inc., Chgo.; founder PUSH-Excel and PUSH for Econ. Justice; lectr. for high schs., colls., prof. audiences in Am., Europe. Interviewer TV program Both Sides with Jesse Jackson. Active Black Coalition for United Community Action, 1969. Recipient Presdl. award Nat. Med. Assn., 1969; Humanitarian Father of Year award Nat. Father's Day Com., 1971; Third Most Admired Man in Am. Gallup Poll, 1985; named one of six new leaders on the rise U.S. News World Report. Address: Rainbow PUSH Coalition 930 E 50th St Chicago IL 60615-2702*

JACKSON, JIMMY JOE, litigation consultant; b. Fabens, Tex., Nov. 27, 1947; s. Andrew Donald and W. Lucille (Briley) J.; children: Robert R., Ruth A. BS in Mgmt., MIT, 1970, MS in Mgmt., 1974; MBA in Fin., So. Ill. U., 1973. Ptnr. Arthur Andersen & Co., S.C., N.Y.C., 1974-91; pres. Jackson Cons., Inc., Washington, 1991—. Capt. USAF, 1970-73. Mem. Am. Statis. Assn. Baptist. Home: Ste 423 1234 Massachusetts Ave NW Washington DC 20005-4535 Office: Ste 423 1234 Massachusetts Ave NW Washington DC 20005

JACKSON, JODY, journalist; b. Milw., Nov. 23, 1954. AA, Hillsborough C.C.; student, U. South Fla. Owner, operator The Old Mill Resort, Okauchee Lake, Wis., 1978-87; dir. mktg. food and beverage Fortune Hotels, St. Petersburg, Fla., 1987-89; talent agt. Dott Burns Talent, Tampa, 1989-91; owner, prodr. JJ Prodns. Inc., Tampa/Miami Beach, Fla., 1991-95; editor, assoc. prodr. Metro Hyde Park News, Inc., Tampa, 1993-96. Mem. Profl. Journalists Soc. of Am., Am. Diabetes Assn. (bd. dirs.), Am. C. of C. Tampa Bay, Ybor City C. of C., South Tampa C. of C., Creative Club of Tampa Bay. E-mail: jjacksol@brill.acomp.usf.edu. Home: 1109 Crescent St Sarasota FL 34242

JACKSON, J(OHN) DAVID, physicist, educator; b. London, Ont., Can., Jan. 19, 1925; came to U.S., 1957, naturalized, 1988; s. Walter David and Lillian Margaret (Ferguson) J.; m. Barbara Cook, June 26, 1949; children: Ian, Nan, Maureen, Mark. BS in Physics and Math., U. Western Ont., 1946, DSc (hon.), 1989; PhD in Physics, MIT, 1949. Rsch. assoc. dept. physics MIT, Cambridge, 1949; from asst. prof. to assoc. prof. math. McGill U., Montreal, Que., Can., 1950-57; from assoc. prof. to prof. physics U. Ill., Urbana, 1957-67; prof. U. Calif., Berkeley, 1967-92, dept. chair, 1978-81, prof. emeritus, 1993—; vis. fellow Cambridge (Eng.) U., 1970; acting head theory group Fermilab, Batavia, Ill., 1972-73; head physics divsn. Lawrence Berkeley Lab., 1982-84; dep. dir. SSC Cen. Design Group, Berkeley, 1985-87; vis. sr. rsch. fellow Oxford (Eng.) U., 1988-89; mem. vis. com. Argonne Nat. Lab., CERN, SSC Lab., Stanford Linear Accelerator Ctr., others. Author: Physics of Elementary Particles, 1958, Classical Electrodynamics, 1962, rev. edit., 1975, 3d edit., 1998, Mathematics for Quantum Mechanics, 1962; also numerous articles; editor Ann. Rev. Nuclear and Particle Sci., 1977-93. J. S. Guggenheim Found. fellow, 1956-57, Ford Found. fellow, 1963-64. Fellow Am. Phys. Soc.; mem. NAS (elected 1990), Am. Acad. Arts and Scis. (elected 1989), ACLU (life). Avocations: mountain hiking, swimming, scientific bibliophily. Address: U Calif Berkeley Dept of Physics Berkeley CA 94720-7300

JACKSON, JOHN EDWARD, educator, logistician, retired naval officer; b. Rapid City, S.D., Feb. 11, 1949; s. William Edward Joseph and Bettye Davis (Williams) J.; m. Valerie Lee McGilton, June 5, 1971; children: Gina Marie, Brian Howard. BA in Univ. Studies, U. N.Mex., 1971; MEd, Providence Coll., 1976; MS in Mgmt., Salve Regina U., 1983, cert. of advanced grad. studies, 1998; grad. mgmt. devel. program, Harvard U., 1997. Commd. USN, 1971, advanced through grades to capt., ret., 1998; disbursing officer USS Hunley AS-31, Charleston, S.C., 1972-74; food svc. officer Naval Edn. and Tng. Ctr., Newport, R.I., 1974-76; supply officer USS Joseph Strauss DDG-16, Pearl Harbor, Hawaii, 1976-78; data processing dept. dir. Nava. Supply Ctr., Pearl Harbor, 1978-80; prof. Ctr. Continuing Edn. U.S. Naval War Coll., Newport, 1980-83, prof. dept. nat. security decision-making, 1994-96, dean Coll. Continuing Edn., 1996—; divsn. dir. Navy Fleet Material Support Office, Mechanicsburg, Pa., 1983-86; curricular officer U.S. Naval Postgrad. Sch., Monterey, Calif., 1986-90; supply officer USS Sierra AD-18, Charleston, 1990-92; exec. officer Naval Supply Ctr., Charleston, 1992-94; mil. chair logistics Naval War Coll., Newport, R.I., 1994—; speechwriter USN, 1978—. *His 27 years of military logistics experience on land and sea included such areas as transportation, distribution, inventory control, information systems, contracting and quality control. His final Navy assignment was as the military chair of logistics at the Naval War College, the college president's principal logistics advisor, and formal liaison with the deputy chief of naval operations. He has taught at the graduate and undergraduate level and now serves as dean of the College of Continuing Education. He is the author of numerous speeches, articles and reviews, and is editor in chief of the "Logistics Leadership Series of Books", detailing logistical theory, history and practice.* Former editor-in-chief newsletter The Oakleaf; editor: Logistics Leadership Series; contbr. articles to profl. jours. Mem. Soc. Logistics Engrs., Navy Supply Corps Assn. (bd. dirs. 1983-96, pres. 1994-96), Naval War Coll. Found., U.S. Naval Inst. (liaison officer). Home: 7 Mast Ct Middletown RI 02842

JACKSON, JOHN HOWARD, lawyer, educator; b. Kansas City, Mo., Apr. 6, 1932; s. Howard Clifford and Lucile (Deischer) J.; m. Joan Leland, Dec. 16, 1962; children: Jeannette, Lee Ann, Michelle. AB, Princeton U., 1954; JD, U. Mich., 1959. Bar: Wis. 1959, Mo. 1959, Calif. 1964, Mich. 1970. Pvt. practice law Milw., 1959-61; assoc. prof., prof. law U. Calif., 1961-66; prof. law U. Mich., 1966-97; univ. prof. law Georgetown U., Washington, 1998—; on leave gen. counsel U.S. Office Spl. Trade Rep., 1973-74, acting deputy spl. rep. for trade, 1974; vis. prof. U. Brussels, 1975-76; vis. fellow Inst. for Internat. Econs., Washington, 1983; Hessel E. Yntema prof. law U. Mich., 1983-97, assoc. v.p. acad. affairs, 1988-89; disting. vis. prof. law Georgetown Law Ctr., Washington, 1986-87, 93; Ford Found. cons. legal edn., vis. prof. U. Delhi, India, 1968-69. Author: World Trade and the Law of GATT, 1969, Contract Law in Modern Society, 1973, 2d edit., 1980, Legal Problems of International Economic Relations, 1977, 3d edit. (with William Davey and Alan Sykes), 1995; (with Jean-Victor Louis and Mitsuo Matsushita) Implementing the Tokyo Round, 1984; (with Edwin Vermulst) Anti-Dumping Law & Practice: Comparative Study, 1989; The World Trading System, 1989, 2d edit., 1997, Restructuring the GATT System, 1990; (with Alan Sykes) Implementing the Urugauy Round, 1997, World Trade Organization, 1998; editor-in-chief Jour. Internat. Econ. Law; bd. editors: Am. Jour. Internat. Law, Jour. Law and Policy in Internat. Bus., others; contbr. articles to profl. jours. With M.I. U.S. Army, 1954-56. Recipient Wolfgang Friedman Memorial award Columbia U., 1992; Rockefeller Found. fellow for study European community law Brussels, 1975-76. Mem. ABA, Am. Soc. Internat. Law (v.p. 1990-92), Am. Law Inst., Council Fgn. Relations, Phi Beta Kappa, Order of Coif. Office: Georgetown U Law Ctr 600 New Jersey Ave NW Washington DC 20001-2022

JACKSON, JOHN JAY, clergyman; b. Chula Vista, Calif., July 13, 1961; s. E. Marvin and Mildred L. Jackson; m. Pamela Harrison, Aug. 18, 1979; children: Jennifer, Dena, Rachel, Joshua. BA in Religion, Chapman U., 1981; MA in Theology, Fuller Theol. Sem., 1983; MA in Ednl. Adminstrn., U. Calif., Santa Barbara, 1984, PhD in Ednl. Adminstrn., 1986. Youth dir. First Bapt. Ch., Buena Park, Calif., 1979-81; min. of youth Oxnard (Calif.) First Bapt., 1981-83, min. of edn., 1983-84, assoc. pastor, 1984-87, sr. pastor, 1988-92; exec. min. Am.-Bapt. Chs. Pacific S.W., Covina, Calif., 1993-97; pastor Carson Valley Christian Ctr., Minden, Nev., 1997—. Bd. dirs. Am. Bapt. Homes of the West, Oakland, Calif., 1993-97, Atherton Bapt. Homes, 1993-97; chair integration adv. com. Oxnard Sch. Dist., 1990-92. Recipient Disting. Svc. award Oxnard Sch. Dist., 1992. Mem. Christian Mgmt. Assn., Oxnard C. of C. (leadership com. 1991, chair edn. com. 1988-90). Office: Carson Valley Christian Ctr PO Box 892 Minden NV 89423-0892

JACKSON, JOHN TILLSON, retired corporate executive; b. Milw., May 13, 1921; s. John F. and Elizabeth (Tillson) J.; m. Suzanne Bartley, Apr. 1953; children: Suzanne Jackson McDevitt, Jennifer Jackson Davies, John Tillson. BS in Adminstrv. Engring, Cornell U., 1942. Jr. engr. George S. Armstrong & Co., Inc., N.Y.C., 1946-48; sr. engr. George S. Armstrong & Co., Inc., 1948-49, v.p., 1949, dir., 1951; asst. to pres. Fed. Telecommunication Labs., 1953-55, ITT, N.Y.C., 1956-57; asst. v.p. ITT, 1957-58, v.p., 1959-60; v.p. Remington Office Equipment div. Sperry Rand Corp., 1960-66, Gen. Waterworks Corp., Phila., 1966-68, IU Internat., Phila., 1968-69; sr. v.p. IU Internat., 1969-72, exec. v.p., chmn. exec. com., 1973-82, vice chmn., 1982-83; chmn. C. Brewer & Co., Ltd. subs., 1975-82; ret.; bd. dirs. ColmacEnergy, Inc. Vice chmn. Acad. Natural Sci., Phila., 1983-86. Served from 2d lt. to maj. AUS, 1942-46. Mem. ASME, Shelter Island Yacht Club (N.Y.), Gulph Mills Golf Club, Merion Cricket Club, Everglades Club, Sailfish Club, Zeta Psi. Home: 210 Ocean Ter Palm Beach FL 33480-3127

JACKSON, JOHN WYANT, medical products executive; b. Corpus Christi, May 25, 1944; s. Donald LeGarde and Marion (McNulty) J; m. Susan Gager, Sept. 6, 1969; children: Alexandra C., Kimberly F., Donald M., Jennifer L. B.A., Yale U., 1967; M.B.A., INSEAD, Fontainbleau, France, 1971; diploma, Institut de Sci. Politique, Paris, 1966. With Merck & Co., Rahway, N.J., 1971-78; dir. med. products Far East Am. Cyanamid Co., Wayne, N.J., 1978-79, dir. med. products Americas and Far East, 1979-81, v.p. Americas and Far East, 1981-83, v.p. internat., 1983-86, pres. device div., 1986-91; pres. Gemini Med., Warren, N.J., 1991-96; chmn., CEO Celgene Corp., Warren, N.J., 1996—; dir. U.S.-Pakistan Econ. Council, N.Y.C., 1981—, U.S.-ROC Econ. Council, Crystal Lake, Ill., 1982-85; chmn. Biotech. Coun. N.J. Treas. Am. Men's Club, Portugal, 1974-75; active Internat. Rotary, Holland, 1976-77. Served to 1st lt. USMCR, 1967-70. Decorated Navy Commendation medal; decorated Purple Heart. Mem. Soc. Paper Money Collectors. Republican. Episcopalian. Office: Celgene Corp Warren NJ 07059

JACKSON, JOHNNY W., minister; b. Shamrock, Tex., Aug. 4, 1933; s. John W. and Faye Leota (Gregory) J.; m. Nancy Jean Howdeshell, June 26, 1953; children: Danny Michael, Stephen Mark, Faye Luanne, Lauree Sue. BA, Abilene Christian U., 1974. Ordained to ministry Chs. of Christ, 1954. Min. Ch. of Christ, Pottsboro, Tex., 1954-55, Morton St. Ch. of Christ, Denison, Tex., 1955-58, Abrams Ch. of Christ, Richardson, Tex., 1958-64, Southside Ch. of Christ, Amarillo, Tex., 1964-66, Cen. Ch. of Christ, Houston, 1966-69, So. MacArthur Ch. of Christ, Irving, 1969-79, Eldridge Rd. Ch. of Christ, Sugar Land, 1979-82, Rolling Hills (Tex.) Ch. of Christ, DeSoto, 1982—; bd. dirs. Cedar Green Living Ctr., DeSoto. Contbr. articles to profl. jours. Mem. Rotary (sec. De Soto chpt. 1986-87). Home: 1408 Richards Cir De Soto TX 75115-2911 Office: Rolling Hills Ch of Christ 115 W Belt Line Rd De Soto TX 75115-4939

JACKSON, JULIAN ELLIS, food company executive; b. Perry, Fla., Oct. 24, 1913; s. Eddie H. and Eva M. (Reid) J.; m. Laurana H. Filson, Oct. 6, 1956; children: Julian Ellis, Eddie King, Robert Allen, Victor Pharis, Julian Ellis IV, Lester Mitchell. Grad., Andrew Jackson High Sch., Jacksonville, Fla., 1931; DSc (hon.), Jones Coll., 1982. With Great Atlantic & Pacific Stores, 1931-43; pres. Jax Meat Co., 1943-58, Jackson's Minit Markets, Inc., 1958-69, Julian Jackson Investment Co., 1955—, Lil' Champ Food Stores, Inc., 1971-98; co-owner Jackson-Cowart Realty Co., 1955-97; dir. Fla. Nat. Bank, Jacksonville, Arlington. Past pres. United Cerebral Palsy, Jacksonville; chmn. Jacksonville Boxing Commn., 1952-71; pres. Gator Bowl Assn., 1957, Fla. Baseball League, 1958-60; bd. dirs. Palmdale Med. Center, Police Athletic League, Jacksonville, Jacksonville Marine Inst., Jones Coll., Jacksonville. Named Super Market Man of Yr., 1960; elected to Fla. Food Inst. Hall of Fame, 1994; recipient Top Mgmt. award Sales and Mktg. Execs. Jacksonville, 1968. Mem. Fla. Super Market Assn. (pres. 1950-59, elected to Fla. Sports Hall of Fame 1994), Fraternal Order of Police, Sportsman Club, Univ. Club (Jacksonville), Univ. Country Club, River Club, Ponte Vedra Club, Masons, Shriners. Home: 7987 Hollyridge Rd Jacksonville FL 32256-7110 Office: Julian Jackson Investment Co 8535 Baymeadows Rd Ste 25 Jacksonville FL 32241

JACKSON, KATHERINE CHURCH, former elementary school educator, reading educator; b. Phila., Apr. 26, 1925; d. John Edward and Katherine Darlington (Short) C.; m. James Kermit Jackson, Dec. 20, 1953; children: James Kermit, Quentin Winfield, Karen A. Jackson White. BS in Edn., Cheyney (Pa.) State Tchrs. Coll., 1946; MEd, Temple U., 1951; DEdin Adminstrn., Nova U., 1981. Cert. elem. sch. tchr., supr., prin., Pa. Elem. tchr. Pub. Schs., Oxford, N. Glenside, Pa., 1946-54; collaborator lang. arts, t.v. tchr. Pub. Schs., Phila., 1956-67, asst. dir., tng. specialist office of sch. vols., 1967-70, dist. supr., dir. reading, 1970-77, elem. prin., 1971-82; asst. prof. Lincoln U., Pa., 1986-87, reading specialist, 1986—. Prodr., photographer: (slide presentation) Parents Help With Reading, 1965; writer, prodr. (t.v. series, script) Reading Inservice for Teachers, 1965; creator, prodr., photographer (slide presentation) PL-142 Works for the Handicapped, 1980. Pres. bd. YWCA, West Chester, Pa., 1984-89; bd. dirs. Cmty. Ctr., West Chester, 1984-91. Recipient Profl. award Bus. and Profl. Women, 1966, Cmty. and Club Svc. award Keystone Federated Women's Club, 1989, Spirit of YWCA, YWCA of Greater West Chester, 1990. Mem. AAUW, Fanny J. Coppin Federated Women's Club (chpt. pres. 1984—, Phila. pres. 1965-69), Bus. Profl. Women. Democrat. Episcopalian. Avocations: reading, singing, opera. Home: 1210 Cheyney Rd West Chester PA 19382-8502 Office: Lincoln U ACT 101/Time Program Lincoln University PA 19352

JACKSON, KENNETH ARTHUR, physicist, researcher; b. Connaught, Ont., Can., Oct. 23, 1930; s. Arthur and Susanna (Vatcher) J.; m. Jacqueline

Della Olyan, June 20, 1952 (div.); children: Stacy Margaret, Meredith Suzanne, Stuart Keith; m. Camilla M. Maruszewski, June 21, 1980 (div.). BS, U. Toronto, 1952, MS, 1953; PhD, Harvard U., 1956. Postdoctoral fellow Harvard U., Cambridge, Mass., 1956-58; asst. prof. metallurgy Harvard U., 1958-62; mem. tech. staff Bell Labs., Murray Hill, N.J., 1962-67; head material physics research dept. Bell Labs., 1967-81, head optical materials research dept., 1981-89; prof. materials sci. and engring. U. Ariz., 1989—; lectr. Welch. Found., 1970, 85; mem. research adv. panel Air Force Office Sci. Research, 1976-82, space application bd. Nat. Acad. Sci., 1974-82. Editor-in-chief Optical Materials, 1999—; contbr. articles to profl. jours. Recipient Mathewson Gold medal AIME, 1966, Crystal growth award AACG, 1993. Fellow AAAS, The Metall. Soc.-AIME, Am. Phys. Soc.; mem. Internat. Orgn. Crystal Growth (treas. 1978-86, Frank prize 1998), Am. Assn. Crystal Growth (pres. 1968-75, coun., award 1993), Materials Rsch. Soc. (v.p. 1975-77, pres. 1977-78, coun.), Am. Soc. Metals, Engring. Coun. for Profl. Devel. (mem. coun.), Fedn. Materials Soc. (trustee). Patentee in field. Office: U Ariz 4715 E Ft Lowell Rd Tucson AZ 85712-1201

JACKSON, KENNETH TERRY, historian, educator; b. Memphis, July 27, 1939; s. Kenneth Gordon and Elizabeth Owen (Willins) J.; m. Barbara Ann Bruce, Aug. 25, 1962; children: Kevan Parish, Kenneth Gordon (dec.). BA magna cum laude, U. Memphis, 1961; MA, U. Chgo., 1963, PhD, 1966. Asst. prof. history Columbia U., N.Y.C., 1968-71, assoc. prof., 1971-76, prof., 1976-87, Mellon prof., 1987-90, Barzun prof., 1990—, chmn. dept. history, 1994-97; vis. prof. Princeton (N.J.) U., 1973-74, George Washington U., 1982-83, UCLA, 1986-87; chair Bradley Commn. on History in Schs., 1987-90; chair Nat. Coun. for History Edn., Inc., 1990-92. Author: The Ku Klux Klan in the City, 1967, Crabgrass Frontier, 1985 (Bancroft prize 1986, Francis Parkman prize 1986), Silent Cities: The Evolution of the American Cemetery, 1989; co-editor: cities in American History, 1972; editor-in-chief Dictionary of American Biography, 1991-95; editor-in-chief, Scribner's Encyclopedia of American Lives, 1996—, Encyclopedia of New York City, 1995; gen. editor Columbia History of Urban Life, 30 vols., 1980—; co-editor American Vistas, 1971, 7th edit., 1995. Trustee South St. Seaport Mus., 1989—, Nat. Coun. Hist. Edn., 1990—, Columbia U. Press, 1994-97, N.Y. Hist. Soc., 1996—, Transp. Alternatives, 1995-97, Skyscraper Mus., 1996—; vestryman Trinity Ch. Wall St., 1997—. Capt. USAF, 1965-68. Recipient Mark Van Doren Teaching award Columbia U., 1989, Outstanding Alumni award U. Memphis, 1989; fellow Woodrow Wilson Found., 1961-62, Guggenheim Found., 1983-84; sr. fellow NEH, 1979-80. Mem. Soc. Am. Historians (pres. 1998—), Orgn. Am. Historians (pres.-elect 1999—), Am. Hist. Assn., Urban Hist. Assn. (pres. 1994), Century Assn., N.Y. State Hist. Assn. (trustee 1996—). Episcopalian. Avocations: skiing, tennis, basketball. Home: 44 Kitchel Rd Mount Kisco NY 10549-4516 Office: Columbia U Dept History 603 Fayerweather Hall New York NY 10027

JACKSON, KINGSBURY TEMPLE, educational contract consultant; b. Newton, Mass., May 15, 1917; s. Ralph Temple and Elizabeth Mesarole (Rhodes) J.; m. June Stewart Cooper, July 29, 1950 (dec. Feb. 1976). B.S., MIT, 1940; postgrad., NYU, 1949-51; M.S., U. Ala., 1964, U. So. Calif., 1969, Pepperdine U., 1975. Registered profl. engr., Calif., Ala. Commd. 2d lt. U.S. Army, 1940, advanced through grades to lt. col., 1961, ret., 1965; comdr. U.S. Army Depot, also Camp Mercer, Korea, 1957-58; project officer, indsl. project dir. U.S. Army Saturn Space Vehicle Program and Pershing Missile System, 1959-61; dir. U.S. Army Missile Command Engring. Documentation Ctr., Redstone Arsenal, Ala., 1962-63; program coordinator NATO-Hawk Missile System, 1963-65; prin. contracting officer, chief European procurement U.S. Army Ordnance, 1964-65; lectr. mgmt. and engring. Grad. Sch., U. So. Calif., L.A., 1965-69; contractual relations supr. L.A. Bd. Edn., 1969-82; pres. Contract Consultants, L.A., 1982—, K.T. Jackson, Gen. Contractors, L.A., 1991—. Author: Engineering documentation Systems Development: Department of Defense and NASA, 1963, Aerospace Propellants and Chemicals: The Manager's Approach, 1968. Vice pres., mem. bd. dirs. Kingsbury Properties Ltd.; corp. sec., bd. dirs. The Concert Singers, Inc. Mem. Am. Soc. Indsl. Engrs., Am. Soc. Mil. Comptrs., Am. Ordnance Assn. (mem. exec. bd. prodn. technique divsn., Army rep. to engring. documentation sect. 1962-65), Soc. Automotive Engrs. (rep. to aerospace gen. stds. divsn. 1962-65), Ret. Officers Assn. (life), Calif. Assn. Sch. Bus. Ofcls., Internat. Assn. Sch. Bus. Ofcls. (emeritus), Aircraft Owners and Pilots Assn., The Concert Singers, Inc., The Planetary Soc., Nat. Space Soc., MIT Club (So. Calif.), A&E Flying Club. Clubs: Mass. Inst. Tech. (So. Calif.); A & E Flying. Office: Contract Consultants PO Box 91161 Los Angeles CA 90009-1161

JACKSON, LAIRD GRAY, physician, educator; b. Seattle, Oct. 10, 1930. BA, Pomona Coll., 1951; MD, U. Cin., 1955. Diplomate Am. Bd. Internal Medicine, Am. Bd. Med. Genetics (bd. dirs.). Rotating gen. intern Sacramento County (Calif.) Hosp., 1955-56; resident in internal medicine Jefferson Med. Coll., Phila., 1959-61, NIH postdoctoral fellow med. oncology, 1961-62, instr. medicine, 1962-64, asst. prof. medicine, 1964-66, assoc. prof., 1966-69, assoc. prof. medicine, pediatrics and ob-gyn, 1969-78, prof., 1978—, dir. div. med. genetics, 1969-78; founder, bd. dirs., treas. Am. Coll. Med. Genetics, 1991-95. Mem. editorial bd. Am. Jour. Med. Genetics, Prenatal Diagnosis, Repository of Human Chromosomal Variants. Capt. USAF, 1956-59. Leukemia Soc. fellow, 1963-65, Leukemia Soc. scholar 1965-70. Fellow ACP; mem. Am. Soc. Human Genetics (social issues com. 1976-80, bd. dirs.), Soc. Pediatric Rsch. Home and Office: 1100 Walnut St Philadelphia PA 19107-5563*

JACKSON, LAMBERT BLUNT, academic administrator; b. Wilmington, Del., July 27, 1940; s. Wendell Ford and Margaret (Blunt) J.; m. Doris Vidal Jackson; children: L. Blunt, Margaret Julia Chantal, Etienne Vidal. BA, U. Del., 1964, MA in Am. Studies, 1965, PhD in History of Am. Civilization, 1976. Master The Marvelwood Sch., Cornwall, Conn., 1965-67; teaching asst. dept. English U. Del., 1970-72, instr. dept. history, 1973-76, interim dir. Am. Studies Program, 1974; rsch. assoc. acad. founds. dept. Rutgers U., Camden, N.J., 1976-77, 78-79; acting dir. Rutgers U., Camden, 1977-78, 80-81, adj. faculty dept. English, 1980-88, asst. dir. acad. founds. dept., 1984-87, acting dir., 1987, dir. Edn. Opportunity Fund Program, 1988—, assoc. dept. urban studies, 1989—, mem. grad. English faculty, 1995—; mgmt. cons. Hispanic Health and Mental Health Assn. of So. N.J., Inc., 1981; supr. student tchr. English Rutgers-Camden Dept. Edn., 1983-85; project dir. City of Camden Youth Commn., 1986; devel. cons. Casa PRAC, Vineland, N.J., 1987; workshop leader Episcopal Diocese of N.J., 1989; cons. Hispanic Family Ctr., Camden, 1988. Author: They Serve: A History of And Salute to Service Clubs in Delaware, 1976, The American Poet, The Prairie Poet. Mem. Urban Coun. of Camden City Episcopal Parishes, 1983—; mem., v.p. Hispanic Task Force of Camden County, 1985-94; mem. Bishop's Hunger Task Force Episcopal Diocese of N.J., 1985, chair, 1986; del. rep. from diocese of N.J. to Nat. Impact Conf., Washington, 1986; mem. bd. trustees William Alexander Procter Found., 1986-92; warden, mem. vestry, clk. Grace Episcopal Ch., Haddonfield, N.J., 1986-90; commn. on ministry Diocese of N.J., Trenton, 1988—, anti-racism commn., 1997—, Hispanic commn., 1997—; trustee, treas. Shepherd's Gate, 1989—; curriculum com. Camden Bd. Edn., 1997—. Grantee N.J. Dept. Higher Edn., 1979-80, 1990—, Pew Charitable Trust, 1987-90, Divsn. of Women, State of N.J., 1988-89, HUD, 1992-94, NSF, 1994-97, Bell Atlantic, 1997-98; recipient Andelot fellowship, 1964-65, 68-69, Univ. fellowship, 1968-69, 69-70, Teaching assistantship, 1970-71, 71-72, Disting. Svc. award Rutgers Adminstrv. Assembly, 1990. Episcopalian. Avocations: collector of Am. and Chinese antiques, hist. restoration, garden design.

JACKSON, LARRY ARTOPE, retired college president; b. Florence, S.C., Feb. 7, 1925; s. Arthur Edward and Rosa (Gilbert) J.; m. Barbara Atwood, June 27, 1953; children: Elizabeth Jackson Eble, Arthur Edward, Barbara Jackson Allen, Charles Rhett. AB, Wofford Coll., 1947, DLitt (hon.), 1976; MDiv, Union Theol. Sem., 1953; MA, U. Pacific, 1973, DD (hon.), 1961; D in Humanities (hon.), Clemson U., 1991. Ordained to ministry United Meth. Ch., 1953; minister chs., 1953-59; prin. Santiago (Chile) Coll., 1959-64; provost Callison Coll. of U. Pacific, Stockton, Calif., 1964-70; v.p. for adminstrn. U. Evansville, 1970-73; pres. Lander Coll., Greenwood, S.C., 1973-92, ret., 1992; vis. fellow Wolfson Coll., Cambridge U., 1985. Mem. Fulbright Commn. for Chile, 1961-64; mem. Commn. on Black Colls. Related to the Meth. Ch., 1973-76. With USAAF, 1943-45; with Am. Friends Svc. Com., 1948-49. Decorated Air medal with 2 oak leaf clusters. Mem. Rotary. Democrat. Home: 604 W Cambridge Ave Greenwood SC 29649-1967 Office: Lander College 300 N Main St Greenwood SC 29649-2099 *Love is the law of life and it is by striving to live under the rule of this law that we find authenticity.*

JACKSON, LARRY C., publishing executive; b. Austin, Tex., Apr. 14, 1944; s. Laurence C. and Mary Ruth (McAngus) J.; m. Susan Blackburn, Dec. 15, 1966; children: Laurence III, Deborah Jackson McClure, Edward. BA in Journalism, U. Tex., 1968. City editor Arlington (Tex.) Daily News, 1967-69; City editor Laredo (Tex.) Times, 1969-71; mng. editor Henderson (Tex.) Daily News, 1971-72; gen. mgr. Austin Citizen, 1972-73; publ. Round Rock (Tex.) Leader, 1973-84, Pecos (Tex.) Enterprise, 1984-87, Corona (Calif.)-Norco Independent, 1987-91; editor, gen. mgr. Wharton (Tex.) Journal-Spectator, 1991—; v.p. River Pubs., Inc., 1994—. Charter pres. YMCA, Round Rock, Tex., 1981; mem. City Charter Commn., Round Rock, 1977; chmn. U.S. Bicentennial Commn., Round Rock, 1975-76; bd. dirs. Tex. Newspaper Found., 1994—. Paul Harris fellow Rotary Internat. Found., 1995; named Citizen of Yr. Round Rock C. of C., 1984. Mem. Tex. Press Assn. (pres. 1998-99), S. Tex. Press Assn. (pres. 1996), Rotary Club (pres. Wharton 1994-95), Wharton (Tex.) C. of C. Republican. Mem. Ch. of Christ. Avocations: tchg. Bible class, playing Oboe, travelling by train. Home: 1203 N Fulton St Wharton TX 77488-3129 Office: Wharton Journal-Spectator 115 W Burleson St Wharton TX 77488-5003

JACKSON, LATRELLE D., psychologist, educator; b. Warner Robins AFB, Ga., Jan. 12, 1966; d. John and Brenda (Johnson) J. BA, U. Ga., 1988, MA, 1991, PhD, 1996. Lic. psychologist, Mich.; lic. profl. counselor, Mich. Resident asst. U. Ga., Athens, 1986-88, grad. asst., 1990-91, grad. resident, 1988-91; transition project dir. A.C.T.I.O.N., Inc., Athens, 1992-94; resident/intern Mich. State U., East Lansing, 1994-95; staff psychologist Pa. State U., University Park, 1995-97; clin. asst. prof. U. Fla., Gainesville, 1997—; owner Time Wise Ent., Athens, 1993-95. Adv. bd. Inst. of Black Culture, U. Fla., 1998—; sec. Pa. State Forum on Black Affairs, 1996-97; radio personality Pa. State U. Cross Cultural Health Program, 1995; evaluation team mem. N.Y. Transition Project, N.Y.C. Pub. Schs., 1994; cons. Ala. transition Project/Birmingham Pub. Schs., 1993-94. Regent's Opportunity scholar, State of Ga., 1991-93. Mem. APA (divsn. 17), Kappa Delta Pi, Psi Chi, Chi Sigma Iota (founder Beta chpt. 1989). Avocations: reading, bowling, family history research, tennis, playing the piano. Office: Univ of Florida Counseling Ctr 301 Peabody Hall Gainesville FL 32611

JACKSON, LEE, artist; b. N.Y.C.; s. Harry and Charlotte (Tallis) J.; m. Adele Grapes, Apr. 11, 1950. Student, Art Students League; with, John Sloan, George Luks. Faculty Sch. for Art Studies, 1947-48, CCNY, 1948-54. One man show Babcock Galleries, 1941, 43, 58, Midtown Gallery, 1989, Midtown Payson Gallery, 1993; exhbns. include Met. Mus. Art, Whitney Mus. Am. Art, Art Inst. Chgo., U. Ill., Corcoran Galleries Art, Va. Mus. Fine Art, Pa. Acad. Art, N.A.D., Mus. City N.Y., Butler Art Inst., Audubon Artists, Nat. Art Mus. Sport, Madison Sq. Garden, 1968, American Drawings 1910-60 Midtown Galleries, 1990, Midtown Payson Galleries, N.Y.C., 1993, others; represented in permanent collections Met. Mus. Art, N.Y.C., Corcoran Galleries Art, Washington, L.A. County Mus. Art, Athens (Ga.) Mus., Walker Art Ctr., Mpls., Art Students League, N.Y.C., Hirchorn Mus. Art, Washington. Guggenheim fellow in painting, 1941; recipient ann. purchase prize Nebr. Art Assn., 1946; spl. invitation prize Salmagundi Club, 1950; Thomas G. Clarke prize NAD, 1951; Grumbacher Prize, 1956, 64; prize for painting in oil NAD, 1961, Grumbacher Purchase prize Audubon Artists, 1964. Mem. Art Student's League, Audubon Artists Am., Artists Equity Assn., Am. Water Color Soc., Nat. Soc. Painters in Casein. Home: PO Box 80 Lumber Ln Bridgehampton NY 11932

JACKSON, LYNN ROBERTSON, lawyer; b. Montgomery, Ala., Nov. 20, 1947; d. Arthur Borders Jr. and Mozelle (Martin) Robertson; m. George Thomas Jackson, Aug. 16, 1969; children: Katherine, William Borders. BS, U. Ala., 1970; JD, Faulkner U., 1979. Bar: Ala. 1981, U.S. Dist. Ct. Ala. 1984. Ptnr. Jackson and Faulk, Clayton, 1981-83, Andrews and Jackson, Clayton, 1983-84; pvt. practice Clayton, 1984-92; ptnr. Jinks, Smithart & Jackson, Clayton, 1992—; chair mandatory legal edn. Ala. State Bar, 1990—; mem. permanent code com., bench and bar rels. com. Ala. State Bar. City atty. City of Clayton, 1984—; bd. trustees Town and County Libr., Clayton, 1990—; trustee Ala. Law Found., 1989—. Mem. ABA, Ala. State Bar Assn. (bar commr. 1985—), Assn. Trial Lawyers Am. Episcopalian. Avocation: raising Arabian show horses and Doberman Pinschers. Home: Licklog Farm Clayton AL 36016 Office: Jinks Smithart and Jackson Court Sq Clayton AL 36016

JACKSON, M. DOROTHY, medical surgical nurse, researcher; b. Ohsweken, Ont., Can., July 12, 1945; d. Charles E. and Effie Irene (Montour) Hill; m. Richard A. Jackson, July 29, 1972; 1 child, Helki Orénda. Diploma in nursing, Greater Niagara Gen. Hosp., Niagara Falls, Ont., 1968; student, Wayne State U., Washtenaw C.C., Ann Arbor, Mich. RN, Can., Mich.; cert. med.-surg. nurse ANA. Staff nurse Fed. Govt. Can., Ottawa, Ont.; nurse clinician III gynecol. and med.-surg. units U. Mich., Ann Arbor, 1992-93; med.-surg. home health care nurse, 1994-95, ret., 1997; staff nurse W.A. Foote Meml. Hosp., Jackson, Mich., 1996—. Mem., chmn. resource com. Women of Colour Task Force, 1987-89, 93-94.

JACKSON, MAE BOGER, executive administrative assistant, office manager; b. Winston-Salem, N.C., May 19, 1963; d. Billy Charles and Leona (Heath) Key; m. John Talbert Jackson, June 13, 1987; 1 child, Thomas William. Student, U. N.C., Charlotte, 1981-83; BS, Johnson Bible Coll., Knoxville, Tenn., 1986. Cert. profl. sec. Adminstrv. asst. The Shelton Cos., Winston-Salem, 1986-88; office automation specialist, personnel mgr. POPI Temp. Svcs., Winston-Salem, 1988-90; exec. asst. Inmar Enterprises, Inc., Winston-Salem, 1990-92, Chesapeake Display and Packaging co., Winston-Salem, 1992—. Mem. NAFE, Profls. Sec. Internat. (treas. 1990, v.p. 1991, pres.-elect 1992, pres. 1993-94, Winston-Salem Sec. of Yr. N.C. divsn. 1991, 96, Winston-Salem Outstanding mem. of Yr. award 1993), Assn. Info. Sys. Profls., Office Automation Soc. Internat. Mem. Christian Ch. (Ch. of Christ). Home: 310 Gatewood Dr Winston Salem NC 27104-2432 Office: Chesapeake Display & Packaging Co 119 Brookstown Ave Ste 200 Winston Salem NC 27101-5245

JACKSON, MARCIA LYNETTE, women's health, pediatrics and geriatrics nurse; b. Cleve., July 14, 1951; d. John Joseph Greenwood and Geraldine Cole; children: Chelisa, Terron. AS, Cuyahoga C.C., Cleve., 1974; BA in Psychology, Cleve. State U., 1988, MEd, 1994. RN, Ohio; cert. instr. CPR. Case mgr. Med. Case Mgmt. Am., 1994—; case mgr. Med. Case Mgmt. Am., 1994—; assessment nurse passport program Western Res. Agy. on Aging, 1991-95; instr. nusring Cuyahoga C.C., 1994—; staff devel. coord. St. Augustine Manor, Cleve., 1995; regional supr. Geric Home Health Care, 1996-98, vis. nurse svc., 1998. Office: St Augustine Manor 7801 Detroit Ave Cleveland OH 44102-2813

JACKSON, MARION LEROY, agronomist, soil scientist; b. Reynolds, Nebr., Nov. 30, 1914; s. Cleve L. and Belle Josephine (Hanson) J.; m. Chrystie Marie Bertramson, Sept. 2, 1937; children—Marjorie Lee, Virginia Lynn (Mrs. Bruce P. Conlon), Stanley Bertram, Douglas Mark. B.S. maxima cum laude with high distinction, U. Nebr., 1936, M.S., 1937, D.Sc. (hon.), 1974; Ph.D., U. Wis., 1939. Land classification aide U.S. Dept. Agr., Lincoln, Nebr., 1936-37; grad. research asst. U. Wis., Madison, 1937-39; postdoctoral fellow U. Wis., 1939-41, instr., 1941-42, asst. prof., 1942-45, asso. prof., 1946-50, prof., 1950-74, Franklin Hiram King Disting. prof. emeritus, 1974—; chemist Purdue U., 1945-46; vis. prof. Cornell U., 1959; disting. vis. prof. U. Wash., Seattle, 1973; mem. panel on disposition radioactive wastes Nat. Acad. Scis., 1976-77; lectr. U.S., Canadian govts., numerous univs. Author: Soil Chemical Analysis, 1958, Soil Chemical Analysis-Advanced Course, 1956, 2d edit., 1969; contbr. articles to profl. jours. Troop chmn. Four Lakes council Boy Scouts Am., 1965, scoutmaster, 1966. Recipient Soil Sci. Achievement award, 1958. Fellow AAAS, Am. Soc. Agronomy, Nat. Acad. Sci., Soil Sci. Soc. Am. (past pres.; Disting. Mem. award 1983, Career award 1986), Mineral Soc. Am.; mem. Clay Minerals Soc. (past pres., Disting. Mem. award 1977), Internat. Soc. Soil Sci., Mineral Soc. London, Phi Beta Kappa, Sigma Xi, Phi Lambda Upsilon, Alpha Zeta, Gamma Sigma Delta, Pi Mu Epsilon. Home: 309 Ozark Trl Madison WI 53705-2534 Office: U Wis 1525 Observatory Dr Madison WI 53706-1207 *Persistent intense curiosity concerning the scientific interrelatedness of inanimate and living things in nature is important. Teaching (sharing) of facts and ideas with students and colleagues, particularly colleagues in seemingly remote but allied disciplines, permits fruitful research and discovery of underlying principles governing soil, healthy nutrition and long life.*

JACKSON, MARY ELLEN, librarian, consultant; b. Oshkosh, Wis., Nov. 20, 1949; d. Lawrence Herbert and Jeanette Lucille (Frohrib) Marten; m. Alan Robert Jackson, Sept. 11, 1971. BA, Carroll Coll., Waukesha, Wis., 1971; MLS, Drexel U., 1974. Libr. searching dept. U. Pa. Librs., Phila., 1973-74, head Rosengarten res., 1974-77, head serials dept., 1977-78, head interlibr. loan dept., 1978-93; access and delivery svcs. cons. Assn. Rsch. Librs., Washington, 1993-98; sr. prog. ofcr. Access Svcs., 1998—; cons. to over 40 librs., consortia and state agys., 1988—; adv. bd., Inst. for Sci. Info., Phila., 1993-96; com. mem. Internat. Fedn. Libr. Assns., The Hague, The Netherlands, 1994—; keynote spkr., workshop leader, conf. organizer for over 150 orgns. in over 10 countries, dir. Natl. Coordinating Com. on Japanese Library Resources, 1998—. Author: Measuring the Performance of Interlibrary Loan Ops. in North Amer. Rsch. and Acad. Libraries, 1998; editor: AMS Studies in Interlibrary Loan, Document Delivery, Access Svcs., and Resource Sharing (ILL/DD), 1998; editor 5 books, Rsch. Access Through New Technology, 1989, RLG Shared Resources Manual, 1992, Advances in Preservation and Access, 1992, Uses of Document Delivery Svcs., 1994, Manging Resource Sharing in the Electronic Age, 1996; contbr. over 70 articles to profl. jours. Recipient cert. of merit Pa. Libr. Assn., 1993. Mem. ALA (Amer. Library Assn., various offices 1978—), Safari Club Internat., Beta Phi Mu. Avocation: sewing. Office: Assn Rsch Librs 21 Dupont Cir NW Ste 800 Washington DC 20036-1118

JACKSON, MARY JANE MCHALE FLICKINGER, principal; b. Cleve., Feb. 23, 1938; d. Thomas William Flickinger and Margaret Julia (Lydon) Flickinger Nichols; m. Robert Lowell Jackson, June 27, 1959; children: Julia Anna Jackson Sommers, Patricia L., Margaret Jacqueline Jackson Tyler. BS in Speech, St. Louis U., 1959; postgrad., U. Copenhagen, 1961-62; MS in Spl. Edn., Southern Ill. U., 1965; EdD, George Washington U., 1977. Cert. tcht. Md. 1972. Tchr. Ritenour Sch. Dist., Overland, Mo., 1959-60; tutor Spl. Sch. Dist. Handicapped, St. Louis, 1960-61; tchr. Rugaards Franske Skole, Copenhagen, Denmark, 1961-62; substitute tchr., primary tchr. St. Louis and Ladue, Mo., 1962-65; tchr. L.A. City Schs., 1966-67, Woodlin Elem. Sch., Silver Spring, Md., 1967-68; various teaching positions, 1968-71, 73-81; asst. prin. Ritchie Park Elem. Sch., Rockville, Md., 1971-73, various supr. positions, 1974-79; asst. prin. Stephen Knolls Sch., Kensington, Md., 1981-88, prin., 1988-97; adj. prof. Trinity Coll., 1997—; v.p. Concerned Citizens Exceptional Edn., Washington, 1968-70; surrogate parent Assn. Retarded Citizens, Washington. Bd. dirs. Archdiocesan of Washington, 1986-91; pres. Bd. Edn., Washington, 1990-91; bd. dirs. United Cerebral Palsy, Montgomery County, 1992—; presenter Young Adult Insts. Internat. Conf., 1994. Recipient Lisa Kane award, 1964. Mem. Wash. Hearing Soc. (bd. dirs. 1969-81), Coun. Exceptional Children (exec. bd., pres. Montgomery county chpt. 1992-93, polit. action coord. for Md. fedn. 1993, exec. com. divsn. of internat. spl. edn. and svcs. 1993), Alexander Graham Bell Assn. (pub. rels. com. 1979—), Rotary. Roman Catholic. Home: 9900 Georgia Ave Apt T-11 Silver Spring MD 20902-5241

JACKSON, MARY L., health services executive; b. Phila., June 25, 1938; d. John Francis and Helen Catherine (Peranteau) Martin; m. Howard Clark Jackson III, Dec. 17, 1954; children: Michael, Mark, Brian, Bert. Student Bucks County C.C., 1977-83. Asst. mgr. retail div. Sears Roebuck & Co., Bensalem, Pa., 1972-77; educator, adminstr., dir. Trevose Behavior Modification Program, Pa., 1975—, leadership tng. workshops, 1979—; participant rsch. studies in field; salesman Makefield Real Estate, Morrisville, Pa., 1977-78; mortgage fin. cons. Tom Dunphy Real Estate, Feasterville, Pa., 1978-81; weight loss cons., Hulmeville, Pa., 1984—, also TV and radio appearances on behavior modification for weight loss and maintenance. Co-author: The Official Calorie Book; pub., columnist monthly newsletter The Modifier, 1977—. Recipient Chapel of Four Chaplain award, 1977. Mem. Assn. Advancement of Behavior Therapy, Bucks County Bd. Realtors, Hulmeville Hist. Soc. (a founder, charter mem.). Democrat. Presbyterian. Avocations: reading, classical music, speed walking, knitting, fishing. Home: 218 Main St Hulmeville PA 19047-5635

JACKSON, MELBOURNE LESLIE, chemical engineering educator and administrator, consultant; b. Wisdom, Mont., Sept. 27, 1915; s. James R. and Adeline (Mallon) J.; m. Elizabeth Clara Ford, Apr. 2, 1944; children: Gary Leslie, Linda Mary, Laurie Elizabeth, Nancy Ruth. BSChemE, Mont. State U., 1941, D in Engring. (hon.), 1980; PhDChemE, U. Minn., 1948. Registered profl. engr., Wash., Idaho. Instr. chem. engring. U. Minn., Mpls., 1944-48; from asst. prof. to assoc. prof. U. Colo., Boulder, 1948-50; head process devel. U.S. Naval Ordnance Test Sta., China Lake, Calif., 1950-53; prof. U. Idaho, Moscow, 1953-65, 70-80, head dept. chem. engring., 1953-65, dean grad. sch., 1965-70, dean Coll. Engring., 1973, 78-80, 83; cons. numerous corps. including James River Corp.; pres. U. Idaho Fed. Credit Union, Moscow, 1972-74. Patentee aeration/flotation devices, 1978, 80; contbr. articles to profl. jours. Chmn. Idaho Air Pollution Control Commn., Boise, 1959-72; chmn., trustee Moscow Sch. Dist., 1957-63. Fellow Am. Inst. Chem. Engrs; mem. Am. Chem. Soc., Am. Soc. Engring. Edn., Sigma Xi. Methodist. Avocations: boating, photography. Home: 625 Ekes Rd Moscow ID 83843-2407 Office: U Idaho Dept Chem Engring Moscow ID 83843

JACKSON, MICHAEL I., hospitality company executive. Beverage mgr., dining rm. supr. Holiday Inn Downtown; asst. gen. mgr. Regina Holiday Inn; gen. mgr. Winnipeg South Holiday Inn, Newfoundland, St. John's Holiday Inn, Newfoundland; v.p. ctrl. region, dir. ops. Atlific Inc., 1986, sr. v.p. ctrl. and Atlantic Can.; exec. v.p., COO Venture Inns Inc.; sr. v.p. ops. Unihost; exec. v.p., COO Commonwealth Hospitality Ltd., Mississauga, Ont., Can., 1998—. Mem. Hotel Assn. of Can. (vice chmn.), IAHI (regional mktg. com.). Office: Commonwealth Hospitality, 5090 Explorer Dr 6th Fl, Mississauga, ON Canada L4W 4T9

JACKSON, MICHAEL JOHN, physiologist, association executive; b. Walton-on-Thames, Eng., Apr. 12, 1938; came to U.S., 1967; s. Leslie William and Mable Maud (Rudd) J.; m. Beryl Ann Tidy, Aug. 20, 1960. B.Sc. with 1st class honors, U. London, 1963; Ph.D, U. Sheffield, Eng., 1966. Lectr. physiology U. Sheffield, 1965-67; asst. prof. George Washington U., Washington, 1967-71, assoc. prof., 1971-77, prof., 1977-90, assoc. dean, 1985-89, dean, 1989-90; exec. dir. Fedn. Am. Soc. Exptl. Biology, 1990—; guest investigator Nat. Inst. Arthritis, Metabolism and Digestive Disease, NIH, 1975-76; cons. USPHS, NIH, 1978, 81, 83, VA, 1978-81. Assoc. editor, Am. Jour. Physiology, 1979-85; contbr. articles to profl. jours. Recipient NIAMDD Research Career Devel. award., 1972-77. Mem. Physiol. Soc. (London), Am. Physiol. Soc., Coun. Eng. Sci. Soc. Execs., Am. Men Women Sci. (mem. adminstrv. bd.), Am. Soc. Assoc. Execs. Home: 6101 Kings Color Dr Fairfax VA 22030-5916 Office: 9650 Rockville Pike Bethesda MD 20814-3998

JACKSON, MICHAEL (JOSEPH), singer; b. Gary, Ind., Aug. 29, 1958; s. Joseph Walter and Katherine Esther (Scruse) J. Student pvt. sch.; LHD (hon.), Fisk U., 1988. Lead singer Jackson-Five (later called The Jacksons), from 1969; performer on numerous TV programs; recs. for Epic Records; performed at Queen Elizabeth's Silver Jubilee, May 1977; appeared in (films) The Wiz, 1978, Moonwalker, 1988, Dangerous the short film, 1993, (TV series) The Jacksons, 1976-77; albums with Jackson-Five include Diana Ross Presents the Jackson Five, 1969, ABC, 1970, Jackson Five Christmas Album, 1970, Third Album, 1970, Goin' Back to Indiana, 1971, Greatest Hits, 1971, Maybe Tomorrow, 1971, Looking Through the Windows, 1972, Farewell My Summer, 1973, Get it Together, 1973, Skywriter, 1973, Dancing Machine, 1974, Moving Violation, 1975, Joyful Jukebox Music, 1976, Boogie, 1980; albums with The Jacksons include The Jacksons, 1976, Goin' Places, 1977, Destiny, 1978, Triumph, 1980, The Jacksons Live, 1981, Victory, 1984; solo albums include Got To Be There, 1972, Ben, 1972, Music and Me, 1973, Forever Michael, 1975, The Best of Michael Jackson, 1975, Off the Wall, 1979, Thriller (listed in Guiness Book of World Records as most successful LP in rec. history), 1982, Bad, 1987, Dangerous, 1991, HIStory: Past, Present and Future, Book 1, 1995; narrator E.T.: The Extra Terrestrial storybook, 1982; videos include: We Are The World, 1990, Black or White, 1991, Leave Me Alone, 1993; leader of Jacksons U.S. tour, 1984; author autobiography Moonwalk, 1988, Dancing the Dream Poems and Reflections, 1992. Recipient gold and platinum record awards; Grammy awards for Record of the Yr. (Beat It), Album of Yr. (Thriller), Pop vocal performer (Thriller), Rock vocal performer (Thriller), World's Best Selling Album of All Time (Thriller), Rock vocal performer for song Beat It, Rhythm and Blues vocal performance (Bille Jean), New rhythm and blues song (Billie Jean), Children's field for narration of E.T., The Innovator's award, Inst. for Musical Arts, 1996, Living Legend award for Best Video for Leave Me Alone, 1993, Cable Ace award, Performance in a Music Special or Series, 1994, World Music award, 1996; named Best Male Artist, MTV-Europe, 1996, Favorite Male Artist Pop-Rock, Am. Music awards, 1996, Artist of a Generation, Brit. Awards., 1996, World's Best Selling R&B Male Artist, World's Best Selling Pop Male R&B Artist, World's Best Selling Male Rec. Artist, World's Best Selling Am. Male Artist, 1997, Jackson Five Induction in the Rock'n Roll Hall of Fame. Office: care Bob Jones 9255 W Sunset Blvd Ste 1100 Los Angeles CA 90069-3308

JACKSON, MICHAEL RAY, baseball player; b. Houston, Dec. 22, 1964. Student, Hill Jr. Coll. With Seattle Mariners, 1988-91, 96, San Francisco Giants, 1992-94; pitcher Cin. Reds, 1995, Cleve. Indians, 1997—. Office: Cleve Indians 2401 Ontario St Cleveland OH 44115-4003*

JACKSON, MICHELLE A., artist; b. Bklyn., Dec. 16, 1969; d. Cordell Hull and Patricia Y. Barrow. BFA, Iowa State U., 1996. Prodn. asst. KUSR Radio, Iowa State U., Ames, 1995-96; rsch. asst. Iowa Ctr. for Emerging Mfg. Tech., Ames, 1996-97; adminstrv. asst. dept. art and design Iowa State U., Ames, fall 1998. Student rep. computer com. dept. art and design Coll. Design, Iowa State U., 1996, peer mentor Student Peer Mentor for New Students, 1996. Ronald B. McNair scholar Grad. Coll., Iowa State U., 1996. Democrat. Episcopal. Avocations: printmaking, painting, writing, tennis, Tae Kwon Do. E-mail: majackson98@hotmail.com.

JACKSON, MICK, film director, producer; b. Aveley, Eng., Nov. 4, 1943. Motion picture and T.V. dir., prodr. Prodr., dir. T.V. films Threads, 1985, The Race for the Double Helix, 1987, (T.V. series) Connections, 1979; dir. films Chattahoochee, 1990, L.A. Story, 1991, The Bodyguard, 1992, Clean Slate, 1994, Volcano, 1997, Josiah's Canon, 1999, others, (T.V. series) The Practice, 1997, Strange World, 1999, (T.V. movies) The Ascent of Man, 1973, A Guide to Armageddon, 1983, Yuri Nosenko, KGB, 1986, Indictment: The McMartin Trial, 1995, others. Office: c/o DGA 7920 Sunset Blvd Los Angeles CA 90046*

JACKSON, MILES MERRILL, retired university dean; b. Richmond, Va., Apr. 28, 1929; s. Miles Merrill and Thelma Eugertha (Manning) J.; m. Bernice Olivia Roane, Jan. 7, 1954; children: Miles Merrill III, Marsha, Muriel, Melia. BA in English, Va. Union U., 1955; MS, Drexel U., 1956; postgrad., Ind. U., 1961, 64; PhD, Syracuse U., 1974. Br. libr. Free Libr., 1955-58; acting libr. C.P. Huntington Meml. Libr., Hampton (Va.) U., 1958-59, libr., 1959-62, asst. prof. libr. sci., 1958-62; territorial libr. Am. Samoa, 1962-64; chief libr. Trevor Arnett Libr., Atlanta U., 1964-69; also lectr. Sch. Libr. Sci.; assoc. prof. State U. N.Y., Geneseo, 1969-75; prof. U. Hawaii, 1975—, dean, 1983-95, chmn. interdisciplinary program in communication and info. scis., 1985-89; cons. in field, 1995—; Fulbright lectr. U. Tehran, Iran, 1968-69; libr., cons. Fiji, Samoa, Papua New Guinea, Micronesia, USIA India, 1993, Pakistan, 1985, Nat. Libr. Edn., 1996, Govt. Am. Samoa, 1997, Hawaii Pub. Libr. Found., 1986-2000; chmn. bd. Hawaii Lit., Inc., 1985-88; commr. Hawaii Libr. Commn., 1996-97. Editor: A Bibliography of Materials on Negro History and Culture for Young People, 1968, Comparative and International Librarianship, 1971, International Handbook of Contemporary Developments in Librarianship, 1981, Pacific Island Studies: Review of the Literature, 1986, Linkages Over Space and Time, 1993; mem. editl. bd. Internat. Jour. Info. Mgmt., Internat. Libr. Rev., 1982-87; founder, editor Pacific Info. and Libr. Svcs. Newsletter; contbr. articles to profl. jours.; book reviewer. Bd. dirs. Cen. YMCA, 1986-94, Hawaii Gov.'s Coun. on Literacy, 1986-96, Hawaii ACLU, 1990-94, office holder in Dem. party of Hawaii, 1992—. With USNR, 1946-48. Recipient Outstanding Alumnus award Va. Union U., 1987; Rsch. grantee Am. Philos. Soc., 1966; Coun. on Libr. Resources fellow, 1970, vis. fellow Republic of China, 1986; Harold Lancour fgn. travel awardee Beta Phi Mu, 1976. Mem. ALA (chmn. Internat. Rels. Roundtable 1988-89), Assn. for Libr. and Info. Sci. Edn. (pres. 1989-90), Coll. Lang. Assn. (hon. mention poetry 1954, 2d prize award short story 1955). Democrat.

JACKSON, MURRAY EARL, academic administrator, educator; b. Dec. 21, 1926. MA, Wayne State U., 1956. Acad. adviser Wayne State U., Detroit, 1955-59, asst. dean for students, 1959-67; founding pres. Wayne County C.C., Detroit, 1967-70; prof. Ctr. for Study of Higher Edn. U. Mich., Ann Arbor, 1971-92. Fax: (313) 393-3808. Home: # 2807 1300 E Lafayette Ave Detroit MI 48207-2926

JACKSON, NAGLE, stage director, playwright; b. Seattle, Apr. 28, 1936; s. Paul Joseph and Gertrude (Dunn) J.; m. Sandra L. Suter, Sept. 15, 1963; children: Rebecca J., Hillary J. BA, Whitman Coll., 1958, LittD (hon.), 1995. Resident dir. Am. Conservatory Theatre, San Francisco, 1967-70; artistic dir. Milw. Repertory Theatre, 1970-76, McCarter Theatre, Princeton, N.J., 1979-90; stage dir. N.J. Opera Festival, Lawrenceville, 1985-91; guest dir. Gorky Theatre, Leningrad, U.S.S.R., 1988, Trøndelag Teater, Trondheim, Norway, 1990. Playwright: At This Evening's Performance, 1985, Opera Comique, 1988, They Shoot Horses, Don't They?-The Musical (book and lyrics), 1992, This Day and Age, 1994, The Quick-Change Room, 1995, Moliere Plays Paris, 1996. Fulbright fellow, Paris, 1958; recipient Prize Onessis Found. Internat. Playwrights Competition, 1997. Mem. Soc. Stage Dirs. & Choreographers, The Dramatists Guild.

JACKSON, NANCY LEE, geography educator; b. Weymouth, Mass, Aug. 28, 1956; d. Sherwood Walter and Barbara Rose (Croker) J.. BA, Clark U., 1978; MS, Antioch/New Eng. Grad. Sch., 1986; PhD, Rutgers U., 1992. Field advisor Rural Cmty. Assistance, Rural Housing Improvement, Inc., Winchendon, Mass., 1979-80, asst. dir., 1980-81, dir., 1981-83; exec. dir. Rural New Eng., Inc., Waldboro, Maine, 1983-87; rsch. asst., IMCS Rutgers U., New Brunswick, N.J., 1987-92; asst. prof. N.J. Inst. of Tech., Newark, 1992-97, assoc. prof., 1997—; dir. Ctr. for Policy Studies, N.J. Inst. of Tech., Newark, 1995-98. Author: Environment Preservation and Pollution Prevention, 1997; contbr. articles to profl. jours. Mem. Planning Bd. Waldboro, 1984-87; bd. dirs. Coastal Econ. Devel. Corp., Bath, Maine, 1986-87, Rural New Eng., Inc., Waldoboro, 1982. Grantee Ford Found., 1984-87, U.S. Dept. of Health and Human Svcs., 1986-87, North Atlantic Treaty Orgn., 1995-98, NOAA N.J. Sea Grant, 1995-98, Deutscher Akademischer Austauschdienst, 1999. Mem. Am. Geog. Soc., Assn. Am. Geographers, Coastal and Marine Specialty Group Orgn. Am. Geographers (bd. dirs. 1994-96), Brit. Geomorphological Rsch. Group. Office: NJ Inst Tech University Heights Newark NJ 07102

JACKSON, NEAL A., lawyer; b. Raleigh, N.C., Sept. 6, 1943; s. Irvine L. and Dorothy A. Jackson; m. Louise M. Reggia (div. 1994); children: Adrienne, Kimberly; m. Sandra Willett, 1995. AB, U. N.C., 1965; JD, Georgetown U., 1968. Bar: D.C. 1968, Md. 1979. Trial atty. USDA, 1968-70; assoc. then ptnr. Macleay, Lynch, Bernhard & Gregg, 1970-76; ptnr. Caldwell & Greene, 1977-78; pvt. practice, 1978-79; mng. ptnr. Adams, McCullough & Beard, Washington, 1980-90; ptnr. Bell, Boyd & Lloyd, Washington, 1990-96; v.p. for legal affairs, gen. counsel & sec. Nat. Pub. Radio, Inc., 1996—. Mem. ABA, Edgemoor Club (pres. 1984-85), Univ. Club. Home: 3408 Reservoir Rd NW Washington DC 20007-2328 Office: Nat Pub Radio Inc 635 Massachusetts Ave NW Washington DC 20001-3753

JACKSON, NONA ARMOUR, writer, illustrator; b. Denison, Tex., Sept. 22, 1939; d. Thomas Jefferson and Novella Mae (Binion) A.; m. R.L. Jackson, Jr., Apr. 16, 1966. Supr., illustrator Diaper Jeans, Inc., Denison, 1959-62; clothing pattern maker, designer Srader's Sportswear, Denison, 1963-65; receptionist Glad Tidings Ch., Sherman, Tex., 1981-84; pastor elderly ministry Glad Tidings Ch., Sherman, 1984-87; author Pottsboro, Tex., 1987—; spkr. in field. Author, illustrator, photographer: The Cotton Mill! Can Anything Good Come from There? Vol. I-IX, 1995, Industries 1973-1981, 1995, Churches 1906-1991, 1995, Schools 1890-1964, 1995, Golden Rule Independent School Extra-Curricular Activities, 1995, Cotton Mill Community, The People: A Biography in Three Volumes, Vols. VI-VIII, 1995, Associates, Vol. IX, Index, Vols. VI-IX, 1995; author, illustrator: Pioneers of North West Grayson County, Texas Mid to Late 19th Century and Early 20th Century: Delaware Bend, Red Branch/Prairie Valley, Rock Creek with Some Dexter, Texas Data, 1996, Pioneers of Central Grayson County, Texas Mid to Late 19th Century and Early 20th Century: Cherrymound and Ambrose, 1996, Pioneers of Central Grayson County, Texas Mid to Late 19th Century and Early 20th Century: Cedar Community, 1996, Pioneers of South East Grayson County, Texas Mid to Late, 19th Century and Early 20th Century: Pilot Grove, 1996; contbr. articles and photographs to pubis. Sec., treas., young people's supt. Sunnyside Bapt. Ch., Denison, 1963-65; Sunday sch. tchr. Glad Tidings Ch., Sherman, 1978-83; tour guide, hostess Grayson County Frontier Village, Inc., Denison, 1978-97. Mem. Grayson County Humane Soc., Nat. Audubon Soc., Nat. Trust Hist. Preservation, Libr. Congress Assoc. (charter). Republican. Assembly of God. Avocations: guitar, art, nature, theology, genealogy. Home: 109 Houston Ave Unit 1 Pottsboro TX 75076

JACKSON, OVID, member of parliament; b. New Amsterdam, Berbice, British Guyana, Feb. 3, 1939; m. Verona Jackson; children: Andrew, Sonja. BA, U. Western Ont.; cert. in tchg., Ont. Coll. Edn., 1968. Field mechanic Ministry of Works and Hydraulics, Guyana, 1959-62; mechanic Jack Barclay's Rolls Royce, 1962-65; automotive mechanic David Foote, Toronto, 1965-67; tech. tchr., automotive specialist West Hill Secondary Sch., Owen Sound, ON, 1968-93; alderman City of Owen Sound, 1974-82, mayor, 1982-83; M.P. for Bruce-Grey House of Commons, 1993—, vice chair standing com. on citizenship and immigration, 1994—, co-vice chair standing com. on health, 1994—, mem. subcom. on HIV/AIDS, 1994—, mem. standing com. on policy devel., 1994—, parliamentary sec. to pres. of treas. bd., 1996-97, mem. parliament, 1997—. Mem. Regional in Cmty. Talks, Good Neighbours Workshop, Regional Police Svcs. Bd. Recipient 125th Can. Commemorative medal for Cmty. Work, St. John Ambulance Priory Vote of Thanks award. Mem. Kiwanis (sec.). Office: House of Commons Rm 217, West Block, Ottawa, ON Canada K1A 0A6*

JACKSON, PATRICIA PIKE, association executive; b. Pasadena, Calif., May 25, 1960; d. William Byrd and Noelle Irene (Schmutz) J. BA in Psychology, Scripps Coll., 1982; MBA, Claremont U., 1990. Asst. mgr. Pacific Bell, San Jose, Calif., 1982-83; asst. dir. ann. giving Scripps Coll., Claremont, 1983-84; dir. campaign activities Claremont McKenna Coll., 1984-86, dir. corp. rels., 1986-88; dir. major and leadership gifts Mt. Holyoke Coll., S. Hadley, Mass., 1988-91; dir. devel. and campaign Wheaton Coll., Norton, Mass., 1991-98; v.p. for edn. Coun. for Advancement and Support Edn., 1998—; mem. Townhall of L.A., 1985—; sec. Coun. for Advancement and Support of Edn., Calif., 1987-88; co-chair Parents Fundraising Conf., N.E. states, 1989-90; v.p. for edn. Coun. for Advancement & Support Edn., Washington, 1998—. Mem. wider rels. Oneonta Congl. Ch., South Pasadena, Calif., 1983-85, stewardship chair, 1985-88; deacon First Congl. Ch., South Hadley, 1988-91. Mem. AAUW (v.p. programs 1990-91), NAFE, NOW, Assocs. for Human Svcs. (bd. dirs.), Bus. and Profl. Women (Young Careerist award 1987). Avocations: reading, hiking, squash, entertaining, writing. Office: CASE 1307 New York Ave Washington DC 20005

JACKSON, PATRICK JOHN, public relations counsel, editor, author, public speaker; b. Grand Rapids, Mich., Sept. 5, 1932; s. Ira William and Edythe Jane (Minnema) J.; children: Richard, Kevin, Pamela, Roberta, Jennie, Alexandra, Jeremy; m. Stacey E. Smith, 1995. Student, Kenyon Coll., 1950-53; M.Ed., Antioch U., 1979. Dir. sports publicity Kenyon Coll., 1951-52; reporter Grand Rapids Press, 1953-54; advt. dir. Beckley (W.Va.) newspapers Corp., 1954-55; v.p. Jackson, King & Griffith, Waynesboro, Va., 1956-59; account exec. Ruder & Finn, N.Y.C., 1958; sr. counsel, co-founder Jackson, Jackson & Wagner, Exeter, N.H., 1959—; editor PR Reporter, 1976—, Who's Who in Pub. Relations, 1976—, Channels, 1982—; adj. prof. public relations Boston U. Sch. Public Communication, 1973-82; vis. prof. Universidad de Segrado Corazon, 1990, Hearst scholar Northern Iowa U., 1995. Editor: N.H. Conservation Directory, 1970-80; ed. Improving Productivity, 1983, co-author: Public Relations Practices: Managerial Case Studies and Problems, 1990, 5th edition, 1994, Actionable, Practical Research for Public Relations Purposes, 1994, A Probing Look at Employee Relations Today, 1998. Chmn. Strafford-Rockingham Regional Coun., 1977-78; chmn. Southeastern N.H. Regional Planning Commn., 1976-77; mem. Gov.'s Com. on N.H. Future, 1978-79; co-founder, legis. agt. Environ. Coalition, 1972-83; mem. Gov.'s Com. on Forest Resources, 1981-82; founder, lobbyist Statewide Program of Action to Conserve our Environment, 1968-93, dir., 1993—; founder Environ. Found., 1975; dir. Granite State Pub. Radio; mng. trustee Richmond Realty Trust, 1973—; trustee Antioch U. 1981-88, First Amendment Congress, 1980-98; chmn. N.H. Agr. Task Force; founder N.Am. Pub. Rels. Coun., 1980—; founder, chmn. Epping Planning Bd., 1967-72; pres. Seacoast Region Assn., 1978-82; bd. dirs. N.H. Social Welfare Coun., 1982-85, Youth Communication, Inc., 1985-93; mem. bd. vis. Def. Info. Sch., 1984-98, chmn., 1989-98; trustee Internat. Bus. Communicators Found., 1991-95, PRSA Found., 1994-98; chmn. pub. rels. adv. bd. Ferris State U., 1988—; trustee Soc. for the Protection of N.H. Forests, 1994—. Recipient Communicator of Yr. award Glassboro State U., 1980, Arthur W. Page award U. Tex., 1984, Vern C. Shrantz award Ball State U., 1982, Gold Anvil award, 1986, Learning & Liberty award, 1987, first winner Pathfinder award Kent State U., 1993; first inductee to Pub. Rels. Hall of Fame Rowan Univ. N.J., 1996. Fellow Pub. Rels. Soc. Am. (pres. New Eng. chpt. 1974-75, nat. dir. 1976-77, nat. sec. 1978, nat. pres.-elect 1979, pres. 1980, Lincoln award for pub. svc. 1978); mem. Am. Assn. Pub. Opinion Rsch., Nat. Sch. Pub. Rels. Assn. (Pres. award 1993), Orgn. Devel. Network, Canadian Pub. Rels. Soc., Arthur W. Page Soc., Internat. Assn. Bus. Communicators, Portsmouth Athanaeum, Delta Kappa Epsilon. Quaker. Home: 51 Central Rd Rye NH 03870-2523 Office: Jackson Jackson Wagner 14 Front St Exeter NH 03833-2795

JACKSON, PATRICK JOSEPH, insurance executive; b. Minn., Mar. 31, 1942; s. Paul Arthur and Lucille Margaret (Cummings) J.; m. Barbara Ann Simpson, July 19, 1964 (div. Apr. 1980); m. Shirley Ann Wellman, Sept. 12, 1982 (div. Oct. 1998); children: Laura Kathleen, Katherine Lucille. BS, Portland State U., 1968. Bank loan officer First Nat. Bank of Oreg., Portland, 1964-68; credit mgr. Meier & Frank Corp., Portland, 1968-70; agt., mgr. Aetna Life, San Jose, Calif., 1970-75; dist. mgr. Calif. Casualty, San Jose, 1975-78; gen. agt. Great So. Life, San Jose, 1978-82; account agt., agy. mgr. Allstate Ins., San Jose, 1982—; instr. Santa Clara (Calif.) U., 1974-76. Author: (monograph) The Affairs of, 1978; newspaper columnist, 1978-82. Mem. ins. subcom. Calif. State Senate, 1978; officer Los Gatos (Calif.) Police Res., 1970-78, treas., 1974-78; mem. Sch. Site Coun., Saratoga, Calif., 1978-80; mem. City Coun., Discovery Bay, Calif., 1991-95, mayor, 1993-94. Named Man of Yr., Los Gatos Youth Unltd., 1978. Mem. San Jose Life Underwriters (bd. dirs. 1974-76), No. Calif. Tollycraft Assn. (sec. 1995-97), Discovery Bay Yacht Club. Republican. Lutheran. Avocations: boating, fishing, shooting, reading. Office: Allstate Ins Co 2923 The Villages Pky San Jose CA 95135-1442

JACKSON, PAUL HOWARD, multimedia producer, educator; b. Topeka, Nov. 10, 1952; s. Dwight Stover and Janice Ilona (Woeltje) J.; m. Elizabeth Ann McGhghy, July 23, 1977; children: Christopher, Jeremy, Catherine, Johanna, Caleb. BA, Washburn U., 1973; MLS, Emporia State U., 1974; MDiv, Concordia Sem., Clayton, Mo., 1979; postgrad., Ind. U., 1993-96; STM, Concordia Theol. Sem., Ft. Wayne, Ind., 1995. Ordained to ministry Luth. Ch.-Mo. Synod, 1979. Pastor St. Paul's Luth. Ch., Wakefield, Nebr., 1979-81, 1st Trinity Luth. Ch., Wayne, Nebr., 1979-81; libr., tchr. Luth. High. Sch. Indpls., 1981-82; libr., prof. St. John's Coll., Winfield, Kans., 1982-85; libr. Winfield (Kans.) Pub. Library, 1985-88; pastor 1st Luth. Ch., Pond Creek, Okla., 1986-88; libr. Concordia Theol. Sem., Ft. Wayne, Ind., 1988-96; multimedia prodr. Concordia Publ. House, St. Louis, 1996—; adj. prof. Concordia U. Wis., Mequon, 1995—. Organizer musical group Celebration, 1982; prodr. W3 Word Witness Worship, 1998, Concordia Self-Study CD-ROM, 1998; contbr. articles to religious jours. Bd. dirs. Trinity Ch. S.E. Asian Mission, Winfield, 1984-86, Wash. Luth. Sch. Assn., 1997—, v.p. 1997-98; co-chair Winfield Com. for Commemorating the Bicentennial of the Constn., Winfield, 1987-88; chmn. Coalition for Purchase and Renovation, St. John's Coll., Winfield, 1988; sec., treas. exec. com. Area 3 Libr. Svc. Authority, Ft. Wayne, 1990-93. Mem. Phi Kappa Phi, Mu Alpha Pi. Republican. Home: 2702 Tallwood Ct Saint Louis MO 63129-4516 Office: Concordia Publ House 35585 Jefferson Ave Saint Louis MO 63118-3968 *All that I am I owe to my Lord and Savior Jesus Christ. What he has done through his life, death, and resurrection far exceeds anything we will ever accomplish.*

JACKSON, PETER VORIOUS, III, retired association executive; b. Butte, Mont., May 18, 1927; s. Peter V. and Besse Portia (McLean) J.; m. Johnneta Pierce, Apr. 29, 1949; children: Ward, Michelle (Mrs. Jerry Vanhour), Johnathan. Wheat and cattle rancher, 1949—; mem. Mont. Ho. of Reps., 1971-72; chief Grass Conservation bur. Mont. Dept. Natural Resources, Helena, 1972-74; supr. Conservation Dist. Madison County, Ennis, Mont., from 1957; past exec. dir. Western Environ. Trade Assn., Helena.; exec. v.p. Soc. for Range Mgmt., Denver, 1983-92; ret., 1992; vol. to develop and implement grazing lands conservation initiative Soil Conservation Soc. USDA, 1992—; mem. Nat. Steering Com. of Grazing Land Conservation Initiative, 1993-98; nat. sec. grazing lands conservation initiative NRCS-USDA. Author: Montana Rangeland Resources Program, 1970. Mem. Madison County Fair Bd.; pres. Grazing Lands Forum, 1988; sec. Nat. Grazing Land Initiative USDA, 1998, 99. Recipient Renner award Soc. Range Mgmt., 1971, Conservation award Mont. Wildlife Fedn., 1966. Mem. Nat. Assn. Conservation Dists. (bd. dirs.), Mont. Assn. Conservation Dists. (exec. v.p. 1974), Soc. for Range Mgmt. (nat. pres., spl. award for outstanding achievement 1992), Masons, Elks, Shriners. Home and Office: PO Box 86 Harrison MT 59735-0086

JACKSON, PHILIP DOUGLAS, professional basketball coach; b. Deer Lodge, Mont., Sept. 17, 1945; m. June; 5 children. Grad., North Dakota, 1967. Basketball player N.Y. Knicks, 1967-78; basketball player N.J. Nets, 1978-80, asst. coach, 1980-82; head coach Albany Patrons (Cen. Basketball Assn.), 1982-87; asst. coach Chicago Bulls, 1987-89, head coach, 1989-98; head coach Los Angeles Lakers, Los Angeles, 1999-. Mem. NBA Championship Team, 1970, 73; coach NBA championship team, 1991, 92, 93,96; named Coach of Yr., NBA, 1996. Office: Los Angeles Lakers P.O.Box 10 3900 W Manchester Blvd Inglewood CA 90306*

JACKSON, PHILLIP ELLIS, cause-related marketing executive, writer; b. Kansas City, Mo., June 4, 1952; s. Phillip Anthony and Lois Irene (Seward) J.; m. Dawn Mutolo Jackson, Aug. 9, 1975; 1 child, Emily Mutolo. AA, Mohawk Valley C.C., 1972; BA magna cum laude in Liberal Arts, SUNY, Albany, 1974; MA in Internat. Rels., SUNY, 1975; PhD in Polit. Sci., U. Chgo., 1981. Speech writer; speech writer, issue com. chmn. Steve Bartlett Congl. Campaign, 1982; sr. v.p. pub. affairs Greater Dallas C. of C., 1982-93; exec. dir. Dallas United, 1984-93; pres. Jackson Gait Creative Enterprises, Inc., Dallas, 1993—; dir. Tex. office Cassidy & Assocs., Dallas, 1993-95; sr. v.p. opers. Jami Charity Brands Svcs. Inc., Dallas, 1995—. Author short fiction. Cons. Dallas Charter Rev. Com., 1989; dir. City of Dallas, Dallas C. of C. N.Am. Free Trade Agreement Labor Secretariat Task Force, 1991-93. Recipient Citizens award Chgo. Police Dept., 1978, Presdl. citations Pvt. Sector Initiatives, 1985, 86, 89; noted Spl. Recognition Dallas City Coun. Home: 6433 Willow Creek Dr Plano TX 75093-8058 Office: Jami Charity Brands Svcs 1 Blue Hill Plz Pearl River NY 10965-3104

JACKSON, POLLY, artist; b. Lubbock, Tex., Aug. 2, 1947. Student, Trinity U., San Antonio, 1965-66, U. Ariz., 1980, Coll. Santa Fe, 1997—. Greeting card designer Sunstone Press, Santa Fe, 1976-79; tile designer Gargoyles, Inc., Santa Fe, 1977-79; slide libr. staff Coll. of Santa Fe, 1997—. Works exhibited in group shows at Armory for the Arts, Santa Fe, 1982, 83, Highlands U., Las Vegas, 1984, 85, 86, Scharf Gallery, Santa Fe, 1985; represented in permanent collections at Capitol Arts Found. Roundhouse, Santa Fe; art work appeared in various mags. Address: 1430 Paseo Norteno Santa Fe NM 87505

JACKSON, R. GRAHAM, architect; b. Sherman, Tex., July 1, 1913; s. Watt J. and Lilly Thompson (Graham) J.; m. Reba Martin, Jan. 6, 1940 (dec. Oct. 1967); m. Violet Stephen Lawrence, May 1, 1971. B.S. in Architecture, Rice U., 1935. With R. Graham Jackson, Architect, 1936-45; ptnr. Jackson & Dill, Architects, Houston, 1946-53, Wirtz, Calhoun, Tungate & Jackson, Architects, Houston, 1953-65, Calhoun, Tungate & Jackson, Architects, Houston, 1965-75, Calhoun, Tungate, Jackson & Dill, 1975-82, CTJ&D, 1983—; asst. prof. architecture U. Houston, part time 1947-51; vis. lectr., critic Rice U., 1963-67. Archtl. works include design Lyndon B. Johnson Spacecraft Center, NASA, Houston, Willford Hall Hosp, Lackland AFB, Tex., Ryon Engring. Bldg., Rice U, Houston, Hankammer Sch. Bus., Baylor U, communications bldg. Tex. Tech. U, Darnall Army Hosp, Ft. Hood, Tex., Burleson acad. quadrangle Baylor U, Waco, Tex., Bergstrom AFB Hosp, Austin, Tex., library and performing arts bldgs. Sam Houston State U, Huntsville, Tex., 2d Bapt. Ch, Houston, Vets. Hosp, Temple, Tex., Coll. Tech., U. Houston, master plan Buckner Children's Village, Beaumont, Tex., Westbury Bapt. Ch, Houston, Chem. and Petroleum Engring. Bldg. U. Tex., Austin, 2d Bapt. Ch., Houston. Mem. founding com. Houston Baptist U.; mem. Rice U. Fund Council, Houston Mus. Fine Arts, Friends of Bayou Bend, Houston Symphony Soc. Fellow Constrn. Specifications Inst. (pres. Houston chpt. 1958-59, region dir. 1961-64, chmn. conv. program com. 1965), AIA (treas. Houston chpt. 1950, pres. 1959, mem. nat. adminstrv. office practice com. 1951-53, 67-73, 78-81); mem. Am. Mgmt. Assn., Am. Arbitration Assn. (panel of arbiters), Rice U. Alumni, Rice U. Assos., Houston Baptist U. Alumni Assn. (hon.), Houston C. of C. (cdn. com. 1950-53). Baptist (deacon). Clubs: Houston, Rice U. Faculty. One of only 12 persons honored by Fellowship in both AIA & CSI. Office: C T J & D Architects 2323 S Voss Rd Ste 440 Houston TX 77057-3812 *I have always wanted to leave to succeeding generations a better world in which to live. Architecture as a profession has offered for me a wonderfully exciting opportunity to accomplish this through design of institutions for learning, healing and worship.*

JACKSON, RANDALL W., geography educator; b. Richland, Wash., Mar. 12, 1954; s. Max Eliot and Wilma Marie (Miller) J.; m. Leslie Marie Pennell, Aug. 11, 1979; children: Adam Douglas, Timothy Clay. BS, U. Utah, 1976; MS, U. Ill., 1980, PhD, 1983. Prof. No. Ill. U., DeKalb, 1983-86; prof. dept. geography Ohio State U., Columbus, 1986—; cons., pres. Bus. & Econ. Geographics, Columbus, 1988—; assoc. dir. rsch. computing Ohio State U., 1990-92. Contbr. articles to profl. jours.; editl. bd. Profl. Geographer, Geographical Analysis, Australasian Jour. Regional Studies, The Profl. Geographer. Mem. Regional Sci. Assn. Internat. (editor nat. newsletter 1997—), Am. Assn. Geographers (bd. dirs. indsl. geog. specialty group 1989-90), Internat. Input-Output Assn. Home: 915 Oxford St Worthington OH 43085-4145 Office: Ohio State U Dept Geography 1036 Derby Hall 154 N Oval Mall Columbus OH 43210-1330

JACKSON, RANDY, computer networking executive; b. Oct. 16, 1944; s. James D. and Carmen (Brown) J.; children: Gail Lynn, Neil Allen. Master cert. netware engr. Pres. Restaurant Technologies, El Segundo, Calif., 1981-88; dir. MIS, Gregory's Restaurants, Anaheim, Calif., 1988-90; ops. mgr. Tricare Inc., Irvine, Calif., 1990-92; dir. tech. Sun Health Corp., Sun City, Ariz., 1992—. Contbr. articles to mags. Del. Ariz. Dem. Nat. Conv., N.Y.C., 1976, del. Utah, 1972. Mem. Networking Profl. Assn. (nat. orgn. chair bd. dirs. 1996, chair univ. rels. 1993-94, local chpt. pres. 1994). Avocation: photography. Home: 15843 N 135th Dr Surprise AZ 85374 Office: Sun Health Corp 10401 W Thunderbird Blvd Sun City AZ 85351-3004

JACKSON, RAYMOND A., federal judge; b. 1949. BA, Norfolk State U., 1970; JD, U. Va., 1973. Capt. U.S. Army JAGC, 1973-77; asst. U.S. atty. Ea. Dist. Va., Norfolk, 1977-93; judge U.S. Dist. Ct. (ea. dist.) Va., Norfolk, 1993—; mem. judicial conf. U.S. Ct. Appeals (4th cir.). Active Day Care and Child Devel. Ctr., Tidewater, 1980-86; bd. dirs. Peninsula Legal Aid Ctr., 1977. Col. USAR, ret. Mem. U.S. Dist. Judges Assn., Va. State Bar, Old Dominion Bar Assn. (pres. 1984-86), Norfolk-Portsmouth Bar Assn., South Hampton Rds. Bar Assn., Am. Inn Ct. (Hoffman-l'Anson chpt.), Va. Law Found., U.S. Judicial Conf. Com. Adminstrn. Magistrate Judge System. Office: 600 Granby St Norfolk VA 23510-1915

JACKSON, RAYMOND CARL, cytogeneticist; b. Medora, Ind., May 7, 1928; s. Thornton Comadore and Flossie Oliva (Booker) J.; m. T. June Snyder, Oct. 24, 1947; children: Jeffrey Wayne, Rebecca June. AB, Ind. U., 1952, AM, 1953; PhD, Purdue U., 1955. Instr. to asst. prof. U. N.Mex., Albuquerque, 1955-58; asst. prof. of Botany U. Kans., Lawrence, 1958-60, assoc. prof. of Botany, 1961-64, prof. of Botany, 1964-71, prof. and chmn.

Botany, 1969-71; prof. and chmn. biol. scis. Tex. Tech U., Lubbock, 1971-78, Horn prof. of Biol. Scis., 1990—; chmn. interdepartmental PhD Program in Genetics, U. Kans., chmn. dept. Botany, U. Kans., 1969-71; speaker and presenter in field. Contbr. numerous articles to profl. jours. Staff sgt. USAF, 1946-49. Mem. Genetics Soc. Am., Genetics Soc. of Can., Soc. for the Study of Evolution, Botanical Soc. of Am. (BSA Merit award 1992), Am. Soc. Plant Taxonomists, Internat. Orgn. of Plant Biosystematists, Delta Phi Alpha, Sigma Xi, Phi Sigma. Republican. Achievements include research on pairing control genes and their comparative effects at the diploid and polyploid levels; genetics, cytogenetics, and gametic selection in Haplopappus gracilis, and in cytogenetics of diploid Triticum species. Home: 7922A Aberdeen Ave Lubbock TX 79424-2808 Office: Dept Biol Scis Tex Tech Univ Lubbock TX 79409

JACKSON, RAYMOND SIDNEY, JR., lawyer; b. Bklyn., Sept. 17, 1938; s. Raymond Sidney and Mary Frost (McInerney) Van Vranken. BA, William Coll., 1960; JD, Harvard U., 1966. Bar: N.Y. 1967, U.S. Dist. Ct. (so. and ea. dists.) N.Y. 1969, U.S. Ct. Appeals (2d cir.) 1969. Assoc. Thacher, Proffitt & Wood, N.Y.C., 1966-76, ptnr., 1976-94, of counsel, 1994—. Mem. South St. Seaport Mus., N.Y.C., 1974—, Gramercy Neighborhood Assocs., N.Y.C., 1974—, Nat. Assn. Coll. and Univ. Attys., 1972. Mem. ABA (vice chmn. admiralty and maritime law com. sect. of tort and ins. practice 1990-92), N.Y. State Bar Assn. (admiralty and maritime com. internat. law and practice sect. 1989-94), Assn. Bar City N.Y. (admiralty com. 1984-85, 88-91), Maritime Law Assn. U.S. (com. on practice and procedure 1976-91). E-mail: RSJacksonJ@aol.com. Office: Thacher Proffitt & Wood 2 World Trade Ctr New York NY 10048-0203

JACKSON, REED MCSWAIN, educational administrator; b. Albemarle, N.C., Apr. 10, 1950; d. Wade Hampton and Louise Reed (Floyd) McSwain; m. William Austin Jackson, July 24, 1984. BA, Coker Coll., 1972; MEd, Francis Marion Coll., 1978; cert. Prin.'s Exec. Program, U. N.C., 1995. Lic. sch. adminstrn., sch. supervision, mentor, reading tchr. 2d grade tchr. Darlington (S.C.) County Schs., 1972-76; 4th grade tchr. Marlboro County Schs., Bennettsville, S.C., 1976-78; chpt. I reading tchr. Halifax (N.C.) County Schs., 1980-90, asst. prin. S.E. Halifax High Sch., 1990-91, dir. testing and secondary edn., 1991-95; accountability/instrnl. specialist Nash-Rocky Mount Schs., N.C., 1995—; mem. steering com. Roanoke Valley Tech Prep Consortium, Weldon, N.C., 1991-95, chairperson mktg. com., 1991-95; cons. So. Assn. Colls. and Schs.; chair Local Option Testing Svcs. governing bd.-N.C. state com. Mem., officer Tar River Embroiderers Guild, Rocky Mount, N.C., 1983-90; mem. Adv. Coun. for Coop. Extension Agy., Halifax, N.C., 1992. Named Halifax County Tchr. of Yr., 1984-85, Eastman Mid. Sch. Tchr. of Yr. 1984. Fellow N.C. Ednl. Policy Fellowship Program; mem. ASCD, Nat. Assn. Secondary Sch. Principals (named Leader 1-2-3 Coach), Phi Delta Kappa. Avocations: gardening, needlework, gourmet cooking, travelling, reading. Home: 4052 Ketch Point Dr Rocky Mount NC 27803-1418 Office: Nash/Rocky Mount Schs 800 N Fairview Rd Rocky Mount NC 27801-6115

JACKSON, REGINALD MARTINEZ, former professional baseball player; b. Wyncote, Pa., May 18, 1946; s. Martinez Jackson; m. Juanita Jackson. Student, Ariz. State U. Outfielder Kansas City, then Oakland Athletics, 1967-75, Balt. Orioles, 1976, N.Y. Yankees, 1977-81; outfielder, designated hitter Calif. Angels, 1982-86; outfielder, designated hitter Oakland Athletics, 1987, advisor, 1988-93; advisor N.Y. Yankees, 1993—; mem. Am. League All-Star Team, 1969, 71-75, 77-82, 84; former commentator ABC Sports. Author: (with Bill Libby) Reggie, 1975, (with Joel Cohen) Inside Hitting, 1975; appearances include (film), The Naked Gun, 1988. Inductee Baseball Hall of Fame, 1993; named Most Valuable Player Am. League, 1973, The Sporting News Major League Player of Year, 1973; Named to The Sporting News Am. League All-Star Team, 1969, 73, 75, 76, 80. Office: care Matt Merola 185 E 85th St Apt 18G New York NY 10028-2146 also: care NY Yankees Yankee Stadium 161st St and River Ave Bronx NY 10451

JACKSON, REGINALD SHERMAN, JR., lawyer; b. Oct. 8, 1946; s. Reginald Sherman and Frances (Holland) J.; m. Joanne Marie Warren, Aug. 31, 1968; children: Reginald Sherman III, Michael W., Adam H. BA, Ohio State U., 1968, JD, 1971. Bar: Ohio 1971, U.S. Supreme Ct. 1976; cert. civil trial advocate Nat. Bd. Trial Advocacy. Mem. Fuller, Henry, Hodge Snyder, Toledo, 1971-76; asst. U.S. atty. no. dist. Ohio U.S. Dept. Justice, 1976-78; ptnr. Connelly, Soutar & Jackson, Toledo, 1978—; adj. prof. trial practice U. Toledo Coll. Law, 1976-89. Fellow Am. Bar Found., Ohio State Bar Found. (trustee 1998—), Toledo Bar Found. (pres. 1993-98); mem. ABA (ho. of dels. 1996-99, litigation sect.), Am. Bd. Trial Advocates, Ohio Bar Assn. (coun. del. 1990—, bd. govs. 1996-99, pres.-elect 1999—), Toledo Bar Assn. (pres. 1989-90), Toledo Country Club (trustee 1981-93, pres. 1991-93), Rotary (trustee 1994-96, 1st v.p.). Home: 2907 River Rd Maumee OH 43537-3740 Office: Connelly Soutar & Jackson 405 Madison Ave Ste 1600 Toledo OH 43604-1214

JACKSON, RENÉE BERNADETTE, English language educator; b. York, Pa., July 20, 1954; d. William Brice and Helen Elizabeth (Webb) J.; 1 child, Karla Janine. BA in Comm., Pa. State Harrisburg, Middletown, 1995, MA in Humanities, 1997; postgrad., Temple U., 1997—. Newsroom intern, journalist Harrisburg Patriot News, 1995; newsroom intern, corr. York (Pa.) Daily Record, 1995-96; rsch. asst. for coord. Master's Humanities Program Pa. State Harrisburg, Middletown, 1995-97; adj. prof. Harrisburg Area C.C., 1997; tchg. asst. African-Am. studies Temple U., Phila., 1997, rsch. asst. broadcasting, telecom. and mass media dept., 1998; adj. English prof. C.C. of Phila., 1999—; GMAT essay evaluator Educl. Testing Svc., Princeton, N.J., 1998—. Mem. AAUW, Assn. for Edn. in Journalism and Mass Comm., Am. Journalism Historians Assn., Nat. Assn. Black Journalists, Assn. for the Study of Afro-Am. Life and History, Assn. Black Women Historians, Soc. Profl. Journalists, Middle-Atlantic Popular Culture Conf. (exec. bd. mem., mem. planning com.). Avocations: historical writing projects, composing piano music, travel. Home: 107 Shelbourne Dr York PA 17403-3821

JACKSON, RICHARD BROOKE, judge; b. Bozeman, Mont., Mar. 5, 1947; s. William T. and Myra (McHugh) J.; m. Elizabeth Ciner, Sept. 19, 1971; children: Jeffrey, Brett, Jennifer. AB magna cum laude, Dartmouth Coll., 1969; JD cum laude, Harvard U., 1972. Bar: Colo. 1972, U.S. Dist. Ct. Colo. 1972, D.C. 1980, U.S. Dist. Ct. D.C. 1980,U.S. Ct. Appeals (10th cir.) 1972, U.S. Ct. Appeals (D.C. cir.) 1980, U.S. Supreme Ct. 1980. Assoc. Holland & Hart, Denver, 1972-78; ptnr. Holland & Hart, Denver and Washington, 1978-98; dist. ct. judge Jefferson County, Golden, Colo., 1998—; instr. in trial practice U. Colo. Law Sch., Boulder, 1984-85, 87, 88, 89, 91, 98, Nat. Inst. Trial Advocacy, 1986, 87, 90, 91. Co-author: Manual for Complex Insurance Coverage Litigation, 1993; editor: A Better New Hampshire, 1968; contbr. articles to profl. jours. Fellow Am. Coll. Trial Lawyers; mem. ABA (former co-chair ins. coverage com. sect. of litigation), Colo. Bar Assn., Denver Bar Assn. Democrat. Avocations: running, golf, reading, travel, Spanish. Home: 5355 Yellowstone St Bow Mar CO 80123-1423 Office: Dist Ct Jefferson Cty 100 Jefferson County Pkwy Golden CO 80401-6002

JACKSON, RICHARD GEORGE, advertising agency executive; b. N.Y.C., Apr. 28, 1940; s. Nicholas and Mary (Vaselina) J.; m. Sandra Thelma LeMere, June 4, 1966; children: Catherine Lynn, Patricia Anne. B.A., Coll. City N.Y., 1961. Creative supr. Wells Rich Greene Inc. (Advt.), N.Y.C., 1967-68; exec. v.p., creative dir. Calderhead Jackson Inc., N.Y.C., 1968-74, Gardner Advt., N.Y.C., St. Louis, 1975; exec. v.p. Morgan, Reitzfeld & Jackson, Inc., N.Y.C., 1976-77; pres., chief exec. officer Altschiller, Reitzfeld & Jackson, N.Y.C., 1977—; chief exec. officer Altschiller, Reitzfeld, Jackson & Solin/NCK, Inc., N.Y.C., 1981-82; pres., chief exec. officer Dick Jackson Inc., N.Y.C., 1982. Recipient N.Y. Internat. Film Festival Bronze award, 1992, Rx Club award, 1991, BPAA Best of Div. award, 1990, AIGA award, 1980, U.S. Comml Festival award, 1980, CLIO award, 1975, Gold, Silver Keys Copywriter's Club award, 1970, One Show award, 1974, 75, 78, 79, 86, 87, Distinctive Merit awards Art Dirs. Show, 1966, 70, 78, 79, 80, 81, Andy award, 1966, 69, 70, 71, 75, 76, 78, 79, 81. Mem. Copy Club N.Y. (v.p. 1974-75, pres. 1975-77), One Club for Art and Copy (pres. 1977-78), N.Y. Advt. Club (dir. Andy awards 1975). Home: 35 E 85th St New York NY 10028-0954 Office: 475 Park Ave S New York NY 10016-6901

JACKSON, RICHARD JOSEPH, epidemiologist, public health physician, educator; b. Newark, Oct. 23, 1945; s. Robert Joseph Jackson and Dorothy C. (Devine) Connolly; m. Joan M. Guilford, June 21, 1975; children: Brendan, Devin, Galen. AB in Biology, St. Peter's Coll., Jersey City, 1969; M in Med. Sci., Rutgers Med. Sch., 1971; MD, U. Calif. San Francisco, San Francisco, 1973; MPH in Epidemiology, U. Calif. Berkeley, Berkeley, 1979. Diplomate Am. Bd. Pediatrics, Am. Bd. Preventive Medicine; lic. physician, Calif. Intern, resident U. Calif., San Francisco, 1973-74, 77-78; resident San Francisco Gen. Hosp. U. Calif., 1974-75; officer Epidemic Intelligence Svc. U.S. Pub. Health Svc., Albany, N.Y., 1975-77; spl. epidemiologist World Health Orgn., Bihar State, India, 1976; med. officer Epidemiol. Studies Sect. Calif. State Dept. Health Svcs., Berkeley, 1979-88; acting chief office environ. health hazard assessment, pub. health med. officer III Calif. State Dept. Health Svcs., Sacramento, 1988-90; chief hazard identification and risk assessment br. Calif. State Dept. Health Svcs., Berkeley, 1990-91; chief hazard identification and risk assessment br. office environ. health hazard assessment Calif. EPA, Berkeley, 1991-92; chief divsn. communicable disease control Calif. State Dept. Health Svcs., 1992-94; dir. Nat. Ctr. Environ. Health, Ctrs. Disease Control and Prevention, Atlanta, 1994—; adj. lectr. U. Calif. San Francisco, 1980—, asst. clin. prof., 1986—. Lt. comdr. USPHS, 1975-77. E-mail: RXJ4@CDC.GOV. Office: Nat Ctr Environ Health Ctrs Disease Control (F-29) 4770 Buford Hwy NE Atlanta GA 30341-3717

JACKSON, RICHARD MONTGOMERY, former airline executive; b. Jacksonville, Fla., Dec. 9, 1920; s. William Kenneth and Katharine (Mitchell) J.; m. Martha Eustis Turner, Sept. 12, 1942; children: Richard Montgomery, Susanne (Mrs. Jeffrey Miller), William Mitchell. B.Sc., Harvard, 1942. With Am. Airlines, Inc., 1945-58; asso. L.S. Rockefeller, 1958-60; with Seaboard World Airlines, Inc., Jamaica, N.Y., 1960-80; pres., chmn. bd. Seaboard World Airlines, Inc., 1960-80; chmn. exec. com. Flying Tiger Line, Jamaica, N.Y., 1980-81; bd. govs., chmn. Internat. Air Cargo Forum. Trustee Village of Lloyd Harbor, N.Y., 1960-68; pres. Lloyd Harbor Sch. Bd., 1957-58; trustee, pres. African Wildlife Found.; bd. govs. Huntington (N.Y.) Hosp., 1960-74. Lt. cmmdr. USNR, WWII. Clubs: Piping Rock (Locust Valley, N.Y.); Island (Hobe Sound, Fla.); Wings (N.Y.C.); Cold Spring Harbor Beach Club (N.Y.). Home: 273 Southdown Rd Lloyd Harbor Huntington NY 11743

JACKSON, ROBBI JO, non-hazardous agricultural products company executive, lawyer; b. Nampa, Idaho, Apr. 12, 1959; d. William R. Jackson and Marilyn K. Samp Jackson Nunez. BS in Fin., U. Colo., Boulder and Denver, 1981; JD, U. Denver, 1987, LLM in Taxation, 1990. Bar: Colo. Asst. office mgr. Jerome Karsh & Co., Denver, 1982; office mgr. Almirall & Assocs., Englewood, Colo., 1983-84; assoc. Moye, Giles, O'Keefe, Vermeire & Gorrell, Denver, 1989-90, Holme Roberts & Owen, Denver, 1990-92; in-house gen. counsel Cmty. Corrections Svcs., Denver, 1992-96; CEO Enviro Cons. Svc., LLC, Evergreen and Lakewood, Colo., 1996—. Mem. staff Adminstrv. Law Rev., Denver, 1985, editor, 1985, mng. editor, 1986-87; co-author course of study materials; presenter in field. Mem. fin. com. Mile-High chpt. ARC, Denver, 1990-92; food delivery person Vols. of Am., Meals-on-Wheels, Denver, 1990-92. Recipient scholarships. Mem. ABA, Colo. Bar Assn. (ethics com.). Republican. Avocations: running marathons and other races, biking, hiking, swimming, piano and organ playing.

JACKSON, ROBERT KEITH, manufacturing company executive; b. South Bend, Ind., Apr. 20, 1943; s. Orval Russell and Dorothy Alice (Gailey) J.; m. Cheryl Dee Bronkhorst, Nov. 6, 1965; children: Jennifer Lynn, Stephen Robert. BS, Western Mich. U., 1966; MBA, Vanderbilt U., 1987. Vocat. tchr. Warren (Mich.) Consol. Schs., 1967-68; mfg. engr. Eaton Corp., Kalamazoo, 1968-77, gen. supt., 1977; gen. supt. Eaton Corp., Kings Mountain, N.C., 1977-80; plant mgr. Eaton Ltd., Manchester, Eng., 1980-84, Eaton Corp., Shelbyville, Tenn., 1984-91; mgr. mfg. and quality assurance Truck Components Ops. Eaton Corp., Kalamazoo, 1991-93; plant mgr. Eaton Corp., Humboldt, Tenn., 1993-96; ops. specialist Eaton Corp., China, 1996-97; gen. mgr. Eaton Truck and Bus. Components (Shanghai) Co., Ltd., 1997—; mem. adv. coun. indsl. studies Mid. Tenn. State U., Murfreesboro, 1985-91, Sch. Bus., 1990-91; mem. machine tool tech. adv. com. Jackson (Tenn.) State C.C., 1994-96; mem. devel. com. U. Tenn. at Martin, mem. mech. engring. adv. bd., 1995-96. Trustee Eaton Pub. Policy Assn., Cleve., 1985-89. Mem. Tenn. Assn. Bus. (bd. dirs. 1989-91), Rotary, Elks, KC. Republican. Roman Catholic. Home: 640 Dogwood Dr Monteagle TN 37356-2010 Office: Super Ocean Fin Ctr, 2168 Yan An West Rd, Shanghai 200335, China

JACKSON, ROBERT LEE, real estate agent; b. Alamogordo, N.Mex., Dec. 31, 1963; s. J.W. Jackson. AA, SUNY, Albany, 1985, BS in Psychology, 1993; BSBA in Adminstrv. Mgmt., U. Ark., Fayetteville, 1986; MBA in Fin., Adam Smith U., 1997; grad., Anthony Robbins Mastery U., 1998; PhD in Fin., Summit U., New Orleans, 1998. Owner Borderman's Reef Apts., Albuquerque, 1986-94, Innovative Concepts, 1995—; agt. Winborn Realtors. Recipient 1st pl. award CNN/U.S.A. Today stock option contest, Atlanta, 1991. Mem. Internat. Assn. Fin. Planners, Exch. Club Am., Louis Rukeyser Wall St. Club (charter mem.), Mercedes Club (charter mem. Ozark chpt., treas. 1998—), Phi Kappa Tau (sec., co-founder 1983-86, treas. Ozark chpt.). Avocations: cars, coin collecting, history, scuba diving. Office: 2367 N Green Acres Rd Ste 118 Fayetteville AR 72703-2832

JACKSON, ROBERT LORING, science and mathematics educator, academic administrator; b. Mitchell, S.D., June 8, 1926; s. Olin DeBuhr and Edna Anna (Hanson) J.; m. Elizabeth Denise Koteski; children: Charles Olin, Catherine Lynne, Cynthia Helen, Aaron J., Hailey E., Adam M.. BS, Hamline U., 1950; MA, U. Minn., 1959; PhD, 1965. Tchr. math. and sci., pub. schs., Heron Lake, Minn., 1950-52; tchr. math. Lakewood (Colo.) Sr. High Sch., 1952-53, Nouassuer Air Force Sch. Casablanca, Morocco, 1953-54, Baumholder (Germany) Elem. Sch., 1954-55, U. Minn. Univ. Lab. Sch., Mpls., 1955-60; asst. prof. sci. and math. edn. U. Minn., Mpls., 1965-66, assoc. prof., 1966-70, prof., 1970-94; emeritus prof. 1994—, head sci. and math. edn., 1980-84, assoc. chmn., dir. undergrad. studies, curriculum and instrn., 1984-88, assoc. chmn., 1989-92; vis. prof. Hamline U., St. Paul, 1958, Mont. State U., Bozeman, 1981, Bethel Coll., St. Paul, 1981, No. Mich. U., Marquette, 1983-84; cons. math. Minn. Dept. Edn., St. Paul, 1960-62. Bd. dirs. Oratorio Soc. Minn., Minn. Chorale, Mpls., 1973-88, pres., 1978-80. With U.S. Army, 1944-46. Decorated Purple Heart; recipient First Alumni award 1988, Disting. Teaching award Coll. Edn., U. Minn., 1984. Mem. Nat. Coun. Tchrs. Math. Methodist. Co-author: (book/man series) Laboratory Mathematics, 1975-76. Home: 810 Purple Sage Ter Henderson NV 89015-5692

JACKSON, ROBERT WILLIAM, utility company executive, retired; b. Beaumont, Tex., June 22, 1930; s. Robert and Elizabeth (Watler) J.; m. Theta Ann Watt, Aug. 14, 1959; 1 child, Robert W. Jr. BBA, U. Tex.; MBA, U. Ill. With Gulf States Utilities Co., Beaumont, Tex., 1955-79, sec., chief fin. officer, 1972-74, sec., treas., chief fin. officer, 1974-75, v.p. fin., chief fin. officer, sec., 1975-79; v.p. fin., chief fin. officer, sec. Cen. Ill. Pub. Svc. Co., Springfield, 1979-80, sr. v.p. fin., chief fin. officer, corp. sec., 1980-95, also bd. dirs.; pres., chief exec. officer CIPSCO Investment Co., Springfield, 1990-95, also bd. dirs.; sr. v.p. CIPSCO Inc., Springfield, 1990, also bd. dirs.; ret., 1995; bd. dirs. 1st Bank of Ill. Co., Springfield, 1st Nat. Bank Springfield, Sangamon State U. Found.; bd. govs. Econs. Am. Mem. bus. adv. coun. U. Ill.; bd. dirs. Springfield Symphony Orch., United Way of Sangamon County; adv. bd. St. John's Hosp., Springfield. Served with U.S. Army, 1953-55. Mem. Am. Soc. Corp. Secs., Fin. Execs. Inst., Edison Electric Inst. (fin. exec. com.). Methodist.

JACKSON, RONALD LEE, II, communications educator; b. Cin., Aug. 4, 1970; s. Ronald Lee, sr. and Sharon Marie (Prather) J.; m. Bereatha Ellynne Gould, June 2, 1995; children: Niayah S., Niles. BA, U. Cin., 1991, MA, 1993; PhD, Howard U., 1996. guest lectr. U. Ga., 1997, Howard U., 1998, Rutgers, 1998, Truman State U., 1999. Author: (book) Negotiation of Cultural Identity, 1999; contbr. articles to profl. jours. Recipient All Am. Scholar award, 1995. Mem. Nat. Comm. Assn. (chmn. black caucus 1999), Ea. Comm. Assn. (chmn. internat. divsn. 1999, chmn. voices of diversity divsn. 2000), Nat. Assn. African Ams., Pa. Black Conf. Highter Edn., Omega Psi Phi. Avocations: tennis, table tennis, racquetball, poetry writing, travel. E-mail: rlj6@psu.edu. Office: Pa State U 234 Sparks Bldg University Park PA 16803

JACKSON, ROY, chemical engineering educator; b. Manchester, Eng., Oct. 6, 1931; married 1957; 2 children. BA, Cambridge U., 1954, MA, 1958; DSc chem. engr., U. Edinburgh, 1968. Lectr. chem. engr. U. Edinburgh, 1961-64, reader, 1964-68; prof. Rice U., 1968-77, U. Houston, 1977-82; prof. chem. engr. Princeton U., 1982—. Mem. Brit Inst.Chem. Engrs., Am. Inst Chem. Engrs. Office: Princeton U Dept Chem Engring Princeton NJ 08544

JACKSON, RUDOLPH ELLSWORTH, pediatrician, educator; b. Richmond, Va., May 31, 1935; s. Samuel and Jennie Sue (Williams) J.; m. Janice Diane Ayer, Dec. 26, 1980; children by previous marriage: Kimberley, Rudolph Ellsworth, Kelley. B.S., Morehouse Coll., Atlanta, 1957; M.D., Meharry Med. Coll., 1961. Asst. in hematology St. Jude Children's Research Hosp., Memphis, 1969-72; asst. prof. pediatrics Sch. Medicine, U. Tenn., Memphis, 1969-72; program coordinator Nat. Sickle Cell Disease Program, HEW; chief sickle cell disease br. Nat. Heart, Lung, Blood Inst.; NIH, Bethesda, Md., 1972-76; assoc. prof. pediatrics and child health, assoc. prof. oncology Howard U. Hosp., Washington, 1976-79; prof., chmn. dept. pediatrics Meharry Med. Coll., Nashville, 1979-83; acting chmn. dept. pediatrics Morehouse Sch. Medicine, Atlanta, 1984-90; cons., mem. research coms. Nat. Heart, Lung, Blood Inst., Nat. Cancer Inst., NIH.; chmn. health task force com. for lead elimination, Washington, 1978-79; mem. sickle cell disease adv. com. to Sec. HEW, 1971-72; mem. adv. coun. Nat. Inst. Arthritis, Diabetes, Digestive and Kidney Diseases, NIH; mem. adv. com. childhood lead poisoning prevention, Ctrs. for Disease Control, Dept. Health and Human Svcs, adv. com. on immune practices, mem HIV panel Agy. for Health Care Policy Rsch. Com., also prevention ctrs.; bd. dirs. Assn. Minority Health Professions Schs. AIDS Rsch. Consortium, 1990—, Zambian HIV/AIDS Prevention Program, 1993—. Contbr. articles to profl. publs. Bd. dirs. Alliance To End Childhood Lead Poisoning and Am. Sudden Infant Death Syndrome Inst., Sickle Cell Found. of Ga., Inc., 1997. With USN, 1962-67. Mem. AMA, Am. Acad. Pediatrics, Nat. Med. Assn., Assn. Med. Sch. Pediatric Dept. Chairmen, Sigma Xi, Alpha Omega Alpha. Democrat.

JACKSON, RYNO MARSHALL, forensic psychologist, consultant; b. Reading, Pa., Oct. 12, 1934; s. Jesse and Helen Adelia (Taylor) J.; m. Jacqueline Estelle Coleman, Aug. 10, 1963; children: Michael, David, Tracy. BA in English Edn., Glassboro State U., 1961; MA, Newark State U., 1972; PsyD, Rutgers U., 1985. Cert. sch. psychologist, N.J.; diplomate Am. Coll. Forensic Examiners, Am. Coll. Psychol. Treating Addictions. English tchr. Scotch Plains-Fanwood, N.J., 1961-70; sch. psychologist Plainfield (N.J.) Bd. Edn., 1970-89; forensic psychologist Forensic Psychology, Flemington, N.J., 1989—; cons. Union County Juvenile and Domestic Rels. Ct., Elizabeth, N.J., 1972-82, Middlesex County Coll., Woodbridge, N.J., 1988-92, Greenbrook Acad., Boundbook, N.J., 1990—; adj. prof. Newark State Coll., Union, N.J., 1992-96. Juvenile conf. com. advisor, Plainfield, 1986-87; search and rescue pilot CAP, Linden, N.J., 1975-85; coach Little League Baseball, Plainfield, 1972-78, Pee Wee Football, 1975-78. Mem. APA, N.J. Psychol. Assn., N.J. Assn. Black Psychologists, Internat. Soc. Police Surgeons, Am. Mensa, Am. Coll. Forensic Psychology. Home: 1208 Salem Rd Plainfield NJ 07060-3323 Office: Assocs in Forensic Psychology 260 Rt 202-31 N Flemington NJ 08822

JACKSON, SAMUEL L., actor; b. Washington, Dec. 21, 1948; m. LaTanya Richardson; 1 child, Zoe. Performances include: (TV series) Movin' On, 1972, Ghostwriter, 1992; (TV movies) The Trial of the Moke, 1978, Uncle Tom's Cabin, 1987, Common Ground, 1990, Dead and Alive: The Race for Gus Farace, 1991, Simple Justice, 1993, Assault at West Point, 1994, Against the Wall, 1994; (films) Together for Days, 1972, Ragtime, 1981, Eddie Murphy Raw, 1987, Coming to America, 1988, School Daze, 1988, (voice-over) Mystery Train, 1989, Do The Right Thing, 1989, Sea of Love, 1989, A Shock to the System, 1990, Def by Temptation, 1990, Betsy's Wedding, 1990, Mo' Better Blues, 1990, The Exorcist III, 1990, Goodfellas, 1990, Return of Superfly, 1990, Jungle Fever, 1991 (Best Actor award Cannes International Film Festival), Strictly Business, 1991, Juice, 1992, White Sands, 1992, Patriot Games, 1992, Johnny Suede, 1992, Jumpin' at the Boneyard, 1992, Fathers and Sons, 1992, National Lampoon's Loaded Weapon 1, 1993, Amos & Andrew, 1993, Menace II Society, 1993, Jurassic Park, 1993, True Romance, 1993, Hail Caesar, 1994, Fresh, 1994, Hail Caesar, 1994, The New Age, 1994, Pulp Fiction, 1994, Losing Isiah, 1995, Kiss of Death, 1995, Fluke, 1995, Die Hard With a Vengeance, 1995, The Great White Hype, 1996, Trees Lounge, 1996, The Search for One Eye Jimmy, 1996, A Time to Kill, 1996, The Long Kiss Goodnight, 1996, 187, 1997, Jackie Brown, 1997, Hard Eight, 1997, Eve's Bayou, 1997, Sphere, 1998, Out of Sight, 1998, The Negotiator, 1998, Rules of Engagement, 1999, Mefisto in Onyx, 1999, Star Wars Episode I: The Phantom Menace, 1999, Deep Blue Sea, 1999, others. *

JACKSON, SHELIA LUCYLE, physical education educator, consultant; b. Newport, Ark., Sept. 28, 1960; d. Charles Wayne Jackson nd Marette McCauley Stiritz. *Parents Charles and Marette received their terminal degrees from the University of Arkansas. Charles, born sixth in a family, was a secondary and college teacher and administrator. He worked for the Arkansas Department of Higher Education, and prior to his death, was the Director of Vocational Technical Programs in Arkansas. Marette, the oldest of six, taught primarily college English for more than forty years and was the President of Arkansas Teachers of English (1978). Siblings Charles Junior (Chuck) and Retta Cauley Zumwalt are teachers in Santiago, Chili and Pea Ridge, Arkansas, respectively.* BSE, So. Ark. U., 1981; MEd, U. Ark., 1984; PhD, Tex. Woman's U., 1988. Tchr. phys. edn. and health Crossett (Ark.) H.S., 1982-83; adapted phys. edn. asst. Richardson Ctr., Fayetteville, Ark., 1983-84; instr. NCAA Youth Sports program U. Ark., Fayetteville, 1984-85; biomechs. lab. asst. Tex. Woman's U., Denton, 1986; adapted phys. edn. cons. Duncanville (Tex.) Sch. Dist., 1987; asst. prof., dir. tennis U. Puget Sound, Tacoma, 1987-90; asst. prof. kinesiology U. N.C., Charlotte, 1990-95, U. Ctrl. Ark., Conway, 1995-98; asst. prof. phys. edn. Ark. Tech. U., Russellville, 1998—; coord. elem. conf. U. Ctr. Ark., 1997; cons. Charlotte Observer. Contbr. chpt. to book, articles to profl. jours. Vl. tchr. First Presbyn. Afterschool Program, Conway, 1995; volleyball marathon team mgr. Easter Seals, Charlotte, 1992-93; event coord. Charlotte Mecklenburg Sr. Games, 1992. Recipient Young Alumni award So. Ark. U., 1999; rsch. and tchg. grantee PEAK Performance Techs., 1997, U. Ctrl. Ark., 1996. Mem. AAHPERD (presider 1993), Ark. Alliance for Health, Phys. Edn., Recreation and Dance, Profl. Disc Golf Assn. (chmn. women's com. 1997-98, Women's Disc Golf Rookie of Yr. award 1995, Women's Disc Golf Master World Champion award 1997), Internat. Soc. Biomechanics in Sports, Internat. Fedn. Adapted Phys. Activity. Christian. Avocations: tennis, volleyball, cycling, backpacking, badminton. Home: 279 Pickles Gap Rd Conway AR 72032-8222 Office: Ark Tech U Dept Phys Edn Russellville AR 72801

JACKSON, SHIRLEY ANN, federal agency administrator, physicist; b. Washington DC; d. George Hiter and Beatrice (Cosby) J.; m. Morris A. Washington; 1 son, Alan. B.S. in Physics, M.I.T., 1968, Ph.D., 1973; DSc (hon.) Bloomfield Coll., 1991, Fairleigh Dickinson U., 1993, hon. degree Dr Laws, Villanova, PA, 1996; Research asso. Fermi Nat. Accelerator Lab., Batavia, Ill., 1973-74, 75-76; vis. scientist European Orgn. for Nuclear Research, Geneva, 1974-75; mem. tech. staff AT&T Bell Labs., Murray Hill, N.J., 1976-91; visitor Stanford Linear Accelerator Center, 1976, Aspen Ctr. for Physics, 1976, 77; prof. physics Rutgers U., 1991-95; chairperson Nuclear Reg. Commn., 1995—; pres. Rensselar Poly. Inst., 1998-; mem. com. edn. and employment women in sci. and engring. Nat. Rsch. Coun., 1980—; cons. NSF, 1977, Nat. Rsch. Coun., 1977—; dir. N.J. Resources Corp., Pub. Service Enterprise Group, PSE&G. Mem. ednl. council M.I.T., 1976-80, trustee, 1975-85, 1987—; trustee Lincoln U. (Pa.), 1980—, Rutgers U., 1986—; mem. N.J. Commn. on Sci. and Tech.; mem. Com. Status of Women in Physics, 1986-88. Recipient Candace award Nat. Coalition 100 Black Women, Salute to Policy Makers award Exec. Women of N.J., 1986, Black Achievers in Industry award Harlem YMCA, 1986, N.J. Gov.'s award, 1993; Martin Marietta Corp. scholar, 1964-68; Prince Hall Grand Masons scholar, 1964-68; NSF trainee, 1968-71; Ford Found. fellow, 1971-73; grantee, 1974-75; Martin Marietta Corp. grad. fellow, 1972-73; mem. Assn. for Advancement of Science, (com. on sci., freedom and responsibility), Fellow, Am. Phys. Soc. (mem. com. on status of women in physics 1986—); Fellow, Am. Acad. Arts & Sci, mem. N.Y. Acad. Scis., Nat. Inst. Sci., Nat. Soc. Black Physicists (pres. 1979—), MIT Alumni Assn. (v.p. 1986—), Sigma Xi, Delta Theta Sigma. Editorial adv. bd. Jour. Sci. Tech. and Human Values, 1982—;

contbr. numerous articles to physics jours. Office: Nuclear Regulatory Commn Chmn of the Commn Washington DC 20555*

JACKSON, STANLEY EDWARD, retired special education educator; b. Washington, Sept. 3, 1918; s. Eugene Edward and Inez Christine (Booth) J. BS, Miner Tchrs. Coll., Washington, 1939; MA, Columbia U., 1947, Profl. Diploma, 1948, EdD, 1958; postgrad., Johns Hopkins U., Peabody Inst. Elem. tchr. D.C. Pub. Schs., 1940-58, elem. sch. prin., 1958-66, dir. spl. edn., 1966-72; gov.-at-large Coun. for Exceptional Children, Reston, Va., 1971-72, asst. exec. dir., membership, 1972-82; lectr. Cath. U., Washington, 1965-66, asst. prof. edn., 1967; instr. D.C. Tchrs. Coll., 1971-72; initiator Tchr. Aide Program Spl. Edn. Classes D.C. Pub. Schs., 1968; founder Juvenile Decency Corps Uplift House, 1964; co-planner Mamie D. Lee Sch. Mentally Retarded, 1968. Author: School Organization for the Mentally Retarded, 1973, Educational Strategies and Services for Exceptional Children, 1976. Pres. Area K Bd. Commrs. Youth Coun., Washington, 1959-65; founder UPLIFT Cmty. House, Washington, 1963, pres. Chpt. 49, 1962-64, 1st pres. Fedn. 524, 1965-66; bd. dirs. Found. for Exceptional Children, 1978. With U.S. Army, 1941-45. Recipient Yes I Care award Found. for Exceptional Children, 1992, Stanley E. Jackson scholarship established in his honor Found. for Exceptional Children, 1980; Plaque for Outstanding Cmty. Svc., Commrs. Coun., Washington, 1963, Outstanding Ret. Tchr. award Jr. Citizens Corps, 1979; Stanley E. Jackson spl. edn. award established in his honor Bd. Edn. D.C. Pub. Schs., 1973, Stanley E. Jackson Scholarships established Peabody Prep., Johns Hopkins U., 1989; decorated four Battle Stars WWII, Naples-Foggia, Rome-Arno, So. France, Rhineland. Mem. NEA, AAUP, NAACP, D.C. Congress Parents and Tchrs. (life), Coun. Exceptional Children, Dept. Elem. Sch. Prins., AMVETS, Urban League, Johns Hopkins Assoc. Program, Kappa Delta Pi, Phi Delta Kappa. Avocations: music, numismatics, writing, philanthropy. Home: Apt 703 One E University Pky Baltimore MD 21218

JACKSON, STANLEY WEBBER, psychiatrist, medical historian; b. Montreal, Que., Can., Nov. 17, 1920; came to U.S., 1952; s. Clarence Stanley and Ada D. (Webber) J.; m. Joan Katherine Currie, Aug. 12, 1946. BCom, McGill U., 1941, MD, CM, 1950; MA, Yale U., 1975. Diplomate Am. Bd. Psychiatry and Neurology. Gen. med. intern Royal Victoria Hosp., Montreal, 1950-51; resident in psychiatry Provincial Mental Hosp, Essondale, B.C., Can., 1951-52; resident in psychiatry Pinel Hosp., Seattle, 1952-54, staff psychiatrist, acting med. dir., 1954-57; diploma San Francisco Psychoanalytic Inst., 1962, Seattle Psychoanalytic Tng. Ctr., 1962; pvt. practice Seattle, 1957-64; rsch. fellow Yale U., New Haven, 1964-66, asst. prof., assoc. prof. psychiatry and history of medicine, 1966-75, prof., 1975—, exec. dir. Yale Psychiat. Inst., 1987-89. Author: Melancholia and Depression: From Hippocratic Times to Modern Times, 1986, Case of the Psyche: A History of Psychological Healing, 1999; editor: Observations on Maniacal Disorders (William Pargeter), 1988, Jour. of History of Medicine and Allied Scis., 1992-96; contbr. numerous articles to book revs. to med. jours., chpts. to books. Flying officer RCAF, 1941-45, ETO, PTO. Fellow Am. Psychiat. Assn. (life); mem. Am. Assn. for History Medicine (pres.). Home: 72 Downs Rd Bethany CT 06524-3616 Office: Yale U Sect History of Med 333 Cedar St New Haven CT 06510-3206

JACKSON, STEVE GLEN, health services administrator; b. Brenham, Tex., June 29, 1947; s. L.W. and Lucille Flora (Symank) J.; m. Phyllis Anne Johnson, Apr. 6, 1968; children: Glen Whitfield, Phillip Ryal, Bryn Aubra, Morgan Blair. BA in Psychology, U. Tex., 1968; MS in Health Care Adminstrn., Trinity U., San Antonio, 1980. Commd. 2d lt. Med. Svc. U.S. Army, 1969, advanced through grades to capt., ret., 1978; chief exec. officer Day County Hosp., Webster, S.D., 1980-81, S.E. Ariz. Med. Ctr., Douglas, 1981-87, S.W. Gen. Hosp., San Antonio, 1987-94; owner, chief exec. officer Premier Homecare, San Antonio, 1994-96; chief exec. officer San Antonio Employers Health Alliance, San Antonio, 1996—; bd. dirs. S.W. Gen. Hosp., 1987-94; mem. curriculum adv. com. dept. health care adminstrn. Trinity U., 1990-93, guest lectr., 1989-96; guest lectr. Bapt. Meml. Health Care Sys. Found., San Antonio, 1996. Intramural basketball coach Stinson Mid. Sch., San Antonio, 1995-96; bd. dirs. S.E. Ariz. Med. Ctr., 1981-87, San Antonio Area Pvt. Industry Coun., 1991-93, Econ. Devel. Corp., Douglas, 1986-87, Ariz. Foster Care Program, Phoenix, 1986. Mem. Greater San Antonio Hosp. Coun., Nat. Bus. Group on Health (bd. dirs.), Tex. Bus. Group on Helath, Am. Coll. Healthcare Execs., Nat. Assn. for Home Health. Mormon. Avocations: photography, camping. Home: 11083 Indian Trl Helotes TX 78023-4223 Office: San Antonio Employers Health Alliance 7990 W Ihio San Antonio TX 78230-4715

JACKSON, STEVEN DONALD, English educator; b. Columbus, Ohio, Sept. 2, 1949; s. Alfred Donald and Ruth Eleanor (Junk) J. BS, Ohio State U., 1971, MA, 1982. Staff libr. Ohio State U., Columbus, 1969-70; tchr. dept. chair Madison Plains Schs., London, Ohio, 1971—. Mem. Nat. Coun. Tchrs. English, Ohio Edn. Assn., Madison Plains Edn. Assn., Ohio State Alumni Assn. Republican. Methodist. Avocations: gardening, genealogy, naval history. Home: 4283 Kelnor Dr Grove City OH 43123-2942

JACKSON, STU, professional sports team executive, former university basketball coach; b. Reading, Pa., Dec. 11, 1955; m. Dr. Janet Taylor; four daughters. BA, business administration and management, Seattle U., 1978. Grad. asst. coach U. Oregon, 1981-82, asst. coach, 1982-83; asst. coach Wash. State U., 1983-85; assoc. coach Providence Coll., 1985-87; asst. coach N.Y. Knicks, 1987-89, head coach, 1989-91; dir. basketball ops. NBA, N.Y.C., 1991-92; head coach Univ. Wisc., Madison, 1992-94; pres., gen. mgr. basketball ops. NBA Vancouver expansion team, B.C., Canada, 1994—. NBA Coach of the Month for December, 1989. Office: Vancouver Grizzlies, 800 Griffiths Way, Vancouver, BC Canada V6B 6G1*

JACKSON, SUSANNE LEORA, creative placement firm executive; b. Rochester, N.Y., June 9, 1934; d. Daniel T. and Gertrude (Grantham) Sherriff; m. David K. Jackson, Mar. 12, 1954; children: Jonnie Sheehan, Jaynette Kettler. Student, Santa Fe Sch. Art, 1952-53, Midwestern U., 1953-55. Supr. ANR Prodn. Co., Houston, 1976-83; v.p. Robinhawk Drafting & Design, Houston, 1983-85; pres., CEO, chmn. bd. Houston Creative Connections, 1985-99; advt. & mktg. dir. Geotech Assn., Houston, 1989-90; past pres. Am. Inst. Design & Drafting, 1984-86; CEO NMASS Comm., 1998, Full Svc. Advt. Agy., 1996-99, Houston Tech. Connections, 1996-99, Outsource and Tech. Placement, 1996-99, Houston Creative Svcs., 1998-99, MicroTeach; bd. dirs. HyperDynamics. Design cons.: (mag.) Urbane, 1989-94. Mem. Mus. Fine Arts, Houston, 1988-98, Greater Houston Partnership, 1989-98; bd. dirs. Literacy Advance, 1993—; pres. bd. Literacy Advance, 1999; mem. com. for advt. Gala for U. Houston-Math and Sci. Dept., 1999—; mem. steering com. W.I.C. , Houston Women Bus. Coun., 1999. Recipient Nat. Multimedia award Am. Advt. Fedn., 1999, also regional award. Mem. NAFE, Houston Advt. Fedn. (Silver and Merit awards 1989, Merit award 1990, Bronze award 1991, 2 Bronze awards 1992, 2 Gold and 4 Merit awards 1992, Gold and Bronze awards 1995, 3 Addys for Interactive 1999, 3 Gold Addys for Multimedia, Nat. Addy award 1999, Houston's Top Women Bus. Owners award 1995, 96, 97, Top Tex. Bus. Women Owner award 1997), Greater Heights C. of C. (bd. dirs. 1994—, vice-chmn. 1996), Galleria C. of C., Rotary (treas. 1992, pres.-elect 1993, pres. 1994), U.S. C. of C. (Blue Chip Enterprise award 1993), Heights C. of C. (chairwoman Women in Action 1997); finalist Ernst & Young Entrepreneur of the Yr., 1998. Republican. Episcopalian. Avocations: oil painting, fishing, cooking. Office: Houston Creative Connection 7026 Old Katy Rd Ste 300 Houston TX 77024-3829

JACKSON, TAMMY, basketball player; b. Dec. 3, 1962. B of Recreation, Fla. State U., 1985. Forward-ctr. Solna, Sweden, Chanson Cosmetics, Shizuoka, Japan; forward-ctr. Schio, Italy, Alcamo, Italy, Ferrara, Italy; forward-ctr. U.Fla; forward-ctr. Limoges, France, St. Andre, Brazil; forward-ctr. WNBA - Houston Comets, 1997—. Recipient U.S. Olypics Team Bronze medal, 1992; named to All-SEC First Team, U.S. Select Team, Nat. Team, World Championship Team, Goodwill Games. Home: 5118 SW 57th Ave Gainesville FL 32608 Office: Houston Comets 2 Greenway Plz Ste 400 Houston TX 77046-0202

JACKSON, THEODORE MARSHALL, retired oil company executive; b. Beaumont, Tex., Oct. 18, 1928; s. Robert and Mary Louise (Watler) J.; m. Maria Pierracou-Dobrowolska Countess de Wernicki de Vladis la Goda, June 19, 1954; 1 child, Mark Andrew. B.B.A. in Engring, U. Tex., Austin, 1951. V.p., sec.-treas. Purvin & Gertz, Inc., Dallas, 1955-71; v.p. treasury and strategic planning New Eng. Petroleum Corp., N.Y.C., 1971-75; v.p. fin. Crown Central Petroleum Corp., Balt., 1975-83; sr. v.p., chief fin. officer Crown Central Petroleum Corp., 1984-91, also bd. dirs. Bd. dirs., treas. Bd. of Child Care; bd. govs. Wesley Theol. Sem. Lt. USNR, 1952-55. Mem. Beta Gamma Sigma, Delta Tau Delta. Republican. Methodist. Home: 8 Wythe Ct Glen Arm MD 21057-9134

JACKSON, THIRSTON HENRY, JR., retired adult education educator; b. Camden, N.J., Mar. 28, 1913; s. Thirston Henry and Elizabeth Loraine (Keck) J.; m. Grace Roberta Ballard, Sept. 26, 1934 (dec. Dec. 1993); 1 child, Diane Jackson Bove. BSEE, Duke U., 1934; MA in Edn., Calif. Luth. U., 1984. Registered profl. engr., Calif.; registered tchr., Calif. Physicist Hughes Aircraft, Hawthorne, Calif., 1932-40; radio engr. Northrop Aviation, Hawthorne, 1940-50; electronic engr. N.Am. Aviation, Inglewood, Calif., 1950-60; sr. design engr. N.Am. Aviation, Downey, Calif., 1960-72; asst. chief engr. Marquardt Aircraft, Van Nuys, Calif., 1972-79; exec. v.p. 21st Century Tech., L.A., 1979-82; tchr. electronics Simi Adult Sch., Simi Valley, Calif., 1982-90; ret., 1990. Patentee automatic navigation device; developer missile navigation heat seeker. Scoutmaster Boy Scouts Am., N.J., 1929-32, N.C., 1932-33, L.A., 1933-54. Mem. Nat. Eagle Scout Assn. (sr.). Avocation: model railroading. Home: 6694 Tremont Cir Simi Valley CA 93063-3945

JACKSON, THOMAS GENE, lawyer; b. N.Y.C., Mar. 9, 1949; s. Alan Clark and Clare Seena (Werther) J.; m. Beatrice Lafrance Korab, June 11, 1972; children: Sarah Ann, Alan Edward. AB magna cum laude in English, Dartmouth Coll., 1971; JD, U. Va., 1974. Bar: N.Y. 1975, U.S. Dist. Ct. (so. and ea. dists.) N.Y. 1975, U.S. Ct. Appeals (2d cir.) 1975, U.S. Ct. Appeals (5th cir.) 1978, U.S. Supreme Ct. 1978, U.S. Ct. Appeals (D.C. cir.) 1986. Editor The Rsch. Group, Charlottesville, Va., 1973-74; assoc. Phillips Nizer Benjamin Krim & Ballon LLP, N.Y.C., 1974-82, ptnr., 1982—; fed. bar coun. com. 2d Cir. Cts., 1997—, chmn. subcom. on tech. in the cts., 1997—. Mem. Village of Irvington Cable TV Adv. Com., N.Y., 1979-91, 95—, chmn. franchise renewal com., 1991-95; sec. Village of Irvington Environ. Conservation Bd., 1983-87, chmn., 1987—; mem. Dartmouth Coll. Alumni Coun., 1986-89. Mem. ABA (sect. antitrust law, Clayton Act com., premerger notification subcom. 1982—), Fed. Bar Coun. (com. 2d cir. cts. 1997—, chmn. subcom. tech. in cts. 1997—), Am. Arbitration Assn. (panel of arbitrators, comml. tribunal 1986—), Assn. of Bar of City of N.Y. (antitrust and trade regulation com. 1988-92, mergers acquisitions and joint ventures subcom. 1991-92), Dartmouth Coll. Club Officers Assn. (exec. com. 1988-91), Dartmouth Coll. Class Secs. Assn. (v.p. 1984-85, pres. 1985-86), Dartmouth Club Westchester (sec. 1984-87, 90—, pres. 1987-90). Home: 32 Hamilton Rd Irvington NY 10533-2311 Office: Phillips Nizer Benjamin Krim & Ballon LLP 666 5th Ave New York NY 10103-0001

JACKSON, THOMAS HAROLD, JR., public relations administrator; b. Atlanta, Dec. 15, 1951; s. Thomas Harold Jackson Sr. and Claire Dickey (Jones) Plymel; m. Sharon Aileen Broome, Nov. 22, 1975; children: Thomas Harold III, Stanley David. AA, Oxford Coll. Emory U., 1971; AB in History, U. Ga., 1973, postgrad., 1973-75; postgrad., Harvard U., 1994. Announcer WLAG AM-FM Radio, LaGrange, Ga., 1970-71; ops. mgr., announcer WGAU/WNGC Radio, Athens, Ga., 1971-74; corr. The Atlanta Constitution, 1974-80; broadcast editor pub. info. dept. U. Ga., Athens, 1974-75; gen. mgr. WLAG/WWCG Radio, LaGrange, 1975-77; news dir. WTRP Radio, LaGrange, 1977-80; reporter, bur. chief WXIA-TV, Atlanta, 1980-88; dir. pub. info. U. Ga., Athens, 1988-97, exec. dir. comm., 1997—; stadium announcer U. Ga. Redcoat Band, Athens, 1974—; pres., bd. dirs. Ga. APBroadcasters, Atlanta, 1986-87, 77-80, 85-88. Del. United Meth. Gen. Conf., St. Louis, 1988, Louisville, 1992; chair Bishop's blue-ribbon study com.; chmn. adminstrv. bd. Athens 1st Meth. Ch., 1993-94, also vice-chmn., lay spkr., mem. fin. coms., staff-parish, stewardship and worship commns.; chmn. Troup Co. Dem. com., LaGrange, 1976-77; mem. U. Ga. Olympic planning com., 1993-96; mem. Athens 96 Olympics coord. com., 1993-96. Recipient reporting awards AP, 1976-82, (10), Pacemaker award AP, 1973, 76, 79, Sch. Bell award Ga. Assn. Educators, 1985; named Disting. Alumnus Oxford Coll. of Emory U., 1989. Mem. Soc. Profl. Journalists, Coun. Advancement and Support of Edn., Athens Area C. of C. (bd. dirs. 1995-97, exec. com. 1995, univ./cmty. rels. com. 1993-94, chair 1994), Phi Kappa Phi, Phi Alpha Theta, Phi Mu Alpha Sinfonia. Avocations: football, reading, writing, singing. Home: 1021 N Rossiter Ter Watkinsville GA 30677-5124 Office: U Ga Comm Alumni House Athens GA 30602

JACKSON, THOMAS HUMPHREY, university president; b. Kalamazoo, June 20, 1950; s. William Humphrey and Louise Longstreth (Cone) J.; m. Bonnie Eileen Gelb; children: Richard, Steven. BA, Williams Coll., Williamstown, Mass., 1972; JD, Yale U., 1975. Bar: N.Y. 1976, Calif. 1979. Law clk. to judge U.S. Dist. Ct. N.Y., 1975-76; law clk. to justice U.S. Supreme Ct., Washington, 1976-77; asst. prof., assoc. prof. to prof. Stanford (Calif.) U. Law Sch., 1977-86; prof. Harvard U. Law Sch., Cambridge, Mass., 1986-88; dean Sch. Law, U. Va., Charlottesville, 1988-91, v.p., provost, 1991-93; pres. U. Rochester, N.Y., 1994—; assoc. Heller, Ehrman, White & McAliffe, San Francisco, 1979-81, spl. counsel, 1981-86; bd. dirs. Rochester Tel.; mem. editl. bd. The Found. Press, Inc. Co-author: (casebooks) Secured Transactions, 1982, 2d edit., 1986, Bankruptcy, 1985, 2d edit., 1990; author: Logic and Limits of Bankruptcy Law, 1986. Trustee George Eastman House; bd. dirs. Kalamazoo Coll. Mem. Nat. Bankruptcy Conf. Office: University of Rochester 240 Wallis Hall Rochester NY 14627-0011

JACKSON, THOMAS PENFIELD, federal judge; b. Washington, Jan. 10, 1937; s. Thomas Searing and May Elizabeth (Jacobs) J. A.B. in Govt., Dartmouth Coll., 1958; LL.B., Harvard U., 1964. Bar: D.C., Md., U.S. Supreme Ct. 1970. Assoc., ptnr. Jackson & Campbell, P.C., Washington, 1964-82; U.S. dist. judge U.S. Dist. Ct. D.C., Washington, 1982—. Vestryman All Saints' Episcopal Ch., Washington, 1969-75; trustee Gallaudet Univ., Washington. Served to lt. (j.g.) USN, 1958-61. Fellow Am. Coll. Trial Lawyers; mem. ABA, Bar Assn. D.C. (pres. 1982-83), Rotary. Republican. Clubs: Chevy Chase, Metropolitan, Lawyers', Barristers. Office: US Dist Ct US Courthouse 3rd & Constitution Ave NW Washington DC 20001

JACKSON, TRACEY LEIGH, health care organization administrator; b. June 6, 1968. BA in Polit. Sci., U. S.C., 1990, MPA, 1998. Exec. dir. Piedmont Care Consortium, Inc., Spartanburg, 1998—. Home: PO Box 4650 Spartanburg SC 29305

JACKSON, VALERIE PASCUZZI, radiologist, educator; b. Oakland, Calif., Aug. 25, 1952; d. Chris A. and Janice (Mayne) Pascuzzi; m. Price A. Jackson, Jr., July 24, 1976; children: Price Arthur III. AB, Ind. U., 1974, MD, 1978. Diplomate Am. Bd. Radiology. Intern, resident in diagnostic radiology Ind. U. Med. Ctr., 1978-82; from asst. prof. radiology to prof. radiology Ind. U. Sch. Medicine, Indpls., 1982-94, John A. Campbell prof. radiology, 1994—; dir. residency program radiology Ind. U. Sch. Medicine, 1994—. Contbr. over 50 articles to profl. jours., chpts. to books. Fellow Am. Coll. Radiology (chair 3 coms.), Soc. Breast Imaging (pres. 1990-92); mem. AMA, Am. Inst. Ultrasound in Medicine, Am. Roentgen Ray Soc., Radiol. Soc. N.Am., Alpha Omega Alpha. Office: Indiana U Sch Med Dept Rad 1001 W 10th St Indianapolis IN 46202-2859

JACKSON, VICTOR LOUIS, retired naturalist; b. Thanh-Hoa, Annam, Vietnam, July 2, 1933; s. Richmond Merrill and Hazel Irene (Peebles) J.; m. Lois Annetta Scott, Apr. 4, 1959 (div. Oct. 1991); children: Nathan Ray, Sharon Ruth (Jackson) Maxwell. B.S., Wheaton Coll., (Ill.), 1955. Sub-dist. ranger Natchez Trace Pkwy., Collinwood, Tenn., 1958-61; park naturalist Gt. Smoky Mountains Nat. Park, Gatlinburg, Tenn., 1961-63; chief park naturalist Organ Pipe Cactus Nat. Monument, Ajo., Ariz., 1963-66; asst. chief naturalist Grand Teton Nat. Park, Moose, Wyo., 1966-73; chief park naturalist Zion Nat. Park, Springdale, Utah, 1973-88; assn. coordinator Zion Natural History Assn., Springdale, 1973-88; ret. Springdale, 1988. Author, photographer: Discover Zion, 1978, in pictures, Zion, The Continuing Story, 1989; editor: Plants of Zion, 1976, Zion Adventure Guide, 1978, Pipe Spring and the Arizona Strip, 1984, The Sculpturing of Zion, 1984, Zion Album, A Nostalgic History of Zion Canyon, 1986, Hiking in Zion National Park: The Trails, 1988, Exploring the Back-country of Zion National Park: Off-Trail Routes, 1988, Zion National Park: Towers of Stone, 1988. Bd. dirs. So. Utah Folklife Festival, 1976-88, God's Refuge, Inc., Dewey, Ariz., 1998-99; vol. naturalist Zion Nat. Pk., 1988-91, Prescott Pines Bapt. Camp, Prescott, Ariz., 1992—; naturalist Prescott Nat. Forest Interpretive Vol. Corps, 1996-98. Capt. Signal Corps U.S. Army, 1955-57. Named Outstanding Interpreter of Yr. in Nat. Park Service, Nat. Parks and Conservation Assn., 1982; recipient Freeman Tilden award, 1982. Republican. Baptist.

JACKSON, W. BRUCE, ophthalmology educator, researcher; b. Peterborough, Ont., Can., May 2, 1943; s. William Herbert and Marjorie Powell (Robinson) J.; m. Mary Lou Sparrow, May 13, 1967; children: David, Julie Alicia. MD, U. Western Ont., 1967. Diplomate Am. Bd. Ophthalmology. Intern Royal Victoria Hosp., Montreal, Que., 1967-68, resident in ophthalmology, 1968-72; prof., chmn. dept. ophthalmology McGill U., Que., 1987-91; prof., chmn. dept. ophthalmology, dir Eye Inst. U. Ottawa, 1991—. Fellow Royal Coll. Physicians and Surgeons. Avocations: skiing, swimming, tennis, golf. Office: U Ottawa Eye Inst, 501 Smyth, Ottawa, ON Canada K1H 8L6

JACKSON, WARD, artist; b. Petersburg, Va., Sept. 10, 1928; s. Julian Bradley and Evie Allen (Jones) J. BFA, Richmond Profl. Inst. of Coll. of William and Mary, 1951, MFA, 1952; postgrad., Hans Hofmann Sch. Fine Arts, 1952. Co-editor Folio mag., 1949-50; instr. art history, dir. Morse Gallery Art Rollins Coll., 1954-55; head of viewing program, archivist Solomon R. Guggenheim Mus., 1955-94; co-editor Art Now: N.Y., 1969-72; adv. editor Art Now Gallery Guide, 1969—. One-man shows include Fleischman Gallery, N.Y.C., 1958-60, Outer Banks Gallery, Kill Devil Hills, N.C., 1958-73, Va. Mus. Fine Arts, Richmond, 1971, 73, Dept. Art, U. Wis., 1967, Atrium Gallery, Seattle, 1965, Graham Gallery, N.Y.C., 1972, Wilhelm Lehmbruck Mus. der Stadt Duisberg, Germany, 1973, Fine Arts Ctr. Gallery, Ocean County Coll., Toms River, N.J., 1973, Stowe Galleries, Cunningham Arts Ctr., Davidson (N.C.) Coll., 1975, Kendall Galllery, N.Y.C., 1985, J.N. Herlin, N.Y.C., 1986, Galerie Adlung & Kaiser, Berlin, 1988, Museum Morsbroich, Stadtisches Museum Leverkusen, 1991, Kunsthalle Bremen, 1992; exhibited in group shows Am. Abstract Artists, N.Y.C., 1949—, New Art Circle J.B. Neumann Gallery, N.Y.C., 1950-52, Contemporary Arts Gallery, N.Y.C., 1953-56, Art USA, 1958, John Daniels Gallery, N.Y.C., 1964-65, The Contemporaries, N.Y.C., 1965, Phoenix Gallery, N.Y.C., 1966, Coll. of William and Mary, 1967, White House, Washington, 1968, Riverside Mus., N.Y.C., 1968-70, French & Co., N.Y.C., 1971, A.M. Sachs Gallery, N.Y.C., 1971, Hall Galleries, Miami, Fla., 1972, Buecker & Harpsichords, N.Y.C., 1973-82, Terrain Gallery, N.Y.C., 1975-79, Arte Fiere, Bologna, Italy, 1978, Galerie Circulus, Bonn, Fed. Republic Germany, 1978, Inst. Contemporary Art, Richmond, 1980, Summit (N.J.) Art Ctr., 1981, City Gallery, N.Y.C., 1982, Anderson Gallery, Richmond, 1982, Moody Art Gallery, Tuscaloosa, ala., 1983, Westherspoon Gallery, Chapel Hill, 1983, A.I.R. Invitational, N.Y.C., 1984-88, Bronx Mus. of the Arts, N.Y.C., 1985, 86, Columbia (S.C.) Mus. Art, 1987-88, Konkret Sieben, Nürnberg, Kunsthaus, Nürnberg, 1987, Todd Capp Gallery, N.Y.C., 1987, participated in Selections from the Am. Abstract Artists, 1988-92, (exhibition travelled throughout Can. and Europe), Centro Cultural de la Villa, Madrid, 1989, Marilyn Pearl Gallery, N.Y.C., 1988-90, Neuberger Mus., Purchase, N.Y., 1989, Solomon R. Guggenheim Mus., N.Y.C., 1987-90, Marymount Manhattan Coll. Gallery, N.Y.C., 1990, Kyusendo Gallery, Kobe, Japan, 1989-90, Edwin A. Ulrich Mus. Art Wichita State U., Kans., 1992, Noyes Art Mus., Oceanville, N.J., 1994, N.J. State Mus., Trenton, 1995, James Howe Gallery, Kean Coll., Union, N.J., 1996, Westbeth Gallery, N.Y., 1996, Castle Gallery, Coll. New Rochelle (N.Y.), 1996, Sidney Mishkin Gallery, Baruch Coll., N.Y.C., 1996, Mary Washington Coll. Gallery, Fredericksburg, Va., 1996, Gibbes Mus. Art, Charleston, S.C., 1997, Sunrise Mus., Charleston, W.Va., 1997, Condeso-Lawler Gallery, N.Y., 1997, Polk Mus. Art, Lakeland, Fla., 1998; represented in permanent collections Nat. Mus. Am. Art, Smithsonian Instn., Elvehjem Art Mus., U. Wis., Bibliotheque Nationale, Paris, Riverside Mus. Collection, Rose Art Mus., Brandeis U., NYU Art Collection, Va. Mus. Fine Arts, Wilhelm Lehmbruck Mus. der Stadt Duisberg, Stowe Galleries, Cunningham Arts Ctr., Davidson Coll., Brit. Mus., London, Solomon R. Guggenheim Mus., Kunsthalle Bremen Met. Mus. Art, Bklyn. Mus., Anderson Gallery, Va. Commonwealth U., N.J. State Mus., Walker Art Ctr., Neuberger Mus., San Francisco Mus. Modern Art, Mus. Fine Arts, Houston, Columbia Mus., S.C., Museum Morsbroich, Stadtisches Museum Leverkusen, Stiftung für Konstructive und Konkrete Kunst, Zurich, Biblioteca di Galleria Nazionale d'Arte Moderna, Rome. Recipient 1st prize for painting N.Y.C. Ctr.Gallery, 1956, cert. of distinction Va. Mus. Fine Arts, 1963, 66, 71, Materials award Com. for Visual Arts, 1985; Nat. Endowment for Arts Artists fellow, 1975-76; Richard A. Florsheim Art Fund grantee, 1991-92. Mem. Coll. Art Assn. Am., Am. Abstract Artists. Home: 152 Forsyth St New York NY 10002-2944

JACKSON, WAYNE SAMUEL, university administrator, communications educator; b. Salem, N.J., Dec. 8, 1958; s. Samuel and Edna (Garlic) J.; m. Rochell Harris, Aug. 27, 1988; children: Taroy, Emmanuel, Joshua. BS in Mass Comm., Norfolk (Va.) State U., 1981; MA in Family Life Edn., Dallas Theol. Sem., 1994. Anchor, beat reporter WTAR-AM, Norfolk, 1983-84, Va. News Network, Richmond, 1984-86; mgr. 2s T-Shirt Emporium, Woodstown, N.J., 1986-87; admissions counselor Mercer County C.C., Trenton, N.J., 1987-94; asst. dir. admissions The Coll. of N.J., Trenton, 1994—; adj. prof. Mercer County C.C., 1993-95, Burlington County Coll., Pemberton, N.J., 1996—; presenter workshops in field. Bd. dirs. Equinox Cmty. Partnership, Pennsauken, N.J., 1994—; tchr. Sunday sch. Christian Stronghold Bapt. Ch., Phila., 1989—, dir. audio/visual ministry, 1998—. Recipient Best Spot News and Best Continuing Story awards UPI, Va., 1984, AP, Va., 1984. Mem. Minority Exec. Coun. (v.p. 1996-98, chair 1998—), Internat. Mentoring Assn., Mid. States Assn. Coll. Registrars and Officers of Admission (planning com. 1992-94). Home: 124 Eastbrook Ln Willingboro NJ 08046-2225

JACKSON, WENDY S LEWIS, social worker; b. Grand Rapids, Mich., May 9, 1965; d. Thomas James and Karen Susan (Kinard) L. BS, U. Mich., 1987, MSW, 1989. Investigator def. D.C. Pub. Defender Officer, Washington, 1985; program asst. Detroit Urban League, 1989; coord. housing Ann Arbor (Mich.) Housing Commn., 1989-90; sr. assoc. United Way, Grand Rapids, 1990-93; program coord. The Grand Rapids Found., 1993-94, program dir., 1994—; mgr. database Kent County Emergency Needs Task Force, Grand Rapids, 1990—, editor, 1990—; sec. Kent County Emergency Food Subcom., Grand Rapids, 1990—; mem. Kent County Domestic Violence Coordinating Com., Grand Rapids, 1990—; mem. pub. affairs com. Mich. League for Human Svcs., Lansing, 1990—; adj. prof. Grand Valley State U. Sch. of Social Work, 1994—. Contbr. articles to profl. jours. Vol. Blodgett Meml. Med. Ctr., Grand Rapids, 1982—; mem. task force Citizens League, Grand Rapids, 1990—; mem. pub. affairs task force United Way, Lansing, 1990—. Recipient Leadership award Kiwanis Club, 1983; Old Kent Bank and Trust scholar, 1983-87. Mem. NASW, Nat. Assn. Black Social Workers, U. Mich. Social Work Govs. (bd. mem. 1991—), U. Mich. Alumni Assn., Women's Leadership Coun., Urban League. Democrat. Episcopalian. Avocations: tennis, racquetball, photography, travel. Home: 16534 Huntington Rd Detroit MI 48219-4072 Office: The Grand Rapids Found 209-C Waters Bldg 161 Ottawa Ave NW Ste 209C Grand Rapids MI 49503-2757

JACKSON, WILFRIED, banker; b. Lima, Peru, Feb. 15, 1955; came to U.S., 1970; s. Jack and Beni (Rivera) J.; m. Lina Belkis Leon, June 18, 1981 (div. June 1984); m. Linda Sue Matheney, Aug. 31, 1985; children: Nichole Brooke, Blake Wilfried. AS, Miami Dade C.C., 1977; BSEE, Fla. Internat. U., South Miami, 1980, BSIE, 1981. Prodn. ops. ACR Electronics, Hollywood, Fla., 1979-80; mgr. field svcs. ops. Modems Plus, Miami Lakes, Fla., 1980-82; mgr. complex sys. integration Timeplex-Unisys, Tampa, Fla., 1982-84; mgr. advanced Telecomm. sys. Bank of Am.-Internat., Miami, 1984-86; mgr. C.I.O. consumer bank Citibank N.A., Ft. Lauderdale, Fla., 1986-95; pres., CEO Citibank Nev., The Lakes, 1995—; bd. dirs. Nev. Devel. Authority, Las Vegas; mem. adv. bd. Nev. Capital Devel. Corp., Las Vegas, 1995—. Contbr. articles to profl. jours. Mem. Nev. Bankers Assn. (bd. dirs. 1996—). Republican. Presbyterian. Avocation: flying. Home: 8309 Opal Cove Dr Las Vegas NV 89128-7701 Office: Citibank (Nev) NA 8725 W Sahara Ave Las Vegas NV 89164-0001

JACKSON, WILLIAM DAVID, research executive; b. Edinburgh, Scotland, May 20, 1927; came to U.S., 1955, naturalized, 1968; s. Joseph and Margaret (Johnston) J.; children—Margaret Eleanor, David Foster. B.Sc., U. Glasgow, Scotland, 1947, Ph.D., 1960; postgrad., U. Strathclyde, Glasgow, 1948. Apprentice English Electric Co., Stafford, 1945-47; research asst. elec. engring. dept. U. Strathclyde, Glasgow, 1948-51; lectr. elec. engring. U. Manchester, Eng., 1951-55, 57-58; vis. lectr. dept. elec. engring. MIT, 1955-57, asst. prof., 1958-62, assoc. prof., 1962-66, lectr. elec. engring., 1968-73; vis. prof. Tech. U., Berlin, Germany, 1966; prof. elec. engring., dept. energy engring. U. Ill., Chgo., 1966-67; prin. research scientist, dir. tech. edn. Avco-Everett Research Lab., Everett, Mass., 1967-72; prof. elec. engring. U. Tenn. Space Inst., Tullahoma, 1972-73; mgr. Electric Power Research Inst., Palo Alto, Calif., 1973-74; mgr. office coal research Interior Dept., Washington, 1974-75; dir. magnetohydrodynamic div. ERDA, Washington, 1975-77; dir. tech. analysis div. Office Energy Research, Dept. Energy, Washington, 1977-79; pres. Energy Cons., Inc., 1979-84, HMJ Corp., 1982—; professorial lectr. George Washington U., 1979-91, vis. prof. 1986-87, adj. prof., 1991—; cons. numerous indsl. firms and govt. agys., 1948—; bd. mem. Hexogon Inc., 1997—; mem. internat. magnetohydrodynamic liaison group, 1966—, chmn., 1969-74, sec., 1986—; coord. coop. program magnetohydrodynamic power generation, U.S.-USSR, 1974-79, mem. numerous govt. and internat. coms. and panels. Editor: Electricity From MHD, 1968; editorial bd.: Internat. Jour. Elec. Engring. Edn, 1962-70; editor-in-chief Magnetohydrodynamics: An Internat. Jour., 1987-92. U.K. Fulbright scholar, 1955-57. Fellow Instn. Elec. Engrs. (past com. sec., chmn.), IEEE (sec.-treas. prof. group biomed. electronics Boston sect. 1962-63, energy devel. subcom. 1973—, chmn. 1988-98, energy devel. and power gen. com. 1986—, mem. steering com. intersoc. energy conversion engring. conf. 1988—, conf. program chair 1989, conf. gen. chair 1996), ASME (past chmn. adv. energy systems divn., energy com. 1986-90); mem. AIAA (Energy Sys. award 1995), AAUP, AAAS, Am. Phys. Soc., Am. Soc. Engring. Edn., Sigma Xi. Office: 2814 Jutland Rd Kensington MD 20895-2840

JACKSON, WILLIAM ELDRED, lawyer; b. Jamestown, N.Y., July 19, 1919; s. Robert Houghwout and Irene Alice (Gerhart) J.; m. Nancy Dabney Roosevelt, Sept. 24, 1944; children—Miranda, Melissa, Melanie, Melinda, Marina. BA, Yale U., 1941; LLB, Harvard U., 1944. Bar: N.Y. 1944, U.S. Supreme Ct. 1952, D.C. 1960. Assoc. Milbank, Tweed, Hadley & McCloy, N.Y.C., 1947-54; ptnr. Milbank, Tweed, Hadley & McCloy, 1954—; chmn. appellate div. 1st Dept. Disciplinary Com., 1985-90; vice chmn. Internat. Ct. Arbitration, 1988-94. Mem. staff Nuremburg trial; trustee Supreme Ct. Hist. Soc., 1987—. Lt. (j.g.) USNR, 1944-46. Mem. Am. Coll. Trial Lawyers, Am. Soc. Internat. Law, Assn. Bar City N.Y. (sec. 1953-54), N.Y. State Bar Assn., ABA, Fed. Bar Coun., Am. Judicature Soc., Coun. Fgn. Rels., Century Club, Downtown Club, Pilgrims Club, River Club. Democrat. Episcopalian. Home: 530 E 72nd St New York NY 10021-4855 Office: Milbank Tweed Hadley & McCloy 1 Chase Manhattan Plz Fl 47 New York NY 10005-1413

JACKSON, WILLIAM GENE, computer company executive; b. Opelika, Ala., Nov. 22, 1946; s. John Willis and Lucy (Jackson) J.; m. Rosalyn Miller, June 17, 1989; children: Verzelia Yvett, Gena Nichole, William Gene, Alisa, Claire Bennett. BS in Mgmt. and Mktg., Syracuse U., 1979, AAS in Mgmt., 1976; postgrad., Pace U. With IBM, 1966—; customer engr. IBM, Huntsville, Ala., 1966-72; sr. customer engr. IBM, Atlanta, 1972-73; field mgr. IBM, Miami, Fla., 1973-75; eastern region ops. analyst IBM, Harrison, N.Y., 1975-76; br. mgr. N.Y.C., 1976; region ops. mgr. region 3 Montvale, N.J., 1977-78; employee rels. program mgr. pers., office products divsn. hdqrs. Franklin Lakes, N.J., 1979; adminstrv. asst. to dir. ops. west, office products divsn. hdqs. Franklin Lakes, 1980; IBM corp. svc. staff Armonk, N.Y., 1981-82; adminstrv. asst. to pres. customer svc. divsn. Franklin Lakes, 1983; region mgr. customer svc. divsn., region 7 Southfield, Mich., 1983-84; dir. svc. support Nat. Svc. divsn. Area 4, 1984-87, regional mgr., 1987-92, dir. quality U.S. Great Lakes area 4, 1992-95, corp. dir. teleops., 1995-98, dir. copr. mktg. global call cttrs., 1998—; mem. Corp. Telecomm. Coun., IBM, Worldwide Call Ctr. Ops. Bd., Steering Bd., Internat. Quality and Productivity Bd. Bd. dirs. spl. affairs Jaycees, Wanaque, N.J., 1978-79; mem. Black exec. exch. program Nat. Urban League. Mem. Am. Mgmt. Assn., Am. Exec. Mgmt. Excellence, Am. Execs. for Mgmt. Excellence, Am. Soc. for Quality Control. Home: 30552 Sunderland Dr Farmington MI 48331-5909 Office: IBM Corp 18000 W 9 Mile Rd Southfield MI 48075-4009

JACKSON, WILLIAM PAUL, JR., lawyer; b. Bexar, Ala., July 7, 1938; s. William Paul and Evelyn Mabel (Goggans) J.; m. Barbara Anne Seignious, Sept. 30, 1966; children: Jennifer Anne, Susan Barrett, William Paul III. BS in Physics, U. Ala., 1960, JD, 1963. Bar: Ala. 1963, D.C. 1969, Va. 1975. Law clk. to judge Ala. Ct. Appeals, Montgomery, 1965; assoc. Bishop and Carlton, Birmingham, Ala., 1965-68, Todd, Dillon and Sullivan, Washington, 1968-70; founding ptnr. Jackson & Jessup, Arlington, Va., 1970-76; pres., sr. atty. Jackson & Jessup, PC, Arlington, Va., 1976—; advisor Oren Harris chair of transp. U. Ark., 1974-91. Comments editor U. Ala. Law Rev., 1962, leading articles editor, 1963; conbtr. articles to profl. jours. V.p. McLean Hunt Homeowners Assn., Va., 1974, pres., 1975-76; bd. dirs. McLean Citizens' Assn., 1976-78; pres. McLean Legal Action Fund, Inc., 1977-81; session mem. Lewinsville Presbyn. Ch., 1981-84; v.p. The Marjoribanks Family, 1994-96, pres., 1996-98; active The Alexandria Chorale, 1985-94. 1st lt. Signal Corps, U.S. Army, 1963-65. Recipient Pub. Service awards Am. Radio Relay League, 1958, Merit award Armed Forces Comm. and Electronics Assn., 1963; Sigma Delta Kappa scholar, 1963. Mem. ABA, Arlington Bar Assn., Fed. Bar Assn., Ala. State Bar, Va. State Bar, D.C. Bar, Va. Bar Assn., Bar Assn. D.C. (chmn. computer tech. com. 1998—), Transp. Lawyers Assn. (chmn. legis. com. 1989-90), Assn. for Transp. Law, Logistics and Policy (nat. pres. 1991-92, chmn. nominating com. 1992-93, chmn. membership com. 1993-99, chmn. D.C. chpt. 1989-90, com. govtl. rels. 1975-90, motor editor Assn. Highlights 1992-98, Presdl. award 1994), Am. Judicature Soc., So. Transp. Logistics Assn. (exec. dir. 1970-99), Ea. Indsl. Traffic League (exec. dir. 1978-88), Bench and Bar Legal Honor Soc. (pres. 1963), Omicron Delta Kappa. Presbyterian (elder). Avocation: amateur radio operator. Home: 1003 Spring Hill Rd Mc Lean VA 22102-1331 Office: Jackson & Jessup PC PO Box 1240 3426 N Washington Blvd Arlington VA 22210-0540

JACKSON, WILLIAM VERNON, library science and Latin American studies educator; b. Chgo., May 26, 1926; s. William Olof and Lillian (Scharenberg) J. B.A. summa cum laude, Northwestern U., 1945; M.A., Harvard U., 1948, Ph.D., 1952; M.S. in L.S, U. Ill., 1951; Diploma honoris causa, U. Central Venezuela, 1968. Tchr. York Community High Sch., Elmhurst, Ill., 1946-47; teaching fellow Harvard U., 1948-50; spl. recruit Libr. of Congress, 1951-52; libr., asst. prof. libr. sci. U. Ill., Urbana, 1952-58; assoc. prof. U. Ill., 1958-62, U. Wis., Madison, 1963-65; faculty rsch. fellow, summers U. Wis., 1963, 64; prof. libr. sci., dir. internat. libr. info. ctr. U. Pitts., 1966-70; prof. libr. sci. George Peabody Coll. for Tchrs., 1970-76; prof. Spanish and Portuguese Vanderbilt U., Nashville, 1970-76; prof. libr. sci. U. Tex. at Austin, 1976-86, prof. emeritus, 1986—, assoc. Inst. Latin Am. Studies, 1976—; vis. lectr. U. Minn. Library Sch., summers 1954-56, Columbia U. Sch. Library Service, summers 1960, 90, Syracuse U. Sch. Libr. Sci., summer 1962, Simmons Coll. Sch. Libr. Sci., summer, 1974, 75, Coll. Librarianship, Aberystwyth, Wales, summer 1977, U. Zulia, Maracaibo, Venezuela, summer 1980, Dominican U. Libr. Sci., summers 1981-84, 86, 89-98, Pratt Inst. Sch. Info. & Libr. Sci., summers 1995-98; vis. prof. Inter-Am. Libr. Sch., U. Antioquia, Medellín, Colombia, 1960, 68, adviser internat. exec. coun., 1961-63; cons. State Dept., 1956, 59, 61, 62, 67, 77, Regional AID Office for C.Am. and Panama, 1965-66, AID Mission to Brazil, 1967-72, AID Mission to Colombia, 1970-71, USIA, 1979-80, 85, 87, 89-92, 94-98, OAS, 1970-71; Coun. Rectors Brazilian Univs., 1972; cons. rsch. libs. N.Y. Pub. Libr., 1965-70, Hispanic Found., Library Congress, Washington, 1964-65; Fulbright research scholar, France, 1956-57; Fulbright lectr. U. Córdoba (Argentina), 1958, adviser, 1970; adviser U. San Marcos, Peru, 1962, 75; external examiner U. West Indies, Jamaica, 1974-78; cons. Bibliothèque Nationale, France, 1979, 81-87; official rep. 350th anniversary Harvard U., 1986; lectr. and researcher various librs. and univs. in Australia, Europe, Egypt, Singapore, Turkey, Latin Am. and U.S., 1987—; sr. fellow Dominican U., 1989—; Windsor lectr., U. Ill., 1990; vis. prof. faculty philosophy and letters U. Buenos Aires, 1991; dir. various activities on the Quin centennial and librs. in Latin Am., 1992; adv. U. Francisco Marroquin, Guatemala, 1992—; U. del Norte, Barranquilla, Colombia, 1993; various univs. and librs. in El Salvador, 1994—, Nat. Libr. and Archives Sch., Mexico City, 1995; pres. Coun. Books and Librs. in L.Am., 1993—; lectr. abroad for Centennial, N.Y. Pub. Libr., 1995-96. Author: Basic Library Techniques, 1955, A Handbook of American Library Resources, 1955, 2d edit., 1962, Studies in Library Resources, 1958, The Foundation Grants Program, 1959, The Libraries of the Associated Colleges of the Midwest, 1960, Aspects of Librarianship in Latin America, 1962, second series, 1992, Library Guide for Brazilian Studies, 1964, The National Textbook Program and Libraries in Brazil, 1967, Resources of Research Libraries, 1969, Steps Toward the Future Development of a National Plan for Library Services in Colombia, 1971, Catalog of Brazilian Acquisitions of Library of Congress, 1964-74, 1977, Resources for Brazilian Studies at the Bibliothèque Nationale, 1980, Library Resources of Harvard University, 1986, Resources of Research Libraries: A Bibliographical Guide to Printed Material, 1998; editor: U. Ill. Library Sch. Assn. News Letter, 1954-56, Assn. Coll. Research Libraries Monographs, 1961-66, Latin Am. Collections, 1974, Reference Publications in Latin American Studies, 1977—, Library and Information Science Education in the Americas: Present and Future, 1981, Library and Information Science in France: A 1983 Overview, 1984, Doce Bibliotecarios Latinoamericanos, 1992; mem. editorial staff Libr. Trends, 1958-62, Ency. Libr. and Info. Sci., 1971—, Jour. Libr. History, 1976-88, Internat. Jour. Revs. in Libr. and Info. Sci., 1985-88; assoc. editor World Librs., 1990—; contbr. articles to profl. jours. and encys. Mem. ALA (chmn. internat. relations round table 1965-66, trustee endowment funds 1977-86), Ill. Library Assn., Assn. Library and Info. Sci. Edn., Bibliog. Soc. Am., Assn. Coll. and Research Libraries, MLA, Am. Assn. Tchrs. Spanish and Portuguese, Theatre Library Assn., Conf. on Latin Am. History, Latin Am. Studies Assn., Sem. on Acquisition Latin Am. Library Materials (pres. 1977-78), Assn. Caribbean Univ. and Research Libraries, Asociación Paceña de Bibliotecarios (hon.; La Paz, Bolivia), Phi Beta Kappa, Beta Phi Mu (pres. 1955-56), Phi Sigma Iota, Sigma Delta Pi (hon.), Phi Lambda Beta (hon.). Clubs: Harvard (Chgo.), Caxton (Chgo.). Home: 196 W Kathleen Dr Park Ridge IL 60068-2618 Office: U Tex Sch Libr and Info Sci SZB 564 Austin TX 78712-1276

JACKSON, WILLIAM WARD, chemical company executive; b. Irvington, N.J., Apr. 19, 1913; s. William Henry and Edwina (Ward) J.; m. Rae M. Applegate, Jan. 1, 1943; 1 dau., Hollace D. (Mrs. Tullman). B.S. in Chem. Engring, Newark Coll. Engring., 1936. Prodn., sales positions Celanese Corp. Am. and affiliates, 1932-51; dist. mgr. Washington Office, Celanese Corp. Am., 1945-47; gen. mgr. indsl. chems. dept. Comml. Solvents Corp., N.Y.C., 1951-53; v.p. petrochem. div. Comml. Solvents Corp., 1953-54, v.p. mktg., 1954-72, v.p. mktg. services and purchasing, 1972-75; also dir.; v.p. IMC Chems. Group, 1975-78, corp. cons., 1978-86; pres. Ward Jackson Assoс., 1978—; dollar-a yr- man WPB, 1941-44, asst. to vice chmn., aircraft cons., 1943-44; mem. exec. mgmt. team Nat. Prodn. Authority, Dept. Commerce, Washington, 1952-53; pres., bd. dirs. Can. Carb Ltd., Medicine Hat, Alta., 1975-86; bd. dirs., mem. exec. com. N.W. Nitro Chem. Corp., Medicine Hat, 1959-71; mem. Aircraft Prodn. Bd., 1941-44. Chmn. bd. dirs. Millburn-Short Hills chpt. ARC, 1956-59, bd. dirs., 1954-60; bd. dirs. Animal Health Inst. Recipient Certificate of Achievement U.S. Army; Certificate of Service Dept. Commerce. Fellow Am. Inst. Chemists, Soc. Chem. Industry; mem. Am. Inst. Chem. Engrs., Mfg. Chemists Assn., Pharm. Mfg. Assn., Am. Chem. Soc., Fertilizer Inst. Sales Exec. Club, Newcomen Soc. N.Am., Am. Def. Preparedness Assn. (v.p., dir.), Inst. Food Technologists, Drug Chem. and Allied Trade Assn. (past pres., treas., dir., chmn. adv. council, exec. com.), Am. Ordnance Assn. (dir.), N.Y. Bd. Trade (past dir., exec. com.), Armed Forces Chem. Assn., past nat. dir., exec. com., v.p., past pres.). Clubs: Short Hills (N.J.); Union League (N.Y.C.), Racquet and Tennis (N.Y.C.), N.Y. Yacht (N.Y.C.), Canadian (N.Y.C.); Capitol Hill (Washington). Patentee in field. Home: 2 Brooklawn Dr Short Hills NJ 07078-2104

JACKSON LEE, SHEILA, congresswoman; b. Queens, N.Y., Jan. 12, 1950; m. Elwyn C. Lee; 2 children. BS, Yale U.; JD, U. Va. Sr. counsel select com. on assassinations U.S. Ho. of Reps., 1977; trial atty. Fulbright and Jaworski, 1978-80; sr. atty. United Energy Resources, Inc., 1980; assoc. judge Houston Mcpl. Ct., 1987-89; mem. Houston City Coun., 1990-94, 104th-106th Congress from 18th Tex. dist., 1995—; mem. judiciary com., sci. com. Democrat. Office: US House Reps 410 Cannon Washington DC 20515-4605*

JACKWIG, LEE M., federal judge; b. 1950. BA, Loyola U. of Chgo., 1972; JD, DePaul U., 1975. Asst. atty. gen. State of Iowa, 1976-79, dep. indsl. commr., 1979-83; asst. U.S. atty. S.D. Iowa, Dept. Justice, 1983-86; bankruptcy judge U.S. Bankruptcy Ct. (so. dist.) Iowa, Des Moines, 1986—. Office: US Courthouse Annex 110 E Court Ave Ste 443 Des Moines IA 50309-2044

JACOB, BERNARD MICHEL, architect; b. Paris; naturalized; s. Paul and Therese (Abase) J.; m. Rosamond Gale Tryon; children: Clara, Paul. Diploma in architecture, Cooper Union, 1955; BArch, U. Minn., 1958. Registered architect, Minn. Sr. designer Ellerbe Assocs., St. Paul, 1958-63; head design Grover Dimond & Assocs., St. Paul, 1963-70; co-founder Team 70 Architects, St. Paul, 1970—, pres., 1977-83; pres. Bernard Jacob Architects Ltd., Mpls., 1983—; mem. constrn. panel Am. Arbitration Assn., 1973—; lectr. Sch. Architecture, U. Minn., Mpls., 1982—. Editor: Architecture Minn. Mag., Minn. Soc. Architects, 1970-80; archtl. criticism columnist: Mpls. Star and Tribune, 1980-83, Corp. Report Mag., 1983; reviewer: (archtl. books) Choice Mag.; co-author: Skyway Typology/Mpls., Pocket Architecture/A Walking Guide to the Architecture Downtown Mpls. and St. Paul, 2d. rev. edit., 1988, Letters to Palladio, 1999. Founding chmn. Heritage Preservation Commn., St. Paul; past mem. St. Paul Planning Bd.; apptd. mem. Minn. State Designer Selection Bd., 1987-90; bd. dirs. Winslow House, 1995-97; chmn. archtl. subcom. Minn. Gov.'s Residence Coun., 1996—. Fellow AIA (chair summer design series com. Minn. chpt. 1992, 93, 94, 95). Office: Bernard Jacob Architects Ltd 412 Foshay Tower 821 Marquette Ave S Minneapolis MN 55402-2915

JACOB, BRUCE ROBERT, law educator; b. Chgo., Mar. 26, 1935; s. Edward Carl and Elsie Berthe (Hartmann) J.; m. Ann Wear, Sept. 8, 1962; children: Bruce Ledley, Lee Ann, Brian Edward. BA, Fla. State U., 1957; JD, Stetson U., 1959; LLM, Northwestern U., 1965; SJD, Harvard U., 1980; LLM in Taxation, U. Fla., 1995. Bar: Fla. 1959, Ill. 1965, Mass. 1970, Ohio 1972. Asst. atty. gen. State of Fla., 1960-62; assoc. Holland, Bevis & Smith, Bartow, Fla., 1962-64; asst. to assoc. prof. Emory U. Sch. Law, 1965-69; rsch. assoc. Ctr. for Criminal Justice, Harvard Law Sch., 1969-70; staff atty. Cmty. Legal Assistance Office, Cambridge, Mass., 1970-71; assoc. prof. Coll. Law, Ohio State U., 1971-73, prof., dir. clin. programs, 1973-78; dean, prof. Mercer U. Law Sch., Macon, Ga., 1978-81; v.p., dean, prof. Stetson U. Coll. Law, St. Petersburg, Fla., 1981-94, dean emeritus and prof., 1994—. Contbr. articles to profl. jours. Mem. Fla. Bar, Sigma Chi. Democrat. Home: 1946 Coffee Pot Blvd NE Saint Petersburg FL 33704-4632 Office: Stetson U Coll Law 1401 61st St S Saint Petersburg FL 33707-3246

JACOB, EDWIN J., lawyer; b. Detroit, Aug. 25, 1927; s. A. Aubrey and Estelle R. (Vesell) J.; m. Constance Dorfman, June 15, 1948; children—Louise B., Beth D., Ellen P. AB cum laude, Harvard U., 1948, JD cum laude, 1951. Bar: N.Y. 1951, U.S. Dist. Ct. (so. dist.) N.Y. 1953, U.S. Dist. Ct. (ea. dist.) N.Y. 1953, U.S. Ct. Appeals (2d cir.) 1954, U.S. Supreme Ct. 1963, U.S. Ct. Appeals (8th cir.) 1981, U.S. Ct. Appeals (10th cir.) 1987. Assoc. Davis Polk Wardwell Sunderland & Kiendl, N.Y.C., 1951-62; ptnr. Cabell, Medinger, Forsyth & Decker, N.Y.C., 1962-69, Lauterstein & Lauterstein, N.Y.C., 1969-72, Jacob, Medinger & Finnegan, LLP, N.Y.C., 1973—; bd. advisors Inst. for Health Policy Analysis, Georgetown U., 1987-90. Contbr. articles to profl. jours. Mem. nat. bd. Assn. Ref. Zionists Am., 1991-97; trustee Stephen Wise Free Synagogue, 1991—, pres., 1994-96. With USN, 1945-46. Mem. Am. Law Inst., Am. Judicature Soc., Assn. Bar City N.Y. Club: Harvard of N.Y.C. Office: Jacob Medinger Finnegan LLP 1270 Ave of Americas New York NY 10020

JACOB, ELIZABETH ANN, elementary education educator; b. Highland Park, Mich., May 14, 1950; d. Theodore George and Helen Mae (Kressbach) J. BS, Ea. Mich. U., 1972; MA, Cen. Mich. U., 1976. Tchr. Tawas City (Mich.) Elem. Sch., 1972—; dir. region II MCTM, 1995. Sunday sch. tchr. Zion Luth. Ch., Tawas City, 1976-89, mem. bd. edn., 1990, mem. bd. fin., 1995-96; instr. water safety Oscoda-Iosco County chpt. ARC, 1979-90; treas., master gardener, Animal Humanitarians Iosco, 1995—. Office: Tawas City Elem Sch 825 2nd St Tawas City MI 48763-9191

JACOB, ELLIS, entertainment company executive; b. Calcutta, India, Oct. 5, 1953; arrived in Can., 1969; s. Raymond and Tryphosa Jacob; m. Sharyn Orzech, July 2, 1978; children: Lauren, Resa. B Commerce, McGill U., Montreal, Que., Can., 1974; M Bus., York U., Toronto, Ont., Can., 1976. Chartered acct., Ont., Que.; cert. mgmt. acct., Ont. Various fin. positions Ford Motor Co., 1977-80; contr. Motorola Can. Ltd., Toronto, Ont., Can., 1981-87; v.p., corp. contr. Cineplex Odeon Corp., Toronto, 1987-88, sr. v.p., 1989, exec. v.p., CFO,, 1989-97; exec. v.p., COO, Cineplex Odeon Can., Toronto, 1997-98; pres., head integration alliance Atlantis Comm. Inc. Laures Cons. Ltd., Toronto, 1998—; bd. dirs. Alliance Atlantis Comm. Inc. Mem. Inst. Chartered Accts., Inst. Mgmt. Accts. Fax: 416-934-6900. Office: Laures Consulting, 53 Harrison Rd, North York, ON Canada M2L 1V7

JACOB, FRANÇOIS, biologist; b. Nancy, France, June 17, 1920; s. Simon and Therese (Franck) J.; m. Lysiane Bloch, Nov. 27, 1947 (dec. 1984); children: Pierre, Laurent, Odile, Henri; m. Geneviève Barrier, 1999. M.D., Faculty of Medicine, Paris, 1947; D.Sc., Faculty of Scis., Paris, 1954; D.Sc. (hon.), U. Chgo., 1965. Asst. Pasteur Inst., 1950-56, head dept. cellular genetics, 1960-92, pres., 1982-88; prof. cellular genetics Coll. of France, 1964-92; prof. emeritus Coll. of France and Inst. Pasteur, 1992—. Author: The Logic of Life, 1970; The Possible and the Actual, 1981, The Statue Within, 1987, Of Flies, Mice and Men, 1997. Recipient Charles Leopold Mayer prize, 1962; Nobel prize in physiology and medicine (with A. Lwoff and J. Monod), 1965. Mem. Académie des Sciences (Paris), Académie française Paris; fgn. mem. Royal Danish Acad. Scis. and Letters, Am. Acad. Arts and Scis., Nat. Acad. Scis. (U.S.), Am. Philos. Soc., Royal Soc. (London), Académie Royale de Médecine de Belgique, Acad. Scis. Hungary, Royal Acad. Scis. Madrid. Rsch. on genetics bacterial cells and viruses; contbr. to mechanisms of info. transfer (messenger RNA) and genetic basis of regulatory circuits, early stages of the mouse embryo. Office: Pasteur Inst, 25 Rue du Dr Roux, 75724 Paris Cedex 15, France

JACOB, MARVIN EUGENE, lawyer; b. N.Y.C., Feb. 4, 1935; s. Sam Jacob and Ann (Garfinkel) Law; m. Atara Binnun, Mar. 27, 1960; children: Shalom J., Aviva, Asher. BA, Bklyn. Coll., 1961; JD cum laude, N.Y. Law Sch., 1964. Bar: N.Y. 1964, U.S. Supreme Ct. 1967. Assoc. regional adminstr. SEC, N.Y.C., 1964-79; ptnr. Weil, Gotshal & Manges, N.Y.C., 1979—; adj. prof. law N.Y. Law Sch., 1975—. Editor: Restructurings, 1993. Mem. ABA, N.Y. State Bar Assn. Office: Weil Gotshal & Manges 767 5th Ave Fl Concl New York NY 10153-0119

JACOB, PAUL BERNARD, JR., electrical engineering educator; b. Columbus, Miss., June 9, 1922; s. Paul Bernard and Sarah Dorsey (Jamison) J.; m. Mildred Evelyn Hammack, Aug. 20, 1946; children: William Boswell, Paul Bernard, III. B.S. in Elec. Engring., Miss. State U., 1944; M.S., Northwestern U., 1948. Registered profl. engr., Miss. Engr., Tenn. Eastman Corp., Oak Ridge, 1944-46; mem. faculty Miss. State U., 1946-88, prof. elec. engring., 1956-88, prof. emeritus, 1988—, assoc. head dept., 1962-88; cons. in field; mem. steering com. Internat. Symposium on High Voltage Engring., 1987—. Author articles on high voltage engring. Recipient Alumnus of Yr. award Miss. State U., 1987, UOP Tech. award Instrument Soc. Am., 1988. Mem. IEEE (life), Power Engring. Soc. (chmn. com., Com. Disting. Svc. award), Am. Soc. Engring. Edn., Sigma Xi, Tau Beta Pi, Eta Kappa Nu (dir. 1962-63, nat. v.p. 1982-83, nat. pres. 1983-84), Phi Kappa Phi, Sigma Alpha Epsilon (bd. dirs. 1961-69, nat. pres. 1969-71, Disting. Svc. award 1975, Highest Effort award for profl. accomplishments 1986, Merit Key award, Order of the True Gentleman 1994), Omicron Delta Kappa. Baptist. Club: Rotary (past pres. Starkville, Miss.). Home and Office: 908 Lakewood Dr Starkville MS 39759

JACOB, ROBERT ALLEN, surgeon; b. Cleve., July 25, 1941; s. John B. and Elaine Irene (Puleo) J.; m. M. Elaine Sheppard, Aug. 23, 1980; children: Kristen Elizabeth, Alexandra Elaine. BA, Case Western Res. U., 1963; MSc, Ohio State U., 1966, MD, 1969. Diplomate Am. Bd. Orthopaedic Surgeons, Am. Acad. Pain Mgmt. Orthopaedic surgeon Bluegrass Orthop. Group PSC, Louisville, 1976—; pres. med. staff Sts. Mary & Elizabeth Hosp., Louisville, 1991—; med. dir. Ky. Pain Therapy Ctr. Contbr. articles to profl. jours. Local fundraising chmn. Orthop. Edn. and Rsch. Found., Sts. Mary & Elizabeth Hosp., 1990-91; bd. dirs. Kentuckiana Hemophilia Found., 1987-89, Hosp. Found., 1991-93. Maj. U.S. Army, 1974-76. Recipient Outstanding Svc. award Kentuckiana Hemophilia Found., 1986, Cert. of Recognition, 1987. Fellow Am. Acad. Orthopaedic Surgeons; mem. Ky. Med. Assn., Southern Med. Assn., Jefferson County Med. Assn., Louisville Orthopaedic Assn., Louisville Soc. Physicians and Surgeons (v.p. 1980, pres. 1984). Republican. Roman Catholic. Avocations: photography, horticulture, scientific instrument collector. Home: 7512 Chestnut Hill Dr Prospect KY 40059-9484 Office: Bluegrass Orthop Group 1900 Bluegrass Ave Ste 203 Louisville KY 40215-1144

JACOB, ROBERT EDWARD, small business and non-profit tax consultant; b. Detroit, June 14, 1954; s. John Joseph and Eleanore Alice (Grates) J.; m. Mary Louise Teran, July 8, 1983; children: Matthew, Autumn, Jason. BA, Mich. State U., 1977; MBA, Wayne State U., 1987. Cert. tax profl., cert. mgmt. acct., cert. practitioner of taxation; enrolled agt.; cert. network adminstr. Gen. ledger acct. Weltronic, Southfield, Mich., 1978-79; acctg. mgr. R.L. Polk, Detroit, 1979-81; chief acct. Family and Neighborhood Svcs., Inkster, Mich., 1981, from contr. to sr. v.p., 1981-90; exec. v.p. ops., CFO Family and Neighborhood Svcs., 1990-93; fin. dir. Warren/Conner Devel. Coalition, Detroit, 1993-95; dep. dir. Wayne Ctr., Detroit, 1996-98; pres. R.E. J.'s Acctg. and Tax Svc. Inc., Southgate 1977—; treas. Tamson Ctr. Inc., Taylor 1983-84; adj. instr. computer sci. Wayne County C.C. Cons. Acctg. Aid Soc., Detroit, 1981—. Mem. Inst. Mgmt. Accts. (Stuart Cameron Soc., nat. dir. 1989-94, pres. Mich. coun. 1988-89, 90-91, pres. Detroit chpt. 1988-89, 90-91, v.p. 1987-88, Jaycee of Month 1979), Nat. Assn. Enrolled Agts., Inst. Cert. Mgmt. Accts., Inst. Cert. Practitioners, Mich. State Alumni Assn., Wayne State Alumni Assn. (treas. 1993—), Aquinas Men's Club, KC. Roman Catholic. Avocations: golf, baseball, chess. Home: 15436 Richmond St Southgate MI 48195-2613

JACOB, ROSAMOND TRYON, librarian; b. Mpls., May 20, 1928; d. Philip Dorn and Rachel Chase (Denison) Tryon; m. Bernard Michel Jacob, Feb. 17, 1951; children: Clara, Paul. BA summa cum laude, Smith Coll., 1949; MA in Libr. Sci., U. Minn., 1974. Sec. Thames & Hudson Pubs., N.Y.C., 1950-51, Columbia Law Sch., N.Y.C., 1952-54, U. Minn., Mpls., 1955-59; libr. St. Paul Pub. Libr., 1976-98; ret.; coun. mem. Depository Libr. Coun. to Pub. Printer, Washington, 1985-88. Co-author: Minnesota State Documents: A Guide for Depository Libraries, 1984; author: (newsletter) Documents/Classified, 1980-96; editor: (newsletter) DOCSOUP, 1980-90. Mem. St. Paul LWV, 1965—. Mem. ALA (Bernadine Abbott Hoduski Founder award govt. documents roundtable divsn. 1994), Minn. Libr. Assn. (Disting. Achievement award 1990).

JACOB, SHARON ROSE, accountant, consultant; b. Beaufort, S.C., Feb. 13, 1953; d. Eddie Velmer and Gertrude (Redmond) Horne; m. Stephen M. Jacob, Sept. 17, 1987; 1 child, Sarah Nicole. BS, U. Md., 1976. CPA, Md. Budget analyst Potomac Electric Power Co., Washington, 1978-80; jr. acct. BCBS of Nat. Capitol Area, Washington, 1976, acct., 1976-78, 80, supr. various acctg depts., 1980-84, subs. coord., 1984-87; prof. acctg. Craven C.C., New Bern, N.C., 1989-90; acct. in pvt. practice, Brandywine, Md., 1990—. Bd. dirs. Md. Ctr. for Youth and Family Devel., Upper Marlboro, 1996-97, treas., 1997-98; mem. Flintstone Elem. Sch. Mgmt. Team, Oxon Hill, Md., 1997-98; bd. dirs. Prince Georges County Bd. Trade, 1992085, treas., 1995-97, sec., 1997-98. Mem. AICPA, Md. Soc. Accts., N.C. Soc CPAs, Nat. Soc. Accts., So. Prince Georges Bus. and Profl. Women (treas. 1994-96, pres.-elect 1996-97). Democrat. Roman Catholic. Avocations: reading, gardening. Office: 12808 Quail Ln Brandywine MD 20613-2506

JACOB, STANLEY WALLACE, surgeon, educator; b. Phila., 1924; s. Abraham and Belle (Shulman) J.; m. Marilyn Peters; 1 son, Stephen; m. Beverly Swarts; children—Jeffrey, Darren, Robert; m. Gail Brandis; 1 dau., Elyse. M.D. cum laude, Ohio State U., 1948. Diplomate: Am. Bd. Surgery. Intern Beth Israel Hosp., Boston, 1948-49; resident surgery Beth Israel Hosp., 1949-52, 54-56; chief resident surg. service Harvard Med. Sch., 1956-

57, instr., 1958-59; asso. vis. surgeon Boston City Hosp., 1958-59; Kemper Found. research scholar A.C.S., 1957-60; asst. prof. surgery U. Oreg. Med. Sch., Portland, 1959-66; asso. prof. U. Oreg. Med. Sch., 1966—; Gerlinger prof. surgery Oreg. Health Scis. U., 1981—. Author: Structure and Function in Man, 5th edit, 1982, Laboratory Guide for Structure and Function in Man, 1982, Dimethyl Sulfoxide Basic Concepts, 1971, Biological Actions of DMSO, 1975, Elements of Anatomy and Physiology, 1989; contbr. to: Ency. Brit. Served to capt. M.C. AUS, 1952-54; col. Res. ret. Recipient Gov.'s award Outstanding N.W. Scientist, 1965; 1st pl. German Sci. award, 1965; Markle scholar med. scis., 1960. Mem. Phi Beta Kappa, Sigma Xi, Alpha Omega Alpha. Achievements include co-discovery of therapeutic usefulness of dimethyl sulfoxide. Home: 1055 SW Westwood Ct Portland OR 97201-2708 Office: Oreg Health Scis U Dept Surgery 3181 SW Sam Jackson Park Rd Portland OR 97201-3011

JACOB, TED MANAS, biomedical and forensic photographer; b. Manila, Philippines, July 10, 1960; s. Doroteo Benitez and Teresa Afring (Manas) J.; m. Maria Teresa Frades Escarcha, Oct. 26, 1991; 1 child, Sarah Marie. Diploma, Brooks Inst., 1984; student, TV broadcasting and rec. scis., L.A. City Coll., 1996. With Brooks Photo Ctr., Santa Barbara, Calif., 1985-88; biomed. photographer Childrens Hosp. L.A., 1989-93, audio-visual comms. specialist, 1993-97; freelance biomed./forensic photographer Milpitas, Calif., 1997—; owner Jacob Comm., Milpitas; humanitarian awards com. Childrens Hosp., L.A. Biblical instr. Logos Christian Fellowship Childrens Hosp., 1996-97. Recipient Humanitarian award Children Hosp. L.A., 1996. Mem. Profl. Photographers Am., Health Scis. Comm. Assn., Ophthalmic Photographes Soc., Internat. Indsl. Photographers Assn. Avocations: reading, swimming, sketching, drawing.

JACOBEY, JOHN ARTHUR, III, surgeon, educator; b. Albuquerque, Oct. 27, 1929; s. John Arthur Jr. and Zelma Mae (Wolfe) Jacobey Mann. AB, Dartmouth Coll., 1951; postgrad., U. Colo., 1951-53; MD, Harvard U., 1956. Diplomate Am. Bd. Surgery, Am. Bd. Thoracic Surgery. Intern Jefferson Davis Hosp., Baylor U., Houston, 1956-57; resident Boston City Hosp., 1957-58, Dartmouth Med. Ctr., Hanover, N.H., 1958-59, Peter Bent Brigham Hosp., 1962-63, St. Mary's Hosp., London, 1963-64, Baylor Affiliated Hosp., Houston, 1964-65; rsch. fellow Harvard Med. Sch., 1959-62; pvt. practice medicine specializing in cardiovascular and thoracic surgery Denver, 1965-71, 72-76; staff surgeon Cheyenne (Wyo.) VA Med. Ctr., 1971-72; asst. prof. clin. surgery SUNY, Stony Brook, 1977-83; pvt. practice medicine specializing in cardiovascular and thoracic surgery Dover, N.J., 1984-92; active cardiothoracic surg. staff Robert Wood Johnson U. Hosp., New Brunswick, N.J., 1992—; clin. instr. surgery U. Colo., Denver, 1965-69; clin. assoc. prof. surgery U. Medicine and Dentistry of N.J., Robert Wood Johnson Med. Sch., New Brunswick, 1984—; leader internat. cardiothoracic surg. delegation to China, Citizen Amb. Program of People to People Internat., 1994. Prin. investigator, author pubs. on cannula counterpulsation, superior mediastinal exploration. Lay reader, chalice bearer Episcopal Ch., Manhasset, N.Y., 1976-83, Mountain Lakes, N.J., 1984-90, Westfield, N.J., 1990—. Fellow Am. Coll. Chest Physicians; mem. AMA, Soc. Thoracic Surgeons, Am. Thoracic Soc., N.J. Soc. Thoracic Surgeons, N.Y. Soc. Thoracic Surgery, N.J. Acad. Medicine, Am. Heart Assn., N.J. Med. Soc., Mass. Med. Soc., Harvard Club (Boston), Univ. Club (Denver). Republican. Avocations: skiing, sailing, tennis, golf. Office: 406B Durham Ctr 4 Ethel Rd Edison NJ 08817-2841

JACOBI, FREDRICK THOMAS, newspaper publisher; b. Neenah, Wis., July 10, 1953; s. H. Paul and Patricia Mary (Steele) J.; m. Kim Lee Muenchow, Aug. 23, 1980; children: James Paul, Steven Thomas. AA in Bus., U. South Fla., 1973; BBA in Fin., Mktg., U. Wis., 1976; MBA in Mktg., U. Wis., Whitewater, 1980. Cert. newspaper circulation. City dist. mgr. Madison (Wis.) Newspapers Inc., 1977-79, city circulation mgr., 1979-80, circulation mgr., 1980-81, mktg. mgr., 1981-82, circulation dir., 1982-85; circulation dir. Gannett Co., Inc., Reno, Nev., 1985-88; regional circulation dir. Gannett Co., Inc., Arlington, Va., 1988-90; pub., pres. Wausau (Wis.) Daily Herald, Gannett Co., Inc., 1990-92, Springfield (Mo.) News-Leader, 1993-96; v.p. Midwest region Gannett Co., Inc., 1993-96; pub., pres. Ft. Myers (Fla.) News-Press, 1996—; com. chmn. Sales and Mktg. Exec., Madison, 1985. Editor Circulation-Central States, 1985. Program chmn. Jr. Achievement of Nev., Reno, 1987-88; pres. Springfield Bus. and Devel. Corp., 1996; bd. dirs. Ozarks Press Assn., Make A Wish Mo., Horizon Econ. Devel., 1997—, Lee County Pub. Schs. Found. Mem. The Exec. Com., Young Pres.'s Orgn., Fla. Press Assn., So. Newspaper Pubs. Assn., Newspaper Assn. Am., Rotary. Republican. Roman Catholic. Avocations: micro-computers, running, gardening. Office: Ft Myers News Press 2442 Martin Luther King Jr Blvd Fort Myers FL 33901

JACOBI, JOE, Olympic athlete, canoeist; b. Bethesda, Md., Sept. 26, 1969. Olympic slalom doubles canoeist Barcelona, Spain, 1992. Recipient Gold medal canoe slalom doubles Olympics, Barcelona, 1992. also: US Canoe and Kayak Team Pan Am Plz 201 S Capitol Ave Ste 610 Indianapolis IN 46225-1026 Address: 12 Grande Ave Copperhill TN 37317-0247*

JACOBI, PETER PAUL, journalism educator, author; b. Berlin, Mar. 15, 1930; came to U.S., 1938, naturalized, 1944; s. Paul A. and Liesbeth (Kron) J.; m. Harriet Ackley, Dec. 8, 1956 (div. 1979); children: Keith Peter, John Wyn. BS in Journalism, Northwestern U., 1952, MS, 1953. Mem. journalism faculty Northwestern U., Evanston, Ill., 1955-81, profl. lectr., 1955-63, asst. prof., 1963-66, assoc. prof., 1966-69, prof. journalism, 1969-81, assoc. dean, 1966-74; communications cons. N.Y.C., 1980-84, Bloomington, Ind., 1985—; prof. journalism Ind. U., Bloomington, 1985—; news assignment editor, newscaster, theatre and music reporter NBC, Chgo., 1955-61; news editor ABC, Chgo., 1951-53; radio commentator on music and opera, 1958-65; theatre and film critic Sta. WTTW, Chgo., 1964-74, arts critic, 1975-77; theatre and film critic Hollister Newspapers Suburban Chgo., 1963-70; music columnist Chicagoan mag., 1973-74; script cons. Goodman Theater, Chgo., 1973-75; syndicated commentator on arts and media N.Am. Radio Alliance, 1978-80; arts corr. Christian Sci. Monitor, 1956-81; music critic, columnist Bloomington (Ind.) Herald-Times, 1985—; columnist Arts Indiana, 1987—, Editors Only, 1994—, Editor's Workshop, 1995—. Author: Writing with Style, The News Story and the Feature, 1982, The Messiah Book-The Life and Times of G.F. Handel's Greatest Hit, 1982, (with Jack Hilton) Straight Talk about Videoconferencing, 1986, The Magazine Article: How to Think It, Plan It, Write It, 1991; contbg. essayist Lyric Opera Companion, 1991; editor Chgo. Lyric Opera News, 1958-61, Music Mag./Musical Courier, Chgo., 1961-62; contbr. articles on writing to Folio, Ragan Report, other mags., articles on arts to Sat. Rev., Chgo. Daily News, N.Y. Times, Highlights for Children, World Book, others. Mem. AAUP, NATAS, Assn. Edn. in Journalism, Soc. Profl. Journalists, Ind. Arts Commn. (chmn. 1990-93), Arts Midwest, Bloomington Arts Commn. Home: 3003 N Browncliff Ln Bloomington IN 47408-1317 Office: Ind U Sch Journalism Bloomington IN 47405

JACOBI, VERONICA ANN, community health nurse, educator; b. L.I., N.Y., Feb. 29, 1944; d. Edward S. and Edna (Morris) Wagner; m. John C. Jacobi Jr., Aug. 23, 1964; 1 child, Tara-Louise. Diploma, Cen. Islip Sch. Nursing, 1965; BSN with honors, SUNY, Brockport, 1982. RN, N.Y. Staff nurse neonatal unit St. Charles Hosp., Port Jefferson, N.Y., 1965-68; staff nurse ob-gyn. Glen Cove (N.Y.) Hosp., 1968-69; staff nurse med./surg. unit Deaconess Hosp., Buffalo, 1969-71; mem. student health svcs. Suffolk County C.C., 1982—. Cen. Islip State Sch. grantee. Mem. Suffolk County Assn. Nurses.

JACOBI, WILLIAM MALLETT, nuclear engineer, consultant; b. Elizabeth, N.J., Apr. 27, 1930; s. Roy H. and Lenore E. (Mallett) J.; m. Maureen Sullivan, Feb. 23, 1963; children: John, Karen, Paul, Michele. BSChemE, Syracuse U., 1951, PhD in Chem. Engring., 1955; MSChemE, U. Del., 1953. Project mgr. Clinch River Breeder Reactor Plant, Oak Ridge, Tenn., 1973-78; gen. mgr. Westinghouse Nuclear Tech. div., Pitts., 1979-81, Westinghouse Nuclear Fuel div., Pitts., 1981-84; v.p. Westinghouse Advanced Power Systems, Pitts., 1984-87; pres. Westinghouse Hanford Co., Richland, Wash., 1987-88; v.p. govt. ops. Westinghouse Electric Co., Pitts., 1988-91; pvt. practice Monroeville, Pa., 1991—; sci. and tech. adv. com. mem. Argonne (Ill.) Nat. Lab., 1980-83; laser exec. rev. com. mem. Lawrence Livermore (Calif.) Nat. Lab., 1990-92. Active bishop's adv. com. Cath. Diocese of Pitts., 1990-92; panel mem. Nat. Rsch. Coun., 1992-93. Mem. Am. Nuc. Soc., Nat. Rsch. Coun. (sub-panel nuc. waste transmutation 1991-95), Greensburg Country Club, Alpha Chi Sigma. Republican. Home and Office: 119 Mt Vernon Dr Monroeville PA 15146-4815

JACOBOWITZ, ELLEN SUE, museum and temple curator, administrator; b. Detroit, Feb. 21, 1948; d. Theodore Mark and Lois Clairesse (Levy) J. BA, U. Mich., 1969, MA, 1970; postgrad. in art history, Bryn Mawr Coll., 1976—; postgrad., Wharton Sch., 1997. Curator Phila. Mus. Art, 1972-90; administr. Cranbrook Inst. Sci., Bloomfield Hills, Mich., 1991-94; adminstr. Temple Emanu-El, Oak Park, Mich., 1995-96; cons. ArtServ Mich., 1997, Home Care Giver, 1998—. Author: The Prints of Lucas Van Leyden, 1983, American Graphics: 1860-1940, 1982. Past bd. dirs. Print Coun. Am., Balt., Netherlands Am. Amity Trust, Washington, 1982-84, Nat. Coun. Jewish Women, Detroit, 1990-91, Mich. Mus. Assn., 1993-94; treas. Sat. Luncheon Club, 1995-96, pres., 1999-2000; active Leadership Oakland, Detroit Inst. Arts. Mem. Am. Jud. Com., Print Coun. Am., U. Mich. Alumni Club, Temple Beth El (archive com.). Avocations: art, tennis, opera, theater, music.

JACOBOWITZ, HAROLD SAUL, lawyer; b. N.Y.C., Aug. 26, 1950; s. William and Miriam (Spector) J.; m. Estrella B. Rivera, Oct. 26, 1972. BA, CUNY, 1972; JD, Rutgers U., 1977. Bar: N.Y. 1977, U.S. Dist. Ct. (so. dist.) N.Y. 1978, U.S. Dist. Ct. (ea. dist.) N.Y. 1978. Assoc. Goldman & Heffernan, N.Y.C., 1977-78, Zola & Zola, N.Y.C., 1978-79, Goldberg & Lysaght, N.Y.C., 1979-82; atty. of record Am. Internat. Group (Jacobowitz, Spessard, Garfinkel & Lesman), N.Y.C., 1982-88, regional mng. atty., 1988-89, chief counsel, 1989-90, v.p., 1990—, chief tech. officer property/casualty claims, 1998—; arbitration panel U.S. Dist. Ct. (ea. dist.) N.Y. Mem. ABA, N.Y. State Bar Assn., Assn. Bar City N.Y., N.Y. County Lawyers Assn., Assn. Trial Lawyers N.Y.C. (bd. dirs.). Office: Am Internat Group 70 Pine St New York NY 10270-0002

JACOBOWITZ, WALTER ERWIN, obstetrician, gynecologist; b. Jersey City, Apr. 2, 1933; s. Morton and Helen Ruth (Weinberger) J.; m. Suzanne Cylinder, Oct. 29, 1958; children: Glenn, Dana, Karen. AB, Princeton U., 1954; MD, NYU, 1958. Diplomate Am. Bd. Ob-Gyn. Rotating intern Phila. Gen. Hosp., 1958-59; resident in ob-gyn. NYU-Bellevue Hosp., N.Y.C., 1959-63; pvt. practice, Morristown, N.J., 1963—; chief dept. ob-gyn. Morristown Meml. Hosp., 1978-80, pres. med.-dental staff, 1996-97; pres. combined med. staffs Atlantic Health Sys., 1998, trustee. Fellow ACOG; mem. Princeton Club N.Y. Democrat. Jewish. Avocations: travel, stamp collecting. Office: Ob-Gyn Assocs of Morris 261 James St Ste 3-c Morristown NJ 07960-6348

JACOBS, ALAN MARTIN, physicist, educator; b. N.Y.C., Nov. 14, 1932; s. Samuel J. and Amelia M. (Ziegler) J.; m. Evelyn Lee Banner, Aug. 7, 1955 (dec. Jan. 1977); children: Frederick Ethen, Heidi Joelle; m. Sharon Lynn Auerbach, Oct. 14, 1978; children: Aaron Michael, Seth Joseph. B.Engring. Physics (John McMullen scholar, LeVerne Noyes scholar, Clevite scholar), Cornell U., Ithaca, N.Y., 1955; postgrad., Oak Ridge Sch. Reactor Tech., 1955-56; M.S., in Physics, Pa. State U., 1958; Ph.D., Pa. State U., 1963. Research asso. nuclear reactor facility Pa. State U., 1956-63; mem. faculty Pa. State U., 1963—, prof. nuclear engring., 1968-80; prof. U. Fla., Gainesville, 1980—, chmn. dept. nuclear engring. scis., 1980-82; chief scientist Future Tech, Inc., Gainesville, 1986-87; cons. to industry. Co-author: Basic Principles of Nuclear Science and Reactors, 1960; patentee dynamic radiography, control of radiation beams by vibrating media, multichannel radiograph, digital x-ray imaging system. NSF sci. faculty fellow, 1960-61; recipient Glenn Murphy award for nuclear sci. edn. ASEE, 1994. Mem. Am. Soc. Nondestructive Testing, Sigma Xi, Tau Beta Pi, Pi Mu Epsilon. Home: 3718 SW 80th Dr Gainesville FL 32608-3662 Office: Dept Nuclear & Radiol Engring U Fla Gainesville FL 32611-8300

JACOBS, ALLAN JOEL, gynecologist, administrator; b. N.Y.C., Feb. 18, 1947; s. Arnold and Pauline (Gluck) J.; m. Pamela Jane Ravin, Mar. 19, 1972; children: Ethan Isaac, Sarah Rachel, Tamara Ruth. BA, Cornell U., 1966; MS, MD, U. So. Calif., 1972. Diplomate Am. Bd. Ob-Gyn. Resident ob-gyn. Parkland Meml. Hosp., Dallas, 1972-76; gynecologic oncology fellow Mount Sinai Hosp., N.Y.C., 1978-80; asst. prof. ob-gyn. Coll. Medicine U. Nebr., Omaha, 1980-83; asst. prof. ob-gyn. Sch. Medicine Washington U., St. Louis, 1983-86; assoc. prof. ob-gyn. Sch. Medicine St. Louis U., 1986-90; chmn. ob-gyn. Beth Israel Med. Ctr., N.Y.C., 1990—; prof. ob-gyn. Albert Einstein Coll. Medicine, Bronx, N.Y., 1994—; adj. prof. ob-gyn. and reproductive sci. Mount Sinai Sch. Medicine, 1994-96, prof. 1990-94; attending phsyician Englewood (N.J.) Hosp., 1993—; assoc. staff Cardinal Glennon Children's Hosp., St. Louis, 1989-90; staff mem. St. Mary's Health Ctr., Clayton, Mo., 1986-90, U. Nebr. Hosp., Omaha, 1980-83; cons. ob-gyn. Jewish Hosp. St. Louis, 1983-86; asst. obstetrician Barnes Hosp., St. Louis, 1983-86; consulting staff Archbishop Bergan Mercy Hosp., Omaha, 1982-83, Nebr. Meth. Hosp., Omaha, 1980-83; courtesy staff Immanuel Hosp., Omaha, 1981-83, Bishop Clarkson Meml. Hosp., Omaha, 1980-83; staff VA Hosp., Omaha, 1980-83. Contbr. articles to profl. jours. Bd. dirs. Jewish Day Sch. Omaha, 1981-83, v.p., 1982-83; bd. dirs. Nebr. divsn. Am. Cancer Soc., 1980-83, profl. edn. com., 1980-83, nominating com., 1981-83; pub. issues com. Mo. divsn. Am. Cancer Soc., 1986-90, profl. edn. com., 1986-90; bd. dirs. Shaare Zedek Synagogue, St. Louis. Maj. U.S. Army, 1976-78. Grantee Am. Cancer Soc., 1987-89, Biogen Rsch. Corp., 1988-89, NeoRx, Inc., 1988-90, Ctr. Disease Control, 1991—, Singer Collaborative, 1993—, Organon, Inc., 1992-93, TAP Pharms., 1992-93. Fellow ACP, Am. Coll. Obstetricians and Gynecologists, European Soc. Gynecologic Oncology (assoc.), N.Y. Acad. Medicine; mem. Western Assn. Obstetricians and Gynecologists, Soc. Gynecologic Oncologists, N.Y. Gynecol. Soc., N.Y. Obstet. Soc., N.Y. County Med. Soc. Jewish. Office: Beth Israel Med Ctr 1st Ave at 16th St New York NY 10003

JACOBS, ANDREW, JR., former congressman, educator; b. Indpls., Feb. 24, 1932; s. Andrew and Joyce Taylor (Wellborn) J.; m. Kim Hood; children: H.B. James Andrew, B.N. Steven Michael. B.S., Ind. U., 1955, LL.B., 1958. Bar: Ind. Practiced in Indpls., 1958-65, 73-74; mem. 89th-92d congresses from 11th Dist., 1965-73, 94th-97th congresses from 11th Dist. Ind., 1975-83, 98th-103rd Congresses from 10th Dist. Ind., 1983-96; Mem. Ind. Ho. of Reps., 1958-60; ranking minority mem. ways & means subcom. on social security; adj. prof. Ind. U., 1996—. Served with USMC, 1950-52. Mem. Indpls. Bar Assn., Am. Legion. Democrat. Roman Catholic. Office: 1201 W 64th St Indianapolis IN 46260-4409*

JACOBS, ANN ELIZABETH, lawyer; b. Lima, Ohio, July 28, 1950; d. Warren Charles and Virginia Elizabeth (Lewis) J.; m. Mark S. Bush, Nov. 26, 1988; 1 child, Whitney Elizabeth. BA, George Washington U., 1972; JD, Cath. U., 1976. Bar: Ohio 1977, Calif. 1977, U.S. Ct. Appeals (D.C. cir.) 1980, U.S. Dist. Ct. (no. dist.) Ohio 1982. Asst. atty. gen. State of Ohio, Columbus, 1977-78; trial atty. EEOC of Ohio, Miami, Fla., 1978-80; sole practice Lima, 1980—; bd. dirs. Allen County Blackhoof Area Legal Svcs. Assn., Marimor Industries, Inc., Lima. Fundraiser Lima Symphony Orch., 1985; trustee Lima Art Assn., YWCA; bd. of Elders, Market St. Presbyn. Ch. Recipient Recognition award US Naval Air Sta., Jacksonville, Fla., 1979. Mem. LWV, Ohio Bar Assn., Calif. Bar Assn., D.C. Bar Assn., Allen County Bar Assn. (chmn. juvenile ct. com. 1993). Avocations: sailing, golf, reading. Home: 1529 Shawnee Rd Lima OH 45805-3801 Office: Jacobs & Von der Embse 558 W Spring St Lima OH 45801-4728

JACOBS, ARNOLD STEPHEN, lawyer; b. N.Y.C., Feb. 26, 1940; s. Charles Edwin and Harriet (Flug) J.; m. Ellen Margaret Kheel, June 10, 1962; children: Beryl Kheel, Arnold Stephen Jr. BME, Cornell U., 1961, MBA, 1963, LLB, 1964. Bar: N.Y. 1964. Assoc. Hughes, Hubbard & Reed, N.Y.C., 1964-65, 1967-71; ptnr. Shea & Gould, N.Y.C., 1971-94, Proskauer Rose LLP, N.Y.C., 1994—; adj. prof. N.Y. Law Sch., 1977-91. Author: The Impact of Rule 10b-5 (3 vols.), 1974, Litigation and Practice Under Rule 10b-5 (6 vols.), 1981—, Manual of Corporate Forms for Securities Practice (4 vols.), 1981—, Opinion Letters in Securities Matters: Text-Clause-Law (3 vols.), 1980—, Section 16 of the Securities Exchange Act (2 vols.), 1989—; contbr. articles to profl. jours. Capt. U.S. Army, 1965-67, Korea. Mem. N.Y. State Bar Assn., Assn. of Bar of City of N.Y. (chmn. securities regulation com. 1982-86), Harmonie Club (N.Y.C.). Home: 108 E 82nd St Apt 7A New York NY 10028-1136 Office: Proskauer Rose LLP 1585 Broadway New York NY 10036-8200

JACOBS, ARTHUR DIETRICH, educator, researcher, health services executive; b. Bklyn., Feb. 4, 1933; s. Lambert Dietrich and Paula Sophia (Knissel) J.; m. Viva Jane Sims, Mar. 24, 1952; children: Archie (dec.), David L. Dwayne C., Dianna K. Hatfield. BBA, Ariz. State U., 1962, MBA, 1966. Enlisted USAF, 1951, commd. 2d lt., 1962, advanced through grades to maj., 1972, ret., 1973; indsl. engr. Motorola, Phoenix, 1973-74; mgmt. cons. State of Ariz., 1974-76, Productivity Internat., Tempe, Ariz., 1976-79; faculty assoc. Coll. Bus. Adminstrn. Ariz. State U., Tempe, 1977-94, sr. lectr., 1995, ret., 1996; productivity advisor Scottsdale (Ariz.) Meml. Health Services Co., 1979-84; researcher U.S. internment of European-Am. aliens and citizens of European ancestry during World War II. Author: The Prison Called Hohenasperg: An American Boy Betrayed by his Government During World War II, 1999; editor, pub. Freedom of Information Times; co-editor: The World War Two Experience-The Interment of German-Americans; Documents, vol. IV; contbr. articles to profl. jours. Bd. dirs. United Way of Tempe, 1979-85. Mem. Am. Soc. Quality Control, Ariz. State U. Alumni Assn. (bd. dirs. 1973-79), Inst. Indsl. Engrs. (pres. Ctrl. Ariz. chpt. 1984-85), Ops. Rsch. Soc. Am., Optimist (life, Tempe), Sigma Iota Epsilon, Beta Gamma Sigma, Delta Sigma Pi.

JACOBS, C. BERNARD, banker; b. Davenport, Iowa, May 15, 1918; s. Henry Bernard and Ruth Alberta (Douglas) J.; m. Irene May Niesen, Mar. 17, 1939; children: Judith, Victoria, Rosemary, Mary Louise, Julie. B.S. in Commerce, Northwestern U., 1948; postgrad. in banking, U. Wis., 1955. V.p. Continental Ill. Nat. Bank, Chgo., 1959-64; exec. v.p. Nat. City Bank, Mpls., 1964-66, pres., 1966-69, chmn. bd., 1969-84; pres., chief exec. officer Nat. City Bancorp, Mpls., 1982-84; chmn. Carney Bank, Boynton Beach, Fla., 1985-96; bd. dirs. Nat. City Bancorp. Chmn. bd. St. Mary's Coll., Winona, Minn., 1973-74. Clubs: Hazeltine Nat. (Chaska, Minn.) (pres. 1973-75); Quail Ridge Country (Boynton Beach, Fla.). Office: Carney Legal Group 1101 N Congress Ave Boynton Beach FL 33426-3308*

JACOBS, CARL EUGENE, printing company official; b. Ft. Wayne, Ind., Nov. 28, 1942; s. Earl Oscar and Marguerite Louise (Unger) J.; m. Linda Maureen Peralta, Sept. 6, 1974; children: Brett, Kim, Kris. BS in Edn., Ball State U., 1965, MA in Speech, 1970. Tchr. Ft. Wayne Community Schs., 1965-70; instr. Ft. Hays (Kans.) State U., 1970-73; dir. pubs. Nat. Collegiate Athletic Assn., Mission, Kans., 1973-77; v.p. sales, mktg. The Lowell Press, Kansas City, Mo., 1977-94; dir. internat. sales Constable-Hodgins Printing Co., Kansas City, Kans., 1994-96; v.p. mktg. Richardson Printing, Inc., Kansas City, Mo., 1996—. Trustee Kansas City Conservatory of Music, 1983-94; bd. dirs. Genesis Sch., Kansas City, 1987; ruling elder, mem. session Southridge Presbyn. Ch., Roeland Park, Kans., 1985-87, 89-91. Mem. Internat. Assn. Bus. Communicators (hon. life chpt. and dist., chpt. pres. 1978, internat. v.p., bd. dirs. 1981, trustee rsch. found. 1990-93), Kiwanis (bd. dirs., v.p. Downtown Kansas City Mo. club 1988-90, pres. 1991-92, Kiwanian of Yr. award 1994, 96), Greater Kansas City People to People, Kansas City Advt. Club. Republican. Avocations: sports, reading, writing. Home: 5720 Willow Pl Parkville MO 64152-6131

JACOBS, CATHERINE HERIOT, financial advisor; b. Shreveport, La., May 22, 1952; d. Walter Byron Jacobs, Jr. and Frances Grey; m. Robert Connell Peterson, June 2, 1973 (div. Nov. 1992); children: Sarah Elizabeth, Robert Connell Jr.; m. John T. Wilson, Dec. 22, 1996. BA, La. State U., 1975. CLU, ChFP, CFP. Financial cons. Larry Thompson & Assocs., Shreveport, La., 1994-96, Lincoln Financial Advs., Shreveport, 5, 1996—. Episcopalian. Avocations: triathlons, reading, kayaking. Office: Lincoln Financial Advisors 401 Edwards St 1100 Shreveport LA 71101

JACOBS, CHARLES NATHAN, editor, writer; b. Paterson, N.J., July 11, 1930; s. Samuel I. and Beatrice J. (Levine) J.; m. Joan Stearns Weiss, May 30, 1953 (div. 1979); children: Julie Gail, JoDee Winger; m. Rosalind H. Eigenfeld, Feb. 21, 1987. BA in Humanities, Columbia Coll., 1952; MS in Journalism, Columbia U., 1953. Reporter N.Y. Jour. Am., N.Y.C., 1950-53; owner Jacobs Dept. Store, Paterson, 1955-80; pub. Garden State Newspapers, San Francisco and Passaic, N.J., 1985-87; pvt. practice editl. cons. Woodcliff Lake, N.J., 1988-90; editor FOCUS Mag., Totowa, N.J., 1990-92; pres., pvt. practice editl. cons. CJ Enterprises, Woodcliff Lake, 1992—. Author: The Business of Writing, 1996. Dep. mayor Paterson, 1966-70; campaign mgr. Kramer for Mayor, Paterson, 1966, 70, 74, 78. Sgt. U.S. Army, 1953-55. Recipient Disting. Svc. award Jaycees, Paterson, 1966, Nat. Vol. award Lane Bryant/U.S. Govt., Washington, 1969, various awards Soc. Profl. Journalists, N.Am. Travel Journalists Assn. Mem. N.Am. Travel Journalists Assn., N.J. Press Club (award winner), Working Press Assn. (award winner). Jewish. Avocations: skiing, tennis, golf, reading, gardening. Home and Office: CJ Enterprises 16 Pinecrest Dr Woodcliff Lake NJ 07675

JACOBS, CHRISTOPHER PAUL, adult education educator, writer; b. Pitts., May 6, 1954; s. Francis Albin and Dorothy Margaret (Caldwell) J. BA in Music/Theatre/Film, U. N.D., 1976, MA in Film Criticism/TV Prodn., 1980. Pub. info. specialist dept. family medicine U. N.D., Grand Forks, 1979-81; newspaper editor, reporter, photographer The Chronicle weekly newspaper, Grand Forks, 1981-83; freelance writer, film critic Grand Forks Herald, 1981, 83-87; theatre mgr. Midcontinent Theatres, Grand Forks, 1985-94; projectionist, asst. mgr. Carmike Cinemas, Grand Forks, 1995—; film instr. U. N.D., Grand Forks, 1995—; film critic High Plains Reader, 1994—; bd. dirs. Greater Grand Forks Symphony, 1985-90, Greater Grand Forks Community Theatre, 1984-86; film. coord. Grand Forks Ctr. for Arts and Humanities, 1980; frequent talk show guest Sta. KFJM pub. radio, KCNN radio, Grand Forks, 1973—; guest instr. film criticism No. Interscholastic Press Assn., Grand Forks, 1980, 85-86. Contbr. articles to pubs.; author: The Treasure of Isis, 1999; co-author: A Guide to the Silent Years of American Cinema, 1999; author/layout designer (hist. brochure) The Empire Theatre, 1986; layout designer newspaper ads for Midco Theatres, 1986-95; writer, producer, dir. (TV movie) School Spirit, 1980; dir. (play) The Children's Hour, 1983; co-dir., actor (play) A Streetcar Named Desire, 1984; lighting designer, co-editor (film) Attentat, 1975 (Silver plaque Chgo. Film Festival 1975); filmmaker several short films, 1969-83; composer 3 choral masses, 1979-90, (string trio) Feb. Trio, 1986; composer, lyricist various pop/rock and jazz/blues songs and jingles, 1990-92; assoc. producer, actor: Dead and Too Stupid To Know It, 1999; co-editor: Introduction to Film Manual and Workbook, 1998; script supervisor (movie): Dead Dogs, 1999. Mem. Soc. Cinephiles (v.p. in charge of newsletter 1986-87, 91-92), U. N.D. Film Soc., Dakota Composers, Greater Grand Forks Arts and Humanities Assn. (bd. dirs. 1983-91, long-range planning com. 1990-91), North Valley Arts Coun. (bldg. com. 1995-98), Phi Beta Kappa, Phi Eta Sigma. Roman Catholic. Avocations: ancient and film history, music, theatre, filmmaking. Office: Carmike 10 Theatre PO Box 13116 2306 32d Ave S Grand Forks ND 58208-3116

JACOBS, DAVID E., federal agency administrator. BA in Polit. Sci., Antioch Coll., 1973; BS in Environ. Health, Oakland U., 1983; MS in Tech. and Sci. Policy, Ga. Inst. Tech., 1988; PhD in Environ. Engring., Kennedy Western U. Cert. indsl. hygienist. With Chrysler Corp., 1975-83, chmn. edn. com. UAW Local 869, 1979-82; cons. S.E. Mich. Com. on Occupl. Safety and Health, 1980-83; teaching asst. quantitative analytical chemistry Oakland U., 1982, lectr., coord. qualitative analytical chemistry, 1983; chemist Nat. Stds. tech. Inc., 1983; environ. rsch. scientist Ga. Inst. Tech., 1983-87, dir. Ga. State Employee Right to Know Program, 1987-88, dir. EPA So. Lead-Based Paint Tng. Consortium, 1989-92; dep. dir. Nat. Ctr. for Lead-Safe Housing, 1992-95; dir. Office Lead-Based Paint Abatement/Poisoning Prevention Office of Lead Hazard Control, Washington, 1995—; bd. dirs. Nat. Lead Abatement Coun., 1993-95. Contbr. numerous articles to profl. jours. Mem. ASTM, APHA, Am. Indsl. Hygiene Assn. (chmn. social concerns com. 1991, nat. nominating com. 1990-92, Ga. sect. sec. 1988, pres. 1989), Am. Acad. Indsl. Hygiene, Soc. for Occupl. and Environ. Health, Nat. Inst. Bldg. Scis. Office: US Dept HUD Lead Hazard Control 451 7th St SW Washington DC 20410-0001*

JACOBS, DELORES HAMM, secondary education educator; b. Tuscaloosa, Ala., Mar. 1, 1947; d. Howard Murphy and Nellie Mae (Booth) Hamm; m. Paul Thomas Jacobs, June 1, 1966; 1 child, Michael Paul. BS in Secondary Edn., U. Ala., 1971; BS in Middle Sch. Edn., Samford U., 1991;

MA in Secondary Edn., U. Ala., Birmingham, 1974. Tchr. English and Title I reading Locust Fork (Ala.) H.S., 1971-85; tchr. speech Pizitz Mid. Sch., Vestavia Hills, Ala., 1985-86, tchr. English,, 1986—, curriculum coord. English dept.; prof. clin. studies U. Ala., Birmingham; student-tchr. sponsor U. Ala., Birmingham, Samford U., Birmingham; co-author Ulyysseus Reading Enrichment Program, Pizitz Mid. Sch.; prof. student tchg. U. Ala., Birmingham. Contbr. poetry to various poetry publs. and editorials to Tuscaloosa News, Vestavia Hills edn. newsletters, Am. Poetic Soc. poetic vols. Bd. dirs. First Ch. of the Nazarene Pre-Sch. and Daycare Sch., Vestavia Hills, 1987-93, ch. organist, 1976—; sch. rep. United Way; rep. Heart Fund, Jefferson County, Ala., vol. Olympic Games, 1996. Mem. NEA, Ala. Edn. Assn., So. Assn. of Schs. (accreditation com., visitation team), Nat. Coun. Tchrs. English, Ala. Reading Assn., Vestavia Hills Garden Club, Chi Delta Phi. Republican. Avocations: golf, water color art, tennis, bowling, music.

JACOBS, DENNIS, federal judge; b. N.Y.C., Feb. 28, 1944; s. Harry N. and Rose J.; m. Judith Weissman. BA, Queens Coll., 1964; MA, NYU, 1965, JD, 1973. Atty. Simpson Thacher & Bartlett, N.Y.C., 1973-92; judge U.S. Ct. Appeals (2d cir.), N.Y.C., 1992—. Office: US Ct Appeals US Courthouse 40 Foley Sq New York NY 10007-1502*

JACOBS, DONALD P., dean, banking and finance educator; b. Chgo., June 22, 1927; s. David and Bertha (Nevod) J.; children: Elizabeth, Ann, David; m. Dinah Nemeroff, May 28, 1978. B.A., Roosevelt Coll., 1949; M.A., Columbia U., 1951, Ph.D., 1956. Mem. research staff Nat. Bur. Econ. Research, 1952-57; instr. Coll. City N.Y., 1955-57; mem. faculty to Morrison prof. fin. Northwestern U. Grad. Sch. Mgmt., 1970-78, chmn. dept., 1969-75, dean, 1975—, Gaylord Freeman Disting. prof. banking, 1978—; Dir. Commonwealth Edison, Hartmarx Corp., Everen Corp., Terex Corp., Prologis, Conf. Savs. and Residential Financing; co-dir. fin. studies Presdl. Commn. Fin. Structure and Regulation, 1970-71; sr. economist banking and currency com. U.S. Ho. of Reps., 1963-64. Editor proc.: Conf. Savs. and Residential Financing, 1967, 68, 69; contbr. articles to profl. jours. Served with USNR, 1945-46. Ford Found. fellow, 1959-60, 63-64. Mem. Am. Econ. Assn., Am. Statis. Assn., Am. Fin. Assn., Econometrics Soc., Inst. Mgmt. Sci. Home: 617 Milburn St Evanston IL 60201-2407 Office: Northwestern Univ J L Kellogg Grad Sch Mgmt 2001 Sheridan Rd Evanston IL 60208-0814

JACOBS, DONALD PAUL, architect; b. Cleve., Aug. 8, 1942; s. Joseph W. and Minnie Mae (Grieger) J.; m. Sharon Daugherty, Apr. 14, 1963 (dec. Feb. 1992); m. Julie Brinkerhoff, Apr. 24, 1993. BS, U. Cin., 1967. Registered architect, Calif., Tex., Ariz., Nev., Ga., Fla., Colo. Draftsman, intern Skidmore, Owings & Merrill, San Francisco, 1967-70; pvt. practice architecture Sea Ranch, 1970-86, chmn. design com., 1975-79; prin. Dorius Archs., Corona del Mar, Calif., 1986-94; pres. JBZ Arch. & Planning, Newport Beach, 1994—. Prin. works represented to numerous newspapers and magazines. Co-chair Project Playhouse, Homeaid, 1993-95. Mem. AIA (chmn. nat. housing com. 1996, awards 1973-74, 77-78, Bay Area Honor Design Excellence award 1974, Homes for Better Living Merit award 1976, Housing Merit award 1978), Sr. Housing Coun. (bd. dirs. Orange County chpt. 1993-94). Democrat. Avocations: tennis, skiing, hiking. Home: 309 Poppy Ave Corona Del Mar CA 92625-3024 Office: JBZ Arch & Planning 5010 Campus Dr Ste 100 Newport Beach CA 92660-2178

JACOBS, ELEANOR, art consultant, retired art administrator; b. N.Y.C., July 25, 1929; d. Samuel and Mary (Praw) Cohen; m. Raymond Jacobs, Dec. 29, 1955; children: Susan, Laura. BA, NYU, 1979. Co-founder, v.p. The Earth Shoe Co., N.Y.C., 1969-79; art adminstr. Print Dept., Sotheby's, N.Y.C., 1980-81; exec. asst. Care, N.Y.C., 1982-84; exec. adminstr. Hirschl & Adler Galleries, N.Y.C., 1984-93; art cons. Recipient Founders Day award NYU, N.Y.C., 1978. Mem. Nat. Arts Club (gov. 1989-97, exhbns. com. 1984—, curatorial com. 1990—, founder, editor exhibiting artists newsletter 1987—, admissions com. 1995—), Nat. Trust for Hist. Preservation, Artists Fellowship, 1985. Avocations: tennis, travel, art cons.

JACOBS, ELEANOR R., retired volunteer; b. N.Y.C., Nov. 19, 1912; d. Leo and Florence May (Schiff) Rosenberger; m. Saul Jacobs, Nov. 29, 1935 (dec. Sept. 1966); 1 child, Diane M. Grad. high sch. Sec. to pres. Kelly Springfield Tire Co., N.Y.C., 1930-34; program dir. USO, Panama Canal Zone, 1953-54; asst. mission chief C.A.R.E., Panama City, Republic of Panama, 1954-56; mil. air transport coord. USAF, Albrook AFB, Panama Canal Zone, 1956; pers. analyst U.S. Army, Ft. Amador, Panama Canal Zone, 1957-58; info. officer U.S. Tropic test Ctr., Ft. Clayton, Panama Canal Zone, 1958-66; info./pub. rels. adminstr. L.Am. reg. office Credit Union Nat. Assn., Panama City, 1966-72; asst. mng. dir. advt. and pub. rels. Credit Union Nat. Assn., Madison, Wis., 1972-76; dir. Nat. Assn. Ret. Credit Union People, 1978-86. Mem. Am. Assn. Ret. Persons, Friend of AAUW, LWV, Common Cause, Amnesty Internat. Christian Scientist. Avocations: weaving, writing, teaching English as a second lang. Home: 606 N Segoe Rd # 316 Madison WI 53705-3110

JACOBS, ELLIOT WILLIAM, plastic surgery; b. N.Y.C., June 23, 1945; s. Charles Philip and Lorraine (Roth) J.; children: Jeffrey, Benjamin. BA, CUNY, 1966; M Med. Scis., Rutgers U., 1968; MD, Mt. Sinai Sch. Medicine, 1970. Diplomate Am. Bd. Plastic Surgery. Pvt. practice, N.Y.C., 1979—. Maj. M.C., USAF, 1977-79. Fellow ACS, Internat. Coll. Surgeons; mem. Am. Soc. Plastic and Reconstructive Surgery, Am. Soc. for Aesthetic Plastic Surgery, Lipoplasty Soc. N.Am., Mensa. Avocations: squash, sailing, garedning, accordion, dancing. E-mail: ewjacobs@mindspring.com. Office: 815 Park Ave New York NY 10021

JACOBS, EUGENE GARDNER, JR., psychiatrist, psychoanalyst, educator; b. Providence, Jan. 3, 1926; s. E. Gardner and Edna Jacobs; m. Alice L. Smith, Apr. 12, 1951 (div. 1980); children: Susan, Nancy, John, Peter. AB, Yale U., 1948; MD, U. Pa., 1952. Diplomate Am. Bd. Psychiatry and Neurology. Intern Pa. Hosp., Phila., 1952-53; resident Neurol. Inst. N.Y., N.Y.C., 1953-54; rsch. fellow Columbia U., N.Y.C., 1954-55; resident N.Y. State Psychiat. Inst., Columbia Presbyn. Hosp., N.Y.C., 1955-58; pvt. practice Phila., 1958—; cons. psychiatrist Pa. Hosp., 1997—; staff psychiatrist Inst. of Pa. Hosp., Phila., 1958-62, sr. attending psychiatrist, 1974-97; chief psychiatrist Student Health Svc., Temple U., Phila., 1973-77; chief dept. psychiatry Phila. Naval Hosp., 1981-85; clin. asst. prof. U. Pa., 1970-81, 97-99, clin. assoc. prof. U. Pa., 1999—; clin. assoc. prof. MCP Hahnemann U., Phila., 1981-98, adj. clin. asst. prof., 1998—. Capt. USNR, ret. Fellow Am. Psychiat. Assn. (life); mem. Phila. Assn. for Psychoanalysis, Am. Psychoanalytic Assn., Phila. Psychiat. Soc. Home and Office: 5400 Wissahickon Ave Philadelphia PA 19144-5223

JACOBS, FERNE KENT, artist; b. Chgo., Sept. 13, 1942; d. Herbert F. and Libby (Astrin) Kent; m. Eugene Jacobs, Oct. 27, 1963 (div. Jan. 1976); 1 child, Peter. MFA, Claremont Grad. Sch., 1976. Exhibited in group shows Mus. Contemporary Crafts, N.Y.C., 1972, Ont. Sci. Ctr., Toronto, Can., 1974, Pacific Design Ctr., L.A., 1976, Cleve. Mus. Art, 1977, Hadler/Rodriguez Galleries, N.Y.C., 1978, Chaffey Cmty. Coll., Alta Loma, Calif., 1980, Craft and Folk Art Mus., L.A., 1981, Gallery Eight, La Jolla, Calif., 1981, Am. Craft Mus., N.Y.C., 1981, Mandell Gallery, 1981, Inst. Contemporary Art, Boston, 1982, Miller/Brown Gallery, San Francisco, 1983, Milw. Art Mus., 1986, The Philbrook Mus. Art, Tulsa, 1987, Palo Alto (Calif.) Cultural Ctr., 1988, Twining Gallery, N.Y.C., 1989, The Sybaris Gallery, Royal Oak, Mich., 1989, 92, 95, Nancy Margolis Gallery, N.Y.C., 1994; represented in permanent collections at Royal Scottish Mus., Edinburgh, The Lannan Found., Palm Beach, Fla., Wadsworth Atheneum, Hartford, Conn., Erie (Pa.) Art Mus., Am. Craft Mus., Detroit Inst. of Arts, R.I. Sch. Design, Oakland (Calif.) Mus., Contemporary Mus., Honolulu; contbr. to books and profl. publs. NEA fellow, 1973-74, 77-78, 90-91, Coll. of Fellows fellow Am. Craft Coun., 1995.

JACOBS, FRANCIS ALBIN, biochemist, educator; b. Mpls., Feb. 23, 1918; s. Anthony and Agnes Ann (Stejskal) J.; m. Dorothy Caldwell, June 5, 1953; children: Christopher, Gregory, Paula, Margaret, John. BS, Regis Coll., Denver, 1939; postgrad, U. Denver, 1939-41; Fellow in Biochemistry, St. Louis U., 1941-49, PhD, 1949. Postdoctoral fellow Nat. Cancer Inst., Bethesda, Md., 1949-51; instr. physiol. chemistry U. Pitts. Sch. Medicine, 1951-52, asst. prof., 1952-54; asst. prof. biochemistry U. N.D. Sch. Medicine, Grand Forks, 1954-56; asso. prof. U. N.D. Sch. Medicine, 1956-64, prof., 1964-87, prof. emeritus, 1987—; dir., research supr. Nat. Sci. Research Participation Program in Biochemistry, 1959-63; advisor directorate for sci. edn. NSF. Contbr. articles to profl. jours. Mem. bishop's pastoral council Diocese of Fargo, N.D., 1979-86. Fellow AAAS, N.D. Acad. Sci. (editor 1967, 68); mem. Am. Soc. for Biol. Chemistry and Molecular Biology, Am. Inst. Nutrition, Soc. Exptl. Biology and Medicine, Am. Chem. Soc. (chmn. Red River valley sect. 1971), AAAS, AMA, Sigma Xi (pres. chpt. 1965-66, Faculty award for Outstanding Sci. Research U. N.D. chpt. 1982, cert. of recognition 1987), Alpha Sigma Nu, Phi Lambda Upsilon. E-mail: fjacobs@medicine.nodak.edu. Home: 1525 Robertson Ct Grand Forks ND 58201-7303 Office: U ND Sch Medicine Dept Biochemistry and Molecular Biology Grand Forks ND 58202 *In teaching and research I find that it is indeed a way of life. Have faith in yourself and your creator. Do what is right, and seek what is true.*

JACOBS, GEORGE, broadcast engineering consulting company executive; b. N.Y.C., July 16, 1924; s. Benjamin and Henrietta (Myerson) J.; m. Beatrice Gregerman, May 27, 1947; children: Michele Jacobs Gordon, Joy Jacobs Kirschbaum. BEE, Pratt Inst., 1949; MSEE, U. Md., 1960. Registered profl. engr., Md., D.C. Govt. exec. Voice of America, USIA, 1949-76; bd. Internat. Broadcasting, Washington, 1976-80; pres. George Jacobs & Assocs., Inc., Silver Spring, Md., 1980—; commr. Commn. Broadcasting to Cuba, 1983; mem. U.S. Del. major ITU Comm. Confs., 1949-92; sr. advisor to chmn. U.S. Del. ITU Conf. on High Frequency Broadcasting, 1984, 87. Co-author: The Shortwave Propagation Handbook, 1976, 80, rev. edit., 1995; also articles. 2d lt. USAF, 1943-46. Decorated Air medal with cluster, 1945; recipient Marconi Gold medal engring. achievement Radio Club of Am., 1977, Superior Honor award U.S. Govt., 1976, Outstanding Performance award 1980; Presdl. Commn. Pres. U.S., 1983; Jack Poppele Broadcast Honor award, 1992, Radio Engring. Achievement award Nat. Assn. Broadcasters, 1997. Fellow IEEE, Radio Club of Am.; mem. Assn. Fed. Comms. Cons. Engrs. Avocations: amateur radio, philately, traveling. Fax: 301-587-8801. E-mail gja@gjainc.com. Home: PO Box 1714 Silver Spring MD 20915-1714 Office: George Jacobs & Assocs Inc 8701 Georgia Ave Silver Spring MD 20910-3713

JACOBS, GRETCHEN HUNTLEY, psychiatrist; b. N.Y.C., July 20, 1941; d. Louis Gordon and Gertrude Mary (Eberz) La Pointe; m. Michael Edward Jacobs, Dec. 26, 1965 (div.); children: Dylan Huntley, Danielle La Pointe. BS, Fordham U., N.Y.C., 1963; MD, SUNY, Bklyn., 1968. Diplomate Am. Bd. Psychiatry and Neurology, Am. Bd. Child and Adolescent Psychiatry. Pediatric intern St. Luke's Hosp., N.Y.C., 1968-69; psychiatry resident George Washington U. Hosp., Washington, 1969-71; child psychiatry resident Beth Israel Hosp., Boston, 1972-73, McLean Hosp. Children's Ctr., Waltham, Mass., 1973-74; coord. health and human devel. Martha's Vineyard Sch. Sys., 1974-80; pvt. practice adult and adolescent/child psychiatry Martha's Vineyard, Mass., 1974—; asst. clin. prof. child psychiatry Tufts U. Med. Sch., Boston, 1974—; staff psychiatrist Martha's Vineyard Hosp., 1974—. Contbr. articles to profl. jours. Cons. Mass. Dept. Pub. Health Svcs. to Multi-Handicapped Children, 1974-75; bd. dirs. Mass. Dept. Social Svcs., 1979-83; founding mem., clin. dir. Vineyard Child Assault Prevention Project, 1986, Com. on Rural Child Psychiatry, 1988-92; active Hospice of Martha's Vineyard Coun. for Young Children. Mem. AMA, Am. Psychiat. Assn., New England Coun. Child and Adolescent Psychiatry, Am. Acad. Child and Adolescent Psychiatry, Mass. Med. Soc., Rotary Internat. (sec. Martha's Vineyard chpt.). Avocations: music, dance, travel, sailing. Home and Office: Tashmoo Farm RR 1 Box 600 Vineyard Haven MA 02568-9733*

JACOBS, HAROLD ROBERT, mechanical engineering educator, practitioner; b. Portland, Oreg., Nov. 19, 1936; s. Harold Henry and Catherine Mae (Gill) J.; m. Georgeen Kirkpatrick, Aug. 26, 1961; children: Sara Catherine, Harold Robert, Kenneth Patrick. BS cum laude, U. Portland, 1958; MS in Mech. Engring., Wash. State U., 1961; PhD in Mech. Engring., Ohio State U., 1965. Registered profl engr., Utah, Wash. Engr. GE, San Jose, Calif., Hanford, Wash., 1958-59, 60; instr. dept. mech. engring. Wash. State U., Pullman, 1959-61; rsch. engr. aerospace divsn. Boeing Co., Seattle, 1961-62, 63; insr. mech engring. Ohio State U., Columbus, 1963-64; mem. tech. staff Aerospace Corp., San Bernadino, Calif., 1964-67; prof. dept. mech. engring. U. Utah, Salt Lake City, 1967-69, from asst. prof. to assoc prof., 1969-74, chmn. fluid mechanics divsn. Coll. Engring., 1974-79, prof. mech. engring., 1974-84, chmn. applied mechanics divsn., 1977-84, chmn. dept. civil engring., 1978-79, assoc. dean rsch., 1981-84; prof. mech engring., head dept. Pa. State U., University Park, 1984-94, prof. emeritus, 1994—; dean Coll. Engring., prof. mech. engring. Colo. State U., Ft. Collins, 1994-99; chief engr. CEEMS, Bothell, Wash., 1999—; mem. summer faculty Sandia Nat. Labs., Livermore, Calif., 1981; vis. prof. U. Strathclyde, Glasgow, Scotland, 1976-77; vis. prof. Imperial Coll., U. London, summer 1992; cons. numerous corps. Mem. internat. adv. bd. Russian Jour. Engring. Thermophysics, 1991—; contbr. numerous articles to profl. jours.; patentee in field; reviewer numerous jours. Ohio State U. fellow, 1962-63. Assoc. fellow AIAA (assoc. adv. coun. Utah sect. 1971-77, treas. 1972-73, chmn. 1974-75, Engr. of Yr. award 1973, numerous coms.); fellow ASME (chmn. gen. papers, coordinating com. heat transfer divsn., chmn. com. on heat transfer in mfg. and material processing 1991-94, mem. numerous coms., tech. editor Jour Heat Transfer 1986-92); mem. ASEE, Am. Inst. Chem. Engrs. (dir. thermal systems divsn. 1994-96, dir. 1994-96, vice chair 1999—), Sigma Xi (Ohio State Outstanding Engring. Alumnus 1991). Office: CEEMS 13816 26th Ave SE Bothell WA 98012

JACOBS, HARVEY COLLINS, newspaper editor, writer; b. Trafalgar, Ind., Sept. 6, 1915; s. Ralph L. and Ruth Marie (Ragsdale) J.; m. Florence Giddings, Apr. 5, 1942 (div. 1979); children: Phillip, Kenneth; m. Charlene Clark, Aug. 7, 1980. A.B., Franklin (Ind.) Coll., 1938, Litt.D., 1974; M.A., Ind. U., 1949; Litt.D., Sussex Coll. Tech., Eng., 1973. Reporter, editorial writer and columnist Franklin Evening Star, 1937-44; dir. pub. relations Franklin Coll., 1941-49, head dept. journalism, 1949-55; asst. editor Rotarian mag., Evanston, Ill., 1955-56; head program div. Rotary Internat., 1956-58, undersec., 1958-63; founder, chmn. dept. journalism and mass communications N.Mex. State U., Las Cruces, 1963-74; dir. Center Broadcasting and Internat. Communications, 1970-74; editor Indpls. News, 1974-92; adj. prof. journalism, disting. editor in residence, Franklin (Ind.) Coll. Author: Rotary: 50 Years of Service, 1955, Seven Paths to Peace, 1959, Adventure in Service, 1961, We Came Rejoicing, 1968, Hugging the Heartland, 1989; cowriter: This Great Land, 1983. Bd. dirs. Ind. Acad. Recipient Disting. Alumnus Citation Franklin Coll., 1957, Nat. Headliner award U. Okla., 1970, Disting. Svc. award N.Mex. Broadcasters Assn., 1971, Carl Towley award Journalism Edn. Assn., 1974, Golden Crown award Columbia U., 1975, Community Svc. award Hoosier Press Assn., 1976, Best Columnist award, 1975, 76, 80, 82, 87, 88, 90, First Elmer Davis award Franklin Coll., 1990; inducted to Ind. Journalism Hall of Fame, 1991. Fellow Pub. Rels. Soc. Am.; mem. Assn. Edn. Journalism, Am. Soc. Newspaper Editors, Authors Guild, Ind. Hist. Soc., Indpls. Press Club, Athletic Club, Rotary (past dist. gov.), Sigma Delta Chi. Home: 524 Leisure Ln Greenwood IN 46142-8315*

JACOBS, HYDE SPENCER, soil chemistry educator; b. Declo, Idaho, May 15, 1926; s. Rex Haynes and Clare Julia (McHale) J.; m. Gareldene Marchant, Aug. 4, 1950; children: Stanalee, Ruth, Julia Jacobs Spresser, Merrie Jacobs Houser, Marcia. MS, U. Idaho, 1954; PhD, Mich. State U., 1957. Cert. profl. agronomist; cert. profl. soil scientist. Prof. soils Kans. State U., Manhattan, 1967-95, asst. dir. ext., 1981-86, asst. to dean of agr., 1986-95, dir. Evapotranspiration Lab., 1964-80; dir. Kans. Water Resources Rsch. Inst., Manhattan, 1964-74, 88-95; liaison rep. Gt. Plains Agrl. Coun., Ft. Collins, Colo., 1987-92; sec. Kans. Food and Agrl. Coun., Manhattan, 1984-92; legis. liaison Agrl. Expt. Sta., Manhattan, 1986-93, Coop. Ext. Svc., 1986-93. Contbr. articles to profl. jours. Fellow Am. Soc. Agronomy, Soil Sci. Soc. Am., Soil and Water Conservation Soc.; mem. Kans. Crop Improvement Assn. (hon. mem.). Mem. LDS Ch.

JACOBS, IRWIN LAWRENCE, diversified corporate executive; b. Mpls., July 15, 1941; s. Samuel and Rose H. Jacobs; m. Alexandra Light, Aug. 26, 1962; children: Mark, Sheila, Melinda, Randi, Trisha. Student pub. schs. Chmn. Genmar Holdings, Inc., Mpls.; chmn. bd. Genmar Industries, Inc., Mpls.; chmn. Jacobs Trading Co., Mpls.; pres., CEO Jacobs Investors, Inc., Mpls.; pres. Jacobs Realty II, Inc., Mpls., 1993—, Jacobs Mgmt. Corp., 1983—, Gateway S/B, Inc., 1993—; chmn. Watkins Inc., Winona, Minn., Operation Bass, Inc., Gilbersville, Ky., 1996—, FLW Tour, Inc., Mpls., 1996—. Clubs: Mpls., Lafayette Country, Oakridge Country. Office: Genmar Holdings Inc 100 S 5th St Ste 2400 Minneapolis MN 55402-1206

JACOBS, JACK BERNARD, judge; b. July 23, 1942; s. Louis K. and Phoebe J.; m. Marion Antiles, Apr. 2, 1967; 1 child, Andrew Seth. AB, U. Chgo., 1964; LLB, Harvard U., 1967. Bar: Del. 1968, U.S. Dist. Ct. Del. 1968, U.S. Ct. Appeals (3d cir.) 1968, U.S. Supreme Ct. 1975. Law clk. Del. Chancery and Superior Cts., 1967-68; assoc. Young, Conaway, Stargatt & Taylor, Wilmington, Del., 1968-71; ptnr. Young, Conaway, Stargatt & Taylor, Wilmington, 1971-85; vice chancellor Ct. of Chancery State of Del., 1985—; adj. prof. Widener U. Sch. Law, 1986—; chmn. Bar-Bench-Media Conf. Del., 1992-93; mem. various faculty continuing legal edn. programs. Contbr. articles to profl. jours. Vice chmn. Nat. Jewish Cmty. Rels. Adv. Coun., 1985-89; bd. dirs. Jewish Fedn. Del., 1981-87, Del. Symphony Assn., 1991-95, Del. Cmty. Found., 1994—, chair grants com., 1998—; pres. Milton & Hattie Kutz Home, 1990-92. Mem. ABA (litigation sect., bus. law sect.), Am. Law Inst., Del. Bar Assn., Harvard Law Sch. Del. (pres. 1986-87), Phi Beta Kappa. Democrat. Jewish. Home: 28 Beethoven Dr Wilmington DE 19807-1923 Office: Ct of Chancery 1000 N King St Wilmington DE 19801-3334

JACOBS, JEFFREY LEE, lawyer, education network company executive; b. Boston, Jan. 20, 1951; s. Philip and Millicent T. (Katz) J.; m. Deborah R. Rath, June 7, 1981; children: Alison, Hannah. BA, U. Pa., 1973; MPA, U. So. Calif., 1979; JD, Pace U., 1985. Bar: Conn. 1985, N.Y. 1988. Asst. to comptroller gen. U.S. Gen. Acctg. Office, Washington, 1976-80; sr. rsch. assoc. Nat. Acad. Pub. Adminstrn., Washington, 1980-83; dir. of seminars Prentice Hall, Clifton, N.J., 1985-87; pres. Profl. Edn. Network, Inc., Westport, Conn., 1987—; lectr. Ga. Tax Inst., Ohio Fed. Tax Inst.; adj. prof. Quinnipiac Coll., U. New Haven; cons. Primedia Workplace Learning. Co-author: GAO: Government Accountability, 1979; producer, writer TV series The CPA Report, 1988-91; producer, writer radio series Legal Practice Alert, 1990—. Trustee Westport Pub. Libr. Mem. ABA (taxation sect.), Acad. Legal Studies in Bus. Home: 16 Janson Dr Westport CT 06880-2568 Office: Profl Edn Network 181 Post Rd W Westport CT 06880-4626

JACOBS, JEREMY M., diversified holding company executive, hockey team owner; m. Margaret Jane Davis; 6 children. DHL (hon.), Canisius Coll.; BA, SUNY, Buffalo; grad. advancement mgmt. program, Harvard U. Chmn., c.e.o. Del. North Cos., Buffalo, NY; former owner Cin. Royals Basketball team; owner, gov. Boston Bruins, NHL,, 1975—; owner Boston Garden, now Fleet Ctr., 1975—. Active United Way, NCCJ, Joint Ctr. for Polit. and Econ. Studies, Internat. Tennis Hall of Fame. Office: Del North Company Inc 1 Del North Pl 438 Main St Ste 1 Buffalo NY 14202-3207 Office: Boston Bruins One Fleet Ctr Ste 250 Boston MA 02214*

JACOBS, JIM, playwright, composer, lyricist, actor; b. Chgo., Oct. 7, 1942; m. Diane Rita Gomez, June 5, 1965 (div. 1974); 1 child, Kristine; m. Denise Nettleton, Apr. 29, 1978. Student, Chgo. City Coll., 1962-63. Appeared in over 50 cmty. and profl. theatre prodns. including Until the Monkey Comes, 1966, Take Me Along, 1967, Flora, The Red Menace, 1968, Entertaining Mr. Sloane, 1969, The Serpent, 1969, Don't Drink the Water, 1970, Jimmy Shine, 1970, all Chgo., No Place to Be Somebody, nat. touring co., 1971, on Broadway, 1971, The Magnolia Club, Chgo., 1975, The Local Stigmatic, Chgo., 1976; dir. The Ruffian on the Stair, Chgo., 1975; actor: (films) Medium Cool, 1969, Love in a Taxi, 1976, (TV series) Open All Night, 1982; author, lyricist, composer: (with Warren Casey) Grease, Broadway, 1972-80, (Tony award nomination 1972, Grammy award nomination 1972), London-West End, 1973, 77, motion picture, 1979, (revival) Grease, London, 1993—(Olivier award nomination), (revival) Broadway, 1994-98 (Tony award nomination), Grease On Ice (Am. Ice Show Tour), 1998—; author: (with Warren Casey) Island of Lost Coeds, 1979; (with Jim Weston) Bats in the Belfry, 1982; (with Jim Weston) Remember the Night, 1988. Recipient Humanitarian of Yr. award Young Adult Inst., N.Y.C., 1992. Mem. Dramatists Guild, Authors League Am., ASCAP, Actors Equity Assn., Screen Actors Guild., AFTRA. Office: care Ronald Taft PC 18 W 55th St New York NY 10019-5315

JACOBS, JOHANN, performing arts company executive. Gen. mgr. Oreg. Ballet Theatre; exec. dir. Ballet West, Salt Lake City, 1998—. Office: Ballet West 50 W 200 S Salt Lake City UT 84101-6922*

JACOBS, JOHN HOWARD, professional society administrator; b. Phila., June 7, 1925; s. Howard Elias and Elizabeth Pauline (Dresel) J.; m. Shirley Elizabeth Salini, Apr. 21, 1960. BS in Econs., N.Mex. State U., 1950; LLD (hon.), Golden Gate U., 1985. Adminstrv. officer U.S. Fgn. Service (NATO), London, Paris, 1951-53; gen. mgr. Vis-a-Pack Corp., Beverly, N.J., 1953-58; exec. dir. Red. Agy., City of Stockton, Calif., 1958-66, San Francisco Planning and Urban Research, 1966-81; exec. dir. San Francisco C. of C., 1981-88, pres., 1988-89; chmn. Pacific Region Nat. Assn. Housing and Redevel. Ofcls., Stockton, 1965-66, mem. nat. bd. govs., San Francisco, 1966-70. Trustee emeritus Fine Arts Mus. San Francisco; bd. dirs. Point Reyes Bird Obs., San Francisco, World Affairs Coun. No. Calif., San Francisco State U. Found.; chmn. pres.'s adv. coun. San Francisco State U.; v.p. San Francisco Devel. Fund. Home: 2823 Octavia St San Francisco CA 94123-4305*

JACOBS, JOHN PATRICK, lawyer; b. Chgo., Oct. 27, 1945; s. Anthony N. and Bessie (Montgomery) J.; m. Linda I. Grams, Oct. 6, 1973; 1 child, Christine Margaret. BA cum laude, U. Detroit, 1967, JD magna cum laude, 1970. Bar: Mich. 1970, U.S. Dist. Ct. Mich. (ea. dist.) 1970, U.S. Ct. Appeals (6th cir.) 1974, U.S. Ct. Appeals (D.C. cir.) 1988, U.S. Supreme Ct. 1978. Law clk. to chief judge Mich. Ct. Appeals, Detroit, 1970-71; assoc., then ptnr. Plunkett & Cooney P.C., Detroit, 1972-92, also bd. dirs.; founding ptnr., prin. mem. O'Leary, O'Leary, Jacobs, Mattson, Perry & Mason P.C., Southfield, Mich., 1992—; investigator Atty. Grievance Com., Detroit, 1975-84; mem. hearing panel Atty. Discipline Bd., Detroit, 1984-87, 94—; adj. prof. law Sch. Law, U. Detroit, 1983-84, faculty advisor, 1984-89, Pres.'s Cabinet, 1982—; elected rep. State Bar Rep. Assembly, Lansing, Mich., 1980-82, 91-92, 93-96; fellow Mich. State Bar Found., 1990-98; treas., mem. steering com. Mich. Bench-Bar Appellate Conf. Com., 1994—; apptd. mem. Mich. Supreme Ct. Com. on Appellate Fees, 1990; spl. mediator appellate negotiation program Mich. Ct. Appeals, 1995—; mem. exec. com. Mich. Appellate Bench-Bar Conf. Found., 1996—; apptd. mem. select com. on improving def. counsel, insurer rels., Mich. State Bar. Biographer The Michigan Lawyer, 1996. Bd. dirs. Boysville of Mich., Clinton, 1988-95, 99—, chmn. pub. policy com., 1993-95, pub. policy liaison, 1999—; apptd. mem. State Bar Mich. Blue Ribbon Com. Improving Def. Counsel-Insurer Rels., 1998-99, spl. amicus curiae counsel to Mich. Supreme Ct., 1999. Recipient Robert E. Dice Med. Malpractice Def. Atty. award Mich. Physicians, 1986; Reginald Heber Smith fellow, 1971-72. Fellow Am. Acad. Appellate Lawyers, Mich. Std. Jury Instn. (subcom. employment law 1984-87); mem. ABA (litigation sect., appellate subcom., torts and ins. practice), Internat. Assn. Def. Counsel (v.p., amicus curiae com., med. and legal malpractice coms., product liability com.), Fedn. Ins. and Corp. Counsel, Mich. Def. Trial Counsel (chmn. amicus curiae com. 1986-88, chmn. future planning com., bd. dirs. 1989—, treas. 1993-94, sec. 1994-95, v.p. 1995-96, program chair 1990, 94, 95, pres., 1996-97), Def. Rsch. Inst. (state rep. 1997-98, Outstanding Performance Citation 1997, appellate com. steering com. 1997—), Cath. Lawyers Soc. (bd. dirs. 1988-98, emeritus dir. 1998—, pres. 1994-95). Democrat. Roman Catholic. Avocations: collecting antique law books, film. Office: O'Leary O'Leary Jacobs Mattson Perry and Mason PC 26777 Central Park Blvd Ste 275 Southfield MI 48076-4167

JACOBS, JOSEPH JOHN, engineering company executive; b. June 13, 1916; s. Joseph and Afiffie (Forzley) J.; m. Violet Jabara, June 14, 1942; children: Margaret, Linda, Valerie. B.S. in Chem. Engring, Poly. Inst. N.Y., Bklyn., 1937, M.S., 1939, PhD., 1942. Registered profl. engr., N.Y., N.J., La., Calif. Chem. engr. Autoxygen, Inc., N.Y.C., 1939-42; sr. chem. engr. Merck & Co., Rahway, N.J., 1942-44; v.p., tech. dir. Chemurgic Corp., Richmond, Calif., 1944-47; pres. Jacobs Engring. Co., Pasadena, Calif., 1947-74; chmn. bd., CEO Jacobs Engring. Group Inc., Pasadena, 1974-92, chmn. bd., 1992—; bd. dirs. Cedars Bank, Digital Gene Techs., Inc. Contbr. tech. articles to profl. jours. Trustee Poly. U. N.Y., Harvey Mudd Coll.; mem.

Assocs. Calif. Inst. Tech.; bd. dirs. Inst. Contemporary Studies, Calif.; bd. visitors Anderson Sch., UCLA. Recipient Herbert Hoover medal United Engrng. Socs., 1983. Fellow AIChE, Am. Inst. Chemists, Inst. for Advancement Engrng.; mem. AAAS, Nat. Acad. Engrng., Am. Chem. Soc., L.A. C. of C., Pasadena C. of C., Annandale Golf Club, Sigma Xi, Phi Lambda Upsilon. Office: Jacobs Engrng Group Inc 1111 S Arroyo Pkwy Pasadena CA 91105-3254

JACOBS, JULIAN I., federal judge; b. Balt., Aug. 13, 1937; s. Sidney and Bernice (Kellman) J.; m. Donna Buffenstein; children: Richard S., Jennifer K. B.A., U. Md., 1958, J.D., 1960; LL.M., Georgetown U., 1965. Bar: Md., 1960. Atty. chief counsel's office IRS, Washington, 1961-65; trial atty. regional counsel's office IRS, Buffalo, 1965-67; assoc. Weinberg & Green, Balt., 1967-69, Hoffberger & Hollander, Balt., 1969-72; assoc. Gordon Feinblatt Rothman Hoffberger & Hollander, Balt., 1972-74, ptnr., 1974-84; judge U.S. Tax Ct., Washington, 1984—; chmn. study commn. Md. Tax Ct., 1978-79, mem. rules com., 1980; mem. spl. study group Md. Gen. Assembly, 1980; adj. prof. grad. tax program U. Balt., 1991-93. Mem. U. Md. Law Rev. Bd. dirs. Md. Research Inst., Inc. Mem. Md. State Bar Assn. (past chmn. taxation sect.), Balt. City Bar Assn. (past chmn. tax legis. subcom.). Office: US Tax Ct 400 2nd St NW Washington DC 20217

JACOBS, KENT FREDERICK, dermatologist; b. El Paso, Tex., Feb. 13, 1938; s. Carl Frederick and Mercedes D. (Johns) J.; m. Sallie Ritter, Apr. 13, 1971. BS, N.Mex. State U., 1960; MD, Northwestern U., 1964; postgrad., U. Colo., 1967-70. Dir. service unit USPHS, Laguna, N.Mex., 1966-67; pvt. practice specializing in dermatology Las Cruces, N.Mex., 1970—; cons. U.S. Army, San Francisco, 1968-70, cons. NIH, Washington, 1983, Holloman AFB, 1972-77; research assoc. VA Hosp., Denver, 1969-70; preceptor U. Tex., Galveston, 1976-77; mem. clin. staff Tex. Tech U., Lubbock, 1977—; asst. clin. prof. U. N.Mex., Albuquerque, 1972—; bd. dirs. First Security Corp. of N.Mex. Author: Breckkan, 1996; contbr. articles to profl. jours. and popular mags. Trustee Mus. N.Mex. Found., 1987-99, mem. bd. regents, 1987-99, pres., 1989-91, 95-99; bd. dirs. Dona Ana Arts Coun., 1992-93, Border Book Festival, 1996—, N.Mex. State U. Found., 1993—. Invitational scholar Oreg. Primate Ctr., 1968; Acad. Dermatology Found. fellow, 1969; named Disting. Alumnus N.Mex. State U., 1985. Fellow Am. Acad. Dermatology, Royal Soc. Medicine, Soc. Investigative Dermatology; mem. AMA, Fedn. State Med. Bds. (bd. dirs. 1984-86), N.Mex. Med. Soc., N.Mex. Bd. Med. Examiners (pres. 1983-84, N.Mex. State U. Alumni Assn. (bd. dirs. 1975-79), Mil Gracias Club (pres. 1972-74) Pres.'s Assocs., Univ. Ambs., Rotary, Phi Beta Kappa, Beta Beta Beta. Democrat. Presbyterian. Home: 3610 Southwind Rd Las Cruces NM 88005-5556 Office: Bldg 15 Ste 106 Las Cruces NM 88011-9148

JACOBS, LAURENCE STANTON, physician, educator; b. Boston, Mar. 24, 1940; s. David W. and Sylvia Dorothea (Berenson) J.; m. Katherine Elizabeth Meyerand, Mar. 24, 1963; children: Karen Emily, Pamela Susan. AB magna cum laude, Harvard U., 1960; MD, U. Rochester, 1965. Diplomate Am. Bd. Internal. Medicine. Intern Barnes Hosp., St. Louis, 1965, resident, 1966-67; research fellow Washington U. Med. Sch., St. Louis, 1967-68, 70-72, asst. prof., 1972-77; assoc. prof. U. Rochester, 1977-82, prof., 1982—, dir. Clin. Research Ctr., 1977-91; assoc. dean Sch. Medicine and Dentistry U. Rochester, N.Y., 1990-94; dir. residency edn. Strong Meml. Hosp., 1990-94; researcher in field; prof. medicine U. Rochester Sch. of Medicine and Dentistry; chmn. merit rev. bd. in endocrinology VA, Washington, 1983-86; mem. study sect. NIH, 1987-91. Contbr. articles to profl. publs., chpts. to books. Served to lt. comdr. USPHS, 1968-70. Mem. Assn. Am. Medical Colls. (northeast group on student affairs), Assn. Clin. Research Ctr. Dirs. (treas., bd. dirs., pres.-elect, pres. 1987-89), Endocrine Soc. (sci. program com. 1983-85), Am. Fedn. for Clin. Research, Am. Soc. for Clin. Investigation, Internat. Soc. for Neuroendocrinology, N.Y. Acad. Scis., Am. Diabetes Assn., Am. Soc. Biochem. and Molecular Biol., Alpha Omega Alpha. Avocations: skiing; ice skating, sailing. Office: U Rochester Sch Medicine PO Box 693 601 Elmwood Ave Rochester NY 14642-0001

JACOBS, LESLIE WILLIAM, lawyer; b. Akron, Ohio, Dec. 5, 1944; s. Leslie Wilson and Louise Frances (Walker) J.; m. Laurie Hutchinson, July 12, 1962; children—Leslie James, Andrew Wilson, Walker Fulton. Student, Denison U., 1962-63; B.S., Northwestern U., 1965; J.D., Harvard U., 1968. Bar: Ohio 1968, D.C. 1980, U.S. Supreme Ct. 1971, Brussels 1996. Law clk. to Chief Justice Kingsley A. Taft Ohio Supreme Ct., 1968-69; assoc. Thompson, Hine and Flory, Cleve., 1969-76, ptnr., 1976—, chmn. antitrust, internat. and regulatory area, 1988—; lectr. Ohio Legal Ctr. Insts., Ohio State Bar Assn. Antitrust and Corp. Counsel Insts., Fed. Bar Assn., ABA, Canadian Inst., Internat. Assn. Young Lawyers, others; mem. Ohio Bd. Bar Examiners, 1990-94. Contbr. articles to profl. jours. Chmn. Cleve. Ctr. Econ. Edn., 1990-93; mem. vis. com. Case Western Res. U. Sch. Law, 1985-91; mem. Leadership Cleve., 1988. Lt. comdr. USNR, 1967-79. Fellow Am. Bar Found. (life), Ohio State Bar Found. (life, trustee 1985-87, Ritter award 1997); mem. ABA (ho. dels. 1986—, antitrust law sect. coun. 1985-88, officer 1991-97, state del. 1995—, nominating com. 1995—), Ohio State Bar Assn. (pres. 1987, Ohio Bar medal 1990), Cleve. Bar Assn. (chmn. jud. selection com. 1982, trustee 1983-85), Am. Law Inst., Nat. Conf. Bar Pres., Internat. Club (Washington), Harvard Club (N.Y.C.), Chagrin Valley Hunt Club, Union Club (Cleve.), Castalia Trout Club. Republican. Presbyterian. Office: Thompson Hine & Flory LLP 3900 Key Ctr 127 Public Sq Cleveland OH 44114-1216

JACOBS, LINDA ROTROFF, elementary school educator; b. Peebles, Ohio, June 10, 1942; d. Joseph Harold Rotroff and Mary Lucille (Peterson) Rotroff Nixon; m. Donald Eugene Jacobs, Nov. 29, 1968; 1 child, Donald Brett. BS in Edn., Ohio State U., 1963; MA in Edn., U. Cin., 1968; postgrad., U. Cin., Miami U., Xavier U., 1968—, Coll. Mt. St. Joseph, 1968—. Cert. tchr., Ohio. Tchr. K-8 Forest Hills Bd. Edn., Cin., 1963-74, 77—; tchr. kindergarten Chillicothe (Ohio) Bd. Edn., 1974-77; tchr. reading adult edn. Cin., 1975; tchr. kindergarten Mercer Elem. Forest Hills, Cin., 1977—; tchr. pupil enrichment program Mercer Elem. Forest Hills, 1997-99; cooperating tchr. student tchrs. Ohio U., U. Cin., No. Ky. U., 1965—; tchr. summer sch. 4th, 5th, and 6th grades math./lang. arts, Cin., 1964-68, kindergarten and 1st grade Forest Hills, Cin., 1978-82; tchr. rep. Head Start, Chillicothe, 1975-77; kindergarten coord. Forest Hills and Hamilton County, Cin., 1965-70, 83-85; mem. supt.'s coun. Forest Hills, Cin., 1979, 82, 88; tchr. rep. PTA, Cin., 1967, 73, 82, 89; facilitator Forest Hills Summer Sch., 1993-96, 97-98; master tchr./advisor entry tchrs. Forest Hills, 1993—; career mentor Ashford-McCarthy Resources, Inc., 1993-94; coord. early entrance screening Hamilton County, 1994, 95, faculty mem. Intervention Based Multifactored Evaluation Com., 1994, 95, mem. Collaboration Team for Inclusion of Spl. Children, 1994, 95; mem. responsive classroom team, 1996-97; mem. steering com. accelerated schs., 1997-98, mem. diversity cadre Accelerated Schs., Great Aspirations pilot program Mercer Elem. Sch. Author: Getting Ready for Kindergarten, 1978, Parenting Tips, 1982, Intervention Assistance Team Handbook, 1992;. Cons. Women Helping Women, Cin., 1989. Recipient Ohio State U. Scarlet and Gray award, 1995; named Hamilton County Tchr. of Yr., 1965. Mem. NEA, Nat. PTA (rep.) Tchrs. Applying Whole Lang., Ohio Edn. Assn. (del. 1965), Southwestern Ohio Edn. Assn., Forest Hills Educators Assn. (sec. 1964-68, Martha Holden Jennings scholar 1976-77), DAR, Ohio State U. Alumni Club of Clermont County (sec. 1995-98), Alpha Kappa Delta (sec. 1975—). Mem. Ch. of Christ. Avocations: interior decorating, writing stories/poems, music, landscaping, reading.

JACOBS, SISTER MARGARET MARY, nurse; b. Cin., Jan. 11, 1945; d. John J. and Elizabeth M. (Brady) J. Diploma, St. Joseph Infirmary Sch., 1967; AB in Biology, Thomas Moore Coll., 1973; BSN, Coll. of Mt. St. Joseph, 1983; MA in Nursing Adminstrn., NYU, 1996, MA in Care of Adult Patient, 1996. RN, Ohio, Ky.; cert. adult nurse practitioner. Nurse St. Joseph Hosp., Lexington, Ky., 1976-77, Our Lady of the Way Hosp., Martin, Ky., 1967-76, St. Francis/St. George Hosp., Cin., Holy Family Home, Melbourne; patient care coord. Hospice of Big Sandy, Paintsville, 1985-93; nurse practitioner Oakhill (Ohio) Cmty. Med. Ctr. Clinics, 1996—, Jackson, Ohio, 1996—; mem. speakers bur. on pain control Purdue Frederick Co. Compiled textbook on basic coronary care. Mem. ANA, Ky. Nurses Assn.

JACOBS, MARIAN, advertising agency owner; b. Stockton, Calif., Sept. 11, 1927; d. Paul and Rose (Sallah) J. AA, Stockton Coll. With Bottarini Advt., Stockton, 1948-50; pvt. practice Stockton, 1950-64; with Olympius Advt., Stockton, 1964-78; pvt. practice Stockton, 1978—; pres. Stockton Advt. Club, 1954, Venture Club, Stockton, 1955; founder Stockton Advt. and Mktg. Club, 1981. Founder Stockton Arts Comms., 1976, Sunflower Entertainment for Institutionalized, 1976, Women Execs., Stockton, 1978; founding dir. Pixie Woods, Stockton; bd. dir. Goodwill Industries, St. Mary's Dining Room, Alan Short Gallery; mem. Calif. Coun. for the Humanities, 1994-95. Paul Harris fellow Rotary Club, 1994; recipient Woman of Achievement award San Joaquin County Women's Coun., Stockton, 1976, Achievement award San Joaquin Delta Coll., Stockton, 1978, Friend of Edn. award Calif. Tchrs. Assn., Stockton, 1988, Stanley McCaffrey Disting. Svc. award, U. of the Pacific, Stockton, 1988, Athena award for Businesswoman of Yr. Greater Stockton C. of C., 1989, Role Model award Tierra del Oro Girl Scouts U.S., 1989; named Stocktonian of the Yr. Stockton Bd. of Realtors, 1978, Outstanding Citizen Calif. State Senate & Assembly, 1978; the Marian Jacobs Writers & Poets Symposium was established in her honor. Republican. Roman Catholic. Avocations: art, photography. Home and Office: 4350 Mallard Creek Cir Stockton CA 95207-5205

JACOBS, MARK NEIL, financial services corporation executive, lawyer; b. Ogdensburg, N.Y., Apr. 2, 1946; s. A. Milton and Alma (Rothwein) J.; m. Susan Ruth Sadowsky, Aug. 17, 1968; children: Melanie Beth, Andrew Lawrence, Jonathan Alexander. B.A., Wagner Coll., 1967; J.D., N.Y. Law Sch., 1971. Bar: N.Y. Law clk. Goldman, Frier & Altesman, N.Y.C., 1971-72; trial atty. U.S. SEC, N.Y.C., 1972-75, supervisory trial atty., br. of enforcement, 1975-77; asst. gen. counsel The Dreyfus Corp., N.Y.C., 1977-82, sec., assoc. gen. counsel, 1982-92, sec., dep. gen. counsel, 1992-94; v.p.-legal, sec., 1994-96, v.p., gen. counsel, sec., 1996—. Mem. ABA. Office: The Dreyfus Corp 8th Fl W 200 Park Ave Fl 7W New York NY 10166-0039*

JACOBS, MARK RANDOLPH, lawyer; b. Columbus, Ohio, June 7, 1953; s. Lee Randolph and Sally Ann (Cummins) J.; m. Linda Beth Rogozinski, Oct. 29, 1983; children: Philip Randolph, Gregory Cummins. BA cum laude with distinction, Yale U., 1979, JD, 1982. Bar: N.Y. 1983, U.S. Dist. Ct. (so. dist.) N.Y. 1983, Conn. 1993. Law clerk Hon. S.W. Kram U.S. Dist. Judge, N.Y., 1983-84; ptnr. Pryor, Cashman, Sherman & Flynn, N.Y., 1988-90, Cadwalader, Wickersham & Taft, N.Y., 1990-92; of counsel Gregory & Adams, Wilton, Conn., 1992-96; ptnr. Jacobs Goldman LLC, Norwalk, Conn., 1997—. Office: Jacobs Goldman LLC Merritt View 383 Main Ave Norwalk CT 06851-1543

JACOBS, MICHAEL JOSEPH, lawyer; b. Bridgeport, Conn., May 17, 1941; s. Joseph Bernard and Edith (Roselund) J.; m. Maureen Anne Collins, Aug. 13, 1966; children: Melanie Anne, Jason Daniel. BS, USCG Acad., 1963; JD with honors, George Washington U., 1971. Bar: Va. 1971, U.S. Ct. Appeals (4th cir.) 1976, U.S. Supreme Ct. 1978, Hawaii 1979, Md. 1983, D.C. 1983, U.S. Dist. Ct. Md. 1983. Enlisted USCG, 1959, advanced through grades to comdr., 1978; legis. counsel USCG, Washington, 1971-74; trial counsel USCG, San Francisco, 1974-77; legal officer USCG, Honolulu, 1977-81; staff atty. USCG, Washington, 1981-83; sr. assoc. Miles & Stockbridge, Easton, Md., 1983-86; ptnr. litigation Miles & Stockbridge A Profl. Corp., Easton, Md., 1986-94; solo practice Easton, 1994-97; ptnr. Jacobs & Barney, Easton, 1997—. Articles editor George Washington Law Rev., 1970-71; contbr. articles to profl. jours. Mem. ABA (sec. gen. practice sect. 1984-85, constabars bar leader of the yr. 1994), Md. State Bar Assn. (mem. coun. gen. practice sect. 1985—, chair 1991-92, mem. task force on solo and small firm practitioners 1992-96, mem. bd. govs. 1995-97, chair standing com. on solo and small firm practice 1997—), Md. Trial Lawyers Assn., U.S. Maritime Law Assn. (proctor 1983—), Talbot County Bar Assn., Rotary, Order of Coif. Democrat. Roman Catholic. Avocations: running, sailing, fishing, whitewater rafting and canoeing. Office: Jacobs & Barney Talbot Landing No 8 295 Bay St Easton MD 21601-2799

JACOBS, NORMAN G(ABRIEL), sociologist, educator; b. N.Y.C., Feb. 28, 1924; s. Joseph and Beatrice (Esserman) J.; m. Margaret Alice Ayres, Aug. 20, 1956; children: Laurie, Charles. BS, CCNY, 1943; AM, Harvard U., 1950, PhD, 1951. Sociologist natural resources sect. SCAP, Tokyo, 1945-46; lectr. Taiwan Normal U., 1955-57; researcher Am. U., 1957-59; community devel. adviser AID, Shiraz, Iran, 1959-61; from asst. prof. to prof. sociology U. Kans., Lawrence, 1962-65; prof. sociology and Asian studies U. Ill., Urbana, 1965-90, prof. emeritus, 1990—; adj. prof. East Asian studies Dickinson Coll., Carlisle, Pa., 1990—; Fulbright prof., Thailand, 1965-66; sr. research scholar Korean Inst. Buddhist Studies, 1975; exchange prof. Keio U., Tokyo, 1968-69. Author: The Origin of Modern Capitalism and Eastern Asia, 1958, 81, Sociology of Development, 1966, Modernization without Development, 1972, The Korean Road to Modernization and Development, 1985, Patrimonial Interpretation of Indian Society, 1989, also articles.; co-author: Japanese Coinage, 1953, 72. With AUS, 1943-46. Mem. Indian Sociol. Soc. (life), Assn. Asian Studies, Pali Text Soc., Internat. Soc. for Japanese Philately, Dai Nippon Soc. of The Netherlands. Theravada Buddhist. Home: 233 Walnut St Carlisle PA 17013-3734 Office: Dickinson Coll Dept East Asian Studies Carlisle PA 17013

JACOBS, NORMAN JOSEPH, publishing company executive; b. Chgo., Oct. 28, 1932; s. Herman and Tillie (Chapman) J.; m. Jeri Kolber Rose, Jan. 2, 1977; 1 son, Barry Herman; children by previous marriage—Carey, Murray, Dale. B.S. in Mktg, U. Ill., 1954. Display salesman Chgo. Daily News, 1954-57; dist. mgr. Davidson Pub. Co., Chgo., 1957-62; v.p. Press-Tech, Inc., Evanston, Ill., 1962-69; pres. Century Pub. Co., Evanston, 1969—; bd. dirs. Chgo. Bulls. Bd. dirs. United Cerebral Palsey Chgo. Served with USNR, 1951-59. Mem. B'nai B'rith, Birchwood Tennis Club, Alpha Delta Sigma, Tau Epsilon Phi. Jewish. Office: Century Pub Co 990 Grove St Evanston IL 60201

JACOBS, PATRICIA LOUISE, geriatrics nurse; b. Battle Creek, Iowa, Feb. 27, 1958; d. John Otto and Mary Ellen (Owens) J. Nurse aide cert., Western Iowa Tech., 1976. CNA. Nurse asst. Beverly Enterprises, Las Vegas, Nev., 1979-80, Hillhaven, West Des Moines, Iowa, 1983-86, Sunrise Manor, Sioux City, Iowa, 1988-89, Countryside Retirement Home, Sioux City, 1989-91, Julia's Valley Manor, Sioux City, 1991-93, Fellowship Village, Inwood, Iowa, 1993-96, Good Samaratin Home, Lennox, S.D., 1996—; mem. spl. care unit Good Samaratin Ctr., Canton, S.D., 1996—; nurse asst. Kimberly Nursing, West Des Moines, 1982-83, 86. Republican. Roman Catholic. Avocations: reading, writing, piano, cross-stitch, needlepoint. Home: 209 S Maple St Inwood IA 51240

JACOBS, PAUL ALAN, lawyer; b. Boston, June 5, 1940; s. Samuel and Sarah (Rodman) J.; m. Carole Ruth Greenstein, Aug. 28, 1962; children: Steven N., Cheryl R., David F., Craig A. BA in Econs. magna cum laude, Tufts U., 1960; JD magna cum laude, U. Denver, 1968. Bar: Colo. 1968, U.S. Dist. Ct. Colo. 1968. Personnel officer First Nat. Bank Denver, 1964-68; assoc. Holme Roberts & Owen, Denver, 1968-73, sr. ptnr., 1973-93; exec. v.p., gen. counsel Colo. Rockies profl. baseball orgn., Denver, 1991-95; ptnr. Jacobs Chase Frick Kleinkopf & Kelley, Denver, 1995—. Bd. dirs. Anti-Defamation League B'nai B'rith, Denver, 1987-95. Served to 1st lt. USAF, 1960-63. Mem. ABA, Denver Bar Assn., Colo. Bar Assn. Jewish. Avocations: skiing, racquetball. Home: 4201 S Narcissus Way Denver CO 80237-2025 Office: Independence Plz 1050 17th St Ste 1500 Denver CO 80265-2078

JACOBS, PETER DANIEL ALEXANDER, architecture and landscape architecture educator; b. Montreal, Que., Can., Dec. 3, 1939; s. Joseph Jacob and Frances (Alexander) J.; m. Ellen-gail Vineberg, Aug. 17, 1967; children: Merav Beth, David Aurum. BA, Antioch Coll., Yellow Springs, Ohio, 1961; MArch, Harvard U., 1964, M Landscape Architect, 1968. Asst. prof. N.S. Tech. Coll., Halifax, Can., 1968-71; assoc. prof. U. Montreal, 1971-80, prof., 1980—; invited prof. U. Aix-Marseille, Aix-en-Provence, France, 1971, U. B.C., Vancouver, Can., 1980, Technion U., Haifa, Israel, 1983, Harvard U., Cambridge, Mass., 1978-90, U. del Valle, Colombia, 1990-93; chmn. environ. planning commn. Internat. Union for Conservation of Nature and Natural Resources, Gland, Switzerland, 1978-90; chmn. pub. adv. com. state of environ. report Govt. of Can., 1989-92. Author: Environmental Strategy and Action, 1981; (with D. Munro) Conservation with Equity, 1986; also articles; co-designer Pl. Berri Urban Pla., Montreal. Pres. Green Spaces Assn., Montreal, 1970-75; v.p. Solomon Schechter Acad., Montreal, 1975-80; chmn. Kativik Environ. Quality Commn., Kuujjuaq, Que., 1980—; bd. dirs. Environ. Choice, Can., 1989-94; pres. Jewish Pub. Libr. of Montreal, 1998—. Recipient E.L. Tammsaare award IUCN, 1988, Gov. Gen.'s medal 125th Ann. of Can. Confedn., Pres.'s medal. Fellow Can. Soc. Landscape Architects (pres. 1978-80), Am. Soc. Landscape Architects; mem. Order Architects Que. Avocations: tennis, squash, photography, reading. Email: Peter.Jacobs@umontreal.ca. Office: Universite de Montreal, U Montreal, CP 6128 Succursale Centre-v, Montreal, PQ Canada H3C 3J7

JACOBS, RANDALL BRIAN, lawyer; b. N.Y.C., July 8, 1951; s. John and Evelyn Jacobs; 1 child, Jillian. BA, Coll. of Idaho, 1972; JD, U. West L.A., 1978. Bar: Calif., D.C., Wis. Lawyer B. Randall Jacobs Law Corp., Brentwood, Calif., 1978—; real estate broker Morgan Reed & Co., Brentwood, 1979—; pvt. investigator Randy Brian Assocs., Brentwood, 1976—. Reserve deputy sheriff, L.A. County Sheriff, L.A., 1979—. Mem. Shom Rim Soc., Nat. Rifle Assn., Masons, Shriners. Office: 522 S Sepulveda Blvd Ste 110 Los Angeles CA 90049-3538

JACOBS, RHODA S., state legislator; b. Bklyn.; m. Jerry Jacobs; 3 children. BA, Bklyn. Coll. Co-founder, formerly co-dir. Bklyn. Coll. Day Care Ctr.; mem. N.Y. State Assembly, 1978—, co-chair task force on homeless, task force New Americans, chair majority program com.; mem. banks com., corps., authorities and commns. com. ins. com., health com., legis. women's caucus. Mem. Bklyn. Women's Polit. Caucus, Nat. Assn. Jewish Legislators (sec., treas.). Office: NY State Assembly Rm 733 LOB Albany NY 12248

JACOBS, RICHARD DEARBORN, consulting engineering company executive; b. Detroit, July 6, 1920; s. Richard Dearborn and Mattie Phoebe (Cobleigh) J.; divorced; children: Richard, Margaret, Paul, Linden. BS, U. Mich., 1944. Registered profl. engr., Ill., Mich., Wis., Miss. Engr. Detroit Diesel Engine divsn. Gen. Motors, 1946-51; mgr. indsl. and marine engine divsn. Reo Motors, Inc., Lansing, Mich., 1951-54; chief engr. Kennedy Marine Engine Co., Biloxi, Miss., 1955-59; marine sales mgr. Nordberg Mfg. Co., Milw., 1959-69, Fairbanks Morse Engine divsn. Colt Industries, Beloit, Wis., 1969-81; pres. R.D. Jacobs & Assocs., cons. engrs., naval arch. & marine engrs., Roscoe, Ill., 1981—. With AUS, 1944-46. Mem. ASTM, Soc. Naval Archs. and Marine Engrs. (chmn. sect. 1979-80), Soc. Automotive Engrs., Am. Soc. Naval Engrs., Soc. Am. Mil. Engrs., Navy League U.S., Propeller Club U.S., Nat. Forensic Ctr., Rockford Polo Club, Masons. Unitarian. Office: 11405 Main St Roscoe IL 61073-9569

JACOBS, RICHARD E., lawyer; b. Lakewood, Ohio. BSBA, Ohio State U., 1976, MBA, 1980, JD, 1980. Bar: Ohio 1980, Ky. 1982. Atty. Ashland Oil, Inc., 1981-86, LEXIS-NEXIS, 1986—; v.p., gen. counsel LEXIS-NEXIS, Dayton, Ohio. Mem. ABA, Ohio Bar Assn., Ky. Bar Assn., Am. Corp. Counsel Assn. Office: LEXIS NEXIS PO Box 933 Dayton OH 45401-0933*

JACOBS, RICHARD E., real estate executive, sports team owner; divorced; 3 children. Ptnr. Jacobs, Visconsi & Jacobs; chmn., chief exec. officer Cleve. Indians. Office: Cleve Indians Jacobs Field 2401 Ontario St Cleveland OH 44115-4003 also: Richard E Jacobs Group 25425 Center Ridge Rd Cleveland OH 44145-4122*

JACOBS, RICHARD JAMES, banker, educator; b. Jamaica, N.Y., Sept. 27, 1941; s. John Beck and Doris Marie (Lewin) J.; m. Jean Anita McIntosh, Aug. 29, 1964; children: Kristine Anne, John McIntosh. BA, Muhlenberg Coll., 1963; MBA, U. Pa., 1965. With Gulf Oil, 1965-72; fin. mgr. Gulf Oil, Balt., 1970-71; mktg. advisor Gulf Oil, Pitts., 1971-72; v.p. mktg. and ops. Finnegans, Inc., Chevy Chase, Md., 1972-73; dir. planning Geico Ins. Co., Chevy Chase, 1973-76; v.p., gen. mgr. G.H. Realty, Annapolis, Md., 1976-78; asst. v.p. mktg. Md. Nat. Bank, Balt., 1978-80, v.p. mktg., 1980-86, sr. v.p. mktg., 1986-88, sr. v.p. wholesale support, 1988-90; chmn., CEO Bottom Line Co., Balt., Md., 1990—; instr. mktg. Md. Banking Sch., Annapolis, 1988—; exec. dir. Wholesale Traders Group, 1981-83; prof. mktg. Johns Hopkins U., Balt., 1990-92. Coord. United Way, Balt., 1979; pres. Amberley Community Assn., Annapolis, 1980; off season job coord. Balt. Colts., 1982. Mem. Bank Mktg. Assn. (adv. coun. 1988-89), Mktg. Info. Group, Mchts. Club, Center Club, Fleet Reserve Club. Roman Catholic. Avocations: boating, fishing, cooking, travel. Home: 1614 Ridout Rd Annapolis MD 21401-5537 Office: Bottom Line Co 1 E Lexington St Baltimore MD 21202-1740

JACOBS, RICHARD MOSS, consulting engineer; b. N.Y.C., Jan. 19, 1925; s. Joseph and Rhoda E. (Levine) J.; m. Esther Rosalyn Siegal, Dec. 19, 1948; children: George Howard, Miriam Wendy, Robert Allan. BS in Indsl. Engring., Syracuse U., 1949, MS in Indsl. Engring., 1952. Registered profl. engr., N.J., Calif., cert. safety profl., quality engr., reliability engr. Mgr. reliability engrng. RCA, Moorestown, N.J., 1951-59; mgr. reliability, quality control, safety Sylvania Electric, Waltham, Mass., 1959-63; asst. dir. reliability Westinghouse Electric Co., Pitts., 1963-69; prof. indsl. engring. N.J. Inst. Tech., Newark, 1969-77; pres. Cons. Services Inst., Inc., Mt. Arlington, N.J., 1970-96, CEO, 1996—; mem. faculty Syracuse U., Villanova U., Drexel U., Boston U., Air Force Inst. Tech.; past internat. sec. reliability com. Internat. Electrotech. Commn., U.S. chief del., chmn. Formal Design Rev.. Com., 1969-93. Mem. editorial rev. bd. Reliability Transactions IEEE, Microelectronics and Reliability. Served with USN, 1943-46. Fellow ASME (chmn. safety engrng. and risk analysis div. 1991-92), Am. Soc. Quality Control, Israel Soc. for Quality Assurance; mem. IEEE (former sec. reliability group), ANSI, ASTM, Am. Soc. Safety Engrs. Democrat. Jewish. Office: Cons Svcs Inst Inc 111 Howard Blvd Ste 204 Mount Arlington NJ 07856-1315

JACOBS, ROBERT ALAN, lawyer; b. Waco, Tex., June 23, 1937; s. Abe and Ruth (Englander) J.; m. Sue C. Braunstein, Aug. 22, 1961; children: Jacqueline Anne, Michelle Keri. BBA, U. Tex., 1957; LLB cum laude, NYU, 1960, LLM in Taxation, 1963. Bar: N.Y. 1961. Assoc. Greenbaum, Wolff & Ernst, N.Y.C., 1961-63; asst. br. chief, chief counsel IRS, Washington, 1963-67; assoc. Paul, Weiss, Rifkind, Wharton & Garrison, N.Y.C., 1967-69; sr. tax mem. Milgrim Thomajan Jacobs & Lee PC, N.Y.C., 1969-87; tax ptnr. Milbank, Tweed, Hadley & McCloy, N.Y.C., 1987—; adj. prof. law NYU, 1976-85; vis. sr. lectr. taxation, U. Calif. Davis, 1977; spl. counsel to sec. treas., Washington, 1965-67. Note and comment editor NYU Law Rev.; contbr. articles to profl. jours. Mem. adv. group Senate Fin. Com. Staff on Subchpt. C. Revision, 1983-85; arbitrator Civil Ct. City of N.Y., 1972—; bd. dirs. Community Action Legal Svcs., 1978-82, MFY Legal Svcs., 1991-98, N.Y. County Lawyers, 1990-93. With U.S. Army, 1960-61. Root-Tilden scholar; recipient commendation medal U.S. Army. Mem. ABA (tax sect., asst. sec. 1987-88, chmn. com. corp. stockholder relationships 1983-85, chmn. task force on pass-through entities 1986-88), Am. Law Inst., Tax Forum (chmn. 1989—), Am. Coll. Tax Counsel, N.Y. State Bar Assn. (tax sect., exec. com. 1980—, sec. 1998), Tax Club (chmn. 1987-88). Office: Milbank Tweed Hadley & McCloy 1 Chase Manhattan Plz Fl 47 New York NY 10005-1413*

JACOBS, RODNEY L., bank executive. Vice chmn., CFO Wells Fargo & Co., San Francisco, 1998—. Office: Wells Fargo and Co 420 Montgomery St San Francisco CA 94104-1205*

JACOBS, ROLLY WARREN, lawyer; b. Nashville, Aug. 26, 1946; s. William Clinton Jr. and Eleanor Olive (Warren) J.; m. Karen Lee Ponist, Sept. 16, 1972; children: Collin Wayne, Tyler Warren. BA in Econs., Washington & Lee U., 1968; JD, U. S.C., 1974. Bar: S.C. 1975, U.S. Dist. Ct. for S.C. 1975. Assoc. Carl R. Reasonover, Camden, S.C., 1975-77; ptnr. Reasonover & Jacobs, Camden, S.C., 1977-80; pvt. practice law Camden, S.C., 1980—; asst. city judge Mcpl. Ct., Camden, 1976-77; master in equity S.C. Jud. Sys., Camden, 1978—; mem. Jud. Coun. for S.C., Columbia, 1989—, Fee Dispute Panel, 1986-93. d. dirs. ARC, Camden, 1976-78, Am. Cancer Soc., Camden, 1976-78, United Way, Camden, 1978-82; active Boy Scouts Am., Camden, 1984-96. Capt. U.S. Army, 1968-72. Recipient Dist. Award of Merit Indian Waters Coun. Boy Scouts Am., 1991. Mem. ABA, VFW, S.C. Bar Assn., Am. Legon, Res. Officers Assn., Elks. Methodist. Avocations: yard work, swimming. Home: 418 Lafayette Way Camden SC 29020-1642 Office: 612 Lafayette St Camden SC 29020-3520

JACOBS, RONALD NICHOLAS, television and motion picture producer/ director; b. Toledo, Nov. 3; s. Ray Joseph and Mary Mae (Popoff) J.; m. Rochelle Margaret Hageman, Oct. 10, 1959; children: Jennifer, Jeff, Jerry. BA, UCLA, 1956. judge best dirs. Acad. Cable Programming; lectr. TV and motion pictures UCLA and U. So. Calif.; presenter in field. Advanced from assoc. producer to exec. in charge of prodn. for various ind. cos. including Daisy Prodn., Sheldon Leonard Prodns., and was associated with shows including The Danny Thomas Show, That Girl, I Spy, The Dick Van Dyke Show, The Mod Squad; films include The Over The Hill Gang, Three On A Date, Samurai; producer films including On The Right Track, Jimmy The Kid, Land of the Free, Running Red; author films including Hanging By A Thread, In The Heat of Passion, Busted; dir. comedy shows, 2d unit action scenes, TV title sequences and commls. Bd. reps. Entertainment Industry Found.; bd. dirs. Jonsson Cancer Ctr., UCLA; trustee St. Jude Children's Rsch. Hosp. Recipient Cir. of Hope award City of Hope, Key to City, Memphis. Mem. NATAS (judge Emmy awards), Nat. Acad. Motion Picture Arts and Scis. (judge Nichol writing fellowships), Dirs. Guild Am. Avocation: tennis. Office: 11350 Ventura Blvd Studio City CA 91604-3140

JACOBS, RUTH HARRIET, poet, playwright, sociologist, gerontologist; b. Boston, Nov. 15, 1924; d. Samuel J. Miller and Jane G. (Miller); m. Neal Jacobs, Aug. 1948 (div.); children: Eli, Edith. B.S., Boston U, 1964; Ph.D, Brandeis U., 1969. Reporter, feature writer Herald-Traveler, Boston, 1943-49; tchr. Mass. Bay Community Coll., Northeastern U., 1961-69; prof. sociology Boston U., 1969-82; prof., chmn. dept. sociology Clark U., Worcester, Mass., 1982-87; vis. rsch. scholar Ctr. for Rsch. on Women Wellesley Coll., Mass., 1985—; prof. human svcs. Springfield Coll., Manchester, N.H., 1988—; lectr. Regis Coll., Weston, Mass., 1989—; vis. prof. Coll. William and Mary, 1990; vis. rsch. scholar Five Colls. Women's Rsch. Ctr., Mount Holyoke Coll., 1992; spkr. in field. Author: Life After Youth: Female, Forty, What Next, 1979, Button, Button, Who Has the Button, 1983, rev. edit., 1996, (manual) Older Women Surviving and Thriving, 1987, Out of Their Mouths, 1988, Be an Outrageous Older Woman: A.R.A.S.P., 1991, rev. edit., 1993, 2d rev. edit., 1997, We Speak for Peace: An Anthology, 1993, Women Who Touched My Life: A Memoir, 1996; co-author: Re-Engagement in Late Life: Re-Employment and Re-Marriage, 1979; contbr. articles to profl. jours., chpts. to books, poetry to anthologies and mags. NIMH grantee, 1972-75; Faculty fellow NSF, 1977-78; recipient Dewing Peace award, Pendle Hill, Walingford, Pa., 1993. Mem. New Eng. Sociol. Assn. (v.p. 1976, Pioneer award 1993). Mem. Soc. of Friends. Home and Office: 75 High Ledge Ave Wellesley MA 02482-1042

JACOBS, SIDNEY J., rabbi, journalist; b. Chgo., May 25, 1917; s. Emanuel and Sarah (Barnett) J.; m. Helen Rosenzweig, Mar. 4, 1951 (div. 1969); children: Nehama Aviva, Michael Ethan, Jonathan Gabriel.; m. Betty J. Lazaroff, July 1, 1971. BSc in Journalism, Northwestern U., 1938; Rabbi, Jewish Inst. Religion, N.Y.C., 1946; MA in Hebrew Letters, Hebrew Union Coll., 1969. Registrar and mem. history faculty Coll. Jewish Studies, Chgo., 1946-49; exec. dir. Chgo. Coun. Am. Jewish Congress, 1949-52; founding rabbi Niles Twp. Jewish Congregation, Skokie, Ill., 1952-70; v.p. Chgo. Bd. Rabbis, 1970-71; mng. editor B'nai B'rith Messenger, L.A., 1971; pres., CEO Jacobs Ladder Pubs., Culver City, Calif., 1985; vis. rabbi Temple Israel, Duluth, Minn., Congregation Beth Israel, Barstow, Calif., Temple Sinai, Cathedral City, Calif., Temple Ner Tamid, Downey, Calif.; lectr. Univ. Inst., Univ. Judaism, L.A., Earl Warren Inst. Ethics and Human Rels. Author: Jewish Word Book, 1982; co-author Clues About Jews for People Who Aren't, 1985, 122 Clues for Jews Whose Children Intermarry, 1988, Jewish Clues to Your Health and Happiness, 1990; editor: High Holiday Services, 1976; contbr. to numerous mags., newspapers including L.A. Mag., Jewish Spectator, The Lutheran, Westways, L.A. Times, Jewish Encyclopedia and others. Incorporator interfaith com. to aid farm workers of Nat. Migrant Ministry; chmn. Niles Twp. Interfaith Clergy Fellowship, Tikvah Inst. for Childhood Learning Disabilities; mem. Amalgamated Clothing and Textile Workers AFL-CIO, clergy adv. com. L.A. Unified Sch. Dist. Supt.; polit. advocate Fund for Animals, Zero Pet Population Growth; founder-mem. World Theol. Assn. for Animal Rights and many other social orgns. Recipient Thomas J. Crowe award for interracial justice, from Cath. Interracial Coun. Chgo, Solomon Schechter award for social action United Synagogue Am.; citations from numerous charitable orgns. and Ill. State Gen Assembly; Emmy award finalist. Mem. Ctrl. Conf. Am. Rabbis, Chgo. Bd. Rabbis (media cons.), Soc. Profl. Journalists, Sigma Delta Chi. Home and Office: Jacobs Ladder Pubs 5003 Cascade Ct Culver City CA 90230-4342

JACOBS, STEPHEN JAY, musician, composer, writer; b. San Francisco, Oct. 7, 1947; s. Martin Phillip and Madeline Louise (Burnley) J. AA in Music, Monterey Peninsula Coll., 1973; postgrad., Calif. State U., Northridge, 1974. Lic. fed. police officer Fed. Law Enforcement Tng. Ctr. Musician, composer Local 47 Am. Fedn. Musicians, L.A., 1973—; writer, poet L.A., 1982—; tchr. life sci. Fauna Edn. Ctr., L.A., 1982; CEO Chui Prodns., L.A., 1982—; police officer U.S. Postal Inspection Svc., L.A., 1995—; ptnr. Jacobs & Jacobs Concepts, L.A., 1996—. *Stephen Jacobs critically acclaimed debut solo album "This World" was recommended for Grammy nomination in 9 categories for 1997 by the NARAS National-Screening committees. The Nationally respected Chicago jazz critic and writer Lofton A. Emenari III rated it as one of the best jazz avant-garde/ alternative albums of 1997. "This World" won a composer's award from ASCAP in 1998. Stephen completed two original screenplays in 1999.* Musician, composer, arranger, writer, narrator, prodr.: (music and text on cassette and CD) This World, 1992; rec. artist Chui Records; contbr. poetry to anthologies (Editors award 1995-96). With U.S. Army, 1965-69, ETO, Vietnam. Mem. NARAS (voting mem.), Internat. Soc. Poets, Am. Fedn. Musicians, Songwriting Guild Am., Fraternal Order Police. Avocations: reading, research, skydiving. Home and Office: Chui Prodns 1259 N Hoover St Los Angeles CA 90029-2009

JACOBS, SUZANNE, author; b. Phila., Nov. 29, 1934; d. Robert and Evelyn (Segal) Gold; m. Barry Stephen Jacobs, June 12, 1952; children: Lynda Beth, Bonnie Dee, Ellen Merle (dec.). Student, Lower Merion Nigh Sch. Owner Offbeat Press, Merion, Pa.; currier Pa. Endocrine Lab., Phila.; dir. Temple Israel Nursery Sch., Phila. Author: Early One Saturday Morning, 1994 (Silver Poet award), World of Poetry, 1995 (Golden Poet award), Twisted Tales, 1996, The Last Tear, 1999; writer polit. commentary for Main Line Times. Coagulator Rep. Party, Phila., 1996; writer, asst. Brith Sholom, 1994-96; writer, dir. plays, entertainment organizer Duke DFC, 1985-90. Recipient KFC Cols. Way award, 1997, Pa. Arts award. Avocations: antiques, collecting art. Office: Offbeat Press PO Box 194 Merion Station PA 19066-0194

JACOBS, TIMOTHY ANDREW, epidemiologist, international health consultant, medical missionary; b. St. Petersburg, Fla., Nov. 5, 1944; s. W. Andrew and Virginia (Ott) J.; m. Carolyn Martin, Nov. 4, 1972; 1 child, Jenny Thuy Ha. BSN, U. Fla., 1970; MS, PNP, U. Utah, 1976; PhD, Internat. Inst. Advanced Studies, 1979; C.T.M., Liverpool (Eng.) Sch. Tropical Medicine, 1982; cert. hosp. epidemiology, U. Iowa, 1985; MPH, Yale U., 1991; cert. in internat. (Spanish) living, Sch. Internat. Tng., Brattleboro, Vt., 1984. Nat. design and media cons. Nat. Assn. Pediatric Nurse Assocs. and Practitioners, Cherry Hill, N.J., 1977-83; asst. prof., co-coord. community health nursing U. N.D., Grand Forks, 1980; vol. epidemiologist, pub. health specialist Vinh Children's Hosp., Vinh City, Vietnam, 1989; pediatric staff nurse I U. Fla. Pediatric Svc., Shands Teaching Hosp., Gainesville, 1970; instr. pediatric nursing U. Utah Coll. Nursing, Salt Lake City, 1976-77; pvt. cons. Internat. Cmty. Health and Epidemiology, New Haven, 1990-94; med. supr., health svcs. mgr. Brown & Root Logcap Med. Clinic, Port-au-Prince, Haiti, 1994-95; med. tech. proposal cons. UN, Rwanda, Angola, 1995; specialist Home Health Care, Tampa, Fla., 1996—; vol. pub. health scientist, cons. Hanoi (Vietnam) Sch. Pub. Health; cons. epidemiologist Vinh and Huong Son, Vietnam, 1993; internat. edn. cons. U. Am., New Orleans, 1994; cons. infectious disease epidemiology, consulate of Nicaragua, Miami, Health for Health Svcs. Hurricane Mitch, 1998; cons. Christian Haitian Outreach Clinics and Orphanages, Jeremie and Mariani, Haiti, 1998—. Contbg. editor Episource, 1991, 97, Resources in Epidemiology; contbr. articles to profl. jours.; contbr. to poetry jours.; anthologies Daybreak on the Land, 1997, Audiotape Sounds of Poetry, 1997. Donor, contbr. Asian Family and Comty. Empowerment Ctr., St. Petersburg, Fla. Capt. Nurse Corps, U.S. Army, 1968-73, Vietnam. Recipient Cert. of Achievement in HIV-AIDS Edn., AIDS Project, New Haven, Conn., 1994, Editor's Choice award for outstanding achievement in poetry Nat. Libr. Poetry, 1997. Fellow Royal Soc. Tropical Medicine and Hygiene (London), Am. Biog. Inst. (advisor, rsch. adv. bd.); mem. AMA, VFW, Am. Legion, Vietnam Vets. Am., Nat. Assn. Pediatric Nurse Assocs. and Practitioners (com. dir. graphics & logos mil. chpt., former chmn. nat. art and exhibits subcom., former mem. pub. rels. com., Cert. Recognition 1983), Am. Pub. Health Assn. (epidemiology sect., internat. healthsect., mem. caucus pub. health and faith cmty.), Internat. Assn. Med. Assistance to Travellers, Fla. Pub. Health Assn., Nat. Adolescent Health Promotion Network, Assn. Mil. Surgeons U.S., Ret. Army Nurse Corps Assn., Liverpool Tropical Sch. Assn. (Eng.), Assn. Yale Alumni in Pub. Health, Consortium for Internat. Nursing Edn., Rsch. & Practice, U.S.-Vietnam Friendship Assn., Doctorate Assn. N.Y. Educators, Fleet Marine Force Corpsman Assn. (former Conn. rep., charter mem.), U.S. Navy Corpsmen United Assn., Am. Assn. Navy Hosp. Corpsmen, U.S. Army (Vietnam) 24th Evacuation Hosp. Assn. (com. asv. reunion 1993), Vets. Vietnam Restoration Project, U.S. Com. Scientific Cooperation with Vietnam, N.Y. Acad. of Sci., Walter Reed Army Med. Ctr. Soc. (charter), Spl. Ops. Med. Assn., Sigma Xi, Sigma Theta Tau (charter mem. Gamma Rho chpt.), Phi Kappa Phi. Home: 11333 Calgary Cir Tampa FL 33624-4804

JACOBS, TRAVIS BEAL, historian, educator; b. N.Y.C., Apr. 22, 1936; s. Albert Charles and Loretta Field (Beal) J.; m. Eleanor Morison (div. 1982); children: Travis Beal, Holmes Morison. AB, Princeton U., 1958; MA, Columbia U., 1960, PhD, 1971. Mem. faculty Middlebury Coll. (Vt.), 1965—, prof. history, 1978-92, Fletcher D. Proctor prof. Am. history, 1992—, chmn. dept. history, 1976-88, 91-95. Co-editor: Navigating The Rapids, 1918-1971, From the Papers of Adolf A. Berle, 1973, America and the Winter War, 1939-40, 1981. Cons. 20th Century Fund, 1972-73; bd. dirs. Psi Upsilon Found., 1971-98, hon., 1998—; trustee Sheldon Mus., pres., 1987-90; pres. Chappaquiddick Island Assn., 1983-86; participant Eisenhower Centennial Programs, 1990. Earhart fellow, 1989-90, 95-96. Mem. Am. Hist. Assn., Ctr. for Study of Presidency, Orgn. Am. Historians, Soc. Historians Fgn. Rels., Vt. Hist. Soc., Princeton Club (N.Y.C.). Episcopalian. Home: 1109 Vt Rte 125 Bridport VT 05734 Office: Dept Hist Middlebury Coll Middlebury VT 05753

JACOBS, WALTER DARNELL, political scientist, educator; b. Lone Wolf, Okla., Mar. 11, 1922; s. John Clayton and Patience Caroline (Goodlander) J.; m. Mary Anderson Stout, Oct. 27, 1978; 1 child, Sara Downs. BS, Columbia U., 1955, MA, 1956, PhD in Pub. Law, 1961. Commd. 2d lt. U.S. Army, 1943, advanced through grades to col., 1964; exch. specialist Libr. Congress, Washington, 1957-59; rsch. specialist Spl. Ops. Rsch. Office, Washington, 1959-61; asst. prof. then prof. U. Md., College Park, 1961-65, assoc. prof., 1965-68, prof., 1968-81; European adv. coun. Dept. State. Author: Modern Governments, 3d edit., 1966, Frunze, The Soviet Clausewitz, 1969, Terrorism in South Africa, 1973, At the Sharp Edge in Africa, 1974, Bewitched Anteater, 1976, African Turmoil and American Interests, 1976, The Flaw in the CAD, 1998; contbr. articles to profl. jours. Chmn. Charleston (S.C.) Rep. Party, 1995-97. Mem. SAR, Am. Africal Affairs Assn. (chmn. 1971-78), Washington Friends Antibolshevik Block Nations, World Peace Soc. (dir. 1967-81), Am. Mil. Inst., Am. Polit. Sci. Assn. Def. Orientation Conf. Assn. (dir. 1971-74), Mukumburu Surf Club, Delta Kappa Epsilon, Pi Sigma Alpha. E-mail: darnell62@msn.com. Home: 62 Smith St Charleston SC 29401-1330

JACOBS, WENDELL EARLY, JR., lawyer; b. Detroit, Nov. 15, 1945; s. Wendell E. and Mildred P. (Horton) J.; m. Elaine M. Lott (div.); children: Wendell Early III, Damon R. BFA, Denison U., 1969; JD, Wayne State U., 1972. Bar: Mich. 1972, U.S. Dist. Ct. (ea. dist.) Mich. 1973, Fla. 1974. Asst. prosecutor Jackson County, Mich., 1973-76; ptnr. Jacobs & Engle, Jackson, 1977—. Mem. Mich. Coun. on Crime and Delinquency. Mem. Nat. Assn. Criminal Def. Lawyers, Criminal Def. Attys. Mich., Jackson County Bar Assn., Eagles Club, Grotto Club, Elks. Avocations: paddleball, motorcycling. Home: 9281 Greenwood Rd Grass Lake MI 49240-9590 Office: Jacobs & Engle 1104 W Michigan Ave Jackson MI 49202-4123

JACOBS, WILLIAM JAY, historian, writer; b. Aug. 23, 1933; s. Louis and Frances Jacobs; m. Susan F. Jacobs, July 20, 1984. BA in History with high honors, U. Cin., 1955, MA in History, 1956; EdD in Curriculum, Am. History, Columbia U., 1963; postgrad., Rutgers U., 1992—. Asst. prof. Hofstra U., 1964-65, Rutgers U., 1965-68; assoc. prof. Hunter Coll. CUNY, 1968-70; prof., dir. div. tchr. edn. and physical edn. Ramapo Coll. N.J., 1970-73; tchr. secondary sch. Hamilton County (Ohio) Schs. and Conn. Pub. Schs., 1975-94; adj. tchr., grad. asst. Rutgers U., Bklyn. Coll., Columbia U., Harvard U., 1967; disting. vis. prof. Ramapo Coll., N.J., 1973-74; reviewer in field. Author 40 books including: Ellis Island: New Hope in a New Land, 1990, Great Lives: Human Rights, 1990, Mother Teresa: Helping the Poor, 1991, revised edit., 1997, Search for Peace: The Story of the United Nations, 1994; contbr. articles to profl. jours. Mem. nat. adv. bd. World Federalist Assn., 1992—; mem. nat. adv. coun. Social Democrats, USA, 1994—. William Howard Taft fellow in history, 1956, World Book Encyclopedia fellow, 1963, Ford Found. fellow, 1967-68, Fulbright fellow, India, 1980, NEH fellow Harvard U., 1983, Woodrow Wilson fellow in History, 1989, Yale U. Vis. fellow in history, 1977-78, 80-81, 89-90, 92—; Urban League Ednl. award, 1983, Acad. Freedom award, 1988.

JACOBS, WILLIAM PAUL, botanist, educator; b. Boston, May 25, 1919; s. Vincent H. and Elizabeth (Kennedy) J.; m. Jane Shaw, Mar. 12, 1949; children: Mark, Anne. A.B. magna cum laude, Harvard U., 1942, Ph.D., 1946. Research assoc. biology Harvard U., 1946-47; jr. prize fellow Harvard Soc. Fellows, 1947-48; faculty Princeton, 1948—, prof. biology, 1962-89, prof. emeritus, 1989—, W.L. Schultz prof. biology, 1969; Mem. com. innovation lab. study Biol. Scis. Curriculum Study, 1959-64; vis. prof. U. Calif.-Berkeley, 1953, U. Oxford, 1962, U. Lausanne, 1967, U. Colo., 1972, U. Bristol (Eng.), 1980. Author: (with C.E. LaMotte) Regulation in Plants by Hormones, 1964, Plant Hormones and Plant Development, 1979; contbr. articles to sci. publs. Served with M.C. AUS, 1942-44. Recipient Morrison prize N.Y. Acad. Scis., 1951; Lalor fellow, 1950-51; NSF sr. postdoctoral fellow, 1957; NSF Faculty fellow, 1962; Guggenheim fellow, 1967; grantee Am. Cancer Soc., NSF, NASA, Office Naval Research, U.S. Army, Hoyt Found. Mem. Soc. Study Devel. and Growth (pres. 1960-61), Bot. Soc. Am. (Dimond prize 1974), Am. Soc. Plant Physiologists (editorial bd. 1968-72, Barnes award for lifetime achievement 1998), Phycological Soc. Am., Internat. Soc. Plant Morphologists, Internat. Phycological Soc., Internat. Plant Growth Substances Assn. Home: 64 Maclean Cir Princeton NJ 08540-5621 Office: Princeton U Dept Molecular Biology Princeton NJ 08544

JACOBS, WILLIAM RUSSELL, II, lawyer; b. Chgo., Oct. 26, 1927; s. William Russell and Doris B. (Desmond) J.; m. Shirley M. Spiegler, Mar. 21, 1950; children: William R. III, Richard W., Bruce Allen. BS, Northwestern U., 1950, JD, 1953. Bar: Ill. 1953, U.S. Dist. Ct. (no. dist.) Ill. 1958, U.S. Ct. Appeals (7th cir.) 1958, U.S. Supreme Ct., 1962. Atty. Continental Casualty Co., Chgo., 1955-58; assoc. Horwitz and Anesi, Chgo., 1958-62; prin. William R. Jacobs and Assocs., Chgo., 1962—; adj. prof. Lewis Coll. Law, Glen Ellyn, Ill., 1975-76; dir., tchr. Ct. Practice Inst., Chgo., 1974—; lectr. Ill. Inst. Continuing Legal Edn., Chgo., 1967—. Elected alderman Des Plaines (Ill.) City Coun., 1953-54; mem. Ill. Bar Assembly, 1973—. 1st lt. inf. U.S. Army, 1946-48. Mem. Ill. State Bar Assn., Am. Acad. Matrimonial Lawyers. Congregationalist. Office: William R Jacobs & Assocs 601 Lee St Des Plaines IL 60016-4616

JACOBSEN, ARNOLD, archivist; b. N.Y.C., Nov. 6, 1913; s. Charles and Sylvia (Rosenfeld) J.; m. Hyla Sernick, 1943 (dec. 1983): children: Maurice, Howard (dec.), m. Elisabeth James. Investigator N.Y. Film Bd. of Trade, N.Y.C., 1933-39; film booker Universal Pictures, N.Y.C., 1940-41; owner Memory Shop, Jackson Hgts., N.Y., 1947-50; publicity and promotions Grand Rapids (Mich.) Stadium, 1951-54; appliance sales Montgomery Ward, Grand Rapids, 1955-61; owner Arnold's Archives, Grand Rapids, 1960—; fin. coord. Consumers Power Co., Grand Rapids, 1962-78; maker of cassettes of over 200,000 out-of-print hist. records for rsch. and ednl. purposes; organizer record catalogues Libr. Congress, 1980's; organizer record info., tapes Smithsonian Instn., 1980's; catalogue supplier of most records of pvt. collection, archivist Chgo. Pub. Libr., 1980—. Libr. commr. E. Grand Rapids Pub. Libr., 1980's; vol. co-prodr. PBS-TV documentary, 1993. Sgt. U.S. Army, 1942-46. Mem. Am. Record Collectors Soc., Mich. Antique Phonograph Soc., Am. Record Collectors Assn. (membership com. 1960). Home and Office: Arnold's Archives 1106 Eastwood Ave SE Grand Rapids MI 49506-3580 *Our great Uncle Monroe Rosenfeld was a song plugger in the early 20th Century. To keep his memory alive, we collect phonograph records and tapes mostly between 1900 & 1955. Almost anyone who recorded between 1900 & 1955 is probably includedand available to be on a cassette. We have categories such as automobile songs, ethnic songs, campaign songs, recordings of original voices (including presidents, kings and many other people). We also have cassettes and lists available such as jazz, big bands, old-time popular songs, and others. We also make cassettes to celebrate birthdays, anniversaries or other events.*

JACOBSEN, EGILL LARS, dentist, educator; b. Copenhagen, Dec. 20, 1940; came to U.S., 1969; s. Haukur and Inge Liss (Kristensen) J.; m. Ruth C. Jacobsen, Aug. 2, 1974; children: Mikael Lars, Anna Liss. BS in Bus., Comml. Coll., Reykjavik, Iceland, 1961; DDS, U. Iceland, Reykjavik, 1967; postgrad., U. Pa., 1972. Lic. dentist, Iceland, Ill. Pvt. practice dentistry Iceland, 1967-69, pvt. practice endodontics, 1973-80; teaching fellow dept. endodontics U. Pa., Phila., 1969-70; asst. prof. dept. endodontics Health Sci. Ctr., U. Conn., Hartford, 1972-73; assoc. prof. endodontics U. Iceland, Reykjavik, 1973-80, U. Ill., Chgo., 1980-97; part-time practice endodontics, Ill., 1983—. Contbr. articles to profl. jours. Fulbright scholar, 1969-72, NATO scholar, 1971-72, Icelandic Rsch. Found. scholar, 1971-72. Mem. Icelandic Dental Assn., Am. Assn. Endodontists, Midwest Soc. Electron Microscopists, Edgar Coolidge Endodontic Study Club.

JACOBSEN, ERIC KASNER, consulting engineer; b. N.Y.C., July 21, 1932; s. Henry and Caroline (Kasner) J.; BSCE, U. Iowa, 1956; m. Dorothy H. Caldwell, Mar. 30, 1957; 1 son, Steven. Registered profl. engr., Ill., N.Y., Iowa, Mo., Wis. Structural engr. Stanley Engring. Co., Muscatine, Iowa, 1956-59; asso. dept. mgr. R. W. Booker & Assos., St. Louis, 1959-63; plant mgr. Tri-Cities Terminal div. Nat. Marine Service, Inc., Granite City, Ill., 1963-65; sr. engr. Monsanto Co., 1965-69; chief structural engr. Weitz-Hettalsater Engrs., Kansas City, 1969-72; supr. structural and archtl. engring. Austin Co., Cleve., 1972-78; mgr. Engring. Mining and Metals div., 1978-87, chief structural engr. western dist., 1987-94; cons. structural engr., 1994—; cons. engr. structural and archtl. engring., 1960—; owner/mgr. Jacobsen Farms. Mem. ASCE, ASME, Chgo. Farmers, Chi Epsilon. Presbyterian. Office: 27 Technology Dr Irvine CA 92618-2364

JACOBSEN, GERALD BERNHARDT, biochemist; b. Spokane, Wash., Nov. 25, 1939; s. Hans Bernhardt and Mabel Grace (Swope) J.; m. Sally-Ann Heimbigner, June 7, 1961 (div. 1976); children: Claire Elise, Hans Edward; m. Jean Eva Robinson, Dec. 5, 1976. BA, Whitman Coll., 1961; MS, Purdue U., 1965, PhD, 1970. Postdoctoral fellow Oreg. State U., Corvallis, 1970-73; rsch. chemist Lamb-Weston, Inc., Portland, Oreg., 1973-85, sr. rsch. chemist, 1985—; presenter at profl. confs. Contbr. articles to profl. jours. Grantee NSF, 1960; NIH grad. fellow, 1965; Herman Frasch postdoctoral fellow Oreg. State U., 1970. Mem. AAAS, Am. Oil Chemists Soc., Am. Chemistry Soc., Assn. Ofcl. Analytical Chemists, Sigma Xi. Achievements include patents for Process for Making A Starch Coated Product, Coated Potato Product Process. Home: 1204 Knollwood Ct Richland WA 99352-9448 Office: Lamb Weston Tech Ctr 2005 Saint St Richland WA 99352-5306

JACOBSEN, HUGH NEWELL, architect; b. Grand Rapids, Mich., Mar. 11, 1929; s. John Edwall and Lucy Ellen (Newell) J.; m. Robin Kearney, Dec. 27, 1952; children: John Edwall, Matthew Christian, Simon Townsend. B.A., U. Md., 1951; B.Arch., M.Arch., Yale, 1955; cert., Archtl. Asso. Sch. Architecture, London, Eng., 1954; L.H.D. (hon.), Gettysburg Coll., 1974, Bradford Coll., 1990; DFA (hon.), U. Md., 1993. Architect with Philip Johnson, New Canaan, Conn., 1955-57, Keyes, Lethbridge & Condon, Washington, 1957-58; prin. Hugh Newell Jacobsen, FAIA, Washington, 1958—; lectr. univs.; vis. prof. U. Cairo, Egypt, 1970. Editor: A Guide to the Architecture of Washington, D.C., 1965; prin. works include Nat. Bldg. Mus., Washington, 1999, others. Mem. Joint Com. Landmarks of Nat. Capital, 1976-82, adv. bd. Internat. Hassan Fathy Inst.; trustee Corcoran Gallery Art. Served with USAF, 1955-57. John Fitzgerald Kennedy Meml. fellow New Zealand Govt., 1971, Silver medal for distinction in design Tau Sigma Delta, 1981. Fellow AIA (Centennial award 1996, nat. AIA honor awards 1969, 74, 78, 80, 85, 88, numerous AIA chpt. awards, 20 Archtl. Record awards, others); mem. NAD (elected), Cosmos Club (Washington), Century Assn., Yale Club (N.Y.C.). Office: 2529 P St NW Washington DC 20007-3024

JACOBSEN, LAREN, programmer, analyst; b. Salt Lake City, June 15, 1937; s. Joseph Smith and Marian (Thomas) J.; B.S., U. Utah, 1963; m. Audrey Bartlett, July 29, 1970 (div.); children—Andrea, Cecily, Julian. Programmer, IBM Corp., 1963-70; systems programmer Xerox Computer Services, 1970-79; pres. Prescient Investments Co., 1975-82; sr. systems analyst Quotron Systems, Los Angeles, 1979-86; programmer/analyst Great Western Bank, 1987-92. Served with USAR, 1961. Mem. Am. Guild Organists (dean San Jose chpt. 1967), Mensa. Home: PO Box 91174 Los Angeles CA 90009-1174

JACOBSEN, LINDA MARY, county official; b. Earling, Iowa, Aug. 28, 1951; d. Leo Virgil and Lillian Kathryn (Kramer) Schaben; m. Merlen John Jacobsen, Aug. 17, 1974 (dec. Feb. 1998); children: Bonnie Kay, Amy Jo. Grad. high sch., Harlan, Iowa. Legal sec. Louis, Moore & Kohorst Attys., Harlan, 1969-79; deputy county recorder Shelby County, Harlan, 1979-87, county recorder, 1988—; mem. initial task force Dept. of Human Svcs., Des Moines, 1997—; mem. initial com. continuing edn. Iowa State Assn. Counties, Des Moines, 1988-94. Sec. Shelby County Rep. Party, Harlan, 1993—; charter mem. Shelby County Rep. Women, 1997—; sec. initial bd. St. Michael's Fin. Coun., Harlan, 1987-90; guild leader, lector St. Michael's Ch., Harlan, 1990—. Mem. Iowa County Recorders Assn. (pres. 1996-97, v.p. 1994-96, treas. 1993-94, sec. 1992-93), Dist. IV Recorders Assn. (pres. 1990-92, legis. del. 1990—). Republican. Roman Catholic. Avocations: bowling, reading, sports and school activities. Home: 1613 Farnam St Harlan IA 51537-1541 Office: Shelby County 612 Court St Rm 201 Harlan IA 51537-1464

JACOBSEN, MAGDALENA GRETCHEN, mediator, federal agency executive; b. N.Y.C., July 26, 1940; d. Carl J. and Helen (Faber) J.; m. Bruce Donald Henricus, Dec. 20, 1986. Cert. labor studies, AFL-CIO, 1971; cert. labor studies, bargaining and arbitration, Harvard U., 1973; cert. indsl. rels., U. Calif., San Francisco, 1975; BS, U. San Francisco, 1987; MS, Golden Gate U., 1989. Sec. CBS TV, Hollywood, Calif., 1962-65; flight attendant Continental Airlines, L.A., 1965-69, mgr. labor rels., 1972-76; local union official, sec.-treas. steward and stewardess divsn. ALPA, Washington, 1966-72; commr. Fed. Mediation and Conciliation Svcs., San Francisco, 1976-89, Portland, Oreg., 1992-93; dir. employee rels. City and County of San Francisco, 1989-92; bd. Nat. Mediation Bd., Washington, 1993—. Mem. Indsl. Rels. Rsch. Assn. (mem. exec. bd. 1980—, pres. San Francisco chpt. 1985-87, Portland chpt. 1992, D.C. chpt. 1997-98). Avocations: golf, swimming, poetry, short-story writing. Office: Nat Mediation Bd 1301 K St NW Ste 250 Washington DC 20005-3317

JACOBSEN, PETER ERLING, professional golfer; b. Portland, Oreg., Mar. 4, 1954. Grad., U. Oreg. Profl. golfer, 1976—. Won Western Australian Open, 1979, Buick-Gooodwrench Open, 1980, Johnnie Walker Cup, Spain, 1981, 82, Colonial Nat. Invitation, Sammy Davis, Jr.-Greater Hartford Open, 1984, Oreg. Open, 1976, Calif. Open, 1986, (with Curtis Strange) Fred Meyer Challenge, 1986, Bob Hope Chyrsler Classic, 1990, Pebble Beach Nat. Pro-Am, Buick Invitational, 1995. Office: care PGA Box 109601 100 Ave of Champions Palm Beach Gardens FL 33410 also: care Cedar Bay Prodns 5119 NE 42d St Seattle WA 98105*

JACOBSEN, RAYMOND ALFRED, JR., lawyer; b. Wilmington, Del., Dec. 14, 1949; s. Raymond Alfred and Margaret (Walters) J.; m. Marilyn Perry, Aug. 4, 1973. BA, U. Del., 1971; JD, Georgetown U., 1975. Bar: D.C. 1975, U.S. Supreme Ct. 1982. From assoc. to ptnr. Howrey & Simon, Washington, 1975-97; dir. Antitrust/Trade Reg. Grp. McDermott, Will & Emery, Washington, 1997-, ptnr., 1997—; adj. prof. internat. anti-trust law Am. U. Law Sch. Spl. projects editor Law & Policy in International Business, 1974-75. Served to capt. U.S. Army, 1975. Mem. ABA (antitrust law sect., adminstrv. law sect., corp. banking and bus. law sect., litigation sect., internat. law sect., pub. contract law sect.), D.C. Bar Assn., U.S. Supreme Ct. Bar Assn. Republican. Club: Army & Navy, City (Washington). Home: 4205 Maple Tree Ct Alexandria VA 22304-1035 Office: McDermott Will & Emery 600 13th St NW Washington DC 20005-3005*

JACOBSEN, RICHARD T, mechanical engineering educator; b. Pocatello, Idaho, Nov. 12, 1941; s. Thorleif (dec.), and Edith Emily (Gladwin) J. dec.); m. Vicki Belle Hopkins, July 16, 1959 (div. Mar. 1973); children: Pamela Sue, Richard T, Eric Ernest; m. Bonnie Lee Stewart, Oct. 19, 1973; 1 child, Jay Michael; stepchild: Erik David Lustig. BSME, U. Idaho, 1963, MSME, 1965; PhD in Engring. Sci., Wash. State U., 1972. Registered profl. engr., Idaho. Instr. U. Idaho, 1964-66, asst. prof. mech. engring., 1966-72, assoc. prof., 1972-77, prof., 1977—, chmn. dept. mech. engring., 1980-85, assoc. dean engring., 1985-90, assoc. dir. Ctr. for Applied Thermodynamic Studies, 1975-86, dir., 1986—, dean engring., 1990-99; dep. R&D dir., chief scientist Bechtel B&W Idaho, Idaho Falls, 1999—; guest rschr. Nat. Inst. Standards Tech., 1979, 86, 99. Author: International Union of Pure and Applied Chemistry, Nitrogen-International Thermodynamic Tables of the Fluid State-6, 1979; Oxygen-International Thermodynamic Tables of the Fluid State-9, 1987, Ethylene-International Thermodynamic Tables of the Fluid State-10, 1988, ASHRAE Thermodynamic Properties of Refrigerants (2 vols.), 1986, (monograph series) Thermodynamic Properties of Cryogenic Fluids, 1997; numerous reports on thermodynamic properties of fluids, 1971—; contbr. articles to profl. jours. NSF sci. faculty fellow, 1968-69; NSF rsch. and travel grantee, 1976-83; Nat. Inst. Standards and Tech. grantee, 1974-91, 95-98, Gas Rsch. Inst. grantee, 1986-91, 1992-98, Dept. Energy grantee, 1991-95. Fellow ASME (faculty advisor 1972-75, 78-84, chmn. region VIII dept. heads com. 1983-85, honors and awards chmn. 1985-91, K-7 tech. com. thermophys. properties 1985—, chmn. 1986-89, 92-95, rsch. tech. com. on water and steam in thermal power systems, 1988—, gen. awards com. 1985-91, chmn. 1988-91, com. on honors 1988-99, vice chmn. 1995-99, mem. bd. on profl. practice and ethics, 1991—, v.p. profl. practice 1998—, Engr. of Yr. 1999), N.W. Coll. and Univ. Assn. for Sci. (bd. dirs. 1990-93), Idaho Rsch. Found. (bd. dirs. 1991-99), Soc. Automotive Engrs. (Ralph R. Teetor Edn. award, Detroit 1968), ASHRAE (co-recipient Best Tech. Paper award 1984), International. Energy Agy. (Annex 18 thermophys. properties environ. acceptable refrigerants 1991-98), Sigma Xi, Tau Beta Pi, Phi Kappa Phi (Disting. Faculty award 1989). Office: Bechtel B&W Idaho Office of Dean 1306 E 17th St Idaho Falls ID 83404

JACOBSEN, SHIRLEY MARIE, editor, songwriter, artist; b. Sioux City, Iowa, Aug. 1, 1944; d. Elmer and Edith Nancy (Lyght) Rich; m. George Allen Archer, Mar. 28, 1965 (div. Feb. 1973); children: David Allen, John Travis; m. Gerald Lee Jacobsen, June 1, 1974; children: Mark Allen, Steven Lee. BCA cum laude, S.W. Assemblies of God U., 1993. Office mgr. Lindsay Soft Water, Fremont, Nebr., 1964; info. asst. Northwestern Bell Telephone Co., Omaha, Nebr., 1964-68; contract acctg. asst. Peter Kiewit Sons, Co., Omaha, 1968-69; asst. pricer Ready Mixed Concrete Co., Omaha, 1971-73; head accounts receivable dept. Lyman Richey Sand and Gravel, Omaha, 1973-74; br. office adminstr. DialAm. Mktg., Omaha, 1984-85; pres. asst. Lyric Co., Omaha, 1985-86; vol. libr. Henderson County Library, Chandler, Tex., 1992-97; mgr. real estate Pvt. Partnership, Nebr. and Tex., 1974—. *The development and leadership of a home-based Bible study has created peace at home. Shirley Jacobsen shares her music with churches, performing artists, and the radio listening audience. She has participated in the expression of Southern Gospel music (defends performing artist's rights), jazz genre and world-wide environmental interests (a forager), and contributed to the World's Poem for Peace. Shirley has experienced the warm hospitality and culture of Israel, England, Canada, and Mexico. Her recent projects are Perfect Peace, When I Read Through the Pages, Jesus Whispers to Me and son et lumière at sea, a sonatina.* Author: Cancer Review, 1983, Successful Telemarketing Business, 1986, A Second Start in Life, 1995, Feelings of the Heart, 1998; songwriter Perfect Peace, He'll Take You Back, 1996, Some Water to Drink, From Thorns to Gems, 1997. S.W. Assemblies God U. divsn. scholar, 1993; named to Internat. Poetry Hall of Fame, 1998. Fellow Internat. Biographical Assn., Am. Biographical Inst.; mem. World Jewish Congress, Broadcast Music, Inc., Women in the Arts, Delta Epsilon Chi (hon.). Avocations: travel, writing, art, music, walking. E-mail: 1stbooks@1stbooks.com. Office: PO Box 1699 Chandler TX 75758-1699 also: 910 Fulton St Falls City NE 68355-3030

JACOBSEN, STEPHEN C., biomedical engineer. BS, U. Utah, 1967, MS, 1970; PhD, MIT, 1973. Prof. U. Utah, 1973—; chmn., CEO Sarcos Inc., Salt Lake City, 1983—; Rsch. prof., dir. ctr. engring. design, U. Utah, 1973—. Bd. dirs. IOMED Inc., 1973—, Sarcos Orgn., 1983—. Recipient Lawrence Poole prize Faculty Med. U. Edinburgh, Scotland, 1982, Becton Dickinson award Assn. Advanced Medical Instrumentation, 1985, Leonardo da Vinci Design award Am. Soc. Mech. Engrs., 1987. Mem. Nat. Acad. Engrs., Nat. Acad. Scis. (Inst. Medicine), Am. Inst. Med. and Biol. Engrs. Home: 360 Wakara Way Salt Lake City UT 84108-1214 Office: Sarcos Inc 360 Wakara Way Salt Lake City UT 84108-1214*

JACOBSEN, THEODORE H. (TED H. JACOBSEN), labor union official, educator; b. N.Y.C., July 27, 1933. BS, Fordham U., 1955; postgrad., Hunter Coll., 1957-80, NYU, 1957-80, Columbia U., 1957-80. Cert. high sch. English tchr., N.Y.C. Tchr. English N.Y.C. Bd. Edn. (on leave), 1957-86; editor Labor News and Trade Union Handbook N.Y.C. Ctrl. Labor Coun., AFL-CIO, N.Y.C., 1986—; mem. exec. bd. Jewish Labor Com., N.Y.C., 1977—, Workers Def. League, N.Y.C., 1986—, Am. Labor ORT, N.Y.C., 1986—; regional v.p. Union Label and Svc. Trades Dept., N.Y., 1980-96; mem. adv. bd. Harry Van Arsdale Jr. Coll. Labor Studies, Empire State Coll., N.Y.C., 1986—; mem. adv. coun. for occupation edn. N.Y.C. Bd. Edn., 1986—, vice-chmn., 1989—; bd. dirs. Nat. Ethnic Coalition Orgns., Inc.; mem. bd. govs. The Forum; sec. N.Y.C. Ctrl. Labor Coun. AFL-CIO. Mem. Cmty. Bd. 8, N.Y.C., 1987-93, N.Y.C. Sch.to-Work Regional Coun. Regional Planning Assn.; mem. exec. bd. Workman's Circle Home-Geriatric Ctr., 1986-89, treas., 1989—; sec. Robert F. Wagner Labor Archives, NYU, 1986—; bd. dirs. Cath. Interracial Coun., 1987—, United Way N.Y., 1988-95, Coun. on Environ., N.Y.C., 1988-95, Italian Acad. Found., Nat. Ethnic Coalition Orgns., Inc., Italic Studies Inst.; trustee Italian Hosp. Soc., ARC in Greater N.Y., 1989—; mem. bd. advisors Transition Ctr., N.Y.C. Bd. Edn., 1991, Svc. Area Planning Group, 1991; mem. exec. bd. Friends A. Philip Randolph Campus H.S. at City Coll., 1990—; mem. Naval War Coll. Found., 1989—; mem. N.Y. State coastal mgmt. adv. com. N.Y. Harbor Maritime Industry, 1988—; charter mem. Battle of Normandy Found., 1988—; chmn. N.Y. Trade Union Coun. for Histadrut, 1992—; mem. Asian Pacific Am. Labor Alliance; life mem. Workmen's Circle Arbeter Ring; patron N.Y.C. Met. Opera; trustee Italian Hosp. Soc., ARC in Greater N.Y., 1989—. Decorated knight Order of Merit (Italy), knight officer Order of Sts. Maurice and Lazarus; recipient Cope awards N.Y. State United Tchrs., 1975, 78, Best Newsletter award, 1974, 75, 79, 80, 81, spl. award educators chpt. Jewish labor Com., 1986, Roberto Clemente award Nat. Assn. for Puerto Rican Civil Rights, 1988, 75th Anniversary Cert. of Appreciaition, U.S. Dept. Labor, 1988, Hurricane Hugo Disaster Relief citation ARC, 1991, 80th Anniversary Exemplar award NAACP, N.Y. br. 1991, Good Scout award Greater N.Y. Couns. Boy Scouts Am., 1992, Spl. Recognition award Hispanic Labor Com., 1992, George Meany award, Leadership Svc. Recognition award United Way of N.Y.C., 1992, Consumer Merit award N.Y. Consumer Assembly, 1992, Torch of Hope award Pride of Judea, 1993, Congl. Ellis Island Medal Honor, 1993, N.Y.C. Coun. Citation, 1993, Coalition of Labor Union Women award, 1994, John LaFarge award for interracial justice Cath. Interracial Coun. N.Y., 1995, N.Y.C. NOVA Ancora Job Tng. Program Award of Appreciation, N.Y.C. Dept. Probation, 1995, Disting. Svc. award Internat. Brotherhood Elec. Workers, Local 3, J Divsn., 1996, Robert Briscoe award Emerald Isle Immigration Ctr., 1996, George Meany award Gtr. N.Y. Couns. Boy Scouts Am.; named Man of Yr., Jewish Heritage Com. and Educators chpt., 1990, Educator of Yr., Assn. Tchrs. of N.Y., 1986; proclamation from Queens borough pres. declaring June 23, 1993 Theodore 'Ted' Jacobsen Day. Mem. AFTRA (bd. govs. 1996—), NATAS (bd. govs. N.Y. chpt.), NAACP (golden life heritage), United Fedn. Tchrs. (editor newsletter, chpt. chmn. 1974-86, mem. P.M. staff 1973—, Eli Trachtenberg award 1966, 74, 77, 81, Albert Lee Smallheiser citation 1976), Order Sons of Italy in Am., Jewish Tchrs. Assn., Cath. Tchrs. Assn., Internat. Labor Comm. Assn., Coalition Labor Union Women, Black Trade Unionists Leadership Com., Jewish Heritage Com., Irish-Am. Studies Com., Irish-Am. Heritage Mus. (charter), Loyal League Yiddish Sons Erin (hon.), U.S. Naval Inst., Internat. Platform Assn., B'nai B'rith (lodge 2201, trustee 1989-96, bd. dirs. Adelstein Family Project HOPE Found. Housing for Elderly 1992—), The Actor's Fund (life), U.S. Holocaust Meml. Mus. (charter), Lower East Side Tenement (hon. commr. 1992—), U.S. Naval Inst., Amigos del Teatro Teresa Carreno (patron Caracas, Venezuela), The Discovery Ctr. (Ft. Lauderdale, Fla.), TV and Radio Working Press Assn., The Asia Soc., Met. Mus. Art, Elks, Nat. Italian-Am. Found. Avocations: theater, opera, travel. Office: NYC Cen Labor Coun AFL-CIO 386 Park Ave S New York NY 10016-8804

JACOBSEN, THOMAS H(ERBERT), banker; b. Chgo., Oct. 15, 1939; s. Herbert Rogde and Catharine (Ball) J.; m. Diane Leisa DeMell. BA, Lake Forest (Ill.) Coll., 1963, LLD, 1995; MBA, U. Chgo., 1968; grad., Advanced Mgmt. Program, Harvard U., 1979. From asst. cashier to v.p. First Nat. Bank Chgo., 1963-76; from v.p. to vice chmn., dir. Barnett Banks, Inc., Jacksonville, Fla., 1976-89; chmn., pres., chief exec. officer Mercantile Bancorp. Inc., St. Louis, 1989—; bd. dirs. TWA, St. Louis, Fed. Res. Bank St. Louis; advisor to bd. dirs. Amiren Corp., St. Louis; past pres. Fed. Res. Systems Fed. Adv. Coun. Life trustee, past chmn. bd. trustees St. Louis Symphony Soc.; trustee Washington U., St. Louis; trustee St. Louis area coun. Boy Scouts Am.; bd. dirs. Nat. Boy Scouts Am.; past chmn. United Way of Greater St. Louis, Inc.; treas. Civic Progress. Mem. Bankers Round Table, Bob O'Link Golf Club (Highland, Ill.), Bogey Club, St. Louis Country Club. Office: Mercantile Bancorp Inc Mercantile Tower PO Box 524 Saint Louis MO 63166-0524

JACOBSEN, THOMAS WARREN, archaeologist, educator; b. Mankato, Minn., Mar. 18, 1935; s. Maurice and Effie (Jensen) J.; m. Kathryn Jane Anderson, Aug. 18, 1956 (dec. June 1978); children: Mark Thomas, Kirsten; m. Susan K. Lehr, Aug. 1, 1981 (div. Dec. 1991); m. Sharyn Anne Elmquist, Jan. 18, 1997. B.A., St. Olaf Coll., 1957; M.A., U. Minn., 1960; postgrad., Am. Sch. Classical Studies, Athens, Greece, 1962-63; Ph.D., U. Pa., 1964. Asst. prof. classics, classical archeology Vanderbilt U., 1964-66; asst. prof. Ind. U., 1966-68, assoc. prof., 1968-75, prof., 1975-92; prof. emeritus, 1992—; chmn. dept. classical studies Ind. U., 1975-78, dir. program in classical archaeology, 1970-85; staff mem. excavations, Porto Cheli, Greece, 1962, 65, 66, field dir., 1967, dir. excavations at Franchthi Cave, Greece, 1967-96, staff excavations, Kea, Greece, 1963; du Pont spl. rsch. fellow Am. Sch. Classical Studies Athens, 1980-81; vis. scholar Tulane U., 1992—. Gen. editor Excavations at Franchthi Cave, Greece, 1985-96; mem. editorial bd. Archaeology, 1988-92. Served with AUS, 1957. Fulbright scholar Greece, 1962-63; Olivia James fellow Archeol. Inst. Am., Greece, 1968-69; Am. Council Learned Socs. fellow, 1973-74; NSF postdoctoral fellow, 1973-74; Am. Philos. Soc. grantee, 1973-74. Mem. AAUP, Archaeol. Inst. Am. (Charles Eliot Norton Meml. lectr. spring 1988), Soc. for Am. Archaeology, Soc. Profl. Archaeologists, Soc. for Preservation of Greek Heritage, Brit. Inst. Archaeology, Ankara Assn. Field Archaeology. Lutheran. Home: 1811 Coliseum St New Orleans LA 70130-5103 Office: Tulane U Dept Classical Studies New Orleans LA 70118

JACOBSEN-THEEL, HAZEL M., historian; b. Becker County, Minn., June 1, 1909; d. Julius and Helma Clara (Klug) Mielke; m. Albert Arthur Jacobsen, June 2, 1933 (dec. June 1984); children: Harry James, Karen Bel; m. Bruce Theel, Jan. 7, 1989 (dec. Dec. 1992). Student, U. Minn., 1926-27; BA in Science and Edn., U. N.D., 1930; postgrad., U. Minn., summers 32-33. Cert. tchr. N.D. and Minn.:. Dining room mgr. Lake Side Hotel, Detroit, 1922-30; tchr. N St. Paul (Minn.) Pub. Sch. system, 1930-33; with Gt. Northern Railway at Glacier Park Entrance Hotel, summer 1932; tchr. Dept. Interior Bur. Ind. Affairs, N.D., 1933-42; mem. aircraft assembly line Higgins Air Craft, La., 1942-45; science tchr. St. Johns (N.D.) Pub. Sch. system, 1945-46; hardware mcht. Jacobsen Hardware Inc., Minn., 1946-73. Contbr. articles to profl. jours. Vol. tour guide of historic places, 1961; life mem., past officer Dakota County Hist. Soc.; charter mem. Dakota County Pioneer Village; tour leader Hastings Area, 1960-89; founder Hastings Vol. Group, 1976-77; established Albert A. and Hazel M. Jacobsen Meml. Fund U. N.D., 1988, Archtl. Treasure Hunt, 1994; supporter Turtle Mountain Indian Mus., Belcourt, N.D., life mem., 1994—; charter mem. gov. apptd. Dakota County Bicentennial Commn., 1976. First woman to be selected Grand Marshall River Town Days and Minn. Aquatennial Miss. River Flotilla, 1992; established Bruce Theel High Sch. Vocat. scholarship meml. for Mt. Pleasant Pub. Sch. Dist. Found., Rolla, N.D. Mem. AAUW, Women's Orgn. Minn. Hist. Soc. (charter mem., officer), Hastings Preservation Commn. (charter mem.), Minn. Territorial Pioneers (Outstanding award 1987), U. N.D. Alumni Assn. (Sioux award 1987), U. Minn. Alumni Assn. (life), Am. Legion Aux. (life), Dakota County Hist. Soc. (rsch. assoc.), Fedn. Women N.D., OES (grand officer N.D.), 1006 Summit Ave. Soc. (life, charter). Avocations: avid bridge player, marathon winner dancing, reading, cooking, foreign travel. Home: 311 Mains St Rolla ND 58367 also: 313 Ramsey St Hastings MN 55033-1222

JACOBS-FUREY, MARILYN SANDRA, television director; b. N.Y.C.; d. Armin and Bertha (Lowenkron) Jacobs; m. Thomas J. Furey, June 28, 1986 (dec. Dec. 1990). BS, NYU, 1950; MA, Western Res., 1951. Sec., receptionist NBC, N.Y.C., 1951-52, prodn. asst., 1952-55, assoc. dir., 1955—; actress Tonight Show and Steve Allen Show, 1955-60; contbr. NBC Nightly News, Meet the Press, Tonight Show, Twenty-One, Concentration, Another World, The Doctors, polit. convs., inaugurations, state funerals, and more. N.Y. County commiteewoman N.Y.C, 1960-62. Recipient Acad. Women Achievers award YWCA, 1985. Mem. Dirs. Guild Am. (bd. dirs. 1975—, chmn. and assoc. dir., stage mgr. coun. 1980-90, asst. sec.-treas 1980—, trustee prodr. pension and health plans 1982—, Franklin Schaffer Lifetime Achievement award 1992), Artists Rights Found. (bd. dirs.), Dirs. Guild Edn. and Benevolent Found. (bd. dirs. 1990—). Avocation: gardening. Home: 311 E 38th St New York NY 10016-2729 Office: NBC 30 Rockefeller Plz Fl 2 New York NY 10112-0036

JACOBSON, ALBERT DALE, pediatrician, accountant; b. Portland, Oreg., Mar. 28, 1942; s. Leonard Dale and Allice Cleo (Wiesendanger) J.; m. Donna Marie Shaw, Aug. 8, 1964; children: Heidi, Craig, Bryan and Chad. BS in acctg., Ariz. State U., 1964; MD, U. Oreg., Portland, 1969. CPA, Oreg.; diplomate Am. Bd. Pediatrics, Am. Bd. Nephrology. Pub. acct. Winn & Co., Eugene, Oreg., 1964-65; intern Good Samaritan Hosp., Phoenix, Ariz., 1970; residency in pediatrics and pediatric nephrology fellowship Naval Hosp., San Diego, 1972, U. Calif., San Diego, 1972; chief pediatrics Naval Regional Med. Clinic, Pearl Harbor, Hawaii, 1972-75; sect. chief pediatric nephrology Tripler Army Hosp., Honolulu, 1972-75; attending staff pediatrician, clin. asst. prof. pediatrics U. Hawaii Med. Sch., Honolulu, 1972-75; pediatrician Health Maintenance Assocs., Phoenix, Ariz., 1975-77; v.p. Health Maintenance Assocs., Inc., Phoenix, Ariz., 1976-77; adminstrv. staff pediatrician, sect. head pediatric nephrology Maricopa County Gen. Hosp., 1977-78; chief pediatric rehab. Barrows Neurological Institution, 1986-88, Children's Med. Ctr., St. Joseph's Hosp., 1986-88; pvt. practice Pediatric Assocs., P.C., Phoenix, Ariz., 1977—; divsn. chmn. Emergency Dept. Children's Hosp., Honolulu, 1972-75; cons. Waimano State Institution for the Retarded, 1972-75, Children's Hosp., Honolulu, 1972-75; advisor Poision Contro Ctr. State of Hawaii, 1972-75; chief of pediatrics Naval Regional Med. Clinics, 1972-75; navy chmn. child abuse com. Tripler Army Hosp., 1972-75; mem. gov.'s adv. bd. Child Protection Soc., 1972-75; media rep., TV appearances on children's health Phoenix Pediatric, 1981-92; host weekly radio program, KTAR Speaking of Kids, 1982-84. Contbr. to profl. jours. Coach Phoenix Little League, 1975-93. Comdr. U.S. Navy, 1970-75. Recipient Best Doctor award Phoenix Mag., 1994; Oreg. State Heart Assn. fellow, 1966; Nat. Pharm. and Drug Mfg. Rsch. fellow, 1968. Fellow Am. Acad. Pediatrics (sec. Ariz. chpt. 1980-82, advisor com. of pediatric practice, 1983-92, chmn. child health finance, 1986-89, exec. com. sect. on adminstrn. and practice mgmt. 1993—, mem. nat. com. on practice and ambulatory medicine 1993—, mem. nat. com. Resource Based Relative Value Scale 1995—, chair sect. adminstrn. and practice mgmt.), Am. Spinal Injury Assn.; mem. AMA, Internat. Soc. Pediatrics, Honolulu and State Hawaii Pediatric Soc. (state chmn. on third party payments), Phoenix Pediatric Soc. (pres. 1996-97), Ariz. Med. Assn., Maricopa County Med. Assn., Maricopa County Pediatric Soc. (pres. elect. 1981-82, pres. 1982-83, com. for the formation of Phoenix Children's Hosp., 1979-83). Avocations: running, tennis, skiing. Office: Pediatric Assocs PC Pointe Corridor Ctr II 7600 N 15th St Ste 130 Phoenix AZ 85020-4347

JACOBSON, ALBERT HERMAN, JR., industrial and systems engineer, educator; b. St. Paul, Minn., Oct. 27, 1917; s. Albert Herman and Gertrude Jacobson; m. Elaine Swanson, June 1960; children: Keith, Paul. BS Indsl. Engring./Adminstrn. cum laude, Yale U., 1939; SM Bus. and Engring. Mgmt., MIT, 1952; MS in Applied Physics, U. Rochester, 1954; PhD in Indsl. and Mgmt. Engring., Stanford U., 1976. Registered profl. engr., Calif. Pers. asst. Yale U., New Haven, Conn., 1939-40; indsl. engr. in electronics Radio Corp. of Am., Camden, N.J., 1940-43; prodn. officer USN BuORD, 1943-44; RINSMAT USN Colonial Radio Corp. (Sylvania), Buffalo, 1944-45; INSORD USN Eastman Kodak Co., Rochester, N.Y., 1945-46; chief engr., dir. quality control Naval Ordnance Office, Rochester, N.Y., 1946-57; staff engr. Space Satellite Program Eastman Kodak Co., Rochester, 1957-59; assoc. dean Coll. Engring. and Architecture Pa. State U., University Park, Pa., 1959-61; v.p., gen. mgr. to pres. Knapic Electro-Physics Inc., Palo Alto, Calif., 1961-62; prof. of indsl. and systems engring. Coll. of Engring. San Jose State U., 1962—, co-founder, coord. Cybernetic Systems grad. program, 1968-88; cons. in field, Calif., Ariz., Ill., 1962—, Lockheed, Motorola, Santa Fe R.R., 20th Century Fox, Alcan-Aluminium Corp., Banner Container, Sci. Mgmt. Corp., No. Telecom, Siliconix, others. Author: Military and Civilian Personnel in Naval Administration, 1952, Railroad Consolidations and Transportation Policy, 1975; editor: Design and Engineering of Production Systems, 1984; contbr. articles to profl. jours. Mem., chmn. Pers. Commn. City of Mountain View, Calif., 1968-78; Eagle Scout, 1931, troop chmn., scoutmaster, mem. Stanford Area Coun. Boy Scouts of Am., Palo Alto, 1970-83; chmn. Campus Luth. Coun. San Jose State U., 1981-86; mem. Santa Clara Valley Luth. Parish Coun., 1991—; pres. N.Y. State Young Adults Coun. YMCA, 1954-55. Lt. comdr. USNR, 1943-46. Recipient commendation USN, 1946; Alfred P. Sloan fellow Program Exec. Devel. MIT, 1951-52; fellow NSF, Stanford U., 1965-66; recipient Scouters Key and Award of Merit Stanford Coun. Boy Scouts Am., 1976. Mem. Am. Soc. Engring. Edn., Inst. Indsl. Engrs., Am. Prodn. and Inventory Control Soc. (bd. dirs. 1975—), Masons, Sigma Xi, Tau Beta Pi. Lutheran. Avocations: orchestra and choir, swimming, tennis, skiing, photography. Home: 1864 Limetree Ln Mountain View CA 94040-4019 Office: San Jose State U Coll Engring 1 Washington Sq San Jose CA 95192-0001

JACOBSON, ALF EDGAR, state legislator; b. Spokane, Wash., Apr. 24, 1924; s. Carl Magnus and Emmy (Bjoresson) J.; m. Sonja Ruth Torstenson; children: Kurt Torsten, Brent Burgess. BS, Northwestern U., 1952; MA, Tufts U., 1954; STB, Harvard U., 1954, STM, 1955, PhD, 1963. Prof. Colby-Sawyer Coll., 1958-86, chmn. social and behavior sci. dept., 1970-77; mem. Dist. 7 N.H. State Senate, 1969-78, asst. majority leader, 1969-70, senate pres., 1975-78; mem. Merrimack County Dist. 2 N.H. State Ho. of Reps., 1982-92, 95—, spkr. pro tem, 1999—. Trustee New London (N.H.) Libr., 1960-63, mem. planning bd., 1965-71, chmn., 1967-69; moderator Kearsarge Regional Sch. Dist., 1968-84, 99—, dir. of welfare, 1993-97; town moderator, New London, 1970-73, selectman, 1973-85, chmn. bd. selectman, 1975-76, 78-79, 81-82, 84-85; del. Rep. Nat. Conv., 1976, 80; mem. Nat. Archive Adv. Commn., 1981-85; mem. Peace Corp Adv. Coun., 1982-84. Recipient Brewer prize Am. Soc. Ch. History, 1965, Bill of Rights award N.H. ACLU, 1994. Mem. Am. Philatelic Soc., Ephemera Soc. Am. Office: House of Reps State House Concord NH 03301

JACOBSON, ALLEN H., economist; b. N.Y.C., July 5, 1939; s. Jack Joseph and Mary (Laxman) J.; m. Gladys Cecile Safier, Sept. 20, 1970; children: Gennifer Ann, Allison Lindsay. BA, NYU, 1962, MA, 1965. Lic. acct. exec. in securities bus., real estate agt. Economist Lional D. Edie & Inc., N.Y.C., 1966-69; sr. economist U.S. Trust Co., N.Y.C., 1969-79; ptnr. Washington Analysis Corp., 1979-87; v.p. NatWest Markets, Washington, 1988-95, Hong Kong Shanghai Bank Corp., Washington, 1995-99; sr. v.p. HSBC Securities, Inc.; ptnr. Washington Analysis Corp., 1999—. Mem. Nat. Economists Club (v.p. 1982-83, 91-92, bd. govs. 1992-93), Nat. Assn. Bus. Economists (coun. nat. chpt. 1985-86), Washington Assn. Money Mgrs., Montgomery County Assn. Realtors, Lakewood Club, Norbeck Club. Avocations: tennis, aerobics, real estate, golf. Home: 13140 Brushwood Way Potomac MD 20854-1025 Office: Washington Analysis Corp Ste 210 1130 Connecticut Ave NW Washington DC 20036-3929

JACOBSON, ANNA SUE, finance company executive; b. Ft. Smith, Ark., Aug. 13, 1940; d. Ray Bradley and Joy Anna (Person) McAlister, (stepfather) Cleve J. McDonald, Sr.; m. Lyle Norman Jacobson, Nov. 23, 1958; children: Lyle Michael, Daniel Ray, Julie Anne, Eric Joseph. Cert. in Fin. Planning, Coll. for Fin. Planning, 1984. Certified fin. paraplanner. Office mgr. Twin Cities Lithographic Inst., St. Paul, 1963-66; sec., St. Paul, Mpls., 1971-78; asst. to pres., office mgr. Planners Fin. Svcs., Mpls., 1978-85, asst. corp. treas., 1987-88; fin. paraplanner McAlmont Investment Co., Mpls., 1985-96, office mgr., 1988-96; registered rep. USR Fin. Svc. Inc., 1996-98; nat. retail mktg. coord. Carlson Leisure Group, Minnetonka, Minn., 1998—; ind. fin. cons.; bd. dir. Planners Fin. Svcs.; mem. bd. advisors Coll. for Fin. Planning, Denver, 1982—; v.p., CFO J&J Specialty Co., 1993—; sr. v.p. AdPro Internat., Inc., Wayzata, Minn., 1996—; speaker various orgns. Co-creator Paraplanning Profession Advisor; mem. firm Fin. Alternatives of Mpls., Wayzata, Minn., 1996—, Mpls., 1985—, nat. retail operation coord. Caylson Cos. Inc., Mpls., 1996—. Del. Dem. Farmer Labor Com., St. Paul, 1980; campaign chmn. mayoral election, Roseville, Minn., 1983, county commr., city coun. election, Roseville, 1980, 84; local chmn. for passage of ERA, Minn.; mem. Am. Lung Assn., St. Paul, Ramsey Found. of Minn., Como conservatory Hist. Soc.; past. pres. PTA, Minn.; mem. exec. coun. Boy Scouts Am., 1977-81; mem. adv. bd. Sch. Dist. 623, Roseville, Minn., 1978-81; fund raising com. mem. Twin Cities Pub. TV Sta., 1975—; mem. ch. coun. deacons St. Michael's Luth. Ch., St. Paul, 1996—, pres. congregation and coun., Roseville, Minn., 1998—, . Recipient Volunteerism award State of Minn., 1981, Cert. of Appreciation Minn. Bicentennial Com., 1976; named 1st Fin. Paraplanner in history of industry. Mem. Internat. Assn. Fin. Planning, Twin Cities Assn. Fin. Planners, Internat. Assn. Bus. and Profl. Women (bd. dirs. 1977-86, pres. 1980-82, Woman of Yr. 1982), Minn. Women's Consortium, Como Conservatory Hist. Soc., Concordia Acad. Booster Club, Beta Sigma Phi Nu Phi Mu Chpt. Democrat. Lutheran. Avocations: tennis, riding, reading, piano, harp. Home: 2171 Dellwood Ave Saint Paul MN 55113-4329 Office: Carlson Leisure Group 701 Lakeshore Pky Minnetonka MN 55441-8207

JACOBSON, ANTONE GARDNER, zoology educator; b. nr. Salt Lake City, May 22, 1929; s. Rufus Ingman and Marvell (Gardner) J.; m. Jacqueline James, July 26, 1962; children: Lauren, Eric. AB, Harvard U., 1951; PhD, Stanford U., 1955. Mem. faculty dept. zoology U. Tex., Austin, 1957—, assoc. prof., 1961-68, prof., 1968-97, prof. emeritus, 1997—; instr. Marine Biol. Lab., Woods Hole, Mass., 1969-70. Contbr. articles to profl. jours. Harvard Nat. scholar, 1947-51, Henry Newell Honors scholar, 1951-55. Mdm. Internat. Soc. Devel. Biologists, Soc. Devel. Biology, Am. Soc. Zoologists, Am. Assn. Anatomists, Sigma Xi. Home: 201 Skyline Dr Austin TX 78746-3610 Office: Univ Tex Dept Zoology Austin TX 78712

JACOBSON, ARLAND DEAN, religion educator; b. Mitchell, S.D., Sept. 25, 1941; s. Olaf Johannes and Ruth Amelia (Gjesdal) J. m. Wilhelmine Treadwell, Aug. 15, 1964; children: Erik Eugene, Karin Inga. BA, Augustana Coll., 1963; student, Div. Sch., U. Chgo., 1964-65; BD, Luther Theol. Sem., St. Paul, 1967; PhD, Claremont Grad. Sch., 1978. Ordained to ministry Evang. Luth. Ch. Am., 1967. Pastor Scranton (N.D.) Luth. Parish, 1967-71, St. Paul Luth. Ch., Humboldt, S.D., 1974-76; vis. prof. Loyola Marymount U., L.A., 1978-79; asst. prof. Concordia Coll., Moorhead, Minn., 1979-83; exec. dir. CHARIS Ecumenical Ctr. and Fargo-Moorhead Communiversity, Moorhead, 1983—; chair bd. Great Plains Inst. Theology, Bismarck, N.D., 1969-71; mem. Faith and Order Commn., Minn. Coun. Chs., Mpls., 1985—. Author: Wisdom Christology in Q, 1978, The First Gospel, 1991, Ecumenical Shared Ministry in the United Methodist Church, 1995; also numerous articles and revs. Chair conf. planning com. Internat. Coalition for Land-Water Stewardship in the Red River Basin, Moorhead, 1983-85, chair edn. com., 1985-87. Scholar Luth. Theol. Sem., 1966, scholar in residence Inst. for Ecumenical and Cultural Rsch., 1990, Harvard Inst. Mgmt. Lifelong Learning, 1992, Tantur Ecumenical Inst., Jerusalem, 1997; Bush fellow, 1992. Mem. Soc. Bibl. Lit., Cath. Bibl. Assn., Soc. for Advancement Continuing Edn. for Ministry (sec. 1996—), The Jesus Seminar, Westar Inst., Kiwanis (bd. dirs. Moorhead club 1989-91), Jazz Arts Group (bd. mem. 1995—). Home: 1915 12th Ave S Moorhead MN 56560-3114 Office: Concordia Coll CHARIS Ecumenical Ctr Moorhead MN 56562

JACOBSON, BARRY STEPHEN, lawyer, judge; b. Bklyn., Mar. 30, 1955; s. Morris and Sally (Ballaban) J.; m. Andrea Jacobson; children: Faith Blair, Matthew Aaron Jacobson. Cert. in drama, Sch. of Performing Arts, N.Y.C., 1973; BA, CUNY, 1977, MA, 1980; JD, Bklyn. Sch. Law, 1980. Bar: N.Y., 1981, U.S. Dist. Ct. (ea. and so. dists.) N.Y. 1981, U.S. Dist. Ct. (we. and no. dists.) N.Y., 1988, U.S. Dist. Ct. D.C., 1988, U.S. Ct. Appeals (2d cir.) 1981, U.S. Ct. Appeals (fed. and D.C. cirs.) 1988, U.S. Supreme Ct. 1984, U.S. Ct. Claims, 1985, U.S. Tax Ct. 1988 and others. Sole practice Bklyn., 1981; asst. corp. counsel N.Y.C. Law Dept., Bklyn., 1981-84; asst. dist. atty. Borough of Queens, Kew Gardens, N.Y., 1984-85; judge adminstrv. law N.Y. Dept. Motor Vehicles, Bklyn., 1985-86, 87-92; assoc. counsel N.Y. State Dept. Health, N.Y.C., 1986; arbitrator N.Y.C. Small Claims Ct., 1986-91; pvt. practice Bklyn., 1992—; gen. counsel Amersfort Flatlands Devel. Corp., Bklyn., 1981-82; arbitrator N.Y.C. Civil Ct. 1987-92; adminstrv. law judge N.Y.C. Parking Violators Bur., 1987-93; mem. Indigent Defenders Appeal Panel, 1988-96; sr. adminstrv. law judge N.Y.C. Parking Violation Bur., 1989-93; leader Nat. Jud. Coll., N.Y. Mem. Roosevelt Dem. Party, Bklyn., 1984-95, mem. adv. bd., 1989-92, treas., 1990-92; active Kings Hwy. Dem. Party, Bklyn., 1982-95, Dem. com. 1986-95; active King's County Young Dems., 1985-86; gen. counsel Bklyn. Coll. Hillel, Bklyn. Coll. Student Govts., 1980-90, also advisor; treas. local div. dept. mtr. vehicles pub. employees fedn. AFL-CIO; coun. ldr. div. #255 Pub. Employee's Fedn., 1989-92, conv. del. 1989, 90, 91; chmn. Bklyn. Traffic Employee Assistance Prog., 1989-92. Named one of Outstanding Young Men Am., 1983, 85, 86, 87, 88. Mem. ABA (judicial sect., spl. const. judges traffic cts. com.), Am. Judges Assn. (hwy. safety com.), Bklyn. Bar Found. (trustee, bd. dirs.), Am. Arbitration Assn. (forums 1988—), Am. Judicature Soc., Assn. Adminstrv. Law Judges (pres.), N.Y. State Dept. Motor Vehicles (v.p.), N.Y. State Adminstrv. Law Judges Assn. (pres. bd. dirs. parking violation com., v.p.), N.Y. State Bar Assn. (pres. for DMV, spl. com. juvenile justice, adminstrv. law jud. coms., jud. adminstrn. com.), Bklyn. Bar Assn. (family ct. com., chmn. young lawyers sect., trustee 1991, chmn. adminstrn. law com.), N.Y. County Lawyers Assn. (family Ct. Com.), Bklyn. Coll. Alumni Assn. (gen. counsel student govt. affiliate 1983-92, bd. dirs. 1985-92), Jaycees, B'nai B'rith, Hillel (bd. dirs. 1983-91, gen. counsel 1987-91), many others. Jewish. Avocations: motorcycling, drama, theatre, target shooting, flying. Home: 342 Coleridge Ln Jericho NY 11753-2605 Office: 26 Court St Ste 810 Brooklyn NY 11242-1108

JACOBSON, CAROLE RENEE, lawyer, educator; b. N.Y.C., Feb. 10, 1935; d. Daniel and Sally (Leader) Gold; m. David S. Jacobson, Jan. 28, 1962; 3 children. BS with honors, U. Pa., 1956; MA English with honors, Columbia U., 1957; JD, Rutgers U., 1979. Bar: Pa. 1980, Fla. 1982, N.J. 1983; cert. English tchr., N.J. Tchr. Manhasset (L.I., N.Y.) High Sch., 1958-62, Westfield (N.J.) High Sch., 1962; dir. social services South Brunswick (N.J.) High Sch., 1976; sr. counsel N.J. Casino Control Commn., Atlantic City, 1981—. Editor N.J. Voter, 1974-75. Elected Hunterdon (N.J.) Cen. Regional Bd. Edn., 1983, 86, 89-92, v.p., 1986-87, pres. 1987-88; mem. Raritan Twp. (N.J.) Bd. Adjustment, 1979-82, vice chmn., 1981; Hunterdon County freeholder candidate, 1975; chmn. legis. subcom. State Consumer Affairs Adv. Com., 1976-82; mem. N.J. State bd. LWV, 1974-75, pres. Hunterdon County, 1972-74, Plainfield, 1968-70; pres. Vol. Bur. Hunterdon County, 1974-76; trustee Hunterdon County Housing Council, 1972-76; mem. Citizens Housing Corp. Raritan Twp. 1971-72; chmn. Hunterdon County Coalition Better Pub. Schs., 1971-72; mem. State Adv. Commn. on the Status of Women, 1991-94. Recipient resolution of appreciation Bd. Adjustment, Raritan Twp., 1982. Home: 1 Pinewood Ct Flemington NJ 08822-4909 Office: Arcade Bldg Tennessee Ave & Boardwalk Atlantic City NJ 08401

JACOBSON, CHARLES ALLEN, aerospace company executive; b. Cresco, Iowa, June 2, 1925; s. Julius and Beulah Rosella (Peterson) J.; m. Marjorie Helen Minear, June 18, 1947; children: Janelle Paige, Charles Allen Jr., Robert Roger, Julian Kent, Joan Leigh. BS in Aerospace Engring., Iowa State U., 1952; postgrad., St. Louis U., 1956-57. Engr. McDonnell Aircraft Corp., St. Louis, 1952-59, group engr., 1959-64, project dynamics engr., 1964-68; dir. Houston ops. McDonnell Douglas Astronautics Co., 1968-84; v.p., gen. mgr. McDonnell Douglas Tech. Svcs. Co., Huntsville, Ala., 1984-85, McDonnell Douglas Space Systems Co., Houston, 1985-90; pres. GB Tech., Inc., Houston, 1990—; bd. dirs. M Bank, Clear Lake, Houston; mem. NASA Johnson Space Ctr. Team Excellence Forum; mem. devel. and adv. coun. U. Houston at Clear Lake, 1987-90; mem. Engring Found. adv. coun., U. Tex., Austin, 1989—; pres. Clear Lake Transp. Partnership, Houston, 1990-95, chmn. bd. dirs., 1995—. Dir. Rotary Nat. Award for Space Achievement, Houston, 1984—; dir. Clear Lake Area Econ. Devel. Found., Houston, 1983-84, 86-89, Clear Lake Symphony, Houston, 1987-89; chmn. Bay Area YMCA, Houston, 1981-82; mem. hon. bd. March of Dimes Walk Am., Houston, 1980; vice chmn. fin. Boy Scouts Am. Baysmore dist., 1987-89; adv. dir. Clear Lake Coun. Tech. Socs., 1989—; vice chmn. aerospace Houston area US Savs. Bonds Campaign, 1988. Lt. cmmdr. USNR, 1943-67. Recipient NASA Pub. Svc. medal, 1981, Profl. Achievement Citation for Engring., Iowa State U., Ames, 1988; named Tech. Adminstr. of Yr., Clear Lake Coun. Tech. Socs., 1984; Rotary Internat. Paul Harris fellow, 1983. Fellow AIAA (assoc., Gemini Achievement award 1966); mem. Armed Forces Comms. and Electronics Assn. (bd. dirs. 1987-89), Nat. Contract Mgmt. Assn., Navy League, South Shore Harbor Country Club (bd. dirs. 1987-89), Space Ctr. Rotary (pres. 1982-83). Republican. Avocations: golf, travel. Home: 2908 Doral Ct League City TX 77573-4412 Office: GB Tech Inc 2200 Space Park Dr Ste 400 Houston TX 77058-3680

JACOBSON, CHARLES EDWARD, JR., urologist; b. Nov. 11, 1910. BS, Trinity Coll., Hartford, Conn., 1931; MD, Cornell U., 1935; MS, U. Minn., 1941. Retired from career as urologist. Mem. numerous nat. and internat. med. socs. Home: 45 Wyllys St Manchester CT 06040

JACOBSON, CRAIG, lawyer. Ptnr. Hansen Jacobson & Teller, Beverly Hills, Calif. Office: Hansen Jacobson & Teller 450 N Roxbury Dr #8 Beverly Hills CA 90210-4022*

JACOBSON, DAVID, rabbi; b. Cin., Dec. 2, 1909; s. Abraham and Rebecca (Sereinsky) J.; m. Helen Gugenheim, Nov. 6, 1938; children: Liz Helenchild, Dottie J. Miller. AB, U. Cin., 1931; Rabbi, Hebrew Union Coll., 1934, DD, 1959; PhD, Cambridge U., 1936; LL.D., Our Lady of Lake Coll., 1964. Instr. Hebrew Union Coll., 1933-34; rabbi West Central Liberal Congregation, London, 1934-36, Indpls. Hebrew Congregation, 1936-38, Temple Beth-El, San Antonio, 1938-76; emeritus Temple Beth-El, 1976—; rabbi Temple Mizpah, Abilene, Tex., 1981-86; chaplain, area mil. installations; chaplain Audie Murphy VA Hosp., 1973-92; chmn. Rabbinical Placement Commn., 1973-78; chmn. discussion program KSAT-TV, 1956-80, KLRN-TV, 1983. Author: Social Background of the Old Testament, 1942, The Synagogue Through the Ages, 1958; contbr. articles to profl. and gen. publs.; also contbr. to: Universal Jewish Ency, 1939-43. Mem. Tex. Senate Com. Welfare Reform, 1970, Tex. State Ethics Commn., 1971, Tex. State Medicaid Task Force, 1977; mem. com. nursing homes Tex. Dept. Human Resources, 1978-80; pres. San Antonio Soc. Crippled Children and Adults, 1963-66, Goodwill Industries San Antonio, 1956-60, Bexar County chpt. Nat. Tb Assn., 1955-57, Community Welfare Council San Antonio, 1951-53, San Antonio Area Found., 1965-69, Research and Planning Council San Antonio, 1966-67, Tex. Social Welfare Assn., 1967-69, San Antonio Manpower Devel. Council, 1968-76, S.W. region Central Conf. Am. Rabbis, 1969-70, Multiple Sclerosis Soc. San Antonio, 1975-78, Nat. Conf. Social Welfare, 1976-77, Am. Inst. Character Edn., 1976-78, Prevent Blindness Soc., San Antonio, 1980-82; mediator San Antonio Printing Trades and Employers, 1968-92; mem. nat. labor panel Am. Arbitration Assn., 1977-92, Fed. Mediation and Conciliation Service, 1981-92; commr. Housing Authority San Antonio, 1954-58; bd. dirs. Our Lady of Lake U., 1966-76, hon. bd. dirs., 1977—; also chmn. adv. bd. Worden Sch. Social Service of coll., 1958-67; founder U. Ind. Hillel Found., 1938, San Antonio Vis. Nurses Assn., 1952, Community Welfare Council San Antonio, 1944; bd. dirs. S.W. Tex. Meth. Hosp., 1956-84, San Antonio Med. Found., 1962—, Alamo council Boy Scouts Am., 1950-90, Children's Hosp. Found., 1964—, Keystone Sch., San Antonio, 1960-80, Ecumenical Center for Religion and Health, 1968—, Alamo chpt. Am. Cancer Soc., 1975-83; chmn. Bexar County Community Corrections Commn., 1979-81; mem. nat. bd. Goodwill Industries Am., 1965-78; bd. overseers Hebrew Union Coll.-Jewish Inst. Religion, 1966-88, bd. govs., 1966-68; mem. Commn. on Social Action of Reform Judaism, 1978-82; mem. nat. bd. Nat. Council on Crime and Delinquency, 1972-88. Served as chaplain with USNR, 1944-46. Recipient Silver Beaver award Boy Scouts Am., 1958, Aristotle-Aquinas award Cath. Coll. Found. S.A., 1959, Golden Deeds award Exch. Club San Antonio, 1959, Keystone award Boys' Club Am., 1962, Lifetime Achievement award B'nai B'rith, 1964, Nat. Humanitarian award, 1975, Edgar Helms award Goodwill Industries, 1972, Outland award Tex. Soc. Prevent Blindness, 1988, Pioneer Peacemakers award San Antonio Bar Found., 1997; named Outstanding Jew NCCJ, 1961, Citizen of Yr. Sembradores de Amistad, 1971, Martin Luther King Disting. Achievement award, 1989; honoree S. Tex. chpt. Prevent Blindness as Person of Vision, 1979. Mem. Ctrl. Conf. Am. Rabbis (chmn. com. Judaism and health 1967-72, chmn. nominating com. 1979), Kallah of Tex. Rabbis (pres. 1950-51, chancellor-historian 1977—), Am. Social Health Assn. (dir. 1969-75, Tex. Congress Parents and Tchrs. (hon. life), Nat. Assn. Retired Reform Rabbis (1st v.p. 1996-97, pres. 1997-98), Rotary (San Antonio), B'nai B'rith (San Antonio) (hon. chmn. 1974), Torch Club (San Antonio) (pres. 1961), Argyle Club (San Antonio), Sigma Alpha Mu, Pi Tau Pi. Home: 207 Beechwood Ln San Antonio TX 78216-7345

JACOBSON, DAVID EDWARD, lawyer; b. Port Chester, N.Y., May 17, 1949; s. Robert Herzel and Ruth Doris (Rosenzweig) J.; m. Debra Ann Denkensohn, Aug. 10, 1975; 1 child, Andrew. B.A. in Econs., U. Rochester, 1971; J.D., SUNY-Buffalo, 1974; LL.M. in Taxation, Georgetown U., 1977. Bar: N.Y. 1975, D.C. 1976, U.S. Tax Ct. 1982, U.S. Ct. Appeals (fed. cir.) 1983. Atty.-adviser Office of Chief Counsel, IRS, Washington, 1974-79; tax counsel com. on fin. U.S. Senate, Washington, 1979-81; assoc. firm Reid & Priest, Washington, 1981-86, ptnr., 1986—. Vol. Income Tax Assistance, Arlington, Va., 1977-81; treas. Overlook Townhouse Homeowners Assn., Arlington. Mem. ABA (mem. tax sect. 1982—, vice-chmn. regulated utilities com. 1988-90, chmn. 1990-92), N.Y. State Bar Assn. Office: Thelen Reid & Priest LLP 701 Pennsylvania Ave NW Ste 800 Washington DC 20004-2625

JACOBSON, (JULIAN) EDWARD, lawyer; b. Chgo., Mar. 18, 1922; s. Lewis Frederick and Pearl (Hoffman) J. BA magna cum laude, Carleton Coll., 1942; Baker Scholar with Distinction, Harvard Bus. Sch., 1943; JD with honors, U. Ariz., 1946; DHL (hon.), Carleton Coll., 1994, Ariz. State U., 1995. Bar: Ariz. 1947, U.S. Dist. Ct. Ariz. 1947, U.S. Ct. Appeals (9th cir.) 1956, U.S. Supreme Ct. 1963. Law clk. to presiding justice Ariz. Supreme Ct., Phoenix, 1947-48; asst. atty. gen. Ariz. Atty. Gen.'s Office, Phoenix, 1948-50; ptnr. Snell and Wilmer, Phoenix, 1950-89, of counsel, 1990—. Author: The Art of Turned Wood Bowls, 1985. Pres. Civic Ctr. Mgmt. Bd., 1960-90, Phoenix Art Mus., 1974-76, Heard Mus., 1962-64, Phoenix Cmty. Coun., 1960-62, Family Svc. Phoenix; mem. Ariz. Commn. on Arts, 1979-88; bd. visitors Coll. Law U. Ariz., Tucson, 1978-80. Recipient Man of Yr. award Phoenix Advt. Club, 1974, Disting. Achievement award Ariz. State U. Law Sch., 1976, Disting. Achievement award Ariz. State U. Coll. Fine Arts, 1982, Gov.'s Arts award State of Ariz., 1983, Centennial Presdl. medal Ariz. State U., 1985, Visionary award Valley Leadership Alumni Assn., 1990, Historymaker award The Hist. League of Ariz. Hist. Soc., 1993. Fellow Ariz. Bar Found. (founding bd. mem. 1980, Walter E. Craig award 1995); mem. ABA, Ariz. Bar Assn., Maricopa County Bar Assn., Law Soc. Ariz. State U. (pres. 1974-75), Am. Judicare Soc., University Club, Phoenix Country Club. Home: 2201 N Central Ave Phoenix AZ 85004-1417 Office: Snell & Wilmer One Arizona Ctr Phoenix AZ 85004-0001

JACOBSON, EDWIN JAMES, medical educator; b. Chgo., June 27, 1947; s. Edwin Julius and Rose Josephine (Jirinec) J.; m. Martha Shanks; 1 child, Emily. BA, U. So. Calif., 1969; MD, UCLA, 1976. Diplomate Nat. Bd. Med. Examiners, Am. Bd. Internal Medicine; lic. physician, Calif. Intern in medicine UCLA Hosp., 1976-77, resident in medicine, 1977-79, fellow in nephrology, 1979-81, chief resident in medicine, 1979-81; asst. clin. prof. of medicine UCLA, 1981-88, assoc. clin. prof. medicine, 1988-94, clin. prof. medicine, 1994—; adj. asst. prof. medicine, UCLA, 1980-81; mem. med. sch. admissions com. UCLA, 1981—; med. staff credentials com., 1984—, med.staff exec. com., 1990-94, med. staff/hosp. adminstrn. liaison com. 1991-94, hosp./med. sch. faculty rels. com., 1991—, nat. kidney found., 1991—, med. adv. bd., 1991—; prin. investigator A/M Group Grant, UCLA Med. Ctr., 1993, Peter Langer Meml. Fund Award, 1993; lectr. in field. Author: Medical Diagnosis: An Algorithmic Approach, 1989; co-author: (with P. Healy) Il Proceso Decisionale nella Diagnosi Medica, 1992; manuscript rev. bd.: Bone Marrow Transplantation, 1988—, Jour. Am. Geriatrics Soc., 1989—; editor for symposia in field; contbr. articles to profl. jours.; editor book chpts. Recipient Upjohn Achievement award, 1977. Mem. ACP, Alpha Omega Alpha. Office: UCLA 100 Ucla Medical Plz Ste 690 Los Angeles CA 90024-6992

JACOBSON, EUGENE DONALD, educator, administrator, researcher; b. Bridgeport, Conn., Feb. 19, 1930; s. Morris and Mary (Mendelsohn) J.; m. Laura Kathryn Osborn, June 9, 1973; children from previous marriage: Laura Ellen, Susan Ruth, Morris David, Daniel Frederick, Miriam Louise. B.A., Wesleyan U., 1951; M.D., U. Vt., 1955; M.S., SUNY-Syracuse, 1960; DrMed (hon.), Jagiellonian U., 1996. Assoc. prof. UCLA Sch. Medicine, 1965-66; prof., chmn. U. Okla. Sch. Medicine, Okla. City, 1966-71, U. Tex. Med. Sch., Houston, 1971-77; vice dean Coll. Medicine U. Cin., 1977-85; dean Sch. Medicine, U. Kans., Kansas City, 1985-88; dean Sch. Medicine, U. Colo., Denver, 1988-90, prof., 1990—; acting head divsn. gastroenterology, 1994; cons. NIH, Bethesda, Md., 1968-72, mem. nat. digestive adv. bd., 1985-87; chmn. Nat. Commn., U.S. Congress, Washington, 1977-79; cons. Upjohn Co., Kalamazoo, 1970-87, G. D. Searle and Co., Chgo., 1984-85. Contbr. 320 articles to profl. jours. Served to maj. U.S. Army, 1956-64. NIH Rsch. grantee, 1967-97. Fellow ACP; mem. AMA (ho. of dels. 1991—), Am. Soc. Clin. Investigation, Assn. Am. Physicians, Am. Physiol. Soc., Am. Gastroenterol. Assn. (pres. 1989-90, Friedenwald medal 1998), Am. Digestive Health Found. (bd. dirs. vice chair 1995-98). Office: U Colo Sch Medicine 4200 E 9th Ave # C-321 Denver CO 80262

JACOBSON, FRANK JOEL, cultural organization administrator; b. Phila., Sept. 14, 1948; s. Leonard and June Anette (Groff) J.; m. Stephanie Lou Savage, July 5, 1970; children: Aaron Jeffery, Adam Michael, Ashley Celeste. BA, U. Wis., 1970; MFA, Boston U., 1973. Mng. dir. Mont. Repertory Theater, Missoula, Mo., 1973-75; asst. prof. drama U. Mont., Missoula, 1973-75; program dir. Western States Arts Found., Denver, 1975-77, dir. programs, 1977-78, gen. mgr. budget/planning, 1978-79; exec. dir. Arvada (Colo.) Ctr. for the Arts & Humanities, 1979-85; dir. theatres and arenas City & County of Denver, 1985-87; pres., CEO Scottsdale (Ariz.) Cultural Coun., 1987—; bd. dirs. Met. Denver Arts Alliance, pres., 1979-85, Rocky Mountain Arts Consortium, pres., 1979-80. Contbr. articles to profl. jours. Mem. panel theater program Nat. Endowment for the Arts, Washington, 1990-92; bd. dirs. Scottsdale Focus, 1988-93, 93-97, Arizonans for Cultural Devel., 1992-97; bd. dirs. Scottsdale Edn. Found., 1994-99, chmn., 1994-96. Mem. Am. Theatre Assn. (bd. dirs. 1976-78), Mont. State Theatre Assn. (bd. dirs., pres. 1974-75), Rocky Mountain Theatre Assn. (bd. dirs., pres. 1976-78), Assn. for Performing Arts Presenters (bd. dirs. 1984-87). Office: Scottsdale Cultural Council 7380 E 2nd St Scottsdale AZ 85251-5604

JACOBSON, GARY STEVEN, lawyer; b. Holyoke, Mass., Sept. 4, 1951; s. Rudolph Milton and Frederika Helena (Vanderryn) J.; m. Sharon W. Turkish, June 16, 1974; children: Lowell Daniel, Lee Stuart. BA cum laude, Wesleyan U., Middletown, Conn., 1973; JD, Northwestern U., 1976. Bar: Conn. 1976, N.Y. 1977, N.J. 1977, U.S. Ct. Appeals (3d cir.) 1981, U.S. Ct. Appeals (2d cir.) 1996. Investigative atty. N.Y. State Commn. on Jud. Conduct, N.Y.C., 1976-77; spl. asst. atty. gen. Office Spl. State Prosecutor, N.Y.C., 1977-79; assoc. Hofheimer, Gartlir, Gottlieb & Gross, N.Y.C., 1979-80; assoc. Kleinberg, Moroney, Masterson & Schachter, Millburn, N.J., 1980-85, ptnr., 1986-90; of counsel Kelley Drye & Warren, N.Y.C., 1990-91, ptnr., 1992-96; ptnr. Farer Siegal Fersko, Westfield, N.J., 1996-98, Jacobson & Brecher LLC, Mountainside, N.J., 1998—. Co-author: Commercial Litigation in New York State Courts, 1995; editor: Judicial Discipline Reporter, 1976. Republican. Jewish. Home: 99 Susan Dr Chatham NJ 07928-1055 Office: Jacobson & Brecher LLC PO Box 1220 608 Sherwood Pkwy Mountainside NJ 07092-0220

JACOBSON, GAYNOR I., retired association executive; b. Buffalo, May 17, 1912; s. Morris and Rose (Fleischman) J.; m. Florence Stulberg, Feb. 22, 1937; children—Margot (Mrs. Harold Gotoff), Helen (Mrs. Murray Levin). *Wife Florence, BA, CSW, MSS in Social Work at the University of Buffalo, N.Y. Four years of social service administration for American Joint District Committee in Czechoslovakia and Hungary. Honorary Doctor of Humane Letters from the State University of New York., 1996. Daughter Margot, BA and MA from University of Michigan, recognized sculptor in glass and bronze with exhibits in Rome, New York City, Tampa, Chigago, Boston, etc. Daughter Helen, BA University of Michigan, MA Boston College, Dean of Pilot High School, Cambridge, Massachusetts. She headed Harvard Law School Nursery and was a bi-lingual counselor at Pilot School before becoming Dean.* B.A., U. Buffalo, 1937, certificate in social work, 1939, M.S.W., 1941; LHD (hon.), SUNY, Buffalo, 1996. Exec. sec. Jewish Community Council, Rochester, N.Y., 1937-40; exec. dir. Jewish Family and Child Care, Rochester, 1938-44, Jewish Child Care Assn., Phila., 1950-51, Am. Technion Soc., 1951-53; country dir. Am. Joint Distbn. Com., Italy, 1944-45, Greece, 1945-46, Czechoslovakia, 1946-47, Hungary, 1947-50; dir. European and N. African ops. HIAS Inc., 1953-54, 61-66, dir. Latin Am. ops., 1955-61, exec. dir., 1966-68, exec. v.p., 1968-81, hon. exec. v.p., 1981—, bd. dirs., 1985—. Sculpture exhibited various galleries in U.S., Hungary, Brazil and France. Coun. overseers United Jewish Appeal Greater N.Y.; mem. Nat. Com. Plastic Arts Brazil Internat. Sculpture Ctr., UNESCO Internat. Assn. Plastic Arts; key activist in rescue of Jews during World War II. Recipient Independence citation and Silver Pin State of Israel, 1973, Disting. Alumni award SUNY at Buffalo, 1995; decorated Nat. Order So. Cross Brazil, 1979; Comdr. Cross of Merit Hungarian Republic, 1948; Gaynor Jacobson Sect. established U.S. Holocaust Mus., 1994; featured in The Secret Alliance: The Extraordinary Story of the Rescue of the Jews Since WWII, 1991. Mem. NASW, Nat. Assn. Jewish Family and Children's Health Svcs. Home (summer): Apt 1106 2373 Broadway New York NY 10024-2837 Home (winter): 17019 N 130th Ave Sun City West AZ 85375-5024 Office: HIAS Inc 333 7th Ave Fl 17 New York NY 10001-5019

JACOBSON, GERALD, psychologist; b. Chgo., Aug. 3, 1929; s. William and Ida (Margolis) J.; children: Kathleen Helton, Mary Wells, Karen Austin, Jerry W. BPS cum laude, Memphis State U., 1982, MS cum laude, 1984. Air crewman USN, 1948-60, from ensign to comdr., 1960-78; with U.S. mil. Binh Thun, Vietnam, 1969-70; intern in pharmacology and psychology Psychiat. Assocs., Memphis, 1979-82; dir. psychology Personal Counseling Ctr., Memphis, 1982—; spkr. in field. Author: In the Face of Fear, Unmasking...Finding the Real You Without a Therapist, Love, Honor and Abuse, 101 Ways to Fool Your Therapist, 1991, From the Valley to the Mountain Top, 1995, The Collision of the Fairy Princess and the Toy Soldier, 1997. Mem. choir 2d Presbyn. Ch., Memphis, 1996-97. Mem. Am. Assn. Marriage and Family Therapists (clin.), Tenn. Assn. Marriage and Family Therapists (clin.), Am. Assn. Christian Counselors (charter clin.), Sch. of Parent Effectiveness Tng. (charter clin.), Sigma Delta PHi, Phi Kappa Phi. Republican. Avocations: music, gardening, poetry, writing, cooking. Home: 1681 Randolph Apt 7 Memphis TN 38120

JACOBSON, GILBERT H., association executive, lawyer; b. Memphis, Feb. 6, 1956; s. Irvin and Edith (Shainberg) J.; m. Shauna Brown, Aug. 23, 1983; children: Yisroel, Esther, Nechama, Mordechai, Avrohom, Doniel. BBA, Memphis State U., 1980; JD, Touro Coll. Sch. Law, Huntington, N.Y., 1983. Bar: N.Y. 1984, Tenn. 1985, Colo. 1986. Tax cons. Rooney, Pace, Inc., N.Y.C., 1983-84; chief fin. officer Denton Mills, Inc., New Albany, Miss., 1984-85; endowment cons. Coun. of Jewish Fedns., N.Y.C., 1986-90; assoc. dir. endowment devel. Coun. of Jewish Fedns., 1990-92, assoc. dir. planned giving and found. rels., 1992-95; dir. Endowment Found. UJA Fedn. Bergen County, River Edge, N.J., 1995-99; assoc. exec. dir. planned giving and endowments UJA-Fedn. N.Y., N.Y.C., 1999—. Contbr. articles to profl. jours. Founding pres. Torah Comty. Project, Denver, 1985-86; officer Congregation Adas Israel, Passaic, N.J., 1987—. Carmi Schwartz fellow Coun. Jewish Fedns., 1993. Mem. Am. Jewish Community Orgn. Personnel, N.Y. State Bar Assn. Avocation: Talmudic study. Office: UJA-Fedn NY 130 E 59th St New York NY 10022

JACOBSON, HAROLD GORDON, radiologist, educator; b. Cin., Oct. 12, 1912; s. Samuel and Regina (Dittman) J.; m. Ruth Enenstein, Aug. 10, 1941; children: Richard, Arthur. B.S., U. Cin., 1934, M.B., 1936, M.D., 1937. Diplomate Am. Bd. Radiology (trustee 1971-82, chmn. written exams com. in diagnostic radiology 1973-81, co-chmn., mem. 1981—, treas. 1976-78, v.p. 1978-80, pres. 1980-82, mem. residency rev. com. 1976-82, vice-chmn. 1979-80, chmn. 1980-82, exec. com. 1976—). Intern Los Angeles County Gen. Hosp., 1936-38; fellow in pathology Longview Hosp., Cin., 1938; resident Mt. Sinai Hosp., N.Y.C., 1939-41, Associated Hosps. U. Tex., 1941-42; asst. in radiology U. Tex., 1941-42; assoc. radiologist New Haven (Conn.) Hosp.; also instr. Yale U., 1952; asst. chief, asso. radiologist VA Hosp., Bronx, N.Y., 1946-50; chief radiology service VA Hosp., 1950-53, cons., 1958—; asst. clin. prof. N.Y. U., 1952-53, clin. prof., 1953-59, prof. clin. radiology, 1959-64; prof. radiology Albert Einstein Coll. Medicine, 1964-71; prof., chmn. Albert Einstein Coll. Medicine of Montefiore Hosp. and Med. Center, N.Y.C., 1972-85; prof. radiology Albert Einstein Coll. Medicine of Montefiore Hosp. and Med. Center, 1985-86, prof. emeritus, chmn., Disting. Univ. Prof. radiology, 1986—; dir. dept. roentgenology Hosp. for Spl. Surgery, N.Y.C., 1953-55; radiologist-in-chief Montefiore Hosp. and Med. Center, N.Y.C., 1955—; sr. cons. in radiology Nat. Bd. Med. Examiners, 1975—, mem. bd., 1979-83; vis. prof. radiology Inst. Orthopaedics, U. London, 1975—; vis. prof., lectr., UCLA Med. Ctr., 1986, 88, various socs., med. schs., univs. in Israel, Brazil, Finland, Cuba, Eastern Europe; vis. prof., lectr., med. ctrs. Republic of China and guest Chinese Radiol. Soc., 1986; named lectures include Felson Lecture, Carman Lecture, Baylin Lecture, Beeler Lecture, Freedman Lecture, Pfahler Lecture, Chamberlain Lecture, Evans Lecture, Sampson Lecture, Wolf Meml. Lecture, Caffey Lecture, Grubbe Lecture, Myron Melamed Lecture; Double Day lectr. U. Tex., 1992, Spl. lectr. N.Y. Roentgen Soc., 1992; head del. of radiologists to Republic of China, 1984. Author: (with Clarence Schein, William Z. Stern) The Common Bile Duct, 1967, Neuroradiology Workshop, Vol. III, 1968, (with Ronald O. Murray) Radiology of Skeletal Disorders: Exercises in Diagnosis, 1971, 2nd edit. 1977, 3rd edit. 1989; co-author: Bone Disease Syllabus, 1972, 2d series, 1976, 3d series, 1980, 4th series 1989, Index for Roentgen Diagnosis, 3d edit. 1975; co-editor in chief Jour. Internat. Skeletal Soc., 1976—; co-chief editor Skeletal Radiology, 1975; mem. editorial bd. Excerpta Medica, 1974—, Jour. AMA, 1979—, others. Served as maj. M.C. AUS, 1942-46. Recipient Gold medal Assn. Univ. Radiologists, 1982, Gold medal Phi Lambda Kappa, 1983, Spl. Excellence award (in lieu of Hon. Doctorate) U. Cin., 1987, Spl. award N.Y. Roentgen Soc., 1993, Alumni Staff Assn. Montefiore Med. Ctr., 1993; spl. named lecture in his honor Roentgen Soc., 1992. Fellow Am. Coll. Radiology (councilor 1960—, bd. chancellors, chmn. com. on radiol. coding 1967—, mem. commn. on credentials 1968—, chmn. commn. on affairs Am. Inst. Radiology 1971—, co-chmn. com. on diagnostic coding index and thesaurus 1973—, Gold medal 1978, selected for video taping as living legend in radiology), Royal Coll. Radiologists (London) (hon.); mem. Am. Roentgen Ray Soc. (Cert. Appreciation 1983, Gold medal 1989), N.Y. Roentgen Soc. (pres. 1959-60, historian 1967—, spl. lecture 1992), AMA, N.Y. State Med. Soc., N.Y. Med. Soc., Soc. of Chairmen Acad. Radiology Depts. (mem. exec. council 1972—, pres. 1973-74), Radiol. Soc. N.Am. (pres. 1966-67, mem. bd. censors 1968—, Diamond Jubilee lectr. 1989, Gold medal 1972), Royal Soc. Medicine (hon.), Internat. Skeletal Soc. (co-founder, pres. 1974-75, chmn., mem. exec. com. 1976—), Chinese Radiol. Soc. (hon.), Cuban Radiol. Soc. (hon.), Alpha Omega Alpha (Rigler lectr. 1964, 70, Crookshank lectr. London 1974, Holmes lectr. Boston 1974, Doubleday lectr. Houston 1991). Home: 3240 Henry Hudson Pky Bronx NY 10463-3212 Office: Montefiore Med Ctr Dept Radiology 111 E 210th St Bronx NY 10467-2401

JACOBSON, HAROLD KARAN, political science educator, researcher; b. Detroit, June 28, 1929; s. Harold Kenneth and Maxine Anna (Miller) J.; m. Merelyn Jean Lindbloom, Aug. 25, 1951; children: Harold Knute, Eric Alfred, Kristoffer Olaf, Nils Karl. AB, U. Mich., 1950; MA, Yale U., 1952, PhD, 1955. Asst. prof. U. Houston, 1955-57; mem. faculty U. Mich., Ann Arbor, 1957—, assoc. prof., 1961-65, prof., 1965—, James Omy Murfin prof. polit. sci., 1977-82, Jesse Siddal Reeves prof. polit. sci., 1984—, rsch. scientist, 1977-97, chmn. dept., 1972-77, acting chmn., 1981, dir. Ctr. for Polit. Studies, 1986-96, interim assoc. v.p. for internat. acad. affairs, 1990-92, sr. rsch. scientist, 1997—; acting dir. Inst. for Social Rsch., Ann Arbor, 1992-93, 94-95; vis. prof. Grad. Inst. Internat. Studies, U. Geneva, 1965-66, 70-71, 77-78; World Affairs Center fellow, 1959-60; vis. research scholar European Center Carnegie Endowment for Internat. Peace, Geneva, 1970-71. Author:

The USSR and the UN's Economic and Social Activities, 1963, Networks of Interdependence, 1979, 84, (with Eric Stein) Diplomats, Scientists, and Politicians, 1966, (with William Zimmerman) The Shaping of Foreign Policy, 1969, (with R.W. Cox and others) The Anatomy of Influence, 1973, (with Dusan Sidjanski and others) The Emerging International Order, 1982, (with David A. Kay and others) Environmental Protection: The International Dimension, 1983, (with Michel Oksenberg) China's Participation in the IMF, The World Bank, and GATT: Toward a Global Economic Order, 1990, (with Peter B. Evans and Robert D. Putnam) Double-Edged Diplomacy: International Bargaining and Domestic Politics, 1993, (with William Zimmerman) Behavior, Culture and Conflict in World Politics, 1994, (with Edith Brown Weiss and others) Engaging Countries: Strengthening Compliance with International Environmental Accords, 1998; editl. bd. Internat. Orgn., 1968-76, 78-90, Am. Jour. Internat. Law, 1979-91, 95—, Internat. Studies Quar., 1980-85, Jour. Conflict Resolution, 1961-72, Am. Polit. Sci. Rev., 1985-88. Mem. U.S. Nat. Commn. for UNESCO, 1980-85. Woodrow Wilson Ctr. fellow, 1984, Ctr. for Advanced Studies in Behavioral Scis. fellow, 1988-89, Ctr. for Internat. Climate and Environ. Rsch. Oslo fellow, 1996. Fellow Am. Acad. Arts and Scis.; mem. AAAS (AAAS Award for Internat. Sci. Cooperation 1995), AAUP, UN Assn. U.S. (bd. dirs. 1980-93), Internat. Social Sci. Coun. (chmn. human dimensions of global environ. change program 1990-94), Internat. Studies Assn. (pres. Midwest div. 1969-70, pres. 1982-83), Internat. Polit. Sci. Assn. (program chmn. 1985-88, v.p. 1988-91), Coun. Fgn. Rels., Detroit Com. Fgn. Rels. (chmn. 1984-86), Am. Polit. Sci. Assn., Midwest Polit. Sci. Assn., Internat. Inst. Strategic Studies (London), Cosmos Club (Washington), Yale Club (N.Y.C.), Club de la Fondation Universitaire (Brussels), Phi Beta Kappa, Phi Kappa Phi. Home: 2174 Delaware Dr Ann Arbor MI 48103-6017 Office: U Mich Inst for Social Rsch PO Box 1248 Ann Arbor MI 48106-1248

JACOBSON, HAROLD LELAND, lawyer; b. Chgo., Oct. 31, 1926; s. Oliver I. and Annabelle (Hershenson) J.; m. Nancee Klein, Aug. 22, 1948; children: Reid, Gary. BS, U. Ill., 1948; JD, Loyola U., 1953. Bar: Ill. 1953, U.S. Dist. Ct. (no. dist.) Ill. 1955. Assoc. ptnr. Schatz, Bush & Jacobson, Chgo., 1953-57; ptnr. Lord, Bissell & Brook, Chgo., 1958—. Served with U.S. Army, 1944-46. Fellow Am. Coll. Trial Lawyers, Am. Bd. Trial Attys., Soc. Trial Lawyers, Am. Bd. Profl. Liability Attys., Fedn. Ins. and Corp. Counsel. Club: Union League. Office: Lord Bissel & Brook 115 S La Salle St Ste 3200 Chicago IL 60603-3972*

JACOBSON, HELEN GUGENHEIM (MRS. DAVID JACOBSON), civic worker; b. San Antonio; d. Jac Elton and Rosetta (Dreyfus) Gugenheim; m. David Jacobson, Nov. 6, 1938; children: Liz Helenchild, Dottie J. Miller. BA, Hollins Coll. With news and spl. events staff NBC, N.Y.C., 1933-38. 1st v.p. San Antonio, Bexar County coun. Girl Scouts U.S.A., 1957-63; Tex. State rep. UNICEF, 1964-69; bd. dirs. U.S. com. UNICEF, 1970-80, hon. bd. dirs., 1980—; bd. dirs. Nat. Fedn. Temple Sisterhoods, 1973-77, Temple Beth-El Sisterhood, Youth Alternatives, Inc.; bd. dirs. Child Guidance Ctr., chmn. bd., 1960-63; bd. dirs. Sunshine Cottage Sch. for Deaf Children, chmn. bd., 1952-54; pres. Cmty Welfare Coun., 1968-70; pres. bd. trustees San Antonio Pub. Libr., 1957-61; trustee Nat. Coun. Crime and Delinquency, 1964-70, San Antonio Mus. Assn., 1964-73; bd. dirs. Cancer Therapy and Rsch. Ctr. South Tex., 1974—, sec., 1977-83; pres. S.W. region Tex. Coalition for Juvenile Justice, 1977-79; chmn. Mayor's Commn. on Status of Women, 1972-74; del. White House Conf. on Children, 1970; mem. Commn. on Social Action of Reform Judaism, 1973-77; chmn. Foster Grandparent project Bexar County Hosp. Dist., 1968-69; sec. Nat. Assembly for Social Policy and Devel., 1969-74; pres. women's com. Ecumenical Ctr. for Religion and Health, 1975-77; chmn. criminal justice planning com. Alamo Area Coun. of Govts., chmn., 1975-77, 1987-88; mem. Tex. Internat. Women's Yr. Coordinating Com., 1977; co-chmn. San Antonio chpt. NCCJ, 1980-84; chmn. United Negro Coll. Fund Campaign, 1983, 84; sec. nat. bd. Avance, Inc., 1991-93; trustee Target 90/Goals for San Antonio, 1986-90; hon. mem. bd. dirs. Witte Mus., 1994—. Recipient Headliner award for civic work San Antonio chpt. Women in Communications, 1958, Nat. Humanitarian award B'nai B'rith, 1975, City of Peace award, 1991; named Vol. Woman of Yr. Express-News, 1959, Spl. Svc. award Tex. Soc. Psychiat. Physicians, 1994; honoree San Antonio chpt. NCCJ, 1970, Nat. Jewish Hosp., 1978; inductee San Antonio Women's Hall of Fame, 1986, others. Mem. Nat. Coun. Jewish Women (Hannah G. Solomon award 1979), Internat. Women's Forum, San Antonio 100, Argyle Club. Home: 207 Beechwood Ln San Antonio TX 78216-7345

JACOBSON, HERBERT LEONARD, licensing executive; b. N.Y.C., Mar. 22, 1940; s. David and Lena (Goldberg) J.; m. Beverly Goldman, Nov. 23, 1961; children: Julie Ellen, Joel Howard. B.S. in E.E., U. R.I., 1961; LL.B., Bklyn. Law Sch., 1965; LL.M., NYU, 1970. Bar: N.Y. 1965, U.S. Patent and Trademark Office 1966, U.S. Supreme Ct. 1969, N.J. 1972. Planning engr. Am. Electric Power, N.Y.C., 1961-66; patent atty. RCA Corp., Princeton, N.J., 1966-74; counsel RCA Corp., N.Y.C., 1974-79, dir. licensing, 1979-83, staff v.p., 1983-86; exec. v.p. GE and RCA Licensing Mgmt. Operation, Inc., Princeton, N.J., 1986—. Home: 42 Yorktown Rd East Brunswick NJ 08816-3325 Office: Gen Electric Co PO Box 2023 Princeton NJ 08543-2023

JACOBSON, HOWARD, classics educator; b. Bronx, N.Y., Aug. 21, 1940; s. David and Jeannette (Signer) J.; m. Elaine Z. Finkelstein, June 10, 1965; children: Michael Noam, Daniel Benjamin, Joel Avram, David Moses. B.A., Columbia U., 1962, Ph.D., 1967; M.A., U. Chgo., 1963. Instr. Greek and Latin Columbia U., 1966-68; asst. prof. classics U. Ill., 1968-73, assoc. prof., 1973-80, prof., 1980—; Lady Davis vis. prof. Hebrew U., Jerusalem, winter 1983; mem. Inst. for Advanced Study, Princeton, N.J., 1993-94. Author: Ovid's Heroides, 1974, The Exagoge of Ezekiel, 1983, A Commentary on Pseudo-Philo's Liber Antiquitatum Biblicarum (2 vols.), 1996; editor for Latin studies: Illinois Classical Studies Supplements. Nat. Endowment for Humanities fellow, 1971-72, 89; assoc. Ctr. for Advanced Study, U. Ill., 1983-84, spring 1994. Mem. Am. Philol. Assn. (Charles J. Goodwin Merit award 1985), Phi Beta Kappa. Jewish. Office: Dept Classics 4072 Foreign Languages Bldg 707 S Mathews Ave Urbana IL 61801-3625

JACOBSON, IRA DAVID, aerospace engineer, educator, researcher; b. Bronx, N.Y., May 28, 1942; s. Abraham and Bertha (Badin) J.; m. Judy Angert; children: Donna, Alan. BS in Aeros. & Astronautics, NYU, 1963; MS in Aero. Engring., U. Va., 1967, PhD in Aero. Engring., 1970. Aerospace engr. NASA, Wallops Island, Va., 1963-67; from asst. to assoc. prof. U. Va., Charlottesville, 1967-93, prof., 1974—, dir. Ctr. for Computer-Aided Engring., 1983-91, dir. Ctr. for Innovative Tech., 1985-91, dir. info. tech. and comm., 1991-93; v.p. for acads. Embry-Riddle Aero. U., Daytona Beach, Fla., 1993-97, exec. v.p., 1997—; cons. various cos. and govt. agys., 1970—. Contbr. over 100 articles to profl. jours. Fellow AIAA (assoc., v.p.-elect edn. 1997, Outstanding Aerospace Educator award 1981); mem. Am. Soc. Engring. Educators (Outstanding Aerospace Educator award 1981), Nat. Computer Graphics Assn., Sigma Xi, Tau Beta Pi, Sigma Gamma Nu. Achievements include development of aircraft ride quality model; first description of fluid mechanical phenomena associated with boundary layer on spinning bodies at angle of attack to predict Magnus effect. Home: 2425 Atlantic Ave Daytona Beach FL 32118

JACOBSON, ISHIER, retired utility executive; b. Worcester, Mass., June 21, 1922; s. Aaron and Mollie (Mallor) J.; m. Maria Bohm, Dec. 18, 1948; children: Joanna M., Jonathan B., Paula R. BA, Clark U., 1946; MSME, Harvard U., 1947, LLB, 1951. Bar: Conn. 1951. Asst. to pres., gen. counsel Connor Engring. Corp., Danbury, Conn., 1951-53; with Citizens Utilities Co., Stamford, Conn., 1954-90; exec. v.p. Citizens Utilities Co., 1970, pres., chief oper. officer, 1970-81, pres., chief exec. officer, 1981-90, also dir.; chmn. bd. dirs. Silver Hill Hosp., New Canaan, Conn. Served to lt. USNR, 1942-46. Home: 326 Four Brook Rd Stamford CT 06903-4605

JACOBSON, JAMES BASSETT, insurance executive; b. San Francisco, Nov. 16, 1922; s. James Peter and Bertha (Bassett) J.; m. Janice Isabel Meilstrup, Aug. 29, 1949; children: Steven Blair, Karen Christine, Richard Barlow. BS, UCLA, 1947; postgrad., U. Pa., 1947-48; MBA, U. So. Calif., 1954. CLU. With Prudential Ins. Co. Am., various cities, 1948-83; v.p. group pension mktg. Prudential Ins. Co. Am., Newark, 1967-70, sr. v.p. in charge group ins., 1970-73; pres., western ops. Prudential Ins. Co. Am., L.A., 1973-83; exec. v.p. CalFed Inc. and Calif. Fed. Savs. & Loan Assn., L.A., 1983-87; chmn., chief exec. officer Beneficial Standard Life Ins. Co., L.A., 1987-88, chmn. bd. dirs., 1984-88; chmn. bd. dirs. Bonneville Internat. Corp., Salt Lake City; bd. dirs. Deseret Trust Co., Salt Lake City, Deseret Trust Co. of Calif., L.A., Galorath, Inc., El Segundo, Calif. Author: An Analysis of Group Creditors Insurance, 1954. V.p. L.A. Philharmonic Assn., 1977-83, bd. dirs., 1975-83; vice chmn. Community TV So. Calif. L.A., 1983, bd. dirs., 1979-83; chmn. bd. dirs. Orthopaedic Hosp., L.A., 1981-84, trustee, 1980-84; chmn. bd. L.A. Ballet, 1974-79, bd. dirs., 1974-83; mem. Calif. Round Table, 1981-83; bd. dirs. Dance Gallery, L.A., 1988-92, NCCJ L.A. Region, 1987—, Criminal Justice Legal Found., 1990—, Sacramento, others. With U.S. Army, 1943-46, 2d lt. res., 1951. Recipient Silver Beaver award Boy Scouts Am., 1984. Mem. Am. Coll. CLUs, UCLA Alumni Assn. (Cmty. Svc. award 1985), Calif. C. of C. (bd. dirs. 1974-83), L.A. C. of C. (bd. dirs. 1981-83), Calif. Club, Lochinvars Club (pres. 1981-84).

JACOBSON, JEFFREY ELI, lawyer, consultant; b. N.Y.C., Aug. 19, 1956; s. Murray and Adele (Ebert) J.; m. Linda Moel, Aug. 11, 1984; children: Justin Myles, Sari Amanda. BA, Fordham U., 1976; JD, N.Y. Law Sch., 1980. Bar: N.Y. 1982, D.C. 1982, U.S. Tax Ct. 1982, U.S. Ct. Internat. Trade 1982, U.S. Dist. Ct. (so. and ea. dists.) N.Y. 1982, U.S. Ct. Appeals (2d cir.) 1988, U.S. Supreme Ct. 1988. Assoc. SESAC, Inc., N.Y.C., 1980-82; sole practice N.Y.C., 1982-85; sr. ptnr. Jacobson & Colfin, P.C., N.Y.C. and L.I., 1985-90; mng. mem. Jacobson & Colfin, P.C., N.Y.C. and Washington, 1991—; v.p., sec. Fifth Ave. Media, Ltd., N.Y.C., 1995—; asst. mgr. Embassy Theatre, N.Y.C., 1975, Victoria Theatre, N.Y.C., 1975; asst. Theatre Confections, Inc., N.Y.C., 1975; mgr. Criterion Theatre, N.Y.C., 1976; mgr., sec. Squirrels Prodns. Ltd., N.Y.C., 1976-88; pres. Aldous Demian Prodns., Ltd., N.Y.C., 1980-82; counsel Box Office Media, N.Y.C., 1982-88, Eggink, N.Y.C., 1982-89, Performance Records, 1988-97, J&J Mus. Enterprises, Ltd., 1982-95, Anamaze Records, 1982-95, Cynthia Entertainment Group, Ltd., 1989-91, Roir Records, 1992—, Super Bubble Music Corp., 1992—, Sergei Artemiev Benefit, 1993, New Riders of the Purple Sage, 1985—, Mick Taylor Music, 1985—, Best Film and Video Corp., 1988-91, Marty Balin, 1988—, Andrew Tosh, 1990—; spkr. CMJ Music Marathon & Musicfest, 1995, Phila. Music Confs., 1993, 94, 95, 96, 97. Mem. editl. bd. Mealey's Intellectual Property Litigation Law Report, 1992-93; contbr. articles to profl. jours.; music and internat. promotion mgmt., 1984-85; columnist IMPS Jour., 1990-95, Replication News, 1998—. Mem. Rep. candidate assembly; v.p. Pelham Pkwy., 1983-88; speaker Songwriter's Guild, N.Y.C., 1983-88, NARAS, 1991; entertainment arbitrator Am. Arbitration Assn., N.Y.C., 1984-95; guest speaker Ctr. for Media Arts, N.Y.C., 1985, Fordham U., N.Y.C., 1986, N.Y. Law Sch., 1987, Detroit Sch. Law, 1991, 93; counsel Pelham Pkwy. Block Assn., Inc., 1991; panelist Mid-Am. Music Conf., Detroit, 1993, Black Radio Exclusive, Econs. of Music, 1993; league player Hewlett-Woodmere Little League, 1994—. Recipient Eagle Scout Silver Palm award Boy Scouts Am., 1972, Cert. of Merit Bronx House, Nathan Burkan award ASCAP, 1980, Plaque of Appreciation, Am. Arbitration Assn., 1985; named Most Admired Men and Women of Yr., 1993, Two Thousand Notable Am. Men, 1993, Man of Yr., 1996. Mem. ABA (chmn. subcom. on satellites, chmn. subcom. on copyright compliance, chmn. subcom. on copyright renewal, mem. patent trademark, copyright law sect., forum com. on entertainment and sports law sects., mem. spl. com. on corp. practice 1992-97, mem. spl. com. on atty. opinions 1994—, mem. spl. com. on internet 1997—), forum com. on comm. law, young lawyer's divsn.; vice chmn. 1992-94, patent, trademark, intellectual property sect. exec. com., 1992-93, media law com., young lawyers divsn., founder Urban Intellectual Property Law seminars 1993-95, dir., 1993-95, mem. com. on atty./client opinions, mem. spl. com. Internet usage), Assn. of Bar of City of N.Y. (entertainment law com. 1992-95, trademark law com. 1997—), Copyright Soc. USA (com. on Bicentennial of copyright, mem. editl. bd. Jour. of Copyright Soc. 1991-93, 97—), Nat. Acad. Rec. Arts and Scis. (edn. com., columnist N.Y. chpt. newsletter 1997—), Rock and Roll Hall of Fame and Museum, Internat. Assn. Entertainment Lawyers, B'nai B'rith (v.p. 1988-91), Order of the Arrow Brotherhood, Sephardic Jewish Brotherhood Am., Audubon Soc. Inc., Phi Delta Phi. Jewish. Avocations: music, photography, swimming, stereo equipment, traveling. Office: Jacobson & Colfin PC 156 5th Ave Ste 434 New York NY 10010-7002

JACOBSON, JEROLD DENNIS, lawyer; b. N.Y.C., Oct. 12, 1940; s. Sidney and Lillian D. (Fink) J.; m. Gertraude M.J. Holle-Suppa, May 4, 1998; children—Diana, Lisa, Pamela. A.B., U. Vt., 1962; J.D., Cornell U., 1965; LL.M. in Labor Law, NYU, 1966. Bar: N.Y. 1966, U.S. Dist. Ct. (so. and ea. dists.) N.Y. 1968, U.S. Dist. Ct. (no. dist.) N.Y. 1981, U.S. Ct. Appeals (2d cir.) 1979, U.S. Ct. Appeals (5th cir.) 1980, U.S. Ct. Appeals (11th cir.) 1981, U.S. Supreme Ct. 1982. Assoc. to gen. counsel ILGWU, AFL-CIO, N.Y.C., 1966-69; assoc. Rains, Pogrebin and Scher, N.Y.C. and Mineola, N.Y., 1969-70; assoc. Guggenheimer & Untermyer, N.Y.C., 1970-74, ptnr., 1975-85; ptnr. Summit, Rovins & Feldesman, N.Y.C., 1986-89, Patterson, Belknap, Webb & Tyler, N.Y.C., 1989-91, Proskauer Rose LLP, N.Y.C., 1991—; lectr. in labor and employment relations law Practising Law Inst., Am. Soc. Law and Medicine, Profl. Edn. Systems, Inc. Bd. dirs. Nassau County chpt. N.Y. State Civil Liberties Union; mem. adv. bd. U. Vt. Holocaust Study Ctr., U. Vt. Coll. Arts and Scis. Mem. ABA, Legal Aid Soc., Am. Arbitration Assn., Am. Acad. Hosp. Attys., Nat. Health Lawyers Assn., N.Y. State Bar Assn. (lectr.) Contbr. articles to profl. jours. Active, Inst. for Internat. Rsch., Coun. on Edn. in Mgmt.; bd. dirs. Nassau County chpt. N.Y. State Civil Liberties Union. Office: Proskauer Rose LLP 1585 Broadway New York NY 10036-8200

JACOBSON, JERRY IRVING, biophysicist, theoretical physicist; b. Bklyn., Jan. 25, 1946; s. Saul Lane and Miriam (Cassin) J.; m. Debra Maria Delso, Aug. 18, 1975; children: Solomon, Jacqueline, Faith, Maria. BA, Bklyn. Coll., 1963-66; DDS, DMD, Temple U., 1970; PhD, CUNY, 1983. Oral surgeon Tremont Med. Group, Bronx, N.Y., 1972-73, University Ave. Med. Group, Bronx, N.Y., 1973-77; pvt. practice Westchester and New City, N.Y., 1972-82; pres. Perspectivism Found., Jupiter, Fla., 1980—, Inst. Theoretical Physics & Advanced Studies for Biophys., Jupiter, 1985—, Alzheimers Rsch. Found., Jupiter, 1990—, Jacobson Resonance Inc., Jupiter, 1991—, Magneto Therapeutics Mfg., Inc., 1994—, Jacobson Resonance Machines Inc., 1995—; prof. rsch., founding dir. microgravity and electromagnetics Inst. Molecular Medicine, U. Calif., Irvine, 1996; CEO, pres. Pioneer Svcs. Internat., Ltd., Deerfield Beach, Fla., 1996—; chmn. dept. applied med. physics and neuromagnetics Nat. Med. and Rsch. Inst., Boca Raton, Fla., 1997—; pres. Pioneer Svcs. Internat. Ltd., Juno Beach, Fla., 1996; chmn. bd., CEO Jacobson Resonance Enterprises, Inc., Juno Beach, Fla., 1998—; spkr. in field. Contbr. articles to profl. jours.; holder med. and plasma physics and dental patents in U.S. and 80 other countries. Served to capt. Army Dental Corps, 1970-72. Mem. Am. Phys. Soc., Bioelectromagnetics Soc., European Bioelectromagnetics Soc., Italian Assn. Biomed. Physics, Internat. Assn. Biologically Closed Electric Circuits (mem. internat. adv. bd.). Avocations: oil painting, musical composition, fiction writing, philosophy. Home and Office: 2006 Mainsail Cir Jupiter FL 33477-1418

JACOBSON, JOHN HOWARD, JR., college president; b. Evanston, Ill., Nov. 6, 1933; s. John Howard and Grace Katharine (Whitney) J.; m. Jeanne G. McKee, Aug. 15, 1954; children: John Edward, Jean Katharine, Jennie Grace, James George. BA with high honors, Swarthmore Coll., 1954; MA, Yale U., 1956, PhD, 1957; LHD (hon.), Empire State Coll.; LittD (hon.), Hope Coll., 1987. Asst. prof. philosophy Hamilton Coll., Clinton, N.Y., 1957-63; assoc. prof. Fla. Presbyn. Coll., St. Petersburg, 1963-67, dean, 1967-72; dean Rochester Ctr. Empire State Coll., N.Y., 1972-74; v.p. acad. affairs Empire State Coll., Saratoga Springs, 1974-87, provost, 1980-87; pres. Hope Coll., Holland, Mich., 1987—. Author: (with others) Logic: A Programmed Text, 1963. Mem. exec. com. Assn. Ind. Colls. and Univs. of Mich. Mem. Am. Philos. Assn., Mich. Intercollegiate Athletic Assn., Holland Area C. of C. (bd. dirs. 1994—), Yale Club N.Y.C., Century Club, Holland Country Club. Mem. Reformed Ch. in America. Home: 92 E 10th St Holland MI 49423-3516 Office: Hope Coll PO Box 9000 141 E 12th St Holland MI 49423-3607

JACOBSON, LAWRENCE SEYMOUR, television executive producer; b. Waterbury, Conn.; m. Alice Bernhard; children: Marlo, Amy. BA, U. Conn. Exec. producer Jim Ameche Prodns.; exec. east coast prodn. Am. Internat. Pictures, 1977-80; pres. Grosso-Jacobson Entertainment Corp., N.Y.C., 1980; exec vp and cfo Fox Inc., Beverly Hills, CA, 1997. Assoc. prodr. Children's Theatre WNBC, N.Y.C., 1961, Emmy Awards NBC, 1962, Connie Francis Spl. ABC, 1963; exec. prodr. Jim Ameche Prodns., 1963-65, Carlton Fredricks Program ABC, 1966-67, Water World, 1971-75, The Racers, 1974-79 (creator), Miss Am. Teenager Pageant, 1977-79, Daytime Star, 1979, Comeback, 1979-80, Baker's Dozen, 1981-82, Night Heat, 1983-88 (Gemini award Best Dramatic TV series 1986, 87, TV Guide award Most Popular program, Can., 1986, 87), Trackdown, 1984, Hot Shots, 1985, Out of the Darkness, 1985 (Christopher award), Diamonds, 1985-87, Gunfighters, 1987, Cop Talk, 1989, True Blue, 1989-90, Family for Joe, 1989-90, Counterstrike USA, 1990—, Top Cops, 1990—, Bellevue Emergency, 1991, Secret Service, 1992, Gangsters, 1992, Police File, 1992, Juvenile Justice, 1994, Remember Me, 1995, While My Pretty One Slept, 1996, The Big Easy, 1996-98. Mem. N.Y.C. Film, Theatre and Broadcasting Adv. Coun. (mayor's 1983-90). Office: Grosso-Jacobson Entertainment 767 3rd Ave New York NY 10017-2023 also: Fox Inc. PO Box 900 Beverly Hills CA 90213-0900*

JACOBSON, LESLIE SARI, biologist, educator; b. N.Y.C., May 22, 1933; d. William and Gussie (Mintz) Goldberg; m. Homer Jacobson, Aug. 18, 1957 (div. Dec. 1995); children: Guy Joseph, Ethan Samuel. BS, Bklyn. Coll., 1954, MA, 1955; postgrad., Columbia U., 1956; postgrad. (NIH fellow), Calif. Inst. Tech., 1960; Ph.D., NYU, 1962. Instr. dept. biology Bklyn. Coll., 1954-57; asst. prof. biology L.I. Coll. Nursing, Bklyn., 1963, prof. biology, 1963-74, dean Grad. Sch., 1973-74; fellow dept. chemistry Bklyn. Coll., 1961-63, prof. health sci., 1974—, dean Sch. Gen. Studies and Continuing Higher Edn., 1974-80, dean Grad. Studies and Continuing Higher Edn., 1980-82, dean Grad. Studies, 1980-88, dean Grad. Studies and Rsch., 1988-89, prof. dept. health and nutritions scis., 1989—, exec. dir. Applied Scis. Inst., 1994-95; awarded Koppelman Endowed Professorship, 1995-97; acting v.p. Rsch. Found. CUNY, N.Y.C., 1998—; instr. dept. nursing L.I. Coll. Sch. Nursing, 1958; nat. program chmn. Assn. Continuing Higher Edn., 1978, nat. bd. dirs., 1978-81, pres.-elect, 1980-81, pres., 1981-82; bd. dirs. Center for Labor and Mgmt., N.Y.; dir. N.Y. Regional Cabinet Adult Continuing Edn., 1982—; mem. adv. com. on minorities Coun. Grad. Schs., 1987-90, svcs. com. Grad. Record Exam. Bd., 1990-93, chmn. Acad. policy com. all-univ. senate CUNY, 1992—; exec. com. univ. com. rsch. awards, CUNY, 1994, vice chmn. com. rsch. awards, 1995-97, co-chair univ. com. rsch. awards, 1996-97; bd. dirs. Hyperion Capital Mgt.; invited speaker at nat. meetings Issues in Higher Edn. V.p. Alpha Sigma Lambda Found., 1983-88; v.p. Mapleton Midwood Cmty. Health Bd. Inc., 1990—; v.p. B'nai B'rith Hillel JACY Assn., 1986-93; exec. mem. Hillel of N.Y., 1986-97; bd. dirs. Meth. Hosp., 1989—; v.p. Am. Lung Assn. of Bklyn.; mem. exec. com. Am. Lung Assn., 1996. Recipient Founders Day award NYU, 1961, N.Y. Outstanding Adult Educator award, N.Y.C., 1978, Nat. Merit award, Assn. Continuing Higher Edn., 1984, Leadership award, 1986, Citation for svc. to community N.Y.C. Coun., 1987, Citation for excellence in edn. Bklyn. Boro Pres., 1987, Citation for outstanding svc. to community N.Y. State Assy., 1987, N.Y. State Senate, 1987. Mem. Sigma Xi, Alpha Sigma Lambda (nat. pres. 1978-80). Rsch., publs. in bacterial virology and endocrine physiology, publs. on issues in higher edn. Office: CUNY Office Rsch Devel Rsch Found 30 W Broadway New York NY 10007-2192

JACOBSON, LLOYD ELDRED, retired dentist; b. Madison, Minn., Mar. 9, 1923; s. Jacob Elton and Hilda Emily (Larson) J.; m. Ruth Solveig Skinsnes, Jan. 26, 1945; children: Rolf, Kathryn, Heidi. Student, St. Olaf Coll., 1943-44, 46-47, U. Chgo., 1945-46; DDS, U. Minn., 1951. Gen. practice dentistry Kenyon, Minn., 1951-91; ret., 1991. Chmn. Am. Luth. Ch. Coun., Mpls., 1972-74; vol. World Brotherhood Exch., Bumbuli, Tanzania, 1965; treas. Kenyon Sch. Bd., 1958-60, Kenyon Devel. Corp., 1955-60. 1st lt. 14th Aif Force (Flying Tigers), USAAF, 1943-45, CBI. Recipient Outstanding Alumni award St. Olaf Coll., 1972, Disting. Alumni award U. Minn. Sch. Dentistry, 1987. Mem. Minn. Dental Assn. (treas. 1980-86), S.E. Dist. Dental Soc. (pres. 1979-80, sec.-treas. 1976-79), Rice County Dental Soc. (pres. 1969). Republican. Lodge: Lions (pres. Kenyon club 1952-54, dist. sec.-treas. 1974, Citizen of Yr. award 1986). Avocations: wood working, golf, stamp collecting. Home: 521 Spring St Kenyon MN 55946-1242

JACOBSON, MARC PETER, art educator; b. Madison, Wis., Aug. 21, 1954; s. James August and Marilyn Joan (LaBrec) J.; m. Nicala Marie Aiello, May 16, 1996. BFA, U. Wis., 1976, MFA, 1985. Instr. Milw. Inst. Art and Design, 1985-90, U. Wis., Milw., 1985-89; asst. prof. fine arts Herron Sch. Art, Indpls., 1993-98; assoc. prof. fine arts Herron Sch. of Art, Indpls., 1998—; vis. asst. prof. found. studies Herron Sch. Art., Indpls., 1990-93. One-man shows include Jan Cicero Gallery, Chgo., 1993, Quincy (Ill.) Art Ctr., 1996; exhibited in group shows at Valdosta State U., 1997 (hon. mention), Fla. State U., 1997, U. Bridgeport, 1998 (hon. mention), Embassy of France, Washington, 1998, Sioux City Art Ctr., Iowa, 1999 (hon. mention). Active Found. in Art, Theory and Edn., 1996—. Recipient Tchg. Excellence award Herron Sch. Art, 1997; Individual Artist grantee Ind. Arts Commn., 1995. Mem. Coll. Art Assn. Avocations: tennis, saxophone, classical and jazz music. Home: 5867 Broadway St Indianapolis IN 46220-2503 Office: Herron Sch Art 1701 N Pennsylvania St Indianapolis IN 46202-1472

JACOBSON, MARIAN SLUTZ, lawyer; b. Cin., Nov. 10, 1945; d. Leonard Doering and Emily Dana (Wells) Slutz; m. Fruman Jacobson, Sept. 21, 1975; 1 child, Lisa Wells. BA cum laude, Ohio Wesleyan U., 1967; JD, U. Chgo., 1972. Bar: Ill. 1972, U.S. Dist. Ct. (no. dist.) Ill. 1972, U.S. Ct. Appeals (7th cir.) 1973. Assoc. Sonnenschein Nath & Rosenthal, Chgo., 1972-79, ptnr., 1979—; vis. com. U. Chgo. Law Sch., 1992-94. Mem. ABA, Chgo. Coun. Lawyers. Office: Sonnenschein Nath & Rosenthal 233 S Wacker Dr Ste 8000 Chicago IL 60606-6342

JACOBSON, MICHAEL FARADAY, consumer advocate, writer; b. Chgo., July 29, 1943; s. Larry and Janet (Siegal) J.; m. Donna Ruth Lenhoff; 1 child, Sonya. BA, U. Chgo., 1965; postgrad., U. Calif., San Diego, 1965-67; PhD, MIT, 1969. Research assoc. Salk Inst. for Biol. Studies, 1970-71; cons. Ralph Nader's Ctr. for Study of Responsive Law, 1970-71; co-founder, exec. dir. Ctr. for Sci. in the Pub. Interest, Washington, 1971—; founder Ctr. for Study Commercialism, 1990. Author: Nutrition Scoreboard, 1975, Eater's Digest, 1972, The Complete Eater's Digest and Nutrition Scoreboard, 1986; (with others) The Booze Merchants, 1983, Salt: The Brand Name Guide to Sodium, 1983, The Changing American Diet, 1983, The Fast Food Guide, 1986, 2d edit., 1991, Marketing Booze to Blacks, 1987, Tainted Booze, 1987, Marketing Disease to Hispanics, 1989, Kitchen Fun for Kids, 1991, Safe Food, 1991; co-editor: Food for People Not for Profit, 1975, Cooking With the Stars, 1992, What Are We Feeding Our Kids?, 1994, Marketing Madness: A Survival Guide for a Consumer Society, 1995. Originator, nat. coord. Food Day, 1975-77. Office: Ctr for Sci in the Pub Interest 1875 Connecticut Ave NW Ste 300 Washington DC 20009-5736

JACOBSON, NATHAN, mathematics educator; b. Warsaw, Poland, Sept. 8, 1910; came to U.S., 1917; s. Charles and Pauline (Rosenberg) J.; married Aug. 25, 1942; children—Michael Sidney, Pauline Ida. A.B., U. Ala., 1930; Ph.D., Princeton U., 1934; D.Sc. (hon.), U. Chgo., 1972. Asst. Inst. for Advanced Study, 1934-35; lectr. Bryn Mawr Coll., 1935-36; NRC fellow U. Chgo., 1936-37; instr. U. N.C., 1937-38, asst. prof., 1938-40, assoc. prof., 1941-42; assoc. prof. Johns Hopkins U., 1943-47; assoc. prof. math. Yale U., New Haven, 1947-49; prof. Yale U., 1949-81, prof. emeritus, 1981—; vis. assoc. prof. Johns Hopkins U., 1940-41; vis. prof. U. Chgo., summer 1947, 65; vis. prof. Tata Inst. Fundamental Research, 1969; vis. prof. Eidgenossisches Technischehochschule, Zurich, 1981; vis. lectr. Japan, Italy, Israel, Peoples Republic China, Taiwan; Sesquicentennial hon. prof. U. Ala., 1981. Author over 10 math. books; contbr. research articles to profl. jours. Served with USN, 1942-43. Fulbright scholar U. Paris, 1951-52; Guggenheim fellow, 1951-52. Mem. Nat. Acad. Scis., Am. Acad. Arts and Scis., Am. Math. Soc. (pres. 1971-73), Internat. Math. Union (v.p. 1972-74), London Math. Soc. (hon.). Avocations: travel; gardening; cinema photography. Home: 2 Prospect Ct Hamden CT 06517-4024 Office: Yale Univ Dept of Math New Haven CT 06520

JACOBSON, NORMAN L., retired agricultural educator, researcher; b. Eau Claire, Wis., Sept. 11, 1918; s. Frank R. and Elma E. (Baker) J.; m. Gertrude A. Neff, Aug. 24, 1943; children: Gary, Judy. B.S., U. Wis., 1940; M.S., Iowa State U., 1941, Ph.D., 1947. Asst. prof. animal sci. Iowa State U., Ames, 1947-49, assoc. prof., 1949-53, prof., 1953, Disting. prof. agr.,

1963-89, assoc. dean Grad. Coll., 1973-88, assoc. v.p. rsch., 1979-88; assoc. provost Iowa State U., 1988-89; dean Grad. Coll. Iowa State U., Ames, 1988-89, emeritus disting. prof. agr., 1989—, interim chair Dept. Food Sci. and Human Nutrition, 1990-92. Contbr. articles to profl. jours., chpts. to books. Served to lt. USN, 1942-46, ETO, PTO. Fellow AAAS, Am. Inst. Nutrition, Am. Soc. Animal Sci. (Morrison award 1970), Am. Dairy Sci. Assn. (pres. 1972-73, Am. Feed Mfrs. Assn. award 1955, Borden award 1960, award of honor 1978, Disting. Svc. award 1989). Presbyterian. Home: 339 Hickory Dr Ames IA 50014-3430 Office: Iowa State U 313 Kildee Hall Ames IA 50011-3150

JACOBSON, PETER LARS, neurologist, educator; b. Englewood, N.J., Feb. 17, 1951; s. George Pershing and Mona (Friedman) J.; m. Karen Joy Frenkel, June 11, 1972; children: Kersten Jenny, Lars Edward II. BA summa cum laude, Princeton U., 1973; MD, Washington U., 1977. Chief resident in neurology U. N.C. Hosp., Chapel Hill, 1980-81; fellow in electroencephalography Mayo Clinic, Rochester, Minn., 1981-82; pres. Pinehurst (N.C.) Neurology, P.A., 1982—; clin. prof. neurology U. N.C., Chapel Hill, 1982—, adj. prof. journalism, 1990—; chmn. dept. neurology Moore Regional Hosp., Pinehurst, 1985-87. Columnist The Pilot, 1989—. Trustee The O'Neal Sch., Southern Pines, N.C., 1992—. Recipient Lange Med. Book prize Washington U., 1976, Samson F. Wennerman award in surgery, 1977, Cert. of Appreciation, State of N.C., 1987; Mosby scholar, 1977. Fellow Am. Acad. Neurology, Am. EEG Soc.; mem. N.C. Neurol. Soc. (pres. 1990-91), Am. Med. Writers Assn., Alpha Omega Alpha, Phi Beta Kappa. Avocations: running, writing. Office: Carolina Headache & Pain Ctr PA 1902 Sandhills Blvd N Ste A Aberdeen NC 28315-2347

JACOBSON, PHILLIP LEE, architect, educator; b. Santa Monica, Calif., Aug. 27, 1928; s. Allen Wilhelm and Greta Percy (Rohde) J.; m. Effie Laurel Galbraith, Nov. 6, 1954; children: Rolf Wilhelm, Christina Lee, Erik Mackenzie. B. Archtl. Engrng. with honors, Wash. State U., 1952; postgrad. (Fulbright scholar), U. Liverpool, Eng., 1952-53; M.Arch., Finnish Inst. Tech., Helsinki, 1969. Field supr. Gerald C. Field Architect, 1950; designer, draftsman John Maloney Architect, 1951, 53-55; designer, project mgr. Young, Richardson, Carleton & Detlie Architects, 1955-56; designer, project architect John Carl Warnecke Architect, San Francisco, Calif., 1956-58; ptnr., design dir. TRA, Seattle, 1958-92; prof. architecture/urban design and planning U. Wash., Seattle, 1962—. Author: Housing and Industrialization in Finland, 1969, The Evolving Architectural Design Process, 1969; contbr. articles to profl. jours.; major archtl. works include Aerospace Research Lab., U. Wash., Seattle, 1969, McCarty Residence Hall, 1960, Highway Adminstrn. Bldg., Olympia, Wash., 1970, Sea-Tac Internat. Airport, 1972, Issaquah (Wash.) High Sch., 1962, State Office Bldg. 2, Olympia, 1976, Sealaska Corporate Hdqrs. Bldg., Juneau, Alaska, 1977, Group Health Hosp., Seattle, 1973, Metro Shelter Program, Seattle, 1977, N.W. Trek Wildlife Preserve, 1976, Rocky Reach/Rock Island Recreation Plan, 1974, master plan mouth of Columbia River, 1976, U. Wash. Biol. Sci. Bldg., 1981, Wegner Hall, Wash. State U., 1982, Wash. Conv. Ctr., 1988, King County Aquatics Ctr., 1990, Albuquerque Airport, 1989, U. Wash. Health Scis. H Wing, 1993. Mem. Seattle Planning and Redevel. Council, 1959-69, v.p., 1966-67; mem. Seattle Landmark Preservation Bd., 1976-81; trustee Pilchuck Sch., 1982—, Northwest Trek Found., 1987-94, AIA/Seattle Archtl. Found., 1986-92. With U.S. Army, 1946-47. Fulbright-Hays Sr. Rsch. fellow Finland, 1968-69; named to Order of White Rose Govt. of Finland, 1985; recipient Silver plaque Finnish Soc. Architects, 1992; recipient numerous design awards. Fellow AIA (pres. Wash. state council 1965, dir. Seattle chpt. 1970-73, sr. council 1970—, Seattle chpt. medal 1994); mem. Am. Inst. Cert. Planners, Phi Kappa Phi, Tau Beta Pi, Tau Sigma Delta, Scarab, Sigma Tau (outstanding alumnus 1967). Home: 3935 51st Ave NE Seattle WA 98105-5243 Office: U of Wash PO Box 355720 Seattle WA 98195-5720

JACOBSON, RAYMOND EARL, electronics company entrepreneur and executive; b. St. Paul, May 25, 1922; s. Albert H. and Gertrude W. (Anderson) J.; BE with high honors, prize for excellence in mech. engrg., Yale U., 1944; MBA with distinction, Harvard U., 1948; B.A. (Rhodes scholar), Oxford U., 1950, M.A., 1954; m. Margaret Maxine Meadows, Dec. 22, 1959 (div. 1986); children: Michael David, Karl Raymond, Christopher Eric. Asst. to gen. mgr. PRD Electronics, Inc., Bklyn., 1951-55; sales mgr. Curtiss-Wright Electronics Div., Carlstadt, N.J., 1955-57; dir. mktg. TRW Computers Co., Los Angeles, 1957-60; v.p. ops. Electro-Sci. Investors, Dallas, 1960-63; pres. Whitehall Electronics, Inc., Dallas, 1961-63, dir., 1961-63; chmn. bd. Gen. Electronic Control, Inc., Mpls., 1961-63, Staco, Inc., Dayton, Ohio, 1961-63; pres. Maxson Electronics Corp., Gt. River, N.Y., 1963-64, Jacobson Assocs., San Jose, Calif., 1964-67; co-founder, pres., chmn., chief exec. officer Anderson Jacobson, Inc., San Jose, 1967-88; chmn. Anderson Jacobson, SA, Paris, 1974-88; chmn. Anderson Jacobson, Ltd., London, 1975-85; chmn. Anderson Jacobson Can., Ltd./Ltée, Toronto, 1975-85, Anderson Jacobson, GmbH, Cologne, 1978-83, CXR Corp., San Jose, 1988-94; bd. dirs. Tamar Electronics, Inc., L.A., Rawco Instruments, Inc., Dallas, 1960-63, Micro Radionics, Inc., L.A., 1964-67, ComputerMan USA, Inc., Reno, 1997—; lectr. engring., UCLA, 1958-60, lectr. bus. adminstrn. U. Calif. Berkeley, 1965-66; mem. underwriting Lloyd's London, 1975-96. Eagle Scout Boy Scouts Am., 1935, committeeman 1968-80. Lt. (j.g.) USNR, 1943-46. Mem. Assn. Am. Rhodes Scholars, Harvard Bus. Sch. Assn., Oxford Soc., Yale Club, Brasenose Soc., Sigma Xi, Tau Beta Pi. Republican. Lutheran. Clubs: Courtside Tennis, Seascape Swim and Racquet. Home: 1247 Montcourse Ln San Jose CA 95131-2420

JACOBSON, RICHARD JOSEPH, lawyer; b. Ft. Benning, July 12, 1943; s. Harold Gordon and Ruth Fern (Enenstein) J.; m. Judy Josephine Dunbar, Sept. 17, 1966; 1 child, David Dunbar. AB, Harvard U., 1965, PhD, 1970; JD, U. Va., 1977. Bar: Ill. 1977, Va. 1977, D.C. 1979, U.S. Dist. Ct. (no. dist.) 1977, U.S. Ct. Appeals (7th cir.) 1991. Asst. prof. English U. Va., Charlottesville, 1970-74; assoc. Keck, Mahin & Cate, Chgo., 1977-83, ptnr., 1984-96; prin. Flaherty & Jacobson, P.C., Chgo., 1996—. Author: Hawthorne's Conception of the Creative Process, 1965; contbr. articles to profl. jours. Pres. North Park Condominium assn., Chgo., 1978-80. Woodrow Wilson Nat. fellow, 1965. Mem. Va. State Bar Assn., D.C. Bar Assn., Assn. Profl. Responsibility Lawyers, Nat. Legal Malpractice Data Ctr. ABA, Cliff Dwellers Club, Legal Club Chgo., Chgo. Literary Club. Home: 850 W Adams St Apt 3D Chicago IL 60607-3088 Office: Flaherty & Jacobson PC 134 N Lasalle St Ste 1600 Chicago IL 60602-1101

JACOBSON, RICHARD LEE, lawyer, educator; b. Los Angeles, Nov. 2, 1942; s. Joseph and Betty (Koenig) J.; children: David, Peter, Michael. S.B., U. Chgo., 1964; J.D., U. So. Calif., 1970. Bar: Calif. 1971, U.S. Ct. Appeals (9th cir.) 1971, D.C. 1980, U.S. Ct. Appeals (4th cir.) 1980, U.S. Ct. Appeals (D.C. cir.) 1980, U.S. Supreme Ct. 1980, U.S. Ct. Appeals (6th cir.) 1983. Law clk. U.S. Ct. Appeals (9th cir.), 1970-71; law clk. to Assoc. Justice William O. Douglas U.S. Supreme Ct., Washington, 1971-72; assoc. Irell & Manella, Los Angeles, 1973-76; mem. trial unit SEC, Washington, 1977-78, spl. counsel to chmn., 1978-79; ptnr. Mayer, Brown & Platt, Washington, 1980-85; spl. counsel Heller, Ehrman, White & McAuliffe, Palo Alto, 1986-88; of counsel Fulbright & Jaworski, Washington, 1988-89, ptnr., 1990—; adj. prof. law Georgetown U. Law Ctr., Washington, 1979-86; mem. bd. advisors, sec. Reform Act Litig. Reporter, 1998—. Exec. editor So. Calif. Law Rev., 1969-70; contbr. articles to profl. jours. Bd. dirs. Washington Lawyers Com. for Civil Rights and Urban Affairs, 1983—. Mem. ABA (chmn. subcom. uniformity of local discovery rules 1983-85, chmn. subcom. securities class actions 1995—, fed. regulation securities com., securities litigation com., 1979—), Am. Law Inst., Washington Coun. Lawyers (bd. dirs. 1982-86, 88—, pres. 1985-86), D.C. Bar Assn. (nominations com. 1984-85, steering com. computer law divsn. 1985-86), Assn. SEC Alumni (pres. 1995-97, dir. 1998—), Order of Coif.

JACOBSON, ROBERT ANDREW, chemistry educator; b. Waterbury, Conn., Feb. 16, 1932; s. Carl Andrew and Mary Catherine (O'Donnell) J.; m. Margaret Ann McMahan, May 26, 1962; children: Robert Edward, Cheryl Ann. BA, U. Conn., 1954; PhD, U. Minn., 1959. Instr. Princeton U., N.J., 1959-62, asst. prof., 1962-64; assoc. prof. Iowa State U., Ames, 1964-69, full prof., 1969—, asst. dean Scis. and Humanities, 1982-85; chemist Ames Lab, Iowa, 1964-69, sr. chemist, 1969—. Contbr. articles to profl. jours. Recipient Wilkinson Teaching award Iowa State U., Ames, 1974, 91. Mem. Am. Chem. Soc., Am. Crystallographic Assn. (chmn. apparatus and standards com. 1982-83). Avocations: gardening; painting. Home: 2732 Thompson Dr Ames IA 50010-4759 Office: Iowa State U 104 Gilman Ames IA 50011

JACOBSON, SANDRA W., lawyer; b. Bklyn., Feb. 1, 1930; d. Elias and Anna (Goldstein) Weinstein; m. Irving Jacobson, July 31, 1955; 1 child, Bonnie Nancy. BA, Vassar Coll., 1951; LLB, Yale U., 1954. Bar: N.Y. 1955, U.S. Supreme Ct. 1960, U.S. Dist. Ct. (so., ea. dists.) N.Y. 1972, U.S. Ct. Appeals (2nd cir.) 1975. Ptnr. Mulligan, Jacobson & Langenus, N.Y.C., 1964-88, Hall, McNicol, Hamilton & Clark, N.Y.C., 1988-92; sole practitioner N.Y.C., 1992—; lectr. in family law. Contbr. articles to profl. jours. and chpts. to books. Mem. ABA (family law sect.), N.Y. State Bar Assn. (family law sect., legis. and exec. com., co-chair lawyer specialization 1999—), N.Y. Women's Bar Assn. (pres. 1989-90, matrimonial and family law com. 1984—, chmn. 1986-88, jud. screening com. 1987-88), Women's Bar Assn. of State of N.Y. (matrimonial com. 1986—, co-chair 1987-89, chair cts. com. 1987-88, amicus com. 1994-96, CLE com. 1998—), Assn. of Bar of City of N.Y. (com. matrimonial law 1984-87, chair 1990-93, com. women in the cts. 1986-96, sec. 1987-90, state cts. of superior juridiction 1987-90, women in the profession 1989-92, judiciary 1995-99, family law 1999—), Westchester County Bar Assn., Am. Acad. Matrimonial Lawyers (chair lawyer specialization com., bd. mgrs. N.Y. chpt. 1987-89, 91-93, 95-98, v.p. 1998—, interdisciplinary com.), Com. to Improve Availability of Legal Svcs., Ind. Jud. Screening Panel, Westchester Women's Bar Assn., Internat. Acad. of Matrimonial Lawyers (bd. govs. U.S. chpt. 1994-97, chair pub. rels. and mktg. com.). Office: 295 Madison Ave New York NY 10017-6304

JACOBSON, SIBYL, insurance company executive. Sr. v.p. external rels. Met. Life Ins. Co., N.Y.C. Office: Met Life Ins Co 1 Madison Ave New York NY 10010-3603*

JACOBSON, SIDNEY, editor; b. N.Y.C., Oct. 20, 1929; s. Reuben and Beatrice (Edelman) J.; m. Ruth Allison, July 4, 1957 (div. Feb. 1975); children: Seth, Kathy Battat; m. Maggi Silverstein, Feb. 26, 1975. BA, NYU, 1950. Exec. editor Harvey Comics, N.Y.C., 1952-83, Marvel Comics, N.Y.C., 1983-89; v.p., editor in chief Harvey Comics Entertainment, L.A., 1989—. Author: Streets of Gold, 1985, Another Time, 1989; writer (comic books) Captain Israel, 1972, The Black Comic Book, 1973, (TV animation series) Johnny Cypher in Dimension Zero, 1975, (TV series) Felix the Cat, 1982, (monthly) You Can't Do That in Comics, 1986; lyricist various popular songs. Mem. Am. Soc. Composers, Authors and Pubs., Am. Guild Authors and Composers, Authors Guild. Home: 2276 S Beverly Glen Blvd Los Angeles CA 90064-2459 Office: Harvey Comics Entertainment 1999 Avenue Of The Stars Los Angeles CA 90067-6022

JACOBSON, SUSANA VIOLA (SUSAN JACOBSON), artist; b. Salt Lake City, Dec. 28, 1947; d. Joseph Stead and Viola Maxine (Nordgren) J. Student, Skowhegan Sch. Painting, Maine, 1970; BFA magna cum laude, U. Utah, 1972; MFA, Stanford U., 1980. Asst. prof. painting Humboldt State U., Arcata, Calif., 1981-85; vis. asst. prof. U. Iowa, Iowa City, 1985-86; asst. prof. painting Yale U. Sch. of Art, New Haven, 1986-89, assoc. prof. painting, 1989-93; acting chair, adj. assoc. prof. art dept. of fine arts Grad. Sch. of Fine Arts, U. of Pa., 1992-93; vis. artist Roswell (N.Mex.) Mus. and Art Ctr., 1981-83, U. Ga., Cortona, Italy, 1983; vis. critic U. Pa., Phila., 1991-93, R.I. Sch. Design, Providence, 1992; critic & lectr. numerous univs. Exhibits throughout the U.S. Grant Ingram-Merrill Found. 1992, Nat. Endowment for Arts 1983-84. Mem. AAUW, AAUP, NOW, U.S. Figure Skating Assn., Southern Poverty Law Ctr., Amnesty Internat., Women's Mus. Washington (charter), Phi Kappa Phi Hon. Soc. Avocation: figure skating. Office: Yale U Sch Art 180 York St New Haven CT 06511-4804

JACOBSON, SVERRE THEODORE, retired minister; b. Loreburn, Sask., Can., Sept. 20, 1922; s. Sverre and Aline Tomina (Joel) J.; m. Phyllis Lorraine Sylte, Sept. 14, 1948; children—Katherine Ann, Paul Theodore. BA, U. Sask., 1946; BD, Luther Theol. Sem., Sask., 1947; postgrad., Luther Theol. Sem., St. Paul, Minn., 1952-53; ThD, Princeton Theol. Sem., 1959. Ordained to ministry Evang. Luth. Ch., 1947. Pastor Lomond, Alta., 1947-53; lectr. Luther Theol. Sem., Saskatoon, Sask., 1956-57; pastor Torquay, Sask., 1958-63; asst. to pres. Evang. Luth. Ch. Can., Saskatoon, 1963-70; pres. Evang. Luth. Ch. Can., 1970-85; interim parish pastor Calgary, Alta., Saskatoon, Weyburn, Elbow and Loreburn, Sask., 1987-98; lectr. Luth. Theol. Sem., Saskatoon, 1987-98. Home: 53 Moxon Crescent, Saskatoon, SK Canada S7H 3B8

JACOBUS, ARTHUR, dance company administrator. BBA, Columbia Coll.; Artist's diploma, Academia di Musica, Italy; M in Arts Adminstrn., Golden Gate U., MBA; M in Human Resources Mgmt., Pepperdine U.; grad. exec. mgmt. program, U. Wash.; grad. strategic perspectives program, Harvard U. Founder, dir. NATO Internat. Band, Naples, 1973-79; pres., gen. mgr. Oakland Symphony, 1979-84; pres., chief exec. officer Pacific N.W. Ballet, Seattle, 1984-93; exec. dir. San Francisco Ballet, 1993—. Mem. Dance/USA. Office: San Francisco Ballet 455 Franklin St San Francisco CA 94102-4471*

JACOBUS, CHARLES JOSEPH, lawyer, title company executive, author; b. Ponca City, Okla., Aug. 21, 1947; s. David William and Louise Graham (Johnson) J.; m. Heather Jeanne Jones, June 6, 1970; children: Mary Helen, Charles J. Jr. BS, U. Houston, 1970, JD, 1973. Bar: Tex. 1973; cert. specialist residential and commerical real estate law Tex. Bd. Legal Specialization. Pvt. practice Houston, 1973-75; staff counsel Tenneco Realty, Inc., Houston, 1975-78; gen. counsel Tenneco Realty, Inc., Deerfield, Ill., 1979-83; chief legal counsel Speedy Muffler King, Deerfield, 1978-79; v.p. Commerce Title Co., Houston, 1983-85; sr. v.p. Charter Title Co., Houston, 1986—; ptnr. Jacobus & Melamed PC, Houston; 1998 Jenkens & Gilchrist, Houston, 1998-99; pvt. practice Bellaire, Tex., 1999—; adv. dir. Heritage Bank, Houston; adj. faculty Tex. A&M U., 1986-90; adj. prof. U. Houston Law Ctr., Houston C.C., Champions Sch. Real Estate; instr. advanced real estate law State Bar Tex., course dir., 1990, Tex. Land Title Assn. Sch. Author: Real Estate Law, 1996, Texas Real Estate, 8th edit., 1998; co-author: Mastering Real Estate Titles and Title Insurance in Texas, 1996, Georgia Real Estate, 1995, Ohio Real Estate, 2d edit., 1990, Calif. Real Estate, 1989, Keeping Current with Texas Real Estate, updated annually, Real Estate Principles, 8th edit., 1996, Real Estate, An Introduction to the Profession, 8th edit., 1996, Texas Title Insurance, updated annually, Texas Real Estate Brokerage and the Law of Agency, 1999; co-author: Real Estate Brokerage Law and Practice; editor: Building Blocks of a Commercial Transaction, 1992, Building Blocks of a Residential Real Estate Transaction, 1994, Texas Real Estate Law Deskbook, 1995; editor-in-chief Tex. Forms Manual. Chmn. Planning and Zoning Commn., Bellaire, Tex., 1976-77; bd. dirs. Tax Increment Fin. Dist., Bellaire, 1984-91; chmn. profl. adv. com. dept. urban and regional planning Tex. A&M U., 1988-89; 1st asst. scoutmaster Boy Scout World Jamboree, Holland, 1995, scoutmaster, Chile, 1998; scoutmaster Nat. Boy Scout Jamboree, 1997; mayor City of Bellaire, 1998—; sec.-treas. Harris County Mayors and Councilman Assn. Recipient Peggy Hayes Tchg. Excellence award TLTA, 1993. Mem. ABA (acquisitions editor books and pubs. com., chmn. brokers and brokerage com. 1986-93), Internat. Wine Food Soc. (host Houston chpt. 1993-94), Am. Coll. Real Estate Lawyers, Nat. Assn. Corp. Real Estate Execs. (chpt. v.p.), Am. Land Devel. Assn. (bd. dirs.), Tex. Land Title Assn. (chmn. forms manual com., TREC earnest money contract task force), Houston Real Estate Lawyers Coun., Real Estate Educator's Assn. (pres. 1987-88), Houston Bar Assn. (chmn. real estate sect. 1987-88), Bellaire/S.W. Houston C. of C. (Real Estate Educator of Yr. 1986, Outstanding Real Estate Educator in Tex. 1986, Outstanding Businessman of Yr. 1990), U. Tex. Mortgage Lending Inst. (faculty), U. Houston Law Alumni Assn. (bd. dirs.). Universal Order Knights of Vine (master barrister Houston chpt.), Les Amis Escoffier, Amici della Vite. Republican. Roman Catholic. Home: 5223 Pine St Bellaire TX 77401-4820 Office: Ste 460 6800 West Loop S Bellaire TX 77401

JACOBY, A. JAMES, securities brokerage firm executive; b. N.Y.C., Jan. 8, 1939; s. D. Paul and Lillian (Jacobson) J.; m. Jayne Wachter, Apr. 16, 1961; children: Karen, Jill, Laurie. AB, Cornell U., 1959; MBA, NYU, 1962. Sr. mng. ptnr. Asiel & Co. LLC, N.Y.C., 1959—; bd. dirs. N.Y. Stock Exch., 1992-98. Mem. Nat. Assn. Securities Dealers (bd. govs., vice chmn. 1983, chmn. nat. bus. conduct com. 1982), Securities Industry Assn. (bd. dirs. 1990-92), Bond Club (bd. govs.). Office: Asiel & Co LLC 20 Broad St New York NY 10005-2601

JACOBY, COLEMAN, scriptwriter; b. Pitts.; s. Harry and Etla (Bernstein) J.; m. Gaby Monet, June 17, 1955; children: Catherine, Antoinette. Grad. high sch., Pitts. Ind. TV scriptwriter, 1950—. Original writer Jackie Gleason Show, creator The Poor Soul, Reggie Van Gleason, Joe the Bartender characters; scriptwriter: (TV series) The Phil Silvers Show (Sgt. Bilko), The Garry Moore Show, Kraft Music Hall, numerous HBO spls., (teleplays) The Wonderful Worls of Burlesque (Emmy award nomination), The Bachelor (Sylvania award). Recipient 4 Emmy awards Nat. Acad. TV Arts and Scis., Christopher award, Sylvania award. Mem. Writers Guild Am. East (life). Democrat. Club: Friars (N.Y.C.). Home and Office: 350 E 84th St New York NY 10028-4405

JACOBY, HENRY DONNAN, economist, educator; b. Dallas, June 25, 1935; s. Henry Harris and Margaret Cameron (Miller) J.; m. Martha Hughes Jacoby, Apr. 4, 1959; children—Daniel Donnan, Caroline Hughes. B.S. in Mech. Engring, U. Tex., Austin, 1957; Ph.D. in Econ, Harvard U., 1967. Systems analyst Tudor Engring. Co., San Francisco, 1959-61; economist Harvard Devel. Adv. Service, Argentina Project, 1963-65; asst. prof. dept. econs. Harvard U., Cambridge, Mass., 1965-69; assoc. prof. polit. economy John F. Kennedy Sch. Govt., 1969-73; prof. mgmt. MIT, Cambridge, 1973—, William. F. Pounds prof. mgmt., 1991—, chmn. faculty, 1988-91; dir. global change program, 1991—; dir. Center for Energy Policy Research, 1978-83; vis. scholar London Bus. Sch., 1983-84; chmn. Mass. Gov.'s Emergy Energy Tech. Adv. Com., 1973-74; mem. Nat. Petroleum Coun., 1975-83. Author: (with F.S. Brooman) Macroeconomics, 1970, (with R. Dorfman and H.A. Thomas, Jr.) Models for Managing Regional Water Quality, 1973, (with J.D. Steinbruner) Clearing The Air, 1973, Analysis of Investment in Electric Power, 1979, (with R. deLucia) Energy Planning for Developing Countries, 1982, (with R.L. Gordon and M.B. Zimmerman) Energy: Markets and Regulation, 1987. Served with USN, 1957-59. Mem. Am. Econ. Assn., Tau Beta Pi. Democrat. Episcopalian. Office: MIT Sloan Sch of Mgmt 50 Memorial Dr Cambridge MA 02142-1347

JACOBY, IRVING, physician; b. N.Y.C., Sept. 30, 1947; s. Philip Aaron and Sylvia Jacoby; m. Sara Kay Vartanian; children: James Tyler, Kathryn Aaryn. BS magna cum laude, U. Miami, Coral Gables, Fla., 1969; MD, Johns Hopkins U., 1973. Diplomate Am. Bd. Internal Medicine, Am. Bd. Infectious Diseases, Am. Bd. Emergency Medicine. Intern Boston City Hosp., 1973-74, resident in medicine, 1974-75, chief resident, 1978-79; resident in medicine Peter Bent Brigham Hosp., Boston, 1975-76, fellow in infectious diseases, 1976-78; asst. dir. emergency med. svcs. U. Mass. Med. Ctr., Worcester, 1979-84; asst. dir. dept. emergency med. U. Calif. Med. Ctr., San Diego, 1984—, assoc. prof. med. surgery, 1988-94; prof. med. surgery, 1994—; disaster control officer, assoc. dir. Hyperbaric Med. Ctr., 1985—; vis. physician, cons. infectious diseases Soroka Med. Ctr., Ben Gurion U., Beer-Sheva, Israel, 1980; flight physician New Eng. Life Flight, Worcester, 1982-84, Life Flight Aeromed. Program U. Calif., 1984-87. Sect. editor for disaster medicine Jour. Emergency Medicine; assoc. editor Undersea and Hyperbaric Medicine, 1996—. Comdr. Disaster Med. Assistance Team CA-4, 1991—. Fellow ACP, Am. Coll. Emergency Physicians; mem. Am. Soc. Microbiology, Infectious Diseases Soc. Am., Nat. Assn. Disaster Med. Assistance Teams (vice chair 1999—), Soc. Acad. Emergency Medicine, Undersea and Hyperbaric Med. Soc., Johns Hopkins Med. and Surg. Assn., Iron Arrow Leadership Soc., Omicron Delta Kappa, Phi Kappa Phi, Alpha Epsilon Delta, Phi Eta Sigma. Office: U Calif Med Ctr 200 W Arbor Dr San Diego CA 92103-8676

JACOBY, JACOB, consumer psychology educator; b. Bklyn., Feb. 17, 1940; s. David and Frances (Berman) J.; m. Renee S. Berkowitz; children: Robin Ann, Jonathan Scott. BA, Bklyn. Coll., 1961, MS, 1963; PhD, Mich. State U., 1966. Prof. consumer behavior Purdue U., West Lafayette, Ind., 1968-81, NYU, 1981—; cons. DuPont, Gen. Electric Co., Gen. Motors Co., Am. Assn. Adv. Agys., Procter and Gamble, Standard Oil, U.S. Senate, FTC, FDA, others. Author: Brand Loyalty, 1978, Miscomprehension of Televised Communication, 1980, The Comprehension and Miscomprehension of Print Communications, 1987. Served to 1st lt. USAF, 1965-68. Recipient Outstanding Contbn. to Advt. award Am. Acad. Advt., 1991, Disting. Sci. Contbn. award Soc. for Consumer Psychology, 1996. Fellow APA (pres. divsn. 23 1973-74, Disting. Sci. Rsch. award 1995), Assn. for Consumer Rsch. (pres. 1975); mem. Am. Mktg. Assn. (H.H. Maynard award 1978), Am. Assn. Pub. Opinion Rsch., Advt. Ednl. Found. (bd. dirs.). Jewish. Office: NYU 44 W 4th St New York NY 10012-1106 Address: 800 West Ave Apt 1018 Miami Beach FL 33139-5539

JACOBY, LOWELL EDWIN, career officer; b. Aug. 28, 1945; m. Celia L. Williams, Dec. 9, 1975. Grad., Aviation Officer Cand. Sch., 1969; student, Navy Postgrad. Sch., 1975; BS in Econs., U. Md.; M in Nat. Security Affairs, Naval Postgrad. Sch. Commd. ensign USN, 1969; advanced through grades to rear admiral, 1994, with fighter sq. 24 USS Hancock (CV-19); intelligence officer seventh fleet detachment Charlie RVN Saigon; current intelligence watchstander, briefing officer, 1973-75; intelligence placement officer, jr. officer assignment officer Naval Mil. Personnel Cmd., 1979-81; head naval ops. br. Navy Field Operational Intelligence Office, dir. Naval Surveillance Info. Ctr.; adminstrv. asst. to dir. naval intelligence, 1983, head, chief naval ops. intelligence plot, 1983; asst. chief of staff, intelligence carrier group eight USS South Carolina, North Atlantic, 1985, USS Nimitz Battle Group, Mediterranean; N2 NATO striking fleet Atlantic, J2 CJTF 120, CJTF 140; head intelligence assignments, placement br. Washington, 1989-90; asst. chief of staff intelligence for comdr. in chief U.S. Pacific fleet, 1990-92; commdg. officer Joint Intelligence Ctr. Pacific, 1992-94; dir. intelligence U.S. Pacific Command, 1994-97, U.S. Navy, 1997—. Decorated 2 Legion of Merit, 2 Navy Commendation Medals, Navy Achievement medal, Nat. Intelligence Medal for Achievement Dir. Ctr. Intelligence, Australian Chief of Def. Commendation. Office: USN 2000 Navy Pentagon Washington DC 20350-2000

JACOBY, ROBERT EDWARD, II, family practice physician; b. DuQuoin, Ill., Mar. 4, 1946; s. Robert Edward and Melba (Scherle) J.; m. Anita Lucille Holder, Sept. 13, 1980; children: Robert Edward III, Daniel Allen. BA in Chemistry, U. Kans., 1968; MD, Johns Hopkins U., 1972. Diplomate Am Bd. Family Practice. Resident U. Kans., 1972-75; clin. asst. prof. family practice U. Kans. Med. Ctr., 1976-80; pvt. practice, Topeka, 1975-76, 84—; mem. staff St. Francis Hosp. and Med. Ctr., Topeka, 1975—, med. dir. family practice group, 1976-83, chmn. family practice dept., 1977-79; mem. staff Stormant-Vail Hosp., Topeka, 1975—; mem. physician utilization panel Blue Cross-Blue Shield Kans., 1976—. Mem. cen. budget com. Greater Topeka United Way, 1978-90; asst. organist 1st Presbyn. Ch. Topeka, 1975—; trustee Shawnee County Hist. Soc., 1976-78; bd. dirs. Counseling and Consultation Svc., Topeka, 1978-82. Mem. Am. Guild Organists (dean Topeka chpt. 1977-78). Avocations: organist, skiing. Home: 3520 NW 43d Ct Topeka KS 66618-2633 Office: Cotton-O'Neil Clinic Stormant-Vail Health Care 901 SW Garfield Ave Topeka KS 66606-1670

JACOBY, ROBERT HAROLD, management consulting executive; b. N.Y.C., June 9, 1942; s. Harold and Ruth (Johnson) J. BA in Econs., Dartmouth Coll., 1964; MA in Polit. Philosophy, Columbia U., 1998. Cert. mgmt. cons. Prin. Albert Ramond & Assocs. Inc., Chgo., 1968-75; pres. Systemetrics Internat. Inc., Indpls., 1975-77; v.p. Theodore Barry & Assocs., London, 1977-82; ptrn. Deloitte Haskins & Sells, N.Y.C., 1982-85; pres. R.H. Jacoby & Assocs. Inc., N.Y.C., 1985—. Contbr. articles to profl. jours. Mem. Acad. Mgmt., Am. Econ. Assn., Am. Water Works Assn., Nat. Assn. Corp. Dirs., Am. Gas Assn., Strategic Mgmt. Soc., Am. Arbitration Assn. (comml. arbitrator 1982—), The Strategic Leadership Forum. Office: RH Jacoby & Assoc Inc 355 South End Ave New York NY 10280-1005

JACOBY, ROBERT OTTINGER, comparative medicine educator; b. N.Y.C., June 20, 1939. DVM, Cornell U., 1963; MS, Ohio State U., 1968, PhD in Pathology, 1969. Asst. prof. pathology Ohio State U., 1969; asst., then assoc. prof. Yale U., New Haven, 1971-87, chmn. sect. comparative medicine, dir. divsn. animal care, 1978—, prof. comparative medicine, 1987—. NIH fellow U. Chgo., 1969-71; recipient Rsch. award Am. Assn. Lab. Animal Sci., 1987, Griffin award, 1993. Mem. AAAS, AVMA, Am. Coll. Vet. Pathologists, Am. Soc. Investigative Pathologists. Achievements include research in pathogenesis of infectious diseases, diseases of laboratory animals, animal models of human disease. Office: Yale U Animal Resources Ctr 333 Cedar St New Haven CT 06510-3289 also: Yale U Sch Medicine Dept Comparative Medicine 375 Congress Ave New Haven CT 06519-1404*

JACOBY, THOMAS S., school system administrator; b. Konigsberg, Fed. Republic Germany, May 13, 1935; came to U.S., 1939; s. Berthold and Anni (Pfingst) J.; m. Adrienne Zacansky, Apr. 14, 1962; children: Michael, Melissa. BS in Edn., West Chester U., 1958; EdM, Temple U., 1961. Cert. health, phys. edn. tchr. Tchr. Sch. Dist. of Phila., 1958-69, dept. head, athletic dir., 1969-71, supr. health and phys. edn., 1971-90, curriculum coord. phys. edn. and athletics, 1990-93, adminstrv. asst. to regional supt., 1993-95, adminstrv. asst. student svcs., 1995—; adj. asst. prof. Temple U., Phila., 1976—; cons. Tech. Adv. Svc. for Attys., Blue Bell, Pa., 1977—; bd. dirs. Lake Owego Camp for Boys, Greeley, Pa. Author: (pamphlets) Physical Education for the Bicentennial, 1976, Street Games of Philadelphia, 1985; contbg. editor: (booklet) Yourself From the Inside Out, 1981. Pres. Phila. Coun. B'nai B'rith, Phila., 1985. Mem. AAHPERD, Pa. State Assn. Health, Phys. Edn., Recreation and Dance (pres. 1980, conv. mgr. 1975, 79, exhibits mgr. Ea. Dist. 1988-92, pres. elect Ea. Dist. 1993, pres. Ea. Dist. 1994, Profl. Honor awards 1973, 90, Elmer B. Cottrell award 1984), ASTM, ASCD, Am. Assn. Sch. Adminstrs., Am. Camping Assn., Phi Delta Kappa. Office: Family Resource Network Adminstrn Bldg 2101 Spring St Philadelphia PA 19103

JACOBY, WILLIAM JEROME, JR., internist, retired military officer; b. Mt. Carmel, Pa., Aug. 9, 1925; s. William Jerome and Florence Marie (White) J.; m. Joeann J. Powroznick, May 5, 1956; children: William Jerome, Teresa Marie. AB, Emory U., 1946; MD, Jefferson Med. Coll., 1950. Diplomate Am. Bd. Internal Medicine. Commd. lt. (j.g.) M.C., USN, 1950, advanced through grades to rear adm., 1972; intern Jefferson Med. Coll. Hosp., Phila., 1950-51, resident in internal medicine, 1951-52, 55-56; Am. Heart Assn. fellow, 1956-57; chmn. dept. medicine U.S. Naval Hosps. Gt. Lakes, Ill., 1964-69, Phila., 1969-72; chmn. dept. medicine, dir. edn. and rsch. Nat. Naval Med. Ctr., Bethesda, Md., 1972-75; comdg. officer Naval Regional Med. Ctr., Portsmouth, Va., 1975-78; dir. med. svcs. VA Cen. Office, Washington, 1978-80, dep. chief med. dir., 1980-83; assoc. clin. prof. Jefferson Med. Coll., 1969—; prof. medicine George Washington U. Med. Sch., 1972, Eastern Va. Sch. Medicine, Norfolk, 1976-78; mem. adv. coun. Nat. Heart, Lung and Blood Inst., NIH, Emergency Med. Svcs. Contbr. articles to profl. jours. Decorated Legion of Merit, Meritorious Svc. medal. Fellow ACP (Laureate award 1996); mem. Assn. Mil. Surgeons (Founders medal 1974), Alpha Omega Alpha, Phi Beta Pi. Roman Catholic. Home: 737 E Tazewells Way Williamsburg VA 23185-6521

JACOME, FELIPE CARLOS, anthropologist. BA in Anthropology, U. Ariz., 1979, MA in Anthropology, 1982. Archeol. field supr. Proyecto Soconusco, Chiapas, Mex., 1981; tchg. asst., cultural resource mgmt. intern Ariz. State Mus., U. Ariz., 1981-82; archeol. techician Archeol. Rsch. Svcs., Inc., 1982; staff archeologist, project dir. Pimeria Alta Hist. Soc. Mus., 1982-84; instr. Pima C.C., 1984-85; dir. programs Episcopal Cmty. Svcs., Ariz., 1985-87; outreach dir. Congressman Kolbe, Ariz., 1987-90; dir. devel. Kino Learning Ctr., Inc., 1980-91, Tucson Mus. Art, 1991-94; cons. Jacome Enterprises, 1994-95, pres., 1997; funding and policy coord. Northern Ariz. U., Tech. Access Program, 1995-97; exec. dir. Ariz. Hist. Soc., Tucson, 1997—. Author: (with Karen Jacome) Intermediate Science Trivial Pursuit: Grades 4-6, 1992; contbr. articles and reports to profl. jours. Coord. vols. Migration and Refugee Svc. Cath. Cmty. Svcs., Ariz., 1984-85; founder, bd. dirs. Tucson Hist. Preservation Found., 1986-87, Ariz. Space Initiative, 1989-92; mem. Ariz. Hunger Adv. Coun., 1987-89, Hispanic Profl. Action Com., 1989-94, Tucson Mus. Art, 1985—, Ariz.-Sonora Desert Mus., 1986, Ariz. Hist. Adv. Coun., 1997—; life mem. Ariz. Aerospace Found., 1991—; commr. Tucson-Pima County Hist. Commn., 1984-91, chmn., 1988-91; chmn. Tucson Mission San Agustin Task Force, 1989-95, Los Descendientes del Presidiio Adv. Coun., 1991-94; bd. dirs. Anza Trail Coalition, 1993-94; commr. Ariz. Space Commn., 1991—. With USAR, 1979-85. Recipient Dr. Martin Luther King, Jr. Dist. Leadership award, 1996. Home: 5170 E Camino Bosque Tucson AZ 85718-4616 Office: Ariz Hist Soc 949 E 2nd St Tucson AZ 85719-4840*

JACOVER, JEROLD ALAN, lawyer; b. Chgo., Mar. 20, 1945; s. David Louis and Beverly (Funk) J.; m. Judith Lee Greenwald, June 28, 1970; children: Aric Seth, Evan Michael, Brian Ethan. BSEE, U. Wis., 1967; JD, Georgetown U., 1972. Bar: Ohio 1972, Ill. 1973, U.S. Ct. Appeals (7th cir.) 1974, U.S. Ct. Appeals (fed. cir.) 1983. Atty. Ralph Nader, Columbus, Ohio, 1972-73, Brinks Hofer, Gilson and Lione, Chgo., 1973—. Mem. ABA, Am. Intellectual Property Law Assn. (com. chmn. 1980-86, bd. dirs. 1994-98), Decalogue Soc. Lawyers, Intellectual Property Law Assn. Chgo. (treas. 1983-84, bd. dirs. 1993-94, 98-99), Intellectual Property Law Assn. Chgo. Ednl. Found. (pres. 1990-93), Am. Techion Soc. (v.p. 1985-91, treas. 1988-91, bd. dirs. 1985—, pres. 1994-97). Home: 1409 Lincoln St Evanston IL 60201-2336 Office: Brinks Hofer Gilson & Lione Ste 3600 455 N Cityfront Plaza Dr Chicago IL 60611-5599

JACOVIDES, LINOS JACOVOU, electrical engineering research manager; b. Paphos, Cyprus, May 10, 1940; s. Jacovos and Zoe (Evangelides) J.; m. Katie McNamee; children: James, Michael, Christina, Julia. BS, U. Glasgow, Scotland, 1961, MS, 1962; PhD, U. London, 1965. Sr. rsch. engr. Def. Rsch. Labs. GM, Calif., 1965-67; sr. rsch. engr. elec. engring. GM Rsch., Warren, Mich., 1967-76; dept. rsch. engr. elec. engring. dept. GM Rsch. Labs., Warren, Mich., 1975-85, asst. dept. head elec. engring. dept., 1985-87, prin. rsch. engr., 1987-88, head elec. and electronics dept., 1988-98; dir. Delphi R&D, Warren, 1999—. Contbr. articles to profl. jours.; editor: Electric Vehicles, 1981. Fellow IEEE; mem. Industry Applications Soc. of IEEE (pres. 1990), Soc. Automotive Engrs. Home: 154 Touraine Rd Grosse Pointe MI 48236-3322 Office: Delphi R&D Mail Stop 480-106-104 30500 Mound Rd Warren MI 48095

JACOX, ADA KATHRYN, nurse, educator; b. Centreville, Mich.; d. Leo H. and Lilian (Gilbert) J. BS in Nursing Edn., Columbia U., 1959; MS in Child Psychiat. Nursing, Wayne State U., 1965; PhD in Sociology, Case Western Res. U., 1969. RN. Dir. nursing Children's Hosp.-Northville State Hosp., Mich., 1961-63; assoc. prof., then prof. Coll. Nursing Univ. Iowa, Iowa City, 1969-76; prof., assoc. dean Sch. Nursing U. Colo., Denver, 1976-80; prof., dir. rsch. ctr. sch. nursing U. Md., Balt., 1980-90, dir. ctr. for health policy rsch., 1988-90; prof. sch. nursing, Independence Found. chair health policy Johns Hopkins U., Balt., 1990-95; assoc. dean for rsch. Wayne State U. Coll. Nursing, Detroit, 1996; co-chmn. panels to develop clin. guidelines for pain mgmt. U.S. Agy. for Health Care Policy and Rsch., 1990-94. Co-author: Organizing for Independent Nursing Practice, 1977 (named Book of Yr., Am. Jour. Nursing); A Process Measure for Primary Care: The Nurse Practitioner Rating Form, 1981 (named Book of Yr., Am. Jour. Nursing). Editor: Pain: A Sourcebook for Nurses, 1977 (named Book of Yr., Am. Jour. Nursing). Chair AIDS study sect. NIH, 1990-92. Recipient Disting. Achievement in Nursing Rsch. and Scholarship, Alumni Assn. Columbia U. Tchrs. Coll., 1975, Disting. award for spl. achievement Nat. Coalition for Cancer Survivorship, 1994, Cameo award for rsch. excellence Sigma Theta Tau, 1996. Rozella Schlotfeldt Leadership award MAIN, 1997; Carver fellow U. Iowa, 1972. Fellow Am. Acad. Nursing; mem. ANA (dir. 1978-82, 1st v.p. 1982-84), AMA (mem. health policy agenda work group 1983-86), Am. Nurses Found. (pres. 1982-85), Am. Acad. Nursing, Nat. Acad. Scis. (com. on nat. needs for biomed. and rsch. pers. 1984-87), Inst. of Medicine, Wayne State U. Alumni Assn. (Disting. alumni award 1994). Office: Wayne State U Coll Nursing 5557 Cass Ave Detroit MI 48202-3615*

JACOX, JOHN WILLIAM, mechanical engineer and consulting company executive; b. Pitts., Dec. 12, 1938; s. John Sherman and Grace Edna (Herbster) J.; 1 child, Brian Erik; m. Roma Jankauskaite, Sept. 3, 1993. BSME in Indsl. Mgmt., Carnegie Mellon U., 1962, BS in Indsl. Mgmt, 1962. Mfg. engr. Nuclear Fuel div. Westinghouse Elec. Co., Pitts., 1962-64; rsch. engr. Continental Can Co. Metal R&D Ctr., Pitts., 1964-65; data processing sales engr. IBM, Pitts., 1965-66; mktg. mgr. nuclear products MSA Internat., Pitts., 1966-72; v.p. Nuclear Cons. Svcs., Inc., Columbus, Ohio, 1973-84; v.p. NUCON Internat., 1981-84; bd. dirs. NUCON Europe Ltd., London, 1981—; pres. Jacox Assocs., Inc., 1984—; cons., lectr. Nat. Ctr. for Rsch. in Vocat. Edn., 1978-84 ; author, presenter, session chmn. DOE/Harvard U. Nuclear Air Cleaning Confs., 1974—; lectr. Harvard U. Sch. Pub. Health Air Cleaning Lab., 1986—; co-chmn. program subcom. Tech. Alliance Cen. Ohio, 1984-85, vice-chmn., chmn.-elect dir. subcom., 1986-87, chmn. bd. trustees, 1986; tech. transfer com. Dayton Area Tech. Network; program com. World Trade Devel. Club; mem. legis. svcs. com. coop. edn. adv. com. Otterbein Coll., 1978-82; industry advisor Franklin U. Grad. Sch. Bus., 1994—. Mem. NRA (patron), ASHRAE (standards com. 3.2 and 9.4), ASTM (chmn. F-21), ASME (code com. nuclear air and gas treatment, main exec. com., chmn. subcom. field test procedures), Am. Nuclear Soc. (pub. info. com.), N.Y. Acad. Scis. (life), Ohio Acad. Sci. (life), Am. Nat. Stds. Inst., Internat. Soc. Nuc. Air Treatment Techs. (co-founder, officer), Columbus Area C. of C. (tech. roundtable 1983), Air Force Assn. (life), Mensa, Sun Bunch (pres. 1980-81), Dayton Area Tech. Network (subcom. on tech. transfer), Tech. Transfer Soc. Home: 5874 Northern Pine Pl Columbus OH 43231-2331 Office: PO Box 29720 Columbus OH 43229-0720

JACOX, MARILYN ESTHER, chemist; b. Utica, N.Y., Apr. 26, 1929; d. Grant Burlingame and Mary Elizabeth (Dunn) J. BA, Syracuse U., 1951; PhD, Cornell U., 1956; ScD (hon.), Syracuse U., 1993. Postdoctoral research assoc. U. N.C., Chapel Hill, 1956-58; fellow in fundamental research Mellon Inst., Pitts., 1958-62; rsch. chemist Nat. Bur. Stds., Washington, 1962—; fellow Nat. Bur. Stds. (now Nat. Inst. Stds. and Tech.), Gaithersburg, Md., 1986-95, sci. emeritus, 1996—. Mem. editorial bd. Revs. Chem. Intermediates, 1984-89, Jour. Chem. Physics, 1989-91; contbr. numerous articles to profl. jours. Recipient gold medal U.S. Dept. Commerce, 1970, Fed. Women's award, 1973, Lippincott award, 1989, Hillebrand prize Chem. Soc. Washington, 1990, WISE lifetime achievement award, 1991. Fellow AAAS, Am. Phys. Soc., Washington Acad. Scis. (Phys. Sci. award 1968); mem. Am. Chem. Soc., Exec. Women in Govt. (sec. 1981, vice-chmn. 1982), Inter-Am. Photochemical Soc. (exec. com. 1978-79), Sigma Xi (pres. elect NBS chpt. 1987-88, pres. 1988-89). Office: Nat Inst Standards & Tech Optical Technology Division Gaithersburg MD 20899-8441

JACQUENEY, STEPHANIE A(LICE), lawyer; b. Freeport, N.Y.; d. Theodore and Mona (Graubart) J. BS, Cornell U., 1979; MPA, JD, Syracuse U., 1982. Bar: N.Y. 1983, U.S. Dist. Ct. (so. and ea. dists.) N.Y. 1983. Law clk. to U.S. atty. U.S. Dist. Ct. (No. Dist.) N.Y., Syracuse, 1981-82; assoc. Olwine, Connelly, Chase, O'Donnell & Weyer, N.Y.C., 1982-84, Cadwalader, Wickersham & Taft, N.Y.C., 1984-87; asst. counsel Manhattan Cable TV, Inc., N.Y.C., 1987-89, gen. counsel, 1989-90, v.p., gen. counsel, 1990-92; v.p. legal dept. Time Warner Cable of N.Y.C., 1992-94; dir. bus. affairs Radio City Prodns., N.Y.C., 1994-97, sr. dir. bus. affairs, 1997-99; v.p. legal and bus. affairs Madison Square Garden, N.Y.C., 1999—. Mem. ABA, N.Y. State Bar Assn., Assn. of Bar of City of N.Y. (com. on arbitration 1984-88, com. on copyright and intellectual property 1996—), N.Y. County Lawyers Assn. Office: Radio City Entertainment Madison Square Garden 2 Penn Plz 16th Flr New York NY 10121

JACQUES, ANDRE CHARLES, financial consultant; b. Verviers, Belgium, July 27, 1921; s. Charles and Adrienne (Nalinne) J.; m. Ghislaine I. Ubaghs, May 4, 1949; children—Patrick, Manoele. License in Fin. and Econs. magna cum laude, Liege U., Belgium, 1943. With Banque Belge pour l'Etranger (Extreme-Orient), Hong Kong and Tientsin, China, 1947-51, Banque Belge et Internationale en Egypte, S.A., Cairo and Alexandria, Egypt, 1951-61, Belgian Am. Banking Corp., N.Y.C., 1961-68; vice chmn. bd. European Am. Bank, N.Y.C., 1968-84; pres. Soc. Générale de Belgique (U.S.) Inc., 1984-88; bd. dirs. Belgian Line, Inc., Am. Tractebel Corp., Chemetals, Inc., Recticel Foam Corp., Wheel Trueing Tool Co., Union Mines, Browning Inc.; mem. adv. bd. Société Générale de Belgique, S.A., Brussels, 1981-88; ret.; active bd. dirs. Universitas Ltd. N.Y., Belgian Am. Ednl. Found., Hoover Found., Brussels. With Belgian Army, World War II. Decorated Officer Order of the Crown (Belgium), Order of Leopold (Belgium). Mem. Belgian Am. C. of C. in U.S. (bd. dirs.). Clubs: Creek (Locust Valley, N.Y.), Cercle Gaulois (Brussels).

JACQUES, JOSEPH WILLIAM, investment advisor; b. Stroudsburg, Pa., Sept. 26, 1953; s. Joseph Francis and Millie C. (Dave) J.; m. Joy Lynn Turner, Dec. 28, 1974; children: Jeffrey, Justin, Joelle, Jeremy. AA in Acctg., Northampton Community Coll., 1973; BS in Acctg., Bloomsburg U., 1974. CPA, Md.; registerd fin. planner master, Md., investment advisor, Md. Auditor U.S. Gen. Acctg. Office, Washington, 1975-82; pres. Coord. Fin. Svcs., Ltd., Bethesda, Md., 1982-84, Joseph W. Jacques, CPA, PA, Rockville, Md., 1985—; ins. agt. Home Life Ins. Co., N.Y.C., 1984—; registerd rep. Comprehensive Fin. Svcs., Severna Park, Md., 1990—. Contbr. articles to profl. jours. Pres. Avery Forest Homeowners Assn., Rockville, 1989-90. Mem. Nat. Assn. Life Underwriters, Internat. Assn. Registered Fin. Planners, Internat. Assn. Fin. Planners, Md. Assn. CPA's. Republican. Roman Catholic. Avocations: tennis, golf, children. Home and Office: 15430 Avery Rd Rockville MD 20855-1711

JACQUETTE, YVONNE HELENE, artist; b. Pitts., Dec. 15, 1934. Student, R.I. Sch. Design, 1952-56; studies with John Frazier, Robert Hamilton, Herman Cherry, Robert Roche. Instr. Moore Coll. Art, Phila., 1972; instr. painting, vis. artist U. Pa., 1972-76, 79-82, instr. Grad. Sch. Fine Arts, 1979-84; instr. Parsons Sch. Design, 1975-78; instr. painting Pa. Acad. Fine Arts Grad. Sch., 1991—, Vt. Studio Ctr., 1993, 97, Huntington (W.Va.) Mus. Art, 1997; vis. artist Nova Scotia Coll. Art, 1974; instr. Skowhegan Sch. of Painting and Sculpture, 1994; artist in residence Harvard U., 1995; represented by DC Moore Gallery, N.Y.C., Mary Ryan Gallery (Prints) N.Y.C. One-woman shows include St. Louis Art Mus., 1983-84, Berggruen Gallery, San Francisco, 1984, Yuracho Seibu-Takanawa Art, Tokyo, 1985, Brooke Alexander Inc., 10 shows 1974-88, 90, 92, 95, N.Y. Mus. Art, Bowdoin Coll. Mus. Art, Maine, 1986, D.C. Moore Gallery, 1997, Mary Ryan Gallery, 1997, Huntington (W.Va.) Mus., 1997; 2-person show Mary Ryan Gallery, 1997; exhibited at Rutgers U. Art Gallery, 1972, Whitney Mus. Art, 1972, N.Y. Cultural Ctr. and U.S. Travelling Show, 1972-73, Internat. Biennial, Tokyo, 1974, Art Inst. Chgo., 1975, Mus. Modern Art, N.Y., 1981-82, Weatherspoon Gallery, N.C., Met. Mus. Art, Mus. Modern Art, Whitney Mus. Am. Art, N.Y., Colby Coll. Mus., Library Congress, Washington, Staatliche Mus., Berlin, Carnegie Inst. Mus. Art, Pitts., Am. Acad. Inst. Arts and Letters, N.Y.; prin. works include painting in oil N. Cen. Bronx Hosp., 1973, five color lithograph Horace Mann Sch., Riverdale, N.Y., 1974, mural for Fed. Bldg. and Post Office, Bangor Maine, 1979-82; prints commissioned by Provincetown Fine Arts Workcenter, 1992, Zimmerli Mus. Rutgers, 1993, Bus. Com. for the Arts, 1994; illustrator Country Rush, Adventures in Poetry, 1982, Aerial, Eyelight Press, 1981, Fast Lanes, 1984; film (with Rudy Burckhardt) Night Fantasies, 1992; set designer Sch. Hardknocks, Dance Theatre Workshop, N.Y.C. and nat. tour, 1989; print commd. by Cleve. Print Club, 1999. Recipient Nat. Acad. Painters award, 1998; Guggenheim Meml. Found. grantee, 1997-98. Mem. Nat. Acad. (Painting award 1998, Print award 1999), Artists Equity Assn., Am. Acad. Arts and Letters (painting award 1990). Office: 50 W 29th St New York NY 10001-4227

JADOT, JEAN LAMBERT OCTAVE, clergyman; b. Brussels, Belgium, Nov. 23, 1909; s. Lambert Paul and Gabrielle Marie (Flanneau) J. D.Philosophie Thomiste, U. Catholique Louvain, Belgium, 1930. Ordained priest Roman Catholic Ch., 1934, consecrated bishop, 1968; parish asst., 1934-39; nat. chaplain Jeunesse Etudiante Catholique, 1939-45; chaplain Ecole Royale Militaire, 1945-52; chief chaplain Force Publique Belgian Congo, 1952-60; nat. dir. Propagation of Faith for Belgium, 1960-68; apostolic pro nuncio in Thailand; also apostolic del. in Laos, Malaysia and Singapore, 1968-71; apostolic pro nuncio in Cameroun and Gabon, also apostolic del. in Equatorial Guinea, 1971-73; apostolic del. to U.S., 1973-80; permanent observer of Holy See to OAS, 1978-80; pro pres. Secretariat for Non Christians at Vatican, 1980-84; titular arch-bishop of Zuri, 1968. Served as chaplain Belgian Army, 1945-52. Decorated Order Leopold. Address: Ave de l'Atlantique 71B12, Brussels Belgium 1150

JADVAR, HOSSEIN, nuclear medicine physician, biomedical engineer; b. Tehran, Iran, Apr. 6, 1961; came to U.S., 1978, naturalized, 1995; s. Ramezan Ali and Fatemeh (Afzal) J.; m. Mojgan Maher, 1995. BS, Iowa State U., Ames, 1982; MS, U. Wis., Madison, 1984, U. Mich., Ann Arbor, 1986; PhD, U. Mich., Ann Arbor, 1988; MD, U. Chgo., 1993. Diplomate Am. Bd. Nuclear Medicine. Rsch. asst. dept. human oncology U. Wis., Madison, 1983-84; rsch. asst. dept. elec. engring. U. Mich., Ann Arbor, 1984-88; sr. rsch. engr. Arzco Med. Electronics, Inc., Chgo., 1988-89; sr. rsch. assoc. Pritzker Inst., Ill. Inst. Tech., Chgo., 1989-92; med. intern U. Calif., San Francisco, 1993-94; resident in radiology Stanford (Calif.) U., 1994-96, resident in nuclear medicine, 1996-98, chief resident in nucelar medicine, 1997-98; fellow in nuclear medicine (positron emission tomography) Harvard Med. Sch., Boston, 1998-99; asst. prof. radiology U. Southern Calif., L.A., 1999—; reviewer study sect. small bus. innovative rsch. program NIH, 1989; session chmn. IEEE/EMBS Ann. Conf., Seattle, 1989. Contbr. articles to profl. jours., chpts. to books. Recipient Resident Rsch. award NIH, 1994. Mem. AMA, IEEE, Am. Roetgeon Ray Soc., Am. Coll. Radiology, Am. Coll. Nuclear Physicians (Resident Rsch. award 1998), Radiol. Soc. N.Am. (Resident Rsch. award 1997), Assn. for Advancement of Med. Instrumentation, Biomed. Engring. Soc., Soc. Nuclear Medicine, Inst. for Clin. PET, Computers in Cardiology (local organizing com. mem. 1990), Tau Beta Pi, Sigma Xi, Eta Kappa Nu. Achievements include patents for esophgeal catheters and method and apparatus for detection of posterior ischemia. E-mail: jadvarúh@nucmed.bidmc.harvard.edu. Home: 1 Longfellow Pl Apt # 414 Boston MA 02114 Office: Mass Gen Hosp Harvard Med Sch Divsn Nuclear Medicine Fruit St Boston MA 02114

JAECKEL, CHRISTOPHER CAROL, memorabilia company executive, antiquarian; b. N.Y.C., Jan. 2, 1941; s. Theodore Ridgway and Yolanda (Benjamin) J.; m. Elizabeth McGreevy Billmire, July 5, 1969; 1 stepchild, Garrett O'Neil Billmire III. BA in English, Princeton U., 1964. Producer, dir. WBAL-TV, Balt., 1966-68, TV news reporter, anchor, 1968-71; pres. Walter R. Benjamin Autographs, Hunter, N.Y., 1971—. Contbr. author: Autographs and Manuscripts, 1978; editor mag./catalog The Collector, 1990. Chmn. Town of Hunter Planning Bd., Tannersville, N.Y., 1978; mem., vice chmn. Bd. Assessment Rev., Hunter, 1980-96; chmn. Rep. Com., Hunter, 1980-82; pres. Hunter Fire Co., 1980-82. Mem. Mountaintop Hist. Soc. (pres. 1978-80), Lions (v.p. Rip Van Winkle club 1980-82). Roman Catholic. Avocations: travel, reading, writing, photography. Office: Walter Benjamin Autographs 664 Scribner Holw Hunter NY 12442

JAEGER, ALVIN A. (AL JAEGER), secretary of state; b. Beulah, N.D., 1943; m. Naomi Berg, 1969 (dec. 1979), m. Kathy Grangaard Anderson, 1986; children: Todd, Stacy, Heidi. Grad., Bismarck State Coll., Dickinson State U.; student, U. N.D., Montana State U. Tchr. Killdeer High Sch., Kenmare High Sch.; with Mobil Oil Corp.; real estate broker; sec. of state N.D., 1993—. With N.D. Army N.G. Named Realtor of Yr. Mem. Nat. Assn. Secs. State (exec. com., com. chmn.), Fargo-Moorhead Area Assn. Realtors (mem. coms. edn., profl. stds., bylaws, multiple listing svc.), N.D. Assn. Realtors (past chairperson state bylaws), Bismarck Kiwanis Club, Charity Luth. Ch. Office: 600 E Boulevard Ave Bismarck ND 58505-0660

JAEGER, DAVID ALLEN, economics educator; b. East Orange, N.J., Mar. 30, 1964; s. Philip Edward and Jean Edna (Van De Mark) J.; m. Alison Isdale Beach, June 30, 1990; children: Andrew, Eliza. BA, Williams Coll., 1986; MA, U. Mich., 1990, 93, PhD, 1995. Rsch. asst. MDRC, N.Y.C., 1986-88; rsch. economist U.S. Bur. Labor Stats., Washington, 1995-97; assoc. prof. Hunter Coll. and CUNY Grad. Sch., N.Y.C., 1997—; vis. assoc. prof. Princeton U., 1999—; rsch. fellow nst. for the Study of Labor, Bonn, Germany, 1998—. Contbr. articles to profl. jours. Mem. Am. Econ. Assn., Am. Statis. Assn., Population Assn. Am., Soc. Labor Economists, Econometric Soc. Office: Hunter Coll Dept Econs 695 Park Ave Dept Econs New York NY 10021-5024

JAEGER, JEFF TODD, professional football player; b. Tacoma, Wash., Nov. 26, 1964. Student, Wash. Coll. With Cleve. Browns, 1987; kicker L.A. Raiders, 1989-96, Chgo. Bears, 1996—. Played in Pro Bowl, 1991; shares single season record for most field goals made (35), 1993. Office: Chgo Bears 1000 Football Dr Lake Forest IL 60045-4829*

JAEGER, KATHLEEN GRACE, French educator; b. Pitts., May 11, 1944; d. Samuel A. and Grace W. McMullan; m. Erwin G. Jaeger, Aug. 7, 1965; 1 child, Erich B. BA in French and Spanish, U. Northern Iowa, 1965, MA in Spanish, 1969, MA in French, 1974; PhD in French, U. Iowa, 1991. Cert. tchr. French, Spanish and English, Iowa. French, Spanish, English tchr. Clinton (Iowa) H.S., 1965-68; French, Spanish tchr. Cedar Falls (Iowa) H.S., 1969-73; French tchr. Ctrl., East, West H.S., Waterloo, Iowa, 1976-86; French instr. Wartburg Coll., Waverly, Iowa, 1988, Cornell Coll., Mount Vernon, Iowa, 1991; French prof. Graceland Coll., Lamoni, Iowa, 1992—; Com. mem. Intercultural Affairs, Graceland Coll., Lamoni, 1993-99, com. mem. gen. edn., 1995-98, faculty sponsor Alpha Mu Gamma, 1992—; translator John Deere Corp., Waterloo, Iowa, 1970-72. Author: Male and Female Roles in the 18th Century, 1994; contbr. articles to profl. jours. Scholarship U. Iowa, 1987, Merchant scholarship U. Northern Iowa, 1987-88. Mem. MLA, Am. Assn. of Tchrs. of French, Iowa Fgn. Lang. Assn. Avocations: reading, traveling, interior decorating. E-mail: kjaeget@graceland.edu. Home: 110 Four Seasons Waterloo IA 50701

JAEGER, KATHLEEN RAE, pediatrics nurse; b. Gt. Falls, Mont., Feb. 24, 1955; d. Peter Paul and Betty Ann (Ostrom) J. BSN, Mont. State U., 1979, MSN, 1989. RN, Mont. Pediatrics staff nurse Mont. Deaconess Med. Ctr., Great Falls, 1979-81, 82-90; staff nurse, intensive care nursery Missoula (Mont.) Community Hosp., 1981-82; staff educator Mont. Deaconess Med. Ctr., Great Falls, 1990-94; clin. instr. Intercollegiate Ctr. Nursing Edn., Spokane, Wash., 1996-97; asst. prof. nursing Northwestern State U., Shreveport, La., 1998—. Mem. Sigma Theta Tau, Phi Kappa Phi. Address: 5316 Meadowsweet Cir Bossier City LA 71112-8642

JAEGER, MARC JULIUS, physiology educator, researcher; b. Berne, Switzerland, Apr. 4, 1929; came to U.S., 1970; s. Francis K. and Jeanne (Perrin) J.; m. Frances Dick, Dec. 1960 (div. 1972); children: Dominic, Olivia; m. Ina Claire Burlingham-Forbes, June 23, 1973. BA, Gymnasium, Berne, 1948; MD, U. Berne, 1954. Diplomate Swiss Bd. Pulmonary Diseases. Resident U. Hosp. of Berne, 1954-63; asst. prof. U. Fribourg, Switzerland, 1963-69; assoc. prof. U. Fla. Coll. Medicine, Gainesville, 1970-76, prof., 1976—. Contbr. over 50 articles to profl. jours., including those on the separation of gases and isotopes such as U235 and deuterium. Democrat. Achievements include five patents for a Method of Separating Solutes and Gases, and for a method to Transport Large Amounts of Heat without Coolant; research in mechanics of breathing, deep sea diving, air pollution and its effects on the lungs, smoking and its effects on the lungs. Home: 5915 SW 36th Way Gainesville FL 32608-5150 Office: U Fla Coll Medicine Gainesville FL 32610

JAEGER, RICHARD CHARLES, electrical engineer, educator, science center director; b. N.Y.C., Sept. 2, 1944; s. O. Fred and Mary Jane (Shatzer) J.; m. Joan Carol Hill, Dec. 28, 1964; children: Peter, Stephanie. BSEE with high honors, U. Fla., 1966, M in Engineering, 1966, PhDEE, 1969. Staff engr. IBM Corp., Boca Raton, Fla., 1969-72, adv. engr., 1972-74, 77-79; rsch. staff mem. IBM Corp., Yorktown Heights, N.Y., 1974-76; assoc. prof. Auburn (Ala.) U., 1979-82, prof. elec. engring. dept., 1982-90, alumni prof., 1983-88, disting. univ. prof., 1990—; dir. Ala. Microelectronics Ctr., Auburn, 1984—; mem. program com. Internat. Solid State Circuits Conf., San Francisco and N.Y.C., 1978-93, program vice chmn., 1992, program chmn., 1993; program co-chmn. Internat. VLSI Cirs. Symposium, Kyoto, Japan, 1989, conf. chmn., Honolulu, 1990; cons. IBM, InSouth, Digital Equipment corp., Control Data Corp. Author: Introduction to Microelectronic Fabrication, 1988, Microelectronic Circuit Design, 1997, Computerization Circuit Analysis Using SPICE Programs, 1997; editor: IEEE Jour. Solid State Cirs., 1995-98; contbr. more than 200 tech. papers to profl. jours.; patentee in field. Grantee NSF, Semicondr. Rsch. Corp., Dept. Def., Ala. Rsch. Inst., 1979—. Fellow IEEE; mem. Solid State Cirs. Coun. IEEE (pres. 1990-91, v.p. 1988-89, sec. 1984-87), IEEE Solid State Cir. Soc., Computer Soc. IEEE (bd. govs. 1985-86, Outstanding Contbn. award 1984, Golden Core award 1996), IEEE Solid-State Cirs. Soc. (adcom mem., Outstanding Contbn. award 1998). Home: 711 Jennifer Dr Auburn AL 36830-7116 Office: Auburn U Ala Microelectronics Ctr 420 Broun Hall Auburn AL 36849-5201

JAEGER, SHARON ANN, chiropractor; b. Adrian, Mich., Feb. 9, 1952; d. Fredrick Adolf and Jean Mary (Theby) J. Student, Western Mich. U., 1970-73; BS, Nat. Coll. Chiropractic, 1975, D in Chiropractic, 1976. Diplomate Am. Chiropractic Bd. of Radiology; lic. chiropractor, Calif., Ill., Ky. Instr. L.A. Coll. Chiropractic, 1978-80; prof. Cleve. Chiropractic Coll., L.A., 1980-

81, 1992-94; cons. Philip C. Runsten Chiropractic, Canoga Park, Calif., 1980-84, Radiology Cons., Chatsworth, Calif., 1984—; pvt. practice North Hollywood, Calif., 1979—. Author: Atlas of Radiographic Positioning, Normal Anatomy and Developmental Variants, 1988; co-author: Case Studies in Chiropractic Radiology, 1990; mem. editl. bd. The Journal of Chiropractic Research, Study of Clinical Investigation, radiology section Journal of Neuromusculoskeletal Sys., Topics in Diagonostic Imaging and the ACA Press; contbr. articles to jours. Mem. Patrons of Children Support Group L.A. Police Dept. Juvenile Disvn., bd. dirs., sec., 1989-92, v.p., 1992-96. Western Mich. U. scholar, Mich. State Chiropractic Aux. scholar, Buccholtz scholar, Springwall scholar; grantee Coun. Roengenology grantee Found. Chiropractic Edn. and Rsch. Fellow Internat. Coll. of Chiropractors; mem. APHA (sec. Radiological Health Sect. 1987-90, sect. coun. 1990-92, Governing coun. 1993-95), Nat. Coll. Chiropractic Alumni Assn., Am. Coll. Chiropractic Radiologists (bd. mem. 1985-91, v.p. 1987-88, pres. 1988-90), Am. Chiropractic Assn., Calif. Chiropractic Assn., Ky. Chiropractic Assn., San Fernando Valley Chiropractic Assn. (2d v.p. 1982-83, edn. chmn. 1984-85, sec. 1988-89), Radiologic Tech. Cert. Com., Coun. Diagnostic Imaging, FCER (bd. dirs. 1991-97, sec., treas., bd. regents, LACC 1993-97), Sigma Chi Psi, Delta Tau Alpha. Office: 4426 Lankershim Blvd North Hollywood CA 91602-2307

JAEHNIG, WALTER BRUNO, JR., communications educator; b. Houghton, Mich., Jan. 11, 1942; s. Walter Bruno and Adele Ruth (Barkkari) J.; m. Jo-Ann Christine DeVries, Sept. 5, 1964 (div. May 1983); children: Johanna Jean, Ella Ruth Catherine, Walter Bruno; m. Kathryn Craig McCullough, Aug. 8, 1985. BS in Journalism, Northwestern U., Evanston, Ill., 1964, MS in Journalism, 1965; PhD in Sociology, Essex (U.K.) U., 1974. Reporter, regional editor The Courier-Jour., Louisville, 1965-68; from asst. prof. to assoc. prof. Ind. U., Bloomington, 1974-81; assoc. prof, dept. head, assoc. dean U. Wyo., Laramie, 1981-87; assoc. prof. So. Ill. U. Sch. Journalism, Carbondale, 1987—, dir., 1987-94. Contbr. articles to profl. jours. Mem. Ill. Press Assn. (bd. dirs. 1994—), Assn. for Edn. in Journalism & Mass Comm., So. Ill. U. Faculty Assn. Avocations: golf, jogging, baseball, English bulldogs. Home: 173 May Apple Ln Carbondale IL 62901-7693 Office: So Ill U Sch Journalism Mailcode 6601 Carbondale IL 62901

JAENIKE, WILLIAM F., retired investment company executive. Degree in elec. engring., Manhattan Coll.; MBA, Pace U. V.p. Depository Trust Co. Inc., N.Y.C., 1974-94, chmn. bd. dirs., CEO, 1994-99; cons. in field. *

JAFEK, BRUCE WILLIAM, otolaryngologist, educator; b. Berwyn, Ill., Mar. 4, 1941; s. Robert William and Viola Mabel (Newstrom) J.; m. Mary Bell Kirkpatrick, Sept. 1, 1962; children: Lynette A., Robert K., Timothy B., Britta C., Kayla E., Kristen M. BS, Coe Coll., 1962; postgrad., U. Omaha, 1962; MD, UCLA, 1966. Instr. dept. otology/laryngology Johns Hopkins Sch. Medicine, Balt., 1971-73; asst. prof. dept. otolaryngology U. Pa. Med. Sch., Phila., 1973-76; prof., dept. chmn. dept. otolaryngology/head and neck surgery U. Colo. Med. Sch., Denver, 1976-98; prof. U. Colo. Med. Sch., 1998—. Served with USPHS, 1971-73. Recipient Fowler award Triologic Soc., 1983. Mem. Triologic Soc. (west region v.p. 1999). Republican. Mem. LDS Ch. Office: U Colo Health Sci Ctr 4200 E 9th Ave # B-205 Denver CO 80220-3706

JAFFA, AYAD A., medical educator, medical researcher. Student, Brunel Tech. Coll., Bristol, Eng., 1975-77; BSc in Biol. Chemistry with honors, U. Essex, Colchester, Eng., 1980, PhD in Biol. Chemistry, 1984. Postdoctoral fellow dept. medicine Med. U. S.C., Charleston, 1984-86, rsch. assoc. dept. medicine, 1986-89, asst. prof. medicine dept. medicine, endocrinology-diabetes-metabolism divsn., 1989-96, asst. prof. pharmacology dept. cell and molecular pharmacology and exptl. therapeutics, 1990-96, mem. grad. faculty, 1991—, assoc. prof. medicine dept. medicine, divsn. endocrinology-diabetes-med. genetics, 1996—, assoc. prof. pharmacology dept. cell and molecular pharmacology and exptl. therapeutics, 1996—; mem. rsch. com. endocrinology-diabetes-med. genetics divsn. Med. U. S.C., Charleston, 1986—; grant reviewer Med. U. Rsch. Com., VA; vis. prof. Cath. U. of Chile, Santiago, 1996; lectr. in field. Manuscript reviewer Am. Jour. Physiology, Kidney Internat., Life Scis., Jour. Pharmacology and Exptl. Therapeutics, Diabetes; contbr. articles to profl. jours. Grantee Med. U. S.C., 1991-92, 92-93, 95-96, VA, 1993—, NIH, 1995—, recipient FIRST award, 1995. Mem. Am. Diabetes Assn. (exec. mem. fund raising com. S.C. affiliate 1992-96, bd. dirs. 1995—, Rsch. and Devel. award 1990, John A. Colwell award 1992, Rsch. award 1996), Am. Fedn. Clin. Rsch. (Henry Christian award 1995). Achievements include research in pathogenesis of diabetic nephropathy, mechanisms of progressive renal disease, renal kallikrein-kinin system, kallikrein and renin gene regulation and expression, growth factors and signal transduction mechanisms, vascular biology. Office: Med U SC Dept Medicine Divsn Endocrinology 171 Ashley Ave Charleston SC 29425-0001*

JAFFA, HARRY VICTOR, political philosophy educator emeritus; b. N.Y.C., Oct. 7, 1918; s. Arthur Sol and Frances (Landau) J.; m. Marjorie Etta Butler, Apr. 25, 1942; children: Donald Alan, Philip Bertran, Karen Louise Jaffa McGoldrick. BA, Yale U., 1939; PhD summa cum laude, New Sch. for Social Rsch., 1951; LLD (hon.), Marietta Coll., 1979, Ripon Coll., 1987. Instr. Queens Coll., CCNY, New Sch. for Social Rsch., 1945-49, U. Chgo., 1949-51, Ohio State U., 1951-64; faculty Claremont (Calif.) McKenna Coll. and Claremont Grad. Sch., 1964-89, Henry Salvatori Rsch. prof. polit. philosophy, 1971-89, prof. emeritus, 1989—; disting. fellow The Claremont Inst., 1989—. Author: Thomism and Aristotelianism: A Study of the Commentary by Thomas Aquinas on the Nicomachean Ethics, 1952, Crisis of the House Divided: An Interpretation of the Issues in the Lincoln-Douglas Debates, 1959, Equality and Liberty, 1965, The Conditions of Freedom, 1975, How to Think About the American Revolution, 1978, American Conservatism and the American Founding, 1984, Original Intent and the Framers of the Constitution: A Disputed Question, 1994; (with Allan Bloom) Shakespeare's Politics, 1964; contbg. author: Shakespeare As Political Thinker, 1981; editor, contbg. author: Statesmanship: Essays in Honor of Sir Winston Churchill, 1982; general editor: Studies in Statesmanship; co-editor: (with Robert Johannsen) In the Name of the People: Speeches and Writings of Lincoln and Douglas in the Ohio Campaign of 1859, 1959. Organizer/dir. Bicycle Racing Program at Claremont Coll., 1976—. Fellow Ford, Rockefeller, Guggenheim, and Earhart founds. Mem. Am. Polit. Sci. Assn., Winston S. Churchill Assn. (founding pres. 1969—). Republican. Jewish. Avocation: cycling. Home: 549 W Baughman Ave Claremont CA 91711-3733 Office: Claremont McKenna Coll Pitzer Hall Dept of Govt Pitzer Hall Claremont CA 91711

JAFFE, ALAN STEVEN, lawyer; b. Portland, Maine, Nov. 11, 1939; s. Herman and Rose (Simon) J.; m. Elizabeth L. Reiss, Nov. 3, 1943; children: David, Robert, Richard. BS cum laude, Cornell U., 1961; LLB cum laude, Columbia U., 1964. Bar: N.Y. 1964. Assoc. Poletti, Freiden, Prashker and Gartner, N.Y.C., 1964-65; asst. chief counsel N.Y.C. Anti-Poverty Program, 1965-66; ptnr. Proskauer Rose LLP, N.Y.C., 1966—, chmn., 1999—; bd. dirs. Lincoln Savs. Bank, N.Y.C., 1984-92. Editor Columbia Law Rev., 1962-64. Bd. dirs., v.p. Coun. Jewish Fedns. N.Am., N.Y.C., 1992-99, Jewish Cmty. Rels. Coun., N.Y., 1987-91; bd. dirs., mem. exec. com. Beth Israel Med. Ctr., 1995—, Am. Jewish Joint Distbn. Com., 1991—; bd. govs. Jewish Agy. for Israel, 1999—; pres. Altro Health and Rehab. Svcs., Inc., N.Y.C., 1983-86, pres. UJA Fedn. of N.Y., 1992-95, bd. dirs. 1980—, chmn. bd. domestic affairs, 1988-91; bd. dirs. N.Y.C. Coalition for Homeless, 1995-98; mem. N.Y.C. Sports Devel. Corp., 1995-98. Office: Proskauer Rose LLP 1585 Broadway New York NY 10036-8200

JAFFE, ANDREW MARK, organization executive, editor, publisher, lecturer; b. Boston, Aug. 2, 1938; s. Henry Leslie and Diana (Gaines) J.; remarried Eileen Ast, 1994; 1 child, Christopher; 1 stepchild, Nicholas. BA, Pomona Coll., 1960; MS in Journalism, Columbia U., 1962. Newsman AP, L.A., 1964-66; corr. Newsweek mag., Atlanta, 1966-69; African bur. chief Newsweek mag., Nairobi, Kenya, 1969-76; bur. chief Newsweek mag., Miami, 1976-77; bus. editor L.A. Herald Examiner, 1978-84; v.p. mktg. Spl. Expdns., N.Y.C., 1984-85; editor Adweek/SouthEast, Atlanta, 1985-88; editorial dir. Adweek mag., N.Y.C., 1988-93; exec. editor, v.p. seminars, directories, new media devel. Adweek Mag. Group, N.Y.C., 1993-97; pub. dir. Adweek Books, N.Y.C., 1995—; exec. dir. Clio Awards Internat., N.Y.C., 1997—; pres. Compass Cons., 1997—; instr. UCLA Extension, 1979-84, Atlanta Portfolio Ctr., 1987-88. Author: (with others) Alaska: Southeast to McKinley, 1986; contbg. editor Atlanta mag., 1987-88. Bd. dirs. Atlanta Virtuosi, 1986-88, Internet Concert Coalition, 1996-98; chmn. bd. Miami Ad Sch., 1993-97. Mem. Am. Bus. Press (bd. dirs. Neal Awards 1995-97), Am. Soc. Mag. Editors, Chinese Gourmet Soc. of N.Y., Overseas Press Club. Avocations: scuba diving, fly fishing, golf. Office: Clio Awards 220 5th Ave Rm 1500 New York NY 10001-7708

JAFFE, ARTHUR MICHAEL, physicist, mathematician, educator; b. N.Y.C., N.Y., Dec. 22, 1937; s. Henry and Clarisse Jaffe; m. Nora Frances Crow, July 24, 1971; 1 child, Margaret Collins; m. Sarah Robbins Warren, Sept. 12, 1992. AB, Princeton U., 1959; BA, Cambridge U., 1961; PhD, Princeton U., 1966. Acting asst. prof. math. Stanford U., 1966-67; asst. prof. physics Harvard U., Cambridge, Mass., 1967-69; assoc. prof. Harvard U., 1969-70, prof. physics, 1970-77, prof. math. physics, 1977-85, Landon T. Clay prof. math. and theoretical sci., 1985—, chmn. dept. math., 1987-90; rsch. fellow Princeton U., 1965-66, Stanford Linear Accelerator Ctr., 1966-67; mem. Inst. for Advanced Study, 1967; vis. prof. Eidgenössische Technische Hochschule, Zurich, 1968; vis. prof. math. physics Princeton U., 1971; vis. prof. Rockefeller U., 1977, U. Rome, 1993; Porter lectr. Rice U., 1982; Hahn lectr. Yale U., 1985; Hendrik lectr. Math. Assn. Am., 1985; mem. pres.'s com. Nat. Medal of Sci., 1997—; scientific bd. Santa Fe Inst., 1998—; pres. Clay Math. Inst. Author: Vortices and Monopoles, 1980, Quantum Physics, 1981, 87, Quantum Field Theory and Statistical Mechanics, Expositions, 1985, Constructive Quantum Field Theory, 1985; Asso. editor: Jour. Math. Physics, 1970-72; editorial council: Annals of Physics, 1975-77; asst. editor, 1977—; editor: Communications Math. Physics, 1976—; chief editor, 1979—; mem. adv. bd.: Letters in Math. Physics, 1975—; editor: Progress in Physics, 1979-86, Selecta Mathematica Sovetica, 1980—, Reviews in Mathematical Physics, 1990; contbr. articles to profl. jours. Alfred P. Sloan Found. fellow, 1968-70; Guggenheim Found. fellow, 1977-78, 92; award Math. and Phys. Scis., N.Y. Acad. Sci., 1979; Dannie Heineman prize for Math. Physics, 1980; NSF fellow, 1961-64; NAS Air Force Office of Scientific Rsch. fellow, 1965-67. Fellow AAAS, Am. Phys. Soc., Am. Acad. Arts and Scis.; mem. Am. Math. Soc. (exec. com. of coun. 1991-95, pres. 1997-98), Internat. Assn. Math. Physics (pres. 1991-96), Coun. of Scientific Soc. Pres. (exec. bd. 1998, chair elect 1999), Joint Policy Bd. for Math. (chair 1998). Home: 27 Lancaster St Cambridge MA 02140-2837

JAFFE, AUSTIN JAY, business administration educator; b. Chgo., Aug. 15, 1952; s. Aaron and Shirley (Davis) J.; m. Lynn Laiken, June 12, 1977; children: Alexander M., Roxanne L. BS in Fin., U. Ill., 1974, MS in Fin., 1975, PhD in Fin., 1978. Fellow Coll. Bus. Adminstrn., U. Ill., Urbana, 1974-75; asst. prof. fin. and real estate Coll. Bus. Adminstrn., U. Oreg., Eugene, 1977-80; vis. asst. prof. Coll. Bus. Adminstrn., Pa. State U., University Park, 1980-81, assoc. prof., 1981-87; rsch dir. Inst. for Real Estate Studies, 1985—; prof. Coll. Bus. Adminstrn., Pa. State U., University Park, 1987-91; Philip H. Sieg prof. bus. adminstrn. Pa. State U., University Park, 1991—, acting chair dept., 1996; vis. prof. dept. real estate econs. Royal Inst. Tech., Stockholm, 1987-88, 96; vis. scholar U. Amsterdam, 1991, vis. prof., 1991, 95; vis. scholar Tel Aviv U., 1992; vis. prof. U. Auckland, 1997, Nat. U. Singapore, 1992, 93, 94, 97, Sw4edish Sch. Econ. and Bus. Adminstrn., Helsinki, 1999; pres. JS & Assocs., State College, Pa., 1987—; advisor Nordic Coun. Mins., 1994, Ea. European Real Property Founds., 1993, World Bank, 1992, 98; external examiner U. Nairobi, 1988, 90. Author: Fundamentals of Real Estate Investment, 3d edit., 1995, Complete Real Estate Investment Handbook, 4th edit., 1988, Analyzing Real Estate Decisions Using Lotus 1-2-3, 1985, Real Estate Investment Decision Making, 1982, Property Management in Real Estate Investment Decision Making, 1979; editor: The Real Estate Reader, 1995; co-editor: Jour. Real Estate Lit., 1991-99; functional editor: Interfaces, 1987-88; spl. editor: Research in Law and Economics, 1987; contbg. editor: Encyclopedia of Housing, 1998; mem. editl. rev. bd. Am. Real Estate and Urban Econ. Assn./Real Estate Econ., 1984-87, 92—, Jour. of Real Estate Fin. and Econs., 1994—, Jour. of Managerial Issues, 1988-91, Jour. Property Valuation and Investment, 1989—, Jour. Real Estate Rsch., 1986—, Rsch. in Real Estate, 1988—, Jour. Property Fin., 1995—, Jour. Property Rsch., 1995—, Jour. Real Estate Edn. and Practice, 1997—, Housing Theory and Soc., 1998—, Internat. Real Estate Rev., 1998—; developer computer software Real Estate Invest Templates, 1987, 88, 91, 92; contbr. articles to profl., internat. and acad. jours. Rsch. grantee Swedish Inst., 1987, S.W. Coun.for Bldg. Rsch./S.W. Fedn. Rental Property Owners, 1988; Homer Hoyt Advanced Studies Inst. fellow, 1988—. Mem. Am. Real Estate and Urban Econs. Assn. (bd. dirs. 1984-86, 89-91, 95-97, 2d v.p. 1992, 1st v.p. 1993, pres. 1994, dir. internat. programs 1998—), Am. Real Estate Soc., Am. Fin. Assn., Am. Law and Econ. Assn., European Network Housing Rsch., Asian Real Estate Soc., European Real Estate Soc., Cato Inst., Conseil Internat. du Bâtiment, Fin. Mgmt. Assn., Nat. Tchg. Faculties, Lincoln Inst. Land Policy, Appraisal Inst., Prudential Realty Group, Soc. Real Estate Appraisers, Urban Land Inst. Jewish. Home: 505 W Nittany Ave State College PA 16801-4059 Office: Smeal Coll Bus Adminstrn Pa State U University Park PA 16802

JAFFE, BERNARD MICHAEL, surgeon; b. N.Y.C.; s. Abner I. and Sylvia (Rothman) J.; m. Marlene Lambert, June 4, 1961; children: Mark Allen, Debra Lynn. B.A., U. Rochester, 1961; M.D., NYU, 1964. Diplomate Am. Bd. Surgery (dir. 1982-88, jr. dir. 1988—, exec. com. 1987-88, rep. to Am. Bd. Med. Specialists 1986-89). Asst. prof. surgery Washington U., St. Louis, 1971-75; asso. prof. Washington U., 1975-77, prof., 1977-79; prof., chmn. dept. surgery SUNY Health Sci. Ctr. at Bklyn., 1979-92; vice-chmn. dept. surgery, chief div. surg. rsch. Tulane U., New Orleans, 1992—. Author: (with Behrman) Methods of Hormone Radioimmunoassay, 1980; editor in chief Surgical Rounds, 1989—. Served to lt. col. USAF, 1972-74. James IV traveling surg. fellow. Mem. ACS, Assn. Acad. Surgery (pres. 1978-79), Soc. Univ. Surgeons (sec. 1979-82, pres. 1983-84), Am. Surg. Assn., Soc. Clin. Surgery, Surg. Biol. Club I (sec. 1982-85), Am. Soc. Clin. Investigation, Soc. for Surgery Alimentary Tract (pres. 1987-88), So. Surg. Assn., Halsted Soc., Transplant Soc., Soc. for Surg. Oncology, Phi Beta Kappa, Alpha Omega Alpha. Office: Tulane Univ Med Ctr 1430 Tulane Ave New Orleans LA 70112-2699

JAFFE, ELLIOT STANLEY, women's clothing retail chain founder, executive; b. Paterson, N.J., May 3, 1926; s. Samuel and Frieda (Wolf) J.; m. Roslyn S. Solomon, July 6, 1952; children: Elise, Richard, David. BS, U. Pa., 1949. Mdse. mgr. R.H. Macy & Co., N.Y.C., 1949-62; founder, CEO, chmn. bd. dirs. The Dress Barn, 1962—; bd. dirs. Smith Barney family of funds, Zweig Total Return Fund. Trustee Coll. Arts and Scis., U. Pa., Tchr.'s Coll. Columbia U.; bd. dirs. Stamford Hosp., 1987—. With U.S. Army, 1943-46. Mem. Nat. Retail Fedn. (bd. dirs.), Harmonie Club. Office: The Dress Barn Inc 30 Dunnigan Dr Suffern NY 10901-4174

JAFFE, ERIC ALLEN, physician, educator, researcher; b. N.Y.C., Apr. 7, 1942; s. Robert Irving and Ruth (Stern) J.; m. Barbara Ruth Little, Feb. 25, 1971; children: Matthew, Alison. Student, Cornell U., 1959-62; MD, SUNY, Bklyn., 1966. Intern then resident Kings County Hosp., Bklyn., 1966-68; resident N.Y. Hosp., N.Y.C., 1968-70, fellow divsn. hematology, 1970-72; instr. medicine Cornell U. Med. Coll., N.Y.C., 1972-73, asst. prof., 1973-77, assoc. prof., 1977-82, prof., 1982-96, adj. prof., 1996—; chmn. dept. of medicine Interfaith Med. Ctr., 1996—; prof. medicine SUNY, Bklyn., 1997—. Editor: The Biology of Endothelial Cells, 1984. Recipient Young Scientist award Passano Found., Balt., 1977. Mem. Am. Soc. Clin. Investigation, Assn. Am. Physicians. Achievements include development of method of culturing endothelial cells. Office: Dept Medicine Interfaith Med Ctr 555 Prospect Pl Brooklyn NY 11238-4204

JAFFÉ, ERNST RICHARD, medical educator and administrator; b. Chgo., Jan. 4, 1925; s. Richard Hermann and Berta (Kohn) J.; m. Anne Jane Sylvestre, Aug. 5, 1950; children: Stephanie Anne Green, Richard Sheridan Jaffé. BS, U. Chgo., 1945, MD, 1948, MS in Pathology, 1948; DHL (hon.), Yeshiva U., 1987. Diplomate Am. Bd. Internal Medicine, Hematology, Nat. Bd. Med. Examiners; lic. physician, N.Y. Intern Med. Presbyn. Hosp., N.Y.C., 1948-50, resident, 1953-55; postdoctoral fellow Albert Einstein Coll. of Medicine, Bronx, N.Y., 1955-57, instr., asst. prof., 1957-62, assoc. prof., 1962-69, prof. medicine, 1969-84, acting dean, 1972-74, 83-84, sr. assoc. dean, 1974-83, 84-91, disting. univ. prof. medicine, 1984-92, disting. univ. prof. medicine emeritus, 1992—; mem. hematology study sect. Nat. Inst. Health, Bethesda, Md., 1972-82, Hirschl Sci. Adv. Com. I.T. Hirschl Trust, N.Y.C., 1974-92, N.Y. Community Trust Blood Disease Panel, N.Y.C., 1978-97; dir. Belfer Inst. for Advanced Biomed. Studies, 1978-92. Co-editor: Seminars in Hematology, 1968—; editor-in-chief Blood, 1975-77; contbr. articles to profl. jours. Nat. bd. govs. ARC, Washington, 1984-90, chmn. blood svcs. com., 1988-90; bd. dirs. Nat. Marrow Donor Program, 1987—; bd. dirs. Henry M. Lillian Stratton Found., 1985-96, pres., 1989-96; trustee Bergen Cmty. Regional Blood Ctr., 1997—. With U.S. Army, 1944-46; capt. USAF, 1951-53. Named Career Scientist, Health Rsch. Coun.; recipient Charles R. Drew award ARC, 1990. Fellow Internat. Soc. Hematology (counselor 1980-88, v.p. 1984-88, historian 1990—); mem. Am. Soc. Hematology (pres. 1983, historian 1993—), Assn. Am. Physicians, Am. Fedn. Clin. Rsch., Am. Soc. Clin. Investigation, Am. Physiol. Soc., Assn. Am. Med. Colls. (emeritus), Coun. Acad. Socs. (adminstrv. bd. 1985-90, chmn. 1989), N.Y. Soc. Study Blood (pres. 1978-80), Soc. for Exptl. Biology and Medicine (pres. 1993-95, past pres. 1995-97), U. Chgo. Alumni Assn. (Profl. Achievement citation 1992), U. Chgo. Med. Alumni Assn. (Disting. Svc. award 1981), Phi Beta Kappa, Sigma Xi, Alpha Omega Alpha. Lutheran. Avocations: philately, photography, reading. Office: Albert Einstein Coll Medicine 1300 Morris Park Ave Bronx NY 10461-1926 *Nothing is more satisfying than to have done a good job and to have earned the affection of your colleagues. However, wife and children are paramount!!.*

JAFFE, F. FILMORE, lawyer, retired judge; b. Chgo., May 4, 1918; s. Jacob Isadore and Goldie (Rabinowitz) J.; m. Mary Main, Nov. 7, 1942; children: Jo Anne, Jay. Student, Southwestern U., 1936-39; J.D., Pacific Coast U., 1940. Bar: Calif. 1945, U.S. Supreme Ct. 1964. Practiced law Los Angeles, 1945-91; ptnr. Bernard & Jaffe, Los Angeles, 1947-74, Jaffe & Jaffe, Los Angeles, 1975-91; apptd. referee Superior Ct. of Los Angeles County, 1991-97, apptd. judge pro tem, 1991-97; ret., 1997; atty. in pvt. practice L.A., 1997—; mem. L.A. Traffic Commn., 1947-48; arbitrator Am. Arbitration Assn., 1968-91; chmn. pro bono com. Superior Ct. Calif., County of Los Angeles, 1980-86; lectr. on paternity. Served to capt. inf. AUS, 1942-45. Decorated Purple Heart, Croix de Guerre with Silver Star, Bronze Star with oak leaf cluster; honored Human Rights Commn. Los Angeles, Los Angeles County Bd. Suprs.; recipient Pro Bono award State Bar Calif., commendation State Bar Calif., 1983. Mem. ABA, Los Angeles County Bar (honored by family law sect. 1983), Los Angeles Criminal Ct. Bar Assn. (charter mem.), U.S. Supreme Ct. Bar Assn., Masons, Shriners. Office: 433 N Camden Dr Ste 400 Beverly Hills CA 90210-4408

JAFFE, GWEN DANER, museum educator; b. N.Y.C., July 8, 1937; d. Izzy and Selma (Hess) Daner; m. Anthony R. Jaffe; children: Thomas, Elizabeth. BA in Art History, Skidmore Coll., 1957; cert. in elem. tchg., Hofstra U., 1960; postgrad., N.Y. Sch. Interior Design, 1964, Columbia U., 1973. Spl. edn. tchr. Payne Whitney Hosp., 1958-65, Bd. Coop. Ednl. Svcs., Westchester, N.Y., 1958-65; designer Jaffe-Halperin Design Firm, N.Y.C., 1965-86; tour guide Walker Art Ctr., Mpls., 1987-89; tchr. Art Express Sch. mus. program Carnegie Mus. of Art, Pitts., 1989—; mem. staff Peace Arts Exch. program Pitts. Children's Mus., 1992-93; designer briefcases and handbags Gwynne Collection, 1993—. Mem. Fiber Arts Guild. Home: 5321 5th Ave Pittsburgh PA 15232-2142

JAFFE, HERB, retired newspaper editor, columnist; b. Newark, Oct. 12, 1932; s. Frank and Adele (Weiner) J.; m. Francine Lozowick, Mar. 30, 1958; children: Steven, Michael. BA in History, Rutgers U., 1954; LLD (hon.), Seton Hall U., 1990. Reporter Newark Star-Ledger, 1954-64, night city editor, 1964-67, legal affairs and investigative writer, 1967-88, op-edit. columnist, 1973-95, legal affairs editor, 1988-95; mem. civil justice reform act adv. com. U.S. Dist. Ct. N.J., 1994-95; adj. asst. prof. journalism NYU, N.Y.C., 1969-74; TV news commentator Sta. WWOR, Channel 9, Secaucus, N.J., 1976-84; mem. N.J. Supreme Ct. Media Rels. Com., Trenton, N.J., 1978-95. Author: Pro Bono Law, 1972 (ABA Cert. Merit award), Liability Crisis, 1987 (ABA Cert. Merit award). With U.S. Army, 1954-55. Recipient Journalism award N.J. State Bar Assn., 1971-78, Scripps-Howard Found. Journalism award, 1974, Nat. Gold Bell award Am. Mental Health Assn., 1975; inductee Rutgers U. Hall of Disting. Alumni, 1991. Mem. N.J. Press Assn. (1st place award for enterprise reporting 1981, 1st place award for investigative reporting 1983), N.J. Alliance for Action (Achievement award 1989), B'nai B'rith (Man of Yr. award Linden N.J. chpt. 1984). Jewish. Avocations: golf, hiking, swimming. Home: 10713 Dover Creek Ave Las Vegas NV 89134-5250

JAFFE, HOWARD LAWRENCE, rabbi; b. N.Y.C., Nov. 7, 1955; s. Nathaniel Herbert and Eleanor Georgine (Arkow) J. BA, CUNY, 1978; MA in Hebrew Lit., Hebrew Union Coll.-Jewish Inst. Religion, 1981. Ordained rabb. 1983. Asst. rabbi Temple Israel, Mpls., 1983-85, assoc. rabbi, 1985-88; rabbi Mountain Jewish Comty. Ctr., Warren, N.J., 1988—, Temple Harshalom (formerly Mountain Jewish Comty. Ctr.); bd. dirs. Assn. Reform Zionists Am., N.Y.C., chmn. Watchung Hills Ministry Assn., Warren, 1988—; chmn. privilege card com. Union Am. Hebrew Congregation, 1989—, trustee United Israel Appeal, N.Y.C., 1989—. Bd. dirs. Somerset Coun. Alcoholism, Sommerville, N.J., 1990, Jewish Family Svcs., Sommerville, 1990; vice-chair UAHC Jr. and Sr. youth com.; mem. N.Am. bd. WUPJ. Mem. Ctrl. Conf. Am. Rabbs, N.J. Assn. Reform Rabbis (pres.). Office: Temple Har Shalom 104 Mount Horeb Rd Warren NJ 07059-5529

JAFFE, JEFF HUGH, retired food products executive; b. Washington, Dec. 25, 1920; s. Henry A. Jaffe and Mildred (Loewenberg) Auslander; m. Natalie Rubin, Dec. 31, 1945; children: Bonita Jaffe Berens, Holly Anne. BS in Archtl. Engring., Va. Poly. Inst. and State U., 1943. Chmn. bd. dirs., pres. The Chunky Corp. (now Ward Candy, Inc.), 1950-69; pres., CEO candy, chocolate and biscuit group Ward Foods Inc., 1969-71, pres., COO, 1971-72; also bd. dirs. Ward Foods, Inc., 1972-74; chmn. bd. dirs., pres. Schutter Candy Co., 1958-67, Klotz Confection Co., 1960-67; pres., CEO The Schrafft Candy Co., 1974-78; v.p. consumer products group Gulf and Western Industries, 1974-78; pres., CEO Bernan Foods, Inc., 1980-85, ret., 1985; bd. dirs. Community Nat. Bank of S.I., N.Y., Ward Foods, Inc., Ward Candy Co., Oxford Energy Co.; guest lectr. Harvard Bus. Sch., 1970-84. Bd. dirs. Young Pres.'s Orgn., Woodmere Acad., Village Hewlett Bay Park (past chmn. and pres.). Mem. Assn. Mfrs. of Confectionery and Chocolate (past chmn.), Candy Execs. Club, Property Owners Assn. (Sailfish Point, Fla., chmn. transition com., chmn. emeritus, CEO). Home: 6500 SE Harbor Cir Stuart FL 34996-1952

JAFFE, LEONARD SIGMUND, financial executive; b. Balt., Oct. 31, 1916; s. Benjamin I. and Anna J. (Berkow) J.; m. Marjorie Dorf, Apr. 24, 1941; children: Carol (Mrs. Fred Levinger), Ellen (Mrs. Robert Davis), Susan A. Jaffe (Mrs. Lisardo Augustin). BA, Johns Hopkins U., 1937; MBA, Harvard U., 1939. Asst. plant mgr. Joseph E. Seagram, N.Y.C., 1942-45, divsn. contr., 1945-56, corp. contr., 1956-58; v.p. fin. Capehart Corp., N.Y.C., 1958-62; v.p. fin., sec.-treas. Rheingold Corp., N.Y.C., 1962-68; v.p. fin. Work Wear Corp., Cleve., 1970-73; exec. v.p. fin. Cook United, Inc., Cleve., 1974-77; pres. Marlen Corp. of Miami, 1978-85, Corp. Fin. Group, Boca Raton, Fla., 1983—; instr. acctg. U. Louisville, 1946-47. Mem. nat. student alumni coun. Johns Hopkins U. Mem. Fin. Execs. Inst., Inst. of Mgmt. Acctg., Harvard Club (N.Y.C.), Oakwood Club (Cleve.), Harvard Bus. Sch. Club, Clevelander Club, Birchwood Country Club (Westport, Conn.), Rotary. E-mail: gaff3509@aol.com. Home: 647 Lakewood Cir E Delray Beach FL 33445-9002 Office: 1515 N Federal Hwy Ste 300 Boca Raton FL 33432-1994

JAFFE, LOUISE, English language educator, creative writer; b. Bronx, N.Y., May 17, 1936; d. Joseph and Anna (Movitz) Neuwirth; m. Steven Jaffe, Aug. 26, 1962 (div. 1975); 1 child, Aaron Lawrence; m. Leo Gerber, 1993. BA, Queens Coll., 1956; MA, Hunter Coll., 1959; PhD, U. Nebr., 1965; MFA, Brooklyn Coll., 1991. Instr. Kingsborough C.C., Bklyn, 1965-67, asst. prof., 1967-70, assoc. prof. English, 1970-88, prof., 1989-95, prof. emeritus, 1995—. Author: Hyacinths and Biscuits, 1985, Wisdom Revisited, 1987, Light Breaks, 1995, The Great Horned Owl's Proclamation and Other Hoots, 1997; author numerous poems and fiction stories; poetry editor New Press Literary Quar., 1997—. Mem. editl. bd. Cmty. Review CUNY, 1984—. Recipient First prize N.Y. Poetry Forum, 1980, First prize, First honorable mention Shelley Soc. N.Y., 1983-84, others. Democrat. Jewish. Avocations:

creative writing, scrabble, crossword puzzles, people-watching, attending and giving poetry readings. Home: 2411 E 3rd St Brooklyn NY 11223-5357 Office: Kingsborough Community Coll Oriental Blvd Brooklyn NY 11235-4906

JAFFE, MARK M., lawyer; b. Paterson, N.J., Sept. 18, 1941; s. Irving and Bertha (Margolis) J.; m. June A. Fisher, June 19, 1977. BS in Econs., U. Pa., 1962; JD, Columbia U., 1985. Bar: N.J. 1965, La. 1968, N.Y. 1970, U.S. Dist. Ct. (ea. dist.) N.Y., U.S. Ct. Mil. Appeals, U.S. Ct. Appeals (2d and 5th cirs.), U.S. Dist. Ct. N.J., U.S. Supreme Ct. Assoc. Hill, Betts & Nash, LLP, N.Y.C., 1969-72; ptnr. Hill, Betts & Nash, N.Y.C., 1972—. Lt. USCGR, 1965-68. Mem. ABA, N.J. Bar Assn., La. Bar Assn., Assn. of Bar of City of N.Y., Am. Judicature Soc., Maritime Law Soc. Home: 377 Rector Pl New York NY 10280-1432 Office: Hill Betts & Nash 1 World Trade Ctr Ste 5215 New York NY 10048-5299

JAFFE, MARVIN EUGENE, pharmaceutical company executive, neurologist; b. Phila., July 16, 1936; s. William Reuben and Ida Dorothy (Weiner) J.; m. Joan Sheila Fineman; children: Jonathan, Matthew, Ondria, Joshua. BS, Temple U., 1956; MD, Jefferson U., 1960. Diplomate Am. Bd. Psychiatry and Neurology. Intern Womack Army Hosp., Ft. Bragg, N.C., 1960-61; resident Jefferson Med. Coll., Phila., 1964-67; neurologist Phila. Gen. Hosp., 1967-70; rsch. physician Merck Sharp & Dohme Rsch. Labs., West Point, Pa., 1970-78, v.p., 1978-87, sr. v.p., 1987-88; pres. R.W. Johnson Pharm. Rsch. Inst., 1988-94; assoc. prof. Jefferson Med. Coll., Phila., 1982—; med. adv. Wilson's Disease Adv. Bd., N.Y.C., 1984—; bd. dirs. Royal Soc. Medicine Found., 1990—, v.p. 1992-95, pres., 1995-98; bd. dirs. Chiroscience P.L.C., Vanguard Medica, P.L.C., Immunomedics, Inc., Titan Pharm., Inc., Matrix Pharms.; mem. vis. com. Whitaker Coll., MIT, 1997—. Contbr. articles to profl. jours. Capt. U.S. Army, 1960-64, Germany. Fellow Am. Acad. Neurology, Am. Heart Assn. (stroke coun.); mem. Alpers Soc. for Clin. Neurology (sec., treas. 1982-88), Pharm. Mfrs. Assn. (steering com. 1983-94, chmn. 1993-94), Am. Physician's Fellowship (nat. dir. 1980—). Office: Cold Cons Svc 20 Seagate Dr Apt 502 Naples FL 34103-2460*

JAFFE, MELVIN, securities company executive; b. N.Y.C., May 20, 1919; s. Benjamin and Zelda (Karp) J.; m. Muriel Hamptman, June 9, 1941 (dec. Mar. 1984); children: Marcy, Meredith; m. Suzanne MacMillan, Jan. 20, 1985; children: Cynthia Johnson, Katie Marsico. BS in Edn., Bucknell U., 1940. Pres. Benjamin jaffe & Son Inc., Bklyn., 1946-68; sr. v.p. investments Dean Witter Reynolds, Garden City, N.Y., 1969—. Pres. Lions Internat., Blkyn., 1965. Staff sgt. U.S. Army, 1942-45, ETO. Mem. Masons. Jewish. Home: 52 Center Ct Roslyn Heights NY 11577-1964

JAFFE, MORRIS EDWARD, insurance executive; b. Bklyn., Apr. 23, 1947; s. Eugene Netter and Sabina (Sensor) J.; m. Laurie F. Lucas, Feb. 14, 1986; children by previous marriage: Shelley Lynne Jaffe Venincasa, James Edward. Student, U. Miami, Fla., 1965-67; BS in Math., U. Md., 1970. CLU, ChFC, CFP, LUTC. Sales, ops. mgr. Levitz Furniture, Rockville, Md., 1972-75; agt. and sales mgr. Metro. Life Ins. Co., Camp Springs, Md., 1975-86; ptnr., ind. ins. agt. Price, Williams, Jaffe & Assocs., Brandywine, Md., 1986-88; ind. ins. agt. So. Md. Ins. Agy., Brandywine, Md., 1988—; mem. pres.'s conf. Metro. Life, Camp Springs, Md., 1977, leader's conf., 1975, 76, 78, 80, pres.'s adv. coun., 1978. Treas., v.p. Gwynn Park High Sch. Parent-Tchr.-Student Assn., Brandywine, 1987-92; mem. Prince Georges Mental Health Assn., Largo, Md., 1988-91, 96—; mem. Regional Inst. for Children and Adolescents-So. Md. Citizens Adv. Bd., Cheltenham, 1988-99, chmn., 1989-96; mem., treas. Friends of RICA, Cheltenham, 1988—; sponsor Boy Scouts Am. Mem. Nat. Assn. Life Underwriters (voting del. to nat. coun. 1986), Md. Assn. Life Underwriters (dir. 1985—, sec./treas. 1999—, named Outstanding Pres. 1986, elected to Hall of Fame 1997), Prince Georges Life Underwriters Assn. (dir. 1977-99, sec. 1981-82, treas. 1982-85, pres. 1985-86, state committeeman 1986-99, Agt. of Yr. 1984), Soc. Fin. Svc. Profls., Life Underwriters PAC (state treas. 1987-90). Office: So Md Ins Agy PO Box 230 Brandywine MD 20613-0230

JAFFE, MURRAY SHERWOOD, surgeon, retired; b. Sept. 29, 1926; s. Lester A. and Rosa (Shor) J.; m. Margery Blum, Mar. 26, 1951; children—Emily, Margaret, Dan. B.S., M.D., U. Cin., 1948. Diplomate Am. Bd. Surgery. Intern Barnes Hosp., St. Louis, 1948-49; resident Cin. Gen. Hosp., 1949-50, 52-56, Cin. VA Hosp., 1949-50, 52-56, Dayton VA Hosp., Ohio, 1949-50, 52-56; practice medicine specializing in surgery Cin., 1958-98; asst. chief surgery VA Hosp., Cin., 1958-82; pres. med. staff Jewish Hosp., Cin., 1978-80; pres. Medco Peer Rev., 1981-84; retired surgeon, 1996. Pres. Ohio div. Am. Cancer Soc., 1970-71. Served with USN, 1945, 50-52. Mem. A.C.S., Cin. Surg. Soc., U. Cin. Grad. Surg. Soc., Phi Beta Kappa, Alpha Omega Alpha. Republican. Jewish. Lodge: Shriners. Home: 56 Tradd St Charleston SC 29401-2540

JAFFE, ROBERT BENTON, obstetrician, gynecologist, reproductive endocrinologist; b. Detroit, Feb. 18, 1933; s. Jacob and Shirley (Robins) J.; m. Evelyn Grossman, Aug. 29, 1954; children: Glenn, Terri. M.S., U. Colo., 1966; M.D., U. Mich., 1957. Intern U. Colo. Med. Ctr., Denver, 1957-58, resident, 1959-63; asst. prof. Ob-Gyn. U. Mich. Med. Ctr., 1964-68, assoc. prof., 1968-72, prof., 1972-74, dir. steroid rsch. unit, 1964-74; prof. U. Calif., San Francisco, 1974—, chmn. dept. ob-gyn and reproductive scis., 1974-96; mem. nat. adv. council, mem. human embryology and devel. and reproductive biology study sect. Nat. Inst. Child Health and Human Devel.; bd. dirs. Population Resource Center. Author: Reproductive Endocrinology: Physiology, Pathophysiology and Clinical Management, 1978, 4th edit., 1998, Prolactin, 1981, The Peripartal Period, 1985; contbr. numerous articles to profl. jours.; mem. editorial bd. Jour. Clin. Endocrinology and Metabolism, 1971-75, Fertility and Sterility, 1972-78; editor-in-chief Obstetric and Gynecologic Survey, 1991—. Josiah Macy Found. faculty fellow, 1967-70, 81; USPHS postdoctoral fellow, 1958-59, 63-64; Rockefeller Found. grantee, 1974-78; Andrew Mellon Found. grantee, 1978-81. Mem. Endocrine Soc. (coun. 1985-86, sec.-treas. 1994-99), Soc. Gynecologic Investigation (pres. 1975-76, Pres.'s Disting. Scientist award 1993), Perinatal Rsch. Soc. (pres. 1973-74), Am. Coll. Obstetricians and Gynecologists (awards), Internat. Soc. Neuroendocrinology, Assn. Am. Physicians, Inst. Medicine Nat. Acad. Scis., Royal Coll. Obstetricians and Gynaecologists (ad eundum). Democrat. Jewish. Home: 90 Mt Tiburon Rd Belvedere Tiburon CA 94920-1512 Office: U Calif Med Sch OB-Gyn & Reproductive Sci San Francisco CA 94143-0556

JAFFE, RUSSELL MERRITT, pathologist, research director; b. Albany, N.Y., Jan. 1, 1947. AB cum laude, Boston U., 1972, MD with honors, 1972, PhD in Biochemistry, 1972. Diplomate Am. Bd. Pathology (clin., chem.), Nat. Bd. Med. Examiners. Med. intern Boston U. Med. Ctr., 1972-73; resident in clin. pathology NIH, Bethesda, Md., 1973-75, sr. staff physician clin. pathology dept., 1973-79, chief resident tng. program clin. chemistry sect., 1976-79; fellow health rsch., practice, policy devel. Health Studies Collegium, 1979—; dir. Serammune Physicians Lab., Sterling, Va., 1987—, Princeton BioCenter, 1989-92; prin. faculty Oriental Med. Strategy in Western Med. Practice, HSC, N.Y.C., 1980-85. Assoc. editor The New Physician, 1971-72, sr. assoc. editor, 1972-73. Bd. govs. Light Found., 1980-99. Comdr. USPHS, 1973-79. Recipient Nat. Rsch. award Am. Acad. Med. Preventics, 1979, J.D. Lane award USPHS, 1975, Excellence in Rsch. award Mead Johnson, 1969, Man of Yr. award Hillel Found., 1967. Fellow Am. Coll. Nutrition, Am. In-Vitro Allergy/Immunology Soc., Am. Soc. Clin. Pathologists; mem. APHA, Am. Assn. Clin. Chemists. Achievements include patent in field. Home: 300 Amwell Rd Hopewell NJ 08525-3116 Office: Serammune Physicians Lab 14 Pidgeon Hill Dr Ste 300 Sterling VA 20165-6133

JAFFE, SIGMUND, chemist, educator; b. New Haven, Mar. 1, 1921; s. Morris and Rose (Blosveren) J.; m. Elaine Leventhal, Aug. 25, 1946; children—Matthew Lee, Paul Jonathan. A.B. with high distinction in Chemistry, Wesleyan U., Middletown, Conn., 1949; Ph.D., Iowa State U., 1953. Research in rare earths Ames (Iowa) Lab., 1949-53; research in carbides, metal and high temperature inorganic reactions, research labs. Air Reduction Corp., 1953-58; prof. chemistry Calif. State U. at Los Angeles, 1958-86, prof. emeritus, 1986—, chmn. dept., 1958-64; part-time prof. Calif. State U. at Los Angeles, Los Angeles, 1986—; vis. prof. Queen Mary Coll., U. London, 1978-79; Research solid propellant fuel systems, 1958-60; photochemistry and gas phase kinetics Jet Propulsion Lab., Calif. Inst. Tech., Pasadena, Calif., 1960-64; NIH fellow Wiezmann Inst. Sci., Israel, 1964-65, vis. prof., 1971-72. Contbr. articles to profl. jours. Served with USNR, 1942-46. Named Outstanding prof. Calif. State U. at Los Angeles, 1973-74. Mem. Am. Chem. Soc., Sigma Xi, Phi Beta Kappa, Phi Lambda Upsilon, Phi Kappa Phi. Home: 14107 Village 14 Camarillo CA 93012-7013 Office: Calif State U Dept Chemistry Los Angeles CA 90032

JAFFE, STANLEY RICHARD, film producer, director; b. N.Y.C., July 31, 1940; s. Leo and Dora (Bressler) J.; m. Melinda Long; children—Bobby, Betsy, Katie, Alexander. B.S. in Econs, Wharton Sch., U. Pa., 1962. With Seven Arts Asso. Corp., 1962-67, exec. asst. to pres., 1964; dir. E. Coast programming Seven Arts TV, 1963-64, dir. programming, 1965-67; pres., chief corp. officer Paramount Pictures Corp., 1969-71; pres. corp., also pres. Paramount TV, 1970-71; pres. Jaffilms, Inc., 1971; exec. v.p. worldwide prodn. Columbia Pictures Corp., 1975-76; pres., chief operating officer Paramount Communications Inc., N.Y.C., 1991-94; gov. N.Y. Rangers, 1991-94, N.Y. Knicks, 1991-94. Creator, writer, assoc. prodr.: The Professionals, 1963; exec. prodr. series for syndication Johnny Cypher, 1965-67; prodr. (films) Goodbye, Columbus, 1968, Bad Company, 1971, Bad News Bears, 1974, Kramer vs. Kramer, 1979 (Oscar award best picture Acad. Motion Picture Arts and Scis., Di Donatello award 1979), Taps, 1981, Fatal Attraction, 1987, The Accused, 1988, Black Rain, 1989, School Ties, 1992; prodr., dir. Without a Trace, 1982; exec. prodr. (films) Man of a Swing, 1973, Racing with the Moon, 1984, Firstborn, 1984. Mem. Acad. Motion Picture Arts and Scis. Club: Variety (N.Y.C.). Office: Lean Bldg 119 10202 Washington Blvd Culver City CA 90232-3119*

JAFFE, SUSAN, ballerina; b. Washington. Student, Md. Sch. Ballet; student, Sch. Am. Ballet, Am. Ballet Theatre Sch. With Am. Ballet Theatre II, 1978-80; with Am. Ballet Theatre, 1980—, soloist, 1981-83, prin., 1983—. Repertoire includes: Le Corsaire, Apollo, La Bayadere, Bouree Fantastique, Carmen, Cinderella, Concerto, Duets, Giselle, The Guards of Amager, Push Comes to Shove, Symphonie Concertante, Ballet Imperial, Coppelia, Etudes, Giselle, Jardin auxLilas, Romeo and Juliet, The Sleeping Beauty, Other Dances, Theme and Variations, Swan Lake, La Sylphide, Undertow, Voluntaries, Dim Lustre, Manon, Gala Performance, Don Quioxte, Cruel World, Sextet, The Snow Maiden, Fall River Legend, Grande Pas Classic, Stepping Stones, Anastasia, others; created role Lynne Taylor-Corbett's Great Galloping Gottschalk, Bruch Violin Concerto No. 1, Serious Pleasures; appeared Spoleto in An Evening of Jerome Robbins Ballets, 1982, Known by Heart (Twyla Tharp); appeared with Kirov Ballet, 1988; guest appearances with The Royal Swedish Ballet, The Royal Danish Ballet, The English Nat. Ballet, La Scala Ballet, Milan, 1997, 98, The Royal Ballet, 1998, Stuttgart Ballet, 1998, The Munich Opera Ballet, The Vienna State Opera Ballet. Recipient N.Y. Woman-Lancome Paris Woman of Yr. award, 1989. Office: Am Ballet Theatre 890 Broadway New York NY 10003-1211

JAFFE, WILLIAM J(ULIAN), industrial engineer, educator; b. Passaic, N.J., Mar. 22, 1910; S. Elias and Ida (Rosensohn) J. *Dr. Jaffe's father, Elias, settled in Passaic, New Jersey in the early 1880's, where he was a founder of that city's first synagogue. His mother, Ida Rosensohn, came from a long rabbinical lineage. His brother, Dr. John Jaffe, was an economist and CPA, professor at the City College of New York, and an honorary member of the American Institute of Certified Public Accountants. His sisters, Sophie G. and Winnifred Jaffe, each spent over half a century in pedagogy in the schools of New York and New Jersey.* BS in Math and Physics, NYU, 1930; MA in Math., Columbia U., 1931, MS in Indsl. Engring., 1941; ScD in Engring., NYU, 1953. Registered profl. engr., Calif. Cons. engring. math. pvt. practice, 1931-41, 45—; naval architect U.S. Navy Phila. Naval Yard, 1941-45; from instr. to disting. prof. N.J. Inst. Tech., Newark Coll. Engring., 1946-75, disting. prof. emeritus, 1975—; mem. bd. standards rev. Am. Nat. Standards Inst., N.Y.C., 1981-89; adj. prof. NYU Grad. Coll. Engring., 1953-54; mem. Clark bd. internat. mgmt. Com. de l'Orgn. Scientifique, 1957-60, chmn. Clark bd., 1960; vis. prof. Sangyo Nohritsu Diagaku, Sanno Inst. Mgmt., Tokyo, 1960. Author: L.P. Alford: Evolution of Modern Industrial Management, (with Lillian M. Gilbreth) Management's Past: A Guide to Its Future; editor: Industrial Engineering Terminology; contbr. numerous articles to profl. jours. Fellow AAAS (coun.), ASME (bd. standardization, codes and standards ednl. commn., Dedicated Svc. award, Centennial award), Inst. Indsl. Engrs., N.Y. Acad. Medicine (chmn. biomed. engring. sect.), Soc. for Advancement of Mgmt.; mem. Am. Math. Soc. (hon., life). Home: 1175 York Ave Apt 9E New York NY 10021-7173

JAFFE-BLACKNEY, SANDRA MICHELLE, special education educator; b. El Paso, Tex., Oct. 6, 1966; d. Stanley Harris and Rhoda (Rosenfield) J.; m. David Charles Blackney, June 26, 1998. BS in Edn., U. Tex., 1990. Lic. cosmetologist, 1985; cert. generic spl. edn. K-12, regular edn. K-8, ESL instr., mediator for cts. With domestics dept. K-Mart, El Paso, 1980-85; work study Regis Coll., El Paso, 1985-87; vol. Austin (Tex.) Ind. Sch. Dist., 1988-90, student tchr., substitute tchr., 1990; tchr. spl. edn. Garland (Tex.) Schs., 1990—, 3d grade ESL tchr., 1995-97, Title I reading specialist, ESL instr., LPAC chair, SCE scribe, 1997-98, ESL tchr. pre-kindergarden, kindergarden, 3d grade, 1998; substitute tchr. Dallas Ind. Sch. Dist., 1990-91; tchr. spl. edn., mentally retarded/learning disabilities/emotionally disabled, Dallas, 1991-94; tchr., tutor Exemplary Ctr. for Reading Instrn., Dallas, 1991-94; instr. ESL for adults. Tchr., trainer, vol. Spl. Olympics, 1993-94; vol. CHAMPS-Children Have and Model Positive Peer Skills, 1994, El Paso Pub. Schs., 1981-82. Recipient Student medals Spl. Olympics, 1993. Mem. NEA, Vocat. Indsl. Clubs Am., Tex. Edn. Assn., Texas Exes (life), Classroom Tchrs. Dallas, Coun. for Exceptional Children, Tex. State Tchrs. Assn. Democrat. Jewish. Avocations: swimming, walking, bike riding, raising poodles, water polo. Home: 2021 Via Corona Carrollton TX 75006-4614 Office: 6929 Town North Dr Dallas TX 75231-8117

JAFFEE, ANNETTE WILLIAMS, novelist; b. Abilene, Tex., Jan. 10, 1945; d. Jules Henry and Evelyn June (Witensky) Williams; m. Dwight M. Jaffee, Aug. 16, 1964 (div. May 1991); children: Jonathan, Elizabeth. BS, Boston U., 1966. Author: Adult Education, 1981, Recent History, 1988, The Dangerous Age, 1998. N.J. Arts Coun. grantee State of N.J., 1985-86, Geraldine Dodge fellow Yaddo, 1991. Mem. PEN.

JAFFE-NOTIER, PETER ANDREW, secondary education educator; b. Holland, Mich., Apr. 9, 1947; s. M. Robert and Ann Jean (Jackson) Notier; m. Vicki Janet Westbrook, Aug. 11, 1971 (div. 1982); children: Andrew Wright Notier, Matthew Westbrook Notier, Timothy Jackson Notier; m. Tamara Jane Jaffe, July 11, 1986; children: Zachary Hayden, Claire Emanuelle. AB cum laude, Dartmouth Coll., 1969; MA, Harvard U., 1972. Cert. secondary tchr. English tchr. Lyons Twp. High Sch., La Grange, Ill., 1973—; English instr. U. Ill., Urbana-Champaign, Ill., 1983-84; sponsor LION sch. newspaper, LaGrange, Ill., 1986—, Menagerie sch. mag., LaGrange, 1986-95; coord. Discovery Ctr., 1991-94. Tchr. Peace Corps Kingdom of Tonga, 1969-71; mem. chair Lyons Twp. Youth Commn., LaGrange, 1975-81; mem., pres. Irving Park Community Food Pantry, Chgo., 1985-88; bd. dirs. Irving Park Homeless Shelter, Chgo., 1986—; mem. Chgo. Sanctuary Alliance, Chgo., 1984-88; mem. Oak Park Farmer's Market Commn., 1990-94. Named Outstanding Young Man in Am. Jaycees, 1971, Outstanding Secondary Tchr. U. Chgo., 1980-82, 86; recipient Community Svc. award Chgo. Fedn. Community Coms., 1975, Gold Crown award Columbia Scholastic Press Assn., 1987-95. Mem. NEA, Nat. Coun. Tchrs. of English, Assn. for Supervision and Curriculum Devel. Mem. Reformed Ch. in Am. Avocations: sailing, cross-country skiing, gardening, woodworking. Office: Lyons Twp High Sch 100 S Brainard Ave La Grange IL 60525-2100

JAFFER, RAHIM, parliamentarian; b. Uganda, Dec. 15, 1971. BA, U. Ottawa. Former legis. asst. Parliament, Can. Ho. of Commons, Ottawa, mem., 1997—; co-owner Grabbajabba franchise, coffee bar in Old Strathcona, Can., bakery cafe, West Edmonton. Mem. Old Strathcona Found., Can. Taxpayers' Fedn. Mem. Edmonton C. of C. Mem. Reform Party of Can. Office: Can Ho of Commons, 111 Wellington St # 612, Ottawa, ON Canada K1A-OA6*

JAFFESON, RICHARD CHARLES, association executive administrator; b. Rochester, N.Y., May 6, 1947; s. Simon and Molly (Schulman) J. BA cum laude, U. Akron, Ohio, 1969; MA, U. Akron, 1971; postgrad., U. Cin., 1971-72. Sr. environ. planner Md.-Nat. Capital Park Planning Commn., Silver Spring, Md., 1972-78; coordinator council progs. Am. Planning Assn., Washington, 1978-82; dir. sci. and tech. Ctr. for Profl. Devel., U. Md., College Park, 1982-90; dir. edn. RBA, 1990-93; exec. dir. Nat. Certification Commn., Chevy Chase, Md., 1993—; ind. rsch. supr. Smithsonian Instn., Bombay Nat. Hist. Soc., 1973-76; exec. dir. Nat. Women's Baseball Hall of Fame, 1998—. Author: Cert. Program Devel. Guide, 1994; creator, editor (mo. bull.) Capital Capsule, 1983-88; creator, prodr. (weekly tape) Event and Employment Recording, 1984-92; exec. editor Capital Comments newsletter, 1985-86; author: Silver Spring Success: An Interactice History of Silver Spring Maryland, 1995, Certification Commentary, vol. 1, 1996; contbr. articles to profl. jours. Mem. Am. Planning Assn. (chpt. v.p. 1978-80, 84-86, Disting. Svc. award 1977, 84, 87, 97), Assn. Am. Geographers (pres. 1976-77, mgr. award fund 1982—, Disting. Svc. award 1983), Am. Econ. Devel. Coun. (dir. basic econ. devel. course 1984-90, bd. regents 1989-91), Am. Inst. Cert. Planners. Avocations: physical fitness, baseball, wildlife. Home: 2003 Hanover St Silver Spring MD 20910-2106

JAFFIN, CHARLES LEONARD, lawyer; b. N.Y.C., Feb. 27, 1928; s. Joseph M. and Rhoda (Abeloff) J.; m. Rosanna Gordon Webster, June 12, 1952; children: David W., Jonathan H., Rhoda E. Murphy, Lora W. Peters, Katherine G. Gibson. A.B., Princeton U., 1948; J.D., Columbia U., 1951. Bar: N.Y. 1951. Assoc. Carter, Ledyard & Milburn, N.Y.C., 1951-55; assoc. Lewis & MacDonald, N.Y.C., 1955-59, ptnr., 1959-60; ptnr. Battle Fowler and predecessor firms, N.Y.C., 1960-93, of counsel, 1994—. Office: Battle Fowler 75 E 55th St New York NY 10022-3205

JAFREE, MOHAMMED JAWAID IQBAL See GEOFFREY, IQBAL

JAGACINSKI, CAROLYN MARY, psychology educator; b. Orange, N.J., Apr. 12, 1949; d. Theodore Edward and Eleanor Constance (Thys) Jagacinski; m. Richard Justus Schweickert, Dec. 27, 1980; children: Patrick, Kenneth. AB with honors in psychology, Bucknell U., 1971; MA in Psychology, U. Mich., 1975, PhD in Psychology and Edn., 1978. Rsch. assoc. U. Mich., Ann Arbor, 1978-79; rsch. assoc. Purdue U., West Lafayette, Ind., 1979-80, vis. asst. prof., 1980-83, rsch. psychologist, 1983-86, vis. lectr., 1986-88, asst. dean, 1988-89, asst. prof. psychology, 1988-94, assoc. prof., 1994—. Contbr. articles to profl. jours. U. Mich. predoctoral fellow, 1977-78, dissertation grantee, 1977-78; Exxon Edn. Found. grantee, 1983-84. Mem. APA, Midwestern Psychol. Assn., Soc. for Judgment and Decision Making, Am. Ednl. Rsch. Assn., Psychonomic Soc., Sigma Xi, Psi Chi. Avocations: tennis, reading. Office: Purdue Univ Dept Psychol Scis West Lafayette IN 47907

JAGENDORF, ANDRE TRIDON, plant physiologist; b. N.Y.C., Oct. 21, 1926; s. Moritz Adolph and Sophie Sheba (Sokolsky) J.; m. Jean Elizabeth Whitenack, June 12, 1952; children: Suzanne E., Judith C., Daniel Z.S. B.A., Cornell U., 1948; Ph.D., Yale U., 1951. Merck postdoctoral fellow UCLA, 1951-53; from asst. prof. to prof. Johns Hopkins U., 1953-66; prof. plant physiology Cornell U., Ithaca, N.Y., 1966—, Liberty H. Bailey prof. plant physiology, 1981-96, Liberty H. Bailey prof. emeritus, 1997—. Author papers, revs. in field. Recipient Outstanding Young Scientist award Md. Acad. Sci., 1961, Kettering Rsch. award, 1963; Weizmann fellow, 1962. Fellow Am. Acad. Arts and Scis., AAAS; mem. NAS, Am. Soc. Plant Physiologists (hon., life, pres. 1967, C.F. Kettering award in photosynthesis, 1978, Charles Reid Barnes award 1989), Am. Soc Biol. Chemists, Am. Soc. Photobiology (councilor 1980), Soc. Gen. Physiologists, Am. Soc. Cell Biology, Japanese Soc. Plant Physiologists. Jewish. Office: Cornell U Plant Biology Sect Plant Sci Bldg Ithaca NY 14853

JAGER, DURK I., marketing agency executive. Pres., chief opers. officer Procter & Gamble, Cin., until 1998, CEO, 1998—. Office: Procter & Gamble Co 1 Procter And Gamble Plz Cincinnati OH 45202-3315*

JAGER, MELVIN FRANCIS, lawyer; b. Joliet, Ill., Mar. 23, 1937; s. Melvin Van Zandt and Lucille Marie (Callahan) J.; m. Virginia Sue Maitland, Aug. 15, 1959; children: Lori, Jennifer, Scott, Christy. BSME, U. Ill., 1962, JD, 1962. Bar: Ill. 1962, D.C. 1962. Assoc. Iron, Birch, Swindler & McKie, Washington, 1962-65; ptnr. Hume, Clement, Brinks, Willian & Olds Ltd., Chgo., 1965-80, Lee, Smith & Jager, Chgo., 1981-83, Niro, Jager & Scavone, Chgo., 1984-85, Brinks, Hofer, Gilson & Lione Ltd., Chgo., 1985—; adj. prof. law No. Ill. U. Sch. Law, 1979-80, John Marshall Law Sch., 1992, U. Ill. Coll. Law, Champaign, 1992—; chmn. Practicing Law Inst. Trade Secret Protection Symposium, 1986, 89. Author: Trade Secrets Law, 1984; editor U. Ill. Law Rev., 1961-62; contbg. author monograph: Sorting Out the Ownership Rights in Intellectual Property: A Practical Guide to Practical Counseling and Legal Representation, 1980. Mem. bd. edn. Glen Ellyn, Ill., 1974-80; chmn. Civic Betterment Party Nominating Com., Glen Ellyn, 1982-88; chmn. Glen Ellyn Environ. Protection Com., 1971-72; chmn. budget rev. com. Glen Ellyn United Fund, 1972, Glen Ellyn Ednl. Loan Fund trust, 1973. Mem. ABA (chmn. litigation sect. intellectual properties and patents com. 1984-88), Ill. State Bar Assn. (chmn. patent, trademark and copyright, coun. 1982-83, editor newsletter 1979-82), Chgo. Bar Assn., Am. Patent Law Assn., Intellectual Property Law Assn. of Chgo. (pres. 1997), Lic. Execs. Soc. (pres. U.S.A./Can. 1993-94), Am. Law Inst., Glen Ellyn Jaycees (life mem., pres. 1972, trustee), Chgo. Law Club, Union League Club, Phi Gamma Delta, Phi Delta Phi. Republican. Roman Catholic. Home: 446 E North Water St Chicago IL 60611-5558 Office: Brinks Hofer Gilson & Lione Ltd Ste 3600 455 N Cityfront Plaza Dr Chicago IL 60611-5599

JAGER, MERLE LEROY, aerospace engineer; b. Eugene, Oreg., Sept. 22, 1942; s. Earl Christian and Alma Marie (Jensen) J.; m. Shannon Kay Jacobsen, Mar. 18, 1967; children: Holly, Peter, Melanie, Marissa,. BS in Mech. Engring., Oreg. State U., 1965; MS in Aeronautical Engring., U. So. Calif., 1967. Aerodynamicist Lockheed-Calif. Co., Burbank, 1965-68; rsch. engr. The Boeing Co., Seattle, 1968-70; aerodynamics engr. Gates Learjet Corp., Torrance, Calif., 1970; project engr. Irvin Industries, Inc., Gardena, Calif., 1971-73; aerodynamics mgr. Northrop Corp., Hawthorne, Calif., 1973-91; mgr. flight mechanics Northrop Corp., Pico Rivera, Calif., 1991-95; aerodynamics mgr. McDonnell Douglas Corp., Long Beach, Calif., 1995—. Patentee in field. Treas. Goldenwest Assn., Westminster, Calif., 1976-78; tribal chief YMCA Indian Princesses Program, Huntington Beach, Calif., 1986-87; bishopric counselor Mormon Ch., Westminster, 1986-95. Mem. AIAA, Tau Beta Pi, Pi Tau Sigma, Sigma Tau. Republican. Home: 6771 Findley Cir Huntington Beach CA 92648-3075 Office: McDonnell Douglas Corp Long Beach CA 90810

JAGER, TOM, Olympic athlete, swimmer. Olympic swimmer Barcelona, Spain, 1992; staff Apple Mountain Swim Camps. Recipient 4x100 meter Medly Relay Gold medal Olympics, 1984, 88, 4x100 Free Relay Gold Medal, 1984, 88, 92, 50m Freestyle Silver medal Olympics, 1988, 50m Freestyle Bronze medal Olympics, Barcelona, 1992. Holder world record 50 meter Freestyle, 1990—, 4x100 meter Freestyle Relay, 1990—. Office: Apple Mountain Swim Camp 64 Ramble Wood Blvd Tijeras NM 87059-8004*

JAGGER, MICK (MICHAEL PHILIP JAGGER), singer, musician; b. Dartford, Kent, Eng., July 26, 1943; s. Joe and Eva Jagger; m. Bianca Perez Morena de Macias, May 12, 1971 (div. Nov. 1979); children: Jade, Karis; m. Jerry Hall, Nov. 21, 1990; children: Elizabeth Scarlett, James Leroy Augustine, Georgia. Student, London Sch. Econs., 1962-64. Mem., lead singer, occasional guitarist Rolling Stones, 1962—, tours of Europe, 1970, 73, 76, 82, U.S., 1966, 69, 72, 75, 78, 81, Australia, 1973, others; Steel Wheels/Urban Jungle tour of U.S., 1989, Europe and Japan, 1990; film appearances include Performance, 1969, Ned Kelly, 1970, Gimmie Shelter, 1970, Sympathy for the Devil, 1970, Ladies and Gentlemen, The Rolling Stones, 1974, Let's Spend the Night Together, 1983, Freejack, 1991; composer songs (with Keith Richards) (I Can't Get No) Satisfaction, Brown Sugar, Honky Tonk Woman, Jumpin' Jack Flash, Sympathy for the Devil, Get Off My Cloud, Paint it Black, 2000 Light Years from Home, Star Star, Have You Seen Your Mother, Baby (Standing in the Shadows), Mother's Little Helper, Ruby Tuesday, Lady Jane, The Citadel, You Can't Always Get What You Want, Fool to Cry, Start Me Up, She's So Cold, As Tears Go By, Wild Horses, many others; albums with Rolling Stones include: The Rolling Stones, 1964, The Rolling Stones II, 1965, The Rolling Stones, Now!, 1965, December's Children (And Everybody's), 1965, 12 x 5, 1965, Out of Our Heads, 1965, Aftermath, 1966, High Tide & Green Grass, 1966, Between the

Buttons, 1967, Flowers, 1967, Got Live If You Want It, 1967, Their Satanic Majesty's Request, 1967, Beggars Banquet, 1968, Let it Bleed, 1969, Through the Past, Darkly, 1969, Get Yer Ya Yas Out, 1970, Stone Age, 1971, Gimme Shelter, 1971, Milestones, 1971, Sticky Fingers, 1971, Hot Rocks, 1972, More Hot Rocks (Big Hits and Fazed Cookies), 1972, Exile on Main Street, 1972, No Stone Unturned, 1973, Goat's Head Soup, 1973, It's Only Rockand Roll, 1974, Metamorphosis, 1975, Rolled Gold, 1975, Made in the Shade, 1975, Black and Blue, 1976, Love You Live, 1977, Some Girls, 1978, Emotional Rescue, 1980, Sucking in the Seventies, 1981, Tatoo You, 1981, Still Life, 1982, Under Cover, 1983, Dirty Work, 1986, Steel Wheels (also co-producer), Flashpoint, 1991, Voodoo Lounge, 1994 (Grammy award Best Rock Album), Striped, 1995, Bridges to Babylon, 1997, No Security, 1999; solo albums: She's The Boss, 1985, Primitive Cool, 1987, Wandering Spirit, 1993; solo singles include Just Another Night of You, Let's Work, (with David Bowie) Dancin' in the Streets; appeared in (films) Freejack, 1992, Bent, 1997. Named to Rock and Roll Hall of Fame, 1989. Office: Virgin Records 338 N Foothill Rd Beverly Hills CA 90210-3611*

JAGJIVAN, BIPIN, radiologist; b. Nairobi, Kenya, Dec. 10, 1954; came to U.S., 1988; MB, ChB, U. Leicester, Eng., 1980. Diplomate Am. Bd. Radiology. Pvt. practice Hartford, Conn.; prof. radiology U. Conn., Farmington, 1989-93; cons. radiologist VA Hosp., Hartford, Conn., 1988-93; attending radiologist U. Conn. Health Ctr., Farmington, 1988-93, St. Francis Hosp., Hartford, 1993—. Contbr. articles to med. jours. Fellow Royal Coll. Radiologists (London); mem. Radiol. Soc. N.Am. Avocations: camping, skiing. Office: Radiol Assocs Hartford 1000 Asylum Ave Hartford CT 06105-1770

JAGLOM, ANDRE RICHARD, lawyer; b. N.Y.C., Dec. 23, 1953; s. Jacob and Irene (Moore) J.; m. Janet R. Stampfl, Apr. 12, 1980; children: Peter Stampfl Jaglom, Wendy Stampfl Jaglom. BS in Mgmt., BS in Physics, MIT, 1974; JD, Harvard U., 1977. Bar: N.Y. 1978, U.S. Dist. Ct. (so. and ea. dists.) N.Y. 1978, U.S. Supreme Ct. 1982, U.S. Ct. Appeals (2d cir.) 1987. Assoc. Paul, Weiss, Rifkind, Wharton & Garrison, N.Y.C., 1977-84; mng. ptnr. Stecher Jaglom & Prutzman LLP, N.Y.C., 1984—; bd. dirs. Cmty. Fund of Bronxville, Eastchester and Tuckahoe, Inc., 1988-94. Computer mktg. and distbn. editor Computer Law Reporter, 1984-90; Am. Law Inst. ABA course of study on product distbn. and mktg., mem. faculty 1983—, chmn., 1989—; contbr. article to law jours.; contbr chpt. to Legal Checklists, 1988—. Trustee bd. edn. Bronxville Union Free Sch. Dist., 1997—. Mem. ABA, Bar Assn. City N.Y. (computer law com. 1986-89, sec. 1990-94, com. on tech. and practice of law 1993-96), Am. Inst. Wine and Food (bd. dirs. N.Y. chpt. 1991—, treas. 1992—. Office: 900 3d Ave New York NY 10022-4728

JAGLOM, HENRY DAVID, actor, director, writer; b. London, Jan. 26, 1941; s. Simon M. and Marie (Stadthagen) J.; m. Victoria Foyt, 1991. Pres. Rainbow Film Co., Los Angeles, Jagfilms, Inc., Los Angeles, Rainbow Releasing, Los Angeles. Writer, dir. (films) A Safe Place, 1971 (selected for N.Y. Film Festival 1971), Tracks (selected for Cannes Film Festival 1976), Sitting Ducks, 1980 (selected for Cannes Film Festival), Can She Bake a Cherry Pie?, 1983 (selected for Berlin Film Festival 1983); actor, writer, dir. (films) Always (But Not Forever), 1985, Someone to Love, 1987 (selected for Cannes Film Festival), New Year's Day, 1989 (selected for Venice Film Festival 1989), Eating (selected for Deauville Film Festival 1990), Venice/Venice, 1991 (selected for AFI/L.A. Film Festival), Baby Fever, 1993, Last Summer in The Hamptons, 1995 (selected for London Film Festival, AFI/L.A. Film Festival), Déjà Vu, 1997; presenter Hearts and Minds, 1973 (Acad. award best documentary 1973). E-mail: rainbow@webstorm.com. Office: Rainbow Film Co 9165 W Sunset Blvd West Hollywood CA 90069-3129

JAGNER, RONALD PAUL, financial administrator, consultant; b. Highland Park, Mich., May 11, 1942; s. Walter Alex and Mary Ann (Stasys) J. BS, U. Detroit, 1965; MBA, Cen. Mich U., 1967. Comml. teller Nat. Bank Detroit, 1962-64; acct. Electronic Bookkeeping, Detroit, 1964-66; asst. div. mgr. Sears Roebuck & Co., Lincoln Park, Mich., 1966; instr. bus. Southwestern Mich. Coll., Dowagiac, 1967-69; mgr. bus. adminstrv. offices Lakeview Sch. Dist., Battle Creek, Mich., 1969-74; bus. mgr. Lakeview Sch. Dist., Battle Creek, 1974-97; adj. instr. econs., acctg., investments Kellogg C.C., Battle Creek, 1970—; fin. chair, trustee Calhoun Mental Health, Battle Creek, 1983-91; asst. treas. Sch. Employees Credit Union, Battle Creek, 1981-90; bd. dirs., treas. Lakeview Bus. Assocs., 1977-83, v.p., 1993-97. EPA accredited asbestos insp., mgmt. planner U. Ill., 1988. Mem. Assn. Sch. Bus. Ofcl. Mich. Sch. Bus. Ofcls., Southwestern Mich. Sch. Bus. Ofcls. (pres. 1977-79), Kiwanis (bd. dirs., treas. Lakeview chpt. 1977-83). Democrat. Roman Catholic. Home: 98 Brookfield Ct Battle Creek MI 49015-4757

JAGNOW, DAVID HENRY, petroleum geologist; b. Dubuque, Iowa, Nov. 24, 1947; s. Albert August and Ardath Helen (Goettsch) J.; divorced; children: Daniel David, Robert Carl, Beth Laura. BA in Geology, U. Iowa, 1970; MS in Geology, U. N.Mex., 1977. Exploration geologist Shell Oil Co., Houston, 1973-77; staff geologist Energy Reserves Group, Denver, 1977-78; exploration mgr. Donald C. Slawson Oil Prodr., Oklahoma City, 1978-82; cons. geologist pvt. practice, Edmond, Okla., 1982-87, Los Alamos, N.Mex., 1987—; venture capitalist Venture Capital Info., Edmond, 1986-87, Venture Calital Info., Los Alamos, 1987—; conservation chair Nat. Speleological Soc., 1995—; dir. Project Underground VA, 1995—; mem. caves and karst task force Bur. Land Mgmt., Carlsbad, N.Mex., 1991-93, Guadalupe caverns geology panel Nat. Park Svc., Carlsbad, 1993. Author: Cavern Development in the Guadalupe Mountains, 1979, Stories From Stones, 1992; mem. adv. bd. Jour. Cave and Karst Studies, 1998—. Conservation chair, chair Pajarito Grotto, Los Alamos, 1998—. Recipient Gov.'s Dist. Svc. award Gov. Iowa, 1970, W.A. Tarr award Sigma Gamma Epsilon, 1970, Lowden prize Geology U. Iowa, 1970. Fellow Nat. Speleological Soc. (Conservation award 1995); mem. Am. Assn. Petroleum Geologists, N.Mex. Entrepreneurs Assn. (bd. dirs. 1988-89), Cave Rsch. Found. (chief scientist 1988-89), Omicron Delta Kappa. Lutheran. Avocations: caving, hiking, rock collecting, cave sci., reading. Home: PO Box 9398 Albuquerque NM 87199-3398 Office: Venture Capital Info Inc 901 18th St # 11300 Los Alamos NM 87544-3009

JAGODA, BARRY LIONEL, media adviser, communications consultant; b. Youngstown, Ohio, Feb. 5, 1944; s. Saul S. and Anne (Fradin) J. B.A., U. Tex., 1966; M.S., Columbia U., 1967. Writer, editor NBC News, Washington, N.Y.C., 1967-69; producer CBS News, N.Y.C., 1969-75; partner Houston, Ritz, Cohen, Jagoda, N.Y.C., 1975; TV advisor Jimmy Carter presdl. campaign, 1976; spl. asst. to the Pres., Washington, 1977-79; cons. Pres., 1979—; pres. Am. Info. Exchange, 1979—; dir. news and pub. affairs George Washington U., 1983-87; v.p. Stackig, Sanderson and White Advt. and Pub. Rels., 1988-93, Shandwick Pub. Affairs, Washington, 1993-97; dir. of comms. IMPAC Corp., 1997—. Recipient Emmy award as producer CBS news special, Watergate 1974. Chmn. bd. dirs. Friends of Raoul Wallenberg Found., 1989—. Ford Found. fellow, 1967. Mem. Nat. Bus. Travel Assn., Sigma Delta Chi. Home: 1650 29th St NW Washington DC 20007-2901 Office: 1250 24th St NW Ste 300 Washington DC 20037-1124

JAGODA, DONALD ROBERT, sales promotion agency executive; b. N.Y.C., Feb. 18, 1929; s. Joseph and Anne (Hollander) J.; m. Sydelle Granoff, Mar. 2, 1952; children—Jeryl, Gwynn, Karyn. B.S. in Mktg., NYU, 1950. Merchandising mgr. Hudson Pulp & Paper Co., N.Y.C., 1953-59; v.p. S.J. Reiner Co., Mineola, N.Y., 1960-62; pres. Don Jagoda Assocs. Inc., Melville, N.Y., 1962—. Served with AUS, 1951-53. Mem. Promotion Mktg. Assn. Am. (Reggie award 1984, 86, 90, bd. dirs., treas.), Mktg. Communications Execs. Internat. (bd. dirs.), Assn. Incentive Mktg. (bd. dirs.), Premium Merchandising Club (pres. N.Y. chpt. 1983), Incentive Federation (bd. dirs.). Office: Don Jagoda Assocs Inc 100 Marcus Dr Melville NY 11747-4229

JAGODZINSKI, RUTH CLARK, nursing administrator; b. N.Y.C., Feb. 24, 1938; d. John Kirkland and Ruth Fishwick Clark; m. Thomas John Jagodzinski, Nov. 1962 (div. 1974); children: Christine Ruth, James Clark. Diploma, Roosevelt Hosp. Sch. Nursing, 1959. RN, Nev., N.Y. Head nurse drug/alcohol detox Sunrise Hosp., Las Vegas, Nev., 1973-75; program coord. careunit North Las Vegas (Nev.) Hosp., 1975-77; co-owner, adminstr. Sunrise Home Health, Las Vegas, 1983-89; dir. pers. PRN Home Health, Las Vegas, 1990-91; dir. home health svcs. Med. Pers. Pool, Las Vegas, 1990-92; dir. profl. svc. Olsten Kimberly Quality Care, Las Vegas, 1992-95; adminstr. Valley Home Health, Las Vegas, 1995-97; regional dir. ops. Integrated Health Mgmt. Svcs., Brunswick, Ga., 1997-98; ind. cons., 1998-99; intake mgr. Olsten Health Svcs., Las Vegas, 1999—; mem. Nev. State Cert. Bd. Substance Abuse Counselors and Program Adminstrs., 1976-86, 90-97, pres., 1980-86. Mem. Nev. Gov.'s Adv. Bd. for Alcohol and Drugs; bd. dirs. We Care Found., 1974—; trustee Community Referral Svcs., 1975-80; bd. dirs. Alcohol Program So. Nev., 1975-85; mem. In-Home Care Svcs. Clark County, 1978-83; bd. dirs. So. Nev. Girls Clubs, 1984-86; mem. adv. bd. Nathan Adelson Hospice, Las Vegas, 1977-89; chmn. nursing subcom. profl. ednn. div. So. Nev. chpt. Am. Cancer Soc., 1989-90, mem. Nev. Bd. Com. on Occupational Excellence, 1989-90. Recipient Community Svc. award Alcohol Program So. Nev., 1978, Svc. award We Care Found., 1989. Mem. Home Health Care Assns. Nev. (life, v.p. 1984-86, 94-95, pres. 1995-98, Svc. award 1999). Fax: (702) 876-6221. Home: 4573 Royal Ridge Way Las Vegas NV 89103-5034 Office: 505 E Capovilla Ste 103 Las Vegas NV 89119

JAGOW, ELMER, retired college president; b. West Bend, Wis., Apr. 25, 1922; s. Bernard and Florence (Kurth) J.; m. Ellen Knief, Oct. 7, 1944 (dec. Apr. 30, 1995); children: Kathryn Jagow Mohrman, Allyson Jagow Weir; m. Joan Geensburg Risberg, Oct. 14, 1995. BS in Edn., Concordia U., 1944; MBA, Northwestern U., 1955; LHD (hon.), Christian Theol. Sem., 1968; LLD (hon.), Ohio U., 1973; LHD (hon.), John Cabot U., 1996. Asst. bus. mgr. Concordia U., River Forest, Ill., 1944-46, bus. mgr., 1946-56; mem. adminstrn. Knox Coll., Galesburg, Ill., 1956-66, treas., bus. mgr., 1956-64, v.p. finance, treas., 1964-66; pres. Hiram (Ohio) Coll., 1966-85, pres. emeritus, 1985—. Former trustee Robinson Meml. Hosp., Heather Hill, Inc., Alzheimer's Ctr., Cleve.; chmn. bd. trustees John Cabot U., Rome, hon. trustee, 1997—. Mem. Garfield Soc., Walden Golf & Tennis Club (Aurora, Ohio). Home: PO Box 7 Hiram OH 44234-0007

JAGR, JAROMIR, professional hockey player; b. Kladno, Czechoslavakia, Feb. 15, 1972. Profl. hockey player Poldi Kladno, Czechosalvakia, 1988-90, Pitts. Penguins, 1990—. Recipient Art Ross trophy, 1994-95; named to Czechoslavakian League All-Star Team, 1989-90, Sporting News and NHL All-Star 1st Teams, 1994-95. Office: c/o Pittsburgh Penguins 66 Mario Lemieux Pl Pittsburgh PA 15219-3501*

JAHANMIR, SAID, materials scientist, mechanical engineer; b. Mar. 18, 1950; married; 2 children. BSME, U. Wash., 1971; MSME, MIT, 1973, PhD in Mech. Engring., 1976. Instr. mech. engring. MIT, 1975-76; lectr. mech. engring. U. Calif., 1976-77; asst. prof. Sibley Sch. Mech. & Aerospace Engring. Cornell U., 1977-80; sr. staff engr. Exxon Rsch. and Engring. Co., Products Rsch. Divsn., 1980-85; program dir. tribology program NSF, 1985-87; mgr. ceramic machining consortium Nat. Inst. Stds. & Tech. (formerly Nat. Bur. Stds.), 1987—; adj. prof. mech. engring. U. Md., 1987-96; presenter in field. Author: Tribology in Manufacturing Processes, 1994, Friction and Wear of Ceramics, 1994; editor Machining Sci. and Tech. Jour.; contbr. articles to profl. jours., chpts. to books; patentee in field. Fellow ASME (chair tribology divsn. 1997—, bd. rsch. and tech. devel. 1995-98, assoc. editor jour. Tribology 1990-93, tribology divsn. exec. com. 1988-90, others, Disting. Svc. award), Soc. Tribologists and Lubrication Engrs. (fellows com. 1993—, edn. com. 1987-95, ceramics and composited com. founding chmn. 1987-89, ann. meeting program com. 1987-91, lubrication fundamentals com. 1986-87, Internat. award); mem. Am. Ceramic Soc. (ann. meeting organizer, chmn. tribology and ceramic maching sessions 1988). Office: Nat Inst Stds & Tech Bldg 223 Rm A329 Gaithersburg MD 20899

JAHN, HELMUT, architect; b. Nurnberg, Germany, Jan. 4, 1940; came to U.S., 1966; s. Wilhelm Anton and Karolina (Wirth) J.; m. Deborah Ann Lampe, Dec. 31, 1970; 1 child, Evan. Dipl. Ing.-Architect, Technische Hochschule, Munich, 1965; postgrad., Ill. Inst. Tech., 1966-67; D.F.A. (hon.), St. Mary's Coll., Notre Dame, Ind., 1980. Registered architect, Ill., Calif., Colo., Fla., Ind., Minn., N.Y., Tex., Va., Nat. Coun. Archtl. Registration Bds. Germany. With P.C. von Seidlein, Munich, 1965-66; with C.F. Murphy Assocs., Chgo., 1967-81, asst. to Gene Summers, 1967-73, exec. v.p., dir. planning and design, 1973-81; prin. Murphy/Jahn, Chgo., 1981-92, pres., 1982—, chief exec. officer, 1983—; mem. design studio faculty U. Ill., Chgo., 1981; Elliot Noyes prof. archtl. design Harvard U., Cambridge, Mass., 1981; Davenport vis. prof. archtl. design Yale U., New Haven, 1983; thesis prof. IIT, Chgo., 1989-92. Prin. works include Kemper Arena, Kansas City, Mo., 1974 (Nat. AIA honor award, Am. Inst. Steel Constrn. award), Auraria Library, Denver, 1975, John Marshall Cts. Bldg., Richmond, Va. 1976, H. Roe Bartle Exhbn. Hall, Kansas City, Mo., 1976, Fourth Dist. Cts. Bldg., Maywood, Ill., 1976, Monroe Garage, Chgo., 1977, Michigan City (Ind.) Library, 1977 (AIA Ill. Council honor award, AIA-ALA First honor award, Am. Inst., Steel Constrn. award), St. Mary's Coll. Athletic Facility, South Bend, Ind., 1977 (AIA Ill. Council Honor award, AIA Nat. honor award, Am. Inst. Steel Constrn. award), Springfield Garage, Ill., 1977, Glenbrook Profl. Bldg., Northbrook, Ill., 1978, Rust-Oleum Corp. Hdqrs., Vernon Hills, Ill., 1978 (Am. Steel Constrn. award), La Lumiere Gymnasium, La Porte, Ind., 1978, Prairie Capital Convention Ctr.-Parking Garage, Springfield, Ill., 1979, W.W. Grainger Corp. Hdqrs., Skokie, Ill., 1979, Xerox Centre, Chgo., 1980, De La Garza Career Ctr., East Chicago, Ind., 1981 (ASHRAE Energy award), Area 2 Police Hdqrs., Chgo., 1981, Oak Brook (Ill.) Post Office, 1981, Commonwealth Edison Dist. Hdqrs., Downers Grove, Ill., 1981 (ASHRAE Energy award), First Source Ctr., South Bend, Ind., 1982, Argonne (Ill.) Program Support Facility, 1982 (Owens-Corning Fiberglass Energy Conservation award), One South Wacker Office Bldg., Chgo., 1982, Addition to Chgo. Bd. of Trade, 1982 (Reliance Devel. Group Inc. award for Disting. Arch., Am. Inst. Steel Constrn. award, Structural Engring. Assn. Ill. award), Mercy Hosp. Addition, Chgo., 1983, 11 Diagonal St., Johannesburg, Republic of South Africa, 1983, U. Ill. Agrl. Engring. Sci. Bldg., Champaign, 1984, Learning Resources Ctr., Coll. of DuPage, Glen Ellyn, Ill., 1984, Plaza East, Milw., 1984 (Disting. Architect award Milw. Art Commn.), Shand Morahan Corp. Hdqrs., Evanston, Ill., 1984, 701 Fourth Ave. S., Mpls., 1984, O'Hare Rapid Transit Sta., Chgo., 1984 (Nat. Honor award), State of Ill. Ctr., Chgo., 1985 (Structural Engring. Assn. Ill. award, AIA Chgo. chpt. award 1986), Parktown Stands, Johannesburg, 1986, Two Energy Ctr., Naperville, Ill., 1986, Hawthorne Ctr. Office Bldg., Vernon Hills, Ill., 1986, Park Ave. Tower, N.Y.C., 1986, 300 E. 85th St. Apts., N.Y.C., Northwestern Terminal, Chgo., 1987 (Structural Engring. Assn. of Ill. award 1987), United Airlines Terminal, 1987 (Structural Engring. Assn. of Ill. award, Nat. AIA Honor award, R.J. Reynolds Meml. award, 1988, AIA Chgo. chpt. award), One Liberty Place, Phila., 1987, Oakbrook (Ill.) Terr. Tower, 1987, O'Hare Internat. Airport, 1988 (AIA Chgo. chpt. award), Merchandise Mart Bridge, Chgo., 1988, Wilshire/Westwood Office Bldg., L.A., 1988, 425 Lexington Ave, N.Y.C., 1989, 750 Lexington Ave., 1989, Cityspire, N.Y.C., 1989, Messe Frankfurt Convention Ctr., Germany, 1989, Barnett Ctr., Jacksonville, Fla., 1990, Messe Frankfurt Tower, Germany, 1991 (AIA Chgo. chpt. award 1992), Livingston Plaza, Bklyn. Hgts., N.Y., 1991, Two Liberty Place, Phila., 1991 (AIA Chgo. chpt. award 1992), 120 N LaSalle, Chgo., 1992 (AIA Chgo. chpt. award 1992), One Am. Plz., Trolley Sta., San Diego, 1992 (AIA Chgo. chpt. award 1992), Mannheim (Germany) Ins. Bldg., 1992 (AIA Chgo. chpt. award 1992), Hyatt Roisy, Paris, 1992, Munich (Germany) Order Ctr., 1993 (AIA Chgo. Chpt. award, Nat. AIA Honor award), Hitachi Tower, Singapore, 1993, Caltex House, Singapore, 1993, Kempinski Hotel, Munich, 1994, (AIA Chgo. Chpt. award), Pallas, Stuttgart, Germany, 1994, 70 KU Damn, Berlin, 1994, (AIA Chgo. Chpt. award, Nat. AIA Honor award), Second Internat. Bangkok Airport, Charlemagne, Brussels, Century 21, Shanghai, China, FKB Airport, Köln, Germany; contbr. to numerous group and solo exhbns. of archtl. drawings and design. Recipient citation Progressive Architecture, 1977, award for Chgo. cen. area plan, 1985, Dean of Architecture award Chgo. design awards, 1991; Arnold W. Brunner meml. prize in architecture, 1982; Chgo. chpt. award AIA, 1975-79, 81-83, 86-88, nat. honor award, 1979, 87, N.Y. State award, 1986; 1st honor award ALA, 1978, energy award ASHRAE, 1981, Presdl. Desirn award Nat. Endowment Arts, 1988, R.S. Reynolds Meml. award, 1988; numerous others. Fellow AIA, Architecture Soc./Art Inst. Chgo., Chgo. Archtl. Club; mem. AIA (numerous Chgo. chpt. awards 1975—). Roman Catholic. Clubs: Comml. of Chgo., Economic of Chgo., Saddle & Cycle. Office: Murphy/Jahn 35 E Wacker Dr Ste 300 Chicago IL 60601-2157*

JAHN, LAURENCE ROY, retired biologist, institute executive; b. Jefferson, Wis., June 24, 1926; s. Roy Johaan and Mabel Marie (Kothlow) J.; m. Helen Florence Faville, Sept. 5, 1947; children: Katharine Marie (Mrs. Ronald J. Cook), Richard Alan. B.S., U. Wis., 1949, M.S., 1958, Ph.D., 1965. Aquatic biologist Wis. Dept. Natural Resources, 1949-59; with Wildlife Mgmt. Inst., Washington, 1959-91; v.p. Wildlife Mgmt. Inst., 1971-87, pres., 1987-91, chmn. bd., 1991-92; chmn. bd. United Conservation Alliance, Washington, 1990-92; liaison officer Nat. Assn. Univ. Fisheries and Wildlife Programs, 1992—; mem. Va. bd. Game and Inland Fisheries, 1992-96, chmn., 1994-95, sci. adv. bd.; chmn. bd. Dept. Def. Strategic Environ. R&D Program, 1992-94; mem. waterfowl adv. com. U.S. Fish and Wildlife Svc., 1968-76, U.S. Implementation Bd., N.Am. Waterfowl Mgmt. Plan, 1988-91, chmn., 1990-91; mem. spl. adv. panel on water resources rsch. Dept. Interior, 1971-73, chmn., 1973, mem. adv. com. on fish, wildlife and parks, 1975-77, mem. adv. com. on outer continental shelf environ. studies, 1975-77; mem. adv. com. on water data for pub. use and working group on river quality assessment U.S. Geol. Survey, 1972-87; mem. wildlife adv. com. Dept. State, 1972-76; mem. adv. com. on natural resources conservation award Sec. Def., 1973, 76, 80, 85, 86; mem. adv. panel on tuna-porpoise Nat. Marine Fisheries Svc., 1974; mem. environ. adv. bd. U.S. Army C.E., 1979-85, chmn., 1983-85; mem. marine fisheries adv. com. NOAA, 1982-84; mem. bd. agr. and renewable resources Nat. Acad. Scis., 1980-83, mem. exec. bd., 1981-83; mem. adv. bd. on wild horse and burro U.S. Dept. Agr. and Interior, 1986-88, Agr./Conservation Coalition, 1981-91, chmn., 1981-86. Author numerous articles in field.; Editor symposia procs. and books. Pres. Horicon (Wis.) Bd. Edn., 1965-67; bd. dirs. Citizens Com. on Natural Resources, 1970-78; mem. steering com. Nat. Watershed Congress, 1971-90, chmn., 1977-90; trustee N.Am. Wildlife Found., 1972-85, sec.-treas., 1974-85; chmn. program com. N.Am. Wildlife and Natural Resources Conf., 1972-88; bd. dirs. Urban Wildlife Rsch. Ctr., 1972-76; mem. bd. Wildfowl Found., 1972-93, sec., 1975-91; mem.-at-large, sec., bd. dirs. Va. Conservation Network, Richmond, 1996-97. With USNR, 1944-46. Recipient certificate merit Nash Conservation Awards Program, 1953; resolution appreciation Miss. Flyway Council, 1970; Outstanding Civilian Service medal Dept. of Army, 1985. Fellow AAAS; mem. Wildlife Soc. (pres. 1979, Trippensie-McPherson award 1984, spl. recognition award 1986, Aldo Leopold Meml. award 1989), Soil Conservation Soc. (commendation 1969), Am. Water Resources Assn. (interim dir. S. Atlantic dist. 1975), Natural Resources Council Am. (exec. com. 1976-86, sec. 1978-81, vice chmn. 1981-83, chmn. 1983-85, hon. mem. 1985, Barbara Swain award of honor 1991), Nat. Audubon Soc., Wilderness Soc., Internat. Assn. Fish and Wildlife Agencies (life), Am. Forests (life), Nat. Wildlife Fedn. (life), Wis. Acad. Scis., Arts and Letters (life), Am. Fisheries Soc., Washington Biologists' Field Club, Whooping Crane Conservation Assn. (life), Wilson Ornithol. Soc. (life), Cosmos Club (admissions com. 1985-88, chmn. 1986-88, awards com. 1991-93, chmn. 1992-93), Boone and Crockett Club. Presbyn. Home and Office: 2435 Riviera Dr Vienna VA 22181-3120

JAHNS, JEFFREY, lawyer; b. Chgo., July 6, 1946; s. Maxim G. and Josephine Barbara (Czernek) J.; m. Jill Metcoff, Sept. 8, 1973; children: Anna Hope, Claire Martine, Elizabeth Grace. AB, Villanova U., 1968; JD, U. Chgo., 1971. Bar: Ill. 1971, U.S. Dist. Ct. (no. dist.) Ill. 1971, U.S. Ct. Appeals (7th cir.) 1973, U.S. Supreme Ct. 1974. Assoc. Roan & Grossman, Chgo., 1971-77, ptnr., 1977-81; ptnr. Seyfarth, Shaw, Fairweather & Geraldson, Chgo., 1981—; mem. tax mgmt. adv. bd. Bur. Nat. Affairs, Washington, 1981--. Co-author: Corporate Acquisition Debt Interest Deduction, 1973; contbr. numerous articles to legal publs., chpts. to books. Trustee, chmn. Chgo. Architecture Found., 1982—; bd. dirs. Prairie Ave. House Mus., 1995-98; trustee Graham Found., 1998—. Ctr. for Urban Studies fellow U. Chgo., 1969-71. Mem. ABA, Chgo. Bar Assn. (chmn. various coms.), Internat. Coun. Shopping Ctrs., Mid-Day Club, Econ. Club Chgo., Lambda Alpha. Office: Seyfarth Shaw Fairweather & Geraldson 55 E Monroe St Ste 4200 Chicago IL 60603-5863

JAHR, ARMIN N., II, clergy member, church administrator. Exec. dir. Luth. Brethren Home Missions, Fergus Falls, Minn. Office: Luth Brethren Home Missions PO Box 655 Fergus Falls MN 56538-0655

JAILLET, MICHAEL ANDRÉ, town administrator; b. Gardner, Mass., Oct. 12, 1952; s. Raymond and Leatrice Jaillet; m. Deborah Patricia Stevens, June 21, 1980; children: Steven, Meghann, Geoffrey. BA in Polit. Sci., Southeastern Mass. U., 1975; MS in Urban Affairs and Policy Analysis, So. Ill. U., Edwardsville, 1980; MA in Econs., So. Ill. U., 1981. Peace Corps vol. Tougan Sols Pretet, Barking Fasso, 1975-77; town planner Town of Clinton, Mass., 1978; instr., analyst So. Ill. U., Edwardsville, 1978-83; mgr., cons. Assessins Dept., Boston, 1983-88; adminstr. Town of Bellingham, Mass., 1985-87; town adminstr. Tow of Westwood, Mass., 1987—; instr. Blackburn Coll., Carlinville, Ill., 1981. Fin. coun. mem. Our Lady of Sorrows Parish, Sharon, Mass., 1983—; exec. com. mem. MMA/MMMA, Boston, 1996—; internat. task force ICMA, Washington, 1997—. Mem. Internat. City Mgrs. Assn. (internat. task force 1997—), Am. Assn. Adminstrv. Profls., Mass. Mcpl. Assn. (local adv. coun. 1997-99, exec. com. mem. 1997-99), Mass. Mcpl. Mgrs. Assn. (nomination com. chmn. 1995, South African exchange com. chmn. 1996-97, at-large rep. 1996, internat. exch. com. chmn. 1997-99, dist. V rep. 1997-99), Westwood Rotary Club. Democrat. Roman Catholic. Avocations: coaching and playing soccer, skiing, golf. E-mail: mjaillet.townhall.westwood.ma.us. Home: 141 Norwood St Sharon MA 02067 Office: Town of Westwood 580 High St Westwood MA 02090

JAIN, ANANT KUMAR, data communications and telecommunications consultant; b. Delhi, India, Apr. 28, 1963; s. Suraj Bhan and Shashi Prabha (Gupta) J.; m. Anju Jain, Jan. 16, 1993; children: Aditi, Abhishek. BSc in Chemistry with honors, U. Delhi, 1983; ME, Indian Inst. of Sci., Bangalore, 1987; postgrad., Northeastern U. Trainee Tata Consultancy Svcs., Delhi, 1987-88, asst. systems analyst and programmer, 1988-90, systems analyst and programmer, 1990-92, sr. system analyst and programmer, 1992-94, asst. cons., 1994-96, assoc. cons., 1996; sr. cons. Tropaion Inc., N.J., 1996-97; mem. tech. staff Lucent Technologies, North Andover, Mass., 1997—; project leader TCS, Delhi, 1992-94, project mgr., 1994-95, cons., 1994-97. Contbr. articles to profl. conf. Mem. IEEE (sr. mem., soc. and tech com. on computer comms., chair Boston comsoc chpt., 1999—, standards coordinating com.-36 on utility com., editor Conference Calendar column, assoc. tech. editor commn. mag.). Avocations: reading, travel, music, movies. Home: GD/35 Pitam Pura, Delhi 110034, India Office: Lucent Technologies Inc 1600 Osgood St North Andover MA 01845

JAIN, NEMI CHAND, chemist, coating scientist, educator; b. Kota, Rajasthan, India, Oct. 15, 1951; came to U.S., 1983, naturalized, 1993; s. Chand Mal and Raj Devi (Nopra) J.; m. Shashi Bala Jain, Jan. 29, 1981; children: Nimisha, Seema. BSc, U. Rajasthan, 1971, MSc, 1973, PhD, 1978; postgrad., N.D. State U., 1990, McCorne Rsch. Inst., 1994, Baldwin-Wallace Coll., 1996. Lectr. chemistry Nat. Coun. of Edn. Rsch. Tng., Ajmer, India, 1976-77; asst. prof. U. Delhi, 1977-83; postdoctoral rsch. assoc. U. Va., Charlottesville, 1983-85; rsch. assoc./assoc. lab. dir. Colo. State U., Ft. Collins, 1985-89; rsch. scientist/team leader Sherwin-Williams Co., Chgo., 1989-96, sr. scientist, 1996—; advisor Truman Coll., Chgo., 1999; cons. and lectr. in field. Developer waterborne coatings; developer coating test course Sherwin-Williams U., 1995; contbr. numerous articles to profl. jours. Judge, Chgo. Sci. Fair, 1992, 95, 97, 98, Competitive Leadership, Profl. Mgmt. Assn., 1997, 98, 1st Responder/Indsl. Med. Tech., 1995—, U. No. Colo, 1989, Am. Chem. Soc. H.S. Edn. Com., 1996—. CSIR fellow, 1973-76, Sardar Patel U. fellow, 1972, Lucknow U. tchr. fellow, 1979; recipient Disting. Nat. award for study abroad Govt. of India, 1983-85, State Govt. Rajasthan merit scholar, 1967-73. Fellow Am. Inst. Chemists; mem. ASTM, Am. Chem. Soc. (mem. h.s. edn. com. 1996-97), Internat. Union Pure and Applied Chemistry, Sigma Xi. Jain. Avocations: reading, walking, cooking, travel, gardening. Fax: (773) 821-2263. E-mail: ncjain@sherwin.com. Home: 10603 S Vicky Ln Palos Hills IL 60465-1925 Office: Sherwin Williams Co 10909 S Cottage Grove Ave Chicago IL 60628-3894

JAIN, PIYARE LAL, physics educator; b. Punjab, India, Dec. 11, 1921; came to U.S., 1949; naturalized, 1961; s. Labh Ch and Maya (Devi) J.; m. Sulakshana Dhawan, Feb. 15, 1966. B.A., Punjab U., 1944, M.A., 1948; Ph.D., Mich. State U., 1954. Research asso. chemistry dept. U. Minn., 1953-54; instr. physics dept. State U. N.Y., Buffalo, 1954-59; asst. prof. State U. N.Y., 1959-61, assoc. prof., 1961-67, prof., 1967—; research asso. U. Chgo., 1959-60, Lawrence Radiation Lab., Berkeley, Calif.; vis. prof., Bristol, Eng.,

1961-62, U. Wash., Seattle, summer 1960; Fulbright vis. prof. Rajasthan U., India, 1965-66; Sci. adviser Am. embassy AID, New Delhi, India, summer 1966. Recipient Excellence award State of N.Y. and United Univ. Professions, Hind Ratten award Govt. of India, 1994. Fellow Am. Phys. Soc. Rsch. in sold state physics, electron and nulcear magnetic reesonance, cosmic radiation and high energy physics, relativistic heavy ion physics. Home: 223 Surrey Run Buffalo NY 14221-3363 Office: Suny At Buffalo Buffalo NY 14214-3001

JAISINGHANI, MANISH KUMAR, manufacturing engineer; b. Bombay, May 14, 1970; came to U.S., 1994.; BS in Indsl. Engring., U. Bombay, 1992; MS in Indsl. Engring., Tex. A&M U., Kingsville, 1996; MBA, Wichita State U., 1997. Prodn. engr. Mukand Steel Co., Bombay, 1992-94; mfg. engr. II, Eaton Corp., Hutchinson, Kans., 1996-98, assembly supervisor, mfg. engr. I, 1998—. Contbr. article to profl. jours. Exxon scholar Tex. A&M U., 1994-96. Mem. Inst. Indsl. Engrs. Avocations: reading, music, skydiving, travel. Home: 1717 E 24th Ave Apt D Hutchinson KS 67502-1150 Office: Eaton Corp 3401 E 4th Ave Hutchinson KS 67501-1969

JAISWAL, DINESH KUMAR, pharmaceutical scientist, educator; b. Howrah, India, Mar. 5, 1947; came to U.S., 1983; s. Jagadish Prasad and Phool Kumari Jaiswal; m. Manju Jaiswal, Feb. 10, 1971; children: Rahul, Kunal. BS in Pharmacy, Banaras Hindu U., Varanasi, India, 1970, MS in Pharmacy, 1972, PhD in Pharmacy, 1978. Assoc. prof. Banaras Hindu U., 1973-75, 78-83; chemist Phoenix Lab., Hicksville, N.Y., 1983-84; sr. chemist Superpharm, Islip, N.Y., 1984-86; mgr. Quad Pharm., Indpls., 1986-90; sr. devel. pharmacist GAF Chem. Co., Wayne, Ind., 1990-93; prin. scientist Mova Pharm., Caguas, P.R., 1993-96, Forest Labs., Inwood, N.Y., 1996—. Contbr. articles to profl. jours., including Jour. Pharm. Scis., PHarm. Rsch., USA, Pharmatech/Manchester. Jr. rsch. fellow UGC, New Delhi, India, 1975, sr. rsch. fellow, 1976, rsch. assoc., 1977. Mem. Am. Assn. Pharm. Scientists, Parenteral Drug Assn. and Controlled Release Soc. Achievements include patent for pharmaceutical tablet with PVP having enhanced drug dissolution rate. Avocations: sports, music, tourism. Home: 4 Birchwood Ct Apt 5L Mineola NY 11501-4514 Office: 300 Prospect St Inwood NY 11096-2035

JAKAB, IRENE, psychiatrist; b. Oradea, Rumania; came to U.S., 1961, naturalized, 1966; d. Odon and Rosa A. (Riedl) J. MD, Ferencz József U., Kolozsvar, Hungary, 1944; lic. in psychology, pedagogy, philosophy cum laude, Hungarian U., Cluj, Rumania, 1947; PhD summa cum laude, Pazmany Peter U., Budapest, 1948; Dr honoris causa, U. Besançon, France, 1982. Diplomate Am. Bd. Psychiatry. Rotating intern Ferencz József U., 1943-44; resident in psychiatry Univ. Hosp., Kolozsvar, 1944-47, resident in neurology, 1947-50; resident internal medicine Univ. Hosp. for Internal Medicine, Pécs, Hungary, 1950-51; chief physician Univ. Hosp. for Neurology and Psychiatry, Pécs, 1951-59; staff neuropathol. rsch. lab. Neurol. Univ. Clinic, Zurich, 1959-61; sect. chief Kans. Neurol. Inst., Topeka, 1961-63; dir. rsch. and edn., 1966; resident psychiatry Topeka State Hosp., 1963-66; asst. psychiatrist McLean Hosp., Belmont, Mass., 1966-67; assoc. psychiatrist McLean Hosp., 1967-74; prof. psychiatry U. Pitts. Med. Sch., 1974-89, prof. emerita, 1989—, co-dir. med. student edn. in psychiatry, 1981-89; dir. John Merck Program, 1974-81; mem. faculty dept. psychiatry Med. Sch., Pecs, 1951-59; asst. Univ. Hosp. Neurology, Zurich, 1959-61; assoc. psychiatry Harvard U., Boston, 1966-69, asst. prof. psychiatry, 1969-74, program dir. grad course mental retardation, 1970-87; lectr. psychiatry, 1974—. Author: Dessins et Peintures des Aliénés, 1956, Zeichnungen und Gemälde der Geisteskranken, 1956, Pictorial Expression in Psychiatry, 1998; editor: Psychiatry and Art, 1968, Art Interpretation and Art Therapy, 1969, Conscious and Unconscious Expressive Art, 1971, Transcultural Aspects of Psychiatric Art, 1975; co-editor: Dynamische Psychiatrie, 1974; editorial bd.: Confinia Psychiatrica, 1975-81; contbr. articles to profl. jours. Recipient 1st prize Benjamin Rush Gold medal award for sci. exhibit, 1980, Bronze Chris plaque Columbus Film Festival, 1980, Leadership award Am. Assn. on Mental Deficiency, 1980; Menninger Sch. Psychiatry fellow, Topeka, 1963-66. Mem. AMA, Am. Psychol. Assn., Am. Psychiat. Assn., Société Medico Psychologique de Paris, Internat. Rorschach Soc., N.Y. Acad. Scis., Internat. Soc. Psychopathology of Expression (v.p. 1959—), Am. Soc. Psychopathology of Expression (chmn. 1965—, Ernst Kris Gold Medal award 1988), Royal Soc. of Medicine (overseas fellow), Internat. Soc. Child Psychiatry and Allied Professions, Internat. Assn. Knowledge Engrs. (v.p. for medicine 1988-95), Deutschsprachige Gesellschaft für Psychopathologie des Ausdruckes (hon. Prinzhorn prize 1967), Hungarian Psychiat. Assn. (hon. 1992), World Psychiat. Assn. (co-chmn. sect. on mass and media and mental health). Home and Office: 74 Lawton St Brookline MA 02446-2501

JAKACKI, DIANE KATHERINE, web production and marketing executive; b. Englewood, N.J., July 27, 1964; d. Bernard and Barbara (Logie) J. BA, Lafayette Coll., 1986. From asst. to mktg. mgr. to website exec. prodr. Home Box Office, N.Y.C., 1987—. Author: (plays) Beowulf: A 20th Century Evening in a 10th Century Mead Hall, 1992, Blocked, 1994, Rubbing Brass, 1996. Youth group leader Congl. Ch., New Canaan, Conn., 1994-96. Avocations: theatre, computers, British history, golf, cycling. Office: HBO 1100 Ave of Americas New York NY 10036

JAKES, JOHN, author; b. Chgo., Mar. 31, 1932; s. John Adrian and Bertha (Retz) J.; m. Rachel Ann Payne, June 15, 1951; children: Andrea, Ellen, John Michael, Victoria. AB, DePauw U., 1953, LittD (hon.), 1977; MA, Ohio State U., 1954; LLD (hon.), Wright State U., 1976; LHD (hon.), Winthrop Coll., 1985, U. S.C., 1993, Ohio State U., 1996. With advt. dept. Abbott Labs., 1954-60; with creative dept. various advt. agencies, 1960-69; creative dir. Dancer Fitzgerald Sample Co., Dayton, Ohio, 1969-70; rsch. fellow dept. history U. S.C., 1989. Author: The Texans Ride North, 1952, A Night for Treason, 1956, Murder He Says, 1958, When the Star Kings Die, 1967, Master of the Dark Gate, 1970, The Kent Family Chronicles: The Bastard, 1974, The Rebels, 1975, The Seekers, 1975, The Furies, 1976, The Titans, 1976, The Warriors, 1977, The Lawless, 1978, The Americans, 1980, North and South Trilogy: North and South, 1982, Love and War, 1984, Heaven and Hell, 1987, California Gold, 1989, Homeland, 1993, In the Big Country, 1993, American Dreams, 1998, (juvenile) Susanna of the Alamo, 1986, (musical) Great Expectations - The Musical, 1999; co-editor anthology: New Trails, 1994. Trustee DePauw U. Recipient Ohio Gov.'s award, 1977, ann. lit. award Friends of Rochester Pub. Libr., 1983, Citizen-Celebrity award for libr. advocacy White House Conf. on Librs., 1995, Disting. Alumni award Ohio State U. Coll. Humanities, 1995, Western Heritage Lit. award Nat. Cowboy Hall of Fame, 1995, Profl. Achievement award Ohio State U. Alumni Assn., 1997, Career Achievement award S.C. Humanities Coun., 1998. Mem. S.C. Acad. Authors, Western Writers Am., Dramatists Guild, Authors Guild, PEN, Century Assn. Office: care Rembar & Curtis Attys 19 W 44th St New York NY 10036-5902

JAKES, LARA CHRISTINE, newspaper reporter; b. Kansas City, Mo., July 8, 1973; d. Robert Alexander Jr. and Jean Throckmorton Jakes. B of Journalism, U. Mo., 1995. Staff writer The Columbia Missourian, Columbia, Mo., 1993-94; Washington corr. The Topeka (Kans.) Capital-Jour., 1994; intern The Washington Times, 1994-95; staff writer The Columbia (Mo.) Daily Tribune, 1995; state reporter The Times Union, Albany, N.Y., 1995—; guest lectr. Coll. of Saint Rose, Albany, 1996—. Recipient 2d Pl. Spot News AP, 1997, Honorable Mention, 1998; writing award Hearst Corp., 1995-97. Mem. Soc. of Profl. Journalists, N.Y. Press Club, Women's Press Club (N.Y.C.). Avocations: creative writing, hiking, running. E-mail: LJAKES@timesunion.com. Home: 108 Dove St Albany NY 12210-1704 Office: The Times Union PO Box 15000 Albany NY 12212-5000 also: LCA Rm 3rd Fl State Capitol Albany NY 12224

JAKES, WILLIAM CHESTER, electrical engineer; b. Milw., May 15, 1922; s. William Chester and Eleanor (Knight) J.; m. Mary Elizabeth Bristle, Sept. 3, 1948; children: Robert, Elizabeth. B.S. in Elec. Engring., Northwestern U., 1944, M.S. in Elec. Engring, 1947, Ph.D., 1949. With Bell Tel. Labs., Inc. (various locations), 1949-87; head radio transmission research dept. Bell Tel. Labs., Inc. (various locations), Holmdel, N.J., 1963-71; dir. Radio Transmission Lab., North Andover, Mass., 1971-87; Mem. sci. adv. bd. Voice of Am., 1957-58. Contbr. articles to profl. jours. With USN, 1944-46. Ph.D. (hon.) Iowa Wesleyan U., 1961; recipient Alumni Merit award Northwestern U., 1962. Fellow IEEE (Paper award 1971, co-recipient Alexander Graham Bell medal 1987); mem. Eta Kappa Nu, Pi Mu Epsilon. Patentee antennas and comm. systems. Home: 58 Wild Rose Dr Andover MA 01810-4620 *Intense dedication to physics and engineering with constant desire for understanding and intellectual honesty, plus the enjoyment of working with others, have been my guiding principles.*

JAKOBE, VIRGINIA ELLIS, retired educator; b. Molino, Mo., Sept. 10, 1922; d. Clyde William and Lucy (Baker) Ellis; m. Henry George Jakobe Sr., Feb. 23, 1963; 1 child, Henry George. BS, NE Mo. State U., 1946; MA, Columbia U., 1960. Cert. elem. art tchr., Mo., N.Y. Tchr. Ellis Sch., Molino, 1941-43; tchr. art and English Marceline Sch., Mo., 1943-44; remedial tchr. Berkley Sch., Mo., 1944-46; tchr. elem. art Maplewood Sch., Mo., 1946-54, Univ. City Schs., Mo., 1954-63, Saranac Lake (N.Y.) Cent. Schs., 1970-90. Editor Show Me Art, 1962-64; originator The Children's Art Exhibit Saranac Lake Cen. Sch., 1970—. Pres. Saranac Lake/N.Y. PTA., 1968-69, St. Louis County Art Tchrs. Assn., 1954-55. Mem. N.Y. State Art Tchrs. Assn., Paint and Palette Artists Assn., Delta Kappa Gamma (sec.). Republican. Episcopalian. Home: 12 Rockledge Rd Saranac Lake NY 12983-1928

JAKOPAC-MILLER, KIM ANN, mental health nurse; b. North Tonawanda, N.Y., Oct. 23, 1957; d. John Walter and Helen May (Hartman) Jakopac; children: Katherine Rose Miller. ASN, Clarion U. Pa., 1990, BSN, 1993; MSN, NP, U. Pitts., 1999. RN, Pa.; cert. mental health nursing ANCC. Mental health nurse child-adolescent unit Clarion (Pa.) Psychiat. Ctr., 1990-91, St. Vincent Health Ctr., Erie, Pa., 1991-93, Braddock (Pa.) Med. Ctr., 1993-95; staff nurse Ctr. for Treatment of Addictive Disorders and acute psychiat. unit VA Med. Ctr., Pitts., 1995-96, nursing supr. acute med. ctr., 1996—. Co-author: Potential for General Systems, 1993. Mem. Hillcrest United Presbyn. Ch., Monroeville, Pa., 1994; participant Crop Walk For Second Harvest Greater Pitts. Cmty. Food Bank. Mem. Phi Eta Sigma, Phi Theta Kappa, Sigma Theta Tau. Democrat. Presbyterian. Avocations: music, art, politics, social reform, psychology. Home: 5562 Hobart St Apt 509 Pittsburgh PA 15217 Office: VA Med Ctr University Dr Pittsburgh PA 15240

JAKSA, DAVID M., wireless network company official; b. Oct. 14, 1946. BSEE, Rose Hulman Inst. Tech., 1968; MBA, U. Iowa, 1982. Mgr. gen. comm. bus. Rockwell Internat., Cedar Rapids, Iowa, 1976-87; dir. satellite bus. Rockwell Internat., Richardson, Tex., Santa Ana, Calif., 1987-91; dir. bus. devel. Rockwell Internat., Richardson, 1991-98; gen. mgr. MMDS, Nortel Networks, Dallas, 1998—. E-mail:djaksa@nortelnetworks.com. Home: 626 Torrey Pines Ln Garland TX 75044-4112 Office: Nortel Networks 19111 N Dallas Pky Ste 200 Dallas TX 75287

JAKSTAS, ALFRED JOHN, museum conservator, consultant; b. Boston, Oct. 30, 1916; s. Walter John and Julia (Barkevich) J.; m. Valerie Jevaraus, Oct. 11, 1942; children: Janet, Julianne. AB, Harvard U., 1938. Teaching fellow Harvard U., 1943-44; conservator Isabella Stewart Gardner Mus., 1943-61; conservator paintings Art Inst. Chgo., 1961-81; lectr., cons., 1981—; Cons. conservation Currier Gallery Art, Mus. Art, R.I. Sch. Design, Wadsworth Atheneum, Springfield Mus. Fine Arts, Notre Dame Gallery, various colls. Recipient IAFA award for outstanding achievement in conservation, 1992-93. Fellow Internat. Inst. Conservation Mus. Objects. Home: 10737 W Welk Dr Sun City AZ 85373-1840 Office: Art Inst Chgo Chicago IL 60603 *The spirit of man must be preserved, as individual bodies pass away.*

JAKUB, PAULA SUE, association administrator; b. Omaha, Nov. 3, 1957; d. Arthur Coulter and Anne Edith (Kabbert) Roxlau; m. Michael Andrew Jakub; children: Neil, Elizabeth. Registered health underwriter. Customer svc. supr. Mut. of Omaha Ins. Co., Omaha, 1978-88; v.p. Am. Fgn. Svcs. Protective Assn., Washington, 1988-90; bd. dirs. Nat. Assn. for Sr. Living Industries, Annapolis. Leader Girl Scouts USA, Washington, 1987-93; bd. dirs. PTO, Dale City, Va., 1991-93, Prince William Softball Assn., Dale City, 1991-96. Mem. Nat. Assn. Health Underwriters. Avocations: reading, interior decorating, sports, crafts, sewing. Home: 6385 Cherry Ridge Ct Manassas VA 20112-3859

JAKUBAUSKAS, EDWARD BENEDICT, college president; b. Waterbury, Conn., Apr. 14, 1930; s. Constantine and Barbara (Narstis) J.; m. Ruth Friz, Aug. 29, 1959; children—Carol, Marilyn, Mark, Eric. B.A., U. Conn., 1952, M.A., 1954; Ph.D., U. Wis., 1961. Economist FPC, 1956, Dept. Labor, 1956-58; instr. U. Wis., 1961-62, asst. prof. econs., 1962-63; asst. prof. Iowa State U., 1963-65, assoc. prof., 1965-66, prof., 1966-71; dean U. Wyo., 1971-76, prof. econs., 1971-79, v.p. acad. affairs, 1976-79; pres. SUNY, Geneseo, 1979-88, Cen. Mich. U., Mt. Pleasant, 1988-92; cons. in higher edn., 1992—. Author: Manpower Economics, 1971. Served with U.S. Army, 1954-56. Mem. Am. Assn. State Univs. and Colls. Mem. United Chs. of Christ.

JAKUBEK, HELEN MAJERCZYK, retired secondary school educator; b. Chgo., Sept. 27, 1931; d. Adolph and Josephine (Majka) Majerczyk; m. Martin F. Jakubek, July 7, 1951; children: Martin M., David R., Mary Ellen, James E. BS in Edn., DeLourdes Coll., 1982; postgrad., U. Ill., Chgo. Cert. K-9 tchr., Ill. Sec. Cmty. Consol. Sch. Dist. 59, Arlington Heights, Ill., 1974-81; tchr. Grove Jr. H.S., Elk Grove Village, Ill., 1982-94. Mem. com. Student at Risk; peer tutoring advisor. Recipient U.S. Tchr. to Japan honor. Mem. Nat. Coun. Tchrs. of English, Phi Delta Kappa. Home: 950 Horne Ter Des Plaines IL 60016-5969

JAKUBOWSKI, THAD J., bishop. Ordained priest Roman Cath. Ch., 1950, bishop, 1988. Apptd. aux. bishop Roman Cath. Ch., Chgo., 1988—; apptd. titular bishop Plestia Roman Cath. Ch., 1988—, consecrated, 1988—. Address: 6002 W Berteau Ave Chicago IL 60634-1630

JALALI, BEHNAZ, psychiatrist, educator; b. Mashad, Iran, Jan. 26, 1944; came to U.S., 1968; d. Badiolah and Bahieh (Shahidi) Samimy; m. Mehrdad Jalali, Sept. 18, 1968. MD, Tehran (Iran) U., 1968. Rotating intern Burlington County Meml. Hosp., Mt. Holly, N.J., 1968-69; resident in psychiatry U. Md. Hosp., Balt., 1970-73; asst. prof. psychiatry dept. psychiatry Sch. Medicine Rutgers U., Piscataway, N.J., 1973-76, Yale U., New Haven, Conn., 1976-81; assoc. clin. prof. psychiatry Yale U., New Haven, 1981-85; assoc. clin. prof. psychiatry dept. psychiatry UCLA, 1985-94, clin. prof. psychiatry dept. psychiatry Sch. Medicine, 1994—; dir. psychotherapy Sch. Medicine Rutgers U., Piscataway, 1973-76; dir. family therapy unit dept. psychiatry Yale U., New Haven, 1976-85; mental health clin. coord., 1987-96, chief clin. svcs., med. student educator West L.A. VA Hosp., 1987—; dir. family therapy clinic W.Va. VA Hosp., 1991—. Author: (with others) Ethnicity and Family Therapy, 1982, Clinical Guidlines in Cross-Cultural Mental Health, 1988; contbr. articles to profl. jours. Fellow Am. Psychiatric Assn., Am. Orthopsychiatry Assn., Am. Assn. Social Psychiatry; mem. Am. Family Therapy Assn., So. Calif. Psychiatric Assn. (chair com. for women 1992), World Fedn. Mental Health. Avocations: photography, hiking, cinema, painting. Home: 1203 Roberto Ln Los Angeles CA 90077-2304 Office: UCLA Dept Psychiatry West LA VA Med Ctr B116a12 Los Angeles CA 90073-1003

JALILI, MAHIR, lawyer; b. Mosul, Iraq, Nov. 22, 1944; s. Ahmad and Khadija Jalili. BS, Leeds U., 1967; MEng., Colo. Sch. Mines, 1971; JD, Loyola U.-Chgo., 1976. Bar: Ill. 1977, Calif. 1993, Colo. 1994. Assoc. Kenyon & Kenyon, N.Y.C., 1977, Graham & James, London, 1977-83; ptnr. Whitman & Ransom, London, 1983-92; counsel Whitman Breed Abbott & Morgan, L.A., 1993-94; English solicitor, 1997. Office: 211 Piccadilly, London WIV-9LD, England

JALLINS, RICHARD DAVID, lawyer; b. L.A., Mar. 21, 1957; s. Walter Joshua and Elaine Beatrice (Youngerman) J.; m. Katherine Sue Pfeiffer, June 12, 1982; children: Stephen David, Rachel Marie. BA, U. Calif., Santa Barbara, 1978; JD, Calif. Western Sch. Law, 1981. Bar: Calif. 1988, U.S. Dist. Ct. (so. dist.) Calif. 1988. Panel atty. Bd. Prison Terms, Sacramento, 1989-96, Appellate Defenders, Inc., San Diego, 1989-91, Calif. Dept. Corrections, Parole Hearings Divsn., Sacramento, 1992-94; dep. commr. Bd. Prison Terms, 1996—. Mem. ABA, San Diego County Bar Assn., Phi Alpha Delta.

JALURIA, YOGESH, mechanical engineering educator; b. Nabha, Punjab, India, Sept. 8, 1949; came to U.S., 1970; s. Jagdishwar and Maya (Verma) J.; m. Anuradha Malhotra, Sept. 9, 1975; children: Pratik, Aseem, Ankur. BS, Indian Inst. Tech., Delhi, 1970; MS, Cornell U., 1972, PhD, 1974. Mem. tech. staff Bell Labs., Princeton, N.J., 1974-76; asst. prof. Indian Inst. Tech., Kanpur, 1976-80; asst. prof. Rutgers U., New Brunswick, N.J., 1980-82, assoc. prof., 1982-85, prof. of mech. engring., 1985-91, prof. II, disting. prof., 1991—; cons. David Sarnoff Lab., SRI, Princeton, 1989-90, Steel Authority, Ranchi, India, 1977-80, others; mem. initiation grants rev. panel, 1987, 90, 93-95, other panels, 1996-98; NSF vis. scientist Indian Inst. Tech., 1988-89; lectr. in field; participant workshop on natural convection NSF, Colo., 1982, Indo-Australian Solar Energy Workshop, New Delhi, 1978, others; assoc. tech. editor J. Heat Transfer, 1993-99; mng. editor Computational Mechanics, 1994—; spkr. in field. Author (with others): Natural Convection Heat and Mass Transfer, 1980, Computational Heat Transfer, 1986, Buoyancy Induced Flows, 1988, (with others) Computer Methods for Engineering, 1988, Design and Optimization of Thermal Systems, 1998, (book chpts.) Natural Convection, 1985, Handbook of Single-Phase Convective Heat Transfer, 1987, Energy Storage Systems, 1989, Handbook of Fire Protection, 1995, numerous others; contbr. numerous articles and papers to profl. jours. and confs. including Rev. Sci. Instrum., Jour. Heat Transfer, Jour. Thermophysics Heat Transfer, Numerical Heat Transfer, Jour. Fluid Mech., Jour. Numerical Meth. Engring.; mem. numerous editorial bds. including mem. editorial adv. bd. Numerical Heat Transfer, 1987—; mem. editorial bd. Internat. Jour. Numerical Meth. Heat and Flow, 1990—; reviewer including Applied Mechanics Rev., Jour. Fluid Mechanics, Jour. Heat Transfer, Jour. Solar Energy Engring.; referee numerous articles. NATO Disting. lectr., 1984, 88; recipient cert. of recognition Dept. of Commerce, 1982, Disting. Alumnus award IIT, 1994. Fellow ASME (chmn. nat. heat transfer conf., coord. com. 1991-92, exec. com. heat transfer divsn. 1998—, Heat Transfer Mem. award 1995, Worcester Reed Warner medal 1999), Am. Phys. Soc., Combustion Inst., India Assn. of East Brunswick (pres. 1985, 91, 94-96), Cornell India Assn. (v.p. 1972-73). Democrat. Hindu. Achievements include patents for Methods and apparatus for heating articles, for Methods and apparatus for avoiding undesirable deposits in crystal growing operations; copyrighted computer software in materials processing and electronics cooling; research in thermal processing of materials, fires, computational heat transfer, natural convection, cooling of electronic equipment and environmental flows, flows rising above finite heated bodies, interaction of buoyant flows with surfaces, buoyant jet flows, mixed convection in enclosures, heat removal from heated elements on a vertical surface, thermal stratification and heat rejection problems, solar energy storage in salt-gradient solar ponds, numerical and experimental simulation of thermal processes in manufacturing systems, computer aided design of thermal systems, knowledge based design methodology, and enclosure fire growth processes. Office: Rutgers U Mech Engring Dept New Brunswick NJ 08901

JAMAIL, JOSEPH DAHR, JR., lawyer; b. Houston, Oct. 19, 1925; s. Joseph Dahr and Marie (Anton) J.; m. Lillie Mae Hage, Aug. 28, 1949; children: Joseph Dahr III, Randall Hage, Robert Lee. B.A., U. Tex., 1950, J.D., 1953. Bar: Tex. 1952. Asst. dist. atty. Harris County, Tex., 1954-55; sole propr. Jamail & Kolius, Houston; prof. tort law U. Tex., 1981. Contbr. articles to profl. jours. Served to sgt. USMCR, 1943-46. Named one of top 25 philanthropists in U.S., 1996; U. Tex. Sch. Law designated Jessie Jones Hall as The Joseph D. Jamail Ctr. for Legal Rsch., U. Tex. Sch. of Law created The Joseph D. Jamail Centennial chair in law and advocacy. Fellow Internat. Acad. Law and Sci., Internat. Soc. Barristers, Internat. Acad. Trial Lawyers, Am. Coll. Trial Lawyers, Inner Circle of Advocates; mem. Am., Houston bar assns., Houston Jr. Bar (dir. 1954-55, treas. 1955-56, v.p. 1956-57, pres. 1957-58), State Bar Tex. (chmn. grievance com. 1963, chmn. town hall task force 1973-74), Assn. Trial Lawyers Am., Am. Judicature Soc., Am. Bd. Trial Advocates, Lawyer-Pilot Bar Assn., Delta Theta Phi. Home: 3682 Willowick Rd Houston TX 77019-1114 Office: Jamail & Kolius 500 Dallas St Ste 3434 Houston TX 77002-4802*

JAMAL, MOEZ AHAMED, banker; b. Mombasa, Kenya, June 15, 1955; s. Ahamed and Shamsultan (Kalyan); m. Nadia Eboo, June 23, 1979; children: Nijhad, Shazia. BA in Econs. with honors, Manchester U., 1976; MBA, NYU, 1979. 1st v.p. Lloyds Bank, N.Y., 1979-85; v.p. Credit Suisse, London, 1985-93; treas. Credit Suisse, N.Y.C., 1993-96; mng. dir., golbal head money markets/funding Credit Suisse First Boston, N.Y.C., 1997—. Mem. R.A.C. Club, Overseas Bankers Club, City Swiss Club. Moslem. Home: 33 High Farms Rd Glen Head NY 11545-2222

JAMAR, STEVEN DWIGHT, law educator; b. Ishpeming, Mich., May 11, 1953; s. Dwight W. and Lorraine (Persgard) J.; m. Shelley June Von Hagen-Jamar, May 19, 1979; children: Alexander S., Eric D. BA, Carleton Coll., 1975; JD cum laude, Hamline U., 1979; LLM with distinction, Georgetown U., 1994. Bar: Minn. 1979, D.C. 1993, U.S. Supreme Ct. 1985. Jud. clk. Minn. Supreme Ct., St. Paul, 1979-80; assoc. Meagher & Geer, Mpls., 1980-86; clin. instr. William Mitchell Coll. of Law, St. Paul, 1987-89; pvt. practice Mpls., 1987-89; vis. asst. prof. law U. Balt., 1989-90; asst. prof. law Sch. Law Howard U., Washington, 1991-94, assoc. prof. law, 1994-96, prof. law, 1996—, dir. legal rsch. and writing program, 1990—; cons. on environ. legal info. sys. project NASA, 1998—. Co-author: Essential Lawyering Skills: Interviewing, Counseling, Negotiation, and Persuasive Fact Analysis, 1999; contbr. articles to profl. jours. Bd. dirs. Legal Advice Clinics, Hennepin County, Mpls., 1980-89, mem. exec. com., 1986-89, sec.-treas., 1988-89; coach Soccer Assn. Columbia, 1991-96. Mem. Legal Writing Inst., 1990— (exec com., 1994-98, pres., 1997-98), ABA, ACLU, Am. Soc. Internat. Law, Amnesty Internat., Computer Law Assn., Assn. Legal Writing Dirs. (bd. dirs., exec. com. 1996-97), Sierra Club, Howard County Go Club. Avocations: canoe camping, soccer, go. Office: Howard U Sch Law 2900 Van Ness St NW Washington DC 20008-1106

JAMBOR, ROBERT VERNON, lawyer; b. Chgo., Aug. 29, 1936; s. Vernon C. and Anne M. (Kohout) J.; m. Arlene M. Gale, Nov. 9, 1957 (dec. Aug. 1993); children: Robyn, Cheryl, Steven; m. Terri J. Skyrme, Jan. 11, 1995. B.M.E., Gen. Motors Inst., Flint, Mich., 1958; J.D., John Marshall Law Sch., Chgo., 1963. Bar: Ill. 1963, U.S. Dist. Ct. Ill. 1963, U.S. Ct. Appeals (7th cir.) 1974, U.S. Ct. Appeals (fed. cir.) 1982, U.S. Supreme Ct. 1983. Product engr. product devel. Electro-Motive div. Gen. Motors Corp., La Grange, Ill., 1958-63; asso. firm Marks & Clerk, Chgo., 1961-63; patent atty. Borg-Warner Corp., Chgo., 1964-69; ptnr. Haight, Hofeldt, Davis & Jambor, Chgo., 1970-87, Dorn, McEachran, Jambor & Keating, Chgo., 1987—; instr. John Marshall Law Sch., 1963-73; arbitrator Am. Arbitration Assn., 1987—. Mem. ABA, Ill. Bar Assn., 7th Cir. Bar Assn., Fed. Cir. Bar Assn., Am. Intellectual Property Law Assn., Intellectual Property Law Assn. Chgo., Internat. Property Owners. E-mail: rjambor@genevaonline. Home: 1173 Terrace Ct Lake Geneva WI 53147-5027 Office: Dorn McEachran Jambor & Keating 55 E Monroe St Ste 2940 Chicago IL 60603-5709

JAMERSON, PATRICIA ANN LOCANDRO, pediatrics nurse, nursing educator; b. East St. Louis, Ill., Dec. 22, 1956; d. Joseph Frank and Theresa (Zavaglia) Locandro; m. William Ross; children: Kyle Andrew, Kirstin Janelle. BSN, U. Ill., Chgo., 1979; MS in Nursing, St. Louis U., 1985; PhD in Nursing, U. Kans., 1998. Cert. Nat. Faculty, AHA-AAP Neonatal Resuscitation, neonatal intensive care nurse, childbirth instr., breastfeeding educator. Med.-surg. staff nurse Mercy Hosp., Urbana, Ill., 1979; staff nurse neonatal ICU, Carle Found. Hosp., Urbana, Ill., 1979-81; staff nurse ICU, Oliver C. Anderson Hosp, Maryville, Ill., 1981; staff nurse neonatal ICU Cardinal Glennon Hosp. for Children, St. Louis, 1981-83, cardiology nurse, 1983-84; chief nurse pediatrics/family practice City of Faith Med. and Rsch. Ctr., Tulsa, 1985-86; outreach coord. St. Francis Hosp., Tulsa, 1986-91; instr., nursing U. Tulsa, 1991-93; asst. prof. Williams Jewell Coll., Liberty, Mo., 1993-94; rsch. asst., tchg. assoc. U. Kans., Kansas City, 1993-95; asst. prof. Avila Coll., Kansas City, Mo., 1995-98; assoc. prof. S.D. State U., 1998—. Contbg. author: Comprehensive Child and Family Nursing Skills, 1991, Nursing Care of Clients with Substance Abuse, 1995, Effective Leadership and Management in Nursing, 1996; editor: Self-Taught Educational Perinatal Program; reviewer Jour. Obstetric, Gynecologic and Neonatal Nursing, 1993, 97, mem. editl. bd., 1995-96. Chair program svcs. com. Greater Kansas City chpt. March of Dimes, 1997-98. Mem. Assn. Women's Health, Obstet. and Neonatal Nursing, Midwest Nursing Rsch. Soc., Sigma Theta Tau. Office: South Dakota State U Box 2275 Brookings SD 57007-0098

JAMES, ALLIX BLEDSOE, retired university president; b. Marshall, Tex., Dec. 17, 1922; s. Samuel Horace and Tannie Etta (Judkins) J.; m. Sue Nickens, Feb. 14, 1945; children: Alvan Bosworth, Portia Veann. AB, Va. Union U., 1944, MDiv, 1946; ThM, Union Theol. Sem. Va., 1949, ThD, 1957; postgrad., Boston U., summer 1951, Pa. State U., summer 1957; LLD, U. Richmond, 1970; DD, St. Paul's Coll., 1980. Ordained to ministry Bapt. Ch., 1942; moderator No. Neck Bapt. Assn., 1950-52; minister Union Zion Bapt. Ch., Gloucester, Va., 1944-53, Mt. Zion Bapt. Ch., Downings, Va., 1945-57, 3d Union Bapt. Ch., King William, Va., 1953-70; dean students Va. Union U., Richmond, 1950-57, dean Sch. Theology, 1957-70, Henderson-Griffith prof. pastoral theology, v.p., 1960-70, pres., 1970-79, pres. emeritus, 1979-85, 93—, chancellor, 1985-93. Author: Calling a Pastor in a Baptist Church, Threescore and Ten Plus—The Pilgrimage of an African-American Educator, 1922-1997; Contbg. editor: The Continuing Quest, 1970. Chmn. Richmond City Planning Commn., 1969-75; dir. Va. Electric and Power Co., Dominion Resources, Inc., Consol Bank and Trust Co.; mem. Commn. on Ch. Family Fin. Planning; mem. scholarship selection com. Philip Morris, Inc.; mem. Mayor's Commn. on Human Rels., 1963-65; pres. Norrell Sch. PTA, 1963-65; mem. exec. com. Ctrl. Va. Ednl. TV; mem. Richmond Independence Bicentennial Commn., Richmond Downtown Econ. and Devel. Commn.; co-chmn. Northside Cmty. Assn., 1964-68; chmn. Univ. Ctr. in Va.; mem. State Bd. Edn. Va., 1975-85, pres., 1980-82; bd. dirs. NCCJ, Va. Inst. Pastoral Care, Task Force for Renewal Urban Strategy and Tng., Richmond chpt. ARC, 1974-75, Better Richmond, Inc., Richmond Downtown Devel. Unltd., Am. Coun. on Edn., 1970-72, Richmond Renaissance, Inc., Met. Richmond Leadership; mem. adv. bd. Inst. for Bus. and Cmty. Devel., U. Richmond; bd. fellows Interpreters House, Lake Janaluska, N.C.; trustee Richmond Meml. Hosp., Nat. Assn. for Equal Opportunity in Edn., v.p.; pres. Richmond Gold Bowl Sponsors, Inc., Nat. Conf. Richmond and Jews, Inc., 1987-90; nat. co-chair Nat. Conf. Christians and Jews, 1994. Recipient Disting. Svc. award Links, Inc., 1971, ednl. achievement award 1985, Good Govt. award Richmond First Club, 1985, Brotherhood award NCCJ, 1975, Mozelle E. Manuel Outstanding Svc. award Met. Bus. League, 1991, Outstanding Leadership award Va. Legislature Black Caucus, 1991, Exemplary Vision award Fullwood Foods, Inc., Balt., 1992, Flame Bearers Edn. award United Negro Coll. Fund, 1997; named Citizen of Yr., Astoria Beneficial Club, 1971, Omega Psi Phi, 1972; Univ. chapel named Allix B. James Chapel in his honor, 1992. Mem. Clergy Assn. Richmond Area (pres.), Am. Assn. Theol. Schs. (pres. 1970-72), Am. Bapt. Conv. (pres. coun. on theol. edn. 1969-72), Bapt. Gen. Conv. VA. (exec. bd.), Soc. for Advancement Continuing Edn. for Mins. (exec. bd.), Greater Richmond C. of C. (bd. dirs.), Alpha Kappa Mu, Alpha Phi Alpha (achievement award 1981, 85). Club: Kiwanis (honoree Richmond area Appreciation Dinner 1993). Office: Va Union U 1500 N Lombardy St Richmond VA 23220-1784

JAMES, BARBARA FRANCES, school nurse, special education educator; b. Elizabeth, N.J., June 29, 1941; d. Edward Joseph and Frances Veronica (Szypula) Turkiewicz; 1 child, John Wayne James. Certificate in group tchg., Kean Coll., 1981; diploma, Elizabeth Gen. Sch. Nursing, 1962; BS magna cum laude, Jersey City State Coll., 1994. Cert. tchr. health edn., cert. sch. nurse, cert. infant specialist, cert. family svc. provider trainer, N.J.; RN, N.J. Oper. room nurse Alexian Bros. Hosp., Elizabeth, 1962-63; obstetrical nurse Rahway (N.J.) Hosp., 1964-65; pvt. duty nurse Alexian Bros., St. Elizabeth and Elizabeth Gen. Hosps., 1964-65; office nurse Stephan S. Halabis, MD, Linden, N.J., 1965-71; tchr. developmentally disabled Assn. for Retarded Citizens, Winfield, N.J., 1971-76; early intervention tchr., home trainer The Arc of Union County/Kohler Child Devel. Ctr., Winfield, 1976—; sch. nurse Kohler Child Dev. Ctr., Winfield, N.J., 1976—; guest lectr. developmental disabilities Kean Coll., Middlesex County Coll., Rutgers U., Jersey City State Coll., Fla. Atlantic U., Union Coll., 1980-92; mem. pres. com. on mental retardation U.S. Dept. Health and Human Svcs., N.J. State Nurses Assn., Elizabeth Pub. Schs. One-woman shows include Elizabeth Gen. Med. Ctr., 1984; exhibited in group shows at N.J. State Mus., Trenton, 1959, Elizabeth Gen. Med. Ctr., 1960-62, Found. Arts and Scis., Long Beach Island, 1981, Kean Coll., Union, N.J., 1981, Woodbridge Mall, 1981; author, illustrator (booklet) Recognizing Childhood Illness, 1973. Mem. legis. com. Union County Protection Coun., Elizabeth, 1975; mem. supervisory com. Winfield Fed. Credit Union, 1977; active Dem. com. Twp. of Winfield, 1978, mem. drug alliance coun., 1990; active local, county and state health fairs. Recipient Health Fair Pub. Svc. award State of N.J., Rutgers U., 1986; Garwood (N.J.) Women's Club scholar, 1959; named Teacher of the Year ARC of Union County, 1981. Mem. Coun. for Exceptional Children, League for Ednl. Advancement of Nurses. Avocation: fine arts painting. Home: 66B Wavecrest Ave Winfield Park NJ 07036-6633 Office: The Arc of Union County Kohler Child Devel Ctr 39 1/2 Wavecrest Ave Winfield Park NJ 07036-6630

JAMES, BRIAN ROBERT, chemistry educator; b. Birmingham, Eng., Apr. 21, 1936; emigrated to Can., 1964, naturalized, 1974; s. Herbert Arthur and Frances Vera (Stride) J.; m. Mary Jane Thompson, Oct. 6, 1962; children: Jennifer Ann, Peter Edward, Sarah Elizabeth, Andrew Francis. B.A., Oxford (Eng.) U., 1958, M.A., 1960, D.Phil., 1960. Research fellow U. B.C., Vancouver, 1960-62; mem. faculty U. B.C., 1964—, prof. chemistry, 1974—; sr. sci. officer U.K. Atomic Energy Authority, Harwell, Eng., 1962-64; NATO Summer Sch. lectr., 1974; mem. catalysis Study group NATO, 1972; mem. chemistry grants com. NRC Can., 1973-77; grad. rsch. fellowships com. Internat. Nickel Co., 1974-77; mem. Can. Nat. Com. IUPAC, 1984-87; cons. in field. Author: Homogeneous Hydrogenation, 1973; editor: Catalysis by Metal Complexes, 17 vols., 1976-95, Biological Aspects of Inorganic Chemistry, 1977; editor Can. Jour. Chemistry, 1978-88; mem. editorial bd. profl. jours.; contbr. 310 articles to profl. jours. Recipient Jacob Biely rsch. prize, 1986, Killam rsch. prize U. B.C., 1988; bursarship Royal Soc. London, 1970; rsch. grantee NRC Can., 1964—, NATO, 1976-78, 82-84, Union Carbide, 1984-86, Battelle, 1984-86, Air Products, 1998—; Guggenheim fellow, 1983, Sr. Killam fellow, 1983, 90, Can. Coun. Killam fellow, 1993-95, Japan Soc. Promotion of Sci. fellow, 1995. Fellow Chem. Soc. London, Royal Soc. Can. (rapporteur 1986, convener 1987), Chem. Inst. Can. (Noranda lectr. 1975, catalysis award 1990, CIC medal 2000); mem. Am. Chem. Soc., N.Y. Acad. Scis., Can. Catalysis Soc. (vice chmn. 1985), Royal Soc. Chem. (award for chemistry of noble metals 1996, E.W.R. Steacie award 1997), Wadham Coll. Soc., Organic Reactions Catalysis Soc. (bd. dirs. 1994—). Home: 4010 Blenheim St, Vancouver, BC Canada V6L 2Y9 Office: U BC, Dept Chemistry, Vancouver, BC Canada V6T 1Z1

JAMES, BRUCE ALLAN, radio station owner, general manager; b. St. Johnsbury, Vt., Sept. 20, 1949; s. Horace Darius and Pauline (Fitch) J.; m. Nancy Leigh Roberts, May 17, 1968; children: Suzanne, Aaren. Student, Lyndon State Coll., 1968-71. Mgr. Music Unltd., Lyndonville, Vt., 1969-74; sr. exec. E.M.A. Agy., Claremont, N.H., 1974-79; pres. Bruce James Co., Lyndonville, Vt., 1979-88; mgr. Lyndonville Printing, 1988-90; owner, mgr. WGMT-FM, Lyndonville, Vt., 1990—, WKXH-FM, St. Johnsbury, Vt., 1998—, WSTJ-AM, St. Johnsbury, 1998—. Adv. bd. Vt. State Mountain Tops Com., Dept. Forest and Parks, Waterbury, 1992-94, mem. planning commn. Town of Lyndon, 1981-83; mem. Town of Lyndon Selectmen, 1986—, chmn., 1989, 91, 92, 94, 97; pres. Stars and Stripes Festival, 1993, 94, 95, 96, 97, 98, 99; commr. N.E. Vt. Baseball, 1999—. Named Commr. of Yr., Babe Ruth Baseball, Vt., 1986, Championship Umpire, Vt. Headmasters, 1990, 92, 93, 94, 95, 96, 97, 98, 99. Mem. Lyndonville Rotary Club (pres. 1989-90), No. Vt. Baseball Umpires (interpretor 1992-95, pres. 1996-98), Vt. Assn. Broadcasters (sec. 1995-97, pres. 1997-99), Vt. Baseball Umpires Assn. (pres. 1999—), Internat. Assn. Approved Basketball Officials, Lyndon C. of C. (pres. 1985-90, hon. lifetime dir. 1992). Avocations: baseball and basketball sports official, photography. Home: PO Box 1387 Lyndonville VT 05851-1387 Office: WGMT-FM PO Box 97 Lyndonville VT 05851-0983

JAMES, CHARLES CLINTON, science education educator, consultant; b. Washington, Nov. 11, 1957; s. Charles Clinton and Harriet Fae (Bempkins) J.; m. Mary Beth Cline; children: Clinton Carty, Mariah Fae. MS in Geology, George Mason U., 1984, EdM, 1986. Chair sci. dept., dir. summer programs St. Patricks Episcopal Sch., Washington, 1982-93; dir. Carnegie Acad. Sci. Edn., Carnegie Instn. Washington, 1993—; edn. and pub. outreach NASA Astrobiology Inst., 1999—; trustee Discovery Creek Childrens Mus., Washington, 1994—. Author: Exploring Together, 1994, Design Connections, 1995. Dir. First Light, Washington, 1989—. Recipient Presdl. Sci. Tchg. award Nat. Sci. Tchrs. Assn., 1991, 94. Episcopalian. Avocations: photography, scuba diving. Office: Carnegie Inst Washington 1530 P St NW Washington DC 20005-1933

JAMES, CHARLES E., JR., lawyer; b. Pontiac, Mich., Sept. 19, 1948. BA, Occidental Coll., 1970; JD with highest distinction, U. Ariz. Bar: Ariz. 1973. Ptnr. Snell & Wilmer, Phoenix, 1990. Mem. ABA, Nat. Assn. Bond Lawyers. Office: Snell & Wilmer 1 Arizona Ctr 400 E Van Buren Phoenix AZ 85004-0001

JAMES, CHARLES FRANKLIN, JR., engineering educator; b. Des Arc, Mo., July 16, 1931; s. Charles Franklin and Beulah Frances (Kyte) J.; m. Mollie Keeler, May 18, 1974; children: Thomas Elisha, Matthew Jeremiah. B.S., Purdue U., 1958, M.S., 1960, Ph.D., 1963. Registered profl. engr., Wis. Sr. indsl. engr. McDonnel Aircraft Co., 1963; asst. prof. U. R.I., 1963-66, prof., chmn. dept. indsl. engring., 1967-82, co-founder, mem Robotics Rsch. Ctr., 1980-83; C. Paul Stocker prof. engring. Ohio U., Athens, 1982-83; dean Coll. Engring. and Applied Sci., U. Wis.-Milw., 1984-95; v.p. academics Milw. Sch. of Engring., 1995—; cons. Asian Productivity Orgn.; arbitrator Fed. Mediation and Conciliation Service, Am. Arbitration Assn.; bd. dirs. Badger Meter Co., Milw. Contbr. articles to profl. jours. With USAF, 1951-55. Recipient Silver medal Tech. U. Budapest, Hungary, 1989. Mem. NSPE, ASME, Wis. Soc. Profl. Engrs. (pres. Milw. chpt. 1993-94, Outstanding Profl. Engr. in Edn. 1993, state-wide treas. 1994-96), Inst. Indsl. Engrs., Am. Soc. Engring. Edn., Soc. Mfg. Engrs., Am. Foundrymen's Soc., Engrs. and Scis. of Milw. (bd. dirs. 1988-95, v.p. 1991-93, pres.-elect 1993-94, pres. 1994-95). Office: Milw Sch of Engring 1025 N Broadway Milwaukee WI 53202-3109

JAMES, CLARITY (CAROLYNE FAYE JAMES), mezzo-soprano; b. Wheatland, Wyo., Apr. 27, 1945; d. Ralph Everett and Gladys Charlotte (Johnson) J. Mus.B., U. Wyo., 1964; Mus.M., Ind. U., 1967. Cert. instr. Radiance Technique. Assoc. prof. voice Radford (Va.) U., 1990—; asst. prof. voice U. Iowa, Iowa City, 1968-72. Debut in opera as Madame Flora in: The Medium, St. Paul Opera, 1971; also sang role with Houston Grand Opera, 1972, Opera Theatre St. Louis, 1976, Augusta (Ga.) Opera Co., 1976; N.Y.C. Opera debut as Baroness in: The Young Lord, 1973; N.Y.C. Opera debut as Widow Begbick in Mahogonny, Opera Co. of Boston, 1973; created role Mother Rainey in: The Sweet Bye and Bye, 1973; Mrs. G. in: Captain Jinks, 1976; Mrs. Cratchit in A Christmas Carol (Musgrave), 1979; created Mrs. Doc in world premiere of A Quiet Place (Leonard Bernstein), Houston, 1983; debut Chgo. Lyric Opera, 1983, Vienna Staatsoper, 1986, National Symphony, 1986, Phila. Orch., 1986; numerous appearances with opera cos. throughout U.S. and fgn. countries including, Dallas Civic Opera, Cin. Opera Co., Netherlands Opera, Amsterdam, Florentine Opera. Rec. artist. Martha Baird Rockefeller grantee, Corbett Found. grantee, 1968; Met. Opera Assn. grantee; recipient Lillian Garabedian award Santa Fe Opera, 1967, Exemplary Alumni award U. Wyo., 1994; named Young Artist Nat. Fedn. Music Clubs, 1972. Office: Radford U Dept Music Radford VA 24142

JAMES, DANIEL J., management consultant; b. Nokomis, Ill., Mar. 21, 1920; s. Daniel and Katie (Lauer) J.; m. Ann Wilder, June 12, 1954; children—Karen Ann, Debra Kay. B.E., Eastern Ill. State U., 1942; M.S., U. Ill., 1946, Ph.D., 1952; Dr. Pedagogy (hon.), Eastern Ill. U., 1958. Chief prodn. scheduling Taylor Instrument Co., Rochester, N.Y., 1946-47; instr. Flint (Mich.) Jr. Coll., 1947-48; asst. prof. Central Mich. Coll., Mt. Pleasant, 1948-50; asst. prof. Atlanta div. U. Ga., 1952-54; prof. marketing U. Ark., Fayetteville, 1954-57; adviser to Govt. of Chile, FAO, UN, 1957-58; program officer AID (formerly ICA), Seoul, Korea, 1959-62; internat. economist Bur. Econ. Affairs, State Dept., 1963; officer in charge politico-econ. affairs Office Near East-South Asian Regional Affairs, 1963-64; econ.-sci. officer Am. Embassy, Taipei, Tawian, 1964-69; polit.-econ., econ.-comml. officer Am. Embassy, New Delhi, India, 1969-72; dep. dir., spl. projects officer Office of Security Assistance and Sales, Bur. Politico-Mil. Affairs, Dept. of State, 1972-78; fgn. policy adviser to comdr.-in-chief U.S. Army Europe and 7th Army, Heidelberg, Germany, 1978-79; internat. economist Office Internat. Security Ops., Bur. Politico-Mil. Affairs, Dept. State, Washington, 1979-80; v.p. Mgmt. Logistics Internat., Ltd., Arlington, Va., 1980-85, sr. assoc., 1986-88; pvt. mgmt. cons. McLean, Va., 1988—. Served to 1st lt. AUS, 1942-45. Home and Office: 723 Lawton St Mc Lean VA 22101-1511

JAMES, DAVID LEE, lawyer, international advisor, author; b. Chgo., Aug. 23, 1933; s. Roy L. and Ethel (Wells) J.; m. Sheila Feagley, May 26, 1962; children: Pamela, James, Winifred, Paul, Brian, Adam. A.B., Harvard U., 1955; J.D., U. Chgo., 1960; grad. exec. program, Stanford U., 1979. Bar: N.Y. 1961, N.J. 1967, Hawaii 1976, Ill. 1987. With various law firms N.Y.C., 1960-67; counsel and asst. gen. counsel, asst. sec. Texasgulf Inc., 1967-75; gen. counsel, sec. Dillingham Corp., Honolulu, 1975-77, v.p., gen. counsel, sec., 1977-84; v.p. legal affairs, sec. Dillingham Corp., San Francisco, 1984-85; asst. gen. counsel, asst. sec. Crown Zellerbach Corp., San Francisco, 1985-86; sr. ptnr., sr. corp. atty. Arnstein & Lehr, Chgo., 1987-90, of counsel, 1990-96; chmn. bus. programs East-West Ctr., Honolulu, 1990-92; chief of party and sr. law devel. advisor USAID and Govt. of Indonesia, Jakarta, Indonesia, 1992-93; pres. Bus. Strategies Internat., San Francisco, Calif., 1993—; hon. consul of Malaysia, Hawaii, 1977-84; adv. bd. Internat. and Comparative Law Ctr., Southwestern Legal Found., Dallas, 1976-91; adv. com. Law of Sea Inst., Honolulu, 1977-84; lectr. in law Stanford U. Sch. Law, 1996-98. Author: Doing Business in Asia, 1993, The Executive Guide to Asia-Pacific Communications, 1995; contbr. various articles on bus. and legal subjects. Bd. dirs. Chgo. Chamber Orch., 1988-90, pres. 1989-90, Jr. Achievement Hawaii, 1976-84, Hawaii Opera Theatre, 1981-84, Friends of East-West Ctr., 1982-84; mem. Morristown (N.J.) Bd. Edn., 1967-68. Served to lt. (j.g.) USNR, 1955-57. Mem. Outrigger Canoe Club (Honolulu), World Trade Club (San Francisco), Harvard Club (N.Y.C.). E-mail: bsicorp@ibm.net. Office: Bus Strategies Internat 44 Montgomery St Ste 500 San Francisco CA 94104-4607

JAMES, DOROTHY LOUISE KING, special education educator; b. Columbus, Miss., Jan. 1, 1952; d. T.B. and Dorothy (Lee) King; m. Willie Earl James, July 7, 1979, children: Ebun, Shantana, Leah, Trinita, Caleb. BS, Harris Stowe Coll., 1979; M in Spl. Edn., U. Mo., 1988; EdD in Guidance Counseling, Lael Coll. and Grad. Sch., 1998. Itinerant resource instr. Northwest High Sch., St. Louis, 1978-80; instr. learning disabilities Cleveland High Sch., St. Louis, 1980-84, Clinton Mid. Sch., St. Louis, 1984-91; resource tchr., unit leader A-team for alternative edn. Stevens Mid. Sch., St. Louis, 1992—; team leader, resource tchr., "A" team unit leader alternative edn. Stevens Mid. Sch. 1988—, Drug Free Schs. and Communities Program, 1993; counselor King-James Enterprises, St. Louis, 1988—, Student Response Team, St. Louis, 1988—. Editor (speech) Internat. Yr. of the Child, 1979 (Bravo award Youth Adv. Comsn. St. Louis County Youth Programs), Clinton Middle School Student Handbook, 1989, team leader Drug Free Schools Community Program. Youth adv. mem. Conflict Mediation, 1992-96; mem. support coun. Stevens Mid. Sch., 1992-96; active New Ebenezer Bapt. Ch. Recipient Excellence in Drug Prevention award U.S. Dept. Edn., 1994, cert. of commendatio, 1994; granteee Power X, The Positive Peer Coalition; winner KPLR-TV Promoting Pers. and Comty Health, 1997. Mem. Coun. for Exceptional Children, Alpha Kappa Alpha. Avocations: reading, walking, stamp collecting, cooking. Home and Office: 2431 Strawberry Fields Ct Florissant MO 63033-1765

JAMES, ELIZABETH JOAN PLOGSTED, pediatrician, educator; b. Jefferson City, Mo., Jan. 15, 1939; d. Joseph Matthew Plogsted and Maxie Pearl (Manford) Plogsted Acuff; m. Ronald Carney James, Aug. 25, 1962; children: Susan Elizabeth, Jason Michael. BS in Chemistry, Lincoln U., 1960; MD, U. Mo., 1965. Diplomate Am. Bd. Pediat., Am. Bd. Neonatal-Perinatal Medicine. Resident in pediat. U. Mo. Hosps. & Clinics, Columbia, 1965-68, fellow in neonatology, 1968-69; dir. neonatal-perinatal medicine Children's Hosp. U. Mo. Hosps. & Clinics, 1971—; fellow in neonatal-perinatal medicine U. Colo. Hosps., Denver, 1969-71; from asst. to assoc. prof. pediatrics and obstetrics sch. medicine U. Mo., 1971-83, prof. child health and obstetrics, 1983—; dir. pediatric edn. program dept. child health sch. medicine U. Mo., Columbia, 1989—. Mem. editl. bd. Mo. Medicine, 1983—; contbr. chpts. to books and articles to profl. jours. Fellow Am. Acad. Pediat. (sect. neonatal-perinatal medicine); mem. Mo. State Med. Assn., Boone County Med. Soc., Alpha Omega Alpha. Roman Catholic. Avocations: classical music, bicycling, herb gardening. Office: U Mo Hosps & Clinics Childrens Hosp 1 Hospital Dr Columbia MO 65201-5276

JAMES, ERNEST WILBUR, lawyer; b. N.Y.C., July 21, 1931; s. Ernest Leaman and Lola Marguerita (Clancy) J.; m. Jane Gallagher; children: Ernest Jude, Sean Patrick, Patrick Logan, Sharon Ann; 1 stepchild, Susan Bartsch. BS, U.S. Naval Acad., 1956; MS in Aero. Engring., U.S. Naval Postgrad. Sch., 1964; JD, St. Louis U., 1979. Bar: Mo. 1979. Title examiner Queens County Registrar's Office, N.Y.C., 1949-51; commd. ensign USN, 1956, advanced through grades to comdr., 1971, designated naval aviator, 1958, aviation maintenance mgr., 1956-69, maintenance mgmt. planning engr., 1969-76, ret., 1976; atty., dir. risk mgmt. Bi-State Devel. Agy., St. Louis, 1979-84; assoc. Haley, Fredrickson and Walsh, 1984-86, ptnr., 1986-88; ptnr. Trakas and James, St. Louis, 1985-88, Stuart, Maue, Mitchell and James, 1988—; adj. prof. safety Cen. Mo. State U. Fellow St. Lous Bar Found. (disting. charter fellow). Home: 7416 Foley Dr Belleville IL 62223-2301

JAMES, ESTELLE, economics educator; b. Bronx, N.Y., Dec. 1, 1935; d. Abraham and Lee (Zeichner) Dinerstein; m. Ralph James (div. 1971); children: Deborah, David; m. Harry Lazer, June 27, 1971 (wid. 1994). BS, Cornell U., 1956; PhD, MIT, 1961. Lectr., econs. dept. U. Calif., Berkeley, 1964-65; acting asst. prof. Stanford (Calif.) U., 1965-67; assoc. prof. SUNY, Stony Brook, 1967-72, prof., 1972-94, provost, div. Social and Behavioral Scis., 1975-79, chmn. dept., 1982-86; vis. scholar Yale U., Australian Nat. U., Tel Aviv U., Brookings Instn., others; cons. World Bank, Washington, 1986-91, sr. economist, 1991-94, lead economist, 1994—. Author: Hoffa and the Teamsters, 1964, The Nonprofit Sector in Market Economies, 1986, Public Policy and Private Education in Japan, 1988, The Nonprofit Sector in International Perspective, 1989, Averting the Old Age Crisis, 1994; contbr. numerous articles to profl. jours. Fellow Woodrow Wilson Internat. Ctr., Washington, 1981-82, Netherlands Inst. for Advanced Study, 1986-87, U.S. Dept. Edn., 1988, Sec. of Navy, 1990, AAUW, Soc. Sci. Rsch. Coun.; Rsch. grants Spencer Found, USAID, NEH, Exxon Edn. Found., NSF; recipient Fulbright award, 1979. Mem. Am. Econs. Assn. Office: World Bank 1818 H St NW Rm Mc3-569 Washington DC 20433-0002

JAMES, FOB, JR. (FORREST HOOD JAMES), former governor; b. Lanett, Ala., Sept. 15, 1934; s. Forrest Hood Sr. and Rebecca (Ellington) J.; m. Bobbie Mae Mooney; children: Forrest Hood III, Timothy E., Patrick F. BSCE, Auburn U., 1955. Mem. Montreal Alouettes, Ont., Can., 1956-57; constrn. supt. Ala., 1958-62; founder, chmn. bd. Diversified Products Corp., 1962-78; gov. State of Ala., 1978-82, 96-98. Active Cystic Fibrosis Found., Boy Scouts Am., Ala. Saftey Coun., Jr. Achievement, Future Farmers Am. Served as lt. U.S. Army, 1957-58. Mem. Young Pres.'s Orgn., Ala. Road Builders Assn. (hon. life), Am. Legion, Spade Honor Soc., Alpha Sigma Epsilon. Republican. Address: 4009 Ballentine Dr Montgomery AL 36106*

JAMES, FRANCIS EDWARD, JR., investment counselor; b. Woodville, Miss., Jan. 5, 1931; s. Francis Edwin and Ruth (Phillips) J.; m. Iris Senn, Nov. 3, 1952; children: Francis III, Barry, David. BS, La. State U., 1951; MS, Rensselaer Poly. Inst., 1966, PhD, 1967. Commd. 2d lt. USAF, 1950, advanced through grades to col., 1972; prof. mgmt. and statistics, chmn. dept quantitative studies Air Force Inst. Tech., Wright Patterson AFB, 1967-71; dir. grad. edn. div. mgmt. programs Air Force Inst. Tech., 1972-74; ret. USAF, 1974; pres. James Investment Rsch., Inc., Alpha, Ohio, 1972—; cons. math. modeling. Author: A Matrix Solution for the General Linear Regression Model; contbr. articles to profl. jours. Mem. coun., bd. overseers Sch. Mgmt., Rensselaer Poly. Inst.; bd. dirs. James Capital Alliance Inc. Decorated Legion of Merit, D.F.C., Air medal, Joint Services Commendation medal, Meritorious Service medal; recipient Outstanding Acad. Achievement award Rensselaer Poly. Inst., 1965, first Alumni Fellow appointment Rensselaer Poly. Inst. Mem. Am. Statis. Assn., Mil. Ops. Research Soc., Am. Fin. Assn., Investment Counsel Assn. Am., Mktg. Technicians Assn., Soc. Logistics Engring. (Eckles award 1973, tech. chmn.), Sigma Iota Epsilon, Epsilon Delta Sigma. Lodges: Masons; Rotary. Home: 2604 Lantz Rd Dayton OH 45434-6627 Office: James Investment Rsch Inc PO Box 8 Alpha OH 45301-0008 *To come up with an outstanding idea is brilliance. To put that idea into action is real genius.*

JAMES, FRANCIS MARSHALL, III, anesthesiologist; b. Phila., Dec. 22, 1935. MD, Hahnemann U., 1961. Intern Phila. Gen. Hosp., 1961-62; resident Hosp. U. Pa., Phila., 1964-67; attending anesthesiologist N.C. Bapt. Hosp., Winston-Salem; prof. Wake Forest U. Bapt. Med. Ctr. Office: Wake Forest U Sch Medicine Dept Anesthesiology Medical Ctr Blvd Winston Salem NC 27157-1009

JAMES, GARY DOUGLAS, biological anthropologist, educator, researcher; b. Norwich, Conn., Dec. 6, 1954; s. Godfrey Merchant and Joan (McIlwaine) J.; m. Kathleen Louise Wilson, July 28, 1979. BA, Wake Forest U., 1976; MA, Pa. State U., 1980, PhD, 1984. Part-time instr. Pa. State U., University Park, 1982-84; postdoctoral assoc. Cornell U. Med. Coll., N.Y.C., 1984-86; asst. prof. physiology and biophysics Med. Coll. Cornell U., N.Y.C., 1986-91, asst. prof. physiology in medicine, 1986-91, assoc. rsch. prof. of physiology in medicine, 1991-98, assoc. rsch. prof. of physiology and biophysics, 1991-98; rsch. prof. Decker Sch. Nursing SUNY, Binghamton, 1998—, dir. Inst. for Primary and Preventative Health Care. Contbr. chpt. to book, articles to profl. jours. Recipient New Investigator Rsch. award NIH, 1986, Internat. Man of the Yr. award Internat. Biog. Ctr., 1993; NIH postdoctoral trainee, 1984. Fellow Human Biol. Assn. (sec.-treas. 1992-96, exec. com. 1996—), Soc. Behavioral Medicine; mem. AAAS, Am. Assn. Phys. Anthropologists, Internat. Platform Assn., Soc. for Study Social Biology, Am. Soc. Hypertension, Soc. for Epidemiol. Rsch., Am. Dermatologlyphics Assn. (exec. com. 1996-98, sec. 1998-99), The Harvey Soc. Lutheran. Office: Decker Sch of Nursing Binghamton Univ/SUNY Box 6000 Binghamton NY 13902-6000

JAMES, GENEVA BEHRENS, secondary school educator; b. Marietta, Minn., Mar. 23, 1942; d. Siegfried and Dora (Schoenrock) Behrens; m. Howard James, Aug. 2, 1963; children: Scott, Dawn. BS, Mankato State U., 1963. Tchr. English Minn. High Schs., 1964-65; instr. acctg. adult continuing edn. Bellevue, Nebr., 1971-75, dir. adult basic edn. ctr., 1974-91; vol. coord. Adult Basic Edn. Ctr., Bellevue, 1983-91; instr. secondary schs. Bellevue, 1980, instr. computer literacy, 1984-91; instr. pilot computer program Bellevue, Nebr., 1987-88; seminar presenter Nebr. State Adult Edn. Assn., 1986, Commn. on Adult Basic Edn., 1987; mem. review bd. English Curriculum Textbook Selection Com. for 10-yr. curriculum, 1996—, Bellevue (Nebr.) Pub. Schs. Computer Utilization Com., 1992—; mem. adv. bd. adult edn., 1993—; mem. student mgmt. team Bellevue West H.S., 1995, mem. disciplinary curriculum team, 1995; developed Jr. Career Project Grade 11, 1998; chmn. North Ctrl. Accreditation Team, 1996; mem. indsl. internship Work Keys-Perkins Grant, 1996. Mem. exec. com. Boy Scouts Am., 1974-80; mem. met. cmty. PLUS task force, 1986-88. Recipient indsl. internship 1997, Careers 2000, scholarship 1998. Mem. AAUW, NEA, PEC (bd. dirs. 1998—), Nat. Assn. Pub. and Continuing Adult Edn., Adult and Continuing Edn. Assn. Nebr., Bellevue Edn. Assn. (bldg. rep. 1997, nat. honor soc. selection com. 1996, dist. scholarship selection com. 1996—, exec. bd. 1998—), Nat. Coun. Tchrs. English (profl. edn. coun. 1998—), WHAR Investment Club (pres.), Alpha Delta Kappa (chmn. scholarship com. 1985-86, 91—). Republican. Lutheran. Home: 1314 Hansen Ave Bellevue NE 68005-3016 Office: Bellevue West HS 1501 Thurston Ave Bellevue NE 68123-2498

JAMES, GEORGE BARKER, II, apparel industry executive; b. Haverhill, Mass., May 25, 1937; s. Paul Withington and Ruth (Burns) J.; m. Beverly A. Burch, Sept. 22, 1962; children: Alexander, Christopher, Geoffrey, Matthew. AB, Harvard U., 1959; MBA, Stanford U., 1962. Fiscal dir. E.G. & G. Inc., Bedford, Mass., 1963-67; fin. exec. Am. Brands Inc., N.Y.C., 1967-69; v.p. Pepsico, Inc., N.Y.C., 1969-72; sr. v.p., chief fin. officer Arcata Corp., Menlo Park, Calif., 1972-82; exec. v.p. Crown Zellerbach Corp., San Francisco, 1982-85; sr. v.p., chief fin. officer Levi Strauss & Co., San Francisco, 1985-98; bd. dirs. Pacific States Industries, Inc., Basic Vegetable Products, Inc., Clayton Group Inc., Crown Vantage Corp (chmn.), Redem Corp., Dresner RCM Capital Corp, Sharper Image, Inc. Author: Industrial Development in the Ohio Valley, 1962. Mem. Andover (Mass.) Town Com., 1965-67; mem. Select Congl. Com. on World Hunger; mem. adv. coun. Calif. State Employees Pension Fund; chmn. bd. dirs. Towle Trust Fund; trustee Nat. Corp. Fund for the Dance, Cate Sch., Levi Strauss Found., Stern Grove

Festival Assn., Zellerbach Family Fund, San Francisco Ballet Assn., Com. for Econ. Devel.; bd. dirs. Stanford U. Hosp., Calif. Pacific Med. Ctr. KQED; vice-chmn. World Affairs Coun.; mem. San Francisco Com. on Fgn. Rels. With AUS, 1960-61. Mem. Pacific Union Club, Bohemian Club, Menlo Circus Club, Harvard Club, N.Y. Athletic Club. Home: 207 Walnut St San Francisco CA 94118-2012

JAMES, GERARD AMWUR, II, lieutenant governor. Lt. gov. U.S. V.I.; commr. ins. and licenses, chmn. Banking Bd. V.I. Fax: (809) 774-6593. Office: Office of Lt Gov 18 Kongens Gade Charlotte Amalie VI 00802*

JAMES, GORDON, III, lawyer; b. Montclair, N.J., Feb. 24, 1947; s. Ernest Gordon Jr. and Betty (Wackerman) J.; m. Adelia Louise Medlin (div. Sept. 1989); children: Deidre Leigh, Diana Catherine, Gordon Daniel; m. Gwen Aline Campanile, Jan. 5, 1991 (div. June 1993). BS, U. Tenn., 1969; JD, Vanderbilt U., 1972. Bar: Fla. 1972, U.S. Dist. Ct. (so. dist.) Fla. 1972, D.C. 1973, U.S. Ct. Appeals (11th cir.) 1980, U.S. Dist. Ct. (mid. dist.) Fla. 1985, U.S. Dist. Ct. (no. dist.) Fla. 1986, U.S. Supreme Ct. 1988. Assoc. Bradford, Williams, Kimbrell, et al, Miami, Fla., 1972-76; ptnr. Druck, Grimmett, Norman, Weaver, Scherer, Ft. Lauderdale, Fla., 1976-77, Druck, Grimmett, Scherer, James, Ft. Lauderdale, 1977-78, Grimmett, Scherer, James, Ft. Lauderdale, 1978-79, Conrad, Scherer, James & Jenne, Ft. Lauderdale, 1979-95, Heinrich Gordon Hargrove Weihe & James, Ft. Lauderdale, 1995—. Eucharistic lay minister, All Saints Episcopal Ch., 1991—. Capt. USAR, 1969-77. Mem. ABA, Fla. Bar Assn. (vice chmn. civil rule of procedure com. 1990-91), Nat. Assn. R.R. Counsel, Am. Acad. Hosp. Attys., Am. Bd. Trial Advs. (cert., chpt. pres. 1998), Def. Rsch. Inst., Fla. Def. Lawyers (pres. 1991-92). Republican. Avocations: fishing, snow skiing, scuba diving, physical and aerobics exercise. Office: Heinrich Gordon Hargrove Weihe & James 500 E Broward Blvd Fort Lauderdale FL 33394-3000

JAMES, HAROLD L(LOYD), geologist; b. Nanaimo, B.C., Can., June 11, 1912; s. Evan and Blodwen (Davies) J.; m. Ruth Graybeal, Feb. 13, 1936; children: David, Robert, Hugh, Herbert. Student, Western Wash. U., 1934; BS with highest honors, Wash. State U., 1938; postgrad., U. Wash., 1938-39; PhD, Princeton U., 1945. Geologist U.S. Geol. Survey, 1938—; instr. geology Princeton (N.J.) U., 1942; prof. U. Minn., Mpls., 1961-64; vis. lectr. Northwestern U., Evanston, Ill., 1953-54. Contbr. articles to profl. jours. Recipient Disting. Service award Dept. of Interior, 1966. Fellow Mineral. Soc. Am. (mem. council 1964-66), Geol. Soc. Am. (mem. council 1959-62); mem. NAS (chmn. geology sect. 1969-72), Soc. Econ. Geologists (mem. council 1962-65, pres. 1971-72, Penrose Medal 1977), Internat. Subcommn. on PreCambrian Stratigraphy (chmn. 1975-84). Avocations: fishing, golf, reading.

JAMES, HENRY THOMAS, former foundation executive, educator; b. Ferryville, Wis., May 19, 1915; s. Harry T. and Alice (Morgan) J.; . Vienna Lewis, June 6, 1939; children: Angelyn Alice (Mrs. Richard J. Grillo), Henry Thomas, Jennifer Lewis (Mrs. Timothy J. Regan), Mary Ellen (Mrs. Robert S. Lewis), Elizabeth Elinor (Mrs. Betty Folliard), Arthur Earl. B.S., Wis. State U., 1938; Ph.M., U. Wis., 1939; Ph.D., U. Chgo., 1958. High sch. tchr. Barron, Wis., 1939-42; supervising prin. Woodville, Wis., 1942-43; counselor U. Wis., Madison, 1946; supt. schs. Augusta, Wis., 1946-49, Whitewater, Wis., 1949-50; asst. supt. pub. instrn. Wis., 1950-54; lectr. U. Mich., 1954; asso. dir. Midwest Adminstrn. Center, asst. prof., asso. prof., dir. field services U. Chgo. Sch. Edn., 1954-58; prof. Stanford Sch. Edn., 1958-70, dean, 1966-70; pres. Spencer Found., Chgo., 1970-85, pres. emeritus, 1985—; cons. in field, 1954—, dir. studies sch. bds. and state sch. finance systems, 1954—; mem. N.Y. Fleischmann Commn., 1969-72, Presdl. Task Force on Edn., 1968, 80; adviser subcom. efficiency and innovation in edn. Com. Econ. Devel.; study dir. The Nation's Report Card, 1986-87; series editor various pub. cos.; chmn. vis. com. Ednl. Testing Svc., 1989-90. Sr. author: School Revenue Systems in Five States, 1961, Wealth, Expenditures and Decision-Making for Education, 1963, Determinants of Educational Expenditures in Large Cities of the United States, 1966, The New Cult of Efficiency and Education, 1969; Editor: Boardmanship, 1961; Editorial adv. bd.: Edn. and Urban Society, 1968—, Contemporary Edn. Rev., 1982—; Contbr. articles to profl. jours. Served to lt. USNR, 1943-46. Recipient Distinguished Service award Nat. Assn. State Bds. Edn., 1973, Viterbo Coll. award for service to higher edn., 1975, Outstanding Service award Am. Edn. Fin. Assn., 1988. Mem. Am. Ednl. Research Assn. (chmn. nominating com. 1964-65, cons. editor jour. 1964-70, program chmn. 1968), Am. Assn. Sch. Adminstrs., AAAS, Nat. Acad. Edn., Univ. Council Ednl. Adminstrn., Chgo. Com., Council on Fgn. Relations, Phi Delta Kappa (bd. editorial cons. 1974-85). Presbyterian. Home: Knollwood Village 1047 Village Sq Altoona WI 54720-2558

JAMES, HERB MARK (JAY JAMES), foundation and insurance executive, free trade consultant; b. Trail, B.C., Can., Jan. 30, 1936; s. George William and Violet Ethyl (Corbin) J. Student, bus. adminstrn. Simon Fraser U., 1965-69; m. Patricia Helen Boyd, Nov. 1, 1958; 1 child, Brad Mark. Founder Internat. Sound Found., Ottawa, Can., 1967—, Blaine, Wash., 1975—; cons. Fed. Bus. Dev. Bank; mem. bus. adv. bd. U.S. Senate, 1981—; pres. Bus. Navigator Svcs.; cons. Can. Internat. Devel. Agy.; founder Better Hearing Better Life projects, Fiji, Kenya, Cayman Islands, Nepal, Costa Rica, Pakistan, Guatemala, Mex., Canassist Mazatlan, Mex., 1995—. Musician B. Pops Orch., South Pacific N.G.O. Group, Ctrl. European Enterprise Devel. Group, North-South Free Trade Adjustment Group; pres. N.W. NAFTA Trade Assn. Govt. of Can. grantee, 1973-83. Mem. Christian Bus. Men's Assn., Can.-Philippines Soc. (co-founder), Conbrio Soc. (hon. dir.), Blaine C. of C., Masons, Shriners, Demolay. Office: Am Bldg PO Box 1587 Blaine WA 98231-1587 also: Ste 970, 104 1015 Columbia St, New Westminster, BC Canada V3M 6V3

JAMES, HERMAN DELANO, college administrator; b. St. Thomas, V.I., Feb. 25, 1943; s. Henry and Frances (Smith) J.; m. Marie Nannie Gray, Feb. 25, 1964; children—Renee, Sybil, Sidney. B.S., Tuskegee Inst., 1965; M.A., St. John's U., N.Y.C., 1967; Ph.D., U. Pitts., 1972; LLD (hon.), Tuskegee U., 1996. Asst. prof. U. Mass., Boston, 1973-78, assoc. provost, 1975-77, asst. chancellor, 1977-78; vice provost Calif. State U.-Northridge, 1978-82; v.p. Rowan Coll. N.J., 1982-84; pres. Rowan U., Glassboro, 1984-98, pres. emeritus, disting. prof., 1998—; bd. dirs. Mid. States Assn., S. Jersey Industries. Contbr. articles to profl. jours. Bd. dirs. Gloucester County (N.J.) United Way; mem. transition team for gov.-elect James Florio, N.J. NIH fellow, 1968-71; recipient Outstanding Achiever award Boston YMCA, 1977, Outstanding Contbr. award Nat. Ctr. for Deafness, 1982, Civic award Cherry Hill Minority Civic Assn., N.J., 1985; Tosney award, Amer. Assn. of Univ. Admin., 1994. Mem. Am. Assn. Higher Edn., Am. Sociol. Assn., N.J. C. of C. (bd. dirs.). Avocation: basketball. Home: 501 Whitney Ave Glassboro NJ 08028-2248 Office: Rowan U 201 Mullica Hill Rd Glassboro NJ 08028-1700

JAMES, HUGH NEAL, video, record, movie producer, director; b. Commerce, Ga., Oct. 10, 1952; s. Carl and Viola (Thomas) J.; m. Debra Lane Taylor, Aug. 19, 1984 (div.). Student, Gainesville Jr. Coll., 1972-73. Pres. Neal James Orgn., Inc., Athens, Ga., 1979—, Cottage Blue Music BMI, Nashville, 1986—, Prodns. Unlimited, Nashville, 1987—; v.p. Video Zine Enterprises Inc., Athens, 1987—; pres. 3d Coast Video Promotions, Nashville, Neal James Music BMI, Hidden Cove Music ASCAP, Millennium II Prodns., Neal James Prodns. Featured songwriter The Nashville Network, 1987; produced projects featuring George Jones, Willie Nelson, Hank Cochran, Dottie West, Merle Haggard, Vern Gosdin, Johnny Paycheck. Recipient 16 nominations for songwriting Country Music Assn., 1984, 85, 87, Producer of Yr. award, 1993. Mem. Am. Fedn. Musician, Music Video Assn., Nat. Entertainment Journalists Assn., Nat. Acad. Rec. Arts and Scis., Country Music Assn., Broadcast Music Inc. Avocations: water skiing, golf, horseback riding, sports cars, real estate, flying, sailing. Home and Office: PO Box 121626 Nashville TN 37212-1626

JAMES, JEANNETTE ADELINE, state legislator, accountant; b. Maquoketa, Iowa, Nov. 19, 1929; d. Forest Claude and Winona Adeline (Meyers) Nims; m. James Arthur James, Feb. 16, 1948; children: James Arthur Jr., Jeannette, Alice Marie. Student, Merritt Davis Sch. Commerce, Salem, Oreg., 1956-57. Payroll supr. Gen. Foods Corp., Woodburn, Oreg., 1956-66; cost acctg., inventory control clk. Pacific Fence & Wire Co., Portland, Oreg., 1966-67, office mgr., 1968-69; substitute rural carrier U.S. Post Office, Woodburn, 1967-68; owner, mgr., acct. and tax preparer James Bus. Svc., Goldendale, Wash., 1969-75, Anchorage, 1975-77, Fairbanks, Alaska, 1977-94; mem. Alaska Ho. of Reps., Juneau, 1993—; chmn. House State Affairs, 1995-98; vice chmn. Legis. Coun., 1995-96; chmn. joint com. Adminstrv. Regulation Rev., 1997-98; cert. workshop and seminar leader, 1989-91; instr. workshop Comm. Dynamics, 1988. Vice chmn. Klickitat County Dems., Goldendale, 1970-74; bd. dirs. Mus. and Art Inst., Anchorage, 1976-80; pres. Anchorage Internat. Art Inst., 1976-78; chmn. platting bd. Fairbanks North Star Borough, 1980-84, mem. Planning Commn., 1984-87; treas., vice chmn. 18th Dist. Reps., North Pole, Alaska, 1984-92; mem. City of North Pole Econ. Devel. Com., 1992-93. Mem. Internat. Tgn. in Comm. (Alaska State winner speech contest 1981, 86), North Pole C. of C., Emblem Club, Rotary (treas. North Pole 1990), Eagles, Women of Moose. Presbyterian. Avocations: bowling, dolls, children. Home: 3340 Badger Rd North Pole AK 99705-6119*

JAMES, JOHN WHITAKER, SR., financial services executive; b. Summit, N.J., Aug. 19, 1942; s. Nathan Whitaker and Dorothy Jane (Laffey) J.; m. Loretta Marie Porter, Dec. 7, 1968; children: John Whitaker Jr., Laurissa Marie, Corinne Helena, Randolph Whitaker. BA in Econs., Princeton U., 1964; MBA in Fin. and Investment cum laude, NYU, 1970. From ofcl. asst., asst. treas. to asst. v.p. Bankers Trust Co., N.Y.C., 1964-72, v.p. equipment leasing, 1972-76; pres., dir. Bankers Trust of Binghamton, N.Y., 1976-80; v.p., divsn. head Bankers Trust Co., N.Y.C., 1980-82; new bus. strategist E.F. Hutton Credit Corp., Greenwich, Conn., 1983-85; sr. ops. mgr. corp. fin. and equipment leasing Chrysler Capital Corp. (formerly E.F. Hutton Credit Corp.), Greenwich, 1985-91; v.p. Chrysler Capital Corp., Stamford, Conn., 1991-97; cons., 1998—, Daimler Chrysler Global Capital Svcs., 1999—. Contbr. articles to profl. jours.; inventor baseball game Diamond Challenge. Campaign chmn. Broome County United Way, Binghamton, 1978; dir., pres. New Canaan chpt. United Way, 1985-90; dir., asst. treas. Family and Children's Svcs., Stamford, 1990-96; dir. New Canaan Cmty. Found., 1991-98, pres., 1998, Family Ctrs. Inc., Greenwich, 1996-97. With USAR, 1966-70. Mem. Societal Inst. Math. Scis. (bd. dirs., v.p., sec., treas. 1993—), David Ackerman Decs. (v.p. 1997-98, pres. 1998—), Assn. Blauvelt Desc., Princeton Club New Canaan (treas. 1985—). Republican. Presbyterian. Avocations: tennis, genealogy. Home: 18 Waterbury Ave Madison CT 06443-3205 Office: Chrysler Capital Corp 225 High Ridge Rd Stamford CT 06905-3000

JAMES, JONI, singer; b. Chgo.; d. Angelo and Mary (Chereso) Babbo; m. Anthony Acquaviva, Dec. 1, 1956 (dec. Sept. 27, 1986); adopted children: Michelangelo, Angela Mia; m. B.A. Schriever, Oct. 5, 1997. One woman show, concerts, TV singer, 1951—; artist MGM Records, N.Y.C., 1952-69; singer Mil. Installations, Internat. Concerts, 1976—; founder, dir., exec. v.p. Virgo Co., Arlington, Va., 1987—; CEO, pres., prodr., artist Joni James Music Co., 1990—; dir., founder, artist Platinum Communications, Palm Beach, Fla., 1986-88. Starred in Theatre Güilds Can Can, concerts, one-woman show, coll. concerts, mil. installations, benefit prodns.; performed Carnegie Hall, N.Y.C., 1998; recs. include 17 LPs, 11 CDs. Recipient 4 Million Sellers Gold Records MGM Records, 1952, 2 Platinum and 2 Million Sellers Gold Records MGM Records, 1953, Platinum 21 Million Sellers Platinum LP award MGM Records, 1960, Platinum LP award MGM Records, 1960, 21 Gold Records, 12 Double Platinum Sellers, 21 Million Seller Platinum LP award MGM Records, 1960, Platinum LP award MGM Records, 1960; 671 singles copyrights and trademarks registered; named Most Played Singer Radio Sta. WNEW, N.Y., 1954; inducted into Big Band Hall of Fame, 1994. Mem. Am. TV and Recording Artists, Am. Guild Variety Artists. Roman Catholic. Avocations: writer, gourmet cook, gardening, needlework, social consciousness causes. Office: Joni James Fan Club Internat PO Box 7207 Westchester IL 60154-7207

JAMES, KANE, economics educator; b. Washington, June 30, 1935; s. Edward Anthony and Mary Agnes (Kerwin) K.; m. Gloria Nancy Verdi, Aug. 27, 1959; children: Laura, Stephen, Edward. BS, Georgetown U., 1957; PhD, MIT, 1960. Rsch. asst. Fed. Res. Bd., 1958, 59; asst. prof. econs. Iowa State U., Ames, 1960-61, Princeton U., 1961-66; assoc. prof., then prof. econs. Boston Coll., 1966-72; Everett D. Reese prof. banking and monetary econs. Ohio State U., Columbus, 1972-92; James F. Cleary prof. fin. Boston Coll., Chestnut Hill, Mass., 1992—; vis. prof. Istanbul U., Turkey, 1966, Simon Fraser U., B.C., Can., 1971, Ariz. State U., 1989, Deakin U., Vic., Australia, 1994; vis. scholar U. Ariz., 1991—; economist Fed. Res. Bank, Boston, 1967-72, Fed. Res. Bank, San Francisco, 1975, Fed. Home Loan Bank Bd., 1972-73, FDIC, 1975-76, U.S. Congress Joint Econ. Com., 1978-80, Office Tech. Assessment, 1982-84, Congl. Budget Office, 1989-91, Fed. Home Loan Mortgage Corp., 1983-84, U.S. Gen. Acctg. Office, 1984-87, Urban Inst., 1988-91, World Bank, 1988-89, 92—; mem. Shadow Fin. Regulatory Com., 1986—; trustee, mem. fin. com. Tchrs. Ins. and Annuity Assn. Am., 1975-87; mem. com. examiners for advanced econs. test Ednl. Testing Svc., 1974-77; rsch. assoc. Nat. Bur. Econ. Rsch., 1979—. Author: Economic Statistics and Econometrics: An Introduction to Quantitative Economic, 1968; The Gathering Crisis in Federal Deposit Insurance, 1985, The S&L Ins. Mess: How Did It Happen? 1989, (with others) Perspectives on Safe and Sound Banking, 1986; co-editor: Inflation, Trade and Taxes: Essays in Honor of Alice E. Bourneuf, 1976; mem. editl. bd. Jour. Fin. Svcs. Rsch., Rev. Social Economy, Jour. Money, Credit and Banking, Quar. Jour. Econs. and Fin., Pacific Basin Finance Jour., Asia-Pacific Jour. Mgmt., Jour. Banking and Fin., Jour. Empirical Fin. Recipient Alumni Disting. Tchg. award Ohio State U., 1981, Outstanding Rsch. award Ohio State U. Coll. Adminstrv. Sci., 1981; Goodyear Corp. fellow, 1958-59, Harold Stonier Found. fellow, 1959-60, Procter & Gamble Corp. fellow, 1962-63, Guggenheim Found. fellow, 1969-70; William Paterson preceptorship, 1964-66; NSF grantee, 1965-66, 67-69, 71-72, 72-74. Mem. Am. Fin. Assn. (pres. 1979, dir. 1978-81), Am. Econs Assn., Am. Statis. Assn., Econometric Soc., Nat. Tax Assn., Tax Inst. Am., Am. Real Estate and Urban Econs. Assn., Midwestern Econs. Assn. (1st v.p. 1982-83), Assn. for Social Econs. (trustee 1991—), Phi Beta Kappa. Roman Catholic. Office: Boston Coll Svc Bldg Chestnut Hill MA 02167

JAMES, KAY LOUISE, management consultant, healthcare executive; b. Little Rock, Feb. 13, 1948; d. Charles Robert and Mary Virginia (Morgan) J. BA, Vanderbilt U., 1970; MBA, U. Chgo., 1986. Diplomate Am. Coll. Healthcare Execs.; CPA, Ill., Mo. Mgr. Wallace Community Mental Health Ctr., Nashville, 1973-78; sr. cons. Ernst & Whinney, Washington, 1978-79; sr. cons. Ernst & Whinney, Chgo., 1979-81, mgr., 1981-84; dir. Am. Hosp. Supply Corp., Evanston, Ill., 1984-85; mgr. Am. Hosp. Supply Fin. Corp., Evanston, 1985-86; sr. mgr. KPMG Peat Marwick, Kansas City, Mo., 1986-89, ptnr., 1989-92; ptnr. Katz, James & Assocs., Inc., Plymouth Meeting, Pa., 1992-93; pres. James Mgmt. Assocs., Inc., Nashville, 1994—; spkr. healthcare topics various grad. programs and profl. assns. Mem. AICPA, Am. Hosp. Assn., Med. Group Mgmt. Assn., Healthcare Fin. Mgmt. Assn., The Healthcare Forum. Democrat. Avocation: tennis. Office: James Mgmt Assocs 3200 W End Ave Ste 500 Nashville TN 37203-1322

JAMES, LOUIS MEREDITH, personnel executive; b. St. Augustine, Fla., June 12, 1941; s. Claire Meredith and Katherine Louise (Colson) J.; m. Karen Lee Libby, Nov. 25, 1966 (div. Mar. 1974); children: Michelle Lee, Kevin Meredith; m. Antoinette Frances Guerrero, Dec. 23, 1978; 1 child, Aaron Teague. BA, U. Minn., 1964. Personnel mgr. Army & Air Force Exch. Svc., worldwide, 1967-77; salary and wage specialist Dept. Def. Wage Staff, Rosslin, Va., 1977-82; dep. chief Dept. Def. Wage Divsn. NAF Br., Arlington, Va., 1982-98, ret., 1998. Commr. Transp. Safety Commn., Vienna, Va., 1986-98, vice chair, 1992-93, chair, 1993-96; mem. Bd. Zoning Appeals, Vienna, 1998-99. Decorated Purple Heart. Mem. DAV (life), VFW (life), Vietnam Vets. Am. (life, local chpt. state coun. and nat. com., bd. dirs., v.p., pres. 1987—, Nat. Mem. of Yr. 1995), Lions (v.p., bd. dirs., chmn. membership com. Vienna chpt.). Republican. Presbyterian. Avocations: fishing, sports, classical music, reading. Home: 6903 Compton Valley Ct Centreville VA 20121-5013

JAMES, MARIA-ELENA, federal judge; b. 1953. BA, U. Calif., Irvine, 1975; JD, U. San Francisco, 1978. Dir. consumer fraud unit Office of Dist. Atty., San Francisco, 1978-80; dep. pub. defender San Francisco, 1980-84, dep. city atty., 1984-88; commr. Calif. Superior Ct., 1988-94; apptd. magistrate judge no. dist. U.S. Dist. Ct. Calif., 1994. Fax: (415) 522-2140. Office: 450 Golden Gate Ave San Francisco CA 94102-3661

JAMES, MARILYN SHAW, secondary education educator, social service worker; b. Chgo., Apr. 6, 1926; d. Harry and Louise A. (Milkey) Shaw; m. Eugene Nelson James, June 17, 1950; children: Jim, Mark, Katherine, Caroline. BS, Carthage Coll., 1947; MA, U. Iowa, 1954. Tchr. home econs. Highland Park (Ill.) High Sch., 1947-50, Hampshire (Ill.) High Sch., 1950-51; instr. home econs. No. Ill. U., DeKalb, 1963-65; tchr. Winkie Bear, Sycamore, Ill., 1970-71; sub. tchr. DeKalb and Sycamore Sch. Dists., 1969—, Hinckley-Big Rock, Ill., 1973-80; homemaker coord. Family Svc. Agy., DeKalb, 1980-88, ret. Stage mgr. Stage Coach Players, DeKalb, 1954—; moderator First Congl. Ch., DeKalb, 1983-84; v.p. Kishwaukee Symphony Assocs., 1988-90, pres., 1990, mem. adv. com. on elder concerns, 1991—, chmn., 1996-97; bd. dirs. Family Svc. Agy., DeKalb, 1971-79. Named Stage Coacher of Yr., Stage Coach Players, 1990. Mem. AAUW (v.p. scholar 1980, 90, 93, 94, 95, 96), LWV (legis. chair 1983), DeKalb County Home Economists, DeKalb Drama Club (pres. 1986-87), Univ. Women's Club (pres. 1991), Family Svc. Aux. (pres. 1998—), DeKalb Women's Club (bd. dirs.), Thursday Arts Lit. Club (pres. 1998—). Democrat. Home: 212 Tilton Park Dr DeKalb IL 60115-1942

JAMES, MARION RAY, magazine founder, editor; b. Bellmont, Ill., Dec. 6, 1940; s. Francis Miller and Lorraine A. (Wylie) J.; m. Janet Sue Tennis, June 16, 1960; children: Jeffrey Glenn, David Ray, Daniel Scott, Cheryl Lynne. BS, Oakland City Coll., Ind., 1964; MS, St. Francis Coll., Fort Wayne, Ind., 1978. Sports and city editor Daily Clarion, Princeton, Ind., 1963-65; English tchr. Jac-Cen-Del High Sch., Osgood, Ind., 1965-66; indsl. editor Whirlpool Corp., Evansville and LaPorte, Ind., 1966-68, Magnavox Govt. and Indsl. Electronics Co., Fort Wayne, 1968-79; editor, pub., founder Bowhunter mag., Fort Wayne, Ind., 1971-88; editor-in-chief Bowhunter mag., Kalispell, Mont., 1989—; instr. Ind.-Purdue U., Ft. Wayne, 1980-88. Author: Bowhunting for Whitetail and Mule Deer, 1975, Successful Bowhunting, 1985, My Place, 1991, The Bowhunter's Handbook, 1997; editor: Pope and Young Book of Bowhunting Records, 1975, 93, 99, Bowhunting Adventures, 1977. Recipient Best Editorial award United Community Svc. Publs., 1970-72; named Alumnus of Yr., Oakland City Coll., 1982, to Hall of Fame, Mt. Carmel High Sch., Ill., 1983. Mem. Outdoor Writers Assn. Am., Fort Wayne Assn. Bus. Editors (Fort Wayne Bus. Editor of Yr. 1969, pres. 1975-76), Toastmasters (Able Toastmaster award), Alpha Phi Gamma, Alpha Psi Omega, Mu Tau Kappa. Home: 2325 Wolftail Pines Whitefish MT 59937-8099 *Read! Being a good reader is the key to good thinking. Develop and expand your mind through active use of the printed word and you will discover a wide world of unlimited possibilities - and ultimate success that comes with self-discovery.*

JAMES, MARY SPENCER, nursing home health administrator; b. London, Ont., Can., July 10, 1949; d. Richard Spencer and Helen Frances (Winterbottom) James; m. Robert Peter Owler, Oct. 4, 1969 (div. June 25, 1975). AA, Norwich U., 1969; Nursing Diploma, Toronto (Ont.) Gen. Hosp., 1973; BA in Psychology, U. Vt., 1975. RN, Calif. Staff nurse Toronto Gen. Hosp., 1973-77, Stanford (Calif.) U. Hosp., 1977-81, B.C. Children's Hosp., Vancouver, 1981-83; sr. staff nurse King Abdul Aziz Mil. Hosp., Tabuk, Saudi Arabia, 1983-84, Charter Med. Ltd./Tawam Hosp., Al Ain, Abu Dhabi, UAE, 1984-87; nurse Dubai Petroleum Co., UAE, 1987-88; nursing dir. Ygia Polyclinic, Limassol, Cyprus, 1988-89; nurse Stat Travelers, Inc., L.A., 1990-91; staff nurse Lucile Salter Packard Children's Hosp. at Stanford, Palo Alto, Calif., 1991-92; case mgr. H.S.S.I. Home Care and Olsten Healthcare, Milbrae and San Francisco, 1992-93; nursing dir. CHS Home Health Agy., San Francisco, 1993-94; liaison nurse coord., pvt. duty supr. United Nursing Internat., San Francisco, 1994-95; nursing supr. Staff Builders Home Care Svcs., Santa Rosa, Calif., 1995; home health coord. Sun Plus Home Health Svcs., Petaluma, Calif., 1995—. Avocations: aerobics, weight training, hiking, reading. Home: 250 C Douglas St Petaluma CA 94952-2577

JAMES, MICHAEL ANDREW, lawyer; b. Indpls., June 8, 1953; s. Joseph Schell and Dorothy Agnes (Meth) J. BA, U. Va., 1975; JD, Yale U., 1978. Bar: N.Y. 1979. Assoc. Chadbourne & Parke, N.Y.C., 1978-80; assoc. Zimet, Haines, Friedman & Kaplan, N.Y.C., 1980-85, ptnr., 1986-95. Vol. gen. counsel People with AIDS Coalition N.Y., 1991-95. Mem. ABA, Phi Beta Kappa. Democrat. Roman Catholic.

JAMES, MICHAEL THAMES, information technology executive, consultant; b. Gulfport, Miss., Feb. 16, 1949; s. William Denning and Christell (Cruthirds) J.; m. Debra Lynn Bryant, May 21, 1983; children: William Bryant, Shelley Christine. BS, U.S. Naval Acad., 1971; MS, U. So. Calif., 1978. Commd. ensign USN, 1971, advanced through grades to lt., 1975, resigned, 1978; mktg. rep. IBM, South Bend, Ind., 1978-79; cons. Price Waterhouse, Houston, 1979-85; internal cons. Shell Oil, Houston, 1985-86; mgr. systems devel. & support Carolina Power & Light, Raleigh, 1986-91; v.p. Sprint Kansas City, 1991-93; ptnr. KPMG Peat Marwick, Dallas, 1994-96; prin. Scott, Madden & Assocs., Dallas, 1996-98; CEO James Cons. Group, Plano, Tex., 1998—; guest lectr. N.C. State U., 1989-91; mem. adv. bd. So. Meth. U. Cox Sch. Bus., 1997—. Mem. computer studies adv. bd. Meredith Coll., 1987-91; adv. bd. Kansas City Met. Spl. Olympics, 1993; mem. industry steering com. Sch. Bus., U. Kans., 1993-94. Mem. Inst. Mgmt. Cons. (sec.-treas. Houston chpt. 1984-85), U.S. Naval Acad. Alumni Assn. (sec.-treas. Triangle area chpt. 1987-91), Stonebriar Country Club, Dallas Corinthian Yacht Club. Republican. Presbyterian. Avocations: golf, tennis, running, sailing. Home: 4525 Emerson Dr Plano TX 75093-7226

JAMES, MILTON GARNET, economist; b. Guyana, Jan. 27, 1937; came to U.S., 1969, naturalized, 1976; s. Reginald Nathaniel and Caroline Elizabeth J.; m. Joyce Fernandes, July 31, 1960; children: Milton Garnet, Michael, Mark. BS, U. London, 1964; MBA, St. John's U., N.Y., 1972; PhD, U. London, 1973. Instr. econs. Baruch Coll. CUNY, 1972-74; asst. prof. mktg. Ramapo Coll., N.J., 1974-77; cons. econs. N.Y.C., 1978—. Chmn. Guyanese Cmty. Coun., U.S., 1976—. Recipient Pub. Svc. award Guyanese Cmty. Coun., 1982. Mem. Am. Econs. Assn., Caribbean Studies Assn., Masons. Episcopalians. Achievements include research in economic development, econometric forecasting, monetary and fiscal policies. Home: 649 E 23rd St Brooklyn NY 11210-1127 Office: Bd Edn 65 Court St Brooklyn NY 11201-4954

JAMES, MURIEL MARSHALL, author, psychotherapist; b. Berkeley, Calif., Feb. 14, 1917; d. John Albert and Hazel (Knowles) Marshall; m. Paul Wesley James (div.); children: Ann, Duncan, John; m. Ernest C. Brawley, June 1964 (dec.). BA with honors, U. Calif., Berkeley, 1956; MDiv, Ch. Divinity Sch. Pacific, 1957; EdD, U. Calif., 1964. Cert. marriage, family & child counselor, Calif. Instr., coord. ARC, San Francisco, 1941-43; safety inspector Kaiser Shipyards, Richmond, Calif., 1943-44; substitute tchr. Oakland (Calif.) Pub. Schs., 1948-52; min. Orinda (Calif.) Cmty. Ch., 1957-59; dean Laymen's Sch. Religion, Berkeley, Calif., 1959-68; instr. U. Calif. Ext., Berkeley, 1966-69; dir., therapist Oasis Edn. & Treatment Ctr., Lafayette, Calif., 1968-73; psychotherapist pvt. practice, Lafayette, Calif., 1969—; lectr. James Inst., Lafayette, 1969—. Author/co-author: Born to Win: Transactional Analysis with Gestalt Experiments, 1971, Winning with People: Group Exercises in Transactional Analysis, 1973, Born to Love: Transactional Analysis in the Church, 1973, Transactional Analysis for Moms and Dads: What Do You Do With Them Now That You've Got Them?, 1974, The Power at the Bottom of the Well, 1974, The OK Boss, 1975, The People Book: Transactional Analysis for Students, 1975, The Heart of Friendship, 1976, Techniques for Psychotherapists and Counselors, 1977, A New Self: Self Therapy with Transactional Analysis, 1977, Marriage is for Loving, 1979, Breaking Free: Self-Reparenting for a New Self, 1981, Winning Ways in Health Care, 1981, It's Never Too Late to Be Happy: The Psychology of Self-Reparenting, 1985, The Better Boss in Multicultural Organizations, 1991, Hearts on Fire: Romance and Achievement in the Lives of Great Women, 1991, Passion for Life: Psychology and the Human Spirit, 1991, Religious Liberty on Trial, 1997, Perspectives in Transactional Analysis, 1998; contbr. chpts. to books, articles to profl. jours. Mem. Interat. Transactional Analysis Assn. (pres. 1980-82). Avocations: friends, family, travel, teaching, creating new books. Fax: 925-283-7013. Address: PO Box 356 Lafayette CA 94549-0356

JAMES, NADINE H., psychiatric nurse, occupational health and home care nurse, nursing administrator, educator; b. Malone, N.Y., Jan. 16, 1943; d. Charles and Iris W. (Reid) Holmes; m. Floyd D. James, Dec. 23, 1961;

children: Kyle T. James, Hope James Grosz. Diploma, Oswego County BOCES, Oswego, N.Y., 1978; ASN, Regents Coll. Degrees, Albany, N.Y., 1981, BS, 1990. RN. Sr. indsl. nurse Stone & Webster Engring. Corp., Oswego; nursing supr. Portamedic Health Care, Liverpool, N.Y.; radiation protection technician Niagara Mohawk Power Corp., Oswego; nurse clinician New Eng. Critical Care, Inc., Westborough, Mass.; utilization rev. analyst Mesa (Ariz.) Luth. Hosp.; psychiat. nurse Benjamin Rush Psychiat. Ctr., Syracuse, N.Y.; nursing instr. Oswego County BOCES Sch. Practical Nursing, Mexico, N.Y., 1995—.

JAMES, PATRICIA ANN, philosophy educator; b. Newberry, Mich., Mar. 17, 1933; d. Albert Michael and Antonette (Sholar) J.; m. James William Dickoff, July 3, 1970; 1 dau., Sara Dorn-Havlik-Dickov. Student, Mich. Coll. Mining Tech., 1951-53; BS, U. Detroit, 1955; MA, Yale U., 1958, PhD, 1962. Research asst. in philosophy and law Yale U., 1959-62, lectr. in philosophy, 1962-64, instr., 1964-65, asst. prof. philosophy, 1965-70; asso. prof. Kent (Ohio) State U., 1970-73, prof., 1973-96, prof. emeritus, 1996—; vis. prof. Sch. Nursing, Oreg. Health Scis. U., 1982-87; adj. prof. Sch. Nursing Kent State U., 1990-91. Fulbright fellow Belgium, 1955-56. Home: 6945 Hudson Rd Kent OH 44240-6070*

JAMES, PATRICK, political science educator; b. Toronto, Ont., Can., Mar. 27, 1957; s. Margaret Elnor; m. Carolyn Cramer, July 6, 1996; 1 child, Ben. BA with honors, U. We. Ont., 1978; PhD, U. Md., 1984. Asst. prof. U. Manitoba, Winnipeg, Can., 1983-84; asst. prof. McGill U., Montreal, 1984-88, assoc. prof., 1988-91; prof. Fla. State U., Tallahassee, 1991-94; prof., chair Iowa State U., Ames, 1994-98, prof., 1997—; minority advisor Cower Acad., Ames, 1997—; Louise Dyer Peace fellow Hoover Instn., Stanford, Calif., 1991; Milton R. Mevill chair Utah State U., Logan, 1997; Lady Davis prof. Hebrew U., Jerusalem, 1999. Author, editor: Politics and Rationality, 1993, Wars in the Midst of Peace, 1997, Peace in the Midst of War, 1998, others; editor Internat. Studies Quarterly, 1999—; mem. editl. bd. Internat. Studies Rev., 1999—; contbr. articles to profl. jours. Mem. Internat. Studies Assn., Internat. Polit. Sci. Assn., Internat. Studies Assn. Midwest (pres. 1999—), Am. Polit. Sci. Assn., Iowa Conf. Polit. Scientists (pres. 1998-99), Peace Sci. Soc. Avocations: chess, golf. E-mail: pjames@instate.edu. Office: Iowa State U Dept Polit Sci Ames IA 50011-1204

JAMES, PERRY EDWIN, III, director Raleigh finance department; b. Wilmington, N.C., Apr. 5, 1951. BS, U. N.C., 1973. CPA, N.C. Asst. dir. fin. dept. City of Raleigh, N.C., 1982-95; dir. fin. dept. City of Raleigh, 1995—. Mem. AICPA, N.C. Assn. CPAs, Govt. Fin. Officers Assn., N.C. Govt. Fin. Officers. Assn. Office: Finance Dept Raleigh Mcpl Bldg Rm 114 222 W Hargett St Raleigh NC 27601-1341

JAMES, PHYLLIS A., lawyer; b. L.I., N.Y., Mar. 23, 1952. BA, Harvard U., 1974, JD, 1977. Bar: Calif. 1978. Mem. Pillsbury Madison & Sutro, San Francisco; corp. counsel City of Detroit Law Dept. Office: City of Detroit Law Dept 1650 First National Building 660 Woodward Ave Detroit MI 48226-3516*

JAMES, P(HYLLIS) D(OROTHY) (BARONESS JAMES OF HOLLAND PARK OF SOUTHWOLD IN COUNTY OF SUFFOLK), author; b. Oxford, Eng., Aug. 3, 1920; d. Sidney Victor and Dorothy May Amelia (Hone) J.; m. Connor Bantry White, 1941 (dec. 1964); children: Clare Bantry, Jane Bantry. Student Brit. schs.; LittD (hons.), U. Buckingham (Eng.), 1992, U. Hertfordshire (Eng.), 1994, U. Glasgow (Scotland), 1995, Durham U., 1998, Portsmouth U., 1999; DLitt, U. London, 1993; D. U. Essex, Eng., 1996. Adminstr. Nat. Health Service, 1949-68; apptd. prin. Civil Svc. Home Office, 1968; prin. Police Dept., 1968-72, Criminal Policy Dept., 1972-79. Author: Cover Her Face, 1962, A Mind to Murder, 1963, Unnatural Causes, 1967, Shroud for a Nightingale, 1971; (with T.A. Critchley) The Maul and the Pear Tree, 1971; An Unsuitable Job for a Woman, 1972, The Black Tower, 1975, Death of an Expert Witness, 1977, Innocent Blood, 1980, The Skull Beneath the Skin, 1982, (play) A Private Treason, 1985, A Taste for Death, 1986, Devices and Desires, 1989, The Children of Men, 1992, Original Sin, 1994, A Certain Justice, 1997, Time to be in Earnest, 1999. Gov. BBC, 1988-93; bd. dirs. Brit. Coun., 1988-93; bd. dirs., chair lit. adv. panel Arts Coun. Gt. Britain, 1988-92. Decorated Order Brit. Empire, 1983; created life peer (Baroness) of U.K., 1991; Assoc. fellow Downing Coll., Cambridge, 1986; hon. fellow St. Hilda's Coll., Oxford, 1996. Fellow Royal Soc. Lit., Royal Soc. Arts; mem. Soc. of Authors (chmn. 1984-86, pres. 1997—), Detection Club. Office: Greene & Heaton Ltd, 37 Goldhawk Rd, London W12 8QQ, England

JAMES, REESE JOSEPH, physician; b. Detroit, July 20, 1953; s. Robert W. and Agnes C. (Gootee) J.; children: Ashley, Kendall, Graham. BS, Western Mich. U., Kalamazoo, 1975, MA, 1976; DO, Univ. Health Scis., Kansas City, Mo., 1981. Diplomate in diagnostic radiology and neuroradiology Am. Osteo. Bd. Radiology. Intern Okla. Osteo. Hosp., Tulsa, 1981-82; resident U. Health Scis., Kansas City, Mo., 1982-85; fellow Meth. Hosp./Baylor Coll. Medicine, Houston, 1985-87; neuroradiologist Pontiac (Mich.) Osteo. Hosp., 1991—, Lapeer (Mich.) Regional Hosp., 1991—; med. dir. Mich. Resonance Imaging, Rochester Hills, 1992—; clin. prof. Mich. State U., Pontiac, 1992—; lectr. and presenter in field. Contbr. articles to profl. jours. Mem. AMA, Am. Soc. Neuroradiology (sr. mem.), Am. Soc. Head and Neck Radiology, Soc. Magnetic Resonance Imaging, Soc. Magnetic Resonance in Medicine, Southeastern Neuroradiol. Soc., Radiol. Soc. N.Am., Am. Osteo. Coll. Radiology, Am. Coll. Radiology, Am. Osteo. Assn., Mich. Radiol. Soc., Mich. Med. Soc., Mich. Assn. Osteo. Physicians and Surgeons, Oakland County Osteo. Assn., Lapeer County Osteo. Assn., Lapeer County Med. Soc., Clin. Magnetic Resonance Soc., Soc. Nuclear Medicine. Republican. Office: Pontiac Osteo Hosp 50 N Perry St Pontiac MI 48342-2217

JAMES, ROBERT BRANDON, social service agency administrator; b. Amesbury, Mass., June 1, 1939; s. Robert Leroy Jr. and Mary Frances (Bacon) J.; m. Carol Ann Goehring, Oct. 19, 1968; children: Michael Brandon, Robin Marie. Student, Haverford Coll., 1957-59; BA, Thiel Coll., 1968; MSW, U. Pitts., 1972. Lic. social worker, Pa. Bus driver Anderson Bus Co., Greenville, Pa., 1963-67; dir. childrens activities St. Pauls Children Home, Greenville, 1967-68; caseworker Mercer (Pa.) County Child Welfare, 1968-70; supr. Butler (Pa.) County Asst. Officer, 1972-78; adminstr. Beaver (Pa.) County Office on Aging, 1978—; bd. mem., treas. Nat. Assn. Area Agys. on Aging, Washington, 1979-82. Bd. mem. Pa. West Soccer Assn., Pitts., 1985-99, pres., 1989-91; mem. Region #1 Championship Com., 1987—; ch. and soc. com. Evangelical Luth. Ch. Am., Pitts., 1996—. Recipient Samuel McCune award for disting. svc. Presbyn. Sr. Care, Pitts., 1996. Mem. Pa. Assn. Area Agys. on Aging (bd. mem. and treas. 1983-98, pres. 1988-89). Avocations: soccer administration and refereeing, genealogy, church, reading. Office: Beaver County Office Aging 500 Market St Beaver PA 15009-2998

JAMES, ROBERT WILLIAM, lawyer, government executive; b. Oakland, Calif., July 5, 1922; s. Reginald William and Antoinette C. E. (Balsden) J.; m. Barbara Jean Zaniboni, Feb. 23, 1962; children: Barbara Marie. A.B., U. Calif.-Berkeley, 1946, L.L.B., 1949. Bar: Calif. 1950. Lawyer State of Calif., Sacramento, 1949-64, asst. chief counsel, 1964-75; dep. dir. Dept. Water Resources, State of Calif., Sacramento, 1975-82, acting dep. dir., 1982-83, chief counsel, 1983—. Contbg. author U. Calif. Law Rev., 1948-49. Served with U.S. Army, 1942-45, Europe. Mem. Phi Betta Kappa. Democrat. Roman Catholic. Lodge: Elks. Home: 5601 Haskell Ave Carmichael CA 95608-1203 Office: Dept Water Resources 1416 9th St Sacramento CA 95814

JAMES, RONALD BRUCE, journalist; b. Cin., Aug. 21, 1956; s. Freeman D. and Ann (Linder) J.; m. Sally Ann Mulcahey, Nov. 11, 1978; children: Tabitha Marie, Nathaniel R. BA in Journalism, Miami U., 1992. Staff writer Register-Herald, Eaton, Ohio, 1994, mng. editor, 1994-95; county adminstr. County of Preble, Eaton, 1995; polit. writer Jour.-News, Hamilton, Ohio, 1995—; bur. chief Thomson Newspapers, 1998. Mem. Soc. Profl. Journalists, Sigma Phi Epsilon. Republican. Methodist. Avocations: golf, fitness, creative writing. Home: 191 W Hendricks St Camden OH 45311-1018 Office: Journal-News 228 Court St Hamilton OH 45011-2820

JAMES, SHARPE, mayor; b. Jacksonville, Fla., Feb. 20, 1936; m. Mary Mattison; 3 children. Grad., Montclair State Coll.; M, Springfield Coll. Former mem. faculty Essex County Coll., Newark, from 1968, then prof.; mayor City of Newark, 1986—. mem. Newark City Council, 1970-86. Served with AUS. Office: City Hall 920 Broad St Ste 200 Newark NJ 07102-2609*

JAMES, SHERYL TERESA, journalist; b. Detroit, MI, Oct. 7, 1951; d. Reese Louis and Dava Helen (Bryant) J.; m. Eric Torgeir Vigmostad, June 15, 1974; children: Teresa, Kelsey. BS in English, Ea. Mich. U., 1973. Staff writer, editor Lansing (Mich.) Mag., 1979-82; staff writer Greensboro (N.C.) News & Record, 1982-86, St. Petersburg (Fla.) Times, 1986-91, Detroit Free Press, 1991—; cons. Poynter Inst., St. Petersburg, 1989—; cons. to high sch. newspapers, St. Petersburg, 1989—. Recipient Penney Missouri Awd. U. Missouri/J.C. Penney, 1985, 1st Pl. Feature Writing Awd. Fla. Soc. Newspaper Editors, 1991, Pulitzer Prize, Feature Writing, 1991, finalist, 1992, Alumna Achievement Awd. Eastern Michigan U., 1992. Democrat. Roman Catholic. Office: Detroit Free Press Knight-Ridder Newspapers 600 W Fort St Detroit MI 48226-2707*

JAMES, SIDNEY LORRAINE, television executive; b. St. Louis, Aug. 6, 1906; s. William Henry and Katherine (Wiese) J.; m. Agnes McCarthy, Oct. 21, 1932 (dec. 1991); children: Christopher, Timothy, Mary, Sidney; m. Donna Petterson, Jan. 14, 1994. Student, Washington U., St. Louis. Mem. editorial staff St. Louis Post-Dispatch, 1928-36; nat. affairs writer Time mag., 1936-38; chief Time, Inc., Chgo., 1938-41; chief Western editorial ops. Time, Inc., 1941-46; v.p. corp. mgmt. Time, Inc., N.Y.C., 1965-67; v.p. Time, Inc., Washington, 1967-70; asst. mng. editor Life mag., 1946-54; founding mng. editor Sports Illus. mag., N.Y.C., 1954-60, pub., 1960-65; chmn. bd. Greater Washington Ednl. TV Assn. (WETA), Inc., 1970—; 1st vice chmn. bd. Pub. Broadcasting Svc. Author: Paper Trail - A Memoir, Press Pass - The Journalist's Tale, 1994; editor: The Wonderful World of Sport, 1967; author forewords Ben Hogan's The Modern Fundamentals of Golf, 1957, Charles Goren's The Book of Bridge, 1961; contbr. articles to Time and Life mags.; co-developer: (radio program) Quiz Kids; dir. first TV broadcast of polit. conv., Life mag. and NBC, 1948; anchor: (TV spl.) We The People, 1953. Mem. Pres.'s Adv. Com. on Youth Fitness; mem. Peabody Awards Bd.; lay trustee Trinity Coll. Recipient George Foster Peabody award for meritorious svc. in broadcasting, 1979. Mem. Def. Orientation Assn., Nat. Inst. Social Scis., U.S. Srs. Golf Assn., Am. Yacht Club, Apawamis Club (Rye, N.Y.), N.Y. Racquet and Tennis Club, Burning Tree Club, 1925 F St. Club, Nat. Press Club, Internat. (Washington). Home: 54993F Paseo Del Lago Laguna Hills CA 92653

JAMES, THOMAS A., investment company executive. Chmn. of bd. Raymond James & Assocs., Raymond James Fin. Inc., St. Petersburg, Fla. Office: Raymond James Fin Inc 880 Carillon Pkwy Saint Petersburg FL 33716-1100*

JAMES, THOMAS NAUM, cardiologist, educator; b. Amory, Miss., Oct. 24, 1925; s. Naum and Kata J.; m. Gleaves Elizabeth Tynes, June 22, 1948; children: Thomas Mark, Terrence Fenner, Peter Naum. BS, Tulane U., 1946, MD, 1949. Diplomate Am. Bd. Internal Medicine (mem. bd. govs. 1982-88), Bd. Cardiovasc. Diseases (bd. dirs. 1972-78). Intern Henry Ford Hosp., Detroit, 1949-50, resident in internal medicine and cardiology, 1950-53, staff, 1959-68; pvt. practice, 1953—; staff U. Ala. Hosps., 1968-87; instr. medicine Tulane U., New Orleans, 1955-58, asst. prof., 1959; prof. medicine U. Ala. Med. Ctr., Birmingham, 1968-87, prof. pathology, 1968-73, assoc. prof. physiology and biophysics, 1969-73, dir. Cardiovasc. Rsch. and Tng. Ctr., 1970-77, chmn. dept. medicine, dir. divsn. cardiovasc. disease, 1973-81, Mary Gertrude Waters prof. cardiology, 1976-87, Disting. prof., 1981-87; prof. medicine, prof. pathology U. Tex. Med. Br., Galveston, 1987—, pres., 1987-97, dir. WHO Cardiovasc. Ctr., 1988-98; U. Tex. Med. Br., Galveston, 1997—; mem. adv. coun. Nat. Heart Lung and Blood Inst., 1975-79; pres. 10th World Congress Cardiology, 1986; mem. cardiology del. invited by Chinese Med. Assn. to China, 1978; Campbell orator Queens U., Belfast, No. Ireland, 1982; Mikamo lectr. Japan Circulation Soc., 1982; Sir Thomas Lewis lectr. Brit. Cardiac Soc., 1983, Einthoven lectr. U. Leiden, The Netherlands, 1993, Bailey K. Ashford lectr. U. P.R., 1995; hon. lectr. U. Padua, 1998. Author: Anatomy of the Coronary Arteries, 1961, The Etiology of Myocardial Infarction, 1963; Mem. editl. bd. Circulation, 1966-83, Am. Jour. Cardiology, 1968-82, Am. Heart Jour, 1976-79; contbr. articles to profl. jours. Capt. M.C. U.S. Army, 1953-55. Fellow ACP (gov. Ala. 1975-79, master 1983); mem. AMA, Am. Clin. and Climatological Assn. (v.p. 1992-93, councillor 1992-93), Assn. Am. Physicians, Am. Soc. Clin. Investigation, Assn. Univ. Cardiologists (pres. 1978-79), Am. Heart Assn. (pres. 1979-80), Am. Coll. Cardiology (v.p. 1970-71, trustee 1970-71, 76-81, First Disting. Scientist award 1982, chmn. publs. com. 1994-97), Am. Soc. Pharmacology and Exptl. Therapeutics, Soc. Exptl. Biology of Medicine, Am. Coll. Chest Physicians, Ctrl. Soc. Clin. Rsch., Internat. Soc. and Fedn. Cardiology (pres. 1983-84), WHO (expert adv. panel on cardiovascular diseases 1988-97), So. Soc. Clin. Investigation, Am. Fedn. Clin. Rsch., Ala. Acad. Honor. Philos. Soc. Tex., Phi Beta Kappa, Sigma Xi, Omicron Delta Kappa, Alpha Omega Alpha, Alpha Tau Omega, Phi Chi. Presbyterian. Clubs: Cosmos, Mountain Brook, Galveston Artillery. Office: U Tex Med Br 301 University Blvd Galveston TX 77555-0175

JAMES, THOMAS W., federal judge. Bankruptcy judge U.S. Bankruptcy Ct., Ill., 1979—. Office: US Dist Ct 756 Dirksen Bldg 219 S Dearborn St Chicago IL 60604-1702

JAMES, TRACEY FAYE, screenwriter; b. Wilmington, Ohio, Feb. 4, 1963; d. James Whitney and Lydia Wanell (Wethington) J. Student, Art Instrn. Schs., 1980, Arlington Career Ctr., 1985. Freelance screenwriter San Antonio, 1981—; sports photographer No. Va. Sun, Arlington, Va., 1988. Author (screenplays): Nights of Terror, 1987, Dark Lords, 1991, Diamond Run, 1996, At the Hands of Mercy, 1997, An Education in Murder, 1999. Recipient award for patriotic svc. U.S. Treasury, 1981. Republican. Episcopalian. Avocations: writing, drawing, bowling, movies, music.

JAMES, VIRGINIA LYNN, contracts executive; b. March AFB, Calif., Feb. 6, 1952; d. John Edward and Azella Virginia (Morrill) Anderson; children: Raymond Edward, Jerry Glenn Jr. Student, Sinclair Community Coll., 1981-83, U. Tex., San Antonio, 1980, Redlands U., 1986, San Diego State U., 1994. With specialized contracting USAF, Wright-Patterson AFB, Ohio, 1973-77; with logistics contracting USAF, Kelly AFB, Tex., 1977-81; contract specialist USAF, Wright-Patterson AFB, Ohio, 1981-84; spl. asst. Peace Log, Tehran, Iran, 1977; acting chief of contracts cruise missile program Gen. Dynamics/Convair, San Diego, 1984-86; contracts mgr. VERAC, Inc., San Diego, 1986-90, Gen. Dynamics, San Diego, 1990-92; mgr. contracts Scientific-Atlanta, San Diego, 1992-93; dir. contracts GreyStone, San Diego, 1993-95; dist. constn. mgr. OHM, San Diego, 1995-98; contract/procurement mgr. Montgomery Watson, Louisville, 1998—; cons. Gen. Dynamics, San Diego, 1985, Efratrom, 1986. Mem. Nat. Assn. Female Execs., Nat. Mgmt. Assn., Nat. Contract Mgmt. Assn. Republican. Office: Montgomery Watson 9016 Taylorsville Rd #237 Louisville KY 40299

JAMES, WAYNE EDWARD, electrical engineer; b. Racine, Wis., Apr. 2, 1950; s. Ronald Dean James and Arlene Joyce (Mickelsen) Dawson; m. Edith Yvonne Cone, Apr. 6, 1997; children: Terry Scott, Kevin Arthur. BS in Electronic Engring. Tech., U. So. Colo., 1976; MS in Computer Sci., Colo. U., 1996. Electronic technician Lawrence Livermore (Calif.) Nat. Lab., 1976-80; electronic technician Inmos Corp., Colorado Springs, Colo., 1980-86, CAD engr., 1986-87; CAD engr. United Techs. Microelectronics Ctr., Colorado Springs, 1988-97, ASIC engr., 1997—. Sec.-treas. Stratmoor Hills Vol. Fire Dept., Colorado Springs, 1983, 84, lt., 1985, capt., 1986. Served with USN, 1968-72. Named Fireman of Yr., Stratmoor Hills Vol. Fire Dept., 1983. Lutheran. Office: UTMC Microelectronic Systems 4350 Centennial Blvd Colorado Springs CO 80907-3701

JAMES, WILLIAM HALL, former state official, educator; b. North Providence, R.I., July 20, 1910; s. John William and May (Hall) J.; m. Virginia Stowell, June 24, 1950, 1 child, Hillery Stowell. Student, U. Lausanne, 1928-29; BPhil, Brown U., 1933; MA, Yale U., 1946, PhD, 1953; LLD, U. New Haven, 1976. Tchr. New Canaan (Conn.) Bd. Edn., 1933-36; teaching prin. Easton (Conn.) Bd. Edn., 1936-42, 46-47, supervising prin., 1947-53, supt. schs., 1953-58; supt. schs. Branford (Conn.) Bd. Edn., 1958-66; staff Commn. Higher Edn., Hartford, Conn., 1966-77; dir. accreditation and scholarships Commn. Higher Edn., Hartford, 1966-77; ret., 1977; cons. Greater New Haven State Tech. Coll., 1977-78, Conn. Commn. Higher Edn., 1980-81; adj. prof. history So. Conn. State Coll., New Haven, 1947-49, adj. prof. econs. and labor-mgmt. rels., 1981-92, adj. prof. labor-mgmt. rels.; adj. prof. internat. rels., Eurasian affairs and history Western Conn. State Coll., Danbury, 1949-58; adj. prof. ednl. adminstrn. U. Bridgeport, Conn., 1958; adj. prof. econs. and indsl. rels. U. New Haven, West Haven, Conn., 1979-90, adj. prof. indls. rels.; adj. prof. labor-mgmt. rels., mgmt. Teikyo Post U., Waterbury, Conn., 1988-93; lectr. in field. Author: The Monetarists and the Current Crisis, 1975. Mem. North Branford (Conn.) Commn. Econ. Devel., 1980-95, chmn., 1981-95; mem. PTA. Maj. USAAF, 1942-46. Recipient Disting. Friend of Greater New Haven State Tech. Coll. award, 1984. Mem. SAR, NEA, Conn. Edn. Assn., Conn. Assn. Pub. Sch. Supts., Conn. Assn. Advancement Sch. Adminstrn., Am. Assn. Sch. Adminstrs., Yale Post-Doctoral Seminar Group (pres. 1968-69), Conn. State Employees Assn., Conn. Coun. Higher Edn. (treas. 1971-77), Am. Assn. Higher Edn., Royal Can. Geog. Soc., Numerical Control Soc., Rotary, Schoolmasters Rotary U.S. (sec.-treas. 1965-69), Am. Legion (post comdr. Easton 1948-49), China-Burma-India Vets. Assn., Exchange Club. Home: 373 Reeds Gap Rd Northford CT 06472-1106

JAMES, WILLIAM J., lawyer. AB, Occidental Coll., Los Angeles, 1966; JD, U. Calif., San Francisco, 1974; LLM, N.Y.U., 1975. Bar: Calif., U.S. Dist. Ct. (ctrl. dist.) Calif. 1976, U.S. Dist. Ct. (no. dist.) Calif. 1992, U.S. Dist. Ct. (ea. dist.) Wis. 1997, U.S. Ct. Appeals (9th cir.) 1976, U.S. Tax Ct. 1979. Asst. U.S. atty. U.S. Atty's Office, L.A., 1976-86; ptnr. Graham & James, LLP, L.A., 1986—; sr. adjunct prof. Golden Gate U., L.A., 1978—. Mem. Fed. Bar Assn. (pres. L.A. chpt. 1991-92), L.A. County Bar Assn. Office: Graham & James LLP 801 S Figueroa St Fl 14 Los Angeles CA 90017-2573*

JAMES, WILLIAM LANGFORD, aerospace engineer; b. Southampton, Va., Jan. 13, 1939; s. Leroy and Worthie (Murphy) J.; m. Elaine Cecilia Reed; children: William Jr., Terri Lynne. Student, Va. State Coll., 1956, Hampton Inst., 1958; BS, Calif. State U., Los Angeles, 1962, MS, 1964; postgrad., U. Nev., Reno, 1984; spl. engring. studies, UCLA, 1970-82. Rsch. engr. non-metallic materials lab. N.Am. Aviation, L.A., 1960-67; rsch. analyst tech. staff The Aerospace Corp., El Segundo, 1967-75, materials engr., 1975-85; project engr. program mgmt. office space launch ops. The Aerospace Corp., El Segundo, Calif., 1985-96; cons. to space ops. The Aerospace Corp., El Segundo, 1996—. Contbr. numerous articles and reports to profl. publs.; patentee in field. Recipient numerous awards for USAF space contributions. Mem. AAAS, Soc. Advancement Material and Process Engring. (vice-chmn. 1987-89). Avocations: traveling, water sports, big game fishing. Home: PO Box 19735 Los Angeles CA 90019-0735 Office: Aerospace Corp M5 712 Los Angeles CA 90009

JAMES, WILLIAM MORGAN, bishop. Bishop Ch. of God in Christ, Toledo. Office: St James Holiness Ch of God in Christ 3758 Chippendale Ct Toledo OH 43607*

JAMES, WILLIAM RAMSAY, cable television executive; b. South Bend, Ind., Oct. 6, 1933; s. William Stubbs and Rose (Ramsay) J.; m. Jane Mehrer, Dec. 29, 1955; children: William Harold, Martha Courtney Quay. BS in Mech. Engring., Princeton U., 1955; MBA, Harvard U., 1960. CPA, Mich. Plant mgr. N. A. Woodworth Co., Ferndale, Mich., 1960-62; ptnr. Touche Ross & Co., Detroit, 1962-69; v.p., gen. mgr. Sta. WJR, Detroit, 1969-80; exec. v.p. Capital Cities Communications, N.Y.C., 1980-86; pres. Cable TV div. Capital Cities Communications, Bloomfield Hills, Mich., 1980-86; pres. James Communications Inc., 1986-87; mng. ptnr. James Communications Ptnrs., Bloomfield Hills, 1988—. Trustee, chmn. William Beaumont Hosp., Royal Oak, Mich. 1st lt. USAF, 1956-58. Mem. AICPA, Mich. Assn. CPAs, AAA Mich. (bd. dirs., chmn.), Country Club (Bloomfield Hills, Mich.), Orchard Lake (Mich.) Country Club, Lost Tree Club (Palm Beach, Fla.), Jupiter (Fla.) Hills Club, Everglades Club (Palm Beach). Republican. Episcopalian. Office: James Communications Ptnrs 710 N Woodward Ave Bloomfield Hills MI 48304-2851

JAMES, WILLIAM W., banker; b. Oct. 12, 1931; s. Will and Clyde (Cowdrey) J.; m. Carol Ann Muenter, June 17, 1967; children: Sarah James Banks, David William. AB, Harvard U., 1953. Cert. trust and fin. advisor. Asst. to dir. overseas divsn. Becton Dickinson & Co., Rutherford, N.J., 1956-59; stockbroker Merrill Lynch, Pierce, Fenner & Smith, Inc., St. Louis, 1959-62; with trust divsn. Boatmen's Nat. Bank, St. Louis, 1962-90, v.p. in charge estate planning, sr. v.p., 1972-90; sr. v.p. Boatmen's Trust Co., St. Louis, 1989-96, fin., trust mktg. cons., 1996—; bd. dirs. Heer-Andres Investment Co., Springfield, 1974-95. Mem. gift and bequest coun. Barnes Hosp., St. Louis, 1963-67, St. Louis U., 1972-78; dir. Mark Twain Summer Inst., St. Louis, 1987-92. Served with U.S. Army, 1953-55. Mem. Estate Planning Coun. St. Louis, Mo. Bankers Assn., Am. Inst. Banking, Harvard Alumni Assn. (bd. dirs. 1987-90), Harvard Club of St. Louis (pres. 1972-73), Harvard Faculty Club (Cambridge, Mass.), Mo. Athletic Club, Noonday Club (St. Louis). Republican.

JAMES-DUNSTON, JANET RENÉE, orchestral music teacher, composer, flutist; b. N.Y.C., Mar. 8, 1954; d. John Wesley and Dorothy Alma (Dorrell) James. BA in Music Edn., Bklyn. Coll., 1976; MA in Music Edn., NYU, 1979; profl. diploma in Ednl. Adminstrn., L.I. U., 1995. Cert. sch. dist. adminstr., N.Y., cert. in orchestral music, N.Y.C., cert. tchr. elem. and secondary schs., N.Y.C. Orchestral music tchr. N.Y.C. Pub. Schs., Bklyn., 1979—. Grantee for jazz composition B.M.I. Jazz Composer's Workshop, N.Y.C., 1995-97. Mem. Duke Ellington Soc., Music Educators Nat. Conf., Internat. Assn. Jazz Educators, Phi Delta Kappa, Kappa Delta Phi. Avocation: travel. Home: 301 Cathedral Pkwy Apt 12D New York NY 10026-4064

JAMESON, ANTONY, aerospace engineering educator; b. Gillingham, Kent, Eng., 1934. BA, Cambridge (Eng.) U., MA in Engring. with honors, 1958, PhD, 1963. Rsch. fellow Trinity Hall, Cambridge, Eng., 1960-63; economist Trades Union Congress, London, 1964-65; chief mathematician missile divsn. Hawker Siddeley Dynamics, Coventry, Eng., 1965-66; staff engr. Grumman Aerospace Corp., Bethpage, N.Y., 1966-72; sr. rsch. scientist Courant Inst. Math. Scis., NYU, N.Y.C., 1972-74, prof. computer sci., 1974-80; prof. mech. & aerospace engring. Princeton (N.J.) U., 1980-82, James S. McDonnell Disting. U. prof. aerospace engring., 1982-96, prof. emeritus, 1996—, dir. program in applied and computational math., 1986-88; prof. aeronautics Stanford (Calif.) U., 1997—. Contbr. articles to profl. jours., chpts. to books. 2nd lt. British Army, 1953-55. Open scholar Trinity Hall, Cambridge, 1955, Hon. fellow, 1990; Alfred P. Sloan Fgn. Post-Doctoral fellow MIT, 1962; named Hon. Prof., Northwestern Polytech. U., Xian, China, 1986, W.R. Sears Disting. lectr. Cornell U., 1992; recipient NASA medal Exceptional Sci. Achievement, 1980, Gold medal Brit. Royal Aero. Soc., 1988, Spirit of St. Louis medal ASME, 1995. Fellow AIAA (Fluid Dynamics award 1993), Royal Soc. London. Office: Stanford U Astronautic Durand Stanford CA 94305-1928

JAMESON, J(AMES) LARRY, chemical company executive; b. Elizabethtown, Ky., 1937; s. William Kendrick and Ruth Helen (Krause) J.; m. Mary Louise Wojcik, June 26, 1965; children: Renee, Jennifer, Julie. BA in Math., Bellarmine Coll., 1959; BS in Chem. Engring., U. Detroit, 1963, MBA, 1970. Tech. mgr. automotive products Rinshed Mason et Cie, Paris, 1965-69; ops. mgr. vinyl coated fabrics Inmont Corp., Toledo, 1969-75; v.p., gen. mgr. European ops. Inmont Corp., London, 1975-79; v.p., gen. mgr. automotive finishes products Inmont Corp., Detroit, 1979-83, sr. v.p. worldwide automotive, 1983-86; pres. Coatings & Colorants div. BASF, Clifton, N.J., 1986-93; pres., CEO Pirelli Cable Corp., Florham Park, N.J., 1993-96; v.p. Ferro Chem. Corp., Cleve., 1996—. Mem. Soc. Automotive Engrs., Orchard Lake Country Club, The Country Club. Avocations: golf, tennis, skiing, hunting. Home: 17181 Hidden Point Dr Chagrin Falls OH 44023-2001 Office: Ferro Corp 1000 Lakeside Ave E Cleveland OH 44114-1147

JAMESON, PAULA ANN, lawyer; b. New Orleans, Feb. 19, 1945; d. Paul Henry and Virginia Lee (Powell) Bailey; children: Paul Andrew, Peter

Carver. B.A., La. State U., 1966; J.D., U. Tex., 1969. Bar: Tex. 1969, D.C. 1970, Va., 1973, N.Y. 1978, U.S. Dist. Ct. D.C. 1970, U.S. Dist. Ct. (ea. dist.) Va. 1976, U.S. Ct. Appeals (D.C. cir.) 1972, U.S. Ct. Appeals (4th cir.) 1976, U.S. Ct. Appeals (5th cir.) 1978, U.S. Supreme Ct. 1973, U.S. Ct. Appeals (2d cir.) 1985. Asst. corp. counsel D.C. Corp. Counsel's Office, 1970-73; sr. asst. county atty. Fairfax County Atty.'s Office, Fairfax, Va., 1973-77; atty. Dow Jones & Co., Inc., N.Y.C., 1977-79, house counsel, 1979-81, asst. to chmn. bd., 1981-83, house counsel, dir. legal dept., 1983-86; sr. v.p., gen. counsel, corp. sec., PBS, Alexandria, Va., 1986-98; ptnr. Arter & Hadden, Washington, 1998—; mem. FCC WRC-2000 Industry Adv. Com.; Advanced TV Tech. Ctr. Inc., (former dir.). Mem. ABA, Fed. Communications Bar Assn., D.C. Bar Assn., Assn. of Bar of City of N.Y., Am. Pub. TV Prodr. Assn. (former chair), Copyright Soc. USA (former trustee). Democrat. Roman Catholic. Office: Arter & Hadden 1801 K St NW Ste 400 Washington DC 20006-1301

JAMESON, RICHARD, magazine editor, film critic; b. New Castle, Pa., Nov. 17, 1944; s. William Theodore and Phoebe Jane (Dufford) J.; m. Kathleen Ann Murphy, May 31, 1973. BA in English with honors, Washington and Jefferson Coll., 1965. Mgr. Edgemont Theater, Edmonds, Wash., 1967-71; editor Movietone News, Seattle, 1971-81; film critic The Weekly, Seattle, 1976-78, 79-86, Pacific Northwest, Seattle, 1986-90, 7 Days, N.Y.C., 1989-90; editor Film Comment, N.Y.C., 1990—; film instr. U. Wash., Seattle, 1969-80. Co-writer (film treatment) The Door in the Jungle, 1978; co-writer, cons. (film script) Heartless, 1986; editor: They Went Thataway: Redefining Film Genres, 1993. Mem. Nat. Soc. Film Critics, Phi Beta Kappa. Democrat. Avocations: video and laserdisc collecting, still photography. Office: Film Soc Lincoln Ctr 70 Lincoln Center Plz New York NY 10023-6548*

JAMESON, SANFORD CHANDLER, education educator; b. Toronto, Ohio, Feb. 12, 1932; s. Sanford Frank and Dorothy Lee (Robinson) J. BS, Miami U., Oxford, Ohio, 1954; MA, Case Western Res. U., 1960; m. Joan Sheridan, June 29, 1963; children: Jennifer Joan, Julie Jo. Asst. dir. admission Case Western Res. U., 1957-60; assoc. dir. admissions Carleton Coll. Northfield, Minn., 1960-63; asst. regional dir. Coll. Entrance Exam. Bd., Evanston, Ill., 1963-66, asst. dir. internat. edn. Central office, N.Y.C., 1966-69, assoc. for internat. edn., 1969-71, dir. internat. edn., Washington, 1971-94, dir. emeritus, 1994—; chmn. Nat. Council Evaluation Fgn. Ednl. Credentials, 1974-78, active, 1964-94; chmn. liaison group for internat. ednl. exchange, 1986-88, active, 1980-94. Lt. USNR, 1954-57. Author, editor workshop reports in field. Recipient 20 Yr. Cert. Appreciation, U.S. Dept. of State, 1992. Mem. SAR, Nat. Assn. Coll. Admission-Counselors, Nat. Assn. Fgn. Student Affairs (bd. dirs., chmn. admission sect., pres. 1976-77, life), Am. Assn. Collegiate Registrars and Admission Officers (Appreciation cert. 1995), Nat. Liaison Com. Fgn. Student Admissions (chmn. 1972-74, sec. 1974-87), Internat. Sch. Svc. (bd. dirs. 1974-81, 83-90, chmn. 1988-90), Soc. Mayflower Descendants, Soc. of the Cin., Masons, (32 deg.), Shriners, Sigma Alpha Epsilon. Presbyterian (elder). Home and Office: 5609 Springfield Dr Bethesda MD 20816-1239

JAMIESON, GRAHAM A., biochemist, organization official; b. Wellington, New Zealand, Aug. 14, 1929; came to U.S., 1956; s. Andrew Wilson and Nan (Graham) J.; m. Barbara MacLachlan, Feb. 20, 1960; 1 child, Brian. BSc, U. Otago, 1949; MSc with first class honors in Organic Chemistry, U. New Zealand, 1951; PhD Lister Inst. Preventive Medicine, U. London, 1954, DSc, 1972. Research fellow dept. biochemistry Cornell U., N.Y.C., 1956; research biochemist Am. Nat. Red Cross, Bethesda, Md., 1961-64; asst. dir. research Am. Nat. Red Cross, 1964-69, dir. research, 1969-78, assoc. dir. blood services, 1978-84, sr. scientist, 1984—; vis. scientist NIH, 1957-61, mem. exptl. hematology study sect., 1978-84; lectr. biochemistry Georgetown U., Washington, 1961, professorial lectr., 1966-74, adj. prof., 1974-96; Winzler Meml. lectr. U. Fla., 1975; mem. adv. com. on blood preservation and substitutes U.S. Army Med. Rsch. and Devel. Command, 1980-92, chmn., 1981-92; vis. prof. U. Sao Paulo, Brazil, 1992, U. Barcelona, Spain, 1993. Editor: (with T.J. Greenwalt) Red Cell Membrane-Structure and Function, 1969, Formation and Destruction of Blood Cells, 1970, Glycoproteins of Blood Cells and Plasma, 1971, The Human Red Cell In Vitro, 1974, Transmissible Disease and Blood Transfusion, 1975, Trace Components of Plasma-Isolation and Clinical Significance, 1976, The Granulocyte: Function and Clinical Utilization, 1977, The Blood Platelet in Transfusion Therapy, 1978, (with D.M. Robinson) Mammalian Cell Membranes, Vol. I, 1978—, Generalizations and Methodology, Vol. II, 1978—, The Diversity of Membranes, Vol. III, 1978—, Surface Membranes of Specific Cell Types, Vol. IV, 1978—, Membranes and Cellular Functions, Vol. V, 1978—, Responses of Plasma Membranes; Interaction of Platelets and Tumor Cells, 1982, Platelet Membrane Receptors: Molecular Biology Immunology, Biochemistry and Pathology, 1988; mem. editorial bds. Thrombosis Rsch., 1978-81, Thrombosis Haemostas, 1989—, Internat. Jour. Hematology, 1989—, Blood, 1996—; contbr. articles to profl. jours. Sir George Grey scholar U. New Zealand., 1951, U. Otago 50; John Edmond fellow. Fellow AAAS; mem. Am. Soc. Biol. Chemists, Am. Chem. Soc., Biochem. Soc. (London), Internat. Soc. Thrombosis and Hemostasis (Shirley Johnson award 1997), N.Y. Acad. Scis., Am. Heart Assn. (exec. com., council on thrombosis), Am. Soc. Hematology, Soc. Exptl. Biology and Medicine, Soc. for Complex Carbohydrates (exec. com.). Home: 5622 Johnson Ave Bethesda MD 20817-3504 Office: Am Nat Red Cross 15601 Crabbs Branch Way Rockville MD 20855-2736

JAMIESON, JAMES BRADSHAW, foundation administrator; b. L.A., June 10, 1931; s. Charles Cameron and Ruth (Bradshaw) J.; m. Perry McNaughton, Dec. 27, 1959; children: Jeffrey McNaughton, Dalton Charles. AA, Citrus Coll., 1950; BA, Claremont Men's Coll., 1955; MA, Claremont Grad. Sch., 1958; PhD, Brown U., 1966. Assoc. prof. polit. studies Pitzer Coll. and Claremont Grad. Sch., 1968-75; rsch. polit. scientist UCLA, 1972-73; v.p. for devel. Pitzer Coll., 1968-72, v.p., 1973-78, prof. polit. studies, 1975-83, exec. v.p., 1979-83, acting pres., 1978-79; prof. govt. Claremont Grad. Sch., 1975-87; v.p. for rsch. Claremont McKenna Coll., 1983-87; exec. dir. Found. for Performing Art Ctr., San Luis Obispo, Calif., 1987-96; pres. SLO Capers, San Luis Obispo, Calif., 1997—; commr. Calif. Postsecondary Edn. Commn., Sacramento, 1987-92; dir. Global Village, Seattle, 1989-95. Contbr. articles to profl. jours. Staff, sec. Ctrl. Coast Performing Arts Ctr. Commn., San Luis Obispo, 1993-95. Sgt. USAF, 1950-52. Fellow Brown U., 1960, 63, tchg. fellow, 1962, fellow Resources for the Future, 1964; rsch. grantee U.S. Dept. Interior, 1972-73; recipient Cal. Poly U. Pres.' Arts award, 1999. Mem. Santa Lucia Flyfishers (bd. dirs. 1988—), Trout Unltd. (bd. dirs. Calif. coun. 1989-94, bd. dirs. nat. bd. 1986-90), Marine's Meml. Club. Avocations: flyfishing, tennis, restoring vintage automobiles. Office: SLO Capers PO 12843 San Luis Obispo CA 93406-2843

JAMIESON, JOHN ANTHONY, engineering consulting company executive; b. London, England, Mar. 16, 1929; came to U.S., 1952; s. John Percival and Jean (Kerr) J.; m. Barbara Armstrong, July 6, 1956; children: John Gordon, Sara Felicity, John Douglas. BS summa cum laude, U. London, 1952; PhD, Stanford U., 1957. Scientist, then mgr. electrooptics div. Aerojet-Gen. Corp., Azusa, Calif., 1957-69; asst. dir. U.S. Army Advanced Ballistic Missile Defense Agy., Washington, 1970-73; pres. Jamieson Sci. & Engring., Inc., Washington, 1973-97; chief scientist Vanguard Rsch., Inc., Fairfax, Va., 1997—; chmn. Sci. & Engring. Support Group to SDIO, Washington, 1985—; mem. sci. adv. bd. USAF, 1990-94; chief scientist Vanguard Rsch., Inc.; bd. dirs. Optelecom, Inc., Gaithersburg, Md., Space Computer Corp., L.A. Author: Infrared Physics & Engineering, 1963; contbr. chpt. in book and articles to profl. jours. Served with RAF, 1947-50. Recipient Space Sys. award AIAA, 1992, award for meritorious civilian svc. U.S. Dept. Air Force, 1990, 94, Thomas B. Dowd Meml. award, 1995, Space-based Infrared Pioneer award USAF, 1999. Republican. Episcopalian. Office: Vanguard Rsch Inc 10400 Eaton Pl Ste 450 Fairfax VA 22030-2208

JAMIESON, JOHN EDWARD, JR., social services administrator, minister, bioethicist; b. Philadelphia, Pa., Mar. 5, 1945; s. John Edward and Frances (Hayes) J.; m. Marilyn T. Haws, June 8, 1968; children: Douglas Stuart, Heather Lynn, Mark Stuart. BA, U. Pa., 1967; MDiv, Ref. Episcopal Sem., Phila., 1970; PhD, Christian Bible Coll., Rocky Mount, N.C., 1990. Ordained to ministry Ref. Episcopal Ch., 1970, Bapt. Ch., 1978. Pastor Trinity Ref. Episcopal Ch., Phila., 1970-73, St. Mark's Ref. Episcopal Ch., Miami, Fla., 1973-75, Hammonton (N.J.) Bapt. Ch., 1978-81; supr. Nepaug Christian Acad., New Hartford, Conn., 1976-78; coord. ops. emergency med. svcs. div. AID Ambulance Svc., Atlantic City, 1982-83; paramedic mobile ICU, West Jersey Health, Camden, N.J., 1983-88; dir. pastoral care Atlantic City Med. Ctr., 1988—; pastor Grace Bible Chapel, Ocean City, N.J., 1988-95; vice chmn. instnl. med. ethics com. Atlantic City Med. Ctr., 1988-96, co-chair, 1996—. Editor Bibl. Bioethics, 1990. Chaplain Somers Point (N.J.) Vol. Rescue Squad, 1987-96, Ocean City Fire Dept.; bd. dirs. Atlantic County unit Am. Cancer Soc., Northfield, N.J., 1988-90, program coord. Cansurmount support program, 1988-90; bd. trustees Ctrl. Ocean City Union Chapel; exec. v.p. Reformed Bible Inst. Delaware Valley. Mem. Am. Assn. Christian Counselors, Nat. Christian Counselors Assn., Assn. Profl. Chaplains, Atlantic-Cape May Pastor's Fellowship (pres. 1990—), N.J. Healthcare Decisions, Delaware Valley Bioethics Com. Network, Jersey Cape Ethics Consortium, So. Jersey Ethics Alliance. Republican. Avocations: travel, photography, reading. Office: Atlantic City Med Ctr 1925 Pacific Ave Atlantic City NJ 08401-6713 *When we concentrate our thoughts on that which is true, noble, right, pure, lovely, admirable and excellent we are lifted above the drudgery of life and open ourselves to the possibility of true greatness.*

JAMIESON, KATHLEEN HALL, dean, communications educator; b. Mpls., Nov. 24, 1946; d. Wayne and Katherine Hall; m. Robert D. Jamieson; children: Robert, Patrick. BA, Marquette U., 1967; MA, U. Wis., 1968, PhD, 1972. From asst. prof. to prof. U. Md., College Park, 1971-86; G.B. Dealey Regents prof. of comm., chair speech comm. dept. U. Tex., Austin, 1986-89; prof. of comm. U. Pa., Phila., 1989—, dean Annenberg Sch. Comm., 1989—, Walter Annenberg deanship, 1993—; polit. commentator Nat. Pub. Radio, 1980-82; dir. comm. House Com. on Aging, U.S. Congress, 1977-78; Presdl. apptd. White House Conf. on Aging, 1980; mem task force NIH Health Message Testing, 1978-80; cons. Nat. Cancer Inst., 1980-84; bd. dirs. Ctr. for Pub. Integrity, 1990—; invited lectr. Mt. Vernon Coll., 1975, U. Calif., Davis, 1976, SUNY, Albany, 1979, The Brent Soc. Lecture, Alexandria, Va., 1980, Harvard U., Cambridge, Mass., 1981, U. Mass., Amherst, 1982, Am. Film Inst. Lecture, 1983, Columbia U., N.Y.C., 1984, AAWU of Hawaii, Honolulu, 1985, Mt. Holyoke, Mass., 1986, Twentieth Century Fund's Theodore White Seminar on Presdl. Debate, Harvard U., 1986, U. Tex., 1987, Clemson U., 1987, The Kenneth Murray Lecture on First Amendment, U. Mich., 1989, William and Mary Coll., 1989, Pa. LWV, 1991, Duke U., Durham, N.C., 1992, Children's Def. Fund, 1992, NEA, Balt., 1992, Smithsonian Inst., Washington, 1992, The Freedom Forum, Columbia U., N.Y.C., 1992, Coll. St. Catherine, St. Paul, 1993, Nat. Conf. Editl. Writers, Phila., 1993, U. Pitts. Inst. Politics, 1993, Eagleton Inst. Politics, Rutgers U., New Brunswick, N.J., 1994, Congl. Clearinghouse on the Future, Washington, 1994, The Penn Club, N.Y.C., 1994, Internat. Women's Media Found., Washington, 1994, and many others. Author: A Critical Anthology of Public Speeches, 1978, Packaging the Presidency: A History and Criticism of Presidential Advertising, 1984 (Golden Anniversary Book award Speech Comm. Assn. 1984), 3rd edit., 1996, Eloquence in an Electronic Age, 1988 (Winans-Wichelns Book award Speech Comm. Assn. 1989), Dirty Politics: Deception, Distraction and Democracy, 1992, Beyond the Double Bind: Women and Leadership, 1995; co-author: Debating Crime Control, 1967, The Interplay of Influence: Media and Their Publics in News, Advertising and Politics, 1983, 3d edit., 1991, Presidential Debates: The Challenge of Creating an Informed Electorate, 1988, Deeds Done in Words: Presidential Rhetoric and The Genres of Governance, 1990, Spiral of Cynicism: The Press and the Public Good, 1997; editor: Age Stereotyping and Television, 1978, Televised Advertising and the Elderly, 1978; co-editor: Form and Genre: Shaping Rhetorical Action, 1978, Communication Research, 1994; assoc. editor QJS, 1975, also book rev. editor, 1975-77, Encoder, 1973-75, Comm. Quar., 1976-78, Comm. Monographs, 1978-80, 89-91, Comm. Edn., 1979-81, Quar. Jour. Speech, 1981-83; regional editor EXETASIS, 1976-80; guest editor The So. States Speech Comm. Jour., 1986, Comm. Edn., 1987; contbr. numerous articles to profl. jours. Knapp fellow, 1967-68, Ford fellow, 1969-71 Fulbright fellow, 1982, East-West Ctr. fellow, 1985, 88; Eli Lily Found. grantee, 1976, Andrew Mellon Found. grantee, 1980, NEH grantee, 1987-88, Woodrow Wilson grantee, 1989, MacArthur grantee, 1992, 93, Markle grantee, 1992, Schuman grantee, 1992, Robert Wood Johnson grantee, 1993-94, Ford Found. Grantee, 1995-96, Carnegie Found. grantee, 1995-96, PEW Charitable Trust grantee, 1996-97; recipient Zeta Phi Eta award, 1979, Past Pres. award for outstanding scholarly achievement Ea. Comm. Assn., 1984, Alumni Merit award Marquette U., 1984, Douglas Ehninger award, 1990, JFK Joan Shorenstein Barone Ctr. Goldsmith award, 1992, Disting. Career in Scholarship award Speech Comm. Assn., 1992, Sara award Phila. chpt. Women in Comm., 1993-94, Murray Edelman Disting. Career award for lifetime contbn. to study of polit. comm. Am. Polit. Sch. Assn. Polit. Comm. Divsn., 1995. Mem. Am. Philosoph. Soc. Office: U Pa Annenberg Sch for Comm 3620 Walnut St Philadelphia PA 19104-6220

JAMIESON, MICHAEL LAWRENCE, lawyer; b. Coral Gables, Fla., Mar. 2, 1940; s. Warren Thomas and Ruth Amelia (Gallman) J.; children: Ann Layton, Thomas Howard; m. Elizabeth Marie Peeples, Dec. 31, 1992. BA in English, U. Fla., 1961, JD with honors, 1964. Bar: Fla. 1964, U.S. Dist. Ct. (mid. dist.) Fla. 1964, D.C. 1998. Teaching asst. U. Fla., 1964; law clk. U.S. Ct. Appeals (5th cir.), 1964-65; assoc. Holland & Knight LLP and predecessor firms, Tampa, Fla., 1965-69; ptnr. Holland & Knight and predecessor firms, Tampa, Fla., 1969—, chmn. bus. law dept., 1992—. Editor-in-chief U. Fla. Law Rev., 1963. Trustee Law Ctr. U. Fla., chmn. bd. dirs., 1986-88; bd. dirs., chmn. Bus. Com. for the Arts Inc., 1989-90; trustee Tampa Bay Performing Arts Ctr. Inc., 1989—, chmn. devel. coun., 1990-91; trustee Cmty. Found. Greater Tampa, 1990-97; chmn. devel. com. Fla. C. of C. Found., 1992-95; mem. Tampa Leadership Conf., Golden Triangle Civic Assn. Recipient Gertrude Brick Law Rev. award, 1963. Fellow Am. Bar Found.; mem. ABA (mem. com on corp. laws, mem. com. on fed. regulation of securities), Am. Law Inst., Hillsborough County Bar Assn., Greater Tampa C. of C. (mem. bd. govs. 1988-91), Com. 100 (mem. policy bd. 1989-92, trustee 1998—), Univ. Club, Tampa Club (bd. dirs. 1985-89, pres. 1987-88), The Down Town Assn., Order of Coif, Phi Kappa Phi.

JAMIESON, STUART WILLIAM, surgeon, educator; b. Bulawayo, Rhodesia, July 30, 1947; came to U.S., 1977; MB, BS, U. London, 1971. Intern St. Mary's Hosp., London, 1971; resident St. Mary's Hosp., Northwick Park Hosp., Brompton Hosp., London, 1972-77; asst. prof. Stanford U., Calif., 1980-83, assoc. prof., 1983-86; prof., head cardiac surgery U. Minn., Mpls., 1986-89, U. Calif., San Diego, 1989—; dir. Minn. Heart and Lung Inst., Mpls., 1986-89; pres. Calif. Heart and Lung Inst., San Diego, 1991-95. Co-author: Heart and Heart-Lung Transplantation, 1989; editor: Heart Surgery, 1987; contbr. over 500 papers to med. jours. Recipient Brit. Heart Found. Fellowship award, 1978, Irvine H. Page award Am. Heart Found., 1979, Silver medal Danish Surg. Soc., 1986. Fellow ACS, Royal Coll. Surgeons, Royal Soc. Medicine, Am. Coll. Chest Physicians, Am. Coll. Cardiology; mem. Royal Coll. Physicians (licentiate), Internat. Soc. for Heart Transplantation (pres. 1986-88), Calif. Heart and Lung Inst. (pres. 1991—). Office: U Calif-San Diego Divsn Cardiothoracic Surgery 200 W Arbor Dr San Diego CA 92103-8892

JAMIL, S. SELINA, eduator; b. Dhaka, Bangladesh, Feb. 3, 1960; d. Syed Altafuddin and Jamilun Nahar Ahmed; m. Nazre Jamil, Nov. 18, 1983; 1 child, Angzhu. BA in English with honors, U. Dhaka, Bangladesh, 1981; MA in English, Mich. State U., 1989, PhD in English, 1997. Lectr. English Jahangirnagar U., Dhaka, Bangladesh, 1985-87; teaching asst. Mich. State U., East Lansing, 1989-95; asst. prof. English U. Hartford, West Hartford, Conn., 1997—; student advisor Hillyer Coll., West Hartford, 1997—. Author of poems; contbr. articles to profl. jours. U. Hartford Internat. Ctr. grantee, 1997; Fulbright scholar, 1987-89. Mem. Modern Lang. Assn., Phi Beta Delta. Avocations: painting, embroidering, writing poetry. Home: 951 Hopmeadow St @11 Simsbury CT 06070 Office: U Hartford 200 Bloomfield Ave West Hartford CT 06117-1599

JAMIN, MATTHEW DANIEL, lawyer, magistrate judge; b. New Brunswick, N.J., Nov. 29, 1947; s. Matthew Bernard and Frances Marie (Newburg) J.; m. Christine Frances Bjorkman, June 28, 1969; children: Rebecca, Erica. BA, Colgate U., 1969; JD, Harvard U., 1974. Bar: Alaska 1974, U.S. Dist. Ct. Alaska 1974, U.S. Ct. Appeals (9th cir.) 1980. Staff atty. Alaska Legal Svcs., Anchorage, 1974-75; supervising atty. Alaska Legal Svcs., Kodiak, Alaska, 1975-81; contract atty. Pub. Defender's Office State of Alaska, Kodiak, 1976-82; prin. Matthew D. Jamin, Atty., Kodiak, 1982; ptnr. Jamin & Bolger, Kodiak, 1982-85, Jamin, Ebell, Bolger & Gentry, Kodiak, 1985-97; part-time magistrate judge U.S. Cts., Kodiak, 1984—; shareholder Jamin, Ebell, Schmitt & Mason, Kodiak, 1998—. Part-time instr. U. Alaska Kodiak Coll., 1975—; active Theshold Svcs., Inc., Kodiak, 1985—, pres., 1985-92, 95-96. Mem. Alaska Bar Assn. (Professionalism award 1988), Kodiak Bar Assn. Office: US Dist Ct 323 Carolyn Ave Kodiak AK 99615-6348

JAMISON, CONNIE JOYCE, sociology educator; b. Nashville, Jan. 4, 1954; d. William Earl and Mary Helen (Fleming) J.; m. Tom Kaardal (div. Nov. 1988). BS in Sociology, Mid. Tenn. State U., 1985, MA in Sociology, 1988; EdD, Tenn. State U., 1997. Prevention coord. Alcohol and Drug Coun., Nashville, 1987-92; adj. prof. sociology Belmont U., Nashville, 1988-94, Trevecca Nazarene U., Nashville, 1993-97; adj. prof. sociology Tenn. State U., Nashville, 1993-97, asst. prof. sociology, 1997—, grad. asst., 1995—. Mem. AAUW, Am. Sociol. Assn., Phi Gamma Mu, Phi Delta Kappa. Home: 2814 Hastings Rd Nashville TN 37214-3222

JAMISON, DAVID DWIGHT, county treasurer; b. Waukee, Iowa, Nov. 20, 1957; s. Dwight Lane and Evelyn Joyce (Whalley) J.; m. Karen Ann Martens, Aug. 1, 1987; children: Kelli Marie, Lauren Michelle, Samuel Marten. BBA, Iowa State U., 1991. Asst. mgr. Kwik Shop, Ames, Iowa, 1981-82; income maintenance mgr. Story County, Nevada, Iowa, 1987-89, income data coord., 1989-94, county treas., 1995—; mem. State Organ Adv. Com., Des Moines, 1997—. Mem. Story County Rep. Ctrl. Com., Ames, 1997—. Sgt. USMC, 1975-80. Recipient Joint Svc. Commendation medal Sec. of Def., 1980. Mem. Nat. Assn. Counties (steering com. 1996—), Iowa State County Treas.'s Assn. (pres. 1997-98), Iowa Statewide Organ Procurement Orgn. (bd. dirs. 1998—), Ames Jaycees (v.p. 1991—), Nevada Rotary (treas. 1994—), Am. Legion, Story County Bull Moose Club. Lutheran. Avocations: golf, co-recreational volleyball, fishing, politics. Home: 3244 Cameron School Rd Ames IA 50014-9396 Office: Story County Treas 900 6th St Nevada IA 50201-2004

JAMISON, DEAN TECUMSEH, economist; b. Springfield, Mo., Oct. 10, 1943; s. Marshall Verdine and Mary Dell (Temple) J.; m. Joanne Leslie, Sept. 14, 1971 (div. 1995); children: Julian C., Eliot A., Leslie S.; m. Kin Bing Wu, Jan. 19, 1997. AB in Philosophy, Stanford U., 1966, MS in Engring. Sci., 1967; PhD in Econs., Harvard U., 1970. Asst. prof. grad. sch. bus. Stanford U., Palo Alto, Calif., 1970-73; economist World Bank, Washington, 1976-88, dir., 1992-93, advisor, 1993-98; dir. Ctr. for Pacific Rim Studies UCLA, 1993—, prof. Sch. Pub. Health, Grad. Sch. Edn. and Info. Studies, 1988—; dir. econs. adv. svc. World Health Orgn., Geneva, 1998—; chmn. ad hoc com. on health R&D for developing countries WHO, Geneva, 1996-97; bd. trustees Drug Strategies, 1994—. Author (with L. J. Lau): Farmer Education and Farm Efficiency, 1982, Disease Control Priorities in Developing Countries, 1993, World Development Report 1993: Investing in Health, 1993; cons. editor AERA Ency. Rsch., 6th edit., 1992. Fellow Woodrow Wilson Found., 1967, NSF, 1968. Mem. Inst. Medicine Nat. Acad. Scis. Avocation: tennis. Fax: (310) 206-4018. E-mail: jamisond@who.ch. Office: UCLA Ctr for Pacific Rim Studies 11-292 Bunche Hall Los Angeles CA 90095-1487

JAMISON, FRANK RAYMOND, communications educator; b. Independence, Mo., Mar. 25, 1938; s. Eldon Verl and Pauline Francis (Mericle) J.; m. Paula Ann Wissing; children: Diana Cherie, Thomas Marshall, Noel Avery. BA, U. Mo., Kansas City, 1960; MS, Syracuse U., 1962; Edn. Specialist, U. No. Colo., 1967. Continuity dir. Sta. WEAR, Syracuse, N.Y., 1961; sales svc. dir. Sta. KCMO-TV, Kansas City, Mo., 1961-62; found., gen. mgr. KUNC-FM-U. No. Colo., Greeley, 1966-67; dir. radio and TV U. No. Colo., 1962-67; mgr. TV svcs. Western Mich. U., Kalamazoo, 1967-84, prof. instnl. media, 1977—, head media svcs., 1984-91; founder, gen. mgr. Edu-CABLE, Kalamazoo, 1989; mgr. video distbn. Western Mich. U., Kalamazoo, 1991—; head audiovisual svcs. King Faisal Specialist Hosp. and Rsch. Ctr., Riyadh, Saudi Arabia, 1977-79; founding ptnr. Lotus Prodns., 1997—; bd. dirs. Southwestern State Employees Credit Union, 1997—; mem. internat. adv. senate Amity Bus. Sch., New Delhi, India, 1995—; mem. nat. convention com. Assn. for Ednl. Comms. and Tech., Washington, 1992. Exec. prodr. TV series Every Child a Wanted Child, 1983 (Cable Ace award 1984); prodr. TV series Poets in Their Time, 1977-79 (Ohio State award 1980); assoc. prodr. radio program Where Are We?, 1969 (Armstrong award 1970); TV prodr. 12th World Scout Jamboree, 1967 (Silver Anvil award). Bd. dirs. New Vic Theatricals, Inc., 1978-82, Arts Coun. Greater Kalamazoo, 1978-82; faculty advisor Students for a Free Tibet, 1995—; founding chair U.S. Postal Svc. Customer Adv. Coun., 1994-98, S.W. Mich. Coun. Boy Scouts Am., 1967-70, 92-95; pres. Buddhist Assn. S.W. Mich., 1990—. Sgt. USAR, 1956-62. Recipient Philo T. Farnsworth award Nat. Fedn. Local Cable Progamming, 1984, Hometown U.S.A. award Nat. Fedn. Local Cable Programming, 1985, Network Founder award SCOLA TV Network, 1990, 50 Yr. Vet. award Boy Scouts Am., 1996, Videographer Award of Excellence for human rights programming, 1997, Videographer Distinction award for creativity, 1999; various grants for acad. projects. Mem. AAUP (various coms.), West Mich. Men's Coun. (sec. bd. dirs. 1994-96), Buddhadharma Soc. (faculty advisor 1991—), Am. Philatelic Soc. (25 Yr. award 1991), Arabian Philatelic Assn., Am. Mensa Ltd. Avocations: philately, videography, international travel, racquetball. Home: 2906 Memory Ln Kalamazoo MI 49006-5535 Office: Western Mich U 1112 Dunbar Kalamazoo MI 49008-5001

JAMISON, FREDERICK WILLIAM, data processing executive; b. St. Louis, Oct. 27, 1947; s. Elmer Bryan and Dolores Josephine (Rivers) J.; m. Linda Kae Hickinbotham, Feb. 13, 1971 (div. Nov. 1981); 1 child, Matthew Edward; m. Sharen Marie Wood, June 5, 1982; children: Brian Michael, Tiffany Leigh. BS in Systems and Data Processing, Washington U., 1980. Draftsman McDonnell Douglas Co., St. Louis, 1966-67, Western Electric Co., St. Louis, 1972-74; constrn. engr. Mo. Pacific R.R. Co., St. Louis, 1974-80; data resource mgr. Southwestern Bell Telephone Co., St. Louis, 1980—; tchr. computers Washington U., St. Louis, 1982-83, Meramec Community Coll., St. Louis, 1980-82; cons. data processing mgmt. Southwestern Bell, St. Louis, 1983—. Designer computer systems; patentee in field. Asst. organizer Harriet Wood for Senator, St. Louis, 1986. Served to sgt. U.S. Army, 1967-70, Vietnam. Decorated Bronze Star, Army Commendation medal. Mem. Smithsonian Inst. (assoc.). Lodge: Masons. Avocations: archery, gardening, the outdoors. Office: Southwestern Bell Telephone Co 1 Bell Ctr Rm 225F Saint Louis MO 63101-3099

JAMISON, GEORGE HILL III, broadcast company executive, writer; b. Richmond, Va., Sept. 18, 1956; s. George Hill Jr. and Joan Aspinwall J.; m. Kathleen Hannan, July 11, 1981; children: Simone, Bernadette, Caroline. BS in Journalism, Boston U., 1978. Dep. dir. pub. affairs Arnold Enring. Devel. Ctr., Tullahoma, Tenn., 1980-81; pub. rels. rep. GE, Washington, 1984-87; media rels. rep. GE, Fairfield, Conn., 1987-91, mgr. internat. comm., 1991-96; v.p. media rels. CNBC, Ft. Lee, N.J., 1996—. Author: Welcome to Club Dad, 1994. Capt. USAF, 1979-84. Roman Catholic. E-mail: george.jamison@nbc.com. Office: CNBC 2200 Fletcher Ave Fort Lee NJ 07024

JAMISON, HARRISON CLYDE, former oil company executive, petroleum exploration consultant; b. St. Louis, Jan. 15, 1925; s. William Clyde and Katherine Maurice (Fitzgerald) J.; m. Beverly Joy Johnson, June 26, 1946; children: Susan, David, Leslie, Daniel, Dale, Nancy, Sara. BA cum laude, UCLA. Geologist Richfield Oil Corp., Bakersfield, Calif., 1950-52, Olympia, Wash., 1952-55; Geologist Richfield Oil Corp., L.A., 1955-60, regional exploration supr., 1961-65; Alaska dist. mgr. Atlantic Richfield Co., Anchorage, 1966-69; Alaska coord. Atlantic Richfield Co., Dallas, 1969-70; mgr. govt. rels. Alyeska Pipeline Svc. Co., 1971-72; chief geologist ARCO Oil & Gas Co., Dallas, 1973-80; v.p. dist. mgr. ARCO Oil & Gas Co., Denver, 1981; pres. ARCO Exploration Co., Dallas, 1981-85; sr. v.p. Atlantic Richfield Co., L.A., 1981-85. Contbr. articles to profl. jours. Former bd. dirs. Tex. Rsch. League, Austin, Dallas Citizens Coun., Mex. Am. Legal Def. and Edn. Fund, Resolution Seismic Svcs. Inc., Wilmington, Del., ARCO Alaska Inc., Thomas Wilson Dibblee Jr. Geol. Found., Hospice of Bend. Fellow Geol. Soc. Am. (former chmn. bd. dirs., trustees GSA Found. 1986-88); mem. Am. Assn. Petroleum Geologists, N.W. Energy Assn. Home and Office: 37615 S Stoney Cliff Ct Tucson AZ 85739-1412

JAMISON, JAMES MARK, cell biologist; b. Warren, Ohio, July 12, 1951; s. James William and Dorothy Mildred (Mocella) J.; m. Cheryl Louise Burgess, Sept. 5, 1992; children: Miguel, Rachel. BSEd, Kent State U., 1973, MS in Ecology, 1981, PhD in Cell Biology, 1986. Postdoctoral fellow N.E. Ohio U. Coll. of Medicine, Rootstown, Ohio, 1986-89; rsch. and forensic scientist Gennan Corp., Akron, Ohio, 1989-91; instr. of microscopic anatomy N.E. Ohio U. Coll. of Medicine, Rootstown, 1992-95, rsch. asst. prof. of microbiology, immunology, 1995-96, rsch. asst., prof. of urology, 1997—. Contbg. author: Progress in Molecular and Subcellular Biology, 1994. Com. chmn. Pack 3274 Cub Scout Pack, Stow, Ohio, 1996-98; dist. tng. chmn. Moecomdws Dist. Cub Scouts, Akron, 1997—; scoutmaster Szow, Ohio, 1998—. Grantee Summa Health System Found., Akron, 1991—, NATO Internat. Coll. Rsch., Brussels, 1994-96, Am. Inst. for Cancer Rsch., Washington, 1998—, Hess, Roth, Kaminsky and Maxon Urol. Rsch. Found., Erie, Pa., 1997—. Mem. Am. Assn. of Anatomists, Am. Soc. for Cell Biology, Electron Microscopy Soc. Am., Internat. Soc. for Interferon Rsch., Am. Soc. Pharmacognosy, Soc. for Basic Urologic Rsch. Office: Dept Urology Neoucom PO Box 95 4209 SR 44 PO Rootstown OH 44272-0095

JAMISON, JAYNE, magazine publisher. Group pub. Child mag., N.Y.C.; pub. Parents mag., N.Y.C.; pub. v.p. Redbook, 1997—. Office: Redbook Mag 224 W 57th St New York NY 10019-3299*

JAMISON, JOHN CALLISON, business educator, investment banker; b. Lafayette, Ind., July 12, 1934; s. John Ruger and Sara (Callison) J.; m. Carol Ann Sansone, July 7, 1979; children: Kelly Elizabeth Supplee, Deborah Louise Jamison. B.S. in Indsl. Econs., Purdue U., 1956; M.B.A., Harvard U., 1961. Assoc. Goldman, Sachs & Co., N.Y.C., 1961-69, ptnr., 1969-82, ltd. ptnr., 1983—; dean Sch. Bus. Adminstrn., John N. Dalton prof. bus. adminstrn. Coll. William and Mary, Williamsburg, Va., 1983-90; pres. bd., CEO The Mariners' Mus., Newport News, Va., 1991-93, trustee, 1991—; bd. dirs. Hershey Foods Corp., Pa., Richfood Holdings Inc., Richmond, The Williamsburg Winery, Va. Bd. govs. Purdue Found., West Lafayette, Ind., 1979-83; bd. dirs. Theatre Devel. Fund, N.Y.C., 1979-83; mem. corp. Hurricane Island Outward Bound Sch., Rockland, Maine, 1983-95; mem. vis. com. Harvard Grad. Sch. Edn., 1983-89. Lt. USN, 1956-59, PTO. Recipient Old Master award Purdue U., 1977; recipient Sagamore of Wabash award Gov. of Ind., 1982. Mem. Rotary, Beta Gamma Sigma. Episcopalian.

JAMISON, JUDITH, dancer; b. Phila., May 10, 1943; d. John J. Student, Fisk U., Phila., Phila. Dance Acad. (now U. of Arts); studied with, Anthony Tudor, John Hines, Delores Brown, John Jones, Joan Kerr, Madame Swaboda. Dancer Alvin Ailey's Am. Dance Theatre, N.Y.C., 1965-80; artistic dir. Alvin Ailey's Am. Dance Theatre, N.Y.C., 1990—; dancer, choreographer touring U.S., Europe, Asia, S.Am., Africa, 1980—; formerly with Maurice Hines Dance Sch., N.Y.C.; founder Jamison Project, 1988-91; vis. disting. prof. Univ. of Arts; guest assoc. artistic dir. 30th ann. tour Alvin Ailey's Am. Dance Theatre, 1990—; guest appearences with Harkness Ballet, Am. Ballet Theatre, San Francisco Ballet, Dallas Ballet. N.Y. dance debut in Agnes DeMille's "The Four Marys", 1965; starring role created for her in Joseph's Legend (John Neumeier), Vienna Opera, Le Spectre de la Rose (Maurice Bejart), Brussels, Paris, N.Y.C.; performed in Maskela Language, 1969, Cry, 1971, Choral Dance, 1971, Mary Lou's Mass, 1971, The Lark Ascending, 1972, The Mooche, 1975, Passage, 1978; star Broadway show Sophisticated Ladies, 1980; choreographer Divining Hymn for Alvin Ailey Am. Dance Theatre, works for Maurice Bejart, Dancers Unltd. Dallas, Washington Ballet, Jennifer Muller/The Works, Alvin Ailey Repertory Ensemble, Ballet Nuevo Mundo de Caracas, Riverside for Alvin Ailey Am. Dance Theatre, also for opera Boito's Mefistofele for Opera Co. Phila.; subject of PBS spl. The Dancemaker; subject of book Aspects of a Dancer; author: Dancing Spirit, 1993. Recipient Dance Mag. award, 1972, Key to the City of N.Y., 1976, Disting. Service award Mayor of N.Y.C., 1982, Disting. Service award Harvard U., 1982, Spirit of Achievement award Nat. Women's Divsn. Yeshiva U. Albert Einstein Coll. Medicine, 1992, Golden Plate award Am. Acad. Achievement, 1993. Address: Alvin Ailey Am Dance Theater 211 W 61st St Fl 3 New York NY 10023-7832*

JAMISON, OLIVER MORTON, retired lawyer; b. Portland, Oreg., Aug. 1, 1916; s. Homer B. and Jean (Allison) J.; m. Margaret Ratcliffe, July 18, 1941; children—Stephen, Thomas, Daniel. A.B., Stanford, 1938, LL.B., 1941. Bar: Calif. bar 1941. Since practiced in Fresno; ptnr. firm then of counsel Thomas, Snell, Jamison, Russell & Asperger P.C. and predecessors, 1941-93; retired, 1994; Lectr. taxation Calif. Bar Continuing Edn. Program, 1948, 51, 54, 64, Am. Law Inst., 1949, 50, 53, U. So. Calif. Inst. Fed. Taxation, 1961; mem. taxation adv. commn. Calif. Bar Legal Splzn. Bd., 1971-74; bd. govs. Calif. State Bar, 1976-79, v.p., 1979. Trustee Calif. State U., Fresno Found., 1973-78, Fresno Community Hosp., 1972-78. Served to capt. AUS, 1942-46. Mem. Fresno County Bar Assn., Fresno County and City C. of C. (pres. 1960), State Bar Calif., Am. Law Inst., Order of Coif, Phi Alpha Delta. Home: 5515 N Fresno St Apt 109 Fresno CA 93710-6093

JAMISON, REX LINDSAY, medical educator; b. Des Moines, July 8, 1933; s. Orin Lindsay and Helen Belle (Buck) J.; m. Dorothy Tufts Lockwood, Mar. 3, 1962; children: Richard Lindsay, John Lockwood. AB, U. Iowa, 1955; BA, U. Oxford, Eng., 1957, MA, 1961; MD, Harvard U., 1960. Intern Mass. Gen. Hosp., Boston, 1960-61, asst. resident in medicine, 1961-62; sr. asst. resident in medicine Columbia-Presbyn. Med. Ctr., N.Y.C., 1962-63; clin. assoc. Lab. Kidney and Electrolyte Metabolism, NIH, Bethesda, Md., 1963-66; instr. in medicine Washington U. Sch. Medicine, St. Louis, 1966-67, asst. prof. medicine, 1967-71, asst. prof. physiology and biophysics, 1968-71; assoc. prof. medicine Stanford (Calif.) U. Sch. Medicine, 1971-82, co-head div. nephrology, 1971-80, chief div., 1980-87, prof. medicine and physiology, 1982-87, acting chmn. dept. medicine, acting physician-in-chief, 1984-86, prof. medicine, 1992—; Charles A. Dewey prof. medicine, chmn. dept. medicine U. Rochester (N.Y.) Sch. Medicine and Dentistry, 1987-90, prof. medicine and physiology, 1990-92; physician-in-chief Strong Meml. Hosp., Rochester, 1987-90; chief renal div. Jewish Hosp. St. Louis, 1966-71, div. nephrology Stanford U. Hosp., 1971-87; vis. prof. Laboratorie de Physiologie Physico-Chimique Centre d'Etudes, Nucleaires de Saclay, Gif-sur-Yvette, France, 1977-78; mem. external monitoring com. modification of diet in renal disease study Nat. Inst. Arthritis, Diabetes and Digestive and Kidney Diseases, 1989-90; med. adv. bd. Nat. Kidney Found. Upstate N.Y., 1987-91, No. Calif., 1992—; mem. Intersoc. Coun., 1988-92; cons. phram. and biotech. cos., 1993—; William C. Smith lectr. UCLA St. Mary Hosp. Author: (with Wilhelm Kriz) Urinary Concentrating Mechanism: Structure and Function, 1982; author, editor: Transplantation in the 1980s: Recent Advances, 1984, (with Serge Jard) Vasopressin, 1991, Nephrology (with Robert Wilkinson), 1997; contbr. numerous articles to profl. jours. Mem. Rhodes Scholar Selection Coms. Vt., Md., Mo., Calif. Dist. V. Rhodes scholar, Markle scholar; John S. Guggenheim Found. fellow; Rsch. Career Devel. grantee USPHS, 1963-66, grantee Calif. Acad. Medicine, Rochester Acad. Medicine; recipient Champion of Hope award Nat. Kidney Found., No. Calif. Fellow ACP, Royal Coll. Physicians (hon.); mem. Am. Heart Assn. (vice chmn. coun. on cardiovascular disease and the kidney 1986-88, chmn. 1988-92), Am. Physiol. Soc., Am. Soc. Clin. Investigation , Am. Soc. Nephrology (chmn. program com. 1984), Assn. Am. Physicians, Assn. Profs. Medicine, Western Assn. Physicians, Western Soc. Clin. Investigation (councilor 1974-77), Peruvian Soc. Nephrology (hon.), Internat. Soc. Nephrology Commn. on Devel. Countries, Phi Beta Kappa. Episcopalian. Avocations: music, golf. Home: 850 Cedro Way Palo Alto CA 94305-1003

JAMISON, RICHARD BRYAN, airport consultant; b. Cumberland, Md., Mar. 13, 1932; s. Harry B. and Eula Jamison; m. Elva J. Taylor, Sept. 25, 1931; three children. BA in History with distinction, U. Mo., 1957, JD, 1965. Broadcaster, news reporter, 1950-51, 54-65; with Am. Airlines, N.Y.C. and Dallas, 1965-85, v.p., 1982-85; dir. Detroit Metro and Willow Run airports County Wayne, Mich., 1985-90. With U.S. Army, 1952-54. Mem. Am. Assn. Airport Execs., Assn. of the Bar of City of N.Y., Tex. Bar Assn., Mo. Bar Assn., Phi Beta Kappa. Methodist. Clubs: Wings (N.Y.). Avocations: broadcasting, reading, hiking, music. Home: 120 Artillery Rd Winchester VA 22602-6945

JAMISON, RICHARD MELVIN, virologist, educator; b. Rayne, La., Oct. 28, 1938; s. Melvin Linwood and Lina Katharine (Muller) J.; children: Richard Wilhelm, Diane Elizabeth, Bonnie Alyssa. M.S. (USPHS fellow), Baylor U. Coll. Medicine, 1962, Ph.D., 1966. Diplomate Am. Bd. Med. Microbiology (trustee 1983-89, 92-99). Rsch. assoc. Oak Ridge Nat. Lab., 1966-67; asst. prof. U. Colo. Med. Center, Denver, 1967-70; virologist La. State U. Med. Center, Shreveport, 1970—; prof. microbiology and immunology La. State U. Med. Center, 1978—, prof. pediatrics, 1987—; pres. gen. faculty, 1992-93; editor Cumitechs, 1998—; cons. Al Fateh U., Socialist People's Libyan Arab Jamahiriya. Vice pres. Shreveport Civic Opera Assn., 1977-79. Fellow Am. Acad. Microbiology; mem. AAAS, Am. Soc. Microbiology, Pan Am. Soc. Clin. Virology, Shreveport Orchid Soc. (pres. 1987-89, treas. 1992-94, v.p. 1995-97). Research in host-virus interactions and picornaviruses, diagnostic and clinical virology. Home: 3005 Meriwether Rd Shreveport LA 71108-5403 Office: PO Box 33932 Shreveport LA 71130-3932

JAMISON, ROGER W., pianist, piano educator; b. Marion, Ohio, June 18, 1937; s. Harold Theodore and Martha Louise (Haas) J.; m. Caroline R. Hansley, Jan. 26, 1957; children: Lisa Renee, Eric Karl. BS, Ohio State U., 1959, MA (scholar), 1961; postgrad. Oberlin Conservatory, Oakland U.; student George Haddad, Columbus, Ohio, Mischa Kottler, Detroit. Piano faculty mem. Detroit Conservatory of Music, 1964-68, Cranbrook Schs., Bloomfield Hills, Mich., 1981-84; performer in one-man mus. presentation Spirits of Great Composers, 1979—; dir. music Birmingham Temple, Farmington Hills, Mich., 1984-95; soloist Brunch with Bach series Detroit Inst. Arts., Detroit Symphony Orch.'s Internat. Brahms Festival; regular soloist Christ Ch., Cranbrook, 1982-95; concert tour of Eng., 1991; condr. All Ohio Piano Ensemble, 1997; cons. Royal Oak Arts Council; adjudicator Am. Coll. Musicians. Mem. Nat. Guild of Piano Tchrs. (past pres. Oakland-Macomb chpt.) Address: 173 W Heffner St Delaware OH 43015-1258

JAMISON, WARREN, writer, lecturer, publisher; b. Mitchell, S.D., Aug. 12, 1924; s. Robert William J.; m. Kitty Sue Wilkerson, Oct. 7, 1961; children: Cynthia Sue, Brian Erik. Co-author: (with Danielle Kennedy) How to List and Sell Real Estate in the 21st Century, 1999; (with Ed McMahon) Ed McMahon's Superselling, 1989, (Literary Guild Selection); (with others) Screw: The Truth About Walpole Prison by the Guard Who Lived It, 1989, (Conservative Book Club Selection), (with Brian Jamison and Josh Gold) Electronic Selling: 23 Steps to E-Selling Profits, 1997; editor: (books) Ed McMahon's The Art of Public Speaking, 1986, How to Master the Art of Selling, Tom Hopkins, 1980, 2d rev. edition, 1982, The Official Guide to Success, 1983, Tom Hopkins, Guide to Greatness in Sales, Tom Hopkins, 1992, Toughness Training for Life, Dr. James E. Loehr, 1993, The New Toughness Training for Sports, Dr. James E Loehr, 1994, The Anti-Diet Book, Jack Groppel, 1995. Mem. Authors Guild, Am. Soc. Journalists and Authors. Home and Office: 2201 S Palm Canyon #202 Palm Springs CA 92264-9341

JAMME, ALBERT JOSEPH, archaeologist, educator; b. Senzeilles, Belgium, June 27, 1916; came to U.S., 1953; s. Alfred and Albine (Roulin) J. S.T.D., Cath. U., Louvain, Belgium, 1946, Dr. Or. Philol. and History, 1952; Lic. Bibl. St., Vatican City, 1948. Faculty Cath. U. Am., 1955—, research prof., epigraphist, archaeologist, 1950—. Author: Miscellanées d'Ancient Arabe, 21 vols., 1971-98. Am. Philos. Soc. grantee, 1960; DeRance Found. grantee, 1979, 80. Mem. Am. Found. for Study of Man (v.p. 1979—), Am. Oriental Soc., Cath. Bibl. Assn., Am. Inst. Yemeni Studies. Roman Catholic. Home: 1624 21st St NW Washington DC 20009-1003 Office: Cath U Am Washington DC 20064

JAMPLIS, ROBERT WARREN, surgeon, medical foundation executive; b. Chgo., Apr. 1, 1920; s. Mark and Janet (McKenna) J.; m. Roberta Cecelia Prior, Sept. 5, 1947; children: Mark Prior, Elizabeth Ann Jamplis Bluestone. BS, U. Chgo., 1941, MD, 1944; MS, U. Minn., 1951. Diplomate Am. Bd. Surgery, Am. Bd. Thoracic Surgery. Asst. resident in surgery U. Chgo., 1946-47; fellow in thoracic surgery Mayo Clinic, Rochester, Minn., 1947-52; chief thoracic surgery Palo Alto (Calif.) Med. Clinic, 1958-81, exec. dir., 1965-81; clin. prof. surgery Stanford U. Sch. Medicine, 1958—; mem. coun. SRI Internat.; chmn. bd. TakeCare Corp.; charter mem., bd. regents Am. Coll. Physician Execs.; mem. staff Stanford Univ. Hosp., Santa Clara Valley Med. Ctr., San Jose, VA Hosp., Palo Alto, Sequoia Hosp., Redwood City, Calif., El Camino Hosp., Mountain View, Calif., Harold D. Chope Cmty. Hosp., San Mateo, Calif.; pres., CEO Palo Alto Med. Found., 1965—; past chmn. Fedn. Am. Clinics; dir. Blue Cross Calif.; varsity football team physician Stanford U. Author: (with G.A. Lillington) A Diagnostic Approach to Chest Diseases, 1965, 2d edit., 1979; contbr. numerous articles to profl. jours. Trustee Santa Barbara Med. Found. Clinic; past pres. Calif. div. Am. Cancer Soc.; past chmn. bd. Group Practice Polit. Action Com.; past mem. athletic bd. Stanford U.; past mem. cabinet U. Chgo.; bd. dirs. Herbert Hoover Boys' Club; past trustee No. Calif. Cancer Program; past bd. dirs. Core Communications in Health, Community Blood Res., others. Served to lt. USNR, 1944-46, 52-54. Recipient Alumni citation U. Chgo., 1968, Nat. Divsn. award Am. Cancer Soc., 1979, Med. Exec. award Am. Coll. Med. Group Adminstrs., 1981, Russel V. Lee award lectr. Am. Group Practice Assn., 1982, Mayo Disting. Alumnus award, 1991. Mem. Inst. Medicine of Nat. Acad. Scis., ACS, Am. Assn. Thoracic Surgery, Am. Surg. Assn., Soc. Thoracic Surgeons (past pres.), Western Thoracic Surg. Assn. (past pres.), Western Surg. Assn., Pacific Coast Surg. Assn., San Francisco Surg. Soc. (past pres.), Portland Surg. Soc. (hon.), Doctors Mayo Soc., Am. Coll. Chest Physicians (bd. govs.), Calif. Acad. Medicine, Am. Fedn. Clin. Research, Am. Group Practice Assn. (past pres.), AMA, Calif. Med. Assn., Santa Clara County Med. Assn., Sigma Xi. Republican. Roman Catholic. Clubs: Bohemian, Pacific Union, Commonwealth of California (San Francisco); Menlo Country (Woodside, (Calif.); Menlo Circus (Atherton, Calif.); Stanford (Calif.) Golf; Rancheros Visitadores (Santa Barbara, Calif.). Office: Palo Alto Med Foundation 300 Homer Ave Palo Alto CA 94301-2726

JAMRICH, JOHN XAVIER, retired university administrator; b. Muskegon Heights, Mich., June 12, 1920; s. John and Mary (Mudry) J.; m. June Ann Hrupka, June 26, 1944; children: June Ann, Marna Mary, Barbara Sue. Student, Milw. State Tchrs. Coll., 1939-40, Ripon Coll., 1940-42; BS, U. Chgo., 1942-43; MS, Marquette U., 1946-48; PhD, Northwestern U., 1951; LHD (hon.), No. Mich. U., 1968. Instr. math. Marquette U., 1946-48; asst. instr. math. U. Wis., 1948-49; asst. dean men Northwestern U., 1949-51; dean students Coe Coll., Cedar Rapids, Iowa, 1951-55; dean faculty, prof. math. Doane Coll., Crete, Nebr., 1955-57; assoc. dir. Legis. Survey Higher Edn. in Mich., 1957-58; prof. higher edn., dir. Center for Study Higher Edn., Mich. State U., 1957-63, assoc. dean Coll. Edn., prof. higher edn., 1963-68; pres. No. Mich. U., 1968-83, adj. prof., 1983—; cons.-examiner N. Central Assn. Colls. and Secondary Schs., 1962—; cons. in field, 1959—; Ford Found. cons. for devel. U. Nigeria, 1964; cons. higher edn. Govt. of Thailand, 1967; dir. Lake Superior & Ishpeming R.R.; chmn. Nat. Adv. Council Fin. Aid to Students, 1975. Author numerous articles in field; co-author several books; piano and vocal music composer. Bd. dirs. Mich. Joint Council on Econ. Edn., 1977—; trustee Marquette (Mich.) Gen. Hosp.; bd. dirs. Bay Cliff Health Camp, Marquette; mem. Mich. Council for Arts, 1969-73. Served to capt. USAAF, 1942-46. Decorated Order Lion Finland; recipient City of Peace award (Israel), World War II Victory medal Russian Govt., 1997, Disting. Svc. medal U.S. Dept. Army, 1983. Mem. Newcomen Soc. N.Am. Home: 523 Governors Green Dr Venice FL 34293-4422

JAMROGIEWICZ, DEBRA LYNN, educational consultant; b. Indpls., Jan. 18, 1953; d. Marion Alfred and Phyllis Ann (Sperback) Fieber; m. Roman Andrew Jamrogiewicz, Mar. 8, 1975; children: Andrew, Peter. BA, Purdue U., 1974. Tchr. All Saints Sch., Ft. Worth, 1975-76; program dir. YMCA, Ft. Worth, 1976-77; office mgr. Canton Corps., Mpls., 1977-79; sch. bd. dirs., chair Wayzata (Minn.) Pub. Schs., 1992—; bd. dirs. N.E. Safe Kids Coalition, Mpls., 1992-96; dir. edn. Ch. of St. Anne, Medina, Minn., 1990-95; pres. Leadership Strategies for Success, Inc., Mpls., 1998—; cons. Hazard, Young, Attea and Assocs., Chgo., 1996—. Bd. dirs. Assn. of Met. Sch. Dists, Mpls., 1995-97; mem. Twin West Women's Network, Mpls., 1996-97; pres. PTA, Wayzata, 1990-91. Mem. Nat. Sch. Bds. Assn., Minn. Sch. Bd. Assn., Twin West-Wayzata-N.W. C. of C. Roman Catholic. Avocations: volunteerism, golf, reading. Office: Wayzata Pub Schs PO Box 660 Wayzata MN 55391-0660

JAMSHEED, JACQUELINE TAHMINEY, financial manager; b. Tehran, Iran, Apr. 15, 1966; d. Rashid and Wendy (Coyle) J; m. Thomas Edward Boldt, Aug. 12, 1995. BA, BS, Syracuse U., 1988; MBA, U. Va., 1995. Asst. editor U.S. Shooting Team, Washington, 1988-92; analyst World Bank, Washington, 1993-94; mgr. Pratt & Whitney, East Hartford, Conn., 1995—. Mem. Potomac Boat Club Crew Team (winner U.S. Club Nats., 1989). Home: 64 Spellmans Point Rd East Hampton CT 06424

JAN, COLLEEN ROSE, secondary school educator; b. Toledo, Ohio, Sept. 1, 1953; d. Robert James and Irene Dolores (Bartnikowski) Kegerreis; children: Brett Robert Jan, Shawna Michele Jan. AA, Monroe County C.C., Mich., 1973; BS, U. Toledo, 1975, JD, 1978, MEd, 1992, postgrad., 1992-98. Cert. in secondary edn., Mich. Sec. Family Planning, Monroe, 1971-73; paralegal Bedford Legal Bldg., Temperance, Mich., 1973-80; tchr. Bedford Pub. Schs., Lambertville, Mich., 1989—, lang. arts chair, 1996, social studies chair, 1996—; union bldg. rep., mem. negotiating team Bedford Pub. Schs., 1997—; mem. NCA Outcomes Visitation Team, Birney Middle Sch., Southfield, Mich., 1993—; mem. dist. assessment and profl. devel. com., 1995-96. Creater video: Winning at the MEAP, 1991. Expository com. co-chair Sch. Improvement/Bedford, Temperance, 1991—, steering com., 1992—; social studies core curriculum mem. Intermediate Sch. Dist., Monroe, 1993-94, Bedford Pub. Schs., 1994—; co-chair NCA steering com., 1994—; co-advisor Students United Against Drugs, Temperance, 1990-96; designer The Cmty. Svc. Alternative, Temperance, 1993-94; facilitator Lion's Club Quest Program, Temperance, 1989-91; campaign mgr. Sch. Bd. Mem., 1987-88; 3d v.p. PTA, Lambertville, Mich., 1998-99; pres. PTSA Bedford Jr. H.S., 1998-99. Mem. AAUW, Nat. Coun. for the Social Studies, Phi Delta Kappa, Phi Kappa Phi. Avocations: travel, reading, woodworking, cards. Office: Bedford Jr High Sch 8405 Jackman Rd Temperance MI 48182-9498

JAN, LILY YEH, physiology, biochemist; b. China, Jan. 20, 1947; came to U.S.; Grad., Nat. Taiwan U., 1968; MSc, Calif. Inst. Tech., 1970, PhD in Biophysics and Physics, 1974. Rsch. fellow Calif. Inst. Tech., 1974-77, Harvard Med. Sch., 1977-79; asst. prof. to prof. physiology U. Calif., San Francisco, 1979-85, prof. physiology and biochemistry, 1985—; rsch. fellow Alfred P. Sloan, 1977-79; lectr. Columbia U., 1988; faculty lectr. U. Calif., San Francisco, 1995. Recipient Kavots Neuroscience Investor award Nat. Inst. Neurol. and Communicable Diseases and Stroke, 1988—; Klingenstein fellow, 1983-86. Mem. NAS. Office: Univ Calif Howard Hughes Med Inst 533 Parnassus Ave San Francisco CA 94143-0724*

JAN, YUH NUNG, biochemistry and physiology educator; b. Shanghai, Republic of China, Dec. 20, 1946; m. Lily Yeh, 1971. BS, Nat. Taiwan U., 1967; MS, Calif. Inst. Tech., 1970. Postdoctoral rsch. fellow Calif. Inst. Tech., 1974-77, dept. neurobiology, Harvard U. Sch. Medicine, 1977-79; asst. prof., then assoc. prof. U. Calif., San Francisco, 1979-85, prof. physiology and biochemistry, 1985—; investigator Howard Hughes Med. Inst., 1984—; fellow Scottish Rite Schizophrenia Rsch. Program, 1974-76, Muscular Dystrophy Assn., 1976-78; W. Alden Spencer lectr., Columbia U., 1988. McKnight scholar, 1978. Mem. Nat. Acad. Sci., Genetics Soc. Am., Soc. Chinese Bioscientists Am., Am. Soc. Cell Biology, Soc. Neurosci., Soc. Develop. Biology. *

JANAIRO, ALTHEA See CARRERE, TIA

JANAVARAS, BASIL JOHN, university business educator, consultant; b. Corinth, Corinth, Greece, Nov. 1, 1943; came to U.S., 1962; s. John Basil and Loukia Demetra (Tzakona) J.; m. Linda Mae Larson, Aug. 19, 1972; children: Loukia Linda, John Basil (dec.). BA, Minot State U., 1967; MS, U. N.D., 1969; EdD, No. Ill. U., 1974. Bus. instr. Mankato (Minn.) State U., 1969-72, asst. prof., 1974-76, assoc. prof., 1977-80, prof., 1980-85; dir. Internat. Bus. Inst., Mankato, 1986-89, chairperson, dir., 1986-91; pres., CEO Ianavaras & Assocs. Internat., Inc., 1990—; dir. internat. bus. studies U. St. Thomas, St. Paul, 1992-96; pres. Odyssey Gift Shops, Mankato, 1978-94; dir. Internat. Bus. Exec. Program, St. Paul, 1988—, Minn. State U. Sys., Vienna, Austria, 1990-92; pres., CEO Janavaras & Assocs. Internat. Inc., Mankato, 1990—. Author: Student Guide to International Business, 1988, Student Resource Manual, 1992, Global Marketing Management System, 1998; contbr. articles to profl. jours. Grantee Mankato State U., 1988-89, U.S. Dept. Edn., 1988-90, So. Minn. Initiative Fund, 1988-90. Mem. Acad. Internat. Bus., Minn. World Trade Week (bd. dirs. 1983—, pres. 1989), Minn. Dist. Export Coun., Minn. World Trade Assn. Home: 27 Capri Dr Mankato MN 56001-4119 Office: Minn State U PO Box 14 Mankato MN 56002-0014

JANCUK, KATHLEEN FRANCES, educational administrator; b. Balt., Apr. 1, 1950; d. Joseph Frank and Dorothy Jane (Lowrey) J. BA in Elem. Edn., Notre Dame Coll., Balt., 1974; MEd in Reading, Towson State U., 1985; MEd in Adminstrn., Loyola Coll., Balt., 1992. Cert. tchr., reading specialist, adminstr. and supr., Md. Substitute tchr. St. Wenceslaus, Balt., 1970-72; tchr. 5th grade St. Boniface, Phila., 1972-77; tchr. 5th grade Cath. C.C., Balt., 1977-82, reading specialist K-5, 1982-88; reading specialist K-8 St. Mary's Elem. Sch., Annapolis, Md., 1988-91; prin. St. Clare Sch., Balt., 1991-97, St. John Neumann Sch., Cumberland, Md., 1997—. Non-voting mem. St. Clare Sch. Bd., Balt., 1991-97; mem. Sch. Sisters of Notre Dame, 1991—; mem. area pastoral coun., 1993-97. Recipient Recognition of Svc. award Archdiocese of Balt., 1993. Mem. ASCD, Elem. Sch. Prins. Assn. (exec. bd. dirs. 1994-97), Nat. Cath. Ednl. Assn., Mid. States Assn. Sch. Evaluation Teams. Democrat. Roman Catholic. Avocations: collecting clowns, puppetry, swimming, singing, playing guitar and piano. Office: St John Neumann Sch Fayette and Smallwood Sts Cumberland MD 21502

JANDER, KLAUS HEINRICH, lawyer; b. Glogau, Ger., May 17, 1940; s. Heinrich Sylvester and Maria Agnes (Widera) J.; m. Deborah I. VanAlst, Aug. 20, 1966; 1 child, Dietrich Alexander Van Alst. BA, CUNY, 1959; JD, Cornell U., 1964; Dipl., U. of the Saar, Ger., 1968. Bar: N.Y., D.C. Assoc. Carter Ledyard & Milburn, N.Y.C., 1964-65; assoc. to sr. ptnr. Alexander & Green, N.Y.C., 1969-89; ptnr. Rogers & Wells, N.Y.C., 1990—; dir. various corps. Contbr. articles to profl. jours.; author: Taking Foreign Corporations Public, 1985, U.S. Subsidiaries of German Companies, 1982. Mem. Cornell Law Sch. adv. coun., 1989—. Col. USAF, 1959-89. Decorated Legion of Merit, Meritorious Svc. medal with oak leaf cluster, Air Force Commendation medal with 2 oak leaf clusters. Fellow Am. Bar Found.; mem. ABA, German Law Assn., Assn. Bar of City of N.Y., Internat. Bar Assn., Germany-Am. Lawyers Assn., Cornell Law Sch. Alumni Assn. (exec. com. 1986-89). Roman Catholic. Avocations: skiing, reading, swimming. Home: 307 Stanwich Rd Greenwich CT 06830-3522 Office: Rogers & Wells 200 Park Ave Fl 8E New York NY 10166-0800 also: Westendstrasse 16-22, 60325 Frankfurt am Main Germany

JANDES, KENNETH MICHAEL, superintendent of schools; b. Berwyn, Ill., Aug. 6, 1943; s. George Jerry and Dorothea Frieda Clara (Grabow) J.; m. RoseMary Patricia Klingebiel, June 18, 1966; children: Michael Jon, Kenneth Mark. BS in Edn., Ill. State U., 1966; MEd, Loyola U., Chgo., 1972; EdD, No. Ill. U., 1984. Cert. tchr., chief sch. bus. official, gen. adminstrv., supt., Ill. Math. tchr. Brook Park Sch., LaGrange Park, Ill., 1966-69, sci. tchr., 1969-74, acting prin., 1972-74; prin. Waterman Sch., South Holland, Ill., 1974-79, Berger-Vandenberg Sch., Dolton, Ill., 1979-95; supt. Lincoln Sch. Dist. # 156, Calumet City, Ill., 1995—; chmn. dept. applied saxophone Am. Conservatory Music, Chgo., 1968-78 ; owner, operator Midwest Music Mart, Riverside, Ill., 1968-73; primary sci. cons. Instructor Mag., Dansville, N.Y., 1969-73; adj. prof. Govs. State U., University Park, Ill., 1985—; performing saxophonist Ken Jandes Dance Orch., Andy Tecson Jazz Ensemble. Composer of numerous choral, band, and orchestral works, 1961—; contbr. articles to profl. jours. Bd. dirs. Community Family Svc. and Mental Health Ctr. La Grange, 1968-74, ECHO Spl. Edn. Coop.; bd. dirs. Thornton Fractional Area Ednl. Coop., v.p., 1998-99; mem. com., treas. Boy Scouts Am., Woodridge, 1985—; baseball coach Woodridges Athletic Assn., 1980-89; active com. on youth traffic safety Ill. Sec. of State, 1987-91; chmn. Thornton Twp. Regional Action Planning Project, 1996—; mem. chancel choir St. Luke Presbyn. Ch., Downers Grove, Ill., 1976—, elder, 1980-86, 92-98. Named one of Outstanding Young Men Am. Jaycees, 1970. Mem. ASCD, Am. Assn. Sch. Adminstrs. (Nat. award 1986), Ill. Assn. Sch. Adminstrs., Ill. Assn. Sch. Bus. Ofcls., Ill. Congress Parents and Tchrs. (hon. life), South Cook County Elem. Sch. Supt.'s Assn. (pres. 1997-98), Calumet City C. of C., Bus. Assocs. Calumet City, MENSA, Lions, Kappa Delta Pi, Phi Mu Alpha Sinfonia, Phi Delta Kappa. Avocations: astronomy, tennis, mathematics, computers, scientific reading, wine and fine dining. Home: 6671 Wheatfield St Woodridge IL 60517-1715 Office: Lincoln Sch Dist 156 410 157th St Calumet City IL 60409-4798

JANDL, HENRY ANTHONY, architect, educator; b. Spokane, July 17, 1910; s. Paul and Marie (Zitterbart) J.; m. Gertrude Ward, June 4, 1940 (dec. 1976); children: Margaret M., H. Ward (dec.); m. Nancy Crater, Oct. 2, 1976. Student, Fontainebleau (France) Sch. Fine Arts, 1933; B.Arch., M.Arch., Carnegie Inst. Tech., 1935; M.F.A. in Architecture, Princeton U., 1937; postgrad., Ecole des Beaux Arts, Paris, 1937-39. Faculty Princeton, 1940-43, 45—, prof. architecture, 1957-75, prof. emeritus, 1975—; acting dir. Princeton (Sch. Architecture), 1964; exec. officer Princeton (Sch. Architecture and Urban Planning), 1968-74; plant engr. Corning Glass Works, N.Y., 1943-45; pvt. practice architecture, 1943—; Vis. critic U. Va., 1957; cons. architect; cons. on phys. facilities to comdg. gen., Fort Monmouth, N.J., 1966-67; archtl. cons. art and architecture com. Diocese of Trenton. Mem., vice chmn. bd. Environ. Design Rev. for Princeton Twp. John Stewardson fellow, 1933; Whitney Warren fellow, 1937; Recipient Princeton prize, 1935; honor award for design of Princeton Borough Hall N.J. chpt. AIA, 1966. Fellow AIA (pres. Capitol chpt. N.J. 1961-62, James River chpt. 1978—, Coll. of Fellows 1971—, AIA Sch. medal 1937); mem. Assn. Collegiate Sch. Architecture, Assn. Princeton Grad. Alumni, Nat. Inst. Archtl. Edn., Alpha Rho Chi (medal for excellence 1935), Phi Kappa Phi, Tau Sigma Delta. Republican. Club: Kennebunk River. Home: 4311 Coventry Rd Richmond VA 23221-3213 also: 229 Island Beach Rd Wells ME 04090-4418

JANDL, JAMES HARRIMAN, physician, educator; b. Racine, Wis., 1925. M.D., Harvard U., 1949. Diplomate Am. Bd. Internal Medicine. Successively intern, asst. resident, research fellow, research assoc., asst. physician, assoc. physician, dir. Thorndike Meml. Lab.; assoc. vis. physician, physician, dir. Harvard Med. unit Boston City Hosp., 1961-74; cons. physician Mt. Auburn Hosp., 1968—; sr. physician Beth Israel Deaconess Med Ctr., 1975—; mem. faculty Harvard Med. Sch., 1952—, assoc. prof. medicine, 1964-68, prof. medicine, 1968—, George R. Minot prof. medicine, 1968—; sr. cons. in medicine Brigham & Women's Hosp., 1987—; vis. prof. MIT, 1973-74. Served with USNR, 1950-52. Mem. Am. Fedn. Clin. Research, Am. Soc. Clin. Investigation, Assn. Am. Physicians. Home: 816 Lowell Rd Concord MA 01742-5514 Office: Harvard Med Sch 25 Shattuck St Boston MA 02115-6027

JANDREAU, JAMES LAWRENCE, information systems executive; b. St. Francis, Maine, Sept. 8, 1943; s. Leon L. and Cora (O'Clair) J.; m. Leslie Kinney, June 2, 1965 (div. Dec. 1981); children: James L., Joel L.; m. Judy K. Ayres, May 23, 1986. BA in Math. and Acctg., U. Maine, Orono, 1965; MBA, George Washington U., 1972. Commd. 2d lt. U.S. Army, 1965, advanced through grades to col., 1992, ret.; with computer ops., plans and programs officer USA Continental Army Command, Ft. Monroe, Va., 1968-70; project/procurement mgr. USA Computer Sys. Support and Evaluation Command, Washington, 1971-73; commdr., pers. officer Regional Pers. Ctr., Darmstadt, Germany, 1974-75; pers. mgr. USA Mil. Pers. Ctr., Schwetzingen, Germany, 1975-78; pers. dir. Dep. Chief of Staff for Pers., Washington, 1978-81; project mgr. Asst. Sec. of the Army, Washington, 1981-83; adjutant gen. 1st Inf. Divsn., Ft. Riley, Kans., 1983-85; chief info. tech. divsn. Joint Chiefs of Staff, Washington, 1986-89; dir. info. sys. USA Pers. Info. Sys. Command, Alexandria, Va., 1989-92; dep. dir., project mgr. Ogden Govt. Svcs., Fairfax, Va., 1992-94; program mgr. Computer Data Sys., Inc., Rockville, Md., 1994-95; asst. v.p., bus. info. systems NISH, Vienna, Va., 1995—. Home: 5835 Post Corners Trl Apt J Centreville VA 20120-6314 Office: NISH 2235 Cedar Ln Vienna VA 22182-5200

JANE, JOHN ANTHONY, neurosurgeon, educator; b. Chgo., Sept. 21, 1931; m. Noella Fortier, Dec. 17, 1960; children: Jane Serrita, Jennie Elizabeth, Katherine Colette, John Anthony Jr. BA cum laude, U. Chgo., 1951, MD, 1956, PhD, 1967. Diplomate Am. Bd. Neurol. Surgeons. Intern Royal Victoria Hosp. McGill U., 1953-56, jr. asst. resident in surgery, 1957-58, sr. fellow and demonstrator in neuropathology, 1959-60; jr. asst. resident in neurosurgery U. Chgo. Clinics, 1957; fellow in neurophysiology Montreal (Can.) Neurol. Inst., NIH, 1958-59; rsch. asst. in neurosurgery St. George's Hosp. and Nat. Hosp., London, 1961; rsch. assoc. dept. psychology Duke U., 1962; sr. resident in neurosurgery, asst. in neurology and neurosurgery U. Ill. Rsch. and Ednl. Hosp. and Ill. Neuropsychiat. Inst., 1963-64; sr. instr. neurosurgery Case Western Res. U. Sch. Medicine, 1965-66, chief neurosurg. div. Cleve. VA Hosp., 1965-66, asst. prof. neurosurgery, asst. neurosurgeon Univ. Hosp. Cleve., chief neurosurg. div. Cleve. VA Hosp., 1967-68; David D. Weaver prof., chmn. dep. neurosurgery U. Va. Health Scis. Ctr., Charlottesville, 1969—; Harry Wilkins lectr. U. Okla., 1983, Samuel Snodgrass lectr. U. Tex. at Galveston, 1983, Herbert Olivecrona lectr. Karolinska Inst. of Stockholm, Sweden, 1985, 29th Ann. Fellows Day lectr. Montreal Neurol. Inst., 1986, Arthur A. Ward lectr. U. Wash., Seattle, 1986, 1st Stuart Rowe lectr. neurosurgery U. Pitts., 1987, E. S. Gurdjian lectr. Wayne State U., Detroit, 1987; mem. neurology B study sect. NIH, 1971-74, neurol. disorders program project rev. B com., 1979-82, spl. study sect. on interdisciplinary studies role of cen. nervous system in hypertension, 1979, sci. adv. com., rev. com. of nat. com. for rsch. on neurol. and communicative disorders, 1981. Author: (with Yashon D.) Cytology of Tumors Affecting the Nervous System, 1969; contbr. numerous articles, abstracts, book chpts. to profl. publs.; editor: (with Winn H.R. and Rimel R.W.) Recent Advances in Neurotrauma Seminars in Neurological Surgery, Jour. Neurosurgery, 1992—; mem. editorial bd. Jour. Neurosurgery, 1984—. Recipient Alumni award for disting. svc. U. Chgo., 1988; grantee NIH.hon guest, Congress of an Neurological Surgeons, 1985. Fellow ACS, Royal Coll. Physicians and Surgeons Can.; mem. Am. Acad. Neurol. Surgery, Am. Assn. Anatomists, Am. Physiol. Soc., Am. Assn. Neurol. Surgeons, AMA, Neurosurg. Soc. Am., Can. Neurosurg. Soc., Rsch. Soc. Neurol. Surgeons (Grass prize and medal 1985), Soc. Neurosci. (chmn. membership com.), Soc. Brit. Neurol. Surgeons, Soc. Univ. Surgeons, So. Neurosurg. Soc., Pavlovian Soc., Med. Soc. Va., Neurosurg. Soc. Virginias, Albemarle County Med. Soc., The Cajal Club. Office: U Va Dept Neurosurgery Box 212 Charlottesville VA 22900-0212*

JANECEK, LENORE ELAINE, insurance specialist, consultant; b. May 2, 1944; d. Morris and Florence (Bear) Picker; m. John Janecek, Sept. 12, 1964; children: Frank, Michael. MAJ in Speech Comms., Northeastern Ill. U., 1972; postgrad., U. Notre Dame, 1979-80; MBA, Columbia Pacific U., 1982; cert. in C. of C. mgmt., U. Colo., 1982. Adminstrv. asst., exec. dir. Ill. Mcpl. Regirement Fund, Chgo.; pres., owner Secretarial Office Svcs., Chgo., 1976-78; founder, pres. Lincolnwood (Ill.) C. of C. and Industry, 1978-85; pres. Lenore E. Janecek & Assocs., Lincolnwood, 1985—; rep. 10th dist. U.S. C. of C., 1978—; appointee Health Care Reform Task Force, 1992—; apptd. by Pres. Bill Clinton Selective Svc. Bd., 1993—; apptd. by Gov. Jim Edgar Ill. Health Care Cost Containment Coun., 1994—; mem. adv. bd. Women Healthcare Execs. Network, Chgo. Artists Coalition, Ill. Lincoln Scholars Series Program, Leadership Ill. Author: Health Insurance: A Guide for Artists, Consultants, Entrepreneurs and Ohter Self-Employed, 1993. Mem. mktg. bd. Niles Twp. Sheltered Workshop; pres. Lincolnwood Sch. Dist. 74 Sch. Bd. Caucus; bd. dirs., officer, founder Ill. Fraternal Order Police Aux.; bd. dirs., officer Lincolnwood Girl's Softball League, PTA; bd. dirs. United Way, 1982-83; mem. sch. curriculum com. Lincolnwood Bd. Edn.; apptd. by Pres. Reagan to Selective Svc. Bd., 1983; pres. United Way Wkokie Valley, Ill., 1989; pres., founder Leadership Ill., 1992—, Twp. Coord. and Health Care advisor, Gov. Jim Edgar, Ill., 1990—. Talent scholar Northeastern Ill. U., 1972; Ill. Assn. C. of C. Execs. scholar, 1979-80; named Disting. Grad. of Yr. Nat. Honor Soc., 1985; chosen one of Top 100 Women Leaders in Am., 1988; recipient Outstanding Women in Healthcare Mgmt. award Women Health Exec. Network, 1994. Mem. Am. Notary Soc., Hadassah. Office: 980 N Michigan Ave # 1400 Chicago IL 60611-7500

JANES, JOSEPH ANTHONY, JR., optometrist; b. El Paso, Tex., Nov. 1, 1951; s. Joseph Anthony and Mildred Caroline (Dechant) J.; m. Janet Elaine Johnson, Jan. 10, 1976; children: Kelly Marie, Michael Harrison, Stephen Christopher. BS in Optometry, U. Houston, 1974, OD, 1976. Optometrist Farah Mfg., El Paso, Tex., 1976-77, Bellaire (Tex.) Eye Assocs., 1977-80; lectr. U. Houston Coll. Optometry, 1978-80, asst. prof., 1980-84; pres., optometrist Bellaire Contact Lens. Assoc., Houston, 1982—; adj. asst. prof. U. Houston Coll. Optometry, 1984-90; adj. assoc. prof. U. Houston, 1991—; v.p., sec. Laser Eye Ctr L.L.C., 1996—; adv. bd. Vistakon Inc., Jacksonville, Fla., 1986; bd. dirs. Laser Eye Inst. Houston, 1996—. Contbr. articles to profl. jours. Fellow Am. Acad. Optometry, Nat. Acad. Eye Surgery; mem. Am. Optometric Assn., Tex. Optometric Assn., Harris County Optometric Assn. (exec. coun. 1997—, v.p. 1998, pres. 1999), Optometric Found., Am. Soc. for Laser Medicine and Surgery, Sigma Nu Frat. (treas. alumni assn. 1981). Avocations: golf. Office: Bellaire Contact Lens Assoc 5420 Dashwood Dr Ste 207 Houston TX 77081-5332

JANES, ROBERT ROY, museum executive, archaeologist; b. Rochester, Minn., Apr. 23, 1948; m. Priscilla Bickel; children: Erica Helen, Peter Bickel. Student, Lawrence U., 1966-68, BA in Anthropology cum laude, 1970; student, U. of the Ams., Mexico City, 1968, U. Calif., Berkeley, 1968-69; PhD in Archaeology, U. Calgary, Alta., Can., 1976. Postdoctoral fellow Arctic Inst. N.Am., U. Calgary, 1981-82; adj. prof. archaeology U. Calgary, 1990—; founding dir. Prince of Wales No. Heritage Centre, Yellowknife, N.W.T., 1976-86, project dir. Dealy Island Archaeol. and Conservation Project, 1977-82; founding exec. dir. Sci. Inst. of N.W.T.; sci. advisor Govt. of N.W.T., Yellowknife, 1986-89; exec. dir., pres., CEO Glenbow Mus. Art Gallery Libr. and Archives, Calgary, 1989—; adj. prof. archaeology U. Calgary, 1990—. Author books, manuscripts, monographs, book chpts.; contbr. articles to profl. jours. mem. First Nations/CMA Task Force on Mus. and First Peoples, 1989-92; bd. dirs. Yoho Burgess Shale Found.; mem. nat. adv. bd. Ctr. for Cultural Mgmt., U. Waterloo. Recipient Nat. Parks Centennial award Environ. Can., 1985, Can. Studies Writing award Assn. Can. Studies, 1989, Disting. Alumni award Alumni Assn. of U. Calgary, 1989, L.R. Briggs Disting. Achievement award Lawrence U., 1991, ACE award for Can. cultural mgmt. Assn. Cultural Execs., 1998; Can. Coun. doctoral fellow, 1973-76; rsch. grantee Govt. of Can., 1974, Social Scis. and Humanities Rsch. Coun. Can., 1988-89. Fellow Arctic Inst. N.Am. (bd. dirs. 1983-90, vice chmn. bd. 1985-89, hon. rsch. assoc. 1983-84, chmn. priorities and planning com. 1983-84, exec. com. 1984-86, assoc. editor Arctic jour. 1987—), Am. Anthrop. Assn. (fgn. fellow); mem. Soc. for Am. Archaeology, Can. Archaeol. Assn. (v.p. 1980-82, pres. 1984-86, co-chmn. fed. heritage policy com. 1986-88), Current Anthropology (assoc.), Can. Mus. Assn. (hon. life mem., cert accreditation 1982, Outstanding award in Mus. Mgmt., Outstanding Achievement award for publ. 1996), Internat. Coun. Mus., Can. Art Mus. Dirs. Orgn. (mem.-at-large bd. dirs.), Mus. West (bd. dirs.), Can. Mus. Assn. (bd. dirs.), Alta. Mus. Assn. (moderator seminars 1990, Merit award 1992, Merit award for Museums and the Paradox of Change 1996), Ranchmens Club, Calgary Philharmonic Soc., Assn. of Cultural Execs. (ACE award for Can. Cultural Mgmt. 1998), Sigma Xi. Home: Box 32 Site 32, RR 12, Calgary, AB Canada T3E 6W3

JANEWAY, BARBARA, public relations executive. Coord. pub. rels. Ralph's Grocery, Compton, Calif. Office: Ralph's Grocery 1100 W Artesia Blvd Compton CA 90220-5186*

JANEWAY, ELIZABETH HALL, author; b. Bklyn., Oct. 7, 1913; d. Charles H. and Jeannette F. (Searle) Hall; m. Eliot Janeway (dec. 1993); children: Michael, William. Student, Swarthmore Coll.; A.B., Barnard Coll., 1935; Ph.D. in Lit. (hon.), Simpson Coll., Cedarcrest Coll., Villa Maria Coll.; D.H.L. (hon.), Russell Sage Coll., 1981, Florida Internat. U., 1988, Simmons Coll., 1989. Assoc. fellow Yale. Author: The Walsh Girls, 1943, Daisy Kenyon, 1945, The Question of Gregory, 1949, The Vikings, 1951, Leaving Home, 1953, Early Days of the Automobile, 1956, The Third Choice, 1959, Angry Kate, 1963, Accident, 1964, Ivanov Seven, 1967, Man's World, Woman's Place, 1971, Between Myth and Morning: Women Awakening, 1974, Powers of the Weak, 1980, Cross Sections: From a Decade of Change, 1982, Improper Behavior, 1987; contbr. to: Comprehensive Textbook of Psychiatry, 2d edit, 1980, Harvard Guide to Contemporary American Writing, 1979, also short stories and critical writing in periodicals and newspapers. Past chmn. N.Y. State Coun. Humanities; past bd. dirs. NOW Legal Def. and Edn. Fund, Fedn. State Humanities Coun.; bd. dirs. Nat. Cultural Alliance. Recipient educator's award Delta Kappa Gamma, 1972; named Disting. Alumna Barnard Coll., 1979; recipient Medal of Distinction, 1981. Mem. Authors Guild (council), Authors League Am. (council), PEN, Phi Beta Kappa (hon.). Home: 350 E 79th St New York NY 10021-9202*

JANEWAY, RICHARD, university official; b. L.A., Feb. 12, 1933; s. Van-Zandt and Grace Eleanor (Bell) J.; m. Katherine Esmond Pillsbury, Dec. 23, 1955; children: Susan Kent, David VanZandt, Elizabeth Anne. AB, Colgate U., 1954; MD, U. Pa., 1958. Diplomate Am. Bd. Psychiatry and Neurology. Intern Hosp. U. Pa., 1958-59; resident N.C. Baptist Hosp., Winston-Salem, 1963-66; mem. faculty Bowman Gray Sch. Medicine (now Wake Forest U. Sch. Medicine), Winston-Salem, 1966—; prof. neurology Wake Forest U., Winston-Salem, 1971—, dir. Bowman Gray Sch. Medicine (Cerebral Vascular Research Center), 1969-71; dean Wake Forest U. Sch. Medicine, Winston-Salem, 1971-85, exec. dean, 1985-94, v.p. health affairs, 1983-90, exec. v.p. health affairs, 1990-97, exec. v.p. health affairs emeritus, 1997—; prof. medicine & mgmt. Wake Forest U., Babcock Grad. Sch. Mgmt., Winston-Salem, 1997—; mem. exec. com. So. Nat. Bank, Winston-Salem, N.C., 1982-92; bd. dirs. BB&T Corp., Castle Springs, Inc.; mem. nat. adv. coun. regional med. programs HEW, 1974-77; mem.-at-large Nat. Bd. Med. Examiners, 1979-87; mem. N.C. Joint Conf. Com. on Med. Care, Inc., 1983—; dir. N.C. Inst. Medicine, N.C. Biotech. Ctr. Mem. Winston-Salem Forsyth County Bd. Edn., 1970-73; bd. dirs. Nat. Assn. for Biomed. Rsch., 1993-96; Ams. for Med. Progress, Inc., 1993-97, Winston-Salem Found., 1994—, chmn., 1997, 98; trustee Colgate U., 1988-95, Winston-Salem State U., 1991-95. Capt. USAF, 1959-63. USPHS fellow, 1956; Markle scholar, 1968-73. Fellow ACP, Am. Acad. Neurology; mem. AMA, Am. Neurol. Assn., Am. Heart Assn. (coun. on stroke), Assn. Am. Med. Colls. (exec. coun. 1977-86, mem. accreditation coun. on grad. med. edn. 1981-85, chmn. coun. of deans 1982-83, exec. com. 1982-86, chmn. 1984-85), Am. Clin. and Climatol. Assn., Inst. Medicine of NAS, Greater Winston-Salem C. of C. (bd. dirs., chmn. 1992), Soc. Med. Adminstrs., Phi Beta Kappa, Sigma Xi, Alpha Omega Alpha. Clubs: Rotary (dir. 1977-80, v.p. 1981-82, pres. 1982-83), Cosmos. Office: Wake Forest U Sch Medicine Medical Center Blvd Winston Salem NC 27157

JANI, SUSHMA NIRANJAN, pediatrics and child and adolescent psychiatrist; b. Gwalior, Madhya, Pradesh, India, Sept. 26, 1959; came to U.S., 1983; d. Kirty Ambalal and Purnima Kirty (Bhatt) Dave; m. Niranjan Natwerial Jani, Mar. 30, 1983; children: Suni Jani, Raja Jani, Roma Jani. Intern Sci., Mithibai Coll., Bombay, India; MB;BS, B.J. Med. Coll., Ahmedabad, India; MD in Adult Psychiatry, Ind. U., 1984; MD in Child Psychiatry, Johns Hopkins U., 1987. Diplomate Am. Bd. Psychiatry and Neurology, sub-bd. Child Psychiatry, Am. Bd. Pediat., Am. Bd. Forensic Examiners. Pediat. emergency physician Merrey Hosp., Balt., 1995-97; child psychiatrist Johns Hopkins Univ. Hosp., Balt.; asst. clin. prof., mem. faculty dept. pediats. and psychiatry Georgetown U. Med. Ctr., Balt., assoc. prof. pediat. and psychiatry; asst. prof. psychiatry Georgetown U.; med. dir. Chesapeake network Devereux Found., Md., Va., W.Va., Washington and Del., 1998—; chief cons. psychiatrist Balt. Detention Ctr., 1988-89, cons. psychiatrist Vets. Hosp., Indpls., 1986-87. Vol. Radha-Krishna Leprosy Camp, Bombay, 1981-83. Mem. AMA, Am. Acad. Child & Adolescent Psychiatry, Am. Psychiatry Assn., Md. Psychiat. Soc., Columbia Assn., India Assn., Am. Acad. Podiatrics. Hindu. Avocations: reading, knitting, sewing, letter-writing. Home: 10485 Owen Brown Rd Columbia MD 21044-3435 Office: 3050 R St Washington DC 20007 also: Hawthorne Office Pl 10770 Hickory Ridge Rd Columbia MD 21044-3646

JANIAK, ANTHONY RICHARD, JR., investment banker; b. Pitts., Sept. 21, 1946; s. Anthony R. and Ann Theresa Janiak; m. Anne Marie McDevitt, Aug. 23, 1969; children: Brian Richard, Carolyn Marie. BS, Pa. State U., 1968; MBA, U. Chgo., 1970. Assoc. Smith Barney & Co., N.Y.C., 1970-74; v.p. Smith Barney Internat., Tokyo, 1974-77; v.p. Smith Barney, Harris Upham & Co., N.Y.C., 1977-78, mng. dir., 1980—, exec. v.p., 1990—; v.p. Smith Barney, Harris Upham Internat., Paris, 1978-80; mng. dir., dir. internat. Smith Barney Inc., N.Y.C., 1995-98; mng. dir. Salomon, Smith Barney, N.Y.C., 1998—; bd. dirs. KEB-Smith Barney Securities, Seoul, Korea, Global Wrap Cons. Group, Tokyo, Soditic Fin., Geneva; mem. adv. com. bus. coun. UN, 1984-90, N.Y.C.; mem. task force on fin. svcs. U.S.-Japan Businessmen's Coun., 1982-83; mem. adv. com. on pub. affairs Japan Soc., N.Y.C., 1986-88; mem. emerging markets adv. com. SEC, 1991-93; exch. ofcl. Am. Stock Exch., 1992—, NASDAQ listing com. Bd. dirs. Town and Village Civic Club of Scarsdale, 1992-95, 98-99. Republican. Roman Catholic. Avocations: tennis, coin collecting, music, golf. Home: 79 Brookby Rd Scarsdale NY 10583-4542 Office: Salomon Smith Barney 388 Greenwich St New York NY 10013-2339

JANIAK, CATHY LYNN, telecommunications industry executive; b. Summit, N.J., Oct. 25, 1950; d. Anthony Tyrone and Jane (LaMaster) Cuva; m. Richard Walter Janiak, Sept. 10, 1968; children: Jacqueline, Jeffrey. BBA, Georgian Ct. Coll., 1986; M of Liberal Studies, Monmouth U., 1996. Teller Supreme Savs. and Loan, Irvington, N.J., 1972-73; with claims svcs. State Farm Ins., Summit, N.J., 1981-83; substitute tchr. Toms River (N.J.) Bd. Edn., 1986-87; sr. svc. analyst N.J. Bell, Toms River, 1982-84, sales cons., 1987-97, asst. mgr., tng. tech. specialist, 1997—. Vol. Artist Guild, Island Heights, N.J., 1982; historian Welcome Wagon, Toms River, 1984-85. Recipient 1st pl. Latin category Star Dust Ball, Meadowlands, N.J., 1992. Avocations: ballroom dancing, antique collecting, gardening, painting, reading. Home: 1119 Kells Ct Toms River NJ 08753-3162 Office: 980 Hooper Ave Toms River NJ 08753

JANICE, BARBARA, illustrator; b. Bklyn., Jan. 25, 1949; d. Irving and Blanche (Lass) Rothman; 1 child, Stacey-Alissa Mirsky. BS in Biology, L.I. U., 1971; studied with, Frank Netter, MD. Staff illustrator Courier-Life Pubs., Bklyn., 1975-78, The Village Voice, N.Y.C., 1978-80; art dir., dept. anatomy SUNY Health Sci. Ctr., Bklyn., 1989-91; freelance illustrator Walt Disney Prodns., N.Y.C., 1990-95, Orlando, Fla., 1990-95; art dir. EuroDisney, Paris, 1990-95; illustrator EuroDisney, Orlando, N.Y.C., 1991-94; art dir. for Donald Duck character EuroDisney, Ft. Lauderdale, Fla., 1994—; sr. sys. specialist for L.Am., Microsoft Corp., 1995-99; cons. Parkland, Fla., 1999—; dir. Barbara Janice Graphics, N.Y.C. and Fla., 1980—, Barbara Janice Cons., Inc., 1999—; guest spkr. Pratt Sch. Art and Design, Bklyn., 1991; art dir. for character Donald Duck, EuroDisney, Paris, 1992—. Illustrator: Current Operative Urology, 6th edit., 1989, A Historical Profile of the Children's Medical Center, 1990, 2d rev. edit., 1992, The Day the Alphabet Was Born, 1991; represented in permanent collections SUNY Health Sci. Ctr., Bklyyn., EuroDisney, Paris, Tokyo Disneyland. Vol. artist Coalition for the Homeless, N.Y.C., 1985, 91, AIDS Coalition, Ft. Lauderdale, N.Y.C., 1992—. Recipient 1st place N.Y. Art Critics award, 1984, 2d place award, 1992. Mem. Assn. Med. Illustrators, Soc. Illustrators (1st place 34th ann. exhbn. 1991, 2d place 33d ann. exhbn. 1990), Graphic Artists Guild (profl. rep.), Am. Biog. Inst. (bd. advisors), Internat. Biog. Ctr. (bd. govs.). Home: 5537 NW 124th Ave Parkland FL 33076-3430

JANICKI, ROBERT STEPHEN, retired pharmaceutical company executive; b. Manette, Wash., Dec. 7, 1934; s. Stephen Walter and Elizabeth Caroline (Gorman) J.; m. I. Jane Betcher, Aug. 18, 1956; children: Robert, Beth, David. BS, Grove City Coll., 1956; MD, Temple U., 1961. Diplomate Nat. Bd. Med. Examiners. Intern U.S. Naval Hosp., Phila., 1961-62; resident in occupl. medicine USN, 1962-63; assoc. dir. clin. rsch. Dow Pharms., Indpls., 1966-68; assoc. med. dir. Neisler divsn. Union Carbide Corp., Sterling Forest, N.Y., 1968-69; assoc. med. dir. regulatory affairs Abbott Labs., North Chicago, Ill., 1969-70; dir. clin. rsch. pharm. products divsn. Abbott Labs., 1970-71, v.p. med. affairs pharm. products divsn., 1971-79, v.p. research pharm. products divsn., 1979-83, corp. v.p. R & D pharm. products divsn., 1983-89, sr. v.p., 1989-90; bd. dirs. Sunpharm Corp., Jacksonville, Fla., Afferon Corp., Wayne, Pa.; cons. New Drug Devel. Contbr. articles profl. to jours. Trustee Grove City (Pa.) Coll. Lt. comdr., M.C. USN, 1961-66. Fellow Am. Coll. Clin. Pharm.; mem. Am. Soc. Clin. Pharmacology and Therapeutics, Coll. Physicians of Phila., Sigma Xi, Alpha Omega Alpha. Home: 138 Anchor Dr Vero Beach FL 32963-2902

JANIGIAN, BRUCE JASPER, lawyer, educator; b. San Francisco, Oct. 21, 1950; s. Michael D. Janigian and Stella (Minasian) Amerian; m. Susan Elizabeth Frye, Oct. 4, 1986; children: Alan Michael, Alison Elizabeth. AB, U. Calif., Berkeley, 1972; JD, U. Calif., San Francisco, 1975; LLM, George Washington U., 1982. Bar: Calif. 1975, U.S. Supreme Ct. 1979, D.C. 1981. Dir. Hastings Rsch. Svcs., Inc., San Francisco, 1973-75; judge adv. in Spain, 1976-78; commr. U.S. Navy and Marine Corps Ct. Mil. Rev., 1978-79; atty. advisor AID U.S. State Dept., Washington, 1979-84; dep. dir., gen. counsel Calif. Employment Devel. Dept., Sacramento, 1984-89; Fulbright scholar, vis. prof. law U. Salzburg, Austria, 1989-90; chmn. Calif. Agrl. Labor Rels. Bd., 1990-95; v.p. Europe, resident dir. Salzburg (Austria) Seminar, 1995-96; U.S. legate European Acad. Scis. and Art, 1996—; Rapporteur World Economic Forum, 1996; of counsel Weintraub Genshlea & Sproul Law Corp., Sacramento, 1998—; prof. law McGeorge Sch. Law, U. Pacific, Sacramento, 1986—, Inst. on Internat. Legal Studies, Salzburg, summer 1987, London Inst. on Comml. Law, summers 1989, 92, 93; vis. scholar Hoover Inst. War, Revolution and Peace, Stanford U., 1991-92; dir. Vienna-Budapest East/West Trade Inst., 1993; vis. prof. law U. Salzburg, 1995-96. Editor: Financing International Trade and Development, 1986, 87, 89, International Business Transactions, 1989, 92, International Trade Law, 1993, 94. Coord. fund raiser March of Dimes, Sacramento, 1987. Capt. USNR, JAGC, 1976-79, mem. Res. Fulbright scholar, 1989-90; decorated Meritorious Achievement medal; recipient USAID Meritorious Honor award. Mem. Calif. Bar Assn., D.C. Bar Assn., Sacamento Bar Assn. (exec. com. taxation sect. 1988-89), Anthony M. Kennedy Am. Inn of Ct. (barrister 1998—), Carnegie Endowment for Internat. Peace, Sacramento Met. C. of C. (award for program contbns. and cmty. enrichment 1989), European Acad. Scis. and Art, World Art Forum, Austro-Am. Soc. (v.p. 1996), Navy League (gen. counsel 1997—), Naval Res. Officers Assn. (life), Marine Meml. Assn., Fulbright Assoc. (life), Knights of Vartan, Phi Beta Kappa. Avocations: cross-country skiing, tennis, bicycling. Home: 1631 12th Ave Sacramento CA 95818-4146 Office: 400 Capitol Mall Fl 11 Sacramento CA 95814-4407

JANIS, ALLEN IRA, retired physicist, educator; b. Chgo., Sept. 11, 1930; s. David M. and Rosa (Ginsburg) J.; m. Phyllis Meyer, Sept. 6, 1953; children: Stuart, Wynne. B.S., Northwestern U., 1951; postgrad., Cornell U., Ithaca, N.Y., 1951-53; Ph.D., Syracuse U., 1957. Mem. faculty U. Pitts., 1957-92, assoc. prof. physics, 1963-68, prof., 1968-92, prof. emeritus, 1993—, sr. research assoc. Philos. Sci. Center, 1967-75, assoc. dir. Philos. Sci. Center, 1975-92; fellow emeritus Philos. Sci. Center, 1993—. Mem. Fedn. Am. Scientists (sec. 1964-65), Am. Phys. Soc., Am. Assn. Physics Tchrs., AAAS, AAUP, Philosophy of Sci. Assn. Home: 425 Garden City Dr Monroeville PA 15146-1258 Office: Univ Pitts Dept Physics Pittsburgh PA 15260

JANIS, CONRAD, actor, jazz musician, art dealer, film producer, director; b. N.Y.C.; s. Sidney and Harriet J.; children: Christopher, Carin; m. Maria Grimm, Nov. 30, 1987. Appeared in numerous Broadway plays including Junior Miss, 1942, Dark of the Moon, 1945, The Next Half Hour, 1945, The Brass Ring, 1951 (World Theater award), Time Out for Ginger, 1952, Visit to a Small Planet, 1957, Sunday in New York, 1961, Marathon '33, 1963, The Front Page, 1969, Same Time Next Year, 1975-76; films include Snafu, 1945, Margie, 1946, That Hagen Girl, 1947, Let's Rock, 1958, Airport '75, The Duchess and the Dirtwater Fox, 1976, The Buddy Holly Story, 1977, Roseland, 1977, Oh, God! Book II, 1979, Nothing in Common, 1987, Sonny Boy, 1987, Mr. Saturday Night, 1992, The Gods Must Be Crazy III, 1992; star, dir. The Feminine Touch, 1995, The Cable Guy, 1995, Addams Family Reunion, 1998; actor, dir. The November Conspiracy, 1996; appeared in over 350 major network TV shows including Suspense, 1950, Highway to Heaven, 1986, Golden Girls, 1987, 89, Murder, She Wrote, 1988, 91, Baywatch, 1996, The New Rockford Files, 1997, Fraiser, 1997, Diagnosis Murder, 1998; numerous TV movies including Miracle on 34th Street, 1973, The Virginia Hill Story, 1974, The Magnificent Magnet of Santa Mesa, 1977, The Gossip Columnist, 1984, The Red Light Sting, 1984, Asimov's Probe, 1987, Caddie Woodlawn, 1988; TV series include I Bonino, Quark, Mork and Mindy, 1978-82; spokesperson TV series on modern art, Appreciating Art, 1991; leader jazz group, 1951—; TV appearances with Johnny Carson, Diana Shore, Mike Douglas, The Late Show with Ross Schaeffer, David Letterman Show, specials include Burt Convy, Juke Box Hits, Jerry Lewis Telethons, others; appeared in major jazz clubs throughout US, jazz festivals, Monterey, Calif., Palm Springs, Calif., Sacramento, Calif., L.A. Classic and many others, concerts at N.Y. Carnegie Hall, Town Hall, Phila. Acad. Music, Nugget Jazz Festival, Playboy Jazz Festival, 1997, others; jazz trombonist with various artists including Roy Eldredge, Coleman Hawkins, Buddy Rich, Bobby Hackett, Hot Lips Page, Wild Bill Davison; leader Beverly Hills Unlisted Jazz Band, 1978—(subject of PBS spl. titled That's A Plenty 1981), The Tuxedo Junction, (PBS spl.) This Joint is Jumpin, 1997; writer, producer, star: (with others) (video spl.) This Joint Is Jumpin', 1997, numerous recs. for many jazz labels; co-owner, Sidney Janis Gallery, N.Y.C.;

co-founder with Maria Grimm, producer Golden Era Pictures (co. now titled MiraCon Pictures), 1988—. Recipient Theatre World award, 1952; named to Playboy Jazz Poll, 1960, 61; Silver Theatre award, 1950. Mem. AFTRA, Acad. Motion Picture Arts and Scis., Actors Equity Assn., Screen Actors Guild, Am. Fedn. Musicians. Club: Nautico (Bilbao, Spain).

JANIS, F. TIMOTHY, technology company executive; b. Chgo., Apr. 11, 1940; s. Fabian M. and Phyllis (Underwood) Janiszewski; m. Kathryn Dickey; children: Mark David, Paul Joseph, Melissa Ann. BS in Chemistry, Wichita State U., 1962, MS in Chemistry, 1963; PhD in Chemistry, Ill. Inst. Tech., 1968. Asst., then assoc. prof. chemistry Ill. Benedictine Coll., Lisle, Ill., 1969-74; asst. acad. dean Franklin (Ind.) Coll., 1974-77; divn. dir. Indpls. Ctr. for Advanced Rsch., 1977-92; founder and pres. ARAC, Inc., Franklin, Ind., 1992—; cons. Argonne (Ill.) Nat. Lab., 1968-74, Office Pers. Mgmt., Denver, 1988-94; mem. adv. bd. R&D Enterprise Asia Pacific, 1999. Co-author: Moving R&D to Marketplace, 1993, rev. edit., 1995, 25 publs. on tech. transfer; internat. editor Tech. Bus. Mag., 1998—; internat. editor Tech. Bus. Mag., 1998—. Mem. Lisle Cmty. High Sch. Bd., 1970-72; bd. dirs. Near North Devel. Corp., Indpls., 1990-94. Named Sagamore of the Wabash, Gov. of State of Ind., 1990. Mem. Tech. Transfer Soc. (treas., pres. 1990-92, exec. dir. 1993-96). Roman Catholic. Avocations: golf, reading, sightseeing, grandchildren. E-mail: arac@iquest.net; url:advicom.net/ ŠARAC; fax: (317) 738-3980. Office: 604 E Davis Dr Franklin IN 46131-2335

JANIS, KENNETH M., physician; b. Bklyn., Aug. 12, 1939; s. Robert and Ida (Sonis) J.; m. Judy Byrnes, Oct. 3, 1992. BA, Colgate U., 1960; MD, NYU, 1964. Intern Boston City Hosp., 1964-65; resident Mass. Gen. Hosp., 1965-67; fellow Stanford (Calif.) U., 1967-68; asst. prof. Harvard U./Mass. Gen. Hosp., Boston, 1972-74; clin. prof. U. Calif., Irvine, 1976-92; assoc. prof. anesthesiology U. N.Mex., Albuquerque, 1992—. Capt. USAF, 1968-70. Avocations: exercise physiology. Office: Univ NMex Dept Anesthesiology Sch of Medicine Albuquerque NM 87131-5216

JANIS, RONALD H., lawyer; b. Buffalo, Apr. 16, 1948. BA, Harvard Coll., 1970; JD, N.Y.U., 1975. Bar: N.J. 1975, N.Y. 1976. With Pitney Hardin Kipp & Szuch, Morristown. Editor NYU Review Law and Social Change, 1974-75; contbr. articles to profl. jours. Mem. ABA (co-chmn. Korea and Japan divsn. Asia Pacific law com. sect. internat. law and practice), N.J. State Bar Assn., N.Y. State Bar Assn., Newark C. of C. (bd. dirs. 1989-94), Korea Soc. *

JANISCHEWSKYJ, WASYL, electrical engineering educator; b. Prague, Czechoslovakia, Jan. 21, 1925; s. Ivan and Hanna (Ravych) J.; m. Emilia Miszczuk; children: Roxolana, Marko. Student, Tech. U. Hannover, Fed. Republic of Germany, 1948-50; B of Applied Sci., U. Toronto, 1952, M of Applied Sci., 1954; Hon. Doctor, Natl. Tech. U. of Ukraine Polytechnical Inst., Kyiv, 1998. Registered profl. engr., Ont. Testing engr. Moloney Electric Co., Toronto, Can., summer 1952; demonstrator/instr. U. Toronto, 1952-55, lectr. to prof., 1959-90, prof. emeritus, 1990—, asst. dept. head elec. engring., 1964-70, assoc. dean faculty of applied sci. and engring., 1978-82; elec. engr. Aluminium Labs., Kingston, Ont., 1955-59; elect. engr. NRC, Ottawa, Ont., Can., summer 1961, Ont. Hydro, Toronto, Can., summers 1962-65. Contbr. over 100 articles to profl. jours. Fellow IEEE; mem. Am. Soc. for Engring. Edn., Internat. Elec. Commn., Internat. Conf. on Large High Vol. Elec. Systems, Can. Elec. Assn., Assn. Profl. Engrs. Ont., Taras Shevchenko Sci. Soc., Ukrainian Free Acad. Scis. Mem. Ukranian Orthodox Ch. Home: 65 Humbercrest Blvd, Toronto, ON Canada M6S 4K6 Office: Univ Toronto, Univ of Toronto, Dept Elec/Computer Engring, Toronto, ON Canada M5S 3G4*

JANKAUSKAS, SAULIUS JURGIS, plastic surgeon; b. Detroit, Feb. 13, 1956; s. Kazys and Marija Jankauskas. BS in Biology, Wayne State U., 1977, MD, 1981. Diplomate Am. Bd. Plastic Surgery and Surgery. Resident in gen. surgery Wayne State U., Detroit, 1981-86; fellow in plastic surgery Med. Coll. Va., Richmond, 1986-88; fellow in aesthetic plastic surgery Los Angeles, 1988-89; pvt. practicw Longwood, Fla., 1989—; chief surgery South Seminole Hosp., Longwood, Fla., 1993-95; clin. rsch. and tchg. staff Health Rsch. Inst., Orlando, Fla., 1994—. Mem. Am. Soc. Plastic and Reconstructive Surgery, Fla. Assn. Plastic and Reconstructive Surgery, Seminole County Med. Soc., So. Med. Assn. (vice chmn. plastic surgery sect. 1998—). Office: Ste 106 521 WSR 34 Longwood FL 32750

JANKE, JOHN ERIC, secondary educator; b. Longview, Wash., Mar. 30, 1960; s. John Charles and Rose Kathryn (Albertson) J. AA, Lower Columbia Coll., 1982; BA in History, Ctrl. Wash. U., 1984, MEd, 1999; BA in Edn., Western Wash. U., 1986. Cert. tchr., Wash. Jr. high tchr. Bd. of Edn., Kelso, Wash., 1986-94, Longview, 1986-94, Spannaway, Wash., 1994-98. Named Alumni of Yr. Ctrl. Wash. U., 1997. Mem. NEA, Wash. Edn. Assn., Bethel Edn. Assn. Avocations: golfing, stamp collecting, pool. E-mail: johnjanke@hotmail.com. Home: 1301 N Chestnut B-3 Ellensburg WA 98926-7643

JANKE, KENNETH, investment consultant; b. Ft. William, Ont., Can., May 13, 1934; s. Adolf Earthman and Julianna (Dika) J.; m. Sally Mildred Roach, June 29, 1957; children: Kenneth Stuart, Laura Lynn, Julie Ann. Student Mich. State U., 1952-56. Asst. mgr. Household Fin. Co., Detroit, 1958-60; gen. mgr. Nat. Assn. Investors, Royal Oak, Mich., 1960-76, pres., CEO, 1976—; bd. dir. Investment Edn. Inst., Royal Oak, 1965—, pres. 1995—; bd. dirs. World Fedn. Investors, Brussels, 1976—, pres., 1995—. Author: Ask Mr. Naic, 1982, Golf Is A Funny Game (But It Wasn't Meant To Be), 1992, Starting and Running a Profitable Investment Club, 1996; co-author: Wit and Wisdom of Golf, 1997; columnist mag. Better Investing. Chmn. Mich. Golf Hall of Fame, Lake Orion; pres. Am. Cancer Soc.-Oakland Country, Southfield, Mich., 1974-75, pres., bd. dirs. NAIC Growth Fund, Royal Oak; bd. dirs. AFLAC, Inc., Columbus, Ga.; Bd. advisors Mich. PGA, West Bloomfield. Served with U.S. Army, 1956-58, ETO. Recipient Disting. Svc. award Investment Edn. Inst., 1972, Founder award Am. Cancer Soc., 1970. Fellow Fin. Analysts Soc. of Detroit (pres. 1984—), Fin. Analysts Fedn.; mem. Nat. Investor Rels. Inst. (pres. Detroit 1985—), Western Golf Assn. (bd. dirs., pres.) Indianwood Golf and Country Club (Lake Orion), Renaissance Club (Detroit), NFL Club (Lauderdale, Fla.), Scalawag's Country Club (Mt. Clemens, Mich.), Masons. Republican. Episcopalian. Avocations: golf; golf collecting. Home: 4305 W Maple Rd Bloomfield Hills MI 48301-2901 Office: Nat Assn Investors Corp 711 W 13 Mile Rd Madison Heights MI 48071-1806

JANKE, RONALD ROBERT, lawyer; b. Milw., Mar. 2, 1947; s. Robert Erwin and Elaine Patricia (Wilken) J.; m. Mary Ann Burg, July 3, 1971; children—Jennifer, William, Emily. B.A. cum laude, Wittenberg U., 1969; J.D. with distinction, Duke U., 1974. Bar: Ohio 1974. Assoc. Jones, Day, Reavis & Pogue, Cleve., 1974-83, ptnr., 1984—. Served with U.S. Army, 1970-71, Vietnam. Mem. ABA (chmn. environ. control com. 1980-83), Ohio Bar Assn., Greater Cleve. Bar Assn., Environ. Law Inst. Office: Jones Day Reavis & Pogue N Point 901 Lakeside Ave E Cleveland OH 44114-1116

JANKLOW, WILLIAM JOHN, governor; b. Chgo., Sept. 13, 1939; s. Arthur W. and LouElla Bernice (Gulbranson) J.; m. Mary Dean Thom, Sept. 3, 1960; children—Russell, Pam, Shonna. B.S.B.A., U. S.D., 1964, J.D., 1966. Bar: S.D. bar 1966, U.S. Supreme Ct. bar 1970. Staff atty. S.D. Legal Services, 1966-67, directing atty., chief officer, 1967-72; chief trial atty. S.D. Atty. Gen's. Office, Pierre, 1973-74; atty. gen. S.D. Atty. Gen's. Office, 1975-78; gov. S.D., 1979-87, 1995—; lectr. in field. Bd. dirs. Nat. Legal Services Corp. Served with USMC, 1956-59. Recipient Nat. award for legal excellence and skill Nat. Legal Aid and Defenders Assn., 1968. Mem. Nat. Assn. Attys. Gen., Am., S.D. trial lawyers assns., Am. Judicature Soc. Republican. Lutheran. Office: Office of the Governor 500 E Capitol Ave Pierre SD 57501-5070

JANKO, MAY, graphic artist; b. N.Y.C., Feb. 27, 1926; d. Jacob and Clara (Schupler) J. BA, Hunter Coll., 1946, MA, 1952; student, Art Students League, 1949-53. Tchr. art N.Y.C. Pub. Schs., 1953-58; textile designer DNE Walter & Co., N.Y.C., 1958-63, Old Deerfield, N.Y.C., 1963-68, M. Lowenstein Corp., N.Y.C., 1968-84. Exhibited in group shows: Libr. of Congress, Washington, 1956, 63, American Prints Today, 1959, Whitney Mus. Am. Art, N.Y.C., 1959, Pa. Acad., Phila., 1959, Bklyn. Mus., 1960, Taipei (Taiwan) Nat. Mus., 1984, 90, 92, Bronx Mus. Arts, 1989, Krasdale Satellite Gallery of Bronx Mus. Arts, 1989, Salmugundi: 13th Ann. Exhbn., 1990; represented in permanent collections: Met. Mus. Art, N.Y.C., Rockefeller Collection, N.Y.C., Cin. Mus. Art, Nat. Gallery, Washington. Recipient Achievement award Hunter Coll., 1956, Leo Meissner award NAD, N.Y.C., 1984, I.B. Markell award in graphics Audubon Artists, N.Y.C., 1961, Daniel Serra y Navas Meml. award, 1994, Art Students League N.Y. Graphics award, 1995. Mem. Soc. Am. Graphic Artists (life; mem. coun. 1977, Henry B. Shope award 1954, Graphic Chem. award 1985), Boston Printmakers, Am. Color Print Soc., Art Students League (life).

JANKOFSKY, KLAUS PETER, medieval studies educator; b. Berlin, Germany, July 8, 1938; came to U.S., 1969; s. Kurt Franz G. and Carola Edith (Wagner) J.; m. Kathleen Marie Kurt, Jan. 4, 1969; children: Kristian, Katia, Kurt. Staatsexamen, U. des Saarlandes, Saarbrücken, Germany, 1958-64, 67-68, Dr. phil. magna cum laude, 1969; Assessor des Lehramts, Seminar f. Studienreferendare, Esslingen, Germany, 1968-69. Asst. Collège d'Enseignement Général, Lons-le-Saunier, France, 1960-61; wissenschaftl. Hilfskraft U. des Saarlandes, 1964-65; instr. Modern Fgn. Langs. Loras Coll., Dubuque, Iowa, 1965-67; studienreferendar Friedrich Schiller Gymnasium, Fellbach, Germany, 1968-69; prof. U. Minn., Duluth, 1969—; asst. dean Grad. Sch. U. Minn., 1978-83; vis. prof. Katholische Universität, Eichstätt, Germany, 1990. Author 2 books and numerous articles in field. Recipient Albert Tezla Scholar/Tchr. award U. Minn., 1990; Bush Found. sabbatical fellow U. Minn., 1984; recipient Horace Morse Alumni Assn. award U. Minn., 1992. Mem. MLA, Carolus Magnus Kreis, Am. Assn. Tchrs. German, Medieval Acad. Am., Internat. Arthurian Soc., Hagiography Soc. Avocations: swimming, cross country skiing, fishing. Office: U Minn Humanities 421 Duluth MN 55812*

JANKOVIC, JOSEPH, neurologist, educator, scientist; b. Teplice, Czechoslovakia, Mar. 1, 1948; came to U.S., 1965; m. Cathy Sue Inselberg, May 26, 1973; children: Jason, Daniel, Zachary. MD, U. Ariz., 1973. Diplomate Am. Bd. Neurology. Med. intern Baylor Coll. Medicine, Houston, 1973-74, asst. prof. neurology, 1977-84, assoc. prof., 1984-88, prof., 1988—; resident in neurology Columbia U., N.Y.C., 1974-76, chief resident in neurology, 1976-77; dir. Parkinson's Disease Ctr. and Movement Disorder Clinic, Houston, 1977—; sr. attending physician Meth. Hosp., Houston, 1988—. Author numerous articles and book chpts. in field; editor/co-editor 18 med. books; mem. editorial bd. jours. Movement Disorders, Clin. Neuropharmacology, Neurology Jour. Chmn. sci. adv. bd. Blepharospasm Rsch. Found.; mem. adv. bd. Dystonia Med. Rsch. Found., Internat. Tremor Found., Tourette's Syndrome Med. Adv. Bd. Grantee disease rsch. founds., pharmaceutical cos., NIH. Fellow Am. Acad. Neurology; mem. AMA, Am. Neurol. Assn., Soc. for Neurosci., Movement Disorders Soc. (pres.-elect 1991-94, pres. 1994-96). Avocations: tennis, family activities, music. Office: Baylor Coll Medicine 6550 Fannin St Ste 1801 Houston TX 77030-2744

JANKOWSKA, MARIA ANNA, librarian, educator; b. Jarocin, Poland, Aug. 12, 1952; d. Tadeusz and Aleksandra (Ruszkowska) Nocun; m. Piotr L. Jankowski, Jan. 14, 1978; children: Pawel Pat, Marta Maja. MA, Sch. Econs., Poznan, Poland, 1975, PhD, 1983; M Libr. Info. Sci., U. Calif., Berkeley, 1989. Rsch. and tchg. asst. Sch. Econs., Poznan, 1976-83, asst. prof., 1983-85; catalog libr., asst. prof. U. Idaho, Moscow, 1989-94, network resources libr., assoc. prof., 1995—. Author: Electronic Guide to Polish Research and University Libraries, 1996, Idaho Geospatial Data Center, 1998; founding editor Green Libr. Jour., 1991-94; gen. editor Electronic Green Jour., 1994—. Guest scholar Smithsonian Inst., Woodrow Wilson Internat. Ctr., Washington, 1985; fellow U Calif., Berkeley Sch. Libr. and Info. Studies, 1989; grantee Rsch. Coun. Grant, U. Idaho, 1990, 95, Internat. Rsch. and Exchs. Bd., Washington, 1995, 96. Mem. ALA (chair task force on environ. 1993-95, 98—), Idaho Libr. Assn., Beta Phi Mu. Office: U Idaho Libr Rayburn St Moscow ID 83844-2350

JANKOWSKI, JOHN EDWARD, JR., government administrator; b. South Bend, Ind., June 2, 1955; s. John and Constance Gay (Maenhout) J.; m. Judy Renee Goldberg, June 25, 1978; children: Kathryn Felice, Jeffrey Ellis. Student, Ind. U., 1973-75; BSFS magna cum laude, Georgetown U., 1977; MA, Johns Hopkins U., 1982. Rsch. asst. Resources for the Future, Washington, 1978-82; asst. dir., strategic & policy analysis Distilled Spirits Coun., Washington, 1982-87; program dir. rsch. & devel. surveys Nat. Sci. Found., Arlington, Va., 1987—. Contbr. articles to profl. jours. Mem. Am. Econ. Assn., Soc. Gov. Econs., Phi Beta Kappa, Sigma Xi. Office: NSF 4201 Wilson Blvd Arlington VA 22230-0001

JANKOWSKI, THEODORE ANDREW, artist; b. New Brunswick, N.J., Dec. 14, 1946; s. Theodore Andrew and Lois (Amarescu) J.; m. Rebecca Buck, July 23, 1983; 1 child, Tito Henry. Student, McMurrough Sch. Art, Indialantic, Fla., 1956-58, 74-75, R.I. Sch. Design, 1972, Cape Sch. of Art, Provincetown, Mass., 1975-76, 79-87, Cen. Fla. U., 1976-77. One-man shows include Eye of Horus Gallery, Provincetown, 1985; exhibited in group shows at Provincetown Art Assn. Mus., 1984, Bethlehem (Pa.) City Hall, 1988, Michael Ingbar Gallery, N.Y.C., 1988, 91; represented in permanent collections at State Mus. at Palace of Peter the Gt., Leningrad, USSR, Mishkan Olemanut Mus. Art, Israel, Novosibirsk (Russia) Picture Gallery, CIGNA Mus., Phila., Johns Hopkins U., Balt., Hiroshima Peace Meml. Mus., Hiroshima Japan - Hunter Mus. of Am. Art, Chattanooga, Holyoke (Mass.) Mus. Art, McGill U., Montreal, Que., Can., Downey (Calif.) Mus. Art, Ark. Art Ctr., Little Rock, Muzeum Niepoldlegosi, Warsaw, Poland, others. Home: PO Box 791 Kapaau HI 96755

JANKURA, DONALD EUGENE, hotel executive, educator; b. Bridgeport, Conn., Dec. 20, 1929; s. Stephen and Susan (Dirga) J.; m. Elizabeth Deborah Joynt, June 20, 1952; children: Donald Eugene Jr., Stephen J., Daria E., Diane E., Lynn M. BA in Hotel Adminstrn., Mich. State U., 1951. Asst. sales mgr. Pick Fort Shelby Hotel, Detroit, 1951-53; steward Dearborn Inn and Colonial Homes, Dearborn, Mich., 1953-54, sales mgr., 1954-60, resident mgr., 1960-62; gen. mgr. Stouffer's Northland Inn, Southfield, Mich., 1962-64; staff adviser Stouffer Motor Inns, Cleve., 1964-66, v.p., 1966-68; v.p. Assoc. Inns & Restaurants Co. Am., Denver, 1968-76, exec. v.p., 1976-81, sr. v.p., 1981-91; pres. Waverly Hospitality Assocs., Parker, Colo., 1991-94; dir. Sch. Hotel and Restaurant Mgmt. U. Denver, 1988-91; disting. spl. lectr. hospitality U. New Haven, Conn.; pres. Am. Hotel Assn. Directory Corp., 1986; guest lectr. Mich. State U., 1964, Fla. Internat. U., 1968, Cornell U., 1983, Denver U., 1986-87; mem. industry adv. bd. U. Denver, Mich. State U.; mem. adv. bd. Acad. Travel and Tourism-Nat. Acad. found., Denver, 1991—, chmn. 1998; commr. Accreditation Commn. Programs in Hospitality Adminstrn., 1995—. Commr. Commn. on Accreditation for Hospitality Mgmt., 1994—; pres. Evergreen Homeowner's Assn., 1994—; mem. USAF Innkeeper Evaluation Team, 1993, 95. Named to Hall of Fame Colo. Hotel and Lodging Assn., 1992, Mich. State U. Sch. Hospitality Bus., 1995, Wall of Fame, 1995; named Alumnus of Yr., Mich. State U. Hotel Sch., 1986. Mem. Am. Hotel and Motel Assn. (dir. 1978-80, vice chmn. industry adv. coun. 1980-81, sec.-treas. 1985, v.p. 1986, pres. 1987—, chmn. host com. 1994, Edn1. Inst. Emeritus award 1995), Colo./Wyo. Hotel and Motel Assn. (dir., bd. dirs. 1984—, Disting. Svc. award 1983), Pinery Country Club, Pres.'s Club, Masons, Phi Kappa Tau. Episcopalian. Avocations: gardening, sailing, cooking, woodworking. Home and Office: 7445 E Windlawn Way Parker CO 80134-5941

JANN, DONN GERARD, minister; b. Eau Claire, Wis., July 17, 1929; s. August William and Dorothy Olive (Nuesse) J.; m. Alice Joan Hartwell, Aug. 29, 1949 (div. 1974); children: Patricia, Scott, Lucinda, Susanna, Todd, Gregg; m. Nancy Ruth Hearn, June 22, 1985. Student, U. Minn., Duluth, 1947-48, BA, Whitworth Coll., 1951; MDiv, Theol. Sem., Princeton, N.J., 1955. Ordained to ministry Presbyn. Ch. (U.S.A.), 1955. Assoc. pastor 1st Presbyn. Ch., Bartlesville, Okla., 1955-59; pastor 1st Presbyn. Ch., Lexington, Nebr., 1960-67, Santa Rosa, Calif., 1967-73; v.p. Presbyn. Ch. Found., N.Y.C., 1973-88; pastor New Hempstead Presbyn. Ch., New City, N.Y., 1988-93; moderator Platte Presbytery, Hastings, Nebr., 1965-66; commr. Presbyn. Gen. Assembly, Portland, Oreg., 1967; chairperson presbytery Christian edn. com. Presbyn. Ch. (U.S.A.), Nebr., 1965-66, presbytery stewardship com., Nebr., 1966-67, synod ch. world interaction com., Calif., 1969-70, presbytery com. on minority candidates, Calif., 1970-71, synod regional budget com., Calif., 1971-72, presbytery com. on spl. gifts, 1989—; chairperson Community Ministries Corp., Lexington, 1966, Profl. Counseling Svcs., Lexington, 1966, County Protestant Community Svcs., Calif., 1969-70; area rep. Ch. Nat. Emergency Convocation on War, Washington, 1968; adj. prof. San Francisco Theol. Sem., San Anselmo, Calif., 1971-72; lectr. Santa Rosa Community Coll., 1972; mem. commn. on stewardship Nat. Coun. Chs., N.Y.C., 1975-88, v.p., chairperson commn. on stewardship, 1984-87, chairperson theol. resource ctr., N.Y., 1986-87. Pres. Coun. Social Svcs., Santa Rosa, 1971. Bd. dirs. Sonoma County (Calif.) chpt. People for Econ. Opportunity, 1968-70; mem. adv. coun. Santa Rosa Sch. Bd.; pres. Coun. Social Svcs., Santa Rosa, 1971; chairperson Interfaith Week of Christian Unity, Calif., 1971-72; active No. Am. Conf. on Christian Philanthropy, N.Y., 1974-87, chair, 1987-88. Mem. Presbytery of Grand Canyon (pres. 1990-93), Area Clergy Assn. (pres. 1990-93). Democrat. Home: 6350 E Kathleen Rd Scottsdale AZ 85254-1980 *It is not what happens to us that necessarily controls our life. The determative factor is what we do with those happenings. And that is what a vibrant faith is all about.*

JANNETTA, PETER JOSEPH, neurosurgeon, educator; b. Phila., Apr. 5, 1932; s. Samuel and Frances (Alfano) J.; m. Diana R. Jannetta, Sept. 9, 1989; children: Susan, Carol, Joanne, Peter, Elizabeth, S. Michael. AB, U. Pa., 1953, MD, 1957. Diplomate Am. Bd. Surgery, Am. Bd. Neurol. Surgery. Intern Hosp. U. Pa., 1957-58, resident in surgery, 1958-63; resident in neurosurgery, asso. UCLA Center for Health Scis., 1963-66; asst. instr. U. Pa., 1958-62, instr., 1960-63, instr. surgery, 1962-63; assoc. prof., chmn. surgery La. State U., 1966-71, prof., chmn. neurosurgery, 1971; prof. neurosurgery U. Pitts., 1971-76, Francis Sergeant Cheever Disting. prof., 1976-98, chmn. dept. neurol. surgery, 1973-98, dir. divsn. neurol. surgery, 1971-73; active staff Presbyn.-Univ. Hosp., Pitts., Children's Hosp. Pitts.; sr. attending staff Montefiore Hosp., Pitts.; sr. cons. VA Hosp., Pitts.; sec. of health Commonwealth of Pa., 1995-96. Co-editor: The Cranial Nerves, 1981, Trigeminal Neuralgia, 1990; contbr. numerous articles to profl. jours. Mem. A.C.S., AMA, AAAS, Am. Surg. Assn., Allegheny County, Pa. med. socs., Assn. Academic Surgery, Am. Assn. Neurol. Surgeons, Congress Neurol. Surgeons, Fellowship Acad. Neurosurgeons, Internat. Assn. Study Pain, Internat. Soc. Pediatric Neurosurgery, Mid-Atlantic, Pa., Pitts. neurosurg. socs., N.Y. Acad. Scis., Pitts. Acad. Medicine, Pitts. Surg. Soc., Ravdin-Rhoads Surg. Soc., Research Soc. Neurol. Surgeons, Soc. Critical Care Medicine, Soc. Neurol. Surgeons, Soc. Neurosci., Soc. Neurosurg. Anesthesia and Neurol. Supportive Care. Office: Presbyn-U Hosp 200 Lothrop St Pittsburgh PA 15213-2546

JANNEY, DONALD WAYNE, lawyer; b. Clinton, N.C., Jan. 9, 1952; s. Wayne Columbus and Bernice (Talley) J.; m. Sydney Louise Rhame, May 28, 1977; children: Taylor Columbus, Camden St. Clair. BA, Furman U., 1974; JD, U. Va., 1978. Bar: Ga. 1978, U.S. Dist. Ct. (no. dist.) Ga. 1978, U.S. Ct. Appeals (11th cir.) 1982. Assoc. Troutman Sanders, Atlanta, 1978-85; ptnr. Troutman Sanders and predecessor firm, Atlanta, 1985—. Bd. dirs. State YMCA Ga., Atlanta, 1980-91. Mem. ABA, Ga. Bar Assn., Atlanta Bar Assn., Lawyers Club Atlanta, Phi Beta Kappa. Baptist. Home: 705 E Morningside Dr Atlanta GA 30324-5220 Office: Troutman Sanders 5200 NationsBank Plz 600 Peachtree St NE Ste 5200 Atlanta GA 30308-2216

JANNEY, PATRA ELLEN, principal; b. Ozark, Ark., Oct. 15, 1932; d. Frank Edward and Elva Cleo (Chandler) Moss; m. William Conrad Janney, Sr., Aug. 10, 1952; children: William C., Jr., DeAnn Patra. BS, W.Va. State Coll., 1965; MA, W.Va. U., 1970; EdD, Va. Poly. Inst. State U., 1984. Cert. edn. adminstr. Va. Poly. Inst. State U.; cert. advanced grad. studies Va. Poly Inst. State U. Tchr. County Line Schs., Branch, Ark., 1951-52, Raleigh County Bd. Edn., Beckley, W.Va., 1962-82; prin. Raleigh County Bd. Edn., Beckley, 1982—; presenter in field. Mem. ASCD (assoc.), Raleigh County Elem. Prin. Assn. Home: Box 786 114 Quietwoods Pl Crab Orchard WV 25827

JANNEY, SALLY BAGGS, civic worker; b. Long County, Ga., Aug. 27, 1936; d. Albert Hall and Thelma Christine (Swindell) Baggs; m. John David Janney, Nov. 17, 1962; children: John David II, Karen Janney Rhodes. Student, Draughons Coll., 1954-55, Armstrong Jr. Coll., Savannah, 1955-57, U. Ga., 1957-59. Adminstrv. asst. to chief profl. svcs. U.S. Army Hosp., Ft. Stewart, Ga., 1956-62; cons. Leggett Dept. Store, Beckley, W.Va., 1980-85; dir. White Gloves and Party Manners program Leggett Dept. Store, Beckley, 1983-89; mgr. Touch of Gold, Beckley, 1990-98. Pres. Aux. to So. Coun. of Optometrists, 1981-82; publicity dir. W.Va. Sports Festival, 1970-74; mem. recreation commn. City of Oak Hill, 1972-80; chmn. LGA White Oak Country Club, 1980-81, 88-90, 99—; cub scout den mother; past pres. Oak Hill Grade Sch. PTA; mem. altar guild, worship com., United Meth. Women, Margaret Stimson Fellowship Oak Hill United Meth. Ch. Mem. Aux. to Am. Optometric Assn. (pres. 1983-84), Oak Hill Jr. Woman's Club (pres. 1966-68, Woman of Yr. 1970-71), Woodland Oaks Garden Club (pres. 1975-79, 99-01), Oak Hill Civic League, Fayette Study Club (pres. 1986-88), Aux. to W.Va. Optometric Assn. (pres. 1978-79, 83-84, treas.), W.Va. Garden Club (life), Aux. to So. Coun. Optometrists (pres. 1981-82). Methodist. Avocations: golf, bridge, travel. Home: 2020 Edgewood Dr Oak Hill WV 25901-2032

JANNEY, STUART SYMINGTON, III, investment company executive; b. Balt., Aug. 30, 1948; s. Stuart Symington and Barbara (Phipps) J.; m. Lynn Mary Buchheit, Oct. 28, 1975; children: Emily, Matthew. BA, U. N.C., 1970; JD, U. Md., 1973. Bar: Md. 1973. Legis. asst. Sen. Charles Mathias U.S. Senate, Washington, 1973-75, fgn. policy asst. Sen. Howard Baker, 1976-77; spl. asst. U.S. Sec. State U.S. State Dept., Washington, 1975-76; ptnr. Niles, Barton & Wilmer, Balt., 1977-86; mng. dir. Alex Brown & Sons, Balt., 1986-94; head Brown Asset Mgmt., Balt., 1986-93; chmn. bd. Bessemer Trust Co., N.Y.C., 1994—, Bessemer Securities Corp., N.Y.C., 1994—; bd. dirs. Md. Million, Inc., Essex Internat., Inc. Vice chmn. bd. Johns Hopkins U., Balt., 1995—; chmn. bd. dirs. Applied Physics Lab., 1991—, Md. Zool. Soc., Balt., 1979—; bd. dirs. Md. Horsebreeders, 1991—, Breeders Cup Ltd.; chmn. Thoroughbred Owners and Breeders Am.; bd. dirs., sec. Nat. Audubon Soc., N.Y.C., 1982-92; steward Jockey Club U.S. Office: Bessemer Trust Co 630 5th Ave New York NY 10111-0100*

JANNING, JOHN LOUIS, research scientist, consultant; b. Dayton, Ohio, Mar. 30, 1928; s. Eugene Alois and Frieda Marie (Kessen) J.; m. Dolores Mary Nartker, Nov. 29, 1952; children: Kathleen, Janet, Theresa, Lawrence, Thomas, Richard, Jacqueline. Electronic technician U. Dayton, 1956-58; cons. engr. NCR Corp., Dayton, 1958-88; liquid crystal display cons. JLJ, Inc., Dayton, 1988—. Contbr. articles to profl. jours.; numerous patents in high tech. field including implantable med. devices; inventor thermal printing wafer, plasma displays, field emission displays and LCDs. With inf. U.S. Army, 1950-52. Recipient Outstanding Profl. Achievement award Affiliate Socs. Coun. Engring. and Sci. Found. Dayton, 1982. Mem. IEEE, Soc. for Info. Display, Inventors Coun. Dayton. Roman Catholic. Avocations: computer, bridge, chess, public speaking. Home and Office: 332 Vindale Dr Dayton OH 45440-3364 also: Lab at 4656 Wilmington Pike Dayton OH 45440

JANNING, SISTER MARY BERNADETTE, nun, retired association executive; b. Custer City, Okla., May 20, 1917; d. Frank R. and Mary Elizabeth (Kreizenbeck) J. R.N., St. Francis Hosp. Sch. Nursing, Wichita, Kans., 1942; B.S. in Nursing Edn, Marquette U., 1951, M.S., 19S2; post-grad., George Washington U., 1972. Joined Sisters of Sorrowful Mother, 1935; asst. dir. St. Johns Sch. Nursing, Tulsa, 1952-56; dir. St. Francis Sch. Nursing, Wichita, 1956-65; provincial superior Tulsa Province, Sisters of Sorrowful Mother, 1965-70; asso. adminstr. St. Francis Hosp., Wichita, 1972-73; pres., chief exec. officer, dir. St. Francis Hosp., 1973-79; exec. dir. Franciscan Villa, Inc., Broken Arrow, Okla., 1979-80, Okla. Cath. Health Conf., 1980-94; ret. Author: Life of a Student Nurse, 1961. Chmn. bd. Kans. affiliate Am. Diabetes Assn., 1974; sec. bd. dirs. Midway Kans. chpt. ARC, 1974—, pres., 1979; chmn. Mid-Central Kans.; adv. bd. KBEZ Stereo 93, Tulsa, Okla., 1982-83. Recipient Twenty-Year Pin award ARC, 1962; Alumni Nurse of Year award St. Francis Sch. Nursing, 1972. Fellow Am. Coll. Health Care Execs.; mem. Am. Coll. Healthcare Adminstrs. (life), Am. Hosp. Assn., Kans. Hosp. Assn. (dir.), Catholic Hosp. Assn., Nat., Kans. leagues nursing, Kans. Hosp. Assn., Kans. Conf. Cath. Health Affairs (pres. 1977), Hosp. Council Met. Wichita, Wichita Hosp. Adminstrs. Office: Okla Cath Health Conf 17600 E 51st St Broken Arrow OK 74012-9231

JANNINI, RALPH HUMBERT, III, electronics executive; b. Boston, Dec. 30, 1932; s. Humbert P. and Marian H. (Roman) J.; m. Pauline T. Occhinto, Feb. 16, 1957; children—Ralph H. IV, Mark L., Lisa M. B.S. Acctg., Bentley Coll., 1957. CPA, Mass. Auditor, New Eng. Electric System, Westboro, Mass., 1957-68, mgr. rates and statistics, 1968-73; asst. to pres. Gas Inc.-Colonial, Lowell, Mass., 1973-76; v.p. Colonial Gas Co., Lowell, 1976-87; pres. James Millen Electronics, Malden, Mass., 1988—; cons. Antennas Etc., Andover, Mass., 1980—; prin. Unadilla/Reyco/InLine Products, 1986—, Andover Book and Collaborative, 1995—. Served with U.S. Army, 1952-53, Korea. Mem. New Eng. Utility Rate Forum (chmn. 1980), New Eng. Gas Assn., Inst. Internat. Auditors. Republican. Roman Catholic. Office: James Millen Electronics 87 Belmont St North Andover MA 01845-2304

JANNUZI, F. TOMASSON, economics educator; b. Pitts., Apr. 23, 1934; s. Frank Humbert and Angela Mary (Tomasson) J.; m. Barbara Lucille Gallagher, Sept. 15, 1957; children: Buell Tomasson, Frank Sampson. AB, Dartmouth Coll., 1955; PhD in Econ., U. London, 1958. Field rep. for So. Asia, E. Africa Found. For Youth and Student Affairs, N.Y.C., 1959-61; asst. rep. The Asia Found., N.Y.C., 1961-62; program officer for So. Asia div. The Asia Found., San Francisco, 1962-65, asst. rep. for India, 1965-68; vis. lectr. in econs. U. Tex., Austin, 1968-72, dir. at the Ctr. for Asian Studies, Nat. Resource Ctr. for So. Asia, 1972-86; assoc. prof. of econs. U. Tex., 1973-79, prof. of econs. and Asian studies, 1979-98, assoc. chmn. dept. econs., 1995-97, prof. emeritus econs., 1998—; pres. Asia Rsch. Assoc. Inc., Austin, Tex., 1985-99; vis. fellow Internat. Devel. Ctr. U. Oxford, Eng., 1989-92; sr. assoc. mem. St. Antony's Coll. Oxford, 1989; vis scholar Ctr. for South Asian Studies, U. Va., 1999—; cons. USAID, Dept. State, Def. Intelligence Coll., The World Bank, 1973—. Author: Agrarian Crisis in India: The Case of Bihar, 1974, India in Transition: Issues of Political Economy in a Plural Society, 1988; India's Persistent Dilemma: The Political Economy of Agrarian Reform, 1994; co-author: (with James T. Peach) The Agrarian Structure of Bangladesh, 1980; contbr. articles to various books, monographs, reports. Dir. Austin Coun. on Fgn. Affairs Inc., Tex., 1987-98; mem. Inst. of Current World Affairs, Hanover, N.H., 1987—; trustee Am. Inst. of Indian Studies, Chgo., 1973-87, chmn. 1979-81. Fellow Ford Found.; mem. Am. Econ. Assn., Asian Econ. Studies (com.), Cosmos Club (Wash.), Phi Beta Kappa. Democrat. Avocations: squash rackets, travel.

JANOFSKY, LEONARD S., lawyer, association executive; b. Los Angeles, Oct. 13, 1909; s. E. and Ida (Schwartz) J.; m. Nancy Nielson, Dec. 29, 1948; children—Annelies Irene Hartzell, John Stephen. B.A., Occidental Coll., 1931, LL.D., 1981; LL.B., Harvard, 1934; LL.D., Pepperdine U., 1979. Bar: Calif. bar 1934. Since practiced in Los Angeles; sr. regional atty. NLRB, 21st Region Ariz. and So. Calif., 1935-36; spl. trial counsel eminent domain proceedings Housing Authority, City Los Angeles, 1950-54; ptnr. firm Paul, Hastings, Janofsky & Walker, 1951—; U.S. State Dept. del. ILO Conf., Geneva, 1969, 70, 85; mem. sr. adv. bd. 9th Cir. Jud. Conf., 1982—; pres. 9th Circuit Hist. Soc., 1987—. Contbr. articles profl. jours. Trustee Occidental Coll., 1963—, chmn., 1969-72; mem. overseers com. to visit Harvard Law Sch., 1969-74; bd. visitors Stanford Law Sch., 1972-75. Served to lt. comdr. USNR, 1942-45. Decorated Orden do Merito Santos Dumont and Ordem das Asas Brancas, Brazilian Air Force; recipient Gold Seal award for outstanding alumnus Occidental Coll., 1973; Medallion award St. Thomas More Law Honor Soc., Loyola U., 1977. Fellow Am. Bar Found., Am. Coll. Trial Lawyers; mem. Am. Law Inst., Internat. Bar Assn., Inter-Am. Bar Assn., ABA (chmn. spl. com. specialization 1970-71, dir. Am. Prepaid Legal Services Inst. 1974—, vice chmn. Commn. Med. Profl. Liability 1975—, ho. of dels. 1975—, chmn. council sect. labor relations law 1975-76, bd. govs. 1978—, pres. 1979-80), Calif. Bar Assn. (pres. 1972-73, gov. 1970-73, exec. com. law in a free soc. 1971-72, 73-77, mem. spl. adv. com. med. malpractice 1975), Los Angeles County Bar Assn. (pres. 1969-70, trustee 1967-69, Shattuck-Price award 1977), Nat. Conf. Bar Presidents (pres. 1973-74, mem. council 1970-75), Nat. Legal Aid and Defender Assn. (dir.), Am. Judicature Soc., Harvard Law Sch. Assn. (2d v.p. 1976-77), Phi Beta Kappa. Club: Chancery (Los Angeles). Home: 661 Thayer Ave Los Angeles CA 90024-3307 Office: 555 S Flower St Los Angeles CA 90071-2300

JANOSKI, HENRY VALENTINE, banker, former investment counselor, realtor; b. Nanticoke, Pa., Feb. 14, 1933; s. Bruce and Marie (Rozmarek) J.; m. Rita Rosemary Ruane, Sept. 27, 1980; children: Maria, Elizabeth. *Parents were proprietors of a wallpaper and paint store. Both grandfathers were coal miners. Antoni Janowski was born in Suwalki province and his wife Anna Krzysztopowicz Janowski in Wilno province of Russian occupied Poland-Lithuania. She arrived with children: Bernard, Anna and Ignacy (Bruce) in 1895 at Philadelphia on the SS Kensington. Jan Rozmiarek and Magdalena Chybki Rozmiarek were born in Poznan province in German occupied Poland. Uncle Charles Rozmarek (Who Was Who) became founding president of the Polish American Congress in 1944. Cousin Marilyn Rozmarek Komosa became a judge in Chicago. Jan and Magdalena had three grandchildren and one great-grandchild who were elected to Phi Beta Kappa* BA magna cum laude, Yale U., 1955; MBA, U. Pa., 1960. Sr. credit analyst Nat. Bank of Detroit, 1960-63; asst. cashier First Nat. Bank, Wilkes-Barre, Pa., 1963-65; sr. v.p. Northeastern Bank, Scranton, Pa., 1965-80; investment counselor, fin. planner, Clarks Summit, Pa., 1980-92; realtor assoc., Clarks Summit, Pa., 1992; chief trust investment officer, Penn Security Bank and Trust Co., Scranton, 1992—; instr. fin. Marywood Coll., Scranton, 1983. Bd. dirs. Community Med. Ctr., Scranton, 1974-97, asst. treas., 1976-91; bd. dirs. Emergency Med. Services Northeastern Pa., Pittston, 1976—, pres., 1985-87; bd. dirs. Polish Am. Congress No. Pa. div., Scranton, 1972—, v.p., 1972-89, pres., 1989—; bd. dirs. Ethics Inst. N.E. Pa., Dallas, 1991-96; bd. dirs., treas. Keystone chpt. Am. Heart Assn., Scranton, 1968-74; chmn. Campaign for Yale U., Northeastern Pa., 1976-78; incorporating dir. Lackawanna County U.S. Constitution Bicentennial Commn., 1987-88; treas. Grove St. Home Sch. Assn., Clarks Summit, 1987-90; lector Christ the King Ch., Dunmore, 1982-87, Our Lady of the Snows Ch., Clarks Summit, 1987—, Ch. of St. Benedict, Newton Twp., 1991—; allocations vol. United Way, 1988-91. 1st lt. AUS, 1955-57. Recipient Assn. of U.S. Army award, 1954, Disting. Military Student award, 1955, Am. Legion award, 1947, 51; Cert. Leadership Lackawanna, 1989. Mem. Am. Bankers Assn., Penn. Bankers Assn., Am. Inst. Banking, Northern Anthracite Bankers Assn., Fin. Analysts of Phila., Fin. Analysts Fedn., Inst. Chartered Fin. Analysts (chartered fin. analyst), Assn. for Investment Mgmt. and Rsch., Estate Planning Coun. Northeastern Pa., Nat. Assn. Realtors, Penn. Assn. Realtors, Greater Scranton Bd. Realtors, Experiment in Internat. Living (France), Le Cercle Francais (treas. 1994—), Ecologia/Ekologiya, Wyo. Hist. and Geol. Soc., Greater Scranton C. of C., Esperanto League for N.Am., Universala Esperanto Asocio, Friends of Poland of Lackawanna County, Polish Nat. Alliance, Polish Falcons Am., Polish Am. Hist. Assn., Kosciuszko Found., Assn. of Yale Alumni (rep. 1988-91), Aircraft Owners and Pilots Assn., Schultzville Airport Pilots Assn., Phi Beta Kappa. Republican. Roman Catholic. Clubs: Westmoreland (Wilkes-Barre), Scranton Club, Yale of Northeastern Pa. (sec. 1985-88, alumni sch. com. interview applicants); Univ. of Pa. (Lackawanna County), Leadership Lackawanna Alumni Assn. Avocations: skiing, flying, travel, languages. Home: 107 Carteret Dr Clarks Summit PA 18411-1009 Office: Penn Security Bank & Trust Co 150 N Washington Ave Scranton PA 18503-1843

JANOSKI, REGINA JANE, nursing educator; b. Norristown, Pa., May 7, 1948; d. Warren T. and Anna M. (Evanik) Dewees; m. John M. Janoski, Aug. 16, 1969; 1 child, Ian C. Diploma, Lankenau Hosp. Sch. Nursing, Phila., 1969; BSN magna cum laude, Eastern Coll., St. David's, Pa., 1987; MSN, Villanova U., 1990. RN, Pa.; cert. med.-surg. nurse. Staff nurse med./surg. Sacred Heart Hosp. and Rehab. Ctr., Norristown, 1969-71, head nurse med./surg., 1972-77, clin. coord. rehab. and med./surg., 1978-83; med.-surg. nursing instr. West Chester (Pa.) U., 1993-96; nursing instr. Montgomery County C.C., Blue Bell, Pa., 1996—; adj. faculty, clin. instr. cmty. health Eastern Coll., St. Davids, Pa., 1990; wound and skin clinician Osteo. Med. Ctr., Phila., 1990-93. Recipient Profl. Nurse Traineeship award, 1989-90. Mem. Sigma Theta Tau. Home: 238 Foulkrod Blvd King Of Prussia PA 19406

JANOSKO, RUDOLPH E. M., psychiatrist; b. Munhall, Pa., Apr. 30, 1930; s. Rudolph E. and Anne (Gerek) J.; m. Audrey M. Nemeth, May 18, 1932; children: Beth, Gwen, Ellen. BS, U. Pitts., 1952, MD, 1956. Cert. in psychiatry Am. Bd. Psychiatry and Neurology. Intern Easton (Pa.) Hosp., 1956-57; resident in psychiatry U. Pitts., 1957-59, 61-62; instr. psychiatry U. Pitts. Sch. Medicine, 1962-65; lectr. U. Pitts. Dept. Spl. Edn., Grad. Sch., 1966-70; clin. asst. prof. psychiatry U. Pitts. Sch. Medicine, 1965-75; mem. attending staff Presbyn.-Univ. Hosp., Pitts., 1962—; faculty Pitts. Psychoanalytic Inst., 1970—; clin. assoc. prof. psychiatry U. Pitts. Sch. Medicine, 1975—; tng. and supervising analyst Am. Psychoanalytic Assn., Pitts. Psychoanalytic Inst., 1979—; pres. Pitts. Psychoanalytic Ctr., 1981-83; dir. Pitts. Psychoanalytic Inst., 1985-86; med. dir. Family Svcs. of Western Pa., Pitts., 1988—; cons. Greater Pitts. Guild for Blind, Bridgeville, Pa., 1964—, Social Security Adminstrn., HHS, Pitts., 1979—. Author in field. Capt. USAF, 1959-61. Recipient Meritorious Distinction award Greater Pitts. Guild for Blind, 1967, Outstanding Tchr. award Western Psychiat. Inst., 1981. Fellow Am Psychiat. Assn.; mem. Am. Psychoanalytic Assn., Pitts. Acad. Medicine, Pitts. Psychoanalytic Soc. (pres. 1983-85), AMA. Republican. Roman Catholic. Avocation: running. Home: 2534 Mt Royal Rd Pittsburgh PA 15217-2542 Office: 161 N Dithridge St Pittsburgh PA 15213-2646

JANOTA, DEBILYN MARIE, school principal; b. Portland, Oreg., Apr. 25, 1953; d. Art Philip and LaVeta Marie (Dozler) Christiansen; m. Joseph Edward Janota III, June 10, 1972; children: Gia Ann, Joseph Ernest IV. BA in Music Edn. K-12, Oreg. Coll. Edn., Monmouth, 1975. Cert. K-12 music specialist. Tchr. Regis H.S., Stayton, Oreg., 1975-77, St. Mary Grade Sch., Stayton, 1978-94; prin. Queen of Peace, Salem, Oreg., 1994—. Chair Chemeketa Cmty. Schs. Kids Track, Stayton, 1983-94. Recipient Support-Cooperation award YMCA, Salem, 1995. Mem. ASCD, AAUW, Archdiocese of Portland in Oreg. Edn., Nat. Cath. Ednl. Assn. (Disting. Grad. 1994), DARE (nat. and county), Willamette Valley Devel. Officers, Salem Area C. of C. Avocations: reading, walking, music, biking, travel. Home: 11632 Shaff Rd SE Aumsville OR 97325-9726 Office: Queen of Peace Sch 4227 Lone Oak Rd SE Salem OR 97302-5700

JANOVER, ROBERT H., lawyer; b. N.Y.C., Aug. 17, 1930; s. Cyrus J. and Lillian D. (Horowitz) J.; m. Mary Elizabeth McMahon, Oct. 23, 1966; 1 child, Laura Lockwood. BA, Princeton U., 1952; postgrad., U. Vienna, 1956; JD, Harvard U., 1957. Bar: N.Y. 1957, U.S. Supreme Ct. 1961, D.C. 1966, Mich. 1973. Practice law N.Y.C., 1957-65; cons. Office of Edn., HEW, 1965; legis. atty. Office of Gen. Counsel, HEW, 1965-66; asst. gen. atty. Mgmt. Assistance Inc., N.Y.C., 1966-71; atty. Ford Motor Credit Co., Dearborn, Mich., 1971-74; mem. firm Freud, Markus, Slavin, Toohey & Galgan, Troy, Mich., 1974-79; pvt. practice Detroit, 1979—, Bloomfield Hills, Mich., 1982—. Contbr. articles to profl. jours. Bd. dirs. Oakland Citizens League, 1976-96, v.p., 1976-79, pres., 1979-96. 1st lt. U.S. Army, 1952-54. Mem. ABA, Mich. State Bar, N.Y. State Bar, Detroit Bar Assn., Bar Assn. D.C., Assn. Bar of City of N.Y., Am. Inns Ct. (master of the bench 1996—), Princeton Club (pres. Mich. 1991-92), Nassau Club (Princeton, N.J.), Harvard Club (N.Y.C.). Home: 685 Ardmoor Dr Bloomfield Hills MI 48301-2415 Office: 100 W Long Lake Rd Ste 200 Bloomfield Hills MI 48304-2774

JANOW, CHRIS, mechanical engineer; b. N.Y.C., Apr. 22, 1953; s. John and Angie (Bizzios) J. BME, CCNY, 1975, MME, 1980. Mech. engr. Fuze Devel. and Engr. Directorate, Picatinny Arsenal, N.J., 1975-80; mech. engr. nuclear and fuze div. Large Caliber Weapons System Lab, Picatinny Arsenal, 1980-84; mech. engr. fuze div. Armament Engring. Directorate, Picatinny Arsenal, 1984-85; systems engr. battlefield mgmt. br., fire control div. Fire Support Armaments Ctr., Picatinny Arsenal, 1985-87; program mgmt. engr. AUS Office of Product Mgr. for Fuzes, Picatinny Arsenal, 1987-88; gen. engr. and assoc. product mgr. for close combat AUS Office of Product Mgr. for Fuzes, 1988-94; assoc. dir. Close Combat Heavy/U.S. Army Fuze Mgmt. Office, 1994—. exec. sec. Fuze Engring. Standardization Working Group, DOD, 1983-85; organizer numerous confs.; tech. cons. U.S. Army Fuze Safety Rev. Bd., 1987—; presenter fuze symposium Am. Def. Preparedness Assn., 1992; U.S. prin. rep. to NATO AC/310 Subgroup II (Fuzes), 1994—. Vice-pres. Greek Orthodox Youth of Am., St. Spyridon Ch., N.Y.C., 1974-75. Mem. Am. Def. Preparedness Assn., Assn. U.S. Army, Picatinny Officers Club, Pi Tau Sigma. Greek Orthodox. Avocations: travel, working out, model making, stamp collecting, golf. Home: 34 Hilltop Ter Bloomingdale NJ 07403-1510 Office: Office of US Army Fuze Mgmt Attn: AMSTA-AR-FZ Picatinny Arsenal NJ 07806

JANOW, LYDIA FRANCES, meeting planner; b. N.Y.C., Dec. 2, 1957; d. John and Angie (Bizzios) J. BA cum laude, CCNY, 1978; grad., CBS Div. Publ., 1984. Cert. meeting planner. Exec. sec. Family Weekly Mag., N.Y.C., 1978-81; asst. mdse. mgr. Family Weekly Mag., 1981-83; spl. events mgr. Family Weekly/USA Weekend, N.Y.C., 1983-86; mgr. meetings & events Mag. Pubs. Assn., N.Y.C., 1986-88; conv. svcs. mgr., sales & catering mgr. Sheraton Heights Hotel, Hasbrouck Heights, N.J., 1989-91; conf. mgr. Aviation Week Group McGraw Hill Inc., N.Y.C., 1991-93, dir. tradeshows and confs., 1993—. Editor: Newsletter Heights Hotel, 1991; contbr. articles to profl. jours. Camp counselor, Hellenic-Am. Neighborhood Action Com., N.Y.C., 1974-78; tchr., Sunday sch., St. Spyridon Ch., N.Y.C., 1974-80. Mem. Internat. Assn. Exhibit Mgrs., Meeting Planners Internat., Assn. Trade Show Exhibitors, Internation Assn. for Exposition Mgmt., Exhibit Mgrs. and Conf. Organizers. Greek Orthodox. Avocations: photography, sports, reading. Home: 29 Levitt Ave Bergenfield NJ 07621-1904

JANOWICH, RON, artist; b. Balt., Apr. 10, 1948; s. Joseph and Rosemary (Reynolds) J.; m. Wendy Wasdahl, Oct. 6, 1974. BFA, Md. Inst., Balt., 1970, MFA, 1972. vis. artist Kent (Ohio) State U., 1992, 96, Cleve. Inst., 1993, 96, Ohio State U., 1996; instr. drawing Parsons Sch. Design, 1984; asst. prof. Lafayette Coll., 1980-85. Solo exhbns. include Lafayette Coll., Easton, Pa., 1981, Artists Space, N.Y.C., 1983, John Davis Gallery, Akron, Ohio, 1984, Wolff Gallery, N.Y.C., 1985, Craig Cornelius Gallery, N.Y.C., 1986, Cava Gallery, Phila., 1986, Germans Van Eck, N.Y.C., 1986, Pamela Auchincloss Gallery, Santa Barbara, Calif., 1987, 90, 92, 94, Lorence Monk Gallery, N.Y.C., 1987, Asher/Faure, L.A., 1987, 89, Galerie Lelong, N.Y.C., 1988, 89, 90, Galerie Hans Strelow, Dusseldorf, Germany, 1988, Knoedler Gallery, London, 1988, Persons & Lindell Gallery, Helsinki, Finland, 1989, Galerie Malmgran, Goteburg, Sweden, 1990, Galleri JMS, Oslo, 1990, Gallery Kuranuki, Osaka, Japan, 1990, Compasse Rose Gallery, Chgo., 1991; group exhbns. include Balt. Mus. Art., 1970, Jacobs Ladder Gallery, Washington, 1972, 73, Aldrich Mus. Contemporary Art, Ridgefield, Conn., 1974, Rosa Esman Gallery, N.Y.C., 1979, Art Galaxy, N.Y.c., 1982, Muhlenberg Coll. Arts, Allentown, Pa., 1983, Newcastle Poly. Art Gallery, Newcastle upon Tyne, England, 1983, Oscarsson Hood Gallery, N.Y.c., 1984, N.Y. Studio Sch., 1984, Nina Freudenheim Gallery, Buffalo, 1984, Susan Montezinos Gallery, Phila., 1984, Lafayette Coll., 1984, Muhlenberg Coll., 1984, Kamikaze, N.Y.C., 1985, Charles Cowles Gallery, N.Y.c., 1985, Condeso/Lawler Gallery, N.Y.C., 1985, Jersey City Mus., 1985, Tibor de Nagy Gallery, N.Y.C., 1985, Dart Gallery, Chgo., 1986, Marilyn Pearl Gallery, N.Y.C., 1986, Max Protetch Gallery, N.Y.C., 1986, Pratt Manhattan Gallery, N.Y.C., 1986, Linda Farris Gallery, Seattle, 1986, Acme Art, San Francisco, 1986, others. NEA fellow, 1976, 89. Avocation: songwriting. Address: 100 W Houston New York NY 10012*

JANOWITZ, HENRY DAVID, gastroenterologist, researcher, medical educator; b. Paterson, N.J., Mar. 23, 1915; s. Sam and Rose (Meyers) J.; m. Adeline R. Tintner, Oct. 31, 1942; children: Mary Rebecca, Anne Francis. BA, Columbia U., 1935, MD, 1939; MS, U. Ill., 1949. Intern Mt. Sinai Hosp., N.Y.C., 1939-41; resident in medicine Mt. Sinai Hosp., 1947-48; pvt. practice N.Y.C., 1956-98; head div. gastroenterology Mt. Sinai Hosp., 1958-83, attending physician gastroenterology, 1961-85, now cons. in gastroenterology, 1985—, clin. prof. medicine, 1967-85; emeritus clin. prof. medicine, 1985—; mem. Am. Bd. Gastroenterology, 1966-70; chmn. program project com., div. arthritis and metabolism NIH, 1969-70. Author: (with D.A. Dreiling and C.V. Perrier) Pancreatic Inflammatory Disease, 1965; Inflammatory Bowel Disease: A Clinical Approach, 1994, Your Gut Feelings, 1987, Indigestion, 1992, Good Food for Bad Stomaches, 1997; contbr. 300 articles to profl. jours.; mem. editl. bd. Proceedings of Soc. for Exptl. Biology and Medicine, 1974-86, Am. Jour. Physiol., 1970-74, Jour. Chronic Diseases, 1966-88. Founder Ileitis and Colitis Found. Am. Served to maj. U.S. Army, 1942-46. Recipient Jacobi medal Mt. Sinai Sch. Medicine, 1974, Clin. Achievement award Am. Coll. Gastroent., 1992. Fellow Royal Soc. Medicine (hon., J. Lester Gabrilove award, 1994); mem. Am. Soc. Clin. Investigation, Assn. Am. Physicians, Am. Phys. Soc., Am. Gastroent. Assn. (pres. 1972-73, Friedenwald medal 1973), N.Y. Gastroent. Assn. (pres. 1968-69), Brit. Soc. Gastroent. (hon.), Royal Soc. Medicine London (hon.).

JANOWSKI, KARYN ANN, artist; b. Milw., Aug. 15, 1958; d. Robert Arthur and Evelyn Rose (Spanbauer) J. BS in Art, U. Wis., 1984. Dir., founder Warehouse Studio for Visual Artists and Musicians, Madison, 1984-86, 88-89; tchg. asst. art therapy seminar U. Wis., 1983; gallery assoc. San Francisco Wome Artists Gallery, 1990-91. Muralist Whitewater (Wis.) Hist. Soc., 1980, Mifflin St. Cmty. Coop Mural, Madison, 1987; contbr. artwork to American Artists, an Illustrated Survey of Leading Contemporaries, The California Art Rev., Art Comm. Internat. Curated Collection I; scenic artist: The Wind in the Willows; collections include Microsoft Image Archive, works at Tralfamadore Coop, Archive of Wis. Regional Primate Rsch. Ctr., Dynamic Resources, Inc., Soc. of Haight-Ashbury Charade, San Francisco, Niels and faith Ingwersen, Jeff Scott Olson, Esq, Hadji Rahimipour,; exhbns. include: Wis. Ctr., Madison, Firehouse 7, DAS Club, The Cannery Bldg., San Francisco, L.A. Mcpl. Art Gallery, George's, L.A., Southampton Cultural Ctr., Hofstra Mus., L.I.; contbr. Dictionary Internat. Biography, Cambridge, Eng. Mem. L.A. Cultural Affairs Slide Registry, 1996—, Artists Space, N.Y.C., L.A.C.E., 1998—. Mem. Washington Soc. of Portrait Artists. Democrat. Avocations: literature, music, nature, family and friends, multimedia/computer animation. Home and Office: 1775 N Orange Dr Apt 202 Los Angeles CA 90028-4334

JANOWSKI, THADDEUS MARIAN, architect; b. Cracow, Poland, Aug. 16, 1923; came to U.S., 1960, naturalized, 1972; s. Stanislaw and Maria (Kijak) J.; m. Zofia K. Owinski, Apr. 19, 1949 (div.); 1 child, Barbara Margaret. MCP in Architecture, Poly. Acad., Cracow, 1949; MArch, U. Ill., 1962; PhD (hon.), Inst. Three Dimensional Perception, 1987. Chief architect Miastoprojekt Cracow, 1949-58; chief cons. So. Poland K.U.A., Warsaw, 1958-60; lectr. Poly Acad. Cracow, 1947-50, 1958-60; instr. U. Ill., 1960-62; assoc. prof. U. Man., Can., 1962-65, Iowa State U., Ames, 1965-71; prof. Syracuse U., N.Y., 1971—; proprietor, dir. Mus. Archtl. Graphics Internat., 1994—; pres. Inst. Three Dimensional Perception, Inc., 1985; chief arch. for Saudi royal family estates, Ga., 1983-89; prin., dir. Mus. Archtl. Graphics Internat., 1991—. Numerous exhbns. in U.S. and Europe, 1949—; built over 6 million sq. ft. constrn. commns. include Interstate Farm Devel., Des Moines, 1967, Settlement of town houses, East Des Moines, 1969. Co-author: Sacred Art in Poland, 1955; The Urban Scale, 1968. Patentee in field. Recipient numerous prizes nat. or internat. competitions including prize Polish Embassy bldg., Peking, China, 1955, 1st prize Polish Pavillion, Brussels, Belgium, 1956, 1st prize astronomy obs. and planetarium Warsaw, 1956, award exptl. bldg., Moscow, 1959, 1st prize sch. bldgs., Poland, 1960, prize Red Rock Hill Devel., San Francisco, 1961, 2d prize campus, Dublin, Ireland, 1964, 1st prize Olympic Stadium, Banff, Can., 1962, 2d and 3rd prizes fall out shelters Office Civil Defense, 1964, 2d prize, 1966; 1st prize Bicentennial medal Iowa, 1972; 1st prize for U.S. Stamp Copernicus Quincentennial; 1st prize and commn. for monument commemorating victims of Katyn Massacre, Toronto, 1979, Syracuse, N.Y., 1985. Fellow World-Wide Acad. Scholars New Zealand, Intercontinental Biographical Assn. (U.K.); mem. Assn. Polish Architects, Assn. Painters, Sculptors and Artists in Poland, Assn. Scientists Hist. Armament, Canadian Assn. U. Tchrs., NRA, Am. Legion. Address: 575 Reynolds Bend Rd SE Rome GA 30161-2546 *On our beautiful planet, architecture is one of the necessary evils. It is a sensor of society's cultural level, therefore the architect determines the dignity of environment by restraint, simplicity, honesty, obviousness, and antiexhibitionism.*

JANSEN, ALLAN W., lawyer; b. Oak Park, Ill., July 22, 1948. BS in Aerospace Engring., U. Ill., 1971; JD, John Marshall Law Sch., 1978. Bar: Calif. 1978, U.S. Dist. Ct. (cen. dist.) Calif. 1978, U.S. Ct. Appeals (9th cir.) 1978, U.S. Patent Office, U.S. Ct. Appeals (fed. cir.) 1986. Ptnr. Lyon & Lyon, L.A., 1986—. Mem. editorial bd. John Marshall Jour. Practice & Procedure, 1977-78. Mem. ABA, Am. Intellectual Property Law Assn., State Bar Calif., L.A. County Bar Assn., L.A. Intellectual Property Law Assn., Phi Delta Phi. Office: Lyon & Lyon 34th Fl 3200 Park Center Dr Ste1200 Costa Mesa CA 92626-7163

JANSEN, ANGELA BING, artist, educator; b. N.Y.C., Aug. 17, 1929; d. Lester and Jean Bing; m. Gunther Jansen, Mar. 8, 1956; children—Edmund, Douglas. B.A., Bklyn. Coll., 1951; M.A., NYU, 1953; student, Bklyn. Mus. Art Sch., 1947-50, Atelier 17, N.Y.C., 1950-52. Tchr. art, public schs. N.Y.C., 1954-60. One-man shows: Madison (Wis.) Art Center, 1977, Gimpel & Weitzenhoffer, N.Y.C., 1974, 78, group shows: Bklyn. Mus., 1950, 70, 76, Library of Congress, Washington, 1969, 71, Ljubljana Internat. Print Biennale, Yugoslavia, 1971, 73, 75, 77, Venice Biennale, 1972, Internat. Exhbn. Drawing, Rejeka, Yugoslavia, 1972 (award), Internat. Print Biennale, Cracow, Poland, 1978; represented in permanent collections: Mus. Modern Art, N.Y.C., Met. Mus. Art, N.Y.C., N.Y. Pub. Library, Art Inst. Chgo., Tate Gallery, London, Victoria and Abert Mus., London, Bibliotheque Nationale, Paris, Bklyn. Mus., Phila. Mus. Art, Fonds d'Art Contemporain, Centre de Recherche et d'Etude de la Sculpture Contemporaine, Mauberge, France, Musée du Petit Format, Couvin, Belgium, Bklyn. Mus., Francine Tyler Art Forum, summer, 1979. Nat. Endowment for Arts grantee, 1974-75.

JANSEN, DANIEL ERVIN, professional speedskater, marketing professional, former Olympic athlete; b. Milw., June 17, 1965; s. Harry William and Geraldine (Grajek) J.; m. Robin Wicker, Apr. 28, 1990; 1 child, Jane Danielle. Student, U. Wis., Milw., 1986, 87, 89. Speed skater U.S. Olympic Com., Colorado Springs, Colo., 1984—; pro tour speedskater, 1994—; sports mktg. profl. Miller Brewing Co., Milw., 1988—. Overall World Cup Champion Internat. Skating Union, 1986, 87, 92, 93, World Sprint Champion, 1988; recipient Gold medal for 1000m men's speedskating Lillehammer Winter Olympic Games, 1994. Roman Catholic. Set world record for 1000m race in 12.43 seconds, Lillehammer Winter Olympic Games, 1994. Home: 4428 S 85th St Milwaukee WI 53228-2806*

JANSEN, DENNIS WILLIAM, economics educator, consultant; b. St. Louis, Oct. 23, 1956; s. Elmer H.V. and Rosemary F. (Sievers) J.; m. Debra J. Hennessey, June 24, 1978; children: Megan, Amy, Mary. AB in Econs. and Math., St. Louis U., 1978; PhD in Econs., U. N.C., 1983. Instr. N.C. State U., Raleigh, 1982-83; vis. scholar Fed. Res. Bank St. Louis, 1988-89; asst. prof. econs. Tex. A&M U., College Station, 1983-88, assoc. prof., 1989-93, prof., 1994—, head dept., 1996—; tchg. fellow U. N.C., Chapel Hill, 1989-94; mem. vis. faculty Cath. U. Louvain, Belgium, 1990, 92, Erasmus U., Rotterdam, the Netherlands, 1990, Ind. U., 1991. Author: Intermediate Macroeconomics, 1994; Money, Banking and Financial Markets, 1995; contbr. articles to profl. jours. Mrs. Victor Humphrey fellow U. N.C., 1978, Earhart Found., Japan, 1988; rsch. fellow PERC, 1992—. Mem. Am. Econ. Assn., Royal Econ. Assn., We. Econ. Assn., So. Econ. Assn. Roman Catholic. Avocations: reading, soccer, coaching little league. Home: 1704 Emerald Pky College Station TX 77845-5543 Office: Tex A&M U Dept Econs College Station TX 77843-4228

JANSEN, DONALD ORVILLE, lawyer; b. Odessa, Tex., Nov. 17, 1939; s. Orville Charles and Dolores Elizabeth (Olps) J.; m. E. Janice Law; children: Donald Orville, Lauren, Christine, David, Margaret. BBA magna cum laude, Loyola U., New Orleans, 1961, JD cum laude, 1963; LLM, Georgetown U., 1966. Bar: La. 1963, Tex. 1965. Ptnr. Fulbright and Jaworski, Houston, 1966—. Served to capt. JAGC, U.S. Army, 1963-66. Mem. ABA, Fed. Bar Assn. State Bar Tex., La. Bar Assn., Am. Coll. Trust and Estate Counsel. Roman Catholic. Home: 5212 Sagesquare St Houston TX 77056-7041 Office: Fulbright & Jaworski 1301 Mckinney St Ste 5100 Houston TX 77010-3031

JANSEN, DONALD WILLIAM, lawyer, legislative administrator; b. Luverne, Minn., Aug. 21, 1948; s. William John and Florence Catherine (Tisdell) J.; m. Jacqueline Skeens, Sept. 30, 1978; children: Christopher Donald, Morgan Whitney, Madison Maarten. BA in Polit. Sci., Ariz. State U., 1970; JD, Gonzaga U., 1975. Bar: Ariz. 1975, U.S. Dist. Ct. Ariz. 1977, U.S. Supreme Ct. 1987, U.S. Ct. Appeals (9th cir.) 1998. Asst. rules atty., counsel to ethics com. Ariz. Ho. of Reps., Phoenix, 1976-83, counsel to majority leader, 1983-87, gen. counsel, 1987; dir. Ariz. Legis. Coun., Phoenix, 1987-92; policy advisor and counsel Ariz. Ho. of Reps., Phoenix, 1992-98, gen. counsel, 1998—. Contbr. to Ariz. State Law Jour., 1988. 1st lt. U.S. Army, 1970-72. Mem. State Bar Ariz., Nat. Conf. State Legislatures, Western Legis. Conf. Roman Catholic. Home: 4389 E Olney Dr Phoenix

AZ 85044-1018 Office: Ariz House of Reps 1700 W Washington St Phoenix AZ 85007-2812

JANSEN, G. THOMAS, dermatologist; b. Manitowoc, Wis., July 16, 1926; s. Gerald M. and Sarah (Grady) J.; m. Frances Bovick, Sept. 6, 1952; children: Mark, Kurt, Anne, Drew, Fran. B.S., U. Wis., Madison, 1948, M.D., 1950. Diplomate: Am. Bd. Dermatology (pres. 1985-86). Intern Med. Coll. of Va., 1950-51; resident in dermatology U. Wis., 1953-54, U. Mich., 1954-56; practice medicine specializing in dermatology Little Rock, 1956—; pres. Little Rock Dermatology Clinic, 1968—; mem. faculty U. Ark. Med. Center, 1956—, prof. dermatology, 1965—, chmn. dept., 1965-82; mem. staff Doctors Hosp., U. Ark. Hosp., St. Vincent Infirmary, Bapt. Hosp.; pres. Am. Dermatology Found., 1980-81. Served as officer M.C. USNR, 1951-54. Recipient Disting. Svc. award Am. Bd. Dermatologists, 1987, Finnerud award Am. Dermatology Found., 1993. Mem. AMA, Am. Dermatol. Assn. (pres. 1993), Am. Acad. Dermatology (asst. sec.-treas. 1980-83, sec.-treas. 1983-85, pres.-elect 1987, pres. 1988, hon. 1991, Master in Dermatology 1991, Everett C. Fox Lectureship award 1995, Gold medal 1997), Soc. Investigative Dermatology, Nat. Program Dermatology, Am. Coll. Chemosurgery, So. Med. Assn. (pres. 1976-77, Disting. Svc. award 1991), Ark. Med. Soc., Ark. Dermatol. Soc., Pulaski County Med. Soc., Alpha Omega Alpha. Roman Catholic. Home: 6601 Pleasant Pl Little Rock AR 72205-2868 Office: 500 S University Ave Ste 501 Little Rock AR 72205-5307

JANSEN, LAMBERTUS, judge; b. Salt Lake City, Oct. 27, 1934; s. Lambertus Christianus and Cobi Maria (van Ekelenburg) J.; m. Rosemary Van Dyke, Aug. 22, 1958 (div. 1969); children: Jackie Lyn, David Scott; m. LaNita Joyce Lindley, Sept. 10, 1982. AA, Westminster Coll., Salt Lake City, 1954, BS, 1959; JD, U. Utah, 1968. Bar: Utah 1968, N.Y. 1983. Tchr. English Jordan Sch. Dist., Sandy, Utah, 1959-62; fraud investigator Utah Job Svc., Salt Lake City, 1962-65; instr. U. Utah, Salt Lake City, 1965-68; lawyer Jansen Law Office, Salt Lake City, 1968-83, Hyatt Legal Svcs., Syracuse, N.Y., 1983-87, Shanley Law Office, Oswego, N.Y., 1987-92; city ct. judge Oswego, 1992—. Dir. Utah Housing Devel. Agy., Salt Lake City, 1969-71; mem. steering com. Oswego County Anti-Drug Program, 1996-97; mem. Oswego County Drug Ct. Program, 1996-97. Mem. Am. Judges Assn., N.Y. State City Ct. Judges Assn., Am. Trial Lawyers Assn., Oswego County Bar Assn., Onondaga County Bar Assn. Roman Catholic. Avocations: skiing, hiking, golf, camping. Home: 30 Talisman Ter Oswego NY 13126-6142 Office: Oswego City Ct 20 W Oneida St Oswego NY 13126-2574

JANSEN, MICHAEL JOHN, hospital administrator; b. Swannanoa, N.C., July 24, 1945; s. Edward John and Mary Bernadette (Haughian) J.; m. Roxanne Shellenberger, June 27, 1970 (div. May 1992); m. Linda Kathryn Hughes, Aug. 21, 1993; children: Kathryn Anne, Victoria Elizabeth. BS in BA, U. S.C., 1967; M. Health Adminstrn., Duke U., 1976. Adminstrv. asst. Watts Hosp., Durham, N.C., 1976-77; asst. dir. Durham County Gen. Hosp., 1977-80; asst. adminstr. St. Joseph's Hosp., Atlanta, 1980-83, sr. v.p., COO, 1983-89; group v.p. SunHealth, Charlotte, N.C., 1989-90; sr. assoc. adminstr., COO Cape Fear Valley Med. Ctr., Fayetteville, N.C., 1991—. Bd. dirs. St. Joseph's Hosp., Atlanta, 1985-89, Fayetteville Symphony Orch., 1993-95, United Way of Cumberland County, Fayetteville, 1993-95; chmn. bd. dirs. Shared Svcs. for So. Hosps., Atlanta, 1986-87. Capt. USAF, 1967-72, Col. USAFR, 1990-96. Recipient Falcon award/Spaatz award Civil Air Patrol, 1967. Fellow Am. Coll. Healthcare Execs. Office: Cape Fear Valley Medical Ctr PO Box 2000 Fayetteville NC 28302-2000

JANSEN, RAYMOND A., JR., newspaper publishing executive. Former pub., CEO Hartford (Conn.) Courant; pub., CEO, pres. Newsday, Melville, N.Y., 1994—. Office: Newsday Inc 235 Pinelawn Rd Melville NY 11747-4250

JANSEN, ROBERT BRUCE, consulting civil engineer; b. Spokane, Wash., Dec. 14, 1922; s. George Martin and Pearl Margaret (Kent) J.; m. Barbara Mae Courtney, Sept. 18, 1943. BSCE, U. Denver, 1949; MSCE, U. So. Calif., 1955. Registered profl. engr., Calif., Colo., Wash. Chief Calif. Div. Dam Safety, Sacramento, 1965-68; chief of ops. Calif. Dept. Water Resources, Sacramento, 1968-71, dep. dir., 1971-75, chief design and constrn., 1975-77; asst. commr. U.S. Bur. Reclamation, Denver, 1977-80; cons. civil engr., 1980—; cons. TVA, Chattanooga, 1981—, So. Calif. Edison Co., Rosemead, 1982—, Pacific Gas and Electric, San Francisco, 1982-93, Hydro-Quebec, Mon., Can., 1986—, Ala. Power Co., Birmingham, 1985—, Ga. Power Co., 1989-94. Author: Dams and Public Safety, 1983; editor: Safety of Existing Dams, 1983; co-author: Development of Dam Engineering in the United States, 1988; editor and co-author: Advanced Dam Engineering for Design, Construction, and Rehabilitation, 1988. Mem. U.S. Com. on Large Dams (chmn.1979-81), ASCE, NAE (elected). Home and Office: 509 Briar Rd Bellingham WA 98225-7811

JANSEN-BROWN, ANGELIKA CHARLOTTE, art museum director; b. Goerlitz, Saxony, Germany, Feb. 19, 1945; came to the U.S., 1968; d. Horst Wolfgang and Charlotte Pratsch; m. PEter Jansen, Apr. 1, 1965 (div.); 1 child, Ingmar; m. Robert Brown, June 23, 1987. BA in Edn. and German, Bklyn. Coll., 1976; PhD in Lit., NYU, 1982. Coord. lang. program NYU, N.Y.C., 1978-91; owner Jansen-Perez Gallery, San Antonio, 1989-95; dir. devel. and alumni affairs Our Lady of the Lake U., San Antonio, 1995-96; exec. dir. San Antonio Art League Mus., 1997—. Fgn. corr. Theatre/Cultural Events, 1976-89. Peer panel mem. City of San Antonio Arts and Cultural, 1989-91; bd. mem. U. Tex., San Antonio, 1992-95, 97—, San Antonio Coun. for Internat. Visitors, 1993—. Mem. World Affairs Coun. (diplomate), Nat. Soc. Arts and Letters, Am. Theatre Critic Assn., San Antonio Mus. Assn. (assoc.), Rotary Downtown. Avocations: performing and visual arts, literature, civil involvement. E-mail: angelikajansen@y-ahoo.com. Home: 701 N St Marys #36 San Antonio TX 78205

JANSMA, THEODORE JOHN, JR., psychologist; b. Phila., Apr. 17, 1943; s. Theodore John and Ruth Virginia (Gezon) J.; m. Jo Bernadette Battiston, June 28, 1969; children: Theodore John III, Christopher Paul. BA, Calvin Coll., Grand Rapids, Mich., 1965; MA, Mich. State U., 1967; PhD, Ill. Inst. Tech., 1971. Lic. psychologist, Mich., Ill. Mental health intern I, II Chgo. State Hosp., 1966-69; mental health counselor II Charles F. Read Zone Ctr., Chgo., 1970-71; dir. Project Talk, Chgo., 1970-71; psychologist III Charles F. Read Zone Ctr., Chgo., 1971-72; staff psychologist Pine Rest Christian Hosp., Grand Rapids, 1972-80, dir. psychology dept., 1977-80; assoc. clin. prof. Coll. Human Medicine Mich. State U., 1976-84; pvt. practice, 1980—; Diplomate Am. Coll. Forensic Examiners. Author: Becoming Kate, 1990. Bd. dirs. Ada (Mich.) Christian Sch. Assn., 1990-96, Ada Christian Sch. Found., 1990-96, pres., 1995, 96. Mem. Am. Psychol. Assn., Mich. Psychol. Assn., Grand Rapids Area Psychol. Assn., Soc. for Clinic. and Experimental Hypnosis, Internat. Soc. for Study Multiple Personality and Dissociation, Internat. Coun. Psychologists, Nat. Bd. for Cert. Clin. Hypnotherapists. Avocations: carpentry, boating, travel. Home: 1669 River Oaks Dr SE Ada MI 49301-9353 Office: 3330 Claystone St SE Grand Rapids MI 49546-7716

JANSON, BARBARA JEAN, publisher; b. Mason City, Iowa, Mar. 7, 1942; d. Harley Arnold and Helen Victoria (Henrickson) J.; m. W. John Shallenberger, Feb. 24, 1963 (div. Sept. 1980); children: Mona, Ann; m. John Batty Henderson, Sept. 8, 1984 (div. 1990); m. Arthur R. Hilsinger, Aug. 31, 1997. BS in Math., Iowa State U., 1965; MS in Math., Trinity Coll., 1970; MBA, U. R.I., 1982. Cert. math. tchr., Iowa, N.Y., Conn. Math. tchr. Pub. High Schs., Avon, Farmington, Bloomfield, Conn., 1966-68, Ulster Acad., Kingston, N.Y., 1971-73; math. instr. Ulster County Community Coll., Kingston, 1973; math. editor Houghton Mifflin Co., Boston, 1974-77; math. instr. Bristol County Community Coll., Fall River, Mass., 1977-78; asst. dir. editorial Am. Math. Soc., Providence, 1978-81, dir. of publ., 1982-85; founder, pres. Janson Publs., Inc. (purchased by Tribune Edn. Group), Providence and Dedham, Mass., 1985-96; pres. Janson Assocs., Dedham, 1996-98; pub. cons. Everyday Learning/Tribune Edn. Group, 1996-98; pres. Janson Assocs., Dedham, 1996—; mem. expert panel materials devel. ref. NSF, 1996—; rep. sci. publ. com. Am. Heart Assn., 1986-90; mem. R.I. State Adv. Commn. on Librs.; mem. R.I. Legis. Commn. for Math. and Sci. Edn., 1991; mem. adv. com. R.I. State Systemic Initiative in Math. and Sci., 1993-94. Editor: Scholarly Publishing: Managing Today, Planning for Tomorrow, 1986. Bd. dirs. Planned Parenthood of R.I., Providence, 1986-87, First Parish Unitarian Ch., Beverly, Mass., 1975-76; mem. steering com. Am. Math. Project, Berkeley, Calif., 1986-92; mem. oversight com. Resources Math. Reform Ednl. Devel. Ctr., Newton, Mass.; adv. mem. R.I. State Coun. on Librs. Recipient Mortar Bd. award Iowa State U., 1965. Mem. AAAS, LWV, Soc. for Scholarly Publishing (bd. dirs. 1986-90, chair ann. meeting 1985), N.Y. Acad. Sci., Am. Math. Soc., Math. Assn. Am., Nat. Coun. Tchrs. Math., Assn. Am. Publishers (jours. com. 1982-85), Nat. Assn. Women Bus. Owners. Unitarian. Home and Office: 8 Jackson Pond Dedham MA 02026-5524

JANSON, PATRICK, singer, actor, conductor, educator; b. Cleve., Oct. 10, 1967; s. Robert L. and Gloria Ann (Dominguez) J.; m. Christine Marie Fondaw, June 8, 1991. MusB, Baldwin-Wallace Coll., 1990. Singer, actor, dir., mus. dir., condr. various theatres and opera cos., 1990—; tchr. music St. Joseph Acad., Cleve., 1990-91, 98—, Univ. Sch., Hunting Valley, Ohio, 1991-92; tchr. Perry-Mansfield Performing Arts Camp, Steamboat Springs, Colo., summer 1993, 95, Usdan Ctr. for the Creative and Performing Arts, L.I., N.Y., summer 1998; prodn. asst. Broadway musical The Life;. Recipient 1st pl. prize Profl. Artists Devel. Competition, 1990. Mem. Actors Equity Assn., Alpha Sigma Phi (pres. interfraternity coun. 1988-89, pres. chpt. 1989-90). Home: 1097 Plainfield Rd South Euclid OH 44121

JANSONS, MARISS, orchestra conductor; b. Riga, Latvia, USSR, Jan. 14, 1943; s. Arvid and Erhayda Jansons; 1 child, Ilona. Diploma, Leningrad Conservatory, Vienna Conservatory. 2d condr. Leningrad Philharm. Orch., USSR, 1973—, assoc. prin. condr., 1985—; music dir. Oslo Philharm. Orch., Norway, 1979—; prof. of conducting St. Petersburg Conservatoire, 1991—; prin. guest condr. BBC Welsh Orch., Cardiff, 1984-88; prin. guest condr. London Philharm., 1992-97; guest condr. Berlin Philharm. Orch., Vienna Philharm. Orch., Royal Concert Gebouw, Amsterdam, also major symphony orchs. in Great Britain, U.S., Can.; music dir. Pitts. Symphony Orch., 1997. Condr. various recordings with Chandos Records, 1984-86, EMI/Angel Records, 1986—, exclusive artist EMI, 1991—. Recipient Royal Norwegian Order of Merit from His Majesty the King of Norway, 1988, with grade Comdr. with Star, 1995; named Artist of the Soviet Union, 1991, EMI Artist of Yr., 1996. Office: Oslo Philharm Orch, Oslo Philharm Orch, PO Box 1607, 0119 Oslo 1, Norway Agent: IMG Artists, IMG Artists, 3 Burlington Lane, London W4 2TH, England Office: Pittsburgh Symphony Orchestra Heinz Hall 600 Penn Ave Ste 1 Pittsburgh PA 15222-3259*

JANSSEN, CHRISTOPHER FRANK, veterinarian; b. Lafayette, La., Feb. 20, 1971; s. George John and Lucille Elena (McGinn) J. BS, Fla. State U., 1993; DVM, La. State U., 1997. Vet. technician Lakeview Vet. Hosp., New Orleans, 1988-91; dive locker technician Fla. State U. Acad. Diving Program, Tallahassee, 1991-93; diver Marine Life Oceanarium, Gulfport, Miss., 1993; zookeeper Zoo World, Panama City, Fla., 1994; rsch. asst. Corcovado, Costa Rica, 1995; clin. veterinarian New Iberia (La.) Rsch. Ctr., 1997—. Office: New Iberia Rsch Ctr 4401 W Adm Doyle Dr New Iberia LA 70560

JANSSEN, JAMES ROBERT, consulting software engineer; b. Frederick, Md., June 14, 1959; s. Robert James and Kathryn Doris (Randolph) J.; m. Deborah June Dellwo, Mar. 15, 1986 (div. Sept. 20, 1988). BSEE, Stanford U., 1981, MSEE, 1982. Simulation technician Varian Assocs., Palo Alto, Calif., 1981; hardware design engr. Fairchild Test Systems, San Jose, Calif., 1982-86, Factron Test Systems, Latham, N.Y., 1986-87; software, sys. designer Schlumberger Technologies Labs., Palo Alto, 1988; software engr. Photon Dynamics, Inc., San Jose, 1989-90, ADAC Labs., Milpitas, Calif., 1990-92; software, system designer ADAC Labs., Aalborg, Denmark, 1992, Milpitas, 1992-94; consulting software engr. self-employed, Sunnyvale, Calif., 1994-96; mem. tech. staff Netscape Comms. Corp., Mountain View, Calif., 1996-99, Am. Online Inc., Mountain View, 1999—; pres., founder Digital Studio Systems, Inc., Sunnyvale, 1990-93. Patentee multiple timing signal generator. Civic vol. City of Sunnyvale, 1993. Mem. Tau Beta Pi. Avocations: motocross racing, guitar playing, auto race driving, auto race spectating. Home and Office: 2028 Lockhart Gulch Rd Scotts Valley CA 95066-2923 *I know enough to know how little I know.*

JANSSEN, LARRY LEONARD, economics educator, researcher; b. Nebraska City, Feb. 21, 1949; s. Harry William and Veletta M. (Windhorst) J.; m. Marcia Kay Parsons, June 30, 1973; children: Matthew Kane, Lara Lindsay, Tiffany Dawn. BS in Agrl. Econs., U. Nebr., 1971; MS, Okla. State U., 1974; PhD, U. Nebr., 1978. NDEA fellow, grad. student Okla. State U., Stillwater, 1971-73; credit analyst-trainee Farm Credit Banks of Omaha, 1973-74; rsch. asst. U. Nebr., Lincoln, 1974-78; asst., assoc. prof. S.D. State U., Brookings, 1978-89; prof. Econ., 1989—; instr. profl. workshops, PRO-ED, Sioux Falls, S.D., 1993—. Contbg. author: Changing Size and Structure of American Farms, 1993, Research in Rural Sociology and Development, 1993; contbr. articles to profl. jours. Pres. First Luth. Ch. Volga, S.D., 1994-95. Recipient Outstanding Young Man of Am., 1986, Outstanding Tchr., 1993, Outstanding Rsch., 1992, S.D. State U. Gamma Sigma Delta. Mem. Am. Agrl. Econ. Assn., Western Agrl. Econ. Assn., Rotary, Sigma Xi, Gamma Sigma Delta. Lutheran. Avocations: hunting, camping, cross country skiing, travel, gardening. Home: 113 Adams Ave Volga SD 57071-9079 Office: South Dakota State Univ 103 Scobey Hall Brookings SD 57007

JANSSEN, PETER ANTON, magazine editor and publisher; b. San Francisco, July 1, 1936; s. Clayton Robson and Florence Ethel (Mohr) J.; m. Kyra Oppermann, Dec. 28, 1958 (div. Nov. 1973); children—Katherine, Kristen; m. Karen Christine Cole, Jan. 20, 1974 (div. Mar. 1990); children—Peter Anton, Elizabeth; m. Renée Starring Cartwright, Mar. 7, 1992. BA in History, Stanford U., 1960; MA, Northwestern U., 1961. Edn. editor Time mag., N.Y.C., 1974-76; sr. editor Money, N.Y.C., 1977-78; editor-in-chief Parent's mag., N.Y.C., 1978, Us Mag., N.Y. Times Co., N.Y.C., 1979-80, Nation's Bus. mag., Washington, 1981; editor-in-chief Motor Boating & Sailing Mag., N.Y.C., 1982-93, editor, pub., 1993—; adj. prof. U. Calif.-Berkeley, 1972; cons. Dept. Transp., HHS, HEW. Contbr. numerous articles to mags. Served with U.S. Army, 1956-58. Recipient Silver Gavel award ABA, 1968. Mem. Am. Soc. Mag. Editors, Edn. Writers Assn. (pres. 1969-71, numerous awards 1965-70), N.Y. Yacht Club, Harbor Found. N.Y. and N.J., Port Washington Yacht Club, Overseas Press Club, U.S. Yacht Racing Union, Am. Powerboat Assn. Presbyterian. Avocations: sailing; boat racing; tennis; skiing. Home: 452 Meadowbrook Rd Fairfield CT 06430-5258 Office: Motor Boating & Sailing Mag 250 W 55th St New York NY 10019-5201

JANSSEN, TOM, state director; b. Crofton, Nebr.. Degree comms., U. Nebr., 1994. Organizational dir. Chuck Hagel U.S. Senate campaign; state dir. U.S. Senator Chuck Hagel. With USAF, 1987-91. Office: 11301 Davenport St Ste 2 Omaha NE 68154

JANSSEN-PELLATZ, EUNICE CHARLENE, healthcare facility administrator; b. Urania, La., Mar. 23, 1948; d. Luther Clarence and Eunice Bobby (Pendarvis) Smith. BS in Nursing, Humboldt State U., 1970; MS in Nursing, Calif. State U., Fresno, 1980. Dir. nurses, asst. adminstr., coord. patient care svcs. Mad River Community Hosp., Arcata, Calif.; nursing supr. Fresno (Calif.) Community Hosp. Mem. Am. Soc. Healthcare Risk Mgmt. Home: 824 Diamond Dr Arcata CA 95521

JANSSENS, JOE LEE, controller; b. Alpine, Tex., Apr. 13, 1964; s. Charles Louis Janssens and Sue Ellen (Cheairs) Ticknor; m. Diana Bookout, Sept. 9, 1995; children: Ryan, Stephanie. BBA in Fin., Tex. A&M U., 1986; BA in Spanish, U. Houston, 1996. CPA, Tex.; cert. mgmt. acct. Staff auditor Price Waterhouse, Houston, 1988-89; consol. acct. Energy Ventures, Inc., Houston, 1989-92; sr. internat. acct. Ashland Exploration, Inc., Houston, 1992-95; contr. Peak Svcs. USA Ltd., Texas City, Tex., 1996-97, Peak USA Energy Svcs., Ltd., Houston, 1997, Tube-Alloy Corp., Houston, 1997-98; fin. dir. Grant Prideco SA de C.V. Veracruz, Mex., 1998—. Mem. Tex. Soc. CPAs, Inst. Mgmt. Accts. Roman Catholic. Avocations: western history, linguistics, scuba diving. Home: 7803 Braesdale Ln Houston TX 77071-1303 Office: 433-5 Carr Mexico-Ver, Veracruz 91690, Mexico

JANTZEN, J(OHN) MARC, retired education educator; b. Hillsboro, Kans., July 30, 1908; s. John D. and Louise (Janzen) J.; m. Ruth Patton, June 9, 1935; children: John Marc, Myron Patton, Karen Louise. A.B., Bethel Coll., Newton, Kans., 1934; A.M., U. Kans., 1937, Ph.D., 1940. Elementary sch. tchr. Marion County, Kans., 1927-30, Hillsboro, Kan., 1930-31; high sch. tchr., 1934-36; instr. sch. edn. U. Kans., 1936-40; asst. prof. Sch. Edn., U. of Pacific, Stockton, Calif., 1940-42; assoc. prof. Sch. Edn., U. of Pacific, 1942-44, prof., 1944-78, prof. emeritus, 1978—, also dean sch. edn., 1944-74, emeritus, 1974—, dir. summer sessions, 1940-72; condr. overseas seminars; mem., chmn. commn. equal opportunities in edn. Calif. Dept. Edn., 1959-69; mem., chmn. Commn. Tchr. Edn. Calif. Tchrs. Assn., 1956-62; mem. Nat. Coun. for Accreditation Tchr. Edn., 1969-72. Bd. dirs. Ednl. Travel Inst., 1965-89. Recipient hon. svd. award Calif. Congress Parents and Tchrs., 1982, McCaffrey disting. Svc. award in recognition of leadership in higher edn., cmty. relationships and internat. svc. San Joaquin Delta Coll., 1996. Mem. NEA, Am. Edn. Rsch. Assn., Calif. Edn. Rsch. Assn. (past pres. 1954-55), Calif. Coun. for Edn. Tchrs., Calif. Assn. of Colls. for Tchr. Edn. (sec., treas. 1975-85), Rotary (Outstanding Rotarian of Yr. award North Stockton 1990, Paul Harris fellow 1980), Stockton Coun. PTA Found., Phi Delta Kappa. Methodist. Home: 117 W Euclid Ave Stockton CA 95204-3122 *I maintain that my success in life is a result of multiple factors, among which the most important are a supportive home environment on a Kansas family farm; a wife who shared her husband's ambitions and supported him fully, often at considerable personal sacrifice; an attempt to serve others through a "power with" attitude rather than a "power over" struggle; and a conviction that one's life transcends the immediacy of the here and now.*

JANULAITIS, M. VICTOR, consulting company executive; b. Augsberg, Ger., Sept. 25, 1945; came to U.S., 1948, naturalized, 1953; s. Vytautas P. Janulaitis; m. Carol L. George, Nov. 23, 1968; children: Victoria C., Michael G. BS, Loyola U., Chgo., 1967; MBA, U. Chgo., 1971. CPA, Ill.; cert. mgmt. cons.; cert. data processor. With IBM, Chgo., 1967-71, Touche Ross & Co., Chgo., 1971-78; v.p. Damon Corp., Boston, 1978-79; part-time instr. Harvard U. Grad. Sch., 1979-80, ind. cons., 1979-80; v.p. Western ops. Index Systems, L.A. and Boston, 1979-82; founder, chief exec. officer Positive Support Rev., Inc., L.A., 1982—; chmn. UCLA Grad. Sch. Mgmt. Assocs. Program, 1986-88, mem. adv. bd.; vis. prof. U. So. Calif. Grad. Sch. Bus., 1996. Author: (with others) Managing the System Development Process, 1980, Information System Position Description Handguide, 1995, Metrics Handguide for the Internet and Information Technology, 1996, PC Policies and Procedures Managment Handguide, 1995, Client Server Management Handguide, 1994. Treas. adv. bd. Malibu Sch., Calif., 1982, 84. Mem. Am. Inst. CPAs, Ill. Soc. CPAs, Am. Prodn. and Inventory Control Soc. (bd. dirs.), Soc. Mgmt. Info. Systems (So. Calif. chpt., chmn.), Inst. Mgmt. Cons. (L.A. chpt.). Office: Positive Support Rev Inc 2500 Broadway Ste 320 Santa Monica CA 90404-3076

JANURA, JAN AROL, apparel manufacturing executive; b. Chgo., May 12, 1949; s. Cornel Harold Charles and Violet Mary Janura. BS, Colo. State U., 1971; MA, Fuller Theol. Sem., 1973; postgrad., Harvard Bus. Sch., 1997. Area dir. Young Life Campaign, Seattle, 1973-76; CEO, dir. Carol Anderson, Inc., L.A., 1977—; CFO Fresh Retail Chain, 1988—, Outdoor Videos Inc., 1988—; dir. Camp Anderson; pres. L.A. Electric Motorcar Co., 1979-80; prin., dir. Pheasant Hill Orchards, Connel, Washington; bd. dirs. Western Leadership Found., Starr Leadership Found., SW Leadership Found., NW Fellowship, Rivergate Fellowship, Crested Butte, Colo., Glendale (Calif.) Young Life Found. Fellowship. Mem. Rep. Nat. Com., 1986, Rep. Presdl. Task Force, 1984-86; trustee Janura Libr., Glendale; founder Smiling Moose Lodge, Cameron, Mont. Weyerhaeuser fellow, 1972-73, Glendale Fellowship Found.; bd. dirs. Palos Verdes Found. Recipient Salesman of Yr. award, 1983, 84,. Mem. Fly Fishermen Am. (life), Trout Unlimited (life), Henrys Fork Found., Calif. Trout, 11-99 Found. (life), Pvt. Aircraft Owners Assn., Beechcraft Owners' Club, Montana and Land Reliance, Friends of Montana Land Reliance, Mammoth Lakes Fly Fisherman, Young Pres.'s Orgn. (L.A. chpt., Beta Forum), Friends of Norris Theater, Snowcreek Athletic Club, L.A. Athletic Club, Wash. Athletic Club, N.Y. Athletic Club, Pres. Pointe Assn. (pres. 1991-96), Admirals Club (life), Solomon Hill Hunt Club, Scootney Farms Hunting Club, Ironwood Country Club, Fly Fisherman Club, Virginia Country Club (Long Beach, Calif.). Office: 18915 S Laurel Park Rd Rancho Dominguez CA 90220-6005

JANZEN, JANET LINDEBLAD, composer; b. Manhattan, Kans., June 25, 1950; d. Oliver and Roberta (Johnson) L.; m. Kenneth Lee Janzen, July 1, 1978; children: Anna Marie, Jacob O. BA, Bethany Coll., 1972. Parish worker St. Paul's Luth. Ch., Wichita, Kans., 1972-74; med. office mgr. Consol. Biomed. Labs., Wichita, 1974-80; freelance composer, writer, musician, 1980—. Author: Songs for Renewal, 1995; composer choir anthems A Cradle Song, 1993, More Like Jesus, 1995, Thou Shalt Know Him, 1997, Drop, Drop, Slow Tears, 1997. Mem. Hymn Soc. U.S. and Can., Scandinavian Soc. Wichita. Avocations: bicycling, camping. Home: 1147 Perry Ave Wichita KS 67203-3057

JANZEN, JEAN WIEBE, poet, educator; b. Dalmeny, Sask., Can., Dec. 5, 1933; d. Henry Peter Wiebe and Anna Schultz; m. Edwin Louis Janzen, July 2, 1954; children: Gail Marie, Scott Matthew, Jill Carol, Peter Barrett. BA, Fresno Pacific Coll., 1968; MA, Fresno State U., 1982. Sec. cardiology Wesley Meml. Hosp., Chgo., 1954-57; pvt. piano tchr. L.A. and Fresno, Calif., 1979-83; poetry writing tchr. Fresno Pacific U., 1989—; poet-in-residence Ea. Mennonite U., Harrisonburg, Va., 1989—; presenter at poetry workshops. Author: (poems) Words for the Silences, 1984, Three Mennonite Poets, 1986, Upside Town Tree, 1992, Snake in the Parsonage, 1995. Mem. Fresno-Madern County Med. Aux., 1962-98; mem. choir Coll. Cmty. Mennonite Brethren Ch., 1962—, chair worship com., leader, 1975-99. Creative writing fellow Nat. Endowment for Arts, 1995. Mem. Fresno Poets Assn. (bd. dirs. 1986-99). Democrat. Avocations: travel, reading, music. E-mail: jjanzen@qnis.net.

JANZEN, LEE, professional golfer; b. Austin, Minn., Aug. 28, 1964. Mem. Ryder Cup Team, 1993. Winner No. Telecom Open, 1992, Phoenix Open, 1993, U.S. Open, 1993, 98; Buick Classic, 1994; The Players Championship, 1995; Kemper Open, 1995; Sprint International, 1995. Office: Sports Link 545-4 Delaney Ave Orlando FL 32801*

JANZEN, NORINE MADELYN QUINLAN, medical technologist; b. Fond du Lac, Wis., Feb. 9, 1943; d. Joseph Wesley and Norma Edith (Gustin) Quinlan. BS, Marian Coll., 1965; med. technologist St. Agnes Sch. Med. Tech., Fond du Lac, 1966; MA, Cen. Mich. U., 1980; m. Douglas Mac Arthur Janzen, July 18, 1970; 1 son, Justin James. Med. technologist Mayfair Med. Lab., Wauwatosa, Wis., 1966-69; supr. med. technologist Dr.'s Mason, Chamberlain, Franke, Klink & Kamper, Milw., 1969-76, Hartford-Parkview Clinic, Ltd., 1976-94, patient svc. ctrs. supr. Med. Sci. Labs., Wauwatosa, Wis., 1994-97, Poole Med. Tech. Med. Sci. Labs, 1997; clin. mgr. Planned Parenthood Wis., 1997—; coord. health in bus. Hartford Parkview Clin., 1990-91, drug program coord., 1991-94; co-chair joint mtg. Clin. Lab. Mgrs. Assn. and Wis. Assn. for Clin. Lab. Scientists, 1993-94. Substitute poll worker Fond du Lac Dem. Com., 1964-65; mem. Dem. Nat. Com., 1973—; coord. Warhawk Band Booster Uniform Project, 1997—. Mem. AAUW (rec. sec. 1996-98, pub. policy chair 1998—) Cmty. League, LWV, Am. Soc. for Clin. Lab. Scientists (people to people clin. lab. scientist del. to People's Republic of China 1989, Mem. of Yr. award 1997), Nat. Soc. Clin. Lab. Scientists (awards com. chair 1984-87, 88-91, nominations com. 1989-92), Wis. Assn. Clin. Lab. Scientists (exec. sec. 1991—, chmn. awards com. 1976-77, 84-85, 86-87, treas. 1977-81, pres.-elect 1981-82, pres. 1982-83, dir. 1977-84, 85-87, Mem. of Yr. award 1982, 95, numerous svc. awards, chair ann. meeting 1987-88), Clin. Lab. Mgmt. Assn. (co-chair joint meeting 1993-94), Milw. Soc. Clin. Lab. Scientists (pres. 1971-72, bd. dir. 1972-73), Communications of Wis. (originator, chmn. 1977-79), Southeastern Suprs. Group (co-chmn. 1976-77), Warhawk Band Boosters (coord. uniform project 1998—), Alpha Delta Theta (nat. dist. chmn. 1967-69, nat. alumnae dir. 1969-71), Alpha Mu Tau. Methodist. Home: N98W17298 Dotty Way Germantown WI 53022-4618 Office: Planned Parenthood 302 N Jackson St Milwaukee WI 53202-5917

JANZEN, TIMOTHY PAUL, family practice physician; b. Salem, Oreg., Dec. 3, 1960; s. Robert Lee and Betty Maude (Youngman) J.; m. Rachel Ann Sauter, Sept. 7, 1985; children: Paul, Marilee, Andrew, Bethany. BS in Chemistry, George Fox Coll., 1983; MD, Oreg. Health Scis. U., 1987. Intern, then resident in family practice Scottsdale (Ariz.) Meml. Hosp., 1987-90; pvt. practice, Portland, Oreg., 1990—. Co-author: The Peters Family

Genealogy, 1995; contbr. articles to profl. publs. Bd. dirs. United Health Network, Portland, 1996. Benson scholar, 1979-83. Fellow Am. Acad. Family Physicians; mem. Christian Med. Soc., Am. Hist. Soc. Germans from Russia, Am. Birding Assn., Oreg. Field Ornithologists. Republican. Baptist. Avocations: birdwatching, family historical research, piano, stamps. Office: South Tabor Family Physicians 10803 SE Cherry Blossom Dr Portland OR 97216-3107

JANZOW, WALTER THEOPHILUS, retired college administrator; b. Ada, Minn., Dec. 18, 1918; s. Frederick William and Emma (Wiegner) J.; m. Frances Enae Snider, June 4, 1944; children—Fred, Frank, Kathleen, Daniel. Student, Concordia Coll., 1935-37; B.A., Concordia Sem., St. Louis, 1941, M. Div., 1944; M.A., So. Ill. U., 1957; Ph.D., Nebr. U., 1970; D.D. (hon.), Concordia Sem., Springfield, Ill., 1965. Ordained to ministry Lutheran Ch., Mo. Synod, 1944; pastor Zion Luth. Ch., Mavie, Minn., 1944-45; pastor Immanuel Luth. Ch., McIntosh, Minn., 1945-51, Murphysboro, Ill., 1951-59; prof. sociology Concordia Tchrs. Coll., Seward, Nebr., 1959-63; pres. Concordia Tchrs. Coll., 1963-77, dir. coll. relations, 1977-83; pres. Concordia Luth. Sem., Edmonton, Alta., Can., 1984-87; Pres. So. Ill. Dist. Luth. Ch. Mo. Synod, 1957-59. Editor: Issues in Christian Education, 1968-70, The Great Breakthrough, 1962; Contbr. articles to religious jours. Bd. dirs. State U. Nebr. Adv. Council, 1973-77. Mem. Am., Midwest Sociol. assns., Nebr. Assn. Ch. Colls. (pres. 1964-65), Nebr. Assn. Colls. and Univs. (pres. 1971-72), Soc. Sci. Study Religion, Luth. Acad. Scholarship, Luth. Human Relations Assn. Am. Home: 7515 Sherman St Lincoln NE 68506-4656

JAOUHARI-MCCUNE, CYNTHIA, nurse, childbirth educator; b. San Francisco, Dec. 11, 1969; d. Hassan El Jaouhari and Rhina Mabel Pineda; m. John David McCune, Jan. 2, 1994. BSN, U. Miami, 1994. RN, Fla. Staff nurse Augusta Med. Ctr., Fishersville, Va., 1995-96, Rockingham Meml. Hosp., Harrisonburg, Va., 1996-97; legal nurse cons. med. malpractice law firm, Harrisonburg, 1997; staff nurse Healthsouth Doctors Hosp., Coral Gables, Fla., 1995, 97—; ob-gyn. office nurse, Coral Gables, 1997—; pvt. tchr. childbirth classes, Miami, Fla., 1998—. Mem. Fla. Nurses Assn., U. Miami Nursing Alumni Assn. Avocations: dance, exercise. Home: 11513 SW 61st Ter Miami FL 33173-1065

JAPP, NYLA F., infection control services administrator; b. Sterling, Colo., Jan. 8, 1948; d. Leonard W. and Eleanor M. (Barnts) J. Diploma, Pikes Peak Inst. Med. Tech., 1970; Assoc. in Nursing, Garden City Community Coll., 1980; diploma, Pikes Peak Inst. Med. Tech., 1970; BS in Human Resources Mgmt., Friends U., 1992; MS in Health Adminstrn., Kennedy Western U., 1997, Kennedy-Western U., 1997. RN, Kans. With surg. unit St. Catherine Hosp., Garden City, Kans.; sanitarian Finney County Commrs., Garden City; mgr. sterile processing St. Catherine Hosp., Garden City, Kans., mgr. infection control; dir. infection control svcs. St. Catherine Hosp.; nurse mgr. U. Kans. Hosp., Kansas City, Kans. Mem. Am. Soc. Hosp. Ctrl. Svc. Pers. (regional bd. dirs., chmn. recognition com., chmn. membership com., mem. tech. cert. com., APIC liaison, AORN liaison, JCAHO liaison, AAMI liaison, regulatory adv. com., Educator of Yr., Tom Samuels rsch. award), Great Plains Soc. Hosp. Ctrl. Svc. Pers. (chmn. program com., mem. newsletter com., chmn. nominating com., rsch. com., pres., bd. dirs.), Nat. Inst. for Cert. Healthcare Sterile Processing and Distbn. Pers. (bd. dirs.), Internat. Assn. Hosp. Ctrl. Svc. Mgmt., Assn. Practitioners in Infection Control. Home: 10325 Earnshaw St Overland Park KS 66215-2233

JAQUA, RICHARD ALLEN, pathologist; b. Fort Dodge, Iowa, Apr. 15, 1938; s. John Franklin and Esther Constance (Rossing) J.; m. Mary Joanne Stewart, Dec. 29, 1969. B.A. magna cum laude, Yale U., 1960; M.D., Harvard U., 1965. Diplomate: Am. Bd. Pathology, Am. Bd. Nuclear Medicine. Teaching fellow pathology Harvard Med. Sch., 1965-67; resident clin. pathology NIH, 1967-69; intern pathology Mass. Gen. Hosp., Boston, 1965-66; fellow tumor pathology Meml.-Sloane Kettering Cancer Center, N.Y.C., 1969-70; asst. prof. pathology U. S.D. Sch. Medicine, Vermillion, 1970-73; assoc. prof. U. S.D. Sch. Medicine, 1973-74, asso. prof., acting chmn. dept. lab. medicine, 1974-77, prof., chmn. dept. lab. medicine, 1977—; dir. U. S.D. Sch. Medicine (Electron Microscopy Lab. and Clin. Virology Lab.), 1979—; pathologist VA Hosp., Sioux Falls, S.D., 1978—; practice medicine specializing in anatomic and clin. pathology and nuclear medicine Lab. Clin. Medicine, Sioux Falls, 1970—. Served with USPHS, 1967-69. Recipient Outstanding Prof. awards U. S.D. Med. Students, 1971, 75, 77, 90; VA grantee, 1980-82. U. S.D. Faculty Recognition award, 1986. Fellow Coll. Am. Pathologists, Am. Soc. Clin. Pathologists; mem. Electron Microscopy Soc. Am., Am. Assn. Cancer Edn., AAAS, Internat. Acad. Pathology, Soc. Nuclear Medicine, Sigma Xi, Alpha Omega Alpha. Home: 27546 483rd Ave Canton SD 57013-5511 Office: USD Health Sci Ctr 1400 W 22nd St Sioux Falls SD 57105-1505

JAQUES, DAMIEN PAUL, theater critic; b. Oak Park, Ill., Nov. 3, 1946; s. Norman Sands and Marion Esther (Werle) J.; m. Patricia A. Mehigan, July 7, 1976 (div. May 1989). BA, Marquette U., 1968. Field organizer, transp. aide Robert Kennedy Presdl. Campaign, Wis., Ind., Calif., 1968; campaign mgr. Carol Bauman Candidate for Congress, Milw., 1968; reporter Sheboygan (Wis.) Press, 1968-69, Evening Press, Binghamton, N.Y., 1969-72; reporter, music critic Milw. Jour., 1972-77, entertainment copy editor, 1977-80, theater critic, 1980—; corr. Back Stage, 1994—; host weekly radio prgm. Milwaukee Presents WHAD. Mem. Am. Theatre Critics Assn. (jurist Outstanding New Play award 1983-93, exec. bd., 1985-88, 1994—, dir. Found., 1994—). Avocations: travel, reading, cooking, fishing. Office: The Milwaukee Journal Sentinel PO Box 371 Milwaukee WI 53201-0371*

JAQUES, THOMAS FRANCIS, librarian; b. Crowley, La., Dec. 25, 1938; s. Robert E. and Frances (Broussard) J.; m. Trudy Seidel, May 16, 1964; children: Michael, Christopher. BSBA, U. Southwestern La., 1960; MS in Libr. Sci., La. State U., 1968. Cert. adminstrv. libr. La. Asst. libr. Rapids Parish Libr., Alexandria, La., 1968-73; asst. state libr. Miss. Libr. Commn., Jackson, 1973-75; state libr. State Libr. La., Baton Rouge, 1975—. Office: Office of State Library PO Box 131 Baton Rouge LA 70821-0131

JAQUITH, GEORGE OAKES, opthalmologist; b. Caldwell, Idaho, July 29, 1916; s. Gail Belmont and Myrtle (Burch) J.; m. Pearl Elizabeth Taylor, Nov. 30, 1939; children: Patricia Ann Jaquith Mueller, George, Michele Eugenie Jaquith Smith. BA, Coll. Idaho, 1938; MB, Northwestern U., 1942, MD, 1943. Intern Wesley Meml. Hosp., Chgo., 1942-43; resident opthalmology U.S. Naval Hosp., San Diego, 1946-48; pvt. practice medicine, specializing in opthalmology Brawley, Calif., 1948—; pres. Pioneers Meml. Hosp. staff, Brawley, 1953, dir. exec. com. Calif. Med. Eye Coun., 1960—, v.p. Calif. Med. Eye Found., 1976—. Sponsor Anza coun. Boy Scouts Am., 1966—, Gold card holder Rep. Assocs., Imperial County, Calif., 1967-68, PTO. Served with USMC, USN, 1943-47. Mem. Imperial County (pres. 1961), Calif. Med. Assn. (del. 1961—), Nat., So. Calif. (dir. 1966—, chmn. med. adv. com. 1968-69), Soc. Prevention Blindness, Calif. Assn. Opthalmology (treas. 1976—), San Diego, L.A. Opthal. Socs., L.A. Rsch. Study Club, Nathan Smith Daivs Soc., Coll. Idaho Assocs., Am. Legion, VFW, Res. Officers Assn., Basenji Assn., Nat. Geneal. Soc., Cuyamaca Club (San Diego), Elks, Phi Beta Phi, Lambda Chi Alpha (Hall of Fame). Presbyterian (elder). Office: PO Box 511 Brawley CA 92227-0511

JARABA, MARTHA E. (BETTY JARABA), secondary school educator; b. San Pedro Sula, Honduras, Feb. 27, 1952; d. G.E. and Francisca L. (Reynaud) Donaldson; m. Jaime I. Jaraba; children: Janine, Jimmy. BA in French, Spanish, La. State U., 1972; M in Ednl. Supervision, Northwestern U., 1998. Cert. tchr. French, Spanish, ESL. Program asst. comms. and bus. partnerships El Paso (Tex.) Ind. Sch. Dist., 1993—; examiner for Ednl. Testing Svc.; mentor New Tchrs. Assistance Program; presenter in field. Published author. Panelist in edn. Tex. Commn. on the Arts; pres. City of El Paso Arts Resource Dept.; bd. dirs. The Opera Co.; mem. standing com. on arts, culture, and recreation for the U.S. Conf. of Mayors. Named Tchr. of Yr., Tex. Tchr. Task Force. Mem. NEA, TESOL, Tex. TESOL, Tex. State Tchrs. Assn., El Paso Tchrs. Assn. Fax: (915) 834-6603. Home: 6629 Camino Fuente Dr El Paso TX 79912-2407

JARAMILLO, CARLOS ALBERTO, civil engineer; b. Medellin, Colombia, Dec. 5, 1952; came to the U.S., 1986; s. Alberto and Maria Jaramillo; children: Daniel J., Nicolas. BCE, U. Nacional, Medellin, 1978; MS, U. Minn., 1980. Registered profl. engr., Wis., Colombia. Engr. Integral S.A., Medellin, 1977-79, sr. design engr., 1980-86; rsch. asst. St. Anthony Falls Lab., Mpls., 1979-80; civil engr. Mead & Hunt Inc., Madison, Wis., 1986-89; sr. geotech. engr. Harza Engring. Co., Chgo., 1989—, jr. ptnr., 1998; prof. Escuela de Ingenieria de Antioquia, Medellin, 1981-86; designer numerous dams & underground structures. Cons. to public utilities, various countries 1994—; contbr. articles to profl. jours. Mem. ASCE (rock mechanics com.), U.S. Com. Large Dams, U.S. Nat. Soc. Soil Mechanics and Found. Engring., Phi Kappa Phi. Avocations: jogging, photography, philately, astronomy. Office: Harza Engring Co Sears Tower 233 S Wacker Dr Chicago IL 60606-6306

JARAMILLO, JUANA SEGARRA, dean; b. San Sebastian, P.R., Mar. 24, 1937; d. Joaquin M. and Carmen M. (Gerena) Segarra; m. Edgar J. Jaramillo, Apr. 13, 1957; children: Jeanette, Yila, Yvonne, Melissa, Edgar Jr. BA, Poly. Inst. P.R., San German, 1956; postgrad., U. Fla., 1956-57; MS, La. State U., 1963. Libr. dir. Inter-Am. U., Aguadilla (P.R.) Regional Coll., 1975-76, cons. libr. and accreditation, 1983—; libr. U.P.R.-Aguadilla Regional Coll., 1976-77, libr. dir., 1983-86, libr., 1986-89, chair steering com. for accreditation, mem. directive coun. honors program, 1989—, dir. instl. planning and rsch., 1989-90, libr. dir., 1990-94; acting assoc. acad. dean, 1994—, dean/dir., 1994—; libr. dir. EDP Coll. P.R., San Sebastian, 1979-83; acting assoc. acad. dean U. P.R., Aguadilla, 1994, dean, dir., 1994—; mem. steering com. nat. edn. program Am. Coun. Edn., P.R., 1982-86, adv. bd. Coun. Higher Edn., P.R., 1982—; external evaluator Middle States Assn. Colls. and Schs., 1997—. Author: Manual bibliografico Electronica, 1987; co-author: El Desarrollo del Pensamiento Critico en Futuros Maestros, 1989; contbr. articles to profl. jours. Mem. Club Civico de Damas, Aguadilla, 1989—. With U.S. Army, 1963-66. Mem. ALA, Am. Assn. Higher Edn., Assn. Caribbean Univs., Rsch. and Instl. Librs., Sociedad de Bibliotecarios de P.R. (pres. continuing edn. 1984-90), Mid. States Assn. Colls. and Schs. (evaluating team mem. 1998—), Rotary-Anns (pres. 1974), Internat. Altrusan, Alpha Delta Kappa. Avocations: cooking, water sports, traveling. Office: UPR Aguadilla PO Box 160 Ramey Aguadilla PR 00604-0160*

JARAMILLO, MARI-LUCI, federal agency administrator; b. Las Vegas, N.Mex., June 19, 1928. BA magna cum laude, N.Mex. Highland U., 1955, MA with honors, 1959; PhD, U. N.Mex., 1970. Tchr. Albuquerque and Las Vegas, N.Mex., 1955-65; asst. prof. U. N.Mex., 1965-72, assoc. prof., chmn. dept. elem. edn., 1972-75, assoc. prof. edn., 1976-77, prof., 1977, spl. asst. to pres., 1981-82, assoc. dean Coll. Edn., 1982-85, v.p. for student affairs, 1985-87; amb. to Republic of Honduras U.S. Dept. State, 1977-80; dep. asst. sec. for Inter-Am. affairs U.S. Dept. State, Washington, 1980-81; asst. v.p., dir. Ednl. Testing Service, Emeryville, Calif., 1987-93; dep. asst. sec. for Inter-Am. affairs Dept. Def., Washington, 1993-95; bd. trustees Tomas Rivera Nat. Policy Ctr., Claremont (Calif.) Coll. Grad. Sch., 1985-93; minority recruiter Dept. State, Washington, 1990—; commr. Calif. Commn. of Post-Secondary Edn., Sacramento, 1990-93; active Coun. Am. Ambs., Washington, 1983—; bd. dirs. Latin Am. Scholarship Program for Am. Univs., Boston, Children's TV Workshop, N.Y.C.; cons. for curriculum, tchr. tng. and sch. reform, 1960—. Contbr. articles to jours., chpts. to books. Bd. dirs. Internat. House, U. Calif., Berkeley, 1989-93; scholar panelist Nat. Latino Comm. Ctr., L.A., 1990—; active Bay area Network L.Am. Women, San Francisco, 1987-93. Decorated Order Francisco Morazan (Honduras), Order of Great Silver Cross (Honduras); recipient Cubberly award Stanford U., 1975, N.Mex. Disting. Svc. award, 1977, Anne Roe award Harvard U. Grad. Sch. Edn., 1986, PRIMERA award Mex. Am. Women's Nat. Assn., 1990; named Outstanding Chicana, 1975, Hon. Honduran Citizen, Govt. of Honduras, 1980, Disting. Woman of Yr., U. N.Mex. Alumni Assn., 1985, Disting. Hispanic lectr. Calif. State U. at Fullerton, 1988, Outstanding Hispanic Educator, 1988, Outstanding Leader in Edn. to Hispanic Cmty., 1991. Mem. Nat. Assn. Bilingual Edn., Latin Am. Assn., Am. Assn. Colls. for Tchr. Edn., Nat. Council La Raza. Home: 4829 Mesa Prieta Ct NW Albuquerque NM 87120-4620

JARBOE, MARK ALAN, lawyer; b. Flint, Mich., Aug. 19, 1951; s. Lloyd Aloysius and Helen Elizabeth (Frey) J.; m. Patricia Kovel, Aug. 20, 1971; 1 child, Alexander. Student, No. Mich. U., 1968-69; AB with high distinction, U. Mich., 1972; JD magna cum laude, Harvard U., 1975. Bar: Minn. 1975, U.S. Dist. Ct. Minn. 1975, U.S. Ct. Appeals (8th cir.) 1975, U.S. Ct. Appeals (7th cir.) 1993. Law clk. to presiding justice Minn. State Ct., St. Paul, 1975-76; from assoc. to ptnr. Dorsey & Whitney LLP, Mpls., 1976-81, ptnr., 1982—; lectr. U. Minn. Law Sch., Hamline U. Sch. Law. Contbr. articles to profl. jours. Pres. parish coun. Ch. of Christ the King, Mpls., 1981-83. Mem. Fed. Bar Assn., Native Am. Bar Assn., Minn. Am. Indian Bar Assn., Mensa, Phi Beta Kappa. Republican. Roman Catholic. Home: 4816 W Lake Harriet Pky Minneapolis MN 55410-1903 Office: Dorsey & Whitney LLP Pillsbury Ctr S 220 S 6th St Minneapolis MN 55402-1498

JARC, FRANK ROBERT, printing company executive; b. Waukegan, Ill., Apr. 4, 1942; s. Frank Joseph and Edith Gertrude (Cankar) J.; m. MeRandy Jarc; 1 dau., Jennifer. BS in Indsl. Engring, U. Mich., 1964; MBA, Harvard U., 1967. Mgmt. trainee Mich. Bell Telephone Co., 1964; with regulatory proceedings dept. United Airlines, Chgo., 1966; fin. analyst Ford Motor Co., Dearborn, Mich., 1967, Freeport Minerals Co., N.Y.C., 1972-73; Fin. analyst Esmark, Inc., Chgo., 1973; controller subs. Swift Grocery Products Co., Chgo., 1973-75; fin. v.p. subs. Estech, Inc., Chgo., 1975-77; v.p. consumer products subs. Estech Gen. Chem. Co., Agrl. Chems. Corp., Chgo., 1977-80; exec. v.p., chief fin. officer Wilson Foods, Oklahoma City, 1980-87; sr. v.p., chief fin. officer United Airlines, Chgo., 1987; exec. v.p., chief fin. officer R.R. Donnelley Co., Chgo., 1987-95; exec. v.p., CFO Viking Office Products, L.A., 1996—. Bd. mgrs. YMCA. Capt. USAF, 1967-71. Mem. Evans Scholarship Alumni Assn., Chgo. Club, Execs. Club Chgo., Chgo. Commonwealth Club, Econ. Club. Home: 302 N Elmwood Ave Waukegan IL 60085-3518 Office: Viking Office Products PO Box 61144 Los Angeles CA 90061-0144

JARCHOW, CRAIG MCHUGH, technology manager; b. L.A., July 20, 1960; s. Brian Hugh and Mary Therese (Craig) J.; m. Angela Marie Wyatt, Dec. 28, 1985; 1 child, Megan Elizabeth. BA in Geol. Scis. with honors, U. Calif. Santa Barbara, 1984; MS in Geophysics, Stanford U., 1987, PhD in Geophysics, 1991. Rsch. geophysicist Amoco Corp., Tulsa, 1991-94; sr. geophysicist Amoco Corp., Denver, 1994-96; bus. devel. Amoco Corp., New Orleans, 1996-97; technology mgr. Apache Corp., Houston, 1997—; assoc. editor Soc. of Exploration Geophysicists, Tulsa, 1995—; founder Stanford Crystal Geophysics Project, 1989; mem. site-selection com. Gas Rsch. Inst., Chgo., 1995-96. Author papers in field. Chmn. pastoral coun. Good Shepherd Parish, Denver, 1995-96, chmn. archbishop's appeal, 1995-96; co-chmn. town hall mtg. Stanford U., Denver, 1995; bd. dirs. Houston and Denver Stanford Alumni Assn., 1993—. Recipient Woodhouse award in Geol. Scis., U. Calif. Santa Barbara, 1984; recipient fellowships/Rhoades, Amoco, Schlumberger, Stanford U., 1985-91; Sloan fellow MIT Sloan Sch. Mgmt. 1998—. Fellow Geol. Soc. Am.; mem. Soc. Exploration Geophysicists (assoc. editor 1995—), European Assn. Geoscientists and Engrs., Am. Assn. Petroleum Geologists, Soc. of Petroleum Engrs., Geophys. Soc. of Tulsa (editor 1992-93). Republican. Roman Catholic. Avocations: family, lang., lit., exercise. Office: Apache Corp 63 Pine Crest Rd Newton MA 02459

JARDETZKY, OLEG, medical educator, scientist; b. Yugoslavia, Feb. 11, 1929; came to U.S., 1949, naturalized, 1955; s. Wenceslas Sigismund and Tatiana (Taranovsky) J.; m. Erika Albensberg, July 21, 1975; children by previous marriage: Alexander, Theodore, Paul. B.A., Macalester Coll., 1950, D.Sc. (hon.), 1974; M.D., U. Minn., 1954, Ph.D. (Am. Heart Assn. fellow), 1956; postgrad., U. Cambridge, Eng., 1965-66; LL.D. (hon.), Calif. Western U., 1978; M.D. (hon.), U. Graz, Austria, 1994; Doctorate (hon.), U. Aix-Marseille II, 1998. Research fellow U. Minn., 1954-56; NRC fellow Calif. Inst. Tech., 1956-57; asso. Harvard U., 1957-59, asst. prof. pharmacology, 1959-66; dir. biophysics and pharmacology Merck & Co., 1966-68, exec. dir., 1968-69; prof. Stanford U., 1969—, dir. Stanford Magnetic Resonance Lab., 1975-97, dir. NMR Center, Sch. Medicine, 1983-84; dir. emeritus Stanford Magnetic Resonance Lab., 1998—; vis. fellow Merton Coll., Oxford (Eng.) U., 1976; cons., vis. prof., lectr. in field; chmn. Internat. Coun. on Magnetic Resonance in Biology, 1972-74; dir. Internat Sch. on Magnetic Resonance in Biology, Ettore Majorana Ctr., Sicily, 1993—; chmn. biotech. panel World Fedn. Scientists, 1998—. Contbr. articles to profl. jours.; mem. editorial bd. Jour. Theoretical Biology, 1961-88, Molecular Pharmacology, 1965-75, Jour. Medicinal Chemsitry, 1970-78, Biochimica Biophypica Acta, 1970-86, Revs. on Bioenergetics, 1972-89, Biomembrane Revs., 1972-80, Jour. Magnetic Resonance in Biology and Medicine, 1986—, Jour. Magnetic Resonance, 1993—. Recipient career devel. award USPHS, 1959-66, Kaiser award, 1973, Von Humboldt award, 1977, Pauling medal, 1984, Grand Gold Honor insignia (Austria), 1993, Founder's gold medal Internat. Coun. Magnetic Resonance in Biology, 1994, Prix Marianne Dessewffy Internat. Conf. of Genealogy and Heraldry, 1998; grantee NSF, 1957—, NIH, 1957—; travel fellow Am. Physiol. Soc., 1959. Fellow AAAS; mem. Am. Chem. Soc., Am. Soc. Biol. Chemistry and Molecular Biology, Biophys. Soc., Assn. Advanced Tech. in Biomed. Scis. (pres. 1981-88), Internat. Soc. Magnetic Resonance (chmn. divns. of biology and Medicine 1986-89), Phi Beta Kappa, Sigma Xi, Alpha Omega Alpha. Home: 950 Casanueva Pl Stanford CA 94305-1068 Office: Dept Molecular Pharmacology Sch Medicine Stanford Univ Stanford CA 94305-5337

JARECKIE, GRETCHEN KINSMAN FILLMORE, retired English language educator; b. Hanover, N.H., Apr. 19, 1927; d. Ernest George and Gretchen Mary (Kinsman) Fillmore; m. Stephen Barlow Jareckie, Aug. 10, 1959. BA cum laude, Syracuse U., 1949; MA, Mt. Holyoke Coll., 1968; Cert. of Advanced Grad. Study, Assumption Coll., 1982. English tchr. Jericho High Sch., Jericho Center, Vt., 1952-53, Meml. Jr. High Sch., Beverly, Mass., 1955-59, Utica (N.Y.) Free Acad., 1959-61, Wachusett Regional High Sch., Holden, Mass., 1961-67; English and music tchr. Brigham Acad., Bakersfield, Vt., 1953-54; asst. prof. English Anna Maria Coll., Paxton, Mass., 1968-74; instr. in English Framingham (Mass.) State Coll., 1974-80; ret., 1980. Author: To the Uttermost Parts of the Earth: Missionaries Who Went Out from Holden's First Congregational Church from 1818 to 1939, 1995. Mem. MLA, Shakespeare Club Worcester, Worcester Mt. Holyoke Club. Democrat. Congregationalist. Avocations: music, research, writing. Home: 47 Mount View Dr Holden MA 01520-2137

JARECKIE, STEPHEN BARLOW, museum curator; b. Orange, N.J., Feb. 18, 1929; s. Eugene Albert and Doris Condit (Brittin) J.; m. Gretchen Kinsman Fillmore, Aug. 10, 1959. BA, Lehigh U., 1951; MA, Syracuse U., 1961. Installation asst. Munson-Williams-Proctor Inst., Utica, N.Y., 1955-60, edn. asst., 1960-61; registrar Worcester (Mass.) Art Mus., 1961-83, assoc. in photography, 1962-69, assoc. curator photography, 1969-73, curator photography, 1973-94, curator of photography emeritus, 1995—; photo. adv. Fitchburg (Mass.) Art Mus., 1996—. Author: WAM catalogue, The Early Republic: Consolidation of Revolutionary Goals, 1976, American Photography: 1840-1900, 1976, Photographers of the Weimar Republic, 1986; contbr. to catalogue, pamphlets, articles to mus. lit. With AUS, 1951-53. Guest Fed. Republic of Germany for study of republic's museums, 1967. Mem. U.S. Naval Inst. (assoc.). Episcopalian. Built scale model original bldgs., grounds of Proctor Inst., 1957-60. Home: 47 Mount View Dr Holden MA 01520-2137 Office: 185 Elm St Fitchburg MA 01420-7503

JAREN, COURTNEY BATES, historian, lawyer, consultant; b. Phila., July 16, 1951; d. James Earl Bates and Laura Louise Courtney; m. Mathias Alfred Jaren, Aug. 25, 1972; children: Olav Reinhard, Laura Bates. BS cum laude, U. Minn., 1982, JD, 1988, PhD, 1998; LLM in Trial Advocacy, Temple U., 1999. Staff adviser to Sen. Warren G. Magnuson, 1979-80; law clk. U.S. Dept. Justice, Mpls., 1985-86; adviser Minn. Regional Health Affiliates Found., 1988-90; rsch. assoc., project mgr. U. Minn., Mpls., 1990-93, asst. to dean liberal arts, 1993-97; legal cons. Applied Engring. Assocs., Conshohocken, Pa., 1997—, Dwyer Real Estate Investments, Ocean City, N.J., 1998—, Gallagher, Schoenfeld, Surkin, & Schuplin, Media, Pa., 1999—, Willig, Williams and Davidson, Phila., 1999—; reader Bodleian Libr., Oxford U., 1997-98, Squires Law Libr., Cambridge U., 1997-98, Harvard Law Sch., 1998-99. Author: (book) America: The 60's and Beyond, 1996, (surveys) Survey Research, 1992, 93. Staff cons., grass roots coord. various polit. campaigns for Dem. candidates, Wash., Minn., Pa., N.J., 1976-96; precinct chair Shorewood dist. King County Dem. Party, Wash., 1978-80; comty. advocate Meth. Ch. Republican. Methodist. Avocation: pianist. E-mail: jaren@bellatlantic.net.

JARES, TERRYL LYNN, musician; b. Berwyn, Ill., Mar. 27, 1954; d. Robert A. and Ruth E. (Shandle) J. MBus, Ill. State U., 1976, BMusEd, 1976. Tchr. string instrument Dist. # 86, Joliet, Ill., 1976-77, Dist # 103, Lyons, Ill., 1977-80; domestic sales mgr. Conquest Sound, Monee, Ill., 1980-84; violinist Rupert's 33 Club, Rolling Meadows, Ill., 1982-87; violinist-violist Auditorium Theatre, Chgo., 1988—; v.p. Artra Artists mgmt., Chgo., 1984—; bd. dirs. Chgo. Fedn. of Musicians Local 10-208, Chgo.; sec./treas. Theater Musicians Assn., Chgo., 1996—. Office: Artra Artists mgmt 555 W Madison St Apt 2110 Chicago IL 60661-2523

JARGALSALKHANY, ENKHSAIKHAN, diplomat; b. Ulaanbaatar, Mongolia, Sept. 4, 1950; came to U.S., 1996; s. Bayaryn Jargalsaikhan and Martha Tserengyin; m. Batgerel Budjavyn; children: Ouyanga, Solongo, Bayarsaikhan, Narangerel, Sarangerel, Ariun. LLD, Moscow State Inst. Internat. Rels., 1979. Sec. legal dept. Ministry Fgn. Affairs, Ulaanbaatar, 1974-79; sec. Permanent Mission Mongolia to UN, N.Y.C., 1979-86; acting head legal and policy planning depts. MFA, Ulaanbaatar, 1986-88; min., counsellor Mongolian Embassy, Moscow, 1988-92; advisor Pres. Mongolia, Ulaanbaatar, 1992-93; exec. sec. Nat. Security Coun. Mongolia, Ulaanbaatar, 1993-96; amb. Permanent Mission Mongolia to UN, N.Y.C., 1996—. Avocations: reading historical books, learning about other countries and cultures. Home and Office: 6 E 77th St New York NY 10021-1704

JARKA, DALE ELIZABETH, surgeon; b. Montreal, Que., Can., July 16, 1957; came to U.S., 1989; d. Frank and Gladys Pearl (Rounds) J.; m. Brian Montgomery Wicklund, Aug. 12, 1988; children: Charlotte Anne Jarka Wicklund, Ian Patrick Wicklund. BS with honors in physiology, McGill U., 1979, MD, CM, 1983. Fellow Royal Coll. Physicians and Surgeons Can.; diplomate Am. Bd. Orthopaedic Surgery. Orthopaedic surgeon The Children's Mercy Hosp., Kansas City, Mo., 1992—. Fellow Royal Coll. Surgeons of Can., Am. Acad. Orthopaedic Surgeons; mem. Mo. State Med. Assn., Pediatric Orthopaedic Soc. N.Am., Ruth Jackson Orthopaedic Soc., Can. Orthopaedic Assn. Avocations: figure skating, singing. Office: The Childrens Mercy Hosp 2401 Gillham Rd Kansas City MO 64108-4698

JARMA, DONNA MARIE, secondary education educator; b. Portsmouth, Va., Aug. 31, 1949; d. Harry A. Sr. and Dreau M. (Schaedel) J. AA, Temple (Tex.) Jr. Coll., 1969; BA, U. Mary-Hardin Baylor, 1971; MA, Tex. Woman's U., 1990, postgrad. in PhD program, 1994—. Tchr. English and Spanish Troy (Tex.) H.S., 1971-77, Howe (Tex.) H.S., 1977—; mem. campus improvement com., Howe Ind. Sch. Dist., 1995-96, mem. curriculum com., 1993; instr. English Grayson County Coll. Contbr. articles to The Leaflet and Inland. Lector and Cath. Christian Doctrine, St. Mary's Cath. Ch., Sherman, Tex., 1988—. Mem. NCTE, Tex. Coun. Tchrs. English (conv. presenter 1994-99, English and Lang. Arts Educator of Yr. 1998-99), Tex. Gifted/Talented (conf. mini-session presenter, Austin, 1993-97). Roman Catholic. Avocations: writing, music, book collecting, bicycling, computers. E-mail: djarm@texoma.net. Home: 416 W Dexter St Sherman TX 75092-2765 Office: Howe ISD 300 Beatrice St Howe TX 75459-4554

JARMAN, DONALD RAY, retired public relations professional, minister; b. Benton Harbor, Mich., May 6, 1928; s. Ray Charles and Grace Marie (Timanus) J.; m. Bo Dee Foster, July 7, 1950 (div. 1985); children: Mark, Katharine Law, Luanne Miller; m. Sharon Lee Becker, Feb. 16, 1991. BA, Chapman U., 1950; MDiv, Lexington Theol. Sem., 1953; DMin, Sch. of Theology, Claremont, 1970. Ordained min. Disciples of Christ, 1950; cert. fundraising exec. Nat. Soc. Fundraising Execs., 1980-89. Pastor Sharpsberg (Ky.) Christian, 1950-53, First Christian Ch., Santa Maria, Calif., 1953-58, St. Claire St. Ch. of Christ, Kirkcaldy, Scotland, 1958-61, So. Bay Christian, Redondo Beach, Calif., 1961-71; dir. human value in health care Eskaton, Charmichael, Calif., 1971-73; exec. dir. Northwestern NBA Svc., Portland, Oreg., 1973-85; dir. pub. relations and mktg. Retirement Housing Found., Long Beach, Calif., 1985-89; part time minister Pico Rivera Christian Ch., 1986-87; dir. community rels. Coscan Davidson Homes, Signal Hill, Calif., 1989-96; interim min. Southgate First Christian Ch., 1994-95; pres. So. Calif. Mins., 1967; chmn. Pacific S.W. Region Christian Ch., 1968; mem. gen. bd. Disciples of Christ, 1969-70; exec. dir. Signal Hill Econ. Devel. Bd., 1992-96. Editor: Reachout, 1973-84, Hill Street News, 1992-95; editor-in-chief:

December Rose, 1985-89; columnist NW Senior News, 1980-84. Pres. Signal Hill C. of C., 1992-93; treas. Hist. Soc., Signal Hill, 1990-94; commr. L.A. County Commn. on Aging, 1994— (Link award for svc., 1998), Signal Hill Commn. Pks. and Recreation, 1996-99; bd. dirs. Bethany Towers, Hollywood, Calif., 1997—. Recipient Master Make-up Technician award Portland Opera, 1983, Outstanding Older American award City of Signal Hill, Calif., 1993, Alumnus of Yr. award Chapman U., 1998. Mem. Rotary (pres. Progress, Oreg. 1983-84, pres. Signal Hill 1993-94, Paul Harris fellow), Chapman U. Alumni Assn. (pres. 1994-95, trustee 1994-96), Los Alamitos Cmty. Art League, So. Calif. Pastel Soc., Lakewood Artist Guild, Masons. Democrat. Avocations: make-up artistry, bread baking, photography, water color, oils and pastels. Home: 1923 Molino Ave Unit 101 Signal Hill CA 90804-1028

JARMAN, JOSEPH, jazz musician; b. Pine Bluff, Ark., Sept. 14, 1937; s. Joseph and Eva (Robinson) J. Student, Chgo. City Jr. Coll., 1958-59, Chgo. Tchrs. Coll., 1958-59, Mil. Inst. Tech., 1959-60, U. Ariz., 1960-61, Am. Conservatory Music, 1966, Aikido Sensei, 1984. Ordained Buddhist priest, 1990. Tchr. Goodman Sch. Music, 1964; lectr. U. Chgo., 1966; pvt. tchr., 1966—; lectr., dir. music and theatre workshop Circle Pine Ctr., Delton, Mich., summer 1968; founder Bklyn Buddhist Assn., Jikishinkan Dojo, Aikido Sensei, 1984. Began performing with Assn. Advancement Creative Musicians, 1965; appeared at Harper Theatre, Chgo., 1965, new-music theatre concert, Chgo., 1966; selected to Detroit Jazz Conf., Wayne State U., 1967, environ. music concert, U. Chgo., 1967; joined Art Ensemble of Chgo., 1969—; instruments include: saxaphone, bassoon, oboe, flute, clarinet, percussion; composer: (songs) Tribute to the Hard Core, 1965, Non-Cognitive Aspects of the City, 1966, Hollows Ecliptic, 1967, Imperfections in a Given Space, 1965, Indifferent Piece for Six, 1967, Homage Song to the New Republic, 1976, Guardians of the Secret Place, 1983, Art of War, 1984, Charm the Rainbow, 1985, Eyes of the Charm Giver, 1986; composed music for Anna Devore Smith's Fires in the Mirror, 1992, Sun and Moon Live in the Sky, 1993, (albums) include Egwin, Song For, Sunbound, Together Alone, As If It Were The Seasons, 1989, The Magic Triangle, Black Sant, Earth Passage Density; others with Art Ensemble of Chgo. Office: PO Box 62 Brooklyn NY 11205-0062

JARMIE, NELSON, physicist, consultant; b. Santa Monica, Calif., Mar. 24, 1928; s. Louis and Ruth (Wydman) J. BS, Calif. Inst. Tech., 1948; PhD, U. Calif., Berkeley, 1953. Staff mem. Los Alamos Sci. Lab., 1953-97; co-founder Pajarito Ski Area, 1957; Los Alamos Sci. Lab. cons. for Dept. Energy regulatory compliance; vis. prof. U. Calif., Santa Barbara, 1960; adj. prof. U. N.Mex., 1957-71; mem. adv. coun. Los Alamos Grad. Ctr., 1958-88; participant Vis. Scientist Program, 1965-71; field mycologist Nat. Park Svc., 1991-98; rsch. on nuclear and particle physics, astrophysics and mycology; cons. for conduct of ops. and quality assurance fed. regulations; taxonomist of macromycetes cons., 1997—. Contbr. numerous articles to sci. jours. and mags.; rsch. in nuclear and particle physics, astrophysics and taxonomic mycology. Mem. Econ. Devel. Council Los Alamos County, N.Mex., 1968. Recipient Disting. Performance award Los Alamos Nat. Lab., 1986. Fellow AAAS, Am. Phys. Soc.; mem. Mycol. Soc. Am., N.Am. Mycol. Soc., Am. Assn. Physics Tchrs., Sigma Xi, Tau Beta Pi. Achievements include research in light-nuclei energy levels; 3-body breakup, nucleon-nucleus scattering, astrophysical reactions; kinematic codes, straggling calculations and infrared laser diagnostics; fundamental properties of antimatter; field surveys of macromycetes.

JARMOLOWICZ, C. RENEE, artist, art educator; b. Detroit, Apr. 27, 1951; d. Russell Richard Bauer and Coramae (Isgrig) Brodeur; m. John Arthur Jarmolowicz, Aug. 20, 1977; children: Monica Joy, Luke Edward. BA, Siena Heights Coll., Adrian, Mich., 1974; attended, Mich. State U., East Lansing, 1977. High sch. art instr. Marlette (Mich) Cmty. Schs., 1975-79; art instr. Cros-Lex Cmty. Edn., Croswell, Mich., 1982-83, 85-86; elem. art. instr. St. Edward on the Lake Sch., Lakeport, Mich., 1985-86, Sts. Peter and Paul Sch., Ruth, Mich., 1990-92; elem. art. cons. for spl. gifted consortium Huron Cty. Intermediate Sch. Dist., Bad Axe, Mich., 1991; pvt. art instr. Our Lady of Lake Huron Sch., Harbor Beach, Mich., 1992-95, Hummingbird's Quill Calligraphy & Design Studio, Deckerville, Mich., 1992-96; instr. Valley Scribes, Midland, Mich., 1997, Mich. Assn. Calligraphers, Royal Oak, 1994—; instr., adj. faculty St. Clair Cty. Cmty. Coll., Port Huron, Mich., 1995—; owner, artist Hummingbird's Quill Calligraphy & Design Studio, Deckerville, Mich., 1991—; spkr., demonstrator Vis. Artist's Day, Ling Elem. Sch., Hemlock, Mich., 1994, Sororian Club, Deckerville, Mich., 1996, Mich. State U. Ext., 4-H Visual Arts and Crafts Workshop, Kettunen Ctr., Tustin, Mich., 1998. Artist: (letter arts-mixed media with calligraphy) Rites of Passage, 1996 (First prize 1996, Juror's Acknowledgement 1996), Untitled, 1997, (Juror's award 1997), (handmade manuscript book-mixed media with calligraphy) Friendship Garden, 1997 (Juror's award 1997, Merit award 1997), Homage to the Creator I - Litany of Trees, 1998 (First place 1998), (handmade book-mixed media) Woods, 1998 (Best of Show 1998), Earth Woman, 1999 (second place 1999). Election inspector Marion Twp. Elections Bd., Deckerville, 1992-98, election inspector, chair, 1996-98. Recipient Second Place award Port Sanilac Art in the Park VIII, 1997, First Place award Lexington Fine Arts Fair, 1997, Internat. Art Fest, 1997. Mem. Mich. Assn. Calligraphers (chair 20th anniversary com. 1997), Assn. for the Calligraphic Arts, Port Sanilac Fine Arts Assn., Valley Scribes. Studio: Hummingbird's Quill Calligraphy Design Studio 4150 Mills Rd Deckerville MI 48427-9390

JARMON, LAWRENCE, developmental communications educator; b. L.A., Nov. 7, 1946; s. Robert and Movella (Young) J. BA, Calif. State U., 1969, MA in Adminstrn. Health and Safety, 1988; MS, U. Wash., 1972; EdD in Edn. Adminstrn., Wash. State U., 1975; MA, Calif. State U., L.A., 1988. Cert. alcohol and drug problems specialist. Athletic dir., instr. dept. phys. edn. L.A. SW Coll., 1975-85, agy. dir. summer programfor disadvantaged youth, 1975-94, asst. dean instruction, 1976, project adminstr. NCAA, 1977-79; instr. health edn. Golden West Coll., Huntington Beach, Calif., 1978; instr. dept. English Calif. State U., L.A., 1986; instr. dept. edn. Nat. U., L.A., 1986-88; prof. devel. comm. L.A. S.W. Coll., 1988—, staff devel. coord., dir. nat. youth sports program, 1992-96, dir. coll. recruitment, adminstr. evening divsn., 1997—, supr. Learning Resource Ctr., 1997—. Author numerous booklets, manuscripts and manuals on sports programs and edn. qualifications and policies. Bd. advisors Scholastic Placement Orgn. for Student Athlete, Mount Laurel, N.J.; bd. dirs. Black Edn. Commn., L.A. Unified Sch. Dist., Calif. State U., L.A. Alumni Assn., Involvement for Young Achievers, L.A., L.A. Police Dept. Football Centurions, Paradise Ch. Found., Inc., L.A., Pop Warner Little Scholars, Inc., Phila.; employee assistance program liaison officer L.A. Cmty. Dist. Named one of Outstanding Young Men of Am., 1980, 81. Mem. AHHPERD, Am. Alliance Health Edn., Am. Assn. Sch. Adminstrs., Calif. State U. Alumni Assn., U. Wash. Alumni Assn., Wash. State Alumni Assn., Calif. Assn. Health, Phys. Edn. and Recreation, Calif. State Athletic Dirs. Assn., L.A. Jr. C. of C., Nat. Interscholastic Athletic Adminstrs. Assn., Phi Delta Kappa, Kappa Alpha Psi. Office: LA SW Coll 1600 W Imperial Hwy Los Angeles CA 90047-4810

JARMUSCH, JIM, director, actor; b. Akron, Ohio. Actor: (films) American Autobahn, 1984, Straight to Hell, 1987, Running Out of Luck, 1987, Helsinki Napoli All Night Long, 1987, Leningrad Cowboys Go to America, 1989, The Golden Boat, 1990, In The Soup, 1992, Iron Horsemen, 1994, Tigrero: A Film That Was Never Made, 1994, Blue in the Face, 1995, Typewriter, the Rifle & the Movie Camera, 1996, Cannes Man, 1996, Sling Blade, 1996, Divine Trash, 1998, (TV series) Fishing With John, 1991, American Cinema, 1994; writer, dir., editor, prodr., composer: Permanent Vacation, 1982 (Joseph von Sternberg prize Mannheim, Internat. Critics prize Figueira da Foz, Portugal 1981); dir., writer, editor: Stranger Than Paradise, 1984 (Camera D'Or Cannes Film Festival 1984, Best Picture of Yr. Nat. Soc. Film Critics 1984); dir., writer: Down By Law, 1986 (Best Film award Locarno, Best Fgn. Film Norway, Denmark and Israel), Mystery Train, 1989 (Highest Artistic Achievement prize Cannes Film Festival), Dead Man, 1995 (World Premiere Cannes Film Festival 1995, Felix award Best Non-European Film 1996, Best Cinematography award N.Y. Critics Cir. 1996), Ghost Dog: The Way of the Samurai, 1999; dir., editor: Coffee and Cigarettes III, 1993 (Golden Palm Cannes Film Festival 1993); exec. prodr.: When Pigs Fly, 1993; dir., cinematographer: Year of the Horse, 1997; writer, cinematographer: You Are Not I, 1981; dir., writer, prodr.: Night on Earth, 1991 (Grand award Best Feature Film Houston Internat. Film Festival 1992, Ind. Spirit award Best Cinematography 1993); dir.: Coffee and Cigarettes, 1986, Coffee and Cigarettes II, 1986.

JARNAGAN, HARRY WILLIAM, JR., project control manager; b. Cedar Rapids, Iowa, Nov. 7, 1953; s. Harry William and Virginia Lillian (Grusy) J.; m. Anne Therese Tompkins, June 7, 1975; children: Douglas William, Michael Patrick, Marianne Virginia. BS, U.S. Mil. Acad., 1975; M of Engring., Tex. A&M, 1984. Registered profl. engr., Tex. Project mgr. Dunbar & Dickson, Inc., Clute, Tex., 1980-83, 84-85; grad. teaching asst. Tex. A&M U., College Station, 1983-84; cost. engr. Bechtel Power Corp., Houston, 1985-87; project control engr. Tenn. Valley Authority, 1987-88, Fluor-Daniel, Inc., Rochester, N.Y., 1988-90, MK-Ferguson Co., Oak Ridge, Tenn., 1990-95; mgr. Avlis project controls U.S. Enrichment Corp., Livermore, Calif., 1995-97; western region project controls mgr. Internat. Tech. Corp., Pleasanton, Calif., 1997-98; program controls mgr. Hatch Mott McDonald, San Jose, Calif., 1998—. Capt. U.S. Army, 1975-80. Mem. Am. Assn. Cost Engrs. (cert., v.p. fin.), Tau Beta Pi. Lutheran. Avocations: running, weight lifting, sky diving. Home: 875 Henderson Way Tracy CA 95376-8944 Office: Hatch Mott McDonald Ste 250 6140 Stoneridge Mall Rd Pleasanton CA 94588

JARNAGIN, TERESA ELLIS, educator, nursing administrator; b. Jackson, Miss., Mar. 11, 1950; d. James Robert and Eloise (Cox) Ellis; m. Nathan O. Jarnagin, Dec. 19, 1970; children: Bethany, Nate. Diploma in nursing, Gilfoy-Miss. Bapt. Hosp., Jackson, 1971; BSN, U. Miss., Jackson, 1993, MSN, 1995; postgrad., LSU, New Orleans, 1997—. RNC, CNA, ANCC; cert. med.-surg. nursing and nursing adminstrn. Staff nurse St. Dominic-Jackson (Miss.) Meml. Hosp., 1975-84, nurse mgr. urology/renal, 1984-93, DON behavioral health svcs., 1993-96; nursing instr. Miss. Coll., 1996—. Recipient first place non-fiction award Gulf Coast Writer's Assn. Contest, 1993. Mem. ANA, Miss. Nurse's Assn. (del. state conv. 1993, 94), Dist. Nurse's Assn. (publicity com. 1992, 93, 94), So. Nursing Rsch. Soc., Sigma Theta Tau, Phi Kappa Phi. Baptist. Avocations: flower gardening, reading, creative writing, needlework. Home: 502 Merganser Trl Clinton MS 39056-6262 Office: Miss Coll Box 4037 Clinton MS 39058

JAROFF, LEON MORTON, magazine editor; b. Detroit, Feb. 27, 1927; s. Abraham and Ruth (Rockita) J.; m. Claire Lynn Fox, Aug. 15, 1954 (div. Nov. 1975); children: Peter, Jill, Susan, Nicholas, Jennifer; m. Mary Katherine Moran, Jan. 10, 1976. B.S. in Elec. Engring. and Math., U. Mich., 1950. Writer Materials and Methods Mag., N.Y.C., 1950-51; researcher, reporter, corr. Life Mag., N.Y.C., Detroit, Chgo., 1951-58; corr., assoc. editor, sr. editor Time Mag., N.Y.C., Detroit, Chgo., 1958-79; scis. editor Time Mag., N.Y.C., 1985-87, contbr., 1988—; founder, mng. editor Discover Mag., N.Y.C., 1980-84; co-chair bd. for student publs. U. Mich., 1992-98. Author: The New Genetics, 1991, also 44 Time mag. cover stories. Trustee Neurosci. Rsch. Found., La Jolla, Calif.; bd. dirs. Rogosin Inst., N.Y.C. With USN, 1944-45. Recipient Robert S. Ball Meml. award Aviation Space Writers Assn., 1978, Excellence award, 1989; Sci. Writing award AAAS/Westinghouse Corp., 1978, Sci. Writing award Am. Inst. Physics/U.S. Steel Corp., 1976, 82, 83; Asteroid 7829 Jaroff named in his honor. Fellow Com. for Sci. Investigation of Claims of the Paranormal; mem. Am. Soc. Mag. Editors (exec. com. 1984-85), Am. Inst. Physics (adv. com. 1982—). Jewish. Avocations: tennis, computers, chess. Home: PO Box 1080 East Hampton NY 11937-0901 Office: Time Mag Time & Life Bldg 1271 Avenue Of The Americas New York NY 10020-1300

JARON, DOV, biomedical engineer, educator; b. Tel Aviv, Oct. 29, 1935; came to U.S., 1958, naturalized, 1972; s. Meir and Sara (Levit) Yarovsky; m. Brooke E. Boberg, Sept. 16, 1978; children: Shulamit, Tamara. B.S. magna cum laude, U. Denver, 1961; Ph.D., U. Pa., 1967. Sr. research asso. Maimonides Med. Center, Bklyn., 1967-70; dir. surg. research Sinai Hosp. of Detroit, 1970-73; asso. prof. elec. engring. U. R.I., Kingston, 1973-77; prof. U. R.I., 1977-79, coordinator biomed. engring., 1973-79; prof. biomend. engring. and sci. Drexel U., Phila., 1979—, dir. Biomed. Engring. and Sci. Inst., 1979-96; Calhoun disting. prof., 1998—; vis. prof. elec. engring. Rutgers U., New Brunswick, N.J., 1968-73; adj. prof. biomed. engring. Wayne State U., 1971-73; adj. prof. physiology Temple U. Sch. Medicine, 1980—; adj. prof. radiology Jefferson Med. Coll., 1983—; dir. Div. Biol. and Critical Systems, NSF, 1991-93; assoc. dir. Nat. Ctr. Rsch. Resources, dir. biomedical tech. NIH, 1996-98. Contbr. articles to sci. jours. NSF, NIH, Office Naval Research, pvt. founds. research grantee. Fellow AAAS, IEEE, Am. Inst. for Med. and Biol. Engring.; mem. AAUP, Internat. Fedn. for Med. and Biol. Engring. (pres.-elect 1997), Biomed. Engring. Soc., Am. Soc. for Engring. Edn., Assn. for Advancement Med. Instrumentation, Internat. Soc. Artificial Organs, Am. Soc. for Artificial Internal Organs, Biophys. Soc., N.Y. Acad. Scis., Engring. in Medicine and Biology of IEEE (pres. 1986-87), Sigma Xi, Tau Beta Pi, Eta Kappa Nu. Achievements include research of cardiac assist devices, cardiovascular dynamics and modeling, biomed. instrumentation. Home: 122 Bethlehem Pike Philadelphia PA 19118-2815 Office: Drexel Univ Biomedical Engring Sci Inst 32nd and Chestnut St Philadelphia PA 19104

JAROS, DEAN, university official; b. Racine, Wis., Aug. 23, 1938; s. Joseph and Emma (Kotas) J. B.A., Lawrence Coll., Appleton, Wis., 1960; M.A., Vanderbilt U., 1962, Ph.D., 1966. Asst. prof. polit. sci. Wayne State U., Detroit, 1963-66; from asst. prof. to prof. polit. sci. U. Ky., 1966-78, assoc. dean Grad. Sch., 1978-80; dean Grad. Sch. No. Ill. U., DeKalb, 1980-84; dean Grad. Sch. Colo. State U., Ft. Collins, 1984-91, assoc. provost, 1991—. Author: Socialization to Politics, 1973, Political Behavior: Choices and Perspectives, 1974, Heroes Without Legacy, 1993, also articles.; Mem. editorial bds. profl. jours. Mem. Exptl. Aircraft Assn. Office: Colo State U Grad Sch Fort Collins CO 80523*

JAROS, ROBERT JAMES, data processing executive; b. Port Reading, N.J., June 30, 1939; s. Michael and Marian (Kurta) J.; m. Margaret Efthin, May 19, 1974; children: Marian Reilly, Jennifer, Christina,. Student, Rutgers U., 1957-65. With Prudential Ins. Co., Newark, 1957-77; sr. sys. analyst, project leader Ins. Svcs. Office, N.Y.C., 1977-81; project mgr. Shearson Lehman Bros. Inc., N.Y.C., 1981-88; cons. G & J Assocs., Middletown, N.J., 1988; commn. Middletown Housing Authority, 1995—; trustee, v.p. Lin-Mid Corp., 1997—. Mem., chmn. Middletown Twp. Transp. Com., 1988—; mem., past pres. Rolling Knolls Civic Soc.; mem. U.S. Power Squadron, Watchung Power Squadron; Rep. County committeeman, Monmouth County, 1989—. With USAR, 1963-68. Fellow Life Mgmt Inst. Soc. of Greater N.Y.; mem. Am. Soc. CLU's, Am. Legion. Roman Catholic. Email: rjaros@juno.com. Home: 12 Jocarda Dr Middletown NJ 07748-3337

JAROSH, ANDREW T., journalist; b. N.Y.C., May 24, 1957; s. Joseph and Anna (Pupshaw) J.; m. Marci M. Boman, Sept. 1986 (div. Sept. 1991); 1 child, Sarah Ann. Student, NYU, 1976-77; BS, U. Wis., Superior, 1979, MA, 1980. Journalist Superior evening telegram, 1978-83, Knight-Ridder, Miami, Fla., 1983-84, Ft. Wayne (Ind.) News-Sentinel, 1984—; instr. journalism Ind. U.-Purdue U., Ft. Wayne, 1980s; journalism trainer Internat. Ctr. for Journalists, Washington, 1996—. Recipient Newswriting awards Inland Press Assn., Hoosier State Press Assn., AP Mng. Editors. Democrat. Avocations: racquetball, model trains, fishing. Home: 1114 Ashwood Dr Auburn IN 46706-3271 Office: Fort Wayne News-Sentinel 600 W Main St Fort Wayne IN 46802-1408

JAROSLOVSKY, ALAN, judge; b. Des Moines, Iowa, May 11, 1948; s. Louis and Ruth (Grossmark) J. BA, UCLA, 1970; JD, Golden Gate U., 1977. Bar: Calif. 1977. Pvt. practice Santa Rose, Calif., 1978-87, U.S. Bankruptcy judge, 1987—. Author: Practical Bankruptcy Procedure, 1993. Dir. Calif. Rural Legal Assistance, 1981. Lt. USN, 1970-73, Vietnam. Mem. Sonoma County Bar Assn. (pres. 1987). Democrat. Jewish. Avocation: astronomy. Office: US Bankruptcy Ct 99 S E St Santa Rosa CA 95404-6527

JARRARD, JAMES PAUL, school program administrator; b. Flint, Mich., July 5, 1951; s. Donald and Virginia Bernadine J. BA with honors, Mich. State U., 1975; MS in Edn., U. So. Calif., University Park, 1982; postgrad., Boston U. Tchr. lang. arts and reading Agrl. Migrant Sch., Immokalee, Fla., 1976-78; tchr. lang. art. and social studies Flint Community Schs., 1978-81; tchr. computer sci., and lang. arts Makiminato Schs. Dept. Def. Schs., Naha, Okinawa, Japan, 1981-84; tchr. computer sci. Mannheim (Fed. Republic Germany) High Sch. Dept. Def. Schs., 1984-86, tchr. computer sci. Munich High Sch., 1986; dist. computer coord. Germany Region Dept. Def. Schs., Bremerhaven, 1986-89; sch. info. mgr. Atlantic Region Dept. Def. Schs., London, 1989-92; mgr. sch. info. sys. devel. Dept. Def. Schs., Arlington, Va., 1992-94; edn. tech. rschr. and developer Dept. Def. Edn. Activity, 1994-96. career tech. coord., 1996-97, coord. electronic comm., 1997—. Mem. ASCD, Overseas Edn. Assn. (NEA). Home: 6917 Lodestone Ct Alexandria VA 22306-1216

JARRARD, LEONARD EVERETT, psychologist, educator; b. Waco, Tex., Oct. 23, 1930; s. Thomas Ivan and Levis Everett (Lasswell) J.; m. Janet Grier Shoop, Aug. 16, 1958; children: Alice Grier, David Frazier, Hugh Everett. B.A., Baylor U., Waco, 1955; M.S., Carnegie Inst. Tech., Pitts., 1957, Ph.D., 1959. Asst. to asso. prof. psychology Washington and Lee U., 1959-66; assoc. prof. to prof. psychology Carnegie-Mellon U., 1966-71; Robert L. Telford prof. psychology Washington and Lee U., Lexington, Va., 1971—; vis. lectr., prof. exptl. psychology U. Oxford, Eng., 1975-76; interim assoc. prof. anatomy U. Fla., 1965-66; acad. visitor Inst. Psychiatry, U. London, 1988-89. Editor: Cognitive Processes of Nonhuman Primates, 1971; cons. editor: Jour. Comparative and Physiol. Psychology, 1970-75, Behavioral Neurosci. Served with USAF, 1952-54. Mem. AAAS, APA, APS; mem. Soc. for Neurosci., Psychonomics Soc., Va. Acad. Sci. So. Soc. Philosophy and Psychology, Phi Beta Kappa, Omicron Delta Kappa, Sigma Xi. Home: PO Box 1067 RR5 Lexington VA 24450-1067 Office: Washington and Lee U Dept Psychology Lexington VA 24450*

JARRARD, MARILYN MAE, nursing consultant, nursing researcher; b. York, Nebr., July 13, 1939; d. Frederick Albert and Esther Marie (Kollmann) Elze; m. William John Jarrard (div.); children: Rebecca Ann, Melissa Linn. Diploma in nursing, Luth. Sch. Nursing, Sioux City, Iowa, 1959. RN, Iowa, Fla.; cert. nutritional support nurse. Staff nurse U. Iowa Hosps. and Clinics, Iowa City, 1959-60, 69-70, minimal care charge nurse, 1971-74, staff nurse medical oncology, 1974-75, hyperalimentation nurse, 1975-79; staff nurse VA Hosp., Iowa City, 1960-65; charge nurse Offutt Air Base Hosp., Omaha, 1965-66; hyperalimentation nurse clinician Northwestern Meml. Hosp., Chgo., 1979-81; nutritional support nurse, team coord. Leila Hosp. and Health Ctr., Battle Creek, Mich., 1981-87; clin. specialist wound care Smith & Nephew Perry, Massillon, Ohio, 1987-89; clin. specialist-I.V. Smith & Nephew, Inc. Wound Mgmt. Divsn., Largo, Fla., 1989—; cons. and rschr. in field. Contbr. numerous articles to profl. jours. With USNG, 1976-79. Mem. Nat. Assn. Vascular Access Networks, Assn. for Profls. in Infection Control and Epidemiology, Inc., Soc. for Healthcare Epidemiology Am., Oncology Nursing, Am. Soc. Parenteral and Enteral Nutrition (nursing faculty 1977), Intravenous Nurses Soc., League Intravenous Therapy Edn. Home: 9209 Seminole Blvd Apt 130 Seminole FL 33772-3127

JARRARD MAHAYNI, MARY MELISSA, psychiatric nurse; b. Vernon, Ala., Nov. 1, 1956; d. Henry Grady and Bonnie Lucille (Hollis) Jarrard; m. Nidai Mahayni, Oct. 5, 1994; 1 child, Chloe Kate Jarrard. BSN, Va. Commonwealth U., 1980; Registered Massage Therapist, Potomac Myotherapeutic Inst., 1984; MS in Psychiat. Nursing, Va. Commonwealth U., 1994. RN, Va., D.C.; registered massage therapist. Nurse asst. in psychiatry MCV Sch. Hosp., Richmond, Va., 1979-80, nurse adolescent med.-surg., 1980-82; cmty. health nurse Kneut-Hanson Hosp., St. Thomas, V.I., 1982-83; trauma nurse Nat. Children's Med. Ctr., Washington, 1983-85; charge nurse Psychiat. Inst. of Richmond, 1985-87; owner myotherapy Massage Therapist, Richmond, 1987-93; counselor Critical Debriefing, Richmond, 1993-94; nursing care mgr. Comprehensive Health Investment Program, 1995-97; clin. nurse specialist behavioral medicine Columbia Retreat Hosp., Richmond, 1997-98; Head Start coord. health, mental health and disabilities VCU Head Start, Richmond, 1998—; cultural diversity mem. MCV Nursing's Cultural Diversity Com., 1993-94. Nurse Traineeship award, 1993, 94. Mem. ANA, Va. Nurses Assn., Child and Adolescent Psychiat. Nursing Assn., Am. Massage Therapy Assn., Virginians Against Handgun Violence (PAC rep. 1993), NOW (polit action com. 1992-93), Nat. Women's Polit Caucus. Democrat. Unitarian. Avocations: mentorship programs, relaxation techniques, swim team mom, exercise. Home: 2125 Stuart Ave Richmond VA 23220-3439

JARRELL, CHARLES MICHAEL, bishop; b. Opelousas, La., May 15, 1940. Student, Immaculata Minor Sem., Cath. U. Ordained priest Roman Cath. Ch., 1967. Ordained priest Lafayette, La., 1967; ordained bishop Diocese of Houma (La.)-Thibodaux, 1993—. Office: Diocese of Houma-Thibodaux PO Box 9077 Houma LA 70361-9077*

JARRELL, DONALD RAY, laboratory administrator; b. Barberton, Ohio, Sept. 25, 1963; s. Paul Everett and Minnie Marie (Aldridge) J.; m. Sandra Leilani Hawkins, May 20, 1989. BS in Chemistry, Marshall U., 1985, MA, 1988. Mgr. receiving Lab. Corp. Am., Research Triangle Park, N.C., 1987—. Mem. Am. Chem. Soc. Democrat. Baptist. Avocations: bowling, swimming, golf, reading. Home: 1362 Hanford Hills Rd Graham NC 27253-3626 Office: Lab Corp Am 1904 Alexander Dr Research Triangle Park NC 27709

JARRELL, IRIS BONDS, elementary school educator, business executive; b. Winston-Salem, N.C., May 25, 1942; d. Ira and Annie Gertrude (Vandiver) Bonds; m. Tommy Dorsey Martin, Feb. 13, 1965; 1 child, Carlos Miguel; m. 2d, Clyde Rickey Jarrell, June 25, 1983; stepchildren: Tamara, Cris, Kimberly. Student, U. N.C., Greensboro, 1960-61, 68-69, U. N.C., Greensboro, 1974-75, Salem Coll., 1976; BS in Edn., Winston-Salem State U., 1983; M in Elem. Edn., Gardner-Webb Coll., 1992. Cert. tchr., N.C. Tchr. Rutledge Coll., Winston-Salem, 1982-84; owner, mgr. Rainbow's End Consignment Shop, Winston-Salem, 1983-85; tchr. elem. edn. Winston-Salem/Forsyth County Sch. Svcs., 1985-96; dir. Knollwood Bapt. Pre-Sch., 1996-97; tchr. gifted/talented students Winston-Salem/Forsyth County Schs., 1998; tchr. Clemmons Elem. Sch., 1998—. Contbr. poetry to mags. Mem. Assn. of Couples for Marriage Enrichment, Winston-Salem, 1984-86, Forsyth-Stokes Mental Health Assn., 1985-86; mem. Winston-Salem Symphony Chorale; mem. Planned Parenthood. Mem. NAFE, NOW, Internat. Reading Assn., N.C. Assn. Adult Edn., Forsyth Assn. Classroom Tchrs., World Wildlife Fund, Greenpeace, KlanWatch. Democrat. Baptist. Avocations: singing, writing, sewing, gardening, reading. Home: 101 Cheswyck Ln Winston Salem NC 27104-2905

JARRELL, WESLEY MICHAEL, soil and ecosystem science educator, researcher; b. Forest Grove, Oreg., May 23, 1948; s. Burl Omer and Edith LaVerne (Sahnow) J.; children: Benjamin George, Emily Theresa. BA, Stanford U., 1970; MS, Oreg. State U., 1974, PhD, 1976. Asst. prof. soil sci. U. Calif., Riverside, 1976-83, assoc. prof., 1983-88; assoc. prof. Oreg. Grad. Inst., Portland, 1988-91, prof., 1991—, dept. head, 1992-94, prof., 1991—, head dept., 1992-94, internat. cons. on agr., 1988; internat. cons. on agr., 1988; internat. cons. on sci. agr. environ., 1988—. Contbr. articles to profl. jours. Mem. AAAS, Soil Sci. Soc. Am., Am. Soc. Agronomy. Mem. AAAS, Soil Sci. Soc. Am., Am. Soc. Agronomy. Democrat. Lutheran. Home: 3036 NW Creekwood Dr Forest Grove OR 97116 Office: Oreg Grad Inst Environ Sci Engring PO Box 91000 Portland OR 97291-1000

JARRETT, ALFRED A., social administration educator, consultant; b. Kalangba, Port Loko, Sierra Leone, Dec. 7, 1950; came to U.S., 1973; AA in Criminal Investigation/Psychology, Muscatine C.C., 1976; MA in Human Devel. Counseling, U. Ill., Springfield, 1979, MA in Child, Family & Cmty. Svcs., 1979; PhD in Social Policy, Ohio State U., 1984. Peer counselor Sangamon State U., Springfield, 1977-78, tchg. asst. human devel. program, 1979; family therapist Sangamon County Youth Svc. Bur., Springfield, 1978-79, clin. coord., 1979-80; grad. rsch. assoc. Coll. Social Work Ohio State U., Columbus, 1980-81, grad. tchg. assoc. Coll. Social Work, 1980-83; adult protective svc. program specialist Tex. Dept. Human Svcs., Dallas, 1987-89; founder, co-dir. Internat. Ctr. on Ethnicity and Gender Grad. Sch. Social Work, U. Arlington, Tex., 1989-91, asst. prof., 1989-91; dir., assoc. prof. social work dept. Paul Quinn Coll., Dallas, 1991-93; assoc. prof., coord. social admin./policy/planning sequence Grad. Social Work Program, Ala. A&M U., Huntsville, 1993—; co-facilitator career prep. program Springfield Urban League, spring 1979; policy analyst and social planner, internat. cons. for developing countries in Africa, 1983—; adj. asst. prof. dept. social work

U. Tex., Arlington, 1987-89; mem. Coun. on Social Work Edn., Alexandria, Va., 1995—; cons. Madison County (Ala.) Commn. Dist. 6, Paul Quinn Coll., Dallas, Dallas Urban League, African Friendship Soc., Sierra Leone Govt.; mem. editl. adv. bd. Collegiate Press, Alta Loma, Calif., 1993—; condr. workshops in field; presenter in field. Author: (books) Social Work Curriculum Design for a National School of Social Work in Sierra Leone, 1984, Curriculum Design for Ethnic Minority Males, 1992, A Case Management Training uide for Social Practitioners, 1993, Self Study for Paul Quinn College Social Work Department, Vols. 1 & 2, 1993, The Rationale for Africa's Retrogression: Militarization and Tribalism, 1994, The Underdevelopment of Africa: Colonialism, Neo-Colonialism and Socialism, 1995, Strategies and Techniques for Building Community Coalitions, 1996, (with Shirley Wesley King) Social Issues Impacting Ethnic Minorities and Gender: Intervention Strategies for Social Practitioners, 1990, (with others) Graduate Social Work Program Self Study for CSWE Accreditation, Vol. 1, 1995; editor: (book) The Impact of Macro Social Systems on Ethnic Minorities in the United States, 1999; contbr. articles to profl. jours.and chpts. to books in field, also book revs., abstracts. Mem. needs assessment com. United Way Madison County, Huntsville, 1994—; mem. task force com. Madison County-Huntsville Drug, Gang and Violence Intervention, Huntsville, 1994—; bd. dirs. Partnership for Drug Free Comty., Huntsville, 1994—, State of Ala. Children First Program, 1999. Recipient Cert. Outstanding Achievement, United Coll. Social Welfare, 1981. Mem. Internat. Student Assn. of Sangamon State U. (founder, pres.), Southwestern Social Sci. Assn., Sangamon State. Internat. Soccer Club (mem. student senate), Phi Beta Delta (Epsilon chpt.), Alpha Delta Mu (Columbus chpt. at Ohio State U.), Phi Alpha. Fax: (205) 851-0749. Office: Ala A&M U Dept Social Work PO Box 302 Normal AL 35762

JARRETT, DALE, professional race car driver; b. Conover, N.C., Nov. 26, 1956; m. Kelley Jarrett; children: Jason, Natalee, Karsyn. Profl. race car driver NASCAR Winston Cup, 1984—; winner 1993 Daytona (Fla.)500, 1995 Miller Genuine Draft 500, Pocono, Pa., 1995, Kmart 400, 1999, Pontiac Excitement 400, 1999. Office: DAJ Racing Inc PO Box 564 Conover NC 28613-0564 Office: c/o Robert Yates Racing 115 Dwelle St Charlotte NC 28208-2929*

JARRETT, KEITH, pianist, composer; b. Allentown, Pa., May 8, 1945. Student, Berklee Sch. Music, 1963. Pianist with groups led by Art Blakey, 1965, Charles Lloyd, 1966-69, Miles Davis, 1970-71; rec. with group led by Art Blakey: Buttercorn Lady, 1966; recs. with groups led by Charles Lloyd: Dreamweaver, Forest Flower, In Europe, The Flowering, 1966, Love In (Live at Fillmore), Journey Within, Live in the Soviet Union, 1967, Soundtrack, 1968; recs. with groups led by Miles Davis: Miles Davis at Fillmore, Live—, Evil, Get Up With It, Directions, 1970; soloist, leader of own groups, 1969—; recs. as leader of own groups or as solo artist: Life Between The Exit Signs, 1967, Restoration Ruin, Somewhere Before, 1968, Gary Burton/Keith Jarrett, 1971, Mourning of a Star, Birth, El Juicio, Ruta and Daitya, Expectations, Facing You, 1971, Fort Yawuh, In The Light, Solo Concerts Bremen & Lausanne, 1973, Treasure Island, Belonging, Luminessence, Death and the Flower, Backhand, 1974, The Koln Concert, Mysteries, Shades, Bob-Be, Byablue, Arbour Zena, 1975, Survivors' Suite, Eyes of The Heart, Staircase, Hymns/Spheres, Sun Bear Concerts, 1976, My Song, 1977, Personal Mountains, Nude Ants, Moth and The Flame, 1979, The Celestial Hawk, Sacred Hymns, Invocations, 1980, Concerts Bregenz and Munich, 1981, Standards Volumes 1 & 2, Changes, 1983, Spirits, Standards Live, 1985, Still Live, Book of Ways, 1986, Dark Intervals, Changeless, 1987, Paris Concert, 1988, Tribute, 1989, Standards In Norway, 1989, The Cure, 1990, Vienna Concert, Bye Bye Black Bird, 1991, At the Dear Head Inn, 1992, Bridge of Light, 1993, At The Blue Note (6 CD set, 1994), La Scala, 1995, Tokyo '96; also recorded with Airto, Freddie Hubbard, Marion Williams, Kenny Wheeler, Gary Peacock, Charlie Haden, Paul Motian; classical recs. include J. S. Bach—Well Tempered Clavier Book 1 (piano), 1987, Book 2 (harpsichord), 1991, Goldberg Variations (harpsichord), 1989, French Suites (harpsicord), 1991, Handel Keyboard Suites, 1993, (with Michala Petri) Handel—Sonatas for Recorder and Continuo, 1990, Bach— Sonatas for Flute and Harpsicord, 1992, (with Dennis Russell Davies/Stuggart Chamber Orch.) Mozart Piano Concerto No. 21, 23, 27, Lou Harrison—Piano Concerto and Suite for violin, piano and orch., 1988, Alan Hohvaness—Lousadzak, 1989, (with Gidon Kremer) Arvo Part—Fratres, 1983, Shostakovitch—24 Preludes and Fugues, Opus 87, 1991; (with Kim Kashkashian) Bach Sonatas for Viola da Gamba, 1991; concert soloist with San Francisco Symphony, Phila. Orch., Boston Symphony Orch., Am. Composers Orch., St. Paul and English Chamber Orch., Rochester and Bklyn, Philharm.; subject of biography: Keith Jarrett: The Man and His Music (Ian Carr), 1991. Decorated officier de L'Ordre des Arts et des Lettres (France); recipient Guggenheim award, 1972, Grand Prix du Disque, Govt. of France, 1972, Prix du Pres. de la Republique (France), 1991; recs. nominated for Grammy award, 1974, 86, 88, 92, 98; recs. named Record of Yr., Time mag., Downbeat mag., Stereo Rev., 1974, N.Y. Times, 1975, 92, Rolling Stone mag., 1976, CD Rev., 1992, Downbeat, 1996; named Pianist/Artist of Yr., Downbeat mag., 1974, 75, 94, 96, 97, 98, Keyboard mag., 1976, 82, 91, Swing Jour. (Japan), 1980, 86, 87, 89, 91, 93, 94, 95, 96; 1st improvising musician to perform Met. Opera, N.Y.C., 1978, Vienna State Opera, 1991, La Scala, Milan, 1995. Mem. Royal Swedish Acad. Music.

JARRETT, LESLIE JOE, video producer; b. Independence, Kans., Oct. 19, 1961; s. Robert Patterson and Betty June (Johnson) J. BS, Ball State U., 1984. News photographer Sta. WIFR-TV, Rockford, Ill., 1984-88, Sta. WTTV, Indpls., 1988-90; prodr., owner Railway Prodns., Indpls., 1990—; co-producer Am. by Rail - The Heartland, 1994, Am. by Rail - West Coast, 1995, Am. by Rail - Winter Wonderland, 1996, Am. by Rail - Route of the S.W. Chief, 1997. Prodr. The Alphabet Train, 1998. Mem. Internat. TV Assn., Nat. Press Photographers Assn. Office: Railway Prodns 8081 Madison Ave Ste 243 Indianapolis IN 46227-6001

JARRETT, NOEL, chemical engineer; b. Long Eaton, Eng., Nov. 17, 1921; came to U.S., 1926, naturalized, 1942; s. John Richard and Lena Eliza (Hexter) J.; m. Violet E. Dipner, Sept. 24, 1949; children: Robert, Kenneth, James, Thomas. B.S. in Chem. Engring, U. Pitts., 1949; M.S. in Chem. Engring, U. Mich., 1951. Lubrication sales engr. Freedom-Valvoline Co., Freedom, Pa., 1949-50; rsch. engr., group leader, asst. chief Alcoa Labs., Aluminum Co. Am., 1951-65, chief div. process metallurgy, 1965-69, asst. dir. metal prodn. labs., 1969-81, tech. dir. smelting rsch. and devel., 1981-82, tech. dir. chem. engring. rsch. and devel., 1982-87; ret., 1987; prin. Noel Jarrett Assocs. Patentee smelting, melting and purification of alumninum. Served with U.S. Army, 1942-45. Fellow Am. Soc. Metals; mem. NAE, Am. Isnt. Chem. Engrs., Minerals, Metals and Materials Soc., VFW, Am. Legion, Masons, Elks, Sigma Xi. Episcopalian. Home and Office: 149 Jefferson Ave New Kensington PA 15068-3127 *I have found that the one who performs the tasks immediately at hand so well that his work cannot be ignored will reap society's rewards without asking.*

JARRETT, POLLY HAWKINS, secondary education educator, retired; b. Columbia, S.C., May 6, 1929; d. William Harold and Ann Beatrice (Carson) Hawkins; m. Nov. 21, 1953 (dec. Aug. 1984); children: William Guy Jr., Henry Carson. Student, Montreat Coll., 1947-49; BS in Secondary Edn., Longwood Coll., 1951. Tchr. 7th grade McDowell County Schs., Marion, N.C., 1951-52; tchr. 8th grade Marion City Schs., 1952-53, Burke County Schs., Morganton, N.C., 1954-56; tchr. 7th grade Wake County Schs., Raleigh, N.C., 1956-58, Durham (N.C.) County Schs., 1958-59; tchr. 7th and 8th grade Raleigh City and Wake County Schs., Raleigh, 1959-79; tchr. social studies Wake County Pub. Schs., Raleigh, 1979-90, ret., 1990; adv. bd. State Employees Credit Union, Raleigh, 1988-92, 94-00. Mem. United Daus. of the Confederacy (chpt. pres. 1978-81, 91-96, divsn. historian 1981-83, dist. VI dir. 1983-85, divsn. chaplain 1986-90, divns. parliamentarian 1994-96, chmn. bd. trustees 1990-91), Delta Kappa Gamma (chpt. pres. 1988-90, regional dir. 1990-92, state 2d v.p. 1997-99), Kappa Delta Pi, Pi Delta Epsilon, Pi Gamma Mu. Democrat. Methodist. Avocations: travel, growing roses, reading, pets. Home: 3405 White Oak Rd Raleigh NC 27609-7620

JARRETT, RONALD DOUGLAS, lawyer, nurse; b. Oceanside, Calif., Oct. 31, 1952; s. W. Douglas and Francia Elizabeth (Ladd) J.; m. Lois Ellen Shurmaster, Dec. 26, 1984; 1 child, Emily Rose. AA, AS in Nursing, Cabrillo Coll., Aptos, Calif., 1981; student Nursing Sci., NYU, 1982-89; JD, Lincoln Law Sch., Sacramento, Calif., 1993. Bar: Calif. 1993, U.S. Dist. Ct. (ea. dist.) Calif. 1993, U.S. Dist. Ct. (no. dist.) Calif. 1994. Law clk. CIGNA Counsel, Sacramento, 1992-94; sole practitioner Sacramento, 1994—; med., legal record rev., pvt. practice, Sacramento, 1992—; computer cons. for lawyers, 1994—. With USN, 1970-73. Mem. ABA, ATLA, Consumer Lawyers Calif., Sacramento County Bar Assn., Million Dollar Advocates Forum (life). Avocations: family, Aikido, Go, flying, history. Office: PO Box 200 Carmichael CA 95609

JARROW, ROBERT ALAN, economics and finance educator, consultant; b. Hackensack, N.Y., June 16, 1952; s. Benjamin Charles and Irene Elizabeth (Kozniewski) Jaworowski; m. Gail Dian Goundry; children: Kyle, Tate, Heather. BA, Duke U., 1974; MBA, Dartmouth Coll., 1976; PhD, MIT, 1979. Prof. fin. and econs. Cornell U., Ithaca, N.Y., 1979—; cons. Bank of Am., San Francisco, 1987-89, Merrill Lunch, 1994—, Kamakura Corp., 1995—. Author: Option Pricing, 1983, Finance Theory, 1988, Modelling Fixed Income Securities and Interest Rate Options, 1996; Derivative Securities, 1996; also articles; assoc. editor Jour. Fin. Quantitative Analysis, 1983—, Rev. Futures Markets, 1987—, Rev. Fin. Studies, 1994—; co-editor: Math. Fin., 1989—, Jour. Derivatives, 1999—. Recipient Pomerance prize Chgo. Bd. Options Exch., 1982; named Fin. Engr. Yr., 1997. Mem. Am. Fin. Assn., Econ. Soc., Ops. Rsch. Soc., Soc. for Promotion Econ. Theory, Math. Assn. Am. Avocations: jogging, soccer, karate. Office: Cornell U Malott Hall Ithaca NY 14853

JARVEY, JOHN A., federal judge. BS, U. Akron, 1978; JD, Drake U., 1981. Law clk. to Hon. Donald E. O'Brien U.S. Dist. Ct. (no. dist.) Iowa, Cedar Rapids, 1981-83; trial atty. U.S. Dept. Justice, Washington, 1983-87; chief magistrate judge U.S. Dist. Ct. (no. dist.) Iowa, Cedar Rapids. Office: 101 1st St SE Cedar Rapids IA 52401-1202

JARVI, NEEME, conductor; b. Tallinn, Estonia, June 7, 1937; came to U.S., 1980; s. August and Elss Jarvi; m. Liilia Jarvi, Sept. 2, 1961; children: Paavo, Kristjan, Maarika. Diploma in Music and Conducting, St. Petersburg (USSR) State Conservatorium, 1960; hon. doctorate, U. Aberdeen, Scotland, Music Conservatory of Talinn, Estonia, Gothenberg (Sweden) U. Condr. Estonian Radio Symphony Orch., 1960-63, chief condr., 1963-76; chief condr. Estonian State Opera, 1963-76, Estonian State Symphony, 1976-80; prin. condr. Gothenburg (Sweden) Symphony Orch., 1982—; prin. condr., music dir., condr. laureate Royal Scottish Orch., Glasgow, 1984-88; music dir. Detroit Symphony Orch., 1990—; prin. guest condr. Birmingham (Eng.) Symphony Orch., 1980-83; guest condr. N.Y. Philharm Orch., Boston Symphony Orch., Phila. Orch., Chgo. Symphony, Royal Concertgebow Amsterdam, The Philharmonia London, London Symphony, all Scandinavian Orchs., several operas at Met. Opera House, N.Y.C.; exclusive rec. contract with Chandos Records of Gt. Britain. Recs. include music of Ellington, Barber, Beach and Ives with DSO; complete symphonies of Sibelius, Stenhammar, Berwald, Dvorak, Gade, Svendsen, Brahms, R. Strauss, Glasounov, Eduard Tubin Schostakovitch, Prokoffiev, Rimski-Korsakov, Part, many others. Decorated knight comdr. North Star Order (Sweden); recipient 1st prize in conducting Accademia Nazionale di Santa Cecilia, 1971. Office: Detroit Symphony Orch Hall 3711 Woodward Ave Detroit MI 48201-2005*

JARVIK, LISSY F., psychiatrist; b. The Hague, Netherlands; m. Murray E. Jarvik, Dec. 19, 1954; children: Laurence A., Jeffrey G. AB cum laude, Hunter Coll., N.Y.C.; MA, Columbia U., PhD; MD, Western Res. U. Diplomate Am. Bd. Pediat. From rsch. asst. to psychiatrist II N.Y. State Psychiat. Inst., N.Y.C.; rotating intern Mt. Sinai Hosp., N.Y.C.; resident in pediatrics Babies Hosp., Columbia Presbyn. Med. Ctr., Vanderbilt Clinic, N.Y.C.; resident in psychiatry N.Y. State Psychiat. Inst., N.Y.C., 1965-68; asst. attending, then attending psychiatrist Vanderbilt Clinic, 1962-72; from rsch. assoc. to assoc. prof. Columbia U. Coll. Phys. and Surg., 1956-72; chief psychogenetic unit West Los Angeles VA Med. Ctr., 1970-82, chief psychogeriatric unit, 1982-87; prof. psychiatry UCLA Med. Sch., 1982-94, prof. emeritus, 1994—; M.S. McLeod vis. prof. U. Adelaide, Australia, 1981; vis. prof. Australian Postgrad. Med. Found., 1981; Disting. Physician Dept. VA, 1987-93, emeritus, 1993—; dir. GetSmart program, 1991—, dir. Upbeat Program, 1993—; cons. in field, mem. numerous task forces. Mem. editl. bd. profl. jours.; founding co-editor Alzheimer Disease and Associated Disorders--An Internat. Jour.; contbr. over 300 articles to profl. jours. Recipient R. Thornton Wilson award, 1967, Woman in Sci. award UCLA, 1981, Group Research award Assn. for Specialists in Group Work, 1984, Research award Alzheimer Disease and Related Disorders Assn., L.A. chpt., 1985, Jack Weinberg Memorial award Am. Psychiatric Assn., 1986, Robert W. Kleemeier award Gerontol. Soc. of Am., 1986, Edward B. Allen award Am. Geriatrics Soc., 1986, Disting. Scientific Achievement award Calif. State Psychol. Assn., 1987, Irving S. Wright award Am. Fedn. for Aging Rsch., 1988, William C. Menninger Meml. award ACP, 1993, Svc. to Psychogeriat. award Internat. Psychogeriat. Assn., 1995, C. Charles Burlingame award The Inst. Living, 1998; named Woman of Achievement, Women's Equality Day, 1980, Woman of Yr., AAUW, Santa Monica, 1985; named to Hunter Coll. Alumni Assn. Hall of Fame, 1991; Foundation fellow Ctr. for Advanced Study in Behavioral Scis., 1988-89. Fellow AAAS, Gerontol. Soc. Am. (Joseph T. Freeman award 1996), Am. Geriatric Soc., Internat. Soc. Twin Studies, Am. Acad. Pediatrics, Am. Psychol. Assn. (div. pres.); mem. Am. Med. Womens Assn., Am. Soc. Human Genetics, Am. Psychopath Assn., Am. Aging Assn., Am. Soc. on Aging, Behavior Genetics Assn., Internat. Assn. Gerontology, Am. Psychiat. Assn. (Disting. Psychiatrist Lectr. 1996), Am. Assn. for Geriat. Psychiatry (past pres., Founders award 1990-91, Sr. Investigator award, 1993), Internat. Psychogeriat. Assn., N.Y. Acad. Scis., West Coast Coll. Biol. Psychiatry, World Psychiat. Assn., Sigma Xi. Office: 760 Westwood Plz Los Angeles CA 90024-1759 Office: VA Med Ctr 11301 Wilshire Blvd # 11L Los Angeles CA 90073-1003

JARVIK, MURRAY ELIAS, psychiatry, pharmacology educator; b. N.Y.C., June 1, 1923; s. Jacob and Minnie (Haas) J.; m. Lissy, Dec. 19, 1954; children—Laurence Ariel, Jeffrey Gil. B.S., CCNY, 1944; M.A., UCLA, 1945; M.D., U. Calif., San Francisco, 1951; Ph.D., U. Calif., Berkeley, 1952. Research technician phys. chemistry Rockefeller Inst., N.Y.C., 1943-44; research assoc. neurophysiology neurology dept. Mt. Sinai Hosp., 1953-55; research assoc. psychopharmacology L.I. Biol. Assn., Cold Spring Harbor, N.Y., 1955-56; asst. prof. pharmacology Albert Einstein Coll. Medicine, 1956-60, assoc. prof., 1960-68, prof., Sadie Danciger Distinguished scholar, 1968, prof. psychiatry, 1969-72; prof. psychiatry, pharmacology U. Calif. at Los Angeles, 1972—; chief psychopharmacology unit Brentwood VA Hosp., 1972—; Vis. asst. prof. physiol. psychology U. Calif. at Berkeley, 1955; adj. asst. prof. N.Y. U., 1957; vis. physician Bellevue Hosp., N.Y.C., 1960; research scientist N.Y. U. Med. Center, 1936-65, sr. research scientist, 1965; mem. adv. com. on abuse of stimulant and depressant drugs Bur. Drug Abuse Control, FDA, 1966—; mem. adv. com. on tobacco habituation Am. Cancer Soc., 1967—. Mng. editor Psychopharmacologia, 1966-71; mem. editorial adv. bd. Behavioral Biology. Recipient Career Scientist award NIMH, 1971, Career Scientist award, 1971-72; fellow Ctr. for Advanced Study in Behavioral Scis. Stanford U., 1988-89. Fellow AAAS, N.Y. Acad. Scis., Am. Psychol. Assn. (div. pres. 1966-68); mem. Am. Coll. Neuropsychopharmacology, Collegium Internatonale Neuro-Psychopharmacologium, Internat. Brain Research Orgn., Am. Psychopath. Assn., Phi Beta Kappa, Sigma Xi. Office: VA Med Ctr Brentwood Los Angeles CA 90073 *A guiding principle in my life has been that psychiatry can and should be a science and not merely an art. The principles of validation and control should be applied to psychiatry just as they are to any other science. I have felt that psychopharmacology and the study of the brain are the pathways one must follow to learn more about behavior. Although great progress is occuring in the understanding of molecular mechanisms, the molar study of behavior is indispensable for a complete knowledge of psychiatry and psychology.*

JARVIS, BARBARA ANN, conference planner, conference manager; b. San Francisco, May 5, 1946; d. Steve and Irma Vivian (Ford) Jarvis; m. Andre Pardow Mitchell (div. Jan. 1973); children: Kristin Dion, Damien Pardow Mitchell; m. Michal Kamionko, Nov. 15, 1987. Student, Skyline City Coll., 1975. Entertainment booking agt. Joe Tex, singer, San Francisco, 1979-82; entertainment booking agt., pres., owner MJM Prodns., San Francisco, Sacramento, 1982-84; dir. transp. Kaiser Permanente Med. Ctr., San Francisco, 1982-95; project mgr., conf. planner Women in Tech. Internat., 1996—; planner WOPAR Designs, San Francisco, 1996—; owner BA Jarvis & Assocs. Event Planning Co., San Francisco, 1997—; v.p. WOPAR Designs, San Francisco, 1996—; asst., event planner Levine Enterprises, 1997—. Bd. dirs. HIV Continuum, San Francisco, 1989; transp. dir. San Francisco Kaiser Neighborhood & Health Plan Mem. Free Svc., 1984-89. Recipient State of Calif. Gov.'s award for best transp. program in Calif., 1990. Mem. Nat. Assn. Health Svcs. Execs., Instl. Mcpl. Parking Assn. (speaker, Award Transp. Excellence IMPC Conv. 1989). Democrat. Roman Catholic. Avocations: European travel.

JARVIS, BILLY BRITT, lawyer; b. Amarillo, Tex., Jan. 9, 1943; s. Billy and Francis Olivia (Beck) J.; m. Linda Jean Holt, Feb. 26, 1965; children: William Britt, Anne Marie, Bonnie Lea. BS in Agrl. Econs., Tex. A&M U., 1965; JD, So. Meth. U., 1968. Bar: U.S. Dist. Ct. (no. dist.) Tex. 1972, U.S. Supreme Ct. 1975. Asst. county atty. Hutchinson County, Borger, Tex., 1968-69; pvt. practice law Spearman, Tex., 1971—. Contbr. articles to profl. jours. Leader Hansford County 4-H, 1976-91. Capt. U.S. Army, 1969-71, Vietnam. Decorated Bronze Star. Mem. Tex. Bar Assn., Panhandle Bar Assn., Tex. Conf. Bar Pres., Phi Delta Phi, Masons, Shriners. Democrat. Avocations: recreational horseback riding. Office: 124 W Kenneth St PO Box 515 Spearman TX 79081-0515

JARVIS, CHARLENE DREW, council member; b. Washington, July 31, 1941; two children. BA, Oberlin (Ohio) Coll., 1962; MS in Psychology, Howard U., 1964; PhD, U. Md., 1971; DSc (hon.), Amherst Coll., 1994. Supr. statis. lab. Howard U., 1965-66, psychol. inst., 1970-71; rsch. psychologist Neuropsychology NIMH, 1971-78; coun. mem. Coun. of the D.C., 1979—, chair task force on the fin. mgmt. system, 1980-81; chair com. on housing and econ. devel. coun. of the D.C., 1981—, chair protem, 1994—; chair bd. dirs. Met. Coun. of Govts.; bd. dirs. Pa. Ave. Devel. Corp., Nat. Health Mus.; mem. steering com. Greater Washington Mktg. Partnership of the Greater Washington Bd. of Trade, 1993—; mem. coms. NIMH, adv. coun., 1993—; mem. breast cancer task force, 1993—; mem. Ronald Reagan Ctr. for Emergency Medicine, George Washington U. Hosp., 1993—. Bd. dirs. Girl Scouts Am., Pvt. Industry Coun., 1986—; mem. Leadership Washington, 1991-92; v.p., exec. com., chair transp. subcom. D.C. chpt. ARC; del. Nat. Dem. Conv., 1980, 84, 88, 92; nat. co-chair Mondale for Pres., 1984, Clinton/Gore campaign, 1992; candidate for mayor, D.C., 1982, 90; chair pro tempore Coun. D.C., 1997—; pres. Southeastern U., 1996—. Named one of 50 Most Powerful Women in the Washington Area Washington Bus. Jour. , 1985, 100 Most Powerful Women in the Washington Area, Washingtonian Mag., 1989, 94, 97. Mem. Nat. Assn. Ind. Colls. and Univs. (bd. dirs.). Home: 1789 Sycamore St NW Washington DC 20012-1030 Office: Coun of the DC 441 4th St NW Rm 708 Washington DC 20001-2714*

JARVIS, DAPHNE ELOISE, laboratory administrator; b. Lithia, Fla., Feb. 18, 1945; d. Grady Edwin and Vera Eloise (Smith) Smith; m. Hubert E. Jarvis, Aug. 1, 1964; 1 child, Jessica Ellen. BS, Blue Mountain Coll., 1966; MA, Spalding U., 1972. Cert. med. technologist with specialist in blood bank. Med. technologist St. Anthony's Hosp., Louisville, 1968-69, Clark County Meml. Hosp., Jeffersonville, Ind., 1969-73; asst. to edn. coord. ARC, Washington, 1973-75; dir. Grace Bapt. Ch. Sch., Bryans Rd., Md., 1978-83; sect. chief blood bank Physicians Meml. Hosp., LaPlata, Md., 1975-76, 83-84; supr. donor blood labs. Southwest Fla. Blood Bank, Tampa, 1984-87, dir., 1987-89; asst. dir. tech. svcs. Ark. Region ARC, Little Rock, 1989-93, dir. tech. svcs./hosp. svcs. Ark. Regional Blood Svcs., 1993-95; mfg. team leader Lifeblood-Midsouth Regional Blood Ctr., Memphis, 1995—; lectr. UAMS Sch. Med. Tech., Little Rock, 1989-95. Children's leader Ingram Blvd Bapt. Ch., West Memphis, Ark., 1995—. Mem. Am. Assn. Blood Banks, South Ctr. Assn. Blood Banks (membership com. 1989-95). Office: Lifeblood Midsouth Reg Blood Ctr 1040 Madison Ave Memphis TN 38104-2198

JARVIS, EDWARD CURTIS, manufacturing and distribution company executive, international business consultant; b. Malden, Mass., Jan. 6, 1951; s. John Albert and Shirley Ann (Fronduto) J.; m. Nancy Jean Cotoia, June 24, 1973; 1 child, Ryan Edward. BA in History and Psychology, Bridgewater State Coll., 1972; postgrad., Salem State Coll., 1973-74; exec. MBA, Suffolk U., 1983. Mfg. and personnel mgr. Cape Dory Yachts, Taunton, Mass., 1974-77; plant mgr. Am. Alumninum Inc., Malden, 1977-80; mgr. human resources Prime Computer, Natick, Mass., 1980-81; orgn. and manpower rep., systems cons. aircraft engine bus. group GE, Lynn, Mass., 1981-83; mgr. profl. compensation and human resources systems Gen. Electric Co., Lynn, Mass., 1983-84; dir. human resources U.S. ops. Scitex Am. Corp., Bedford, Mass., 1984-85; corp. dir. worldwide human resource planning Scitex Corp. Ltd., Herzlia, Israel, 1985-86; corp. v.p., corp. dir. human resources Towle Mfg. Co., Burlington, Mass., 1986-88; exec. v.p., gen. mgr. Demakes Enterprises, Lynn, Mass., 1988-89, chief exec. officer, 1989-95; pres., CEO One XCEL, Inc., Danvers, Mass., 1995-97; pres. One XCEL, Inc., Foothill Ranch, Calif., 1997-98; pres., CEO SportTech Industries Inc., Boxford, Mass., 1998—; clin. prof. Entrepreneurial Studies, Sawyer Bus. Sch., Boston, MA, 1998—; internat. bus. cons.; exec. bd. dirs. Bus. Edn. Found. Bd. dirs. Lynn Bus./Edn. Found., 1990-97; v.p. Prevent Blindness Mass., 1995—, Bridgewater State Coll. Found., Bridgewater, Mass., 1995—; bd. advisors Nat. Youth Sports Found.; mem. bus. adv. com. Bridgewater State Coll., 1998—. Mem. Beach Club, Ipswich Country Club. Roman Catholic. Avocations: tennis, basketball, golf, sailing, travel. Home: PO Box 156 West Boxford MA 01885-0156 Office: Suffolk Univ Sawyer Bus Sch Beacon Hill 8 Ashburton Pl Boston MA 02108-2770

JARVIS, ELBERT, II (JAY JARVIS), employee benefits specialist; b. Washington, N.C., Sept. 20, 1944; s. Elbert J. Sr. and Laura F. (Lilley) J.; m. Anita Kleinfeld, Nov. 28, 1968 (div. Nov. 1983); 1 child, Elbert J. III; m. Audrey H. Liebross, July 28, 1991; 1 child, Benjamin Grover. A of Bus. Adminstrn., No. Va. C.C., 1972; BSBA, George Mason U., 1974. Sales mgr. Baumgarten Co., Washington, 1970-71; sales rep. Mass Mut., Washington, 1974-84; pres. The Pers. Dept., Inc., Annandale, Va., 1983—; founder No. Va. Group Health Alliance, No. Va. C. of C., 1998. Editor: (student handbook) Focal Point, 1973, Beth El Temple 1995-97, bd. dirs. Directory chair, 1990, 91, 92, 94. Scoutmaster, Webelos leader Boy Scouts Am., Clifton and Arlington, Va., 1970-71, 85-86; mem. county com., state del. Arlington Rep. Party, 1975-85; pres., sec. Arlington Jaycees, 1980-82; pres., bd. dirs. Lafayette Village Cmty. Assn., Annandale, Va., 1994-95; bd. dirs. Beth El Hebrew Congregation, 1994-97, founder, chmn. bd. dirs. No. Va. C. of C., 1998—. Mem. Am. Compensation Assn., Health Underwriters Assn. (sec. No. Va. chpt. 1996-97), Washington chpt. Cert. Employee Benefit Specialists (assoc.), Arlington C. of C. (chmn. comms. com. 1983, bd. dirs. 1988-92, 92-94, chmn. sml. bus. coun. 1990, 92, chmn. expo com. 1991, chmn. awards and small bus. week 1994, Disting. Svc. awards 1989), Soc. Employee Benefits Profls., Alexandria C. of C. (mem. advantage program com. 1993-96), Fairfax County C. of C. (vice chmn. small bus. awards 1993-94, mem. team captain 1996), Lafayette Village Comm. Assn. (pres.). Jewish. Avocations: canoeing, camping, photography. Home: 7828 Ashley Glen Rd Annandale VA 22003-1556 Office: The Pers Dept Inc 4330M Evergreen Ln Annandale VA 22003

JARVIS, GILBERT ANDREW, humanities educator, writer; b. Chelsea, Mass., Feb. 13, 1941; s. Vernon Owen and Angeline M. (Burkard) J.; m. Carol Jean Ganter, Jan. 26, 1963; children: Vicki Lynn, Mark Christopher. BA, St. Norbert Coll., De Pere, Wis., 1963; MA, Purdue U., 1965, PhD, 1970. Prof. Ohio State U., Columbus, 1970-95, chmn. humanities edn., 1980-83, assoc. chmn. dept. ednl. theory and practice, 1983-87, chmn. dept. ednl. studies, 1987-95, dir. ESL programs, 1994—, chmn. prof. emeritus, 1995—; cons. Internat. Edn. Program, U.S. Dept. Edn., Washington, 1977-84, many schs., agys. and pub. cos. Author: Et Vous?, 1983, 86, 89; Invitation, 1979, 2d edit., 1984, 3d edit., 1988, 4th edit., 1993, Y tu?, 1986, 2d edit., 1988, Connaitre et se connaitre, 3d edit., 1986, Invitation Essentials, 1991, 3d edit., 1999; editor: The Challenge for Excellence, 1984; mem. editl. bd. Modern Lang. Jour., 1979-86; adv. bd. Can. Modern lang. Rev., 1982—. Mem. Am. Coun. Tchg. Fgn. Langs., Phi Delta Kappa. Avocations: travel, photography. Home: 8337 Evangeline Dr Columbus OH 43235-1136 Office: English as a Second Lang Programs 1945 N High St Columbus OH 43210-1201

JARVIS, J. ANDREW, architectural firm executive. BA, U. Pa., 1974, MArch, 1976. Registered architect Ariz., Washington, Ky., Mo., N.J., N.Y.,

Pa., Tex., Wash. Project prin. Ewing Cole Cherry Brott, Phila., CEO, 1999—. Mem. AIA, Phi Beta Kappa. Office: Ewing Cole Cherry Brott Fed Res Bldg 100 N 6th St Philadelphia PA 19106-1590*

JARVIS, JAMES HOWARD, II, judge; b. Knoxville, Tenn., Feb 28, 1937; s. Howard F. and Eleanor B. J.; m. Martha Stapleton, June 1957 (div. Feb. 1962); children—James Howard III, Leslie; m. Pamela K. Duncan, Aug. 23, 1964 (div. Apr. 1991); children: Ann, Kathryn, Louise; m. Gail Stone, Sept. 4, 1992. BA, U. Tenn., 1958, JD, 1960. Bar: Tenn. 1961, U.S. Dist. Ct. (ea. dist.) Tenn. 1961, U.S. Ct. Appeals (6th cir.) 1965. Assoc. O'Neil, Jarvis, Parker & Williamson, Knoxville, Tenn., 1960-68, mem., 1968-70; mem. Meares, Dungan, Jarvis, Maryville, Tenn., 1970-72; judge Law and Equity Ct., Blount County, Tenn., 1972-77, 30th Jud. Cir. Ct., Blount County, 1977-84, U.S. Dist. Ct. (ea. dist.) Tenn., Knoxville, 1984-91, chief judge, 1991—. Past bd. dirs. Maryville (Tenn.) Coll.; mem. and past chmn. fin. com. St. Andrews Episc. Ch.; past bd. dirs. Detoxification Rehab. Inst. of Knoxville; mem. com. on codes of conduct Jud. Conf. U.S. Mem. ABA (com. ethics and profl. responsibility), Tenn. Bar Assn. (bd. govs. 1983-84), Am. Judicature Soc., Tenn. Trial Judges Assn. (past mem. exec. com.), Tenn. Jud. Conf. (pres. 1983-84), Blount County Bar Assn., Knoxville Bar Assn., Great Smoky Mountains Conservation Assn., Phi Delta Phi, Sigma Chi (significant Sigma Chi). Republican. Home: 6916 Stone Mill Rd Knoxville TN 37919-7431 Office: Howard H Baker Jr US Courthouse 800 Market St Knoxville TN 37902-2303

JARVIS, JOHN CECIL, lawyer; b. Clarksburg, W.Va., May 11, 1949; s. James M. and Maud Lee (Duncan) J.; m. Rebecca Ann Ullom; children: Amy, Jennie, Brian. BS in Civil Engring., Lehigh U., 1971; JD, Vanderbilt U., 1975. Bar: W.Va. 1975. Ptnr. McNeer, Highland, McMunn and Varner L.C., Clarksburg, 1975—; vice chmn., bd. dirs. W.Va. United Health Sys., Inc.; bd. dirs. One Valley Bank Inc. Democrat. Methodist. Office: McNeer Highland et al PO Box 2040 Clarksburg WV 26302-2040

JARVIS, MARY G., principal. Prin. Smoky Hill High Sch., Aurora, Colo., 1988—. Recipient Blue Ribbon Sch. award, 1990-91. Office: Smoky Hill High Sch 16100 E Smoky Hill Rd Aurora CO 80015-1751*

JARVIS, RICHARD S., academic administrator; b. Nottingham, Eng., Feb. 13, 1949; came to U.S., 1974; s. John Leslie and Mary Margaret (Dodman) J.; m. Marilou Thompson, Nov. 7, 1986; stepchildren: Kimberly Nipko, Christopher Healey. BA in Geography, Cambridge (Eng.) U., 1970, MA, 1974, PhD in Geography, 1975. Lectr. Durham (Eng.) U., 1973-74; assoc. prof. SUNY, Buffalo, 1975-87, asst. to pres., 1986-87; v.p. acad. SUNY, Fredonia, 1987-90, prof. geoscis., 1987-90; vice provost SUNY Sys., Albany, 1990-94; chancellor Univ. and C.C. Sys. Nev., Reno and Las Vegas, 1994—; mem. adv. bd. Bechtel Nev., Las Vegas, 1995-97, NTS Devel. Corp., Las Vegas, 1997, INC, Las Vegas, 1997. Editor: River Networks, 1983; contbr. articles to profl. jours. Trustee United Way, Reno, 1996—, EDAWN, Reno, 1996—. Office: Univ and CC Sys Nev Syss Adminstrn N 2601 Enterprise Rd Reno NV 89512-1666 also: Syss Adminstrn S 5550 W Flamingo Rd Ste C1 Las Vegas NV 89103

JARVIS, WILLIAM ESMOND, retired Canadian government official; b. Gladstone, Man., Can., Dec. 10, 1931; s. Frederick Roberts and Dorothy Wells (Tuckwell) J.; m. Leona Mae Jarvis; children: Cheryl, Darrell, Dennis, Morgan. B.Sc., U. Man., 1950-55; M.Sc., Mich. State U., 1960. With Dept. Agr. Province of Man., Can., 1955-67; dept. minister Dept. Agr. Province of Man., 1962-67; asst. dept. minister Govt. Can., Ottawa, Ont., 1967-75; coord. Grains Group Dept. Industry Trade and Commerce, 1971-75, assoc. dep. minister, 1975-77; chief commr. Can. Wheat Bd., Winnipeg, Man., 1977-90; Can. high commr. to New Zealand Wellington, 1990-94. Recipient U. Man. Alumni Assn. Jubilee award, 1981. Mem. Agrl. Inst. Can., Man. Inst. Agrologists.

JASCOURT, HUGH D., lawyer, arbitrator, mediator; b. Phila., Mar. 25, 1935; s. Jacquard A. and Gladys Mae (Bregen) J.; m. Resa B. Zall, Nov. 28, 1963; children: Stephen, Leigh. AB, U. Pa., 1956; JD, Wayne State U., 1960. Bar: Mich. 1961, U.S. Supreme Ct. 1965, D.C. 1967. Atty. advisor U.S. Dept. Labor, Washington, 1960-64; asst. dir. employee-mgmt. rels. Am. Fedn. Govt. Employees, Washington, 1964-65; atty. advisor Nat. Labor Rels. Bd., Washington, 1965-66; exec. dir. Fed. Bar Assn., Washington, 1966-67; house counsel Am. Fedn. of State, County, & Mcpl. Employees, Washington, 1967-69; sr. labor-law counsel Bd. of Gov. Fed. Reserve Bd., Washington, 1969-72; dir. Pub. Employment Rels. Rsch. Inst., Washington, 1972-74; asst. solicitor U.S. Dept. of Interior, Washington, 1974-82; sr. labor-law counsel U.S. Dept. Commerce, Washington, 1982-90; pres. Agency for Dispute Resolutions and Synergistic Rels., Greenbelt, Md., 1991—; lectr. George Washington U. Law Sch., Washington, 1970-75; chmn. unfair labor practice panel Prince George County Employee Rels. Bd., Upper Marlboro, Md., 1972-83, mem. Greenbelt (Md.) Employee Rels. Bd., 1984—; arbitrator/mediator, 1973—. Author, editor: Trends in Public Sector Labor Relations, 1973, Government Labor Relations, 1979; author: (with others) Labor Relations, 1978-82; Collective Bargaining, 1980; labor rels. editor Jour. Law and Edn., 1972—. Pres. Road Runners Club Am., 1962-66, Prince George County (Md.) Fedn. of Recreational Couns., 1969, Prince George County Coun. of PTAs, 1989-90; coach U.S. track and field team AAU So. Games, Trinidad, 1964, Internat. Cross Country Championship, Morocco, 1966; v.p. Am. Running and Fitness Assn., 1968-84. Inductee Road Runners Club Am. Hall of Fame, 1986; initial inductee D.C. Road Runners Club Hall of Fame, 1994. Fellow Coll. of Labor and Employment Lawyers; mem. ABA (com. on state and local labor employment and law, chmn. subcom. 1982—, co-chmn. com. on fed. svc. labor and employment law 1985-97, mem. mediation com., sect. on dispute resolution), ASPA, Soc. Fed. Labor Rels. Profls. (bd. dirs. 1992-93), Soc. Profls. in Dispute Resolution (charter mem.), Indsl. Rels. Rsch. Assn., Internat. Pers. Mgmt. Assn., Am. Arbitration Assn., Md. Coun. on Dispute Resolution. Office: Agency Dispute Resolution & Synergistic Rels 18 Maplewood Ct Greenbelt MD 20770-1907

JASEN, MATTHEW JOSEPH, state justice; b. Buffalo, Dec. 13, 1915; s. Joseph John and Celina (Perlinski) Jasinski; m. Anastasia Gawinski, Oct. 4, 1943 (dec. Aug. 1970); children: Peter M., Mark M., Christine (Mrs. David K. Mac Leod), Carol Ann, (Mrs. J. David Sampson); m. Gertrude O'Connor Travers, Mar. 25, 1972 (dec. Nov. 1972); m. Grace Yungbluth Frauenheim, Aug. 31, 1973. Student, Canisius Coll., 1936; LLB, U. Buffalo, 1939; post-grad., Harvard U., 1944; LLD (hon.), Union U., 1980; LL.D. (hon.), N.Y. Law Sch., 1981. Bar: N.Y. 1940. Ptnr. firm Beyer, Jasen & Boland, Buffalo, 1940-43; pres. U.S. Security Rev. Bd., Wurttemberg-Baden, Germany, 1945-46; judge U.S. Mil. Govt. Ct., Heidelberg, Germany, 1946-49; sr. ptnr. firm Jasen, Manz, Johnson & Bayger, Buffalo, 1949-57; justice N.Y. Supreme Ct. (8th jud. dist.), 1957-67; judge N.Y. Ct. Appeals, 1968-85; U.S. Supreme Ct. spl. master S.C. v. U.S., 1987-88; spl. master Ill. vs. Ky. U.S. Supreme Ct., 1989-95; of counsel Moot & Sprague, Buffalo, 1986-90; counsel Jasen, Jasen & Sampson, P.C., Buffalo, 1990-99, Jasen & Jasen, P.C., Buffalo, 1999—; mem. N.Y. State Jud. Screening Com., 1996—. Contbr. articles to profl. jours. Mem. council U. Buffalo, 1963-66; trustee Canisius Coll. Chair of Polish Culture, also, Nottingham Acad. Served to capt. AUS, 1943-46, ETO. Fellow Hilbert Coll.; recipient Disting. Alumnus award SUNY-Buffalo Sch. Law, 1969, Disting. Alumnus award Alumni Assn., 1976, Disting. Alumnus award Canisius Coll., 1978, Edwin F. Jaeckle award SUNY-Buffalo Sch. Law, 1982. Mem. Nat. Conf. Appellate Judges, State U. N.Y. at Buffalo Law Sch. Alumni Assn. (pres. 1964-65), Am., N.Y. State, Erie County bar assns., Am. Law Inst., Am. Judicature Soc., Lawyers Club Buffalo (pres. 1961-62), Nat. Advocates Club, Profl. Businessmen's Assn. Western N.Y. (pres. 1952), Phi Alpha Delta, DiGamma Soc. Roman Catholic (mem. Bishop's Bd. Govs., Buffalo diocese 1951—). Clubs: K.C. (4 deg.). Home: 26 Pine Ter Orchard Park NY 14127-3928 Office: Ste 700 69 Delaware Ave Buffalo NY 14202-3866

JASHEL, LARRY STEVEN (L. STEVEN ROSE), entrepreneur, media consultant; b. Dayton, Ohio, Jan. 21, 1950; s. Joseph John and Ruth Margarete (Race) J. Student, Harper Coll., Palatine, Ill., 1968-70. Pub.'s asst. Pub.'s Devel. Corp., Chgo., 1971-73; pub. rels. dir. Ill. Entertainer/Chgo. Star/Bankers' Guide, Chgo., 1973-76; v.p. Internat. Media Prodns., Inc., Chgo., 1976-78, Microdynamics Corp., Chgo., 1978-80; exec. v.p. Calif. Aqua Tech, Inc., The Solar Generation, L.A., 1980-82; pres., CEO Ra-Tel Comms. Corp., Ra-Tel Entertainment Corp./Cable Radio, Chgo., 1982-88; founder Steven Rose Prodns. and L.S. Jashel Assocs., Chgo., 1988-98; founder, CEO Spuppets, Ltd., 1996, Children's Cultural Network, 1998—; exec. dir. Superior Benefit Solutions, 1998—; TV producer, dir., writer Ind. Broadcasting, Chgo., 1982—; radio producer, on-air personality Nat. Pub. Radio, Chgo. and Washington, 1982—, WJRC-AM, Chgo., 1987-88; music producer for ind. rec. artists, Chgo., 1982—; cons. Corp. for Pub. Broadcasting, 1982—; speaker in field. Musician, singer, composer 177 copyrighted songs; author: Song of a New Age, 1990, A Bakers Dozen, 1995; (book and TV script) Lovestar--The Exciting Adventures, 1994-95; author, producer, director Spuppets (puppets in space), 1997; author: (with others) Morning Song, 1997, The Best Poems of 1997; (book) Planet Medieval, 1998; (musical acts) The Detours, Sudden, The Amboy Dukes, The Yellow Brick Road, J.J. Lee and the Radiants, 1964-72. Recipient Blue Ribbon Athlete award, Midwest Sports Assn., 1968, Film Festival award 1984, Am. Svc. award Am. Svc. Corp., 1988, Editor's Choice award Nat. Libr. Poetry, 1992, Nat./Internat. award of Distinction for children's video and packaging, 1998, Videographer award, 1998; named delegation rep. to Presdl. Inauguration Ball, Washington, 1980. Mem. Am. Soc. of Composers, Artist and Pubs. (award 1998-99), Nat. Assn. Rec. Arts and Scis. (Grammy awards 1982, 87—), Nat. Assn. Pvt. Enterprise, Smithsonian Instn. (nat. assoc.), Nat. Cable TV Assn., Internat. Assn. Bus., Eckankar, Children's Entertainment Assn. Avocations: writing for children, bicycling, camping, hiking. Office: Steven Rose Prodns 15519-B Keating Ave Oak Forest IL 60452

JASICA, ANDREA LYNN, investor, former mortgage banking executive; b. Orlando, Fla., Aug. 21, 1945; d. Walter S. and Florence E. Jasica. AA in Pre Bus. Adminstrn. cum laude, Orlando Jr. Coll., 1965; BS with honors, Rollins Coll., 1976. Sec. Am. Mortgage Co. Fla. Inc., Orlando, 1965-68; closing specialist Charter Mortgage Co., Orlando, 1968-70, Gen. Guaranty Mortgage Co. Inc., Winter Park, Fla., 1971; sr. loan processor C.E. Brooks Mortgage Co. Inc., Orlando, 1971-79; v.p. mktg. Twin Homes Ltd., Orlando, 1980-83; asst. v.p., mgr. region Atlantic Mortgage and Investment Corp. subs. Atlantic Nat. Bank, Orlando, 1984-86; v.p. Commerce Nat. Mortgage Co., Winter Park, 1987-88; supr. Bur. of Census, U.S. Dept. Commerce, Orlando, 1990; investor, 1990—; real estate assoc. Atlantic-to-Gulf Realty Inc., 1972-73, Medel Inc., Maitland, Fla., 1973-74; instr. Mortgage Personnel Svcs. Inc. Contbr. articles to profl. jours. Home: 1011 E Harwood St Orlando FL 32803-5706

JASIEWICZ, RONALD CLARENCE, anesthesiologist, educator; b. Suffern, N.Y., June 8, 1964; s. Clarence William and Adele Helen (Rucki) J. AAS in Sci., Math., SUNY, Rockland, 1984; BS in Life Sci., N.Y. Inst. Tech., 1987; DO, N.Y. Coll. Osteo. Medicine, 1992; AAS in Emergency Med. Tech., SUNY, Rockland, 1993. Diplomate Nat. Bd. Osteo. Med. Examiners, AM. Bd. Anesthesiologists. Unit asst. Good Samaritan Hosp., Suffern, 1980-87; paramedic Empress Ambulance Svc., Yonkers, N.Y., 1985-86, Nyack (N.Y.) E.M.S., 1986-87; intern in medicine and surgery Wilson Meml. Regional Med. Ctr., Johnson City, N.Y., 1992-93; asst. clin. instr. Stony Brook (N.Y.) Med. Sch., 1993-96; resident in anesthesiology Univ. Med. Ctr., 1993-96; fellow pediatric anesthesiology Children's Hosp. of Buffalo, 1996-97; clin. instr. Buffalo Med. Sch., 1996-97; pediatric anesthesiologist U. Med. Ctr. Stony Brook, N.Y., 1997—; asst. prof. anesthesiology SUNY Sch. Medicine, Stony Brook, 1997—; mem. admission com. SUNY Stony Brook Med. Sch., 1998—, also treas. Bd. mgrs., treas. Stonington at Port Jefferson-Condominium II, 1998—; bd. dirs. Stonington at Port Jefferson HOA, 1998—. Med. corps. U.S. Naval Res., 1998—. Am. Osteo. Coll. Anesthesiologists, Am. Osteo. Assn., Sigma Omicron. Roman Catholic. Avocations: downhill skiing, travel, rollerblading, physical fitness, the arts. Home: 69 Commodore Cir Port Jefferson Station NY 11776-2298 Office: U Med Ctr at Stony Brook Dept Pediatric Anes Stony Brook NY 11794-8480

JASINSKI-CALDWELL, MARY L., company executive; b. Chester, Pa., May 8, 1959; d. A. Robert and Helen M. Jasinski; m. William A. Caldwell, Aug. 4, 1990; children: Helaina M., Anna L. Student, Loyola Coll., Balt., 1980; BS, Goldey Beacom Coll., Wilmington, Del., 1983. Registered orthotic fitter; cert. sr. pharmacy technician. Gen. mgr. pension plan City Pharmacy of Elkton (Md.), Inc., 1975-96, treas., 1987-96, jr. ptnr., 1994, v.p., 1996—; founder, pres. City Home Health Care, Inc., Elkton, 1997—; disc jockey, promoter Garfield's Restaurant, Elkton; editl. writer local newspapers; pro-life columnist KC newsletter. Creator ednl. program PARTICIP.A.A.T.E For Life. Bd. dirs. Cecil County chpt. ARC, 1996—, Mission Am., Inc., Md. Right to Life, 1993-94, co-chair Cecil County chpt.; adv. Cecil County Pregnancy Ctr., Cecil County Bd. Edn. Textbook Adoption Policy Com., 1995; pro-life educator City Pharmacy of Elkton, Inc. Speaker of March For Life of Md., 1997-98, Md. Pub. TV, 1997. Alpha Chi scholar, Lindback scholar; recipient J.W. Miller award, Outstanding Achievement in Excellence award K.C., 1994, named Family of Yr., 1995; named to Honor Roll of Best 250 Independents in U.S., Drug Topics, 1992. Mem. NAFE, Am. Mgmt. Assn., Nat. Fedn. Ind. Bus., Am. Assn. Pharm. Technicians, Nat. Right to Life Com., Am. Life League, Internat. Platform Assn., Pro-Life Md., Christian Coalition, Cath. Alliance, Cecil County C. of C., Stopp Internat., Human Life Internat., Concerned Women for Am., Movement for a Better Am., Pharmacists for Life, Goldey Beacom Coll. Alumni Assn., Movement for a Better America, Alpha Chi. Republican. Roman Catholic. Avocations: home improvement, gardening, social concerns, pro-life education, reading. Office: City Pharmacy Inc 723 N Bridge St Elkton MD 21921-5398

JASIORKOWSKI, ROBERT LEE, real estate broker, computer consultant; b. Milw., Nov. 17, 1954; s. Thomas Joseph and Alice Rosemary (Lee) J. BA, U. Wis., Milw., 1987. Real estate broker, info. sys. mgr., property mgr. Nat. Realty Mgmt., Inc., Milw., 1990—; real estate broker ERA Worth Realty, Inc., Glendale, Wis., 1991-94; computer cons. Hometrak Realty, Milw., 1986-90. Mem. Nat. Assn. Realtors, Nat. Assn. Real Estate Appraisers (cert.), U. Wis.-Milw. Alumni Assn. (life). Republican. Avocations: photography, astronomy. Home: 3561 S Honey Creek Dr Milwaukee WI 53220-1246 Office: Nat Realty Mgmt Inc 1155 Quail Ct Pewaukee WI 53072-3703

JASKIEWICZ, DAVID WALTER, optometrist; b. Beaver Falls, Pa., Aug. 28, 1956; s. Walter John and Edith Marie (Maljevec) J.; m. Cynthia Marie Frederick, Sept. 22, 1984; 1 child, Calista Marie Frederick-Jaskiewicz. BSME, U. Notre Dame, 1978; BS in Gen. Scis., Pa. Coll. Optometry, Phila., 1980, OD, 1983. Lic. optometrist, Pa. Assoc. Optometric Care, Aliquppa, Pa., 1983-85; assoc., jr. ptnr. Eye Care Assocs., Erie, Pa., 1985-88; assoc. Pearle Vision, Pitts., 1988-90; owner Valley Vision Ctr., Monaca, Pa., 1990-92; assoc. Walmart Vision Ctr., Monaca, 1992—; chairperson Walmart Optometric Adv. Bd. Mem. U. Notre Dame Alumni Club (Pitts. chpt.). Roman Catholic. Avocations: swimming, biking, hiking, reading, music. Home: 340 Pinkerton Rd Wexford PA 15090-8678 Office: Rt 18 Monaca PA 15061

JASKOT, JOHN JOSEPH, insurance company executive; b. Allentown, Pa., Dec. 5, 1921; s. George W. and Anna (Kuzma) J.; m. Joyce Ranck, May 25, 1946; children: Lisa Anne, Philip Ross. Student, Muhlenberg Coll., Allentown, 1947-49; J.D. with honors, George Washington U., 1951, LL.M., 1953. Bar: D.C. 1951. Exec. v.p., gen. counsel, corp. sec. United Svcs. Life Ins. Co., Washington, 1953-88; v.p., legal counsel United Svcs. Gen. Life Co., 1968-87; v.p. Bankers Security Life Ins. Soc., 1985-88, also bd. dirs.; sec. Provident Life Ins. Co., 1983-86, United Olympic Life Ins. Co., 1984-86; sec., sr. v.p. USLICO Corp., 1984-88; ret., 1988. With USCGR, 1942-46, PTO. Mem. Am. Arbitration Assn. (arbitrator 1988—). Home: 15101 Interlachen Dr # 920 Silver Spring MD 20906-5620 *True success should only be measured by an individual's own assessment of his accomplishments.*

JASKULA, JANET, pediatrics nurse, educator; b. Chgo., Mar. 9, 1951; d. John J. and Katheryn O. (Cheatham) J. Diploma, Ill. Masonic Med. Ctr., Chgo., 1973; BSN cum laude, Sonoma State U., Rohnert Park, Calif., 1983; MS, U. Calif., San Francisco, 1986. Cert. pub. health nurse. Staff nurse Rush Med. Ctr., Chgo., 1973-75, Kentfield (Calif.) Hosp., 1976-78, R.K. Davies Hosp., San Francisco, 1978-80, Marin Gen. Hosp., Greenbrae, Calif., 1983-86; clin. nurse in pediatrics U. Calif., San Francisco, 1980-86, clin. nurse III, in pediatric surgery, 1986-94, asst. clin. prof. dept. family health care nursing; pediatric clin. instr. Coll. San Mateo, Calif., 1994—; clin. specialist pediatric nephrology U. Calif., San Francisco, 1995—. Mem. Calif. Nurses Assn., Golden Gate Nurses Assn., U. Calif. San Francisco Nursing Alumni Assn., Sigma Theta Tau.

JASMIN, GAETAN, pathologist, retired educator; b. Montreal, Que., Can., Nov. 24, 1924; s. Horace and Antoinette (Piquette) J.; m. Suzanne Dupont, Oct. 18, 1952; children: Eve, Luc, Pierre. B.A., Coll. St. Laurent, 1945; M.D., U. Montreal, 1951, Ph.D., 1956. Intern Hotel Dieu, Montreal, 1950; asst. prof. exptl. medicine U. Montreal, 1952-55, prof., 1955—, chmn. dept. pathology, 1970-82, now emeritus prof.; research assoc. Md. Research Council Can., 1958-69. Bd. dirs. J.F. Morgan Found. Mem. Soc. Exptl. Biology and Medicine, Am. Physiol. Soc., Can. Soc. Clin. Investigation, Histochem. Soc., Muscular Dystrophy Assn. Can., Fedn. Can. Socs. Biology, Cercle Français Pathologie Ultrastructurale, Royal Coll. Physicians and Surgeons Can., Internat. Acad. Pathology. Office: U Montreal Dept Path Faculty Med, PO Box 6128, Montreal, PQ Canada H3C 3J7

JASNY, GEORGE ROMAN, retired energy company executive; b. Katowice, Poland, June 6, 1924; came to U.S., 1940; s. Maurice and Irene (Heiman) J.; m. Gloria Jane Jones, June 23, 1951 (dec. 1998); children—Elizabeth Pruitt, Thomas Paul; m. Martha Adler, Jan. 9, 1999. B.S.Ch.E., U. Wash., 1949; M.S.Ch.E., MIT, 1952. Mem. tech. staff Union Carbide Nuclear Div., Oak Ridge, 1950-73; dir. engring. Union Carbide Nuclear Div., 1973-80, v.p. engring. and computing, 1980-84; v.p. tech. ops. Martin Marietta Energy Systems, Inc., Oak Ridge, 1984-89; ret., 1989; mem. bd. engring. advisors Tenn. Tech. U., Cookeville; past mem. engring. adv. coun. U. Tenn., Knoxville, 1985. Past chmn. bd. dirs. Meth. Med. Ctr. Oak Ridge, 1985; chmn. bd. dirs. Oak Ridge Utility Dist.; past chmn. Meth. Hosp. Found., Pellissippi State Tech. Comm. Coll. Found. With USN, 1943-46, PTO. Fellow AIChE (Robert E. Wilson award); mem. NAE, Am. Soc. Engring. Mgmt. (pres. 1984), Sigma Xi, Tau Beta Pi. Democrat. Lodge: Rotary. Avocations: reading; hiking; jogging; gardening. Home: 128 Indian Ln Oak Ridge TN 37830-4044

JASON, J. JULIE, money manager, author, lawyer; b. Owensboro, Ky., May 14, 1949; d. Richard and Grazina Pauliukonis; m. Marius J. Jason, Dec. 19, 1970; children: Ilona, Leila. BA, Baldwin-Wallace Coll., 1971; JD, Cleve. State U., 1974; LLM, Columbia U., 1975. Bar: Ohio 1974, N.Y. 1976, U.S. Dist Ct. (so. dist.) N.Y. 1976, U.S. Ct. Appeals (2d cir.) 1976, U.S. Supreme Ct. 1978. Pvt. practice N.Y.C., 1974-78; asst. gen. counsel Paine Webber, N.Y.C., 1978-83; pres. P.W. Trust and Paine Webber Futures Mgmt. Co., N.Y.C., 1983-88; sr. fin. svcs. atty. Donovan, Leisure, Newton & Irvine, N.Y.C., 1988-89; co-founder, mng. dir. Jackson, Grant & Co., Stamford, Conn., 1989—; arbitrator NYSE; mediator U.S. Bankruptcy Ct., 1997. Author: You and Your 401(K), 1996, The 401(K) Plan Handbook, 1997; weekly columnist "401-OK" Times Mirror Publ., 1998—. Mem. ABA, AAUW (chair scholarship com. 1992-93), Nat. Assn. Securities Dealers (cert. arbitrator, cert. mediator), Am. Soc. Journalists & Authors, Investment Co. Inst. (sec. regulation com. 1978-83), The Corp. Bar, Columbia U. Alumni Club of Fairfield County (pres. 1993-94, chair pres.'s coun. 1994-96). Office: Jackson Grant & Co 1177 High Ridge Rd Stamford CT 06905-1211

JASON, MARY L., librarian; b. Aug. 2, 1959. Adminstrv. libr. Bradford (Ill.) Libr. Dist., 1991—; kindergarten tchr., supv. Country Christian Acad., Bradford, Ill., 1996—. Home: 111 S Peoria St Bradford IL 61421

JASON, PHILIP KENNETH, English language educator; b. N.Y.C., Dec. 25, 1941; s. Leon Abraham and Esther (Bookbinder) J.; m. Ruth Epstein, Jan. 28, 1962; children: Hope Jason Bell, Daniel. BA, New Sch., N.Y.C., 1963; MA, Georgetown U., 1965; PhD, U. Md., 1971. From instr. to asst. prof. Georgetown U., Washington, 1966-73; from asst. to full prof. U.S. Naval Acad., Annapolis, Md., 1973—; bd. dirs. The Writer's Ctr., Bethesda, Md. Author: (poetry) Thawing Out, 1979, Near the Fire, 1983, The Separation, 1995, (anthologies) Anais Nin Reader, 1973, Shaping: New Poems in Traditional Prosodies, 1978, Fourteen Landing Zones: Approaches to Vietnam War Literature, 1991, The Critical Response to Anais Nin, 1996, Open Door: A Poet Lore Anthology 1980-96, 1997, Retrieving Bones: Stories and Poems of the Korean War, 1999; editor Poet Lore, 1979—; contbr. articles to profl. jours. Mem. MLA, Popular Culture Assn. Home: 12823 Valewood Dr Naples FL 34119-8502 Office: US Naval Acad English Dept 107 Maryland Ave Annapolis MD 21402-1316

JASPERSEN, FREDERICK ZARR, economist; b. Phila., Sept. 23, 1938; s. Frederick Franklin and Jean Lorraine (Zarr) J.; m. Margie C. Trainor, Oct. 10, 1965. B.A. in Internat. Relations, Dartmouth Coll., 1961; M.A. Peace Corps fellow, Ind. U., 1965, Ph.D. in Econs., 1969. Mem. Peace Corps, Colombia, 1961-63; teaching asst. fellow Ind. U., Bloomington, 1964-65; Harvard U. econ. advisor Ministry Fin., Chile, 1968-69; economist Standard Oil N.J., N.Y.C., 1969-70, Am. Embassy Brazil, 1970-71; sr. economist World Bank, Washington, 1978-86, lead economist macroecon. adjustment policy and growth, 1987-91; chief devel. policy rsch. divsn. Inter-Am. Devel. Bank, Washington, 1991-95; sr. advisor Internat. Fin. Corp., Washington, 1995-98; dir. Latin Am. Inst. of Internat. Fin., Washington, 1999—; lectr. econs. Chile, Brazil, Ind. U. Contbr. author: World Development Report, 1981, Adjustment Experience and Growth Prospects of the Semi-Industrial Countries, 1981; co-editor: Pathways to Growth: Comparing Latin America and East Asia, 1997. V.p. Sidwell Friends Sch. Alumni Assn., 1978-80. Ford Found. Latin Am. teaching fellow Fletcher Sch., Tufts U., 1967-68. Mem. Am. Econ. Assn., World Affairs Coun. Clubs: Dartmouth (Washington), Cosmos (Washington). Home: 5013 Randall Ln Bethesda MD 20816-1959 Office: 1818 H St NW Washington DC 20433-0001

JASSO, GUILLERMINA, sociologist, educator; b. Laredo, Tex., July 22, 1942; d. José Jasso-Rodríguez and Guillermina de los Santos-Lozano. BA, Our Lady of the Lake Coll., 1962; MA, U. Notre Dame, 1970; PhD, Johns Hopkins U., 1974. Asst. prof. Barnard Coll. and Columbia U., N.Y.C., 1974-77; spl. asst. to commr. U.S. Immigration and Naturalization Svc., Washington, 1977-79; dir. rsch. U.S. Select Commn. on Immigration and Refugee Policy, Washington, 1979-80; asst. prof. U. Mich., Ann Arbor, 1980-82; assoc. prof. U. Minn., Mpls., 1982-86, prof., 1986-87; prof., dir. theory workshop U. Iowa, Iowa City, 1987-91; prof. NYU, N.Y.C., 1991—, dir. methods workshop, 1991-97; mem. study sect. on social sci. and population NIH, 1991-95; mem. U.S. Com. for Internat. Inst. for Applied Sys. Analysis, 1993—; mem. various programs NSF, 1987-96, 98-99; mem. panel on demographic and econ. impacts of immigration NAS, 1995-97; mem. population rsch. subcom. Nat. Inst. Child Health and Human Devel., NIH, 1998—; vis. prof. Zentrum Umfragen, Methoden, und Analysen, Mannheim, Germany, 1995, U. Leipzig, Germany, 1996; mem. core rsch. team bination study on migration between Mex. and U.S., U.S. Commn. on Immigration Reform, 1995-97; mem. editl. bd. Social Justice Rsch., 1985—, Jour. Math. Sociology, 1985—; dep. editor Am. Sociol. Rev., 1996-99; disting. alumni lectr. U. Notre Dame, 1987; univ. pub. lectr. Our Lady of the Lake U., 1989. Author: The New Chosen People, 1990; contbr. articles to profl. jours. Grantee Russell Sage Found., 1983-85, Rockefeller Found., 1985-86, NSF, 1994-97, NIH, 1995-99; fellow Ctr. for Advanced Study in Behavioral Scis., Stanford, Calif., 1999—. Fellow Johns Hopkins Soc. Scholars; mem. Am. Sociol. Assn. (chair internat. migration sect. 1996-99, chair theory sect. 1996-99), Sociol. Rsch. Assn. E-mail: gjl@is3.nyu.edu. Office: NYU Dept Sociology 269 Mercer St 4th Fl New York NY 10003-0831

JASSO, WILLIAM GATTIS, public relations executive; b. Akron, Ohio, Mar. 2, 1953; s. Joseph and Jean E. (Gattis) J.; m. Jeanne Marie Taylor, Aug. 20, 1977; 1 child, Megan Elizabeth. BA in Communications, U. Akron; student Crisis Mgmt. Sch. and Advanced Pub. Affairs Sch., Fed. Emergency Mgmt. Agy.; student, Mich. State Sch. Bus., 1993. News dir. Sta. WHLO, Akron, 1972-81; news anchor, editor Sta. WNEO-TV, Northeast Ohio, 1978-81; govt. affairs mgr. Warner Cable Communications, Dublin, Ohio, 1981-83, corp. dir. pub. rels., 1983-85; v.p. communications Nat. Golf. Found., Jupiter, Fla., 1985-88; asst. to mayor City of Akron, 1988-94; dir. govt. affairs and media rels. Time Warner Cable N.E. Ohio, Akron, 1994-95; dir. pub. affairs Time Warner Cable N.E. Ohio, 1995-96; v.p. pub. affairs, 1996—; guest lectr. U. Akron, Kent State U., 1988—; pub. rels. chmn. Ohio Sports Fest, 1988-90; motivator Youth Motivation Task Force, Akron, 1989—; City of Akron liaison NEC World Series of Golf, 1988-94; nat. selection panel mem. Golf Digest 100 Best Golf Courses in U.S., 1987—; organizer 1st Golf Summit, Westchester C. of C., N.Y., 1986;

producer nat. launch Time Warner Inc.'s Road Runner high-speed online svc., 1996. Editor: Golf Curriculum Kit, 1987, Golf Driving Range Manual, 1987, (mag.) GolfMarket Today, 1986-88, The Spirit of Akron, 1989; producer, reporter (documentary) John Lennon--Beatle Without A Country, 1975. Committeeman Great Trail coun. Boys Scouts Am., 1989-91; trustee All-Am. Soap Box Derby, Canton Cmty. Forum; mem. 1993-94 class Leadership Akron; bd. dirs. Akron Child Guidance Ctr., 1995—; mem. pub. affairs com. Akron Regional Devel. Bd. Recipient 6 awards AP, 1975-81, 8 awards Akron Press Club, 1974-81, 4 Image awards Ohio Cable TV Assn., 1994-99. Mem. Pub. Rels. Soc. Am. (accredited pres. Akron chpt. 1990-91, Presdl. Citation award 1993), Cable TV Pub. Affairs Assn. (2 Beacon awards 1994-99). Avocations: golf, writing, public speaking, guitar. Office: Time Warner Cable NE Ohio 530 S Main St Ste 1751 Akron OH 44311-1090

JASSY, EVERETT LEWIS, lawyer; b. N.Y.C., Feb. 4, 1937; s. David H. and Florence A. (Pollak) J.; m. Margery Ellen Rose; children: Katherine Savitt Lennon, Andrew Ralph, Jonathan Scott. AB, Harvard U., 1957, JD, 1960. Bar: N.Y. 1960, D.C. 1975. Assoc. Dewey Ballantine, N.Y.C., 1960-68, ptnr., 1968—, chmn. mgmt. com., 1996—. Mem. ABA, N.Y. State Bar Assn., Assn. of Bar of City of N.Y., The Tax Club, Harmonie Club (bd. govs. 1999—), Fairview Country Club, Washington Athletic Club. Avocations: golf, travel. Home: 20 Tompkins Rd Scarsdale NY 10583-2838 Office: Dewey Ballantine LLP 1301 Avenue Of The Americas New York NY 10019-6022

JASTROW, ROBERT, physicist; b. N.Y.C., Sept. 7, 1925; s. Abraham and Marie (Greenfield) J. A.B., Columbia, 1944, M.A., 1945, Ph.D., 1948; postdoctoral fellow, Leiden U., 1948-49, Princeton Inst. Advanced Study, 1949-50, 53, U. Calif. at Berkeley, 1950-53; D.Sc. (hon.), Manhattan Coll., 1980, N.J. Inst. Tech., 1987. Asst. prof. Yale, 1953-54; cons. nuclear physics U.S. Naval Research Lab., Washington, 1958-62; head theoretical div. Goddard Space Flight Center NASA, 1958-61, chmn. lunar exploration com., 1959-60, mem. com., 1960-62; dir. Goddard Inst. Space Studies, N.Y.C., 1961-81; adj. prof. geology Columbia, 1961-81, dir. Summer Inst. Space Physics, 1962-70; adj. prof. astronomy Columbia (Summer Inst. Space Physics), 1977-82; adj. prof. earth sci. Dartmouth, 1973-92; pres. G.C. Marshall Inst., 1985—; dir., chmn. of bd. Mt. Wilson Inst., 1991—. Author: The Evolution of Stars, Planets and Life, 1967, Astronomy: Fundamentals and Frontiers, 1972, Until the Sun Dies, 1977, God and the Astronomers, 1978, 2d edit., 1992, Red Giants-White Dwarfs, 1991, The Enchanted Loom, 1981, How To Make Nuclear Weapons Obsolete, 1985, Journey to the Stars, 1989; editor: Exploration of Space, 1960; co-editor: Jour. Atmospheric Scis., 1962-74, The Origin of the Solar System, 1963, The Venus Atmosphere, 1969. Recipient Medal of Excellence Columbia, 1962, Grad. Faculties Alumni award, 1967; Arthur S. Flemming award, 1965; medal for exceptional sci. achievement NASA, 1968. Fellow Am. Geophys. Union, A.A.A.S., Am. Phys. Soc.; mem. Internat. Acad. Astronautics, Council Fgn. Relations, Leakey Found., Nat. Space Soc. (bd. govs.). Clubs: Cosmos, Explorers, Century. Office: Mt Wilson Observatory Hale Solar Lab 740 Holladay Rd Pasadena CA 91106-4115

JASZAROWSKI, KELLY ANN, nurse, enterostomal therapy specialist; b. N.J., Jan. 9, 1962; d. Michael Thomas and Karen Bernice (Frosco) Foran; m. James Keith Jaszarowski, June 30, 1984; children: Patrick James, Eric Daniel, Angela Marie. Diploma, Jewish Hosp. Sch. Nursing, St. Louis, 1983; BSN with honors, Sangamon State U., 1989; diploma in enterostomal therapy, Abbott Northwestern Program, Mpls., 1990; MSN in Primary Healthcare, Ind. U. Cert. enterostomal therapist, 1990. Staff nurse Jewish Hosp. St. Louis; staff nurse ICU/CCU St. Francis Med. Ctr., Peoria, Ill., enterostomal therapy nurse; nurse specialist in enterostomal therapy Lafayette (Ind.) Home Hosp.; mem. faculty Ind. U., Purdue U., Spoon River Coll., Ill. Mem. ANA, Ill. State Nurses Assn., Wound, Ostomy and Continence Nurses Soc., United Ostomy Assn., Sigma Theta Tau.

JASZCZAK, RONALD JACK, physicist, researcher, consultant; b. Chicago Heights, Ill., Aug. 23, 1942; s. Jacob and Julia (Gudowicz) J.; m. Nancy Jane Bober, Apr. 15, 1967; children: John, Monica. BS with highest honors, U. Fla., 1964, PhD, 1968. Staff physicist Oak Ridge Nat. 1969-71, AEC postdoctoral fellow, 1968-69; prin. rsch. scientist Searle Diagnostics, Inc., 1971-73, sr. prin. rsch. scientist, 1973, rsch. group leader, 1973-77, chief scientist, 1977-79; assoc. prof. radiology Duke U. Med. Ctr., Durham, N.C., 1979-89, prof., 1989—, assoc. prof. biomedical engring., 1986-91, prof., 1992—; rsch. prof. Inst. of Stats. and Decision Scis., 1992-93; founder, chmn. bd. dirs. Data Spectrum Corp., Hillsborough, N.C.; investigator Nat. Cancer Inst. Grant, 1983—, Dept. Energy Grant, 1989—. Contbr. articles to profl. jours.; patentee in field. Fellow NASA, 1964-67, U. Fla., 1967-68; RCA scholar, 1963-64. Fellow IEEE; mem. IEEE Nuclear and Plasma Scis. Soc. (pres. 1997—), Soc. Nuclear Medicine, Am. Phys. Soc., AAAS, Am. Assn. Physicists in Medicine, Soc. Photo-Optical Instrumentation Engrs., Sigma Xi, Phi Beta Kappa, Phi Kappa Phi, Tau Sigma, Sigma Pi Sigma. Home: 2307 Honeysuckle Rd Chapel Hill NC 27514-1716 Office: Duke U Med Ctr DUMC 3949 Durham NC 27710

JATLOW, PETER I., pathologist, medical educator, researcher; b. New Brunswick, N.J., Feb. 12, 1936; s. Daniel and Anne (Davis) J.; m. Stephanie Bea Yager, Dec. 22, 1959; children—Allison, Julia. B.S., Union Coll., Schenectady, 1957; M.D., SUNY Downstate Med. Ctr., Bklyn., 1961; M.S. (hon.), Yale U., 1976. Intern Montefiore Hosp., Bronx, N.Y., 1961-62; resident Yale-New Haven Hosp., 1962-66; asst. prof. lab. medicine Yale U., New Haven, 1968-73, assoc. prof. lab. medicine, 1973-76, prof. lab. medicine, 1976—, chmn. dept. lab. medicine, 1984—; cons. FDA, Washington, 1978-82; mem. biomed. research rev. com. USPHS, Nat. Inst. Drug Abuse, Rockville, Md., 1982-86; mem. test material deve. subcom. FLEX Program Nat. Bd. Med. Exam., Philly, 1990-91. Editor: Methodology in Analytical Toxicology, vol. II, 1982; editorial bd. Clin. Chemistry, 1973-83, Selected methods in Clin. Chemistry, 1976-79, Jour. Analytical Toxicology, 1978-79, Therapeutic Drug Monitoring, 1979-86, 90—, Clinica Chimica Acta, 1984-90, Am. Jour. Clin. Pathology, 1988—; contbr. numerous articles to profl. jours. Served to surgeon USPHS, 1966-68. Recipient Irving Sunshine award in clin. toxicology Internat. Assn. Therapeutic Drug Monitoring and Toxicology, 1993. Fellow Coll. Am. Pathologists; mem. AAAS, Acad. Clin. Lab. Physicians and Scientists (pres. 1983-84, Gerald T. Evans award 1988), Am. Soc. Clin. Pathology, Am. Assn. Clin. Chemistry (award for outstanding contbns. to clin. chemistry in selected area of rsch. 1985, award for outstanding contbns. in edn. 1995). Home: 617 Saddle Ridge Rd Orange CT 06477-2024 Office: Yale U Sch Medicine Dept Lab Medicine 333 Cedar St Dept Lab New Haven CT 06510-3289

JAUDES, RICHARD EDWARD, lawyer; b. St. Louis, Feb. 22, 1943; s. Leo August Jr. and Dorothy Catherine (Schmidt) J.; m. Mary Kay Tansey, Sept. 22, 1967; children: Michele, Pamela. BS, St. Louis U., 1965, JD, 1968. Bar: Mo. Supreme Ct. 1968, U.S. Dist. Ct. (ea. dist.) Mo. 1973, U.S. Ct. Appeals (8th cir.) 1973, U.S. Supreme Ct. 1990. With Peper, Martin, Jensen, Maichel & Hetlage, St. Louis, 1973-97, mng. ptnr., 1990-93; lawyer, co-chair labor and employment practice group Thompson Coburn, St. Louis, 1997—, mem. mgmt. com. Vol. Civic Entrepreneurs Orgn., St. Louis, 1990; vol. counsel St. Louis chpt. MS Soc., 1990, exec. com. Lt. USN, 1968-73; comdr. USNR, ret. Office: Thompson Coburn One Mercantile Ctr Saint Louis MO 63101-1693

JAUDES, WILLIAM E., retired lawyer; b. St. Louis, 1937; s. August William and Gertrude Johanna (Simon) J.; m. Carol Joan Hurtgen, June 30, 1961; children: Phyllis Anne, Richard William, Suzanne Louise. AB, U. Mo., 1958; JD, St. Louis U., 1962, MBA, 1969. Bar: Mo. 1962, Ill. 1964, U.S. Dist. Ct. (ea. dist.) Mo. 1962, U.S. Supreme Ct. 1966, U.S. Ct. Appeals (8th cir.) 1980. Atty. Union Electric Co., St. Louis, 1963-73, gen. atty., 1973-80, gen. counsel, 1980-85, v.p. gen. counsel, 1985-88. Author: introduction to Mo. Bar Assn. book, Adminstrative Law, 1979. Mem. Mo. Bar Assn., Ill. Bar Assn., Am. Corp. Counsels Assn., Edison Electric Inst. Legal Com. Mem. United Grace Ch. Christ. Home: 3873 Holly Hills Blvd Saint Louis MO 63116-3134 Office: American Corporation 1901 Chouteau Ave Saint Louis MO 63103-3003

JAUDON, VALERIE, artist; b. Greenville, Miss., Aug. 6, 1945; d. Baize R. and Gladys E. (Hill) J.; m. Richard Kalina, Oct. 23, 1979. Student, Miss. State Coll. for Women, 1963-65, Memphis Acad. Art, 1965, U. of Americas, Mexico, 1966-67, St. Martins Sch. Art, London, 1968-69. One-woman shows of paintings include, Holly Solomon Gallery, N.Y.C., 1977-79, 81, Pa. Acad. Fine Arts, Phila., 1977, Galerie Bishofberger, Zurich, Switzerland, 1979, Galerie Hans Strelow, Dusseldorf, Fed. Republic Germany, 1980, Corcoran Gallery, Los Angeles, 1981, Sidney Janis Gallery, N.Y.C., 1983, 85, 86, 88, 90, 93, 96, Quadrat Mus., Bottrop, Fed. Republic Germany, 1983, Amerika Haus, Berlin, 1983, Dart Gallery, Chgo., 1983, Fay Gold Gallery, Atlanta, 1985, Macintosh/Drysdale Gallery, Washington, 1985, Barbara Scott Gallery, Bay Harbor Islands, Fla., 1994, Miss. Mus. Art, Jackson, 1996, Betsy Senior Gallery, N.Y.C., 1998; numerous group shows, earlies being, Mayor Gallery, London, 1979, Galerie Habermann, Cologne, Germany, 1979, Galerie Hans Strelow, Dusseldorf, 1979, Galerie Modern Art, Vienna, Austria, 1980, Mus. Modern Art, Oxford, Eng., 1980, Greenberg, Gallery, St. Louis, 1980, Sidney Janis Gallery, N.Y.C., 1980, San Francisco Art Inst., 1980, Mus. Modern Art, N.Y.C., 1980, Leo Castelli Gallery, N.Y.C., 1980, Thomas Segal Gallery, Boston, 1980, Venice (Italy) Biennale, 1980, Nat. Gallery of Art, Washington, 1980, Chgo. Art Inst., 1981, Mus. Fine Arts, Boston, 1982, Neuberger Mus., Purchase, N.Y., 1982, Hudson River Mus., Yonkers, N.Y., 1983, Berkshire Mus., Pittsfield, Mass., 1983, La Jolla Mus., Calif., 1983, Margo Leavin Gallery, Los Angeles, 1984, Bronx Mus., 1985, Am. Ctr., Paris, 1986, Dayton Art Inst., 1987, Cin. Art Mus., 1989, Tel Aviv Mus. Art, 1992, Robert McClain Gallery, Houston, 1996, Turner/Runyon Gallery, Dallas, 1997; executed ceramic mural Equitable Bldg., N.Y.C., 1988, brick and granite plaza Police Plaza, N.Y.C., 1989; Blue Pools Courtyard Birmingham (Ala.) Mus. Art, 1993; mosaic floor Washington Nat. Airport, 1997; represented in permanent collections including Hirshhorn Mus., Washington, Mus. Modern Art, N.Y.C., Albright-Knox Art Gallery, Buffalo, N.Y., Fogg Art Mus., Cambridge, Mass.,Sammlung-Lugwig Mus., Aachen, Fed. Republic Germany, Dayton (Ohio) Art Inst., National Museum of Women in the Arts, Wash. D.C., St. Louis Art Mus., Ludwig Mus., Budapest, Hungary, Miss. Mus. Art, Jackson. Recipient 1st prize award So. Contemporary Arts Festival, 1967, Art award Miss. Inst. Arts and Letters, 1981, 97, Excellence in Design award N.Y.C. Art Commn., 1988, civic Spirit award Women's City Club of N.Y., Merit award Am. Soc. Landscape Architects Ala. chpt., 1994; N.Y. State CAPS grantee for graphics, 1980; Visual Arts Fellowship grant Nat. Endowment Arts, 1988; N.Y. Found. for Arts grantee in painting, 1992. Address: 795A Accabonac Rd East Hampton NY 11937-1807

JAUDZEMIS, KATHLEEN A., judge; b. Omaha, Nebr., Jan. 18, 1949. BA, Univ. of Nebr., 1971, MA, 1976; JD, Univ. of Nebr. Law Coll., 1982. Bar: Nebr., U.S. Dist. Ct. Nebr., U.S. Ct. Appeals (8th cir.). Tchr. St. Paul pub. schs., Nebr., 1971-74, Lincoln pub. schs., Nebr., 1974-79; atty. Cline, Williams, Wright, Johnson & Oldfather, 1982-91; magistrate judge U.S. Dist. Ct. Nebr., 8th circuit, Omaha, 1992—. Mem. ABA, Nebr. Bar Assn., Fed. Magistrate Judges Assn. Avocations: swimming, reading, travel. Office: Edward Zorinsky Fed Bldg PO Box 336 215 N 17th St Omaha NE 68102-4970

JAVACHEFF, CHRISTO VLADIMIROV See CHRISTO

JAVID, MANUCHER J., retired neurosurgery educator; b. Tehran, Iran, Jan. 11, 1922; came to U.S., 1944, naturalized, 1957; s. Asdolah and Touba (Ahdiyeh) J.; m. Lida Emma Fabbri, Oct. 19, 1951; children—Roxane, Daria, Jeffrey, Claudia. M.D., U. Ill., 1946. Diplomate: Am. Bd. Neurosurgery. Intern Augustana Hosp., Chgo., 1946-47; resident gen. surgery Augustana Hosp., 1947-48, resident neurosurgery, 1948-49; asst. in neuropathology Ill. Neuropsychiat. Inst., Chgo., 1948-49; fellow in neurosurgery Lahey Clinic, Boston, 1949; resident neurosurgery New Eng. Med. Center, Boston, 1950; clin. research fellow neurosurgery Mass. Gen. Hosp., Boston, 1950; asst. resident Mass. Gen. Hosp., 1951, sr. resident neurosurgery, 1952; teaching fellow in surgery Harvard, 1952; instr. Med. Sch. U. Wis., Madison, 1953-54; asst. prof. Med. Sch. U. Wis., 1954-57, asso. prof., 1957-62, prof. neurosurgery, 1962-98, endowed named prof. neurol. surgery, 1998, emeritus prof., 1998—, chmn. dept. neurosurgery, 1963-95; cons. neurosurgeon VA Hosp., Madison, 1956—. Contbr. articles profl. jours. Mem. AMA, ACS, AAUP, AAAS, Soc. Neurol. Surgeons, Am. Assn. Neurol. Surgeons, Am. Assn. Med. Colls., Soc. for Neurosci., Central Neurosurg. Soc. (pres. 1964), Internat. Intradiscal Therapy Soc. (treas. 1987-90, pres.-elect 1990—, pres. 1991), N.Y. Acad. Scis., Xeiron, Sigma Xi, Phi Beta Pi, Alpha Omega Alpha.. Mem. Baha'i Faith. Club: Rotarian. Introduced clin. use of urea for reduction intracranial and intraocular pressure. Home: 4750 Lafayette Dr Madison WI 53705-4865 *Since I was a small child, I wanted to be a doctor and help the sick. As I grew older, the Baha'i Faith, served as a guideline to achieve this goal. Its teachings have helped me to appreciate the oneness of God, the oneness of religion, the oneness of humanity, and the sanctity of life.*

JAVID, NIKZAD SABET, dentist, prosthodontics educator; b. Kashan, Iran, May 24, 1934; s. Salam and Pika (Farhang) Javid-S.; m. Mahnaz Zolfaghari, Oct. 22, 1942; children: Nikrooz, Behrooz, Farnaz. DMD, U. Tehran, Iran, 1958; cert., U. Chgo., 1970; MSc, Ohio State U., 1971; MEd, U. Fla., 1981. Asst. prof. U. Tehran, 1959-69, prof., dean, 1975-79; asst. prof. Ohio State U., 1971-73, assoc. prof., 1973-74; assoc. prof. removable prosthodontics U. Fla., 1974-75, prof., 1982; pvt. practice dentistry specializing in prosthodontics, Gainsville, Fla., 1980—; cons. in field; guest lectr. numerous internat. meetings. Author books, including: Stress Breaker in Partial Denture, 1966, Cleft Palate Prosthetics, 1968, Complete Denture Construction, 1974, (with Sara Nawab) Essentials of Complete Denture Prosthodontics, 1988; contbr. numerous articles to profl. jours. Named Outstanding Clin. Instr. of Yr. Student Dental Council, Columbus, Ohio, 1973, Outstanding Tchr. of Yr. 1990, Excellent Clin. Prof., U. Fla., 1994, Most Outstanding Prof. of Yr., 1996, Disting. Prof. of Yr., 1998. Fellow Internat. Coll. Dentists, Internat. Coll. Prosthodontics, Am. Coll. Prosthodontics, Am. Acad. Maxillofacial Prosthetics, Royal Soc. Health (Eng.); mem. Iranian Dental Assn. (dir. 1975-78), ADA, Internat. Assn. Dental Research (sec.-treas. Iran div. 1978). Lodge: Lions. Home: 3941 NW 67th Pl Gainesville FL 32653-8351 Office: U Fla PO Box 100435 Gainesville FL 32610-0435

JAVITS, ERIC MOSES, lawyer; b. N.Y.C., May 24, 1931; s. Benjamin Abraham and Lily (Braxton) J.; m. Margaretha Espersson, May 24, 1979; children by previous marriage: Jocelyn Ingrid, Eric Moses. Student, Stanford U., 1948-49; A.B., Columbia U., 1952, J.D., 1955. Bar: N.Y. 1955, U.S. Supreme Ct. 1959. Temp. cons. Office Def. Moblzn., Washington, 1951; assoc. firm Javits & Javits, N.Y.C., 1955-58; mem. firm to ptnr. Javits & Javits, 1958-82; sr. ptnr. Javits, Robinson, Brog, Leinwand & Reich, P.C. (and successor firms), 1984-89; cons. to Dept. State, amb.-designate to Venezuela, 1989-90; sr. counsel Robinson, Brog, Leinwand, Reich, Genovese & Gluck, P.C. (and successor firms), 1993—; ind. gen. ptnr. ML Venture Ptnrs., 1982-96; spl. dep. to N.Y. Atty. Gen. Elections Frauds Bur., 1958-59; counsel N.Y. Senate Com. on Affairs of City N.Y., 1959; mem. N.Y.C. Commn. for Protocol, 1994—; bd. dirs. N.Y. State Conv. Ctr. Oper. Corp., 1995—; past dir. N.Y. Stock Exch., Am. Stock Exch., over the counter cos. Author: SOS New York, 1961. Mem. numerous charitable coms.; bd. govs. N.Y. Young Rep. Club, 1955-58, v.p., 1957-58, bd. advisers, 1958-64; trustee French Inst./Alliance Francaise, 1995—, Cardozo Law Sch., 1997—; mem. exec. com. Jacob K. Javits campaigns, 1954-80; mem. N.Y. Rep. County Com., 1960-64; mem. exec. com. Nat. Rep. Club, 1962-70; exec. sec. U.S. Paper Exporters Coun., Inc., 1964-72; mem. bd. Spain-U.S.A. C. of C., 1993—; chmn. emeritus Spanish Inst., N.Y.C.; bd. dirs. Fair Return League, Inc., pres., 1975—; chmn. Republican Eagles, 1996—. Decorated Order of Isabel La Catolica (Spain), 1981, 89; recipient Spanish Inst. Gold medal, 1994. Mem. Assn. Bar City N.Y., New York County Lawyers Assn., Am., N.Y. State bar assns., Nat. Inst. Social Scis., Am. Judicature Soc., World Peace Through Law Center (charter), Phi Beta Kappa, Beta Theta Pi, Phi Alpha Delta, Nacoms. Jewish. Office: 31st Fl 1345 Avenue Of Americas New York NY 10105-0302

JAVITS, JOSHUA MOSES, lawyer; b. N.Y.C., Jan. 2, 1950; s. Jacob Koppel and Marian (Borris) J.; m. Sabina Paula Golding, May 25, 1985. BA, Yale U., 1972; JD, Georgetown U., 1978. Bar: D.C. 1979, Calif. 1983. Trial atty. NLRB, L.A., 1978-83; assoc. Mullholland & Hickey, Washington, 1983-85, Cades, Schutte, Fleming & Wright, Washington, 1985-87; arbitrator Washington, 1985-88; mem., chmn. Nat. Mediation Bd., Wshington, 1988-93; ptnr. Ford & Harrison, Washington, 1993—. Mem. ABA, Indsl. Relations Rsch. Assn., Soc. Fed. Labor Relations Profls., Soc. Profls. in Dispute Resolution. Office: Ford & Harrison 1920 N St NW Ste 200 Washington DC 20036-1623

JAVITT, JONATHAN C., physician, health policy analyst, writer; b. N.Y.C., Nov. 7, 1956; s. Norman B. and Suzanne (Markovits) J.; m. Marcia C. Fishman, June 29, 1986; children: Zachary, Matthew, Gabrielle. AB with honors, Princeton U., 1978; MD, Cornell U., 1982; MPH, Harvard U., 1984. Diplomate Am. Bd. Ophthalmology. Intern Lenox Hill Hosp., N.Y.C., N.Y., 1982-83; resident Wills Eye Hosp., Phila., 1984-87; fellow Johns Hopkins Hosp., Balt., 1988-89; instr. Johns Hopkins U., 1987-90, asst. prof., 1990-99; prof. Johns Hopkins U., Balt., 1999—; asst. prof. Georgetown U., Washington, 1990-93, assoc. prof., 1993-96; prof. Sch. Medicine, prof. sch. Pub. Policy Georgetown U., Washington, Md., 1996—; founder, chmn. Certitude, Inc., Mpls., 1994—; sr. v.p., nat. med. dir. United Health Care/Applied Health Care Informatics, Mpls., 1997-98; chmn., chief tech. officer Health Directions LLC, Bethesda, 1998—; expert cons. Health Care Fin. Adminstrn., Balt., 1987—; spl. employee The White House Health Reform Task Force, Washington, 1992; cons. Nat. Eye Inst./NIH, 1990—, Nat. Inst. Diabetes Digestive and Kidney Disease/NIH, 1991—, Agy. for Health Care Policy Rsch., 1994—, The World Bank, Washington, 1993—, Swedish Coun. on Tech. Improvement, 1997, Japanese Min. of Health, 1993, Australia Min. of Health, 1994—. Editor Archives of Ophthalmology, 1993—, Ophthalmology Times, 1993—; author more than 200 books, chpts., articles; patentee in field. Com. chair Nat. Health Policy Coun., Washington, 1992—; cmty. speaker on health care The White House, 1992—. Recipient Cert. of Appreciation, USAF, 1991, Physician Scientist award Nat. Eye Inst., 1988; U.S. Presdl. Letter of Appreciation, 1993; Kellogg Found. fellow, 1983; guest of honor Japanese Glaucoma Soc., 1996, New England Ophthalmologic Soc., 1997. Fellow Am. Acad. Ophthalmology (Honor award 1990), Am. Glaucoma Soc.; mem. AMA, Assn. for Rsch. in Vision and Ophthalmology, Assn. for Health Svc. Rsch., Am. Glaucoma Soc., Royal Ocean Racing Club. Republican. Jewish. Avocations: sailing, flying. Office: Health Directions LLC 7201 Wisconsin Ave Ste 620 Bethesda MD 20814-4849

JAVITT, NORMAN B., medical educator, researcher; b. N.Y.C., Mar. 9, 1928; s. Bernard and Zara (Hillman) Jakubovitz; m. Suzanne Markovits, June 5, 1955; children: Jonathan Chaim, Daniel Coleman, Joel Israel, Gail Hannah. AB cum laude, Syracuse U., 1947; PhD in Physiology, U. N.C., 1951; MD, Duke U., 1954. Diplomate Am. Bd. Internal Medicine; lic. physician, N.Y. Predoctoral fellow USPHS, Chapel Hill, N.C., 1949-51; intern Mt. Sinai Hosp., N.Y.C., 1954-55, asst. resident, 1957-58, chief resident, 1959-60, Sara Welt fellow in medicine, spl. USPHS, 1961-62; asst. physician, advanced fellow Am. Heart Assn. Vanderbilt Clinic, Columbia Coll. Physicians and Surgeons, N.Y.C., 1957-58; instr. dept. medicine NYU Sch. Medicine, 1962-64, asst. prof., 1964-68; assoc. prof. Cornell U.Med. Coll., N.Y.C., 1968-73, prof., 1973-83; assoc. attending physician N.Y. Hosp., N.Y.C., 1968-73, attending physician, 1973-83; prof. medicine, prof. pediatrics NYU Med. Ctr., N.Y.C., 1983—, dir. divsn. hepatic diseases, 1983—, assoc. dir. clin. rsch. unit, 1985-90; cons. Meml. Sloan-Kettering Cancer Ctr., N.Y.C., 1970-83; vis. prof. Rockefeller U. Hosp., 1970-76; cons. medicine VA Hosp., Bklyn., 1977-83; chief divsn. gastroenterology Cornell-N.Y. Hosp. Med. Ctr., 1973-81, chief divsn. hepatic diseases, acting chief divsn. gastroenterology, 1981-83; cons. Tisch Hosp., NYU Med. Ctr., 1983—; mem. tng. grant study sect. Nat. Inst. Arthritis, Metabolic & Digestive Diseases, NIH, 1978-85; mem. steering com. Nat. Cooperative Gallstone Study, 1973-80, chmn. clin. mgmt. com., 1974-78; gen. medicine study Section A, NIH, 1976-80. Mem. editl. adv. bd. Hosp. Practice, 1969-93; assoc. editor Jour. Lipid Rsch., 1977-78, 86—, editl. bd., 1983—; author, editor 2 books; contbr. articles to profl. jours. Capt., M.C., U.S. Army, 1955-57. Fellow ACP; mem. Am. Physiol. Soc., Am. Soc. Pharmacology and Exptl. Therapeutics, Am. Fedn. Clin. Rsch., Am. Soc. Clin. Investigation, Am. Assn. Study of Liver Disease, Am. Gastroenterol. Assn., Am. Soc. Clin. Pharmacology and Therapeutics, Am. Soc. Biol. Chemists, Am. Pediatric Soc., Am. Soc. Parenteral and Enteral Nutrition, Harvey Soc., Sigma Xi, Alpha Omega Alpha. Jewish. Avocation: grandparenting. Home: 501 E 79th St New York NY 10021-0735 Office: NYU Med Ctr Divsn Hepatic Disease New York NY 10016

JAVORE, GARY WILLIAM, lawyer; b. San Antonio, Apr. 3, 1952; s. Fred Walter and Glennice Jean (Gilbert) J. BA, Kent (Ohio) State U., 1975; JD, Cleve. State U., 1978. Bar: Tex. 1978, U.S. Dist. Ct. (we. dist.) Tex. 1981, U.S. Ct. Appeals (5th cir.) 1981, U.S. Supreme Ct. 1981. Atty. Bexar County Legal Aid, San Antonio, 1979-81; prin. Johnson, Christopher, Javore & Cochran, San Antonio, 1981—; bd. dirs. Bexar County Legal Aid, San Antonio, 1986—. Author, speaker legal seminars. Mem. Leadership San Antonio Class XXIV. Fellow Tex. Bar Found., San Antonio Bar Found.; mem. San Antonio Trial Lawyers Assn. (bd. dirs. 1986—, treas. 1991, pres. 1993, Outstanding Young Lawyer award 1986), Greater San Antonio Builders Assn. (cons., exec. bd. 1990—, v.p. assoc. coun. 1993), Tex. Trial Lawyers Assn., Order of Barristers. Avocations: wood carving, tennis, scuba diving. Office: Johnson Christopher Javore & Cochran 5802 Northwest Expy San Antonio TX 78201-2851

JAW, ANDREW CHUNG-SHIANG, software analyst; b. Tainan, Taiwan, Feb. 10, 1953; came to U.S., 1978; s. Ping-Tsen and Pey-Yuh Jaw; m. Amy Chi, July 30, 1979; children: Andrew, Anfin, Audrey. BS in Mech. Engring., Tatung Inst. Tech., Taipei, Taiwan, 1974; MS in Metallurgical Engring., Poly. Inst. N.Y., 1981; MSEE, Syracuse U., 1987. Engr. Tatung Co., Taipei, 1976-78; sr. assoc. engr. IBM Corp., Endicott, N.Y., 1980-89, Rochester, Minn., 1990-91; software cons. A BOC Health Care Co., Madison, Wis., 1991-92; sr. software engr. A Rockwell Internat. Co., Milw., 1992-94; lead programmer analyst Am. Mobile Satellite Corp., Lincolnshire, Ill., 1998; lead tech. programmer analyst Am. Mobile, 1998—. Patentee in field. Recipient Cert. of Merit, Assembly of the State of N.Y., 1985; rsch. fellow Poly. Inst. N.Y., 1979. Mem. IEEE.

JAY, BURTON DEAN, insurance actuary; b. Sparta, Ill., Jan. 16, 1937; m. Eva May Eudy, Aug. 10, 1958; children—Cynthia Ann, Sylvia Ruth Putnam, Jon Russell. B.A. in Math, Ripon Coll., 1959. Actuarial student Northwestern Nat. Life Ins. Co., Mpls., summers 1957-59; various actuarial positions United of Omaha Life Ins. Co., Omaha, 1962-67, exec. v.p., chief actuary, 1967-91; sen., v.p. actuary Mut. of Omaha Ins. Co., 1991—. Bd. dirs. Omaha Ballet, 1986-95, exec. com., 1988-89, v.p. fin., 1988-89. 1st lt. AUS, 1959-62. Fellow Soc. Actuaries (part VI com. 1967-73, chmn. 1969-73, program com. 1975-80, chmn. 1980, planning com. 1986-88, task force on long term care valuation methods 1991-95, bd. govs. 1982-86, 88-90, v.p. 1985-86, 88-90, chmn. com. on health fin. issues 1993-98); mem. Am. Acad. Actuaries (com. on life ins. fin. reporting principles 1975-82, chmn. 1980-82, bd. dirs. 1981-88, treas. 1983-86, v.p. 1986-88, state health com. 1997—, chmn. health orgn. risk based capital task force 1997—, valuation task force 1997—), Life Ins. Mktg. Rsch. Assn. (fin. mgmt. rsch. com. 1974-78, chmn. 1977-78), Am. Coun. Life Ins. (actuarial com. 1983). Methodist (adminstrv. bd.). Home: 3056 Armbrust Dr Omaha NE 68124-2723 Office: Mutual of Omaha Ins Co Mutual Of Omaha Plz Omaha NE 68175

JAY, CHARLES DOUGLAS, religion educator, college administrator, clergyman; b. Monticello, Ont., Can., Oct. 10, 1925; s. Charles Arthur and Luella Gertrude (McPherson) J.; m. Ruth Helen Crooker, Jan. 30, 1948; children—David, Ian, Garth. B.A., Victoria Coll., U. Toronto, Ont., 1946; M.A., U. Toronto, Ont., 1948; M.Div., Emmanuel Coll., 1950; Ph.D., U. Edinburgh, 1952; D.D. (hon.), Queen's U., 1971, Wycliffe Coll., 1976, Regis Coll., 1980, U. St. Michael's Coll., 1983, Victoria U., 1999. Ordained to ministry United Ch. of Can., 1951. Lectr. dept. philosophy Queen's U., 1946-47; pastor Elk Lake-Matachewan Ch., Ont., 1952-54, Trafalgar-Sheridan Ch., Oakville, Ont., 1954-55; asst. prof. philosophy of religion and Christian ethics Emmanuel Coll. U Toronto, 1955-58, assoc. prof., 1958-63, prof. philosophy of religion and ethics, 1963-91, registrar, 1958-64, prin., 1981-90; prof. emeritus Emmanuel Coll., 1991—; founding dir. Toronto Sch. Theology, 1969-80; R.P. McKay meml. lectr., various univs., colls. across Can., 1966-67; spl. lectr. Hankuk Theol. Sem., Seoul, Korea, 1978, Fed. Theol. Sem., Pietermaritzburg, Republic of South Africa, 1981, Union Sem., Manila and Nanjing Theol. Sem., Nanjing, People's Republic of China, 1991; mem. working group Dialogue with People of Living Faiths and Ideologies, World Council Chs., 1970-83; chmn. div. world outreach United Ch. of Can.,

1975-82; mem. commn. on accreditation Am. Assn. Theol. Schs., 1962-68. Contbr. chpts. to various books. Served with Can. Officers Tng. Corps, 1953-54, as chaplain Royal Can. Navy Res., 1956-59. Decorated Order of Can. Fellow Am. Theol. Schs., 1963. Mem. Assn. Theol. Schs. U.S. and Can. (v.p. 1976-78, pres. 1984-86), Am. Soc. Christian Ethics, Can. Theol. Soc. Office: Emmanuel Coll, 75 Queen's Park Crescent, Toronto, ON Canada M5S 1K7

JAY, CHERYL ANN, neurology educator; b. Nov. 12, 1960. BS in Biochemistry, UCLA, 1982; MD, Columbia U., 1986. Med. staff fellow Nat. Insts. of Health, Bethesda, Md., 1990-92; asst. clin. prof. U. Calif. (Irvine), Dept. of Neurology, Orange, 1992-95, U. Calif. Dept. of Neurology, San Francisco, 1995—. E-mail: cajay@itsa.ucsf.edu. Office: Neurology Ser 4M62 San Francisco Gen Hosp 1001 Potrero Ave San Francisco CA 94110-3594

JAY, CHRISTOPHER EDWARD, stockbroker; b. Walla Walla, Wash., May 2, 1949; s. Orville Elmo and Juanita Hope (Beckius) J.; m. Mardra Marguerite Jones, July 25, 1981; children: Pohaku Kepano, Hope Lauren, Christopher James. BS, Lewis and Clark Coll., 1972; MA, U. Nev., 1975. 1st v.p. Merrill Lynch & Co., Anchorage, 1975—, now 1st v.p. Dist. chair Rep. Cen. Com., Anchorage, 1980-81; bd. trustees Lewis and Clark Coll., Portland, Oreg., 1988—; bd. dirs. Anchorage Mus. History and Art Found., 1988-90, KSKA Pub. Radio, Anchorage, 1991-93, Alaska Pub. Broadcasting Inc., Anchorage, Providence Hosp. Found., Anchorage; bd. dirs., treas. Anchorage Symphony Orch.; active 1st Presbyn. Ch., Anchorage. Named one of nation's top brokers, Registered Rep. mag., 1995, 1998 Broker Hall of Fame, Rsch. Mag., 1998; recipient disting. alumni award Lewis and Clark Coll., 1996. Mem. Rotary (pres. Anchorage chpt. 1989-90, Paul Harris fellow 1989, co-chmn. dist. conv. 1997). Republican. Presbyterian. Avocations: reading, walking, travel, civic activities. Home: 11060 Hideaway Lake Dr Anchorage AK 99516-1183 Office: Merrill Lynch & Co 3601 C St Fl 14 Anchorage AK 99503-5925

JAY, FRANK PETER, writer, educator; b. Bklyn., Feb. 12, 1922; s. Frank G. and Harriet Ann (Niffer) J.; m. Jayne Marie Charles, Aug. 15, 1947; children—Jennifer, Christopher, Alison, Angela, Jonathan, Melissa, Bryan, Nicole, Matthew. A.B., Fordham U., 1943; M.A., Columbia U., 1946. Mem. faculty Fordham U., 1946-92, prof. English, 1948-92; editor-in-chief reference books Funk & Wagnalls, N.Y.C., 1963-65, exec. editor, 1968-73; editor-in-chief reference books Reader's Digest, N.Y.C., 1965-66; editor-in-chief IEEE Dictionary, 1977, 84, 88. Author: Jack: The Story of a Pretty Good Donkey, 1970, also articles, short stories; editor-in-chief: The New Internat. Year Book, 1963, 64, 65, Internat. Everyman's Ency., 20 vols, 1970. Served with USAAF, 1942-43. Mem. Overseas Press Club (N.Y.C.), Princeton Club (N.Y.C.), Manhasset Bay Yacht Club, Kappa Delta Pi. Home: 3 Huntington Rd Port Washington NY 11050-3510

JAY, JERRY LEON, SR., retired publishing executive, industrial engineer; b. Jenkins, Mo., Mar. 22, 1951; s. George Henry and Mary Louisa J.; children: Jerry L. Jr., Drake Allen. Journeyman Seneca Controls, Fraser, Mich., 1978-81; maintenance mgr. Kent-Moore Corp., Detroit, 1981, S.R. of Tenn., Riply, 1982-85; ret. Jerry L. Jay Publ., Verona, Mo., 1985; Author: Patent Applications Simplified, 1996; patentee pneumatic desedimentiation machine improvement, process and apparatus for separating plastics from contaminants, pneumatic desedimentation machine. Home: 277 Old Aurora Rd Verona MO 65769-9210 Address: PO Box 128 Verona MO 65769

JAY, MICHAEL ELIOT, radiologist; b. Bklyn., Nov. 29, 1949; s. Leon and Ruth (Zucker) J.; m. Susan C. Champagne; children: Melissa, Zachary. BS with honors, SUNY, Stonybrook, 1971; MD, Georgetown U., 1975. Diplomate in diagnostic radiology, vascular and interventional radiology Am. Bd. Radiology. Rotating internship Nassau County Med. Ctr., East Meadow, N.Y., 1975-76, resident in diagnostic radiology, 1976-79; fellow in cardiovascular radiology Brigham Woman's Hosp., Boston, 1979-80, staff radiologist, 1980—; assoc. chief dept. radiology West Roxbury (Mass.) VA Med. Complex, 1980—; instr. radiology Harvard Med. Sch., Boston, 1980-86, asst. clin. prof. radiology, 1986—; lectr. in field. Author: Plain Film in Heart Disease, 1992, (chpt.) Oxford Handbook of Medicine, U.S. edit., 1999; mem. editl. bd. Jour. Cardiovascular Medicine, 1985-86, Primary Cardiology, 1986-87, Choices in Cardiology, 1987-94; contbr. articles to profl. jours. Mem. New England Cardiovascular Interventional Radiology Soc., Radiology Soc. N. Am. Jewish. Avocations: skiing, ice skating, classical and pop music, travel. Office: VA Med Ctr VFW Hwy Revere MA 02151

JAY, NORMA JOYCE, artist; b. Wichita, Kans., Nov. 11, 1925; d. Albert Hugh and Thelma Ree (Boyd) Braly; m. Laurence Eugene Jay, Sept. 2, 1949; children: Dana Denise, Allison Eden. Student Wichita State U., 1946-49, Art Inst. Chgo., 1955-56, Calif. State Coll., 1963. Illustrator Boeing Aircraft, Wichita, Kans., 1949-51; co-owner Back Door Gallery, Laguna Beach, Calif., 1973-88. One-woman shows include Milcir Gallery, Tiburon, Calif., 1978, Newport Beach City Gallery, 1981; group shows include Am. Soc. Marine Artists ann. exhbns., 1978-98, Peabody Mus., Salem, Mass., 1981, Mystic Seaport Mus. Gallery, Conn., 1982-95, Grand Cen. Galleries, N.Y., 1979-84, The Back Door Gallery, Laguna Beach, Calif., 1973-88, Mariners' Mus., Newport News, Va., 1985-86, Nat. Heritage Gallery of Fine Art, Beverly Hills, Calif., 1988—, Md. Hist. Mus., 1989, Kirsten Gallery, Seattle, 1991-97, R.J. Schaefer Gallery Mystic (Conn.) Seaport Mus., 1992, Vallejo Gallery, Newport Beach, Calif., 1992, Caswell Gallery, Troutdale, Oreg., 1994-95, Columbia River Maritime Mus., Astoria, Oreg., 1994, 95, Coos Art Mus., Coos Bay, Oreg., 1994-98, Arnold Art Gallery, Newport, Conn., 1994, Mystic Internat. Exhbn., Mystic, Conn., 1995, Lu Martin Galleries, Laguna Beach, Calif., 1996—, Frye Art Mus., Seattle, 1997, Cummer Mus. Art & Gardens, Jacksonville, Fla., 1997-98; represented in permanent collections including James Irvine Found., Newport Beach, Niguel Art Assn., Laguna Niguel, Calif., Deloitte, Haskins & Sells, Costa Mesa, Calif., M.J. Brock & Sons Inc., North Hollywood, Calif., others. Recipient Best of Show award Ford Nat. Competition, 1961, First Pl. award Traditional Artists Exhbn., San Bernadino County Mus., 1976, Artist award Chriswood Gallery Invitational Exhbn., Rancho California, Calif., 1973, Dirs. Choice award, People's Choice award, Coos Art Mus. Marine Exhbn., 1996, featured guest artist, 1998, 1st Place award Maritime Art Exhibit, Newport Harbor Nautical Mus., Newport Beach, Calif., 1998-99. Fellow Am. Soc. Marine Artists (charter); mem. Niguel Art Assn. (first pres. 1968, hon. life mem. 1978), Artists Equity, Am. Artists Profl. League. Democrat.

JAY, PETER AUGUSTUS, writer, farmer; b. N.Y.C., Nov. 27, 1940; s. Peter and Gertrude (McGinley) J.; m. Stephanie Gerard, Oct. 27, 1967 (div. Dec. 1972); children: William, Sarah. BA, Harvard U., 1962. Vol. Peace Corps, Peru, 1962-64; journalist The Aegis, Bel Air, Md., 1964-65, The Washington Post, 1965-73; columnist The Balt. Sun, 1974-98; owner, editor, pub. The Record, Havre de Grace, Md., 1973-89; family farm operator Havre de Grace, Md., 1988—; Nieman fellow Harvard U., 1972-73. Author, editor: Havre de Grace: An Informal History, 1986; contbr. articles to profl. publs. Recipient numerous awards. Avocations: farmer, horseman, professional charterboat captain. E-mail: pajay@juno.com. Office: 100 St John St PO Box 696 Havre De Grace MD 21078

JAYABALAN, VEMBLASERRY, nuclear medicine physician, radiologist; b. India, Apr. 3, 1937; came to U.S., 1970; s. Parameswaran and Janakay (Amma) Menon; m. Vijayam Jayabalan, May 2, 1963; children: Kishore, Suresh. B.Sc., Madras Christian Coll., India, 1955; M.B., B.S., U. Madras, 1961; Diploma in Med. Radioagnosis, U. Liverpool, Eng., 1967. Diplomate: Am. Bd. Radiology, Am. Bd. Nuclear Medicine. Intern Jipmer Hosp., Pondicherry, India, 1961-62; resident in cariology K.E.M. Hosp., Bombay, India, 1962-63; resident in radiology Mt. sinai Hosp., Chgo., 1970-72; fellow in nuclear medicine Michael Reese Hosp., Chgo., 1972-73; dir. nuclear medicine Hurley Med. Ctr., Flint, Mich., 1973—; assoc. clin. prof. radiology Mich. State U. Fellow Internat. Coll. Physicians; mem. Genesee County Med. Soc., Mich. Med. Soc., Radiol. Soc. N.Am., Am. Coll. Nuclear Physicians, Soc. Nuclear Medicine, Am. Coll. Internat. Physicians. Home: 6286 W Cimarron Trl Flint MI 48532-2018 Office: Hurley Med Ctr Flint MI 48503

JAYE, DAVID ROBERT, JR., retired hospital administrator; b. Chgo., Aug. 15, 1930; s. David R. and Gertrude (Gibfried) J.; m. Mary Ann Scanlan, June 6, 1953; children—David, Jeffery, Kathleen. B.S., Loyola U. at Chgo., 1952; M.H.A., Northwestern U., 1954. Adminstrv. asst. Chgo. Wesley Meml. Hosp., 1953-54; asst. adminstr. Sharon (Pa.) Gen. Hosp., 1957-60, St. Joseph Hosp., Joliet, Ill., 1960-65; adminstr. Sacred Heart Hosp., Allentown, Pa., 1965-69; pres., chief exec. officer St. Joseph's Hosp., Marshfield, Wis., 1969-90; cons. Marshfield, 1990—; regional v.p. Sisters of Sorrowful Mother Ministry Corp., Milw., 1989-91; bd. dirs. Marshfield Savs. and Loan; cons. Marshfield, Wis., 1991—. Past pres. North Central Wis. Hosp. Council; mem. Wis. State Health Policy Council; bd. dirs. Wis. Blue Cross, Marshfield Devel. Corp. Served as lt., Med. Service Corps USAF, 1954-57. Fellow Am. Coll. Hosp. Adminstrs. (coun. regents); mem. Am. Hosp. Assn. (coun. fed. rels., ho. of dels.), Cath. Hosp. Assn. (past trustee), Wis. Hosp. Assn. (past chmn. bd. trustees), Rotary, Elks, KC. Home and Office: 1125 Ridge Rd Marshfield WI 54449-1734

JAYME, WILLIAM NORTH, writer; b. Pitts., Nov. 15, 1925; s. Walter A. and Catherine (Ryley) J.; student Princeton, 1943-44, 47-49. With Young & Rubicam Advt., Inc., 1949, Charles W. Gamble & Assos., 1949-50; asst. circulation promotion mgr. Fortune mag., 1950-51, Life mag., 1951-53, copy dir., sales and advt. promotion CBS Radio Network, N.Y.C., 1953-55; sr. copywriter McCann-Erickson, Inc., 1955-58; established own advt. creative service, 1958-71; pres. Jayme, Ratalahti, Inc., 1971-97; lectr. direct mktg. Stanford U., Radcliffe Coll., worldwide mktg. confs. Producer U.S. Army radio program Music Motorized, 1945-46; editor, producer Time, Inc. TV programs Background for Judgment, 1951, Citizen's View of '52; script editor CBS Radio-UPA motion picture Tune in Tomorrow, 1954; creator promotions that launched Smithsonian, New York, Bon Appetit, Food & Wine, American Health, Worth, Saveur, Civilization, other nat. mags.; author script adaptations for Studio One and other TV programs, articles and stories in periodicals. Served as sgt., 2d Armored Div., AUS, 1944-46. Democrat. Episcopalian. Club: Century Assn.,(N.Y.C.). Author: (with Roderick Cook) Know Your Toes and Other Things to Know, 1963; (with Helen McCully, Jacques Pepin) The Other Half of the Egg, 1967; (opera libretto, with Douglas Moore) Carry Nation. Address: 1033 Bart Rd Sonoma CA 95476-4707

JAYNE, CRISTINA MARSH, retired elementary education educator; b. Mar. 15, 1935. BS in Elem. Edn., Ohio U., 1958. Cert. elem. tchr., Ohio. Tchr. grade 2 Kingston (Ohio) Sys., 1956-59; tchr. grade 3 and 4 Chillicothe City, Ohio, 1960-67, tchr. grade 5, 1974-98; ret., 1998. Address: 459 West Fifth St Chillicothe OH 45601-3014

JAYNE, CYNTHIA ELIZABETH, psychologist; b. Pensacola, Fla., June 5, 1953; d. Gordon Howland and Joan (Rockwood) J. AB, Vassar Coll., 1974; MA, SUNY, Buffalo, 1978, PhD, 1983. Lic. psychologist, Pa. Instr. dept. psychiatry Temple U. Sch. Medicine, Phila., 1982-84, asst. prof., 1984-85, asst. dir. outpatient svcs., asst. dir. residency tng., 1982-85, clin. asst. prof., 1985—; pvt. practice psychology Phila., 1985—; adj. prof. Chestnut Hill Coll., 1994—. Contbr. articles to profl. jours. Soc. for Sci. Study Sex scholar, 1981; Sigma Xi grantee, 1981, Kinsey Inst. Dissertation award, 1983. Mem. Ea. Psychol. Assn., Soc. for Sci. Study Sex (bd. dirs. 1984-86).

JAYNE, EDWARD RANDOLPH, II, executive search consultant; b. Kirksville, Mo., Sept. 24, 1944; s. Edward Randolph and Marietta (Jonas) J.; m. Nancy Elizabeth King, June 18, 1966; children: Kathryn Eden, Matthew Randolph. BS, USAF Acad., 1966; PhD, MIT, 1969. Officer, pilot USAF, 1966-77; staff nat. security coun. The White House, Washington, 1976-77; assoc. dir. nat. security and internat. affairs Office of Mgmt. and Budget The White House, Washington, 1977-80; v.p. Gen. Dynamics Corp., St. Louis, 1980-87; pres. McDonnell Douglas Missile Sys. Co., St. Louis, 1987-93; pres., COO Insituform Mid-Am., St. Louis, 1993-94; ptnr. Heidrick & Struggles, Vienna, Va., 1996—; bd. dirs. The Falcon Found., USAF Acad., Colo. Maj. gen. Air Nat. Guard. NSF fellow, 1966-69; White House fellow, 1973-74. Office: Heidrick & Struggles 8000 Towers Crescent Dr Ste 555 Vienna VA 22182-6205

JAYNE, FRED EUGENE, financial planner. BA in Polit. Sci., Brigham Young U., 1976, MPA, 1978. Fiscal analyst Office of Legis. Fiscal Analyst, Salt Lake City, 1978-89; dir. budget, fin. Utah Ct. Adminstrn., Salt Lake City, 1989—. Home: 9614 S Saphire Cir Sandy UT 84094

JAYNE, THEODORE DOUGLAS, technical research and development company executive; b. Painesville, Ohio, Dec. 3, 1929; s. Earl Douglas and Mary Griffin (Erskine) J.; m. Penelope Sanders, Mar. 7, 1959 (div. Sept. 1980); children—Douglas T., Virginia M., Jillanne M. B.A., U. Chgo., 1950; postgrad. Case Inst. Tech., 1950-54. Head materials, instr. labs. Rand Devel. Corp., Cleve., 1950-64; dir. labs. Gen. Tech. Services, Upper Darby, Pa., 1964-69; tech. dir., prin. T. Jayne Co., Painesville, 1969—. Patentee in field. Office: T Jayne Co 10234 Johnnycake Ridge Rd Painesville OH 44077-2055

JAYNES, ROBERT HENRY, JR., retired military officer; b. Greeneville, Tenn., Feb. 6, 1948; s. Robert Henry and Della Mae (Broyles) J.; m. Peggy Jane Farmer, Dec. 24, 1981. BS, East Tenn. State U., 1970. Pilot 57th assault helicopter co. U.S. Army, Republic of Vietnam, 1972-73; advanced through grades to lt. col. U.S. Army, 1988; co. commdr. U.S. Army, Ft. Jackson, S.C., 1976-78; aviation tng. developer/evaluator for dir. evaluation U.S. Army, Ft. Rucker, Ala., 1978-80; battalion advisor Alaska NG U.S. Army, Kotzebue, 1980-81; exec. officer recruiting battalion U.S. Army, San Juan, P.R., 1981-84; officer-in-chg. Chief of Staff of Army's Allied Office Hall of Fame U.S. Army Command and Gen. Staff Coll., Ft. Leavenworth, Kans., 1984-85; exec. officer U.S. Army Space Initiatives Study U.S. Army Space Coun., Washington, 1985; student and staff group leader Command and Gen. Staff Coll. U.S. Army, Ft. Leavenworth, Kans., 1986-87; program mgr. U.S. Army enlistment incentives Office of Dep. Chief of Staff for Personnel/The Pentagon, Washington, 1988-93; ret. U.S. Army, 1993; mgr., dir. fed. programs Network Computing Devices, Bethesda, Md., 1993-95; bus. devel. mgr. Computer Assocs. Internat., Inc., Reston, Va., 1995—. Contbr. articles to profl. jours. Founding mem. Leavenworth Computer Coun., pres. 1986-87. Decorated Bronze Star and Legion of Merit. Mem. Assn. U.S. Army, Army Aviation Assn. Am. (v.p. mem. 1975-76, v.p. student affairs 1986-87), Recreational Equipment Assn., Scabbard & Blade, Pentagon Personal Computer User Group (founder, program chmn., vendor rep., newsletter editor 1987-89, chmn. 1989-91). Avocations: hunting, fishing, camping, computers, automobiles. Office: Computer Assocs Internat Reston Exec Ctr Bldg 3 12120 Sunset Hills Rd Reston VA 20190-3231

JAYSON, LESTER SAMUEL, lawyer, educator; b. N.Y.C., Oct. 25, 1915; s. Morris and Mary (Gardner) J.; m. Evelyn Sylvia Lederer, Feb. 6, 1943; children: Diane Frankie, Jill Karen Jayson Ladd. BSS with spl. honors in History and Govt., CCNY, 1936; JD (bd. student advisers), Harvard U., 1939. Bar: N.Y. 1940, U.S. Supreme Ct. 1952, D.C. 1976. With firm Oseas and Pepper, N.Y.C., 1939-40, Marshall, Bratter & Seligson, N.Y.C., 1940-42; spl. asst. to atty. gen. U.S., 1942-50; trial atty. Dept. Justice, 1951-56, chief torts sect. civil div., 1957-60; sr. specialist Am. pub. law, chief Am. law div. Congl. Research Service, Library of Congress, 1960-62, dep. dir. service, 1962-66, dir., 1966-75; prof. law Potomac Sch. Law, 1975-81; Vice chmn. Interdeptl. Fed. Tort Claims Com., 1958-60; rep. Justice Dept. to legal div., air coordinating com. Internat. Civil Aviation Orgn., 1959-60; mem. com. exec. privilege Justice Dept., 1956-60; adv. statutory studies group Commn. Govt. Procurement, 1970-72; mem. adv. council Office Tech. Assessment, 1973-75; cons. govt. relations com. Nat. Assn. Theatre Owners, 1978-79. Author: Handling Federal Tort Claims: Judicial and Administrative Remedies, 1964-95; also articles; supervising editor: The Constitution of the United States of America-Analysis and Interpretation, 1964, 72. Mem. ABA, Fed. Bar Assn. (chmn., then vice chmn. fed. tort claims com. 1963-66, 70-74, chmn. 1967-68, mem. nat. council 1967-73), Am. Friends of Wilton Park, Assn. Trial Lawyers Am., Pi Sigma Alpha (hon.). Clubs: Cosmos (Washington), Harvard (Washington). Home: 7512 Newmarket Dr Bethesda MD 20817-6622

JAYSON, MELINDA GAYLE, lawyer; b. Dallas, Sept. 29, 1956; d. Robert and Louise Adelle (Jacobs) J. BA, U. Tex., 1977, JD, 1980. Bar: Tex. 1980, U.S. Dist. Ct. (no. dist.) Tex. 1980, U.S. Ct. Appeals (5th and 11th cirs.) 1981, U.S. Dist. Ct. (so. dist.) Tex. 1989, U.S. Ct. Appeals (8th cir.) 1990, U.S. Supreme Ct. 1991. Assoc. Akin, Gump, Strauss, Hauer & Feld, Dallas, 1980-86, ptnr., 1987-96; ptnr. Melinda G. Jayson, P.C., 1996—; comml. arbitrator, mem. regional adv. coun. Am. Arbitration Assn.; arbitrator, mediator N.Y. Stock Exch., and NASD Regulation, Inc.; mediator, arbitrator Dispute Solutions, Inc.; mediator U.S. EEO Commn. Named one of Outstanding Young Women Am., 1983. Mem. Tex. Bar Assn., Dallas Bar Assn., State Bar of Tex. (mem. dist. 6A grievance com. 1997—, mem. professionalism enhancement com. 1997—). Office: Ste 2015 5445 Caruth Haven Ln Dallas TX 75225-8166

JAY-Z (JIGGA) (SEAN CARTER), music company executive; b. Bklyn.. CEO Roc-A-Fella Records, N.Y.C., 1996—. First started rapping with ptnr. The Jaz, 1990; debut solo album "Reasonable Doubt," 1996; co-founder Roc-A-Fella Records with Damon Diggs and Kareem "Biggs" Burke; wrote, directed and starred in short autobiographical film "Streets is Watching"; other albums include "In My Lifetime Vol. 1," 1997, "Vol. 2 Hard Knock Life (Edited Version)," 1998, "Vol. 2 Hard Knock Life," 1998. Office: Roc A Fella Records 5th Fl 79 5th Ave New York NY 10003*

JAZAYERY, MOHAMMAD ALI, foreign languages and literature educator emeritus; b. Shushtar, Iran, May 27, 1924; came to U.S., 1951; s. Mohammad Kazem and Batul J. J. Lic., U. Tehran, 1950; postgrad., U. Mich., 1953, Georgetown U., 1954; PhD, U. Tex., 1958. Tchr. English high sch., Ahvaz, Iran, 1950-51; tchg. asst. in English U. Tex., Austin, 1953-54, instr., 1955-57, lectr., 1957-58, vis. assoc. prof. lingustics and English, 1962-65, assoc. prof. linguistics, 1965-68, prof., 1968-70, prof. Persian dept. Oriental and African langs. and lits., 1970-89, prof. emeritus, 1990—; asst. dir. Ctr. for Mid. Ea. Studies, 1966-73, dir., 1981-87; acting chmn. dept., 1973, chmn., 1976-84; linguistic rschr. Am. Coun. Learned Socs., Washington, 1954-55; assoc. prof. English U. Tehran, 1958-59; lectr. Persian U. Mich., Ann Arbor, 1959-62; vis. prof. Johns Hopkins U. Sch. of Advanced Internat. Studies, Washington, 1957, Harvard U., 1958, Utah State U., Logan, 1961, Princeton U., 1967, NYU, 1968, Portland State U.(Oreg.), 1972; translator Voice of Am, Washington, 1954,55,56; U.S. Office Edn. linguistic rschr. in Persian U. Mich., 1959-62; dir. lang. tng. for Iran programs U.S. Peace Corps, Logan, Austin, 1962-65; cons. in field. Author: The Abuses of Our Society, 1947, (with Herbert H. Paper) English for Iranians, 1955, Writing System of Modern Persia, 1955, Elementary Lessons in Persian, 1968, Farhangestan: La Academia Irania de la Lengua, 1979; translator: Practical Psychology in Plain Language, vols. 1-7, 1949-50; editor: (with Peter Avery, Massud Farzan and Paper) Modern Persian Reader, vols. 1-3, 1963, (with Edgar C. Plomè and Werner Winter) Linguistic and Literary Studies in Honor of Archibald A. Hill, vols. 1-4, 1978-79, (with Winter) Languages and Cultures: Studies in Honor of Edgar C. Plomè, 1988; bd. editors Lit. East and West, 1970-80, acting editor, 1974-75; contbr. articles to profl. jours. Iran, Europe, U.S., Ency. of Islam, 2nd edit., Ency. Iranica, Ency. of Modern Mid. East, Ency. of Historians and Hist. Writing. U. Tehran fellow, 1947-50, Fulbright fellow, 1951-52; grantee Am. Coun. Learned Socs., 1953, 54, HEW, 1969-70, U. Tex. Spl. Faculty Assignments, 1985, 87. Mem. Am. Oriental Soc. (nominating com. 1965-67), Linguistic Soc. Am. (life), Soc. Linguistica Europaea, Mid. East Studies Assn. N.Am. (life, mem. program com. 1968), Soc. Iranian Studies (mem. coun. 1978-83). Home: 705 Laurel Valley Rd Austin TX 78746-3509 Office: U Tex Dept Mid Ea Langs-Cultures Austin TX 78712

JEAN, KENNETH, conductor; b. N.Y.C.. Studied violin, San Francisco State U.; studied conducting with Jean Morel, Juilliard Sch. Music. Conducting debut Carnegie Hall with Youth Symphony Orch. N.Y.; European debut with Internat. Festival Youth Orchs., Aberdeen, Scotland, 1980; music dir. Youth Symphony Orch. N.Y.; conducting asst. Cleve. Orch.; resident condr. Detroit Symphony Orch., 1978-85; prin. guest condr. Hong Kong Philharm.; music dir. Fla. Symphony Orch.; assoc. condr. Chgo. Symphony Orch., 1986—; has appeared with numerous other U.S. Orch., Scottish Chamber Orch., Orch. Swiss Radio, Park Theater Orch., Stockholm, Belgrade Strings, S.W. German Radio Orch. (Donaueschinger Festival); has recorded works of Chinese composers, also Brahms Hungarian Dances with Hong Kong Philharm. Recipient Leopold Stokowski Conducting award Am. Symphony Orch., 1984, Seaver/Nat. Endowment Arts Condr. award, 1990. Office: Chgo Symphony Orch 220 S Michigan Ave Chicago IL 60604-2501 also: Fla Symphony Orch 1900 N Mills Ave Ste 3 Orlando FL 32803-1444

JEAN, LOREN, state legislator; b. Nashua, N.H., Feb. 27, 1938; m. Shirley Jean; one child; three stepchildren. Grad. H.S., Nashua. Bldg. contractor; mem. Dist. 17 N.H. Ho. of Reps., mem. pub. protection and vet. affairs coms. Mem. Litchfield Planning Bd., 1989—; commr. Regional Planning Commn., 1990—, Commn. for Human Rights, 1991—, Conservation Commn., 1992—. Mem. Amvets Post 1. Office: NH Ho of Reps State Capitol Concord NH 03301*

JEAN, PATRICIA ANNE, medical center administrator; b. Methuen, Mass., Sept. 15, 1946. Diploma in Nursing, Worcester (Mass.) City Hosp., 1967; BSN magna cum laude, U. Lowell (Mass.), 1984; MSN in Nursing Adminstrn., U. Mass., 1992. cert. critical care unit nurse. Grad. profl. nurse Boston City Hosp., 1967; staff nurse Holy Family Hosp. and Med. Ctr., Methuen, Mass., 1967-69, charge nurse ICU, 1969-70, asst. head nurse, 1970-83; nurse mgr. cardiac sect. Holy Family Hosp. and Med. Ctr., Methuen, Mass., 1983-93; dir. cardiology Cath. Med. Ctr., Manchester, N.H., 1993-94, nurse mgr., 1993-94, dir. cardiology, 1994-95; dir. cardiology Cath. Med. Ctr. and Elliott Hosp., Manchester, 1995-96; adminstr. cardiac svcs. Optima Healthcare, Manchester, 1996—. Contbr. articles to profl. jours. Mem. Am. Orgn. Nurse Execs. (affiliate), Am. Coll. Cardiovasc. Adminstrs., U. Lowell Nursing Honor Soc., Sigma Theta Tau. Home: 412 Forest St Methuen MA 01844-1939

JEANLOZ, ROGER WILLIAM, biochemist, educator; b. Berne, Switzerland, Nov. 3, 1917; came to U.S., 1947, naturalized, 1953; s. William M. and Rose (Poisat) J.; m. Dorothea A.H. de Passavant, Dec. 20, 1945; children: Patrick Marc (dec.), Claude-André, Raymond François, Danielle Renée, Sylvie Anne. Baccalaureate, Coll. Geneva, Switzerland, 1936; Chem.E., U. Geneva, 1941, D.Sc., 1943; A.M. (hon.), Harvard, 1961; D.Sc. (hon.), U. Paris, 1980. Research asso. U. Geneva, 1943-45, U. Basel, 1945-46; asst. U. Montreal, 1946-47; sr. research fellow NIH, 1947-48; sr. scientist Worcester Found. Exptl. Biology, 1948-51; asso. biochemist Mass. Gen. Hosp., Boston, 1951-61; biochemist Mass. Gen. Hosp., 1961—; research asso. Harvard Med. Sch., 1951-57, asso. organic chemistry, 1957-60, asst. prof. biol. chemistry, 1960-61, asso. prof., 1961-69, prof., 1969-88, emeritus prof. biol. chemistry and molecular pharmacology, 1988—; biochemist Shriver Ctr. for Mental Retardation, 1992—; mem. study sect. physiol. chemistry div. research grants NIH, 1964-68, 69-70; mem. physiol. chemistry B. research study com. Am. Heart Assn., 1971-74. Author: (with Balazs) The Amino Sugars, 4 vols, 1965, (with Gregory) Glycoconjugate Research, 2 vols, 1979; Editor: Carbohydrate Research; editorial bd. Connective Tissue Research, Molecular Biology, Biochemistry and Biophysics, Biochimie, Glycoconjugate Jour.; contbr. articles to profl. jours. Recipient medal Société de Chimie Biologique de France, 1960, medal U. Liege, 1964, Prix Jaubert U. Geneva, 1973, Stratton award Am. Friends of Switzerland, 1981, Alexander von Humboldt Sr. Scientist award, 1983; Guggenheim fellow, 1976-77. Fellow AAAS; mem. Am. Soc. Biol. Chemists, Am. Chem. Soc., Swiss Chem. Soc., Royal Chem. Soc. (London), French Biochem. Soc., Biochem. Soc., Soc. for Glycobiology, Am. Coll. Rheumatology. Fax: (781) 893-4018. E-mail: jeanloz@fas.harvard.edu. Home: 42 Ruthven Rd Newton MA 02458-2316 Office: Shriver Ctr for Mental Retardation 200 Trapelo Rd Waltham MA 02452-6332

JEAN-MARY, JOSEPH BELLADERE, educator; b. Dessalines, Haiti, Dec. 11, 1944; came to U.S., 1970; s. Dorcius and Marie Eleide J.; children: Brian, Kassim, Alain. BS, Kean U., 1992; MPA, Rutgers U., 1997. Warehouseman Aquatherm Products, Rahway, N.J., 1970-72; chem. operator Ashland Chems., Newark, 1972-90; substitute tchr. Elizabeth (N.J.) Pub. Schs., 1990-98; tchr. St. Anthony H.S., Jersey City, N.J., 1998—. Mem. Am. Soc. Pub. Adminstrn., North Ctrl. Jersey Assn. Realtors. Home: 30 Young Ave Hillside NJ 08306

JEANNE, ROBERT LAWRENCE, entomology educator; b. N.Y.C., Jan. 14, 1942; s. Armand Lucien and Ruth (Stuber) J.; m. Louise Grenville Bluhm, Sept. 18, 1976; children: Thomas Lucien, James McClure. B.S. in Biology, Denison U., 1964; postgrad., Justus-Liebig U., Giessen, Fed.

Republic Germany, 1964-65; M.A., Harvard U., 1968, Ph.D. in Biology, 1971. Instr. biology U. Va., Charlottesville, 1970-71; asst. prof. biology Boston U., 1971-76; asst. prof. entomology U. Wis., Madison, 1976-79, assoc. prof., 1979-83, prof., 1983—. Research, numerous publs. on social insects. Rotary Found. fellow in internat. understanding, 1964-65; NSF grantee, 1972—; Guggenheim Meml. fellow, 1986-87. Mem. Assn. Tropical Biology, Internat. Union for Study Social Insects (assoc. editor Insectes Sociaux), Animal Behavior Soc., Wis. Acad. of Scis., Arts and Letters, Phi Beta Kappa, Sigma Xi. Achievements include field rsch. on insects in U.S., Mexico, Costa Rica, Panama, Surinam, Brazil, Venezuela, Peru, India, Australia. Office: U Wis Dept Entomology 1630 Linden Dr Madison WI 53706-1520

JEANNERET, PAUL RICHARD, management consultant. BA in Psychology, U. Va., 1962; MA in Psychology and Sociology, U. Fla., 1963; PhD in Indsl. and Orgnl. Psychology, Purdue U., 1969. From cons. to sr. cons. Lifson, Wilson, Ferguson & Winick, Inc., Houston, 1969-73; v.p. PAQ Svcs., Inc., 1972-90, pres., 1990—; prin. LWFW, Inc., Houston, 1974-76, mng. prin., 1977-81; mng. prin. Jeanneret & Asscos., Houston, 1982—; grad. rsch. asst. Purdue U., 1967-69; instr. physiol. and introductory psychology Old Dominion Coll., Norfolk, Va., 1965-67; adj. prof. psychology dept. U. Houston, 1982—. Cons. editor: Jour. Applied Psychology, 1989-94; panel editor: Pers. Psychology, 1994-98. Lt. (j.g.) USNR, 1964-67. Fellow APA (divsn. indsl. and orgnl. psychology, divsn. cons. psychology), Soc. Orgnl. Behavior; mem. Am. Compensation Assn., Soc. Indsl. and Orgnl. Psychology (elected officer 1995-98), Disting. Profl. Contbns. award 1990), Tex. Indsl/Orgnl. Psychologists, Houston Area Indsl. and Orgnl. Psychologists (past exec. com.), Sigma Xi. Office: Jeanneret & Assocs Inc 601 Jefferson St Ste 3900 Houston TX 77002-7913

JEANSON, CEDRIC, film company executive; b. Paris, Jan. 6, 1956; came to U.S., 1989; s. Dominique and Nicole (Jansse) J. MS in Internat. Mgmt., Internat. Mgmt. Inst. Paris, 1987; MBA, Northwestern U., Evanston, Ill., 1991. Mgr. internat. distbn. Dino de Laurentiis Comm., Beverly Hills, Calif., 1991-93; dir. internat. Miramax Film Corp., L.A., 1993-95, v.p. internat. sales, 1995-97; sr. v.p. Miramax Film Corp., N.Y.C., 1997—. Mem. Brit. Acad. Film and TV Arts, Am. Film Mktg. Assn., Am. Film Inst. Avocations: film, music, soccer, tennis, skiing. Office: Miramax Film Corp 99 Hudson St New York NY 10013-2815

JEAVONS, NORMAN STONE, lawyer; b. Cleve., Apr. 18, 1930; s. William Norman and Mildred (Stone) J.; m. Kathleen Taze, Oct. 18, 1936; children: Kathleen Stone, Ann Lindsey. B.A., Dartmouth Coll., 1952; LL.B., Case Western Res. U., 1958. Bar: Ohio 1958. Atty. firm Baker & Hostetler, Cleve., 1958—, ptnr., 1968—. Mem. policy com., trustee Laurel Sch., Shaker Hts., Ohio, 1980—, Beech Brook, Cleve., 1972—, Storm King Sch., Cornwall-on-Hudson, N.Y. Served to lt. j.g. USCG, 1952-55. Mem. ABA, Ohio Bar Assn., Cleve. Bar Assn., Order of Coif, Ct. of Nisi Prius. Republican. Clubs: Univ. (Cleveland); Cleveland Racquet (Pepper Pike). Home: 32555 Creekside Dr Pepper Pike OH 44124-5223 Office: Baker & Hostetler 3200 National City Ctr 1900 E 9th St Ste 3200 Cleveland OH 44114-3475*

JECKLIN, LOIS UNDERWOOD, art corporation executive, consultant; b. Manning, Iowa, Oct. 5, 1934; d. J.R. and Ruth O. (Austin) Underwood; m. Dirk C. Jecklin, June 24, 1955; children: Jennifer Anne, Ivan Peter. BA, State U. Iowa, 1992. Residency coord. Quad City Arts Coun., Rock Island, Ill., 1973-78; field rep. Affiliate Artists, Inc., N.Y.C., 1975-77; mgr., artist in residence Deere & Co., Moline, Ill., 1977-80; dir. Vis. Artist Series, Davenport, Iowa, 1978-81; pres. Vis. Artists, Inc., Davenport, 1981-88; pres., owner Jecklin Assocs., 1988—. asst. to exec. dir. Walter W. Naumburg Found., N.Y.C., 1990—; cons. writer's program St. Ambrose Coll., Davenport, 1981, 83, 85; mem. com. Iowa Arts Coun., Des Moines, 1983-84; panelist Chamber Music Am., N.Y.C., 1984, Pub. Art Conf., Cedar Rapids, Iowa, 1984; panelist, mem. com. Lt. Gov.'s Conf. on Iowa's Future, Des Moines, 1984; trustee Davenport Mus. Art, 1975-98, hon. trustee, 1998; trustee Nature Conservancy Iowa, 1987-88; mem. steering com. Iowa Citizens for Arts, Des Moines, 1970-71; bd. dirs. Tri-City Symphony Orchestra Assn., Davenport, 1968-83; founding mem. Urban Design Council, HOME, City of Davenport Beautification Comm., all Davenport, 1970-72; bd. gov. Am. Craft Mus., N.Y.C., 1995—; mem. devel. coun. U Iowa Mus. Art, 1996—. Recipient numerous awards Izaak Waltton League, Davenport Art Gallery, Assn. for Retarded Citizens, Am. Heart Assn., Ill. Bur. Corrections, many others; LaVernes Noyes scholar, 1953-55. Mem. Am. Symphony Orch. League, Crow Valley Golf Club, Outing Club, Rotary. Republican. Episcopalian. Home and Office: 2717 Nichols Ln Davenport IA 52803-3620

JEDAN, DIETER, language educator; b. Oct. 1, 1944. BA, Carthage Coll., 1969; MA, U. Kans., 1971, PhD, 1973. Instr. Ill. Wesleyan U., Bloomington, 1972-76; dir. tchg. assts., prof. dept. German UCLA, 1976-85; from assoc. prof. to prof. Murray State U., Murray, Ky., 1985-93; prof., chair S.E. Mo. State U., Cape Girardeau, 1993—. E-mail: djedan@semovm.semo.edu. Office: 1508 Sylvan Ln Cape Girardeau MO 63701

JEDLOVIC, GARY J., meteorologist, remote sensing scientist; b. Berwyn, Ill., Oct. 21, 1957; s. Robet F. and Lois M. J.; m. Kathleen Bridge Caragher, Mar. 15, 1980; children: Benjamin, Phillip, Dylan. BS, St. Louis U., 1979, MS, 1981; PhD, U. Wis., 1987. Atmospheric scientist NASA, Huntsville, Ala., 1987—; adj. prof. U. Ala., Huntsville, 1988—, Fla. State U., Tallahassee, 1989-95; project mgr. NASA, Huntsville, 1991-93, br. chief, 1994-95, prin. scientist, 1995—. Contbr. articles to sci. jours. Bd. dirs. Friends of the Playgrounds, Huntsville, Ala., 1997-99. Mem. Am. Meteorol. Soc. (com. satellite meteorology, Boston, 1993-98), Am. Geophys. Union, Am. Soc. Phogrammetry and Remote Sensing. Roman Catholic. Avocations: elem. and middle sch. basketball coach, gardening. E-mail gary.jedlovec@msfc.nasa.gov. Home: 128 Oldwood Rd Huntsville AL 35811-0200 Office: NASA/GHCC 977 Explorer Blvd Huntsville AL 35806

JEDZINIAK, LEE PETER, lawyer, educator, state insurance administrator; b. Springfield, Mass., June 1, 1956; s. Leo Stanley and Helena (Ludwin) J. BA in Polit. Sci., The Citadel, 1978; JD, U.S.C., 1981. Bar: S.C. 1981, U.S. Dist. Ct. S.C. 1982, U.S. Ct. Appeals (4th cir.) 1982, U.S. Ct. Appeals (11th and D.C. cirs.) 1983, U.S. Ct. Appeals (3d, 5th and 10th cirs.) 1984, U.S. Tax Ct. 1985, U.S. Ct. Appeals (9th cir.) 1985, U.S. Supreme Ct. 1985. Law clk. to presiding judge 15th Jud. Cir. Ct., Conway, S.C., 1981-83; atty. consumer advs. office State of S.C., Columbia, 1983-85, staff counsel dept. ins., 1985-88, gen. counsel dept. ins., 1988-95, dir. ins., 1995-99; v.p. compliance S.C. Farm Bur. Ins. Cos., West Columbia, 1999—; profl. lectr. MPA and MBA depts. Golden Gate U., 1984-90, St. Leo Coll., 1990-93, Troy State U., 1991—. Mem. S.C. Bar Assn., Citadel Alumni Assn. Roman Catholic. Office: SC Farm Bur Ins Cos PO Box 2124 West Columbia SC 29171-2124

JEEP, JOHN MICHAEL, German studies educator; b. Quebec, Can., July 3, 1954; came to U.S., 1954; s. Charles W. Jr. and Winifred (Gohl) J.; m. Lynda Hoffman, Apr. 18, 1975; 1 child, Cariña. MA, U. Münster, 1985; PhD in German Lang., U. Chgo., 1990. German lectr. U. Osnabrück, 1985-86, U. Münster, 1986; instr. of German Loyola U., Chgo., 1986-87, 90-91; German tchr. Lab. Schs. U. Chgo., 1987-90, 91; vis. prof. German Miami U., Oxford, Ohio, 1992-93, asst. prof. German, 1993-98; dir. Intensive German Summer Program, German dept. Miami U., Oxford, 1993, 98, dir. Austrian Scholars Program, 1997, 99, assoc. prof. German, 1998—; cons. Houghton-Mifflin Pub., Boston, 1995-96; reviewer grant proposals Nat. Endowment for the Humanities, Washington, 1995, 96, 97. Author: Alliterating Word-Pairs in Old High German, 1995, Stabreimende Wortpaare bei Notker Labeo, 1987; bibliographer Med. Feminist Index, 1997—; An Encyclopedia: contbr. articles to profl. jours.; reviewer of profl. jours. Summer rsch. grant Nat. Endowment for the Humanities, 1991. Mem. MLA (bibliographer Germanic studies 1992—), German Studies Assn., Soc. for German Philology, Am. Assn. Tchrs. German. Avocations: sports, travel, reading. Office: Miami U German Russia & East Asian Irvin Hall 140 400 E Spring St Oxford OH 45056-1859

JEFF, MORRIS F.X., JR., muncipal or county official; m. Florence Calvin; children: Dean, Byron, Janine. BS, Xavier U.; MSW, Atlanta U.; D of Social Work, Tulane U. Case worker Children's Divsn. Cook County Dept. Pub. Aid, Chgo., 1960-65; exec. House Movement, Louisville, 1965-74; dir. Dept. Human Svcs. City of New Orleans, 1974—; adj. prof. Tulane U., So. U. New Orleans; vis. prof. U. New Orleans; co-owner Counseling and Diagnostic Family Inst., New Orleans. Bd. dirs. Nat. Violence Prevention Collaborative. Mem. New Orleans Assn. Black Social Workers, 100 Black Men of New Orleans (program chmn.). Fax: 504 565-7662. Office: City of New Orleans Dept Human Services 5730 Saint Bernard Ave New Orleans LA 70122-1320*

JEFFAY, HENRY, biochemistry educator; b. Bklyn., Feb. 9, 1927; s. Alexander and Dora (Soloman) J.; m. Ana Idalia Muniz, Feb. 9, 1957; children: Randall, Kevin, Jason, Stefanie, Susan. B.S., U. Wis., 1948, M.S., 1949, Ph.D., 1953. Instr. U. P.R. Sch. Medicine, 1955; research assoc. U. Ill. Coll. Medicine, 1955, asst. prof. biochemistry, 1956, assoc. prof., 1961-67, prof., 1967—, prof. biochemistry, 1980-92, asst. dean, 1970-76; dean U. Ill. Coll. Medicine (Sch. Basic Med. Sci.), 1976-80; ret., prof. emeritus U. Ill. Coll. Medicine, 1992—; dir. basic med. scis. Rockford (Ill.) Sch. Medicine, 1974-76; cons. FTC, West Side VA Hosp., Chgo., Norwegian Am. Hosp., Chgo.; dir. med. edn. Roosevelt Meml. Hosp., Chgo. Contbr. articles to profl. jours. Trustee Glen Ellyn (Ill.) Pub. Libr., 1970-76; bd. dirs. Am. Cancer Soc., 1987-91, mem. com. on chemoprevention, Ill. divsn., 1987-92. With AUS, 1945-46. Recipient research award Chgo. Dental Soc., 1959. Mem. Am. Soc. Biol. Chemists, AAAS, Internat. Assn. Dental Research. Home: 4313 N Placita De Susana Tucson AZ 85718-7437

JEFFE, SIDNEY DAVID, automotive engineer; b. Chgo., May 6, 1927; s. J.I. Jeffe; children: Robert A., Leslie A. BSME with honors, Ill. Inst. Tech., 1950; MS in Automotive Engring. with honors, Chrysler Inst. Engring., 1952; postgrad., Carnegie-Mellon U., 1968. With Chrysler Corp., 1950-80, v.p. engring. and rsch., 1976-80; sr. v.p. ops. Sheller Globe Corp., Detroit, 1982-86; prof. mech. engring. Ohio State U., 1980-82; sr. v.p. internat. bus. and tech. devel. and implementation, head customer and govt. rels. activities Sheller Globe Corp., Detroit, 1986-90; v.p. internat. bus. and tech. devel. Mesnel S.A.- Schlegel Corp., Madison Heights, Mich., 1990-92; internat. bus. and tech. cons., expert witness, 1992—; exec. dir. Transp. Rsch. Ctr. Ohio, E. Liberty; sec.-treas. Transp. Rsch. Bd. Ohio, 1980-82; sr. v.p. internat. bus. and tech. devel. United Tech. Engineered Sys. Divsn., 1990; bd. dirs. J.L. French Automotive Castings Inc. Responsible for devel. Chrysler's first front-wheel drive cars- Omni, Horizon, K cars and Minivans, 1976-80; author papers in field. Served with AUS, 1945-47. Fellow Engring. Soc. Detroit, Soc. Automotive Engrs. (Russell Springer award 1957, Coll. Fellows 1985); mem. Tau Beta Pi (Outstanding New Mem. award 1948), Pi Tau Sigma (Outstanding New Mem. award 1949). Unitarian. Clubs: DC Ranch Country (Scottsdale, Ariz.), Orchard Lake Country, Detroit Athletic, Ren Cen. Home: 3673 Quail Holw Bloomfield Hills MI 48302-1250

JEFFERIES, JOHN TREVOR, astronomer, astrophysicist, observatory administrator; b. Kellerberrin, Australia, Apr. 2, 1925; came to U.S., 1956, naturalized, 1967; s. John and Vera (Healy) J.; m. Charmian Candy, Sept. 10, 1949; children: Stephen R., Helen C., Trevor R. MA, Cambridge (Eng.) U., 1949; DSc, U. Western Australia, Nedlands, 1962. Sr. research staff High Altitude Obs., Boulder, Colo., 1957-59, Sacramento Peak Obs., Sunspot, N.Mex., 1957-59; prof. adjoint U. Colo., Boulder, 1961-64; prof. physics and astronomy U. Hawaii, Honolulu, 1964-83, dir., Inst. Astronomy, 1967-83; dir. Nat. Optical Astronomy Obs., Tucson, 1983-87; astronomer Nat. Optical Astronomy Obs., 1987-92; cons. Nat. Bur. Stds., Boulder, 1960-62; disting. vis. scientist Jet Propulsion Lab., 1991-94. Author: (monograph) Spectral Line Formation, 1968; contbr. articles to profl. jours. Guggenheim fellow, 1970-71. Mem. Internat. Astron. Union, Am. Astron. Soc. Home: 1652 E Camino Cielo Tucson AZ 85718-1105

JEFFERIES, MICHAEL JOHN, retired electrical engineer; b. London, Feb. 2, 1941; came to U.S., 1967; s. Charles William and Dorothy Eleanor (Bates) J.; m. Mary Ann Cenci, May 27, 1969; children: Carlyn, Kevin. B.Sc. in Elec. Engring., Nottingham U., 1963, Ph.D., 1967. With Gen. Electric Co., Schenectady, 1967-76; mgr. cryogenics br. corp. research and devel. Gen. Electric Co., 1976-77, mgr. elec. systems and tech. lab., 1977-80, R&D mgr. engring. physics labs., 1980-87; gen. mgr. tech. Gen. Electric Motors, Ft. Wayne, Ind., 1987-90; faculty elec. engring. tech. Purdue U., 1990-93; v.p. tech. and mfg. Carrier Corp., Syracuse, N.Y., 1993-95, ret. Contbr. articles to profl. jours. Fellow IEEE; mem. Instn. Elec. Engrs. (U.K.). Home: 4315 Hepatica Hill Rd Manlius NY 13104-8714

JEFFERIES, ROBERT AARON, JR., diversified manufacturing executive, lawyer; b. Richmond, Ind., June 30, 1941; s. Robert Aaron and Roberta June (Hart) J.; m. Sylvia Mae Gilmore, Apr. 16, 1962; children—David E., Michael S., Stephen R. A.B. with honors in Govt, Earlham Coll., Richmond, 1963; J.D. with distinction (Herman C. Krannert scholar 1963-65), Ind. U., 1966. Bar: Ohio bar 1966, Ind. bar 1966, Ill. bar 1970, Mo. bar 1970. Assoc. firm Shumaker, Loop & Kendrick, Toledo, 1966-69; asst. gen. counsel, asst. sec. May Dept. Stores Co., St. Louis, 1969-77; v.p., gen. counsel, sec. Leggett & Platt, Inc., Carthage, Mo., 1977-90, sr. v.p., gen. counsel, sec., dir. mergers, acquisitions and strategic planning, 1990-92, sr. v.p. mergers, acqusitions, strategic planning, 1993—; also bd. dirs. Leggett & Platt, Inc., Carthage Mo., 1991—; bd. visitors Ind. U. Sch. of Law. Contbr. articles to legal jours.; bd. editors law jour., Ind. U., 1965-66. Mem. Am. Bar Assn., Ind. Bar Assn., Ohio Bar Assn., Ill. Bar Assn., Mo. Bar Assn., St. Louis Bar Assn., Am. Corp. Counsel Assn., Order of Coif. Office: Leggett & Platt Inc PO Box 757 Carthage MO 64836-0757

JEFFERIES, WILLIAM MCKENDREE, internist, educator; b. Richmond, Va., Oct. 1, 1915; s. Richard Henry and Mary Adeline (Harris) J.; m. Jeanne Telfair Mercer, Dec. 28, 1946 (dec. Dec., 1991); children: Richard Mercer, Scott McKendree, Colin Tucker, Leslie McLaurin. BA summa cum laude, Hampden Sydney Coll., 1935; MD, U. Va., 1940. Diplomate Am. Bd. Internal Medicine. Instr. in Math., Physics, Chemistry McGuires Univ. Sch., Richmond, Va., 1936; resident Mass. Gen. Hosp., Boston, 1940-42; flight surgeon San Antonio Aviation Cadet Ctr., 1942; post surgeon India China Div. Air Transport Command, 1943-45, divsn. med. inspector, 1945; rsch. fellow Am. Cancer Soc. Com. on Growth NRC Harvard Med. Sch., Boston, 1946-49; from instr. to asst. prof. medicine Case Western Reserve Med. Sch., Cleve., 1949-92; clin. prof. medicine U. Va. Sch. of Medicine, Charlottesville, 1993—; mem. internship com. Univ. Hosps., Cleve., 1955-65; bd. dirs. Brush Found., 1966-67; mem. com. for human investigation Luth. Med. Ctr., Cleve., 1977-92; chmn. diabetes adv. com. Euclid Gen. Hosp., Cleve., 1979-82. Author: (med. books) Safe Uses of Cortisone, 1981, Safe Uses of Cortisol, 1996; contbr. articles to profl. jours., chpts. to books. Com. mem. Boy Scouts Am., Shaker Heights, Ohio, 1957-68; past chmn. coun. of deacons, bd. of ministry and fellowship Plymouth Ch. of Shaker Heights. Lt. col. med. corps U.S. Army (attached to air force) India Burma Theatre. Fellow ACP; mem. AAAS, SAR, AMA, N.Y. Acad. Scis., Albemarle County Med. Soc., Am. Thyroid Assn. (Van Meter award 1949), Clin. Immunology Soc., Endocrine Soc., Am. Fertility Soc., Am. Fedn. for Clin. Rsch., Ctrl. Soc. for Clin. Rsch., Friends of Nat. Libr. of Medicine, Am. Legion, Cheshire Cheese Club, Raven Soc., Phi Beta Kappa, Omicron Delta Kappa, Alpha Omega Alpha, Kappa Alpha, Phi Beta Pi. Avocations: golf, fly fishing, skiing. *Anything worth doing is worth doing to the best of your ability.*

JEFFERS, BEN, political organization executive. Chmn. La. Dem. Party, 1997—. Office: PO Box 4385 Baton Rouge LA 70821-4385*

JEFFERS, DONALD E., retired insurance executive, consultant; b. Louisville, Ill., Aug. 21, 1925; s. Byron V. and Alice B. (Burgess) J.; m. Marion D. Benna, Aug. 14, 1948 (dec.); 1 son, Derek; m. Janice C. Smith, Apr. 21, 1979 (dec.). B.S. in Accountancy, U. Ill., 1948. C.P.A., Ill., D.C. Sr. acct. Coopers & Lybrand, CPAs, N.Y.C. and Chgo., 1948-56; asst. v.p. Continental Casualty Co., Chgo., 1956-64; dep. comptr. First Nat. Bank Boston, 1965-67; exec. v.p., treas. Interstate Nat. Corp., Chgo., 1967-74; pres., chief exec. officer Interstate Nat. Corp., 1974-85, also dir.; chmn., dir. Interstate Ins. Group and Geo. F. Brown & Sons Inc.; chmn. Jeffers & Assocs., Inc., San Diego, 1985—; former sec., dir. Ill. Ins. Info. Service; underwriting mem. Lloyd's London, 1977—. Served with inf. AUS, 1943-45. Decorated Purple Heart. Mem. AICPA, Ill. Soc. CPAs, Econ. Club (Chgo.). Home: 500 W Harbor Dr Apt 1021 San Diego CA 92101-7727 Office: 501 W Broadway Ste 339 San Diego CA 92101-3536

JEFFERS, IDA PEARLE, management consultant, volunteer; b. Houston, Tex., Sept. 5, 1935; d. Stanford Wilbur and Ida Pearle (Kinkead) Oberg; m. Samuel Lee Jeffers, Aug. 29, 1956; children: John Laurence (dec.), Julie Elizabeth Flynn, Melinda Leigh. Student, U. Colo., 1953-56; BA in History, U. N.Mex., 1957. Asst. to mayor City of Albuquerque, 1978, dir. capital improvements, 1979-81; pres. Orgn. Plus, 1988-98; guest lectr. U. N.Mex. Albuquerque Pub. Sch., 1968-71. Chmn. Comprehensive Plan Rev., Bond Issue, various coms., Albuquerque, 1968-98; mem. Middle Rio Grand Coun. Govts., Albuquerque, 1972-74; mem. Environ. Planning Commn., Albuquerque, 1972-77, chmn. 1975-76; chmn. Citizen Adv. Group, Community Devel., Albuquerque, 1974-75; mem. Jr. League, Albuquerque, 1966-97, bd. dirs. 1970-76; mem. N. Mex. Architect, Engrs. Joint Practice Bd. 1978-85, chmn. 1983-85; treas. St. Mark's Episcopal Ch., 1983-86; pres. Eldorado High Sch. Parents, Albuquerque, 1985-86; pres. Regional Conservation Land Trust, Albuquerque, 1987-91; trustee Found., Study and Care of Organic Brain Damage, Houston, 1972-82, pres. 1982-94; mem. Urban Transp. Planning Policy Bd., 1972-74; chmn. community advisors Albuquerque Youth Symphony, 1985-91; founder, chair Friends of Sandia (N.Mex.) Sch., 1965-68, chmn. devel. pre-sch. bd., 1974; mentor Leadership Albuquerque, 1987-91; bd. dirs. Good Govt. Group, Albuquerque, 1988-92, treas. 1988-92; mem., treas. Albuquerque Arts Alliance, 1988-91; mem. Albuquerque All Faiths, All Faith's Receiving Home Aux., 1964-68, sec. 1966, Jr. Women Club, 1963-66, Chaparral Coun. Girl Scouts leaders, 1971-73, selections chmn., 1973-74, Albuquerque Tutorial Coun., 1967-69; foundation bd. Albuquerque Youth Symphony, 1995-97. Recipient Disting. Pub. Svc. award, State of N. Mex., 1975, Disting. Woman of N. Mex. award, N.Mex. Women's Polit. Caucus, 1976, Golden Talon award Eldorado High Sch., Albuquerque, 1985, Panhellenic Coun. Disting. Alumnae award 1979. Mem. Rotary, Delta Gamma (pres. 1963-67, chmn. collegiate adv. bd. 1968-71, Cable and Shield awards 1970, 77). Republican. Episcopalian. Avocations: gardening, sewing, skiing, music.

JEFFERS, KEVIN ALLEN, vocalist; b. South Milwaukee, Wis., Mar. 11, 1961; s. Carrold Aurthur Jeffers and May (Allen) Arndt. MusB cum laude, Heidelberg Coll., 1983; MusM cum laude, Northwestern U., 1984; DMA, U. Wis., 1991. Prof. voice U. Wis., Platteville, 1992-93; pvt. voice instr., Evanston, Ill., 1983-85, Madison, Wis., 1985-90; teaching staff U. Wis., Madison, 1986-91; composer of classical vocal lit., 1985-90; McLean Artist resident Musical Theatre Works, 1998-99. Singer (Edward Rutledge) 1776, 1985, (John Proctor) The Crucible, (Virgil Thomson) Mother of Us All, 1986, (Boatswain) H.M.S. Pinafore, 1986, (Second Critic) Tightrope, 1985, (Maletesta) Don Pasquale, 1987 (recitalist, lectr.) Am. Mus. Theatre, 1988, (Melichor) Amahl and the Night Visitor, 1988, (Danilo) The Merry Widow, 1988, (Count Almaviva) Marriage of Figaro, 1988, (Carl-Magnus) A Little Night Music, 1989, Life's Cycle, (Baritone) Hodie, 1990, (Jack Point) Yeoman of the Guard; composer (music, book, lyrics) Life's Cycle, 1990, Starry Messenger, 1992, Spoon River, 1994, If It Happens in the Song, 1996, Caught in the Net, 1997; composer over 250 songs. Eckstein grantee Northwestern U., 1983; recipient Madison Civic Opera award, 1985. Mem. Pi Kappa Lambda. Episcopalian. Avocations: fitness, reading, philosophy, sports. Home: 1173A 2nd Ave # 190 New York NY 10021-8277

JEFFERS, MICHAEL BOGUE, lawyer; b. Wenatchee, Wash., July 10, 1940; s. Richard G. and Betty (Ball) J. BA, U. Wash., 1962, LLB, 1964; LLM in Taxation, NYU, 1970. Bar: Wash. 1964, N.Y. 1970, Calif. 1988. Ptnr. Hughes & Jeffers, Wenatchee, 1964-65, 68, Hill, Betts & Nash, N.Y.C., 1970-72, Battle Fowler, N.Y.C., 1973-88, Buchalter, Nemer, Fields & Younger, Newport Beach, Calif., 1988-89, Riordan & McKinzie, Costa Mesa, Calif., 1989-90, Phillips, Haglund, Haddan & Jeffers, Newport Beach, 1991-93, Jeffers, Wilson Shaff & Falk, LLP, Newport Beach, Calif., 1994—; sec. Thornburg Mortgage Asset Corp., Hi-Shear Tech., Inc. Alumni trustee U. Wash., 1970-73; bd. dirs. Ballet Pacifica. Mem. ABA, Calif. Bar Assn., Orange County Bar Assn., Wash. State Bar Assn., U. Wash. Alumni Assn. (pres. Greater N.Y. chpt. 1972-88), Pacific Club, Nat. Wild Turkey Fedn., Explorers Club, Phi Gamma Delta. Office: Jeffers Wilson Shaff & Falk LLP 18881 Von Karman Ave Ste 1400 Irvine CA 92612-1562*

JEFFERSON, DAVID, computer scientist; b. Pasadena, Calif., Dec. 21, 1938; s. Benjamin Fleetwood and Helen (Kenoss) J.; m. Patricia Elaine Pounds, Jan. 7, 1967 (dec. Oct. 1994); children: Eric (dec.), Kimberly; m. Neva Marie Carlson, May 17, 1997. BS, Calif. Inst. Tech., 1960; AM, Columbia U., 1962; PhD, U. Mich., 1969. Computer scientist Naval Surface Warfare Ctr., Dahlgren, Va., 1960-72, 1973-74; vis. prof. Naval Postgrad. Sch., Monterey, Calif., 1972-73; mgr. info. system design David Taylor Rsch. Ctr., Carderock, Md., 1974-82; mgr. database architecture Nat. Bur. Standards, Gaithersburg, Md., 1982-87; chief info. system engring. div. Nat. Inst. Standards and Tech. (formerly Nat. Bur. Standards), Gaithersburg, Md., 1987-96, cons., 1996—; lectr. U. Md., College Park, 1977-82; database rapporteur Internat. Orgn. for Standardization, 1986—. USN fellow Columbia U., 1961, U. Mich., 1964, NSF fellow U. MIch., 1965; recipient Bronze medal U.S. Dept. Commerce, 1986, Silver medal, 1991. Mem. IEEE, Assn. Computing Machinery, Sr. Exec. Svc., Sr. Execs. Assn., Sigma Xi. Episcopalian. Office: Nat Inst of Stds and Tech Bldg 101 Rm A434 Gaithersburg MD 20899*

JEFFERSON, JAMES WALTER, psychiatry educator; b. Mineola, N.Y., Aug. 14, 1937; s. Thomas Hutton and Alice (Withers) J.; m. Susan Mary Cole, June 25, 1965; children: Lara, Shawn, James C. BS, Bucknell U., 1958; MD, U. Wis., 1964. Cert. Am. Bd. Psychiatry and Neurology, Am. Bd. Internal Medicine. Asst. prof. psychiatry U. Wis. Med. Sch., Madison, 1974-78, assoc. prof., 1978-81, prof., 1981-92; disting. sr. scientist Dean Found. for Health, Rsch. and Edn., Madison, 1992-98; clin. prof. psychiatry U. Wis. Med. Sch., Madison, 1992—; disting. sr. scientist Madison Inst. Medicine, 1998—; pres. Healthcare Tech. Sys., Madison, 1998—; co-dir. Lithium Info. Ctr., Madison, 1975—, Obsessive Compulsive Info. Ctr., Madison, 1990—; dir. Ctr. Affective Disorders, Madison, 1983-92. Co-author: Neuropsychiatric Features of Medical Disorders, 1981, Lithium Encyclopedia for Clinical Practice, 1983, 2nd edit., 1987, Depression and Its Treatment, 1984, 2nd edit., 1992, Anxiety and Its Treatment, 1986, Handbook of Medical Psychiatry, 1996. Served to maj. U.S. Army, 1968-71. Fellow ACP, Am. Psychiat. Assn.; mem. Collegium Internat. Neuropsychopharmacologium, Am. Soc. Clin. Psychopharmacology (nat. bd. trustees 1996—). Avocations: bicycling, travel. Office: Madison Inst Medicine 7617 Mineral Point Rd Madison WI 53717-1623

JEFFERSON, KURT WAYNE, political science educator; b. Macomb, Ill., Jan. 17, 1966; s. Robert Wayne and Sally Ann (Wallace) J.; m. Lori Jeanene Merriman, Aug. 8, 1992; children: Kelly Lynn, Megan Leigh. BA in Polit. Sci. magna cum laude, Western Ill. U., 1988; MA in Polit. Sci., U. Mo., 1989, PhD in Polit. Sci., 1993. Grad. tchg. asst. dept. polit. sci. U. Mo., Columbia, 1988-91, instr. dept. polit. sci., 1992; instr. dept. social and cultural studies Stephens Coll., Columbia, 1992-93; asst. prof. polit. sci. dept. polit. sci. Westminster Coll., Fulton, Mo., 1993-99, assoc. prof. polit. sci. dept. polit. sci., 1999—, chair dept. polit sci., 1999—; vis. asst. prof. polit. sci. dept. polit. sci. U. Mo., Columbia, summer 1993; dir. Churchill Acad., Westminster Coll., Fulton, 1996—, coord. leadership studies, 1997—; cons. U. Mo. Rsch. Bd., U. Mo. Sys., St. Louis, 1996; edit. adv. bd. Collegiate Press, Alta Loma, Calif., 1997—. Contbr. articles to profl. jours. Dir. men's ministry United Pentecostal Ch., Columbia, 1995—; soccer coach Columbia Soccer League, 1993-94. Mem. Am. Polit. Sci. Assn., Brit. Politics Group. Avocations: Bible reading, sports, banjo playing, reading, baseball card collecting. Fax: 573-592-5217. E-mail: jefferk@jaynet.wcmo.edu. Home: 3701 Triple Crown Dr Columbia MO 65202-4849 Office: Westminster Coll 501 Westminster Ave Fulton MO 65251-1230

JEFFERSON, MARGO L., journalist; b. Chgo., Oct. 17, 1947. BA in English and Am. Lit. cum laude, Brandeis U., 1968; MS, Columbia U., 1971. Editor Newsweek, 1973-78; asst. prof. dept. journalism NYU, 1979-83, 89-91; contbg. editor Vogue, 1984-89, 7 Days, 1984-89; lectr. Am. Lit., performing arts & criticism Columbia U., N.Y.C., 1991-93; critic culture desk The New York Times, 1993-95, Sunday theater critic, 1995-97, cultural corr., 1997—. Recipient Pulitzer Prize for criticism, 1995. Office: The New York Times 229 W 43rd St New York NY 10036-3959*

JEFFERSON, PEGGY LEE, English educator; b. Whittier, Calif., Oct. 19, 1949; d. James A. and Mary Lee Rea; m. Kit D. Jacoby, June 15, 1978 (div.

Sept. 1991); children: Jenifer, Chip, Dale; m. Bucky Jefferson, July 3, 1997; children: Karissa, Nicole Jefferson. BA in English, Calif. State U., Chico, 1993. Cert. secondary tchr., Calif. ROP bus. tchr. Butte Valley H.S., Dorris, Calif., 1988-91; English tchr. Weed (Calif.) H.S., 1995; English/ROP bus. tchr. Happy Camp H.S., Calif., 1995—. Avocation: reading. Office: Happy Camp High Sch 234 Indian Creek Rd Happy Camp CA 96039

JEFFERSON, RALPH HARVEY, international affairs consultant; b. Rochester, N.Y., Aug. 6, 1927; s. Charles Frederic and Mabel Florence (Thomas) J.; m. Jenny Chaapel Clark, Oct. 29, 1960; children: Edward Clark, Jenny Chaapel, Alexandra Victoria. BA, Yale U., 1949; LLB, Harvard U., 1952; cert., Inst. d'Etudes Politiques, Paris, 1956. Bar: N.Y. 1952. Treas. Harvard Legal Aid Bur., 1950-52; atty. Root, Ballantine, Harlan, Bushby and Palmer, N.Y.C., 1952-55; legal adviser to def. adviser U.S. Mission to NATO, Paris, 1960-63; atty. Office of Asst. Gen. Counsel, Office Sec. of Def., Washington, 1957-60, 63-66; acting spl. adviser for prisoner of war affairs Office of Asst. Sec. Def., Washington, 1970-71, dep. dir. in Europe-NATO Directorate, 1967-70, 72-78; civil dep. comdt., dir. studies NATO Def. Coll., Rome, 1978-82; dir. for NATO policy Office Asst. Sec. Def., Washington, 1982-88; sr. rsch. fellow Nat. Def. U., Washington, 1988-89; internat. affairs cons. Washington, 1994—. Bd. dirs. Chol Chol Found. for Human Devel. With USN. Mem. Diplomatic and Consular Officers Ret. (assoc.). Avocations: piano, tennis, sailing. Home and Office: 507 Epping Forest Rd Annapolis MD 21401-6562

JEFFERSON, SANDRA TRAYLOR, choreographer, ballet coach; b. Tarboro, N.C., Feb. 28, 1942; d. Charles Labon and Doris Vivian (Parker) Traylor; m. Milton Franklin Jefferson, July 2, 1960; children: Mark Franklin, Todd Christopher. Student, Parks Sch. Dance, Petersburg, Va., 1947-58, Sch. of the Richmond (Va.) Ballet, 1958-60; diploma, Julia Mildred Harper Sch. Dance, Richmond, 1960; studied with Robert David Brown, Sterling, Va., 1978-80. Soloist Ballet Impromptu, Richmond, 1958-60; freelance dance instr. Chantilly, Va., 1968-70; ballet coach Artistic Skating Club of Sterling, 1980; founder, dir. Ballet for Skaters, Manassas, Va., 1980-89; artistic dir., cons. in choreography No. Va. Artistic Skating Club, Manassas, 1986-89; artistic dir. Skating Club of Manassas, 1989; founder, dir. Ballet for Skaters, Seabrook, Md., 1989-94; choreographer, ballet coach Nat. Capitol Dance and Figure Club, Seabrook and Washington, 1989-94; founder, dir. Ballet for Figure Skaters, Sterling, Va., 1993-94; students include nat. medalists in the U.S. and Can. and mems. Can. World Team, U.S. Olympic Sports Festival Team; freelance choreographer, ballet coach, Sterling, 1993—. Developer: Brosano Technique Vocabulary of Movement, 1986, Free Form Ballet, 1993; co-developer (artistic skating technique) Brosano Technique, 1981. Social dir. Jaycee-ettes, Winchester, Va., 1963-67. Recipient Achievement award Jaycee-ettes, 1963, 64, 65, 66, 67, U.S. S.E. Soc. Roller Skating Tchrs. Am. award, 1988, World Decoration of Excellence award Am. Biog. Inst., 1989. Mem. Profl. Dance Tchrs. Assn. Methodist. Avocations: art, music. Home and Office: 507 S Maple Ct Sterling VA 20164-2710

JEFFERSON, WILLIAM L. (JEFF JEFFERSON), congressman; b. Lake Providence, LA, Mar. 14, 1947. BA, Southern Univ., 1969; JD, Harvard U., 1972; LLM, Georgetown U, 1996. U.S. Ct. Appeals law clerk, lawyer; legislative asst. to Sen. Johnston; state sen., 1981-90; mem. 102nd-105th Congresses 2nd dist. La. U.S. Ho Reps., 1991—; mem. Ways and Means Com., Dem. Steering Com., subcoms. Human Resources and Trade. Served AUS, Judge Advocate General Corps. Office: US Ho of Reps 240 Cannon Bldg Ofc Bldg Washington DC 20515-1802

JEFFERY, GEOFFREY MARRON, medical parasitologist; b. Dundee, N.Y., May 13, 1919; s. Joseph Ewart and Augusta (Knapp) J.; m. Jane Wicker, Aug. 16, 1941; children: Janet A. Harrison, Thomas W., Sarah V. Houghton, Susan E. Tosh. AB, Hobart Coll., 1940; MA, Syracuse U., 1942; ScD, Johns Hopkins U., 1944; MPH, Yale U., 1961. Biol. aide health and safety dept. TVA, 1944; commd. officer USPHS, 1944, scientist dir., 1960; tech. aid, cons. malaria control in war areas TVA, 1944-45; assigned divsn. lab. svcs. Communicable Disease Ctr., 1945-46; charge br. lab. Sch. Tropical Medicine Communicable Disease Ctr., San Juan, P.R., 1946-47; asst. prof. biology U. Bridgeport, Conn., 1947-48; charge Malaria Rsch. Lab., NIH, Milledgeville, Ga., 1948-54; mem. staff Lab. Tropical Diseases-Lab. Parasite Chemotherapy, NIAID, NIH, Columbia, S.C., 1954-63; head sect. epidemiology Lab. Tropical Diseases-Lab. Parasite Chemotherapy, NIAID, NIH, 1961-63; asst. chief Lab. Parasite Chemotherapy, NIAID, NIH, Bethesda, 1963-66, acting chief, 1966, chief, 1967-69; chief C.Am. Malaria Rsch. Sta., San Salvador, El Salvador, 1969-74; asst. dir. Bur. Tropical Diseases, Ctr. Disease Control, Atlanta, 1974-75; dir. vector biology and control div. Bur. Tropical Diseases, 1975-81; asst. dir. divsn. parasitic diseases Ctr. for Infectious Diseases, Ctrs. for Disease Control, 1982-84; Mem. expert adv. panel on malaria WHO, 1963—; assoc. mem. commn. malaria Armed Forces Epidemiol. Bd., 1965-69, mem., 1969-73; Del. Internat. Congress Tropical Medicine and Malaria, Lisbon, 1958, Rio de Janeiro, 1963, Teheran, Iran, 1968; Del. Internat. Congress Parasitology, Rome, Italy, 1964, Washington, 1969; Del. Internat. Conf. on Protozoology, London, 1965, Latin Am. Congress Parasitology, Medellin, Colombia, 1973; mem. sci. group on chemotherapy of malaria WHO, Geneva, 1967, mem. sci. group on parasitology, Teheran, 1968; cons. on status of malaria in Africa AID, 1979; mem. sci. working group on applied field rsch. in malaria WHO, Geneva, 1979, mem. steering com., 1981-86; cons. on malaria U.S.-China Health Agreement, 1980; del. Asia and Pacific Conf. on Malaria, Honolulu, 1985; temp. advisor meetings WHO, Kuala Lumpur, 1981, Albuquerque, 1982, Nairobi, 1983, Bangkok, 1984; invited participant concerted action 1st plenary meeting on malaria modelling European Union, Tuebingen, Germany, 1998. Contbr. numerous articles to sci. jours. tropical medicine and parasitology. Recipient Pub. Health Svc. Commendation medal, 1966, Dept. Army cert. of appreciation patriotic civilian svc., 1973. Fellow Royal Soc. Tropical Medicine (local sec. 1984-89); mem. Am. Soc. Tropical Medicine and Hygiene (sec.-treas. 1961-67, v.p. 1971, pres. 1975, Bailey K. Ashford award 1959), Am. Soc. Parasitologists, Assn. Southea. Biologists (editor bull. 1959-60, exec. com. 1962-66), Tropical Medicine Assn. Washington, Southea. Soc. Parasitologists, S.C. Acad. Sci. (mem. council 1960, 62, Jefferson award 1952, 56, 60), Commd. Officers Assn. USPHS, Sigma Xi, Kappa Sigma. Presbyterian. Home: 1093 Blackshear Dr Decatur GA 30033-2612 Office: Center Disease Control Atlanta GA 30333

JEFFERY, JAMES NELS, protective services official; b. Torrance, Calif., May 16, 1944; s. Daryl Fredrick and Mildred Evelyn (Sogard) J. AA, Long Beach City Coll., 1964; student, Calif. State U., Long Beach, 1964-65, Calif. State U., Sacramento, 1979-80. Capt., firefighter L.A. Fire Dept., 1965-87; dir. Long Beach (Calif.) Search & Rescue Unit, 1968—; asst. chief fire divsn. Calif. Office Emergency Svcs., Riverside, 1987-97; rep. Firescope Communications, Riverside, 1979—. Co-author emergency plans. Chmn. svc. com. Boy Scouts Am., Long Beach, 1979-81, tng. com., 1982—; bd. dirs. Long Beach Community Episepsy Clinic, 1971-72. Recipient Disting. Svc. award Long Beach Jaycees, 1977, Community Svc. award Long Beach Fire Dept., 1978, Silver Beaver award Boy Scouts Am., 1983, Commendation Mayor City of L.A., 1985. Mem. Calif. State Firemen's Assn., Calif. Fire Chiefs Assn., Nat. Coord. Coun. on Emergency Mgmt., Nat. Eagle Scout Assn., So. Calif. Assn. Foresters and Fire Wardens, Lions, Elks. Republican. Lutheran. Avocations: vol. work, camping, hunting. Home: 3916 Cerritos Ave Long Beach CA 90807-3608 Office: PO Box 92257 Long Beach CA 90809-2257

JEFFERY, PETER GRANT, musicologist, fine arts educator; b. N.Y.C., Oct. 19, 1953; s. Grant Turner and Mathilde (Matano) J.; m. Margot Fassler, 1983; children: Joseph Jeffery Fassler, Francis Fassler Jeffery. BA cum laude, Bklyn. Coll., CUNY, 1975; MFA, Princeton U., 1977, PhD, 1980. Cataloguer, editor Hill Monastic Manuscript Libr., St. John's U., Collegeville, Minn., 1980-82; Mellon faculty fellow Harvard U., Cambridge, Mass., 1982-83; mem. faculty N.Y. Sch. Liturgical Music, N.Y.C., 1983-84; asst. prof. U. Del., Newark, 1984-87, assoc. prof., 1987-92; prof. Princeton U., 1993—; vis. scholar Ctr. for Lit. and Cultural Studies, Harvard U., 1990-92, Boston Coll., 1992-93; vis. prof. Harvard U., 1992-93. Author: Re-envisioning Past Musical Cultures, 1992; contbr. articles to jours. in field; mem. editorial bd. Plainsong and Medieval Music (Cambridge, Eng.), 1991—, Ethiopian Christian Liturgical Chant, 1993-97. NEH rsch. grantee, 1986-88, John D. and Catherine T. MacArthur Found. fellow, 1987-92. Mem. Am. Musicological Soc. (coun. 1986-88, Alfred Einstein award 1985), Medieval Acad. Am., N.Am. Acad. Liturgy, Soc. Bibl. Lit., Soc. for Ethnomusicology. Roman Catholic. Office: Princeton U Dept Music Princeton NJ 08544

JEFFERY, WILLIAM RICHARD, developmental biology educator, researcher; b. Chgo., June 9, 1944; s. William and Marjorie (Gross) J. BS, U. Ill., Chgo., 1967; PhD, U. Iowa, 1971. Rsch. assoc. U. Wis., Madison, 1971-72, Sch. Medicine, Tufts U., Boston, 1972-74; asst. prof. biophysics U. Houston, 1974-77; asst. prof. zoology U. Tex., Austin, 1977-80, assoc. prof., 1980-85, prof., 1985-87, J.F. Miescher Regents prof., 1987-90; prof. zoology U. Calif., Davis, 1990-93, prof. molecular and cellular biology, 1993-96; prof., head biology Pa. State U., University Park, 1997-99; prof., chair biology U. Md., College Park, 1999—; co-dir. embryology course Marine Biology Lab., Woods Hole, Mass., 1983-87, active, 1975—. Mem. editl. bd. Devel., 1987—, Jour. Exptl. Zoology, 1989—, Seminars in Devel. Biology, 1990-96, Seminars in Cell and Devel. Biology, 1997—, Biol. Bull., 1985-90, Cell Motility and the Cytoskeleton, 1985-86, Internat. Jour. Devel. Biology, 1989—, Animal Biology, 1991—; N.Am. editor Zygote, 1993-96. Fellow AAAS; mem. Am. Soc. Zoologists (divsn. chmn. 1988-90, Outstanding Svc. award 1990), Soc. Devel. Biologists (trustee 1987-89, 1995-97, pres. 1995-96), Am. Soc. Cell Biology, Sigma Xi. Home: 714 Tanley Rd Silver Spring MD 20904 Office: Univ Md Dept Biology 1200 Bio/Psych Bldg College Park MD 20742

JEFFORDS, JAMES MERRILL, senator; b. Rutland, Vt., May 11, 1934; s. Olin Merrill and Marion (Hausman) J.; m. Elizabeth Daley; children: Leonard Olin, Laura Louise. BS, Yale U., 1956; LLB, Harvard U., 1962. Bar: Vt. 1962. Law clk. to Judge Ernest Gibson Vt. Dist., 1962; ptnr. Bishop, Crowley & Jeffords, Rutland, 1963-66, Kenney, Carbine & Jeffords, Rutland, 1966-69; atty. gen. State of Vt., 1969-72; ptnr. George E. Rice, Jr. and James M. Jeffords, 1973-74; mem. 94th-100th Congresses from Vt., mem. agr. com., ranking minority mem. edn. and labor com., chmn. environ. study conf., 1978-79, a founder Congl. solar coalition, mem. Congl. tourism caucus, mem. Nat. Commn. on Employment and Unemployment Stats., 1979-89, U.S. senator from Vt., 1989—, chmn. health, edn., labor and pensions com., labor/human rels. com., vet. affairs com., fin. com.; spl. com. on aging; mem. New Eng. Congl. Caucus, N.E.-Midwest Coalition; town agt. Shrewsbury, 1964-68, zoning adminstr., 1966-68, zoning adminstr., 1966-68; mem. Jud. Selection Bd., 1967-68; chmn. Hwy. Dept. Investigating Com., 1968; mem. Vt. Senate, 1967-68. With USNR, 1956-59; capt. Res. (ret.). Mem. Am. Bar Assn., Vt. Bar Assn., Rutland County Bar Assn., Am. Judicature Soc. (dir. 1973-76), VFW. Republican. Congregationalist (trustee). Lodges: Lions, Elks. Office: US Senate 728 Hart Bldg Washington DC 20510-4503*

JEFFREDO, JOHN VICTOR, aerospace engineer, manufacturing company executive, inventor; b. Los Angeles, Nov. 5, 1927; s. John Edward and Pauline Matilda (Whitten) J., m. Elma Jean Nesmith (div. 1958); children: Joyce Jean Jeffredo Ryder, Michael John; m. Doris Louise Hinz, (div. 1980); children: John Victor, Louise Victoria Jeffredo-Warden; m. Gerda Adelheid Pillich, 1980. *John Jeffredo's Great Grandfather Francis Jeffredo left Brittany in 1861, landing in Mexico with Napoleon III's French troops, then heading to California in 1863. He married Great Grandmother Jeffredo, A Native American Santa Catalina Islander, in 1865. His Great Grandfather Juan Matias Sanchez, born of an English mother and Spanish father in Spain during Wellington's Peninsula Campaign against Napoleon, left England in 1835. He reached California in 1836, acquiring large tracts of land in the Los Angeles, California area. John's Great Grandfather Thomas Hunter arrived in California with the Mormon Battalion in 1847. He married John's Great Grandmother, Paulina Wala, a Native American San Clemente Islander, in 1851.* Grad. in aeronautical engring., Cal-Aero Tech. Inst., 1948; AA machine design, Pasadena City Coll., 1951; grad. in electronics, The Ordnance Sch. U.S. Army, 1951; postgrad, U. So. Calif., 1955-58, Palomar Coll., 1977-96; MBA, La Jolla U., 1980, PhD in human rels., 1984. Design engr. Douglas Aircraft Co., Long Beach and Santa Monica, Calif., 1955-58; devel. engr. Honeywell Ordnance Corp., Duarte, Calif., 1958-62; cons. Honeywell Devel. Labs, Seattle, 1962-65; supr. mech. engring. dept. aerospace divsn. Control Data Corp., Pasadena, Calif., 1965-68; project engr. Cubic Corp., San Diego, 1968-70; supr. mech. engring. dept. Babcock Electronics Co., Costa Mesa, Calif., 1970-72; owner, operator Jeffredo Gunsight Co., Fallbrook, Calif., 1971-81; chief engr. Western Designs, Inc., Fallbrook, Calif., 1972-81, exec. dir., 1981-88, CEO, 1988-96, owner, operator, 1981-87; owner, operator Western Design Concepts, Inc., 1987-94; exec. dir. JXJ, Inc., San Marcos, Calif., 1981-88, CEO, 1988—; mgr. Jeffredo Gunsight divsn., 1981-94, chief engr. JXJ, Inc., 1987-92 (merger JXJ, Inc. and Western Design Concepts, Fallbrook, Calif.), prin. 1992—, owner, mgr., Energy Assocs., San Diego, 1982-86, pres. Jeffredo Internat., 1984-88, founder, CEO John-Victor Internat., San Marcos, Calif., Frankfurt, Fed. Rep. Germany, 1988—, The Jeffredo Solution, Fallbrook, 1996—, engring. cons. Action Instruments Co., Inc., Gen. Dynamics, Alcyon Corp., Systems Exploration, Inc. (all San Diego), Hughes Aircraft Co., El Segundo, Allied-Bendix, San Marcos, bd. dirs.Indian World Corp., JXJ, Inc., John-Victor Internat. Author: Gabrieleño, New Perspective on the Island Gabrielino, The Ocean People, Wildcatting; contbr. articles to trade jours. and mags.; guest editl. writer Town Hall, San Diego Union; narrator: (film) The Sacred Desert, 1994; spkr. in field; patentee agrl. frost control, vehicle off-road drive system, recoil absorbing system for firearms, telescope sight mounting system for firearms, breech mech. sporting firearm, elec. switch activating system, 37 others, others pending. Mem. San Diego County Border Tsk Force on Undocumented Aliens, 1979-80, 81-82, mgr., rep. Island Gabrieleno Group, NAGPRA repatriation project, 1995—, historian Maritime Shoshone, 1995—, spokesman Island Shoshone, 1995—, chmn. Native Californian Coalition, 1982—, bd. dirs. Nat. Geographic Soc., 1968. With U.S. Army, 1951-53. Recipient Superior Svc. Commendation award U.S. Naval Ordnance Test Station, Pasadena, 1959. Mem. AIAA (sr.), NRA (life), Soc. Automotive Engrs., San Diego Zool. Soc., Sierra Club (life), The Wilderness Soc., Pechanga Band of Luiseno Indians (life), Cova, Catalina Island Mus. Soc., The Planetary Soc., Soc. for Calif. Archaeology, North County Scots. Avocations: chess, music, archaeology, conservation, sculpture. Home: 1629 Via Monserate Fallbrook CA 92028-9305 Office: PO Box 669 San Marcos CA 92079-0669

JEFFRESS, CHARLES N., government agency administrator; b. Feb. 25, 1948. BA, U. N.C., 1971; grad. Program for Sr. Execs. in Govt., Harvard U., 1990. Asst. commr. N.C. Dept. Labor, 1977-92, dep. commr., 1993-97; asst. sec. of labor for occupl. safety and health U.S. Dept. Labor, Washington, 1997—. Mem. Phi Beta Kappa. Office: OSHA/Dept Labor 200 Constitution Ave NW Washington DC 20210-0001*

JEFFREY, CHRISTINA FAWCETT, political scientist, educator; b. El Paso, Tex., July 14, 1947; d. John Rutherford and Patricia Alsop (Kelly) Fawcett; m. Fredrick Dale Price, July 4, 1966 (div. Dec. 1988); children: Fredrick, William, Patricia Michelle, Christina Crawford; m. Robert C. Jeffrey Jr., Mar. 22, 1989; 1 child, Marjorie. Student, Vassar Coll., 1965-66; AB, Plano U., 1969; MA, U. Ala., Tuscaloosa, 1973, PhD, 1984. NDEA fellow U. Ala., Tuscaloosa, 1969-72, grad. tchg. asst., 1970-73, asst. dir. aquatics, 1973, dir. internat. student affairs, 1973-77, dir. student affairs Capstone Coll. Nursing, 1977-80; mgr. internat. trade, exec. sec. Ala. World Trade Assn., Birmingham, Ala., 1980-82; asst. prof. polit. sci. Troy State U., Weisbaden, Germany, 1984-85, Troy (Ala.) State U., 1985-87; assoc. prof. Kennesaw (Ga.) State U., 1987—; mem. Ala. Commn. Yr. of the Child, 1979-80, Ala. Wmen's Commn., 1987-91; mem. acad. adv. bd. Ga. Pub. Policy Found., Atlanta, 1992-99; mem. strategic planning coun. Nonprofit Resource Ctr., Marietta, Ga., 1997—. Contbr. articles to profl. jours. Grass roots reporter Prodigy Network, 1996—; historian U.S. Ho. of Reps., Washington, 1995; founder, pres. Operation Integrity, 1996—; candidate for Congress, Ga., 1999. Fellow Intercollegiate Studies Inst., Phila., 1969; Nat. Def. Edn. Act fellow, 1969-72; recipient fellowship Operation Integrity, 1999. Mem. ASPA (pres. Ga. chpt. 1994-96, policy issues commn. 1995—, chmn editl. bd. PATimes 1998—). Roman Catholic. Avocations: swimming, tennis. Office: Kennesaw State U 1000 Chastain Rd NW Kennesaw GA 30144-5588

JEFFREY, FRANCIS, software developer, forecaster; b. Calif., 1950. *Francis Jeffrey arrived into a life marked by events from World War II. His father Jess, a US Marine hero, was wounded and traumatized in the fierce battle of Iwo Jima, and a grandfather was lost at sea. Francis grew up in a family business headed by his aunt Connie, a banker, and uncle Joseph Busco, a gifted industrial engineer and entrepreneur, who built Photic Corporation into the fastest growing industrial employer in San Diego County. One cousin, Marie Francesca Busco is a scholar and author in European art. His other cousins, Tom, Paul and James Dowdy, are academics, and his sister, Janice Diskan, is a horticulturist.* BA in Computational Neurophysiology, U. Calif., Berkeley, 1972. Research assoc. U. Calif., San Diego, 1972-73; cons. Sci. Applications, Inc., La Jolla, Calif., 1973-75; entrepreneur Big Sur, Calif., 1973-77; cons. Alive Systems Info. Scis., San Francisco, 1978-87; founder, pres., chief exec. officer Alive Systems, Inc. and Elfnet, Inc., Malibu, Calif., 1987—; cons. Inst. for Advanced Computation, Sunnyvale, Calif., 1973-75, Human-Dolphin Found., 1980-82, 87-89, Esalen Inst., 1982-83. *ELFNET embodies his Patent Cooperation Treaty International Publication WO97/24663 (1997), a system providing for programming and communication of programs as an integral part of cultural transmission and human communication, based on teleportable packages of relationship, "clumplets," that are swatches of virtual brain tissue transplantable between neuronal environments called "clumps" hosted on conventional computers--So we have a robust cultural medium that can also form the basis for programming in the 21st Century, with its emphasis on network communication as interactive multipersonal environment. After the "2000 Bug" debacle, ELPHIN will replace the opacity of current technology with a lucid humanistic paradigm.* Author: (with others) Handbook of States of Consciousness, 1986, John Lilly So Far, 1990, (with others) Voices from The Edge, 1995, Patent Cooperation Treaty International Publication WO 97/24663, 1997, Japanese edit., 1998 ; originator Malibu civic dolphin protection resolution, 1992, whales as living cultural resources resolution, 1994; designer com. co-piloting; creator symposium Radical Connectionism and the Visualization of Networkk Programs, 1999—. Co-founder New Forum, Monterey, Calif., 1984, Gt. Whales Found., San Francisco, 1986, chmn., CEO, Malibu (Calif.) Dolphin Recovery Ctr., 1996—; co-founder Big Sur chpt. L5 Nat. Space Soc.; creator Annual Malibu (Calif.) Symposium on Radical Connectionism and the Visualization of Network Programs, 1999—. Mem. AAAS, IEEE, Assn. for Computing Machinery, Am. Soc. for Cybernetics (founding, control sys. group), Amnesty Internat. (leadership group), Cousteau Soc. (life mem.), Raoul Wallenberg Inst. Ethics (adv. bd.). Achievements include invention of conscious networks system and "adverteasing". E-mail: francis@elfi.com. Home and Office: PO Box 6844 Malibu CA 90264-6844

JEFFREY, RICHARD CARL, philosophy educator; b. Boston, Aug. 5, 1926; s. Mark M. and Jane (Markovitz) J.; m. Edith Kelman, Jan. 2, 1955; children—Daniel, Pamela. Student, Boston U., 1943-44; M.A., U. Chgo., 1951; Ph.D., Princeton U., 1957. Logical designer computers MIT Digital Computer Lab. also Lincoln Lab., 1952-55; asst. prof. elec. engring. MIT, 1958-59; asst. prof. philosophy Stanford U., 1959-63; vis. mem. (Inst. for Advanced Study), 1963; assoc. prof. philosophy CCNY, 1964-67; prof. philosophy U. Pa., 1967-74, Princeton U., 1974—. Author: The Logic of Decision, 1965, 2nd edit, 1983, Formal Logic: Its Scope & Limits, 1967, 3d rev. edit., 1990, (with George Boolos) Computability and Logic, 1974, 3d edit., 1989, Probability and the Art of Judgement, 1992; editor: (with Rudolf Carnap) Studies in Inductive Logic and Probability, 1970, vol. 2, 1979. Served with USNR, 1944-46. Mem. Am. Philos. Assn., Assn. for Symbolic Logic, Philosophy of Sci. Assn. (pres.), Am. Acad. Arts and Scis. Home: 55 Patton Ave Princeton NJ 08540-5251

JEFFREY, ROBERT CAMPBELL, university dean; b. San Antonio, Nov. 11, 1927; s. John George and Mary (Anderson) J.; m. Marjorie Louise Carspecken, Feb. 9, 1947 (div. 1973); children: Robert Campbell, Paula, Douglas, Nora, Margaret; m. Phillis Jane Hopkins Rienstra, Nov. 1, 1974. B.A., U. Iowa, 1949, M.A., 1950, Ph.D., 1957. Asst. prof. Cornell Coll., Mt. Vernon, Iowa, 1950-53; instr. U. Iowa, Iowa City, 1953-54; asst. prof. speech communication U. Va., Charlottesville, 1954-59; assoc. prof. Ind. U., Bloomington, 1959-68; prof., chmn. dept. U. Tex., Austin, 1968-79, dean Coll. Communication, 1979-93, Allan Shivers Centennial chair in communication, 1983—, Walter Cronkite Regents chair in communication, 1991-93; sr. fellow Freedom Forum Media Studies Ctr., N.Y., 1993-94; cons. Assn. Comm. Adminstrn., Washington, 1976-84. Co-author: Legislature Procedures in the General Assembly of the State of Indiana, 1969, Speech: A Text with Adapted Readings, 3d edit., 1980, Speech: A Basic Text, 3d edit., 1989. Parliamentarian Ind. Senate, Inpls., 1964-68; pres. Ind. U. Employees Fed. Credit Union, 1966-67; bd. dirs. Paramount Theatre, Austin, 1980-87; bd. govs. Headliners Found., Austin, 1990-93. Served with USNR, 1945-46, PTO. Mem. Nat. Speech Comm. Assn. (exec. sec. 1960-63, pres. 1973, Disting. Svc. award 1991), Tex. Speech Comm. Assn. (exec. sec. 1970-80, Outstanding Svc. award 1980), Assn. Comm. Adminstrn. (pres. 1977), Golden Key Nat. Honor Soc., Phi Kappa Phi. Democrat. Home: 2001 Robinhood Trl Austin TX 78703-2131 Office: Coll Comm U Tex Austin TX 78712

JEFFREY, ROBERT GEORGE, JR., industrial company executive; b. Bronx, N.Y., Oct. 2, 1933; s. Robert George and Ethel Ruth (Rohrbeck) J.; m. Linda L. Nardone; children: Diana, Christine, Jennifer, Joseph. B.B.A., Pace U., 1959; M.B.A., NYU, 1966. CPA, N.Y., N.J. Sr. acct. Deloitte & Touche, N.Y.C., 1959-65; asst. mgr. corp. acctg. Union Camp Corp., Wayne, N.J., 1965-66; asst. to comptr. Union Camp Corp., 1966-69, mgr. corp. acctg., 1969-70, dir. fin. planning, 1970-72, corp. comptr., 1972-79; exec. v.p. Huntington Mgmt. Corp., 1980-82; v.p. fin. Rudco Industries Inc., 1982-84, sr. v.p., 1984-87; ptnr. R.G. Jeffrey, CPA, Wayne, 1987—; adj. prof. taxation William Paterson U., 1993—; bd. dirs. The Corby Group. Trustee Wayne Twp. Bd. Edn., 1975-78. Served with USAF, 1952-56. Mem. AICPA, N.Y. State Soc. CPAs, N.J. Soc. CPAs (bd. dirs. Passaic County chpt.), Fin. Execs. Inst. Home: 28 Pelham Rd Wayne NJ 07470-2873 Office: 61 Berdan Ave Wayne NJ 07470-3229

JEFFREY, SHIRLEY RUTHANN, publisher; b. Durant, Okla., Aug. 5, 1936; d. Hubert D. and Pauline (Blain) Carr; m. Dwight W. Jeffrey, Oct. 6, 1966; children: Robin Kimberly Reese, Paula Cherie Lyon, Michelle Jolie Jeffrey. AA, El Camino Coll., Gardena, Calif., 1962; BA, U. So. Calif., L.A., 1966. Cert. Ikebana tchr., Tokyo. Publisher Pelican Publs., Denton, Tex.; self-employed polit. cons. and spkr. Co-author: Gesneriad Judges Manual, 1989; author/editor: Internat. Cookbook, 1990, Episcias, 1990; contbr. articles to various jours. Hdqs. worker Denton County Rep. Com., 1988, coord. vols., 1993-94, mem. exec. com., precinct chmn., 1993—, polit. campaign mgr., 1995—, cons., 1997—, 1st vice chmn., 1996-98; bd. dirs. Am. Cancer Soc., Denton, 1975-77; referee U.S. Soccer Fedn., Denton, 1980-81; Rep. polit. cons., and campaign mgr., 1998—; campaign mgr. for Hayes for chmn. Rep. Com., 1995-96, 97-98, Russell campaign for city coun., 1997, Judge Vahlenkamp campaign for jdge Denton County Criminal Ct., 1997-98. Mem. U.S. SEC, Gesneriad Soc. Internat. (pres. 1987-90), North Tex. African Violet Judges Coun. (pres. 1975-76), First African Violet Soc. of New Orleans (pres. 1973-74), Nat. Assn. Parliamentarians, Tex. Assn. Parliamentarians, Am. Gloxinia and Gesneriad Soc. (sr. judge), Am. Assn. Ret. Persons (chpt. bd. dirs. 1992-97), others. Episcopalian. Avocations: Japanese flower arranging, flower arranging/pottery/bonsai, terrariums, landscaping design. Home: 1918 Williamsburg Row Denton TX 76201-2227 Office: Pelican Publs PO Box 720 Denton TX 76202-0720

JEFFREYS, CHARLES WAYNE, advertising executive; b. Fort Worth, Feb. 18, 1945; s. Charles T. and Bessie V. (Chance) J.; m. Penny L. Howell, June 15, 1968; 1 child, William T. BBA, Tex. Christian U., 1967. Salesman Fort Worth Star-Telegram, 1967-68; asst. mgr. All Ch. Press, Fort Worth, 1968-70; v.p. Dally Inc., Dallas, 1970—. Scoutmaster Boy Scouts Am., Arlington, Tex.; past chmn. N.W. Christian Ch., Arlington. Mem. Advt. Club Fort Worth, Rotary (chair pub. rels. Arlington chpt. 1976—). Avocations: church activities, family activities, civic activities. Home: 2001 Candlewood Dr Arlington TX 76012-2207 Office: Dally Inc 500 Main St Fort Worth TX 76102-3937

JEFFREY-SMITH, LILLI ANN, biofeedback specialist, educator, administrator; b. Bedford, Ind., 1944; d. Charles Constantine and Adelai (Malon) Jeffrey-Smith. Grad. Ind. Bus. Coll., 1963; B.S., Ind. U., 1973; grad. Psychosomatic Medicine Clinic, Berkeley, Calif. (accredited by Albert Einstein Coll. Medicine); PhD in Behavioral Sci., Kennedy-Western U., 1988.

Diplomate Am. Bd. Disability Analysts (sr.); cert. biofeedback specialist. Project assoc., stress mgmt. clinician City of Indpls., 1973-79; cons. Airport Med. Clinic, Indpls., 1981; outreach coord. Abbot-Northwestern Hosp., Mpls., 1981; dir. biofeedback dept. Sister Kenney Inst., Mpls., 1979-81, Noran Neurol. Clinic, Mpls., 1981-83; instr., dir. Biofeedback Tng. and Treatment Ctr., Edina, Minn., 1979—; pres. Biofeedback Rsch. and Devel. Co. Ltd., Edina, 1983—; cons. to biofeedback depts. St. Joseph Hosp., Mankato, Minn., 1984—, Lakeview Clinic, Waconia, Minn., 1983, Psychiat. Clinic of Mankato, 1983—, Fairview Ridges Hosp., Burnsville, Minn., 1987—. Author, narrator health and wellness tape series. Mem. Republican Presdl. Task Force, 1984—, NSC, 1985; co-chmn. Mayor's Handicapped Task Force, Indpls., 1975; founder, pres. Miss Wheel Chair of Ind., Inc. Named Hon. Lt. Gov., State of Ind., 1978; given Key to the City of Indpls., 1973, Flag of the City of Indpls., 1975. Mem. ABDA, NAFE, AAUW, AAAS, Am. Inst. Stress, N.Y. Acad. Sci., Edina C. of C., Minn. Women's Network, Biofeedback Soc. Am., Biofeedback Soc. Minn., Am. Assn. Control Tension, Am. Assn. Behavioral Therapists, Am. Assn. Biofeedback Clinicians, Nat. Assn. Women Bus. Owners, Soc. Open Focus and Tng. Rsch., Am. Assoc. of U. Woman, Nat. Assoc. of Female Execs., Assn. Trainers in Clin. Hypnosis, Internat. Stress and Tension Control Assn., Minn. Assn. Rehab. Providers, Nat. Assn. Exec. Women, Internat. Platform Assn. Avocations: music, stamp collecting, shooting, poetry. Office: Biofeedback Tng & Treatment Ctr 7300 France Ave S Ste 200 Minneapolis MN 55435-4542

JEFFRIES, CHARLES DEAN, microbiology educator, scientist; b. Rome, Ga., Apr. 9, 1929; s. Andrew Jones and Rachel Lucinda (Ringer) J.; m. Virginia Mae Alford, Sept. 6, 1953. BS, N. Ga. Coll., 1950; MS, U. Tenn., 1955, Ph.D., 1958; postgrad., Purdue U., 1955-56. Technician Ga. Pub. Health Dept., Rome, 1950-51; instr. microbiology Wayne State U., Detroit, 1958-60, asst. prof., 1960-65, assoc. prof., 1965-70, prof., 1970-96, prof. emeritus, 1996—, acting chmn. dept., 1972-73, assoc. dermatology, 1968—, asst. dean for curriculum affairs, dir. grad. programs Sch. Medicine, 1975-80, prof. (voluntary) dept. biol. scis., 1990—; prof., chair dept. microbiology and immunology Ross U. Sch. of Medicine, Roseau, Commonwealth of Dominica, West Indies, 1996—, dean basic scis., 1997-98, dean, 1998—; guest researcher Ctr. for Disease Control, USPHS, Dept. HHS, Atlanta, 1980-81; Fulbright-Hays lectr., Cairo, 1965-66; examiner bacteriology Bd. Basic Scis., State of Mich., 1967-72; v.p., 1970-72; cons. VA Med. Ctr., Allen Park, Mich., 1989-92. Contbr. articles to profl. jours. Councilor Am. Assn. Basic Sci. Bds., 1970-72; mem. sci. adv. bd. Mich. Cancer Found., 1970-79; mem. Am. Inst. Biol. Scis.-EPA adv. panel, 1979-80; pres. acad. senate Wayne State U., 1989-92. Served with AUS, 1951-53. Grantee NIH, 1958-70, NSF, 1959-69. Fellow Am. Acad. Microbiology; mem. Am. Soc. for Microbiology (councilor 1976-78, chmn. med. mycology div. 1977-78), Nat. Registry Microbiologists, Internat. Soc. Human and Animal Mycology, Sigma Xi. Office: Ross U Sch of Medicine, Box 266, Roseau Commonwealth of Dominica, West Indies

JEFFRIES, RICHARD HALEY, physician, broadcasting company executive; b. Harrisburg, Pa., June 7, 1941; s. Richard Lawrence and Jeanette Ruth (Haley) J.; 1 child, Richard Straley. BS, Pa. State U., 1963; DO, Kirksville Coll. Osteo. Medici, 1968. Diplomate Am. Coll. Osteo. Internists. Intern Cmty. Gen. Osteo. Hosp., Harrisburg, 1968-69, resident in internal medicine, 1969-72, attending staff dept. internal medicine, 1972—, dir. coronary and intensive care units, 1983-86, chmn. dept. medicine, 1986-98, v.p. med. staff, 1977-79, pres., chief of staff, 1979-82; pvt. practice Harrisburg, 1972—; founder, pres. Quaker State Broadcasting, Inc., WTPA-FM, Mechanicsburg, Pa., 1982—; founder, sec. Midstate Comm., Inc., 1990-97; vice chmn. dept. medicine Pinnacle Health Sys., 1998—; sr. clin. instr. Phila. Coll. Osteo. Medicine, 1977-81, clin. asst. prof., 1981—; clin. asst. prof. Hahnemann Med. Coll., Phila., 1977—, N.Y. Coll. Osteo. Medicine, N.Y.C., 1981-84; adj. asst. prof. U. Osteo. Medicine and Health Scis., Des Moines, 1990—; regional clin. faculty Kirksville (Mo.) Coll. Osteo. Medicine, 1993; trustee Cmty. Gen. Osteo. Hosp., Harrisburg, 1979-84, mem. staff exec. com., 1974-84, 86—, chmn. staff exec. com., 1979-82; sr. flight surgeon FAA, 1975—; med. dir. Ecumenical Home of Harrisburg, Beverly Preferred Choice Hospice Program, Harrisburg, 1995—, Blue Ridge Haven East Nursing Home, Harrisburg. Contbr. articles to profl. jours. Chmn. fundraising dr. Dauphin County Retarded Citizens Assn., 1984; founding mem., bd. dirs., past pres. Dauphin Residences, Inc., 1974-81; mem. Allied Arts Fund, Physicians Divsn., 1992, 93, 94; alumni bd. Kirksville Coll. Osteo. Medicine, 1997—. Mem. Am. Osteo. Assn., Pa. Osteo Med. Assn., Am. Coll. Osteo. Internists, Am. Soc. Critical Care Medicine, Pa. Soc. Critical Care Medicine (founding mem.), Am. Heart Assn. (bd. dirs. South Ctrl. Pa. chpt. 1976-79), Daguerreian Soc., Alpha Chi Sigma. Republican. Methodist. Avocations: photography, photographic collection, fly fishing, travel. Home: 2902 Parkside Ln Harrisburg PA 17110-1238 Office: Bronstein-Jeffries PA 4830 Londonderry Rd Harrisburg PA 17109-5240

JEFFRIES, ROBERT JOSEPH, retired engineering educator, business executive; b. Norwalk, Conn., Jan. 6, 1923; s. Charles William and Christine (Jacobsen) J.; m. Anna Darling Cumming, Oct. 13, 1945; children: Christine Darling, Bruce Cumming. BS, U. Conn., 1944, MS, 1946; DEng, Johns Hopkins U., 1948. Engr. NACA, 1944-46; instr. Johns Hopkins U., 1946-48; research assoc. N.C. State Coll., 1948-49; assoc. prof. Mich. State U., 1949-54; tech. planning adviser Schlumberger Instrument Co., 1954-55; asst. to pres. Daystrom, Inc., 1955-57; pres., founder Data-Control System, Inc., 1957-66, chmn. bd., 1966-68; prof. U. Bridgeport, Conn., 1968-75, ret.; founder, dir. Ednl. & Tech. Cons., Inc., 1953-57; v.p., dir. TJB Resources Inc., 1972-88; dir. emeritus Evergreen Fund Family; v.p., founder Found. Instrumentation Edn. and Rsch., 1958-66; fellow-in-residence Edgar Cayce Found., Virginia Beach, Va., 1981-88; prof. Atlantic U., 1986-90. Editor Jour. Instrument Soc. Am., 1953-54; contbr. tech. papers. Trustee Am. Unitarian Assn., Cmty. Ch. Coll., Sun City Ctr., Tampa Bay Cmty. Found., sec. coun. Recipient Disting. Alumnus award U. Conn., Disting. Alumnus award John Hopkins U. Fellow NRC; mem. Instrument Soc. Am. (pres. 1957-58), Assn. Rsch. and Enlightenment (trustee), Conn. Commn. for Higher Edn. (vice chmn.), U. Conn. Engring. Alumni Assn. (pres. 1969-71), Sigma Xi, Tau Beta Pi, Eta Kappa Nu. Home: 2118 New Bedford Dr Sun City Center FL 33573-6160

JEFFRYES, MARK ALLEN, elementary school educator, administrator; b. Wakefield, Nebr., Nov. 10, 1953; s. James A. Jeffryes and Martha G. Wright; m. Theresa McClary Jeffryes. BA, U. Colo., 1977; MA in Curriculum and Instrn., U. Colo., Denver, 1991; grad., Nat. Geographic Inst., 1992. Cert. tchr., Colo. Elem. tchr. Douglas County Schs., Highlands, Colo., 1998—; presenter Midwest Regional Geography Conf., Greeley, Colo., 1993; dean of students/sch. tech. coord., 1995—. Vol. tutor Denver Pub. Schs., 1987. Profl. Alternative Consortium for Tchrs. intern fellow U. Colo., Denver, 1990-91. Mem. ASCD, NEA, Colo. Geographic Alliance (tchr. cons. 1992—, grad. Summer Geography Inst. 1992), Internat. Tech. Edn. Assn. Democrat. Avocations: travel, reading, tennis, cycling, skiing. Home: 7862 W Glasgow Pl Littleton CO 80128-4846 Office: Bear Canyon Elem Sch 9660 Salford Ln Highlands Ranch CO 80126

JEFFS, THOMAS HAMILTON, II, banker; b. Grosse Pointe Farms, Mich., July 11, 1938; s. Thomas Raymond and Geraldine (Bogan) J.; m. Patricia Lucas, June 20, 1964; children—Leslie, Laura, Caroline. BBA in Gen. Bus., U. Mich., 1960, MBA, 1961. With NBD Bank, 1962—, pres., chief oper. officer; vice chmn., bd. dirs. First Chgo. NBD Corp., 1995; bd. dirs. MCN Energy Group, Inc., Detroit, Intermet Corp., Local Initiatives Support Corp. Bd. dirs. Detroit Symphony, Econ. Club Detroit; chmn. New Detroit, Inc.; dir. Detroit Renaissance, Inc. With U.S. Army, 1962-62. Mem. Bankers Roundtable, Detroit Athletic Club, Detroit Club (pres. 1982), Detroit Country Club, Yondotega Club, Grosse Pointe Club. Republican. Episcopalian. Home: 27 Fair Acres Dr Grosse Pointe MI 48236-3101 Office: NBD Bank 611 Woodward Ave Detroit MI 48226-3408

JEGEN, SISTER CAROL FRANCES, religion educator; b. Chgo., Oct. 11, 1925; d. Julian Aloysius and Evelyn W. (Bostelmann) J. BS in History, St. Louis U., 1951; MA in Theology, Marquette U., 1958, PhD in Religious Studies, 1968; hon. degree, St. Mary of the Woods, Terra Haute, Ind., 1977. Elem. tchr. St. Francis Xavier Sch., St. Louis, 1947-51; secondary tchr. Holy Angels Sch., Milw., 1951-57; coll. tchr. Mundelein Coll., Chgo., 1957-91; prof. pastoral studies Loyola U., Chgo., 1991—; adv. coun. U.S. Cath. Bishops, Washington, 1969-74; trustees Cath. Theol. Union, Chgo., 1974-84. Author: Jesus the Peace Maker, 1986, Restoring Our Friendship with God, 1989; co-author: (with Byron Sherwin) Thank God, 1989; editor: Mary According to Women, 1985. Participant Nat. Farm Worker Ministry, Fresno, Calif., 1977—; mem. Pax Christi, U.S.A., 1979—, Jane Addams Conf., Chgo., 1989. Recipient Loyola Civic award Loyola U., Chgo., 1981, Chgo. medallion for Excellence in Catechesis, 1996; named one of 100 Women to Watch Today's Chgo. Woman, 1989. Mem. Cath. Theol. Soc. Am., Coll. Theology Soc., Cath.-Jewish Scholars Dialog, Liturgical Conf. Democrat. Roman Catholic. Avocations: music, gardening. Home: Wright Hall 6364 N Sheridan Rd Chicago IL 60660-1700 Office: Loyola U Inst Pastoral Studies 6525 N Sheridan Rd Chicago IL 60626-5385

JEGEN, LAWRENCE A., III, law educator; b. Chgo., Nov. 16, 1934; s. Lawrence A. and Katherine M. (Stibgen) J.; m. Janet M. Holmberg, Aug. 30, 1958; children: Christine M., David L. BA, Beloit Coll., 1956; JD, U. Mich., 1959, MBA, 1960; LLM, NYU, 1963. Bar: Ill. 1959, U.S. Dist. Ct. (no. dist.) Ill. 1959, U.S. Dist. Ct. (so. dist.) Ind. 1962, Ind. 1966, U.S. Tax Ct. 1966, U.S. Ct. Appeals (7th cir.) 1980, U.S. Supreme Ct. 1980. Tax cons. Coopers & Lybrand, N.Y.C., 1960-62; asst. prof. law Ind. U., Indpls., 1962-64, assoc. prof., 1964-66, prof., 1966—, Thomas F. Sheehan prof. tax law and policy, 1982—, prof. philanthropic studies Ctr. Philanthropy, 1992—; co-founder Annual Tax Inst. for Colls. and Univs.; spl. counsel Ind. Dept. Revenue, 1963-65, Gov.'s Commn. on Med. Edn., 1970-72; mem. commr.'s adv. com. IRS, 1981-82; mem. Ind. Corps. Survey Commn., 1965—; commr. Nat. Conf. Uniform State Laws, 1981-91; dir. N.Am. Wildlife Assn., 1981-90. Author: Indiana Will and Trust Manual, 1967—; Lifetime and Estate, Personal and Business Planning, 1987; Estate Planning and Administration in Indiana, 1979, numersous other books, articles, chpts. Chmn. bd. dirs. Ind. Bar Ednl. Sys. Tchrs., 1988-89; mem. adv. bd. Ind. U. Ctr. on Philanthropy. Recipient Spl. Alumni Tchg. award Ind. U. Alumni Assn., 1970, 76, 80, 85, Most Outstanding Prof. award Sch. Law, Ind. U., 1970, 80, 85, 89, 99, Tchr. of Significance award Ind. U., 1980, Disting. Tchg. award Ind. U., 1989, Internat. Tchg. award Assn. Con. Legis. Adminstrn., 1990, Excellence in Tax award Quality for Taxpayers, Inc., 1990, Excellence in Taxation award for improvement tax adminstrn. State of Ind. Quality for Ind. Taxpayers, Inc., 1990, The Thomas Hart Benton Mural medallion, 1993, 4 Sagamore of the Wabash awards State Ind.; named hon. sec. of state State of Ind., 1967, 80, hon. dep. atty. gen., 1968; hon. state treas., 1969; Ford fellow, 1963. Fellow Am. Bar Found. (life), Am. Coll. Probate Counsel, Am. Coll. Tax Counsel; mem. ABA, FBA, Mid-West Inst. Estate and Tax Planning (adv. bd.), Ind. Bar Assn. (chmn. taxation sect. 1969-70, presdl. citation 1971), Indpls. Bar Assn., Ind. Trial Lawyers Assn. (corp. taxation, estate taxation, state and local taxation). Office: Indiana Univ Sch Law 735 W New York St Indianapolis IN 46202-5222

JEHANI, AHMED, lawyer; b. Beghazi, Libya, Oct. 15, 1946; came to U.S., 1972; s. Mohamed and Massauda (Kadiki) J.; m. Mariem Ghrairi, Nov. 12, 1994; 1 child, Lyn. LLM, Harvard U., 1973; MA, Tufts U., 1976, MALD, 1977, PhD, 1978. Legal cons. Boston, 1975-79; gen. counsel Ageco, B.P., Benshazi, Libya, 1967-75; sr. counsel World Bank, Washington, 1979—. Office: World Bank 1818 H St NW Washington DC 20433-0002

JEHLE, MICHAEL EDWARD, financial executive; b. Lawrence, Kans., Apr. 2, 1954; s. Edwin Paul and Catherine Claire (Cragoe) J.; m. Kimberly Ellen Davis, Aug. 4, 1979; children: Kathryn Anne, Christine Michelle. BS, S.W. Mo. State U., 1976; JD, Stanford U., 1979. Bar: Calif., Ill., Pa. Atty. The First Nat. Bank of Chgo., 1979-84, sr. atty., 1984-86; v.p., gen. counsel Equibank, Pitts., 1986-87, sr. v.p., gen. counsel, sec., 1987; sr. v.p., gen. counsel, sec. Equimark Corp., Pitts., 1987-89, exec. v.p., chief fin. officer, 1989-90; pres. Strategic Adv. Group, Pitts., 1990-95, Strategic Healthcare Advisors, Pitts., 1993-95; dir. rsch. MED 3000 Group, Inc., Pitts., 1995-96; pres. THI, Inc., Pitts., 1996—. Co-author: Sovereign Lending, 1984. Mem. ABA, Nat. Health Lawyers Assn., Healthcare Fin. Mgmt. Assn. Republican. Methodist. Avocation: wine collecting. Home: 411 Maple Ln Sewickley PA 15143-1021 Office: THI Inc 411 Maple Ln Sewickley PA 15143-1021

JEKEL, JAMES FRANKLIN, physician, public health educator; b. St. Louis, Oct. 14, 1934; s. Oscar Henry and Frances Sarah (Newell) J.; m. Janice Marilyn Clark, Aug. 30, 1958; children: Clifford R., Mark R., Linda F., Timothy W. AB, Wesleyan U., 1956; MD, Washington U., St. Louis, 1960; MPH, Yale U., 1965. House officer Hartford (Conn.) Hosp., 1960-62; epidemiologist Ctrs. for Disease Control, Atlanta, 1962-67; asst. prof. pub. health Yale U. Sch. Medicine, New Haven, 1967-71, assoc. prof., 1971-80, prof., 1980-97; prof. emeritus Yale U. Sch. Medicine, New Haven, Conn., 1997—; C.E.A. Winslow prof. pub. health Yale U. Sch. Medicine, New Haven, 1982-97, dir. residency program in gen. preventive medicine, 1975-93; asst. dir. Robert Wood Johnson Scholar Program Robert Wood Johnson Clin. Scholar Program, New Haven, 1976-95; dir. sect. preventive medicine and cmty. health Griffin Hosp., Derby, Conn., 1996—. Pres. Bd. Health Quinnipiack Valley Health Dist., Hamden, Conn., 1986-91. Lt. comdr. USPHS, 1962-67. Fulbright Faculty fellow The Bahamas, 1985-86; recipient various rsch. grants, 1968—. Fellow Am. Coll. Preventive Medicine, Am. Sci. Affiliation; mem. Am. Pub. Health Assn., Christian Med./Dental Soc. Presbyterian. Office: Yale U Sch Med Box 208034 60 College St New Haven CT 06520-8034

JELDERKS, JOHN A., federal judge; b. 1938. Apptd. magistrate judge U.S. Dist. Ct. Oreg., 1991. Fax: (503) 326-7788. Office: 512 US Courthouse 620 SW Main St Portland OR 97205-3037

JELGERHUIS, JANE MARIE, legislative staff member; b. Waupon, Wis., Jan. 1, 1962; d. Thomas Christian and Delores May Vanden Heuvel; m. Drew G. Jelgerhuis, Aug. 3, 1984; children: Jessica, Ross, Keeley. BBA, Dordt Coll., 1984. Pvt. piano tchr. Holland, Mich., 1978-97; choral accompanist Faith Christian Reformed Ch., Holland, 1993-95; spl. projects coord. Rep. Peter Hoekstra, Holland, 1993—. Bd. dirs. Holland Christian Schs. Band, Orch., Choir, 1997—, Holland Cmty. Chorale, 1998—; mem. congl. campaign com. Pete Hoekstra campaign, Holland, 1992—; chmn. Allegan County (Mich.) Reps., 1994-97. Mem. Toastmasters (v.p. pub. rels. 1998—). Presbyterian. Avocations: music, performance, organ, piano, violin. E-mail: jane.jelgerhuis@mail.house.gov. Home: 897 Ottawa Ave Holland MI 49423 Office: Congl Office of Peter Hoekstra 31 E 8th St Ste 320 Holland MI 49423

JELINEK, FREDERICK, electrical engineer, educator; b. Prague, Czechoslovakia, Apr. 18, 1932; came to U.S., 1949, naturalized, 1955; s. William and Trudy (Kocmanek) J.; m. Milena Tobolova, Feb. 4, 1961; children—Hannah, William. B.S., MIT, 1956, M.S., 1958, Ph.D., 1962. Instr. MIT, Cambridge, 1959-62; lectr. Harvard U., Cambridge, 1962; asst. prof. Cornell U., Sch. Elec. Engring., Ithaca, N.Y., 1962-66; assoc. prof. Cornell U., Sch. Elec. Engring., 1966-72, prof., 1972-74; vis. scientist MIT, Lincoln Lab., 1964, 65, IBM, 1968-69; sr. mgr. continuous speech recognition IBM, T.J. Watson Research Center, Yorktown Heights, N.Y., 1972-93; prof., dir. Ctr. Lang. and Speech Processing Whiting Sch. Engring. Johns Hopkins U., Balt., 1993—. Author: Probabilistic Information Theory, 1968, Statistical Methods for Speech Recognition, 1998; contbr. articles to profl. jours. Chmn. Liberal Party, Ithaca, N.Y., 1970-72, mem. state exec. com., 1971-73. Recipient Outstanding Achievement in the Field of Speech Comm. European Speech Comm. Assn.; named One of top 100 innovators in speech recognition by Tech. Mag., 1981. Fellow IEEE (life, pres. Info. Theory Group 1977, bd. govs. 1970-79, 81-86, Info. Theory Group best paper award 1971, Soc. award Signal Processing Soc. 1998, Golden Jubilee Paper award Info. Theory Soc. 1998). Office: Johns Hopkins U Ctr Lang and Speech Processing Barton Hall 3400 N Charles St Baltimore MD 21218

JELINEK, JOHN JOSEPH, public relations executive; b. San Pedro, Calif., Sept. 3, 1955; s. Joseph Francis and Patricia Valerie (Powers) J.; m. Christl Michele Schneider, June 1986 (div. July 1997). BA, Loyola U., 1977; MA, Loyola-Marymount U., 1983. Assoc. editor E-Go Enterprises, Sherman Oaks, Calif., 1976-77; advt. dir. Select Promotions, Irvine, Calif., 1977-78; editor SCORE Internat., Westlake Village, Calif., 1978-79; exec. editor Petersen Pub. Co., L.A., 1979-82, editor, 1982-85; pub. rels. account exec. Hill and Knowlton Inc., L.A., 1985-87; acct. supr. Freeman/McCue Pub. Rels., Newport Beach, Calif., 1987-88; account supr. tech. div. Fleishman Hillard Inc., L.A., 1988-89; rep. pub. affairs corp. news dept. Ford Motor Co., Dearborn, Mich., 1989-90; product info. mgr. Ford of Can., Oakville, 1990-92; car product devel., pub. affairs mgr. Ford Motor Co., Dearborn, Mich., 1993-96; product devel., pub. affairs mgr. Ford Motor Co., Dearborn, 1996-98, dir. pub. affairs Large and Luxury Vehicle Ctr., 1998—. Author: (with others) Consumer's Guide to 1978 Trucks, 1978, Consumer's Guide to 1980 Trucks, 1979, Complete Guide to Used Cars, 1981, How to Buy the Best Compact Truck, 1984; columnist Guns & Ammo Mag., 1980-84, Petersen's Hunting Mag., 1986-87. Capt. Calif. State Mil. Res. 1982-89. Recipient 1st place award Calif. Newspaper Pub. Assn., 1977. Mem. NRA (life), L.A. County Mus. Natural History-Automobile Collection Coun., Aircraft Owners and Pilots Assn., Nat. Aeronautical Assn., Detroit Inst. Art. Republican. Roman Catholic. Avocations: travel, flying, skiing, cooking. Office: Ford Motor Co Product Devel MD 1239 20000 Rotunda Dr Bldg 2 Dearborn MI 48121

JELINEK, VERA, university director; b. Kosice, Czechoslovakia, Dec. 16, 1935; came to U.S., 1947; d. Joseph and Margit (Lefkovits) Schnitzer; m. Josef E. Jelinek, June 19, 1960; children: David, Paul. BA in History, CUNY, 1956; MA, Johns Hopkins U., 1958; PhD in Modern European History, NYU, 1977; diploma, Sch. Advanced Internat. Study, Bologna, Italy. Translator Rockefeller Bros. Fund, N.Y.C., 1958-59; exec. dir. U.S. Youth Coun., N.Y.C., 1959-63; dir. internat. programs, social and natural scis. NYU, N.Y.C., 1985—; adv. com. N.Y.C.-Budapest Sister City Program, 1991-94; prin. dir. pilot tng. program for new UN diplomats NYU, 1996-97. Author audio cassette: Before You Go-Italy, 1985. Mem. internat. adv. com., edn. com. Mus. Am. Folk Art, N.Y.C. Recipient fellowship Ford Found., 1960, grant NYU Curriculum Challenge Fund, 1989, 90, Phillip E. Frandson award Nat. Univ. Continuing Edn. Assn., 1991. Mem. Am. Folk Art Soc., Carnegie Coun. on Ethics and Internat. Affairs, Fgn. Policy Assn., Women's Fgn. Policy Group, Phi Beta Kappa. Democrat. Avocations: tennis, jogging, folk art, cooking, travel. Office: NYU SCPS Internat Programs 48 Cooper Sq New York NY 10003-7154

JELKS, GLENN WILLIAM, plastic surgeon; b. South Gate, Calif., Oct. 21, 1943; s. William Harold and Parthena Imogene Jelks; m. Elizabeth Anne Brady, Sept. 4, 1965; children: Jennifer, Deborah, Michael. BA, U. Calif., Berkeley, 1965; MS, Mich. State U., 1973, MD, 1973. Diplomate Am. Bd. Ophthalmology, Am. Bd. Plastic and Reconstructive Surgery, Nat. Bd. Med. Examiners. With med. edn., mktg. and sales dept. Merck, Sharp and Dohme divsn. Merck and Co., Inc., San Francisco, 1965-69; med. rsch. fellow dept. interdepartmental curriculum Mich. State U.-Biomed. Comm. Ctr., East Lansing, 1971-73; grad. asst., clin. sci. instr. Mich. State U., East Lansing, 1973; intern straight surgery UCLA, 1973-74, resident gen./orthopaedic surgery, 1974-75; resident ophthalmology UCLA-Jules Stein Eye Inst., 1975-78; resident Inst. Reconstructive Plastic Surgery, NYU Med. Ctr., N.Y.C., 1978-80; assoc. prof. ophthalmology, assoc. prof. plastic surgery NYU Med. Ctr., N.Y.C.; attending plastic surgeon Bellevue Hosp., N.Y.C., Manhattan Eye, Ear and Throat Hosp., N.Y.C., The Valley Hosp., Ridgewood, N.J., Lenox Hill Hosp., N.Y.C.; adj. attending in ophthalmology and plastic surgery N.Y. Eye and Ear Infirmary, N.Y.C.; examiner Am. Bd. Plastic Surgeons, 1995, 96; mem. continuing med. edn. adv. com., surg. case rev. com., oper. rm. com. N.Y. Eye and Ear Infirmary; mem. laser com. NYU Med. Ctr.; mem. audiovisual com. Manhattan Eye, Ear and Throat Hosp.; vis. prof. Mass. Eye and Ear Infirmary, Boston, 1989, Robert H. Ivy Soc., Phila., 1990, UCLA, 1992, Yale U., New Haven, Conn., 1992. Consulting editor Ophthalmic Plastic and Reconstructive Surgery, Plastic Surgery Outlook, Ophthalmic Plastic and Reconstructive Surgery Jour; assoc. editor Annals of Plastic Surgery, 1995-96. Recipient Rsch. Travel award Am. Coll. Cardiology, 1970, Sci. Exhibit award AMA Conv., San Francisco, 1972, Lester T. Jones award for excellence in surg. anatomy Am. Soc. Ophthalmic Plastic and Reconstructive Plastic Surgeons 1986, Arthur L. Garnes Lectr. award Harlem Hosp., N.Y., 1987; NIH Cardiovas. trainee Mich. State U., 1969; Student Rsch. fellow Mich. Heart Assn., 1970, 71. Fellow Am. Acad. Ophthalmology; mem. AMA (Continuing Edn. award 1976, 79, 82, 85, 88), Internat. Soc. Craniofacial Surgeons, European Soc. Opthalmic Plastic and Reconstructive Surgery, Am. Acad. Ophthalmology, Am. Soc. Plastic and Reconstructive Surgeons, Am. Coll. Surgeons, Am. Soc. Maxillofacial Surgeons (mem. continuing med. edn. com. 1995-96), Am. Soc. Aesthetic Plastic and Reconstructive Surgery (mem. edn. commn. 1994, traveling prof. 1995), Am. Assn. Plastic Surgeons (mem. time and place com. 1995-96), Northeastern Soc. Plastic Surgeons (chmn. membership com. 1994-95, mem. nominating com. 1994-95, sec. 1995-96), N.Y. State Med. Soc., N.Y. County Med. Soc., N.Y. Regional Soc. Plastic and Reconstructive Surgeons, N.Y. Acad. Medicine, N.Y. Orbit Soc. E-mail: parkprac@aol.com. Office: 875 Park Ave New York NY 10021

JELKS, MARY LARSON, retired pediatrician; b. Galva, Ill., 1929. MD, U. Nebr., 1955. Diplomate Am. Bd. Pediats., Am. Bd. Allergy and Immunology. Intern Johns Hopkins Hosp., Balt., 1955-56, resident, 1956-57, 58-60; resident Grace-New Haven Hosp., 1957; fellow U. Fla. Tchg. Hosp., 1960-61; clin. asst. prof. U. South Fla.; ret., active aerobiology, 1985—. Fellow Am. Acad. Allery and Immunology, Am. Acad. Pediats.; mem. AMA. E-mail address: marysneeze@aol.com. Achievements include active research in aerobiology. Home: 1930 Clematis St Sarasota FL 34239-3813

JELLEMA, JON, state legislator; b. Bloomington, Ind., Dec. 7, 1943; s. William Harry and Frances (Peters) J.; m. Betsy Zevalkink; children: Frances, Kate, Jon R., Elizabeth. BA, Calvin Coll., 1966; MA and ABD, Mich. State U., 1972. Prof. Grand Valley State U., Allendale, Mich., 1972-94; asst. dean William James Coll., Grand Valley State U., Allendale, 1986-87; dir. liberal studies program Grand Valley State U., Allendale, 1988-89, chmn. English dept., 1989-91, prof. English dept., 1991-94; mem. Mich. Ho. of Reps., Lansing, 1994—; vice-chmn. appropriations com., vice chmn. sub-com. on transp., chmn. joint capital outlay comm., chmn. policy comm., mem. edn. commn. states, mem. urban caucus. Pres. Grand Haven (Mich.) Pub. Sch. Bd., 1972-84; founder North Ottawa Cmty. Coalition. Mem. Assn. for Values in Higher Edn., Phi Kappa Phi. Avocations: sailing, skiing. Home: 510 Park Ave Grand Haven MI 49417-2107 Office: 67 Capitol Lansing MI 48909

JELLEN, EDWARD D., federal judge; b. 1946. BA, U. Calif., Berkeley, 1967; JD, U. Calif., 1971. With legal dept. Bank of Am., 1972-78; with Jellen & Holman, 1978-82, Jellen & Assocs., 1982-87; apptd. bankruptcy judge no. dist. U.S. Dist. Ct. Calif., 1987, apptd. chief judge, 1997. Office: 1300 Clay St Rm 215 Oakland CA 94612-1425

JELLEY, SCOTT ALLEN, microbiologist; b. Tarrytown, N.Y., July 22, 1960; s. Alfred Paul and Nadine Elaine (Scott) J. BS in Biology, Bucknell U., 1982; MS in Microbiology, Va. Poly. Inst., 1985. Grad. teaching asst. Va. Poly. Inst., Blacksburg, 1983-85, lab. specialist, 1985; scientist Pfizer Cen. Rsch., Groton, Conn., 1986-88; microbiologist Findley Rsch., Inc., Fall River, Mass., 1988-90; microbiologist sterilization scis. group Johnson & Johnson Profl., Inc., Raynham, Mass., 1990—. Contbr. articles to Applied and Environmental Microbiology. Mem. Assn. for Advancement Med. Instrumentation (sterilization resuable med. devices com.). Achievements include development of sterilization validation techniques for medical devices. Office: Johnson & Johnson Profl Inc 325 Paramount Dr Raynham MA 02767-5110

JELLICORSE, JOHN LEE, communications and theatre educator; b. Bristol, Tenn., Nov. 1, 1937; s. Harold Lee and Kathleen (Nickels) J.; m. Lenah Mary Lawrence, July 21, 1961 (div. 1980); 1 child, Jennifer Lee; m. Delayna Maxine Jordan, June 28, 1992; 1 child, John Adam. AB, U. Tenn., 1959; PhD, Northwestern U., 1967. From instr. to assoc. prof. Northwestern U., Evanston, Ill., 1962-69; assoc. prof. U. Tenn., Knoxville, 1969-74; prof., head dept. communication and theatre U. N.C., Greensboro, 1974-88, dir. theatre div., 1988-90, dir. broadcasting/cinema div., 1990-91; dean Sch. Comm. Hong Kong Bapt. U., 1991-94; prof. U. N.C., Greensboro, 1994—; cons. Wroclaw Tech. U., Poland. Contbr. chpts. to books, articles to profl. jours. Recipient Outstanding Tchr. award Northwestern U., 1968; So. Fellowship Fund fellow, 1959-62. Mem. AEJMC, Assn. for Communication Adminstrn., Am. Film Inst., Internat. Communication Assn., So. Communication Assn., Southeastern Theatre Conf., Carolinas Speech Communication Assn., Speech Communication Assn., Whitmanian. Office: 10 Forest Lake Cir Greensboro NC 27407-5008

JELLIFFE, ROGER WOODHAM, cardiologist, clinical pharmacologist; b. Cleve., Feb. 18, 1929; s. Russell Wesley and Rowena (Woodham) J.; m. Joyce Miller, June 12, 1954; children: Susan, Amy, Elizabeth, Peter. BA, Harvard U., 1950; MD, Columbia U., 1954. Diplomate Am. Bd. Internal Medicine, Am. Bd. Cardiovascular Disease. Intern Univ. Hosps., Cleve., 1954-56; also jr. asst. resident in medicine; Nat. Found. Infantile Paralysis exptl. medicine fellow Case Western Res. U., Cleve., 1956-58; staff physician in medicine VA Hosp., Cleve., 1958-60; resident in medicine VA Hosp., 1960-61; instr. medicine U. So. Calif. Sch. Medicine, L.A., 1961-63; asst. prof. U. So. Calif. Sch. Medicine, 1963-67, assoc. prof., 1967-76, prof. medicine, 1976—; developer Lab. Applied Pharmacokinetics, 1973—, The USC*PACK Computer Programs, 1973—; cons. Dynamic Scis., Inc., Van Nuys, Calif., 1976-93, Simes S.P.A., Milan, 1979-97, IVAC Corp., San Diego, 1983-88, Bionica, Sydney, Australia, 1987-94. Author: Fundamentals of Electrocardiography, 1990; cons. editor Am. Jour. Medicine, 1972-78, Current Prescribing, 1974-79, Am. Jour. Physiology, 1984-91, Computers in Biology amd Medicine, 1994—, Therapeutic Drug Monitoring, 1995—; contbr. articles to profl. jours.; patentee in field. Advanced Rsch. fellow L.A. County Heart Assn., 1961-64; recipient Rsch. Achievement award Clin. Scis. Am. Assn. Pharm. Scis., 1997. Fellow ACP, Am. Coll. Med. Informatics, Am. Coll. Clin. Pharmacology, Am. Heart Assn. Coun. on Clin. Cardiology; mem. Am. Soc. Clin. Pharmacology and Therapeutics (chmn. pharmacometric sect. 1995-97), Am. Fedn. Clin. Rsch., Am. Med. Informatics Assn. Achievements include research on optimal mgmt. of drug therapy; development of computer programs for optimal mgmt. of drug therapy; population pharmacokinetic modeling; development of intelligent infusion devices. Office: U So Calif Sch Medicine CSC 134-B 2250 Alcazar St Los Angeles CA 90033-1004

JELLINEK, GEORGE, broadcast executive, writer, music educator; b. Budapest, Hungary, Dec. 22, 1919; came to U.S., 1941; s. Daniel and Jolan Jellinek; m. Hedy Dicker, July 29, 1942; 1 child, Nancy Berezin. Student, Lafayette Coll., 1943; MusD (hon.), L.I. U., 1984. Dir. program services SESAC, Inc., N.Y.C., 1955-64; rec. dir. Muzak, Inc., N.Y.C., 1964-68; music dir. Sta. WQXR, N.Y.C., 1968-84; asst. prof. music NYU, N.Y.C., 1976-91. Author: (biography) Callas, Portrait of a Prima Donna, 1960, 2d edit. 1986, (opera librettos) (music by Eugene Zador) The Magic Chair, 1966, The Scarlet Mill, 1968; contbg. editor: Stereo Rev. mag., 1958-74, Ovation mag., 1974-88; author: (book) History Through the Opera Glass, 1994; contbr. articles to the N.Y. Times, Musical America, The Opera Quar. Trustee Bagby Found. Served to 1st lt. M.I., U.S. Army, 1942-46. Recipient Maj. Armstrong Broadcast award, 1978, Ohio State award, 1978, Gabriel award, 1982, Gold medal Internat. Radio Festival, 1995, Grammy award, 1996. Mem. ASCAP, AFTRA. Office: Sta WQXR 122 5th Ave New York NY 10011-5605

JELLINEK, MICHAEL STEVEN, psychiatrist, pediatrician; b. N.Y.C., Sept. 30, 1948; s. Kurt and Kate (Jacoby) J.; m. Barbara A. Jellinek, June 14, 1970; children: David M., Abraham R., Isaiah T., Hanna R. BA, Columbia Coll., 1970; MD, Albert Einstein Coll. Medicine, 1973. Diplomate Nat. Bd. Med. Examiners, Am. Bd. Pediatrics; diplomate in psychiatry and child psychiatry Am. Bd. Psychiatry and Neurology. Instr. pediatrics Montefiore Hosp. & Med. Ctr., N.Y.C., 1976-79; chief child psychiat. svcs. Mass. Gen. Hosp., Boston, 1979—, asst. in pediat., 1979-81, asst. pediatrician, 1981-83, dir. outpatient psychiatry, 1984-93, assoc. pediatrician, 1984-86, assoc. psychiatrist, 1984-86, pediatrician, 1986—, psychiatrist, 1986—, asst. gen. dir. ambulatory svcs., 1992—, sr. v.p. ambulatory svcs., 1994—, sr. v.p. adminstrn., 1995—; assoc. prof. psychiatry (pediatrics) Harvard U., Boston, 1987-96, prof. psychiatry and pediatrics, 1996—; asst. instr. Columbia U., N.Y.C, 1970; cons. Shriner Burns Inst., Boston, 1979—. Dir. Camp Rainbow, Croton-on-Hudson, 1977-81. Fellow Am. Acad. Pediat., Am. Acad. Child Psychiatry (treas. 1991-93, Simon Wile award 1993); mem. Soc. Prof. Child Psychiatry, New Eng. Coun. Child Psychiatry, Inst. Soc. Ethics and Life Scis. Democrat. Jewish. Avocations: running, soccer coach, carpentry. Home: 132 Pleasant St Newton MA 02459-1828 Office: Mass Gen Hosp Fruit St Bulfinch 351 Boston MA 02114

JELLINEK, MILES ANDREW, lawyer; b. Phila., Dec. 27, 1947; s. Alfred Marquis and Rena Elizabeth (Felberg) J.; m. Annabelle Francis O'Leary, Apr. 9, 1976; children—Beth Elise, Laura Anne. B.A., U. Pa., 1969, J.D., 1974. Bar: Pa. 1974, N.J. 1987. Law clk. Ct. Common Pleas, Phila., 1974-75; sr. mem. Cozen and O'Connor, Phila., 1975—. Republican. Jewish. Club: Germantown Cricket (Phila.). Avocations: tennis, squash, golf. Office: Cozen & O'Connor 1900 Market St Philadelphia PA 19103-3527

JELLINEK, PAUL S., foundation executive, health economist; b. Madison, Wis., Dec. 25, 1951; s. Joseph S. Jellinek and Elvira Myers; m. Janice Susan Kissling, Dec. 23, 1972; children: Lisa, Michael, Amy, Robert. BA, U. Pa., 1972, U. So. Fla., 1978; MS in Pub. Health, U. N.C., 1980, PhD, 1983. Copy editor Sarasota (Fla.) Herald-Tribune, 1973; reporter Wayne County Reporter, Monticello, Ky., 1974; med. health tech. St. Joseph's Hosp., Tampa, Fla., 1975-78; program officer Robert Wood Johnson Found., Princeton, N.J., 1983-91, v.p., 1991—; dir. Grantmakers in Health, Washington, 1993-99; mem. Gov.'s Task Force on Child Abuse, Trenton, N.J., 1988-94. Contbr. articles to profl. jours. Mem. social justice com. Our Lady of Sorrows Ch., Mercerville, N.J., 1989—. Bush Inst. for Child and Family Policy fellow, 1982-83. Mem. Am. Econ. Assn., Am. Pub. Health Assn. Avocation: blues band. Office: Robert Wood Johnson Foundation PO Box 2316 Princeton NJ 08543-2316

JELLINEK, ROGER, editor; b. Mexico City, Jan. 16, 1938; came to U.S., 1961; s. Frank Louis Mark and Marguerite Lilla Donne (Lewis) J.; m. Margherita DiCenzo, Dec. 22, 1963 (div. 1984); children: Andrew Mark, Claire; m. Eden-Lee Murray, 1984; 1 child, Everett Peter Murray. Student, Bryanston Sch., Dorset, Eng., 1951-56; MA, Cambridge U., Eng., 1961. Assoc. editor Random House, 1963-64; editor Walker & Co., 1964-65; editor N.Y. Times Book Rev., 1966-70, dep. editor, 1970-73; editor in chief Times Books, Quadrangle/N.Y. Times Book Co., 1974-78, sr. editor, 1978-81, editor Lamont newsletter and yearbook, 1981-91; pres. Clairemark, Ltd., 1981—, Jellinek & Murray Literary Agy. Editor Atlantic Realm Project, 1983-93; publisher Hawaii map series. Pres. ArtMaps Ltd., 1996—. With Royal Marines, 1956-57, 2d lt. Brit. Intelligence Corps, 1957-58. Mellon fellow Yale U., 1961-63. Home and Office: 109 Nawiliwili St Honolulu HI 96825-2041

JELLOWS, TRACY PATRICK, software engineer; b. Quincy, Mass., Oct. 15, 1951; d. Henry David and Dorothy Margret (Joyce) J. BS in Physics, Bridgewater (Mass.) State Coll., 1981; postgrad., U. Mass., Boston, 1982. Software engr. Lotus Devel. Corp., Cambridge, Mass., 1984-85, sr. software engr., 1985-89; prin. engr. 1-2-3 Graphics Lotus Devel. Corp., 1989-90; prin. engr. Edsun Labs., Waltham, Mass., 1990-91; prin. engr., cons. Saturn Software, Brockton, Mass., 1991-96; prin. engr. Thomson Fin. Svcs., Boston, 1996-98; cons. engr. Saturn Software, Brockton, Mass., 1998—. Mem. IEEE, Assn. Computing Machinery, Aircraft Owners and Pilots Assn., Mensa. Democrat. Roman Catholic. Avocations: music, computer software and hardware, boating, general aviation. Home: 9 Toby Rd Brockton MA 02302-1947

JELUS, SUSAN CRUM, writer, editor; b. Cin., Sept. 14, 1952; d. Robert Malcolm and Jean Moses Crum; m. Raymond Jelus, Aug. 1, 1975 (div. Dec. 1989). BA, Miami U., Oxford, Ohio, 1974. Continuity mgr. Sta. WLWT TV, Cin., 1975-77; traffic mgr. Sta. WCKY-WWEZ, Cin., 1977-79; advt. coord. Cintas Corp., Cin., 1979-80; audio-visual writer-prodr. Dayton, 1981-84; tech. writer Sinclair C.C., Dayton, 1984-86; sr. instrnl. developer The Reynolds & Reynolds Co., Dayton, 1986-95; publs./on-line help author Rsch. Computer Svcs., Dayton, 1995—; editor, pub. New Song Press, Dayton, 1995—. Editor: (lit. jour.) A New Song, 1996—; contbr. poetry to anthologies. Bd. dirs. Hist. Dist. Archtl. Rev. Bd., Germantown, Ohio, 1990-93; campaign tng. chairperson United Way, Dayton, 1987; dir. Jr. Handbell Choir, South Park United Meth. Ch., Dayton, 1995. Recipient Commendation award for poetry Chester H. Jones Found., 1995, Award of Merit, Soc. for Tech. Comm., 1989. Mem. Soc. Am. Poets. Democrat. Avocations: watercolor painting, acoustic guitar, children's music, song lyricist. E-mail: nsongpress@aol.com. Office: New Song Press PO Box 629 Dayton OH 45409-0629

JEMAL, LAWRENCE, retail executive. CEO Nobody Beats the Wiz, Carteret, N.J. Office: Nobody Beats the Wiz 1300 Federal Blvd Carteret NJ 07008-1095

JEMELIAN, JOHN NAZAR, management consultant; b. N.Y.C., May 10, 1933; s. Nazar and Angel (Jizmejian) J.; m. Rose Melkonian, Nov. 22, 1958; children: Sheri, Lori, Brian, Joni. BS, U. So. Calif., 1956. Mgr. audit staff Price Waterhouse & Co., Los Angeles, 1958-64; treas. The Akron, Los Angeles, 1964-82; v.p. fin. The Akron, 1976, exec. v.p., 1977-82; v.p., gen. mgr., dir. Acromil Corp., City of Industry, Calif., 1982-85; sr. v.p. fin. and adminstrn., chief fin. officer, sec., treas. World Vision Inc., 1985-98; pres. Claremont Facilities Corp., 1990-98, Pasadena Resources Corp., 1990-94; dir. D.L. Engring., Inc.; fin. adviser African Enterprises, 1966-68. Bd. dirs. Pasadena Christian Sch., 1965-67, 69-70, treas., 1965-67; deacon Lake Ave. Congregrational Ch., 1964-68, trustee, 1970-73, chmn. bd. trustees, 1972-73, chmn. ch. com. 1974; bd. dirs. Forest Home Christian Conf. Ctr., 1972-75, 78-81, 84-88, 1992-95; chmn. bd. Media Ministries, Inc., 1975-95, Donor Automation, 1975—; trustee Haigazian Coll., Beirut, 1974-78, Narramore Christian Found., 1976-93, Met. Ministries, 1979-80; chmn. Christian Bus. Men's Com., 1979-81, 86-87, Sahag Mesrob Armenian Christian Sch., 1980-85; deacon, elder Ch. on the Way. With F.A., U.S. Army, 1956-58. Named Boss of Year Beverly Hills chpt. Nat. Secs. Assn., 1970. Mem. Am. Inst. C.P.A.s, Calif. Soc. C.P.A.s, Retail Controllers Assn. (dir. 1973-74), Delta Sigma Pi, Beta Alpha Psi, Beta Gamma Sigma. Clubs: Los Angeles Athletic, Toastmasters-Windjammers (Los Angeles) (pres. 1963). Home: 261 Sharon Rd Arcadia CA 91007-8044 Office: PO Box 5051 Monrovia CA 91016-3198

JEN, FRANK CHIFENG, finance and management educator; b. Shanghai, May 15, 1931; came to U.S., 1957; s. Seybold E. and Susan (Lin) J.; m. Daisy Chi, Aug. 26, 1962; children: Amy K., Wendy K., Edward K. B.S., N. Central Coll., 1959; M.B.A., U. Wis., 1960, Ph.D., 1963. Asst. prof. finance SUNY, Buffalo, 1964-66, assoc. prof., 1966-68, prof., 1968-97, chmn. dept. fin., 1967-70, Mfrs. & Traders Trust Co.'s prof. banking/fin. to emeritus, 1972-97, 97—, chmn. dept. fin., 1967-70, chmn. dept. operating analysis, 1970-77, dir. bank mgmt. inst. and advanced comml. lending program, 1977-97, co-dir., dir. China MBA program, 1984-91; vis. prof. Dalian (China) U. Tech., 1980—; Am. dir. Consulting and Rsch. Ctr. Nat. Mgmt. Ctr., Dalian U. Tech., 1995—. Contbr. articles to profl. jours. Mem. Am. Fin. Assn., Am. Econ. Assn., Soc. Econ. and Fin. Mgmt. in China (pres. 1985-88), Pi Gamma Mu, Beta Gamma Sigma. Home: 287 Forestview Dr Buffalo NY 14221-1439 Office: SUNY Buffalo Sch Mgmt Jacobs Ctr Amherst NY 14260

JENCKS, CHRISTOPHER SANDYS, public policy educator; b. Balt., Md., Oct. 22, 1936; s. Francis Haynes and Elizabeth (Pleasants) J. B.A., Harvard U., 1958, M.Ed., 1959; postgrad., London Sch. Econs., 1959-61; LL.D., Kalamazoo Coll., 1969; D.Litt., Columbia Coll., 1983. Assoc. editor New Republic mag., 1961-63; fellow Inst. Policy Studies, Washington, 1963-67, Cambridge Policy Studies Inst., 1968-75; mem. faculty Harvard U., 1967-80, 96—, prof., 1973-80, 96—; John D. MacArthur prof. sociology and urban affairs Northwestern U., Evanston, Ill., 1980-96; Malcolm Wiener prof. social policy, 1998—; vis. prof. U. Chgo., 1994-95. Author: (with David Riesman) The Academic Revolution, 1968, (with others) Inequality, 1972, Who Gets Ahead?, 1979, (with Paul Peterson) The Urban Underclass, 1991, Rethinking Social Policy, 1992, The Homeless, 1994, (with Meredith Phillips) The Black-White Test Score Gap, 1998. Guggenheim fellow, 1967-68, 82-83, Inst. for Advanced Study fellow, 1985-86, Russell Sage Found. fellow, 1991-92, Ctr. for Advanced Study in Behavioral Scis., 1997-98. Office: Harvard U Kennedy Sch Govt Cambridge MA 02138

JENCKS, WILLIAM PLATT, biochemist, educator; b. Bar Harbor, Maine, Aug. 15, 1927; s. Gardner and Elinor (Melcher) J.; m. Miriam Ehrlich, June 3, 1950; children: Helen Esther, David Alan. Grad., St. Paul's Sch., Balt., 1944; MD, Harvard U., 1951. Intern Peter Bent Brigham Hosp., Boston, 1951-52; postdoctoral fellow Mass. Gen. Hosp., Boston, 1952-53, 55-56; postdoctoral fellow chemistry Harvard U., 1956-57; mem. faculty Brandeis U., Waltham, Mass., 1957—, prof. biochemistry, 1963—. Served as 1st lt., M.C. AUS, 1953-55. Recipient ASBMB-Merck award Am. Soc. Biochem. and Molecular Biology, 1992. Fellow Royal Soc.; mem. NAS, AAAS, Am. Chem. Soc. (award in biol. chemistry 1962, James Flack Norris award in phys.-organic chemistry 1995, Repligen award 1996), Am. Philos. Soc., Am. Soc. Biol. Chemists, Am. Acad. Arts and Scis., Alpha Omega Alpha. Home: 11 Revere St Lexington MA 02420-4419 Office: Brandeis U Grad Dept Biochemistry Waltham MA 02254

JENDEN, DONALD JAMES, pharmacologist, educator; b. Horsham, Sussex, Eng., Sept. 1, 1926; came to U.S., 1950, naturalized, 1958; s. William Herbert and Kathleen Mary (Harris) J.; m. Jean Ickeringill, Nov. 18, 1950; children: Tricia Jenden Billes, Peter Donald, Beverly Jean Jenden Riedlinger. BSc in Physiology with 1st class honours, Kings Coll. London, 1947; MB, BS with honours, U. London, 1950; PhD in Pharm. Chemistry (hon.), U. Uppsala, Sweden, 1980. Demonstrator pharmacology U. London, 1948-49; lectr. pharmacology U. Calif.-San Francisco, 1950-51, asst. prof. pharmacology, 1952-53; mem. faculty UCLA, 1953, assoc. prof., 1956-60, prof. pharmacology, 1960—, prof. pharmacology and biomath., 1967—, chmn. dept. pharmacology, 1968-89; Wellcome vis. prof. U. Ala., Birmingham, 1984; mem. brain research inst. UCLA, 1961—. Contbr. articles in field. Served to lt. comdr. M.C., USNR, 1954-58. USPHS Postdoctoral fellow, 1951-53, NSF Sr. Postdoctoral fellow; hon. research assoc. Univ. Coll., London, 1961-62; Fulbright Short-Term Sr. Scholar award, Australia, 1983; recipient Univ. Gold medal U. London, 1950. Fellow Am. Coll. Neuropsychopharmacology, West Coast Coll. Biol. Psychology (charter); mem. AAAS, Am. Soc. Pharmacology and Exptl. Therapeutics, Am. Physiol. Soc., Physiol. Soc. (London), Soc. Neurosci., Am. Chem. Soc., Western Pharmacology Soc. (pres. 1970), Assn. for Med. Sch. Pharmacology, Am. Soc. Neurochemistry, Internat. Union Pharmacology. Home: 3814 Castlerock Rd Malibu CA 90265-5625

JENES, THEODORE GEORGE, JR., retired career officer; b. Portland, Oreg., Feb. 21, 1930; s. Theodore George and Mabel Marie (Moon) J.; m. Beverly Lorraine Knutson, Jan. 29, 1953; children—Ted, Mark. BS, U. Ga., 1956; MS, Auburn U., 1969; grad., Army Command and Gen. Staff Coll., Armed Forces Staff Coll., Air War Coll.; LLD (hon.), U. Akron, 1986. Enlisted U.S. Army, 1951, commd. 2d lt., 1953, advanced through grades to lt. gen., 1984, various assignments, 1953-75; comdr. 3d Brigade, 2d Inf. Div., Republic of Korea, 1975-76, 172d Inf. Brigade, Ft. Richardson, Alaska, 1978-81; dep. commdg. gen. U.S. Army Tng. Ctr., Ft. Dix, N.J., 1976-78; comdr. 4th Inf. Div., Ft. Carson, Colo., 1982-84; dep. commdg. gen. U.S. Army Combined Arms Combat Devel. Activity, Ft. Leavenworth, Kans., 1981-82; comdg. gen. 3d U.S. Army, Ft. McPherson, Ga., 1984-87; commander U.S. Army Forces Ctrl. Command, Ft. McPherson, Ga., 1984-87; dep. comdg. gen. hdqrs. U.S. Army Forces Command, Ft. McPherson, Ga., 1984-87, ret., 1987; cons. Burdeshaw and Assocs., 1987-88; gen. mgr. Seattle Tennis Club, 1988-94. Decorated D.S.M., Legion of Merit, Bronze Star, Meritorious Service medal, Air medal, Army Commendation medal, Vietnamese Cross of Gallantry with Silver Star. Mem. Assn. of U.S. Army, Rotary. United Methodist. Fax: 425-745-8068. Avocations: reading military history; cycling; skiing, golf. Home: 809 169th Pl SW Lynnwood WA 98037-3307

JENG, TZYY-WEN, biochemist; b. Taichung, Taiwan, Nov. 2, 1947; came to U.S., 1974; s. Ching-Po and Yu-Ju (Wong) J.; m. Kwan-Yee Sum; children: Howard L., Way A. BS, Nat. Taiwan U., Taipei, 1970; PhD, U. Calif., Berkeley, 1978. Rsch. assoc. U. Ariz., Tucson, 1979-84, rsch. asst. prof., 1984-86, rsch. specialist and rsch. asst. prof., 1986-88; sr. rsch. biochemist Abbott Labs., Abbott Park, Ill., 1988-90, rsch. investigator, 1991-92, assoc. rsch. fellow, 1992—. Author: Natural Toxins, 1980; contbr. articles to Jour. Molecular Biology. Wilhelm Bernard Fund grantee Internat. Congress on Electron Microscopy, 1982. Mem. N.Y. Acad. Scis. Achievements include patents in field. Office: Abbott Labs AP 20 100 Abbott Park Rd Apt 20 Abbott Park IL 60064-3502

JENKIN, DOUGLAS ALAN, computer consultant; b. Dovercourt, England, Sept. 14, 1932; came to U.S., 1973; s. William Douglas and Violet Foss (Harvey) J.; m. Rosemary Joan Finch, Oct. 28, 1961 (dec.); children: Paul, Sally, Richard, Christopher; m. Billie Maxine Willmon, Mar. 14, 1998. BA in Natural Sci., Oxford, England, 1956, MA, 1959. Chartered engr. Process engr., planner Esso Petroleum Co., Fawley, England, 1956-63; econs. engr. Altona Petrochem. Co., Altona, Victoria, Australia, 1963-65; systems analyst C-E-I-R Ltd., London, 1965-68; programmer C-E-I-R, Inc., Washington, 1968-69; mgr. math. program Scicon Ltd., London, 1969-73; lectr. computer sci. Birkbeck Coll., London, 1970-73; examiner computer sci. London U., 1970-73; mgr. North Am. Scicon Ltd., Houston, 1973-74; v.p. Bonner and Moore Assocs., Inc., Houston, 1974-91; sr. cons. AspenTech. (formerly Setpoint Inc.), Houston, 1991-99; mng. dir. Jenkinternatl. Assoc., 1999—. Contbr. articles to profl. jours. Served as pilot officer RAF, 1951-53, England. Fellow British Computer Soc.; mem. Inst. for Ops. Rsch. and the Mgmt. Scis. Avocations: scuba diving, windsurfing, jogging. Home: 213 Elkins Lk Huntsville TX 77340-7305 Office: 213 Elkins Lane Huntsville TX 77340-7305

JENKIN, JAMES THOMAS, videotape editor; b. Monclair, N.J., Apr. 28, 1964; s. David Alan and Dolores Ann (Hyland) J. Student, Raritan Valley Coll., Somerville, N.J., 1987-88; cert. advanced non-linear editing, Avid Sch. Forman Rising Sun Coatings, Flemington, N.J., 1985-89; with dept. videotape playback Picsonic Prodns., N.Y.C., 1989-91, videotape editor, 1991—. Contbr. articles to mags. Recipient various Telly awards, 1991, 92, 95, Communicator award, 1997, Videographer award, 1998. Mem. Internat. TV Soc. Avocations: music composition, softball, tennis, movie research. Office: Picsonic Prodns 25 W 45th St New York NY 10036-4902

JENKINS, ALBERT FELTON, JR., lawyer; b. Madison, Ga., Jan. 18, 1941; s. A. Felton and Jimmie Lucille (Davis) J.; m. Julie Richardson Green, Apr. 16, 1966; children: A. Felton III, Emily Green, Alan Davis. AB, U. Ga., 1963, LLB, 1965. Bar: Ga. 1965, U.S. Dist. Ct. (no. dist.) Ga. 1965, U.S. Ct. Appeals Ga. 1965, U.S. Ct. Appeals (4th cir.) 1981, U.S. Ct. Appeals (5th cir.) 1966, U.S. Ct. Appeals (11th cir.) 1981, U.S. Ct. Appeals (D.C. cir.) 1987, U.S. Supreme Ct. 1968. Assoc. King & Spalding, Atlanta, 1965-70, ptnr., 1971-92, ret. ptnr., 1992—; chmn. bd. visitors U. Ga. Law Sch., Athens, 1974; mem. Gov.'s Appellate Jud. Selection Com., Atlanta, 1972-73, Gov.'s Jud. process Rev. Com., Atlanta, 1984-85, Ga. Joint Study Commn. on Revenue Structure, 1992-95, Ga. Agrl. Exposition Authority; dir. Dundee Mills, Inc., 1994-95. Co-author: (2 vol. treatise) Georgia Civil Procedure Forms-Practice, 1988. Sec. U. Ga. Bd. Trustees, 1979-85; chmn., pres. Atlanta Unit Am. Cancer Soc., 1982-83; trustee Atlanta Fulton Pub. Libr. Sys., 1995-97. Sgt. Air Nat. Guard, 1965-71. Fellow Am. Bar Found.; mem. State Bar of Ga. (pres. Young Lawyers 1972-73, bd. govs. 1983-91), Piedmont Driving Club (Atlanta), Phi Beta Kappa, Omicron Delta Kappa. Methodist. Office: King & Spalding 191 Peachtree St SW Ste 4100 Atlanta GA 30303-3637

JENKINS, ALEXANDER, III, business executive; b. Weymouth, Mass., Feb. 17, 1934; s. Alexander and Eva Gladys (Price) J.; m. Judith H. Switzer, Jan. 4, 1975; children: Alexander Tuxbury, Edith Garland, Charles Jordan. BS, Yale U., 1956; MBA, Harvard U., 1961. Rsch. asst. Harvard Bus. Sch., Boston, 1961-62; treas. Ocean Rsch. Equip., Inc., Falmouth, Mass., 1962-65, 77-78; treas. Orion Research, Inc., Cambridge Mass., 1962-70, exec. v.p., 1970-71; pvt. practice cons., 1971-79; v.p., Adcole, 1972-77; pres. Jenkins Trading, Inc., Everett, Mass., 1973-91, prin. Sormani Calendars div., 1991—; treas., dir. Pintek, Inc., 1979-81; div. mgr. Spectra Physics, 1980-81; pres., CEO Orion Rsch., Inc., Cambridge, 1981-88, chmn., chief exec. officer, 1988-89; pvt. cons., 1989—, treas. Jenkins Trading Inc. (dba Sormani Calendars) 1991—; bd. dirs. Reagecon Diagnostics Ltd. Served with USN, 1956-59. Episcopalian. Home: 37 Breakwater Dr Chelsea MA 02150-4024 Office: 7 Charlton St Everett MA 02149-2432

JENKINS, ANTHONY CHARLES, correspondent; b. London, Apr. 13, 1956; came to U.S., 1986; s. Victor Silberstein and Anne Elizabeth Jenkins de Blanes; m. Jayne H. Tsuchiyama, Jan. 5, 1995; 1 child, Max. BA, Durham U., U.K., 1978. Sr. account exec. Internat. Mktg., London, 1980-82; Nicaragua corr. Guardian Newspaper, London, 1982-85, sr. corr. Central Am. and Caribbean, 1985-86; N.Y. corr. Expresso, Lisbon, Portugal, 1986-89, N.Am. bur. chief, 1989—. Author: Nicaragua and the U.S.A. Years of Conflict, 1989, Nicaragua A Decade of Rebellion, 1991; contbr. articles to profl. jours. Pres. Durham Students' Union, 1978-79; gen. sec. Fgn. Corr. Assn., Nicaragua, 1984-86. Recipient Gazeta Prize, Journalists' Assn., Portugal, 1988. Fellow Ctr. Internat. Policy; mem. UN Corrs. Assn. Avocations: skiing, sailing, flying. Home: 40 E 72nd St New York NY 10021-4228 Office: Expresso Rm S-360 UN New York NY 10017

JENKINS, ANTHONY CURTIS, sales executive; b. Kirkwood, Mo., Apr. 16, 1958; s. Allen C. and Phyllis K. (Kley) J.; m. Angela K. Roberts, Sept. 17, 1983. BS, Maryville U., 1982, MS, 1985. Merchandising mgr. CMC Corp., St. Louis, 1980-87; v.p. Cellular Hotline, St. Louis, 1988-89; sr. v.p. sales GPX, Inc., St. Louis, 1990—; officer exec. com., Hagemeyer Consumer Electronics, Inc. Roman Catholic. Avocations: hunting, fishing.

JENKINS, BILLIE BEASLEY, film company executive; b. Topeka, June 27, 1943; d. Arthur and Etta Mae (Price) Capelton; m. Rudolph Alan Jenkins, Nov. 1, 1935; 1 child, Tina Caprice. Student, Santa Monica City Coll., 1965-69. Exec. sec. to v.p. prodn. Screen Gems, L.A., 1969-72; exec. asst. Spelling/Goldberg Prodns., 1972-82; dir. adminstrn. The Leonard Co./Mandy Films, 1982-85, v.p., 1985-87; exec. asst. to pres. and chief oper. officer 20th Century Fox Film Corp., L.A., 1986-87, dir. adminstrn., 1987-90, dir. prodn. svcs. & resources Fox Motion Pictures div., 1990-92; program coord. Am. Film Inst. Gary Hendler Minority Filmmakers Program, 1990-93; pres., CEO Masala Prodns., Inc., 1991—. Asst. to exec. producer: (films) War Games, 1984, Spacecamp, 1986; (movies for TV) Something about Amelia, 1984, Alex, The Life of a Child, 1985; (series) Paper Dolls, 1985, Cavanaughs, 1987, Charlie's Angels, Rookies, others; exec. prodn. cons. (documentary) The Good, The Bad, The Beautiful, 1995-96. Commr. L.A. City Cultural Heritage Commn., 1992-93. Named 1991 Woman of Excellence, Boy Scouts Am.; honored First African-Am. Women Pioneers of So. Calif. Top Ladies of Distinction City of Angels chpt. L.A., 1999. Mem. NAFE, Women in Film Assn. (pres. 1991, 92, advisor to exec. bd. 1993-95), Black Women's Network, Am. Film Inst., Ind. Feature Prodns./West, Motivating Our Students Through Experience (exec. bd. mem.), Top Ladies of Distinction (City of Angels chpt.- L.A.). Avocations: photography, gardening, writing.

JENKINS, BRENDA GWENETTA, early childhood/special education specialist; b. Durham, N.C., Aug. 11, 1949; d. Brinton Alfred and Ophelia Arden (Eaton) Jenkins. BS, Howard U., 1971, MEd, 1972; postgrad., Trinity Coll., Am. U., U. D.C., Marymount Coll., 1976—. Cert. Advanced Grad. Studies Spl. Edn., 1975, aerobics instr., Nat. Dance Exercise Instr.'s Tng. Assn. Cheerleading coach Howard U., Washington, 1971-86; aerobics instr. D.C. Pub. Schs., Washington, 1982-97; tchr. D.C. Pub. Schs., Washington, 1972—; v.p. Nerdlihc Corp., Washington, 1985—; co-owner Fantasia Early Learning Acad., Washington, 1985-98; ptnr. Jenkins, Trapp-Dukes and Yates Ptnrship., Washington; instr. aerobics Washington Dept. Recreation, Washington, 1988-93; instr. You Fit, Inc. Nat. Children's Ctr. Washington, Washington, 1991-93, Anthony Bowen YMCA, Washington, 1992-93; instr. health, nutrition support Rockville, Md., 1992; instr., coach Maryvale PomPom/cheerleaders, Montgomery County, Md., 1992-94; tchr., collabrative program asst. chair Maryvale PomPom/cheerleaders, Montgomery County, 1994-95, co-chair program com., 1995-96; fitness instr. Oxedine Performing Arts Acad., Montgomery County, 1995-96; Goals 2000 english, lang. arts, history writer D.C. Pub. Schs., 1995-96; aerobic instr. handicapped Coun. Exceptional Children, Washington, 1982, recreation svcs., City of Rockville, 1986—; developer My Spl. Friend program, 1984, BJ's Thinking Cap, 1991, Learning Creations, 1994, Girlfriends; bldg. rep. Washington Tchrs. Union AFT, AFL-CIO, 1987-89, 91-94, 1996, asst. bldg. rep., 1990-91, 94-95, 97-99; supr. foster grandparent program Sharpe Health Sch., 1988—; trainer AIDS in Workplace, 1990, Early Childhood Substance Abuse Project Tng., 1992-93, SAPE, 1995, Metro Foster Grandparent Program, Washington, 1992-93; mem. preschool adv. bd. D.C. Pub. Schs., 1992-93, coordinating curriculum coun., 1994-96; master tchr. Coop. Tchr. Corp., 1993; curriculum writer, 1993; v.p. spl. edn. Washington Tchrs. Union Local # 6, 1994-2001; stds. specialist, 1997—; presenter in field; del. 75th convention Am. Fed. Tchrs., 1998; mem. adv. bd. Supt.'s Tchr. Affairs, 1999; mem. Spl. Edn. State Adv. Panel, Washington, 1998-2000, D.C. Parent Tng. and Info. Ctr., ARC, Inc. Adv. Panel; exec. bd. dirs. Assembly of Petworth,

1998-99. Active D.C. Spl. Edn. Adv., 1998, Coun. Exceptional Children, 1998, ASCD, 1998; presenter AFT Civil, Human, Women's Rights Conf., 1998; Internat. Space Camp, Huntsville, Ala., 1998. Recipient Outstanding Svc. award Kappa Delta Pi, 1978, 79, 81, 82, 84, citation Washington Tchrs. Union, 1985; named D.C. Tchr. of Yr. Coun. Chief State Sch. Officers, 1998; grantee spl. edn. D.C. Pub. Sch. state office, 1993, Citibank, 1994; named to Hall of Fame Bison Found. Inc., Howard U., 1995. Mem. Am. Fed. Tchrs., D.C. Parents and Friends Children Spl. Needs (bd. dirs.), Howard Alumni Cheerleaders Assn. (co-founder 1977, pres. 1990-94, v.p. 1998-99, Outstanding Recognition award, 1984, renamed The Brenda G. Jenkins award, 1987); Theta Alpha chpt. Kappa Delta Pi (exec. com.). Democrat. Avocations: alumni cheerleading, fashion design, cooking, dancing, poetry writing.

JENKINS, BRUCE, sportswriter; b. Oct. 4, 1948; s. Gordon Jenkins; m. Martha Jane Stanton; 2 children. Degree in Journalism, U. Calif., Berkeley, 1971. With San Francisco Chronicle, 1973—, sports columnist, 1989—. Author: Life After Saberhagen, 1986, North Shore Chronicles, 1990. Recipient nat. awards AP, UPI, Basketball Writers Assn.; nominated Pulitzer Prize for columns Barcelona Olympics, 1992. Office: San Francisco Chronicle 901 Mission St San Francisco CA 94103-2905*

JENKINS, BRUCE STERLING, federal judge; b. Salt Lake City, Utah, May 27, 1927; s. Joseph and Bessie Pearl (Iverson) J.; m. Margaret Watkins, Sept. 19, 1952; children—Judith Margaret, David Bruce, Michael Glen, Carol Alice. BA with high honors, U. Utah, 1949, LLB, 1952, JD, 1952. Bar: Utah 1952, U.S. Dist. Ct. 1952, U.S. Supreme Ct. 1962, U.S. Circuit Ct. Appeals 1962. Pvt. practice Salt Lake City, 1952-59; assoc. firm George McMillan, 1959-65; asst. atty. gen. State of Utah, 1952; dep. county atty. Salt Lake County, 1954-58; bankruptcy judge U.S. Dist. Ct., Utah, 1965-78, judge, 1978—, chief judge, 1984-93; adj. prof. U. Utah, 1987-88, 96—. Research, publs. in field; contbr. essays to Law jours.; bd. editors: Utah Law Rev, 1951-52. Mem. Utah Senate, 1959-65, minority leader, 1963, pres. senate, 1965, vice chmn. commn. on orgn. exec. br. of Utah Govt., 1965-66; Mem. adv. com. Utah Tech. Coll., 1967-72; mem. instl. council Utah State U., 1976. Served with USN, 1945-46. Named Alumnus of Yr. award Coll. Law Univ. Utah, 1985; recipient Admiration and Appreciation award Utah State Bar, 1995, Emeritus Merit of Honor award U. Utah Alumni Assn., 1997. Fellow Am. Bar Found.; mem. ABA, Am. Inn Ct., Utah State Bar Assn. (Judge of Yr. 1993), Salt Lake County Bar Assn., Fed. Bar Assn. (Disting. Jud. Svc. awrd Utah chpt. 1993), Order of Coif, Phi Beta Kappa, Phi Kappa Phi, Phi Eta Sigma, Phi Sigma Alpha, Tau Kappa Alpha. Democrat. Mormon. Office: US Dist Ct 462 US Courthouse 350 S Main St Ste 150 Salt Lake City UT 84101-2180

JENKINS, C(ARLE) FREDERICK, religious organization executive, minister, lawyer; b. Orange, N.J., Nov. 18, 1931; s. Carle Brong and Euphemia (Repp) J.; m. Jane Shearer, Sept. 15, 1956; children: Elizabeth Ruth, Jonathan Thomas (dec.), Timothy Carle, Jeffrey Anson, Katharine Ann. AB, Amherst Coll., 1953; MDiv, Yale U., 1956; MA, Case Western Res. U., 1972; JD, Cleve. State U., 1982. Ordained to ministry Presbyn. Ch. USA, 1960; bar: Ohio, 1982, N.J., 1985. Urban min., community worker Inner City Protestant Parish, Cleve., 1956-65; pastor Phillips Ave. Presbyn. Ch., East Cleveland, Ohio, 1965-69; exec. presbyter Presbytery of Monmouth, Tennent, N.J., 1984-90; dir. constl. svcs. Presbyn. Ch. (USA), Louisville, 1990—, assoc. stated clk., 1993; interim pastor Northminster Presbyn. Ch., Lorain, Ohio, 1972; stated clk. Presbytery of Western Res., Cleve., 1973-83; interim min. Westlake (Ohio) Presbyn. Ch., 1978-79, East Side Presbyn. Ch., Ashtabula, Ohio, 1982-83; sec. com. on reorgn. of presbytery Greater Cleve. Coun. Chs., 1972-73, bd. dirs. 1969-70; sec. Gen. Coun. Presbytery, 1973-83. Trustee Winding Brook Condominium Assn., 1986-88, Wessex Pl. Community Assn., Louisville. Recipient Resolution of Appreciation Cleve. City Coun., 1965. Mem. ABA. Democrat. Home: 9520 Wessex Pl Louisville KY 40222-5043 Office: Presbyn Ch (USA) 100 Witherspoon St # 4416 Louisville KY 40202-1396

JENKINS, CLAUSTON LEVI, JR., college president; b. Durham, N.C., Mar. 4, 1938; s. Clauston Levi Sr. and Mary (Asbill) J.; m. Elizabeth H. Boney, Dec. 11, 1993. AB, U. N.C., 1960; MA, U. Va., 1963, PhD, 1966; JD, U. N.C., 1975. Tchr. English Broughton High Sch., Raleigh, N.C., 1961; asst. prof. U. Wis., Madison, 1966-68, asst. dir. acad. programs, 1968-70; coord. instnl. studies N.C. State U., Raleigh, 1970-73, univ. counsel, 1976-86; pres. St. Mary's Coll., Raleigh, 1986—. Mem. Raleigh C. of C. (bd. dirs.), Phi Beta Kappa, Phi Eta Sigma. Home: 1209 College Pl Raleigh NC 27605-1802 Office: St Marys Coll 900 Hillsborough St Raleigh NC 27603-1610*

JENKINS, DARRELL LEE, librarian; b. Roswell, N.Mex., Aug. 12, 1949; s. Lindon C. and Joyce (King) J.; m. Susan Jenkins. BA, Ea. N.Mex. U., 1971; MLS, U. Okla., 1972; MA, N.Mex. State U., 1976. Asst. edn., psychology, gift libr. N.Mex. State U., Las Cruces, 1972-73, edn. psychology libr., 1973-74, asst. reference libr., 1974-75, asst. catalog libr., 1975-76, asst. serials libr., 1976-77, acting head reference dept., 1977; adminstrv. svcs. libr. So. Ill. U., Carbondale, 1977-82, dir. libr. svcs., 1982-91, social studies libr., 1992—; cons. U.S. Naval Base, So. Ill. U., Groton, Conn., 1985-91; chmn. bd. dirs. CEC Comm., Inc., 1997-99. Author: Specialty Positions in ARL Libraries, 1982; co-author: Library Development and Fund Raising Capabilities, 1988; contbr. articles to profl. jours. Mem. ALA (chmn. libr. orgn. mgmt. sect. 1985-86), Am. Soc Info. Sci., Ill. Libr. Computer System Orgn. (pres. 1985-86), Phi Kappa Phi, Beta Phi Mu, Phi Alpha Theta. Republican. Mem. Ch. Assembly God. Avocations: tennis, swimming. E-mail: jenkins@midamer.net.

JENKINS, DONALD JOHN, art museum administrator; b. Longview, Wash., May 3, 1931; s. John Peter and Louise Hazel (Pederson) J.; m. Mary Ella Bemis, June 29, 1956; children—Jennifer, Rebecca. B.A., U. Chgo., 1951, M.A., 1970. Mus. asst. Portland (Oreg.) Art Mus., 1954-56, asst. curator, 1960-69, curator, 1974-75, dir., 1975-87, curator Asian art, 1987-98, curator, 1998—; assoc. curator oriental art Art Inst. Chgo., 1969-74; mem. gallery adv. com. Asia House Gallery, N.Y.C., 1977-91; application reviewer NEH, Washington, 1984-86; lectr. various museums and art orgns., 1969—. Author: (exhbn. catalogues) Ukiyo-e Prints and Paints, 1971, The Ledoux Heritage, 1973, Masterworks/China and Japan, 1976, Images of Changing World, 1983, The Floating World Revisited, 1993. Mem. Pittock Mansion Adv. Com., Portland, 1975-87, chmn., 1983-84; chmn. NW Regional China Coun., Portland, 1980-89; mem. art selection com. Performing Arts Ctr., Portland, 1983-89. Recipient Uchiyama Susumu Meml. award Japan Ukiyo-e Soc., 1993, Order of Rising Sun with gold rays and rosette Japanese Govt., 1994, Flying Horse Cmty. Svc. award N.W. China Coun., 1996. Mem. Am. Assn. Mus., Soc. for Japanese Arts, Assn. Asian Studies, Classical Chinese Garden Soc. (chmn. bd. 1991-97), Japan-Am. Soc. Oreg. (chmn. cultural affairs com. 1987—), The Internat. House of Japan. Home: 16418 NW Rock Creek Rd Portland OR 97231-2406 Office: Portland Art Mus 1219 SW Park Ave Portland OR 97205-2486

JENKINS, EDWARD BEYNON, research astronomer; b. San Francisco, Mar. 20, 1939; s. Francis Arthur and Henrietta Beynon (Smith) J.; m. Myrna Dean Stewart, June 29, 1963; children: Brian Francis, Eric Dean. AB, U. Calif., Davis, 1962; PhD, Cornell U., 1966. Rsch. assoc. Princeton (N.J.) U., 1966-67, mem. rsch. staff, 1967-73, rsch. astronomer, 1973-79, sr. rsch. astronomer, 1979—; mem. mgmt. and ops. working group NASA, Washington, 1976-79, 88-91, mem. astrophysics subcom., 1992-93; mem. com. on space astronomy and astrophysics NAS, Washington, 1986-89; co-investigator Space Telescope Imaging Spectrograph, 1985—, Far Ultraviolet Spectroscopic Explorer, 1989—. Contbr. numerous articles to Astrophys. Jour. Recipient Rsch. award Alexander von Humboldt Found., 1992-93. Mem. Am. Astron. Soc. (v.p. 1996-99), Internat. Astron. Union (pres. Commn. 44, 1988-91). Democrat. Unitarian. Office: Princeton U Obs Astronomy Dept Princeton NJ 08544

JENKINS, ELAINE PARKER, secondary school educator; b. Charleston, S.C., Sept. 25, 1950; d. William Lucius and Nancy Stevenson (Beaty) Parker; m. Marshall Pinckney Sherard, Jr. (div.); children: Marshall Pinckney III, Jessica Parker; m. Howard Claude Jenkins, June 14, 1986; children: David Wayne, Kristen Michelle. BA in English and Edn., Presbyn. Coll., 1971; postgrad., Clemson U., 1976, 84, U. N.C., Charlotte, 1986, N.C. State U., 1987-89, U. N.C., 1995, 97. Tchr. English Blythewood (S.C.) Jr. H.S., 1972-74, McDuffie H.S., Anderson, S.C., 1976-78, G.B.S. Hale H.S., Raleigh, N.C., 1987-90, East Wake H.S., Wendell, N.C., 1990-95, So. Wayne H.S., Dudley, N.C., 1995-1997; tchr. English Clayton (N.C.) H.S., 1997—, head English dept., 1997—; yearbook tchr. various secondary schs. Bd. dirs. Faith Luth. Sch., Raleigh, 1995-97; tchr. Lord of Life Luth. Ch., 1986-97. Mem. Nat. Coun. of Tchrs. of English, N.C. Tchrs. of English, N.C. Assn. Educators/NEA, N.C. Scholastic Media Assn. (v.p. yearbook divsn.), N.C. Assn. Educators, Thomas Wolfe Soc. Home: 4612 Winterlochen Rd Raleigh NC 27603-3868 Office: Clayton HS 600 S Fayetteville St Clayton NC 27520-2716

JENKINS, ELIZABETH A., federal judge; b. 1949. BA, Vanderbilt U.; JD, U. of Fla. Coll. of Law. Bars: Fla., D.C. Atty. advisor U.S. Dept. of Justice, 1976-78; asst. U.S. atty. Middle Dist. of Fla., Orlando, FLa., 1978-82, Southern Dist. of Fla., West Palm Beach, Fla., 1983-85; magistrate judge U.S. Dist. Ct. (mid. dist.) Fla., 1985—. Office: US Courthouse 801 N Florida Ave Ste 1135 Tampa FL 33602

JENKINS, ELLEN JANET (JAN JENKINS), historian, history educator; b. Austin, Tex., Sept. 11, 1952; d. Neal and Melissa (Harwell) J.; m. W.E. Whittaker, III, Aug. 18, 1972 (div. July 1982); 1 child: William Barry. BA, U. Tex., Dallas, 1977; MA, U. North Tex., 1983, PhD, 1992. Tchr. Garland (Tex.) Ind. Sch. Dist., 1977-81; tchg. fellow history U. North Tex., Denton, 1982-86; rsch. asst. Rsch. Laboratory Archeology and History of Art, Oxford U., Eng., 1984; asst. prof. history U. Ark., Monticello, 1992-97; asst. prof. history, dir. U. Honors Ark. Tech. U., Russellville, 1997—; fundraising, restoration St. Matthew's Ch., Harwell, Eng. 1981, 84; editl. bd. Drew County Hist. Jour., Monticello, 1994-96. Author: (with John M. Fletcher) The Harwell Trail, 1981; contbr. (book reviews) Teaching History, 1992-94, (essay) Encyclopedia of Propaganda, 1997. Bd. dirs. Drew County Hist. Mus., Monticello, 1993-95; spkr. various civic orgns., Dallas, 1988-97, Monticello, 1992-97, Russellville, 1997-98. Rsch. grantee U. Ark., 1993, 94, 96, Tchg. Project grantee Ark. Humanities Coun., 1995-96. Mem. Assn. St. Cross Coll. at Oxford U., Ark. Assn. Coll. History Tchrs., So. Hist. Assn., European Hist. sect. of So. Hist. Assn. (nominating com. 1998—), Phi Alpha Theta. Democrat. E-mail: ssjj@catuvm.atu.edu. Office: Ark Tech U Social Scis and Philosophy WPN 267 Russellville AR 72801

JENKINS, FERGUSON ARTHUR, JR. (FERGIE JENKINS), former baseball player; b. Chatham, Ont., Can., Dec. 13, 1942; s. Ferguson Arthur Sr. and Delores Jenkins; m. Kathy Williams, Feb., 1965 (div.); children: Kelly, Delores, Kimberly; m. Maryanne Jenkins (dec.); 1 stepson, Raymond; 1 child, Samantha; m. Lydia Farrington, Dec. 1993. With various minor league teams, 1962-65; pitcher Phila. Phillies, 1965-66, Chgo. Cubs, 1966-73, 82-83, Tex. Rangers, 1974-75, 78-81, Boston Red Sox, 1976-77; former pitching coach minor league team Tex. Rangers; pitching coach Chgo. Cubs. Inductee Baseball Hall of Fame, 1991; recipient Cy Young award, 1971, Am. League Comeback Player of Yr. Sporting News, 1974; named to All-Star team, 1967, 71, 72, Sporting News All-Star team, 1967, 71, 72; named Nat. League Pitcher of Yr. Sporting News, 1971. Address: Nat Baseball Hall of Fame PO Box 590 Cooperstown NY 13326*

JENKINS, FRANCES OWENS, retired small business owner; b. Leonard, Tex., Nov. 12, 1924; d. R. Melrose and Maureen (Durrett) Owens; m. William O. Jenkins (div. 1961); children: Steven O., Tamara. Student theatre arts, East Tex. State U., 1939-42, Ind. U., 1945-48, U. Tenn., 1954-56. Fashion model Rogers Modeling Agy., Boston, 1950-52, Rich's, Knoxville, Tenn., 1955-60; owner, instr. Arts Sch. Self-Improvement and Modeling, Knoxville, 1959-69; onwer, pres. Fran Jenkins Boutique, Knoxville, 1964-95; ret., 1995; cons. Miss Am. Pageant, Knoxville, 1958-66. Actress Carousel Theatre, Knoxville, 1955-58. Home: 8833 Cove Point Ln Knoxville TN 37922-6402 also: 71 Pelican Cir Panama City Beach FL 32407

JENKINS, GEORGE, stage designer, film art director; b. Balt., Nov. 19, 1908; s. Benjamin Wheeler and Jane (Clarke) J.; m. Phyllis Adams, May 6, 1955; 1 dau by previous marriage, Jane Jenkins Dumais; 1 stepdau., Alexandra Kirkland Marsh (dec.). Student architecture, U. Pa., 1931. Cons. theatre U. Pa., Anenberg Theatre; vis. prof. motion picture design UCLA, 1985-87, 88. Set designer Broadway prodns. including I Remember Mamma, 1944, Dark of the Moon, 1945, Lost in the Stars, 1949, Bell, Book and Candle, 1950, The Bad Seed, 1954, Happiest Millionaire, 1956, Miracle Worker, 1959, Wait Until Dark, 1966, Only Game in Town, 1968, Night Watch, 1972, Sly Fox, 1976; art dir. films including Best Years of Our Lives, 1946, Secret Life of Walter Mitty, 1948, Mickey One, 1965, Up the Down Staircase, 1966, Wait Until Dark, 1967, No Way to Treat a Lady, 1967, Subject Was Roses, 1968, Klute, 1970, 1776, 1971, The Paper Chase, 1972, Parallax View, 1973, Funny Lady, 1974, All the President's Men, 1977, Comes A Horseman, 1978, China Syndrome, 1978, Starting Over, 1979, The Postman Always Rings Twice, 1980, Roll Over, 1981, Sophie's Choice, 1982, Dream Lover, 1984, Orphans, 1987, See You in the Morning, 1989, Presumed Innocent, 1990; TV programs including Annie Get Your Gun, NBC TV, 1957, The Dollmaker, ABC-TV, 1983; art dir. in charge color, CBS-TV, 1953-54. Recipient Donaldson award for I Remember Mama, Billboard Publs., 1946, Acad. award for All the President's Men, 1977, nominated for Acad. award for China Syndrome, 1978. Mem. Delta Phi. Office: 740 Kingman Ave Santa Monica CA 90402-1336

JENKINS, GEORGE L., lawyer, fast food company executive; b. Wheeling, W.Va., Jan. 30, 1940; s. George Addison and Mildred Irene (Liggett) J. AB magna cum laude, Kent State U., 1963; JD with honors, U. Mich., 1966. Bar: Ohio 1966. Assoc. Vorys, Sater, Seymour & Pease, Columbus, Ohio, 1966-71, ptnr., 1975—; first asst. atty. gen. State of Ohio, Columbus, 1971-75; dir. Fleagane Enterprises, Inc., Columbus, 1977—, JMHS, Inc., 1984—, Impex Logistics, Inc., 1993—, Nat. Am. Logistics, Inc., 1994—. Mem. ABA, Ohio State Bar Assn., Columbus Bar Assn. (chmn. various coms. 1966—), Columbus Athletic Club, Muirfield Country Club, Desert Mountain Club. Democrat. Methodist. Avocations: tennis, jogging, travel, reading, golf. Office: Vorys Sater Seymour & Pease PO Box 1008 52 E Gay St Columbus OH 43215-3161

JENKINS, HOWARD M., supermarket executive; b. 1951. MBA, Emory U. With Publix Supermarkets, Inc., Lakeland, Fla., 1966—, v.p. rsch., exec. v.p., 1976-90, chmn. bd. dirs., CEO, 1990—. Office: Publix Supermarkets Inc PO Box 407 Lakeland FL 33802-0407 also: 1936 George Jenkins Blvd Lakeland FL 33815-3760*

JENKINS, JAMES WILLIAM, osteopath, medical consultant; b. Columbus, Ohio, May 15, 1953; s. William Harvey and Irene Barbara (Kacsor) J.; m. Deborah Susan Dorrance, June 16, 1987. BA in Biology, Calif. State U., Fullerton, 1976; DO, Coll. Osteopathic Med. Pacific, 1984; diploma in emergency medicine, Ohio State U., 1988. Cert. correctional health profl. Intern Warren (Ohio) Gen. Hosp., 1984-85; resident in emergency medicine Meml. Osteopathic Hosp., York, Pa., 1985-87; rsch. fellow, clin. instr. Coll. Medicine, Ohio State U., Columbus, 1987-88; clin. emergency physician, med. edn. coord. emergency dept. Dr.'s Hosp., Columbus, 1988-89; med. dir. emergency dept. Greenfield (Ohio) Area Med. Ctr., 1989-93, clin. emergency/trauma physician, 1991-93; med. dir. Chillocothe (Ohio) Correctional Inst., 1993-96; clin. physician, healthcare cons. Ross Correctional Inst., Chillicothe, 1996—; emergency med. svc. med. advisor Franklin Twp. Fire Dept., Columbus, 1988-89; clin. asst. prof. Coll. Osteo. Medicine Pacific, Pomona, Calif., 1989. Contbr. articles to profl. publs., chpt. to book. Mem. CPR com. ARC, Santa Ana, Calif., 1978-81; instr. trainer Am. Heart Assn., Santa Ana, 1972-80; instr., course coord. basic trauma life support Am. Coll. Emergency Physicians, Columbus, 1988—. Rsch. grantee Emergency Medicine Found., 1988, Kellogg Found., 1979-80; recipient rsch. fellow award Emergency Medicine Residents Ohio, 1988, Armstrong Lit. award, 1980. Mem. Am. Assn. Physician Specialists, Beta Beta Beta. Avocations: collecting books, martial arts.

JENKINS, JOHN ANTHONY, lawyer; b. Cin., Apr. 11, 1926; s. John A. and Norma S. (Snyder) J.; m. Margery N. Jenkins, May 24, 1997; children: Julie Anne, John Anthony III. BEE, Ohio State U., 1951, JD, 1953. Bar: Ohio, 1954, U.S. Supreme Ct. 1963. Assoc. Knepper White Richards & Miller, Columbus, Ohio, 1954-58, ptnr., 1958-78; ptnr. Arter & Hadden, Columbus, 1978-94, of counsel, 1995—; mem. mgmt. com. Arter & Hadden, Cleve., 1984-89; dir. Gen. Exploration Co., Dallas, 1972-80; gen. ptnr. Columbus Lasher P/S, Columbus, Ohio, 1976—, Indian Bend Ltd. P/S, Phoenix, 1978—; pres. Mummy Mountain Devel., Phoenix, 1978-89. Author: Ohio Public Contract law, 1989, 3d edit., 1994; contbr. articles to profl. jours. Trustee Citizens Rsch., Inc., Columbus, 1960-72; pres. Columbus Kiwanis Found., 1973-76; pres. Beta Theta Pi Bldg. Assn., Columbus, 1972-76. With U.S. Army, 1944-46. Fellow Am. Bar Found.; mem. ABA (chmn. com.), Ohio Bar Assn. (chmn. com.), Columbus Bar Assn. (chmn. com.), Capital Club, Muirfield Village Golf Club, Scioto Country Club, Golf Club (Gahanna, Ohio), Desert Mountain Club (Scottsdale, Ariz.) Masons, Shriners. Republican. Avocation: golf. Home: 10692 EHoney Mesquito Dr Scottsdale AZ 85262 Office: Arter & Hadden 10 W Broad St Ste 2100 Columbus OH 43215-3422

JENKINS, JOHN EDWARD, JR., electronics executive, engineering educator; b. Charlotte, N.C., Aug. 14, 1937; s. John Edward and Ruby (Killian) J.; m. Leslie Blyth, Mar. 27, 1969; children: Isabel Margaret Jenkins Bader, Iain Edward. BSEE, Duke U., 1958; MBA, Harvard U., 1960; PhD, Edinburgh (Scotland) U., 1970. Registered profl. engr., N.C. Projects coord. Astra, Inc., Raleigh, N.C., 1960-63; ops. analyst Rsch. Triangle Inst., Rsch. Triangle Park, N.C., 1963-65; lectr. elec. engring. Edinburgh U., 1965-71, U. N.C., Charlotte, 1971—; v.p. Jenkins Electric Co., Charlotte, 1971-95, pres., 1995—; chmn. engring. commn. Elec. Apparatus Svc. Assn., St. Louis 1988-90. Assoc. editor Electrical Insulation, 1990-96; contbr. chpt. to Handbook of Electric Motors, 1995; inventor, patentee in field. Mem. IEEE (sr., dir. 1975-76, Outstanding Engr. N.C. 1980). Republican. Presbyterian. Avocation: walking. Office: Jenkins Electric Co Inc 5933 Brookshire Blvd Charlotte NC 28216-3386

JENKINS, JOHN SMITH, academic dean, lawyer; b. Pittston, Pa., Dec. 11, 1932; s. Walter Hershel and Mildred (Lewis) J.; m. Marilyn Lewis, Aug. 23, 1958; 1 child, John Smith Jr. B.A., Lafayette Coll., Easton, Pa., 1954; J.D. with honors, George Washington U., 1961; M.A., Am. U., 1967. Bar: Va. 1961, U.S. Ct. Appeals for the Armed Forces, 1964, U.S. Supreme Ct. 1982. Commd. ensign U.S. Navy, 1955, advanced through grades to rear admiral, 1978; stationed at naval communications sta. Pearl Harbor, Hawaii, 1955-56; duty on U.S.S. Rochester, 1956-57; with Bur. Naval Personnel Washington, 1957-62; with Hdqrs. 1st Naval Dist. Boston, 1962-64; staff Office Navy JAG, 1964-65; staff Office Legis. Affairs Washington, 1969-71; staff Office of Asst. Sec., 1971-73, spl. counsel to sec. Office of Sec., 1973-76, asst. civil law JAG, 1976-78, dep. JAG, 1978-80, JAG, 1980-82; asst. dean Nat. Law Ctr. George Washington U., Washington, 1982-86, assoc. dean, 1986—. Decorated D.S.M. Legion of Merit. Fellow Am. Bar Found.; mem. ABA (ho. of dels., chair standing com. on lawyers in the armed forces 1991-94, mem. standing com. on delivery of legal svcs. 1997—), FBA, Judge Advs. Assn., Army and Navy Club (gov. 1988), Farmington Country Club. Episcopalian. Home: 5809 Helmsdale Ln Alexandria VA 22315-4138 Office: George Washington U Law Sch 2000 H St NW Washington DC 20006-4234

JENKINS, JOHNIE NORTON, research geneticist, research administrator; b. Barton, Ark., Nov. 3, 1934; married, 1959; 2 children. BSA, U. Ark., 1956; MS, Purdue U., 1958, PhD in Genetics, 1960. Rsch. assoc. in agronomy U. Ill., Urbana, 1960-61; rsch. geneticist Agrl. Rsch. Svc., USDA, 1961-80; dir. Crop Sci. Rsch. Lab. Agrl. Rsch. Svc., USDA, Mississippi State, Miss., 1980—; prof. crop sci. and mem. grad. faculty Miss. State U., 1964—. Recipient Mobay Cotton Rsch. Recognition award. Fellow AAAS, Am. Soc. Agronomy, Crop Sci. Soc. Am. Achievements include research on host plant resistance to cotton insects and nematodes; investigations of basic causes of insect and nematode resistance in cotton plants and development of factors which will confer resistance. Office: USDA-ARS Crop Sci Rsch Lab PO Box 5367 Mississippi State MS 39762-5367

JENKINS, KENNETH VINCENT, literature educator, writer; b. Elizabeth, N.J.; s. Thomas Augustus and Rebecca Meredith (Williams) J.; 4 children. AB, MA, Columbia Coll.; postgrad., Columbia U. Tchr. South Side Sr. High Sch., Rockville Centre, N.Y., 1953-72, chmn. dept. English, 1965-72; prof. Afro-Am. lit. Nassau Community Coll., Garden City, N.Y., 1972—, chmn. Afro Am. studies dept., 1975—, supr. adj. faculty, 1974-82; cons. in English, N.Y. State Dept. Edn., Albany, 1965-72; mem. Regents Question Com. in English, Albany, 1966-71. Author: Last Day in Church, 1955, Teaching African Literature, 1960; contbr. revs., poems to profl. publs. Chmn. bd. dirs., founder Target Youth Ctrs., Inc., 1973-76, African-Am. Book Ctr., 1982—; mem. nat. bd. Pacifica Found., 1973-79, chmn., 1975-76, pres., 1976-78; bd. dirs. Sta. WBAI-FM, N.Y.C., 1972-85, Nassau County Youth Bd., 1976—, chmn., 1978—; mem. N.Y. Gov.'s Commn. on Youth, 1984-94; bd. dirs. L.I. Cmty. Found., 1989-98, N.Y. State Youth Support, Inc., 1990-93. Pennington grantee, 1953, community, county, state awards, M.L. King award Celebration Com. Nassau County, 1990; mem. bd. Schomburg Ctr., N.Y.C., 1990—. Mem. Afro-Am. Inst., Assn. Study of Afro-Am. Life and History, Mensa, Phi Delta Kappa. Office: Nassau C C Garden City NY 11530

JENKINS, LEROY, violinist, composer; b. Chgo., Mar. 11, 1932; m. Linda Harris; 1 child, Chantille Kwintana. Student with, Walter Dyett, Chgo.; BA, Fla. A&M U., 1961. Mem. Assn. for Advancement of Creative Musicians, Chgo., 1965-69; composer-in-residence, Assessore Cultura, Italy. Formed trio with Anthony Braxton and Leo Smith, 1968; also played with Albert Ayler, Archie Shepp, Alice Coltrane, Cecil Taylor; formed Revolutionary Ensemble, 1971-77; performed solo violin concerts; formed trio with Muhal Richard Abrams and Andrew Cyrille; also performed duets with Oliver Lake; artistic dir. Composers Forum, 1986—; mem. adv. bd., co-founder Meet the Composer; appeared in jazz festivals including Ann Arbor, 1973, Newport Jazz Festival, 1974, numerous others; performed at Carnegie Hall, 1985, Kennedy Ctr., 1986; albums and CD's include Space Minds, New Worlds Survival of America, Vietnam 1 & 2, Manhattan Cycles, The People's Republic, Creative Construction Company, Urban Blues, For Players Only, Mixed Quintet, Ei Glatson, Swift are the Winds of Life, Leroy Jenkins Live!, Monkey on the Dragon for Violin and Chamber Ensemble, Dream of Dreams for Home for Baritone, Flute, and Viola; compostions include Themes and Improvisations on the Blues, 1985, Out of the Mist, String Quartet, Concerto for Improvised Violin and Chamber Orchestra, 1983; opera and theater pieces Mother of Three Sons, 1991, Off-Duty Dryad, 1991, Fresh Faust, The Negroes Burial Ground, The Three Willies, 1997, among others; recording with Cleve. Chamber Symphony: "Wonderlust", 1998, other solo concerts, 1998; commd. for baritone and piano for N.Y.C. performance, Equal Interest Tours, 1999, Spolletto Festival at Chgo. Cultural Ctr., pieces for trio: violin, trumpet and piano, string quarter, others; solo violin tour in Fla. and La. NEA grantee, 1973, 74, 78, 83, 86, N.Y. Found. for the Arts, The Rockefeller Found.; recipient Downbeat poll award, 1974-83, Lila Wallace/Meet the Composer award. Mem. Assn. for the Advancement of Creative Musicians. Office: 276 Prospect Pl Brooklyn NY 11238-3901*

JENKINS, LINDA FAYE, executive secretary; b. Houston, Apr. 23, 1948; d. Lewis Carr Whatley and Rose Leona Shook; m. Henry Thomas Puckett, Feb. 3, 1968 (div. Aug. 1972); 1 child, Mark Thomas; m. Lester R. Jenkins, May 31, 1974; 1 child, Rebecca Rose. BA in Mgmt., Our Lady of the Lake U., 994. Legal sec. Houston Natural Gas Corp., 1972-87; exec. asst., gen. counsel ENRON, Houston, 1987-91, exec. asst. internat. regulatory and environ. affairs, 1998—, exec asst. govt. affairs, 1994-97; exec. sec. Transwestern Pipeline, Houston, 1991-94. Mem. Women Profls. Govt. (membership chair 1994-95). Roman Catholic. Avocations: genealogy, scrapbooks, volunteer. Office: ENRON Internat 333 Clay St Houston TX 77002-7369

JENKINS, LOUIS (WOODY), television executive, state legislator; b. Baton Rouge, Jan. 3, 1947; s. Louis and Doris Laverne (Rowlett) J.; m. Diane Carole Aker, June 15, 1968; children: Margaret Ann, Elizabeth Ann, David Aker, Catherine Ann. BA in Journalism, La. State U., 1969, JD, 1972. Newsman Sta. WLCS, Baton Rouge, 1964-65; announcer Sta. WAFB-TV, Baton Rouge, 1965-66; pub., editor North Baton Rouge Jour., Baton Rouge, 1966-69; pres. Great Oaks Co., 1972—; CEO WBTR-TV, Baton Rouge; chmn. Sta. WBTR-TV, Baton Rouge, 1987—, Sta. KADO-TV, Shreveport, 1997—, KMNO-TV, Monroe, La., 1998—, WSTY-TV, Hammond, La., 1998—; mem. La. Ho. of Reps., Baton Rouge, 1972—, chmn. com. on labor, 1988-92; mem. Emerald Direct, Amway Corp., 1994—; chmn. bd. dirs. Royal St. Gallery, New Orleans, 1998—. Author: Declaration of Rights, Louisiana Constitution of 1974. Del. La. Constl. Conv., Baton

Rouge, 1973-74; Pres. Reagan's adv. Com. for Trade Negotiations, 1982-84; exec. dir. Coun. for Nat. Policy, 1981-85, bd. dirs. 1990—; founder, chmn. Friends of the Ams., 1984—; co-founder, chmn. Am. Legis. Exch. Coun., 1977-78; hon. chmn. La. delegation Rep. Nat. Conv., 1996; Rep. nominee U.S. Senate from La., 1996. Named Legislator of Yr., Nat. Taxpayers Union, 1978, Eagle Forum, 1990; recipient Outstanding Editorial Writing award La. Press Assn., 1969, Prodr. Best Local TV News Program in U.S. award Community Broadcasters Assn., 1992, Samuel Adams award Local Govt. Coun., 1999. Mem. Nat. Assn. TV Program Execs., Cmty. Broadcasters Assn. (bd. dirs.), Am. Conservative Union (bd. dirs. 1994—). Office: WBTR-TV 914 N Foster Dr Baton Rouge LA 70806-1807

JENKINS, LOUISE SHERMAN, nursing researcher; b. Normal, Ill., Jan. 19, 1943; d. Fred and Zylpha Louise (Garrett) Sherman; m. Gary L. Jenkins, Oct. 30, 1965 (div. July 1976). Diploma, Evanston Hosp. Sch. Nursing, 1963; BS, No. Ill. U., 1979; MS, U. Md., Balt., 1982, PhD, 1985. Asst. head nurse intensive care Community Meml. Hosp., LaGrange, Ill., 1963-65; head nurse coronary care Luth. Gen. Hosp., Park Ridge, Ill., 1965-69; nurse clinician hemodialysis unit Evanston Hosp., Evanston, Ill., 1969-74; head nurse Skokie Valley Community Hosp., Skokie, Ill., 1974-75; faculty dept. continuing edn. Northwest Community Hosp., Arlington Heights, Ill., 1975-80; Walter Schoeder chair nursing rsch. U. Wis. Milw. Sch. Nursing and St. Luke's Med. Ctr., Milw., 1987-96; mem. faculty Sch. Nursing U. Md., Balt., 1996—, acting dir. grad. studies, 1997-98; dir. grad. studies U. Md., 1998—. Mem. editl. bd. Jour. Cardiopulmonary Rehab., Nursing Rsch., Jour. Cardiovasc. Nursing; mem. rev. panel Am. Jour. Health Behavior. Chmn. Coun. Cardiovasc. Nursing, Dallas, 1995-97, Am. Heart Assn., Milw., 1988-95, exec. bd. dirs. Wis. affiliate, 1995-96; fellow coun. on cardiovasc. nursing. Fellow, clin. nurse scholar Robert Wood Johnson Found., U. Calif., San Francisco, 1985-87. Mem. Am. Assn. Cardiovasc. and Pulmonary Rehab. (bd. dirs.-at-large 1993-95), Wis. Nurses Assn. (bd. dirs. 1988-90, Excellence in Nursing Rsch. award 1995), Midwest Nursing Rsch. Soc. (gov. bd. 1993-95), Coun. Nursing Rsch., N.Am. Soc. Pacing and Electrophysiology, Sigma Xi, Sigma Theta Tau. E-mail: jenkins@umaryland.edu. Office: Sch Nursing U Md Ste 731 655 W Lombard St Baltimore MD 21201-1512

JENKINS, MARGARET BUNTING, human resources executive; b. Warsaw, Va., Aug. 3, 1935; d. John and Irma (Cookman) Bunting; children: Sydney, Jr., Terry L. Student, Coll. William and Mary, 1952; AA in Bus. Adminstrn., Christopher Newport U., 1973; BA in Human Resource Devel., St. Leo Coll., 1979; M in Adminstrn., George Washington U., 1982; PhD in Human Rsch. Mgmt., Columbia Pacific U., 1986. Rehab. counselor, tchr. York County Schs., Yorktown, Va.; mgr. Waterfront Constrn. Co., Seafood Corp., Seaford, Va., 1960-72; labor rels. specialist Naval Weapons Sta., Yorktown, 1974-77; staffing specialist NWS, Yorktown, 1977-78; position classification specialist Supr. Shipbldg. & Repair, & Naval Weapons Sta., Newport News, Va., 1978-81; supr. pers. mgmt. specialist SupSHIP, Newport News, 1981-90; pers. mgmt. specialist Naval Weapons Sta., Yorktown and Cheatham, Va., 1990-94; bd. dirs. various health orgns.; owner Jenkins Consulting. Author: Organizational Impact on Human Behavior, 1996; (poetry) Heron Haven Reflections, 1996; poetry published in Mists of Enchantment, 1995, Treasured Poems of America, 1996, Poets of the 90's. Recipient Navy Meritorious Civilian Svc. award SUPSHIP, Newport News, 1990, 2 Navy commendations, others. Mem. Soc. for Human Resource Mgmt., Fedn. Women's Clubs, Sierra Club, Audubon Soc., Nature Conservancy, Classification and Compensation Soc. (pres. 1984), 4-Alumni Assn., Toastmasters Internat. (pres. 1985-87, various offices, award), Internat. Soc. of Poets (Disting. mem. 1996), Internat. Platform Assn. Methodist. Avocations: reading, creative writing, art. Home and Office: PO Box 203 Seaford VA 23696-0203 *Excel beyond the norm. Be a risk-taker, and blaze a trail so others may follow. Allow creativity to flourish.*

JENKINS, MARGARET CONSTANCE, elementary education educator; b. Hanover, N.H., Feb. 5, 1946; d. Elmer Marten and Christine Hilda (Woodward) J.; m. Samuel Bernard Cromwell, Aug. 13, 1988. BE, Plymouth State Coll., 1968. Cert. elem. tchr., N.H. 1st grade tchr. Bedford (N.H.) Sch. Dist., 1969—; early childhood devel. workshop presenter, Mass., N.H., 1977-83; real estate agt. Marketplace Realty, Bedford, 1985-87; Here's Looking at You 2000 trainer, 1990—. Computer grantee State of N.H., 1989. Mem. NEA (N.H. exec. bd. 1987-89, regional sec. 1985-93), Bedford Edn. Assn. (sec. 1983-89, parent sch. vol. program trainer 1996—, curriculum developer 1996—, intern supr. 1997—, organizer, facilitator adult women's readers' club 1997—), Tchrs. as Readers Club. Congregationalist. Avocations: reading, swimming, travel, sailing. Home: 16 Norton Ave Manchester NH 03109-4419

JENKINS, MARGIE LITTLE, human relations specialist, psychotherapist; b. Cin., May 28, 1923; d. C. Roy and Mabel Hope Little; m. Robert Russell Jenkins, Aug. 21, 1946; children: Toby Howard Gilbert, Richard Roy, Susan Beth, Robert Houston. BS, U. Cin., 1945; MSW, U. Houston, 1976. Lic. prof. counselor, Tex. Tchr. YWCA, Mpls., 1945-46, William Woods Coll., Fulton, Mo., 1946-47; therapist Interface Counseling Ctr., Houston, 1976-81; counselor Meml. Dr. Presbyn. Ch., Houston, 1978-81; pvt. practice human rels. cons., psychotherapist Houston, 1981—; designer, leader seminars in field. Contbr. columnist Life Lessons to Ky. Post, 1992—. Elder Meml. Dr. Presbyn. Ch., 1974—. Mem. NASW, Internat. Soc. Retirement Planning, Am. Soc. Aging, Tex. Assn. Marriage and Family Therapists, Tex. Counseling Assn. Republican. Avocations: writing, gardening, swimming, reading, entertaining. Home: 13407 St Mary's Ln Houston TX 77079 Office: 8955 Katy Freeway # 205 Houston TX 77024

JENKINS, MARIE P., art educator; five children. Secretarial cert., Armstrong Bus. Coll., 1959. Cert. art specialist. Pvt. vocal tchr. Grace, Idaho, 1962-99; pvt. piano tchr. Grace, 1970-99; pvt. art tchr. Intermountain Area, Idaho, 1980-99; art tchr., specialist K-12 Soda Springs (Idaho) Pub. Sch. Dist. 150, 1992-93; owner Jenkins Arts and Solfelt Music; fine art artist in mediums of watercolor, oil, acrylic, Utah and Idaho and travelling shows; music dir. Broadway musical prodns. for Caribou County Theatre Guild. Polit. cartoonist, 1969-70; illustrator children's books, 1990-91. Bd. dirs. Caribou County Theatre Guild, 1975-77; vocal soloist. Sudden Opportunity grantee Idaho Arts Coun. Mem. Idaho Watercolor Soc., Utah Watercolor Soc. Avocations: gardening, cross country skiing, composing inspirational music, directing and producing church and community concerts and variety shows. E-mail: artsmusic12@juno.com.

JENKINS, MARK GUERRY, cardiologist; b. Charleston, S.C., July 6, 1957; s. Oliver Hart and Lois (Metze) J.; m. Kathy Ann Moses, June 20, 1980; children: Anne Elizabeth, Andrew Guerry. BA, U. Va., 1979; MD, Med. U. S.C., 1983. Diplomate Am. Bd. Internal Medicine, Am. Bd. Cardiovascular Diseases, Am. Bd. Clin. Cardiac Electrophysiology. Resident in internal medicine U. Va., Charlottesville, 1983-86; fellow in cardiology U. N.C., Chapel Hill, 1986-89; cardiologist Cardiovascular Cons., P.C., Savannah, Ga., 1989—; dir. clin. cardiac electrophysiology Meml. Med. Ctr., 1989—, chief cardiology sect., 1993-96, 97—; asst. clin. prof. medicine Med. Coll. Ga., 1997—. Contbr. articles to profl. jours. Fellow Am. Coll. Cardiology; mem. AMA, AHA (sec. 1st dist. med. soc. 1993—), Alpha Omega Alpha, Phi Beta Kappa. Avocation: sailing. Office: Cardiovascular Cons PC 4750 Waters Ave Ste 302 Savannah GA 31404-6268

JENKINS, MCKAY BRADLEY, English language educator, journalist; b. Middletown, Conn., Feb. 1, 1963; s. Donald Chase and Carla Swan (Donkin) J. BA, Amherst Coll., 1985; MS, Columbia U., 1987; PhD, MA, Princeton U., 1996. Reporter Annapolis (Md.) Capital, 1987-88, Seattle Times, 1988, Atlanta Constn., 1988-92; asst. prof. English, U. Del., Newark, 1996—; book critic Newark Star-Ledger, 1996—. Author: The South in Black and White, 1999. Mem. Assn. for Study Lit. and Environ. (sec. 1997—). Buddhist. Office: U Del English Dept Memorial Hall Newark DE 19716-2595

JENKINS, MELVIN LEMUEL, lawyer; b. Halifax, N.C., Oct. 15, 1947; s. Solomon Green and Minerva (Long) J.; m. Wanda Joyce Holly, May 20, 1972; children—Dawn, Shelley, Melvin, Holly Rae-Ann. B.S., N.C. Agrl. and State U., 1969; J.D., U. Kans., 1972. Bar: Nebr. 1973. U.S. Dist. Ct. Nebr. 1973. Atty., Legal Aid Soc., Kansas City, Mo., 1972, HUD, Kansas City, 1972-73; regional atty. U.S. Commn. on Civil Rights, Kansas City, Mo., 1973-79; regional dir. U.S. Commn. on Civil Rights, Kansas City, Mo., 1979—. Chmn. A.M. Roundtable, Kansas City, 1981-83; mem. Kansas City Human Relations Commn., 1980; Mem. Mo. Black Adoption Adv. Bd., Kansas City, 1981—; bd. dirs. Joan Davis Spl. Sch. Mem. Nebr. Bar Assn., ACLU, Nat. Bar Assn., Fed. Bar Assn., ABA, Urban League. African Methodist Episcopalian. Lodge: Masons (master mason for civil rights 1979). Home: 8015 Sunset Cir Grandview MO 64030-1461 Office: 911 Walnut St Kansas City MO 64106-2017 Office: Commission on Civil Rights Central Regional Office 4th & State Ave #908 Kansas City KS 66101

JENKINS, ORVILLE WESLEY, retired religious administrator; b. Hico, Tex., Apr. 29, 1913; s. Daniel Wesley and Eva (Caldwell) J.; m. Louise Cantrell, June 29, 1939; children—Orville Wesley, Jan (Mrs. John Calhoun), Jeanne (Mrs. David Hubbs). Student, Tex. Tech U., 1929-34; B.A., Pt. Loma Nazarene Coll., 1938; student, Nazarene Theol. Sem., 1946-47; D.D., So. Nazarene U., 1957. Ordained to ministry Ch. of Nazarene, 1939; pastor Dinuba, Calif., 1938-42, Fresno, Calif., 1942-45, Topeka, 1945-47, Salem, Oreg., 1947-50, Kansas City, Mo., 1959-61; supt. West Tex. Dist. Ch. of Nazarene, 1950-59, Kansas City Dist., 1961-64; exec. sec. dept. home missions Ch. of Nazarene, Kansas City, 1964-68; gen. supt. Ch. of Nazarene, 1968-85. Author: The Church Winning Sunday Nights, 1961; contbr. articles to ch. publs. Former trustee So. Nazarene U. Home: 2309 W 103rd St Leawood KS 66206-2334 Office: 6401 Paseo Blvd Kansas City MO 64131-1213 *The Christian life has brought meaningful and purposeful existence and has led to a wonderful sense of fulfillment in living. It is a joy to follow the day-to-day excitement of this life.*

JENKINS, PAUL, artist; b. Kansas City, Mo., July 12, 1923; s. William Burris and Nadyne (Fellers) J.; m. Esther Ebenhoe, 1944 (div.); 1 child, Hilarie Paula; m. Alice Baber, 1964 (div.); m. Suzanne Donnelly, 1979. Student, Art Students League, N.Y.C., 1948-52; Hum.D., 1973. Author: play Strike the Puma, 1966; co-author: Observations of Michel Tapié, 1956, Shaman to the Prism Seen, 1987, Anatomy of a Cloud, 1983, Seven Aspects of Amadeus and the Others, 1992, Shaman to the Prism Moon, 1994; also articles; film The Ivory Knife, 1965 (Golden Eagle award Venice Biennale 1966); exhbns. include Studio Paul Facchetti, Paris, 1954, Gimpel Weitenzhoffer Gallery, N.Y.C., Karl Flinker Gallery, Paris, Georges Fall Gallery, Paris, Galerie Patrice Trigano, Paris, Galerie Sapone, Nice, Gimpel Fils Gallery, London, Gallery Art Point, Tokyo, Martha Jackson Gallery, N.Y.C., Assoc. Am. Artists, N.Y.C., Samuel Stein Gallery, Chgo., Galerie Proarta, Zurich, Chateau-Musée de Cagnes Sur Mer, Joseph Rickards Gallery, N.Y.; one-man retrospective, Mus. Fine Arts, Houston, San Francisco Mus. Art, Palm Springs Desert Mus., Musée Picasso, Antibes, Mus. Nice, France; rep. permanent collections, Mus. Modern Art, Whitney Mus., Guggenheim Mus., N.Y., Corcoran Gallery, Washington, Tate Gallery, London, Musee D'Art Moderne, Paris, Centre Georges Pompidou, Paris, Fondation Maeght, St-Paul-de-Vence, Musée Picasso, Antibes, Stedelijk Mus., Amsterdam, Netherlands, Mus. Western Art, Tokyo, others. Served with USNR, 1943-45. Decorated Commandeur des Arts et Lettres France; recipient Silver medal Corcoran Gallery Art, 1967, Art Dir.'s award for Anatomy of a Cloud, 1984, Life Achievement award Butler Inst. Am. Art, 1997, medal City of Paris, 1997. Mem. Royal Cambrian Acad. (hon.; Wales), Nat. Acad. N.Y. (elected). Studio: Imago Terrae PO Box 6833 Yorkville Sta New York NY 10128

JENKINS, PAUL RANDALL, poet, editor; b. Des Moines, Apr. 9, 1942; s. Richard T. and Rachael (Holmes) J.; m. Barbara Benda, Aug. 14, 1964 (div. 1971); 1 child, Eve; m. Ellen K. Watson, July 9, 1977; 1 child, Della. BA, Grinnell Coll., 1964; MA, Phd, U. Wash., 1969. Asst. prof. English U. Mass., Amherst, 1969-76; assoc. prof. Am. lit. Fed. U. Brazil, 1980-82; assoc. prof. English Elms Coll., Chicopee, Mass., 1983-89; assoc. prof. poetry Hampshire Coll., Amherst, 1987—. Author: (poetry) Forget the Sky, 1980, (history) The Conservative Rebel, 1983, (poetry) Radio Tooth, 1997; editor: The Mass. Rev., 1984—, (jour.) Latin Am.: A Special Issue, 1986; contbr. poetry to jours. Archivist Town of Greenfield, Mass., 1977-78; writer, historian, 1978-80. Fulbright lectr. U.S., Brazil, 1980-82. Office: Mass Rev U Mass South Coll Box 37140 Amherst MA 01003-7140

JENKINS, RANDALL DAVID, accountant; b. Waynesboro, Miss., Nov. 7, 1961; s. Kennie L. and Mary Helen (Stanley) J. Grad., Hobson Tech. Coll., 1982. Rural carrier assoc. U.S. Postal Svc., Waynesboro, 1988-90; asst. Jackie Griffin, CPA, Chatom, Ala., 1991-97; owner Jenkins Tax Svc., Silas, Ala., 1984—. Mem. New Orleans Mus. Art, Meridian Mus. Art, Mobile Mus. Art. Home: PO Box 49 Silas AL 36919-0049

JENKINS, RICHARD ERIK, patent lawyer; b. Newport News, Va., Jan. 12, 1946; s. Willard Erette and Ina Beatrice (Porter) J.; m. Susan Rankin Thurston, Aug. 24, 1968 (div. Nov. 1991); 1 child, Anna. BS, N.C. State U., 1968, M in Stats. and Econs., 1971; JD, U. N.C., 1975. Engr. Celanese Corp., Charlotte, N.C., 1971-72; assoc. atty. Stevens, Davis, Miller & Mosher, Washington, D.C., 1975-76, Bell, Seltzer, Park & Gibson, Charlotte, N.C., 1976-78; ptnr. Adams &Jenkins, Charlotte, 1978-80; asst. patent counsel Burlington Industries, Inc., Greensboro, N.C., 1980-84; sr. ptnr. Jenkins & Wilson, Durham, N.C., 1984—; adj. assoc. prof. Duke U., Durham, 1989—, N.C. State U., Raleigh, N.C., 1992—. Trustee N.C. Ctrl. U., Durham, 1992-95; bd. govs. Univ. Club, Durham, 1994-98; bd. dirs. Coun. Entrepreneurial Devel., 1988-90. Mem. AMA, N.C. Bar Assn., Rotary, Hope Valley Country Club, Univ. Club, Carolina Club. Republican. Presbyn. Avocations: golf, yard, reading, sports cars. Office: Jenkins & Wilson PA 3100 Tower Blvd Ste 1400 Durham NC 27707-2575

JENKINS, RICHARD LEE, manufacturing company executive; b. Lynchburg, Va., July 20, 1931; s. Robert Julian and Beulah Vivian (Crews) J.; m. Doris E. Rucker, Dec. 24, 1958; children: Terena M., Richard C. BA, Lynchburg Coll., 1957; MBA, U. Mass., 1970. Various fin. mgmt. positions Gen. Electric Co., Lynchburg, Schenectady, N.Y., and Pittsfield, Mass., 1957-72; controller, mgr. Mfg. Transformer div. Allis-Chalmers, Pitts., 1972-75; gen. mgr. Indsl. Pump div. Allis-Chalmers, Cin., 1975-79; sr. v.p. Lynchburg Foundry, 1979-81; gen. mgr. service div. Siemens-Allis, Inc., Atlanta, 1981-84; sr. v.p. adminstrn. and internat. ops., chief fin. officer Diversified Products Corp., Opelika, Ala., 1984—; treas., bd. dirs. Micah Corp. of Berkshire County, Pittsfield, 1968-72; bd. dirs. Va. Nat. Bank, Lynchburg, 1979-81. Auditor ARC, Pittsfield, 1966; bd. dirs., exec. on loan United Community Services, Pittsfield, 1972; campaign chmn. Piedmont Heart Assn., Lynchburg, 1980. Served with USN, 1950-54, Korea. Clubs: Cherokee Country (Atlanta), Saugahatchee Country (Opelika). Home: 2245 Springwood Dr Auburn AL 36830-7231 Office: Diversified Products Corp 309 Williamson Ave Opelika AL 36804-7313

JENKINS, ROBERT BERRYMAN, real estate developer; b. Evanston, Ill., Oct. 11, 1950; s. Clive Ridley and Genevieve (Brown) Crawford J.; m. Carol Lynn Lealey, Sept. 22, 1984; children: Paul Brown, Leighanne Kealey. BEE, Cornell U., 1972; postgrad., U. W. Fla., 1974. Cert. Profl. Solar Technology, 1984. Owner Fothergill's Outdoor Sportsman, Aspen, Colo., 1978-81; owner, engr. Sophisticated Solar, Aspen, 1983-85; owner/pres. Sandhill Devels., Gulf Breeze and Aspen, 1985—; owner, pres. Roaring Fork Liquors, Inc., Glenwood Springs, Colo., 1992—. Grad. Leadership Santa Rosa County, Fla., 1988-89. Recipient U.S. Dept. Energy Nat. Award for Energy Innovation, 1987, Gov.'s Energy award Fla. Gov., 1987; named Man of Yr., Gulf Breeze, 1991. Mem. Internat. Coun. Shopping Ctrs., Trout Unltd. (life). Republican. Methodist. Avocations: snowskiing, flyfishing, windsurfing, whitewater rafting. Office: Sandhill Devels 400 Gulf Breeze Pky Ste 305 Gulf Breeze FL 32561-4458

JENKINS, ROBERT EMERSON, coach; b. Chatham, N.J., Jan. 12, 1962; m. Cindy Jenkins; children: Zachary, Liam. BA, Duke U., 1984; MA, U. Va., 1988. Lic. coach U.S. Soccer Fedn. Coach soccer, tchr. history Pingry Sch., Martinsville, N.J., 1984-86; grad. asst., asst. coach soccer U. Va., 1986-92; head coach soccer Am. U., Washington, 1992—. Office: Am Univ 4400 Massachusetts Ave NW Washington DC 20016-8001*

JENKINS, ROBERT GORDON, retired air force officer, technology executive; b. Charlottesville, Va., Dec. 14, 1941; s. Charles Gordon and Rosa Lee (Berry) J.; m. Nicki Jean Mitchell, Aug., 1966; children: Lara Elizabeth, Christopher Scott. BS, Va. Poly. Inst. and State U., 1964; MS, W.Va. U., 1967. Commd. USAF, 1968—, advanced through grades to brig. gen.; fighter pilot USAF, Vietnam, Thailand, 1968-75; comdr. 22d Tactical Fighter Squadron, Bitberg Air Base, Germany, 1981-82; asst. chief staff ADC Allied Air Forces Ctrl. Europe, Boerlink, Germany, 1982-84; dep. comdr. for ops. Tactical Air Warfare Ctr., Eglin AFB, Fla., 1984-85; comdr. Air Forces Iceland, Keflavik, 1985-87; vice comdr. 354 Tactical Fighter Wing, Myrtle Beach, S.C., 1987-88, comdr., 1988-90; dep. dir. gen. purposes forces HQ USAF, Pentagon, Washington, 1990-92, dep. dir. ops., 1992; comdr. 51st Fighter Wing, Osan Air Base, Korea, 1992-94; vice comdr. 7th Air Force, Osan Air Base, Korea, 1994-95; dir. logistics HQ Pacific Air Force, 1995-97; pres. Exco Techs. Inc., 1997—. Decorated Legion of Merit with cluster, DFC, 2 Meritorious Svc. medals, 2 Air medals, 2 Commendation medals, Disting. Flying Cross, Disting. Svc. medal. Mem. Order of Daedalians. Home: 9853 Hidden Estates Cv Vienna VA 22181-6090

JENKINS, ROBERT NORMAN, newswriter, editor; b. Washington, Oct. 22, 1943; s. Jack Julian and Mina Lorraine (Katz) J.; m. Dianne Ruth Lang, June 1966 (div. June 1973); children: Kirsten Rose, Joshua Matthew; m. Dianne Carol Dearmin, Dec. 14, 1974; children: Michael Robert, Ryan Robert. BA in Journalism, Mich. State U., 1965. Newspaper reporter Grand Rapids (Mich.) Press, 1965-67; newspaper reporter, editor Newsday, Garden City, N.Y., 1967-69, St. Petersburg (Fla.) Times, 1969—. Recipient First Place News Section Design, Fla. Soc. Newspaper Editors, 1974, Winner Lowell Thomas Travel competition SATW, 1996, Gold award, Silver award, 1998, Bronze award, 1998. Mem. Soc. Am. Travel Writers (chmn. Editors Coun.), Hon. Coaches Mich. State U. Office: St Petersburg Times 490 1st Ave S Saint Petersburg FL 33701-4204

JENKINS, ROBERT ROWE, lawyer; b. Norwalk, Ohio, Aug. 8, 1933; s. Robert Leslie and Millie Leona (Rowe) J.; m. Francis Jean Cline, June 12, 1955 (div. July 1972); children: Diane Elaine, Katherine Eileen; m. Jean Dingus, July 9, 1972. Student, Lebanon Valley Coll., 1951-55; BS in Chemistry, Eastern Coll. (now U. Balt.), 1967; JD, U. Balt., 1975. Bar: Md. 1976, U.S. Dist. Ct. Md. 1976, U.S. Ct. Appeals (4th cir.) 1979, U.S. Supreme Ct. 1979. Atty. Social Security Adminstrn., Balt., 1975-76; trial atty. Nelson R. Kandel, Balt., 1976-77; sole practice Balt., 1977-81; ptnr. Jenkins Block & Mering, Balt., 1981—; faculty continuing profl. edn. of lawyers Md. Inst., Balt., 1986—. Ruling elder Faith Christian Fellowship Presbyterian Ch. Am., Balt., 1982—. Served with U.S. Coast Guard, 1955-59. Mem. ABA, Md. Bar Assn., Balt. City Bar Assn., Assn. Trial Lawyers Am., Md. Trial Lawyers Assn., Christian Legal Soc., Nat. Orgn. Social Security Claimant's Rep. (exec. com.). Republican. Avocations: fishing, boating. Home: 1003 Travers St Cambridge MD 21613-9100 Office: Jenkins Block and Assocs 711 W 40th St Ste 235 Baltimore MD 21211-2186 also: 1011 E Main St Ste 212 Richmond VA 23219-3537 also: 516 Poplar St Cambridge MD 21613-1834 also: 33 W Franklin St Ste 102 Hagerstown MD 21740-4826

JENKINS, ROYAL GREGORY, manufacturing executivve; b. Springville, Utah, Dec. 11, 1936; s. Chester W. and Sarah E. Jenkins; m. Donna Jeanne Jones, Aug. 3, 1957; children: Brad, Kent. BS in Engring., San Jose State U., 1959; MBA, U. Santa Clara, 1968. With Lockheed Corp., Sunnyvale, Calif., 1959-64; contr. ICORE Industries, Sunnyvale, Calif., 1964-68; divsn. v.p. fin. Dart Industries, L.A., 1968-74; dir. planning, divsn. v.p. Avery label group Avery Internat., L.A., 1974-81; group v.p. materials group Avery Internat., Painesville, Ohio, 1981-87; sr. v.p. tech. and planning Avery Internat., Pasadena, Calif., 1987-88; sr. v.p. fin., CFO Avery Dennison Corp., Newport Beach, Calif., 1988-97. Republican. Avocation: golf.

JENKINS, RUBEN LEE, chemical company executive; b. Beggs, Okla., Nov. 27, 1929; s. William Arnold and Myrtle (Kimble) J.; m. Sylvia Griffin, July 17, 1956; children: Amy, Kimble Lee, William Griffin. BA, U. Okla., 1952, LLB, 1956; LLM, NYU, 1959. Bar: Okla. 1956. Law clk. to presiding justice U.S. Dist. Ct. (we. dist.) Okla., Oklahoma City, 1956; clk. U.S. Ct., Oklahoma City, 1956-58; research asst. in internat. law NYU, N.Y.C., 1958-59; assoc. Allende & Brea, Buenos Aires, Argentina, 1959-60; exec. v.p., gen. counsel White Eagle Internat., Midland, Tex., 1960-65; v.p. corp. devel. Plough, Inc., Memphis, 1965-71, dir, 1970, sr. v.p. hdqrs., 1972-73, exec. v.p., 1973-76, pres., 1976-89; dir. Schering-Plough Corp., Madison, N.J., 1971-89, sr. v.p., 1976-80, exec. v.p., 1980-89; bd. dirs. Nat. Commerce Bancorp., Memphis. Bd. dirs. Chickasaw coun. Boy Scouts Am., Memphis; trustee Memphis U. Sch. Capt. USMC, 1952-54. Mem. ABA, Tenn. Bar Assn., Okla. Bar Assn., Non-Prescription Drug Mfrs. Assn. (bd. dirs. 1976-89), Palm Beach Polo & Country Club, Tournament Players Club Southwind (Memphis). Presbyterian. Office: 6075 Poplar Ave Ste 431 Memphis TN 38119-0115

JENKINS, SPEIGHT, opera company executive, writer; b. Dallas, Jan. 31, 1937; s. Speight and Sara (Baird) J.; m. Linda Ann Sands, Sept. 6, 1966; children: Linda Leonie, Speight. B.A., U. Tex.-Austin, 1957; LL.B., Columbia U., 1961; DMus (hon.), U. Puget Sound, 1992; HHD, Seattle U., 1992. News and reports editor Opera News, N.Y.C., 1967-73; music critic N.Y. Post, N.Y.C., 1973-81; TV host Live from the Met, Met. Opera, N.Y.C., 1981-83; gen. dir. Seattle Opera, 1983—; classical music editor Record World, N.Y.C., 1973-81; contbg. editor Ovation Mag., N.Y.C., 1980—, Opera Quar., Los Angeles, 1982—. Served to capt. U.S. Army, 1961-66. Recipient Emmy award for Met. Opera telecast La Boheme TV Acad. Arts and Scis., 1982. Mem. Phi Beta Kappa Assocs. Presbyterian. Home: 903 Harvard Ave E Seattle WA 98102-4561 Office: Seattle Opera Assn PO Box 9248 Seattle WA 98109-0248

JENKINS, STANLEY MICHAEL, stockbroker; b. Charleston, S.C., Feb. 21, 1940; s. Ben and Esther Lea (Brofsky) J.; m. Helen Iris Feinberg, May 12, 1963 (div. May 3, 1977); children: Lori, Susan. AB in English, The Citadel, 1962. Registered investment adviser, securities prin., options prin., fin. ops. prin., govt. bond prin; cert. fund specialist. Acct. exec. Merrill Lynch, Palm Beach, Fla., 1963-73; v.p. Dean Witter Reynolds, Palm Beach, 1973-78, Paine Webber, Palm Beach, 1978-83; sr. v.p. Donaldson Lufkin Jenrette, Miami, 1983-85; pres. William M. Stanley, Lake Worth, Fla., 1985-88; v.p. Smith Barney, West Palm Beach, 1988-90; sr. v.p. Stuart, Coleman & Co. Inc., West Palm Beach, 1990-92, Am. Trust Securities, Inc., Delray Beach, Fla., 1992-94; pres. Stanley M. Jenkins & Assoc., West Palm Beach, Fla., 1994—; exec. v.p. The Computer Channel, Inc., Delray Beach. Bd. dirs. Palm Beach Mental Health, West Palm Beach, 1980-85, Palm Beach Habilitation Ctr., 1975-80, North Palm Beach Country Club, 1970-75. Comdr. USN, ret. Mem. ABA, Am. Arbitration Assn. (panel arbitrators), Internat. Assn. Fin. Planners, Nat. Assn. Securities Dealers (bd. arbitrators), N.Y. Futures & Options Soc., Internat. Assn. Fin. Planners, Econ. Soc. South Fla., Vietnam Vets Am., Palm Beach Fraternal Order Police, Am. Jewish Com. (past pres. 1977), Palm Beach C. of C., Assn. of Citadel Men, Assn. Former Intelligence Officers, Palm Beach Pundits. Republican. Avocations: tennis, boating, jogging. Home: 3711 37th Way West Palm Beach FL 33407 Office: Stanley M Jenkins & Assoc 222 Lakeview Ave Ste 160-164 West Palm Beach FL 33401-6145

JENKINS, THOMAS LLEWELLYN, physics educator; b. Cambridge, Mass., July 16, 1927; s. Francis A. and Henrietta (Smith) J.; m. Glen Pierce, July 8, 1951; children: Gale F., Phillip P., Matthew A., Sarah E. B.A., Pomona Coll., 1950; Ph.D., Cornell U., 1956. Physicist Lawrence Radiation Lab., Livermore, Calif., 1955-60; faculty Case Western Res. U., Cleve., 1960—, prof. physics, 1968-94, prof. emeritus physics, 1994—. Sci. and Engring. Research Council fellow Southampton U., (Eng.), 1983. Mem. Am. Phys. Soc., AAAS, Phi Beta Kappa, Sigma Xi. Home: 869 Belwood Dr Cleveland OH 44143-3239 Office: Case Western Res Univ Physics Dept Cleveland OH 44106

JENKINS, WALTER DONALD, real estate executive; b. Lockport, N.Y.; s. Walter Kimball and Mary Elizabeth (Erler) J.; m. Teda Anne Yelton, May 21, 1977; children: Benjamin Donald, Andrew Kimball, Natalie Anne. BA, U. Ill., 1976. Draftsman Skidmore, Owings & Merrill, Chgo., 1976; constrn. sales Ramm Brick and Material, La Grange, 1976-77; supt., project mgr. U.S. Home Corp., Hanover Park, 1977-78; asst. project mgr. Morse Diesel Inc., Chgo., 1979-81; project mgr. La Salle Ptnrs. Inc., Chgo., 1981-86, Inland Constrn. Co., Chgo., 1986-89; M.W. region constrn. mgr. Embrey Investment Inc., 1989-91; sr. v.p. Equis Project Mgmt., Chgo., 1991-98; sr. mng. dir. CB Richard Ellis Project Mgmt., Rosemont, Ill., 1998—. Deacon 1st Congregational Ch., LaGrange, Ill. Mem. The Phoenix Soc., La Grange Hist. Soc. Republican. Avocations: renovation of older homes, reading, basketball. Office: CB Richard Ellis 6133 N River Rd Rosemont IL 60018

JENKINS, WILLIAM E., business executive; b. L.A., Sept. 30, 1949; m. Catherine D. Jenkins; children: Laura J. Gann, Richard M. Jenkins. BS, No. Ariz. U., 1974; MS, U. Ariz., 1976. Cert. safety profl. Safety engr. Am. Smelting & Refining Co., Tucson, 1976-78; loss prevention engr. Mobil Oil S.E. Inc., New Orleans, 1978-80; supr. environ. health and safety engring. Mobil Exploration Norway Inc., Stavanger, 1980-82; supr. engring. P.T. Arun NGL Co., Lhok Seumawe, Indonesia, 1982-83; supr. loss prevention engring. Mobil Saudi Arabia, Jeddah, 1983-85; mgr. internat. environ., health & safety engring. Mobil Exploration & Production Divsn., Dallas, 1985-88; mgr. environ., health & safety divsn. Mobil North Sea Ltd., Aberdeen, Scotland, 1988-94; mgr. environ., health & safety sys. & strategic planning Mobil Exploration & Prodn. Inc., Dallas, 1995; mgr. global environ., health & safety risk mgmt. Mobil Oil Corp., Dallas, 1995-96; mgr. environ., health & safety ctr. for risk mgmt. Mobil Oil Corp., Fairfax, Va., 1996-97; v.p. Mobil Oil Shipping and Transp., Fairfax, 1997—. Contbr. articles to profl. jours. Mem. Am. Soc. Safety Engrs., U.K. Inst. Occupational Safety & Health, Soc. Petroleum Engrs. Achievements include development of first comprehensive environ. health and safety management system in oil and gas industry, first competency-based professional development system for loss prevention engineers in oil and gas industry.

JENKINS, WILLIAM L. (BILL JENKINS), congressman; b. Rogersville, Tenn.. Farmer, Rogersville, atty.; circuit ct. judge 3d jud. dist. State of Tenn., 1990-96; mem. 105th-106th Congress from 1st Tenn. Dist., Washington, 1997—; former dir. Home Fed. Savs. and Loan, Tenn. Bd. dirs. TVA, 1972-78; mem. Tenn. Ho. of Reps., 1963-70, spkr. of House, 1968-70; commr. Tenn. Dept. Conservation; policy advisor energy and legis. issues to gov. State of Tenn.; chmn. Tenn. Heart Assn., Cancer Crusade. Mem. Hawkins County Farm Bur., Am. Legion, Masons. Republican. Baptist. Avocations: hunting, fishing. Office: US House of Reps 1708 Longworth House office Bldg Washington DC 20515-4201 also: PO Box 769 320 W Center St Kingsport TN 37660-3658*

JENKS, DENNIS, publishing executive. Pres. Osborne/Jenks Prodns., Wethersfield, Conn. Office: care Osborne/Jenks Prodns 936 Silas Deane Hwy Wethersfield CT 06109-4273*

JENKS, FREDERICK LYNN, English educator, university program administrator; b. Buffalo, Jan. 3, 1942; s. Frederick L. and Mary Jane (Space) J.; m. Constance Diane Shryock, Feb. 6, 1965 (div. Mar. 1980); 1 child, Andrew Thomas. BA in Modern Langs., Grove City (Pa.) Coll., 1963; MA in Spanish and Psychology, Case Western Res., 1966; PhD in Lang. Edn., Wayne State U., Detroit, 1971. Lang. tchr. Warren (Pa.) Area H.S., 1964-65; asst. dir. admissions and fin. aid Oberlin (Ohio) Coll., 1966-68; instr. edn. Wayne State U., 1968-71; asst. prof. multilingual/multicultural edn. Fla. State U., Tallahassee, 1971-75, assoc. prof., 1975-81, prof., 1981—; dir. Ctr. for Intensive English Studies, Fla. State U., 1979—, dir. coll. programs, 1996—, chair coun. for internat. edn., 1997—; mem. lang. and instrn. com. TOEFL-Ednl. Testing Svc., Princeton, N.J., 1996—, mem. TOEFL policy com., 1987-90; disting. vis. scholar U. Tenn., Martin, 1987; mem. Fulbright Selection Com.-Langs., 1995—. Contbr. chpts. to books. Sr. scholar Fulbright Commn., Heredia, Costa Rica, 1993. Mem. TESOL (Found. com. 1996—), Assn. Internat. Educators. Avocations: soccer, bicycling, philately. Home: 406 Audubon Dr Tallahassee FL 32312-1601 Office: Fla State U 918 W Park Ave Tallahassee FL 32304-8030

JENKS, THOMAS EDWARD, lawyer; b. Dayton, Ohio, May 31, 1929; s. Wilbur L. and Anastasia A. (Ahern) J.; m. Marianna Fischer, Nov. 10, 1961; children—Pamela (dec.), William, David, Christine, Daniel, Douglas. Student, Miami U., Oxford, Ohio, 1947-50; J.D. cum laude, Ohio State U., 1953. Bar: Ohio 1953, U.S. Dist. Ct. (so. dist.) Ohio 1961, U.S. Supreme Ct. 1971, U.S. Ct. Appeals (6th cir.) 1984. Sole practice Dayton, 1955—; of counsel Jenks, Surdyk & Cowdrey, Dayton; lectr. med. malpractice law. Served to 1st lt. USMC, 1953-55. Fellow Am. Coll. Trial Lawyers, Am. Bar Found., Ohio Bar Found.; mem. ABA (ho. of dels. 1985-88), Dayton Bar Assn. (pres. 1978-79), Ohio Bar Assn. (mem. bd. govs. litigation sect., 1990-98), Internat. Assn. Def. Counsel, Ohio Assn. Civil Trial Attys., Am. Bd. Trial Advs. (adv.), Nat. Conf. Bar Pres., Kettering C. of C. (past pres.), Kettering Holiday at Home Found. (past pres.), Order of Coif, Phi Delta Phi, Sigma Chi. Republican. Roman Catholic. Clubs: Dayton Lawyers (pres. 1999—), Optimist (past pres. Oakwood chpt.). Office: Jenks Surdyk & Cowdrey 900 1st Nat Plz Dayton OH 45402-1501

JENKS, TOM, writer; b. Temple, Tex., Aug. 23, 1950; s. Edwin Riley and Ouida (Baxter) J.; m. Carol Louise Edgarian, Aug. 21, 1993; children: Richard, Anne Riley, Lucy Honor. BA magna cum laude, U. Va., 1980; MFA, Columbia U., 1983. Contbg. editor The Paris Rev., N.Y.C., 1980—; assoc. fiction editor Esquire mag., N.Y.C., 1983-85; sr. editor Scribners, N.Y.C., 1985-87; lit. editor GQ mag., N.Y.C., 1987-91; vis. lectr. Iowa Writer's Workshop, Iowa City, 1989; Hurst prof. Washington U., St. Louis, 1990; vis. prof. U. Calif., Davis, 1990-93; editor Writer Nights Lincoln Ctr., N.Y.C., 1986-88. Author: Our Happiness, 1990; editor: American Short Story Masterpieces, 1987; editor: (with Raymond Carver) Hemingway's The Garden of Eden, 1986, (with Carol Edgarian) The Writer's Life, 1997; contbr. articles to profl. jours. Mem. Poets Editors Novelists Am.

JENKS-DAVIES, KATHRYN RYBURN, retired daycare provider and owner, civic worker; b. Lynchburg, Va., Oct. 9, 1916; d. Charles Arthur and Jessie Katherine (Moorman) Ryburn; m. Thomas Edgar Jenks Jr., Sept. 9, 1941 (dec. June 1975); children: Thomas Edgar III, Jessika, Timothy; m. Robert E. Davies, Dec. 27, 1986 (dec. Mar. 1996). *Ancestors on mother's side of family were Quakers from England and large landowners. Great-grandfather Moorman married into Chilton family that came over on the Mayflower. Grandfather was tobacco auctioneer and landowner. Grandmother graduated from Martha Washington College in Abington, Virginia. Mother graduated from Memphis Conference Female Institute. Daughter, Jessika, graduated from Longwood College, Farmville, Virginia. Father owned Boyd-Ryburn Lumber Co. in Erwin, Tennessee. He also owned, with his brothers, the Blair Hard Wood Lumber Farm in Glade Spring, Virginia. Son, Ted, graduated Virginia Military Institute. Son, Tim, graduated University of Tennessee and is now a computer specialist.* BS, State Tchr. Coll., 1938; postgrad., Mary Washington Coll., 1947-48, U. Va., 1957-58, William and Mary Coll., 1967-68, Va. Commonwealth U., 1969-70. Elem. tchr. various schs., Grundy, Va., 1939-41; phys. therapist U.S. Army, Ft. Bragg, N.C., 1942; operator motor pool U.S. Army, Ft. Still, Okla., 1943-44; occupational therapist U.S. Army, Augusta, Ga., 1944-45; instr. phys. edn. King George (Va.) High Sch., 1947-48; instr. phys. edn. Stafford (Va.) High Sch., 1949-50, substitute tchr., 1950-53; owner, dir. Kay's Kindergarten, Fredericksburg, Va., 1959-83; ret., 1983. Featured in Fredericksburg Times mag., The Free Lance-Star and Richmond Newspapers. Counselor Girl Scouts U.S.A., Grundy, Va., 1939-41; life mem. Kenmore Assn., 1949—; mem. Hist. Fredericksburg Found., Inc., 1953—, vol. Garden Week and Christams Open House; mem. Mental Health Bd., 1978-84; founder Ford Franklin Found., 1968-78; mem. Fredericksburg Clean Cmty. Commn., 1987—; rep. United Way, Fredericksburg; instr. art ceramics Cmty. Ctr. Fredericksburg, 1950-80; bd. dirs. Miss Fredericksburg Fair Pageant, 1965-88; participant cmty. parades; coord. Fredericksburg Agrl. Fair 18th Century Craft People and Artisans, 1988-93, also others; bd. dirs. Antique Farm Implements, Gas and Steam Engines, 1989-93, Fredericksburg Fair, 1994-96; active State Fair of Va., 1981-95, Am. Heritage Showcase Endl. Reenactment Pioneer Farmstead, 1981-96. Recipient Virginia Ellison Vol. Svc. award Fredericksburg Clean Community Commn., 1976-87, Recognition of Svc. award, 1983-84, 1st, 2nd. and 3rd pl. trophies cmty. parades, awards radio Stas. WFLS and WFVA, 1949-89; honored by Kiwanians for travelogue for fund raiser, 1995—, vol. award, 1997. Mem. AAUW (advt. chmn. travelogue 1971-89, Donor Honoree award 1983, 98, bd. dirs. 1971-79), Lioness Club (bd. dir. 1968-87, Lioness Tamer 1984—, bd. dirs. 1996-97, Tongue Wagger 1985, 96—), Soroptimist Internat. Fredericksburg (life mem., sec. 1971-73, pres. 1973-75, bd. dirs. 1971-78, co-chmn. Soroptimist Travelogue 1991-93, First Class Pub. Recognition Trophy 1986, Women Helping Women award 1982, named 1 of 5 who have made a difference in cmty. 1994), Order of Eastern Star (hostess 1995, 96, 97, 98), Nat. League of Fredericksburg (bd. dir., Svc. Recognition Trophies 1963, 69, 80), Izaac Walton League (bd. dir. Dog Mart parade 1965-72). Republican. Episcopalian. Avocations: ceramics, drama, dancing, travel, golf. Home: 8 Blair Rd Fredericksburg VA 22405-3025

JENNE, ARTHUR KIRK, secondary school educator; b. Pikeville, Ky., Jan. 15, 1942; s. William Kendrick and Robina Laurie (Kirk) J.; m. Linda Louise Morris; children: Karen Jenne Stevens, Arthur Kirk II. BS, Towson (Md.) State Coll., 1970; MEd, Western Md. Coll., 1973. Instr. Balt. County Pub. Schs., Towson, 1970—; designer computer learning ctr. Balt. County Pub. Schs., 1986. Author: Read, Study, Think...Reading Comprehension, 1973, Computer Utilization of T.G., 1987. Pres. St. Matthew's Ch. Coun., Pleasant Valley, Md., 1994, Carroll County U.C.C. Lay fellowship, 1994-96. With USMC, 1961-65. Mem. Md. Instructional Computer Coord., State of Md. Internat. Reading Assn., Marine Corps. League, Valley Lions (pres. 1991-92), Am. Legion. Home: 2110 Hughes Shop Rd Westminster MD 21158-2923

JENNEMAN, KAREN S., federal judge. Bankruptcy judge U.S. Bankruptcy Ct. (mid. dist.) Fla., Orlando, 1993—. Fax: 407-648-6692. Office: Ste 950 135 W Central Rd Orlando FL 32801

JENNER, WILLIAM ALEXANDER, meteorologist, educator; b. Indianola, Iowa, Nov. 10, 1915; s. Edwin Alexander and Elizabeth May (Brown) J., m. Jean Norden, Sept. 1, 1946; children: Carol Beth, Paul William, Susan Lynn. AB, Cen. Meth. Coll., Mo., 1938; certificate meteorology U. Chgo., 1943; MEd, U. Mo., 1947; postgrad. Am. U., 1951-58. Instr. U. Mo., 1946-47; rsch. meteorologist U.S. Weather Bur., Chgo., 1947-49; staff Hdqrs. Air Weather Svc., Andrews AFB, Md., 1949-58, Scott AFB, Ill., 1958-84, dir. tng., 1960-84. Mem. O'Fallon (Ill.) Twp. High Sch. Bd. Edn., 1962—, sec., 1964-71, pres., 1971-83, 1985-87, 93—, v.p., 1990-93; mem. gov. bd. Belleville Area Spl. Svcs. Coop., 1996—; pres. St. Clair County Regional Vocat. System Bd., 1986-89, active, 1986—; vice chmn. southwestern div. Ill. Assn. Sch. Bds., 1987-89, chmn., 1989-95, dir., 1994—; comdr. 507th Fighter Group Assn. Inc., 1987-89; mem. O'Fallon Planning Commn., 1973-84, sec., 1979-81, sub-div. chmn., 1978-84; alderman City of O'Fallon, 1984-93. With AUS, 1942-46. Recipient Disting. Svc. award O'Fallon PTA, 1968, Disting. Svc. award City of O'Fallon, 1985, Community Svc. award O'Fallon Toastmasters Club, 1991, Master Bd. Mem. award Ill. Assn. Sch. Bds., 1991, award of Excellence O'Fallon C. of C., 1991. Merit cert. St. Clair County, 1987, Exceptional Civilian Svc. award Dept. Air Force, 1984, Jenmer Award established by Air Weather Svc., 1984, Spl. Recognition award Ill. State Bd. of Edn., 1995, Lifetime Disting. Svc. award, 1998, Disting. Alumni award Ctrl. Meth. Coll., 1999. Fellow Am. Meteorol. Soc.; mem. APA, Am. Psychol. Soc., Wilson Ornithol. Soc., Am. Philatelic Soc., Am. Philatelic Congress, Am. Meteorol. Soc., AAAS, Nat. Soc. Study Edn., Ill. Assn. Sch. Bds. (bd. dirs. 1994—), Nat. Audubon Soc., Nat. Arbor Day Found., Tree City USA, Nat. Parks and Conservation Assn., Nat. Wildlife Fedn., Nat. Resources Defense Coun., Nature Conservancy, Vt. Inst. Natural Sci., Leadership St. Louis., Focus St. Louis, The World Wildlife Fund, N.Y. Acad. Scis., Internat. Platform Assn., Am. Legion, The Wilderness Soc., The Wildlife Conservation Soc., Rails to Trails Conservancy, Phi Delta Kappa, Psi Chi. Club: O'Fallon Sportsmen's. Lodges: Masons, Shriners, Sierra. Home: 307 Alma St O'Fallon IL 62269-2449

JENNERICH, EDWARD JOHN, university official and dean; b. Bklyn., Oct. 22, 1945; s. William James and Anna Johanna (Whicker) J.; m. Elaine Zaremba, May 27, 1972; children—Ethan Edward, Emily Elaine. B.A., Trenton State Coll., 1967; M.S.L.S., Drexel U., 1970; Ph.D., U. Pitts., 1974. Cert. tchr., learning resources specialist. Tchr. U.S. history Rahway High Sch., N.J., 1967-70; librarian Westinghouse High Sch., Pitts. Pub. Sch., 1970-74; adminstrv. intern U. Pitts, 1973; chmn. dept. library sci. Baylor U., Waco, Tex., 1974-83; dean Sch. Library Sci. So. Conn. State U., New Haven, 1983-84; v.p. acad. affairs Va. Intermont Coll., Bristol, 1984-87; grad. dean Seattle U., 1987-89; assoc. provost for acad. adminstrn., dean Grad. Sch., 1989—; pres. Knowledge N.W. Inc., 1997—; mem. rev. panel Fulbright Adminstrv. Exch., 1983-86. Co-author: University Administration in Great Britain, 1983, The Reference Interview as a Creative Art, 1987, 2d edit., 1997; contbr. articles to profl. jours. Bd. dirs. Waco Girls Club, Tex., 1977-83. Mem. ALA (office for libr. pers. resources 1980-82), Am. Assn. Univ. Adminstrs. (bd. dirs. 1980-82, 83-86, 89-93, 94—, v.p. 1996—, exec. com. 1982-87, chmn. overseas liaison com. 1982-87, Eileen Tosney Adminstrv. Excellence award 1985), Assn. for Coll. and Rsch. Librs. (exec. bd. dirs. 1984-88), Phi Delta Kappa. Republican. Episcopalian. Avocations: collecting and painting military miniatures, reading, travel, outdoor sports, sailing. Home: 6935 NE 164th St Kenmore WA 98028-4282 Office: Seattle U Office of Assoc Provost Seattle WA 98122*

JENNERMANN, DONALD L., humanities educator; b. Ladysmith, Wis., Dec. 20, 1939. BA, U. Wis., 1963, MA, 1964; PhD, Ind. U., 1974. Instr. humanities Ind. State U., Terre Haute, 1964-69, asst. prof., 1969-75, assoc. prof., 1976-82, prof., 1982—, chmn. dept., 1988—, dir. honors, 1978—; mem. Nat. Collegiate Honors Coun., 1978—. Editor: The Fair, (poetry), 1966-70, Literature for Living, 1978, The Writer and the Past, 1981, The Poem of the Mind, 1999; Author: Born of a Cretan Spring, 1982, Bearing North, 1996 The Insistent Second, 1999. Lilly open faculty fellow Lilly Found., 1984-85. Mem. Mid-East Honors Assn. (pres. 1992), Golden Key, Eta Sigma Phi, Phi Kappa Phi. Office: Ind State U Root Hall Terre Haute IN 47809

JENNETT, SHIRLEY SHIMMICK, home care management executive, nurse; b. Jennings, Kans., May 1, 1937; d. William and Mabel C. (Mowry) Shimmick; m. Nelson K. Jennett, Aug. 20, 1960 (div. 1972); children: Jon W., Cheryl L.; m. Albert J. Kukral, Apr. 16, 1977 (div. 1990). Diploma, Rsch. Hosp. Sch. Nursing, Kansas City, Mo., 1958. RN, Mo., Colo., Tex., Ill. Staff nurse, head nurse Rsch. Hosp., 1958-60; head nurse Penrose Hosp., Colorado Springs, Colo., 1960-62, Hotel Dieu Hosp., El Paso, Tex., 1962-63; staff nurse Oak Park (Ill.) Hosp., 1963-64, NcNeal Hosp., Berwyn, Ill., 1964-65, St. Anthony Hosp., Denver, 1968-69; staff nurse, head nurse, nurse recruiter Luth. Hosp., Wheat Ridge, Colo., 1969-79; owner, mgr. Med. Placement Svcs., Lakewood, Colo., 1980-84; vol., primary care nurse, admissions coord., team mgr. Hospice of Metro Denver, 1984-88, dir. patient and family svcs., 1988, exec. dir., 1988-94; pres. Care Mgmt. & Resources, Inc., Denver, 1996—. Mem. NAFE, Nat. Women Bus. Owners Assn., Nat. Hospice Orgn. (bd. dirs. 1992-95, coun. former bd. mems. 1995—), Nat. Orgn. Profl. Geriatric Care Mgrs., Denver Bus. Women's Network. Mem. Ch. of Religious Sci. Avocations: reading, walking, golf. Office: Care Mgmt & Resources Inc 2055 S Oneida St #150 Denver CO 80224

JENNEWEIN, JAMES JOSEPH, architect; b. New Rochelle, N.Y., July 20, 1929; s. Carl Paul and Gina (Pirra) J.; m. Edith Joan Wilson, Nov. 28, 1953; children: James Christopher, Gina Louise, Donald Andrew, Jonathan Paul. BArch, Syracuse U., 1952. Fulbright scholar Stuttgart U. (Technische Hochschule), Federal Republic of Germany, 1955-56; draftsman McCoy & Blair Architects, White Plains, N.Y., 1956-57; designer Harrison & Abramovitz Architects, N.Y.C., 1957-60; prin./ptnr. Jennewein Architects, N.Y.C., 1961-62; prin. McElvy, Jennewein, Stefany & Howard, Architects, Tampa, Fla., 1962-84, Jennewein, Archtl. Planning, Tampa, 1984; prin., ptnr. Jennewein Schemmer and Assocs., Tampa, 1985-91; ptnr. Ruyle and Masters Plus Jennewein, Architects, P.A., Tampa, 1992—; pres. Fla. State Bd. Architecture, 1969-72. Trustee Brookgreen Gardens, Murrells Inlet, S.C., 1983—; chmn. Gasparilla Art Show, Tampa, 1977, Tampa C. of C. Environ. Com., 1987; pres. Tampa Bay Art Ctr., 1975, Tampa Mus. Art, 1985. Lt. (j.g.) USN, 1952-55. Recipient House of Yr. award Archtl. Record, N.Y.C., 1963, Ybor Sta. P.O. award Hillsborough County Planning Commn., Tampa, 1989. Fellow AIA; mem. Fla. Assn. AIA (pres. 1985-86, Pullara award 1985), Fla. Cen. Chpt. AIA (pres. 1967-68, Honor medal 1985), Nat. Sculpture Soc. (allied profl.), Tampa Yacht Club, University Club, Ye Mystic Krewe of Gasparilla, Tampa. Republican. Episcopalian. Avocations: fishing, sailing. Home: 4710 W Clear Ave Tampa FL 33629-5512 Office: Ruyle and Masters Plus Jennewein Architects 3333 W Kennedy Blvd Ste 203 Tampa FL 33609-2959

JENNI, DONALD ALISON, zoology educator; b. Pueblo, Colo., June 20, 1932; s. George Luis and Genevieve Agnes (Cox) J.; m. Mary Anne Hovland, Aug. 16, 1956; children—Robert Walter, William George, Karen Elizabeth, Thomas Iver; m. Catherine Brinckerhoff Cory, Jan. 3, 1986. B.S., Oreg. State U., 1953; M.S., Utah State U., 1955; Ph.D., U. Fla., 1961. Asst. prof. zoology U. Fla., 1961-62; asst. prof. Eastern Ill. U., 1962-64; vis. scientist U. Leiden, Netherlands, 1964-66; assoc. prof. U. Mont., 1966-71, prof., 1971—, chmn. dept. zoology, 1972-75, 85-88, dean biol. scis., 1988-91; vis. prof. Cornell U., 1975, U. Wash., 1979. Served with USAF, 1955-57. NIH fellow, 1964-66; NSF research grantee, 1970, 73, 74, 85; NATO and NRC travel grantee, 1970-72; Boone and Crockett Club research grantee, 1981-83; Camp Fire Research Fund grantee, 1983-87; NSF Young Scholars grantee, 1991, 92; NSF Travel grantee, 1985, 92. Mem. Am. Ornithologists Union, Animal Behavior Soc., Ecol. Soc. Am., Assn. Tropical Biology, Wilson Ornithol. Soc., Cooper Ornithol. Soc., N.Am. Ornithol. Assn. (organizing host 1994 conf.). Office: U Mont Div Biol Scis Missoula MT 59812

JENNINGS, A. DRUE, utility company executive. Pres. Kansas City Power and Light Co., 1987-99, chief exec. officer, 1988—, chmn. bd. dirs., 1991—. Office: Kansas City Power & Light Co 1201 Walnut St Kansas City MO 64106-2117

JENNINGS, ALFRED HIGSON, JR., music educator, actor, singer; b. Danbury, Conn., Dec. 24, 1959; s. Alfred Higson and Linda (Keating) J. BS, U. Conn., 1982, MMus, 1984. Cert. profl. educator, Conn. Teaching asst., choral dept. U. Conn., Storrs, 1982-84; tchr. music Danbury Pub. Schs., 1985—; ptnr. Jennings Oil Co., 1999—; asst. condr. Concert Choir/Chamber Singers, U. Conn., 1982-84, asst. dir. Annual Elizabethan Christmas Dinner Concert, 1983; musical dir. for theatrical prodns. Danbury High Sch., 1985-88; bariton soloist St. Matthew Episcopal Ch. Choir, Wilton, Conn., 1986—. Vocal dir. plays The Sound of Music, 1986, Camelot, 1988, Annie, 1990, others; actor in plays Godspell, 1985, South Pacific, 1987, Oklahoma!, 1988, You're a Good Man, Charlie Brown, 1988, Into the Woods, 1991, Assassins, 1992, others; actor Amahl and the Night Visitors, 1998. Named Tchr. of Yr., South St. Elem. Sch., 1990, 97, Roberts Ave. Elem. Sch., 1997; recipient Project Redesign grant Danbury Pub. Schs., 1991-92, Exemplary Program award, Conn. Assn. Schs., 1997. Mem. NEA, Musicals at Richter, Inc. (sec. 1987-88, v.p. 1988-89, program editor 1991-94), Orff-Schulwerk Assn., Conn. Edn. Assn. Avocations: singing, conducting, theatre. Home: 8 Cipolla Ln Brookfield CT 06804-1511 Office: Danbury Pub Schs 63 Beaver Brook Rd Danbury CT 06810-6211

JENNINGS, ALSTON, lawyer; b. West Helena, Ark., Oct. 30, 1917; s. Earp Franklin and Irma (Alston) J.; m. Dorothy Buie Jones, June 12, 1943; children: Alston, Eugene Franklin, Ann Buie. A.B., Columbia U., 1938; J.D., Northwestern U., 1941. Bar: Ark. 1941. Practiced law Little Rock, 1947—; spl. agt. intelligence unit Treasury Dept., 1946; asso. Wright, Harrison, Lindsey & Upton, 1949-51, mem., 1951-60; mem. Wright, Lindsey, Jennings, Lester & Shults, 1960-65, Wright, Lindsey & Jennings, 1965—. Bd. dirs. Community Chest Greater Little Rock; mem. adv. bd. Salvation Army, Pulaski County. Served to lt. USNR, 1941-45. Fellow Am. Bar Found.; mem. ABA, Ark. Bar Assn., Pulaski County Bar Assn. (past pres.), Internat. Assn. Def. Counsel (pres. 1972-73), Am. Coll. Trial Lawyers (regent 1975-79, treas. 1979-80, pres.-elect 1980-81, pres. 1981-82). Home: 1801 Beechwood St Little Rock AR 72207-2001 Office: 200 W Capitol Ave Little Rock AR 72201-3605

JENNINGS, CAROL, marketing executive; b. Marion, Ohio, Oct. 2, 1945; d. Richard P. and Mary (LeMaster) J.; m. John Putnam Merrill Jr., Jan. 3, 1981. BA, Miami U., Oxford, Ohio, 1967. News editor Penton Pub. Inc., Cleve., 1967-69; pub. rels. exec. Cen. Nat. Bank, Cleve., 1969-71; dir. pub. rels. New Eng. Conservatory of Music, Boston, 1971-74, Bklyn. Acad. Music, N.Y.C., 1974-75; account exec., supr. Hill and Knowlton, N.Y.C., 1975-81, from v.p. to mng. dir., 1981-87; sr. v.p., gen. mgr. Hill, Holliday, Connors, Cosmopolus, Boston, 1987, Hill and Knowlton, Boston, 1987-90; dir. corp. communications Bain and Co., Boston, 1991-93; dir. mktg. Heidrick and Stuggles, Inc., Atlanta, 1995-97; mktg. and pub. rels. cons. Palm Beach, Fla., 1997—. *

JENNINGS, CHARLES ROBERT, educator; b. N.Y.C., May 14, 1963; s. Norman Laurie and Nellie Mae (Lewis) J. BS, U. Md., 1986; MS, CUNY, 1990; MRP, Cornell U., 1994, PhD, 1996. Project mgr. Tridata Corp., Arlington, Va., 1988-91; asst. prof. pub. mgmt. John Jay Coll Criminal Justice, CUNY, N.Y.C., 1997—; cons. in field. Chair, mem. Bd. Fire Commrs., Ithaca, N.Y., 1993-96. Mem. Am. Planning Assn., Am. Statis. Assn., Nat. Fire Protection Assn., Regional Sci. Assn. Internat., Urban and Regional Info. Systems, Inst. Fire Engrs. (assoc.). Home: 445 W 59th St New York NY 10019-1104

JENNINGS, COLEMAN ALONZO, theatre educator; b. Granger, Tex., Nov. 21, 1933; s. V.R. and Elsie Jennings; m. Lola Hanawalt; children: Coleman Charles, Adrienne Elise. BFA, U. Tex., 1958, MFA, 1961; grad., Lutz and Carr Theatre Mgmt. Course, N.Y.C., spring 1968; EdD, N.Y.U., 1974. From instr. to prof. drama U. Tex., Austin, 1963—; Jesse H. Jones Endowed Prof. in Fine Arts U. Tex., 1985; chmn. dept. theater and dance, 1980-92; vis. lectr. and advisor to numerous comns., confs. and univs.; cons. Performing Arts Repertory Theatre, N.Y.C., 1972-74, Rockefeller Found., 1974, So. Methodist U., 1987, Tex. Edn. Agy., 1981 and others; adj. Alliance of Arts Edn.; appointed mem. UNESCO (rep. Am. Theatre Assn.), 1969-75 (exec. com. 1973-75). Dir. numerous works include Rapunzel & The Witch, Sinbad the Sailor, 1965, The Ice Wolf, 1970, Rags to Riches, 1971, You're A Good Man Charlie Brown, 1972, Steal Away Home, 1975, Sacramento Fifty Miles, 1978, The Honorable Urashima Taro, 1979, The Arkansaw Bear, 1980, The Magician's Nephew, 1983, Charlotte's Web, 1986, Cells of Freedom, The Early Life of Louis Braille, 1989, In My Grandmother's Purse, 1996; editor: Six Plays For Children by Aurand Harris, 1977; producer: Round-Up Revue, 1981, Centennial Revue, 1983, and others; author: The Honorable Urashima Taro, 1968, rev. edit., 1999; co-author: (with Lola H. Jennings) Braille: The Early Life of Louis Braille, 1989, (with Lola H. Jennings) Johnny Tremain, 1992; editor: Theatre for Young Audiences: 20 Great Plays for Children, 1998; co-editor Plays Children Love, 1981, vol. II, 1988, Theatre for Youth: Twelve Plays with Mature Themes, 1986, Eight Plays for Children: The New Generation Play Project, 1999. Recipient Charlotte Chorpenning Nat. award Children's Theatre Assn. Am., 1962, 65, spl. citation Mayor of Austin, 1976, Founders award Tex. Ednl. Theatre Assn., 1986, Campton Bell Lifetime Achievement award Am. Alliance for Theatre Edn., 1997; fellow NDEA, Sam S. Schubert fellow; grantee Tex. Commn. on Arts and Humanities, 1975, U. Tex. President's Assocs. Fund, 1975, Austin Jr. League, 1977. Fellow Coll. Fellows Am. Theatre; mem. Am. Assn. Theatre for Youth, Children's Theatre Found. Am. (bd. dirs. 1995—), Internat. Assn. Theatre for Children and Youth, S.W. Theatre Conf., Tex Ednl. Theatre Assn. Office: U Tex Dept Theatre Dance Austin TX 78712

JENNINGS, DEBRA VERA, lawyer; b. Meridian, Miss., Oct. 20, 1960; d. Rudolph and Fannie Mae (Cole) J. BA in Polit. Sci., U. Houston, 1981; JD, South Tex. Coll., 1986. Officer U.S. EEOC, Houston, 1986-89; loan adminstr. First City Nat. Bank, Houston, 1989-91; atty. Debra Jennings & Assocs., Houston, 1991—. Bd. dirs. Lawndale Art and Performance Ctr., Houston, 1993—, Milam House AIDS hospice, Houston, 1993. Kellogg scholar, 1981, scholar South Tex. Coll. Law Alumni Assn., 1985. Mem. Alpha Kappa Alpha, Inc. Baptist. Avocations: playing tennis, traveling, photography. Office: Debra Jennings & Assocs 3401 Louisiana St Ste 110 Houston TX 77002-9546

JENNINGS, DENNIS RAYMOND, accountant; b. Coleman, Tex., Sept. 28, 1942; s. Raymond Earl and Montie Elizabeth (Moore) J.; m. El Wanda Key, Oct. 31, 1964; children: Jon Marc, Jamie Dennis, Amy Elizabeth. BBA cum laude, Tex. Tech U., 1970. CPA, Tex. Mgr. Peat, Marwick, Mitchell & Co., Dallas, 1970-77, PricewaterhouseCoopers, L.L.P., Tulsa, 1977-79; ptnr. PricewaterhouseCoopers, L.L.P., New Orleans, 1979-88, Dallas, 1988—; quality control team leader PricewaterhouseCoopers LLP, 1981-85, nat. quality control cord. West region, 1988-89, Atlantic region, 1990-91, chmn. pers. com. S.W. region, 1983-84, mem. pers. com., 1985—, oil and gas com., 1985—; co-chmn. Nat. Energy Practice, 1994—, internat. advisor, 1996—. Contbg. author: Montgomery's Auditing, 11th and 12th edits., 1990, 97; co-author: Petroleum Accounting, Principles, Procedures & Issues, 4th edit., 1996; contbg. author: (brochure) The Revised Petroleum Accounting Rules, 1980, Survey of Accounting Practices in the Oil and Gas Industry, 1994, 97; contbr., editor: PricewaterhouseCoopers, L.L.P. Energy Industry Newsletter; editor Devels. in Fin. Acctg. and Reporting, Petroleum Acctg. and Fin. Mgmt. Jour., 1990—. Bd. dirs. U. New Orleans Oil and Gas Conf., 1985-88; mem. acctg. adv. coun. A.B. Freeman Sch. of Bus. Tulane U., New Orleans, 1986-88; mem. audit adv. com. New Orleans Parish Sch. Bd., 1980-83; mem.

acctg. adv. com. Tex. Tech U., 1991-93, chmn., 1992. Named Disting. Acctg. Alumni, Tex. Tech U., 1997. Mem. AICPA, Tex. Soc. CPAs, La. Soc. CPAs (bd. dirs. New Orleans chpt., cert. of merit 1985, 87), New Orleans C. of C. (chmn. govtl. affairs com. 1984-88, mem. West Bank coun. edn. com. 1985-86, mem. exec. com. 1987, Outstanding Svc. award 1985), Open, Inc. (bd. dirs., vice chmn., treas., chmn. fin. com.), Coun. Petroleum Accts. Soc. of Dallas (pres., mem. exec. com., chmn. FASB-SEC reporting com., program chmn. N.Am. Petroleum Acctg. Conf., chmn. program chmn., bd. dirs.), Aurora Garden Club, Petroleum Club, Royal Oaks Country Club, Chaparral Club. Republican. Avocations: tennis, golf, jogging, photography. Office: PricewaterhouseCoopers LLP Ste 1800 2001 Ross Ave Dallas TX 75201-2997

JENNINGS, EMMIT M., surgeon; b. Tucumcari, N.Mex., Oct. 12, 1922; s. Felix Carlow and Rose (Wich) J.; m. Laura-Jean Cameron, Sept. 23, 1950; children: Katherine, John, Patrick, Teresa, Margaret, Colleen, Maureen. BS, Notre Dame, 1945; MD Sch. of Medicine, St. Louis U., 1946. Diplomate Am. Bd. Surgery, Am. Coll. Surgeons. Physician family practice, Tucumcari, 1950-51; chief of surgery U.S. Army, Ft. Huachuea, 1951-53; fellowship thoraci surgery, L.A., 1953-54; pvt. practice Gen. Surgery, Roswell, N. Mex., 1954-93; pres. N.Mex. Med. Soc., 1967-68, N.Mex. Physicians Liability Co., Albuquerque, 1986-93, N.Mex. Physicians, 1986—; del. from N.Mex. AMA, 1968-76. Mem. City Coun. of Roswell, 1960-64, commr. Chaves County, 1989-92; senator State of N.Mex., Santa Fe, 1993-96. Capt. U.S. Army, 1943-46, 51-53. Recipient A.H. Robbins award for Cmty. Svc., 1980; named Man of the Yr. Jaycees, Roswell, 1957, Citizen of Yr., 1999. Mem. Am. Legion, Knights of Columbus, Elks. Republican. Roman Catholic. Avocation: golf. Home: 2001 Brazos St Roswell NM 88201-3361 Office: 218 W 1st St Roswell NM 88201-4602

JENNINGS, FRANCIS P., historian, writer; b. Pottsville, Pa., Sept. 19, 1918; s. James and Della (Biermann) J.; m. Joan Woollcott, Dec. 6, 1940 (dec. 1989); three children. BS, Temple U., 1939, MEd, 1951; PhD, U. Pa., 1965. Tchr. h.s. Phila., 1941-54; asst. prof. Delaware Valley Coll., Doylestown, Pa., 1961-63; assoc. prof. Glassboro (N.J.) State Coll., 1963-66; dir. divsn. social sci. Moore Coll. Art, Phila., 1966-68; chair history Cedar Crest Coll., Allentown, Pa., 1968-76; dir. Ctr. for History of Am. Indian Newberry Libr., Chgo., 1976-81. Author: The Invasion of America; Indians, Colonialism, and the Cant of Conquest, 1975, The Ambiguous Iroquois Empire: The Covenant Chain Confederation of Indian Tribes with English Colonies, 1984, Empire of Fortune: Crowns, Colonies, and Tribes in the Seven Years War in America, 1988, The Founders of America, 1993, Benjamin Franklin, Politician, 1996; co-editor: The History and Culture of Iroquois Diplomacy, 1985; contbr. articles to profl. jours. Mem. Soc. Am. Historians, Orgn. Am. Historians, Pa. Hist. Soc., Am. Soc. Ethnohistory (pres. 1973). Home: 1555 Oak Ave # 505 Evanston IL 60201-4233

JENNINGS, FREDERIC BEACH, JR., economist, consultant, saltwater flyfishing guide; b. Boston, Dec. 29, 1945; s. Frederic Beach III and Ellen (Osgood) J.; m. Lucille Candace Giglio, Aug. 15, 1975; children: Frederic Beach V, Thomas Chapin. BA magna cum laude, Harvard U., 1968; MA in Econs., Stanford U., 1980, PhD in Econs., 1985. Jr. medicare acct. Blue Cross-Blue Shield, Boston, 1968-69; ind. rsch. fellow Inst. Humane Studies, Menlo Park, Calif., 1969-71, 77-78; asst. mgr. Globe Bag Co., South Boston, 1972-73; rsch. asst. Charles River Assocs., Cambridge, Mass., 1973-74; rsch. and teaching fellow Stanford (Calif.) Dept. Econs., 1974-79; instr. econs. Tufts U., Medford, Mass., 1979-83; asst. prof. Bentley Coll., Waltham, Mass., 1985-87; sr. econ. cons. The Mac Rsch. Group, Cambridge, 1987-88, Charles River Assocs., Boston, 1988-91; sr. mgr. Econ. Analysis Group Office of Fed. Tax Svcs. Arthur Andersen & Co., Washington, 1991-92; pres. EconoLogistics, Ipswich, Mass., 1992—; owner Peak Dawn Anglers, Ipswich, 1996—; founder Ctr. Ecol. Econ. and Ethical Edn., Ipswich, 1998—; chmn., rep. Stanford Grad. Student Coun., 1974-76; senator Stanford Student Senate, 1975-76; co-pres. Associated Students Stanford U., 1976-77; founder Stanford Grad. Students Assn., 1978-79, The Bentley Participants, Waltham, 1986-87, Full Circle Discussion Group Tufts U., Medford, 1981-84; resident assoc. Residential Edn., Stanford, 1978-79. Author: Democracy in Disarray, 1978, Mystical Tides, 1996, (paper) Value, Exchange and Profit, 1966, (essays) Academy, Society and Personal Growth, 1983, Whither Our Education?, 1983. Mem. Am. Econ. Assn., Cliometrics Soc., Indsl. Orgn. Soc., Western Econ. Assn., Atlantic Econ. Soc., Kress Soc., Harvard Travellers Club, Rotary. Avocations: fly fishing, sailing, skiing, tennis, golf. Home: 261 Argilla Rd Ipswich MA 01938-2615 Office: EconoLogistics 59 Market St Ipswich MA 01938-2212 also: Peak Dawn Anglers PO Box 946 Ipswich MA 01938-0946

JENNINGS, HENRY SMITH, III, cardiologist; b. Atlanta, May 16, 1951; s. Henry Smith Jr. and Elizabeth (Martin) J.; m. Polly Cooper; 1 child, Mary Bailey. BS summa cum laude, Davidson Coll., 1973; MD, Vanderbilt U., 1977. Diplomate Am. Bd. Internal Medicine, subspecialty cardiovascular diseases, Nat. Bd. Med. Examiners; lic. physician and surgeon, Tenn., Ky. Intern internal medicine Vanderbilt U. Affiliated Hosps., Nashville, 1977-78, resident internal medicine, 1978-80; fellow clin. cardiology divsn. cardiology dept. medicine Vanderbilt U., Nashville, 1980-82; clin. instr. medicine Vanderbilt U. Sch. Medicine, Nashville, 1982-89, asst. clin. prof. medicine, 1989-97, assoc. clin. prof. medicine, 1997—; med. dir. Cardiac Rehab. Ctr. St. Thomas Hosp., Nashville, 1984—; mem. active staff St. Thomas Hosp., Nashville; vis. staff Vanderbilt U. Med. Ctr., Nashville; mem. courtesy staff Centennial Med. Ctr., Nashville; mem. cons. staff Bapt. Hosp., Nashville. Contbr. articles to profl. jours. Bd. dirs. Heart Inst., St. Thomas Hosp., Nashvile, 1992-94, Tenn. Heart Inst., 1989-91. Justin Potter med. scholar Vanderbilt U. Sch. Medicine, Nashville, 1973-77. Fellow ACP, Am. Coll. Cardiology, Am. Coll. Chest Physicians, Coun. Clin. Cardiology Am. Heart Assn., Soc. Cardiac Angiography and Interventions (cert. of proficiency in diagnostic cardiac catheterization and angioplasty 1989-92, 92-95, 96-99); mem. Internat. Soc. Heart Transplantation, Am. Heart Assn., So. Med. Assn., Tenn. Med. Assn., Nashville Acad. Medicine, Nashville Cardiovasc. Soc. (trustee 1992—). Methodist. Fax: 615-222-5188. Home: Northumberland 3 Castle Rising Nashville TN 37215 Office: Fredi Hall & Jennings PC 4230 Harding Pike Ste 401 Nashville TN 37205-4900

JENNINGS, IRMENGARD KATHARINA, academic administrator; b. L.A., May 20, 1957; d. Walter Heinrich and Annemarie (Bauer) Brandes; m. Grant Andrew Jennings, May 25, 1979 (dec. May 1991); 1 child, Marcus Joseph. MusB, U. Redlands, 1979, MusM, 1994. Sales clk. Sliger's Music, Redlands, Calif., 1979-81; tchr. music Montessori in Redlands, 1983; sec. cmty. sch. music & arts U. Redlands, 1984-88, sec. sch. music, 1984-95, asst. to dir. sch. music, dir. cmty. sch. music & arts, 1995—; assoc. dir. Cmty. Chorus Redlands, 1984-97, U. Redlands Choir, 1984-97. Interim organist Trinity United Meth. Ch., Pomona, Calif., 1983-84; dir. music United Meth. Ch., Yucaipa, Calif., 1984-88; sec. Ch. of Christ, Redlands, 1983-84; dir. handbells, assoc. dir. music Trinity Episcopal Ch., Redlands, 1988-97; organist Faith Luth. Ch., Yucaipa, 1997—, adj. prof. of Oragan, Univ. of Redlands, 1999—. Mem. Sigma Alpha Iota (scholastic award 1978), Pi Kappa Lambda. Avocations: sewing, reading, gardening, snging. Office: U Redlands Sch Music PO Box 3080 1200 E Colton Ave Redlands CA 92374-3755

JENNINGS, JAMES NORBERT, JR., marketing executive, entrepreneur; b. Boston, Feb. 4, 1961; s. James Norbert Jennings and Lynn Thorn Trainor; m. Colleen Elizabeth Gerle, May 8, 1993; children: Sarah, Joanna; stepchild: Elizabeth Morgan. AA in Bus. with honors, Cypress (Calif.) Coll., 1988; Cert. of Entrepreneurship, Calif. State U., Fullerton, 1992. Cert. tutor, Calif.; lic. property and casualty, variable annuities, health and life agt., mortgage broker. Asst. supr. customer svc. T-Shirt City, Cin., 1983-84; customer svc. mgr. Harry Rosenblatt & Sons, L.A., 1984-85; credit mgr. Starlite Safety Supply Co., La Mirada, Calif., 1986-88; nat. sales mgr. The Svc. Warehouse, Gardena, Calif., 1989-91; pres., CEO Com-Net Telecom, Inc., Cin., 1992-98; dist. leader Primerica Fin. Svcs., 1998—; amb. and key man Promise Keepers; inside sales Cintas, Mason, Ohio, 1997; mng. exec. Kaire Internat., Longmont, Colo. Keyman Vineyard Cmty. Ch., Cin., 1994-97. Office: Com-Net Telecom Inc & LSE 9749 Winton Rd Cincinnati OH 45231-2618

JENNINGS, JERRY D., communications company executive; b. Flint, Mich., July 2, 1940; s. C. Oren and Retha S. (Wood) J.; m. Misako Sonoda, Oct. 10, 1976; children: Catherine, Victoria, Elizabeth. Student, Mott Community Coll., Flint, Mich., 1958-59, U. Mich., 1960; BS, Ea. Mich. U., 1961; student, John Jay Coll., CUNY, 1970-71, Harvard U., 1987. Intelligence officer CIA, Washington and S.E. Asia, 1965-68; spl. agt. FBI, Memphis, N.Y.C., 1968-72; spl. asst. to dir. Office Nat. Narcotics Intelligence Dept. Justice, Washington, 1972-73; staff mem. NSC, Washington, 1973-82; exec. dir. Office of Sci. and Tech. Policy, Washington, 1982-86, White House Sci. Coun., Washington, 1982-86; acting dir. SSS, Washington, 1987, dep. dir., 1988-90; acting dir. Fed. Emergency Mgmt. Agy., Washington, 1990, dep. dir., 1991-92; chmn., chief exec. officer Phoenix Comm. and Rsch. Co., McLean, Va., 1993—. Served to Capt. USMC, 1961-65. Mem. SAR, The Army and Navy Club (Washington), Am. Legion, Mil. Order Carabao. Baptist. Avocations: tennis, skiing, chess. Office: Phoenix Comm Rsch Co Mc Lean VA 22103-4832

JENNINGS, JOHN CECIL, lawyer, minister, career officer; b. San Antonio, Oct. 25, 1935; s. Cecil Vance and Jonnye Carmen (Moore) J.; m. Norma Jean Ray, June 2, 1956; children: Tracey Lynne, Brenda Ann, John Philip. BBA, U. Tex., 1958, JD, 1961. Bar: Tex. 1961; ordained min. Bapt. Bible Fellowship. Atty. Tex. Employment Commn., Austin, 1961-96, Tex. Work Force Commn., Austin, 1996—. Col. Tex. State Guard, 1978—. Mem. NRA, State Bar Tex. Republican. Baptist. Avocations: handgun instructor, weightlifter, bicyclist, motorcyclist. Home: 607 Quail Run Rd Pflugerville TX 78660-4380 Office: Tex Work Force Commn 101 E 15th St Austin TX 78701-1442

JENNINGS, JOSEPH ASHBY, banker; b. Richmond, Va., Aug. 12, 1920; s. Joseph Ashby and Leone (Bishop) J.; m. Anne Barrow Hatcher, Oct. 29, 1960; children: Joseph Ashby III, Ashby Anne. B.S., U. Richmond, 1949, DSc (hon.), 1980; grad. certificate, Stonier Grad. Sch. Banking, Rutgers U., 1952; LLD (hon.), Va. Union U., 1991. With United Va. Bank, Richmond, 1949-85; v.p. United Va. Bank, 1956-66, sr. v.p., 1966-67, exec. v.p., 1967-71, pres., 1971, chmn. bd., 1972-85; also dir.; vice chmn. bd. United Va. Bankshares, Inc., 1972-75, pres., 1975-76, chief adminstrv. officer, 1972-76, chmn. bd., chief exec. officer, 1976-85, chmn. bd., 1985-86. Trustee emeritus U. Richmond. Served with USAAF, 1942-46. Mem. Fin. Analysts Fedn. (past exec. v.p., dir.), Phi Beta Kappa, Omicron Delta Kappa, Phi Delta Theta, Beta Gamma Sigma. Presbyterian.

JENNINGS, LA VINIA DELOIS, educator; b. Jan. 11, 1957. BS, Va. Commonwealth U., 1979; MA, Longwood Coll., 1981; PhD, U. N.C., 1989. Assoc. prof. U. Tenn., Knoxville, 1989—; Fulbright sr. lectr. Fulbright Program, Málaga, Spain, 1998.

JENNINGS, LANE EATON, futurist writer, editor, translator; b. Wilmington, Del., Sept. 4, 1944; s. Robert Kimmel and Edith (Eaton) J.; m. Margaret Ann Stone, Sept. 12, 1970 (div. March 1987); m. Cheryl Ann Laughery, Oct. 7, 1987. BA cum laude, Williams Coll., 1966; MA, Harvard U., 1968, PhD in German Lit., 1970. Escort-interpreter U.S. Dept. State, Washington, 1970-71; asst. dir. internat. dept. Nat. Savs. & Loan League, Washington, 1971-76; staff editor The Futurist World Future Soc., Bethesda, Md., 1976-78, editor WFS Bull., 1978-84, prodn. editor Future Survey, 1979—, rsch. dir., 1978—; head writer, later v.p. creative ops. SAI TV Prodns., Annapolis, Md., 1984-89; freelance editor/writer for various clients, Washington area, 1989—; lit. translator, interpreter Goethe Haus/German Embassy, Washington, 1995, 99, also Libr. of Congress; mem. FY2000 lit. adv. panel Md. State Arts Coun., Balt., 1998—. Author: Virtual Futures, 1996, Fabrications, 1998; contbg. author: MacMillan Encyclopedia of the Future, 1996; editor: Futures Research directory, 1993-94. Program leader poets group Iona Sr. Svcs., Washington, 1992—. Fulbright scholar, Munich, 1966-67; Harvard travelling fellow, Berlin, 1970. Mem. MLA, The Writers ctr., World Futures Studies Fedn. E-mail: lanejen@aol.com. Home: 6373 Barefoot Boy Columbia MD 21045 Office: World Future Soc 7910 Woodmont Ave Ste 450 Bethesda MD 20814

JENNINGS, MARCELLA GRADY, rancher, investor; b. Springfield, Ill., Mar. 4, 1920; d. William Francis and Magdalene Mary (Spies) Grady; student pub. schs.; m. Leo J. Jennings, Dec. 16, 1950 (dec.). Pub. relations Econolite Corp., Los Angeles, 1958-61; v.p., asst. mgr. LJ Quarter Circle Ranch, Inc., Polson, Mont., 1961-73, pres., gen. mgr., owner, 1973—; dir. Giselle's Travel Inc., Sacramento; fin. advisor to Allentown, Inc., Charlo, Mont.; sales cons. to Amie's Jumpin' Jacks and Jills, Garland, Tex. Investor. Mem. Internat. Charolais Assn., Los Angeles County Apt. Assn. Republican. Roman Catholic. Home and Office: 509 Mount Holyoke Ave Pacific Palisades CA 90272-4328

JENNINGS, MARK RUSSELL, biologist; b. Santa Paula, Calif., May 25, 1956; s. Roy Fay and Helen Virginia (Sowers) J. AA in Life Scis., Ventura (Calif.) Coll., 1976; BS in Fisheries, Humboldt State U., 1978, MS in Natural Resources, 1981; PhD in Wildlife and Fisheries Sci., U. Ariz., 1986. Fisheries staff Humboldt State U., Arcata, Calif., 1979-81; grad. student asst. Calif. Dept. Fish & Game, Red Bluff, Calif., 1981; rsch. assoc. U. Ariz., Tucson, 1982-86; rsch. fishery biologist U.S. Fish and Wildlife Svc., Dixon, Calif., 1986-90; rsch. fish and wildlife biologist U.S. Fish and Wildlife Svc., San Simeon, Calif., 1992-93, Nat. Biol. Svc., San Simeon, 1993-96, U.S. Geol. Survey, San Simeon, 1996—; rsch. assoc. Calif. Acad. Sci., San Francisco, 1987—, Calif. Poly. State U., San Luis Obispo, 1994—; asst. adj. prof. U. Calif., Santa Barbara, 1993—; asst. in agrl. experiment sta. U. Calif., Davis, 1995—. Contbr. articles to profl. jours. Bank of Am. Award winner, 1974; recipient Spl. Achievement award for superior svc. U.S. Fish and Wildlife Svc., 1987, Conservation award Southwestern Herpetologists Soc., 1991, Spl. Achievement award for superior svc. Nat. Biol. Svc., 1994. Mem. Am. Fisheries Soc. (cert. fisheries scientist, newsletter co-editor 1978—), Am. Soc. Ichthyologists and Herpetologists (soc. historian 1978—), Soc. for Study of Amphibians and Reptiles, Herpetologists League, Am. Inst. of Fishery Rsch. Biologists, The Wildlife Soc. Avocations: history, genealogy, numismatics, hunting, fishing. Office: US Geological Survey Biol Resources Divsn PO Box 70 San Simeon CA 93452-0070

JENNINGS, PAUL CHRISTIAN, civil engineering educator, academic administrator; b. Brigham City, Utah, May 21, 1936; s. Robert Webb and Elva S. (Simonsen) J.; m. Millicent Marie Bachman, Aug. 28, 1981; m. Barbara Elaine Morgan, Sept. 3, 1960 (div. 1981); children: Kathryn Diane, Margaret Ann. BSCE, Colo. State U., 1958; MSCE, Calif. Inst. Tech., 1960, PhD, 1963. Prof. civil engring., applied mechanics Calif. Inst. Tech., Pasadena, 1966—; chmn. divsn. engring. Calif. Tech. Inst., Pasadena, 1985-89, v.p., provost, 1989-95, acting v.p. for bus. and fin., 1995, 98-99; mem. faculty bd. Calif. Tech. Inst., 1974-76, steering com., 1974-76, chmn. nominating com., 1975, grad. studies com., 1978-80; cons. in field. Author: (with others) Earthquake Design Criteria. Contbr. numerous articles to profl. jours. 1st lt. USAF, 1965-66. Recipient Honor Alumnus award Colo. State U., 1992, Achievement in Academia award Coll. Engring., 1992; Erskine fellow U. Canterbury, New Zealand, 1970, 85. Fellow AAAS, New Zealand Soc. Earthquake Engring.; mem. ASCE (Walter Huber award 1973, Newmark medal 1992), Seismol. Soc. Am. (pres. 1980), Earthquake Engring. Rsch. Inst. (pres. 1981-83), Athenaeum Club. Avocations: fly fishing; running. Home: 640 S Grand Ave Pasadena CA 91105-2423 Office: Calif Inst Tech Mail Code 212-31 Pasadena CA 91125

JENNINGS, PETER CHARLES, television anchorman; b. Toronto, Ont., Can., July 29, 1938; s. Charles and Elizabeth (Osborne) J.; children: Elizabeth, Christopher. Student, Trinity Coll. Sch., Port Hope, Ont., Carleton U., Ottawa, Ont.; LLD, Rider (N.J.) Coll. Began career with Sta. CFJR, Ont.; formerly with CBC, Montreal, Que., CJOH-TV, Ottawa; former parliamentary corr., network anchorman Canadian TV, Ottawa; network anchorman, nat. corr. ABC News, N.Y.C., from 1964; London anchorman World News Tonight, until 1983, anchorman, sr. editor, 1983—; also involved with prodn. numerous network documentaries.; anchorman Peter Jennings Reporting, 1990—; moderator news spls. for children; anchorman Capital to Capital; anchor TV series The AIDS Quarterly, PBS. Recipient 9 Emmy awards for news reporting, Alfred I. DuPont-Columbia U. award. Mem. Internat. Radio and TV Soc., Overseas Press Club (awards). Office: ABC Press Relations 47 W 66th St Rm 800 New York NY 10023-6290*

JENNINGS, REBA MAXINE, critical care nurse; b. Gainesville, Mo., Oct. 28, 1936; d. William Claude and Osa Marie (Whillock) Loftis; m. Robert Wayne Jennings, Nov. 10, 1953; children: Sherry Anita, Robert Allen, Lalia Marie. Diploma, Burge Sch. Nursing, Springfield, Mo., 1983. ACLS; RN, Mo., Alaska. Med-surg. staff nurse AMI-Springfield Community Hosp., 1983-84; pvt. duty nurse Western Med. Svcs., Springfield, 1984; staff nurse in CCU, ICU, emergency dept. Tri-County Sisters of Mercy Hosp., Mansfield, Mo., 1984-85; cardiac telemetry staff nurse St. John's Regional Health Ctr., Springfield, 1985-93; nurse obs. unit Valley Hosp., Palmer, Alaska, 1993-94; nurse PCU Alaska Regional Hosp., Anchorage, 1994; PCU nurse Providence Alaska Med. Ctr., Anchorage, 1995-98.

JENNINGS, ROBERT BURGESS, experimental pathologist, medical educator; b. Balt., Dec. 14, 1926; s. Burgess Hill and Etta (Crout) J.; m. Linda Lee Sheffield, June 28, 1952; children—Carol L., Mary G., John B., Anne E., James R. B.S., Northwestern U., 1947, M.S., B.M., 1949, M.D., 1950. Diplomate Am. Bd. Pathology (trustee 1976-87, pres. 1986-87). Intern Passavant Meml. Hosp., Chgo., 1949-50; resident pathology Passavant Meml. Hosp., 1950-51; mem. faculty Northwestern U. Med. Sch., 1953-75, prof. pathology, 1963-75, Magerstadt prof. and chmn. pathology dept., 1969-75; prof., chmn. dept. pathology Duke U. Med. Sch., Durham, N.C., 1975-89, James B. Duke prof., 1980—; vis. scientist Middlesex Hosp. Med. Sch., London, 1961-62; cons. VA Rsch. Hosp., Chgo.; mem. attending staff Northwestern Meml. Hosp., Chgo., 1963-75; mem. pathology A Study sect. USPHS, 1960-65; mem. clin. cardiology adv. com. NIH, 1976-80, mem. cardiovascular and renal study sect., 1992-95. Mem. editl. bd. Lab. Investigation, 1967-95, Archives Pathology, 1970-80, Jour. Molecular and Cellular Cardiology, 1972-89, Exptl. and Molecular Pathology, 1973—, Circulation, 1988-91, 93-96, Circulation Rsch., 1976-82, Histopathology, 1977-92, Am. Jour. Pathology, 1983-92, Jour. Applied Cardiology, 1986-90, Cardiosci., 1990-95, Trends in Cardiovascular Medicine, 1991-92, Cardiovascular Pathology, 1991-95. Served as lt. (j.g.) USNR, 1951-53. Recipient Peter Harris award Internat. Soc. Heart Rsch., 1992, Disting. Achievement award Soc. Cardiovasc. Pathology, 1996; Markle scholar med. scis., 1958-63. Office: Duke U Med Ctr Dept Pathology Durham NC 27710

JENNINGS, ROBERT LEE, aircraft maintenance executive; b. N.Y.C., May 6, 1946; s. Leo William and Ruth Helen (Fehrenbach) J.; children: David Robert, Robert Michael. Grad., Teterboro (N.J.) Sch. Aeros., 1971. Line serviceman Atlantic Aviation Corp., Teterboro, 1970-74; supr. aircraft maintenance Dart & Kraft, Inc., Teterboro, 1974-84; pres., CEO, Big A Flying Club, Inc., Teterboro, 1974—; chief maintenance Am. Standard, Inc., Teterboro, 1984-87; dir. maintenance Damin Jet Inc., Teterboro, 1987-89; dir. aircraft maintenance Am. Bus. Jet, Inc., Teterboro, 1989-90, Brunswick Air Svc., Teterboro, 1985-87, Jet Air Internat. Seagull Aircraft Corp., Teterboro, 1990-99, Jet Svcs., L.L.C., Teterboro, 1996-97; dir. aircraft maintenance AeroLeasing Group Geneva (U.S. Aeroleasing Charter Inc.), 1993-94). Mem. Profl. Aircraft Maintenance Assn., Nat. Bus. Aircraft Assn., Am. Inst. Econ. Rsch., Les Amis du Vin, German Wine Soc. Republican. Roman Catholic. Home: 920 W Walnut Dr Newton NJ 07860-4621 Office: 333 Industrial Ave Teterboro NJ 07608-1022

JENNINGS, STEPHEN GRANT, academic administrator; b. Indpls., Dec. 6, 1946; s. Grant Orville and Helen Zura (MacDonald) J.; m. Sarah Ferguson, Apr. 26, 1969; children: Amy Jennings Bishop, Meredith Zoe. BA, Trinity U., 1968; MS, Miami U., Oxford, Ohio, 1970; PhD, U. Ga., 1976; diploma, Harvard U., 1982; LLD, Coll. Ozarks, Point Lookout, Mo., 1997; LHD, Simpson Coll., 1998. Asst. dean for resident life So. Meth. U., Dallas, 1970-73; asst. dir. housing U. Ga., Athens, 1973-76; assoc. dean students Tulane U., New Orleans, 1976-80; v.p. student svcs. Furman U., Greenville, S.C., 1980-83; pres. Coll. of Ozarks, Point Lookout, Mo., 1983-87, Simpson Coll., Indianola, Iowa, 1987-98, Oklahoma City U., 1998—; instnl. cons. Am. Coll. in London, 1995; bd. dirs. Quail Creek Bank, Oklahoma City. Bd. dirs. United Way of Cen. Iowa, Iowa Sci. Ctr., Greater Des Moines com., Coun. of Ind. Colls. Mem. Coun. Ind. Colls., Nat. Assn. Schs., Colls. and Univs. (bd. dirs. 1993—), Nat. Assn. Intercollegiate Athletics (coun. of pres. 1983-87), So. Assn. Colls. and Schs. (vis. teams 1982—), North Cen. Assn. Colls. and Schs. (vis. teams 1989—), So. Assn. Coll. Student Pers. (pres. 1983), Harvard U. Alumni Assn. (class rep.), Rotary (treas. Branson club 1986-87, Indianola club 1987—), Sigma Alpha Epsilon. Avocations: racquet sports, golf, reading. Office: Office of Pres Oklahoma City Univ 2501 N Blackwelder Ave Oklahoma City OK 73106-1402

JENNINGS, SUSAN JANE, lawyer; b. Providence, June 23, 1952; d. John Edward and Betty Jean (Frost) Stedman; m. James Albert Jennings, Jan. 2, 1982; children: Olivia Arden, Caroline Alexis, Susan Alexandra. BA, Ind. U., 1973; JD, Tex. Tech U., 1978; LLM in Taxation, So. Meth. U., 1985. Bar: Tex. 1978, U.S. Dist. Ct. (no. dist.) Tex. 1979, U.S. Tax Ct. 1986. Advanced mktg. cons. Southwestern Life Ins., Dallas, 1978-81; asst. gen. counsel Res. Life Ins., Dallas, 1981-85; gen. counsel, corp. sec., v.p. Life Ins. Co. SW, Dallas, 1986—; of counsel Erhard, Ruebel and Jennings, Dallas, 1981—; bd. dirs. Tex. Legal Res. Ofcls. Assn., 1994-95. Contbr. articles to profl. jours. Mem. ABA (editor Tort and Ins. Law Jour. 1996—), Dallas Bar Assn. (chmn. corp. counsel sect. 1996-97, immediate past chair 1998), Kappa Delta (pres. Dallas alumnae 1983-84), Phi Delta Phi. Republican. Presbyterian. Avocations: swimming, cycling, cooking, music. Home: 4001 Miramar Ave Dallas TX 75205-3129 Office: Life Ins Co SW 1300 W Mockingbird PO Box 47421 Dallas TX 75247

JENNINGS, THOMAS PARKS, lawyer; b. Alexandria, Va., Nov. 16, 1947; s. George Christian and Ellen (Thompson) J.; m. Shelley Corrine Abernathy, Oct. 30, 1971; 1 child, Kathleen Eayre. BA in History, Wake Forest U., 1970; JD, U. Va., 1975. Bar: Va. 1975. Assoc. Lewis, Wilson, Lewis & Jones, Arlington, Va., 1975-78; atty. First Va. Banks, Inc., Falls Church, 1978-80, gen. counsel, 1980—, sec., 1993—, sr. v.p., 1995—; adj. prof. George Mason U. Sch. Law, Arlington, 1987-88. Trustee Arlington Cmty. Found., 1998—; dir. Rixey St. Found., Inc., 1997—; deacon Georgetown Presbyn. Ch., Washington, 1979-82, elder, 1982-85, 95-97, trustee, 1988-90. With U.S. Army, 1970-71. Mem. ABA, Am. Soc. Corp. Secs., Va. State Bar Assn., Va. Bankers Assn. (legal affairs com.), Fairfax County Bar Assn., Am. Corp. Counsel Assn., Washington Met. Area Corp. Counsel Assn. (bd. dirs. 1984-87). Avocations: bridge, kayaking. Office: First Va Banks Inc 6400 Arlington Blvd Ste 420 Falls Church VA 22042-2336

JENNINGS, SISTER VIVIEN ANN, English language educator; b. Jersey City; d. Eugene O. and Alice (Smith) J. BA, Caldwell Coll.; MA in English, Cath. U. Am.; MS in Telecommunications, Syracuse U.; PhD in English, Fordham U.; EdD (hon.), Providence Coll.; LittD (hon.), Caldwell Coll.; postgrad., Oxford (Eng.) U., 1994. Prof. English Caldwell Coll., 1960-69; major supr. Dominican Sisters-Caldwell, 1969-79; instr. broadcasting writing Syracuse U., 1979-80; with community affairs dept. Sta. WIXT TV, Syracuse, N.Y., 1980; dir. telecommunications Barry U., 1982-83; dir. pub. affairs Cath. Telecommunications Network Am., 1983-84; pres. Caldwell Coll., 1984-94, prof. English, 1995—; originator, designer campus TV studios Caldwell Coll., Barry U.; curriculum planner, coord. new grad.-level curriculum in telecommunications Barry U.; lectr. on edn. and media issues. Producer: Centenary Journey, 1981, Advent Vesper Chorale, 1981, American Immigrant Church, 1982, Las Casas: Ministry of Presence, 1987; coproducer: The Boat People, 1980. Founder, dir. Children's TV Experience; founder Project Link Ednl. Ctr., Newark. Recipient Gov.'s Pride N.J. Albert Einstein award for edn., 1989. Office: Caldwell Coll 9 Ryerson Ave Caldwell NJ 07006-6145*

JENNINGS, WILLBUR, musician, popular. Songwriter (with James Horner) "My Heart Will Go On" for movie Titanic, 1997 (Grammy award 1999, Academy award Oscar 1998, Golden Globe award 1998, Golden Satellite award 1998), (with Jack Nitzsche and Buffy Sainte-Marie) "Up Where We Belong" for movie Officer and a Gentleman, 1982 (Academy award Oscar 1983, British Academy award BAFTA 1984, Golden Glove award 1983), (with Lalo Schifrin) "People Alone" for movie The Competition, 1980 (nominated for Oscar 1981), (with James Horner) "Dreams to Dream" for movie An American Tale: Fievel Goes West, 1991 (nominated for Golden Globe award 1992), (with Eric Clapton) "Tears in Heaven" for movie Rush, 1991 (nominated for Golden Globe award 1992). Office: c/o BMI Writer/Publisher Relations 3rd Fl W 8730 Sunset Blvd Los Angeles CA 90069*

JENNINGS, WILLIAM R., state agency administrator; m. Anne Gurley; two children. BS in Engring., U. S.C., postgrad. vice-chmn. athletic adv. coun. Irmo/Chapin Recreation Commn. Former state parks planner to dir. Divsn. Engring./Planning S.D. Dept. Parks Recreation and Tourism, 1971-75, 91-97, exec. dir., 1997—. Bd. dirs. S. C. Wildlife Fedn., Gov.'s Cup Billfishing Series; adv. com. S.C. Sporting Dogs and Field Trial Commn.; mem. Conservation, Edn., Comm. adv. bd. Dept. Natural Resources; former vice-chmn. bd. deacons, chmn. personnel com. Chapin Bapt. Ch. Mem. Nat. Assn. Recreation Planners, Nat. Recreation and Parks Assn. Office: SC Dept Parks/Recreation 1205 Pendleton St Columbia SC 29201-3731*

JENNINGS, WIRT HOLMAN, JR., retired marketing executive; b. Newberry, S.C., Oct. 5, 1927; s. Wirt Holman and Dorothy Elizebeth (Suber) J.; m. Carrie Lucille Braswell, Oct. 26, 1947; children: Michael Earl, Martha Jane, Dorothy Elizebeth. BS in Math. and Chemistry, Newberry Coll., 1949; grad., Lynhurst U., 1958. Area rep. to mgr. T.A. Edison, Inc., West Orange, N.C., 1949-52; sales trainee Esso Std. Oil, N.J., Columbia, S.C., 1952-55; sales rep. Esso Std. Oil, N.J., Bennettsville, S.C., 1955-56; sales supr., asst. dist. mgr. Esso, Humble, Enco, Columbia, 1956-64; dist. mgr. Esso, Humble, Enco, Birmingham, Ala., 1964-67; project coord. Esso, Humble, Enco, Memphis, 1967-68; nat. project coord. Exxon Co. USA, Houston, 1968-75; innovative project coord. Exxon Co. USA, Charlotte, N.C., 1975-80, Memphis, 1980-83, Houston, 1983-85; pres. Mktg. Expeditors, Inc., Houston, 1985-93; councilman Newberry County Coun., 1997—. Co-founder, pres. Cayce/West Columbia (S.C.) Jaycees, 1956; pres. Ala. Petredeum Coun., Birmingham, 1966; v.p. AARP, Newberry, 1997—; pres. Rep. Party, Newberry, 1997—; mem. founding bd. dirs. Nat. Ins. Automotive Svc. Excellence, Washington, 1972-74. With USN, 1945-46. Mem. Newberry Coll. Home Guard (comdr. 1997—), Columbia Exxon Annuitant Club (ex-officio, pres. 1998—). Avocations: fishing, hunting, golfing. Home: 51 Jennings Point Rd Prosperity SC 29127

JENNISON, BRIAN L., environmental specialist; b. Chelsea, Mass., June 13, 1950; s. Lewis L. and Myra S. (Piper) J. BA, U. N.H., 1972; PhD, U. Calif., Berkeley, 1977; cert. hazardous materials mgr., U. Calif., Davis, 1986. Teaching, rsch. asst. U. Calif., Berkeley, 1972-77; staff rsch. assoc. Dept. of Molecular Biology, Berkeley, 1978-80; instr. dept. biology Calif. State U., Hayward, 1977; sr. biologist San Francisco Bay Marine Rsch. Ctr., Emeryville, Calif., 1980-81; inspector I Bay Area Air Quality Mgmt.Dist., San Francisco, 1981-83, inspector II, 1983-88; enforcement program specialist Bay Area Air Quality Mgmt. Dist., San Francisco, 1988-92; dir. air quality mgmt. div. Washoe County Dist. Health Dept., Reno, Nev., 1992—; cons. U.S. Army Corps of Engrs., L.A., 1980, San Francisco, 1981; instr. U. Calif., Berkeley ext., 1990-93, Assoc. Bay Area Govs., 1990-92; adj. prof. U. Nev., Reno, 1994—. Contbr. articles to profl. jours. Postdoctoral fellow, Harbor Br. Found., 1977-78. Mem. AAAS, Air and Waste Mgmt. Assn. (chmn. Ea. Sierra chpt. 1994-96), Navy League of U.S. (life), Phi Beta Kappa. Avocations: railroad history, photography. Office: Washoe County Dist Health Dept PO Box 11130 Reno NV 89520-0027

JENNRICH, JUDITH A., critical care nurse, nursing educator; b. Chgo., May 19, 1949; d. Kenneth W. and Arlene J. Diploma, Mt. Sinai Hosp. Sch. Nursing, Chgo., 1971; BSN, U. Ill., Chgo., 1973; MSN, Loyola U., Chgo., 1976; PhD, Loyola U., 1992. RN, Ill. Staff nurse Mt. Sinai Hosp., Chgo., head nurse, clin. critical care nurse specialist; faculty NIEHOFF Sch. Nursing Loyola U., Chgo. Contbr. to profl. articles. Fulbright scholar, 1995. Mem. ANA, AACCN (cert. critical care nurse), Am. Assn. Holistic Nurses, Sigma Theta Tau (Alpha Beta chpt.). Home: 1975 Parkside Dr Apt 2A Park Ridge IL 60068-1059

JENRETTE, JOSEPH MALPHUS, III, radiation oncologist; b. Raleigh, Feb. 24, 1951; s. Joseph Malphus and Helen Bell (Broughton) J.; m. Elizabeth Chandler, Dec. 24, 1954; children: Emma Chandler, Elliott Broughton. BA, U. N.C., 1973; MD, Med. U. S.C., 1979. Diplomate Am. Bd. Radiology. Resident in radiation oncology Med. U. S.C., Charleston, 1979-83, instr. radiation oncology, 1983-86, asst. prof., 1986-89, assoc. prof., 1989—, acting chmn. dept. radiation oncology, 1989-94. Contbr. articles to profl. jours. Pres. S.C. divsn. Am. Cancer Soc., 1989-90; exec. com. Hollings Cancer Ctr., Charleston, 1990—; pres. Charleston Symphony Orch., 1990-92; pres., founder Over the Rainbow Arts, Charleston, 1988—; v.p. Am. Classical Homes Found., N.Y.C., 1993—, Charleston Preservation Soc., 1990-92; bd. dirs. The Cmty. Found., 1996—; bd. trustees Ashley Hall Sch., 1996-98; bd. visitors Coll. of Charleston, 1997—. Recipient Carolopolis award Preservation Soc., 1989, Pace Leadership awardee Am. Cancer Soc., 1985, Danforth Leadership awardee Danforth Found., 1969. Mem. AMA, S.C. Med. Soc., Am. Coll. Radiation Oncology, S.C. Oncology Soc. (pres. 1992-93), Radiol. Soc. N.Am., Am. Soc. for Therapeutic Radiology and Oncology, Charleston Men's Book Club, Order of Holy Grail. Avocations: swimming, reading, fishing, travel, child rearing. Office: Medical University of SC Dept Radiation Oncology Charleston SC 29425

JENRETTE, THOMAS SHEPARD, JR., music educator, choral director; b. Roanoke, Va., Feb. 1, 1946; s. Thomas Shepard and Virginia Catherine (Harris) J. BA, U. N.C., 1968, MusM, 1970; D of Mus. Arts, U. Mich., 1976. Choral dir. Cummings High Sch., Burlington, N.C., 1969-72; dir. cultural arts Burlington (N.C.) City Schs., 1972-73; dir. choral activities S.W. State U., Marshall, Minn., 1976-79, East Tenn. State U., Johnson City, 1979—; dir. music First Christian Ch., Johnson City, 1981-84, Covenant Presbyn. Ch., Johnson City, 1991—; dir. East Tenn. State U. Chorale European Tour, 1985, 98; guest condr. choral festival N.C. High Sch., Raleigh, 1987, Govs. Sch. for Arts, Murfreesboro, Tenn., 1987, Nat. Seminar of Intercollegiate Men's Choruses, Inc., 1992; guest condr. N.C. All-State Male Choir, 1997, All-East Tenn. H.S. Male Choir, 1998. Grantee East Tenn. State U., 1988, 90, 96. Mem. Am. Choral Dirs. Assn. (life, conductor 1986, 88, 94, so. div. convs., 89, 99 nat. conv.), Tenn. Music Educators Assn. (conductor state convs. 1990, 91, 94, dir. White House, Christmas 1989, Canticum Novum Festival, Caracas, Venezuela, 1996), Internat. Fedn. Choral Music, Nat. Assn. Tchrs. Singing, The Coll. Music Soc. (life), Music Educators Nat. Conf. (condr. so. divsn. conv. 1997), Phi Mu Alpha (hon.), Omicron Delta Kappa, Pi Kappa Lambda. Home: 2734 E Oakland Ave Apt C-25 Johnson City TN 37601-1887

JENS, ELIZABETH LEE SHAFER (MRS. ARTHUR M. JENS, JR.), civic worker; b. Monroe, Mich., Jan. 25, 1915; d. Frank Lee and Mary (Bogard) Shafer; m. Arthur M. Jens, Jr., Aug. 14, 1937; children: Timothy V., Christopher E., Jeffrey A. Student, Kalamazoo Coll., 1932-34, U. Wis., 1935, Northwestern U., 1934-36; BS, Northwestern U., 1936; postgrad., Wheaton Coll., 1965; Lic. Practical Nurse, Triton Coll., 1968-69. Gray lady Hines (Ill.) Hosp., 1948-49, 51-53; vol. Elgin (Ill.) State Hosp., 1958-72; writer Newsletter Vol. Planning Coun., 1960-62. Writer column Mental Health and You for Press Publs., 1969-90, Life Newspapers, 1982-93, Pioneer Newspapers, 1984, Herald Newspapers, 1986-94; author: The Jewelled Flower: The True Account of a Courageous Young Man's Life and Death By His Own Hand, 1987. Mem. Family Svc. Assn. DuPage County; vol. coord., organizer, chmn. bd. dirs., treas. Thursday Evening Club, social club for recovering mental patients DuPage County, 1966—; vol. FISH orgn., 1973-84; bd. dirs. DuPage County mental Health Soc., 1962-68, sec., 1963-64, 65-68, chmn. forgotten patient com., 1963-68, chmn. new projects, 1965-68; co-chmn. Glen Ellyn unit Ctrl. DuPage Hosp. Assn. Women's Aux., 1959-60; bd. dirs. chmn. com. on pesticides, Ill. Audubon Soc., 1963-73; mem. Ill. Pesticide Control Com., 1963-73, Citizens Com. Dutch Elm Disease, Glen Ellyn, 1960; bd. dirs. Natural Resources Coun. Ill., 1961-67, sec., 1961-64; bd. dirs. DuPage Art league, 1958-68, chmn. bd., 1961-63, Paint-out chairperson, 1968-84, 91—, chmn. new bldg. com., 1968-75, Best in Show award 1991; bd. dirs. mem. planning com., publicity chmn. DuPage Fine Arts Assn., 1965-67; bd. dirs. Friends Libr. Glen Ellyn, 1967-68; mem. adv. bd. Rachel Carson Trust for Living Environment 1971-74; bd. dirs. Mental Health Assn. of DuPage, 1973—, sec., 1973-75, pres., 1980-81, chmn. cmty. liaison, 1981—, chmn. action group, 1976—; mem. DuPage Subarea adv. coun. Suburban Cook County-DuPage County Health Sys. Agy., 1977-83; bd. dirs. DuPage County Comprehensive Health Planning Agy., 1976, DuPage County Bd. of Health, 1987-95; mem. DuPage County Mental Health Adv. Bd., 1977—; mem. com. on midlife and older women Ill. Commn. on Status of Women, 1978-85; bd. dirs., publicity chmn. DuPage County Coun. Vol. Coords., 1977-78; bd. dirs., membership chmn. Homemakers Equal Rights Assn. in DuPage County, 1979-84; pubclicity chmn., v.p. Homemakers Coalition for Equal Rights, 1984-97; mem. ERA Ill. Bd., 1987—, v.p., 1994-97; mem. DuPage County Health Planning Coun., 1984-94, chairperson task force on residencies for mentally ill, 1990-93; mem. Community Care Coalition of DuPage County, 1988-93, NAACP; mem. pub. rels. com. Bethlehem Ctr. Food Bank of DuPage County, 1987-89; tour guide Stacy's Tavern-Glen Ellyn Hist. Mus., 1986-96; chmn. Grass Roots Com. to Pass Ill. Marital Property Act, 1982-97; mem. adv. bd. Older Adult Inst. Coll. DuPage, 1989—; del. for Mental Health Assn. DuPage to DuPage County Consortium, 1989—, DuPage Consortium, Prevention and Intergenerational Task Force, 1991-97; vol. Hospice of DuPage, 1990—; bd. dirs. Willowbrook Wildlife Found., 1992-96, v.p., 1992-94; bd. dirs. DuPage area Older Women's League, chairperson publicity, 1992-96 (recipient Wonderful Older Woman ann. award 1990); with Clown Min. Fox Valley Unity Ch., 1991-95; vol. Ill. Dept. Mental Health, DuPage County. Recipient Pathfinders award, ERA Ill., 1965; hon. mention in Nat. Sonnet contest, 1967; Vol. of Yr. Ill Mental Health Assn., 1975; Svc. award Ill. Rehab. Assn., 1980; named DuPage County Outstanding Woman Leader in Arts and Culture W. Suburban YWCA, 1984, Friend of the Mentally Ill, Alliance for the Mentally Ill of DuPage County Ann. award, 1988, Adade Wheeler award Coll. of DuPage, 1994, Mental Health Person of Yr., Mental Health Assn. of Ill., 1995, Pub.. Svc. award Ill. State Med. Soc., 1996; vol. DuPage County Health Dept. Mental Health Svcs., 1999—. Mem. Mental Health Assn. DuPage, Wilderness Soc., Humane Soc. U.S., Nat. Trust for Hist. Preservation, DuPage County Hist. Soc. (life) Glen Ellyn Hist. Soc. (life), Nat. Audubon Soc., Nat. Writers Club (monthly meeting chmn. Midwest chpt. 1973-74, 4th award Ann. Mag. Contest 1978), DuPage Art League (hon. life, Best of Show award 1991), Defenders of Wildlife, Theosophical Soc. Am. (Quest Study Group 1992—), Nature Conservancy Ill. (hon.), Chgo. Art Inst. (life), Ill. Assn. Mental Health (dir. 1966-68), Amnesty Internat., Pi Beta Phi. Home: 22 W 210 Stanton Rd Glen Ellyn IL 60137-7111

JENSEN, ADOLPH ROBERT, former chemistry educator; b. Elmhurst, Ill., Apr. 14, 1915; s. Adolph George William and Marie (Diener) J.; m. Nelle B. Willams, Sept. 5, 1950; children—Robert, Margaret. B.S., Wheaton Coll., Ill., 1937; M.S., U. Ill., 1940, Ph.D., 1942; postgrad., Ohio U., summer 1959, Rensselaer Poly. Inst., summer 1962, Purdue U., summer 1970, Duke, summer 1971. Head analytical chemistry sect. Lewis Flight Propulsion Lab., NASA, Cleve., 1942-46; prof. chemistry Baldwin-Wallace Coll., Berea, Ohio, 1946-83; prof. emeritus Baldwin-Wallace Coll., 1983—, chmn. dept. chemistry, 1956-71; vis. scientist Ohio Acad. Sci., 1960-64. Fellow AAAS; mem. Am. Chem. Soc., Ohio Acad. Sci. (v.p. chemistry sect. 1969-70), AAUP, Lutheran Acad. Scholarship, Sigma Xi, Phi Lambda Upsilon, Sigma Pi Sigma. Home: 25527 Butternut Ridge Rd North Olmsted OH 44070-4505 Office: Baldwin-Wallace Coll Wilker Hall Berea OH 44017

JENSEN, ANDREW ODEN, retired obstetrician, gynecologist; b. El Paso, Tex., Aug. 30, 1920; s. Andrew Rudolph and Annie Laura (Oden) J.; m. Patricia deMaret Steele, May 10, 1952; children: Elise Ann Jensen Murphy, Nancy Marie Jensen Souter, Andrew Oden Jr. BA, So. Meth. U., 1941; MD, U. Tenn., Memphis, 1949. Diplomate Am. Bd. Ob-Gyn. Intern Episcopal Hosp., Phila., 1949-50; resident in ob-gyn. Hermann Hosp., Houston, 1950-53; clin. instr. Baylor U. Coll. Medicine, Houston, 1951-53; chief ob-gyn Med. Arts Clinic, Brownwood, Tex., 1954-55; pvt. practice Denison, Tex., 1955-74, Temple, Tex., 1975-86; locum tenens, 1986-96, ret., 1996; cons. in ob.-gyn. Lake Cumberland Dist. Health Dept., Somerset, Ky., 1974-75, Perrin AFB, Sherman, Tex., 1956-69; lectr., del. people-to-people program Nat. Congress Ob-Gyn in China, 1984. Bd. dirs. Brownwood Jr. C. of C., Denison C. of C., 1959-62. Fellow Am. Coll. Obstetricians and Gynecologists, Tex. Assn. Ob-Gyn; mem. AMA, Soc. Med. Soc., Grayson County Med. Soc. (pres. 1969-70), Cen. Assn. Obstetricians and Gynecologists, Am. Fertility Assn., West Tex. Ob-Gyn Soc., Rotary (pres. Denison 1966-67, Paul Harris fellow 1990), Delta Chi, Phi Chi. Republican. Anglican. Avocations: photography, golf. Home: 3330 Wimbledon Dr Cibolo TX 78108-2162

JENSEN, ANNE TURNER, automobile service company executive; b. Upper Providence Twp., Pa., Sept. 15, 1926; d. Ellwood Jackson and Elizabeth Addis (Downing) Turner; student Hood Coll., 1944-45, Phila. Coll. Pharmacy and Sci., 1945-46, 47-48; m. Harry Frederick Jensen, Jr., Apr. 13, 1946; children—Frederick Howard, Richard Jordan, Peter Hielm. Legal sec. Robertson & Turner, Media, Pa., 1950-51; sec. Luncheon-is-Served, Media, 1951-53; asst. sec., treas. Delvale Realty Corp., Media, 1955-59; bookkeeper Turner Realty Co., 1960-64, William H. Turner, Atty., 1960-64, Media Auto Service, 1957-74; sec. Media Auto Service, Inc., 1957—. Capt. Heart Fund Dr., 1958-60. Republican. Presbyterian. Clubs: DAR (chpt. regent 1971-74, state corr. sec. 1977-80, nat. chmn. 1974-77), Daughters of Am. Colonists, Daughters of Colonial Wars (state treas. 1974-77, 80-83), Magna Carta Soc., Daus. of 1812, Navy League U.S. (N.Y. Coun.), Am. Legion.

JENSEN, ARTHUR ROBERT, psychology educator; b. San Diego, Aug. 24, 1923; s. Arthur Alfred and Linda (Schachtmayer) J.; m. Barbara Jane DeLarme, May 6, 1960; 1 child, Roberta Ann. BA, U. Calif., Berkeley, 1945; PhD, Columbia U., 1956. Asst. med. psychology U. Md., 1955-56; research fellowInst. Psychiatry U. London, 1956-58; prof. ednl. psychology U. Calif., Berkeley, 1958-94; prof. emeritus, 1994—. Author: Genetics and Education, 1972, Educability and Group Differences, 1973, Educational Differences, 1973, Bias in Mental Testing, 1979, Straight Talk about Mental Tests, 1981, The g Factor, 1998; contbr. to profl. jours., books. Guggenheim fellow, 1964-65, fellow Ctr. Advanced Study Behavioral Scis., 1966-67. Fellow AAAS, Am. Psychol. Assn., The Glaton Inst., Am. Psychol. Soc.; mem. Psychonomic Soc., Am. Soc. Human Genetics, Soc. for Social Biology, Behavior Genetics Assn., Psychometric Soc., Sigma Xi. Office: U Calif Sch Edn Berkeley CA 94720

JENSEN, ARTHUR SEIGFRIED, consulting engineering physicist; b. Trenton, N.J., Dec. 24, 1917; s. Emil Anthony and Emma Anna (Lund) J.; m. Lillian Elizabeth Reed, Aug. 9, 1941; children: Deane Ellsworth, Alan Forrest, Nancy Lorraine. *Son Deane Ellsworth, an audio electronic engineer, established Jensen Transformers, Inc., North Hollywood, CA. The company designed and sold high fidelity audio transformers for recording to radio and TV studios including Disney World and Disneyland. He was inducted in Mix Magazine's TEC Hall of Fame for lifetime achievement. In 1994, daughter Nancy Lorraine, an aerospace engineer/chemist, was presented by NASA Goddard Space Flight Center with its Exceptional Achievement Award for outstanding work modifying the Electroless Nickel Plating process which improved mirror performance for use in Geostationary Operational Environmental Satellites (GOES).* BS, U. Pa., 1938, MS, 1939, PhD, 1941; diploma in advanced engring., Westinghouse Sch. Applied Sci., 1972, diploma in computer sci., 1977. Registered profl. engr., Md. Research physicist U.S. Naval Research Labs., Washington, 1941; research physicist RCA Labs., Princeton, N.J., 1945-57; mgr. spl. electron devices Westinghouse Electronic Tube Div., Balt., 1957-65; sr. adv. physicist Electronics Systems Ctr., Balt., 1965-91; cons. physicist Westinghouse Electronic Systems Ctr., Balt., 1991-94; co-owner, chief engr. Jensen Cons. Engring., 1994—; mem. Md. State Bd. Registration Profl. Engrs., 1979-86, vice chmn., 1983-86; cons. Nat. Acad. Sci., 1970. *The true miracle of creation is that fewer than thirty laws of nature suffice to determine the course of the universe since its beginning. While it is highly doubtful that an infinitely wise Creator would ever have had need to suspend any of these laws, yet the statistical nature of the Second Law of Thermodynamics and the Uncertainty Principle provide means for the Creator to influence our lives without violating any law, by affecting our thoughts and perceptions. Co-inventor: 1948 first practical random access memory (RAM) electron tube, used in early computers, first computerized telephone central office, over-the-horizion radar, airborne moving target radar, and DEW line radar analysis, which was licensed by RCA; 1960 infrared TV camera tube which aided aerodynamic design of SR-71 supersonic plane; 1975 light valve electron tube that projected large, bright, live TV picture display; 1980 low noise integrated circuit for camera photoplane detector chip. Contributed to conceptual designs of military meteorological satellite sensor systems.* Contbr. articles to profl. jours.; 25 patents. Mem. Endowed Sons of Norway Found., Nancy Lorraine Jensen Meml. Scholarship Fund. Served to capt. USN, 1941-46, USNR, 1946-77, ret., 1977—. Hector Tyndale fellow, 1939, George Lieb Harrison fellow, 1940; recipient outstanding svc. award Engrs. Coun. Md., 1986, Gov.'s citation, 1986, Westinghouse spl. patent award, 1972; endowed Sons of Norway Found., Nancy Lorraine Jensen Meml. Scholarship Fund. Fellow IEEE (life), Washington Acad. Scis.; mem. AAAS, AIAA, Res. Officers Assn., Ret. Officers Assn., Naval Res. Assn., Am. Phys. Soc., Am. Assn. Physics Tchrs., Soc. Photo-Optical Instrumentation Engrs., Optical Soc. Am., N.Y. Acad. Scis., Md. Acad. Scis. (chmn. awards com.), Nat. Coun. Engring. Examiners (chmn. internat. rels. com.), Infrared Info. Symposium, Am. Legion, Fleet Res. Assn., Sons of Norway, Nat. Eagle Scout Assn., Sigma Xi, Pi Mu Epsilon, Kappa Phi Kappa. Club: U.S. Naval Acad. Officers and Faculty. Achievements include patents in field. Home and Office: Chapel Gate 1104 Oak Crest Village 8820 Walther Blvd Parkville MD 21234-0922

JENSEN, BAIBA, principal. Prin. Hawkins Elem. Sch., Brighton, Mich. Recipient Elem. Sch. Recognition awards U.S. Dept. Edn., 1989-90. Office: Hawkins Elem Sch 8900 Lee Rd Brighton MI 48116-2000*

JENSEN, CHERRYL KAY, writer, public relations consultant; b. Maquoketa, Iowa, Dec. 27, 1949; d. Lewis Leroy and Mary Virginia (Rowan) J.; 1 child, Aschleigh Farynn Jensen-Eldridge. BA in English Lit., U. Iowa, 1972; MA in Journalism, Ctrl. Mich. U., 1981. Editorial asst. U. Iowa, Iowa City, 1972-73; writer Ctrl. Mich. U., Mt. Pleasant, 1973-79, news bur. dir., 1979-84; asst. dir. pub. rels. Mich. State U., East Lansing, 1984-90; dir. univ. rels. Iowa State U., Ames, 1990-94; dir. comm. Heritage Coll., Toppenish, Wash., 1994-98; owner CK Jensen Comms., Yakima, Wash., 1998—. Mem. Coun. for the Advancement and Support of Edn. (chair instnl. rels. track dist. V conf. 1987, conf. program chair dist. VI 1994). E-mail: ckjensen@nwinfo.net. Office: CK Jansen Comms 1302 Spokane St Yakima WA 98902

JENSEN, CHRISTIAN EDWARD, family practice physician; b. Newark, July 7, 1933; s. Anrold Vang Jensen and Helen Marie Palme; m. Gail Lillian Baxter, Oct. 31, 1957; children: Christian J., Wendy Joy. BS, Rutgers U., 1954, MA, 1955; MD, Duke U., 1972; MPH, Med. Coll. Wis., 1989. Diplomate Am. Bd. Family Practice, Am. Bd. Preventive Medicine in Occupl. Medicine. Self-employed bus. exec. Middletown, N.J., 1957-65; pvt. practice specializing in family medicine Denton, Md., 1973-82; med. supr. E.I. DuPont de Nemours, inc., Seaford, Del., 1982-90; med. dir., pres. Delmarva Found. for Med. Care, Easton, Md., 1991-93, assoc. med. dir., 1998—; dir. occupl. medicine U.S. Naval Acad., Annapolis, Md., 1993-97. Author: Physicians of Caroline County Maryland, 1774-1984. Deacon Calvary Bapt. Ch., Denton, Md., 1976—. Capt. USNR, 1955-97. Fellow Am. Acad. Family Physicians, Am. Coll. Occupl. and Environ. Medicine, Am. Coll. Physician Execs. Home: 8950 Pealiquor Landing Dr Denton MD 31629

JENSEN, D. LOWELL, federal judge, lawyer, government official; b. Brigham, Utah, June 3, 1928; s. Wendell and Elnora (Hatch) J.; m. Barbara Cowin, Apr. 20, 1951; children: Peter, Marcia, Thomas. A.B. in Econs, U. Calif.-Berkeley, 1949, LL.B., 1952. Bar: Calif. 1952. Dep. dist. atty. Alameda County, 1955-66, asst. dist. atty., 1966-69, dist. atty., 1969-81; asst. atty. gen. criminal div. Dept. Justice, Washington, 1981-83, assoc. atty. gen., 1983-85, dep. atty. gen., 1985-86; judge U.S. Dist. Ct. (no. dist.) Calif., Oakland, 1986—; mem. Calif. Council on Criminal Justice, 1974-81; past pres. Calif. Dist. Atty.'s Assn. Served with U.S. Army, 1952-54. Fellow Am. Coll. Trial Lawyers; mem. Nat. Dist. Atty.'s Assn. (victim/witness commn. 1974-81), Boalt Hall Alumni Assn. (past pres.). Office: US Dist Ct 1301 Clay St Rm 490C Oakland CA 94612-5217

JENSEN, DALLIN W., lawyer; b. Afton, Wyo., June 2, 1932; s. Louis J. and Nellie B. Jensen; m. Barbara J. Bassett, Mar. 22, 1958; children: Brad L., Julie N. BS, Brigham Young U., 1954; JD, U. Utah, 1960. Bar: Utah 1960, U.S. Dist. Ct. Utah 1962, U.S. Ct. Appeals (10th cir.) 1974, U.S. Ct. Appeals D.C. 1980, U.S. Supreme Ct. 1971. Asst. atty. gen. Utah Atty. Gen., Salt Lake City, 1960-83, solicitor gen., 1983-88; shareholder Parsons, Behle & Latimer, Salt Lake City, 1988—; alt. commr. Upper Colo. River Commn., 1983—; mem. Colo. River Basin Salinity Adv. Council, 1975—; spl. legal cons. Nat. Water Commn., Washington, 1971-73; mem. energy law center adv. council U. Utah Coll. Law, 1976—. Mem. editl. bd. Rocky Mountain Mineral Law Found., 1983-85. Author: (with Wells A. Hutchins) The Utah Law of Water Rights, 1965. Contbr. articles on water law and water resource mgmt. to profl. jours. Served with U.S. Army, 1955-57. Mem. LDS Ch. Home: 3565 S 2175 E Salt Lake City UT 84109-2902 Office: PO Box 45898 Salt Lake City UT 84145-0898

JENSEN, DENNIS MARK, marketing executive; b. Lawrence, Kans., Oct. 26, 1946; s. Keith E. and Betty M. (Gardner) J.; m. Wendalyn A. Dennis, Mar. 21, 1969 (div. Nov. 1987); 1 child, Michael Shawn; m. Mary Forbes Russell, Aug. 21, 1996; 1 child, Russell Forbes. Student, Ind. State U., 1964, Ind. U., 1964-66; BA, Adrian Coll., 1968; MA, U. Fla., 1970; postgrad., U. Mo., 1970-71, 74-77. Teaching asst. English U. Fla., Gainesville, 1968-70; teaching asst. speech and dramatic art U. Mo., Columbia, 1970-71, 74-77; project analyst Pfizer Pharms., N.Y.C., 1977-80, mgr. communications devel., 1980-81; mgr. tech. com. Pfizer Inc., N.Y.C., 1981-86; mgr. profl. rels. Pfizer Internat., N.Y.C., 1986-89, sr. mgr. profl. rels., 1989-96, mktg. mgr., 1996—. Elder Pleasantville Presbyn. Ch., N.Y., 1981-83. With USN, 1971-74. Recipient tng. grants NIH, USPHS, Ind. U. Med. Ctr., 1964, Am. Cancer Soc. Adrian Coll., 1966. Mem. AAAS, Am. Soc. Microbiology. Methodist. Office: Pfizer Internat 235 E 42nd St New York NY 10017-5755

JENSEN, DICK LEROY, lawyer; b. Audubon, Iowa, Oct. 25, 1930; s. A.B. and Bernice (Fancher) J.; m. Nancy Wilson, June 30, 1956; children: Charles F., Sarah R. (dec.). LL.B., U. Iowa, 1954. Bar: Iowa 1954. Practice in Audubon, Iowa, 1958-60; gen. counsel, sec. Walnut Grove Products, Co., Atlantic, Iowa, 1960-64; legal staff W.R. Grace & Co., Atlantic, 1964-66; gen. counsel, v.p., sec. Spencer Foods, Inc., Iowa, 1966-72; dir. Spencer Foods, Inc., 1968-72; mem. Dreher, Simpson and Jensen, Des Moines, 1972—. Notes and legis. editor: Iowa Law Rev, 1953-54. Pres. S.W. Iowa Mental Health Inst., 1964-66. Served to lt. USNR, 1955-58. Mem. Masons, Sigma Nu, Phi Delta Phi. Republican. Presbyterian. Home: 3901 River Oaks Dr Des Moines IA 50312-4638 Office: Dreher Simpson & Jensen 1500 Hub Tower 699 Walnut St Des Moines IA 50309-3929

JENSEN, EDMUND PAUL, retired bank holding company executive; b. Oakland, Calif., Apr. 13, 1937; s. Edmund and Olive E. (Kessell) J.; m. Marilyn Norris, Nov. 14, 1959; children: Juliana L., Annika M. BA, U. Wash., 1959; postgrad., U. Santa Clara, Stanford U., 1981. Lic. real estate broker, Oreg., Calif. Mgr. fin. plan and evaluation Technicolor, Inc., Los Angeles, 1967-69; group v.p. Nat. Industries & Subs, Louisville, 1969-72; v.p. fin. Wedgewood Homes, Portland, 1972-74; various mgmt. positions U.S. Bancorp, Portland, 1974-83; pres., COO U.S. Bancorp, Inc., Portland, 1983-93; vice chmn., COO U.S. Bancopr, Inc., Portland, 1993-94; pres., CEO Visa Internat., 1994-98; ret., 1998; bd. dirs. U.S. Nat. Bank of Oreg., U.S. Bank Washington. Chmn. United Way, 1986, N.W. Bus. Coalition, 1987; bd. dirs. Saturday Acad., Portland, 1984—, Visa U.S.A., Visa Internat., Marylhurst Coll., Oreg. Bus. Coun., Oreg. Downtown Devel. Assn., Oreg. Ind. Coll. Found., 1983—, treas., 1986—, chmn., 1988—; bd. dirs. Portland Art Mus., 1983—, vice chmn., 1989—. Mem. Portland C. of C. (bd. dirs. 1981—, chmn. 1987), Assn. Res. City Bankers, Assn. for Portland Progress (pres. 1988), Waverly Country Club, Multnomah Athletic Club, Arlington Club. Office: US Bancorp PO Box 8837 Portland OR 97208-8837

JENSEN, EDWARD CHARLES, forestry educator; b. Morrison, Ill., Mar. 7, 1949; s. Gilbert Lee Jensen and Regina Winifred Fitzpatrick-Jensen; m. Linda Marie Lahey, June 16, 1973; children: Christopher Edward, Nicholas Charles, Courtney Lynn. BS, U. Ill., 1973; MS, U. Wash., 1976; PhD, Oreg. State U., 1989. Faculty rsch. asst. U. Ill., Urbana, 1973-74; instr. Oreg. State U., Corvallis, 1990-96, asst. prof., 1990-96, assoc. prof., 1996—; sci. proposal reviewer Sci. Coun. B.C., Vancouver, Can., 1995—; reviewer Jour. Forestry, Bethesda, Md., 19976. Co-author: Trees to Know in Oregon, 1994, Manual of Oregon Trees and Shrubs, 1990, (CD-ROM) Conifers of the Pacific Northwest, 1998; contbr. articles to profl. jours. Judge State H.S. Forestry Skills, Corvallis, 1990-98, Oreg. State Fair, Salem, 1980-86; coach Boys and Girls Club, Corvallie, 1990-91, Corvallis Parks and Recreation, Am. Youth Soccer Orgn., 1986-90;. Recipient Golden ARC Best of Show award Agrl. Resources Coun., 1995, Excellence in Coll. and Univ. Tchg. award USDA-NASULGC, 1997. Mem. Soc. Am. Foresters (com. chair 1976—, Carl A.

Schenck award for tchg. excellence 1997), Phi Kappa Phi, Xi Sigma Pi. Avocations: nature, nature photography, organized sports, outdoor sports. Fax: (541) 737-3759. E-mail: jensene@ccmail.orst.edu.

JENSEN, ELWOOD VERNON, biochemist; b. Fargo, N.D., Jan. 13, 1920; s. Eli A. and Vera (Morris) J.; m. Mary Welmoth Collette, June 17, 1941 (dec. Nov. 1982); children: Karen Collette, Thomas Eli; m. Hiltrud Herborg, Dec. 21, 1983. AB, Wittenberg U., 1940, DSc (hon.), 1963; PhD, U. Chgo., 1944; DSc (hon.), Acadia U., 1976, Med. Coll. Ohio, 1991; MD (hon.), U. Hamburg, 1994. Mem. faculty U. Chgo., 1947-90, assoc. prof. biochemistry Ben May Inst. Cancer Rsch., 1954-60, prof., 1960-63, Am. Cancer Soc. research prof. physiology, 1963-69, dir. Ben May Inst., 1969-82, dir. Biomed. Ctr. Population Research, 1972-75, prof. physiology, 1969-73, 77-84, prof. biophysics, 1973-84, prof. biochemistry, 1980-90, Charles B. Huggins disting. svc. prof., 1981-90, emeritus prof., 1990—; research dir. Ludwig Inst. for Cancer Research, 1983-87; scholar-in-residence Fogarty Internat. Ctr. NIH, 1988, Cornell U. Med. Coll., 1990-91; prof. Inst. for Hormone and Fertility Rsch. U. Hamburg, Fed. Republic Germany, 1992-97; Nobel vis. prof. Karolinska Inst., Huddinge, Sweden, 1998; STINT vis. scientist Karolinska Inst., 1998-99; vis. prof. Max-Planck-Inst. für Biochemie, Munich, Germany, 1958; mem. chemotherapy rev. bd. Nat. Cancer Inst., 1960-62, bd. sci. counselors, 1969-72; mem. Nat. Adv. Coun. Child Health and Human Devel., 1976-80; mem. adv. com. biochemistry and chem. carcinogenesis Am. Cancer Soc., 1968-72, coun. for rsch. and clin. investigation, 1974-77; mem. assembly life scis. NRC, 1975-78; mem. com. on sci., engring. and public policy Nat. Acad. Scis., 1981-82; mem. rsch. adv. bd. Clin. Rsch. Inst. of Montreal, 1987-96, Klinik für Tumor Biologie, Freiburg, 1993—, Strang Cancer Prevention Ctr., 1994—; cons. Rockefeller U. Hosp., 1990-92. Mem. editl. adv. bd. Perspectives in Biology and Medicine, 1966—, Archives of Biochemistry and Biophysics, 1979-84; mem. editl. bd. Biochemistry, 1969-72, Life Scis., 1973-78, Breast Cancer Rsch. and Treatment, 1980—, Endocrine-Related Cancer, 1994—, Jour. Biol. Markers, 1998—; assoc. editor: Jour. Steroid Biochemistry, 1974-94; contbr. articles to profl. jours. Recipient D.R. Edwards medal, 1970, La Madonnina prize, 1973, Pap award, 1975, prix Roussel, 1976, Nat. award Am. Cancer Soc., 1976, Gregory Pincus Mem. award, 1978, Gairdner Found. award, 1979, Lucy Wortham James award, 1980, Charles F. Kettering prize, 1980, Golden Plate award, 1980, Nat. Acad. Clin. Biochemistry award, 1981, Scientist of Yr. award Achievement Rewards for Coll. Scientists Found., 1981, Pharmacia award, 1982, Hubert H. Humphrey award, 1983, Rolf Luft medal, 1983, Renzo Grattarola medal, 1984, Fred C. Koch award, 1984, Axel Munthe award, 1985, Humboldt Sr. Rsch. prize, 1992, Joseph Bolivar DeLee award Chgo. Lying-In Hosp., 1995; Guggenheim fellow, 1946-47. Mem. NAS (council 1981-84), AAAS (Amory prize 1977), Am. Soc. Biochemistry and Molecular Biology, Am. Chem. Soc., Am. Assn. Cancer Rsch. (G.H.A. Clowes award 1975), Endocrine Soc. (pres. 1980-81), Am. Gyn/Ob Soc. (hon.), St. Paul Surg. Soc. (hon.), EORTC Receptor and Biomarker Group (hon.). Address: Karolinska Inst Dept Med, Nutrition Novum, S-141 86 Huddinge Sweden

JENSEN, ERIK HUGO, pharmaceutical quality control consultant; b. Fredericia, Denmark, June 27, 1924; came to U.S. 1950; s. Alfred Marinus and Clara Krista (Sorensen) J.; m. Alice Emy Olesen, Oct. 8, 1949; children: Ian Peter, Lisa Joan, Linda Anne. BS, Royal Danish Sch. Pharmacy, Copenhagen, 1945, MS, 1948, PhD, 1954. Head product development AB Ferrosan, Malmo, Sweden, 1955-57; research scientist Upjohn Co., Kalamazoo, Mich., 1957-62, head quality control, 1962-63, mgr. quality control, 1963-66, asst. dir. quality control, 1966-81, dir. quality control, 1981-85, exec. dir. control devel. and adminstrn., 1985-86; pres., cons. Jensen Enterprises, 1986—. Author: A Study on Sodium Borohydride, 1954; contbr. articles to profl. jours.; patentee in field. Bd. dirs. Kalamazoo Inst. Arts, 1971-73, treas., 1973-74, pres., 1974-75. Mem. Pharm. Mfr.'s Assn. (quality control sect. recorder 1971-78, vice chmn. 1978-80, chmn. 1980-83), Acad. Pharm. Scis. (vice chmn. 1968-69, chmn. 1971-72) Lodge: Kiwanis (treas. 1962-65). Avocations: painting, sculpting, photography.

JENSEN, GERTRUDE EILEEN, librarian; b. Jan. 17, 1928. Student, U. No. Iowa, 1946, 47. Tchr. Armstrong-Wallingford (Iowa) Country Schs., 1946-48, 50-51; dir. Armstrong Pub. Libr., 1997—. Home: 1820 540th Ave Armstrong IA 50514-7513

JENSEN, HANS WILLIAM, library director; b. Sept. 8, 1953. BA in Math, History, U. Wis., 1975, MALS, 1977. Asst. dir. Sun Prairie (Wis.) Pub. Libr., 1978-83; dir. Portage (Wis.) Pub. Libr., 1983—. E-mail: hjensen@scls.lib.wi.us. Office: Portage Pub Libr 253 W Edgewater St Portage WI 53901-2117

JENSEN, HAROLD LEROY, physician; b. Mpls., Aug. 17, 1926; s. Harold Hans and Nell Irene (Cameron) J.; m. Nancy Elizabeth Scharff, Sept. 9, 1950 (div. 1976); children—Eric Richard, Kris Ann, Beth Susan; m. 2d, Sandra Lee Steinel, Oct. 18, 1976. B.S., U. Ill., 1950, M.D., 1955. Intern Ill. Central Hosp., Chgo., 1955-56, resident, 1956-57; practice medicine specializing in internal medicine Flossmoor, Ill., 1957-87; mem. staff Ingalls Meml. Hosp., Harvey, Ill., dir. continuing med. edn., 1979-87, v.p. med. affairs, 1987—; asst. clin. prof. medicine U. Ill.; guest lectr. Gov.'s State U., University Park, Ill.; bd. dirs. HealthChicago HMO, 1989-92. Mem. editorial bd. Chgo. Healthcare, 1990-93; contbr. articles to profl. jours. Pres. bd. dirs. Homewood (Ill.) Pub. Libr., 1970-76; mem. policy bd. Cook County Healthcare Summit, 1990; chmn. Ill. Med. Polit. Action Com., 1990-92; chmn. Met. Chgo. Health Info. Network, 1995—. With U.S. Army, 1944-46. Mem. AMA (del. 1983-95), Cho. Med. Soc. (pres. 1985-86), Ill. Med. Soc. (trustee 1983-86, sec.-treas. 1986, trustee 1988-96, chmn. bd. trustees 1988-90), Chgo. Health Econs. Coun. (vice chmn. 1981-85), Edn., Am. Coll. Physicians Execs., Am. Coll. Utilization Rev. Physicians (cert., bd. dirs. 1985-89), Ill. State Med. Inter-Ins. Exch. (bd. govs. 1986—, vice chmn. 1990-91, chmn. 1991—), Flossmoor Country Club (pres. 1972-73), Ill. Med. Physicians' Svc. Orgn. (bd. dirs. 1995-96). Republican. Office: Ill State Med Inter-Ins Exch 20 N Michigan Ave Chicago IL 60602-0008

JENSEN, HELENE WICKSTROM, retired nutritionist, educator; b. Carthage, Mo., Mar. 3, 1929; d. Frank Emil and Lois (Stroup) Wickstrom; m. Robert Gordon Jensen, Dec. 20, 1947; children: Gordon Lee, Jeffrey Alan. BS, U. Mo., 1951; MS, U. Conn., 1983; PhD, Century U., 1996. Registered dietitian; cert. dietitian/nutritionist. Dietitian-in-charge U. Mo., Columbia, 1952-56; therapeutic dietitian Windham Community Meml. Hosp., Willimantic, Conn., 1967, dir. food service, 1967-72; dir. sch. lunch program Windham Pub. Schs., Willimantic, 1963-66; lectr. U. Conn., Storrs, 1972-78, leader edn1. outreach program, 1979-92; cons. Storrs, 1992-97; ret., 1992. Recipient award Met. Life Ins. Co., 1985, Czajowski Nutrition award U. Conn., 1989, Disting. Alumna award U. Conn. Agr. and Natural Resources Alumni Assn., 1989. Mem. Am. Dietetic Assn. (presenter), Am. Sch. Food Svc. Assn. (exec. bd. 1989-91, presenter), Soc. Nutrition Edn., Conn. Sch. Food Svc. Assn. (com. mem.), Conn. Nutrition Coun. (presenter), Conn. Dietetic Assn. (presenter, Dietitian of Yr. 1987), Phi Kappa Phi, Gamma Sigma Delta. Home: 186 Chaffeeville Rd Storrs Mansfield CT 06268-2637

JENSEN, JACK MICHAEL, publishing executive; b. Salt Lake City, June 5, 1951; s. W. Donald and Catherine Ann (Hearley) J.; m. Cathleen Ann O'Brien, Sept. 15, 1985; children: Grace Ann, Ned Michael. BA, Ft. Wright Coll. of the Holy Names, 1974. Bookseller Dayton Hudson, 1972-76; salesman Chronicle Books, San Francisco, 1976-82, mktg. dir., 1983-86, gen. mgr., 1987-89, pub., 1989—, pres., 1996—; mem. faculty Stanford Pub. Course, 1988-89.

JENSEN, JAMES E., director congressional and government affairs; b. Santa Monica, Calif., Oct. 26, 1953. BA, U. Calif., Berkeley, 1976. Aid to Rep. Jim Lloyd Calif., 1978-79; adjunct prof. Johns Hopkins U., 1978-79; aid to Senator Al Gore, 1980-87; dir. congressional pub. affairs Office of Tech. Assessment, Washington, 1987-95; dir. congressional, govt. affairs Nat. Acad. Scis., Washington, 1995—. Fellow Nat. Ctr. Atmospheric Rsch. Office: National Academy of Sciences 2101 Constitution Ave NE Washington DC 20418-7307*

JENSEN, JAMES ROBERT, dentist, educator; b. Mpls., Mar. 17, 1922; s. Ernest William and Edith Ann (Norstedt) J.; m. Alvern Halverson, Mar. 24, 1945; children: Thomas, Mark, James, Elizabeth. B.A., U. Minn., 1944, D.D.S., 1946, M.S., 1950. Diplomate Am. Bd. Endodontics. Teaching asst. U. Minn., 1948-50, asst. prof., 1950-53, asso. prof., 1953-57, prof., chmn. div. operative dentistry and endodontics, 1957-69, asst. dean acad. affairs, 1969-74, asso. dean acad. affairs, 1974-90, chmn. dept. restorative scis., prof., dir. div. endodontics, 1990-92, prof. emeritus, 1992—; cons. endodontics VA Hosp., Mpls.; team leader operative dentistry and endodontics Project Vietnam of AID; cons. dental health Pan Am. Health Orgn., WHO; curriculum cons. U. North Sumatra, Indonesia, 1986-87; mem. staff King Saud U., Riyadh, Saudi Arabia, 1987—, U. Autonoma, Neuva Leon, Mex., 1974—; postgrad. faculty U. Autonoma de Neuva Leon, Monterrey, Mex. Author: (with Thomas P. Serene and Fernando Sanchez) Fundamentos Clinicos de Endodoncia, 1977, (with Thomas P. Serene) Fundamentals of Clinical Endodontics, 8th edit., 1984, Japanese edit., Effective Dental Assisting, 7th edit., 1991; contbr. articles to profl. jours. Served with U.S. Army, 1943-44; as capt. Dental Corps, 1946-48; res. dental surgeon USPHS and Assn. Res. Officers. Fellow Am. Coll. Dentists, Internat. Colls. Dentists; mem. ADA, Minn. Dental Assn., Mpls. Dist. Dental Soc., Am. Assn. Endodontists. Home: 2167 Rosewood Ln N Saint Paul MN 55113-5324

JENSEN, JOHN ROBERT, lawyer; b. Rapid City, S.D., Aug. 9, 1946; s. Edwin Robert and Roxina Althier (Hollinger) J.; m. Susan McClelland, Aug. 27, 1977; children: Margaret Marie, Jennifer Jo, Edwin Robert II, James Peder. BA, Calif. State U.-Northridge, 1971; JD, Baylor U., 1976. Bar: Tex. 1977, U.S. Dist. Ct. (no. dist.) Tex. 1977, U.S. Ct. Appeals (5th cir.) 1982. Asst. ins. dir. Groesbeck Fin., Los Angeles, 1971-73; v.p. Capital Cons., Dallas, 1973-74; assoc. McConnell & Assocs., Arlington, Tex., 1977; sole practice, Arlington, 1978-84; ptnr. Jensen & Jensen, Arlington, 1984—. Author: Checklist for Texas Lawyers, 1979, 81. Served with U.S. Army, 1966-68, Vietnam. Decorated Army Commendation medal. Mem. Arlington Bar Assn., Baylor Order Barristers, Tex. Bd. Legal Specialization (cert. personal injury trial law), Nat. Bd. Trial Adv. (cert. civil trial adv.), Delta Theta Phi (treas. Baylor chpt. 1976). Lutheran. Office: Jensen & Jensen 6025 Interstate 20 W Arlington TX 76017-1077

JENSEN, JOLI, communicatons educator; b. Bad Kreuznach, Germany, Feb. 23, 1954; d. Donald D. and Janet (Kepner) J.; m. Craig Allan Walter, July 13, 1985; children: Charles William, Thomas Craig. BA in Psychology, U. Nebr., 1975; MA in Journalism, U. Ill., 1977, PhD in Communication, 1985. Asst. prof. U. Va., 1983-85, U. Tex., 1985-91; assoc. prof. U. Tulsa, 1991—; writing cons. MCI/Worldcom, Okla., 1992—. Author: (books) Redeeming Modernity, 1990, The Nashville Sound, 1998. Recipient univ. fellowship NEH, 1993, faculty tchg. grant U. Tulsa, 1992-98, faculty fellowship U. Tex., 1997. E-mail: joli-jensen@utulsa.edu. Office: Faculty of Communication U Tulsa Tulsa OK 74104

JENSEN, JUDY DIANNE, psychotherapist; b. Portland, Oreg., Apr. 8, 1948; d. Clarence Melvin and Charlene Augusta (Young) J.; m. Frank George Cooper, Sept 4, 1983; stepchildren: Pamela Cooper, Brian Cooper. BA in Sociology and Anthropology with honors, Oberlin Coll., 1970; MSW, U. Pitts., 1972; postgrad., U. Wis., 1977. Lic. clin. social worker, marriage and family therapist, Oreg. Social worker Day Hosp. Western Psychiat. Inst. and Clinic, Pitts., 1972-73, South Hills Child Guidance Ctr., Pitts., 1973-74; mem. drug treatment program Umatilla County Mental Health Clinic, Pendleton, Oreg., 1975-77; social worker Children's Services Div. State of Oreg., Pendleton, 1978-80, therapist intensive family services project, 1980—, dir. intensive family services project, 1986—; pvt. practice Pendleton, 1980—. NIMH grantee, 1970-72; NDEA fellow 1977; Gen. Motors scholar Oberlin Coll., 1966-70. Mem. Am. Assn. Marriage and Family Therapists (clin.), Nat. Assn. Social Workers. Avocations: fgn. travel, aviation, jogging, photography, personal jour. and poetry writing. Home: 325 NW Bailey Ave Pendleton OR 97801-1604 Office: PO Box 752 Pendleton OR 97801-0752

JENSEN, KATHRYN PATRICIA (KIT), public radio station executive; b. Fairbanks, Alaska, June 20, 1950; d. Edward Leroy and Doris Patricia (Fee) Bigelow; 1 child, Alexander Morgan. BA, U. Alaska, 1974. Sta. mgr., program dir. Sta. KUAC-FM, U. Alaska, Fairbanks, 1976-82; gen. mgr. Sta. KUAC-FM-TV, U. Alaska, Fairbanks, 1982-87; pres., gen. mgr. Sta. WCPN-FM, Cleve. Pub. Radio, 1987—; founding mem. Alaska Pub. Radio Network, 1978-85; bd. dirs. Nat. Pub. Radio, 1983-89, Pub. Radio Internat., 1997—. Recipient Elaine B. Mitchell award Alaska Pub. Radio Network, 1988, Oebie award, 1992, 95, William H. Kling Innovation and Entrepreneurship award Pub. Radio Internat., 1995, Leadership in Non-profit Mgmt. award Case We. Res. U., Mandel Ctr. Non-Profit Orgns., 1999. Episcopalian. Avocations: reading, gardening. Office: WCPN-90.3 FM 3100 Chester Ave Ste 300 Cleveland OH 44114-4604

JENSEN, KLAVS FLEMMING, chemical engineering educator. MSc in Chem. Engring., The Tech. U. of Denmark, 1976; PhD in Chem. Engring., U. Wis., 1980. Rsch. and teaching asst. dept. chem. engring. U. Wis., Madison, Wis., 1976-79, rsch. asst. Math. Rsch. Ctr., 1979-80; asst. prof. dept. chem. engring. and materials sci. U. Minn., 1980-84, assoc. prof. dept. chem. engring. and materials sci., 1984-88, fellow Minn. Supercomputer Inst., 1986-89, prof. dept. chem. engring. and materials sci., 1988-89; prof. materials sci. and engring. MIT, Cambridge, Mass., 1989—, prof. dept. chem. engring., 1989—, Joseph R. Mares career devel. chair dept. chem. engring., 1989-94, Lammot du Pont Prof. dept. chem. engring., 1994—; vis. prof. Tech. U. Aachen, Germany, 1988; mem. internat. adv. bd. on Chem. Vapor Deposit, 1990—. Editl. bd. mem.: Chemtronics, 1988-91, ACS Journal I&EC Research, 1988-91, Oxford U. Press Topics in Chemical Engineering, 1992—; adv. editorial bd. ACS Journal Chemistry of Materials, 1988-96; contbr. over 250 articles to profl. jours. Recipient Outstanding Junior faculty award Arco Oil and Gas Co., 1981, Shell Faculty Career Initiation award, 1982, Young Author's award Electrochemical Soc., 1983, Young Chem. Engr. of the Yr. award AIChE Twin City Section, 1984, Presdl. Young Investigator award NSF, 1984-89, Allan P. Colburn award Am. Inst. Chem. Engrs., 1987; Camille and Henry Dreyfus Tchr. Scholar grant, 1985-90; John Simon Guggenheim fellow, 1987. Mem. AIChE (chmn. electronic materials sect. 1989-91, dir. materials divsn. 1990-94, C.M.A. Stine award Materials Engring. and Scis. divsn. 1995, chair 1997-98), Soc. Indsl. and Applied Math., Am. Chem. Soc., Materials Rsch. Soc., Electrochem. Soc. Research interest include processing and characterization of electronic materials, chemical kinetics and transport phenomena, microfabricated chemical systems. Office: MIT 66-566 77 Massachusetts Ave Cambridge MA 02139-4301*

JENSEN, MARION PAULINE, singer; b. Glendale, Calif., June 29, 1931; d. Paul Morton and Marion (Grus) Bellows; m. Maynard I. Jensen, Aug. 15, 1959; children: Clare, Steven, Jeannetta, Lauretta, Paul, Tony, Phil. Studied voice with, Barbara Burk Prosper, San Francisco Opera, Christina Carlson, Edward Schick, Robert Kyber, Gibner King, David Jimerson; currently studies voice with, Christine Meadows. Pvt. tchr. music. Profl. performer of stage, concert, radio and TV; piano bar entertainer; author: So You Want To Sing, 1983; opera/stage roles include mother in Amahl and the Night Visitors, Kate in Brigadoon, Olga Navakovich in Merry Widow, Tuptim in The King and I, Mable in Pirates of Penzance, Bride in trial by Jury, Josephine in H.M.S. Pinafore, Sherry in Paint Your Wagon, Dolly in Rio Rita, others; opera cos. performed with include Oregon Light Opera, Pacific Theatre Arts, Oreg. Opera Ensemble, Vancouver Civic Theatre, Portland Opera; numerous concerts and recitals in L.A., San Francisco, various cities in Wash., Oreg.; strolling entertainer Nendels Inn, Sylvia's Downtown Restaurant; singer/hostess Frontier Room; singer Portland Hilton, others. Tchr. English Laubach (Oreg.) Literacy, 1972—. Mem. Internat. Assn. Musicians, Nat. Assn. Tchrs. Singing, Music Tchrs. Nat. Assn., Oreg. Music Tchrs. Assn., Nat. Fedn. Music Clubs of Am. (state chmn. student auditions). Democrat. Roman Catholic. Avocations: raising birds, designing and sewing, writing and illustrating children's books. Home: 10230 N Tyler Ave Portland OR 97203-1251

JENSEN, MARK KEVIN, foreign language educator; b. Bethesda, Md., Aug. 13, 1951; s. Harold Boyd and Annabelle Bertha Jensen; m. Agnès Guichard, Dec. 20, 1976; 1 child, Gregory. BA, Princeton U., 1974; MA, U. Calif., Berkeley, 1983, PhD, 1989. Assoc. prof. French, Pacific Luth. U., Tacoma, 1989—. Co-author: The Traveler in the Life and Works of George Sand, 1994, Mélanges sur L'Oeuvre de Paul Bénichou, 1995; translator: Émile Zola's J'Accuse, 1992, Paul Bénichou's The Consecration of the Writer, 1999; contbr. articles to profl. jours. Pres. Cercle Français de Tacoma, 1993-95; co-founder, v.p. Anna Comstock Dinner Club and Literary Union, 1993—. Mem. MLA, AAUP, Am. Assn. Tchrs. French, Assn. Internat. des Etudes Françaises, Assn. des Amis D'Alfred de Vigny, Washington Assn. Fng. Lang. Tchrs. Home: 3110 N 31st St Tacoma WA 98407-6411 Office: Pacific Luth U Dept Langs and Lits Tacoma WA 98447

JENSEN, MARVIN ELI, retired agricultural engineer; b. Clay County, Minn., Dec. 23, 1926; s. John M. and Inga C. (Haugness) J.; m. Doris A. Lundberg, Sept. 4, 1947; children: Connie, Jeffrey, Eric. BS in Agr., N.D. State U., 1951, MS in Agrl. Engring., 1952, DSc (hon.), 1988; PhD in Civil Engring., Colo. State U., 1965. Instr., asst. prof. N.D. State U., Fargo, 1952-55; agrl. engr. Soil and Water Rsch. divsn. USDA, Bushland, Tex., 1955-58; head irrigation and drain sect. Soil and Water Rsch. divsn. USDA, Ft. Collins, Colo., 1959-61; investigation leader Soil and Water Rsch. divsn. USDA, Ft. Collins and Kimberly, Idaho, 1961-68; dir. Snake River Conservation Rsch. Ctr. Agrl. Rsch. Service USDA, Kimberly, 1969-78; nat. program leader Agrl. Rsch. Service USDA, Ft. Collins and Beltsville, Md., 1979-87; dir. Colo. Inst. for Irrigation Mgmt. Colo. State U., Ft. Collins, 1987-92; ret.; pres. Internat. Commn. Irrigation and Drainage, New Delhi, 1984-87. Editor: (monograph) Design and Operation of Farm Irrigation Systems, 1980; sr. editor: (manual) Evapotranspiration and Irrigation Water Requirements, 1990. Recipient Disting. Svc. award USDA, 1983, W.E. Morgan Alumni Achievement award, 1990, Disting. Svc. award Colo. State U., 1994. Fellow Am. Soc. Agrl. Engrs. (tech. v.p. 1983-86, John Deere Gold medal 1982); mem. NAE, ASCE (hon., chmn. irrigation and drainage div. 1976-77, Tipton award 1982, Arid Lands Hydraulic Engring. award 1990, State-of-the-Art award, 1992). Avocations: golf, photography.

JENSEN, MICHAEL CHARLES, journalist, lecturer, author; s. Stanley Charles and Billie Jane (Cooke) J.; m. Jane Rice Woodruff, July 23, 1960; children: Heidi, Michael Charles Jr. A.B., Harvard U., 1956; M.S., Boston U., 1961. Reporter Boston Herald-Traveler, 1960-63, exec. fin. editor, 1963-64; reporter, editor N.Y. Times, N.Y.C., 1970-78; chief. fin. corr. NBC Nightly News, Today program, N.Y.C., 1978—; lectr. in field. Author: The Financiers, 1976; contbg. author: Corporations and Their Critics, 1980; contbr.: articles to Saturday Rev., Harvard Bus. Rev. Served to lt. (j.g.) USNR, 1957-60. Recipient Page One award Newspaper Guild N.Y., 1973, Deadline Club award N.Y.C. profl. chpt. Sigma Delta Chi, 1976, media awards for econ. understanding, 1980, Janus awards for excellence in fin. broadcasting, 1981, 88, award for best news documentary San Francisco Film Festival, 1984, Gabriel awards Assn. Cath. Broadcasters, 1988, 89, 93, Disting. Alumnus award Boston U., 1989, EDI award Nat. Easter Seal Soc., 1991, Nat. News Emmy, 1993; named best econs. and bus. corr. in Am., TV Guide, 1988. Mem. Am. Soc. Bus. Press Editors (pres. N.Y. chpt. 1965-66), Am. Bus. Press (dir. 1967). Club: Harvard of N.Y. Office: NBC 30 Rockefeller Plz Fl 2 New York NY 10112-0036

JENSEN, OLIVER ORMEROD, editor, writer; b. Ithaca, N.Y., Apr. 16, 1914; s. Gerard E. and Dorothea H. (Ormerod) J.; m. Alison Pfeiffer Hargrove, Feb. 21, 1970; stepchildren: Christopher, Stephen, Penelope. BA, Yale U., 1936. With J. Walter Thompson Co., 1937-38; asst. mng. editor Judge mag., 1938-39; with Benton & Bowles, 1939-40; writer Life mag., 1940-41, 46-50, articles editor, mem. bd. editors, 1946-50; a founder Thorndike, Jensen & Parton, Inc. (publishers), 1950; a founder Am. Heritage mag., 1954, mng. editor, 1954-59, editor, 1959-76, sr. editor, 1976-80, 83-86, contbg. editor, 1986—; editorial bd. Horizon mag., 1958-76; pres. Conn. Valley R.R. Co., Essex, 1971-74, 76-80, chmn. bd., 1980-87, dir., 1988—; chief div. prints and photographs Library of Congress, Washington, 1981-83. Author: Carrier War, 1945, The Revolt of American Women, 1952, A College Album, 1974, The American Heritage History of Railroads in America, 1975, America's Yesterdays, 1978; co-author: American Album, 1968, High Honor, 1989; editor: America and Russia, 1962, Great Crimes and Trials, 1974, The U.S. Navy, An Illustrated History, 1977, Bruce Catton's America, 1979, Connecticut Railroads, 1986, The Miracle of Connecticut, 1992; corrd. sec. Yale Alumni mag., 1991—. Mem. Andover Alumni Council, 1962-65. Ensign to lt. USNR, 1942-45. Recipient James Gordon Bennett prize Yale, 1936. Mem. Am. Assn. State and Local History (mem. council 1957-76), Soc. Am. Historians, Am. Antiquarian Soc., Eastern Nat. Park and Monument Assn. (bd. dirs.1986-92), Phi Beta Kappa. Clubs: Yale (N.Y.C.), Century (N.Y.C.); Acorn (Conn.). Address: PO Box 620 Old Saybrook CT 06475-0620

JENSEN, PAUL EDWARD TYSON, business educator, consultant; b. New Orleans, Apr. 27, 1926; s. Paul Christian and Nena Laura (Robertson) J.; m. Jule Valerie Geisenhofer, Jan. 10, 1953; children: Christian, Elena, Constance. BS in Physics, Tulane U., 1947, BBA, 1949; MBA, Golden Gate U., 1976. Asst. mgr. Cuban Atlantic Sugar Co., Lugareño, Cuba, 1952-55; sr. engring. specialist GTE, Mountain View, Calif., 1955-82; sr. staff engr. TRW, Inc., Sunnyvale, Calif., 1982-92; dean Sch. of Bus., Northwestern Poly. U., Fremont, Calif., 1988—, also bd. trustees; cons. geog. info. sys. TRW, Inc., Sunnyvale, 1993-94. Capt. USMCR, 1945-61, WWII, Korea. Fellow Soc. Tech. Comm. (assoc.); mem. IEEE (life, sr. mem.), Am. Phys. Soc., Soc. Computer Simulation, World Future Soc., Assn. Old Crows. Presbyterian. Avocations: amateur radio, jogging, photography, travel. Home: 8033 Regency Dr Pleasanton CA 94588-3131 Office: Northwestern Poly U 117 Fourier Ave Fremont CA 94539-7482

JENSEN, PAUL ERIK, marketing executive; b. Washington, Oct. 15, 1948; s. Albert Erik and Helen Lorraine (Schrader) J.; m. Ilene LaFollette, June 30, 1973 (div. Aug. 1984). Lic., Balt. Nav./Engring. Sch., 1970; student, Taipei (Taiwan) Lang. Inst., 1973-75; tchg. cert., U. Mich., 1976; AB in Asian Studies, Ind. U., 1978. 3d officer Swedish Gulf Line AB, Goethenburg, 1970; English tchr. Taipei Lang. Inst., 1974-75; dir. transp. Cmty. Action Program, Bloomington, Ind., 1978-79; mgr. China projects Weyerhaeuser Co., Tacoma, 1979-84; dir. export mktg. Plum Creek Timber Co., Seattle, 1984-88; pres. Jensen Internat., Alexandria, Va., 1988—; guest lectr. George Washington U., Washington, 1992-94, lead instr., 1994, adj. assoc. prof., 1995-97; vis. prof. Shanghai U. of Fin. and Econs., 1997; adj. prof. Webster U., Shanghai, 1997, 99; sr. exec. trainer China-Brit. Mgmt. Inst., Beijing, 1998, 99; expert witness, spkr. in field. Author: Marketing Strategies for Forest Products-Pacific Rim Opportunities, 1992; editor: Operations and Production Management, 1999; contbr. articles to profl. and acad. publs. Vol. counselor Listening Line, Bloomington, 1976-78; vol. driver disaster team ARC, Bloomington, 1977-79; vol. cons. for internat. child kidnapping case, Washington, 1994-95. With USN, 1966-69. Recipient Svc. cert. ARC, 1978, Letter of Appreciation, U.S. Dept. Commerce, 1989. Mem. Global Bus. Access Ltd. (profl. assoc.). Avocations: private aircraft pilot, scuba diving, sailing. Office: Jensen Internat PO Box 253 Tall Timbers MD 20690-0253

JENSEN, PETER SCOTT, psychiatrist, public health service officer; b. Logan, Utah, Nov. 14, 1949; s. Jay David and Amy Elizabeth (Hillyard) J.; m. Cornelia Denise Myers, Dec. 22, 1973; children: Rebekah, David, Jonathan, Elisabeth. BS in Psychology, Brigham Young U., 1974; MD, George Washington U., 1978. Diplomate Nat. Bd. Med. Examiners, Am. Bd. Psychiatry and Neurology. Resident in psychiatry Letterman Army Med. Ctr., San Francisco, 1978-81; fellow in child psychiatry U. Calif., San Francisco, 1981-83; asst. chief child-adolescent-family psychiatry Eisenhower Army Med. Ctr., Augusta, Ga., 1983-86, chief child-adolescent-family psychiatry, 1986-88; rsch. psychiatrist Walter Reed Army Inst. of Rsch., 1988-89; chief Child and Adolescent Disorders Rsch Br. Nat. Inst. Mental Health, Washington, 1989-97; assoc. dir. child and adolescent rsch. Nat. Inst. Mental Health, 1997—. Contbr. articles to profl. jours. Recipient Kenyon Joyce Rsch. award No. Calif. Psychiatric Soc., 1983, Norbert Regier Rsch. award, 1989, 96. Mem. Am. Acad. Child Adolescent Psychiatry (sec. 1995-96, McGavin award 1996, Ittelsen award 1998), Am. Psychiat. Assn., Coun. for Children, Adolescents, and Families. Mem. LDS Ch. Office: Nat Inst Mental Health Office of Dir Bethesda MD 20892

JENSEN, REUBEN ROLLAND, former automotive company executive; b. Ainsworth, Nebr., Dec. 22, 1921; s. Jens Christian and Amy Caroline (Boyer) J.; m. Janet A. McCann, Oct. 19, 1974; children: Shannon (Mrs. Roger Santora), Bruce, Scott. Student, U. Nebr., 1938-41. With Gen. Motors Corp., Detroit, 1946; jr. engr. Hydra-Matic div. Gen. Motors Corp., 1965-67, gen. mgr. Hydra-Matic div., 1967-70, gen. mgr. Allison div., 1970-72, v.p., group exec., 1972-74, exec. v.p., 1974-84; Mem. adv. bd. Chem.

Bank Internat., 1973-86. Served with USNR, 1943-45. Recipient Silver Beaver, Disting. Eagle, Silver Buffalo, Boy Scouts Am., 1973. Mem. Assn. U.S. Army, Navy League U.S., Am. Ordnance Assn., Alpha Tau Omega. Clubs: Quail Ridge Country, Pine Tree Country (Boynton Beach, Fla.); Meadowbrook Country (Northville, Mich.). Lodge: Masons. Home: 3609 Chinaberry Ter Boynton Beach FL 33436-4528 Home: 18500 Sheldon Rd Northville MI 48167-9535

JENSEN, RICHARD CURRIE, lawyer; b. Flushing, N.Y., June 5, 1939; s. David T. and Isabel (Currie) J.; m. Leslie Dodge, Jan. 9, 1965; children: Tracy, Richard, David, Meredith, Lauren, Christopher. BS in Social Studies, Villanova U., 1961; JD, Fordham U., 1964. Bar: N.Y. 1965. Staff atty. Comml. Union Ins. Co., N.Y.C., 1965-67; ptnr. Morris, Duffy, Ivone & Jensen, N.Y.C., 1967-85, Ivone, Devine & Jensen, Lake Success, N.Y., 1985—. Mem. ABA, N.Y. State Bar Assn., Nassau County Bar Assn., Am. Soc. Law & Medicine. Republican. Roman Catholic. Office: Ivone Devine & Jensen 2001 Marcus Ave Ste 100N New Hyde Park NY 11042-1024

JENSEN, RICHARD DENNIS, librarian; b. Payson, Utah, Oct. 20, 1944; s. Ruel Whiting and Ethel Josepha (Otte) J.; m. Maxine Swasey, Apr. 21, 1966; children: Shaun, Craig, Todd, Jana, Brad, Kristine, April, Lynne. BS in Zoology, Brigham Young U., 1971, MLS, 1976. Asst. sci. libr. Brigham Young U., Provo, Utah, 1971-76, life sci. libr., 1976-84, dept. chair sci. and tech. libr., 1985—. Co-author: Agricultural and Animal Sciences Journals and Serials: An Analytical Guide, 1986, (indexes) Great Basin Naturalist, 50 Year Index, 1991, BYU Geology Studies, Cumulative Index, vol. 1-37, 1954-1991, 1992. Mormon. Avocations: farming, sports, camping. Office: Brigham Young U Libr Sci & Maps Dept 2324 HBLL Provo UT 84602-2734

JENSEN, RICHARD JORG, biology educator; b. Sandusky, Ohio, Jan. 17, 1947; s. Aksel Carl and Margaret (Wolfe) J.; m. Faye Robertson, May 30, 1970. BS, Austin Peay State U., 1970, MS, 1972; PhD, Miami U., 1975. Asst. prof. Wright State U., 1975-79; prof. St. Mary's Coll., 1979—; guest prof. U. Notre Dame, Ind., 1981—, dir. Greene-Nieuwland Herbarium, 1988—; sr. rsch. fellow Ctr. for Field Biology, Austin Peay State U., 1986-88; vis. scholar dept. botany Miami U., 1987; panelist systematic biology program NSF, 1983-87. Assoc. editor Am. Midland Naturalist, 1988—; mem. exec. com. Am. Midland Naturalist, 1989—; mem. editl. bd. Plant Systematics and Evolution, 1990-96; assoc. editor Systematic Botany, 1996—. Recipient Award for outstanding tchg. Wright State U., 1978, Maria Pieta award for outstanding tchg. St. Mary's Coll., 1997; named to Austin Peay State U. Acad. Hall of Fame, 1998; NSF grantee, 1973, 79, 85, 87, 95, Rsch. Corp. grantee, 1984, Eli Lilly grantee, 1990. Fellow Ind. Acad. Sci. (co-chair program com. 1988, fellow com., biol. survey com., publ. com., grantee, 1983, 91); mem. Am. Soc. Plant Taxonomists (treas. 1991-96, rsch. com. 1987-90, chmn. 1989-90, Disting. Svc. award 1996), Bot. Soc. Am., Internat. Assn. Plant Taxonomy, Soc. Systematic Biology, Internat. Oak Soc. (bd. dirs. 1997—), Sigma Xi (grantee 1974). Democrat. Avocations: reading, computing, baseball card collecting. Home: 2044 Carrbridge Ct South Bend IN 46614-3514 Office: St Mary's Coll Dept Biology Notre Dame IN 46556 also: Greene-Nieuwland Herbarium Univ of Notre Dame Dept Biology Notre Dame IN 46556

JENSEN, ROBERT GRANVILLE, geography educator, university dean; b. Seattle, June 16, 1935; s. John Granville and Eva Phyllis (Watson) J.; m. Nansie Jean Gilfillan, June 8, 1957; children: Carolyn, Maryann, Paul. BS, Oreg. State U., 1957; MA, U. Wash., Seattle, 1962, PhD, 1964. Acting asst. prof. Portland (Oreg.) State U., summer 1963; from asst. prof. to assoc. prof. geography Syracuse (N.Y.) U., 1964-78, prof., 1979—, chmn. dept., 1973-90, interim dean Grad. Sch., 1989-90, dean Grad. Sch., 1990-94, interim dean Coll. Arts and Scis., 1993-94, dean Coll. Arts and Scis., 1994—, dir. Soviet and East European Studies, 1968-75; del. Soviet-Am. Seminar on Cities, Moscow, 1975. Contbr., editor: (with Shabad and Wright) Soviet Natural Resources in the World Economy, 1983 (Geog. Soc. Chgo. award 1984, named one of outstanding acad. books, Choice 1984-85); assoc. editor Soviet Geography, 1983-87; co-editor Soviet Economy, 1984-88; contbr. articles to profl. jours. Mem. Commr.'s Doctoral Coun. N.Y. State Dept. Edn., 1989-92. Served to 1st lt. USMC, 1957-60. Fgn. Area fellow to USSR Am. Council Learned Socs., 1965-66; Fulbright-Hays faculty research fellow to USSR, 1970-71; Sr. Exchange scholar Internat. Research and Exchanges Bd., 1970-71; NSF grantee, 1977-80. Mem. Am. Assn. for Advancement Slavic Studies, Am. Geog. Soc., Assn. Am. Geographers (chmn. splty. group 1980-81, 83-84, honors award for contbns. to Soviet and East European scholarship 1993). Democrat. Avocations: alpine skiing, tennis. Home: 304 Scott Ave Syracuse NY 13224-1726 Office: Syracuse U Office of Dean Arts & Scis 300 Hall of Langs Syracuse NY 13244-1700

JENSEN, ROBERT TRAVIS, physician, educator, researcher; b. Minot, N.D., Mar. 19, 1926; s. John and Katherine N. (Arnold) J.; m. Rosemary Elizabeth McEachern; children: Janet, Katherine, Tova Marie. Student, Concordia Coll.; BA, Denison U., 1946; MD, U. Minn., 1949; Diploma in Tropical Medicine and Hygiene, London Sch. Hygiene and Tropical Medicine, 1958; MPH, Johns Hopkins U., 1967. Diplomate Am. Bd. Internal Medicine, Am. Bd. Preventive Medicine. Commd. capt., physician officer Med. Corps U.S. Army, Japan, Korea, 1950-51; advanced through grades to col. U.S. Army, Md., 1967, ret., 1976; physician officer Med. Corps. U.S. Army, Korea, Japan, 1950-51; physician officer Brooke Army Hosp., Walter Reed Inst. Rsch. U.S. Army, 1952-55; physician officer Ft. Meade Hosp. U.S. Army, Md., 1955-57; chief dept. pub. health Acad. Health Sci. U.S. Army, San Antonio, Tex., 1971-76; missionary physician Luth. Ch., Tanzania, 1957-66; chief dept. health, edn. and welfare U.S. Civil Adminstrn., Okinawa, Ryuku Isls., 1969-71; supt. state chest hosps. Dept. Health State of Tex., San Antonio, 1977-82; assoc. prof. dept. family practice Health Scis. Ctr. U. Tex., San Antonio, 1983-97, ret., 1997; pvt. practice in internal medicine, 1997-98, ret., 1998; lectr., cons. in field. Contbr. articles to med. jours. Decorated Silver Star, Bronze Star. Fellow Am. Coll. Physicians, Am. Coll. Preventive Medicine; mem. Am. Soc. Tropical Medicine and Hygiene. Republican. Presbyterian.

JENSEN, ROBERT TRYGVE, lawyer; b. Chgo., Sept. 16, 1922; s. James T. and Else (Uhlich) J.; m. Marjorie Rae Montgomery, Oct. 3, 1959 (div. June 1973); children: Robert Trygve, James Thomas, John Michael; m. Barbara Mae Wilson, Aug. 5, 1974. Student, U. N.C., 1943; LL.B., J.D., Northwestern U., 1949, B.S., 1949; LL.M., U. So. Calif., 1955. Bar: Calif. 1950. Asst. counsel Douglas Aircraft Co., Inc., 1950-52, 58-60, counsel El Segundo div., 1952-58; gen. counsel Aerospace Corp., El Segundo, 1960-84; asst. sec. Aerospace Corp., 1961-67, sec., 1967-85. Founding mem. World Assn. Lawyers of World Peace Through Law Center. Served with AUS, 1942-46, PTO. Mem. Alpha Delta Phi, Phi Delta Phi.

JENSEN, RODNEY H., hotel executive. V.p. Nat. 9 Inns, Salt Lake City, 1985—. Office: National 9 Inns 2285 S Main St Ste 9 Salt Lake City UT 84115-2640*

JENSEN, RONALD H., medical educator; b. Chgo., Nov. 25, 1938; s. Gunner Charles and Elizabeth (Rowley) J.; m. Judith Ann Miller, Dec. 27, 1958; children: Montgomery Allen, Gregory Joel, Heather Lee. BS in Chemistry, Lawrence Coll., 1960; PhD in Chemistry, Calif. Inst. Tech., 1964. Rsch. fellow Calif. Inst. Tech., Pasadena, 1964-67; rsch. biochemist Internat. Mineral and Chem. Corp., Libertyville, Ill., 1967-69; sr. investigator Smith Kline and French Lab., Phila., 1970-75; biomed. scientist Lawrence Livermore (Calif.) Nat. Lab., 1975-91; prof. lab. medicine U. Calif., San Francisco, 1991—; biophysicist Lawrence Berkeley (Calif.) Lab., 1994—; mem. sci. adv. coun. Ministry of Scis. of Russia, Moscow, 1995—; mem. working group NCI Study of Leukemia among Clean-up Workers in Ukraine following Chernobyl, 1993—; sci. advisor Italian-Ukranian Coop. Program on Children's Health following Chernobyl, 1993—. Contbr. articles to profl. jours. Grantee NCI, 1992—. Mem. Soc. for Analytical Cytology, Am. Assn. Cancer Rsch. Avocations: fishing, golf. Office: U Calif San Francisco Cancer Ctr Box 0808 202340 Sutter St San Francisco CA 94115

JENSEN, SAM, lawyer; b. Blair, Nebr., Oct. 30, 1935; s. Soren K. and Frances (Beck) J.; m. Marilyn Heck, June 28, 1959 (div. Jan. 1987); children: Soren R., Eric, Dana; m. Carmen Patton, Apr. 7, 1990. BA, U. Nebr., 1957, JD, 1961. Bar: Nebr. 1961. Mem. Smith Bros., Lexington, Nebr., 1961-63, Swarr, May, Smith and Andersen, Omaha, 1963-83, Erickson & Sederstrom, P.C., Omaha, 1983—; chmn. bd. dirs., v.p. bd. dirs. Omaha Public Power Dist., 1979-81; chmn. Nebr. Coordinating Commn. for Postsecondary Edn., 1976-78. Del. Nat. Rep. Conv., 1960, mem. Nebr. Rep. Ctrl. Com., 1968-70; mem. Regents Commn. Urban U., U. Nebr., Omaha, chmn. Task Force on Higher Edn.; mem. Hwy Commn. State of Nebr., 1989-95; vice chmn. Opera Omaha, 1992-95, v.p., 1994-96. Recipient Disting. Service award U. Nebr., 1981. Mem. Omaha Bar Assn. (past exec. com.), Nebr. Bar Assn. (chmn. com. public relations 1973-76), Am. Bar Assn., U. Nebr. Alumni Assn. (pres. 1976-78), Beta Theta Pi, Phi Delta Phi. Clubs: Rotary, Omaha, Racquet. Clubs: Rotary, Omaha. Office: 1 Regency Westpointe 10330 Regency Parkway Dr Omaha NE 68114-3708

JENSEN, SUZANNE E., artist, art educator; b. Fort Wayne, Ind., Apr. 8, 1961; d. Harold R. and Madeliene M. J.; m. Daniel P. Daily (div.1995); m. Patrick Janson; 1 child, Covey. BFA, Ind. State U., 1983; MFA, Tulane U., 1985. Art instr. Ursuline Acad. H.S., New Orleans, 1985-86; adj. instr. Tulane U., New Orleans, 1985-86; assoc. prof. art Auburn U., Montgomery, Ala., 1987—. Office: Auburn U. Montgomery 7300 University Dr Montgomery AL 36117-3531

JENSEN, TOM, political party executive, lawyer; b. Cin., Dec. 29, 1948; s. Carl and Martha Jensen; m. Nannette Jensen; children: Natalie, Laura. Student, Cumberland Coll., 1972, No. Ky. U., 1978. Rep. State of Ky., 1985-96, Ky. Ho. of Reps.; minority floor leader, 1991-94; pvt. practice London, Ky., 1994—. Active Just Say No to Drugs Program; del. Mexico for Am. Coun. Young Polit. Leaders; chmn. Laural County Rep. Com.; legal counsel Mem. Rep. Ho. of Reps., 1988; chmn. Ky. State Rep. Party. Mem. Masons, Shriners. Presbyterian. Office: 303 S Main St London KY 40741-1906*

JENSEN, WILLIAM PHELPS, chemistry educator; b. Mpls., May 22, 1937; s. William Lee and Doris (Phelps) J.; m. Margie Bilsland, Aug. 11, 1962; children: Barbara Jensen Ahlstrom, David, Paul. B Chemistry, U. Minn., 1959; MS, U. Iowa, 1962, PhD, 1964. Rsch. chemist Pitts. Plate Glass Co., New Martinsville, W.Va., 1963-66; vis. asst. prof. La. State U., Baton Rouge, 1966-67; asst. prof. chemistry S.D. State U., Brookings, 1967-72, assoc. prof., 1972-76, prof., 1976—; bd. dirs. S.D. NSF-State-Wide Systemic Initiative, Pierre, 1991—; mem. adv. bd. McRel, Aurora, Colo., 1992—. Recipient award for svc. to students S.D. State U., 1989. Home: 1305 Forest St Brookings SD 57006-3231 Office: SD State U Chemistry Dept Brookings SD 57007

JENSEN-CARTER, PHILIP SCOTT, advertising and architectural photographer, medical photographer; b. N.Y.C., Aug. 9, 1950; s. Jerry and Phoebe (Nortman) Carter; m. Lyndsay Jensen, Jan. 8, 1983. BFA, Md. Inst. Coll. Art, 1972; grad., Scarborough Sch. Studio mgr. Geroge Hausman, Inc., N.Y.C., 1973-76; CEO Jensen-Carter Photographer, Bedford Hills, N.Y., 1976—. Mem. Advt. Club Westchester (Gold award of excellence 1990, 95, 96, Silver award of excellence 1990, 95, 96, 97, Bronze award of excellence 1997), Women in Comm. (Clarion award Westchester chpt. 1997, 98, 99, Bronze and Silver awards 1997). Democrat. Avocations: golf, cycling, antiquing, restoration, traveling. Home: 33 Fairmount Rd Golden Brg NY 10526-1110 Office: Jensen-Carter Photographer PO Box 479 Bedford Hills NY 10507-0479

JENSEN-WHITE, TERESA ELAINE, financial planner; b. Honesdale, Pa., Aug. 11, 1948; d. James Bernard Jensen and LaVaughn Beatrice (Tomlinson) Nixon; m. Leo H. White. Student, San Antonio Coll., 1966-67. Cert. fin. planner; registered investment advisor. V.p. Outdoor Sports Ctr., San Antonio, 1968-73; tchr. New Age Sch., San Antonio, 1973-76; organizer, negotiator Nat. Maritime Union, Galveston, Tex., 1973-76; agt., sales mgr. B&B Assocs., San Antonio, 1977-78; pvt. practice San Antonio, 1978-80; pres. Money Mgrs. Inc., San Antonio, 1981—; adj. instr. Coll. Fin. Planning, Denver, 1985—, St. Mary's U., San Antonio, 1985—; expert witness for legal community. Mem. Big Sister Alamo Area Big Bros. & Big Sisters, San Antonio, 1981, bd. dirs. 1985. Recipient Presdl. Citation C. of C., 1982. Mem. Inst. Cert. Fin. Planners (v.p. Cen. Tex. soc. 1986-87, pres. 1987-88, chmn. 1988-89, state chmn. 1991—), Internat. Assn. Fin. Planners, Internat. Bd. Standards and Practices for Cert. Fin. Planners. Republican. Office: Money Mgrs Inc The Lincoln Center 7800 W Ih 10 Ste 636 San Antonio TX 78230-4750

JENSH, RONALD PAUL, anatomist, educator; b. N.Y.C., June 14, 1938; s. Werner G. and Dorothy (Hensle) J.; m. Ruth Eleanor Dobson, Aug. 18, 1962; children: Victoria Lynn, Elizabeth Whitney. BA, Bucknell U., 1960, MA, 1962; PhD, Jefferson Med. Coll., 1966. Instr. in anatomy Thomas Jefferson U., Phila., 1966-68, assoc. in radiology, 1966-68, asst. prof. radiology and anatomy, 1968-74, assoc. prof. radiology, 1968-92, assoc. prof. anatomy, 1968-74, prof. anatomy, 1982-94, vice chmn., 1984-94, prof. pathology, anatomy and cell biology, 1994—, assoc. prof. pediatrics, 1992—, chmn. curriculum com., 1987-93; head anatomy div. Coll. Allied Health Scis. Thomas Jefferson U., 1975-88, co-dir. pre-doctoral tng. program, 1971-79, course coord. histology, 1988-93; mem. staff Op. Concern Inc., Cherry Hill, N.J., 1970-72; cons. reproductive biology Bio-Search Inc., Argus Research Lab. Inc., Ortho Research Found. Contbr. articles to sci. jours. Mem. task force com. on communications S. Jersey Methodist Conf., 1974-80; chmn. Learning Resources Ctr., Haddonfield United Meth. Ch. (N.J.), 1976-79. Recipient Christian R. and Mary F. Lindback Found. Disting. Teaching award, 1978, Disting. Alumnus award, 1985, Faculty Achievement award Burlington Northern Found., 1989, Jefferson Med. Coll. Portrait, 1994, Award for Disting. Alumnus in a Chosen Profession, Bucknell U., 1997. Mem. AAAS, Am. Soc. Zoologists, N.Y. Acad. Scis., Teratology Soc. (treas. 1989-92), Behavioral Teratology Soc. (pres. 1985-86), Am. Assn. Anatomists, Soc. Am. Mus. Natural History, Inst. Social Ethics and Life Scis., Jefferson Med. Coll. Alumni Assn. (hon. life), Phi Beta Kappa, Sigma Xi, Psi Chi, Phi Sigma. Home: 230 E Park Ave Haddonfield NJ 08033-1835 Office: 562 Jefferson Alumni Hall 1020 Locust St Philadelphia PA 19107-6731

JENSON, JON EBERDT, association executive; b. Madison, Wis., Aug. 1, 1934; s. Theodore Joel and Gertrude Beatrice (Edberdt) J.; m. Jeannette Marie Hasman, May 1, 1976; children: James, Peter. BS, U. Wis., 1956; postgrad., Goethe U., Frankfort, Germany, 1956; diploma, U. Cologne, West Germany, 1957. From staff rep. to dir. mktg. and tech. svcs. Forging Industry Assn., Cleve., 1959-75; exec. v.p., sec. Am. Metal Stamping Assn., Cleve., 1975-80; pres. Precision Metalforming Assn., Richmond Heights, Ohio, 1980—; exec. dir., sec. Forging Industry Ednl. and Research Found., Cleve., 1967-75; lectr. N.Y. U., 1973-75; Ohio bd. advisors Liberty Mut. Ins. Co. Author: Forging Industry Handbook, 1966; editor: Metal Forming mag, 1975-90, pub. 1990—. Bd. regents Insts. Orgn. Mgmt., U.S. C. of C., 1977-83, vice chmn., 1982, chmn., 1983; mem. bd. regents Marycrest Sch., Independence, Ohio, 1979-86; bd. dirs. Cleve. Conv. and Visitors Bur., 1988. With USNR, 1958-59. Rotary Internat. fellow, 1956. Mem. Am. Soc. Assn. Execs. (cert. assn. exec.), Cleve. Soc. Assn. Execs., Rockwell Springs Trout Club, Capitol Hill Club. Home: 5700 Brookside Rd Cleveland OH 44131-6013 Office: 6363 Oak Tree Blvd Independence OH 44131-2556

JENSON, PAULINE ALVINO, retired speech and hearing educator; b. Orange, N.J.; m. Bernard A. Jenson; 1 child, Mark J. BS, Trenton State Coll., 1948; MA, Columbia U., 1950, PhD, 1969. Lic. speech pathologist and audiologist, N.J. Tchr. English and history Bordentown (N.J.) H.S., 1948-49; tchr. Lexington Sch. for Deaf, N.Y.C., 1950-51, with rsch. dept., 1969-70; tchr. N.J. Sch. for Deaf, West Trenton, 1951-56, 58-61, St. Mary's Sch. for Deaf, Buffalo, 1956-58; speech pathologist Hunterdon Med. Ctr., Flemington, N.J., 1959-60, dir. speech and hearing, 1960-62; asst. prof. Trenton (N.J.) State Coll., 1962-65; instr., lectr. Teacher's Coll., Columbia U., N.Y.C., 1966-69; prof. dept. speech pathology and audiology Trenton (N.J.) State Coll., 1970-95; Yrbk Dedica, 1978; prof. dept. lang. and comm. sci. Coll. N.J. (formerly Trenton State Coll.), 1995-98, chmn. dept., 1991-94, retired, 1998; cons. Universal Films & Visual Arts, N.Y.C., 1968-70, State Agys. and Schs. for Handicapped, N.J., N.Y., 1976-98; evaluator Coun. on Edn. of Deaf, Washington, 1979-83. Author: (with others) Speech for the Deaf Child, 1971; inventor cueing system for deaf speakers, 1976; editor: (info. booklets) Topics, Princeton, N.J., 1980-86. Help line vol. N.J. Assn. for Children with Hearing Impairments, Princeton, 1973-95; co-author, cons. Senate Bills on Deafness, Trenton, 1979—; commr. Legislative Commn. to Study Svcs. for Hearing Impaired Children, Trenton, 1988-90. Recipient post masters scholarship U.S. Office Edn., Teacher's Coll., Columbia, U., 1965, Pauline Jenson award The Coll. of N.J., 1996—; grantee N.J. Dept. Edn., 1973, N.J. Dept. Human Svcs., 1992-96. Mem. N.J. Assn. for Children with Hearing Impairment (founder, exec. dir. 1973-95, Pauline Jenson award at Trenton State Coll. named in her honor, 1996), N.J. Speech, Lang. and Hearing Assn. (life, Disting. Svc. award 1985, Disting. Clin. award 1998), Am. Speech, Lang. and Hearing Assn. (cert., life). Avocation: bibliophily. Office: PO Box 1336 Princeton NJ 08542-1336

JENSON, WILLIAM G., federal agency adminstrator; b. Hartford, Conn.. BA in History, Hobart Coll., 1970; JD, Suffolk U., 1975. Bar: Mass., 1975. Atty. Office Gen. Counsel USDA, Washington, 1976-96, jud. officer, 1996—; instr. USDA, 1980—, mem. grad. sch.'s paralegal com., 1987. Mil. intelligence specialist U.S. Army, Vietnam, 1970-72. Mem. ABA (vice chairperson adminstv. law and regulatory practice-agr. sect. 1996—), Mass. Bar Assn. Office: Dept Agr Office Jud Officer South Bldg Rm 1104 Washington DC 20250

JENSSEN, WARREN DONALD, microbiologist; b. Woodbridge, N.J., Aug. 23, 1942; s. Joseph and Lillian (Anderson) J.; m. Donna M. Larson; children: Kirsten E., Erik C. BA, Rutgers U., 1965, PhD, 1970; MS, Purdue U., 1966. Diplomate Am. Acad. Microbiology, Am. Bd. Bioanalysis. Tchg. fellow Purdue U., W. Lafayette, Ind., 1965-66; rsch. fellow Rutgers U., New Brunswick, N.J., 1966-70, 84-87; postdoctoral fellow Rutgers Med. Sch., New Brunswick, N.J., 1983-84; adj. prof. Union County Coll., Cranford, N.J., 1969-70, asst. prof., 1970-74, assoc. prof., 1974-79, prof., 1979-85; sr. prof. Union County Coll., 1985—; adj. prof. Kean Coll., Union, N.J., 1972-75; clin. microbiology cons. JFK Med. Ctr., Edison, N.J., 1973-76, Raritan Bay Med. Ctr., Perth Amboy, N.J., 1976-98, VA Med. Ctr., Lyons, N.J., 1989-96; dir. health svcs. lab. Union County Coll., 1974-82, Union County Pub. Health Lab., 1977-82; pub. health bacteriologist N.J. Dept. Environ. Protection, 1973—; assoc. med. staff Raritan Bay Med. Ctr., 1985—; clin. lab. dir. N.J. Bd. Med. Examiners, 1985—; adj. clin. instr. Robert Wood Johnson Med. Sch., 1985-91; adj. prof. biomed. careers program Univ. Medicine and Dentistry of N.J., 1999—; recycling coord., Califon, 1988-92, Hunterdon County Health Adv. Com., 1985-88, Hunterdon County Mcpl. Officers Assn., 1987-89. Contbr. articles to profl. jours. Den leader, asst. scoutmaster Boy Scouts Am., Califon, N.J., 1980-84; vice chmn. Bd. Health, Califon, 1983-89; mem. Environ. Comm., Califon, 1985-89. Mem. Theobald Smith Soc., Am. Soc. Microbiology, N.J. Link for Microbiology (program chair 1983-85), AAUP (exec. bd. 1973—). Achievements include antibiotic action on membrane-associated polyribosomes of Streptococcus faecalis, photoinduction of sporulation in Trichoderma viride, computerized compilation of antimicrobial susceptibility data, fatal septicemia due to CDC-DF2 in a splenectomized patient, a novel insertion of a resistance transposon in methicillin-resistant Staphylococcus aureus, prevalence of MLS resistance and erm gene classes among clinical strains of staphylococci and streptococci, molecular epidemiology of MLS resistance in staphylococus aureus and coagulate-negative staphylococci. Avocations: boating, fishing, hiking, camping. Home: 83 River Rd Califon NJ 07830-4371 Office: Union County Coll 1033 Springfield Ave Cranford NJ 07016-1528

JENTZ, GAYLORD ADAIR, law educator; b. Beloit, Wis., Aug. 7, 1931; s. Merlyn Adair and Delva (Mullen) J.; m. JoAnn Mary Hornung, Aug. 6, 1955; children: Katherine Ann, Gary Adair, Loretta Ann, Rory Adair. BA, U. Wis., 1953, JD, 1957, MBA, 1958. Bar: Wis. 1957. Pvt. practice law Madison, 1957-58; from instr. to assoc. prof. bus. law U. Okla., 1958-65; vis. instr. to vis. prof. U. Wis. Law Sch., summers 1957-65; asso. prof. to prof. U. Tex., Austin, 1965-68, prof., 1968-98, prof. emeritus, 1998—, Herbert D. Kelleher prof. bus. law, 1982-98, chmn. gen. bus. dept., 1968-74, 80-86. Author: (with others) Business Law Text and Cases, 1968, Business Law Text, 1978, Texas Uniform Commercial Code, 1967, rev. edit., 1975, West's Business Law: Alternate Edition, 7th edit., 1999, Legal Environment of Business, 1989, Texas Family Law, 7th edit., 1992, West's Business Law: Text and Cases, 7th edit., 1998, Fundamentals of Business Law, 5th edit., 2000, Business Law Today, 5th edit., 2000, Business Law Today-Comprehensive Edition, 5th Edit., 2000, Business Law Today-The Essentials, 5th edit., 2000, Business Law Today-Alternate Essentials Edition, 4th edit., 1997; dep. editor Social Sci. Quar., 1966-82, editl. bd., 1982-94; editor-in-chief Am. Bus. Law Jour., 1969-74, adv. editor, 1974—. Served with AUS, 1953-55. Recipient Outstanding Tchr. award U. Tex. Coll. Bus., 1967, Jack G. Taylor Tchg. Excellence award, 1971, 89, Joe D. Beasley Grad. Tchg. Excellence award, 1978, CBA Found. Adv. Coun. award, 1979, Grad. Bus. Coun. Outstanding Grad. Bus. Prof. award, 1980, James C. Scorboro Meml. award for outstanding leadership in banking edn. Colo. Grad. Sch. Banking, 1983, Utmost Outstanding Prof. award, 1989, CBA award for excellence in edn., 1994, Banking Leadership award Western States Sch. Banking, 1995, U. Tex. Civitatis award, 1997; named to CBA Hall of Fame, 1999. Mem. Southwestern Fedn. Adminstrv. Disciples (v.p. 1979-80, pres. 1980-81), Am. Arbitration Assn. (nat. panel 1966-96), Acad. Legal Studies in Bus. (pres. 1971-72, exec. com. 1989-94, Faculty award of excellence 1981), So. Bus. Law Assn. (pres. 1967), Tex. Assn. Coll. Tchrs. (pres. Austin chpt. 1967-68, exec. com. 1979-80, state pres. 1971-72), Wis. Bar Assn., Omicron Delta Kappa, Phi Kappa Phi (pres. 1983-84). Home: 4106 N Hills Dr Austin TX 78731-2826 Office: U Tex CBA 5.202 MSIS Dept Austin TX 78712

JEPPSON, LAWRENCE SMITH, publisher fine arts, consultant; b. Logan, Utah, June 5, 1926; s. Robert Baird and Elsie (Smith) J.; m. Frances Bennett, Nov. 5, 1952; children; Marian J. Stoddard, Carolyn J. Richards, Morgan B., Alison J. Hyde, Anne J. Bradham, Bryan B. Cert. civil engring., Oregon State U., 1946; BS, U. Utah, 1948; MS, Boston U., 1952. Missionary, mag. editor Church of Jesus Christ of Latter-day Saints, France, Belgium, Paris,, Geneva,, Switzerland, 1948-51; pub. rels. dir. Washington, 1952-56; pres., owner Lawrence Jeppson Pub. Rels. Svc., Industries Agy., Advt., Washington, 1951-80; pres. Jeppson Galleries and Lawrence Jeppson Assocs. Fine Arts, Bethesda, Md., 1958—; editor, publ. contemporary art Bethesda, Md., 1964-68; co-founder and art mgr. Collectors' Investment Fund, Washington, L.A., 1970-80; pres., owner Art Circut Svcs., Bethesda, 1965—; pres., chmn. Mathieu Matégot Found. for Contemporary Tapestry, Washington, Bethesda, 1989—; owner, publ. AcroEditions & Legacy Press, Bethesda, 1978—; lectr. in field. Author: Murals of Wool, 1960, The Fabulous Frauds...Great Art Forgeries, 1970, The Neo-Iconography of Tsing-fang Chen, 1978, Un Coup d'Oeil Honnête Sur Les Mormons, 1951, The Spirit of Liberty, 1986, The Art of Dr. T.F. Chen: Neo-Iconography, 1990, Ecstasies in Wool, 1998; editor, publ. Contemporary Art Reports; TV and radio appearances; contbr. articles to profl. jours. Bd. visitors U. Md. Pub. Rels. Dept., 1957, Citizen Adv. bd. Montgomery Co. Dept. Recreation, 1980; ofcl. U.S. del. ARCO, Madrid, 1987. Recipient fellowship rsch. Cultural Ministry, France, 1970. Republican. LDS. Avocations: writing, traveling. Home: 9004 Honeybee Ln Bethesda MD 20817-6927 Office: Lawrence Jeppson Assoc 9004 Honeybee Ln Bethesda MD 20817-6927

JEPSEN, MARY LOU, optical scientist, business executive; b. Windsor, Conn., Apr. 5, 1965; d. Donald Allen and Jane Anne (Barry) J. BS, Brown U., 1987, PhD, 1996; MS, MIT, 1989. Asst. prof. computer sci. Royal Melbourne Inst. Tech., Australia, 1991; invited fellow Kunsthochscule für Medien Köln, Cologne, Germany, 1992; rsch. scientist Advanced Environ. Rsch. Group, Providence, 1993; NASA fellow R.I. Space Grant Program, Providence, 1993-94; tech. dir. Brown U. Multimedia Lab., Providence, 1994-95; v.p. optics and materials MicroDisplay Corp., San Pablo, Calif., 1996-98; sr. mem. rsch. staff Philips Rsch., Briarcliff Manor, N.Y., 1998—; cons. Note Printing Australia, 1991, Brown U. Graphics Group, 1993-96. Organizer, contbr. numerous techno-art shows worldwide, 1987-96; contbr. numerous articles to profl. jours. Recipient NASA Space Act Monetary award, 1994, othrs. Mem. SPIE, Optical Soc. Am. (Scholarship award 1987). Achievements include co-creation of world's first holographic video system; creation of world's biggest display hologram (city-block size); invention of lunar projection system for Moon-TV. Home: 101 West 23rd St New York NY 10011 Office: Philips Rsch 345 Scarborough Rd Briarcliff Manor NY 10510

JEPSEN, PETER LEE, court reporter; b. Virginia, Minn., Dec. 23, 1952; s. Peter Frederick and Delores Audrey (Sorenson) J.; m. Valerie Lynn Tow, Mar. 20, 1976; children: Sarah Jo, Jennifer Lynn, Elizabeth Ann. Student, St. Cloud State U., 1971, Mankato State U., 1972, Southwestern AVTI, Jackson, Minn., 1978. Registered profl. reporter; chartered shorthand reporter. Freelance ct. reporter Carney & Assocs., Rochester, Minn., 1978-79; ofcl. ct. reporter State of S.D., Sioux Falls, 1979-80; part owner, reporter Carney & Assocs., Rochester, 1980-83; realtime captioner Can. Captioning Devel. Agy., Toronto, Ont., 1984-85, mgr. live captioning services, 1985-87; captioning trainer and cons. XScribe Corp., San Diego, 1987-88, mgr. captioning products and services, 1988-91; dir. U.S. Senate Office of Captioning Svcs., Washington, 1991-92; v.p. U.S. Captioning, Inc., San Diego, 1992-93; dir. U.S. Senate Office Captioning Svcs., Washington, 1994—. Lutheran. Avocations: reading, music, aviation. Office: St-54 The Capitol Washington DC 20510

JEPSON, HANS GODFREY, investment company executive; b. Spencer, W.Va., July 24, 1936; s. Hans G. and Juanita Imogene (Shears) J.; m. Barbara Gayle Keller, Dec. 3, 1966. A.B. magna cum laude, Princeton U., 1958. Exec. editor Arnold Bernhard & Co., N.Y.C., 1961-68; v.p., research dir. Dominick & Dominick, Inc.,, N.Y.C., 1968-70; dir., sr. v.p., research dir. Alliance Capital Mgmt. Corp., N.Y.C., 1970-76; exec. v.p., chief investment officer U.S. Trust Co. N.Y., N.Y.C., 1976-80; pres. Valquest Assocs., Inc., N.Y.C., 1980—, Lafayette Enterprises, Inc., N.Y.C., 1983—, The Stanton Corp., Del., 1994—; dir. United News & Media, Inc., Del. Bd. dirs. J. Aron Charitable Found, The 1331 Found. 2d lt. U.S. Army, 1958-59, capt. USAR, 1959-66. Mem. Assn. for Investment Mgmt. and Rsch., N.Y. Soc. Security Analysts, Dial, Elm and Cannon Club (Princeton, N.J.), Princeton Club (N.Y.C.), Econ. Club (N.Y.C.), La Boule New Yorkaise (N.Y.C.), Fedn. Petanque USA, Inc. Home: 11 5th Ave New York NY 10003-4342 Office: Lafayette Enterprises Inc 126 E 56th St Fl 23 New York NY 10022-3639

JEPSON, ROBERT SCOTT, JR., international investment banking specialist; b. Richmond, Va., July 20, 1942; m. Alice Finch Andrews, Dec. 28, 1964; children: Robert Scott, John Steven. BS, U. Richmond, 1964, M of Commerce, 1975; JD (hon.), Gonzaga U., 1986; DCS (hon.), U. Richmond, 1987; DH (hon.), Hamline U., 1988; LLD (hon.), Tusculum Coll., 1989, Ashland U., 1990, Elmhurst Coll., 1991; DSC in Bus. Adminstrn., Franklin U., 1996. With Va. Commonwealth Bankshares, Richmond, 1966-68; v.p. corp. fin. Birr Wilson & Co., Inc., San Francisco, 1968-69; pres. Calif. Capital Mgmt. Corp., Irvine, 1970-73; v.p., dir. corp. fin. Cantor Fitzgerald & Co., Beverly Hills, Calif., 1973-75; dir. corp. planning and devel. Campbell Industries, San Diego, 1975-77; v.p., mgr. merger and acquisition divsn. Continental Ill. Bank, Chgo., 1977-82; sr. v.p., group head U.S. Capital Markets Group, 1st Nat. Bank Chgo., 1982-83; chmn., CEO The Jepson Corp., Chgo., 1983-89, Jepson Assoc. Inc., Savannah, Ga., 1989—; chmn. Jepson Vineyards Ltd., Ukiah, Calif., 1985—, Coburn Optical Industries Inc., Tulsa, 1992-98; chmn., CEO Kuhlman Corp., Savannah, Ga., 1993-99; bd. advisors Jepson Found., Chgo., 1988—; bd. dirs. Circuit City Stores, Inc., Richmond, Va.; asst. prof. fin. Nat. U., 1976. Bd. trustees Gonzaga U., Spokane, Wash., 1982-86, Hamline U., St. Paul, Minn., 1987-92; bd. trustees, vice rector U. Richmond, 1992-95, Marine Mil. Acad., Harlingen, Tex., 1993—; mem. bd. advisors Franklin U., Columbus, 1996—; lectr. numerous schs. including U. Richmond, U. Chgo., Northwestern U., Kansas U., Luther Coll., Wake Forest U. 1st lt. M.I., AUS, 1964-66. Recipient Citation Honor Founders medal Elmhurst Coll., Ill., 1994, Volunteerism and Philanthropy award Coun. Ind. Colls., 1997. Mem. Commonwealth Club (Richmond), Savannah Yacht Club, Oglethorpe Club (Savannah), Chatham Club (Savannah), Plantation Club (Savannah), Omicron Delta Kappa, Alpha Kappa Psi, Beta Gamma Sigma (Entrepreneur of Yr. medallion 1996), Phi Gamma Delta. Republican.

JERACE, CHARLOTTE LOUISE, writer, consultant; b. Rockland, Maine, Nov. 17, 1942; d. Max and Ida (Shapiro) Gopan; m. Harvey Cohen, Aug. 22, 1964 (div. Oct. 1971): children: Scott, Melissa; m. Michael Crawley Jerace, July 12, 1986. MEd, Antioch U., 1981. pres. Coast-to-Coast Prodns., Truro, Mass., 1990—. Agt. Aetna Life Ins. Co., Boston, 1975-80; mng. editor Employee Comm. Svcs., Natick, Mass., 1980-85; sr. mgr. KPMG Peat Marwick, Boston, 1985-94; prin. Buck Consultants, Boston, 1994—. Author: A Survivor's Manual, 1978, Facing the Future, 1980, Secret Hiding Places, 1994, Voice Like an Angel, 1997; author short story; screenwriter Secret Hiding Places, 1997. Chmn. Truro Beach Commn., 1993—; pres. Boston chpt. Eleanor Roosevelt group Hadassah, 1968-70, mem., 1966—. Recipient Telly award, 1990, 91, 92, Award of Excellence Bus. Ins. Mag., 1993. Mem. Internat. Assn. Bus. Communicators (Award of Excellence 1992), New. Eng. Employee Benefits Coun. Democrat. Jewish.

JERDEE, THOMAS HARLAN, business administration educator, organization psychology researcher and consultant; b. Mpls., Aug. 30, 1927; s. Thomas Elias and Agnes (Christensen) J.; m. Marian Alice Raether, July 26, 1953; children—William Hans, Robert Gustaf. B.A., Gustavus Adolphus Coll., 1950; M.A., U. Minn., 1956, Ph.D., 1960. Asst. prof. bus. adminstrn. U. N.C., Chapel Hill, 1959-63, assoc. prof., 1963-68, prof., 1968—; cons. Dannie J. Moffie and Assocs., 1975—; prof. emritus U. N.C., Chapel Hill, 1991—. Co-author: Older Employees, 1985, Becoming Aware, 1976; contbr. articles to profl. jours. Treas. Triangle Greenways Coun., Research Triangle, N.C. With USN, 1952-54. Avocations: hiking; bicycling; canoeing; skiing. Home: 210A Spring Ln Chapel Hill NC 27514-3540

JERGE, DALE ROBERT, small business owner; b. Buffalo, Oct. 15, 1951; s. Herbert L. and Ruth R. (Maxson) J.; m. Susan B. Rinaldo, Jan. 22, 1983; 1 child, Nicholas D. AAS, Erie Community Coll., Amherst, N.Y., 1972; BA in Sociology, SUNY, Buffalo, 1974, MS in Social Scis., 1976, postgrad., 1988, M in Social Preventative Medicine, 1998. Cert. occupl. health and safety technologist; cert. hazardous materials supr.; cert. indsl. pulmonary technologist; cert. safety and security dir.; cert. occupl. hearing conservationist; registered environ. profls.; registered hazardous and chem. materials mgr.; nat. registered environ. profls. Loss control specialist Twin Fair, Buffalo, 1975-79; indsl. hygienist Continental Ins. Tech. Svcs., Buffalo, 1979-1997; owner, pres. Indsl. Hygiene & Occupl. Health, Inc., Buffalo, 1997—; adj. prof. Niagara County C.C., Lockport, N.Y., 1989—, OSHA Tng. Inst., Ea. Mich. U., Ypsilanti, 1997—. Mem. APHA, Am. Soc. Safety Engrs., Am. Insl. Hygiene Assn., World Safety Orgn. (affiliate mem., cert. safety and security profl., cert. hazardous materials supr.), Coun. for Accreditation in Occupational Hearing Conservation (cert.). Office: SUNY Sch Medicine & Biomed Scis Buffalo NY 14221

JERGE, MARIE CHARLOTTE, minister; b. Mineola, N.Y., Dec. 26, 1952; d. Charles Louis and Helen Marie (Scheld) Scharfe; m. James Nelson Jerge, Aug. 27, 1977. AB, Smith Coll., 1974; MDiv, Luth. Theol. Sem. of Phila., 1978. Pastor St. Mark Evang. Luth. Ch., Mayville, N.Y., 1978-88; co-pastor Zion Evang. Luth. Ch., Silver Creek, N.Y., 1983-88; asst. to the bishop Upstate N.Y. Synod, Buffalo, 1988—; dir. Acad. of Preachers, Phila., 1995-99, also bd. dirs.; bd. dirs. Acad. Preachers, Phila., 1982-99. Chairperson Chautauqua County Commn. of Family Violence and Neglect, Mayville, 1981-82, bd. dirs., 1978-88. Named one of outstanding Young Women in Am., 1980. Avocations: needlework, aerobics, tennis, golf. Home: 370 Borden Rd Buffalo NY 14224-1713 Office: Upstate NY Synod 49 Linwood Ave Buffalo NY 14209-2203

JERGER, EDWARD WILLIAM, mechanical engineer, university dean; b. Milw., Mar. 13, 1922; s. Nickolaus and Ann (Huber) J.; m. Dorothy Marie Post, Aug. 2, 1944 (dec. 1981); children: Betty Ann Murphy, Barbara Lee Smyth; m. Elizabeth Cordiner Sweitzer, Mar. 27, 1982. B.S. in Mech. Engring, Marquette U., 1946; M.S., U. Wis., 1948; Ph.D., Iowa State U., 1951. Registered profl. engr., Iowa, Ind. Process engr. Wis. Malting Co., Manitowoc, 1946-47; asst. prof. mech. engring. Iowa State U., 1948-55; asso. prof. mech. engring. U. Notre Dame, 1955-61, prof., head mech. engring., 1961-68, asso. dean, 1968-82, prof. mech. engring., 1982-97, prof. emeritus, 1989—; cons. U. Madre De Maestra Santiago, Dominican Republic, 1965-71. Served with USAAF, 1943-46. Mem. ASME, Am. Soc. Engring. Edn., Nat. Soc. Profl. Engrs., Internat. Assn. Housing Sci. (dir.), Nat. Fire Protection Assn., Internat. Assn. Arson Investigators, Sigma Xi, Phi Kappa Phi, Pi Tau Sigma (nat. v.p. 1969-74, pres. 1974-78), Tau Beta Pi. Home: 4 Coburn Ct Okatie SC 29910-4560 Office: Univ Notre Dame Coll Engring Notre Dame IN 46556-5637

JERMAIN, ALAN, advertising executive. Exec. dir. media Lowe & Ptnrs./SMS, N.Y.C., 1988—. Office: Lowe & Ptnrs/SMS 1114 Avenue Of The Americas New York NY 10036-7703*

JERMIASON, JOHN LYNN, elementary school educator, farmer, rancher; b. Rochester, Minn., Jan. 9, 1958; s. Orlyn and Evelyn S. Jermiason; m. Ann M. Gebhardt, July 30, 1990. BA in Music, Psychology, St. Olaf Coll., 1981; AS in Agr., N.D. State U., 1982; BS in Edn., Minot State U., 1990. Sales rep. Century 21 Real Estate, Minot, N.D., 1989; ind. farmer, rancher Minot, 1982—; substitute elem. tchr. Minot Pub. Schs., 1993—. Prin. violist Minot Symphony Orch., 1983—, bd. dirs., 1996—; mem. ch. coun. Augustana Luth. Ch., Minot, 1989-91. Mem. Elks, Phi Mu Alpha, Kappa Delta Pi. Avocations: string music ensembles, church choir. Home: PO Box 452 Minot ND 58702-0452

JERNBERG, SANDRA KAY, elementary education educator; b. Mpls., Dec. 6, 1958; d. Roy H. and Betty L. (Bonn) Whitney; m. Dale John Jernberg, Aug. 5, 1985. BS in Elem. Edn., U. Minn., 1984; MA in Curriculum and Instrn., U. St. Thomas, Minn., 1993. Cert. tchr., Minn. Tchr. Mpls. Pub. Schs., 1985, Andersen Comtemporary Sch., Mpls., 1985-89, Chiron Middle Sch., Mpls., 1989-91, Pillsbury Math. Sci./Tech., Mpls., 1991—; mem. math. leadership team for bldg. Mpls. Schs. and U. Minn., 1990—; mem. SciMath. Minn. Team. Featured tchr. in book, I Am A Teacher, 1990; named finalist in U.S. West Outstanding Tchr. Program, 1992; recipient Minn. State award of excellence in math./sci. teaching, 1994, 95, Minn. Presdl. award for excellence in math. and sci., 1995; Venture grantee, 1992, 94, Imagination Fund grantee, 1995, 96, 97, 98. Mem. ASCD, NSTA, Nat. Coun. Tchrs. Math., Minn. Coun. Tchrs. Math. Avocations: gardening, traveling, reading. Home: 4231 Harriet Ave Minneapolis MN 55409-1835 Office: Pillsbury Math/Sci/Tech 2250 Garfield St NE Minneapolis MN 55418-3927

JERNIGAN, JOHN G., career officer. BS, USAF Acad., 1970; MD, U. Okla., 1974, MPH, 1976; grad., Indsl. Coll. Armed Forces, 1986. Commd. 2d lt. USAF, 1970, advanced through grades to brig. gen., 1996; chief aeromed. svcs. USAF Clinic, Randolph AFB, Tex., 1977-80, USAF Hosp., Mather AFB, Calif., 1980-83; chief aeromed. svcs. then acting hosp. comdr. USAF Hosp., Royal Air Force, Upper Heyford, Eng., 1983-85, then chief aerospace medicine, 1983-85; dep. comdr. aeromed. evacuation 375th Aeromed. Airlift Wing, Scott AFB, Ill., 1986-88; command surgeon, hosp. comdr. USAF Hosp., USAF Air Force Acad., Colorado Springs, Colo., 1988-91; dep. command surgeon, dir. profl. svcs. Hdqs. Mil. Airlift Command, Scott AFB, 1991-92; comdr. USAF Med. Ctr., Scott AFB, 1992-93; command surgeon Hdqs. Pacific Air Forces, Hickam AFB, Hawaii, 1993-95, U.S. Transp. Command and Air Mobility Command, Scott AFB, 1995-97; comdr. Human Sys. Ctr., Brooks AFB, Tex., 1997-98, 311th Human Sys. Wing, Brooks AFB, 1998—. Decorate Legion of Merit with oak leaf cluster. Office: HSC/CC 2510 Kennedy CIR Ste 116 Brooks AFB TX 78235-5120

JERNIGAN, MADELEINE ANNETTA, medical/surgical nurse; b. Taos, N.Mex., Aug. 17, 1926; d. Marvin and Bessie Ruth (Hodges) Barnett; m. Cecil Eugene Jernigan, Sept. 11, 1948; children: Tiffany Pamela Susan, Douglas Samuel. AA, Jefferson Davis, Houston, 1948, U. Houston, 1948; cert., Hospice of Mercy, Fairfield, Tex. Staff nurse head nurse Freestone County Coop. Hosp., Fairfield; head nurse, asst. dir. Wortham (Tex.) Hosp.; head nurse, staff nurse Mexia (Tex.) Mmel. Woul-Harris Meth.; head nurse mobile nursing Home Health Svcs., Mexia. Mem. ANA, Tex. Nurses Assn.

JERNIGAN, ROBERT WAYNE, statistics educator; b. Jacksonville, fla., Feb. 4, 1951; s. Belton Karl and Ruth (Warren) J.; m. Rose Marie Receveur, Aug. 4, 1973; children: Nicholas, Laura. PhD, U. South Fla., 1978. Asst. prof. stats. Am. U., Washington, 1978-82, assoc. prof. stats., 1982-86, prof. stats., 1986—, chair dept. math. and stats., 1991-93, 96-97; sr. statistician U.S. EPA, Washington, 1984-91. Contbr. monograph, articles to profl. jours. Fellow Wash. Acad. Scis. (sci. achievement award for math. and computer sci. 1986); mem. AAAS, Soc. for Study of Evolution, Am. Statis. Assn., Math. Assn. Am., Inst. Math. Stats., Sigma Xi, Phi Kappa Phi, Pi Mu Epsilon. Office: Am U Dept Math & Stats 4400 Massachusetts Ave NW Washington DC 20016-8001

JERNSTEDT, KENNETH ELLIOTT, lawyer; b. Rockeville Center, N.Y., Feb. 27, 1944; s. Kenneth Allen and Laura Jean (Elliott) J.; m. Sandra Reece, Aug. 20, 1967; children: Erik, Matt, Kaitlin. BA in History, Stanford U., 1966; JD, U. Calif., Berkeley, 1969. Bar: Calif. 1970, Oreg. 1970, U.S. Dist. Ct. Oreg., U.S. Ct. Appeals (9th cir.), U.S. Supreme Ct. 1977. Assoc. Spears, Lubersky, Campbell, Bledsoe & Young, Portland, Oreg., 1970-75; ptnr. Spears, Lubersky, Campbell, Bledsoe & Young, Portland, 1975-80; ptnr., exec. com. Bullard, Korshoj, Smith & Jernstedt, Portland, 1980—. Bd. dirs. Vis. Nurses Assn., Portland, 1973-82; mem. Oreg. Fish and Wildlife Commn., 1987-92, chmn., 1988-90; basketball coach Sellwood Boys Club, Portland, 1981-87, West Sylvan Sch., Portland, 1987-90; coach S.E. Soccer Assn., Portland, 1981-90; coach Lake Oswego Soccer Assn. 1992; coach youth basketball YMCA, 1992-93; pres., coach Lake Oswego Youth Traveling Basketball Assn., 1995-97. Mem. ABA (labor sect.), Calif. Bar Assn., Oreg. State Bar Assn. (exec. bd. labor sect. 1975), Multnomah Athletic Club, Stanford Club (pres. 1974-75). Republican. Avocations: skiing, fishing, hunting, biking, running. Office: Bullard Korshoj Smith & Jernstedt 1000 SW Broadway Ste 1900 Portland OR 97205-3071

JERNSTEDT, RICHARD DON, public relations executive; b. McMinnville, Oreg., Feb. 26, 1947; s. Don and Catherine (Anderson) J.; m. Jean Diane Woods, Dec. 28, 1969; children—Ty Parker, Tiffin Kay. BS, U. Oreg., 1969. Mgr. mktg. com. Container Corp. Am., Chgo., 1976-78; exec. v.p. Golin/Harris, Chgo., 1983-85, pres., 1988-91; CEO Golin/Harris Comm., Chgo., 1991—; bd. dirs. Internat. Pub. Rels. Bd. dirs. Off the St. Club, Chgo., 1984—; trustee U. Oreg. Found., 1991—, bd. govs. 410 Club, 1991—. Lt. (j.g.) USNR, 1968-72. Recipient Golden Trumpet award Publicity Club of Chgo.; named Outstanding Jr., U. Oreg., 1968. Mem. Internat. Assn. Bus. Communicators, Pub. Rels. Soc. Am. (Silver Anvil award 1986), Internat. Pub. Rels. Assn., Coun. Pub. Rels. Firms (bd. dirs.). Republican. Presbyterian. Avocations: sports, music, photography, traveling. Office: 111 E Wacker Dr Chicago IL 60601-3713

JEROME, FRED LOUIS, science organization executive; b. N.Y.C., Feb. 10, 1939; s. Victor Jeremy and Alice Rose (Hamburger) J.; m. Jocelyn Beatrice Boyd, May 1, 1963; children: Rebecka, Mark, Daniel. B.A. magna cum laude, CCNY, 1960. Staff writer Wilmington Star-News (N.C.), 1961, Augusta Herald (Ga.), 1962, AP, San Francisco, 1967-71; assoc. editor Pub. Employees Press, N.Y.C., 1963; editorial asst. Newsweek mag., N.Y.C., 1964-66; pub. rels. writer St. Lukes Hosp., N.Y.C., 1975; pub. info. dir. Scientists Inst. Pub. Info., N.Y.C., 1975-95, dir. Media Resource Svc., 1980-92, exec. v.p., 1988—; lectr. environ. health SUNY-Empire State Coll., 1975, 96; adj. prof. grad. divsn. SUNY-Stony Brook, 1976; adj. prof. writing CUNY, 1981; prof. journalism Sch. Visual Arts, 1982; adj. prof. journalism NYU, 1983; adj. prof. environ. reporting Columbia Journalism Sch., 1991, 94; adj. prof. English Empire State Coll., 1994-96; cons. Ctr. Biomed. Edn. CUNY, 1983; chmn. task force soc. at large NRC, 1984; mem. vis. com. to evaluate NAS News Office, 1993; chmn. awards com. Lewis Thomas Sci. Writing awards; cons. Sigma Xi, 1996—, Ctr. for CUNY, 1983, 96-97. Author articles for profl. and gen. publs.; editor SIPIscope, 1975-95, Current Controversy, 1982-86; mem. adv. bd. Tech. Rev., 1985-90; mem. editorial adv. bd. The Scientist, 1986-92. Mem. Nat. Assn. Sci. Writers (awards com., membership com.), Internat. Sci. Writers Assn., Soc. Profl. Journalists, N.Y. Acad. Sci., AAAS (com. pub. understanding of sci. 1986-92), Am. Inst. Physics (pub. info. com. 1987, children's book com. 1988), Coun. for Advancement Sci. Writing (bd. dirs.), Inst. of Medicine (com. on responsible conduct of rsch. 1989), Phi Beta Kappa. Home: 230 W 79th St New York NY 10024-6210

JEROME, JERROLD V., insurance company executive. BS, Linfield Coll., 1952; MBA, Stanford U., 1959. V.p. Teledyne, Inc., L.A., 1962-90; pres., CEO Unitrin, Inc., Chgo., 1990-92, vice chmn., 1992-94, chmn., 1994—. Office: Unitrin Inc 1 E Wacker Dr Chicago IL 60601-1802*

JEROME, JOSEPH WALTER, mathematics educator; b. Phila., June 7, 1939; s. Joseph Walter and Hermena Josephine (Ostertag) J.; divorced. B.S. in Physics, St. Joseph's U., 1961; M.S., Purdue U., 1963, Ph.D., 1966. Vis. asst. prof. U. Wis., Madison, 1966-68; asst. prof. Case Western Res. U., Cleve., 1968-70; faculty Northwestern U., Evanston, Ill., 1970—; assoc. prof. Northwestern U., 1972, prof. math., 1976—; vis. fellow Oxford (Eng.) U., 1974-75; vis. prof. U. Tex., Austin, 1978-79, Rush Med. Coll., Chgo., 1994—; cons. Bell Labs., N.J., 1981—; vis. scientist, 1982-83; vis. scholar U. Chgo., 1985. Author: (with S. Fisher) Springer Lecture Series Math. 479, 1975, Approximation of Nonlinear Evolution Systems, 1983, Analysis of Charge Transport, 1995. Br. Sci. Coun. sr. vis. fellow Oxford, 1974-75; NSF rsch. grantee, 1970—; recipient disting. alumnus award Purdue U. Sch. Sci., 1996. Mem. Am. Math. Soc., Soc. for Indsl. and Applied Math. Roman Catholic. Office: Northwestern U 2033 Sheridan Rd Evanston IL 60208-0830

JEROME, NORGE WINIFRED, nutritionist, anthropologist; b. Grenada, Nov. 3, 1930; came to U.S., 1956, naturalized, 1973; d. McManus Israel and Evelyn Mary (Grant) J. B.S. magna cum laude, Howard U., 1960; M.S., U. Wis., 1962, Ph.D., 1967. Cert. nutrition specialist; fellow Am. Coll. Nutrition. Asst. prof. U. Kans. Med. Sch., Kansas City, 1967-72, asso. prof., 1972-78, prof., 1978-95, dir. cmty. nutrition divsn., 1981-95, prof. emeritus, 1996—; dir. Office of Nutrition, AID, Washington, 1988-91; sr. rsch. fellow Univ. Ctr., AID, Washington, 1991-92; assoc. dean for minority affairs U. Kans. Sch. Medicine, 1996-98; mem. tech. adv. group The Nat. Ctr. for Minority Health; dir. ednl. resource centers U. Kans. Med. Center, 1974-77, head community nutrition labs., 1978-95; cons. Children's TV Workshop, 1974-77; chairperson adv. bd. Teenage Parents Center, 1971-75; mem. planning and budget council, children and family sers. United Community Services, 1971-80; mem. panel on nutrition edn. White House Conf. on Food, Nutrition and Health, 1969; mem. bd. dirs., health care com. Prime Health, 1976-79; bd. dirs. Council on Children, Media and Merchandising; mem. consumer edn. task force Mid-Am. Health Systems Agy., 1977-79; commr. N.Am. working group Commn. Anthropology Food and Food Habits, Internat. Union Anthrop. and Ethnol. Scis., 1979-80; chmn. com. nutritional anthropology Internat. Union Nutritional Scis., 1979-80; mem. lipid metabolism adv. com. NIH, 1978-80; mem. nat. adv. panel multi-media campaign to improve children's diet U.S. Dept. Agr., 1979-81; bd. advisers Am. Council on Sci. and Health, 1985-88. Sr. author: Nutritional Anthropology, 1980; asso. editor: Jour. Nutrition Edn, 1971-77; adv. council, 1977-80; editor: Nutritional Anthropology Communicator, 1974-77; editorial adv. bd.: Med. Anthropology: Cross Cultural Studies in Health and Illness, 1976-88; adv. bd.: Internat. Jour. Nutrition Planning, 1977-88, Nutrition and Cancer: An Internat. Jour, 1978—, Jour. Nutrition and Behavior, 1981-86; contbr. articles to profl. jours. Mem. com. man-food sys. NRC, 1980-83; bd. dirs. Kansas City Urban League, 1969-77, Crittenton Ctr., Kansas City, Mo., 1979-80; mem. awards com. in nutrition edn. Met. Life Found., 1983-85; pres. Assn. for Women in Devel., 1991-93; trustee U. Bridgeport, Conn., 1992—; trustee Child Health Found., 1992—, chmn. bd. dirs., 1996—; bd. dirs. Black Health Care Coalition of Kansas City, 1993—, Solar Cookers Internat., 1992—, (pres. 1998, 99). Decorated Dau. Brit. Empire.; Recipient First Higuchi/Irvin Youngberg Research Achievement award U. Kans., 1982. Fellow Am. Soc. for Nutritional Scis., Am. Anthrop. Assn. (chairperson com. on nutritional anthropology 1974-77, founder com. nutritional anthropology 1974), Soc. Applied Anthropology, Am. Coll. Nutrition, Soc. Med. Anthropology, Am. Soc. Nutritional Scis., 1998; mem. Am. Public Health Assn. (food and nutrition council 1975-78, governing council 1982-85), Am. Inst. Nutrition (program com. 1983-86), Am. Soc. Clin. Nutrition, Am. Men and Women of Sci., Nat. Acad. Scis. (world food and nutrition study panel), N.Y. Acad. Scis., Inst. Food Technologists, Am. Dietetic Assn., Assn. for Women in Devel. (pres. 1991-93), Soc. Behavioral Medicine, Club of Rome (U.S. assoc.). Office: U of Kans Med Ctr 3901 Rainbow Blvd Kansas City KS 66160-0001 *Creative blending appears to have been the key for me—the melding of multiple traditions and styles, the melding of philosophies and strategies, and most importantly, the melding of ancient and modern thought and practices.*

JERREL, BETTYE LOU, science educator; b. Evansville, Ind., Oct. 29, 1930; d. John Brill and Georgia (Howell) Baird; m. Bryan Leigh Jerrel, Sept. 8, 1949; children: Cindy Miller Anderson, John Bryan Jerrel. BA in Biology and Econs., U. Evansville, 1962, MA in Biology and Econs. Cert. tchr., Ind. Tchr., adminstr. Evansville/Vanderburgh Sch. Corp., 1962-97, ret.; mem. State Bd. of Edn., 1973-89. Pres. Vanderburgh County Coun., Evansville, 1991-96; commr. Vanderburgh County Commn., Evansville, 1997—; pres. Bd. of Park Commrs., Evansville, 1972-80; mem. Ind. Public Defenders Commn., 1991—. Mem. Evansville Assn. of Retarded Citizens (v.p. 1997—), Ind. Assn. of Counties, Phi Kappa Pi. Republican. Avocations: biking, tennis. Home: PO Box 2544 Evansville IN 47728-0544 Office: County Commn 1 Martin Luther King Blvd Evansville IN 47708

JERRITTS, STEPHEN G., management consultant; b. New Brunswick, N.J., Sept. 14, 1925; s. Steve and Anna (Kovacs) J.; m. Audrey Virginia Smith, June 1948; children: Marsha Carol, Robert Stephen, Linda Ann; m. 2d, Ewa Elizabet Rydell-Vejlens, Nov. 5, 1966; 1 son, Carl Stephen. Student, Union Coll., 1943-44; B.M.E., Rensselaer Poly. Inst., 1947, M.S. Mgmt., 1948. With IBM, various locations, 1949-58, IBM World Trade, N.Y.C., 1958-67, Bull Gen. Electric div. Gen. Electric, France, 1967-70, merged into Honeywell Bull, 1970-74; v.p., mng. dir. Honeywell Info. Systems Ltd., London, 1974-76; group v.p. Honeywell U.S. Info. Systems, Boston, 1977-80; pres., chief operating officer Honeywell Info. Systems, 1980-82, also bd. dirs.; pres., chief exec. officer Lee Data Corp., 1983-85; with Storage Tech. Corp., 1985-88, pres., chief operating officer, 1985-87, also bd. dirs., vice-chmn. bd. dirs., 1988; pres., chief exec. officer NBI Corp., 1988-92, also bd. dirs.; corp. sr. v.p., pres. Latin Am., bd. dirs. Wang Labs. Inc., 1994-98; mgmt. cons. Bd. dirs. Guthrie Theatre, 1980-83, Charles Babbage Inst., 1980-92, Minn. Orch., 1980-85; trustee Rensselaer Poly. Inst., 1980-85, mem. adv. bd. Lally Sch. Mgmt., 1994—. With USNR, 1943-46. Mem. Computer Bus. Equipment Mfrs. (dir. exec. com. 1979-82), Assoc. Industries Mass. (dir. 1978-80). Home and Office: 650 College Ave Boulder CO 80302-7136

JERRYTONE, SAMUEL JOSEPH, trade school executive; b. Pittston, Pa., Mar. 21, 1947; s. Sebastian and Susan Teresa (Chiampi) J.; children: Sandra, Cheryl, Samuel, Sebastian. Assoc. in Bus., Scranton (Pa.) Lackawanna Jr. Coll., 1966. Mgr. House of Jerrytone Beauty Salon, West Pittston, Pa., 1967-68; regional sales dir. United Republic Life Ins., Harrisburg, Pa., 1970-76; night instr. Wilkes-Barre (Pa.) Vo-Tech High Sch., 1976-78; spl. sales agt. Franklin Life Ins. Co., Wilkes-Barre, 1978-80; instr. Jerrytone Beauty Sch., Pittston, Pa., 1968-69, supr., 1969-95; prof. sch. evaluator Nat. Accrediting Com. Arts and Scis., 1974-95; mem. adv. craft com. Wiles-Barre Vo-Tech H.S., 1988—. Mem. com. Rep. Presdl. Task Force, Washington, 1984, mem. parish coun. Guardian Angel Cathedral, Las Vegas, 1997. Mem. Pa. Hairdressers Assn., Nat. Accrediting Com. Cosmetology, Am. Coun. Cosmetology Educators, Masons (3d degree award 1983, 32d degree award Lodge Coun. chpt. consistory 1984), Shriners (Irem temple). Roman Catholic. Avocations: reading, golf, bowling, music, video filming.

JERSILD, THOMAS NIELSEN, lawyer; b. Chgo., Dec. 12, 1936; s. Gerhardt S. and Martha M. (Beck) J.; m. Colleen Gay Campbell, June 15, 1963; children: Karen, Paul. BA, U. Chgo., 1957, JD, 1961. Bar: Ill. 1961, U.S. Dist. Ct. (no. dist.) Ill. 1961. Ptnr. Mayer, Brown & Platt, Chgo., 1969—. Author: Illinois Corporate and Business Forms, 2 Vols., 1989, with ann. supplements, Foreign Investment in U.S. Oil and Minerals, 1987; editor: U. Chgo. Law Rev., 1959-61. Past chmn. Ill. Sec. of State's Corp. Acts Adv. Com. Mem. ABA, Chgo. Bar Assn. (past chmn. corp. law com., past chmn. pub. utility law com.), Ill. State Bar Assn. (corp. and securities law sect.), Ea. Mineral Law Found., Legal Club Chgo. (past pres.), Law Club Chgo. (bd. dirs.). Office: Mayer Brown & Platt 190 S La Salle St Ste 3100 Chicago IL 60603-3441

JERVEY, EDWARD DREWRY, retired history educator; b. Orange, N.J., Oct. 30, 1929; s. Louis Paschal and Adelaide Esmond (Drewry) J.; m. Thora Jo Thompson, June 12, 1951; children: David Drewry, Warren Lee, Charles Thompson. AB, Emory U., 1950; STB, Boston U., 1953, AM, 1955, PhD, 1958. Assoc. prof. history Lambuth Coll., Jackson, Tenn., 1958-61; prof. history Radford (Va.) U., 1961-91. Author: History of Methodist Church in Southern California & Arizona: 1850-1950, 1960, Prison Life Among the Rebels, 1990; contbr. articles to profl. jours. Elected mem. Raford City Coun., 1980-84; vol. Carilion Radford Hosp., Radford, 1986—. Phi Beta Kappa. Methodist. Avocations: travel, tennis, walking. Home: 135 Greenbrier Dr Radford VA 24141-3809

JERVEY, HAROLD EDWARD, JR., medical education consultant, retired; b. Charleston, S.C., Dec. 3, 1920; s. Harold Edward and Stella (White) J.; m. Lillian Pearce Hair, July 13, 1946; children: Harold Edward, III, Nancy Middleton, Margaret Pearce, Harriett Beachum, Helen White, Charles Stewart, Lillian Hair. BS, U. S.C., 1941; MD, Med. U. S.C., 1949. Diplomate Am. Bd. Med. Examiners (mem.). Intern Greenville (S.C.) Gen. Hosp., 1949-50; house officer Bapt. Hosp., Columbia, S.C., 1951-54; gen. practice medicine Columbia, 1951-74; acting head health facilities U. S.C., 1968-70; asst. prof. Med. U. S.C., 1970-77; pres. Fedn. State Med. Bd. U.S., Ft. Worth, 1960-61, exec. v.p., sec., 1978-84; sec., treas. Edit. Bull., 1961-78; med. cons. S.C. Law Enforcement Agy., 1958-61, S.C. Vocat. Rehab. Dept., 1961-63, S.C. Indsl. Commn., 1963-68, S.C. Dept. Family Practice, 1971-74; med. adv. S.C. Gov. Health and Social Devel., 1973-75; mem. S.C. Bd. Med. Examiners, 1952-72, sec., 1954-56, vice chmn., 1962-64, bd. dirs. Fedn. Assn. Health Regulatory Bds., 1977-80; mem. adv. bd. Am. Bd. Med. Specialties, 1959-70; pres., chmn. bd. Ednl. Commn. Fgn. Med. Grads., 1978-80; past pres. Gen. Practitioners Club Central S.C., pres.Columbia Med. Club; del. Congress Dels. Am. Acad. Gen. Practitioners, 1958-62. Author articles in field. Contbg. editor: Med. Economics. Episc. lay reader, past vestryman; active Richland County Bd. Health, 1992-93; mem. Bishop's Commn. on Aging, 1997—. Lt. comdr. USNR, WWII, 1941-45, capt. M.C., USNR. Decorated Bronze Star, 16 battle stars, Presdl. unit citation. Fellow Am. Acad. Family Practice; mem. AMA (coms.), S.C. Med. Assn., S.C. Med. Soc., S.C. Acad. Family Practice, Columbia Med. Soc., Soc. of Cincinnati, S.C. Hist. Soc., S.C. Writers Workshop, Sertoma, Rotary (v.p. centuring U. So. Calif. grads. 1998—). Episcopalian. 2d in command in boarding party which seized the only Japanese ship captured in WWII, July/Aug. 1945. Address: 4819 Quail Ln Columbia SC 29206-4622

JERVIS, DAVID THOMPSON, political science educator; b. Bryn Mawr, Pa., Mar. 16, 1954; s. Walter T. and Mary Charlotte (Abernethy) J. BA, Eastern Coll., St. Davids, Pa., 1976; MA, Villanova U., 1978; PhD, Temple U., 1985. Asst. prof. Washburn U., Topeka, 1985-92, assoc. prof. polit. sci., 1992-96, prof., 1996—, asst. dir. Internat. Ctr., 1991—; vis. prof. U. Orebro, Sweden, 1995, U. Witwatersrand, South Africa, 1995. Contbr. articles to profl. jours. Bd. dirs. Internat. Ctr. Topeka, 1988—. Fulbright scholar U. Zagreb, 1997-98. Mem. Internat. Studies Assn., Pi Sigma Alpha, Phi Alpha Theta, Phi Kappa Phi, Phi Beta Delta. Avocations: reading, sports, travel. Office: Washburn U Dept Polit Sci Topeka KS 66621

JERVIS, JANE LISE, college official, science historian; b. Newark, N.J., June 14, 1938; d. Ernest Robert and Helen Jenny (Roland) J.; m. Kenneth Albert Pruett, June 20, 1959 (div. 1974); children: Holly Jane Pruett, Cynthia Lorraine Pruett; m. Norman Joseph Chonacky, Dec. 26, 1981; children: Philip Joseph Chonacky, Joseph Norman Chonacky. AB, Radcliffe Coll., 1959; MA, Yale U., 1974, MPhil, 1975, PhD in History of Sci., 1978. Freelance sci. editor and writer, 1962-72; lectr. in history Rensselaer Poly. Inst., 1977-78; dean Davenport Coll., lectr. in history of sci. Yale U., 1978-82; dean students., assoc. prof. history Hamilton Coll., 1982-87; dean coll., lectr. in history Bowdoin Coll., 1988-92; pres. Evergreen State Coll., Olympia, Wash., 1992—. Author: Cometary Theory in 15th Century Europe; contbr. articles to profl. jours.; book reviewer; presenter in field. Trustee Maine Hist. Assn., 1991-92, Stonehill Coll., 1996—, Providence St. Peter's Hosp., 1997—; chair Maine selection com. Rhodes Scholarship Trust, 1990-92, chair N.W. selection com., 1992-93; commr. N.W. Assn. Schs. and Colls. Commn. on Colls., 1994—. Office: Evergreen State Coll Office of President Olympia WA 98505

JERVIS, ROBERT, political science educator; b. N.Y.C., Apr. 30, 1940; s. Herman and Dorothy J.; m. Kathe Weil, June 19, 1967; children: Alexa, Lisa. BA, Oberlin Coll., 1962; MA, U. Calif.-Berkeley, 1963, PhD, 1967. Asst. prof. govt. Harvard U., 1968-73, assoc. prof., 1973-75; vis. assoc. prof. polit. sci. Yale U., 1974-75; prof. polit. sci. UCLA, 1975-80; prof. polit. sci. Columbia U., N.Y.C., 1980—, Adlai E. Stevenson prof. of internat. rels., 1989—, chair exec. com. of faculty arts and scis., 1993-94, acting assoc. v.p. arts and scis. for planning, 1994-95; Lady Davis vis. prof. Hebrew U., Jerusalem, spring 1977. Author: Perception and Misperception in International Politics, 1976, The Illogic of American Nuclear Strategy, 1984, Psychology and Deterrence, 1985, The Logic of Images in International Relations, 2d edit., 1989, The Meaning of the Nuclear Revolution, 1989, System Efects: Complexity in Political and Social Life, 1997; editor: Perspectives on Deterrence, 1989, Dominoes and Bandwagons, 1990, Soviet American Relations after the Cold War, 1991, Coping with Complexity in the International System, 1992; contbr. articles to prof. jours. Guggenheim fellow, 1978-79; recipient Grawemeyer award Ideas Improving World Order, Nevitt Sanford Career Achievement award Internat. Soc. Polit. Psychology, 1992, Lionel Trilling award, 1998. Fellow AAAS; mem. Am. Polit. Sci. Assn. (v.p. 1988-89, pres.-elect 1999—, Best Book in Polit. Psychology award 1998), Internat. Studies Assn. (Security Studies award 1996), Coun. on Fgn. Rels. (fellow 1970-71). Democrat. Home: 1170 5th Ave New York NY 10029-6527 Office: Columbia U Dept Polit Sci New York NY 10027

JERVIS, ROBERT E., chemistry educator; b. Toronto, May 21, 1927; s. Bertram Charles and Mary Elizabeth (Gibbings) J.; m. Frances Jane (Jean) McCourt, Dec. 30, 1950; children: Ann K., Peter R. BA, U. Toronto, 1949, MA, 1950, PhD, 1952. Registered profl. engr., Ont. Rsch. chemist Atomic Energy Can., Chalk River, 1952-58; prof. applied chemistry and chem. engring. U. Toronto, 1958-92, prof. emeritus, 1992—, dir. nuclear reactor, 1970-93, assoc. dean rsch. faculty engring., 1974-78, chmn. rsch., 1981-85; vis. prof. radio chemistry U. Tokyo, 1965-66; vis. prof. Cambridge U., 1978, Nat. U. Malaysia, 1979; cons., dir. Chem. Engring. Research Cons., Ltd., Toronto; chmn. nat. com. Adv. Com. Nuclear Safety, 1989—. Co-author: Nuclear Methods of Crime Investigation; contbr. 225 articles to profl. jours. Bd. dirs. Inter Varsity Christian Fellowship Can., 1959-82. Recipient Ressovsky medal Russian Acad. Scis., 1992, Ehman award Am. Nuc. Soc., 1998. Fellow Chem. Inst. Can., Indian Acad. Forensic Sci. (hon.), Can. Nuclear Soc. (W.B. Lewis medal 1991, R.E. Jervis award named in his honor), Royal Soc. Can., Can. Sci. Christian Affiliation/Am. Sci. Affiliation. E-mail: robert.jervis@utoronto.ca. Home: 30 Chestergrove Crescent, Agincourt, ON Canada M1W 1L4 Office: U Toronto, Dept Chem Engring & Chemistry, Toronto, ON Canada M5S 3E5 *Applying science to community problems is of special interest to me because I see my science as a type of service. I am a religious man and like to think that my work is an expressive and integral part of my life of thought and faith.*

JESBERG, ROBERT OTTIS, JR., science educator; b. Springfield, Ill., Nov. 17, 1947; s. Robert O. Sr. and Catharine I. (Patton) J.; m. Ruth Marie Andreas, Aug. 21, 1971; children: Kate Debra, Amy Lyn. BA in Biology, Susquehanna U., 1969; MEd, Temple U., 1971, secondary prin. cert., 1974. Cert. secondary biology and gen. sci. tchr., secondary sch. prin. Sci. tchr. Centennial Schs., Warminster, Pa., 1969—, asst. prin., 1979, 85, 88; sci. cons. K'NEX Industries, Inc., Hatfield, Pa., 1994—; sci. coord. Centennial Schs., Warminster, Pa., 1996-98; mem. adv. com. Gov.'s Sci. Inst. Carnegie Mellon U., 1999—; site dir., instr. Lawrence Hall of Sci., NSF Summer Insts., U. Calif., Berkeley, 1990-92; sci. cons. Singapore Am. Schs., 1993; dir. adult edn. Centennial Schs., Warminster, Pa., 1984-97, staff devel. trainer, 1985—; instr. Pa. Commonwealth Excellence in Sci. Tchg. Alliance, Franklin Inst. Mus., Phila., 1996—. Author: (with others) K'NEX Racer Energy Educator Guide, 1996, K'NEX Bridges Educator Guide, 1996, K'NEX Educator Guide, 1995. Elder Lenape Valley Presbyn. Ch., New Britain, Pa., 1988—. Recipient Outstanding Sci. Supr. in Pa. Pa. Sci. Suprs. Assn., 1989; named Outstanding Educator in Bucks County, Pa. Bucks County ASCD, 1987, Outstanding Contbn. and Svc. to Bucks County ASCD, 1987. Mem. Nat. Sci. Tchrs. Assn., Pa. Math/Sci. Eisenhower Consortium (chairperson 1997-98), Bucks County Sci. Tchrs. Assn. (pres. 1992—). Republican. Home: 116 Blue Jay Rd Chalfont PA 18914-3104 Office: Log College Mid Sch 730 Norristown Rd Warminster PA 18974-2626

JESCHKE, THOMAS, gifted education educator. Dir. spl. edn. Des Moines Pub. Schs., 1975-93, exec. dir. student svcs., 1993—. Recipient Coun. of Admin. of Spec. Edn. Outstanding Admin. award, 1994. Office: Des Moines ISD Adminstrv Office 1800 Grand Ave Des Moines IA 50309-3310*

JESINSKY, SUSAN GAIL, special education educator; b. Las Cruces, N.Mex., Mar. 3, 1947; d. Joseph Hartful and Georgia Miram (Cothern) Arnold; m. Dennis Randolph Jesinsky, July 15, 1967; 1 child, Amber Elizabeth. BS in Secondary Edn., N.Mex. State U., Las Cruces, 1969, MA in Edn. Specialities, 1982. Cert. spl. edn. tchr., instrnl. leader, ednl. diagnostician, N.Mex. Social worker N.Mex. Dept. Human Svcs., Dona Ana County, 1969-71, social work supr., 1971-76; social worker III Children in Need of Supervision, N.Mex. Dept. Human Svcs., Dona Ana County, 1976-77; special edn. tchr. Gadsden Independent Schs., Anthony, N.Mex., 1980-82, edn. diagnostician, 1982-85, special edn. tchr.-behavior disorders, 1985-97; edu. diagnostician Ysleta Ind. Sch. Dist., El Paso, Tex., 1997—. Mem. Coun. for Exceptional Children, Phi Delta Kappa. Democrat. Baptist. Avocation: horses. Home: PO Box 353 Santa Teresa NM 88008-0353 Office: Ysleta Ind Sch Dist Spl Edn Dept 9600 Sims Dr El Paso TX 79925-7200

JESKE, CHARLES MATTHEW, lawyer; b. Bartlesville, Okla., July 16, 1964; s. Arnold Carl and Maudie Marie (Matthews) J.; m. Pamela Kay Paholek, May 20, 1989. BBA in Fin./Acctg., Tex. A&M U., 1986; JD, South Tex. Coll. Law, Houston, 1989. Bar: Tex. 1989, U.S. Dist. Ct. (so. dist.) Tex. 1990, U.S. Ct. Appeals (5th cir.) 1990. Briefing atty. 14th Dist. Ct. of Appeals Tex., Houston, 1989-90, 90-91; sr. assoc. atty. Renneker & Assocs., Houston, 1991-96; pvt. practice Houston, 1996—; Contractor, investment analyst Jeske Homes, Bryan, Tex., 1986—. Trustee, officer Meml. Hollow Citizens, Inc., Houston, 1994-96. Mem. Houston Bar Assn., Houston Young Lawyers Assn., Tex. A&M U. Former Students Assn., Phi Alpha Delta Alumni Assn. Republican. Lutheran. Avocations: photography, travel. Home and Office: 12407 Barryknoll Ln Houston TX 77024-4113

JESKE, HOWARD LEIGH, retired life insurance company executive, lawyer; b. York, Nebr., Sept. 25, 1917; s. Charles W. and Sina (Hanna) J.; m. Bettyclaire Barton, Nov. 23, 1943; children: Vaughn C., Craig B., Lynn Ellen Braziel, Laurel Claire McFarland. A.B., Cornell Coll., Mt. Vernon, Iowa, 1940; LL.B., McGeorge Coll. Law, Sacramento, 1951. Bar: Calif. 1951. Capt. USAAF, 1942-45. Mem. ABA, Calif. Bar Assn., Sutter Club (Sacramento). Republican. Home: 4035 Eagles Nest Auburn CA 95603-5922

JESSEN, CHRIS MICHAEL, music educator; b. Rolla, Mo., Nov. 25, 1972; s. Clark e. and Mary Ann (Knight) J. BS in Music Edn., Quincy (Ill.) U., 1995; MS in Ednl. Adminstrn., Columbia State U., Metairie, La., 1998, PhD in Ednl. Adminstrn., 1998. Lic. funeral dir. Dir. music North Wood R-IV Sch., Salem, Mo., 1996—; music min. Salem (Mo.) United Meth. Ch., 1995-98. Mem. NEA, Mo. Farm Bur., Masons,(K.T.), Shriners, Odd Fellows, St. Louis Area Assn. Jaguar Automobile Club N.Am. Democrat. Anglican. Home: RR 4 Box 466 Salem MO 65560-9224

JESSEN, DAVID WAYNE, accountant; b. Albuquerque, Jan. 13, 1950; s. Irving Matthew and Lucille Barbara (Huber) J.; m. Melissa Meyer, Oct. 4, 1975; children: Jennifer Leigh, Kimberly Paige. BBA in Acctg., U. N.Mex., 1972. CPA, N.C., N.Mex. Staff acct. local CPA firm, Albuquerque, 1971-74, jr. partner, 1974-75; mgr. in charge Santa Fe office Alford, Meroney & Co., CPA's, 1975-80, prin. in charge Santa Fe office, 1980-82; dir. taxes N.Mex. offices Arthur Young & Co., Albuquerque, 1980-86, tax ptnr., 1984—, ptnr.-in-charge, Raleigh, N.C., 1987-89; mem. Arthur Young Nat. Real Estate Com., 1988, mem. nat. hightech com., 1988-94; ptnr., dir. entrepreneurial svcs. Ernst & Young, Raleigh, 1989—, S.W. region dir. entrepreneurial svcs., 1992-94, dir. tax dept., 1995—. Asst. scoutmaster Boy Scouts Am.; bd. dirs. St. Joseph Hosp. Health Care Found., 1986-87; bd. dirs. N.C. Mus. Art Found., 1992—, treas., 1994—, Kiwanis Found. Eagle Scout., N.C. Mus. Art, 1994—, Bus. Friends Coun., N.C. Soc. to Prevent Blindness; mem. Ch.- Congregation at Duke U. Chapel; chmn. pres.'s cir. young exec. com. Wake Med. Ctr. Found., 1995—, bd. dirs., 1997—. Mem. AICPA (nat. com. small bus. taxation), Coun. for Entrepeneurial Devel. (treas. 1989-92, bd. dirs.), Nat. Assn. Accts. (Raleigh chpt., v.p., bd. dirs. 1989-91), N.Mex. Estate Planning Council, N.Mex. Soc. CPAs (taxation com., pub. relations com., v.p. Santa Fe chpt. 1980), N.C. Assn. CPAs, Santa Fe C. of C., Albuquerque C. of C., Raleigh C. of C., Santa Fe Jaycees, Albuquerque Jaycees, Alpha Kappa Psi. Lutheran. Lodges: Elks, Kiwanis, West Raleigh Rotary. Home: 4921 Misty Oak Dr Raleigh NC 27613-6349

JESSER, BENN WAINWRIGHT, chemical engineering and construction company executive; b. N.Y.C., June 10, 1915; s. Edward Arthur and Vera Wainwright (Benn) J.; m. Alice Forster Abeel, July 3, 1939 (dec.); m. Dorothea Potter Coogan, Aug. 29, 1954 (div.); children: Wendy, Penny, Bonnie Benn, John, Dorothea.; m. Barbara Gill Jenter, June 6, 1982. B.S. in Chem. Engring, Princeton U., 1936, M.S., 1941. Control engr. du Pont Co., Gibbstown, N.J., 1936-38; instr. Princeton U., 1938-42; v.p. ops. M.W. Kellogg, N.Y.C./London, 1942-71; pres. Hoechst-Uhde Corp., Englewood Cliffs, N.J., 1971-80, chem. engring. cons., 1980—. Contbr. articles to profl. jours. Chmn. bd. trustees Stoneleigh Burnham Sch.; bd. dirs. coun. Girl Scouts U.S.; trustee Saddle River Country Day Sch. Mem. Am. Inst. Chem. Engrs., ASME, Princeton Engring. Assn. (pres.), Class '36 Princeton (pres.), Com. Engring. Law, Princeton Alumni of Nantucket (pres.), Sigma Xi, Tau Beta Pi. Republican. Episcopalian. Clubs: Sankaty Head Golf, Amelia Island Plantation, Nantucket Yacht, Fox Meadow Tennis; Princeton (N.Y.C.). Home: 83 Sea Marsh Rd Amelia Island FL 32034-5040 *One of the most important characteristics for both happiness and success isenthusiasm. Enthusiasm is both contagious and catalytic. People around an enthusiastic person join in the enthusiasm for a project, a game or a trip. And enthusiasm has a catalytic effect in enhancing the chance of success of the event.*

JESSER, ROGER FRANKLYN, former brewing company engineering executive, consultant; b. Fort Collins, Colo., Mar. 8, 1926; m. Sarah Joanna Sunderland, June 16, 1946; children: Jan Karl, Robin Kay Jesser Bull. BSCE, Colo. State U., 1949. Lic. profl. engr., Colo., La., Va. Engr. U.S. Bur. Reclamation, Loveland, Colo., 1950-52, Western Engring. Co., Denver, 1952-54, Al Ryan Cons. Engr., Denver, 1954-55; engr. constrn. supr. Adolph Coors Co., Golden, Colo., 1955-76, v.p. constrn., 1976-81, v.p. engring. constrn., 1981-88, ret., 1988; cons. engr. Evergreen, Colo., 1988—; mem. engring. dean's coun. Colo. State U., 1987—, pres., 1992. Sec.-treas. Good Samaritan Health Svcs., 1986-87; mem. exec. com., bd. dirs. Luth. Med. Ctr., Wheatridge, Colo., 1980-99; commr. Jefferson County Housing Auth., 1990-96; mem. fgn. trip com. Denver Mus. Natural History, 1994—; bd. dirs. Hiwan Homeowners Assn., 1999. With USAAF, 1944-46. Mem. NSPE (bd. dirs. 1987-93, 97—), Profl. Engrs. Colo. (pres. 1984-85), Colo. Engring. Coun. (pres. 1989), Denvoys-Denver C. of C. (mem. exec. com. 1982—). Republican. Lutheran. Home: 2588 S Medinah Dr Evergreen CO 80439-8905

JESSERER, HENRY L., III, lawyer; b. Rochester, N.Y., Apr. 5, 1946. AB, John Carroll U., 1969; JD, U. Akron, 1973. Bar: N.Y. 1974, U.S. Dist. Ct. (we. dist.) N.Y. 1974, U.S. Supreme Ct. 1977. Mem. Harris, Beach & Wilcox, Rochester. Mem. Trevett, Lenweaver, & Salzer. Office: Trevett Lenweaver & Salzer 700 Reynolds Arcade 16 E Main St Rochester NY 14614-1808

JESSOR, RICHARD, psychologist, educator; b. Bklyn., Nov. 24, 1924; s. Thomas and Clara (Merkin) J.; m. Shirley Glasser, Sept. 27, 1948 (div. 1982); children: Kim, Tom; m. Jane Ava Menken, Nov. 13, 1992. Student, CCNY, 1941-43; BA, Yale U., 1946; MA, Columbia U., 1947; PhD, Ohio State U., 1951. Intern, clin. psychology trainee VA/Ohio State U., Columbus, 1947-50; asst. prof. psychology U. Colo., Boulder, 1951-56, assoc. prof., 1956-61, prof., 1961—, dir. rsch. program problem behavior Inst. Behavioral Sci., 1966-97, dir. Inst. Behavioral Sci., 1980—; dir. MacArthur Found. Rsch. Network on Successful Adolescent Devel. Among Youth in High Risk Settings, 1987-96; cons. Nat. Inst. on Drug Abuse, 1975-76, Nat. Inst. on Alcohol Abuse and Alcoholism, 1976-80, WHO, Geneva, 1976-80; cons. in field. Author: (with T.D. Graves, R.C. Hanson & S.L. Jessor) Society, Personality, and Deviant Behavior: A Study of a Tri-Ethnic Community, 1968, (with S.L. Jessor) Problem Behavior and Psychosocial Development: A Longitudinal Study of Youth, 1977, (with J.E. Donovan and F. Costa) Beyond Adolescence: Problem Behavior and Young Adult Development, 1991; co-editor: Contemporary Approaches to Cognition, 1957, Cognition, Personality and Clinical Psychology, 1967, Perspectives on Behavioral Science: the Colorado Lectures, 1991, Ethnography and Human Development: Context and Meaning in Social Inquiry, 1996; editor: New Perspectives on Adolescent Risk Behavior, 1998; cons. editor Jour. Cons. and Clin. Psychology, 1975-77, Cmty. Mental Health Jour., 1974-78, Alcohol Health and Rsch. World, 1981-90, Alcohol, Drugs and Driving, 1985—, Adolescent Medicine: State of the Art Revs., 1989—; cons. editor Sociometry, 1964-66, assoc. editor, 1966-69; contbr. articles to profl. jours. Served with USMC, 1943-46, PTO. Decorated Purple Heart; Social Sci. Rsch. Coun. pre-doctoral fellow Ohio State and Yale U., 1950-51; Social Sci. Rsch. Coun. fellow Ohio State U., 1954, Social Sci. Rsch. Coun. postdoctoral fellow U. Calif.-Berkeley, 1956-57, NIMH spl. rsch. fellow Harvard-Florence Rsch. Project, Italy, 1965-66, Ctr. for Advanced Study in the Behavioral Scis. fellow Stanford U., 1995-96; recipient Faculty Rsch. Lectureship award U. Colo., 1981-82; Gallagher lectr. Soc. Adolescent Medicine, 1987. Fellow APA, Am. Psychol. Soc. (charter fellow); mem. Soc. for Psychol. Study of Social Issues, Am. Sociol. Assn., Soc. for Study of Social Problems. Avocations: mountain climbing, running marathons. Home: 402 Hapgood St Boulder CO 80302-6911 Office: U Colo Inst Behavioral Sci CB 483 Boulder CO 80309

JESSUP, EDWIN HARLEY, III, aerospace engineering executive; b. New Haven, Mar. 5, 1947; s. Edwin Harley Jr. and Patricia Ann (Potter) J.; m. Laura French Lally, May 22, 1975; children: Todd Benjamin, Brian Arthur. BS in Aerospace Engring., Brown U., 1968; MS in Aero. Engring., USAF Inst. Tech., Wright-Patterson AFB, Ohio, 1976. Commd. 2nd lt. USAF, 1968, advanced through grades to lt. col., 1992; pilot USAF, various locations, 1968-75; program mgr. USAF, Wright-Patterson AFB, 1976-80; dir. tng. USAF, Loring AFB, Maine, 1980-84; dir. operational testing and evaluation USAF, Edwards AFB, Calif., 1984-90; ret., 1990; aerospace engring. mgr. Delex Sys., Inc., California, Md., 1991—; USAF Avionics Lab. rep. Joint Technical Coord. Group/Joint Munitions Effectiveness Manual, 1982-84. Named Project Engr. of Yr. Wright Aero. Labs., Wright-Patterson AFB, 1980. Mem. Air Force Assn., Order of Daedalians (chpt. adjutant 1984—), Ret. Officers Assn., Tau Beta Pi. Roman Catholic. Avocations: private piloting, sailing. Home: 2460 Abigail Ct Prince Frederick MD 20678 Office: Delex Systems Inc 44425 Pecan Ct Ste 152 California MD 20619

JESSUP, JAN AMIS, arts volunteer, writer; b. Chgo., Aug. 10, 1927; d. Herman Harvey and Anita (Lincoln) Sinako; m. Everett Orme Amis, Dec. 20, 1970 (dec. Nov. 1981); m. Joe Lee Jessup, Apr. 16, 1989. BA, U. Minn., 1948; postgrad., Rutgers U., 1969-70. bd. dirs., exec. com. Broward Ctr. for Performing Arts Pacers, Fort Lauderdale, Fla., 1985-88, pres., 1987-88; speaker U. Internat. Bus., Beijing, 1985. Active not-for-profit orgns. including Girl Scouts U.S., Boy Scouts Am., Presbyn. Ch.; beautification com. Lighthouse Point, Fla., 1978-89, sec., 1988-91; rep. to Fla. Art Orgns., 1987-88; bd. dirs. Archways, Ft. Lauderdale, 1987-91; trustee Miami City Ballet, 1991-94; adv. bd. Guild of the Palm Beaches, 1994-95; bd. govs. Fla. Philharm. Orch., 1981—, v.p. representing all affiliates, 1985-87, 92, 94-96, exec. com., 1989-93, v.p. individual giving, 1991-92, bd. dirs., 1994—, chmn. affiliate com., 1994-95, v.p. vols., 1995-96, chmns. adv. coun., 1996-98; bd. trustees The Harid Conservatory, Boca Raton, 1997—, mem. steering com. The Harid Conservatory Sch. Music at Lynn U., Fla. Grand Opera, 1993—, Concert Assn. Fla., Inc., 1995-98; mem. Palm Beach Cultural Coun., 1993—; advisor Friends of Philharm., 1996-97; pres. pro-tem The Harid Guild of The Harid Conservatory, 1998-99; mem. bd. dirs. The Harid Guild. Mem. Nat. Soc. Arts and Letters, Am. Symphony Orch. League (vice chmn. 1989-90, sec. vol. coun. 1986-87, v.p. 1987-88, pres. 1989-90, advisor 1990-91, assoc. Resource Devel. Inst. 1996—, bd. dirs. 1998—), The Opus Soc. (bd. dirs., m. exec. com. 1981—, chmn. 1981-85), Ft. Lauderdale Philharm. Soc. (bd. dirs. 1986—), Opera Soc. (sec. 1986-87, v.p. pub. rels. 1987-88), Royal Palm Dinner Theatre (bd. dirs., 1998—), Gold Coast Jazz Soc. (bd. dirs. 1992-98, v.p. 1994-98), Royal Dames of Cancer Rsch. (bd. trustees 1995-97), Boca Raton Resort and Club , Royal Palm Yacht and Country Club, Royal Palm Yacht and Country Club Women's Club, Sea Grape Garden Club (past pres.). Republican. Avocations: music listening, boating, fishing, writing, bridge playing. Home: 133 Coconut Palm Rd Boca Raton FL 33432-7975

JESSUP, JOE LEE, business educator, management consultant; b. Cordele, Ga., June 23, 1913; s. Horace Andrew and Elizabeth (Wilson) J.; m. Janet Amis, Apr. 16, 1989. BS, U. Ala., 1936; MBA, Harvard U., 1941; LLD (hon.), Chung-Ang U., Seoul, Korea, 1964. Sales rep. Proctor & Gamble, 1937-40; liaison officer bur. pub. rels. U.S. War Dept., 1941; spl. asst. and exec. asst. Far Ea. div. and office exports Bd. Econ. Warfare, 1942-43; exec. officer to chief of staff Svcs. of Supply-Europian Theatre, 1943-44; exec. officer, office deptl. adminstrn. Dept. State, 1946; exec. sec. adminstr.'s adv. coun. War Assets Adminstrn., 1946-48; v.p. sales Airken, Capitol & Service Co., 1948-52; assoc. prof. bus. adminstrn. George Washington U., 1952, prof., 1952-77, prof. emeritus, 1977—, asst. dean Sch. Govt., 1951-60; pres. Jessup and Co., Ft. Lauderdale, Fla., 1957—; bd. dirs. Giant Food, Inc., Washington (audit comm. 1974-75), 1971-75, Am. Equity Investors, Inc., 1986-87, Hunter Assn. Labs, Fairfax, Va., 1964-69 (exec. comm. 1966-69, exec. v.p. 1967, gen. mgr. 1969), coordinator Air Force Resources Mgmt. program, 1951-57; del. in edn. 10th Internat. Mgmt. Conf., Sao Paulo, Brazil, 1954, 11th Conf., Paris, 1957, 12th Conf., Sydney and Melbourne, Australia, 1960, 13th Conf., Rotterdam, Netherlands, 1966, 14th Conf., Tokyo, 1969, 15th Conf., Munich, Germany, 1972; mem. Md. Econ. Devel. Adv. Commn., 1973-75. Mem. Civil Svc. Commn., Arlington County, Va., 1952-54; mem. nat. adv. coun. Ctr. for Study of Presidency, 1974—; mem. bd. overseers Lynn U., Boca Raton, 1991—; mem. adv. bd. Youth Automotive Tng. Ctr., Hollywood, Fla., 1993—; mem. Atlanta regional panel for selection of White House fellow, 1990-95, mem. Miami regional panel, 1994-95; trustee Tng. Within Industry Found., Summit, N.J., 1954-58, Philharm Orch., Fla., 1986-91; mem. Chaine des Rotisseurs, 1987-92, 94—. Decorated Bronze Star; recipient cert. of appreciation Sec. of Air Force, 1957. Mem. Harvard Club (N.Y.C.), Univ. Club (Washington), Royal Palm Yacht and Country Club. Home: 133 Coconut Palm Rd Boca Raton FL 33432-7975

JESSUP, JOHN BAKER, lawyer; b. N.Y.C., July 30, 1921; s. Henry Herbert and Eugenia Griffin (Baker) J.; m. LaVerle J. Jessen, July 29, 1989; 1 child from previous marriage, John M. BA, Yale U., 1942, LLB, 1948. Bar: N.Y. 1948, Conn. 1955. Assoc. Winthrop Stimson Putnam & Roberts, N.Y.C., 1948-58, ptnr., 1959-93; counsel, 1994—. Mem. Zoning and Planning Commn., Ridgefield, Conn., 1958-65. Lt. USN, 1942-46, PTO. Mem. N.Y. State Bar Assn., Conn. Bar Assn., Down Town Assn., N.Y. Yacht Club. Republican. Episcopalian. Avocation: sailing. Office: Winthrop Stimson et al 1 Battery Park Plz New York NY 10004-1405

JESSUP, PAUL FREDERICK, financial economist, educator; b. Evanston, Ill., Apr. 16, 1939; s. Paul S. and Gertrude (Strohmaier) J.; m. Johanna A.M. Friesen, June 27, 1970; children: Christine Marieke, Paul Charles Friesen. BS, Northwestern U., 1960, PhD, 1966; AM, Harvard U., 1963; BA, U. Oxford, Eng., 1963; M.A., U. Oxford, 1983. Economist com. banking and currency U.S. Ho. of Reps., Washington, 1963-64; faculty U. Minn., Mpls., 1967-82; prof. fin. U. Minn., 1973-82; with Jessup & Co., Inc., St. Paul, 1982—; William Kahlert prof. mgmt. and econs. Hamline U., St. Paul, 1988—; dir. Gerbill Inc.; Sabbatical prof. in residence Fed. Res. Bank, Mpls., 1973-74. Author: The Theory and Practice of Nonpar Banking, 1967, (with Roger B. Upson) Returns in Over-the-Counter Stock Markets, 1973, Competing for Stock Market Profits, 1974, Modern Bank Management: A Casebook, 1978, Modern Bank Management, 1980; editor: Innovations in Bank Management: Selected Readings, 1969; contbr. articles to profl. jours. Bd. dirs. St. Mark's Found., Assocs. of the James Ford Bell Libr. Mem. Midwest Fin. Assn. (past pres.). Clubs: Skylight (Mpls.); Univ. Club (Chgo.). Home: 1979 Shryer Ave W Saint Paul MN 55113-5414 Office: Hamline U 1536 Hewitt Ave Saint Paul MN 55104-1284

JESSUP, PHILIP CARYL, JR., lawyer, museum executive; b. Utica, N.Y., Aug. 30, 1926; s. Philip C. and Lois K. (Kellogg) J.; m. Dorothy A. Kerr, Jan. 15, 1951 (div.); children: Timothy, Nancy, Margaret; m. Helen I. Ibbitson, Jan.24, 1969; stepchildren: Genevieve, Lucinda, Francesca, Alexander. B.A., Yale Coll., 1949; J.D., Harvard U., 1952. Bar: N.Y. 1954. Atty. Whitman, Ransom & Coulson, N.Y.C., 1952-58; legal officer Internat. Nickel Co., Inc., N.Y.C., 1958-63; gen. solicitor internat. Inco Ltd., N.Y.C., 1963-68; chief legal officer, sec., dir. Inco Europe Ltd., London, 1968-72; pres., mng. dir. P.T. Internat. Nickel Indonesia, Jakarta, 1972-78; v.p., gen. counsel and sec. Inco Ltd., N.Y.C., Toronto, Can., 1978-84; sec., gen. counsel Nat. Gallery Art, Washington, 1985—; dir. Biogen N.V., Geneva, 1981-85; chmn. bd. Inco Gulf, E.C., Bahrain, 1980-84. Trustee Oberlin, Internat. Book Inst. Inc., Phila., 1978—, sec.-treas., 1989-96, chmn. bd., 1996—; mem. adv. commn. H.H. Humphrey Fellowship Program, 1984-89;

trustee Asia Soc., 1991-99, sec., 1993-99, mem. adv. com. Washington Ctr., 1985—, chmn. adv. com., 1989—; pres. Friends of Hosp. for Sick Children, Toronto, 1985—; mem. Coun. on Fgn. Rels., N.Y.C., 1972—; pres. West Brooklyn Ind. Dems., 1956-58. Served to staff/sgt. C.E., U.S. Army, 1944-46. Mem. ABA, Assn. of Bar of City of N.Y., Century Assn. (N.Y.C.). Democrat. Home: 3415 O St NW Washington DC 20007-2817 Office: Nat Gallery Art Washington DC 20565

JESSUP, R. JUDD, health care executive; b. San Francisco, Oct. 15, 1947; s. R. Bruce and Adaline (Brown) J.; m. Jeanne Bannash, Sept. 7, 1968 (div. Dec. 1987); children: Jarrett, Jody, Rik, Alycia; m. Charlene Massei, May 19, 1990. BA, Knox Coll., 1969; MBA, U. Denver, 1971. Dir. mktg. svcs. Blue Cross-Blue Shield Colo., Denver, 1972-78, dir. alternate delivery systems, 1978-80; pres. HMO Colorado, Inc., Denver, 1980-87, TakeCare Health Plan, Concord, Calif., 1987-94, TakeCare, Inc., 1991-94; pres. HMO divsn. F.H.P. Internat., Fountain Valley, Calif., 1994-96; pvt. investor, 1996—; bd. dirs. Adesso Specialty Svcs. Orgn., Corvel Corp., Novamed Eyecare Svcs., Pacific Dental Benefits, U.S. Labs., Inc., Millennium Health, Inc. Avocation: golf. Home: 30962 Via Serenidad Trabuco Canyon CA 92679-4002

JESSUP, WARREN T., retired lawyer; b. Eureka, Calif., Aug. 1, 1916; s. Thurman W. and Amelia (Johnson) J.; m. Evelyn Via, Sept. 13, 1941; children: Thurman W., Paul H., Stephen T., Marilyn R. Jessup Huffman. B.S., U. So. Calif., 1937; J.D., George Washington U., 1942. Bar: D.C. 1941, Calif. 1947, U.S. Dist. Ct. (cen., so., no. dists.) Calif. 1947, U.S. Ct. Appeals (Fed. cir., 9th cir.) 1947, U.S. Supreme Ct. 1947. Engr. Gen. Electric Co., 1937-38, patent dept., 1938-42; mem. patent div. USN, 1944-46; patent counsel 11th Naval Dist., 1946-50; mem. Huebner, Beehler, Worrel & Herzig, 1950-56; ptnr. Herzig & Jessup, 1957-59; individual practice law, 1959-68; mem. firm Jessup & Beecher, Sherman Oaks, also, L.A., 1968-85, Jessup Beecher & Slehofer, Westlake Village, Calif., 1985-93, Jessup & Slehofer, Westlake Village, Calif., 1993-94; ret.; patent expert, cons., 1994—; instr. patent law, grad. div. Law Sch. U. So. Calif.; instr. bus. law U. Calif. at L.A. Author: Patent Guide for Navy Inventors, 1950; Contbr. to: Ency. of Patent Practice and Invention Mgmt. Chmn. citizens adv. com. Point Mugu State Pk., 1973; active Ventura County Mental Health Bd.; mem. Ventura County Mental Health Adv. Bd., 1977-82, chmn., 1979. Lt. comdr. USN, 1942-46, comdr. Res. Mem. Patent Law Assn. Los Angeles (pres. 1974-75), NSPE, Am. Intellectual Property Law Assn., Conejo Valley Bar Assn. (pres. 1987), Conejo Valley Hist. Soc. (bd. dirs. 1971-83), Order of Coif, Tau Beta Pi, Eta Kappa Nu, Phi Kappa Phi, Phi Delta Phi. Baptist. Home: 1697 W Potrero Rd Thousand Oaks CA 91361-5022 *"Have no anxiety about anything; for all things work together for good to them that love God." Many times the limitations in human faith make it impossible to believe that. But it is true and will materialize whenever faith is strong enough to let God rule.*

JESTER, JACK D., lawyer; b. Columbus, Ohio, Jan. 31, 1946. BS, Ohio State U., 1968, JD, 1971; LLM, U. Mo., 1972. Bar: Ohio 1971, Ill. 1978. Gen. counsel, atty. inspector Ohio Divsn. Securities, 1973-74; mem. Coffield, Ungaretti & Harris (now named Ungaretti & Harris), Chgo.; spl. counsel City Counselors Office, Kansas City, Mo., 1971-72; counsel Mayor's Environ. Control Task Force, Kansas City, 1971-72. Contbr. articles to profl. jours. Mem. ABA, Urban Land Inst., Mortgage Bankers Assn., Nat. Assn. Bond Lawyers, Ill. State Bar Assn., Ohio State Bar Assn., Internat. Coun. Shopping Ctrs. Office: Ungaretti & Harris 3500 Three 1st Nat Plz Chicago IL 60602*

JESTIN, HEIMWARTH B., retired university administrator; b. Montreal, Que., Can., Sept. 24, 1918; s. Emil Ernst and Rosa (Ege) J.; m. Catherine M. Townshend, Oct. 14, 1944; children—Loftus, Jennifer, Carolyn. B.S., Central Conn. State Coll., 1947; M.A., Yale, 1949, Ph.D., 1954. Head English dept., tchr. history Thomaston (Conn.) High Sch., 1947-50; prin. Canton High Sch., Collinsville, Conn., 1951-53; supt. schs. Canton, Conn., 1953-62; prof. philosophy and edn. Central Conn. State Coll., 1956-65, dean coll., 1965-67, v.p. acad. affairs, 1967-85; provost Conn. State U., 1985-87; prof. U. Hartford, 1961-63. Author: Critical Experiences During the Early Years of Superintendency, 1955, The Canton Evaluation Plan, 1960, Role of the Superintendent of Schools in Connecticut, 1967, Ecology Holds Key to Man's Destiny, 1969, Well-Educated Barbarians, 1970, Higher Education Direction, 1971, Year Round Schooling Keyed to Modern Need, 1972, For a New State University System, 1977, They Know a Lot, But are They Educated?, 1977, Crucial Year for Higher Education, 1978, Enrollments Not Nose Diving, 1979, To Improve Higher Education, a Two-Tier University System, 1980, For a State University System, 1981; co-editor: The Connecticut Study of the Role of the Public School, 1960. Trustee Roaring Brook Nature Center; bd. mgrs., life mem. Conn. PTA. Served with AUS, 1941-46. Decorated Order Brit. Empire. Mem. Conn. Council Sch. Coll. Rels. (hon.). Home: 180 Garden St Farmington CT 06032-2208

JESUP, CYNTHIA SMITH (CINDY JESUP), elementary education educator; b. Beaumont, Tex., Sept. 3, 1956; d. Rayburn E. and Lula Delle (Fancher) Smith; m. Richard Douglas Jesup, Sept. 9, 1978; children: Alexis, Derrick. BS, Auburn (Ala.) U., 1979; M, Nova U., Ft. Lauderdale, Fla., 1994. Cert. tchr. art K-12, exceptionalities K-12, phys. edn. K-8, 6-12, Fla. Tchr. phys. edn., coach Trantwood Elem., Virginia Beach, Va., 1980-82; tchr. phys. edn./health, coach Huntsville (Ala.) City Schs., 1983-88; tchr. art, exceptional student edn., elem. resource, phys. edn. Samsula Elem., New Smyrna Beach, Fla., 1992—; trainer Fla. B.A.L.A.N.C.E. Fla. Diagnostic Learning Resources, Daytona Beach, 1995—; Fla. chair visual arts lesson plans/electronic curriculum Fla. Dept. Edn., 1996; vol. tchr. family art workshops, 1993—; tchr., founder Art Through the Ages art camp, 1997. Contbr. articles to 1994 Elem. Resource Guide. Sch. improvement chair Samsula Elem., 1995—; vol., instr., mem. Mus. of Arts and Sci., Daytona Beach, 1992-96; workshop leader Very Spl. Arts Festival, Daytona Beach, 1992—; sch. rep. Dist. Adv. Coun., Volusia County, Fla., 1994-95; rep. Parent Adv. Coun. Spruce Creek H.S., 1996—; bd. dirs., mem. PTA, Huntsville and Volusia City, 1987—. Named Fla. Elem. Art Tchr. of Yr., Fla. Art Edn. Assn., 1996; recipient Edn.'s Unsung Heroes award No. Life, 1996, Crystal Apple award S.E. C. of C., Volusia, 1995; Fulbright fellow Inst. Internat. Edn., Japan, 1997; grantee Futures, 1993, 95, 96, 97, 98, 99, Fla. Dept. Edn. Bus. Partnership, 1994, 96, S.E. Kiwanis, 1994, 96, 97, New Smyrna Rotary, 1994, Bryant Foods, 1994, Jr. League, 1995, Port Orange Kiwanis, 1996, 97. Mem. Coun. for Exceptional Children (pres., internat. del., grantee 1996, award of excellence, FFCEC pres. award), Nat. Art Edn. Assn. (del. elem. divsn.), Fla. Art Edn. Assn. (dir. elem. divsn.), Volusia Art Assn. (pres.), Internat. Reading Assn., Volusia County Reading Coun., Art Haus (program com.), Phi Delta Kappa. Office: Samsula Elem Sch 248 N Samsula Dr New Smyrna Beach FL 32168-8762

JETER, DEREK, baseball player; b. Pequannock, N.J., June 26, 1974. Baseball player N.Y. Yankees, 1995—. Named Am. League Rookie of Yr. Baseball Writers Assn. of Am., 1996, Minor League Player of Yr. The Sporting News, 1994. Achievements include member of World Series Champions, 1996. Office: NY Yankees Yankee Stadium E 161st and River Ave Bronx NY 10451*

JETER, KATHERINE LESLIE BRASH, lawyer; b. Gulfport, Miss., July 24, 1921; d. Ralph Edward and Rosa Meta (Jacobs) Brash; m. Robert McLean Jeter, Jr., May 11, 1946. BA, Newcomb Coll. of Tulane U., 1943; JD, Tulane U., 1945. Bar: La. 1945, U.S. Dist. Ct. (we. dist.) La. 1948, U.S. Tax Ct. 1965, U.S. Supreme Ct. 1971, U.S. Dist. Ct. (ea. dist.) La. 1975, U.S. Ct. Appeals (5th cir.) 1981, U.S. Dist. Ct. (mid. dist.) La. 1982. Assoc. Montgomery, Fenner & Brown, New Orleans, 1945-46, Tucker, Martin, Holder, Jeter & Jackson, Shreveport, 1947-79; ptnr. Tucker, Jeter, Jackson and Hickman and predecessors, Shreveport, 1980—; judge pro tem 1st Jud. Dist. Ct., Caddo Parish, La., 1982-83; mem. adv. com. to joint legis. subcom. on mgmt. of the community; pres. YWCA of Shreveport, 1963; hon. consul of France; Shreveport, 1982-91; pres. Little Theatre of Shreveport, 1966-67; pres. Shreveport Art Guild, 1974-75; mem. task force crim justice La. Priorities for the Future, 1978; pres. LWV of Shreveport, 1950-51. Recipient Disting. Grad. award Tulane U., 1983. Mem. Am. Law Inst., La. State Law Inst. (mem. coun. 1980—, adv. com. La. Civil Code 1973-77, temp. ad hoc. com. 1976-77, sr. officer 1993—), Am. Law Inst., Pub. Affairs Rsch. Coun. (bd. trustees 1976-81, 91—, exec. com. 1981-84, area exec. committeeman Shreveport area 1982), ABA, La. Bar Assn., Shreveport Bar Assn. (pres. 1986), Nat. Assn. Women Lawyers, Shreveport Assn. for Women Attys., C. of C. Shreveport (bd. dirs. 1975-77), Order of Coif, Phi Beta Kappa. Author: (with Fredricka Doll Gute) Historical Profile, Shreveport 1850, 1982; author: A Man and His Boat, The Civil War Career and Correspondence of Lieutenant Jonathan H. Carter, 1996; contbr. articles on law to profl. jours. Home: 3959 Maryland Ave Shreveport LA 71106-1021 Office: 401 Edwards St Ste 905 Shreveport LA 71101-5509

JETER, WAYBURN STEWART, retired microbiology educator, microbiologist; b. Cooper, Tex., Feb. 16, 1926; s. Joseph Plato and Beulah (Stewart) J.; m. Margaret Ann McDonald, May 30, 1947; children—Randall Mark, Monette Ann, Marcus Kent. B.S., U. Okla., 1948, M.S., 1949; Ph.D., U. Wis., 1950. Diplomate: Am. Bd. Microbiology. Mem. faculty U. Iowa, 1950-63, assoc. prof., 1958-63; prof. microbiology U. Ariz., Tucson, 1963-89, prof. microbiology emeritus, 1989—, prof. pharmacology and toxicology, 1983-91, prof. pharmacology and toxicology emeritus, 1991—, head dept. microbiology and med. tech., 1967-83, dir. lab. cellular immunology, 1976-91; dir. med. tech. program U. Ariz., 1976-79; vis. prof. immunology and med. microbiology U. Fla., 1980; pres. Scientific Rels. Svcs., Inc., 1988—. Contbr. articles profl. jours. Served with USNR, 1943-46. Fellow AAAS; mem. Am. Acad. Microbiology, Am. Assn. Immunologists, Ariz. Acad. Sci., Am. Soc. Microbiology (mem. council 1975-77), Soc. Exptl. Biology and Medicine, Sigma Xi. Democrat. Presbyterian. Home: 5140 N Via Sempreverde Tucson AZ 85750-5966

JETT, DENNIS COLEMAN, foreign service officer; b. Waltham, Mass., June 26, 1945; s. Clifton H. and Helen (Driscoll) J.; children: Brian, Allison, Noa; m. Lynda Schuster, Dec. 31, 1989. BA, U. N.Mex., 1967, MA, 1969; PhD in Internat. Rels., U. Witwatersrand, 1998, postgrad. Political officer U.S. Embassy, Buenos Aires, Argentina; watch officer Operations Ctr. Dept. of State, Washington, 1975-76; economist Econ. Bureau Dept. of State, Washington, 1976-80; sci. attache U.S. Embassy, Tel Aviv, Israel, 1980-83; deputy chief of mission U.S. Embassy, Lilongwe, Malawi, 1986-89, Monrovia, Liberia, 1989-91; exec. asst. to under sec. for polit. affairs Dept. of State, Washington, 1992-93; acting spl. asst. to the President Nat. Security Coun., Washington, 1993; amb. to Mozambique U.S. Embassy, Maputo, 1993-96; amb. to Peru U.S. Embassy, Lima, 1996—. Lt. USNR, 1965-72. Recipient Disting. Honor award, 1991, Cobb award, 1999. Mem. Am. Fgn. Svc. Assn. (Christian A. Herter award 1995). Office: Am Embassy Lima APO AA 34031

JETT, STEPHEN CLINTON, geography and textiles educator, researcher; b. Cleve., Oct. 12, 1938; s. Richard Scudder Jett and Miriam Ida (Horn) Greene; m. Mary Frances Manak, Aug. 7, 1971 (div. 1977); 1 child, Jennifer Frances; m. Lisa Sue Roberts, June 17, 1995. AB, Princeton U., 1960; postgrad., U. Ariz., 1962-63; PhD, Johns Hopkins U., 1964. Instr. geography Ohio State U., Columbus, 1963-64; asst. prof. U. Calif., Davis, 1964-72, assoc. prof., 1972-79, prof., 1979—, chmn., 1978-82, 88-89. Author: Navajo Wildlands, 1967 (1 of 50 Books of Yr., Am. Inst. Graphic Arts 1967, 1 of 20 Merit Award Books, Western Book Pubs. Assn. 1969), House of Three Turkeys, 1977, Navajo Architecture, 1981 (1 of Outstanding Acad. Books, Choice mag. ALA 1981); (monograph) Tourism in the Navajo Country, 1966; editor jour. Pre-Columbiana; contbr. numerous articles to profl. jours. and chpts. to books. Mem. Hist. and Landmarks Commn., Davis, 1969-73; vice chmn. Gen. Plan Noise Element Study Com., Davis, 1974-76, chmn. ad hoc citizens noise com., 1997-98; mem. exec. coun. Univ. Farms Unit Number 1 Neighborhood Assn., Davis, 1987-90. Fellow Am. Geog. Soc., Explorers Club; mem. AAAS, Assn. Am. Geographers (chair Am. Indian spltty. group 1989-91), Soc. Am. Archaeology, Epigraphic Soc. (bd. dirs. 1996—), Inst. for Study of Am. Cultures (bd. dirs. 1996—). Avocations: travel, photography, textiles and other ethnographic arts, French language and culture. Office: U Calif Davis Divsn Textiles and Clothing 1 Shields Ave Davis CA 95616-5270

JETT, TERRI RENEE, educator; b. Oakland, Calif., Dec. 7, 1963; d. Kenneth Alonzo and Beatrice Jett; children: Akilah Jenee Shahid, Talib Isaac Shahid. BA, Calif. State U., Hayward, 1991, MPA, 1994; PhD, Auburn U., 1998. Grad. tchg. asst. Auburn (Ala.) U., 1994-98, instr., 1998—. Grad. Equity fellow Calif. State U., Hayward, Affirmative Action Office, 1992-94; Pres. Grad. fellow Auburn U., 1994-98. Mem. ASPA, Am. Polit. Sci. Assn., Auburn Black Caucus (Grad. Student of Yr. 1992). Democrat. Presbyterian.

JETTE, ERNEST ARTHUR, lawyer; b. Nashua, N.H., Apr. 19, 1945; s. Fernand Ernest and Jeannette M. (Thibodeau) J.; m. Bridget Belton, Sept. 4, 1977; 1 child, Alexandra. BA, Boston Coll., 1967, JD, 1970. Bar: N.H. 1970, U.S. Dist. Ct. N.H. 1971, U.S. Tax Ct. 1972; diplomate Trial Practice Inst. Mng. atty. N.H. Legal Assistance, Nashua, 1970-72; ptnr. Janelle, Nadeau & Jette, Nashua, 1972-81; dir. Hamblett & Kerrigan, P.A., Nashua, 1981-93; pvt. practice Nashua, 1993—; lectr. paralegal studies Rivier Coll., Nashua, 1977-78. Chmn. Nashua Regional Planning Commn., 1981-82; mem. Town of Merrimack (N.H.) Master Plan Com., 1981, dir. Nashua Youth Coun., Inc., 1975-80, pres., 1978-79; dir. NEEDS, Inc., 1972-75; chmn. Heart Sunday, N.H. Heart Assn., 1973; mem. pub. affairs com. N.H. Assn. Commerce and Industry, 1983-93; mem. sch. bd. Bishop Guertin H.S., 1994-96. Capt. U.S. Army, 1970. Mem. ABA (state com. disaster legal assistance 1973-75, litigation, tort and ins. practice sects.), N.H. Bar Assn. (past mem. law related edn., coop. with the cts., profl. responsibility coms.), N.H. Bar Found., N.H. Trial Lawyers Assn., Nashua Bar Assn. (pres. 1990-91), Greater Nashua C. of C. (dir. 1985-96), Four Seasons Property Owners' Assn. (pres. 1977-78), Rotary Club Nashua (dir. 1978-79, pres. 1992-93). Home: 9 Westbrook Dr Nashua NH 03060-5314 Office: 7 Concord St Nashua NH 03060-2328

JETTER, ARTHUR CARL, JR., insurance company executive; b. Omaha, Oct. 9, 1947; s. Arthur Carl and Virginia Ann (Turner) J.; m. Jennifer Ann Jochim, Mar. 30, 1974; children: Arthur Carl III, Sarah Ann. BBA, Dana Coll., 1974. Registered health underwriter; CFP, CLU; registered employee benefits cons.; FLMI. Sales rep. life ins. Guarantee Mut., Omaha, 1974-81; pres. Art Jetter & Co., Omaha, 1981—, Employers Mut. Acceptance Co., Omaha, 1981—. Capt. inf. U.S. Army, 1968-72, Vietnam. Fellow Life Mgmt. Inst.; mem. CLU (cert., edn. chmn. Omaha chpt. 1984-91), Nat. Assn. Health Underwriters (pres. 1991-92, Gordon Meml. award 1995, Health Ins. Industry person of yr. 1995). Republican. Lutheran. Home: 13624 Parker Cir Omaha NE 68154-3829 Office: Art Jetter and Co 11305 Chicago Cir Omaha NE 68154-2636

JETTKE, HARRY JEROME, retired government official; b. Detroit, Jan. 2, 1925; s. Harry H. and Eugenia M. (Dziatkiewicz) J.; B.A., Wayne State U., 1961; m. Josefina Suarez-Garcia, Oct. 22, 1948; 1 child, Joan Lillian Clark. Owner, operator Farmacia Virreyes/Farmacia Regina, Toluca, Mex., 1948-55; intern pharmacist Cunningham Drug Stores, Detroit, 1955-63; drug specialist, product safety specialist FDA, Detroit, 1963-73; acting dir. Cleve., U.S. Consumer Product Safety Commn., 1973-75, compliance officer, 1975-78, supr., investigations, 1978-82, regional compliance officer, 1982-83, sr. resident, 1983-90; ret., 1990. Served with Fin. Dept., U.S. Army, 1942-43. Drug specialist FDA. Mem. Am. Soc. for Quality Control (sr., chmn. Cleve. sect. 1977-78, cert. quality technician, cert. quality engr.), Asociación Nacional Mexicana de Estadistica y Control de Calidad, Ohio Gun Collectors Assn., Cleve. Fed. Exec. Bd. (policy com.), 1985. Roman Catholic. Home: 25715 Yeoman Dr Cleveland OH 44145-4745

JETTON, GIRARD REUEL, JR., lawyer, retired oil company executive; b. Washington, Feb. 19, 1924; s. Girard Reuel and Hallie (Grimes) J.; m. Mera Riddell, Sept. 4, 1948 (dec. Dec. 1997); children: Mera Elizabeth, Robert Girard, James Thomas. BS in Engring., George Washington U., 1945, BA, 1947; JD, Harvard U., 1950. Bar: D.C. 1951, Md. 1959, Ohio 1960. Elec. engr. in rsch., 1944-45; patent atty. Washington, 1950-51; atty. IRS, Washington, 1951-54; trial atty. Dept. Justice, Washington, 1954-55; atty. then ptnr. McClure & McClure, Washington, 1955-60; with Marathon Oil Co., Findlay, Ohio, 1960-85, asst. to chmn. bd., 1969-73, corp. sec., 1973-85; pvt. practice Findlay, 1985—. With USNR, 1945-46. Mem. Bar Assn. D.C., Findlay/Hancock County Bar Assn., Met. Club (Washington). Home and Office: 170 Orchard Ln Findlay OH 45840-1130

JETTON, STEVE, newspaper editor. Met. edito The Houston Chronicle. Office: Houston Chronicle 801 Texas St Houston TX 77002-2996

JEUB, MICHAEL LEONARD, financial executive; b. Mpls., Mar. 2, 1943; s. Leonard M. and Florence J.; m. Alice Ann Linden (div. 1980); children: Christopher Michael, Annette Michelle; m. Julia Jean Stephenson, Feb. 4, 1983; children: Michael Leonard Jr., Robert. BS in Acctg. Calif. State Poly. U., 1966. CPA, Tex., Calif. Staff acct. Ernst & Whinney, L.A., 1966-70; CFO Internat. Clin. Lab., Inc., Nashville, 1970-85, pres. east, 1985-88; pres. August Enterprises, 1988-91; pres., COO, CFO MICA, San Diego, 1991-93; exec. v.p., CFO, treas. Nat. Health Labs., Inc., 1993-94; sr. v.p., CFO, Jenny Craig Internat., 1994—. Office: 11355 N Torrey Pines Rd La Jolla CA 92037-1013

JEUNET, JEAN-PIERRE, film director; b. Avignon, France, 1955. Dir., writer: Delicatessen, 1991 (Tokyo Gold award Tokyo Internat. Film Festival 1991, César awards best writing, best direction 1991, Catalonian Internat. Film Festival best dir. award and prize of Screenwriter's Critic and Writer's Catalan Assn. 1991; nominated BAFTA Film award Brit. Acad. Awards for Best Film not in the English Lang., 1991), La Cité des enfants perdus, 1995 (nominated Golden Palm, Cannes Film Festival, 1995, nominated Ind. Spirit award for Best Fgn. Film, 1996); dir. L'Évasion, 1978, Le Manège, 1980 (César award best short animation film 1981), Le Bunker de la dernière rafale, 1981, Pas de repos pour Billy Brakko, 1984, Foutaises, 1989 (Golden Palm, Cannes Film Festival, best short film 1989), Alien: Resurrection, 1997 (nominated Saturn award Acad. Sci. Fiction, Horror and Fantasy Films, 1997), Ulysse 31, 1999. Office: c/o DGA 7920 Sunset Blvd Los Angeles CA 90046*

JEW, HENRY, pharmacist; b. Hong Kong, June 10, 1950. BS in Pharmacy, U. Ga., 1974. Preceptor to externship program So. Sch. of Pharmacy, U. Ga., 1974-78; researcher Brompton's Mixture, 1977-78; pharmacist VA Med Ctr, Decatur, Ga., VNS Inc., Atlanta.

JEWELER, ROBIN, lawyer; b. Washington, Sept. 11, 1951; d. David Baer and Jeanne Carolyn (Weiss) J.; m. Laurence Donald Wiseman, May 29, 1978; children: Justin Jeweler, David Baer. BA with honors, U. Md., 1973; JD, George Washington U., 1976. Bar: Md., Washington. Jud. clk. Supreme Ct. Appeals, Charleston, W.Va., 1977-78; atty. Matthew Bender, Inc., N.Y.C., 1978-79; legis. atty. Congrl. Rsch. Svc., Libr. Congress, Washington, 1980—. Contbr. articles to profl. jours. Bd. dirs. Jewish Hist. Soc., Washington, 1996-98, sec., 1999; pres. Bells Mill PTA, 1993. Mem. Internat. Women's Insolvency and Restructuring Confedn., Fed. Bar Assn., Am. Bankruptcy Inst. Fax: 202-707-8595. E-mail: rjeweler@crs.loc.gov. Home: 10621 Democracy Ln Potomac MD 20854-4016 Office: Libr Congress 101 Independence Ave SE Washington DC 20540-0002

JEWELL, GEORGE HIRAM, lawyer; b. Fort Worth, Jan. 9, 1922; s. George Hiram and Vera (Lee) J.; m. Betty Jefferis, July 21, 1944; children: Susan Jewell Cannon, Robert V., Nancy Jewell Wommack. BA, U. Tex., 1942, LLB, 1950. Bar: Tex. 1950. With Baker & Botts, Houston, 1950—, sr. ptnr., 1960-90, counsel, 1990—. Trustee Tex. Children's Hosp., Houston, 1977—, pres., 1982-83, chmn., 1984-86; bd. dirs. Schlumberger Found., N.Y.C., 1982—. Lt. USNR, 1943-46, 50-53. Fellow Am. Coll. Tax Counsel, Am. Bar Foun.; mem. ABA, Houston Country Club, Coronado Club (pres. 1976-77), Old Baldy Club (chmn. 1993-98), Eldorado Country Club (pres. 1995-96), Order of Coif, Phi Beta Kappa, Phi Delta Phi. Home: 6051 Crab Orchard Rd Houston TX 77057-1447

JEWELL, H. RICHARD, English language educator; b. Monmouth, Ill., Jan. 21, 1949; s. Louis C. and Helen I. (Stevens) J. BA in Philosophy, Monmouth Coll., 1970; MA in Theology, San Francisco Theol. Seminary, 1972, MDiv, 1973; MA in English, St. Cloud State U., 1985. Freelance writer Little Falls, Minn., 1977-85; instr. dept. English St. Cloud (Minn.) State U., 1985-90, North Hennepin C.C., Brooklyn Park, Minn., 1989-93, Anoka (Minn.) Ramsey C.C., 1993-96; edn. specialist in composition dept. English U. Minn., Mpls., 1996—. Mem. MLA, The Loft Writers' Orgn., Nat. Coun. Tchrs. of English, Midwest MLA, Minn. Coun. Tchrs. of English. Democrat. Congregationalist. Avocations: creative writing, academic writing, camping, reading, travel. Home: 410 Groveland Ave Apt 401 Minneapolis MN 55403-3208 Office: Undergrad Writing Program U Minn 207 Church St SE Minneapolis MN 55455-0134

JEWETT, GEORGE FREDERICK, JR., forest products company executive; b. Spokane, Wash., Apr. 10, 1927; s. George Frederick and Mary Pelton (Cooper) J.; m. Lucille Winifred McIntyre, July 11, 1953; children: Mary Elizabeth, George Frederick III. BA, Dartmouth Coll., 1950; MBA, Harvard U., 1952. Asst. sec., asst. treas. Potlatch Corp., 1955-62, v.p. adminstrn., 1962-68, corp. v.p. adminstrn., 1968-71, sr. v.p., 1972-77, vice chmn. bd. adminstrn., 1977-78, vice chmn., 1979—, also dir. Trustee Calif. Pacific Med. Found.; trustees coun. Nat. Gallery Art, 1994. Clubs: St. Francis Yacht, N.Y. Yacht, Bohemian, Pacific Union, San Diego Yacht. Home: 2990 Broadway St San Francisco CA 94115-1062 Office: 1 Maritime Plz Ste 1640 San Francisco CA 94111-3506

JEWETT, JOHN RHODES, real estate executive; b. Indpls., Nov. 24, 1922; s. Chester Aten and Grace (Rhodes) J.; m. Marybelle Bramhall, June 12, 1946; children: John R., Jane B. B.A., DePauw U., 1944. Econ. research analyst Eli Lilly & Co., Indpls., 1946-48; with Pitman-Moore Co., Indpls., 1948-65; v.p., asst. to pres. Pitman-Moore Co., 1959-65; with F.C. Tucker Co., Inc., Indpls., 1965—; v.p. F.C. Tucker Co., Inc., 1978—; pres. Market Sq. Arena, 1974-79, Ind. Pacers (profl. basketball team), 1977-79. Chmn. Marion County Heart Assn.; dir. Marion County Child Guidance Clinic, ARC; trustee Meth. Hosp., Indpls.; committeeman Republican Precinct. Served with AUS, 1943-46. Mem. Met. Indpls. Bd. Realtors, Ind. Assn. Realtors, Nat. Assn. Realtors, Indpls. C. of C. Clubs: Meridian Hills Country, Kiwanis. Home: 8504 Bent Tree Ct Indianapolis IN 46260-2348 Office: 2500 One American Sq Indianapolis IN 46282

JEWISON, NORMAN FREDERICK, film producer, director; b. Toronto, Ont., Can., July 21, 1926; s. Percy Joseph and Irene (Weaver) J.; m. Margaret Ann Dixon, July 11, 1953; children: Kevin Jefferie, Michael Philip, Jennifer Ann. Student, Malvern Collegiate Inst., Toronto, 1940-44; BA, Victoria Coll., U. Toronto, 1944; LLD (hon.), U. Western Ont., 1974, U. Trent, 1985, Ryerson Inst., 1986. With CBC, 1952-58, CBS, 1958-61, Universal Studios, 1961-64; freelance film dir., producer, exec. producer, 1965—; presenter student film award CNE, 1980-81; dir. Harry Belafonte, Jackie Gleason, Andy Williams, Judy Garland, Danny Kaye TV shows; produced 1981 Acad. Awards; pres. of jury Avoriaz Film Festival, France, 1981. Dir.: (TV films) 40 Pounds of Trouble, The Thrill of it All, 1963, Send Me No Flowers, 1964, (feature films) Art of Love, The Cincinnati Kid, 1965, In the Heat of the Night, The Thomas Crown Affair, 1967, Gaily, Gaily, 1968; producer, dir.: (films) The Russians are Coming, 1966, Fiddler on the Roof, 1970, Jesus Christ Superstar, 1972, F.I.S.T., 1977, And Justice For All, 1979, Best Friends, 1982, Only You, 1994; producer: (films) The Landlord, 1969, Billy Two Hats, 1972, Rollerball, 1974; exec. producer: (films) Dogs of War, 1980, Iceman, 1983, The January Man, 1988; exec. producer, dir.: (films) A Soldiers Story, 1984, Agnes of God, 1985, Moonstruck, 1988, In Country, 1989; co-producer, dir. (film) Other People's Money, 1991. Served with Royal Can. Navy, 1945-46. Decorated companion Order of Can., 1982; named Dir. of Yr., Nat. Assn. Theatre Owners, 1982, Best Dir. Berlin Film Festival, 1988; recipient Can. Liberty award, 1958, Irving G. Thalberg Meml. award, 1999, Emmy award, 1960, Emmy award nominations, 1961-62, TV Dirs. award, 1961, Golden Globe award, 1966, Acad. award nominations, 1966-67, 72, 74, 84, 88; honored by Calif. ACLU, 1984. Mem. Can. Ctr. for Advanced Film Studies (founder, co-chmn. 1986), Dirs. Guild Am. (goals and purposes com. 1982, award nominations 1966, 67, Outstanding Directorial Achievement award nomination 1984). Avocations: skiing, yachting, tennis. Office: Yorktown Prodns Ltd 300 W Olympic Blvd Santa Monica CA 90404 Office: care Boaty Boatwright 40 W 57th St New York NY 10019*

JEWITT, DAVID WILLARD PENNOCK, retired banker; b. Cleve., Feb. 22, 1921; s. Homer Moore and Helen Katherine (Pennock) J.; m. Margaret Van Pelt Cool, Apr. 13, 1957; children: Andrea, Joel. BA, Amherst Coll.,

1943; Amherst Meml. fellow, Harvard, 1946-47; LLD (hon.), Fairfield U., 1980. With Irving Trust Co., N.Y.C., 1947-51, Chem. Bank, N.Y.C., 1951-59; with Conn. Nat. Bank, Bridgeport, 1959-86; exec. v.p. Conn. Nat. Bank, 1977-86. Trustee emeritus Am. Seamen's Friend Soc., N.Y.C., Mystic Seaport Mus., Gaylord Hosp., Wallingford, Oak Lawn Cemetery Assn., Fairfield; trustee Fairfield U., chmn. bd. trustees, 1972-78, trustee emeritus, 1980. Lt. USNR, WWII. Decorated comdr. Order Ruben Dario (Nicaragua); recipient medal of merit Fairfield U., 1968, Julilee medal, 1992. Mem. Theodore Gordon Flyfishers, Fairfield County Beagles, Nat. Beagle Club, The Pilgrims, Army and Navy Club (Washington), Squadron A Assn. (N.Y.C.), Royal Bermuda Yacht Club, Royal Swedish Yacht Club, Flyfishers Club (London). Episcopalian. Home: 239 Crosslands Dr Kennett Square PA 19348-2023

JEWLER, SARAH, magazine editor; b. Washington, May 18, 1948; d. Samuel and Esther Jewler. BA, George Washington U., 1970. Prodn. mgr. Benwill Pub., Boston, 1975-79; asst. prodn. mgr. Rolling Stone, N.Y.C., 1980-81; editl. prodn. freelancer N.Y.C., 1981-83; art prodn. mgr. Cuisine Mag., N.Y.C., 1983-84; mng. editor Manhattan Inc., N.Y.C., 1984-89, The Village Voice, N.Y.C., 1989-94, New York Mag., N.Y.C., 1994—. Office: New York Magazine 444 Madison Ave Fl 14 New York NY 10022-6999

JEYDEL, RICHARD K., lawyer; b. Livingston, N.J., Jan. 10, 1950; m. Ellen C. Ebert, Aug. 30, 1981; children: Patricia, Peter. AB, Sarah Lawrence Coll., 1972; JD, Harvard U., 1975. Bar: N.J. 1975, N.Y. 1983, U.S. Ct. Appeals (3d and 5th cirs.) 1983. Assoc. McCarter & English, Newark, 1976-79; corp. counsel Kanematsu-Gosho (USA), Inc., N.Y.C., 1979-85, v.p., gen. counsel, 1985-91; sr. v.p., sec., gen. counsel Kanematsu USA Inc., N.Y.C., 1991—; past mem. ethics com. Supreme Ct. Dist. XIII; mem. panel of arbitrators and mediators, large complex case program arbitrator and mediator Am. Arbitration Assn. Capt. U.S. Army, 1975-76. Mem. ABA, Am. Corp. Counsel Assn. (bd. dirs. 1996—), N.J. Bar Assn., N.J. Corp. Counsel Assn. (bd. dirs. 1986-90, 93—, pres.), Am. Arbitration Assn. (panel arbitrators and mediators, bd. dirs. 1996—). Office: Kanematsu USA Inc 114 W 47th St Fl 23 New York NY 10036-1574

JEYNES, MARY KAY, college dean; b. Miami, Fla., Oct. 31, 1941; d. Nasrallah and Martha (Jabaly) Demetry; m. Paul Jeynes, Sept. 30, 1978. BS, Fla. State U., 1963. Program dir. Orange County YMCA, Orlando, Fla., 1964-69, Ea. Queens YMCA, Belrose, N.Y., 1970-73; regional coord. N.Y. State Park and Recreation Commn., N.Y.C., 1974-77; dir. health, fitness and recreation YWCA of N.Y.C., 1978-79; dean continuing edn. and adult programs Marymount Manhattan Coll., N.Y.C., 1980—. Mem. East Manhattan C. of C. (pres. 1996-97, chmn. bd. dirs. 1998—). Office: Marymount Manhattan Coll 221 E 71st St New York NY 10021-4501

JEZL, BARBARA ANN, chemist, automation consultant; b. Pitts., June 7, 1947; d. James L. and Elizabeth (Bannister) J. BS in Chemistry, U. Del., 1969, PhD in Organic Chemistry, 1974. Jr. chemist Am. Cyanamid, Pearl River, N.Y., 1969-70; NSF postdoctoral assoc. U. Cin., 1974-76; inst. application specialist E.I. DuPont de Nemours & Co., Wilmington, Del., 1976-79, mem. computing staff, 1979-84, staff specialist, 1985-93, sr. rsch. chemist scientific computing divsn., 1993—. Author: Science, 1990; contbr. articles to profl. jours. Bd. dirs. Unitarian-Universalist Fellowship of Newark, 1981-85, pres., chmn. bd., 1986-87, rep. Delaware Valley Area Coun., Phila., 1983-85, v.p. Fellowship of Newark, 1984-85. Mem. AAAS, IEEE Computer Soc., Am. Chem. Soc., Soc. for Computing Machinery, Macintosh Sci. and Tech. Assn. (bd. dirs., co-chmn. tech. adv. com. 1990-99, conf. co-chair eSEAM 97, Apple customer adv. bd. 1997—). Avocations: equestrian, agrarian, aviation. Home: 5448 W Pinehurst Dr Wilmington DE 19808-2619 Office: EI duPont de Nemours & Co Exptl Sta PO Box 80320 Wilmington DE 19880-0320

JEZUIT, LESLIE JAMES, manufacturing company executive; b. Chgo., Nov. 4, 1945; s. Eugene and Tillie (Fleszewski) J.; m. Janet Diane Bushlus, Oct. 12, 1968; children—Douglas Blake, Kevin Lane. B.S. in Mech. and Aerospace Engring., Ill. Inst. Tech., 1969, M.B.A., 1974. Mgr. engring. graphic systems group Rockwell Internat., Chgo., 1968-74; dir. comml. systems Rockwell Internat., Cicero, Ill., 1974-75; v.p. mktg. and sales Mead Digital Systems, Dayton, Ohio, 1975-80; v.p. mktg. and sales Signal div. Fed. Signal Corp., University Park, Ill., 1980-81, pres. Signal div., 1981-85; v.p. corp. devel. Fed. Signal Corp., Oak Brook, Ill., 1985-86; div. mgr. power distbn. div. Eaton Corp., Milw., 1986-87, gen. mgr. indsl. control and power distbn. div., 1987-88, v.p., 1988-91; pres., chief oper. officer Robertshaw Controls Co., Richmond, Va., 1991-95; pres., CEO, bd dirs Quixote Inc., Chgo., 1995—; chmn. Transp. Mgmt. Techs., LLC, Chgo., 1998—; instr. Keller Sch. Mgmt., Chgo., 1982-83. Patentee in field. Active United Way, Chgo., 1983-85; mem. Chgo. Crime Commn.; bd. dirs. Better Bus. Bur. of Milw., 1986, United Performing Arts Found of Milw., 1986, Greater Milw. Com., 1991-92. Mem. Gas Appliance Mfrs. Assn. (bd. dirs. 1994-96), Will County Local Devel. Co. (v.p. 1984-85, Bus. Man of Yr. award 1985), South Suburban C. of C., Monee C. of C. Republican. Club: Metropolitan (Chgo.). Avocations: boating; fishing; photography; cross country skiing. Home: 26576 Countryside Lake Dr Mundelein IL 60060-3342 Office: Quixote Inc 1 E Wacker Dr Chicago IL 60601-1802

JHABVALA, RUTH PRAWER, author; b. Cologne, Germany, May 7, 1927; lived in India, 1951-75; came to U.S., 1975; d. Marcus and Eleonora (Cohn) Prawer; m. Cyrus S. H. Jhabvala, 1951; 3 children. MA, London U., 1951, DLitt (hon.), 1986, LHD (hon.), 1995, D Arts (hon.), 1996. Author: (novels) To Whom She Will, 1955, The Nature of Passion, 1956, Esmond in India, 1957, The Householder, 1960, Get Ready for Battle, 1962, A Backward Place, 1965, A New Dominion, 1972, Heat and Dust, 1975 (Booker award for fiction Nat. Book League 1975), In Search of Love and Beauty, 1983, Three Continents, 1987, Poet and Dancer, 1993, Shards of Memory, 1995; (short story collections) Like Birds, Like Fishes and Other Stories, 1964, A Stronger Climate: Nine Stories, 1968, An Experience of India, 1971, How I Became a Holy Mother and Other Stories, 1976, Out of India: Selected Stories, 1986, East Into Upper East, 1998; (film scripts) The Householder, 1963 (with James Ivory), Shakespeare Wallah, 1965 (with Ivory), The Guru, 1968, Bombay Talkie, 1970, Autobiography of a Princess, 1975, Roseland, 1977, Hullabaloo over Georgie and Bonnie's Pictures, 1978, The Europeans, 1979, Jane Austen in Manhattan, 1980, Quartet, 1981, Heat and Dust, 1983, The Bostonians, 1984, A Room With a View, 1986 (Writers Guild of Am. award for best adapted screeplay 1986, Acad. award for best adapted screenplay 1986), (with John Schlesinger) Madame Sousatzka, 1988, Mr. and Mrs. Bridge, 1990, Howards End, 1992 (Acad. award for best adapted screenplay 1992), Remains of the Day, 1993 (Acad. award nomination for best adapted screenplay 1993), Jefferson in Paris, 1995, Surviving Picasso, 1996, (with James Ivory) A Soldier's Daughter Never Cries, 1998. Guggenheim fellow, 1976; Neil Gunn. Internat. fellow, 1979; MacArthur Found. fellow, 1984-89; named Comdr. Br. Empire, 1998. Home: 400 E 52d St New York NY 10022-6404

JHAMB, INDAR MOHAN, physician; b. New Delhi, Oct. 10, 1952; came to U.S., 1978; s. Suraj Bhan and Kaushalya (Tandon) J.; married, 1978; 2 children. MBBS, U. Delhi, New Delhi, 1970, MD, 1974. Diplomate Am. Bd. Allergy and Immunology, Am. Bd. Pediatrics. Resident U. Delhi, 1975-78; resident U. Louisville, 1979-81, fellow, 1981-83; pvt. practice Bowling Green, Ky. Fellow Am. Coll. Allergy, Asthma and Immunology, Am. Acad. Pediatrics; mem. Am. Assn. Cert. Allergists. Avocations: tennis, martial arts, music, soccer, pool. Office: 1228 Ashley Cir Bowling Green KY 42104-5803

JHIN, MICHAEL KONTIEN, health care executive; b. Hong Kong, Jan. 26, 1950; came to U.S., 1958; s. Paul Y. and Monica J. BSME, Rensselaer Poly. Inst., 1971; MBA, Boston U., 1974. Adminstrv. asst. St. Vincent Hosp., Worcester, Mass., 1974-76; asst. dir. Thomas Jefferson U. Hosp., Phila., 1976-79, assoc. dir., 1979-84; exec. dir., CEO Temple U. Hosp., Phila., 1984-88; exec. v.p. Long Beach (Calif.) Meml. Health Sys., 1988-90; pres., CEO St. Luke's Episcopal Hosp., Houston, 1990—, St. Luke's Episcopal Health Sys., Houston, 1995—. Bd. dirs. Greater Houston Partnership, 1999—, Houston World Affairs Coun., 1998—, Jr. Achievement, 1992—, Houston Forum, 1996—, Tex. Hosp. Assn., 1993-96, Tex. Heart Inst., 1998—, United Way Tex. Gulf Coast, 1999—; bd. dirs. Houston Hosp. Coun., 1991-96, chmn. bd., 1994-95. Fellow Am. Coll. Healthcare Execs., Joint Commn. on Accreditation of Healthcare Orgn. (bd. dirs. 1998—), Rensselaer Alumni Assn. (pres. 1996-97, bd. dirs. 1991-98), Am. Hosp. Assn. (regional policy bd. 1992-95); mem. Young Pres.'s Orgn. Office: St Luke's Episcopal Health Sys 6720 Bertner St Houston TX 77030-2604

JI, ZHENGHUA, computer engineer; b. Yangzhou, China, Oct. 9, 1955; came to U.S., 1985; m. Han Zou, June 21, 1986; 1 child, Leeann H. BS, Harbin U. Polytech, China, 1981; MS, Beijing U. Aerospace, 1983; PhD, U. Pitts., 1990. Asst. prof. Beijing U. Aerospace, 1983-85; rsch. assoc. Stevens Inst. Tech., Hoboken, N.J., 1989-91; hardware engr. Hewlett-Packard Co., Wilmington, Del., 1991—. Contbr. articles to profl. jours. Mem. ASME. Office: Hewlett-Packard Co 2850 Centerville Rd Wilmington DE 19808

JIALAL, ISHWARLAL, medical educator; b. Durban, Natal, South Africa, Oct. 13, 1953. B in Medicine, B in Surgery, U. Natal, South Africa, 1976, MD, 1983. Registered med. practitioner, specialist in chem. pathology South African Med. and Dental Coun.; Diplomate Royal Coll. Pathologists (Eng.), Am. Bd. Internal Medicine, Am. Bd. Clin. Chemistry. Intern in medicine and surgery King Edward VIII Hosp., U. Natal Med. Sch., Durban, South Africa, 1977, resident in endocrinology and metabolism divsn., 1978-82; resident dept. chem. pathology U. Natal, 1978-82, sr. lectr./specialist depts. medicine and chem. pathology, 1984-87; fellow divsn. diabetes and metabolism Harvard Med. Sch., E.P. Joslin Rsch. Lab., Joslin Diabetes Ctr., Boston, 1983-84; dir. clin. pathology R.K. Khan Hosp., U. Natal Med. Sch., 1984-87; assoc. prof./sr. specialist dept. chem. pathology and medicine U. Natal Med. Sch., 1987; sr. fellow divsn. metabolism, endocrinology and nutrition, dept. medicine U. Wash., Seattle, 1987-88; asst. prof. depts. clin. nutrition, internal medicine and pathology U. Tex. Southwestern Med. Ctr., Dallas, 1988-92, co-dir. Lipid Clinic, 1990—, assoc. prof. dept. pathology, internal medicine and clin. nutrition, 1992—, dir. clin. chemistry dept. pathology, 1992—, sr. investigator Ctr. Human Nutrition, 1992—, prof. internal medicine and pathology, 1997—, assoc. dir. divsn. clin. pathology, 1997—; dir. divsn. clin. chemistry Parkland Meml. Hosp.; attending physician, co-dir. Lipid Disorders Clinic, Parkland Meml. and Aston Ambulatory Care Ctr.; attending physician endocrinology & metabolism Parkland Meml. and Zale Lipshy Hosps.; cons. chem. pathologist VA Med. Ctr., Dallas; vis. scientist dept. chem. pathology and metabolic disorders St. Thomas Hosp. Med. Sch., London, 1984; cons. chem. pathologist Dallas VA Med. Ctr., 1995—. Clin. Rsch. grantee Am. Diabetes Assn., 1996. Home: 7214 Rustic Valley Dr Dallas TX 75248-2312 Office: U Tex Southwestern Med Sch Dept Pathology 5323 Harry Hines Blvd Dallas TX 75235-9073*

JIANG, BAI-CHUAN, optical educator; b. Hongzhou, Zhejiang, China, June 21, 1944; came to the U.S., 1987; s. Gaoquan and Yueru (Zhao) J.; m. Wei-Fen, Feb. 4, 1970; 1 child, Alexander Xingzhi. BS, Fudan U., 1966; MS, Chinese Acad. Scis., Shanghai, 1982; PhD, Acad. Sinica, Shanghai, 1986. Optics engr. Shanghai Camera Factory, 1967-78; rsch. asst. Acad. Sinica, Shanghai, 1978-81; rsch. assoc. Chinese Acad. Scis., Shanghai, 1982-86; vis. scientist physiology dept. U. Toronto, Ont., 1986-87; postdoctoral fellow psychology dept. Pa. State U., University Park, 1987-88; postdoctoral fellow U. Houston Coll. Optometry, 1988-89; asst. prof. U. Houston Coll. Optometry, 1990-97, assoc. prof., 1998—. Contbr. articles to profl. jours; patentee in field. Recipient Outstanding Young Scientist grant Chinese Acad. Scis., 1985-86, Rsch. fellowship Nat. Rsch. Coun. Can., 1988, Rsch. fellowship Med. Rsch. Coun. Can., 1989, NIH grant, 1991—, Rsch. grant Bausch & Lomb InVision Inst., 1993. Fellow Am. Acad. Optometry; mem. AAAS, Assn. for Rsch. in Vision and Ophthalmology, Human Factor and Ergonomics Soc., Sigma Xi. Avocations: photography, travel, writing.

JIANG, HE, biomedical scientist, entrepreneur; b. Chengdu, Sichuan, China, Feb. 13, 1958; came to U.S., 1994; s. Xintian Jiang and Youbai Shan; m. Kang Rao, Aug. 1, 1983; children: Kelen T., Lan T. MD, Luzhou (China) Med. Coll., 1982; MSc, 3d Mil. Med. U., Chongqing, China, 1985; PhD, U. Man., 1994. Lic. MD, Chinese Ministry Health and Ednl. Com. Asst. prof. 3d Med. U., Chongqing, China, 1985-87; vis. prof. faculty medicine U. Man., Winnipeg, 1987-88, rsch. scientist dept. physiology, 1988-90; guest rschr. NIH, Bethesda, Md., 1994—; chmn. Kela Global Exchange, Ltd., 1998. Rsch. in molecular motor, asthma, diagnostics; contbr. articles to profl. jours., chpts. to books. Recipient 3d Natural Scis. Rsch. award China State Nature and Sci. Com., Chongqing, 1987, Vis. Scholarship award China State Edn. Com., Can., 1987-88, Studentship award Man. Health Rsch. Coun., Can., 1988, 89, Man. Lung Assn., Can., 1988, Major Student Rsch. award, 1990, 94, St. Boniface Gen. Hosp. Rsch. Found., 1988, Man. Med. Svc. Found. award, 1989, Sigma Xi Student Rsch. award U. Man., 1991. Fellow Med. Rsch. Coun. Can. (Postdoctoral fellowship 1990-94, 94-97); mem. Nat. Soc. Med. Scientists (Top Ten Young Med. Scientists in U.S. award), Biophys. Soc., Am. Physiol. Soc., Can. Ctrs. Excellence Respiratory (affiliate), Chinese Pathophysiol. Soc., N.Y. Acad. Scis. Avocations: volleyball, photography, trade, multimedia and animation design, music and singing. Office: Lab Molecular Cardiology NIH 8N202/10 9000 Rockville Pik Bethesda MD 20892

JIANG, JOHN JIANZHONG, materials engineer; b. Kaiping, Guangdong, People's Republic China, May 7, 1960; came to U.S., 1985; s. Dong and Laiwa (Chu) J. BS in Elec. Engring., South China Inst. Tech., 1982; MS in Ceramic Engring., Alfred U., 1987. Technician Sanbu Micro Electric Motor Works, Kaiping, 1976-78, asst. engr., asst. project planner, 1982-84, tech. svc. engr., 1984-85; with Canton (People's Republic China) Research Inst. Electronics, 1982-85; rsch. and devel. engr., 1987, sr. devel. engr., 1988-89, prin. engr., 1989-91, engring. mgr., 1991-92, v.p. engring., 1993-94; chief tech. officer Am. Electronic Materials, Inc., San Diego, 1987-95; prin. devel. engr. Vitramon, Inc., Monroe, Conn., 1996; project mgr. Vishay Vitramon Inc., Roanoke, Va., 1997—; speaker profl. meetings. Contbr. articles to profl. jours. and EMC Ency.; inventor of multilayer ceramic chip inductor process. Mem. IEEE, IEEE-Electromagnetic Compatibility Soc., IEEE Engring. Mgmt. Soc., Materials Rsch. Soc., Am. Phys. Soc., Am. Ceramic Soc. Avocations: reading, table tennis, volleyball, badminton. Office: Vishay Vitramon Inc PO Box 11786 Roanoke VA 24022-1786

JIANG, LONGZHI, mechanical engineer; b. Anqing, Anhui, People's Republic of China, Feb. 1, 1962; s. Yuhua and Xianqin (Chen) J.; m. Yufei Hong, Dec. 29, 1991; 1 child, Christine. MS, Hefei U. of Tech., 1986, Clarkson U., 1995; PhD, Purdue U., 1998. Rsch. asst. Hefei U., 1983-86, asst. prof., 1986-91; rsch. asst. Clarkson U., 1992-94, Purdue U., 1995-98; rsch. engr. GE Co., Florence, S.C., 1998—; advisor sr. students SeniHefei U.; asst. dir. engring. mechanics Dept. Civil Engring., Hefei U. of Tech., advisor 1987-91. Contbr. articles to profl. publs. Recipient Disting. Young Rschr. award Chinese Assn. of Sci. and Tech., 1992. Mem. ASME, Chinese Soc. of Hydraulic Engring., Chinese Soc. of Mechanics. Fax: 843-664-1671. E-mail: longzhi.jiang@med.ge.com. Office: GE Co 3001 W Radio Dr Florence SC 29501

JIBBEN, LAURA ANN, state agency administrator; b. Peoria, Ill., Oct. 1, 1949; d. Charles Otto and Dorothy Lee (Skaggs) Becker; m. Michael Eugene Hagan, July 7, 1967 (div. Apr. 1972); m. Louis C. Jibben, July 14, 1972. BA in Criminal Justice, Sangamon State U., 1984; MBA, Northwestern U., 1990. Asst. to chief of adminstrn. Ill. Dept. Corrections, Springfield, 1974-77, exec. asst. to dir., 1977-80, dep. dir., 1980-81; mgr. toll services Ill. Tollway Dept., Oak Brook, 1981-86; chief adminstrv. officer Regional Transp. Authority, Chgo., 1986-90, fund mgr. loss financing plan, 1987-90, also chmn. pension trust; exec. dir. Regional Transp. Authority, 1990-96; v.p., gen. mgr. MTA, Inc., Chgo., 1996—; cons. labor studies Sangamon State U., Springfield, 1981; bd. dirs. Chgo. Found. for Women. Apptd. mem. transp. adv. bd. City of Naperville, 1988-90; bd. dirs. Family Shelter Svcs., 1990-91; bd. dirs., chair devel. com. Govt. Assistance Program, 1997—; mem. surface transp. adv. panel U. Ill., 1997—; mem. nat. adv. bd. Women's Transp. Seminar, 1996—. Recipient Appreciation award VFW, Chgo., 1983, award Ill. State Toll Hwy. Authority, 1986; named Woman of Yr., Nat. Women's Transp. Seminar, 1991, AAUW, 1991. Mem. NAFE, Women's Transp. Seminar (Woman of Yr. award Chgo. chpt. 1991, Nat. Woman of Yr. 1991), Beta Sigma Phi (treas., v.p., corr. sec. Naperville and Easton, Ill. chpts.), Lambda Alpha. Avocations: reading, jogging, gardening. Office: MTA Inc 111 N Canal St Ste 915 Chicago IL 60606-7204*

JILER, WILLIAM LAURENCE, publisher; b. Bridgeport, Conn., Oct. 16, 1925; s. Jacob and Sarah J.; m. Jan Gardner, Oct. 14, 1956; children: Wendy Jo, James Paul. B.S., Bates Coll., Lewiston, Maine, 1948; postgrad., U. So. Calif., 1950. With E.R. Squibb & Co., New Brunswick, N.J., 1948-50; with Commodity Research Bur., Inc., N.Y.C., now Jersey City, 1950-64, 69-85; pres. Commodity Research Bur., Inc., 1969-85; with Standard & Poor's Corp., 1964-69, dir., 1964-69; mem. econ. adv. com. Commodity Futures Trading Commn., 1975-76. Author: How Charts Can Help You in the Stock Market, 1962; assoc. editor: Commodity Year Book, 1951-80; created the CRB Commodity Futures Index Traded as a Futures Contract on the New York Futures Exchange. Served to 2d lt. USAAF, 1943-45. Mem. Nat. Assn. Bus. Economists, Market Technicians Assn., N.Y. Soc. Security Analysts. *Find a need and fulfill it to the best of your ability.*

JILHEWAR, ASHOK, gastroenterologist; b. Nanded, Maharashtra, India, Jan. 30, 1947; came to U.S., 1977; naturalized 1987; BS, Marathwada U., Aurangabad, India, 1970; MB, Marathwada U., 1970; MD, Govt. Med. Coll., Aurangabad, 1970. Diplomate Am. Bd. Internal Medicine, Am. Bd. Gastroenterology, Am. Bd. Geriatric Medicine, Am. Bd. Quality Assurance and Utilization Rev. Physicians. Rotatory intern Med. Coll. Hosp., Aurangabad, India, 1968-70; resident St. Luke's Hosp. and Royal infirmary, Huddersfeild, Bolton, Eng., 1970-72; med. registrar internal medicine Gen. Hosp., Sligo, Ireland, 1973-77; chief resident PG1 and internal medicine U. Health Scis.-Chgo. Med. Sch. and VA Hosp., 1977-79; clin. instr. U. Heath Scis.-Chgo. Med. Sch., 1978-79; fellow in gastroenterology Michael Reese Hosp., Chgo., 1980-81; mem. exec. com. Meth. Hosp., Chgo, 1985-90, chmn. dept. med., 1988-90; mem. staff dept. medicine Grant Hosp., Chgo., 1986—; lectr. preventive and social medicine Med. Coll., Aurangabad, 1970; mem. exec. com. Meth. Hosp. Chgo., 1985-90, v.p. med. staff, 1987-88, treas., sec. 1985-87, chmn. dept. medicine, 1988-90; med. dir. approved homr for intermediace care nursing home, 1986-95; med. advisor Office Hearings and Appeals, HHS, 1985—; med. reviewer Ill. Med. Rev. Orgn., 1993—, Crescent Cmty. Found. for Med. Care, 1994—. Fellow Royal Coll. Physicians Can., Am. Coll. Internat. Physicians; mem. AMA, ACP, Am. Gastroenterol. Assn., Royal Coll. Physicians U.K., Royal Coll. Physicians Ireland, Ill. State Med. Assn., Chgo. Med. Soc. (PRO study com., fee mediation subcom. 1992). Office: North Park Stomach Clinic 5393 N Milwaukee Ave Chicago IL 60630-1251

JIMENEZ, BETTIE EILEEN, retired small business owner; b. LaCygne, Kans., June 8, 1932; d. William Albert and Ruby Faye (Cline) Montee; m. William R. Bradley, Aug. 21, 1947 (div. Sept. 1950); 1 child, Shirley; m. J.P. Jimenez, Feb. 20, 1951 (div. Nov. 1978); children: Pamela, Joe Jr., Robin Michelle. Student, Ft. Scott Jr. Coll., Paola, Kans., 1979-81. Reporter LaCygne Jour., 1943-45; union recorder I.L.G.W.U., Paola, 1956-57; mgr. Estes Metalcraft, Osawatomie, Kans., 1977-82; owner El Rey Tavern, Osawatomie, 1980-95; ret., 1995. Home: 516 Walnut Ave Osawatomie KS 66064-1254

JIMÉNEZ, EMILIO, corporate lawyer; b. San Juan, Puerto Rico, Feb. 27, 1967; s. Emilio and Ana Lidia (Colón) Jiménez; m. Alicia María Alvarez, Mar. 30, 1996. BA cum laude, Harvard Coll., 1989; JD, NYU, 1992. Bar: N.Y. 1993, Mass. 1992. Assoc. Jones, Day, Reavis & Pogue, N.Y.C., 1992-93, Brown & Wood, N.Y.C., 1993-95; asst. v.p., legal and compliance dept. CSFP Capital, Inc., N.Y.C., 1995-97; v.p., asst. gen. counsel J.P. Morgan & Co. Inc., N.Y.C., 1997—. Staff editor NYU Law Review, 1990-92. Mem. Am. Bar Assn., N.Y. State Bar Assn., Fly Club, Harvard Club of N.Y.C. Republican. Roman Catholic. Avocations: golf, marksmanship. Home: 422 E 72nd St Apt 6F New York NY 10021-4618 Office: JP Morgan & Co Inc 60 Wall St New York NY 10005-2888

JIMENEZ, JOSEPHINE SANTOS, portfolio manager; b. Lucena, Quezon, Philippines, June 6, 1954; came to U.S., 1972; d. Jose Hirang and Virginia Villapando (Santos) J. BS, NYU, 1979; MS, MIT, 1981. Securities analyst Mass. Mut. Life Ins. Co., Springfield, 1982-83; investment officer One Fed. Asset Mgmt., Boston, 1984-87; sr. analyst, portfolio mgr. Emerging Markets Investors Corp., Washington, 1988-91; mng. dir., portfolio mgr. Montgomery Asset Mgmt., San Francisco, 1991—; founding ptnr. Montgomery Emerging Markets Fund; trustee M.I.T. Corp. Mem. Inst. Chartered Fin. Analysts. Office: Montgomery Asset Mgmt 101 California St San Francisco CA 94111-5802

JIMÉNEZ, LEONARDO, popular accordionist; b. San Antonio, Mar. 11, 1939. Accordionist with his own conjunto (group) mid-50s; recorded for many local labels, with Anglo musician, Doug Sahm for Atlantic, 1972; appeared in Les Blank/Chris Strachwitz documentary, (film) True Stories: Chulas Fronteras, 1974; toured and recorded with Ry Cooder and Peter Rowan; mem. Tex. Tornados band; albums include Entre Humo y Botellas, 1989, Un Mojado Sin Licencia, 1993, Flaco Jimenez, 1994, Ay Te Dejo En San Antonio, El Sonido de San Antonio, Flaco's Amigos, Y Su-Conjunto. Recipient Best Mex.-Am. Performance Grammy award, 1996, Grammy for Arhoolie LP: Ay Te Dejo En San Antonio, 1987. Studio: 10911 Highway 16 S San Antonio TX 78224

JIMENEZ, LUIS ALFONSO, JR., sculptor; b. El Paso, Tex., July 30, 1940; s. Luis Alfonso and Alicia (Franco) J.; m. Susan Brockman; children: Elisa Victoria, Luis Adan, Juan Orion, Sarah Alicia Xochil. B.S. in Art and Architecture, U. Tex., Austin, 1964; postgrad., Ciudad U., Mexico City, 1964. Exhibited in one-man shows, including, Graham Gallery, N.Y.C., 1969-70, O.K. Harris Works of Art, N.Y.C., 1972-75, Contemporary Arts Mus., Houston, 1974, Mus. of N.Mex., Santa Fe, 1980, Frumkin Struve, Chgo., 1981, Adeliza's Candy Store Gallery, Folsom, Calif., 1983, Phyllis Kind Gallery, N.Y.C., 1984, Moody Gallery, Houston, 1987, 95, Scottsdale Cultural Arts Ctr., Nat. Mus. Am. Art, Washington, 1994, Marsha Mateyka Gallery, Washington, 1994, Adair Margo Gallery, El Paso, Tex., 1995, A.C.A. Galleries, N.Y.C., 1998, Working Class Heroes: Images from the Popular Culture, traveling retrospective, opened Dallas, Dallas Mus. Art 1997, Palm Springs Mus. Art, 1998, Blaffier Mus., Tex., 2 Albuquerque Mus. Art; exhibited in group shows, including, Human Concern Personal Torment, Whitney Mus., N.Y., 1969, Nat. Mus. Am. Art, Washington, 1980, Albuquerque Mus., 1980, Edinburgh (Scotland) Festival, 1980, Walker Art Center, Mpls., 1980, U. Minn., Mpls., 1981, Roswell Mus. and Art Ctr., N. Mex., 1984, Albright-Knox Art Mus., Buffalo, N.Y., Hirshhorn Mus. and Sculpture Garden, Smithsonian Instn., Washington, Hispanic Art in the U.S., 1988, Hispanic Arts in the U.S. traveling show, 1987-89, Latin Am. Spirit in the U.S., 1989, Committed To Print, Mus. Modern Art, N.Y.C., 1989, Whitney Biennial, N.Y.C., 1991, New Mus., N.Y.C., Art of the Other Mex. traveling exhibit, 1993, 20 Yrs. of Landfall Prints, Whitney Mus., 1997; represented in permanent collections, Nat. Mus. Am. Art, Anderson Mus. Contemporary Art, Roswell N.M., Witte Mus., San Antonio, Long Beach (Calif.) Mus., New Orleans Mus. Art, Roswell (N. Mex.) Mus. and Art Center, Sheldon Meml. Gallery, Lincoln, Nebr., Art Inst. Chgo., Met. Mus. Art, N.Y.C., Smithsonian Instn., Mus. Modern Art, Albuquerque Mus. Art, Fed. Reserve Bank, Dallas, Fine Arts Mus., Santa Fe, U. Texas, San Antonio, U. New Mex., Albuquerque, others, also pvt. collections; works include Vaquero Sculpture, Moody Park, Houston, 1977; Nat. Endowment for Arts and City Housing Authority commn. Sodbuster sculpture, Fargo, N.D., 1977; Southwest Pietà, Nat. Endowment for Arts commn. Art in Pub. Places, City of Albuquerque, 1981; Steel Worker, Nat. Endowment for Arts, La Salle Sta., Buffalo, N.Y.; Niagara Frontier, Transp. Authority Commn., VA Hosp., 1982; Flag Raising, Oklahoma City Sculpture Commn.; Howl, Wichita State U., Kans., 1983; Border Crossing, Otis Art Inst. of Parsons Sch. Design, Los Angeles, 1984; Fiesta Dancers, Gen. Services Adminstrn., Otay Mesa, Calif., 1986; sculpture commn. NEA and City of El Paso, 1986, Plaza de los Lagartos, Omni Hotel, San Diego, 1986, City of Las Vegas, 1989, New Denver Airport, 1991, City of N.Y. Cultural Affairs, Hunt's Point Market, Bronx, N.Y., Firefighter, Cleve., 1996, sculpture commn. U. OK, Norman, OK, 1998. Recipient Steuben Glass award 1972, Hassam Fund award Am. Acad. Arts and Letters, 1977, Awards in Visual Arts, 1985, Greenburger Found. award, 1987, Skowhegan sculpture award, 1989, Gov.'s award State of N.Mex., 1993, Award of Distinction Nat. Coun. of Art Adminstrs., 1995, disting. alumni U. Tex., Austin; named goodwill amb. City of Houston, 1993, 98, Tex. Artist of Yr., Houston Art League, 1998, Distinguished Alumni, Univ. Tex. and Austin; fellow Nat. Endowment Arts, 1987, 88, Am. Acad. in Rome, 1979, La Napoule Art Found. and Nat. Endowment Arts residency fellow, 1990. *I am a traditional artist in the sense* *that I give form to my culture's icons. I work with folk sources; the popular culture and mythology, and a popular material; fiberglass, shiny finishes, metal flake, and at times with neon and illuminated. In the past the important icons were religious, now they are secular.*

JIMÉNEZ, ONILDA A., Spanish educator; b. Fomento, Cuba, Dec. 24, 1926; came to U.S., 1965; d. Ricardo Jiménez and Ana Francisca Pineda. PhD, U. Havana, Cuba, 1955; MA, Columbia U., 1968; PhD, NYU, 1979. Prof. U. Masénica, Havana, 1957-59; consul Cuban Ministry of Fgn. Affairs, Caracas, Venezuela, 1960-61; prof. Spanish N.J. City U., Jersey City, 1968-96, Spanish advisor, 1978-96, prof. emeritus, 1998—. Author: Gabriela Mistral, 1982, La Mujer en Martí, 1999; editor: On the Road, 1985. Scholar Cultural Hispánica, 1964-65, Am. Coun. for Emigres in the Professions, 1967-68. Mem. MLA, Círculo de Cultura (mem. adv. bd. 1992-93), Centro Cultural Cubano, Instituto Literario Hispánico, Instituto Cervantes, Nat. Assn. Cuban Educators. Republican. Roman Catholic.

JIMENEZ, SERGIO A., internist, science educator; b. Cuzco, Peru, Feb. 21, 1942; s. Julio Alexandre and Bertha Margarite (Astete) J. BS, Nat. U. San Marcos, Lima, Peru, 1959, MD, 1964; MS, U. Pa., 1984. Diplomate Am. Bd. Internal Medicine. Asst. prof. dept. medicine U. Pa., Phila., 1974-80, asst. prof. dept. orthop. surgery, 1978-80, assoc. prof. medicine and orthop. surgery, 1980-86, prof., 1986-87; prof. medicine, dir. rheumatology rsch. Thomas Jefferson U., Phila., 1987-92, prof. biochemistry and molecular biology, 1987—, dir. divsn. rheumatology, 1992—, Dorrance H. Hamilton prof. medicine, 1992—; hon. adj. fellow Benjamin Franklin Inst., Phila., 1981—; chmn. med. adv. bd. Scleroderma Rsch. Found., Mid-Atlantic Chpt., 1979—; mem. rsch. scholarships com., Ea. Pa. chpt. Arthritis Found., 1981-84; mem. med./sci. bd. Scleroderma Fedn., 1994—; mem. Nat. Inst. Health Gen. Medicine A Study Sect., 1990-94, mem. spl. rev. com., 1995—; Nat. Inst. Health Peer Review Oversight Group, 1998—. Author over 200 articles to med. jours., 300 abstracts in procs. worldwide sci. jours., 90 editls., revs., and chpts. to jours. and books. Bd. dirs. Washington Square West Civic Assn., Phila., 1978-82, v.p., 1981-82, trustee, 1988—; mem. Phila. Hispanic C. of C., 1990—. Capt. Peruvian Army Res., 1964-65. Recipient Gerald P. Rodnan award for excellence in scleroderma rsch., U. Pitts., 1986; program project for rsch. on osteoarthritis, NIH, 1992—. Fellow Soc. for Molecular Medicine; mem. Am. Coll. Rheumatology, Am. Soc. Biol. Chemistry and Molecular Biology, Osteoarthritis Rsch. Soc. (exec. bd. 1994—, pres.-elect 1997—), Internat. Soc. for Matrix Biology (founding mem.). Republican. Roman Catholic. Avocations: fine arts, sculpture, opera, anthropology, archeology. Home: 900 Spruce St Philadelphia PA 19107-6131 Office: Thomas Jefferson Univ 233 S 10th St Ste 509 Philadelphia PA 19107-5541

JIMMAR, D'ANN, elementary education educator, fashion merchandiser; b. Leighton, Ala., Dec. 10, 1942; d. Harry D. Qualls and Lillian Jimmar. BS in Elem. Edn., Ala. A&M U., 1965, MS in Urban Studies, 1973; PhD in Higher Edn., Iowa State U., 1986. Elem. tchr. Limestone County Bd. Edn., Athens, Ala., 1966-68, Huntsville (Ala.) City Bd. Edn., 1968-71; instr. dept. community planning and urban studies Ala. A&M U., Huntsville, 1973-78; rsch. asst. dept. sociology and anthropology Iowa State U., Ames, 1978-79, rsch. aide, 1980-81, 82-83; ednl. aide, substitute tchr. Ames Community Sch. Dist., 1983-86; coord. practicums Nova U., Ft. Lauderdale, Fla., 1986-87; tchr. Downtown Adult Edn. Ctr., Ft. Lauderdale, 1987-88, Apollo Mid. Sch., Hollywood, Fla., 1988-89, Greenview Elem. Sch., Columbia, S.C., 1989-91; dir. rsch. edn. NuWAE Ent., Houston, 1991-92; cosmetic cons., counter mgr. Elizabeth Arden Foley's/May Co., 1992—. Sec.-treas. Ames Tenant Landlord Svcs., 1982-83, bd. dirs. 1982-, 83, 84-85, chmn., 1984-85. Recipient svc. award Local Govt. Study Commn., Huntsville, 1972, Ms. Alumni award Ala. A&M U., 1978. Mem. ASCD, Ala. A&M U. Alumni Assn. (chaplain 1977-78), Phi Delta Kappa, Delta Sigma Theta. Home: 8001 W Tidwell Rd Apt 416 Houston TX 77040-5536

JIMMINK, GLENDA LEE, retired elementary school educator; b. Lamar, Colo., Feb. 13, 1935; d. Harold Dale and Ruth Grace (Ellenberger) Fasnacht; m. Gary Jimmink, Oct. 24, 1964 (div. 1984); 1 child, Erik Gerard. BA, U. LaVerne, Calif., 1955. Tchr. elem. grades Pomona (Calif.) Unified Sch. Dist., 1955-61, Palo Alto (Calif.) Unified Sch. Dist., 1961-65, San Rafael (Calif.) Sch. Dist., 1966-95; ret.; mem. curriculum coun. San Rafael Sch. Dist., 1983-90, 94-95, mentor tchr., 1989-90, mem. social studies steering com., 1990-95; charter mem. Marin County Curriculum Connection, 1991-95. Artist, pub. (calendar) Dry Creek Valley, 1987; author: World Geography Resource Handbook for Tchrs., 1990, others. Mem. Marin Arts Coun., San Rafael, 1988-95, Big Bros.-Big Sisters, San Rafael, 1986-93, Earthwatch, 1990—. Mem. Colored Pencil Soc. Am., Mendocino Art Assn., Nat. Wildlife Soc., Richmond Art Ctr., Sierra Club, Gualala Arts Assn., Berkeley Art Ctr/. Avocations: art, reading, horticulture, travel.

JINDRA, CHRISTINE, editor; b. Cleve., Sept. 18, 1947; d. Lad Joseph and Ann Frances (Makar) J.; m. Peter J. Junkin, Aug. 1, 1970 (div. Dec. 1987); children: William Patrick, Michael Lad. BS in Journalism, Ohio State U., 1969. City reporter Buffalo News, 1969-70; metro reporter Plain Dealer, Cleve., 1970-82, assignment editor, nat. reporter, 1982-84, state editor, 1984-86, metro editor, 1986-88, feature editor, 1988-92, asst. mng. editor, 1992—. Mem. Women's Cmty. Found., Women's City Club. Avocations: skiing, gardening, traveling, cooking. Office: Plain Dealer 1801 Superior Ave E Cleveland OH 44114-2198

JINKS, ROBERT LARRY, retired newspaper publisher; b. Mt. Pleasant, Tex., Jan. 26, 1929; s. Leon Carlton and Mary (Cunnyngham) J.; m. Anne Claire van Ravesteyn, May 8, 1971; children by previous marriage: Laura Beth, Daniel Carlton, Beau Pottorff. BJ, U. Mo., 1950; MS, Columbia, 1956. News editor Muskogee (Okla.) Times-Democrat, 1950-51; reporter Greensboro (N.C.) Daily News, 1953-55; reporter, city editor Charlotte (N.C) Observer, 1950-60; mem. staff Miami (Fla.) Herald, 1960-77, mng. editor, 1966-72, exec. editor, 1972-77; editor, v.p. San Jose (Calif.) Mercury News, 1977-81; sr. v.p. news and ops. Knight-Ridder Corp., Miami, Fla., 1981-89; pub. San Jose (Calif.) Mercury News, 1989-94, ret., 1994; pres. AP Mng. Editors, 1975-76, Fla. Soc. Newspaper Editors., 1975; bd. mem. McClatchy Newspapers, Inc.; chmn. journalism adv. com. Knight Found. With AUS, 1951-53. Named to 50th anniversary honors list Columbia Grad. Sch. Journalism, 1963, Disting. Grad., 1983; Disting. Grad. award U. Mo., 1990. Mem. Am. Soc. Newspaper Editors (dir. 1980-86).

JINNETT, ROBERT JEFFERSON, lawyer; b. Birmingham, Ala., May 9, 1949; s. Bryan Floyd Jr. and Elizabeth Coleman (Borders) J.; m. Doreen S. Ziff, Aug. 2, 1975; children: Brynn Leigh, Maren Alexandra. BA, Harvard U., 1971; JD, Cornell U., 1975. Bar: N.Y. 1976, U.S. Dist. Ct. (no. dist.) N.Y. 1976, U.S. Dist. Ct. (so. dist.) N.Y. 1978, U.S. Dist. Ct. (ea. dist.) N.Y. 1979, U.S. Supreme Ct. 1988. Law clk. N.Y. State Ct. Appeals, Albany, 1975-77; assoc. Rogers & Wells, N.Y.C., 1977-82, LeBoeuf, Lamb, Greene & MacRae, N.Y.C., 1983-85; ptnr. LeBoeuf, Lamb, Leiby & MacRae, N.Y.C., 1986-94; ptnr. LeBoeuf, Lamb, Greene & MacRae, L.L.P., N.Y.C., 1994, of counsel, 1995—; pres. LeBoeuf Computing Techs., LLC., N.Y.C., 1996—; sr. cons. Cutter Consortium Year 2000 Adv. Svc. Co-editor: Year 2000 Law Deskbook, 1999; contbr. articles to profl. jours. Recipient 3d nat. prize Nathan Burkan Meml. Competition, ASCAP, 1974; German Acad. Exch. Svc. fellow U. Heidelberg, Germany, 1971-72. Mem. S.R., Jamestowne Soc. Republican. Episcopalian. Avocation: poetry. Office: LeBoeuf Lamb Greene MacRae 125 W 55th St New York NY 10019-5369

JINRIGHT, NOAH FRANKLIN, vocational school educator; b. Banks, Ala., Dec. 5, 1936; s. William Carroll and Ila Marie (Garrett) J.; m. Sarah Ann (Graham) Nickolson, Nov. 21, 1959 (div. Sept. 1974); children: Charlene M., Lisa A., Michael D.; m. Frances Lenora Gaskins, June 11, 1978; children: Diana Carol, Jonathan Franklin. Cert. archtl. and mech. drafting, Columbus (Ga.) Tech., 1971, cert. plate and pipe welder, 1984, CNC, 1983. Lic. ins. agent, Ga. Operator scale Bibb Textiles, Columbus, 1954-56; operator press and share Columbus Iron Works, 1957-58; ins. agt. Interstate Life, Columbus, 1958-61; winder starter/generator Joe Hooten, Inc., Columbus, 1960; fireman City of Columbus, 1960-66; advt. rep. Jinright Enterprises, Columbus, 1966; ins. agt. Security Life of Ga., Columbus, 1966; operator share and press Pascoe Steel, Columbus, 1966-67; machinist Goldens' Foundry and Machine Works, Columbus, 1967; carpenter, roofer Muscogee County Sch. Dist., Columbus, 1968-72; pattern maker Pekor Iron Works, Columbus, 1972-78; instr. metals tech. Kendrick H.S., Columbus, 1978—; past mfg. rep. printing and advtg. specialties; cons. Voc. Tng. and Rsch. Inst., Seoul, Korea, 1989-90. sponsor Spencer H.S. AWS Club, 1979-81; exec. trainer Precision Metalforming Assn., 1996; past trustee Epworth United Meth. Ch., ch. usher. Sgt. USAFR, 1963-65. Recipient recruiting cert. for outstanding recruiting students USAF, 1991-92. Mem. Internat. Soc. Welding Educators (program adv. bd.), Am. Foundry Soc., Am. Welding Soc., Vocat. Indsl. Clubs Am. (advisor, cert. of appreciation region VIII 1996), Trade and Indsl. Educators Ga. (mem. West Ga. Sch. to work-evaluation team 1994—). Methodist. Avocations: fishing, hunting, camping, model building, photography. Home: 2040 Lee Rd 427 Phenix City AL 36867 also: PO Box 63 Columbus GA 31902-0063 Office: Kendrick HS 6015 Georgetown Dr Columbus GA 31907-4611

JIRAUCH, CHARLES W., lawyer; b. St. Louis, Apr. 27, 1944; s. Mary K. (Horan) J.; m. Sally J. Costello, June 1, 1968 (div. Mar. 1977); m. Dana K. Bowen; children: Melissa, Mathew, Kathleen. BSEE, Washington U., 1966; JD, Georgetown U., 1970. Bar: Ill. 1971, Ariz. 1975, Nev. 1991, , Calif. 1993, Colo. 1993, U.S. Patent Office 1970, U.S. Supreme Ct. 1978. Atty. Leydig, Voit & Mayer, Chgo., 1970-71, McDermott, Will & Emery, Chgo., 1971-75, Streich Lang, Phoenix, 1975—. Bd. dirs. Valley Big Bros./Big Susters, 1980-86, pres. bd. dirs., 1985-86, pres., 1988-92; bd. advisors to dean Ariz. State U. Sch. Engring., 1988—. Mem. ABA, Ariz. Bar Found., Maricopa County Bar Found., Am. Judicature Soc., Am. Intellectual Property Law Assn., Ariz. Dem. Coun., Ariz. Civil Liberties Union, Az. chap. Am. Electronic Assn., 1998—; bd. advs. Sch. Engring. Az. State U., 1998—, bd. dirs. Valley Big Brothers/Sisters, 1980-86 (pres. 1985-86, 88-92). Democrat. Roman Catholic. Office: Streich Lang 2 N Central Ave Fl 2 Phoenix AZ 85004-2391

JIRKA, BRAD PAUL, sculptor, art educator; b. Chgo., Feb. 25, 1954; s. Donald H. and Doris M. (Zonsius) J.; m. Katherine Ann Jones, Oct. 18, 1980. Student, U. Colo., 1972-73; BFA, Mpls. Coll. Art and Design, 1976. Co-founder, officer Midwest Ctr. Rsch. and devel. of Elec. Art, Mpls., 1976-78; ptnr. B. Jirka/N. Andersen Neon, Mpls., 1976-80; owner, artist B. Jirka & Assocs., Northfield, Minn., 1976—; co-founder, lead instr. Am. Sch. Neon, Mpls., 1994-95; gen. ptnr. St. Elmo's Kitchen Ltd. Partnership, Mpls., 1984-89; v.p. design St. Elmo's Inc., Mpls., 1990—; asst. prof. fine arts divsn. Mpls. Coll. Art and Design, 1980—; cons. design engr. Neon Dynamics Inc., Minnetonka, Minn., 1987-94; lectr., presenter Lightfair Internat., Chgo., 1995; vis. artist Minn. State Arts Bd., North High, Mpls., 1984, Vine, Park H.S., Cottage Grove, Minn., 1985; vis. lectr. Walker Art Ctr., Mpls., 1985. Artist neon mural Riverplace, 1982 (Ctr. Urban Environ. 1984), installation commn. Minn. State Arts Bd., 1993-94, Duluth Pub. Arts Commn., 1995-96, sculpture commn. Cray Rsch., 1990-91; artist archtl. neon installation Opus Tower/Target Ctr., 1984, 88, 90. Ford faculty grantee Mpls. Coll. Art & Design, 1983; recipient 1st pl. comml. neon Nat. Electric Sign Assn., Mpls., 1987. Mem. Internat. Sculpture Ctr., Minn. Sign Assn. (chair std. practice com. 1987-92, bd. dirs. 1986-97, v.p. 1998, pres. 1999), Chgo. Yacht Club. Avocations: sailing, skiing, wooden boat restoration, antique scientific instruments. Studio: 2688 89th Ct W Northfield MN 55057-4767 Office: Minn Coll Art & Design 2501 Stevens Ave Minneapolis MN 55404-4347

JIRKANS, MARIBETH JOIE, school counselor; b. Cleve., May 3, 1945; d. Raymond Wenceslaus and Elsie Koryta J.; children: Annemarie Gurchik, Keith Robert Gurchik. Student, U. Vienna, Austria, 1965; BS in Elem. Edn., Coll. Mt. St. Joseph, 1967; MEd in Ednl. Counseling, Cleve. State U., 1984; postgrad., U. Akron, 1986-88, Kent State U., 1989—. Cert. elem., spl. edn. and adult edn. tchr., counselor. Tchr. North Olmstead (Ohio) City Schs., 1967-76; tchr. adult edn. Polaris Vocat. Sch., Middleburg Heights, Ohio, 1978; tchr. adult edn., ESL Lakewood (Ohio) City Schs., 1978-79; tchr. 2d grade St. Rose Sch., Lakewood, 1979-80; tchr. learning disabilities Cleve. Pub. Schs., 1980-85; tutor handicapped Cleve. Christian Home, 1982-84; elem. sch. counselor Cleve. Pub. Schs., 1985-97; tchr. Kent (Ohio) State U., 1997-98; sch. psychologist asst. PSI Assocs. Inc., 1998—; counselor West Side Community Mental Health Ctr., Cleve., 1983-84; sales mgr. Field Enterprises Inc., Cleve., 1977-82. Contbr. articles to newspapers. Vol. Fairview Gen. Hosp., Cleve., 1959-63, Cerebral Palsy Camp, 1959-63, Allen Halfway House for Children, Cin., 1963-67; co-founder Westshore Separated, Divorced and Remarried Caths., Cleve., 1975-85; chair North Olmsted Jr. Women's Club; mem. parish coun. St. Brendan Ch., North Olmstead, 1975-87; mem. com. Cleve. Symphony, Cleve. Art Mus. Recipient Speaker's United Torch award United Way, Cleve., 1st Pl. prize in clothing design Stretch & Sew, 1975, 1st Pl. prize in needlepoint Framemakers Art, 1983. Mem. AACD, AAUW, Am. Assn. Marriage and Family Therapists, N.E. Ohio Counselor Assn., Ohio Counselors Assn., Ohio Assn. Counseling and Devel., Coun. for Exceptional Children, Am. Sch. Counselor Assn., ASCD, Gestalt Inst., Audubon Soc., Cleve. Mus. Art, Cleve. Natural History Mus., Cleve. Tchrs. Union, Gestalt Inst., Am. Aerobics and Fitness Assn., Edgewater Yacht Club, English Speaking Union, Holden Arboretum, Pi Lambda Theta, Chi Sigma Iota. Democrat. Avocations: aerobics, art, cycling, dancing, gardening. Home: 727 Tollis Pky Cleveland OH 44147-1813

JIROUSEK, CHARLES EDWARD, small business owner; b. Mpls., Aug. 10, 1941; s. Edward Harold and Marjorie Tildon (Davis) J.; m. Carole Ann Torreano, Feb. 28, 1977; children: Jesse Charles, Terri Marie. AA, U. Minn., 1961, BS in Forestry, 1967. With U.S. Forest Svcs., Young, Ariz., 1963-64; surveyor, draftsman City of Mpls., 1965-67; surveyor Foley Bros., Red Wing, Minn., 1967-68; with Belville & Hoffman, Mpls., 1971; owner Arrowhead Music, Duluth, Minn., 1972-86, Safety Harbor, Fla., 1986—. Mem. Guild of Am. Luthiers. Avocations: playing country blues on 12-string guitar; entertainer Fla. State Folk Festival.

JIRSA, JAMES OTIS, civil engineering educator; b. Lincoln, Nebr., July 30, 1938; s. Otis Frank and Anna Marie (Skutchan) J.; m. Marion Ansley Coad, Aug. 7, 1941; children: David, Stephen. BS, U. Nebr., 1960; MS, U. Ill., 1962, PhD, 1963. Registered profl. engr., Tex. Asst. prof. civil engring. U. Nebr., Lincoln, 1964-65; asst. prof. then assoc. prof. Rice U., Houston, 1965-72; assoc. prof. then prof. U. Tex., Austin, 1972-82, Finch prof. engring., 1982-84, Ferguson prof. civil engring., 1984-88, dir. Ferguson Structural Engring. Lab., 1985-88, Janet S. Cockrell Centennial chair in engring., 1988—, chmn. dept. civil engring., 1996—; research engr. Portland Cement Assocs., 1965; engr. H.J. Degenkolb Assocs., San Francisco, 1980. Contbr. articles to profl. jours. Fulbright scholar U. Paris, 1963-64; recipient Rsch. award Japanese Soc. for Promotion Sci., 1980, 94, J.A. Boase award Reinforced Concrete Rsch. Coun., 1993. Fellow Am. Concrete Inst. (TAC chmn. 1985-88, bd. dirs. 1987-90, v.p. 1998—, Alfred Lindau award 1986, Wason medal 1977, Reese award 1977, 79, Bloem award 1990); mem. NAE, ASCE (com. chmn. 1972-81, Reese award 1970, 91, Huber Rsch. prize 1978), Earthquake Engring. Rsch. Inst. (bd. dirs.), Structural Engring Assn. Tex., Internat. Assn. for Bridge and Structural Engrs., Nebr. Czech Orgn. (King Charles award 1983). Office: U Tex Dept Civil Engring Cockrell Hall Ste 4.2 Austin TX 78712

JISCHKE, MARTIN C., academic administrator; b. Chgo., Aug. 7, 1941; m. Patricia Fowler; children: Charles, Marian. BS in Physics with honors, Ill. Inst. Tech., 1963; MS in Aeronautics and Astronautics, MIT, 1964, PhD in Aeronautics and Astronautics, 1968. Engr. Rand Corp., Santa Monica, Calif., 1965; research engr. Battelle N.W. Lab., Richland, Washington, 1970; research fellow Donald W. Douglas Lab., Richland, 1971, Nat. Aeronautics and Space Adminstrn., Moffett Field, Calif., 1973; from asst. prof. to prof. aerospace, mech. and nuclear engring. U. Okla., 1968-75, prof., dir. Sch. Aerospace, Mech. and Nuclear Engring., 1977-81, interim pres., 1985, dean Coll. Engring., 1981-86, mem. various coms., 1985; White House fellow, spl. asst. to sec. of transp. U.S. Dept. Transp., Washington, 1975-76; chancellor U. Mo., Rolla, 1986-91; pres. Iowa State U., Ames, 1991—; bd. dirs. Kerr McGee Corp., Mo. Alliance for Sci., The Keystone Found., Mo. Corp. for Sci. and Tech., vice-chmn., 1990-91; participant Japanese Econ. Found. Vis. Leaders Program, 1983; mem. Gov.'s Coun. on Sci. and Tech. State of Okla., 1983-84, Gordon Rsch. Conf. on Geophysics; mem. planning com. for 80's Okla. State Regents for Higher Edn.; mem. organizing com. 14th Midwestern Mechanics Conf.; mem. adv. com. for engring. sci. NSF Engring. Directorate, 1985-88; mem. com. on statewide postsecondary telecomm. policy Mo. Coordinating Bd. for Higher Edn., 1987-91; chmn. Congrl. Aero. Adv. Com., 1987-89; sci. adviser to Gov. of Mo., 1990-91; mem. Am. Coun. on Edn. Com. on Math. and Sci., 1990-91. Contbr. articles and reports to profl. publs. Civilian aide Sec. of Army, State of Mo. East, 1987-91; bd. dirs. Bankers Trust, 1995—, Iowa Spl. Olympics, Am. Coun. on Edn., 1996—, Nat. Merit Scholarship Corp., 1997—; mem. Kellogg Commn. on the Future of State and Land-Grant U., 1995—. Recipient Ralph Teetor award Soc. Automotive Engrs., 1971, Brandon H. Griffith award U. Okla., U. Okla. Regents award for superior teaching, 1975, IIT Prof. Achievement award, 1992, Delta Tau Delta Achievement award, 1992, Engrs. Club St. Louis Achievement award, 1991, Dept. Army Outstanding Civilian Svc. medal, 1991; NASA fellow, 1966; NSF fellow, 1965; AEC/NORCUS summer faculty fellow, 1970-71, NASA/ASEE fellow, 1973. Fellow AAAS, AIAA (assoc., sec.-treas. Okla. chpt., vice chmn., chmn.); mem. ASME, AAUP (v.p., pres. Okla. chpt.), NSPE, Am. Phys. Soc., Am. Soc. Engring. Edn. (Centennial Medallion 1993), Nat. Assn. State Univs. and Land Grant Colls. (bd. dirs., chair 1997—), Assn. Big Twelve Univs. (pres. 1994—), Mo. Soc. Profl. Engrs., Rotary, Phi Beta Kappa, Tau Beta Pi, Sigma Xi, Pi Tau Sigma, Sigma Gamma Tau, Sigma Pi Sigma, Phi Eta Sigma. Home: The Knoll Iowa State U Ames IA 50014 Office: Iowa State U Office of Pres 117 Beardshear Ames IA 50011-2035

JOBE, LARRY ALTON, financial company executive; b. Knox City, Tex., Jan. 12, 1940; s. Lloyd Alton and Georgia (Swift); m. Suzanne Marie Storch, Aug. 2, 1980; 1 dau., Jennifer Marie; children by previous marriage: Lorrie Aileen, Lezlie Amee, Lowell Alton, Lloyd Alan, Leland Austin, Llewyn. B.B.A., U. North Tex., 1961, postgrad., 1961-65. CPA, Tex. Joined Grant Thornton, Dallas, 1961; mgr. Grant Thornton, 1967-69, ptnr., 1968-69; mng. ptnr., mem. exec. com. Grant Thornton, Dallas, 1973—, S.W. regional mng. ptnr., 1983-91; chmn. Legal Network, Inc., 1991—; pres. Nat. Corporate Network, 1997—; asst. sec. commerce Washington, 1969-72; v.p. fin. Dart Industries, 1972-73; mem. acctg.adv. bd. U. North Tex., U. Tex.; bd. dirs. Ind. Nat. Bank. Contbr. articles to profl. jours. Bd. dirs. Dallas Citizens Coun., Eisenhower World Affairs Inst.; chmn. bd. trustees Dallas Theol. Sem.; mem. Chief Execs. Roundtable; chmn. bd. Dallas Alliance for Minority Enterprise, Dallas Minority Bus. Ctr., Profl. Devel. Inst. of U. North Tex.; mem. pres.'s coun. North Tex. State U. Recipient Excellence in Acctg. award Haskins and Sells Found., 1960; Outstanding Alumni award U. North Tex., 1965, Pres.' Svc. award, 1986; U.S. Interagy. Audit Tng. award, 1970, Outstanding Svc. award, 1st Place Author's award Fed. Govt. Accts. Assn., 1970. Mem. AICPA, Tex. Soc. CPAs, Fed. Govt. Accts. Assn., Dallas C. of C. (dir., vice chmn.), Blue Key, Phi Eta Sigma, Alpha Chi, Alpha Lambda Pi, Beta Alpha Psi. Office: 600 N Pearl St Ste 2100 Dallas TX 75201-2825

JOBS, STEVEN PAUL, computer corporation executive; b. 1955; adopted s. Paul J. and Clara J. (Jobs); m. Laurene Powell, Mar. 18, 1991. Student, Reed Coll. With Hewlett-Packard, Palo Alto, Calif.; designer video games Atari Inc., 1974; co-founder Apple Computer Inc., Cupertino, Calif., chmn. bd., 1975-85, former dir.; pres. NeXT, Inc., Redwood City, Calif., 1985—; chief exec. officer NeXT, Inc., Redwood City; interim CEO Apple Computer, Cupertino, Calif., 1997—; chmn., chief exec. officer Prixar Animation Studios. Co-designer: (with Stephan Wozniak) Apple I Computer, 1976. Recipient Nat. Medal Tech. presented by Pres. Ronald Reagan, Entrepreneur of the Decade award, Inc. Mag., Jefferson award for Pub. Svc. Office: Pixar Animation Studios 1001 W Cutting Blvd Ste 200 Richmond CA 94804-2028*

JOBSON, KATHLEEN MILLER, nurse midwife; b. Hutchinson, Kans., Feb. 24, 1960; d. Mahlon and Fannie Miller; m. Darrell Jobson, July 3, 1992; children: Sara Miller Jobson, Meghan Miller Jobson. ADN, Hesston Coll., 1989; B in Nursing, Bethel Coll., 1992; MSN, U. N.Mex., 1995. Cert. nurse midwife, lic. Am. Coll. of Nurse-Midwivery. RN in pediatrics Hutchinson (Kans.) Hosp. Corp., 1989-90; RN in labor and delivery HCA Wesley Med. Ctr., Wichita, Kans., 1990-92; RN in labor and delivery Lovelace Med. Ctr., Albuquerque, 1992-95, cert. nurse midwife, 1995-97, 98—; RN in labor, delivery Pratt (Kans.) Regional Med. Ctr., 1999—; substitute instr. nursing porgram Pratt C.C. and Area Vocat. Sch., 1999. Vol. svc. worker Amish Mennonite Aid, El Salvador, Cen. Am., 1984-86, sch. tchr., svc. worker, Belize, Cen. Am., 1982-84. Grantee Mennonite Women's Missionary and Svc. Commn., 1994, U. N.Mex., 1994. Mennonite. Avocations: gardening, photography, quilting, hot air ballooning, fgn. langs.

JOCHIM, MICHAEL ALLAN, archaeologist; b. St. Louis, May 31, 1945; s. Kenneth Erwin and Jean MacKenzie (Keith) J.; m. Amy Martha Waugh, Aug. 12, 1967; children: Michael Waugh, Katherine Elizabeth. BS, U. Mich., 1967, MA, 1971, PhD, 1975. Lectr. anthropology U. Calif., Santa Barbara, 1975-77, asst. prof., 1979-81, assoc. prof., 1981-87, prof., 1987—, dept. chmn., 1987-92; asst. prof. Queens Coll. CUNY, Flushing, 1977-79; mem. archaeology rev. panel NSF, Washington, 1988-90. Author: Hunter-Gatherer Subsistence and Settlement, 1976, Strategies for Survival, 1981, A Hunter-Gatherer Landscape, 1998; editor (series) Interdisciplinary Contributions to Archaeology, 1987—. Chmn. Community Adv. Com. for Spl. Edn., Santa Barbara County, 1980-82. Grantee NEH, 1976, NSF, 1980, 81, 83, 89, 91, 94, Nat. Geog. Soc., 1987, 97, Wenner-Gren, 1999. Fellow Am. Anthrop. Assn.; mem. Soc. for Am. Archaeology, Sigma Xi. Office: Univ of Calif Dept Anthropology Santa Barbara CA 93106

JOCHNER, MICHELE MELINA, lawyer; b. Naperville, Ill., May 19, 1966. BA summa cum laude, Mundelein Coll., Chgo., 1987; JD with honors, DePaul U., 1990, LLM in Taxation Law, 1992. Bar: Ill. 1990, U.S. Dist. Ct. (no. dist.) Ill. 1990, U.S. Ct. Appeals (7th cir.) 1996, U.S. Supreme Ct. 1996. Law clk. U.S. Securities & Exch. Commn., Chgo., 1989; legal rsch. asst. to prof. Marlene Nicholson DePaul U. Sch. Law, Chgo., 1989-91; legal rsch. asst. to assoc. dean Vincent Vitullo DePaul U. Sch. Law, 1989-91; law clk. extern U.S. Dist. Ct. (no. dist.) Ill., Chgo., 1989-90; judicial law clk. Cir. Ct. of Cook County, Chgo., 1991-92; staff atty. Cir. Ct. of Cook County, 1992-93, sr. staff atty., 1993-95, acting supr. legal rsch. divsn., 1995-96; staff atty. permanency project child protection divsn. Cir. Ct. Cook County, Chgo., 1996-97; jud. law clk. to Hon. Mary Ann G. McMorrow Ill. Supreme Ct., Chgo., 1997—; mem. subcom. money transfers and adminstrv. regulations Ill. Supreme Ct., 1995-96; adj. prof. law John Marshall Law Sch., Chgo., 1994—, judge Herzog moot ct.competition, 1997—; adj. prof. law DePaul U. Coll. Law, 1998—; spkr. in field. Contbr. articles to profl. jours. Recipient Harold A. Shertz award Film, Air & Package Carriers Conf., Alexandria, Va., 1990. Mem. ABA, Ill. Bar Assn. (Lincoln award 2d pl. 1994, 97, 1st pl. 1996, 99, mem. gen. practice sect. coun.), Fed. Bar Assn., Chgo. Bar Assn., U.S. Supreme Ct. Hist. Soc., Order of Coif, Kappa Gamma Pi, Phi Sigma Tau. Avocations: writing fiction, non-fiction.

JOCHUM, LESTER H., dentist; b. Chgo., Nov. 19, 1929; s. J. Harry and Hilma O. (Swanson) J.; m. Anne Elizabeth Cannon, Sept. 20, 1952 (div. Apr. 1983); 1 child, David S. Student U. Wyo., 1947-48; BS in Bus. Adminstrn. with honors, Oreg. State U., 1952; pre-dental student Portland State Coll., 1959-60; B.S. with honors in Sci., U. Oreg., 1963, D.M.D., 1964. Staff acct. Pacific Telephone and Telegraph Co., San Francisco, 1952-59; gen. practice dentistry, San Jose, Calif., 1965-83; dental cons. Delta Dental Plan of Calif., Sacramento, 1983-98, ret., 1998; ptnr. Trinity Imports, 1985-93. Contbr. articles Calif. Wine Press; also others. Asst. chief Santa Clara Reserve Police Dept., Calif., 1976-83. Active No. Calif. diocese Episc. Ch. Served with U.S. Army, 1952-54. Mem. Sacramento Dist. Dental Soc., Calif. Dental Assn., ADA, Phi Kappa Phi, Psi Omega, Alpha Phi Omega, Lambda Chi Alpha (ritual chmn. 1951, soc. chmn. 1952). Republican.

JOCHUM, VERONICA, pianist; b. Berlin; d. Eugen and Maria (Montz) J.; m. Wilhelm V. von Moltke, Nov. 15, 1961. MusM, Staatliche Musikhochschule, Munich, 1955, Concert Diploma, 1957; pvt. study with Edwin Fischer, Josef Benvenuti, 1958-59, Rudolf Serkin, Phila., 1959-61. Faculty Settlement Sch. Music, Phila., 1959-61, New Eng. Conservatory Music, Boston, 1965—, Berkshire Music Center, Tanglewood, 1974, Radcliffe Inst., Cambridge, Mass. Recorded albums with Laurel, Deutsche Grammophon, Philips, Golden Crest, Pro Arte, GM Recordings, CRJ, Tudor; Numerous tours, throughout N. and S. Am., Asia, Europe and, Africa; as soloist with world renowned orchs., including Boston Symphony, Balt. Symphony, London Philharmonic, Los Angeles Chamber Orch., London Symphony, Mpls. Symphony, Berlin, Hamburg and Munich Philharmonics, Bavarian and Bamberg Symphonies, Munich Chamber Orch., radio orchs. of Hamburg, Munich, and Frankfurt, Orch. Maggio Musicale, Florence, La

Fenice Orch., Venice, RAI-Orch., Naples, Mozarteum Orch., Salzburg, Concertgebouw Orch., Amsterdam, The Hague Philharmonic, Venezuelan Symphony, Caracas, Jerusalem Symphony, others; appearances on radio and TV, recitals in more than 50 countries on 4 continents; participant, Marlboro Music Festival, Montreux Festival, Bregenz Festival, Festival de Vallonie (Belgium), Tanglewood, Ea. Music Festival, Chambermusic East. Bd. mem. Berkshire Inst. Theology and the Arts. Recipient Cross of the Order of Merit award German Pres., 1994, fellowship Bunting Inst. of Radcliffe Coll., 1996-97. Office: New Eng Conservatory Music 290 Huntington Ave Boston MA 02115-5018*

JOCK, PAUL F., II, lawyer; b. Indpls., Jan. 25, 1943; s. Paul F. and Alice (Sheehan) J.; m. Gail A. Webre, Sept. 16, 1967; children: Craig W., Nicole L. BBA, U. Notre Dame, 1965; JD, U. Chgo., 1970. Bar: Ill. 1970, N.Y. 1990. Ptnr. Kirkland & Ellis, Chgo. and N.Y.C., 1970—; v.p. legal affairs Tribune Co., Chgo., 1981. Assoc. editor U. Chgo. Law Rev., 1969-70. Served to lt. USN, 1965-67. Mem. ABA, Chgo. Bar Assn., Assn. of the Bar of City of N.Y. Office: Kirkland & Ellis 200 E Randolph St Fl 54 Chicago IL 60601-6636 also: Citicorp Ctr 153 E 53rd St New York NY 10022-4611

JOCKETTY, WALT, professional sports team executive; m. Sue Jocketty; children: Ashley, Joey. BBA, U. Minn., 1974. Dir. minor league, scouting/asst. gen. mgr./player personnel Oakland A's, 1980-93; v.p., gen. mgr. St. Louis Cardinals, 1994—. Office: St Louis Cardinals 250 Stadium Plz Saint Louis MO 63102-1722*

JOCKUSCH, CARL GROOS, JR., mathematics educator; b. San Antonio, July 13, 1941; s. Carl Groos and Mary English (Dickson) J.; m. Elizabeth Ann Northrop, June 17, 1964; children—William, Elizabeth, Rebecca. Student, Vanderbilt U., 1959-60; B.A. with highest honors, Swarthmore Coll., 1963; Ph.D., M.I.T., 1966. Instr. Northeastern U., 1966-67; asst. prof. math. U. Ill., Urbana-Champaign, 1967-71; asso. prof. U. Ill., 1971-75, prof., 1975—. Contbr. articles to profl. jours.; editor Jour. Symbolic Logic, 1974-75, Proc. Am. Math. Soc., 1997—. NSF research grantee. Mem. Assn. Symbolic Logic, Am. Math. Soc., Math. Assn. Am. Home: 704 E McHenry St Urbana IL 61801-6846 Office: Univ Ill Dept Math 1409 W Green St Urbana IL 61801-2943

JODOCK, DARRELL HARLAND, minister, religion educator; b. Northwood, N.D., Aug. 15, 1941; s. Harry N. and Grace H. (Hansen) J.; m. Janice Marie Swanson, July 8, 1972; children: Erik Thomas, Aren Kristofer. BA summa cum laude, St. Olaf Coll., 1962; BD with honors, Luther Theol. Sem., 1966; postgrad., Union Theol. Sem., N.Y.C., 1966-67; PhD, Yale U., 1969. Ordained to ministry Am. Luth. Ch., 1973, Luth. Ch. in Am., 1978. Instr. Luther Theol. Sem., St. Paul, 1969-70, asst. prof., 1970-73, 75-78; asst. pastor Grace Luth. Ch., Washington, 1973-75; prof. dept. religion Muhlenberg Coll., Allentown, Pa., 1978-99, head dept. of religion, 1978-92, Class of 1932 rsch. prof., 1989; disting. prof. religion Gustavus Adolphus Coll., St. Peter, Minn., 1999—; chmn. various coms. N.E. Pa. Synod Evang. Luth. Ch. in Am., 1979-99, del. to nat. assembly, 1995, 97, 99; adv. bd. Berman Ctr. for Jewish Studies, 1985-92; founder, chmn. bd. Inst. for Jewish-Christian Understanding, 1988-99. Author: The Church's Bible: Its Contemporary Authority, 1989; translator: Luther and the Peasants' War (Hubert Kirchner), 1972; editor and co-author: Ritschl in Retrospect: History, Community and Science, 1995, Catholicism Contending with Modernity: Roman Catholic Modernism and Anti-Modernism in Historical Context, 1999; contbr. articles to profl. jours. Del. Dem. Farm Labor Party, Rochester, Minn., 1972, St. Paul, 1976. Recipient Paul C. Empie Meml. award Muhlenberg Coll., 1987; Danforth Found. fellow 1962-69, Inst. for Ecumenical and Cultural Rsch. fellow, 1982-83. Mem. Am. Acad. Religion (pres. 19th Century theology group 1981-86, 97—), Am. Soc. Ch. History, Soc. for Values in Higher Edn., Internat. Schleiermacher Soc., Internat. Bonhoeffer Soc., Søren Kierkegaard Soc., Phi Beta Kappa, Omicron Delta Kappa (campus leadership 1985—). Office: Gustavus Adolphus Coll Dept Religion 800 W College Ave Saint Peter MN 56082

JOE, THOMAS, think-tank. Founder and dir. Ctr. for the Study of Social Policy, Washington, D.C., 1979—. Office: Ctr Study Social Policy 1250 I St NW Ste 503 Washington DC 20005-3922*

JOEHL, RAYMOND JOSEPH, surgeon, educator; b. Alton, Ill., July 20, 1948; m. Julia Nelle Garrels, Aug. 28, 1970; children: Jacob, Samuel, Hillarie, Sarah, Claudia, Hannah. BA, U. Pa., 1970; MD, St. Louis U., 1974. Diplomate Am. Bd. Surgery. Resident in surgery Pa. State U., Hershey, 1974-79, rsch. fellow, 1979-80, from asst. to assoc. prof. surgery, 1980-85; from assoc. prof. to prof. surgery Northwestern U., Chgo., 1985-91, James R. Hines prof. surgery, 1993—; chief divsn. gen. surgery and dir. residency in surgery, attending surgeon Northwestern Meml. Hosp., VA Chgo. Health Care Sys.-Lakeside divsn., 1985—, Hershey Med. Ctr., 1980-85; chief surg. svc. VA Lakeside Med. Ctr., Chgo., 1987-95. Fellow ACS, Am. Surg. Assn.; mem. Soc. Univ. Surgeons, Soc. for Surgery Alimentary Tract, Alpha Omega Alpha. Episcopalian. Avocations: children, advocate for disabled especially blind, teaching. Office: Northwestern U Divsn Gen Surg Tarry 11-703 300 E Superior St Chicago IL 60611-3010

JOEL, AMOS EDWARD, JR., telecommunications consultant; b. Phila., Mar. 12, 1918; s. Amos Edward and Anna (Potsdamer) J.; m. Rhoda Ethel Fenton; children: Jeffrey, Stephanie, Andrea. BEE, MIT, 1940, MEE, 1942. Registered profl. engr., N.Y. Mem. tech. staff Bell Tel. Labs., N.Y. and N.J., 1940-52; supr. Bell Tel. Labs., Whippany, N.J., 1952-54, dept. head, 1954-61; dir. Bell Tel. Labs., Holmdel, N.J., 1961-67, cons., 1967-83, ret., 1983.; cons., 1983—; cons. AT&T Bell Comm. Rsch., GTE, IBM, Contel, Pacific Tel.; lectr. in field of switching sys. Author: Electronic Switching Central Office Systems of the World, 1976, Electronic Switching: Digital Central Office Systems of the World, 1982, History of Science and Technology in the Bell System-Switching Technology, 1982; author: (with others) Fundamentals of Digital Switching, 1983, 2d edit., 1990, Electronics, Computers and Telephone Switching, 1990, Future of the Central Office, 1991; contbr. articles to encys. and profl. jours.; holder more than 70 patents. Co-recipient Outstanding Patent award N.J. R & D Coun., 1972, Stuart Ballantine medal Franklin Inst., 1981, Century prize Internat. Telecom. Union, 1983, Columbian medal City of Genoa, Italy, 1984, Kyoto prize in advanced tech., 1989, Nat. Med. of Tech., 1993; named N.J. Inventor of Yr., 1989. Fellow IEEE (life, co-recipient Alexander Graham Bell medal 1976, IEEE medal of honor 1992, nat. medal tech. 1993), Am. Acad. Arts and Scis.; mem. NAE, AAAS, Comm. Soc. of IEEE (pres. 1973-75), Assn. for Computing Machinery, Sigma Xi. Avocations: organ and keyboard music, railroading. Home: 131 N Wyoming Ave South Orange NJ 07079-1529

JOEL, BILLY (WILLIAM MARTIN JOEL), musician; b. Bronx, N.Y., May 9, 1949; s. Howard and Rosalind (Nyman) J.; m. Christie Brinkley, Mar. 23, 1985 (div. Aug. 1994); 1 child, Alexa Ray. LHD (hon.), Fairfield U., 1991; HMD (hon.), Berklee Coll. Music, 1993. Popular rec. artist, 1972—; songs include Just the Way You Are, 1978 (Grammy award for record of yr., Grammy award for song of yr.), Honesty, 1979 (Grammy nomination for song of yr.) We Didn't Start the Fire, 1989 (Grammy nominations for record of yr., song of yr. best pop vocal performance, male); albums include Piano Man, Streetlife Serenade, Turnstiles, The Stranger, 52nd Street (Grammy awards for best album, best male vocal performance 1979), Glass Houses, 1980 (Grammy award for best rock male vocal performance, Am. Music award for album of yr.), Songs in the Attic, The Nylon Curtain, 1982 (Grammy nomination for album of yr.), An Innocent Man, Greatest Hits, Vols. I and II, 1985, Vol. III, 1997, The Bridge, 1986, Concert: Live from the Soviet Union, 1987, Storm Front, 1989, River of Dreams, 1993 (4 Grammy nominations); summer tour with Elton John, 1994, spring tour with Elton John, 1995, Asian and European tour with Elton John, 1998. Recipient Grammy nomination Best Pop Vocal Performance Male and Producer of Yr., 1990, Grammy Legend award, 1990, Am. Music Awards award of merit, 1999; inducted into Songwriters Hall of Fame, 1992, Rock and Roll Hall of Fame, 1999. Premiered first prodn. tour of the USSR by an Am. popular artist, 1987. Office: Maritime Music Inc 2d Fl 280 Elm St Fl 2D Southampton NY 11968-3464

JOEL, WILLIAM LEE, II, interior and lighting designer; b. Richmond, Va., Feb. 23, 1933; s. J. Alton and Dorothy Joel; m. Merry Pick, June 5, 1955; children: Taryn, Dana, Wendy, Holly. Student, R.I. Sch. Design, 1953-55; AB, Brown U., 1955; postgrad., N.Y. Sch. Interior Design, 1956, Pratt Inst., 1958-61. Cert. interior designer Commonwealth of Va. Draftsman Mills Denmark Inc., N.Y.C., 1957-58; with sales and interior design Lord & Taylor's Inc., N.Y.C., 1958-61; pres., interior designer Richmond (Va.) Art Co. Inc.; instr. Va. Commonwealth U. (formerly Richmond Profl. Inst.), 1963-67; set designer Barksdale Theatre, Hanover, Va., 1977-88; mem. adv. bd. interior design program Va. Poly. Inst and State U., 1986-90; speaker numerous orgns., radio and TV programs. *In the past decade the direction of world responsibility demands that all disciplines be more effective and efficient in the use of all natural resources,none are more responsible than the disciplines that dictate the use of interior environment. To this end we have focused on better coordination of interior space planning with the latest technology of lighting and controls. To demonstrate these principles we publish a series of lighting articles on the Web. We changed from a retail and design studio in 1995 to an online Website combining both retail and interior-lighting design services.* Prin. works include Culpepper (Va.) Hosp., The Curles Neck Pl., Richmond, Dominion Nat. Bank, Richmond, Gary, Stoch, Walls offices, Richmond, Gov.'s Exec. Mansion, Commonwealth Va., 1976, Hello Inc., Richmond, Hill Bldg., Richmond, Hunter House Mus., Norfolk, Va., Richmond, Fredericksburg and Potomac R.R. Co. corp. hdqrs., Rolph Clark Stone Packaging Co. offices, Straub and Dalch office complex, Westminster Canterbury House, Richmond, Wickham Valentine House, Willow Oaks Country Club, Continental Cablevision, Richmond, St. Paul Episcopal Ch., Richmond, numerous residences; author: articles published bi-monthly in Rich Art website. Co-chmn. com. for cert. Va. Interior Designers, 1982-90; mem. Downtown Mktg. Com., chmn. subcom. Xmas Sound and Lighting, Richmond, 1988-91, mem. prodn. Richmond Forum sets and lighting design, 1989-95; bd. visitors Found. for Interior Design Edn. and Rsch., 1977-84, mem. accreditation com., 1984-88; mem. Va. Mus. Fine Arts, City of Richmond Christmas Candlelight Com., edn. com. Retail Mchts. Assn., 1980-85; mem. urban design com. Ctrl. Richmond Assn., 1993. 1st lt. USMC, 1952-57. Recipient award Va. Mus. Fine Arts, Richmond, 1970, Cert. Distinction, 1973; named contest winner Richmond Symphony Orch., 1975. Fellow Am. Soc. Interior Designers (cert., pres. Va. chpt. 1970-72, 80-81, mem. nat. bd. 1972-74, 76-77, regional v.p. 1976-77, nat. com. 1976); mem. Nat. Fire Protection Assn. Avocations: sailing, canoeing, electronics, sport cars. Home: 8905 Sierra Rd Richmond VA 23229-7828 Office: Richmond Art Co 115 N 1st St Richmond VA 23219-2125

JOELSON, MARK RENE, lawyer; b. Paris, Oct. 23, 1934; came to U.S., 1941, naturalized, 1947; s. Michael and Helen (Streicher) J.; m. Anastasia Whelan, June 4, 1967; children: Helen, Daniel, Marisa. BA, Harvard U., 1955, LLB, 1958; diploma in law, Oxford U., Eng., 1962. Bar: D.C. 1958, U.S. Supreme Ct. 1959. Atty. U.S. Dept. Justice, Washington, 1958-63; assoc., then ptnr. Arent, Fox, Kintner, Plotkin & Kahn, Washington, 1963-80; ptnr. Wald, Harkrader & Ross, Washington, 1980-85, Morgan, Lewis & Bockius LLP, Washington, 1986-97; mem. adv. com. internat. investment, tech. and devel. U.S. Dept. State, 1978-87; cons. UN Conf. Trade and Devel., 1977-79; adj. prof. Georgetown U., Washington; arbitrator U.S.-Can. Free Trade Agreement. Author: (with Earl W. Kintner) An International Antitrust Primer, 1974; editor: (with others) Current Legal Aspects of Doing Business in the E.E.C., 1978, Enterprise Law of the 80's, 1980, Joint Ventures in the United States, 1988. Fulbright scholar Oxford U., 1961-62. Mem. ABA (chmn. sect. internat. law and practice 1983-84, del. Internat. Bar Assn. coun. 1984-92), Internat. Bar Assn., Fed. Bar Assn. (pres. D.C. chpt. 1976-77), Washington Inst. Fgn. Affairs, Cosmos Club (Washington).

JOERGER, JAY HERMAN, psychologist, entrepreneur; b. Freeport, N.Y., Sept. 23, 1957; s. Herman Alexander and Ellen Rose (Becker) J.; m. Diana Botero, Mar. 27, 1993; children: Nicholas Alexander, Richard Andrew. BS, Union U., 1980; MA, Colgate U., 1981; EdD, Columbia U., 1987. Diplomate Am. Bd. Profl. Disability Cons., Wellness Profl., Substance Abuse Psychology, Clin. Psychology, Psychology Assessment, Evaluation and Testing, Child Custody Evaluation; lic. psychologist, N.Y.; cert. addiction specialist, bd. cert. forensic examiner; bd. cert. in forensic medicine; registered hypnotherapist. Drug abuse counselor Drug Abuse Coun., Norwich, N.Y., 1980-81; vocat. rehab. counselor Community Workshop, Glens Falls, N.Y., 1981-83; assoc. psychologist N.Y. State, Wingdale, N.Y., 1986-96; pres. Mentors Resource and Devel. Corp., 1991—; mem. group practice Ctr. Stress Reduction, 1993-97, Carmel Psychol. Assocs., 1993-94; admission and hosp. privileges Four Winds Hosp., Katonah, N.Y., 1995—; cons., Somers, N.Y., 1988—; adj. asst. prof. Iona Coll., 1993-95; adj. prof. Lehman Coll., 1994—; founding coord. Alcoholism and Drug Abuse Counselor Tng. Program Lehman Coll., 1996; bd. dirs. Rapid Rabbit, Inc.; forensic psychol. cons. and expert witness. Author: A Participant Manual for Mentally Ill Chemical Abusers, 1989, Living Successfully: A Self-Study Guide, 1993; co-author: The Physical, Psychological and Social Effects of Chemical Abuse - A Clinician's Workbook, 1994, 2d edit., 1995, Substance Abuse: Evaluation and Treatment Training Program, 1995; (book, audio tape) Living Successfully: Relax and Enhance Your Life, 1996. Amateur radio operator, mil. affiliate radio operator Westchester Emergency Comm. Assn., Westchester County, 1983—; bd. dirs. Hudson Valley Fedn., Clintondale, N.Y., 1987-88. Recipient Excellence in Psychology award Med. Staff Orgn., Harlem Valley Psychologists, 1990. Mem. Am. Coll. Forensic Examiners (life), Am. Bd. Profl. Disability Cons., N.Y. State Psychol. Assn. (sec.-treas. addiction divsn. 1993-95, liaison managed care task force 1994-95), Westchester County Psychol. Assn. (pres. indsl. orgn. divsn. 1992-95). Avocations: amateur radio, motorcycling, cooperatives, martial arts. Home and Office: Rural Rte 2 120 Krystal Dr Somers NY 10589-3039

JOFEN, JEAN, foreign language educator. BA, Bklyn. Coll., 1943; MA, Brown U., 1945; PhD, Columbia U., 1960; MS, Yeshiva U., 1961. Cert. sch. psychologist, N.Y. Teaching fellow Brown U., 1943-44; lectr. adult edn. Bklyn. Coll., 1951-61; assoc. prof. Yeshiva U., N.Y.C., 1955-62; assoc. prof., chmn. dept. Germanic and Slavic langs. Bernard M. Baruch Coll., N.Y.C., 1962-77, prof., 1977—, chmn. dept. modern langs., 1977-83, chmn. dept. Germanic, Hebraic and Oriental langs., 1983—, bd. govs., 1973—; mem. adv. bd. Jewish Studies CUNY, 1986; lectr., speaker various sci., civic and religious orgns. and socs. in U.S. and Europe; scholar abroad, Vienna, Austria, 1991. Author: A Linguistic Atlas of Eastern European Yiddish, 1964, rev. edit., 1967, Das letzte Geheimnis (in German), 1972, The Jewish Mystic in Kafka, 1987, (textbooks) Yiddish for Beginners, 1963, Yiddish Literature for Beginners, 1972, (with Y. Kerstein) Hebrew for Beginners, 1975, (with E. Mok) Chinese for Beginners, 1980; editor Elizabethan Concordance series: The Concordance of The Works of Christopher Marlowe, 1979, A Concordance to The Shakespeare Apocrypha, 3 Vols., 1987; Nat. Endowment for Humanities; assoc. editor Jour. Evolutionary Psychology; contbr. numerous articles to profl. jours. Recipient Nat. Jewish Culture Found. award, 1963, Kohut Found. award, 1966, Bernard M. Baruch Coll. medal for 35 yrs. svc., AAUW award, 1968, 69, others; fellow Inst. for Yiddish Lexicological Rsch. CUNY, 1963—; grantee Ford Found., 1970, Population Coun. Rockefeller Inst., 1970-71, Rsch. Found. CUNY, 1985, Lucius N. Littauer Found., 1986, Austrian Fed. Ministry for Sci. and Rsch., 1991. Fellow Jewish Acad. Arts and Scis.; mem. Am. Assn. Tchrs. German, MLA, AAUP, Am. Assn. Profs. Yiddish (pres.), Am. Psychol. Assn., Marlowe Soc. Am. (founder 1975, pres. 1975-84, organizer 1st. Internat. Congress in Eng. 1983), Mich. Acad. Arts and Scis., Acad. Scis. and Humanities CUNY, Sigma Alpha. Address: 409 Avenue I Brooklyn NY 11230-2619

JOFFE, BARBARA LYNNE, computer applications systems manager, computer artist, project management professional; b. Bklyn., Apr. 12, 1951; d. Lester L. and Julia (Schuelke) J.; m. James K. Whitney, Aug. 25, 1990; 1 child, Nichole. BA, U. Oreg., 1975; MFA, U. Mont., 1982. Cert. project mgr. IBM; cert. project mgmt. profl. Project Mgmt. Inst. Applications engr., software developer So. Pacific Transp., San Francisco, 1986-93; computer fine artist Barbara Joffe Assocs., San Francisco, Englewood, Colo., 1988—; instr. computer graphics Ohlone Coll., Fremont, Calif., 1990-91; adv. programmer, project mgr.-client/server Integrated Sys. Solutions Corp./IBM Global Svcs. So. Pacific/Union Pacific Railroads, Denver, 1994-97; applications sys. mgr. IBM Global Svcs./CoBank, Greenwood Village, Colo., 1997—. Artwork included in exhibits at Calif. Crafts XIII, Crocker Art Mus., Sacramento, 1983, Rara Avis Gallery, Sacramento, 1984, Redding (Calif.) Mus. and Art Ctr., 1985, Euphrat Gallery, Cupertino, Calif., 1988, Computer Mus., Boston, 1989, Siggraph Traveling Art Shown, Europe and Australia, 1990, 91, 4th and 7th Nat. Computer Art Invitational, Cheney, Wash., 1991, 94, Visual Arts Mus., N.Y.C., 1994, 96, IBM Golden Circle, 1996. Recipient IBM Project Mgmt. Excellence award, 1998. Mem. Assn. Computing Machinery, Project Mgmt. Inst. (cert.). Avocations: art, gardening, hiking. Home: 7271 S Jersey Ct Englewood CO 80112-1512

JOFFE, BENJAMIN, mechanical engineer; b. Riga, Latvia, Feb. 23, 1931; came to U.S., 1980, naturalized, 1985; s. Alexander and Mery (Levenson) J.; m. Frida Erenshteyn, Aug. 6, 1960; children: Alexander, Helena. ASME, Mech. Tech. Sch., Krasnoyarsk, USSR, 1951; BSME, Polytechnic Inst. Moscow, 1959; MSME, Polytechnic Inst. Riga, 1961; PhD, Acad. Scis., Riga, 1969. Design engr. Electromachine Mfg. Corp., Riga, 1955-59, head engrng. dept., 1959-62; sr. design engr. Acad. Scis., Riga, 1962-67; sr. scientist Inst. Physics, Riga, 1967-78; chief design engr. Main Design Bur., Riga, 1978-80; sr. design engr. Elec-Trol, Inc., Saugus, Calif., 1980-81; sr. design engr. VSI Aerospace divsn. Fairchild, Chatsworth, Calif., 1981-85; mech. engrng. mgr. Am. Semiconductor Equipment Tech., Woodland Hills, Calif., 1985-90; mem. tech. staff Jet Propulsion Lab. Calif. Inst. Tech., Pasadena, 1991-97; staff scientist aerospace/comm. divsn. ITT, Ft. Wayne, Ind., 1997—; presenter numerous papers in field. Author: (booklets) Mechanization and Automatization of Punching Presses at the Plants of the Latvian SSR, 1963, Mechanization and Automatization Processes of Plastic Parts Production at the Plants of the Latvian SSR, 1964, Mechanization and Automatization of Control and Measuring Operations, 1966, Electromagnetic Identification and Orientation of Parts (EMAGO), 1976, (books) Inventions in Soviet Latvia in the Field of Technology and Means of Production of Apparatus and Machines, 1965, Inventions in Soviet Latvia: Production of Apparatus and Machines, 1971, Orientation of Parts by Electromagnetic Field, 1972, Inventions in Soviet Latvia: Elements of Automatics, Calculating and Control-Measuring Systems, 1973, Inventions in Soviet Latvia: Elements and Mechanisms of Apparatus and Machines, Technology and Means of Their Production, 1977, among others; contbr. articles to profl. jours. Recipient Honored Inventor award Latvian Republic, Riga, 1967, 1st prize Latvian Acad. Scis., 1972, Latvian State award in engrng. scis., 1974, certs. of recognition NASA, 1996, 97. Mem. Planetary Soc. Republican. Achievements include more than 230 patents for discovery of physical and engineering basis for noncontact techniques of orientation, identification and assembly of parts by electromagnetic fields; mechanisms and machines design for semiconductive and spacecraft industries. Fax: (219) 451-6033. E-mail: bjoffe@itt.com. Office: ITT Aerospace/Comm Divsn MS 613 PO Box 3700 Fort Wayne IN 46801-3700

JOFFE, ROBERT DAVID, lawyer; b. N.Y.C., May 26, 1943; s. Joseph and Bertha (Pashkovsky) J.; children by prior marriage: Katherine, David; m. Virginia Ryan, June 20, 1981; stepchildren: Elizabeth DeHaas, Ryan DeHaas. A.B., Harvard U., 1964, J.D., 1967. Bar: N.Y. 1970, U.S. Dist. Ct. (so. and ea. dists.) N.Y. 1971, U.S. Ct. Appeals (2d cir.) 1972, U.S. Supreme Ct. 1973. Maxwell Sch. Africa Pub. Svc. fellow (funded by Ford Found.) Republic of Malawi, 1967-69, state counsel, 1968-69; assoc. Cravath, Swaine & Moore, N.Y.C., 1969-75, ptnr., 1975—, dep. presiding ptnr., 1997-98, presiding ptnr., 1999—; apptd. to bd. dirs. by Pres. Clinton, Romanian Am. Enterprise Fund, 1994—. Bd. dirs. Lawyers Com. for Human Rights; bd. dirs. The Jericho Project, 1985-97; chair Harvard Law Sch. Nat. Fund, 1995-97, Dean's Adv. Bd., 1997—. Mem. ABA, N.Y. Bar Assn., Assn. of the Bar of the City of N.Y. (chmn. trade regulation com. 1980-83, exec. com. 1995-99), Coun. on Fgn. Rels., Human Rights Watch/Africa (adv. com.), Harvard Club. Home: 300 W End Ave Apt 13A New York NY 10023-8156 Office: Cravath Swaine & Moore 825 8th Ave Fl 46 New York NY 10019-7475

JOFFE, ROLAND, film director; b. London, Nov. 17, 1945. Student, Manchester (Eng.) U. With YYoung Vic, the Nat. Theatre and the Old Vic, 1973-78; dir. Nat. Theatre, 1978, Granada TV, Thames, BBC. Dir. (documentaries) Rope, Ann, No Mama No, 1979, (plays) The Spongers, 1978, Tis Pity She's a Whore, The Legion Hall Bombing, 1978, United Kingdom (co-writer), 1981, (series) Coronation Street, Bill Brand, The Stars Look Down, (films) The Killing Fields, 1984, The Mission, 1986, Fat Man and Little Boy, 1989, City of Joy, 1992 (also co-prodr.), The Scarlett Letter; prodr.: Made in Bangkok, Super Mario Bros. Office: William Morris Agy 151 El Camino Drive Beverly Hills CA 90212

JOGLEKAR, PRAFULLA NARAYAN, information systems management educator, consultant; b. Dhulia, India, May 12, 1947; s. Narayan D. and Nirmala N. (Parchure) J.; m. Suvarna V. Lagu, Oct. 15, 1951; children: Aditya, Ajinkya. BSc, Nagpur (India) U., 1966; MBA, Indian Inst. Mgmt., Ahmedabad, India, 1968; MS, U. Pa., 1972, PhD, 1978; postgrad., U. Rochester, U. Minn., Ind. U. Staff analyst Dept. Atomic Energy, Bombay, India, 1968-69; systems analyst Voltas (PVT) Ltd., Bombay, 1969-70; mgmt. research analyst U. Pa., Phila., 1970-72; from instr. to full prof. La Salle U., Phila., 1972-87, chmn. mgmt. dept., 1973-77, 79-82, dir. applied research ctr., 1979-85, Lindback prof. bus. adminstrn., 1987-89, Lindback prof. prodn. and ops. mgmt., 1991—; mgmt. cons. various pvt. firms, govt. agys., nonprofit orgns., Phila., 1972—; expert witness fed. court, Montreal, Can., 1985. Contbr. articles to profl. jours. and confs.; editor Varta, Indian Students Assn., Phila., 1975-76. Pres. Marathi Mandal, Phila., 1980-81; mem. People to People Systems Engrng. Delegation, Peoples Republic China, 1986. Nat. Merit scholar Govt. of India, Nagpur and Ahmedabad, 1962-68, D.C.M. scholar Indian Inst. Mgmt., Ahmedabad, 1968; grantee La Salle U., 1977, 89, 80, 82, 87, 90, 92, 93, 96, 97, 98; NASA/ATEE faculty summer fellow, 1993, 94. Mem. Inst. Mgmt. Scis., Am. Mgmt. Assn., Nonprofit Mgmt. Assn. (bd. dirs. 1985-90). Hindu. Avocations: travel, bridge, puzzles. E-mail: joglekar@Lasalle.edu. Home: 202 Lenape Ave Elkins Park PA 19027-3514 Office: La Salle U 1900 W Olney Ave Philadelphia PA 19141-1199

JOHANNES, JOHN ROLAND, political science educator, academic administrator; b. Milw., Dec. 15, 1943; s. Jerome Fridolin and Teresa (Stoiber) J.; m. Frances Virginia Slater, Aug. 5, 1967; children: Teresa, Michael, James. BS, Marquette U., 1966; AM, Harvard U., 1968, PhD, 1970. Asst. prof. polit. sci. Marquette U., Milw., 1970-75, assoc. prof., 1975-84, prof., 1984-95, chmn. dept. polit. sci., 1980-88, dean Coll. Arts and Scis., 1988-93; v.p. acad. affairs Villanova (Pa.) U., 1995—; chmn. Bradley Inst. for Democracy and Pub. Values, 1988-93. Author: Policy Innovation in Congress , 1972, To Serve the People, 1984; co-editor and contbr. editor Money, Elections, and Democracy, 1990; contbr. articles to profl. jours. Am. Philos. Soc. grantee, 1978; Everett Dirksen Ctr. grantee, 1981, 82, NEH grantee, 1972. Mem. Am. Polit. Sci. Assn., Midwest Polit. Sci. Assn., So. Polit. Sci. Assn., Assn. Am. Colls. and Univs. Home: 840 Galer Dr Newtown Square PA 19073-3517 Office: Villanova U Office Acad Affairs 800 E Lancaster Ave Villanova PA 19085-1603

JOHANNES, ROBERT J., lawyer; b. Milwaukee, Wis., July 31, 1952. BA summa cum laude, Marquette U., 1974; JD, U. Chgo., 1977. Bar: Wis. 1977. Mem. Michael, Best & Friedrich LLP, Milw., 1977—. Mem. ABA, Wis. Bar Assn., Phi Beta Kappa. Office: Michael Best Friedrich LLP 100 E Wisconsin Ave Ste 3300 Milwaukee WI 53202-4108

JOHANNES, VIRGIL IVANCICH, electrical engineer; b. Omaha, Feb. 7, 1930; s. Tolomeo Ivancich and Albertine (Canino) J.; m. Rachelina Joan Del Pizzo, Aug. 31, 1962; 1 child, Laura. BSEE, CCNY, 1953; MS, Columbia U., 1954, D Engring., 1961. Registered profl. engr., N.J. Lectr. CCNY, 1953-58; prof., chmn. elec. engrng. dept. Fairleigh Dickinson U., Teaneck, N.J., 1962-63; mem. tech. staff Bell Labs., Murray Hill, N.J., 1963-64; supr. repeater cirs. group Bell Labs., Holmdel, N.J., 1964-68, head digital line dept., 1968-72, head digital multiplex dept., 1972-78, head earthstation tech. dept., 1978-83; head undersea systems Devel. dept. AT&T Bell Labs., Holmdel, N.J., 1983-89; vice chmn. study group XVIII Internat. Tel. and Telegraph Consultative Com., Geneva, Switzerland, 1978-92; pres. Virgil I. Johannes, Inc., Holmdel, 1989—. Contbr. numerous articles to profl. jours.; author sects. of Electronic Engineers Handbook; patentee in field. Mem. IEEE (chair accreditation policy com. 1994-96, mem. engrng. accreditation com. of accreditation bd. for engrng. and tech. 1994-96), N.Y.-N.J. Trail Conf. Avocations: hiking, scuba diving, water and cross-country skiing. Home and Office: 230 Balfour Dr Winter Park FL 32792-3450

JOHANNESON, GERALD BENEDICT, office products company executive; b. 1940. BS, N.D. State U., 1962. With Internat. Harvester, Chgo., 1962-83, Uniroyal, Troy, Mich., 1983-85; exec. v.p. Haworth Inc., Holland,

Mich., 1985-87, exec. v.p., chief oper. officer, 1987—, pres., COO, 1994-97; pres., CEO Haworth Inc., Holland, 1997—. Office: Haworth Inc 1 Haworth Ctr Holland MI 49423-9570

JOHANNS, MICHAEL O., governor; b. Osage, Iowa, June 18, 1950; s. John Robert Sr. and Adeline Lucy (Royek) J.; m. Constance J. Weiss, June 10, 1972 (div. Dec. 1985); children: Justin Michael, Michaela Susan; m. Stephanie A. Suther, Dec. 24, 1986. BA, St. Mary's Coll., Winona, Minn., 1971; JD, Creighton U., 1974. Jud. law clk. Nebr. Supreme Ct., Lincoln, 1974-75; assoc. lawyer Cronin & Hannon, O'Neill, Nebr., 1975-76; ptnr. Office of Nelson Johanns, Lincoln, 1976-91; mayor City of Lincoln, 1991-98; gov. State of Nebr., 1999—. Mem. Lancaster County Bd., Lincoln, 1983-87; mem. City Coun. Lincoln, 1989-91. Mem. Nebr. Bar Assn. Roman Catholic. Avocations: skiing, biking, reading. Office: Office of Gov PO Box 94848 Lincoln NE 68509-4848*

JOHANNSEN, CHRIS JAKOB, agronomist, educator, administrator; b. Randolph, Nebr., July 24, 1937; s. Jakob J. and Marie J. (Lorenzsen) J.; m. Joanne B. Rockwell, Aug. 16, 1959; children: Eric C., Peter J. BS, U. Nebr., Lincoln, 1959, MS, 1961; PhD, Purdue U., 1969. Program leader lab. for applications of remote sensing Purdue U., 1966-69, from asst. prof. to assoc. prof. agronomy, 1969-77, dir. ag data network, 1985-87, dir. lab. for applications of remote sensing, 1985—; prof. U. Mo., Columbia, 1977-84, dir. geogrpahic resources ctr., 1981-84; dir. Ag Data Network, Purdue U., 1985-87, Lab. for Applications of Remote Sensing, 1985—, Nat. Resources Rsch. Inst., 1987-93, Environ. Scis. and Engring. Inst., West Lafayette, 1994-96; vis. prof. U. Calif., Davis, 1980-81; cons. Lockheed Electronics, Houston, 1975-76, NOAA, Columbia, Mo., 1978-80, FAO UN, Nairobi, Kenya, 1983, 87, Rome, 1987, U.S. Agy. Internat. Devel., Eastern Africa, 1983, USDA-Soil Conservation Svc., Washington, 1984, 95-96, Space Sci. Corp., Washington, 1984-85, IBM, 1991, Ball Aerospace Corp., 1995; space imaging EOSAT, 1996—, Rhone Poulenc, 1998—; bd. dirs. Ecologistics Ltd.; vis. chief scientist Space Imaging Inc., 1996-97. Pres. coun. St. Andrew's Luth. Ch., Columbia, 1975-77; asst. scoutmaster Boy Scouts Am., Gt. Rivers coun., Columbia, 1979-84, West Lafayette, 1985-91; pres. Purdue Luth. Ministry, 1989-95. Recipient Tech. Innovation Rsch. award NASA, 1979, Disting. Svc. award Mo. Assn. Soil and Water Conservation Dists., 1982, Agr. Alumni Merit award U. Nebr., 1995. Fellow Am. Soc. Agronomy, Soil Sci. Soc. Am., Soil Conservation Soc. Am. (pres. 1982-83); mem. World Assn. of Soil and Water, Am. Soc. Photogrammetry and Remote Sensing (Outstanding Svc. award 1992), Internat. Soc. Soil Sci., Geosci. and Remote Sensing Soc. of IEEE, Ind. Acad. Scis., Rotary (Lafayette chpt. bd. dirs. 1995-98), Epsilon Sigma Phi. Home: 209 Cedar Hollow Ct West Lafayette IN 47906-1671 Office: Lab Applications Remote Sensing 1202 POTR Hall Purdue U West Lafayette IN 47907-1202

JOHANNSEN, SONIA ALICIA, retired county official; b. Glasgow, Mont., Dec. 30, 1935; d. Rudolph H. and Maude Agnes (Millis) Skonord; m. H. Douglas Johannsen, June 5, 1954 (dec. Nov. 1977); children: Tara Lee, Jodi Jean; m. Edward J. Bunz, Jan. 11, 1980; stepchildren: Barbara Ann, Diane Marie, Susay Kay. Clk. City of LaPorte, Iowa, 1967-69, mayor, 1970-75; elected Black Hawk County Bd. Supervisors, Waterloo, Iowa, 1977-88, 94-98. Active mem. Black Hawk County Rep. Women, Iowa Citizens Foster Care Rev. Bd.; pres. Village Aux. Mem. LWV, Am. Legion Aux. Lutheran. Office: Black Hawk County 540 F Park Ln Waterloo IA 50703-4712

JOHANSEN, BOB, think-tank executive. BS, U. Ill.; PhD, Northwestern U. Staff Inst. for the Future, Menlo Pk., Calif., 1973; dir. New Info. Techs. Program Inst. for the Future, pres.; rsch. affiliate at MIT in Ctrs. for Info. Systems Rsch. and Coordination Sci. Author: Teleconferencing and Beyond: Communications in the Office of the Future, Upsizing the Individual in the Downsized Organization (with Rob Swigart), 1994, Global Work (with Mary O'Hara-Devereaux), 1994; contbr. articles to profl. jours.; led NSF project to evaluate the effects of computer conferencing on the productivity of energy rschrs.; prin. investigator of the Intermedia Project, which compared audio, video and computer-based teleconferencing (results published as Electronic Meetings: Technical Alternatives and Social Choices--a basic reference work on teleconferencing); spkr. in field; recognized as one of the world's leading experts on groupware and related technologies. Office: Inst for the Future 2744 Sand Hill Rd Menlo Park CA 94025

JOHANSEN, EIVIND HERBERT, special education services executive, former army officer; b. Charleston, S.C., Mar. 7, 1927; s. Andrew and Ruth Lee (Thames) J.; m. Dolores E. Klockmann, June 9, 1950; children: Chris Allen, Jane Elizabeth. BS, Tex. A&M U., 1950; MS, George Washington U., 1968; postgrad., Harvard U., 1955, Army Command and Gen. Staff Coll., 1963, Naval War Coll., 1968, Advanced Mgmt. Program, U. Pitts., 1971. Quartermaster officer U.S. Army, 1950-79, advanced through grades to lt. gen., 1977; strategic planner Office Joint Chiefs of Staff, 1968-69, group comdr., 1969-70; army dir. distbn., 1970-72, army dir. materiel, 1972-75; comdg. gen. Army Aviation Systems Command, St. Louis, 1975-77; army dep. chief staff for logistics Washington, 1977-79; ret., 1979; pres., CEO Nat. Industries for Severely Handicapped, Inc., 1979-92; mem. exec. council, chmn. mgmt. improvement com. Fed. Exec. Bd., St. Louis, 1975-77; bd. advs. Am. Def. Preparedness Assn., St. Louis, 1975-77, tech. and mgmt. adv. bd., Washington, 1977-79; chmn. Army Logistics Policy Council, 1977-79; bd. advs. Army Logistic Mgmt. Coll., 1978-79, Army Mgmt. Engring. Coll., 1978-79. Contbr. articles to profl. jours. Mem. President's Com. for Purchase from Blind and Other Severely Handicapped, Washington, 1973-74, chmn., 1975; mem. President's Com. on Employment of Handicapped; bd. dirs., chmn. ind. ops. com. Mo. Goodwill Industries, 1975-77; chmn. youth program Jr. Achievement, St. Louis, 1975-77; sponsor Air Explorer Post, Boy Scouts Am., 1975-77; bd. dirs. Q.M. Found., 1979-88, 92-93. Decorated DSM, Legion of Merit with two oak leaf clusters, Bronze Star, numerous others; recipient Tex. A&M Disting. Alumnus award, 1985, Hall of Honor award Tex. A&M, 1997, Disting. Svc. award Nat. Industries for Severely Handicapped, 1992, Disting. Career award Nat. Assn. Rehab. Facilities, 1992; named to Quartermaster Hall of Fame, U.S. Army, 1992. Mem. Assn. U.S. Army (bd. advisors St. Louis 1975-77), Am. Helicopter Soc., Army Aviation Assn. Am., Ret. Officers Assn., Nat. Rehab. Assn., Tex. A&M Alumni Assn. Washington (exec. bd. 1974, 78-79, pres. 1975, bd. dirs. 1993-95), George Washington U. Alumni Assn., U. Pitts. Alumni Assn., Harvard U. Alumni Assn., Toastmasters. Home: 6310 Windpatterns Trl Fairfax Station VA 22039-1207

JOHANSEN, JOHN MACLANE, architect; b. N.Y.C., June 29, 1916; s. John Christen and Jean (MacLane) J.; m. Beate Gropius; children from previous marriage: Deborah, Christen. B.S., Harvard U., 1939; MArch, Harvard Grad. Sch. Design, 1942. Prin. Johansen-Bhavnani, N.Y.C., 1973-89; pvt. practice N.Y.C., 1989—. Author: A Life in the Continuing Modern Architecture. Fellow AIA (honor award 1972, medal of honor N.Y. 1976); mem. Am. Acad. in Rome, NAD, Am. Acad. Arts and Letters (Brunner award 1968), Archtl. League (N.Y. pres. 1968-70). Address: 821 Broadway New York NY 10003-4708

JOHANSEN, KAREN LEE, retired sales executive; b. Sheldon, Iowa, Dec. 5, 1945; d. Alvin Anthony and Marjory Gertrude (Kuiper) Eich; m. Pete Brunsting, May 15, 1964 (div. Dec. 1983); children: Jeffrey Brunsting, Keri Wallenstein; m. Alan Brockberg, Oct. 30, 1988 (div. Apr. 1991); m. Alan Johansen, Aug. 21, 1993. Student, Sioux Valley Hosp. Sch. Nsg., 1963-65; grad., S.D. Police Acad., 1978; postgrad., Phoenix Paralegal Inst., 1981-82. Owner Redwood Steak House and Lounge, White, S.D., 1975-76; dep. sheriff Brookings (S.D.) County Sheriff's Office, 1978-79; clk. of ct. City of Gillette, Wyo., 1980-82; child support enforcement officer Campbell County, Gillette, 1982-84; jud. asst. Wyo. Dist. Ct., Sheridan, 1984-85; office mgr. Felt & Martin Law Firm, Billings, Mont., 1985-87; owner paralegal svcs. office, Pipestone, Minn., 1987-89; dist. agt. Prudential Ins. Co. Am., Pipestone, 1989-91; sales mgr. Prudential Ins. Co. Am., Austin, Minn., 1991-93; mgr. S.W. Minn. Prudential Ins. Co., Worthington, Minn., 1993-94; cons. Aanenson Agy., Inc., Fulda, Slayton, Minn., 1994-95; estate planner, agt. Farm Bur. Ins. Co., Slayton, Minn., 1994-96, Prudential Ins., Slayton, Minn., 1996-97; ret. Asst. Campaign to Re-Elect Andy Steensma, Pipestone, 1990; mem. Ihlen (Minn.) City Coun., 1990; chair Brookings Summer Art Festival, 1976-79, chair, 1977-79, chair entertainment, 1976. Mem. Nat. Assn. Life Underwriters, Nat. Assn. Security Dealers. Democrat. Avocations: reading, travel, animals.

JOHANSEN, ROBERT JOHN, electrical engineer; b. S.I., N.Y., Mar. 30, 1952; s. Odd Ingvold and Theresa Florence (Stanislawiszyn) J. Grad. h.s., Staten Island, N.Y., Staten Island, N.Y., 1970. Comm. technician AAT Electronics Corp., S.I., 1975-78; engr. ITT Mackay Corp., Elizabeth, N.J., 1978-85; product engr. Panasonic Co., Secaucus, N.J., 1985-94; cons. comm. systems S.I., N.Y., 1994-96; sr. tech. assoc. Lucent Technologies-Wireless Tech. Prodn. Ctr., Piscataway, N.J., 1997—; tech. staff Philips Consumer Comms.-Lucent Techs., 1998—; test engr. Motorola, Piscataway, N.J., 1999—. Contbr. articles to profl. jours. Active People for Perot Campaign, S.I., 1992, United We Stand Am., 1992. Mem. IEEE, Am. Amateur Radio League, S.I. Amateur Radio Assn. (pres. 1989-91, mem. exec. coun.), Radio Club Am. Home: 61 Burnside Ave Staten Island NY 10302-2302

JOHANSEN, ROBERT JOSEPH, consulting actuary; b. N.Y.C., May 2, 1922; s. Irving Joseph and Margaret (McKee) J.; m. Mary Carroll Hayes, June 27, 1964; children: Mary Carroll, Robert Hayes, David McKee. BA, Manhattan Coll., 1943; MA, Columbia U., 1974. With Met. Life Ins. Co., N.Y.C., 1947-82, 3d v.p., 1964-68, 2d v.p., 1968-69, v.p. personal ins. adminstrn., 1969-70, v.p., 1970-72, v.p., actuary, 1972-82; cons. actuary, 1982—; sec. Coun. Profl. Assns. on Fed. Stats., 1980-83, chmn., 1984; vice chmn. exec. com. Ins. Guaranty Corp. N.Y., 1974-82. Contbr. articles to profl. jours. Trustee Dominican Coll., Blauvelt, N.Y., 1970-87; former pres. Van Cortlandt Terr. Assn.; mem. Mayor's Com. for Cmty. Rels., Yonkers, N.Y., 1978-86. Served with USAAF, 1943-46. Fellow Soc. Actuaries (treas. 1980-83, gen. chmn. edn. and exam com. 1970-71, chaired coms. the produced the 1983 Table A annuity valuation mortality table, mem. com. on rsch. mgmt. 1998-91, com. on experience studies 1988-91); mem. Am. Acad. Actuaries (com. on life ins. rsch. 1993—, chmn. 1997—, chmn. task force on mortality guarantees in variable products 1996—), Am. Statis. Assn., Internat. Actuarial Assn., N.Y. Actuaries Club (treas. 1978-81), Actuarial Studies in Non-Life Ins., N.Y. Acad. Scis. Roman Catholic. Office: Life Actuarial Svcs 56 Pershing Ave Yonkers NY 10705-3631

JOHANSON, DONALD CARL, physical anthropologist; b. Chgo., June 28, 1943; s. Carl Torsten and Sally Eugenia (Johnson) J.; m. Lenora Carey, 1988; 1 child, Tesfaye Meles. BA, U. Ill., 1966; MA, U. Chgo., 1970, PhD, 1974; DSc (hon.), John Carroll U., 1979; D.Sc. (hon.), Coll. of Wooster, 1985. Mem. dept. phys. anthropology Cleve. Mus. Natural History, 1972-81, curator, 1974-81; pres. Inst. Human Origins, Berkeley, Calif., 1981-97; dir. Inst. Human Origins, Tempe, Ariz., 1997—; prof. anthropology Stanford U., 1983-89, Ariz. State U., 1997; adj. prof. Case Western Res. U., 1978-81, Kent State U., 1978-81. Co-author: (with M.A. Edey) Lucy: The Beginnings of Humankind, 1981 (Am. Book award 1982), Blueprints: Solving the Mystery of Evolution, 1989, (with James Shreeve) Lucy's Child: Discovering a Human Ancestor, 1989, (with Kevin O'Farrell) Journey from the Dawn: Life with the World's First Family, 1990, (with Lenora Johanson and Blake Edgar) Ancestors: In Search of Human Origins, 1994, (with Blake Edgar) From Lucy to Language, 1997; host PBS Natures Series; prodr. (film) Lucy in Disguise, 1982; host, narrator NOVA series In Search of Human Origins, 1994 (Emmy nomination 1995); contbr. numerous articles to profl. jours. Recipient Jared Potter Kirtland award for outstanding sci. achievement Cleve. Mus. Natural History, 1979, Profl. Achievement award U. Chgo., 1980, Gold Mercury Internat. ad personem award Ethiopia, 1982, Humanist Laureate award Acad. of Humanism, 1983, Disting. Svc. award Am. Humanist Assn., 1983, San Francisco Exploratorium award, 1986, Internat. Premio Fregene award, 1987, Alumni Achievement award U. Ill., 1995; grantee Wenner-Gren Found., NSF, Nat. Geog. Soc., L.S.B. Leakey Found., Cleve. Found., George Gund Found., Roush Found. Fellow AAAS, Calif. Acad. Scis., Rochester (N.Y.) Mus., Royal Geog. Soc.; mem. Am. Assn. Phys. Anthropologists, Internat. Assn. Dental Research, Internat. Assn. Human Biologists, Am. Assn. Africanist Archaeologists, Soc. Vertebrate Paleontology, Soc. Study of Human Biology, Societe de l'Anthropologie de Paris, Centro Studi Ricerche Ligabue (Venice), Founders' Coun., Chgo. Field Mus. Natural History (hon.), Assn. Internationale pour l'etude de Paleontologie Humaine, Mus. Nat. d'Histoire Naturelle de Paris (corr.), Explorers Club (hon. dir.), Nat. Ctr. Sci. Edn. (supporting scientist). Office: Inst Human Origins Ariz State U P.O. Box 874101 Tempe AZ 85287-4101

JOHANSON, MARTHA CECILIA, elementary educator; b. Tumbes, Peru, Mar. 3, 1963; came to U.S., 1991; d. Danilo and Judith (Cardenas) J.; m. Lawrence Cesnik. BEd, Cath. U. Peru, Lima, 1984; MEd, U. Inca Garcilazo, Lima, 1989; MS in Counseling, Ind. U., 1995; postgrad., Columbia U., 1996—. Program asst. child devel. Naval Tng. Ctr., Orlando, Fla., 1992, Ft. Benjamin Harrison, Indpls., 1992-93; bilingual sr. kindergarten tchr. Park Tudor Sch., Indpls., 1993-95; tchr., coord. early childhood Project Reach Youth, Bklyn., 1996—; sr. coord. early intervention Graham-Windham, N.Y.C., 1996-97; bilingual elem. guidance counselor N.Y.C. Bd. Edn., 1997, interim dir. pupil pers. svcs., 1997—; mental health specialist intern Migrant Head Start, Indpls., 1995; ednl. rsch. cons. Children's TV Workshop, N.Y.C., 1995-96. Cultural rep. Fiesta, Indpls., 1994-95; bd. dirs. Hispanic Ctr., Indpls., 1994. Martha Johanson Day proclaimed by Mayor of Indpls., 1993; recipient cert. of recognition Ind. Migrant Head Start, 1995; grad. scholar Ind. U., 1993-94, Elliot Jaffe scholar Columbia U., 1997-98; ednl. leadership grantee Christel de Hahn, 1993=94. Mem. ACA, AAUW, Nat. Assn. for Young Children, Nat. Assn. for Bilingual Edn., Internat. Early Childhood Assn., Ind. U. Alumni Assn. Avocations: tennis, ping-pong, biking, reading, classical music. Home: 206 Shearwater Ct W Apt 33 Jersey City NJ 07305-5420

JOHANSON, ORIN WILLIAM, social worker, school counselor, consultant; b. Salt Lake City, June 23, 1946; s. Nephi E. and Margaret (Bauman) J.; m. Agnes Lindstrom, Oct. 8, 1986; children: Chad Zierenberg, Jason Zierenberg, Amanda. BA in Sociology, U. Utah, 1971, MSW, 1973. Lic. clin. social worker, cert. social worker, marriage and family counselor, Utah; cert. grief counselor; cert. mediator. Youth counselor Utah Boy's Ranch, Salt Lake City, 1970-73; caseworker Ettie Lee Homes for Boys, Fontana, Calif., 1973-74; social worker Salt Lake City Schs., 1974-97; program coord. peer leadership team West H.S., 1986—, sch. counselor, 1997—; assoc. prof. U. Utah Grad. Sch. Social Work, Salt Lake City, 1975-76, Westminster Coll., Salt Lake City, 1988; cons. on drug and alcohol edn., 1977—; prevention specialist Utah Div. Substance Abuse, Salt Lake City, summer 1982; cons. Ctr. for Ednl. Devel., San Antonio, 1980-86, Kans. Sch. Team Tng., Wichita, 1980-86; trainer Improv Teen Theatre, Salt Lake City, 1980—, K-12 Drug and Alcohol Edn., Salt Lake City, 1978—, Parent-Teen Alternative Program, Salt Lake City, 1984—. County and state del. Salt Lake County Dem. Com., 1968-73; bd. dirs. Community Counseling Ctr., Salt Lake City, 1982-85, Utah Assn. for Children's Therapy, 1980. Mem. NEA, Utah Edn. Assn., Salt Lake Tchrs. Assn., Collegiate Assn. for Devel. and Renewal Educators, Kans. Assn. for Prevention Profls. Avocations: sports, camping, music, travel. Home: 1226 Moray Ct Park City UT 84060-6901 Office: West H S 241 N 300 W Salt Lake City UT 84103-1120

JOHANSON, PATRICIA MAUREEN, artist, architect, park designer; b. N.Y.C., Sept. 8, 1940; d. Alvar Einar and Elizabeth (Deane) J.; m. E.C. Goossen (dec.); children: Alvar Deane, Gerrit Hull, Nathaniel James. Student, Bklyn. Mus. Art Sch., 1958, Art Students League, 1961; A.B., Bennington Coll., 1962; M.A., Hunter Coll., 1964; B.S., B.Arch., City Coll. Sch. Architecture, 1977; DFA (hon.), Mass. Coll. of Art, 1995. vis. prof. art SUNY-Albany, 1969; vis. artist MIT, 1974, Oberlin (Ohio) Coll., 1974, Alfred (N.Y.) U., 1974, West Tex. State U., 1988, Yale U., 1989, Mass. Coll. Art, Boston, 1994; Southworth lectr. Colby Coll., Waterville, Maine, 1981; cons. Mitchell-Giurgola Assocs., architects, N.Y.C., Phila., 1972—, Oikos, Seoul, South Korea, 1996, Yukong Ltd., Ulsan, South Korea, 1996, Nat. Endowment for Arts, Washington, 1988, City of Petaluma, Calif., 1999; artist-in-residence N.Y. Found. for Arts, 1987—; del. Survival and the Arts, Sundance Inst., Utah, 1991; del. Global Forum Gen. Assembly, Kyoto, Japan, 1993, Art & Environ., Ankara, 1997, Year 2000 Symposium, Dumbarton Oaks, Washington. One-man shows Tibor de Nagy Gallery, N.Y.C., 1967, SUNY at Albany, 1969, Montclair (N.J.) State Coll., 1974, Rosa Esman Gallery, N.Y.C., 1978, 79, 81, 83, Dallas Mus. Art, 1982, Philippe Bonnafont Gallery, San Francisco, 1984, New Arts Program, Kutztown, Pa., 1987, Albany Acad., 1987, Painted Bride Art Ctr., Phila., 1991; National Museum of Kenya, Nairobi, 1996—, retrospectives, Bennington Coll., 1973, 91, Twining Gallery, N.Y.C., 1987, Berkshire Mus., Pittsfield, Mass, 1987; group shows, Hudson River Mus., Yonkers, N.Y., 1964, Bennington Coll., 1964, 84, Stable Gallery, N.Y.C., 1966, Tibor de Nagy Gallery, N.Y.C., 1966, 68, Larry Aldrich Mus., Ridgefield, Conn., 1968, Mus. Modern Art, N.Y.C., 1968, Grand Palais, Paris, 1968, Kunsthaus Zurich, 1969, Tate Gallery, London, 1969, Vassar Coll., 1969, Finch Coll. Mus., 1971, Everson Mus., Syracuse, N.Y., 1971, Detroit Inst. Arts, 1973, MIT, 1974, 83, Casa Thomas Jefferson, Brasilia, Brazil, 1975, Pa. Acad. Fine Arts, Phila., 1975, Greenwich (Conn.) Library Art Gallery, 1977, Bklyn. Mus., 1977, 80, New Gallery Contemporary Art, Cleve., 1977, Cleve. State U., 1977, Cooper-Hewitt Mus., N.Y.C., 1978, Mus. Modern Art, N.Y.C., 1979, Berkshire Mus., Pittsfield, Mass., Newark Mus., 1979, Graham Gallery, N.Y.C., 1980, U. Mass., Amherst, 1980, Mus. Contemporary Art, Chgo., 1981, Sotheby-Parke Bernet, N.Y.C., 1980, Centro de Documentación de Arte Actual, Barcelona, Spain, 1980, 81, Galeria O'Patacón la Coruña, Spain, 1981, SUNY, Old Westbury, 1981, Rosa Esman Gallery, 1981, 82, 83, Miami U., 1981, Met. Mus. Art, N.Y.C., 1982, 83, Berkshire Mus., 1982, 86, Laumeier Sculpture Park, St. Louis, 1982, 93, 94, Teatro Contadino, Naples, 1982, Dallas Mus. Natural History, 1982, 93, Suzanne Gross Gallery, Phila., 1984, Harvard U., 1984, Stamford Mus., Conn., 1985, 89, Md. Inst. Art, 1985, Bard Coll., N.Y., 1985, 90, U. Calif., La Jolla, 1985, Ark. Art Ctr., Little Rock, 1985, Warwick Mus., R.I., 1985, Marisa Del Re Gallery, N.Y.C., 1986, Am. Acad. Arts and Letters, N.Y.C., 1986, Hunter Coll. Art Gallery, 1986, 91, 93, Stamford Mus., Ct., 1989, Albany Inst. History and Art, 1988, Kouros Gallery, N.Y., 1988, L.I. U., 1989, Blum-Helman Gallery, N.Y., 1989, Murray State U., Ky., 1989, N.Y. State Mus., 1989, Burchfield Art Ctr., Buffalo, 1990, Grand Rapids (Mich.) Art Mus., 1990, U. North Tex., Denton, 1990, Hofstra U. Art Mus., 1990, Salina (Kans.) Art Ctr., 1991, U. Houston, 1991, Crocker Art Mus., Sacramento, 1991, Laguna (Calif.) Art Mus., 1991, 94, Centro Insular de Cultura, Spain, 1991, San Jose State U., 1991, Nat. Theater, Brasilia, Brazil, 1992, Queens (N.Y.) Mus. of Art, 1992, Whatcom Mus., Bellingham, Washington, 1993, Calif. Crafts Mus., San Francisco, 1993, 94, Nat. Mus. of Fine Arts, Rio De Janeiro, 1993, La Defense, Paris, 1993, San Jose Mus. of Art, Calif., 1993, U. Pa., 1993, Salt Lake Art Ctr., Utah, 1993, Madison (Wis.) Art Ctr., 1993, La Virreina, Barcelona, Spain, 1994, Longwood Art Ctr., Va., 1994, De Cordova Mus., Mass., 1994, Ctr. for the Arts, Miami, 1994, Dahl Fine Arts Ctr., S.D., 1994, Gallery Nikko, Tokyo, 1994, 96, Soho 20 Gallery, N.Y.C., 1994, Internat. Sculpture Ctr., Washington, 1994, Pratt Manhattan Gallery, N.Y.C., 1994, Skidmore Coll., 1996, Brickbottom Gallery, Sommerville, Mass., 1996, Michael Fuchs Gallery, Berlin, 1997, City Coll. N.Y., 1997; represented in permanent collections, Detroit Inst. Arts, Dallas Mus. Art, Mus. Modern Art, Met. Mus. Art, N.Y.C., Nat. Mus. Women in Arts, Washington, Berkshire Mus., N.Y. State Council on Arts Film Collection, Syracuse, Storm King Art Ctr., Mountainville, N.Y., Crawford and Chester Sts. Park, Cleve., Oberlin Coll., Bennington Coll., Brandeis U., U. Mass., Amherst, also pvt. collections; films The Art of the Real, USIA, 1968, Stephen Long, CBS-TV, 1968, Patricia Johanson: Cyrus Field, 1974, The City Project: Cleveland, 1977, A Conversation with Patricia Johanson, Heritage Cablevision, 1985, Patricia Johanson, Berks (Pa.) Community TV, 1990, Patricia Johanson: The Leonhardt Lagoon, 1992, Patricia Johanson: A Sense of Place, 1992, Patricia Johanson: Multilevel Designs, Aesthetic, Ecological, Functional, Cedar Arts Forum, Iowa, 1994, Q&A with Patricia Johanson, PBS, 1998, Chicken Scratch with Patricia Johanson, Petaluma, California Cmty. TV, 1999; author: Art and Survival: Creative Solutions to Environmental Problems, 1992; works include park design, sculpture, ecological landscapes, street furniture, pavement designs, site planning for Consol. Edison Co., Yale U., Columbus East High Sch., Ind., House and Garden mag., Internat. Yr. of Child Commn., Fair Park Lagoon, Dallas, Corning Preserve, Albany, Cathedral Sq., Sacramento, Calif., Pelham Bay Pk., N.Y.C., Candlestick Pt. State Park, San Francisco, Omame Project, Brasilia, Brazil, Park for a Rainforest, Amazonas, Brazil, Nairobi River Park, Kenya, Ulsan Dragon Park, Ulsan, Korea, The Rocky Marciano Trail, Brockton, Mass., Pub. Art Master Plan, Rockland County, N.Y., 1990, Ecol. Master Plan Greater Boston Metropolitan Region, 1994—. Bd. dirs. New Arts Program, Pa., 1988—; bd. advisors Artists Representing Environ. Arts, Inc., N.Y.C., 1991—. Guggenheim fellow, 1970, 80, NEA fellow, 1975, Olesen fellow Bennington Coll., 1991; Alolph & Esther Gottlieb Found. grantee, 1998; recipient 1st prize Environ. Design Competition, Montclair State Coll., 1974, Internat. Womens Yr. award, 1976, Gold medal Acad. Italia delle Arti, Parma, 1979; Townsend Harris medal CCNY, 1994; named to Hunter Coll. Hall of Fame, 1987; named to Mepham H.S. Hall of Fame, 1998. Mem. Global Forum Arts Group. Home: 179 Nick Mush Rd Buskirk NY 12028-3202 *Let problems be your inspiration.*

JOHANSSON, NILS A., information services executive; b. 1948. Grad., U. Uppsala, Sweden, 1972; MBA, U. Ill., 1975. With Am. Hosp. Supply Corp., 1973-81; group contr. Bell & Howell Co., Skokie, Ill., 1981-87, treas., 1987-88, treas., v.p., 1988-89, bd. dirs., 1990—; v.p. fin., CFO Bell & Howell Co., Skokie, 1989—; bd. dirs., 1990, sr. v.p. fin., CFO, 1992—; exec. v.p., CFO Bell & Howell Co., Skokie, Ill., 1994—. Office: Bell & Howell Co 5215 Old Orchard Rd Skokie IL 60077-1076*

JOHN, CHRIS, congressman; m. Payton Smith. BBA, La. State U. Mem. La. Ho. of Reps., 1987-97; mem. 105th Congress from 7th La. dist., 1997—, mem. agr. resources com. Democrat. Office: US House of Reps 1504 Longworth Washington DC 20515 also: 566 Jefferson St Ste 100 Lafayette LA 70501-6906 also: 1011 Lake Shore Dr Ste 306 Lake Charles LA 70601-9415

JOHN, ELTON HERCULES (REGINALD KENNETH DWIGHT), musician; b. Pinner, Middlesex, Eng., Mar. 25, 1947; s. Stanley and Sheila Eileen (Farebrother) Dwight. Student, Royal Acad. Music, London, 1959-64. Singer, songwriter, musician; began playing piano, 1951; joined group Bluesology, 1965; appeared in movie Tommy, 1975; toured America 10 times 1970-76; composer, performer: Empty Sky, 1969, Elton John, 1970, Tumbleweed Connection, 1971, 11.17.70, 1971, Friends, 1971, Madman Across The Water, 1971, Honky Chateau, 1972, Don't Shoot Me I'm Only The Piano Player, 1973, Goodbye Yellow Brick Road, 1973, Caribou, 1974, Greatest Hits, 1974, Empty Sky, 1975, Captain Fantastic and the Brown Dirt Cowboy, 1975, Rock of the Westies, 1975, Here and There, 1976, Blue Moves, 1976, Greatest Hits Vol. II, 1977, A Single Man, 1978, Victim of Love, 1979, 21 at 33, 1980, Jump Up, 1982, Too Low For Zero, 1983, The Fox, 1983, Breaking Hearts, 1984, Ice on Fire, 1985, Leather Jackets, 1986, Your Songs, 1986, Live in Australia, 1987, Reg Strikes Back, 1988, Sleeping with the Past, 1989, The Thom Bell Sessions, 1989, To Be Continued, 1990, The One, 1992, Duets, 1993, Made in England, 1995, The Big Picture, 1997, Elton John & Tim Rice's AIDA (toured with Billy Joel), 1998-99; composer, performer singles: Lady Samantha, 1969, From Denver to L.A., 1970, Take Me to the Pilot/Your Song, 1970, Border Song, 1970, Friends, 1971, Levon, 1971, Tiny Dancer, 1972, Rocket Man, 1972, Honky Cat, 1972, Crocodile Rock, 1972, Daniel, 1973, Saturday Night's Alright for Fightin', 1973, Goodbye Yellow Brick Road, 1973, Step into Xmas, 1973, Bennie and the Jets, 1974, Don't Let the Sun Go Down on Me, 1974, The Bitch Is Back, 1974, Lucy in the Sky with Diamonds, 1974, Philadelphia Freedom, 1975, Someone Saved My Life Tonight, 1975, Island Girl, 1975, I Feel like a Bullet (In the Gun of Robert Ford), 1976, Don't Go Breaking My Heart, 1976, Sorry Seems to Be the Hardest Word, 1976, Bite Your Lip (Get Up and Dance), 1977, Ego, 1978, Song for Guy, 1979, Mama Can't Buy You Love, 1979, Victim of Love, 1979, Part-Time Love, 1979, Johnny B Goode, 1979, Little Jeannie, Song for Guy, 1978, Are You Ready for Love, 1979, Little Jeannie/Conquer the Sun, 1980, Don't Ya Wanna Play This Game No More?, 1980, Chloe, 1981, Empty Garden (Hey Hey Johnny), 1982, Blue Eyes, 1982, I'm Still Standing, 1983, Kiss the Bride, 1983, I Guess That's Why They Call It the Blues, 1983, Sad Songs (Say So Much), 1984, Who Wears These Shoes, 1984, Wrap Her Up, 1986, Nikita, 1986, Heartache All Over the World, 1986, Candle in the Wind, 1987, I Don't Wanna Go on with You Like That, 1988, Town of Plenty, 1988, Candle in the Wind (live), 1988, A Word in Spanish, 1988, Healing Hands, 1989, Sacrifice, 1990, You Gotta Love Someone, 1991, Easier to Walk Away, 1991, Don't Let the Sun Go Down on Me, 1991, The One, 1992, Believe, 1995, Made in England, 1995; composer music (film) The Lion King, 1994 (Best Original Song Acad. award for "Can You Feel the Love Tonight?"); albums include Love Songs, 1996. Chmn. Watford Football Club, 1976-90, pres. Watford Football Club, 1990—; established Elton John Aids Found., 1993. Recipient Gold Discs for all albums composed; played to over 2 million people across 4 continents, 1984, 86; first popular Western singer to perform in USSR, 1979; Best British Male Artist Brits award, 1991; Grammy award, 1981; inducted into Rock & Roll Hall of Fame, 1994. Office: care John Reid Enterprises Ltd, care John Reid Enterprises, 32 Galena Rd, London W6 OLT, England also: MCA Records 70 Universal City Plz Universal Cty CA 91608-1011*

JOHN, FRANK HERBERT, JR., real estate appraiser, real estate investor; b. Georgetown, Guyana, Mar. 4, 1961; s. Frank Herbert Clement John and Doris Marian Schofield Jones; m. Barbara Jean Stewart, June 2, 1989; 1 child, Andre Nicholas John. BBA, Howard U., 1984. Lic. real estate appraiser. Intern IBM, N.Y.C., 1983; account rep. IBM, Washington, 1984-92; pres. Washington Appraisal, Bethesda, Md., 1993—, 1993—. Bd. dirs. Concerned Black Men, Washington, 1990-93, chmn. internat. awareness program, 1990-93. Mem. Nat. Assn. Real Estate Investors, Nat. Assn. Realtors, Greater Washington Bd. Trade, D.C. C. of C., Delta Sigma Pi, Beta Gamma Sigma. Baptist. Office: Washington Appraisal 4650 E West Hwy Ste 206 Bethesda MD 20814-3409

JOHN, GERALD WARREN, hospital pharmacist, educator; b. Salem, Ohio, Feb. 16, 1947; s. Harold Elba and Ruth Springer (Pike) J.; m. Jean Ann Marie Orris, Nov. 5, 1977; children: Patrick Warren, Jeanette Lynn. BS in Pharmacy, Ohio No. U., 1970; MS, U. Md., 1974. Registered pharmacist, Ohio, S.C. Staff pharmacist North Columbiana County Cmty. Hosp., Salem, 1970-72; asst. resident in hosp. pharmacy U. Md. Hosp., Balt., 1972-73, sr. resident, 1973-74, chmn. patient care pharmacies, 1974-76; dir. pharmacy Ohio Valley Hosp., Steubenville, 1976-97; exec. dir. Tri-State Health Svcs., Inc., 1997—; mem. adv. bd. Contemporary Pharmacy Practice, 1977-83; preceptor profl. externship program Ohio No. U. Sch. Pharmacy, 1977—; adj. clin. instr. practical experience program Duquesne U. Sch. Pharmacy, 1976—; adj. clin. instr. Ohio State U. Sch. Pharmacy, 1988-99; dir. of pharmacy Trinity Med. Ctr., Steubenville, 1997—. Columnist Weirton Daily Times, 1990-94. Trustee, v.p. Valley Hospice Inc., 1985-98. Named Hosp. Pharmacist of Yr., Md. Soc. Hosp. Pharmacists, 1976, Outstanding Young Man of Am., U.S. Jaycees, 1977. Fellow Am. Soc. Con. Pharmacists; mem. Am. Soc. Hosp. Pharmacists, Ohio Soc. Hosp. Pharmacists, Jefferson County Acad. Pharmacy, Southeastern Ohio Soc. Hosp. Pharmacists (pres. 1985-87), Rho Chi, Phi Eta Sigma. Methodist.

JOHN, HUGO HERMAN, natural resources educator; b. Natoma, Kans., Feb. 13, 1929; s. Lorenz Louis and Clara Marie (Doehrmann) J.; m. Prudence Patricia Shuck, Sept. 9, 1950; children: Patrick, Peter, Sarah. BS, U. Minn., 1959, MS, 1961, PhD, 1964. From asst. prof. to assoc. prof. Coll. Forestry U. Minn., St. Paul, 1964-69, prof., 1969-72; prof. Coll. Forestry, Wildlife and Range Scis., assoc. dean U. Idaho, Moscow, 1972-74; dean, prof. Sch. Natural Resources U. Vt., Burlington, 1974-83; dean Coll. Agriculture and Natural Resources, dir. Agrl. Expt. Sta. and Coop. Extension U. Conn., Storrs, 1983-87, prof. natural resources, 1987-94, prof. emeritus, 1994—; forestry expert UN Food and Agr. Orgn., Puerto Cabezas, Nicaragua, 1965-66, Nat. Univ. Medellin, Colombia, 1969-71; cons. Taconic Found., N.Y.C., Internat. Paper Co., N.Y.C., 1981-84; sr. cons. UN Devel. Programme, Humane Soc. of U.S., 1993—; devel./planning cons. Internat. Exec. Svcs. Corps., Zimbabwe, 1996, Ukraine, 1998. Contbr. articles to profl. jours. Mem., treas. bd. dirs. Smokey House Project, Danby, Vt., 1976—; bd. dirs. Merek Forest Found., Rupert, Vt., 1980-83, Ea. States Expn., West Springfield, Mass, 1989—, mem. Conn. trustees, 1984—, chmn., 1989—. With U.S. Army, 1950-52. Mem. Soc. Am. Foresters (chmn. accreditation com. 1981-84), Am. Forestry Assn. Avocations: gardening, woodworking. Home: Box 732 501 4th Ave SE Mapleton MN 56065-9782

JOHN, JUDITH A., literature educator; b. May 30, 1951. BS in Edn., Mo. Western U., 1986; MA, Kansas State U., 1989, PhD, 1992. Assoc. prof. lit. Southwestern Mo. State U., Springfield, Mo., 1992—. E-mail: jaj225f@mail.smsu.edu.

JOHN, LEWIS GEORGE, political science educator; b. Waco, Tex., Nov. 25, 1936; s. Lewis Hervin and Margaret Reese J.; m. Annette Louise Church, June 3, 1961; children: Andrew Lewis, Christopher Donald. BA, Washington & Lee U., 1958; M in Pub. Affairs, Princeton U., 1961; PhD, Syracuse U., 1973. Asst. dean students, dir. fin. aid and placement Washington & Lee U., Lexington, Va., 1963-66, assoc. dean students, 1968-69, dean students, prof. politics and adminstrn., 1969-90, prof. politics and adminstrn., 1969—; leader workshops and seminars, various colls., 1981-85; presenter symposia and confs. Contbr. articles to profl. jours. and chpts. to books. Chmn. Lexington Sch. Bd. 1979-80; pre-law adviser NCAA Faculty Athletics Rep. Served to 1st lt. US Army, 1961-63. Woodrow Wilson fellow Princeton U., 1959-60; Fulbright scholar U. Edinburgh, 1958-59. Mem. ASPA, Nat. Assn. Student Personnel Adminstrs. (bd. dirs. 1977-79, 87-89, region III exec. bd. 1980-85, chmn. career devel. and profl. standards div. 1987-89, Disting. Svc. award 1982), Va. Assn. Student Personnel Adminstrs. (pres. 1975, Outstanding Profl. award 1983), Am. Polit. Sci. Assn., Phi Beta Kappa, Beta Gamma Sigma, Omicron Delta Kappa (faculty sec. Washington and Lee chpt. 1987-90, 98—, faculty advisor 1990-98), Omicron Delta Epsilon, Pi Sigma Alpha. Democrat. Presbyterian. Avocation: sports. Home: 8 Edmondson Ave Lexington VA 24450-1904 Office: Washington & Lee U Commerce Sch 125-B Lexington VA 24450

JOHN, MERTIS, JR., record company executive; b. Detroit, May 22, 1932; s. Mertis and Lillie G. (Robinson) J.; m. Essie M. Wincher, June 16, 1957; 1 child, Darryl E. AA, Wayne Coll., 1978. Songwriter King Records, Cin. and N.Y.C., 1955-67; founder Mertis Music Co., Detroit, 1962—; founder, pres. Meda Records, 1981—; corr. mem. Broadcast Music Inc. Author: Speaking from the Heart, 1996, My Life and My Experiences in the Entertainment World; author (poem) A World of Freedom, 1989; co-prodr. Inside Music, 1977; songwriter This Is Your Day, 1996; musician; composer over 300 songs. With U.S. Army, 1952-54, Korea. Recipient Golden Poet award World of Poetry, 1989, 90. Mem. Detroit Soc. Musicians and Entertainers (chmn. bd. dirs. 1984—), Nat. Acad. Rec. Arts and Scis., Am. Fedn. Musicians, Masons (32d degree). Baptist. Fax: (313) 862-5882.

JOHN, NANCY R., librarian, writer; b. Bklyn., Feb. 1, 1948; d. Rex K. and Gwendolyn K. J.; m. Edward J. Valauskas, May 3, 1980. AB, Stanford U., 1969; MLS, UCLA, 1973. Cataloger Nat. Gallery Art, Washington, 1974-77; catalog libr. U. Ill. Chgo. Cir., 1978-79, asst. univ. libr., 1980—; internet advisor U.S. Mission to Internat. Orgns., Geneva, Switzerland, 1995-96; cons. U. Arts, Phila., 1991-93. Co-author: Internet Troubleshooter, 1994; co-editor: Internet Initiative, 1995; editor: (by K.G. Saur) Libri, 1995—. Recipient Esther J. Piercy award ALA, 1982. Mem. ALA (pres. ALCTS 1989-90), Internat. Fedn. Libr. Assn. and Instns. (profl. bd. 1989-93, 2d v.p. 1997-99). Avocation: golf, needlework. Fax: 312/413-0424. E-mail: nrj@uic.edu. Home: 5050 S Lake Shore # 3214 Chicago IL 60615 Office: UIC Univ Libr Box 8198 m/c 234 Chicago IL 60680

JOHN, RALPH CANDLER, retired college president, educator; b. Prince Frederick, Md., Feb. 18, 1919; s. Byron Wilson and Gladys Bennett (Thomas) J.; m. Dorothy Corinne Prince, Aug. 17, 1943; children: Douglass Prince, Byron Wilson II, Alan Randall. B.A., Berea Coll., 1941; student, Duke U., 1941-43; S.T.B., Boston U., 1943, S.T.M., 1944; Ph.D., Am. U., 1950; L.H.D., Iowa Wesleyan U., 1968; Litt.D., Simpson Coll., 1972; DHL, Western Md. Coll., 1997. Ordained to ministry United Methodist Ch., 1941; asso. minister Foundry Meth. Ch., Washington, 1945-49; chmn. dept. philosophy and religion Am. U., 1949-51, dean students, 1955-58, dean Coll. Arts and Scis., 1958-63, hon. lifetime prof. philosophy, 1963—; pres. Simpson Coll., Indianola, Iowa, 1963-72; pres. Western Md. Coll., Westminster, 1972-84, pres. emeritus, 1984—; dir. Princor Mut. Funds, Fair Lanes, Inc., Jiffy Lube Internat., Inc., Shore Stop of Berlin, Inc.; chmn. adv. com. Washington Internat. Ctr., 1959-63; mem. commn. on instrl. affairs Assn. Am. Colls. Del., World Meth. Conf., London, 1966; dir. Student Aid Internat., Inc., 1975-86. Trustee Randolph-Macon Acad., 1959-81. Served to capt. AUS, 1951-53; maj. Res. Recipient Alumni Recognition award Am. U., 1968, Disting. Alumnus award Boston U., 1969, Disting. Alumnus award Berea Coll., 1976, Disting. Civilian Service medal Dept. Army, Citation for Disting. Service, Gov. of Md., Disting. Svc. to Higher Edn. award, Berea Coll.; Paul Harris fellow Rotary Internat. Mem. Am. Council on Edn. (commn. on edn. and internat. affairs 1959-63), Am. Philos. Assn., Am. Acad. Religion, Am. Acad. Polit. and Social Sci., Md. Ind. Coll. and Univ. Assn. (chmn. bd., exec. com.), Iowa Assn. Pvt. Colls. and Univs. (chmn. bd., exec. com.), Newcomen Soc. N.Am., Phi Beta Kappa, Phi Kappa Phi, Omicron Delta Kappa, Pi Gamma Mu, Pi Sigma Alpha. Clubs: Prairie (Des Moines); Center (Balt.); Cosmos (Washington); Ocean Pines.

JOHN, RICHARD C., enterprise development organization executive; b. Milw., Mar. 17, 1950; s. Richard C. and Mary W. (Widrig) J.; m. Carolyn H. Finn, June 2, 1973; children: Catherine M., Yuri G., Meredith C. BBA, U. Wis., 1972; MBA, Northwestern U., 1982. CPA. Supr. sr. acct. Price Waterhouse, N.Y.C., 1972-78; with Amoco Corp., Chgo., 1978-83; supr. fin. contr. Amoco Prodn. Co. Internat., Chgo., 1983-84; mgr. acctg. Amoco Oil Co., Chgo., 1984-85; staff dir. budgets Amoco Corp., Chgo., 1985-87; mgr. fin. & adminstrn. Amoco Chem. Co., Houston, 1987-89; contr. Amoco Performance Products, Atlanta, 1989-93; mgr. Amoco Corp., Chgo., 1993-96; v.p. fin. and adminstrn., CFO Opportunity Internat., Oak Brook, Ill., 1996—. Bd. dirs. Flagstaff Mission to the Navajos, 1996—; deacon 4th Presbyn. Ch., 1979-87; elder, treas. Clear Lake Presbyn. Ch., 1988-89; officer, mem. choir Johnson Ferry Bapt. Ch., 1990-93; missions com. Wheaton Bible Ch., 1994—. Mem. AICPA, Fin. Execs. Inst. Office: Opportunity Internat 2122 York Rd Oak Brook IL 60523-1930

JOHN, RICHARD RODDA, transportation executive; b. Berlin, Mar. 31, 1929; came to U.S., 1938; s. Richard R. and Margaret G. (Howard) J.; m. Suzanne L. Heckman, June 7, 1958; children: Richard Rodda, Margaret Louise, Robert Edward. BS in Engring. Physics magna cum laude, Princeton U., 1951, MSME, 1952, MS in Aero. Engring., 1953, PhD in Aero. Engring., 1957. Dir. Aerophysics lab. AVCO Corp., Wilmington, Mass., 1958-70, chief mech. engring. div., 1971-76, dir. Office Energy and Environment, 1976-82, dep. dir., chief scientist, 1982-89; dir. John A. Volpe Nat. Transp. Systems Ctr., Cambridge, Mass., 1990—; mem. adv. com. on space power and electric propulsion, NASA, 1965-70, aero. engring. dept. adv. coun. Princeton U., 1972-78. Contbr. articles to profl. jours. Recipient Presdl. Meritorious Rank award, 1987, Presdl. Disting. Rank award, 1990; Howard C. Phillips fellow Princeton U., 1952, Guggenheim fellow, 1953. Fellow AIAA (assoc., chmn. electric propulsion com. 1965-70); mem. Soc. Automotive Engrs. (rsch. exec. bd. 1978-85), Phi Beta Kappa, Sigma Xi. Congregationalist. Avocations: gardening, golf, 20th century print collecting, classical music. Home: 19 Saddle Club Rd Lexington MA 02420-2102 Office: Dept Transp John A Volpe Nat Transp Systems Ctr 55 Broadway-Kendall Sq Cambridge MA 02142

JOHN, ROBERT MCCLINTOCK, lawyer; b. Phila., May 21, 1947; s. Lewis Timothy and Marie (McClintock) J.; m. Barbara Ann Weand, May 10, 1975; children: Jennifer, Ryan. BA, Villanova U., 1969, JD, 1972. Bar: Pa. 1972, U.S. Dist. Ct. (ea. dist.) Pa. 1973, U.S. Ct. of Appeals (3d cir.) 1998, U.S. Ct. Appeals (3d cir.) 1998. Atty. Schneider, Nixon & John, Hatboro, Pa., 1972-74, ptnr., 1975-93, sole proprietor, 1993—. Scoutmaster Boy Scouts Am., Hatboro, 1972—, long range planning com., 1979; lectr. and student loan com. Hatboro-Horsham High Sch., 1972-95, co-chmn. Tip of the Hat Cavalcade of Bands, 1994, 95, 96; co-prs. Hatters for Music, 1997-99; prodr. multi media banquet show Marching Hatters, 1994-98; mgr. Little League, Horsham, Pa., 1985-96, girls' sr. tournament coach, 1993; referee Hatboro-Horsham Youth Basketball Assn., 1990-91, mgr., 1991-94. Recipient award Hatboro-Horsham Sch. Bd., 1979, medal Hatboro YMCA Triathlon, 1983, Silver Beaver award Boy Scouts Am., 1981, Scoutmaster's award of Merit, 1989, Nat. God and Svc. award, 1991, Hatboro-Horsham H.S. Prin.'s Golden Apple award, 1997, Martin Luther King Humanitarian award Upper Moreland Mid. Sch., 1997, others. Mem. Pa. Bar Assn., Montgomery County Bar Assn., Greater Hatboro C. of C. (pres. 1983, Honored Citizen Svc. to Youth award 1984, judge advocate 1984—, chmn. awards com. and prod. multimedia awards ceremony biannual borough ball, 86, 89, 97, 99), Navy League (sec. southeastern Pa. coun. 1975-88, pres. 1989, S.E. Pa. Coun. Svc. to Youth and Community award 1990, Willow Grove naval Air Sta. svc. award 1986), Rotary (pres. 1984, Dist. Gov.'s Outstanding Pres.'s award 1984, host family foreign exch. students). Republican. Roman Catholic. Avocations: scouting, swimming, cycling, backpacking. Home: 83 Home Rd Hatboro PA 19040-1830 Office: Schneider Nixon & John 76 Byberry Ave # 698 Hatboro PA 19040-3419

JOHN, SARAH A., emergency medicine physician; b. Chgo., Dec. 4, 1946; d. Erwin Roy and Eve Evelyn (Spiro) John; m. Eldon Clare Roberts Jr., July 8, 1988; children: Elena and Milena (twins). AB, Brandeis U., Waltham, Mass., 1968; MD, N.Y. Med. Coll., N.Y.C., 1975. Diplomate Am. Bd. Emergency Medicine. Bd. dirs. Health Systems Agy. No. Va., Fairfax, 1996-98. Fellow Am. Coll. Emergency Physicians (bd. dirs. Va. chpt. 1994-98, treas. 1998-99); mem. Am. Assn Women Emergency Physicians (bd. dirs. 1995-98, pres. 1997, immediate past pres. 1998). Office: Am Assn Women Emer Phys 2857 Pine Spring Rd Falls Church VA 22042-1315

JOHN, SUSAN V., state legislator; b. Nov. 20, 1957. BA, George Washington U.; JD, Syracuse U. Bar: N.Y. Atty. firm Phillips, Lytle, 1983—; mem. N.Y. State Assembly, mem. jud. com., edn. com., govt. ops. com., also mem. energy com., librs. and edn. tech. com., chair com. on govt. ops., chair subcom. on pub. sch. violence. Mem. Greater Rochester Assn. Women Attys. Office: 274 Goodman St N Ste C-254 Rochester NY 14607-1154 Office: NY State Assembly Rm 621 LOB Albany NY 12248

JOHNOPOLOS, STEPHEN GARY, commission representative; b. Chgo., Jan. 3, 1950; s. Alexander and Anna (Poncher) J. BS, De Paul U., 1973. Cons., writer music, advt., pub. rels. Saxton, Pa., 1972-83; program coord., grantsman Huntingdon County Commrs., Huntingdon, Pa., 1983-85; human svcs. dir. Huntingdon County Commrs., 1985-87; program dir., grantsman Employment & Tng., Inc., Huntingdon, 1988; commn. rep. So. Alleghenies Planning and Devel. Commn., Altoona, Pa., 1989—; lectr. and speaker in field of creative arts. Author: Proposals and Grants: A Comprehensive Curriculum, 1987, One Branch, 1988, Writing Proposals That Sell, 1988. Pres. Tussey Mountain Sch. Dist., Saxton, 1984-85, Weatherization, Inc., Huntingdon, 1987, Employment and Tng. Inc., Huntingdon, 1987, Mental Health/Mental Retardation Citizens Adv. Bd., 1990-91. Recipient Past Pres. award of appreciation Weatherization Bd. Dirs., 1988, Tussey Mountain Sch. Dist., 1985, Tussey Mountain Jaycees, 1978, Poetry Award of Merit, 1989, Golden Poety award, 1989, Silver Poet award, 1990. Avocations: choreography, personal fitness tng, martial arts, national level jazz piano performer. Office: So Alleghenies Pl-Devel Com 541 58th St Altoona PA 16602-1158

JOHN PAUL, HIS HOLINESS POPE, II (KAROL JOZEF WOJTYLA), bishop of Rome; b. Wadowice, Poland, May 18, 1920; s. Karol and Emilia (Kaczorowska) W. Student, Jagiellonian U., Krakow, 1937-39, ThD, 1949; studied in underground sem., Krakow, 1942-46; D. ethics, Pontifical Angelicum U., Rome, 1948; Dr. (hon.), J. Guttenberg U., Mainz, Fed. Republic Germany, 1977. Ordained priest Roman Cath. Ch., 1946; pastor St. Florian's Parish, Krakow, 1948; student chaplain Jagiellonian U., 1949; prof. moral theology Krakow, 1953; prof. ethics, then chmn. dept. philosophy Cath. U. of Lublin, 1954-58, dir. ethics inst., 1956-58; aux. bishop of Krakow, 1958, archbishop of Krakow, 1964-78; great chancellor Pontifical Theol. Faculty, Krakow; created cardinal by Pope Paul VI, 1967; elected Pope, Oct. 16, 1978, installed, Oct. 22, 1978. Author of: books, poetry, plays, including The Goldsmith's Shop; Play Easter Vigil and Other Poems, 1979, Love and Responsibility, 1960, The Acting Person, 1969, Foundations of Renewal, 1972, Sign of Contradiction, 1976; encyclicals: The Redeemer of Man, 1979, On Human Work, 1981, The Apostles of the Slavs, 1985, The Lord, the Giver of Life, 1986, Redemptoris Mater, 1987, Sollicitudo Rei Socialis, 1987, Dives in Misericordia, 1989, Crossing the Threshold of Hope, 1994; contbr. articles on philosophy, ethics and theology to various jours. Mem. Polish Acad. Scis. Address: Palazzo Apostolico, Vatican City 00120, Vatican City*

JOHNS, BEVERLEY ANNE HOLDEN, special education administrator; b. New Albany, Ind., Nov. 6, 1946; d. James Edward and Martha Edna (Scharf) Holden; m. Lonnie J. Johns, July 28, 1973. BS, Catherine Spalding Coll., Ky., 1968; MS, So. Ill. U., 1970; postgrad., Western Ill. U., 1973-74, 79-80, 82, U. Ill., 1984-85. Cert. adminstr., tchr. Ill. Demonstration tchr. So. Ill. U., Carbondale, 1970-72; instr. MacMurray Coll., Jacksonville, Ill., 1977-79, 90-93; intern Ill. State Bd. Edn., Springfield, 1981; program supr. Four Rivers Spl. Edn. Dist., Jacksonville, Ill., 1972—; chmn. Ill. Special Edn., 1982—; conf. coord. Ill. Alliance, Champaign, 1982-94; bd. dirs. Jacksonville Area Assn. Retarded Citizens, v.p., 1993-94, sec. 1996—; lectr. to profl. confs.; cons. in field. Author: Report on Behavior Analysis in Edn., 1972, (with V. Carr) Techniques for Managing Verbally and Physically Aggressive Students, 1995, (with V. Carr and C. Hoots) Reduction of School Violence: Alternatives to Suspension, 1995, (with J. Keenan) Techniques for Managing a Safe School, 1997; editor: Position Papers of Ill. Council for Exceptional Children, 1981; contbr. articles to profl. jours. Govt. rels. chmn. Internat. Council Exceptional Children, 1984-87; fed. liason Ill. Adminstrs. Spl. Edn., 1985-86. So. Ill. U. fellow, 1968; resolution honoring Beverly H. Johns 60th Ann. Internat. Coun. for Exceptional Children Conv., 1982; cert. of recognition Ill. Atty. Gen., 1985. Recipient Lifetime Achievement award Ill. Coun. for Exceptional Children, 1989; named Jacksonville Woman of the Yr. Bus. and Profl. Women, 1988, First Lady Ill. Coun. Exceptional Children, 1993, Unsung Hero Jacksonville Jour.-Courier, 1993. Mem. ASCD, Assn. Retarded Citizens (com. 1982—), Ill. Coun. for Children With Behavioral Disorders (founder, past pres., presdl. award 1985), pres. Ill. div. for learning disabilities 1991-92, Ill. Alliance for Exceptional Children (v.p 1982-94), Learning Disabilities Assn. (bd. dir.), Ill. Coun. Exceptional Children (past pres., chmn. govt. rels. com. 1982-95, 97-98, governing bd. 1984-95, Presdl. award 1983), Internat. Coun. for Children With Behavioral Disorders (pres. 1997), West Cen. Assn. for Citizens with Learning Disabilities (founder, com. chair 197—), Internat. Pioneer Press (editor CEC pioneer divsn., pres.- elect divsn. internat. pioneers), Internat. Divsn. Learning Disibilities (exec. bd.), Delta Kappa Gamma (chpt. pres. 1988-90, state exec. bd. 1991—), Phi Delta Kappa. Roman Catholic. Avocation: world travel. Home: PO Box 340 Jacksonville IL 62651-0340 Office: Four Rivers Spl Edn Dist 936 W Michigan Ave Jacksonville IL 62650-3113

JOHNS, DIANA, secondary education educator. BS, Mich. State U.; MS, U. Mich. Jr. high sch tchr. Crestwood Dist. Schools, Dearborn Heights, Mich., sr. high sch. tchr., sci. dept. chair. Outstanding Earth-Sci. Tchr. award, 1992, Tchr. of the Year award Crestwood Sch. Dist., Scholarship award Crestwood High Sch. Chpt. NHS. Mem. Nat. Assn. Geology Tchrs., Mich. Earth Sci. Tchrs. Assn. Office: Crestwood Sr High Sch 1501 N Beech Daly Rd Dearborn Heights MI 48127-3403*

JOHNS, EMERSON THOMAS, chemical company executive; b. Phila., June 24, 1947; s. Charles and Sophia (Milak) J.; m. Marlene Catherine Giorello, Oct. 9, 1971; children: Tracey, Jeffrey. BS in Acctg., Mt. St. Mary's Coll., 1969; MBA in Fin., Widener U., 1980. Auditor DuPont Co., Atlanta, Parlin, N.J., Wilmington, N.C., Beamont, Tex. and, Clinton, Iowa, 1969-77; fin. analyst internat. dept. DuPont Co., Wilmington, Del., 1978-80, mgr. acctg. and internal controls, 1981-82; mgr. acctg. and bus. analysis dept., petrochems. dept. Savannah River plant Dupont Co., Aiken, S.C., 1983-85; mgr. adminstrv. svcs. atomic energy div. DuPont Co., Wilmington, 1986-89, mgr. govt. contracting fin. dept., 1989—; fin. mgr. engring. Engring. DuPont Fin., Wilmington, 1990; fin. mgr. integrated ops. DuPont Engring., Wilmington, 1992; global fin. mgr. Engring. Svcs. and Security, Safety, Health, Environ., Wilmington, 1994, Asset Productivity and Bus. Svcs., Wilmington, 1999—; instr. bus. edn. St. John the Beloved. Bd. dirs. St. Mary Help of Christians Sch., Aiken, 1985, chmn.-elect, 1986; bd. dirs. Foxchase Civic Assn., Aiken, 1986; advisor Jr. Achievement, Wilmington, 1987-90, in-sch. instr., 1989-90; mem. Christian formation St. John the Beloved, Wilmington, 1988-89, com. chmn., 1989-90; spl. funds solicitor United Way, 1995-98. Mem. Foxchase Swim Club (pres. 1985). Roman Catholic. Avocations: golf, personal computers, travel. Home: 1105 Kelly Dr Yeatman Estates Newark DE 19711 Office: DuPont Co Fin 1007 S Market St Wilmington DE 19801-5227

JOHNS, JANET SUSAN, physician; b. Chgo., July 18, 1941; d. Nicholas C. and Doris Ann (Douglas) J.; m. Harlan R. Bullard; children: George, Sam. AB, Ind. U., 1963, MD, 1966. Diplomate Am. Acad. Family Practice. Intern Meml. Hosp., South Bend, Ind. Home: 3510 Woodcliff Dr Lafayette IN 47905-8834 Office: Purdue U Student Health 1826 Push West Lafayette IN 47905

JOHNS, JASPER, artist; b. Augusta, Ga., May 15, 1930; s. Jasper and Jean (Riley) J. Student, U. S.C., 1947-48. One-man exhbns. include, Leo Castelli Gallery, N.Y.C., 1958, 60, 61, 63, 66, 68, 76, 81, 84, Minami Gallery, Tokyo, 1965, 75, Galerie Rive Droite, Paris, 1959, 61, Galleria D'Arte Del Naviglio, Milan, 1959, Ileana Sonnabend, Paris, 1963, Columbia Mus. Art (S.C.), 1960, Jewish Mus., N.Y.C., 1964, White-chapel Gallery, London, 1964, Pasadena Mus. (Calif.), 1965, Smithsonian Instn. Nat. Collection Fine Arts, 1966, Arts Council Gt. Britain, 1974-75, Whitney Mus. Am. Art,1977, Kunsthalle, Cologne, 1978, Centre Pompidou, Paris, 1978, Hayward Gallery, London, 1978, Seibu Mus., Tokyo, 1978, San Francisco Mus. Modern Art, 1978, Kunstmuseum, Basel, 1979, Des Moines Art Ctr., 1983, St. Louis Art Mus., 1985, Mus. Modern Art, 1986, Kunsthalle, 1986, Wight Art Gallery UCLA, 1987, Galerie Daniel Templon, Paris, 1987, Mus. Contemporary Art, L.A., 1987, Am. Pavillion 43rd Biennale, Venice, 1988, Phila. Mus. Art, 1988, Walker Art Ctr., Mpls., 1990, Mus. Fine Arts, Houston, 1990, Fine Arts Mus. San Francisco, 1990, Montreal Mus. Fine Arts, 1990, Nat. Gallery Art, Washington, 1990, Kunstmus. Basel, 1990, Hayward Gallery, London, 1990, St. Louis Art Mus., 1991, Ctr. for Fine Arts, Miami, 1991, Denver Art Mus., 1991, Brooke Alexander Edits., N.Y.C., 1991, Whitney Mus. Am. Art, N.Y.C., 1991, Harvard U. Art Mus., 1992, San Diego Mus. Art, 1992, Cana Art Gallery, Seoul, 1991, Gagosian Gallery, N.Y., 1992, Palaus de Luppe, La Fondation Vincent Van Gogh, Arles, France, 1992, Milw. Art Mus., 1992, Galeria Weber Alexander Cobo, Madrid, 1992, Nat. Acad. Design, N.Y.C., 1996; represented in permanent collections Mus. Modern Art, Albright-Knox Art Gallery, Buffalo, Tate Gallery, London, Moderna Museet, Stockholm, Stedelijik Mus., Amsterdam, The Netherlands, Whitney Mus., N.Y.C., Kunstmuseum, Basel, Centre Pompidou, Art Inst. Chgo., Balt. Mus. Art, Cleve. Mus. Art, Kunsthaus Zurich, Mpls. Inst. Art, Nat. Gallery Art, San Francisco Mus. Modern Art, Va. Mus. Fine Arts, Richmond, Walker Art Ctr. Recipient 1st prize Print Biennale Ljubljana, Yugoslavia, prize IX Sao Paulo (Brazil) Biennale, Skowhegan medal for Painting Skowhegan Sch. of Painting and Sculpture, Skowhegan medal for Graphics, Mayors award of Honor for Arts and Culture City of N.Y., Wolf prize for Painting, Wolf Found., Internat. prize Venice Biennale, 1988, Nat. Medal of Arts, The White House; named to S.C. Hall of Fame, 1989. Mem. Am. Acad. Arts and Letters (Gold medal for graphic art), Royal Acad. Arts, Nat. Inst. Arts and Letters, Am. Acad. Arts and Scis. Office: care Leo Castelli Gallery 420 W Broadway New York NY 10012-3764*

JOHNS, MARGARET BUSH, neuroendocrinologist, researcher, educator; b. Boston, July 31, 1928; d. Ernest William Bush and Ellinor (Brennan) Gazik; m. D. Craig Johns, Jan. 15, 1953 (div. 1982); children: Katherine Adrian, Sara Elizabeth; m. H. Peter Stern, May 30, 1985. *Grandmother, Katherine T. Meagher Brennan, Milton, Massachusetts, educator, helped Blessed Mother Katharine Drexell, founder Order Blessed Sacrament, Philadelphia. Grandfather, James Augustus Brennan, Athletic League, 1870s, played chamber music with Victor Herbert. Mother was a diarist. Stepfather, L. Martin Gazik, helped create Liberia's first map, 1954-56. Father, Ernest William Bush, DO, Still College Osteopathy, 1902, practiced Southern Pines, N.C., 1905-74. Daughters Katherine A. Johns, AIA, Old Chatham, N.Y., Sara Johns Griffen, executive director Olana, Hudson, N.Y. Grandchildren Julia and Christopher Shaw, Emily and Stephen Griffen. Husband H. Peter Stern, violinist and chairman of Storm King Art Center, Mountainville, N.Y., vice chairman World Monuments Fund.* Student, George Washington U., 1945-47, NYU, 1951-53; BA, Hunter Coll., N.Y.C., 1971; PhD, Rutgers U., 1979. Postdoctoral NIH rsch. fellow Mt. Sinai Med. Sch., N.Y.C., 1978-81; instr. dept. biol. scis. Hunter Coll., N.Y.C., 1982-83; rsch. scientist NYU, N.Y.C., 1985; ind. rschr. in neuroendocrinology Mountainville, N.Y., 1985—; cons. Lederle Labs., 1984; reviewer NIH, NSF, 1982—. Contbr. articles to Nature, Endocrinology, Annals of N.Y. Acad. Sci. Vol. tutor non-English-speaking children N.Y. Pub. Sch. Sys., N.Y.C., 1964; vol. landscape coord. Neighbors United for Justice in Housing, Newburgh, N.Y., 1988—, vol. edn. cons. Harlem Valley Secure Ctr., Wingdale, N.Y., 1998—. Fellow The Endocrine Soc. Democrat. Achievements include the first to discover a function of the vomeronasal organ in mammalian physiology; first to discover specific and saturable in vitro uptake of serotonin in gonadotrophs in the anterior pituitary of rats and humans. Avocations: pastel painting, gardening, travel. Home: 192 6th Ave New York NY 10013-1228 Office: H Peter Stern Residence Otterkill Rd Mountainville NY 10953

JOHNS, MICHAEL DOUGLAS, government relations executive, policy analyst, health care consultant; b. Allentown, Pa., Sept. 8, 1964; s. Glenn Franklin and Nancy Louise (Hummel) J.; m. Nicole Denise Miles, Sept. 30, 1995 (div. 1999); 1 child, Michael Douglas Jr. Student, Cambridge (Eng.) U., 1984; BBA in Econs., U. Miami, 1986. Editl. intern Nat. Journalism Ctr., Washington, 1983; Lyndon Baines Johnson intern Congressman Don

Ritter, Washington, 1984; asst. editor Policy Rev. Mag., Washington, 1986-88; fgn. policy analyst The Heritage Found., Washington, 1988-91; spl. asst. to pres. Drew U., Madison, N.J., 1991-92; speechwriter to Pres. of U.S. The White House, Washington, 1992; speechwriter to U.S. Sec. Commerce U.S. Dept. Commerce, Washington, 1992-93; dir. rsch. Internat. Rep. Inst., Washington, 1993-94; mgr. corp. comm., sr. writer Eli Lilly and Co., Indpls., 1994-95; pub. policy analyst, cons., writer Fairfax, Va., 1995-97; aide to U.S. Senator Olympia J. Snowe U.S. Senate, Washington, 1997; dir. rsch. and tech. S.R. Wojdak & Assocs., Phila., 1997-98, sr. assoc., 1998—; fgn. policy group advisor Dole for Pres., Inc., Washington, 1996; authored speeches and ofcl. statements for former pres. George Bush, including July 4th nat. TV address to the nation, departure statement with Japanese Prime Minister, speeches to Office of Nat. Drug Control Policy, Nat. Inst. for Responsible Fatherhood and Family Devel., Am. Legion/Boys Nation, others; sr. advisor to global devel. projects Internat. Rep. Inst., Kuwait, Turkey, other nations, 1993-94; directed and contributed to nat. and internat. mktg. and comms. strategies for cancer, cardiovascular, ctrl. nervous sys., endocrine, and infectious disease pharm. products Eli Lilly and Co., 1994-95; govt. rels. and strategic bus. devel. counsel to numerous nat. and Pa. based hosps., nursing homes, pharmaceutical mfrs. and other corp., health care and non-profit clients S.R. Wojdak & Assocs., 1997—; guest polit. and pub. policy analyst for numerous TV and radio programs including MacNeil/Lehrer News Hour, C-SPAN, CNBC, PBS Nightly Bus. Report, Fox Morning News, Voice of Am., BBC, others; guest lectr. UN, Vassar Coll., U. N.C., Chapel Hill, others; U.S. adv. coun. Mozambique Inst., London; bd. trustees Ctr. Internat. Rels., Washington; participant various seminars. Author: U.S. and Africa Statistical Handbook, 1990, 2d edit., 1991; contbg. author: Freedom in the World: The Annual Survey of Political Rights and Civil Liberties, 1993, Finding Our Roots, Facing Our Future: America in the 21st Century, 1997; contbg. editor USSR Monitor newsletter, The Heritage Found., 1989-91; peer reviewer The Harvard Internat. Jour. of Press/Politics Harvard U.; alumni bd. advisors Campus mag. Intercollegiate Studies Inst., Wilmington, Del.; contbr. articles to profl. jours., mags., newspapers including Wall St. Jour., Christian Sci. Monitor, Chgo. Tribune; reported from Africa, Asia, L.Am., Middle East, Persian Gulf and former Soviet Union. Active Luth. Ch. of the Holy Spirit, Emmaus, Pa., The Coca-Cola Co. Civic Action Network, Emmaus (Pa.) Fire Co. Recipient Shell Oil Co.'s Century III Leadership award, 1981, Svc. award Kiwanis, 1982, cert. appreciation Spl. Olympics, 1983, award of appreciation Lao Vets Am., 1995, numerous citations in Congl. Record, U.S. Congress. Mem. Nat. Journalism Ctr. Alumni Coun., Pa. Assn. for Govt. Rels., Iron Arrow Honor Soc. U. Miami, Assn. on Third World Affairs, Reagan Alumni Assn., Bush/Quayle Alumni Assn., Puente de Jovenes Profls. Cubanos, Washington Ind. Writers, Lambda Chi Alpha (Internat. Hall of Fame 1996). Republican. Lutheran. Home: 1500 Locust St #2719 Philadelphia PA 19102-4328

JOHNS, MICHAEL MARIEB EDWARD, otolaryngologist, academic administrator; b. Detroit, Jan. 27, 1942; s. Trina Lou DelCampo; children: Christina, Michael. BS, Wayne State U., 1964, Grad. Biol. Sci., 1965; MD with distinction, U. Mich., 1969. Diplomate Am. Bd. Otolaryngology. Intern Univ. Hosp., Ann Arbor, Mich., 1969-70, resident in otolaryngology, 1971-75; resident in gen. surgery St. Joseph's Mercy Hosp., Ann Arbor, 1970-71; asst. prof. U. Va. Med. Ctr., Charlottesville, 1977-79, assoc. prof., 1979-82, prof., 1982-84; prof. Johns Hopkins U. Sch. Medicine, Balt., 1984-96, dean med. faculty, v.p. medicine, 1990-96; exec. v.p. health affairs Emory U., Atlanta, 1996—; co-chmn. Md. Sci. Week Blue Ribbon Panel, Balt., 1992—' chmn-elect Coun. of Deans. Co-author: Head and Neck Cancer, 1990; contbr. articles to profl. jours. Grantee Robert Wood Johnson Found., 1992, NIH, 1995. Mem. Inst. Medicine, Cosmos Club, Ctr. Club. Office: Emory U Robert W Woodruff Health Scis Ctr 1440 Clifton Rd NE Ste 400 Atlanta GA 30322-1053*

JOHNS, RICHARD JAMES, physician, educator; b. Pendleton, Oreg., Aug. 19, 1925; s. James Shanard and Pearl (McKenna) J.; m. Carol Greacen Johnson; children: Richard Clark, Robert Shanard, James Ashmore. BS, U. Oreg., 1947; MD, Johns Hopkins U., 1948. Diplomate Am. Bd. Internal Medicine. Intern Johns Hopkins Hosp., Balt., 1948-49, asst. resident, 1951-53, fellow in medicine, 1953-55, resident, 1955-56, instr., 1955-57, physician, 1956—, asst. prof., 1957-61, assoc. prof., 1961-66, asst. dean admissions, 1962-66, prof. medicine, 1966—, dir. subdept. biomed. engring., 1966-70, mem. adv. bd., prin. profl. staff Applied Physics Lab., 1967—, prof., dir. dept. biomed. engring., 1970-91, disting. svc. prof., 1991—; bd. visitors Sch. Engring., Duke U., 1986—; chmn. adv. com. Divisional Health Scis. and Tech. Harvard-MIT, 1987-92; mem. com. sci., engring. and pub. policy NAS, 1988-90; mem. sci. adv. com. GM, 1991-97. Sec., vice chmn., chmn. med. bd. Myasthenia Gravis Found.; trustee Am. Bd. Clin. Engring., pres., 1976-83; bd. dirs. Whitaker Found., 1991-94. Capt. M.C. AUS, 1949-51. Fellow ACP, AAAS, Am. Inst. for Biol. & Med. Engring. (founding), Royal Soc. Medicine; mem. Am. Clin. and Climatol. Assn. (v.p. 1977-78, sec.-treas. 1979-85, pres. 1986-87), Am. Soc. Clin. Investigation, Assn. Am. Physicians, Biomed. Engring. Soc. (bd. dirs. 1972-75, pres. 1978-79), IEEE (pres. group on engring. in medicine and biology 1970-72), Inst. Medicine NAS (coun. 1987-90), Johns Hopkins Med. Soc. (pres. 1968-69), Interurban Clin. Club (pres. 1980-81), Peripatetic Club, Caduceus Club, Sigma Xi, Alpha Omega Alpha, Phi Kappa Psi, Nu Sigma Nu, Tau Beta Pi. Clubs: Annapolis Yacht; Elkridge; Johns Hopkins (v.p. 1969-70). Home: 203 E Highfield Rd Baltimore MD 21218-1105 Office: Johns Hopkins U Sch Med Ste 2-300 1830 E Monument St Baltimore MD 21205-2100

JOHNS, RICHARD SETH ELLIS, lawyer; b. Eugene, Oreg., Apr. 23, 1946; s. Frank Errol Jr. and Emily Elizabeth (Ellis) J.; m. Eleanor Lee Kuntz, Mar. 8, 1981. BA in English, U. Calif., Santa Barbara, 1968; JD, U. Calif., San Francisco, 1971. Bar: Calif. 1971, Ill. 1972. Instr. law U. Chgo., 1972-73; assoc. Atchison, Topeka & Santa Fe RR, Chgo., 1973-75, Furth, Fahrner, Bluemle & Mason, San Francisco, 1975-84; of counsel Maier, Dimitriou & Ross, San Francisco, 1984; ptnr. Rubenstein, Bohachek & Johns, San Francisco, 1985-88, Kipperman & Johns, San Francisco, 1988—. Contbr. articles to Calif. Law Rev. Bd. dirs. Congregation Beth Shalom, San Francisco, 1982-92, Bay Area sect. Am. Jewish Com., 1984—; leader Family Policy Task Force, 1987-88; guest of Christian Dem. Union, Konrad Adenhauer Stiftung-German-Am. Jewish Exchange Program, Fed. Republic Germany, 1985; dir. Mus. of the City of San Francisco, 1996-97, v.p., 1997—. 1st lt. U.S. Army, 1972-75. Mem. ABA, Calif. Bar Assn., Concordia-Argonaut Club, Ill. State Bar. Office: Kipperman & Johns 3 Embarcadero Ctr 28th Fl San Francisco CA 94111

JOHNS, ROY (BUD JOHNS), publisher, author; b. Detroit, July 9, 1929; s. Roy and Isabel Johns; m. Judith Spector Clancy, 1971 (dec. 1990); m. Frances Moreland, 1992. BA in English and Econs., Albion (Mich.) Coll., 1951. Various editorial positions Mich. and Calif. daily newspapers, 1942-60; bur. chief Fairchild Pubs., 1960-69; dir. corp. communications Levi Strauss & Co., 1969-81, corp. v.p., 1979-81; pres. Synergistic Press, Inc., San Francisco, 1968—; bd. dirs. Applewood Books, Bedford, Mass.; founder, ptnr. Apple Tree Press, Flint, Mich., 1954-55; cons. on comms., pub., and related areas. Author: The Ombibulous Mr. Mencken, 1968, What is This Madness?, 1985; co-editor, author: Bastard in the Ragged Suit, 1977; scriptwriter, exec. producer: What is This Madness?, 1976; exec. producer: The Best You Can Be, 1979 (CINE Golden Eagle award 1980); editor: Old Dogs Remembered, 1993, paperback edit., 1999; free-lance writer numerous mag. articles. Mem. Nat. Coun. of Mus. of Am. Indian, N.Y.C., 1980-90; dir. The San Francisco Contemporary Music Players, 1981—, Greenbelt Alliance, San Francisco, 1982—, pres., 1990-95; dir. Save San Francisco Bay Assn., 1996-97, San Francisco Performing Arts Libr. and Mus., 1998—. Inventor sport of ride and tie racing, 1971. Home and Office: 3965 Sacramento St San Francisco CA 94118-1627

JOHNS, WARREN LEROI, lawyer; b. Nevada, Iowa, June 9, 1929; s. Varner Jay and Ruby Charlene (Morrison) J.; m. Elaine C. Magnuson, July 24, 1955 (div. June 1983); children: Richard Warren, Lynn Cherie Johns-Pence; m. Ruth Page Scott, Sept. 29, 1985. BA, La Sierra U., 1950; MA, Andrews U., 1951; JD, U. So. Calif., 1958. Bar: Calif. 1959, U.S. Dist. Ct. (cen. dist.) Calif. 1959,U.S. Supreme Ct. 1963, Md. 1976, D.C. 1976, U.S. Dist. Ct. Md. 1976, U.S. Dist. Ct. D.C. 1976, U.S. Tax Ct. 1976, U.S. Ct. Appeals (4th cir.) 1976, U.S. Ct. Appeals (10th cir.) 1977, U.S. Ct. Customs and Patent Appeals 1979. Gen. counsel So. Calif. Conf. Seventh-day Adventists, Glendale, 1959-63, Pacific Union Conf. Seventh-day Adventists, Glendale and Sacramento, 1964-69; pvt. practice Sacramento, 1969-75; gen. counsel Gen. Conf. Seventh-day Adventists, Washington, 1975-92, trustee; pvt. practice Brookeville, Md., 1992-98; mem. adv. bd. Ctr. for Ch./State Studies, De Paul U. Coll. Chgo., 1987-93, spl. counsel to gen. conf., 1992-95; spl. counsel Adventist HealthCare Corp., Columbia Union HealthCare Corp., 1992-97. Author: Dateline Sunday USA, 1967, Ride to Glory, 1999; founding editor JD, 1978-92. Chmn. bd. dirs., pres. Sacramento Area Econ. Opportunity Coun., 1974. Recipient Frank Yost award Ch. State Coun., Glendale, Alumnus of Achievement award Andrews U., 1981, Alumnus of Yr. award La Sierra U., 1994. Mem. AAAS, ABA (vice-chmn. com. on torts, non-profit, charitable and religious orgns., sect. of tort and ins. practice 1990-91). Democrat. Avocations: sports, photography, book collecting. Office: 21320 Georgia Ave Brookeville MD 20833-1132

JOHNSEN, EUGENE CARLYLE, mathematician and educator; b. Mpls., Jan. 27, 1932; s. Bernhardt Thorwald and Esther Elvira (Eklund) J.; m. Marjorie Marie Wacklin, Aug. 31, 1957. BChem, U. Minn., 1954; PhD, Ohio State U., 1961. NAS/NRC Rsch. Assoc. Nat. Bur. Stds., Washington, 1962-63; lectr. math. U. Calif., Santa Barbara, 1963-64, asst. prof., 1964-68, assoc. prof., 1968-74, prof., 1974-94, prof. emeritus, 1994—, dir. summer sessions, 1981-94, 94-97; vis. lectr. in math. U. Mich., Ann Arbor, 1968-69; vis. scholar in sociology Harvard U., Cambridge, Mass., 1984-85; mathematician Sperry Rand, St. Paul, 1956, 57; instr. chem. and math. U. Minn., 1956-57; instr. math. Ohio State U., Columbus, 1962. Contbr. numerous articles to profl. jours.; mem. editl. bd. Jour. Math. Sociology. Mem. Los Angeles County Mus. Art, 1985—, L.A. Music Ctr. Opera League, 1986—; mem. Santa Barbara C. of C./U. Calif. Santa Barbara Bus. Adv. Com., 1979-84. Grantee USAFOSR, NSF, Dept. Edn.; Fulbright fellow U. Tübingen, 1969; fellow NSF, 1959. Mem. AAAS, AAUP, Am. Math. Soc., Math. Assn. Am., Am. Statis. Assn., Soc. Indsl. and Applied Math., Internat. Network for Social Network Analysis, Am. Sociol. Assn. (acting chairperson, then chairperson math. sociology sect. 1995-97), U. Calif. Santa Barbara Faculty Club, Am.-Scandinavian Found., Sons of Norway (pres. Ivar Aasen Lodge 1999—), Phi Beta Kappa, Sigma Xi, Phi Lambda Upsilon, Pi Mu Epsilon. Avocations: music, opera, tennis, travel. Home: 1603 Paterna Rd Santa Barbara CA 93103-1826 Office: U Calif Dept Math Santa Barbara CA 93106

JOHNSEN, NIELS WINCHESTER, ocean shipping company executive; b. New Orleans, May 9, 1922; s. Niels Frithjof and Julia Anita (Winchester) J.; m. Millicent Alva Mercer, Sept. 9, 1944; children—Niels Mercer, Ingrid Christina Johnsen Barrett, Gretchen Anita Johnsen Bryant. Student, Tulane U., 1939-42. V.p. States Marine Lines, N.Y.C., 1946-56; v.p. Central Gulf Lines, Inc., N.Y.C., 1947-65, vice chmn., 1965-71, chmn., 1971-98; chmn. Internat. Shipholding Corp., N.Y.C., 1979—, Waterman Steamship Corp., N.Y.C., 1989-97; dir. Reserve Fund, Inc., N.Y.C., 1970-97. Bd. mgrs. Seamens Ch. Inst., N.Y.C., 1974-90. Served to lt. (j.g.) U.S. Maritime Service, 1942-45. Recipient award Marine Soc., 1993, medal of honor Ellis Island, 1994, Internat. Hall of Fame award Maritime Assn., 1993; named Entrepreneur of Yr., 1996. Mem. Nat. Cargo Bus. (bd. dirs. 1970-96), Am. Bur. Shipping (bd. mgrs. 1967-92), Seamens Ch. Inst. (hon. bd. mem., Silver Bell award 1988, Admiral of the Ocean Sea award 1993), India House (bd. dirs. 1962-98), Rumson Country Club (pres. 1985), Seabright Beach Club. Republican. Presbyterian. Avocations: golf; skiing. Office: Internat Shipholding Corp 1 Whitehall St New York NY 10004-2109*

JOHNSEN, PEGGY WINCHELL, education administrator; b. Wynne, Ark., Dec. 22, 1936; d. Hubbard H. and Nadine (Jackson) Winchell; m. W.E. Johnsen, Feb. 14, 1987; 1 child, Susan Dowell Benson. BS in Edn., U. Ctrl. Ark., 1957; MS, U. Tenn., 1966; Edn. Specialist, U. Ark., 1979, EdD, 1984. Instr. grad. sch. U. Tenn., Knoxville, 1964-66; tchr. various secondary schs., Bigelow, Lake Village, Ark., 1957-64; ednl. coord. Ark. Dept. of Edn., Little Rock, 1966-80; coord. industry tng. Ark. Power & Light Co., Little Rock, 1980-86; with ops. planning divsn. Lockheed Missile & Space, Vandenberg AFB, Calif., 1987-93; dir. tech. prep. Cuesta Coll., San Luis Obispo, Calif., 1994-98; assoc. faculty Allen Hancock Coll., 1999—; vice-chmn. vocat. adv. coun. Pulaski County, Little Rock, Pulaski County, 1981-84; chmn. vocat. adv. coun. Little Rock Sch. Dist., 1982-84. Author: (booklet) Performance Based Training, 1995, Basic Stained Glass: A Competency Based Instructor's Manual; editor: (curriculum guide) Word Processing: A Competency Based Guide, 1995. Edn. dir., v.p. Civitan, Little Rock, 1985-86. Mem. Los Padres Artist Guild (bd. dirs. 1994—), Am. Vocat. Assn., Minerva Club, Delta Kappa Gamma. Lutheran. Avocation: teaching art of stained glass. Home: 931 E Boone St Santa Maria CA 93454-6342

JOHNSON, ABIGAIL, investment company executive. BA in Art History, Hobart and William Smith Colls, 1984; MBA, Harvard U., 1988. Rsch. assoc. Booz, Allen and Hamilton; portfolio mgr. Fidelity Investments, Boston, 1988—, assoc. dir., 1998—, sr. v.p., 1998—; bd. dirs. FMR Corp. Office: Fidelity Investments 82 Devonshire St Boston MA 02109-3614*

JOHNSON, ADELE CUNNINGHAM, marina executive; b. Vineland, N.J., May 14, 1934; d. Charles and Lorraine (Durand) Cunningham; m. Carl H. Johnson Jr., May 14, 1955; children: C. Howard III, Lorraine Johnson Bonifield, Charles Victor. BS, Syracuse U., 1955. Owner, mgr. Avalon (N.J.) Anchorage Marina, 1984—; mem. U.S. Power Squadron, 1968—; capt. lic., USCG, 1985; adv. bd. Bank of N.J., Vineland, 1970-75. Organizer, dir. Millville (N.J.) Youth Week, 1956; organizer Millville Hosp. Vol. Svcs., 1966, dir., 1966-70; bd. dirs. United Way Millville, Millville YMCA Swim Team, 1969-77; v.p. Millville YMCA, 1970-75; mem. Newcomb Hosp. Found., Vineland, 1981-88; pres. Cumberland County Coll. Found., Vineland, 1986—. Mem. N.J. Marine Trades Assn., Millville Womens Club, State Fedn. Womens Clubs (2d dist. v.p. 1982-84), Avalon C. of C., Cape May County C. of C., Zonta. Republican. Methodist. Home: 403 20th St Avalon NJ 08202-2103 Office: Avalon Anchorage Marina 885 21st St Avalon NJ 08202-2116

JOHNSON, ALAN, retired window/patio door manufacturer. Exec. v. pres., sec. Andersen Corp., Bayport, Minn., 1958—. Office: Andersen Corp 100 4th Ave N Bayport MN 55003-1096

JOHNSON, ALAN B., advertising executive. Sr. v.p., media svcs. dir. Mullen Advertising Inc., Wenham, Mass. Office: Mullen Advertising Inc 36 Essex St Wenham MA 01984-1799*

JOHNSON, ALAN BOND, federal judge; b. 1939. BA, Vanderbilt U., 1961; JD, U. Wyo., 1964. Pvt. practice law Cheyenne, Wyo., 1968-71; assoc. Hanes, Carmichael, Johnson, Gage & Speight P.C., Cheyenne, 1971-74; judge Wyo. Dist. Ct., 1974-85; judge U.S. Dist. Ct. Wyo., 1986-92, chief judge, 1992—; part-time fed. magistrate U.S. Dist. Ct. Wyo., 1971-74; substitute judge Mcpl. Ct., Cheyenne, 1973-74. Served to capt. USAF, 1964-67, to col. Wyo. Air N.G., 1973-90. Mem. ABA, Wyo. State Bar, Laramie County Bar Assn. (sec.-treas. 1968-70), Wyo. Jud. Conf. (sec. 1977-78, chmn. 1979), Wyo. Jud. Council. Office: US Dist Ct O'Mahoney Fed Ctr 2120 Capitol Ave Ste 2242 Cheyenne WY 82001-3666

JOHNSON, ALAN GERHARD, English educator; b. Pune, India, Aug. 11, 1961; came to U.S., 1979; s. Gerhard Tilman and Virginia Wehr Johnson; m. Margaret Prasangi, Jan. 5, 1989; children: Nishant, Shirin, Roshin. BA in English, So. Ill. U., 1984; MA in English, U. Va., 1988; PhD in English, U. Calif., Riverside, 1998. H.S. English tchr. Schutz Am. Sch., Alexandria, Egypt, 1988-89, St. Matthias H.S., Huntington Park, Calif., 1989-91; tchg. asst. in English U. Calif., Riverside, 1992-97, lectr. in English, 1997-98; asst. prof. English Wharton (Tex.) County Jr. Coll., 1998—. Co-editor jour. The Globe, 1984; contbr. articles, poetry to profl. publs. T.L. Kellogg scholar, 1983, 84; Humanities grad. student rsch. grantee U. Calif., Riverside, 1994, 95; Writing fellow U. Calif., Riverside, 1994-95. Mem. MLA. Avocations: writing, sketching, singing, travel, hiking. E-mail: chaijohnson@webmail.com. Home: 302 Tennie St Wharton TX 77488 Office: Wharton County Jr Coll Wharton TX 77488

JOHNSON, ALBERT WESLEY, consultant on governance; b. Insinger, Sask., Can., Oct. 18, 1923; s. Thomas William and Louise Lillian (Croft) J.; m. Ruth Elinor Hardy, June 27, 1946; children: Andrew, Frances, Jane, Geoffrey. B.A., U. Sask., 1942; M.A., U. Toronto, Ont., Can., 1945; M.P.A. (Littauer fellow), Harvard U., 1950, Ph.D. (Littauer fellow), 1963; LL.D. (hon.), U. Regina, 1977, U. Sask., 1978, Mt. Allison U., 1982, Queen's U., 1992, Carleton U., 1999. Dep. provincial treas. Govt. of Sask., Regina, 1952-64; asst. dep. minister fin. Govt. of Can., Ottawa, Ont., 1964-68; econ. adviser to prime minister on constn. Govt. of Can., 1968-70, sec. treasury bd., 1970-73, dep. minister nat. welfare, 1973-75; pres. CBC, Ottawa, 1975-82; Skelton-Clark fellow Queens U., 1982-83; prof. polit. sci. U. Toronto, 1983-89, prof. emeritus, 1989—; sr. fellow Can. Centre for Mgmt. Devel., Ottawa, 1989-91; cons. on governance Internat. Monetary Fund, Indonesia, 1988, 91, S. Africa, 1992-99; chmn. task force on univ. programs, Sask., 1992-93. Contbr. articles to profl. publs.; editorial bd.: Can. Public Policy, 1974-75. Bd. dirs. Nat. Film Bd., 1970-82, U. Sask. Hosp., 1957-64; mem. Nat. Arts Centre, 1975-82; bd. govs. U. Sask., Saskatoon, 1952-63. Recipient Gold medal Profl. Inst. of Pub. Svc. of Can., 1975; decorated Companion of the Order of Can., 1997. Mem. Ottawa Polit. Economy Assn. (pres. 1969-70), Inst. Public Adminstrn. Can. (pres. 1962-63, Vanier medal 1976, nat. council 1951-69), Can. Polit. Sci. Assn. (exec. council 1963-64). Mem. United Ch. of Can.

JOHNSON, ALBERTA CLARK, psychology educator; b. Chattanooga, Apr. 19, 1942; d. William Ross and Helen W. Clark; m. John Burlin Johnson, Mar. 12, 1965; children: Sonya K., Roxanne Johnson Dingman. BA, U. N.C., Greensboro, 1964; MS, U. Ariz., 1979, PhD, 1988. Cert. family life educator, Nat. Coun. Family Rels. Membership dir. Tucson Area Coun. Camp Fire, 1981-83; asst. dir. Ext. Winter Sch., Tucson, 1984-87; human devel. specialist U. Ariz. Coop. Ext. Svc., Tucson, 1983-87; assoc. faculty Pima C.C., Tucson, 1987-88; family life specialist U. Ariz. Coop. Ext. Svc., 1989-92, U. Ark. Coop. Ext. Svc., Little Rock, 1989-92; cons. Little Rock, 1992-93; asst. prof. psychology and edn. Floyd Coll., Rome, Ga., 1993-97, assoc. prof. psychology, 1997—. Contbr. articles to profl. jours. Sec., governing state bd. dirs. Parents Anonymous of Ariz., Phoenix, 1983-84; mem. Gov.'s Coun. on Children, Youth and Families, Phoenix, 1983-84; pres. bd. dirs. Pima County chpt. Parents Anonymous, Tucson, 1985-86; v.p. Women's Info. Network, Inc., Rome, 1997. Named Woman of Excellence, 1998, Women in Mgmt. and Greater Rome C. of C. Mem. AAUP, Nat. Coun. on Family Rels., Nat. Assn. for Edn. of Young Children, Coun. Tchrs. of Undergrad. Psychology, Ga. Assn. for Young Children, Psi Beta, Kappa Omicron Nu, Pi Lambda Theta. Avocations: photography, hiking, camping, reading. Office: Floyd Coll PO Box 1864 3175 Highway 27 N Rome GA 30162-1864

JOHNSON, ALEX CLAUDIUS, English language educator; b. Freetown, Sierra Leone, Aug. 14, 1943; came to U.S., 1991; s. Eunice Angela (Thorpe) J.; m. Daphne Marvel Taylor; children: Marvin, Joyemi. BA in English Lang. and Lit. with honors, U. Durham, Eng., 1968; MA in English and Am. Lit., U. Kent, Canterbury, Eng., 1971; MPhil in Linguistics, U. Leeds, Eng., 1974; PhD in English, U. Ibadan, Nigeria, 1982. Tchr. various h.s., Freetown, Sierra Leone, 1966-69, 71-72; sr. lectr., lectr. English dept. Fourah Bay Coll., Sierra Leone, 1974-88, sr. lectr., acting head classics/philosophy dept., 1987-88, assoc. prof., head English dept., 1988-91; prof. English lang. and Creole studies U. Bayreuth, Germany, 1982-84; vis. prof. S.C. State U., Orangeburg, 1991-92, prof., 1992; acting vice prin. Fourah Bay Coll., summer 1989, 90, dean faculty of arts, 1989-91; cons. UNESCO, 1985-89; external assessor U. Cape Coast, Ghana, 1988. Contbr. articles to internat. profl. jours., papers to internat. confs. and symposia. Chief examiner West Africa Examinations Coun., Accra, Ghana, 1978-91, Inst. Edn., U. Sierra Leone, 1980-91; chair Nat. Primary Curriculum Revision Com., 1981. Mem. AAUP, Coll. Lang. Assn., African Lit. Assn., West African Linguistic Soc. (sec., organizer 13th West African Langs. Congress, Freetown, 1978), West African MLA (exec. com. 1981-82). Episcopalian. Home: 767 Windmill Way NW Orangeburg SC 29118-2838

JOHNSON, ALFRED CARL, JR., former navy officer; b. Joliet, Ill., Oct. 2, 1930; s. Alfred Carl and Frances (Wright) J.; m. Beverly Jean Raisler, Dec. 27, 1953; children: Sheri Lynn, David Craig, Laura Lee. Student, U. Ill., 1948-51, Naval Post Grad. Sch., 1958-59, Naval War Coll., 1964-65; BS in Systems Analysis, George Washington U., 1968. Enlisted USN, 1952, advanced through grades to capt., 1974; served as head systems analysis Nat. Mil. Command System, Joint Chiefs of Staff, Washington, 1965-68; air ops. officer USS J.F. Kennedy CVA-67, Norfolk, Va., 1968-70; squadron comdr. Composite Squadron 5, Okinawa, Japan, 1970-71; ops. officer USS Midway CVA 41, San Francisco, 1971-73; dir. programming and budget Naval Aviation, Chief of Naval Ops., Washington, 1973-77; air wing comdr. Airwing 6, Pensacola, Fla., 1977-79; chief staff Naval Edn. Tng., Pensacola, 1979-84; ret., 1984—. Contbr. articles to jours. Scout leader Boy Scouts Am., 1961—. Decorated Legion of Merit with two gold stars, Bronze Star. Mem. Assn. Naval Aviation, Rotary (Paul Harris fellow), Psi Upsilon, Am. Security Coun. Avocations: sailing, camping, community service. Home: 4984 Prieto Dr Pensacola FL 32506-5381

JOHNSON, ALICE ELAINE, retired academic administrator; b. Janesville, Wis., Oct. 9, 1929; d. Floyd C. and Alma M. (Walthers) Chester; m. Richard C. Johnson, Sept. 25, 1948 (div. 1974); children: Randall S., Nile C., Linnea E. BA, U. Colo., 1968. Pres., administrator Pikes Peak Inst. Med. Tech., Colorado Springs, Colo., 1968-88; mem. adv. com. to Colo. Commn. on Higher Edn., 1979-80, State Adv. Coun. on Pvt. Occupational Schs., Denver, 1978-86; mem. tech. adv. com. State Health Occupations, 1986-88; bd. dirs. All Souls Unitarian Ch., Colorado Springs, 1990—, mem. celebration team, 1990-91, pres. bd. trustees, 1991-93. Mem. Colo. Pvt. Sch. Assn. (pres. 1981-82, bd. dirs. 1976-88, Outstanding Mem. 1978, 80), Phi Beta Kappa. Democrat. Unitarian. Avocations: writing, travel, reading. *We must review and renew our committment, as a nation, to true freedom of religion, and resist current tendencies to mix church and state.*

JOHNSON, ALLEN, Olympic athlete; b. Washington, Mar. 1, 1971. Grad. h.s., Burke, Va. 3rd place in hurdles NCAA Championship, 1992, 2nd place in hurdles, 1993, 3rd place USATF, 1994, 2nd place World Cup, 1994, 1st place USATF Indoor Title, 1995, World Indoor Title, 1995, Gold medal, track and field, 110 meter hurdles, Olympic Games, Atlanta, 1996. Office: USA Track & Field PO Box 120 Indianapolis IN 46206-0120*

JOHNSON, ALLEN DRESS, cardiologist; b. Evansville, Ind., Jan. 30, 1941; m. Eliane Emilie Mangassar; children: Nicole, Kristina. Student, Haverford Coll., 1958-60; BA, Johns Hopkins U., 1962, MD, 1965. Diplomate cardiovascular diseases Am. Bd. Internal Medicine. Intern, asst. resident Johns Hopkins Hosp., Balt., 1965-67, sr. resident, 1969-70; exchange resident Sch. Medicine, Am. U. Beirut, 1966; clin. assoc. Nat. Inst. Child Health and Human Devel., Gerentology Rsch. Ctr. NIH, Balt., 1967-69; NIH postdoctoral fellow in cardiology U. Calif. Sch. Medicine, San Diego, 1970-72; asst. prof. U. Calif., San Diego, 1973-78, assoc. prof., 1978-97; dir. critical care svcs. Scripps Clinic and Rsch. Found., La Jolla, Calif., 1979-81, head div. cardiovascular diseases, 1981—, vice chmn. dept. medicine, 1984-89, dir. Heart-Lung-Vascular Ctr., 1985—; clin. prof. medicine U. Calif., San Diego, 1997—. Author, editor books, numerous articles and abstracts. Fellow ACP, Am. Coll. Cardiology, Am. Heart Assn., Coun. Clin. Cardiology of Am. Heart Assn.; mem. Am. Fedn. Clin. Rsch., Laennec Soc., San Diego County Heart Assn., Calif. Heart Assn. Office: Scripps Clinic & Rsch Found 10666 N Torrey Pines Rd La Jolla CA 92037-1092

JOHNSON, ALONZO BISMARK, city official, court administrator; b. Natchez, Miss., Aug. 1, 1958; s. Albert Zena and Bettie Dee (Brown) J. Student, Xavier U., 1976-78; MusB Edn., Alcorn State U., 1980. Piano instr. Houston's Sch. Music, New Orleans, 1977-78; dep. dist. ct. clk. Dallas County Dist. Clks. Office, 1981-84; probation officer I Dallas County Adult Probation Dept., 1984-89; regional civil rights compliance specialist Tex. Dept. Human Svcs., Arlington, 1989-90; min. of music Good Shepherd Bapt. Ch. Irving, Tex., 1989-94; court adminstr. IV-D Family Court of Dallas, 1992—; tng. registrar Comp USA, 1994-98; residential housing mgr. Dallas Housing Authority, 1999—. Guest pianist Sta. WYES-TV, New Orleans, 1977, Jackson (Miss.) Symphony Orch., 1979, 80; founder Youth Inspirational Interdenominational Choir, Fayette, Miss., 1978; mem. nat. chpt. Edwin Hawkins Music and Arts Seminar, Inc./Love Fellowship Conv.; min. music West Mt. Horeb Bapt. Ch., Dallas, 1994, St. Luke Christian Ctr., Duncanville, Tex., 1997—. Recipient Outstanding Music award Dallas Metroplex Temple of Elks #1305, 1984, 85; B-Sharp Music scholar Xavier U., 1977, Fine Arts scholar Alcorn State U. Mem. NAACP, EHMAS (treas. local chpt.), Dallas Assn. Ct. Adminstrn., Heroines of Jericho, Mason, Phi

Mu Alpha Sinfonia (charter mem. 1977, sec. 1977-78). Baptist. Avocations: reading, traveling, music. Home: 2007 Maryland Ave Dallas TX 75216-1929

JOHNSON, A(LYN) WILLIAM, chemistry educator, writer, researcher, consultant; b. Calgary, Alta, Can., Dec. 16, 1933; came to U.S., 1954, naturalized, 1981; s. Alyn C. and Irene (Johnston) J.; m. Joan Auger, July 26, 1956; children: Patricia, Nancy, Robert, Katherine. BS, U. Alta., 1954; PhD, Cornell U., 1957. Research fellow Mellon Inst., Pitts., 1957-60; asst., then asso. prof. chemistry U. N.D., 1960-65; asso. prof., chmn. dept. chemistry U. Sask. Regina, 1965-67; dean Grad. Sch., prof. chemistry U. N.D., Grand Forks, 1967-75, 77-88, dir. R & D, 1967-75, prof. chemistry, 1988-94, emeritus prof., 1995—; vis. prof. U.S. Mil. Acad., West Point, N.Y., 1994-95, U. Mass., Amherst, 1989; dir. N.D. regional environ. assessment program N.D. Legis. Coun., Bismarck, 1975-77. Author: Ylid Chemistry, 1966, Ylides and Imines of Phosphorus, 1993, Invitation to Organic Chemistry, 1998, also over 50 articles to profl. jours. Fellow AAAS, Chem. Inst. Can.; mem. Am. Chem. Soc. (cons. C3s program), Rotary (local pres. 1989-90), Sigma Xi. Episcopalian. Home: 9 Tanyard Ln Bella Vista AR 72714-2450

JOHNSON, ANDREW MYRON, pediatric immunologist, educator; b. Brundidge, Ala., Aug. 15, 1935; s. Andrew Foman and Verdie Lee (Hildreth) J.; m. Mary Winne Sherwood, June 30, 1962 (div. June 1981); children: Helen Lee, Andrew Sherwood. AB, Asbury Coll., Wilmore, Ky., 1955; MD, Vanderbilt U., 1959. Diplomate Am. Bd. Pediatrics. Assoc. chief pediatrics Charles V. Chapin Hosp., Providence, 1965-66; practice medicine specializing in pediatrics Barrington, R.I., 1966-68; from asst. to assoc. prof. pediatrics Sch. Medicine U. N.C., Chapel Hill, 1970-83; investigator Ctr. for Blood Research, Boston, 1983-86; investigator, dir. R.D.L. Found. for Blood Research, Scarborough, Maine, 1986-89; dir. pediatric teaching svc. Moses H. Cone Meml. Hosp., Greensboro, N.C., 1989-97; prof. pediatrics U. N.C. Sch. Medicine, Chapel Hill, 1989—, dir. maternal serum screening lab., 1997—; sci. cons. Atlantic Antibodies, Scarborough, 1973-88; cons. Sorin Biomedica, Turin, Italy, 1986-87; med. dir. CBR Labs., Boston, 1983-87; tchr. adult edn. Old South Ch., Boston, 1985-86. Contbr. chpts. to books, numerous articles to profl. jours. Capt. USAF, 1962-64. Recipient Spl. Fellowship Blood Grouping Lab. USPHS, Boston, 1968, 69, 70. Fellow Am. Acad. Pediatrics; mem. Am. Pediatric Soc., Soc. Pediatric Rsch., Electrophoresis Soc., Am. Assn. Clin. Chemists, Bel Canto Co., Sigma Xi, Alpha Omega Alpha (pres., v.p. 1958-59). Presbyterian. Avocations: photography, music, bicycling. Office: Univ NC Sch Medicine Prenatal Screening Ob-gyn CB # 7570 Chapel Hill NC 27599-7570

JOHNSON, ANDREW W., secondary education educator; b. Abington, Pa., May 5, 1975; s. Ralph Walton and Catherine H. Johnson; m. Heather Marie Arnold, June 27, 1998. BS in Math., Ursinus Coll., Collegeville, Pa., 1997. Instrnl. 1 cert. for secondary schs., Pa. Teller, info. cons. Harleysville (Pa.) Nat. Bank, 1994-98; tchr. math. Souderton (Pa.) Area Sch. Dist., 1997—; WWW home-page designer Ursinus Coll., 1994-96; mentor Indian Valley Mid. Sch., Harleysville, 1999—. Mem. Phi Beta Kappa. Republican. Mennonite. Avocations: singing in choirs, listening to Mahler's music. Office: Indian Valley Mid Sch 130 Maple Ave Harleysville PA 19438

JOHNSON, ANGELA, children's book author; b. Tuskegee, Ala., June 18, 1961; d. Arthur and Truzetta (Hall) J. Author: Tell Me a Story, Mama, 1989 (Sch. Libr. Jour. Best Books list 1989), Do Like Kyla, 1990, When I Am Old with You, 1990 (Ezra Jack Keats award U.S. Bd. on Books for Young People 1990, Coretta Scott King Book award 1990), One of Three, 1991, The Leaving Morning, 1992, The Girl Who Wore Snakes, 1993, Julius, 1993, Toning the Sweep, 1993 (Young Adult Libr. Svcs. Assn. Best Book for young adults list 1994), Shoes Like Miss Alice's, 1994, Joshua By the Sea, 1994, Joshua's Night Whispers, 1994, Mama Bird, Baby Bird, 1994, Rain Feet, 1994. Child development worker, vol. Svc. to Am., Ravenna, Ohio, 1981-82. Office: care Orchard Books 7th Fl 95 Madison Ave New York NY 10016-7801

JOHNSON, (MARY) ANITA, physician, medical service administrator; b. Clarksburg, W.Va., Oct. 18, 1926; d. Paul F. and Mary Elizabeth (Harris) J.; m. Lawrence J. Ciessau, Aug. 22, 1959 (div. 1974); children: Matthew A., Susan E., Sharon L., Mark A.; m. Ralph Allen Fretwell, Dec. 18, 1976. BS, North Tex. U., 1946; MD, Woman's Med. Coll. Pa., 1950. Intern Baylor U. Hosp., Dallas, 1950-51, resident, 1951-54; practice medicine specializing in internal medicine Dallas, 1954-58, Chgo., 1958—; instr. internal medicine Southwestern Med. Coll., U. Tex., Dallas, 1954-58; med. dir. YWCA, Dallas, 1955-58; physician for infant welfare Chgo. Bd. Health, 1960-63; house physician, emergency physician St. Mary of Nazareth Hosp. Ctr., Chgo., 1963-81, instr. nurses ICU, 1963-80, asst. cardiologist, 1963-86, sec. med. staff, 1974-75, treas. med. staff, 1980, pres. med. staff, 1982, 84; med. dir. Family Care Ctr., 1973-74, chief med. clinics, 1977-78, chmn. credentials com., 1982-92, chief internal medicine, 1983-92; clin. instr. medicine U. Health Scis., Chgo. Med. Sch., North Chicago, Ill., 1982-95; nat. med. dir. Nat. Cath. Soc. Foresters Ins. Co., Chgo., 1975-77; chmn. ann. benefit com. St. Mary of Nazareth Hosp. Ctr., 1992; cons. internal medicine Lisbaon VA Hosp., Dallas, 1955-56; lectr. to cmty. elem. sch. students on opportunities in health field, 1967—; gov. bd. St. Mary Nazareth Hosp. Ctr., 1991-94, life trustee, 1994—. Named Med. Woman of Yr., St. Mary of Nazareth Hosp. Ctr., 1973. Mem. ACP, AMA (del. hosp. med. staff sect. 1980-92), Ill. Soc. Internal Medicine (councillor 1990-93, cons. 1993—), Am. Soc. Internal Medicine, Am. Coll. Angiology, Am. Med. Women's Assn. (S.W. regional dir. 1955-58, nat. chmn. publicity and pub. rels. 1991-93, pres.-elect br. 2, 1981, 82, 89, 90, pres. 1983-85, 91-94, regional gov. Midwest sect. 1985-91, bd. dirs. 1985-91, 92—, v.p. fin. 1997-98, cmty. svc. award 1991, nat. chmn. retirement issues com. 1993—, nat. pres.-elect 1998—, Pres.'s Recognition award 1998), Ill. Med. Soc. (trustee 1987-90, com. on CME accreditation 1987-96, coun. on pub. rels. on membership svcs 1992, govt. affairs com. 1991—), Chgo. Med. Soc. (councillor 1980—, chmn. malpractice ins. com., del. to Ill. Med. Soc. 1981—, pres. Northside br. 1985-87, chmn. practice mgmt. com. 1990-93, nominating com., Midwest Clin. Conf. 1991—, Cook County jud. panel 1995—, chmn. sr. physicians com. 1997—, chmn. subcom. continuing med. edn. 1997-98, chmn. presdl. ad hoc com. sr. physicians 1997-99, chmn. continuing med. edn. com. 1998—), Zeta Phi. Home and Office: 6226 Edgebrook Ln W Indianhead Park IL 60525-6983 *Learning to look beyond today has been one of the greatest lessons I've learned. Long term is what matters, whether one is talking about relationships, money or goals one sets for oneself.*

JOHNSON, ANITA, Spanish language educator; b. Boston, Apr. 22, 1951; d. Robert Edward and Rita Louise (Campbell) J.; m. Robert Sanford Garland, Jan. 8, 1994. BA, Carlow Coll., 1973; MA, Middlebury Coll., 1976; PhD, U. Wis., 1988. Instr. Marquette U., Milw., 1985-86, Tufts U., Medford, Mass., 1986-87; asst. prof. Spanish, Colgate U., Hamilton, N.Y., 1987-93, assoc. prof., 1994—; dir. study abroad Colgate U., Madrid, 1989-95. Book rev. editor Estreno, 1996-99; contbr. articles to profl. jours. Mem. AAUP, N.E. MLA. Democrat. Avocations: skiing, running. E-mail: ajohnson@mail.colgate.edu. Office: Colgate U 13 Oak Dr Hamilton NY 13346

JOHNSON, ANNE ELISABETH, medical assistant; b. Springfield, Mass., Nov. 3, 1955; d. Michael Francis Xavier and Miriam Rose (Coombs) Gigliotti. NSCC, Beverly, Mass., 1976. Cert. med. transcriptionist; cert. med. asst. Home health aide Sr. Home Care Svcs., Gloucester, Mass., 1974-76; lab asst., EKG technician, phlebotomist Addison Gilbert Hosp., Gloucester, Mass., 1976-80; exec. asst. MGA Inc., Gloucester, Mass., 1980-83, 85-94; med. asst. Cape Ann Med. Ctr., Gloucester, 1983-85; med. transcriptionist, med. sec., orthopedic asst. Orthopedic Assocs. of Cape Ann, P.C., Gloucester, 1996—; dance instr., 1973-80. Sec. Am. Cancer Soc., Gloucester, 1978-79; polit. asst. Dem. Party, Gloucester, 1974-85; active People for the Ethical Treatment of Animals. Mem. NAFE, Mass. Soc. for Prevention of Cruelty to Animals, Doris Day Animal League, Surfrider Found. Roman Catholic. Avocations: ballet, jazz, tap, modern dance. Home: 27 Exchange St Gloucester MA 01930-3449 Office: Anne Elisas Profl Svcs Gloucester MA 01930

JOHNSON, ANTHONY O'LEARY (ANDY JOHNSON), meteorologist, consultant; b. Tampa, Fla., Apr. 19, 1957; s. Paul Bryan and Katie Hobbs (Nunez) J. BS in Meteorology, Fla. State U., 1979. Cert. cons. meteorologist. Courthouse runner Gregory, Cours, et. al., Tampa, 1977; water resources planner S.W. Fla. Water Mgmt. Dist., Brooksville, 1978; staff meteorologist Sta. WTVT-TV, Tampa, 1979-82, systems mgr., 1982-89, weather office mgr., 1989—; meterol. cons. Gulf Coast Weather Svc.-Weather Vision, Tampa, 1979—; software devel. mgr. TTI Techs. Inc., Tampa, 1989-92; site coord. Space Sci. and Engring. Ctr. U. Wis., Madison, 1989—. Active capital improvements com. Plantation Homeowners Assn., Tampa, 1991; judge Hillsborough Regional Sci. Fair, Tampa, 1990, 91, 92, 96; fundraiser Dunedin Youth Guild, 1992, Northside Mental Health Hosp. Aux., 1993, 94, Children's Home, Pinellas Aux., 1993, 94, 95; vol. Sch. Enrichment Vols. in Edn. (SERVE), 1992. Mem. AAAS, Am. Meteorol Soc. (Seal of Approval for TV weathercasting 1982—, v.p. West Fla. chpt. 1984-85, pres. 1989-92, 94—), Internat. Platform Assn., Phi Beta Kappa, Pi Mu Epsilon, Chi Epsilon Pi. Republican. Achievements include development of quantitative predictive methods of energy delivery interruption in severe Florida freezes; research on temporal and spatial climatological anomalies on landfalling hurricanes in West Central Florida. Home: 11003 Brightside Dr Tampa FL 33624-7010 Office: Sta WTVT-TV Weather Svc 3213 W Kennedy Blvd Tampa FL 33609-3006

JOHNSON, ANTHONY PETER, minister; b. N.Y.C., Mar. 22, 1949; s. Fred and Thelma Clementine (Calogero) J.; 1 child, Elizabeth Erling. BA, Boston U., 1971; MDiv, Harvard U., 1977; MS, New Sch. for Social Rsch., N.Y.C., 1990. Ordained by Unitarian Fellowship, Burbank, Calif., 1977; cert. ministerial fellowship for parish and community, Unitarian Universalist Assn. Dir. religious edn. First Parish, Kingston, Mass., 1976-77; minister Unitarian Fellowship, Burbank, 1977-80, Unitarian Soc., New Brunswick, N.J., 1981-86; coord. Ozanam Men's Shelter, New Brunswick, 1986-87; cons. minister, 1986—; exec. dir. It's Time . . . Inc., N.Y.C., 1989-95; min. First Unitarian Universalist Ch. of Essex County, 1996—; mem. adj. faculty New Sch. for Social Rsch., N.Y.C., 1993, Monmouth U., West Long Branch, N.J., 1997—; cons./coord. Coalition for a Nuclear-Free Harbor, N.Y.C., 1986. Contbr. articles to profl. jours./publs. Bd. dirs. UU Counseling and Edn. Svc., Belle Mead, N.J., 1984-86, Assn. for Neighborhood and Housing Devel., N.Y.C., 1990-93, NOVA Opportunity Ctr., Burbank, 1977-78; mem. steering com. Citizens Commn. on Police Repression, L.A., 1978-80; mem. N.J. Immigration Policy Network, Newark, 1984-86, 98—; mem. task force N.Y. Immigration Coalition, N.Y.C., 1993-95. Mem. Unitarian Universalist Ministers Assn. (pres. Metro N.Y. Chpt. 1983-85, 98—), Inst. for Religion in An Age of Sci. Avocations: hiking, writing. Home: 279 Cleveland Ave Long Branch NJ 07740-6140 Office: 47 Cleveland St Orange NJ 07050-2709

JOHNSON, ANTONIA AXSON, corporate executive; b. Sept. 6, 1943; d. Axel Axson and Antonia Johnson; m. P. Göran Ennerfelt; children: Alexandra Mörner, Caroline Mörner, Axel Mörner, Sophie Mörner. Student, Radcliffe Coll., 1963-64; MA in Psychology and Econs., U. Stockholm, 1971. With Nordstjernan AB, 1971-79; with Axel Johnson AB, Stockholm, 1979—, chmn., 1982—; chmn. bd. Axel Johnson Inc., Stamford, Conn., Hemkopskedjan AB, Sweden, City Mission of Stockholm; bd. dirs. Axel Johnson Internat., Sweden, Nordstjernan AB; chmn. The Axel and Margaret Axson Johnson's Found., Nordic Constrn. Co., Stockholm Environ. Inst.; mem. IVA-Royal Swedish Acad. of Engring. Scis., Xerox Corp.; chmn. World Childhood Found.; chmn. World Childhood Found. Mem. adv. coun. Grad. Sch. Bus., Stanford U. Named Profl. Woman of Yr., 1987, Fin. Woman of Yr., 1988; named # 1 of Am.'s Top 25 Women Bus. Owners, Nat. Found. for Women Bus. Owners and Working Woman, 1992, named # 4 of Am.'s Top 50 Women Bus. Owners, 1993. Mem. IVA-Royal Swedish Acad. Engring. Scis., Internat. Inst. Indsl. Environ. Econs. Office: Axel Johnson AB, Villagatan 6 / PO Box 26008, S-100 41 Stockholm Sweden also: Axel Johnson Inc 300 Atlantic St Stamford CT 06901-3522

JOHNSON, ARLENE LYTLE, government agency official; b. Pitts., Jan. 20, 1937; d. Willis and Minnie Lee (Blackman) Neal; m. William Dalois Johnson, Aug. 27, 1971; children: Robin Gerome Lytle, Cheryl Rose Lytle Campbell. Student various profl. courses. Clk.-typist, Pa. Dept. Revenue, Harrisburg, 1955; office sec. Akron (Ohio) Jewish Center, 1956-57; clk.-stenographer Pa. Employment Service, Pitts., 1960-61; Dept. Treasury, Washington, 1961; sec.-stenographer HEW, Washington, 1961-70, exec. sec. to dir. Bur. Community Health Services, Health Services Adminstrn., Rockville, Md., 1970-81; staff asst. to dep. asst. sec. for children and families HHS, 1981-93, staff asst. to asst. sec. for children and families, 1993—. Recipient Spl. Recognition award USPHS, 1991, Superior Service award Health Services and Mental Health Adminstrn., 1973; Sustained Superior Service award HHS, 1984-90, 93, Spl. Recognition award Human Devel. Svcs. Adminstrn. for Children and Families, 1989, 91. Jehovah's Witness. Home: 5945 Addison Rd Capitol Hgts MD 20743-2166 Office: Aerospace Bldg Rm 610 370 Lenfant Promenade SW Washington DC 20447-0001

JOHNSON, ARNOLD IVAN, civil engineer; b. Madison, Nebr., June 3, 1919; s. Casten Henry and Awilda May (Reeves) J.; m. Betty Lou Spencer, June 3, 1941; children: Robert Arnold, Brucy Gary, Carmen Sue. BSCE, U. Nebr., 1949, AB in Math., 1950, postgrad., 1950-54; PhD in Geohydrology (hon.), Hacettepe U., Ankara, Turkey, 1995. Registered profl. engr., Colo., D.C.; cert. profl. hydrologist. With U.S. Geol. Survey, 1948-79; asst. chief Office Water Data Coordination U.S. Geol. Survey, Washington, 1971-79; water resources cons. Woodward-Clyde Cons., Denver, 1979-84; pres. A. Ivan Johnson, Inc. Cons., Arvada, Colo., 1984—; faculty affiliate Colo. State U., 1969-70; bd. dirs. Renewable Natural Resources Found., 1971-81, Water Ctr. for Humid Tropics L.Am. and the Caribbean, Panama, 1994—; chmn. bd. trustees Inst. for Standard Rsch., 1989-91; pres. Internat. Commn. Ground Water, 1972-75, Internat. Commn. Remote Sensing and Data Transmission, 1980-87; chmn. IAHS Divsn. on GIS, 1991—; v.p. U.S. nat. commn. Internat. Union Geodesy and Geophysics, 1976-79. Author, editor over 130 reports and books in field. With USNR, 1942-44. Recipient award of merit Dept. Interior, 1962, Meritorious Svc. award, 1977, Engr. of Yr. award Profl. Engrs. in Govt., 1969, John Wesley Powell award U.s. Geol. Survey, 1992, Finnegan award Am. Nat. Stds. Inst., 1993. Fellow ASCE (chair com. on metrication 1978-95, chair irrigation drain divsn. 1988-89, chair tech. coun. codes and stds. 1982-85, mem. mng. group F on codes and stds. 1995-97, chair spl. stds. divsn. 1991-94, chair stds. com. on artificial recharge 1989—, Outstanding Svc. award 1991, hon. mem. award 1992, Royce Tipton award 1992), ASTM (bd. dirs. 1989-91, hon. mem. 1987, fellow award of Merit 1982, Reinhart award 1983, William T. Cavanaugh Meml. award 1987, Spl. Svc. award 1990, 91, 93, 94, 95, 96, 97, 50 Yr. Active Svc. award 1992, D18 A. Ivan Johnson Outstanding Svc. award dedicated 1995), Am. Water Resources Assn. (pres. 1972, rep. to NAS 1971-79, Icko Iben award 1986, fellow 1976—, rep. to OAS Interam. Water Resources Network 1994—); mem. Am. Geophys. Union (life, sec., sect. on hydrology 1973-77, EOS editor 1984-90), Am. Inst. Hydrology (adv. com. 1987—, C.B. Theis award 1995), Nat. Water Well Assn. (spl. recognition award 1989), Assn. Engring. Geologists, Internat. Assn. Hydrological Scis. (life hon. pres. 1987—, U.S. nat. commn. 1991—), U.S. Nat. Com. Hydrol. Sci., OAS Coun. for Interam. Water Resources Network, Internat. Soc. Soil Sci., Internat. Soc. Soil Mechanics and Found. Engring., Am. Soc. Photogram and Remote Sensing, Internat. Assn. Hydrogeologists (U.S. nat. commn.), Assn. Geoscientists Internat. Devel., NSPE (chpt. pres. 1970-71), Archaeol. Soc. Am., Bibl. Archaeol. Soc. Achievements include research in hydrologic processes, land subsidence, artificial recharge and laboratory methods. *

JOHNSON, ARNOLD RAY, public relations executive; b. Baton Rouge, Sept. 15, 1955; came to U.S., 1954; s. Hillery and Sedonia (Celestine) J. BA, Xavier U., 1977. Chmn., CEO U.S.A. Pub. Rels., Baton Rouge, 1989—, Inter-Continental Transp., New Orleans, 1989—; pres. U.S. Nat. Airlines, Diamond "J" Ranch, Tex., United Internat. Found., Inc.; active internat. program on negotiation Harvard U., internat. forum Wharton Sch. Active Knights Peter Clare Cath. Orgn., UN Internat. Drug Program. Named Amb. of Goodwill; recipient Regional Businessman of Yr. Ernest & Young. Mem. Internat. Plimsoll Club, Internat. Club, World Trade Assn. (v.p.), Beta Rho Omega. Republican. Roman Catholic. Home: 2480 78th Ave Baton Rouge LA 70807-5613 Office: Inter-Continental Transport Inc 1 Canal St Ste 2500 New Orleans LA 70130-1152

JOHNSON, ARNOLD WILLIAM, mortgage company executive; b. Axtell, Kans., June 5, 1916; s. William and Hilda Elizabeth (Hedstrom) J.; m. Bertha Mildred Scott, Oct. 9, 1940; 1 child, Jill Lynn. BSBA, Kans. U., 1940. Pres., prin. Arnold W. Johnson Ins. Agy., Topeka, 1940—, also chmn.; pres., prin. C.R. Scott Mortgage Co. Inc., Topeka, 1956—, chmn.; bd. dirs. Preferred Fire Ins. Co., Topeka, 1950-75, Capitol Abstract and Title Co., Topeka, 1965-75, Pioneer Nat. Life Ins. Co., Topeka, 1967-83, treas., Kans. Mut. Ins. Co., Topeka, 1979—, dir. Fidelity State Bank and Trust Co., Topeka. Active adv. bd. Topeka Capitol Cty Ctrl. Bus. Dist. Redevel., 1984-90, Kans. Watertower Place Redevel., 1984-90; trustee, deacon, treas. First Congl. Ch. With USN, 1942-45. Recipient Silver Found. award YMCA, 1989, Outstanding Svc. award Kans. Mut. Ins. Co., 1987. Mem. Topeka Bd. Realtors, Kans. Bd. Realtors, Nat. Bd. Realtors, Profl. Ins. assn., Topeka C. of C., Downtown Topeka Inc., Topeka Retail Credit Bur. and Better Bus. Bur., Knife and Fork Club Internat., Cosmopolitan Club Internat., Moose, Elks, Masons, Shriners, Royal Order Jesters, VFW, Am. Legion, Alpha Kappa Psi. Republican. Avocations: golf, reading, travel. Home: 1531 SW Lakeside Dr Topeka KS 66604-2529 also: 534 S Kansas Ave Ste 420 Topeka KS 66603-3426

JOHNSON, ARTHUR GILBERT, microbiology educator; b. Eveleth, Minn., Feb. 1, 1926; s. Arthur Gilbert and Selma (Niemi) J.; m. Mildred Louise Anderson, June 15, 1951; children: Susan, Sally, Gary, Peter. B.A., U. Minn., 1950, M.Sc., 1951; Ph.D., U. Md., 1955. Biochemist Walter Reed Army Inst. Research, Washington, 1952-55; asst. prof. U. Mich., 1956-62, asso. prof., 1962-66, prof. microbiology, 1966-78; prof., head dept. med. microbiology/immunology U. Minn. Sch. Medicine, Duluth, 1978—; mem. pre, postdoctoral and spl. fellowships study sect. NIH, 1968-70; mem. nat. adv. dental rsch. coun. NIH, 1972-75; mem. Nat. Bd. Med. Examiners, 1980-84; mem. bacteriology and mycology study sect. NIH, 1983-87, chmn., 1986-87; cons. microbiology. Editor Infection and Immunity, 1977-86. Served with US Merchant Marine, 1943-46. Mem. Am. Assn. Immunologists, Am. Soc. Microbiology, Infectious Diseases Soc. Am., Soc. Biol. Therapy, Immunocomprised Host Soc., Internat. Endotoxin Soc., Assn. Med. Sch. Microbiology and Immunology Chairs (pres. 1991-92). Rsch. on immunology. Home: 209 Rockridge Cir Duluth MN 55804-1857

JOHNSON, ARTHUR MENZIES, retired college president, historian, educator; b. Waltham, Mass., July 24, 1921; s. Frederick P. and Florence (Bishop) J.; m. Emily Ann Wilford, Dec. 28, 1946; children—Robert Menzies, Nancy Revell. B.A., Harvard U., 1944, M.A., 1948; Ph.D. Vanderbilt U., 1954. Instr. Thayer Acad., Braintree, Mass., 1946-47; instr. Cambridge Sch., Weston, Mass., 1948-50; asst. prof. U.S. Naval Acad., 1954-58; mem. faculty Grad. Sch. Bus. Adminstrn. Harvard U., 1958-70, prof. bus. history, 1966-70; Univ. prof. U. Maine, Orono, 1969-70, A & A Bird prof. Am. history, 1970-84, pres., 1984-86; trustee Bangor Savs. Bank, 1976-94; sec., pres. New Eng. Econ. Edn. Coun., 1966-68, pres. Bus. History and Econ. Life program, 1968-70, chmn., 1970-75; chmn. Bigelow Lab. for Ocean Scis., Boothbay Harbor, Maine, 1982-84, 88-89. Author: Development of American Petroleum Pipelines, 1956; Government Business Relations, 1965; Petroleum Pipelines and Public Policy, 1967; (with Barry E. Supple) Boston Capitalists and Western Railroads, 1967; Winthrop W. Aldrich, Lawyer, Banker, Diplomat, 1968; The American Economy, 1974; The Challenge of Change, 1983. Vice chmn. Maine Coun. on Econ. Edn., 1969-84; mem. adv. com. Eleutherian Mills-Hagley Found., 1967-70, trustee, 1973-85; trustee Husson Coll., 1977-85, Maine Maritime Mus., 1987-92, Miles Health Care, 1989-97, chmn., 1995-97; trustee Farnsworth Art Mus., 1990-93; mem. Maine Sci. and Tech. Bd., 1984-86; overseer Mt. Desert Island Biol. Lab., 1984-88; bd. dirs. Maine Cmty. Found., 1984-93, Maine Devel. Found., 1985-86; bd. of advisors Maine Maritime Acad., 1986-88; chmn. Maine Commn. to Commemorate Bicentennial U.S. Constn., 1986-88; mem. Maine Marine Rsch. Bd., 1990-92; chmn. Maine Indian Tribal State Com., 1992-93. Served with USAAF, 1943-46, to capt. USAF, 1951-53. Home: Bristol Rd Damariscotta ME 04543

JOHNSON, ARTHUR V., II, secondary education educator. BA in Math. and History, Tufts U., 1967; postgrad., Lowell U., 1968-74, MEd in Curriculum and Adminstrn., 1977; postgrad., Northeastern U., 1977-79, U. N.H., 1984-88, Boston U., 1990-91. Tchr. jr. high sch. Nashua, N.H., 1967-69, tchr. sr. high sch., 1969—; dir. digital computer bus program, 1984; dir., instr. Critical Skills Insts., 1985—; instr. geometry Inst. at Groton Sch., 1990, 91; instr. geometry seminar U. N.H., 1991; instr. geometry and patterns seminar Nat. Coun. Math., 1993—; mem. F.I.P.S.E. Program, U. N.H., 1986-88, NSF Inst. U. N.H., 1986-88, Tsongas Ctr., U. Lowell, 1990. Author Math That Matters, 1991, Mathematics History for the Classroom, 1992; contbr. articles to profl. jours.; host videotape series MATH: The Basics, Ky. Ednl. TV, 1990. Family ch. counselor, 1980—; instr. Kid's Kollege, 1984-90; instr., avdisor Challenge Program, River Coll., 1986-91. Recipient N.H. award Taxpayer Edn. Program, 1990, Presdl. Excellence in Teaching award, 1992; named N.H. Tchr. of Yr., 1992. Mem. Nat. Coun. Tchrs. Math. (chmn. joint articulation com. with Math. Assn. Am. 1985-87, chair publs. Boston regional conf. 1988, chair publicity Nasha regional conf. 1991), Pi Lambda Theta (hon.). Home: 7 Steadman St Chauncer MA 03051 Office: Nashua Sr High Sch 36 Riverside Dr Nashua NH 03062-1312*

JOHNSON, ARTHUR WILLIAM, JR., planetarium executive; b. Steubenville, Ohio, Jan. 8, 1949; s. Arthur William and Carol (Gilcrest) J. BMus, U. So. Calif., 1973. Lect. Griffith Obs. and Planetarium, 1969-73; planetarium writer, lectr. Mt. San Antonio Coll. Planetarium, Walnut, Calif., 1970-73; dir. Fleischmann Planetarium U. Nev., Reno, 1973—; apptd. Nev. state coord. NSTA/NASA Space Sci. Student Involvement Program, 1994. Writer, prodr. films (with Donald G. Potter) Beautiful Nevada, 1978, Riches: The Story of Nevada Mining, 1984. Organist, choirmaster Trinity Episcopal Ch., Reno, 1980—; bd. dirs. Reno Chamber Orch. Assn., 1981-87, 1st v.p., 1984-85. Nev. Humanities Com., Inc. grantee, 1979-83. Mem. Am. Guild Organists (dean No. Nev. chpt. 1984-85, 96-99), Internat. Planetarium Soc., Cinema 360 (treas. 1985-90, pres. 1990-98), Pacific Planetarium Assn. (pres. 1980), Lions (pres. Reno Host Club 1991-92), Large Format Cinema Assn. (v.p. 1996-99). Republican. Episcopalian. Office: Fleischmann Plantarium U Nev Mail Stop 272 Reno NV 89557-0010

JOHNSON, AUDREY ANN, options trader, stockbroker; b. Chgo., June 7, 1954; d. Elmer and Diane Ann (Vassiv) J. Student, North Ctrl. Coll., 1972-75, U. Ill. Registered stockbroker, real estate salesperson, Ill. Real estate salesperson Century 21 Cahill Bros., Chgo., 1975-80; stockbroker Charles Schwab, Chgo., 1980-87; Chgo. Bd. Options Exch. floor trader Drexel Burnham, Chgo., 1987-90; pvt. practice specializing in futures, options, indexes and equities Chgo., 1990—; options broker, stockbroker Profl. Trader's Inst. Securities, Chgo., 1990—; real estate broker Realty Execs., Orland Park, Ill., 1995; arbitrator Chgo. Bd. Options Exch., 1989-92; guest spkr. Chgo. TV Channel 26, 1993-94; participant NAFTA. Mem. Nat. Assn. Securities Dealers, Ind. Floor Members Assn., Chgo. Bd. Options Exch., Palos Hills Horseman's Assn. Democrat. Roman Catholic. Home: 9174 South Rd Palos Hills IL 60465-2135

JOHNSON, BADRI NAHVI, sociology educator, real estate business owner; b. Tehran, Iran, Dec. 1, 1934; came to U.S., 1957; d. Ali Akbar and Monir Khazraii Nahvi; m. Floyd Milton Johnson, July 2, 1960; children: Robert, Rebecca, Nancy, Shahla. BS, U. Minn., 1967, MA, 1969; postgrad., 1994—. Stenographer Curtis 1000, Inc., St. Paul, 1958-62; lab. instr. U. Minn., Mpls., 1966-69, teaching asst., 1969-72; chief exec. officer Real Estate Investment and Mgmt. Enterprise, St. Paul, 1969—; instr. sociology Anoka-Ramsey Community Coll., Coon Rapids, Minn., 1973—; pub. speaker, bd. dirs., sponsor pub. radio KFAI, Mpls., 1989-93; established an endowed scholarship for women Anoka Ramsey C.C., 1991. Radio talk show host KCW, Brookline Parks, Minn., 1993. Organizer Iranian earthquake disaster relief, 1990; bd. dirs. dist. 7 Cmty. Coun., 1996-98. Recipient Earthquake Relief Orgn. citation Iranian Royal Household, 1968. Mem. NEA, Nat. Soc. Scis. Assn., Minn. Edn. Assn., Sociologists of Minn., U. Minn. Alumni Assn., Minn. Club, St. Petersburg Yacht Club. Avocations: world travel, classical and historical novels, exotic food, gardening. Home: 1726 Iowa Ave E Saint Paul MN 55106-1334 Office: Anoka-Ramsey Community Coll 11200 Mississippi Blvd NW Minneapolis MN 55433-3470 Also: U Minnesota Soc Dept Minneapolis MN 55455

JOHNSON, BARBARA ANN, health services educator; b. Rochester, N.Y., July 3, 1953; d. Ray Clifford and Helen Frances (Lindgren) J.; m. William A. Perison, Feb. 28, 1986 (dec. 1998); 1 child, Alyssa Ann. BSEd, Worcester State COll., 1975; MA, U. Mass., 1977; PhD, U. Fla., 1982. Lic. speech-lang. pathologist, Tex., La., N.Y., Calif. Speech therapist Killingly Pub. Schs., Danielson, Conn., 1975-76; grad. tchg. asst. dept. comm. disorders U. Mass., Amherst, 1976-77; level II trainee VA Med. Ctr., Gainesville, Fla., 1977-78; grad. tchg. asst. Eng. Lang. Inst. U. Fla., Gainesville, 1978-79, grad. tchg. asst. speech dept., 1980-81; pvt. practice speech-lang. pathologist North Ctrl. Fla., 1980-81; asst. prof. speech sci., pathology and audiology dept. St. Cloud (Minn.) State U., 1983-84; dir. speech-lang. pathologist South County Speech-Hearing-Learning Ctr., Gilroy, Calif., 1984-85; vis. asst. prof. speech dept. Nat. Inst. for Deaf Rochester (N.Y.) Inst. Tech., 1985-90; asst. prof. speech dept. La. Tech. U., Ruston, 1990-92; assoc. prof., chair/dir. dept. comm. disorders U. Tex.-Pan Am., Edinburg, 1992-96, interim dean, assoc. prof. Coll. Health Scis. & Human Svcs., 1996-98, prof., chair dept. comm. disorders, 1998—; presenter, mentor in field. Author: Language Disorders in Children: An Introductory Clinical Perspective, 1996; contbr. articles to profl. publs. Grantee Crippled Children's Soc. Santa Clara County, 1985, U.S. Dept. Edn., 1993, 94, U. Tex.-Pan Am., 1994, Pro-Tec Equipment, 1995, Health Career Opportunity Program, 1996—. Mem. Am. Speech-Lang.-Hearing Assn. (cert. clin. competence, Svc. Recognition award 1993, mem. profl. svcs. bd. 1991-93, multi-site com. 1991-93), Tex. Speech-Lang.-Hearing Assn., Coll. Health Deans, Tex. Soc. Allied Health Professions, Coun. Grad. Programs in Comm. Scis. and Disorders, Coun. Suprs. in Speech-Lang. Pathology and Audiology (pres. 1997), Kappa Delta Pi. Office: U Tex Pan Am 1201 W University Dr Edinburg TX 78539-2909

JOHNSON, BARBARA ELAINE SPEARS, education educator; b. Chgo., May 24, 1932; d. William Everett and Sadie Mae (Fennoy) Spears; m. John Gilbert Johnson, July 29, 1967 (dec. Jan. 1985); children: Steven W., Jeri-Lynn Johnson Jackson. AB, U. Chgo., 1952; EdB, Chgo. Tchrs. Coll., 1954; EdM, Loyola U., Chgo., 1967; EdS, U. Ill., Chgo., 1982; MSEd in counseling, Chgo. State U., 1986. Tchr. Chgo. Pub. Schs., 1954-64, counselor, 1964-70; evening tchr. Chgo. Pub. High Schs., 1964-66; dir. resource skills City Colls. of Chgo., 1970-84, dir. audio visual, 1985-86, coordinator academic support ctr., 1986-87, prof. acad. support, 1988-93, prof. emeritus, 1993—; faculty coun. City Colls. of Chgo., v.p. 1989-90, pres. 1990-91. Coordinator food ministry Cosmopolitan Community Ch., Chgo., 1983—. Recipient Dedication to Youth award McCosh Sch. Council, 1985, citations of recognition Ill. Community Coll. Bd., 1982, 84. Fellow Ill. Com. Black Concerns in Higher Edn. (plaque 1984); mem. Ill. C.C. Faculty Assn. (life, exec. bd. 1979—, pres. 1981-82, plaque 1982), Ill. Assn. Personalized Learning Programs (exec. bd., treas. 1975-85, Outstanding Contbn. award 1985), U. Ill. Mothers Assn. (chair 1977-81), Ill. C.C. Annuitants Assn. (exec. bd. dirs. 1993—, pres. 1995-97), Alpha Kappa Alpha. Home: 8610 S Vernon Ave Chicago IL 60619-6015

JOHNSON, BARBARA JEAN, retired lawyer, judge; b. Detroit, Apr. 9, 1932; d. Clifford Clarence and Orma Cecile (Boring) Barnhouse; m. Ronald Mayo Johnson, June 24, 1965; 1 dau., Belinda Etezad. B.S., U. So. Calif., 1953, J.D., 1970. Bar: Calif. 1971. Ptnr. Anglea, Burford, Johnson & Tookay, Pasadena, Calif., 1970-77; judge L.A. Mcpl. Ct., 1977-81; judge L.A. Superior Ct., 1981-97; ret., 1997; lectr. U. So. Calif. Law Sch. profl. program; adj. prof. Southwestern U. Law Sch. Recipient Ernestine Stahlhut award, 1981. Mem. Calif. Judges Assn., Nat. Assn. Women Judges, Calif. Women Lawyers Assn. (pres. 1976-77), Women Lawyers Assn. L.A. (pres. 1975-76), Internat. Assn. Women Judges, World Jurist Assn. Home: 1000 Prospect Blvd Pasadena CA 91103-2810

JOHNSON, BARBARA JEAN, rehabilitation nurse, gerontology nurse; b. Pottsville, Pa., Sept. 14, 1948; d. Guy F. and Rachel S. (Schwenk) Boger; m. Ronald L. Johnson, Apr. 25, 1970; children: Jennifer E., Roxanne M. Diploma in nursing, Reading (Pa.) Sch., 1967. LPN, Pa.; cert. intravenous nurse. Pvt. duty nurse Health Care InCorp, Auburn, Pa., 1982-83; staff nurse med.-surg. unit St. Joseph's Hosp., Reading, 1967-69; staff nurse Visiting Nurse Assn. of Reading and Berks County, 1969-73; team leader skilled unit Laurel Living Ctr. (name now Laurel Ctr.), Hamburg, Pa., 1983—. Home: 1457 Summer Hill Rd Auburn PA 17922-9027

JOHNSON, BENJAMIN ARLEN, religious studies educator; b. Melby, Minn., June 29, 1937; s. Benjamin Arvid Johnson and Ruth Ulrika Werner; m. Suzanne Frances Wasgatt, May 13, 1960; children: Samuel, Jennie Ruth, Krister, Jesse. BA, Gustavus Adolphus Coll., 1959; MDiv, Luth. Sch. Theology, 1961; ThD, Harvard U., 1966. Ordained minister Evangelical Luth. Ch. Am., 1965. Mem. faculty Hamma Sch. Theology, Wittenberg U., Springfield, Ohio, 1965-78, Trinity Luth. Sem., Columbus, Ohio, 1978-80; sr. pastor Salem Luth. Ch., St. Cloud, Minn., 1980-92; mem. faculty Luth. Bible Inst., Irvine, Calif., 1992-96, pres., 1996—; mem. exec. com. Minn. Coun. Chs., Mpls., 1985-87; cons. Luth. World Fedn., Geneva, 1967, 82; lectr. Diocese of W.Va., 1978—. Author: Holy Week, 1973, Built on a Rock, 1982 (Concordia Hist. Inst. award); contbr. articles to profl. jours. Trustee Gustavus Adolphus Coll., 1982-89. Fellow Danforth Found., 1959-65, Soc. for Values in Higher Edn., 1971-72, Assn. Theol. Schs., 1971; recipient Outstanding Cmty. award St. Cloud Times, 1987. Office: Luth Bible Inst 5321 University Dr Ste H Irvine CA 92612

JOHNSON, BENJAMIN ERSKINE, psychologist, health care administrator, consultant; b. Birmingham, Ala., Nov. 7, 1948; s. Jim and Oneida Alice J.; m. Alice Johnson, Feb. 14, 1985. BA, U. Wash., 1971; MA, Wayne State U., 1979; D in Psychology, Forest Inst., Springfield, Mo., 1995. Lic. psychologist, Mo.; registered counselor, Wash. Psychologist St. Louis State Hosp., 1984-82, Shasta County Mental Health, Redding, Calif., 1992-93; system planner King County Mental Health, Seattle, 1993-96; health svc. adminstr. King County Pub. Health, Seattle, 1996—; psychologist Johnson/Clark Assocs., Renton, Wash., 1997-98, Progressive Psychol. & Behavioral Health Svcs., Seattle, 1998—; adj. faculty City Univ., Renton, 1995—, Antioche U., Seattle. Mem. APA, Am. Mental Health Counselor Assn. Office: Progressive Psychol & Behavioral Svcs 304 Main Ave S Renton WA 98055-2758

JOHNSON, BENJAMIN F., VI, real estate developer, consulting economist; b. Kingston, N.Y., Sept. 17, 1952; s. Benjamin F. and Alice (Terry) J.; B.A. in Econs., U. South Fla., 1974; M.S. in Econs., Fla. State U., 1977, Ph.D. in Econs., 1982. Sr. utility analyst Office of Public Counsel, State of Fla., 1974-77; pres., cons. economist Ben Johnson Assos., Inc., Tallahassee, Fla., 1977—; pres. Coastal Devel. Cons., Inc., St. George Island, Fla., 1991—. Mem. Am. Econ. Assn., Urban Land Inst. Contbr. articles to N.Y. Times, Public Utilities Fortnightly, profl. jours. Office: Ben Johnson Assoc Inc 1234 Timberlane Rd Tallahassee FL 32312-1792

JOHNSON, BERNADETTE JOSHUA, state supreme court justice. Former civil ct. judge La. Dist. Ct., New Orleans; assoc. justice Supreme Ct. La., New Orleans, 1994—. Office: Supreme Ct 301 Loyola Ave New Orleans LA 70112-1814*

JOHNSON, BETH ANN, pediatric nurse, gerontology nurse; b. Rochester, Minn., June 15, 1960; d. Robert D. and Mary Ann (Postier) Senjem; children: Sara Johnson, Kristen Johnson. ADN, Rochester Community Coll., 1989. RN, Minn. Charge nurse Bethany Samaritan Heights, Rochester; home health aide Joseph Postier, Byron, Minn.; pediatric nurse Shamrock Nursing Svc., Dodge Center, Minn.; staff nurse Hiawatha Homes, Rochester, 1993, asst. health svcs. dir., 1994, health svcs. dir., 1995-96; clin. nurs. Fed. Med. Ctr., Rochester, 1996—.

JOHNSON, BETH EXUM, lawyer; b. Beaumont, Tex., July 4, 1952; d. James Powers Jr. and Betty Jean (Clement) Exum; m. Walter William Johnson, Apr. 25, 1981; children: Stratton William, Jacqueline Clement, Jacob Claiborne. BA in Psychology, Tulane U., 1974; JD, Loyola U., New Orleans, 1985; LLM in Energy and Environ., Tulane U., 1989. Bar: La. 1985, Tex. 1993, U.S. Dist. Ct. (ea. dist.) La. 1985, U.S. Dist. Ct. (we. and mid. dists.) 1989. Paralegal McCloskey, Dennery, Page & Hennesy, New Orleans, 1975-80; oil and gas abstractor of title Frawley, Wogan, Miller & Co., New Orleans, 1980-82; assoc. trust counsel, asst. v.p. and trust officer Hibernia Nat. Bank, New Orleans, 1985-95; legal cons. New Orleans, 1995-96; assoc. Gelpi and Assocs., PLC, New Orleans, 1996—; mem. faculty succession practice Tulane U., New Orleans, 1990-94, 97, environ. law practice, 1991-94; mem. fundraising com. and atty. honor roll New Orleans Pro Bono Project. Mem. New Orleans Estate Planning Coun. Mem. ABA, La. Bar Assn., New Orleans Bar Assn., Jr. League New Orleans, Friends City Park, La. Children's Mus., Audubon Zoo, Aquarium and La. Nature Ctr., Phi Alpha Delta, Kappa Alpha Theta. Avocations: tennis, Thoroughbred horse racing, interior decorating, travel. Home: 959 Harrison Ave New Orleans LA 70124-3837 Office: 203 Carondelet St Ste 907 New Orleans LA 70130-3087

JOHNSON, BETH MICHAEL, school administrator; b. New Orleans, Dec. 7, 1938; d. Carney Leon and Amy Juanita (Monju) J. BA, St. Mary's Dominican, 1963; MEd, U. New Orleans, 1978. Cert. elem. tchr., prin., sch. supt., supr. student teaching, parish supr. of instruction, La. Tchr. Holy Rosary, New Orleans, 1959-68, Cath. High, New Roads, La., 1968-69; prin. St. Ignatius, Grand Coteau, La., 1969-71; asst. prin. Lourdes Community, New Orleans, 1972-74, prin., 1974-77; asst. prin., guidance counselor Our Lady of Prompt Succor, Westwego, La., 1977-78; prin. Our Lady of Perpetual Help, Belle Chasse, La., 1978-85; asst. prin. Archbishop Chapelle H.S., Metairie, La., 1985-89, prin., 1989-97, pres., 1997—. Author: (workbook) A Study Guide of Europe, 1983. Recipient Exemplary Sch. award U.S. Dept. Edn., 1986, 91. Mem. ASCD, Nat. Cath. Edn. Assn. Secondary Prin. Assn. (exec. bd. 1991—, pres. 1993—), Nat. Assn. Secondary Sch. Prins. (pres. 1993), Elem. Prins. Assn. (exec. bd. 1974-80, pres. 1976-80). Democrat. Roman Catholic. Avocation: travel. Office: Archbishop Chapelle High Sch 8800 Veterans Memorial Blvd Metairie LA 70003-5235

JOHNSON, BETSEY LEE, fashion designer; b. Hartford, Conn., Aug. 10, 1942; d. John Herman and Lena Virginia J.; m. John Cale, Apr. 4, 1966; 1 child, Lulu; m. Jeffrey Olivier, Feb. 7, 1981. Student, Pratt Inst., N.Y.C., 1960-61; B.A., U. Syracuse, 1964. Editorial asst. Mademoiselle mag., 1964-65; ptnr., co-owner Betsey, Bunky & Nini, N.Y.C., from 1969; owner retail stores N.Y.C, L.A., San Francisco, Coconut Grove, Fla., Venice, Calif., Boston, Chgo., Seattle. Prin. designer: Paraphernalia (owned by Puritan Fashions, Inc.), 1965-69; designer, Alvin Duskin Co., San Francisco, 1970; head designer: Alley Cat by Betsey Johnson, div. LeDamor, Inc., 1970-74; freelance designer for, Jr. Womens div. Butterick Pattern Co., 1971, Betsey Johnson's Kids Children Wear for new div, Shutterbug, Inc., 1974-77, Betsey Johnson for, Jeanette Maternities, Inc., 1974-75; designer first line womens clothing for, Gant Shirtmakers, Inc., 1974-75; Tric-Trac by Betsey Johnson, Womens Knitwear, 1974-76; children's wear for Butterick's Home Sewing catalog, from 1975; head designer jr. sportswear co.: childrens wear for Star Ferry by Betsey Johnson and Michael Milea, 1975-77; owner, head designer, B.J., Inc., designer wholesale co., N.Y.C., 1978, pres., treas., B.J. Vines, N.Y.C., owner, Betsey Johnson store, N.Y.C., from 1979 (Recipient Mademoiselle mag. Merit award 1970, Coty award 1971, 2 Tommy Print awards 1971); owner 3 retail stores in N.Y.C., 3 in L.A., 1 San Francisco, 1 in Miami, 1 in Chgo., 1 in Seattle. Mem. Coun. Fashion Designers Am., Women's Forum. also: 110 E 9th St Ste A889 Los Angeles CA 90079-1889

JOHNSON, BETTY LOU, secondary education educator; b. Stockwell, Ind., Apr. 4, 1927; d. Paul Stanley Jones and Ethel Leona (Royer) J.; m. Kenneth Odell Johnson, Aug. 5, 1950; children: Cynthia Jo (Mrs. James P. Greaton), Gregory Alan. BS in Home Econs., Purdue U., 1948; postgrad., Northwood Inst. Culinary Arts, 1981, 83. Cert. home economist. Tchr. LaCrosse (Ind.) Jr.-Sr. High Sch., 1948-49, Wendell L. Willkie High Sch., Elwood, Ind., 1949-51, Thomas Carr Howe High Sch., Indpls., 1951-57; substitute tchr. Gt. Oaks Joint Vocat. Sch. Dist., Cin. Mem. AAUW, Am. Home Econs. Assn. (life), Ohio Home Econs. Assn. (life), John Purdue Club, Purdue Pres.'s Coun., Purdue U. Alumni Assn. (life), Gamma Sigma Delta. Home: Indian Hill Village 8360 Arapaho Ln Cincinnati OH 45243-2718

JOHNSON, BEVERLY PHILLIPS, chairman, bank officer; b. Richmond, Va., May 14, 1963; d. Harold Thomas and Betty Lucille (Trammell) Phillips; m. Robert Mark Johnson, Nov. 29, 1985; children: Margaret Elizabeth, Laura Ellen. BS, Lee Coll., Cleveland, Tenn., 1985. Comptroller Frank White Co., Cleveland, Tenn., 1983-86; credit analyst 1st Am. Nat. Bank, Chattanooga, 1986-88; mortgage banker 1st Am. Nat. Bank, Cleveland, Tenn., 1988-89; comml. real estate banker 1st Am. Nat. Bank, Chattanooga, 1989-92; comml. lender, v.p. SunTrust Bank, Cleveland, Tenn., 1992-98; chmn. Franco, Inc., Cleveland, Tenn., 1996—. Divsn. campaign chairperson United Way, Bradley County, Cleveland, 1987-90, 93, 96, 97; treas. Cleveland Cmty. Concert Assn., 1989-95, pres., 1995—; mem. Leadership Cleveland, 1991-92; bd. dirs. Am. Heart Assn., blockwalkers capt., 1993; bd. dirs. Cleveland Family YMCA, 1993—, treas., 1995-97, chmn., 1998; bd. dirs. 1st United Meth. Child Devel. Ctr., 1992—; trustee First United Meth. Ch. Mem. Main St. Cleveland (treas. 1995-98), Rotary, Cleveland Country Club (assoc.), Civitan (bd. dirs. Cleveland chpt. 1984-91, 93-98, Chattanooga chpt. 1991-92), United Way Pillars Club, Lee Coll. Pres. Cir., Cleveland/Bradley C. of C. (econ. devel. coun. 1992-98). Republican. United Methodist. Avocations: golf, tennis, racquetball. Home: 1220 Bramblewood Trl NW Cleveland TN 37311-4107 Office: Suntrust Bank PO Box 1149 Cleveland TN 37364-1149

JOHNSON, BOINE THEODORE, instruments company executive, mayor; b. N.Y.C., Dec. 17, 1931; s. Boine Theodore and Emma (Hall) J.; children: Boine Theodore III, Marc Ian, Jordan James, Jann Louise; m. Kathleen Piaggesi, July 11, 1992. B.A. cum laude, Williams Coll., 1953; M.B.A. with high distinction (Baker scholar), Harvard, 1958. Instr. Harvard Bus. Sch., 1958-59; asst. to dir. corporate planning AMF Corp., N.Y.C., 1959-62; mgr. mgmt. cons. div. Commonwealth Services Inc., N.Y.C., 1962-66; mgr. corporate planning Gen. Electric Co., 1966-68; sr. v.p. corporate devel., gen. mgr. chem. div. Technicon Corp., Tarrytown, N.Y., 1968-79; v.p. Perkin Elmer Corp., Norwalk, Conn., 1979-81; v.p., gen. mgr. Capintec, Inc., Montvale, N.J., 1981-82; pres. Voland Corp., Hawthorne, N.Y., 1982-88; pres., chmn. Texture Techs. Corp., Scarsdale, N.Y., 1988—; dir. Datamedic, Inc., Peoples Bank for Savs. of New Rochelle, Meditron, Inc. Trustee, mayor Village of Scarsdale, N.Y., 1971-77; bd. dirs., vice chmn. Westchester County Assn. Served to lt., C.E. USNR, 1953-56. Mem. Sci. Apparatus Makers Assn., Theta Delta Chi (trustee edn. found. 1968-72, pres. Founders' Corp. 1966-87, pres. grand lodge 1969-71), Williams Club, Amateur Comedy Club (N.Y.C.), Town Club (Scarsdale), St. Botolph Club (Boston). Republican. Presbyterian. Home and Office: 18 Fairview Rd Scarsdale NY 10583-2136*

JOHNSON, BONNIE SUE, piano educator; b. Macon, Ga., Aug. 17, 1958; d. Herbert Franklin and Betty Jean (Gattis) Green; m. Michael Marwood Johnson, July 10, 1982; children: Pamela Elaine, Phillip Michael. B of Music Edn., Wesleyan Coll., 1980. Ch. pianist Lynmore Meth. Ch., Macon, 1985-86, Cross Keys Bapt. Ch., Macon, 1986-87, Park Meml. Meth. Ch., Macon, 1987-97, Bass United Meth. Ch., Macon, 1997-98. Composer (tape) Unspoken Melodies, 1996, S & S Cafeteria comml., 1996, (song) Macon's Cherry Blossom, 1996. Accompanist grand chorus 1st Bapt. Ch., 1997—. Fellow Macon Music Tchrs. Assn. (v.p. membership 1996-98, publicity chmn. 1999); mem. Music Tchrs. Nat. Assn., Morning Music Club. Avocations: walking, swimming, reading. Home: 4731 Leo Pl Macon GA 31210-3001

JOHNSON, BRIAN CURTIS, poet, educator; b. Mt. Pleasant, Mich., Sept. 16, 1960; s. Keith Ashley and Diane (Cassone) J. BA in English with highest honors, U. Calif., Berkeley, 1983; MFA in Creative Writing, Brown U., 1993. Asst. editor The Prose Poem: An Internat. Jour., Providence, 1995—; vis. lectr. Brown U., Providence, 1994, Yale U., New Haven, 1997—; adj. prof. Providence Coll., 1995-96, So. Conn. State U., New Haven, 1997—. Contbr. poems to various lit. publs. Recipient prize Acad. Am. Poets, 1992. Mem. MLA. Avocations: tennis, history of religions. Home: 31 Clark St New Haven CT 06511-3801

JOHNSON, BRIAN KEITH, electrical engineering educator; b. Madison, Wis., Mar. 11, 1965; s. Alston Cornelius and Virginia Rae (Kroener) J.; m. Elizabeth M. Williams, Jan. 3, 1998; 1 child, Erica Pearl. BS, U. Wis., 1987, MS, 1989, PhD, 1992. Registered profl. engr., Wis., Idaho. Teaching asst. U. Wis., Madison, 1988, rsch. asst., 1988-92; engr. Lawrence Livermore Nat. Labs., Livermore, Calif., 1989; asst. prof. U. Idaho, Moscow, 1992-97, assoc. prof., 1997—; instr. Coll. Engring. Tchg. Asst. Tng., U. Wis., Madison, 1988, Engring. prof. devel., 1992-98; co-advisor Iron Cross Leadership Soc., Madison, 1988-92, U. Idaho IEEE Student Chpt., 1995—; dir. Western Virtual Engring., 1996-99. Lodge chief Order of the Arrow, Boy Scouts Am., 1982-84, dir. Brownsea Double 2Course, Madison, 1987, advisor, 1990-92. Recipient Vigil Hon. Membership, Order of the Arrow, Boy Scouts Am., 1988, Leadership award, Exploring Boy Scouts Am., 1986, Outstanding Young Faculty award U. Idaho Coll. Engring., 1985. Mem. IEEE, Nat. Soc. Profl. Engrs., Am. Soc. Engring. Edn., Wilderness Soc., CIGRE, USNC. Lutheran. Avocations: cross country ski racing, bicycling, backpacking. Office: U Idaho Dept Elec Engring Moscow ID 83844

JOHNSON, BRUCE, engineering educator; b. Hawarden, Iowa, Sept. 4, 1932; s. York and Dorothy Ellen (DeBruce) J.; m. Dorothy Jane Rylander, Aug. 27, 1955; children: Sharon Lee, Kristen Kay. B.S. in Mech. Engring., Iowa State U., 1955; M.S. in Mech. Engring., Purdue U., 1962, Ph.D., 1965. Instr. U.S. Naval Acad., Annapolis, Md., 1957-59, assoc. prof., 1964-70, project dir. model basin, 1968-76, prof., 1970—, Naval Sea Systems Command prof. hydrodynamics, 1975-87, dir. Hydromechanics Lab., 1976-87, dir. ocean engring. program, 1996—; instr. Purdue U., 1959-64; chmn. 18th Am. Towing Tank Conf., 1977, U.S. Rep. Info. Com. Internat. Towing Tank Conf., 1975-84, chmn. symbols and terminology group, 1985—, editor, pub. ITTC Symbols and Terminology List, 1996—. Author: (with T. Gillmer) Introduction to Naval Architecture, 1982, (with D. Newman) Engineering Economic Analysis, 1994; editor: (with B. Nehrling) Proc. of 18th Am. Towing Tank Conf, 1977; contbr. articles to profl. publs. Trustee Bauman Bible Telecasts, 1970-93, fin. chmn., 1990-93; mem. Bowie State U. Found., 1995-97. Served with USN, 1955-59. Recipient award for excellence in engrng. teaching Western Electric Fund, 1971, Navy Meritorious Civilian Svc. award, 1994, 96, Navy Superior Civilian Svc. award, 1998, Svc. Excellence award Naval Acad. Alumni Assn., 1998; Ford Found. grantee, 1962-64. Mem. ASME, Am. Soc. Engring. Edn., Soc. Naval Architects and Marine Engrs. (chmn. Chesapeake Sailing Yacht Symposium 1985, 87), Am. Soc. Naval Engrs. (chmn. scholarship com. 1983-89, nat. coun. 1986-88, 89-91), Md. Capital Yacht Club (bd. dirs. 1986-93, commodore 1992), Naval Acad. Sailing Squadron, Chesapeake Bay Yacht Racing Assn. (pres. 1990). Methodist. Rsch. in hydrodynamics. Home: 12600 Kilbourne Ln Bowie MD 20715-2647 Office: Dept Naval Architecture and Ocean Engring US Naval Acad Annapolis MD 21402

JOHNSON, BRUCE ALAN, financial company executive; b. Portland, Maine; s. John H. and Berta C. (Langstroth) J.; m. Shirley A. Knight, Feb. 20, 1953; children: Jacquelyn, Craig, Keith, Mark. BS with honors, U. Md., 1970. Commissioned 2nd lt. U.S. Army, 1953; promoted to lt. col. U.S. Army, Vietnam, 1968; ret. U.S. Army, 1970; dir. mktg. Textile Assn. Am., Hallandale, Fla., 1970-77; regional dir. Holden Fin., Ft. Lauderdale, Fla., 1977-85; regional v.p. Integrated Resources, Ft. Lauderdale, 1985-88; sr. v.p. Zurich Kemper Investments, Ft. Lauderdale, 1988—. Decorated Bronze Star with seven battle stars, Legion of Merit, Purple Heart, Presdl. Citation. Mem. Nat. Assn. Securities Dealers, Bd. of Arbitrators, Internat. Assn. Fin. Planners, Mil. Order Purple Heart, Ret. Officers Assn. Avocations: golf, tennis.

JOHNSON, B(RUCE) CONNOR, biochemist, educator, consultant; b. Regina, Sask., Can., Apr. 28, 1911; came to U.S., 1937; s. Wilfred Connor and Edna Pearl (Young) J.; m. Elizabeth Marie Peterson, Sept. 1, 1940 (div.); children: Bruce Connor II, Peter Young, Stephen Paine, Elizabeth Carter (dec.), Christina Marie; m. Halina Victoria Bogdanska, Oct. 25, 1966; 1 child, Margaret Edna. BA in Chemistry, McMaster U., 1933, MA in Chemistry, 1934; PhD in Biochemistry, U. Wis., 1940. Chemist Can. Canners, Hamilton, Ont., 1934-37; DuPont fellow U. Ill., Urbana, 1940-42; rsch. biochemist Golden State Co., San Francisco, 1942-43; from asst. prof. to assoc. prof. U. Ill., Urbana, 1943-51, prof. biochemistry, 1951-65; prof., head dept. biochemistry and molecular biology U. Okla. Health Scis. Ctr., Oklahoma City, 1965-79, prof., 1979-82, prof. emeritus, 1982—; disting. career scientist Okla. Med. Rsch. Found., Oklahoma City, 1982—; rsch. scientist Inst. de Chimie Biologique, U. Strasbourg, France, 1971; mem., head biochemistry sect. Okla. Med. Rsch. Found., Oklahoma City, 1966-73, head vitamins and nutrition rsch., 1973-81; rsch. scientist dept. pediats. Coll. Medicine, U. South Fla., St. Petersburg, 1985-87; mem. nutrition study sect. NIH, 1962-66; cons. Can. Sci. Svc., Winnipeg, Man. and Ottawa, Can., 1952, 64, Armour & C., Cen. Rsch. Labs., Chgo., 1957-63, Agrl. Rsch. Coun., Fedn. Rhodesia and Nyasaland, 1962, N.Mex. State U., Las Cruces, 1975, others; ofcl. U.S. del. Pres. Eisenhower's 2d Atoms for Peace Mission to S.Am., 1956, 2d UN Atoms for Peace Conf., Geneva, Switzerland, 1958, USAF, Dept. of Def. Symposium on Arctic Biology and Medicine, Fairbanks, Alaska, 1965, White House Conf. on Food and Nutrition, Washington, 1969, others; invited participant to numerous symposia including Gordon Conf. on Vitamins & Metabolism, New London, N.H., 1956, Workshop on Vitamin K Function, Internat. Nutrition Congress, San Diego, 1981, Internat. Conf. on Post-Translational Covalent Modification of Proteins for Function, Oklahoma City, 1982. Author: Methods of Vitamin Determination, 1948; editor: Post-Translational Modifications of Proteins, 1983; contbr. chpts. to 25 books, 1955-86; mem. editl. bd.: Jour. Nutrition, 1966-70; mem. sci. adv. bd.: Nat. Vitamin Found., 1953-56; contbr. numerous papers on nutrition and biochemistry to profl. publs. Pres. 1st Unitarian Ch. Oklahoma City, 1972, Alliance Française d'Oklahoma City, 1980. Recipient Nutrition Coun. award Am. Feed Mfrs. Assn., 1960, Purkyne medal Czech Acad. Sci., 1969; Guggenheim Found. fellow U. Reading, Eng., 1955, NSF sr. fellow Inst. de Chimie des Substances Naturelles, Nat. Ctr. Sci. Rsch., Gif-sur-Yvette, U. Paris, France, 1961-62, U. Uppsala, Sweden, 1962. Mem. AAAS, Am. Assn. Med. Colls., Internat. Haemostasis and Thrombosis Soc., Endocrine Soc., Biochem. Soc. (Gt. Britain), Am. Soc. for Biochemistry and Molecular Biology, Am. Soc. Nutritional Scis., Am. Chem. Soc., Soc. Exptl. Biology and Medicine. Avocations: philately, ancient and world history, travel, canoeing. Fax: (405) 271-3980. E-mail: connor-johnson@omrf.uokhsc.edu. Office: Okla Med Rsch Found 825 NE 13th St Oklahoma City OK 73104-5005

JOHNSON, BRUCE EDWARD HUMBLE, lawyer; b. Columbus, Jan. 22, 1950; s. Hugo Edward and M. Alice (Humble) J.; m. Paige Robinson Miller, June 28, 1980; children: Marta Noble, Winslow Collins, Russell Scott. AB, Harvard U., 1972; JD, Yale U., 1977; MA, U. Cambridge, Eng., 1978. Bar: Wash. 1977, Calif. 1992. Atty. Davis Wright Tremaine LLP, Seattle, 1977—; King County Gov. Access Channel Oversight com., 1996—. Bd. dirs. Seattle Repertory Theatre, 1993—, pres., 1999—. Mem. ABA (tort and ins. practice sect., media law and defamation torts com. chair 1999—). Home: 711 W Kinnear Pl Seattle WA 98119-3621 Office: Davis Wright Tremaine LLP 2600 Century Sq 1501 4th Ave Seattle WA 98101-1688

JOHNSON, BRUCE MARVIN, English language educator; b. Chgo., Apr. 29, 1933; s. George A. and Elsie L. (Clausing) J.; m. Jean C. Kruger, June 29, 1957; 1 son, Abram. A.B., U. Chgo., 1952; B.A., Northwestern U., 1954, M.A., 1955, Ph.D., 1959. Instr. English U. Mich., 1958-62; asst. prof. English U. Rochester (N.Y.), 1962-68, assoc. prof., 1968-76, prof., 1976-92, prof. emeritus, sr. faculty assoc., 1992—, chmn. dept. English, 1981-84. Author: Conrad's Models of Mind, 1971, True Correspondence: A Phenomenology of Thomas Hardy's Novels, 1983. Sr. fellow NEH, 1974-75; fellow Guggenheim Found., 1977-78. Democrat. Home: Apt 407 16540 Heron Coach Way Fort Myers FL 33908-5523 Office: U Rochester Dept English Rochester NY 14627

JOHNSON, BRUCE ROSS, elementary education educator; b. La Porte, Ind., May 18, 1949; s. Egbert Johannes Daniel and Ruth Elvera (Johnson) J. BS, Ball State U., Muncie, Ind., 1971; ME, Valparaiso U., 1975; postgrad., Nat. Coll. Edn., Evanston, Ill., 1974, Beijing Normal U., 1988, Western Mich. U., U. Va., Ind. U., Purdue U., Antioch U., Seattle, Antioch U., Seattle, Calif State U. Cert. elem. sch. tchr., Ind. Vol. tchr. Peace Corps, St. Vincent, W.I., W.I., 1971-72; tchr. South Ctrl. Sch., Union Mills, Ind., 1972-76, 77—; tchr. gifted and talented Purdue U., 1995—, guest lectr. dept. edn., 1995—; missionary tchr. Luth. Ch., Liberia, West Africa, 1976-77; vis. instr. U. London, 1974, U. Moscow, 1974, U. Paris, 1974; edml. seminar China, 1988, Japan, 1990, Australia, 1993. Contbr. articles to newspapers. Pres. People to People Internat., La Porte, Ind., 1981-83, trustee, Kansas City, Mo., 1983-88; bd. dirs. La Porte County Libr. Leasing Corp., 1988—; mem. ch. coun. Bethany Luth. Ch., La Porte, 1983-86, 90-93; LaPorte County Bicentennial Commn., 1976-76; v.p. Friends of La Porte County Libr., 1984-86, pres., 1986-88; chmn. books and coffee meet the author series LaPorte County Pub. Libr., 1985—; trustee La Porte County Hist. Soc., 1985-92, 94—; v.p. N.W. Ind. Geneal. Soc., 1981-82; pres. Cmty. Concert Assn., La Porte, 1984; mem. Pan Am. Games Com., 1986-87; mem. steering com. La

Porte County Spelling Bee, 1979-91, chmn., 1981, 85, 90, 99; LaPorte County Leadership, Inc., 1986-87; chmn. Miss. Valley coun. People-to-People, 1983-88; mem. bicentennial com. Bill of Rights, 1989-90; bd. dirs. LaPorte Literacy Coalition, 1997—. Named one of Outstanding Young Men Am., 1985, State finalist NASA Tchr.-in-Space project, 1985; Ind. State Tchrs. Assn. scholarship, 1970, Dean Earl A. Johnson Outstanding Svc. award Ball State U., 1971; cert. of merit Ind. Dept. Edn., 1985. Mem. NEA (life), Ind. State Tchrs. Assn., Amateur Music Club (pres. 1982-83), Little Theater Club (bd. dirs. 1980-83, 89-92), Lions (bd. dirs. 1983—), Phi Delta Kappa (life). Avocations: performing in musical theater, collecting foreign coins, traveling, gardening. Home: 2012 Village Rd La Porte IN 46350-7874 Office: South Cen Community Schs 9808 S 600 W Union Mills IN 46382-9600

JOHNSON, BYRON JERALD, retired state supreme court judge; b. Boise, Idaho, Aug. 2, 1937; s. Arlie Johnson and V. Bronell (Dunten) J.; children: Matthew, Ethan, Elaine, Laura; m. Paticia G. Young, 1984. AB, Harvard U., 1959, LLB, 1962. Bar: Idaho, 1962. Justice Idaho Supreme Ct., Boise, 1988-98; ret., 1998.

JOHNSON, C. TERRY, lawyer; b. Bridgeport, Conn., Sept. 24, 1937; s. Clifford Gustave and Evelyn Florence (Terry) J.; m. Suzanne Frances Chichy, Aug. 24, 1985; children: Laura Elizabeth, Melissa Lynne, Clifford Terry. AB, Trinity Coll., 1960; LLD, Columbia U., 1963. Bar: Ohio 1964, U.S. Ct. Appeals (6th cir.) 1966, U.S. Dist. Ct. (so. dist.) Ohio 1970. Legal dep. probate ct. Montgomery County, Dayton, Ohio, 1964-67; head probate dept. Coolidge Wall & Wood, Dayton, 1967-79, Smith & Schnacke, Dayton, 1979-89, Thompson, Hine and Flory, Dayton, 1989-92; head estate planning and probate group Porter, Wright, Morris & Arthur, Dayton, 1992—; frequent lectr. on estate planning to various profl. orgns. Contbr. articles to profl. jours. Fellow Am. Coll. Trust and Estate Counsel; mem. ABA, Ohio Bar Assn. (bd. govs. probate and trust law sect., chmn. 1993-95), Dayton Bar Assn. (chmn. probate com. 1992-94), Ohio State Bar Found. (trustee 1995-99), Ohio CLE Inst. (trustee 1995—, chair 1998-99), Dayton Legal Secs. Assn. (hon.), Dayton Racquet Club, Dayton Bicycle Club. Home: 8307 Rhine Way Centerville OH 45458-3017 Office: Porter Wright Morris & Arthur 1 S Main St Ste 1600 Dayton OH 45402-2028

JOHNSON, CAGE SAUL, hematologist, educator; b. New Orleans, Mar. 31, 1941; s. Cage Spooner and Esther Georgianna (Saul) J.; m. Shirley Lee O'Neal, Feb. 22, 1968; children: Stephanie, Michelle. Student, Creighton U., 1958-61, MD, 1965. Intern U. Cin., 1965-66, resident, 1966-67; resident U. So. Calif., 1969-71; instr. U. So. Calif., L.A., 1971-74, asst. prof., 1974-80, assoc. prof., 1980-88, dir. Comprehensive Sicle Cell Ctr., 1991—, prof., 1988—; chmn. adv. com. Calif. Dept. Health Svcs., Sacramento, 1977—; dir. Hemoglobinopathy Lab., L.A., 1976—; bd. dirs. Sicke Cell Self-Help Assn., L.A., 1982-86. Contbr. numerous articles to profl. jours. Dir. Sickle Cell Disease Rsch. Found., L.A., 1986-94; active Nat. Med. Fellowships, Inc., Chgo., 1979—; chmn. rev. com. NIH, Washington, 1986-91; chmn. adv. com., 1995-97, mem. adv. coun., 1997—. Major U.S. Army, 1967-69, Vietnam. Fellow N.Y. Acad. Scis., Am. Coll. Angiology; mem. Am. Soc. Hematology, Am. Fedn. Clin. Rsch., Western Soc. Clin. Investigation, Internat. Soc. Biorheology, E.E. Just Soc. (sec.-treas. 1985-93, pres. 1994-95, sec. 1996—). Avocation: restoring antique automobiles. Office: U So Calif 2025 Zonal Ave Los Angeles CA 90033-1034

JOHNSON, CAMILLE, media executive. Sr. v.p., media dir. Goldberg Moser O'Neill, San Francisco. Office: Goldberg Moser ONeill 77 Maiden Ln San Francisco CA 94108-5414*

JOHNSON, CANDICE ELAINE BROWN, pediatrics educator; b. Cin., Mar. 21, 1946; d. Paul Preston and Naomi Elizabeth Brown; m. Thomas Raymond Johnson, June 30, 1973; children: Andrea Eleanor, Erik Albert. BS, U. Mich., 1968; PhD Microbiology, Case Western Reserve U., 1973, MD, 1976. Diplomate Am. Bd. Pediat., 1981. Intern, resident in pediat. Rainbow Babies and Children's Hosp./Met. Gen. Hosp., Cleve., 1976-78; fellow in ambulatory pediatrics Met. Gen. Hosp., 1978-79; asst. prof. pediat. Case Western Res. U., Cleve., 1980-90, assoc. prof., 1990-97; prof. pediat. U. Colo., Denver, 1997—; pediatrician Children's Hosp., Denver, 1997—; mem. rev. panel NIH, Washington, 1993; faculty sen. Case Western Res. U., 1988-91. Contbr. articles profl. jours. Mem. Am. Acad. Pediat., Ambulatory Pediatric Assn., Soc. for Pediatric Rsch., So. Utah Wilderness Alliance, Sierra Club. Home: 2290 Locust St Denver CO 80207-3943 Office: Child Health Clinic B032 1056 E 19th Ave Denver CO 80218-1007

JOHNSON, CARL FREDERICK, marriage and family therapist; b. July 18, 1947. BA in Psychology, Northwestern U., 1969; MA in Clin. Psychology, Ga. State U., 1975. Lic. marriage and family therapist, Ga. Grad. tchg. asst. Ga. State U., Atlanta, 1972-73; family therapist Bridge Family Ctr., Atlanta, 1973-80; pvt. practice The Family Workshop, Atlanta, 1979—; adj. instr. Dekalb C.C., Clarkston, Ga., 1981-82; appointee Ga. Composite Bd. Profl. Counselors, Social Workers and Marriage and Family Therapists, 1985-93; exec. dir. Ga. Assn. Marriage and Family Therapy, Atlanta, 1997—. Contbr. articles to profl. jours. Fellow Am. Assn. for Marriage and Family Therapy (Divnsl. Contbn. award 1993); mem. Ga. Assn. for Marriage and Family Therapy (Outstanding Ctbn. award 1983, 85, 93, Lifetime Achievement/Disting. Svc. award 1996, chair legis. affairs com. 1980-85, 93-95), Assn. Marital and Family Therapy Regulatory Bds. (founder, pres. 1987-91, coord. devel. nat. licensing exam in marital and family therapy 1989-92). Home: 751 N Parkwood Rd Decatur GA 30030-5023 Office: Family Workshop Ste 410 2957 Clairmont Rd NE Atlanta GA 30329-1647

JOHNSON, CARL RANDOLPH, chemist, educator; b. Charlottesville, Va., Apr. 28, 1937. BS, Med. Coll. Va., 1958; PhD in Chemistry, U. Ill., 1962. NSF rsch. fellow chemistry Harvard U., 1962; from asst. to prof. chemistry Wayne State U., Detroit, 1962-90, Disting. prof., 1990—, chair dept. chemistry, 1997—; Humboldt sr. scientist, 1991; bd. dirs. Organic Syntheses, Inc. Mem. adv. bd. Jour. Organic Chemistry, 1976-81. Alfred P. Sloan fellow, 1965-68. Mem. Am. Chem. Soc. (assoc. editor jour. 1984-89, Harry and Carol Mosher award 1992), Royal Soc. Chemistry. Achievements include research in organic sulfur chemistry, especially sulfoxides and sulfoximines, exploratory synthetic chemistry, synthesis of compounds of potential medicinal activity, organometallic chemistry, synthesis of natural products, enzymes in synthesis. Office: Wayne State Univ Dept Chemistry Detroit MI 48202

JOHNSON, CAROL LYNN, secondary school counselor; b. Wooster, Ohio, Dec. 17, 1951; d. John K. and Marge M. (Reese) Coffey; m. Robert B. Johnson, June 19, 1950; children: Katie Johnson, Russell Johnson. BS in Edn., U. Akron, 1973; MA in Edn., Colo. State U., 1982, PhD in Edn., 1995. Cert. tchr., Colo. Tchr. North Ctrl. Sch. Dist., Creston, Ohio, 1972-78; tchr./counselor Estes Park (Colo.) H.S. Park R-3 Sch. Dist., 1978—. Mem. AAUW, ASCD, Colo. Assn. Sch. Execs., Delta Kappa Gamma, Phi Delta Kappa. Home: 169 1/2 Stanley Circle Dr Estes Park CO 80517-6304 Office: Estes Park HS 1600 Manford Ave Estes Park CO 80517

JOHNSON, CAROL R., school system administrator. BA in Elem. Edn., Fisk U., 1969; MA in Curriculum and Instrn., U. Minn., 1980, D in Edn. Policy and Adminstrn., 1997. Elem. tchr. Washington Pub. Schs., 1969; elem. tchr., coord. career opportunities Mpls. Pub. Schs., 1970-76; coord. R&D, project dir. tng. urban educators U. Minn., Mpls., 1976-86; prin., asst. prin. elem. schs. Mpls. Pub. Schs., 1986-89, asst. to assoc. supt. elem. edn., assoc. supt., 1989-95; supt. St. Louis Park (Minn.) Schs., 1995-97, Mpls. Pub. Schs., 1997—. Spkr. in field. Bd. dirs. The Found., Health Sys. Minn., Boy Scouts Am. Viking Coun., adv. com. Learning for Life; commn. mem. Golden Valley Police, Civil Svc., 1990—, chair, 1994-95, U. Minn. Alumni Assn., comm. and fin. com. Bush Leadership fellow, 1993-94; recipient Apple for Teacher award Iota Phi Lambda, 1992-93, Leadership award Omega Psi Phi, 1996. Mem. ASCD (Minn. chpt.), NAS/Nat. Rsch. Coun. (strategic edn. rsch. program feasibility study 1996—), Am. Assn. Sch. Adminstrs., Minn. Assn. Sch. Adminstrs. (edn. policy com. 1996-97), LWV Golden Valley, Mpls. Links, Inc. (St. Paul chpt.), Jack and Jill, Inc. (Mpls. chpt.), Children First Exec. Com. and Vision Team St. Louis Park, Delta Sigma Theta. Office fax: 612 627-2005. Home fax: 612 541-0080. Home: 416 Turnpike Rd Golden Valley MN 55416-1155 Office: Mpls Pub Schs 807 Broadway St NE Minneapolis MN 55413-2332*

JOHNSON, CAROLINE JANİCE, insurance company executive; b. Chgo., Jan. 6, 1941; d. LeRoy Paine and Johnetta Louise (Brock) Collins; m. Charles Robert Rice (divorced); 1 child, Robert Michael; m. James Arthur Lunningham (divorced); 1 child, Mark LeRoy; m. George Bolds (div. 1970); 1 child, Troy Andrew; m. Howard Edward Johnson Sr., May 4, 1985 (separated 1997). Sec. Roosevelt U., Chgo., 1959-60; police steno Chgo. Police Dept., Chgo., 1960-62; sec., dental asst. Dr. Lucien Holman, Joliet, Ill., 1962-64; sec. Amoco Chems., Joliet, Ill., 1964-68; ins. sales Allstate, Joliet, Ill., 1978-85; dept. mgr., ins. sales Beneficial Ins. Co., Chgo., 1985-86; agy. mgr. Heritage Agy. Inc., Chgo., 1987-88; owner Ins. Coun., Inc., Chgo., 1988—. Mem. Chgo. Assn. Ins. Women (bd. dirs. communication Chgo. chpt. 1989—), Internat. Horsemen's League (Chgo. pres. 1987-88, 97—, bus. mgr. 1988-97, pres. 1997—). Democrat. Avocations: riding and showing horses. Home: 4524 Heartland Dr Apt 27D Richton Park IL 60471-2407 Office: Ste 202 1353 S Wabash Ave Apt 202 Chicago IL 60605-2596

JOHNSON, CAROLYN JEAN, law librarian; b. Beaver Dam, Wis., Nov. 7, 1938; d. Henry William and Bernice Mae (Haas) Krueger; m. Robert Edward Johnson, June 19, 1960; children: Eric Steven, Kristin Elizabeth. BS in Edn., Wartburg Coll., 1960. Tchr. various locations, 1960-64, Hennepin County Library, 1972-81; libr. 3M Tech. Libr., St. Paul, 1981-86; law libr. 3M Ctr. Law Libr., St. Paul, 1986—. Mem. Am. Assn. Law Libraries, Minn. Assn. Law Libraries. Lutheran. Avocations: reading, walking, cooking. Office: 3M Co Ctr Law Library PO Box 33355 Saint Paul MN 55133-3355

JOHNSON, CARYN See GOLDBERG, WHOOPI

JOHNSON, CATHY ADAMS, educational administrator; b. Detroit; m. Donald M. Johnson, Jr., Sept. 1993; 1 child, Donald M. III. BA, U. Mich., 1984; MA, Wayne State U., 1988, EdD, 1996. Ednl. continuing cert., Mich. Tchr. Bloomfield Hills (Mich.) Schs., 1984-88; art asst. Wayne State U., Detroit, 1988-91; tchr. Children's Mus., Detroit Pub. Schs., 1991-96, curriculum supr., 1996—. Mem. ASCD, Nat. Coun. for Social Studies, Wayne State U. Alumni Assn. (bd. govs. 1996-99), Phi Delta Kappa (sec. 1997-98), Delta Kappa Gamma, Alpha Kappa Alpha. Avocations: painting, drawing. Home: 13150 E Outer Dr Detroit MI 48224 Office: Detroit Pub Schs 5057 Woodward Rm 832 Detroit MI 48202

JOHNSON, CHARLENE DENISE LOGAN, medical/surgical and pediatric nurse; b. Portsmouth, Ohio, Jan. 31, 1955; d. Paul Franklin and Rhoedna (Dawson) Logan; m. Edwin Christopher Johnson Sr., July 29, 1994. ADN, Morehead (Ky.) State U., 1986. RN, Ky. Staff nurse Our Lady of Bellefonte Hosp., Ashland, Ky., 1986-87; charge nurse St. Claire Med. Ctr., Morehead, 1988—. Home: RR 1 Box 103 Vanceburg KY 41179-9700 Office: St Claire Med Ctr 222 Medical Cir Morehead KY 40351-1180

JOHNSON, CHARLES BARTLETT, mutual fund executive; b. Montclair, N.J., Jan. 6, 1933; s. Rupert Harris and Florence (Endler) J.; m. Ann Demarest Lutes, Mar. 26, 1955; children: Charles E., Holly, Sarah, Gregory, William, Jennifer, Mary (dec.). BA, Yale U., 1954. With R.H. Johnson & Co., N.Y.C., 1954-55; pres. Franklin Distbrs., Inc., 1957—; pres., CEO Franklin Resources, Inc., 1969—; bd. dirs. various Franklin and Templeton Mut. Funds; bd. govs. Investment Co. Inst., 1973-88. Trustee Crystal Springs Uplands Sch., 1984-92; bd. dirs. Peninsula Cmty. Found., 1986-96, San Francisco Symphony, 1984—; bd. overseers Hoover Instn., 1993—. Mem. Nat. Assn. Securities Dirs. (bd. govs. 1990-92, 96-98, chmn. 1992), Burlingame Country Club, Pacific Union Club (San Francisco), Commonwealth Club of Calif. (bd. dirs. 1995-97). Office: Franklin Resources Inc PO Box 7777 San Mateo CA 94403-7777*

JOHNSON, CHARLES COLTON, English educator, dean; b. Watseka, Ill., Oct. 18, 1938; s. Fred and Helen Gladys (Risley) J.; m. Jean Lynn Murphy, June 14, 1960; children: Sarah Augusta, Catharine Olivia. BA, Northwestern U., 1960, MA, 1961, PhD, 1967. Prof. English Vassar Coll., Poughkeepsie, N.Y., 1965—, dean of studies, 1975-91, dean of coll., 1991—. Author: Uncollected Prose of W.B. Yeats, 1975; contbr. articles, revs. to profl. jours. Bd. dirs. Coll. Venture, Providence, 1978—. Recipient Charles A. Dana award for pioneering achievement in higher edn. Charles A. Dana found., 1991. Avocations: hiking, squash. Home: 46 Livingston St Rhinebeck NY 12572-1533 Office: Vassar Coll Dept English Poughkeepsie NY 12604

JOHNSON, CHARLES FLOYD, television executive, producer; b. Camden, N.J., Feb. 12; s. Orange Maull and Bertha Ellen (Seagers) J.; m. Sandra Brashears, June 4, 1966 (div. 1971); m. Anne Burford, June 18, 1983; 1 child, Kristin. BA, Howard U., 1962, JD, 1965; student, U. Del., 1960. Bar: D.C., 1968. Atty., advisor U.S. Copyright, Washington, 1967-70; assoc. Howard Berg Law Offices, Wilmington, Del., 1970-71; prodn. coordinator Universal TV, Universal City, Calif., 1971-74, assoc. producer The Rockford Files and Baa Baa Black Sheep, 1974-76, producer The Rockford Files, Simon and Simon (pilot), Hellinger's Law, 1976-80, supervising producer Magnum P.I., 1982-86, co-exec. producer Magnum P.I., 1986-88, exec. producer Revealing Evidence, 1990; producer Bret Maverick Warner Bros. TV, Burbank, Calif., 1981-82; producer Voices of Our People (In Celebration of Black Poetry) Sta. KCET/Pub. Broadcasting System, L.A., 1981-82; co-exec. producer B.L. Stryker Blue Period Prodns., L.A., 1988-90; vice chmn. Media Forum, L.A., 1980-85; bd. dirs. Comm. Bridge, L.A., 1981-89. Author: (bull.) Copyright & Developing Countries, 1967; co-author: Black Women in Television, 1990; co-exec. producer Quantum Leap, 1992-93, JAG, 1996—; exec. producer The Rockford Files movies, 1993-96. Bd. dirs. Ind. Video and Filmmakers, 1985-90, Kwanza Found., 1985—, Crossroads Theatre Acad., 1990-98, Mediascope, 1994—. With U.S. Army, 1965-67. Recipient Stony Brook Coll. Preparatory award, 1979, Horward U. Alumni Assn. award, 1982, 85. Mem. AFTRA, SAG, Writers Guild Am., Acad. TV Arts and Scis. (student activities com., Emmy award 1978, 1981 (2), 7 Emmy nominations), Caucus for Producers, Writers and Dirs. (steering com.), Producers Guild Am. (treas. 1996-98, sec. 1998—), Am. Film Inst., Omega Psi Phi (treas. local chpt. 1961-62). Democrat. Methodist. Avocations: bicycling, traveling. Office: Paramount Studios 5555 Melrose Ave Los Angeles CA 90038

JOHNSON, CHARLES JOSEPH, telecommunications executive, computer engineer; b. Saint Louis, Mo., Oct. 11, 1966; s. Charles Arnold and Barbara Paulette (Maloney) J.; m. Lori Ann Burford, Sept. 24, 1994. Student, Southeast Mo. State U., Cape Girardeau, 1985-87; DSC Switch, Translations, DSC Technical, Dallas, 1993. Owner, operator DES, Inc., Cape Girardeau, 1985-88; design tech., CAD Annis Constrn., Cape Girardeau, 1988-91; sys. devel. engr. Epic Corp., Jackson, Mo., 1990-91; computer tech. Advanced Tech.-Radio Shack, Jackson, Mo., 1992; tech. mgr., network adminstr., Internet svc. provider LDD, Inc., Cape Girardeau, 1992—; owner DES, Inc./FBN, LLC; computer cons. WAN/LAN cons. Cape Girardeau Fire Dept., 1985-86; pres. Drafting and Design Club, Cape Girardeau, 1987-88, Soc. Mfg. Engrs., Cape Girardeau, 1988-89. Roman Catholic. Avocations: martial arts, moto-cross, basketball, volleyball, football. E-Mail: joeyj@flybynite.com. Home: RR 1 Box 3D Benton MO 63736-9701 Office: Stark Truss Co 3284 Pcr 806 Perryville MO 63775-7187

JOHNSON, CHARLES L., II, military officer. BSCE, USAF Acad., 1972; MS in Engrng. Adminstrn. and Law, George Washington U., 1976; grad., Air Command and Staff Coll., 1986, Air War Coll., 1991, Def. Sys. Mgmt. Coll., 1993. Commd. 2d lt. USAF, 1972, advanced through grades to brigadier gen., 1997; UH-1N/CH-3E instr. pilot, chief scheduling and tng. 89th Mil. Airlift Wing, Andrews AFB, Md., 1973-78; AB-212 instr. pilot Joint DOD Helicopter Tech. Asst. Field Royal Saudi Air Force, Taif Air Base, Saudi Arabia, 1978-79; C-141 flight examiner, chief pilot, chief current ops. 60th Mil. Airlift Wing, Travis AFB, Calif., 1980-83; chief spl. actions and studies group Airlift and Trainers Sys. Program Office, Wright-Patterson AFB, Ohio, 1983-85; chief C-17 program divsn. Mil. Airlift Command, Scott AFB, Ill., 1986-90; mil. asst. to asst. sec. of Air Force for acquisition The Pentagon, Washington, 1991-92; comdr. 97th Ops. Group 97th Air Mobility Wing, Altus AFB, Okla., 1992-93; dir. C-141 Sys. Program Office Warner Robins Air Logistics Ctr., Robins AFB, Ga., 1993-96; program dir. C-17 Sys. Program Office Aero. Sys. Ctr., Wright-Patterson AFB, Ohio, 1996—. Decorated Meritorious Svc. medal with 5 oak leaf clusters. Office: ASC/YC 2590 Loop Rd W Wright Patterson AFB OH 45433

JOHNSON, CHARLES LAVON, JR., clinical neuropsychologist, consultant; b. Raleigh, N.C., Aug. 31, 1954; s. Charles Lavon Sr. and Edna Louise (Schaaf) J.; m. Janet Andrews, June 23, 1990. BA, N.C. State U., 1976, MS in Sociology, 1979, MS in Psychology, 1983; PhD, Fielding Inst., Santa Barbara, Calif., 1989. Lic. practicing psychologist. Instr., sch. psychologist N.C. State U., Raleigh, 1983-84; contractual psychologist Wake County Pub. Sch. System, Raleigh, 1985-86; clin. psychology intern John Umstead Hosp., Butner, N.C., 1988, staff psychologist, 1989; cons. psychologist Springmoor Life Care Retirement Community, Raleigh, 1988-90; sr. psychologist Dorothea Dix Hosp., Raleigh, 1989-91; contractual psychologist Cumberland County Pub. Sch. System, Fayetteville, N.C., 1989-91; cons. psychologist Disability Determination Svcs., Raleigh, 1991—; pvt. practice, 1990—; cons. clin. neuropsychologist Coastal Plan Hosp., Rocky Mount, 1991-93, Tenth Jud. Dist. Juvenile Ct., Raleigh, 1990-91, Dartmouth Clinic, Southern Pines, N.C., 1990-92), clin. instr. dept. psychiatry U. N.C. Sch. Medicine, Chapel Hill, 1990-94. Contbr. articles to profl. jours. Mem. West Raleigh Citizens Adv. Coun., Raleigh, 1985-90. Avocations: music, golf, antiques. Office: Disability Determination PO Box 243 Raleigh NC 27602-0243*

JOHNSON, CHARLES LESLIE, aerospace physicist, consultant; b. Ashland, Ky., Mar. 1, 1962; s. Charles Leslie and June Mays (Gesling) J.; m. Carol Elaine Peck, May 7, 1988; children: Carl Stuart, Leslie Arlene. BA in Chemistry and Physics, Transylvania U., 1984; MS in Physics, Vanderbilt U., 1986; grad., Internat. Space U., 1991. Rsch. physicist Gen. Rsch. Corp., Huntsville, Ala., 1986-90; aerospace physicist NASA-Marshall Space Flight Ctr., Huntsville, 1990-98; mgr. Interstellar Propulsion Rsch. NASA, Huntsville, Ala., 1998—; cons. Gen. Rsch. Corp., Huntsville, 1990-91; co-chmn. space symposium Tech. and Bus. Exhbn. and Symposium, 1994; chmn. STEDTRAIN (Sci. Tech. Edn. and Tng.) symposium, 1995. Tech. cons.: (motion picture) Lost in Space, 1998; contbr. articles to profl. jours. Deacon 1st Christian Ch., Huntsville, 1989-91. Named Profl. of Yr., Huntsville Assn. Tech. Socs., 1998. Mem. AIAA (chmn. space programs and techs. conf., advanced techs. and applications symposium 1996), Nat. Space Soc., World Future Soc. (pres. North Ala. chpt. 1998-99, prin. investigator propulsive small expendable deployer space experiment 1998—), Am. Geophysical Union. Republican. Office: Interstellar Propulsion Rsch NASA Marshall Space Flight Ctr Huntsville AL 35812

JOHNSON, CHARLES N., elementary education educator. Tchr., vice prin. Morgan (Utah) Middle Sch.; prin. Clinton (Utah) Elem., 1997—. Recipient Tchr. Excellence award Internat. Tech. Edn. Assn., 1992. Office: Clinton Elem 1101 W 1800 N Clinton UT 84015-8999*

JOHNSON, CHARLES NELSON, JR., physicist; b. Mt. Hope, Kans., June 17, 1915; m. Ruth E. Berry; children: Janet A. LaMotte, Diane G. Lee, Charles B. Jr. AB, Friends U., 1938; PhD, Johns Hopkins U., 1941. Jr. instr. engring. physics Johns Hopkins U., Balt., 1938-41; physicist Bur. Ord., USN, 1941-42, Norfolk Navy Yard, Va., 1942-46; sr. physicist Aviation Ord. Dept., 1946-51, Ballistic Instrumentation Dept., Naval Proving Ground, 1951-55; supervisory rsch. physicist U.S. Army Engr. Rsch. and Devel. Ctr., 1955-67; chief detection br. Intrusion, Detection & Sensor Lab., 1967-71; chief phys. sci. group Countermine-Counter Intrusion Dept., 1971-73; cons. physicist Environ. Rsch. Inst. Mich., Searle Consortium, Arlington, Va., 1974—. Sci. fair judge Fairfax County H.S. Fellow AAAS; mem. Am. Phys. Soc., Sigma Xi. Office: 3100 N Oxford St Arlington VA 22207-5352

JOHNSON, CHERYL (CJ), newspaper columnist. Gossip columnist Mpls. Star Tribune. Office: Mpls Star Tribune 425 Portland Ave Minneapolis MN 55488-1511

JOHNSON, CHRISTINE ANN, nurse; b. Omaha, Nebr., Aug. 23, 1951; d. Ralph James and Marlene (Marlenee) Matney; m. Timothy Carl Johnson, Aug. 1, 1970; children: Erik Carl, Christine Nicole. Cert. practical nurse, Met. Tech. Community Coll., 1973; BA cum laude, Creighton U., 1989. LPN, Nebr.; cert. pregnancy exercise instr.; cert. lactation cons. EKG technician Bishop Clarkson Meml. Hosp., Omaha, 1971-74, lic. practical nurse, 1978—, instr. pregnancy exercise, 1984-86, instr. sibling preparation, 1985-86, instr. breastfeeding, 1985-95; LPN Cons. in Cardiology, P.C., Omaha, 1974-78; tchr. asst. Creighton U. Dept. Psychology, Omaha, 1987-88; lactation cons. Bergan Mercy Med. Ctr., Omaha, 1994—; teaching asst. dept. psychology, child psychology, adolescent psychology, devel. psychology Creighton U., 1987-88. Assoc. editor (cons.' corner) Jour. Human Lactation, 1994-96. Sec. United Meth. Women First United Meth. Ch., 1984-85, chmn. 1985-86; vol. Radio Talking Book, 1985; mem. Omaha Pub. Schs. Superintendent's Task Force on Human Growth and Devel., 1986, Project Linus, 1997—; vol. Paws for Friendship, 1997—, Dresses for Humanity Durham Western Heritage Mus., Omaha, 1999. Mem. Internat. Lactation Cons. Assn., Psi Chi. Methodist. Home: 4618 N 129th Ave Omaha NE 68164-1708 Office: Bergan Mercy Med Ctr 7500 Mercy Rd Omaha NE 68124-2319

JOHNSON, CHRISTOPHER GARDNER, technology educator; b. Akron, Ohio, Aug. 18, 1954; s. Francis McWhorter and Ann (Gardner) J.; m. Ingrid Novodvorsky, Dec. 1, 1990. BA in Secondary Edn., U. Ariz., 1976, MEd in Edn. Media, 1978, PhD in Secondary Edn., 1987. Cert. tchr. cmty. coll. Assoc. site dir. lab. for computer based instrn. U. Ariz., Tucson, 1980-85, dir. humanities computing and tech., 1985—; assoc. faculty Pima Cmty. Coll., Tucson, 1978; cons. Control Data Corp., 1983, 86, Apple Computer Inc., 1991-94; adj. asst. prof. ednl. psychology, 1995—, Nat. Assn. Sec. Sch. Prins., 1998—; adj. asst. prof. ednl. leadership, 1996—, process improvement facilitator/quality focal point, 1995-97, CORE ptnr. Office of Continuous Orgnl. Renewal, 1995-97. Contbr. articles to profl. jours. Mem. Assn. Supervision and Curr. Devel., Internat. Soc. for Technol. in Edn., Ariz. Ednl. Media Assn. (S.E. regional dir. 1994-96, pres.-elect 1996, pres. 1997-98, 1992 Spl. Svc. award 1992), Tucson Area Coun. for Tech. (chair 1994—, pres. 1994-97). Avocations: scuba diving, hiking, bicycling, traveling. Office: Univ Ariz Humanities Computing & Tech PO Box 210067 Tucson AZ 85721-0067

JOHNSON, CLARENCE RAY, minister; b. Port Arthur, Tex., Jan. 31, 1943; s. Ervin Ray and Mina Frances (Cox) J.; m. Betty Olene Mears, Nov. 22, 1962; children: Gregory Clarence, Garemy Kevin, Darren Kendall, Sherry Lynn. Ordained to ministry Ch. of Christ, 1962. Min. Hwy. 29 Ch. of Christ, Liberty Hill, Tex., 1962-63, Jonestown Ch. of Christ, Leander, Tex., 1963-70, Springhill (La.) Ch. of Christ, 1970-75, La Porte (Tex.) Ch. of Christ, 1975-84, Exton (Pa.) Ch. of Christ, 1984-91, Shiloh Ch. of Christ, Mexia, Tex., 1991-97, Susquehanna Ch. of Christ, Marietta, Pa., 1997—; tchr., counselor Sabinal (Tex.) Bible Camp, 1978-80. Author: (with others) Is It Lawful?, 1989, Psalms to Sing, 1995, series of tracts, 1983-94, series of Bible study work books, 1995-97; news editor Gospel Guardian, 1971-73; contbr. articles to profl. jours. Trustee Liberty Hill Ind. Sch. Dist., 1968-70; panel mem. life issues seminar La. State U. Med. Coll., Shreveport, 1973. Republican. Home and Office: 323 W High St Elizabethtown PA 17022-2141 *Your child's first concepts of his heavenly Father are almost certain to be based on what he has seen, heard, and experienced at the hand of his physical father. May God help us strike that delicate balance between strictness and mercy, and provide a loving, secure atmosphere where our children may properly grow "in wisdom and stature, and in favor with God and men."*

JOHNSON, CLARENCE TRAYLOR, JR., circuit court judge; b. Trenton, Fla., Aug. 16, 1929; s. Clarence Traylor and Jessie Granade (Wilson) J.; m. Shirley Ann Traxler, Aug. 30, 1957; children: James Waring, Robert Dale, Douglas Earl, Jan Elizabeth. BSBA, U. Fla., 1955, JD, 1958. Ptnr. Cone, Wagner, Nugent, Johnson, McKeown & Dell, West Palm Beach, Fla., 1958-71; cir. ct. judge 18th Jud. Cir. of Fla., Brevard and Seminole Counties, 1971-92; chmn. Fla. Conf. of Cir. Judges, 1990-91; mem. Fla. Bench Bar Commn., State of Fla., 1990-92; faculty Fla. Jud. Coll., 1988-90; mem. Fla. Fed.-State Jud. Coun., 1989-91, Jud. Coun. Fla., 1989-91. Pres. Jr. C. of C., Cocoa, Fla., 1963-64; chmn. bd. Cen. Brevard YMCA, Cocoa, 1965-66; pres.

YMCA, Brevard County, 1968-71, Rotary, Cocoa, 1965-66; charter pres. Vassar B. Carlton Am. Inn of Ct., 1992-93. With USAF, 1950-54. Recipient Disting. Svc. award Cocoa Jaycees, 1965, Jud. Achievement award Acad. Fla. Trial Lawyers, 1987. Mem. ABA, Brevard County Bar Assn. (pres. 1969-70), The Fla. Bar (bd. govs. 1970-71). Lutheran. Avocation: fishing. Home: 600 Heron Dr Merritt Island FL 32952-4022

JOHNSON, CLARICE P., materials procurement executive; b. Madison, N.C., Dec. 15, 1941; d. George Taylor and Betty Mae Penn; m. William Howard Johnson, June 22, 1962; children: William Jr., Renata. BS in Biology, Upsala Coll., 1974, BSBA, 1983; MS, N.J. Inst. Tech., 1990. Mfg. biologist Organon, Inc., West Orange, N.J., 1975-80, prodn. supr., 1980-84, mfg. supr., 1982-84, sr. regulatory assoc., 1984-85, mgr. prodn. and inventory control, 1985-89, mgr. procurement and materials planning, 1989—; edn. counselor, Organon, Inc., 1988—; lectr., guest cons. Jersey City (N.J.) State Coll., 1990, Cenogenics, Old Bridge, N.J., 1989; mem. Organon Gender Focus Group, West Orange, 1993—. Author: Vendor Certification, 1990. Pres. College Park Neighborhood Assn., South Orange, N.J., 1983-87; mem. South Orange Community Rels. Bd., 1981-88; tutorer Essex County C.C., Newark, 1989. Mem. Am. Prodn. and Inventory Control Soc. (pres. No. N.J. chpt., exec. v.p. 1995-96, v.p. edn. 1994, v.p. membership 1993, Mem. of Yr. 1993, CPIM, company coord. 1992-93, Company of Month award 1992, pres. 1996-97, region II dir. edn.), Nat. Assn. Purchasing Mgmt., Am. Soc. Quality Control, AAAS, Internat. Soc. Pharm. Engrs., People to People Internat., Delta Sigma Theta. Democrat. Avocations: reading, dancing, theater, travel. Home: 429 Wilden Pl South Orange NJ 07079-2518 Office: Organon Inc 375 Mount Pleasant Ave West Orange NJ 07052-2724

JOHNSON, CLARION ELLIS, physician; b. Bklyn., Dec. 31, 1950; s. Clarion and Eddye Pride Scott J.; m. Heather Lee Mitchell, June 26, 1976; children: Clarion Ellis III, Sarah Elizabeth. BA, Sarah Lawrence Coll., 1972; MD, Yale U., 1976. Diplomate Am. Bd. Internal Medicine, Nat. Med. Bd. Examiners, Am. Bd. Preventive Medicine. Intern Downstate Med. Ctr., Bklyn.; resident Harlem Hosp. Ctr., N.Y.C.; dir. CCU/ICU, staff cardiologist, dir. Echocardiography Lab. Kimbrough Army Cmty. Hosp., Ft. Meade, Md., 1981-83; staff rschr. dept. microwave rsch. Walter Reed Army Inst. Rsch., Washington, 1984-86, staff cardiologist, 1984-86; dir. critical care support lab., asst. prof. dept. medicine Howard U. Sch. Medicine, Washington, 1986-87; sr. med. officer, rschr. Evaluation Rsch. Corp. Internat., Fairfax, Va., 1987-88; assoc. clin. dir. Mobil Corp., Fairfax, 1988-93, clin. dir., 1993-94, sr. clinic dir., 1994-98, acting dir. med. clinics, co-lead med. leadership team, 1998, gen. mgr., med. dir. Global Med. Svcs., 1998—; asst. prof. dept. medicine Uniformed Svcs. U. Health Scis., F. Edward Hebert Med. Sch., Bethesda, Md., 1982—; attending physician Fairfax (Va.) Hosp., 1990—; adv. bd. Ctr. for Sci. and Tech. in the Media, Washington, 1991-94; vol. Washington Free Clinic, 1995—; bd. dirs. Mobil Found. Contbr. articles to profl. jours. Pres. bd. dirs. City Lights Sch. Maj. U.S. Army, 1979-86. Walter Reed Army Med. Ctr. fellow, 1979-81, 83-84. Mem. ACP (assoc.), Va. Occupl. Med. Soc. (bd. mem. 1995, conf. com. 1996), Bio-Electro Magnetic Soc., Yale Club N.Y.C. Democrat. Roman Catholic. Avocations: marathon running, martial arts. Home: 5504 Dorset Ave Chevy Chase MD 20815 Office: Mobil Oil Co Med Dept 3225 Gallows Rd Fairfax VA 22037

JOHNSON, CLARK EVERETTE, JR., judge; b. Jacksonville, Ala., Oct. 2, 1923; s. Clark Everette and Nora Lee (Kelley) J.; m. Arlene Washam, Feb. 23, 1952; children: David Terrel, Paul T., Clark Everette III. BS in Commerce, U. Ala., 1947, LLB, 1948. Bar: Ala. 1948. Pvt. practice Albertville, Ala., 1948-71; asst. dist. atty. Marshall County, 1952-53; cir. judge 27th Jud. Cir., Marshall County, 1971-88; tchr. Sunday sch. local Meth. ch., 1950—. Candidate for Ala. legis., 1958, 62. With AUS, 1943-46. Decorated Purple Heart. Mem. Ala. Bar Assn., Marshall County Bar Assn. Home: 5 Wright Rd Albertville AL 35951-4130

JOHNSON, CLARKE COURTNEY, financial consultant, educator; b. Wisconsin Rapids, Wis., July 11, 1936; s. Julius and Esther (Larsen) L. B.S.E.E., U. Wis., 1958; M.S.I.M., Purdue U., 1962, Ph.D., 1972. Asst. prof., asst. dean U. Wis.-Milw., 1966-72; vis. prof. Boston U. Sch. Mgmt., 1973-75; assoc. prof., assoc. dean DePaul U. Coll. Commerce, Chgo., 1975-77; prof., dean Iona Coll. Sch. Bus., New Rochelle, N.Y., 1977-79; prof. fin. Pace U. Grad. Sch. Bus., N.Y.C., 1979-98, chmn. dept., 1985-98, chmn. faculty coun. Sch. Bus., 1996-98; ret., 1998; pres. C. Johnson and Assocs., 1998—; cons. in field. Contbr. articles to profl. jours. Served with USAF, 1958-61. Mem. Am. Fin. Assn., Am. Econs. Assn., Fin. Mgmt. Assn., Eta Kappa Nu, Beta Gamma Sigma. Home: 333 E 79th St Apt 20Y New York NY 10021-0961 Office: 333 E 79th St Apt 20-Y New York NY 10021-0961

JOHNSON, CLAUDIA ANDERSON, psychologist; b. Duluth, Minn., June 15, 1940; d. Carl Engwald and Irma Rose (Seymour) Anderson; m. Loyd D. Andrew, Apr. 1975 (div. 1985); children: Jean Marie, Julie Ann. BA summa cum laude, U. Minn., 1968; MA, U. Utah, 1971, PhD, 1974. Surveyor Joint Commn. on Accreditation of Hosps. Orgn., Chgo., 1978-80; pvt. practice Roanoke, Va., 1981-91, Richmond, Va., 1991-97, Woodbridge, Va., 1997—; quality assurance coord. VA Med. Ctr., Salem, Va., 1980-85; asst. prof. Med. Coll. Va., 1992—. Mem. Inter Regional Soc. Jungian Analysts (candidate 1991—, candidate rep. 1996-97). Avocations: reading, gardening, writing, fishing.

JOHNSON, CLIFFORD VINCENT, college administrator; b. New Orleans, Nov. 15, 1936; s. William James and Floy (Wade) J.; m. Margaret Klavins, Feb. 5, 1960; children: William, Stephen, Lisa, Mara. BA, Dillard U., 1957; MAT, Harvard U., 1970. Rsch. asst. U. Ill., Chgo., 1958-59, Childrens Hosp.-U. Chgo., 1959-61; biochemistry researcher Université de Paris, 1962-68; dir. spl. tutorial program Tufts U., Medford, Mass., 1969-70; sr. program assoc. Inst. for Svcs. to Edn., Washington, 1970-76, dir. curriculum and faculty devel., 1976-79; spl. asst. to the pres. Clark Coll., Atlanta, 1982-83; exec. dir. I've Known Rivers, Inc., New Orleans, 1983-84; v.p. for devel. Dillard U., New Orleans, 1985-98; pres. Johnson Assocs., New Orleans, 1998—; dir. devel. Amistad Rsch. Ctr. Tulane U., New Orleans, 1998—; cons. Nat. Adv. Coun. on the Edn. of Blacks in Am., 1980, Media Assocs., Inc., Washington, 1979-81, Bronx (N.Y.) Community Coll., 1979-80, NEH, Washington, 1981-85. Contbg. author: Best Short Stories by Black Writers, 1967; exec. producer (documentary film) New Orleans Concerto, 1978; prodn. supr. (documentary film) In Search of Improvisation, 1983. Bd. dirs. Arts Media Svcs., Inc., Washington, 1981-83, New Orleans Mus. Art, 1990-96, Odyssey House, La., 1999—; mem. adv. coun. New Orleans Jazz and Heritage Festival Found., 1990-99; mem . cmty. adv. bd. WWOZ-FM; mem. La. State Police Commn., 1991-94. Recipient Creative Program award Nat. Univ. Extension Assn., 1973, Spl. Appreciation award S.C. State U., 1976; Martin Luther King Jr. fellow Harvard U., 1968. Mem Nat. Soc. Fund Raising Execs. (v.p. La. chpt. 1988-91, Outstanding Fund Raiser of Yr. award 1992, bd. dirs., found. bd. dirs. 1993—). Avocations: jazz collecting, travel. Home: 5511 St Roch Ave New Orleans LA 70122-5252 Office: Tulane U Amistad Rsch Ctr Tilton Hall New Orleans LA 70118-5698

JOHNSON, CONOR DEANE, mechanical engineer; b. Charlottesville, Va., Apr. 20, 1943; s. Randolph Holaday and Louise Anna (Deane) J.; m. Laura Teague Rogers, Dec. 20, 1966; children: William Drake, Catherine Teague. BS in Engring. Mechanics, Va. Poly. Inst., 1965; MS, Clemson U., 1967, PhD in Engring. Mechanics, 1969. Registered profl. engr., Calif. With Anamet Labs., Inc., 1973-82; sr. structural analyst Anamet Labs., Inc., Dayton, Ohio, 1973-75; prin. engr. Anamet Labs., Inc., San Carlos, Calif., 1975-81, v.p., 1981-82; program mgr. Aerospace Structures Info. and Analysis Ctr., 1975-82; co-founder, pres. CSA Engring., Inc., Palo Alto, 1982—; tech. dir. damping conf., exec. com. N.Am. Conf. on Smart Materials and Structures. Contbr. articles to profl. jours. Capt. USAF, 1969-73. Mem. AIAA (structural dynamics tech. com.), ASME (adaptive structures tech. com., structures and materials award 1981), N.Am. Smart Structures and Materials Conf. (mem. exec. com., tech. chmn. Damping confs. 1991, 93, 95, 96), Gourmet Cooking Club, Sigma Xi. Methodist. Home: 3408 Beresford Ave Belmont CA 94002-1210 Office: CSA Engring Inc 2565 Leghorn St Mountain View CA 94043

JOHNSON, CORWIN WAGGONER, law educator; b. Hamlet, Ind., Oct. 5, 1917; s. Lonnie Edmund and Nora Lee (Drake) J.; m. July 24, 1942; m. Evelyn Banks; children: Kent Edmund, Kirk Allan. B.A., U. Iowa, 1939, J.D., 1941; postgrad. (Sterling fellow), Yale U. Law Sch., 1941, 46. Bar: Iowa 1941, Calif. 1946, Tex. 1957. Spl. agt. FBI, Dept. Justice, 1942-46; instr. in law U. Iowa, 1946-47; asst. prof. law U. Tex., Austin, 1947-49; asso. prof. U. Tex., 1949-54, prof., 1954—. Co-author: Cases and Materials on Property, 7th rev. edit., 1996, Principles of Property, 3d rev. edit., 1989; contbr. articles to law revs. Mem. Austin Planning Commn., 1954-56. Mem. ABA, Tex. Bar Assn., Am. Law Inst., Order of Coif, Phi Beta Kappa. Democrat. Methodist. Home: 3425 Monte Vista Dr Austin TX 78731-5722 Office: U Tex Law Sch 727 E Dean Keeton St Austin TX 78705-3224

JOHNSON, CRAIG NORMAN, investment banker; b. Warren, Pa., Jan. 8, 1942; s. Norman Andrew and Edice (Rieder) J.; m. Sally Van Dusen, May 23, 1969; children: Maria Pepper, Anna Sergeant, Samantha Bennett. BS, U. Pa., 1963, MBA, 1968. Cert. mgmt. cons. Inst. Mgmt. Cons. Prin. William E. Hill & Co. Inc., N.Y.C., 1968-72; v.p. INA Properties, Phila., 1972-75; sr. prin. Hay Assocs., Phila., 1975-80; pres. Lavino Shipping Co., Phila., 1980-90; pres., dir. Maritrans Inc., Phila., 1990-93; mng. dir. Glenthorne Capital Inc., 1994—; bd. dirs. The Phila. Contributorship, Blair Corp., We Love Country. Mem. Com. of Seventy, Phila., 1975-97; bd. dirs. Acad. Natural Scis., Phila.; trustee Springside Sch., 1994-98; assoc. trustee U. Pa., 1990-96. Repubican. Episcopalian. Office: Glenthorne Capital Inc 1525 Locust St Philadelphia PA 19102-3732

JOHNSON, CRAIG THEODORE, portfolio manager; b. Chgo., Oct. 1, 1955; s. C. Theodore and Dorothy (Lind) J.; m. Dianne Lee Eggen, Oct. 12, 1985; children: Juliana, Kyle. BSBA, Drake U., 1977. Asst. mgr., asst. buyer Marshall Field & Co., Chgo., 1977-80; asst. mgr. Wickes Cos., Wheeling, Ill., 1980-82; salesman John Hancock, Des Plaines, Ill., 1982-83; portfolio mgr. Leonetti & Assocs., Inc., Buffalo Grove, Ill., 1983—. Mem. Nat. Assn. Investors, World Future Soc. Republican. Lutheran. Avocations: reading, sports, gardening, astronomy. Office: Leonetti & Assocs Inc 1130 W Lake Cook Rd Ste 300 Buffalo Grove IL 60089-1976

JOHNSON, CREIGHTON ERNEST, insurance company executive, retired; b. Thomasville, Ga., Dec. 8, 1925; s. William Daniel and Ida Rosa (Jarvis) H.; m. M. Lucille McWhirter, July 30, 1948; children: Judith, Nancy, Janice. BA, U. Miami, 1949. Chartered life underwriter. Life ins. agent So. Life & Health Ins. Co., Miami, Fla., 1949-54; dist. mgr. So. Life & Health Ins. Co., Mobile, Ala., 1954-60; dist. mgr. So. Life & Health Ins. Co., New Orleans, 1960-61, regional mgr., 1961-63; divsn. mgr. So. Life & Health Ins. Co., Birmingham, Ala., 1963-80; v.p. So. Life & Health Ins. Co., Birmingham, 1981-90; ret., 1990—. Mem. edn. com. docent coun. Birmingham Mus. Art, 1995—, docent chair, 1997-98. With USAF, 1944-46, 50-51. Mem. Birmingham Com. Fgn. Rels., Nat. Docent Symposium Coun. (ins. chmn. 1994—). Avocations: painting. Home: 3708 Country Club Dr Birmingham AL 35213-2816

JOHNSON, CRYSTAL MARIA, primary school educator; b. Franklin, Pa., July 21, 1952; d. Shaler Theodore and Marjourie Louise Johnson; m. Elie Rothenberg, Aug. 1979 (div. June 1989); 1 child, Aaron S. BA, U. Fla., 1975; MS, U. North Fla.; specialist, U. Fla. Cert. tchr., Fla. Thcr., title I lead Duval Sch. Bd., Jacksonville, Fla., 1975-82, primary specialist, 1982-88; adminstrv. tng. Duval County Sch., Jacksonville, Fla., 1989-91; tchr. Duval County Sch., Jacksonville, 1991-97, AASP tchr., 1997—. Vice chair Share Decision Making, Jacksonville, 1997-98; mem. School Improvement Team, Jacksonville, 1997-98; vol. Am. Cancer Soc., Heart Fund, Jacksonville, 1996-99. Mem. ASCD, Duval Tchrs. United, Sierra Club, Planned Parenthood, PC Users, Kappa Delta Pi. Democrat. Jewish. Avocations: writing, travel, needlework, home improvement. E-mail: jxcrystal@aol.com. Home: 7938 Naranja Dr W Jacksonville FL 32217 Office: duPont Middle Sch 2710 duPont Jacksonville FL 32217

JOHNSON, CURTIS LEE, publisher, editor, writer; b. Mpls., May 26, 1928; s. Hjalmar N. and Gladys (Goring) J.; m. Jo Ann Lekwa, June 30, 1950 (div. 1974); children: Mark Alan, Paula Catherine; m. Rochelle Miller Hickey, Jan. 11, 1975 (div. 1980); m. Betty Axelrod Fox, Aug. 28, 1982 (div. 1990); m. Necia Tesla Wakefield, Nov. 17, 1998. B.A., U. Iowa, 1951, M.A., 1952. Mag. and ency. editing and writing Chgo., 1953-60, textbook and ednl. editing and writing, 1960-66; editor, pub. December Press, 1962—, pres., 1985—; free-lance editing and writing, 1966-72, 78—; mng. editor Aldine Pub. Co., 1972-73; v.p. St. Clair Press, 1973-77; sr. writer Bradford Exchange, 1978-81; mng. editor Regnery Gateway, 1981-82. Author: (with George Uskali) How to Restore Antique and Classic Cars, 1954; novels Hobbledehoy's Hero, 1959, Nobody's Perfect, 1973, Lace and a Bobbitt, 1976, The Morning Light, 1977, Song for Three Voices, 1984; The Mafia Manager, 1991, (with R. Craig Sautter) Wicked City Chicago, 1994, Thanksgiving in Vegas, 1995, 500 Years of Obscene...and Counting, 1997; editor: (with Jarvis Thurston) Stories from the Literary Magazines, 1970, Best Little Magazine Fiction, 1970, (with Alvin Greenberg), 1971, (with Jack Conroy) Writers in Revolt, 1973, (with Diane Kruchkow) Green Isle in the Sea, 1986, Who's Who in Writers, Editors & Poets, 1985-97; essays The Forbidden Writings of Lee Wallek, 1978; also fiction, articles; cons. editor: Panache mag, 1967-76. Served with USN, 1946-48. Nat. Endowment Arts writing grantee, 1973, 81. Mem. Nat. Writers Union, Phi Beta Kappa, Phi Eta Sigma. Office: December Press PO Box 302 Highland Park IL 60035-0302

JOHNSON, CURTIS SCOTT, engineer; b. Faribault, Minn., Aug. 15, 1954; s. Robert Alfred and Alice Lucille (Backstrom) J.; m. Elaine Marlys Fitzner, Dec. 4, 1976; children: Erik, Scott. BSEE, Iowa State U., 1976. Registered profl. engr., Iowa. Engr. in tng. Iowa So. Utilities, Centerville, Iowa, 1976-78; distbn. engr. Cedar Falls (Iowa) Utilites, 1978-81, asst. mgr. engring., 1981-89, mgr. dept. engring., 1989-98; pres. C.S. Johnson & Associates, P.C., Cedar Falls, 1998—. Asst. cubmaster Cub Scout Pack 179, Cedar Falls, 1990-92, cubmaster, 1992-94, chmn., 1994-96; bd. govs. Iowa Maths. Coalition, Des Moines, 1991-95. Mem. NSPE (v.p. Iowa chpt. 1989-95, pres. 1995-96, John Dunlap-Sherman Woodward award 1987), IEEE, Cedar Falls C. of C. (bd. dirs. 1995-98). Republican. Lutheran. Avocations: golf, camping, fishing. Home: 3036 Pheasant Dr Cedar Falls IA 50613-1684 Office: CS Johnson and Assocs PC 3036 Pheasant Dr Cedar Falls IA 50613-1684

JOHNSON, CYRUS EDWIN, grain farmer, former food products executive; b. Alton, Ill., Feb. 18, 1929; s. Cyrus L. and Jennie C. (Keen) J.; m. Charlotte E. Johnson; children: Judie M., Renee B. B.S., U. Ill., 1956, M.A., 1959. Dist. traffic mgr. Ill. Bell Telephone Co., Chgo., 1970-71, dist. comml. mgr., 1971-73; v.p. social action Gen. Mills, Inc., Mpls., 1973-78, v.p. dir. corp. personnel, 1978-80, v.p. human resource environment, 1980-81, v.p., dir. facilities and services, 1981-91; grain farmer Alton, Ill., 1977-91; dir. Ault, Inc., Mpls., Life-Span, Inc., Mpls. 1982-88. Bd. dirs. United Way Mpls. Area, 1975-86; active Nat. YMCA, 1973-79; mem. citizens adv. com. Mpls. Tech. Inst., 1981-84; mem. deans adv. council Coll. Bus., U. Ill., Chgo., 1981-84; past pres. Harvard U. Bus. Sch. Assn., Boston, 1978-79; mem. adv. coun. div. bus. Bethune-Cookman Coll.; bd. dirs. Greater Mpls. area Girl Scouts U.S., 1983-90, nat. bd. dirs., 1990—; bd. dirs. W.Va. State Coll. Found., 1989-91. Served with U.S. Army, 1950-52. Recipient Old Masters Program award Purdue U., 1975; recipient Chgo. Defender Roundtable of Commerce award, 1963. Baptist. Lodges: Rotary; Masons.

JOHNSON, DANIEL M., provost; b. Springfield, Ohio, June 10, 1940; m. Elaine Clark Johnson; children: Brent, Darin. BA, Tex. Christian U., 1963, MA, 1965; PhD, U. Mo., 1973. Instr. dept. sociology Blackburn Coll., Carlinville, Ill., 1965-67, chmn. dept. sociology, chmn. divsn. social scis., 1970-73; instr. dept. sociology Christian Coll., Columbia, Mo., 1967-69; asst. prof. sociology, dir. sociology honors program Wichita (Kans.) State U., 1969-70; assoc. prof. sociology and pub. affairs Sangamon State U., Springfield, Ill., 1973-78, dir. Ctr. for Study and Pub. Affairs, 1975-79, prof. sociology and pub. affairs, 1978-79; assoc. prof. sociology, co-dir. Va. Commonwealth U., Richmond, 1979-80, chmn. dept. sociology and anthropology, 1980-83, prof. sociology, 1980-91, interim assoc. dean Coll. of Humanities and Scis., 1987-88; dean Sch. of Cmty. Svc., prof. sociology U. North Tex., Denton, 1991-97; provost U. of Alaska, Anchorage, 1997—; vis. asst. prof. sociology Lincoln U., Jefferson City, Mo., 1968, 69, 70; founder, dir. Survey Rsch. Lab., Va. Commonwealth U., Richmond, 1983-88; spkr. in field.; cons. in field. Author: (with others) Metropolitan Universities: An Emerging Model in Higher Education, 1995, Black Migration in America: A Social Demographic History, 1981, The Middle Size Cities of Illinois: Their People, Politics and Quality of Life, 1980, Churches in Transitional Neighborhoods: Options for Local Congregations, 1992, Cities and Sickness: Health Care in Urban America, 1983; contbr. numerous articles to profl. jours. Fellowship NSF, 1971; recipient numerous grants. Mem. Met. Univs. Coalition, Coun. for the Arts and Scis. in Urban Univs., Am. Sociol. Assn., Population Assn. of Am., Phi Kappa Phi. Home: 7321 East Chester Heights Anchorage AK 99504 office: U Alaska Anchorage Office Acad Affairs 3211 Providence Dr Anchorage AK 99508-8054

JOHNSON, DAVE, Olympic athlete, track and field. Olympic track and field participant Barcelona, Spain, 1992. Recipient Decathlon Bronze medal Olympics, Barcelona, 1992. Office: US Track & Field 1 Rca Dome Ste 140 Indianapolis IN 46225-1023*

JOHNSON, DAVEY (DAVID ALLEN JOHNSON), baseball team manager; b. Orlando, Fla., Jan. 30, 1943; children: Dave Jr., Dawn, Andrea. Student, Johns Hopkins U.; B.S., Trinity U. Baseball player Balt. Orioles, 1965-72; baseball player Atlanta Braves, 1973-75, Phila. Phillies, 1977-78, Chgo. Cubs, 1978; mgr. Inter-Am. League, Miami, 1979, Jackson League, Tex., 1981, Tidewater, Internat. League, 1983, N.Y. Mets, N.Y.C., 1984-90, Cin. Reds, 1993-96, Balt. Orioles, 1996-97, L.A. Dodgers, 1999—. Recipient Am. Gold Glove, 1969-71; mem. Am. League All-Star Team, 1968, 70, Nat. League All-Star Team, 1973; mgr. Nat. League All-Star Team, 1986, World Series championship team, 1986. Co-holder single season record most home runs by second baseman (42), 1973. Office: Los Angeles Dodgers 1000 Elysian Park Ave Los Angeles CA 90012-1199

JOHNSON, DAVID, medical administrator. Dir. divsn. oncology, hematology Vanderbilt Clinic, Nashville. Office: Vanderbilt Clinic 1956 Vanderbilt Divsn Hematology/Oncology Nashville TN 37232-5536*

JOHNSON, DAVID BLACKWELL, safety engineer; b. Annapolis, Md., June 16, 1954; s. Charles McCoy and Jane (Ingling) J.; m. Jacalyn Benjamin, Aug. 7, 1976; children: Sarah Ingling, Jeffrey Blackwell, Kevin Berington. BA, Drew U., 1976; postgrad., NYU, 1976-78. Cert. safety profl. Am. Bd. Cert. Safety Profls. Rsch. assoc. NYU Med. Ctr., 1978-79; safety engr., indsl. hygienist Burroughs Corp., Plainfield, N.J., 1979-80; mgr. safety and indsl. hygiene Unisys Corp., Plainfield, 1980-81; corp. supr. hazardous materials Revlon, Inc., Edison, N.J., 1981-82; mgr. safety and health Revlon, Inc., 1982-84; mgr. indsl. hygiene and safety Celanese Engring. Resins, Inc., Chatham, N.J., 1984-87; corp. dir. environ., health and safety affairs Hoechst Celanese Corp., Somerville, N.J., 1987-96; v.p. environ., health and safety affairs Givaudan-Roure Corp., Clifton, N.J., 1996—; bd. dirs., Celanese Emergency Brigade Tng. Ctr., Rock Hill, S.C., 1987—. Adviser safety com. City of Summit, N.J., 1985; pres. Summit Regional Bd. Health. Mem. Am. Indsl. Hygiene Assn. (treas. N.J. sect. 1984-85), Am. Soc. Safety Engrs., Nat. Safety Mgmt. Assn., Am. Pub. Health Assn., Kiwanis. Episcopalian. Avocations: baseball, fishing, golf. Home: 25 Waldron Ave Summit NJ 07901-2805 Office: Givaudan-Roure Corp 155 Passaic Ave Fairfield NJ 07004

JOHNSON, DAVID KENNETH, historian; b. Keene, N.H., Dec. 31, 1960; s. Kenneth R. and Julia (Lewis) J. BA, Georgetown U., 1983; MA, U. Chgo., 1987; PhD candidate, Northwestern U., 1992—. Historian History Assocs. Inc., Rockville, Md., 1988-92; fellow history dept. Northwestern U., Evanston, Ill., 1992-96, adj. lectr., fellow history dept., 1997—; fellow Smithsonian Instn., Washington, 1996-97. Author: (with others) Creating a Place for Ourselves, 1997, Leaders From the 1960s, 1994; contbr. articles to profl. jours. Pres. Northwestern U. Gay & Lesbian Univ. Union, 1995-96. Fellow Smithsonian Instn., 1996-97; Dissertation Year fellow Northwestern U., 1997-98. Mem. Orgn. Am. Historians, Am. Hist. Assn. Office: Northwestern Univ Dept Hist Harris Hall 202 Evanston IL 60208

JOHNSON, DAVID LYNN, materials scientist, educator; b. Provo, Utah, Apr. 2, 1934; s. David Elmer and Lucile (Maughan) J.; m. Rolla LaRae Page, June 26, 1959; children: Jeannette, David Page, Brice Aaron, Jeffrey Lynn, Karyn Rae. B.S., U. Utah, 1956, Ph.D., 1962. Mem. faculty dept. materials sci. and engring. Northwestern U., Evanston, Ill., 1962—; prof. Northwestern U., 1971—, chmn. dept. materials scis. and engring., 1982-87, Walter D. Murphy Disting. prof., 1987—; cons. in field. Contbr. articles to profl. jours. NSF grantee, 1971-77, 79—. Fellow Am. Ceramic Soc. (chmn. basic sci. div. 1978-79, trustee 1980-81, 1990-93); mem. AAAS, Acad. Ceramics (charter), Metall. Soc., Materials Research Soc., Internat. Inst. for Sci. of Sintering, Am. Powder Metallurgy Inst., Sigma Xi, Alpha Sigma Mu, Phi Eta Sigma, Phi Kappa Phi, Tau Beta Pi. Mem. LDS Ch. Achievements include demonstration of ultra-rapid sintering of ceramics in high temperature gas plasmas; development of advanced sintering models. Office: Northwestern U Dept Materials Sci/Engring 2225 N Campus Dr Evanston IL 60208-3108 *The pursuit of truth engenders the excitement of discovery, but living, working, growing and being with one's fair wife, children and grandchildren reflect the joys of the eternities, for herein can be found the true meaning of life.*

JOHNSON, DAVID PORTER, infectious diseases physician; b. Cin., Oct. 21, 1939; s. Frederic William and Frances MacNeil Johnson; m. Caryle Anne Richardson, Oct. 26, 1985; children: Laurel, Andrew, Daniel, Gabriela. BA, Yale U., 1960, MD, 1964. Mem. faculty Sch. Medicine Yale U., New Haven, 1970-71; pvt. practice Middletown, Conn., 1971-91; chief infectious disease sect. VA Med. Ctr., Bay Pines, Fla., 1991—; mem. faculty Yale U., 1970-78, U. Conn., Hartford, 1978-91, U. South Fla., Tampa, 1991—. Contbr. articles to profl. publs. Lt. comdr. USNR, 1968-70. Peter Parker fellow Yale U., 1963. Fellow ACP; mem. Am. Soc. Microbiology, Am. Assn. History of Medicine, Infectious Disease Soc. Am. Republican. Roman Catholic. Office: Dept Vet Affairs Med Ctr 10,000 Bay Pines Blvd Bay Pines FL 33504*

JOHNSON, DAVID RAYMOND, lawyer; b. Bartlesville, Okla., Sept. 12, 1946; s. Lloyd Theodore and Mary Pauline (Auten) J.; m. Marion Frances Monroe, May 14, 1977; children: Marc, Meredith. BA, Tulane U., 1968; JD, U. Va., 1971. Bar: Tex. 1971, D.C. 1977, U.S. Dist. Ct. D.C. 1979, U.S. Ct. Appeals (D.C. cir.) 1981, U.S. Supreme Ct. 1982, U.S. Claims Ct. 1984. Assoc. Fulbright & Jaworski, Houston, 1971-72; assoc. Fulbright & Jaworski, Washington, 1974-78, ptnr., 1978-87; atty.-advisor Office of Gen. Counsel of Air Force, Washington, 1972-74; ptnr. Gibson, Dunn & Crutcher, LLP, Washington, 1987—. Trustee Washington Episcopal Sch., 1991-93, McLean Sch. Md., 1994-96. Capt. USAF, 1972-74. Mem. D.C. Bar Assn., Phi Beta Kappa, Raven Soc., Order of Coif, Congresional Country Club. Office: Gibson Dunn & Crutcher LLP 1050 Connecticut Ave NW Ste 900 Washington DC 20036-5306

JOHNSON, DAVID SELLIE, civil engineer; b. Mpls., Apr. 10, 1935; s. Milton Edward and Helen M. (Sellie) J. BS, Mont. Coll. Mineral Sci. Tech., 1958. Registered profl. engr., Mont. Trainee Mont. Dept. Hwys., Helena, 1958-59, designer, 1959-66, asst. preconstrn. engr., 1966-68, regional engr., 1968-72, engring. specialities supr., 1972-89, preconstrn. chief, 1989-93, forensic engr., 1965—, traffic accident reconstructionist, 1978—; dir. mktg. Sverdrup Civil, Inc., Helena, 1994—; consulting engr., 1985—. Contbr. articles on hwy. safety to profl. jours. Adv. bd. mem. Helena Vocat.-Tech. Edn., 1972-73. Fellow Inst. Transp. Engrs. (expert witness coun.); mem. NSPE, Nat. Acad. Forensic Engrs. (diplomate), Mont. Soc. Profl. Engrs., Transp. Rsch. Bd. (geometric design com., tort liability com.), Wash. Assn. Tech. Accident Investigators, Corvette Club, Treasure State Club (pres. Helena 1972-78, sec. 1979-82), Shriners. Avocations: photography, sports car racing. Home and Office: 1921 E 6th Ave Helena MT 59601-4766

JOHNSON, DAVID SIMONDS, meteorologist; b. Porterville, Calif., June 29, 1924; s. Frank David and Wanda (Simonds) J.; m. Margaret T. McFarland, Nov. 29, 1974 (dec. Dec. 1987). Student, U. Calif.-Berkeley, 1942-43, Reed Coll., 1943-44, Harvard U., 1945, AB, UCLA, 1948, MA, 1949. Meteorol. aide U.S. Weather Bur., Boise, Idaho, 1946-47; rsch. asst. to asst. meteorologist UCLA, 1947-52; assoc. meteorologist Pineapple Rsch. Inst., Honolulu, 1952-56; with U.S. Weather Bur., 1956-65, dir. Nat. Weather Satellite Ctr., 1964-65; dir. Nat. Environ. Satellite Ctr. Environ. Sci. Svcs. Adminstrn., Washington, 1965-70, Nat. Environ. Satellite Svc. NOAA, 1970-80; asst. adminstr. for satellites NOAA, 1980-82; spl. asst. to pres. Univ.

Corp. for Atmospheric Rsch., Washington, 1982-83, also cons.; pres. Damar Internat., 1984-86; sr. program officer NAS-NRC, 1986-94; ret., 1994; mem. working group II com. space rsch. Internat. Coun. Sci. Unions, 1965-69; chmn. panel neutral atmosphere, 1966-69; mem. working group VI com. space rsch., 1965-78; mem. panel edn. and manpower com. atmospheric scis. NAS, 1967-69, com. for study of nation's weather observation system, 1986-87; mem. Gov. Md. Sci. Resources adv. bd., 1963-67; exec. com. panel on satellites World Meterol. Orgn., 1973-82, cons. to sec.-gen., 1982-86. Co-author: Studies of the Structure of the Atmosphere over the Eastern Pacific Ocean in Summer, 1961. With USAAF, 1943-46. Recipient Gold medal Dept. Commerce, 1965, Satellite Silver medal, 1985, Exceptional Svc. award NASA, 1966, award Nat. Civil Svc. League, 1974, William T. Pecora award, 1978, Presdl. Meritorious Svcs. award, 1980, recognition award Space Tech. Hall of Fame, 1992. Fellow AIAA (assoc.), Am. Meterol. Soc. (pres. 1974, councilor 1963-65, 68-70, 73-76, 81-83, exec. com. 1969-70, 73-75, 81-83, planning commn. 1989-93, ad hoc com. on chpts. 1993-96, chmn. com. atmospheric measurements 1965-68, com. on AMS programs in support of sci. and edn. 1995—, Brooks award 1982), Am. Geophys. Union, Am. Astronautical Soc. (bd. dirs. 1988-93, exec. com. 1988-93, nominating and fellows coms. 1990, Achievement award 1982, Lovelace award 1992); mem. AAAS, Internat. Acad. Astronautics, Cosmos Club, Sigma Xi. Mem. United Ch. of Christ. Home: 1133 Lake Heron Dr Apt 3A Annapolis MD 21403-3566

JOHNSON, DAVID W. (DAVE), hotel facility executive; b. Decatur, Ga., May 20, 1961. BA, Northea. Ill. U., MA. Corp. dir. sales and mktg. Wyndham Hotel and Resorts, 1987-89; hotel mgr. Wyndham Harbour Island, 1989-90; gen. mgr. Wyndham Garden Hotel, Bloomington, 1990-92; regional v.p. ops. Midwest Wyndham Garden Hotels, 1992-94, v.p. ops. Ea. U.S., 1994-95, sr. v.p., 1995-97; pres. Wyndham Garden Hotels and Wyndham Grand Heritage Hotels, Dallas, 1997—. Address: Grand Heritage Hotels Internat 1950 Stemmons Fwy Ste 6001 Dallas TX 75207

JOHNSON, DAVID WILFRED, JR., ceramic scientist, researcher; b. Windber, Pa., Sept. 23, 1942; s. David W. Sr. and Vanessa J. (Shoff) J.; m. Bonnie Kay Respet, June 20, 1964; children: Analee J., Bradley D. BS in Ceramic Sci., Pa. State U., 1964, PhD in Ceramic Sci., 1968. Tech. staff Bell Telephone Labs., Murray Hill, N.J., 1968-83; supr. advanced ceramic processing AT&T Bell Labs., Murray Hill, N.J., 1983-88; head metallurgy and ceramics rsch. dept. Bell Labs Lucent Techs., Murray Hill, N.J., 1988—; adj. prof. Stevens Inst. Tech., Hoboken, N.J., 1982—, Nat. Acad. Engring., 1993; Taylor lectr. Pa. State U., University Park, 1989. Contbr. over 125 articles to profl. jours. Chmn. Bedminster (N.J.) Twp. Zoning Bd. of Adjustment, 1991-92, 96—. Fellow Am. Ceramic Soc. (v.p. 1990-92, treas. 1992, pres. 1994, Ross Coffin Purdy award 1978, Fulrath award 1984, John Jeppson award 1998), Am. Soc. Materials; mem. AAAS, NAE, Materials Rsch. Soc., Acad. Ceramics. Achievements include over 30 patents for ceramic processing; research in ceramic powder processing as applied to ferrites, ceramic substrates, sol-gel silica glass and high temperature superconductors. Office: Bell Labs 700 Mountain Ave Rm 1f-206 New Providence NJ 07974-1208

JOHNSON, DAVID WILLIS, food products executive; b. Tumut, New South Wales, Australia, Aug. 7, 1932; came to U.S., 1976; s. Alfred Ernest and Eileen Melba (Burt) J.; m. Sylvia Raymonde Wells, Mar. 12, 1966; children: David Ashley Lawrence, Justin Christopher Kendall, Harley Alistair Kent. B in Econs., U. Sydney, Australia, 1954, diploma in Edn., 1955; MBA, U. Chgo., 1958. Exec. trainee Ford Motor Co., Geelong, Australia; mgmt. trainee Colgate-Palmolive, Sydney, 1959-60, product mgr., 1961, asst. to mng. dir., 1962, brands mgr., 1963, gen. products mgr., 1964-65; asst. gen. mgr., mktg. dir. Colgate-Palmolive, Johannesburg, Republic of South Africa, 1966, chmn., mng. dir., 1967-72; pres. Warner-Lambert/Parke Davis Asia, Hong Kong, 1973-76; pres. personal products div. Warner-Lambert Co., Morris Plains, N.J., 1977, pres. Am. Chicle Div., 1978; exec. v.p., gen mgr. Entenmann's div. Warner-Lambert Co., Bay Shore, N.Y., 1979; pres. specialty foods group Warner-Lambert Co., Morris Plains, 1980-81, v.p., 1980-82; pres., CEO Entenmann's div. Warner-Lambert Co., Bay Shore, 1982; v.p. Gen. Foods Corp., White Plains, N.Y., 1982-87; exec. officer Entemann's, Inc., Bay Shore, 1982-87; chmn., pres., CEO Gerber Products Co., Fremont, Mich., 1987-89, chmn., CEO, 1989-90; pres., CEO, dir. Campbell Soup Co., Camden, N.J., 1990-97, chmn. bd., 1993—; bd. dirs. Colgate-Palmolive Co.; exec. adv. bd. Donaldson, Lufkin & Jenrette Mcht. Banking Ptnrs.; mem. adv. coun. U.Notre Dame Coll. Bus. Adminstrn., U. Chgo. Grad. Sch. Bus. Recipient Disting. Alumnus award U. Chgo., 1992, Dir. of Yr.award Nat. Assn. Corp. Dirs., 1997. Mem. Am. Bakers Assn. (past bd. dirs.), Nat. Food Products Assn. (past bd. dirs.), Grocery Mfrs. Am. (past bd. dirs.). Office: Campbell Soup Co World Hdqrs Campbell Pl Camden NJ 08103*

JOHNSON, DAVID WOLCOTT, psychologist, educator; b. Muncie, Ind., Feb. 7, 1940; s. Roger Winfield and Frances Elizabeth (Pierce) J.; m. Linda Mulholland, July 7, 1973; children: James, David, Catherine, Margaret, Jeremiah. BS, Ball State U., 1962; MA, Columbia U., 1964, EdD, 1966. Asst. prof. ednl. psychology U. Minn., Mpls., 1966-69, assoc. prof., 1969-73, prof., 1973—, Emma Birkmaier prof. in ednl. leadership, 1994—; orgnl. cons., psychotherapist. Author: Social Psychology of Education, 1970, (with Goodwin Watson) Social Psychology: Issues and Insights, 1972, Reaching Out, 1972, 6th edit., 1997, Contemporary Social Psychology, 1973, (with F. Johnson) Joining Together, 1975, 6th edit., 1997, (with D. Tjosvold) Porductive Conflict Management, 1983, Circles of Learning, 1984, 4th edit., 1993, (with R. Johnson) Learning Together and Alone, 1975, 5th edit., 1998, Human Relations and Your Career, 1978, 3d Edit., 1991, Educational Psychology, 1979, Cooperative Learning, 1984, 7th edit., 1998, Structuring Cooperative Learning, 1987, Creative Conflict, 1987, Leading the Cooperative School, 1989, 2d edit., 1994, Cooperation and Competition: Theory and Research, 1989, Teaching Students to be Peacemakers, 1991, 3d edit., 1995, also film, 1991, Active Learning: Cooperative Learning in the College Classroom, 1991, Learning Mathematics and Cooperative Learning, 1991, Creative Controlversy, 1992, 3d edit., 1995, (with R. Johnson, E. Holubec) Advanced Cooperative Learning, 1988, 3d edit., 1998, (with R. Johnson, K. Smith) Cooperative Learning: Increasing College Faculty Instructional Productivity, 1991, Academic Controversy, 1997, Cooperation in the Classroom, 1984, 7th edit., 1998, Positive Interdependence, 1992, (video) 1992, (with R. Johnson and E. Holubel) The Nuts and Bolts of Cooperative Learning, 1994, (with R. Johnson) Meaningful and Manageable Assessment Through Cooperative Learning, 1996, (with R. Johnson) Learning to Lead Teams, 1997, Human Relations: Valuing Diversity, 1999; editor Am. Ednl. Rsch. Jour., 1981-83; contbr. over 350 articles to profl. jours. Bd. dirs. Walk-In Counseling Ctr., 1971-74. Recipient Gordon Allport award Soc. for Psychol. Study of Social Issues, 1981, Helen Plante award Am. Soc. Engring. Edn., 1984, Outstanding Rsch. award Am. Pers. and Guidance Assn., 1972, Nat. Coun.l for the Social Studies Rsch. award, 1986, Outstanding Rsch. award Am. Assn. Counseling and Devel., 1988, award for Outstanding Contbn. Am. Edn. Minn. Assn. for Supervision and Curriculum Devel., 1990, Outstanding Alumni of Yr. award Ball State U., 1990, Rsch. and Practice award S.W. Ohio Planning Coun. for Insvc. Edn., 1990, Excellence in Tchg. award Dept. Def. Schs., Panama, 1994, Emma Birkmaier Prof. in Ednl. Leadership Coll. Edn. U. Minn., 1994-97. Fellow Am. Psychol. Assn.; mem. Am. Sociol. Assn., Am. Ednl. Rsch. Assn. (award for Outstanding Contbn. to Coop. Learning 1996), Am. Mgmt. Assn., Am. Assn. for Counseling and Devel., Nat. Rsch. Coun. Home: 7208 Cornelia Dr Minneapolis MN 55435-4160 Office: U Minn 330 Burton Hall Minneapolis MN 55455 *Success is a combination of focus, perseverance, and pain-endurance.*

JOHNSON, DEAN LALANDER, mayor; b. Norwalk, Ohio, Mar. 28, 1943; s. Verner LaLander and Marianne Virginia (Halvorson) J.; m. Sally Ann Mayer, June 14, 1969; children: Kevin L., Eric A., Stuart R. BA, Wash. State U., 1965. Economist FMC, Washington, 1965; transport economist CAB, Washington, 1968-84; transp. specialist U.S. Dept. Transp., Washington, 1985-97; city coun. City of Annapolis, Md., 1989-97; mayor City of Annapolis, 1997—. Pres., v.p. Colonial Players Theater, 1974-83 (bd. dirs.), Ann Arurdel County Trst, 1975—, Adm. Heights Imp. Assn. 1982-87. Capt. U.S. Army, 1965-70. Republican. Presbyterian. Home: 480 Schley Rd Annapolis MD 21401-2261 Office: City of Annapolis 160 Duke Of Gloucester St Annapolis MD 21401-2517

JOHNSON, DEBORAH CROSLAND WRIGHT, mathematics educator; b. Winston-Salem, N.C., July 17, 1951; d. Clayton Edward and Elizabeth Elliott (Bradley) Crosland; married; children: Jacqueline, Stephanie. BS in Math. Edn. magna cum laude, Appalachian State U., 1973; MEd in Math., U. N.C., Greensboro, 1976, cert., 1984. Cert. tchr., N.C., academically gifted. Tchr. math. Mt. Tabor H.S., Winston-Salem, 1973-76, McDowell H.S., Marion, N.C., 1976-78, Ctrl. Cabarrus H.S., Concord, N.C., 1978-81, Walter M. Williams H.S., Burlington, N.C., 1981—; mem. sch. improvement team Walter M. Williams H.S., 1989-92. Active First Presbyn. Ch., Burlington, 1988—. Mem. NEA, N.C. Assn. Educators, Nat. Coun. Tchrs. Math., N.C. Coun. Tchrs. Math., N.C. Assn. Gifted and Talented, Alpha Delta Kappa (hon. tchrs. sorority). Democrat.

JOHNSON, DEBORAH VALERIE GERMAINE, parish administrator; b. Bakersfield, Ca., Jan. 16, 1957; d. Joseph Harvey and Fern (Stoker) J.; m. Robert Arthur Richmond, Jr., Oct. 2, 1982; children: Abelard, Neville, Bane. BA, U. Calif., Davis, 1979; MA, Sch. for Internat. Tng., Brattleboro, Vt., 1981; PhD, Loyola U., L.A., 1988. Life cert. Master Catechist, Calif. Conf. Cath. Bishops; life credential Adult Edn. Philos. and Theology, Calif. Legis. analyst 94th Congress, Washington, 1976-78; adult edn. analyst Orgn. Am. States, Washington, 1979-80; adult edn. dir. Diocese of Fresno, Bakersfield, Calif., 1988-91; lit. and philos. prof. Cerro Coso Coll., Kern Valley, Calif., 1989-98; philos. prof. Porterville (Calif.) Coll., 1997-98; parish adminstr. St. Joseph's Ch., Bakersfield, Calif., 1997—; master prof. U. Phoenix, Bakersfield, Calif., 1996—; reconnaissance adv. Buzirnan Acad., Bakersfield, Calfi., 1992—; fibonacci forcaster Furman, Jameson & Rumpole, Dover, 1993—; devel. analyst Nayler and Naylor, Mt. Eldora, Calif., 1997—; sr. assoc. Togrone Excursians, Bakersfield, Calif., 1998—. Author: Volcan, 1989, Freirean Andragogy, 1991, Wittgenstein, 1993, General Systems Theory, 1994. Mem. Audubon Soc., Bakersfield, Calif., 1994—, Sequoia Forest Alliance, Kernville, Calif., 1994—, Internat. Human Rights Campaign, N.Y.C., 1995—; lay assoc. Sisters of Mercy, Burlingame, Calif., 1988—. Named Tchr. of Yr. Cerro Coso Coll., Kern Valley, Calif., 1990, Kern C.C., Bakersfield, Calif., 1992; recipient Prof. Achievement award Hoyden Found. Mt. Eldora, Calif., 1995, Innovation in Andragogy award Synesthetic Soc., Bakersfield, Calif., 1998. Mem. AAUP, APA, Asakawa Assn. Calif., Johnson Garry Partnership Ltd., Internat. Herge Ecolier, Mt. Eldora Decartes Excursions. Roman Catholic. Avocations: cricket, arboreal architectonics, fractal snergy, hagiography, gastronomy. Office: St Joseph's Church 1515 Baker St Bakersfield CA 93305

JOHNSON, D'ELAINE ANN HERARD, artist; b. Puyallup, Wash., Mar. 19, 1932; d. Thomas Napoleon and Rosella Edna (Berry) Herard; m. John Lafayette Johnson, Dec. 22, 1956. BFA, Ctrl. Wash. U., 1954; MFA, U. Wash., 1958, postgrad., 1975—; postgrad. U. London, 1975—. Instr. art Seattle Pub. Schs., 1954-78, instr. art workshops, 1960-70; instr. Mus. History and Industry, Seattle, 1954-56; art dir., instr. Martha Washington Sch. for Girls, Seattle, 1955-58; dir. Mt. Olympus Estate, Edmonds, Wash., 1971; cons. art groups, Wash. State, 1954—; lectr. Ctrl. Wash. State U., Seattle PTA, Creative Arts Assn., Everett, Everett C.C., Women's Caucus for Art, Seattle, Llubs Art Gallery d'Elaine, Edmonds, Wash., 1957-62, numerous others; pvt. art instr., Seattle, 1960-68; served as art juror for numerous shows. Founder Mt. Olympus Preserve for Arts, Edmonds, Wash., 1971, sponsor art events, 1971—; active Wash. Coalition Citizens with Disabilities; lectr. in field. Exhibited in group shows: Fry Art Mus., Seattle, 1964, Seattle Art Mus., 1959, Henry Art Gallery, Seattle, 1972, Vancouver Maritime Mus., B.C., Can., 1981, N.S. Art Mus., Can., 1971, Whatcom Mus., Bellingham, Wash., 1975, State Capitol Mus., Olympia, Wash., 1975, Corvallis State U., Oreg., 1982, Newport Mus., Oreg., Nat. Artist Equity, 1972, Belluvue Art Mus., Seattle, 1989, Rosicrusian Egyption Mus., San Jose, Calif., 1990, St. Mark's Cathedral, Seattkem 1991, Sidney Mus. and Arts Assn., Port Orchard, Wash., 1991, Bellvue Art Mus., 1992, Pacific Arts Ctr. Hauberg Gallery, Seattle, 1992, Bon Marche Gallery, Seattle, 1992, Northeast Trade and Exbn. Hall, 1993, Edmonds (Wash.) Art Mus., 1993, Ilwaco (Wash.) Heritage Mus., 1993, Robert Frey Gallery, Seattle, 1994, Northlight Gallery, Everett, 1995, Newmark Gallery, Seattle, 1995, Corvallis Art Ctr., Oreg., 1995, Maryhill Mus., Goldendale, Wash., 1996; 482 exhibits 1950—, over 1200 paintings through 1970; illustrator: The Bing Crosby Family Music Books for Children, 1961; TV art instr. TV-9 U. Wash., 1968. Elected to Wash. State Art Commn. Registry, Olympia, 1982; recipient numerous awards. Mem. Nat. Artist Equity, Internat. Soc. Artists, The Cousteau Soc., Am. Coun. for Arts, Nat. Women's Studies Assn., Assn. Am. Culture, Internat. Platform Assn., Nat. Pen Women Assn., Retired Tchrs.' Assn., Kappa Delta Pi, Kappa Pi. Avocations: scuba diving, camping, travel, violin, writing. Home and Office: 16122 72nd Ave W # D Edmonds WA 98026-4517

JOHNSON, DENISE REINKA, state supreme court justice; b. Wyandotte, Mich., July 13, 1947. Student, Mich. State U., 1965-67; BA, Wayne State U., 1969; postgrad., Cath. U. of Am., 1971-72; JD with honors, U. Conn., 1974. Bar: Conn. 1974, U.S. Dist. Ct. Conn. 1974, Vt. 1980, U.S. Ct. Appeals (2d cir.) 1983, U.S. Dist. Ct. Vt. 1986. Atty. New Haven (Conn.) Legal Assistance Assn., 1974-78; instr. legal writing Vt. Law Sch., South Royalton, 1978-79; clerk Blodgett & McCarren, Burlington, Vt., 1979-80; chief civil rights divsn. Atty. Gen.'s Office, State of Vt., 1980-82; chief pub. protection divsn. Atty. Gen.'s Office, Montpelier, Vt., 1982-88; pvt. practice Shrewsbury, Vt., 1988-90; assoc. justice Vt. Supreme Ct., Montpelier, 1990—. Chair Vt. Human Rights Commn., 1988-90. Mem. Am. Law Inst. Office: Vt Supreme Ct 109 State St Montpelier VT 05609-2700*

JOHNSON, DENNIS D., elementary school principal. Prin. Pine Tree Elem. Sch., Kent, Wash., 1986—. Recipient Elem. Sch. Recognition award U.S. Dept. Edn., 1989-90. Office: Pine Tree Elem Sch 27825 118th Ave SE Kent WA 98031-8778*

JOHNSON, DENNIS RAY, utility supply executive; b. Ft. Worth, Tex., Aug. 26, 1946; s. Ray W. and Joe Ann (Yeargan) J.; m. L.S. Longley Davis, July 14, 1964 (div. Oct. 1976); children: Dennis R. Jr., Bradley Todd. Diploma, Brantley Draughon Coll., Ft. Worth, 1969; cert., Tarrant County Jr. Coll., Ft. Worth, 1970. Pres. Atlas Utility Supply Co., Ft. Worth, 1967—; bd. dirs. Colleyville Econ. Devel. Corp., Mercantile Bank Ft. Worth. Mem. Am. Water Works Assn., Water and Sewer Distbrs. Am., Tex. Water Utilities Assn., The Distbn. Group (dir.), Masons. Lutheran. Avocations: golf, legends racing, skiing. Office: Atlas Utility Supply Co 2301 Carson St Fort Worth TX 76117-5212

JOHNSON, DEWEY, JR., biochemist; b. Sapulpa, Okla., Sept. 23, 1926; s. Dewey and Maude (Hickey) J.; m. Patricia R. Rodgers, Feb. 14, 1953; children: Joseph D., Paul D., Mary Ann, Richard E. BS, Colo. State U., 1950; MS, U. Conn., 1955; PhD, Rutgers State U., 1958. Nutritionist Limecrest Rsch. Lab., Newton, N.J., 1958-63; biochemist Equitable Life, N.Y.C., 1963-79; biochemist Met. Life, N.Y.C., 1980-90, disability underwriter, 1990-92; chemist EPA, Edison, N.J., 1993—. Contbr. rsch. articles to profl. jours. Avocations: gardening, woodworking. Home: 59 Dunnell Rd Maplewood NJ 07040-1333

JOHNSON, DEWEY E(DWARD), JR., dentist; b. Charleston, S.C., Mar. 19, 1935; s. Dewey Edward and Mabel (Momeier) J.; A.B. in Geology, U. N.C., 1957, D.D.S., 1961. Pvt. practice dentistry, Charleston, 1964-92, assoc. to Stanley H. Karesh, Charleston, D.D.S., 1970-77, tech. market rschr., designer, Charleston, 1970-90, indsl. designer, various orgns., 1965, 75, 77, 88, 91, 92. Served to lt. USNR, 1961-63. Mem. Royal Soc. Health, Charleston C. of C. (cruise ship com. 1969), ADA, Charleston Dental Soc., Hibernian Soc., Charleston Museum, Internat. Platform Assn., Charleston Library Soc., S.C. Hist. Soc., Gibbes Art Gallery, Preservation Soc. of Charleston, Navy League of U.S., Phi Kappa Sigma, Sigma Gamma Epsilon, Psi Omega. Congregationalist. Club: Optimist. Achievements include various scientific and engineering designs; patent in dental matrix device. Home: 112 Folly Road Blvd Charleston SC 29407-7509

JOHNSON, DIANA ATWOOD, business owner, innkeeper; b. Rochester, N.Y., Nov. 3, 1946; d. Edwin Havens and Barbara (Field) A.; m. Kenneth Durant Milne, June 10, 1967 (div. Apr. 1982); m. Howard Samuel Tooker, May 5, 1985 (div. Aug. 1994); m. John Samuel Johnson, June 2, 1996. BA, Skidmore Coll., 1968. Owner, innkeeper Old Lyme (Conn.) Inn, 1976—; vice-chmn., bd. dirs. Maritime Bank & Trust, Essex, Conn., 1995-99; adv. bd. Webster Bank, 1999—; incorporator Lawrence Meml. Hosp., New London, Conn., 1990-95. Trustee Conn. River Mus., Essex, 1976—, pres., 1989-94, chmn., 1994-96; trustee Lyme Hist. Soc., Old Lyme, 1985-87, Lyme Acad. Fine Arts, Old Lyme, 1980—, chmn. 1996—, treas., 1992-96; vice chmn. Mystic Coast Travel and Leisure Coun., 1992-94, chmn. 1994-96; bd. dirs. Conn. chpt. Nature Conservancy, 1994—; mem. adv. bd. Norwich Navigators, 1995—; dir. Southeastern Conn. Enterprise Region, 1995—; del. Rep. Nat. Conv., San Diego, 1996; mem. Rep. Town Com., 1997—, vice chmn., 1998-99; mem. Conn. Rep. Fin. Com., 1997—. Mem. Nat. Restaurant Assn., Conn. Restaurant Assn. (bd. dirs. 1991-93, 99—), Prof. Assn. Innkeepers, Gray Gables Croquet Club (founder), U.S. Croquet Assn. Republican. Presbyterian. Avocations: American antiques, antique house restoration, croquet. Home: 12 Tantummaheag Rd Old Lyme CT 06371-1137 Office: Old Lyme Inn Inc PO Box 787 85 Lyme St Old Lyme CT 06371-2336

JOHNSON, DIANE JONES, librarian; b. Youngstown, Ohio, Oct. 23, 1956; d. Wilbur Hudson and Barbara Jean Jones; m. Paul David Taylor, Sept. 27, 1975 (div. Nov. 1989); children: Noel Thomas Taylor, Sara Elizabeth Taylor; m. Ray Johnson, Dec. 30, 1989. BS summa cum laude, Youngstown State U., 1978; MLS, East Carolina U., 1985. Cert. libr. assoc., Md.; cert. pub. libr., N.C. Print svcs. Canfield (Ohio) H.S., 1978-80; media specialist Poland (Ohio) Mid. Sch., 1980-82; libr. Sheppard Meml. Libr., Greenville, N.C., 1982-90; catalog technician St. Mary's Coll., St. Mary's City, Md., 1990-93; pub. svcs. libr. Charles County Pub. Libr., La Plata, Md., 1993-97, acting dir., 1997, br. mgr., 1997—. Cons.: (book) Senior High School Catalog, 1985-89. Youngstown Edn. Found. scholar Youngstown State U., 1975-78. Mem. ALA, Md. Libr. Assn., Pub. Libr. Assn. Baptist. Avocations: reading, walking, traveling, needlework. Home: 1309 Leicester Dr La Plata MD 20646 Office: Charles County Pub Libr 2 Garrett Ave La Plata MD 20646

JOHNSON, DOLORES DEBOWER, consultant; b. Schuyler, Nebr., Nov. 8, 1932; d. Ernest Edward and Edna Cecelia (Stone) DeBower; m. Richard Allan Johnson, Sept. 3, 1952 (dec. 1983); children: Erik, Kristi, Kurt. BA summa cum laude, U. Minn., 1972; cert., Harvard U., 1975. Mgr. St. Paul Chamber Orchestra, 1973-77, Houston Symphony, 1977-80; gen. mgr. Minn. Opera, St. Paul, 1980-81; dir. devel. Walker Art Ctr., Mpls., 1981-84; mng. dir. Houston Grand Opera, 1984-96; adj. lectr. Goucher Coll., Balt., 1998—. Bd. dirs. Cultural Arts Coun. Houston, 1986-90, Bus. Vol. in Arts, 1991-96. Bush Found. fellow, 1975. Mem. Minn. Composers Forum (pres. 1982-84). Fax: 402-352-2598. Home: 707 Banner St Schuyler NE 68661-2230 Office: PO Box 162 Schuyler NE 68661-0162

JOHNSON, DON EDWIN, lawyer; b. Decatur, Ill., Jan. 29, 1939; s. B. Edwin and Mary Louise (Pitzer) J.; m. Suzanne Curtis, Aug. 23, 1959; children: Jennifer, Marc Wade. BA cum laude, Millikin U., 1959; LLB, U. Ill., 1961, JD, 1968. Bar: Ill. 1961, U.S. Dist. Ct. (so. dist.) Ill. 1961, U.S. Tax Ct. 1986. Law clk. Ill. Supreme Ct., Springfield, 1961-63; assoc. Hohlt, House & DeMoss, Pinckneyville, Ill., 1961-66; ptnr. Johnson Seibert & Bigham, Pinckneyville, 1966—; state's atty. Perry County, Ill., Pinckneyville, 1968-72; bd. dirs. 1st Nat. Bank, Pinckneyville, First Perry Bancorp, Pinckneyville. Contbr. articles to profl. jours. City atty. DuQuoin, Ill., 1965-68, Pinckneyville, 1983—; bd. dirs. Rend Lake Coll. Found., Ina, Ill., 1981-90; bd. visitors U. Ill. Coll. Law, 1984-88. Fellow Am. Coll. Trust and Estate Counsel, Am. Bar Found., Ill. Bar Found. (chmn. 1986-87); mem. Ill. State Bar Assn. (chmn. fed. tax sect. 1983-84, chmn. mineral law sect. 1984-86, 94-95, 96-97), Ea. Mineral Law Found. (trustee 1985—), Nat. Acad. Elder Law Attys., Pinckneyville C. of C. (pres. 1968), So. Ill. Golf Assn. (pres.), USGA (com.), Rotary (pres. 1966, 76), Elks, Scottish Rite, Shriners, Chaine des Rotisseurs. Republican. Presbyterian. Avocations: golf, travel, stamp and coin collecting. Home: 605 W South St Pinckneyville IL 62274-1236 Office: Johnson Seibert & Bigham One N Main St Pinckneyville IL 62274

JOHNSON, DON ROBERT, religious organization leader, administrator; b. Salina, Kans., Oct. 8, 1942; s. Ben Henry and Bertha Lucile (Armstrong) J.; m. Judith Mae Skelton, Apr. 12, 1980; children: Jennifer, Monica, Anaise, Rebekah. AA, S.W. Bapt. Coll., 1962; BA, East Tex. Bapt. Coll., 1964; MDiv, Midwestern Theol. Sem., 1968; postgrad., U. Iowa, 1969-70. Ordained to ministry So. Bapt. Conv., 1966, United Meth. Ch., 1970. Pastor various Meth. chs., Iowa, 1968-74, Calvary United Meth. Ch., Waterloo, Iowa, 1974-82; chaplain Stephens Coll., Columbia, Mo., 1982-86; sr. leader N.Y. Soc. for Ethical Culture, N.Y.C., 1986-98; dir. Metzger Price Fund, N.Y.C., 1987—; advisor Ctr. for Urban Well-Being, Carmel, Calif., 1988-97; spkr. Contbr. articles to jours. Chmn. multi-cultural com. Mid Mo. Assn. of Colls. and Univs., Columbia, 1984-86; pres. Neighborhood Housing Svcs., Inc., Waterloo, Iowa, 1978-82; chmn. People's Community Health Clinic, Waterloo, 1978-80. Mem. Nat. Leaders Coun. (pres. 1994-98), Am. Ethical Union (cert.), Internat. Humanist and Ethical Union. Avocations: walking, reading, music, travel, collecting antiques. *I believe in the centrality of ethics in human life, the uniqueness of each individual and their right to dignity, the significance of relationships, and the human responsibility to create a better world.*

JOHNSON, DONALD CLAY, librarian, curator; b. Clintonville, Wis., Aug. 19, 1940; s. Everett Clay and Gertrude Edna Dorthea (Learmann) J. BA, U. Wis., 1962, PhD, 1980; MA, U. Chgo., 1967. Curator S.E. Asia Collection Yale U., New Haven, 1967-70; head reference libr. No. Ariz. U., Flagstaff, 1971-72; asst. libr. reader svcs. Nat. U. Malaysia, Kuala Lumpur, 1972-74; head reader svcs. Coll. William and Mary, Williamsburg, Va., 1980-87; curator Ames Libr. South Asia, U. Minn., Mpls., 1987—. Author: Southeast Asia: A Bibliography, 1970, Guide to Reference Materials on Southeast Asia, 1970, Index to Southeast Asian Journals, 1982. Scholar Ford Found., 1963-64; rsch. grantee Am. Inst. Indian Studies, 1989, 90, 94. Mem. ALA (life), Assn. for Asian Studies (editor Resources for Scholarship series 1997-98). Avocation: textiles in South and Southeast Asia. Office: U Minn Ames Libr South Asia 309 19th Ave S Minneapolis MN 55455-0438

JOHNSON, DONALD HARRY, JR., government official, educator; b. Chgo., May 30, 1950; s. Donald Harry and Dorothy Wright (Millard) J.; m. Kathryn Elizabeth Wiersum, June 24, 1972 (div. Aug. 1987); children: Eric Donald, Christine Melin. BA Elem. Edn. and History, Carthage Coll., Kenosha, Wis., 1972; postgrad., Harvard U., 1977; MA Higher Edn. Adminstrn., U. Mich., 1979, MA Polit. Sci., 1980, PhD, 1982; diploma, Inst. (Fair Housing) John Marshall Law Sch., 1998. Cert. tchr. K-8, social scis., Ill., Wis., Colo., V.I. Equal opportunity specialist/civil rights analyst U.S. Dept. HUD, Chgo., 1988—; elem. edn. tchr. All Sts. and V.I. Pub. Schs., St. Thomas, 1972-75; commr. V.I. Athletic Assn., 1973-75; higher edn. adminstr. Carthage, Suomi Coll., Springfield (Ill.) Coll., U. Mich., 1975-83; dir. admissions Suomi Coll., 1977-78; adminstr. Disabled Student Newsletter, U. Mich., 1978-79; adminstrv. asst. Office of Minority Svcs., U. Mich., 1978-79, admissions officer U. Mich., 1979-81; dean coll. Springfield (Ill.) Coll., 1981-83; exec. coun. Ctrl. Ill. Fgn. Lang. Coll. Consortium, 1981-83, chmn. internat. studies group, 1981-83; cons. polit. candidates, Ann Arbor, Washington, Chgo., 1979—; polit. sci. prof. U. Mich., Lincolnland Coll., U. Ill.-Springfield, Coll. DuPage, Triton Coll., Elmhurst Coll., Aurora (Ill.) U., 1980-90; rsch. affiliiate Caribbean Rsch. Inst., U. V.I., 1980-82; rsch. cons. Afro-Am. Thematic Project, U. Ill.-Springfield, 1983-85; chmn. HUD Disabled Employee Adv. Com., Chgo., 1988—, labor/mgmt. exec. coun., 1996-98; cons. colls. and univs.; lectr. in field. Contbg. author: Theory and Practice of 3rd World Solidarity, 1998; guest commentator NBC Today, 1982, Nat. Pub. Radio, 1984; author, ERIC, Nat. Inst. Edn., Boulder, Colo., 1982; editor: Disabled Student Newletters, U. Mich., 1978-79. Disting. guest Embassy of Finland, Washington, 1995; candidate local sch. coun., Chgo., 1994; ednl. guest speaker Com. of Ill. State Bd. Edn., Chgo., 1994; mem. com. ACCESS LIVING, Chgo., 1991—, ednl. com. Chamber of Commerce, Springfield, 1982; disability trainer to pub. and pvt. sector individuals, 1978—. Named Disting. Young Alumnus award Carthage Coll., Kenosha, Wis., 1982; Rackham grantee U. Mich., 1980-82, others.; recipient HUD Superior Achievement award 1998. Mem. Am. Fedn. Govt. Employees (election chmn. 1991, exec. coun. 1997—). Lutheran. Avocations: freelance writing, bicycling, scuba diving. Home: 2206 W Morse Ave Chicago IL 60645-4820 Office: US Dept HUD 77 W Jackson Blvd Ste 2101 Chicago IL 60604-3511

JOHNSON, DONALD RAYMOND, lawyer; b. N.Y.C., June 26, 1960; s. Donald Francis and Jacqueline E. (Barnett) J. BA, Liberty U., 1982, MA, 1984; JD, Washington and Lee U., 1989; postgrad., Va. Polytech. Inst., Yale U., U. Va. Bar: Va. 1989, D.C. 1991, N.Y. 1995, U.S. Dist. Ct. (so. and ea. dists.) N.Y., U.S. Dist. Ct. (ea. and we. dists.) Va., U.S. Ct. Appeals (fed. cir.), U.S. Supreme Ct. Pvt. practice Charlottesville, Va., 1989-96; dir., pres. Internat. Brokerage & Investment Co., Charlottesville, 1991—; dir., v.p. Internat. Investment Svcs., Inc., Charlottesville, 1991—; pvt. practice N.Y.C., 1995—. Bd. dirs. Excellence in Edn., Charlottesville, 1990-92, Heritage Soc., Charlottesville, 1990-92; U.S. del. German-Am. Multiplicitorian Seminars. Named one of Outstanding Young Men of Am.; recipient numerous awards and honors for ednl., civic, and social activities. Mem. ABA, ATLA. Republican. Baptist. Avocations: running, sailing, tennis. Fax: (212) 352-2701. E-mail: drjohnson@ibm.net. Home: 126 Atlantic Ave Massapequa Park NY 11762 Office: 9th Fl 49 W 24th St New York NY 10010-3206

JOHNSON, DONALD WAYNE, lawyer; b. Memphis, Feb. 2, 1950; s. Hugh Don and Oline (Rowland) J.; m. Jan Marie Mullinax, May 12, 1972 (div. 1980); 1 child, Scott Fitzgerald; m. Cindy L. Walker, Dec. 10, 1988; children: Trevor Christian, Mallory Faith. Student Memphis State U., 1968, Lee Coll., 1968-72; JD, Woodrow Wilson Coll. of Law, 1975. Bar: Ga. 1975, U.S. Dist. Ct. (no. dist.) Ga. 1975, U.S. Ct. Appeals (5th cir.) 1976, U.S. Tax Ct. 1978, U.S. Ct. Claims 1978, U.S. Supreme Ct. 1979, U.S. Ct. Appeals (11th, 9th, Fed., D.C. cirs.) 1984. Ptnr. Barnes & Johnson, Dalton, Ga., 1975-77, Johnson & Fain, Dalton, 1977-80; pvt. practice, Dalton, 1975-85, Atlanta, 1985—; city atty. City of Forest Park, Ga., 1996-97. Bd. dirs. Pathway Christian Sch., Dalton, 1978-85, Jr. Achievement of Dalton, 1978-84, Dalton-Whitfield County Day Care Ctrs., Inc.; legal counsel Robertson for Pres. Com., Ga., 1988; bd. chmn. Ga. Family Coun., 1990-97; Rep. chmn. Clayton County, 1993-95; Rep. gen. counsel 3rd Congl. Dist., 1993-95, Clayton County Rep. Com., 1995-96; Rep. candidate for Ga. Senate, 1998. Recipient Power of One award Ga. Family Coun., 1997. Mem. ATLA, Ga. Trial Lawyers Assn. (bd. govs. 1984), Ga. Bar Assn., Christian Legal Soc. Mem. Ch. of God. Office: PO Box 187 Fayetteville GA 30214-0187

JOHNSON, DORIS ANN, educational administrator; b. Marinette, Wis., Dec. 4, 1950; d. Jerome Louis and Jean Fern (Henry) La Plant; m. Daniel Lee Leonard, June 10, 1972 (div. June 1987); children: Jeremiah Daniel, Erica Leigh, Wesley Cyril; m. Paul Robert Johnson, Oct. 21, 1989; stepchildren: Kindra Michelle, Tanya Mari. Student, U. Wis., Oshkosh, 1969-70; BA in Edn., U. Wis., Eau Claire, 1973; MS in Edn., U. Wis., Whitewater, 1975; postgrad., Oreg. State U., 1988. Reading specialist Brookfield (Wis.) Cen. High Sch., 1975-79; lead instr. N.E. Wis. Tech. Coll., Marinette, 1979-87; dir. adult basic edn. Umpqua C.C., Roseburg, Oreg., 1987-95, dir. developmental edn., 1995—; founding bd. dirs. Project Literacy, Umpqua Region, Roseburg, 1989-98; mem. adv. bd. Umpqua Cmty. Action Network, Roseburg, 1987-94; mem. State Dirs. of Adult Edn., Oreg., 1987—, vice chair, 1992-93, chair, 1993-94; mem. Adminstrn. Assn., Roseburg, 1989—, chair, 1993-94, 94-95; bd. dirs. Greater Douglas United Way, 1994—; adv. bd. Oreg. Litaracy Line, 1994-96. Co-author literacy module Communication Skills, 1988; author ednl. curriculum. Founding mem., bd. dirs. St. Joseph Maternity Home, Roseburg, 1987-90; mem. Literacy Theater, Roseburg, 1988-95; bd. dirs. Greater Douglas United Way, 1994—; mem. Project Leadership, Roseburg, 1988-89; mem. adv. bd. Oreg. Literacy Line, 1994-96; mem. Roseburg Valley Rep. Women, 1994-96. State legalizatoin assistance grantee Fed. Govt., 1988-93, homeless literacy grantee Fed. Govt., 1990-91, family literacy grantee Fed. Govt., 1991-93, intergenerational literacy grantee State of Oreg., 1991, literacy expansion grantee Fed. Govt., 1992-95, literacy outreach grantee Fed. Govt., 1992—, staff devel. spl. projects grantee Fed. Govt., 1992-93. Fellow TESOL, Inst. Inst. Leadership Devel., Am. Assn. Adult and Continuing Edn., Oreg. Assn. Disabled Students, Oreg. Developmental Edn. Studies, Oreg. Assn. for Children with Learning Disabilities, Western Coll. Reading and Learning Assn., Am. Assn. Women in Coll. and Jr. Coll., Roseburg Valley Rep. Women, Altrusa Internat. Club of Roseburg (chair literacy com. 1993-97), Rep. Women. Republican. Lutheran. Avocations: peer counseling, reading, hiking, cooking, running support groups. Home: 761 Garden Grove Dr Roseburg OR 97470-9670 Office: Umpqua CC PO Box 967 Roseburg OR 97470-0226

JOHNSON, DOROTHY CURFMAN, elementary education educator; b. Smithsburg, Md., Nov. 21, 1930; d. Paul Frank and Rhoda Pearl (Witmer) Curfman; m. Robert Nelson Johnson, Jan. 24, 1952 (div. Dec. 1965); children: Gregory Nelson, Eric Paul. Student, Gettysburg Coll., 1948-50, Waynesboro Bus. Coll., 1950, Broward C.C., Ft. Lauderdale, Fla., 1967; BS in Edn., Fla. Atlantic U., 1969. Cert. tchr., Fla. Sec. to prodn. mgr. Westinghouse Elec. Corp., Sunbury, Pa., 1951-53; sec. to v.p., sales Metal Carbides Corp., Youngstown, Ohio, 1966; tchr. Sch. Bd. of Broward County, Ft. Lauderdale, 1969-93, curriculum specialist, 1993-96; Masters in Edn. Prog., 1973-74, team coord. Sanders Park Elem., Pompano Beach, Fla., 1985-96; mem. North Area Adv. Bd., Pompano Beach, 1990-96; sec. Sanders Park PTA, Pompano Beach, 1994-96. Sec.-treas. Georgen Arms Bd. of Dirs., Pompano Beach, 1997—; dir. Georgen Arms Condo, Inc., Pompano Beach, 1974—; mem. Jr. League, Youngstown. Recipient Master Tchr. award State of Fla., 1981-82. Mem. Alpha Xi Delta. Lutheran. Home: 280 S Cypress Rd Apt 5 Pompano Beach FL 33060-7038

JOHNSON, DOROTHY PHYLLIS, retired counselor, art therapist; b. Kansas City, Mo., Sept. 13, 1925; d. Chris C. and Mabel T. (Gillum) Green; BA in Art, Ft. Hays. State U., 1975, MS in Guidance and Counseling, 1976, MA in Art, 1979; m. Herbert E. Johnson, May 11, 1945; children: Michael E., Gregory K. Art therapist High Plains Comprehensive Mental Health Assn., Hays, Kans., 1975-76; art therapist, mental health counselor Sunflower Mental Health Assn., Concordia, Kans., 1976-78, Pawnee Mental Health Svcs., 1978-91, co-dir. Project Togetherness, 1976-77, coord. partial hospitalization, 1978-82, out-patient therapist, 1982-91; pvt. practice, 1991-97, ret., 1997; dir. Swedish Am. State Bank, Courtland, Kans., 1960—, sec., 1973-77. Mem. Kans., Am. art therapy assns., Am. Mental Health Counselors Assn., Am. Counseling Assn., Kans. Counseling Assn., Assn. for Humanistic Psychologists, Assn. Transpersonal Psychologists, Assn. Specialists in Group Work, Phi Delta Kappa, Phi Kappa Phi. Contbr. articles to profl. jours. Home: PO Box 200 Courtland KS 66939-0200

JOHNSON, DOUG, advertising and public relations executive; b. Watertown, N.Y., Aug. 16, 1919; s. H. Douglas and Clare (Lane) J.; m. Geraldine Evans, Aug. 11, 1943; children: Andrew (dec.), Molly E., Faith D. Student pub. schs. Pres. Doug Johnson Assos. (pub. relations), Syracuse, N.Y., 1949-61, Barlow/Johnson, Inc. (advt. and pub. relations), Syracuse, 1961-80, Johnlow Corp., Fayetteville; chmn. bd. Nowak Barlow Johnson, Fayetteville, 1980-82; v.p. mktg. Edward Joy Co., Inc., Syracuse, 1982-84; playwright, pres. 10 Co. Mktg.; dir. Agway Indemnity Ins. Co., Dewitt, N.Y., Key Bank of Central N.Y., Syracuse, Syracuse Baseball Club, Inc.; chmn. exec. com. Agway Ins. Co., Dewitt. Home sec. to congressman, 1949-65; bd. dirs., v.p. Community Gen. Hosp. Syracuse, N.Y. State Coll. Forestry Found.; bd. dirs., past pres. Syracuse Boys Club ; v.p. N.Y.C. Assoc. Artists; pres. L.W. Artists Assn., 1997-98. Served with AUS, 1941-45. Decorated Purple Heart with 3 oak leaf clusters, Bronze Star, Combat Infantry Badge with Silver Star. Mem. Pub. Rels. Soc. Am. (cert. bus. communicator), Syracuse C. of C. (pres. 1968-69). Club: Century (gov.). Home and Office: 1444 Leisure World Mesa AZ 85206-2304

JOHNSON, DOUGLAS WAYNE, church organization official, minister; b. nr. Carlyle, Ill., Aug. 21, 1934; s. Noel Douglas and Laura Margaret (Crocker) J.; m. Phyllis Ann Heinzmann, June 8, 1956; children: Kirk Wayne, Heather Renee, Kirsten Joy, Tara Carlynne. Student, So. Ill. U., 1952-53; BA, McKendree Coll., 1956; STB, Boston U., 1959, MA, 1963; PhD, Northwestern U., 1968. Ordained to ministry as elder United Meth. Ch., 1959. Pastor Pullman Meth. Ch., Chgo., 1960-64; dir. rsch. No. Ill. conf. United Meth. Ch., Chgo., 1964-66; assoc. for planning and rsch. Nat. Coun. Chs. in Christ in the USA, N.Y.C., 1968-75; exec. dir. Inst. Ch. Devel., 1975-85; dir. rsch. Gen. Bd. Global Ministries United Meth. Ch., N.Y.C., 1985—; mem. faculty Western Conn. State Coll., Danbury, 1969-73; mem. rsch. adv. com. United Meth. Ch., gen. bd. of global ministries. Author: Managing Change in the Church, 1974; (with George Cornell) Punctured Preconceptions, 1972; The Care and Feeding of Volunteers, 1978; (with others) Religion in America, 1978; The Challenge of Single Adult Ministry, 1982, Computer Ethics, 1984, Growing Up Christian in the Twenty-First Century, 1984, The Tithe: Challenge or Legalism, 1984, Lets Be Realistic About Your Church Budget, 1984, Ministry to Young Couples, 1985, Secretary's Guide to Church Office Procedures, 1985, Using Computers in Mission, 1985, Finance in the Church, 1986; (with Alan K. Waltz) Facts and Possibilities, 1988; Vitality Means Church Growth, 1989, Empowering Lay Volunteers, 1991, Don't Know Much About Being a Leader in the Church, 1996; contbr. articles to ch. periodicals. Teaching fellow Garret Theol. Sem. Northwestern U., 1967-68; recipient Svc. award Nat. Coun. Chs., 1973, Svc. award Gen. Bd. of Global Ministries United Meth. Ch., 1995. Mem. Soc. Sci. Study of Religion, Religious Rsch. Assn., Am. Sociol. Assn., Rural Sociol. Soc. Office: 475 Riverside Dr New York NY 10115-0122

JOHNSON, DOUGLAS WAYNE, secondary education educator; b. Rochester, Pa., July 26, 1952; s. Fred P. and Jean O. (Henry) J.; children: Megan, Matthew, Marcie. Student, U. Valencia, Spain, 1973; BS, Slippery Rock U., 1974; elem. edn. cert., Geneva Coll., Beaver Falls, Pa., 1978. Cert. instrnl. II, Pa. Spanish tchr. Ingomar Mid. Sch. North Allegheny Schs., Pitts., 1985—; part-time driver edn. coord. C.C. Allegheny County-North Campus, Pitts., 1984—; part-time dir. edn. Ingomar United Meth. Ch., Pitts., 1983-93; mem. Carson Total Quality Team, Pitts., 1995-97; rep. North Allegheny profl. devel. com., Pitts., 1993—. Treas. QUALITY, Pitts., 1988-90; pres., v.p. Monaca (Pa.) Borough Coun., 1975-79; mem. Monaca Vol. Firemen, 1974-79; pres. Ingomar Elem. PTA, 1995-97; student council advisor Ingomar Mid. Sch., 1997—; mem. Pa. Dist. # 3 Student Coun. Bd. Mem. Assn. for Supervision and Curriculum Devel., Pa. State Modern Lang. Assn., North Allegheny Fedn. Tchrs. (state rep. 1994, 96, exec. coun. mem. 1993-97, bldg. rep. 1993-97), Slippery Rock Alumni Assn. (homecoming rep. 1974—), Leotha Hawthorne Reading Coun. Republican. Methodist. Home: PO Box 149 Ingomar PA 15127-0149 Office: North Allegheny Sch Dist 200 Hillvue Ln Pittsburgh PA 15237-5344

JOHNSON, DOUGLAS WELLS, lawyer; b. Denver, May 31, 1949; s. Robert Douglas and Mildred Irene (Fehr) J.; m. Kathryn Ann Hoberg, Oct. 18, 1980. BA, U. Denver, 1971, JD, 1974. Bar: Colo. 1974, U.S. Dist. Ct. Colo. 1974, U.S. Ct. Appeals (10th cir.) 1974; U.S. Supreme Ct. 1977, Ill. 1980, U.S. Dist. Ct. (no. dist.) Ill. 1980, U.S. Ct. Appeals (7th cir.) 1981, D.C. 1981, U.S. Ct. Internat. Trade 1981, U.S. Dist. Ct. (ea. dist.) Mich. 1983, U.S. Ct. Appeals (6th cir.) 1984, U.S. Ct. Appeals Fed. Cir. 1984, U.S. Dist. Ct. (no. dist.) Ind. 1986, U.S. Ct. Appeals (4th and 8th cirs.) 1986. Ptnr. Mellman, Mellman & Thorn, Denver, 1974-80; sr. atty. Amoco Corp., Chgo., 1980-91, mgr. real estate Amoco Oil Co., Chgo., 1991-4; sr. atty. Amoco Corp., Chgo., 1994-98; prin. legal counsel Amoco Pipeline Co., 1998—. U. Denver Alumni scholar, 1967-71. Mem. ABA, Ill. Bar Assn., D.C. Bar Assn., Chgo. Bar Assn., Kappa Delta Pi. Office: BP Amoco Corp 200 E Randolph St Ste 1907B Chicago IL 60601-6436

JOHNSON, DOUGLAS WILLIAM, physician, radiologist, oncologist; b. Westpoint, NY, July 23, 1977; s. Andrew Larson and Barbara Joan (Rosborough) J.; m. Susan Mary Friedman, July 23, 1977; children: Danielle, Michael. BS in Biology, Va. Polytechnic Inst., Blacksburg, Va., 1976; MD, Med. Coll. Va., Richmond, 1979. Chmn. radiation oncology David Grant USAF Med. Ctr., Travis AFB, Calif., 1983-87; ptnr. Fla. Radiation Oncology Group, Jacksonville, Fla., 1987—; asst. prof. radiation-oncology Stanford Med. Ctr., Stanford U., Calif., 1983-87; asst. prof. oncology Mayo Clinic Med. Sch., Rochester, Minn., 1995—; fellow Am. Coll. Radiology, Phila., 1995. Patentee in field. Col. USAF, 1975—. Fellow Am. Coll. Radiology; mem. Am. Soc. Therapeutic Radiology & Oncology. Avocation, aviation. Office: Baptist Regional Cancer Ctr 1235 San Marco Blvd Ste 3 Jacksonville FL 32207-8560

JOHNSON, DUANE P., academic administrator; b. Wadena, Minn., Mar. 19, 1937; s. Julian C. and Lillian M. (petri) J.; m. Mary E., Oct. 22, 1960; children: Michael D., Gregory P. BS, Iowa State U., 1959; MEd, Colo. State U., 1970. County extension agt. 4-H Oreg. State U., Gresham, 1959-70; ext. specialist 4-H and youth devel. Oreg. State U., Corvallis, 1970-80, state leader 4-H, 1980-94, prof. adult edn., ext. specialist program devel., 1994—. Contbr. numerous articles to profl. jours. Mem. Nat. Assn. Ext. 4-H Agts., Assn. Vol. Adminstrn., ASCD, Oreg. State U. Ext. Assn. Office: Oreg State U Ballard Extension Hall Rm 105 Corvallis OR 97331-3608

JOHNSON, DWIGHT ALAN, lawyer; b. Huntington, W.Va., Sept. 26, 1945; s. Oliver Frederick and Garnette (Taylor) J.; m. Bonny Libbey, Nov. 15, 1969; children: Claire L., Daniel F., Philip T. BA, Princeton U., 1968; JD, Yale U., 1974. Bar: Conn. 1975, D.C. 1975, U.S. Ct. Appeals (D.C. cir.) 1976. Assoc. Jones, Day, Reavis & Pogue, Washington, 1974-77; assoc. Murtha, Cullina, Richter and Pinney LLP, Hartford, Conn., 1977-80, ptnr., 1980—, chmn. exec. com., 1990-95; bd. dirs. Phonon Corp., Simsbury, Conn. Sec., bd. dirs. Conn. Capitol Region Growth Coun., Hartford, 1992-97; bd. dirs. Conn. Sci. Mus., 1978-84, pres., 1982-83; bd. dirs. Parents Anonymous Conn., Inc., 1981-87, pres., 1983-85; bd. dirs. Tutu Found. Devel. and Relief South Africa, 1986-89, Lyme Disease Found., 1990-94; bd. dirs. Hartford Symphony Orch., 1991—, pres., 1994-96; trustee World Affairs Coun., 1998—; trustee Conn. Energy Found., 1984-90, Conn. Policy Econ. Coun., 1996—. With U.S. Army, 1968-71, Vietnam. Decorated Bronze Star. Mem. Conn. Bar Assn. (mem. exec. com. pub. utilities law sect. 1979—). Office: Murtha Cullina Richter and Pinney LLP City Pl 185 Asylum St Hartford CT 06103

JOHNSON, E. ERIC, insurance executive; b. Chgo., Feb. 7, 1927; s. Edwin Eric and Xenia Alice (Waisanen) J.; m. Elizabeth Dewar Brass, Sept. 3, 1949; children: Christal L. Johnson Neal, Craig R. BA, Stanford U., 1948. Dir. group annuities Equitable Life Assurance Soc., San Francisco, 1950-54; div. mgr. Equitable Life Assurance Soc., L.A., 1955-59; v.p. Johnson & Higgins of Calif., L.A., 1960-67, dir., 1968-87, chmn., 1986-87; chmn. TBG Fin., L.A., 1988—; bd. dirs. Am. Mutual Fund; exec. v.p. Johnson & Higgins, N.Y.C., 1984-87, Law Environ. Group, Showscan Corp. Bd. dirs. Sta. KCET, pub. TV, L.A., 1977-95, chmn., 1992-94; mem. adv. bd. UCLA Med. Ctr., 1983—, chmn. 1995-97; bd. dirs. Jonsson Comprehensive Cancer Ctr., UCLA, 1985—, Stanford U. Grad Sch. Bus., 1986-91; trustee Nuclear Decommissioning Trust, Rosemead, Calif., 1986-94, Calif. State Dept. Mental Hygiene, Calif. Coun. for Econ. Edn. Mem. Calif. Club, L.A. Country Club, Vintage Club, Riviera Tennis Club, Links Club N.Y.C., Beach Club, So. Calif. Tennis Assn. (v.p.), Tehama Golf Club. Avocations: golf, tennis, contemporary art, spectator sports. Office: TBG Fin 2029 Century Park E Los Angeles CA 90067-2901

JOHNSON, E. SCOTT, lawyer; b. Washington, June 28, 1951; s. William and Dorothy (Young) J.; m. Karen Colaianni, May 15, 1969 (div. 1972); 1 child, Scott Adrian; m. Cindy Ward, Feb. 14, 1986; 1 child, Tracy Elizabeth. BA summa cum laude, Md. U., 1985; JD cum laude, Georgetown U., 1988. Studio musician Blue Seas Studios, Balt., 1973-75; record producer Flite III Studios, Balt., 1975-80; atty. Ober, Kaler, Grimes & Shriver, Balt., 1988—; legal intern Nat. Assn. Broadcasters, 1987. Editor-in-chief Public Domain Report, 1993—; contbr. articles to profl. jours.; producer LP's including Portal of Antrim, 1976, Rivers of Memory, 1979, Portraits, 1978; Doncha Hide It, 1978, co-producer North Mountain Velvet, 1978. Pres. Md. Lawyers for the Arts, Balt., 1990—; pres. Young Audiences Md., Balt., 1994-97; bd. dirs. Mid-Atlantic Arts Found., 1997. Recipient First Prize: Nathan Burkan Copyright Law Competition ASCAP, Georgetown, 1987, Second Prize: Stephen G. Thompson Nat. Writing Competition Communications Law. Mem. ASCAP, Nat. Acad. Recording Arts & Scis., Washington Area Music Assn., Md. Bar Assn., Am. Bar Assn.

JOHNSON, EARL, JR., judge, author; b. Watertown, S.D., June 10, 1933; s. Earl Jerome and Doris Melissa (Schwartz) J.; m. Barbara Claire Yanow, Oct. 11, 1970; children: Kelly Ann, Earl Eric, Agaarn Yanovitch. B.A. in Econs., Northwestern U., 1955, LL.M., 1961; J.D., U. Chgo., 1960. Bar: Ill. 1960, U.S. Ct. Appeals (9th cir.) 1964, D.C. 1965, U.S. Supreme Ct. 1966, Calif. 1972. Trial atty., organized crime sect. Dept. Justice, Washington, Miami, Fla. and Las Vegas, Nev., 1961-64; dep. dir. Neighborhood Legal Services Project, 1964-65; dep. dir. OEO Legal Services Program, 1965-66, dir., 1966-68; vis. scholar Center for Study of Law and Soc., U. Calif., Berkeley, 1968-69; assoc. prof. U. So. Calif. Law Center, Los Angeles, 1969-75, dir. clin. programs, 1970-73; prof. law U. So. Calif. Law Center, 1976-82, dir. Program Study Dispute Resolution Policy, Social Sci. Research Inst., 1975-82; assoc. justice Calif. Ct. Appeal, 1982—; co-dir. Access to Justice Project, European U. Inst., 1975-79; vis. scholar Inst. Comparative Law, U. Florence, Italy, 1973, 75; Robert H. Jackson lectr. Nat. Jud. Coll., 1980; adv. panel Legal Svcs. Corp., 1976-80; legis. impact panel Nat. Acad. Scis., 1977-80; faculty Asian Workshop on Legal Svcs. to Poor, 1974; mem. Internat. Legal Ctr., Legal Svcs. in Developing Countries, 1972-75; founder, bd. mem. Action for Legal Rights, 1971-74; pres., trustee Western Ctr. on Law and Poverty, 1972-73, 76-80; v.p., chmn. exec. com. Calif. Rural Legal Assistance Corp., 1973-74; exec. com. Nat. Sr. Citizens Law Ctr., 1980-82; sec. Nat. Resource Ctr. for Consumers of Legal Svcs., 1974-82; chair Nat. Equal Justice Libr. Com., 1989-92; pres., bd. dirs. Consortium for Nat. Equal Justice Libr., Inc., 1992-95, bd. mem., 1995—; chair Calif. Access to Justice Working Group, 1993-96; mem. Calif. Commn. on Access to Justice, 1997—. Author: Justice and Reform: The Formative Years of the American Legal Services Program, 1974, 2d edit., 1978, Toward Equal Justice: A Comparative Study of Legal Aid in Modern Societies, 1975, Outside the Courts: A Survey of Diversion Alternatives in Civil Cases, 1977, Dispute Processing Strategies, 1978, Dispute Resolution in America, 1985, California Trial Guide, 7 vols., 1986, Texas Trial Guide, 6 vols., 1989, New York Trial Guide, 5 vols., 1990, Florida Civil Trial Guide, 5 vols., 1990, Ill. Civil Trial Guide, 5 vols., 1991, Fed. Trial Guide, 5 vols., 1992, Indiana Civil Trial Guide, 5 vols., 1992, California Family Law Trial Guide, 5 vols., 1992, Pennsylvania Civil Trial Guide, 5 vols., 1992, Mich. Trial Guide, 5 vols., 1993, N.C. Civil Trial Guide, 5 vols., 1993, California Criminal Trial Guide, 3 vols., 1994; editor U. Chgo. Law Rev, 1960; mem. editl. bd. Jour. Law and Social Inquiry, 1987—; contbr. articles to books and periodicals. Bd. dirs. Beverly Hills Bar Found., 1972-73, Nat. Legal Aid and Defenders Assn., 1987-91; trustee Los Angeles Legal Aid Found., 1969-71; mem. Los Angeles County Regional Planning Commn., 1980-81; bd. visitors U. San Diego Law Sch., 1983-86. Served with USNR, 1955-58. Recipient Dart award for acad. innovation U. So. Calif., 1971, Loren Miller Legal Services award Calif. State Bar, 1977, Appellate Justice of the Yr. award Los Angeles Trial Lawyers Assn., 1989, Outstanding Jud. Achievement award Calif. Trial Lawyers Assn., 1991; named So. Calif. Citizen of Week, 1978; Ford Found. fellow, 1960; Dept. State lectr., 1975; grantee Ford Found.; grantee Russell Sage Found.; grantee Law Enforcement Assistance Adminstrn.; grantee NSF. Fellow Am. Bar Found. (rsch. adv. com. 1995—); mem. ABA (com. chmn. 1972-75, spl. com. resolution minor disputes 1976-83, coun. sect. of individual rights and responsibilities 1990-91, consortium on legal svcs. and the pub. 1991-94), Calif. Bar Assn., L.A. Bar Assn. (neighborhood justice ctr. com. 1976-81), Law and Soc. Assn., Nat. Legal Aid and Defender's Assn. (bd. dirs. 1968-74), Am. Acad. Polit. and Social Sci., Calif. Judges Assn. (appellate cts. com. 1983-87, 93—, ethics com. 1985-89), Internat. Assn. Procedural Law, Order of Coif. Democrat. Office: Ct Appeals Calif 2d Appellate Dist 300 S Spring St Los Angeles CA 90013-1230 *I have profound faith in the power of ideas to shape American society and in the special significance of one fundamental concept—equal justice, in its full meaning.*

JOHNSON, EARLE BERTRAND, insurance executive; b. Otter Lake, Mich., May 3, 1914; s. Bert M. and Blanche (Sherman) J.; m. Frances Pierce, 1940 (dec.); children: Earle Bertrand, Victoria, Julia, Sheryl; m. Peggy Minch Rust, Apr. 30, 1972. B.S., U. Fla., 1937, J.D., 1940. With State Farm Ins. Cos., Bloomington, Ill., 1940-95; regional agy. dir. State Farm Ins. Cos., 1958-60, regional v.p., 1960-65, v.p., sec. State Farm Mut. Automobile Ins. Co., 1965-80, dir., 1967-88; sr. v.p., treas. State Farm County Mut. Ins. Co. Tex., 1965-80, treas., 1963-80; chmn. State Farm Life Ins. Co., 1970-86, dir., mem. exec. com., 1965-88; v.p., mem. exec. com. State Farm Fire & Casualty Co., 1965-80, dir., 1965-95; dir. State Farm Investment Mgmt. Corp.; v.p., sec. State Farm Internat. Svcs., Inc., 1967-81; mem. exec. com. State Farm County Mut. Ins. Co. Tex., 1970-86. Mem. Agy. Officers Round Table (exec. coms.), Am., Fla. bar assns., Soc. Former FBI Agts., Life Ins. Mktg. and Research Assn. (dir. 1975-78), Life Underwriter Tng. Council (trustee 1974-77), Phi Alpha Delta, Phi Kappa Tau. Home: 59 N Country Club Pl Bloomington IL 61701-3450 Office: State Farm Life Ins Co One State Farm Plaza Bloomington IL 61701

JOHNSON, EARVIN (MAGIC JOHNSON), professional sports team executive, former professional basketball coach; b. Lansing, Mich., Aug. 14, 1959; s. Earvin and Christine Johnson; m. Cookie Kelly; 1 son, Earvin. Student, Mich. State U., 1976-79. Basketball player L.A. Lakers, 1979-91, 95-96; sportscaster NBC-TV, 1993-94; chmn. Johnson Devel. Corp., 1993—; head coach L.A. Lakers, 1994, v.p., co-owner, 1994—; chmn. Magic Johnson Entertainment, 1997—; talk show host The Magic Hour, 1998—; gold medalist, U.S. Olympic Basketball Team, 1992. Author: (autobiography) Magic, 1983; (autobiography, with Roy S. Johnson) Magic's Touch, 1989; What You Can Do to Avoid AIDS, 1992; My Life, 1992. Recipient Citizenship award, 1992, All-Around Contbns. to Team Success award IBM, 1984; mem. NCAA Championship Team, 1979, NBA All-Star Team, 1980, 82-92, MVP NBA All-Star Game, 1990, 92, NBA Championship Team, 1980, 82, 85, 87, 88; named MVP NBA Playoffs, 1980, 82, 87, NBA, 1987, 89, 90, All-Star Game, 1990, 92, Player of the Year, Sporting News, 1987; recipient Schick Pivotal Player award, 1984; named to All-NBA first team, 1983-91, second team, 1982, NBA All-Rookie Team, 1980. Holder NBA playoff record most assists (2320); NBA Finals single-series record highest assists-per-game avg. (14), 1985, highest assists per game, rookie (8.7), 1980, NBA Finals single game record most points by rookie (42), 1980, NBA Finals single game recored most assists one quarter (8), NBA single game record most assists (22). Office: Magic Johnson Found Ste 1080 1600 Corporate Pointe Culver City CA 90230 also: Johnson Devel Corp 9100 Wilshire Blvd Beverly Hills CA 90212 also: FX Networks Inc 1440 S Sepulveda Blvd Los Angeles CA 90025-3458*

JOHNSON, EDDIE BERNICE, congresswoman; b. Waco, Tex., Dec. 3, 1935; d. Lee Edward and Lillie Mae (White) J.; m. Lacy Kirk Johnson, July 5, 1956 (div. Oct. 1970); 1 child, Dawrence Kirk. Diploma in Nursing, St. Mary's Coll. of South Bend, 1955; BS in Nursing, Tex. Christian U., 1967; MPA, So. Meth. U., 1976; LLD (hon.), Bishop Coll., 1979, Jarvis Coll., 1979, Tex. Coll., 1989, Houston-Tillotson Coll., 1993, Paul Quinn Coll., 1993. Chief psychiat. nurse psychotherapist Vets. Hosp., Dallas, 1956-72; state rep. Tex. Ho. Reps. Dist. 33-0, Dallas, 1972-77; regional dir. HEW, Dallas, 1977-79; exec. asst. to adminstr. for primary health care policy HEW, Washington, 1979-81; v.p. Vis. Nurse Assn. of Tex., Dallas, 1981-87; mem. Tex. State Senate, dist. 23, 1986-93, U.S. Congress from 30th Tex. dist., Washington, 1993—; mem. sci., transp. and infrastructure coms. U.S. Congress from 30th Tex. dist.; cons. div. urban affairs Zales Corp., Dallas, 1976-77; exec. asst. personnel div. Neiman-Marcus, Dallas, 1972-75; pres. Eddie Bernice Johnson & Assocs., Inc., Metroplex News, Dallas-Ft. Worth Airport. Bd. dirs. ARC. Recipient Citizenship award Nat. Conf. Christians and Jews, 1985; named an Outstanding Alumnus St. Mary's Coll. of Nursing, 1986. Mem. Alpha Kappa Alpha. Office: US Ho of Reps 1123 Longworth HOB Washington DC 20515

JOHNSON, EDGAR MCCARTHY, psychologist; b. Jacksonville, Fla., Oct. 29, 1941; s. James Mack Johnson and Dorothy (Vickers) Logue; m. Fatima Nunes, Sept. 9, 1967; children: Victoria C., David M. BS in Applied Psychology, Ga. Inst. Tech., 1964; MS in Exptl. Psychology, Tufts U., 1967, PhD in Exptl. Psychology, 1969. Research psychologist U.S. Army Research Inst., Alexandria, Va., 1970-78, chief human factors sect., 1978-80, dir. systems research lab., 1980-82, tech. dir. U.S. Army Research Inst., 1982-93, dir., 1993—; chief psychologist U.S. Army, 1982—. Served to capt. U.S. Army, 1968-70. NDEA fellow, 1965-67. Fellow Am. Psychol. Assn., Am. Psychol. Soc., Human Factors and Ergonomics Soc., Washington Acad. Sci. (Sci. Achievement award 1980); mem. IEEE (Franklin V. Taylor award 1984), Ergonomics Soc., Sigma Xi. Club: Cosmos (Washington). Home: 5315 Renaissance Ct Burke VA 22015-2194 Office: US Army Rsch Inst 5001 Eisenhower Ave Alexandria VA 22304-4841

JOHNSON, EDITH SCOTT, English educator, writing consultant; b. Nashville, Ga., Mar. 25, 1943; d. James O'Leary and Edith Scott (Strother) Fuller; m. David James Moore, Feb. 4, 1961 (div. Sept. 1968); children: Meg Moore Bragdon, Marijim Moore Reeves; m. James Carter Johnson, Nov. 22, 1969 (div. June 1975); 1 child, James Carter III. BA in Art and English, Valdosta (Ga.) State Coll., 1968; MA in English, U. Nev., Reno, 1990; PhD in English, Ga. State U., Atlanta, 1997. Test code writer Westinghouse Air

Brake Co., Lexington, Ky., 1962-64; rsch. asst. U. Ky., Lexington, 1964-67; songwriter, recording artist Dove and Commanchee Records, Nashville, 1967-74; adminstrv. coord. devel. studies Ga. State U., Atlanta, 1976-80; asst. dir. PACE program U. Nev., Reno, 1985-88, asst. dir. writing ctr., 1988-90, adj. instr. English, 1989-91; asst. prof. English Abraham Baldwin Coll., Tifton, Ga., 1991—; writing cons. Crisp Area Arts Alliance, Cordele, Ga., 1996-97; resident poet Abraham Baldwin Coll., 1995-97; rschr. Ga. State U., Atlanta, 1991-97. Author: Driftwood and Wintergreen, 1996 (Internat. Poet award Internat. Soc. Poets 1996), Cold Hearts and Glass Eyes, 1997 (1st class award Ga. State U. 1997), Images of Love and Ice, 1998, The Evening Wolves, 1998; contbg. poet: World of Poetry, 1985 (Golden Poet award 1985), Iliad Press, 1995-96 (Poet of Yr. award 1995-96); performer Arts Experiment Sta., Tifton, 1996-97; poetry reader The Magpie Shop, Art Dept. Cornwall (Eng.) Coll., 1996. Tchr. bible Trinity United Meth. Ch., Tifton, 1997. Collected works dedicated in her honor Crisp Area Arts Alliance, Cordele, 1997. Mem. Nat. Coun. Tchrs. English, Nat. Assn. for Devel. Edn. (presenter, presider 1991-97), Nat. Authors' Registry, Order Ea. Star (organist 1986-91, grand choir 1990). Republican. Avocations: dulcimer, piano, guitar, singing, landscape and portrait art. Home: 609 12th St E Tifton GA 31794-4043 Office: Abraham Baldwin Coll 2802 Moore Hwy # Sta50 Tifton GA 31794-2605

JOHNSON, EDNA RUTH, editor; b. Sturgeon Bay, Wis., Dec. 23, 1918; d. Charles Frederick and Georgina (Knutson) Johnson; m. Al Larson, 1955. BA, U. So. Fla., 1971. With The Churchman, 1950-89; editor The Human Quest (formerly The Churchman), St. Petersburg, Fla., 1968—; tchr. ballroom dancing to Eckerd Coll. Students, St. Petersburg, Fla., 1995-96. Editor, Friendship News (USA-USSR), N.Y.C., 1975-88; mem. editorial bd. The Humaist, Amherst, N.Y., 1980—. Bd. dirs. ACLU, Nat. Emergency Civil Liberties Com., N.Y.C. Named Fla. Humanist of Yr. Am. Humanist Assn. Fla., 1975, Pres. Soc. of Fine Arts Arts, Pinellas Park, Fla., 1970-90. Mem. Acad. Sr. Profls. at Eckerd Coll. Avocation: ballroom dancing, ballet, painting. Home and Office: Palm Shores Apt 2B 830 N Shore Dr NE Saint Petersburg FL 33701-2002

JOHNSON, EDWARD CROSBY, III, financial company executive; b. Boston, June 29, 1930; s. Edward Crosby and Elsie (Johnson) J.; m. Elizabeth Bishop Hodges, Oct. 8, 1960; children: Abigail Pierrepont, Elizabeth Livingston, Edward Crosby. A.B., Harvard U., 1954. With Fidelity Investments, Boston, 1957—, pres., chief exec. officer, 1972-77; chmn. bd., chief exec. officer parent co. FMR Corp., 1977—. Bd. dirs. Ctr. for Neurologic Diseases; hon. trustee Mus. Fine Arts, Boston. Served with AUS, 1954-56. Fellow Am. Acad. Arts and Scis.; mem. Mass. Hist. Soc. Office: Fidelity Investments 82 Devonshire St Boston MA 02109-3614

JOHNSON, EDWARD ROY, library director; b. Denver, Nov. 29, 1940; s. Burton Clifford and Bonnie Jean (Daughtry) J.; m. Benita Irene Hulbert, June 14, 1964; 1 son, Elliot Hulbert. B.A., U. Colo., 1964; M.A., U. Wis., 1966; Ph.D., 1974. Library asst. Univ. Colo., Boulder, 1964-65; ref. librarian Univ. Iowa, Iowa City, 1966-67; bus. librarian Univ. Iowa, 1967-69; asst. dean libraries Pa. State Univ., State College, 1972-79; dir. librs. North Tex. State Univ., Denton, 1979-87; dean of librs. Okla. State U., Stillwater, 1987—. Author: (with Stuart H. Mann) Organization Development for Academic Libraries, 1980. Pres. Jewish Community Center, State College, 1977-79, Jewish Congregation, Denton, Tex., 1981-84. Recipient U.S. Dept. Health, Edn., Welfare fellowship, 1969-72; Research grant Council Library Resources, 1977-78. Mem. ALA, AAUP, Tex. Library Assn., Am. Philatelic Soc., Phi Alpha Theta, Beta Phi Mu. Clubs: Kiwanis, B'nai B'rith. Home: 5020 W 10th Ave Stillwater OK 74074-1411 Office: Edmon Low Libr Okla State U Stillwater OK 74075

JOHNSON, EINAR WILLIAM, lawyer; b. Fontana, Calif., Apr. 6, 1955; s. Carl Wilbur and Judith Priscilla (Orcutt) J.; m. Cynthia Jeanne Bailey, Oct. 9, 1976; children: Brian Mark (dec.), Carl Einar, Gregory Daniel, Christopher James, Shaun Curtis, Bradford Keith. BA in Speech Communications, Brigham Young U., 1980; JD, J. Reuben Clark Law Sch., Provo, Utah, 1983. Bar: Calif. 1983, U.S. Dist. Ct. (cen. dist.) Calif. 1984, U.S. Ct. Appeals (9th cir.) 1986, U.S. Supreme Ct. 1987. Asst. debate coach Brigham Young U., Provo, Utah, 1979-80; fin. committeeman Jed Richardson for Congress, Provo, 1980; sales mgr./salesman Ortho Mattress, Orem, Utah, 1979, 81; law clk. Acret & Perrochet, L.A., 1982; jud. clk. U.S. Cts., Salt Lake City, 1983-84; litigation atty. Smith & Hilbig, Torrance, Calif., 1984-90; litigation ptnr. Smith & Hilbig, 1990-93; owner, founder Johnson and Assocs., 1993—; editor Moot Ct. program J. Reuben Clark Law Sch., 1982-83. Contbr. articles to profl. jours. Missionary, leader Ch. of Jesus Christ of Latter Day Saints, Denver, 197476, Sunday sch. tchr., L.A., 1986-89, stake high counselor, 1989-92, 1st counselor ward bishopric, 1992-93, pres. elders quorum, 1993-94, high counselor, 1994—. Recipient A.H. Christensen award, Am. Jurisprudence awards Bancroft-Whitney, 1981. Mem. ABA, Calif. Bar Assn., L.A. County Bar Assn., Assn. Trial Lawyers Am., Internat. Platofrm Assn., Order Barristers, Kappa Tau Alpha. Republican. Mormon. Avocations: photography, guitar, fishing, house remodeling, automobile restoration. Office: Johnson & Assocs 3655 Torrance Blvd Ste 470 Torrance CA 90503-4848

JOHNSON, ELAINE MCDOWELL, retired federal government executive, educator; b. Balt., June 28, 1942; d. McKinley and Lena (Blue) McDowell; m. Walter Johnson; children: Nathan H. Murphy Jr., Michael W. Murphy. BA, Morgan State U., Balt., 1965; MSW, U. Md., 1971, PhD, 1988. Drug abuse adminstr., acting regional dir. State Md. Drug Abuse Adminstrn., Balt., 1971-72; social sci. analyst, pub. health advisor Nat. Inst. Drug Abuse, Rockville, MD, 1972-76, dep. dir., dir. div. community assistance, 1976-82, dep. assoc. dir. for policy devel., 1981-82, dir. div. prevention and communications, 1982-85; exec. asst. to adminstr. Alcohol, Drug Abuse & Mental Health Adminstrn., Rockville, Md., 1985; dep. dir. Nat. Inst. on Drug Abuse, Rockville, MD, 1985-88; dir. Ctr. for Substance Abuse Prevention, 1988-96; acting adminstr. Alcohol, Drug Abuse and Mental Health Adminstrn., Rockville, Md., 1992, Substance Abuse and Mental Health Svcs. Adminstrn., Rockville, Md., 1992-94; expert cons. in substance abuse, treatment, and mental health fields; prof. Morgan State U., Balt. *Elaine Johnson has twenty-eight years of successful experience, including over twenty years of Federal service, administering research, prevention and treatment services programs in the alcohol, drug abuse and mental health fields; in developing, coordinating, implementing, and evaluating comprehensive service delivery systems; in managing complex financial and human resources; and in establishing and maintaining collaborative relationships with executive and legislative bodies at the Federal, State, and local levels; private sector groups and organizations; professional organizations; international groups; and community agencies and leaders. In serving as acting administrator for both the Alcohol, Drug Abuse and Mental Health Administration (ADAMHA) and the Substance Abuse and Mental Health Services Administration (SAMHSA), she maintained the agencies budgets in excess of $2 billion.* Active United Meth.Ch., Balt., 1994—. Recipient Outstanding Leadership in Improving Health Care in Black Cmty. award Nat. Med. Assn., 1989, Secretary's commendation HHS, 1989, Disting. Svc. award, 1990, Nat. Coun. on Alcoholism and Drug Dependence Ind., Pres. award for outstanding fed. leadership, 1991, Presdl. Meritorious Exec. Rank award, 1991, Presdl. Meritorious Disting. Rank award, 1993. Mem. NASW, Am. Coll. Mental Health Adminstrn., Sr. Execs. Assn. Office: Morgan State U Jenkins Behavioral Scis Ctr Rm 434 Cold Spring Ln and Hillen Rd Baltimore MD 21251

JOHNSON, ELIZABETH ERICSON, retired educator; b. Rockford, Ill., Oct. 5, 1927; d. Gunnar Lawrence and Victoria Amelia (Carlson) Ericson; m. Barent Olaf Johnson, June 2, 1951; children: Ann E. Arellano, Susan M. Taber. BA, U. Ill., 1949; MSEd, No. Ill. U., 1969. Tchr. Sch. Dist. 205, Rockford, Ill., 1949-53, 65-92. Mem. Ct. Appointed Spl. Advocate, Rockford, 1992—. Mem. AAUW, LWV (bd. dirs. 1994-96, local bd.), Winnebago Ret. Tchrs. Assn. (various bds.), Phi Delta Kappa. Avocations: musician, violist. Home: 1902 Valencia Dr Rockford IL 61108-6818

JOHNSON, ELLEN RANDEL, real estate broker; b. Canton, Miss., May 9, 1916; d. Robert Colquhoun and Laura Arabella (Taylor) Randel; m. Floyd Everett Johnson Sr.; children: Dolly Mae Johnson Day, Floyd Everett Johnson Jr. Student, Blue Mountain Coll., 1934-35; course in real estate, Miss. Realtors Inst., 1976-77. Bookkeeper E. Constantin, Jr., Yazoo City, Miss., 1951-54, 56-59; draftsman Miss. State Hwy. Dept., Yazoo City, 1955; office mgr. Miss. Chem. Corp. Fed. Credit Union, Yazoo City, 1963-66; freelance journalist Yazoo Herald, 1970-74; broker, owner Ellen Johnson Realty, Yazoo, 1977; broker, assoc. Phyllis Waltman Realtors and Century 21 Beard & McMahan Realtors, Hattiesburg, Miss., 1978-79; broker, owner Ellen Johnson, Realtor, Hattiesburg, 1979-91. Author: The Dining Table for Candida Patients, 1988, Yesterday, Today, For Tomorrow: A Family History, Colquhoun/Calhoun and Their Ancestral Homelands, 1993; contbr. articles to profl. jours. Charter dir. Yazoo Arts Council, 1973-75; chmn. civic quiz Am. Bus. Women's Assn., Hattiesburg, 1987. Mem. Nat. Assn. Realtors (Omega Tau Rho medal 1984), Nat. Women's Council Realtors, Miss. Women's Council Realtors (gov. 1984, v.p. 1983-84, by-laws chmn. 1984, Realtor of Yr. 1984), Hattiesburg Women's Council Realtors (v.p. 1982-83, Realtor of Yr. 1984), Miss. Assn. Realtors (by-laws com.), Hattiesburg Bd. Realtors (bd. dirs., com. chmn. 1979, 81, 84, v.p. multiple listing service 1982-83, pres. 1983-84, treas. 1987, Realtor of Yr. 1984). Republican. Baptist. Clubs: Mozart (Yazoo City) (pres. 1969); Miss. Music (Jackson) (jr. festival chmn. 1973-75). Avocations: genealogy, music, writing, watching TV. Home and Office: 1302 Estelle Ave Hattiesburg MS 39402-2719

JOHNSON, ELLIS LANE, mathematician; b. Athens, Ga., July 26, 1938; s. Glenn Irvin and Edna Marshall (Volberg) J.; m. Anne Hall , Dec. 30, 1962 (div. June, 1978); children: Michael Glenn, Catherine Lane; m. Huiling Gan, Sept.12, 1987; 1 child, Frederick Gan. BS, Ga. Inst. Tech., 1960; MA, U. Calif., Berkeley, 1962, PhD, 1965. Asst. prof. Yale U., New Haven, 1964-68; rsch. staff mem. IBM T.J. Watson Rsch. Ctr., Yorktown Heights, N.Y., 1968-93; Coca-Cola prof. Ga. Inst. Tech., Atlanta, 1989—; adj. prof. U. Waterloo, Ont., Can., 1970-77, SUNY, Stony Brook, 1983-87. Author: (rsch. monograph) Integer Programming: Facets, Subadditivity and Duality, 1980; co-editor: Studies in Integer Programming, 1977, Discrete Optimization, 1979; contbr. numerous articles to profl. jours. Recipient Sr. Scientist award Alexander von Humboldt Found., 1980, George B. Dantzig prize Math. Programming Soc./ Soc. Insdl. and Applied Math., 1985; IBM fellow, 1990. Mem. NAE, Math. Programming Soc., Inst. for Ops. Rsch. and Mgmt. Sci. Office: Ga Inst Tech Sch Indsl & Sys Engring Atlanta GA 30332-0205

JOHNSON, ELMER HUBERT, sociologist, researcher in criminology; b. Racine, Wis., Apr. 10, 1917; s. Elmer Dumguard and Lucinda (Hinderholtz) J.; m. Carol Catherine Holmes, June 19, 1943; children: Joy Marjorie Boyden, Jill Catherine Lewis. BA, U. Wis., 1946, MA, 1948, PhD, 1950. Reporter Racine Jour. Times, 1935-40; from asst. prof. to prof. N.C. State U., Raleigh, 1949-66; asst. dir. N.C. State Prison Dept., Raleigh, 1958-60; prof. So. Ill. U., Carbondale, 1966-87, Disting. prof., 1984, emeritus, 1987—; bd. dirs. Joint Commn. on Corrections, Washington, 1965-70; vis. fellow Max Planck Inst., Freiburg, Germany, 1978, Nat. Inst. Law Enforcement and Criminal Justice, Washington, 1979, UN Asia and Far East Inst., Tokyo, 1985, others. Author: Crime, Correction and Society, 1965; editor: International Handbook of Contemporary Development in Criminology, 2 vols., 1983; editor: Handbook on Crime and Delinquency Prevention, 1987, Japanese Corrections: Managing Convicted Offenders in an Orderly Society, 1996, Criminalization and Prisoners in Japan: Six Contrary Cohorts, 1997, Community and Corrections in Japan: Nature and Challenges, 1999. Served to capt. USAAC, 1941-46, with USAF Res. Mem. Internat. Soc. Criminology, Internat. Sociol. Assn., Am. Soc. Criminology (bd. dirs. 1975-80), Acad. Criminal Justice Scis., Am. Sociol. Assn. Avocations: scholarly reading, international contacts, music appreciation. Home: 451 E Clayton Rd Carbondale IL 62901-7104

JOHNSON, EMERY ALLEN, physician; b. Sioux Falls, S.D., Apr. 16, 1929; s. Emery Albert and Florence Emily J.; m. Nancy Mourning, June 19, 1954; children: Steven, Scott, Jennifer, Jill. B.S., Hamline U., 1951; M.D., U. Minn., 1954; M.P.H., U. Calif., Berkeley, 1964. Commd. med. officer USPHS, 1955-81; Indian health area dir. USPHS, Billings, Mont., 1964-66; asst. and dep. dir. Indian Health Service USPHS, Rockville, Md., 1966-69; dir. Indian Health Service USPHS, 1969-81, asst. surgeon gen., 1969-81; cons. in pub. health and med. care adminstrn., 1981—; cons. Peace Corps, WHO, AID, Nat. Med. Center, Liberia; U.S. del. UNICEF Exec. Bd., 1978. Recipient Rockefeller Public Service award, 1979; Excellence in Public Service award Am. Acad. Pediatrics; medals USPHS. Mem. APHA (chmn. health adminstrn. sect.), Am. Acad. Family Practice, AMA. Office: 13826 Dowlais Dr Rockville MD 20853-2658

JOHNSON, ERIC, legislative administrator; b. Phila., Mar. 19, 1971. AA, Palm Beach C.C., 1993. Dep. chief of staff to Rep. Robert Wexler U.S. Ho. of Reps., Washington, 1997—. Office: US Ho of Reps 213 CHOB Washington DC 20515

JOHNSON, ERNEST FREDERICK, chemical engineer, educator; b. Jamestown, N.Y., Apr. 4, 1918; s. Ernest Frederick and Esther Marie (Engstrom) J.; m. Marjorie Ruth McMullin, July 15, 1944; children: David S. (dec.), Carolyn L. Walton, Arthur B., Melissa A. Bonner. BS, Lehigh U., 1940; PhD, U. Pa., 1949. Rsch. engr., tech. supr. synthetic organic chem. mfr. Barrett div. Allied Chem. Corp., Phila., 1940-46; asst. prof. dept. chem. engring. Princeton U., 1948-54, assoc. prof., 1954-59, prof., 1959-86, acting chmn. dept. chem. engring., 1959-60, chmn. dept., 1977-78, assoc. dean faculty, 1962-66, clk. of faculty, 1983-86, assoc. Plasma Physics Lab., 1955-86, prof. emeritus, 1986—, sr. advisor to pres., 1988-91; cons. petroleum, chem., engring., environ., food processing firms, govt. agys., 1949—; bd. dirs. Autodynamics Inc. 1968-85; mem. adv. bd. Indsl. and Engring. Chemistry, 1964-67. Author: Automatic Process Control, 1967; contbr. Advances in Chemical Engineering, 1958, Ency. Chemistry, Chemistry of Fusion Power Development, 1972; contbr. articles to sci. jours. Trustee Associated Univs., Inc., 1962-68, chmn. bd., 1965-67; trustee Westminster Found., 1973-79. Recipient Nat. Engrs. Week Engring. Edn. award, 1994. Fellow AAAS, AIChE (exec. com. Cen. Jersey sect. 1972—), Am. Inst. Chemists; mem. Am. Chem. Soc. (exec. com. div. indsl. and engring. chemistry 1965-67, coun. 1976-78), Princeton Engring. Assn. (sec.-treas. 1954-57, exec. com. 1954—), Adirondack Mountain Club, Appalachian Mountain Club, Tärnavrá Yacht Club, Sigma Xi, Tau Beta Pi, Phi Eta Sigma. Presbyterian (elder). Home: 90 Lambert Dr Princeton NJ 08540-2319 also: Indian Point Rd Stonington ME 04681-9702

JOHNSON, EUGENE CLARE, data processing company executive; b. Whitehall, Wis., Nov. 19, 1940; s. Paul Reuben and Clara Theresa (Severson) J.; m. Livia Ann Baynes, Sept. 23, 1967; children: Andrew Paul, Anthony Alexander. Student, Madison Coll., 1959, Pasadena Coll., 1961, Purdue U., 1962, Harvard U., 1974. Vol. Peace Corps, Chile, 1962-64; acct. Am. Ins. Underwriters, N.Y.C., 1964-66; advanceman to Pres. Richard M. Nixon N.Y.C., 1966-68; asst. treas. Bristol-Myers Co., N.Y.C., 1968-69; spl. asst. to Gov. Nelson Rockefeller N.Y.C., 1969-77; mgr. advanced systems div. U.S. Postal Service, Washington, 1971-80; with govt. relations dept. ITT, Washington, 1980-85; exec. v.p., chief operating officer TCom Systems, Inc., Washington, 1985-88; v.p. market devel. Diversified Data and Communications Inc., Washington, 1988-90; pres., chief exec. officer Bus. Mail Express, Inc., Washington, 1990-95, Mail 2000, Washington, 1995—; founder Electronic Funds Transfer Assocs., Washington, 1977. Patentee performance analyzer. Sr. adviser Reagan Presdl. Transition Team, 1980; presdl. appointee U.S. Archtl. and Transp. Barriers Compliance Bd., 1988-90; adv. bd. Peace Corps., 1990-92. Club: Kenwood Golf and Country (Bethesda, Md.) (chmn. bd. dirs. 1987). Avocations: tennis, golf, jogging. Home: 5525 Chamberlin Ave Chevy Chase MD 20815-6643 Office: Mail 2000 Inc 5420 Butler Rd Bethesda MD 20816

JOHNSON, EUGENE LAURENCE, lawyer; b. Wisconsin Rapids, Wis., Nov. 30, 1936; s. Elmer Hilding and Clarabell May (Staffeld) J.; m. Barbara Dell Braley, June 18, 1960; children: Mark, Ben, Christopher. BSCE, U. Wis., 1960, JD, 1962. Bar: Minn. 1963, Calif. 1965, U.S. Patent Office 1963. Atty. Pillsbury Co., Mpls., 1962-64; assoc. Mellin, Hanscom & Hursh, San Francisco, 1964-66, Dorsey & Whitney, Mpls., 1966-98; ptnr. Eugene L. Johnson, PA, Mpls., MN, 1998—; adj. prof., program founder intellectual property law William Mitchell Coll. of Law, 1967-75. Capt. C.E. USAR, 1960. Mem. Minn. Bar Assn. (past bd. govs.), Am. Intellectual Property Law Assn., Minn. Intellectual Property Law Assn. (past pres.), Mpls. Athletic Club, Lafayette Country Club. Republican. Office: Eugene L Johnson PA 1500 Bohns Point Rd Wayzata MN 55391-9309

JOHNSON, EUGENE WALTER, mathematician, editor; b. El Paso, Tex., May 25, 1939; s. Walter Albert and Lillian Ann (Martinets) J.; m. Sandra Sue Gilbert, Oct. 16, 1959; 1 dau., Catherine Mary. Student, Riverside City Coll., 1958-60; BA, U. Calif., Riverside, 1963, MA, 1964, PhD, 1966. Asst. prof. Eastern N.Mex. State U., 1966; asst. prof. math. U. Iowa, Iowa City, 1966-70; asso. prof. U. Iowa, 1970-75, prof., 1975—, chmn. dept., 1976-79. Author: Linear Algebra with Maple, 1993, Linear Algegra with Mathematics, 1995; co-author: Maple Flight Manual, 1992; contbr. articles to profl. jours. Mem. Am. Math. Soc., Math. Assn. Am. Democrat. Home: 4320 Oakridge Trl NE Iowa City IA 52240-7735 Office: Univ Iowa Dept Math Iowa City IA 52242

JOHNSON, EVELYN BRYAN, flying service executive; b. Corbin, Ky., Nov. 4, 1909; d. Edward William and Myme Estelle (Fox) Stone; m. Wyatt J. Bryan, Mar. 21, 1931 (dec. 1963); m. Morgan N. Johnson, Feb. 25, 1965 (dec. Mar. 1977). Grad., Tenn Wesleyan Jr. Coll., 1929; student, U. Tenn., 1930-32. With Morristown (Tenn.) Flying Svc., Inc., 1947—, chief flight instr., 1949—, sec.-treas., 1949-62, pres., 1962-82; mgr. Moore Murrell Airport, 1962—; gov.'s appointee Tenn. Aero. Commn., 1983-86, vice-chmn., 1987-89, chmn., 1989, 94-96, 96—. Recipient Carnegie Hero medal, 1958, Svc. to Mankind award Morristown Sertoma Club, 1981, Kitty Hawk award, FAA, 1991, Friends of Aviation award Tenn. Aviation Assn., 1992, Stewart G. Potter Aviation Edn. award Aviation Distbrs. and Mfrs. Assn., 1992, Elder Statesman of Aviation award Nat. Aeronautics Assn., 1993; named Flight Instr. of Yr., Nashville Dist. 1973, 79, So. region 1979, Nat., 1979 (all FAA), Outstanding Alumnus Tenn. Wesleyan Coll., 1981, Inductee Women in Aviation Pioneers Hall of Fame, 1994, Hamblen Women Hall of Fame, 1997, Flight Instr. Hall of Fame, FAA Air Adventure Mus., Oshkosh, 1997. Mem. CAP, Morristown Area C. of C., Nat. Assn. Flight Instrs. (bd. dirs., treas 1987-88, award 1992), Ninety-Nines, Whirly Girls (plaque 1992), Aircraft Owners and Pilots Assn. Silver Wings (bd. dirs. 1987—, Woman of Yr. 1981, Carl Fromhagen award 1992, Ninety Nines award of merit 1994). Republican. Baptist. Holder of record most flying time for women pilots, 1995, Guiness Book of Records 1995-96, 97, 98, 99. Home: RR 1 Jefferson Cy TN 37760-9801 Office: PO Box 1013 Morristown TN 37816-1013

JOHNSON, EWELL CALVIN, research and engineering executive; b. Tampa, Fla., Apr. 18, 1926; s. Ewell Calvin and Alice Elizabeth (Reitz) J.; m. Elaine Hixon, Sept. 30, 1967; 1 dau., Cynthia Ann. BEE, Ga. Inst. Tech., 1947; MS, MIT, 1949, DSc, 1951. V.p. engring. and rsch. Bendix Corp., Detroit, 1951-73; v.p rsch. and devel. Gould Inc., Chgo., 1973-75; pres. Vincent Corp., Tampa, 1980-85; dir. rsch. and devel. Aerosonic Corp., Clearwater, Fla., 1988-89; mem. corp. staff UBC Inc., Tampa, 1989—. Contbr. articles to profl. jours. Patentee in field. Named Outstanding Young Engr., Engring. Soc. Detroit, 1955, Outstanding Young Alumnus, Ga. Inst. Tech., 1961, Outstanding Mich. Inventor, Mich. Patent Law Assn., Detroit, 1963. Fellow IEEE; mem. Rotary Club, Palma Ceia Golf Club (Tampa), Alpha Tau Omega (pres. 1946-47). Home: PO Box 18751 Tampa FL 33679-8751 Office: UBC Inc 6101 Johns Rd Tampa FL 33634-4482

JOHNSON, EYDITH G. IVORY, poet; b. South Bend, Ind., Sept. 13, 1960; d. Fred and Willa (Ivory) Riley; m. Gary Johnson, May 21, 1994; children: Eric, Ericia. Student, Ind. U., South Bend, 1991. Cert. nurse aid, medication asst. Patient care asst. Meml. Hosp., South Bend, 1990-91; program asst. Logan Industries, South Bend, 1992-94; detention monitor, tchr.'s aide Sch. Corp. of South Bend, 1994-95. Author: (book of poetry) Wings, Women's Thoughts Poetry, 1996, Voices After Wards, 1996, (non-fiction) Where Are My People?, 1997. Recipient Alive with Svc. awards, C. of C., South Bend, 1996, 97. Avocations: writing, drawing, writing.

JOHNSON, FENG-LING MARGARET, English educator; b. Fengshan, Taiwan, Republic of China, Apr. 25, 1963; came to U.S., 1987; d. Ren-tsuo and Yu-ehn (Huang) Chang; m. Timothy Arnold Johnson, Dec. 28, 1991; children: Daniel R., Jonathan H. BA, Nat. Taiwan U., 1985; MA, Ohio U., 1989; PhD, U. Ill., 1995. Cert. 2d lang. acquisition and tchr. edn. English writer and translator English Today Mag., Taipei, Taiwan, 1985; sales rep. Lien-I Textile Co., Taipei, 1985-86; tchr. English MingDao H.S., Taichung, Taiwan, 1986-87; instr. Chinese various positions, Independence, Iowa, 1992-96; asst. prof. ESL Northwestern Coll., St. Paul, Minn., 1996—; presenter in field. Recipient Leadership Mentoring Program award Tchrs. English Spkrs. Other Langs., 1999. Mem. TESOL, Inc., Minn. TESOL (co-editor newsletter 1999), Internat. Reading Assn., Am. Assn. Applied Linguistics, Phi Kappa Phi. Office: Northwestern Coll 3003 Snelling Ave N Saint Paul MN 55113

JOHNSON, FRANCES SWIGON, English educator; b. Jersey City, Oct. 8, 1947; d. Joseph Thomas and Helen Catherine (Malayter) Swigon; m. Carl Frederick Johnson; children: Matthew Waters, Mark Waters, Justin Waters, Wesley Johnson. BA in English, Christopher Newport U., 1982; MA in English, Old Dominion U., 1984; PhD in English, U. Okla., 1996. Grad. tchg. asst. English Old Dominion U., Norfolk, Va., 1982-84, info. officer, 1984-85; instr. English Old Dominion U., Norfolk, 1985-89, lectr., computer lab. dir., 1989-94; asst. to dir. composition U. Okla., Norman, 1991-93, interim dir. Writing Ctr., 1994-96; asst. prof. college writing Rowan U., Glassboro, N.J., 1996—; radio show host Cmty. Voices, Rowan U., Glassboro, 1998—. Contbr. articles to profl. jours. Mem. Home and Sch. Assn., Pitman, N.J., 1995—; presenter County In-Svc. Edn. Day, Gloucester County, Franklinville, N.J., 1998. Recipient scholarship U. Okla., 1991. Mem. MLA, Nat. Coun. Tchrs. English, Rhetoric Soc. Am., Coalition Women Scholars in Rhetoric and Composition, Assn. Tchrs. Tech. Writing, Phi Kappa Phi, Sigma Tau Delta. Avocations: reading, gardening, cooking, pro football. Office: Rowan U 201 Mullica Hill Rd Glassboro NJ 08028

JOHNSON, FRANCIS SEVERIN, physicist; b. Omak, Wash., July 20, 1918; s. Ralston Severin and Elizabeth (Gruenes) J.; m. Maurine Marie Green, Sept. 12, 1943; 1 dau., Sharan Kaye. B.Sc. with honors in Physics, U. Alta., Can., 1940; M.A. in Physics and Meteorology, UCLA, 1942, Ph.D. in Meteorology, 1958. Head, high atmosphere research sect. U.S. Naval Research Lab., Washington, 1946-55; mgr. space physics research Lockheed Missiles & Space Co., 1955-62; head, atmospheric and space scis. div. S.W. Center Advanced Studies, Dallas, 1962-64; dir. earth and planetary scis. lab. S.W. Center Advanced Studies, 1964-69; acting pres. U. Tex. at Dallas, 1969-71; dir. Center for Advanced Studies, 1971-74, Cecil H. and Ida M. Green honors prof. natural sci., 1974-89, prof. emeritus, 1989—, exec. dean grad. studies and research, 1976-79; asst. dir. astron., atmosphere, earth and ocean scis. NSF, Washington, 1979-83; cons. ionospheric physics subcom., space scis. steering com. NASA, 1960-62, mem. planetary atmospheres subcom., space scis. steering com., 1962-67, chmn. lunar atmospheric measurements team, Apollo sci. planning teams, 1964-67, mem. adv. bd. Mars space missions, 1964-67, mem. lunar and planetary missions bd., 1967-71; mem. adv. panel atmospheric scis. NSF, 1962-67; mem. working group IV COSPAR, 1965-80, v.p., 1975-80; mem. Nat. Acad. Scis. panel adv. to central radio propagation lab. Nat. Bur. Standards, 1962-65, mem. panel weather and climate modification Nat. Acad. Scis., 1964-70, mem. space sci. bd., 1969-81, mem. geophysics research bd., 1971-77, mem. bd. on atmospheric scis. and climate, 1984-87, mem. Nat. Acad. Scis. com. adv. to NOAA, 1966-71, mem. climate research bd., 1977-79; mem. adv. com. research to coordinating bd. Tex. Coll. and Univ. System, 1966-67; mem. sci. advisory bd. USAF, 1968-79; mem. nat. adv. com. Oceans and Atmosphere, 1971-73; pres. Spl. Com. on Solar Terrestrial Physics, 1974-77; mem. Aerocibo adv. bd. and vis. com. Nat. Astronomy and Ionsphere Ctr. Cornell U., 1985-88. Author: Satellite Environment Handbook, 1965; also numerous articles. Served with USAAF, 1942-46. Decorated Bronze Star medal; recipient Henryk Arctowski award NAS, 1972, Exceptional Sci. Achievement medal NASA, 1973, Meritorious Civilian Service award USAF, 1979, Disting. Tex. Sci. award Tex. Acad. Scis., 1984. Fellow Am. Geophys. Union (vice chmn. sect. geomagnetism and aeronomy 1964-68, pres. sect. solar planetary relationships 1970-72, John Adam Fleming award 1977), AAAS (council mem. 1968-72), Am. Meteorol. Soc. (councilor 1976-78), IEEE, AIAA (chmn. tech. com. space and atmospheric physics 1961-64, Space Sci. award 1966); mem. Internat. Assn. Geomagnetism and Aeronomy (exec. com. 1967-71), Internat. Union Radio Sci. (chmn. U.S. Commn. IV 1964-67, sec. U.S. nat. com. 1967-70, vice chmn. 1970-73, chmn. 1973-76), Internat. Union Geodesy and Geophysics (U.S. nat. com. 1973-76), Sigma Xi. Office: U Tex At Dallas MS FO22 PO Box 830688 Richardson TX 75083-0688

JOHNSON, FRANK, retired state official, educator; b. Ogden, Utah, Mar. 12, 1928; s. Clarence Budd and Arline (Parry) J.; m. Maralyn Brewer, Aug. 15, 1950; children: Scott, Arline, Laurie, Kelly, Edward. BS, U. Utah, 1955; MS, U. Ill., 1958, PhD, 1960. Instr. U. N.D., Grand Forks, 1955-56; teaching asst. U. Ill., Urbana, 1956-59; rsch. asst. prof. U. Del., Newark, 1959-60; prof. U. Utah, Salt Lake City, 1960-93, assoc. dean, 1970-77; dir. divsn. pub. utilities State of Utah, Salt Lake City, 1989-95; cons. Gen. Foods, Sears, Magnavox, Albertsons, Zion Bank, Nat. Food Brokers Assn., others; owner, part-owner Old Post Office Bldg., Ogden, Utah, Seventeenth St. Storage; bd. dirs. Enterprise Mentors Internat. Legis. Utah House of Reps., Salt Lake City, 1982-88. Republican. Avocations: mountains, boating, travel, reading, public service. Home: 2373 Dayspring Ln Salt Lake City UT 84124-1887

JOHNSON, FRANKLYN ARTHUR, academic administrator; b. Rochester, N.Y., Nov. 6, 1921; s. Robert Barnes and Olyve Cole (Eckler) J.; m. Emily Bernetta Lingle, Aug. 15, 1945 (div. Aug. 1978); children: Franklyn Arthur (dec.), Terri A. Cochran, Sandra C. Fox; m. Elena Senese, Sept. 27, 1991. BA, Rutgers U., 1947; MA, Harvard U., 1949, PhD, 1952; LHD (hon.), Jacksonville U., 1961; DLitt (hon.), Mt. Senario Coll., Ladysmith, Wis., 1971; LLD (hon.), Flagler Coll., St. Augustine, Fla., 1976; DCL (hon.), Drury Coll., Springfield, Mo., 1976; HHD (hon.), Mo. Valley Coll., 1978. Intelligence officer CIA, Washington, 1949-51; asst., assoc. prof. govt. Rollins Coll., Winter Park, Fla., 1952-56; pres., prof. govt. Jacksonville U., Fla., 1956-63, Calif. State U., Los Angeles, 1963-65; asst. sec., dir. Job Corps OEO, Washington, 1965-67; pres., chmn., trustee Wm. H. Donner Found., N.Y.C., 1967-70; dir. Arthur Vining Davis Founds., Coral Gables, Fla., 1970-78; prof. adminstrn. Fla. Atlantic U., Boca Raton, 1970-87; pres., prof. mgmt. S.W. Fla. Coll., Naples, 1987—; trustee Inst. for Am. Univs., Aix-en-Provence, France, 1967-97, Eckerd Coll., St. Petersburg, Fla., 1978-90; chmn. S.E. Coun. Founds., Atlanta, 1975-77. Author: Defence by Committee, 1960, Defence by Ministry, 1980, 81, One More Hill, 1949, rev. edits., 1982, 88, Santori, 1990, Castro: The Last Hurrah, 1992, The Periled Presidency, 1995, Here and There, 1995, After Thoughts, 1996, D. S. Nemenoff, Maestro, 1996, A Chance Encounter, 1996, Odds and Ends, 1996, The Gods That Failed, 1997, Pearls Are a Girl's Best Friend, 1997, The 22nd Amendment, 1998, The Reluctant Presidents, 1999, Santori Island of Evil; also articles on def., civil and mil. rels., adminstrn. Mem. U.S. Com. United World Colls., N.Y.C., 1975-85, Fla. Gov.'s Coun. on Indian Affairs, Tallahassee, 1975-80, exec. adv. coun. Fla. Atlantic U., chmn.; bd. dirs. Collier Cultural and Ednl. Ctr., Naples; v.p., dir. Beachwood Assn., Inc., 1992-94; pres. Francobollo Press. Lt. U.S. Army, 1942-45, ETO. Decorated Croix deGuerre (France), Silver Star, 5 Bronze Stars, 3 Purple Hearts, Conspicuous Svc. Cross; recipient George Washington honor medal Freedoms Found., Valley Forge, 1956, Profl. Achievement award Barry U., Miami, Fla., Eric Fenby lectr., 1991; named Champion Ind. Higher Edn. in Fla., Ind. Colls. Fla., 1992 Svc. Medallion, N. Fla. Jr. Coll., Madison, Fla. Fellow Inter-U. Seminar on Armed Forces and Soc.; mem. Delius Assn. Am. (life, founding pres.), Can. Inst. Strategic Studies, Phi Beta Kappa, Phi Alpha Theta, Pi Alpha Alpha (pres.), Phi Kappa Phi. Republican. Presbyterian. Avocations: classical music, writing fiction. Home: PO Box 1873 Bonita Springs FL 34133-1873

JOHNSON, FREDA S., public finance consultant; b. N.Y.C., Mar. 17, 1947; m. J. Chester Johnson, May 7, 1989. BA in Polit. Sci., CUNY, 1968; grad. Advanced Mgmt. Program, Harvard U., 1986. Analyst mcpl. div. Dun & Bradstreet Corp., N.Y.C., 1968-71; sr. analyst Moody's Investor Svc., Inc. (subs. Dun & Bradstreet), N.Y.C., 1972, v.p., assoc. dir. mcpl. dept., 1973-79, sr. v.p., dir. mcpl. dept., 1979-81, exec. v.p., 1981-90; pres. Govt. Fin. Assocs., Inc. pub. fin. adv. co., 1992—; mem. Anthony Commn. for Pub. Fin.; former sr. credit advisor Ecolink, joint Soviet-Am. pub. fin. project; Congl. testifier U.S. Senate Com. on Banking, Housing and Urban Affairs, subcom. fiscal affairs and health U.S. Ho. of Reps., U.S. Senate Com. Govtl. Affairs, Joing Econ. Com. Congress; bd. dirs. MBIA Inc., Nat. Assn. Ind. Pub. Fin. Advisors, 1993-95, Queens Coll. Corp. Adv. Bd.; bd. govs. Coun. Mcpl. Performance, 1984-86; instr. New Sch. for Social Rsch., 1982-83; mem. adv. bd. City Almanac, 1982-84; trustee Citizens Budget Com.; spkr. numerous profl. orgns., univs.; adj. prof. Grad. Sch. Bus. Adminstrn. Columbia U., spring 1991. Avocations: theater, museums, basketball fan. Office: Govt Fin Assocs 63 Wall St Fl 16 New York NY 10005-3001

JOHNSON, FREDERICK CARROLL, federal government executive; b. Sheridan, Wyo., Oct. 23, 1940; s. Carroll Luverne and Edna Elizabeth (Berg) J.; m. Pamela Ann Windsor, May 30, 1964 (dec. Feb. 1974); 1 child, Christian; m. Marla Starr Poore, Apr. 19, 1996. BS, U. N.D., 1962; postgrad., U. Tex., 1962-64; MS, U. Wash., 1966, PhD, 1966. Sr. scientist DBA Sys., Lanham, Md., 1966-68; sr. mathematician Boeing Sci. Rsch. Labs., Seattle, 1968-73; mathematician Nat. Bur. Standards, Gaithersburg, Md., 1973-77, divsn. chief, 1977-82, 1984-89; ptnr. Natural Resource Cons., Seattle, 1982-84; assoc. dir. for computing Nat. Inst. Standards and Tech., Gaithersburg, 1989—. Recipient Silver medal Dept. Commerce, 1977, others. Mem. IEEE, Soc. for Indsl. and Applied Math., Assn. for Computing Machinery, Cray Users Group, Nat. Fisheries Soc. Office: NIST Bldg 820 Rm 601 Gaithersburg MD 20899

JOHNSON, GARY EARL, governor; b. Minot, N.D., Jan. 1, 1953; s. Earl W. and Lorraine B. (Bostow) J.; m. Dee Simms, Nov. 27, 1976; children: Seah, Erik. BA in Polit. Sch., U. N.Mex., 1975. Pres., CEO Big J Enterprises, Albuquerque, 1976—; gov. State of N.Mex., 1995-98, 98—. Bd. dirs. Entrepreneurship Studies at U. N.Mex., 1993-95. Named to list of Big 50 Remodelers in the USA, 1987; named Entrepreneur of Yr., 1995. Mem. LWV, C. of C. Albuquerque (bd. dirs. 1993-95). Republican. Lutheran. Avocations: rock-climbing, mountain climbing, skiing, pilot, triathlete. Office: Office of Gov Rm 400 State Capitol Santa Fe NM 87503

JOHNSON, GARY KEITH, pediatrician; b. Chgo., Aug. 26, 1951; s. John Edward and Dorothy Lucille (Rudder) J. AB, Dartmouth Coll., 1973; MD, U. Ill., Chgo., 1979, MPH, 1985. Diplomate Am. Bd. Med. Examiners, Am. Bd. Pediatrics. Intern Columbus Hosp., Chgo., 1980, resident in pediatrics, 1980-83; fellow in ambulatory pediatrics Cook County Hosp., Chgo., 1983-85; dir. ambulatory pediatrics Hurley Med. Ctr., Flint, Mich., 1986-92; clin. pediatrician McCree North Health Ctr., Flint, 1992-95; participant scholars program Mich. Pub. Health Leadership Inst., Flint, 1995-96; med. dir. Genesee County Health Dept., 1995—; asst. prof. pediatrics Mich. State U., East Lansing, 1986—, tchr. med. ednl. program Coll. Human Medicine and U. Affiliated Hosp. of Flint (Mich.), Inc., 1986—; presenter in field. Contbr. numerous articles to profl. jours. and cmty. newspapers. Chairperson Early On program Genesee County, 1993-94. Primary Care Faculty Devel. fellow Mich. State U., 1988-89. Fellow Am. Acad. Pediatrics (Mich. chpt. exec. com. cmty. access to child health, state facilitator 1990-98); mem. AMA, Genessee County Med. Soc., Mich. State Med. Soc., Ambulatory Pediatric Assn., Am. Pub. Health Assn. Democrat. Presbyterian. Avocations: swimming, bicycling. Office: Genesee County Health Dept 630 S Saginaw St Flint MI 48502-1525

JOHNSON, GARY KENT, management education company executive; b. Provo, Utah, Apr. 16, 1936; s. Clyde LeRoy and Ruth Laie (Taylor) J.; m. Mary Joyce Crowther, Aug. 26, 1955; children: Mary Ann Johnson Harvey, Gary Kent, Brent James, Jeremy Clyde. Student Brigham Young U., 1954-55, U. Utah, 1955-58, 60-61, U. Calif.-Berkeley, 1962. Sales rep. Roche Labs., Salt Lake City, 1958-61, sales trainer, Denver, 1962, sales trainer, Oakland, Calif., 1962, div. mgr., Seattle, 1962-69; sec.-treas. Western Mgmt. Inst., Seattle, 1969-71; pres. WMI Corp., Bellevue, Wash., 1971-96, pres. GKJ Corp., 1996—, Provisor Corp., 1983-86; speaker, cons. various nat. orgns. Bd. dirs. Big Bros.; del. King County Republican Com. Served with U.S. N.G., 1953-61. Walgreen scholar, 1955-58; Bristol scholar, 1958. Mem. Am. Soc. Tng. and Devel., Internat. Platform Assn., Bellevue Athletic Club. Phi Sigma Epsilon. Mem. LDS Ch. Author: Select the Best, 1976; Antitrust Untangled, 1977; The Utilities Management Series, 1979; Performance Appraisal, A Program for Improving Productivity, 1981, QSE Quality Service Everytime, 1990, Continuous Performance Improvement, 1993. Office: GKJ Corp 1416 W Lake Sammamish Pkwy SE Bellevue WA 98008-5218

JOHNSON, GARY LEROY, publisher; b. Mpls., Aug. 19, 1938; s. Maurice Fred and Alta Elizabeth J.; m. Carol Ann Schlisler, Sept. 8, 1962. Diploma, Bethany Coll. of Missions, Mpls., 1959; student, Augsburg Coll., 1960-63. Mgr. Bethany Book Shop, Mpls., 1960-63, Bethany Printing Div., Mpls., 1963-76; pub. Bethany House Pubs., Mpls., 1963—. Writer songbooks: Come Songbook, 1979, Thanks Songbook, 1979, Reminded of His Goodness Songbook, 1981. Avocations: songwriting, photography. Office: Bethany House Pubs 11300 Hampshire Ave S Minneapolis MN 55438-2455

JOHNSON, GARY M., lawyer; b. 1947. BS, Gustavus Adolphus Coll., 1969; JD, NYU, 1973. Law clk. to justice U.S. Ct. Appeals (3d cir.), Phila., 1973-74; assoc. Dorsey & Whitney, Mpls., 1974-79, ptnr., 1980—. Fellow Am. Coll. Trust and Estate Counsel; mem. ABA, Internat. Bar Assn., Minn. Bar Assn., Hennepin County Bar Assn., Order of Coif. Office: Dorsey & Whitney 220 S 6th St Ste 2200 Minneapolis MN 55402-1498

JOHNSON, GARY R., corporate lawyer. MA, Ohio State U.; JD, U. Minn. Bar: Minn. 1974. V.p. law Northern St. Power Co., v.p., gen. counsel, 1991—. Office: Northern St Power Co PO Box 5th Fl 414 Nicollet Mall Minneapolis MN 55401-1927*

JOHNSON, GARY ROBERT, political scientist, editor; b. Shenandoah, Iowa, June 30, 1949; s. Glen Robert and Norma Jean (Otte) J.; m. Margaret Delaina Maddox, Aug. 30, 1975; children: Samuel Maddox, Katherine Elizabeth. BA, Augustana Coll., Rock Island, Ill., 1972; MA, U. Cin., 1975, PhD, 1979. Teaching asst., rsch. asst. U. Cin., 1972-78; rsch. cons. Frost & Jacobs, Attys.at Law, Cin., 1976; instr., then asst. prof. polit. sci. Lake Superior State U., Sault Ste. Marie, Mich., 1978-84, assoc. prof. polit. sci., 1984-90, head dept. social scis., 1981-89, prof. polit. sci., 1990—; vis. lectr. Drake U., Des Moines, 1986-87; manuscript referee various jours., pubs., 1986—; mem. faculty workgroup on undergrad. instrnl. quality Gov.'s Commn. on Future of Higher Edn. in Mich., 1984. Bibliography co-editor Politics and the Life Scis. jour., 1986-91, editor, 1991—; contbr. articles, book revs. to profl. jours., edited books. Recipient Disting. Tchr. award Lake Superior State U., 1998; grantee State of Mich., 1987. Mem. AAAS, Am. Polit. Sci. Assn. (panel discussant, chair 1989—, sect. program chair 1990-91), Assn. Politics and Life Sci. (exec. dir. 1996—, conf. chair 1998), Internat. Soc. Polit. Psychology, Internat. Soc. Human Ethology, Human Behavior and Evolution Soc. Avocations: genealogy, old books, racquetball. Home: 924 Johnston St Sault Sainte Marie MI 49783-3324 Office: Lake Superior State U Dept Polit Sci 650 W Easterday Ave Dept Polit Sault Sainte Marie MI 49783-1626

JOHNSON, GARY THOMAS, lawyer; b. Chgo., July 26, 1950; s. Thomas G. Jr. and Marcia (Lunde) J.; m. Susan Elizabeth Moore, May 28, 1978; children: Christopher Thomas, Timothy Henry, Anna Louisa. AB, Yale U., 1972; Hons. BA, Oxford U., 1974, MA, 1983; JD, Harvard U., 1977. Ba: Ill. 1977, U.S. Dist. Ct. (no. dist.), Ill. 1977, U.S. Ct. Appeals (7th cir.) 1985, U.S. Supreme Ct. 1986, N.Y. 1993. Assoc. Mayer, Brown & Platt, Chgo., 1977-84, ptnr., 1985-94; ptnr. Jones, Day, Reavis & Pogue, Chgo., 1994—; mem. Spl. Commn. on Adminstrn. of Justice Cook County, Chgo., 1984-88; v.p. Criminal Justice Project of Cook County, 1987-91; bd. dirs. Lawyers' Com. for Civil Rights Under Law, 1992—, trustee, 1994—, regional vice chair, 1996—; mem. Ill. Supreme Ct. Spl. Commn. on the Adminstrn. of Justice, 1992-94. Bd. dirs. Chgo. Lawyers' Com. for Civil Rights Under Law, 1981-90, Legal Assistance Found., Chgo., 1987-96, pres., 1994-96. Rhodes scholar Oxford U., 1972-74. Fellow Am. Bar Found. (life), Ill. Bar Found.; mem. ABA (Ho. of Dels. 1991-97), Internat. Bar Assn., Chgo. Bar Assn., Chgo. Coun. Lawyers (pres. 1981-83), Am. Judicature Soc. (bd. dirs. 1987-91). Democrat. Office: Jones Day Reavis & Pogue 77 W Wacker Dr Chicago IL 60601-1692

JOHNSON, GARY WILLIAM, environmental scientist; b. Warwick, R.I., Feb. 23, 1957; s. Donald Milton and Elaine Carin (Soderlund) J.; m. Diane Lynn Farrell, Aug. 1, 1992; children: Danielle Lynn, Kelsey Ann. BA in Biology, U. R.I., 1979; MS in Environ. Sci., U. New Haven, 1987. Cert. instr. Inst. Nuclear Power Operators; OSHA cert. safety trainer. Rschr. Nat. Marine Fisheries Svc., Narragansett, R.I., 1978-79; asst. scientist N.E. Utilities, Waterford, Conn., 1979-84; assoc. scientist N.E. Utilities, Berlin, Conn., 1984-86; scientist N.E. Utilities, Rocky Hill, Conn., 1986-97; sr. scientist, environ. coord. N.E. Nuclear Energy Co., Waterford, Conn., 1997—; prin. scientist Ecologic Risk Mgmt. Svcs., Monroe, Conn., 1989-94; guest lectr. U. New Haven, 1990-96; lectr. in field. Contbr. articles to profl. jours. Vol. sci. guide East Lyme (Conn.) Jr. High Sch., 1983-96; guide, lectr. Audubon Soc., Jamestown, R.I., 1983-85; mem. Waterford Conservation Commn., 1997—. Mem. Edison Electric Power Industry Biologists, Nat. Environ. Tng. Assn. Achievements include development of state of the art computer models to perform quantitative analysis of ecologic and human health risk from exposure to toxic materials, implementation of environ. mgmt. sys. for a nuclear power generating facility; research in condenser biofouling control. Home: 2 Melanie Dr Waterford CT 06385-1600 Office: NE Nuclear Energy Co Millstone Nuclear Power Sta PO Box 128 Waterford CT 06385-0128

JOHNSON, GEORGE, JR., physician, educator; b. Wilmington, N.C., Apr. 6, 1926; s. George W. and Evelyn (Hill) J.; m. Marian Patterson Ritchie, July 1, 1950; children: Sally Hope, George William, David Ritchie, Robert Hill. BS, U. N.C., 1949, certificate medicine, 1950; MD, Cornell U., 1952. Intern, resident surgery N.Y. Hosp., 1952-59; pvt. surg. practice, 1959-62; asst. prof. to prof. U. N.C., 1961—, chief gen. surgery svcs., 1969-93; vice-chmn. dept. surgery, 1969—; Roscoe B.G. Cowper disting. prof. in surgery U. N.C., 1973—; mem. adv. com. N.C. Emergency Med. Svcs., chmn., 1973—, N.C. Gov.'s Hwy. Safety Com., 1977-89. Mem. editorial bd. Jour. of Trauma, 1980—, Jour. Vascular Surgery, 1983—; contbr. chpts. to books, articles to profl. jours. Served to 1st lt. inf. AUS, 1944-46. Mem. AMA (rep. to ho. of dels. from SCVS 1994), Univ. Assn. Emergency Med. Svcs. (pres. 1973), Am. Soc. Surg. Assns., N.C. Bd. Med. Examiners, Internat. Cardiovascular Soc. (v.p. 1989-93), Internat. Soc. Cardiovascular Surgery (pres. 1985-86), ACS (pres. N.C. chpt., gov. 1977-83, 91-96, trauma com. 1974-81, exec. bd. trauma com. 1977-81), So. Univ. Surgeons, So. Assn. Vascular Surgery (sec.-treas. 1981-85, pres.-elect 1986, pres. 1987), Durham-Orange County Med. Soc. (pres. 1971), Halsted Soc., Am. Venous Forum (pres. 1992). Club: Rotary. Home: 217 Mill Race Dr Chapel Hill NC 27514-3130*

JOHNSON, GEORGE H., financial services company executive; b. Boston, Aug. 30, 1941; s. Harry G. and Josephine (Grenda) J.; m. Marguerite Anne Harrington, Aug. 12, 1967; 1 child, Heather Diana. BS, Northeastern U., Boston, 1966. CLU, ChFC; cert. internal auditor; enrolled agt. IRS; cert. tax preparer; fellow life office mgmt. Sr. internal auditor U.S. Life Corp., N.Y.C., 1970-76; dir. internal audit, treas. Consumers United Group, Inc., Washington, 1976—, also bd. dirs.; former bd. dirs., chair World Hunger Edn. Svc., Washington. Participant blood bank donor program ARC, Washington, 1977—. Mem. Inst. Internal Auditors, Md. Soc. Accts., Am. Soc. CLU and ChFC, Cert. Tax Preparers, Washington Inst. Internal Auditors. Home: 11805 Bunchberry Ln Gaithersburg MD 20878-2315

JOHNSON, GEORGE TAYLOR, training and manufacturing executive; b. Kansas City, Mo., Jan. 12, 1930; s. George Dewey and Geneva (Van Leu) J.; m. Pamela Kay Cole, Aug. 30, 1981; children: Van L., Victoria Johnson-Beineke, Wendell O., Marcella Johnson-Stewart, Julia I. BA, Columbia U., 1977. Enlisted U.S. Army, 1947; chief instr. rotary wing sect. U.S. Army Transp. Sch., Ft. Eustis, Va., 1965-67; ret. U.S. Army, 1967; group leader aerospace publs. Beech Aircraft Corp., Wichita, Kans., 1968-79, adminstr. aerospace logistics programs, 1979-87, staff asst. program mgmt., 1987-88, staff adminstr. program mgr., 1988-92, ret., 1992; pres., CEO Diversified Ednl. Tng. and Mfg. Co., 1992—. Founder U.S. Army Black Pilots Reunions, U.S. Army Black Aviators Assn.; mem. Cmty. Action Agy., Wichita, 1973-75, State of Kans. Aviation Adv. Com., 1991—, Pvt. Industry Coun., Wichita, 1994—; Kans. del. White House Conf. on Small Bus., Washington, 1995. Decorated DFC, Air medal with V and four oak leaf clusters; named Welfare to Work Small Bus. Owner of Yr., SBA, 1999. Mem. NAACP, VFW, Army Aviation Assn. Am., 9th and 10th Cav. Assn., Wichita C. of C. (bd. dirs. 1996-99), Wichita Ind. Bus. Assn. (bd. dirs. 1996—), Rotary Internat. Baptist. Home: 9430 Cross Creek St Wichita KS 67206 Office: 2102 E 21st St N Wichita KS 67214-1943

JOHNSON, GEORGE WILLIAM, retired academic administrator; b. Jamestown, N.D., July 5, 1928; s. George Carl and Mathilde (Trautman) J.; m. Joanne Ferris, June 11, 1955; children: Robert Craig, William Garth. BA, Jamestown Coll., 1950; MA, Columbia U., 1953, PhD, 1960. Asst. chmn. dept. English Temple U., Phila., 1964-66; assoc. dean liberal arts Temple U., 1966-67; chmn. dept. English, 1967-68, dean liberal arts, 1968-78; pres. George Mason U., Fairfax, Va., 1978-96; pres. emeritus George Mason U., Fairfax, 1996—. Contbr. articles to scholarly jours. Bd. dirs. Elizabethtown Coll., 1989—. With U.S. Army, 1950-52. Named Washingtonian of Yr., 1984. Mem. Am. Assn. State Colls. and Univs. (mem. com. state rels. 1981-85, Va. rep. 1985-89, mem. mission to Mex. 1979, mem. mission to China 1984), Am. Council Edn., Bus. Higher Edn., Va. C. of C. (bd. dirs. 1993—), Golden Key Nat. Honor Soc. Roman Catholic. Office: George Mason U Office of Pres Fewick Libr 4400 University Dr 2d Fl Fairfax VA 22030-4422*

JOHNSON, GERALD, III, cardiovascular physiologist, researcher; b. Liberty, Tex., Aug. 16, 1945; s. Gerald Jr. and Jimmie Leah (Hensley) J.; m. Delynda Juanice Wall, Sept. 20, 1985. MS, U. Okla., 1971; PhD, U. Okla., Oklahoma City, 1980. NIH stipendiary U. Okla., Oklahoma City, 1972-76, rsch. assoc., 1979-80; electrophysiologist Childrens Med. Ctr., Tulsa, Okla., 1980-82; post-doct. fellow Oral Roberts U. Sch. Medicine, Tulsa, 1982-84, asst. prof., 1984-88; sr. rsch. fellow Jefferson Med. Coll., Phila., 1988-90; assoc. prof. dept. medicine, rsch. health scis. ctr. U. Okla., 1990-98, prof. dept. medicine, 1998—; dir. cardiovasc. lab. W.K. Warren Med. Rsch. Inst., Tulsa, 1990—; cons. McGee Rehab. Inst., Phila., 1990, Dept. Pediatrics City of Faith Hosp., Tulsa, 1982, Aerobics Ctr. Oral roberts U., Tulsa, 1981; rsch. asst. to assoc. VA Hosp., Oklahoma City, 1970-72, Cen. State Hosp., Norman, Okla, 1969-70, U. Okla. Health Scis. Ctr., Oklahoma City, 1979-80; mem. numerous coms. Oral Roberts U., 1984-88; adj. assoc. prof. physiology dept. pharmacology and physiology Okla. State U. Coll. Osteo. Medicine, Tulsa; mem. faculty 3d Internat. Conf. Nuc. Cardiology, Florence, Italy, 1997. Contbr. numerous articles to profl. jours.; reviewer Jour. Nuc. Cardiology, Jour. Nuc. Medicine, Life Scis.; presenter in field. Grantee The Hearst Found., 1981-82, Am. Heart Assn., 1985-86, 97; recipient Travel award Biofeedback Soc. Am., 1981, Citation Paper awards, 1981, 82, Best Basic Rsch. Paper award Jour. Nuc. Cardiology, 1997. Fellow Coun. on Circulation; mem. AAAS, Internat. Soc. for Heart Rsch. (Am. sect.), Am. Heart Assn., Am. Physiol. Assn., Am. Soc. Nuc. Cardiology (founding), Fedn. Am. Socs. for Exptl. Biology, Soc. Nuc. Medicine, Okla. Soc. Physiologists (pres.), N.Y. Acad. Scis., Soc. of Sigma Xi, Phi Kappa Phi. Achievements include research on protective effects of exercise training in shock, adrenoceptor relationships in hypertension, morphologic differences in vasculature during hemorrhagic hypotension, protective effects of nitric oxide and sodium nitrite in ischemia/reperfusion, role of endothelium in myocardial ischemia/reperfusion. Office: W K Warren Med Rsch Inst 6465 S Yale Ave Ste 1010 Tulsa OK 74136-7812

JOHNSON, GERALDINE ESCH, language specialist; b. Steger, Ill., Jan. 5, 1921; d. William John Rutkowski and Estella Anna (Mannel) Pietz; m. Richard William Esch, Oct. 12, 1940 (dec. 1971); children: Janet L. Sohngen, Daryl R., Gary Michael; m. Henry Bernard Johnson, Aug. 23, 1978 (dec. 1988). BSBA, U. Denver, 1955, MA in Edn., 1958, MA in Speech Pathology, 1963; vocat. credential, U. No. Colo., 1978, postgrad.; postgrad., Metropolitan State Coll., U. Colo., Colo. State U., Colo. Sch. of Mines, U. Hawaii. Cert. speech therapist, Colo.; cert. tchr., class A counselor, tchr. educationally handicapped, Colo. Tchr. music Judith St. John Sch. Music, Denver, 1946-52; tchr. West High Sch., Denver, 1955-61, chmn. bus. edn. dept., 1958-61, reading specialist, 1977-78; speech therapist, founder South Denver Speech Clinic, 1965-71; tchr. Educationally Handicapped Resource Rm., Denver, 1971-74, Diagnostic Ctr., The Belmont Sch., Denver, 1974-77; speech-lang. specialist elem. and jr. high schs., Denver, 1978-86; itinerant speech-lang. specialist various elem. and jr. high schs., Denver, 1978—; ret. Denver Pub. Sch. System, 1986; home lang tchr. Early Childhood Edn., Denver, 1975; mem. Ednl. TV Adv. com., Colo.; sec. Cen. Bus. Edn. Com., Colo; tchr. letter writing clinics, local bus., Denver, 1960—. Former judge Colo. State Speech Festivals; demonstrator, lectr. Speech-Lang. and Learning Disabilities area Colo. Edn. Assn., 1971-73; vol. communications and prereading skills tchr. YMCA (10 years). Recipient Spl. Edn. award Denver Pub. Schs., 1986. Mem. Speech-Lang.-Hearing Assn. (cert.), U. Denver Sch. Bus. Alumni Bd., Beta Gamma Sigma, Kappa Delta Pi, Delta Pi Epsilon. Home: 14050 E Linvale Pl Apt 502 Aurora CO 80014-3735

JOHNSON, GLENDON E., retired insurance company executive; b. 1924. BS, U. Utah, 1948; JD, Harvard U., 1952. In charge Wash. office Am. Life Convention, Washington, 1959-68; pres. Great Southern Life Ins. Co., Houston, 1968-70; pres., chmn. bd. dirs., CEO Am. Nat. Ins. Co. Inc., Galveston, Tex., 1970-77; law ptnr. Routier & Johnson P.C., Washington, 1978-84; pres., CEO John Alden Ins. Co., Inc., 1984-87; chmn. bd., CEO John Alden Fin. Corp., Miami, Fla., 1987-98; pres., chmn. bd., CEO John Alden Life Ins. Co., 1984-98. Mem. nat. bd. Boy Scouts Am., 1971-77, 1981—, nat. exec. com., 1981—, nat. v.p., chmn. audit com., mem. nominating com., 1994—, mem. exec. bd. Fla. coun., chmn. nat. Cub Scout com., 1981-83, chmn. nat. program group, 1983-86, chmn. mktg. and relationships com., 1987-91, chmn. pers. com., 1992-93 (Silver Beaver award 1971, Silver Antelope award 1974, Silver Buffalo award 1993, Good Scout award 1993). *

JOHNSON, GLENN THOMPSON, judge; b. Washington, Ark., July 19, 1917; s. Floyd and Reola (Thompson) J.; m. Elaine Bailey, May 26, 1993; children: Evelyn A., Glenn T. B.S., Wilberforce U., 1941; J.D., John Marshall Law Sch., 1949, LL.M., 1950; grad., Nat. Coll. State Trial Judges, 1971, Appellate Ct. Judges Seminar, N.Y. U., 1974; LL.D. (hon.), Ark. Bapt. Coll., 1978. Bar: Ill. 1950. Pvt. practice law, 1950-57; asst. atty. gen. Ill., 1957-63; sr. asst. atty. Met. San. Dist. Chgo., 1963-66; assoc. judge Cir. Ct., Cook County, Chgo., 1966-68, judge, 1968-73; justice Ill. Appellate Ct., Chgo., 1973—. Trustee John Marshall Law Sch. Served with AUS, 1942-46. Recipient merit award John Marshall Law Sch., 1970; Merit award Beatrice Caffrey Youth Service, 1976. Mem. Nat. Bar Assn. (merit award 1970), ABA, Ill. Bar Assn., Chgo. Bar Assn., Cook County Bar Assn. (awards 1967, 73, pres. 1964-66), Am. Acad. Matrimonial Lawyers (gov.). Methodist. Home: #2203-S 5050 S Lake Shore Dr Apt 2203 Chicago IL 60615-3217

JOHNSON, GLORIA JEAN, counseling professional; b. St. Louis, Jan. 30, 1945; d. Willie Jr. and Ruby Bernice (Haynes) Stevens; m. Louis W. Johnson, Dec. 2, 1963; children: Anthony Kenneth, Marvin Louis, Andre Darnell. MS in Counseling, Evang. Sem., PhD in Marriage and Family Counseling, 1993. Dir. counseling dept. EC Bible Coll., St. Louis, 1987-88; cons. in field St. Louis, 1987-94; founder, exec. dir. Life Source Cons., Inc., St. Louis, 1994—. Vol. counselor CMC C-Star Program, St. Louis, 1992-93; bd. dirs. Mo. Coalition Against Domestic Violence, Jefferson City, 1995—, Mo. Coalition Against Sexual Assault, 1998—; chair Women of Color Task Force Against Domestic Violence State of Mo., 1996-97; mem. St. Louis County Domestic and Family Violence Coun., 1996—, St. Louis City Family Violence Coun., 1998—, Family Support Task Force, 1998—; mem. adv. coun. Sexual Assault Ctr., 1982—; founder Christian Women Against Abuse, 1998. Mem. ACA, Am. Assn. Christian Counselors, Nat. Black Women's Health Project, Internat. Assn. Marriage and Family Counselors. Office: Life Source Cons Inc PO Box 5752 Saint Louis MO 63121-0752

JOHNSON, GOODYEAR See O'CONNOR, KARL WILLIAM

JOHNSON, GORDON GILBERT, religion educator, minister; b. St. Paul, Nov. 19, 1919; s. Gilbert Oliver and Myrtle Isabel (Bjorklund) J.; m. Alta Fern Borden, May 21, 1945; children: Gregg A., Gayle E. Johnson Boyd. Cert., Moody Bible Inst., 1941; AA, Bethel Coll., St. Paul, 1943; student, Harvard U., 1944, 45; BA, U. Minn., 1945; BD, Bethel Theol. Sem., 1946; ThM, Princeton Theol. Sem., 1950; ThD, No. Bapt. Theol. Sem., 1960. Ordained to ministry Bapt. Gen. Conf., 1946. Pastor 1st Bapt. Ch., Milltown, Wis., 1946-48, Bethel Bapt. Ch., Montclaire, N.J., 1948-51, Central Ave. Bapt. Ch., Chgo., 1951-59; v.p., dean, prof. preaching Bethel Theol. Sem., St. Paul, 1959-84; interim sr. pastor Trinity Bapt. Ch., St. Paul, 1972-73; assoc. pastor, intrim sr. pastor College Ave. Bapt. Ch., San Diego, 1984-89; interim dean Bethel Sem. West, San Diego, 1990-91; interim sr. pastor Clairemont Emmanuel Bapt. Ch., San Diego, 1990-91, First Bapt. Ch.,

Lakewood, Long Beach, Calif., 1991-92, New Life Ch., Woodbury, Minn., 1993, Elim Bapt. Ch., Mpls., 1995-96; chmn. bd. publ. Bapt. Gen. Conf., Chgo., 1948-53, pres. bd. trustees, 1953-55, chmn. world mission bd., 1955-60, moderator, 1957-58, 85-86; mem. gen. coun. Bapt. World Alliance, Washington, 1965-85; lectr. in field; del. to World Congress on Evangelism, Berlin, 1965; educator for elderhostels for Bethel Coll., Minn., 1992-98; vis. prof. Regent Coll., Vancouver, 1976; pres. Minn. Sem. Consortium, 1979-81. Author: My Church; contbr. articles to profl. jours. With USN, 1944-45. Rsch. scholar Yale U. Div. Sch., 1969. Mem. Acad. Homileticians, Religious Speech Assn. *In a capricious and sometimes explosive world an underlying confidence in the gracious providence of a loving God gives peace and wholeness of life. That makes possible an optimism about life.*

JOHNSON, GORDON JAMES, artistic director, conductor; b. St. Paul, 1949. BS, Bemidji State U., 1971; MS, Northwestern U., 1977; D in Mus. Arts, U. Oreg.; studied with Leonard Bernstein, Erich Leinsdorf, Herbert Blomstedt. Music dir., condr. Great Falls (Mont.) Symphony Assn., 1981—, Glacier Orch. and Chorale, Mont., 1982-97; artistic dir., condr. Flathead Music Festival, Mont., 1987-96; music dir., condr. Mesa (Ariz.) Symphony Orch., 1997—; grad. teaching fellow U. Oreg., 1979-81; artist in residence Condr's Guild Inst., W.Va. U., condr. orch., 1984; condr. Spokane Symphony at The Festival at Sandpoint; guest condr. St. Paul Chamber Orch., 1971, Spokane Symphony, 1983, 86, Dubuque (Iowa) Symphony, 1985, Charlotte (N.C.) Symphony, 1985, Lethbridge (Alberta, Can.) Symphony, 1986, Cheyenne (Wyo.) Symphony, 1986, West Shore (Mich.) Symphony, 1988, Bozeman (Mont.) Symphony, 1989, Kumamoto Symphony (Kyshu, Japan), 1991, Kankakee (Ill.) Symphony, 1993, Toulon (France) Symphonies, 1994, Guam Symphony, 1995, Tokyo Lumiere Orch., 1995, Fort Collins (Colo.) Symphony, 1995, Wilmslow (Eng.) Symphony Orch., 1997; guest ballet condr. Alberta Ballet, 1986, Oakland (Calif.) Ballet, 1988, Eugene (Oreg.) Ballet, 1993, David Taylor Ballet, Colo., 1994, St. Petersburg (Russia) Ballet, 1995, Western Ballet Theater, Oreg., 1996; spkr. regional conf. Am. Symphony Orch. League, 1987, nat. conf., 1988; mem. adj. faculty U. Great Falls, 1981—, U. Mont., 1996—; lectr. U. Guam, 1995; condr. seminars L.A. Philharmonic Inst., 1983, Condr.'s Guild Inst., 1984, Festival at Sandpoint, Condr.'s Program, 1986, Am. Symphony Orch. League's Am. Condr.'s Program, N.Y. Philharmonic, 1987, Condr.'s Guild "Bruckner Seminar", Chgo. Symphony Orch., 1989, Carnegie Hall Tng. Program for Condrs., Cleve. Orch., 1993. Philharmonic Condr.'s scholar St. Paul Chamber Orch., 1971; L.A. Philharmonic Inst. fellow, 1983; named to Highland Park High Sch. Hall of Fame, St. Paul, 1997. Mem. ASCAP. Office: Great Falls Symphony Assn PO Box 1078 Great Falls MT 59403-1078

JOHNSON, GORDON SELBY, consulting electrical engineer; b. Petersburg, Ind., July 25, 1918; s. Basil Orvil and Lillian May (Selby) J.; m. Frances Marie Overstreet, June 15, 1940; children: Lowell, Anne, Judith, Martha, Carol, Gordon, Mary. BSEE, Purdue U., 1939. Registered profl. engr., Wis. Engr. Sunbeam Electric Mfg. Co., Evansville, Ind., 1939-41; engr. Kohler (Wis.) Co., 1941-48, dept. head, 1948-55, chief engr., 1955-65, mgr. engring., 1965-76, sr. staff engr., 1976-85, cons. engr., 1985-87; pvt. practice cons. Dundee, Fla., 1987—; dir. communications and tech. assistance Elec. Generating Systems Assn., Boca Raton, Fla., 1986-92, tech. dir., 1993—, pres., 1983-84. Author: Kohler Tech. Series, 1976-85; editor: Elec. Grounding, 1992, On-Site Power Generation, 1990, 2d edit., 1993, 3rd edit., 1998; editor Powerline mag., 1986-92, tech. editor, 1993—; contbr. numerous articles to profl. jours. Pres. Sheboygan (Wis.) County Coun. of Chs., 1965-67; lay leader N.E. Wis. Dist. United Meth. Ch., 1975-76; chmn. adv. com. Lakeshore Tech. Coll., Sheboygan, 1970-80; adv. high sch. sci. seminars. With U.S. Mcht. Marine, 1944-45, ETO, NATOUSA. Recipient L.H. Carpenter Outstanding Svc. award Elec. Generating Systems Assn., 1973. Fellow IEEE (sect. chmn. 1953-54); mem. NSPE, Soc. Automotive Engrs., Nat. Fire Protection Assn. Avocations: competitive running, bicycling, gardening. Home and Office: 306 7th St Dundee FL 33838-4328

JOHNSON, GRACE ALEXANDER, anthropologist, curator; b. May 14, 1937. MA, San Diego State U., 1995. Curator Lat. Am. ethnography San Diego Mus. of Man, 1975—. E-mail: grace johns@aol.com. Home: 1350 El Prado San Diego CA 92101-1616 Office: San Diego Mus fo Man San Diego CA 92101

JOHNSON, GRANT LESTER, lawyer, retired manufacturing company executive; b. Virginia, Minn., Aug. 16, 1929; s. Ernest and Anna Elizabeth (Nordstrom) J.; m. Esther Linnea Nystrom, June 16, 1956 (dec. July 1985); children: Karen Elisabeth, Elise Ann; m. Amy Rowe Fetzer, July 18, 1992. AB, Cornell U., 1951; LLB, Harvard U., 1957. Bar: Ohio 1958, Ill. 1972. Assoc. Squire, Sanders & Dempsey, Cleve., 1957-58; atty. Pickands Mather & Co., Cleve., 1958-71, assoc. gen. counsel, 1967, gen. counsel, 1968-71, sec., 1969-71; corporate counsel Interlake, Inc., Chgo., 1971-73, v.p. law, 1974-78, v.p. law and adminstrn., 1978-84, sr. v.p., gen. counsel, 1984-86; sr. v.p., gen. counsel The InterLake Corp., 1986-91, ret., 1991. Lt. (j.g.) USN, 1951-54. Home: 4 Oakbrook Club Dr Apt G-205 Oak Brook IL 60523-1328

JOHNSON, GREGORY KENT, dentist, educator; b. Concordia, Kans., Mar. 19, 1950; s. Herbert Eugene and Dorothy Phyllis (Green) J.; m. Mary Ann Head, Nov. 19, 1976. BS, Ft. Hays (Kans.) State U., 1972; DDS with distinction, U. Mo., Kansas City, 1976; MA, Antioch U., 1984. Commd. USN, advanced through grades to comdr.; dental officer Naval Air Sta., Corpus Christi, Tex., 1976-79, Naval Sta., Subic Bay, Philippines, 1979-81, Naval Air Sta., Atlanta, 1981-83; resident gen. dentistry Naval Dental Sch., Bethesda, Md., 1983-84; dental officer USS Holland, Charleston, S.C., 1984-86; br. dir. Marine Corps Fin. Ctr., Kansas City, 1986-91; clin asst. prof. surgery U. Mo.-Kansas City Sch. Dentistry, 1990-91; head operative dentistry dept., staff clinic Naval Dental Ctr., Orlando, Fla., 1991-94; clinic dir. 21st Dental Co., Kaneohe Bay, Hawaii, 1994-97. Fellow Acad. Gen. Dentistry; mem. ADA, Acad. Operative Dentistry. Home: 5802 Manor Dr Parkville MO 64152-6062 Office: U Mo Sch Dentistry Dept Restorative Dentistry 650 E 25th St Kansas City MO 64108-2716

JOHNSON, GREGORY L., lawyer. BA, Fordham U.; MBA, Columbia U.; JD. Bar: N.Y. 1973. V.p., gen. counsel Warner Lambert Co., Morris Plains, N.J.; lawyer. BA Fordham U.; MBA Columbia U., JD. Bar: N.Y. 1973. Vice pres., gen. counsel Warner Lambert Co., Morris Plains, N.J. Office: Warner-Lambert Co 201 Tabor Rd Morris Plains NJ 07950-2693*

JOHNSON, GUY CHARLES, music educator, musician; b. Marinette, Wis., Nov. 8, 1933; s. Everton Ellsworth and Anna Mae (Brazier) J. BFA, U. Wis., Milw., 1955; MusM, Ind. U., 1956. Asst. prof. piano Drury Coll., Springfield, Mo., 1956-57, Luther Coll., Decorah, Iowa, 1959-68; assoc. prof. music Friends U., Wichita, Kans., 1968-95; impresario Lewis and Selma Miller Recital series, Wichita, 1976-86. Recital debut Athenaeum Hall, Milw., 1955; appearances with numerous symphonies including Rochester (Minn.) Symphony, Milw. Symphony, Santa Barbara (Calif.) Symphony; accomapnist for various operas, ballet cos. Mem. Wichita-Sedgwick County Hist. Mus. Mem. Wichita Area Piano Tchrs. League (pres. 1969, 90—), Kans. Music Tchrs. Assn., Nat. Guild Piano Tchrs., Wichita Art Assn. Home: 640 N Rock Rd Wichita KS 67206-1794

JOHNSON, HARMER FREDERIK, art appraiser; b. Faversham, Kent, England, Jan. 21, 1943; s. Stanley George and Lorna Mary (Clark) J.; m. Judith Rose Fischman, July 14, 1970; children: Jesse, Joanna, Eliza. Dept. asst. Sotheby & Co., London, 1961-66; dept. head, v.p. Sotheby Parke-Bernet Co., N.Y.C., 1966-73; pres. Harmer Johnson Books Ltd., N.Y.C., 1975—, Harmer Johnson Co., N.Y.C., 1973—. Author: (books) American Indian Art Magazine, Guide to the Arts of the Americas: Pre-Columbian, American Indian, 1992. Mem. Appraisers Assn. Am. (pres. 1986-88, cert.). Avocations: music, theatre. Office: Harmer Johnson 146 E 84th St New York NY 10028-2026

JOHNSON, HAROLD EARL, human resources specialist; b. Lincoln, Nebr., July 11, 1939; s. Earl W. and Evelyn Jean (Sipp) J.; m. Carol Louise Schmidt, Aug. 17, 1971 (div.); children: Andrew Brian, Daniel Earl. BS, U. Nebr., 1961. From indsl. relations trainee to mgr. profl. employment Am. Can Co., 1961-68; dir. recruitment/devel. metal mining div. Kennecott Copper Corp., 1968-73; v.p. personnel Am. Medicorp Inc., 1973-75; v.p. employee relations. devel., then sr. v.p. employee relations and corp. adminstrn. INA Corp., 1975-79; sr. v.p. human resources Federated Dept. Stores, Inc., Cin., 1979-85; sr. v.p. corp. personnel and adminstrn. The Travelers Cos., Hartford, Conn., 1985-89; mng. ptnr. Korn/Ferry Internat., N.Y.C., 1989-92; exec. search and human resources Norman-Broadbent Internat., N.Y.C., 1992-96; sr. ptnr., bd. dirs. The Cabot Group, Washington, 1996—. Mem. Am. Mgmt. Assn., Conf. Board, Sky Club (N.Y.C.), Univ. Club (N.Y.C.), Country Club at Landfall (Wilmington, N.C.), Winged Foot Golf Club (Mamoroneck, N.Y.), Econ. Club (N.Y.C.). Republican. Presbyterian. Office: LAI Worldwide Inc 200 Park Ave New York NY 10166

JOHNSON, HAROLD GENE, lawyer; b. St. Louis, July 20, 1934; s. Edward Henry Johnson and Betty (Burton) Pallister; m. Susan Ann Giesecke, Oct. 10, 1953; children: H. Mark, Deborah S. Johnson Schnitzer, Michael R., Laura A. Johnson Schwent, Mitchell D. BSBA, Washington U., St. Louis, 1961, LLB, 1962. Bar: Mo. 1962, U.S. Dist. Ct. (ea. dist.) Mo. 1964, U.S. Ct. Appeals (8th cir.) 1981. Assoc. Schomburg, Marshall & Craig, St. Louis, 1962-63, Green & Raymond, St. Louis, 1963-64; ptnr. Johnson & Hayes, St. Louis, 1978-85, Law Offices Mitchell D. Johnson, St. Louis, 1988-93, Johnson & Johnson, 1993—. Judge mcpl. ct. City of Bridgeton, Mo., 1973-85. Served with U.S. Army 1954-56. Recipient Spl. Service award City of Bridgeton, 1985; Honored with ann. presentation of The Judge Harold Johnson award Pro-Life Direct Action League, 1985. Bar: Mo. Bar Assn., Met. Bar St. Louis, St. Louis County Bar Assn. Avocation: woodworking. Office: 500 Northwest Plz Ste 715 Saint Ann MO 63074-2222

JOHNSON, HARRY WATKINS, defense analyst; b. Richmond, Va., Dec. 16, 1945; s. Harry Watkins and Ellen Katherine (Arvin) J.; m. Judith Indie Isbell, Sept. 6, 1969; children: Katherine Elizabeth, Blair Lawrence. BS, Va. Poly. Inst. and State U., 1968; MEd, Boston U., 1974. Commd. 2d lt. U.S. Army, 1968, advanced through grades to lt. col., 1985; staff officer U.S. Army, Ft. Pickett, Va., 1970-74; petroleum officer U.S. Army, Germersheim, Germany, 1974-77; asst. prof. mil. sci. U. Pitts., 1977-80; readiness officer U.S. Army, Nurnberg, Germany, 1980-81, exec. officer 501 S&T Batallion, 1981-83; dept. G-4 1st Armored Divsn. U.S. Army, Ansbach, Germany, 1983-84; chief logistics initiatives U.S. Army Logistics Ctr., Ft. Lee, Va., 1984-88; chief logistics concepts Quartermaster sch. U.S. Army, Ft. Lee, Va., 1988-91; project mgr. Mil. Profl. Resources, Inc., Ft. Lee, 1991—; v.p. Highty Tighty Alumni Inc., Blacksburg, Va., 1992—. Asst. scoutmaster Boy Scouts Am., Chester, Va., 1990—. Decorated Legion of Merit, bronze Star medal. Mem. Nat. Sojourners Inc. (pres. 1989-90), Sons of Confed. Vets., Masons, Shriner. Presbyterian. Avocations: woodcarving, camping. Home: 11440 Marsden Rd Chester VA 23831-1817 Office: Mil Prof Resources Inc PO Box 5203 Fort Lee VA 23801-0203

JOHNSON, HARVEY, JR., mayor; b. 1946. BA, Tenn. State U., 1968; MA, U. Cin., 1970. Small town/human devel. office mgr. Miss. Rsch. and Devel. Ctr., 1976-79; exec. dir. Miss. Inst. for Small Towns, 1979-97; assoc. commr. Miss. State Commn., 1990-96; dir. Miss. Ctr. for Tech. Transfer, 1986-90; asst. prof. Jackson (Miss.) State U., 1985-90; mayor City of Jackson, Miss., 1997—. Mailing Address: PO Box A Jackson MS 39205-0017 Office: Office of Mayor City Hall 219 S President St Jackson MS 39201-4308

JOHNSON, HAYNES BONNER, author, journalist, television commentator; b. N.Y.C., July 9, 1931; s. Malcolm Malone and Ludie (Adams) J.; m. Julia Ann Erwin, Sept. 21, 1954 (div.); children—Katherine Adams, David Malone, Stephen Holmes, Sarah Brooks, Elizabeth Haynes. BJ, U. Mo., 1952; MS, U. Wis., 1956; HHD (hon.), Wheeling Jesuit U., 1997; LHD (hon.), U. Mo., 1999. Reporter Wilmington (Del.) News-Jour., 1956-57; with Washington Star, 1957-69, reporter, copy editor, to asst. city editor, night city editor to spl. assignments corr.; nat. corr. Washington Post, 1969-73, asst. mng. editor, 1973-77, columnist, 1977-94; prof. polit. comm. and journalism George Washington U., Washington, 1994-96; Knight chair, prof. journalism U. Md., 1998—; Ferris prof. journalism and pub. affairs Princeton U., 1975-78; TV commentator PBS Washington Week in Rev., 1967-94, The News Hour with Jim Lehrer, 1994—; guest scholar Brookings Instn., 1987-91; Regents lectr. U. Calif., Berkeley, 1992; lectr. in field. Author: Dusk at the Mountain, 1963, The Bay of Pigs, 1964; (with Bernard M. Gwertzman) Fulbright: The Dissenter, 1968; (with George C. Wilson) Army in Anguish, 1972; (with Richard Harwood) Lyndon, 1973, The Working White House, 1975, In the Absence of Power, 1980; (with Howard Simons) The Landing, 1986, Sleepwalking Through History, 1991, Divided We Fall, 1994; (with David S. Broder) The System, 1996; editor: The Fall of a President, 1974. Served to 1st lt. AUS, 1952-55. Recipient Pub. Svc. prize and Grand award for reporting Washington Newspaper Guild, 1962, 68, Interpretive Reporting award, 1965, Nat. Reporting award, 1968, Pulitzer prize for nat. reporting, 1966, Headliners award for nat. reporting, 1968, Sigma Delta Chi gen. reporting award, 1969; fellow in comm. Duke U., 1973-74; profl. in residence Annenberg Sch., 1993. Mem. Nat. Acad. Pub. Adminstrn. Clubs: Gridiron (Washington); Nassau (Princeton); Fed. City (Washington). Office: Coll Journalism U Md Journalism Bldg 3900 Watson Pl NW Apt 3D College Park MD 20742-7111

JOHNSON, HEIDI SMITH, science educator; b. Mpls., June 1, 1946; d. Russell Ward and Eva Ninette (Holmquist) Smith; m. Alan C. Sweeney, Dec. 21, 1968 (div. 1977); m. Robert Allen Johnson, July 17, 1981. BA, U. Calif., Riverside, 1969; MA, No. Ariz. U., 1992. Park ranger U.S. Nat. Parks Svc., Pinnacles Nat. Monument, 1972-73; aide Petrified Forest Mus. Assn., Ariz., 1973-75; dispatcher police dept. U. Ariz., Tucson, 1975-76; communications operator II dept. ops. City of Tucson, 1976-78; dispatcher Tucson Police Dept., 1978-82, communications supr., 1982-85, communications coord., 1985; substitute tchr. Bisbee (Ariz.) Pub. Schs., 1985-91; instr. English Cochise Community Coll., Douglas, Ariz., 1990-92; tchr. English/creative writing Bisbee H.S., 1992-93; tchr. earth sci. and hist. geology Lowell Mid. Sch., Bisbee, 1993—; GEd tchr. Cochise County Jail, 1988-89; owner Johnson's Antiques and Books, Bisbee, 1990—. Trustee Bisbee Coun. on Arts and Humanities, 1986-88; pres. Cooper Queen Libr. Bd., Bisbee, 1988-91; book sales chmn. Shattuck Libr., Bisbee Mining Mus., 1987-92; founder Riverside (Calif.) chpt. Zero Population Growth, 1968. Mem. Mid-Am. Paleontol. Soc., Sierra Club (mem. nat. wilderness study com. 1969-72, wilderness survey leader 1969-72), Paleontol. Soc., Nat. Ctr. Sci. Edn., The Nature Conservancy. Roman Catholic. Avocations: paleontology, flower gardening, book collecting. Home: PO Box 1221 Bisbee AZ 85603-2221

JOHNSON, HENRY BREAVOID, occupational therapist, career officer; b. Newport News, Va., Nov. 15, 1964; s. Henry Jr. and Jetsie Louise (White) J.; m. Mariquit Lopez, July 07, 1997. BS in Rehab. Svcs., Va. Commonwealth U., Richmond, 1989; cert. in occupl. therapy, Temple U., Phila., 1994. 2d lt. med. corps USAR, 1997—. Mem. Am. Occupl. Therapy Assn., Pa. Occupl. Therapy Assn., Minority Recruitment Retention Com. (vice chmn. 1996-98, chmn. 1998—). Avocations: fitness, martial arts, reading.

JOHNSON, HERBERT ALAN, history and law educator, lawyer, chaplain; b. Jersey City, Jan. 10, 1934; s. Harry Oliver and Magdalena Gertrude (Diemer) J.; m. Barbara Arlene Balcerak, Sept. 24, 1955 (dec. Nov. 1980); children: Amanda Blair, Vanessa Paige.; m. Jane McCue, June 4, 1983. AB, Columbia U., 1955, MA, 1961, Ph.D. (Schiff fellow), 1965; LLB, N.Y. Law Sch., 1960; postgrad., Luth. Theol. So. Sem., 1981-84. Bar: N.Y. 1960, U.S. Supreme Ct 1965, D.C. 1967, S.C. 1983; ordained vocat. deacon, 1991. Jr. clk. First Nat. City Bank of N.Y., N.Y.C., 1955; adminstrv. asst. Chase Manhattan Bank, N.Y.C., 1957-60; practiced in N.Y.C., 1960-67; research asst. Papers of John Jay, Columbia U., 1961-63, asso. sem. on history of legal polit. thought, 1966-77, asso. sem. on early Am. history, 1967-77; lectr. Hunter Coll. City U. N.Y., 1964-65, asst. prof. history, 1965-67; asso. editor Papers of John Marshall, Inst. Early Am. History and Culture, Williamsburg, Va., 1967-70; co-editor Papers of John Marshall, Inst. Early Am. History and Culture, 1970-71, editor, 1971-77; prof. law and history U. S.C., Columbia, 1977-90, Ernest F. Hollings prof. constl. law, 1991—; lectr. Coll. William and Mary, Williamsburg, 1967-77; Bostick vis. rsch. prof. So. studies program U. S.C., 1976, 77; mem. com. rsch., publs. Heritage '76 Com. Am. Revolution Bicentennial Commn., 1972-73; mem. bd. adjustments, appeals, Williamsburg, 1970-77; trustee Fund for Preservation of John Marshall House, 1972-74, Fund Coop. Editl. Rsch. Am. Antiquarian Soc., 1972-76; vis. prof. faculty law U. Birmingham, Eng., 1998. Author: The Law Merchant and Negotiable Instruments in Colonial New York, 1664-1730, 1963, John Jay, 1745-1829, 1970, Imported Eighteenth-Century Law Treatises in American Libraries 1700-1799, 1978, Essays on New York Colonial Legal History, 1981, History of Criminal Justice, 1988, 2nd edit., 1995, John Jay: Colonial Lawyer, 1989, The Chief Justiceship of John Marshall, 1997; co-author: Historical Courthouses of New York State-18th and 19th Century Halls of Justice Across the Empire State, 1977, Foundations of Power-John Marshall, 1801-15, vol. 2, History of the Supreme Court of the United States, 1981; editor: The Papers of John Marshall, Vol. 1, 1974, Vol. II, 1977, South Carolina Legal History, 1980, American Legal and Constitutional History: Cases and Materials, 1994; gen. editor Chief Justiceships of the U.S. Supreme Court Series, 1989—; contbr. articles to profl. jours. Chaplain assoc. Bapt. Med. Ctr., Columbia, 1983—, hospice legal svcs. vol., 1986—; mem. ethics com. S.C. Episcopal Home, Still Hopes, 1989—. 1st lt. USAF, 1955-57; col. Res. ret. Recipient William P. Lyons Masters' Essay award Loyola U., 1962, Paul S. Kerr History prize N.Y. State Hist. Assn., 1970; Am. Council Learned Socs. fellow, 1974-75, Inst. Humane Studies fellow, 1981, 85; vis. fellow Centre for Comparative Constl. Studies, U. Melbourne Law Faculty, 1992; vis. rsch. scholar U. Toronto Law Faculty, 1995. Mem. Am. Hist. Assn. (Littleton-Griswold com. 1976-81, mem. interim com. Bicentennial era 1976-77), Selden Soc. (state corr. for S.C. 1988—), Stair Soc., Osgoode Soc., Air Force Assn., Am. Law Inst., Assn. Am. Law Schs. (chmn. legal history sect. 1979), Am. Soc. Legal History (pres. 1974-75, del. Am. Coun. Learned Socs. 1977-80, bd. dirs. 1999—), U. South Caroliniana Soc., Res. Officers Assn., Coll. of Chaplains, Nat. Eagle Scout Assn. Episcopalian. Home: 615 LaBruce Ln Columbia SC 29205-2858 Office: U SC Sch Law Columbia SC 29208

JOHNSON, HERBERT FREDERICK, sales executive, former university administrator, librarian; b. St. Paul, Aug. 1, 1934; s. Herbert Oscar and Hazel Grace (Otto) J.; m. Delores Elaine Madson, Aug. 21, 1955; children: Steven F., Eric L., Kirsten M. B.A., U. Minn., 1957, M.A., 1959; postgrad., Kursverksamheten Vid Lunds Universitet, Betyg, 1975. Libr. U.S. Govt., Washington, 1959-61; asst. bus. libr. Columbia U., 1961-64; head libr., assoc. prof. Hamline U., 1964-71; libr., prof. Oberlin Coll., 1971-78; libr. Oberlin Pub. Library, 1971-78; dir. librs. Emory U., 1978-88, mem. faculty adv. com. Jimmy Carter Ctr. for Policy Studies, 1982-84; sales & svc. rep. Active Mobility of Ga., Marietta, 1988-91; sr. regional mgr. Williams/Howard Assocs., 1989-91; regional v.p. Primerica Fin. Svcs., Marietta, Ga., 1991—; registered prin. PFS Investments, Inc., 1991—; project dir. Nat. Drug Info. Ctr. Nat. Families in Action Inc., 1989-90; lectr. U. Minn. Libr. Sch., 1967; vis. prof. Atlanta U. Sch. Libr. Svcs., 1979; charter bd. Cooperating Librs. in Consortium, St. Paul, 1969-71; libr. adv. com. Minn. Higher Edn. Coordinating Commn., 1970-71; mem. com. input standards Ohio Coll. Libr. Ctr., 1972-73, chmn. com. patron input, 1973-75; chmn. Ohio Multitype Interlibr. Cooperation Com., Ohio State Libr. Bd., 1976-78; mem. adv. and steering com. Ohio Pre-White House Conf. on Libr. and Info. Services, 1977-78; bd. dirs. Assn. Rsch. Librs., 1983-88, pres., 1987-88; chmn. librs.adv. com. Univ. Center in Ga., Atlanta, 1979-80, 85-86; del. users council OCLC Online Computer Libr. Ctr. Inc., 1981-83, 85-88; bd. dirs. Southeastern Libr. Network, 1980-83, chmn. bd., 1981-83; bd. govs. Rsch. Librs. Group, 1986-87. Contbr. articles to profl. jours. Mem. com. on internat. programs Nat. Student YMCA's, 1962-64; mem. Minn. Republican Task Force on Edn., 1966; pres., treas. Lord of Life Lutheran Ch., Lorain, Ohio, 1972-75; mem. Lorain Coop. Luth. Ministry Bd., 1976-78; v.p. St. Luke Luth. Ch., Atlanta, 1979-80, 81-82; bd. dirs. Nat. Families in Action, 1979-89, 90—, pres. 1987-88, v.p., 1990-93; mem. adv. com. DeKalb/Rockdale counties of Met. Atlanta chpt. ARC, 1981-88, Cobb/Douglas counties of Met. Atlanta chpt. ARC, 1988-92, emergency community svcs. com., 1990-94; bd. dirs. Scandinavian Am. Found. Ga., 1983—, v.p. 1993—; bd. dirs. Swedish Coun. Am. 1987—, chair Glenn T. Seaborg Nobel prize travel award com., 1990—, jr. achievement classroom cons., 1993-94. Decorated Army Commendation medal, Meritorious Service medal; George Williams fellow, 1957; Council on Library Resources fellow, 1974-75; NSF grantee, 1967-71. Mem. ALA, Am. Scandinavian Found., Am. Swedish Inst., Ga. Libr. Assn., Southeastern Libr. Assn., Atlanta Zool. Soc., Chattahoochee Nature Ctr., Common Cause, Minn. Libr. Sch. Alumni Assn. (chmn. 1967), Wildlife Preservation Trust, Nat. Trust Hist. Preservation, Scandinavian Am. Found. Ga., Sierra Club, High Mus. Art, Rotary (dist. 6900 youth exch. com. 1994-97, treas. 1995-97, sec. North Dekalb, Ga. club 1981-82, pres. 1984-85), East Cobb (Ga.) Bus. Assn. (mem. bd. 1996—), The Res. Officers Assn., Nordic Lodge 708, Vasa Order of Am., Beta Phi Mu. Office: Primerica Fin Svcs 700 Sandy Plains Rd Ste A7 Marietta GA 30066-6392 *Too many folks have given up realizing their dreams, yet with the Lord's help, anyone has the capacity to make their dreams a reality. The toughest part of thestruggle is winning the battle between the ears - that is in believing in oneself. There is no greater thrill than having helped another win that struggle and having made a difference in that person's life!.*

JOHNSON, HERMAN JAMES, correctional facility administrator; b. Savannah, Ga., Feb. 4, 1953; s. Herman James and Dotha Lee (Owens) J.; m. constance Ellen Bryan, Dec. 1, 1977; 1 child, Jacqueline Clarise. AS, Armstrong State Coll., 1975, BS, 1976; MEd, U. Ga., 1980. Probation officer State of Ga., Dept. Corrections, Savannah, 1976-80, supt. Savannah Transitional Ctr., 1980-90; warden Putnam State Prison State of Ga., Dept. Corrections, Eatonton, 1990-91; warden Montgomery State Prison State of Ga., Dept. Corrections, Mt. Vernon, 1991-93; warden Telfair State Prison State of Ga., Dept. Corrections, Helena, 1993-96; warden Macon State Prison State of Ga., Dept. Corrections, Oglethorpe, 1996-98; warden dept. correction Jack T. Rutledge State Prison, Columbus, Ga., 1998—; chmn. Chatham County Criminal Justice Adv. Coun., Savannah, 1986-87; cons. Action Inc., Athens, Ga., 1992-93. Advisor Fanak Callens Boys Club, Savannah, 1989-90; chmn. Touching Childrens Lives Positively, Savannah, 1987-88. Mem. Am. Corrections Assn., Ga. Prison Wardens Assn., So. States Corrections Assn., Alpha Phi Alpha. Methodist. Avocations: reading, basketball, bowling. Home: 6508 Natha Ave Columbus GA 31909-3251 Office: Jack T Rutledge State Prison Manor Rd Columbus GA 31906

JOHNSON, HERMAN LEONALL, research nutritionist; b. Whitehall, Wis., Apr. 1, 1935; s. Frederick E. And Jeanette (Severson) J.; m. Barbara Dale Matthews, July 3, 1960 (dec. May 1971); m. Barbara Ann Badger, Apr. 3, 1976. BA in Chemistry, North Cen. Coll., Naperville, Ill., 1959; MS in Biochemistry & Nutrition, Va. Poly. Inst. and State U., 1961, PhD in Biochemistry and Nutrition, 1963. Rsch. biochemist S.R. Noble Found., Ardmore, Okla., 1963-65; nutrition chemist U.S. Army Med. Rsch., Denver, 1965-74; nutrition physiologist Letterman Army Rsch., Presidio San Francisco; 1974-80, Western Human Nutrition Rsch. Ctr. USDA, Presidio San Francisco, 1980—. Contbr. numerous articles to profl. jours. Trustee 1st Meth. Ch., Ronnert Park, Calif., 1985-94, mem. fin. com., 1994—. With Med. Svc. Corps U.S. Army, 1954-56. Named one of Outstanding Young Men of Am., 1975; NIH traineeship Va. Poly. Inst. and State U., Blacksburg, 1961-63. Mem. AAAS, Am. Inst. Nutrition, Am. Soc. Clin. Nutritionists, Am. Coll. Nutritionists, Am. Coll. Sports Medicine, Sebastopol Spinners, Sigma Xi, Phi Lambda, Phi Sigma. Republican. Achievements include research on human nutrition. Home: 256 Alden Ave Rohnert Park CA 94928-3704 Office: USDA Western Human Nutrition Rsch Ctr PO Box 29997 San Francisco CA 94129-0997

JOHNSON, HOLLIS EUGENE, III, foundation executive; b. Nashville, June 24, 1935; s. Hollis Eugene Jr. and Jennie Frances (Settle) J.; m. Marie Celeste Morrison, Nov. 19, 1960; children: Hollis Eugene IV, Martha Settle. BA, Vanderbilt U., 1956. With First Am. Nat. Bank, Nashville, 1959-76, v.p., trust officer, until 1976; exec. sec.-treas. So. Bapt. Found., Nashville, from 1976, now pres. Chmn. bd. trustees Franklin Rd. Acad., 1986-88, 95—; pres. Nashville Residence for Young Women, 1973, Nashville Area Jr. C. of C., 1965; chmn. Cumberland Valley Girl Scout investment coun., 1976-79; deacon Belmont Heights Bapt. Ch., 1974—, chmn., 1984, 89. With USNR, 1956-59. Mem. Assn. Bapt. Found. Execs. (pres. 1982), Nashville Soc. Fin. Analysts, Assn. for investment mgmt and rsch. Home: 5308 Confederate Dr Nashville TN 37215-5202 Office: So Bapt Found 901 Commerce St Nashville TN 37203-3697*

JOHNSON, HOLLIS RALPH, astronomy educator; b. Tremonton, Utah, Dec. 2, 1928; s. Ellwood Lewis and Ida Martha (Hansen) J.; m. Grete Margit Leed, June 3, 1954; children: Carol Ann Harrison, Wayne L., Lyle David, Charlotte Willian, Lise Marie Tyner, Richard L. BA in Physics, Brigham Young U., 1955, MA in Physics, 1957; PhD in Astrogeophysics, U. Colo., 1960. NSF postdoctoral fellow Paris Obs., 1960-61; rsch. assoc. Yale U., 1961-63; assoc. prof. astronomy Ind. U., Bloomington, 1963-69, prof.,

1969-94, prof. emeritus, 1994—, chmn. dept. astronomy, 1978-82, 90-93; NAS/NRC sr. fellow NASA Ames Rsch. Ctr., 1982-83; vis. scientist High Altitude Obs., Boulder, Colo., 1971-72; F.C. Donders vis. prof. U. Utrecht, The Netherlands, 1989; vis. prof. Niels Bohr Inst., Copenhagen, 1990, 1994-97; bd. dirs. Assn. Univs. for Rsch. in Astronomy, 1991-94. Contbr. articles to profl. jours. Served with U.S. Army, 1951-53. Mem. Internat. Astron. Union, Am. Astron. Soc., AAAS, AAUP, Sigma Xi. Mem. LDS Ch. Office: Ind U Dept Astronomy Swain W 319 Bloomington IN 47405

JOHNSON, HORACE RICHARD, electronics company executive; b. Jersey City, Apr. 26, 1926; s. Horace Adam and Grace (Lower) J.; m. Mary Louise Kleckner, July 29, 1950; children: Lucinda Louise, Karen Ann, Richard Adam, Russell Kleckner, David Thorp. BEE with distinction, Cornell U., 1946, postgrad., 1947; PhD in Physics, M.I.T., 1952. Mem. tech. staff Hughes Aircraft Co., 1952-57; co-founder Watkins-Johnson Co., Palo Alto, Calif., 1958; pres. Watkins-Johnson Co., 1967-87, vice chmn. bd. dirs., 1988—; lectr. engring. UCLA, 1956-57, Stanford U., 1958-68; chmn. Los Angeles Profl. Group on Electron Devices, 1955-56; dir. WEMA, 1971-72, Vols. Internat. Tech. Assistance, 1971-73. Patentee in field; contbr. articles to profl. jours. Pres. Stanford Area council Boy Scouts Am., 1968-70, bd. mem., 1967-77; campaign chmn. Palo Alto-Stanford chpt. United Fund, 1967. Served with USNR, 1943-46. Research Lab. for Electronics fellow, 1947-51. Fellow IEEE; mem. Nat. Acad. Engring., NAM (dir. 1983-90), Am. Phys. Soc., Newcomen Soc. North Am., Commonwealth Club Calif., Tau Beta Pi, Phi Kappa Phi, Gamma Alpha, Sigma Xi, Eta Kappa Nu. Office: Watkins-Johnson Co 3333 Hillview Ave Palo Alto CA 94304-1223

JOHNSON, HORTON ANTON, pathologist; b. Cheyenne, Wyo., Nov. 12, 1926; s. Horton Antonius and Katharine Mary (Tidball) J.; m. Caryl Abell Daly, Nov. 20, 1970; children by previous marriage: Katherine, Kristin, Margaret, Ann, Gregory, Marjorie. AB, Colo. Coll., 1949; MD, Columbia U., 1953. Diplomate: Am. Bd. Pathology. Intern Univ. Hosp., Ann Arbor, Mich., 1953-54; resident in pathology Univ. Hosp., 1954-57, Pondville Cancer Hosp., Walpole, Mass., 1957-58; scientist Brookhaven Nat. Lab., 1958-60, 63-70; asst. prof. pathology U. Utah, 1960-63; prof. pathology SUNY, Stony Brook, 1970-72, Ind. U., 1972-75; prof., chmn. dept. pathology Tulane U., New Orleans, 1975-84; prof. pathology Columbia U., N.Y.C., 1984-91; dir. pathology St. Luke's-Roosevelt Hosp. Ctr., N.Y.C., 1984-91. Served with USNR, 1944-46. Recipient Lederle Med. Faculty award, 1961. Fellow Coll. Am. Pathologists; mem. Am. Assn. Pathologists, Internat. Acad. Pathology, Biophys. Soc., Radiation Research Soc., N.Y. Acad. Scis., Assn. Clin. Scientists, Soc. Health and Human Values, Phi Beta Kappa, Alpha Omega Alpha. Rsch. on radiation injury, aging, theoretical biology. Home: 39 N Cove Rd Old Saybrook CT 06475-2538 Office: 3 Lincoln Ctr Ste 47C New York NY 10023-6566

JOHNSON, HOWARD ARTHUR, JR., corporate executive, operations analyst, financial officer; b. Indpls., July 25, 1952; s. Howard Arthur Sr. and Joy (Nelson) J.; m. Teresa Thirsk, Aug. 11, 1979, 1 child, Jamie E. BA in Polit. Sci. and Ops. Rsch. Analysis, U. Kans., 1974; MA in Internat. Studies and Mgmt., U. Wyo., 1984. Ops. rsch. analyst Armament Systems, Inc., Ft. Walton Beach, Fla., 1980-81, EG&G InterTech, Inc., Arlington, Va., 1981-84, dep. to U.S. Dir. Plans and Budgets, Royal Saudi Navy, Saudi Arabian Ministry Def. and Aviation, Riyadh, Saudi Arabia, 1981-82; ops. rsch. analyst FMC Corp., Mpls., 1984-85; ops. rsch. analyst Honeywell, Inc., 1985-92, sr. prin. systems staff engr., systems engring. mgr., 1985-92; CFO, co-founder, chief corp. security SEER, Inc., Eden Prairie, Minn., 1992—; cons. USN, Colorado, 1977-78, FMC Corp., 1992—, Embassy Suites, 1993; Sustaining mem. Nat. Com., Washington, 1984—. Lt. USN, 1974-78. Grad. acad. scholar U. Wyo., 1983-84. Mem. AAAS, IEEE, Ops. Rsch. Soc. Am., Acad. Internat. Bus., Inst. Mgmt. Scis., Fgn. Policy Rsch. Inst., Mil. Ops. Rsch. Soc., Armed Forces Communications Electronics Assn., Washington Ops. Rsch. Mgmt. Sci. Coun., Tau Kappa Epsilon. Office: SEER Inc 10409 Huntington Dr Ste 200B Eden Prairie MN 55347-4938

JOHNSON, HOWARD PAUL, agricultural engineering educator; b. Odebolt, Iowa, Jan. 27, 1923; s. Gustaf Johan and Ruth Helen (Hanson) J.; m. Patricia Jean Larsen, June 15, 1952; children: Cynthia, Lynette, Malcolm. BS, Iowa State U., 1949, MS in Agrl. Engring., 1950; MS in Hydraulic Engring., U. Iowa, 1954; PhD, Iowa State U., 1959. Engr., Soil Conservation Service, Sioux City, Iowa, 1949; instr. Iowa State U., Ames, 1950-53, 54-59, asst. prof., 1959-60, assoc. prof., 1960-62, prof. agrl. engring., 1962-80, head dept., 1980-88, prof. emeritus; cons., 1960-80. Contbr. numerous articles, papers to profl. lit. Co-editor Hydrologic Modeling, 1981. Patentee flow meter. Pres., Sawyer Sch. PTA, Ames, 1965; precinct rep. Republican party, Ames, 1980. Served with AUS, 1943-46, ETO. Recipient Iowa State U. Gamma Sigma Delta Merit award, 1983; EPA grantee, 1975-80; Anson Marston Disting. Prof. Engring., 1986. Fellow AAAS, Am. Soc. Agrl. Engrs. (div. chmn. 1969-70, tech. coun. 1974-76, Engr. of Yr. Iowa sect. 1981, Mid-Central sect. 1982, John Deere medal 1994). Baptist. Lodge: Rotary. Avocations: reading, photography, fishing, writing. Office: Iowa St U Dept Agrl Engring 100 Davidson Hall Ames IA 50014

JOHNSON, HOWARD WESLEY, former university president, business executive; b. Chgo., July 2, 1922; s. Albert H. and Laura (Hansen) J.; m. Elizabeth J. Weed, Feb. 18, 1950; children: Stephen Andrew, Laura Ann, Bruce Howard. B.A., Central Coll., Chgo., 1943; MA, U. Chgo., 1947; cert., Glasgow (Scotland) U., 1946; LLD (hon.), Harvard U., U. Miami, 1966, U. Mass., 1969, Oklahoma City U., 1970, U. Cin., 1973, Babson Coll., 1978; ScD (hon.), Lowell Tech. Inst., Tufts U., Bryant Coll., 1967; LHD (hon.), Northea. U., 1966, Roosevelt U., 1969; LittD (hon.), Clarkson Coll. Tech., 1973. From asst. to assoc. prof., dir. mgmt. rsch. U. Chgo., 1948-51, 53-55; asst. to v.p. pers. adminstrn. Gen. Mills, Inc., 1952-53; assoc. prof., dir. exec. programs, assoc. dean Sloan Sch. Mgmt., MIT, 1955-59, prof., dean, 1959-66; pres. MIT, 1966-71; chmn. corp., 1971-83, hon. chmn. corp., 1983-90, life mem. corp., 1983-97, life mem. emeritus, 1997—; exec. v.p. Federated Dept. Stores, 1966; chmn. Fed. Res. Bank Boston, 1968-69; trustee Putnam Funds, 1961-71; mem. Pres.'s Adv. Com. on Labor-Mgmt. Policy, 1966-68; chmn. Environ. Studies Bd. NAS-NAE, 1973-75; mem. sci. adv. com. Mass. Gen. Hosp., 1968-70; mem. Nat. Manpower Adv. Com., 1967-69, Nat. Commn. on Productivity, 1970-72; trustee Com. Econ. Devel., 1968-71, Wellesley Coll., 1968-86, trustee emeritus 1986—; trustee Radcliffe Coll., 1973-79; hon. trustee Aspen Inst. for Humanistic Studies, Inst. Deaf Analyses, 1971-79; mem. corp. Woods Hole (Mass) Oceanog. Instn. Author: Holding the Center: Memoirs of a Life in Higher Education, 1999. Trustee WGBH Ednl. Found., 1966-71, Henry Francis du Pont Winterthur Mus., 1984-87, Dibner Inst., 1992-97; mem. corp. Mus. Sci., Boston; overseer Boston Symphony Orch., 1968-72; mem.-at-large Boy Scouts Am.; pres. Boston Mus. Fine Arts, 1975-80, trustee 1971-72, chmn. bd. overseers, 1980-83, chmn. exec. com., 1983-87, hon. life trustee 1992—; trustee Alfred P. Sloan Found., 1982-95, chmn. bd. 1988-95; bd. dirs. Nat. Arts Stablzn. Found., 1983-87, Museo de Arte de Ponce, 1983-87. With AUS, 1943-46. Recipient Alumni medal U. Chgo., 1970. Fellow AAAS, Am. Acad. Arts and Scis.; mem. Coun. Fgn. Rels., Am. Philos. Soc., Century Assn. (N.Y.C.), Comml. Club (Boston), Tavern Club (Boston), St. Botolph Club (Boston), Phi Gamma Delta. Office: MIT 77 Massachusetts Ave Cambridge MA 02139-4307

JOHNSON, INGOLF BIRGER, retired electrical engineer; b. Bklyn., Sept. 29, 1913; s. Johan Ingevald and Antonie (Hansen) J.; m. Johanna Charlotte Mortensen, Sept. 6, 1942; children: Bruce Edward, Richard Birger. BEE, Poly. Inst. Bklyn. (now Poly. U.), 1937, MEE, 1939. Registered profl. engr., N.Y. Engr. Gen. Electric Co., Pittsfield, Mass., 1939-42; engring. tchr., mgr. Gen. Electric Co., Schenectady, 1942-78; cons. elec. engr. Schenectady, 1978-92; cons. Nuclear Regulatory Commn., Washington, 1980-86. Contbr. articles to profl. jours.; patentee in field. Recipient Steinmetz award, 1975. Fellow IEEE (Habirshaw medal 1966, Centennial medal 1984, Lamme medal 1986), AAAS; mem. Nat. Acad. Engring., Internat. Conf. High Voltage Systems (U.S. rep. 1963-68, Attwood assoc. 1986), Profl. Engring. Soc. Lutheran. Clubs: Elfun Soc., Cotillion (pres. 1984-85); Niskayuna Brush and Pallette (v.p. 1986-88, pres. 1988-90); Benedicts; GE Co. Quarter Century. Lodges: Scandinavian Forum of Tri-Cities (pres. 1984-85), Ret. Men's Frat. Albany. Avocations: oil painting, dancing, gardening, fishing, swimming. Home: 1508 Barclay Pl Niskayuna NY 12309-4120

JOHNSON, IRVING STANLEY, pharmaceutical company executive, scientist; b. Grand Junction, Colo., June 30, 1925; s. Walter Glen and Frances Lucetta (Tuttle) J.; m. Alwyn Neville Ginther, Jan. 29, 1949; children: Rebecca Lyn, Bryan Glenn, Kirsten Shawn, Kevin Bruce. AB, Washburn U., Topeka, 1948; PhD, U. Kans., 1953. With Lilly Rsch. Labs., Indpls., 1953-88, v.p. rsch., 1973-88; mem. profl. edn. com. Am. Cancer Soc., 1972-82; active rschr. cancer, virus, genetic engring.; mem. Recombinant Adv. Com., NIH, 1985-88; mem. UCLA Symposia Bd., 1986-89; cons. biomed. rsch., 1989—; bd. dirs. Allelix Biopharms., Ligand Pharms., Athena Neuroscis., 1989-96; sci. adv. bd. Elan Corp., 1996—, Warner-Lambert, 1999—; trustee La Jolla Cancer Rsch. Found., 1990-93; advisor to biomed. rsch. cos., venture capital groups. Mem. sci. adv. bd. Biotech., 1986—; mem. editorial bd. Chemico-Biol. Interactions, 1968-73; contbr. articles to profl. publs. With USNR, 1943-46. Recipient 1st ann. Congl. award for sci. and tech., 1984. Fellow AAAS; mem. Am. Assn. Cancer Rsch. (Cain Meml. award for outstanding preclin. rsch. in cancer chemotherapy 1986), Am. Soc. Cell Biology (mem. pub. policy com.), Environ. Mutagen Soc., Internat. Soc. Chemotherapy, N.Y. Acad. Scis., Soc. Exptl. Biology and Medicine, Am. Soc. Immunologists (mem. sci. adv. bd. biotech), Soc. for Neurosci., Sigma Xi, Phi Sigma. Episcopalian. Patentee in field.

JOHNSON, IVER CHRISTIAN, valuation company executive; b. N.Y.C., Oct. 21, 1928; s. Rudolph Albert and Mae Sophia (Bernhardt) J.; m. Ann E. Wells, May 15, 1954 (div. Apr. 1978); children: Christian Robert, Roberta Dawn, Brad Milton; m. Rochelle Valene Wehrheim, Dec. 6, 1986. BSME, N.Y.U., 1950; MBA, Northwestern U., 1958. Registered profl. engr. Engr. Yale & Towne Mfg. Co., Chgo., 1952-54; computer sales engr. GE, Phoenix, 1958-60; comml. broker O'Malley Investment & Realty Co., Phoenix, 1960-64; v.p. Investors Trust & Realty Co., Inc., Phoenix, 1964-66; ptnr. Shuart Bros. Constrn. Co., Phoenix, 1966-69; pres. Iver C. Johnson & Co., Ltd., Phoenix, 1970-95; del. mem. Citizen Amb. Program Econ. Mgmt. Delegation to Soviet Union, Moscow, Kiev and Odessa, USSR, 1990. Chmn., mem. bd. appeals Ariz. State Land Dept., 1989-95; exec. com. Ariz. Appraiser Coalition, 1989-92. 1st lt. USAF, 1954-56; mem. Ash Grove (Mo.) City Coun., 1997—. Mem. Am. Soc. Appraisers (sr., pres. 1985-86, ASA award 1981, Outstanding Mem. award 1990), Inst. Indsl. Engrs., Internat. Right of Way Assn. (SRWA award 1990), Am. Mktg. Assn. (profl.). Republican. Lutheran. Avocations: instrument piloting, freelance writing. Home and Office: 904 E Auburn Dr Ash Grove MO 65604-9100

JOHNSON, J. B., JR., federal judge; b. 1936. JD, U. Ky., 1961. Pvt. practice, 1965-86; judge 34th jud. cir. Ky. Cir. Ct., 1973-84; part-time magistrate judge ea. dist. U.S. Dist. Ct. Ky., 1977-86, apptd. magistrate judge ea. dist., 1996. With USAF, 1961-64. Fax: (606) 549-5270. Office: 310 Main St Williamsburg KY 40769-1124

JOHNSON, J. CHESTER, financial executive, poet; b. Chattanooga, Sept. 28, 1944; m. Freda Stern; children: Juliet Christina, Guilbert Roland. Student, Harvard U., 1962-65; BSE, U. Ark., 1967. Sr. analyst Moody's Investors Svc., 1968-71; head pub. fin. rsch. and adv. group The Morgan Bank, 1972-77; dep. asst. sec. U.S. Treasury Dept., Washington, 1977-78; chmn., prin. Govt. Fin. Assocs., Inc., N.Y.C., 1979—; bd. dirs., chair fin. com. N.Y. State Environ. Facilities Corp., 1991-95; chmn. Fed. Task Force to create Nat. Devel. Bank; chmn. Fed. Inter-agy. Task Force for Improvement Govtl. Fin. Reporting; chmn. Fund to Assure Pub. Infrastructure Fin., Nat. Infrastructure Bond Coalition, 1988-91; interviewed on pub. fin. Cable News Network, ABC Morning News Feature, PBS News Roundup, NBC Nightly News, others. Author: (poetry) OH America!, January 12th, 1967, 2d edit., 1975, Family Ties, Internecine Interregnum!, 1981, For Conduct and Innocents, 1982, Shorts: For Fun, Not for Instruction, 1985, It's a Long Way Home, An American Sequence, 1985, Shorts: On Reaching Forty, 1985, Exile/Martin, 1986, The Professional Curiosity of a Martyr, 1987, Freda's Appetite, 1991, Lazarus, Come Forth, 1993, Plain Bob (Unbehaved), 1993; (with W.H. Auden) revised psalms in The Book of Common Prayer of The Episcopal Church, 1971-77; co-author: Original Disclosure Guidelines for Securities' Offerings by State and Local Governments, 1976, The Future of Boston's Capital Plant, 1980, Mayor's Financial Management Handbook, 1985: contbr. numerous articles to profl. jours. Recipient Young So. Poets award, Internat. Poets award. Mem. Nat. Assn. Ind. Pub. Fin. Advisors (pres. 1989-91), Nat. Soc. Mcpl. Analysts, Nat. Fedn. Mcpl. Analysts (Disting. Lifetime Contbn. award 1988). Office: Govt Fin Assocs Inc 63 Wall St Fl 16 New York NY 10005-3001

JOHNSON, J. M. HAMLIN, manufacturing company executive; b. Ridgway, Pa., Oct. 10, 1925; s. Manferd H. and Esther (Hallstrom) J.; m. Sara N. Richardson, Sept. 11, 1948; children: Stephanie (Mrs. William G. Cox), Robert H., Elizabeth E., Lara, David L., Christine M. (Mrs. Thomas Syzmanski), Shawn J. B.S., Grove City Coll., 1949; student, Pa. State U., 1969. With Stackpole Corp., St. Mary's, Pa., 1950—, supr. acctg., to 1960, operational auditor, 1960-64, mgr. acctg., 1964-68, asst. treas., 1968-71, treas., asst. sec., 1971-79, v.p., treas., asst. sec., 1979-84; v.p., treas. asst. sec., dir. Stackpole Corp., 1984-88, v.p., treas., sec., dir., 1988; ret., 1990; bd. dirs. Hamlin Bank & Trust Co., Cmty. Nurses of Elk & Cameron Counties Inc., Home Health Svcs. Past mem. Ridgway Area Sch. Bd.; trustee Stackpole-Hall Found., 1983—; chmn., bd. dirs. St. Marys Regional Med. Ctr.; bd. dirs., past treas., past pres. ELCAM Vocat. Rehab. Ctr.; bd. dirs. United Fund St. Marys. With USAAF. Mem. Nat. Assn. Accts. (pres. 1958-59), Bavarian Hills Club. Home: 517 Center St Saint Marys PA 15857-1001

JOHNSON, J. MITCHELL, communications executive; b. Dallas, May 12, 1951; s. J. Edward and Blanche (Dabney) J.; 1 child, Philip Louis. BS, U. Tex.; MS, U. So. Calif. Prodn. asst. Guggenheim Prodns., Washington, 1975-77; pres. Ft. Worth Prodns., 1977—; CEO J. Mitchell Johnson Prodns., Ft. Worth, 1986—; publisher Fodor's Video Guides, Ft. Worth, 1986-93; CEO Abamedia, LP, Ft. Worth and Moscow, 1995—; pres. Archive Media Project, Ft. Worth and Moscow, 1996—; official trade rep. Russian State Film and Photo Archives, Krasnogorsk. Producer 14 films for Fodor's, 1986-93; 20 TV programs for Ostankino Russian TV; Co-production ABC News N.Y. 1994-95; Producer, dir. TV films including Gymnast, Pub. Broadcasting System, 1980 (JQ award 1981); Artist and Athlete, ABC, 1980; producer TV films Moses Pendleton Presents Moses Pendleton, ABC, 1983 (1st place award San Francisco Film Festival 1984), Mondale for America, 1984, Yanks for Stalin (History Channel) 1999, Red Files (PBS Series) 1999. Exec. producer Mondale for Am.-Cons. '84, Washington, 1984; chmn. Budapest, Hungary-Ft. Worth Sister Cities Internat. Com., chmn. media panel Tex. Commn. for Arts and Humanities, Austin, 1986, chmn. Citizens Cable Bd., City of Ft. Worth, 1990-91. Recipient Gold award N.Y. TV Film Festival, 1981, Golden Eagle award Council on Internat. Nontheatrical Events, Washington, 1983, Best Documentary and Film awards N.Mex. Film Festival, Albuquerque, 1984, Best Documentary award USA Film Festival, Dallas, 1984. Mem. Internat. Music Ctr. (pres. 1987-88), Motion Picture Producers Tex. (pres. 1987-88), Found. for Social Innovations Moscow-N.Y. (bd. dirs.), Ft. Worth Club. Democrat. Methodist. Avocations: travel, music, electronics. Office: J Mitchell Johnson Prodns Inc PO Box 125 Fort Worth TX 76101-0125

JOHNSON, JACQUELINE, Native American program administrator. Student, Utah State U., Snow Coll., U. Alaska S.W. From rsch. asst. to exec. dir. Tlingit-Haida Regional Housing Authority; dep. asst. sec. Native Am. Programs, U.S. Dept. Housing and Urban Devel., Washington; appointed by Pres. Clinton to fund adv. bd. Nat. Cmty. Devel. Fin. Instn.; mem. Nat. Commn. on Am. Indian, Alaska Native, and Native Hawaiian Housing; chairperson Nat. Am. Indian Housing Coun., 1994. Dir. Native Youth Culture Camp, 1985—; mem. Raven/Sockeye Clan of Tlingit Tribe; sec. Juneau Tlingit and Haida Cmty. Coun. FAX: 202-401-7909. Office: Office Native Am Programs Housing and Urban Devel 451 7th St SW Rm 4126 Washington DC 20410-0001

JOHNSON, JAMES, principal; b. July 20, 1945. EdD, Pacific Western U., 1996. Tchr. Meriden (Conn.) Pub. Schs., 1978-94; prin. High Meadows Sch. Unified Sch. Dist. II, Holmdel, Conn., 1994—. E-mail: docjay@erols.com. Home: 601 Gracey Ave Meriden CT 06451

JOHNSON, JAMES A., financial organization executive; b. Benson, Minn., Dec. 24, 1943; s. Alfred I. and Adeline (Rasmussen) J.; m. Katherine Marshall, Feb. 15, 1969 (div. 1973); m. Maxine Isaacs, Jan. 12, 1985; 1 child, Alfred Isaacs. BA, U. Minn., 1965; MA, Princeton U., 1968. Spl. asst. to Sen. Walter Mondale U.S. Senate, Washington, 1972; dir. pub. affairs Dayton Hudson Corp., Mpls., 1973-76; exec. asst. to v.p. Walter Mondale The White House, Washington, 1977-81; pres. Pub. Strategies, Washington, 1981-85; mng. dir. Lehman Bros., N.Y.C., 1985-89; vice-chmn. Fannie Mae, Washington, 1990-91, CEO, 1991—, also chmn. bd. dirs. Chmn. John F. Kennedy Ctr. for Performing Arts, Fannie Mae Found.; chmn. bd. trustees The Brookings Instn.; bd. dirs. Alliance to Save Energy, Carnegie Corp., N.Y., Carnegie Endowment for Internat. Peace, Dayton Hudson Corp., The Enterprise Found., Kaufman & Broad Home Corp., Nat. Alliance to End Homelessness, Nat. Housing Endowment, United Healthcare Corp., mem. bus. coun. Democrat. Avocations: tennis, golf, travel. Office: Fannie Mae 3900 Wisconsin Ave NW Washington DC 20016-2892*

JOHNSON, JAMES ARNOLD, business consultant, venture capitalist; b. Detroit, June 15, 1939; s. Waylon Z. and Elsie Jean (Peuser) J.; 1 child, Stephanie Louise. BA, Stanford U., 1961; MBA, U. Chgo., 1968. CPA, Calif. Asst. cashier internat. banking First Nat. Bank of Chgo., 1965-68; ptnr.-in-charge mgmt. cons. Peat, Marwick, Mitchell & Co., Honolulu, 1968-79, ptnr.-in-charge small bus. services, 1977-80; pres. Johnson Internat., Inc., Incline Village, Nev., 1980—; pres. BioEngring. Applications, Inc., Honolulu, 1981-90; bd. dirs. KSH Systems, Inc., Incline Village, 1984-96, pres. Pflueger Group, Inc., 1985-87; gen. ptnr. numerous investment partnerships; mem. bd. dirs. TransData Internat., Inc., 1995—; CFO TransData Internat., Inc., 1995—, Ad Epress Canada Inc., 1996—. Served to lt. USNR, 1962-65. Mem. AICPA, Calif. Soc. CPAs. Home: 685 Wilson Way Incline Village NV 89450 Office: PO Box 6898 Incline Village NV 89450-6898

JOHNSON, JAMES BEK, JR., library director; b. Sommerville, Mass., Oct. 1, 1943; s. James Bek and Esther Elizabeth (Cummings) J.; m. Deborah Marie Clawson, Oct. 21, 1972; children: Kirsten Eliska, Jessica Cummings. BA in History, La. State U., New Orleans, 1966; MS in LS, La. State U., Baton Rouge, 1968. Libr. La. State Penitentiary, Angola, 1968-70; cons. S.C. State Libr., Columbia, 1972-73, dir. dept. for handicapped, 1973-79, dep. dir., 1979-90, dir., 1990—. Contbr. articles to profl. jours. Mem. S.C. Gov.'s Com. on Employment of Handicapped, 1977—; vol. coach Columbia Recreation Dept., 1983-91; pres. Quail Creek Neighborhood Assn., Hopkins, S.C., 1986-90; mem. improvement coun. Lower Richland High Sch., Hopkins, 1991-93. With USMC, 1970-72. Mem. ALA (various coms.), Southeastern Libr. Assn., S.C. Libr. Assn. (chmn. pub. libr. sect.), Chief Officers State Libr. Agys. (legis. com. 1990-96, sec. 1994-96), Staff Liaison, Governor's info. resource ctr. Democrat. Episcopalian. Avocations: gardening, collecting opera records, baseball. Office: SC State Libr PO Box 11469 Columbia SC 29211-1469

JOHNSON, JAMES DAVID, concert pianist, organist, educator; b. Greenville, S.C., Aug. 7, 1948; s. Theron David and Lucile (Pearson) J.; m. Karen Elizabeth Jacobson, Feb. 1, 1975. MusB, U. Ariz., 1970, MusM, 1972, D of Mus. Arts, 1976; MusM, Westminster Choir Coll., 1986. Concert pianist, organist Pianists Found. Am., Boston Pops Orch., Royal Philharm., Nat. Symphony Orch., Leningrad Philharmonic, Victoria Symphony, others, 1961—; organist, choirmaster St. Paul's Episcopal Ch., Tucson, 1968-74, First United Meth. Ch., Fairbanks, Alaska, 1974-89, All Saints Episc. Ch., Omaha, 1995—; prof. music U. Alaska, Fairbanks, 1974-96, chair music dept., 1991-94; Isaacson prof. of music U. Nebr., Omaha, 1994—. Recordings include Moszkowski Etudes, 1973, Works of Chaminade Dohnanyi, 1977, Mendelssohn Concerti, 1978, Beethoven First Concerto, 1980, Beethoven, Reinecke, Ireland Trios with Alaska Chamber Ensemble, 1988, Kabalevsky Third Concerto, Muczynski Concerto, Muczynski Suite, 1990, Beethoven Third Concerto, 1993. Recipient Record of Month award Mus. Heritage Soc., 1979, 80; finalist mus. amb. program USIA, 1983. Mem. Music Tchrs. Nat. Assn., Phi Kappa Phi, Pi Kappa Lambda. Episcopalian. Avocations: painting, woodworking. Office: U Nebr Dept Music Omaha NE 68182

JOHNSON, JAMES DOUGLAS (JIM JOHNSON), lawyer; b. Crossett, Ark., Aug. 20, 1924; s. Thomas William and Maudie Myrtle (Long) J.; m. Virginia Morris, Dec. 21, 1947; children: Mark Douglas, John David and Joseph Daniel (twins). LL.B., Cumberland U., 1947. Bar: Ark. 1948. Practice in Crosset, 1948-58; assoc. justice Supreme Ct. Ark., 1958-66; practice law Little Rock, 1966—; Ark. Senate 22d Senatorial Dist., 1950-54. Served with USMCR, World War II. Mem. Ark. Jud. Council, Lamda Chi Alpha. Republican. Christian Scientist. Home: PO Box 1086 Conway AR 72033-1086

JOHNSON, JAMES E., airport executive. Sr. dir. airports Hillborough County Aviation Authority, Tampa, Fla., Tampa Internat. Airport. Office: Tampa Internat Airport PO Box 22287 Tampa FL 33622-2287*

JOHNSON, JAMES ERLING, insurance executive; b. Waseca, Minn., May 19, 1942; s. Erling Olaf and Geneva Eleanor (Nyberg) J. BA cum laude, Carleton Coll., 1964; MS, U. Iowa, 1966. Sr. asst. health svcs. officer USPHS, 1966-68; with Minn. Life Ins. Co., St. Paul, 1968—, 2d v.p., actuary, 1976-79, v.p., actuary, 1979-90, sr.v.p., actuary, 1990—; pres., chief exec. officer Minn. Fire & Casualty, Minnetonka, 1984-97, also bd. dirs.; pres., chief exec. officer Adjustable Life Ins. Co., St. Paul, 1988-93, also bd. dirs. Mem. alumni bd. Carleton Coll., Northfield, Minn., 1987-90, coun., 1988-89, bd. trustees 1999—; campaign cabinet St. Paul United Way, 1988-89; bd. dirs. Minn. Landmarks, 1988—, treas., 1989-91, chmn., 1991-96; trustee ECH Found., 1989-95, asst. treas., 1990-91, treas., 1991-95; bd. dirs. Alliance of Am. Insurers, 1994-95, vice chmn., 1994-95, Saint Paul Chamber Orch., 1998—, co-chair indivdual gifts com., 1998—; mem. adv. bd. Minn. Ctr. for Ins. Rsch., 1995—. U. Iowa fellow, 1964-66. Fellow Soc. Actuaries; mem. Am. Acad. Actuaries, Twin Cities Actuarial Club (chmn. 1978-79), Minn. (St. Paul) Club, Decathlon Athletic Club, Flagship Athletic Club, University Club (St. Paul), Minn. Assn. of Mutual Ins. Cos. (bd. dirs. 1984-97, pres. 1992-94), Nat. Assn. of Secondary Sch. Prins. (trustee Trust to Reach Edn. 1999—), Phi Beta Kappa, Pi Mu Epsilon. Episcopalian. Avocations: travel, reading, running, swimming. Home: 2034 Lower Saint Dennis Rd Saint Paul MN 55116-2833 Office: Minn Life Ins Co 400 Robert St N Saint Paul MN 55101-2098

JOHNSON, JAMES GIBSON, JR., community recycling specialist; b. Flagstaff, Ariz., Feb. 26, 1938; s. James Gibson and Inga Anette J.; m. Faye Bodian, Aug. 23, 1973; children: Jill Johnson, Ginger Johnson, Jonathan Johnson. BA, U. Colo., 1960. Editor, pub. Town and Country Rev., Boulder, Colo., 1963-78; owner James G. Johnson and Assocs., Boulder, Colo., 1978-87; exec. dir. Eco Cycle Recycling, Boulder, Colo., 1987-89; community recycling specialist Office of Energy Conservation, State of Colo., Denver, 1989-97; recycling cons. James G. Johnson Assoc., Boulder, 1997—; Colo. mgr. Southwestern Pub. Recycling Assn., Tuscon, 1999—. Mem. Open Space Bd. Trustees, Boulder, 1980-85, chmn., 1984-85; mem. Boulder County Pks. and Open Space Bd., 1985-93; chmn., 1987-89; mem. Boulder County Planning Commn., 1993—. Democrat. Avocations: running, skiing. Home: 630 Northstar Ct Boulder CO 80304-1021 Office: 630 Northstar Ct Denver CO 80304

JOHNSON, JAMES HAROLD, lawyer; b. Galesburg, Ill., May 3, 1944; s. Harold Frank and Marjorie Isabel (Liby) J.; m. Judith Eileen Moore, June 5, 1966; children: Todd James, Tiffany Nicole. BA, Cole Coll., 1966; JD, U. Tex., 1969. Bar: N.Y. 1970, Colo. 1971, Tex. 1975. Assoc. Winthrop, Stimson, Putnam & Roberts, N.Y.C., 1969-70, Sherman & Howard, Denver, 1970-72; corp. counsel Tex. Instruments, Inc., Dallas, 1972-85; v.p., gen. counsel, sec. Am. Healthcare Mgmt., Dallas, 1985-86, Ornda Healthcorp, Dallas, 1986-94; shareholder Jenkens & Gilchrist, PC, Dallas, 1994-97; ast. gen. counsel Sulzer Medica Inc., Houston, 1997—. Mem. ABA, Tenn. Bar Assn., Am. Soc. Corp. Secs., Tex. Bar Assn., Nat. Health Lawyers Assn. Republican. Methodist. Avocations: skiing, horseback riding. Home: 3907 N Kimball Ct Missouri City TX 77459-6230 Office: Sulzer Medica 3 E Greenway Plz Ste 1600 Houston TX 77046-0391

JOHNSON, JAMES J., lawyer. BA, U. Mich.; JD, Ohio State U. Bar: Ohio 1972. V.p., gen. counsel Proctor & Gamble Co., Cin., 1991—, now sr. v.p., gen. counsel, 1991—. Office: Procter & Gamble Co 1 Procter And Gamble Plz Cincinnati OH 45202-3393*

JOHNSON, JAMES JOSEPH SCOFIELD, lawyer, judge, educator, author; b. Washington, Apr. 28, 1956; s. Richard Carl and Harriette (Benson) J.; m. Sherry Bekki Hall; children: Andrew Joel Schaeffer Johnson. AA with high honors, Montgomery Coll., Germantown, Md., 1980; BA with honors, Wake Forest U., 1982; JD, U. N.C., 1984; ThD with highest honors, Emmanuel Coll. Christian, 1996; PhD with highest honors, Cambridge Grad. Sch., Springdale, Ark., 1996, MSc, M of Liberal Arts, 1999. Bar: Tex. 1985, U.S. Dist. Ct. (no. dist.) Tex. 1986, U.S. Dist. Ct. (ea. dist.) Tex. 1987, U.S. Ct. Appeals (5th cir.) 1989, U.S. Dist. Ct. (we. and so. dists.) Tex. 1990; bd. cert. bus. bankruptcy law Tex. Bd. Legal Specialization, 1990, 95, Am. Bankruptcy Bd. Cert., 1992; cert. water quality monitor Tex. Natural Resource Conservation Commn., 1994. Assoc. various orgns., Dallas, 1985—; pvt. practice law Dallas, 1993—; adj. prof. LeTourneau U., Dallas, 1991—, Dallas Christian Coll., 1995—; lectr. History, Ecology, Culture, Norwegian Cruise Lines, 1998—. Author: Introduction to Environmental Studies, 1995, 98, Doxological Zoology and Zoogeography, 1998; sr. editl. staff N.C. Jour. Internat. Law and Comml. Regulation, 1983-84; conf. issue editor Harvard Jour. Law & Pub. Policy, 1984; contbr. articles to profl. jours. Protestant chaplain Boy Scouts Am., Goshen, Va., 1976; libr. vol. N.W. Bible Ch., Dallas, 1991-98; cmty. program dir. Southwestern Legal Founds. Conf. on Internat. and Am. Law, 1991-92; active mem. Pro Bono Coll. State Bar Tex., Dallas, 1992—98; scripture chmn. Gideons Internat., North Dallas, Tex., 1993-94. Recipient award for excellence in biblical studies and biblical langs. Am. Bible Soc., 1982. Mem. Coun. Cert. Bankruptcy Specialists (cert.), Tex. River & Reservoir Mgmt. Soc., Soc. Christian Philosophers, Sangre de Cristo Mountain Coun., Creation Rsch. Soc., Evangel. Theol. Soc. Republican. Avocations: reading, writing, birding, traveling, hiking. Office: PO Box 2952 Dallas TX 75221-2952

JOHNSON, JAMES M., orchestra executive; b. Puyallup, Wash., June 15, 1963; s. E. Marvin and Virginia G. (Isvick) J.; m. Jennifer B. Katz, Apr. 17, 1994. BA cum laude, Pacific Luth. U., 1985; MBA, So. Meth. U., 1988, MA in Arts Adminstrn., 1988. Publicist, computer systems mgr. Pantages Ctr. Performing Arts, 1985-86; programming asst. N.Y. Internat. Festival Arts, 1988; gen. mgr. Martha Graham Ctr. Contemporary Dance, N.Y.C., 1988-94; dir. ops. Orch. of St. Luke's, N.Y.C., 1994—. Office: Orch of St Lukes 330 W 42nd St Fl 9 New York NY 10036-6902

JOHNSON, JAMES MYRON, psychologist, educator; b. Sauk Centre, Minn., Aug. 4, 1927; s. Walfred and Sophie Catherine (Koelzer) J.; m. Constance Mary Blodgett, Apr. 15, 1950; children: Kathryn, Peter, Donna, Daniel, Amy, Linda, Eric, Christian. B.A., U. Minn., 1948; M.A., Clark U., 1950; Ph.D., Columbia, 1958; ME (hon.), Stevens Inst. Tech., 1986. Staff psychologist Lever Bros. Co., 1955-64; Adj. prof. Grad. Sch. Indsl. Engring., N.Y.U., 1963-66; dep. dir. lab. psychol. studies Stevens Inst. Tech., 1964-67, dir., 1967-73, prof. mgmt. sci. and psychology, 1966-89, prof. emeritus, 1989—, assoc. dean acad. affairs, 1972-76, dir. tech. and soc. curriculum, 1972-75; dir. Center for Mgmt. of Organizational Resources, 1976-81; sr. partner Organizational Scis. Assocs., 1980-88; v.p. G. W. Fotis Assocs., Inc., 1982-88, head, dept. of mgmt., 1988-89; cons. to industry. Producer film The Man Who Revolutionized Mangement: Frederick Winslow Taylor. Pres. Darien (Conn.) Mental Health Assn., 1961-64, 68-70; mem. Darien Democratic Town Com.; bd. dirs. Gateway, Inc., 1979-86. Served with USNR, 1945-46. Mem. Am. Psychol. Soc., Met. N.Y. Assn. Applied Psychology (pres. 1963-64), Sigma Xi (treas. 1984-89), Old Lyme Country Club. Democrat. Roman Catholic. Home: 4 Tantummaheag Rd Old Lyme CT 06371-1137

JOHNSON, JAMES P., religious organization executive. Pres. Christian Ch. Found., Inc., Indpls. Office: Christian Ch Found Inc 130 E Washington St PO Box 1986 Indianapolis IN 46206-1986*

JOHNSON, JAMES ROBERT, ceramic engineer, educator; b. Cin., Jan. 2, 1923; s. Charles William and Della Ramona (Schubert) J.; m. Virginia M. Bowen, Apr. 3, 1945; children: Cathy (Mrs. Edward Spear), Barbara (Mrs. Charles Kallusky), Randy, John, Jamie (Mrs. J.R. Myers), Brian. BS, Ohio State U., 1947, MS, 1948, PhD, 1950; DSc (hon.), U. Wis., 1993. Asst. prof. U. Tex., 1950-51; tech. adviser ceramics Oak Ridge Nat. Lab., 1951-56; lab. mgr., dir., exec. scientist Minn. Mining & Mfg. Co., St. Paul, 1956-79, cons., 1979—; William L. McKnight prof. U. Minn., Duluth, 1988-89; adj. prof. U. Wis.-Stout, U. Minn., 1979—. Contbr. articles to profl. jours.; patentee in field. Served with C.E. AUS, 1943-46. Recipient Distinguished Alumnus award Ohio State U., 1970, 3M Carlton award, 1970, Prakken award Internat. Tech. Edn. Assn., 1989, James R. Johnson award established in his honor, U. Wis. Stout, 1983, Nelva Runnalls Rsch. award, U. Wis. Stout, 1989. Fellow Am. Ceramic Soc. (pres. 1973-74, disting. life mem.), Wis. Acad. Scis., Arts and Letters (pres. 1988); mem. NAE, Nat. Inst. Ceramics Engrs. (Pace award 1959, Greaves-Walker award 1985), Am. Soc. for Metals Engring. (Materials Achievement award 1980), Research Engring. Soc. Am. Pioneer in auto catalytic converters, high temperature nuclear fuel materials. Home: 1189 Tamarind Way Boca Raton FL 33486-5554

JOHNSON, JAMES TERENCE, college chancellor; b. Springfield, Mo., Oct. 25, 1942; s. Clifford Lester and Margaret Jeanne (Wallace) J.; m. Martha Susan Mitchell, May 2, 1964; children: Jennifer Jeanne, Emily Jill. BA, Okla. Christian Coll., 1964; JD, So. Meth. U., 1967; LLD (hon.), Pepperdine U., 1980. Staff counsel, asst. prof. Okla. Christian Coll., Oklahoma City, 1968-72; v.p. Okla. Christian U., 1972-73; exec. v.p. Okla. Christian U. of Sci. and Arts, 1973-74, pres., 1974-95, chancellor, 1995—; min. Okla., Tex., 1961—; pvt. practice law Oklahoma City, 1969—; cofounder Enterprise Sq., U.S.A., 1982. Mem. Okla. Bar Assn., Phi Delta Theta. Office: Okla Christian U PO Box 11000 Oklahoma City OK 73136-1100

JOHNSON, JAMES WILLIAM, English educator, author; b. Birmingham, Ala., Mar. 1, 1927; s. James Terry and Maude Belle (Brown) J.; m. Nan Heffelfinger, Oct. 5, 1957; children—Miranda, Reed. B.A. cum laude, Birmingham-So. Coll., 1950; M.A. (Am. Council Learned Socs. fellow), Harvard U., 1950; Ph.D., Vanderbilt U., 1954; Fulbright scholar, Univ. Coll., U. London, 1954-55. Instr. English Vanderbilt U., 1953-54; instr. English U. Rochester, N.Y., 1955-58; asst. prof. U. Rochester, 1958-61, assoc. prof., 1961-65, prof. English, 1965-97, univ. orator, 1989-96, prof. emeritus, 1998; cons. various pubs. Author: Logic and Rhetoric, 1962, The Formation of English Neo-Classical Thought, 1967, Utopian Literature, 1968, The Plays of John Dennis, 1980; Contbr. articles to scholarly jours. Bd. dirs. Opera Theatre of Rochester; mem. Friends of Eastman Opera Theater. Served with USN, 1945-46. Folger Library fellow, 1963; Am. Council Learned Socs. fellow, 1966-67; Guggenheim fellow, 1970-71. Mem. MLA, English Inst., Am. Soc. for 18th Century Studies, North Eastern Am. Assn. for 18th Century Studies (v.p. 1979, pres. 1980-81), Landmark Soc. Western N.Y., Friends Univ. Librs. (pres. 1991-94), Alpha Tau Omega. Democrat. Home: 400 East Ave #611 Rochester NY 14607-1649 *I subscribe to two maxims: The end of all public ambition is to be happy at home (Samuel Johnson), and Happiness is nobody sick and no bill collectors at the door (Chinese proverb).*

JOHNSON, JAMES WILSON, pastor; b. Benson, N.C., Apr. 11, 1942; s. Roy Allen and Edna Mavoreen (Allen) J.; m. Charlotte Marie Smith, Aug. 15, 1964; children: Donna Marie, Johnnie Allen. BA in History and Edn., Meth. Coll., Fayetteville, N.C., 1964; postgrad., East Carolina U., 1964, Southeastern Bapt. Sem., Wake Forest, N.C., 1964—. Lic. to ministry So. Bapt. Conv., 1964, ordained, 1987. Interim pastor 15 chs., N.C., 1964-86; pastor Albertson (N.C.) Bapt. Ch., 1986-97, Concord Bapt. Ch., Rose Hill, N.C., 1997—; driver edn. specialist N.C. Divsn. Motor Vehicles, Raleigh, 1968—; dir. brotherhood Ea. Bapt. Assn., Warsaw, 1987-91, chmn. nominating com., 1988-90, vice moderator, 1989-91, moderator, 1991-93, mem. numerous coms., 1968—. Bd. dirs. Duplin County Assn. for Retarded Citizens, 1969-79, v.p., 1975-77, pres., 1977-79. Mem. N.C. State Employees Assn. Home and Office: Concord Bapt Ch 519 Boney St Wallace NC 28466

JOHNSON, JANE OLIVER, artist; b. Fresno, Calif., Jan. 3, 1929; d. Evan Donaca Oliver and Adaline Dorinda (Nelson) Edwards; m. Vernon Reddinger Allen, Aug. 11, 1946 (div. 1963); children: Lue Elizabeth, Mark Laroy, Stuart Vernon; m. Loren Theodore Johnson, Mar. 8, 1981. Student, Fresno City Coll., 1952-55, Fresno State, 1955-60, Hayward State Coll., 1965-70. Tech. artist Hughes, Northrup, Lockheed, Magnavox, L.A., 1972-84; artist Neighborhood Gallery, L.A., 1976-80. Works exhibited at Beyond Baroque, San Jose Mission, Tribal Treas., Calico Gallery. Mem. state ctrl. com. Calif. Dem. Party, 1993; active 34th Assembly Dist. Exec. Bd., 1993, sec. 1997; elected San Bernardino County Dem. Ctrl. Com., 1994, re-elected, 1996; mem. First Congl. Ch. L.A., 1973—. Mem. ACLU, High Desert Cultural Arts, So. Poverty Law Ctr., Mus. of Tolerance, L.A. County Mus. Art, Stockford Dem. Club (mem. environ. women's caucus 1993, pres. 1995). Avocations: writing philosophy, hiking. Home: PO Box 1323 Lucerne Valley CA 92356-1323

JOHNSON, JANE PENELOPE, freelance writer; b. Danville, Ky., July 1, 1940; d. Buford Lee Carr and Emma Irene (Coldiron) Sebastian; m. William Evan Johnson, July 15, 1958; children: William Evan Jr., Robert Anthony. Grad., Famous Writer's Sch. Fiction, Westport, Conn., 1967; grad. writer's div., Newspaper Inst. Am., N.Y.C., 1969; LittD (hon.), The London Inst. Applied Rsch., 1997. Freelance writer Lexington, Ky., 1969—. Contbr. poetry to Worldwide Poetry Anthologies, Sparrowgrass Poetry Forum; contbr. articles to mags.; author song lyrics: Everlasting Freedom, Answered Prayer, Glory Bound; recs. include America, 1997-98, The Light of the World, 1998-99. Patron Menninger. Ennobled by Prince John, The Duke of Avram, Tasmania, Australia; semifinalist N.Am. Poetry Open; finalist Poetry Open Poetry Guild N.Y.; recipient 28 Editor's Choice awards for poetry Nat. Libr. of Poetry, 1994; inductee Internat. Poetry Hall of Fame, 1996. Fellow The World Lit. Acad. Eng.; mem. NAFE, Smithsonian Assocs., Peale Ctr. for Christian Living, Sweet Adelines, Internat. Soc. Poets (life, advisor), Internat. Platform Assn., Charles Menniger Soc. (life), Internat. Order of Merit, Nat. Writer's Club, Poetry Guild N.Y. Democrat. Avocations: swimming, skating, dancing, piano. Office: PO Box 8013 Gardenside Br Lexington KY 40504

JOHNSON, JANET HELEN, Egyptology educator; b. Everett, Wash., Dec. 24, 1944; d. Robert A. and Jane N. (Osborn) J.; m. Donald S. Whitcomb, Sept. 2, 1978; children: J.J., Felicia. BA, U. Chgo., 1967, PhD, 1972. Instr. Egyptology U. Chgo., 1971-72, asst. prof., 1972-79, assoc. prof., 1979-81, prof., 1981—; dir. Oriental Inst., 1983-89; research assoc. dept. anthropology Field Mus. of Natural History, 1980-84, 94—. Author: Demotic Verbal System, 1977, Thus Wrote Onchsheshonqy, 1986, 2d revised edit., 1991, (with Donald Whitcomb) Quseir al-Qadim, 1978, 80; editor: (with E.F. Wente) Studies in Honor of G.R. Hughes, 1977, Life in a Multi-Cultural Society, 1992. Smithsonian Instn. grantee, 1977-83; NEH grantee, 1978-81, 81-85; Nat. Geog. Soc. grantee, 1978, 80, 82. Mem. Am. Rsch. Ctr. in Egypt (bd. govs. 1979—, exec. com. 1984-87, 90-96, v.p. 1990-93, pres. 1993-96). Office: U Chgo Oriental Inst 1155 E 58th St Chicago IL 60637-1540

JOHNSON, JANET LEANN MOE, statistician, engineering professional; b. Mpls., July 19, 1941; d. Arnold Olvin and Ruby Victoria (Nelson) Moe; m. Donald Michael Johnson, Sept. 4, 1965; children: Michael John, Jennifer Kay. BA, U. Minn., 1962; MS, Rochester (N.Y.) Inst. Tech., 1983. Teaching asst. dept. maths. U. Minn., Mpls., 1960-62; mathematician Corning (N.Y.) Inc., 1962-63; sci. forecaster Corning (N.Y.) Glass Works, 1963-66, sci. programmer, 1966-70, sr. statis., 1970-79, sr. devel. engr., 1979-85; sr. project engr. Corning Inc., 1985-96, engring. assoc., 1996—. Author: An Analysis of the Low-Level Performance Channel Multiplier Arrays, 1969, Effects of Vacuum Space Charge in Channel Multipliers, 1969. Asst. troop leader Webelos, Boy Scouts Am., Painted Post, N.Y., 1979; troop leader Girl Scouts U.S., Painted Post, 1982-83. Fellow Royal Statis. Soc.; mem. Am. Soc. for Quality Control (sr.), Am. Statis. Assn., Soc. Women Engrs. (sr., past sec. rep. and pres. Twin Tiers chpt. 1978—, Engr. of Yr. 1988). Achievements include patent in glass ceramics for dental constructs; research on non-traditional machining, chemical vapor deposition coating and optical fiber. Office: Johnson Technologies Ltd Corning NY 14831

JOHNSON, JANET LOU, real estate executive; b. Boston, Aug. 22, 1939; d. Donald Murdoch and Helen Margaret (Slauenwhite) Campbell; m. Walter R. Johnson, Mar. 31, 1962; children—Meryl Ann, Leah Kathryn, Christa Helen. Student, Gordon Coll., Hamilton, Mass., 1962-64. Adminstr., account exec. Fuller/Smith & Ross, Boston, 1958-63; adminstr. Walter R. Johnson, P.E., Gloucester, 1970-76; broker Realty World, Gloucester, 1976-77, Hunneman & Co., Gloucester, 1977-79; pres., owner Janet L. Johnson Real Estate, Gloucester, 1979—. Mem. Mass. Assn. Realtors (bd. dirs. 1985-87), Nat. Assn. Realtors, Cape Ann C. of C., Cape Ann Bd. Realtors (pres. 1984-85, state dir. 1985-86), North Shore Assn. Bd. Realtors. Home: 35 Norseman Ave Gloucester MA 01930-1026 Office: Janet L Johnson Real Estate 79 Rocky Neck Ave Gloucester MA 01930-4180

JOHNSON, JANIS KAY, pharmacist; b. Hibbing, Minn., June 28, 1947; d. Vernon Lawrence and Irene May (Dall) Nelson; m. Robert Anthony Zupancich, June 28, 1969 (div. June 1972); m. Stephen Charles Johnson, Apr. 26, 1974. BS in Pharmacy, N.D. State U., 1970. Registered pharmacist, Minn., N.D., Ariz. Pharmacy intern Steele Rexall Drug, Tomah, Wis., 1970-72; staff pharmacist Nordby Drug, Grand Rapids, Minn., 1972-75, Kare Drug, Grand Rapids, 1976-77, Thrifty-White Pharmacy, Winona, Minn., 1983-85, Applewood Apothecary, LaCrescent, Minn., 1986-87, Reed Drug, Grand Rapids, 1987-91, Thrifty-White Pharmacy, Grand Rapids, 1991-94, Wal-Mart Pharmacy #1609, Grand Rapids, 1994—. Vice pres. Am. Cancer Soc.-Itasca, Grand Rapids, 1976, pres., 1977-78; chmn. recruitment Relay for Life, Am. Cancer Soc., 1995-97. Avocations: flying, reading, swimming, counted cross-stitch, travel. Home: 20400 Crystal Springs Lp Grand Rapids MN 55744-9592 Office: Wal-Mart Pharmacy 1400 S Pokegama Ave Grand Rapids MN 55744-4266

JOHNSON, JAY L., career officer; b. Great Falls, Mont., 1946; m. Garland Hawthorne; 1 child, Cullen. Grad., U.S. Naval Acad., 1968. Cert. naval aviator. Commd. ensign USN, 1968, advanced through grades to adm., served on USS Oriskany, 1969, former asst. chief naval pers. Bur. Naval Pers., comdr. Carrier Group Eight, Theodore Roosevelt Battle Group, 1992, comdr. 2d Fleet, Striking Fleet Atlantic, Joint Task Force 120, 1994; from vice chief naval ops. to chief naval ops. USN, Washington, 1996—; former comndng. officer VF-84 USN, former comdr. Carrier Air Wing One, former asst. chief of staff for ops. comdr. 6th fleet, former sr. air wing comdr. Carrier Air Wing One, former chief naval pos. strategic study group. Decorated Def. Dist. Svc. medal, Def. Superior Svc. medal, 4 Legion of Merit awards, Def. Meritorious Svc. medal, 8 Air medals, others. Office: Chief Naval Ops 2000 Navy Pentagon Washington DC 20350-2000*

JOHNSON, JAY WITHINGTON, former congressman; b. Bessemer, Mich., Sept. 30, 1943; s. Ruben W. and Catherine W. (Withington) J.; m. Jane Sholtz (div.); m. Jo Lee Works, June 26, 1982; stepchildren: Christopher, Joanna. AA, Gogebic Community Coll., 1963; BA, No. Mich. U., 1965; MA, Mich. State U., 1970. Disk jockey Sta. WFMK, Lansing, Mich., 1968-69; news anchorman Sta. WILX-TV, Lansing, 1969-70; radio news reporter Sta. WOWO, Ft. Wayne, Ind., 1970-73; news anchorman Sta. WPTV-TV, West Palm Beach, Fla., 1973-76; radio news reporter Sta. WVCG/WLVE-FM, Miami, Fla., 1976; TV producer Sta. WPLG-TV, Miami, 1976; news anchorman, mng. editor Sta. WPEC-TV, West Palm Beach, 1977-80; news anchorman Sta. WOTV-TV, Grand Rapids, Mich., 1980-81, Sta. WFRV-TV, Green Bay, Wis., 1981-87, Sta. WLUK-TV, Green Bay, 1987-96; mem. 105th Congress from 8th Wis dist., 1997-98, mem. agrl., transp. and infrastructure coms.; acting dep. asst. sec. congl. rels. USDA, 1999—. Vol. Big Bros./Big Sisters, Green Bay, 1982-87 (Vol. of Yr. 1985); pres., bd. dirs. Family Violence Ctr., Green Bay, 1982-87; v.p. communications United Way, Green Bay, 1987—; adv. bd. Libertas Alcohol Treatment Ctr., 1989—. With U.S. Army, 1966-68. Recipient Gov's award Gov. Tommy Thompson, 1988; named Citizen of Yr. Masons, 1987. Home: 2553 Trevino Dr Green Bay WI 54311-6390 Office: USDA 213 A Admin Bldg 1400 Independence Ave Washington DC 20250*

JOHNSON, JEAN ELAINE, nursing educator; b. Wilsey, Kans., Mar. 11, 1925; d. William H. and Rosa L. (Welty) Irwin. B.S., Kans. State U., 1948; M.S. in Nursing, Yale U., 1965; M.S., U. Wis., 1969, Ph.D., 1971; DS (hon.), Univ. Wis., 1998. Instr. nursing Iowa, Kans. and Colo., 1948-58; staff nurse Swedish Hosp., Englewood, Colo., 1958-60; in-svc. edn. coord. Gen. Rose Hosp., Denver, 1960-63; rsch. asst. Yale U., New Haven, 1965-67; assoc. prof. nursing Wayne State U., Detroit, 1971-74, prof., 1974-79; dir. Ctr. for Health Rsch., 1974-79; assoc. dir. oncology nursing Cancer Ctr. U. Rochester, N.Y., 1979-93; prof. nursing U. Rochester, 1979-95, prof. emerita, 1995—; Rosenstadt prof. health rsch. Faculty Nursing U. Toronto, 1985; vis. prof. U. Utah Coll. Nursing, 1996-97, U. Wis., Madison, 1998. Author: Self-Regulation Theory: Applying Theory to your Practice, 1997; contbg. author: Handbook of Psychology and Health, vol. 5, 1984; contbr. articles to profl. jours. Recipient Bd. Govs. Faculty Recognition award Wayne State U., 1975, award for disting. contbn. to nursing sci. Am. Nurses Found. and ANA Coun. for Nurse Rschrs., 1983, Grad. Teaching award U. Rochester, 1991, Disting. Rschr. award Oncology Nursing Soc., 1992, Outstanding Contbns. to Nursing and Psychology award divsn. of health psychology APA, 1993; NIH grantee, 1972-95. Fellow AAAS, APA (Outstanding Contbns. to Nursing and Psychology award 1993), Acad. for Behavioral Medicine Rsch., Am. Psychol. Soc.; mem. ANA (chmn. coun. for nurse rschrs. 1976-78, commn. for rsch. 1978-82), Inst. Medicine NAS (com. on patient injury compensation 1976-77, membership com. 1981-86, gov. coun. 1987-89), Sigma Xi, Omicron Nu, Phi Kappa Phi. Home: 1412 East Ave Rochester NY 14610-1619 Office: U Rochester Box 80N 601 Elmwood Ave Rochester NY 14642-0001

JOHNSON, JEFFREY CARL, elementary education educator; b. Apr. 14, 1962. BS in Animal Sci., Iowa State U., 1985; MAT in Elem. Edn., Nat. Louis U., 1996. Co-thcr. kindergarten and pre-kindergarten Hubbard Wood Sch. Dist. 36, Winnetka, Ill., 1994-95, computer tchr., 1995—. Email: johnjeff@nttc.org. Address: 461 Chukker Ct Wheeling IL 60090

JOHNSON, JEH VINCENT, architect; b. Nashville, July 8, 1931; s. Charles Spurgeon and Marie Antoinette (Burguette) J.; m. Norma Edelin, Dec. 28, 1956; children—Jeh Charles, Marguerite Marie. A.B., Columbia U., 1953, M.Arch., 1958. Architect/designer Paul R. Williams, Los Angeles, 1956; designer Adams & Woodbridge, N.Y.C., 1957-62; asso. Gindele & Johnson (P.C. Architects and predecessors), Poughkeepsie, N.Y., 1967-69; partner Gindele & Johnson (P.C. Architects and predecessors), 1969-71, pres., 1971-80; ptnr. LeGendre Johnson McNeil Assos., 1980-90; pvt. practice architecture Wappingers Falls, N.Y., 1990—; sr. lectr. in art Vassar Coll., 1964—, lectr. in urban studies, 1995—; mem. N.Y. State Bd. for Architecture, 1974-84, chmn., 1980-82; mem. Nat. Commn. Urban Problems, 1967-69; nat. master grader Nat. Coun. Archtl. Registration Bds., 1984-91; bd. dirs. The Bank of the Hudson. Designer: Dutchess County (N.Y.) Mental Health Ctr., 1969, Lagrange (N.Y.) Town Hall, 1969, Newburgh (N.Y.) Houses on the Lake, 1970, Whitney Young Health Ctr., Albany, N.Y., 1973, St. Simeon Apts. for Elderly, Poughkeepsie, 1973, 93, Bedford-Stuyvesant Comml. Ctr., N.Y.C., 1978, Camp of Tomorrow, Girl Scouts U.S.A., Mt. Pleasant, N.Y., 1985, Millbrook (N.Y.) Ch. Alliance Housing, Ctrl. Bapt. Ch., Salt Point, N.Y., Hillcrest House, Poughkeepsie, 1992, The Intercultural Ctr. at Vassar Coll, 1993, St. Anna Apts., Poughkeepsie, 1996. Mem. Dutchess County Planning Bd., 1988-92; bd. dirs. Scenic Hudson, Inc., 1995—. William Kinne Fellows traveling fellow, 1958. Fellow AIA (mem. nat. task force on affordable housing, Students medal 1958); mem. Nat. Orgn. Minority Architects (charter), AAUP, NAACP, Nat. Coun. Archtl. Registration Bds., Sigma Pi Phi. Club: Masons. Home and Office: 14 Edgehill Rd Wappingers Falls NY 12590-1228

JOHNSON, JENNIE, chaplain, social worker; b. Houston, Sept. 18, 1952; d. James L.C. and Marilyn Mildred (Frazier) J.; 1 child, Thomas. BS in Social Work, Tex. Woman's U., 1976; postgrad., Bishop's Sch. of Theology, Denver, 1979-80, Samaritan Theol. Sem., L.A., 1982-84, Episcopal Theol. Sem., Austin, Tex., 1986-87. Cert. social worker, Tex.; oblate Order of St. Benedict, 1998. Comdr. 94th Ord. Det. USAR, Ft. Carson, Colo., 1978-80; evaluator 1st maneuver tng. command USAR, Denver, 1980-81; prodn. control planner Elmo Semiconducter, L.A., 1981-83; quality control planner TRW Def. and Space Guidance, L.A., 1983-84; dir. chpt. svcs. Greater Amarillo (Tex.) Red Cross, 1985-86; chaplain Austin State Hosp., 1987-88, Brackenridge Hosp., Austin, 1988-91, Hospice Austin, 1992-95; asst. dir. Centex Chpt. ARC, Austin, Tex., 1995-96; chaplain Seaton Medical Ctr., Austin, 1998—; conveener Integrity Austin, 1989-90, 92-94, 96-97; conf. presenter Nat. Episcopal AIDS Coalition, Cin., 1990, mem., 1990—. Founding bd. dirs. Out Youth Austin/YWCA, 1990-92; mem. Tex. AIDS Network, Austin, 1992—; foster parent Casey Family Program, Austin, 1992-94; diocesan del. St. Michael's Episcopal Ch., Austin, 1988—, jr. warden, 1993-95, mem. vestry, 1993-97, mem. divsn. for spiritual devel. of diocese Mentor Edn. for Ministry; mem.-at-large Women for Social Witness Network, Nat. Episcopal Ch., 1992-96; mem. Episcopal Womens Caucus, 1992-97, Nat. Hospice Orgn., 1993—, Tex. Hospice Orgn., 1992—, presenter state conf., 1995, Order of St. Luke the Physician, 1984—. 1st lt. U.S. Army, 1975-80. Democrat. Avocations: paleontology, needlework, reading, fishing, camping.

JOHNSON, JENNIFER LUCKY, psychotherapist; b. Paso, Wash., Oct. 22, 1938; d. Carl Eilert Leslie and Doris Christine (Westby) Lucky; m. Robert Eugene Johnson, Aug. 11, 1962; children: Nathan Robert, Douglas Eugene, Jeffrey Carl. BSN, St. Olaf Coll., 1960; M in Pastoral Ministry, Seattle U., 1990. RN, Wash.; lic. advanced nurse practitioner; cert. clin. specialist in adult mental health/psychiat. nursing. Staff nurse ICU U. Minn., Mpls., 1960-61, U. Wash., Seattle, 1961-62; psychiat. nurse Am. Lake VA Hosp., Tacoma, Wash., 1962; Indian pub. health nurse U.S. Pub. Health Hosp., Harlem, Mont., 1963-66; geriatric nurse Christian Rest Home, Lynden, Wash., 1983-93; dir. social svcs. and psychiat. cons. Christian Rest Home, Lynden, 1988-93; pvt. practice therapist Bellingham, Wash., 1992—; prescribing psychiat. nurse Whatcom Counseling and Psychiat. Clinic, Bellingham, 1994-97; adj. faculty Seattle U., 1996—; chair social svcs. forum Wash. Assn. Homes for the Aging, Seattle, 1992-94; mem. adv. bd. Wash. Dept. Health and Social Svcs., Mental Health and Aging, Olympia, 1993; dementia trainer in field. Co-author: (tng. manual for profls.) Prosthetic Care for the Person with Dementia: A Holistic Approach, 1993. Bd. mem. Whatcom Symphony, Bellingham, 1984-85, Mt. Baker Meadows, Ferndale, Wash., 1990-92. Recipient Light of Love award Alzheimer's Soc. Wash., Bellingham, 1993. Mem. Wash. State Nurses Assn., Coalition Mental Health Profls. and Consumers. Lutheran. Avocations: reading, walking on the beach, singing, attending concerts. Office: 1909 Broadway Bellingham WA 98225-3237

JOHNSON, JEROME LINNÉ, cardiologist; b. Rockford, Ill., June 19, 1929; s. Thomas Arthur and Myrtle Elizabeth (Swanson) J.; m. Molly Ann Rideout, June 27, 1953; children: Susan Johnson Nowels, William Rideout. BA, U. Chgo., 1951; BS, Northwestern U., 1952, MD, 1955. Diplomate Nat. Bd. Med. Examiners. Intern U. Chgo. Clinics, 1955-56; resident Northwestern U., Chgo., 1958-61; chief resident Chgo. Wesley Meml. Hosp., 1960-61; mem., v.p. Hauch Med. Clinic, Pomona, Calif., 1961-88; pvt. practice cardiology and internal medicine Pomona, 1988—; clin. assoc. prof. medicine, U. So. Calif., L.A., 1961—; mem. staff Pomona Valley Hosp. Med. Ctr., chmn. coronary care com. 1967-77; mem. staff L.A. County Hosp. Citizen ambassador, People to People; mem. Town Hall of Calif., L.A. World Affairs Coun. Lt. USNR, 1956-58; bd. dirs. Claremont chpt. ARC, 1993—; bd. dirs., health com. Mt. San Antonio Gardens Retirement Home, 1993—. Fellow Am. Coll. Cardiology, Am. Geriatrics Soc., Royal Soc. Health; mem. Galileo Soc., Am. Heart Assn. (bd. dirs. L.A. County div. 1967-84, San Gabriel div. 1963-89), Am. Soc. Internal Medicine, Inland Soc. Internal Medicine, Pomona Host Lions. Avocations: photography, swimming, bicycling, medical and surgical antiques, travel. Home: 648 Delaware Dr Claremont CA 91711-3457

JOHNSON, JERRY DOUGLAS, biology educator; b. Salina, Kans., Sept. 1, 1947; s. Maynard Eugene and Norma Maude (Moss) J.; m. Kathryn Ann Johnson, May 12, 1973; children: George Walker, Brett Arthur. BS in Zoology, Fort Hays State U., 1972; MS in Biology, U. Tex., El Paso, 1975; PhD in Wildlife Sci., Tex. A&M U., 1984. Teaching asst. biology dept. U. Tex., El Paso, 1973-75; instr. biology El Paso C.C., 1975—; adj. asst. prof. U. Tex., El Paso, 1984—; Piper prof. El Paso Community Coll., 1989-90; councilor bd. scientists Chihuahuan Desert Rsch. Inst., Alpine, Tex., 1991—. Co-author: Middle American Herpetology, 1988; contbr. articles to profl. jours. Bd. dirs. Meml. Park Improvement Assn., 1987—, El Paso Coun. for Internat. Visitors, 1988—, v.p., 1996, Parks and Recreation Bd., El Paso, 1991-94. Grantee Soc. Sigma Xi, 1974, Theodore Roosevelt Found. Am. Mus. Natural History, 1979, Exline Corp., 1980, NSF, 1992—, NIH, 1992—, Tex. Pks. and Wildlife Dept., 1998; recipient El Paso Natural Gas Faculty Achievement award, 1995-96, Nat. Inst. Staff and Orgnl. Devel.

Tchg. Excellence award, 1995-96. Mem. NSF, Nat. Ctr. for Acad. Achievement, Nat. Inst. Gen. Med. Sci., Soc. for Study of Amphibians and Reptiles (elector 1980, assoc. editor Geog. Distbn. Herpetol. Rev. 1993—), Southwestern Assn. Naturalists (assoc. editor 1977-85, bd. govs. 1985-89), Tex. Herpetol. Soc. (v.p., pres. 1995-96), El Paso Herpetol. Soc. (pres. 1993-95), Herpetologists League, others. Home: 3147 Wheeling Ave El Paso TX 79930-4321 Office: El Paso CC Biology Dept PO Box 20500 El Paso TX 79998-0500

JOHNSON, JIMMY, professional football coach; b. Port Arthur, Tex., July 16, 1943. BA, U. Ark., 1965. Asst. coach Louisiana Tech. U., LA, 1965, Wichita State U., KS, 1967, Iowa State U., IA, 1968-68, U. Oklahoma, Norman, OK, 1970-72, U. Arkansas, AR, 1973-76, U. Pittsburg, 1977-78; head coach Oklahoma State U., OK, 1979-83, U. Miami, Miami, FL, 1983-88, Dallas Cowboys, Dallas, TX, 1989-94; sports commentator, football analyst Fox Network, 1994-95; head coach, gen. mgr. Miami Dolphins, 1996—. Coach NCAA Divsn. I championship team, 1987, Super Bowl (XXVII, XXVIII) championship team, 1992-93; named Coach of Yr. Walter Camp Found., 1986-87, NFL Coach of Yr. Coll. & Pro Football Newsweekly, 1990, UPI, 1990, AP, 1990, Football Digest, 1991; recipient Seattle Gold Helmet award, 1986. Office: Miami Dolphins 7500 SW 30th St Davie FL 33314-1020*

JOHNSON, JOAN BRAY, insurance company consultant; b. Kennett, Mo., Nov. 19, 1926; d. Ples Green and Mary Scott (Williams) Bray; m. Frank Johnson Jr., Nov. 6, 1955; 1 child, Victor Kent. Student, Drury Coll., 1949-51, Cen. Bible Inst. and Coll., 1946-49. Staff writer Gospel Pub. Co., Springfield, Mo., 1949-51; sec. Kennett Sch. Dist. Bd. Edn., 1951-58; spl. features corr. Memphis Press-Scimitar, 1959-60; sec. to v.p. Cotton Exchange Bank, Kennett, Mo., 1959-60; proposal analyst Aetna Life Ins. Co., El Paso, Tex., 1960-64, pension adminstr., 1964-71; office mgr. Brokerage div. Aetna Life Ins. Co., Denver, 1971-78; office adminstr. Life Consol. div. Aetna Life Ins. Co., Oakland, Calif., 1979-82; office adminstr. PFSD div. Aetna Life Ins. Co., Walnut Creek, Calif., 1983-86; office adminstr. PFSD-Health Mktg. div. Aetna Life Ins. Co., Sacramento, Calif., 1986-89; regional adminstr. Aetna Life Ins. Co., Hartford, Conn., 1989-91; cons. Aetna Life Ins. Co., Santa Ana, Calif., 1991—, Met-Life Ins. Co., Dallas, 1998—. Officer local PTA, 1964-71; prs. Wesley Svc. Guild, 1968-71; den mother Boy Scouts Am.; fin. sec. Green Valley United Meth. Ch., 1992—. Recipient Tex. Life Svc. award PTA, 1970. Fellow Life Office Mgmt. Assn. (instr. classes); mem. DAR (regent Silver State Nev. chpt. 1994-96, Nev. state treas. 1998—, bd. dirs. Nev. 1996-2000), Assn. Bus. and Profl. Women, Life Underwriters Assn., Clark County Heritage Mus., Last Monday Club, Opti-Mrs., Allied Arts Club. Democrat. Fax: 702-547-1803. Home: 2415 La Estrella St Henderson NV 89014-3608

JOHNSON, JOE See JOHNSON, WILBUR CORNEAL

JOHNSON, JOEL W., food products executive. With General Foods Corp.; exec. v.p. sales and mktg. Hormel Foods Corp., 1991-92, pres., 1992-93, chief operating officer, chief exec. officer, 1993-95; chmn. bd., CEO, pres. Hormel Foods Corp., Austin, Minn., 1995—; bd. mem. Overseers of The Carlson Sch. Mgmt. U. Minn.; trustee Hamilton Coll. Office: Hormel Foods Corp 1 Hormel Pl Austin MN 55912-3680*

JOHNSON, JOHN, broadcast journalist; b. N.Y.C., June 20, 1938; s. John Edward and Irene Elizabeth (Tutt) J.; children: Eric Justin, Cydney Patricia, Anthony Lawrence, Christina Rachel. BA, CUNY, 1961, M Art Edn., 1963; DHL (hon.), St. Thomas Aqunias Coll., 1991. Tchr., asst. prin. N.Y.C. Bd. Edn., 1960-67; assoc. prof. fine arts Lincoln U., 1967-68; prodr., dir., writer documentary unit ABC News, N.Y.C., 1968-71; corr. ABC Evening News, N.Y.C., 1971-72; reporter WABC-TV News, N.Y.C., 1972-85, sr. corr., anchor, 1985-95; anchor WCBS-TV News, N.Y.C., 1995-96; anchor, sr. corr. WNBC-TV News, 1996—. Essayist: The Black Power Revolt, 1968. Recipient Best Enterprise Reporting award AP, 1977, Emmy award for Best Sports Programming, 1978, Best Documentary award AP, 1979, Emmy award for Best Investigative Reporting, 1983, Emmy award for Best Spot News, 1982, Emmy award for Best Svc. News, 1982, Nat. Broadcast award for Outstanding Spot News, UPI, 1982. Mem. AFTRA, Dirs. Guild Am. Office: WNBC TV News 30 Rockefeller Plz New York NY 10112-0002*

JOHNSON, JOHN A., communications company executive; b. Milw., 1915; s. John W. and Amy (Nelson) J.; m. Harriet Nelson, Sept. 11, 1938; children: Barbara (Mrs. James A. Groff), John Vance, Susan (Mrs. Don H. Boatwright), Richard Bailey. AB, DePauw U., 1937; JD, U. Chgo., 1940; LLM, Harvard U., 1946. Bar: Ill. 1946, D.C. 1979. Gen. counsel USAF, 1952-58, NASA, 1958-63; v.p. internat. Comm. Satellite Corp. (COMSAT), 1964-73, sr. v.p., 1973-74; pres. COMSAT Gen. Corp., 1973-77, chmn. bd., CEO, 1977-80; chmn. Satellite TV Corp., 1980-81; U.S. rep. interim comm. satellite com. INTELSAT, 1964-73, chmn. 1964-69, bd. govs., 1973-74, INMARSAT Coun., 1979; dir. World Christian Broadcasting Corp., 1981-91. Contbr.: articles to profl. jours., also to Ency. Brit. Active Falls Church (Va.) Sch. Bd., 1949-56, chmn. 1951-56; mem. exec. bd. Va. Sch. Bds. Assn., 1953-56; trustee Northeastern Christian Jr. Coll., 1955-85, chmn. bd. trustees, 1958-73; bd. visitors Coll. of U. Chgo., 1966-71, Western Res. Law Sch., 1964-67; bd. dirs. Pan Am. Devel. Found., 1986-92, Health Talents Internat. Lt. (j.g.) USNR, 1943-46. Recipient Exceptional Civilian Service award Dept. Air Force; Outstanding Leadership medal NASA; Alumni citation for pub. service U. Chgo.; Alumni citation DePauw U. Mem. Am. Soc. Internat. Law, Inter-am Bar Assn., Internat. Acad. Astronautics. Mem. Ch. of Christ. Home: 3643 N Nelson St Arlington VA 22207-5319

JOHNSON, JOHN ANDREW, construction executive; b. Grand Rapids, Mich., Apr. 10, 1942; s. Arnold L. and Ione A. (Christenson) J.; m. Peggy J. Ruckman, June 12, 1971 (dec. Apr. 1996); children: Perry T., John C-G. (dec.); m. Luisa Moncada Ruiz, June 30, 1997; 1 child, Andrew L. Assoc. in Engring., Mich. State U., E. Lansing, 1964; diploma, U.S.A. Signal Sch., Ft. Monmouth, 1966, Detroit Diesel Allison, Indpls., 1972. Tech. writer Massey-Ferguson, Inc., Indpls., 1965-66, 1969-70; svc. rep. Massey-Ferguson, Inc., Akron, Ohio, 1970-73; regional svc. mgr. Massey-Ferguson, Inc., Detroit, 1973-78; regional sales mgr. Massey-Ferguson, Inc., Columbus, Ohio, 1978-84; pres. Johnson and Assocs., Ind., 1984-86; svc. mgr. Hanomag Baumaschinen GmbH, Hannover, Fed. Republic Germany, 1986-90, Samsung Constrn. Equipment, Seoul, Republic of Korea, 1990-98; dir. Internat. Cons., Pierceton, Ind., 1998-99, Volvo Constrn. Equip. N.Am. Inc., Ashville, N.C., 1999—. With U.S. Army, 1966-69. Mem. Soc. Automotive Engrs., Profl. Photographers Assn., Pierceton C. of C., Am. Legion. Republican. Lutheran. Avocations: golf, fishing, hunting, photography. Home: 205 E Tulip St Pierceton IN 46562-9479 Office: Volvo Construction Equip N Amer 1 Volvo Drive Asheville NC 28803

JOHNSON, JOHN BRAYTON, editor, publisher; b. Watertown, N.Y., Dec. 14, 1916; s. Harold Bowtell and Jessie R. (Parsons) J.; m. Catherine Amelia Common, June 21, 1941; children: John Brayton, Ann Johnson Kaiser, Deborah Johnson, Harold Bowtell II. A.B., Princeton, 1939; L.H.D., St. Lawrence U., 1978. Reporter Watertown (N.Y.) Daily Times, 1939-41, 46-49, editor and pub., 1949—; Chmn. Coun. to Health Sci. Ctr., Syracuse, 1955-98. trustee N.Y. State Dormitory Authority, Elsmere, 1956—; trustee emeritus St. Lawrence U., Canton, N.Y. Served with M.I. AUS, 1941-46. Mem. AIA (hon.), Princeton Club N.J., Black River Valley. Republican. Presbyterian. Home: 221 Flower Ave W Watertown NY 13601-3936 Office: Johnson Newspaper Corp 260 Washington St Watertown NY 13601-3301

JOHNSON, JOHN DOUGLAS, newspaper publisher; b. St. Clair, Mich., June 29, 1949; s. Calvin E. and Donna E. (Beedon) J.; m. Cathy Ruhstorfer, Jan. 22, 1972 (div. July 25, 1992); children: Jennifer, Laura, Heather; m. Cherie Stabnick, Aug. 17, 1996. AA, St. Clair County C.C., Port Huron, Mich., 1969; BA, Ctrl. Mich. U., 1972. Pub. Sanilac Publishing, Sandusky, Mich., 1976—; ptnr. J&E Mgmt., Sandusky, 1984—; pub. Sanilac Web Printing, Sandusky, 1986—, Richmond (Mich.) Newspaper Group, 1992—; owner Sanilac Ctr. Banquet Hall, Sandusky, 1992—, Sandusky Mini-Storage, 1996—; bd. dirs. Mich. Newspapers, Inc., Lansing, Mich., 1994—. Pres. Big Brothers, Big Sisters, Sanilac County, Mich., 1980-81, Sandusky Lions Club, 1982-83; v.p. Richmond C. of C., 1986—. Avocations: golf, tennis, racquetball, diving, classic cars. Home: 370 W Sanilac Rd Sandusky MI 48471-1084 Office: Sanilac Publishing Inc 432 S Sandusky Rd Sandusky MI 48471-9300

JOHNSON, JOHN EDWIN, orthodontist; b. Waverly, Ky., Aug. 9, 1931; s. Richard Spalding and Margaret (Vize) J.; m. Margaret Josephine Smith, Dec. 29, 1956; children: Catherine Margaret, Michael John. DDS, St. Louis U., 1956. Diplomate Am. Bd. Orthodontics (charter mem. coll. diplomates). Pres. John E. Johnson, DDS, DP Corp., New Albany, Ind., 1956—; bd. dirs., sec. DePaul Sch. for Dyslexia, Louisville, 1974-78. Contbr. articles to profl. publs. Capt. U.S. Army, 1956-58. Mem. ADA, Am. Assn. Orthodontists, European Orthodontic Soc., So. Assn. Orthodontists, South Ctrl. Dental Soc., Ind. Dental Soc. (pres. south ctrl. component 1968-69), Rotary (pres. New Albany, Ind. club 1992-93, founder and chmn.), Big Springs County Club, Pendennis Club. Roman Catholic. Avocations: golf, photography, horticulture. Office: 215 E Spring St New Albany IN 47150-3422

JOHNSON, JOHN GRAY, retired university chancellor; b. Irwin, Pa., Aug. 8, 1924; s. John Arthur and Elizabeth (Gray) J.; m. L. Jane Wyncoop, Aug. 28, 1948; children: Scott Raymond, Lynn. B.S., Carnegie Mellon U., 1949; LL.D. (hon.), U. Indpls. (formerly Ind. Central U.), 1980. Alumni dir. Carnegie Mellon U., 1955-60; exec. dir. Am. Alumni Council, Washington, 1960-64; v.p. devel. Butler U., Indpls., 1964-66, pres., 1978-88, chancellor, 1989-90; v.p. for devel. Carnegie Mellon U., Pitts., 1966-78. With AUS, 1943-46. Decorated Air medal. Named Sagamore of the Wabash. Mem. Ind. C. of C. (life), Oasis Tutoring, Kiwanis, Oro Valley Country Club, Phi Kappa Phi, Omicron Delta Kappa. Home: 14326 N Green Meadow Ln Tucson AZ 85737-7120

JOHNSON, JOHN H., publisher, consumer products executive; b. Arkansas City, Ark., Jan. 19, 1918; m. Eunice Johnson; children: John Harold (dec.), Linda Johnson Rice. Student, U. Chgo., Northwestern U., Howard U.; LL.D., Central State Coll., Shaw U., N.C. Coll., Benedict Coll., Carnegie-Mellon Inst., Morehouse Coll., N.C. A. and T. State U., Syracuse U., Eastern Mich. U., Hamilton Coll., Lincoln U., Malcolm X Coll., Upper Iowa Coll., Wayne State U., Pratt Inst., Chgo. State U., Northeastern U., Am. U., Ctrl. State Coll., Clark Atlanta U., DePaul U., Harvard U., NYU, Northwestern U., Roosevelt U., U. Ark., Pine Bluff, U. D.C., U. Ill., U. So. Calif., Wilberforce U. Pub., chmn. chief exec. officer Johnson Pub. Co., Inc., Chgo. N.Y.C., L.A., Washington, 1942—; pub., editor Ebony, Jet, Ebony South Africa; pres. Sta. WLOU, Louisville, Fashion Fair Cosmetics, Chgo., Supreme Beauty Products; pub., chmn., CEO Johnson Pub. Co., Chgo.; chmn., chief exec. officer Supreme Life Ins. Co., Chgo.; bd. dirs. Greyhound Corp., Dillard Dept. Stores, Inc., The Dial Corp.; mem. adv. bd. 1st Comml. Bank of Little Rock. Author: Succeeding Against the Odds, 1989. Trustee Art Inst., Chgo. Named Outstanding Young Man U.S. Jaycees, 1951, Communicator of Yr. U. Chgo. Alumni Assn., 1974, Chicagoan of Yr., Chgo. Boys Club, 1983; recipient Horatio Alger award, 1966; John Russwurm award Nat. Newspaper Pubs. Assn., 1966, Spingarn medal NAACP, 1966, Henry Johnson Fisher award Mag. Pubs. Assn., 1971,Columbia Journalism award, 1974, Honors Disting. Accomplishment United Negro Coll. Fund, 1983, Robie award Jackie Robinson Found., 1985, Disting. Contbrn. to Journalism award Nat. Press Found., 1986; named to Acad. Disting. Entrepreneurs Babson Coll., 1979; Chgo. Bus. Hall of Fame, 1983; named to Entrepreneur of Decade Black Enterprise Mag., 1987; inducted into Black Press Hall of Fame, 1987, Pub. Hall of Fame Folio Ednl. Trust Inc., 1987, Ill. Bus. Hall of Fame, 1989, Nat. Sales Hall of Fame, 1989, Chgo. Journalism Hall of Fame, 1990; recipient Harold H. Hines Jr. Benefactors' award United Negro Coll. Fund, 1988, Excel award Internat. Assn. Bus. communicators, Founders award NCCJ, 1989, Disting. Svc. award Harvard U. Grad. Sch. Bus. Adminstrn., 1991, Salute to the Media award Impact Publs., Africa's Future award UNICEF, 1992, Booker T. Washington Speaker's award Booker T. Washington Bus. Assn., Heritage award Exec. Leadership Coun., 1992, Dow Jones Entrepreneurial Excellence award Dow Jones and the Wall Street Jour., 1993, Monarch award for Comms., Alpha Kappa Alpha, 1993, Comm. award Ctr. for Comm., Inc., 1995, Presdl. medal of Freedom, 1996, Corp. Pioneer award Bus. Policy Rev. Coun., 1996, Lifetime Achievement award Am. Advt. Found., 1996, Nat. Bus. Hall of Fame award Nat. Jr. Achievement, 1997; inductee Entrepreneurship Hall of Fame, U. Ill.-Chgo., 1993. Fellow Sigma Delta Chi; mem. U.S. C. of C. (dir.), Mag. Pubs. Assn. Office: 1270 Avenue Of The Americas New York NY 10020-1700

JOHNSON, JOHN IRWIN, JR., neuroscientist; b. Salt Lake City, Aug. 18, 1931; s. John Irwin and Ann Josephine (Freeman) J. A.B., U. Notre Dame, 1952; M.S., Purdue U., 1955, Ph.D., 1957. Instr., then asst. prof. Marquette U., Milw., 1957-60; USPHS spl. research fellow U. Wis., Madison, 1960-63; Fulbright-Hays research scholar U. Sydney, Australia, 1964-65; assoc. prof. biophysics, psychology and zoology Mich. State U., E. Lansing, 1965-69; prof. Mich. State U., 1969-81, prof. anatomy, 1981—, chmn. dept. biophysics, 1973-78; vis. fellow psychology dept. Yale U., New Haven, 1975-76. Recipient Career Devel. award NIH, 1965-72, research grantee, 1966-79; research grantee NSF, 1969-71, 71-73, 73-76, 78-89, 91—; 3d hon. life mem. Anat. Assn. Australia and N.Z., 1973. Mem. Soc. Neurosci., Am. Assn. Anatomists, Soc. for Comparative and Intergrative Biology, Am. Soc. Mammalogists, Animal Behavior Soc., AAUP, ACLU, Sigma Xi. Home: 2494 W Grand River Ave Okemos MI 48864-1447 Office: Mich State U Dept Anatomy 519A E Fee Hall East Lansing MI 48824-1316*

JOHNSON, JOHN J., historian, educator; b. White Swan, Wash., Mar. 26, 1912; s. George E. and Mary (Whitford) J.; m. Maurine Amstutz, June 8, 1942; 1 son, Michael G. B.A., Central Wash. Coll., 1940; M.A., U. Calif.-Berkeley, 1943, Ph.D., 1947; postgrad., U. Chgo., 1943-44, U. Chile, 1946. Tchr. pub. schs. Wash., 1935-39; mem. faculty Stanford U., 1946-78, prof. history, 1958-78, emeritus prof., 1977—; chmn. com. Latin Am. studies, 1966-72; prof. U. N.Mex., Albuquerque, 1980-85; acting chief S. Am. br., div. research Am. Republic, State Dept., 1952-53; lectr. U. Ariz. Summer Sch., Guadalajara, Mex., 1955, 58, 61; cons. to industry and govt., 1959—; Fulbright lectr. U. Auckland, New Zealand, 1974; vis. prof. U. N.Mex., 1977, 79, Ariz. State U., 1980. Mng. editor Hispanic Am. Hist. Rev., 1980-85. Author: Pioneer Telegraphy in Chile, 1948, Political Change in Latin America; The Emergence of the Middle Sectors, 1958, The Military and Society in Latin America, 1964, Simon Bolivar and Spanish American Independence: 1783-1830, 1967, 2d edit., 1992, Latin America in Caricature, 1980, 2d edit., 1993, A Hemisphere Apart: The Foundations of United States Policy Toward Latin America, 1990; editor, contbr.: Role of the Military in Underdeveloped World, Continuity & Change in Latin America, 1964. Recipient Bolton prize Conf. Latin Am. History, 1959, Disting. Alumnus award Cen. Wash. U., 1977, Disting. Service award Conf. Latin Am. History, 1987; fellow Nat. Humanities Ctr., 1985-86. Mem. Am. Hist. Assn. (mem. council 1976-79, chmn. conf. Latin Am. history 1961), Latin Am. Studies Assn. (pres. 1970, 1st Kalman Silvert Pres.'s prize 1983). Home: 71 Pearce Mitchell Pl Stanford CA 94305-8533 Office: Stanford U History Dept Stanford CA 94305

JOHNSON, JOHN PATRICK, neurosurgeon, educator; b. Great Falls, Mont., Apr. 16, 1956; s. Alexander Charles and Jane (Koepper) J.; m. Nancy Tripp, Oct. 11, 1993; 1 child, Alexander Charles. BS, The Citadel, 1978; MD, Oreg. Health Scis. U., 1981, Oreg. Health Scis. U., 1986. Intern in surgery UCLA Med. Ctr., 1986-87, resident in neurosurgery, 1987-92; fellow Nat. Hosp. Neurology and Neurosurgery, Queen Square, Eng., 1991, Spine fellow dept. neurosurgery, 1992; staff neurosurgeon Harbor/UCLA Med. Ctr., Torrance, Calif., 1992—, Wadsworth VA Med. Ctr., L.A., 1992—; chief adminstrv. and clin. affairs divsn. neurosurgery Olive View/UCLA Med. Ctr., Sylmar, Calif., 1993-97; co-dir. UCLA Comprehensive Spine Ctr., L.A., 1994—; dir. UCLA Spinal Neurosurgery Fellowship Program, L.A., 1995—; co-dir. UCLA Ctr. Autonomic Disorders, L.A., 1996—; asst. prof. divsn. neurosurgery UCLA Sch. Medicine, L.A., 1993—; tech. cons. Depuy-Motech, Wabash, Ind., 1996. Contbr. articles to profl. jours. Rsch. grantee UCLA Acad. Senate Grant, L.A., 1994-95, 95-96, Radionics, Inc., Burlington, Mass., 1996—; rsch. fellow N.Am. Spine Soc., 1994-95. Mem. AMA, ACS, Am. Assn. Neurol. Surgeons, N.Am. Spine Soc., Congress Neurol. Surgeons, Calif. Assn. Neurol. Surgeons. Avocations: skiing, hunting, fishing, family ranch business, traveling. Office: UCLA Med Ctr Divsn Neurosurgery 10833 LeConte Ave Los Angeles CA 90095-6901

JOHNSON, JOHN PRESCOTT, philosophy educator; b. Tumalo, Oreg., Apr. 24, 1921; s. John Edward and Caroline Prescott (Eaton) J.; m. Mable Alice Dougherty, June 9, 1943; children: Grace Beth Johnson Booth), John Paul, Carol Ruth Johnson Hull. AB, Pitts. State U., 1947, MS, 1948; PhD, Northwestern U., 1959. Asst. prof. philosophy Bethany (Okla.) Nazarene Coll., 1949-57; asst. prof. U. Okla., Norman, 1957-62; assoc. prof. philosophy Monmouth (Ill.) Coll., 1962-69; prof. philosophy Monmouth (Ill.) Coll., 1969-86; chmn. dept. philosophy Monmouth (Ill.) Coll., 1967-86, emeritus prof. philosophy, 1986—; Vis. asst. prof. Northwestern U., summer 1961; Cons. research project student values U.S. Office Edn., 1967. Contbr. articles to philos. jours. Mem. Am. Philos. Assn., Ill. Philos. Assn. (sec.-treas. 1967-69, pres. 1971-73).

JOHNSON, JOHN RANDALL, SR., religious organization administrator; b. Marion, Va., July 26, 1945; s. Marvin Roy and Ida Alice (Roe) J.; m. Margaret Mae Sullivan, Aug. 8, 1965; children: John Jr., Brian, Joanna. BS in Mgmt., Va. Poly. Inst. and State U., 1971; MS in Mgmt., So. Nazarene U., 1984. Sec., treas., Christian edn. dir. Stoneville (N.C.) Internat. Pentecostal Holiness Ch., 1970-75; Sunday Sch. tchr. Bloomfield Dr. Internat. Pentecostal Holiness Ch., Macon, Ga., 1975-77, deacon, 1975-77, assoc. pastor, 1977-78; pastor Warner Robins (Gas.) Internat. Pentecostal Holiness Ch., 1978-79; contr. Internat. Pentecostal Holiness Ch., Oklahoma City, 1979—, sec.-treas., bd. dirs. Ext. Loan Fund, 1993—; adj. prof. Southwestern Coll. Christian Ministries, Bethany, Okla., 1985-90. Elder N.W. Christian Ctr., Oklahoma City, 1990—. Mem. Am. Mgmt. Assn., Nat. Assn. Evangelicals (mem.-at-large affiliate Christian Stewardship Assn. 1981—), Inst. Mgmt. Accts. Republican. Office: Intl Pentecostal Holiness Church 7300 NW 39th Expy Bethany OK 73008-2340

JOHNSON, JOHN WARREN, retired association executive; b. Mpls., Jan. 29, 1929; s. Walter E. and Eileen L. J.; m. Marion Louise Myrland; children—Daniel Warren, Karen Louise, Nancy Marie. B.A., U. Minn., 1951. CEO Am. Collectors Assn., Inc., Mpls., 1955-96; ret., 1996; dir. Western Nat. Ins. Group, 1998—. Author: Political Christians, 1979, You Can Manage Your Money, 1981, 38 Days to Cape Town, 1981; Credit Guide for Collectors, 1984, The Pearls of Saigon, 1987, The Use of Humor in Public Speaking Is No Joke!, 1991, 53 Days to Beijing, 1991, The Strange Blood of East Africa, 1995. Mem. Mpls. City Coun., 1963-67; mem. Minn. State Ho. of Reps., 1967-74, asst. majority leader, 1972-74; Republican candidate for Gov. of Minn., 1974. With USNR, 1947-53. Mem. Am. Soc. Assn. Execs. (chmn. bd. 1986-87), U.S. C. of C. (chmn. bd. regents 1973, bd. dirs. 1990-92), Minn. Soc. Assn. Execs. (past pres.). Lutheran. Office: 4121 W 50th St Ste 1 Minneapolis MN 55424-1206

JOHNSON, JOHN WILLIAM, JR., executive recruiter; b. St. Petersburg, Fla., Dec. 10, 1932; s. John William and Elizabeth (Lowitz) J.; m. Cecelia Lynn Wescott, Feb. 6, 1960; children: William Wescott, James Robert, Gayle McCrimmon. A.B., Wesleyan U., Middletown, Conn., 1954; postgrad., NYU, 1958-59. With Benton and Bowles, Inc., N.Y.C., 1958-82, v.p., account supr., 1963-70, sr. v.p., mgmt. supr., 1970-82, adminstr. profit sharing plan, 1969-82, dir., 1977-82; with Webb, Johnson Assocs., N.Y.C., 1982—, founder, former pres., 1982-95, mng. dir., 1995—. Mem. Scarsdale Planning Bd., 1984-88, Scarsdale Non-Partisan Jud. Qualifications Com., 1987-92, Scarsdale Bd. Ethics, 1995—; pres. Rainsford House Assn., N.Y.C., 1964-66, bd. dirs., 1962-70; bd. mgrs. Jacob Riis Settlement, 1963-89; bd. dirs. St. Christopher's Inc., 1965—; mem. parents steering com. Coll. William and Mary, 1987-91; warden Ch. St. James the Less, Scarsdale, 1993-95. Pilot USNR, 1954-58. Decorated Air medal; co-honoree Scarsdale Hist. Soc. award, 1996. Mem. Winged Foot Golf Club, Sky Club, Union League Club, Mid Ocean Club, Harbour Ridge Club. Home: 43 Axtell Dr Scarsdale NY 10583-5601 Office: 280 Park Ave New York NY 10017-1216

JOHNSON, JOHNNIE, bishop. Bishop Ch. of God in Christ, Goose Creek, S.C. Office: Calvary Ch of God in Christ 302 Jeffs Cir Goose Creek SC 29445-7603*

JOHNSON, JOHNNIE DEAN, investor relations consultant; b. Wells County, Ind., Aug. 18, 1938; s. William Clayton and Anna Sarah (Woods) J.; m. Jean Johnson, June 26, 1960 (div. Aug. 1986); 1 child, Judith; m. Geraldine U. Foster, Mar. 5, 1988. BA, U. Findlay (Ohio), 1960; MBA, Bowling Green (Ohio) State U., 1976. CPA, Ohio. Spl. asst. to pres. Marathon Oil (acquired by U.S. Steel 1982), 1978-82; asst. fin. vice chmn., chief fin. officer U.S. Steel, 1982-84, asst. corp. comptr., investor, strategic planning, 1984-85, asst. corp. comptr. investor rels., 1985-86; mng. dir. Georgeson & Co. Inc., N.Y.C., 1987-91; founder, chmn., CEO Johnnie D. Johnson & Co. Inc., N.Y.C., 1991-98; chmn., CEO Strategic IR, Inc., N.Y.C., 1998—. Trustee U. Findlay (Ohio), 1989—. Mem. Nat. Investor Rels. Assn. (chmn. 1985-86), Petroleum Investor Rels. Assn. (pres. 1979-80), Investor Rels. Assn. (treas. 1988-90). Congregationalist. Home: 6 Tantummaheag Rd Old Lyme CT 06371-1137 Office: 530 Fifth Ave 20th Fl New York NY 10036

JOHNSON, JOHNNY RAY, mathematics educator; b. Chatham, La., Dec. 19, 1929; s. Dave Ernest and Bessie (Morris) J.; m. Betty Ann Moore, Oct. 21, 1960 (div. May 1982); children: Todd Michael, John Fitzgerald, Shauna Renee; m. Barbara F. Kennedy, June 1, 1990. B.S., La. Tech U., 1951; M.S., Auburn U., 1953, Ph.D., 1959. Asst. prof. math. La. Tech U., 1958-62; assoc. prof. math. Appalachian State U., 1962-63; prof. elec. engring. La. State U., Baton Rouge, 1963-83; prof. emeritus La. State U., 1983—; prof. math. U. North Ala., 1984-95, prof. emeritus, 1995—; adj. prof. elec. engring. U. Fla., Gainesville, 1976-77; mem. staff Combat Ops. Research Group, Ft. Monroe, Va., summer 1957; mathematician Boeing Co., New Orleans, summer 1965; engring. specialist Gen. Dynamics, 1983-84. Author: (with David E. Johnson) Mathematical Methods in Engineering and Physics, 1965, Graph Theory with Engineering Applications, 1972, Introductory Electric Circuit Analysis, 1981, Linear Systems Analysis, 1975; (with David E. Johnson and John L. Hilburn) Basic Electric Circuit Analysis, 1978, 3d edit., 1986, 4th edit., 1990, (with David E. Johnson, John L. Hilburn and Peter D. Scott) 5th edit., 1995, (with David E. Johnson and Harry P. Moore) A Handbook of Active Filters, 1980, (with David E. Johnson) A Funny Thing Happened on the Way to the White House, 1983, (with David E. Johnson and John L. Hilburn) Electric Circuit Analysis, 1989, 2d edit., 1991, Introduction to Digital Signal Processing, 1989, (with David E. Johnson, John L. Hilburn & Peter D. Scott) Electric Circuit Analysis, 3d edit., 1997. Pres. Wildwood PTA, 1973-74. Served with AUS, 1954-56. Mem. IEEE (sr. 1968-93), U. North Ala. Inst. for Learning in Retirement (v.p., chmn. curriculum com. 1997-98, treas. 1998-99), Sigma Xi, Tau Beta Pi, Phi Kappa Phi, Eta Kappa Nu, Pi Mu Epsilon, Kappa Mu Epsilon. Home: 222 S Meadowcrest Dr Florence AL 35630-1430

JOHNSON, JON E., magazine editor and publisher; b. St. Cloud, Minn., Sept. 13, 1963; s. Walter Ernest and Irene June (Brown) J. BA Comm., Sch. Comm. Arts, Mpls., 1983. Editor Movie Collector's World, Fraser, Mich., 1985-88; co-founder Discoveries Mag. Inc., Pt. Townsend, Wash., 1988-93; dir. Time Peace Archives, Mpls., 1993—. Author: Make Your Own Kind of Music: A Career Retrospective of Cass Elliot, 1989; R&B/soul editor: Your Hit Parade, American Top Ten, 1994, Dream a Little Dream: The Cass Elliot Collection, 1997. Honoree S.E. Tex. Musical Heritage Mus., Port Arthur, 1989. Mem. Am. Swedish Inst., Värmlandsförbundet. Democrat. Lutheran. Avocation: photography. Home: PO Box 58 Annandale MN 55302-0058

JOHNSON, JON L., advertising executive. Chmn., CEO, dir. Publicis, Salt Lake City. Office: Publicis 110 Social Hall Ave Salt Lake City UT 84111-1504

JOHNSON, JONAS TALMADGE, otolaryngology educator; b. Ravenna, Ohio, Jan. 3, 1947; s. J. Norman and K. Alice (Harkørader) J.; m. Janis, Dec. 22, 1968; children: Olin T., Rurik C., Ivar N. MD, SUNY, Syracuse, 1972; postgrad., Dartmouth Coll., 1965-68. Cert. Am. Bd. Otolaryngology. Asst. prof. U. Pitts., 1979-84, assoc. prof., 1984-87, prof., 1987—, vice chmn., 1982—; active staff Montefoire Hosp., Pitts., 1987—, Western Pa. Hosp., 1996—, U. Pa. Med. Ctr. Southside Hosp., 1996—; cons. VA. Med. Ctr., Pitts., 1979-80, Children's Hosp., Pitts., 1980-89. Editor. Am. Jour. Otolaryngology, 1992—; co-editor: Infectious Diseases and Antimicrobial Therapy of the Ears Nose and Throat, 1997, Carcinoma of the Thyroid,

1999, Tracheotomy, 1999; mem. numerous editl. bds., 1984—; contbr. articles to med. jours. Maj. M.C., USAF, 1977-79. Recipient Ben Shuster award Am. Acad. Facial Plastic and Reconstructive Surgery, 1976. Mem. AMA, ACS, Am. Acad. Otolaryngology-Head and Neck Surgery (bd. dirs. 1992-94, coord. for continuing edn. 1995—, Merit award in clin. rsch. 1976, Honor award 1982, Disting. Svc. award 1994), Am. Laryngol. Soc. (v.p. ea. sect. 1999—), Rhinol., and Otol. Soc., Am. Diopter and Decibel Soc., Am. Bronchoesophagologic Soc., Triological Soc., Am. Head and Neck Soc. (sec. 1998—), Am. Rhinol. Soc., Am. Assn. Cancer Rsch., Am. Soc. Clin. Oncology, Am. Radium Soc. Office: Eye and Ear Inst UPMC 200 Lothrop St Ste 500 Pittsburgh PA 15213-2546

JOHNSON, JONATHAN EDWIN, II, lawyer; b. Whittier, Calif., May 1, 1936; s. Roger Edwin and Louise (Thompson) J.; m. Clare Hardy, June 23, 1963 (dec. 1995); children: Joanthan III, Hardy, Benjamin, Adam, Rufus, Bradford, Roger, Ralph. BChemE, Cornell U., 1959, MBA, 1960; JD with honors, George Washington U., 1963. Bar: Calif. 1964; cert. specialist family law, Calif. Assoc. Tuttle & Taylor, LA., 1963-65; pvt. practice, L.A., 1965-67; ptnr. Johnson & Jarvis, L.A., 1967-68, Johnson, Poulson, Coons & Slater, L.A., 1968—; instr. paralegal probate U. West L.A. Sch. Law, 1974; mem. clergy adv. com. to supt. edn., City of L.A., 1978-81. Fellow Am. Acad. Matrimonial Lawyers; mem. Calif. State Bar Assn. (mem. legis. com. family law sect. 1978-88, chmn. 1980), Beverly Hills Bar Assn. (mem. exec. com. family law sect. 1977-82, 86-88, 91—), Inter-stake Bus. and Profl. Assn. L.A. (pres. 1974), Cornell Club of So. Calif. (pres. 1966-68), Order of Coif, Sigma Chi, Phi Delta Phi. Mem. LDS Ch. Home: 1094 Acanto Pl Los Angeles CA 90049-1604 Office: Johnson Poulson Coons Et Al 10880 Wilshire Blvd Ste 1100 Los Angeles CA 90024-4112

JOHNSON, JONE E., clergy member; b. May 15, 1951. BA in Mgmt., Mundelein Coll., 1981; MDiv, Meadville/Lombard Theol. Sch., 1991. Ordained to ministry Unitarian Universalist Ch. Various tng. and edn. mgmt. positions, 1980-90; Unitarian Universalist min. Berrien U. U. Fellowship, St. Joseph, Mich., 1991-93; ethical culture leader Chgo. Ethical Humanist Soc., 1991-96, No. Va. Ethical Soc., Vienna, Va., 1997—. E-mail: jj@pbat.com.

JOHNSON, JOSEPH CLAYTON, JR., lawyer; b. Vicksburg, Miss., Nov. 15, 1943; s. Joseph Clayton and Rose Butler (Levy) J.; m. Cherrian Frances Turpin, Oct. 24, 1970; children: Mary Clayton, Erik Cole. BS, La. State U., 1965, JD, 1969. Bar: La. 1969, U.S. Dist. Ct. (ea. dist.) La. 1969, U.S. Dist. Ct. (mid. dist.) La. 1969, U.S. Dist. Ct. (we. dist.) La. 1979, U.S. Ct. Appeals (5th cir.) 1982. Ptnr. Taylor, Porter, Brooks & Phillips, Baton Rouge, 1969—; mem. civil justice reform act com. U.S. Dist. Ct. (mid. dist.) La., 1995-97, chmn. 1996-97; mem. La. Atty. Disciplinary Bd., 1997—. Bd. Editors Oil and Gas Reporter. Pres. Baton Rouge area Am. Cancer Soc., 1987-88. With U.S. Army, 1969-75. Mem. ABA, La. Bar Assn. (mem. ho. of dels. 1979-92, council rep. mineral law sect. 1986-94, chmn. mineral law sect. 1992-93), La. State Law Inst. (mineral code com.), Baton Rouge Bar Assn., Dean Henry George McMahon Am. Inn of Ct. Republican. Methodist. Office: PO Box 2471 Baton Rouge LA 70821-2471

JOHNSON, JOSEPH EGGLESTON, III, physician, educator; b. Elberton, Ga., Sept. 17, 1930; s. Joseph Eggleston Jr. and Marie (Williams) J.; m. Judith H. Kemp, Jan. 21, 1956; children: Joseph Eggleston IV, Judith Ann, Julie Marie. BA cum laude, Vanderbilt U., 1951, MD, 1954. Diplomate Am. Bd. Internal Medicine (bd. govs. 1977-83, exec. com. 1981-83), Am. Bd. Allergy and Immunology. Intern Johns Hopkins Hosp., Balt., 1954-55, resident, 1957-61, physician, 1961-66; mem. faculty Johns Hopkins Med. Sch., Balt., 1961-66, asst. dean, 1963-66; chief infectious diseases U. Fla. Coll. Medicine, Gainsville, 1966-72, assoc. dean, 1970-72; prof., chmn. dept. Bowman Gray Sch. Medicine, Winston-Salem, N.C., 1972-85; chief med. service N.C. Baptist Hosp., mem. residency rev. com. internal medicine, 1978-83, chmn. residency rev. com. internal medicine, 1983-85; dean Med. Sch., prof. medicine U. Mich., Ann Arbor, 1985-90, prof. internal medicine, 1985-93; accreditation commn. on grad. med. edn., 1988-93; sr. v.p. membership and spl. advisor to exec. v.p. Am. Coll. Physicians, Phila., 1993—, interim exec. v.p., 1994-95; adj. prof. of medicine U. Pa., 1994—. Contbr. articles to profl. jours. Served to lt. USNR, 1955-57. John and Mary R. Markle scholar, 1962-67; Mead-Johnson postgrad. scholar, 1960-61. Fellow ACP (sci. program com. 1979-85, chmn. sci. program com. 1982-85, chmn. elect bd. govs. 1985, chmn. bd. govs., bd. regents 1985-93, gov.-elect N.C. 1981-82, gov. N.C. 1982-86, treas. 1991-93, interim exec. v.p. 1994—), Am. Acad. Allergy, Royal Soc. Medicine (travelling fellow 1970-71); mem. AMA (chmn. Med. Sch. sect. 1990-91, alternate del. 1996—), Am. Fedn. Clin. Rsch., Assn. Am. Physicians, Infectious Diseases Soc. Am., Soc. Exptl. Biology and Medicine, N.Y. Acad. Scis., Am. Assn. Immunologists, So. Soc. Clin. Investigation, Am. Soc. for Microbiology, Assn. Profs. Medicine (sec.-treas. 1978-81, pres.-elect 1981-82, pres. 1982-83), Am. Clin. and Climatol. Assn., Société Française de la Tuberculose et des Maladies Respiratoires, Assn. Program Dirs. in Internal Medicine (exec. coun. 1980-83), Assn. Am. Med. Colls. (exec. coun. 1983-85), Coun. Acad. Socs. (adminstrv. bd. 1978-85), Federated Coun. for Internal Medicine (vice chmn. 1981-82, chmn. 1982-83), Johns Hopkins Soc. Scholars, Phi Beta Kappa, Sigma Alpha Epsilon, Phi Chi, Omicron Delta Kappa, Alpha Omega Alpha. Office: Am Coll Physicians Independance Mall West Sixth St at Race Philadelphia PA 19106

JOHNSON, JOSEPH H., JR., lawyer; b. Dothan, Ala., July 14, 1925. Student, La. Poly. Inst.; LLB, U. Va., 1949. Bar: Ala. 1949. Of counsel Lange, Simpson, Robinson & Somerville, Birmingham, Ala. Recipient Bernard P. Friel medal for disting. svc. in pub. fin., 1997. Mem. ABA (mem. coun. 1962-66, 68-72, 73-77, chmn. 1981-82, sec. of urban, state and local govt. law), Assn. of Bar of City of N.Y., Birmingham Bar Assn. (chmn. com. on profl. ethics 1978-79), Ala. State Bar, Nat. Assn. bond Lawyers (pres. 1988-89), Am. Coll. Bond Counsel (bd. dirs. 1998—). Office: Lange Simpson Robinson & Somerville 1700 Regions Bank Bldg # A Birmingham AL 35203-3217

JOHNSON, JOY ANN, diagnostic radiologist; b. New Richmond, Wis., Aug. 16, 1952; d. Howard James and Shirley Maxine (Eidem) J.que. BA in Chemistry summa cum laude, U. No. Colo., 1974; D of Medicine, U. Colo., 1978. Diplomate Am. Bd. Radiology, Nat. Bd. Med. Examiners; cert. added qualification pediatric radiology. Resident in radiology U. Colo., 1978-81, fellow in radiology, 1981-82; asst. prof. diagnostic radiology and pediatrics, chief sect. pediatric radiology Clin. Radiology Found. U. Kans. Med. Ctr., Kansas City, 1982-87; radiologist Radiology Assocs. Ltd., Kansas City, Mo., 1987-92; mem. staff Bapt. Med. Ctr., Kansas City, Mo., 1987-92; radiologist Children's Mercy Hosp., Kansas City, 1992-95, Leavenworth-Kansas City Imaging, 1996—; assoc. prof. U. Mo., Kansas City, 1992—; speaker Radiol. Soc. Republic of China, 1985. Contbr. articles to med. jours. Nat. Cancer Inst. fellow, 1982. Mem. AMA, Am. Coll. Radiology, Radiol. Soc. N.Am., Am. Inst. Ultrasound in Medicine (mem. program com. Kansas City 1984), Soc. Pediatric Radiology, Am. Assn. Women in Radiology, Lambda Sigma Tau. Avocations: horseback riding, jumping, physical fitness, sports, reading. Office: Leavenworth-Kansas City Imaging 9201 Parallel Pkwy Kansas City KS 66112-1528*

JOHNSON, JOYCE MARIE, psychiatrist, epidemiologist, public health officer; b. Baton Rouge, Jan. 30, 1952; d. Gene Addison and Helen Marie (Kalcik) J.; m. James Albert Calderwood, Mar. 28, 1987; 1 child, James. BA, Luther Coll., Decorah, Iowa, 1972; MA, U. Iowa, 1974; DO, Mich. State U., 1980. Cert. in psychiatry, pub. health and preventive medicine, and clin. pharmacology. Cooking instr. Kirkwood C.C., Iowa City, Iowa, 1974-76; health planner Iowa Regional Med. Program, Iowa City, 1974-76; commd. USPHS, advanced through grades to rear adm.; intern USPHS Hosp., Balt., 1980-81; med. epidemiologist Hepatitis Labs., Ctrs. Disease Control, Phoenix, 1981-83, AIDS, Ctrs. Disease Control, Atlanta, 1983-84; resident in psychiatry NIMH, 1984-87, staff psychiatrist, 1987-88; epidemiologist, acting div. dir. Food and Drug Adminstrn., 1988-93; asst. surgeon gen. USPHS, 1995—; dir. divsn. nat. treatment demonstrations, Substance Abuse and Mental Health Svcs. Adminstrn., 1993-97; chief med. officer USCG, 1997—. Med. Perspectives fellow, New Guinea and Thailand, 1978-79; mem. clin. faculty Mich. State U., 1983-93, Georgetown U. Med. Ctr., 1988—, Uniformed Svcs. U. of the Health Scis. Mem. Mensa, Cosmos Club. Office: 5518 Western Ave Bethesda MD 20815-7122

JOHNSON, JOYCE MARIE, marketing and communications executive; b. Akron, Ohio, July 8, 1962; d. Bob R. and Karin B. (Mehl) J.; m. Don Ostapowicz, May 19, 1990; children: Peter Joseph, Kevin David, Jackson Thomas. BS, Ohio U., 1994. Reporter, anchor WAKC-TV, Akron, 1986-89; news dir. WQMX, Akron, 1989-96; dir. mktg. and comms. Family Svcs., Akron, 1996—; drama tchr. Weathervane Theatre 1986-93. Fundraising chmn. First Night; v.p. bd. dirs. Love Fund. Recipient Ohio Media award, 1995. Mem. Human Soc. Greater Akron (trustee). Office: Family Svcs 160 W Grayling Dr Akron OH 44333-2848

JOHNSON, JOYCE THEDFORD, state agency administrator; b. Hazelhurst, Miss., June 27, 1956; m. Leo Kleb Johnson; 1 child, Harmony Saige. Student, Hinds Jr. Coll.; BA, U. Miss., 1979. Lic. social worker. Divsn. sec. Temple Industries, Port Gibson, Miss., 1975; coord. programs North Miss. Retardation Ctr., Oxford, 1976-77; sec. dept. edn. U. Miss., 1977-78, office mgr. mineral rsch. inst., 1978-80; from analyst to rsch. asst. to legis. asst. Miss. State Senate, Jackson, 1980-93; dir. divsn. family and children svcs. Miss. Dept. Human Svcs., 1993-94; ops. cons. Sta-Home Home Health Agy., 1995-96, Medshares Mgmt. Svcs., Inc., 1996—; coord. Ho. and Senate Joint Indigent Care Study Com., Joint Resdl. Child Care Study Com.; Senate Interim Study Coms. Rural Health and Sunset; mem. staff reorgn. com., steering com. Kellogg Initiative, children's advisory coun., disabilities prevention coun.; chairperson infant mortality task force, Pres. Nat. Adv. com. Rural Health; mem. Robert Wood Johnson Adv. Com.; facilitator various nat. assn. and fed. govt. meetings. Vol. Mother's March, Spl. Olympics; sponsor Luth. Youth Group; cheerleader sponsor Exchange Club; room mother Rankin County Schs.; bd. dirs. Rankin County PTO; active Nativity Luth. Ch., Brandon, Miss. Recipient Outstanding Young Women of Am., 1980, Outstanding Career Women in Miss., 1991. Mem. U. Miss. Alumni Assn., Alpha Omicron Pi. Address: PO Box 1231 Oxford MS 38655

JOHNSON, JUDITH MISNER, educator; b. Hasbrouck, N.Y., Apr. 19, 1935; d. Milford Misner and Lillian Ora Lawrence; m. John Johnson, Jan 29, 1957 (div. Apr. 1984); children: Daniel, Amy, Meredith. BS in Elem. Edn., SUNY, Fredonia, 1956; MA in Edn., U. Conn., 1977. Lic. tchr., N.Y. Elem. tchr. Ellenville (N.Y.) Ctrl. Sch., 1969-94; curriculum coord., designer and writer, bd. advisor Creative Response to Conflict, Inc., Nyack, N.Y., 1994—; adj. prof. women's studies Sullivan County C.C., Lock Sheldrake, N.Y., 1990-94; curriculum devel. cons. Sunburst, Pleasantville, N.Y., 1994. Author: Violence Prevention Through Conflict Resolution, 1995, CCRC's Friendly Classroom Mediation Manual, 1997, CCRC's Friendly Classrooms and Communities for Children, 1998. Mediator Ulster Sullivan Mediation, Highland, N.Y., 1984—. N.Y. State Bd. Regents scholar, 1954, Delta Kappa Gamma grad. scholar, 1976. Mem. ASCD, Nat. Assn. Mediation in Edn., Phi Delta Kappa. Avocations: writing poetry and memoirs, book collecting, music, theater. Fax: (914) 358-4924. E-mail: ccrcnyack@aol.com. Office: Creative Response to Conflict Inc 521 N Broadway Nyack NY 10960

JOHNSON, JUDY DIANNE, elementary education educator; b. Houston, Oct. 1, 1947; d. Thomas Hunter and Roxie Pauline (Swink) Mitchell; m. Dennis Carlton Johnson, June 4, 1971; children: Juli Lyn, Jill Nicole. BS, U. Houston, 1969; MEd, Stephen F. Austin U., 1981. Cert. supr., tchr., Tex. Elem. tchr. Humble (Tex.) Independent Sch. Dist., 1969-92, Katy Ind. Sch. Dist., Tex., 1992—. Mem. Assn. Tex. Profl. Educators, Katy Profl. Educators, Coun. for Advancement of Math. Teaching, Asns. for Supervision and Curriculum Devel., Tex. Coun. Tchrs. Math. Baptist. Avocation: reading. Office: Bear Creek Elem Sch 4815 Hickory Downs Dr Houston TX 77084-3654

JOHNSON, JULIE MARIE, lawyer/lobbyist; b. Aberdeen, S.D., Aug. 7, 1953; d. Howard B. and Jerauldine (Dilly) J.; m. Bryan L. Hisel. BA in Govt., Comm., U. S.D., 1974, MA in Polit. Sci., 1976, JD, 1976. Bar: S.D. 1977, U.S. Dist. Ct. S.D. 1977. Assoc. Siegel, Barnett Law Firm, Aberdeen, 1977; law clk. Fifth Judicial Circuit Ct., Aberdeen, 1977-78; ptnr. Maloney, Kolker, Fritz, Hogan & Johnson, Aberdeen, 1978-84; dep. sec. S.D. Dept. Labor, Aberdeen, Pierre, 1983-84, sec. Gov.'s Cabinet, 1985-87; pres. Industry and Commerce Assn. of S.D., Pierre, 1987-95; sec., Gov.'s Cabinet S.D. Dept. Revenue, Pierre, 1995; exec. dir. S.D. Rural Devel. Coun., Pierre, 1995—. Treas. S.D. Cmty. Found., Pierre, 1987-95; mem. Pvt. Industry Coun., 1985-87, S.D. Coun. on Vocat. Edn., 1985-87; bd. dirs. Mo. Shores Women's Resource Ctr., Pierre, 1988-89; chmn. S.D. Main St. Adv. Coun., 1987-91; bd. dirs. United Way, 1988-96, chmn., 1991; mem. Shortgrass Arts Coun., 1987—, South Dakotans for the Arts, 1981—, Solid Waste Mgmt. Plan Task Force, 1990, S.D. Citizens Adv. Coun. on Hazardous Waste, 1991-92, gov.'s adv. coun. on health care reform, 1992-93; bd. dirs. Hist. S.D. Found., 1996-99; founding mem., legal counsel Outdoor Women of S.D., Inc., 1995—; bd. trustees USD Found., 1992—, Dakota Wesleyan U., 1996—; founding mem., treas. S.D. Discovery Ctr. and Aquarium, Inc., bd. dirs., 1988-92; mem. S.D. Water Congress, 1990—, bd. dirs., 1987-95; bd. dirs. Nyoda Girl Scout Coun., 1997-99; mem. adv. bd. W.O. Farber Ctr. for Excellence in Civic Leadership, 1998—; bd. dirs. Farber Fund, 1987—; founding mem. S.D. Chambers & Econ. Devel. Coun., 1989—; mem. network mgmt. team Nat. Rural Devel. Partnership, 1998—. RJR Nabisco fellow Women Execs. in State Govt., Harvard, 1986; named Outstanding Young Citizen Jaycees, Aberdeen, 1982, S.D. Jaycees, 1983. Mem. S.D. Bar Assn., Industry and Commerce Assn. S.D. (bd. dirs. 1985-87), U. S.D. Alumni Assn. (exec. com. 1987-96, pres. 1990-92), AAUW, Bus. and Profl. Women U.S.A. (nat. legis. chmn. 1987-88, 92-94, nat. chmn. issues mgmt. 1991-93, pres. S.D. 1984-85, Woman of Yr. award Aberdeen chpt. 1982), Women Execs. in State Govvt. (bd. didrs. 1985-87), Coun. State Mfrs. Assn., S.D. Mining Assn. (bd. dirs. 1991-95), Nat. Indsl. Coun., Coun. State C.'s of C., Ducks Unltd., Rotary, Zonta, ABC Investment Club, Rocky Mountain Elk Found. Republican. Lutheran. E-mail: juliej@state.sd.us. Office: 1100 E Church St # 352 Pierre SD 57501-2399 Office: Capitol Lake Plz 711 E Wells Ave Pierre SD 57501-3335 Office: SD Rural Devel Coun 75 S Harmon Dr Mitchell SD 57301-6250

JOHNSON, KARLA ANN, county official; b. Heber City, Utah, July 27, 1957; d. Henry Edward and Twila Faun (Jacobson) Kohler; m. Arthur Que Johnson, Sept. 22, 1977; children: Russell, Kohler Scott, Marc. Cattle rancher Kanab, Utah, 1981—. Bd. dirs. S.W. Utah Dept. Health, St. George; bd. dirs., pres. Kanab C. of C.; charter mem. Nat. Coun. Women's Adv. to Congress, Washington; ambassador Mountain Am. Credit Union, St. George; sec. County Rep. Party, Kanab, Utah; pres. PTA, Kanab. Mem. Internat. Assn. Clks., Recorders, Election Ofcls., Treas., Friendship and Cultural Exch. Soc., Coalition of Resources and Economies, Utah Assn. Counties (bd. dirs.).

JOHNSON, KATHARYN PRICE (MRS. EDWARD F. JOHNSON), civic worker; b. Smyrna, Del., Mar. 24, 1897; d. Lewis M. and Jennie Cairl (Smithers) Price; grad. Centenary Coll., 1915, LHD (hon.), 1997; student Goucher Coll., 1915-18; m. Edward F. Johnson, Nov. 16, 1920; children: Edward A., Jane Cairl Johnson Kent. With Liberty Loan Com. for Md. and Liberty Loan Assn. of Balt., 1918-20; dir. Scarsdale Woman's Club, 1933-36; dir. White Plains Thrift Shop, 1930-43, pres., 1936-43; mem. exec. com. Scarsdale Community Fund, 1934-38; active Scarsdale council Girl Scouts, 1937-53, commr., 1939-41, now hon. mem. Scarsdale-Hartsdale council, 1953-69; mem. region 2 com. Girl Scouts U.S.A., 1942-56, mem. nat. bd., exec. com., 1947-55, chmn. orgn. and mgmt. dept., 1952-55, mem. nat. field com., 1943-55, mem. equipment service com. 1956-69, mem. internat. com., 1956-60, mem. gifts com., 1974-81; mem. Bd. Edn., Scarsdale, N.Y., 1943-46; disaster chmn. Scarsdale chpt. ARC, 1942-45; mem. Commn. Human Rights, 1958-69, Commn. Status of Women, 1957-69; rep. World Assn. Girl Guides and Girl Scouts to UN, 1957-71, mem. NGO com. on UNICEF, 1965-72, sec., 1968-70; participant World Confs., World Assn. Girl Guides and Girl Scouts, Greece, 1960, Denmark, 1963, Japan, 1966, Finland, 1969, Can., 1972, Eng., 1975, Iran, 1978, World Conf., U.S., 1984. Recipient Juliette Low World Friendship medal Girl Scouts USA, 1984. Mem. Nat. Coun. Women U.S., Scarsdale Hist. Soc., Olave-Baden-Powell Soc. (founder), Pi Beta Phi. Republican. Presbyterian. Clubs: Scarsdale Woman's (life), Scarsdale Golf, Nat. Women's Republican; Shenorock Shore. Home: 165 Brewster Rd Scarsdale NY 10583-2021

JOHNSON, KATHERINE ANNE, health research administrator, lawyer; b. Medford, Mass., Apr. 20, 1947; d. Lester and Eileen Anne (Henaghan) J. BS, La. State U., 1969; MSA, George Washington U., 1972; JD, Cath. U., 1985. Bar: Md. 1985. Pub. health adviser HHS, Washington, 1970-76; dir. plan implementation SE Colo. Health Sys. Agy., Colorado Springs, 1976-78; sr. mng. assoc. CDP Assocs., Inc., Atlanta, 1978-87, dir. legal affairs, 1986-87; v.p. Cancer CarePoint Inc., Atlanta, 1987; sr. mgr. Salick Health Care, Inc., Bethesda, Md., 1987-89; pvt. practice atty. cons., Potomac, Md., 1989-90; assoc. dir. for adminstrn. San Antonio Cancer Inst., 1990-96; assoc. dir. planning and adminstrn. CTRC Rsch. Found., San Antonio, 1996-97, v.p., 1997-98; COO Inst. Drug Devel., San Antonio, 1997-98; prin. biomed. program devel. consulting Inst. Drug Devel., 1998—; spkr. in field. Contbr. articles to profl. jours. Vol. Ct.-Apptd. Spl. Adv. for Abused Children. Mem. Md. Bar Assn., Am. Health Lawyers Assn., Leadership Tex. Class of 1996, Soc. Rsch. Adminstrs. Avocations: skiing, reading, antique collecting. Office: 15228 Antler Creek Dr San Antonio TX 78248-2009

JOHNSON, KATHERINE HOLTHAUS, health care marketing professional; b. Denver, Mar. 19, 1961; d. William Philip and Barbara Kristine (Nielsen) Holthaus; m. Robert Scott Johnson; children: Katie Maree, Brian David, Kiersten Rose. B in Applied Math. Engring., U. Colo., 1983; MBA, U. Denver, 1992. Acctg. intern Cooper, Haugen & Co., CPAs, Englewood, Colo., 1982-84; market analyst mktg. dept. Porter Meml. Hosp., Denver, 1985-88; account exec. Tallant LaPointe & Ptnrs., Inc., Englewood, 1988-92; advt. mgr. Micromedex, Inc., Denver, 1992-93; mktg. cons. Highlands Ranch, Colo., 1993-96; product mgr. Micromedex, Inc., Englewood, Colo., 1996-98; mktg. cons. Highlands Ranch, Colo., 1999—. Judge, vol. 4-H Clubs, Met. Denver, 1979—; supt. Sunday sch. Ascension Luth. Ch., Littleton, Colo., 1985-87. Recipient 2 Advantage awards Adventist Health System, 1987. Mem. Soc. for Healthcare Planning and Mktg., Am. Hosp. Assn., Acad. for Health Svcs. Mktg., Am. Mktg. Assn., Alpha Chi Omega. Republican. Avocations: bicycling, swimming, aerobics, reading, baking.

JOHNSON, KAY DURBAHN, real estate manager, consultant; b. Crookston, Minn., Apr. 4, 1937; d. Wilbert John and Frieda (Johnson) Durbahn; m. Ray Arvin Johnson, May 14, 1960; children: Sherry Kay Johnson Johnston, Diane Rosalind Johnson Peterson, Laura Faye Johnson. BA, U. Minn., 1959. Reference analyst Indsl. Rels. Ctr. U. Minn., Mpls., 1959-61; real estate mgr. Minnetonka, Minn., 1976—; ptnr. Broadmoor Plantation Investors, Fargo, N.D., 1976—; v.p. D&T Property, Inc., Minnetonka, 1990—, also bd. dirs.; tax reduction cons. R.A. Johnson & Assocs., Minnetonka, 1985—. City of Minnetonka Planning Commn., 1972-74, vice chair, 1973-74; mem. Land Use Task Force, 1972-74; liaison Ridgedale Devel.; various coun. positions Minnetonka Luth. Ch., mem. choir; mem. GMC Motorcoach Assn. Mem. Mpls. Inst. Arts. Republican. Avocations: art, music, camping, traveling. *For greater happiness try to balance your life by making time for all aspects of living, including activities to meet social, spiritual, physical, family, work, and intellectual needs.*

JOHNSON, KEITH LIDDELL, chemical company executive; b. Darlington, England, July 22, 1939; came to U.S., 1948, naturalized, 1958; s. Arthur Henry and Beatrice (Liddell) J.; m. Margaret Elaine Meston, Aug. 29, 1959; children: Leslie Margaret, Kevin Liddell, Gregory Norman, Kathleen Elaine; 1 ward, Ann Louise Warwick. BA, U. Mich., 1960. Chem. technician Ajem Labs., Livonia, Mich., 1956-60; rsch. chemist labs. Swift & Co., Chgo., 1960-63, project mgr., 1963-67; group leader R&D ctr. Swift & Co., Oak Brook, Ill., 1967-71; adminstrv. asst. to exec. v.p. Swift & Co., Chgo., 1971-72, quality assurance dir., 1974-78, group mgr. plant quality assurance, 1978-82; quality assurance mgr. refinery divsn. Swift Edible Oil Co. subs. Swift & Co., Chgo., 1972-73, corp. quality assurance mgr., 1973-74; tech. dir. Norman Fox & Co., L.A., 1982-83, br. mgr., 1983-88, gen. mgr., 1988—, exec. v.p., dir., 1989—, pres., 1993—; bd. dirs. Lexard Corp., L.A., v.p. 1990—; mem. Chgo. Manpower Area Planning Com., 1971; mem. industry adv. bd. South Coast Air Quality Mgmt. Dist., Calif., 1982-84. Contbr. articles to profl. jours. V.p., dir. St. Martha's Sr. Care Ctr., West Covina, Calif., 1993—, chmn. bd., 1995—, vestry St. Martha's Episcopal Ch., sr. warden 1991-96, 98—; bd. dirs. St. Martha's Episcopal Sch., 1999—. Mem. Chgo. Chemists Club, Chem. Art Forum Chgo. (v.p. 1980, pres. 1981), Am. Chem. Soc., Soc. Cosmetic Chemists (membership chmn. Bay area chpt. 1985, chmn. 1987-88), Am. Oil Chemists Soc., Jr. Assn. Commerce and Industry (dir. 1968, v.p. 1969, exec. v.p. 1970, pres. 1971), Chem. Mktg. Assn. So. Calif., U.S. Jr. C. of C. (dir. 1972), Ill. Jr. C. of C. (v.p. 1972). Episcopalian. Achievements include 17 U.S. and 25 fgn. patents. Home: 342 Amberwood Dr Walnut CA 91789-2473 Office: PO Box 58727 Los Angeles CA 90058-0727

JOHNSON, KELLY HAL, performance analyst; b. Temple, Tex., July 17, 1968; s. Kenneth Walter and Joye Elynne Johnson. BBA in Fin., Baylor U., 1990; MBA in Internat. Bus., George Washington U., 1995, cert. program, 1999. Intermediate trading acct. Mobil Oil Corp., Fairfax, Va., 1990-92, supply and trading acct., 1992-95, crude scheduler, 1995-96, gas and distillate scheduler, 1996-97, global perforamance analyst, 1998—. Mem. pastoral searchcom. Westminster Presbyn. Ch., Alexandria, Va., 1996-98, mem. pers. com., 1998—. Mem. Internat. Policy Inst., World Affairs Coun., UN Assn., Jr. Area C. of C. (chaplain). Presbyterian. Avocations: choral performance, guitar, international events, travel. E-mail: KellyúHúJohnson@email.Mobil.com. Home: 202 W Taylor Run Pkwy Alexandria VA 22314 Office: Mobil Oil Corp 3225 Gallows Rd Fairfax VA 22037

JOHNSON, KENNETH F., lawyer; b. Ft. Bragg, Calif., June 10, 1938; s. Frank W. and Gertrude Johnson; m. Jane Perry Drennan, June 11, 1961; children: Erik Allan, Mark. BSCE, U. Calif., Berkeley, 1962; JD, U. Calif., Hastings, 1969. Bar: Calif. 1970. V.p., shareholder Crosby, Heafey, Roach & May, Oakland, Calif., 1969—. Note and comment editor: Hastings Law Jour., 1968-69. With USNR, 1962-66. Scholar U. Calif. Hastings, 1967-68, 68-69. Mem. ABA, ATLA, Calif. Bar Assn., Alameda County Bar Assn., Contra Costa County Bar Assn., Bar Assn. San Francisco, Calif. Bus. Trial Lawyers Assn., Assn. Def. Counsel, Order of Coif. Office: Crosby Heafey Roach & May 1999 Harrison St Fl 26 Oakland CA 94612-3572

JOHNSON, KENNETH HARVEY, veterinary pathologist; b. Hallock, Minn., Feb. 17, 1936; s. Clifford H. and Alma (Anderson) J.; Sept. 17, 1960; children: Jeffrey, Gregory, Sandra. BS, U. Minn., 1958, DVM, 1960, PhD, 1965. Jr. asst. health officer NIH, Bethesda, Md., 1958; practice vet. medicine Edina, Minn., 1960; USPHS-NIH non-service fellow U. Minn., St. Paul, 1960-65; asst. prof. dept. vet. pathology and parasitology U. Minn., 1965-69, assoc. prof., 1969-73, prof., 1973-98, prof. emeritus, 1998—, head, sect. pathology, dept. vet. biology, 1974-76, chmn. dept. vet. pathobiology Coll. Vet Medicine, 1976-83; cons. Minn. Mining & Mfg. Co., Medtronic Inc., Natural-Y Surg. Specialties; principle and co-investigator several NIH grants, 1965—. Mem. editl. bd. Amyloid, the Internat. Jour. of Exptl. and Clin. Investigation; contbr. chpts.: Veterinary Clinics of North America, 1971, Spontaneous Animal Models of Human Disease, 1979, Kirk's Current Veterinary Therapy; contbr. articles to sci. jours. Councilman Nativity Lutheran Ch., St. Anthony Village, Minn., 1972-75. Recipient Tchr. of Yr. award, 1968-69, Norden award for disting. tchr. in vet. medicine, 1970, Beecham award for rsch. excellence, 1989, Ralson Purina Small Animal Rsch. award, 1990, Phi Zeta faculty achievement award, 1992. Mem. AAUP, Am. Soc. for Investigative Pathology, Minn. Vet. Med. Assn., Am. Coll. Vet. Pathologists (hon. mem.), Sigma Xi, Phi Zeta, Gamma Sigma Delta. Home: 3510 Skycroft Dr Minneapolis MN 55418-1780 Office: Univ Minn Coll Vet Medicine Dept Vet Patho Biol Saint Paul MN 55108

JOHNSON, KENNETH LANCE, baseball player; b. Lincoln Heights, Ohio, July 6, 1963. Student, Triton Coll., Ill. Baseball player St. Louis Cardinals, 1984-88, Chgo. White Sox, 1988-95, N.Y. Mets, 1995-97, Chgo. Cubs, 1997—. Named Am. Assn. MVP, 1987. Achievements includes holding major league record for most consecutive years leading league in triples (21), hits (227), Am. League single-season record for fewest errors by outfielder who led league in errors, share Am. League single-game record for most triples. *

JOHNSON, K(ENNETH) O(DELL), aerospace engineer; b. Harville, Mo., Aug. 31, 1922; s. Kenneth D. and Polly Louise (Wilson) J.; B.S. in Aero. Engring., Purdue U., 1950; m. Betty Lou Jones, Aug. 5, 1950; children—Cynthia Jo, Gregory Alan. Engr., design, quality and production mgmt. Gen. Lamp Co., Elwood, Ind., 1950-51; mem. staff aircraft gas turbine engine design Allison div. Gen. Motors Corp., Speedway, Ind., 1951-66; mem. turbofan aircraft engines plus marine, indsl. gas turbine engine design mgmt. staff Gen. Electric Co., 1966-86, cons. aerospace engrng. Belcan Corp., Cin., 1986—. Served to capt. USAF, 1942-45. Assoc. fellow AIAA. Republican. Methodist. Holder over 20 patents in field. Recipient UDF Pioneer & Extraordinary Service award for unducted fan invention and patent, Gen. Electric Co., 1985, cert. recognition NASA, 1987; named to Gen. Electric Aircraft Engines Propulsion Hall of Fame, 1987. Home: 8360 Arapaho Ln Cincinnati OH 45243-2718 Office: Belcan Corp Dept Engring 10200 Anderson Way Cincinnati OH 45242-4718*

JOHNSON, KENNETH OSCAR, oil company executive; b. Center City, Minn., Apr. 11, 1920; s. Oscar W. and Sigrid (Hollsten) J.; m. Margery Wheeler, Apr. 18, 1945; 1 child, Eric W. B.S. in Chem. Engring., U. Minn., 1942. With Exxon Corp., Houston, 1942-74; heavy fuels mgr. supply dept. Exxon Corp., 1968-72, wholesale fuels sales mgr., mktg. dept., 1972-74; chmn., chief exec. officer Belcher Oil Co., Miami, Fla., 1974-88; sr. v.p. Coastal Corp., Houston, 1988—, also bd. dirs.; bd. dirs. Petroleum Industry Found. Patentee in field. Club: Petroleum (Houston). Home: 845 Admiralty Parade Naples FL 34102-7874 Office: Coastal Corp 9 E Greenway Plz Houston TX 77046-0905

JOHNSON, KENNETH PETER, neurologist, medical researcher; b. Jamestown, N.Y., Mar. 12, 1932; s. Kenneth Peter and Nina (Bengtson) Johnson; m. Jacquelyn Johnson, June 23, 1956; children: Peter, Thomas, Diane, Douglas. B.A., Upsala Coll., East Orange, N.J., 1955; M.D., Jefferson Med. Coll., Phila., 1959. Diplomate: Am. Bd. Psychiatry and Neurology. Intern Buffalo Gen. Hosp., 1959-60; resident Hosp. of Cleve., 1963-65; asst. prof. neurology Case Western Res. U., Cleve., 1968-71, assoc. prof., 1971-74; prof. U. Calif., San Francisco, 1974-81; prof., chmn. U. Md., Balt., 1981—; chief neurology VA Hosp., Balt., 1981-83. Editor: Neurovirology, 1984; contbr. numerous articles in field to profl. jours. Served to lt. U.S. Navy, 1961-63. Recipient Weil award Am. Assn. Neuropathology, 1967; recipient Research Ctr. Devel. award NIH, 1968-73; Zimmerman lectr. Stanford U., 1981. Fellow Am. Neurol. Assn.; mem. Am. Acad. Neurology, Am. Soc. Virology, Am. Congress Rehab. Medicine, Am. Soc. Neurorehab., Internat. Soc. for Neuroimmunology. Lutheran. Office: U Md Hosp Neurology Dept N4W46 22 S Greene St Baltimore MD 21201-1544*

JOHNSON, KENNETH STUART, publisher, printer; b. Chgo., Aug. 22, 1928; s. William Moss and Lucille (Carsellio) J.; student Wright Jr. Coll., 1949-50, U. Ill., 1951-52; m. Joanne Barbaria Johnson; children: Cynthia Diane, Randall, Andrew, Peter. Dir., chmn. Free Press, Inc., Carpentersville, Ill., 1965-92; pres. Johnson Enterprises Inc. Served with U.S. Army, 1946-47. Named Man and Boy of Year, 1963. Mem. Cook County Pubs. Assn. (pres. 1963, dir.), Profl. Journalistic Soc., Sigma Delta Chi. Home: 44 Park Ln Park Ridge IL 60068-2830

JOHNSON, KENNETT CONRAD, advertising agency executive; b. Crystal City, Mo., Feb. 5, 1927; s. Robert Winthrop and Gladys Agnes (Butler) J.; m. Noreen Ellen Driscoll, July 25, 1953; children: Lydia, Burke. BA in Journalism, U. Mo., 1950. State editor Binghamton Press, N.Y., 1950-55; advt. supr. Southwestern Bell, St. Louis, 1955-59; sr. v.p. Gardner Advt., St. Louis, 1959-63, 69-75, N.Y.C., 1963-64, 65-69; v.p. Butler & Gardner Ltd., London, 1964-65; exec. v.p. Kenrick Advt., St. Louis, 1975-77; exec. v.p. BHN Advt. and Pub. Relations Inc. (formerly Batz Hodgson Neuwoehner), St. Louis, 1977-81, pres., chmn., chief exec. officer, 1981-88, chmn., 1988-89; founder, pres. The Kennett Mktg. Cos., Inc., St. Louis, 1989—. Vice chmn. pub. rels. commn. City of Town and Country, Mo.; campaign comms. chmn. United Way, St. Louis, 1981-83, co-chmn., 1984-89, bd. dirs., 1982-92; bd. dirs. Arts and Edn. Coun. Greater St. Louis, 1988-94, chmn. pub. rels. com., 1989-91, BBB Ea. Mo. and So. Ill., 1985-87, chmn. advt. rev. com., 1985-88; chmn. mktg. comms. 74th PGA Am. championship, Bellerive, 1992. With CIC, 1946-47, Japan. Recipient Clio award Am. TV and Radio Commls. Festival N.Y., 1971. Mem. Am. Assn. Advt. Agys. (chmn. Mo. coun. 1973-74), Am. Advt. Fedn. (gov. 9th dist. 1988-89, chmn. 1989-90, Advt. Man of Yr. 1986, Ad Club Silver medal 1988), Bellerive Country Club (St. Louis). Home and Office: 1798 Ivy Pointe Ct Naples FL 34109-3377

JOHNSON, KERMIT DOUGLAS, minister, retired military officer; b. Mpls., Sept. 2, 1928; s. J. Anton Uno and Anna Judith (Goranson) J.; m. Carolyn Marie Johanson, Dec. 22, 1951; children: Karin Joy, Christopher Douglas. BS, U.S. Mil. Acad., 1951; MDiv, Princeton Theol. Sem., 1960; grad., Command Gen. Staff Coll., 1969, U.S. Army War Coll., 1976. Ordained to ministry, Presbyn. Ch., 1960. Commd. 2d lt. U.S. Army, 1951; infantry co. comdr. U.S. Army, Korea, 1952-53; resigned U.S. Army, 1955, recommd. as chaplain, 1960, advanced through ranks to maj. gen., 1979, served in Vietnam, two tours Federal Republic of Germany; dep. chief of chaplains U.S. Army, Washington, 1978-79, chief of chaplains, 1979-82, ret., 1982; assoc. dir. Ctr. for Def. Info., Washington, 1983-86. Author: Realism and Hope in a Nuclear Age, 1988, Ethics and Counterrevolution: American Involvement in Internal Wars, 1997, chpts. in 5 books on mil. ethics, nuclear issues and just war; contbr. articles to various periodicals. Decorated Bronze Star with oak leaf cluster. Home and Office: 64 Glade Cir E Rehoboth Beach DE 19971-4115 *In this world so full of tragedy, I believe the only cure for an inhuman aloofness from suffering is in our attempt to discern the good news and join with it.*

JOHNSON, KEVIN MAURICE, professional basketball player; b. Sacramento, Mar. 4, 1966. Student, U. Calif., 1987. Basketball player Cleveland Cavaliers, 1987-88, Phoenix Suns, 1988—. Named to Dream Team II, 1994, NBA Most Improved Player, 1989, All-NBA Second Team, 1989-91, 94, All-NBA Third Team, 1992. Office: care Phoenix Suns 201 E Jefferson St Phoenix AZ 85004-2412*

JOHNSON, KEVIN ORLIN, publisher, writer. BA, So. Ill. U., 1974; MA, St. Louis U., 1977; PhD, U. Ill., 1988. CEO Pangaeus Cos., Dallas. Author: Rosary: Mysteries, Meditations, and the Telling of the Beads, 1997, Why Do Catholics Do That? A Guide to Teachings and Practices of the Catholic Church, 1994 (best seller award Pubs. Weekly 1995), Apparitions: Mystic Phenomena and What They Mean, 1998; editor: Missal: The Order of Mass in English, 1997; writer, producer (film series) SeedTime: Saving the World's Future Food in America's Home Gardens, 1997; contbr. articles to profl. jours. Recipient Grand award news writing, med. Coun. Advancement & Support Edn., 1985, Journalism award Cath. Press. Assn., 1988, Gold award Dallas Advt. League TOPS. 1988, 89, Excellence award Comm. Arts Mag., 1989, Best show award AR100 Award Show, 1990. Mem. Seed Savers, Friends of Poplar Forest. Avocations: gardening, native plant conservation. Office: Pangaeus Cos PO Box 670127 Dallas TX 75367-0127

JOHNSON, KEVIN RAYMOND, lawyer, educator; b. Culver City, Calif., June 29, 1958; s. Kenneth R. Johnson and Angela J. (Gallardo) McEachron; m. Virginia Salazar, Oct. 17, 1987; children: Teresa, Tomás, Elena. AB in Econs. with great distinction, U. Calif., 1980; JD magna cum laude, Harvard U., 1983. Bar: Calif. 1985, U.S. Dist. Ct. (no., ea. and so. dists.) Calif. 1985, U.S. Ct. Appeals (9th cir.) 1985, U.S. Supreme Ct. 1991. Rsch asst. to Charles Haar prof. Harvard U., Cambridge, Mass., 1982-83, instr. legal writing, 1982; law clk. to Hon. Stephen Reinhardt U.S. Ct. Appeals (9th cir.), L.A., 1983-84; atty. Heller Ehrman White & McAuliffe, San Francisco, 1984-89; acting prof. law U. Calif., Davis, 1989-92, prof. law, 1992—, assoc. dean for acad. affairs, 1998—; instr. civil procedure, complex litigation, immigration law, refugee law, acting dir. clin. legal edn., spring 1992; mem. legal del. to El Salvador, 1987. Author: How Did You Get To Be Mexican? A White/Brown Man's Search for Identity, 1999; editor: Harvard Law Review, 1981-83; contbr. articles to profl. jours. Bd. dirs. Legal Svcs. No. Calif., 1996—, exec. com., 1997—; bd. dirs. Yolo County ACLU, 1990-93, chmn. legal com., 1991-93; magistrate merit selection panel U.S. Dist. Ct. for Ea. Dist. Calif.; vol. Legal Svcs. Program, San Francisco, Sacramento, Calif.; mem. Lawyers Com. for Civil Rights of the San Francisco Bay Area, 1991—; various pro bono activies. Recipient Commendation, Calif. State Bar, 1985-90, Disting. Tchr. award U. Calif. Davis Sch. of Law, 1993. Mem. ABA (coordinators com. immigration 1998—), Calif. Bar Assn. (standing com. legal svcs. for poor 1992-94, gov. com. continuing edn. bar 1993-98), U. Calif. Alumni Assn. (class sec. Class of 1980), Harvard Club San Francisco, Phi Beta Kappa. Democrat. Roman Catholic. Office: U Calif Sch Law King Hall Davis CA 95617

JOHNSON, KEVIN ROGERS, systems analyst, journalist; b. Dallas, Aug. 10, 1975; s. Dan Rogers and Susan (Hearn) J. BBA, Baylor U., 1997. Electronic editor Baylor Lariat, Waco, Tex., 1994, staff writer, copy desk chief, 1995, city editor, 1996; copy editor intern Rochester (Minn.) Post-Bull., 1996; editor-in-chief Baylor Lariat, 1996, staff photographer, 1997; analyst Frito-Lay, Plano, 1997—. Mem. Assn. Info. Tech. Profls., Soc. Profl. Journalists, Golden Key, Gamma Beta Phi. Avocations: camping, hiking, biking, train riding, road trips.

JOHNSON, KEVIN TODD, physician; b. Mpls., Feb. 26, 1953; s. John Edward and Jeanne Marilyn (Ness) J.; m. Karen Ann Paulson, Aug. 1, 1981; children: Matthew, Elizabeth, Erik. BA magna cum laude, Augustana Coll., Rock Island, Ill., 1975; MD, St. Louis U., 1979; postgrad., Maryville U., St. Louis, 1996—. Resident in internal medicine Med. Coll. Wis., Milw., 1980-82, chief resident, 1982-83, fellow in pulmonary medicine, 1983-85; dir. pulmonary rehab. DePaul Health Ctr., Bridgeton, Mo., 1985—; pulmonologist, internist Northway Internist, 1985—; mem. quality assurance com. Physicians Health Plan, St. Louis, 1992-94; bd. dirs. DePaul Physicians Orgn., Bridgeton, 1994—. Contbr. articles to profl. jours. Active Trinity Luth. Ch., St. Louis, 1987—; bd. dirs. DePaul Cmty. Adv. Bd., St. Louis, 1995—. Fellow Am. Coll. Chest Physicians; mem. Am. Thoracic Soc., Soc. Critical Care Medicine, Am. Coll. Physician Execs., Phi Beta Kappa. Office: Northway Internist 12255 De Paul Dr Ste 550 Bridgeton MO 63044-2510*

JOHNSON, KEYSHAWN, professional football player; b. L.A., July 22, 1972. W. L.A. Coll., U. So. Calif. Wide receiver N.Y. Jets, 1996—. Named wide receiver coll. All-Am. first team The Sporting News, 1995. First round draft pick (1st pick overall) NFL, 1996; mem. AFC Ea. Conf. championship team, 1998. Office: NY Jets 1000 Fulton Ave Hempstead NY 11550*

JOHNSON, KIRSTEN DENISE, elementary education educator; b. L.A., Sept. 21, 1968; d. Daniel Webster Johnson and Marinella Venesia (Ishem) Johnson Miller; 1 child, Khari Malik Manning-Johnson. BBA in Ins., Howard U., 1990; student, Southwestern Sch. Law, L.A., 1991-92, Calif. State U., Dominguez Hills, 1994-97. Asst. Ctr. for Ins. Edn. Howard U., Washington, 1988-89; intern Cigna Ins. Co., L.A., 1989; agt. asst. McLaughlin Co., Washington, 1989-90; legal sec. Harris & Baird, L.A., 1990-92; legal asst. Hamrick & Garrotto, L.A., 1992-94; tchr. 5th grade L.A. Unified Sch. Dist., 1993—; intern Travelers Cos., 1987—; free-lance writer Calif. Mus. Sci., L.A., 1994—; workshop presenter in field. Participant UCLA/CSP Sci. Project; tutor Delinquent Teenage Group Home Residents, 1998—. Nat. Dean;s List, 1987, 88, All Am. scholar, 1989, John Schumacher scholar, 1991, Martin Luther King Jr. scholar, 1996. Mem. NEA (RA del.), UTLA (mem. ho. of reps.), CTA, Internat. Soc. Poets. Democrat. Avocations: reading, traveling, movies, weight lifting.

JOHNSON, KRAIG NELSON, lawyer, mediator; b. Landstuhl, Germany, July 8, 1959; came to U.S., 1966; s. Howard Arthur and Joy Anne (Nelson) J.; m. AmberJade F. Leca, Nov. 13, 1993. BA with honors, Eckerd Coll., 1981; M in Internat. Mgmt., Am. Grad. Sch. Internat. Mgmt., Glendale, Ariz., 1982; JD, Baylor U., 1992. Bar: Fla. 1993; cert. mediator and arbitrator Supreme Ct. of Fla. Mktg. mgr. Jack Eckerd Corp., Clearwater, Fla., 1982-85; mktg. systems mgr. NCS, Inc., Houston, 1985-87; dir. ops. Petro, Inc., El Paso, 1987-90; atty. and shareholder Zimmerman, Shuffield, Kiser & Sutcliffe, P.A., Orlando, Fla., 1992—. Editor: Florida Workers' Compensation Practice, 1994; contbr. articles to profl. jours. Mem. internat. trade and investment adv. bd. Econ. Devel. Commn. of Mid-Fla., Orlando, 1997—; mem. Task Force on Title IX, Baylor U. Bd. of Regents, Waco, 1992-93; bd. dirs. Asian-Am. C. of C., Orlando, 1994-95. Fellow Soc. of Antiquaries of Scotland; mem. Am. Immigration Lawyers Assn., St. Andrew's Soc. of Ctrl. Fla. (bd. dirs., v.p. 1996-98, pres. 1998—), Fla. Bar Assn. (sect. on internat. law and litig.), Order of Barristers. Avocations: sailing, flying, shooting sports, languages, Mandarin Chinese and German. Home: 509 N Hampton Ave Orlando FL 32803 Office: Zimmerman Shuffield Kiser & Sutcliffe PA 315 E Robinson St Ste 600 Orlando FL 32802

JOHNSON, LADY BIRD (MRS. LYNDON BAINES JOHNSON), widow of former President of U.S.; b. Karnack, Tex., Dec. 22, 1912; d. Thomas Jefferson Taylor; B.A., U. Tex., 1933, B.Journalism, 1934, D.Letters, 1964; LL.D., Tex. Woman's U., 1964; D.Letters, Middlebury Coll., 1967; L.H.D., Williams Coll., 1967, U. Ala., 1975; H.H.D., Southwestern U., 1967; m. Lyndon Baines Johnson (36th Pres. U.S.), Nov. 17, 1934 (died Jan. 22, 1973); children: Lynda Bird Johnson Robb, Luci Baines. Mgr. husband's congl. office, Washington, 1941-42; owner, operator radio-TV sta. KTBC, Austin, Tex., 1942-63, cattle ranches, Tex., 1943—. Hon. chmn. Nat. Headstart Program, 1963-68, Town Lake Beautification Project; also cotton and timberlands, Ala. Mem. Advisory council Nat. Parks, Historic Sites, Bldgs. and Monuments; bd. regents U. Tex., 1971-77, mem. internat. conf. steering com., 1969; trustee Jackson Hole Preserve, Am. Conservation Assn., Nat. Geog. Soc.; founder Nat. Wildflower Research Ctr., Austin, 1982. Recipient Togetherness award Marge Champion, 1958; Humanitarian award B'nai B'rith, 1961; Businesswoman's award Bus. and Profl. Women's Club, 1961; Theta Sigma Phi citation, 1962; Disting. Achievement award Washington Heart Assn., 1962; Industry citation Am. Women in Radio and Television, 1963; Humanitarian citation Vols. of Am., 1963; Peabody award for White House TV visit, 1966; Eleanor Roosevelt Golden Candlestick award Women's Nat. Press Club; Damon Woods Meml. award Indsl. Designers Soc. Am., 1972; Conservation Service award Dept. Interior, 1974; Disting. award Am. Legion, 1975; Woman of Year award Ladies Home Jour., 1975; Medal of Freedom, 1977; Nat. Achievement award Am. Hort. Soc., 1984. Life mem. U. Tex. Ex-Students Assn. Episcopalian. Author: A White House Diary, 1970. Address: LBJ Libr 2313 Red River St Austin TX 78705-5702*

JOHNSON, LAEL FREDERIC, lawyer; b. Yakima, Wash., Jan. 22, 1938; s. Andrew Cabot and Gudney M. (Fredrickson) J.; m. Eugenie Rae Call, June 9, 1960; children: Eva Marie, Inga Margaret. AB, Wheaton (Ill.) Coll., 1960; JD, Northwestern U., 1963. Bar: Ill. 1963, U.S. Dist. Ct. (no. dist.) Ill. 1964, U.S. Ct. Appeals (7th cir.) 1966. V.p., gen. counsel Abbott Labs., Abbott Park, Ill., 1981-89, sr. v.p., sec., gen. counsel, 1989-94; of counsel Schiff Hardin & Waite, Chgo., 1995—. Mem. Chgo. panel CPR Inst. for Dispute Resolution; chair Northwestern U. Law Sch. Bd. Mem. ABA, Chgo. Bar Assn., Assn. Gen. Counsel. Office: Schiff Hardin & Waite 6600 Sears Tower Chicago IL 60606

JOHNSON, LAMONT, composer, musician, producer, consultant; b. N.Y.C., Oct. 1, 1941; s. James Arthur and Katie Mae (Mathis) J.; m. France Ellis, may 25, 1978 (div. 1985); children: Astrid-Brett, Neil Collin-Keith, Rand. Student, Manhattan Coll., Syracuse U. Pianist various, 1963—; producer motion pictures various, 1965—, composer, motion picture scores, 1968-82, composer classical works, 1967-76; bd. dirs. Artisan Filmworks; cons. Anheuser-Busch. Pianist/soloist Charley Parker meml. Album, 1964, numerous other recordings including Sun, Moon and Stars, Speed of Light, Aces and Kostelanetz Plays the Academy Award Winner, (with others) Jackies Blues Bag (winner Jazz Showcase Nat. TV Competition 1995, 96), New and Old Gospel; developer several ethnic pieces for prodn. at Lincoln Ctr., N.Y., 1967, in assn. with Maestro Leonard Bernstein and Choreographer Jerome Robbins, classical works including Interstellar Suite, performed by the LaMirada Symphony Orch., 1974-75 and Symphony Number Two in Blues, performed by various symphonic orchs., 1974-76, light operatic works including Everycat and Silas; pianist album Burned By the Passion, 1992 Riverside Jazz Festival; performances for Music Dept. U. Calif. Riverside; contbr. articles to profl. jours. With USAF, 1959-62. Recipient numerous music and film awards including Jazz Heritage Found., Duke Ellington Award for Composer/Arranger, Los Angeles, 1977, Nat. Negro Scholarship Found., 1958, Video Showcase award Nat. Jazz Svc. Orgn., 1993. Mem. ASCAP (recipient standard award, 1977—), Acad. Performing Arts and Scis., Writers Guild of Am., Jazz Heritage Soc. Avocations: gardening, auto restoration. Home: PO Box 120621 San Diego CA 92112-0621

JOHNSON, LARRY DEMETRIC, professional basketball player; b. Tyler, Tex., Mar. 14, 1969. Student, Odessa Jr. Coll.; grad., U. Nevada, Las Vegas, 1991. Basketball player Charlotte Hornets, 1991-96, N.Y. Knicks, 1996—. Recipient John R. Wooden award NCAA, 1991, Naismith award, 1991; named NBA Rookie of Yr., 1992, NBA All-Rookie team, 1992, Sporting News Coll. Player of Yr., 1991, Sporting News All-Am. First Team, 1990-91; mem. NBA All-Star team, 1993, 94, Dream Team II, 1994. Mem. NCAA Divsn. I Championship Team, 1990. Office: NY Knicks Two Pennsylvania Plz New York NY 10121-0091*

JOHNSON, LARRY WALTER, lawyer; b. Princeton, Minn., May 21, 1934; s. Alfred Herbert and Lillian Martha (Wetter) J.; m. Mary Ann Lindstrom, June 14, 1958; children: Lawrence W. II, Kristin Jane. BS in Law, U. Minn., 1957, LLB, 1959. Bar: Minn. 1959. Assoc. Dorsey & Whitney, Mpls., 1961-66, ptnr., 1967-95, of counsel, 1996—. Co-author, co-editor Minnesota Estate Administration, 1968. Bd. dirs. Minn. Bus. Found. Excellence in Edn., St. Paul. 1981-85, Walker Sponsor's Fund, Mpls., 1987; trustee Walker Meth. Residence and Health Services, Inc., Mpls., 1985-86. Served to 1st lt. U.S. Army, 1959-61. Fellow Am. Coll. of Trust and Estate Counsel, mem. Minn. Bar Assn., Hennepin County Bar Assn., Mpls. Athletic Club. Republican. Congregationalist. Avocation: handball. Home: 5400 Highwood Dr W Minneapolis MN 55436-1225 Office: Dorsey & Whitney 220 S 6th St Ste 2200 Minneapolis MN 55402-1498*

JOHNSON, LAURENCE F., college executive; b. Corpus Christi, Tex., Dec. 17, 1950; s. Howard E. and B. Louise (Franklin) J.; m. Maria Guadalupe Cisneros-Solís, Dec. 15, 1979; children: Alexis Elizabeth, Laurence Alejandro. BA, U. Tex., 1975, PhD, 1993; MBA, S.W. Tex. State U., San Marcos, 1988. Divsn. chair Austin C.C., 1983-93; assoc. dir. League for Innovation in the C.C., Mission Viejo, Calif., 1994-96; exec. v.p. Terra C.C., Fremont, Ohio, 1996—; mem. adv. bd. Invest Learning, Inc., San Diego, 1994-96; postdoctoral trainee Inst. for Ednl. Mgmt., Harvard U., 1998. Author: Embracing the Tiger, 1997; contbr. articles to profl. jours.; editor: Leadership Abstracts, 1994-96, Learning Without Limits, 1996, Common Ground, 1996; gen. editor C.C. Jour. Rsch. and Practice, Denton, Tex., 1994-97. Mem. Tri-County Mental Health Bd., Fremont, Ohio. Recipient Sloan Rsch. award Am. Assn. C.C.s, Washington, 1996, Goodman Malamuth award Am. Assn. Univ. Adminstrs., Washington, 1994, Internat. Tchg. Excellence award Nat. Inst. for Staff and Orgnl. Devel., 1991; named to Exec. Leadership Inst., League for Innovation, Costa Mesa, Calif., 1995. Mem. Nat. Coun. Instrnl. Adminstrs., Continuous Quality Improvement Network (instl. rep.), Nat. Learning Infrastructure Initiative (instl. rep.), Phi Kappa Phi, Kappa Delta Pi. Avocations: music, scuba, skiing, reading. Office: Terra C C 2830 Napoleon Rd Fremont OH 43420-9670

JOHNSON, LAVERNE ST. CLAIR, retired elementary school educator; b. Danville, Va.; d. Emanuel Linwood and Lula St. Clair (Yarbrough) White; m. Cornell A. Johnson, Apr. 10, 1955 (div. Apr. 1982); children: Cassandra St. Clair, LeBrahne Cornell. Student, Howard U., 1950-55, Allen U., 1955; BA, Queens Coll., 1977, MA, 1986. Cert. and lic. in reading edn., common br., N.Y. Asst. tchr. 1st Hebrew Day Nursery, Bklyn., 1967-75; tchr. United Youth Action Day Care, Bklyn., 1977-80, Charles R. Drew Day Care Ctr., Queens Village, N.Y., 1980-83, N.Y.C. Bd. Edn., Bklyn., 1983-95; ret., 1995. Composer childrens' music; author: (childrens' poems) Fall Time Fall Time, 1974. Mem. Com. to Eliminate Media Offensive to African People, St. Albans, N.Y., 1988—, Dem. Club, St. Albans, Bklyn. Philharmonic Chorus, St. Albans Congl. Ch. choir, Howard U. Choir, Carr-Hill Singers, Cambria Heights Civic Assn., other choral groups. Mem. United Fedn. Tchrs. Howard U. Alumni Club (sec. L.I. chpt. 1970-79), Lioness (v.p. Cambria Heights, N.Y. 1980-82, cert. of appreciation 1980-89). Avocations: musical composition, poetry, aerobics, church activities, community groups.

JOHNSON, LAWRENCE ALAN, cereal technologist, educator, administrator; b. Columbus, Ohio, Apr. 30, 1947; s. William and Wyoma (Swift) J.; m. Bernice Ann Miller, June 15, 1969; children: Bradley, David. BS, Ohio State U., 1969; MS, N.C. State U., 1971; PhD, Kans. State U., 1978. Rsch. chemist Durkee Foods div. SCM Corp., Strongsville, Ohio, 1973-75; assoc. rsch. chemist Food Protein R&D Ctr. Tex. A&M U., College Station, 1978-85; prof.-in-charge Ctr. for Crops Utilization Rsch. Iowa State U., Ames, 1991—; mem. rsch. com. Am. Soybean Assn., St. Louis, 1987-91, Nat. Corn Grower's Assn., St. Louis, 1990-91. Author: (with others) Handbook of Cereals, 1991; editor: (book/procs.) Technologies for Value-Added Products from Proteins and Co-Products, 1989; contbr. more than 130 articles to profl. jours. 1st lt. U.S. Army, 1971-73, Vietnam. Recipient Rsch. award Corn Refiners Assn., 1998. Mem. Am. Assn. Cereal Chemists (assoc. editor jour. 1982-85), Am. Soc. Agrl. Engrs., Am. Oil Chemists Soc. (assoc. editor jour. 1989—, Archer Daniels Midland Rsch. award 1986), Royal Swedish Acad. Agr. and Forestry (fgn. mem. 1999), Inst. Food Techs. Republican. Lutheran. Achievements include 11 patents. Home: 2226 Buchanan Dr Ames IA 50010-4368 Office: Ctr Crops Utilization Rsch Iowa State U Ames IA 50011

JOHNSON, LAWRENCE EUGENE, lawyer; b. Morrison, Ill., Sept. 26, 1937; s. Frederick Eugene and Ruth Helen (Lorke) J.; m. Debby Karen McCaleb, June 17, 1961; children: Mark Lawrence, Eric Eugene, Lori Ann Johnson Purtzer. BS, No. Ill. U., 1960, MS, 1962; JD, U. Ill., 1965. Bar: Ill. 1965, U.S. Dist. Ct. (ctrl. dist.) Ill. 1965, U.S. Ct. Appeals (7th cir.) 1965; lic. pilot. Pvt. practice, 1965-68; states atty. County of Champaign, Ill., 1968-72; pvt. practice Champaign, 1972—; spl. asst. atty. gen. litigation Ill. Dept. Revenue, 1982-86, Ill. Dept. Labor, 1982-86, Ill. Dept. Transp., 1986-90, Ill. Dept. Conservation, 1988-90, Ill. Dept. Nuclear Safety, 1989-90. Bd. mem. Ill. State Bd. Elections, 1990-95, vice chmn., 1993-95; chmn. Ill. Liquor Control Commn., 1972-73; hearing officer Ill. State Bd. Elections, 1988-90; mem. airport hazard zoning task force divsn. aeronautics Ill. Dept. Transp., 1987-88. With U.S. Army, 1955-57. Mem. U.S. Pilots Assn. (bd. dirs. 1989—), Ill. Pilots Assn. (pres. 1991-93, v.p., bd. dirs. 1989-91), Illini Area Pilots Assn. (pres. 1989-91), Ill. Trial Lawyers Assn., Champaign Urbana Kiwanis Early Risers, Champaign Urbana Ambucs, AMVETS (life). Office: Johnson & Assocs PO Box 1127 202 W Hill St Champaign IL 61824-1127

JOHNSON, LAWRENCE M., banker; b. 1940. Student, U. Hawaii. With Bank of Hawaii, Honolulu, 1963—, exec. v.p., 1980-84, vice chmn., 1984-89, pres., 1989—, now chmn. bd., CEO; pres. Pacific Century Fin. Corp. Office: Bancorp Hawaii Inc 130 Merchant St PO Box 2900 Honolulu HI 96846-0001 Office: Pacific Century Fin Corp Financial Plz of the Pacific 130 Merchant St Honolulu HI 96813-4450

JOHNSON, LAWRENCE WILBUR, JR., lawyer; b. Columbia, S.C., Apr. 17, 1955; s. Lawrence Wilbur and Ruth (Cooper) J.; m. Cindy Ann Small, May 26, 1979. BS in Acctg., U. S.C., 1976, JD, 1979. Bar: S.C. 1979, U.S. Dist. Ct. S.C. 1979, U.S. Ct. Appeals (4th cir.) 1980. Jud. clk. 3d Jud. Cir. Ct., Bishopville, S.C., 1979-80; ptnr. Robinson, McFadden, Moore, Pope, Williams, Taylor & Brailsford, P.A., Columbia, 1980-87; shareholder Adams, Quackenbush, Herring & Stuart, P.A., Columbia, 1987-94; ptnr. Young, Clement, Rivers & Tisdale, LLP, Columbia, 1994-96, Johnson Law Firm, Columbia, 1996—. Mem. S.C. Bar Assn., Richland County Bar Assn. (pres. bankruptcuy law sect. 1982-85), S.C. Bankruptcy Law Assn. (bd. dirs.), S.C. Bar Ho. of Dels., Greater Columbia C. of C. (bd. dirs.), Com. of 100 (chmn.), Forest Lake Club , U. S.C. Alumni Assn. (bd. dirs. 1980-82), Chi Psi, Omicron Delta Kappa. Republican. Baptist. Avocation: golf. Home: 415 Sesqui Trl Columbia SC 29223-2938 Office: Johnson Law Firm PA 1728 Main St Ste 221 Columbia SC 29201-2844 also: PO Box 883 Columbia SC 29202-0883

JOHNSON, LAYMON, JR., management analyst; b. Jackson, Miss., Sept. 1, 1948; s. Laymon and Bertha (Yarbrough) J.; m. Charlene J. Johnson, Nov. 13, 1982. B in Tech., U. Dayton, 1970; MS in Sys. Mgmt., U. So. Calif., 1978. Mem. tech. staff Rockwell Internat., Canoga Park, Calif., 1975-77; sr. dynamics engr. Gen. Dynamics, Pomona, Calif., 1978-83; fin. sys. specialist Northrop Corp., Pico Rivera, Calif., 1983-90; utility budget analyst dept. water and power City of L.A., 1991-97; mgmt. analyst L.A. Police Dept., 1997—. Lt. comdr. USNR, 1970-92. Mem. Am. Philatelic Soc., Libr. Congress Assocs., So. Calif. Crime Analysts Assn., L.A. County Mus. Art, Music Ctr. L.A., ISSM Triumvirate, Trojan Club, Tau Alpha Pi. Democrat. Roman Catholic.

JOHNSON, LELAND "LEE" HARRY, social services administrator; b. Moscow Twp., Wis., Jan. 30, 1947; s. Amos Sanford and Bethellen (Otto) J.; m. Laurel Landry; children: Najib, Zack, Jessica, Karine. B degree, Gettysburg Coll., 1969; M degree, Ind. U.-Purdue U., 1971. Supr. psychiat. social work Rock County Guidance Clinic, Beloit, Wis., 1971-73; acting adminstr. Rock County Guidance Clinic, Janesville, Wis., 1974; program dir., coord. Rock County Mental Health Svcs., 1974-75; program dir. Columbia County Home & Unified Bd., Portage, Wis., 1975; svcs. program dir. Columbia County Home & Unified Bd., Portage, Wyocena, Wis., 1975-77; dir. human svcs. Columbia County Health Svcs., Portage, 1977; exec. dir. Navajo County Guidance Clinic, Winslow, Ariz., 1977-78, Coconino Community Guidance Ctr. Inc., Flagstaff, Ariz., 1978-85; human svcs. dir Eau Claire (Wis.) County Human Svcs., 1985-89; from dep. dist. adminstr. to dist. adminstr. Fla. Dept. Children and Families, Jacksonville, 1989—. Mem. NASW, Acad. Cert. Social Workers. Home: 219 Segovia Rd Saint Augustine FL 32086-6447 Office: Dept Children and Families 5920 Arlington Expy Jacksonville FL 32211-7156

JOHNSON, LENNART INGEMAR, materials engineering consultant; b. Mpls., Dec. 23, 1924; s. Sixten Richard Wilhem and Marie Augusta Johnson; m. Muriel Grant, Oct. 7, 1961; 1 child, Sandra Lee. BS in Chem. Engring., U. Minn., 1948. Petroleum engr. Northwestern Refining Co., New Brighton, Minn., 1948-49; sr. engr. Ordnance Div. Honeywell, Hopkins, Minn., 1949-67, prin. materials engr. Def. Sys. Div., 1967-69, supr. engring. Def. Sys. Div., 1969-87; staff engr. Armament Sys. Div. Honeywell Inc., Hopkins, Minn., 1987-88; cons. Soc. Automotive Engring., Warrandale, Pa., 1989—; cons. Ecubed Assocs., Inc., 1993—; forum leader and presenter, U. Wis. Engring. Inst., Madison, 1965. Contbr. articles to profl. jours. Mem. credentials com. Hennepin County Rep. Conv., Minn., 1972, alt. del., 1974. Recipient Prize Paper award, Inst. Elec. Engrs. Fellow Am. Inst. Chemists; mem. Soc. Automotive Engrs. (sec. composites com. 1986-87, chmn. 1987-88), Am. Inst. Chem. Engrs. Achievements include development of and research in injection molding technology, urethane and epoxy casting resins, and urethane foaming resins; preparation of numerous Aerospace Material Specifications published by Society of Automotive Engineers. Home and Office: 14109 Mount Ter Minnetonka MN 55345-3826

JOHNSON, LEONARD GUSTAVE, research mathematician, consultant; b. Neguanee, Mich., Mar. 12, 1918; s. Werner Leonard and Sophia (Larsson) J.; m. Taimi Marie Lappi, July 5, 1944; 1 child, Virginia. BA, No. Mich. U., 1940; MA, U. Mich., 1941. Math. tchr. Channing (Mich.) H.S., 1941-42; rsch. mathematician Gen. Motors Corp., Detroit, 1945-74; seminar leader Detroit Rsch. Inst., Grosse Pointe Farm, Mich., 1958-98. Author: The Statistical Treatment of Fatigue Experiments, 1964, Theory and Technique of Variation Research, 1964; editor Statis. Bull. Detroit Rsch. Inst., 1961-98. State Coll. scholar U. Mich., 1940-41. Fellow Am. Soc. Quality (cert. reliability engr.); mem. Soc. Automotive Engrs., Indsl. Math. Soc. (treas. 1950-51, pres. 1994-97, Gold award 1991), Kappa Delta Pi, Phi Beta Kappa. Avocations: writing poetry, computer software development. Home and Office: 31811 Bretz Dr Warren MI 48093-1670

JOHNSON, LEONARD HJALMA, lawyer; b. Thomasville, Ga., May 22, 1957; s. Hjalma Eugene and Laura Nell (McLeod) J.; m. Nancy Louise Brock, Dec. 13, 1981; children: Brock Hjalma, Paige McLeod. BSBA, U. Fla., 1978, JD, 1980. Assoc. Dayton, Sumner, Luckie and McKnight, Dade City, 1981-83, Greenfelder and Mander, Dade City, 1983-84; pres. East Coast Bank Corp., Ormond Beach, Fla., 1982—; pvt. practice Dade City, 1984-89; ptnr. Schrader, Johnson, Auvil & Brock, P.A., Dade City, 1990—; vice chmn. Bank of Madison (Fla.) County, 1985-88, N. Fla. Bank Corp., Madison, 1985-88, Bank at Ormond By-the-Sea, 1983—; vice chmn. Lake State Bank, 1989-96. Bd. dirs. Downtown Dade City Main St. Inc., 1987-96, East Pasco Habitat for Humanity, 1998—; trustee Dade City Hosp., 1994-96, chmn., 1996; mem. Leadership Fla. Mem. ABA, Fla. Bar Assn., Pasco County Bar Assn. (sec. 1982-83), Young Pres. Orgn. (edn. chmn. Fla. chpt. 1997-98, chpt. chmn. 1998-99), Dade City C. of C., Fla. Blue Key. Republican. Methodist.

JOHNSON, LEONARD JAMES, lawyer; b. Belmond, Iowa, May 25, 1951. BA in Govt., St. Johns U., Collegeville, Minn., 1974; JD, U. Iowa, 1977. Bar: Mo. 1977, U.S. Dist. Ct. (we. dist.) Mo. 1977, Kans. 1978, U.S. Dist. Ct. Kans. 1978, U.S. Ct. Appeals (10th cir.) 1985, U.S. Ct. Appeals (8th cir.) 1986 . Assoc. Morrison & Hecker LLP, Kansas City, Mo., 1977-82, ptnr., 1982—; mem. fed. practice com. Western Dist. Mo., Kansas City, 1986-93. Mem. ABA, Mo. Bar Assn., Def. Research Inst. Home: 4330 W 207th St Bucyrus KS 66013-9647 Office: 2600 Grand Blvd Kansas City MO 64108-4613

JOHNSON, LEONARD MORRIS, pediatric surgeon; b. Gowanda, N.Y., June 11, 1931; s. Leonard Brynolf and Helen Berdena (Morris) J.; m. Ann Marie Homer, Mar. 30, 1968; children: H. Leif B. Johnson, Nils A.C. Johnson. BA, Haverford Coll., 1954; MD, U. Pa., 1958; MS in Surgery, U. Minn., Mayo Grad. Sch., Rochester, 1966. Diplomate Am. Bd. Gen. Surgery; cert. special competence in pediatric surgery. Intern Colo. Gen. Hosp., Denver, 1958-59; fellow in gen. surgery Mayo Clinic, Rochester, 1959-63; fellow in pediatric surgery Children's Mercy Hosp., Kansas City, Mo., 1964-65; vis. pediatric surgeon Acad. Hosp., Uppsala, Sweden, 1967; registrar in pediatric urology Alder Hey Children's Hosp., Liverpool, Eng., 1967-68; gen. surgeon SS Hope (Project Hope), Guayaquil, Ecuador, 1964; gen. and pediatric surgeon SS Hope (Project Hope), Conakry, Guinea, 1965, Nicaragua, Colombia, Sri Lanka, 1965-68; pediatric surgeon Children's Hosp., Oakland, Calif., 1969—; chief of dept. of surgery Children's Hosp., Oakland, 1989-92. Bd. dirs. Children's Hosp., Oakland, Calif., 1982-91; bd. trustees Children's Hosp. Found., Oakland, 1986-95; mem. exec. bd. Mt. Diablo-Silverado Coun. Boy Scouts Am., 1996—. Recipient Order Ruben Dario, Pres. Republic of Nicaragua, Managua, 1966; recipient Bronze Bambino award Children's Hosp., Oakland, 1990. Fellow Am. Coll. of Surgeons, Surgical fellow Am. Acad. of Pediatrics; mem. AMA, Am. Trauma Soc. (founding mem.), Am. Pediat.-Surg. Assn., Pacific Assn. Pediatric Surgeons, Brit. Assn. Pediat. Surgeons, Calif. Med. Assn., Alameda-Contra Costa Med. Assn. Republican. Avocations: photography, hiking, skiing, travel, music.

JOHNSON, LEONARD R., industrial engineer, educator; b. Mar. 22, 1946. BS, Mont. State U., 1968, MS, 1970; PhD, W.Va. U., 1984. Rsch. indsl. engr. U.S. Forestry Svc., Morgantown, W.Va., 1970-73; rsch. engr. Mont. State U., Bozeman, 1974; prof., dept. head U. Idaho, Moscow, 1974—; interim dean U. Idaho, 1994-95. E-mail: ljohnson@uidaho.edu.

JOHNSON, LESLIE CAROLE, editor, publisher; b. Mpls., June 16, 1942; d. Lester Carl and Lillian Irene (Barrette) Lindstrom; m. Dennis Arthur Johnson, Aug. 8, 1964 (div. Sept. 2, 1988); children: Anthony James, Renee Denise; m. Willard Bromberg Shapira, Feb. 3, 1996; stepchildren: Eve Shapira Roycraft, Joel Shapira, Stephen Shapira. BA in Journalism, U. Minn., 1964. Freelance writer Mpls., 1964-73; editor, pub. The Mississippi Rag, Mpls., 1973—. Pres. Twin Cities Jazz Soc., Mpls., St. Paul, 1982-84, bd. dirs., 1978-84; arts adv. com. bd. dirs. Met. Coun./Regional Arts Coun., St. Paul, 1986-89; vol. driver Meals on Wheels, Mpls., 1986-89; vol. cook Loaves & Fishes, Mpls., 1988-94; vol. Midwest Cmty. Hospice, Mpls., 1991—. Mem. NAFE, Internat. Assn. Jazz Educators. Democrat. Roman Catholic. Avocations: reading, walking, music appreciation. Home: 5644 Morgan Ave S Minneapolis MN 55419-1525 Office: The Mississippi Rag 9448 Lyndale Ave So Ste 100 Bloomington MN 55420

JOHNSON, LESTER FREDRICK, artist; b. Mpls., Jan. 27, 1919; s. Edwin August and Helma Marie (Holmes) J.; m. Josephine Valenti, Feb. 12, 1949; children: Leslie Maria, Anthony Edwin. Student, Mpls. Art Inst., 1939-41, St. Paul Art Sch., 1939-41, Art Inst. Chgo., 1943. Prof. painting Yale U., 1964—, dir. studies, 1968—; Mem. Milford (Conn.) Fine Arts Council, 1972-73; mem. art adv. com. Housatonic Community Coll., Stratford, Conn., 1969-87. One-man shows, Zabriskei Gallery, N.Y.C., Martha Jackson Gallery, N.Y.C., Donald Morris, Detroit, Walter Moos Gallery, N.Y.C., Toronto, Can., David Barnett Gallery, Milw., Mpls. Art Inst., Dayton Art Inst., Fort Worth Art Inst., Yale Univ. Mus., Gimpel Fils Gallery, London, Gimpel Hanover Gallery, Zurich, Switzerland, Westmoreland Mus. Art, Greenburg, Pa. (traveling), Augustana Coll. Centennial Hall Gallery, Pa. Acad. Fine Arts, Newport Harbor Art Mus., Edward Thorpe Gallery, N.Y.C., Gimpel-Weitzenhofer Gallery, N.Y.C., Peter Findley Gallery, N.Y.C., Denise Dade' Gallery, N.Y.C., Joseph Rickards Gallery, N.Y.C.; exhibited in numerous group shows; represented in permanent collections, Albright Knox Mus., Dayton Art Inst., Met. Mus. Art, N.Y.C., Mus. Modern Art, New Sch. for Social Research, Phoenix Art Mus., U. Nebr., Walker Art Mus. Recipient fellowship Trumbull Coll., 1966—; Creative Arts award Brandeis U., 1978; Guggenheim fellow, 1973. Mem. Nat. Acad. Design (elected assoc., coun.). Home: PO Box 7582 Greenwich CT 06836-7582 Office: Yale U Sch Art York And Chapel St New Haven CT 06520

JOHNSON, LINDA ARLENE, petroleum and flatbed semi-freight transporter; b. Sparta, Wis., Mar. 6, 1946; d. Clarence Julius and Arlene Mae (Yahnke) Jessie; children: Darrick, Larissa. With Union Nat. Bank & Trust Co., Sparta, 1964-69, Hill, Christensen & Co., CPA's, Tomah, Wis., 1969-75; owner Johnson of Wis. Oil Co., Inc., Tomah, 1969-95; with Larry's Express, Inc., Tomah, 1975-78; owner Johnson Rentals, 1979—, Johnson of Wis. Transport Co., Inc., Tomah, 1982—. Mem. St. Paul's Luth. Ch., Tomah. Mem. Petroleum Marketers Assn. Am., Nat. Assn. Convenience Stores, Am. Trucking Assn., Wis. Assn. Convenience Stores, Petroleum Marketers Assn. Wis., Tomah Area C. of C., Tomah Area Credit Union (bd. dirs. 1993—, sec. 1993-94), Rotary Club Tomah (dir. 1997—). Home and Office: 24011 Flatter Ave Tomah WI 54660-4424

JOHNSON, LINDA THELMA, information specialist; b. New Britain, Conn., May 18, 1954; d. Oren and Lois Elizabeth (Armstrong) J.; 1 child, Portia Lauren. BS in Econs., Va. State U., 1978; cert. in computer programming, Morse Sch. Bus., 1978; cert. in legal assisting, Morse Sch. Bus., Hartford, Conn., 1994. Programmer analyst Vitro Automation Industries, Silver Spring, Md., 1980-83; sr. analyst Sci. Mgmt. Corp., Lanham, Md., 1984-86; sr. programmer analyst Applied Mgmt. Scis. Inc., Silver Spring, 1986; programmer analyst Computer Data Systems Inc., Rockville, Md., 1986-88; project leader systems cert. dept. Arbitron Co., Laurel, Md., 1988-90; systems analyst Engring. and Econ. Rsch., Inc., Vienna, Va., 1990; computer cons. Comsys Tech. Svcs. Inc., Rockville, 1990, CPU Inc., Fairfax, Va., 1991; quality assurance cons. Cigna Corp., Bloomfield, Conn., 1992; info. systems specialist The Travelers Ins. Group, Hartford, Conn., 1994-96; mem. rsch. bd. advisors The Am. Biographical Inst., Inc. Mem. NAFE, NAACP, Am. Bus. Women's Assn. Democrat. Baptist. Avocations: crossword puzzles, horseback riding. Home: 386 Park Ave Bloomfield CT 06002-3106

JOHNSON, LINNEA RUTH, federal judge; b. 1946. BA, U. Ga.; JD, Stetson U., 1971. Asst. state atty. Dade County, Fla.; asst. U.S. atty. So. Dist. Fla.; magistrate judge U.S. Dist. Ct. (so. dist.) Fla., 1987—. Office: 131 US Courthouse 300 NE 1st Ave Miami FL 33132-2126

JOHNSON, LOERING M., design engineer, historian, consultant; b. Dickinson, N.D., Sept. 22, 1926; s. Bertel C. and A.S. Victoria (Worra) J.; m. Maral Austin, June 21, 1952; children: Mairi Victoria, Maureen Kay, Marc Douglas, Mara Elizabeth. BSEE, U. N.D., 1952; MS in Engring. Sci., Rensselaer Poly. Inst., 1961. Lic. profl. engr., Conn. Engring. trainee Argonne Nat. Lab. E.I. duPont, Chgo., 1952-53; engr. E.I. duPont de Nemours, Inc., Aiken, S.C., 1953-55; design engr. Combustion Engring., Inc., N.Y.C., Windsor, Conn., 1955-57; supr. analog computer Combustion Engring., Inc., Windsor, 1957-59, supr., mgr. Inst. Controls Elec. Design, 1959-70, mgr. standards, records and office automation, 1979-85; cons. engr. LMJ Enterprises, Tariffville, Conn., 1985—; adj. asst. prof. U. Hartford, West Hartford, Conn., 1986-93. Author: (with others) Standard Handbook for Electrical Engineers, 1987; contbr. articles to profl. jours. Chmn. Constitutional Bicentennial Com., Simsbury, Conn., 1987-88; historian Simsbury Hist. Soc., 1989-95. With U.S. Army, 1946-48. Named Engr. of Yr. Conn. Soc. Profl. Engrs., Hamden, 1983, Hometown Hero Town of Simsbury, 1989. Cellow IEEE (life, stds. bd. 1978-81, chmn. environ. quality com. 1982-83, Stds. medallion nuclear power engring. com. 1975); mem. NSPE (life, nat. dir. 1981-84), VFW (dist. 3 judge adv. 1985-87), Toastmasters Internat. (dist. 53, area B lt. gov. 1980-81, Toastmaster of Yr. 1983), Conn. Assn. Mcpl. Historians (pres. 1991-94, Citizenship and Cmty. Svc. award 1999), Sons of Norway, Sigma Xi. Republican. Episcopalian. Avocations: writing, photography. Office: LMJ Enterprises PO Box 372 Tariffville CT 06081-0372

JOHNSON, LOLA NORINE, advertising and public relations executive, educator; b. Austin, Minn., Dec. 28, 1942; d. Alton E. and Evelyn M. (Quast) Milbrath; m. Dennis D. Johnson, June 15, 1963 (div. July 1973); children: Brenda J., Erik B. Attended, Coll. of St. Thomas. Pub. rels. account rep. Kerker & Assocs. Advt. and Pub. Rels., Bloomington, Minn., 1973-78; comm. mgr. Norwest Bank Mpls., 1978-83; dir. media rels., account supr. Edwin Neuger & Assocs. Pub. Rels., Mpls., 1983-85; v.p., mng. dir. The Richards Group, Mpls., 1985-86; owner, pres. PR Plus, Edina, Minn., 1986—; mem. cmty. faculty, instr., counselor Met. State U., Mpls., St. Paul, 1980-93. Cons. comm. United Way, Mpls., 1982. Recipient Gold award United Way Mpls., 1982. Home and Office: PR Plus 7151 York Ave S Apt 807 Minneapolis MN 55435-4435

JOHNSON, LOWELL C., state commissioner; b. Dodge County, Nebr., June 12, 1920; B.S. in Mech. Engring., U. Nebr., 1942; m. Ruth Marion Sloss, June 21, 1943; children: Mark C., Kent R., James S., Nancy L. Farm and property mgmt. exec.; pres. Johnson-Sloss Land Co., North Bend, Nebr.; mem. Nebr. Legislature, 1980-93, vice-chmn. legis. appropriations com., mem. com. on coms.; commr. Nebr. Pub. Svc. Commn., 1995—; former bd. dirs. Equitable Fed. Savs. Bank, Fremont, Nebr.; former trustee Meml. Hosp. Dodge County; former mem. adv. council Nebr. Dept. Labor; mem. behavioral scis. adv. com. Immanuel Hosp., Omaha; former mem. County Sch. Reorgn. Com.; former field rep. Congressman Charles Thone; former pres. bd. dirs. North Bend Sr. Citizens Home. Mem. Am. Legion, Fremont and North Bend C. of C. Clubs: Masons, Shriners, Rotary. Office: PO Box 370 North Bend NE 68649-0370

JOHNSON, LUAN, disaster management consultant; b. Provo, Utah, Apr. 27, 1956; d. Jack R. and Colleen (Kesler) J. BA, Brigham Young U., 1981, MA, 1984; PhD, U. Wash., 1994. Dir. Teaching Resource Ctr., Provo, 1980-84; teaching asst. communications dept. Brigham Young U., Provo, 1982-83; counselor Master Acad., Salt Lake City, 1985; ednl. designer, program mgr. City of Sunnyvale, 1986-90; tchg. asst., rsch. asst., speech comm. dept. U. Wash., Seattle, 1991-93; program mgr. City of Seattle, 1993—. Recipient Best Ednl. Campaign award Internat. Assn. of Emergency mgrs., 1998. Pres. Youth Assn. Retarded Children, Brigham City, 1976-77. Recipient Nat. League of Cities Award for Innovators, 1990, Nat. Coord. Coun. on Emergency Mgmt. Best Newsletter award, 1996, 98, 1st pl.-best ednl. campaign Internat. ASsn. Emergency Mgrs., 1998. Mem. Phi Kappa Phi. Mem. LDS Ch. Avocation: collecting and flying kites. Home: 21329 76th Ave W Apt 11 Edmonds WA 98026-7534 Office: SPAN 23632 Hwy 99 Ste F322 Edmonds WA 98026-9206

JOHNSON, LYNNE A., lawyer; b. Oct. 25, 1951; d. Gaylar Winton and Donna Lucille (Tolford) J. AB in Econs. with departmental honors and distinction, Vassar Coll., 1973; JD, Yale U., 1976. Bar: Ga. 1977, N.Y. 1981. Asst. to gen. counsel Sys. and Technics, S.A., Gland, Switzerland, 1976-77; assoc. Powell, Goldstein, Frazer & Murphy, Atlanta, 1977-79; assoc. Fried, Frank, Harris, Shriver & Jacobson, N.Y.C., 1979-97, spl. counsel, 1997—, dir. corp. adminstrn., 1998—. Contgb. author: Exit Age: Reconsidering Compulsory Education for Adolescents: Studies in Law, Education and Social Science, 1981. Hon. grad. fellow for legal studies, 1973-74. Mem. ABA, Am. Soc. Internat. Law, Internat. Bar Assn., Inter-Am. Bar Assn., Assn. Immigration and Nationality Lawyers, N.Y. County Lawyers' Assn., State Bar Assn., N.Y. State Bar Assn., Soc. Univ. Patent Adminstrs., Lotus Club. Office: One New York Pla New York NY 10004

JOHNSON, MADELINE MITCHELL, retired administrative assistant; b. Cleve., Oct. 24, 1930; d. Maidlon and Katherine (Reynolds) Mitchell; m. Elvyn Frank Johnson, Dec. 4, 1954. BS, Case Western Res. U., 1976. Adminstrv. asst. Fed. Res. Bank Cleve., 1950-92, tng. coord. data svcs., 1988-92, ombudsman rep., 1989-92; ret., 1992; mem. tng. task force bd. govs. FRS, Washington, 1987-92. Chair bd. trustees Affinity Bapt. Ch., 1990-93; trustee N.E. Ohio Cmty. Mental Health Ctr. Mem. Am. Bus. Women's Assn. (pres. 1986-88, Women of Yr. Cleve. chpt. 1987), Nat. Coun. Negro Women, Top Ladies of Distinction (Woman of Yr. Cleve. chpt. 1993-94, pres. 1995-97), Am. Bapt. Women (treas.). Avocations: golf, swimming, reading. Home: 33705 Wellingford Ct Solon OH 44139-6600

JOHNSON, MAGIC See JOHNSON, EARVIN

JOHNSON, MALCOLM CLINTON, JR., publishing consultant; b. Jersey City, Sept. 4, 1925; s. Malcolm Clinton and Edna Menard (Freeman) J.; m. Jean Anne Guinane, Dec. 28, 1963 (div. 1974); children: Clinton, Brian. Student, Harvard U., 1943-44, Amos Tuck Sch. Bus. Adminstrn., 1944-45; A.B., Dartmouth Coll., 1946; M.S., U. Ill., 1947. Editor, McGraw Hill Book Co., N.Y.C., 1949-60; sr. editor McGraw Hill Book Co., 1960-62, editor in chief engring. and sci., 1962-65; editor, pub. coll. dept. Time Life Books, N.Y.C., 1965-67; v.p. publ. W.A. Benjamin Inc., N.Y.C., 1967-70; v.p., editorial dir. book div. R.R. Bowker, N.Y.C., 1970-73; dir. NYU Press, N.Y.C., 1973-80; pres. Malcolm Johnson Assos. (Publ. Cons.), N.Y.C., 1980—. Served to lt. (j.g.) USNR, 1943-45. Mem. Coll. Publs. Group (chmn. 1968-69), N.Y. Acad. Scis., Motovun Group European Publs., Chi Phi. Clubs: Harvard, Yale, NYU (N.Y.C.); Saltaire Yacht (N.Y.); Potlach (Eluthera, B.W.I.); Publishers Lunch (sec.-treas. 1978-79).

JOHNSON, MARC JAY, judge; b. Syracuse, N.Y., Dec. 3, 1954; s. Alfred Loomis and Rose (DePhillips) J.; m. Kristi Ann Griffith, Nov. 5, 1988; children: Courtney Rose, Brianna Lynn. B, St. Lawrence U., 1977; JD, Western New England Coll., 1980. Atty. pvt. practice, N.Y., 1985-94; adminstrv. law judge Workers Compensation Bd., N.Y., 1994—. Author: In the East, 1994. Capt. U.S. Army, 1981-89. Decorated Army Commendation medal, Army Achievement medal. Mem. Am. Philatelic Soc., Syracuse Stamp Club (Grand award 1991). Avocations: Iaido, postal history, reading, travel. Office: NY State Workers Compensation Bd 935 James St Syracuse NY 13203

JOHNSON, MARGARET ANN (PEGGY), library administrator; b. Atlanta, Aug. 11, 1948; d. Odell H. and Virginia (Mathiasen) J.; m. Lee J. English, Mar. 4, 1978; children: Carson J., Amelia J. BA, St. Olaf Coll., 1970; MA, U. Chgo., 1972; MBA, Met. State U., 1990. Music cataloger U. Iowa Librs., Iowa City, 1972-73; analyst Control Data Corp., Bloomington, Minn., 1973-75; br. libr. St. Paul Pub. Librs., 1975-77; head tech. svcs. St. Paul Campus Librs., U. Minn., 1977-86; collection devel. office U. Librs., U. Minn., Mpls., 1987-90; asst. dir. St. Paul Campus Librs., U. Minn., 1987-95; planning officer U. Librs. U. Minn., Mpls., 1993-97, asst. univ. libr., 1997—; libr. cons. Mekerere U., Kampala, Uganda, 1990, U. Nat. Rwanda, 1990, Inst. Agriculture and Vet. Hassan II, Rabat, Morocco, 1992—. Author: Automation and Organizational Change in Libraries, 1991, The Searchable Internet, 1996; editor: New Directions in Technical Services, 1997; author bimonthly column Technicalities Jour.; editor Guide to Tech. Svcs. Resources, 1994, Recruiting, Educating and Tng. Librarians for Collection Devel., 1994, Collection Mgmt. and Devel., 1994; contbr. articles to profl. jours. Recipient Samuel Lazerow Rsch. fellowship Assn. Coll. and Rsch. Librs., Inst. for Sci. Info., 1987. Mem. ALA, Minn. Libr. Assn., Internat. Assn. Agrl. Librs. and Documentalists, Assn. for Internat. Agrl. and Extension Edn., U.S. Agrl. Info. Network, Assn. for Libr. Collections and Tech. Svcs. (v.p. 1998—). Office: U of Minn Librs 499 Wilson Libr 309 19th Ave S Minneapolis MN 55455-0438

JOHNSON, MARGARET H, welding company executive; b. Chgo., June 3, 1933; d. Harold W. and clara J. (Pape) Glavin; m. Odean Jack Johnson, Nov. 18, 1950; children: Karen Ann, Dean Harold. Student, Moody Bible Inst., 1976-78. V.p., sec. Seamline Welding, Inc., Grayslake, Ill., 1956-96, also bd. dirs. Author: Living Faith, 1973, 80, Lord's Ladder of Love, 1976, God's Rainbow, 1982; contbr. articles to religious mags. Trustee SWCEPS, Grayslake, 1963-99; life mem. Rep. presdl. Task Force, 1982—; trustee, 1986-88; charter founder Ronald Reagan Rep. Ctr., 1987; mem. lake View Neighborhood Group, Chgo., Cmall Group Ch. Cmty.; active Mary, Seat of Wisdom Cath. Women's Club, 1970-90, renew facilitator, 1986-88, co-chairperson, 1986-88; Sunday sch. tchr.; Mem. parish coun. St. Gilbert parish, 1995-99, evangelization chair, 1995—, hospitality chair, 1995—, welcome home program, 1998-99. Mem. AARP, ASCAP, Fedn. Ind. Small Bus., Internat. Platform Assn., Women's Aglow Fellowship, Grayslake c. of C., Exch. Club of Grayslake, Grayslake Devel. Corp. Home: 20 Hawley Ct Grayslake IL 60030-1517

JOHNSON, MARGARET KATHLEEN, business educator; b. Baylor County, Tex., Oct. 30, 1920; d. George W. and Julia Rivers (Turner) Higgins; m. Herman Clyde Johnson, Jr., July 27, 1949 (dec.); 1 child, Carolyn Kay. BS, Hardin-Simmons U., 1940; M in Bus. Edn., North Tex. State U., 1957, EdD, 1962. Clk. Farmers Nat. Bank, Seymour, Tex., 1940-41; adminstrv. sec. U.S. Navy, Corpus Christi, Tex., 1941-46; adminstrv. asst. Hdqrs. 8th Army, Yokohama, Japan, 1946-49; instr. Coll. Bus. Adminstrn., U. Ark., 1957-60; teaching fellow Sch. Bus. Adminstrn., North Tex. State U., 1960-62, instr., 1962-63; asst. prof. bus., tchr. edn. and secondary edn. Tchrs. Coll., U. Nebr., Lincoln, 1963-65; asso. prof. Tchrs. Coll., U. Nebr., 1966-70, prof., 1970—; guest lectr. U. N.Mex., 1967, Curriculum Devel. in Bus. Edn., N.S. Dept. Edn., 1969, North Tex. State U., 1970, East Tex. State U., 1972; in Policies Commn. for Bus. and Econ. Edn., 1979-83; mem. bd. devel. Hardin-Simmons U., 1994-97. Author: Standardized Production Typewriting Tests series, 1964-65, National Structure for Research in Vocational Education, 1966; co-author: Introduction to Word Processing, 1980, 2d edit., 1985, Introduction to Business Communication, 1981, 2d edit., 1988, Business Communication Principles and Applications, 1996; editor: Nat. Bus. Edn. Assn. Yearbook, 1980. Recipient United Bus. Edn. Assn. award as outstanding grad. student in bus. edn. North Tex. State U., 1957; award for outstanding service Nebr. Future Bus. Leaders Am., 1968; Mountain-Plains Bus. Edn. Leadership award, 1977; merit award Nebr. Bus. Assn., 1979. Mem. Nat. Bus. Edn. Assn. (exec. bd. 1975, 76-78), Mountain-Plains Bus. Edn. Assn. (exec. sec. 1970-73, pres. 1975), Nebr. Bus. Edn. Assn. (pres. 1966-67), Nebr. Council on Occupational Tchr. Edn., Delta Pi Epsilon. Office: U Nebr 529 Hill St Lincoln NE 68502-3318

JOHNSON, MARIE-LOUISE TULLY, dermatologist, educator; b. N.Y.C., July 26, 1927; d. James Henry and Mary Frances (Dobbins) Tully; m. Kenneth Gerald Johnson, June 10, 1950. AB, Manhattanville Coll., 1948; PhD, Yale U., 1954, MD, 1956. Intern, then resident Yale-New Haven Med. Ctr., 1956-59; asst. prof. medicine, dermatology Yale U., 1961-67, clin. prof. dermatology, 1980—; chief dermatologist med. svc. Atomic Bomb Casualty Commn., Hiroshima, Japan, 1964-67; assoc. prof. dermatology NYU, 1967-70, 74-76, prof. dermatology, 1976-80; assoc. prof. dermatology, coordinator continuing med. edn. Dartmouth Coll., Hanover, N.H., 1971-74; chief dermatology Bellevue Hosp., N.Y.C., 1974-80; dir. med. edn. Benedictine Hosp., Kingston, N.Y., 1980-93; cons. Health and Nutrition Exam. Survey I, II, Health Stats., Washington, 1967-84. Contbg. author: Cecil's Textbook of Medicine, 15th edit., 1979, 16th edit., 1982, 17th edit., 1985, Dermatology in General Medicine, 2d edit., 1979. Mem. Cardinal Cooke Pro-Life Commn., Albany, N.Y., 1986-87; bd. dirs. Maternity and Early Childhood Found., Albany, 1985—, pres., 1987—. Named Disting. Alumna, Manhattanville Coll., 1977. Fellow Am. Acad. Dermatology (master, bd. dirs. 1976-80; mem. Am. Dermatol. Assn. (bd. dirs. 1986-92, v.p. 1991-92), NAS Inst. Medicine, Internat. Physicians for Prevention of Nuclear War (del. 1982, 83, 87, 88, 89). Roman Catholic. Home: 15 Strawberry Bank Rd High Falls NY 12440-5128 Office: Kingston Hosp Med Arts Bldg Ste 202 368 Broadway Kingston NY 12401-5144*

JOHNSON, MARILYN, obstetrician, gynecologist; b. Houston, May 7, 1925; d. William Walton and Marilyn (Henderson) J.; B.A., Rice Inst., 1945; M.D., Baylor U., 1950. Intern, New Eng. Hosp. Women and Children, Boston, 1950-51; resident Meth. Hosp., Houston, 1951-53; resident in gynecology M.D. Anderson Tumor Inst., Houston, 1954, fellow, 1955; fellow in gynecol. pathology Harvard Med. Sch., 1952-53; practice medicine specializing in ob-gyn, Houston, 1954-81, Fredericksburg, Tex., 1981-97, ret., 1997; mem. staffs St. Joseph's, Meml., Meth., Park Plaza, Hill Country Meml. Rosewood, South Austin Community, Comfort (Tex.) Community hosps.; clin. instr. ob-gyn Coll. Medicine, Baylor U., 1954—, Postgrad. Sch. Medicine, U. Tex., 1954—; gynecologist De Pelchin Faith Home, Houston, 1954—, also Rice U., Richmond State Sch.; med. dirs. Birthright, Inc., Houston, 1973—; chief med. staff Hill Country Meml. Hosp., Fredericksburg, Tex., 1990-92; cons. Tex. bd. Blue Cross Blue Shield; pro-life public speaker. Bd. dirs. Right to Life, Houston, Found. for Life. Sandoz Labs. grantee, 1973, 75, Delbay Pharm. Co. grantee, 1977. Fellow Am. Coll. Obstetricians and Gynecologists; mem. AMA, Am. Soc. Colposcopic Pathologists, Tex. Med. Assn., Am. Med. Women's Assn., Internat. Infertility Assn., Harris County Med. Soc., Postgrad. med. Assembly S. Tex., Houston Ob-Gyn Soc., Tex. Folklore Soc. Republican. Baptist. Clubs: Zonta; Fredericksburg Rockhounds. Home: 2301 Lakeside Ct Rockport TX 78382-3519

JOHNSON, MARK ALAN, lawyer; b. Marysville, Ohio, June 5, 1960; s. Neil Raymond and Elizabeth Johnson; m. Deborah Anne Hillis, Sept. 21, 1984. BA, Otterbein Coll., 1982; JD, Ohio State U., 1985. Bar: Ohio 1985, U.S. Dist. Ct. (so. dist.) Ohio 1985, U.S. Ct. Appeals (6th cir.) 1987, U.S. Dist. Ct. (no. dist.) Ohio 1991. Assoc. Baker and Hostetler LLP, Columbus, Ohio, 1985-92, ptnr., 1993—. Mem. ABA (litigation sect., mem. bus. torts litigation com., comml. and banking litigation com.), Ohio Bar Assn., Columbus Bar Assn., Indsl. Truck Assn. (mem. lawyers com.). Office: Baker & Hostetler LLP 65 E State St Ste 2100 Columbus OH 43215-4260

JOHNSON, MARK ANDREW, lawyer; b. Plainville, Kans., Feb. 27, 1959; s. Delton Lee and Margaret Ellen (McCracken) J. BA in Chemistry, Reed Coll., 1982; JD, U. Calif., Berkeley, 1987. Bar: Oreg. 1987, U.S. Supreme Ct. 1991. Jud. clk. U.S. Dist. Ct. Oreg., Portland, 1987-88, Oreg. Ct. of Appeals, Salem, 1988-89; assoc. Gevurtz, Menashe, Larson, Kurshner & Yates, PC, Portland, 1989-93; ptnr. Findling & Johnson LLP, Portland, 1993-99; of counsel Bennett, Hartman & Reynolds, Portland, 1999—. Mem. ABA, Nat. Gay and Lesbian Law Assn. (co-chmn. 1994-95), Oreg. Gay and Lesbian Law Assn. (co-chair 1990-92), Oreg. State Bar (pres.). Office: Bennett Hartman & Reynolds 300 Jefferson Sta 851 SW 6th Ave Ste 1600 Portland OR 97204

JOHNSON, MARK CYRUS, financial planner, tax preparer; b. Lenoir, N.C., May 6, 1943; s. Roy Leonard and Violet G. (Smith) J.; m. Willie R. Spoon, Feb. 25, 1967; 1 child, Christy Yvette Johnson Cooper. AB, Lenoir Rhyne, 1965; MDiv, Luth. Theol. So. Sem., Columbia, S.C., 1969; MEd, U. N.C., Greensboro, 1976. CFP; enrolled agt., IRS. Pres. Mark C. Johnson, CFP, Oak Ridge, N.C., 1990—. Mem. Coll. Health Care Adminstrs. (treas. 1980-98), Inst. CFPs, Accredited Tax Preparers, Jaycees, Rotary. Home and Office: 4532 Peeples Rd Oak Ridge NC 27310-9763

JOHNSON, MARK D., college administrator; b. Bklyn., July 3, 1945; s. Emil A. and Mary Jane (Jennings) J.; m. Carla Bergstrom, Sept. 13, 1968; children: Rebecca, Katrina. BA, U. Rochester, 1967; MA, U. Chgo., 1969; EdD, Pa. State U., 1976. Sr. planning analyst Pa. State U., University Park, 1976-78; dir. instnl. rsch. Allegheny Coll., Meadville, Pa., 1978-79; assoc. coord. Wash. State Coun. for Postsecondary Edn., Olympia, 1979-82; asst. commr. Conn. Dept. Higher Edn., Hartford, 1982-93; dep. dir. Ark. Dept. Higher Edn., Little Rock, 1993-94; dir. planning Pulaski Tech. Coll., North Little Rock, Ark., 1994-97, dean adminstrn., 1997—; cons. editor Rsch. in Higher Edn.; chair ann. conf. State Higher Edn. Acad. Officers, Boston, 1993. Contbr. articles to profl. jours. Mem. City Planning Commn., Olympia, 1979-81; bd. dirs. Serving to Equip People, North Little Rock, 1995—. 1st lt. U.S. Army, 1969-72. Mem. Assn. for Instnl. Rsch., Soc. for Coll. and Univ. Planning. Office: Pulaski Tech Coll 3000 W Scenic Dr North Little Rock AR 72118-3347

JOHNSON, MARK EUGENE, lawyer; b. Independence, Mo., Jan. 8, 1951; s. Russell Eugene and Reatha (Nixon) J.; m. Vicki Ja Lane, June 11, 1983. AB with honors, U. Mo., 1973, JD, 1976. Bar: Mo. 1976, U.S. Dist. Ct. (we. dist.) Mo. 1976, U.S. Ct. Appeals (8th cir.) 1984, U.S. Supreme Ct. 1993. Ptnr. Morrison & Hecker, LLP, Kansas City, Mo., 1976—. Editor: Mo. Law Rev., 1974-76. Pres. Lido Villas Assn., Inc., Mission, Kans., 1979-81. Mem. ABA, Mo. Bar Assn., Kansas City Bar Assn., Lawyers Assn. Kansas City, Def. Research Inst., Internat. Assn. Defense Counsel, Mo. Orgn. Def. Lawyers, Carriage Club, Order of Coif, Phi Beta Kappa, Phi Eta Sigma, Phi Kappa Phi, Omicron Delta Kappa. Republican. Presbyterian. Home: 4905 Somerset Dr Shawnee Mission KS 66207-2230 Office: Morrison & Hecker LLP 2600 Grand Blvd Ste 1200 Kansas City MO 64108-4606

JOHNSON, MARK MATTHEW, museum administrator; b. Dec. 10, 1950; s. Charles Michael Jr. and Jean Lee (Reid) J.; m. Amy Joy Schneider, March 10, 1984; children: Rachel Amelia, Sarah Jean. BA, U. Wis., Whitewater, 1974; cert. Art Mus. Studies, U. Ill., 1976, MA in Art History, 1976. Tchg. asst. art and design U. Ill., Urbana Champaign, 1974-75; rsch. assoc. Krannert Art Mus., Champaign, 1975; asst. dir., curator Krannert Art Mus., 1981-85; lectr. dept. mus. edn. Art Inst. Chgo., Champaign, 1975-77; curator dept. art history and edn. Cleve. Mus. Art, 1977-81; dir. Muscarelle Mus. Art. Coll. William and Mary, Williamsburg, Va., 1985-94; lect. dept. fine arts Muscarelle Mus. Art. Coll. William and Mary, 1985-94; dir. Montgomery (Ala.) Mus. Fine Arts, 1994—. Author: Idea to Image: Preparatory Studies from the Renaissance to Impressionism, 1980, Romeyn de Hooghe, 1989, Literacy Through Art, 1990, Nissan Engel: Nouvelles Dimensions, 1994, Hans Grohs: An Ecstatic Vision, 1996, (English and French edits.) Nissan Engel, 1998; organized, curated numerous exhbns., 1980—. Rsch. and travel grantee various mus. Mem. Assn. Art Mus. Dirs., Internat. Coun. Mus., Coll. Art Assn., Am. Assn. Mus. (accreditation com.). Office: Montgomery Mus Fine Arts PO Box 230819 One Museum Dr Montgomery AL 36123-0819

JOHNSON, MARK PAUL, obstetrics and gynecology educator, geneticist; b. Fargo, N.D., Sept. 28, 1953; s. Milton Leslie Johnson and Jean Nora (Edhlund) McNeil; m. Christine Marie Jerpbak, May 5, 1984; children: Jennifer, Erik, Rolf. BA in Biology magna cum laude, Concordia Coll., Moorhead, Minn., 1976; MS in Med. Genetics, U. Minn., 1980, MD, 1984. Diplomate Am. Bd. Ob-Gyn., Am. Bd. Med. Genetics. Grad. rsch. fellow dept. lab. medicine and pathology U. Minn. Med. Ctr., Mpls., 1979-80; resident in ob-gyn. U. Mich. Med. Ctr., Ann Arbor, 1984-88; fellow in med. genetics, clin. instr. ob-gyn. Wayne State U. Sch. Medicine, Detroit, 1988-90, clin. instr. dept. molecular biology and genetics, 1988-90, asst. prof. ob-gyn., molecular medicine-genetics, pathology, 1990-96, assoc. prof. ob-gyn., molecular medicine-genetics, pathology, 1997-98, assoc. dir. div. reproductive genetics, 1990-98, assoc. dir. Ctr. for Fetal Diagnosis and Therapy, 1990-98, assoc. dir. grad. program in genetic counseling, 1996-98; assoc. prof. ob-gyn., surgery, pediats. U. Pa., Phila., 1998—; dir. obstetrics svcs., divsn. fetal surgery Children's Hosp., Phila., 1998—; vis. asst. prof. ob-gyn. Med. Coll. Ohio, Toledo, 1991-93; numerous presentations, condr. workshops in field; dir. obstetrical svcs., divsn. fetal surgery Children's Hosp. Phila. Editor: (with others) Maternal Genetic Disease, 1995, Invasive Outpatient Procedures in Reproductive Medicine, 1996; mem. editl. bd. Fetal Diagnosis and Therapy, 1991—; contbr. numerous articles, abstracts and revs. to med. jours., chpts. to books. Recipient Bronze Beeper award Galens Med. Soc., 1987, 1st place award for outstanding rsch. paper Wayne State U.-Hutzel Hosp., 1990, Faculty Achievement award Alpha Omega Alpha, 1998; grantee March of Dimes Birth Defects Found., 1991, Nat. Inst. Child Health and Human Devel., 1994-97. Fellow ACOG (1st place award for outstanding rsch. paper 1990), Am. Coll. Med. Genetics (founding); mem. AMA, Am. Soc. Human Genetics, Internat. Fetal Medicine and Surgery Soc. (pres. 1997), Soc. Perinatal Obstetricians, Ctrl. Assn. Obstetricians and Gynecologists, Mich. Med. Soc. (med. ethics com. 1995), Wayne County Med. Soc. (med. ethics com. 1993-98), Sigma Xi, Alpha Omega Alpha. Avocations: sailing, fly fishing, classic cars. Office: Pediatric Gen and Thoracic Surgery Childrens Hosp of Phila 34th and Civic Ctr Blvd Philadelphia PA 19104

JOHNSON, MARK S., umpire; b. Louisville, Nov. 18, 1950. Student, E. Ky. U. Former umpire Gulf Coast League, Fla. State League, Instrnl. League, So. League, Ariz. Instrnl. League, Dominican Republic League, Puerto Rico League, Pacific Coast League; umpire maj. league baseball Am. League, N.Y.C., 1984—; with Umpires Union, Phila. Sgt.-at-arms legislature Ky. State, 1974-76. Avocations: fishing, golfing. Office: Am League 350 Park Ave New York NY 10022 also: Umpires Union 1735 Market St Philadelphia PA 19103

JOHNSON, MARK STEVEN, public health administrator; b. Rockford, Ill., July 18, 1949; s. Mark F. and Rita M. (Petersen) J.; m. Deborah K. Nelson/Gill, Dec. 22, 1969 (div. Dec. 1983); m. Betty J. Johnson, May 7, 1988; stepchildren: Shannon C. Sexton, Cramer M. Sexton. BA, No. Ill. U., 1971; MPA, U. Alaska S.E., Juneau, 1987. Substitute tchr. Harlem Sch. Dist., Rockford, 1971-72; caseworker Ill. Dept. Pub. Aid, Rockford, 1972-74; EMS health planner Comprehensive Health Planning of N.W. Ill., Rockford, 1974-78; EMS coord. Physicians Svcs. of Fairbanks, Alsaks, 1978-79; chief emergency med. svcs. sect. Alaska Dept. Health and Social Svc., Juneau, 1979-95, chief cmty. health and EMS, 1996—; dir. EMS for Children project, dir. Injury Prevention project Alaska Dept. Health and Social Svcs., 1990—. Mem. editorial bd. Prehosp. and Disaster Medicine, 1993—; author book chpt. and articles. Mem. Alaska Safety Adv. Coun., 1997—. Named EMS Adminstr. of Yr., Gov. Hickel and Alaska Coun. on EMS, 1993. Mem. Nat. Assn. State EMS Dirs. (exec. bd. 1985-88), Am. Soc. for Circumpolar Health, Alaska Pub. Health Assn. (exec. bd. 1988, Barbara Berger award 1995), State and Terr. Injury Prevention Dirs. (v.p. 1996-98, pres.-elect 1999), Alaska State Emergency Response Commn. Avocations: travel, hiking, fishing. Home: 10726 Horizon Dr Juneau AK 99801-7625 Office: Cmty Health and EMS Dept Health and Social Svcs 410 Willoughby St Juneau AK 99810-0616

JOHNSON, MARLENE M., nonprofit executive; b. Braham, Minn., Jan. 11, 1946; d. Beauford and Helen (Nelson) J.; m. Peter Frankel. BA, Macalester Coll., 1968. Founder, pres. Split Infinitive, Inc., St. Paul, 1970-82; pres., bd. dirs. Face to Face Health and Counseling Clinic, 1977-78; with Working Opportunities for Women, 1977-82; lt. gov. State of Minn., St. Paul, 1983-91; sr. fellow Family Support Project, Ctr. for Policy Alternative, 1991-93; assoc. adminstr. for adminstrn. GSA, Washington, 1994-95; v.p. for people and strategy Rowe Furniture Corp., McLean, Va., 1995-97; CEO NAFSE: Assn. Internat. Educators, 1998—; founder, past chmn. Nat. Leadership Conf. Women Execs. in State Govt.; mem. exec. com., midwestern chair Nat. Conf. Lt. Govs.; bd. dirs. AFS-USA, Inc., 1992-98, Nat. Capitol Region coun. Girl Scouts U.S., 1997—; mem. adv. bd. Ctr. for Children in Poverty, Columbia U.; mem. commn. on internat. edn. Am. Coun. for Edn., 1999—. Chmn. Minn. Women's Polit. Caucus, 1973-76, Dem.-Farmer-Labor Small Bus. Task Force, 1978, Child Care Task Force, 1987; dir. membership sect. Nat. Women's Polit. Caucus, 1975-77; vice chmn. Minn. Del. to White House Conf. on Small Bus., 1980; co-founder Minn. Women's Campaign Fund, 1982; bd. dirs. Nat. Child Care Action Campaign; chair Children's 2000 Commn., 1990; candidate for Mayor St. Paul, 1993. Recipient Outstanding Achievement award St. Paul YWCA, 1980, Disting. Svc. award St. Paul Jaycees, 1980, Disting. Citizen citation Macalester Coll., 1982, Disting. Contbns. to Families award Minn. Coun. on Family Rels., 1986, Minn. Sportfishing Congress award, 1986, Royal Order of Polar Star Govt. Sweden, 1988, Children's Champion award Def. Fund, 1989, Jane Preston award Minn. State Coun. on Vocat. Tech. Edn., 1989, Legis. Leadership award Am. Fedn. Tchrs., 1991; named One of Ten Outstanding Young Minnesotans, Minn. Jaycees, 1980; Swedish Bicentennial Commn. grantee, 1987. Mem. Nat. Assn. Women Bus. Owners (past pres.).

JOHNSON, MARSHALL HARDY, investment company executive; b. Raleigh, N.C., Sept. 7, 1923; s. William Thompson and Evie (Barnes) J.; m. Mary Lynn Lewis, June 24, 1947 (div. 1977); children: Marshall Hardy, Lynn Lewis Johnson-Titchener, Carter Johnson Overton; m. Beverly Ray Johnson, June 2, 1984. Student, U. N.C., 1942-43, 45-46; IBA, U. Pa., 1955-57. Reporter, analyst Dunn & Bradstreet, Raleigh, 1946-47; chmn., pres., CEO McDaniel Lewis & Co., Greensboro, N.C., 1947—; v.p. Scott & Stringfellow, Inc., Richmond, Va., 1993-96; mem. Midwest Stock Exch., Chgo., 1960-77; bd. dirs. First Citizen Bank & Trust, Greensboro, Mcpl. Coun., Raleigh; adv. dir. Friends Home, 1985-93. Contbr. articles to profl. jours. Dir. Young Dems., Greensboro, 1962-66, Jr. C. of C., Greensboro, 1964-70; deacon First Bapt. Ch., Greensboro. With USN, 1942-46. Fellow Fin. Fedn. Am.; mem. Am. Arbitration Assn. (nat. panel bd. 1963—), Nat. Assn. Securities Dealers (nat. panel arbitration 1985—), Securities Industries Assn. (Mid-Atlantic exec. com. 1986-93), Securities Dealers of Carolinas (pres. 1976), Magna Charta Baron, Odd Fellows, Kiwanis (Hixon award 1998), Greensboro Country Club, City Club, Alpha Tau Omega. Avocations: tennis, golf, swimming. Home: 310 Kimberly Dr Greensboro NC 27408-5018 Office: McDaniel Lewis & Co PO Box 9 Greensboro NC 27402-0009 *I've learned that our quality of life is largely determined by our own choices.*

JOHNSON, MARTIN ALLEN, publisher; b. Bklyn., Aug. 20, 1931; s. Ellis A. and Estelle (Rudnick) J.; m. Suzanne Cornbleet, Dec. 12, 1964 (div. Feb. 1979); 1 dau., Sarah; m. Diane Schlesinger Krull, Aug. 19, 1981. A.B., Bard Coll., 1954. Asso. editor Am. Printer and Lithographer mag., N.Y.C., 1956-57; mng. editor Am. Printer and Lithographer mag., 1957-58, editor, 1958; mng. editor Printing Impressions mag., Phila., also; Delaware Valley Printing Impressions, 1958-61; pub. PTM mag., Chgo., 1959-67; v.p. Ednl. Screen and Audio Visual Guide, Chgo., 1962-67; pres. Trade Periodical Co., Chgo., 1967—, Pub. Dynamics, Inc., Stamford, Conn., 1968—, U.S. Indsl. Publs., Inc., Stamford, 1971—, U.S. Graphics Corp., Stamford, 1974—, Landmark Comms. Corp., Stamford. Contbr. articles to profl. jours. Served with AUS, 1954-56. Recipient Justin P. Allman award Wallcoverings Assn., 1993. Mem. Typophiles (N.Y.C.), Ams. for Music Library in Israel, Am. Soc. Interior Designers. Jewish. Clubs: Chgo. Press, Executives (Chgo.); Landmark (Stamford); Wellington (London). Avocations: poetry, objective biblical history, painting. Office: Pub Dynamics Inc 5030 Champion Blvd Ste 6-227 Boca Raton FL 33496-2473

JOHNSON, MARTIN CLIFTON, physician; b. Santa Fe, Nov. 16, 1933; s. Henry J. and Dorothy (Clifton) J.; m. priscilla Bollam, June 13, 1959; children: Martin Clifton II, Kurt B., Kirsten L. Ustach, Katharine E. AB, Stanford U., 1955, MD, 1959. Diplomate Am. Bd. Neurol. Surgery, Am. Bd. Pediat. Neurosurgery, Am. Bd. Forensic Examiners, Am. Bd. Forensic Medicine. Intern in surgery Palo Alto (Calif.) Stanford U. Hosp., 1959-60; fellow in neurosurgery Mayo Found., Rochester, Minn., 1960-61; asst. resident gen. surgery Presbyn. Med. Ctr., San Francisco, 1963-64; asst. resident, sr. resident, chief resident in neurosurgery U. Cin., 1964-68; pvt. practice neurosurgery/pediat. neurosurgery Portland, Oreg., 1968—; mem. staff Emanuel Hosp.; neurosurg. cons. Shriners Hosp. for Crippled Children. Col. MC. USAR; lt. comdr. USNR, 1961-63. Fellow ACS, Am. Acad. Pediats.; mem. AMA, Portland Met. Med. Soc., Oreg. Med. Soc., Congress Neurol. Surgeons, Am. Assn. Neurol. Surgeons, Soc. Critical Care Medicine, N.W. Pediatric Soc., Oreg. Neurosurg. Soc., Internat. Soc. for Pediatric Neurol. Surgery, Am. Assn. Pediatric Neurosurgery, Portland Acad. Pediatrics, Multnomah Athletic Club, Columbia Edgewater Country Club, Columbia Aviation Club. Home: 31870 SW Country View Ln Wilsonville OR 97070-7476 Office: Pacific Northwest Neurol Assocs PC 501 N Graham St Ste 350 Portland OR 97227-2005

JOHNSON, MARTIN WAYNE, lawyer; b. Portland, Oreg., Nov. 9, 1946; s. David S. and Elsie Jane (Kalmen) Johnson; m. Kathleen Umrein, Mar. 27, 1977; children: Jessica, Brian, Douglas. BA, Lewis & Clark Coll., 1968; JD, U. Calif., 1974. Bar: Calif. 1974. Assoc. Wilson, Elser, Moskowitz, Edelman & Dicker, San Francisco, 1982-86, ptnr., 1987—. Assoc. editor Calif. Law Review, U. Calif., 1972-74. Dir. Sleepy Hollow Homes Assn., San Anselmo, Calif., 1991-93. Lt. (j.g.) USNR, 1968-71. Mem. Order of Coif. Democrat. Presbyterian. Avocations: backpacking, fishing, gardening. Office: Wilson Elser Moskowitz Edelman & Dicker 650 California St Ste 1400 San Francisco CA 94108-2718

JOHNSON, MARVIN MERRILL, chemical engineer, chemist; b. Salt Lake City, Mar. 21, 1928; s. John Ivan and Hildur Elizabeth (Johnson) J.; m., Apr. 8, 1951; children: Mark, Jennifer, Lorelie, Maryanne. BS in Chem. Engring., U. Utah, 1950, PhD in Chem. Engring., 1958. Sr. rsch. chemist Phillips Petroleum, Bartlesville, Okla., 1956-68, rsch. chemist, 1968-74, sr. rsch. assoc., 1974-75, sr. scientist, 1978-86; prof. chem. engring. Okla. State U., Stillwater, 1986-89; sr. scientist Phillips Petroleum, 1989-91, rsch. & devel. rsch. fellow, 1991—. Contbr. articles to profl. jours.; patentee in field. Named Inventor of Yr. Okla. Bar Assn., 1981. Fellow AICE; mem. Nat. Acad. Engring., Am. Chem. Soc. (Okla. Chemist 1982, Southwest Regional award 1982, Nat. Medal Tech. 1985, IRI Achievement award 1993, hero of chemistry ACS, 1998), Sigma Xi. Home: 4413 Woodland Rd Bartlesville OK 74006-5340 Office: c/o Phillips Petroleum Co 354 Pl Phillips Rsch Ctr Bartlesville OK 74004

JOHNSON, MARVIN RICHARD ALOIS, architect; b. Humphrey, Nebr., Aug. 13, 1916; s. Otto Henry and Reenste (Berends) J. A.B., U. Nebr., 1943, B.A. in Architecture, 1943; M.Architecture, Harvard U., 1948. Designer, draftsman firm Clark & Enersen, Lincoln, Nebr., 1946-47, 48-50; cons. architect div. sch. planning N.C. Dept. Public Instrn., Raleigh, 1950-80; architect, cons. ednl. facilities, 1981—; cons. HEW, Washington, 1960. Contbr. articles to profl. jours. Served with USNR, 1943-46. Fellow AIA (recipient Distinguished Service citation N.C. chpt. 1960, v.p. N.C. chpt. 1977-78, pres.-elect 1979, pres. 1980); mem. Council Ednl. Facility Planners, Am. Assn. School Adminstrs., N.C. Mus. Art, Phi Beta Kappa. Democrat. Lutheran. Home: 3113-215 Charles Root Wynd Raleigh NC 27612-5375

JOHNSON, MARY, museum director. Acting dir. Dept. Libr. and Pub. Records, Phoenix, now dep. dir. Office: Dept Libr Archives and Pub Records 1700 W Washington St Ste 200 Phoenix AZ 85007-2812*

JOHNSON, MARY ANN, computer training vocational school owner; b. Joliet, Ill., June 26, 1956; d. Truly and Pearlie Mae (Bell) J.; m. Russell Alan Jackson, May 18, 1976 (div. 1983); children: Pamela Ann, Russell Alan Jr. AA, Joliet (Ill.) Jr. Coll., 1990; student mgmt. info. systems, Governor State U. Student intern Argonne (Ill.) Nat. Lab., 1972-79, sec. II, 1979-82; word processor specialist SunGard Corp., Hinsdale, Ill., 1982-86; desktop designer, adminstrn. Amoco Chem. Corp., Naperville, Ill., 1988-89; desktop designer Travelers Corp., Naperville, 1989-90; adminstrv. sec., computer operator Metromail Donnelly, Lombard, Ill., 1990-91; owner, mgr. Tech. Soft Svcs., Joliet, 1991—; lectr., condr. seminars on running small bus. Author: Running a Small Business, 1996. Mem. Women Bus. Devel., Joliet Region C. of C. Avocations: self-defense, computer and software edn. Office: Tech Soft Svcs 160 E Illinois St Ste 603 Chicago IL 60611*

JOHNSON, MARY ELIZABETH, retired elementary education educator; b. St. Louis, Sept. 17, 1943; d. Richard William Blayney and Alice Bonjean (Taylor) Blayney Needham; m. Clyde Robert Johnson, Aug. 31, 1963; children: Brian (dec. 1991), Elizabeth Johnson Meyer, David. BS cum laude, U. Ill., 1966; MA, Maryville U., 1990; postgrad., So. Ill. U., 1990. Cert. elem. tchr., Ill., Mo. Tchr. Hazelwood Sch. Dist., Florissant, Mo., 1971-93, positive intervention tchr., 1989-91; Author play: Say No to Drugs, 1991. Author: Secret Study Skills for Third Graders, 1990. Mem. Hazelwood Schs. Music Boosters, 1980-88; mem. coms. Townsend PTA, Florissant, 1976—; contbr. Schlarship Run-Walk, 1982—; mem. Children's United Rsch. Effort in Cancer, 1986—; vol. Spl. Love, Inc., camp for children with cancer, 1986—; active The Children's Inn, Bethesda, Md., 1990—, Bailey Scholarship Fund, U. Ill., 1994—. Fred S. Bailey scholar, 1962-66, Edmund J. James scholar, 1964-65; named Townsend Tchr. of Yr., 1989-90. Mem. NEA, Internat. Platform Assn., Kappa Delta Pi, Alpha Lambda Delta, Phi Kappa Phi. Baptist. Avocations: travel, reading, crafts, writing, music. Home: 2016 Bay Tree Sun City Summerlin NV 89134-5235

JOHNSON, MARY ELIZABETH, editor, author; b. Brewton, Ala., Sept. 5, 1944; d. James Wallace and Helen Louise (Pearson) J.; B.S., U. Ala., 1966, M.S., 1970. Writer, Simplicity Pattern Co., N.Y.C., 1968-70; writer Singer Co., N.Y.C., 1970-71; editor Coats & Clark, Inc., N.Y.C., 1972-73; asso. editor Reader's Digest Gen. Books, N.Y.C., 1973-75; sr. editor Oxmoor House, Birmingham, 1976-79; editor-in-chief Decorating and Craft Ideas Mag., Birmingham, 1979-82; mgr. eponymous imprint Black Belt Press, Montgomery, 1993-96; writer, editor, pub. cons., 1996—. Author books including: Prize Country Quilts, 1976; Pillows: Designs, Patterns Projects, 1977; Country Quilt Patterns, 1977; Times Down Home, 1978; Rugs: Designs, Patterns, Projects, 1979; (with Katherine Pearson) Nature Crafts, 1980; (with Zuelia Ann Hurt) Needlecraft Designs from Our Best Quilts, 1978, A Garden of Quilts, 1984, Star Quilts, 1992, 2d edit., 1996, The American Quilt: A History of Cloth and Comfort, 1750-1950, 1993. Home: 1283 Westmoreland Ave Montgomery AL 36106-2017

JOHNSON, MARY ELIZABETH SUSAN, consulting engineer; b. Cobourg, Ont., Can., Mar. 28, 1947; d. Albert David Houston and Phyllis Mary (Austen) Smith; m. John Henry Johnson, Aug. 31, 1969; children: Anne, Judith, Andrew. B in applied sci., U. Toronto, 1970, postgrad., 1973. Registered profl. engr., New Brunswick, Can. Indsl. engr. North York Gen. Hosp., Willowdale, Ont., 1970-71; adminstrv. resident The Princess Margaret Hosp., Toronto, 1972-73; cons. Alta. Hosp. Assn., Edmonton, 1973-75; dir., mgmt. systems Calgary Gen. Hosp., Calgary, Alta., 1975-79; planning coord. Saint John (New Brunswick) Regional Hosp., 1979-93; prin. Johnson Engineered Solutions Ltd., Saint John, N.B., 1995—. Mem. editorial bd. Sci. Med. Bulletin, 1986-88. Leader Girl Guides of Can., 2nd Saint John Brownies, 1981-86, 18th Saint John Brownies, 87-92, 2nd Saint John Pathfinders, 1992—, mem. Nat. Coun., 1996-98. Fellow Am. Coll. Health Care Execs.; mem. Assn. Profl. Engrs. Province New Brunswick (2d v.p. 1995-96), Inst. Indsl. Engrs. (sr.).

JOHNSON, MARY KATHERINE, elementary education educator; b. Prescott, Wis., June 12, 1945; d. Walter Frank and Mary Jane (Larson) Johnson; m. William F. Hilton, June 23, 1968 (div. 1985); children: Bradley Eric, Karin Louise. BA, Mich. State U., 1967, MA, 1970; postgrad., U. Calif., Berkeley, 1970—. Cert. elem. tchr., Calif. Tchr. East Lansing (Mich.) Pub. Schs., 1967-68, Hall's Crossroads Sch., Aberdeen, Md., 1968-69, Oakland (Calif.) Pub. Schs., 1970-82; tchr., cons. Bay Area Writing Project, Berkeley, 1978—, Bay Area Math. Project, Berkeley, 1994—, Bay Area Calif. Arts Project, Berkeley, 1997—; cons. Child Devel. Project, San Ramon, Calif., 1985; tchr. Berkeley Unified Sch. Dist., 1986—; coord. pub. programs, math. edn. program Lawrence Hall of Sci., U. Calif., Berkeley, 1996-98; mem. MATHTEQ U. Calif., Berkeley, 1987-90; mem. com. of credentials Commn. for Tchr. Preparation and Licensing, Sacramento, 1974-76; spkr. Asilomar Math. Conf., 1991, 94-98, mem. program com., 1995; spkr. Wine Country Math. Conf., 1992, Calif. chpt. Assn. for Persons with Severe Handicaps Conf., 1992, 94, 97, 98, bd. dirs., 1997—; spkr. Assn. for Persons with Severe Handicaps Internat. Conf., 1993, Supported Life Conf., 1992; rep. No. Regional Spl. Edn. Local Plan Area Com., Region III Full Inclusion Task Force for State of Calif., 1994-98; participant Calif. Rsch. Inst., 1992; mem. adv. task force on tchr. preparation in mainstreaming Calif. Commn. on Tchr. Credentialling, 1996. Contbg. author: Portfolio Assessment in Mathematics, 1990, Teacher Handbook on Homework, C.M.C. Communicator, 1993. Coord. children's coun. Epworth Meth. Ch., Berkeley, 1985-88, 96-98, Youth Coun., 1993-95; cert. lay spkr. Bay View dist. Calif.-Nev. United Meth. Ch., Berkeley, 1989—, bd. trustees, 1994-96, 98—; pres. bd. trustees Maya's Music Therapy Fund, 1994—. Named Math. Tchr. of Yr. Alameda/Contra Costa Counties Math. Educators, 1996; Berkeley Pub. Edn. Found. grantee, 1988, 89, 90, 92, 94, 95, 98, In Dulce Jullibo Inc. grantee, 1989, 90, 92, 94, 95, BAMP grantee, 1995, Calif. Math. Coun. grantee, 1995; fellow Bay Area Math. Project, 1994, Oakland-Bay Area Writing Project, 1977, Bay Area Writing Project, 1978, 98, Bay Area Calif. Arts Project, 1997. mem. Nat. Coun. Tchrs. English, Nat. Coun. Tchrs. Math., Calif. English Coun., Calif. Math. Coun., P.E.O.;bd. dirs. CA Chpt. Assn. Persons with Severe Handicaps, 1997—. Democrat. Avocations: singing, jogging, swimming, gourmet cooking, sewing. Home: 1016 Keeler Ave Berkeley CA 94708-1404 Office: Oxford Sch 1130 Oxford St Berkeley CA 94707-2624

JOHNSON, MARY LOU, lay worker; b. Moline, Ill., July 15, 1923; d. Percy and Hope (Aulgur) Sipes; m. Blaine Eugene Johnson, May 30, 1941 (dec.); children: Vivian A. Johnson Sweedy, Michael D. (dec.), Amelia Johnson Harms Thomas, James Michael (dec.). Grad. high sch., Moline. Chmn. Christian edn. 1st Christian Ch., Moline, 1971-73, 77-79, 84-86, elder, 1973-76, 77-80, chmn. official bd., 1979-81, dir. Christian edn., 1988-93, ret., 1993; Sunday sch. tchr. 1st Christian Ch, Moline, 1958-84; cluster del. Christian Chs. Ill. and Wisc., Moline, 1988-89. Author: (poem) What Is A Mother?, 1965. Officer various positions PTA, Moline, 1972-75, hon. life mem. State of Ill., 1972; leader, dist. dir. Girl Scouts U.S., Moline, 1955-65; skywatcher USAF Ground Observer Corps, Moline, 1955-57; vol. telethon coord. Muscular Dystrophy Assn., Moline, 1971-94; del. lt. gov.'s Commn. on Aging, Springfield, Ill., 1990. Recipient numerous appreciation awards Muscular Dystrophy Assn., 1964-94. Republican. Home: 2014 9th St Moline IL 61265-4779 *Life hands us many challenges. I find them interesting and always have been willing to accept them. Not all my efforts have been successful; however, each attempt has helped me grow to be a better person.*

JOHNSON, MARY MURPHY, social services administrator, writer; b. N.Y.C., Mar. 5, 1940; d. Richard and Nora (Greene) Murphy; m. Noel James Johnson, Oct. 8, 1961 (dec.); children: Valerie Johnson Powell, Donna Homan, Noreen Marie Pettitt, Richard. BA in English/History magna cum laude, Jacksonville State U., 1983, BS in Social Work magna cum laude, 1983, MA in History, 1984, B in Social Work magna cum laude, 1988. Cert. gerontology specialist. Asst. activities dir. Jacksonville (Ala.) Nursing Home, 1985-86; social services dir. Beckwood Manor, Anniston, Ala., 1987—; Cons. in field. Editor: Vladivostak Diary, 1987. Mem. AAUW, Ala. Archaeol. Soc., Coosa Valley Archaeol. Soc. (sec. 1982-87), Soc. Ala. Archivists, Human Svcs. Coun., Vietnam Vets. Am., Soc. for Creative Anachronism (Reeve, Canton of the Peregrine), Phi Eta Sigma, Phi Alpha Theta, Sigma Tau Delta, Omicron Delta Kappa. Russian Orthodox. Avocations: collecting antiques and depression glass, hiking, reading, archaeology.

JOHNSON, MARY PERRINE, musician, educator; b. Centralia, Ill., Apr. 21, 1929; d. David bates and Fanny Eliza (French) Perrine; m. Robert Royce Johnson, Dec. 30, 1953; children: Perrine Johnson Anderson, Royce W., Allegra F. Johnson Pitera. BS, Cornell U., 1951. Rsch. asst. Harvard U., Cambridge, Mass., 1951-52, Calif. Inst. Tech., Pasadena, 1952-55; mem. Recorders Court, Detroit, 1966-80, Good Company, Detroit, 1979-87, Musica Reservata of Utah, Logan, 1988—; workshop faculty Mideast Workshop recorders, Baroque flute, viola da gamba, Irish whistle, Pitts., 1980—; workshop leader various recorder socs., Mich., N.Y., Utah; artist in edn. Utah Arts Coun., Salt Lake City, 1990-94. Reviewer Music Rev., 1996—. Music dir. Salt Lake Recorder Soc., 1988—; breast cancer awareness com., vol. Am. Cancer Soc., Salt Lake City, 1993—. Mem. Am. Recorder Soc. (cert. tchr.), Viola da Gamba Soc. Am., PEO, Univ. of Utah Women's Club (pres. 1990-91), Sigma Xi. Avocation: tennis. Home: 3857 Eagle Point Dr Salt Lake City UT 84109-3822

JOHNSON, MARY SUSAN, transportation company professional; b. Bloomingdale, Ind., Nov. 19, 1937; d. William Blaine Shade and Goldina VandaVeer (Newlin) Brown; children: Roger, Tisa, Julia, Angela, Robert, William. Grad. high sch., Rockville, Ind. Sec., treas. Tri-State Transport, Inc., 1968-73; road driver Roadway Express, Chicago Heights, Ill., 1977—, safety team capt., 1991-92, 94; completed Passport Tour (Abate), 1990, 94; mem. Roadway Express Dist. Road Team Dist. 12, 1995-97. Mem newsletter com. focus group Roadway Express; mem. focus group Kenworth Driver's Bd., 1992—; active Motorcycle Safety Found., Motorcycle Rider Course; instr. for abate of Ind., Ind. Dept. of Edn. Recipient rodeo awards, 3d place 8/48 rally Motorcycle Endurance Rider's Assn., 1996; 1st woman to finish on a Harley-Davidson motorcycle World Famous Iron Butt Rally, 1995, finished 6th place out of 78 starts and 61 finishers in 8th Iron Butt Rally, 1997. Mem. Am. Motorcycle Assn., Am. Bikers Aim Toward Edn., Am. Radio Relay League, Chgo. Women in Trade Group, Stars Radio Club, Harley Owners Group (newsletter editor Calumet region chpt. 1994-96, Hammond, Ind., asst. dir. Calumet region chpt. 1996-99), Ladies of Harley. Avocations: motorcycle endurance riding, amateur radio. Home and Office: PO Box 316 Griffith IN 46319-0316

JOHNSON, MARY ZELINDA, artist; b. Hopkinton, Mass., June 3, 1914; d. Pietro and Ida (Sora) Sabettini; m. Paul Y. Johnson; 1 child, Paula Johnson Cooper. Student, AIC, Springfield, Mass., 1945-46, Sarah Whitney Olds, Patchogue, N.Y., 1947-49, Edna Ross, Patchogue, N.Y., 1949-51, Emile Gruppe, Gloucester, Mass., 1948, Pratt Inst., Bklyn., 1952-54, L'Acad. Julien, Paris, 1957-58, U. Fine Arts, Bangkok, 1960-62, Khiem Yemsiri/Royal Sculptor a, Sch. Fine Arts, Bangkok, 1961-62. Dir. Swinburne Sch., Newport, R.I., 1970-73. Art exhbns. include: Brookhaven, N.Y., 1948, Patchogue, L.I., 1949, Stoney Brook Mus., 1951, Athens, Greece, 1955, Casablanca, Morocco, 1958, Arts Club/Washington, 1959, 22nd Met. Exhibit at Smithsonian, Washington, 1959, Nat. Mus. of Bangkok, 1961, Bangkok Art Ctr., 1961, Tourist Orgn. of Thailand, 1961, Panamanian N.A. Assn., Panama City, 1963, Naval Officer's Club, Newport, 1972, Wharf Gallery, Newport, 1972, Swinburne Sch., 1972, Springfield Coll. Hastings Gallery, 1986, Westfield Atheneum Jasper Rand Gallery, 1990, Biltmore Studio, Washington, 1984, Nat. Greek Art Exhbns., Springfield, 1990, Washington Arts Club, 1993, others; internal. artist and sculptor/multimedia and woodcuts. Vol. USO, Portland, Maine, 1942-43, Ft. Hancock, N.J., 1941-42; driver Red Cross Motorcorps, Charleston, S.C., 1943-45, Springfield, 1945-46, others. Recipient 1st prize in State Dept. Bridge Tournament, worldwide, 1964. Mem. Arts Club/Washington, Young Artists Group/Bangkok, Am. Fgn. Svc. Assn., Washington Arts Club, Siam Soc./Bangkok, Naval Officers Wives Club/Washington, USIA Alumni Assn. Republican. Roman Catholic. Avocations: internat. cuisine, bridge, tennis, swimming, horseback riding. Home: Vinson Hall # 105 6251 Old Dominion Dr Mc Lean VA 22101-4818

JOHNSON, MARYANNA MORSE, business owner; b. Oxford, Miss., Dec. 21, 1936; d. Hugh McDonald and Anna Sullivan (Virden) Morse; children: Julianna, Hunter, Cynthia, Capp. Student, Miss. U. for Women, 1957; BSN cum laude, Tex. Woman's U., 1986. RN, Tex. Owner MM Johnson Network India, Boulder, Colo., 1968—; health promotion cons., 1986—. Mem. Sigma Theta Tau. Home: 3102 Bell Dr Boulder CO 80301-2277

JOHNSON, MARYL RAE, cardiologist; b. Fort Dodge, Iowa, Apr. 15, 1951; d. Marvin George and Beryl Evelyn (White) J. BS, Iowa State U., 1973; MD, U. Iowa, 1977. Diplomate Am. Bd. Internal Medicine; diplomate of Subspeciality of Cardiovascular Diseases. Intern, U. Iowa Hosps., Iowa City, 1977-78, resident 1978-81, fellow, 1979-82; assoc. in cardiology U. Iowa Hosps. and Clinics, Iowa City, 1982-86, asst. prof. medicine cardiovascular divsn., 1986-88; asst. prof. medicine Med. Ctr. Loyola U., 1988-92, assoc. prof. 1992-94; assoc. prof. Rush U., 1994-97, Northwestern U. Med. Sch., 1998—; med. dir. cardiac transplantation U. Iowa Hosp., 1986-88, assoc. med. dir. cardiac transplantation Loyola U., 1988-94; assoc. med. dir. Rush Heart Failure and Cardiac Transplant Program, 1994-97; dir. Heart Failure Cardiac Transplant Program, Northwestern U. Med. Sch., 1998—. Mem. Nat. Heart Lung and Blood Adv. Coun., Bethesda, Md., 1979-83, biomed. rsch. tech. rev. com. NIH, 1990-93 (chairperson 1992-93). Assoc. editor: Jour. Heart and Lung Transplantation, 1995—. Barry Freeman scholar, 1974; recipient Jane Leinfelder Meml. award U. Iowa Coll. Medicine, 1977, Clin. Investigator award NIH, 1981, New Investigator Research award, NIH, 1986. Mem. AMA, AAAS, ACP, Internat. Soc. Heart and Lung Transplantation, Am. Heart Assn., Am. Fedn. Clin. Rsch., Am. Coll. Cardiology, Am. Soc. Transplant Physicians, Ill. State Med. Soc., Chgo. Med. Soc., Order of the Rose, Alpha Lambda Delta, Phi Kappa Phi, Iota Sigma Pi, Alpha Omega Alpha. Office: Northwestern U Med Sch 250 E Superior St Ste 520 Chicago IL 60611-2958

JOHNSON, M(AURICE) GLEN, political science educator; b. Pikeville, Ky., Nov. 18, 1936; s. Marvin Forrest and Norcie (Wicker) J.; m. Sipra Bose, July 13, 1963; children: Denise Bose, Robert Alexander. BA, Georgetown Coll., Ky., 1958; MA, U.N.C., 1961, PhD, 1966. Instr. polit. sci. U. Ky., Lexington, 1963-64; instr. Vassar Coll., Poughkeepsie, N.Y., 1964-66, asst. prof., 1966-72, assoc. prof., 1972-77, prof., 1977—; Shirley Ecker Boskey chair in internat. rels., 1999—; dir. program of internat. studies Vassar Coll., Poughkeepsie, N.Y., 1985-89, acting pres., 1997-98; dir. Am. Studies Rsch. Ctr., Hyderabad, India, 1990-93. Author: (with others) Beyond the Water's Edge, 1975, Consensus at the Crossroads, 1972, La Dèclaration Universelle des Droits de l'Homme, 1991, Ah, Columbus! The Indian Discovery of America, 1993, The Universal Declaration of Human Rights 1948-1993, 1994, The Universal Declaration of Human Rights: A History of its Creation and Implementation, 1998; editor Indian Jour. Am. Studies, 1990-93; contbr. articles to profl. jours. Trustee Poughkeepsie Day Sch., 1968-72, 85-88, pres. bd. trustees, 1986-88; trustee Eleanor Roosevelt Ctr. at Val-Kill, 1986-90, 94—, v.p., 1989-90, 95-97, pres., 1997—; mem., bd. dirs. Friends of Fulbright in India, 1995—. Named Sr. Fulbright lectr. U. Poona, India, 1977-78, sr. Fulbright lectr. India, 1990-93. Mem. Am. Polit. Sci. Assn., Assn. for Asian Studies, Internat. Studies Assn. Home: 39 Garfield Pl Poughkeepsie NY 12601-4321 Office: Vassar Coll Box 376 124 Raymond Ave Poughkeepsie NY 12604-0376

JOHNSON, MAURICE VERNER, JR., agricultural research and development executive; b. Duluth, Minn., Sept. 13, 1925; s. Maurice Verner Sr. and Elvira Marie (Westberg) J.; m. Darlene Ruth Durand, June 23, 1944; children: Susan Kay, Steven Dale. BS, U. Calif., 1953. Registered profl. engr. From research engr. to dir. research and devel. Sunkist Growers, Ontario, Calif., 1953-84; v.p. research and devel. Sunkist Growers, Ontario, 1984-90, ret., 1990—; v.p., dir. Calif. Citrus Quality Council, Claremont. Contbr. articles to profl. pubs.; patentee in field. Sgt. U.S. Army, 1944-46, ETO. Fellow Am. Soc. Agrl. Engrs. (dir. 1969-70); mem. ASME, Am. Inst. Indsl. Engrs., Am. Assn. Advancement Sci., Nat. Soc. Profl. Engrs., Tau Beta Pi. Republican. Avocation: golf. Office: Sunkist Growers 760 E Sunkist St PO Box 3720 Ontario CA 91761-0993

JOHNSON, MELBA EDWARDS, secondary education educator; b. Jefferson, N.C., Mar. 28, 1947; d. Lee Swanson Edwards and Mabel (Wilson) Worley; children: Andrea Reeves, Chan Badger; m. James Steven Johnson, Dec. 27, 1986. BA in English and Edn., U. N.C., 1969; MS in English and Edn., N.C. A&T U., 1987. Tchr. English Durham (N.C.) H.S., 1969-70, Alleghany H.S., Sparta, N.C., 1970-87; tchr. English, SAT Prep West Brunswick H.S., Shallotte, N.C., 1987—; instr. Kaplan's Ednl. Testing Ctr., Shallotte, 1996-97; instr. English Brunswick C.C., Supply, N.C., 1995-96, Princeton Rev. SAT Testing Ctr. Pianist Jennie's Br. Ch., Shallotte, 1992-99. Recipient Svc. to Mankind award Sertoma Club, Ocean Isle Beach, N.C., 1997; named Tchr. of Yr. Brunswick County, 1997-98. Mem. N.C. English Tchrs. Assn. (Outstanding English Tchr. 1996-97), N.C. Assn. Edn., Brunswick County Assn. Educators (innovative learning group/thinking maps trainer). Baptist. Avocations: piano playing, reading, walking, tutoring. Home: 39 Fairway Dr Shallotte NC 28470-4422 Office: Brunswick County Schs PO Box 189 35 Referndum Dr NE Bolivia NC 28422-0189

JOHNSON, MELISSA ANN, early childhood educator; b. Washington, Nov. 30, 1973; d. Walter Dave and Ann Elizabeth (Griffin) Wyatt; m. Carson Alexander Johnson, May 31, 1996. BS in Edn., Valdosta (Ga.) State U., 1996. Cert. educator, Ga. Shift mgr. Wellington Foods, Tifton, Ga., 1989-92, RTM/Arby's, Valdosta, 1992-95; paraprofl., team tchr. St. John Cath. Sch., Valdosta, 1995-96; technician child devel. program RAF, Lakenheath, Eng., 1997—; substitute tchr. Dept. Def. Ednl. Activities, RAF Lakenheath, 1997; tchr. Valdosta State U. Summer Dream Sch., 1996. RTM scholar, Valdosta, 1994-95. Fellow Student Assn. Ga. Educators; mem. Profl. Assn. Ga. Educators. Avocations: fine arts, sculpture, sketching, computers, travel. Home: Psc 41 Box 6146 APO AE 09464-6146 also: 7404 Northgate Dr W Tifto GA 31794

JOHNSON, MICAH WILLIAM, television newscaster, director; b. Pitts., July 23, 1963; s. William T. and Joann K. (Pierce) J. Student, Indiana U. Pa., 1981-84. Announcer WLEM-AM/WQKY-FM, Emporium, Pa., 1978-81; news dir., anchorman WIUP-TV, Indiana, Pa., 1981-84; anchorman, reporter WSEE-TV, Erie, Pa., 1984-85; anchorman, mng. editor WVVA-TV, Bluefield, W.Va., 1985-86; news dir., anchorman WKYN-TV, St. Mary's, Pa., 1986-87; anchorman television and radio news Cable News Network, Atlanta, 1987-89; anchorman, corr. NBC-TV News, Washington, 1989-90; sr. producer radio & TV U.S. Senate, Washington, 1990; anchorman, news dir. Sta. KTSM-TV-AM-FM, El Paso, Tex., 1990-93, Sta. WTOV-TV, Steubenville, Ohio, 1993-94; dir. news Sta. WBRE-TV, Wilkes-Barre, Pa., 1994-96; news dir. Sta. WPXI-TV, Pitts., 1996-97; dir. news and prodn. WVIT-TV Paramount Pictures, Hartford, Conn., 1997-98; pres., CEO Mediastars Internat.; talk show host Sta. KTSM Newsradio, El Paso, 1990-93; adj. prof. Dekalb Coll., Clarkston, Ga., 1987-89; bd. dirs. Conn. Assoc. Press. Vol. fireman Morris Twp. Fire Co., Morrisdale, Pa., 1980—, Erie Emergency Med. Svcs., 1984-85; dir. choir Morrisdale United Meth. Ch., 1982-87; bd. dirs. El Paso Humane Soc., El Paso Zool. Soc.; mem. adv. bd. Salvation Army. With Pa. N.G., 1981—. Recipient Presdl. Citation for Cmty. Svc., 1992, Best of the Best award/Cmty. Svc. Nat. Assn. Broadcasters, 1992, AP award, 1985, 86, 87, 90, 91, 92, 93, 94, 95, 96, 97, 98, Nat. Pianist award Am. Coll. Musicians, 1973-79, Ind. U. Disting. Alumni award, 1990, Gold medal award Internat. Radio Festival N.Y, 1990, Gavel award State Bar of Tex., 1992, Tex. Gov.'s award/Cmty. Svc., 1992, Outstanding Contbn. to Law Enforcement award combined law enforcement assns. of Tex., 1991-92, Spl. Recognition award U.S. Marshal's Svc., 1992, Pub. Safety award Pa. Gov., 1996; nominee Emmy award for Best Newscast, 1994, 95, 96, 97; recipient Emmy award for Best Newscast, 1997. Mem. NATAS, Nat. Press Club, Radio-TV News Dirs. Assn. (Overall Excellence in News award), Conn. Assoc. Press Bd. Dirs. (v.p.), Nat. Radio Broadcasters Assn., El Paso Police Officers Assn. (hon.), White House Corrs. Assn., Nat. Wildlife Fedn. (bd. dirs. Ind. U. mag.), El Paso Humane Soc. (bd. dirs.), El Paso Zool Soc. (bd. dirs.) Nat. Press Club, El Paso Downtown Lions Club, Masons. Avocations: dogsled racing, fishing, travel, piano. Office: 15626 N 54th Place Scottsdale AZ 85254

JOHNSON, MICHAEL, track and field Olympic athlete; b. Dallas, Sept. 13, 1967. Student, Baylor U., 90. Recipient Gold medal 200 meters Goodwill Games, 1990, 94, 4 x 100 relay Barcelona Olympics, 1992, 200 meters and 400 meters Summer Olympics, Atlanta, 1996, Jesse Owens award, 1994; winner 200 meters World Athletic Championships, 1991, 400 meters, 1993; U.S. Nat. champion 200 meters, 1990-92, 95; named Athlete of Yr. USA Track & Field, 1993-94; world record holder indoor 400 meters, 200 meters at 1996 Olympics; gold medal for 400 meters World Championship, 1997. Office: USA Track & Field PO Box 120 Indianapolis IN 46206-0120*

JOHNSON, MICHAEL DENNIS, lawyer; b. Upper Darby, Pa., Sept. 2, 1948; s. Peter Joseph and Gloria Veronica (Magro) Caruso; 1 child, Monica Ann. BA in political sci., Washington State Univ., 1970; JD, Univ. Washington, 1973. Bar: Wash., Ct. of Appeals Bar (5th cir.), Ct. of Appeals Bar (8th cir.). Trial lawyer Civil Rights Divsn., Washington, 1973-76; sr. trial lawyer Criming Sect. Civil Rights Divsn., Washington, 1976-84; sr. litigation counsel U.S. Dept. Justice, Little Rock, Ark., 1984-93, first asst. U.S. atty., 1993—; adj. prof. Univ. Ark., Little Rock, 1985—; instr. Nat. Inst. of Trial Advocacy, So. Bend, Ind., 1988—, U.S. Dept. Justice Advocacy Inst., Washington, 1980—, Criminal Justice Inst., Little Rock, 1993-97. Author: Management of Civil Rights Allegation, 1994. Recipient Cert. of Appreciation ATF, 1986, 88, 97, Spl. Recognition award, 1988, LECC, 1993, Outstanding Svc. award IRS, 1992, Exceptional Svc. award FBI, 1989, Cert. of Achievement award Ark. Trial Lawyers Assn., 1991, Ark. Investigation, 1990, DOJ Trial Advocacy, 1987, Outstanding Achievement award Secret Svc., 1998. Mem. William R. Overton Inn of Ct. Avocations: photography, travel, athletics. Office: US Atty Office 425 W Capitol Ave Ste 500 Little Rock AR 72201-3405

JOHNSON, MICHAEL EDWARD, communication consultant, magician; b. Escondido, Calif., Jan. 14, 1959; s. Harold W. and Joan C. (Donkin) J.; m. Cynthia Lee Tunget, Sept. 3, 1994. AA in Liberal Scis., Palomar Coll., San Marcos, Calif., 1979; BA in Speech Comm., San Diego State U., 1981. Journalist cons. Aztec Shops Ltd., San Diego, 1979-83; mktg. rep. Commuter Computer, San Diego, 1984-86; ridesharing coord. Assn. Monterey Bay Area Govts., Monterey, Calif., 1986-89; editor Paul Kagan Assocs., Inc., Carmel, Calif., 1989-91; account exec. Commuter Computer, San Diego, 1991-92; pub. info. specialist Air Pollution Control Dist., San Diego, 1992-93; pres. Michael E. Johnson & Assocs., San Diego, 1993—; chmn. Telecommuting Strategic Planning team, San Diego, 1994; vice chair Commute Mgmt. Adv. Com., Sacramento, 1989. Editor jour. The Astrophile, 1995-97; editor newsletters Autograph Rsch., 1991—, Space Autograph News, 1993—, Celebrity Home Adress Newsletter, 1995—. Recipient Bronze medal Aviacion y Espacio, 1996, 1st place high jump Mt. San Antonio Relays, 1979. Mem. Soc. Am. Magicians, Universal Autograph Collectors Club. Avocations: magic, writing, off-road skateboarding. Office: Michael E Johnson & Assocs 862 Thomas Ave San Diego CA 92109-3940

JOHNSON, MICHAEL KENNETH, chemistry educator; b. Tonbridge, Kent, Eng., Mar. 8, 1953; came to U.S., 1980; s. Thomas Sydney and Eileen (Heath) J.; m. Carole Ann Woodhouse, Aug. 21, 1976; children: Caroline Louise, Thomas Michael. BA, Cambridge U., 1974, MA, 1977; MSc, U. East Anglia, 1975, PhD, 1977. Postdoctoral fellow U. East Anglia, Norwich, 1977-80; postdoctoral rsch. assoc. Princeton (N.J.) U., 1980-82; asst. prof. chemistry La. State U., Baton Rouge, 1982-86; assoc. prof. chemistry U. Ga., Athens, 1987-91, prof. chemistry, 1991-98, rsch. prof. chemistry, 1998—, dir., 1993-97; mem. biophysics grant rev. panel NSF, Washington, 1990-95. Editor: Electron Transfer in Biology and the Solid State, 1990; contbr. over 130 rsch. articles to profl. jours. Alfred P. Sloan fellow, 1986; recipient rsch. grants NIH, 1984, 87, 94, NSF, 1986, 90, 94, 98. Mem. Am. Chem. Soc., Phi Kappa Phi. Home: 1100 Double Bridges Rd Winterville GA 30683-4830 Office: U Ga Dept Chemistry Athens GA 30602

JOHNSON, MICHAEL LEWIS, psychiatrist; b. Louisville, May 17, 1941; s. Ralph L. and Bee (Burr) J.; children: Kirstin, Aaron, Jessica; m. Frances Bourne. AB, Earlham Coll., Richmond, Ind., 1963; MD, Ind. U., 1968. Diplomate Am. Bd. Psychiatry and Neurology. Intern Marion County Gen. Hosp., Indpls., 1968-69; resident in psychiatry Wash. U. Barnes Hosp., St. Louis, 1969-72; staff psychiatrist U.S. Naval Hosp., Portsmouth, Va., 1972-74, South Cen. Community Mental Health Ctr., Bloomington, Ind., 1974-80; psychiatrist pvt. practice, Bloomington, Ind., 1974-83; unit dir. Milford-Whitinsville (Mass.) Regional Hosp., 1983-85; staff psychiatrist Harvard Vanguard Med. Assocs., Cambridge, Mass., 1985—, Peabody, Mass., 1997—; instr. in psychiatry Harvard Med. Sch., Cambridge, 1985—, Cambridge Hosp., 1985-92, Brigham and Women's Hosp., 1993—; mem. HPHC credentials com., HVMA psychopharmacology com., HVMA CENT Psychiat. Consultation Svc. Author: (book chpt.) Psychotherapists Guide to Pharmacotherapy, 1989; subject of docudrama Virtuoso, 1991. Quaker. Subject of stage play, Virtuoso, 1996. Office: Harvard Vanguard Med Assocs 1611 Cambridge St Cambridge MA 02138-4302

JOHNSON, MICHAEL MARION, judge; b. Long Beach, Calif., Feb. 12, 1951. BA in Polit. Scis. magna cum laude, UCLA, 1973; JD with honors, U. Calif., San Francisco, 1976. Bar: Calif. 1976, U.S. Ct. Appeals (9th and 3d cts.), U.S. Dist. Ct. (no. dist., ctrl. dist., ea. dist. and so. dists.) Calif. 1979, U.S. Supreme Ct. 1980. Ptnr. and assoc. Baker & Hostetler, L.A., 1976-84, L.A. ptnr. in charge of lawyer hiring, 1984-87, ptnr., 1984-97, mem. exec. com., 1988-91; judge L.A. County Superior Ct., 1997—. Commr. Calif. Fair Employment and Housing Commn., 1987-91, 1995-97; bd. dirs. So. Calif. Employment Round Table, Inc., 1992-97. Calif. State scholar UCLA, 1973, U. Calif. Towne scholar, 1976. Mem. ABA (sects. on litig. and labor and employment), Calif. State Bar Assn. (chair labor and employment sect. 1995-96), Calif. Judges Assn., L.A. County Bar Assn. (sect. on labor law), Phi Beta Kappa, Pi Gamma Mu. Office: LA Superior Ct PO Box 151 Main Post Office Los Angeles CA 90053-0151*

JOHNSON, MICHAEL PAUL, history educator; b. Ponca City, Okla., July 6, 1941; s. Howard W. and Maybelle P. (Fetrow) J.; m. Anne E. Thompson, June 2, 1962; children: Ian Michael, Sarah Elizabeth. AB in Chemistry cum laude, Knox Coll., 1963; MA in History, Stanford U., 1967, PhD in History, 1973. Asst. prof. LeMoyne Coll., Memphis, 1967-68; instr. San Jose (Calif.) State U., 1970-71; asst. prof. history U. Calif., Irvine, 1971-77, assoc. prof., 1977-84, prof., 1984-94; prof. Johns Hopkins U., Balt., 1994—. Author: Toward a Patriarchal Republic, 1977, Black Masters, 1984, No Chariot Let Down, 1984, The American Promise, 1998, Reading the American Past, 2 vols., 1998. Fellow Am. Coun. Learned Socs., 1977, NEH, 1982. Mem. Am. Hist. Assn., Orgn. Am. Historians, So. Hist. Assn., Phi Beta Kappa. Office: Johns Hopkins U Dept History Baltimore MD 21218

JOHNSON, MICHAEL RANDY, insurance company executive; b. York, Nebr., Jan. 29, 1946; s. Sheldon Albert and Mary Lynn (Barbur) J.; m. Virginia L. Allgood, Apr. 5, 1975; children: Cory Michael, Scott Alan, Adam Todd. Student, Doane Coll., 1964-66, U. Nebr., 1966-68. Farmer Geneva, Nebr., 1968-84; field reporter Agrl. Stabilization and Constrn. Svc., Geneva, 1973-80; adjuster Fed. Crop Ins. Corp., Kansas City, Kans., 1979-81, North Ctrl. Crop Ins., Eau Claire, Wis., 1981-84, Acceptance-Redland Ins. Co./Am. Agrisurance-Agrijusters, Council Bluffs, Iowa, 1984-86; field supr. Acceptance-Redland Ins. Co./Am. Agrisurance-Agrijusters, Council Bluffs, 1986-88, tng. supr., 1988-90, regional claims supr., 1990-92, v.p., asst. claims mgr., 1993-94, claims mgr., sr. v.p., 1994-98, dir. claims, sr. v.p., 1998—; cons. Segura La Comml., Monterey, Mex., 1988-92, Segures Am., Mexico City, 1988-92; contbg. bd. mem. Code of Ethics Bd. Nat. Crop Ins. Svc., Overland Park, Kans., 1992—; speaker in field. Author: (reference handbook) Grop Growth Patterns and Loss Adjustment, Mexico, 1991; editor: Crop Adjusting Manual, 1990, '91, '92. Mem. Masons. Methodist. Avocations: reading, fishing, platform speaking, plant studies. Home: 810 Elm St Missouri Valley IA 51555-1141 Office: Acceptance-Redland Ins Co Am Agrisurance-Agrijusters 535 W Broadway Council Bluffs IA 51503-0812 also: PO Box 7 Missouri Valley IA 51555-0007

JOHNSON, MICHAEL WARREN, international relations specialist; b. Mpls., Oct. 2, 1948; s. Warren Redy and Lorraine Agnes (Capistran) J.; BS, U.S. Mil. Acad., 1970; MA in Internat. Relations, U. So. Calif., 1973; PhD in Polit. Sci., MIT, 1985; postgrad., Harvard U., 1987; m. Jeanine Ann Tyldesley, Feb. 6, 1971 (div. 1991); children: Benjamin T., Joseph A., Katherine E.; m. Deborah V. Matthews, July 26, 1991; children: Maximilian N., Scott M. Commd. 2d lt. U.S. Army, 1970, advanced through grades to capt., 1974, resigned, 1975; sr. middle east analyst U.S. Army Mil. Intelligence, 1975; stockbroker Merrill Lynch, Pierce, Fenner & Smith, Inc., Boston, 1975-81; v.p. Thomson McKinnon Securities Inc., Boston, 1981-82; 1st v.p. Jefferies & Co., Boston, 1982-84; sr. v.p. Moseley, Hallgarten, Estabrook & Weeden, Inc., Boston, 1984-88; internat. rels. cons. Geopolitical Strategist, Inc., 1984—. Fgn. policy adviser to Congl. candidate, 1980. Mem. Assn. of Grads. U.S. Mil. Acad.

JOHNSON, MIKKEL BORLAUG, physicist; b. Waynesboro, Va., Jan. 2, 1943; s. Wallace A. and Anne D. (Davies) J.; m. Lynne McFadden, June 14, 1966; children: Kara Marit, Krista Lynne. BS, Va. Poly. Inst., 1966; MS, Carnegie Mellon U., 1968, PhD, 1970. Rsch. assoc. Cornell U., Ithaca, N.Y., 1970-72; staff mem., fellow Los Alamos (N.Mex.) Nat. Lab., 1972—; vis. prof. SUNY, Stony Brook, 1981-82, Carnegie Mellon U., 1997-98. Editor: Relativistic Dynamics and Quark-Nuclear Physics, 1986, Nuclear and Particle Physics on the Light Cone, 1989, LAMPF Workshop on (Pi,K) Physics, 1991; assoc. editor Nuclear Physics, 1975-97. Lab. fellow Los Alamos Nat. Lab, 1991; recipient Humboldt award for Sr. U.S. Scientist, Humboldt Found., 1986. Fellow Am. Phys. Soc. Home: 118 Piedra Loop Los Alamos NM 87544-3828 Office: Los Alamos Nat Lab P-Div Ms H846 Los Alamos NM 87545

JOHNSON, MILDRED SNOWDEN, retired nursing educator; b. Elgin, Tex., Nov. 15, 1915; d. Milton Foy and Pearl Mae (DeLoach) Snowden; children: Roy B. Johnson, Betty Carol Johnson. BSN, U. Tex., Galveston, 1965; MSN, U. Tex., Austin, 1972. Cert. clin. nurse spl. adult psychol./mental health. Psychiatric nurse tech. State Hosp., Austin, 1959-63; head nurse Holy Cross Hosp., Austin, 1967, St. David's Hosp., Austin, 1968-69; acting dir. Ctrl. Tex. Coll., Kileen, Tex., 1969-70; asst. prof. nursing U. Tex., Galveston, 1970-93; ret., 1993. Mem. ANA, Nat. League Nursing, Tex. Nurses Assn., Tex. League Nursing, Sigma Theta Tau Internat. Home: 2116 Fordham Ln Austin TX 78723-1332

JOHNSON, MILLARD WALLACE, JR., mathematics and engineering educator; b. Racine, Wis., Feb. 1, 1928; s. Millard Wallace and Marian Manilla (Rittman) J.; m. Ruth Pugh Gifford, Dec. 26, 1953; children: Millard Wallace III, Jeannette Marian Brooks, Charles Gifford, Peter Allen. BS in Applied Math. and Mechanics, U. Wis., 1952, MS, 1953; PhD in Math, MIT, 1957. Rsch. asst. MIT, 1953-57, lectr., 1957-58; mem. staff Math. Rsch. Ctr. U. Wis., Madison, 1958-94, prof. mechanics, 1958-63, prof. mechanics and math., 1964-94, mem. staff Rheology Rsch. Ctr., 1970—; mem. Engine Rsch. Ctr. U. Wis., 1985—; prof. emeritus U. Wis., Madison, 1994—. Contbr. articles to profl. jours. Adv. bd. Internat. Math. and Statis. Libra. (IMSL), 1971-92. With USN, 1946-48. Fellow ASME; mem. Soc. Rheology, Soc. Indsl. and Applied Math., Am. Acad. Mechanics, Brit. Soc. Rheology, Phi Beta Kappa. Home: 802 Blue Ridge Pkwy Madison WI 53705-1148 Office: U Wis Dept Eng Phys 1500 Engineering Dr Madison WI 53706-1609

JOHNSON, MORGAN BURTON, artist, writer; b. Santa Monica, Calif., Nov. 25, 1952; s. Arnold and Roma (Burton) J. BA in Psychology, U. Calif., San Diego, 1974; Cert. Fgn. Studies, Lycee du Universite, Dijon, France, 1968. Mgr. Coronet Stores, Las Vegas, Nev., 1975; mgr., chef Diver's Cove Restaurant, Long Beach, Calif., 1977-80; prodn. control asst. Century Plastics, Compton, Calif., 1980; prodn. supr. Analytichem Internat., Harbor City, Calif., 1980-81; sr. planner Sci. Mfg./Am. Hosp., Emeryville, Calif., 1982-85; materials mgr. Applied Biosys. (Perkin-Elmer), Foster City,

Calif., 1985-90; owner, pres. Two Bears Restoration, 1990—. Exhibited in group shows at Medford (Oreg.) Ctr., 1993, Mills House Art Gallery, Garden Grove, Calif., 1979, San Bernardino Mus. Art, 1980-81, Calif. Poly. State U., San Luis Obispo, 1985, West Coast Biennial, Pacific Grove Art Ctr., 1985, Cunningham Meml. Art Show, Bakersfield, Calif., 1985, The Rogue Gallery, Medford, 1984, 85, 90, 91, C. Erickson Gallery, Half Moon Bay, Calif., 1986-90, Britt Music Festival, Jacksonville, Oreg., 1994; solo shows include Daleo Farms, Sams Valley, Oreg., 1995, Cache Salon, Walnut Creek, 1996, First Congl. Ch., Long Beach, 1996; included in pvt. collections; author: Trees of Other Colors, 1994, Condemned to a Life of Painting Pretty Pictures, 1994, Circle of the White Buffalo, 1996; published in Nat. Libr. Poetry Anthology, 1997, 98. Mem. So. Oreg. Arts Coun., Medford, 1990—, San Francisco Artist's Coop, 1980-83; fin. sec. Long Beach Art Assn., 1978-79; hanging com. mem. San Diego Art Inst., 1974-76. Recipient 1st prize Recreation and Parks Dept., L.A., 1965, 66, Long Beach Art Assn., 1977, 3d pl. award Downey Mus. Art, 1977, 78, So. Oreg. Lambda Excellence award for art, 1998. Avocations: hiking, skiing, gardening. Home and Office: 2130 Capital Ave Medford OR 97504-6944

JOHNSON, MURRAY H., optometrist, researcher, consultant, lecturer; b. Montreal, Que., Can., Jan. 29, 1956; came to U.S., 1980; s. William and Leah (Bedzowski) J.; m. Linda Fluxman, Apr. 30, 1978; children: Warren Natan, Tanya Yael, Arielle Carly. Diploma in Optometry, Witwatersrand Coll., Johannesburg, 1977; postgrad., U. Montreal, 1980; BS, U. Houston, 1981, OD, 1981, MSc in Physiol. Optics and Vision Sci., 1984; postgrad., U. Tex. Health Ctr., 1983. Lic. optometrist, Tex., therapeutic lic., Tex.; cert. ocular therapeutics for treatment and mgmt. ocular disease U. Houston. Clin. instr. U. Houston, 1981-85, postdoct. fellow, 1981-84; researcher Inst. contact Lens Rsch., Houston, 1983-88; pvt. practice optometry specializing in contact lenses Eye & Contact Lens Assocs. North Tex., Dallas, 1985—; vis. asst. prof. U. Houston, 1984-85, adj. asst. prof., 1985-89; cons., clin. investigator Metro Optics, Inc., Dallas, 1989—; premktg. clin. evaluator, cons. and investigator to various contact lens and pharm. mfrs., 1989—; clin. investigator Paragon Optical, Mesa, Ariz., 1992; cons. Unilens Corp., Largo, Fla., 1989; clin. examiner Nat. Bd. Clin. Skills Exam., Nat. Bd. Examiners in Optometry, 1997—. Contbr. articles to profl. jours. Mem. clin. care com. Global Vision Inst., Global Vision Dallas, 1996; mem. edn. com. Akiba Acad. Dallas, 1986-88, bd. dirs., 1986-97, long range planning com., 1987-88, devel. com., 1993, v.p., treas., 1993-94, budget com., 1993-96, scholarship com., 1994—; bd. dirs. Congregation Share Tefilla, Dallas, 1988-92; steering com. B'nai B'rith, 1986-88, treas., 1987-88; bd. dirs., assoc. bd. dirs. Equitable Bank, Dallas, 1994-96. Postdoctoral fellow U. Houston, 1981-84, grantee 1981, 82; Ezell Rsch. fellow Am. Optometric Found., 1983. Fellow Am. Acad. Optometry; mem. AAAS, Assn. Rsch. in Vision and Ophthalmology, Am. Pub. Health Assn. (vision care sect.), Am. Optometric Assn. (contact lens sect.), Tex. Optometric Assn., Dallas County Optometric Soc., Am. Optometric Found. (Ezell fellows club), Sigma Xi. Jewish. Avocations: walking, swimming, racquetball. Office: Eye & Contact Lens Assocs N Tex 18111 Preston Rd Ste 180 Dallas TX 75252-5481

JOHNSON, NANCY ANN, education educator; b. Worcester, Mass., May 12, 1932; d. Arthur Eugene and Anna Evelyn (Erickson) J.; BA, Clark U., 1955, MA in Edn., 1957; EdD, Boston U., 1977. Tchr., public schs., Auburn, Mass., 1956-63; reading supr., public schs., Groton, Mass., 1963-68; asst. prof. edn. Worcester State Coll., 1968-78, assoc. prof., 1978, prof., 1982, chair dept. edn., 1982-84, 91, coord. student teaching, 1980-83; adv. bd., local sch. Mem. pastoral com. Peoples Ch., Worcester, 1973-80, Christian edn. com., 1978-91, sec., 1990-94, ch. libr. extension 1992-93, adult edn. coord.; coll. rep. Teen Access-City Worcester Project; mem. exec. bd. Friends of Worcester Public Libr., 1980—, sec., 1981-82; coord. book sale vols.; corporator Worcester YMCA; mem. state lit. coun.; bd. dirs. Brittan Sq. Neighborhood Coun.; docent Worcester Hist. Mus., 1995—; sec. Clark Alumnae Coun., 1961-66; grant writer tree project City of Worcester-Brittan Sq. Neighborhood Assn.,; vol. Worcester Hist. Mus . Recipient Cmty. Improvement award. Brittan Sq. Neighborhood Coun. Mem. AAUW, Mass. Assn. Tchr. Educators (pres. 1987-88), Delta Kappa Gamma (sec. Tau chpt. 1974-76, 1st v.p. chpt. 1976, pres. 1990-92), Pi Lambda Theta (pres. Alpha Gamma chpt. 1979-81, mem. exec. bd. chpt. 1975-79), Phi Delta Kappa (Educator of Yr. 1993, advisor ctrl. chpt. chair rsch. ctrl. Mass. chpt., found. rep., scholarship chair), Kappa Delta Pi (co-counselor), Boston U. Womens Club (pres.), Boston U. Alumni Club Worcester County (pres. 1992-94, nominating chair, scholarship chair). Office: 486 Chandler St Worcester MA 01602-2832

JOHNSON, NANCY K., judge; b. Cin.. BA, Univ. of Cin., 1975, JD, 1978. Bar: Ohio 1978, Tex. 1980. Asst. atty. gen. Ohio, 1978-80, Tex., 1980-81; asst. U.S. atty. Tex. So. Dist., 1982-90; magistrate judge U.S. Dist. Ct. (Tex. so. dist.), 5th circuit, 1990—. Mem. Fed. Bar Assn., Houston Bar Assn. Office: Federal Bldg 515 Rusk St Ste 7019 Houston TX 77002-2604

JOHNSON, NANCY LEE, congresswoman; b. Chgo., Jan. 5, 1935; d. Noble Wishard and Gertrude Reid (Smith) Lee; m. Theodore H. Johnson, June 27, 1932; children—Lindsey Lee, Althea Anne, Caroline Reid. B.A., Radcliffe Coll., 1957; postgrad., U. London, 1957-58. Vice chmn. Charter Commn. New Britain, Conn., 1976-77; mem. Conn. Senate from 6th dist., 1977-82, 98th-105th Congresses from 6th Conn. dist., Washington, 1983—; mem. ways and means com., subcom. health, chair oversight com. Pres. Friends of Libr., New Britain Pub. Libr., 1973-76, Radcliffe Club Northern Conn., 1973-75; bd. dirs., pres. Sheldon Cmty. Guidance Clinic, 1974-75; dir. religious edn. Unitarian Universalist Soc. New Britain, 1967-72; bd. dirs. United Way New Britain, 1976.79. Recipient Outstanding Vol. award United Way, 1976; English Speaking Union grantee, 1958-59. Republican. Home: 141 S Mountain Dr New Britain CT 06052-1511 Office: Ho of Reps 343 Cannon Bldg Washington DC 20515-0706

JOHNSON, NAOMI BOWERS, nurse; b. Ft. Benning, Ga., Aug. 17, 1954; d. Bob and Henrietta Violet (Hoomalu) Bowers; m. James William Johnson, Dec. 7, 1973 (div.); children: Amelia, Melissa, Charity, James-William. ADN, Troy State U., Montgomery, Ala., 1974. Office supr., lab. supr., nursing coord. physician's office, Selma, Ala.; patients care coord. West. Ala. Home Health Agy., Selma; discharge planning/social svcs., SOBRA and clin. case mgmt. coord. Vaughan Regional Med. Ctr. Hosp., Selma; DON Dunn Nursing Home, Selma, Capitol Hill Health Care Ctr.; dir. mktg. and admissions Mariner Post Acute Health Care Network, Montgomery, Ala.

JOHNSON, NED (EDWARD CHRISTOPHER JOHNSON), publishing company executive; b. Lexington, Mass., Dec. 6, 1926; s. Edward J. and Mary A. (MacInnes) J.; m. Irma Di Lonardo, Mar. 13, 1946; children—Dana Elizabeth, Blair Christopher. B.S., Boston U., 1948. Vice pres. Moore Pub. Co., N.Y.C., 1948-57; sr. v.p. Cahners Pub. Co., Boston, 1957-88; pub. Design News mag., 1977-88; founder, chmn. Cahners Advt. Research Reports, 1976-88. Served with USNR, 1944-46. Mem. Am. Bus. Publs., Bus. and Profl. Advt. Assn. Democrat. Clubs: Boston Yacht (Marblehead, Mass.); Univ. (Boston); Jackson (N.H.); Ski and Tennis. Home: Black Mountain Rd PO Box 296 Jackson NH 03846-0296 *I thoroughly believe in the principle that each of us can accomplish anything we wish to accomplish, once the desire for accomplishment is firmly established and recognized within. I also believe that each of us has a responsibility to create an atmosphere among our fellow workers which will make it possible for each individual to accomplish the level of excellence within himself.*

JOHNSON, NICHOLAS, writer, lawyer, lecturer; b. Iowa City, Sept. 23, 1934; s. Wendell A.L. and Edna (Bockwoldt) J.; m. Karen Mary Chapman, 1952 (div. 1972); children: Julie, Sherman, Gregory; m. Mary Eleanor Vasey, 1991. B.A., U. Tex., 1956, LL.B., 1958; L.H.D., Windham Coll., 1971. Bar: Tex. 1958, D.C. 1963, U.S. Supreme Ct. 1963, Iowa 1974; lic. radio amateur. Law clk. to judge John R. Brown, U.S. 5th Circuit Ct. Appeals, 1958-59; law clk. to U.S. Supreme Ct. Justice Hugo L. Black, 1959-60; acting assoc. prof. law U. Calif. at Berkeley, 1960-63; assoc. Covington & Burling, Washington, 1963-64; adminstr. Maritime Adminstrn., chmn. Maritime Subsidy Bd. U.S. Dept. Commerce, 1964-66; commr. FCC, 1966-73; adj. prof. law Georgetown U., 1971-73; Poynter fellow Yale U., 1971; vis. prof. U. Ill., Champaign-Urbana, 1976, U. Okla., Norman, 1978, Ill. State U., Normal, 1979, U. Wis., Madison, 1980, Newhouse Sch., Syracuse U., 1980, U. Iowa Coll. Law, 1981—; vis. prof. dept. communications studies U. Iowa, 1982-85; vis. prof. Western Behavioral Scis. Inst., U. Calif., San Diego, 1986-91; vis. prof. Calif. State U., Los Angeles, 1986; co-dir. U. Iowa Inst. for Health, Behavior and Environ. Policy, 1990-93; chmn., dir. Nat. Citizens Comm. Lobby, 1975—, Nat. Citizens Com. for Broadcasting, 1974-78; pub. access, 1975-77; commentator Nat. Pub. Radio, 1975-77, 83-86, Sta. WRC-AM, Washington, 1977, Sta. WSUI, Iowa City, 1982-87; presdl. advisor White House Conf. on Libraries and Info. Services, 1979; exec. com. World Acad. Art and Sci., 1993-97. Author: Cases and Materials on Oil and Gas Law, 1962, How to Talk Back to Your Television Set, 1970, Japanese transl., 1971, Life Before Death in the Corporate State, 1971, Test Pattern for Living, 1972, Broadcasting in America, 1973, Cases and Materials on Communications Law and Policy, 1981, 82, 83, 84, 85, 86, Readings for Law of Electronic Media, 1993-94, (with David Loundy) Law of Electronic Media in a Cyberspace Age, 1996; syndicated columnist: Gannett News Service, 1982-84, Register and Tribune Syndicate, 1984, Cowles Syndicate, 1985-86, King Features Syndicate, 1986; contbr. to legal, gen., internat. publs.; contbg. editor, host PBS The New Tech Times, 1983-84. Dem. candidate for U.S. Ho. of Reps. from 3d Iowa Dist., 1974; bd. dirs. Internat. Soc. Gen. Semantics, Iowa City Cmty. Sch. Dist., Vols. in Tech. Assistance (VITA); mem. adv. bd. Ctr. for Media Edn., Cultural Environ. Movement, Fairness and Accuracy in Reporting, Inst. for Pub. Accuracy, Planet Ctrl. TV, Hightower and Assocs., Project Censored, War and Peace Found., Working Assets Long Distance; mem. Broadband and Telecom. Commn., Iowa City, 1981-87. Named One of 10 Outstanding Young Men in U.S., U.S. Jaycees, 1967, recipient New Republic Pub. Defender award, 1970, Civil Liberties Award Ga. ACLU, 1972, DeWitt Carter Reddick award U. Tex., 1977, George Stoney award Nat. Fedn. Local Cable Programmers, 1987; fellow World Acad. Art and Sci., 1991—. Mem. D.C., Iowa bar assns., State Bar Tex., Golden Key, Order of Coif, Phi Beta Kappa, Phi Delta Phi, Phi Eta Sigma, Pi Sigma Alpha. Democrat. Unitarian. Home and Office: PO Box 1876 Iowa City IA 52244-1876

JOHNSON, NIEL MELVIN, archivist, historian; b. Galesburg, Ill., July 28, 1931; s. Clarence Herman and Frances Albertina (Nelson) J.; m. Verna Gail Applegate, May 1, 1952; children: Kristin, David. BA, Augustana Coll., 1953; MA, State U. Iowa, 1965, PhD, 1971. Tchr. Unit #115, Biggsville, Ill., 1954-57; asst. historian U.S. Army Weapons Command, Rock Island, Ill., 1957-60, chief historian, 1960-63; instr. Augustana Coll., Rock Island, Ill., 1967-69; asst. prof. Dana Coll., Blair, Nebr., 1969-74; vis. asst. prof. U. Nebr., Omaha, 1975-76; archivist, historian Harry S. Truman Libr., Independence, Mo., 1977-92; pres. Portal to the Plains, Inc., Blair, Nebr., 1973-77, Am. Friends of Emigrant Inst. Sweden, East Moline, Ill., 1984-89. Author: George S. Viereck: German-American Propagandist, 1972, Portal to the Plains, 1974; co-author: Rockford Swedes: American Stories, 1993; contbr. articles in field to profl. jours., newspapers. coord. New Sweden '88 com. of Greater Kansas City, Mo.; chmn. Historic Trails City Com., Independence, 1988-93. Recipient Commendation, Concordia Hist. Inst., St. Louis, 1977. Mem. Orgn. Am. Historians, Midwestern Archives Conf., Jackson County Hist. Soc., Scandinavian Assn. (pres. 1987-89). Democrat. Lutheran. Avocations: painting, writing, photography, golf, impersonator of Harry S. Truman. Home: 15804 Kiger Cir Independence MO 64055-3750

JOHNSON, NILS, JR., minister; b. Balt., Apr. 3, 1930; s. Nils and Hazel Margaret (Caulk) J.; m. E. Marian Baker, June 10, 1950 (div. Dec. 30, 1971); children: Nils III, Leif Todd, Marta Kristine, Peter Kurt; m. Crystal Ann Wolfe, June 22, 1979; children: Thomas Ned Wolfe, Timothy Marlowe Wolfe (dec.). BS, Ind. U., 1955; B in Divinity, Oberlin Coll., 1958; postgrad., Drew U., 1963-67. Ordained clergy Evangelical Luth. Ch. in Am. Pastor Florence (Ohio) Congregational Ch., 1958-60; assoc. pastor St. Jacobs Luth. Ch., Miamisburg, Ohio, 1960-63; pastor Epiphany Luth. Ch., Warren, N.J., 1963-72; campus pastor Kutztown (Pa.) U., 1972-92; chaplain Muhlenberg Coll., Allentown, Pa., 1993-96; campus ministry cons. NEPA Synod Evangelical Luth. Ch. Am., Wescosville, Pa., 1981-93, divsn. for edn., Chgo., 1993-96. Pres. bd. dirs. Reading (Pa.)-Berks Campfire Girls, 1975-76; exec. bd. dirs. Friend, Inc., Berks County, Pa., 1985-92; bd. dirs. Reading-Berks Pa. Habitat for Humanity, 1999—. Monroe fellow, 1958-89. Avocations: woodworking, sailing. Home: 8 Curtis Rd Kutztown PA 19530-9205

JOHNSON, NOBLE MARSHALL, research scientist; b. San Francisco, Feb. 23, 1945. BSE cum laude, U. Calif., Davis, 1967, MSE, 1970; PhD, Princeton U., 1974. Mem. rsch. staff SRI Internat., Menlo Park, Calif., 1974-76; mem. rsch. staff Xerox Palo Alto (Calif.) Rsch. Ctr., 1976-85, prin. scientist Electronic Materials Lab., 1987—; mgr. Blue laser Diode Area, 1999—; vis. lectr. Princeton (N.J.) U., 1986, U. Erlangen-Nürnberg, Germany, 1987. Co-editor: 4 books; contbr. more than 275 articles to profl. jours.; patentee in field. Recipient Disting. Sr. U.S. Scientist award, Alexander von Humboldt Found., Germany, 1987; Nat. Def. Grad. fellow, Princeton U., 1969-72. Fellow Am. Phys. Soc.; mem. IEEE (sr.), Materials Rsch. Soc. (coun. 1986-88), Sigma Xi. Office: Xerox Palo Alto Rsch Ctr Electronic Materials Lab 3333 Coyote Hill Rd Palo Alto CA 94304-1314

JOHNSON, NOEL LARS, biomedical engineer; b. Palo Alto, Calif., Nov. 11, 1957; s. LeRoy Franklin and Margaret Louise (Lindsley) J.; m. Elise Lynnette Moore, May 17, 1986; children: Margaret Elizabeth, Kent Daniel. BSEE, U. Calif., Berkeley, 1979; ME, U. Va., 1982, PhD, 1990. Mgr. R&D Hosp. Products divsn. Abbott Labs., Mountain View, Calif., 1986-99; CEO Calorie Mgmt. Sys., Inc., 1999—. Contbr. articles to profl. jours. Fellowship NIH 1980-85; rsch. grantee Abbott Labs. 1989. Mem. IEEE, Biomed. Engring. Soc., Sigma Xi, Delta Chi (founder, 1st pres. chpt. U. Calif. at Berkeley). Achievements include invention of respiratory monitor, patented automated drug delivery system, pharmacokinetic drug infusion, and critical care disposables. Fax: 408-867-9395. Home: 14586 Aloha Ave Saratoga CA 95070-6004

JOHNSON, NORMA HOLLOWAY, federal judge; b. Lake Charles, La.; d. H. Lee and Beatrice (Williams) Holloway; m. Julius A. Johnson, June 18, 1964. B.S., D.C. Tchrs. Coll., 1955; J.D., Georgetown U., 1962. Bar: D.C. 1962, U.S. Supreme Ct. 1967. Pvt. practice law Washington, 1963; atty. civil divsn. Dept. Justice, Washington, 1963-67; asst. corp. counsel Office of Corp. Counsel, Washington, 1967-70; judge D.C. Superior Ct., 1970-80; judge U.S. Dist. Ct. (D.C. dist.), Washington, 1980-97, chief judge, 1997—. Bd. dirs. Judiciary Leadership Devel. Coun. Fellow Am. Bar Found.; mem. Nat. Bar Assn., Fed. Judges Assn., Am. Judicature Soc., Supreme Ct. Hist. Soc., Am. Inns of Ct. (William Bryant inn). Office: US Dist Ct US Courthouse 333 Constitution Ave NW Washington DC 20001*

JOHNSON, NORMA LOUISE, accountant; b. Cin., June 21, 1951; d. Raymond and Geneva (Cheesbrough) Banks; m. Raymond D. Johnson, Aug. 31, 1973; children: Raymond, Rhea, Amos, Dorian. AD summa cum laude, Southwestern Coll. Bus., 1992; cert., H&R Block; BA, Union Inst., 1998. Confidential sec. NCR, Dayton, Ohio, 1969-70; receiving clk. Delco Products, Dayton, 1972-73; sr. clk. GM Assembly, Cin., 1973-74; primary order clk. AC Delco, Cin., 1974-76; with customer svc. dept. Nacom, Cin., 1982; acctg. clk. CCSI, Cin., 1993; pres. Johnson's Fin., Cin., 1994—. Avocation: writing poetry. Home: 1126 Waycross Rd Cincinnati OH 45240-3026

JOHNSON, NORMAN JAMES, physician, lawyer, medicological consultant; b. Bklyn., Apr. 15, 1921; s. James Henry and Florence Gertrude (Crilley) J.; m. Bernadette Frances Lowe, Jan. 17, 1948; children: Michael Lowe, Christopher Day, Mark HUghes, David Hughes. AB magna cum laude, Fordham U., 1942; MD, SUNY, 1945; JD, U. Ga., 1979. Bar: Ga. 1981; cert. Am. Bd. Pediat., Am. Bd. Emergency Medicine. Intern Kings County Hosp., Bklyn., 1945-46; intern pediatrics The L.I. Coll. Hosp., Bklyn., 1948-49; resident cardiology Irvington House, Irvington-on-Hudson, N.Y., 1949-50; resident pediatrics Cin. Children's Hosp., 1950-51, chief resident pediatrics, 1951-52; assoc. prof. pediatrics U. Ark., Little Rock, 1952-56; chief pediatrics. Miners Meml. Hosp., Williamson, W.Va., 1956-59; asst. prof. pediatric medicine U. Tenn. Med. Sch., Memphis, 1959-61; from asst. chief to chief pediatrics Met. Hosp., Detroit, 1961-71; practice medicine specializing in pediats. Athens, Ga., 1972-77; clin. dir emergency medicine St. Mary's Hosp., Athens, 1976-86; with emergency medicine Hilton Head Hosp., Hilton Head Island, S.C., 1986-87; with Newton Gen. Hosp., Covington, Ga., 1987-95; instr. pediatrics U. Cin. , 1951-52, assoc. prof. pediatrics U. Ark., Little Rock, 1952-56, asst. prof. pediatrics U. Tenn., Memphis, 1959-61. Contbr. articles to profl. jours. Pres. PTA, Athens, 1975-76, Friends of Ga. Mus. of Art, Athens, U. Ga., 1985-86, 95-96. Capt. U.S. Army, 1946-48, PTO. Mem. Am. Acad. Pediatrics, Am. Coll. Emergency Physicians, Irish and Am. Pediat. Soc. Democrat. Roman Catholic. Avocations: singing, running. Home and Office: PO Box 305 Watkinsville GA 30677-0008

JOHNSON, OLIN CHESTER, education educator; b. Phila., Sept. 19, 1941; s. Benjamin F. and Eva M. J.; B.S., Cheyney State Coll., 1965; M.Ed., Temple U., 1969; M.S., U. Pa., 1972; m. Vernetta Dudley, Nov. 22, 1964; children—Quanda, Olin Jr. Cert. elem. edn., social studies, elem. prin., secondary prin., supt., Pa. Tchr., Phila. Sch. Dist., 1965-68, supr., 1968-72, dir., coordinator urban career ednl. ctr., 1973-75, prin., 1976—, prin. William Bryant Sch., 1977-80, Charles R. Drew Sch., 1981—; mem. secondary sch. com. U. Pa., Phila.; adj. asst. prof. Drexel U., Phila., 1989—, mem. ednl. adv. com. Chmn., Community Concern 13, Inc., 1970—; chmn. B.F. Johnson Scholarship Fund, 1971—; vice-chmn. Phila. M.H. Multi-Purpose Learning Center, 1975-85; bd. dirs. Open Door Bapt. Ch. Recipient award Nat. Tchr. Corp., 1970, Four Chaplains Community Service award, 1971, 73, Phila. Prin. Merit award Phila. Sch. Dist. #1, 1978, OIC commendation, 1973, Pa. dept. of edn. Planning and Testing Citation, 1987; Prin. Outstanding Leadership C.R. Drew Sch. award, 1987; Ford Found. fellow U. Pa., 1971-74. Mem. Am. Assn. Sch. Adminstrs., Pa. Congress Sch. Adminstrs., Phi Delta Kappa, Kappa Alpha Psi.

JOHNSON, OLIVER THOMAS, JR., lawyer; b. San Antonio, July 3, 1946; s. Oliver Thomas and Joan Elizabeth (Edwards) J.; m. Susan Caroline Nelson, Nov. 6, 1976; children: Caroline Elizabeth, Thomas Christian. Student, U. Redlands, 1964-65; BA, Stanford U., 1968, JD, 1971. Bar: Calif. 1972, D.C. 1975, U.S. Ct. Internat. Trade 1983, U.S. Supreme Ct. 1991. Atty. office of legal adviser U.S. Dept. State, Washington, 1971-73, spl. asst. to legal adviser, 1973-75; assoc. Covington & Burling, Washington, 1975-80, ptnr., 1980—. Co-author: The Registration of Foreign Agents in the United States, 1981, Private Investors Abroad: Problems and Solutions, 1987, The North American Free Trade Agreement: Issues, Options, Implications, 1992, The International Lawyer's Deskbook, 1996; contbr. articles to profl. jours. Bd. dir. U.S.-Azerbaijan Coun., Washington, 1995. Mem. ABA, Am. Soc. Internat. Law, Washington Inst. Fgn. Affairs, U.S. Coun. for Internat. Bus., Met. Club, Order of Coif. Office: Covington & Burling 1201 Pennsylvania Ave NW Washington DC 20004-2401

JOHNSON, OMOTUNDE EVAN GEORGE, economist; b. Freetown, Sierra Leone, Mar. 27, 1941; came to U.S., 1961; s. Evan George and Elizabeth O. (Allen) J.; m. Octavia Olayemi John, Oct. 30 1965; children: Olatunde Cheryl, Omoyemi Evan, Olubayo Darryl. BA, UCLA, 1965, MA, 1967, PhD, 1970. Lectr. in econs. Calif. State U., Long Beach, 1967-69; lectr. U. Sierra Leone, Freetown, 1969-73; vis. asst. prof. U. Mich., Ann Arbor, 1973-74; economist IMF, Washington, 1974-79, sr. economist, dep. div. chief, 1979-92, advisor, 1992-94, divsn. chief, 1994-98, asst. dir., 1998—; vis. rsch. fellow U. Oxford, Eng., 1996-97; resident rep. IMF, Ghana, 1987-90. Contbr. numerous articles to profl. jours. Mem. Am. Econ. Assn., U.S. Chess Fedn., Royal Econ. Soc. U.K., Nat. Symphony Orch. Assn., Washington Performing Arts Soc., Met. Opera Guild. Episcopalian. Avocations: chess, piano, classical music, reading. Home: 6401 Oak Meadow Way McLean VA 22101 Office: IMF 700 19th St NW Washington DC 20431-0001

JOHNSON, ONALEE H., retired nursing educator; b. Elkland, Pa., Jan. 14, 1921; d. Charles Raymond and Maude Louise (King) Hoffa; divorced; children: Leif C., Erik N. (dec.). Diploma, E.J. Meyer Meml. Hosp. Sch., Buffalo, 1942; BSN, cert. in supervision of obstetrics, U. Colo., 1954, M in Nursing Adminstrn., 1965; postgrad., SUNY, Buffalo, 1973-74. Lic. nurse, Ariz. Clin. instr. obstet. nursing St. Luke's Hosp. Sch. Nursing, Denver, 1962-63; dir. ADN program North Cen. Mich. Coll., Petoskey, 1965-67; assoc. dir. nursing St. Vincent's Hosp., Portland, Oreg., 1969-70; asst. prof. Sch. Nursing, SUNY, Buffalo, 1970-76; coord. continuing edn. ANA, Kansas City, Mo., 1976-80; dir. faculty devel. in nursing edn. project So. Regional Edn. Bd., Atlanta, 1981-82; assoc. dir. W.K. Kellogg Found. nat. edn. project, assoc. U. Tenn., Chattanooga, 1982-84; vis. asst. prof., coord. joint BSN program with W.Va. U. Sch. Nursing and Glenville (W.Va.) State Coll., 1984-88; participant facilitator tng. workshop Hamilton County Health Dept., Chattanooga, 1983; cons. part-time Southeast Ariz. Area Health Edn. Ctr., 1991-92; participant various profl. confs. on continuing nursing edn. Contbg. author: Systematic Nursing Assessment: A Step Toward Automation, 1972. Apptd. mem. N.Y. State Coun. Continuing Edn., 1973-76. 1st lt. Nursing Corps, U.S. Army, 1944-46, ETO. Pub. Health Ednl. grantee. Mem. ANA (participant convs., mem. coun. on continuing edn. ann. conf. 1972-76, 78-79, 81), NLN (participant ann. conf. Ga. chpt. 1981-82, participant nat. conv. 1981). Home: 320 N Camino Del Vate Green Valley AZ 85614-3134

JOHNSON, OPAL M., retired nurse assistant; b. Gayville, S.D., Dec. 26, 1926; d. LeRoy Lester Mincks and Helen Ruth Browning; m. Nathan L. Johnson Jr., Sept. 24, 1949; children: Janice L., James Robert. With Montgomery Ward Credit Dept., Omaha, 1947-51; nursing asst. Clarkson Hosp., Omaha, 1967-82; ret. Compiler: Benge Family Collection, 1997. Home: 12505 A St Omaha NE 68144-4136

JOHNSON, ORA J., clergyman; b. Oakland City, Ind., Aug. 31, 1932; s. Ora F. and Thelma Pauline (Julian) J.; B.S., Oakland City U., 1971, MS, 1996, DD, 1996; m. Wanda Mae Lockamy, Aug. 11, 1952; children—David Russell, Kent Alan, Vicki Jeanne. Ordained to ministry Baptist Ch., 1966; sales rep., staff sales mgr. Western & So. Ins. Co., Evansville, Ind., 1956-70, also pastor Corydon (Ky.) Gen. Bapt. Ch., 1965-68, Wadesville (Ind.) Gen. Bapt. Ch., 1968-70, North Haven Gen. Bapt. Ch., Evansville, 1970-75; nat. dir. evangelism and ch. growth Gen. Bapt. Hdqrs., Poplar Bluff, Mo., 1976-82; pastor 1st Gen. Bapt. Ch., Malden, Mo., 1982-88, Howell Gen. Bapt. Ch., Evansville, Ind., 1988-90; asst. v.p. for denomination rels. Oakland City U., 1990-93, exec. v.p., 1995—; pastor 1st Gen. Bapt. Ch., Owensboro, Ky., 1993-95; moderator Gen. Assn. of Gen. Bapts. Nat. Conv., 1991; producer, dir. weekly TV program Moments of Worship, 1973-74; pres. Greater Evansville Sunday Sch. Assn., 1975; pres. Gen. Bapt. Home Mission Bd., 1972-73, Gen. Bd. Gen. Bapts., 1972-73; pres. Evansville Clergy Assn., 1975-76. Named Outstanding Theolog of 1971, Gen. Bapt. Brotherhood; recipient Good Shepherd award Boy Scouts Am., 1980. Mem. Christian Resource Assoc., Evangelization Forum, Nat. Assn. Evangelicals, Malden Ministerial Alliance (pres. 1983), Malden C. of C. (pres. 1985-86). Club: Malden Optimist, Kiwanis (bd. dirs. Evansville club 1975, Poplar Bluff club 1981-83, pres. 1997-98). Home: 110 N Lucretia St Oakland City IN 47660-1038 Office: Oakland City U 143 N Lucretia St Oakland City IN 47660-1037

JOHNSON, ORRIN WENDELL, lawyer; b. Mpls., Nov. 7, 1920; s. Elmer Godfrey and Lydia (Carlson) J.; m. Patsy Elizabeth Coons, Apr. 2, 1951; children: Forrest, Wendell, Carol, Laura. BA cum laude, U. Tex., 1942, JD cum laude, 1947. Bar: Tex. 1947, U.S. Ct. Appeals 1948, U.S. Supreme Ct. 1964. Assoc. Karl Gibbon, Harlingen, Tex, 1947-49; ptnr. Gibbon, Coneway, Johnson, Harlingen, 1949-51, Gibbon & Johnson, Harlingen, 1951-53; pvt. practice law Harlingen, 1953-67; ptnr. Johnson & Davis, Harlingen, 1967-95; of counsel Rodriguez, Colvin and Chaney, Brownsville, Tex., 1995—. Assoc. editor Tex. Law Rev., 1946-47; contbr. articles to profl. jours. Pres. Cameron County Good Govt. League, 1979-82, bd. dirs., 1980-86; trustee Marine Mil. Acad., 1964-91, v.p., 1982-86, pres., 1986-89; adv. dir. Valley Baptist Hosp., 1964-72. Maj. USMCR, 1942-57. Recipient Pub. Service Achievement award Common Cause, 1981. Fellow Am. Coll. Trial Lawyers, Am. Coll. Trust and Estate Attys., Tex. Acad. Trust and Probate Lawyers, Am. Bar Found., Tex. Bar Found. (trustee 1977, chmn. fellows 1980-81, sustaining life mem., Lola Wright Found. award 1989); mem. ABA (del. Tex. chpt. 1989-90), State Bar Tex. (bd. dirs. 12th dist. 1972-75, pres. 1982-83, chmn. rules ethics com. 1986-88, Pres.' award 1986, Frank J. Scurlock award 1983, trustee Tex. Ctr. for Legal Ethics and Professionalism 1990-94), Immigration Law Reform Inst. (bd. dirs., exec. com. 1987-90), Order of Coif, Masons, Phi Delta Phi. Methodist. Office: Law Offices of Orrin Johnson 402 E Van Buren St Harlingen TX 78550-6834

JOHNSON, OWEN VERNE, program director; b. Madison, Wis., Feb. 22, 1946; s. Verner Lalander Johnson and Marianne Virginia (Halvorson) Muse; m. Marta Kucerova, July 17, 1969; children: Eva, Hana. BA in History with distinction, Wash. State U., 1968; MA in History, U. Mich., 1970, cert. in Russian Ea. European Studies, 1978, PhD in History, 1978. Reporter Pullman (Wash.) Herald, 1961-67; reporter, announcer Sta. KWSU Radio-TV, Pullman, 1965-68; reporter, editor, producer Sta. WUOM, Ann Arbor, Mich., 1969-77; adminstrv. asst. Ctr. for Russian and Ea. European Studies U. Mich., Ann Arbor, 1978-79; asst. prof. sch. journalism So. Ill. U., Carbondale, 1979-80; asst. prof. Ind. U., Bloomington, 1980-87, assoc. prof., 1987—, acting dir. Polish studies, 1989-90, dir. grad. studies, 1990-91, dir. Russian and Ea. European Inst., 1991-95; lectr. U. Mich., 1978-79; mem. Studia Academica Slovaca, Comenius U., Bratislava, Czechoslovakia, 1973; mem. Modern Sweden Seminar, Uppsala, 1967; field advisor journalism Am. Coun. Tchrs. of Russian, 1993-96; adj. prof. history Ind. U., Bloomington, 1996—. Author: Slovakia 1918-38: Education and the Making of a Nation, 1985; co-author: Eastern European Journalism Before, During and After Communism, 1999; contbr. articles to profl. jours.; corr. editor: Journalism History, 1985—; mem. editorial bd. Slovakia, 1978-89, Journalism Monographs, 1986-88, Kosmas, 1996—; cons. editor Slavic Rev., 1985-91. Capt. USAR, 1971-79. Grantee Nat. Coun. for Soviet and East European Rsch., 1988-90, Am. Coun. Learned Socs./Social Sci. Rsch. Coun. Joint Com. on Ea. Europe, 1983, Internat. Rsch. and Exchs. Bd., 1973-89; recipient Excellence in Journalism award Sigma Delta Chi, 1966. Mem. Am. Hist. Assn., Am. Assn. for Advancement of Slavic Studies (edn. com. 1988-90), Assn. for Edn. in Journalism and Mass. Comm. (head history divsn. 1985-86), Czechoslovak History Conf. (editor newsletter 1980-84, exec. com. 1988-92, Stanley Pech award 1987-88), Internat. Assn. for Media Comm. Rsch., Orgn. Am. Historians, Slovak Studies Assn. (pres. 1988-91). Democrat. Presbyterian. Fax: (812) 855-0901. E-mail: johnsono@indiana.edu. Office: Ind U Sch Journalism 222C Ernie Pyle Hall Bloomington IN 47405

JOHNSON, PAM, newspaper editor. Mng. editor Ariz. Republic, Phoenix, 1993-96, v.p. news, exec. editor, 1996—. Office: Ariz Republic PO Box 1950 Phoenix AZ 85001-1950

JOHNSON, PATRICIA LYN, mathematics educator; b. Upper Sandusky, Ohio, June 28, 1957; d. Chester Ellsworth and Judith Lyn (Adams) Geary; m. James Walter Johnson III, June 12, 1976. BS, Ohio State U., 1981, MS, 1983. Grad. teaching assoc. math. dept. Ohio State U., Columbus, 1980-87, lectr., 1987-88; supr. Math. Learning Ctr., instr. math. Ohio State U., Lima, 1988—; judge math. counts Lima (Ohio) Soc. Profl. Engrs., 1989—; judge Math. Awareness Week, Joint Policy Bd. for Math., Lima, 1990—; grader Ohio Coun. Tchrs. Math. Ann. Contest, 1998—. Mem. Am. Math. Soc., Math. Assn. Am., Am. Math. Assn. of Two-Yr. Colls., Assn. for Women in Math., Ohio Math. Assn. of 2-Yr. Colls. Methodist. Office: Ohio State U 4240 Campus Dr Lima OH 45804-3576

JOHNSON, PATRICIA MARY, publisher; b. Evanston, Ill., Mar. 14, 1937; d. Harold W. and Florence M. (Miller) J.; children: William, Nancy, Richard. Student, Art Inst. Chgo., 1970-73; Degree in Interior Design, LaSalle U., 1972. Interior design communicator, prodr., host weekly syndicated cable tv program on interior design, 1980-86; owner Design Comms., R&D Splsts., Rosenhayn, N.J., 1976; exec. dir., founder Corp. for Disabled/Handicapped, 1985—, A Positive Approach. Author: Eliminating Barriers From Your Lifestyle, 1988, Guide to Securing Housing for People with Developmental Disabilities, 1993, numerous children's books, 1996—; pub. (mags.) A Positive Approach, 1985-96, An Approach to Barrier Free Design, 1992; prodr.: A Guide to Securing Independent Housing for Individuals with Disabilities, 1994. Recipient award N.J. Gov., 1985, Practitioner of Yr. award N.J. Rehab. Assn., 1987, Humanitarian Svc. award United Cerebral Palsy, 1987, Jefferson award, NBC, 1988, Healing Cmty. UN Pub. award, 1989, Cmty. Svc. award Pres. George Bush, 1991.

JOHNSON, PATRICK, JR., lawyer; b. New Orleans, June 6, 1955; s. Patrick and Louise (Durand) J.; m. Gayle Marie Daniel, Feb. 24, 1979; children: Patrick III, Daniel Hartman, Michael Joseph. BS, U. New Orleans, 1977; JD magna cum laude, Tulane U., 1979; diploma with distinction, U. Stockholm, 1980. Bar: La. 1980, U.S. Dist. Ct. (ea. and mid. dists.) La. 1980, U.S. Ct. Appeals (5th and 11th cirs.) 1981, U.S. Supreme Ct. 1985, U.S. Dist. Ct. (we. dist.) La. 1986. Assoc. Lemle & Kelleher, L.L.P., New Orleans, 1980-85; ptnr. Lemle & Kelleher, New Orleans, 1985—; lectr. in field. Articles editor Tulane U. Law Rev., 1978-79, mem. bd. student editors, 1977-78. Mem. ABA (bus. bankruptcy com., chpt. 11 and secured creditors subcom.), Am. Bankruptcy Inst., La. Bar Assn. Home: 403 Atherton Dr Metairie LA 70005-3809 Office: Lemle & Kelleher LLP Pan-Am Life Ctr 21st Fl 601 Poydras St New Orleans LA 70130-6029

JOHNSON, PAUL BRETT, writer, illustrator; b. Mousie, Ky., May 19, 1947; s. Paul and Harriet Johnson. MA in Edn., U. Ky., 1970. Author, illustrator: (children's picture books) The Cow Who Wouldn't Come Down, 1993, Lost, 1995, Farmers' Market, 1997, A Perfect Pork Stew, 1998, others. Recipient Best Book award Sch. Libr. Jour., 1993, 96, Notable Book award Smithsonian Instn., 1997. Mem. Soc. Children's Book Writers and Illustrators. Avocation: traveling. Home: 444 Fayette Park Lexington KY 40508

JOHNSON, PAUL EUGENE, telecommunications engineer, consultant; b. Portsmouth, Ohio, Sept. 11, 1950; Life ptnr. Kevin Warren Wadsworth. Student electronic data processing, Mata Coll., Columbus, Ohio, 1971. Asst. v.p., data ctr. mgr. Crocker Nat. Bank, San Francisco, 1978-87; 1st v.p., data ctr. mgr. First Nationwide Bank, Daly City/Folsom, Calif., 1987-92; consulting systems engr. Bank Am., Concord, Calif., 1993—. Mem. Solano County (Calif.) Reps., 1982, El Dorado County (Calif.) Reps., 1992, 94; mem. AIDS Walk Striders Club, San Francisco, 1996. Named Outstanding Volunteer, Vol. Ctr. of Dorado County, Placerville, Calif., 1993. MCC. Avocation: gardening.

JOHNSON, PAUL OREN, lawyer; b. Mpls., Feb. 2, 1937; s. Andrew Richard and LaVerne Delores (Slater) J.; m. Georgene Howalt, July 1, 1961; children: Scott, Paula, Amy. BA, Carleton Coll., 1958; JD cum laude, U. Minn., 1961. Bar: Minn. 1961. Atty. Briggs & Morgan, St. Paul, 1961-62; atty. Green Giant Co., Le Sueur, Minn., 1961-66, asst. sec., 1967-74, sec., 1975-79, v.p., gen. counsel, 1971-79, v.p. corporate rels., 1973-79, mem. mgmt. com., 1976-79; gen. counsel H.B. Fuller Co., St. Paul, 1979-84, sr. v.p., sec., 1980-90, mem. mgmt. com., 1981-90; bd. dirs. Lectec Corp., Compatible Techs., The Fulcrum Group, chmn. bd. dirs.; nat. bd. dirs. Self Help for Hard of Hearing People. Coun. v.p., exec. com. Boy Scouts Am.; bd. dirs. Rep. County Com., 1965; bd. dirs. Minn. State U., 1979-82, v.p., 1980-82; chmn. bd. dirs. Minn. Com. Serving Deaf and Hard of Hearing; bd. dirs. Hearing Soc. of Minn. Office: The Riverwood 307 1015 Sibley Memorial Hwy Saint Paul MN 55118-3680

JOHNSON, PENELOPE ANNE, university dean; b. Fullerton, Calif., Feb. 24, 1952; d. Laurence Steven and Martha Sue Johnson; m. Lloyd Arthur Shaw. BA in Sociology, U. Calif., Davis, 1974; MS in Counseling, San Francisco State U., 1980. Career ctr. mgr. San Francisco State U., 1980-83; asst. dean Golden Gate U., San Francisco, 1983-89; coll. rels. mgr. Cooper & Lybrand, San Francisco, 1989-90; interim dean Mills Coll., Oakland, Calif., 1990-91; dir. student devel. Cabrillo Coll., Aplos, Calif., 1991-95; student svcs. dean Evergreen Valley Coll., San Jose, Calif., 1995-97; dean counseling and student svcs. Fotohill Coll., Los Altos Hills, Calif., 1997—. Home: 11 Sea Crest Ct Half Moon Bay CA 94019-4220 Office: Foothill Coll 12345 El Monte Rd Los Altos Hills CA 94022

JOHNSON, PETER FORBES, transportation executive, business owner; b. Salem, Mass., May 7, 1934; s. William Bennett and Sarah Loraine (Nee) J.; m. Mikell Kraus, Oct. 11, 1958; children: Krista, Todd, Karyn, Jennifer. BS, U.S. Mcht. Marine Acad., 1957. Deck officer Texaco, Port Arthur, Tex., 1958-63; from deck officer to master Reynolds Metals Co., Corpus Christi, Tex., 1963-65, port capt., 1965-68, operating mgr., 1968-71; internat. marine mgr. Gulf Miss. Marine Corp., New Orleans, 1971-72; cons. Peter F. Johnson & Assocs., New Orleans, 1972-73; exec. v.p. Pyramid Marine, Inc., New Orleans, 1973-76; pres., chief exec. officer, owner, chmn. bd. Pacific-Gulf Marine, Inc., New Orleans, 1976—; trustee Am. Maritime Officers, Dania, Fla. Lt. (j.g.) USNR, 1959-63. Mem. Coun. Am. Master Mariners, Soc. Naval Architects and Marine Engrs., Propeller Club U.S. (Maritime Man of Yr. 1986), U.S. Navy League, Southern Yacht Club, English Turn Country Club. Republican. Roman Catholic. Avocations: fly fishing, golf, hunting, sailing. Home: 3 Lakeway Ct New Orleans LA 70131-3322 Office: Pacific Gulf Marine Inc PO Box 6479 New Orleans LA 70174-6479

JOHNSON, PETER RAY, minister; b. Beatrice, Ala., Apr. 28, 1933; s. Mack Lawrence and Minnie Mae (Malone) J.; m. Doris Burney; children: Lorraine, Loretta, Eric. *Loretta Doris Johnson, born June 10, 1962. She is the daughter of Reverend Peter and Doris Johnson. She has a twin sister and one brother. Father is a minister and mother Doris Johnson is a retired school teacher. They live in Raleigh, North Carolina. Loretta received her BA degree from Morris Brown College in Atlanta. Her MA in Counseling came from the University of Washington D.C. She has 14 years of experience as an elementary school teacher in bilingual education and special education in Washington D.C. public school system. She also assisted in organizing a program for battered women and their children.* BA, Shaw U., 1966, MD, 1993. Road car inspector N.Y.C. Transit Authority, 1966-86; ret., 1986; prison minister State of N.C., Raleigh, 1995—; minister New Bethel Bapt. Ch., Raleigh, 1995—. sport dir. Raleigh YMCA, Bible tchr.; basketball coach N.Y. Park Assn.; chaplain Sertoma Club, Raleigh; served with Martin Luther King, Jr. in bus boycott, Montgomery, Ala., 1955; counselor Sr. Citizens Assn., Raleigh, 1992, 96; builder Homes for the Poor, Raleigh, 1991-97; headed com. which fed 5,000 people Allen AME Ch., Jamaica, N.Y., 1982-89, others. Sgt. USMC, 1952-56, Korea. Recipient Korean Pub. citation USMC, others. Mem. Ministerial Alliance (pres. local chpt. 1990-92), Am. Assn. Ret. Persons. Democrat. Avocations: basketball, golf, bowling. Home: 213 N Trail Dr Raleigh NC 27615-7223

JOHNSON, PHILIP, investment banking executive; b. Decatur, Ill., Mar. 3, 1947; s. Raymond Avis and Mary Alice (Trolia) J.; m. Lucia Elizabeth Sontag, Nov. 24, 1978; children: Christian Phelps, Alice Tyler, Hope Elizabeth. AB, Cedarville Coll., 1970; postgrad., Harvard U., 1973-75. Securities analyst State St. Rsch. & Mgmt., Boston, 1976-80; instnl. sales-fixed income salesman Boettcher & Co., Denver, 1980-81; instnl. salesman Morgan Stanley & Co., Chgo., 1982-86, Goldman Sachs Inc., Boston, 1986-88; br. mgr. L.F. Rothschild & Co., Boston, 1989-90; nat. sales mgr. NationsBanc Capital Markets, Charlotte, N.C., 1990-96; v.p. syndications Key Global Fin., Boston, 1997—. With USMC, 1966-68, Vietnam. Mem. The Country Club, Brookline, Mass., Harvard Club Boston. Republican. Evangelical. Avocations: theological studies, tennis, sailing.

JOHNSON, PHILIP LESLIE, lawyer; b. Beloit, Wis., Jan. 24, 1939; s. James Philip and Christabel (Williams) J.; m. Kathleen Rose Westover, May 12, 1979; children: Celeste Marie, Nicole Michelle. AB, Princeton U., 1961; JD, U. South Calif., 1973. Bar: Calif. 1973, U.S. Ct. Appeals (9th cir.) 1975, U.S. Ct. of Military Appeals, 1978, U.S. Supreme Ct. 1980. Pilot U.S. Marine Corps., 1961-70; assoc. Law Office Wm. G. Tucker, L.A., 1973-78; ptnr. Engstrom, Lipscomb & Lack, L.A., 1978-92; judge pro tem Calif. State Bar Ct., 1990-95; ptnr. Lillick & Charles, Long Beach, Calif., 1993-99, Cogswell Woolley Nakazawa & Russell, Long Beach, 1999%; chmn. aerospace law com. Def. Rsch. Inst. Contbr. articles to profl. jours. Pres., bd. dirs. U. So. Calif. Legion Lex, 1992-93; chmn. com. to nom. alumni trustees Princeton U., 1996-97, mem. exec. com. of alumni coun., 1996-97; chmn. Marine Corps Scholarship Found. L.A. Ball, 1997-99. Mem. ABA, (aviation & space law com., torts & ins. practice section), Princeton Club (So. Calif., bd. dirs.). Avocations: flying, snow skiing, jazz. Home: 5340 Valley View Rd Rancho Palos Verdes CA 90275-5089 Office: Cogswell Woolley Nakazawa & Russell 111 W OceanBlvd #2000 Long Beach CA 90802

JOHNSON, PHILIP MCBRIDE, lawyer; b. Springfield, Ohio, June 18, 1938. AB with honors, Ind. U., 1959; LLB, Yale U., 1962. Bar: Ill. 1962, D.C. 1983, N.Y. 1984. Ptnr. Kirkland & Ellis, Chgo., 1962-81; chmn. Commodity Futures Trading Commn., Washington, 1981-83; ptnr. Wiley, Johnson & Rein, Washington, 1983-84, Skadden, Arps, Slate, Meagher & Flom, Washington, 1984—; lectr. on commodities regulation U. Va. Law Sch., 1993—; spkr. panelist on Commodity Exch. Act Fed. Bar Assn., others; mem. adv. com. definition and regulation Commodity Futures Trading Commn., adv. com. state jurisdiction and responsibility; adv. com. regulatory coordination, adv. com. fin. products Commodity Futures Trading Commn. Author: Commodities Regulation, 2 vols., 1997, Derivatives: A Manager's Guide to the World's Most Powerful Financial Instruments, 1999; mng. editor Yale U. Law Jour, 1962, Agrl. Law Jour; contbr. articles to legal jours. Mem. ABA (founder, chmn. com. on futures regulation 1975-81, mem. governing coun. sect. on bus. law 1981-83), Futures Industry Assn. (bd. dirs. 1980-81, 86-87), Internat. Bar Assn. (founder, chmn. subcom. on commodities, futures and options law 1986-90), N.Y. Stock Exch. (mem. regulatory adv. com. 1988—). Office: Skadden Arps Slate Meagher & Flom Ste 700 1440 New York Ave NW Washington DC 20005-6000

JOHNSON, PHILIP WAYNE, lawyer; b. Greenwood, Ark., Oct. 24, 1944; s. John Luther and Flora (Joyce) J.; m. Carla Jean Newsom, Nov. 6, 1970; children: Betsy, Carl, Jeff, Laura, Philip. B.A., Tex. Tech. U., 1965, J.D., 1975. Bar: Tex. 1975, U.S. Dist. Ct. (no. and we. dists.) Tex. 1976, U.S. Ct. Appeals (5th cir.) 1984, U.S. Supreme Ct. 1984; cert. in civil trial and personal injury trial law, Tex. Bd. Legal Specialization. Assoc. Crenshaw Dupree & Milam, Lubbock, Tex., 1975-80; ptnr. Crenshaw Dupree & Milam, 1980-98; justice Tex. State Ct. of Appeals (7th dist), Amarillo, 1999—; mem. pattern jury charge and state judiciary rels com. State Bar Tex. Bd. dirs., pres. Lubbock County Legal Aid Soc., Tex., 1977-79; bd. dirs., chmn. Trinity Christian Schs., Lubbock, 1978-83, 85-89; bd. dirs., pres. S.W. Lighthouse for Blind, Lubbock, 1978-85. Served to capt. USAF, 1965-72. Decorated Silver Star, D.F.C.; Cross of Gallantry (Vietnam). Fellow Am. Bar Found., Tex. Bar Found. (life); mem. ABA, Tex. Bar Assn., Amarillo Bar Assn., Lubbock County Bar Assn. (pres. 1984-85), Phi Delta Phi. Home: 2301 60th St Lubbock TX 79412-3304 Office: Seventh Ct of Appeals 501 S Fillmore St Ste 2 A Amarillo TX 79101

JOHNSON, PHILLIP EUGENE, mathematics educator; b. Bostic, N.C., Feb. 25, 1937; s. Lin Joe and Gertrude (Pitman) J.; m. Carolyn Roberta Long, Dec. 23, 1959; 1 son, Philip Marc. B.S., Appalachian State U., 1959; M.A., Am. U., 1966, Vanderbilt U., 1963; Ph.D., Vanderbilt U., 1968; postgrad., N.C. State U., 1971, Cambridge U., 1973. Tchr. math. Fredericksburg, Va., 1960-61, Fairfax County, Va., 1961-63; faculty U. Richmond, 1963-65, Vanderbilt U., 1966-71; prof. math. U. N.C., Charlotte, 1971—. Author: A History of Set Theory, 1972; Contbr. articles to profl. jours. Served with USMCR, 1960. Grantee NSF, 1960-63, summers 1961-63; Grantee Ga. U. summer, 1965. Mem. Math. Assn. Am., Nat., N.C. councils tchrs. math., AAUP, Pi Mu Epsilon. Home: 336 Beaver Creek Estates Dr West Jefferson NC 28694 Office: ASU Math Dept Math Dept Boone NC 28608

JOHNSON, PHYLLIS ELAINE, chemist; b. Grafton, N.D., Feb. 19, 1949; d. Donald Gordon and Evelyn Lorraine (Svaren) Lanes; m. Robert S.T. Johnson, Sept. 12, 1969; children: Erik, Sara. BS, U. N.D., 1971; PhD, 1976. Instr. chemistry Mary Coll., Bismarck, N.D., 1971-72; postdoctoral rsch. fellow U. N.D., Grand Forks, 1975-79, chemist, 1977-79; rsch. chemist USDA Human Nutrition Rsch. Ctr., 1979-87, rsch. leader for nutrition, biochemistry and metabolism, 1987-91; assoc. dir. Pacific West Area USDA-ARS, 1996-97; dir. Beltsville Area USDA, ARS, 1997—; Disting. Chemistry Alumni lectr. U. N.C., 1998. Editor: Stable Isotopes in Nutrition, 1984; mem. editl. bd. Jour. Micronutrient Analysis, 1988-91, Jour. Nutrition, 1998—; contbr. articles to profl. jours. Chmn. Parents of Gifted and Talented, 1984-86. Recipient Arthur S. Flemming award Outstanding Sci. Achievement, 1989, Women in Sci. and Engring. award, 1993, Sioux award N.D. Alumni Found., 1998, Fed. Energy and Water Mgmt. award, 1998. Mem. Am. Soc. Clin. Nutrition, Am. Chem. Soc., Am. Inst. Nutrition, Internat. Soc. Trace Element Rsch. in Humans (sec. 1992-98), Exec. Women in Govt., Sr. Exec. Assn., Soc. Exptl. Biology Medicine, Phi Beta Kappa, Sigma Xi, Gamma Sigma Delta, Sons of Norway (dist. v.p. 1984-86, dist. pres. 1986-88, internat. bd. dirs. 1988-92). Lutheran. Avocations: cooking, skiing, needlework, camping. Home: 7868 Manet Way Severn MD 21144-1649 Office: USDA Bldg 003 Rm 223 10300 Baltimore Ave Beltsville MD 20705-2350

JOHNSON, QULAN ADRIAN, software engineer; b. Great Falls, Mont., Sept. 17, 1942; s. Raymond Eugene and Bertha Marie (Nagengast) J.; m. Helen Louise Pocha, July 24, 1965; children—Brenda Marie, Douglas Paul, Scot Paul, Mathew James. B.A. in Psychology, Coll. Gt. Falls, 1964. Lead operator 1st Computer Corp., Helena, Mont., 1966-67; v.p., sec.-treas. Computer Corp. of Mt., Great Falls, 1967-76, dir., 1971-76; sr. systems analyst Mont. Dept. Revenue, Helena, 1976-78; software engr. Mont. Systems Devel. Co., Helena, 1978-80; programmer/analyst III info. systems div. Mont. Dept. Adminstrn., Helena, 1980-82; systems analyst centralized services Dept. Social and Rehab. Services State of Mont., 1982-87, systems and programming mgr. info systems, Blue Cross and Blue Shield of Montana, Helena, 1987-98, project coord., 1998—. Mem. Mensa, Assn. Info. Tech. Profls. Home: 2231 8th Ave Helena MT 59601-4841 Office: Blue Cross & Blue Shield Info Systems 404 Fuller Ave Helena MT 59601-5006

JOHNSON, RALPH RAYMOND, ambassador, federal agency administrator; b. Portland, Oreg., Mar. 31, 1943; s. Ralph Wilson and Margaret Mary (Munly) J.; m. Ann Frances Huetter, Aug. 19, 1967; children: David, Timothy. BA in Polit. Sci., Seattle U., 1963; MA in Internat. Rels., Columbia U., 1965. Mgmt. trainee Seattle First Nat. Bank, 1968-69; vice-consul U.S. Embassy, Georgetown, Guyana, 1969-71; econ. officer U.S. Embassy, Warsaw, Poland, 1973-76, La Paz, Bolivia, 1977-79; asst. chief indsl. and strategic materials U.S. Dept. State, Washington, 1979-81, chief trade agreements div., 1981-83, office dir. European regional polit./econ. affairs, 1985-86, dep. asst. sec. state, 1986-91, prin. dep. asst. sec. state, 1991-93, coord., aid to Eastern Europe with rank of amb., 1993-95; U.S. amb. to Slovak Republic, 1995-99; dep. trade rep. bilateral affairs Japan-Europe U.S. Trade Rep.'s Office, Washington, 1983-85; prin. dep. High Rep. Sarajevo, Bosnia, 1999—. Sgt. U.S. Army, 1965-68. Mem. Am. Fgn. Svc. Assn., Seattle U. Alumni Assn. (Disting. Pub. Svc. award 1994). Roman Catholic. Avocations: photography, building furniture, running, scuba diving.

JOHNSON, RALPH THEODORE, JR., physicist; b. Salina, Kans., Apr. 29, 1935; s. Ralph Theodore and Mary Alice (Wallerius) J.; m. Ruth Elaine Rohrer, Jan. 25, 1958; children: Barbara A., Thomas T., Gregory E., Janet E. MS in Physics, Kans. State U., 1959, PhD, 1964. Staff mem. GE, Cin., 1957-58; rsch. and teaching asst. Kans. State U., 1958-63; from rsch. scientist to mgr. Sandia Nat. Lab., Albuquerque, 1965-97; mem. N.Mex. Govs. Energy Task Force, 1974; mem. assessment panel Nat. Rsch. Panel, 1978-90; mem. Am. Nat. Std. Writing Com., 1990-97. Contbr. articles to profl. jours. Pres., bd. dirs. Marriage Enrichment Nonprofit Corp. 1st lt. USAF, 1963-65. Achievements include patent for neutron radiation detector; memory phenomenon in amorphous semiconductors; ionic conduction in solid electrolytes; radiation effects in semiconductors and electronics; metrology program development; marriage program development. Home: 6601 Arroyo Del Oso Ave NE Albuquerque NM 87109-2733

JOHNSON, RANDALL C., mortgage banker; b. Tulsa, Okla., Feb. 12, 1949; s. Clyde O. and Barbara Grace Johnson; m. Mary Dan Peck Hewlette, June 25, 1971 (div. Aug. 1981); 1 child, Paul C.; m. Frances Evelen Wigelious, Oct. 1, 1982; 1 child, Tyler B. BA, U. Miami, Coral Gables, Fla., 1971. V.p. Baker Mortgage Co., Miami, Fla., 1971-75; S.E. U.S. regional mgr. Gen. Electric Credit Corp., Coral Gables, Fla., 1975-77; pres., CEO Equitable Mortgage Resources, Inc., Clearwater, Fla., 1977-89; chmn., CEO Market St. Mortgage Co., Clearwater, 1989—; mem. adv. bd. Avondale Funding Corp., Chgo., 1998—, Residential Funding Corp./GM Acceptance, Bloomington, Minn., 1999. Contbr.: Real Estate Financing Desk Book, 1977. Pres. Mental Health Assn. Pinellas County, Clearwater, 1986-89; participant Leadership Pinellas, Clearwater, 1988-98; dir. Clearwater Marine Sci. Ctr., 1990-91; vice chmn. Mortgage Bankers Polit. Action Com., Washington, 1996-98. Named Outstanding Young Men in Am., JCs Internat., 1979, Floridans to Watch in the Next Ten Years, Fla. Trend Mag., Miami, 1980, Significant Sig, Sigma Chi Nat. Fraternity, Evanston, Ill., 1998; faculty fellow Sch. Mortgage Banking, Washington, 1988. Mem. Mortgage Bankers Assn. Am. (cert. mortgage banker, profl. mem., bd. govs. 1995—, Legion of Honor 1999), Mortgage Bankers Assn. Fla. (profl. mem., pres. 1987-88), Belleair Country Club (mem.-guest tournament champion 1994), Carlouel Yacht Club. Republican. Episcopalian. Avocations: spending time with my family, golfing, fishing. E-mail: JohnsonMSM@aol.com and rjohnson@msmc.net. Fax: 727-791-4136. Home: 2800 Countryside Blvd Clearwater FL 33761 Office: Market St Mortgage Corp Ste 200 2650 McCormick Dr Clearwater FL 33759

JOHNSON, RANDALL DAVID (RANDY JOHNSON), professional baseball player; b. Walnut Creek, Calif., Sept. 10, 1963. Student, U. So. Calif. With Montreal (Can.) Expos, 1985-89; pitcher Seattle Mariners, 1989-98, Houston Astros, 1998-99, Ariz. Diamondbacks, 1999—. Named to All-Star Team, 1990, 93-95; recipient Cy Young award, 1995; named Pitcher of Yr. Sporting News, 1995; Am. League strikeout leader, 1995. Leader in Am. League Strikeouts., 1992. Office: c/o Ariz Diamondbacks BankOne Ballpark 401 E Jefferson Phoenix AZ 85003*

JOHNSON, REVERDY, lawyer; b. N.Y.C., Aug. 24, 1937; s. Reverdy and Reva (Payne) J.; m. Marta Schneebeli, Apr. 4, 1970 (div.); children: Deborah Ghiselin, Reverdy Payne; m. Robbie M. Williams, Feb. 20, 1994. AB cum laude, Harvard U., 1960, LLB, 1963. Bar: Fla. 1963, Calif. 1964, N.Mex. 1997. Assoc. Brobeck, Phleger & Harrison, San Francisco, 1963-66; from assoc. to ptnr. Pettit & Martin, San Francisco, 1966-95; of counsel Steinhart & Falconer LLP, San Francisco, 1995—, Scheuer Yost & Patterson, Sante Fe, NMex., 1996—; co-owner Johnson Turnbull Vineyards, Napa Valley, Calif., 1977-93; mem. tech. adv. com., com. open space lands Calif. Joint Legislature, 1968-69, chmn., 1969-70. Bd. dirs. Planning and Conservation League, 1966-72, League to Save Lake Tahoe, 1972-77, Found. for San Francisco's Archtl. Heritage, 1975-84, San Francisco Devel. Fund, 1986-96. Mem. Urban Land Inst. (vice chmn. recreational devel. council 1975-78, comml. and retail devel. council 1980—), Napa Valley Vintners Assn. (bd. dirs. 1985-88, v.p. 1987, pres. 1988), Am. Coll. Real Estate Lawyers, Lambda Alpha. Office: PO Drawer 9570 333 Market St Fl 32 San Francisco CA 94105-2102 also office: Scheuer Yost & Patterson 125 Lincoln Ave Ste 223 Santa Fe NM 87501-2053*

JOHNSON, REX RAY, automotive education educator; b. Buckhannon, W. Va., June 27, 1949; s. Virgil Melvin and Vesta Matilda (Carpenter) J.; m. Beverly Ann Ashcraft, Aug. 18, 1973. BA in Edn., Fairmont State Coll., 1972. Welder T & T Machine Co., Morgantown, W.Va., 1971; tchr. Norwood (Ohio) City Schs., 1972; technician Cecil Jackson Equipment, Oakland, Md., 1973-76; asst. prof. automotive tech. Allegany Community Coll., Cumberland, Md., 1976—; dir. Automotive Tech. and Transp., Cumberland, 1984—. Recipient Miriam D. Sanner award for Outstanding Teaching, 1989-90. Mem. (charter) Nat. Assn. Coll. Automotive Tchrs., Inc., Md. Tchrs. Assn., I-Car Assn., (chair. 1989-90). Avocation: drag racing. Office: Allegany Community Coll Willowbrook Rd Cumberland MD 21502

JOHNSON, RICHARD ARLO, lawyer; b. Vermillion, S.D., July 8, 1952; s. Arlo Goodwin and Edna Marie (Styles) J.; m. Diane Marie Zephier, Aug. 18, 1972 (div. Jan. 1979); m. Sheryl Lavonne Mader, June 5, 1981; 1 stepchild, Chadwick O. Wagner; 1 child, Sarah N. BA, U. S.D., 1974, JD, 1976. Bar: S.D. 1977, U.S. Dist. Ct. S.D. 1977. Ptnr. Pruitt, Matthews, Muilenberg & Strange, Sioux Falls, S.D., 1977-92, Strange, Farrell & Johnson, P.C., Sioux Falls, 1992—. Mem. Pub. Defender Adv. Bd., Sioux Falls, 1983-98; mem. S.D. Dental Peer Rev. Com. S.E. Dist. Fellow Am. Acad. Matrimonial Lawyers; mem. ATLA, ABA, S.D. Trial Lawyers Assn., State Bar S.D. (chmn. family law com. 1989-92), Phi Delta Phi (pres. 1976-77), Masons, Shriners. Democrat. Lutheran. Home: 409 E Lotta St Sioux Falls SD 57105-7109 Office: Strange Farrell & Johnson PC 141 N Main Ave Ste 200 Sioux Falls SD 57104-6429

JOHNSON, RICHARD ARNOLD, statistics educator, consultant; b. St. Paul, July 10, 1937; s. Arnold Verner and Florence Dorothy J.; m. Roberta Anne Weinard, Mar. 21, 1964; children—Erik Richard, Thomas Robert. B.E.E., U. Minn., Mpls., 1960, M.S. in Math., 1963, Ph.D. in Stats., 1966. Asst. prof. stats. U. Wis., Madison, 1966-70, assoc. prof., 1970-74, prof. stats, 1974—, chmn. dept. stats., 1981-84; head Greentree Statis. Consulting, Madison, Wis., 1978—; cons. industry, Dept. Energy; cooperating scientist Dept. Agr. Co-author: Statistical Concepts and Methods, 1977, Applied Multivariate Statistical Analysis, 1982, 4th edit., 1998, Probability and Statistics for Engineers (4th edit. 1990, 5th edit. 1994, 6th edit. 00), Statistics-Principles and Methods, 1985, 3d edit., 1996, Business Statistics-Decision Making with Data, 1997, Statistical Reasoning and Methods, 1998. Recipient Frank Wilcoxon prize, 1991; NATO sr. postdoctoral fellow, 1972; numerous grants NSA, NSF, ONR, Air Force, NASA. Fellow Inst. Math. Stats. (program sec. 1980-86, mem. of council 1980-86), Am. Statis. Assn. (sect. rep. to council 1980-82), Royal Statis. Soc.; mem. Internat. Statis. Inst. Lutheran. Avocations: fishing, cross-country skiing. Office: Greentree Statis Cons 7122 Valhalla Trl Madison WI 53719-3039

JOHNSON, RICHARD AUGUST, English language educator; b. Washington, Apr. 18, 1937; s. Cecil August and Esther Marie (Nelson) J.; m. Michaela Ann Memelsdorff, Aug. 20, 1960; children—Nicholas, Patrick, Hong, Loeun. B.A., Swarthmore Coll., 1959; Ph.D., Cornell U., 1965. Instr. English U. Va., Charlottesville, 1963-65; asst. prof. Mt. Holyoke Coll., South Hadley, Mass., 1965-71, assoc. prof., 1971-74, prof., chmn. dept., 1974-80, 1988-91, prof. Alumnae Found., 1980-86, Lucia, Ruth and Elizabeth MacGregor prof. English, 1986—; vis. prof. Amherst Coll., 1979, 84-88. Author: Man's Place: An Essay on Auden, 1973; co-author: Common Ground: Personal Writing and Public Discourse, 1992; contbr. articles to profl. jours. Mem. MLA, AAUP, Phi Beta Kappa. Democrat. Episcopalian. Home: 27 College St Apt 2 South Hadley MA 01075-1501 also: 40 Hammond St Providence RI 02909-1230 Office: Mount Holyoke Coll Dept English South Hadley MA 01075*

JOHNSON, RICHARD CARL, philosophy educator, humanities educator; b. Chgo., Sept. 2, 1933; s. Carl Helmer and Ann Catherine (Johnson) J.; m. Ann Elizabeth Faust, July 1, 1958 (Feb. 1974); children: Eric Richard, Tawny Elizabeth; m. Margaret Ann Wodetzki, May 23, 1984. BA, U. Chgo., 1954, UCLA, 1958; MA, U. Colo., 1962. Advising asst. to acad. dean U. Colo., Boulder, 1963-65; dean students Tougaloo (Miss.) Coll., 1965-67, asst. prof. philosophy, 1967-89, chair humanities divns., 1986-88, acting asst. acad. dean, 1988, chair dept. philosophy, 1967—; mem. instnl. review bd. U. Med. Ctr., Jackson, Miss., 1993—; mem. adv. bd. Sta-Home Home Health, Jackson, 1985—. Actor, story teller Mississippi, Freedom!, 1992, 96. Pres. bd. Jackson area Human Rels. Coun., 1969-71; state affiliate pres. ACLU, Jackson, 1977-80, nat. bd. dirs., N.Y.C., 1980-82; pres. bd. dirs. Common Cause, Jackson, 1995—. With U.S. Army, 1954-56, Korea. Mem. AAUP (chpt. pres. 1992-97), Am. Philos. Assn., Miss. Philos. Soc. (pres. 1978-79). Democrat. Avocations: bicycling, motorcycling, running. Home: 550 Launcelot Rd Jackson MS 39206-4815 Office: Tougaloo Coll 500 W County Line Rd Tougaloo MS 39174

JOHNSON, RICHARD CLARK, lawyer; b. Knoxville, Tenn., Feb. 5, 1937; s. Paul R. and Bernice (Whittaker) J.; m. Suzanne M. O'Meara, Apr. 13, 1969. AB magna cum laude, Harvard U., 1958, JD magna cum laude, 1962. Bar: Mass., D.C. Asst. and acting exec. dir. FPC, Washington, 1966-68; assoc., then ptnr. Vom Baur, Coburn, Simmons & Turtle, Washington, 1968-79; ptnr. Seyfarth, Shaw, Fairweather & Geraldson, Washington, 1979-94, mng. ptnr., 1983-94; ptnr. Jenner & Block, Washington, 1995—. Served to capt. USAF, 1962-65. Fulbright scholar U. Bonn, Fed. Republic Germany, 1958-59. Mem. ABA, Mass. Bar Assn., D.C. Bar Assn., Nat. Def. Indsl. Assn. Clubs: Harvard (Boston); University, Metropolitan (Washington). Avocations: civil war studies, gardening, distance running, watercolor painting, languages. Office: Jenner & Block 601 13th St NW Ste 1200S Washington DC 20005-3823

JOHNSON, RICHARD CLAYTON, engineer, physicist; b. Eveleth, Minn., May 9, 1930; s. Elvin and Sadie (Abramson) J.; m. Sallie Staples Hairston, Aug. 2, 1958 (div. 1971); children: Karen Louise, Diana Elizabeth.; m. Margaret R. Campbell, Jan. 1, 1984. B.S. in Physics, Ga. Inst. Tech., 1953, M.S., 1958, Ph.D., 1961. Registered profl. engr., Ga. Co-op student Ga. Power Co., 1949-51; with Ga. Inst. Tech., 1952-87, prin. research engr., 1967-87, assoc. dir. Engring. Expt. Sta., 1975-79; pres. Micro-J, Inc., 1987—; cons. to govt. and industry, 1966—; mem. sci. adv. group for U.S. Army Missile Command, 1975-78. Author: Designer Notes for Microwave Antennas, 1991; editor: Antenna Engineering Handbook, 3d edit., 1993; contbr. rsch. papers., chpt. to book. Served to lt. (j.g.) USNR, 1953-55. Fellow IEEE (editor newsletter Antennas and Propagation Soc. 1975-77, v.p. Antennas and Propagation Soc. 1979, pres. 1980, Disting. lectr. 1978-79, mem. adminstrv. com. 1978-84, leader study group to China 1980); mem. Am. Phys. Soc., Antenna Measurement Techniques Assn. (Disting. Achievement award 1989), Sigma Xi, Phi Kappa Phi, Tau Beta Pi, Phi Eta Sigma, Sigma Pi Sigma, Phi Kappa Sigma. Patentee in field. Home and Office: 8592 Roswell Rd Apt 316 Atlanta GA 30350-1869

JOHNSON, RICHARD DAVID, retired librarian; b. Cleve., June 10, 1927; s. Robert Emanuel and Emma (Lindhorst) J.; m. Harriett Herzog, Sept. 8, 1956; children: Ruth Ellen, Royce Emanuel. BA, Yale U., 1949; MA in Internat. Rels., U. Chgo., 1950, MALS, 1957. Libr. Nat. Opinion Rsch. Ctr. U. Chgo., 1956-57; reference libr. Stanford, 1957-59; cataloger Stanford U., 1959-60, 61-62, adminstrv. asst. to dir., 1960-61, head acquisitions, 1962-64, chief undergrad. libr. project, 1964-67, chief libr. tech. svcs., 1967-68; dir. librs. Claremont (Calif.) Colls., 1968-73, SUNY, Oneonta, 1973-94; ret., 1994. Editor: Calif. Libr., 1966-68, Coll. and Rsch. Librs., 1974-80, Choice, 1982, Lexington Books series on librs., 1981-87, N.Y. Libr. Assn. Bull., 1986-91, Assn. Libr. Collections and Tech. Svcs. Newsletter, 1989-91, Glimmerglass Opera Guild Newsletter, 1995—; mng. editor: Jour. Libr. Automation, 1980. Trustee Four County Libr. System, Binghamton, N.Y., 1978-88, South Cen. Rsch.Libr. Coun., Ithaca, 1986-90. With inf. AUS, 1952-54. Decorated Bronze Star; recipient Acad./Rsch. Libr. of Yr. award Assn. Coll. and Rsch. Librs., 1984, Trustees award for outstanding svc. South Ctrl. Rsch. Libr. Coun., 1994. Mem. ALA, Calif. Libr. Assn. (pres. 1972), N.Y. Libr. Assn. (pres. acad. and spl. librs. sect. 1981-82, 2d v.p. 1982, Spirit of Librarianship award 1992), Beta Phi Mu. Presbyterian. Home: 2 Walling Blvd Oneonta NY 13820-1918

JOHNSON, RICHARD DEAN, pharmaceutical consultant, educator; b. DeKalb, Ill., July 8, 1936; s. Arthur Dean Johnson and Evelyn Alice (Telford) Williams; m. Paula Marcellus Jennings, Nov. 3, 1942; children: Janet Telford, Julie Tess, Richard Dean Jr., Jennings Brodie. *Maternal Granfather E.D. Telford, AB 1896 McKendree College, LLB 1899 Georgetown U., was a three term Illinois State Senator and Republican candidate for Congress in 1926. Daughter Janet Telford Johnson, AB 1994 Duke U., MBA 2000 Anderson School of Business, University of California Los Angeles, has accepted a sales position with Goldman Sachs. Daughter Julie Tess Johnson, AB summa cum laude 1997 Bowdoin College, is a portfolio associate with Trillium Asset Management. Son Richard Dean Johnson Jr., AA 1998 Tacoma Community College, is currently a theater arts major at the University of Puget Sounds and appeared in the 1998 film 10 Things I Hate About You.* BS, U. Calif., Berkeley, 1960; PharmD, U. Calif., San Francisco, 1961, MS, 1962, PhD, 1965; MBA, Rockhurst Coll., Kansas City, Mo., 1984. Pharmacy lic., Calif., 1960; cert. tchr., Calif., 1967. Sect. head R&D Allergan Inc., Irvine, Calif., 1965-67; dir. regulatory affairs Syntex Labs., Inc., Palo Alto, Calif., 1967-73; mng. dir. licensing Marion Labs., Inc., Kansas City, Mo., 1973-79; v.p. licensing Marion Labs., Inc., Kansas City, 1980-82, v.p. corp. devel., 1983-87, v.p. bus. alliances, 1987-89; corp. v.p. Marion Merrell Dow, Inc., Kansas City, 1989-91; ret., chmn., CEO KC Pharma, LLC, Mo., 1991—; adj. prof. Sch. Pharmacy, U. Mo., Kansas City, 1991-95, R&D coun., 1993—, adj. grad. prof., 1995—; bd. dirs. Dey Labs., Inc., Concord, Calif., Tanabe-Marion Labs., Kansas City, U.S. Biosci., Inc., Blue Bell, Pa., ImmunoPharmaceutics, Inc., San Diego, Lovelace Respiratory Rsch. Inst., Albuquerque, Micrologix Biotech Inc., Vancouver, B.C., mem. comp. and audit coms.; guest lectr. U. S.C. Sch. Bus. Adminstrn., Columbia, 1975-79. *Over 35 years Dr. Johnson has gained executive experience in the U.S. pharmaceutical industry leading to corporate officer status in two Fortune 500 companies as well as numerous company and community board director and trusteeships. A major contribution to U.S. medicine included his patent licensing role in Japan of two major new drugs, a life saving cardiovascular agent and a gastrointestinal antiulcer product, achieving combined sales of more than $1.5 billion. He is currently an Adjunct Graduate Professor in the School of Pharmacy, University of Missouri-Kansas City.* Contbr. articles to pharm. jours. Presdl. exch. exec. White House, Washington, 1970-71, U.S. Pharmacopeia Com. of Rev., 1990-94, 95—; trustee U. Mo., Kansas City Pharmacy Found., 1993—, v.p., 1994-96, pres., 1996-98, pres. emeritus, 1998—, chmn. devel. com., 1994-96, chmn. exec. and fin. coms., 1996-98, dean's adv. bd., 1995—; trustee Kansas City Cmty. Found., 1993—, U. Kansas City Bd., Mo., 1996—; mem. fin. and real estate coms., 1998—; mem. dean's adv. bd. Sch. Pharmacy U. Calif., San Francisco, 1994-97, bd. counsellors, 1997—; mem. dean's adv. bd. Sch. Pharmacy U. Mo., Kansas City, 1995—; trustee Conservatory of Music, U. Mo., Kansas City, 1998—; Henry W. Bloch Sch. Bus. and Pub. Adminstrn. exec. roundtable U. Mo., Kansas City, 1998—; active Internat. Rels. Coun., Kansas City, 1998—; active De La Salle Sch. Devel. Com., 1993—, St. Lukes Hosp. Stroke Com., 1993—, U.S. Pharmacopeia Drug Nomenclature Com., 1990-94, 95—, vet. drug com., 1998—, ARC, Kirkwood Soc. Recipient Grad. award Borden Co., 1962; NIH Pub. Health Svc. Tng. grantee, 1962-65; Am. Found. for Pharm. Edn. fellow, 1962-64, Sir Henry S. Wellcome Meml. fellow, 1962-63, Am. Inst. Chemists fellow, 1965-70. Mem. AAAS, ACS, ARC Kirkwood Soc., Am. Found. for Pharm. Edn. Centurion, Am. Assn. Pharm. Scis., Am. Pharm. Assn., Acad. Pharm. Sci., N.Y. Acad. Sci., Pharm. Mfrs. Assn., Fedn. Internat. Pharmacy, Licensing Exec. Soc., Balboa Bay Club (Newport Beach, Calif.), Hallbrook Country Club (Kansas City, Mo.), La Jolla (Calif.) Beach and Tennis Club, Carriage Club (Kansas City, Mo.), Sigma Xi, Rho Chi, Phi Lambda Sigma. Home: 5330 Ward Pky Kansas City MO 64112-2369 Office: KC Pharma LLC 222 W Gregory Blvd Kansas City MO 64114-1110 also: 8486 El Paseo Grande La Jolla CA 92037-3013

JOHNSON, RICHARD FRED, lawyer; b. Chgo., July 12, 1944; s. Sylvester Hiram and Naomi Ruth (Jackson) J.; m. Sheila Conley, June 26, 1970; children: Brendon, Bridget, Timothy, Laura. BS, Miami U., Oxford, Ohio, 1966; JD cum laude, Northwestern U., 1969. Bar: Ill. 1969, U.S. Dist. Ct. (no. dist.) Ill. 1969, U.S. Ct. Appeals (7th cir.) 1977, U.S. Supreme Ct. 1978, U.S. Ct. Appeals (2d cir.) 1980, U.S. Ct. Appeals (9th cir.) 1991, U.S. Ct. Appeals (5th cir.) 1993. Law clk. U.S. Dist. Ct. (no. dist.) Ill., Chgo., 1969-70; assoc. firm Lord, Bissell & Brook, Chgo., 1970-77, ptnr., 1977—; lectr. legal edn. Contbr. articles to profl. jours. Recipient Am. Jurisprudence award, 1968. Mem. Chgo. Bar Assn., Union League. Home: 521 W Roscoe St Chicago IL 60657-3518 Office: Lord Bissell & Brook 115 S La Salle St Ste 3200 Chicago IL 60603-3972

JOHNSON, RICHARD JAMES VAUGHAN, newspaper executive; b. San Luis, Potosi, Mex., Sept. 22, 1930; s. Clifton Whatford and Myrtle Louise (Hinman) J.; m. Belle Beraud Griggs, Aug. 6, 1955; children: Shelley Beraud, Mark Hinman. B.B.A., U. Tex., Austin, 1954. Asst. to exec. dir. Tex. Daily Newspaper Assn., 1955-56; with Houston Chronicle Pub. Co., 1956, v.p. sales and mktg., 1971, exec. v.p., 1972, pres., 1973-87, pub., 1987, chmn. and pubr., 1990—; adv. dir. Chase Bank Houston, dir. Am. Gen. Corp., Mut. Ins. Co. Ltd. Bd. dirs. Tex. Med. Ctr., Greater Houston Partnership; chmn., CEO, and dir. Robert A. Welch Found.; bd. visitors M.D. Anderson Cancer Ctr., Meth. Hosp. With U.S. Army, 1952-54. Mem. Tex. Daily Newspaper Assn. (pres. 1978), Am. Newspaper Pubs. Assn. (past pres. and chmn.), River Oaks Club, Houston Club, Coronado Club. Unitarian. Office: Houston Chronicle 801 Texas St Houston TX 77002-2996

JOHNSON, RICHARD KARL, hospitality company executive; b. Gaylord, Minn., May 27, 1947; s. Karl S. and Mildred (Tollefson) J.; m. Eva Margaret Wick, Oct. 12, 1973; children: Michelle, Richard, Ryan. BA, Gustavus Adolphus U., St. Peter, Minn., 1969. Gen. mgr. Green Giant Restaurants, Inc., Mpls., 1969-71, Mpls. Elks Club, Mpls., 1971-73; dir. concept devel. Internat. Multifoods, Mpls., 1972-75; v.p. concept devel. A&WFood Svcs. Can., North Vancouver, B.C., 1975-81; dir. food and beverages Ramada, Reno, 1981-82; pres., owner R.K. Johnson & Assoc., Reno, 1981—; owner D.J. Mgmt., 1990—; asst. gen. mgr. Gold Dust West Casino, Reno, 1983-85; gen. mgr. P&M Corp., Reno, 1985-86; v.p. ops. C.P.S.W. Inc., Reno and Tempe, Ariz., 1986-87, Lincoln Fairview, Reno, 1987-89; v.p. corp. affairs Myers Realty, 1991—. Mem. Aircraft Owners and Pilots Assn., Nat. Restaurant Assn., Nev. Realtor, Elks Club. Lutheran. Avocations: flying, scuba diving. Home and Office: RK Johnson & Assoc 825 Meadow Springs Dr Reno NV 89509-5913

JOHNSON, RICHARD KENT, publishing executive; b. Moberly, Mo., Mar. 22, 1952; s. Edward Quivron and Elizabeth Jane (Barber) J.; m. Susan Dale Fersh, Sept. 4, 1976; children: Alexis Sarah, Claire Danielle. BA, Am. U., 1974. TV prodn. specialist Smithsonian Inst., Washington, 1974-77; dir. pub. rels. Congl. Info. Svc., Bethesda, Md., 1977-80, dir. advt. and promotion, 1980-83, dir. communications, 1983-89, dir. mktg., 1989-90, v.p. mktg., 1990-96; v.p. mktg. Univ. Publs. Am., Bethesda, 1990-96; sr. v.p. Congl. Info. Svc. and Univ. Pubs. Am., 1997-98; enterprise dir. Scholarly Pub. and Acad. Resources Coalition, Washington, 1998—. Recipient Echo Leader award Direct Mktg. Assn., 1986, Mktg. Achievement award Info. Industry Assn., 1985, 89, 90. Home: 5622 Lamar Rd Bethesda MD 20816-1350

JOHNSON, RICHARD T., neurology, microbiology and neuroscience educator, research virologist; b. Grosse Pointe, Mich., July 16, 1931; s. Horton and Katharine (Tidball) J.; m. Frances W. Johnson, Sept. 18, 1954; children: Carlton, Erica, Matthew, Nathan. AB cum laude, U. Colo., Boulder, 1953; MD, U. Colo., Denver, 1956. Diplomate Am. Bd. of Psychiatry and Neurology. Intern Stanford U. Hosps., San Francisco, 1956-57; clin. pathologist dept. virus diseases Walter Reed Army Inst. of Research, Washington, 1957-58, asst. chief dept. of virus diseases, 1959; asst. resident in neurology Mass. Gen. Hosp., 1959-60, clin. fellow neuropathology, 1959-61, sr. resident neurology, 1961-62; teaching fellow in neurology Harvard Med. Sch., Boston, 1959-60, teaching fellow neuropathology, 1959-61; teaching fellow neurology Harvard Med. Sch., 1961-62; exchange teaching fellow, 1st asst. in neurology Med. Sch. of King's Coll., U. Durham, Newcastle-Upon-Tyne, 1962; hon. fellow dept. microbiology Australian Nat. U., Canberra, 1962-64; assoc. neurologist Cleve. Met. Gen. Hosp., 1964-69; asst. prof. neurology Case Western Res. U., Cleve., 1964-68, assoc. prof. neurology, 1968-69; assoc. prof. microbiology Johns Hopkins U. Sch. of Medicine, Balt., 1969-74, Dwight D. Eisenhower prof. neurology, 1969-88, prof. microbiology, 1974—, prof. neurosci., 1983—; joint appointment dept. molecular microbiology & immunology Johns Hopkins U. Sch. Hygiene and Pub. Health, 1984—; neurologist Johns Hopkins Hosp., Balt., 1969—, neurologist-in-chief, 1988-97, prof., dir. dept. neurology, 1988-97; cons. neurology Balt. City Hosps., 1974; vis. prof. U. Peruana Cayetano Heredia, Lima, Peru, 1971, Imperial Coll. of Health Scis., Teheran, Iran, 1974, Inst. fur Virologie und Immunobiologie, U. Wurzburg, 1976; vis. prof. neurology and neuropathology Mahidol U., Bangkok, 1984; vis. scientist Armed Forces Research Inst. of Med. Scis., Bangkok, Thailand, 1984; dir. Nat. Neurosci. Inst., Singapore, 1997—. Author: (with others) Amotrophic Lateral Sclerosis: Recent Research Trends, 1976, Infections of the Nervous System, 1987, Viral Infections and the Developing Nervous System, 1988; author: Viral Infections of the Nervous System, 1982, 88, Current Therapy in Neurologic Diseases, 1985, Current Therapy in Neurologic Diseases, Vol. 2, 1987, Vol. 3, 1990; mem. editorial bd. 10 profl. jours.; editor Annal Neurol. Mem. adv. coun. James A. Baker Inst. for Animal Health, Cornell U., 1977-89; program dir. Pew Neurosci. Program, Pew Charitable Trusts, 1985-91; mem. adv. bd. Nat. Multiple Sclerosis Soc., 1971—, exec. com., 1981—, chmn. 1985-89. Recipient Jean Martin Charcot award Internat. Fedn. of Multiple Sclerosis Socs., 1985, Smadel medal Infectious Disease Soc. of Am., 1986, Multiple Sclerosis Soc. medal Assn. of Brit. Neurologists, 1986; comendador Order of Hipolito Unanue, 1981, numerous others. Fellow Am. Acad. of Neurology (2d v.p. 1975-77); mem. Assn. of Am. Physicians, Am. Soc. for Virology, Australian Assn. of Neurologists (hon.), Interurban Clin. Club, Acad. Brasileira de Neurologia, Assn. for Research in Nervous and Mental Diseases, Internat. Brain Research Orgn., Peripatetic Club, Soc. for Neurosci., Soc. Peruana de Psiquiatria, Johns Hopkins Med. Soc. (pres. 1970-71), Balt. Neurol. Soc. (pres. 1973-74), Am. Soc. for Clin. Investigation, Am. Neurol. Assn. (councillor 1977-81, v.p. 1984-85, pres. 1986-87), Am. Assn. of Neuropathologists (assoc.), World Fedn. of Neurology (chmn. research group on neuroimmunology and virology 1979—), Am. Soc. for Microbiology, AAAS, Philippine Neurol. Assn. (hon. fellow), Internat. Soc. for Antiviral Research, Inst. of Medicine of the Nat. Acad. of Sci., Am. Fedn. of Clin. Research, Alpha Omega Alpha, Phi Beta Kappa. Avocations: photography, travelling. Office: Johns Hopkins U Sch Medicine Dept of Neurology 600 N Wolfe St Meyer 6-181 Baltimore MD 21205

JOHNSON, RICHARD TENNEY, lawyer; b. Evanston, Ill., Mar. 24, 1930; s. Ernest Levin and Margaret Abbott (Higgins) J.; m. Marilyn Bliss Meuth, May 1, 1954; children: Ross Tenney, Lenore, Jocelyn. AB with high honors, U. Rochester, 1951; postgrad., Trinity Coll., Dublin, Ireland, 1954-55; LLB, Harvard, 1958. Bar: D.C. 1959. Trainee Office Sec. Def., 1957-59; atty. Office Gen. Counsel. Dept. Def., 1959-63; dep. gen. counsel Dept. Army, 1963-67, Dept. Transp., 1967-70; gen. counsel CAB, 1970-73, mem., 1976-77; gen. counsel NASA, 1973-75, ERDA, 1975-76; chmn. organizational integration Dept. Energy Activation, Exec. Office of Pres., 1977; ptnr. firm Sullivan & Beauregard, 1978-81; gen. counsel Dept. Energy, 1981-83; ptnr. Zuckert, Scoutt, Rasenberger & Johnson, 1983-87; prin. Law Offices of R. Tenney Johnson, Esq., Washington, 1987—; gen. counsel Assn. of Univs. for Rsch. in Astronomy, 1987—. Lt. USNR, 1951-54. Mem. ABA, Fed. Bar Assn., Cosmos Club, Phi Beta Kappa, Theta Delta Chi. Office: 2121 K St NW Ste 800 Washington DC 20237-1801

JOHNSON, RICHARD TURNER, television producer, consultant; b. Seattle, Mar. 21, 1933; s. B.E. and Marie (Turner) J.; m. Joyce Loraine McLeod, Dec. 1, 1957; children: Rick, Mark. BA in Theater Arts, UCLA, 1959, MA in Theater Arts, 1961. TV stage mgr., set designer Sta. KHJ-TV Channel 9, L.A., 1962-67, producer, dir., 1967-72, prodn. mgr., 1972-81, asst. program dir., exec. producer, 1981-90; exec. dir. Conejo Players Theater, Thousand Oaks, Calif., 1968—; arts commr. City of Thousand Oaks, 1986-92. Exec. producer: (TV program) Off-Hand (L.A. Emmy 1982, 86, 88), Teen Talk (L.A. Emmy 1983, 89), Taking 'High' Out of High School, 1985 (L.A. Emmy 1985), School Beat, 1986 (L.A. Emmy 1986); dir. plays including Carousel, Kiss Me Kate, Peter Pan, Guys & Dolls, Tribute, Pipe Dream, How to Succeed in Business, Mikado, Champagne General, Amorous Flea, A Thousand Clowns, The Most Happy Fellow, Big River. Mem. Cultural Ctr. Planning Com., Thousand Oaks, 1985-86. With USNR, 1954-57. Mem. Acad. TV Arts and Scis., Arts Coun. Conejo Valley, Alliance for the Arts (campaign dir. 1990-96), UCLA Theater Arts Alumni Assn. Avocations: painting, carpentry, swimming, skiing.

JOHNSON, RICHARD WALTER, entrepreneur; b. Mpls., Oct. 2, 1928; s. Walter Benjamin and Evelyn (Peterson) J.; m. Marlys Jean Tiller, Feb. 21, 1988; children: Richard Walter, William Charles, Nancy Ann, Thomas Gregory, Michael Richard. B.B.A. with distinction, U. Minn., 1949. C.P.A., Nebr., Ill. With Arthur Andersen & Co. (C.P.A.'s), 1949-74; mng. partner Arthur Andersen & Co. (C.P.A.'s), Omaha, 1960-74; chmn. bd., chief exec. officer Western Securities Co. of Del., Omaha, 1975—; pres., CEO Modern Equipment Co., Omaha, 1975—. Bd. dirs., exec. com. Jr. Achievement Omaha, 1962—, pres., 1966-67; gen. campaign chmn. Heart of the Midlands United Way, 1972, chmn. pacemaker sect. fund raising campaign, 1964, chmn. corporate standards com., 1966, assoc. gen. chmn., 1968, treas., mem. exec. com., 1969; bd. dirs. Fontenelle Forest Nature Ctr. Assn. Mid-Am. council Boy Scouts of Am., Omaha Symphony Assn., Omaha Big Bros. Assn., Omaha Playhouse Assn.; Trustee Creighton U. Pres.'s Council. Recipient One of Outstanding Young Men in Am. award, 1965, Gifford award Fontenelle Forest Assn., 1997. Mem. AICPA, Nebr. Soc. CPAs, Newcomen Soc. N.Am., Omaha C. of C. (chmn. membership rels. com. 1962—, bd. dirs. 1965-76, mem. exec. com., v.p. 1968-72), Omaha Club, Omaha Country Club, Garden of the Gods Club (Colorado Springs), Masons, Shriners, Rotary Internat., Beta Gamma Sigma, Beta Alpha Psi. Home: 1323 N 98th Ct Omaha NE 68114-2112 Office: 2000 Cuming St Omaha NE 68102-4324

JOHNSON, ROBERT ALAN, lawyer; b. Harrisburg, Pa., June 18, 1944; s. Harry Andrew and Minna Melissa (Ebert) J.; m. Selina Braham Pedersen, Aug. 25, 1979; children: Isabella P., Robert A. Jr. BA, Washington and Jefferson Coll., 1966; JD, Harvard U., 1969. Bar: Pa. 1969. Assoc. Buchanan Ingersoll, Pitts., 1969-76, ptnr., 1977—. Contbr. legal articles to profl. jours. Pres. Bach Choir Pitts., 1979-81; bd. dirs. Pitts. Opera, 1985-94, River City Brass Band, Pitts., 1986-95, Renaissance and Baroque Soc., Pitts., 1994—, Friends of the Music Libr., Carnegie Libr. of Pitts., 1995—. Fellow Am. Coll. Tax Counsel; mem. ABA, Am. Arbitration Assn. (panel arbitrators), Allegheny County Bar Assn., Allegheny Tax Soc. (chmn. 1982-83), Pitts. Tax Club, Duquesne Club. Presbyterian. Avocation: avid collector classical music recs. Home: 601 St James St Pittsburgh PA 15232-1434 Office: Buchanan Ingersoll 301 Grant St Ste 20 Pittsburgh PA 15219-1410

JOHNSON, ROBERT ALLISON, life insurance company executive; b. Canandaigua, N.Y., Sept. 8, 1928; s. Allison Fisher and Thelma Marie (Beers) J.; m. Suzanne Amundsen Stone, Dec. 18, 1951; children—Pamela Suzanne, Carol Alison, Elizabeth Stone, Cynthia Marie. B.A. in History, Harvard U., 1950; M.B.A., Western New Eng. Coll., 1963. With Mass. Mut. Life Ins. Co., Springfield, 1951—; employment mgr. Mass. Mut. Life Ins. Co., 1958-72, dir. personnel, 1972-76, sr. v.p., 1976—. Active ARC. Served with U.S. Army, 1951-53. Mem. Life Office Mgmt. Assn., Am. Soc. C.L.U.'s. Home: 8920 Shipwatch Dr Wilmington NC 28412-3536 Office: 1295 State St Springfield MA 01111-0001

JOHNSON, ROBERT ARNOLD, physician, cardiologist, poet; b. Caldwell, Idaho, May 31, 1942; s. Robert Lyle and Ellen Lora (Salisbury) J.; m. Judith Suzanne Gibson, Sept. 7, 1962 (div. Apr. 1989); children: Heidi Johnson Judge, Heather, Erin; m. Susan Eileen Pickett, Apr. 29, 1989. BS in Zoology, Wash. State U., 1964; MD, U. Wash., 1969. Intern, then resident in medicine Beth Israel Hosp., Boston, 1969-73; fellow in cardiology Mass. Gen. Hosp., Boston, 1971-74; from instr. to asst. prof. medicine/cardiology Mass. Gen. Hosp./Harvard Med. Sch., Boston, 1974-83; cardiologist Walla Walla (Wash.) Clinic, 1983-97; med. dir. cardiac svcs. St. Mary Med. Ctr., Walla Walla, 1997—. Author, co-editor: The Practice of Cardiology, 1980, 2d edit., 1988; author book-length epic poem; contbr. articles to profl. jours. Bd. dirs., chair fundraising Walla Walla Symphony Soc., 1994-97. Mem. Am. Heart Assn. (fellow coun. on clin. cardiology), Acad. Am. Poets, Nat. Assn. Advancement of Sci., Phi Beta Kappa, Alpha Omega Alpha. Democrat. Avocations: music (audience, criticism), travel (Italy), cooking, wine tasting. Home: 362 S 3rd Ave Walla Walla WA 99362-3037 Office: St Mary Physician Group 401 W Poplar St Walla Walla WA 99362-2846

JOHNSON, ROBERT BRITTEN, geology educator; b. Cortland, N.Y., Sept. 24, 1924; s. William and Christine (Hofer) J.; m. Garnet Marion Brown, Aug. 30, 1947; children: Robert Britten, Richard Karl, Elizabeth Anne. Student, Wheaton (Ill.) Coll., 1942-43, 46-47; AB summa cum laude, Syracuse U., 1949, MS, 1950; PhD, U. Ill., 1954. Asst. geologist Ill. Geol. Survey, 1951-54; asst. prof. geology Syracuse U., 1954-55; sr. geologist and geophysicist C.A. Bays & Asso., Urbana, Ill., 1955-56; from asst. prof. to prof. engring. geology Purdue U., 1956-66, head, engring. geology dept., 1964-66; prof. geology DePauw U., 1966-67, head, dept. geology, 1966-67; prof. geology Colo. State U., 1967-88, acting chmn. dept. geology, 1968, chmn. dept., 1969-73, prof. in charge geology programs, dept. earth resources, 1973-77, acting head dept. earth resources, 1979-81, prof. emeritus, 1988—; regional geophysicist U.S. Bur. of Reclamation, 1967-76; geologist U.S. Geol. Survey, 1976-88; cons. in field, 1957—; instr. Elderhostel programs, 1991—. Active local Boy Scouts Am., 4-H Club, Sci. Fair, dist. schs.; VITA vol. Served with USAAF, 1943-46. Fellow Geol. Soc. Am. (sr. fellow, E.B. Burwell Jr. Meml. award 1989); mem. Assn. Engring. Geologists (Claire P. Holdredge Outstanding Publ. award 1990), Phi Beta Kappa. Republican. Home: 2309 Moffett Dr Fort Collins CO 80526-2122

JOHNSON, ROBERT BRUCE, historic preservationist; b. Salina, Kans., Dec. 14, 1941; s. Robert Alexander and Virginia Belle (Keen) J.; m. Dora Koundakjian, May 14, 1966 (div. May 1986); children: Martin, Alicia; m. Genevieve Whittemore, Oct. 18, 1986; 1 child, James Trevor Johnson. BA, Wheaton Coll., 1964; JD, Cath. U. Sch. of Law, Washington, 1976. Orgnl. sales leader The Southwestern Co., Nashville, 1963-65; asst. housing mgr. Nat. Capitol Housing Authority Housing Urban Devel., Washington, 1966-67; project dir. Archdiocese of Washington Office of Edn., Washington, 1967-70; dep. dir. Dept. Labor Youth Svcs., Washington, 1970-75; pres. Intown Properties Inc., Washington, 1977-81, Mt. Vernon Realty Inc., Washington, 1981-86, Premier Realty Svcs. Inc., Washington, 1986-90; sr. v.p. AmeriFund Inc., Washington, 1990-95; devel. dir. Patrick Henry Inst., Lynchburg, Va., 1995-98; cons. Nat. Trust for Hist. Preservation, Washington, 1982-83, New Covenant Schs., Lynchburg, Va.; ptnr. Towne Ctr. Assocs., Staunton, Va., 1979-92, Capitol Link Devel. Assocs., Wshington, 1986-89, Coolidge House Assocs., Washington, 1987-94. Contbr. articles to profl. jours. Treas., co-founder New City Montessori Sch., Washington, 1969-73; mem. Cmty. Advisors on Equal Employment, Washington, 1967-70; patron Nat. Children's Choir, 1979-89, treas., initiator Bottle Bill Initiative Campaign, Washington, 1985-86. Recipient Silver Palm Eagle Scout

Boy Scouts Am., 1957. Mem. Nat. Trust for Hist. Preservation, Hist. Staunton Found. (ann. preservation award 1982, 83), Victorian Soc. Am., Lynchburg Acad. Music Theatre. Home: Villa Mozart 517 Washington St Lynchburg VA 24504

JOHNSON, ROBERT BRUCE, company director; b. 1944. MS, U. Ariz., 1980, BS, 1968. Hydrologist W.S. Gookin & Assocs., Scottsdale, Ariz., 1972-75; hydrologist II City of Tucson, 1975-78, chief hydrologist, 1978-97, lead adminstr., 1997-98, asst. dir., 1998—. Office: City of Tucson PO Box 27210 Tucson AZ 85726-7210

JOHNSON, ROBERT CHARLES, medical administrator; b. Madison, Wis., Nov. 1, 1963; s. Gordon Dale and Gretta June (Davidson) J.; m. Cindi Kalin, May 30, 1992; 1 child, Benjamin Kalin. BS in Elec. Engring. and Computer, Kans. State U., 1985; MD, U. Kans., 1993. Bd. cert. in radiation oncology. Med. dir. Heartland Cancer Ctr., St. Joseph, Mo., 1993—; co-chmn. cancer com. Heartland Regional Med. Ctr., St. Joseph, 1993-96, chmn., 1996—. Dir. Am. Cancer Soc., St. Joseph, 1993—. Mem. Am. Coll. Radiology, Am. Coll. Radiation Oncology, Am. Soc. of Therapeutic Radiation Oncologists. Methodist. Avocations: trumpet, home remodeling. Office: Heartland Cancer Treatment Ctr 902 N Riverside Rd Ste 201 Saint Joseph MO 64507*

JOHNSON, ROBERT CLYDE, theology educator; b. Knoxville, Tenn., Aug. 17, 1919; s. Robert Clyde and Lucille (Davis) J.; m. Elizabeth Childs, June 26, 1942; children—Robert Clyde III, Richard Albert, Catherine Barton, Anne Elizabeth. B.S., Davidson Coll., 1941, D.D., 1963; postgrad., Princeton Theol. Sem., 1941-43; B.D., Union Theol. Sem., N.Y.C., 1944, S.T.M., 1953; M.A., Columbia U., 1947; M.A. (hon.), Yale U., 1963; D.D., Tusculum Coll., 1953; Ph.D., Vanderbilt U., 1957. Ordained to ministry Presbyn. Ch., 1943. Minister in Shrewsbury, N.J., 1943-47, Greeneville, Tenn., 1947-55; asst. prof. theology Pitts. Theol. Sem., 1955-57, prof., 1957-63; Noah Porter prof. theology Yale Div. Sch., 1963-90, Noah Porter prof. theology emeritus, 1990—, dean, 1963-69; fellow Ezra Stiles Coll., Yale, 1963-83; lectr. Yale Div. Sch., 1991-94. Author: The Meaning of Christ, 1958, Authority in Protestant Theology, 1959, The Church and Its Changing Ministry, 1962. Served as chaplain USNR, 1944-46. Home: 77 Lake Dr New Milford CT 06776-4135 also: 141 Garfield Ave North Haven CT 06473-4322

JOHNSON, ROBERT DALE, marketing technology administrator; b. Greensburg, Ind., May 25, 1965; s. Lester Wilburn and Mildred Louise (Sidwell-Ray) J. Assoc. in Elec. Engring., ITT Tech. Inst., 1985, BS in Automation, 1986; BSBA, Ind. Wesleyan U., 1989. GTE Midwestern Tel. Ops. GTE Midwestern Telephone Ops., Westfield, Ind., 1984-87; computer network specialist Midwestern Tel. Ops./GTE North, Carmel, Ind., 1987-89; mktg. adminstr. GTE Telecom, Indpls., 1988-89; tech. svcs. coord. GTE North/GTE Data Svcs., Westfield, Ind., 1989; data products salesman GTE Telecom, Muskegon, Mich., 1989-90; products divsn. mgr. Genzink Steel Corp., Holland, Mich., 1992-95; mgr. mktg. tech. Haworth Inc., Holland, Mich., 1996—; pres. Trinity Cons. for Sys. and Svcs. Inc., Spring Lake, Mich., 1990—; instr. Ind. U.-Purdue U., Indpls., 1989. Mem. Soc. Mfg. Engring. (past chmn.), U.S. Space Found., Bass Anglers Sportsman Soc. Republican. Wesleyan. Avocations: fishing, boating, art, taxidermy, golf. Home: 9255 Jackson Rd Clarksville MI 48815 Office: One Haworth Ctr Holland MI 49423

JOHNSON, ROBERT EUGENE, historian, academic administrator; b. N.Y.C., Aug. 7, 1943; s. Robert E. and Eileen Mary (Holden) J.; m. Laura Zoe Climenko; children: Byron, Alexander. BA, Antioch Coll., 1965; PhD, Cornell U., 1975. History lectr. Erindale Coll. U. Toronto, 1971-74, asst. prof. history, 1975-79, assoc. prof. history, 1979-95; prof., 1995—; dir. Ctr. for Russian and East European Studies U. Toronto, 1989—. Author: Peasant and Proletarian, 1979, The Seam Allowance, 1982, Contadini e Proletari, 1993; editor: The 1937 Census of USSR, 1992. Rsch. grantee Social Sci. and Humanities Rsch. Coun. Can., Toronto and Moscow, 1994-99. Mem. Am. Hist. Assn., Am. Assn. for Advancement of Slavic Studies, Can. Assn. Slavists (v.p. 1985-86). Avocations: mycology, cross-country skiing, canoeing. Office: U Toronto, 130 St George St Rm 14335, Toronto, ON Canada M5S 1A5

JOHNSON, ROBERT EUGENE, physiologist; b. Conrad, Mont., Apr. 8, 1911; s. Arthur D. and Florence May (Disbrow) J.; m. Margaret Hunter, Jan. 11, 1935; children: Thomas Arthur, Charles William, Katherine Helen (dec.). B.S. in Chemistry, U. Wash., 1931; B.A. in Physiology (Rhodes scholar), U. Oxford, Eng., 1934, D.Phil. in Biochemistry, 1935; M.D., Harvard U., 1941. Research asst. advancing to asst. prof. indsl. physiology Harvard Fatigue Lab., 1935-46; expert cons. QMC 3, AUS, 1941-46; dir. U.S. Army Med. Nutrition Lab., Chgo., 1946-49; prof. physiology U. Ill. at Urbana, 1949-73, head dept., 1949-60, dir. univ. honors program, 1959-67, acting dean Grad. Coll., 1952-53; prof. biology Knox Coll., Galesburg, Ill., 1973-79; coordinator Knox Coll.-Rush U. Med. Program, 1973-79; sci. cons. Presbyn.-St. Luke's Hosp., Chgo., 1973-83; pres. Horn of the Moon Enterprises, Montpelier, Vt., 1980—; vis. prof. physiology U. Vt., 1983—. Co-author: Metabolic Methods, 1951, Physiological Measurements of Metabolic Functions in Man, 1963; author: Sir John Richardson, 1976; also articles in profl. jours. NSF Sr. Postdoctoral Research fellow, 1957-58; Guggenheim Meml. Found. fellow, 1964-65. Mem. Am. Soc. Clin. Investigation, Am. Physiol. Soc., Nutrition Today, History of Sci. Soc., Phi Beta Kappa, Sigma Xi. Home and Office: 5 East Terr South Burlington VT 05403-6145 *These I believe: Work hard. Deal honestly and straightforwardly with everyone. Be temperate in all aspects of life. Respect the rights and privileges of all living creatures.*

JOHNSON, ROBERT GLENN, geology and geophysics educator; b. Iowa, Dec. 12, 1922; m. Elizabeth Louise Gulliver, July 17, 1949. BS, Case Western Res. U., 1947; PhD, Iowa State U., 1952. Project engr. Bendix Aviation Inc., Red Bank, N.J., 1952-55; scientist Honeywell Inc., Mpls., 1955-74, staff scientist, 1974-90; adj. prof. dept. geology and geophysics U. Minn., Mpls., 1990—. Contbr. articles to profl. publs. Achievements include 23 patents on control technology sensors; pioneering research in silicon microstructure sensor technology; key contributions to understanding of glacial climate change mechanisms. Office: U Minn Dept Geology-Geophys 310 Pillsbury Dr SE Minneapolis MN 55455-0219

JOHNSON, ROBERT HENRY, political science educator; b. Hannaford, N.D., Jan. 23, 1921; s. Albert Idan and Alma (Peterson) J.; divorced; children: Mark Olin, Eric Lowell, Hilary Jean. BA, Concordia Coll., Moorhead, Minn., 1942; MS, Syracuse U., 1943; PhD, Harvard U., 1949. Tchg. fellow Harvard U., 1948-49, instr. govt., 1949-51; asst. to exec. sec. NSC, 1951-54, mem., sec. spl. staff, 1954-59, dir. planning bd. secretariat, 1959-61, mem. sr. staff, 1961-62; mem. policy planning coun. State Dept., 1962-67; sr. fellow Brookings Instn., 1966-68, guest scholar, 1970, 71, 73, 80; Harvey Picker prof. internat. rels. Colgate U., 1968-71, 80-84, Charles Evans Hughes prof. govt., 1971-80, chmn. dept. polit. sci., 1979-82, 83-84; vis. fellow Overseas Devel. Coun., 1974-75, 76-77, 84-86, 87-88; sr. fellow Nat. Policy Assn., 1988—; cons. to dir. internat. divsn. GAO, 1978-82; resident assoc. Carnegie Endowment for Internat. Peace, 1982-83, 86-87. Author: Improbable Dangers, U.S. Conceptions of Threat in the Cold War and After, 1994; contbr. articles to profl. jours. and newspapers. With USNR, 1943-46. Recipient Rockefeller Pub. Svc. award, 1958; Alumni Achievement award Concordia Coll., 1975; fellow Social Sci. Rsch. Coun., 1948-49; Ford Found. grantee, 1966. Mem. Am. Polit. Sci. Assn., Coun. on Fgn. Rels. Congregationalist. Home: 3120 Wellington Rd Alexandria VA 22302-2228 Office: Nat Policy Assn 1424 16th St NW Washington DC 20036-2211

JOHNSON, ROBERT L., broadcast executive; m. Sheila; 2 children. BS, U. Ill.; MS in Internat. Affairs, Princeton U. Urban League, Washington, Corp. for Pub. Broadcasting, Washington; Press sec. for Hon. Walter E. Fauntroy Congl. Del. D.C., Washington; v.p. Govt. Rels. Nat. Cable TV Assn., Washington, 1976-79; founder, chmn. and CEO BET Holdings, Inc., Washington, 1980—; bd. dirs. U.S. Airways, Hilton Hotels Corp., United Negro Coll. Fund, Nat. Cable TV Assn.'s Acad. Cable Programming, Am. Film Inst., Advtg. Coun. Recipient 1997 Broadcasting & Cable mag. Hall of Fame award, CTAM's Grand Tam award, Cablevision mag.'s 20/20 Vision award, an NAACP Image award, Nat. Women's Polit. Caucus' Good Guys award, Disting. Alumni award from Princeton U., Pres.'s award from Nat. Cable TV Assn. Office: BET Holdings Inc 1 BET Plz 1900 W Pl NE Washington DC 20018-1211*

JOHNSON, ROBERT LEE, JR., physician, educator, researcher; b. Dallas, Apr. 28, 1926; s. Robert L. and Doris (Miller) J.; m. Aileen Johnson, 1952; children: Stephen Lee, Robert Edward. BS, So. Meth. U., 1947; MD, Northwestern U., 1951. Intern Cook County Hosp., Chgo., 1951-52; resident in internal medicine Parkland Meml. Hosp., Phila., 1952-55; fellow nat. foun. infantile paralysis and clin. instr. U. Tex. Southwestern Med. Ctr., Dallas, 1955-56; fellow dept. physiol. and pharmacology Grad. Sch. Medicine U. Pa., Phila., 1956-57; asst. prof. U. Tex. Southwestern Med. Ctr., Dallas, 1959-65, assoc. prof., 1965-69, prof. medicine, 1969—; vis. staff Parkland Meml. Hosp., Dallas, 1957—, Zale Lipshy U. Hosp., Dallas, 1989—; cons. chest diseases VA Hosp., Dallas, 1966—; dir. chest medicine clinic Parkland Meml. Hosp., 1983—; mem. parent rev. com. Nat. Heart, Lung, and Blood Inst. for Spl. Ctrs. of Rsch. proposals, 1983-85; mem. Nat. Heart, Lung, and Blood Rsch. Rev. Com., 1985-89; mem. respiratory and applied physiology study sect. NIH, 1991-94. Mem. editl. bd. Jour. Clin. Investigation, 1972-77, Jour. Applied Physiology, 1980-82, 96—, Circulation, 1996—; guest referee editor Jour. Applied Physiology, Am. Jour. Physiology, Chest, Circulation, Circulation Rsch., Am. Rev. Respiratory Disease, Am. Jour. Med. Sci., Jour. Clin. Investigation, Early Human Devel., Kidney Internat.; contbr. articles to profl. jours. With Naval ROTC, 1945-46; with USNR, 1944-46; maj. USAR, 1962. Mem. Am. Heart Assn. (cardiopulmonary coun. exec. com. mem. 1990-92, nominating com. cardiopulmonary coun. 1989-93, chmn. 1990-92), Am. Thoracic Soc. (planning com. mem. 1987-90, com. proficiency standards 1985-94, Scientific Accomplishment award 1996, recipient Scientific Accomplishment award 1996), Am. Coll. Chest Physicians, Am. Fedn. Clin. Rsch., Am. Physiol. Soc., Am. Soc. Clin. Investigation, Assn. Am. Physicians, Cen. Soc. Clin. Rsch., So. Soc. Clin. Rsch., Soc. Sigma Xi. Fax: 214-648-8027. E-mail: robert.johnson@email.swmed.edu. Office: UT Southwestern Med Ctr 5323 Harry Hines Blvd Dallas TX 75235-9034

JOHNSON, ROBERT LEWIS, JR., retail company executive; b. Chgo., June 17, 1935; s. Robert Lewis Sr. and Gladys (Cherry) J.; m. Rose Harris; children—Rhonda, Rosalyn. B.A., Roosevelt U., 1958. Asst. mgr. Chgo. Housing Authority, 1960-65; v.p. concessions and contract sales Sears, Roebuck and Co., Chgo., 1965-91; chmn., chief exec. officer Johnson Bryce Inc., Memphis, 1991—; dir. Rymer Corp., Chgo., Fed. Reserve Bd. St. Louis Dist., 1998. Bd. dirs. Evanston Hosp., Ill., 1983-87, Suburban United Way, Chgo., 1987-91, Voices for Ill. Children, 1987-91, Rising Tide Found., Memphis C. of C.; chmn. Evanston Civil Service commn., 1981-88; trustee Roosevelt U., Chgo., 1986—, mem. alumni bd., 1984-88; mem. Sch. of Bus. Round Table Fla. A&M U., 1987—. Served with U.S. Army, 1958-60; Fedr. Res. Bd., St. Louis, 1998; bd. trustees Lemoyne Own Coll., Memphis, 1997. Club: Druids. Home: 310 Barton Ave Evanston IL 60202-3302 Office: Johnson Beyce Inc 3861 Delp St Memphis TN 38118-6123

JOHNSON, ROBERT LOUIS, cable television company executive; b. Hickory, Miss., Apr. 8, 1946; m. Sheila Crump, Jan. 19, 1969. BA in History, U. Ill., 1968; M in Pub. Affairs, Princeton U., 1972. Press sec. Hon. Walter E. Fauntroy, Congl. del. from Washington, 1973-76; v.p. govt. rels. Nat. Cable TV Assn., 1976-79; founder, pres. Black Entertainment TV, Washington, 1979—, Dist. Cablevision, Inc., 1980—; chmn., pres., CEO BET Holdings, Inc. (formerly Black Entertainment TV), Washington, 1993—. Recipient Image award NAACP, 1982, Bus. of Yr. award D.C. C. of C., 1985, Exec. Leadership Coun. award Turner Broadcasting, 1993, 20/20 Vision award Cablevision Mag., 1995, Hall of Fame award Broadcasting and Cable Mag., 1997, Good Guys award Nat. Women's Polit. Caucus, 1998, Disting. Alumni award Princeton U., 1998. Office: BET Holdings Inc 1900 W Pl NE Washington DC 20018-1211

JOHNSON, ROBERT MAX, lawyer; b. Thomas, Okla., Aug. 20, 1942; s. Claude L. and Jesse C. (Stimmel) J.; m. Virginia A. LeForce, May 31, 1964; children: Kelli Brook, Brent Matthew. BS, Okla. State U., 1964; JD, U. Okla., 1967. Bar: Okla. 1967. Shareholder Crowe & Dunlevy, Oklahoma City, 1967—, pres., 1985-87, exec. com., 1992—; spl. lectr. in land fin. and real estate contracts U. Okla. Coll. of Law, Norman, 1973, 84. Mng. editor: Oklahoma Environmental Law Handbook, 1992-96; contbr. to book: The Law of Distressed Real Estate, 1987; case editor Okla. Law Rev., 1966. Bd. dirs. Redbud Found., Oklahoma City, 1987-96, Myriad Gardens Conservatory, Oklahoma City, 1987-89, Myriad Gardens Found., 1993-96, ARC, 1994-96, Arts Coun. Oklahoma City, 1994—, Am. Heart Assn., 1999—; chmn. Oklahoma City Festival of Arts, 1993-94, Murrah Fed. Bldg. Meml. Task Force, 1995-96, Oklahoma City Nat. Meml. Found., 1996-98, Oklahoma City Nat. Meml. Trust, 1998—. Capt. U.S. Army, 1968-70. Fellow Am. Coll. Mortgage Attys. (bd. regents, pres. 1994-95, chmn. exec. com. 1995-96); mem. Am. Coll. Real Estate Lawyers, Oklahoma City Golf and Country Club (bd. dirs. 1981-82, sec. 1982), Phi Delta Phi (magister 1966-67), Lambda Alpha. Avocations: golf, quail hunting, fly fishing, skiing. Home: 1511 Guilford Ln Oklahoma City OK 73120-1208 Office: Crowe & Dunlevy 1800 Mid Am Tower Oklahoma City OK 73102

JOHNSON, ROBERT WALTER, marine engineer, priest; b. Houston, Aug. 10, 1958; s. Bob J. and Ruth Ovella (Rotenberry) J. Student, S.W. Tex. State U., 1977-81. Pres., CEO The Traveller, Unltd., Engring. & Environ. Cons., Webster, Tex., 1994—. Active Christian Coalition, Rep. Nat. Com.; mem. Citizens Com. for Right To Keep and Bear Arms. With USN, 1982-86. Mem. NRA (life), Am. Maritime Officers, Seafarers Internat. Union, 100 Club Houston. Mem. LDS Ch. E-mail: traveler@wt.net.

JOHNSON, RODNEY DALE, retired law enforcement officer, photographer; b. Montebello, Calif., May 14, 1944; s. Albert Gottfreid and Maxine Elliot (Rogers) J.; m. Karen Rae Van Antwerp, May 18, 1968; 1 child, Tiffany Nicole. AA, Ela C.C., 1973; postgrad. law enforcement specialist, FBI Acad., 1976; BA, U. LaVerne, 1978. Cert. tchr. police sci., Calif. Dep. Los Angeles County Sheriff's Dept., 1969-75, dep. IV, 1976-78, sgt., 1978-99; ret., 1999; fire arms inst., Hacienda Heights, Calif., 1975-94; photographer Weddings and Portraits, 1983-94; photography instr., Hacienda Heights, 1983-94; pres. Wheelhouse Enterprises, Inc., Whittier, 1971-86; instr. State Sheriff's Civil Procedural Sch. Los Medanos Coll., Concord, Calif., 1985-88. Creator, actor Cap 'n Andy, 1973-80; song writer for Cap 'n Andy theme, 1972. Sgt. USMC, 1965-69, Vietnam, master gunnery sgt. USMCR, 1969-94, ret.; intelligence chief, Persian Gulf. Recipient Svc. award Trinity Broadcasting Network, 1979. Mem. Profl. Peace Officers Assn., Sheriff's Relief Assn., Assn. Photographers Internat., Marine Corps. Intelligence Assn., Inc., Faithbuilders Club (pres. 1981-87). Republican. Mem. Assembly of God.

JOHNSON, ROGER CHRISTIE, environmental engineer; b. Belmond, Iowa, Aug. 12, 1925; s. Elmer Adolph and Goldie Evelyn (Christie) J.; m. Constance Jean Benson, July 26, 1953; children: Christie Clark, Gregary, Jamie, Bradley, Wade, Eric. BS in Chemistry, Calif. Inst. Tech., Pasadena, 1949. Qualified environ. profl., Iowa waste water operator. Lab technician Gen. Mills, Belmond, 1956-61; asst. quality assurance mgr. Gen. Mills, West Chgo., Ill., 1961-63; plant chemist Ctrl. Soya, Belmond, 1963-66, quality assurance mgr., 1966-83; environ. engr. Eaton Corp., Belmond, 1983—. Cubmaster, Webelos leader Cub Scouts Am., Belmond, 1964-69; bd. dirs. Belmond Cmty. Retirement Apts., 1970—; chair, vice chair Wright County (Iowa) Dems., 1972-98. With U.S. Army, 1943-45. Mem. honor roll NIACC, 1994. Mem. LEPC (region V), Am. Chem. Soc., Am. Indsl. Hygiene Assn., Air and Waste Mgmt. Assn., Water Environ. Fedn., Am. Water Works Assn., Iowa Environ. Coun., Iowa Water Pollution Control Assn., Inst. of Profl. Environ. Practice, Union of Concerned Scientists, Wildlife Fedn., Sierra Club, Nat. Resources Def. Coun. Congregationalist/United Ch. of Christ. Home: 312 4th Ave NE Belmond IA 50421-1314 Office: Eaton Corp 700 Luick Ln S Belmond IA 50421-1785

JOHNSON, ROGER LEE, minister; b. Anniston, Ala., Dec. 6, 1941; s. Paul Lee and Margie Ree (Malone) J.; m. Virginia Ruth Grubb, June 3, 1947; children: Sheri Leigh, Stephanie Michelle. BA, Harding U., 1964; MA in Religion, Harding Grad. Sch., Memphis, 1987. Min. Ch. Christ, Lebanon, Va., 1964-65, Northwest Ch. Christ, Durant, Okla., 1965-67, Ch. Christ, Caledonia, Miss., 1967-68, Broadway Ch. of Christ, Garland, Tex., 1968-72, Garden Ridge Ch.Christ, Lewisville, Tex., 1972-77, Sharpstown Ch. Christ, Houston, 1977-83, Union Ave Ch. Christ, Memphis, 1983-94, Woodland Hills Ch. of Christ, Cordova, Tenn., 1994-96, Northport (Ala.) Ch. of Christ, 1996—. Contbr. articles to religious jours. Mem. Evang. Theol. Soc. Republican. Home: 2217 Yorktown Dr Tuscaloosa AL 35406-1632 Office: Northport Ch of Christ PO Box 333 Northport AL 35476-0333 *To live honorably is to live with dignity. To treat others kindly is to live compassionately. To live in faith and love for God is to live supremely.*

JOHNSON, ROGER WARREN, chemical engineer; b. Huntsville, Ala., Oct. 25, 1960; s. Frederic Allen and Joan (Bickum) J.; m. Margaret Jane Major, June 16, 1984. BChemE, Auburn U., 1984. Process engr. fibers divsn. E.I. DuPont de Nemours & Co., Waynesboro, Va., 1984-86; devel. engr. imaging systems E.I. DuPont de Nemours & Co., Brevard, N.C., 1986-87; R & D engr. Hercules Inc.-A&TP, Oxford, Ga., 1987-92; account mgr. Hercules Inc.-Absorbents and Textile Products, Oxford, Ga., 1992-95; product mgr. Hercules Inc.-A&TP, Oxford, Ga., 1995-96; staple II plant mgr. FiberVisions LLC, Oxford, Ga., 1997-98; fiber tech. svc. mgr. Amoco Polymers, Alpharetta, Ga., 1998—. Mem. Auburn Alumni Assn., Phi Kappa Phi. Home: 1410 Mclendon Ave NE Atlanta GA 30307-2129 Office: Amoco Polymers 4500 McGinnis Ferry Rd Alpharetta GA 30005-2203

JOHNSON, ROGERS BRUCE, retired chemical company executive; b. Boston, Apr. 8, 1928; s. Rogers Bruce and Dorothy Squires (Aiken) J.; m. Margery Ruth Howe, June 25, 1951 (div. July 1997); children: Wynn, Carol, Stephen, Herrick; m. Alexandra Caroline Luckes Lee, Nov. 28, 1998. B.A., Harvard U., 1949, M.B.A., 1955. Field salesman Dow U.S.A., Pitts., 1956-61; mgr. molding materials Dow Europe, Zurich, Switzerland, 1961-65; bus. mgr. styrene polymers Dow U.S.A., Midland, Mich., 1965-70; corp. products dir. Dow Chem. Co., Midland, Mich., 1970-76; v.p. supply, distbn. and planning Dow Chem. U.S.A., Midland, Mich., 1976-81, group v.p. adminstrv. services, 1981-89; dir. Dow Can., Sarnia, Ont., Can., 1973-77, Dow Pacific, Hong Kong, 1973-77; bd. dirs. Strategic Planning Inst., 1987-88. Bd. dirs. Midland Community Tennis Ctr., (Mich.), 1974-89, Mich. Citizens' Research Council, 1985-89; pres. Midland Community Tennis Ctr. (Mich.), 1975-78, treas., 1972-76, 79-80; pres. Midland County Growth Council, 1985-89. Served to 1st lt. USAF, 1951-53. Decorated Bronze Star. Republican.

JOHNSON, ROLANDA LANETTA, medical/surgical nurse, educator; b. Nashville, Sept. 17, 1963; d. James Vince and Mary Louise (Brown) P. BSN, Tuskegee U., 1985; MS in Nursing, Troy State U., 1990; PhD in Nursing Sci., Vanderbilt U., 1998. RN, Ala.; cert. clin. specialist, med.-surg. nurse. Relief supr. Fairview Med. Ctr., Montgomery, 1985, charge nurse; staff nurse Jackson Hosp. & Clinic, Montgomery, 1989-89, nurse clinician, 1989-90; ednl. instr. Jackson Hosp. & Clinic, 1990-93; staff nurse Jackson Hosp. and Clinic, 1993—; asst. prof. Vanderbilt U., 1998—; rsch. cons., analyst Vanderbilt U. Med. Ctr., Nashville, Tenn., 1994-98. Mem. ANA, Ala. Nurses Assn., Sigma Theta Tau, Chi Eta Phi, Delta Sigma Theta. Home: 104 N West St Macon MS 39341-2630

JOHNSON, RONALD CARL, chemistry educator; b. Milw., Sept. 5, 1935; s. Carl Walter and Valeska Ella (Schulz) J.; m. Susan Nancy Anderson, Aug. 27, 1960; children: Erica Susan, Laura Karen. BS, Lawrence Coll., 1957; PhD, Northwestern U., 1961. From asst. prof. to prof. Emory U., Atlanta, 1961-75, prof., 1975—. Author: Coordination Chemistry, 1964, 2d edit. 1987; Descriptive Chemistry, 1965, General Chemistry, 1974. Mem. AAAS, AAUP, Am. Chem. Soc. (chair Ga. sect. 1974-75, counselor 1977-80), Ga. Acad. Sci. (pres. 1977-78), Phi Beta Kappa, Sigma Xi. Presbyterian. Avocations: jogging, racquetball, bridge. Office: Emory U Dept Chemistry Atlanta GA 30322

JOHNSON, RONALD CHARLES, psychology educator; b. Duluth, Minn., July 18, 1927; s. Bror Asas and Mabel Irene J.; m. Carol Marie Anderson, Nov. 1, 1953 (dec. Mar. 1981); children: Roni, Steven, Christopher. BA, U. Minn., Duluth, 1949; MA, Denver U., 1950; PhD, U. Minn., 1959. Instr. U. Minn., Mpls., 1956-57; from asst. prof. to assoc. prof. San Jose (Calif.) State Coll., 1957-62; assoc. prof. U. Hawaii, Honolulu, 1962-65, prof. emeritus, 1970—; from assoc. prof. to prof. U. Colo., Boulder, 1965-70. Author: Child Psychology, 1965, 3d edit., 1974, The Roots of Individuality, 1978; editor: Conscience Contract, 1972. With USNR, 1944-46, PTO. Recipient Disting. Rsch. award Hawaii Psychol. Assn., 1993. Mem. AAAS, Behavior Genetics Assn. (Dobzhansky award 1996), Soc. Study Social Biology. Democrat. Avocations: reading, writing, travel. Home: 23 Kalaka Pl Kailua HI 96734

JOHNSON, RONDA JANICE, professional not-for-profit fundraiser; b. Muleshoe, Tex., Sept. 28, 1943; d. Randolph Revere and Betty Jo (Pool) J. BS in Edn., U. Tex., Austin, 1966; MBA, Houston Bapt. U., 1980. Cert. fund raising exec. Tchr. Galena Park Ind. Sch. Dist./Houston Ind. Sch. Dist., 1966-68; adminstrv. asst. Houston-Galveston Area Coun., 1968-69, Johns Hopkins U. Applied Physics Lab., Columbia, Md., 1969-73; dir. adminstrn. Edmondson Coll. Bus., Chattanooga, 1973-76; dir. Branell Women's Coll., Atlanta, 1976-78; dir. devel. U. Tex. Health Sci. Ctr., Houston, 1978-84, Houston Symphony Orch., 1984-85, Houston Child Guidance Ctr., 1985-87; pres. ctrl. divsn. Douglas M. Lawson Assocs., Inc., Houston, 1987-96; sr. cons. Cargill Assocs., Ft. Worth, 1996-97; vice chancellor instnl. advancement Tex. Tech. U., Health Scis. Ctr., Lubbock, 1997—; instr. Vol. Support Ctr., Houston, 1992, continuing edn. div. Rice U., Houston, 1992-95. Adv. bd. Houston Achievement Pl., 1992; bd. dirs. Escape Ctr., Houston, 1992-94. Named Woman of the Yr. by S.W. Houston News, 1994. Mem. Nat. Soc. Fundraising Execs. (bd. dirs. 1989—, pres. 1994-95; mem. found. bd. 1997—), Planned Giving Coun., Houstonian Network. Republican. Avocations: reading, photography, travel, cooking, gardening. Office: Texas Tech Office of Devel PO Box 41081 Lubbock TX 79409-1081 Address: 407 Utica Dr Lubbock TX 79416-4928

JOHNSON, ROSEMARY WRUCKE, personnel management specialist; b. Leith, N.D., Sept. 21, 1924; d. Rudolph Aaron and Metta Tomina (Andersen) Wrucke; m. Robert Johnson Jr., Sept. 28, 1945 (div. 1964). Student, George Washington U., 1944-45, 47, Nat. Art Sch., Washington, 1943-45. Supr. Displaced Persons Commn., Frankfurt, Germany, 1950-52, FBI, Washington, 1952-81; cons. position mgmt. orgn. design Arlington, Va., 1981—. Mem. NAFE, Classification and Compensation Soc., Soc. FBI Alumni (membership chmn. 1985-91), Internat. Platform Assn. Lutheran. Avocations: painting, sketching. Home and Office: 2525 10th St N Apt 820 Arlington VA 22201-1968

JOHNSON, ROY RAGNAR, electrical engineer; b. Chgo., Jan. 23, 1932; s. Ragnar Anders and Ann Viktoria (Lundquist) J.; m. Martha Ann Mattson, June 21, 1963; children: Linnea Marit, Kaisa Ann. BSEE, U. Minn., 1954, MS, 1956, PhD, 1959. Rsch. fellow U. Minn., 1957-59; from rsch. engr. to sr. basic rsch. scientist Boeing Sci. Research Labs., Seattle, 1959-72; prin. scientist KMS Fusion, Inc., Ann Arbor, Mich., 1972-74; dir. fusion expts. KMS Fusion, Inc., 1974-78, tech. dir., 1978-91, dept. head for fusion and plasmas, 1985-88; tech. dir. Innovation Assocs., Inc., Ann Arbor, 1992; inertial confinement fusion classification/records mgr. Lawrence Livermore Nat. Lab., 1992—; vis. lectr. U. Wash., Seattle, 1959-60; vis. scientist Royal Inst. Tech., Stockholm, 1963-64; cons. Dept. Edn., Washington, 1995, 98. Author: Nonlinear Effects in Plasmas, 1969, Plasma Physics, 1977, Research Trends in Physics, 1992; contbr. articles to profl. publs.; patentee in field. Bd. advisors Rose-Hulman Inst. Tech., 1982—. Decorated chevalier Order of St. George; comdr. Order of Holy Cross of Jerusalem. Fellow Am. Phys. Soc.; mem. AAAS, AIAA, IEEE (life), Nuclear Plasma Scis. Soc. of IEEE (exec. com. 1972-75), N.Y. Acad. Scis., Am. Def. Preparedness Assn., Assn. of Old Crows, Vasa Order Am., Am. Swedish Inst. (chmn. Svea lodge), Torpar Riddar Orden, Swedish Pioneer Hist. Soc., Swedish Coun. Am., Detroit Swedish Coun., Swedish Club of Detroit, Swedish Am. Hist. Soc., Eta Kappa Nu, Gamma Alpha. Lutheran. Home: 1141 Concannon Blvd Livermore CA 94550-6451 Office: Livermore Nat Lab PO Box 808 Livermore CA 94551-0808

JOHNSON, RUBY LAVERNE, retail executive; b. Ada, Okla., Oct. 31, 1917; d. James Lee and Minta Estelle (Speights) Eppler; m. Albert Howard Johnson, Dec. 22, 1938; children: Phyllis, Richard, Jim, Bruce. With So. Bell Telephone, Ada, 1936-38; founder, owner, buyer Johnson's Furniture,

Bossier City, La., 1963—. Mem. La. Home Furniture Assn., Bossier City C. of C., Univ. Club Shreveport. Avocations: gardening, shopping, travel, camping. Home: 3376 Jon Rd Shreveport LA 71119-2236 Office: Johnsons Furniture 921 Westgate Ln Bossier City LA 71112-3595

JOHNSON, RUFUS WINFIELD, lawyer; b. Montgomery County, Md., May 1, 1911; s. Charles L. and Margaret (Smith) J.; m. Rosena L. Allen, June 21, 1939 (div. May 1971); m. Vaunda Louise Griffith, May 29, 1971; step-children: Yvonne, Jackie, Karen, Rodney, Michelle. AB, Howard U., 1934, postgrad., 1934-36, LLB, 1939. Bar: Calif., Ark., Supreme Ct. Ark., Supreme Ct. Calif., D.C. Dist. Ct., U.S. Ct. Appeals, D.C., U.S. Supreme Ct., Supreme Ct. Korea; cert. counsel Judge Advocate Gen. Sch., Washington. Pvt. practice D.C., Calif., Ark., 1945—; originator Lawyer's Pro Bono Svc. Ret. lt. col. USAR. Recipient Combat Infantry badge, U.S. Army, 1944, Purple Heart, 1944, Bronze Star, 1944, Spl. Citation Bravery, 1944. Mem. VFW (life), Am. Judicature Soc., Am. Acad. Polit. and Social Sci., Mil. Order Purple Heart, Internat. Soc. Poets, Am. Kempo Karate Assn., Sr. Citizens Coalition, Ret. Officers Assn., Am. Legion, Masons, Am. Karate Assn. (5th degree Shorin-Ryu Black Belt), Lions. Baptist. Home: PO Box 776 Mason TX 76856-0776

JOHNSON, RUPERT HARRIS, JR., finance company executive. BA, Washington and Lee U., 1962. With Franklin Resources, Inc., San Mateo, Calif., 1965—, exec. v.p., chief investment officer, dir.; sr. v.p., asst. sec. Franklin Templeton Distbrs., Inc.; pres. Franklin Advisers, Inc.; mem. exec. com., bd. govs. Investment Co. Inst.; trustee Santa Clara U., Washington and Lee U.; chmn. bd. dirs. Franklin Mgmt., Inc.; exec. v.p., sr. investment officer Franklin Trust Co.; dir. various Franklin Templeton funds; portfolio mgr. Franklin DynaTech Fund. With USMC, 1962-65. Mem. Nat. Assn. Securities Dealers (dist. conduct com.). Office: Franklin Resources Inc Templeton Group 777 Mariners Island Blvd San Mateo CA 94404-1585

JOHNSON, RUTH CRUMLEY, economics educator; b. Bristol, Tenn., Feb. 13, 1936; d. Glenn Fine and Marian Grace (Thomas) Crumley; m. Robert William Johnson, June 10, 1971 (dec. May 1995); m. Edwin Douglas Smiley, Aug. 2, 1998. BS, U. Tenn., 1970, MS, 1971, PhD, 1981. Grad. rsch. asst. U. Tenn., Knoxville, 1978-79; rsch. assoc. Oak Ridge (Tenn.) Nat. Lab., 1979-80, Oak Ridge Associated Univs., 1980-82; pres., co-founder Econ. Sys. Analysis, Inc., Oak Ridge, 1983-85; economist Sci. & Tech., Inc., Oak Ridge, 1986-88; mem. adj. faculty Pellissippi State Tech. C.C., Knoxville, 1988—; mem. People to People Internat. del. of economists to USSR, 1989. Contbr. articles to profl. jours. Chairperson Anderson County Youth Workers Coun., Oak Ridge, 1977; bd. dirs. Anderson County Health Coun., Oak Ridge, 1975-77, Anderson County Cmty. Action Commn., Clinton, Tenn., 1972-74; chairperson bd. dirs. United Ch., Oak Ridge, 1997. Mem. AAUW, Am. Econ. Assn., Phi Kappa Phi, Gamma Sigma Delta, Omicron Nu. Avocations: gardening, hiking, travel, genealogy. Home: 105 Adelphi Rd Oak Ridge TN 37830-7807

JOHNSON, RUTH JEANNETTE, nursing administrator; b. Brainerd, Minn., Jan. 18, 1927; d. Jacob and Oleanna Margit (Berg) Thoe; m. Paul Leonard Johnson, Aug. 3, 1950; childre: Patricia Johnson Schultenover, Christopher, Jayne. Student, Brainerd Jr. Coll., 1944-45; diploma, Kahler Hosp. Sch. Nursing, Rochester, Minn., 1948. RN, Minn. Pub. health nurse Merced (Calif.) County Health Dept., 1951-53; head nurse Rochester (Minn.) Meth. Hosp., 1969-70, 72-80, head clinic nurse, 1970-71; operating rm. supr. Boulder (Colo.) Community Hosp., 1971-72; retired. Mem. Assn. Operating Rm. Nurses. Home and Office: 2217 20th St NW Rochester MN 55901-0769

JOHNSON, SALLY A., nurse, educator; b. Rockford, Ill., Apr. 24, 1923; d. Herbert A. and Aileen (Peyton) Johnson; m. Bion D. Vickerman, 1994; children: Ann Elizabeth Scannell, Stacey Aileen Lerager. *Husband Bion David Vickerman is an engineer for Clark Equipment for 20 years. He received a degree from Pittsburgh Technical Institute. Daughter, Ann Scannell, ND, RNC, CS, graduated Villanova University with a BSN in 1975, an MSN from Catholic University in Washington, D.C. in 1977 and a doctorate in nursing from Case Western Reserve University in 1996. She is an assistant professor at Fitchburg State College. She has traveled abroad in Italy, Russia and the Netherlands presenting and lecturing from 1996-98. Daughter, Stacey Lerager, is a nurse practitioner at Brighton Marine Public Health Center in Boston. She received her BS and RN at Villanova University in 1979 and her MA at Simons College in Boston in 1985. She is also a part-time instructor at Simons.* RN Good Samaritan Hosp., 1945; nurse obstetrics delivery Women's Hosp., N.Y.C., 1947-49, St. Francis Hosp., Evanston, Ill., 1953; charge, head nurse Broward Gen. Hosp., Ft. Lauderdale, Fla., 1968; night supr. Ashbrook Convalescent and Nursing Hosp., Scotch Plains, N.J., 1968—; owner Thomas A. Edison Brick Co., Sally Johnson Franz Enterprises. Coun. chmn. Betty Merit Tchrs. Scholarship, 1962; area nat. organizer Girl Scouts U.S.A., 1962-65; Westfield (N.J.) Round-Up and Health chmn., 1962-63; pres. Tamaques Sch., 1965, adviser Parent Tchr. Orgn., 1966, fgn. relationship chmn., 1967-68; exec. bd. chmn. Westfield High Sch. PTA Newsletter, 1968-70; chmn. Nat. Space Edn., Westfield, 1964; Westfield chmn. fgn. nurses Overlook Hosp., Summit, N.J., 1964-69. Recipient scholarship to Harvard U. Coll. Bus. Mem. Nat. Assn. Investors Corp., Nat. Dist. Nurses Assn., NOW (N.J. coord. 1967-68), Am. Contract Bridge League, Bridge Tchrs. Assn., Naples Investment Club (sec. 1995-96). Republican. Inventor holder for marking devices. Home: 50 Quiche Ct Fort Myers FL 33912-2162

JOHNSON, SAM D., federal judge; b. Hubbard, Tex., Nov. 17, 1920; s. Sam D. and Flora (Brown) J.; m. June Page, June 1, 1946; children: Page Johnson Harris, Janet Johnson Clements, Sam. J. B.B.A., Baylor U., 1946; LL.B., U. Tex., 1949. Bar: Tex. 1949. Pvt. practice law Hillsboro, Tex., 1949-53; county atty. Hill County, Tex., 1953-55; dist. atty. and dist. judge 66th Jud. Dist. of Hill County, Tex., 1955-65; judge 14th Ct. Civil Appeals, Houston, 1967-72; assoc. justice Supreme Ct. Tex., Austin, 1973-79; sr. judge U.S. Ct. Appeals (5th cir.), 1979—; Bd. dirs. Houston Legal Found. 1965-67. Served with AUS, 1942-45. Recipient Disting. Alumnus award Baylor U., 1978-79. Mem. ABA (chmn. appellate judges conf. 1976-77, bd. govs. 1979-82), Am. Bar Found., Am. Judicature Soc., Tex. Bar Assn., Houston Bar Assn., Baylor Ex-Students Assn. (pres. 1972-73). Democrat. Office: US Ct Appeals Homer Thornberry Judicial Bldg 903 San Jacinto Blvd Rm 400 Austin TX 78701-2450*

JOHNSON, SAMMYE LARUE, communications educator; b. Dallas, Oct. 8, 1946. BS in Journalism with distinction, Northwestern U., 1968, MS in Journalism with highest distinction, 1969. Asst. editor Where Mag., Chgo., 1969; feature writer Chicago Today newspaper, Chgo., 1969-71, editor Sunday mag., 1971-73; comms. dir. VIA Met. Transit Sys., San Antonio, Fed. Rep. Germany, 1979; asst. prof. journalism William Allen White Sch. Journalism U. Kans., Lawrence, 1979-80; assoc. prof. comm. Trinity U., San Antonio, 1980-91; prof. comm. U. Kans., Lawrence, 1991—; Carlos Augustus de Lozano chair journalism Trinity U., San Antonio, 1998—, prof. comm., 1991—, Carlos Augustus de Lozano chair journalism, 1998—; cons. pub. rels. Community Guidance Ctr., San Antonio, 1985-88, Funding Info. Ctr., San Antonio, 1983—, Bexar County Women's Ctr., San Antonio, 1984—. Contbr. articles to profl. jours., consumer and trade mags., newspapers. Named Today's Woman of Achievement San Antonio Light Newspaper, 1981, Pub. Rels. Educator of Yr. Tex. Pub. Rels. Assn., 1984-85. Mem. Women in Comms. (dir. 1978-80, pres. chopt. 1983-84, Proliner award 1981, 82, 83, 86, 87, 88, 90, 93, 96, 97, Comms. Headliner of Yr. 1984), Internat. Assn. Bus. Communicators (bd. dirs. 1979, Gold Quill award 1979, named Communicator of Yr. 1981, numerous other awards 1976-96), Assn. for Edn. in Journalism and Mass Comms. (sec., vice chair, chair mag. divs. 1985-89, Mag. Educator of Yr. 1997), Kappa Tau Alpha. Home: 7523 Bridgewater Dr San Antonio TX 78209-3113 Office: Trinity U Dept Communication 715 Stadium Dr San Antonio TX 78212-7200

JOHNSON, SAMUEL (SAM JOHNSON), congressman; b. San Antonio, Tex., Oct. 11, 1930; m. Shirley L. Melton; children: James R., Gini Mulligan, Beverly Briney. BBA, So. Meth. U., 1951; M in Internat. Affairs, George Washington U.; grad., Armed Forces Staff Coll., Nat. War Coll. Joined USAF, 1950; fighter pilot USAF, Korea, Vietnam; prisoner of war USAF, 1966-73, former dir. Air Force Fighter Weapons Sch., former mem. Thunderbirds, wing commdr., air div. commdr., ret., 1979; founder home bldg. co., 1979; mem. Tex. Ho. of Reps., 1984-91, 102d-106th Congresses from 3d Tex. dist., Washington, D.C., 1991—; mem. ways and means subcom. Health, Social Security Coms., mem. edn. and the workforce com.; mem. Edn. and the Workforce com., early childhood, youth and families subcom. Chmn. Conservative Action Team. Decorated 2 Silver Stars, Disting. Flying Cross, 4 Air medals, 2 Purple Hearts. Office: 1030 Longworth HOB Washington DC 20515 also: 801 E Campbell Rd Ste 425 Richardson TX 75081-1890*

JOHNSON, SAMUEL CURTIS, wax company executive; b. Racine, Wis., Mar. 2, 1928; s. Herbert Fisk and Gertrude (Brauner) J.; m. Imogene Powers, May 8, 1954; children: Samuel Curtis III, Helen Johnson-Leipold, Herbert Fisk III, Winifred Johnson Marquart. BA, Cornell U., 1950; MBA, Harvard U., 1952; LLD (hon.), Carthage Coll., 1974, Northland Coll., 1974, Ripon Coll., 1980, Carroll Coll., 1981, U. Surrey, 1985, Marquette U., 1986, Nijenrode U., 1992. With S.C. Johnson & Son, Inc., Racine, 1954—, internat. v.p., 1962-63, exec. v.p., 1963-66, pres., 1966-67, chmn., pres., chief exec. officer, 1967-72, chmn., chief exec. officer, 1972-88, chmn., 1988—; bd. dirs. Deere & Co., Moline, Ill., H.J. Heinz Co., Phila., Mobil Corp., N.Y.C.; chmn. bd. dirs. Johnson Worldwide Assocs., Inc., Johnson Internat. Inc. Trustee Am. Mus. Natural History, N.Y.C.; trustee emeritus The Mayo Found., Cornell U., presdl. councillor; chm Johnson's Wax Fund, Inc., Johnson Found., Inc.; founding chmn. emeritus Prairie Sch., Racine; chmn. adv. coun. Cornell U. Grad. Sch. Mgmt.; regent emeritus Smithsonian Instn.; hon. mem. Bus. Coun.; mem. nat. bd. govs. The Nature Conservancy. Mem. Chi Psi. Clubs: Cornell (N.Y.C., Milw.); Univ. (Milw.); Racine Country. Home: 4815 Lighthouse Dr Racine WI 53402-2666 Office: S C Johnson Wax 1525 Howe St Racine WI 53403-2236*

JOHNSON, SAMUEL FREDERICK, English and literature educator emeritus; b. Pitts., July 22, 1918; s. Samuel Frederick and Estella Helen (Kitsch) J. BA, Haverford Coll., 1940; MA, Harvard U., 1941, PhD, 1948; postgrad., Ind. U., 1943, The Sorbonne, 1945-46. Instr. Harvard U., Cambridge, Mass., 1948-49; asst. prof. NYU, N.Y.C., 1949-54; from asst. prof. to prof. English and comparative renaissance lits. Columbia U., N.Y.C., 1954-84, prof. emeritus, 1984—; vis. prof. Washington U., St. Louis, 1963; mem. supervising com. English Inst., N.Y.C., 1957-59. Editor: Julius Caesar, 1960, rev. edit., 1969; author: Early Elizabethan Tragedies of the Inns of Court, 1987; festschrift: Shakespeare and Dramatic Tradition, 1989. With U.S. Army, 1942-46. Guggenheim fellow, 1954; Huntington Libr. grantee, 1972. Mem. MLA (asst. sec., editor 1951-52), Renaissance Soc. Am. (assoc. editor 1967-84), Shakespeare Assn. Am. (assoc. editor 1956-57, mem. edit. bd. Shakespearean Internat. Yearbook 1996—), Phi Beta Kappa. Democrat. Avocations: chamber music, opera. Home and Office: 285 Riverside Dr Apt 7C New York NY 10025-5227

JOHNSON, SANDRA ANN, elementary educator educator; b. Houston, Apr. 27, 1958; d. Johnnie and Area (Bradford) J. AA, Houston C.C., 1991; BBA, Tex. So. U., 1994; MEd, Prairie View A&M U., 1998; postgrad., Tex. So. U., 1998—. Tchr. computers Houston Sch. Dist., 1981—; instr. North Harris Coll., Houston, 1996—. Vol. Herman Hosp., Houston, 1987-88; counselor Vision of Hope Women, Houston, 1996-97; contact person Houston Mayor's Camp, 1997. Named Disting. Role Model of Houston, North Main Ch. of God in Christ, 1998. Mem. Chi Sigma Iota. Democrat. Baptist. Avocations: tennis, golf, jogging, reading, racquetball. Office: Mary Bethune Acad 1500 S Victory Dr Houston TX 77088-7102

JOHNSON, SANDRA LYNN, education consultant; b. Mesa, Ariz., Apr. 14, 1942; d. Kenneth Cade and Merlyn Grace (Mattes) Terry; m. Olin Neal Johnson, June 2, 1961; children: Diane Lynn Johnson McLean, Keith Terry. BS, Tex. Tech U., 1967; MA, U. Tex., 1983, PhD, 1994. Cert. secondary, elem., kindergarten, and gifted edn. tchr., Tex. Tchr. various pvt. schs., Austin, Tex., 1969-84, Austin Ind. Sch. Dist., 1974-76; dir. University Avenue Early Learning Ctr., Austin, 1976-84; cons. Johnson Cons., Austin, 1984-91, ednl. cons., 1998—; cons. region XIII, Edn. Svc. Ctr., Austin, 1991-98; adj. faculty U. Tex., Austin, 1998—; trainer AP Environ. Sci. for Coll. Bds., 1996—. Editor: Hands Across Texas, 1991, Fulfilling a Dream, 1997, And There Was Light, 1998. Sunday sch. tchr. University Avenue Ch. of Christ, Austin, 1975-83; master tchr. Nat. Tchr. Tng. Inst. for PBS. Scholar Nat. Honor Soc., 1960, Hardin Simmons U., 1960, Abilene C. of C., 1960; Advanced Micro Devices grantee, 1997, Eisenhower grantee, 1997. Mem. Nat. Sci. Tchrs. Assn., Nat. Sci. Assn. for Rsch. in Sci. Tchg., Nat. Assn. for Gifted Children, Austin Assn. for Edn. Young Children (v.p. 1971-73, pres. 1973-74, chmn. Week of Young Child 1974-75, newsletter editor 1975-76, historian 1983-86, rep. to Tex. Classroom Tchrs. Assn. 1975-76, conf. chmn. 1971-72), Tex. State Tchrs. Assn., Phi Kappa Phi, Kappa Delta Pi. Democrat. Avocations: swimming, reading, painting, hiking, camping, yoga. Office: Johnson Cons 604 E Covington Dr Austin TX 78753

JOHNSON, SANKEY ANTON, manufacturing company executive; b. Bremerton, Wash., May 14, 1940; s. Sankey Broyd and Alice Mildred (Norum) J.; m. Carolyn Lee Rogers, Nov. 30, 1968; children: Marni Lee, Ronald Anton. B.S. in M.E, U. Wash.; M.B.A., Stanford U. V.p., gen. mgr. Cummins Asia Pacific, Manila, Philippines, 1974-78; v.p. automotive Cummins Engine Co., Columbus, Ind., 1978-79; v.p. North Am. Bus., 1979-81; pres., chief exec. officer Onan Corp., Mpls., 1981-85; exec. v.p. Pentair Inc., St. Paul, from 1985, chief operating officer, 1985—, pres., 1986-89; pres., chief exec. officer Hidden Creek Industries, Mpls., 1989—; trustee Mfr.'s Alliance. Bd. advisors Stanford Grad. Sch. Bus. Mem. Minneapolis Club, Lafayette Club. Home: 2310 Huntington Point Rd W Wayzata MN 55391-9743 Office: Hidden Creek Industries 4508 Ids Ctr Minneapolis MN 55402

JOHNSON, SCOTT LOREN, sales executive; b. Detroit, July 13, 1963; s. Ronald Fred Johnson and Barbara Ruth (Everett) Dahm. A in Bus. Adminstrn., Oakland C.C., Auburn Hills, Mich., 1989; BBA cum laude, Walsh Coll., 1997. Sales engr. Wilson Agy., Inc., Troy, Mich., 1983-87; pres. Metalex, Inc., Troy, 1987-88; regional sales mgr. Mascotech, Inc., Fraser, Mich., 1988-92; sales dir. Mascotech, Inc., Fraser, 1992-95, sales mgr., 1995-99; dir. sales new venture fear Maseotech, Inc., Royal Oak, Mich., 1999—. Avocations: alpine skiing, golf, boating.

JOHNSON, SHARON DENISE, executive; b. Kans. City, Mo., Nov. 18, 1947; d. Leland Earl and Leona (Gover) Dailey; m. Herbert Johnson, Oct. 27, 1973. AA in Studio Art, Met. C.C., Kans. City, Mo., 1967; BA in Studio Art, U. Mo., Kans. City, 1969, MPA, 1976. Draftsman, stat. analysis JBM & Assoc., Kans. City, 1969-73; office mgr., adminstr. Felix Camera & Video, Overland Park, Kans., 1976-93; v.p., treas. Hedlund & Assoc., Overland Park, Kans., 1993—. Chair fin. com. Luth. Ch. of Resurrection, Prairie Village, Kans., 1992-95, chair computer com., 1993—, mem. coun., 1991-95, bd. mem. Leawood Police Community Leadership League. Mem. Inst. Mgmt. Accts., William Jewell Fine Arts Guild, Phi Kappa Phi. Republican. Avocations: reading, needlework, computers, photography. Home: 8404 Meadow Ln Leawood KS 66206-1422 Office: Hedlund & Assoc 7219 Metcalf Ave Overland Park KS 66204-1974

JOHNSON, SHARON MARGUERITE, social worker, clinical hypnotherapist; b. San Diego, July 23, 1962; d. James Hugh and Efstathia (Bliziotis) J.; m. Sandy L. Scott, July 6, 1995; children: Devon, Rocky, Madonna, Sadie, Audre, Maya, Yoko. AAS, So. Maine Tech. Coll., South Portland, 1983; BA in Social Work, U. Maine, Orono, 1992, MSW, 1993. Lic. clin. social worker, mental health rehab. technician IV, transformational breath facilitator. Head cook Meals for Maine, Inc., Bangor, 1985-88; instr. ARC, Bangor, 1987-92; counselor assoc. substance abuse Wellspring, Inc., Bangor, 1987-93; counselor aide Onward Program U. Maine, Orono, 1989-92; intensive case mgr. Cmty. Health and Counseling Svc., Bangor, 1993-95, mental health therapist, 1993-97; consultation liaison clinician Acadia Hosp., Bangor, 1997—; pvt. practice psychotherapy, 1997—; adj. social work faculty U. Maine, Orono, 1995; adj. mem. human svc. faculty U. Coll., Bangor, 1997—; field interviewer Rsch. Triangle Inst., 1997. Mem. edn. com. Peace and Justice Ctr. Eastern Maine, Bangor, 1993-96, mem. steering com., 1995-96; mem. admissions com. U. Maine Sch. Social Work, Orono, 1994-95; asst. to vol. coord. Maine Won't Discriminate, Bangor, 1995. Mem. NASW (Maine chpt. chair clin. com. 1995-96, BASW student rep. 1991-92, pres.-elect 1994-95, BASW Ray Dow Meml. award 1992, named MSW Outstanding Student 1993), Am. Assn. Profl. Hypnotherapists (cert.), No. New Eng. Soc. Clin. Hypnotherapists. Democrat. Avocations: metaphysics, pet therapy, guitar. Home: PO Box 147 Winterport ME 04496-0147 Office: The Acadia Hosp Stillwater Ave Bangor ME 04401

JOHNSON, SHELLI WRIGHT, lawyer; b. LaPorte, Ind., Apr. 1, 1953; d. Burdette Baxter and Doris Dunfee (Childs) Wright; m. James Alan Johnson, May 22, 1980; children: Andrew James, Scott Robert, Jenna Marie. BS, Ball State U., 1975; JD, Valparaiso U., 1979. Bar: Ind. 1979, U.S. Dist. Ct. (no. and so. dists.) Ind. 1979. Tchr. lang. arts Coffee County Schs., Douglas, Ga., 1975-76; assoc. Law Offices of Larry W. Rogers, Portage, Ind., 1979-83, Harper & Rogers, Valparaiso, Ind., 1983-85, Law Offices of James A. Johnson, Portage, 1985-89, Law Offices Shelli Wright Johnson, Valparaiso, 1989—; tchr. family law, bankruptcy Sawyer Bus. Coll., Merrillville, Ind., 1990. Fundraiser Valparaiso U. Community-Univ. Fund Raising Campaign; com. mem. 4-H Celebration Sale; founder, adminstr. Doris Wright Meml. Scholarship Fund. Mem. ABA, Ind. Bar Assn. (family and juvenile law sect., bankruptcy and creditors rights sect.), Porter County Bar Assn., Porter County Am. Inns of Ct., Northwest Ind. Archeol. Assn., The Civil War Trust, Porter County Celebration Sale Auction Com., Ball State U. Found. (philanthropy adv. com.), Concordium Found. (bd. avd.), Delta Theta Phi. Home: 555 N County Rd 300 E Valparaiso IN 46383 Office: 304 E Us Highway 6 Valparaiso IN 46383-9754

JOHNSON, SHIRLEY AMAGNA, systems analyst; b. Santa Rosa, The Philippines, Apr. 16, 1959; came to U.S., 1980; d. Federico Fontalera Amagna Jr. and Lourdes Dayan Barriga; m. Mark James Johnson, Mar. 25, 1982; children: Farrell, Mark Jr., Craig. BS in Commerce, Ctrl. Philippines U., Iloilo City, 1980; MBA, Drury Coll., 1990; postgrad., U. So. Calif., 1994—. Acct. U. Mo., Rolla, 1987-90; acctg. sys. analyst County of San Luis Obispo, Calif., 1990-99; project mgr. Wellpoint Health Networks, Inc., Thousand Oaks, Calif., 1999—. Bd. dirs. Ctrl. Coast Women's Polit. Com., San Luis Obispo, 1995-96; founding mem. Clean Campaign Com., San Luis Obispo, 1996—; mem. adv. bd. Citizens Transp. Adv. Com., San Luis Obispo, 1998-99; mem. San Luis Obispo Leadership Program, 1999—. Mem. ASPA, Inst. Mgmt. Accts. E-mail: shirley.johnson@wellpoint.com. Office: 1 Wellpoint Way Thousand Oaks CA 91362

JOHNSON, SHIRLEY ELAINE, management consultant; b. Terre Haute, Ind., Sept. 15, 1946; d. Mervil Ray and Sarah Kathryn (Tucker) W.; children: Richard Alan, Gary Michael. BA, DePaul U., 1991. Sec. to v.p. fin. Cenco Inc., Oak Brook, Ill., 1972-74, exec. asst. to group pres., 1974-75, asst. to chmn., 1975-77, corp. personnel/office mgr., 1977-80; corp. sec. Acadia Petroleum Corp., Denver, 1980-82; mgr. office Chapman, Klein & Weinberg, PC, Denver, 1982-84; asst. to chmn. The Heidrick Ptnrs., Inc., Chgo., 1984-92, v.p., 1992-98; assoc. Heidrick & Struggles Inc., Chgo., 1998—. Mem. NAFE, Am. Mgmt. Assn., Exec. Women Internat., The River Club, Rsch. Roundtable. Home: 820 Mckenzie Station Dr Lisle IL 60532-5807 Office: Heidrick & Struggles Inc 233 S Wacker Dr Ste 7000 Chicago IL 60606

JOHNSON, SIDNEY MALCOLM, foreign language educator; b. New Haven, Aug. 17, 1924; s. Everett Caswell and Eleanor (Eckman) J.; m. Lora Louise Dunbar, Sept. 29, 1945; children: Thomas Malcolm, Frederick William, Karl Everett. B.A., Yale U., 1944, M.A., 1948, Ph.D., 1953. Asst. instr. Yale U., 1946-51; instr. U. Kans., 1951-53, asst. prof., 1953-58, asso. prof., 1958-62, prof., 1962-65; prof. German, chmn. dept. Emory U., Atlanta, 1965-72; prof. German, Ind. U., Bloomington, 1972-93; chmn. dept. Ind. U., 1972-78, 91-92, prof. emeritus, 1993—; dir. Ind.-Purdue U. Study Program, U. Hamburg, W.Ger., 1978-79. Translator: (with M.E. Gibbs) Willehalm (Wolfram von Eschenbach), 1984, Titurel and the Songs (Wolfram von Eschenbach), 1988, Kudrun, 1992; author: (with M.E. Gibbs) Medieval German Literature. A Companion, 1997; contbr. articles on medieval German lit. to profl. jours. Served to lt. (j.g.) USNR, 1943-46. Research grantee Am. Philos. Soc., 1963. Mem. MLA, Am. Assn. Tchrs. German, AAUP, Wolfram von Eschenbach Gesellschaft, Internat. Assn. Germanic Studies, Medieval Acad. Home: 2320 E Covenanter Dr Bloomington IN 47401-5402

JOHNSON, SILAS R., JR., air force officer; b. Ft. Worth, Jan. 29, 1945; s. Silas Robert and Lucille (Burns) J.; m. Paulette Kamykowski, Apr. 12, 1968; children: Jennifer, Tyler. BBA, U. Miami, Coral Gables, Fla., 1967; MPA, Pepperdine U., 1979; postgrad., Air U., Montgomery, Ala., 1975, 83, 89. Commd. 2d lt. USAF, 1968, advanced through grades to major gen., 1998; co-pilot, aircraft comdr. 416 Bombardment Wing, Griffiss AFB, N.Y., 1969-74; spotlight officer, chief of tanker assigments Strategic Air Command, Offutt AFB, 1974-77; RF-4C pilot 363d Tactical Reconnaissance Wing, Shaw AFB, S.C., 1977-80; co-pilot, aircraft comdr., flight comdr. 60th Bombardment Squadron, Anderson AFB, Guam, 1981-83; air staff action officer to asst. dir. air force issues team USAF Hdqrs./The Pentagon, Washington, 1983-86; comdr. 46th Bombardment Squadron/319th Bombardment Wing, Grand Forks AFB, N.D., 1986-88; dir. Joint Flag Officer Warfighting Course, Maxwell AFB, Ala., 1989-90; asst. dep. comdr. maint., later vice comdr. 319th Bombardment Wing, Grand Forks AFB, 1990-91; vice comdr. 4th Wing, Seymour Johnson AFB, N.C., 1991-92; comdr. 93d Bomb Wing, Castle AFB, Calif., 1992-94, 552d Air Control Wing, Tinker AFB, Okla., 1994-96; dep. dir. ops. joint chiefs of staff The Pentagon, Washington, 1996-98; vice comdr. 21st Air Force, McGuire AFB, N.J., 1998—. Decorated Legion of Merit with 2 oak leaf clusters, Air medal with 2 oak leaf clusters, Air Force Commendation medal, Vietnam Svc. medal; recipient Moeller Trophy for outstanding wing comdr. in air combat command, 1996. Mem. Daedalians (chpt. pres.), Sigma Chi. Avocations: golf, reading.

JOHNSON, SONDRA LEA, accountant; b. Kansas City, Mo., May 11, 1952; d. Albert John Oscar and Dorothy Mae (Hudgens) J. AA, Longview Coll., 1972; BSBA cum laude in Acctg., Cen. Mo. State U., 1974, MBA, 1980. CPA, Mo. Acct. Farmland Industries, Kansas City, 1974-76; acct., auditor Ernst & Whinney, Kansas City, 1976-79, Laventhol & Horwath, Kansas City, 1980-81; corp. acct., mgr. Butler Mfg. Co., Kansas City, 1981-84; audit supr. Grant Thornton Internat., Kansas City, 1984-89; sr. fin. analyst Hoechst Marion Roussel, Kansas City, 1989-95; with fin. reporting dept. UtiliCorp United, Inc., Kansas City, 1996—; specialized instr. nat. continuing edn. tng. program, Grant Thornton Internat., various locations U.S.A.; acctg. instr. Cen. Mo. State U., Warrensburg, 1979-80, Rockhurst Coll., Kansas City, 1981-82, Avila Coll., Kansas City, 1989-90. Mem. AICPAs, Inst. Mgmt. Accts., Mo. Soc. CPAs, Women's C. of C. of Kansas City, Phi Kappa Phi. Democrat. Lutheran. Avocations: travel, collecting ltd. edition figurines, spectator sports, music. Office: UtiliCorp United Inc 10700 E 350 Hwy Raytown MO 64138

JOHNSON, STANFORD LELAND, marketing educator; b. Mapleton, Utah, July 31, 1924; s. Leland Stanford and Mary Alice (Thompson) J.; m. Lucy E. Watts, Sept. 14, 1945 (div. 1976); children: Janet, Debbie, Stanford Leland, Robert, Gregory, Kent; m. Heidi G. Ivanoff, Jan. 1977 (div. 1996); m. Linda M. Sartain, Oct., 1998. B.S. in Bus. and Social Sci., Utah State U., 1949; M.S. in Mktg. and Retailing, NYU, 1950; Ph.D. in Bus, N.Y. U., 1965. Cert. comml. pilot. Field research Dept. Commerce, 1949-51; asst. mgr. Wickel's Men's Wear Store, Logan, Utah, 1951-52; asst. prof. Sch. Bus., Utah State U., 1951-54; asst. dean, instr. N.Y. U., 1954-64; mem. faculty San Francisco State U., 1964-89, prof. mktg., transp. and world bus., 1968-89, chmn. dept., 1972-76; cons. to industry, 1960—; lectr. U. Calif. Med. Sch., Pharm. Adminstrn., 1969-85. Editorial cons., McGraw-Hill Book Co., Houghton Mifflin Co., Wadsworth Pub. Co., Sci. Research Assos. Bd. dirs., acad. adviser Schiller Internat. U., Heidelberg, Germany, 1969—. Served as pilot USAAF, 1943-45. Ins. fellow Am. Assn. U. Tchrs., 1953; Forum and Finance fellow, 1954; Found. for Econ. Edn. fellow, 1955; recipient Founder's Day award NYU, 1965. Mem. Sales and Mktg. Execs. Assn. Republican. Mem. Ch. of Jesus Christ of Latter Day Saints. Home: 4609 Park Woods Dr Pollock Pines CA 95726-9508

JOHNSON, STEPHEN PHILIP, educational administrator; b. DuBois, Pa., Oct. 26, 1945; s. Andrew Rudolph and Mildred Virginia J.; m. Lorraine Sandra Ponzi, Nov. 29, 1968; children: Christopher Andrew, Marc Ronald. BA with honors, Pa. State U., 1967; MPA, Syracuse U., 1969. Adminstrv. intern, tchr. Syracuse (N.Y.) City Sch. Dist., 1968-72; coop. ext. specialist Cornell U., Alton, N.Y., 1972-76; program coord. Cornell U., Ithaca, N.Y., 1976-78; assoc. pub. policy Cornell U., Ithaca, 1978-84, dir. govt. affairs, 1984-87, 1987—. Contbr. articles to profl. jours. Mem. friends scouting Boy Scouts Am., Ithaca, 1990—; founding mem. Alcoholism Coun., Newark, 1972-76; bd. dirs. Cmty. Action Self Help, Sodus, N.Y., 1973, Program Funding Inc., Rochester, N.Y., 1973-77, Daycare and Child Devel. Coun., 1981-83, Bd. Zoning Appeals, Lansing, N.Y., 1982-88, Rural Schs. Program, Ithaca. Mem. Tompkins County C. of C. (mem. com. 1983-91), Univ. Club, Cornell Club N.Y., Epsilon Sigma Phi. Avocations: jogging, football fan, reading. Office: Cornell U 114 Day Hall Ithaca NY 14853

JOHNSON, STERLING, JR., federal judge; b. 1934. BA, Bklyn. Coll., 1963; LLB, Bklyn. Sch. Law, 1966. With N.Y.C. Police Dept., 1957-67; asst. U.S. atty. U.S. Atty. Office (ea. dist.) N.Y., 1967-70; atty. civilian complaint rev. bd. U.S. Atty. Office (so. dist.) N.Y., 1970-74, atty. drug enforcement adminstrn., 1974-75, spl. narcotics prosecutor, 1975-91; fed. judge U.S. Dist. Ct. (ea. dist.) N.Y., Bklyn., 1991—; active Second Cir. Task Force on Gender, Racial, and Ethnic Fairness in Cts.; mem. Nat. Conf. Fed. Trial Judges Exec. Com. Bd. dirs. Bedford Stuyvesant Restoration Corp., Cardinal Cook Com. on Substance Abuse; active Police Athletic League, Pres. Drug Adv. Coun. With USMC, 1952-55, USNR, 1975—. Mem. ABA, N.Y. State Bar Assn., Nat. Black Prosecutors Assn., Nat. Orgn. Black Law Enforcement Execs., N.Y. State Dist. Attys. Assn. Office: US Dist Ct 225 Cadman Plz E Rm 432 Brooklyn NY 11201-1818*

JOHNSON, STEWART WILLARD, civil engineer; b. Mitchell, S.D., Aug. 17, 1933; s. James Elmer Johnson and Grace Mahala (Erwin) Johnson Parsons; m. Mary Anis Giddings, June 24, 1956; children: Janelle Chiemi, Gregory Stewart, Eric Willard. BSCE, S.D. State U., 1956; BA in Bus. Adminstrn. and Polit. Sci., U. Md., 1960; MSCE, PhD, U. Ill., 1964. Registered profl. engr., Ohio. Commd. 2d lt. USAF, 1956, advanced through grades to lt. col.; prof. mechs. and civil engring. Air Force Inst. Tech. USAF, Dayton, Ohio, 1964-75; dir. civil engring. USAF, Seoul, Republic of Korea, 1976-77; chief civil engring. research div. USAF, Kirtland AFB, N.Mex., 1977-80; ret. USAF, 1980; prin. engr. BDM Corp., Albuquerque, 1980-94, Johnson and Assocs., Albuquerque, 1994—; cons. in site surveys, found. design, constrn. of ground stas. for satellite comm. sys., 1992-96; cons. space sci. and lunar basing NASA, U. N.Mex., N.Mex. State U., Los Alamos Nat. Labs., 1986—; adj. prof. civil engring. U. N.Mex., 1987—; prin. investigator devel. concepts for lunar astron. obs. U. N.Mex., N.Mex. State U., NASA, 1987-94; tech. chmn. Space '88, Space '90, Space '94 and Space '96 Internat. Confs., Albuquerque; vis. lectr. Internat. Space U., Japan, 1992, Huntsville, Ala., 1993, Barcelona, Spain, 1994, Stockholm, 1995; mem. panel on siting lunar base European Space Agy., 1994; gen. chair Space 96 and RCEII Conf., Albuquerque, 1996; gen. chmn. Space Conf., Albuquerque, 1998, Robotics Conf., Albuquerque, 1998. Editor Engineering, Construction, and Operations in Space, I, 1988, II, 90, V, 96; contbr. articles to profl. jours. Pres. ch. coun. Ch. of Good Shepherd United Ch. of Christ, Albuquerque, 1983-85, chmn. bd. deacons, 1991-93, moderator, 1996-97; S.W. Conf. (United Ch. Christ) del. to Gen. Synod XIX, St. Louis, 1993, Gen. Synod XX, Oakland, Calif., 1995, Gen. Synod XXI, Columbus, Ohio, 1997; trustee Lunar Geotech. Inst., 1990—; mem. adv. bd. Lab. for Extraterrestrial Structures Rsch., Rutgers U., 1990—. Fellow Nat. Acad. Scis. NRC, 1970-71; recipient World Bar Assn. Space Humanitarian award, 1996. Mem. AIAA (space logistics com., Engr. of Yr. region IV 1990), ASCE (chmn. exec. com. aerospace divsn. 1979, tech. activities com. 1984, chmn. com space engring. and constrn. 1987—, mem. nat. space policy com. 1988—, chmn. 1990—, Outstanding News Corr. award 1981, Aerospace Scis. and Tech. Applications award 1985, 90, Edmund Friedman Profl. Recognition award 1989), Soc. Am. Mil. Engrs., Am. Geophys. Union, Soc. Am. Milit. Engrs., Sigma Xi, Pi Sigma Alpha. Republican. Mem. United Ch. of Christ. Avocations: photography, swimming, walking, gardening, hiking.

JOHNSON, SYLVIA S., retired secondary school educator; b. Jefferson City, Tenn., Sept. 20, 1937; d. David and Agnes Marie (Ingram) Barnett; m. Charles Johnson Jr., Aug. 28, 1960; 1 child, Sylvia Charlene. BS in Home Econs, Berea Coll.; MS in Family Life, Wayne State U. Tchr. Pershing High Sch., Detroit, 1967-74, 1980-96; counselor Murray Wright Day Care, Detroit, 1974-80; ret., 1996. Vol. tchr. ARC, Detroit, 1980—; sec. Can-Do Block Club, Detroit, 1987—; mem. pres.'s coun. Berea Coll., 1987—. Democrat. Methodist. Avocations: tennis, basketball. Home: 19335 Greydale Ave Detroit MI 48219-1889

JOHNSON, SYLVIA SUE, university administrator, educator; b. Abiline, Tex., Aug. 10, 1940; d. SE Boyd and Margaret MacGillivray (Withington) Smith; m. William Ruel Johnson; children: Margaret Ruth, Laura Jane, Catherine Withington. BA, U. Calif., Riverside, 1962; postgrad., U. Hawaii, 1963. Elem. edn. credential, 1962. Mem. bd. regents U. Calif.; mem. steering com. Citizens Univ. Com., chmn., 1978-79; bd. dirs., charter mem. U. Calif.-Riverside Found., chmn. nominating com., 1983—; pres., bd. dirs. Friends of the Mission Inn, 1969-72, 73-76, Mission Inn Found., 1977—, Calif. Bapt. Coll. Citizens Com., 1980—; bd. dirs. Riverside Cmty. Hosp., 1980—, Riverside Jr. League, 1976-77, Nat. Charity League, 1984-85; mem. chancellors blue ribbon com., devel. com. Calif. Mus. Photography. Named Woman of Yr., State of Calif. Legislature, 1989, 91, Citizen of Yr., C. of C., 1989. Mem. U. Calif.-Riverside Alumni Assn. (bd. dirs. 1966-68, v.p. 1968-70).

JOHNSON, TERRY CHARLES, biologist, educator; b. St. Paul, Aug. 8, 1936; s. Roy August and Catherine (McKigen) J.; m. Mary Ann Wilhelmy, Nov. 23, 1957; children: James, Gary, Jean. BS, Hamline U., 1958; MS, U. Minn., 1961, PhD, 1964. Postdoctoral fellow U. Calif., Irvine, 1964-66; asst. prof. Med. Sch., Northwestern U., Chgo., 1966-69, assoc. prof., 1969-73, prof., 1973-77; prof. div. biology Kans. State U., Manhattan, 1977—, dir. div. biology, 1977-92, Univ. Disting. prof., 1989; dir. Konza Prairie Rsch. Area, Manhattan, 1977-92, Ctr. for Basic Cancer Rsch., Manhattan, 1980—, Ctr. for Space Life Scis., Manhattan, 1990-92; co-dir. Bioserve Space Techs., Manhattan, 1989—. Recipient Outstanding Tchr. of Yr. award Med. Sch., Northwestern U., 1975, Outstanding Tchr. award Ill. Coll. Pediatric Medicine, 1976, Disting. Grad. Faculty award Kans. State U., 1987, Outstanding Sci. award Sigma Xi Kans. State U. chpt., 1993. Mem. AAAS, Am. Soc. for Gravitational and Space Biology, Am. Soc. for Microbiology, Am. Soc. for Neurochemistry, Am. Soc. for Cell Biology, N.Y. Acad. Sci. Avocation: reading. Home: 205 Drake Dr Manhattan KS 66503-3029 Office: Kans State U Div Biology Ackert Hall Manhattan KS 66506

JOHNSON, TESLA FRANCIS, data processing executive, educator; b. Altoona, Fla., Sept. 2, 1934; s. Tesla Farris and Ruby Mae (Shockley) J.; m. Eleanor Mary Riggs, Oct. 17, 1975. BSEE, U. S.C., 1958; MS in Ops. Rsch., Fla. Inst. Tech., 1968; PhD in Adminstrv. Mgmt., Walden U., Mpls., 1990. Machinist apprentice Seaboard Airline Ry., 1952-54; asst. computer engr. So. Ry. System, Washington, 1958-61; sr. sci. programmer NCR, Dayton, Ohio, 1961-66; staff programmer IBM, East Fishkill, N.Y., 1966-72; mgr. Jay Turner Co., Grace, Idaho, 1973-74; programmer, analyst Ccybernetics & Systems, Inc., Jacksonville, Fla., 1974-77; systems analyst 1st Nat. Bank Md., Balt., 1977-78; sr. systems analyst GM, Detroit, 1978-80; tech. analyst Sunbank Data Corp., Orlando, Fla., 1980-81; mgr. data adminstrn. dept. Martin Marietta Corp., Orlando, 1981-92; dir. technology Computer Bus. Assocs., 1993-96; program mgr. Computer Horizons, 1997—; adj. prof. bus. adminstrn. Valencia C.C., Orlando, 1989-94, Orlando Coll., 1990-92, Fla. Inst. Tech., Melbourne; mentor grad. sch. of computer resource mgmt. Webster U., 1993-94. Recipient cert. of appreciation NASA, 1969, Excalibur award. Mem. Acad. Internat. Bus., Tau Beta Pi, Sigma Phi Epsilon. Republican. Baptist. Avocations: stamp and coin collecting, organ. Home and Office: 26203 Corkwood Ct Land O'Lakes FL 34639-5624

JOHNSON, THEA JEAN, internet and intranet security service provider; b. Conshohocken, Pa.; d. Andrew Edward and Mary Rachel (Hillyard) Lewis; m. Lewis Edward Johnson, Apr. 30, 1966; 1 child, Vanessa Rachel. BS in Indsl. Mgmt., Temple U., 1968; Diploma in Computer Systems Engring., IBM Edn. Ctr., N.Y.C., 1968; AMA Cert., Villanova U., 1976. Internet/Intranet security svc. provider RGI, Falls Church, Va., 1981-84; pres. NESS, Reston, Va., 1984—. Facilitator/co-author: (book) Lifelong Learning, 1992 (plaque 1992), others. Bd. dirs. Reston Community Assn., 1988-89; mem. Fairfax County Commn., 1989-92; nat. del. Dem. Nat. Conv., San Francisco, 1984; chair Fairfax County Coun. Arts, 1993; fgn. rels. commr. Internat. Children's Festival, Wolf Trap; deacon Martin Luther King Ch.; co-chairperson Va. del. White House Conf. on Small Bus., 1995; mem. White House Conf. on Small Bus. Summit, 1996; founder IBM Acad Tng. Program for Phila. h.s. children at risk. Recipient Svc. award U.S. Dept. Health and Human Svcs., Washington, 1992, citation Outstanding Vol. Reagan/Bush, Washington, 1985, Outstanding Contbn. to White House Conf. on Small Bus. Pres. William J. Clinton, others. Mem. Network Entrepreneurial Women (charter mem.), LWV (exec. bd. Reston chpt. 1989-91), Va. Assn. Female Execs. (adv. bd. 1989-93), Alpha Kappa Alpha. Democrat. Baptist. Avocations: intergenerational community programs, gourmet cooking, tennis, puzzles, decorating. Office: NESS Inc 2022 Swans Neck Way Ste 2B Reston VA 20191-4035

JOHNSON, THEODORE, retired physician; b. Ames, Iowa, Apr. 30, 1925; s. Birger Lars and Elizabeth (Schulze) J.; m. Hope Polishuk, Aug. 1951; children: Theodore E., Jeffrey L., Christian E. BS, Mont. State U., 1948; MD, Temple U., 1953. Intern Thomas D. Dee Hosp., Ogden, Utah, 1954; physician Weber County, Ogden, Utah, 1954-59; pvt. practice Ogden, 1955-59; asst. editor JAMA AMA, Chgo., 1959-60; pvt. practice Glenview, Ill., 1964-77; asst. dir. AMA Commn. Cost of Med. Care, Chgo., 1960-63; med. dir. Raleigh Hills Hosp., Spokane, Wash., 1977-84; pvt. practice Spokane, 1977-84; clin. dir. LOU Wash. State Hosp., Medical Lake, 1986-88, clin. dir. ITA, 1990-93; ret., 1994; clin. instr. Abraham Sch. Medicine, Chgo., 1975-77; asst. physician Alcohol Treatment Ctr., Luth. Gen. Hosp., Park Ridge, Ill., 1967-77, chmn. dept. family practice, 1969; chmn. med. staff Wash. State Hosp., Medical Lake, 1987-89. Pub. health officer Glenview, Ill., 1964-67. Lt. USN, 1943-46, USNR, 1946-66. Mem. AMA, Wash. Med. Assn., Spokane Med. Soc. (pres. 1985), Am. Soc. Addiction Medicine.

JOHNSON, THEODORE MEBANE, investment executive; b. Denver, Jan. 25, 1934; s. Harold Theodore and Flora Luella (Cunningham) J.; m. Sandra Hall, May 23, 1970. B.S., U. Denver, 1956; postgrad. Advanced Mgmt. Program, Harvard U. Partner, Hornblower Weeks-Hemphill, Noyes, 1961-78; sr. v.p., dir., exec. com. Hornblower Weeks-Hemphill, until 1978; exec. v.p., dir. Eastern group, mgr. PaineWebber, Inc., N.Y.C., 1978—; chmn. bd. Cross Match Techs. Co-founder, past dir. N.Am. Housing Corp. Served to lt. (j.g.) USNR, 1956-57. Mem. Securities Industry Assn. (govt. rels. com., past chmn. Mid-Atlantic chpt.). Presbyterian. Clubs: Bond (Washington), Congressional Country (Washington), Univ. (Washington), City Tavern (Washington), N.Y. Athletic, Robert Trent Jones Country (Manasas, Va.), Iselworth Golf and Country (Windemre, Fla.). Home: 140 Atlantic Ave Palm Beach FL 33480

JOHNSON, THOMAS DAVID, pharmacologist; b. Hammond, Ind., Jan. 19, 1951; s. Kathrine Florence (Basham) J.; m. R. Luanne Novak, Jan. 20, 1984; 1 child, Anna Novak Johnson. BS, Pan Am. U., 1973, MS in Biology, 1974; PhD of Pharmacology, U. Houston, 1984. Instr. rsch. Baylor Coll. Medicine, Houston, 1984-86, asst. prof. rsch., 1987-98, rsch. scientist, 1998—. Contbr. articles to profl. jours. Office: Baylor Coll Medicine Dept Anesthesiology One Baylor Plz Houston TX 77030*

JOHNSON, THOMAS FLOYD, former college president, educator; b. Detroit, June 1, 1943; s. Edward Eugene and Adella Madeline (Norton) J.; m. Michele Elizabeth Myers, Mar. 26, 1965; children: Jason, Amy, Sarah. BPh, Wayne State U., 1965; BD, Fuller Theol. Sem., 1968; ThM, Princeton Sem., 1969; PhD, Duke U., 1979. Pastor Presbyn. Ch. U.S.A., Pa., Mich., 1969-76; asst. prof. U. Sioux Falls, S.D., 1978-83; acad. dean Sioux Falls (S.D.) Coll., 1981-83, pres., 1988-97; prof. N.Am. Baptist Sem., Sioux Falls, 1983-88; dean Western Even. Sem., prof. biblical theology George Fox U., Newberg, Oreg., 1997—; interim pres. George Fox U., Newberg, 1997-98. Contbr. 9 articles to Internat. Standard Bible Ency., 1988; author: 1, 2, and 3 John New International Biblical Commentary, 1993. Bd. dirs. Children's Home Soc. S.D., Sioux Falls, 1980-86, S.D. Symphony Orch., 1988-92, Carroll Inst., 1989-93, Coalition Christian Colls. and Univs., 1992-97. Mem. Am. Bapt. Assn. Colls. and Univs. (pres. 1992-94), Soc. Bibl. Lit., Sioux Falls C. of C. (bd. dirs. 1992-95), Rotary (bd. dirs. Downtown Club 1991-95, pres. 1993-94). Office: George Fox Univ 12753 SW 68th St Portland OR 97223 *Every day, with all its tasks and relationships, is a gift from God. Our response is to live thankfully, in service to God and God's world.*

JOHNSON, THOMAS STEPHEN, banker; b. Racine, Wis., Nov. 19, 1940; s. H. Norman and Jane Agnes (McAvoy) J.; m. Margaret Ann Werner, Apr. 18, 1970; children: Thomas Philip, Scott Michael, Margaret Ann. AB in Econs., Trinity Coll., 1962; MBA, Harvard U., 1964. Instr. Grad. Bus. Sch. Ateneo de Manila U., Philippines, 1964-66; spl. asst. to contr. U.S. Dept. Def., Washington, 1966-69; with Chem. Bank, N.Y.C., 1969-89, pres., dir., 1983-89; pres., dir. Manufacturers Hanover Trust Co.; pres., dir. Mfrs. Hanover Corp., N.Y.C., 1989-91, resigned, 1991; chmn., CEO GreenPoint Fin. Corp., GreenPoint Bank, N.Y.C., 1993—; bd. dirs. Alleghany Corp., R.R. Donnelley & Sons, Inc., Online Resources & Comm. Corp., Inst. Internat. Edn. Trustee, treas. Asia Soc.; chmn. bd. trustees Trinity Coll.; trustee U.S. Japan Found., United Way of N.Y.C.; bd. dirs. Cancer Rsch. Inst., Channel 13-WNET. Mem. Coun. on Fgn. Rels., Montclair Golf Club, Palm Beach Polo and Country Club, River Club N.Y.C., Links N.Y.C., Harvard Club N.Y.C. Democrat. Roman Catholic. Office: GreenPoint Fin Corp 90 Park Ave Fl 4 New York NY 10016-1301

JOHNSON, THOMAS STUART, lawyer; b. Rockford, Ill., May 21, 1942; s. Frederick C. and Pauline (Ross) J. BA, Rockford Coll. 1964, LLD, 1989; JD, Harvard U., 1967. Bar: Ill. 1967. Pres.Williams & McCarthy, Rockford, 1967—; lectr. in field. Contbr. numerous articles to profl. jours. Chmn. bd. trustees Rockford Coll., 1986-89; trustee Eastern Ill. U., 1996—; chmn. bd. dirs. Ill. Inst. Continuing Legal Edn., Chgo., 1984-86; trustee Emanuel Med. Ctr., Turlock, Cal., 1984-86, trustee Swedish Covenant Hosp., Chgo., 1984-86; treas. Lawyers Trust Fund of Ill., Chgo., 1984-86; trustee, Lincoln Acad. of Ill., 1999—, mem. bd. govs., 1985-90, Regent's Coll., London, 1985-89; bd. dir. benevolence bd. Covenant Ch. Am., Chgo., 1984-86; chmn. Regent's Found. for Internat. Edn., London. With U.S. Army, 1965-67. Fellow Am. Bar Found., Am. Coll. Trust and Estate Counsel; mem. ABA (ho. dels. 1982-89, chmn. commn. on advt. 1984-88), Ill. Bar Assn. (bd. govs. 1976-82, sec. 1981-82, medal of honor 1997), Winnebago County Bar Assn. (pres. 1990), Am. Judicature Soc. (bd. dirs. 1986-90), Rockford Country Club, Rotary (pres. Rockford 1992-93). Republican. Home: 913 N Main St Rockford IL 61103-7068

JOHNSON, THOMAS WEBBER, JR., lawyer; b. Indpls., Oct. 18, 1941; s. Thomas W. and Mary Lucinda (Webber) J.; m. Sandra Kay McMahon, Aug. 15, 1964 (div. 1986); m. Deborah Joan Collins, May 17, 1987 (div. 1990); m. Barbara Joyce Walter, Mar. 13, 1992. BS in Edn., Ind. U., 1963, JD summa cum laude, 1969. Bar: Ind. 1969, Calif. 1970. Law clk. Ind. Supreme Ct., Indpls., 1968-69; assoc. Irell & Manella, L.A., 1969-76; ptnr. Irell & Manella law firm, L.A., 1976-84, Newport Beach, Calif., 1984—; chair Com. on Group Ins. Programs for State Bar of Calif., San Francisco, 1978-79; adj. prof. law UCLA, 1996—; lectr. for Practicing Law Inst., Calif. Continuing Edn. of the Bar, Calif. Judges Assn., seminars on ins. and bus. litigation. Editor-in-chief: Ind. Law Review, 1968-69; contbr. articles to profl. jours. With USNR, 1959-65. Named Outstanding Grad. Province XII, Phi Delta Phi legal fraternity, 1969. Mem. ABA (lectr. chair ins. coverage litigation com., tort and ins. practice sec. 1995-96), Calif. Bar Assn., Orange County Bar Assn., Masons, Newport Beach Country Club. Republican. Mem. Christian Ch. Office: Irell & Manella Ste 400 840 Newport Center Dr Newport Beach CA 92660-6324

JOHNSON, TIMOTHY AUGUSTIN, JR., lawyer; b. Clearwater, Fla., Dec. 17, 1945; s. Timothy Augustin and Ruth (Brown) J.; m. Clair Smith, Aug. 23, 1967; children: Chester Wolcott, Kathryn Elizabeth. BA, U. Fla., 1966, JD, 1969. Bar: Fla. 1969, U.S. Dist. Ct. (mid. dist.) Fla. 1970, U.S. Ct. Appeals (5th cir.) 1972, U.S. Supreme Ct. 1972. Assoc. Carlton, Fields et al., Tampa, Fla., 1969-73; ptnr., shareholder Johnson, Blakely, Pope, Bokor, Ruppel & Burns P.A., Clearwater, 1973—; mem. Fla. Bd. Bar Examiners. Pres. PACT, 1986-88; mem. Leadership Fla., 1983-84; chmn. Clearwater Long Range Econ. Devel. Commn., 1988-89; mem. bd. trustees Tampa Prep. Sch., 1985-90; trustee, chmn. investment subcom. U. South Fla. Found.; chmn. Clearwater Charter Rev. Com. Name 1 of 5 Outstanding Young Men, Jr. C. of C., Fla., 1979, Friend of the Arts, Arts Coun., Pinellas County, Fla., 1986. Mem. Fla. Bar (pres. young lawyers sect., bd. govs.). Republican. Avocations: fitness, hiking, boating. Office: Johnson Blakely Pope Et Al 911 Chestnut St Clearwater FL 33756-5643

JOHNSON, TIMOTHY PETER, senator; b. Canton, S.D., Dec. 28, 1946; s. Vandal Charles and Ruth Jorinda (Ljostveit) J.; m. Barbara Brooks, June 6, 1969; children: Brooks Dwight, Brendan Vandal, Kelsey Marie. BA, U. S.D., 1969, MA, 1970, JD, 1975; postgrad., Mich. State U., 1970-71. Bar: S.D. 1975, U.S. Dist. Ct. S.D. 1976. Fiscal analyst Legis. Fiscal Agy., Lansing, Mich., 1971-72; pvt. practice Vermillion, S.D., 1975-86; mem. S.D. Ho. of Reps., 1978-82, S.D. Senate, 1982-86, U.S. Ho. of Reps., 1987-97; U.S. senator from S.D. S.D., 1997—; adj. inst. U. S.D., Vermillion, 1974-83; mem. S.D. Code Commn., Pierre, 1982-86. Mem. Vermillion City Planning Commn., 1977-78; treas. Clay County Dem. Com., Vermillion, 1978; del. Dem. Nat. Conv., 1988, 92, 96. NSF grantee, 1969-70. Mem. S.D. Bar Assn., Clay County Bar Assn., Phi Beta Kappa, Omicron Delta Kappa. Democrat. Lutheran. Office: 324 Russell Senate Ofc Bldg Washington DC 20510-4101 also: PO Box 1554 Aberdeen SD 57402*

JOHNSON, TOD STUART, market research company executive; b. Mpls., June 6, 1944; s. David Z. and Helen R. (Connor) J.; m. Cindy Schwartz, Aug. 28, 1966; children—Scott, Stacey. B.S., Carnegie Mellon U., 1966, M.S.I.A., 1967. Vice pres. Market Sci. Assocs., Inc., Des Plaines, Ill., 1967-71; pres., chief exec. officer NPD Research, Inc., Port Washington, N.Y., 1971-89, Home Testing Inst., Inc., Port Washington, N.Y., 1980-89, OPOC Computing, Inc., Port Washington, N.Y., 1980-89, NPD Group, Port Washington, N.Y., 1982—, The NPD Group Inc. (merger of NPD Rsch. Inc., Home Testing Inst. Inc., and OPOC Computing), Port Washington, N.Y., 1989—; chmn., dir. NPD/Nielsen, Inc., 1987-91; chmn. ISL Internat. Surveys Ltd., Toronto, 1990—; mng. dir. GFK Mktg. Svcs. Europe GmbH, 1995—; chmn., CEO Media Metrix Inc., Port Washington, 1998—; bd. dirs. Advt. Rsch. Found., N.Y.C., sec., 1988, vice chmn., 1989, chmn., 1990; founding co-chmn. Coun. Mktg. and Opinion Rsch., 1992-94. Contbr. articles to profl. jours.; patentee in field. Trustee Carnegie-Mellon U., Pitts., 1980—, chmn., trustee student affairs com., 1982-85, co-chmn. devel. com., 1993—; trustee Coun. for Arts in Westchester, 1987-90; assoc. trustee North Shore U. Hosp., Manhasset, N.Y., 1984-90. Mem. Young Pres. Orgn., Am. Mktg. Assn. Republican. Jewish. Home: 10 Heathcote Rd Scarsdale NY 10583-4414 Office: NPD Group 900 W Shore Rd Port Washington NY 11050-4624

JOHNSON, TOM, broadcasting executive. Pres., chmn., CEO CNN and Headline News, Atlanta. Office: Turner Broadcasting Sys PO Box 105366 Atlanta GA 30348-5366*

JOHNSON, TOM MILROY, academic dean, medical educator, physician; b. Northville, Mich., Jan. 16, 1935; s. Waldo Theodore and Ruth Jeanette (Christensen) J.; m. Emily Chapin Rhoads, June 13, 1959 (div. Aug. 1983); children—Glenn C., Heidi R.; m. Jane Susan Robb, June 10, 1987; 1 stepchild, Elizabeth K. B.A. in Psychology with honors, Coll. of Wooster, 1956; M.D., Northwestern U., 1961; postgrad. in health systems mgmt., Harvard U., 1974. Rotating intern Detroit Receiving Hosp., 1961-62; resident in internal medicine U. Mich. Med. Ctr., Ann Arbor, 1962-65; fellow in pulmonary disease U. Mich. Med. Ctr., 1967-68; asst. prof. internal medicine Mich. State U., East Lansing, 1968-71; assoc. prof., asst. dean Coll. of Medicine Mich. State U., Grand Rapids, 1971-77; prof. medicine, dean Sch. of Medicine U. N.D., Grand Forks, 1977-88; prof., assoc. dean Coll. Human Medicine, Mich. State U., 1988-94; campus dean, CEO Kalamazoo Ctr. for Med. Studies Mich. State U., 1994-98; prof. emeritus medicine Mich. State U., East Lansing, Mich., 1999—; Bd. Dir. Health Share Grp., Petosky, MI, 1994—. Contbr. articles to profl. jours. Capt. M.C., USAF, 1965-67. Recipient Outstanding Tchr. awards Mich. State U., 1969-70, 71, 73, U. N.D. Sch. of Medicine, 1984; A. Blaine Brower Traveling scholar ACP, 1977; Tom M. Johnson lecture hall named in his honor Grand Rapids Med. Ctr., 1982. Fellow ACP; mem. AMA, Mich. State Med. Soc., Studebaker Drivers Club, Antique Automobile Club of Am., Alpha Omega Alpha. Club: Cosmos (Washington). Avocation: restoration of antique automobiles and older farm houses. Home & Office: 4815 Barton Rd Williamston MI 48895-9305

JOHNSON, VAHE DUNCAN, lawyer; b. Providence, Dec. 18, 1938; s. Vahe D. and Katharine (Simpson) J.; m. Diana E. Lepow, Apr. 13, 1964; children: Alexandra, Mark Adam. AB, Harvard U., 1960, LLB, 1963. Bar: R.I. 1964. From assoc. to ptnr. Edwards & Angell, Providence, 1963—; bd. dirs. Fleet Nat. Bank, Fleet Bank of Mass., N.A., Fleet Bank, N.A. Trustee Providence Found., 1985, Providence Pub. Libr, 1988, Miriam Hosp., Providence, 1990, Lifespan Corp., Capitol Ctr. Commn., Sturbridge Village, 1995. Office: Edwards & Angell 2800 Bank Boston Plazar Providence RI 02903*

JOHNSON, VERNON EUGENE, history educator, educational administrator; b. Norfolk, Va., Oct. 25, 1930; s. Ellis Moses and Maude Louvenia (Wilkins) J.; m. Barbara Lucy Wynder, June 6, 1959; children: Kevin Bertram, Troy Eugene, Stacy Yvette. AB with distinction, Va. State Coll., 1951; MA, U. Pa., 1964; diploma with honors U.S. Army Command and Gen. Staff Coll., 1968; postgrad. Old Dominion U., 1977-78; advanced cert. in edn. Coll. William and Mary, 1979, EdD, 1982. Commd. 2d lt. U.S. Army, 1951, advanced through grades to lt. col., 1966, ret., 1979; adminstr., univ. collection mgr., adj. instr. Hampton (Va.) U., 1980-96; sr. prof. Tidewater Va. Ctr.; St. Leo Coll. of Fla., 1980—. Active Boys' Clubs. Decorated Legion of Merit with oak leaf cluster; recipient Brotherhood award, 1981, Jefferson Cup, 1982; named Man of Yr., 1981. Mem. Am. Assn. of Higher Edn., Am. Hist. Assn., Assn. for the Study Higher Edn., Nat. Hist. Assn., Assn. U.S. Army, Alpha Kappa Mu, Phi Alpha Theta, Omega Psi Phi (3d dist. rep.). Methodist. Club: Beau Brummell Civic and Social.

JOHNSON, VICKI KRISTINE, rehabilitation nurse; b. Kansas City, Kans.; d. Samuel Gustave Johnson and Loretta M. (Sweezy) Harrington; m. Dennis Reid Altman, May 7, 1993. Diploma, Rsch. Med. Ctr. Sch. Nursing, 1981; BSN, U. Mo., 1992. Nurse The Rehab. Inst., Kansas City, 1986—. Mem. ANA, Nat. League for Nursing, Am. Assn. Spinal Cord Injury Nurses. Office: 3011 Baltimore Ave Kansas City MO 64108-3403

JOHNSON, VICKI R., insurance company executive; b. Glens Falls, N.Y., June 19, 1952; d. Leonard H. and Rose (Petrosky) J. AB, Franklin and Marshall Coll., 1974; postgrad., U. Portland, 1979-80; MBA, UCLA, 1986, MPH, 1996. ChFC, CLU. Acct. exec. The Prudential, San Diego, 1974—; mem. Oreg. Accident and Health Claim Assn., 1976-81. Pres. Ridgeview Condominium Assn., 1978-81; mem. L.A. Olympic Organizing Com., 1984; active San Diego Employee Benefit Coun. Fellow Life Mgmt. Inst.; mem. AAUW (Del Mar-Leucadia br.), Nat. Health Underwriters, UCLA Alumni Bd. (dir. at large, exec. MBA 1986-94), Neptune Cove Home Owners Assn. (pres. 1995-98). Presbyterian. Home: 1691 Neptune Ave Encinitas CA 92024-1051 Office: 9171 Towne Centre Dr Ste 380 San Diego CA 92122-6213

JOHNSON, VICKI VALEEN, paramedic, technical advisor movie studios; b. Houston, May 26, 1958; d. Louis Reginald and Nobie Jeanine (Johnson) Vanderburg; 1 child, Jacqueline Monique. Cert EMT, U. Tex., San Antonio, 1991; cert. paramedic, Ctrl. Tex. Coll., 1993; cert. advanced life support, Metroplex Hosp., Kileen, Tex., 1993; cert. CPR instr., ARC, Burnet, Tex. Cert. paramedic, EMT, Tex.; cert. CPR, ARC. Free lance film, spl. events and commercials paramedic, tech. advisor various studios including Warner Bros., CBS, 20th CenturyFox, L.A., 1994—; paramedic Internat. Olympics Diving Competition, Atlanta, 1996; event dir. Sea World of Tex., San Antonio, 1995; health supr. Girl Scouts Am. of Tex., 1998. Named Princess of Kingsland, Kingsland, Tex. C. of C., 1978, Imperial Miss Houston, 1981-82; Miss Imperial Houston Exhibit, San Antonio Livestock Show and Rodeo, 1996, Outstanding Young Women of Am., Atty. Gen.'s Office, Tex.; elected to San Antonio chpt Women's Hall of Fame, 1994. Mem. Internat. Alliance Stage and Theatrical Employees Union 484 (med. com. 1995-97), Tex. Assn. Film and Tape Profls., Order of Ea. Stars. Democrat. Methodist. Avocations: writing, travel, movies, spending time with daughter. Home: PO Box 1121 Kingsland TX 78639-1121

JOHNSON, VICKIE, professional basketball player; b. Apr. 15, 1972. B of Sociology & Psychology, La. Tech. Inst., 1996. Guard-forward Tarbes, France, 1996-97, WMBA - N.Y. Liberty, N.Y.C., 1997—. Named NCAA Tournament All-Final Four, 1994, Sun Belt Conf. Player of Yr., MVP, Kodak All-Am., 1995, Street & Smith All-Am., 1996, La. Player of Yr.,

1996. Avocations: movies, shop, friends, tennis. Office: NY Liberty 2 Penn Plz New York NY 10121-0001*

JOHNSON, VICTOR CHARLES, association executive; b. Pitts., July 24, 1941; s. Anne M. Byers; children: Christine Johnson Payne, Timothy Mark. BA, Whitworth Coll., 1963; MA, San Francisco State U., 1971; PhD, U. Wis., 1975. Tng. assoc. Ford Found., Bogota, Colombia, 1967-69; subcom. staff assoc. U.S. Ho. of Reps., Washington, 1975-81, subcom. staff dir., 1981-93; assoc. dean internat. edn. Jacksonville U., 1997-98; sr. dir. pub. affairs NAFSA: Assn. of Internat. Educators, Washington, 1998—. Vol. U.S. Peace Corps, Liberia, West Africa, 1963-65, regional dir. internat.-Am. ops., 1993-97. Office: NAFSA Assn of Internat Educators 1307 New York Ave NW Washington DC 20005

JOHNSON, VICTOR LAWRENCE, banker; b. Phila., Feb. 8, 1928; s. Paul J. and Eleanor (Moskowitz) J.; m. Joan Markovitz, Dec. 4, 1955; children: Linda E., Sally A. Grad., Phillips Exeter Acad., 1945; B.A., Haverford Coll., 1949; M.B.A., Wharton Sch. of U. Pa., 1951. Vice pres. Ocean City Mfg. Co., Phila., 1953-58; pres. Johnson Computing Co., Phila., 1958-68; chmn. bd., dir. Johnson Computing Co., 1968—; with Provident Nat. Bank, Phila., 1969—; sr. v.p. Provident Nat. Bank, 1971—; pres., dir. Allen Data Systems, Inc., Phila., 1970; pres. JCI Data Processing Inc., 1976—; bd. dirs. Sircom Knitting Co., Spring City, Pa., pres., 1980-81; chmn. Wordco Data Systems Inc., 1992. Bd. dirs., mem. budget com. Phila. United Fund, 1954-67; bd. dirs. Nicetown Club Boys and Girls, Phila., 1954-57, Huntingdon Valley (Pa.) Civic Assn., 1956-64; bd. dirs., exec. com. Rydal/Meadowbrook (Pa.) Civic Assn., 1969—; mem. planning and devel. com. Germantown Friends Sch., 1970-73; vol. trustee Not-For-Profit Hosps. Bd., v.p., 1984-87, chmn. planning com., 1987-89; vice chmn., 1989-96, trustee, exec. com. Albert Einstein Med. Ctr., 1973—, vice chmn., 1980, chmn. bd. govs. No. divsn., 1981-84, chmn. bd. dirs., 1987-90; chmn. bd. trustees Health Care Found., 1987-90; dir. Jefferson Health System, 1998; sec., treas. Delaware Valley Hosp. Couns., 1982-95; chmn. bd. Delaware Valley Health, Edn. and Rsch. Found., 1982-85; bd. dirs. Phila. Festival Theatre for New Plays, 1989-94. With U.S. Army, 1951-52. Mem. Pa. Bankers Assn., Bank Automation Assn. Delaware Valley, Am. Hosp. Assn. (coun. governing bds. 1989), Hosp. Trustees Assn. Pa. (vice chmn. bd. 1991-92, chmn. bd. 1992). Clubs: Locust (Phila.); Philmont Country (Huntingdon Valley) (bd. dirs., exec. v.p.). Home: Hidden Glen Meadowbrook PA 19046 Office: 200 Route 130 S Cinnaminson NJ 08077-2892

JOHNSON, VIRGIL ALLEN, retired agronomist; b. Newman Grove, Nebr., June 28, 1921; s. Oscar Johannas and Fairy Bell (Johnson) J.; m. Betty Ann Tisthammer, July 29, 1943; children: Karen, Leslie (dec.), Reed, Scott. B.S. with distinction, U. Nebr., 1948, Ph.D. (Regents Grad. fellow, Ak-Sar-Ben grad. fellow, Sears, Roebuck Grad. fellow), 1952. Agt. Agrl. Research Service, U.S. Dept. Agr., Lincoln, Nebr., 1951-52; research agronomist Agrl. Research Service, U.S. Dept. Agr., 1954-75, supervisory research agronomist, 1975-78; asst. agronomist U. Nebr., Lincoln, 1952-54; asso. prof. U. Nebr., 1954-63, prof. agronomy dept., 1963-86, emeritus, 1986—, leader wheat research, 1978-86; cons. Gt. Plains Wheat, Inc.; mem. Nat. Wheat Improvement Com.; mem. tech. com. Wheat Quality Council. Contbr. articles to profl. publs. Served in inf. U.S. Army, 1940-43; Served in U.S. Army AC, 1943-45. Decorated D.F.C., Air medal with 3 oak leaf clusters; recipient Agrl. Achievement award Ak-Sar-Ben, 1970, Disting. Service award Dept. Agr., 1981; Internat. Agronomy award, 1984; Crop Sci. Disting. Career award, 1985; Agronomic Service award ASA, 1987; inductee Agr. Rsch. Svc. Sci. Hall of Fame USDA, 1990, Nebr. Hall of Agrl. Achievement, 1991; AID grantee, 1966-79. Fellow Am. Soc. Agronomy, AAAS; mem. Crop Sci. Soc. Am. (Crop Sci. award 1975, pres. 1978), Sigma Xi, Gamma Sigma Delta (Internat. award 1969), Alpha Zeta. Lutheran. Co-developer 28 varieties of hard red winter wheat. Home: 128 N 13th St Lincoln NE 68508-1561 Office: U Nebr East Campus 169 Plant Sci Bldg Lincoln NE 68583

JOHNSON, VIRGIL EVANS, JR., research scientist; b. Tampa, Fla., Feb. 26, 1927; s. Virgil Evans Sr. and Opal Florence (Harper) J.; m. Emma Frances Kinard, Nov. 20, 1948; children: Cynthia Latimer, Lynn Langer, Shirley Brott. BEE, Ga. Inst. Tech., 1949; SM, MIT, 1955; PhD, Johns Hopkins U., 1988. Hydraulics engr. U.S. Waterways Exptl. Sta., Vicksburg, Miss., 1949-50, 52-53; rsch. asst. Hydrodynamics Lab., MIT, Cambridge, 1953-55; aero. rsch. scientist Nat. Adv. Com. for Aeronautics-NASA Langley, Hampton, Va., 1955-60; from chief engr. to pres. Hydronautics Inc., Laurel, Md., 1960-83; chief engr. Tracor Hydronautics Inc., Laurel, 1983-91; v.p., chief scientist, co-founder Hydronautics Rsch. Inc., Fulton, Md., 1991—. Contbr. articles to profl. jours.; inventor and patentee in field. With USN, 1945-46, PTO; capt. U.S. Army, 1950-52, Korea. Republican. Methodist. Avocations: fishing, sailing. Home: 24011 Woodfield Rd Gaithersburg MD 20882-2827 Office: Hydronautics Rsch Inc 7210 Pindell School Rd Fulton MD 20759-9752

JOHNSON, VIRGINIA GAYLE, secondary education educator; b. Lincoln, Ill., June 6, 1946; d. Charles William and Mary Jane (Gayle) Anderson; m. Kenneth Paul Johnson, Dec. 17, 1967; children: Darren Nils, Teri Lynn. BS, Ill. State U., 1968; MS, U. Ill., 1993, Western Ill. U., 1993; adminstrv. degree, Western Ill. U., 1994. Tchr., home econs. Hillcrest High Sch., Country Club Hills, Ill., 1968-70; tchr., home econs. Rock Falls (Ill.) High Sch., 1970-89, learning disabilities resource tchr., 1989-91, spl. edn. coord., 1992—. Chmn. bd. dirs. Select Employees Credit Union; mem. St. John's Luth. Ch. Mem. ASCD, Ill. Vocat. Assn., Ill. Edn. Assn., Rock Falls High Sch. Assn. (pres. 1975, Mem. of Yr. 1989), Coun. for Exceptional Children (LD and EMH divsns.), Sterling Athletic Booster Club (treas.). Avocations: quilting, cross stitch, sewing. Home: 3809 Hickory Hills Rd Sterling IL 61081-9265 Office: Rock Falls High Sch 101 12th Ave Rock Falls IL 61071-1099

JOHNSON, W. TAYLOR, physician; b. Suffolk, Va., Jan. 17, 1936; s. Walter Taylor and Ethel (Storey) J.; m. Bettie Ann Orenduff; children: Elizabeth Ann, Patricia Ellen. Grad., Duke U., 1957, MD, 1961. Diplomate Am. Bd. Dermatology, Am. Bd. Dermatopathology. Commd. ensign USN, 1954; advanced through grades to capt. Nat. Naval Med. Ctr., 1975; intern Nat. Naval Med. Ctr., Bethesda, Md., 1961-62; resident in dermatology U.S. Naval Hosp., San Diego, 1964-66; fellow in dermatopathology Armed Forces Inst. Pathology, Washington, 1967-68; staff physician U.S. Naval Tng. Ctr., San Diego, 1962-64; staff dermatologist Nat. Naval Med. Ctr., Bethesda, 1967-72, asst. chief of dermatology, 1972-78, chief of dermatology, 1978-81, ret., 1981; asst. prof. medicine Georgetown U., Washington, 1969-88; pvt. practice Gaithersburg, Md., 1981—. Contbr. articles to profl. jours. Mem. AMA, Assn. Mil. Dermatologists (pres. 1979), Washington, D.C. Soc. Dermatology (pres. 1983), Am. Acad. Dermatology, Am. Soc. Dermatopathology, Montgomery County, Md. Med. Soc., Med. and Chirurgical Faculty of Md., Internat. Soc. for Dermatol. Surgery. Republican. Presbyterian. Avocations: tennis, computers. Home: 12301 Rivers Edge Dr Potomac MD 20854-1072 Office: Ste A-28 19201 Mont Village Ave Gaithersburg MD 20879

JOHNSON, W. THOMAS, JR., media executive; b. 1941. BJ, U. Ga., 1963; MBA, Harvard U., 1965. With Tex. Broadcasting Corp., Dallas, 1965-75; exec. v.p. Tex. Broadcasting Corp., 1965; pub. Dallas-Herald Times, 1975; with L.A. Times, 1975—, pres., 1977, pub., 1980, sr. v.p., 1986, vice chmn., chmn. bd. dirs.; pres., bd. dirs. Cable News Network, 1990—; chmn. bd. dirs. Times Mirror Newspaper mgmt com.; v.p. Turner Broadcasting Sys., Atlanta. Dep. press sec., spl. asst. Pres. Lyndon B. Johnson, 1969. White House fellow, 1965; named Pub. of Yr., Adweek Mag., 1984, Cable Exec. of Yr., Adweek Mag., 1991; Recipient Horatio Alger Distinguished Am. award, 1987. Mem. Stanford Profl. Journalism Fellowship Program (chmn.), Lyndon B. Johnson Found. (chmn.), Mayo Found. (bd trustees), Knight Found. (bd. trustees). Office: Cable News Network 1CNN Ctr NW PO Box 105366 Atlanta GA 30348-5366*

JOHNSON, WAINE CECIL, dermatologist; b. Mt. Vernon, Tex., Sept. 30, 1928; s. Tulley Bell and Lizzie J.; m. Deanna Glutz, Dec. 1973; children: Susan Lynn, Carol Ann, Sandra Kay. B.S., E. Tex. State U., 1949; M.D., U. Tex., 1953. Intern Brooke Army Hosp., 1953-54; resident in dermatology Walter Reed Army Hosp., 1955-58; fellow in dermal pathology Armed Forces Inst. Pathology, 1960-61; mem. staff Skin and Cancer Hosp., Phila., 1962-78; asst. dir. lab. Skin and Cancer Hosp., 1962, dir., 1970-78; mem. faculty Temple U. Med. Sch., Phila., 1962-78; prof. dermatology Temple U. Med. Sch., 1970-78; clin. prof. U. Pa. Med. Sch., 1978—; chmn. dept. dermatology Grad. Hosp. U. Pa., 1978-98; pres. Dermatology Assns., 1990—; mng. ptnr. Del. Valley Dermatopathology LLP, 1998—. Author numerous papers in field.; Co-editor: Dermal Pathology, 1974. Served to maj. M.C. USAR, 1953-62. Recipient Gold medal sci. exhibit Am. Soc. Clin. Pathologists-Coll. Am. Pathologists, 1962. Mem. AMA, ACP, Am. Acad. Dermatology (chmn. com pathology 1976-80), Am. Dermatol. Assn., Internat. Acad. Pathology, Am. Registry Pathology (sec. 1982-85, treas. 1985), Am. Soc. Dermatopathology (pres. 1988) Soc. Investigative Dermatology, Histochem. Soc., Phila. Dermatol. Soc. (pres. 1979-80), Atlantic Dermatol. Conf. (pres. 1979-80), Coll. Physicians of Phila. (chmn. dermatology sect. 1994-97). Home: 744 Crosswicks Rd Rydal PA 19046-3004 Office: 137 S Easton Rd # 8 Glenside PA 19038-4535

JOHNSON, W(ALKER) REED, nuclear engineering educator; b. Chattanooga, Sept. 3, 1931; s. Albert Walker and Mary (Reed) J.; m. Vivien Rowland, June 17, 1956; children—Dorothy, Mary Reed, V. Ross. B.S. in Physics, Va. Mil. Inst., 1953; cert., Oak Ridge Sch. Reactor Tech., 1954; Dr. Sci. in Engrng. Physics, U. Va., 1962. Shielding engr. Electric Boat div. Gen. Dynamics, Groton, Conn., 1954-55; nuclear engr. Alco Products Co., Inc., Schenectady, N.Y., 1955-57; project engr. nuclear engrng. dept. U. Va., Charlottesville, 1958-60, mem. faculty nuclear engrng. dept., 1962—, lectr. nuclear engrng., 1964-66, assoc. prof. nuclear engrng., 1966-68, prof. nuclear engrng., 1968-85, research prof. nuclear engrng., 1985-92, prof. emeritus, 1992—; adminstrv. judge U.S. NRC, Atomic Safety and Licensing Appeal Bd., Bethesda, Md., 1974-91. Contbr. tech. articles on radiation shielding and nuclear engineering to profl. jours. Mem. Com. on Fgn. Relations, Charlottesville. Fellow Am. Nuclear Soc. (chmn. radiation protection and dosimetry div. 1973-74, Va. sect. 1991-92), Tau Beta Pi, Omicron Delta Kappa. Episcopalian. Avocation: tennis. Office: Univ of Virginia Nuclear Engrng Dept Reactor Facility Charlottesville VA 22903

JOHNSON, WALLACE, retired army officer; b. Oklahoma City, Aug. 8, 1939; s. Carroll Wallace and Pauletta (Bibbs) J.; m. Lela Mae Johnson, Dec. 25, 1959; children: Wallace, Steven, Valerie Lynne, Sharon Denise. BS, U. Okla., 1961; MBA, Ala. A&M U., 1973. Commd. 2d lt. U.S. Army, 1961, advanced through grades to lt. col., 1978; lt. inf. platoon leader, exec officer 1/58th Inf. (Mech), Ft. Benning, Ga., 1962-64; detachment comdr. Co. A-29 C 10th spl. forces Bad Tolz, West Germany, 1964-66, detachment comdr. A333, 5th spl. forces group, Republic Vietnam, 1966-67; br. chief instr. USAMMCS Redstone Arsenal, Ala., 1969-71; security plans, ops. officer 23d support group, Republic Korea, 1971-72; chief orgn. br. USAMMCS, Redstone Arsenal, 1973-75; exec. officer 101st Ordnance Bn., Heilbronn, W. Ger., 1976-78; surety insp. Office of Insp. Gen., Heidelberg, W. Ger., 1978-79; sr. logistics instr. Command and Gen. Staff Coll., Ft. Leavenworth, Kans., 1979-84; chief materiel and logistics systems div. Army Ordnance Missile and Munition Ctr. and Sch., 1984-85; sr. program analyst CAS, Inc., 1985-86; mgr. logistics integration Acustar, Inc. Mil.-Pub. Electronic Systems, 1986-88, mgr. bus. devel. dept., automatic test equipment (ATE)/test program sets (TPS) and electroluminescent display products Chrysler Corp., 1986-91; dir. mktg. Automation Rsch. Systems Ltd., 1991-93, program mgr., 1993-94 GMU, 1994—; dir., mentor-protege program; instr. U.S. Army server shcs.; sr. parachutist, jump master. Decorated Combat Inf. Badge, Bronze Star. Mem. Assn. U.S. Army, Am. Def. Preparedness Assn., Internat. Platform Assn., Soc. Logistics Engrs., Unmanned Vehicle Assn., Spl. Forces Assn. Republican. Baptist. Club: Jaywalkers of Ft. Leavenworth (v.p. 1980-81), Kiwanis, Nat. Space Club (vice chmn.). Lodge: Sertoma (Leavenworth chpt. pres. 1981-84). Home: 9513 Retriever Rd Burke VA 22015-4515 Office: George Mason U Fairfax VA 22030-3409

JOHNSON, WALTER CURTIS, electrical engineering educator; b. Weikert, Pa., Jan. 6, 1913; s. David C. and Mary (Ely) J.; m. Carolyn Shirk, Sept. 1, 1934; children: Walter Curtis, William Stanford, David Edward. B.S., Pa. State Coll., 1934; student in advanced engrng., Gen. Electric Co., 1934-37; E.E., Pa. State Coll., 1942. Instr., dept. elec. engring. Princeton, 1937, prof. elec. engrng., 1948—, Arthur LeGrand Doty prof. engrng., 1963-81, Arthur LeGrand Doty prof. emeritus, 1981—, chmn. dept., 1950-65; engrng. cons. various cos.; resident visitor Bell Telephone Labs., 1968. Author: Mathematical and Physical Principles of Engineering Analysis, 1944, Transmission Lines and Networks, 1950, (with P.R. Clement) Electrical Engineering Science, 1960; articles tech. and sci. publs. Recipient Western Elec. award for excellence in engrng. edn.; Am. Soc. Engrng. Edn., 1967; Nat. award for Best Initial Paper Am. Inst. Elec. Engrs., 1939. Fellow IEEE, AIEE, IRE; mem. Am. Soc. Engrng. Edn. (chmn. elec. engrng. div. 1955-56), Am. Phys. Soc., Sigma Xi. Presbyterian. Home: 31 Meadow Lks # O7 Hightstown NJ 08520-3372

JOHNSON, WALTER EARL, geophysicist; b. Denver, Dec. 16, 1942; s. Earl S. and Helen F. (Llewellyn) J.; m. Ramey Kandice Kayes, Aug. 6, 1967; children: Gretchen, Roger, Aniela. Grad. in Geophys. Engrng., Colo. Sch. of Mines, 1966. Registered profl. engr., Colo.; cert. geologist, Colo. Geophysicist Pan Am. Petroleum Corp., 1966-73; seismic processing supr. Amoco Prodn. Co., Denver, 1973-74, marine tech. supr., 1974-76, divsn. processing cons., 1976-79; geophys. supr. No. Thrust Belt, Denver, 1979-80; chief geophysicist Husky Oil Co., Denver, 1981-82; exploration mgr. Rocky Mountain and Gulf Coast divsn., Denver, 1982-84; geophys. mgr. ANR Prodn. Co., Denver, 1985—; pres. Sch. Lateral Ditch Co.; cons. engr. Bd. dirs. Rocky Mountain Residence. Mem. Denver Geophys. Soc., Soc. Exploration Geophysicists. Republican. Baptist. Office: 600 17th St Ste 800 Denver CO 80202-5402

JOHNSON, WALTER KLINE, civil engineer; b. Mpls., Aug. 28, 1923; s. Horace Edward and Ida Axelina (Kline) J.; m. Geneva Lorraine Olson, Sept. 2, 1950; children: Kristine Idelle, Karen Margaret, Konstance Louise. BCE, U. Minn., 1948, MS, 1951, PhD, 1963. Registered profl. engr., Minn. With Greeley and Hansen, Chgo., 1948-49, Infilco, Inc., Tucson, 1951-52, Toltz, King, Duvall, Anderson & Assocs., St. Paul, 1952-55; faculty U. Minn., Mpls., 1955—, assoc. prof. civil engrng., 1965-74, prof., 1974-75; dir. planning Met. Waste Control Commn., St. Paul, 1975-89; mgmt. cons. in environ. engrng. St. Paul, 1989—. Patentee wastewater sampler. Capt. USAAF, 1943-46. EPA rsch. fellow Brit. Water Pollution Rsch. Lab., 1971. Fellow ASCE (pres. N.W. sect. 1972-73), Am. Water Works Assn., Cen. State Water Environment Assn.; mem. Am. Acad. Environ. Engrs. (diplomate). Lutheran. Rsch. on biol. waste water treatment, sludge bulking, nitrogen removal by denitrification. Home: 5321 29th Ave S Minneapolis MN 55417-2010

JOHNSON, WALTER L., transportation company executive; b. Flint, Mich., Aug. 31, 1927; s. Fred T. and Nellie L. (Niswonger) J.; m. Ida E. Laukonen (div.); children: Eric, Mary, David; m. Rozann Randazo. BA in Math., U. Mich., 1950. Indsl. engr. Kaiser Motors, Willow Run, Mich., 1951-53; various positions including N.Am. coordinator Brazil Kaiser-Willys, Toledo, 1953-68; gen. mgr. plant AM Gen., South Bend, Ind., 1968-74; v.p. mfg. automotive group Midland Ross, Southfield, Mich., 1974-76; exec. v.p. ops. Midland Steel Products, Cleve., 1976-79; pres. Midsco div. Lamson & Sessions, Cleve., 1979-85, exec. v.p. transp. equipment products, 1985-88, also bd. dirs. Served with USN, 1945-46. Home: 590 Wedgewood Way Naples FL 34119-1811

JOHNSON, WARREN DONALD, retired pharmaceutical executive, former air force officer; b. Blackwell, Okla., Sept. 2, 1922; s. Charles Leon and Vera Ruth (Tucker) J.; children: Richard Johnson, Patricia Suzanne Johnson Peak, Lindabeth Johnson Brown, Ross Anthony. Student, Oklahoma City U., 1940-41. Served to 1st lt. U.S. Army, 1942-45; commd. 1st lt. USAAF, 1945; advanced through grades to lt. gen. USAF, 1972; chief of staff SAC Offutt AFB, Nebr., 1971-73; dir. Def. Nuclear Agy., Washington, 1973-77; ret., 1977; corp. v.p. Baxter Internat. Inc., Deerfield, Ill., 1977-91; cons., tchr. Lake Forest Grad. Sch. Mgmt., 1991—. Decorated D.S.M., Legion of Merit with 2 oak leaf clusters, Joint Commendation medal.

JOHNSON, WATTS CAREY, lawyer; b. Chgo., June 21, 1925; s. Carey R. and Leone (VanMechelen) J.; m. Claire Hayes Johnson, June 4, 1950; children: Gregory, Philip, Carolyn, Brian, Barbara. BA, Western Mich. U., 1947; JD, Northwestern U., 1950. Bar: Ill. 1950, U.S. Supreme Ct. 1967. Justice of the peace Princeton Twp., Bureau County, Ill., 1952-56; asst. state's atty. State's Atty. Office, Bureau County, 1957-64; ptnr. Peterson, Johnson & Martin, 1960-69, Johnson, Martin & Russell, Princeton, Ill., 1969-88; ptnr. Johnson, Martin, Russell, English, Scoma & Beneke, Princeton, Ill., 1988-95, ret., 1995; of counsel Johnson, Martin, Russell, English, Scoma & Beneke, Princeton, 1995-97, Russell, English, Scoma & Beneke, P.C., Princeton, 1997—; mem. rules commn. Ill. Supreme Ct., 1977-95; commr. State of Ill. Ct. of Claims, 1989-95; ret. 1996; mem. Atty. Registration and Disciplinary Commn. State of Ill., 1973-92, inquiry divsn., 1973-76, hearing divsn., 1976-78, rev. bd., 1979-90, commr., 1991-95. Pres. Bureau County chpt. ARC, 1959-62; pres. Princeton Jaycees, 1954; chmn. Bureau County Merit Commn., 1985-88. Fellow Am. Coll. Trust and Probate Counsel; mem. Ill. Cts. Commn., Ill. Appellate Lawyers Assn., Ill. Def. Counsel, Internat. Assn. Def. Counsel. Republican. Baptist. Avocation: computers. Office: Russell English Scoma & Beneke PC 10 Park Ave W Princeton IL 61356-2019

JOHNSON, WAYNE D., gas industry executive; b. Winterset, Iowa, Sept. 20, 1932; s. Leslie E. and Ruth N. J.; m. Lynne Alice Brouwer, June 15, 1963; children: Christopher W., Kevin B. BA, U. Nebr., 1954; LLB, Harvard U., 1959. Bar: Ill. bar 1959. Assoc., then ptnr. Ross, Hardies, O'Keefe, Babcock & Parsons, Chgo., 1959-72; asst. gen. counsel Peoples Gas Co., Chgo., 1972-75; sr. v.p., gen. counsel Entex, Inc., Houston, 1975-78; pres. Entex, Inc., 1978-86, utility cons., 1986-87; pres. United Tex. Transmission Co., 1987-93, Am. Natural Gas Power, Inc., Houston, 1993-97; utility cons., 1997—; dir. Simmons & Co. Past chmn. Galveston Bay Found.; vice chmn. Sam Houston Area Coun., Boy Scouts Am. With U.S. Army, 1954-56. Woodrow Wilson fellow, 1954. Mem. Am. Gas Assn., So. Gas Assn. (past chmn.), Legal Club (Chgo.). Home: 12 Tiel Way Houston TX 77019-1510

JOHNSON, WAYNE EATON, writer, editor, former drama critic; b. Phoenix, May 9, 1930; s. Roscoe and Marion (Eaton) J.; children: Katherine, Jeffrey. BA, U. Colo., 1952; postgrad., Duke U., 1952-53; postgrad. (KLM polit. reporting fellow 1957), U. Vienna, Austria, 1955-56; MA, UCLA, 1957. Reporter Internat. News Service, Des Moines, 1958, Wheat Ridge (Colo.) Advocate, 1957; Pueblo (Colo.) Chieftain, 1959; reporter Denver Post, 1960, editl. writer, music critic, 1961-65; arts and entertainment editor Seattle Times, 1965-82, drama critic, 1980-92; instr. journalism Colo. Woman's Coll., 1962. Author: Show: A Concert Program for Actor and Orchestra, 1971, America! A Concert of American Images, Words and Music, 1973, From Where the Sun Now Stands: The Indian Experience, 1973, Let's Go On: Pacific Northwest Ballet at 25, 1997; editor, co-pub.: Secrets of Warmth, 1992, Footprints on the Peaks, 1995, The Burgess Book of Lies, 1995. With CIC AUS, 1953-55, Korea. Home: 11303 Durland Pl NE Seattle WA 98125-5926

JOHNSON, WAYNE HAROLD, librarian, county official; b. El Paso, Tex., May 2, 1942; s. Earl Harold and Cathryn Louise (Greeno) J.; m. Patricia Ann Froedge, June 15, 1973; children: Meredith Jessica (dec.), Alexandra Noëlle Victoria. BS, Utah State U., 1968; MPA, U. Colo., 1970; MLS, U. Okla., 1972. Circulation libr. Utah State U., Logan, 1968, adminstrv. asst. libr., 1969; with rsch. dept. Okla. Mgmt. and Engring. Cons., Norman, 1972; chief adminstrv. svcs. Wyo. State Libr., Cheyenne, 1973-76, chief bus. officer libr. archives and hist. dept., 1976-78, state libr., 1978-89; county grants mgr. Laramie County, Wyo., 1989—. Trustee Bibliog. Ctr. for Rsch., Denver, pres., 1983, 84; mem. Cheyenne dist. Longs Park coun. Boy Scouts Am., 1982-86; active Cheyenne Frontier Days, 1975—; mem. admissions and allocation com. United Way, 1991-94; mem. Ho. of Reps., Wyo. Legislature, 1993—; chmn. Transp. Hwys. Com., 1999—. Served with USCG, 1960-64. Mem. Aircraft Owners and Pilots Assn., Cheyenne C. of C. (chmn. transp. com. 1982, 83, military affairs com. 1994—), Am. Legion. Republican. Presbyterian. Club: No. Colo. Yacht. Lodges: Masons, Kiwanis (bd. dirs. 1986, 87). Office: 309 W 20th St Cheyenne WY 82001-3601

JOHNSON, WEYMAN THOMPSON, JR., lawyer; b. Atlanta, July 13, 1951; s. Weyman Thompson Sr. and Dixie LaNé (Peevy) J.; m. E. Allison Forkner, July 13, 1974; children: Chloe Forkner, Willa Rose. BA, Mercer U., 1973; JD, U. Ga., 1979. Bar: Ga. 1979, U.S. Dist. Ct. (no. dist.) Ga. 1979, U.S. Ct. Appeals (4th and 11th cir.) 1983, U.S. Supreme Ct. 1989. Reporter Columbus (Ga.) Ledger Newspaper, 1973-75; assoc. Fisher & Phillips, Atlanta, 1979-83, ptnr., 1984; assoc. Paul, Hastings, Janofsky & Walker, Atlanta, 1984-88, ptnr., 1988—. Author: Plant Closing Law, 1989. Bd. deacons First Bapt. Ch., Decatur, 1984—, chmn., 1998; chmn. Ga. chpt. Nat. Multiple Sclerosis Soc., Atlanta, 1990-94, bd. dirs., 1995—. Mem. ABA, Ga. Bar Assn., Atlanta Bar Assn. (chmn. labor sect. 1989-90, bd. dirs. 1991-92), Indsl. Rels. Rsch. Assn., Ga. Def. Lawyers Assn., Nat. M.S. Assn. (bd. dirs. 1995—, v.chmn. 1998—), Eagles Landing Country Club. Home: 49 Sorrow Rd Stockbridge GA 30281-1841 Office: Paul Hastings Janofsky & Walker 600 Peachtree St NE Fl 24 Atlanta GA 30308-2265

JOHNSON, WILBUR CORNEAL (JOE JOHNSON), biologist; b. Kalamazoo, Nov. 16, 1941. BS, Mich. State U., 1964, MS, 1967. Cert. wildlife biologist. Wildlife technician W.K. Kellogg Bird Sanctuary, Mich. State U., Augusta, 1964-85, chief wildlife and bird sanctuary mgr., 1985—. Recipient Miles B. Pirnie Meml. award Mich. Duckhunters Assn., 1993. Mem. Wildlife Soc., Pheasants Forever (nat. bd. 1988—). Office: WK Kellogg Bird Sanctuary Mich State Univ 12685 E C Ave Augusta MI 49012-9707

JOHNSON, WILLARD CHAPIN, surgeon, researcher; b. Waterbury, Conn., Nov. 4, 1937; s. Edward Oscar and Dorothy (Graves) J.; m. Elsie Ernest, Dec. 16, 1964 (dec. Nov. 1994); children: Karen, Thomas, David; m. Regina Ruth Kobett, Jan. 5, 1996. BS, MIT, 1959, MS, 1960; MD, Tufts U., 1964. Diplomate Am. Bd. Surgery. Intern Phila. Gen. Hosp., 1964-65; resident Boston City Hosp., 1965-70; chief vascular surgery Boston VA Med. Ctr., 1982—, chief surgery, 1988—; prof. surgery Tufts U. Sch. Medicine, Boston, 1982-92; prof. surgery Boston U. Sch. Medicine, 1992—, vice chmn. dept. surgery, 1998—. Comdr. USN, 1970-72. Mem. ACS, Soc. Vascular Surgery, Internat. Soc. Cardiovascular Surgery, New Eng. Surg. Soc., New Eng. Soc. Vascular Surgery, Boston Surg. Soc. Office: Boston VA Med Ctr 150 S Huntington Ave Boston MA 02130-4817

JOHNSON, WILLARD RAYMOND, political science educator, consultant; b. St. Louis, Nov. 22, 1935; s. Willard and Dorothy (Stovall) J.; m. Vivian Robinson, Dec. 15, 1957; children: Caryn L., Kimberly E. BA, UCLA, 1957; MA, Johns Hopkins U., 1961; PhD, Harvard U., 1965. Asst. prof. polit. sci. MIT, Cambridge, Mass., 1964-69, assoc. prof., 1969-73; prof. polit. sci. MIT, 1973-96, prof. emeritus, 1996—; vis. assoc. prof. Harvard U. Sch. Bus., Cambridge, 1969; exec. dir. Circle Inc., Roxbury, Mass., 1968-70; adj. prof. Fletcher Sch., Medford, Mass., 1971-82; cons. U.S. Nat. Commn. for Minority Enterprise, Washington, 1969; bd. dirs. Interfaith Housing Corp., Boston, 1970; chmn. bd. Circle Inc. subs, Greater Roxbury Devel. Corp., 1970; mem. U.S. Commn. for UNESCO, Washington, 1960-66. Author: The Cameroon Federation, 1970, (with Vivian R. Johnson) West African Governments and Volunteer Development Organizations, 1990; contbr. articles to Daedalus, 1973-82; New Eng. dir. Jour. African Civilizations, 1979-82, Jour. Modern African Studies, 1983; mem. editorial bd. Africa Today, 1975—. Bd. dirs. TransAfrica and TransAfrica Forum, Washington, 1978-95, chmn., 1984-86, pres. Boston chpt., 1980-84, 89-90; chmn. Africa Policy Task Force, McGovern for Pres. campaign, 1972; sr. adv. bd. Boston Pan-African Forum, Inc., 1997—. Recipient M.L. King Jr. award MIT Pres.'s Office, 1982—, YMCA Black Achiever's award, 1988; fellow and grantee Ford Found.; grantee Social Sci. Research Council, 1975, Rockefeller Found., 1977; Fulbright grantee, 1987; resident fellow Rockefeller Study Ctr., Bellagio, Italy, Sept. 1987; Fulbright scholar Indonesia, summer 1991. Mem. Coun. Fgn. Rels., Assn. Concerned African Scholars (bd. dirs. 1977—, nat. co-chmn. 1984-89), African Studies Assn., Nat. Conf. of Black Polit. Scientists. Democrat. Baptist. Office: MIT Dept Polit Sci 30 Wadsworth St Cambridge MA 02142-1320 *I believe that personal and social health is based on responsible engagement, creative action, reflective credulity, disciplined energy, and mutual respect.*

JOHNSON, WILLIAM A., JR., mayor. BA in Polit. Sci., Howard U., MA in Polit. Sci.; LHD (hon.), Keuka Coll., 1990. Instr. polit. sci. C.S. Mott C.C., Flint, Mich., 1967; dep. exec. dir. Urban League of Flint, 1971; pres.,

CEO Urban League of Rochester, N.Y., 1972-93; mayor City of Rochester, N.Y., 1994—; spkr. in field. Recipient Disting. Minett Prof. award RIT Coll. Continuing Edn., 1993-94. Office: Office of the Mayor 307A City Hall 30 Church St Rochester NY 14614-1206*

JOHNSON, WILLIAM ALEXANDER, clergyman, philosophy educator; b. Bklyn., Aug. 20, 1934; s. Charles Raphael and Ruth Augusta (Anderson) J.; m. Carol Genevieve Lundquist, June 11, 1955; children—Karin Ruth, Karl William, Krister Frederick. B.A., Queens Coll., City U. N.Y., 1953; B.D. (Univ. fellow, Morrow Meml. fellow, Daniel Delaplaine fellow), Union Theol. Sem., 1956; Teol. Kand., Lund U., 1957, Teol. Lic., 1958, Teologie Doktor, 1962; M.A., Columbia U., 1958, Ph.D. (Univ. fellow, Rockefeller Bros. fellow), 1959. Ordained deacon Meth. Ch., 1955, priest Episcopal Ch., 1968. Profl. baseball player N.Y. Giants, 1949-51; dir. Boys Club, Salvation Army, Jamaica, N.Y., 1952-54; minister Mt. Hope and Teabo Meth. chs., Wharton, N.J., 1954-56; elder Meth. Ch., 1956; minister Immanuel and Union Meth. chs., Bklyn., 1957-59; asst. in instrn. Columbia U., N.Y.C., 1957, Union Theol. Sem., N.Y.C., 1958; instr., asst. prof. religion Trinity Coll., Hartford, Conn., 1959-63; lectr. philosophy and theology Hartford Sem. Found., 1961-62; assoc. prof. religion, chmn. dept. religion Drew U., Madison, N.J., 1963-66; research prof. religion NYU, N.Y.C., 1966; vis. lectr. Union Theol. Sem., N.Y.C., 1966; vis. prof. religion Princeton (N.J.) U., 1966-68; prof., chmn. dept. religion Manhattanville Coll., Purchase, N.Y., 1967-71; vis. prof. Christian ethics Gen. Theol. Sem., N.Y.C., 1970; Albert V. Danielsen prof. Christian thought, prof. philosophy and history of ideas Brandeis U., Waltham, Mass., 1971—, prof. Near Ea. and Jewish studies, 1988—; canon residentiary Cathedral Ch. of St. John The Divine, N.Y.C., 1973—; vis. Prof. Protestant theology N.Am. Coll., Vatican City, 1969-75; vis. prof., Tokyo, Stockholm, 1979, U. Gothenburg, Sweden, 1979, U. Copenhagen, 1994-95, Univ. Perth, Australia, 1997; examining chaplain Diocese of Arctic, 1982; lectr., Europe, Asia, Africa, S.Am., Australia, Caribbean, Arctic. Author: The Philosophy of Religion of Anders Nygren, 1958, Christopher Polhem: The Father of Swedish Technology, 1963, Nature and the Supernatural in the Theology of Horace Bushnell, 1963, On Religion: A Study of Theological Method in Schleiermacher and Nygren, 1964, Problems in Christian Ethics, 1965 (with Nels F.S. Ferré) Swedish Contributions to Modern Theology, 1966, The Search for Transcendence, 1974, The Christian Way of Death, 1974, Invitation to Theology, 1979, Philosophy and the Gospel, 1979, (with Moorhead Kennedy) Christianity and Terrorism, 1986, O Boundless Salvation, 1987; also articles; debut as Popolo in Aida, Met. Opera, 1989, Tosca, 1990, La Boheme, 1992. Democratic committeeman Hartford, 1960-63; mem. exec. com. Am. Friends Service Com., Coll. Div., 1966-70; bd. dirs. Queens Coll. CUNY; priest-in-charge Korean Episc. Ch., N.Y.C., 1992—. Recipient David F. Swenson-Kierkegaard Meml. award, 1964, Harbison award for Tchr. of Yr. Danforth Found., 1965; named Outstanding Young Man in Am. Jr. C. of C., 1964; Disting. Alumnus Queens Coll., 1980; Scandinavian-Am. Found. fellow, 1956, 85; Fulbright scholar U. Copenhagen, 1957-58; Dempster Grad. fellow Meth. Ch., 1958; Am. Philos. Soc. fellow, 1971, 85. vis. rsch. fellow Princeton, 1972; Guggenheim fellow for study in Rome, Italy, 1972; NSF grantee, 1978; Rockefeller fellow Aspen Inst., 1978, fellow Aspen Inst., Jerusalem, 1982; Nat. Endowment Humanities grantee, 1978, 86; grantee Arthur Vining Davis Found., 1981; grantee Trinity Ch. of N.Y.C., 1982, 84; grantee Tauber Inst. Study of European Jewry; named All-Am. Baseball Player, Amateur Athletic Assn., 1952, 53, All-Am. Soccer Player, Amateur Athletic Assn., 1953. Mem. Am. Acad. Religion, Asia Soc., Japan Soc., Scandinavian-Am. Heritage Soc., Am. Philos. Assn., Danforth Assos., Soc. for Sci. Study Religion, Soc. for Religion in Higher Edn. (Kent fellow 1959), Soc. Anglican Theologians, Vasa Order Am., Am. Soc. Christian Ethics, Swedish Pioneer Hist. Soc., Soc. for Scandinavian Study, Danish-Am. Soc., Australian Am. Soc., Willa Cather Pioneer Meml. Found., Authors Guild, Episcopal Churchmen for S.Africa, New Haven Theol. Group, Westchester Inst. Psychiatry and Psychoanalysis (dir.), Ecumenical Found. for Christian Ministry, English Speaking Union, Ch. Soc. for Coll. Work, Paris Am. Club, Columbia University Club, Met. Opera Club, The Pilgrims, The Coffee House, Lotos Club, Century Club, Explorer's Club, Phi Beta Kappa, Pi Gamma Mu, Phi Sigma Tau. Democrat. Episcopalian. Home: 27 Fox Meadow Rd Scarsdale NY 10583-2903 also: 44 Pascal Ave Rockport ME 04856-5918 Office: Brandeis U Rabb Grad Ctr Waltham MA 02154 *I have attempted in my life to fulfill the simple prayer of St. Francis: Lord, make me an instrument of your peace/Where there is hatred . . . let me sow love/Where there is injury . . . pardon/Where there is doubt . . . faith/Where there is despair . . . hope/Where there is darkness . . . light/Where there is sadness . . . joy. For it is giving that we receive; it is pardoning that we are pardoned; and it is dying that we are born to eternal life.*

JOHNSON, WILLIAM DAVID, retired university administrator; b. Bloomington, Ind., Aug. 9, 1924; s, Ben and Ida Grace (Garlock) J.; m. Audrey Aelise Thurston; 1 child, Sheryn Aelise Johnson Peters. B.S., Ind. U., 1946. Asst. bursar U. Va., Charlottesville, 1947-54; comptroller George Washington U., 1954-69, dir. planning and budgeting, 1969-82, assoc. provost, 1982-84, provost, 1984-89. Served to 1st lt. U.S. Army, 1943-46; ETO. Mem. Fin. Exec. Inst. (chpt. pres. 1969-70), Eastern Assn. Coll. and Univ. Bus. Officers, Nat. Assn. Coll. and Univ. Bus. Officers, Omicron Delta Kappa, Delta Chi. Republican. Presbyterian. Avocations: woodworking; golf; skeet shooting. Home: 500 Ivy Cir Alexandria VA 22302-4001

JOHNSON, WILLIAM DEAN, power company executive; b. Pa., Jan. 9, 1954. BA, Duke U., 1978; JD, U. N.C., 1982. Law clk. Hon. J.D. Philips Jr., U.S. Ct. Appeals, 4th Cir., 1982-83; assoc. Hunton & Williams, 1983-90, ptnr., 1990-92; assoc. gen. counsel Carolina Power & Light, Raleigh, 1992-95, v.p., corp. sec., 1995—. Mem. ABA, N.C. Bar Assn. Office: Carolina Power & Light Co 411 Fayetteville Street Mall Raleigh NC 27601-1748*

JOHNSON, WILLIAM HARRY, international management consultant; b. Ridley Park, Pa., Oct. 1, 1941; s. Harry Brown and Florence Lydia (Round) J.; m. Anna Marie Castellanos, Oct. 19, 1984. BS, Drexel U., Phila., 1963; MBA, Drexel U., 1967. Mgmt. exec. DuPont Co., Wilmington, Del., 1963-69; bus. analysis mgr. Imperial Chem. Ind., Wilmington, 1970-76; mgr. analysis and acquisitions Fluor Daniel Corp., Irvine, Calif., 1976-78; fin. analysis mgr. Alexander Proudfoot, Chgo., 1978-79; exec. v.p., chief fin. officer Sego Internat., Niagara Falls, Ont., Can., 1980-82; exec. v.p., gen. mgr. Sci. Mgmt. Corp., Basking Ridge, N.J., 1982-87; exec. mgr. Boeing, Long Beach, Calif., 1987—; bd. dirs. A.M.T. Inc., Pierrefonds, Que., Can., CRA, Inc., Clariton, Pa., Madden Assocs., Buffalo Grove, Ill., KABB Inc., El Segundo, Calif., Sego Internat., Productivity Cons., Inc., Montreal, Commonwealth Cos., London. Author: Explosives Distributors, 1967, Maintenance Productivity - It Can Be Achieved, 1988, Facilities Work Order Guide, 1989, Participative Management in Facilities Operations, 1991, Productivity Expectations with International Business, 1993; contbr. articles to profl. jours. Mem. Rep. Nat. Com., Washington, El Segundo Residents Assn. Recipient Aerospace Quality Achievement award McDonnell Douglas, 1997, Presdl. Achievement award, Rep. Nat. Com., 1988, Outstanding Achievement award, Sego Internat., 1981. Mem. Inst. Indsl. Engrs., Am. Mgmt. Assn., Nat. Productivity Assn. of Can. (dir. 1980-95), Nat. Assn. Accts., Nat. Petroleum Refinery Assn., Am. Mktg. Assn., Internat. Productivity Orgn., Drexel U. Alumni Assn. (bd. dirs.), Highlander Clan, Lions (Kowloon, Hong Kong), K & C Clans Assn. (Hong Kong), Internat. Bus. Assocs. (Sydney, Australia). Republican. Presbyterian. Avocations: dogs, international traveling, tennis, swimming. Home: 807 Hillcrest St El Segundo CA 90245-2025 Office: Boeing Airlift & Tankers Program Mail Code C078-0317 2401 E Wardlow Rd Long Beach CA 90807-5309

JOHNSON, WILLIAM HOWARD, agricultural engineer, educator; b. Sidney, Ohio, Sept. 3, 1922; s. Russell Earl and Dollie (Gamble) J.; m. Wyoma Jean Swift, Oct. 2, 1943; children: Lawrence Alan, Cheri Ellen, Dana Sue. B.S., Ohio State U., 1948, M.S., 1953; Ph.D., Mich. State U., 1960. Registered profl. engr. Mem. faculty Ohio Agrl. Expt. Sta., Wooster, 1948-64; mem. faculty Ohio Agrl. Research and Devel. Center, Wooster, 1964-70; prof., asso. chmn. dept. agrl. engring. Ohio Agrl. Research and Devel. Center, 1959-70; part-time prof. Ohio State U., 1964-70; prof., head dept. agrl. engring. Kans. State U., Manhattan, 1970-81; dir. Engring. Experiment Sta. Kans. State U., 1981-87; cons. farm equipment cos. Author: (with B.J. Lamp) Principles, Equipment and Systems for Corn Harvesting, 1966; also articles. Recipient Distinguished Alumnus award Coll. Engring., Ohio State U., 1974; named to Coll. Engring. Kans. State U. Hall of Fame, 1992; recipient Cyrus Hall McCormick-Jerome Increase Case medal Am. Society of Agricultural Engineers, 1994. Fellow Am. Soc. Agrl. Engrs. (pres. 1986-87, McCormick-Case Gold Medal award 1994), Kans. Engring. Soc. (pres. 1985-86), Sigma Xi, Tau Beta Pi. Achievements include research on soil-plant-machine relationships, harvesting, design for soiltillers, planters, harvesters. Home: 1532 Williamsburg Manhattan KS 66502-0408 Office: Kans State Univ Dept Agrl Engring Seaton Hall Manhattan KS 66506

JOHNSON, WILLIAM HUGH, JR., state official, hospital administrator; b. N.Y.C., Oct. 29, 1935; s. William H. and Florence P. (Seinsoth) J.; m. Gloria C. Stube., Jan. 23, 1960; children: Karen A., William H. III. BA, Hofstra U., 1957; MEd, U. Hawaii, 1969. Commd. 2d lt. U.S. Army, 1957, advanced through grades to lt. col., 1972, health adminstr., world wide, 1957-77, health adminstr., world wide, ret., 1977; CEO U. N. Mex. Hosp., Albuquerque, 1977-97; asst. prof. U.S. Mil. Acad., West Point, N.Y., 1962-65; mem. clin. faculty U. Minn., Mpls., 1980-83; preceptor Ariz. State U., Tempe, 1982-83; pres. Albuquerque Area Hosp. Coun., 1980; v.p. strategic alliances U. N.Mex. Health Scis. Ctr.; adminstr. Horizon Splty. Hosp., Albuquerque, 1997; adj. prof. cabinet sec. N. Mex. Dept Human Svcs., Santa Fe, 1997-99; bd. dirs. Bank Am. of N.Mex., Tri West, Inc.; sec. human svcs. State N.Mex., 1997-98; adj. prof. U. N.Mex., 1999. Mem. exec. bd. Albuquerque Com. on Devel.; v.p. Vis. Nurse Svc., Albuquerque, 1979; pres. Magnifico Arts Fiesta; bd. dirs. ACCION (Microlender), 1999, Goodwill N.Mex., bd. dirs. Albuquerque Conv. and Visitors Bur., mem. exec. com., 1994—, chmn., 1997-98. Decorated Army Commendation Medal with 2 oak leaf clusters, Order of Merit (Rep. of Vietnam), Legion of Merit. Mem. Am. Hosp. Assn. (governing bd. met. hosp. sect. 1982-86, chmn. com. AIDS, mem. regional policy bd. 1982-86, 88—), Am. Coll. Hosp. Adminstrs., Coun. Tchg. Hosps. (bd. dirs.), N.Mex. Hosp. Assn. (bd. dirs. 1983, chmn. 1995—), Nat. Assn. Pub. Hosps. (bd. dirs. Tri West Inc., Vita S.W.), Greater Albuquerque C. of C. (bd. dirs., econ. planning coun., v.p.), N.Mex. Assn. Commerce and Industry (treas.). Roman Catholic. Home: 7920 Sartan Way NE Albuquerque NM 87109-3128 Office: NMex Dept Human Svcs Bolton Plz 2009 S Pacheco St Santa Fe NM 87505-5473

JOHNSON, WILLIAM JENNINGS, marketing consultant, entrepreneur, estate planner; b. Sioux Falls, S.D., Sept. 16, 1955; s. Jennings Pearson and Donna E. (Kelley) J.; m. Suzanne Reando, Mar. 8, 1980; children: Krista Marie, Daniel William. BSBA, Black Hills State U., 1978. Salesman Met. Life, Rapid City, S.D., 1978-79, EMSCO Industries, Rapid City, 1979-80; salesman, pres., founder, chmn. Diversified Fin. Svcs., Inc., Rapid City, 1981—; co-owner Sibco Inc., Rapid City, 1984—; pres., co-founder Success Inc., Rapid City, 1991—; guest authority spkr. Paul Strassels Radio Talk Show Annuities, 1990; mktg. cons. Control Tech. Internat., Rapid City, 1994; group conf. mktg. facilitator S.D. Bus. 20, 1994. Co-author: (sales tng. guide) Moneytalks, 1991. Active Rimrock Evang. Free Ch. Recipient cert. merit S.D. SBA, 1978, Key Club Desting. Sales award Keystone Mass Distbrs., Inc., Boston, 1983, Million Dollar Premium Prodr. award Am. Investors Life Ins., Topeka, 1988, Chmn.'s Club award Life USA Ins. Co., Mpls., 1989, 90, 91, 92, 93, Nat. Sales Achievement award Nat. Assn. Life Underwriters, 1992; named Million Dollar Round Table Ct. of the Table, 1992, 97, 98. Mem. Million Dollar Round Table. Republican. Avocations: golf, fishing, reading. Office: Diversified Fin Svcs Inc 1508 Mt View Rd Ste 101 Rapid City SD 57702-4349

JOHNSON, WILLIAM POTTER, newspaper publisher; b. Peoria, Ill., May 4, 1935; s. William Zweigle and Helen Marr (Potter) J.; m. Pauline Ruth Rowe, May 18, 1968; children: Darragh Elizabeth, William Potter. AB, U. Mich., 1957. Gen. mgr. Bureau County Rep., Inc., Princeton, Ill., 1961-72; pres. Johnson Newspapers, Inc., Sebastopol, Calif., 1972-75, Evergreen, Colo., 1974-86, Canyon Commons Investment, Evergreen, 1974—; pres. Johnson Media, Inc., Granby, Colo., 1987—. Author: How the Michigan Betas Built a $1,000,000 Chapter House in the '80s. Alt. del. Rep. Nat. Conv., 1968. Lt. USNR, 1958-61. Mem. Colo. Press Assn., Nat. Newspaper Assn., Maple Bluff Country Club, Madison Club, Bishops Bay Country Club, Bal Harbour Club, Beta Theta Pi. Home: 5302 Lighthouse Bay Dr Madison WI 53704-1114 Office: PO Box 409 Granby CO 80446-0409

JOHNSON, WILLIAM R., state supreme court justice; b. Oct. 21, 1930; married; 2 children. Student, Dartmouth Coll., Harvard U. Pvt. practice law Hanover; state senator N.H. Gen. Assembly, Concord, state rep.; judge N.H. Superior Ct., Concord, 1969-85; assoc. judge N.H. Supreme Ct., Concord, 1985—; instr. law Dartmouth Coll., Hanover. Office: NH Supreme Ct One Noble Dr Concord NH 03301*

JOHNSON, WILLIAM RAY, insurance company executive; b. West Union, Ohio, Feb. 12, 1930; s. A. Earl and Helen (Walker) J.; m. Anne Abrams, Mar. 27, 1954; children: Elizabeth Anne, William Randall. BS in Edn., Wilmington Coll., 1951. Tchr., theatre dept. Miami U., Oxford, Ohio, 1951; divsn. mgr. Prudential Ins. Co. of Am., Waco, Tex., 1956-60; nat. tng. cons., gen. agt. Paul Revere Life Ins. Co., Dallas, 1960-65; health and accident ins. cons. Dallas, 1965-68; ptnr. Wiedemann & Johnson, Cos., Dallas, 1965-93; mem. exec. com. Cullen Frost Bank, Dallas, 1986-94, mem. trust com., 1986-94, chmn. 1991-94; bd. dirs. Gulles Frost Bank, Dallas, 1986-94. Bd. dirs. Suicide Prevention of Dallas, 1973-81, pres. 1975-76; bd. dirs. Routh St. Ctr., 1975-78, Turtle Creek Manor, 1977-79, Sr. Citizens of Greater Dallas, Inc., 1977-81, Dallas Child Guidance Clinic, 1977-83; mem. Bishops Adv. Com. on Planning and Devel., Episcopal Diocese of Dallas, 1976-81; sr. warden St. Michael's Episcopal Ch., 1979-81; trustee Episcopal Theol. Sem. of SW, Austin, Tex., 1981-87, mem. exec. com., 1984-86; mem. bd. theol. edn. Episcopal Ch., N.Y.C., 1982-88; mem. exec. coun. Episcopal Diocese of Dallas, 1983-86, standing com., 1987-90; trustee St. Michael Sch., 1989-91, Greater Dallas Community of Chs., 1986-89, mem. exec. com. 1987-88. Served to 1st lt. USAF, 1951-55. Mem. Multiple Sclerosis Soc. (bd. dirs. N. Texas Divsn. 1987-89), Anglican Sch. Theology (bd. trustees 1986-89, 98—, chmn. 1988-89), Dallas Country Club.

JOHNSON, WILLIAM S., financial planning company executive, educator; b. Elmhurst, Ill., May 11, 1957; s. Raymond J. and Nancy A. (Zinns) J.; m. Lisa Ann Grundy, July 14, 1990; 1 child, William Chase. BS in Bus. and Acctg., Ind. U., 1979; MBA in Fin., Mercer U., 1986. CPA, Calif.; CFP. Auditor, sr. auditor Ernst & Young, CPA's, Indpls., 1979-80; various fin. and acctg. positions Am. Hosp. Supply Co., Evanston, Ill., 1980-86; v.p. fin., dir. acctg. Abbey Med./Beaverbrook Group, Costa Mesa, Calif., 1987-91; corp. fin. mgr. Severin Group, Ivrine, Calif., 1991-94; corp. contr., CFO, Earle M. Jorgensen Co., Brea, Calif., 1994—; mem. adj. faculty U. Phoenix, Fountain Valley, Calif., 1998—. Mem. AICPA, Calif. Soc. CPA's, Inst. CFP's. Home: 116 Via Yella Newport Beach CA 92663-5537*

JOHNSON, WILLIAM W., dental educator; b. Monroe, Wis., Jan. 31, 1952; s. Herbert T. and Edna (Goecks) J.; m. Veronica A. Hartman, Aug. 4, 1973. DDS, Marquette U., 1977, MS, 1989. Pvt. dental practice Lancaster, Wis., 1977-79, Monroe, Wis., 1979-90; assoc. prof. U. Tenn., Memphis, 1990-97, Minn. State U., Mankato, 1997—; adj. asst. prof. Marquette U., Milw., 1989—, chmn. and assoc. prof. Minn. State U., Mankato, 1997—. Contbr. articles to profl. jours. Pres. faculty orgn. U. Tenn. Coll. of Dentistry, memphis, 1994-95. Mem. Wis. Dental Assn. (rep. to mem. svcs. divsn. 1985-90), Green CountyDental Soc. (pres. 1985-88), Am. Assn. Dental Schs., Am. Dental Assn., Acad. Gen. Dentistry, Acad. Operative Dentistry, Chgo. Dental Soc., Internat. Assn. Dental Rsch., memphis Dental Soc., Tenn. Dental Assn., Omicron Kappa Upsilon, Alpha Sigma Nu. Office: Minn State Univ Dept Dental Hygiene 3 Morris Hall Mankato MN 56001

JOHNSON, WILLIE SPOON, quality management consultant; b. Burlington, N.C., Apr. 14, 1943; d. William Luther and Ruth Viola (Baldwin) Spoon; m. Mark C. Johnson, Feb. 25, 1967; 1 child, Christy. Diploma in nursing, Watts Hosp. Sch. Nursing, Durham, N.C., 1964; BS, Pheiffer Coll., Misenheimer, N.C., 1971; MPH, U. N.C., 1983. RN, N.C., S.C., Calif.; cert. profl.in healthcare quality. Staff nurse med.-surg. Wesley Long Hosp., Greensboro, N.C., 1964-66; pub. health nurse Guilford County Health Dept., Greensboro, 1966-68; staff nurse ARC, L.A., 1967-68; pub. health nurse Health Dept., Sanford and Albemarle, N.C., 1968-72; dir. practical nurse edn. Sandhills C.C., Carthage, N.C., 1971-77; quality assurance/DRG coord. Humana Hosp. Greensboro, 1977-88; dir. quality mgmt. Women's Hosp. Greensboro, 1988-98; pvt. practice Oak Ridge, N.C., 1998—; mem. utilization rev. bd. Upjohn Health Care, Greensboro, 1980-92; cons. Quality Mgmt. Resources, Duluth, Ga., 1993—. Bd. mem. Health System Agy., 1976-77. Mem. Nat. Assn. Healthcare Quality (N.C. del. 1991, 93), Am. Soc. Healthcare Risk Mgmt., Healthcare Quality Certification Bd. (bd. mem. region III rep. 1993-96, sec.-treas. 1995-96), N.C. Assn. Healthcare Quality (bd. mem. 1989-94, co-chair edn. com. 1990-93). Lutheran. E-mail: m-wjohnson@worldnet.att.net. Fax: 336-664-0495. Home and Office: 4532 Peeples Rd Oak Ridge NC 27310-9763

JOHNSON, WYATT THOMAS, JR. (TOM JOHNSON), cable news executive; b. Macon, Ga., Sept. 30, 1941; s. Wyatt Thomas and Josephine Victoria (Brown) J.; m. Edwina Mac Chastain, Dec. 29, 1963; children: Wyatt Thomas III, Christa Johnson Shaffer. A.B. in Journalism, U. Ga., 1963; M.B.A., Harvard, 1965. Reporter, mgmt. trainee Macon Telegraph and News, 1957-65; White House fellow, 1965-66; asst. press sec. to Pres. U.S., 1966, dep. press sec., 1967; spl. asst. to Pres., 1968, exec. asst., 1969-70; exec. v.p., dir. Tex. Broadcasting Corp., Sta. KTBC-AM-FM-TV, Austin, 1970-73; exec. editor, v.p., dir. Dallas Times Herald, 1973-75, publisher, 1975-77; pres. Los Angeles Times, 1977-80, publisher, 1980-89, also chief exec. officer; vice chmn. Times Mirror Co., 1989-90; pres. CNN, Atlanta, 1990—; mem. Pres.'s Commn. on White House Fellows, 1979 ; pres. adv. bd. Henry W. Grady Sch. Journalism, 1974-75. Co-author: Automating Newspaper Composition, 1965. Bd. dirs. Mayo Found.; chmn. bd. Lyndon B. Johnson Found., John S. and James Knight Found. Named Nat. Man of Year Sigma Nu, 1962, Outstanding Young Man of Ga. Jr. C. of C., 1967, One of Five Outstanding Young Texans Tex. Jaycees, 1969, One of 10 Outstanding Men of U.S., 1975. Mem. Ga. Alumni Soc. (pres. 1979), Coun. on Fgn. Rels. N.Y., Sigma Nu. Office: CNN PO Box 105366 1 Cnn Center Plz Atlanta GA 30335-4200*

JOHNSON, YVONNE AMALIA, elementary education educator, science consultant; b. DeKalb, Ill., July 1, 1930; d. Albert O. and Virginia O. (Nelson) J. *Albert and Virginia spent their lifetimes farming. Albert's father returned to DeKalb after the Gold Rush. He homesteaded land which later became the family farm. Albert's mother was charter member of 1st Lutheran Church in DeKalb in 1858. Virginia's father was a blacksmith and made one of the first firewagons for DeKalb. Albert was a charter member of the DeKalb County Farm Bureau when it was established in 1912. Virginia did missionary work for Lutheran Church. Elaine, Yvonne's sister, was teacher and later worked in the poultry division of DeKalb Agricultural Association. Elaine's husband, Leo, was the communications director for DeKalb Agricultural Association and developed the company logo.* BS in Edn., No. Ill. State Tchrs. Coll., 1951; MS in Edn., No. Ill. U., 1960. Tchr. Love Rural Sch., DeKalb, 1951-53, West Elem. Sch., Sycamore, Ill., 1953—; Ill. honors sci. tchr., ISU, 1985-87. Contbr. articles to profl. publs. Bd. dirs. Sycamore Pub. Libr., 1974-98, pres. bd. dirs., 1984-98, chmn. maj. fund drive for addition to libr., 1994-98; founder Dekalb County Excellence in Edn. award, 1999. Named DeKalb County Conservation Tchr., 1971, Gov.'s Master Tchr., State of Ill., 1984, Outstanding Agrl. Tchr. in the Classroom Dekalb County Farm Bur., 1993; grantee NSF, 1961, 62, 85, 86, 87, NASA, 1988; Sci. Lit. grantee State of Ill., 1992-94. Mem. NEA, ASCD, NSTA (cert. in elem. sci.), Ill. Sci. Tchrs. Assn., Ill. Edn. Assn., Sycamore Edn. Assn., Coun. for Elem. Sci. Internat. Office: West Elem Sch 240 Fair St Sycamore IL 60178-1641

JOHNSON, ZANE QUENTIN, retired petroleum company executive; b. Bristow, Okla., Mar. 5, 1924; s. Sylvester B. and Meta B. (Biggs) J.; m. Nila Jean Caylor, June 4, 1949; children: Zane Quentin, Mark Caylor, Janis Lyn. B.S. in Chem. Engring, U. Okla., 1947. With Gulf Oil Corp. (and subs. cos.), from 1947; pres., chief operating officer Gen. Atomic, Inc., San Diego, 1969-70; exec. v.p. Gulf Oil Corp., Pitts., 1970-75; pres. Gulf Sci. & Tech. Co., Pitts., from 1975, now ret.; faculty Sch. Chem. Engring., U. Okla. Mayor, Port Arthur, Tex., 1957-58; bd. dirs. United Community Services of San Diego County, 1969-70, Boy Scouts Am., Duquesne U.; trustee Shadyside Hosp. Served to 1st lt. USAAF, PTO. Decorated Air medal with three oak leaf clusters; recipient U. Okla. Coll. Engring. Hall of Fame award. Mem. AIChE, Am. Petroleum Inst., Port Royal Club, Naples Yacht Club, Royal Poinciana Golf Club, Hound Ears Golf Club (Blowing Rock, N.C.). Republican. Presbyterian. Home: 8410 Abbington Cir # A-34 Naples FL 34108-7733

JOHNSON-BROWN, HAZEL WINFRED, nurse, retired army officer; b. West Chester, Pa., Oct. 10, 1927; d. Clarence Lemont and Garnett (Henley) J. RN diploma, Harlem Hosp., N.Y.C., 1950; BSN, Villanova U., 1959; MSN, Tchr.'s Coll., Columbia U., 1963; PhD in Ednl. Adminstrn., Cath. U. Am., 1978. 1st lt. U.S. Army Nurse Corps, 1955, advanced through grades to brig. gen., 1979; mem. staff U.S. Army Med. R&D Command, Washington, 1967-73; dir. Walter Reed Army Inst. Nursing, Washington, 1976-78; asst. for nursing Office of Surgeon Med. Command, Korea, 1978-79; chief Army Nurse Corps Office of Surgeon Gen. Dept. of the Army, Washington, 1983-86; dir. govtl. affairs office Am. Nurses Assn., 1986-96; prof. Coll. Nursing and Health Sci. George Mason U., 1989-96; dir. Ctr. for Health Policy George Mason U., 1996—; cons. Nursing Edn. Health Policy, Health Adminstrn. Decorated Disting. Svc. medal, Legion of merit, Meritorious Svc. medal, Army Commendation medal; recipient Evangeline G. Bovard Army Nurse of Yr. award Letterman Army Med. Ctr., San Francisco, 1964, Dr. Anita Newcomb McGee award DAR, Washington, 1971. Mem. Assn. Balck Nursing Faculty, Black Women United for Action, Assn. U.S. Army, Nat. Assn. Military Family, Am. Nurses Assn., Nat. League Nursing, Sigma Theta Tau.

JOHNSON-CHAMP, DEBRA SUE, lawyer, educator, writer, artist; b. Emporia, Kans., Nov. 8, 1955; d. Bert John and S. Christine (Brigman) Johnson; m. Michael W. Champ, Nov. 23, 1979; children: Natalie, John. BA, U. Denver, 1977; JD, Pepperdine U., 1980; postgrad., U. So. Calif., 1983-84. Bar: Calif. 1981. Pvt. practice Long Beach, Calif., 1981-82, L.A., 1981-87, Woodland Hills, Calif., 1993-99; of counsel Greenbaum & Champ, 1999—; legal reference librarian, instr. Southwestern U. Sch. Law, L.A., 1982-88; adj. prof. law, 1987-88; atty. Contos & Bunch, Woodland Hills, 1988-93; free lance writer/artist; owner The Purple Iguana, 1997—. Editor-in chief: Southern Calif. Assn. Law Libraries Newsletter, 1984-85; mem. law rev. Pepperdine U., 1978-80; contbr. articles to profl. jours. Trustee United Meth. Ch., Tujunga, Calif., 1986-88. West Pub. Co. scholar, 1983; recipient H. Wayne Gillis Moot Ct. award, 1980, Vincent S. Dalsimer Best Brief award 1979. Mem. ABA, So. Calif. Assn. Law Libr., Am. Assn. Law Libr., Calif. Bar Assn., Southwestern Affiliates, Friends of the Libr. L.A. Democrat. Home and Office: 5740 Valerie Ave Woodland Hills CA 91367-3967

JOHNSON MACDOWELL, TINA, elementary education educator; b. Denver, Apr. 2, 1947; d. Ernest Harold and Hildegard (Kranefeld) J. BA, Trinity U., San Antonio, 1969; MA, U. Colo., 1980. Colo. profl. tchr. license. Tchr. Jefferson County Schs., Arvada, Colo., 1969-98; retired, 1998; mem. master tchr. program Jefferson County Schs., Arvada, 1982-85, mem. peer coaching program, 1984-85, mentor tchr. induction program, 1996; off campus coll. instr. Colo. State U., Arvada, 1992—. Co-author: Around the World in 180 School Days, 1994, Geography Too, 1994. Active Holy Cross Luth. Ch., Wheatridge, Colo., 1958—. Recipient Honorable Mention Colo. Tchr. of Yr., Colo. Dept. Edn. and Colo. State Bd. Edn., 1985; Colo. Venture grantee Jefferson Found., 1990-91; Delta Kappa Action Rsch. grantee for geography, 1990-91. Mem. NEA, Colo. Edn. Assn., Jefferson County Edn. Assn., Colo. Geog. Alliance, Delta Kappa Gamma, Phi Delta Kappa. Avocations: traveling, bicycling, gardening, gourmet cooking. Home: 130 Lake St Dallas PA 18612-1015

JOHNSON VELAZCO, NANCY RUTH, marketing professional; b. Phila., Feb. 4, 1948; d. Samuel Blaine and Ruth Dorothy (Carpenter) Johnson; m. Julio Horacio Velazco, Dec. 6, 1982 (div. Oct. 1984); 1 child, Cristine. BA in Spanish, Ursinus Coll., Collegeville, Pa., 1970; MA in Spanish, Villlanova U., 1974; MBA, U. Pa., 1978. Secondary tchr. Spanish, William Penn Sch. Dist., Lansdowne, Pa., 1970-76; indsl. rsch. analyst indsl. rsch. unit Wharton Sch., U. Pa., Phila., 1976-78; sales rep. pharms. Eli Lilly & Co., Providence, 1978-79; market rsch. analyst Eli Lilly & Co., Indpls., 1979-80; mktg. mgr. Eli Lilly & Co., Buenos Aires, 1980-82; Intron product mgr., bus. devel. mgr. Schering Plough Corp., Miami, Fla., 1983-84, regional mktg. dir. for L.Am., 1984-89; dir. respiratory, dermatology and antifungals Schering Plough Corp., Kenilworth, N.J., 1989-90, sr. mktg. dir. global mktg., 1991—.

Author: The Political, Economic and Labor Climates in Mexico, 1977, The Political, Economic and Labor Climates in Peru, 1978. Chmn. party events Children's Specialized Hosp., Mountainside, N.J., 1994—. Mem. Nat. Soc. DAR (treas. Westfield chpt. 1995—). Republican. Home: 727 Glen Ave Westfield NJ 07090-4326 Office: Schering-Plough Corp 2000 Galloping Hill Rd Kenilworth NJ 07033-1328

JOHNSSON, HILLARY CRUTE, soloist, opera singer; b. N.Y.C., Apr. 12, 1959; d. Samuel and Helena A. (Barker) Johnson; m. Reginald Crute, Sept. 11, 1989. Student, Am. Inst. Music, Graz, Austria, 1978, 79; BFA, CCNY, 1979; student, Mozarteum, Salzburg, Austria, 1981, Met. Opera Young Artists Program, N.Y.C., 1984-87. Opera singer Opera Ebony, Opera North, Phila., 1982, Memphis Opera, 1986, Little Orch. Soc., N.Y.C., 1987, Opera Orch. N.Y., N.Y.C., 1987, N.J. State Opera, Newark, 1984, N.J. Lyric Opera Co., Trenton, 1985, El Paso (Tex.) Symphony Orch., 1987, Chgo. Symphony, 1986, 87, Met. Opera Co., N.Y.C., 1985—, World Premiere and Am. Premiere Dvorah by Paul Schoenfield, 1998, Haifa Symphony, 1998, Nat. Symphony, 1998; adjudicator Leontyne Price Vocal Arts Competition, 1991, 93, 94, 95. Soloist Salzburg (Austria) Festival, 1995, Grace Bumbry Black Music Vocal Ensemble, 1994—, Bregenzer Festspiele, 1998; recorded: (Am. opera) Eventide, Joseph Fennimore; world premiere D'Vorah, Haifa, Israel, 1998, Am. premiere, Washington, 1998. Recipient awards Liederkranz Found., N.Y.C., 1983, Sullivan Found., N.Y.C., 1983, Leontyne Price Vocal Arts award, Negro Bus. and Profl. Women, Washington, 1988, Bregenz Summer Festival, 1997, 1st Pl. award Amato Opera Assn., N.Y.C., 1984. Mem. Am. Guild Mus. Artists. Democrat. Office: Met Opera House Lincoln Ctr New York NY 10023

JOHNSTON, BERNARD FOX, author, foundation executive; b. Taft, Calif., Nov. 19, 1934; s. Bernard Lowe and Georgia Victoria (Fox) J.; m. Audrey Rhoades, June 9, 1956 (div. Sept. 1963); 1 child, Sheldon Bernard. BA in Creative Arts, San Francisco State U., 1957, MA in World Lit., 1958. Lectr. philosophy Coll. of Marin, Kentfield, Calif., 1957-58; lectr. humanities San Francisco State U., 1957-58, 67-68; instr. English Contra Costa Coll., San Pablo, Calif., 1958-63; Knowles Found. philosophy fellow, 1962; fellow Syracuse (N.Y.) U., 1964-66; freelance writer Piedmont, Calif., 1968-77; pres. Cinema Repertory, Inc., Point Richmond, Calif., 1978-89; pres., exec. dir. Athena Found., Tiburon-Truckee, Calif., 1990—; exec. prodr. (TV series) The Heroes of Time, (TV documentary) The Shudder of Awe; CEO The Athena Found., Inc., 1997, Mahler Festival, U. Colo., Boulder, 1998. Author: (screenplay) Point Exeter, 1979, Ascent Allowed, 1988 (award); author, editor: Issues in Education: An Anthology of Controversy, 1964, The Literature of Learning, 1971; festival pianist Lake Tahoe Internat. Film Festival, 1998; resident pianist Tahoe-Chrysler Corp., 1998. Arts grantee Silicon Valley Community Found., 1998. Mem. Dirs. Guild Am., Writers Guild Am., Coun. for Basic Edn., Wilson Ctr. Assocs., Assn. Lit. Scholars and Critics, Smithsonian Instn., Donner Land Trust, Nat. Assn. Scholars, Calif. Assn. Scholars, San Francisco State Alumni Assn., Commonwealth Club of Calif. Avocations: classical piano, backpacking, softball. Office: Athena Found 11679 Mougle Ln Truckee CA 96161-6117

JOHNSTON, BETTY, writer; b. El Paso, Tex., Sept. 19, 1925; d. Robert Blaine and Mary Augusta (Schmidt) Anderson; m. E.M. Johnston, Mar. 18, 1956; stepchildren: Jess, Mark. BA, U. Ariz., 1947. Copywriter Radio Sta. KOPO, Tucson, 1947-49, San Francisco, 1949-50; sales copy writer Sta. K60-TV, San Francisco, 1950-52; dir. advt. and publicity Paramount Picture Theatres Corp., L.A., 1952-57; writer, office mgr., casting dir. Flagg Films, L.A., 1957-62; lifestyle editor Laguna Beach (Calif.) News Post, 1967-70; reporter, editor The Vista (Calif.) Press, 1970-86; Village Life editor The Enterprise, Fallbrook, Calif., 1986-91, editor, 1991-96; zone editor N.C. Times, San Diego, 1995-96; writer, columnist North County Times, 1996—. Mem. Friends of Fallbrook Libr., Fallbrook Hist. Soc., Angel Soc. Republican. Office: Fallbrook Enterprise Bldg 232 S Main St Fallbrook CA 92028-2850

JOHNSTON, BRUCE FOSTER, economics educator; b. Lincoln, Nebr., Sept. 24, 1919; s. Homer Klotz and Ethel Matilda (Hockett) J.; m. Harriet L. Pollins, Mar. 31, 1944; children—Bruce C., Patricia C. B.A., Cornell U., 1941; M.A., Stanford U., 1950, Ph.D., 1953. Agrl. mktg. adminstr. Dept. Agr., 1941-42; chief food br. econ. and sci. sect. SCAP, Tokyo, 1945-48; agrl. economist Food and Agr. div. U.S. Mission to NATO and European Regional Orgn., Paris, 1952-54; assoc. prof. econs., assoc. economist Food Research Inst., Stanford U., Calif., 1954-59, prof. econs., economist, 1959—; cons. World Bank, FAO, others. Author: (with Tomich and Kilby) Transforming Agrarian Economies: Opportunities Seized, Opportunities Missed, 1995, (with Clark) Redesigning Rural Development: A Strategic Perspective, 1982, (with Anthony, Jones and Uchendu) Agricultural Change in Tropical Africa, 1979, (with Kilby) Agriculture and Structural Transformation: Economic Strategies in Late-Developing Countries, 1975; co-editor:, contbr.: (with Ohkawa and Kaneda) Agriculture and Economic Growth: Japan's Experience, 1969. Guggenheim fellow, 1962, Internat. Inst. Applied Systems Analysis fellow, 1978-79, Adminstr.'s fellow AID, 1991. Fellow Am. Agrl. Econs. Assn.; mem. Am. Econ. Assn., African Studies Assn., Phi Beta Kappa, Phi Kappa Phi. Home: 613 Walnut St Pacific Grove CA 93950-3932 Office: Stanford U Food Rsch Inst Stanford CA 94305

JOHNSTON, CAROLYN JUDITH, construction engineer; b. Atlanta, Nov. 24, 1961; d. Lynn H. and Doris S. (Lacy) J.; m. Paul William Miller, July 20, 1996. BS in Constrn. Mgmt., So. Tech. U., 1990; MS in Constrn. Mgmt., Clemson U., 1997. Cert. profl. constructor. Journeyman plumber Quality Mech., Norfolk, Va., 1984-86; asst. supt. R.G.Moore Bldg., Virginia Beach, Va., 1986-87; asst. field engr. Holder Constrn., Atlanta, 1987-89; clk. of works Sharondale Constrn., Atlanta, 1989-90; constrn. engr. Bechtel, Aiken, S.C., 1990-95; project engr. R.W. Allen & Assocs., Augusta, Ga., 1995-97; project mgr. York Internat., Aiken, S.C., 1997—. Nat. Assn. Women Constrn. scholar, Atlanta, 1990. Mem. Am. Inst. Constructors, Profl. Constrn. Estimators (sec. 1996—, newsletter editor 1996—), Nat. Mgmt. Assn. Office: York International 704-68F Savannah River Site Aiken SC 29803

JOHNSTON, CATHERINE V., magazine publisher. Former pub. Mirabella mag., N.Y.C.; now pub. Mademoiselle mag., N.Y.C., 1995-96; exec. v.p. Conde Nast Publs., N.Y.C., 1997. Office: Conde Nast Publs 350 Madison Ave Fl 17 New York NY 10017-3704*

JOHNSTON, CYRUS CONRAD, JR., medical educator; b. Statesville, N.C., July 16, 1929; m. Marjorie Tarkington, Feb. 20, 1960; 2 children. BA, Duke U., 1951, MD, 1955. Diplomate Am. Bd. Internal Medicine. Intern Duke Hosp., Durham, N.C., 1955-56; resident in medicine Barnes Hosp., St. Louis, 1956-57; rsch. fellow in endocrinology and metabolism Ind. U., Indpls., 1959-61, instr. medicine, 1961-63, asst. prof., 1963-67, assoc. prof., 1967-69, prof. medicine, 1969-97, disting. prof. medicine, 1997—; assoc. dir. Gen. Clin. Rsch. Ctr. Ind. U. Med. Ctr., Indpls., 1962-67, program dir., 1967-72, prin. investigator, 1968-88, dir. divsn. endocrinology and metabolism, 1968-94; mem. aging rev. com. Nat. Inst. Aging, 1982-85, chmn. geriatrics rev. com., 1985-86; mem. nursing sci. rev. com. NIH, 1988-89; mem. com. for protection of human subjects Ind. U.-Purdue U., Indpls., 1966—, chmn., 1978—; chmn. Nat. Osteoporosis Found. Sci. Adv. Bd., 1986—; med. adv. panel Paget's Disease Found., 1989—; v.p. Nat. Osteoporosis Found., 1992—; mem. Nat. Adv. Coun. on Aging, 1992-95. Assoc. editor Bone and Mineral, 1985-94, Bone, 1995—; editl. bd. Jour. Bone and Mineral Rsch., Jour. Clin. Endocrinology and Metabolism, 1988-91. Capt. USAF, 1957-59. Recipient Career Rsch. Devel. award USPHS, 1963-68, Sandoz prize Internat. Assn. Gerontology, 1993. Mem. ACP, AAAS, AMA, Am. Assn. Clin. Endocrinologists (Yank D. Coble, Jr. M.D. Disting. Svc. award 1998), Am. Fedn. Clin. Rsch., Am. Soc. for Bone and Mineral Rsch. (Frederic C. Bartter award 1996), Am. Clin. and Climatological Soc., Ctrl. Soc. for Clin. Rsch., Endocrine Soc., Sigma Xi. Office: Indiana Univ Dept Medicine Emerson Hall 545 Barnhill Dr Rm 421 Indianapolis IN 46202-5112

JOHNSTON, DALE, member of parliament; m. Dianne Friestad; children: Dalene, Michelle. Farmer Cretomere Dist. Ponoka County, 1967—; councillor County of Ponoka, 1986-92, reeve, chmn., bd. edn., 1989-92; M.P. for Wetaskiwin House of Commons, 1993—, mem. standing com. on human resources devel., 1994, critic for human resources devel., 1994, dept. critic for human resources devel., 1995, reform party labour critic, 1996, reform party shadow critic for labour, 1997, vice chair, standing com. on human resources devel., 1997—, mem. com. status on persons with disabilities, 1997—. Bd. dirs. Ponoka Gen. Hosp., 1986-92. Office: House of Commons, 106 E Block, Ottawa, ON Canada K1A 0A6*

JOHNSTON, DAVID LLOYD, academic administrator, lawyer; b. Sudbury, Ont., Can., June 28, 1941; s. Lloyd Allen and Dorothy Isobelle (Stonehouse) J.; m. Sharon Jean Downey, Aug. 29, 1964; children: Deborah Nicole, Barbara Alexandra, Sharon Elisabeth, Jenifer Joan, Catherine Ives. AB, Harvard U., 1963; LLB, Cambridge U., 1965, Queen's U., 1966; LLD (hon.), 10 univs., 1991. Bar: Called to Ont. bar 1969. Asst. prof. law Queen's U., Kingston, Ont., 1966-68; prof. U. Toronto, Ont., 1968-74; prof., dean U. Western Ont., London, 1974-79; prin., vice chancellor, prof. McGill U., Montreal, Que., Can., 1979-94, prof. law, 1979-99; pres., vice chancellor U. Waterloo, 1999—. Author: Canadian Securities Regulation, 1977, 2nd edit. 1998, Business Associations, 1979, Canadian Companies and the Stock Exchanges, 1979, If Quebec Goes: The Real Cost of Separation, 1995, Getting Canada On-Line: Understanding the Information Highway, 1995, Cyberlaw, 1997. Mem. Law Soc. Upper Can., Can. Bar Assn. Anglican. Office: McGill U, 3690 Peel St, Montreal, PQ Canada H3A 1W9

JOHNSTON, DENNIS ROY, computer systems integrator; b. Wahoo, Nebr., June 29, 1937; s. Roy Alfred and Wilma Jean (Weidensall) J.; Student U. Nebr., 1955-56, 57-58, U. Colo., 1961-64; m. Dorothy McLay Carr, June 19, 1965; children: Kristin Anne, Ami Carr. City planner Denver Urban Renewal Authority, 1965-69; dir. graphics Haines, Lundberg & Waehler, N.Y.C., 1969-72; sr. v.p., sr. project mgr. LCP Assos., Inc., N.Y.C., 1972-90; prin., computer cons. Chatham (N.J.) Cons. Group, 1990—. Mem. Am. Mgmt. Assn., Adminstrv. Mgmt. Soc. (cert. of merit), Nat. Computer Assn., Chatham Area C. of C., Fish and Game Assn. Chatham. Republican. Methodist. Home and Office: 3 Sussex Ave Chatham NJ 07928-2038

JOHNSTON, D.R.M. See MOENICH, DAVID RICHARD

JOHNSTON, EDWARD ALLAN, lawyer; b. Balt., Sept. 25, 1921; s. William Henry and Hattie Frisby (Sanner) J.; m. Dorothy Janet Swart, June 23, 1951 (dec. Jan. 1994); children: Elizabeth Janet, Jean Taylor; m. Mary Ellen Kinnaird, Apr. 15, 1995. B.B.A., U. Balt., 1942, B.S., 1947, LL.B., 1949, LL.M., 1957. Bar: Md. 1949; C.P.A., Md. Assoc. Whiteford, Taylor & Preston, Balt., 1954-62; ptnr. Whiteford, Taylor & Preston, 1962—; lectr. taxes U. Balt., 1948-65; bd. dirs. Dunbar Armored Express Inc. Pres. Dickeyville Assn., 1960; bd. dirs. Contact-Balt., 1974-80, chmn. bd., 1976-80; trustee Asbury Found., 1970—; trustee The Wesley Home, Inc., 1985-92; v.p., gen. counsel Soc. of Srs., 1983—; gen. counsel Ea. Srs. Golf Assn., Inc., 1988—; chmn. of adminstrv. bd. Meth. Ch., 1965-69, 88-90, trustee, chmn. bd., 1977-87. Recipient Alumnus of Yr. award U. Balt., 1980. Mem. U. Balt. Alumni Assn. (pres. 1975-76), Md. Golf Assn. (v.p. 1960-67, pres. 1968), Mid. Atlantic Golf Assn. (v.p. 1978-81, pres. 1982, gen. counsel 1983—), Balt. Country Club (golf com., house commn., bd. govs. 1989-95, exec. com., treas. fin. com. 1991-95, v.p. 1992-93, pres. 1993-95). Home: 4104 Ravenhurst Cir Glen Arm MD 21057-9767 Office: Whiteford Taylor & Preston 210 W Pennsylvania Ave Ste 400 Baltimore MD 21204-5332

JOHNSTON, F. BRUCE, JR., educator; b. Pitts., May 10, 1950; s. F. Bruce and (Mrs.) Johnston Sr.; m. Sue S. Johnston, July 20, 1974; children: Stuart, Megan, Ellen. BA, Westminster Coll., 1972; MA, Bowling Green (Ohio) State U., 1973; EdD, Western Mich. U., 1989. Dir. student housing West Liberty (W.Va.) State Coll., 1973-77; asst. dean of students Hope Coll., Holland, Mich., 1977-90; v.p. student life, dean of students Lyon Coll., Batesville, Ark., 1990—; field reader U.S. Dept. of Edn., Washington, 1991—. Elder First Presbyn. Ch., Batesville, 1994—; Eastman scholarship com. Ark. Eastman Corp., Batesville, 1993—; supt. search com. Batesville Pub. Schs., 1993. Mem. Nat. Assn. Student Personnel Adminstrs., Ark. Coll. Pers. Assn. Presbyterian. Avocations: running, reading, tennis.

JOHNSTON, FRANCIS CLAIBORNE, JR., lawyer; b. Richmond, Va., Jan. 6, 1943; s. Francis Claiborne and Virginia (Williams) J.; m. Carolyn Satterfield, Dec. 5, 1970; children: Angier Williams, Francis Claiborne III. AB magna cum laude, Princeton U., 1964; LLB, U. Va., 1967. Bar: Va. 1967, U.S. Dist. Ct. (ea. dist.) Va. 1968, U.S. Ct. Appeals (4th cir.) 1968. Assoc. Mays & Valentine, Richmond, 1968-72; ptnr. Mays & Valentine LLP, Richmond, 1972—; mng. ptnr. Mays & Valentine, Richmond, 1987-91; adj. asst. prof. T.C. Williams Sch. Law, U. Richmond, 1974-76; bd. dirs. Eskimo Pie Corp. Mem. session and diaconate 1st Presbyn. Ch., Richmond; bd. dirs. 1st Presbyn. Ch. Endowment Fund, Inc., 1972—, pres., 1993—; bd. dirs. Westham Civic Assn., 1984-86, Westminster-Canterbury Found., 1986-91, Westminster-Canterbury Corp., 1996—, vice-chmn. 1999; bd. dirs. Va. Post-Conviction Assistance Project, 1991, pres., 1996-98; bd. dirs. Libr. of Va., 1997—; trustee Valentine Mus., Richmond, 1980-89. Fellow Am. Bar Found., Va. Law Found. (bd. dirs. 1991-94); mem. ABA (Ho. Dels. 1992-98), Va. Bar Assn. (chmn. exec. com. 1988, pres. 1990), Richmond Bar Assn., Assn. of Bar of City of N.Y., Am. Law Inst., Commonwealth Club, Country Club Va., Forum Club, Farmington Country Club. Home: 7009 Lakewood Dr Richmond VA 23229-6933 Office: Mays & Valentine 1111 E Main St Richmond VA 23219-3531 also: PO Box 1122 Richmond VA 23218-1122

JOHNSTON, FRANK C., psychologist; b. West Hartford, Conn., June 21, 1955; s. Frank C. and Chris (Butler) J.; m. Susan H. Leffert, July 26, 1981; 1 child, Daniel Frank. *Father Frank C. Johnston Sr. was a graduate of the Class of 1945 at the U.S. Naval Academy. He was a research engineer with General Electric Co. and received several patents in the area of power engineer. Wife Susan Leffert Johnston is a Phi Beta Kappa graduate of SUNY Albany. She received her MA and EdM from Columbia University. In 1984, she obtained her PhD from SUNY Albany. She is a licensed psychologist in independent practice. In 1995, she was awarded the President's Early Career Distinguishment Award by the New York State Psychological Association.* BA, Fairfield U., 1977; MEd, Columbia U., 1979, MA, 1979; PhD, SUNY, Albany, 1984. Sch. psychologist bd. coop. ednl. svcs. Herkimer, N.Y., 1979-80; intern Counseling Ctr., SUNY, Buffalo, 1983-84; psychologist Family Svc. Rochester, N.Y., 1985-87, Child and Youth div. Rochester Mental Health Ctr., 1988; pvt. practice Rochester, 1988—; cons. Brockport (N.Y.) Day Care Ctr., 1989-90, Learning Devel. Ctr., Rochester Inst. Tech., 1989-90; co-founder Behavioral Health Consortium Rochester, 1996. Mem. APA, N.Y. State Psychol. Assn. (managed care task force), Genesee Valley Psychol. Assn. (mem. legal legis com. 1988-90, mem. ins. com. 1990-92, chmn. ins. com. 1990, 93, pres. 1994, past pres. 1995, mem. psychology subcom. 1988—, mem. mental health task force preferred care 1999—), Rochester Area Assn. Clin. Psychologists, Nat. Register Health Svc. Providers in Psychology. Office: 480 White Spruce Blvd Rochester NY 14623-1608

JOHNSTON, GEORGE W., lawyer; b. Syracuse, N.Y., Aug. 8, 1950; s. Norman Fero and Mary Jane (Innes) J. BA, Johns Hopkins U., 1972; JD, Georgetown U., 1975. Bar: Md. 1975. Law clerk U.S. Dist. Ct., Balt., 1975-76; atty. Venable, Baetjer & Howard, Balt., 1976—; chief oper. officer Venable, Baetjer & Howard, LLP, 1999—; lectr. in field. Author: BNA Aids Guide, 1990, Affirmative Action Workbook, 1992, Maryland Employer's Guide, 1991; contbr. articles to profl. jours. Vice chmn. Md. Citizens for the Arts. Mem. ABA, FBA, Md. Bar Assn., Balt. City Bar Assn. Office: Venable Baetjer & Howard 1800 Mercantile Bank 2 Hopkins Plz Ste 2100 Baltimore MD 21201-2982

JOHNSTON, GERALD SAMUEL, physician, educator; b. Johnstown, Pa., Aug. 4, 1930; s. Fleurence Gerald and Lorna Freda (Lawhead) J.; m. Dorothy Anna Jones, June 18, 1956; children: Joy Johnston Biciocchi, Jill A. Verna, Jana S. Moritzkat, Gerald S. Jr., Amy L. Tapparo, Douglas S. BS, U. Pitts., 1952, MD, 1956. Diplomate Am. Bd. Internal Medicine, Am. Bd. Nuclear Medicine. Intern Walter Reed Gen. Hosp., Washington, 1956-57; resident in internal medicine Brooke Gen. Hosp., San Antonio, 1958-61; commd. med. officer U.S. Army, 1955-71, advanced through grades to col., 1971; capt. USPHS, 1971-82; surgeon 358 Gen. dispensary, Seoul, Korea, 1961-62; chief nuclear medicine Walter Reed Gen. Hosp., Washington, Md., 1963-69, Letterman Gen. Hosp., San Francisco, 1969-71, NIH, Bethesda, Md., 1971-82; chief nuclear medicine U. Md., Balt., 1982-93, acting chmn. dept. radiology, 1989-92, prof. medicine, radiology and oncology, 1982-93; chmn. dept. nuclear medicine Washington Hosp. Ctr., 1993—. Author two books; contbr. over 250 articles to profl. jours. Decorated Legion of Merit, 1970. Fellow ACP, Am. Coll. Radiology; mem. AMA, AAUP, Am. Coll. Nuclear Medicine, Soc. Nuclear Medicine, Soc. of Chmn. of Acad. Radiology Depts. Republican. Avocations: carpentry (home crafts), history, philosophy, observer, running. Office: Washington Hosp Ctr 110 Irving St NW Washington DC 20010-2975

JOHNSTON, HAROLD S(LEDGE), chemistry educator; b. Woodstock, Ga., Oct. 11, 1920; s. Smith L. and Florine (Dial) J.; m. Mary Ella Stay, Dec. 29, 1948; children: Shirley Louise, Linda Marie, David Finley, Barbara Dial. AB, Emory U., 1941, ScD (hon.), 1965; PhD, Calif. Inst. Tech., 1948. Instr. to assoc. prof. chemistry Stanford (Calif.) U., 1947-56; assoc. prof. Calif. Inst. Tech., Pasadena, 1956-57; prof. U. Calif., Berkeley, 1957—, dean, coll. chemistry, 1966-70; vis. prof. U. Rome, 1964; adv. com. Calif. Statewide Air Pollution Rsch.Ctr., 1969-73, Nat. Ctr. Atmospheric Rsch., 1975-78, FAA High Altitude Polution Program; vis. adv. com. Brookhaven Nat. Lab., 1970-73; faculty rsch. lectr. U. Calif., Berkeley, 1989. Author: Gas Phase Reaction Rate Theory, 1966, Gas Phase Reaction Kinetics of Neutral Oxygen Species, 1968, Reduction of Stratospheric Ozone by Nitrogen Oxide Catalysts from Supersonic Transport Exhaust, 1971; contbr. articles to profl. jours. Recipient Tyler prize Environ. Achievement, 1983, Disting. Alumni award Calif. Inst. Tech., 1985, NAS award for Chemistry in Service to Society Nat. Acad. of Sciences, 1993, Nat. Medal of Scis., 1997; grantee Materials and Molecular Rsch. divsn. Lawrence Berkeley Lab., 1966—. Fellow AAAS, Am. Chem. Soc. (Gold Medal award Calif. sect. 1956, Pollution Control award 1974, award in the Chemistry of Contemporary Technol. Problems 1985), Am. Phys. Soc., Am. Geophys. Union (Roger Revelle medal 1998), Nat. Acad. Scis. (adv. panel to Nat. Bur. Standards, 1965-67, com. Motor Vehicle Emissions, 1971-75, Svc. to Soc. award in chemistry 1993), Am. Assn. Arts and Scis., Sigma Xi (nat. lectr. 1973). Home: 132 Highland Blvd Berkeley CA 94708-1023 Office: U Calif Dept Chemistry Berkeley CA 94720

JOHNSTON, HARRY A., II, former congressman; b. West Palm Beach, FL, Dec. 2, 1931; m. Mary Otley; children: Victoria, Rebecca. Ed., Va. Mil. Inst., 1953, U. Fla. Law Sch., 1958. Mem. Fla. Senate, former pres.; ptnr. Jones Foster Johnston & Stubbs, 1958-91, 96—; mem. 101st-104th Congresses from 14th (now 19th) Fla. dist., 1989-96; mem. fgn. affairs com., subcom. Africa, internat. ops., econ. policy, trade and environment, budget com. Mem. United Fund Palm Beach County, Norton Gallery, Girl Scouts U.S. With U.S. Army, 1953-55. Named Most Valuable Senator Fla. Press Corps, 1981. Mem. Palm Beach Bar Assn. (former pres.), Rotary (former pres. Greater West Palm Beach). Democrat. Presbyterian. Office: Jones Foster Johnston & Stubbs 505 S Flagler Dr STe 1100 West Palm Beach FL 33401-3475

JOHNSTON, JAMES JOEL, foreign service officer, publisher; b. Little Rock, Mar. 20, 1936; s. William Carleton and Capitola (Treece) J.; m. Margaret Zoe Grant, Aug. 11, 1962; children: William Grant, David Alexander. BA, U. Okla., 1958, MA, 1963; MA, Ohio State U., 1979. Fgn. svc. officer Dept. State, Washington, 1963-88; pub., owner Searcy County Publs., Marshall, Ark., 1991—. Author: Searcy County to 1850, 1991, Shootin's Obituaries, Politics, 1991; editor, pub. Searcy County Ancestor Info Ex, 1990—; creator Ancestor Fair, 1990. Sec. Searcy County Indsl. Devel. Corp., Marshall, Ark., 1991-92; pres. Searcy County Hist. Assn., Marshall, 1993-96. Lt. USN, 1958-61, PTO. Fellow Soc. Antiquaries; mem. Scottish Soc. (pres. N.W. Ark. 1994-97), Fgn. Svc. Assn., Rotary (pres. 1996-97). Republican. Presbyterian. Avocations: Arkansas history. Home: 2333 N East Oaks Dr Fayetteville AR 72703-6106 Office: Searcy County Publs PO Box 65 Marshall AR 72650-0065

JOHNSTON, JAMES MONROE, III, air force officer; b. Stamford, Tex., Jan. 19, 1940; s. James Monroe Jr. and Dollie Katherine (Crider) J.; m. Sallie Trail, Aug. 27, 1960; children: James Blake, Kendell Kay, Lance Michael. BBA in Retailing, Tex. Tech U., 1962; grad., Air Command and Staff Coll., Maxwell, Ala., 1972, Nat. War Coll., Washington, 1982. Commd. 2d lt. USAF, 1962, advanced through grades to brig. gen., 1988, ret. brig. gen., 1992; fighter pilot 31 Tactical Fighter Wing, Homestead AFB, Fla., 1964-65; fighter pilot, advisor Vietnamese Air Force, Danans, 1965-66; instr. pilot Eglin AFB, Fla., 1966-70; comdg. officer USAF Acad., Colorado Springs, Colo., 1970-73; ops. officer, comdr., various assignments Thailand, Eng., 1973-82; div. chief Pentagon, Washington, 1982-84; wing comdr. Luke AFB, Hill AFB, Utah, 1984-87; insp. gen. Tactical Air Command, Langley AFB, Va., 1987-88; dir. aerospace safety Hdqrs. Air Force Inspection and Safety Ctr., Norton AFB, Calif., 1988-90; vice comdr. 5th Air Force, Yokota AFB, Japan, 1990-92; investment advisor Multi-Fin. Securities Corp., Colorado Springs, Colo., 1993—. Dep. dir. West Pacific coun. Girl Scouts U.S., Tokyo, 1990-92, West Pacific coun. Boy Scouts Am., 1990-92. Decorated DSM, Legion of Merit, DFC, Air medal (10), Meritorious Svc. medal (3). Mem. Air Force Assn., Far East Coun. on Internat. Rels. (exec. dir. 1990-92), Order of Daedalians, Sertoma Internat., Colorado Springs C. of C. (chmn. mil. affairs coun. 1997-98). Presbyterian. Avocations: skiing, golf.

JOHNSTON, JAMES ROBERT, library director; b. Wheaton, Ill., June 3, 1947; s. Robert W. and Elizabeth S. (Townsend) J.; m. Carol Ann Trezza, June 14, 1969; children: Steven J., Julie M. BA, U. Notre Dame, 1969; MLS, Fla. State U., 1973. Head librarian Grande Prairie Library Dist., Hazel Crest, Ill., 1973-76; chief librarian Joliet (Ill.) Pub. Library, 1976—; pres. bd. dirs. Ill. Library Employees Benefit Plan; mem. automation com. Heritage Trail Libr. Sys., Shorewood, Ill.; pres. Ill. Libr. Employees Benefit Plan, Joliet; bldg. cons. Co-author: Illinois Library Trustees Association Booklet "Selecting Consultants", 1986; contbr. speeches and articles in field. Mem. Joliet Ctr. for Econ. Devel. Owners and Mgrs. Assn. (chmn.), Interlibrary Cooperative Subcom. Ill. State Libr. Assn. (Pub. Libr. sect. 1977-78, legis. devel. com. 1977-82, jr. members. rountable 1976-77), Beta Phi Mu (Gamma chpt.). Mem. Ill. Library Assn. (Pub. Library sect. 1977-78, legis. devel. com. 1977-82, jr. members. roundtable 1976-77, regional planning com. 1996, Ill. State Libr. Title III rev. com. 1996—), Beta Phi Mu (Gamma chpt.). Lodge: Kiwanis. Avocations: HO guage model railroading, softball, bowling, golf. Home: 15 Wheeler Ave Joliet IL 60436-1529 Office: Joliet Pub Library 150 N Ottawa St Joliet IL 60432-4192

JOHNSTON, JAMES WESLEY, retired tobacco company executive; b. Chgo., Apr. 11, 1946; s. Ted and Irma (Hacker) J.; m. Beverly S. Cline, Nov. 10, 1967; children: Amanda E., Emily S. BS in Accountancy, U. Ill., 1967; MBA, Northwestern U., 1971. C.P.A., Ill. Fin. analyst Ford Motor Co., 1967-69; with N.W. Industries, 1969-79, dir. corp. devel., 1973-75, v.p. mktg., 1975-79; exec. v.p. Asia/Pacific R.J. Reynolds Tobacco Internat. Inc., 1979; pres., chief exec. officer Asia/Pacific R.J. Reynolds Tobacco Internat. Inc., Hong Kong, 1979-81; exec. v.p. R.J. Reynolds Tobacco Co., U.S., 1981-84; divsn. exec. consumer banking N.E. U.S. Citicorp, N.Y.C., 1984-89; chmn. CEO R.J. Reyolds Tobacco Co., Winston-Salem, N.C., 1989-95; chmn. R.J. Reynolds Tobacco Worldwide, Winston-Salem, N.C., 1993-96; vice chmn. RJR Nabisco, Inc., 1995-96, ret., 1996; bd. dirs. Sealy Corp., Cleve. Treas., trustee, pres. Village of Bolingbrook, Ill., 1973-75; bd. dirs. Winston-Salem Bus. Inc., 1989—, N.C. Citizens for Bus. and Industry, Raleigh, 1989—; mem. mktg. com. Nat. Multiple Sclerosis Soc., N.Y.C., 1986—; active N.C. Bus. Coun. Mgmt. and Devel., Raleigh, 1989—; trustee Wake Forest U., Winston-Salem, 1991—; mem. bd. visitors Bowman Gray-Bapt. Hosp. Med. Ctr., Winston-Salem, 1991—. Mem. Greater Winston-Salem C. of C. (bd. dirs. 1989—), Old Town Club, Piedmont Club. Office: 380 Knollwood St Ste 570 Winston Salem NC 27103-1865

JOHNSTON, JEFFERY W., publishing executive; b. Lockport, N.Y., Dec. 14, 1951; s. Sidney W. and Barbara (Jeffery) J.; m. Marcia Lynn Paca, Aug. 3, 1974; children: Paul W., Sarah E., David P. BA, Dartmouth Coll., 1974. Sales rep. John Hancock Ins., Boston, 1974-76; from sales rep. to editor edn., coll. textbooks Allyn Bacon Publ., Rochester, N.Y., 1976-85; from editor edn., coll. textbooks to exec. editor Merrill Publ., Columbus, Ohio, 1985-90; v.p., editor-in-chief Merrill Imprint-Macmillan Publ., Columbus, 1990-94; v.p., publisher Merrill Imprint-Prentice Hall, Columbus, 1994—. Republican. Avocations: running, reading. Office: Prentice Hall 445 Hutchinson Ave Columbus OH 43235-5677*

JOHNSTON, JOCELYN STANWELL, paralegal; b. Evanston, Ill., Feb. 16, 1954; d. Gerald and Dorothy Jeanne (Schoenfield) Stanwell; m. Thomas Patrick Johnston, Nov. 28, 1986. BA, U. Minn., 1981; cert., Phila. Inst. Paralegal Tng., Phila., 1986. Paralegal Fredrikson & Byron P.A., Mpls., 1981-84, Reed, Smith, Shaw and McClay, Phila., 1984-85, McCausland, Keen & Buckman, P.C., Radnor, Pa., 1985-86, Harris, Guenzel, Meier & Nichols, P.C., Ann Arbor, Mich., 1986-87, Conner & Bentley, P.C., Ann Arbor, 1987-88, Cichocki & Armstrong, Ltd., Oak Park, Ill., 1988-90, Bishop and Bishop, Oak Brook, Ill., 1994-95, Martin, Breen & Merrick, Oak Park, 1994-95, Saitlin, Patzik, Frank & Samotny, Ltd., Chgo., 1995, Bryson R. Cloon, Esquire, Leawood, Kans., 1996—. Mem. Kans. Bar Assn. Democrat. Home: 14501 Marty St Overland Park KS 66223-2300 Office: Bryson R Cloon Esquire 11350 Tomahawk Creek Pkwy Leawood KS 66211

JOHNSTON, JOHN BENNETT, JR., former senator; b. Shreveport, La., June 10, 1932; m. Mary Gunn, 1956; children: Bennett, Hunter, Mary, Sally. Student, Washington and Lee U., U.S. Mil. Acad.; LL.B., La. State U., 1956. Bar: La. 1956. Mem. firm Johnston, Johnston & Thornton, 1959; mem. La. House Reps., 1964-68, La. Senate, 1968-72; U.S senator from La., 1972-96; chmn. Dem. senatorial campaign com., 1975-76; ptnr. Johnston & Assocs., 1996—; mem. appropriations com., ranking minority subcom. on energy and water devel., ranking minority com. on energy and natural resources, mem. budget com., mem. spl. com. on aging, mem. select com. on intelligence. Served to 1st lt. U.S. Army, 1956-59. Democrat. Office: Johnston & Assocs Ste 200 1455 Pennsylvania Ave NW Washington DC 20004-1024*

JOHNSTON, JOHN DEVEREAUX, JR., law educator, retired; b. Asheville, N.C., Oct. 1, 1932; s. John D. and Marion R. (Green) J.; m. Beryl R. Watson, Dec. 21, 1952; m. Diana Armatage, June 10, 1972; children: Catherine, Patricia, Sharon, Laura, Jackie, John. A.B., Duke U., 1954, LL.B., 1956. Bar: N.C. 1956, U.S. Ct. Appeals (4th cir.) 1969, U.S. Supreme Ct. 1969. Mgmt. trainee J.P. Morgan & Co., 1956-58; pvt. practice Asheville, 1959-62; asst. prof. Duke U. Law Sch., Durham, N.C., 1963-64, asst. dean, 1963-65, assoc. prof., 1965-67, prof., 1968-69; prof. law NYU Law Sch., N.Y.C., 1969-89, prof. law emeritus, 1990—; vis. prof. Vanderbilt U., 1972, UCLA, 1975, Washington U., St. Louis, 1981, Hastings Coll. Law U. Calif., San Francisco, 1984. Author: (with G. Johnson) Land Use Control, 1977; contbr. articles to profl. jours. Home: 21 Stuyvesant Rd Asheville NC 28803-3022 *As a young law teacher, I was mentored by two wise elders. One emphasized preparation: Don't ever go into class without knowing where you intend to take it. The other counselled flexibility: Be prepared for anything, and let student input determine how the class will unfold. A third elder provided a synthesis: Never overestimate what your students already know, nor underestimate what they are capable of learning.Applying that maxim, I determined to introduce new subjects slowly and carefully, even spoon-feeding the students for a while. Thereafter, development of the topic proceeded at their speed. After they reached a level of sophistication well beyond my expectations, I concluded that the third elder was the wisest.*

JOHNSTON, JOHN THOMAS, engineering executive; b. St. Louis, Jan. 24, 1930; s. Herbert Johnston and Mabel (Farris) Seeley; m. Shirley Wiladean Trulove, Nov. 25, 1950; children: John David, Thomas Daniel. Cert. in mech. tech., Washington U., St. Louis, 1960, BS in Physics, 1963; MBA, Lindenwood Coll., 1978. Structural engr. McDonnell Aircraft, St. Louis, 1955-66, 67-70, project engr., 1970-83, integrator-engr., 1983-87; chief engr. Lear Jet, Wichita, Kans., 1966-67; mgr. aero tech. E-Systems, Greenville, Tex., 1987-92, mem. tech. staff, 1992-93; pvt. practice cons. Greenville, Tex., 1993—; pres. Tech. Engrng. Cons., Greenville, Tex., 1995—; designated engrng. rep. FAA, Kansas City, Mo., 1967-75; chief exec. officer Midwest Travel Inst., St. Peters, Mo., 1985-90. Contbr. articles to profl. pubs.; patentee in field. Fundraiser Lindenwood Coll., St. Charles, Mo., 1987; organizer Jr. Achievement, St. Charles, 1975; juvenile officer Jud. Dist. 11, St. Charles, 1970's. Sgt. U.S. Army, 1950-53. Mem. AIAA. Home and Office: 3 Thornhill Dr Greenville TX 75401-9404

JOHNSTON, KENNETH JOHN, astronomer, scientific director naval observatory; b. N.Y.C., Oct. 9, 1941; s. Marion Nugent Johnston; m. Therese M. Clasen, June 25, 1966. BEE, Manhattan Coll., 1964; PhD, Georgetown U., 1969. NAS, NRC postdoctoral assoc. Naval Rsch. Lab., Washington, 1969-71, radio astronomer, 1971-80, supr. physicist, 1980-90, chief scientist ctr. for advanced space sensing, 1990-92, supt. remote sensing divsn., 1992-93; sci. dir. U.S. Naval Observatory, Washington, 1993—. Contbr. over 400 articles to Astron. and Astrophys. Lit. Recipient NRL Sigma Xi Pure Sci. award, 1985, Alexander von Humboldt Sr. Scientist award, 1985, Max Planck Soc. Rsch. award, 1990. Mem. Internat. Astron. Union, Union of Radio Sci., Royal Astron. Soc., Am. Astron. Soc. Achievements include development of a program that applied interferometric techniques for high resolution imaging at optical and radio wavelengths; directed a pioneering effort to develop the first imaging optical interferometer to be located at Flagstaff, Ariz.; established a global inertial reference frame at optical/ radio wavelengths; developed radio techniques to probe the surface of asteroids, and the first images of interstellar masers. Office: US Naval Observatory 3450 Massachusetts Ave NW Washington DC 20392-0001

JOHNSTON, LAURANCE SCOTT, foundation director; b. St. Paul, Aug. 4, 1950; s. Scott D. and Laura L. (Wallace) J. BS, Hamline U., 1972; MS, Northwestern U., 1973, PhD, 1976; MBA, George Mason U., 1985. Postdoctoral fellow Chgo. Med. Sch., 1977-78; regulatory scientist Bur. Foods, FDA, Washington, 1978-81; exec. sec. NIH, Bethesda, Md., 1981-86; dir. div. sci. rev. Nat. Inst. Child Health and Human Devel., NIH, Bethesda, 1986-92; dir. spinal cord rsch. and edn. founds. Paralyzed Vets. of Am., 1992-97, cons. in biomed. and disability rsch., 1997—. Contbr. articles to profl. jours. Damon Runyon/Walter Winchell Cancer Found. fellow, 1978. Home: PO Box 118 Indian Hills CO 80454-0118

JOHNSTON, LAWRENCE D., career officer; b. Okla., Apr. 28, 1947. BS in Econ., Okla. State U., 1970; grad., Squadron Officer Sch., 1975; MS in Mgmt., Troy State U., 1979; grad., Air Command and Staff Coll., 1982; student, Nat. Def. U., 1982; MS in Nat. Security and Strategic Studies, Naval War Coll., 1990; Sr. Officials in Nat. Security, Harvard U., 1992, Sr. Execs. in Nat./Internat. Security, 1997. Commd. 2d lt. USAF, 1970, advanced through grades to brig. gen., 1996; F-4 flight leader, fast forward air controller 388th Tactical Fighter Wing, Korat Royal Thailand AFB, 1971-72; F-4 instr. 35th Tactical Fighter Wing 35th Tactical Fighter Wing, George AFB, Calif., 1972-75; F-4 fighter weapons instr., flight comdr. and chief wing weapons and tactics 347th Tactical Fighter Wing, Moody AFB, Ga., 1975-78; fighter weapons instr., chief weapons tng. 406th Tactical Fighter Tng. Wing, Zaragoza AFB, Spain, 1978-79; staff action officer Hdqs. USAF in Europe, Ramstein AFB, W. Germany, 1980-81; chief wing weapons and tactics, asst. ops. officer 474th Tactical Fighter Wing, Nellis AFB, Nev., 1982-87, chief wing maintenance tng. div., ops. officer, F-16 squadron comdr., 1982-87; dir. assignments Hdqs. Tactical Air Command, Langley AFB, Va., 1987-89; comdt. USAF Fighter Weapons Sch., Nellis AFB, Nev., 1990-91; vice-comdr. 363rd Fighter Wing, Shaw AFB, S.C., 1991-93; comdr. various AFB's, 1993-98; dir. plans and programs Hdqs. Air Combat Command, Langley AFB, 1998—. Decorated Legion of Merit with oak leaf cluster, D.F.C. with three oak leaf clusters, Purple Heart, Air medal with 17 oak leaf clusters. Office: USAF HQ ACC/XP 204 Dodd Blvd Ste 202 Langley AFB VA 23665-5001

JOHNSTON, LINDA TIDWELL, municipal official. BA in Psychology, U. Fla., 1969. Tchr. English, speech and drama Cocoa H.S., Rockledge, Fla., 1969-70; exec. trainee Burdines Dept. Store, West Palm Beach, Fla., 1970-72; adminstrv. asst., counselor Fortune Personnel, Cocoa Beach, 1972-73; social worker State of Fla., Cocoa Beach, 1973-74; dir. ret. sr. vol. program City of Raleigh, 1974-79, dir. citizen involvement divsn., 1979-91, divsn. dir. cmty. svcs. dept., 1991-96, dir. neighborhood svc. divsn. cmty. svcs. dept., 1996-98, sr. cmty. specialist neighborhood svcs. div. cmty. svcs., 1998—. Mem. Nat. Assn. Human Rights Workers, N.C. Assn. Vol. Adminstrs., Woman's Club Raleigh. Office: Cmty Svcs Dept 310 W Martin St # 201 Raleigh NC 27601-1326

JOHNSTON, LLOYD DOUGLAS, social scientist; b. Boston, Apr. 18, 1940; s. Leslie D. and Madeline B. (Irvin) J.; 1 child, Douglas Leslie. B.A. in Econs., Williams Coll., 1962; M.B.A., Harvard U., 1965, postgrad., 1965-66; M.A. in Social Psychology, U. Mich., 1971, Ph.D., 1973. Research asst. Grad. Sch. Bus. Adminstr., Harvard U., Boston, 1965-66; asst. study dir. Inst. Social Research, U. Mich., Ann Arbor, 1966-73, asst. research scientist, 1973-75, assoc. rsch. scientist, 1975-78, sr. rsch. scientist and program dir., 1978-98; disting. sr. rsch. scientist Inst. Social Rsch., U. Mich., Ann Arbor, 1998—; chmn. exec. com. U. Mich. Substance Abuse Rsch. Ctr. Excellence, 1990-95, acting dir., 1994-95; prin. investigator Monitoring the Future: A Continuing Study of Lifestyles and Values of Am. Youth, 1975—, Youth, Education and Society, 1996—, also other nat. and internat. survey studies; cons. to WHO, UN, EEC, Coun. of Europe, Pan Am. Health Orgn., White House, U.S. Congress, various founds., numerous fgn. govts., fed. agys, univs., rsch. insts., TV networks, Nat. Partnership for Drug Free Am., 1975—; chmn. tech. planning group; mem. Resource Group for Goal Seven, Nat. Ednl. Goals Panel, 1991—; mem. extramural sci. adv. bd. Nat. Inst. on Drug Abuse, 1990-94; mem., also chmn. prevention subcom., Nat. Adv. Coun. on Drug Abuse, 1982-86, Presdl. appointee White House Conf. for a Drug-Free Am., 1987-88, Presdl. appointee Nat. Commn. for Drug Free Schs., 1989-90; chmn. drug epidemiology sect. Internat. Coun. on Alcohol and Addictions, 1982—; mem. Com. on Problems of Drug Dependence, 1982-86; mem. or chmn. various adv. coms. various univs., founds.; mem. various working groups NAS; mem. various coms. and adv. groups Nat. Inst. Drug Abuse, 1975—; mem. or chmn. 6 working groups WHO, 1975-96; invited lectr. nat. and internat. confs. and convs.; testimony before Congress and fed. regulatory agys. Author: Drugs and American Youth, 1973, Student Drug Use in America, 1975-81, 82, Nat. Survey Results on Drug Abuse from the Monitoring the Future Study 1975-1997, vol. 1 and 2, 1998, 29 other books and monographs on drug use and lifestyles of Am. secondary sch. students and young adults, 1972—, 21 reference vols.; editor: Conducting Follow Up Research on Drug Treatment Programs, 1977; contbr. over 75 chpts. to books, articles to profl. jours. Recipient Nat. Pacesetter award in rsch. Nat. Inst. on Drug Abuse, 1982, 1st Sr. Rsch. Scientist award and lectureship U. Mich., 1987. Fellow Coll. on Problems of Drug Dependence; mem. APA, Soc. for Psychol. Study Social Issues (sec.-treas. 1976-79), Am. Sociol. Assn., Am. Pub. Health Assn. Home: 5538 Lawrence Ct Pinckney MI 48169-9257 Office: U Mich Inst Social Rsch Ann Arbor MI 48109

JOHNSTON, LOGAN TRUAX, III, lawyer; b. New Haven, Dec. 9, 1947; s. Logan Truax Jr. and Elizabeth (Josey) J.; m. Celeste Linguere; children: Charlotte Hathaway, Logan Truax IV, Owen Conrad, Oritse J., Gboyega P. BA, Yale U., 1969; JD, Harvard U., 1973. Bar: Ill. 1973, Ariz. 1984, U.S. Ct. Appeals (2d cir.) 1982, U.S. Ct. Appeals (7th cir.) 1973, U.S. Ct. Appeals (9th cir.) 1986, U.S. Ct. Appeals (fed. cir.) 1990, U.S. Supreme Ct. 1991. Assoc. Winston & Strawn, Chgo., 1973-79, ptnr., 1979-83; ptnr. Winston & Strawn, Phoenix, 1983-89; mng. ptnr. Johnston Maynard Grant & Parker, Phoenix, 1989-97, Johnston & Dodd, Phoenix, 1997—; spl. asst. state's atty. Du Page County, Ill., Wheaton, 1976-77; cons. Community Legal Svcs., Phoenix, 1984—. Contbg author: Arizona Appellate Handvook, Vol. III. Served with U.S. Army N.G., 1970-76. Mem. ABA, Maricopa County Bar Found., Maricopa County Bar Assn., Ariz. Bar Found., Ariz. State Bar Assn., Phoenix Heroes Endowment Fund. Presbyterian. Avocations: books, movies, golf, hiking, travel. Office: Johnston & Dodd PLC One N 1st St Phoenix AZ 85004

JOHNSTON, MALCOLM CARLYLE, bank executive; b. Glasgow, Scotland, July 10, 1934; s. Malcolm and Margaret Brown (MacPherson) J.; m. Anna Maria Bindels, Sept. 7, 1963; children: Margareta J.M., Malcolm H.A. Grad., Kelvinside Acad., Glasgow. With Standard Bank of Ghana Ltd, 1955-62, Standard Bank of Nigeria Ltd., 1962-69, The Bank of Nova Scotia, 1969-97; asst. agt. The Bank of Nova Scotia, N.Y.C., 1969-72; spl. rep. The Bank of Nova Scotia, Hong Kong, 1972-74; mgr. The Bank of Nova Scotia, Kuala Lumpur, Malaysia, 1974-76, Kingston, Jamaica, 1976-78; from asst. gen. mgr. to gen. mgr. The Bank of Nova Scotia, Caribbean region, 1979-83; sr. v.p. comml. credit The Bank of Nova Scotia, Toronto, 1983-86, exec. v.p. internat. banking, 1986-97; pres., CEO The Bank of N.T. Butterfield & Son, Hamilton, Bermuda, 1997—; also bd. dirs. Mil. Svc. The Royal Highland Regiment, The Black Watch. Fellow Inst. Can. Bankers (gold medal 1983); mem. Chartered Inst. Bankers, Nat. Club (Toronto), Hong Kong Club, Kelvinside Academicals, Glasgow. Office: The Bank of Nova Scotia, Bank Butler Field Bermuda, PO Box HM 195, Hamilton, ON Canada M5H 1H1

JOHNSTON, MARGUERITE, journalist, author; b. Birmingham, Ala., Aug. 7, 1917; d. Robert C. and Marguerite (Spradling) J.; m. Charles Wynn Barnes, Aug. 31, 1946; children: Susan, Patricia, Steven, Polly. A.B., Birmingham-So. Coll., 1938. Reporter Birmingham News, 1939-44; Washington corr. Birmingham News, Birmingham Age-Herald, London Daily Mirror, 1945-46; columnist Houston Post, 1947-69, fgn. news editor, mem. editorial bd., 1969-85, assoc. editor editorial page, 1972-77, asst. editor editorial page, 1977-85; lectr. in field, 1947—; instr. creative writing U. Houston, 1946-47, lectr. feature writing, 1965-66; lectr. Baker Coll., Rice U., 1977-78; del. Asian Am. Women Journalists Conf., Honolulu, 1965, 1st World Conf. Women Journalists, Mexico City, 1969. Author: Public Manners, 1957, A Happy Worldly Abode, 1964, Houston: The Unknown City, 1836-1946, (Winedale Historical Ctr. Ima Hogg award, Otis Lock award East Tex. Historical Assn.), 1991. Bd. dirs. Tex. Bill of Rights Found., 1962-64; bd. dirs. Planned Parenthood, 1953-55, Population Inst., 1985-91; mem. Mcpl. Art Commn., 1971-76, Houston Com. Fgn. Relations. Recipient Theta Sigma Phi Headliner award, 1954, 1st ann. award of merit Houston Com. Alcoholism, 1956, cert. of merit Gulf Coast chpt. Am. Soc. Safety Engrs., 1960, Agnese Carter Nelms award Planned Parenthood, 1968, Sch. Bell award Tex. State Tchrs. Assn., 1974, 75, Gold Key award Nat. Council Alcoholism, 1975, Global award Population Inst., 1981. Mem. Tex. Soc. Architects (hon.), Philos. Soc. Tex., Phi Beta Kappa, Pi Beta Phi. Home: 5319 Cherokee St Houston TX 77005-1701

JOHNSTON, MARILYN FRANCES-MEYERS, physician, medical educator; b. Buffalo, Mar. 30, 1937; B.S., Dameon Coll., 1966; Ph.D., St. Louis U., 1970, M.D., 1975. Diplomate Am. Bd. Pathology, Diplomate Nat. Bd. Med. Examiners. Fellow in immunology Washington U., St. Louis, 1970-72; resident in pathology Washington U. Hosp., St. Louis, 1975-77, St. John's Mercy Med. Ctr., St. Louis, 1977-79; research fellow hematology St. Louis U. Sch. Medicine, 1979-80; instr. biochemistry St. Louis U., 1972-75, asst. prof. pathology, 1980-87, assoc. prof. 1987-92, prof., 1992—, dir. transfusion service, 1980—; med. dir. Mo./Ill. Regional Red Cross, 1983-88; area chmn. for inspection and accreditation Am. Assn. Blood Banks, Arlington, Va., 1984. Author: Transfusion Therapy, 1985. Recipient Transfusion Medicine Acad. award Nat. Heart, Blood and Lung Inst., 1984; Goldberger fellow AMA, 1979. Mem. Am. Assn. Blood Banks, Am. Assn. Immunologists, Internat. Soc. Blood Transfusion, Am. Soc. Clin. Pathologists, Sigma Xi. Office: St Louis U Hosp 16560 Chesterfield Airport Rd Chesterfield MO 63017

JOHNSTON, MARY ELLEN, nursing educator; b. Roswell, N.Mex., June 4, 1951; d. E. Bernard and Jane (Shugart) J. BSN, Baylor U., 1973; MSN, Oral Roberts U., 1982. Staff nurse crit. care dept. Tucson Med. Ctr., 1973-74; charge nurse med. unit St. Mary's Hosp., Roswell, 1975; instr. nursing Ea. N.Mex. U., Roswell, 1975—. Mem. ANA (cert. med.-surg. nurse), N.Mex. Nurses Assn. (past pres. dist. V), Baylor U. Nurses Alumni Assn., Philanthropic and Ednl. Orgn., Daus. of Am. Colonists, Altrusa Club Roswell, DAR, Sigma Theta Tau. Republican. Methodist. Home: 2715 N Kentucky Ave Apt 16 Roswell NM 88201-5868 Office: Ea NMex U PO Box 6000 Roswell NM 88202-6000

JOHNSTON, MAXINE, retired librarian; b. Gillham, Ark., Dec. 21, 1928. Student, Lamar Coll., 1946-51; BS, Sam Houston State U., 1953; MLS, U. Tex., 1958. Adminstrv. asst. Beaumont Pub. Libr. (formerly Tyrell Pub. Libr.), 1947-53; asst. libr. South Park H.S., 1953-55; reference libr. Lamar U., 1955-68, acting dir., 1968-69, assoc. dir., 1970-80, dir., 1980-88. Contbr. articles to profl. jours. Mem. ALA (life), Tex. Libr. Assn. (life, dist. vice chair 1960-61, nominating com. chair 1965-66, reference round table 1967-69, vice chair, chair 1967-69, legis. com. 1973-75, coll. & univ. divsn. vice-chair, chair 1984-86), Tex. Info. Exch. (bd. chair 1971-72), Tex. Coun. State Univ. Librs. (state contract com. chair 1983-86), Big Thicket Assn. (life, com. mem. 1966-81, v.p. 1971-73, pres. 1973-75, 94-98, newsletter editor 1971-81, 99—), Big Thicket Conservation Assn. (bd. dirs. 1993-99), Tex. Com. Natural Resources (task force chair 1987-92), LWV, Nat. Parks and Conservation Assn. (Margery Stoneman Douglas Citizen Conservationist of Yr. award 1996), Sierra Club (exec. com. Lone Star chpt. 1994-96, Spl. Svc. award 1989), Tex. Folklore Soc., Tex. Gulf Hist. Soc., Nature Conservancy, Alpha Chi, Beta Phi Mu, Phi Kappa Phi. Home: 9715 Main St Batson TX 77519-7938

JOHNSTON, (WILLIAM) MICHAEL, political science educator, university administrator; b. Omaha, Nebr., Nov. 1, 1949; s. William M. and Margaret Mary (Ryan) J.; m. Bette Bennett, 1976; children: Michael Joseph, Patrick Brendan Ryan. BA in Polit. Sci summa cum laude, Macalester Coll., St. Paul, 1971; MPhil in Polit. Sci., Yale U., 1974, PhD in Polit. Sci., 1977. Teaching fellow, acting instr. Yale U., 1972-76; instr. U. Pitts., 1976-77, asst. prof., 1977-82, assoc. prof., 1982-86; assoc. prof. Colgate U., 1986-90, acting chair, Spring 1988, prof., 1990—, chmn. dept. polit. sci., 1990-96; dir. Geneva program, 1996; vis. lectr. politics, vis. fellow Ctr. Urban and Regional Rsch., U. Glasgow, Scotland, 1983-84; vis. fellow dept. politics and Inst. Rsch. in Social Scis., U. York, Eng., 1991; vis. fellow St. Aidan's Coll., 1997, dept. politics U. Durham (Eng.), 1997; rsch. cons. Conn. Joint Legis. Commn. Sch. Fin., Hartford, 1974; rsch. assoc. Cogen, Holt and Assocs., New Haven. 1974-75; Pitts. on-site coord. cmty. devel. block grants evaluation ABT Assocs., Cambridge, Mass., 1979-80; cons., expert witness N.Y. State Commn. Govt. Integrity, 1989; cons. Assocs. for Rural Devel., Washington, 1992, tng. program U.S. Agy. Internat. Devel. Democratization and Governance, 1996; tng. cons. Inst. Internat. Econs., Washington, World Bank, Washington, The Asia Found., San Francisco, 1997—; cons., participant anti-corruption confs. Italy, Princeton U., China, Colombia, Mex., Ctrl. Am., Eng., France, Thailand; guest lectr. U. Santiago de Compostela, Spain, Inst. des Hautes Etudes de la Justices, Paris, U. Durham, People's U. China, Beijing, Oxford (Eng.) U., Staffordshire (Eng.) Poly., U. York, U. Glasgow, Providence Coll., Hamilton Coll., W.Va. Wesleyan U.; plenary spkr., participant Ditchley (Eng.) Conf. on Corruption in Dem. States, 1995; participant, working group chair Ditchely (Eng.) Conf., 1998; bd. dirs., coun. governance Transparency Internat. USA; lectr., spkr. in field; participant 9th Ann. Bank Conf. Devel. Econs. World Bank, Washington, 1997; co-organizer program on governance and democratization 2nd Convention European Assn. Advancement Social Scis., Cyprus, 1997. Author: Political Corruption and Public Policy in America, 1982, Fraud, Waste and Abuse in Government, 1986, Political Corruption: A Handbook, 1989; contbr. articles to profl. jours. NSF fellow, 1972-76; grantee U. Pitts., 1983, Nuffield Found., 1984, Fulbright/British Coun. Higher Edn., 1984, Colgate U. Rsch. Coun. Maj. Grants com., 1987, New Liberal Arts program Colgate U./Sloan Found., 1988, 90, Leverhulme Trust/Social and Cmty. Planning Rsch., 1998. Mem. Internat. Polit. Sci. Assn. (sec. rsch. com.), Phi Beta Kappa, Pi Sigma Alpha. Democrat. Roman Catholic. Avocations: computing, baseball, trains. E-mail: mjohnston@mail.colgate.edu. Fax: 315-228-7883. Home: 41 E Main St Earlville NY 13332-3215 Office: Colgate U Dept Polit Sci 13 Oak Dr Hamilton NY 13346-1383

JOHNSTON, NANCY DAHL, data processing specialist, paralegal; b. Waco, Tex., Sept. 18, 1954; d. Howard Edward and Gladys Marie (Haynes) Dahl; children: Russell Edward, Dennis Aaron. Student, Tex. Woman's U., Denton, Victor Valley Coll., Victorville, Calif., U. So. Maine, Portland; cert., Nat. Acad. Paralegal Studies, 1991. Data processing coord. Denton County, 1986-89; customer svc. mgr. Jet-Line Svc., Inc., Portland, Maine, 1989-92; exec. sec. to state court adminstr. State of Maine, Portland, Maine, 1993-95; risk mgmt. technician UNUM Corp., Portland, Maine, 1996—. Vol. Maine Audubon Soc., Global Response, Com. for Responsible Transp. Mem. NAFE, Maine Assn. Paralegals, Mcpl. Software Users Group (sec. 1988-89), Greenpeace. Avocations: camping, winter sports. Home: 5121 Heatherstone Ct Kissimmee FL 34741

JOHNSTON, NORMAN JOHN, architecture educator; b. Seattle, Dec. 3, 1918; s. Jay and Helen May (Shultis) J.; m. Lois Jane Hastings, Nov. 22, 1969. B.A., U. Wash.-Seattle, 1942; B.Arch., U. Oreg., 1949; M. in Urban Planning, U. Pa.-Phila., 1959, Ph.D., 1964. Registered architect, Wash. City planner Seattle City Planning Commn., 1951-55; asst. prof. arch. U. Oreg.-Eugene, 1956-58; assoc. prof. architecture and urban planning U. Wash.-Seattle, 1960-64, prof., 1964-85, prof. emeritus, 1985—, assoc. dean, 1964-76, 79-84, chmn. dept. architecture, 1984-85; mem. nat. examinations com. Nat. Coun. Archtl. Registration Bds., Washington, 1970-81, 88—; vis. prof. Tokyo Inst. Tech., 1991, 98. Author: Cities in the Round, 1983, Washington's Audacious State Capitol and its Builders, 1988 (Gov.'s Book award 1984, 89), The College of Architecture and Urban Planning, 75 Years at the University of Washington: A Personal View, 1991, The Fountain and the Mountain - The University of Washington Campus, 1895-1995, 1995; editor: NCARB Architectural Registration Handbook, 1980; contbr. articles to profl. jours. Commr. King County Policy Devel. Commn., Seattle, 1970-76; mem. Capitol campus design adv. com. State of Wash., Olympia, 1980—, chmn., 1980-88, 96; trustee Mus. History & Industry, 1997—. Recipient Wash. Disting. Citizen award, 1987. Fellow AIA (pres. Seattle chpt. 1981, AIA medal Seattle chpt. 1991, Washington Coun. medal 1997); mem. State of Wash. Architects Registration Bd. (chmn. 1992-93, 98-99), Phi Beta Kappa, Sigma Chi, Tau Sigma Delta. Presbyterian. E-mail: njjo@u.washington.edu. Home: 900 University St Apt Au Seattle WA 98101-1778 Office: U Wash C Architecture & Urban Planning PO Box 355726 Seattle WA 98195-5726

JOHNSTON, OLIVER MARTIN, JR., animator; b. Palo Alto, Calif., Oct. 31, 1912; s. Oliver Martin and Arclissa Florence (Boggs) J.; m. Marie Estelle Worthey, Jan. 23, 1943; children: Richard Oliver, Kenneth Andrew. Student, Stanford U., 1931-34, U. Calif., Berkeley, 1932, Chouinard Art Inst., 1934-35. Directing animator Walt Disney Co., Burbank, Calif., 1935-78; lectr., spkr. in field. Asst. animator Snow White and the Seven Dwarfs, 1937; animation supr. Fantasia, 1940, Bambi, 1942; animator Pinnochio, 1940, The Fox and the Hound, 1981, Victory Through Air Power, 1943, The Three Calleros, 1945, Make Mine Music, 1946; directing animator Song of the South, 1946, Melody Time, 1948, The Adventures of Ichabod and Mr. Toad, 1949, Cinderella, 1950, Alice in Wonderland, 1951, Peter Pan, 1953, Lady and the Tramp, 1955, Sleeping Beauty, 1959, 101 Dalmatians, 1961, Sword in the Stone, 1963, Mary Poppins, 1964, The Jungle Book, 1967, The Aristocats, 1970, Robin Hood, 1973, Rescuers, 1977, also shorts and TV cartoons; author: Disney Animation -- The Illusion of Life, 1981, Too Funny For Words, 1987, Bambi-the Story and the Film, 1990, Jungle Book Portfolio, 1992, The Disney Villain, English edit., 1993, French edit., 1995; contbg. editor sketch book series; subject of documentary Frank and Ollie; drawings exhibited in Whitney Mus., N.Y.C., 1981. Guest spkr. Russian Govt. and Soyuzmultifilm, 1976, other East European Countries, U.S. Info. Agy. Cultural Exch. Program, 1986. Recipient Pioneer in Film award Delta Kappa Allpha, 1978, honor award Mus. Modern Art, 1978, Annie award Internat. Animated Film Soc., 1980, Disney Legend award, 1989, Grand Prix of the Ams., 1995. Avocations: trains, reading, studying, sports. Address: 748 Flintridge Ave Flintridge CA 91011

JOHNSTON, OSCAR BLACK, III, lawyer; b. Tulsa, Oct. 1, 1941; s. Oscar Black Jr. and Carol (VanDerwiele) J.; m. Ruth Archdeacon Darrough; children: Eric Oscar, David Darrough. BBA, Baylor U., 1963; JD, U. Tulsa, 1966. Bar: Okla. 1966, U.S. Dist. Ct. (no., ea., we. dists.) Okla., U.S. Ct. Claims, U.S. Ct. Appeals (10th cir.), U.S. Supreme Ct. Asst. U.S. attorney U.S. Dist. Ct. (we. dist.) Okla., 1970-76; ptnr. Logan & Lowry, L.L.P., Vinita, Okla., 1979—. Assoc. editor Tulsa Law Review, 1964-66. Presiding judge divsn. 54 Okla. Temp. Ct. Appeals, 1980-81, judge divsn. XIV, 1991-93; presiding judge panel VI Lawyer-Staffed Ct. Appeals, 1992. Capt. JAGC, U.S. Army, 1966-70. Fellow Am. Bar Found., Okla. Bar Found. (trustee 1988-96, pres. 1995); mem. ABA (sects. litigation, family law and criminal), Fed. Bar Assn. (pres. Oklahoma City chpt. 1975), Craig County Bar Assn. (pres. 1986-88), Okla. Bar Assn. (adminstrn. of justice, bench and bar coms.), Okla. Trial Lawyers Assn., Rotary (pres. Vinita 1983-84), Phi Alpha Delta. Republican. Methodist. Office: Logan & Lowry PO Box 558 Vinita OK 74301-0558 Home: 116 Westwood Ave Vinita OK 74301-2703

JOHNSTON, OTTO WILLIAM, German language and literature educator; b. Feb. 26, 1942. BA, Wagner Coll., 1963; MA, Columbia U., 1966; PhD, Princeton U., 1969; postgrad., U. Heidelberg, Germany, 1961-62, U. Vienna, Austria, 1962-63, U. Göttingen. Prof. Germanic langs. and lits. U. Fla.,

Gainesville, 1969—, chmn. dept. Germanic and Slavic studies, 1978-83, 98—. E-mail: ot1942@nersp.nerdc.ufl.edu. Office: U Fla 263 Dau Hall GS11 Gainesville FL 32611

JOHNSTON, PATRICK RICHARD, risk management specialist, county official; b. Elizabethtown, N.Y., May 15, 1957. BS in Indsl. Risk Mgmt., Ea. Ky. U., 1982, MS in Loss Prevention Adminstrn., 1989. Ins. engr. III United Svc. Agy. Inc., Lexington, Ky., 1984-90; mgr. health, safety Valvoline Co. and SuperAm. Group Ashland, Inc., Lexington, 1990-96; dir. risk mgmt. Performance Assocs., Inc., Cin., 1996-97, Lexington-Fayette Urban County Govt., Lexington, 1997—. Home: 1001 Doe Meadow Ct Lexington KY 40509-2064 Office: Lexington-Fayette Urban County Govt 121 N Martin Luther King Blvd Lexington KY 40507-1542*

JOHNSTON, RICHARD ALAN, lawyer; b. Buffalo, Mar. 18, 1950; s. Richard W. and Virginia (Holmes) J.; m. Patricia Downing, Aug. 28, 1971; children: Matthew, Sarah, Elizabeth, Michael. BA, Cornell U., 1972; JD, Harvard U., 1976. Bar: Mass. 1977, U.S. Dist. Ct. Mass. 1977, U.S. Ct. Appeals (1st cir.) 1977. Law clk. to presiding justice Mass. Ct. Appeals, Boston, 1976-77; assoc. Hale and Dorr LLP, Boston, 1977-82, ptnr., 1982—. Co-chmn. North Area Task Force, Charlestown, Mass., 1981—; trustee Dennis (Mass.) Conservation Trust, 1988—, pres., 1995—; mem. transition team Mass. Gov. William Weld, 1990-91; internat. election observer Internat. Human Rights Law Group, Nepal, 1991; dir. Friends of City Square Park, 1993—; trustee Hockey Humanitarian Award Found., 1997—; pres. Friends of Tanzanias Schs., Inc., 1997—. Mem. ABA, Internat. Bar Assn., Boston Bar Assn., Nat. Health Lawyers Assn., Mass. Bar Assn. Home: 43 Monument Ave Charlestown MA 02129-3323 Office: Hale & Dorr LLP 60 State St Boston MA 02109-1816

JOHNSTON, RICHARD BOLES, JR., pediatrician, educator, biomedical researcher; b. Atlanta, Aug. 23, 1935; s. Richard Boles and Jane (Dillon) J.; m. Mary Anne Claiborne, Aug. 13, 1960; children: Richard B. III, S. Claiborne, Kristin M. BA, Vanderbilt U., 1957, MD, 1961; MS (hon.), U. Pa., 1986. Diplomate Am. Bd. Pediatrics, Am. Bd. Pediatric Infectious Disease. Resident in pediatrics Vanderbilt U., 1961-63, Harvard U., 1963-64; fellow in pediatric immunology Harvard U., Boston, 1967-70; asst. prof., assoc. prof. depts. pediatrics and microbiology U. Ala. Med. Ctr., Birmingham, 1970-76; vis. assoc. prof. Rockefeller U., N.Y.C., 1976-77, vis. prof., 1983-84; prof. pediatrics Sch. Medicine U. Colo., Denver, 1977-86; chmn. dept. pediatrics Nat. Jewish Ctr. Immunology and Respiratory Medicine, Denver, 1977-86; chmn. dept. pediatrics Sch. Medicine U. Pa., Phila., 1986-90, Wm. H. Bennett prof. pediatrics Sch. Medicine, 1986-92; med. dir. March of Dimes Birth Defects Found., White Plains, N.Y., 1992-98; adj. prof. pediat, chief sec. pediat. immunology Yale U. Sch. Medicine, 1992-98; prof. pediatrics Sch. Medicine U. Colo., Denver, 1999—; bd. trustees Internat. Pediatric Rsch. Found., 1983-87, 95-98, chmn. 1984-87, 97-98; sci. adv. com. Pediatric Pharms. Inc., 1988-90; chmn. adv. bd. for vaccines and related biols. FDA, Bethesda, Md., 1990-93; chmn. com. vaccine safety, Inst. Medicine, 1992-93, chmn. com new rsch. in vaccines, 1993-94, chmn. forum vaccine safety, 1995—, chmn. com. asthma and indoor air, 1998-99, mem bd. health promotion disease prevention, 1994—. Mem. editl. bds. of 7 biomed. jours., 1978—; contbr. numerous articles in area of immunology to scholarly and profl. jours.; editor: Current Opinion in Pediatrics, 1997—. Capt. M.C., U.S. Army, 1964-66. Recipient faculty scholar award Josiah Macy Jr. Found., 1976-77, commr. citation and Wiley medal FDA, 1994. Fellow Am. Assn. Advancement Sci.; mem. Inst. Medicine NAS, Am. Soc. Clin. Investigation, Am. Pediat. Soc. (pres. 1996-97), Assn. Am. Physicians, Soc. Pediat. Rsch. (pres. 1980-81). Office: Nat Jewish Med and Rsch Ctr Birth Defects Found 1400 Jackson St Denver CO 80206

JOHNSTON, RICHARD FOURNESS, biologist; b. Oakland, Calif., July 27, 1925; s. Arthur Nathaniel and Marie (Johnson) J.; m. Lora Lee Bliler, Feb. 7, 1948; children: Regan, Janet, Cassandra. B.A., U. Calif.-, Berkeley, 1950, M.A., 1953, Ph.D., 1955. Asst. prof. dept. biology N.Mex. State U., 1956-58; mem. faculty depts. zoology and ecology U. Kans., Lawrence, 1958—, prof., 1968-92, prof. emeritus, 1992—, chmn., 1979-82, editor mus. publs., 1974-76, 86-91; program dir. systematic biology NSF, Washington, 1968-69; editor Ann. Rev. Ecology and Systematics, 1968-92, Current Ornithology, 1981-87. Mem. adv. panel biol. scis. Smithsonian Fgn. Currency Program, 1969-71. Served with AUS, 1943-46. Am. Acad. Arts and Scis. grantee, 1957; nat. Acad. Sci. grantee, 1959; NSF grantee, 1959-83. Fellow Am. Ornithol. Union (Coues award 1975), AAAS, mem. Ecol. Soc. Am., Soc. Systematic Zoology (editor jour. 1967-70, pres. 1977), Soc. Study Evolution. Home: 615 Louisiana St Lawrence KS 66044-2337 Office: U Kans Mus Natural History Lawrence KS 66045 *Variability or heterogeneity or pluralism is present in nearly everything humans do or to which they are exposed.*

JOHNSTON, ROBERT ATKINSON, psychologist, educator; b. Allentown, Pa., July 8, 1931; s. Robert and Marion (McBride) J.; children: Robert Paul, Kenneth Moffett, Scott Andrew; m. Janet Persing. A.B., Haverford Coll., 1952; M.A., State U. Iowa, 1954, Ph.D., 1955. Intern VA Hosp., Knoxville, Iowa, 1955-56; staff psychologist VA Hosp., Coatesville, Pa., 1956; asso. prof. psychology, dir. Univ. Center for Psychol. Services, U. Richmond, 1957-63; prof. psychology, asso. dean faculty Coll. William and Mary, 1963-74, dept. psychology, 1974—, chair, 1994—. Pres. Williamsburg PTA Council, 1967-69; chmn. bd. dirs. Williamsburg Pre-sch. for Spl. Children, 1968-69. Mem. Am., Eastern psychol. Assn., Va. Acad. Sci., AAUP, Am. Physiol. Assn. Home: PO Box 455 Williamsburg VA 23187-0455 Office: Coll William and Mary Williamsburg VA 23187-8795

JOHNSTON, ROBERT FOWLER, venture capitalist; b. Phila., Aug. 15, 1936; s. William S. and Elinor (Fowler) J.; m. Lynn Dixon, Feb. 5, 1972; children: William McCord, Bradford Dixon, Alexandra Fowler. BA, Princeton U., 1958; MBA, NYU, 1964. With F.S. Smithers & Co., N.Y.C., 1960-61, Smith Barney & Co., N.Y.C., 1963-67; pres. Johnston Assocs. Inc., Princeton, N.J., 1967—; bd. dirs. Envirogen Inc., Lawrenceville, N.J., Immunicon corp., Huntington Valley, Pa., Praelux Inc., Lawrenceville, Janus Pharmas. Inc., N.Y.C. Co-author: Entrepreneural Science: New Links Between Corporations, Universities and Government. Mem. adv. coun. Princeton U. Dept. Molecular biology, 1983—; mem. exec. com. Friends of Inst. Advanced Study, Princeton, 1992—, chmn., 1998—; founder Edn. Ventures Found. With USAF, 1961-62. Mem. Nat. Venture Capital Assn., Univ. Club of N.Y.C. Avocations: archaeology, art. Home: Sycamore Creek 48 Elm Ridge Rd Pennington NJ 08534 Office: Johnston Assoc Inc 181 Cherry Valley Rd Princeton NJ 08540-7911

JOHNSTON, ROBERT JAKE, federal magistrate judge; b. Denver, Sept. 30, 1947; m. Julie Ann Black; children: Jennifer, Robert, Jr., Michelle. BS, Brigham Young U., 1973; JD, U. Pacific, 1977. Bar: Nev. 1977, U.S. Dist. Ct. Nev. 1978, U.S. Ct. Appeals (9th cir.) 1984. Law clk. to Hon. Merlyn Hoyt Nev. 7th Judicial Dist., Ely, 1977-78; dist. atty. White Pine County, Ely, 1979-82; pvt. practice Johnston & Fairman, Ely, 1979-82; deputy dist. atty. Office Clark County Dist. Atty., Las Vegas, Nev., 1983-84; asst. U.S. atty. Office U.S. Atty., Las Vegas, 1984-87; chief civil div. Office U.S. Atty., 1986-87; U.S. magistrate judge U.S. Dist. Ct., Las Vegas, 1987—. Dir. Boy Scouts Am. Boulder Dam Area Coun., Las Vegas. With U.S. Army, 1967-70. Mem. Nev. Bar Assn., Clark County Bar Assn., Fed. Magistrate Judicial Assn. (dir. 1990-92), Las Vegas Track Club, 9th Jud. Cir. Hist. Soc., Southwest Oral History Soc., 9th Cir. Conf. Exec. Com. Office: US Dist Ct 300 Las Vegas Blvd S Ste 4650 Las Vegas NV 89101-5883

JOHNSTON, RONALD CHARLES, chemistry educator; b. Erie, Pa., Nov. 3, 1941; s. Earl Clair and Mary Elizabeth Johnston. BA, Washington & Jefferson Coll., 1964; MEd, U. Maine, 1989. Chmn. sci. dept. Hun Sch. of Princeton, N.J., 1971-91, Flint Hill Sch., Oakton, Va., 1991-96; head sci. dept. Trinity Sch., N.Y.C., 1996—. Mem. Nat. Sci. Tchrs. Assn., Nat. Marine Educators Assn. Democrat. Roman Catholic. Avocations: reading, photography. E-mail: rjohnston@trinity.nyu.ny.us. Home: 201 Bridge Pla N #12-B Fort Lee NJ 07024 Office: Trinity Sch 101 W 91st St New York NY 10024

JOHNSTON, ROY G., consulting structural engineer; b. Chgo., Jan. 7, 1914; s. Karl Gunnar and Esther M. (Youngberg) J.; m. Naomi Harmon, July 30, 1936 (dec.); children—Judith R., Robert K.; m. Lucille Peterson, Dec. 28, 1991. B.S.C.E., U. So. Calif., 1935. Cert. civil and structural engr., Calif. Plan checker County of Los Angeles, 1935; structural designer C. Devel., Los Angeles, 1936-44; structural engr. Lummis Co., Los Angeles, 1944-45, Brandow & Johnston, Los Angeles, 1945-64; v.p., structural engr. Brandow & Johnston Assocs., Los Angeles, 1964—; mem. structural safety com. VA, 1973-91; mem. Calif. Bd. Registration Engrs., 1971-78, pres., 1975-76; past chmn. Bldg. Seismic Safety Coun., Washington, 1982-85; mem. State Bldg. Stds. Commn., Calif., 1985-94; mem. steering com. 8th World Conf. Earthquake Engring., 1984; cons. U.S.-Japan Seismic Rsch. Program, 1980-87; lectr. earthquake engring. seminars. Contbr. articles to profl. jours. Trustee Westmont Coll., 1964—, chmn., 1972-88. Recipient Disting. Alumni award U. So. Calif., 1972, 82, George Washington award Inst. Advancement Engring., L.A., 1985; named Constrn. Man Yr., Constrn. Industry so. Calif., 1981, Engr. of Yr. SEOSC, 1990, Pres. Award Tall Bldg. Coun., 1994. Fellow ASCE, Am. Concrete Inst.; mem. NAE, Earthquake Engring. Rsch. Inst. (bd. dirs., v.p.), Structurals Engr. Assn. (Calif. pres.), Structurals Engrs. So. Calif. (pres., engr. of Yr. 1990), Nat. Acad. Engrs. Republican. Avocations: travelling; golf. Office: Brandow & Johnston Assocs 1660 W 3rd St Los Angeles CA 90017-1138

JOHNSTON, SHERYL L., communications executive; b. Portland, Oreg., Feb. 18, 1944; d. Frank F. and Edith A. (Vallereux) Neels; m. Robert K. Johnston, Feb. 14, 1973; 1 child, James Patrick. Student, Portland State U., 1962-65, 67-68, Sch. of the Art Inst., Chgo., 1972-74, Northwestern U., 1975; BA, Columbia Coll., Chgo., 1993. Adminstrv. asst. Art Inst. Chgo., 1971-75; asst. editorial dir. Sta. WLS-TV, Chgo., 1975-76; dir. pub. rels. Prime Time Sch. TV, Chgo., 1976-77; v.p. J. Walter Thompson Co., Chgo., 1977-82; pres. Sheryl Johnston Communications, Chgo., 1982—; tchr. Columbia Coll., 1991, 95, 96. Mem. Country Music Assn. (pub. rels. com. 1981, 82, 85). Democrat. Episcopalian. Avocations: dancing, exercising, writing. Office: 623 W Oakdale Chicago IL 60657-5309

JOHNSTON, STANLEY HOWARD, JR., curator of rare books, bibliographer; b. Cleve., Apr. 28, 1946; m. Carol Ann Lewis, June 19, 1976. BA, Columbia Coll., 1968; MA,, U. Western Ontario, London, Ontario, Can., 1970, PhD, 1977; MS in Libr. Sci., Case Western Reserve U., 1979. Tchg. asst. U. Western Ontario, London, Can., 1971-72; asst. to editors Spenser Newsletter, London, Ontario, Can., 1972-73; bibliographer Cleve. Herbals Project, Cleve, 1984-90; curator of rare books Holden Arboretum, Kirtland, Ohio, 1990—; internet columnist Coun. on Botanical and Horticultural Librs., 1995—; libr. adv. com. The Herb Soc. Am., Kirtland, Ohio, 1997—. Author: The Cleveland Herbal, Botanical and Horticultural Collections, 1992, Cleveland's Treasures from the World of Botanical Literature, 1998; contbr. articles to profl. jours.; internet columnist. Mem. MLA, Bibliographical Soc. Am., Soc. for History of Natural History, Am. Libr. Assn. (rare books and manuscripts sect.), The Bibliographical Soc., Coun. on Botanical and Horticultural Librs. (mem. publs. com., electronic comm. com., 1996—, documentation strategy com., long term planning com., 1997—), Renaissance Soc. Am., Medieval Acad. Am., Am. Philatelic Soc., No. Ohio Bibliophilic Soc. Republican. Presbyterian. Avocations: philately, collecting mysteries, fantasy, sci.-fiction. Home: 7226 Grant St Mentor OH 44060-4704 Office: The Holden Arboretum 9500 Sperry Rd Kirtland OH 44094-5149

JOHNSTON, STEPHEN EDWARD, clinical information systems coordinator, educator; b. Beaufort, S.C., Aug. 17, 1949; s. William Joseph and Florence Martha (Boineau) J.; children: Sarah Ellen, Matthew Ford. ASN, Trident Tech. Coll., Charleston, S.C., 1985; BSN, U. State of N.Y., Albany, 1990; MSN, Med. U. S.C., 1994. Staff nurse in emergency rm. Charleston Meml. Hosp., 1985-86; staff nurse, trauma Med. U. S.C., Charleston, 1986; staff nurse surg. ICU VA Med. Ctr., Charleston, 1987-88, nurse mgr., 1988-91, quality mgmt. clin. specialist, 1991—; mem. faculty Med. U. S.C. Coll. Nursing, 1994-96. Vestryman Ch. of Holy Communion, Charleston, 1994-96. Mem. ANA. Episcopalian. Avocations: water skiing, golf, tennis. Office: Ralph H Johnson VA Med Ctr 109 Bee St Charleston SC 29401-5703

JOHNSTON, SUMMERFIELD K., JR., food products executive; b. 1954. V.p. Johnston Food Group, Inc., 1983-85; officer Cleveland (Tenn.) Coca-Cola, 1986-87; v.p., gen. mgr. Midwest Coca-Cola (subsid. Johnston Coca-Cola Bottling Co.), Mpls., from 1987, pres., regional ops., 1987—; chmn., CEO Coca-Cola Enterprises, Inc., Atlanta, GA. Office: Coca-Cola Enterprises PO Box 723040 Atlanta GA 31139-0040*

JOHNSTON, THOMAS MCELREE, JR., church administrator; b. Coral Gables, Fla., June 10, 1934; s. Thomas McElree and Lorine (Davis) J.; m. Anna Youel Armstrong, July 2, 1960; children: Kathryn Armstrong, Timothy Armstrong, Sara Helen. BA, Amherst Coll., 1956; MDiv, Yale U., 1959; ThM, Princeton Theol. Sem., 1963; D of Ministry, San Francisco Theol. Sem., 1978. Ordained to ministry Presbyn. Ch., 1959. Assoc. coord. religious affairs N.C. State U., Raleigh, 1959-62; min. community svc. Tabernacle Presbyn. Ch., Phila., 1963-66; organizer, head of staff Ch. of the Reconciler, Clearwater, Fla., 1966-78; assoc. Presbytery devel. Synod of the Covenant, Columbus, Ohio, 1978-85, assoc. exec., 1985-88; exec. Synod of the Trinity, Camp Hill, Pa., 1988—; pres. Pa. Coun. Chs., Harrisburg, 1995-98; mem. Pa. Coun. Interch. Cooperation, Harrisburg; chair Synod Exec. Forum, 1997; chmn. gen. assembly Synod Staff Forum, 1997; corr. mem. Gen. Assembly Coun., Louisville, 1993-94. Publisher: (newspaper) Trinitarian. Pres., organizer Religious Cmty. Svcs., Inc. Clearwater, 1968-70; pres. Pinellas County Head Start, Inc., Clearwater, 1968-72; mem. Pinellas County Sch. Bd., Pinellas County Coun., Clearwater, 1972-76; bd. dirs. Cmty. Svcs. Found., Largo, Fla., 1969-78. Named Vol. of Yr., Civic Coun., Pinellas County, Fla., 1972; recipient Humanitarian award Lions Club, 1975. Mem. Rotary Internat. Home: 1041 Country Club Rd Camp Hill PA 17011-1049 Office: Presbyn Ch Synod of the Trinity 3040 Market St Camp Hill PA 17011-4539

JOHNSTON, TIMOTHY SIDNEY, computer engineer; b. Royal Oak, Mich., Nov. 30, 1966; s. Sidney Charles and Kathleen Ann (Backer) J. BS with high honors, Rochester Inst. Tech., 1991. Data processing clk. City of Madison Hts., Mich., 1987; maint. programmer Compuware Corp., Farmington Hills, Mich., 1988; tech. assoc. AT&T Bell Labs., Naperville, Ill., 1989; archtl. verification software team mem. Semiconductor Engring. Group, DEC, Hudson, Mass., 1991; project engr. Applied Computer Engring., Inc., Warren, Mich., 1992-94; software engr. Brendan Sci. Corp., Grosse Pointe Farms, Mich., 1994-98; info. analyst Elec. Data Systems, Troy, Mich., 1998—; part-time tchr. Am. Sign Lang., 1992—. Staff mem. Deaf Teen Club Youth Leadership Tng. Program, Pontiac, Mich., 1991—; staff writer The Deaf Nation Newspaper, Waterford, Las Vegas, 1992—; Bible study group leader Our Savior Luth. Ch. of the Deaf, Farmington Hills and Holly, Mich.; dir. Miss. Deaf Mich. Pageant. Mem. Mich. Deaf Assn., Phi Beta Kappa, Alpha Sigma Lambda, Phi Kappa Phi, Tau Alpha Pi, Kappa Phi Theta. Avocations: in-line skating, woodburn drawings, hiking, swimming, reading, travel. Office: EDS MS 501 300 E Big Beacer Ave Troy MI 48083

JOHNSTON, VAN ROBERT, management educator; b. Sudbury, Can., Feb. 23, 1945; s. Olaf Wesley and Bernice Everlyn (Mullen) J.; m. Suzanne Marie Simpson, July 26, 1969; children: David A., Erik W., Jacqueline M. BA in Polit. Sci., Loyola U., L.A., 1967; M of Pub. Adminstrn., U. Southern Calif., 1974, PhD, 1976. Sr. lifeguard, trainer, instr. L.A. County, 1963-68; rsch. assoc., instr. U. Southern Calif., L.A., 1975-76; dir. prof. mgmt. program U. Denver, 1986-88, chair bus. and pub. policy, 1986-91, prof. mgmt. policy, 1976—; disting. vis. prof. mgmt. strategy USAF Acad., Colorado Springs, 1991-93; faculty assoc. Intermodal Transp. Inst., Denver, 1997—; profl. cons., trainer, rschr. numerous orgns., 1975—. Co-editor Policy Studies Rev., 1997—; contbr. numerous articles to profl. jours. Marshall internat. golf tournament Profl. Golf Assn., 1986, 87; coach, soccer Cherry Creek Soccer Assn., 1977-84; active Boy Scouts Am., 1979-89. Recipient Outstanding Young Men of Am. U.S. Jaycees, 1979, Program and Mgmt. award Nat. Am. Soc. of Pub. Adminstrs., 1984, Univ. Tchg. award Mortar Bd. Nat. Honor Soc., U. Denver, 1997. Mem. Am. Soc. for Pub. Adminstrs. (exec. com. 1997-98, nat. coun. 1997-98, sect. chair 1997—, publs. com. 1996—, Outstanding Svc. award 1998), Pinery County Club, Colo.-Am. Soc. for Pub. Adminstrn. (pres., v.p., Leadership award 1983). Avocations: golf, ranch, Siberian Husky, photography, exercise. Office: U Denver Daniels Coll of Bus Dept of Mgmt Denver CO 80208

JOHNSTON, VIRGINIA EVELYN, editor; b. Spokane, Wash., Apr. 26, 1933; d. Edwin and Emma Lucile (Munroe) Rowe; student Portland C.C., 1964, Portland State U., 1966, 78-79; m. Alan Paul Beckley, Dec. 26, 1974; children: Chris, Denise, Rex. Proofreader, The Oregonian, Portland, 1960-62, teletypesetter operator, 1962-66, operator Photon 200, 1966-68, copy editor, asst. women's editor, 1968-80; spl. sects. editor (UPDATE), 1981-83, 88-95; editor FOODday, 1982—; pres. Matrix Assocs., Inc., Portland, 1975—, chmn. bd., 1979—; pres. Bones & Brew Inc.; bd. dir. Computer Tools Inc. Cons. Dem. Party Oreg., 1969, Portland Sch. Dist. No. 1, 1978. Mem. Eating and Drinking Soc. Oreg. (past pres.), We. Culinary Inst. (mem. adv. bd.), Internat. Food Media Conf. (past mem. adv. bd.). Democrat. Editor Principles of Computer Systems for Newspaper Mgmt., 1975-76. Home: 4140 NE 137th Ave Portland OR 97230-2624 Office: Oregonian Pub Co 1320 SW Broadway Portland OR 97201-3499

JOHNSTON, WALDO CORY MELROSE, museum director; b. Cooperstown, N.Y., Sept. 21, 1913; s. Waldo Cory and Marie (Jones) J.; m. Elinor Doolittle, July 1, 1939; children: Waldo Cory Melrose, Elinor (Mrs. Gilbert Vincent), Carol (Mrs. Amos Galpin), James Andrews Melrose. AB, Yale U., 1937; postgrad., Harvard U., 1938. Tchr. Pomfret (Conn.) Sch., 1939-41, asst. headmaster, 1946-51; exec. sec. Yale Alumni Bd., New Haven, 1951-59, dir. com. on enrollment and scholarships, 1960-65, assoc. dir. alumni rels., 1960-65; dir. Mystic (Conn.) Seaport Mus., 1965-78, dir. emeritus, 1978—, trustee, 1978; headmaster Berkshire Sch., 1978-79, headmaster emeritus, 1979—. Contbr. articles to profl. jours. Mem. adv. com. South St. Seaport Mus., N.Y.C., 1969-93; trustee Sail Edn. Assn., Woods Hale, Mass., 1971—, Conn. River Found, 1982-88; bd. govs. Chesapeake Bay Maritime Mus., St. Michaels, Md., 1971-82; mem. adv. com. Eleutherian Mills-Hagley Found., Wilmington, Del., 1974-77, adv. coun. Soc. for Preservation New Eng. Antiquities, Boston, 1976-93; bd. dirs. Am. alumni Coun., 1953-60, sec. treas., 1953-58, pres., 1960-61; mem. bd. admissions Yale U., 1955-65; dir. Dwight Hall, 1952-65; bd. dirs. New Haven Coun. Social Agys., 1952-65, Cooperstown Art Assn.; pres. Cooperstown Art Assn., 1955-56, hon., 1961—; trustee Berkshire Sch., Sheffield, Mass., 1956-78, 79-89, trustee emeritus, 1989—, exec. com. 1963-78; bd. incorporators Lawrence and Meml. Hosps., New London, Conn., 1965-79, Conn. Blue Cross, 1973-74; bd. dirs. Conn. Blue Cross, 1974-79; trustee Nat. Trust for Hist. Preservation, Washington, 1974-80, mem. exec. com., 1975-80, chmn. maritime preservation com., 1976-82; mem. Maritime Task Force, 1982-88; mem. adv. bd. Hartford Nat. Bank, 1965-78. Served from 2d lt. to lt. col. USAAF, 1941-45. Fellow Davenport Coll., Yale U. Mem. Am. Assn. Museums, Coun. Am. Maritime Museums (pres. 1973-78, hon. fellow 1978—), Am. Assn. State and Local History, Newcomen Soc. (hon.), Internat. Congress Maritime Museums (exec. com. 1974-81, hon. founding fellow 1981—), N.Y. State Hist. Assn., Conn. Antiquarian Soc., Am. Sail Tng. Assn., Am. Catboat Assn. (hon.), Scroll and Key, Yeamans Hall Club, Charleston, S.C., N.Am. Sta. Royal Scandinavian Yacht Club (gov. 1973-78), N.Y. Yacht Club, The Century Assn. (N.Y.C.), Mory's Assn. (New Haven), Essex Club (Conn.), Yacht Club, Off Soundings Club (Conn.), Cruising Club Am. Home: 10 Hanna Ln Essex CT 06426-1007 Office: Mystic Seaport Mystic CT 06355

JOHNSTON, WILLIAM DAVID, biotechnology executive; b. Chgo., Nov. 5, 1944; s. Samuel David and Jeanne (Williams) J.; m. Susan Diane Ward, Aug. 19, 1966; children: Kimberly Dawn Sites, Kirk David, Tiffany Dee Hansen, Kyle Donald, Ryan Daryl. BS in Chemistry, Brigham Young U., 1969, PhD in Organic Chemistry, 1974. V.p. Parish Chem. Co., 1973-75; mgr. materials control Baxter Healthcare Corp., 1975-80; group mgr., polymer rsch. and material control Travenol Labs., Inc., 1980-84, v.p. Material and Membrane Tech. Ctr., 1984-86, v.p. applied scis., 1987-93; v.p., gen. mgr. gene therapy div. Baxter Healthcare Corp., Round Lake, Ill., 1993-97; pres., CEO Inhibitex, Inc., Atlanta, 1997—; mem. adv. bd. Ill. Jr. Acad. Sci., Springfield, 1984-86; bd. dirs. Ill. Hi-Tech. Assn., 1990-92; mem. adv. bd. Coll. Engring., U. ill., Chgo., 1988-92, dept. chem. engring. Northwestern U., Evanston, Ill., 1989-98. Contbr. articles to profl. jours.; patentee in field. Stake pres. LDS Ch., Buffalo Grove, Ill., 1988-97; exec. coun. N.E. Ill. coun. Boy Scouts Am., 1989-97; chmn. bd. LDS Social Svcs., Naperville, Ill., 1990-97; bd. dirs. Neocrin Co., 1992-96. Brigham Young U. scholarship. Mem. AAAS, Am. Chem. Soc., Internat. Soc. for Artificial Organs, Internat. Soc. Blood Purification (exec. bd. 1991-96), Soc. for Biomaterials, Internat. Soc. of Cell Transplantation, Sigma Xi. Home: 1422 Spyglass Hill Dr Duluth GA 30097-5948

JOHNSTON, WILLIAM FREDERICK, emergency services administrator; b. Oakridge, Tenn., Mar. 4, 1945; s. Leonard E. and Helene C. (Spicker) J.; m. Kathleen Jo Hotaling, Nov. 17, 1988; 1 child, Lindsey Anne. BS, U. Wash., 1969, MS, 1971, MD, 1974, MBA, 1998. Diplomate Am. Bd. Emergency Medicine. Med. intern U. Wash. Affiliated Hosps., Seattle, 1974-75; emergency medicine resident Valley Med. Ctr. Fresno/U. Calif. San Francisco, Fresno, 1975-77; pres., CEO N.W. Emergency Physicians, Seattle, 1977-81; med. dir. emergency svcs. N.W. Hosp., Seattle, 1977—; bd. dirs. First Choice Helath Plan, Inc., First Choice Health Network, Inc., Washington Casualty Co., N.W. Healthcare Ins. Svcs. Contbr. articles to med. jours. Fellow Am. Coll. Emergency Physicians. Avocations: skiing, hiking, flying, kayaking, computers. Home: 4731 Beach Dr SW Seattle WA 98116-4340 Office: N W Hosp 1550 N 115th St Seattle WA 98133-8498

JOHNSTON, WILLIAM J., JR., neurosurgeon; b. Sept. 11, 1945. BS, U. Southwestern La., 1969; MD, La. State U., 1973. Neurol. surgeon Neurosurg. Assocs., Metairie, La., 1979—; chief of staff E. Jefferson Gen. Hosp., Metairie, 1992. Office: 4228 Houma Blvd Ste 220 Metairie LA 70006-3006

JOHNSTON, WILLIAM MEDFORD, artist, retired educator; b. Atlanta, Mar. 2, 1941; s. William P. and Sara (Medford) J.; m. Loraine Presley, Aug. 17, 1968. BA, Ga. State U., 1965; MFA, Fla. State U., 1967. Prof. emeritus Ga. State U., Atlanta, 1967-97. Exhibited in group shows at The Red Clay Survey 4th Biennial Exhbn. of Contemporary So. Art, 1994 (Merit award 1994), Am. Drawing Biennial 6, Pulp Fictions: Works on Paper, 1996 (Merit award 1996), Nexus Contemporary Art Ctr., Atlanta, 1998, Muscarelle Mus. of Art, The Coll. of Wm. and Mary, Williamsburg, Va., 1998; solo exhbn. Sandler Hudson Gallery, Atlanta, 1998-99. Regional fellow So. Arts Fedn., Nat. Endowment for the Arts, 1990, fellow Hambidge Ctr., 1994. Mem. Contemporary Art Soc. (bd. dirs.). Avocations: travel, reading, cooking.

JOHNSTON, WILLIAM WEBB, pathologist, educator; b. Statesville, N.C., Aug. 26, 1933; s. Jesse Clyde and Pauline Elizabeth (Massey) J. B.S., Davidson Coll., 1954; M.D., Duke U., 1959. Diplomate Am. Bd. Pathology, Am. Bd. Cytopathology, Internat. Bd. Cytopathology. Intern Duke U., 1959-60, resident in pathology, 1960-63, mem. faculty, 1963—, prof. pathology, 1972-97, dir. div. cytopathology and cytotechnology tng. program, 1966—; ret., 1996; bd. dirs. Anatomical Pathology Svc.; cons. pathologist Durham VA Hosp., Duncan County Hosp.; chmn. Internat. Bd. Cytopathology, 1992-98. Author: (with W.J. Frable) Respiratory Cytopathology, 1974; Diagnostic Respiratory Cytopathology, 1979; (with S.H. Bigner) The Cytopathology of the Central Nervous System, 1981, 2d edit., 1994, Pulmonary Cytology (with James Linder), 1992; assoc. editor Acta Cytologica, 1978—, sr. mem. editorial bd., 1992; editor: Masson Monographs in Cytopathology; mem. editorial bd. Am. Jour. Clin. Pathology, 1986; editorial cons. Masson Publs., N.Y.C.; mem. editorial adv. bd. Jour. Nat. Cancer Inst. Fellow Internat. Acad. Cytology (Maurice Goldblatt award 1995), Am. Soc. Clin. Pathologists, Coll. Am. Pathologists, Royal Soc. Medicine; mem. AMA (del. 1982-96), Am. Soc. Cytology (rev. bd., pres. 1981-82, Papanicolaou award 1986), Am. Assn. Pathologists, Arthur Purdy Stout Soc. Surg. Pathology, Internat. Acad. Pathology, Am. Assn. for Cancer Rsch. Republican. Presbyterian (organist). Home: 8200 Bromley Rd Hillsborough NC 27278-9709

JOHNSTON, YNEZ, artist; b. Berkeley, Calif., May 12, 1920. BFA, U. Calif., Berkeley, 1941, MFA, 1946. Lectr. art U. Calif., Berkeley, 1950-51, Colorado Springs Fine Arts Center, 1954, 55, Chouinard Art Inst., 1956, Calif. State U., Los Angeles, 1966, 67, U. Judaism Sch. Fine Arts, Los Angeles, 1967, Otis Art Inst., Los Angeles, 1978-81; artist-in-residence Fullerton Coll. (Calif.), 1982. One-man exhbns. include: San Francisco Mus. Art, 1943, Redlands U., 1947, Santa Barbara (Calif.) Mus. Art, 1952, 57, Pasadena (Calif.) Mus. Art, 1955, 62, Colorado Springs (Colo.) Fine Arts Center, 1955, Calif. Palace Legion of Honor, 1956, The O'Hana Gallery,

London, 1958, Paul Kantor Gallery, Los Angeles, 1952, 53, 55, 57, 58, 61-62, 63, Beloit (Wis.) Coll., 1961, Barbara Cecil Gallery, New Orleans, 1963, Mex., 1959, Occidental Coll., Los Angeles, 1955, Esther Bear Gallery, 1967, Ball State U., 1967, Stewart-Verde Galleries, San Francisco, 1966, San Francisco Mus. Art, 1967, Mekler Gallery, Los Angeles, 1970-82, 84, 89, Tokyo Shoten Gallery, N.Y.C., 1976, Mitsukoshi Gallery, Tokyo, 1977, Wiener Gallery, N.Y.C., 1977, Worthington Gallery, Chgo., 1982, 85, 88, Mekler Gallery, 1987, 89, Tomlyn Gallery, Fla., 1990-99, Fresno Mus. Art, 1992, Tortue Gallery, Santa Monica, 1994-96, Tobey Moss Gallery, L.A., 1994, Kennedy Museum, Athens, Ohio, 1997, Lyman Allyn Mus. New London, CT, 1998, Schmidt-Bingham Gallery, N.Y.C., 1998, Santa Cruz Mus., CA. 1998; also exhibited numerous group shows including: Whitney Mus. Am. Art, 1953-56, Mus. Modern Art, 1952, 54, Carnegie Inst., 1951, 55, I.F.A. Gallery, Washington, 1963, 100 Prints of the Year, N.Y.C., 1963, Bklyn. Mus., 1966, Vancouver (B.C., Can.) Print Internat., World Print Competition, San Francisco, 1977, Met. Mus., 1978, Los Angeles County Mus., 1980-81, Drawings from Their Collection, Nat. Gallery Smithsonian, Washington, Wight Gallery UCLA, 1988, Nat. Gallery Modern Art, New Delhi, 1988, Memory Gallery, Nagoya, Japan, 1990, Gallery IV, L.A., 1990, Worcester Art Mus., 1991, Amon Carter Mus., 1991, Women's Art Mus., Washington, 1994, Met. Mus. Fresno, Calif., 1994, Brigitie Haasner Gallery, Wiesbaden, Germany, others; represented in permanent collections numerous museums including, Santa Barbara Mus. Art, Mus. Modern Art, Philbrook Art Center, Los Angeles County Mus., City Art Mus. St. Louis, Whitney Mus. Am. Art, Phila. Mus. Art, San Diego Mus. Art, U. Ill., Met. Mus. Art, Hirshhorn Collection, Herbert F. Johnson Collection (Cornell U.), San Francisco Mus. Art, Otis Art Inst., Milw. Art Center, Worcester Art Mus. (travelling print exhbn. to Terra Mus., Chgo., Amon Carter Mus., Ft. Worth, 1990), Santa Fe Mus. of Fine Art, The Nat. Mus. Israel, Jerusalem, Gift Gardens Bot./Sculpture Pk., Fla., Norton-Simon Mus., numerous schs. and colls., other museums, also pvt. collections. Recipient San Francisco Mus. Art award oil painting, 1946; awards Calif. State Fair, 1951, 61, 62; award etching Los Angeles County Mus., 1950; exhbn. first award Met. Mus. Art, 1952; purchase award Exhbn. Fgn. Artists, Rome, Italy, 1952; purchase award Otis Art Inst., 1963; purchase award Los Angeles Municipal Art Dept., 1967; also commns.; John Simon Guggenheim Found. grantee, 1952; Louis Comfort Tiffany grantee, 1955, 56; Huntington Hartford grantee, 1957; James Phelan grantee, 1958; MacDowell Colony grantee, 1959; Tamarind workshop fellow, 1966; Nat. Endowment Arts painting grantee, 1976, 85. Address: 579 Crane Blvd Los Angeles CA 90065-5019

JOHNSTONE, DEBORAH BLACKMON, lawyer; b. Birmingham, Ala., Jan. 26, 1953; d. T.C. Blackmon and Joan (Thompson) Ryals; m. David Johnstone, July 26, 1968 (div. 1976); children: Pamela, Robin. A.S., Jefferson Sch. Nursing, Birmingham, 1976; BA, Birmingham-So. Coll., 1982; JD, Birmingham Law Sch., 1986. Bar: Ala. 1986. Nurse Carraway Med. Ctr., Birmingham, 1976-86; assoc. Emond & Vines, Attys., Birmingham, 1986-88; atty., med.-legal cons. Am. Internat. Group, Bedford, Dallas, Ft. Worth, 1988—. Founder, v.p. Burleson Animal Soc., 1998—. Mem. ABA, ATLA, ACLU, AAAS, Ala. Trial Lawyers, Ala. State Bar, Tex. Bd. Nurse Examiners, Ala. Bd. Nursing, Consumers Union. Democrat. Roman Catholic. Avocations: history, golf, writing non-fiction, jewelry design. Office: 849 E Renfro St Burleson TX 76028-5019

JOHNSTONE, EDWARD HUGGINS, federal judge; b. 1922. J.D., U. Ky., 1949. Bar: Ky. 1949. Ptnr. firm Johnstone, Eldred & Paxton, Princeton, Ky., 1949-76; judge 56th Cir. Ct. Ky, 1976-77; judge U.S. Dist. Ct. (we. dist.) Ky., 1977—, chief judge, 1985-90; sr. judge, 1993—. Mem. ABA, Ky. Bar Assn. Office: US Dist Ct 219 Fed Bldg 501 Broadway St Paducah KY 42001-6856 Also: 262 US Courthouse 601 E Broadway Louisville KY 40202-1709*

JOHNSTONE, IRVINE BLAKELEY, III, lawyer; b. Newark, Dec. 21, 1948; s. Irvine Blakeley Jr. and Ruth (Morton) J.; m. Phyllis Nevins, Oct. 16, 1983. BA with honors, Lehigh U., 1972; JD, Duke U., 1975. Bar: N.J. 1975, U.S. Dist. Ct. N.J. 1975, U.S. Ct. Appeals (3d cir.) 1979, N.Y. 1981. Assoc. Riker, Danzig, Scherer & DeBevoise, Newark, 1975-76, Shanley & Fisher, Newark, 1976-80; ptnr. Johnstone, Skok, Loughlin & Lane, Westfield, N.J., 1980—. Mem. bd. of govs. Blair Acad., 1978-84; atty. Rahway Lifers Group (N.J.) State Prison, 1980-85, Planning Bd., Clark, N.J., 1981-82, Bd. of Adjustment, Clark, 1982-84. Mem. ABA, N.J. Bar Assn., Union County Bar Assn., Def. Rsch. Inst., Union County Arbitration Bd. (cert. civil trial atty. N.J. Supreme Ct.), N.J. Trial Lawyers Assn., Am. Trial Lawyers Assn., R.J. Hughes Am. Inns of Ct. (master 1995—). Republican. Presbyterian. Club: Baltusrol (Springfield, N.J.). Avocations: flying, golf, sports. Home: 5 Bartles Rd Lebanon NJ 08833-4606

JOHNSTONE, JAMES GEORGE, engineering educator; b. LaPorte, Ind., July 29, 1920; s. Arthur Paul and Lydia Henrietta (Werremeyer) J.; m. Louise Moffit, Aug. 24, 1946; 1 child, Nancy Louise Johnstone Ratay. Student, Western Ky. State U., 1939-41; Geol. Engr., Colo. Sch. Mines, 1948; M.S. in Engring, Purdue U., 1952. Registered profl. engr., Ind., Colo. Plant engr. Ford Motor Co., Detroit, 1942-45; asst. prof. geology Purdue U., Lafayette, Ind., 1948-55; project engr. Geophoto Services, Denver, 1955-57; prof. engring. Colo. Sch. Mines, Golden, 1957-83, prof. emeritus, 1983—; partner Colo. Central Narrow Gauge R.R., Georgetown, 1970—; cons. engr. Ind. Toll Rd., Dewline, Mass. Turnpike, Colo. Dept. Hwys.; mem. Colo. Bd. Registration Profl. Engrs. and Land Surveyors, 1971-79, chmn., 1978-79. Mem. Wheatridge (Colo.) Incorporation Commn., 1968-69, Wheatridge St. Commn., 1969-71; mem. Jefferson County Housing Authority Bd., 1986—, chmn., 1989-92. Named Colo. Profl. Engr. of Year, 1967, 79; recipient Mines medal Colo. Sch. Mines, 1986. Mem. NSPE (bd. dirs. 1967-74, 77-79, nat. v.p. 1974-76), ASCE, Am. Soc. Engring. Edn., Nat. Coun. Engring. Examiners, Profl. Engrs. Colo. (pres. 1965-66, bd. dirs. 1967-74, 76-94, trustee, treas. Edn. Found. 1990—), Engrs. Coun. for Profl. Devel. (coun. 1975-79), Colo. Sch. Mines Alumni Assn. (pres. 1990), Order of Engr. (nat. chmn. 1991), Sigma Xi, Tau Beta Pi, Sigma Gamma Epsilon. Republican. Methodist. Home: 1805 S Balsam St Apt 177 Lakewood CO 80232-6779

JOHNSTONE, JOHN WILLIAM, JR., retired chemical company executive; b. Bklyn., Nov. 19, 1932; s. John William and Sarah J. (Singleton) J.; m. Claire Lundberg, Apr. 14, 1956; children: Thomas Edward, James Robert, Robert Andrew. BA, Hartwick Coll., Oneonta, N.Y., 1954; DSc (hon.), Hartwick Coll., 1990; grad. advanced mgmt. program, Harvard U., 1970. With Hooker Chem. Corp., 1954-75, group v.p., 1973-75; pres. Airco Alloys divsn. Airco, Inc., 1976-79; v.p., gen. mgr. indsl. products, then sr. v.p. chems. group Olin Corp., 1979-80; corp. v.p., pres. chems. group Olin Corp., Norwalk, Conn., 1980-85, pres., 1985-87, chief operating officer, 1986-87, chmn., pres., CEO, 1988-96, chmn. of bd., 1996, bd. dirs., ret., 1996; bd. dirs. Phoenix Home Life Ins. Co., Rsch. Corp. Techs., Inc., Am. Brands, Inc., McDermott Internat., Inc., Arch Chem. Inc. Trustee Hartwick Coll., 1983-91, 92—. Mem. Soc. Chem. Industry, Soap and Detergent Assn. (former chmn. bd. dirs.), Chem. Mfrs. Assn. (chmn. bd. dirs. 1991), Woodway Country Club, Blind Brook Club, Links Club, Chemist Club. Episcopalian.

JOHNSTONE, JOYCE VISINTINE, education educator; b. Columbus, Ohio, Nov. 12, 1943; d. James Joseph and Virginia (Vogel) Visintine; m. James S. Luckett, Nov. 27, 1965 (dec. May 1969); children: Anne, Robert; m. William E. Kuhn, Sept. 1, 1995. BA, Cath. U. Am., 1965; MA, Butler U., 1974; PhD, Ind. U., 1994. Tchr. Columbus Pub. Schs., 1965-68, Hawaii Pub. Schs., Wahiawa, 1968-69, Montgomery County (Md.), Wheaton, 1969-70; chair edn. dept. Marian Coll., Indpls., 1975-98; assoc. dir. grad. program in edn. U. Notre Dame, South Bend, 1998—, fellow Inst. for Ednl Initiative, 1998—; dir. Ind. Cath. Prins. Inst., 1989-94. Cath. Prins. Inst. grantee Lilly Endowment, Indpls., 1990, Project Enhance grantee Ind. Bell, Indpls., 1991, 95; Parent Partnership grant Danforth Found., 1995-97. Mem. ASCD, Assn. Tchr. Educators (pres. 1990-91, Turkey Run Outstanding Educator 1990), Ind. Assn. Colls. for Tchr. Edn. (pres., 1990-92, Outstanding Svc. award 1995). Roman Catholic. Office: Inst Ednl Initiative Univ Notre Dame Notre Dame IN 46556

JOHNSTONE, KENNETH ERNEST, electronics and business consultant; b. L.A., Sept. 13, 1929; s. John Ernest and Lorena Hayes (Patterson) J.; m. Edna Mae Iverson, Aug. 20, 1950; children: Bruce, Kent, Anita, Christian, Daniel, Carol, Karen. BSEE, U. Wash., 1966. Registered profl. engr., Wash. Electronics technician The Boeing Co., Seattle, 1955-66, engr., 1966-75; engring. mgr. Boeing Aerosystems Internat., Seattle, 1975-85; ptnr. North Creek Engring., Lynnwood, Wash., 1985-87; pres. SensorLink Corp., Lynnwood, 1987-90; electronics and bus. cons. Bellingham, Wash., 1991—; internat. cons., lectr. in field. Mem. IEEE (sr.), Tau Beta Pi. Avocations: sailing, amateur radio, languages. Home and Office: 3765 E Smith Rd Bellingham WA 98226-9573

JOHNSTONE, PAULA SUE, medical technologist; b. Springfield, Mo., July 5, 1947; d. Nathan Paul and Ima Louise (Glenn) Johnstone. BS, S.W. Mo. State U., 1969. Cert. med. technologist Am. Soc. Clin. Pathologists. Vol., Cox Med. Ctr., Springfield, 1964-68; lab., office aide Springfield Med. Lab., 1964-68; chief technologist Springfield Gen. Osteo. Hosp., 1969-73; staff technologist St. John's Regional Health Ctr., Springfield, 1973-75, evening supr., 1975-76, asst. adminstrv. dir., 1976-86, clin. lab. coord., 1986-89, lab. computer coord., 1989-96, hosp. LIS coord., 1996-98, lab. quality improvement technologist, Health Sys. Dir., Glidewell Bapt. Ch. Tng., Springfield, 1984-85, chmn. budget and fin. com. 1986-87; pres. MER class Broadway Bapt. Ch., 1993-94, 95-96, 97—. Mem. NAFE, Am. Soc. for Clin. Lab. Sci., Mo. Soc. Med. Technologists (pres. 1976-77, columnist newsletter 1976-77), S.W. Mo. State U. Alumni Assn. Baptist. Clubs: Nat. Travel, Frommer's Dollarwise Travel Club. Avocations: Internat. travel, reading, knitting, house plants. Home: 1384 E Arlington St Springfield MO 65803-3768 Office: St Johns Regional Health Ctr 1235 E Cherokee St Springfield MO 65804-2203

JOHNSTONE, PHILIP MACLAREN, lawyer; b. Sharon, Conn., Mar. 24, 1961; s. Rodney Stuart and Frances Louise (Davis) J.; m. Elizabeth Laird McGovern, Sept. 10, 1988. BA in Econs. magna cum laude, Duke U., 1983; JD, U. Pa., 1986. Bar: Mass. 1986, Conn. 1987, U.S. Dist. Ct. Conn. 1988, R.I. 1998. Ptnr. Waller, Smith & Palmer, P.C., New London, Conn., 1997—; bd. dirs. J Boats, Inc., Newport, R.I., 1987—. Mem. ABA, Mass. Bar Assn., Conn. Bar Assn., R.I. Bar Assn. Republican. Episcopalian. Avocations: tennis, golf. Home: 17 Cliff St Stonington CT 06378-1249 Office: Waller Smith and Palmer PC 52 Eugene Oneill Dr New London CT 06320-6324

JOHNSTONE, QUINTIN, law educator; b. Chgo., Mar. 29, 1915; s. Quintin and Wegia (Metsker) J.; m. Nancy McMullen; children: Robert Dale, Katherine Mary. A.B., U. Chgo., 1936, J.D., 1938; LL.M., Cornell U., 1941; J.S.D., Yale U., 1951; DHL, Quinnipiac Coll., 1993. Bar: Ill. 1939, Oreg. 1948. Pvt. practice Chgo., 1939-41; atty. OPA, 1941-47; mem. law faculty Wilamette U., 1947-50, U. Kans., 1950-55; mem. law faculty Yale U., 1955—, Justus S. Hotchkiss prof., 1969-85, prof. emeritus, 1985—; dean law, prof. Haile Selassie I U., Ethiopia, 1967-69; prof. N.Y. Law Sch., 1985—. Author: (with D. Hopson) Lawyers and Their Work, 1967; (with C. Berger) Land Transfer and Finance, 4th edit., 1993; (with M. Wenglinsky) Paralegals, 1985; contbr. articles to profl. jours. Mem. ABA, Conn. Bar Assn., Oreg. Bar Assn. Home: 22 Morris St Hamden CT 06517-3423 Office: Yale Law Sch PO Box 208215 New Haven CT 06520-8215

JOHNSTONE, ROBERT PHILIP, lawyer; b. Bellefonte, Pa., Dec. 1, 1943; s. B. Kenneth and Helene (Hetzel) J.; m. Susan Alice Hardy, June 22, 1968; children: Natalie, Nancy. BS with honors, Denison U., 1966; JD magna cum laude, U. Mich., 1969. Bar: Ind. 1969. Assoc. Barnes, Hickam, Pantzer & Boyd, Indpls., 1969-75, ptnr., 1976-82; ptnr. Barnes & Thornburg, Indpls., 1982—; chmn. litigation dept. Barnes & Thornburg, 1988-89, mem. mgmt. com., 1988-89; lectr., panelist legal seminars and trial advocacy programs. Sec.-treas. Contemporary Art Soc. of Indpls. Mus. of Art, 1983-84; v.p., mem. of bd. Friends of Herron Gallery, Herron Sch. of Art, 1981-85. Fellow Am. Coll. Trial Lawyers (state com. 1992—, state chair 1995-96, com. on spl. problems in the adminstrn. of justice 1995—, award for courageous adv. com. 1996—); mem. U.S. 7th Fed. Cir. Bar Assn., Ind. Bar Assn., Fed. Bar Assn., Indpls. Bar Assn., Order of the Coif, Woodstock Club (Indpls., bd. dirs. 1988-90, v.p. 1989, pres. 1990), Indpls. Art Ctr. (bd. dirs. 1991-97), Dramatic Club (Indpls.), Phi Beta Kappa, Omicron Delta Kappa. Home: 1065 W 52nd St Indianapolis IN 46228-2463 Office: Barnes & Thornburg 11 S Meridian St Indianapolis IN 46204-3506

JOHNSTONE, ROSE MAMELAK (MRS. DOUGLAS JOHNSTONE), biochemistry educator; b. Lodz, Poland, May 14, 1928; d. Jacob Shea and Esther (Rotholz) Mamelak; m. Douglas Johnstone, Aug. 9, 1953; children: Michael, Eric. BSc, McGill U., 1950, PhD, 1953. Nat. Cancer Inst. of Can. fellow Nat. Inst. for Med. Rsch., London, Strangeway Rsch. Lab., Cambridge, Eng., 1954-56; rsch. assoc. McGill-Montreal Gen. Hosp. Rsch. Inst., 1956-60; faculty McGill U., Montreal, Que., Can., 1961-97; assoc. prof. biochemistry McGill U., 1967-76, prof., 1977-97; prof. emeritus, 1997—; chmn. dept. McGill U., 1980-90; Gilman Cheney chair biochemistry McGill U., Montreal, 1985-96, emeritus chair, 1997—. Contbr. articles to profl. jours. Grantee Nat. Cancer Inst. Can., 1965-67, Med. Rsch. Coun. of Can., 1965—, NIH, 1987-90, 92-96. Fellow Royal Soc. Can. (treas. 1991-94); mem. McGill Assn. U. Tchrs. (membership sec. 1967-70, treas. 1995-96), Biol. Chemists Am., Can. Biochem. Soc. (pres. 1985-86), Internat. Assn. Women Bioscientists (sec. 1985-88). Home: 4064 Oxford, Montreal, PQ Canada H4A 2Y4 Office: McGill Univ McIntyre Med Sci Ctr, Dept Biochemistry 3655 Drummond, Montreal, PQ Canada H3G 1Y6

JOHNSTONE, STOWELL, former state agency administrator. Grad., U. Idaho, 1953, MA in Edn./Adminstrn., 1960. Tchr. Moscow (Idaho) High Sch., 1956-58; tchr., dir. driver edn. Moscow Sch. Dist. # 28, 1957-66; acting prin. Moscow Mid. Sch., 1958-59; prin. Moscow Jr. High, 1959-61; dir. secondary curriculum Moscow Sch. Dist., 1961-62, adminstrv. asst. to supt. schs., 1962-64; prin. Moscow High Sch., 1964-67, West Anchorage (Alaska) High Sch., 1967-70; dir. audio-visual svcs., libr. processing and TV prodn. Anchorage Sch. Dist., 1970-71, dir. secondary edn., 1971-78, asst. dep. supt. secondary sch. mgmt., 1978-81, asst. dep. supt. ednl. planning, 1981-82; chair Alaska Bd. Edn., Juneau, 1994-98; instr. U. Idaho, 1958-60; part time supr. maintenance pers. Moscow Sch. Dist., 1963-67; part time instr. U. Alaska, Anchorage, 1956-85, Anchorage C.C.; trustee Alaska Coun. Econ. Edn., 1977-85. Active exec. com. Jr. Achievement of Alaska, 1966-85; chmn. Alaska Pub. Broadcasting Commn., 1969-83; bd. dirs. Alaskan of Yr. Com., 1979-82; v.p., mem. Alaska Repertory Theatre Statewide Bd., 1979-85; v.p. Alaska March of Dimes Bd., 1988-89. With USAF, 1953-56, col. Res. ret. Recipient Outstanding Young Men of America award, Disting. Svc. award, Moscow, 1966, Gov.'s award for Outstanding Svc. to Alaska, 1979, Disting. Svc. award Alaska Assn. Secondary Sch. Prins., 1980, Exec. of Yr. award City of Anchorage, 1980. Mem. Northwest Assn. Schs. and Colls. (chmn. Alaska com. 1973-78, pres. commn. schs. 1978-82, sec. 1983—, pres. 1991-94), Northwest Assn. of Schs. and Colls. *

JOHNTING, WENDELL, law librarian; b. Winchester, Ind., Aug. 30, 1952; s. Ernest K. and Jewell G. (Browning) J. AB, Taylor U., 1974; MLS, Ind. U., 1975. Asst. dir. tech. svcs. Ind. U. Sch. Law Libr., Indpls., 1975—; project dir. Indpls. Law Cataloging Consortium, 1980-92; vis. libr. Cambridge U., Squire Law Libr., Cambridge, Eng., 1985; founding mem. Info. Online Project Leaders, 1987-90; spkr. in field. Libr. vol. Beech Grove (Ind.) Pub. Libr., 1993-95; reader, vol. Marion County Health Care Home, Indpls., 1989. Mem. Ohio Region Assn. Law Librs. (exec. bd. 1982-85, sec. 1982), Ind. U. Librs. Assn. (v.p. 1986-87, exec. bd. 1982-85), Dramatic Order Knights Khorassen, Knights of Pythias (chancellor comdr. 1997), Beta Phi Mu, Chi Alpha Omega, Alpha Phi Gamma. Republican. Baptist. Avocations: gardening, astronomy, cooking. Home: 420 N 23rd Ave Beech Grove IN 46107-1032 Office: Ind U Sch Law Libr 735 W New York St Indianapolis IN 46202-5222

JOICE, NORA LEE, clinical dietitian; b. Kearney, Nebr., Mar. 5, 1948; d. Frank Rogers and Clarrisa Blanche (Drinnan) Jackson; m. David Wayne Joice, Dec. 21, 1973. BS, U. Ariz., 1971. Registered dietitian; lic. dietitian. Clin. dietitian St. Francis Hosp., Tulsa, 1972-76; pub. health nutritionist Tulsa City County Health Dept., 1976-81; clin. dietitian City of Faith Hosp., Marriott Corp., Tulsa, 1982-84, asst. chief dietitian, 1984-86, chief clin. dietitian, 1986-87, clin. nutrition specialist, 1987-89; cons. dietitian in long-term health facilities Marriott Corp., Tulsa, 1990-92; pvt. practice cons. dietitian Tulsa, 1992—; clin. dietitian Broken Arrow (Okla.) Med. Ctr., 1993-94; outpatient clin. dietitian St. John's Med. Ctr., Tulsa, Okla., 1995—. Mem. Okla. Dietetic Assn., Am. Dietetic Assn., Okla. Cons. Dietitians in Health Care Facilities, Dietitians in Gen. Clin. Practice. Democrat. Pentecostal. Avocations: crafts, painting, piano. Home and Office: 2320 S Urbana Ave Tulsa OK 74114-3627

JOINER, CHARLES WYCLIFFE, judge; b. Maquoketa, Iowa, Feb. 14, 1916; s. Melvin William and Mary (von Schrader) J.; m. Ann Martin, Sept. 29, 1939; children: Charles Wycliffe, Nancy Caroline, Richard Martin. BA, U. Iowa, 1937, JD, 1939. Bar: Iowa 1939, Mich. 1947. With firm Miller, Huebner & Miller, Des Moines, 1939-47; part-time lectr. Des Moines Coll. Law, 1940-41; faculty U. Mich. Law, 1947-68, assoc. dean, 1960-65, acting dean, 1964-65; dean Wayne State U. Law Sch., Detroit, 1968-72; U.S. dist. judge, sr. judge, 1972-99, ret., 1999; assoc. dir. Preparatory Commn. Mich. Constl. Conv., 1961, co-dir. research and drafting com., 1961-62; civil rules adv. com. U.S. Jud. Conf. Com. Rules Practice and Procedure, 1959-70, evidence rules adv. com., 1965-70; rep. Mich. Atty. Gens. Com. Ct. Congestion, 1959-60. Author: Trials and Appeals, 1957, Civil Justice and the Jury, 1962, Trial and Appellate Practice, 1968; Co-author: Introduction to Civil Procedures, 1949, Jurisdiction and Judgments, 1953, (with Delmar Karten) Trials and Appeals, 1971. Mem. charter rev. com. Ann Arbor Citizens Council, 1959-61; mem. Mich. Commn. on Uniform State Laws, 1963—; Mem. Ann Arbor City Council, 1955-59. Served to 1st lt. USAAF, 1942-45. Fellow Am. Bar Found. (chmn. 1977-78); mem. ABA (chmn. com. specialization 1952-56, spl. com. uniform evidence rules fed. cts. 1959-64, adv. bd. jour. 1961-67, spl. com. on specialization 1966-69, ethics com. 1961-70, council mem. sect. individual rights and responsibilities 1967-77, chairperson 1976-77), State Bar Mich. (pres. 1970-71, chmn. joint com. Mich. procedural revision 1956-62, commr. 1964—), Am. Judicature Soc. (chmn. pubs. com. 1959-62), Am. Law Student Assn. (bd. govs.), Am. Law Inst., Scribes (pres. 1963-64).

JOINER, ELIZABETH GARNER, French language educator; b. Atlanta, Feb. 15, 1939; d. Albert Ross and Bessie Mae (Sessions) Garner; m. Lawrence Don Joiner, June 8, 1964 (dec. July 1981); m. George Buford Norman, Aug. 8, 1996. BA, LaGrange Coll., 1959; MA, U. Ga., 1964; PhD, Ohio State U., 1974. Tchr. French and English Franklin County H.S., Carnesville, Ga., 1959-60, Winder (Ga.)-Barrow H.S., 1960-62; grad. tchg. asst. U. Ga., Athens, 1962-64, instr. French, 1964-65; instr. French Winthrop Coll., Rock Hill, S.C., 1965-68, asst. prof. French, 1968-74; asst. prof. French U. S.C., Columbia, 1974-77, assoc. prof. French, 1977-84, prof. French, 1984—. Author: (textbook) First-Year French, 1977, Departs, 1978, Horizons, 1984, Video-Verite, 1994, (monograph) The Older Foreign Language Learner, 1981; editor: Developing Communication Skills, 1978; contbr. chpts. to scholarly books including Developing Language Teachers for a Changing World, 1974—; contbr. articles to scholarly jours. Decorated Chevalier des Palmes Academiques, French Govt., 1991; NDEA fellow U.S. Govt., 1971-72. Mem. MLA, Am. Assn. Tchrs. of French, Am. Coun. on Tchg. of Fgn. Langs. (chair Birkmeier Award com. 1990-91), S.C. Fgn. Lang. Tchrs. Assn. (pres. 1977-78), Phi Kappa Phi, Phi Beta Kappa. Home: PO Box 448 Columbia SC 29202-0448 Office: U S C Dept French and Classics Columbia SC 29208

JOINER, LORELL HOWARD, real estate development and investment executive; b. Temple, Tex., Nov. 27, 1945; s. Burt Lawrence and Geneva Evelyn (Howard) J.; m. Cynthia Ann Morin, Mar. 30, 1968. BEcons., Trinity U., San Antonio, 1967; MArch, U. Tex., 1977. Registered architect, Tex. Exec. v.p. Tex. Diversified Properties, San Antonio, 1964-68; exec. v.p. Gen. Properties Devel., San Antonio, 1970-76, pres., chief exec. officer, 1976—; pres., chief exec. officer Gen. Properties Investment Inc., San Antonio, 1979—; bd. dirs. Internat. Modelbau GMBH, Geneva, 1986—. Author: Reliable Trackwork Construction, 1986; contbr. articles to profl. publs.; author script, narrator TV programs, Computer Show, 1987, Real Time Interface, 1987. Bd. dirs. San Antonio Community Theater, 1986-89, Tex. Transp. Mus., San Antonio, 1978—; vol. San Antonio Big Bros./Big Sisters, 1986—; mem. com. Muscular Dystrophy Assn. 1st lt. U.S. Army, 1968-70. Named Master Archtl. Model Builder, Nat. Model Bldg. Assn., 1980. Fellow Internat. Modelbau (bd. dirs. 1986—); mem. AIA (assoc., 1st place award for design 1980), Royal Automobile Club, Rolls Royce Owner's Club. Avocations: collecting Rolls Royces, Chinese porcelain, books and wine, rail transportation. Home: 7507 Shadylane Dr San Antonio TX 78209-2738 Office: Gen Properties Investment 18985 Marbach Ln San Antonio TX 78266-2132

JOKL, ALOIS LOUIS, electrical engineer; b. Vienna, Austria, Mar. 16, 1924; came to the U.S., 1939; s. Samuel and Ernestine (Fischer) J.; m. Agnes Antoinette Wozniak, Dec. 29, 1951; children: Justine Ann, Martin Louis, James Anthony. B in Engring., U. So. Calif., 1944; PhD, U. Colo., 1973. Registered profl. engr., Va., N.Y. Elec. engr. Westinghouse Electric Corp., Buffalo, 1946-51; chief elec. engr. R&D div. Continental Motors Corp., Detroit, 1955-64; br. chief power tech. div. USA Belvoir RDE Ctr., Ft. Belvoir, Va., 1964-72, chief power generation div., 1972-88, sr. scientist logistics equipment, 1988-89; cons. Alexandria, Va., 1989—; lectr. Cath. U. Am., Washington, 1981—; mem., chief U.S. delegation Quadripartite Working Group Elec. Power Sources, London, Auckland, New Zealand, 1983-89; judge Sch. Sci. Fairs, Alexandria, 1980-91. Contbr. articles to profl. jours. With U.S. Army, 1944-46, ETO. Mem. IEEE (sr. life), Sigma Xi (v.p. Belvoir chpt. 1983-85). Roman Catholic. Achievements include four patents; research in magnetic field calculations, electrical machinery design methods, waveform predictions. Home and Office: 2607 N Stevens St Alexandria VA 22311-1512

JOKLIK, GÜNTHER FRANZ, mining company executive; b. Vienna, Austria, May 30, 1928; came to U.S., 1953; s. Karl Friedrich and Helene (Giessl) J.; m. Pamela Mary Fenton, Dec. 22, 1962; children: Carl Duncan, Katherine Pamela, Paul Richard. B.Sc. with 1st class honors, U. Sydney, Australia, 1949, Ph.D., 1953; DSc (hon.), U. Utah, 1994. Exploration geologist Kennecott Corp., N.Y.C., 1954-62; exploration mgr. Australia div. AMAX, Inc., Greenwich, Conn., 1963-71, v.p., 1972-73; v.p. Kennecott Corp., 1974-79, pres., CEO, 1980-93; ret., 1993; sr. v.p. metals Std. Oil Co. (parent), Cleve., 1982-89; pres., CEO MK Gold Co., Salt Lake City, 1995—; dir. First Security Corp., Salt Lake City, Cleve. (Ohio)-Cliffs, Inc.; mem. Nat. Strategic Materials Adv. Com., 1984-89; hon. consul for U.K., Salt Lake City, 1995; pres., CEO, MK Gold Co., 1995. Fulbright scholar Columbia U., 1953-54; recipient Giant In Our City award Salt Lake Area C. of C., 1994. Mem. Nat. Acad. Engring, Copper Club (Man of Yr. 1989), Alta Club (Salt Lake), The Country Club. Avocations: skiing; tennis. Office: Eagle Gate Tower # 2100 60 E South Temple Salt Lake City UT 84111-1004

JOKLIK, WOLFGANG KARL, biochemist, virologist, educator; b. Vienna, Austria, Nov. 16, 1926; s. Karl F. and Helene (Giessl) J.; m. Judith Vivien Nicholas, Apr. 9, 1955 (dec. Apr. 1975); children: Richard G., Vivien H.; m. Patricia Hunter Downey, Apr. 23, 1977. B.Sc. with 1st class honors, U. Sydney, Australia, 1948, M.Sc., 1949; D.Phil. (Australian Nat. U. scholar), U. Oxford, Eng., 1952. Australian Nat. U. research fellow Copenhagen, Denmark, 1953, Canberra, Australia, 1954-56; fellow, 1957-62; assoc. prof. cell biology Albert Einstein Coll. Medicine, Bronx, N.Y., 1962-65; prof. cell biology Albert Einstein Coll. Medicine, 1965-68, Siegfried Ullmann prof. biochem. virology, 1966-68; prof., chmn. dept. microbiology and immunology Duke U. Med. Ctr., Durham, N.C., 1968-92, James B. Duke Disting. prof. microbiology and immunology, 1972-92, James B. Duke prof. microbiology, 1992-96, James B. Duke prof. emeritus, 1996—. Sr. author: Zinsser Microbiology, 15th, 16th, 17th, 18th, 19th, 20th edits.; editor-in-chief Virology, 1975-93, Microbiological Rev., 1991-95; contbr. articles to profl. jours. Recipient Sr. U.S. award Alexander Humboldt Found., 1985, ICN Internat. prize for virology, 1991. Mem. NAS, Inst. Medicine of NAS, Am. Soc. Virology (pres. 1982-83), Am. Soc. Microbiology, Am. Soc. Biol. Chemists. Address: Duke U Med Ctr Dept Microbiology PO Box 3020 Durham NC 27710

JOLAS, BETSY, composer, educator; b. Paris, Aug. 5, 1926; d. Eugene and Maria (MacDonald) J.; m. Gabriel Illouz, Aug. 27, 1949; children: Frederic, Claire, Antoine. BA, Bennington Coll., 1946; student, Conservatoire Nat. Paris, 1946. Replaced Olivier Messiaen Paris Conservatory, 1971-74, prof. advanced analysis and composition, 1975—; prof. composition Tanglewood, 1976-77, SUNY, Buffalo, 1976, Yale U., 1979, 82, Boston U., 1985, Darius Milhaud prof. Mills Colls., Fromm prof. Harvard, 1994; residnet Am. Acad.,

Rome, 1999. Compositions include Points d'or for one saxophonist playing four saxophones and ensemble, 1982, Episode Sixiéme pour alto, 1983; Trois Duos Pour Tuba et Piano, 1983; O Wall, for wind quintet, 1976; Well Met, for ensemble, 1973; Tales of a Summer Sea, for orch., 1977, Stances, for piano and orch., 1978, Points D'Aube, for ensemble and viola solo; Preludes Fanfares Interludes Sonneries, for wind orch. and percussion, 1983; Trois Rencontres, for orch., 1973, Sonate á 12, for 12 voice soloists a capella, 1970; Motet II, for choir and orch., 1965; Caprice á deux voix, for soloists without accompaniment, 1978; Quatuor II for solo voice and string trio, 1964; Le pavillon au bord de la riviére, chamber opera in 4 acts, 1975; Le Cyclope, chamber opera in one act, 1986; Schliemann opera in 3 acts, 1989; Frauenleben 9 Lieder for viola and orch., 1992, Prix Internat. Maurice Ravel, 1992, Personnalité de l'année, 1993, Prix SACEM de la Meileure Créátion, 1994, Sigrancia Ballade for baritone and orch., 1995, Lumor 7 sacred lieder for saxophone and orch., 1996, Petite Symphonie Concertante for violin and orch., 1997; many recs.; contbr. articles to profl. jours. Performer French Radio, Paris, 1955-65. Decorated chavelier de l'Ordre Nat. du Mérite, Commandeur des Arts et Lettres, chevalier de la Legion d'honneur; recipient Internat. Conducting Competition prize, Besancon, 1953, Copley Found. Chgo. award, 1954, ORTF award, 1961, Am. Acad. Arts award, 1973, Grand Prix de la Music, 1974, Grand Prix de la Ville de Paris, 1981, Grand Prix de la SACEM, 1982, Koussevitsky Found. award, 1974. Mem. Am. Acad. Arts and Letters, Am. Acad. Arts and Scis. Office: Conservatoire Nat Supérieur de Musique, 209 Ave Jean Jaures, 75019 Paris France

JOLICOEUR, PAUL, molecular biologist; b. Beauceville, Que., Can., Jan. 4, 1945; s. Philippe Jolicoeur and Eva Rodrigue; m. Claudine Tremblay, Apr. 10, 1976. BA, Laval U., Que., 1964, MD, 1968, PhD, 1973. Intern Royal Victoria Hosp., Montreal, Que., Can., 1968-69; med. dir Lama-Kara Hosp. (SUCO), Togo, Africa, 1968-79; pvt. practice Gaspésie, P.Q., 1970; postdoctoral fellow MIT, Cambridge, 1973-76; dir. lab. molecular biology Clin. Rsch. Inst. Montreal, Que., 1976—. Contbr. articles to profl. jours. Recipient medal Lt. Gov. of Que., 1964. Mem. Med. Rsch. Coun. (study sect. 1978-81, Centennial fellow 1975-76), Nat. Cancer Inst. (study sect. 1982-84, 96—, adv. com. on rsch. 1984-88). Fax: 514-987-5794. Home: 5296 Durocher, Outremont, PQ Canada H2V 3Y1 Office: Montreal Inst Clin Rsch, 110 W Ave des Pins, Montreal, PQ Canada H2W 1R7

JOLISSAINT, STEPHEN LACY, pathologist; b. Honolulu, Oct. 7, 1951; s. John Mire and Joyce Marie (Lacy)) J.; m. Belle Kamille Bowen, Dec. 29, 1988; children: Taylor Elise, Stephen Lacy Jr., Barrett Claire. BS, La. State U., Baton Rouge, 1973; MD, La. State U., New Orleans, 1976. Intern, then resident U.S. Army, Fitzsimons Army Med. Ctr., Aurora, Colo., 1976-80; staff pathologist U.S. Army, 1980-82; pathologist Pecot, Padgett & Jolissaint, APMC, Opelousas, La., 1982-97, Pathology Group of La., Baton Rouge, 1997—; staff pathologist Our Lady of the Lake (La.) Med. Ctr., 1997—, Woman's Hosp. La., 1997—, Summit Hosp., 1997—. Fellow Am. Coll. Pathologists (keyperson 1986-88), Am. Soc. Clin. Pathology; mem. AMA (del. young physicians sect. 1986-91), La. Med. Soc. (del. 1985-88, 90-91, chmn. young physicians com. 1988-91), La. Pathology Soc., St. Landry Parish Med. Soc. (pres. 1985-86), Thoroughbred Owners and Breeders Assn., Alpha Omega Alpha. Roman Catholic. Avocations: thoroughbred racing, saltwater fishing. Home: 202 Mill Valley Run Lafayette LA 70508-7052

JOLLES, IRA HERVEY, lawyer; b. N.Y.C., Dec. 12, 1938; s. Harry and Hannah Ruth (Rapaport) J.; m. Andrea Lopen, May 7, 1967; children: Adam, Noah. AB, Columbia U., 1959; JD, Harvard U., 1962. Bar: N.Y. 1963. Assoc. Breed, Abbott & Morgan, N.Y.C., 1963-66; dir. N.Y.C. Income Tax Bur., 1966-68; assoc. Berlack, Israels & Liberman, N.Y.C., 1968-70, ptnr., 1971-89; sr. v.p., gen. counsel GPU, Inc., Morristown, N.J., 1990—; adj. prof. law Bklyn. Law Sch., 1984-89; bd. dirs. GPU Svc. Inc., Morristown, GPU Internat. Inc., Parsippany, N.J., GPU Electric, Inc., Parsippany, GPU Power, Inc., Parsippany, LRB Ltd., London, GPU Powernet Pty Ltd., Melbourne, Australia, Midlands Electricity PLC, Worcester, U.K., Utilities Mut. Ins. Co., Parsippany, Empresa Distribuidora Electrica Regional S.A., Empresa Distribuidora San Luis S.A., Empresa Distribuidora del Electricidad de La Rioja S.A., Empresa Distribuidora de Electricidad de Salta S.A. Bd. dirs. Rashi Assn., N.Y.C., Cahnman Found., N.Y.C., Regional Plan Assn., N.Y.C. Mem. ABA, Assn. Bar City N.Y., Harvard Club, Phi Beta Kappa. Jewish. Home: 610 West End Ave New York NY 10024-1605 Office: GPU Inc PO Box 1911 300 Madison Ave Morristown NJ 07962-6118

JOLLES, JANET KAVANAUGH PILLING, lawyer; b. Akron, Ohio, Sept. 5, 1951; d. Paul and Marjorie (Logue) Kavanaugh; m. Martin Jolles, Mar. 6, 1987; children: Madeleine Sloan Langdon Jolles, Jameson Samuel Rhys Jolles. BA, Ohio Wesleyan U., 1973; JD, U. Mo., 1976; LLM, Villanova U., 1985. Bar: Pa. 1976, U.S. Tax Ct. 1976, U.S. Dist. Ct. (ea. dist.) Pa. 1976, Ohio 1996. Atty. Schnader, Harrison, Segal & Lewis, Phila., 1976-83; gen. counsel Kistler-Tiffany Cos., Wayne, Pa., 1983-95; lawyer Janet Kavanaugh Pilling Jolles & Assocs., Berea, Ohio, 1996—. Mem. Phila. Estate Planning Coun., Estate Planning Coun. Cleve. Mem. ABA, Ohio State Bar Assn., Cleve. Bar Assn., Cuyahoga County Bar Assn., Phila. Bar Assn. (probate sect., tax sect.), Pa. Bar Assn., Berea Women's League, Phi Beta Kappa, Phi Delta Phi. Office: 43 E Bridge St Ste 101 Berea OH 44017-1909

JOLLY, BRUCE DWIGHT, manufacturing company executive; b. Wheeling, W.Va., Aug. 27, 1943; s. Edward and Martha Elizabeth (Glass) J.; m. Alice Marie O'Beirne, May 25, 1974 (div. Sept. 1997); children—Mara O'Beirne, Brock Thomas. A.B., Dartmouth Coll., 1965; M.B.A., U. Va., 1967. Systems engr. IBM Corp., Richmond, Va., 1967-68; fin. analyst Keystone Consol. Industries, Peoria, Ill., 1970-73; contr. HON Industries, Inc., Muscatine, Iowa, 1973-76, sec., treas., 1976-79; v.p. fin. Hawkeye Steel Products, Inc., Waterloo, Iowa, 1979-83, Cosco, Inc., Columbus, Ind., 1983-90; chief fin. officer Kiel Bros. Oil Co. Inc., Columbus, Ind., 1990-96; v.p. fin. Riverton Investment Corp., Winchester, Va., 1996—. With AUS, 1968-70, Vietnam. Decorated Bronze Star. Mem. Rotary, Phi Kappa Psi. Republican. Presbyterian. Home: 1420 Ramseur Ln Winchester VA 22601-6738 Office: Riverton Investment Corp 158 Front Royal Pike Ste 305 Winchester VA 22602-4324

JOLLY, BRUCE OVERSTREET, retired newspaperman; b. Bay City, Tex., July 2, 1912; s. Irvin and Alice Gretchen (Overstreet) J.; m. Sarah Clark Tate Jeffress, Jan. 22, 1946; children—Bruce Overstreet, Jr., Edwin Jeffress. AB in English and Journalism, Franklin Coll., 1938. Reporter, Indpls. News, 1938-40, Post Tribune, Gary, Ind., 1940-42, 47-48; Washington corr. Daily News, Greensboro, N.C., 1949-65; with pub. relations dept. So. Ry., Washington, 1965-72. Author: The First Hundred Years, 1977; Keeping Up With Yesterday, 1985, A Century of Progress, 1990, Travels With Barbara, 1992, Midst the Shifting Winds (The South and Civil Rights--Truman to Johnson), 1998; editor: The Brightness of His Presence, 1980. Bd. dirs. Sheltered Occupational Ctr. No. Va., Arlington, 1984-94; mem. planning commn. N.C. Tercentenary Celebration, 1962. With USAF, 1942-46, CBI. Recipient Cert. of Merit, State of N.C., 1963; alumni citation Franklin Coll., 1977. Mem. Nat. Press Club, Soc. of the South Pole (correspondent Antartic, 1963), Soc. Profl. Journalists, Arlington Knights of the Round Table (pres. 1982-83). Episcopalian. Avocations: golf, swimming, travel. Home: 4800 Fillmore Ave Apt 458 Alexandria VA 22311-5055

JOLLY, CHARLES NELSON, lawyer, pharmaceutical company executive; b. New Brunswick, N.J., Aug. 14, 1942; s. Nelson Frederick and Marie Mercedes (Montemayor) J.; m. Laurie Cherie Puryear, Feb. 5, 1992; children: T. Christopher, Susan Noel. BS, Holy Cross Coll., 1964; LLB, George Washington U., 1967. Bar: D.C. 1968, Tenn. 1984. Atty. Swift & Co., 1966-70, Miles Labs., 1970-71; dir. legis. affairs Miles Labs., Washington, 1971-75; assoc. gen. counsel Miles Labs., Elkhart, Ind., 1975-77; v.p., sec., gen. counsel, bd. dirs. Chattem Inc., Chattanooga, 1977-94; of counsel Chamblis, Bahner and Stophel, Chattanooga, 1994—. Cand. for U.S. Congress, 1994, 96; bd. dirs. Sr. Neighbors of Chattanooga, Inc., Tenn. Conservation League. Mem. ABA, Tenn. Bar Assn., Chattanooga Bar Assn., D.C. Bar Assn., Non-Prescription Drug Mfrs. Assn. (past dir., vice chmn. exec. com.), Coun. Better Bus. Burs. U.s. (past dir.), Better Bus. Bur. of Chattanooga (past chmn., bd. dirs.), Van Buren County C. of C. (bd. dirs.), The Narrows Club (McConnelsburg, Pa.), Middle Tenn. Amateur Retriever Club (sec.), Chattanooga Retriever Club (dir.).

JOLLY, DANIEL EHS, dental educator; b. St. Louis, Aug. 25, 1952; s. Melvin Joseph and Betty Ehs (Koehler) J.; m. Paula Kay Haas, 1972 (div.); 1 child, Farrell; m. Karen Lynn Small, 1998; stepchildren: Ryan, Ariel. *Daniel Ehs Jolly is descended from signatories of the Magna Charta. The Shelton family ancestors sheltered a child, the future Queen Elizabeth I from death threats by her sister, the then Queen Mary, in their home, Shelton Hall south of Norwich. The family was then invited to reside with the Royal Family after Elizabeth ascended to the throne. The Shelton family left England in the early 1600's for the Colonies and subsequently fought in the Revolutionary War for independence from England. Dr. Jolly, a dentist, is a member of the Sons of the American Revolution and the Magna Charta Barons.* BA in Biology and Chemistry, U. Mo., Kansas City, 1974, DDS, 1977. Resident in hosp. dentistry VA Med. Ctr., Leavenworth, Kans., 1977-78; pvt. practice Newcastle, Wyo., 1978-79; asst. prof. U. Mo., Kansas City, 1979-87; chief restorative dentistry Truman Med. Ctr., Kansas City, 1979-87; dir. dental oncology Trinity Luth. Hosp., 1982-87; assoc. prof., dir. gen. practice residency program Ohio State U., Columbus, 1987—; prof., dir. gen. practice residency program, 1993—; dir. Honduras Clinic Project, 1992—; bd. dirs. Rinehart Found., U. Mo. Dental Sch., Kansas City, 1985-87; cons. Lee's Summit (Mo.) Care Ctr., 1984-87, Longview Nursing Ctr., Grandview, Mo., 1986-87; sec. Combined Hosp. Dental Staff, Columbus, 1989-90, v.p., 1990-91, pres., 1991-92. *Daniel E. Jolly, DDS, is a Professor of Dentistry and Director of the Graduate training in Hospital Dentistry at the Ohio State University College of Dentistry. He is internationally recognized in the field of dental care for hospital and medical patients, the handicapped, and geriatric individuals. He has served as President of the International Association of Dentistry for the Handicapped, President of the American Academy of Dentistry for Persons with Disabilities, and as the Chairman of the Federation of Special Care Organizations in Dentistry. His clinical and educational skills are much sought after in Ohio and internationally.* Author: (manual) Hospital Dental Hygiene, 1984, Hospital Dentistry, 1985, OSU Manual of Hospital Dentistry, 1989—, (booklet) Nursing Home Dentistry, 1986, Dental Oncology, 1986. Mem. regional coun. Easter Seal Soc., Kansas City, 1985-87, mem. profl. adv. coun. Nat. Easter Seal Soc., 1986-92; sec. bd. dirs. Easter Seal Rehab. Ctr., Columbus, 1990-93; pres. Health Profls. Serving Humanity. With U.S. Naval Sea Cadet Corps, 1998-99. Recipient Alumni Achievement award in dentistry U. Mo., Kansas City, 1995, Ohio Dental Assn. Humanitarian award, 1998. Fellow Acad. Dentistry Internat., Am. Soc. Dentistry for Children, Am. Assn. Hosp. Dentists (regional v.p. 1993—, sec.), Acad. Gen. Dentistry, Am. Soc. Geriatric Dentistry, Acad. Dentistry for Handicapped (pres. 1992), Am. Coll. Dentistry, Pierre Fauchard Acad.; mem. ADA, Internat. Assn. Dentistry for Handicapped (pres. 1994-96, past pres. 1996-98, editor 1998—), Mo. Dental Assn., Internat. Assn. Dental. Handicap, Greater Kansas City Dental Soc., Fedn. Spl. Care Orgns. in Dentistry (chmn. 1992-93), Southwest Oncology Group, Internat. Soc. for Oral Oncology, Ohio Dental Assn. (Humanitarian award 1998). Club: Magna Charta Barons. Avocations: photography, skiing, scuba diving, swimming, horses. E-mail: jolly.4@osu.edu. Home: 1326 Glenn Ave Columbus OH 43212-3281 Office: Ohio State U Coll Dentistry 305 W 12th Ave Columbus OH 43210-1267

JOLLY, E. GRADY, federal judge; b. 1937. BA, U. Miss., 1959, LLB, 1962. Trial atty. NLRB, Winston-Salem, N.C., 1962-64; asst. U.S. atty. No. Dist. Miss., 1964-67; trial atty. Dept. Justice Tax Div., Washington, 1967-69; pvt. practice Jolly, Miller & Milam, Jackson, Miss., 1969-82; judge U.S. Ct. Appeals (5th cir.), Jackson, 1982—. Office: US Ct Appeals James O Eastland Courthouse 245 E Capitol St Rm 202 Jackson MS 39201-2409*

JOLLY, JOHN RUSSELL, JR., lawyer; b. Charlotte, N.C., Sept. 7, 1942; s. John Russell and Mildred Inez (Hovis) J.; m. Mary Angela Blanton, Dec. 28, 1963 (div. 1987); children: John R. III, Christopher E. BA, U. N.C., 1964, JD with honors, 1967. Bar: N.C. 1967, U.S. Ct. Appeals (4th cir.) 1970, U.S. Dist. Ct. (ea., mid. & we. dists.) N.C. 1970, U.S. Supreme Ct. 1972. Ptnr. Poyner & Spruill, Raleigh, Charlotte, N.C., Rocky Mount, N.C., 1967-79, 82—; superior ct. judge N.C. Gen. Ct. of Justice, 1979-82. Mem. Nat. Assn. Railroad Trial Counsel, N.C. Bar Assn., N.C. Assn. Def. Attys. (pres., bd. dirs. 1988-91). Democrat. Episcopalian. Avocations: boating, golf, exercise. Office: Poyner & Spruill PO Box 10096 Raleigh NC 27605-0096

JOLLY, WILLIAM THOMAS, foreign language educator; b. Helena, Ark., Apr. 8, 1929; s. Sidney Eugene and Eva (Jones) J. BA, Southwestern at Memphis, 1952; MA, U. Miss., 1958; PhD, Tulane U., 1968. Assoc. ancient langs., chmn. dept. Millsaps Coll., Jackson, Miss., 1959-65; assoc. prof. Greek and Latin Rhodes Coll., Memphis, 1965-75, prof., 1975-94, chmn. dept. fgn. langs., 1975-79, prof. emeritus, 1994—. With USN, 1953-55. Recipient Clarence Day award Day Found., 1991. Mem. Am. Philol. Assn/, Linquistic Soc. Am., Archaeol. Inst. Am., Classical Assn. Mid. West & South, Tenn. Classical Assn., Tenn. Philol. Assn., Am. Classical Legue. Democrat. Methodist. Home: 697 University St Memphis TN 38107-5138 Office: Rhodes Coll 2000 N Parkway Memphis TN 38112-1690

JONAITIS, ALDONA CLAIRE, museum administrator, art historian; b. N.Y.C., Nov. 27, 1948; d. Thomas and Demie (Genaitis) J. BA, SUNY, Stony Brook, 1969; MA, Columbia U., 1972, PhD, 1977. Chair art dept. SUNY, Stony Brook, 1983-85, assoc. provost, 1985-86, vice provost undergrad. studies, 1986-89; v.p. for pub. programs Am. Mus. Natural History, N.Y.C., 1989-93; dir. U. Alaska Mus., Fairbanks, 1993—. Author: From the Land of the Totem Poles, 1988; editor, author: Chiefly Feasts: The Enduring Kwakiutl Potlatch, 1991; editor: A Wealth of Thought: Franz Boas on Native American Art History, 1995, Looking North: Art from the University of Alaska Museum, 1998. Mem. Native Am. Art Studies Assn. (bd. dirs. 1985-95). Office: U Alaska Mus 907 Yukon Dr Fairbanks AK 99775

JONAS, GARY FRED, health care center executive; b. N.Y.C., Apr. 26, 1945; s. Otto and Hilde (Levy) J.; m. Rosalyn Ethel Levy; children: Lauren, Rachel. BS in Ops. Rsch., Columbia U., 1966; MBA, Harvard U., 1968. Mgmt. cons. Fry Cons., Washington, 1968-69; div. dir. Univ. Rsch. Corp. Ctr. Human Svcs., Chevy Chase, Md., 1970-73, exec. v.p., 1973-75, pres., chief exec. officer, 1975-85, chmn., chief exec. officer, 1985-88, also bd. dirs.; pres., chief operating officer The Earle Palmer Brown Cos., Bethesda, Md., 1988-93, also bd. dirs.; pres., CEO 20/20 Laser Ctrs., Inc., Bethesda, 1993-97, also bd. dirs.; exec. v.p., dir. TLC The Laser Ctr. Inc., Bethesda, 1997—; bd. dirs. Laser Sight Inc., Color Me Beautiful Inc., Herndon Va.; faculty assoc. Johns Hopkins U., 1999—. Contbr. articles to profl. jours. Mem. Inst. Mgmt. Cons. (cert.), Profl. Svcs. Coun. (past bd. dirs., v.p.), Nat. Contract Mgmt. Assn., Conf. Bd., Am. Soc. Tng. and Devel., Washington Bd. Trade, Young Pres.'s Orgn. (exec. com., chmn. Washington metro chpt. 1987-88), Harvard Club, Harvard Bus. Sch., Woodmont Country Club. Home: 6716 Melody Ln Bethesda MD 20817-3115 Office: TLC The Laser Ctr Inc 6701 Democracy Blvd Ste 200 Bethesda MD 20817-7516

JONAS, HARRY S., professional society administrator; b. Kirksville, Mo., Dec. 3, 1926; s. Harry S. and Sarah (Laird) J.; m. Connie Kirby, Aug. 6, 1949; children—Harry S., III, William Reed, Sarah Elizabeth. BA, Washington U., St. Louis, 1949, MD, 1952. Intern St. Luke's Hosp., St. Louis, 1952-53; resident Barnes Hosp., St. Louis, St. Louis Maternity Hosp., St. Luke's Hosp., 1952-56; practiced medicine specializing in ob-gyn Independence, Mo., 1956-74; prof. ob-gyn, chmn. dept. ob-gyn Truman Med. Center; asst. dean U. Mo-Kansas City Sch. Medicine, 1975-78, dean, 1978-87; asst. v.p. med. edn. AMA, Chgo., 1987—. Mem. Independence City Council, 1964-68; mem. Jackson County (Mo.) Legislature, 1973-74. Mem. Am. Coll. Obstetricians and Gynecologists (pres. 1986-87), Central Assn. Obstetricians and Gynecologists, Assn. Profs. Gynecology and Obstetrics, Assn. Am. Med. Colls., A.C.S., AMA, Mo. State Med. Assn., Jackson County Med. Soc., Kansas City (Mo.) Gynecol. Soc., Chgo. Gynecol. Soc. Home: 420 E Ohio St Apt 38E Chicago IL 60611-4670 Office: AMA 515 N State St Chicago IL 60610-4325

JONAS, JIRI, chemistry educator; b. Prague, Czechoslovakia, Apr. 1, 1932; s. Frantisek and Jirina (Vondrak) J.; m. Ana M. Masiulis, June 1, 1968. BSc, Tech. U. Prague, 1956; PhD, Czechoslovak Acad Sci., 1960. Research assoc. Inst. Organic Chemistry, Czechoslovak Acad. Sci., Prague, 1960-63; vis. scientist, dept. chemistry U. Ill., Urbana, 1963-65, from asst. to assoc. prof., 1966-72, prof., 1972—, dir. sch. chem. scis., 1983-93; dir. Beckman Inst. Advanced Sci. and Tech., 1993—; sr. staff mem. Materials Research Lab. U. Ill., Urbana, 1970-93, prof. Ctr. for Advanced Study, 1996—. Mem. editl. bd. Jour. Magnetic Resonance, 1975—, Jour. Chem., 1980-83, Jour. Chem. Physics, 1986-89, , Ann. Rev. Phys. Chemistry, 1991-95, Accts. of Chem. Rsch., 1990-93; assoc. editor Jour. of Am. Chem. Soc.; contbr. more than 300 articles in field of chem. phys. to profl. publs. J.S. Guggenheim fellow, 1972-73, Alfred P. Sloan fellow, 1967-69; Univ. Sr. scholar U. Ill., 1985-88; recipient U.S. Sr. Scientist award Alexander von Humboldt Found., 1988. Fellow Am. Acad. Arts and Scis., AAAS, Am. Phys. Soc.; mem. Nat. Acad. Scis., Am. Chem. Soc. (Joel Henry Hildebrand award 1983), Materials Research Soc. Roman Catholic. Clubs: U. Ill. Tennis; NBTC (Naples, Fla.). Office: Univ of Ill Beckman Inst 405 N Mathews Ave Urbana IL 61801-2325

JONAS, MANFRED, historian, educator; b. Mannheim, Germany, Apr. 9, 1927; came to U.S., 1937, naturalized, 1944; s. Walter and Antonie (Dannheisser) J.; m. Nancy Jane Greene, July 19, 1952; children: Andrew Miles, Kathryn Leslie, Emily Susan, Matthew Greene. B.S., CCNY, 1949; A.M., Harvard U., 1950; Ph.D. (Teaching fellow), Harvard, 1959. Mil. intelligence analyst U.S. Dept. Def., 1951-54; teaching fellow Harvard, 1954-59; vis. prof. Am. history Free U., Berlin, 1959-62; asso. prof. PMC Colls., 1962-63; faculty Union Coll., Schenectady, 1963-96; dir. grad. program Am. studies Union Coll., 1964-74, prof. history, 1967-81, chmn. dept. history, 1970-81, chmn. div. social sci., 1971-74, Washington Irving prof. modern lit. and hist. studies, 1981-86, John Bigelow prof. history, 1986-96, prof. emeritus, 1996—, chmn. dept. history, 1970-81, chmn. div. social sci., 1971-74; lectr. CCNY, 1950, U. Md. Extension, 1954, Northeastern U., 1958; dir. NDEA Insts. for Advanced Study in History, 1966-68; cons. U.S. Office Edn., 1966, NEH, 1985; sr. Fulbright-Hays lectr. U. Saarland, Germany, 1973; Charles Warren fellow Harvard U., 1977-78; Salgo vis. prof. Eôtvôs Lorand U., Budapest, 1983-84. Author: Die Unabhângigkeitserklärung der Vereinigten Staaten, 1964, Isolationism in America, 1935-41, 1966, 90, American Foreign Relations in the Twentieth Century, 1967, The United States and Germany, 1984; co-editor: Roosevelt and Churchill: Their Secret Wartime Correspondence, 1975, 90, New Opportunities in a New Nation, 1982; editorial bd. Diplomatic History, 1980-83; contbr. articles profl. jours. Mem. N.Y. State Regents Exam. Com. in Am. History, 1970-87; moderator Forum 17 WMHT-TV, 1965; bd. dirs. Freedom Forum, Inc., 1965-76, chmn., 1969-70, 75-76. Served with USNR, 1945-46. Mem. Am. Hist. Assn., Orgn. Am. Historians, Soc. for Historians Am. Fgn. Relations, AAUP (pres. chpt. 1969-71, chair conf. com. 1988-93), Phi Beta Kappa (pres. Alpha chpt. N.Y. 1990-92, 93-95), Phi Alpha Theta. Home: 33 Front St Schenectady NY 12305-1301

JONAS, RICHARD ANDREW, medical educator; b. Adelaide, South Australia, Nov. 28, 1951; came to U.S., 1982; s. Lyall Richard Jonas; m. Dianne E. Wearne, Apr. 12, 1980 (div. May 1996); children: Andrew William, Michael Richard. MBBS with honors, U. Adelaide, 1974; MA, Harvard U., 1994. Gen. surgery resident Royal Melbourne (Australia) Hosp., 1975-79; cardiac surgery resident Green Lane Hosp., Auckland, New Zealand, 1980-82; resident in cardiac surgery Brigham & Women's Hosp., Boston; surg. fellow Brighman and Women's Hosp., Boston, 1982-83; chief resident in cardiac surgery Children's Hosp., Boston, 1983-84; prof. surgery Harvard Med. Sch., Boston, 1994—; chief of cardiac surgery Children's Hosp., Boston, 1994—. Author: Cardiopulmonary Bypass in Neonates and Infants, 1994, Brain Injury and Cardiac Surgery, 1995; assoc. editor Jour. of Thoracic and Cardiovascular Surgery, 1994. Fellow ACS, Soc. of Neurosci.; mem. Am. Assn. of Thoracic Surgery, Soc. of Thoracic Surgery, Am. Surg. Assn. Episcopalian. Avocations: snow skiing, mountain treckking. Office: Dept Cardiac Surgery Children's Hosp 300 Longwood Ave Boston MA 02115-5724

JONAS, RUTH HABER, psychologist; b. Tel Aviv, Aug. 24, 1935; d. Fred S. and Dorothy Judith (Bernstein) Haber; m. Saran Jonas, Sept. 16, 1956; children: Elizabeth, Frederick. AB, Barnard Coll., 1957; MA, New Sch. for Social Rsch., 1977, PhD, 1987; grad. psychotherapy and psychoanalysis, NYU, 1996. Lic. psychologist, N.Y. 1st and 2d yr. intern clin. psychology NYU Med. Ctr.-Bellevue Hosp., N.Y.C., 1985-87; postdoctoral rsch. fellow NYU Med. Ctr., N.Y.C., 1987-88; clin. instr. psychiatry NYU Sch. Medicine, N.Y.C., 1987, clin. asst. prof. psychiatry, 1991; sr. psychologist forensic svc. Bellevue Hosp., N.Y.C., 1988—; pvt. practice psychology N.Y.C., 1988—. Fellow Am. Orthopsychiat. Assn.; mem. APA, N.Y. State Psychol. Soc., Manhattan Psychol. Assn., Am. Heart Assn. (fellow stroke coun.). Office: 200 E 33d St Ste 10B New York NY 10016-4827

JONAS, SARAN, neurologist, educator; b. N.Y.C., June 24, 1931; s. Myron and Margaret (Wurmfeld) J.; m. Ruth Haber, Sept. 16, 1956; children: Elizabeth Ann, Frederick Jonathan. B.S., Yale U., 1952; M.D., Columbia U., 1956. Diplomate Am. Bd. Psychiatry and Neurology, Am. Bd. Internal Medicine. Intern Bellevue Hosp., N.Y.C., 1956-57; resident and fellow in medicine and neurology Bellevue Hosp., 1957-62; practice medicine specializing in neurology N.Y.C., 1964—; from clin. instr. to assoc. prof. clin. neurology NYU Sch. Medicine, 1964-77, prof. clin. neurology, 1977—, acting chmn. dept. neurology, 1987-91; assoc. dir. neurology NYU Hosp., 1970-87, dir., 1987-91, dir. electroencephalography, 1969-94; acting dir. neurology Bellevue Hosp., N.Y.C., 1987-91, assoc. dir., 1991—, dir. electroencephalography, 1994—. Served with USN, 1962-64. N.Y. State fellow in rheumatic diseases, 1962-64. Mem. Am. Acad. Neurology, Assn. for Rsch. in Nervous and Mental Diseases, Am. Heart Assn. (Stroke Coun., Epidemiology Coun.), Am. Epilepsy Soc. Office: 530 1st Ave New York NY 10016-6481

JONAS, STEVEN, public health physician, medical educator, writer; b. N.Y.C., Nov. 22, 1936; s. Harold Jacob and Florence Jane (Kyzor) J.; m. Josephine Gear, June 19, 1964 (divorced); m. Linda Sue Friedman, Nov. 23, 1971 (div.); children: Jacob Henry, Lillian Sara; m. Adrienne Weiss, July 4, 1993 (div.). BA cum laude, Columbia Coll., 1958; MD, Harvard U., 1962; MPH, Yale U., 1967; MS, NYU, 1997. Diplomate Am. Bd. Preventive Medicine-Pub. Health. Intern Lenox Hill Hosp., N.Y.C., 1962-63; postdoctoral rschr. London Sch. Econs., 1964-65, resident in preventive medicine and pub. health, 1965-67; dist. health officer, 1967-68; dir. Ambulatory Care Planning and Devel./N.Y.C. Dept. Health, 1969; dir. dept. social medicine Morrisania City Hosp., Bronx, N.Y., 1969-71; asst. prof. Albert Einstein Coll. Medicine, Bronx, 1969-71;; lectr. Mt. Sinai Sch. Medicine, N.Y.C., 1969-89; asst. prof. dept. cmty. medicine SUNY Stony Brook Health Scis. Ctr., 1971-74; coord. ambulatory svcs. Univ. Hosp., 1971-74, assoc. prof. dept. cmy. and preventive medicine, 1974-83, prof. dept. preventive medicine, 1983—; attending physician Nassau County Med. Ctr., East Meadow, N.Y., 1973-86; cons. Dept. Medicine, Winthrop-U. Hosp., Mineola, N.Y., 1979-93; adj. assoc. prof. Columbia U. Sch. Architecture, 1977-79; adj. assoc. prof. med. edn. Tex. Coll. Osteo. Medicine, Ft. Worth, 1980—; adj. prof. legal edn. Touro Coll. Sch. of Law, Huntington, N.Y., 1998—. Author: Quality Control of Ambulatory Care: A Task for Health Departments, 1977, Medical Mystery: The Training of Doctors in the United States, 1978, Triathloning for Ordinary Mortals, 1986, 2nd edit., 1999, An Introduction to the U.S. Health Care System, 3d edit., 1992, 4th edit., 1998, The New Americanism, 1992, Take Control of Your Weight, 1993, Regular Exercise: A Handbook for Clinical Practice, 1995, The Essential Triathlete, 1996; editor, co-author: Health Care Delivery in the United State (Book of Yr. award Am. Jour. Nursing 1982), 1977, 81, 86, co-editor, 1999; co-author: Pacwalking: The Balanced Way to Aerobic Health, 1988, The "I Don't Eat (But I Can't Lose)" Weight-Loss Program, 1989, Just the Weigh You Are, 1997, Help Your Man Get Healthy, 1999; assoc. editor: Health Promotion and Disease Prevention in Clinical Practice, 1996; chief editor: (Springer series) Health Care and Society, 1976-79, Medical Education, 1978—; assoc. editor Preventive Medicine, 1983—, Am. Jour. of Preventive Medicine, 1987-92, mem. editl. bd., 1987—; book rev. editor Am. Jour. Preventive Medicine, 1991-92; mem. editl. bd. Am. Med. Athletics Assn. Quarterly, 1988—, Health Promotion in Clinical Practice, 1998—, ACSM's Health & Fitness Jour., 1999—; contbr. articles and revs. to numerous profl. jours.; reviewer for several med. jours. Sr. advisor U.S. Preventive Svcs. Task Force, 1984-89. Fellow Am. Pub. Health Assn., Am. Coll. Preventive Medicine (com. chmn. 1979-82), N.Y. Acad. Medicine (med. edn. com. 1983-92); mem. AMA, Am. Hosp. Assn., Assn. Am. Med. Colls., Profl. Ski Instructors Am. (cert. level I 1995), Assn. Tchrs. Preventive Medicine (pres. 1977-78), Phi Beta Kappa. Democrat. Jewish. Avocations: cycling, pacewalking and running, weight lifting, triathlon competition, skiing. Home: 105 Washington Ave Prt Jefferson NY 11777-2003 Office: SUNY Sch Med Stony Brook NY 11794-8036

JONAS, TONY, television executive. Dir. dramatic series Aaron Spelling Prodns.; v.p. dramatic series and long form programming MGM/UA TV Group; sr. exec. in charge of devel. Winkler/Rich Prodns., Paramount; v.p. devel. Disney TV; sr. v.p. drama devel. Warner Bros. TV (previously Lorimar TV), 1989-91, exec. v.p. creative affairs, 1991-95, pres., 1995-98; pres. Tony Jonas Prodns., Burbank, Calif., 1999—. Office: Tony Jonas Prodns Bldg 17 Rm J 4000 Warner Blvd Burbank CA 91522*

JONASSEN, GAYLORD D., computer company executive, new products and market development; b. East Orange, N.J., Oct. 13, 1932; s. Jonas M. and Alma M. (Stelter) J.; B.S. in M.E., Ariz. State U., 1960; m. Shirley Ann Christophel, June 15, 1956; children—Glenn, Brenda. Cert. profl. cons. Devel. engr. Motorola Semiconductor, Phoenix, 1956-60; plant and facilities research and devel. engr. Western Electric, N.Y.C., 1960-65; new products mgr. Deutsch Relays, Long Island, N.Y., 1965-67; new product mktg./sales mgr. Kinemotive Corp., Farmingdale, N.Y., 1967-69; div. mgr. Atlantic Sci. Corp., Plainview, N.Y., 1969-70; exec. v.p., tech. dir. Telecommunications Industries, Inc., Copaigue, N.Y., 1970-73; founder, pres., Internat. Protein Industries, Inc., Hauppauge, 1973-84, chmn. bd., 1973-84; mgmt. cons. Gaylord Jonassen Assocs., 1984-85; computer systems engring. project engring. program mgmt. Norden Systems, UTC, 1985-91; Gaylord D. Jonassen/ Group, 1991—; founder, pres. Scan-trol Sys., Inc., 1997—. Served with U.S. Navy, 1950-54. Recipient Disting. Achievement award, Coll. Engring. and Applied Sci., Ariz. State U., 1982; ASTM fellow, 1958. Mem. L.I. Assn. Commerce and Industry. Patentee in field. Contbr. articles to various publs. Home: 9 Wood Ln Smithtown NY 11787-4931

JONASSEN, JAMES O., architect; b. Aberdeen, Wash., July 23, 1940; s. James E. and Marjorie E. (Smith) J.; m. Patricia E. Glen, June 9, 1958 (div. Oct. 1975); m. Marilyn Joan Kampa, June 11, 1977; children—Christian A., Steven E. B.Arch., U. Wash., 1964; M.S. in Architecture, Columbia U., 1965. Registered architect, Ala., Alaska, Ariz., Calif., Colo., Fla., Ga., Idaho, Ill., Kans., La., Minn., Mo., Mont., Nebr., Nev., N.Mex., N.D., N.C., Ohio, Okla., Oreg., S.D., Tex., Wash., Utah, Wis., D.C., Del., Mass., Miss., N.H., N.Y., R.I., Vt., P.R., British Columbia, Can. Designer NBBJ Group, Seattle, 1965-70, ptnr., 1970-83, chief exec. officer, 1983—. Prin. works include Battelle Meml. Lab., Richland, Wash., 1965, (lab. of year award, 1968), Heath Profl. Bldg., 1970, Children's Orthopedic Hosp., Seattle, 1972, (AIA Honor award 1976), St. Mary's Hosp. Surg. Pavilion, Rochester, Minn., 1982, St. Vincent Med. Office Bldg., Portland, Oreg., 1983, Scottsdale Meml. Hosp. N., Ariz., 1984, Seattle VA Hosp., 1985, Stanford U. Hosp., 1986, St. Joseph Hosp. Med. Ctr., 1988, Providence Med. Ctr., Seattle, 1990 (AIA Merit award), David Grant Med. Ctr., Fairfield, Calif., 1986 (USAF Honor award 1989, Spl. citation DOD 1988, Type 1 Honor award USAF 1989, Excellence in Design award DOD 1991). Bd. dirs. Health Facilities Rsch. and Edn. Project, 1991—, Swedish Med. Ctr. Found., 1993, Sch. Zone Inst., 1990—; pres. bd. Architecture and Children Project, 1990-92. Naramore Found. fellow, 1969; Columbia U. scholar, 1964; Recipient Seattle Newsmaker Tomorrow award Time Mag., 1978. Fellow AIA (chmn. steering com. 1983-85, nat. com. architecture for health, mem. Nat. Life Cycle Task Force 1977, bd. dirs. Seattle chpt. 1985-87); mem. Am. Hosp. Assn., Western Hosps. Assn. (chmn. architects sect. 1973), Wash. Athletic Club, Columbia Tower Club, Rotary. Office: NBBJ 111 S Jackson St Seattle WA 98104-2881*

JONASSOHN, KURT, sociologist, educator; b. Cologne, Germany, Aug. 31, 1920; emigrated to Can., 1940, naturalized, 1946; s. Richard and Frieda; m. Pearl Pepper, Jan. 26, 1956; children—Frieda, Joseph David. B.A., Sir George Williams Coll., 1953; M.A. (Samuel Lapitsky fellow), McGill U., 1955; postgrad. (Univ. scholar), U. Chgo., 1955-56. Asst. study dir. U. Chgo., 1957-59; research sociologist Directorate of Personnel Planning, RCAF Hdqrs., Ottawa, Ont., Can., 1959-61; asst. prof., then prof. sociology Sir George Williams U. (now Concordia U., Sir George Williams campus), Montreal, Que., Can., 1961—; co-founder, dir. Montreal Inst. for Genocide and Human Rights Studies, 1986—. Author: (with Frank Chalk) The History and Sociology of Genocide: Analyses and Case Studies, 1990, Genocide and Gross Human Rights Violations in Comparative Perspective, 1998; co-editor ISA Bull., 1974-82; contbr. articles and revs. to profl. jours. and books. Bd. dirs. Can. Youth Hostels Assn., 1975-77; bd. dirs. Hostelling Tours Agy., Inc., pres., 1976-77; mem. coun. Inst. on the Holocaust and Genocide, Israel, 1995—; assoc. Genocide Studies Ctr., Australia, 1993—. Imperial Oil grad. research fellow, 1955-58. Mem. Internat. Sociol. Assn. (dep. exec. sec. 1974-78, exec. sec. 1978-82), Can. Sociology and Anthropology Assn. (sec.-treas. 1971-74), Am. Sociology Assn. Jewish. Office: Concordia U Dept Sociology SGW Campus, 1455 de Maisonneuve Blvd W, Montreal, PQ Canada H3G 1M8

JONASSON, OLGA, surgeon, educator; b. Peoria, Ill., Aug. 12, 1934; d. Olav and Swea C. (Johnson) J. MD, U Ill., Chgo., 1958; DSc, Newberry (S.C.) Coll., 1982. Diplomate Am. Bd. Surgery (bd. dirs. 1988-94). Intern and resident U. Ill. Rsch. & Ednl. Hosps., 1959-64; prof. surgery U. Ill., 1975-87; chief of surgery Cook County Hosp., Chgo., 1977-86; chmn., prof. dept. surgery Ohio State U., Columbus, 1987-93; mem. staff U. Ill. Hosps., Chgo., 1993—. Markle scholar John & Mary Markle Found., 1969. Fellow ACS; mem. Am. Surg. Assn. Office: Am Coll Surgeons Surg Svcs Dept 633 N Saint Clair St Chicago IL 60611-3234

JONCKHEERE, ALAN MATHEW, physicist; b. Howell, Mich., Feb. 12, 1947; s. August Peter and Elizabeth Gertrude (Nash) Jonckheere; m. Barbara Jean Minter, Aug. 16; children: Jessica, Susan, Laura Jean and Amanda Jean (twins). B.S., Mich. State U., 1969; M.S., U. Wash., 1970, Ph.D., 1976. Instr. physics dept. Fermi Nat. Accelerator Lab., Batavia, Ill., 1976-78, staff physicist, 1978—, assoc. dept. head meson dept., 1981-83, assoc. dept. head exptl. areas, 1983-84, Beams group coordinator, 1984-85, accelerator div. exptl. support dept., 1985-89, researcher div. D0 dept., 1989—; researcher elem. particle physics Stanford Linear Accelerator Ctr., Lawrence Berkeley Lab., Calif. Contbr. papers to physics publs. Office: Fermi Natl Accelerator Lab PO Box 500 Batavia IL 60510-0500

JONDAHL, TERRI ELISE, importing and distribution company executive, medical equipment company executive; b. Ukiah, Calif., May 6, 1959; d. Thomas William and Rebecca (Stewart) J. AA in Bus. Adminstrn., Mendocino Coll., 1981; BA in Adminstrn. and Mgmt., Columbia Pacific U., 1993. Sec. to planning commn. County of Mendocino, Ukiah, Calif., 1977-80; office systems analyst County of Mendocino, Ukiah, 1980-83; micro systems analyst Computerland of Annapolis, Md., 1983-84; controller Continental Mfg. Inc., Nacogdoches, Tex., 1984-87; mktg. mgr. Continental Mfg. Inc., Nacogdoches, 1987-89, dir. sales and mktg., 1989-95; exec. v.p. CAB Inc., Norcross, Ga., 1995—; pres., CEO PIE* Med. Corp., Duluth, Ga., 1998—; Mem. JSEC Com. Tex. Employment Commn., 1990-93. Co-author: National Federation of Business & Professional Women Local Organization Revitalization Plan, 1989. Mem. NAFE, Tex. Fedn. Bus. and Profl. Women (state pres. 1994-95), Nacogdoches Bus. and Profl. Women (pres. 1987-88), Ukiah Bus. and Profl. Women (pres. 1981-82), Nacogdoches County C. of C. (small bus. adv. com. 1990), Decatur Bus. and Profl. Women, Peachtree Corners/Norcross Rotary, Gwinnett County C. of C. (CEO exec. roundtable). Home: 1587 Martin Nash Rd SW Lilburn GA 30047-1941 Office: CAB Inc # G 5964 Peachtree Corners E Norcross GA 30092-2407

JONER, BRUNO, aeronautical engineer; b. Oskarstrom, Sweden, Dec. 17, 1921; came to U.S., 1962, naturalized, 1967; s. Algot and Hanna (Erickson) J.; m. Ingrid Gustafsson, Oct. 3, 1953; children: Peter, Eva, David. BS in Aero. and Mech. Engring., Stockholm Inst. Tech., 1940. Tech. dir. Ostermans Aero AB, Stockholm, 1946-52; devel. engr. mgr. STAL Finspong, Sweden, 1952-57; mgr. aviation dept. Salen & Wicander, AB, Stockholm, 1957-62; project engr. Boeing Vertol Co., Phila., 1962-77, Boeing Marine Systems Co., Seattle, 1977-88, Boeing Huntsville (Ala.) Internat. Space Sta., 1988-96, Boeing Rotorcrafts, Phila., 1997—. Author papers in field; co-author: Feasibility Study of Modern Airships. With Swedish Air Force, 1942-43. Assoc. fellow AIAA; mem. U.S. Naval Inst., Nat. Assn. Unmanned Vehicle Systems (charter). Office: PO Box 16858 Philadelphia PA 19142-0858

JONES, A. DURAND, park administrator. Chief supt. Rocky Mountain Nat. Park, Estes Park, Colo. Office: Rocky Mountain Nat Park Estes Park CO 80517*

JONES, ABBOTT C., investment banking executive; b. Lexington, Ky., Aug. 14, 1934; s. John Catron and Lois (Sauters) J.; m. Carol Donahue, June 29, 1957; children: Cynthia, Alison, Hilary. B.A., Principia Coll., 1956; M.B.A., Harvard U., 1958. Salesman Carnation Co., 1959-60; account exec. Benton & Bowles, N.Y.C., 1960-63; with Ogilvy & Mather, N.Y.C., 1963-77, sr. v.p., dir., 1973-77; sr. v.p., gen. mgr. Foote, Cone & Belding, N.Y.C., 1977-82; pres. Foote, Cone & Belding, Associated Communications Cos., N.Y.C., 1982-86; pres., chief operating officer Foote, Cone, Belding Communications, Inc., N.Y.C., 1986-89; pvt. cons. practice Greenwich, Conn., 1989-90; mng. dir. AdMedia Corp. Advisors, Inc., N.Y.C., 1990—. Served with U.S. Army, 1958-59. Clubs: University, Belle Haven (Greenwich, Conn.). Office: 19th Flr 444 Madison Ave New York NY 10022-6903

JONES, AIDAN DREXEL, lawyer; b. Wilmington, Del., Dec. 17, 1945; s. Richard Leonard and Dorothy Drexel (Walsh) J.; m. Kathleen Dellert, Aug. 19, 1972; 4 children. BA, Wesleyan U., 1967; JD, Georgetown U., 1974. Bar: D.C. 1975, U.S. Supreme Ct. 1984, Md. 1996. Law clk. U.S. Dist. Ct., Washington, 1974-75; assoc. Edward Greensfelder Jr. P.C., Washington, 1975-77, Haight, Gardner, Poor & Havens, Washington, 1977-83; ptnr. Finley, Kumble, Wagner, Heine, Underberg, Manley, Myerson & Casey, Washington, 1983-87, Laxalt, Washington, Perito & Dubuc, Washington, 1988-90, Washington, Perito & Dubuc, Washington, 1990-91, Graham & James, Washington, 1991-95. Contbr. articles to profl. jours. Mem. nat. alumni com. Wesleyan U., Middletown, Conn., 1987-89, 1967 class agt., 1985-92; trustee River Road Unitarian Ch., 1992-94; co-treas. Sidwell Friends Sch. Parents Assn., 1995-97, v.p., 1997-98, pres. 1998-99. Lt. USN, 1968-71. Mem. ABA (vice chmn. aviation and space law com. 1985-91). Office: 1818 N St NW Ste 700 Washington DC 20036-2477

JONES, ALAN PORTER, JR., food manufacturing executive; b. Milw., Feb. 27, 1925; s. Alan Porter and Eleanor Pratt (Bright) J.; m. Jean Drummond, Sept. 12, 1953; children: Richard, Susan, Cynthia, Alexandra. BA, Harvard U., 1948, MBA, 1950. With Jones Dairy Farm, Ft. Atkinson, Wis., 1950—, asst. treas., 1953-61, treas., 1961-74, v.p., treas., 1974-93, also bd. dirs.; pres. Uncle Josh Bait Co., 1978—; bd. dirs. Johnson Bank. Dir. Dwight Foster Pub. Libr., 1952-87, Wis. Livestock and Meat Coun., 1981-97, Ft. Atkinson C. of C., 1985-88; mem. Ft. Atkinson Sch. Bd., 1968-69, Wis. Gov.'s Adv. Com. on Internat. Trade, 1981-97, Wis. Internat. Trade Coun., 1997—, Wis. Citizens Environ. Coun., 1980-84, Wis. Radioactive Waste Policy Coun., 1984-87; trustee Ripon Coll., Wis., 1974-77; bd. dirs. Wis. Nature Conservancy, 1992-95. With Inf. U.S. Army, 1943-45. Decorated Bronze Star, Combat Inf. Badge. Mem. Nat. Audubon Soc., Sierra Club, Nature Conservancy, Wilderness Soc., Am. Legion. Republican. Home: 433 Adams St Fort Atkinson WI 53538-1401 Office: Jones Dairy Farm PO Box 808 Fort Atkinson WI 53538-0808

JONES, ALEX S., journalist, writer, broadcaster; b. Greeneville, Tenn., Nov. 19, 1946; m. Susan E. Tifft, Sept. 21, 1985. BA, Washington and Lee U., 1968. Editor Greeneville (Tenn.) Sun, 1978-83; press reporter N.Y. Times, 1983-92; host On the Media Nat. Pub. Radio, 1993-97; host, exec. editor Media Matters PBS, 1995—; Eugene C. Patterson prof. Practice Journalism Duke U., 1996—; sr. commentator On the Media, 1997—; sr. fellow Media Studies Ctr., 1996-97. Author: (with Susan E. Tifft) The Patriarch: The Rise and Fall of the Bingham Dynasty, 1991, The Trust: The Private and Powerful Family Behind The New York Times, 1999. Recipient Pulitzer prize for specialized reporting, 1987; Nieman fellow, 1981-82. Home: 225 W 86th St Apt 309 New York NY 10024-3355

JONES, ALLISON, basketball coach. BA, St. John's U., 1981. Asst. coach women's basketball Yale U., New Haven, 1981-84, Columbia U., N.Y.C., 1984-86; head coach women's basketball Pace U., 1986-92, U. Hartford, Conn., 1992—. Named All-Am. Coach Am. Women's Sports Fedn. Mem. NCAA (legis. com.), Women's Basketball Coaches Assn. Office: U Hartford Dept Athletics Sports Info 200 Bloomfield Ave West Hartford CT 06117-1545*

JONES, ANITA KATHERINE, computer scientist, educator; b. Ft. Worth, Mar. 10, 1942; d. Park Joel and Helene Louise (Voigt) J.; m. William A. Wulf, July 1, 1977; children: Karin, Ellen. AB in Math., Rice U., 1964; MA in English, U. Tex., 1966; PhD in Computer Sci., Carnegie Mellon U., 1973, D in Sci. and Tech. (hon.), 1999. Programmer IBM, Boston, Washington, 1966-69; assoc. prof. computer sci. Carnegie-Mellon U., Pitts., 1973-81; founder, v.p. Tartan Labs. Inc., Pitts., 1981-87; free-lance cons. Pitts., 1987-88; prof., head computer sci. dept. U. Va., Charlottesville, 1988-93, prof., 1997—; dir. def. rsch. and engring. Dept. Def., Washington, 1993-97; univ. prof. U. Va., Charlottesville, 1997—; mem. Def. Sci. Bd., Dept. Def., 1985-93, 98—, USAF Sci. Adv. Bd., 1980-85, Nat. Sci. Bd., 1998—; governing bd. Nat. Sci. Found.; bd. dirs. Sci. Applications Internat. Corp.; trustee Mitre Corp., 1989-93. Editor: Perspectives on Computer Science, 1977, Foundations of Secure Computation, 1971. Recipient Air Force Meritorious Civilian Svc. award, 1985, Medal for Disting. Pub. Svc. Dept. of Def., 1996, Disting. Svc. award Computing Rsch. Assn., 1997. Fellow ACM (editor-in-chief Transactions on Computer Sys. 1983-91), IEEE; mem. Nat. Acad. Engring., Sigma Xi. Avocation: gardening.

JONES, ANNE, librarian; b. St. Louis, Mo., July 29, 1934; d. Bernard Joseph and Mary Christina (DeRubertis) Muller-Thym. BA in English, CUNY, 1958. Libr. J.H. Whitney & Co., N.Y.C., 1957-67; reference libr. Am. Mgmt. Assn., N.Y.C., 1967-86, libr., database adminstr., 1986-89, mgr. info. resource ctr., 1989—. Author: Celebrate the Journey: History of the West End Presbyterian Church, 1988. Democrat. Presbyterian. Avocations: reading, writing poetry. Office: American Management Assn 1601 Broadway New York NY 10019-7420

JONES, ANTHONY RAY, military career officer; m. Nancy Erwin; children: Regan, Erin, Holly. BS in Bus., Ind. U., 1970; M in Sys. Mgmt., U. So. Calif., L.A., 1982; grad., Army Command/Gen. Staff Coll., U.S. Army War Coll. Commd. 2nd lt. U.S. Army Infantry, 1970, advanced through grades to maj. gen., 1998; inf. platoon leader, co. exec. officer 1st bn. 30th Inf. U.S. Army Infantry, Schweinfurt, Germany; aviation platoon leader, HHC co. comdr. 9th inf. divsn. U.S. Army Infantry, Ft. Lewis, Wash.; exec. officer 213th Aviation Co. U.S. Army Infantry, Camp Humphreys, Korea; co. comdr. E Co., task force 160 U.S. Army Infantry; exec. officer 160th Spl. Ops. Aviation Group U.S. Army Infantry, Ft. Campbell, Ky.; comdr. 3d bn., 227th Aviation Regiment, 3d Armored Divsn. U.S. Army Infantry, Ft. Hood, Tex.; comdr. Combat Aviation Brigade, 24th Inf. Divsn. U.S. Army Infantry, Ft. Stewart, Ga.; chief ops. and contingency plans, dep. chief staff ops. U.S. Army Infantry, Washington, dep. dir. ops. J3 Joint Staff; asst. divsn. comdr.-forward 1st Armored divsn. U.S. Army Infantry, Tuzla, Bosnia-Herzegovina; asst. ops. officer, test concepts and project officer U.S. Army Aviation Bd., Ft. Rucker; ops. rsch., sys. analysis for force modernization office U.S. Army Mil. Pers. Ctr., Alexandria, Va.; aviation ops. officer Spl. Ops. Office, dep. chief of staff U.S. Army, Washington. Decorated Def. Superior Svc. medal, Legion of Merit with oak leaf cluster, Bronze Star, Meritorious Svc. medal with seven oak leaf clusters, Air medal, Army Commendation medal with oak leaf cluster, Nat. Def. Svc. medal with oak leaf cluster, Armed Forces Expeditionary medal, S.W. Asia Svc. medal, Kuwait Liberation medal, Joint Meritorious Unit award with oak leaf cluster. Office: US Army Aviation Ctr Fort Rucker AL 36362

JONES, ARBURTA ELIZABETH, development specialist; b. Jersey City, N.J., Dec. 5, 1957; d. William Benjamin Cowherd and Willie Arburta DeShong; m. James Lee Jones, Feb. 27, 1982; children: Darnell Sinclair, Cedric Armstrong. BA in Social Work, U. Pitts., 1980; MPA, Rutgers U., 1997. Cert. social worker; cert. supervisory mgmt. Child care worker Group Homes of Camden County, N.J., 1980-81; program coord. Neighborhood Ctr., Camden, 1981-82; social worker II N.J. Div. Devel. Disabilities, Vineland, N.J., 1982-83; family svc. specialist II and III N.J. Div. Youth and Family Svcs., Camden, 1983-86; resource devel. specialist N.J. Div. Youth and Family Svcs., Hammonton, N.J., 1986-88; supervising family svc. specialist N.J. Div. Youth and Family Svcs., Camden, 1988-97; supervising program devel. specialist N.J. Div. Devel. Disabilities, Trenton, N.J., 1997—. Pres. United Meth. Women, Parkside United Meth. Ch., 1997—, chairperson pastor-parish rels. com., 1998—. Mem. NAACP, Am. Soc. of Pub. Adminstrs., Nat. Assn. Negro Bus. Profl. Women, Pi Alpha Alpha, Gamma Sigma Sigma. Democrat. Avocations: bible study, reading, sewing. E-mail: ajones1@dhs.state.nj.us. Home: 1351 Decatur St Camden NJ 08104 Office: NJ Divsn of Youth and Family Svcs Policy and Planning Unit 50 East State St Trenton NJ 08625

JONES, ARTHUR EDWIN, JR., library administrator, English and American literature educator; b. Orange, N.J., Mar. 20, 1918; s. Arthur Edwin and Lucy Mabel (Alpaugh) J.; m. Rachel Evelyn Mumbulo, Apr. 24, 1943; 1 child, Carol Rae Jones Jacobus. BA, U. Rochester, 1939; MA, Syracuse U., 1941, PhD in English, 1950; MLS, Rutgers U., 1964. Instr. English Syracuse U., N.Y., 1946-49; Instr. English Drew U., Madison, N.J., 1949-52, asst. prof., 1952-55, assoc. prof., 1955-60, prof. English and Am. lit., 1960-86, dir. libraries, 1956-85, prof., libr. emeritus, 1986—; evaluator Middle States Assn. Colls., Phila., 1955-85. Author: Darwinism and American Realism, 1951; contbr. articles to profl. jours.; book reviewer Library Jour., 1956-75, Choice, 1969—. Trustee Madison Pub. Library, N.J., 1958-79, pres., 1976-79. Served to 1st lt. U.S. Army, 1941-46. Named to U. Rochester Athletic Hall of Fame, 1997; Lilly Endowment scholar Am. Theol. Libr. Assn., 1963-64. Mem. MLA, Nat. Coun. Tchr. of Eng., ALA (councillor 1970-71), Am. Theol. Libr. Assn. (pres. 1967-68), AAUP, Lions Club, Habitat for Humanity. Democrat. Home: 400 Avinger Ln Apt 409 Davidson NC 28036-9718

JONES, AUDREY BEYER, dietitian; b. Madison, Wis., Feb. 1, 1921; d. Adelbert John and Hazel Mae (Crocker) B.; m. Frank C. Jones, July 11, 1954; children: Philip Lynn, Paul Douglas, David Scott. BS, Milw.-Downer Coll., 1941; BA, U. Wis., 1947; Tchg. Cert., U. Corpus Christi, Tex., 1962. Lic. dietitian, Tex. Dietitian Charity Hosp., New Orleans, 1942-43, 12th Evac Hosp./U.S. Army, 1943-44, VA Hosp., Wood, Wis., 1948-51; clinic dietitian VA Reg. Office, Milw., 1951-53; chief dietitian Kuakini Hosp., Honolulu, 1954-55; nutrition cons. various hosps. Corpus Christi, 1964—. Docent Art Mus. So. Tex., Corpus Christi, 1990-93. 1st lt. U.S. Army, 1943-44; ETO. Mem. AAUW (pres. Corpus Christi br. 1994-96), Am. Dietetic Assn. (registered dietitian), Tex. Dietetic Assn., Corpus Christi Dietetic Assn. (pres. 1972). Republican. Lutheran. Avocations: travel, birding, reading, crossword puzzles, bridge. Home: 4621 Monette Dr Corpus Christi TX 78412-2344

JONES, BARBARA DEAN, substance abuse counselor; b. Taunton, Mass., Dec. 11, 1931; d. Laurence Franklin and Amy Laura (Harrington) Dean; m. Rial Cooper Jones, Aug. 31, 1957 (div. July 1987); children: Dean Michael, Mark Jackson, Amy Winifred. Student, Duke U., 1952; BA, U. Mass., 1953; MEd in Human Svcs., Boston U., 1983. Cert. in alcohol education and prevention, Fla., 1981; lic. real estate agt., Va., 1979, Calif., 1984. Psychiat. social worker Alcohol Rehab. Ctr., Butner, N.C., 1953-55; social case worker Granville County Dept. Pub. Welfare, Oxford, N.C., 1955-56; dist. dir. Bright Leaf Girl Scout Coun., Durham, N.C., 1956-57; kindergarten tchr. Sasebo, Japan, 1961; social worker Assn. for the Blind, Charleston, S.C., 1962-63; tchr. Am. Studies Ctr., Naples, Italy, 1980-82; alcohol rehab. counselor Navy Regional Med. Ctr., Naples, 1982-83; family counselor Parkside Recovery Ctr., Oceanside, Calif., 1987-89; human rels. cons. Decorating Den, Anaheim, Calif., 1989-90; alcohol facilitator Navy Alcohol Safety Action Program, Naples, 1980-83. Bd. dirs. Fairfax (Va.) Ballet Co., 1978, YWCA, Glendora, Calif., 1972; pres. Naval Officers Wives Club, Charleston, 1964; lay min. St. Michael's Episcopal Ch., Carlsbad, Calif., 1966; chmn. alcohol and drug abuse com. Self Esteem Task Force of San Diego County, 1990; mem. San Diego Mus. Art, Mingei Mus. World Folk Art; v.p. Camino Real Assn., 1996-97, pres., 1997-98. Recipient cert. of appreciation U.S. Navy, 1983; Yale U. Summer Sch. of Alcohol Studies fellow, 1955. Mem. AAUW, Latin Am. Arts Assn., Women's Internat. Ctr., Oceanside Newcomer's Club (chmn. cultural arts 1996, 97, pres. elect 1997-98, pres. 1998-99, 99—). Republican. Avocations: travel, golf, arts, bridge. Home and Office: 3421 Summerset Way Oceanside CA 92056-3208

JONES, BARBARA EWER, school psychologist, occupational therapist; b. Marion, Ind., Jan. 28, 1942; d. J. Bertrand and Audrey May (Carter) Ewer; m. Jan Alden Fowler. BS, Ind. U., 1965, MS, 1970; MS, Ind. U.-Purdue U., Indpls., 1977; postgrad., U. Indpls., 1986-93. Tchr. Marion Sch. Sys., 1965-66, Decatur Twp. Sch. Sys., Indpls., 1967-71; contract substitute tchr. San Bernardino (Calif.) Sch. Sys., 1967; dir. Univ. Early Childhood Sch., Indpls., 1971-75; psychologist occupl. therapist master level Monroe County Cmty. Sch. Corp., Bloomington, Ind., 1977—, also consultation and insvc. trainer, rschr.; lectr. evening divsn. Butler U., Indpls., 1974-81; mem. com. for study of children of alcoholics in sch. environ., Bloomington, 1990—. Co-editor, author The Special Needs Child in American Schools, 1995; contbr. articles to profl. jours. Recipient awards for photography, sculpture, and watercolors, 1978, 86-89. Mem. Am. Occupl. Therapy Assn., Ind. Occupl. Therapy Assn. Home: 4788 S Lick Creek Rd Morgantown IN 46160-9598

JONES, BARCLAY GIBBS, III, investment banker; b. Berkeley, Calif., Oct. 14, 1960; s. Barclay Gibbs and Anne (Tompkins) J.; m. Jean Murray Dyer, Nov. 11, 1989; children: Barclay, Katherine, August. BS in Econs., U. Pa., 1982. Asst. to pres. W.P. Carey & Co., Inc., N.Y.C., 1982-86, v.p., 1986-87, sr. v.p., 1987-88, mng. dir., 1988-97, vice chmn., 1997-99; mng. dir. Barlow Ptnrs., N.Y.C., 1999—. Mem. Racquet and Tennis Club, The Brook Club, St. Elmo Club, Cold Spring Harbor Beach Club, Piping Rock Club. Office: Barlow Ptnrs 370 Park Ave New York NY 10020-1605

JONES, BENJAMIN ANGUS, JR., retired agricultural engineering educator, administrator; b. Mahomet, Ill., Apr. 16, 1926; s. Benjamin Angus and Grace Lucile (Morr) J.; m. Georgeann Hall, Sept. 11, 1949; children: Nancy Kay Jones-Richardson, Ruth Ann Jones-Sommers. BS, U. Ill., 1949, MS, 1950, PhD, 1958. Registered profl. engr., Ill. Asst. prof., asst. ext. engr. U. Vt., Burlington, 1950-52; instr., agrl. engr. U. Ill., Urbana, 1952-54, asst. prof., agrl. engr., 1954-58, assoc. prof., agrl. engr., 1958-64, prof., agrl. engr., 1964-92, prof. emeritus, 1992—, assoc. dir., agrl. exptl. sta., 1973-92; assoc. dir. emeritus, 1992—, U. Ill., Urbana, 1992; cons. various Ill. Drainage Dists., 1958—. Co-author: (textbook) Engineering Application in Agriculture, 1973; contbr. articles to Jour. Soil & Water Conservation, Encyclopedia Britannica, Agrl. Engring., Transactions of ASAE, Proceedings of ASCE, Soil Sci. Soc. Am. Proceedings, Crops and Soils, Jour. Hydrology, Water Resources Bulletin. Merit badge examiner Boy Scouts Am., Burlington, 1950-52; lay mem. Cen. Ill. Con. United Meth. Ch., 1978-81. With USN, 1944-46. NSF fellow. Fellow Am. Soc. Agrl. Engrs. (bd. dirs., trustee); mem. Soil and Water Conservation Soc., Am. Soc. for Engring. Edn., Sigma Xi, Gamma Sigma Delta, Alpha Epsilon. Home: 2012B Eagle Ridge Ct Urbana IL 61802-8617 Office: U Ill Agrl Exptl Sta 211 Mumford Hall 1301 W Gregory Dr Urbana IL 61801-3608

JONES, BETTY KAY, academic adminstrator; b. Pomeroy, Ohio, May 27, 1951; d. Harold Verland and Helen Morrow Watson; m. Barry William Jones, July 4, 1998; 1 child, Jennifer Morrison. BA, Ky. Christian Coll., 1973; MA, Morehead (Ky.) State U., 1976, Morehead (Ky.) State U., 1979; PhD, Ohio U., 1997. Prof. Ky. Christian Coll., Grayson, Ky., 1976-95; assoc. prof. La. Coll., Pineville, 1996-97; lab mgr. Ohio U., Athens, 1997-98; asst. prof. U. Ga., Athens, 1998—; graphics cons. Milledge Ave. Bapt. Ch., Athens, 1998—; judge Peabody awards U. Ga., 1999. Recipient Disting. Alumni award Ky. Christian Coll., 1989. Mem. Soc. Profl. Journalists, Assn. of Educators of Journalism, Delta Epsilon Chi, Kappa Tau Alpha. E-mail: betjones@arches.uga.edu. Office: Henry W Grady Coll Journalism U Ga Athens GA 30602-3018

JONES, BEVERLY ANN MILLER, nursing administrator, retired patient services administrator; b. Bklyn., July 14, 1927; d. Hayman Edward and Eleanor Virginia (Doyle) Miller; m. Kenneth Lonzo Jones, Sept. 5, 1953 (dec.); children: Steven Kenneth, Lonnie Cord. BSN, Adelphi U., 1949. Chief nurse regional blood program ARC, N.Y.C., 1951-54; asst. dir., acting DON M.D. Anderson Hosp. and Tumor Inst., Houston, 1954-55; asst. DON Sibley Meml. Hosp., Washington, 1959-61; assoc. dir. nursing svc. Anne Arundel Gen. Hosp., Annapolis, Md., 1966-70; asst. adminstr. nursing Alexandria (Va.) Hosp., 1972-73; v.p. patient care svcs. Longmont (Colo.) United Hosp., 1977-93; pvt. cons., 1993-99, ret.; instr. ARC, 1953-57, chmn. nurse enrollment com. D.C. chpt., 1959-61; mem. adv. bd. Boulder Valley

Vo.-Tech. Health Occupations Program, 1977-80; del. nursing adminstrs. good will trip to Poland, Hungary, Sweden and Eng., 1980. Contbr. articles to profl. jours. Mem.-at-large exec. com. nursing svc. adminstrs. sect. Md. Nurses' Assn., 1966-69; bd. dirs. Meals on Wheels, Longmont, 1978-80, Longmont Coalition for Women in Crisis, Applewood Living Ctr., Longmont; mem. utilization com. Boulder (Colo.) Hospice, 1979-83; mem. task force on nat. commn. on nursing Colo. Hosp. Assn., 1982, mem. coun. labor rels., 1982-87; mem. U. Colo. Task Force on Nursing, 1990; vol. Champs program St. Vrain Valley Sch. Dist. Mem. Am. Orgn. Nurse Execs. (chmn. com. membership svcs. and promotions, nominee recognition of excellence in nursing adminstrn.), Colo. Soc. Nurse Execs. (dir. 1978-80, 84-86, pres. 1980-81, mem. com. on nominations 1985-86). Home: 853 Wade Rd Longmont CO 80503-7017

JONES, BILL, state official, rancher; b. Coalinga, Calif., Dec. 20, 1949; s. C.W. and Cora Jones; m. Maurine Abramson, Aug. 29, 1971; children: Wendy, Andrea. BS in Agribus. and Plant Sci., Calif. State U., Fresno, 1971. Ptnr. ranch, nr. Firebaugh, Calif.; mem. Calif. Assembly, Sacramento, 1983—, Rep. leader, 1991—; Sec. of State State of California, 1994—. Former chmn. Fresno County Rep. Cen. Com. Named Outstanding Young Farmer, Fresno C. of C. Mem. Fresno County and City C. of C. (past bd. dirs.). Methodist. Avocations: horseback riding, golf, flying, travel. Home: 2254 W Dovewood Ln Fresno CA 93711-2810 Office: Office Sec State 1500 11th St Sacramento CA 95814-5701

JONES, BILL T., dancer, choreographer; b. Bunnell, Fla., Feb. 15, 1952. Student, SUNY, Binghampton, 1970; PhD (hon.), Bard Coll., 1996. Co-founder Am. Dance Asylum, 1973; co-founder, artistic dir. Bill T. Jones/Arnie Zane & Co. (now Bill T. Jones/Arnie Zane Dance Co.), 1982—. Author: Last Night on Earth, 1995; choreographer, soloist Negroes for Sale, 1973, Track Dance, 1974; (with Arnie Zane) Pas de Deux for Two, 1974, Across the Street, 1975, Everybody Works/All Beasts Count, 1976, Whosedebabedolbabedoll, 1977, De Sweet Streak to Loveland, 1977, The Runner Dreams, 1978, Stories, Steps and Stomps, 1978, Progresso, 1979, Echo, 1979, Naming Things Is Only the Intention to Make Things, 1979, Floating the Tongue, 1979, Monkey Run Road, 1979, Blauvelt Mountain, 1980, Sisyphus, Act I and II, 1980, Open Spaces, 1980, Tribeca, Automation, Three Wise Men, Christmas, 1980, Secret Pastures, 1984, History of Collage, 1988, D-Man in the Waters, 1989 (Bessie Award 1989), Dances 1989, Last Supper at Uncle Tom's Cabin/The Promised Land, 1991, Love Defined, 1991, Aria, 1992, Last Night on Earth, 1992, Fête, 1992, Achilles Loved Patroclus, 1993, War Between the States, 1993, Still/Here, 1994, We Set Out Early...Visibility Was Poor, 1997; dir., choreographer operas including New Year, 1990, The Mother of Three Sons, Lost in the Stars; dir. (with Rhodessa Jones) Perfect Courage, 1990 (Izzy award 1990). Recipient (with Arnie Zane) N.Y. Dance and Performance award (Bessie) choreographer/creator category, given for freedom of information, 1986, Dorothy B. Chandler Performing Arts award, 1991, Dance Mag. award, 1993, Edinburgh Festival Critics' Award (presented to company), 1993, Creative Artists Public Svc. Award, 1979; MacArthur Genius fellowship, 1993. Office: Bill T Jones/Arnie Zane Co 853 Broadway Ste 1706 New York NY 10003-4703*

JONES, BILLY ERNEST, dermatology educator; b. Daytona Beach, Fla., Jan. 29, 1933; s. Bibb Ernest and Marjorie (Eyre) J.; m. Hannah Warren, June 12, 1958; children: Alan W., Lawrence W., Marjorie E. BS, The Citadel, 1954; MD, Duke U., 1958. Diplomate Am. Bd. Dermatology. Commd. 2d lt. U.S. Army, 1958, advanced through grades to maj., 1964; intern William Beaumont Hosp. U.S. Army, El Paso, Tex., 1958-59; gen. med. officer Henry Barracks U.S. Army, Cayey, P.R., 1959-61; resident in dermatology The Presidio U.S. Army, San Francisco, 1961-64; chief dermatology U.S. Army, Ft. Gordon, Ga., 1964-67; resigned U.S. Army, 1967; practice medicine specializing in dermatology Greenville, N.C., 1967-80; prof. medicine East Carolina U., Greenville, 1991-97, ret., 1997. Recipient Clin. Tchr. award Sr. Class, 1983, 84, 88, Teaching Recognition award 1st yr. residents, 1982, 3d yr. residents, 1985 Med. Sch. East Carolina U. Fellow Am. Acad. Dermatology; mem. AMA, N.C. Med. Soc. Republican. Episcopalian. Avocations: barbershop singing, yachting, horticulture.

JONES, BOISFEUILLET, JR., lawyer, newspaper executive; b. Atlanta, Nov. 14, 1946; s. Boisfeuillet and Laura (Coit) J.; m. Barbara Frost Pendleton, Sept. 13, 1969; children: Lindsay Pendleton, Theodore Boisfeuillet. A.B., Harvard U., 1968, J.D., 1974; D.Phil., Oxford U., 1981. Bar: Mass. 1974, D.C. 1979. Law clk. Judge Levin H. Campbell, U.S. Ct. Appeals (1st cir.), Boston, 1974-75; atty. Hill and Barlow, Boston, 1975-80; v.p., counsel Washington Post, 1980-95, pres., gen. mgr., 1995—; dir. Bowater Mersey Paper Co., Ltd., N.S., Robinson Terminal Warehouse Corp., Alexandria, Va., Fed. City Coun., Washington, Eugene & Agnes Meyer Found., Washington, Greater Washington Bd. Trade, St. Albans Sch., Washington. Rhodes scholar Rhodes Trust, 1968. Episcopalian. Home: 4331 Forest Ln NW Washington DC 20007-1137 Office: Washington Post 1150 15th St NW Washington DC 20071-0002

JONES, BONNIE DAMSCHRODER, special education specialist; b. Cocoa, Fla., Dec. 20, 1945; d. Eugene Edward and Lu Jeanette (Hufford) Damschroder; m. Robert Kirk Jones, June 8, 1968; children: Kelly Anne, Jennifer Graham. BS in Edn., Capital U., Columbus, Ohio, 1967; MS in Edn., George Mason U., 1976; transition specialist cert., U. Hawaii, 1988; EdD, Columbia U., 1999. Tchr. mental retardation Waterford (Conn.) Pub. Schs., 1967-68; tchr. mentally retarded Escambia County Schs., Pensacola, Fla., 1968-70; tchr. learning disabilities Fairfax County Schs., Fairfax, Va., 1975-78; curriculum specialist Newport News (Va.) Pub. Schs., 1978-80; program coord. Peninsula Area Coop. Ednl. Svcs. Day Treatment Regional Sch., Newport News, 1980-81; dist. transition coord. Hawaii Dept. Edn., Honolulu, 1984-88; program specialist Kans. Dept. Edn., Topeka, 1988-90; rsch. asst. Columbia U. Tchrs. Coll., N.Y.C., 1991-92; tchr. learning disabilities Fairfax County Pub. Schs., Fairfax, Va., 1992-94, tchr., dept. chairperson, 1994-96; program specialist U.S. Dept. Edn. Office of Spl. Edn. Programs, 1997—; adj. faculty George Mason U., Fairfax, 1976, 97—, Baruch Coll., 1992; supervising tchr. Hampton (Va.) Inst., 1981, U. Hawaii, Honolulu, 1988, George Mason U., 1996; mem. exceptional needs standards com. Nat. Bd. for Profl. Tchg. Standards, 1994-98, nat. adv. com. on assessment of exceptional needs standards, 1998—. Co-author: Identifying Handicapping Conditions, 1978, Career Awareness for Students with Handicaps, 1986, Implementing Transition Goals, 1992, 2d edit., 1999. Mem. Jr. League, Portland, Maine, Honolulu, and Topeka, 1983—; pres. USCG Officers' Wives Club, Portland, 1983, bd. dirs. Newport News, 1978-79, Honolulu, 1984-88, N.Y.C., 1991; co-chmn. carnival booth Punahou Sch., Honolulu, 1987, 88; treas. Red Hill Sch. PTA, Honolulu, 1985-87; bd. dirs. Internat. Divsn. Career Devel., 1989-94, treas., 1992-94; pres. Kans. Divsn. Career Devel., 1989-90. Recipient cert. of appreciation USCG, Boston, 1983, community svc. award, N.Y.C., 1991; Vocat. Educator of Yr. award Hawaii Vocat. Edn. Assn., 1987, Outstanding Contbn. to Transition award Kans. Div. on Career Devel., 1990, Outstanding Alumni award George Mason U. Grad. Sch. Edn., 1998. Mem. ASCD, Am. Ednl. Rsch. Assn., Coun. for Exceptional Children (subcom. on knowledge and skills profl. standards com. 1990-94), Phi Delta Kappa. Home: 7726 Silver Sage Ct Springfield VA 22153-2126

JONES, BRENDA GAIL, school district administrator; b. Winnipeg, Man., Can., Nov. 5, 1949; d. Glen Allen and Joyce Catherine (Peckham) McGregor. BA, San Francisco State U., 1972; MA, U. San Francisco, 1983. Cert. tchr., sch. adminstr., Calif. Tchr. Lakeport (Calif.) Unified Sch. Dist., 1973-82, asst. prin., 1982-88, dir. ednl. svcs. and spl. projects, 1988—; instr. English Mendocino Coll., Ukiah, Calif., 1977-82. Mem. Assn. Calif. Sch. Adminstrs. (past pres. 1987, Lake County charter), Order Ea. Star (past matron Clear Lake chpt. 1995, dep. grand matron 1999). Democrat. Episcopalian. Avocations: tole painting, physical fitness, calligraphy, travel, skiing. Home: 1315 20th St Lakeport CA 95453-3051 Office: Lakeport Unified Sch Dist 100 Lange St Lakeport CA 95453-3297

JONES, BRENDA K., health facility administrator; b. Columbia, Tenn., Nov. 4, 1954; d. G.J. and Betty Jo (Jennings) Brown; m. Steven Allen Jones, July 26, 1975; children: Ashley Erin, Christopher Michael, Kaitlyn Rebecca. ADN, Ea. N.Mex. U., 1974; BSCHA, St. Joseph's U., 1987. Dir. Corp. Home Care, Carlsbad, N.Mex.; owner, mgr. Home Care Connection, Carlsbad, 1997. Recipient commendation ARC.

JONES, BRIAN, television station executive. BS in Radio, TV and Film, U. Tex., 1992. V.p., gen. mgr. Sta. KTVT-TV, Ft. Worth, 1995—. Bd. dirs. Better Bus. Bur.; mem. United Way, Cystic Fibrosis. Mem. Nat. Assn. TV Program Execs., Tex. Assn. Broadcasters. Office: Sta KTVT-TV PO Box 2495 Fort Worth TX 76113-2495

JONES, C. PAUL, lawyer, educator; b. Grand Forks, N.D., Jan. 7, 1927; s. Walter M. and Sophie J. (Thorton) J.; m. Helen M. Fredel, Sept. 7, 1957; children—Katherine, Sara H. B.B.A., U. Minn., 1950, J.D., 1950; LL.M., William Mitchell Coll. of Law, 1955. Assoc. Lewis, Hammer, Heaney, Weyl & Halverson, Duluth, Minn., 1950-51; asst., chief dep. Hennepin County Atty., Mpls., 1952-58; asst. U.S. atty. U.S. Atty's. Office, St. Paul, 1959-60; assoc. Maun & Hazel, St. Paul, 1960-61; ptnr. Dorfman, Rudquist, Jones, & Ramstead, Mpls., 1961-65; state pub. defender Minn. State Pub. Defender's Office, Mpls., 1966-90; adj. prof. law William Mitchell Coll. of Law, St. Paul, 1953-70, prof. law, 1970—, assoc. dean for acad. affairs, 1991-95; adj. prof. U. Minn., Mpls., 1970-90; mem. adv. com. on rules of criminal procedure Minn. Supreme Ct., 1970—. Author: Criminal Procedure from Police Detention to Final Disposition, 1981; Jones on Minnesota Criminal Procedure, 1955, 64, 70, 75; Minnesota Police Law Manual, 1955, 67, 70, 76. Mem. Minn. Gov.'s Crime Commn., St. Paul, 1970s, Minn. Fair Trial-Free Press Assn., Mpls., 1970s, Citizens League, Mpls., 1955—, Mpls. Aquatennial Assn., Mpls., 1955-60, Minn. Citizens Coun. on Crime and Justice, 1991—. Recipient Reginald Heber Smith award Nat. Legal Aid and Defender Assn., 1969. Fellow Am. Coll. Trial Lawyers; mem. Am. Bd. Trial Advs., ABA, Minn. State Bar Assn., Hennepin County Bar Assn., Ramsey County Bar Assn., Nat. Legal Aid & Defender Assn. Democrat. Lutheran. Clubs: Suburban Gyro of Mpls., Mpls. Athletic. Lodge: Rotary. Avocations: fishing; hunting; golfing; desert watching. Home: 5501 Dewey Hill Rd Edina MN 55439-1906 Office: William Mitchell Coll Law 875 Summit Ave Saint Paul MN 55105-3030

JONES, CARLETON SHAW, information systems company executive, lawyer; b. N.Y.C., Sept. 8, 1942; s. Carlyle Herman and Virginia Ann (Sloat) J.; m. Dona Baker VanArsdale, July 15, 1972; children: Emily Baker, Timothy Dustin. BA, Denison U., 1964; LLB, Yale U., 1967. Bar: Ohio 1967, Fla. 1971, D.C. 1973. Law clk. to chief judge U.S. Ct Appeals (6th cir.), Akron, Ohio, 1967; dep. gen. counsel Price Commn., Exec. Office of Pres., Washington, 1971-73; assoc. Shaw, Pittman Potts & Trowbridge, Washington, 1973-77, ptnr., 1978-91; sr. v.p., counsel Sysorex Info. Sys., Fairfax, Va., 1992, pres., 1992-97, also bd. dirs.; pres. Vanstar Govt. Sys. (formerly Sysorex Info. Sys.), Fairfax, 1997-99; spkr. on fed. high-tech. procurement issues. Lt. (j.g.) USNR, 1967-71. Mem. ABA, FBA, Nat. Contract Mgmt. Assn., Chevy Chase Club.

JONES, CAROLE MOODY-ANDERSON, retired outreach representative; b. Terre Haute, Ind., Sept. 19, 1929; d. Willard and Constance (Hathecock) Moody; m. Orville Merle Anderson, Mar. 27, 1948 (div. 1963); children: Larry Joe (dec.), Orville M., Dorian Trent, Younte Pierre, Peter Shawn; m. Pleasant Thomas Jones, June 13, 1969 (dec. 1986); 1 child, H. Mina. Student, Ind. State U., 1948, 63, 79. Nurse asst. St. Anthony H.S., Terre Haute, 1950-61; file clk. customer svc. Columbia Record, Terre Haute, 1961-67; long distant operator Gen. Tel., Terre Haute, 1967-68; libr. and tchr. asst. Clay Cmty. Schs., Brazil, Ind., 1968-72; clk. J.C. Penney, Terre Haute, 1974-76; field agt. Purdue Co-op Ext., Brazil, Ind., 1976-87; outreach rep. Health Care Excel, Terre Haute, 1988-96; ret., 1996. Active with props, makeup and costumes, actress Terre Haute Cmty. Theater, 1963-67; PTA mem., v.p. PTO, Brazil, 1969-79; pres. Ind. State U.-Adv. Bd. Upward Bound., 1976-79; asst. Girl Scouts Am., Brazil, 1977-80; bd. mem. Rose Southside Day Care, Terre Haute, 1988-96; presenter ch. workshops, 1942—. Recipient Nat. Beneficiary Svcs. Merit award Health Care Fin. Adminstrn., Balt., 1995, Lifetime Achievement award Ky. Consol. Health Sys., Louisville, 1995, Nat. Mature Media Program award Mature Market Resource, Am. Custom Pub. Co., 1995. Mem. NAACP, Order Ea. Star, Am. Assn. of Ret. Persons, United Sr. Action Fund, Pioneer Post 340 Aux., Alpha Pi Chi (Alpha Beta chpt.). Avocations: reading, walking, writing speeches, research. Home: 210 S Lambert St Brazil IN 47834-3210

JONES, CAROLINE ANN, art historian, educator, curator; b. Durham, N.C., Apr. 21, 1954; d. Edward Ellsworth and Virginia (Sweetnam) J.; m. Peter Louis Galison, Jan. 11, 1987; children: Samuel Alexander, Sarah Maria. AB magna cum laude, Harvard-Radcliffe Coll., 1977; postgrad., NYU, 1979-83; PhD, Stanford U., 1992. Studio asst. Hobo Rd. Graphic Design, London, Eng., 1975-76; grants officer Mus. Modern Art, N.Y.C., 1977-79, asst. coord. exhbns., 1979-81, assoc. coord., 1981-83; asst. dir. for curatorial affairs Art Mus. Harvard U., Cambridge, Mass., 1983-85; asst. prof. art history Boston U., 1992-98, assoc. prof. art history, 1998—; lectr. Tel Aviv U., CAA San Francisco, 1989, L.A. County Mus., 1989, U. Minn., Mpls., 1990, Stanford U., 1990, Met. Mus. Art, 1991, Stanford Humanities Ctr., 1992, CAA, Chgo., 1992, Mus. Contemporary Art, L.A., 1992, Centre Georges Pompidou, Paris, 1993, Boston U., 1994, 98, CUNY Grad. Ctr., 1994, Harvard U., 1994, Princeton U., 1995, Max Planck Inst., Berlin, 1995, CAA Boston, 1996, Internat. Congress of History of Art, Amsterdam, 1996, Whitney Mus. Am. Art, 1997, Brit. Assn. Art History, London, 1997, Internat. Forum on Contemporary Art Theory, Guadalajara, 1997, U. Kans., 1997, Brown U., 1996-98, Mus. Fine Arts/Addison Gallery, 1998, among others. Author: Modern Art at Harvard, 1985, Bay Area Figurative Art, 1990 (Commonwealth Club award), Machine in the Studio, 1996; contbr. articles to profl. jours. including Critical Inquiry, Harvard mag.; filmmaker, dir. Frank Stella at the Fogg, 1984, prodr. The Secret of Nancy Drew, 1982; freelance curator of exhbns. San Francisco Mus. Modern Art, 1989, 90, 91, Hara Mus., Tokyo, 1989-90, Stanford Art Mus., 1988, Boston U. Art Gallery, 1996-97. Vol. educator Cambrige (Mass.) Pub. Sch., 1996, 97, 98, Radcliffe Children's Ctr., Cambridge, 1998. Grantee U. Minn., 1988-91. Mem. AAUW, AAUP, Am. Assn. Mus. (regional rep. 1993—), Coll. Art Assn., Art Table, Inc. Office: Boston U CAS Rm 302 725 Commonwealth Ave Boston MA 02215-1401

JONES, CAROLINE ROBINSON, advertising executive; b. Benton Harbor, Mich.; d. Ernest and Mattie Robinson; 1 child, Anthony R. BA, U. Mich., 1963. Copywriter J. Walter Thompson, N.Y., 1963-68, v.p., co-creative dir. Zebra Assocs., Inc., N.Y., 1968-71; copywriter Kenyon & Eckhardt, N.Y., 1971-74; ptnr., creative dir. Black Creative Group, N.Y., 1974-77; v.p., creative group head Batten, Barton, Durstine & Osborn, Inc., N.Y., 1977; exec. v.p., creative dir. Mingo-Jones Advt., N.Y., 1978-86; pres. Caroline Jones Advt. Inc., N.Y.C., 1986-95, Caroline Jones, Inc., N.Y.C., 1995-95, pres. 1995—. Bd. dirs. Advt. Council, Eureka Cmtys. Recipient creative advt. awards Clio, One Show, ANNY, NYMRAD, Art Dirs., CEBA, Ad Woman of Yr., 1990, Ellis Island award of honor, 1997 and others, Matrix award Women in Comm.; mem. Com. of 200. Mem. N.Y.C. Partnership, N.Y. Mem. N.Y. Women's Forum, Smithsonian Instn. Office: Caroline Jones Inc 641 Lexington Ave Fl 21 New York NY 10022-4503 Address: 200 E 66th St # C-204 New York NY 10021-6728

JONES, CAROLYN ELLIS, retired employment agency and business service company executive; b. Marigold, Miss., Feb. 21, 1928; d. Joseph Lawrence and Willie Decelle (Forrest) Peeples; m. David Wright Ellis, May 30, 1945 (div. 1966); children—David, Lyn, Debbie, Dawn; m. Frank Willis Jones, Jan. 1, 1980. Student La. State U., 1944-49. Owner, mgr. Personnel and Bus. Service, Inc., Greenwood, Miss., 1962-88, now v.p.; owner Honor Pub. Co., Greenwood, 1988—. Author: The Lottie Moon Storybook, 1985; Editor: An Old Soldier's Career, 1974. Contbr. articles to religious and gen. interest publs. Mem. adv. bd. career edn. Greenwood Pub. Schs., 1975-76, mem. adv. bd. vocat.-tech. dept., 1975-88; conf. leader Miss. Bapt. Convention Singles Retreat, 1980; Mission Service Corps del. Home Mission Bd., So. Bapt. Conv., Hawaii, 1979. Mem. Greenwood C. of C. (edn. com. 1980—, guest speaker career day program local high sch.), Mothers Against Drunk Drivers, Altrusa Internat., Nat. Fedn. Ind. Bus., Miss Delta Rose Soc., Miss. Native Plant Soc., Gideon Aux. (pres. 1986-88). Avocations: writing, rose exhibitions, wildflowers. Office: Honor Pub 802 W President Ave Greenwood MS 38930-3326

JONES, CAROLYN EVANS, speaker, writer, small business owner; b. Middleboro, Mass., Sept. 5, 1931; d. King Israel and Kleo Estelle (Hodges) Evans; m. John Homer Jones, Sept. 9, 1966 (dec. July 1986); 1 child, David Everett. BA in English, Tift Coll., 1952; M Religious Edn., Carver Sch. Missions and Social Work, 1958; BA in Art, Mercer U., 1982. Cert. secondary tchr., Ga. Tchr. McDuffie County Bd. Edn., Thomson, Ga., 1952-53, Colquitt County Bd. Edn., Norman Park, Ga., 1953-55; missionary Home Mission Bd. SBC, New Orleans and Macon, 1958-66; spl. edn. tchr. Bibb County Bd. Edn., Macon, 1968-70, 75-79; owner, operator Laney Co. Imprinted Specialties, Macon, 1986-97; owner Creative Imprints, Macon, 1997—; distbr. Nikken, Inc., 1998—. Contbr. numerous articles and poems to profl. jours. Bible tchr. YWCA, Macon, 1980-85; deacon 1st Bapt. Ch., Macon. Mem. Alumnae Assn. Tift Coll. (bd. dirs.). Democrat. Avocations: church work, travel. Office: Creative Imprints 2451 Kingsley Dr Macon GA 31204-1718

JONES, CATESBY BROOKE, retired banker; b. Lexington, Va., Mar. 7, 1925; s. Catesby and Elizabeth (Cox) J.; m. Margaret Gordon Gaffney, June 13, 1953 (dec. Apr. 1995); children: Catesby II, Margaret Brooke, Elizabeth Gordon; m. Barbara Jeffreys Webb, Mar. 16, 1996. Grad., St. Paul's Sch., 1943; B.A. in Econs, Yale, 1949; grad., Stonier Grad. Sch. Banking, Rutgers U., 1956, U. Va. Grad. Sch. Bus., 1961. With United Va. Bank, Richmond, 1949-85; sr. v.p., head nat. div. United Va. Bank, 1965-85; fin. cons. Marsh & McLennan Inc., 1985-88; former pres., dir. Buffalo Creek & Gauley R.R. Co.; former dir. Spindale Mills, Inc.; bd. dirs. Regency Bank. Chmn. fin. com., bd. dirs. Richmond Area Community Coun., 1959-63; div. chmn. United Givers Fund, 1965, 72; treas., bd. dirs. MCV Hosp. Hospitality House, 1985-92. 1st Lt. AUS, 1944-46. Mem. Va. C. of C. (treas., dir. 1964-67), Richmond C. of C. (chmn. membership relations com. 1957-59), Soc. Colonial Wars in Va. (gov. 1976), Soc. Cincinnati (pres. Va. chpt. 1979-82, gen. pres. 1983-86), Jamestown Soc., Newcomen Soc., Beta Theta Pi. Episcopalian. Clubs: Yale of Va. (past pres.); Country of Va. (Richmond); Edgartown Golf. Home: 2 Chatham Sq 6161 River Rd Richmond VA 23226-3318

JONES, CATHERINE ELAINE, educational administrator; b. Dec. 28, 1947. BA, Norfolk State U., 1968; MA, George Washington U., 1993, EdS, 1995. Asst. prin. York H.S., Yorktown, Va. E-mail: cjones@yhs.ycsd.york.va.us.

JONES, CHARLES CALHOUN, estate and business planning consultant; b. Bedford, Pa., Jan. 12, 1940; s. Charles Stauffer and Marjorie Vesta (Calhoun) J.; m. Patricia Jean Diehl, Aug. 12, 1960; children: Kathryn Lynn, Suzanne Elizabeth, Christopher Andrew. BS in Econs., Widener U., 1961. CLU; fin. mgmt. advisor. Field dir. Bus. Men's Assurance, Kansas City, Mo., 1970-76; pres. Agrl. Bus. Adminstrn., Kansas City, 1976-78; br. mgr. E.F. Hutton, Raytown, Mo., 1978-79; pres. C.C.J. Inc., Kansas City, 1979-90; chmn. coun. John Hancock Mut. Life Ins. Co., 1992-98, mem. agts. adv. com., mktg. chmn., 1992—; chmn. bd. dirs. Pentrust—; advisor Nat. Cattleman's Assn., Denver, 1976-79. Author: Financial Management PenTrust, 1987; contbr. articles to profl. jours. Gov. Am. Royal, Kansas City, 1981; mem. adminstrv. bd. and coun. Luth. Ch., Kans. Mem. Lees Summit C. of C. (econ. devel. com. 1982-85), CLU Soc. (bd. dirs. 1998—), Assn. Internat Fin. Planners (bd. dirs. 1976-80), Planned Giving Coun. (charter), Rotary Internat., Loch Lomond Club (Luss, Scotland), Am. Soc. CLU, Blue Hills C.C. Avocation: golf. Office: Pen Trust Advisors 6800 College Blvd Ste 270 Overland Park KS 66211-1532

JONES, CHARLES EDWARD, mechanical engineer; b. Bklyn., Apr. 20, 1920; s. Charles Edward and Mary Margaret (Decker) J.; m. Noel Catherine McDonald, Feb. 12, 1944; children—Claudia, Geoffrey, Kathryn, Jonathan. BME, CCNY, 1947; MS, Tex. A&M U., 1951; PhD, Cornell U., 1957. Lectr. mech. engrng. CCNY, 1947-49; asst. prof. Tex. A&M U., 1949-52; instr. Cornell U., 1952-54; rsch. engr. B & W Rsch. Ctr., Alliance, Ohio, 1954-59, mgr. R & D lab., 1959-67, asst. dir., 1967-68, dir., 1968-71; v.p. ops. Bailey Meter Co., Wickliffe, Ohio, 1971, pres., 1971-75; asst. to group v.p. Babcock & Wilcox Indsl. Products Group, N.Y.C., 1975-80. Contbr. articles in field to profl. jours. Trustee Euclid Gen. Hosp., 1972-75, ASME Found., 1993-95. Capt. USAR, 1943-66. Fellow ASME (pres. 1980-81, life), Sigma Xi, Tau Beta Pi, Phi Kappa Phi, Pi Tau Sigma; mem. United Engrs. Trustees (trustee, chmn. fin. com., treas. 1986-90, 2d v.p. 1990-91, 1st v.p. 1991-93, pres. 1993-94). Home and Office: 15 Tradewinds Way Salem SC 29676-4029

JONES, CHARLES EDWIN, historian, bibliographer, chaplain; b. Kansas City, Mo., June 1, 1932; s. Dess Dain and Dove (Barnwell) J.; m. Beverly Anne Lundy, May 30, 1956; 1 child, Karl Laurence. BA, Bethany-Peniel Coll., 1954; MALS, U. Mich., 1955; MS, U. Wis., 1960, PhD, 1968; postgrad., Episcopal Div. Sch., Cambridge, Mass., 1975-76. Ordained to ministry Reformed Episcopal Ch. as deacon, 1990. Libr. Park Coll., 1961-63; manuscript curator Mich. Hist. Coll. U. Mich., Ann Arbor, 1965-69; assoc. prof. history Houghton Coll., 1969-71; hist. cataloguer Rockefeller Libr. Brown U., 1971-76; chaplain-in-residence Quail Creek Nursing Ctr., Oklahoma City, 1989-98. Author: Perfectionist Persuasion, 1974, Guide to the Study of the Holiness Movement, 1974, Guide to the Study of the Pentecostal Movement, 1983, Black Holiness, 1987, The Charismatic Movement, 1995; contbr. articles to scholarly jours. With U.S. Army, 1956-58. Mem. Am. Theol. Libr. Assn., Can. Ch. Hist. Soc. Democrat. Mem. Reformed Episcopal Ch. Home: 12300 Springwood Dr Oklahoma City OK 73120-1724

JONES, CHARLES ERIC, JR., lawyer; b. Phila., Dec. 21, 1957; s. Charles Eric and Janith (Van Orden) J.; m. Ronda Nolen, May 16, 1981; children: Charles Eric III, Courtney Elaine, Camille Elizabeth. BBA, U. Tex., 1980; JD, St. Mary's U., 1983. Bar: Tex. 1983, U.S. Dist. Ct. (no. dist.) Tex. 1985, U.S. Dist. Ct. (we. dist.) Okla. 1986, U.S. Dist. Ct. (we. and ea. dists.) Ark. 1987, U.S. Supreme Ct. 1988, U.S. Ct. Appeals (5th cir.) 1988, U.S. Dist. Ct. (ea. dist.) Tex. 1992. Briefing atty. Tex. Ct. Criminal Appeals, Austin, 1983-84; assoc. Nunn Griggs & Wetsel, Sweetwater, Tex., 1984; ptnr. Nunn, Griggs, Wetsel & Jones, Sweetwater, 1985-88, 1985-89; ptnr. Nunn, Griggs, Jones & Sheridan, Sweetwater, 1989-91, Jones & Edwards, L.L.P., Sweetwater, 1992-94, Jones, Edwards & Young, L.L.P., Sweetwater, 1995, Jones & Young, LLP, Sweetwater, Tex., 1995-97, Charles E. Jones, Jr. & Assocs., 1997—; chmn. St. Mary's Legal Rsch. Bd., San Antonio, 1982-83; student instr. St. Mary's U., San Antonio, 1982-83, The Order of Barristers, 1983. Bd. dirs. Nolan County Hospice, Inc., Sweetwater, 1984-92, Nolan County Crimestoppers, Inc., Sweetwater, 1985-90, chmn., 1987-89; dir. adminstrv. bd. United Meth. Ch., Sweetwater, 1985-88; chmn. Nolan County United Way, 1985-87; co-chmn. City Coun. Libr. Bd., 1987—. Mem. ABA, Assn. Trial Lawyers Am., Tex. Bar Assn., Tex. Trial Lawyers Assn., Tex. State Bar Coll., Order of Barristers, Tex. Assn. Banking Counsel, Indp. Bankers Assn. Tex., Tex. Bd. of Legal Specialization (bd. cert. civil trial law). Avocations: flying, scuba diving, skiing, golf. Home: 804 Josephine St Sweetwater TX 79556-3312 Office: Charles E Jones Jr & Assocs PO Box 188 Sweetwater TX 79556-0188

JONES, CHARLES HILL, JR., banker; b. N.Y.C., July 14, 1933; s. Charles Hill and Susan Roy (Johnston) J.; grad. Groton (Mass.) Sch., 1952; BA in Econs., U. Va., 1956; m. Hope Haskell, Jan. 28, 1961; children: Hope H., Charles Hill III, Henry M.T. With Wood, Struthers & Winthrop, Inc., N.Y.C., 1956-73, gen. ptnr., 1968-69, v.p., dir., dir. rsch., 1969-73; sr. v.p., chief investment officer Midlantic Nat. Bank, Edison, 1974-87; gen. ptnr. Edge Ptnrs., 1987—; bd. dirs. Home Port Bancorp, 1992—, Jefferson Savs. & Loan, 1992-95, Green Fund Realty, 1993—, N.J. Title Ins. Co., 1995—, NJT Holdings, 1995—. Treas., N.Y. chpt. R.E. Lee Meml. Found., 1964-69; trustee, chmn. fin. com. Monmouth Med. Center, 1975-81; pres. bd. trustees Rumson (N.J.) Country Day Sch., 1982-85. Trustee Hampden-Sydney Coll., 1995—. Mem. Inst. Chartered Fin. Analysts, Bond Club, City Midday Club (trustee, treas. 1965-71, v.p. 1972-74). Author: (with Joseph D. Davis) Toll Road Bonds, 1959, The Growth Rate Appraiser, 1968. Home: 218 Via Linda Palm Beach FL 33480-3405 Office: Edge Ptnrs PO Box 7511 Shrewsbury NJ 07702-7511

JONES, CHARLES IRVING, bishop; b. El Paso, Tex., Sept. 13, 1943; s. Charles I. Jr. and Helen A. (Heyward) J.; m. Ashby MacArthur, June 18, 1966; children: Charles I. IV, Courtney M., Frederic M., Keith A. BS, The Citadel, 1965; MBA, U. N.C., 1966; MDiv, U. of the South, 1977, DD, 1989. CPA. Pub. acctg. D.E. Gatewood and Co., Winston-Salem, N.C., 1966-72; dir. devel. Chatham (Va.) Hall, 1972-74; instr. acctg. U. of the South, Sewanee, Tenn., 1974-77; coll. chaplain Western Ky. U., Bowling

Green, 1977-81; vicar Trinity Episcopal Ch., Russelville, Ky., 1977-85; archdeacon Diocese of Ky., Louisville, 1981-86; bishop Episcopal Diocese of Mont., Helena, 1986—; bd. dirs. New Directions Ministries, Inc., N.Y.C.; mem. standing com. Joint Commn. on Chs. in Small Communities, 1988-91, Program, Budget and Fin., 1991-94; v.p. province VI Episcopal Ch., 1991-94, mem. Presiding Bishop's Coun. Advice, 1991-94. Author: Mission Strategy in the 21st Century, 1989, Total Ministry: A Practical Approach, 1993; bd. editors Grass Roots, Luling, Tex., 1985-90; contbr. articles to profl. jours. Founder Concerned Citizens for Children, Russelville, 1981; bd. dirs. St. Peter's Hosp., Helena, 1986—; bd. dirs. Christian Ministry in Nat. Parks, 1992—. With USMCR, 1961-65. Mem. Aircraft Owners and Pilots Assn. Avocations: running, flying, writing, skiing. Office: Diocese Mont 515 N Park Ave Helena MT 59601-2703

JONES, CHARLES J., transportation executive, firefighter; b. Marshfield, Oreg., Jan. 29, 1940; s. Charles J. Cotter and Lois C. (Smith) Meltebeke; m. Sharon S. Madsen, Mar. 29, 1969; children: Mary E., Judith A., Kari C., April M., Autumn C. AS in Fire Sci. Tech., Portland Community Coll., 1974; BS in Fire Adminstrn., Eastern Oreg. State Coll., 1983; diploma, Nat. Fire Acad., 1983, 85; MPA, Lewis and Clark Coll., 1989. Cert. class VI fire officer, Oreg., hazardous materials instr., fire instr. I; lic. real estate agt., Oreg., lic. tax preparer. From firefighter to capt. Washington County Fire Dist., Aloha, Oreg., 1964-74, battalion chief, 1974-81, dir. comms., dir. research and devel., 1981-85, dir. strategic planning, 1986-88; cons. Tualatin Valley Fire & Rescue, Aloha, 1989-90; pres., CEO Jones Transp., 1989—; basic and advanced 1st aid instr. ARC, 1965-80; cons. Washington County Consol. Communications Agy., 1983-86, chmn. 9-1-1 mgmt. bd., 1982-83; mem. adv. bd. Washington County Emergency Med. Svcs., 1981-86; owner/instr. Internat. Vocat. Inst. and Family Tree Learning Ctrs. Jones Internat., Ltd., 1990-95. Editor local newsletter Internat. Assn. Firefighters, 1970; contbr. articles on fire dept. mgmt. to jours. Active Community Planning Orgn., Washington County, 1979-90, chmn. 1988-89. With USAF, 1957-59. Mem. Oreg. Fire Chiefs Assn. (chmn. seminar com. 1982-83, 89, co-chmn. 1981, 84, 86, 87, 88). Republican. Mem. Infinity Universal Ch. Avocations: photography, genealogy, antique auto restoration, traveling, writing. Office: Jones Transp PO Box 7206 Aloha OR 97007-7206

JONES, CHARLES T., principal; b. Hackensack, N.J., Oct. 12, 1947; s. Charles H. and Lillian K. J.; m. Candace Jones, Sept. 30, 1971; children; Melissa, Brad. BA, Ctrl. Coll. U., 1969; MA, Seton Hall U., 1975. Tchr. HAckensack (N.J.) Pub. Schs., 1970-80, asst. prin., 1980-93, prin., 1993—; supr. enrichment program Hackensack Pub. Schs., 1984-88. Elder 2d Presbyn. Ch., Hackensack, 1999—; coach Hackensack Little League Baseball, 1975-90. With U.S. Army Res., 1970-76. Recipient Edn. award Nat. Assn. Negro Bus. & Profl. Women's Club, 1998; named Tchr. of Yr. Bergen County Coun. PTA's, 1981. Mem. ASCD, Nat. Coun. Tchrs. Math., Nat. Coun. Reading Tchrs., Nat. Sci. Tchrs. Assn., Hackensack Assn. Sch. Adminstrs. (pres. 1980—), Hackensack Troast Athletic Club. Avocations: golf, sports, dining, reading, stamp collecting. Home: 293 Euclid Ave HAckensack NJ 07601 Office: Fanny Meyer Hillers Sch 56 Longview Ave Hackensack NJ 07601

JONES, CHARLES WELDON, biologist, educator, researcher; b. Providence, May 25, 1953; s. Charles Weston and Evelyn Lois (Hall) J. AB, Harvard U., 1975, AM, 1977, PhD, 1980. Helen Hay Whitney postdoctoral fellow Stanford (Calif.) U., 1980, postdoctoral fellow, 1980-82; asst. prof. Bethel Coll., St. Paul, 1982-85, assoc. prof., 1985-90, prof., chair, 1990—; vis. scholar Harvard U., Cambridge, Mass., 1988-89; councilor Coun. Undergrad. Rsch., Washington, 1990—; vis. scientist Mayo Clinic, 1995-96. Author: (with others) Levels of Genetic Control in Development, 1981; contbr. articles to Science, Cell, Nature. Fellow NSF, 1976, NIH, 1995; grantee Rsch. Corp., 1982, NSF, 1984, 85, 90; named Minn. Prof. of Yr. Carnegie Found. Advancement Teaching, 1995. Mem. AAAS, Nat. Biology Tchrs. Assn., Assn. Biology Lab. Edn., Sigma Zeta (pres. 1987-88). Achievements include first fusion of animal/plant cells. Home: 1667 Brueberry Ln Arden Hills MN 55112-1780 Office: Bethel Coll 3900 Bethel Dr Saint Paul MN 55112-6902

JONES, CHARLES WILLIAM, association executive; b. Montgomery, Ala., Mar. 20, 1936; s. Charles W. and Flaria (Duke) J.; children: Beth, Charles P. BS in Acctg., U. Ala., 1958. CPA, Ala. Ptnr. Aldridge Borden & Jones CPA, Montgomery, Ala., 1958-69; pres. Ring Around Products, Montgomery, 1969-77; assoc. gen. dir. Montgomery YMCA, 1978-94; exec. dir. Blue and Gray Assn., Montgomery, 1980—. Active Montgomery Bd. Edn., 1968-74. Mem. AICPA, Montgomery Lions Club (Lion of Yr. 1991), Montgomery Country Club. Office: Blue and Gray Assn 771 S Lawrence St Ste 106 Montgomery AL 36104-5005*

JONES, CHERYL BROMLEY, English language and humanities educator; b. Attleboro, Mass., Apr. 12, 1947; d. C. Chester and Lillian P. (Griffin) Bromley; married, Aug. 5, 1972. BA in English, State Coll. Bridgewater, 1969, MAT; postgrad., Lesley Coll., Boston Coll. English tchr. Oliver Ames H.S., North Easton, Mass., 1969-70, Easton Jr. H.S., North Easton, 1970-88; English. social studies tchr. Sandwich (Mass.) H.S., 1988-94; English, writing, humanities tchr. Plymouth (Mass.) North H.S., 1994—; assoc. prof. U. Mass., Boston, 1998; assoc. cons. Rsch. Better Tchg./Tchrs., Acton, Mass., 1997—; tchr., facilitator summer residency Poetry ALive!, Asheville, N.C., 1990—; literacy cons., Buzzard's Bay, Mass., 1988—; creator, dir. student poetry reading Lang. Art Consortium Educator Student Celebratory Poetry Reading, 1989—. Author: (book series) Teaching with Panache, 1991. Lucretia Cocker fellow Mass. Dept. Edn., 1989-90; recipient Peter Faraldy award MASCD, 1995-96. Mem. Nat. Coun. Tchrs. English (election com., support tchg. & learning English 1991), Mass. Coun. Tchrs. English (liaison 1996—, pres. 1992-96), Lucretia Crocker Acad. Tchg. Fellows (bd. alt. 1995-98). Roman Catholic. Avocations: race walking, cooking, traveling. Home: 12 Woodside Ave Buzzards Bay MA 02532-4727 Office: Plymouth North HS 41 Obery St Plymouth MA 02360-2195

JONES, CHRISTINE MASSEY, retired furniture company executive; b. Columbus, Ga., Nov. 7, 1929; d. Lewis Everett and Donia (Spivey) Massey; divorced; children—James Raymond, Jr., James David. Student, Ga. Southwestern Coll., 1947-48. With Muscogee Mfg. Co., Columbus, Ga., 1948-56; sec. to pres. Muscogee Mfg. Co., 1956; sec. to pres. and treas., corp. sec. Haverty Furniture Cos., Inc., Atlanta, 1956-59, sec. to pres. and treas., 1959-63, sec. to pres., 1963-72, sec. to pres., adminstrv. asst., 1972-74, sec. to pres., admintrv. asst., asst. corp. sec., 1974-78, corp. sec., 1978-86, corp. sec., asst. v.p., 1986-93; v.p. stockholder rels., sec. Haverty Furniture Cos., Atlanta, 1993-97, ret., 1997. Mem. Am. Soc. Corp. Secs. (securities industry com.).

JONES, CHRISTOPHER, advertising company executive; m. Sara Jones; children: Laura, Gus. Former co-pres., exec. v.p. Worldwide Agy. Ops. J. Walter Thompson Co., N.Y.C., former mng. dir. multinational accounts; chief exec. J. Walter Thompson, London, 1989-92; CEO J. Walter Thompson Co., N.Y.C., 1997—. Office: J Walter Thompson Co 466 Lexington Ave New York NY 10017-3140*

JONES, CHRISTOPHER PRESTIGE, classicist, historian; b. Kent, U.K.; s. William Prestige and Irene May (McCreddie) J. BA, Oxford U., 1962; PhD Classical Philology, Harvard U., 1965. From lectr. to prof. U. Toronto, Can., 1965-92, chair dept. classics, 1986-90; prof. classics and history Harvard U., Cambridge, 1992-97, George Martin Lane prof. classics and history, 1997—; vis. lectr. Harvard U., 1968; assoc. prof. Ecole Normale Supérieure de Jeunes Filles, Paris, 1979, Ecole Normale Supérieure, Paris, 1992; acting vice dean Faculty Arts and Scis., U. Toronto, 1985-86. Author: Philostratus: Life of Apollonius of Tyana, 1971, Plutarch and Rome, 1971, The Roman World of Dio Chrysostom, 1978, Culture and Society in Lucian, 1986; co-editor: Le Martyre de Pionios, prêtre de Smyrne, 1994, Kinship Diplomacy in the Ancient World, 1999; contbr. numerous articles to profl. jours. Fellow Royal Soc. Can., Am. Numismatic Soc.; mem. Am. Philol. Assn. (chair subcom. epigraphical bibliog. 1981-89, subcom. cartography 1986-90), Am. Acad. Arts and Scis., German Archeol. Inst. (corr. mem. 1992—), Am. Philos. Soc. Home: Apt 107 130 Mount Auburn St Cambridge MA 02138 Office: Harvard U Boylston Hall Cambridge MA 02138

JONES, CLAIRE BURTCHAELL, artist, teacher, writer; b. Oakland, Calif.; d. Clarence Samuel and Florence Mallett (Hinchman) Burtchaell; m. E.C. Jones; children: Holland Mallett, Lela Claire, S. Evan. AB, Stanford U.; postgrad., Laguna Beach Sch. Art, 1972-73, San Diego Art Acad., 1980-82. Freelance art tchr. Park Ridge, Ill., 1967; tchr. Jade Fon Group, Pacific Grove, Calif., 1972-73, Merced Coll., Sierra Mountains, Calif., 1973; freelance pvt. workshop, painting for commns. and galleries Calif., 1973—. Author: First The Blade (anon. collection), 1939, Arrows in the Air, 1947-51, Utah Sings, 1953; editor: Watercolor West Newsletter, 1978-83; contbr. articles to profl. jours. Recipient numerous awards for artwork. Mem. Nat. Mus. Women in the Arts (founding mem.), Assn. Western Artists (bd. dirs. 1970-71), Watercolor West (bd. dirs. 1978-81, 86—, membership chmn. 1988-96), Stanford Alumni Assn., Literati West (founder, sec.-treas. 1994—).

JONES, CLARIS EUGENE, JR., botanist, educator; b. Columbus, Ohio, Dec. 15, 1942; s. Claris Eugene and Clara Elizabeth (Elliott) J.; m. Teresa Diane Wagner, June 26, 1966; children: Douglas Eugene, Philip Charles, Elizabeth Lynne. B.S., Ohio U., 1964; Ph.D., Ind. U., 1969. Asst. prof. botany Calif. State U., Fullerton, 1969-73, assoc. prof., 1973-77, prof. botany, 1977—, chmn. dept. biol. sci., 1989—, dir. Fullerton Arboretum, 1970-80, dir. Faye MacFadden Herbarium, 1969—; disting. faculty mem. Sch. Natural Sci. and Math., 1999—. Author: A Dictionary of Botany, 1980; editor: Handbook of Experimental Pollination Biology, 1983; contbr. articles to profl. jours. Mem. Am. Inst. Biol. Sci., AAAS, Bot. Soc. Am., Internat. Assn. Plant Taxonomy, Am. Soc. Plant Taxonomists, Soc. Study Evolution, Systematics Assn., Ecol. Soc. Am., Calif. Bot. Soc., Sigma Xi. Methodist. Office: 800 N State College Blvd Fullerton CA 92831-3547

JONES, CLARK POWELL, JR., financial services executive; b. Gainesville, Fla., Nov. 1, 1964; s. Clark Powell and Mary Evelyn (Eddins) J.; m. Patricia Ann Pagli, Sept. 26, 1993; children: Kylie Elizabeth, Erin Nicole. BA in Econs. and Polit. Sci., Emory U., 1986; MBA in Fin., NYU, 1994. Cert. cash mgr. Corp. svcs. officer First Am. Corp., Nashville, Tenn., 1986-89; v.p. Berkshire Capital Corp., N.Y.C., 1989-95; sr. mgr.-bus. svcs. group Barnett Banks, Inc., Jacksonville, Fla., 1995-98; v.p. alliance mgmt. and devel. Fleet Fin. Group, 1998—; bd. dirs. Eddins Broadcasting Co., Inc. Mentor INROADS, 1998, Jr. Achievement, 1998. Mem. Emory Univ. Alumni Assn. Republican. Methodist. Avocations: reading, golf. Office: Fleet Fin Group Bus/Entrepren Svcs Group 5 Whittier St 2nd Fl Framingham MA 01701

JONES, CLIFFORD AARON, SR., lawyer, international businessman; b. Long Lane, Mo., Feb. 19, 1912; s. Burley Monroe and Arlie (Benton) J.; children: Clifford A. Jones II, Joni Lee Jones Ryan; m. Marilyn T. Hayes, May 1, 1995. LL.B., U. Mo., 1938, J.D., 1969. Bar: Nev. 1938, U.S. Dist. Ct. Nev. 1939, D.C. 1982, U.S. Ct. Appeals (9th and D.C. cirs.) 1983, U.S. Supreme Ct. 1983. Founder, sr. ptnr. Jones Vargas (formerly Jones, Jones, Close & Brown), Las Vegas, Nev., 1938-93, retired, 1993; majority leader Nev. Legislature, 1941-42; judge 8th Jud. Dist., Nev., 1945-46; lt. gov. State of Nev., 1946-54; owner, builder, chmn. bd. Thunderbird Hotel, Inc., Las Vegas, 1948-64; founder Valley Bank of Nev., 1953; founder, sec., bd. dirs. First Western Savs. and Loan Assn., 1964-66; pres., chmn. bd. Caribbean-Am. Investment Co., Inc., 1960-78; pres., bd. dirs. Income Investments, Inc., 1963-65; sr. v.p., bd. dirs. Barrington Industries, Inc., 1966-70; chmn. bd., pres. Cen. African Land Co. Mem. Clark County (Nev.) Democratic Central Com., 1940-80, chmn., 1948; nat. committeeman from Nev. Dem. Party, 1954; mem. Nev. Dem. State Central Com., 1945-60; 4 time del. Dem. Nat. Conv. Served as lt. col. F.A. U.S. Army, 1942-46, ETO. Mem. ABA (past mem. tax sect.), Am. Coll. Trust and Estate Counsel, Nev. Bar Assn., D.C. Bar Assn., Am. Legion, VFW, Phi Delta Phi, Kappa Sigma. Clubs: United Nations Lions (N.Y.C.); Elks (Las Vegas), Lions (Las Vegas) (past pres.).

JONES, CLYDE ADAM, art educator, artist; b. Cobleskill, N.Y., Nov. 10, 1924; s. Lester L. and Myra (Karker) J.; BFA, Syracuse U., 1948, MA, 1954; EdD, Pa. State U., 1961. Tchr. art North High Sch., Binghamton, N.Y., 1948-49, 1950-56; instr. ceramics Jr. League of Binghamton, 1950-53; guest instr. ceramics Rehab. Guild, Saranac Lake, N.Y., 1951-54; asst. prof. art edn. Edinboro (Pa.) State Coll., 1956-58; instr. Creative Arts Workshop, Cornell U., Ithaca, N.Y., summer, 1958; asst. prof. child devel. U. Conn., Storrs, 1961-66, asst. dean Sch. Home Econs. and Family Studies, 1976-79, trustee Syracuse U. Libr. Assocs., 1970, assoc. prof. human devel. and family rels., 1966—; prof. emeritus, 1985—; cons. Head Start program, Conn., 1965-66. Mem. Gov.'s Commn. on Status or Women, 1965-67; bd. dirs. Greater Mansfield Arts Coun., 1986—, mem. adv. bd., 1989—; mem. governing bd. Nat. Assn. for Creative Children and Adults, 1986—; mem. Cobleskill (N.Y.) Hist. Soc., newsletter editor, 1993. With AUS, 1943-45. Recipient Honorable Mention Ceramic Nat. Exhbn., 1954. Mem. Conn. Assn. for Edn. of Young Children (v.p. 1970-72), New Eng. Assn. for Edn. of Young Children (publs. com. 1980—, editor newsletter 1963-65), Hartford Assn. for Edn. of Young Children (pres. 1967-69), Nat. Assn. for Edn. of Young Children, Soc. for Rsch. in Child Devel., Nat. Soc. for Study of Edn., Nat. Art Edn. Assn. (rsch. trainee 1965), Internat. soc. for Edn. thru Art, Assn. for Childhood Edn. Internat., Conn. Home Econs. Assn. (del., dir. 1978-82, newletter editor 1984—, named Home Economist of Yr. 1992), Am. Home Econs. Assn., Phi Delta Kappa. One man shows: Rehab. Guild, Saranac Lake, N.Y., Windham Hosp., Willimantic, Conn., Art Bldg, Pa. State U., Student Union U. Conn.; group shows include: Roberson Meml., Binghamton, N.Y., Erie (Pa.) Art Mus., Munson-Williams-Proctor Inst., Utica, N.Y., Mus. of Fine Arts, Syracuse, Norwich (Conn.) Art Mus., Schoharie Couty Arts Coun., Albany Inst. of History and Art, Essex (Conn.) Art Assn., Rochester (N.Y.) Meml. Art Gallery; illustrations for history volumes of Sch. of Home Econs. and Family Studies and Sch. of Nursing, U. Conn. Home: 52 Storrs Heights Rd Storrs Mansfield CT 06268-2322 Office: U Conn Sch Family Studies Storrs Mansfield CT 06269

JONES, CLYDE WILLIAM, anesthesiologist; b. Barbados, West Indies, Sept. 29, 1929; came to U.S., 1947; s. Lewis F. and Albertha B. (Lewis) J.; m. Norma Anita, Sept. 14, 1963; children: Michael W., Ronald C., Stephen T. BS, City Coll., N.Y.C., 1954; MD, Howard U., 1958. Diplomate Am. Bd. Anesthesiology. Capt. U.S. Navy, 1959-79, med. officer, 1959-63; resident in anesthesiology U.S. Naval Hosp., San Diego, 1963-66; staff anesthesiologist U.S. Naval Hosp., Camp Pendleton, Calif., 1966-67, chief of anesthesiology, 1967-69; chief of anesthesiology 1st Hosp. Co., Danang, Vietman, 1968, U.S. Naval Hosp., Marianas Island, Guam, 1969-71; staff anesthesiologist Naval Regional Med. Ctr., San Diego, 1971-73, chief of anesthesiology, 1973-79; staff anesthesiologist Kaiser Permanente Med. Ctr., San Diego, 1979-81, 87—, chief of anesthesiology, 1981-87. Contbr. articles to profl. jours. Acolyte lay reader, sub Deacon All Sts. Episcopal Ch., San Diego, 1971—; bd. dirs. Bishop's Sch., San Diego, 1980-81, San Diego Civic Light Opera, Inc., 1980-83. Recipient Meritorious Svc. medal, certificate of merit Surgeon Gen. U.S. Navy, 1979. Fellow Am. Coll. Anesthesiologists; mem.Am. Soc. Anesthesiologists (delegate), Assn. Mil. Surgeons of U.S., Am. Soc. Clin. Hypnosis, Internat. Anesthesia Rsch. Soc., Naval Inst., Sigma Pi Phi. Democrat. Avocations: hypnosis, coin collecting, medical volunteer. Home: 5201 Countryside Dr San Diego CA 92115-2136 Office: Kaiser Permanente Med Ctr 4647 Zion Ave San Diego CA 92120-2507

JONES, COBI, professional soccer player; b. Detroit, June 16, 1970. Student, UCLA. Midfielder Coventry City, 1994-95, Vasco da Gama, 1995-96, L.A. Galaxy, 1996—; with gold medal U.S. team, Pan Am. Games, 1991, U.S. Olympic Team, 1992, U.S. Nat. Team, 1992-95, including victory over Ivory Coast, 1992; tied for all-time assist lead, with 18. Host (TV show) Megadose (MTV) 1997; guest appearance (TV show) Beverly Hills 90210, 1994. Office: c/o US Soccer Fedn 1801-1811 S Prairie Ave Chicago IL 60616 and: LA Galaxy 1640 S Sepulveda Blvd Los Angeles CA 90025*

JONES, COLLETTE ANN, artist; b. Dallas, July 29, 1941; d. Leo Lawrence Wisley and Thelma Lorraine Lindley; m. Joe Bailey Lee, June 25, 1961 (div. Nov. 1964); m. Clinton Lee Jones, Mar. 4, 1967; children: Lori Hennington, Randy, Chad. BFA in Interior Design, U. North Tex., 1975; EdB in Elem. Edn., Tarleton State U., 1994. Interior designer Unispace Design, Dallas, 1975-79; art tchr. The Old Craft Store, Carrollton, Tex., 1983-86, MJ Designs, Carrollton, 1986-87; elem. tchr. Itasca (Tex.) I.S.D., Itasca, Tex., 1993-94, Happy Hill Farm, Granbury, Tex., 1994-95; artist Granbury, 1995-; bd. dirs. Cross Timbers Fine Arts Coun., Stephenville, Tex. Coord. Rio Brazos Art Festival, Granbury, 1997--. Recipient first prize, hon. mention Lake Granbury Art Assn., 1996, Rio Brazos Art Festival, 1997; hon. mention Richardson Civic Art Soc., 1998. Mem. Southwest Watercolor Soc., Soc. of Layerists in Multimedia, Internat. Soc. of Exptl. Artists, Soc. Watercolor Artists, Ctrl. Tex. Art Assn. Republican. Roman Catholic. Avocations: quilting, reading. E-mail: cjcj@itexas.net. Home and Office: Artresource Studio 5203 Wedgefield Granbury TX 76049

JONES, CRAIG WARD, lawyer; b. Pitts., June 14, 1947; s. Curtis Edison and Margaret (McFarland) J.; m. Sarah Dowding; children: Laura McFarland, Rebecca Long, Nancy Harper. BA, Carleton Coll., 1969; JD, U. Pitts., 1976. Bar: Pa. 1976, U.S. Dist. Ct. (we. dist.) Pa. 1976, U.S. Ct. Appeals (3d cir.) 1981. Ptnr. Reed, Smith, Shaw & McClay, Pitts., 1976—. Served to lt. USNR, 1969-73. Mem. Allegheny County Bar Assn. Presbyterian. Home: 208 Cornwall Dr Pittsburgh PA 15238-2639 Office: Reed Smith Shaw & McClay Mellon Sq 435 6th Ave Ste 2 Pittsburgh PA 15219-1886

JONES, CYNTHIA RECTOR, artist; b. Washington, Apr. 27, 1951; d. George Harry and Patricia (Twohy) Rector; m. Kelly Chapman Jones, June 12, 1971; children: Grace, Kelly, Laura. BA, Stratford Coll., 1971. Tchr. North Shore Pvt. Sch., Norfolk, Va., 1971-73, First Presbyn. Presch., Norfolk, 1985-90. Exhbns. include Edenton Gallery, Norfolk, 1994, Smithfield Gallery, Norfolk, 1994, Suffolk Mus., Norfolk, 1994, Agora Gallery, 1997, Va. Wesleyan Coll. City union rep. King's Daughters Hosp., Norfolk, 1976, 80, 95; parish coun. Sacred Heart Catholic Ch., Norfolk, 1983-85; pres. St. Mary's Infant Home, Norfolk, 1993-95. Mem. Jr. League Norfolk, Harborfront Garden Club (pres. 1987-88).

JONES, CYNTHIA TERESA CLARKE, artist; b. Bklyn., Aug. 12, 1938; d. Arthur Ottio and Emma (Gibbs) Clarke; m. Robert H. Jones. Apr. 21, 1968 (div. Sept. 1977); 1 child, Kim Marie. Student, Bklyn. Mus., 1954-57, Art Career Sch., 1958, Hunter Coll., N.Y.C., 1963-65. One woman shows include Queens Borough Pub. Libr., Jamaica, N.Y., 1986, Baruch Coll., 1972; exhibited in group shows Queens Coun. on Arts Exhibit at Gertz Dept. Store, 1972, Queens Coll. Arts Festival, 1972, Dist. Coun. 37, First Art Exhbn., 1972, Artist Equity Group Shows Union Carbide, 1975, 77, Queensborough Community Coll. Invitational Show at Holocaust Resource Ctr., 1985, Pen and Brush, 1990, AQA Gallery, 1990, AQA at Chung Cheng Gallery at St. Johns U., 1987-90, Lowenstein Libr. Gallery Fordham U., 1989, Arlington Arts Ctr., 1991, Pursuit of Peace Ceres Gallery, 1991; designer cover Rsch. Papers Stats. Dept. Bernard M. Baruch Coll., 1973; works reprinted in Locally Speaking Local 384 newsletter. Donator work to MUSE Gallery, 1990, to Hale House Ctr., Inc.; active Women's Caucus for Art. Recipient Joseph Grumbacher Co. award, 1958, Scholastic Art award and key, 1957, Fine Arts award Queensboro Soc., 1973, Outstanding Painting award, 1973, France Lieber Meml. award Nat. Assn. Women Artists, Inc., 1992, two certs. of merit Latham Found., 1956-58; scholar Latham Found., 1958. Mem. Artists Equity Assn., Inc. N.Y., Alliance of Queens Artists, Coll. Art Assn., Queens Coun. on Arts, Ind. Arts Assn., Arlington Arts Ctr. Va., Queensboro Coll. Art Gallery (assoc.), Nat. Assn. Women Artists (The Kreindler Meml. award 1995) Print Club, Guild Am. Papercutters. Office: 11332 Mayville St Jamaica NY 11412-2410

JONES, D. PAUL, JR., banker, lawyer; b. Birmingham, Ala., Sept. 26, 1942; s. D. Paul and Virginia Lee (Mount) J.; m. Charlene Dale Angelich, Aug. 1964; children: Holly, Allison, Paul, III. B.S., U. Ala., 1964, J.D., 1967; LL.M., N.Y. U., 1968. Bar: Ala. Mem. firm Balch, Bingham, Baker, Hawthorne, Williams & Ward, Birmingham, 1970-78, of counsel, 1978-86; exec. v.p., gen. counsel, dir. Compass Bancshares, Inc., Birmingham, 1978-84, vice chmn., 1984-89, pres., COO, 1989-91, chmn., CEO, 1991—; bd. dirs. Compass Bank, Golden Enterprises, Inc., Russell Lands Co., Fed. Res. Bank Atlanta, Bus. Coun. Ala., Compass Bancshares, Inc., Region 2020, Inc.; exec. com. Pub. Affairs Rsch. Coun. Ala.; mem. Internat. Fin. Conf. Chmn. Ala. Bus. Charitable Trust Fund; mem. adv. bd. Better Bus. Bur. Birmingham; adv. bd. Salvation Army, Birmingham; bd. visitors Sch. Commerce and Bus. Adminstrn., U. Ala.; mem. pres.'s coun. U. Ala., Birmingham, pres.'s cabinet; mem. pres.'s coun. Ala. Inst. Deaf and Blind; ptnr. Econ. Devel. Partnership Ala.; grad. bd. trustees Leadership Birmingham; grad. Leadership Ala.; adv. bd. Juvenile Diabetes Found., Ala.; co-chmn. Advantage 21 Leadership Coun.; mem. adv. coun. Nat. Multiple Sclerosis Soc. Mem. ABA, Ala. Bar Assn. (chmn. sect. corp., banking and bus. law 1973-75, bd. bar examiners 1975-78), Birmingham Bar Assn., Am. Bankers Assn. (mem. govt. rels. coun. 1985-88), Ala. Bankers Assn. (pres. 1989-90, chmn. fin. com. 1990-91, exec. coun.), Fin. Svcs. Roundtable (banking and fin. markets com.), Newcomen, Birmingham C. of C., Birmingham C. of C. Found., Birmingham Bus. Leadership Group, Svc. Corps Ret. Execs. (adv. bd.), The Club, Old Overton, Country Club Birmingham, Willow Point Golf and Country Club (Alexander City), Rotary. Home: 3148 Guilford Rd Birmingham AL 35223-1217 Office: Compass Bancshares Inc PO Box 10566 Birmingham AL 35296-0001 also: Compass Bancshares Inc 15 20th St S Birmingham AL 35233-2000

JONES, DALE CHERNER, marketing executive, consultant; b. Chgo., Apr. 22, 1948; d. Morrie and Rose (Fidelman) Cherner; m. Jerome J. Jones, Dec. 16, 1973 (div. Feb. 1985); m. Edward Louis Kathrein, Oct. 24,1987; stepchildren: Janet Kirkwood, Brian Kathrein. BA, Northwestern U., 1968, M in Mgmt., 1986. Manuscripts librarian Chgo. Hist. Soc., 1968-69; mktg. coord. Perkins & Will Architects & Engrs., Chgo., 1969-73; owner Mktg. & Mgmt. Cons., Evanston, Ill., 1974-77; mktg. adminstr. Grumman-Butkus (formerly Enercon Ltd.), Evanston, 1977-79; assoc., mktg. dir. H.W. Lochner, Inc., Chgo., 1979-82; prin., owner JCS, Inc., Evanston, 1982-83; prin., dir. mktg. Schirmer Engrng. Corp., Deerfield, Ill., 1983-88; pres., COO, ptnr. R.E. Timm & Assocs., Hinsdale, Ill., 1990-95; owner Jones Consulting, 1995—; v.p. AMKA/DLM Archs., Ltd., 1997—; mktg. advisor Chgo. chpt. Ill. Soc. Profl. Engrs., 1980—. Contbr. articles to profl. jours. Fellow Soc. for Mktg. Profl. Svcs. (founder Chgo. chpt., nat. bd. dirs. 1984-86, pres. 1979-82, Cert. of Achievement 1982); mem. AIA (affiliate; mem. adv. coun. 1984-86, Cert. 1985), Assn. Bus. Women Am. (founder Chgo. chpt., treas. 1973-74, pres. 1974-75, Bus. Woman of Yr. 1974), Kellogg Alumnae Club, Northwestern Club of Chgo., Kellogg Club of Chgo. Avocations: travel, books, public speaking.

JONES, DALE EDWIN, public defender; b. Rahway, N.J., Oct. 22, 1948; s. Horatio Gates and Audrey Irma (Morgan) J.; m. Karen Anne Woodhall, June 19, 1971; children: Sharon, Michael, Stephan; m. Maria D. Noto, Aug. 2, 1987 (div. 1989); m. Joan E. DiTullio, Oct. 18, 1991; 1 child, Trevor. BA, Rutgers U., 1970, JD, 1973. Bar: N.J. 1973, U.S. Dist. Ct. N.J. 1973, U.S. Supreme Ct. 1977, N.Y. 1983. 1st asst. pub. defender Office Pub. Defender, Newark, 1974-84; dep. pub. defender in charge of capital litigation Office Pub. Defender, 1984-87; asst. pub. defender Office of Pub. Defender, Trenton, N.J., 1987—; mem. model jury charge com., N.J. Supreme Ct., 1983-88, criminal practice com., Trenton, 1983—, com. media rels., 1987-89, strategic planning com., 1996-98, rules of evidence com., 1998—. Mem. editorial bd. N.J. Lawyer. Mem. ACDL-N.J., Nat. Assn. Criminal Def. Lawyers (cert. criminal atty.), Amnesty Internat. Democrat. Office: Pub Defender Office RJ Hughes Justice Complex PO Box 850 Trenton NJ 08625

JONES, DAN BRIGMAN, ophthalmologist, educator; b. Raleigh, N.C., June 12, 1936; m. Marilyn Woodall; children: Danny Brigman Jr., Allen Walker. BA, Duke U., 1958, MD, 1962. Diplomate Am. Bd. Ophthalmology. Intern Duke Hosp., Durham, 1962-63; resident in ophthalmology Bascom Palmer Eye Inst., U. Miami (Fla.) Sch. Medicine, 1965-69; fellow in cornea and external disease Moorfields Eye Hosp., Inst. Ophthalmology, London, 1967-68; asst. prof. then assoc. prof. ophthalmology dept. surgery Vanderbilt U. Sch. Medicine, Nashville, 1969-71; assoc. prof. then prof. ophthalmology Cullen Eye Inst., Baylor Coll. Medicine, Houston, 1972-78; Sid W. Richardson prof., chmn. dept. ophthalmology Cullen Eye Inst., Baylor Coll. Medicine, 1981—, Margarett Root Brown chair ophthalmology, 1991—; mem. staff, then chief ophthalmology svc. Ben Taub Gen. Hosp., 1972—, Meth. Hosp., Houston, 1972—; mem. staff St. Luke's Episcopal Hosp., Houston, 1973—, M.D. Anderson Hosp. and Tumor Inst., Houston, 1978—; chief ophthalmology sect. VA Hosp., Houston, 1973-78; mem. sci. adv. com. Knights Templar Eye Found., Inc., 1984—; mem. various coms. and couns. Nat. Eye Inst., 1975—; mem. adv. panel on ophthalmology U.S. Pharmacopeial Conv., 1980-84; mem. ophthalmic drugs adv. com. FDA, 1975-78; cons. in field; vis.

prof. to numerous schs., including Johns Hopkins U., Balt., 1975, 79, Washington U., St. Louis, 1975, Tipler Army Hosp., Honolulu, 1974, Yale U., New Haven, 1988, others; lectr. in field. Contbr. numerous articles to profl. jours. Bd. dirs. William C. Connor Found., Tex. Christian U., 1981—, Tex. Soc. to Prevent Blindness, 1981—; bd. dirs. The Lighthouse of Houston, 1981-89, mem. adv. coun., 1989—; mem. exec. med. com. Lions Eye Bank of Tex., 1981—, bd. dirs., 1989—. Epidemic intelligence officer USPHS, 1963-65. Recipient Honor award in Edn. Am. Acad. Ophthalmology and Otolaryngology, 1976; grantee NIH, 1978—, Sid W. Richardson Found., 1977-82. Mem. AMA (mem. program com. sect. ophthalmology 1970-73), Am. Acad. Ophthalmology (mem. faculty of basic and clin. sci. course 1970-76, mem. ophthalmology knowledge assessment com. 1972-80, mem. adv. com. 1973-77, mem. long range planning com. 1976-80, mem. program adv. com. 1986-89, sec. instrn. 1989—, trustee 1989—, Sr. Honor award 1986), Am. Ophthalmol. Soc., Am. Soc. for Microbiology, Assn. for Rsch. in Vision and Ophthalmology, Assn. Univ. Profs. Ophthalmology (chmn. resident and fellowship edn. com. 1986-88, chmn. edn. com. 1988—, trustee 1988—, pres. bd. trustees 1993—), Harris County Med. Soc., Houston Ophthal. Soc. (pres. 1979-80), Ocular Microbiology and Immunology Group, Inc. (exec. sec. 1973-89, bd. dirs. 1989—), Pan Am. Assn. Ophthalmology, Tex. Ophthal. Assn. (mem. bd. councillors 1982-85), Tex. Soc. Infectious Diseases, Baylor Ophthalmology Alumni Assn., Inc., Bascom Palmer Alumni Assn., Phi Beta Kappa, Phi Eta Sigma, Alpha Omega Alpha. Office: Cullen Eye Inst 6565 Fannin NC 205 Houston TX 77030

JONES, DAN LEWIS, psychologist; b. Halifax, Va., Oct. 8, 1951; s. Ernest Lewis and Mary Elizabeth (Francis) J.; m. Temple Kiger Jones, Aug. 17, 1974; children: Natalie Temple, Layla Michelle. BA, Appalachian State U., 1974; MA, West Ga. Coll., 1976; PhD, U. Kans., 1986. Lic. psychologist, N.C., Calif., Va.; diplomate in counseling psychology Am. Bd. Profl. Psychology; cert. treatment of alcohol and other psychoactive substance use disorders, APA Coll. of Profl. Psychology. Instr. psychology N.C. Ctrl. U., Durham, 1976-79; counselor Adult Life Resource Ctr., U. Kans., Lawrence, 1979-84; psychology intern Counseling Ctr. U. Calif., Irvine, 1984-85; acting dir. adult life resource ctr. U. Kans., 1985-86; staff psychologist Counseling Ctr. Utah State U., Logan, 1986-88; psychologist Counseling Ctr. East Tenn. State U., Johnson City, 1988-89; sr. psychologist, dir. tng., asst. dir. Counseling and Psychol. Svcs., Appalachian State U., Boone, N.C., 1989-97; dir. Counseling and Psychol. Svcs., Appalachian State U., Boone, 1996—, 1997—; part-time pvt. practice; cons. IRS, 1985, Bristol (Tenn.) Mental Health Ctr., 1989, N.C. Ct. Counseling Svcs., 1979. Author: (with others) Counseling Adults, 1985, (editor; author (manual) The Stress management Workshop, 1985, (with others) AACD Stress Workshop Manual, 1985. Fellow Acad. of Counseling Psychology; mem. APA (chmn. spl. interest group on coll. counseling ctrs. divsn. 17, mem. program com. divsn. 29), Am. Coll. Pers. Assn. (directorate commn. VII), Soc. of Psychotherapy Integration. Democrat. Avocations: racquetball. Home: 357 Fawn Dr Boone NC 28607-8461

JONES, DANIEL EDWIN, JR., bishop; b. Westcliffe, Colo., Jan. 31, 1942; s. Daniel Edwin and Vivian Mary (Falkenberg) J. BA, Carroll Coll., Helena, Mont., 1964; MA, Am. Coll., Louvain, Belgium, 1968. Ordained priest Roman Cath. Ch., 1968; ordained to ministry Ch. of Jesus Christ, 1994, now consecrated bishop; mem. Order of Magnificat of Mother of God (3d order mem.). Parish priest Diocese of Pueblo, Colo., 1968-72; itinerant mission priest Traditional Cath. Movement, Westcliffe, Colo., 1972-93; itinerant bishop Ch. of Jesus Christ, St. Jovite, Que., Can., 1994—; third order mem. Order of the Mother of God, 1994. Editor/pub. Sangre de Cristo Newsnotes, 1973—. Avocations: rockhounding, golf, hunting, fishing. Office: Sangre de Cristo Newsnotes PO Box 89 Westcliffe CO 81252-0089

JONES, DANIEL HAMILTON, optometrist; b. Nashville, Dec. 1, 1961; s. George William and Garnell (Hamilton) J.; m. Peggy Jean Schenck, May 19, 1984; children: Haley, Kelsey. BA, William Jewell Coll., 1984; OD, U. Mo., St. Louis, 1989. Cert. optometrist Mo. Bd. Optometry. Chemist Midwest Rsch. Inst., Kansas City, Mo., 1984-85; optometrist Chapman, Waterman & Jones, Liberty, Mo., 1989—. Commr. Liberty Planning and Zoning Commn., 1995—. Mem. Am. Optometric Assn., Mo. Optometric Found., Mo. Optometric Assn., Greater Kansas City Optometric Soc. (bd. mem. 1995—), Richmond Rotary Club, Liberty Sertoma Club (treas. 1990—).

JONES, DANIEL HARE, librarian, consultant; b. Charleston, S.C., Jan. 18, 1949; s. Daniel Hare and Maria Clare (Duffy) J.; m. Rajia Christina Tobia, Dec. 15, 1979; children: Andrew Duffy, Patrick Joseph. BS, Clemson U., 1971; MLS, Emory U., 1977. Tchr. pub. schs. Blackville, S.C., 1971-73; tchr. Peace Corps., Malaysia, 1973-74; libr. Biomed. Libr. U. So. Ala., Mobile, 1977-79; libr. Briscoe Library U. Tex. Health Sci. Ctr., San Antonio, 1979-98; pres. Libr. Cons. NA, Inc., Mobile, Ala., 1998—; indexer publs. Nat. Inst. Arthritis, Metabolism and Digestive Diseases, 1978; cons. Georgetown U., Washington, 1985-87, S.W. Found. for Biomed. Rsch., 1994-95; mem. libr. adv. coun. Springer-Verlag Pub. Co., 1992-96; dir. R & D for N.Am. representing Otto Harrassowitz, Wiesbaden, Germany, 1998—. Mem. editl. bd. Serials Rev., 1991-97, Newsletter on Serial Pricing Issues, 1990—. Mem. ALA, Acad. Health Info. Profls. (disting.), Med. Libr. Assn., Tex. Libr. Assn. Roman Catholic. Avocations: swimming, gardening. Home: 223 Clearview Dr San Antonio TX 78228-1940 Office: Library Consultants NA Inc Ste 4B 820 University Blvd S Mobile AL 36609

JONES, DANIEL LEE, software development company executive; b. Sterling, Colo., Feb. 17, 1954; s. Gerald Dean and Joyce Elaine (Pyle) J.; m. Laurie Elaine Ganong, Sept. 6, 1975; 1 child, Jonathon Alexander. AB cum laude, Dartmouth Coll., 1976; MA in Physics, U. Calif., Davis, 1977, PhD in Physics, 1979. Assoc. in physics U. Calif., Davis, 1976-79; physicist Argonne (Ill.) Nat. Lab., 1979-82; mem. tech. staff TRW, Inc., Redondo Beach, Calif., 1982-84; chief scientist, co-founder Affine Scis. Corp., Newport Beach, Calif., 1984-85; chief scientist Peripheral Systems, Inc., Van Nuys, Calif., 1985-89; dir. info. systems Jones & Jones, Sterling, Colo., 1989-92; v.p., co-founder Jones Techs. Inc., Sterling, 1991-92, also bd. dirs.; chief scientist Sykes Enterprises, Inc., Tampa, Fla., 1992-99; pres. D.L. Jones, Inc., 1999—; sec. Jones Techs. Inc., Sterling, 1991-92; cons. Davis Polk & Wardwell, N.Y.C., 1987-91. Author (newspaper column) Your Computer, 1991-93; contbr. articles to profl. jours. Dist. accountability com. RE-1 Valley Schs., Sterling, 1991-94, dist. tech. com., 1991-94; mem. Northwestern Jr. Coll. Found. Bd., 1995—. Recipient Rufus Choate scholar Dartmouth Coll., 1972, Outstanding Contbrn. Inst. of Internal Auditors, 1987-88; tech. transfer grantee TRW, Inc., 1982. Mem. IEEE, IEEE Computer Soc., Assn. for Computing Machinery, Soc. for Indsl. and Applied Math. Republican. Methodist. Avocations: reading, writing, mathematics. Home: 510 Glenora St Sterling CO 80751-4642 Office: Sykes Enterprises Inc 777 N 4th St Sterling CO 80751-3244

JONES, DAVID ALLEN, health facility executive; b. Louisville, Aug. 7, 1931; s. Evan L. and Elsie F. (Thurman) J.; m. Betty L. Ashbury, July 24, 1954. BS, U. Louisville, 1954; JD, Yale U., 1960. Bar: Ky. 1960. Founder Humana Inc. (formerly Extendicare Inc.), Louisville, 1961-97, also chmn., dir.; ptnr. Greenebaum, Doll and McDonald and predecessor, Louisville, 1965-69, of counsel, 1969-74; dir. Abbott Labs. Served as lt. (j.g.) USN, 1954-57. Mem. Louisville Area C. of C. Office: Humana Inc 500 W Main St Ste 300 Louisville KY 40202-4268*

JONES, DAVID ALWYN, geneticist, botany educator; b. Colliers Wood, Surrey, Eng., June 23, 1934; came to U.S., 1989; s. Trefor and Marion Edna Jones; m. Hazel Cordelia Lewis, Aug. 29, 1959; children: Catherine Susan, Edmund Meredith, Hugh Francis. BA, MA in Natural Scis., U. Cambridge, Eng., 1957; DPhil in Genetics, U. Oxford, Eng., 1963. Chartered biologist, UK. Lectr. genetics U. Birmingham, Eng., 1961-73; prof. genetics U. Hull, Eng., 1973-89, head dept. plant biology and genetics, 1983-88; prof. botany U. Fla., Gainesville, 1989—, chmn. dept. botany, 1989-98; chmn. membership com. Inst. of Biology, London, 1982-87. Co-author: Variation and Adaptation in Plant Species, 1971, Analysis of Populations, 1976, What is Genetics?, 1976, Zmiennosc i przystosowanie roslin, 1977; contbr. over 100 articles to profl. jours. Fellow Linnean Soc., Inst. Biology; mem. AAAS, Am. Soc. Naturalists, Bot. Soc. Am., Internat. Soc. Chem. Ecology (coun. 1983-84, 89-91, keynote spkr. ann. meeting 1984, pres. elect 1986-87, pres. 1987-88, past pres. 1988-89, co-editor Jour. Chem. Ecology 1994—), Brit. Assn. Advancement of Sci. (chmn. coord. com. for cytology and genetics 1974-87), Genetical Soc. Gt. Britain (convenor ann. meetings profs. of genetics 1983-88), Ecol. Genetics Group, Population Genetics Group, Soc. for Study of Evolution, Gamma Sigma Delta, Sigma Xi (pres.-elect U. Fla. chpt. 1999—). Achievements include research in practical population biology especially in ecological genetics and chemical ecology of cyanogenic plants. Home: 7201 SW 97th Ln Gainesville FL 32608-6378 Office: U Fla Dept Botany 220 Bartram Hall Gainesville FL 32611-8526

JONES, DAVID CHARLES, retired air force officer, former chairman Joint Chiefs of Staff; b. Aberdeen, S.D., July 9, 1921; s. Maurice and Helen Alice (Meade) J.; m. Lois M. Tarbell, Jan. 23, 1942; children: Susan Jones Coffin, Kathy Jones Franklin, David Curtis. Student, U. N.D., Minot State Coll.; grad., Flying Sch., Roswell, N.Mex., 1943, Nat. War Coll., Washington, 1960; H.L.D., U. Nebr., 1974, La. Tech. U., 1975, Minot State Coll., 1979, Boston U., 1980, Troy State U. Commd. 2d lt. U.S. Air Force, 1943, advanced through grades to gen., 1971; dep. comdr. ops. Vietnam; vice comdr. 7th Air Force; comdr.-in-chief U.S. Air Force Europe; comdr. 4th Allied Tactical Air Force; chief of staff U.S. Air Force, Washington, 1974-78; chmn. Joint Chiefs of Staff, Dept. Def., Washington, 1978-82, ret., 1982; bd. dirs. SRA Internat., Inc., Servus Fin. Inc. Decorated Def. D.S.M., Air Force D.S.M., Navy D.S.M., Army D.S.M., Legion of Merit, D.F.C., Bronze star, Air medal, numerous others. Mem. Air Force Assn., Alfalfa Club. Clubs: Alfalfa, Army-Navy Country, Bohemian.

JONES, DAVID CHARLES, international financial and management consultant; b. Cowes, Eng., Feb. 8, 1935; came to U.S., 1970; s. Charles Alfred and Alice Elizabeth (Rickman) J.; m. Gabrielle Clara Mabey, Sept. 28, 1957; children: Stephen Charles, Philip Simon (dec.), Catherine Claire. Cert. in acctg. and fin. mgmt., Chartered Inst. Pub. Fin. and Accountancy, London, 1961. Cert. acct., Eng. Clk. Brit. Rail, London, 1951-55, Isle of Wight (Eng.) County Coun., Newport, 1955-56; acct. Petworth (Eng.) Dist. Coun., 1956-59; chief acct. Kingswood (Eng.) Dist. Coun., 1959-61; sr. acct. Luton (Eng.) Borough Coun., 1961-63; tech. asst. Govt. of U.K., Entebbe, Uganda, 1963-68, Blantyre, Malawi, 1968-70; sr. fin. analyst World Bank, Washington, 1970-80, fin. adviser, 1980-87; cons. Internat. Fin. and Mgmt. Cons., Annandale, Va., 1987—, World Bank, Internat. Monetary Fund, 1987—; vis. lectr. Grad. Sch. Design, Harvard U., Cambridge, Mass., 1987—, rsch. fellow, 1994—, Grad. Sch., George Mason U., Fairfax, Va., 1990—; v.p. Internat. Devel. Tng. Inst., Washington, 1988-95; sr. assoc. cons. Internat. Mgmt. Cons. Ltd., Eng.; expert testimony D.C. Com., U.S. Ho. of Reps. Author: Municipal Accounting for Developing Countries, 1984; contbr. articles to profl. jours. Cpl. R.A.F., 1953-55, Eng. Fellow Chartered Assn. of Cert. Accts.; mem. Chartered Inst. Pub. Fin. and Accountancy, Internat. Consortium on Govtl. Fin. Mgmt. (bd. dirs. 1980—). Episcopalian. Avocations: amateur poet, music composer, classical music, meditation, railways. Home: 4936 Andrea Ave Annandale VA 22003-4180

JONES, DAVID JOHN, III, preventive medicine physician, medical executive; b. Ellwood City, Pa., Jan. 1, 1933; s. David John Jr. and Margaret Sarah (Liebendorfer) J.; m. Marie Anne Butler, Aug. 13, 1955; children: Sharon Jones Olszewski, David John IV, Marcie Jones Walsh. BS in Chemistry cum laude, Grove City Coll., 1954; MD, Jefferson Med. Coll., Phila., 1958; MPH in Med. Care Adminstrn., U. Pitts., 1965. Diplomate Am. Bd. Preventive Medicine. Intern Western Pa. Hosp., Pitts., 1958-59; resident in preventive medicine U. Pitts., Pa. Dept. of Health, 1963-65; pvt. practice Sharon, Pa., 1961-63; asst. prof. cmty. health U. Mo., Columbia, 1965-69; assoc. prof. medicine, dir. cmty. medicine U. Md. Sch. Med., Balt., 1969-76; dir. cmty. medicine York (Pa.) Hosp., 1969-76; v.p. Pa. Blue Shield, Camp Hill, 1976-83, Silver Spring Health Plan, Mechanicsburg, Pa., 1984-87; med. dir. All Health, Harrisburg, Pa., 1987—; bd. dirs. Vision Benefits of Am., Pitts.; bd. trustees Presbyn Homes, Inc. Editor Am. Jour. Med. Quality, 1986—. Lt. cmdr. (sr. surgeon), USPHS, 1959-61. Milbank Faculty fellow, N.Y.C., 1967. Fellow Am. Coll. Med. Quality (disting.; v.p., pres.-elet, pres., 1992—, Disting. Svc. award), Masons. Republican. Presbyterian. Avocations: music, art, gardening, bridge. Home: 1455 Virginia Ave York PA 17403-3629 Office: All Health 4750 Lindle Rd Harrisburg PA 17111-2428

JONES, DAVID M., zoological park director; b. Cheshire, Eng., Aug. 14, 1944; came to U.S., 1994; m. Janet Jones; 3 children. BSc in Zoology, Royal Vet. Coll., London, 1966; B Vet. Medicine, Royal Veterinary Coll., London, 1969. 1st resident vet. surgeon Whipsnade pk. Zool. Soc. London, Eng., 1969-75; sr. vet. officer Zool. Soc. London, 1975, responsible for animal collection London and Whipsnade, 1981, dir. zoos London and Whipsnade, 1984, chief exec., 1991; dir. conservation and consultancy London and Whipsnade, 1993; dir. N.C. Zool. Park, Asheboro, 1994—, Dept. Environ. Health, Natural Resources State of N.C., 1994—; chmn. Fauna and Flora Internat., London, 1987-94; chmn. conservation com. World Wide Fund for Nature, 1988-94, bd. trustees; chmn. Brooke Hosp. for Animals, London, Pakistan, India, 1990-98, Yadkin Pee-Dee Lakes Project, 1998—, Uwharrie Heritage LLC, 1998—; mem. coun. World Wildlife Fund U.S., 1996—, U.K., 1997—. Contbr. articles to profl. jours. Bd. trustees World Wide Fund for Nature, U.K., chmn. conservation com.; chmn. Brooke Hosp. for Animals. Fellow Inst. Biology; mem. Royal Coll. Vet. Surgeons. Home: 1688 Sylvan Way Asheboro NC 27203-2546 Office: NC Zool Park 4401 Zoo Pkwy Asheboro NC 27203-1425

JONES, DAVID MILTON, economist, educator; b. Newton, Iowa, June 22, 1938; s. Charles Raymond and Mary Evelyn (Corrough) J.; m. Becky Ann Jones Strait, Aug. 4, 1962; children: David, Jennifer, Stephen. BA with honors, Coe Coll., 1960; MA, U. Pa., 1961, PhD, 1969. Economist Fed. Res. Bank N.Y., N.Y.C., 1963-68; v.p., fin. economist Irving Trust Co., N.Y.C., 1968-72; vice-chmn., chief economist, bd. dirs. Aubrey G. Lanston & Co., Inc., N.Y.C., 1972—; advisor panel Fed. Res. Bank N.Y., 1982-93, cons. bd. govs., 1996—; mem. econ. adv. bd. Columbia U., 1982-87; former dir. pub. interest Suffolk County Savs. and Loan, Centerreach, N.Y.; bd. dirs. Aubrey G. Lanston & Co., Inc., Coe Coll., Union Theol. Sem. Author: Fed Watching and Interest Rate Projections: A Practical Guide, 1986, The Politics of Money: The Fed under Alan Greenspan, 1991, The Buck Starts Here: How the Federal Reserve Can Make or Break Your Financial Future, 1995. Chmn. fin. and investment com. United Ch. Bd. for World Ministries, N.Y.C., 1975-86; mem. bond com. Twp. of Montclair, 1982-83. Woodrow Wilson Found. fellow, 1960; NDEA fellow, 1960. Mem. Nat. Assn. Bus. Economists, Econ. Club of N.Y., Nat. Econ. Club (bd. dirs.). Home: 168 Gates Ave Montclair NJ 07042-2009 Office: Aubrey G Lanston & Co Inc 1 Chase Manhattan Plz New York NY 10005-1401

JONES, DAVID PROCTOR, academic administrator; b. Eugene, Oreg., Apr. 16, 1970; s. John Edwin Jones and Mary Elizabeth (Proctor) Brown. BA in Secondary Edn., SUNY, Oswego, 1992; MS in Counseling, U. Nebr., Kearney, 1995. Tchr. Carlisle (Iowa) H.S., 1993; residence hall dir. U. Nebr., Kearney, 1993-95; area dir. office of residence life Coll. of William and Mary, Williamsburg, Va., 1995—; mem. program com. Upper Midwest Region-Assn. of Coll. and Univ. Housing Officers. Author computer program R.A. Train, 1995; contbr. articles to profl. publs. and jours. Dance-A-Thon organizer Habitat for Humanity, Kearney, 1993-94. Recipient Pres. Scholarship award Upper Midwest Region-Assn. of Coll. and Univ. Housing Officers, 1994, Outstanding New Profl. award, 1994, Assn. of Coll. and Univ. Housing Officers, 1997. Mem. Southeastern Assn. Housing Officers (newcomers workshop chair 1996-98, membership svcs. com. chair 1998, author jour. 1995, 98, case study winner 1996), Order of Omega, Sigma Tau Chi. Republican. Roman Catholic. Avocations: reading, sports, juggling, writing. Office: Coll of William and Mary Office of Residence Life Campus Ctr 212 Williamsburg VA 23187

JONES, DAVID RHODES, retired newspaper editor, consultant; b. Connellsville, Pa., Sept. 13, 1932; s. David Rhodes and Ruth Elizabeth (Dillon) J.; m. Mary Lee Lauffer, Oct. 8, 1955; 1 dau., Elizabeth Lee. B.A., Pa. State U., 1954; M.A., N.Y. U., 1961. Reporter Wall Street Jour., N.Y.C., 1957-61; bur. chief Wall Street Jour., Pitts., 1961-63; with N.Y. Times, 1963—, corr., Detroit, 1963-65, nat. labor reporter, Washington, 1965-68; asst. nat. editor, N.Y.C. N.Y. Times, N.Y.C., 1969-72; nat. editor N.Y. Times, 1972-87, editor nat. editions, 1987-97, asst. mng. editor, 1989-97; cons. N.Y. Times. Trustee Pa. State U. Served to 1st lt. USAF, 1955-57. Mem. Sigma Delta Chi, Tau Kappa Epsilon. Office: NY Times Co 229 W 43rd St New York NY 10036-3959

JONES, DAVID ROBERT, zoology educator; b. Bristol, Eng., Jan. 28, 1941; came to Can., 1969; s. William Arnold and Gladys Margery (Parker) J.; m. Valerie Iris Gibson, Sept. 15, 1962; children: Melanie Ann, Vivienne Samantha. B.Sc., Southampton U., 1962; Ph.D., U. East Anglia, Norwich, Eng., 1965. Rsch. fellow U. East Anglia, Eng., 1965-66; lectr. zoology U. Bristol, Eng., 1966-69; prof. zoology U. B.C., Vancouver, B.C., Can., 1969—. Contbr. numerous articles to profl. jours. Fellow Killam Found. Can., 1973, 89; recipient Killam Rsch. prize, 1993. Fellow Royal Soc. Can.; mem. Soc. Exptl. Biology, Am. Physiol. Soc., Can. Zool. Soc. (Fry medal 1992). Office: U BC, 6270 University Blvd, Vancouver, BC Canada V6T 1Z4

JONES, DAVID R(USSELL), not-for-profit executive; b. Bklyn., Apr. 30, 1948; s. Thomas Russell and Bertha Jones; m. Valerie King, June 2, 1978; children: Russell King-Jones, Vanessa King-Jones. BA, Wesleyan U., 1970; JD, Yale U., 1974; MA (hon.), Wesleyan U., 1983; LHD (hon.), CUNY, 1999. Bar: N.Y. 1975. Litigation assoc. Cravath, Swaine & Moore, N.Y.C., 1975-79; spl. advisor Mayor of N.Y.C., 1979-83; exec. dir. N.Y.C. Youth Bur., Bklyn., 1983-86; pres., CEO Cmty. Svc. Soc., N.Y.C., 1986—; chmn. bd. dirs. Carver Fed. Savs. Bank, N.Y.C., 1989—; mem. bd. Jobs For the Future, Boston, 1990-98; mem. adv. bd. JFK Sch. Govt., Cambridge, Mass., Barnard Columbia Ctr. Leadership Pub. Policy, N.Y.C. Columnist N.Y. Amsterdam News, 1992—; TV host CUNY-TV, 1993—. Mem. bd. Health & Hosps. Corp., N.Y.C., 1993-98, N.Y. Found., 1996—; vice chair Primary Health Care Devel. Corp., N.Y.C., 1993-95; trustee Wesleyan U., Middletown, Conn., 1984-96; mem. bd., mem. exec. com., Upper Manhattan Empowerment Zone, N.Y.C., 1996—. Thomas J. Watson fellow, 1970. Mem. Black Agy. Execs. (pres. 1987-94). Avocations: bike riding, travel, reading, carpentry. Office: Cmty Svc Soc NY 105 E 22d St New York NY 10010

JONES, DEAN CARROLL, actor; b. Decatur, Ala., Jan. 25, 1931; s. Andrew Guy and Nolia Elizabeth (Wilhite) J.; m. Mae Inez Entwisle, Jan. 1, 1954 (div.); children: Carol Elizabeth, Deanna Mae; m. Lory Basham, June 2, 1973; 1 child, Michael David. Student, Asbury Coll. Blues singer, New Orleans; performances include: (Broadway) There Was A Little Girl, 1960, Under the Yum Yum Tree, 1961, Company, 1970, Into the Light, 1986; (films) The Opposite Sex, 1956, Tea and Sympathy, 1956, These Wilder Years, 1956, Somebody Up There Likes Me, 1956, The Great American Pastime, 1956, The Rack, 1956, Until They Sail, 1957, Jailhouse Rock, 1957, 10,000 Bedrooms, 1957, Designing Woman, 1957, Torpedo Run, 1958, Handle With Care, 1958, Imitation General, 1958, Never So Few, 1959, Night of the Quarter Moon, 1959, Under the Yum-Yum Tree, 1963, New Interns, 1964, That Darn Cat, 1965, Two On a Guillotine, 1965, The Ugly Dachshund, 1966, Any Wednesday, 1966, Monkeys, Go Home, 1967, The Horse in the Grey Flannel Suit, 1968, Blackbeard's Ghost, 1968, The Love Bug, 1969, Mr. Superinvisible, 1970, The $1,000,000 Duck, 1971, Snowball Express, 1972, The Shaggy D.A, 1976, Herbie Goes to Monte Carlo, 1977, Born Again, 1978, St. John in Exile, 1986, Other People's Money, 1991, Beethoven, 1992, Clear and Present Danger, 1994, Kickboxer 5, 1994, A spasso nel tempo, 1996, That Darn Cat, 1997, (voice) Batman & Mr. Freeze: SubZero, 1998, (TV series) Ensign O'Toole, 1962-63, What's It All About, World?, 1969 (host), The Chicago Teddy Bears,1971, Herbie, The Love Bug, 1982, Beethoven (animated), 1994, (voice) Jonny Quest: The New Adventures, 1996; (TV movies) The Great Man's Whiskers, 1971, Guess Who's Been Sleeping in My Bed, 1973, Once Upon a Brothers Grimm, 1977, When Every Day Was the 4th of July, 1978, The Long Days of Summer, 1980, Fire and Rain, 1989, Saved By the Bell: Hawaiian Style, 1992, The Computer Wore Tennis Shoes, 1995, Special Report: Journey to Mars, 1995, The Love Bug, 1997; appeared on TV series Wagon Train, Murder She Wrote, Superman. With USN Air Corps, 1950-54. Mem. Acad. Motion Picture Arts and Scis., Acad. TV Arts and Scis., Acad. Rec. Arts and Scis. *

JONES, DEANNA ELAINE, mathematics educator; b. Flint, Mich., Dec. 10, 1964; d. William Louis Jones and Glenowyn Lorraine Tice. BS, Cen. Mich. U., 1987, MA, 1993. Cert. in elem. continuing tchg., Mich.; cert. in elem. adminstrn., Mich.; cert. in ednl. tech. Tchr. Gerrish-Higgins Sch. Dist., Roscommon, Mich., 1988—, sys. operator, 1993-95; North Ctrl. Accreditation/steering com. Gerrish-Higgins Sch. Dist., Roscommon, 1995—. Mem. ASCD, Nat. Coun. Tchrs. of Math., Mich. Coun. Tchrs. Math., Delta Kappa Gamma. Avocations: computers, reading, traveling, music.

JONES, DEBRA K., accountant; b. Liberal, Kans., Dec. 25, 1955; d. Donald F. and Q. Joyce (Rolf) Ewing; m. Thomas W. Jones III, Aug. 3, 1974; children: Heather Michelle, Ryan Thomas. BS, Pratt (Kans.) C.C., 1974, Kans. State U., 1976. Acct. Harold Coulter Acctg., Pratt, 1976-78, Patton, Cramer & LaProd, Chartered, Pratt, 1978—. Spkr. chmn. scholarship com. Pratt H.S., 1995-97; asst. leader Girl Scouts U.S., 1984-94; fin. com. United Meth. Ch., Pratt, 1994—. Avocations: quilting, fishing, cooking, needlework, surfing internet. Home: 306 N Ninnescah St Pratt KS 67124-1843

JONES, DENNIS PAUL, food and consumer goods company executive; b. Columbus, Ohio, Jan. 16, 1952; s. Paul David and Irma Rosella (Seabright) J.; m. Kathy Kirby, June 26, 1983. BS, Miami U., Oxford, Ohio, 1974; MBA, U. Miami, Coral Gables, Fla., 1976. Sys. mktg. rep. Sci. Bur. Co. divsn. IBM, Chgo., 1976-78; sys. analyst Beatrice Cos., Chgo., 1978-80, dir. stragetic planning, 1980-82, v.p. strategic planning, 1982-87; v.p. bus. planning and devel. TLC Beatrice Internat., N.Y.C., 1987-89, sr. v.p. bus. planning and devel., 1989-93, exec. v.p. ops., 1993—; bd. dirs. subs. of TLC Beatrics, France, Spain, Italy, Germany, Ireland, Belgium, The Netherlands, Thailand. Mem. Chgo. Coun. on Fgn. Rels., Coun. Fgn. Rels., N.Y., Sheffield Preservation Assn., Chgo. Mem. U.S. Belgium C. of C. Republican. Lutheran. Office: TLC Beatrice Europe SA, 22 rue du Capucines, 75002 Paris France also: TLC Beatrice Internat 9 W 57th St Ste 3910 New York NY 10019-2701

JONES, DIANA WYNNE, writer; b. London, Aug. 16, 1934; d. Richard Aneurin Jones and Marjorie (Jackson) Hughes; m. John Anthony Burrow, Dec. 22, 1956; children: Richard, Michael, Colin. BA, St. Anne's Coll. U. Oxford, Eng., 1956. Free-lance writer part-time Essex, Oxford, Eng., 1944-70; full-time writer Oxford, Bristol, Eng., 1970—; panel judge Guardian Award for Children's Books, London, 1979-83, Whitbread Prize for Lit., Children's Sect., London, 1988. Author: (children's and young adults' books) Wilkins' Tooth (in U.S. Witch's Business), 1973, The Ogre Downstairs, 1974, Eight Days of Luke, 1975, Cart and Cwidder, 1975, Dogsbody, 1975, Power the Three, 1976, Drowned Ammet, 1977, Charmed Life, 1977 (Guardian award 1978), Who Got Rid of Angus Flint, 1978, The Spellcoats, 1979, The Magicians of Caprona, 1980, The Homeward Bounders, 1981, The Time of the Ghost, 1981, Witch Week, 1982, Warlock at the Wheel, 1984, Archer's Goon, 1984 (Boston Globe/Horn Book award), Fire and Hemlock, 1985, Howl's Moving Castle, 1986 (Boston Globe/Horn Book award), A Tale of Time City, 1987, The Lives of Christopher Chant, 1988, Chair Person, 1989, Wild Robert, 1989, Hidden Turnings, 1989, Castle in the Air, 1990, Black Maria, 1991, A Sudden Wild Magic, 1992, The Crown of Dalemark, 1993, Stopping for a Spell, 1993, Hexwood, 1993, Fantasy Stories, 1994, Everard's Ride, 1995, The Tough Guide to Fantasyland, 1996, Minor Arcana, 1996, Deep Secret, 1997, Dark Lord of Derkholm, 1998, (retelling of) Puss n' Boots, 1999. Recipient, Mythopoaic Soc. Awd., 1995, 99. Mem. Soc. of Authors. Avocations: cooking, hiking, owning a cat. Home: 9 The Polygon, Bristol England BS8 4PW Office: care Greenwillow Books 105 Madison Ave New York NY 10016-7418

JONES, DON CARLTON, insurance agent; b. Jacksonville, Tex., Aug. 6, 1943; s. Carlton P. and Sue (Galledge) J.; m. Pat Jones; children: Carlton, Vicki, Staci. BS, Sam Houston State U. Casualty underwriter Am. Gen. Ins. Co., San Antonio, 1967-69; spl. agt. Trinity Universal Ins. Co., Houston, 1969-73; sec., treas. Crockett (Tex.) Ins. Svc., 1973-82, pres., 1990—; pres. Hociston-Walken County Ins. Svc., Crockett, 1982—, Trinity (Tex.) Ins. Agy. Mem. Houston County Airport Commn., Crockett, 1985—; pres. Indsl. Devel. Authority, Crockett, 1986-90. Served with U.S. Army. Mem. Lions Club (past pres.), C. of C. (past pres.), Nat. C. of C. Ind. Ins. Agts. Tex., Cert. Ins. Counselors Tex., Soc. Cert. Ins. Counselors, Crockett C. of C. (pres. 1981—). Office: Crockett Ins Svc 206 S 5th St Crockett TX 75835-2029

JONES, DONALD KELLY, state agency executive; b. Fresno, Calif., Aug. 9, 1944; s. Chester Henry and Helen Edith (Summers) J.; m. Carolyn Wray Dolly, Mar. 23, 1979. BA in History, Stanford U., 1966; M Internat. Affairs, Johns Hopkins U., 1968. Asst. prof. Davidson (N.C.) Coll., 1973-75; sr. economist GM Corp., N.Y.C., 1975-84; dir. internat. trade Am. Paper Inst., N.Y.C., 1984-86; sr. mgr. bus. devel. Nissho Iwai Am. Corp., N.Y.C., 1986-95; dep. commr., sr. v.p., chief adminstrv. officer, bd. dirs. Empire State Devel. Corp., N.Y.C., 1995—; mem. U.S. bus./industry adv. com. OECD, N.Y.c., 1977-84. Author: Structure of American Government, 1975. Rep. Party candidate for N.Y. State Assembly, 1992; chmn. Change-N.Y., Albany, 1992-95; pres. Taxpayers' Alliance of N.Y., Hartsdale, N.Y., 1994—; bd. dirs. Columbia Sch. Internat. Bus., N.Y.C., 1995—; mem. Westchester County Budget Adv. Com., White Plains, N.Y., 1995—; apptd. mem. N.Y.C. Dist. Export Coun., 1996—. Recipient Recognition of Svc. award UN Internat. Bus. Coun., 1984, Outstanding Svc. award Cleve. World Trade Assn., 1993. Mem. Am. Enterprise Inst., Heritage Found., Cato Inst., Johns Hopkins U. Alumni Assn. (bd. dirs. 1994—), Eastside Conservative Club. Republican. Avocations: classical music, politics, travel. Home: 10 Hawthorne Way Hartsdale NY 10530-3005

JONES, DONALD LEE, religious studies educator; b. Xenia, Ohio, Aug. 7, 1938; s. Dana Dalphon and Alice Lenore (Lewis) J.; m. Susan Alicia Haas, Aug. 19, 1961; children: Douglas Haas, Kevin Scott Jones, Darin Andrew. BA, Ohio Wesleyan U., 1960; MDiv, Meth. Theol. Sch. in Ohio, 1963; PhD, Duke U., 1966. Asst. prof. religion Earlham Coll. and Sch. Religion, Richmond, Ind., 1966-67; asst. prof. religion U. S.C., Columbia, 1967-70, assoc. prof. religion, 1970-75, prof. religious studies, 1975—, chmn. relgious studies, 1980-89, grad. dir. religious studies, 1986-92, 95—. Contbr. articles to profl. jours. Bd. dirs. Richland County Guardian Ad Litem Project, Columbia, 1990-97, chair 1994-95; bd. dirs. Family Svc. Ctr., Columbia, 1990-96, chair 1994-95; chair pastoral counseling svc. com. Trenholm Road United Meth. Ch., Columbia, 1979—, trustee Ministry Resources Found., 1990—; pres. Columbia Kiwanis Club, 1991-92; chmn. Atlas Road Elem. Sch. adv. coun., Columbia, 1983; founding mem. Christian-Jewish Congress of S.C., 1976; mem. S.C. Coun. for Human Rights, 1968-70. Mem. Soc. of Biblical Lit. (S.E. chair regional secs. 1984), Columbia Torch Club Internat. (pres. 1996-97), Soc. of Biblical Lit. (nat. coun. 1981-84, S.E. pres. 1972-73, regional sec. 1981-87), S.C. Acad. of Religion (pres. 1975-76). Democrat. United Methodist. Avocations: golf, reading, music. Home: 848 Malibu Dr Columbia SC 29209-2446 Office: Dept Religious Studies U SC Columbia SC 29208

JONES, DONNA LEE NOBLE, emergency nurse; b. Bryan, Tex., Feb. 4, 1953; d. Kathryn MacLean Noble; m. Alan Jones. ADN with honors, North Shore Community Coll., Beverly, Mass., 1982. RN, Mass., Calif.; CEN, cert. trauma nurse, mobile intensive care nurse. Med.-surg. nurse Salem (Mass.) Hosp., 1982-86; emergency nurse Beverly Hosp., 1986-90; neurol. nurse Mass. Gen. Hosp., Boston, 1990-91; emergency nurse Level I Trauma Ctr. Valley Med. Ctr., Fresno, Calif., 1991-93, Petaluma Valley, 1993-96, 98—, Sonoma Valley, 1993—, San Francisco Gen. Hosp., 1997—; med. advisor Human Rights Com. Bass River, Beverly, 1983-84; adj. faculty paramedic edn. Northeastern U., Boston, 1989-90. Educator Project RAP, Unit Against Sexual Assault, Beverly, 1988-90; EMT educator North Shore Ambulance, Salem, 1989; educator Emergency Nurses Care Program, Mass., 1987. Mem. Emergency Nurses Assn. (sec. Mariner chpt. 1989-90), Sonoma County Bar Assn, Alpaca Owners Breeders Assn. (citizen ambassador del. emergency medicine 1990, 93). Avocations: photography, travel, forensics, medical legal issues, alpacas.

JONES, DONNA MARILYN, real estate broker, legislator; b. Brush, Colo., Jan. 14, 1939; d. Virgil Dale and Margaret Elizabeth (McDaniel) Wolfe; m. Donald Eugene Jones, June 9, 1956; children: Dawn Richter, Lisa Shira, Stuart. Student, Treasure Valley Community Coll., 1981-82; grad., Realtors Inst. Cert. residential specialist. Co-owner Parts, Inc., Payette, Idaho, 1967-79; dept. mgr., buyer Lloyd's Dept. Store, Payette, Idaho, 1979-80; sales assoc. Idaho-Oreg. Realty, Payette, Idaho, 1981-82; mem. dist. 13 Idaho Ho. of Reps., Boise, 1987-90, mem. dist. 10, 1990-94, mem. dist. 9, 1995-98; assoc. broker Classic Properties Inc., Payette, 1983-91; owner, broker ERA Preferred Properties Inc., 1991-98; mem. dist. 9 Idaho Ho. of Reps., 1992-98. Co-chmn. Apple Blossom Parade, 1982; mem. Payette Civic League, 1968-84, pres. 1972; mem. Payette County Planning and Zoning Commn., 1985-88, vice-chmn. 1987; field coordinator Idaho Rep. Party Second Congl. Dist., 1986; mem. Payette County Rep. Cen. Com. 1978—; precinct II com. person, 1978-79, state committeewoman, 1980-84, chmn. 1984-87; outstanding county chmn. region III Idaho Rep. Party Regional Hall of Fame, 1985-86; mem. Payette County Rep. Women's Fedn., 1988—, bd. dirs., 1990-92; mem. Idaho Hispanic Commn., 1989-92, Idaho State Permanent Bldg. Adv. Coun., 1990-98; bd. dirs. Payette Edn. Found., 1993-96, Western Treasure Valley Cultural Ctr., 1993-96; nat. bd. dirs. Am. Legis. Exchange Coun., 1993-98; mem. legis. adv. coun. Idaho Housing Agy., 1992-97; committeeperson Payette County Cen.; chmn. Ways and Means Idaho House of Reps., 1993-97, House Revenue & Taxation Com., 1997-98; mem. Multi-State Tax Compact, 1997-98; Idaho chmn. Am. Legis. Exchange Coun., 1991-95; exec. dir. Idaho Real Estate Commn., 1998—. Recipient White Rose award Idaho March of Dimes, 1988; named Payette/Washington County Realtor of Yr., 1987. Mem. Idaho Assn. Realtors (legis. com. 1984-87, chmn. 1986, realtors active in politics com. 1982-98, polit. action com. 1986, polit. affairs com. 1986-88, chmn. 1987, bd. dirs. 1984-88), Payette/Washington County Bd. Realtors (v.p. 1981, state dir. 1984-88, bd. dirs 1983-88, sec. 1983), Bus. and Profl. Women (Woman of Progress award 1988, 90, treas. 1988), Payette C. of C., Fruitland C. of C., Wiesr C. of C.. Republican. Avocations: reading, interior decoration. Home: 1911 1st Ave S Payette ID 83661-3003 Office: Idaho Real Estate Commn 633 N 4th St Boise ID 83720-0077

JONES, DOROTHY F., judge; b. Sept. 3, 1946; d. Birl Floyd Madden and Aszie (Brown) Madden Simpson; m. Raymond Wilkerson (div. Jan. 1972); 1 child, Vicky; m. Allen J. Jones, Aug. 15, 1987 (dec. Aug. 1997); 1 stepchild, Felicia. BA, DePaul U., 1974, JD, 1979. Bar: Ill. 1979, U.S. Dist. Ct. (no. dist.) Ill. 1980, U.S. Supreme Ct. 1983. Acct. Allied Radio, Chgo., 1962-68, Atlantic Richfield, Chgo., 1968-72; tchr. Chgo. Pub. Schs., 1974-80; asst. pub. defender Cook County Pub. Defender's Office, Chgo., 1980-92; elected cir. judge Daley Ctr. Cir. Ct. Cook County, Chgo., 1992—, retained, 1998; legal adviser 28th Ward alderman, Chgo., 1982-83. Chmn. prin.'s com. Suder Sch., Chgo., 1978, rec. sec. cmty. coun., 1979; adviser Westside People for Progress, Chgo., 1982; bd. dirs. Chgo. Youth Ctrs.; founder Concerned Citizens, Mother's House. Recipient certs. merit Clemente H.S. Bilingual Dept., Chgo., 1979, Kinsey Elem. Sch., Chgo., 1980, Kennedy H.S., Chgo., 1980. Mem. ABA, Ill. State Bar Assn., Chgo. Bar Assn., Cook County Bar Assn. (bd. dirs. 1982-84, rec. sec. young lawyers sect. 1982-83, Merit award 1982, cert. of appreciation 1998), Am. Arbitration Assn., Nat. Assn. Criminal Def. Attys., Ill. Judges Assn., Ill. Jud. Coun., Austin Cmty. Club, Mix Bowling League. Democrat. Methodist. Home: 133 S Waller Ave Chicago IL 60644-3948 Office: Richard J Daley Ctr Cir Ct Cook County 50 W Washington St Chicago IL 60602-1305

JONES, DOROTHY JOANNE, social services professional; b. L.A.; d. Joseph Anthony and Florence (Chaffin) Ghiotto; divorced; children: Teri McKane, Carole Shroll, Christopher Jones. BA, La Verne U., 1980; MS, Calif. State U., Fullerton, 1983. Lic. marriage, family/child counselor. Dep. sheriff L.A. County Sheriff Office, 1972-76; dir. A.I.C., L.A., 1976-80; mgr. McDonnell Douglas, Long Beach, Calif., 1980-93; pvt. practice Los Alamitos, Calif., 1985—; cons. L.A. County, 1993-94. Author: When to SayNo, 1983; contbr. poems to lit. publs. Mem. Ctr. for Performing Arts, L.A., 1976&, Transpacific Mgmt., Long Beach, 1982-83. Recipient Spl. Svc. award Assn. Labor and Mgmt., Orange County, Calif., 1983. mem. Employee Assistance Profls. Assn. (pres. 1980-82), Alcoholism Info. Ctr. (v.p. 1980-91), Counseling Assocs. (v.p. 1976-83), Calif. Assn. Marriage and Family Tehrapists (cons. Los Angeles County 1993—). Democrat. Episcopalian. Avocations: dancing, swimming, sailing.

JONES, DOROTHY VINCENT, diplomatic historian; b. Washington, Dec. 14, 1927; d. Guy Morgan and Margaret Hildora (Magnusen) Vincent; m. Robert R. Jones, Sept. 3, 1947; children: Daniel R., Mark A. BA, Washburn Mcpl. U., 1949; MA, U. Mo.-Columbia, 1971; PhD, U. Chgo., 1979. Past mem. staff Belleville (Kas.) Telescope, stringer, 1950-51; past co-publisher Lebanon (Kas.) Times, stringer, 1952-55; stringer Shorewood (Wis.) Herald, 1963-67; ind. scholar, 1979—; curator 2 exhibits U. Chgo. Libr., 1982-85; vis. scholar U. Chgo., 1986-91; scholar-in-residence The Newberry Libr., Chgo., 1986—; assoc. history dept. Northwestern U., Evanston, Ill., 1991—; cons. to editors of Peace/Mir, Syracuse U. Press, 1992; cons. Peace Task Force, Evang. Luth. Ch. in Am., 1992; mem. editl. adv. bd. for Ethics & Internat. Affairs, N.Y., 1993—; bd. trustees Carnegie Coun. on Ethics & Internat. Affairs, 1996—. Author: Code of Peace, 1991 (Gelber award 1991), Splendid Encounters, 1984, License for Empire, 1982; co-author: Traditions of International Ethics, 1992, On Cultural Ground, 1994, Ethics and Statecraft, 1995, The Dumbarton Oaks Conversations and the United Nations, 1998; contbr. articles to profl. jours. Recipient Saxton fellowship Harper Pub., 1961-62, Excellence in Writing award Western History Assn., 1970, Grad. fellowship U. Chgo., 1972-73, MacArthur fellowship MacArthur Found., 1986-88. Democrat. Baptist. Avocation: gardening. Home and Office: 1213 Main St Evanston IL 60202-1650

JONES, DOUG, travelog producer; b. Kansas City, Kans., June 25, 1948; s. Harold Paul and Edith Maxine (Ellis) J. BA, U. Mo., Kansas City, 1970. Owner Internat. Travel Films, L.A., 1968—. Producer feature travel films, videos including Great Alaska Cruise, Great World The Great Canadian Train Ride (over 1,000,000 copies sold), Cruise of Queen Elizabeth 2, Portraits of the Great Far East, Great Cities of Europe, Queen Elizabeth 2 Sails New Zealand and Australia, Portraits of America-The National Parks, San Francisco-The City at the End of the Rainbow, The Hawaiian Adventure, Magic of Venice, Royal London; host syndicated show The Travel Show with Doug Jones; 39 lectr. appearances Nat. Geog. Soc. Mem. Internat. Lectr. and Motion Picture Assn. (pres. 1986-87), Internat. Travel Adventure Film Guild (pres. 1984-85), Soc. Am. Travel Writers. Democrat. Avocations: boating, flying, theatre. Office: Internat Travel Films PO Box 39402 Los Angeles CA 90039-0402

JONES, DOUGLAS EPPS, natural history museum director; b. Tuscaloosa, Ala., May 28, 1930; s. Walter Bryan and Hazel Lucile (Phelps) J.; m. Bonnie A. Cook, June 4, 1955; children: Susan, Elizabeth, Walter B. II. BS in Geology, U. Ala., 1952; MS in Geology, La. State U., 1956, PhD in Geology, 1959. Research geologist La. Geol. Survey, Baton Rouge, 1954-58; asst. prof. geology U. Ala., Tuscaloosa, 1958-61, assoc. prof., 1961-66, prof., 1966-98, dean Coll. Arts & Scis., 1968-84, dean univ. libraries, 1984-86, acad. v.p., 1988-90; dir. Ala. Mus. Natural History U. Ala. Mus., Tuscaloosa, 1986-98, ret. Served to 1st lt. U.S. Army, 1952-54. Mem. Kiwanis, Sigma Xi. Presbyterian. Avocations: antique gun collecting, hunting, fishing. Home: 823 Overlook Rd N Tuscaloosa AL 35406-2120*

JONES, DOUGLAS GORDON, retired literature educator; b. Bancroft, Ont., Can., Jan. 1, 1929; s. Gordon Wilfred and Arlene (Ford) J.; m. Betty Jane Kimbark, Sept. 23, 1950 (div.); children: Stephen, Skyler, Tory Joanne, North; m. Monique Baril, Dec. 1, 1976; 1 stepson, Nicolas Grandmangin. BA in English, McGill U., 1952; MA in English, Queen's U., 1954; DLitt (hon.), Guelph U., 1982. Instr. Royal Milit. Coll., Kingston, Ont., 1954-55, Ont. Agrl. Coll., Guelph, 1955-61, Bishop's U., Lennoxville, 1961-63; prof. dept. letters and comm. U. Sherbrooke, Que., Can., 1963-94; vis. prof. U. Victoria, B.C., 1978, U. Canadienne en France, Villefranche-sur-Mer, 1987; mem. arts adv. panel, juries Can. Coun. Author: (poetry) Frost on the Sun, 1957, The Sun is Axeman, 1961, Phrases from Orpheus, 1967, Under the Thunder the Flowers Light Up the Earth, 1977 (Gov. Gen. award for poetry 1977, A.J.M. Smith award for poetry 1977), A Throw Particles: New and Selected Poems, 1983, Balthazar and Other Poems, 1988 (QSPELL prize for poetry 1989), A Thousand Hooded Eyes, 1991, The Floating Garden, 1995 (QSPELL prize for poetry 1995), Wild Asterisks in Cloud, 1997; translator The Terror of the Snows: Selected Poems of Paul-Marie Lapointe, 1976, The Fifth Season: Poems by Paul Marie Lapointe, 1985, Normand de Bellefeville Categorics, One, Two & Three, 1993 (Gov. Gen. award for translation 1993), Emile Martel, For Orchestra and Solo Poet, 1996; editor, contbg. translator: The March to Love: Selected Poems of Gaston Miron, 1986, Esprit de Corps: Quebec Poetry of the Late Twentieth Century in Translation, 1997; founding editor, mem. editl. adv. bd. Ellipse; contbr. articles to profl. jours. Mem. Assn. for Can. and Que. Lits., Royal Soc. Can., League Canadian Poets. Home: 120 Houghton St Box 356, North Hatley, PQ Canada J0B 2C0 Office: PO Box 356, North Hatley, PQ Canada J0B 2C0

JONES, DOUGLAS RAYMOND, farming executive, state legislator; b. Twin Falls, Idaho, Mar. 24, 1949; s. Leslie Raymond and Charlotte Jones; m. Mary Elizabeth Morris, June 11, 1972; children: Jennifer, Heather, Douglas Jr. BS in Agr., U. Idaho, 1972. V.p. Leslie R. Jones, Inc., Twin Falls, 1972-86, pres., 1986—; rep. Idaho Ho. of Reps., Boise, 1985—, chmn. agrl. affairs com., 1997—; chmn. edn. com. Nat. Conf. State Legislators, 1994-95, mem. exec. com., 1995—. Mem. Gov.'s Task Force on Agr., Boise, 1979-80; mem. exec. com. Agrl. Cons. Coun., U. Idaho, Moscow, 1984-96; pres. Twin Falls County Farm Bur., 1980-82; bd. dirs. young farmers Idaho Farm Bur., Boise, 1978-80; troop fin. chmn. Boy Scouts Am., Twin Falls, 1972-94; v.p. Twin Falls Zoning and Planning Bd., 1984-85; mem. Nat. Edn. Goals Panel, 1994—; mem. adv. bd. for standards for excellence in edn. project Coun. for Basic Edn., 1995-97. Recipient Golden Apple award Idaho Edn. Assn., 1988, Terry Reilly Dedication to Young Children with Disabilities award Assn. for Early Childhood Learning, 1989, Friends of Coops. award, Idaho Coop. Coun., 1992. Mem. Twin Falls C. of C. (chmn. agrl. com. 1982-85), Rotary (Blue Lakes chpt.), Alpha Zeta. Republican. Avocation: private pilot. Office: Leslie R Jones Inc 3653 Highway 93 Twin Falls ID 83301-0237*

JONES, DOUGLAS W., lawyer; b. Fort Lauderdale, Fla., 1948. AB, Princeton U., 1970; JD, Harvard U., 1973. Bar: N.Y. 1974. Mem. Milbank, Tweed, Hadley & McCloy LLP, N.Y.C. Mem. ABA, Assn. of the Bar of the City of N.Y. Office: Milbank Tweed Hadley & McCloy LLP 1 Chase Manhattan Plz New York NY 10005-1413

JONES, E. STEWART, JR., lawyer; b. Troy, N.Y., Dec. 4, 1941; s. E. Stewart and Louise (Farley) J.; m. Constance M., Dec. 28, 1968; children: Christopher, Brady, Erin. BA, Williams Coll., 1963; JD, Albany Law Sch., 1966. Bar: N.Y. 1966, U.S. Dist. Ct. (no. dist.) N.Y. 1966, U.S. Dist. Ct. (so. and ea. dist.) N.Y. 1994, U.S. Dist. Ct. (we. dist.) N.Y. 1987, U.S. Claims Ct. 1991, U.S. Ct. Appeals (2d cir.) 1976, U.S. Supreme Ct. 1976. Asst. dist. atty. Rensselaer County (N.Y.), 1968-70, spl. prosecutor, 1974; ptnr. E. Stewart Jones, Troy, 1974—; lectr. in field; mem. com. on profl. standards of 3d jud. dept. State of N.Y., 1977-80, mem. 3d jud. screening com., Albany County; mem. merit selection panel for selection and appointment of U.S. magistrate for No. Dist. N.Y., 1981, 91; bd. dirs. Univ. Found. at Albany, trustee Troy Savs. Bank. Contbr. numerous articles to profl. jours. Trustee The Albany Acad., Albany Law Sch.; active Nat. Alumni Coun. Albany Law Sch. With USNG. Fellow Am. Bar Found., Am. Inns Ct., Internat. Acad. Trial Lawyers, Am. Bd. Criminal Trial Lawyers (Upstate N.Y. chmn. 1998—), Am. Coll. Trial Lawyers, Inner Circle of Advs., Am. Bd. Profl. Liability Attys. (diplomate), Internat. Soc. Barristers (chmn. upstate N.Y. 1998—); mem. N.Y. State Bar Assn. (Outstanding Practitioner award 1980, mem. exec. com. of criminal justice sect. 1977-90, mem. exec. com. trial lawyers sect. 1981-94, mem. spl. com. med. malpractice, other coms.), N.Y. State Trial Lawyers Assn. (bd. dirs. 1982-91, dir. emeritus 1991), Capital Dist. Trial Lawyers Assn. (bd. dir. 1973-76), ABA (numerous coms.) Calif. Attys. for Criminal Justice, Practising Law Inst., Am. Judicature Soc. (sustaining), Rensselaer County Bar Assn., Am. Soc. Law and Medicine, Albany County Bar Assn., N.Y. State Defenders Assn., Am. Arbitration Assn. (nat. panel of arbitrators), Dispute Resolutions, Inc. (nat. panel of arbitrators), Fed. Bar Coun., Upstate Trial Attys. Assn., Inc., Nat. Bd. Trial Advocacy (diplomate), Nat. Assn. Criminal Def. Lawyers, N.Y. State Assn. Criminal Def. Lawyers, Am. Bd. Trial Advocates (advocate), Inst. for Injury Reduction (founder), Trial Lawyers for Pub. Justice (founder), Civil Justice Found. (founding sponsor), Schuyler Meadows Club, Troy Country Club, Troy Club, Steuben Athletic Club, Ft. Orange Club, Stone Horse Yacht Club (Harwich Port, Mass.), Equinox Country Club (Manchester, Vt.), Williams Club (N.Y.C.). Home: 46 Schuyler Rd Loudonville NY 12211-1447 Office: 28 2nd St Troy NY 12181-3986

JONES, E. THOMAS, lawyer; b. Buffalo, July 19, 1950; s. Thomas Kenneth and Marian Arlene (Turk) J.; m. Jennifer Dee Lowery, Oct. 19, 1974; children: Evan Thomas III, Courtney Bree. BA, SUNY, Buffalo, 1972; JD, Cleve. State U., 1981. Bar: N.Y. 1982, U.S. Dist. Ct. (we. dist.) N.Y. 1982, U.S. Ct. Appeals (2d cir.) 1987. Mem. mgmt. staff Marine Midland Bank, Buffalo, 1971-76, M&T Bank, Buffalo, 1976-78, 81-82, Nat. City Bank, Cleve., 1978-81; sole practice Buffalo, 1982—. Committeeman Amherst Rep. Party, N.Y., 1984—; fire fighter Getzville Fire Co., Inc., Amherst, 1988-91; town councilman, Amherst, 1990-91; coach, bd. dirs. Amherst Youth Hockey Assn.; dep. town atty. Town Amherst, N.Y., 1996—. Mem. ABA, Erie County Bar Assn. Home: 1375 N French Rd Amherst NY 14228

JONES, EDDIE J., professional football team executive. Pres., COO Miami Dolphins, Fla. Office: Miami Dolphins 7500 SW 30th St Davie FL 33329-1020*

JONES, EDITH HOLLAN, judge; b. Phila., Apr. 7, 1949; BA, Cornell U., 1971; JD with honors, U. Tex., 1974. Bar: Tex. 1974, U.S. Supreme Ct. 1979, U.S. Ct. Appeals (5th and 11th cirs.), U.S. Dist. Ct. (so. and no. dists.) Tex. Assoc. Andrews & Kurth, Houston, 1974-82, ptnr., 1982-85; judge U.S. Ct. Appeals (5th cir.), Houston, 1985—. Gen. counsel Rep. Party of Tex., 1981-83. Mem. ABA, State Bar Tex. Presbyterian. Office: US Ct Appeals Bob Casey US Courthouse 515 Rusk Ave Rm 12505 Houston TX 77002*

JONES, EDITH IRBY, physician; b. Conway, Ark., Dec. 23, 1927; d. Robert and Mattie (Buice) Irby; m. James Beauregard Jones, Apr. 16, 1960 (dec. Oct. 1989); children: Gary, Myra, Keith. BS, Knoxville Coll., 1948; MD, U. Ark., 1952. Intern Univ. Hosp., Little Rock, Ark., 1952-53; gen. practice medicine Hot Springs, Ark., 1953-59; resident in internal medicine Baylor Coll. Medicine, Houston, 1959-62; practice medicine specializing in internal medicine Houston, 1962—; mem. staff Meth. Hosp., Houston, Hermann Hosp., Houston, Riverside Gen. Hosp., Houston, St. Elizabeth Hosp., Houston, St. Anthony Ctr., Houston, St. Joseph Hosp., Houston, Thomas Care Ctr., Houston; mem. staff Town Park, Houston, chief of staff; clin. asst. prof. medicine Baylor Coll. Medicine, U. Tex. Sch. Medicine, Houston; dir. Prospect Med. Lab.; bd. dirs., sec. Mercy Hosp. Comprehensive Health Care Group; ptnr. Jones, Coleman and Whitfield; grand med. examiner Ct. Calanthe Jurisdiction, Tex.; cons. Social Security Agy., Tex. Pub. Welfare Dept., Vocat. Rehab. Assn., Tex. Rehab. Commn.; bd. dirs. Standard Savs. Assn., Houston; numerous others. Contbr. articles to profl. jours. Bd. dirs. Houston Internat. U., Drug Addiction Rehab. Enterprise, March of Dimes, Houston, Odessey House, Houston; mem. adv. bd. Houston Council on Alcoholism; mem. com. for revising justice code, Harris County, Tex.; chmn. bd. trustees Knoxville Coll.; impartial hearing officer Houston Ind. Sch. Dist.; trustee Mut. Assn. for Profl. Service; mem. Community Welfare Planning Assn., Friends of Youth, Human Services Adv. Council, Houston; mem. bd. visitors U. Houston; numerous others. First black to receive BS and MD degrees from U. Ark; Dr. Edith Irby Jones Day proclaimed by State of Ark., 1985, City of Little Rock, 1985, City of N.Y.C., 1986; named One of 30 Most Influential Black Women Houston, 1984; inducted into Tex. Black Women's Hall of Fame, 1986; commended by Calif. Senate, 1969; proclaimation by city council, Houston, 1985, Mayor of Houston, 1986; recipient cert. of citation Ho. of Reps. State of Tex., 1986; portrait placed in entrance hall U. Ark. for Med. Scis., 1985; numerous others. Mem. AMA, Am. Med. Women's Assn. (v.p. Houston chpt.), Nat. Med. Assn. (past pres.), Lone Star Med. Assn., Harris County Med. Assn., Houston Med. Forum, Tex. Assn. Disability Examiners, Bus. and Profl. Women, Nat. Council of Negro Women, Inc. (v.p. Dorothy Height chpt.), NAACP, PTA, YMCA, Alpha Kappa Mu, Delta Sigma Theta, Eta Phi Beta. Democrat. Clubs: Links, Inc., Top Ladies of Distinction, Girl Friends, Inc., Women of Achievement, Inc. (Hall of Fame 1985). Lodge: Order Eastern Star. Avocations: travel, walking, swimming. Home: PO Box 14207 Houston TX 77221-4207 Office: 2601 Prospect St Houston TX 77004-7737

JONES, EDWARD, physician, pathologist; b. Wellington, Kans., Mar. 21, 1935; s. Thomas S. and Grace M. (Sydebotham) Imel; m. Barbara A. Blount, Aug. 30, 1956; children—Kimberly Riegel, Sheila, Matt, Tom. A.B. in Chemistry, U. Kans., 1957, M.D., 1961. Diplomate Am. Bd. Anatomic Clin. Pathology. Intern St. Francis Hosp., Wichita, Kans., 1951-62; sr. asst. USPHS, Yuma, Ariz., 1962-64; gen. practice, medicine Lawrence Meml. Hosp., Kans., 1964-65; resident in pathology St. Luke's Hosp., Kansas City, Mo., 1965-69; pathologist Central Kans. Med. Ctr., Great Bend, 1969—; physician cons. Hoisington Luth. Hosp., Kans., 1969—, St. Joseph's Meml. Hosp., Larned, Kans., 1969—, Edwards County Hosp., Kinsley, Kans., 1969—; dir. Central Kans. Med. Center, Great Bend, 1974-76, pres., 1976-78. Bd. dirs. Cedar Park Place, Great Bend, 1980-88. Fellow Coll. Am. Pathologists (del., foreman 1978-87), Am. Soc. Clin. Pathologists; mem. Kans. Soc. Pathologists (pres. 1980-81). Republican. Congregationalist. Club: Great Bend Community Theater. Avocations: theater, musical theater. Home: 3208 Broadway St Great Bend KS 67530-3716 Office: Cen Kans Med Ctr 3515 Broadway Ave Great Bend KS 67530-3633

JONES, EDWARD GEORGE, neuroscience professor, department chairman; b. Upper Hutt, Wellington, N.Z., Mar. 26, 1939; came to U.S., 1972; s. Frank Ian and Theresa Agnes (Riordan) J.; m. Elizabeth Suzanne Oldham, Apr. 27, 1963; children: Philippa Emilie, Christopher Edward. MD, U. Otago, Dunedin, N.Z., 1962; PhD, U. of Oxford, Eng., 1968. Med. and surg. intern Tauranga Hosp., New Zealand, 1963; demonstrator to assoc. prof. dept. anatomy U. Otago Med. Sch., Dunedin, New Zealand, 1964-72; Nuffield Dominions demonstrator and lectr. Balliol Coll., U. of Oxford, Eng., 1964-72; assoc. prof. to prof., dept. anatomy and neurobiology Washington U. Sch. Medicine, St. Louis, 1972-84, George H. and Ethel Ronzini Bishop scholar, 1981-84, dir. div. exptl. neurology, 1981-84; prof. and chmn. dept. anatomy and neurobiology U. Calif., Irvine, 1984-98; dir. Ctr. Neurosci. U. Calif., Davis, 1998—; cons. NIH, 1972—; dir. Neural Systems Lab., Frontier Rsch. Program in Neural Mechanisms of Mind and Behavior, Riken, Japan, 1988-96; vis. sr. rsch. fellow St. John's Coll. at U. Oxford, Eng., 1989-90. Author: The Thalamus, 1984; co-author: The Thalamus and Basal Telencephalon, 1982; co-editor: (book series) Cerebral Cortex, 1984—; author, reviewer numerous sci. and hist. articles, chpts. in books, 1964—. Mem. Pres.'s Adv. Bd. Calif. State U., Long Beach, 1986-90. Recipient Rolleston Meml. prize U. Oxford, 1970; rsch. grantee NIH, 1971—; named one of 1000 most cited biol. scientists, Sci. Citation Index, 1982. Mem. Soc. for Neurosci. (com. chair 1978-81, 88-89, pres.-elect 1997-98, pres. 1998-99), Am. Assn. Anatomists (Cajal medal 1989), AAAS, Anat. Soc. Great Britain and Ireland (Symington Meml. prize 1968). Democrat. Avocations: reading, writing, carpentry. Office: U Calif Ctr Neurosci 1544 Newton Ct Davis CA 95616

JONES, EDWARD LOUIS, historian, educator; b. Georgetown, Tex., Jan. 15, 1922; s. Henry Horace and Elizabeth (Steen) J.; m. Dorothy M. Showers, Mar. 1, 1952 (div. Sept. 1963); children: Cynthia, Frances, Edward Lawrence; Lynne Ann McGreevy, Oct. 7, 1963; children Christopher Louis, Teresa Lynne. BA in Philosophy, U. Wash., 1952, BA in Far East, 1952, BA in Speech, 1955, postgrad., 1952-54; JD, Gonzaga U., 1967. Social worker Los Angeles Pub. Assistance, 1956-57; producer, dir. Little Theatre, Hollywood, Calif. and Seattle, 1956-60; research analyst, cons. to Office of Atty. Gen., Olympia and Seattle, Wash., 1963-66; coordinator of counseling SOIC, Seattle, 1966-68; lectr., advisor, asst. to dean U. Wash., Seattle, 1968—; instr. Gonzaga U., Spokane, Wash., 1961-62, Seattle Community Coll., 1967-68; dir. drama workshop, Driftwood Players, Edmonds, Wash., 1975-76. Author: The Black Diaspora: Colonization of Colored People, 1988, Tutankhamon: Son of the Sun, King of Upper and Lower Egypt, 1978, Black Orators' Workbook, 1982, Black Zeus, 1972, Profiles in African Heritage, 1972, From Rulers of the World to Slavery, 1990, President Zachary Taylor and Senator Hamlin: Union or Death, 1991, Why Colored Americans Need an Abraham Lincoln in 1992, Forty Acres and a Mule: The Rape of Colored Americans, 1994; editor pub. NACADA Jour. Nat. Acad. Advising Assn., more. V.p. Wash. Com. on Consumer Interests, Seattle, 1966-68. Served to 2d lt. Fr. Army, 1940-45. Recipient Outstanding Teaching award U. Wash., 1986, Tyee Inst. Yr. U. Wash., 1987, appreciation award Office Minority Affairs, 1987, acad. excellence award Nat. Soc. Black Engrs., 1987, Appreciation award Fla. chpt. Nat. Bar Assn., 1990; Frederick Douglass scholar Nat. Coun. Black Studies, 1985, 86. Mem. Nat. Assn. Student

Personnel Adminstrs., Smithsonian Inst. (assoc.), Am. Acad. Polit. and Social Sci., Nat. Acad. Advising Assn. (bd. dirs. 1979-82, Cert. of Appreciation 1982, editor Jour. 1981—, award for Excellence 1985), Western Polit. Sci. Assn. Democrat. Baptist. Avocations: travel, research, chess. Office: Univ Wash Ethnic Cultural Ctr Seattle WA 98195

JONES, EDWIN CHANNING, JR., electrical engineering educator; b. Parkersburg, W.Va., June 27, 1934; s. Edwin Channing and Helen M. J.; m. Ruth Carol Miller, Aug. 14, 1960; children: Charles, Cathleen, Helene. BSEE, W.Va. U., 1955; Diploma, U. London, 1956; PhD, U. Ill., 1962. Lic. profl. engr., W.Va. Engr. GE, Syracuse, N.Y. and Bloomington, Ill., 1955, 62, Westinghouse Electric Co., Balt., 1959; asst. prof. elec. engring. U. Ill., Urbana, 1962-66; asst. prof. Iowa State U., Ames, 1966-67, assoc. prof., 1967-72, prof., 1972—, univ. prof., 1995—, assoc. chair dept., 1997; mem. Accreditation Bd. Engring. Tech., N.Y.C., 1984-87. Author handbook chpts. on electronic engring. Served as lt. U.S. Army, 1956-58. Recipient Faculty citation Iowa State U., Ames, 1986. Fellow AAAS, IEEE (pres. edn. soc. 1975-76, mem. ednl. activities bd. 1975-76, 78-81, 84-87, accreditation activity award), Am. Soc. Engring. Edn.; mem. Soc. History of Tech., Sigma Xi, Tau Beta Pi, Eta Kappa Nu, Phi Kappa Phi, Phi Beta Delta. Avocations: photography, slide rule collecting. Home: 111 Hunziker Cir Ames IA 50010-5022 Office: Iowa State U 2210 Coover Hall Ames IA 50011

JONES, EDWIN MICHAEL, lawyer, former insurance company executive; b. Bridgeport, Conn., May 15, 1916; s. Edward Henry and Mary Ellen (Carroll) J.; m. Alberta Irene Conway, Aug. 21, 1948; children: Michele, Karen, Alberta, Edwin, Marianne. B.A., Yale U., 1937; LL.B., NYU, 1942, LL.M. in Taxation, 1951. Bar: N.Y. 1943, Conn. 1947, U.S. Supreme Ct. 1959. Security analyst Goodbody & Co., N.Y.C., 1937-42; economist War Prodn. Bd., Washington, 1942-43; assoc. firm Root, Ballantine, Harlan, Bushby & Palmer, N.Y.C., 1946-48; pvt. practice N.Y.C., 1948-52; pres., dir. Talisman Corp., N.Y.C., 1952—; atty., officer N.Y. Life Ins. Co., N.Y.C., 1952-72; ptnr. firm Shea & Gould, N.Y.C., 1972-81, Lane & Mittendorf, N.Y.C., 1981-82; exec. dir. Pension Benefit Guaranty Corp., Washington, 1982-84; of counsel Finley, Kumble, Wagner et al, N.Y.C., 1984-88; prin. Bentley, Mosher, Babson & Lambert, P.C., Stamford and Greenwich, Conn., 1988-93, of counsel, 1994—; mem. adv. coun. on employee welfare and pension benefits U.S. Sec. Labor, Washington, 1991-93; pres., trustee Nat. Ctr. for Automated Info. Retrieval, N.Y.C., 1972-83. Contbr. articles to profl. jours. Mem. Adv. Council of Non-Pub. Sch. Secular Edn., Conn., 1971-72; pres. Fairfield (Conn.) Found. of Diocese of Bridgeport, 1973-86, bd. dirs. 1973— . Served to maj. USAAF, 1943-46. Decorated Army Commendation medal. Mem. ABA (chmn. ins. com. 1960-82, employee benefits com. tax sect. 1976-82), N.Y. State Bar Assn. (chmn. tax sect. 1966-67, govt. practice com. lawyers and accts. 1972-87), Assn. Bar City N.Y. (employee benefits com. 1988-92), Assn. Life Ins. Counsel, Yale Club (N.Y.C.), Belle Haven Yacht Club (vice commodore, bd. dirs. 1970-75). Roman Catholic. Office: Bentley Mosher Babson & Lambert PC 321 Railroad Ave Greenwich CT 06830

JONES, ELAINE HANCOCK, humanities educator; b. Niagara Falls, N.Y., Feb. 17, 1946; d. Roy Elmer and June Edna (Clark) Hancock; m. Ralph Jones III, Oct. 9, 1971 (div. June 1981). AAS in Comml. Design, U. Buffalo, 1962; BFA, SUNY, Buffalo, 1971, MFA in Painting, 1975; postgrad., Fla. State U., 1993—. Med. illustrator Roswell Park Meml. Inst., Buffalo, 1967-70; designer, animator Acad. McLarty Film Prodns., Buffalo, 1970-73; publs. designer Buffalo/Erie County Hist. Soc., 1974-78; dir. publs. Daemen Coll., Amherst, N.Y., 1978-80; owner, art dir. Plop Art Prodns., Melbourne, Fla., 1981-86; instr. humanities Brevard C.C., Melbourne, 1986—; prof. humanities Brevard campus Rollins Coll., Melbourne, 1995—. One-woman shows include SUNY, Buffalo, 1974, Upton Gallery, N.Y., 1975, Gallery Wilde, Buffalo, 1978; exhibited in group shows at Fredonia Coll., N.Y., 1975, Upton Gallery, 1975, Brevard Art Mus., Melbourne, Fla., 1987. Mem. docent program Art Mus./Sci. Ctr., Melbourne, 1983-84, mem. edn. com., 1995—; officer Platinum Coast chpt. Sweet Adelines Internat., 1984-90. Nat. Merit scholar, 1971-75; recipient cert. of merit Curtis Paper Co., 1977; N.Y. State Coun. on Arts grantee, 1975. Republican. Home: 2240 Sea Ave Indialantic FL 32903-2524 Office: Brevard CC Liberal Arts Dept 3865 N Wickham Rd Melbourne FL 32935-2310

JONES, ELAINE R., civil rights advocate; b. Norfolk, Va., Mar. 2, 1944. AB, Howard U., 1965; LLB, U. Va., 1970. Pres., dir.-counsel, atty. NAACP Legal Def. and Ednl. Fund, Washington; mem. panel arbitration Am. Stock Exch. Recipient Recognition award Black Am. Law Student Assn, 1974, Spl. Achievement award Nat. Assn. Black Women Attys., 1975. Mem. Nat. Bar Assn., Internat. Fedn. Women Lawyers, Old Dominion Bar Assn., Va. trial Lawyers Assn., Delta Sigma Theta. Office: NAACP Legal Defense & Ednl Fund 99 Hudson St Fl 16 New York NY 10013-2897*

JONES, ELIZABETH NORDWALL, county government official; b. Glendale, Calif., Sept. 1, 1934; d. Darrell Robert and Rosita (Hopps) Nordwall; m. William Maurice Jones, Jan. 28, 1956; children: Kevin Scott, Sigrid Elizabeth, Kimberly Anne. Student, DePauw U., 1952-54; BA, U. So. Calif., 1956; EdS, MA, U. Fla., 1975. Outreach librarian Santa Fe Regional Library, Gainesville, Fla., 1966-72; testing coordinator CETA Program, Gainesville, 1974-75; supr. Alachua County Crisis Ctr., Gainesville, 1975-79, dir., 1979-84; dir. Dept. Vol. Services, Gainesville, 1983-89, Dept. Human Svcs., Gainesville, 1989-91; Dept. Community Svcs., 1991-97; retired, 1997. Trustee Santa Fe Community Coll., Gainesville, 1974-85; mem. Fla. Adv. Council on Libraries, Talahassee, 1977-87; mem. State community Coll. Coordinating Bd., Tallahassee, 1983-84. Bd. dirs., pres. Friends of Five Pub. TV; pres. Girls Club of Alachua County, United Way of Alachua County; bd. dirs. North Ctrl. Fla. Health Planning Coun., Inc.; county ct. mediator. Mem. Am. Assn. Suicidology (nat. treas. 1983-85, nat. bd. dirs. 1985-87, nat. pres. 1987-88, nat. cert. examiner 1991-94), Fla. Assn. C.C. (past state bd. dirs.), Altrusa Internat. (pres. Gainesville chpt. 1983-84), LWV (past pres. Gainesville chpt.), Women's Forum Gainesville, Rotary (chpt. sec. 1994, bd. dirs. 1995), Leadership Fla. Class XIV, Alpha Chi Omega. Avocations: reading mysteries, camping, fishing. Home: 5915 NW 27th Ave Gainesville FL 32606-6440

JONES, ELIZABETH SELLE, minister; b. L.A., May 15, 1926; d. Raymond Martin Louis and Claire (Holley) Selle; m. James Latimer Jones, Dec. 22, 1945; children: Stephen, Nancy, David, Susan. BA, U. Calif., Santa Barbara, 1970; MDiv, Starr King Sch. for Ministry, Berkeley, Calif., 1980; DMin, San Francisco Theol. Sch., 1994. Ordained to ministry Unitarian Universalist Ch., 1980. Minister Unitarian Universalist Ch. in Livermore (Calif.), 1981-96, minister emerita, 1996—; trustee Starr King Sch. for the Ministry, Berkeley, 1989-97; del. gen. assembly Unitarian Universalist Assn. of Congregations, 1974-91. Pres. Glendale (Calif.) PTA, 1958-60. Mem. Unitarian Universalist Ministers Assn. (exec. com. 1987-89), Amnesty Internat., NOW, Greenpeace, Nat. Peace Inst., LWV, Habitat for Humanity, Neighbor to Neighbor, Planned Parenthood. Democrat.

JONES, ELIZABETH WINIFRED, biology educator; b. Seattle, Mar. 8, 1939; d. Kenneth Clifford Harris and Dorothea (Dowty) J. BS, U. Wash., 1960, PhD, 1964. Postdoctoral fellow MIT, Cambridge, 1964-67, instr. in biology, 1967-69; asst. prof. Case Western Res. U., Cleve., 1969-74; assoc. prof. Carnegie Mellon U., Pitts., 1974-82, prof., 1982--; vis. scientist Sch. Medicine Wash. U., 1981-82; adj. prof. in psychiatry U. Pitts., 1985—; mem. genetics tng. com. NIH, Bethesda, Md., 1972-73, mem. genetics study sect., 1976-80, 84-86, chair, 1990-93. Co-author: (with D.L. Hartl) Genetics: Principles and Analysis, 1998, (with D.L. Hartl) Essential Genetics, 1999; editor: Molecular Biology of the Yeast Saccaromyces, 2 vols., 1981, 82, Molecular and Cellular Biology of the Yeast Saccaromyces, 3 vols., 1991, 92, 97; assoc. editor Genetics, 1980-96, editor-in-chief 1997—; assoc. editor Yeast, 1984—, Ann. Rev. of Genetics, 1990—; mem. editl. bd. Molecular Biology of the Cell, 1992—. Recipient Rsch. Career Devel. award NIH, 1971-74, 75-77. Fellow AAAS; mem. Am. Soc. Microbiology, Am. Acad. of Microbiology, Am. Soc. Cell Biology (coun. 1992-95), Genetics Soc. Am. (pres. 1987), Am. Soc. Human Genetics. Office: Carnegie Mellon U 4400 5th Ave Pittsburgh PA 15213-2617

JONES, ELLEN CAROL, English educator; b. Columbus, Ohio, Jan. 22, 1952; d. Russell William and Harriet Elizabeth J.; m. Morris Beja, June 18, 1990. BA cum laude, Ohio State U., 1979, MA, 1980; MA, Cornell U., 1984, PhD, 1989. Asst. prof. English Purdue U., Lafayette, Ind., 1987-94, St. Louis U., 1994—; vis. scholar Willamette U., Portland, Oreg., 1992. Editor: The Politics of Modernism, Virginia Woolf, Feminist Readings of Joyce/Modern Fiction Studies, 1989, 92, Joyce: Feminism/Post/Colonialism/European Joyce Studies, 1998; co-editor: Feminism and Modern Fiction/Modern Fiction Studies, 1988; contbr. articles to spl. jours. and books. Mellon Found. grantee, 1995-98. Mem. MLA (del. 1990-92), Internat. James Joyce Found., Am. Conf. Irish Studies, Virginia Woolf Soc. Office: St Louis U Dept English 221 N Grand Blvd Saint Louis MO 63103-2006

JONES, EUGENE GORDON, pharmaceutical company executive; b. Lookout, W.Va., June 26, 1929; s. Alphus Raymond and Mona Blanche (Bobbitt) J.; m. Nancy Lee Hall, Aug. 19, 1951; children: Gene Douglas, Michael Gordon, Rebecca Lee, Jody Lynn. BS, Va. Tech. U., 1951. Med. rep. The Upjohn Co., Charlottesville, Va., 1956-60; profl. svcs. mgr. The Upjohn Co., Washington, 1960-63; sr. med. rep. The Upjohn Co., Roanoke, Va., 1963-68; hosp. med. rep. The Upjohn Co., Richmond, Va., 1968-70; dist. sales mgr. The Upjohn Co., Va., 1970-73; tng. specialist The Upjohn Co., Kalamazoo, Mich., 1973-76, tng. mgr., 1976-87, nat. tng. dir., 1987-90; pres. Global Meeting Planners, 1991—. Author: (self instrn. course) Managed Health Care, 1985, Arthritis Primer, 1976. Pres. Am. Diabetes Assn., Roanoke chpt., 1967, Richmond chpt., 1971, state del., 1970; bd. dirs. United Way, Kalamazoo, 1990, 91, Mich. Diabetes Assn., Detroit, 1979; deacon River Rd. Presbyn. Ch.; mem. Rep. Presdl. Task Force. Lt. U.S. Army, 1951-53, Korea, capt. USAR, 1953-60. Mem. VFW, Nat. Soc. Pharm. Sales Trainers (hon., pres. Western chpt. 1980-81, pres. nat. orgn. 1987-88, dir. 1985-90, founder newsletter 1987), Meeting Planners Internat., Internat. Meeting Planners, Mil. Order World Wars (treas. 1964-68), Kalamazoo Air History Mus., Charles Garfield Group (hon.), Korean War Vets. Assn. Avocations: volunteering, golf, reading, walking, travel. Home: 2828 Kalarama Rd Kalamazoo MI 49024-2321

JONES, EUINE FAY, architect, educator; b. Pine Bluff, Ark., Jan. 31, 1921; s. Euine Fay and Candie Louise (Alston) J.; m. Mary Elizabeth Knox, Jan. 6, 1943; children: Janis Fay, Jean Cameron. BArch, U. Ark., 1950; MArch, Rice U., 1951; DFA (hon.), Kans. State U., 1984; LHD (hon.), Drury Coll., 1985, Hendrix Coll., 1991; DHL (hon.), U. Ark., 1990, Lindsey Wilson Coll., 1997. Asst. prof. architecture U. Okla., 1951-53; Frank Lloyd Wright Taliesin fellow, 1953; prof. architecture U. Ark., 1953-88, chmn. dept., 1966-74, dean Sch. Architecture, 1974-76; pvt. practice architecture, 1953—; Rome Prize fellow in architecture and design, 1981; dean, u. prof. emeritus U. Ark., 1988. Served as lt., naval aviator USNR, 1942-45. Recipient nat. awards for archtl. design, Gold medal for distinction in archtl. design Tau Sigma Delta, 1984, Disting. Alumnus award U. Ark., 1982, Rice U., 1989; subject of book by Robert Ivy, Jr., AIA Press, 1992. Fellow AIA (Gold medal for Lifetime Achievement 1990); mem. Assn. Collegiate Schs. Architecture (Disting. Prof. award 1985), Soc. Archtl. Historians. Home: 1330 Hillcrest Ave Fayetteville AR 72703-1924

JONES, EVELYN GLORIA, medical technologist, educator; b. Roanoke, Va., Aug. 13, 1940; d. William Darnell and Elizabeth (Harris) Powell; m. Theodore Joseph Jones, Aug. 21, 1965. BS in Biology, Tenn. State U., 1973; cert. in med. tech., Vanderbilt U., 1974; MEd in Adminstrn. and Supervision, Tenn. State U., 1993. Cert. clin. lab. scientist Nat. Cert. Agy. Med. Lab Pers. Med. technologist Metro Gen. Hosp., Nashville, 1974-78, Vanderbilt Med. Ctr., Nashville, 1978-97; microbiologist Tenn. Dept. Health Lab. Svcs., Nashville, 1997—; tech. cons. Vanderbilt Point of Care Program, 1993-96; lectr. St. Thomas Program Med. Tech., Nashville, 1991-94, Tenn. State U./Meharry Med. Tech. Program, Nashville, 1991—. Bd. dirs. Tenn. Valley Region ARC Blood Svcs., 1996—; asst. sec. The Links, Inc., 1997—. Mem. AAAS, Am. Soc. Clin. Pathologist (assoc., cert. med. technologist), Phi Delta Kappa, Alpha Kappa Alpha. Roman Catholic. Home: 1003 Cross Bow Dr Hendersonville TN 37075-9403 Office: Tenn Dept Health Lab Svcs Dept Microbiology Nashville TN 37202

JONES, EVERETT RILEY, JR., oil company executive; b. Leitchfield, Ky., July 28, 1918; s. Everett Riley and Margie (Hatfield) J.; m. Lois Gibbins, July 15, 1950; children: Stacey Rae, Rande Leigh. Student, Spencerian C.C., 1936-37, U. Louisville, 1946-47. Lic. pub. acct., Ky. Sec. treas., dir. Lafitte Oil Corp., Louisville, 1947-49; ptnr. Fryer & Hanson Drilling Co., Dallas, 1950-58; pres., dir. Bengal Producing Co., Dallas, 1959—; dir. Dallas County Small Bus. Devel. Ctr., Inc. Trustee S.W. Engring. Found. Served to capt. USAAF, 1942-45. Decorated D.F.C., Air medal with 4 oak leaf clusters. Mem. Engrs. Club Dallas (past pres.) Dallas Petroleum Club (past pres.), Royal Air Force Club in London. Episcopalian. Home: 8002 Glen Albens Cir Dallas TX 75225-1822 Office: 8080 N Central Expy Dallas TX 75206-1838

JONES, FARRELL, judge; b. Chgo., May 6, 1926; s. Farrell and Kathryn (Crum) J.; BA, Lincoln U., 1950; JD, N.Y. U., 1957; m. Audrey E. Howard, June 16, 1951 (dec.); children—Joanne Kathryn and Jacqueline Elinor (twins). Social investigator N.Y.C. Dept. Social Svcs., 1957-58; Bar: N.Y., 1958. Asst. counsel Gov. Harriman's Com. to Rev. N.Y. State Parole System, 1958; field rep. N.Y. State Commn. for Human Rights, 1958-60, sr. field rep., 1960-61, regional dir. L.I. region, 1961-63; exec. dir. Nassau County (N.Y.) Commn. on Human Rights, 1963-70; dep. county exec. Nassau County, 1970-71; assoc. dir., clin. asst. prof. div. alcoholism and drug dependence State U. N.Y. Downstate Med. Ctr., 1971; 1st dep. adminstr. N.Y.C. Human Resources Adminstrn., 1971-74; asst. v.p. Blue Cross and Blue Shield Greater N.Y., 1974-88; sole practice, Port Washington, N.Y., 1988-90; judge adminstrv. law N.Y. State Workers Compensation Bd., 1990—; bd. dirs. Mental Health Assn. Nassau County, 1991—, Health Watch Info. & Promotion Svcs, Bklyn, N.Y. (nat.); cons. N.Y. State Dept. Edn. on Intergroup Rels.; cons. L.I. Sch. Dists.; pres. Sci. Mus. L.I., Plandome, N.Y., 1984—; bd. dirs. Am. Com. on Africa. Bd. dirs. Family Svc. Assn. Nassau County, N.Y.C. Comprehensive Health Planning Agy., 1971-74, Cow Bay Housing, Port Washington, 1975-85; chmn. Nassau County Econ. Opportunity Commn., 1971-72; pres. Nassau County Law Svcs. Com., 1969-71; bd. dirs. Health and Welfare Coun. of Nassau County, Nassau County Community Econ. Devel. Corp., Nassau Community Health Svcs. Found., 1966-69, Community Health Plan of Suffolk County, N.Y., 1981-86, chmn. labor com., 1981-86; mem. Nassau County Crime Coun., 1966-71; trustee Adelphi U., mem. adv. bd. Sch. Social Work, 1964—, chmn., 1970—; assoc. trustee North Shore Hosp., 1991—; trustee Port Washington Pub. Libr., 1976—, Urban League L.I., 1976—; mem. Nassau County Youth Bd., 1964-71; life mem., pres. North Shore Br. NAACP, 1983-87; mem. adv. coun. Hofstra U., 1967-72, v.p., 1971-72; pres. Levitt Found, 1994—. With AUS, 1951-53. Recipient Brotherhood award NCCJ, 1982. Mem. One Hundred Black Men (exec. bd. Nassau-Suffolk chpt. 1983-87), Nassau County Bar Assn., Alpha Phi Alpha. Unitarian. Address: 9 The Quarter Deck Port Washington NY 11050-1431

JONES, FERDINAND TAYLOR, JR., psychologist, educator; b. N.Y.C., May 15, 1932; s. Ferdinand Taylor and Esther (Haggie) J.; m. Antonina Laub, Sept. 26, 1953 (div. Mar. 1967); children: Joanne Esther, Terrie Lynn; m. Myra Jean Rogers, Nov. 25, 1967. AB, Drew U., 1953; PhD, U. Vienna, Austria, 1959. Staff psychologist Riverside Hosp., Bronx, N.Y., 1959-62; chief psychologist Westchester County Community Mental Hosp. Bd., White Plains, N.Y., 1962-67; tng. cons. Lincoln Hosp. Mental Health Services, Bronx, 1967-69; tchr. psychology Sarah Lawrence Coll., Bronxville, N.Y., 1968-72; prof. psychology Brown U., Providence, 1972-97, prof. emeritus, 1997, dir. psychol. svcs., 1972-1992; scholar-in-residence The Schomburg Ctr. for Rsch. in Black Culture, 1987; cons. St. Peter's Head Start, Yonkers, N.Y., 1967-71, Bronx State Hosp., 1969-72; vis. prof. U. Dar es Salaam, Tanzania, 1993, Oberlin Coll., 1997, 98, U. Cape Town, 1999. Bd. dirs. Am. Orthopsychiat. Assn., 1984-87. Served with AUS, 1953-56. Mem. Am. Psychol. Assn., Am. Orthopsychiat. Assn. (pres. 1989-90), Ea. Psychol. Assn., Westchester County Psychol. Assn. (past pres.), Assn. Black Psychologists, Soc. Psychol. Study Social Issues. Developed (with Myron W. Harris) small group method for reduction of distance and dissonance in interracial communication. Home: 30 Langham Rd Providence RI 02906-3548 Office: Brown U 79 Waterman St Providence RI 02912-9079 *Dedicated to channeling a lifelong fascination with people into skilled understanding of human behavior and the alleviation of problems in human functioning.*

JONES, FLETCHER, JR., automotive company executive. CEO Fletcher Jones Mgmt., Las Vegas, Nev., pres. Office: Fletcher Jones Mgmt 175 E Reno Ave Ste C-6 Las Vegas NV 89119-1102*

JONES, FLORENCE M., music educator; b. West Columbia, Tex., Apr. 11, 1939; d. Isaiah and Lu Ethel (Baldridge) McNeil; m. Waldo D. Jones, May 29, 1965; children: Ricky, Wanda, Erna. BS, Prairie View A&M U., 1961, MEd, 1968; postgrad., Rice U., 1988, U. Houston, 1980. Cert. tchr. elem. edn., math. Tchr. English and typing Lincoln High Sch., Port Arthur, Tex., 1961-62; tchr. grades three and four Houston Ind. Sch. Dist., 1963-90, tchr. gifted and talented, 1990-94; tchr. piano Windsor Village Liberal Arts Acad., Houston, 1994—; dist. tchr. trainer Houston Ind. Sch. Dist., 1985-90; shared decision mem. Sch. decision Making Team, 1993-94; coord. gifted/talented program, Petersen Elem. Sch., Houston, 1990-94; participant piano Recital Hartzog Studio, 1985-88; film previewer Houston Media Ctr. Curriculum writer Modules to Improve Science Teaching, 1985; author sci. pop-up book, 1980, gifted/talented program, 1994; contbr. poems to lit. jours. Youth camp counselor numerous non-denominational ch. camps, U.S., 1961-89; active restoration of Statue of Liberty, Ellis Island Found., N.Y.C., 1983-85; lay minister Ch. of God, 1961-94. Recipient Letter of Recognition for Outstanding Progress in Edn., Pres. Bill Clinton, 1994, Congresswoman Sheilia Jackson Lee, Tex. Gov. George Bush, State Rep. Harold V. Sutton Jr., Houston Mayor Bob Lanier, Tex. Gov. Ann Richards; Gold Cup/Highest Music award Hartzog Music Studio, 1987, Diamond Key award Nat. Women of Achievement, 1995, Editors Choice award Nat. Library Poetry, 1995, others. Mem. NEA, Houston Assn. Childhood Edn. (v.p. 1985-88), Assn. for Childhood Edn. (bd. dirs. 1979-91), Houston Zool. Soc., World Wildllife Fund, Nat. Storytelling Assn., Tejas Storytelling Assn. (life), Soc. Children's Book Writers and Illustrators, Nat. Audubon Soc., Am. Mus. Natural History, Tex. Ret. Tchrs. Assn. (life), Internat. Soc. Poets (disting. life mem.), others. Democrat. Avocations: writing, reading, storytelling, collecting sea shells, arts and crafts. Home: 3310 Dalmatian Dr Houston TX 77045-6520

JONES, FLORESTA D., English educator; b. Hopewell, Va., Dec. 24, 1950; d. William A. Sr. and Florine (Brown) Jones. BA, Berry Coll., 1972; MA, Mich. State U., 1975; doctoral student, Rutgers, The State U. Assoc. dir. ednl. opportunity program, instr. Georgian Court Coll., Lakewood, N.J.; co-dir. Learning Through Writing Project Brookdale C.C., Lincroft, N.J., prof. English; adj. faculty in modern langs. and history depts.; faculty coord. for Diversity across Curriculum; faculty participant N.J. Project on Inclusive Scholarship, Curriculum, and Tchg.; Nat. Site coord. Brookdale Am. Assn. Colls. and Univs. Contbr. articles to profl. jours. FICE matching-funds grantee, 1986-88. Mem. AAUW, Nat. Coun. Tchrs. English, N.J. Edn. Assn., N.J. TESOL (bilingual edn.). Home: 64 Jefferson Dr Spotswood NJ 08884-1240 Office: Brookdale CC Newman Spring Rd Lincroft NJ 07738

JONES, FLOYD A., municipal official; b. Leavenworth, Kans., Oct. 13, 1946. BA, Washburne U., 1975. Dir. Cedar Rapids (Iowa) Civil Rights Commn., 1981-90; field supr. Kans. Commn. on Civil Rights, Topeka, 1975-81; athletic instr., corrections officer Kans. Dept. of Corrections, Topeka, 1968-75; dir. Human Rights Commn./City of Des Moines, 1990—. Mem. Internat. Assn. of Ofcl. Human Rights Agys. (mem. planning com.), Iowa Assn. of Human and Civil Rights Agys. (v.p., treas.), NAACP, Kappa Alpha Psi (mem. alumni chpt.). Office: Dir Human Rights Commn Armory Bldg/602 E First St Des Moines IA 50309*

JONES, FRANK CATER, lawyer; b. Macon, Ga., June 19, 1925; s. Charles Baxter and Carolyn (Cater) J.; m. Annie Gantt Anderson, Mar. 31, 1951; children: Eugenia Anderson Henderson, Annie Gantt Blattner, Carolyn Corley, Frank Cater. BBA, Emory U., 1947; LLB, Mercer U., 1950, LLD (hon.), 1996. Bar: Ga. 1950. Pvt. practice Macon, 1952-77; mem. firm Jones, Cork & Miller (and predecessor), 1952-77, King & Spalding, Atlanta, 1977—; bd. dirs. So. Trust Corp., Century South Banks, Inc. Trustee Wesleyan Coll., Macon, 1966—, chmn. bd. dirs., 1981-86; pres. Atlanta Symphony Orch. League, 1982-84; chmn. Ga. Gt. Park Authority, 1980-83, Ga. Pub. Telecom. Commn., 1983-98, Met. Atlanta chpt. ARC, 1987-88; bd. dirs., exec. com. Carter Ctr., Emory U., 1987—; chmn. Michael C. Carlos Mus., 1991-96; trustee Emory U., Atlanta, 1991-95, trustee emeritus, 1995—. Fellow ACTL (bd. regents 1986—, sec. 1990-92, pres. 1993-94); mem. ABA (ho. of dels. 1972-94), Macon Bar Assn. (pres. 1954), Ga. Bar Assn. (pres. young lawyers sect. 1956-57), State Bar of Ga. (pres. 1968-69), U.S. Supreme Ct. Hist. Soc. (v.p.), Greater Macon C. of C. (pres. 1965), Rotary. Home: 77 E Andrews Dr NW Apt 242 Atlanta GA 30305-1331 Office: King & Spalding 191 Peachtree St Atlanta GA 30303-1763

JONES, FRANK GRIFFITH, lawyer; b. Houston, Sept. 11, 1941; s. A. Gordon and Grace (Griffith) J.; m. Deborah Ann Young, July 5, 1969; children: Russell G., Sarah G., Christopher Y. BS, Rice U., 1963; JD, U. Tex., 1966. Bar: Tex. 1966, U.S. Dist. Ct. (so., no. and ea. dists.) Tex., U.S. Ct. Appeals (5th and 8th cirs.); cert. civil trial specialist. Ptnr. Fulbright & Jaworski, Houston, 1966—; chmn. Fulbright & Jaworski Employment Commn., 1988-92. Mem. Fulbright and Jaworski policy com., litigation mgmt. com., head litigation practice devel. com., exec. com., 1992-94; chmn. troop com. Boy Scouts Am., Houston, 1986-88; mem. Rice U. Fund Coun., Houston, 1987-93; pres. Baker Coll., Rice U., 1962-63; bd. dirs. Houston Symphony, Holly Hall. Lt. (j.g.) USNR, 1967-72. U. Tex. Law Sch. Keeton fellow, 1993—. Fellow Am. Coll. Trial Lawyers (ADR com. 1986-96, chmn. 1992-94, ethics com. 1996—), Internat. Acad. Trial Lawyers; mem. ABA, Am. Bd. Trial Advs., Internat. Assn. Def. Counsel, Houston Bar Assn., Houston Young Lawyers Assn. (pres. 1972-73), Tex. Bar Assn., Tex. Bar Found., Houston Bar Found., Am. Bar Found., Houston Assn. Cert. Civil Trial and Appellate Specialists, Tex. Assn. Def. Counsel, Am. Counsel Assn., Def. Rsch. Inst., Tex. Assn. Cert. Civil Trial Specialists, Products Liability Adv. Coun., Houston City Club, Courthouse Club, Rotary, Phi Delta Phi (past pres.). Avocations: tennis, travel. Office: Fulbright & Jaworski 1301 Mckinney St Houston TX 77010-3031

JONES, FRANK WYMAN, management consultant, mechanical engineer; b. Ironton, Ohio, Jan. 20, 1940; s. Kylius and Kathleen (McDonald) J.; m. Margaret Kwitek, Sept. 1, 1962; children: Kelly, Connie, Katie, Colleen, Carolyn. BSME, U. Cin., 1963; MBA, Ind. U., 1965. V.p., gen. mgr. G & L Machine Tool Divsn., Fond du Lac, Wis., 1976-80; exec. v.p. Giddings & Lewis Inc., Fond du Lac, Wis., 1980-81, pres., CEO, 1982-86; mgmt. cons. Tucson, 1987—; bd. dirs. Modine, Racine, Wis., Jason Inc., Milw., Ingersoll Milling Machine Co., Rockford, Ill., Star Cutter Co., Farmington Hills, Mich., Gardner Publs., Inc., Cin. Gen. Tool Co., Cin., D.T. Industries, Springfield, Mo. Mem. Am. Mgmt. Assn., Nat. Assn. Corp. Dirs. Republican. Roman Catholic. Home: 6740 N Saint Andrews Dr Tucson AZ 85718-2619

JONES, FRANKLIN ROSS, education educator; b. Charlotte, N.C., Jan. 3, 1920; s. William Morton and Olive Ruth (Moser) J.; divorced; children: Franklin Ross, C. Morton, Susan Noel. AB, Lenoir Rhyne Coll., 1941; MA, U. N.C., 1951; DEd, Duke U., 1960. Tchr. schs. N.C., 1944-48; prin. Jr. High Sch., Henderson, N.C., 1948-54; dist. sch. prin. Wake County, N.C., 1954-56; dist. supt. Roxboro (N.C.) schs., 1956-58; chmn. dept. edn. Randolph-Macon Coll., Ashland, Va., 1959-64; interim dean U. Richmond (Va.), 1962; dean Sch. Edn. Old Dominion U., 1964-69; Eminent prof. Old Dominion U., 1974-94; founder Child Study Center, 1965, disting. prof., 1969—, social founds. program leader, 1973-77, doctoral program liaison rep., 1974-77, faculty chmn., 1981—; dir. Forest Ridge Corp., 1985; vis. rsch. scholar Duke U., 1967; cons. HEW, State Sch. Sys. and Colls.; lectr. in field; mem. com. White house Conf. Children and Youth, 1968-71, Ea. regional chmn., 1968-71; mem. Va. Gov.'s Com. Implementation, 1971-73; spkr. 25th Internat. Congress of Psychology, Brussels, 1992; symposium chmn. European Congress of Psychology, Athens, Greece, 1995; cons. to dean on test score stats., Old Dominion U., 1995—. Author: Psychology of Human Devel., 1969, 2d edit. 1985, 3d edit. 1992, Handbook on Testing, 1972, Understanding the Middlescent Years, 1978, Theory of Adult Development, 1980, Radio series Sta. WTAR, Norfolk, 1973-75; test item writer for N.Y. Regency exams, 1987, Ednl. Testing Svc., 1989; guest editor of Education, 1990—. Mem. Norfolk Urban Coalition, 1969-73; chmn. March of Dimes, Person County, N.C., 1956-57; mem. adv. bd. Tidewater Rehab. Ctr., 1967-69; chmn. Hull Scholarship Fund, 1983-85; coord. U. Joy Fund Drive, 1974-95; univ. chmn. United Fund, 1982, 84; chmn. assessment com. Va. Reading to Learn Program, 1990-91; cons. to sch. systems, ETS, HEW, Coll. 1966—; dir. Praxis Ctr., 1993—; adminstr. Nat. Bd. for Cert. Counselors Ctr. Recipient Dean's Svc. award Old Dominion U., 1984, Univ. award for Fund RAising, 1994, Heritage Found. award, 1996. Mem. Am. Psychol. Soc. (charter), S.E. Psychol. Assn., Va. Assn. U. Profs. (dir. 1962-64), South Atlantic Philosophy Edn. Soc. (pres. 1966-69, dir. 1969—), Va. Assn. Rsch. in Edn. (Disting. Rsch. awards 1972, 73, 78),N.C. Edn. Assn. (pres. North Cen. chpt. 1951, pres. North Cen. Prins. 1956), Ea. Ednl. Rsch. Assn., Nat. Urban Edn. Assn., Bicycle Relay Jr. Marathon World's Record Team, 1933, Alpha Tau Kappa, Kappa Delta Pi, Phi Delta Kappa, Phi Kappa Phi, Pi Gamma Mu (sec. 1962-64). Club: Harbor (Norfolk). Lodges: Lions, Rotary. Home: 1026 Manchester Ave Norfolk VA 23508-1243

JONES, FREDERICK CLAUDIUS, English language and linguistics educator; b. Freetown, Sierra Leone, Apr. 9, 1943; m. Olivia Erica Metzger, July 17, 1982; children: Yvonne, Charlene, Lallie, Raymond. BA in English Lang. and Lit. magna cum laude, U. Durham, Eng., 1966; diploma in edn., U. Sierra Leone, 1967; MA in Linguistics and English, U. Leeds, Eng., 1972, PhD in Linguistics and Phonetics, 1983. Asst. prof. English lang. and lit. Milton Margai Advanced Tchrs. Coll., Freetown, 1970-75; supr. teaching practice U. Sierra Leone, 1973-84, asst. prof. English, dir. English dept. lang. lab., 1975-85; asst. prof. Inst. Linguistics, Tech. U. Berlin, 1985-90; assoc. prof. English St. Augustine's Coll., Raleigh, N.C., 1990—, dir. honors program, 1994—; part-time instr. U. Sierra Leone, 1972-75; part-time newsreader Sierra Leone Broadcasting Svc., 1969-85; examiner to chief examiner The Nat. Examinations Bd. at Standardized High Sch. Level; cons. YWCA, 1978. Editorial bd. publs. com. Ministry of Edn., Sierra Leone, 1978-85; contbr. articles to profl. jours.; editorial asst. A Krio-English Dictionary, 1980; co-producer, co-dir. (video): Insights into Writing Across the Curriculum, 1992. Mem. The West African Linguistic Soc., Australian Linguistic Soc., Soc. Linguistica Europaea, The Linguistic Soc. Am., Soc. Pidgin and Creole Studies, Conf. on Coll. Composition and Comms., Nat. Coun. Tchrs. of English, Sigma Tau Delta. Methodist. Avocations: reading, theater, journalism, travel. Home: 1005 Mockingbird Dr Raleigh NC 27615-6125 Office: St Augustines Coll 1315 Oakwood Ave Raleigh NC 27610-2247

JONES, G. DOUGLAS, prosecutor. U.S. atty. no. dist. State of Ala., Birmingham, 1997—. Office: Robert S Vance Fed Bldg Courthouse 1800 5th Ave N Birmingham AL 35203-2111*

JONES, GALEN RAY, physician assistant; b. Salt Lake City, Feb. 1, 1948; s. Leonard Ray and Veda (Whitehead) J.; m. Patricia Ann Poulson, Jan. 21, 1972; children: Brian, Marci, Natalie. Grad., Med. Field Svc. Sch. Ft. Sam Houston, San Antonio, 1971; BS, U. Utah, 1982. Missionary Ch. of Jesus Christ of Latter Day Saints, Alta., Sask., Can., 1967-69; asst. mgr. Cowan's Frostop Hamburger Stand, Salt Lake City, 1969-70; with Safeway Stores, Inc., Salt Lake City, 1970; o.r. tech. Latter Day Saint Hosp., Salt Lake City, 1973-75; physician asst. Lovell Clinic Inc., Lovell, Wyo., 1975-77, Family Health Care, Inc., Tooele, Utah, 1977-86, West Dermatology and Surgery Med. Grp., Redlands, Calif., 1986-95; with blood and marrow transplant program Univ. Hosp. and Primary Childrens Med. Ctr. U. Utah, Salt Lake City, 1996-98; physician asst. D. Edgar Allen Dermatology, Ogden, 1998—; maturation lectr. Tooele Sch. Dist., 1978-86; course dir., instr. EMT, North Big Horn County Search and Rescue, 1976; instr. EMT, Grantsville Ambulance Inc., 1979-85; lectr. on skin care and changes to sr. citizen groups, hosp. auxs., health fairs, 1986—; high sch. sophomore sem. tchr. religion, 1991-96; owner Adventureland and TopHat Video, Magna, Utah, 1982-96. Author: (with others) The P.A. Clinical Practice, 1995. Chmn. County Health Teen Pregnancy Prevention Project, Tooele, 1980-81; adv. bd. State Dept. Health-Rural Health Network, Salt Lake City, 1985-86; health lectr. County Health & Edn. Dept. Progs., Tooele, 1977-86; mormon bishop/pastor Lakeview Ward, Latter Day Saints Ch., Tooele, 1982-86; mem. Utah Acad. Physician Assts. (pres. 1980-81, editor newsletter 1979-80). With U.S. Army, 1971-73. U. Utah grantee, 1966, 67, 69. Fellow Am. Acad. Physician Assts., Utah. Acad. Physicians Assts. Republican. Mem. LDS Ch. Avocations: gardening, hiking, camping, skiing, photography, travel. Home: 2670 Willow Wick Dr Sandy UT 84093-1929 Office: D Edgar Allen Dermatology 3860 Jackson Ave Ogden UT 84403-1956

JONES, GEOFFREY MELVILL, physiology research educator; b. Cambridge, Eng., Jan. 14, 1923; s. Benett and Dorothy Laxton (Jotham) J.; m. Jenny Marigold Burnaby, June 21, 1953; children—Katharine, Francis, Andrew, Dorothy. B.A., Cambridge U., 1944, M.A., 1947, MB, BCh, 1949. House surgeon Middlesex Hosp., London, Eng., 1949-50; sr. house surgeon Addenbrookes Hosp., Cambridge, Eng., 1950-51; sci. med. officer Royal Air Force Inst. Aviation Medicine, Farnborough, Eng., 1951-55; sci. officer Med. Research Council, Eng., 1955-61; assoc. prof. physiology, dir. aviation med. rsch. unit McGill U., Montreal, Que., Can., 1961-68, prof., dir., 1968-88, Hosmer research prof., 1978-91; emeritus prof. physiology McGill U., Montreal, Que., 1991—; adj. prof. clin. neuroscis. U. Calgary, Alta., Can., 1991—, Coll. France, 1979, 95; vis. prof. Stanford U., 1971-72. Author: (with another) mammalian Vestibular Physiology, 1979; editor: (with another) Adaptive Mechanisms in Gaze Control, 1985; contbr. numerous articles to profl. jours. Served to squadron leader Royal Air Force, 1951-55. Sr. rsch. assoc. Nat. Acad. Sci., 1971-72; recipient Skylab Achievement award NASA, 1974, 1st recipient Dohlman medal Dohlman Soc. Toronto U., 1987, Quinquennial Gold medal Barany Soc. Internat., 1988, Ashton Graybiel award U.S. Naval Aerospace Labs., 1989, Wilbur Franks Annual award Can. Soc. Aerospace Medicine, Buchanan-Barbour award Royal Aeronautical Soc., 1991, Mc Laughlin Medal, 1991, Royal Soc. Can. Fellow Can. Aeronautics and Space Inst., Aerospace Med. Assn. (Harry Armstrong award 1968, Arnold D. Tuttle award 1971), Royal Soc. Can. (McLaughlin medal 1991), Royal Soc. London, Royal Aeronautical Soc. London (Stewart Meml. award 1989, Buchanan Barbour award 1990); mem. U.K. Physiol. Soc., Can. Physiol. Soc., Can. Soc. Aerospace Med. Soc., Internat. Collegium Otolaryngology, Soc. Neurosci. Avocations: tennis, sailing, outdoor activities, reading, choral singing. Office: U Calgary Dept Clin Neuroscis, 3330 Hospital Dr NW, Calgary, AB Canada T2N 4N1

JONES, GEORGE EDWIN, private investigator; b. Red Bank, N.J., Nov. 13, 1923; s. William T. and Margaret (Maloney) J.; m. Joan Frances Layden, Aug. 9, 1952; children: George Edwin Jr., Joan Frances Canning, Patricia Michelle Mullin, Michael P. BSS, Georgetown U., 1947, postgrad., 1948-49. Lic. pvt. investigator, N.J. Spl. agt. FBI, various locations, 1951-78; security cons. Shepherd Security Svcs., Inc., Freehold, N.J., 1980—; contract investigator U.S. Dept. Justice, 1989—, U.S. Treasury Dept., U.S. Customs Svc., 1989—, M.V.M. Inc., Falls Church, Va., 1990—. Exec. reservist FEMA, Washington, 1982—; mem. Provost Marshal's Guild, Ft. Monmouth, N.J., 1972-84. Mem. Am. Legion, St. Vincent dePaul Soc., Nat. Assn. Ret. Fed. Employees, Soc. of Former Spl. Agts. of the FBI, Inc., Assn. of Former Intelligence Officers, Fed. Law Enforcement Officers Assn., Internat. Police Assn. Republican. Roman Catholic. Home: 225 Sycamore Ave Shrewsbury NJ 07702-4512

JONES, GEORGE FLEMING, foundation executive; b. San Angelo, Tex., June 27, 1935; s. George Fleming and Cora (Brewer) J.; m. Maria Rosario Correa, Apr. 23, 1960; children: George III, Robert, Michael, Mary Louise. AB magna cum laude, Wabash Coll., 1955; AM, Tufts U., 1956; MA, Stanford U., 1967. Joined Fgn. Svc., Dept. State, 1956; with Econ. Bur., Dept. State, Washington, 1956-58; with Am. Embassy, Ecuador, 1958-60, Ghana, 1961-63, Venezuela, 1963-66; officer in charge Venezuelan affairs Dept. State, Washington, 1967-69, officer in charge Colombian affairs, 1969-71; polit. advisor U.S. Mission to IAEA, Vienna, Austria, 1971-74; counselor for polit. affairs Am. Embassy, Guatemala, 1974-77; student Nat. War Coll., Washington, 1977-78; Latin Am. adviser U.S. del. U.S.-Soviet Conventional Arms Talks, 1978; dep. dir. office Latin Am. regional polit. affairs Dept. State, 1978-80, dir., 1980-82; dep. chief of mission Am. Embassy, Costa Rica, 1982-85, Chile, 1985-89; sr. adviser for Latin Am. and Caribbean affairs U.S. del. UN Gen. Assembly, N.Y.C., 1990, 95; amb. to Republic of Guyana Georgetown, 1991-95; dir. programs for the Ams., Internat. Found. for Election Sys., Washington, 1996—. Recipient Superior Honor award Dept. State, 1987. Mem. Am. Fgn. Svc. Assn. (v.p. 1989-90), Sr. Fgn. Svc. Assn. (bd. dirs. 1990-92). Home: 3804 Acosta Rd Fairfax VA 22031-3804 Office: Internat Found for Election Sys 1101 15th St NW Washington DC 20005-5002

JONES, GEORGE HILTON, retired history educator, writer; b. Baton Rouge, Jan. 11, 1924; s. William Carruth and Elizabeth Fly (Kirkpatrick) J. BA, La. State U., 1947; DPhil, Oxford (Eng.) U., 1950. Instr. Hofstra Coll., Hempstead, N.Y., 1950-51; asst. prof. Ind. U., Bloomington, 1951-52; asst. editor Am. Book Co., N.Y.C., 1953-54; asst. prof. Washington Coll., Chestertown, Md., 1954-56, Tex. Technol. Coll., Lubbock, 1958-61, Kans. State U., Manhattan, 1961-64; assoc. prof. Olivet (Mich.) Coll., 1964-66; from assoc. to full prof. Ea. Ill. U., Charleston, 1966-89, prof. emeritus, 1989—; bd. dirs. R.J. Best, Inc., San Francisco. Author: The Main Stream of Jacobitism, 1955, Charles Middleton, The Life and Times of a Restoration Politician, 1968, Convergent Forces, Immediate Causes of the Revolution of 1688 in England, 1991, Great Britain and the Tuscan Succession Question, 1999; co-author: Southern Regional Education Board, 1960. Cpl. U.S. Army, 1943-45. Rhodes scholar, Oxford, 1947-50; fellow Newberry Libr., Chgo., summer 1959, Guggenheim Found., London, 1960-61. Fellow Royal Hist. Soc.; mem. AAUP, N.Am. Conf. on Brit. Studies, United Oxford and Cambridge Univ. Club. Democrat. Avocation: writing light verse. Home: 1530 3rd St Charleston IL 61920-3312

JONES, GEORGE HUMPHREY, retired healthcare executive, hospital facilities and communications consultant; b. Kansas City, Mo., July 10, 1923; s. George Humphrey and Mary R. (Marrs) J.; m. Peggy Jean Thompson, Nov. 23, 1943; children: Kenneth L., Daniel D., Kathleen Jones Smith, Carol R. Jones Johnson, Janet S. Jones Fitts. Student, U. Mo., Kansas City, 1940-43, Wis. State U., Oshkosh, 1943. Police officer Kansas City (Mo.) Police Dept., 1947-51; elec. contr. Paramount Elec. Svc., Kansas City, 1947-50; electrician Automatic Temp. Control Co., Kansas City, 1951-57; pres., chief ops. George H. Jones Co., Kansas City, 1957-65; sales mgr. Nycon Inc., Lee's Summit, Mo., 1965; design engr. Midland Wright Corp., Kansas City, 1966; dist. sales mgr. Comm. Electronics, Kansas City, 1967; plant ops. supr. Rsch. Med. Ctr., Kansas City, 1968-77; dir. plant ops. and comm. Rsch. Med. Ctr., 1977-90; hosp. facilities and comm. cons. Overland Park, Kans., 1990—; guest lectr. Nat. U., San Diego, 1987. Vol. Salvation Army Emergency Svcs.; bd. dirs. Camellot Fine arts Acad., 1974-76, v.p. bd. dirs., 1975-76; adv. dir. Rsch. Med. Ctr., 1990—; mem. Confederate Air Force. With USAAF, 1942-46, U.S. Army, 1950-51. Fellow Am. Soc. Hosp. Engring., Healthcare Info. and Mgmt. Systems Soc.; mem. Kansas City Area Hosp. Engrs. (pres. 1985, bd. dirs. 1985-89), Am. Legion, Alpha Phi Omega. Presbyterian. Avocations: fishing, photography. Home and Office: 6022 W 86th St Shawnee Mission KS 66207-1521

JONES, GEORGIA ANN, publisher; b. Ogden, Utah, July 6, 1946; d. Sam Oliveto and Edythe June Murphy; m. Lowell David Jones; children: Lowell Scott, Curtis Todd. Sculptor, 1964-78, journalist, 1968-80; appraiser real property Profl. Real Estate Appraisal, San Carlos, Calif., 1980-95; online columnist, 1995-97; owner, pub. Ladybug Press, San Carlos, 1996—; leader workshops for writers, 1994—. Author: A Garden of Weedin', 1997, Write What You Know: A Writer's Adventure, 1998; sculptor, 1964-78; patentee Scruples-tag, 1980; editor, pub. Women on a Wire, 1996; author, playwright, A Stitch in Time, 1995, The Usual Suspects, 1995. Mem. Internat. Friends of Lit. and Culture (bd. dirs., U.S. chpt., Pave Peace keynote spkr. internat. congress 1999). Avocations: drawing, designing and building homes, landscape gardening. Office: Ladybug Press 751 Laurel St Ste 223 San Carlos CA 94070-3113

JONES, GERALD EDWARD, religion educator; b. Gettysburg, S.D., June 20, 1933; s. Otis Clinton and Alma May (Gorman) J.; m. Joyce Nadine Lindstrom; children: Eric Otis, JanEtta, Angela, Nadine, Sylvia, Gerald. BS, Brigham Young U., 1957, MA, 1960, PhD, 1972; postgrad., U. Minn., U. Iowa. Seminary prin. LDS Ch. Ednl. System, St. Johns, Ariz., 1957-59, Grantsville, Utah, 1960-63, Rexburg, Idaho, 1964-66, Pocatello, Idaho, 1966-67; dir. Inst. Religion U. Wyo., Laramie, 1967-70, U. Calif., Berkeley, 1971-85, Stanford U., Palo Alto, Calif., 1985-92, Yale U., New Haven, Conn., 1992-95; tour dir. Brigham Young U., Provo, Utah, 1978-80; lectr., cons. various orgns. Utah, Calif., Idaho, 1970-90; bd. dirs. Internat. Network for Religion and Animals, No. Wales, Pa. Author: Animals and the Gospel, 1980; contbg. editor: Between the Species Jour., Berkeley, 1984—; contbr. articles to profl. jours. Bd. govs. Nat. Coun. of Christians and Jews, San Franciscio, 1986-92, nat. trustee, N.Y.C., 1988-92; pub. policy expert Heritage Found., Washington, 1982-94. Recipient commendation Merritt Hosp., Oakland, Calif., 1984. Mem. S.D. Hist. Soc. (life), Utah Hist. Soc. (life), U. Wyo. Sch. Religion (pres. 1969-70). LDS. Avocations: world travel, book collector, church activities. Home: 1311 Edinburgh Ct Concord CA 94518-3918

JONES, GERALDINE MARY FLORENCE, journalist; b. Nov. 15, 1968. AA, Pitt C.C., Greenville, N.C., 1994; BS in Sci., Appalachian State U., 1996. Art cons., framer Larson-Juhl, Fla., Univ. Art Gallery, Greenville, N.C., Hickory's (N.C.) Finest; journalist Hickory Daily Record, 1998—. Home: 2061 Wall St Morganton NC 28655

JONES, GLENN EARLE, property management executive; b. Greensboro, N.C., May 11, 1946; s. Harold Clifford and AnnaBelle (Goodwin) J. B.S., Cornell U. Sch. Hotel and Restaurant Mgmt., 1968. Asst. to gen. mgr. Warwick Hotel, Houston, 1968-69; Northeastern Ohio sales rep. L.G. Balfour Co., Attleboro, Mass., 1969-72; resident mgr. Chase Park Plaza Hotel, St. Louis, 1972-74; gen. mgr. Holiday Inn, Steamboat Springs, Colo., 1974, Santa Fe Hilton Inn, 1975, Sheraton Inn, New Orleans, 1976-79; pres. Landmark Systems, Inc., New Orleans, 1979—; chmn. Sheraton, So. Regional Owners and Mgrs. Council, 1981—. Mem. com. membership Greater New Orleans Tourist and Conv. Commn.; mem. dist. com. United Fund. Mem. New Orleans Hotel and Motel Assn. (treas.), Cornell Soc. Hotelmen, Am. Hotel Mgmt. Assn. (cert., mem. fund devel. com. Ednl. Inst.). Episcopalian. Home: 636 Lang St New Orleans LA 70131-5226

JONES, GLENN ROBERT, cable systems executive; b. Jackson Center, Pa., Mar. 2, 1930. BS in Econs., Allegheny Coll.; JD, U. Colo.; diploma exec. program, Stanford U.; LHD (hon.), Allegheny Coll. CEO, chmn. Jones Intercable Inc., Englewood, Colo. Author: (poetry) Briefcase Poetry of Yankee Jones, vol. I, 1978, vol. II, 1981, vol. III, 1985, Jones: Dictionary of Cable Television Terminology, 1973, 2d edit., 1976, 3d edit., 1987. Mem. World Future Soc., Nat. Cable TV Assn. Office: Jones Internat Ltd 9697 E Mineral Ave Englewood CO 80112-3446*

JONES, GORDON EDWIN, horticulturist; b. Lorraine, N.Y., Feb. 1, 1921; s. Griffith Edwin and Mary Edna (Green) J. B.S., Cornell U., 1943; M.S., Hofstra U., 1961; m. Thelma Dolores Popp, Dec. 27, 1946; children: Susan D., Thomas E., Robin A., Peter G. Mgr. flower seed div. and trial grounds Robson Seed Co., Hall, N.Y., 1945-56; asst. prof. ornamental horticulture dept. N.Y. State A&T Coll., Farmingdale, 1957-65; dir. Planting Fields Arboretum, Oyster Bay, N.Y., 1958-93 (ret. 1993). Trustee, Planting Fields Found.; past bd. dirs. Rhododendron Species Found.; past dist. commr. Boy Scouts Am. Capt. U.S. Army, 1943-46, ETO. Recipient Silver Achievement medal Nat. Council award Federated Garden Clubs, 1975; named Man of Yr., L.I. Nurserymen's Assn., 1979; Gold Medal of Hort. award N.Y. State Nurserymen's Assn., 1985; Sidney M. Shapiro Meml. Adminstrv. Award, 1987. Mem. Am. Rhododendron Soc. (gold medal, bronze medal), Am. Assn. Bot. Gardens and Arboreta (past bd. dir.), Assn. Interpretive Naturalists, Hort. Soc. N.Y. (past bd. dir.), N.Y. Hortus Club (sec.-treas.), Pi Alpha Xi, Alpha Gamma Rho. Club: Oyster Bay Rotary (pres. 1980-81). Editor: Rhododendrons and Their Relatives, 1971; contbr. articles to profl. jours. Home: 3378 Seneca Castle Rd Stanley NY 14561-9545

JONES, GORDON KEMPTON, dentist; b. Rochester, N.Y., July 22, 1946; s. Joseph Kempton and Eunice (Patten)J.; m. Kathleen Anne FitzSimmons, July 24, 1971; children: Bryan Kempton, Brendan Austin, Graeme Meghan, Michael Cameron, Meredith Hunter, Mallory Sterling. BA in Chemistry, U. N.C., 1968, DDS, 1976; MS in Restorative Dentistry, U. Mich., 1984. Lic. dentist, Ill., N.C. Commd. lt. USN, 1976, advanced through ranks to capt., 1993; resident Naval Regional Med. Ctr., Camp Pendleton, Calif., 1977; dentist U.S.S. Holland USN, Holy Loch, Scotland, 1977-80; dentist regional med. ctr. USN, Great Lakes, Ill., 1980-82; head dept. operative dentistry Naval Dental Clinic, Great Lakes, Ill., 1984-90, 93-97, Naval Dental Ctr., Norfolk, Va., 1990-93; cons. operative dentistry Naval Dental Clinic, Great Lakes, Ill., 1984-90, 93-96; dir. managed care Naval Dental Ctr., Great Lakes, Ill., 1993-97, clinic dir., 1996-97; cons. operative dentistry Naval Dental Ctr., Norfolk, 1990-93; comdg. officer Naval Dental Rsch. Inst., 1997—; splty. leader for dental rsch. Surgeon Gen. U.S. Navy, 1997—; cons. Naval Hosp. Great Lakes, 1984-86, 93—; asst. clin. prof. Northwestern U. Dental Sch., Chgo., 1985-90, 95-98; quality assurance coord., head advanced clin. program in gen. dentistry, Norfolk, 1990-93; com. chmn. Am. Bd. Operative Dentistry, 1987—, pres., 1996—, mem. exec. coun., 1996—. Contbr. articles to profl. jours.; speaker in field. Course dir. ARC, Great Lakes, 1984-90. Fellow Internat. Coll. Dentists; mem. ADA, Acad. Operative Dentistry (mem. jour. editl. bd. 1993-95, 96—), Internat. Assn. Dental Rsch., Acad. Gen. Dentistry, Am. Assn. Dental Schs., Am. Legion, Omicron Kappa Upsilon, Alpha Phi Omega, Delta Sigma Delta. Avocations: computer science, reading, jogging. Home: 1541 N Mckinley Rd Lake Forest IL 60045-1377

JONES, GRAHAM ALFRED, mathematics educator; b. Brisbane, Queensland, Australia, Oct. 29, 1937; came to U.S., 1991; s. Charles Henry and Doris Beatrice (Powell) J.; m. Marion Rose Rudge, Dec. 15, 1962; children: Timothy Charles, Cameron Philip. BSc, U. Queensland, 1960, BEd with 1st honors, 1964; MA, San Diego State U., 1968; PhD, Ind. U., 1974. Tchr. Cavendish Rd. High Sch., Brisbane, 1961-66; Fulbright Exch. tchr. John Francis Poly., L.A., 1966-67; head dept. math. Kelvin Grove Tchrs. Coll., Brisbane, 1968-71; head dept. math. Kelvin Grove Coll. Advanced Edn., Brisbane, 1974-76, dean of sci., 1976-82; campus prin. Brisbane Coll. Advanced Edn., Carseldine campus, Brisbane, 1982-85; pro-vice chancellor, prof., dir. Gold Coast (Australia) Univ. Coll., Griffith U., 1985-91; prof. math. Ill. State U., Normal, 1991—; mem. Bd. Tchr. Edn., Brisbane, 1982-86; chair Math. Adv. Com. of Queensland, Brisbane, 1968-71, 74-76. Author monographs, reports and rsch. articles. NSF scholar, 1967-68. Fellow Australian Inst. Mgmt., Australian Coll. Edn.; mem. Math. Edn. Rsch. Group of Australasia (life, founding pres. 1980-84), Am. Ednl. Rsch. Assn., Nat. Coun. Tchrs. Math. (reviewer for jours. 1991—). Presbyterian. Avocations: surfing, wind-surfing, theatre, tennis, cryptic crosswords. Home: 705 Kathleen Dr Normal IL 61761-4031 Office: Ill State U Dept Math Stevenson Bldg Normal IL 61790-4520

JONES, GRANT RICHARD, landscape architect, planner; b. Seattle, Aug. 29, 1938; s. Victor Noble and Iona Bell (Thomas) J.; m. Ilze Grinbergs, 1965 (div. 1983); 1 child, Kaija. Student, Colo. Coll., 1956-58; BArch, U. Wash., 1962; M in Landscape Arch., Harvard U., 1966, postgrad. (Frederick Sheldon fellow), 1967-68. Draftsman Jones Lovegren Helms & Jones, Seattle, 1958-59; assoc. Richard Haag Assos., Seattle, 1961-65; rsch. assoc. landscape architecture rsch. office Harvard U., 1966-67; state conservation planner Eckbo Dean Austin & Williams, Honolulu, 1968-69; prin. Jones & Jones, Seattle, 1969—; lectr. and spkr. in field; chmn. landscape archtl. registration bd., State of Wash., 1974-79; mem. coun. Harvard U. Grad. Sch. Design, 1978-82, 91-96; vis. com. Harvard U. Grad. Sch., 1993—, U. Wash. Coll. Architecture, 1990—; bd. dirs. Scenic Am., Waterfront Ctr., Arcade Mag. Author: The Nooksack Plan: An Approach to the Investigation and Evaluation of a River System, 1973; (with B. Gray and J. Burnham) A Method for the Quantification of Aesthetic Values for Environmental Decision Making, 1975, Design as Ecogram, 1975; (with J. Coe and D. Paulson) Woodland Park Zoo: Long Range Plan, Development Guidelines and Exhibit Scenarios, 1976, Landscape Assessment. . .Where Logic and Feelings Meet, 1978, Design Principles for Presentation of Animals and Nature, 1982, What Are Zoos?, 1984, An Arboretum on a Landfill, 1984, Beyond Landscape Immersion to Cultural Resonance, 1989, Some Thoughts on Power and Influence, 1993; prin. works include Nooksack River Plan, Bellingham, Wash.; Yakima (Wash.) River Regional Greenway, Union Bay Teaching and Research Arboretum, U. Wash., Seattle, Newhalem Campground, North Cascades Nat. Park, Woodland Park Zool. Gardens, Seattle, Washington Park Arboretum, U. Wash., Seattle, zoo master plans for Kansas City, Roanoke, Va., Detroit and Honolulu, Dallas Arboretum and Bot. Garden, Toledo Zoo African Savannah Complex, Thai Elephant Forest at Woodland Park Zoo, Singapore Bot. Gardens, Paris Pike Hist. Hwy, Denver Commons, others. Recipient Nat. award Am. Assn. Zoos and Pub. Aquaria, 1981-84. Fellow Am. Soc. Landscape Architects (chmn. Wash. chpt. 1972-73, trustee 1979—, v.p., 1988-90, Merit award in community design 1972, Honor award in regional planning 1974, Merit award in regional planning 1977, Merit award in park planning 1977, Merit award in instnl. planning 1977, Pres.'s award of excellence 1980, merit awards in landscape planning), Nature Conservancy, Am. Hort. Soc., Am. Assn. Bot. Gardens and Arboreta, Wash. Environ. Council, Phi Gamma Delta. Office: Jones & Jones 4th Fl 105 S Main St Ste 400 Seattle WA 98104-2578*

JONES, GWENYTH ELLEN, director publishing information systems/technology; b. Omaha, Sept. 21, 1952; d. Robert Lester and Mary Ellen (Ouren) J.; m. William F. Knoff Jr.. BA, U. Va., 1974, MA in English, 1982. Mktg. dir. John Wiley & Sons, N.Y.C., 1986-89, pub., 1989-90, dir. info. systems and tech., 1990-97, dir. pub. info. systems & techs., 1997—. Mem. Assn. Am. Pubs. Avocations: dancing, tennis. Office: John Wiley and Sons 605 3rd Ave Fl 6 New York NY 10158-0012

JONES, GWYNETH, soprano; b. Pontnewynydd, Wales, Nov. 7, 1936; d. Edward George and Violet (Webster) J.; m. Till Haberfeld, Mar. 7, 1969. Student, Royal Coll. Music, London, Accademia Chigiana, Siena, Italy, Internat. Opera Ctr., Zurich, Switzerland; Dr. h.c. musica, U. Wales and Glamorgan. Mem. Royal Opera, Covent Garden, Eng., 1963—, Vienna (Austria) State Opera, 1966—, Deutsche Opera Berlin, 1966, Munich Bavarian State Opera, 1967—. Guest performances in numerous opera houses including Hamburg, Bayreuth, Dresden, Paris, Zurich, Rome, Chgo., San Francisco, Los Angeles, Tokyo, Buenos Aires, Munich, La Scala, Milan, Met. Opera, N.Y.C., Bayreuth Festival, Salzburg Festival, Verona; appeared in 50 leading roles including Tosca, Minnie, Turandot, Leonora in Il Trovatore, Desdemona in Otello, Lady MacBeth, Fidelio, Aida, Senta, Sieglinde, Marschallin, Isolde, Ortrud, Salome, Brunnhilde, Medea, Kundry, Madame Butterfly, Elizabeth/Venus in Tannhauser, Ariadne, Farberin, Elektra, Helena in Aegyptische Helena, Poppea, Santuzza, Hannah Glawari, Erwartung, La Voix Humaine; court singer, Bavaria, Austria; rec. artist for Decca, Deutsche Grammophon, Philips, EMI, CBS; films, TV and concert appearances. Recipient Shakespeare Prize Hamburg, 1987, Verdienst Kreuz I Klasse Fed. Republic Germany, 1988, Golden Medal Honour, 1991, Decorated dame comdr. Order Brit. Empire, 1986, Commandeur Des Arts Et Lettres, 1992, Verdienst-Krenz T. Klasse, Austria, 1998, numerous other European decorations. Fellow Royal Coll. Music. Address: Box 556, CH-8037 Zurich Switzerland

JONES, HAROLD ANTONY, banker; b. Bklyn., Nov. 5, 1943; s. Harold Edward and Marie Albertine (Schwietering) J.; m. Jo Ann T. Titone, Oct. 8, 1966; children: Christopher, Gregory. BA, Pace Coll., 1968; postgrad., Am. Inst. Banking, 1970; A.A.S., Grad. Sch. Savs. Banking, Brown U., 1975; grad., Exec. Mgmt. Program, U. Mass., 1977. With Mfrs. Trust Co., N.Y.C., 1961-64; with Lincoln Savs. Bank, N.Y.C., 1964-90; dir. mktg. Lincoln Savs. Bank, 1978-79, sr. v.p., corp. sec., 1979-81, dir. retail banking div., 1980-90; sr. v.p. bank adminstrn. Ridgewood Savs. Bank, N.Y.C., 1990—; guest lectr. money and banking NYU; guest lectr. corp. social responsibility Columbia U.; pres. N.Y. Savs. Banks Life Ins. Council, 1985. Named Outstanding Banker in Community Revitalization Brighton Beach Neighborhood Assn., 1978, Banker of Yr. Manhattan C. of C., 1990. Mem. Fin. Advt. and Mktg. Assn. N.Y. (dir.), Bank Mktg. Assn., Savs. Banks Assn. N.Y. State (com. on pub. info.), Thrift Inst. Mktg. (chmn. exec. com.), Harbour Green Assn. (pres. 1992). Office: Ridgewood Savings Bank 71-02 Forest Ave Ridgewood NY 11385-5647

JONES, HAROLD C., director agriculture; b. Pahokee, Fla., Oct. 22, 1947. BS, U. Fla., 1969, MS, 1971. Agent Agrl. Dept. Coop. Ext. Svc., Jacksonville, Fla., 1971-96, dir., 1996—. Mem. Nat. Assn. County Agrl. Agents (Svc. award 1984, Fla. chpt. Svc. award 1984), Fla. Turf Grass Assn. (Wreath of Grass award 1992). Office: Agricultural Dept Cooperative Extension Svc 1010 N Mcduff Ave Jacksonville FL 32254-2031*

JONES, H(AROLD) GILBERT, JR., lawyer; b. Fargo, N.D., Nov. 2, 1927; s. Harold Gilbert and Charlotte Viola (Chambers) J.; m. Julie Squier, Feb. 15, 1964; children: Lenna Lettice Mills Jones Carroll, Thomas Squier, Christopher Lee. B of Engring., Yale U., 1947; postgrad., Mich. U., 1948-49; JD, UCLA, 1956. Bar: Calif. 1957. Mem., ptnr. Overton, Lyman & Prince, L.A., 1956-61; founding ptnr. Bonne, Jones, Bridges, Mueller & O'Keefe,

L.A., 1961-89, of counsel, 1990-92; of counsel Lewis, D'Amato, Brisbois & Bisgaard, 1992—. Bd. dirs. Wilshire YMCA, 1969-75. With U.S. Army, 1950-52. Fellow Am. Coll. Trial Lawyers (Calif. Trial Lawyer of Yr. 1996), Am. Bd. Trial Advs. (nat. pres. 1988-89, nat. exec. com. 1990, 92, 96, nat. bd. dirs. 1977—, pres. L.A. chpt. 1980), Internat. Acad. Trial Lawyers: mem. ABA, Calif. Bar Assn., Los Angeles County Bar Assn. (past. chmn. legal-med. rels. com.), Orange County Bar Assn., So. Calif. Assn. Def. Counsel, Jonathan Club, Transpacific Yacht Club (commodore 1996-98), Newport Harbor Yac ht Club (commodore 1998), Cruising Club Am., L.A. Yacht Club, Univ. Athletic Club, Ctr. Club. Home: 818 Harbor Island Dr Newport Beach CA 92660-7228 Office: 650 Town Center Dr Ste 1400 Costa Mesa CA 92626-7128

JONES, HARVEY ROYDEN, JR., neurologist; b. Plainfield, N.J., Nov. 18, 1936; m. Mary Elizabeth Norman, Mar. 18, 1961; children: Roy, Kathryn, Frederick, David. BS, Tufts U., 1958; MD, Northwestern U., 1962. Diplomate in Neurology and Clin. Neurophysiology Am. Bd. Psychiatry and Neurology; diplomate Am. Bd. Electroencephalography, Am. Bd. Electrodiagnostic Medicine. Intern Phila. Gen. Hosp., 1962-63; resident in internal medicine Mayo Grad. Sch. Medicine, Rochester, Minn., 1963-65; resident in neurology Mayo Grad. Sch. medicine, Rochester, Minn., 1965-66; chief neruology svc. U.S. Army Hosp., Bad Connstatt, Germany, 1966-70; resident in neurology/clin. neurophysiology Mayo Grad. Sch. medicine, Rochester, Minn., 1970-72; from clin. instr. to clin. prof. neurology Harvard Med. Sch., Boston, 1972—; staff neurologist, Jaime Ortiz-Patino chair neurology Lahey Clinic, Burlington, Mass., 1972—; assoc. in neurology, assoc. divsn. neurophysiology Children's Hosp. Med. Ctr., Boston, 1977—; bd. dirs. Am. Bd. Psychiatry and Neurology, 1997—. Contbr. numerous articles to profl. jours.; editor, author: CIBA Collection, Nervous System Part II, 1986, Pediatric Clinical Electromyography, 1996. Fellow Am. Acad. Neurology; mem. Am. Neurol. Assn. E-Mail: Royden.Jones@Lahey.org. Home: 22 Woodridge Rd Wellesley MA 02482-7033 Office: Lahey Clinic 41 Mall Rd Burlington MA 01805-0001

JONES, HENRY EARL, dermatologist, direct patient care educator; b. Detroit, Jan. 24, 1940; s. Henry Clay and Treva Jewel (Jones) J.; m. Hilda Ann Skagfield; children: Gregory, Laronda, Tamara, Hanna, Meredith. B.S., Murray State U., 1961; M.D., Tulane U., 1965. Diplomate Am. Bd. Dermatology. Intern, Tripler Gen. Hosp., Honolulu, 1965-66; resident in dermatology Letterman Gen. Hosp. and U. Calif.-San Francisco, 1966-69; asst. chief div. dermatology Letterman Army Inst. Research, San Francisco, 1970-73; asst. prof. dermatology and head immunodermatology U. Mich., 1973-76; prof. dermatology, chmn. dept. Emory U., 1976-84, clin. prof., 1984—, dir. Emory affiliated dermatology tng. program, 1976-84; clin. prof. medicine (dermatology) U. South Ala. Sch. Medicine, Mobile, 1992—; bd. dirs. SID, 1980-85. Served as lt. col. U.S. Army, 1965-73. Decorated Bronze star; recipient John Herr Musser Meml. award Tulane U., 1965, Disting. Alumnus award Murray State U., 1990. Am. Acad. Dermatology, Am. Dermatol. Assn., Alpha Omega Alpha. Home: 12500 Lookingglass Rd Roseburg OR 97470-9067 Office: 201 Medical Loop Ste 170 Roseburg OR 97470-8835

JONES, HENRY L., JR., federal judge. BA, Yale U., 1967; JD, U. Mich., 1972. Law clk. to Hon. G. Thomas Eisele U.S. Dist. Ct. (ea. dist.) Ark., 1973; law clk. to Hon. Gerald Heaney U.S. Ct. Appeals (8th cir.), 1973-74; atty. Walker, Hollingsworth and Jones (and predecessor firms), 1974-78; magistrate judge U.S. Dist. Ct. (ea. dist.) Ark., Little Rock, 1978—; atty. Washtenaw County Legal Aid Soc., 1970; instr. trial practice U. Ark., Little Rock, 1981. Mem. U.S. Jud. Conf. Office: 521 US Courthouse 600 W Capitol Ave Little Rock AR 72201-3329

JONES, HENRY WAYNE, secondary education educator; b. Pickens, S.C., Feb. 15, 1954; s. Wayne Arthur and Essie Mae (Patterson) J.; m. Margaret E. Waldrep, May 5, 1979. BS in Econ., Clemson U., 1995. Soils lab tech. Duke Power Co., Seneca, S.C., 1973-91, environ. mgmt. scientist, 1991-94; youth apprenticeship coord. Morgan County Bd. Edn., Madison, Ga., 1996—. Com. mem. Vendor Regulation Com., Madison, Ga. 1995-96, Downtown Bus. Coun., Madison, 1996—; commn. mem. Hist. Preservation Commn., Madison, 1997—; steering com. Madison Safekids Coalition, 1997—. Named Explorer Leader of Yr. Oconee Dist. Boy Scouts, 1993. Mem. Profl. Assn. Diving Instrs., Phi Kappa Phi. Democrat. Avocations: scuba diving (cert. instr.), snow skiing. Home: PO Box 770 Madison GA 30650-0770 Office: Morgan County HS 1231 College Dr Madison GA 30650-1462

JONES, HERBERT CORNELIUS, III, otolaryngologist; b. 1936. MD, Ind. U., 1961. Intern Brook Gen. Hosp., San Angonio, 1961-62; resident in otolaryngology H&NS U. Ill. Coll. Medicine, 1965-68; mem. staff S.W. Cmty. Hosp., Atlanta, 1968—; clin. assoc. prof. otolaryngology Sch. Medicine Morehouse, Atlanta, 1986—; mem. staff Ga. Bapt. Hosp., Atlanta, 1982—. Mem. Am. Acad. Otolaryngology Head and Neck Surgery, Nat. Med. Assn. Office: Jones Otolaryngology 2600 Martin Luther King Jr Dr Atlanta GA 30311-1636*

JONES, HERMAN OTTO, JR., corporate professional; b. Jacksonville, Fla., Dec. 1, 1933; s. Herman Otto Sr. and Esther (Powell) J.; m. Marjorie Seaver, June 4, 1955 (dec. June 1996); two children (dec.); m. M. Beth Seaver, May 10, 1997. BSA, U. Fla., 1956. V.p. Oak Crest Hatcheries, Inc., Jacksonville, 1956-71; v.p. Oak Crest Enterprises, Inc., Jacksonville, 1958-71; dir. sales Diversified Imports, Inc., Lakewood, N.J., 1971-73, BEC Ltd., Winchester, Eng., 1973-78; sales rep. Paul Revere Ins. Co., Jacksonville, 1978-81; v.p. Anitox Corp., Buford, Ga., 1981-85; pres. Gateway Suppliers, Inc., Jacksonville, 1986-98; v.p. Sales Agritek Bio Ingredients Corp., Montreal, Quebec, Can., 1993-97; pres. Gateway Bio-Nutrients, Inc., 1998—. Contbr. articles to profl. jours. Vice chmn. bd. deacons Riverside Bapt. Ch., 1988-89, deacon, 1991-94, sec. of deacons, 1991-92, dir. Sunday Sch., 1992-93; bd. dirs. South Shore Condos, 1998—, treas., 1998—. Named Outstanding Mem., Fla. Poultry Fedn., 1965, Southeastern Poultry and Egg Assn., 1963, State Outstanding Young Farmer, Fla. Jaycees, 1968; recipient Disting. Service award, Jacksonville Jaycees, 1970. Mem. Greater Jacksonville Fair Assn., Rotary (bd. dirs. South Jacksonville 1989-91), Masons (master), Shriners, Jesters, Order Ea. Star (past patron). Republican. Avocations: golf, travel. Home: CND #703 1551 1st St S Jacksonville Beach FL 32250-6360

JONES, HIRAM L. (DOC), career officer, chaplain. BS, Sam Houston State U., 1959; MDiv, So. Meth. U., 1963; DD (hon.), Wiley Coll., 1974; postgrad., Washington Sch. Psychiatry, 1976, Calif. Family Study Inst., 1976, Georgetown U., 1978; grad., Air Command and Staff Coll., 1982. Ordained to ministry Meth. Ch. Commd. capt. USAF, 1970, advanced through grades to brig. gen., 1997; Protestan chaplain Kincheloe AFB, Mich., 1969-72, Andrews AFB, Md., 1974-78, Kalkar Kaserne, W. Germany, 1978-79; sr. Protestant chaplain Bergstrom AFB, Tex., 1979-81; chaplain, faculty mem. Air Command and Staff Coll., Maxwell AFB, Ala., 1982-85; chief plans and program div. Office Command Chaplain Hdqs. Pacific Air Forces, Hickam AFB, Hawaii, 1985-88; chief budget and logistics div. Office Command Chaplain Hdqs. Air Tng. Command, Randolph AFB, Tex., 1988-91; sr. chaplain Bolling AFB, D.C., 1991-93; command chaplain Hdqs. USAF in Europe, Ramstein AFB, W. Germany, 1993-95, Hdqs. Air Combat Command, Langley AFB, Va., 1995-97; dep. chief Air Force Chaplain Svc. Hdqs. USAF, Washington, 1997—. Decorated Legion of Merit. Mem. Tex. Annual Conf. United Meth. Ch. Office: HQ USAF/HC 112 Luke Ave Ste 313 Bolling AFB DC 20332-9050

JONES, HOUSTON GWYNNE, history educator; b. Yanceyville, N.C., Jan. 7, 1924; s. Paul Hosier and Lemma Sue (Fowlkes) J. BS, Appalachian State Coll., 1949; MA, George Peabody Coll., 1950; postgrad., NYU, 1951-52; cert. archival adminstrn., Am. U., 1957; PhD, Duke U., 1965. Prof. history Oak Ridge (N.C.) Mil. Inst., 1950-53; chmn. div. soc. scis. West Ga. Coll., Carrollton, 1955-56; state archivist of N.C. State Dept. Archives & Hist., Raleigh, N.C., 1956-68; dir. State Dept. Archives & History, Raleigh, N.C., 1968-74; adj. prof. history U. N.C., Chapel Hill, 1974-94, dir. N.C. Coll., 1974-94, Thomas W. Davis rsch. historian, 1994—; mem. Nat. Hist. Publs. and Records Commn., Washington, 1978-86, N.C. Hist. Commn., Raleigh, 1977—. Author: Books For History's Sake, 1966, The Records of a Nation, 1969, Local Government Records, 1980, North Carolina Illustrated, 1983, North Carolina History: An Annotated Bibliography, 1995, Historical Consciousness in the Early Republic, 1995; editor-in-chief N.C. Hist. Rev., 1968-74; gen. editor: North Caroliniana Society Imprints, 1978—. Chmn. Am's. 400th Anniversary Com., Raleigh, 1978-80; sec.-treas. North Caroliniana Soc., Chapel Hill, 1975—; sec. Joint Commn. on Status of Nat. Archives, Washington, 1967-68. Recipient Disting. Alumnus award Appalachian State U., 1971, Cannon Cup hist. preservation N.C. Soc. for Preservation of Antiquities, 1971, Univ. Svc. award U. N.C. Gen. Alumni Assn., 1990, Disting. Svc. award in documentary publ. and preservation Nat. Hist. Publs. and Records Commn., Washington, 1990. Fellow Soc. Am. Archivists (pres. 1968-69, Waldo G. Leland prize 1967, 81), Soc. North Caroliniana (Soc. award 1994); mem. N.C. Literary and Hist. Assn. (sec. 1969-75, pres. 1975-76, Crittenden Meml. award 1977), N.C. Writers Conf. (chmn. 1982, Conf. award 1994), Am. Assn. for State and Local History (sec. 1978-82, award of merit 1968, award of distinction 1989), Nat. Assn. State Hist. Preservation Officers (com. chmn. 1972-74), Hist. Soc. N.C. (pres. 1979-80, R.D.W. Connor award 1956), Carolina Club. Democrat. Home: 302 Country Club Rd Chapel Hill NC 27514-3906 Office: U NC Libr NC Collection Chapel Hill NC 27599-3930

JONES, HOWARD LANGWORTHY, retired educational administrator, consultant; b. Pelham, N.Y., Nov. 16, 1917; s. Dyer Tillinghast and Margaret (Langworthy) J.; m. Margaret Irene Lloyd, Apr. 27, 1940; 1 son, D. Lloyd. A.B., Colgate U., 1939; M.A., Syracuse U., 1948, Ed.D., 1951; LL.D., Colgate, 1969. Tchr., coach secondary sch. East Hampton, N.Y., 1939-42; mem. faculty Colgate U., 1947-61, prof., 1947-55, v.p., 1956-61; pres. Northfield (Mass.) Mt. Hermon Sch., 1961-79; spl. asst. to pres. Colgate U., Hamilton, N.Y., 1979—; ptnr. Joerger, Jones, & Krehel; dir. Imagetics Corp., Greenfield.; Bd. dirs. A Better Chance, Inc., Boston, 1962—, Elderhostel Inc.; trustee Good Hope Sch., St. Croix, V.I., 1966-73, Cushing Acad., Asburnham, Mass., 1967-73, Colgate U., 1969—, Coll. V.I., 1962—. Served as pilot USAAF, 1943-47. Mem. Am. Mgmt. Assn. (dir. 1965-71), Nat. Assn. Ind. Schs. (dir. 1971—), Phi Delta Kappa, Phi Kappa Tau. Clubs: Univ. (N.Y.C.). Home: 22 E Pleasant St Hamilton NY 13346-1330

JONES, HOWARD ST. CLAIRE, JR., electronics engineering executive; b. Richmond, Va., Aug. 18, 1921; s. Howard St. Claire and Martha Lillian (Mason) J.; m. Evelyn Mercer Saunders, Nov. 27, 1946. BS, Va. Union U., 1943, DSc (hon.), 1971; cert. engring., Howard U., 1944; MSEE, Bucknell U., 1973; DHL (hon.), Trinity Coll., Hartford, Conn., 1997. Registered profl. engr., D.C., Va., Md. Indsl. engring. aid Bur. Ships USN, Washington, 1943; electro mech. engring. aide U.S. Bur. Standards, Washington, 1944; electronic physicist U.S. Bur. Standards, 1946-53; electronic scientist, engr., supervisory phys. scientist Harry Diamond Labs., AUS, Washington, 1953-80; tech. cons. microwave electronics, 1980—; Tchr. radio physics Hilltop Radio-Electronics Inst., Washington, 1946-52; assoc. prof. elec. engring. Howard U., 1958-63, adj. prof., 1982; cons. microwave engring., 1965-69; cons. univ. relations, 1983—. Contbr. tech. reports and publs. Served as instr. mech. engring. AUS, 1944-46. Recipient four Sustained Superior Performance or Spl. Act awards Harry Diamond Labs AUS, 1956, 68, 70, 75, Inventor of Year award, 1972; Sec. Army Fellowship award, 1972; Army Research and Devel. award, 1975; Meritorious Civilian Service award, 1976, 80. Fellow IEEE (Harry Diamond Field award 1985), AAAS, Washington Acad. Sci.; mem. ASEE, NAE (elect mem.). Achievements include holding 31 U.S. patents microwave field. Home and Office: 3001 Veazey Ter NW Washington DC 20008-5454

JONES, HUGH RICHARD, lawyer; b. New Hartford, N.Y., Mar. 19, 1914; s. Hugh Richard and Anna (Jones) J.; m. Jean McMillen, July 3, 1937; children: Hugh Richard, Anne E., Thomas McM., Jean C., David B. AB, Hamilton Coll., 1935, LLD, 1974; JD, Harvard U., 1939; LLD, Albany Law Sch., 1981, Syracuse U., 1995; DD, Gen. Theol. Sem., 1987. Bar: N.Y. 1940, U.S. Supreme Ct. 1963. Instr. Am. U. at Cairo, 1935-36; assoc. Burke & Burke, N.Y.C., 1939-42, Miller, Hubbell & Evans, Utica, N.Y., 1945; ptnr. Miller, Hubbell & Evans, to 1953, Evans, Pirnie & Burdick, Utica, 1953-69, Evans, Burdick, Severn & Jones, Utica, 1970-72; assoc. judge N.Y. Ct. Appeals, Albany, N.Y., 1973-84; resident counsel Hiscock & Barclay, Syracuse, N.Y., 1985-91; advisor Restatement of Trusts, 3d, 1994-97, Prudent Investor Rule, 1987-90. Mem. N.Y. State Bd. Social Welfare, 1959-69, chmn., 1964-69, dir. local health and welfare agys., Utica; trustee Hamilton Coll., 1967—, SUNY, 1969-72; chancellor to presiding bishop Episcopal Ch., 1986-91, chancellor to Bishop of Cen. N.Y. 1957—; chmn. Gov. Cuomo's Adv. Commn. on Liability Ins., N.Y., 1986; chm. Temp. State Commn. on Exec., Legis. and Jud. Compensation, 1987-88; chmn. Constl. Commn. Jud. Nomination, 1992-97. Served to lt. comdr. USNR, 1942-45. Decorated Bronze Star with Combat V.; recipient Humanitarian award for services to Spanish Speaking Cmty. of N.Y. State, 1969; Civic award Colgate U., 1970; William R. Hopkins Bronze medal St. David's Soc. State of N.Y., 1974; Bishop's Cross, Diocese of Cen. N.Y., 1986, 94. Fellow Am. Bar Found.; mem. ABA, N.Y. State Bar Assn. (pres. 1971-72, Root-Stimson award 1978, Gold medal 1985), Oneida County Bar Assn. (pres. 1962), Assn. Bar City N.Y., Am. Law Inst., Am. Judicature Soc. (Herbert Harley award 1987), New York County Lawyers Assn. (hon.). Home: Acacia Village Apt 205 509 Coolidge Rd Utica NY 13502*

JONES, J. GILBERT, research consultant; b. San Francisco, June 1, 1922; s. Enoch Roscoe L. Sr. and Remedios (Ponce de Leon) J.; student U.S. Mcht. Marine Acad., 1942-44, San Francisco City Coll., 1942-44, 46-47; AB, U. Calif., Berkeley, 1949, MA, 1952. Lic. pvt. investigator. Ins. insp. Ins. Cos. Insp. Bur., San Francisco, 1959-62; pub. rels. cons., San Francisco, 1962-67; ins. insp. Am. Svc. Bur., San Francisco, 1967-72; propr., mgr. Dawn Universal Internat. San Francisco, 1972—, Dawn Universal Security Svc., San Francisco, 1983—. Mem. SAR, Libr. of Congress Assocs., Sons. Spanish-Am. War Vets. Soc., World Affairs Coun. N. Calif., U. Calif. Alumni Assn., Commonwealth Club of Calif. Republican. Office: PO Box 424057 San Francisco CA 94142-4057

JONES, J. KENLEY, journalist; b. Greenville, S.C., Feb. 24, 1935; s. J. Clyde and Mildred Idel (Smith) J.; m. Margaret Jean McPherson, Dec. 11, 1965; children—Stephanie, Jason, Eleanor. Student, Furman U., 1953-55; B.S. in Speech, Northwestern U., 1957, M.S. in Journalism, 1963; postgrad., Columbia U., 1964-65. Reporter City News Bur. of Chgo., 1962; reporter, cameraman KRNT-TV, Des Moines, 1963-64, WSB-TV, Atlanta, 1965-69; fgn. corr. NBC News, Asia, 1969-72; corr. NBC News (Southeast Bur.), Atlanta, 1972-98. Served with USNR, 1958-61. Recipient Overseas Press Club award for best television reporting from abroad, 1970. Mem. AFTRA, Nat. Acad. Television Arts and Scis. Presbyterian. Office: 100 Colony Sq Ste 1140 1175 W Peachtree St NW Atlanta GA 30309-3432

JONES, J. KENNETH, art dealer, former museum administrator; b. Syracuse, N.Y., Jan. 1, 1945; s. John Paul and Esther Elizabeth (Auborn) J. B.F.A., Ringling Sch. Art, Sarasota, Fla., 1969. Designer Southeastern Galleries, Charleston, S.C., 1969, designer, warehouse mgr., display coordinator, 1973; designer Engel Bros. Furnitue, Charleston, 1969-70; designer, buyer Maxwell Bros. Furniture, Charleston, 1970-73; curator decorative arts and cultural history Charleston Mus., 1973-84; curator Henry Morrison Flagler Mus., Palm Beach, Fla., 1984-85; asst. dir. Henry Morrison Flagler Mus., Palm Beach, 1985-91; owner The Estate Agts. Antiques, Asheville, N.C., 1991—; mgr. Antique Market Gallery, Asheville, N.C., 1998—. Mem. Mayor's Com. for Econs. of Amenity, Charleston, 1982-84; mem. Save the Ft. Sumter Flag Com., Ft. Moultrie, Sullivans Island, S.C., 1983. Episcopalian. Address: 73 Cumberland Ave Asheville NC 28801-2237

JONES, J. TODD, veterinarian; b. Birmingham, Ala., Sept. 3, 1969; s. James Harold and Sandra Gayle (Peoples) J. BS in Microbiology, Auburn U., 1992, DVM, 1995. Lic. veterinarian, Ala., Ky., Ga. Veterinarian Caldwell Mill Animal Clinic, Birmingham, 1995-96, Gainesway Animal Clinic, Lexington, Ky., 1996-98, N. Cobb Animal Clinic, Kennesaw, Ga., 1998—. Mem. AVMA, Am. Assn. Animal Hosp., Ala. Vet. Med. Assn., Ky. Vet. Med. Assn., Ga. Vet. Med. Assn., Greater Atlanta Vet. Medicine Assn., Auburn Alumni Assn. Republican. Baptist. Office: North Cobb Animal Clinic 2680 N Cobb Pkwy Kennesaw GA 30152

JONES, JACK DELLIS, oil company executive; b. Carnegie, Okla., Mar. 3, 1925; s. Henry Clifford and Dora Dean (Dellis) J.; m. Sally Kramer, Dec. 19, 1953; children—Margaret K., Elizabeth D., Susan L. B.S., U.S. Naval Acad., 1947; J.D., U. Tulsa, 1955. Bar: Okla. 1955, Tex. 1960, Calif. 1962. Engr. Sunray Oil Co., 1953-55; asst. county atty. Tulsa County, 1955-56; with Getty Oil Co., 1956-84, v.p., 1966-80, group v.p., 1980-84; pres. Getty Refining and Mktg. Co., Tulsa, 1973-84; also dir.; dir. First Nat. Bank & Trust Co., Tulsa, Banks Mid-Am. Trustee Hillcrest Med. Ctr., Tulsa, 1977-86; bd. dirs. Tulsa Salvation Army, 1977—, Ark. Basin Devel. Assn., 1978-85. Served with U.S. Navy, 1943-50, 51-53. Mem. Calif. Bar Assn., Tex. Bar Assn., Okla. Bar Assn., Am. Petroleum Inst. (bd. dirs. 1980-84), Met. Tulsa C. of C. (bd. dirs. 1977-86), Southern Hills Country Club, Shriners, Rotary. Episcopalian.

JONES, JAMES ARTHUR, retired utilities executive; b. Anderson, S.C., Sept. 18, 1917; s. James Rol and Maude Magdalene (Pendleton) J.; m. Clara Melba Sharpe, May 7, 1942; children: Elva Jones Summerlin, James Roland, Michael Arthur, Robert Franklin, William Lawrence. BS, N.C. State U., 1951. With Carolina Power & Light Co., Wilmington and Raleigh, N.C., 1951—; v.p. Raleigh, 1969-70, sr. v.p., 1970-73, exec. v.p., 1973—, chief oper. officer, 1976, vice chmn., 1981, also bd. dirs. Past pres. N.C. State U. Engring. Found. Named Disting. Engring. Alumnus, N.C. State U., 1974, Watauga medal, 1993, Outstanding Engr., Raleigh Engrs., 1976. Fellow ASME; mem. NSPE, Am. Soc. Nuclear Engrs., Am. Inst. Indsl. Engr., N.C. Soc. Engrs. (Outstanding Engr. award 1974), N.C. Health Physics Soc., Masons, Pi Tau Sigma, Phi Kappa Phi. Home: 200 W Cornwall Rd Apt 107 Cary NC 27511-3865

JONES, JAMES CURTISS, surgeon; b. Dillon, S.C., Apr. 25, 1943; s. Samuel and Eunice Irene (Mallett) Jones; m. Dianne McAdams, Oct. 18, 1986; children: Lashawn, James II, Eunicia, Jette, Morgan. BS, Morehouse Coll., 1965; MD, U. Calif., San Francisco, 1969. Diplomate Am. Bd. Surgery, Am. Bd. Thoracic Surgery. Commd. maj. U.S. Army, 1979, advanced through grades to col., 1992; chief thoracic surgeon Malcolm Grow USAF Med. Ctr., Andrews AFB, Md., 1979-83; staff thoracic surgeon Landstuhl (Germany) U.S. Army Med. Ctr., 1983-86; chief thoracic surgeon Madigan Army Med. Ctr., Ft. Lewis, Wash., 1986-90; staff thoracic surgeon Letterman Army Med. Ctr., Presidio Army Base, Calif., 1990; chief thoracic surgeon 8th Evacuation Hosp., Saudi Arabia, 1990-91; staff thoracic surgeon Brooke Army Med. Ctr., Ft. Sam Houston, Tex., 1991-92; chief thoracic surgery Womack Army Med. Ctr., Ft. Bragg, N.C., 1992-96; pvt. practice Fayetteville, N.C., 1997—. Active Friends of Pacific Luth. U., Tacoma, 1987-90, Friends of Weymouth, Southern Pines, N.C., 1995-96. Nat. Med.-Sloan fellow Nat. Med. Fellowships, 1965-69. Fellow ACS, Am. Coll. Chest Physicians; mem. Soc. Thoracic Surgeons, So. Thoracic Surg. Assn., Fayetteville Symphony Orch. Assn., Omega Psi Phi. Baptist. Avocations: swimming, listening to music, hiking, mountaineering. Office: 517 Owen Dr Fayetteville NC 28304-3433

JONES, JAMES EARL, actor; b. Arkabutla, Miss., Jan. 17, 1931; s. Robert Earl and Ruth (Williams) J.; m. Cecilia Hart, Mar. 15, 1982; 1 child, Flynn Earl. BA, U. Mich., 1953, LHD (hon.), 1970; diploma, Am. Theatre Wing, 1957; studied with Lee Strasburg, Ted Danielewsky; DFA (hon.), Princeton U., 1980, Yale U., 1982; LHD (hon.), Columbia Coll., 1982; ArtsD (hon.), NYU, 1994. Appeared in plays: Much Ado About Nothing, 1955-59, 1961, Stalag 17, 1955-59, The Caine Mutiny, 1955-59, Arsenic and Old Lace, 1955-59, The Desperate Hours, 1955-59, Othello numerous appearances (Drama Desk award for best performance, 1964, Vernon Rice award, 1965), Egghead (Broadway debut), Sunrise at Campobello, 1958, The Big Knife, 1959, , King Henry V, 1960, Measure for Measure, 1960, Richard II, 1961, A Midsummer Night's Dream, 1961, The Apple (Obie award best actor) 1961, Clandestine on the Morning Line (Obie award best actor) 1961, Richard III, 1961, Taming of the Shrew, 1961, Moon on a Rainbow Shawl (Obie award best actor) 1962, The Merchant of Venice, 1962, The Tempest, 1962, Toys in the Attic, 1962, Macbeth, 1962, The Winter's Tale, 1963, The Emperor Jones, 1964, 1967, Baal (Obie award best performance) 1965, Coriolanus, 1965, Troilus & Cressida, 1965, The Great White Hope, 1969 (Drama Desk award outstanding performance 1969, Golden Globe award new male star of yr. 1971, Tony award for best actor, Antoinette Perry award best actor in a dramatic play, 1969), Les Blancs (Drama Desk award outstanding performance) 1970, Hamlet (Drama Desk award outstanding performance) 1973, King Lear, 1973, The Cherry Orchard (Drama Desk award outstanding performance) 1973, The Iceman Cometh, 1973, Of Mice and Men, 1974, Paul Robeson, 1977, Hedda Gabler, 1980, Master Harold and The Boys, 1982-83, Fences, 1985-87 (Drama Desk award, Antoinette Perry award, Outer Critics Circle award for Best Actor, 1987, Tony award for Best Actor, Drama Critics award); appeared in movies: Dr. Strangelove, 1963, The Great White Hope, 1970 (Acad. Award nom. best actor 1970, Golden Globe award new male star of 1971), King: A Filmed Record Montgomery to Memphis, 1970, The Man, 1972, Malcolm X, 1972, Claudine, 1973 (Image award best actor NAACP, 1974, Golden Glove award non. best actor in a musical or comedy, 1974) The River Niger, 1975, The Bingo Long Traveling All-Stars and Motor Kings, 1976, Star Wars, 1977 (voice of Darth Vader), The Greatest, 1977, A Piece of the Action, 1978, The Empire Strikes Back, 1980 (voice of Darth Vader), Conan the Barbarian, 1982, Return of the Jedi, 1983 (voice of Darth Vader), Soul Man, 1986, Allan Quartermain & the Lost City of Gold, 1987, Matewan, 1987, Gardens of Stone, 1987, Coming to America, 1988, Field of Dreams, 1989, The Hunt For Red October, 1990, Sneakers, 1991, Patriot Games, 1992, Meteor Man, 1993, Sommersby, 1993, The Sandlot, 1993, The Lion King, 1994 (voice), Clear and Present Danger, 1994, Cry The Beloved Country, 1995, A Family Thing, 1996, Looking for Richard, 1996, Gang Related, 1997, Summer's End, 1998, Undercover Angel, 1999, Quest for Atlantis, 1999; TV movies include: The Cay, 1974 (Golden Gate award, Golden Hugo award, Gabriel award, 1975), King Lear, 1974, Jesus of Nazareth, 1977, Roots: The Next Generation, 1979, Guyana Tragedy: The Story of Jim Jones, 1980, The Atlanta Child Murders, 1985, The Last Elephant (Ace nomination) 1990, Heatwave, 1990 (Ace award, best actor in a supporting role, Emmy award best supporting actor in a spl. or mini-series 1991), By Dawn's Early Light, 1990 (Emmy award nomination outstanding supporting actor 1991), The Vernon Johns Story, 1993, What the Deaf Man Heard, 1997; TV series: (narrator) Malcolm X, 1972, (host) Black Omnibus, 1973, (host) Vegetable Soup, 1975, Sojourner, 1975, Third and Oak (Ace award); star TV series Paris, 1979-80, Gabriel's Fire, 1990 (Outstanding Lead Actor in Dramatic Series Emmy award 1991), Pros & Cons, 1991 (Emmy award best actor in a drama series, Best Actor NAACP), Under One Roof, 1995; appeared on TV shows Guiding Light, As The World Turns, The Defenders, East Side, West Side, Dr. Kildare, Tarzan, Highway to Heaven, L.A. Law, Homicide: Life on the Street, Lois & Clark: The New Adventures of Superman, Frasier, Law & Order, Touched by an Angel, Picket Fences, (voice) The Simpsons, Garfield and Friends; appeared, narrated TV specials including Black Omnibus: Negro in the Arts, 1973, (narrator) Beauty & The Beast CBS Library Misunderstood Monsters, 1981, Aladdin & His Wonderful Lamp Fairie Tale Theatre, 1986, Wonderworks, 1986, Soldier Boys CBS Schoolbreak Special, 1987, The 41st Annual Tony Awards, 1987, Square One Television, 1987, America Picks The All-Time Favorite Movies, 1988, Teach 109 American Playhouse, 1988, (narrator) A Hard Road to Glory: The Black Athlete, 1988, (narrator) Michael Jackson: Motown on Showtime, 1988, (host, narrator) The Way We Hear Smithsonian World, 1988, (host narrator) Who Lives Who Dies, 1988, Saturday Night with Connie Chung, 1989, Third and Oak: The Pool Hall American Playwrights Theatre, 1989, The 43rd Annual Tony Awards, 1989, Reflections on the Silver Screen with Prof. Richard Brown, 1990, America's All Star Tribute to Oprah Winfrey, 1990, World Series, 1990, 44th Annual Tony Awards, 1990, Golden Glove awards, 1990, Nat. Meml. Day Concert, 1990, 42d Annual Primetime Emmy Awards, 1991, A Party for Richard Pryor, 1991, 17th Annual People's Choice Awards, 1991, 12th Annual Ace Awards, 1991, (narrator) Visitors from the Unknown, 1991, Muhammad Ali, Biography, 1991, Portrait of Castro's Cuba, 1991, Twenty-Third Annual NAACP Image Awards, 1991, When It Was A Game, 1991, (narrator) The Creative Spirit, 1992, AFI Salute to Sidney Poitier, 1992, Shelly Duvall's Bedtime Stories, 1992, (narrator) Ivory Wars: Lincoln Memorial Day Concert, 1993, 47th Annual Tony Awards, 1993, The Second Civil War, 1996, Alone, 1997, Lincoln Memorial Day Concert, 1997; recordings include: Great American Documents (with Orsen Welles, Henry Fonda, Helen Hayes), 1976, The People Could Fly, Oedipus Rex, To be Young, Gifted and Black, Poems from Black Africa, The Emperor Jones, Native Son, The Great White Hope, John Henry, The New Testament, Portraits of Freedom; appeared in Bell Atlantic Commercials; the voice behind CNN Lincoln Portrait, 1993; vocal introduction 3rd Rock from the Sun; co-author: (with

Penelope Niven) James Earl Jones: Voices and Silences, 1993. Recipient The Village Voice Off-Broadway award, 1962, Theatre World award, 1962, Hon. Doctoral Degree Black Am. Culture Festival, 1969, Grammy award, 1976, medal for spoken lang. Am. Acad. Arts and Letters, 1981, Office of Black Ministries Toussaint medallion, 1982, Theater Hall of Fame award, 1985, Emmy award for performance in children's programming, Soldier Boys, CBS Schoolbreak Spl., 1987-88, L.A. Film Tchrs. Assn. Jean Renoir award, 1990, Commonwealth award Disting. Svc. in the Dramatic Arts, Bank of Del., 1991, Nat. Medal of Arts for outstanding contbn. to cultural life of country, 1992, Hall of Fame Image award for great contbn. to arts, NAACP, 1992, UCLA medal, 1993; named Disting. Artist, L.A. Music Ctr. Club, 1994, John Houseman award The Acting Co., 1995; numerous other acting awards, nominations-Obie, Drama Desk, Tony, Golden Globe, Outer Critics Cir., ACE, others. Mem. Nat. Council of Arts (Presdl. appt. to adv. bd. 1962, presdl. appointee 1970-76), Actors' Equity Assn., SAG, Am. Fedn. TV and Radio Artists, Theatre Comm. Group (bd. dirs. 1962);. Address: Horatio Prodns PO Box 610 Pawling NY 12564-0610*

JONES, JAMES EDWARD, JR., retired law educator; b. Little Rock, June 4, 1924. B.A., Lincoln U., Mo., 1950; M.A., U. Ill. Inst. Labor and Indsl. Relations, 1951; J.D., U. Wis., 1956. Bar: Wis., U.S. Supreme Ct. Indsl. relations analyst U.S. Wage Stabilization Bd., Region 7, 1951-53; legis. atty. Dept. Labor, Washington, 1956-63, counsel for labor relations, 1963-66, dir. office labor mgmt., policy devel., 1966-67, assoc. solicitor labor div. labor relations and civil rights, 1967-69; vis. prof. law and indsl. relations U. Wis.-Madison, 1969-70, prof., 1970-93, Bascom prof. law, 1983-91, Nathan P. Feinsinger prof. labor law, 1991-93, prof. emeritus, 1993—; dir. Inst. Relations, Research Inst., 1971-73, assoc. Inst. for Research on Poverty, 1970, dir. Ctr. for Equal Employment and Affirmative Action, Indsl. Relations Research Inst., 1974-93; mem. research and edn. staff Pulp, Sulphite and Paper Mill Workers, AFL-CIO, 1958; mem. Fed. Service Impasses Panel, 1978-82; mem. pub. rev. bd. Internat. Union UAW, 1970—; mem. adv. com. NRC Nat. Acad. Scis., 1971-73; mem. Wis. Manpower Planning Council, 1971-76; mem. spl. com. on criminal justice, standards and goals Wis. Council Criminal Justice, 1975-76; bd. dirs. labor law sect. Wis. State Bar, 1976; mem. Fed. Mediation and Conciliation Arbitration Panel, 1975—; spl. arbitrator U.S. Steel and United Steel Workers, 1976-86; mem. expert com. on family budget revision Dept. Labor Series, 1978-79; cons. in field. Mem. Madison Police and Fire Commn., 1973-77, 94-95, pres., 1976-77. Recipient Sec. Labor Career Svc. award Dept. Labor, 1963, Hilldale award (Social Sci. Divsn.), 1990-91, Wis. Law Alumni Disting. Svc. award, 1995, tchr. of yr. award Soc. Am. Law Tchrs., 1998, disting. alumni award U. Ill., 1996; John Hay Whitney fellow, 1953, 54. Mem. Labor Law Group Trust (chmn. editorial policy com. 1978-82), Indsl. Relations Research Assn. (treas. Washington chpt. 1968-69, exec. bd. 1977-80), Fed. Bar Assn. (chmn. labor law com. 1967-69, dep. chmn. council on labor law and labor relations 1979-80), State Bar Wis., Nat. Bar Assn. (nat. adv. com. of equal employment clin. project 1970-79), Nat. Acad. Arbitrators, Order of Coif, Phi Kappa Phi. Office: Univ Wisconsin Sch of Law Madison WI 53706

JONES, JAMES FLEMING, JR., college president, Roman language and literature educator; b. Atlanta, Apr. 9, 1947; s. James F. and Sarah Kate (Smith) J.; m. Jan Sheets, Nov. 15, 1969; children: Jennifer, Justin, Jason. BA, U. Va., 1969; MA, Emory U., 1972; cert., U. Paris-Sorbonne, 1972; MPhil, Columbia U., 1974, Ph.D., 1975. Tchr., chmn. dept. fgn. langs. Woodward Acad., College Park, Ga., 1969-72; preceptor Columbia U., 1973-75; prof. Romance langs. and lit. Washington U., St. Louis, 1975-91, chmn. dept. Romance langs., 1982-91; vice provost, dean Dedman Coll., So. Meth. U., Dallas, 1991-96; pres. Kalamazoo Coll., 1996—; sr. visitor for Hilary term, Oxford, 1987. Precentor, Ch. of St. Michael and St. George, Clayton, Mo., 1978-91. Decorated chevalier Ordre des Palmes Académiques; recipient Avis Blewett award Am. Guild Organists, 1989, Faculty award Washington U., 1990, Disting. Alumnus award Ga. Mil. Acad.-Woodward Acad. Alumni Assn., 1990; NEH fellow, 1976, Folger Inst. fellow, 1982. Mem. MLA, Am. Assn. Tchrs. of French, Am. Soc. 18th Century Studies, Soc. Rousseau Studies, Soc. Prévost d'Exiles. Office: Kalamazoo Coll Office of Pres 1200 Academy St Kalamazoo MI 49006-3268*

JONES, JAMES PARKER, federal judge; b. Tampa, Fla., July 3, 1940; s. Edmund Leroy and Nellie (Parker) J.; m. Mary Duke Trent, June 24, 1964; children: J. Trent, Benjamin P., Jonathan E. AB, Duke U., 1962; LLB, U. Va., 1965. Bar: Va. 1965. Asst. atty. gen. Va. Atty. Gen., Richmond, 1965-66; law clk. U.S. Ct. Appeals, Richmond, 1966-68; atty. Penn, Stuart, Eskridge & Jones, Abingdon and Bristol, Va., 1968-96; judge U.S. Dist. Ct., Abingdon, Va., 1996—; bd. dirs. Va. Ctr. for Innovative Tech., Reston, Va., 1987-90. State senator Commonwealth of Va., 1983-88; mem. Dem. Nat. Com., 1982-92; mem. State Bd. Edn., 1990-96, pres., 1992-96. Fellow Am. Coll. Trial Lawyers (mem. Va. state com. 1995-96); mem. The Nature Conservancy (trustee Va. chpt. 1988-96). Democrat. Espicopalian. Home: 107 Hillside Dr NE Abingdon VA 24210-2013 Office: US Dist Ct 180 E Main St Abingdon VA 24210-2839

JONES, JAMES REES, retired oil company executive; b. Britton, S.D., Nov. 26, 1916; s. Buell Fay and Florence (Bockler) J.; m. Betty Jane Preston, May 28, 1943; children—Quentin Buell, Newton James, Preston Lee. B.S. in Accountancy, U. Ill., 1938. From accountant to sr. accountant Ernst & Ernst (C.P.A.'s), Detroit and Kalamazoo, 1938-41, 46-48; auditor, then div. auditor, chem. plant office mgr. Pan Am. Petroleum Corp., 1948-56; comptroller Amoco Chems. Corp., Chgo., 1956-62; mgr. auditing Standard Oil Co., Ind., 1962-63; controller Murphy Oil Corp., El Dorado, Ark., 1963-74; v.p. Murphy Oil Corp., 1974-75; also dir.; chmn., mng. dir. Canam Offshore Ltd., Hamilton, Bermuda, 1975—; pres., dir. Mentor Ins. Ltd., Hamilton, 1975—; controller Ocean Drilling & Exploration Co., El Dorado, 1963-66, also; dir.; controller, dir. Deltic Farm & Timber Co., Inc., El Dorado, 1963-72, v.p., 1963-75. Past mem. El Dorado Water Utilities Commn.; past pres., bd. dirs. United Campaign El Dorado. Served to capt. AUS, 1941-46. Mem. Fin. Execs. Inst., Am. Petroleum Inst., Mid-Continent Oil and Gas Assn., Phi Kappa Psi. Home: 905 Kings Ct Russellville AR 72801-5719

JONES, JAMES RICHARD, business administration educator; b. Saginaw, Mich., May 25, 1940; s. George B. and Rena Jones; m. Sheila I. Jones; children: Kimme Ann, Kriste Gay, Kelle Lyn, Karme Jill. B.A., Mich. State U., 1962, M.B.A., 1964; PhD, Ariz. State U., 1969. Research analyst Mich. Public Service Commn., Lansing, 1962; systems analyst Allis-Chalmers Mfg. Co., West Allis, Wis., 1964-65; asst. prof. transp. U. Houston, 1967-70; asso. prof. mktg. U. Ga., Athens, 197—72; spl. asst. Dept. Transp., Washington, 1972-74; transp. economist Dept. Transp., 1974-76; Disting. prof. transp. Memphis State U., 1976-81; George R. Brown Disting. prof. bus. Trinity U., San Antonio, 1981—; cons. in field. Author books in field; contbr. articles to profl. jours.; bd. editors: Jour. Mktg. Theory and Practice, 1992—. Keeshin fellow, 1963. Mem. Am. Soc. Traffic and Transp., Am. Mktg. Assn., Council Logistics Mgmt., Transp. Research Forum, Transp. Research Bd., So. Mktg. Assn., Assn. Mktg. Theory and Practice, Am. Inst. Decision Scis. Home: 1711 Brush Creek Dr San Antonio TX 78248-2003 Office: Trinity U 715 Stadium Dr San Antonio TX 78212-3104

JONES, JAMES ROBERT, ambassador, former congressman, lawyer; b. Muskogee, Okla., May 5, 1939; m. Olivia Barclay, 1968; children—Geoffrey Gardner, Adam Winston. AB in Journalism and Govt., U. Okla., 1961; LLB, Georgetown U., 1964. Bar: Okla. 1964, D.C. 1964. Legis. asst. to Congressman Ed Edmondson, 1961-64; spl. asst. to Pres. Lyndon Johnson, 1965-69; mem. 93d-99th congresses from 1st Dist. Okla., 1973-87; chmn. budget com. 97th and 98th Congress; chmn. social security subcom. 99th Congress; ptnr. Dickstein, Shapiro & Morin, Washington, 1987-89; chmn. bd., chief exec. officer Am. Stock Exch., N.Y.C., 1989-93; U.S. amb. to Mexico, 1993-97; pres. Warnaco Internat., 1997-98; bd. dirs. Kaiser Family Found., Grupo Modelo, Kansas City So. Ind., Am. Red Cross, Anheuser Busch, Keyspan, Inc., co-chmn. U.S.-Mex. Bus. Com. Chmn. Am. Bus. Conf. Served as capt. CIC AUS, 1964-65. Mem. Okla. Bar Assn., D.C. Bar Assn. Office: 544 E-86 #14E New York NY 10028 *In essence, I try to follow the admonition of Thomas Aquinas, "To work as if everything depends upon you, and pray as if everything depends on God.*

JONES, JAMES THOMAS, JR., tobacco company executive; b. Beverly Manor, Va., June 14, 1946; s. James Thomas and Irene Celestine (Baldwin) J.; m. Vionia Ann Fisher, July 5, 1966; children: James T. III, Vionia Jr., Veronica. Field sales rep. R.J. Reynolds Tobacco Co., Camden, N.J., 1973-76; asst. div. mgr. R.J. Reynolds Tobacco Co., Phila., 1976-80; div. mgr. R.J. Reynolds Tobacco Co., Newark, 1980-84; regional tng. and devel. mgr. R.J. Reynolds Tobacco Co., N.Y.C., 1984-88; nat. trade rels. mgr., minority markets R.J. Reynolds Tobacco Co., Winston-Salem, N.C., 1988-90; chain accounts mgr. R.J. Reynolds Tobacco Co., Edison, N.J., 1990-95; regional mgr. air purification equipment Plymovent, Edison, 1996—; cons., Sioux IndianTribe, Marty, S.D., 1989—. Mem. Internat. Platform Assn., S.C. Legis. Black Caucus, S.C. Legis. Corp. Roundtable. Republican. Baptist. Avocations: model railroading, gardening, swimming, tennis. Home: 80 Highland Ridge Rd Manalapan NJ 07726-8640 Office: Plymovent 375 Raritan Center Pkwy Edison NJ 08837-3920 also: J & V Consulting Group 80 Highland Ridge Rd Manalapan NJ 07726-8640

JONES, JAMES WILSON, physician, cell biologist, ethicist; b. Muskogee, Okla., Oct. 13, 1941; s. James C. and Hildred L. Jones; m. Joan Wachna, Aug. 24, 1983; children: James A., Misty A., Cyndra L., Jena S. Student, U. Tulsa, 1959-62; MD, Tulane U., 1966, PhD, 1979, postgrad., 1981-82. Diplomate Am. Bd. Surgery, Am. Bd. Thoracic Surgery, Am. Bd. Critical Care. Intern Phila. Gen. Hosp., 1966-67; resident in surgery Mayo Grad. Sch. Medicine, 1969-70; resident in gen. surgery Charity Hosp. La., 1971-73, 74-75, resident in thoracic surgery, 1973-74, 75-76, asst. clin. dir., co-dir. surg. intensive care unit, 1976-83; resident in thoracic surgery Ochsner Clinic, 1976; asst. prof. surgery sch. medicine Tulane U., New Orleans, 1976-83; chief surg. svc. VA Med. Ctr., Houston, 1983-85, 89-98; prof. surgery, cell biology and med. ethics Baylor Coll. Medicine, Houston, 1983-85, 89-98; surg. dir. Ritter Heart Inst., Toledo, 1985-89; W. Alton Jones Disting. prof. Columbia Hosp.-U. Mo., 1998—, Hugh E. Stephenson chair surgery, 1998—; mem. student affairs com. med. sch. Tulane U., 1977-82; mem. hosp. bylaws com. Tulane Med. Ctr., 1978-79, mem. transfusion com., 1980-81; mem. transfusion com. Charity Hosp. La., 1978-80, mem. tracheotomy audit, 1980-81; mem. clin. exec. bd. VA Med. Ctr., 1983-85, 89-98, mem. various coms.; sr. cardiac surgeon King Faisal Hosp., Riyadh, Saudi Arabia, 1984; mem. med. ethics com. St. Mary Hosp., Port Arthur, Tex., 1987; mem. trustee's cardiovascular com. Toledo Hosp., mem. critical care com.; mem. high sch. adv. com. health care professions Baylor Coll. Medicine, 1990-92, chmn. allied health com., 1992-97; mem. Regional Cardiology Adv. Com., 1993-94; mem. sub-com. indsl. rels. Annals Thoracic Surgery; cons., presenter in field. Author: Autotransfusion: Therapeutic Principles & Trends, 1993; mem. editorial bd. Internat. Rev. Anesthesiology, 1990-94; contbr. articles to profl. jours.; patentee in field. Lt. comdr. M.C., USNR, 1967-69. Recipient ann. svc. award, Mended Hearts; grantee NIH, 1963, 64, New Orleans Cancer Soc., 1965, Haemonetics Corp., 1988, Ortho Pharm., 1989, Berlex, 1990, Baxter-Edwards, 1991, 93, Sandoz Pharms., 1992, Cardiogenesis, 1996, VA Merit Rev., 1997; rsch. fellow Am. Cancer Soc., 1975-76, 77-78, Soc. Surg. Oncology, 1977; Hawthorne scholar, 1964-65, 65-66. Fellow ACS, Am. Coll. Cardiology, Am. Coll. Chest Physicians; mem. Am. Assn. Thoracic Surgery, Am. Heart Assn., Soc. Am. Inventors, Southeastern Surg. Congress, Southwestern Surg. Congress, So. Thoracic Surg. Assn., Internat. Cardiovascular Soc. (N.Am. chpt.), Michael E. DeBakey Internat. Surg. Soc., Soc. Thoracic Surgeons, So. Surg. Assn., Tex. Surg. Assn., Houston Surg. Soc., Soc. Critical Care Medicine, Mayo Alumni Assn., Sigma Xi, Alpha Kappa Kappa, Alpha Omega Alpha. Avocations: Civil War history, history of medicine, wreck diving (master diver). Office: U Mo Columbia Hosp Dept Surgery Rm M580 1 Hospital Dr Columbia MO 65212

JONES, JAN LAVERTY, mayor. B degree, Stanford U. Dir. human resources S.M.C. Restaurants, Menlo Park, Calif., 1972-74; dir. R & D Thriftmart Corp., 1976-85; CEO Jan-Mar Corp., 1985-89; Mayor City of Las Vegas, Las Vegas, Nev., 1991—; former pres. Fletcher Jones Mgmt. Group; bd. dirs. Bank of Am., Nev., Desert Springs Hosp., Pub. Edn. Found. Founder, chair Mayor's Com. for a Better Cmty.; adv. bd. U. Nev. Las Vegas Law Sch., Nathan Adelson Hospice, Lied Discovery Mus., Shade Tree Shelter for Homeless Women and Children. E-mail: mayor-jjjones@ci.las-vegas.nv.us. Office: Office of Mayor City Hall 10th Fl 400 E Stewart Ave Las Vegas NV 89101-2927*

JONES, JANET DULIN, writer, film producer; b. Hollywood, Calif., Sept. 6, 1957; d. John Dulin and Helen Mae (Weaver) J. BA, Calif. State U., Long Beach, 1980. Developer mini-series and TV series Embassy Comm., L.A., 1981-84; assoc. to producer Hotel Aaron Spelling Prodns., L.A., 1984-85; writing intern Sundance Film Inst., L.A., 1985; feature film story analyst Carson Prodns., L.A., 1985-86; freelance screenplay and play writer, L.A. and N.Y.C., 1986—. Author (screenplays) Fad Away, 1986, Alone in the Crowd, 1987, Story of the Century, 1988, The Long Way Home, 1989 (play) Cousin Judy, 1989, The Set-up, 1990, Roommates, 1991, Local Girl, 1991, Dickens and Crime, 1992, (books) Little Bear Books, Vols. 1-5, A Weighty, Waity Matter-My Adventures with India (screenplays), 1992, Coming and Going, 1993, Watching the Detectives, 1994, The Ambassadors, 1994, Words of Love, 1995, Map of the World, 1995, Katherine, 1996, Vanity Fair, 1996, Sarah's Mark, 1998; dir. Words of Love, 1998, Custom of the Country (edith Wharton), 1999. Bd. dirs. Sterling Cir. of Aviva Ctr. for Girls, 1990; bd. dirs., recording sec., steering com. The Creative Coalition, 1991-92. Mem. ACLU, WOmen in Film, Earth Communication Office (TV and film coms.), Writers Guild Am., Ind. Feature Project, Am. Film Inst., Sundance Film Inst. (pre-selection com. 1985-87), People for Am. Way, Habitat for Humanity, Anmesty Internat., Delta Gamma. Address: 6137 Lindenhurst Ave Los Angeles CA 90048

JONES, JANET VALERIA, psychiatric nurse, clinical nurse educators; b. Detroit, June 14, 1942; d. Frederick Leopold and Anne Elizabeth (Doege) J.; m. Calvin L. Jones, Dec. 12, 1960; children: Cherie L., Mark A., Kevin D. ASN, U. Guam, 1974; BSN with honors, Stephen F. Austin State U., 1982; MS in Allied Health, U. Tex., Tyler, 1985; MSN in Nurse Adminstrn., Tex. Women's U., Dallas, 1991. RN, Calif., Tex. Staff nurse Barstow (Calif.) Cmty. Hosp.; instr. Stephen F. Austin State U., Nacogdoches, Tex., Tyler Jr. Coll., Rusk, Tex.; nurse III Tex. Dept. Corrections, Tenn. Colony, Tex.; nurse supr. geriatric-med. unit Rusk (Tex.) State Hosp.; asst. DON, clin. nurse educator Terrell (Tex.) State Hosp.; lectr., speaker and presenter in field. Author: Nurses Celebrate the Past Envision the Future, 1996; contbr. poems to poetry jour. Mem. ANA, Tex. Nurses Assn., Am. Psychiat. Nurses Assn. Home: 252 Rainbow Dr Apt 15210 Livingston TX 77399-2052

JONES, JAY, II, radio station executive. Pres. KISS-FM, San Antonio. Office: KISS-FM 8930 Fourwinds Dr Ste 500 San Antonio TX 78239-1973*

JONES, JAY PAUL, environmental engineer; b. Wilmington, Del., Sept. 17, 1953; s. H. Walton and Eleanor Jane (Slaybaugh) J.; m. Cecilia A. Betts, Mar. 9, 1970; children: Jay Paul Jr., Stephanie Camille, Shaun M. BS in Agr. Engring. Technology, U. Del., 1975. Registered profl. engr. Del. Lectr. engring. U. Del., Newark, 1976-79; water resources engr. Water Resources Del. DNREC, Dover, 1979-87; program mgr. Hazardous Waste Mgmt. br. Del. DNREC, Dover, 1987-89; regional dir. James C. Anderson Assocs., Inc., Dover, 1989-95; mktg. dir. CABE Assocs., Inc., Dover, 1995—. Author: Hazardous Wastes in Delaware, 1991, 93. Core group leader, mem. Holy Cross Home Prayer Ctrs., Dover, 1990—; leader Holy Cross Visitation Ministry, Dover, 1993-94, confirmation instr., 1991-97, RCIA sponsor, 1996-97, Holy Cross Development Campaign, 1995, Holy Cross Completion Campaign, 1998; pres. Dover H.S. Basketball Boosters, 1992; campaign mem. Com. to Elect Pat Lynn, Dover, 1992; instr. Jr. Achievement, 1996-97. Mem. NSPE, Del. Engring. Soc. (pres. 1995-96, v.p. 1994-95, 99— Kent Sussex chpt.), Ctrl. Del. Econ. Devel. Coun., Air and Waste Mgmt. Assn., Capitol City Rotary, Maple Dale Country Club (chmn. membership com. 1997). Republican. Roman Catholic. Avocations: hunting, golf. Home: 180 Merion Rd Dover DE 19904-2323 Office: CABE Assocs Inc PO Box 877 Dover DE 19903-0877

JONES, JEAN CORREY, organization administrator; b. Denver, Jan. 12, 1942; d. Robert Magnie and Elizabeth Marie (Harpel) Evans; m. Stewart Hoyt Jones, Aug. 3, 1963; children: Andrew and Correy. BS in History, Social Studies and Secondary Edn., Northwestern U., 1963. Cert. non-profit mgr. History tchr. Glenbrook South H.S., Glenview, Ill., 1963-65; outreach rsch. dir. Episc. Diocese of Denver, 1977-80; pub. affairs adminstr. United Bank of Denver, 1980-82; exec. dir. Mile Hi coun. Girl Scouts U.S., Denver, 1982—; substitute tchr. Denver Pub. Schs., 1965-80. Active Minoru Yasui Cmty. Vol. Award com., 1979-99, Women's Forum of Colo., 1989-99, Leadership Denver (Member of Yr., 1988), 1988—; pres. Jr. League, Denver, 1979-80, Rotary, Denver, 1995—, pres., 1995-96, commr., chair Colo. Civil Rights commn., Denver, 1987-96, vice chair Health One, Denver, 1996; bd. dirs. Hist. Denver, Inc., 1994—, Samaritan Inst., Denver, 1999; vice chair, trustee Colo. Trust, 1999; pres. Women's Forum of Colo. Inc., 1999—. Named Profl. Woman of Achievement Colo. Women's Leadership Coalition and Colo. Easter Seal Soc., 1995. Mem. Denver Metro C. of C., Univ. Club. Republican. Episcopalian. Avocations: swimming, tennis, reading. Office: Girl Scouts Mile High Coun PO Box 9407 Denver CO 80209-0407

JONES, JEAN GRACE, speech educator; b. Paterson, N.J., Aug. 16, 1954; d. Robert L. and Diane E. (Patri) J.; children: Cheryl Schoonmaker, Adam Schoonmaker. BS, Wright State U., Dayton, Ohio, 1988, MA, 1989; PhD, U. Pitts., 1995. Cert. secondary English and speech tchr., Ohio; cert. secondary English and comm. tchr., Pa. Tchg. asst. Wright State U., 1987-89; tchg. fellow U. Pitts., 1990-95; asst. prof. dept. speech and comm. studies Edinboro U. Pa., 1995—. Recipient grad. rsch. writing award Ohio U. Comm. Rsch. Conf., 1993, Excellence in Tchg. award Internat. Comm. Assn., 1994. Fellow Western Pa. Writing Project; mem. Nat. Comm. Assn. (conf. top paper award 1992), Ea. Comm. Assn., Inst. for Ethics and Values in Edn. Democrat. Avocations: piano, aerobics, camping. Office: Edinboro U Pa Dept Speech-Comm Studies Edinboro PA 16444

JONES, JEANNE PITTS, director early childhood school; b. Richmond, Va., Oct. 19, 1938; d. Howard Taliaferro and Anne Elizabeth (Warburton) Pitts; m. Jack Hunter Jones, Nov. 17, 1962; children: Jack Hunter, Jr., Judith Anne, James Howard, Jon Martain. BA, Marshall U., 1961, post-grad. studies, 1962 summer; postgrad. studies, Presbyn. Sch. Christian Edn., Richmond, 1974, 94, Va. Commonwealth U., 1987-88; postgrad. in edn., Va. Commonwealth U., 1996—. Cert. tchr. Va. Tchr. Richmond (Va.) Pub. Schs., 1961-65; founder Bon View Sch. for Early Childhood Edn., Richmond, 1971, teacher, 1971-91, dir., 1971—; validator Nat. Assn. for Edn. of Young Children, 1993—, mentor, 1994—; acad. affairs chmn. Good Shepherd Episcopal Sch. Bd., Richmond, 1985-88; mentor Ecumenical Child Care Network Nat. Coun. Chs., Washington, 1990-92. Chmn. room parents Crestwood Sch. PTA Bd., Richmond, 1974-80; publicity chmn. Va. Swimming, Richmond, 1978-88, children's coord. Bon Air United Meth. Ch., Richmond, 1985-93, v.p. Bon Air United Meth. Women, 1991-94; dir. Camp Friendship, Bon Air UMC, Richmond, 1992—; Va. Children's Action Network, Va. Conf. of United Meth. Ch., rep., 1993-95; Va. Conf. United Meth. Ch., weekday com. 1992-94. Recipient Spl. Mission recognition Bon Air United Meth. Women, Richmond, 1987. Mem. Richmond Early Childhood Assn. (mem.-at-large 1994-96, rec. sec. 1996-98), Presch. Assn. Ch. Ednl. Dirs. (pres. 1993-95), Chesterfield Coalition Early Childhood Educators (bd. dirs. 1993-97). Republican. Avocations: aerobics, reading. Home: 9103 Whitaker Cir Richmond VA 23235-4053 Office: Bon View Sch Early Childhood Edn 1645 Buford Rd Richmond VA 23235-4274

JONES, JEFFERY LYNN, software engineer; b. Aug. 5, 1960; s. Robert Meryl and Ione Dell (Eaves) J. Ptnr., co-owner Megabyn Assocs (previously JJ Enterprises), Oklahoma City, 1982—; v.p., co-owner Oklahoma Digital Techs., Inc., Oklahoma City, 1987—; ptnr. Nighthawk Bus. Ideas, Jones, Okla.; contract cons. Bank Tech Inc., Oklahoma City, 1985-86, Phillips Petroleum Corp., Bartlesville, Okla., 1986-87; cons. Union Oil Co. of Calif., Oklahoma City, 1989—. Co-author: (software) PetroTrak 2000 Lease/Production Petroleum Tracking System, 1991. Pres. Atari Computer Club, Oklahoma City, 1983-84. With USAF, 1978-80. Recipient Paul Harris award Rotary Internat., 1991. Achievements include co-design of PXI 512 Medical Image Processing System and CompuLanx Computerized Forklift Data System; software engineer for international manufacturer of high speed video webb inspection systems. Home and Office: Nighthawk Bus Ideas 7833 NE 95th St Jones OK 73049-5801

JONES, JEFFREY FOSTER, lawyer; b. Phila., Apr. 24, 1944; s. Richard L. and Dorothy A. (Shaw) J.; m. Susan Craft, Aug. 22, 1970; children: Amanda, Michael. BA, Williams Coll., 1966; JD, Harvard U., 1973. Bar: Mass. 1973, U.S. Dist. Ct. Mass. 1974, U.S. Dist. Ct. Appeals (1st cir.) 1974. Law clk. Supreme Jud. Ct., Boston, 1973-74; assoc. Palmer & Dodge, Boston, 1974-80, ptnr., 1980-88, mng. ptnr., 1998—; chmn. bd. Law Firm Resources Project., 1981—. Overseer Boys and Girls Clubs of Boston, 1974-93, sec., bd. dirs., 1993—; trustee Radcliffe Coll., 1995—, Sterling and Francine Clark Art Inst., 1995-98. Lt. USN, 1966-70. Mem. ABA, Nat. Assn. Coll. and Univ. Attys., Boston Bar Assn., Mass. Bar Assn. Democrat. Avocations: racquetball, golfing, reading. Office: Palmer & Dodge 1 Beacon St Ste 22 Boston MA 02108-3190

JONES, JENK, JR., editor, educator; b. Tulsa, June 24, 1936; s. Jenkin Lloyd and Juanita Rose (Carlson) J.; m. Carol Beatrice Jaros, June 27, 1959; children: Janette Lloyd Jones Strickland, Landon Lloyd. BA in Polit. Sci., U. Colo., 1958. Sports writer Mpls. Tribune, 1959; reporter, news editor Anchorage Times, 1959-61; state capital corr. Tulsa Tribune, Oklahoma City, 1961-62, Washington corr., 1962-63, copy editor, Tulsa, 1963-64; chief copy desk, 1964-65, asst. city editor, 1965-66, asst. mng. editor, 1966-67, mng. editor, 1968-74, exec. editor, 1974-88, editor, 1988-91, editor, pub., 1991-92; chief copy editor, writer, photographer South Ctrl. Golf Mag., 1993—, Hurricane Tracker Mag., 1995—; part-time prof. journalism Okla. State U., 1993-95, part-time prof. polit. sci. Rogers U. at Tulsa, 1995— ; consulting editor The Tulsa Sentinel, 1992-93; juror Pulitzer Prize, 1982-83. Served with USAFR, 1958-64. Unitarian. Home: 6447 S Louisville Ave Tulsa OK 74136-1532

JONES, JENKIN LLOYD, retired newspaper publisher; b. Madison, Wis., Nov. 1, 1911; s. Richard Lloyd and Georgia (Hayden) J.; m. Ana Maria de Andrada Rocha, July 30, 1976; children: Jenkin Lloyd, David, Georgia; stepchildren: Maria Alice Glaser, Paulo Rocha. PhB, U. Wis., 1933; various hon. degrees. Reporter Tulsa Tribune, 1933, mng. editor, 1938, editor, 1941-88, pub., 1963-1991; ret., 1992. Author: The Changing World, 1966. Served to lt. comdr. USNR, 1944-46, PTO. Recipient William Allen White award Okla. Hall of Fame, 1957; Fourth Estate award Am. Legion, 1970; Freedom Leadership award Freedoms Found., 1969; Disting. Service award U. Wis., 1970; Disting. Service award U. Okla., 1971; Disting. Service award Okla. State U., 1972. Mem. Am. Soc. Newspaper Editors (pres. 1957), Inter Am. Press Assn., U.S. C. of C. (pres. 1969), Internat. Press Inst. Republican. Unitarian. Clubs: So. Hills Country (Tulsa). Home: 6683 S Jamestown Pl Tulsa OK 74136-2616

JONES, JENNIFER, actress; b. Tulsa, Mar. 21, 1919; d. Philip R. and Flora Mae (Suber) Isley; m. Robert Walker, Jan. 2, 1939 (div. June 1945); children: Robert Hudson, Michael Ross; m. David O. Selznick, July 13, 1949 (dec. 1965); 1 dau., Mary Jennifer; m. Norton Simon, May 30, 1971. Ed., pub. schs., Dallas; student, Monte Cassino Jr. Coll., Northwestern U., Am. Acad. Dramatic Arts. Appeared stock cos.; actress in motion pictures, 1943—, The Song of Bernadette, Since You Went Away, Cluny Brown, Love Letters, Duel in the Sun, We Were Strangers, Madame Bovary, Portrait of Jennie, Carrie, Wild Heart, Ruby Gentry, Indiscretion of an American Wife, Beat the Devil, Love is a Many-Splendored Thing, Good Morning, Miss Dove, The Man in the Gray Flannel Suit, The Barretts of Wimpole Street, A Farewell to Arms, Tender Is The Night, The Idol, The Towering Inferno, Eagles over London. Pres. Norton Simon Mus., Pasadena, Calif., 1989—. Recipient Acad. Motion Pictures Arts and Scis. award for best performance by an actress (for work in Song of Bernadette), 1943; Winged Victory award France, 1948; Triunfo award Spain, 1953; Film Critics Award Japan, 1953; First Ann. Audience award, 1955; winner Nat. Critics Poll, 1955; award Stars and Stripes citation for war work ARC; medal and citation for work at front during Korean War. Office: care Norton Simon 411 W Colorado Blvd Pasadena CA 91105-1825*

JONES, JERRY (JERRAL WAYNE JONES), professional football team executive; b. L.A., Oct. 13, 1942; m. Gene Jones; children: Stephen, Charlotte, Jerry Jr. Grad., U. Ark., 1965, MBA, 1970. Exec. v.p. Modern Security Life, Springfield, Mo., 1965-69; prin. oil and gas bus., 1970—; pres., gen. mgr. Dallas Cowboys, 1989—. Active Nat. Paralysis Assn., Boys Clubs Am. Avocations: hunting, fishing, playing tennis, water and snow skiing. Office: Dallas Cowboys 1 Cowboys Pkwy Irving TX 75063-4999*

JONES, JERRY LEE, computer educator; b. Glade Spring, Va., Nov. 24, 1947; s. William and Mary (Waugh) J. BS, Va. State U., 1969, MEd, 1973; EdD, Va. Poly. Inst. and State U., 1979. H.S. tchr. Balt. City Pub. Schs., 1969-74; prof. J. Sargeant Reynolds C.C., Richmond, Va., 1974—; part-time instr. Marymount Cath. H.S., Richmond, Va., 1987-89. Author textbook: Structured Programming Logic, 1985. Methodist. Avocations: piano, organ. Home: 3514 Patterson Ave Apt 5 Richmond VA 23221-2133 Office: J Sargeant Reynolds CC 1651 E Parham Rd Richmond VA 23228-2327

JONES, JOAN MEGAN, anthropologist; b. Laramie, Wyo., Sept. 7, 1933; d. Thomas Owen and Lucille Lenoir (Magill) J. BA, U. Wash., 1956, MA, 1968, PhD, 1976. Mus. educator Burke Mus. U. Wash., Seattle, 1969-72; anthropologist Quinault Indian Nation, Taholah, Wash., 1976-77; researcher, corp. officer Profl. Anthropology Consulting Team/Social Analysts, Seattle, 1977-79; research assoc. dept. anthropology U. Wash., Seattle, 1982-91; research investigator Dept. Social and Health Services State of Wash., Seattle, 1977; vis. lectr. Dept. Anthropology U. B.C., Vancouver, 1978; research specialist Artsplan Arts Alliance Wash. State, Seattle, 1978; vis. instr. Dept. Anthropology Western Wash. U., Bellingham, 1981; cons. in field. Author: Northwest Coast Basketry and Culture Change, 1968, Basketry of Quinault, 1977, Native Basketry of Western North America, 1978, Art and Style of Western Indian Basketry, 1982, Northwest Coast Indian Basketry Styles. Wenner-Gren Found. Anthrop. Research fellow, 1967-68; Ford Found. fellow, 1972-73; Nat. Mus.'s. Can. grantee, 1973-74. Fellow Am. Anthrop. Assn., Soc. Applied Anthropology; mem. Nat. Assn. Practicing Anthropologists, Assn. Women in Sci., Skagit Valley Weavers Guild (v.p. Skagit County chpt. 1985-86, 89-90, corr. sec. 1988-89), Whidbey Weavers. Avocations: handweaving, hand spinning, knitting.

JONES, JOEL MACKEY, academic administrator; b. Millersburg, Ohio, Aug. 11, 1937; s. Theodore Ra nd Edna Mae (Mackey) Jones; children: Carolyn Mae, Jocelyn Corinne. BA, Yale U., 1960; MA, Miami U., Oxford, Ohio, 1962; PhD, U. N.Mex., 1966. Dir. Am. studies U. Md., Balt., 1966-69; chmn. Am. studies U. N.Mex., Albuquerque, 1969-73, asst. v.p. acad. affairs, 1973-77, dean faculties, assoc. provost, prof. Am. studies, 1977-85, v.p. adminstrn., 1985-88; pres. Ft. Lewis Coll., Durango, Colo., 1988-99; interim supr. of schs. Durango Pub. Schs., 1999; bd. dirs. 1st Nat. Bank. Contbr. numerous essays, articles and chpts. to books. Founder Rio Grande Nature Preserve Soc., Albuquerque, 1974—; bd. dirs., mem. exec. com. United Way, Albuquerque, 1980-83; na. bd. cons. NEH, 1978—; bd. dirs. Mercy Hosp., 1990-94; mem. ACE Commn. on Leadership. Farwell scholar Yale U., New Haven, 1960; sr. fellow NEH, 1972; adminstrv. fellow Am. Coun. Edn., Washington, 1972-73. Mem. Am. Studies Assn., Am. Assn. Higher Edn., Am. Assn. State Colls. and Univs. (chair com. on cultural diversity, Colo. state rep. 1994—). Home: Box 428 Durango CO 81302 Office: Ft Lewis Coll 214 Reed Libr Durango CO 81301-3999

JONES, JOHN ANDERSON, JR., school system administrator; b. New Orleans, June 15, 1940; s. John Anderson and Irene Wells (Bennett) J.; divorced; children: Cheryl Lynn Jones Williams, Cyril Ivan Jones. BS in Social Studies, So. U., 1962, MA in African-Am. Studies, 1972; postgrad., La. State U., 1971, U. New Orleans, 1975, Tulane U., 1975, Harvard U., 1989. Cert. tchr., prin., supr., adminstr., supt., La. Rsch. asst. La. Dept. Edn., Baton Rouge, 1976-77; tchr. New Orleans Pub. Schs., 1962-75, supr. social studies, 1977-84, supr. instrs., 1984-85, spl. asst. prin., 1985-86, assoc. dir., 1990-98, dir. govtl. liaison, 1992-98; ret., 1998; cons., presenter in field; teaching asst. Tulane U., New Orleans, 1976-77, Xavier U., New Orleans, 1989, So. U., New Orleans, 1990, U. New Orleans, 1992; rschr. Consortium for Internat. Studies for West Africa, New Orleans, 1981; chmn. bd. dirs. New Orleans Home Mortgage Authority, 1989-95; book reviewer in field. Co-author: Educating Black Male Youth: A Moral and Civic Imperative, 1988; also contbr. to profl. publs. Res. dep. civil sheriff Res. Dep. Civil Sheriffs Assn., New Orleans, 1984; mem. Commn. on Excellence in Inner City Schs., La. Legislature, Baton Rouge, 1990; chmn. bd. New Orleans Home Mortgage Authority, 1989-95; mem. La. Gov.'s Edn. Transition Team, 1991; mem. pub. rels. com. United Way; mem. New Orleans Human Rels. Commn., 1998; trustee New Orleans chpt. PUSH/Excel. 1st lt. U.S. Army, 1963-65. Named Tchr. of Yr., Fortier H.S., 1974, 75; recipient cert. of appreciation ABA, 1981, young lawyers sect. La. Bar Assn., 1989, trophy Cox Cable and New Orleans Pub. Schs., 1991; also others; scholar Tulane U., 1976-77; fellow Close Up Found., 1979, 80, 82, 83, 86-90; grantee Harvard U., 1989. Mem. Nat. Coun. for Social Studies (plaque 1980), La. Coun. for Social Studies (plaque 1984), Nat. Social Studies Suprs. Assn., La. Coun. on Econ. Edn. (trustee 1984—, plaque 1990), Profl. Pers. Assn. (organizing, co-chmn.), Phi Delta Kappa, Pi Gamma Mu, Omega Psi Phi (reporter 1989-90). Democrat. Baptist. Avocations: billiards, travel, chess, sports. Home: 7001 Cove Dr New Orleans LA 70126-3032 Office: New Orleans Pub Schs 1815 Saint Claude Ave New Orleans LA 70116-1440

JONES, JOHN ARTHUR, lawyer; b. San Antonio, Fla., Oct. 9, 1921; s. Charles Garfield and Catherine Magdalene (Smith) J.; m. Margarette Lorraine (Sally) Johnson, Nov. 17, 1949; children: Matthew, Lisa, Malcolm, Darby. AA, U. Fla., 1947, JD with honors, 1949. Bar: Fla. 1949, U.S. Dist. Ct. (so. dist.) Fla. 1952, U.S. Ct. Appeals (11th cir.) 1982, U.S. Supreme Ct. 1978. Assoc., Holland & Knight and predecessors, Tampa, Fla., 1949-54; ptnr., 1954—; faculty Fla. Sch. of Banking, 1969-81. Served in U.S. Army, 1940-46; lt. col., USAR. Decorated Bronze Star. Fellow Am. Coll. Trust and Estate Counsel; mem. ABA, Fla. Bar Assn. (cert. wills, trusts and estates, chmn. real property probate and trust law sect. 1980-81), Hillsborough County (Fla.) Bar Assn., Internat. Acad. Estate and Trust Lawyers, Am. Coll. Real Estate Lawyers, Am. Bar Found., Masons, Shrine, Tampa Club, Univ. Club. Editor, contbr.: How To Live and Die With Florida Probate, 1972, Basic Practice Under Florida Probate Code, 1976, 97. Home: 5027 W San Miguel St Tampa FL 33629-5428 Office: Holland & Knight PO Box 1288 400 N Ashley Dr Ste 2300 Tampa FL 33602-4322

JONES, JOHN BAILEY, federal judge; b. Mitchell, S.D., Mar. 30, 1927; s. John B. and Grace M. (Bailey) J.; m. Rosemary Wermers; children: John, William, Mary Louise, David, Judith, Robert. BSBA, U. S.D., 1951, LLB, 1953. Bar: S.D. 1953. Sole practice Presho, S.D., 1953-67; judge Lyman County, Kennebec, S.D., 1953-56; mem. S.D. Ho. of Reps., Pierre, 1957-61; judge S.D. Cir. Ct., 1967-81, U.S. Dist. Ct. S.D., Sioux Falls, 1981—; now sr. judge. Mem. Am. Judicature Soc., S.D. Bar Assn., Fed. Judges Assn., VFW, Am. Legion. Methodist. Lodges: Elks, Lions. Avocation: golf. Office: US Dist Ct # 302 400 S Phillips Ave Sioux Falls SD 57104-0961*

JONES, JOHN COURTS, wildlife biologist; b. Washington, Oct. 3, 1913; s. Copeland Page and Marie Louise (Wood) J.; m. Wilma Irene Aho, Feb. 22, 1940 (dec. Feb. 1988); m. Joanne Quear Buehler, Oct. 12, 1991; 1 child, Scott Robert Buehler. BA, U. Minn., 1934; MA, George Washington U., 1937. Cert. hazard control mgr., safety mgr., wildlife biologist. Wildlife biologist U.S. Bur. Biol. Survey, Washington, 1936-37, Bur. of Game, Conservation Dept., Albany, N.Y., 1938-42; animal control biologist U.S. Fish & Wildlife Svc., Washington, 1946-56, safety mgr., 1964-65; staff specialist Bur. Sport Fish & Wildlife, Washington, 1957-63, chief office of safety, 1966-75; dir. BioDynamic Systems, Bethesda, Md., 1975—. Author: Food Habits of the American Coot, 1940, Manual of Rodent Control, 1947, Rat Control Methods, 1947, (with others) The Ruffed Grouse, 1947. Vice-pres. Glen Mar Park Civic Assn., Bethesda, Md., 1974-78. With Sanitary Corps., 1943-46. Recipient Orgn. Award of Honor Nat. Safety Coun., 1972, 73. Mem. Am. Ornithologists Union, Am. Soc. of Mammalogists, Cooper Ornithol. Soc., Nat. Safety Mgmt. Soc., Nat. Safety Mgmt. Soc., The Wildlife Soc., Wilson Ornithol. Soc. Avocations: photography, woodworking. Home and Office: BioDyanamic Systems 5810 Namakagan Rd Bethesda MD 20816-2346

JONES, JOHN EVAN, medical educator; b. Mt. Pleasant, Utah, Oct. 29, 1930; s. Aaron Eugene and Malinda May (Flowers) J.; m. Judith Carolyn Watson, Dec. 22, 1954; children: Malinda Anne, Evan Alan, Nathan Keith. AA, Coll. Eastern Utah, 1950; BS, U. Utah, 1952, MD, 1955. Diplomate Am. Bd. Internal Medicine, Am. Bd. Endocrinology and Metabolism. Intern U. Minn. Hosps., Mpls., 1955-56, resident, 1956-57, 59-60; dir. tng. endocrinology USPHS, Mpls. and Morgantown, W.Va., 1959-61; mem. faculty W.Va. U., Morgantown, 1961-91, assoc. prof. medicine, 1967-70, prof. medicine, 1970—, chmn. div. metabolism and endocrinology, 1970-74; dean W.Va. U. (Sch. Medicine), 1974-82, v.p. for health scis., 1982-91; v.p. for health scis. Med. Coll. Va./Va. Commonwealth U., Richmond, Va., 1991-97, spl. asst. to the pres., 1997—. With USNR, 1957-59. Fellow ACP (gov. for W.Va. 1975-79); mem. Endocrine Soc., Alpha Omega Alpha. Home: 13904 Beechwood Point Cir Midlothian VA 23112-2538

JONES, JOHN FRANK, retired lawyer; b. Carrington, N.D., Feb. 24, 1922; s. Dwight Frank and Veronica Esther (Sheehy) J.; m. Sally Oppegard; children: Janna Jones Bellwin, John M., Jeramy Ridder, Jill Jones Nester, Julie, Jeffrey, J. David. BS, U. N.D., 1946; MS in Organic Chemistry, U. Wis., 1953; JD, U. Akron, 1956. Bar: Ohio 1956, U.S. Patent Office, U.S. Ct. Appeals. Patent atty. B. F. Goodrich Co., Akron, Ohio, 1956-62; sr. patent atty. Standard Oil Co., Cleve., 1962-70, patent counsel, 1970-81, food and drug atty. Vistron Corp. subs. Standard Oil Co., Cleve., 1968-81, ret., 1981; cons. to Standard Oil Co., Cleve. and Ashland Chem. Co. (div. Ashland Oil Co.), Columbus, Ohio, 1981-95, B.F. Goodrich Co. Served with USAAF, 1943-46. Decorated D.F.C., Air medal. Mem. Am. Chem. Soc., Ohio Bar Assn., ABA, Cleve. Intellectual Property Law Assn., CBI Hump Pilots Assn. Republican. Patentee in chem. and polymer fields; contbr. articles on polymer sci. to profl. jours. Home and Office: 2724 Cedar Hill Rd Cuyahoga Falls OH 44223-1226

JONES, JOHN HARDING, photographer; b. Pitts., Apr. 28, 1923; s. John F. and Emma Eleanor (West) J.; 1 child, Blair Harding. BFA, Rochester Inst. Tech., 1949; MBA, Pepperdine U., 1978; PhD, U. London, 1983; M in Photography (hon.), Brantridge Forest, Eng.; DLitt (hon.), Ky. Christian U.; EdD, St. John's U. Seaman U.S. Naval Air, 1940, advanced through grades to comdr., 1948; ret., 1963; chief photographer U.S. Steel Corp., Pitts.; mgr. art & photo dept. Magnavox Corp., Urbana, Ill.; chief photographer rehab. medicine sect. U.S. Vet. Adminstrn., L.A.; coord. rehab. medicine domiciliary sect. Wadsworth VA Hosp., L.A.; tchr. Carnegie Mellon Inst., Pitts., Earl Wheeler Schs., Pitts., Seattle U., Art Inst. Pitts.; dir., owner The Little Studio, Panorama City, Calif., 1989—, The Little Studio West, Panorama City, 1994—; owner The Little Studio, Pitts., The Little Studio West. *Dr. Jones enlisted in the United States Naval Air 1940 as Apprentice Seaman. Raised through the ranks (Mustang) to Commander (Naval Aviator and Naval Flight Officer), he retired in 1963. He served aboard the U.S.S. Lexington CV-2, lost at the Battle of Coral Sea, May 8, 1942. He also served aboard U.S.S. Saratoga CV-3 and CV-60, Lexington CV-16, and the Leyte CV-32. He was awarded Distinguished awards for his aerial reconnaissance over enemy held territory and Naval Intelligence work. He was awarded 21 medals, among which are Distinguished Service Medal, Legion of Merit and the Purple Heart. He is still actively involved with 18 Military and Veterans organizations and publisher of a news letter called "The Howling".* Author: Photography, 1972, The Correspondence Educational Directory, 1976, 79, 84, 94, Correspondence Courses for High School Credit & GED Preparation, 1994. Comdr. USNR, ret. Recipient award Writers Guild, 1977, Merit award Cooking, 1986; elected to Am. Police Hall of Fame, 1996. Mem. Profl. Photographers Am., Masons, Shriners, Order of the Eastern Star (worthy patron 1986). Presbyn. Avocations: bowling, writing, travel, civic activities, stamp collecting. Home: 5320 Zelzah Ave Apt 203 Encino CA 91316-2214

JONES, JOHN HARRIS, lawyer, banker; b. New Blaine, Ark., Apr. 9, 1922; s. Ira Burton and Byrd (Harris); m. Marjorie Crosby Hart, 1983. A.B., U. Central Ark., 1941; postgrad., George Washington U. Law Sch., 1941-42; LL.B., Yale, 1947. Bar: Ark. 1946, U.S. Supreme Ct. 1963. Comms. clk. FBI, 1941-42; practice in Pine Bluff, 1947—; spl. judge Circuit Ct., 1950; spl. chief justice Ark. Supreme Ct., 1997; chmn. bd. Pine Bluff Nat. Bank, 1964-77, pres., 1966-76; Mem. Ark. Bd. Law Examiners, 1953-59; Republican nominee for U.S. Senate, 1974; Rep. presdl. elector, 1980; v.p., dir. John Rust Found., 1953-60. Served to 1st lt. USAAF, 1943-45. Decorated Purple Heart, Air medal. Mem. Ark. Bar Assn., Jefferson County Bar Assn. (pres. 1959-60). Mem. Christian Ch. (elder 1963-65, trustee 1965-71, 78-84). Clubs: Eden Park (Pine bluff), Capital (Little Rock). Home: 4001 S Cherry St Pine Bluff AR 71603-7156 Office: 104 S Main St Pine Bluff AR 71601-4320

JONES, JOHN LOU, arbitrator, retired railroad executive; b. Garnavillo, Iowa, July 22, 1929; s. Ira S. and Myrtle C. (Flagel) J.; m. Nancy H. Sikes, Feb. 2, 1953; children—Nanette, Robert, Eleanor, Stefani, Amanda, Jennifer, Eric. B.A., Luther Coll., 1950; M.S., MIT, 1954; A.M.P., Harvard U., 1974. Staff engr. Chrysler Corp., Detroit, 1957-59; br. chief USAF, 1959-63; dir. computer activities So. Ry. Co., Washington, 1963-64, asst. v.p.-data processing, Atlanta, 1964-69, v.p.-mgmt. info. services, 1969-82; exec. v.p.-adminstrn. Norfolk So. Corp., Va., 1982-87; bd. dirs. Norfolk & Western Ry., Roanoke, Va., So. Ry. Co., Atlanta; also bd. dirs. various ry. subs.; arbitrator in massive dispute on intellectual property rights between IBM and Fujitsu Co., 1985-97. Bd. dirs. Va. Symphony, 1986-92, Urban League of Hampton Roads, 1985-87. Capt. USAF, 1951-57. Bd. dirs. Cultural Alliance of Greater Hampton Rds., 1984-87. Recipient Disting. Svc. award Luther Coll., 1976. Mem. Conf. on Data System Langs. (chmn. 1967-85), COBOL Devel. Com. (chmn. 1960-67), Am. Assn. R.R.s (data systems div.) (chmn. 1969-70), Am. Mgmt. Assn. (v.p. planning council 1970-72, Disting. Service award 1972), Better Bus. Bur. Norfolk (bd. dirs. 1983-87), Council Better Bus. Burs. (bd. dirs. 1984-90). Lutheran. Office: 909 Unicorn Trl Chesapeake VA 23322-7365

JONES, JOHN MARTIN, JR., lawyer; b. Balt., Dec. 31, 1928; s. John Martin and Nannalee (Rogers) J.; m. Dayle Fort Nesbitt, July 27, 1969; children—David Mallory, Kelly Anne Klein, Jeffrey Wallace Arthur, Kathleen Celeste Silvester; stepchildren—Martha Nesbitt Dewey, William Fort Nesbitt, Howard Scott Nesbitt. AB, U. Md., 1951, LLB, 1953. Bar: Md. 1953, U.S. Dist. Ct. Md. 1953, U.S. Ct. Appeals (4th cir.) 1954, U.S. Supreme Ct. 1959. Assoc. Piper & Marbury, Balt., 1954-59, ptnr., 1960-86; pvt. practice, 1986—; asst. atty. gen. State of Md., 1959-60; mem. Md. Gov.'s Commn. to Study Tax Laws. Mem. Balt. Area council Boy Scouts Am.; publ. adv. Regional Planning Council, Greater Balt., 1977. Mem. ABA, Md. Bar Assn., Bar Assn. Balt. City, Am. Judicature Soc. (life), Am. Law Inst. (life), Order of Coif, Delta Theta Phi, Delta Kappa Epsilon. Clubs: Center, Yale of N.Y.C, DKE of N.Y.C, Rule Day; Le Conta. Mem. adv. com. in drafting and preparation of Am. Law Inst.'s Model Land Development Code, 1970-77. Home: 8025 Strauff Rd Baltimore MD 21204-1834 Office: 200 Saint Paul Pl Ste 2121 Baltimore MD 21202-2004 *Palma Non Sine Pulvere.*

JONES, JOHN PAUL, probation officer, psychologist; b. Blanchard, Mich., July 23, 1944; s. Lawrence John and Thelma Blanche (Eldred) J.; m. Joan Margaret Bruder, Aug. 18, 1972; children: Jason John, Justin John, Jessica Joan-Margaret. BS, Cen. Mich. U., 1970, MA, 1974; PhD, Wayne State U., Detroit, 1980. Diplomate Am. Bd. Forensic Medicine, Am. Bd. Cert. Forensic Examiners, Am. Bd. Psychol. Specialties, Am. Acad. of Experts in Traumatic Stree; cert. addictions counselor. Mgr. F. W. Woolworth Co., Bay City, Mich., 1970; probation officer Oakland County Cir. Ct., Pontiac, Mich., 1970-74, probation officer supr., 1974-78, dir. spl. probation program, 1978-80; chief probation officer County of Oakland, Pontiac, 1980-93; outpatient clin. dir. Auro Med. Ctr., Bloomfield Hills, 1993—; lectr. Oakland U., Rochester, Mich., 1978-82; lic. psychologist Psychol. Svcs. of Bloomfield Hills, Mich., 1980-82, Family Treatment Ctr., Pontiac, Mich., 1983-84, Associated Profls., Bloomfield Hills, 1984-85, Auro Med. Ctr., Bloomfield Hills, 1985—. Pres. Pontiac Lions Club, 1986-87; study subcom. Oakland County Jail, 1982-84; mem. Oakland County Child Sexual Abuse Task Force, 1982-83. With U.S. Army, 1966-68. Mem. APA (bd. govs.), Internat. Neuropsychol. Assn., Am. Correctional Psychologist Assn., Am. Acad. Experts in Traumatic Stress, Am. Coll. Forensic Examiners (BCFE, BCFM), Mich. Corrections Assn., Mich. Assn. Probation Officers Svcs., Mich. Psychol. Assn., Fraternal Order of Police, Cen. Mich. U. Alumni Assn. (bd. dirs. Mt. Pleasant chpt. 1989-93), Mich. Neuropsychol. Soc., Am. Psychol. Assn. Republican. Avocations: travel, horseback riding, reading, fencing. Home: 2915 Masefield Dr Bloomfield Hills MI 48304-1951 Office: Auro Med Ctr Ste 102 1711 S Woodwood Ave Bloomfield Hills MI 48302

JONES, JOHN STANLEY, director special projects, Tucson; b. Scranton, Pa., Mar. 25, 1947. BA, SUNY, Stony Brook, 1968; MS, U. Ariz., 1977. Prin. planner Pima County, Tucson, 1979-84; planning cons. pvt. practice, Tucson, 1984-89; dir. devel. svcs. ctr. City of Tucson, 1989-90, dir. devel. svcs. dept., 1990-93, acting water dir., 1993-94, dir. spl. projects, 1995—. Recipient Local Official award, Nat. Assn. Homebuilders, 1995. Mem. Am. Planning Assn., Am. Inst. Cert. Planners. Office: City of Tucson PO Box 27210 Tucson AZ 85726-7210

JONES, JOHN WESLEY, entrepreneur; b. Wenatchee, Wash., Nov. 15, 1942; s. Richard F. and Hazel F. (Hendrix) J.; m. Melissa L. Meyer, June 22, 1968 (div. 1982); children: John E., Jennifer L.; m. Deborah G. Matthews, Apr. 24, 1993. BA in Bus./Econs., Western Wash. U., Bellingham, 1966. Trainee Jones Bldg., Seattle, 1967-69; mgr. Jones Bldg., 1969-78; owner/mgr. N.W. Inboards, Bellevue, Wash., 1974-78, Jones Bldg., Seattle, 1978-86; pvt. investor Bellevue, 1987—; owner/mgr. J. Jones Enterprises, 1994—; trustee BOMA Health & Welfare Trust, 1982-86, chmn. 1986; mem. Seattle Fire Code Adv. Bd., 1979-86. With USMCR, 1966-72. Mem. Seattle Bldg. Owners and Mgrs. Assn. (trustee 1979-86), Bldg. Owners and Mgrs. Internat., N.W. Marine Trade Assn., Am. Assn. Individual Investors, Composite Fabricators Assn., Soc. Naval Architects and Marine Engrs., Boat U.S., Seattle Yacht Club, NRA, Internat. Show Car Assn., Nat. Street Rod Assn., Specialty Equipment Mktg. Assn. Republican. Avocations: boating, water skiing, snow skiing, automobiles, photography. Home: 61 Skagit Key Bellevue WA 98006-1021 Office: PO Box 52745 Bellevue WA 98015

JONES, JOIE PIERCE, acoustician, educator, writer, scientist; b. Brownwood, Tex., Mar. 4, 1941; s. Aubrey M. and Mildred K. (Pierce) J.; m. Kay Becknell, June 12, 1965. B.A. (Jr. fellow 1961-63), U. Tex., Austin, 1963, M.A., 1965; Ph.D., Brown U., 1970. Sr. scientist Bolt Beranek & Newman, Inc., Cambridge, Mass., 1970-75; assoc. prof., dir. ultrasonics research lab. Case Western Res. U. Sch. Medicine, Cleve., 1975-77; prof., chief med. imaging, dir. grad. studies, dept. radiol. scis. U. Calif., Irvine, 1977—; cons. acoustics; pres. Computer Sci. Systems, 1978—; founding gen. ptnr. Of Food and Wine, 1982—, Meditherm Assocs., Ltd., 1983-85, Spar Techs., 1987-90, Surgisonics Inc., 1991—; proposal reviewer NSF/NIH, 1974—; appointee sci. and tech. adv. com. Pres. Carter, 1977-81. Author 3 books; mem. editorial bd. Ultrasound in Medicine and Biology, 1976—; contbr. over 200 articles to profl. jours.; 15 patents in field. Active vol. local govt. Fellow Am. Inst. Ultrasound in Medicine; mem. IEEE, AAAS, Acoustical Soc. Am., Am. Phys. Soc., Am. Assn. Physicists in Medicine, Calif. Wine and Food Soc., Phi Beta Kappa. Democrat. Home: 2094 San Remo Dr Laguna Beach CA 92651-2628 Office: U Calif Dept Radiol Sci Irvine CA 92697-5000

JONES, JOSEPH HAYWARD, lawyer; b. Shamokin, Pa., July 9, 1924; s. Joseph H. and Anna Elizabeth (Lippiatt) J.; m. Grace Loretta Hicks, Mar. 17, 1951; children: Elizabeth Christie, Joseph H. Jr., Gregory H. BA, Ursinus Coll., 1947, LLD (hon.), 1987; JD, Dickinson Sch. Law, Carlisle, Pa., 1950; LLM, NYU, 1954. Bar: Pa. 1950, U.S. Supreme Ct. 1959. Ptnr. Williamson, Friedberg & Jones, Pottsville, Pa., 1950—; mem. Pa. Judicial Reform Commn., 1987. Past pres. Appalachian Trail coun. Boy Scouts Am., Hawk Mountain coun. Boy Scouts Am.; sec., past pres. Schuylkill Econ. Devel. Corp.; pres. Pottsville Area Devel. Corp., 1986; bd. dirs. Salvation Army, Pa. Lawyers Trust Account Bd., 1989-96. Lt. (j.g.) USN, 1942-45, PTO. Recipient Silver Beaver award Boy Scouts Am., Disting. Citizen award Pa. State U., Schuylkill, 1987, Citizen of Yr. award St. David's Soc. Schuylkill and Carbon Counties; named Young Man of Yr., Pottsville Area Jaycees, Vol. of Yr., So. Schuylkill United Fund, 1972. Mem. Pa. Bar Assn. (pres. 1987-88, recipient Pa. Bar medal, chmn. task force legal svcs. to poor 1989-90, recipient ADL torch of Liberty 1997), Pa. Bar Found. (pres.), Masons (33 deg.), Lions (past pres.). Home: 2100 Mahantongo St Pottsville PA 17901-3112 Office: Williamson Friedberg & Jones Ten Westwood Rd Pottsville PA 17901

JONES, JOSEPH W., foundation administrator. Chmn. Robert W. Woodruff Found. Inc., Atlanta, Joseph B. Whitehead Found., Atlanta, 1977—. Office: Robert W Woodruff Found Inc 50 Hurt Plz Atlanta GA 30303*

JONES, JULIA PEARL, elementary school educator; b. Kesler, W.Va., Nov. 22, 1942; d. Wallace Leon and Wilda Thelma (Doss) Frazier; m. James Victor Jones, Jr., Nov. 26, 1961; children: Julie Lorraine Lynch, Jamie Lynn Dunston Smith. BS in Elem. Edn. cum laude, Memphis State U., 1979; MEd cum laude, U. Va., 1986; MLS summa cum laude, James Madison U., 1998. Cert. elem./mid. sch. prin., supr., K-7th grade tchr., art tchr. Tchr. 4th grade Spotsylvania County (Va.) Schs., 1979-91, reading resource specialist, 1991-96, sch. libr., 1996—. Mem. ASCD, Nat. Tchrs. Assn., Va. Edn. Assn., Spotsylvania Edn. Assn., Nat. Congress of Parents and Tchrs., Internat. Reading Assn., Va. Reading Assn. Rappahannock Reading Coun. (past pres., Reading Tchr. of Yr. 1993-94), Va. Edn./Media Assn., Christian Bus. and Profl. Women, Internat. Platform Assn., Order Ea. Star, Kappa Delta Pi, Phi Delta Kappa. Methodist. Avocation: art. Home: 5414 Jamie Ct Fredericksburg VA 22407-1618

JONES, K. C., professional basketball coach; b. Taylor, Tex., May 25, 1932. Ed., U. San Francisco. Player Boston Celtics, NBA, 1958-67; coach Brandeis U., Waltham, Mass., 1967-71; asst. coach Los Angeles Lakers, NBA, 1971-72; coach San Diego Conquistadores, Am. Basketball Assn., 1972-73, Capital Bullets (later Washington), 1973-76; asst. coach Boston Celtics, NBA, 1977-83, coach, 1983-88, v.p. basketball ops., 1988-89; asst. coach, cons. player pers. dir. Seattle SuperSonics, NBA, 1989-90, head coach, 1990-92; asst. coach Boston Celtics, 1995-07; head coach New Eng. Blizzard, ABL, Hartford, Conn., 1997—; mem. gold medal U.S. Olympic Basketball Team, 1956; mem. NCAA Championship Team, 1955, NBA Championship Team, 1959-66; coach NBA All-Star Game, 1975, 84, 86. Served with U.S. Army, 1956-58. Coach NBA Championships, 1984, 86; named to San Francisco Bay Area Sports Hall of Fame, 1989, Naismith Meml. Basketball Hall of Fame, 1989. Office: care New Eng Blizzard 179 Allyn St Ste 403 Hartford CT 06103-1421*

JONES, KACY DOUGLAS, accountant; b. Lancaster, Ohio, Feb. 6, 1955; s. Jack Victor and Barbara Jean (Unkle) J.; m. Lisa Marie Elliott Bells, 1981 (div. 1987); 1 child, Paul Andrew. BS, Franklin U., 1986. CPA, Ohio. Acct. Capital Tax Planning, Columbus, Ohio, 1986-87; tax assoc. Coopers & Lybrand, Columbus, 1988-91; acctg. supr. Ameriflora '92, Columbus, 1992-93; acctg. mgr. Rite Rug, Columbus, 1993-97, TS Trim Industries, Inc., Canal Winchester, Ohio, 1997—. Chamber scholar Columbus Area C. of C., 1986. Mem. Ohio Soc. CPAs, Masons. Democrat. Methodist.

JONES, KATHARINE JEAN, research physicist; b. Torrance, Calif., Feb. 18, 1940; d. Harold Thomas and Olive Katharine (Hume) Holtom; m. Noel Duane Jones, June 29, 1963; children: Evan Edward, Leonard L. BA, Pomona Coll., 1961; PhD magna cum laude, U. Berne, Switzerland, 1966; BS in Math. and Physics, Purdue U., 1976, MS in Physics, 1978. Rsch. asst. Labs. Linus Pauling Calif. Inst. Tech., Pasadena, 1963; rsch. assoc. biochemistry dept. Ind. U. Sch. Medicine, Indpls., 1967-70; teaching asst. physics dept. Purdue U., West Lafayette, Ind., 1976-78, rsch. asst. indsl. engring. dept., 1978; rsch. physicist Naval Air Warfare Ctr., Indpls., 1978-95; rsch. physicist dept. math. Rice U., 1995—. Contbr. articles to profl. jours.; patentee in field. Fellow NIH, 1964-66, 68-70. Mem. AAAS, IEEE, Soc. for Photo-optical Instrumentation Engrs. (SPIE), Optical Soc. Am., Sigma Pi Sigma. Avocations: orchids, skiing. Home: 3 Flagstone Path Spring TX 77381-6621

JONES, KATHRYN CHERIE, pastor; b. Breckenridge, Tex., Nov. 26, 1955; d. Austin Thomas and Margaret May (Mohr) J. BA, U. Calif., San Diego, 1977; MDiv, Fuller Theol. Sem., 1982. Assoc. pastor La Jolla (Calif.) United Meth. Ch., 1982-84; pastor in charge Dominguez United Meth. Ch., Long Beach, Calif., 1984-88, San Marcos (Calif.) United Meth. Ch., 1988-90; dir. Resource Initiatives & Interpretation, Nashville, 1990—; coord. chaplains Pacific Hosp., Long Beach, 1986-88. Bd. dirs. So. Calif. Walk to Emmaus Cmty., L.A., 1987-88, San Diego chpt., 1988-90. Mem. Christian Assn. Psychol. Studies, Evangs. for Social Action. Democrat. Office: The Upper Room 1908 Grand Ave PO Box 189 Nashville TN 37202-0189

JONES, KAYLIE ANN, writing educator, writer; b. Paris; came to U.S., 1974; d. James R. and Gloria J.; m. Kevin Michael Heisler, Aug. 12, 1995; 1 child, Eyrna Holland Heisler. BA, Wesleyan U., 1981; MFA, Columbia U., 1983; degree in Russian Lang. (hon.), Pushkin Inst., Moscow, 1987. Grants coord. Poets and Writers, N.Y.C., 1983-84, asst. to dir. devel., 1984-87; instr.

writing The Writer's Voice, N.Y.C., 1988-95; prof. Southampton campus L.I. U., 1995—; writers in residence N.Y.C. pub. schs. Tchrs. and Writers, 1991—. Author: As Soon As It Rains, 1985, Quite the Other Way, 1989, A Soldier's Daughter Never Cries, 1990, Faded Midnight, 1999; cons., writer (film) A Soldier's Daughter Never Cries, 1998. Mem. James Jones Lit. Soc. (bd. dirs., chmn. 1st novel, Fellowship award), Phi Beta Kappa. Avocations: scuba diving, yoga, weight lifting. E-mail: kayliej@mindspring.com. Office: Humanities Southampton Coll Montauk Hwy Southampton NY 11968

JONES, KEITH ALDEN, lawyer; b. Tulsa, July 11, 1941; s. Leonard Virgil and Bernadine (Hutchison) J.; m. Renata Skuta, June 15, 1974; children: Emily Isobel, Alden Rivendale. BA, Harvard U., 1963, LLB, 1966. Bar: Mass. 1966, D.C. 1978, U.S. Supreme Ct. 1972. Asst. prof. Boston U. Law Sch., 1966-67; lectr. Harvard U. Law Sch., 1967-68; assoc. Ropes & Gray, Boston, 1968-70; minority counsel U.S. Senate Select Com. on Small Bus., 1970-72; asst. to Solicitor Gen. of U.S., 1972-75; dep. solicitor gen., 1975-78; ptnr. Fulbright & Jaworski, Washington, 1978-94; of counsel Beck, Redden & Secrest, Houston, 1995—. Mem. ABA, Am. Law Inst.

JONES, KELLEY SIMMONS, therapist, social worker; b. Shaker Heights, Ohio, May 2, 1965; d. Horace Bly Simmons and Sandra Gail (Pagana) Wright. BA in Psychology/Bus. magna cum laude, Ursuline Coll., Pepper Pike, Ohio, 1989; M in Counseling Psychology, St. Martin's Coll., Lacey, Wash., 1997. Adminstrv. asst. Stanspec Corp., Cleve., 1986-89; primary counselor, family therapist New Directions, Pepper Pike, Ohio, 1986-90; children's care specialist Adventure Nature Program, Yelm, Wash., 1991-93; exec. dir., founder Monarch Therapeutic Learning Ctr., Lacey, 1993—; regional assoc. trainer Developmental Therapy-Developmental Tchg., 1998—; vice-chair adv. bd. Partnership for Children, Youth, Families, Olympia, Wash., 1996—; mem. at large adv. bd. Ptnrs. for Prevention, Olympia, 1995—; bd. mem. Child Protective Team, Thurston County, Wash., 1994—; mem. homeless child care policy task force Thurston County, Lacey, 1996-98; mem. Elem. Sch. Health Planning Team, North Thurston, 1997-98; mem. Child Abuse Task Force, 1998—. Mem. Therapeutic Child Devel. Assn. Avocations: art, reading, camping, travel, advocating for children. Office: Monarch Therapeutic Learning Ctr PO Box 3541 Lacey WA 98509-3541

JONES, KENNETH BRUCE, surgeon; b. Scottsville, Ky., Apr. 17, 1953; s. Kenneth C. and Betty (Miller) J.; m. Carol Jean Munger, June 28, 1980; children: Daniel, Christopher, Elizabeth. BS, U. Ky., 1974; MD, Vanderbilt U., Nashville, 1978. Diplomate Am. Bd. Surgery; cert. advanced trauma life saving. Surg. intern and resident U. Louisville Med. Sch., 1978-80; resident in surgery East Tenn. U. Med. Sch., Johnson City, 1980-82, chief resident, 1983; surgeon Claiborne Surg. Group, Tazewell, Tenn., 1983-84, N.E. Ark. Surg. Clinic, Jonesboro, Ark., 1984—; sec. med. staff Meth. Hosp., 1986-87, chief of surgery, 1988-90, vice chief of staff, 1989-91, chief of staff, 1992-94; chief of surgery St. Bernard's Regional Med. Ctr., 1996-97; asst. clin. prof. surgery U. Ark. Area Health Edn. Ctr., Jonesboro, 1985—; cancer liaison of Am. Coll. Surgeons Commn. on Cancer to St. Bernard's, 1996—. Contbr. articles on surgery to profl. jours. Active sch. bd., 1993-98; deacon So. Bapt. Ch. Justin Potter med. scholar, 1974-78. Mem. ACS (cancer liaison physician commn. on cancer), Am. Soc. Gen. Surgery, So. Med. Assn., Ark. Med. Assn., Soc. Am. Gastrointestinal Endoscopic Surgeons, Am. Soc. Bariatric Surgery, NRA, Ark. Wildlife Fedn., Ducks Unltd., Quail Unltd., Wildlife Forever, Nat. Sporting Clays Assn., Phi Beta Kappa. Baptist. Avocations: hunting, sporting clays shooting, jogging. Home: 2600 Nix Lake Dr Jonesboro AR 72404-0917 Office: NE Ark Surg Clinic 800 S Church St Ste 104 Jonesboro AR 72401-4154

JONES, KENNETH D., secondary education educator, coach; b. May 23; s. James C. and Lucille M. Jones. BS in Edn. in Math. Edn., U. Ill., 1982; MA in Ednl. Adminstrn., Ea. Ill. U., 1993. Tchr. math. Casey (Ill.)-Westfield Schs., 1989-91, Edinburg (Ill.) Sch. Dist., 1983-89, 91—. Scholar FMC Corp., 1980. Mem. NEA, Nat. Coun. Tchrs. Math., Ill. Edn. Assn., Ill. H.S. Assn. (ofcl.), Edinburg Athletic Club. Avocation: youth sports. Office: Edinburg Sch Dist 100 E Martin St Edinburg IL 62531

JONES, KENSINGER, advertising executive; b. St. Louis, Oct. 18, 1919; s. Walter C. and Anna (Kensinger) J.; m. Alice May Guseman, Oct. 7, 1944; children: Jeffrey, Janice A. Jones Geary. Student, Washington U., St. Louis, 1938-39. TV writer, advt. agy. supr. Leo Burnett Co., 1952-57; exec. v.p., creative dir. Campbell-Ewald Co., Detroit, 1957-68; sr. v.p., creative dir. D.P. Brother & Co., Detroit, 1968-70; sr. v.p., exec. creative dir. Leo Burnett Co., Inc., Chgo., 1970-73; regional creative dir. Leo Burnett Pty. Ltd., Sydney, Australia, 1973-75, Leo Burnett, SE Asia, 1975-77; creative supr. Biggs/Gilmore, 1981-83; lectr. Mich. State U., 1982-95; emeritus, 1996; bd. dirs. Cello-Foil, Inc.; vis. lectr. People's Republic China, 1988, Taipei, Taiwan, Jakarta, Indonesia, 1990, Dalhousie U., N.S., 1992. Author: Enter Singapore, 1974, Looking For the Best, 1994; co-author: Cable Advertising-New Ways to New Business, 1986, A Call From the Country, 1989, Love Poems of a Business Man, 1997; writer; radio series Land We Live IN, 1945-52; contbr. poems and articles to mags. Chmn. Barry County Planning and Zoning Commn., Parks and Recreation Commn.; county grants coord. Barry County, 1977-78, mem. futuring steering com., 1988—; mem. Econ. Devel. Action Group, 1988—, Mich. State U. Dean's Cmty. Coun. on the Arts, 1993-96, Mich. State U. Co-op. Ext. Adv. Coun., 1990-94; mem. communications com. Nat. Coun. Boy Scouts Am., 1966-92; bd. dirs. World Med. Relief, Inc., 1961-92, dir. emeritus, 1993. Recipient Silver Beaver award Boy Scouts Am., Silver Salute Mich. State U., 1982, award Freedoms Found., 1984, Positive Action for Tomorrow award Barry County, 1995. Mem. The Players Club, Circumnavigators Club, Adcraft Club of Detroit. Home: 425 Pritchardville Rd Hastings MI 49058-9328 *The opportunity to absorb, examine, synthesize and then utilize facts and experience is what makes creative endeavor fascinating. Somehow the individual mind finds new and meaningful relationships between previously unrelated data. An idea is born. It becomes an advertising campaign, a book or movie, a new product. Trying to find those new relationships makes life rewarding in so many ways. Dissatisfaction with the status quo is the prod toward all progress. Use your talents broadly. Not just to make a living, but to improve your life, your environment, your society. By doing so you'll improve your talents.*

JONES, KENT ALBERT, economist; b. Wilmington, Del., May 5, 1953; s. Albert Hyatt and Sylvia Esther (Phelps) J.; m. Tonya Diantha Price, May 21, 1977; children: Ana-Lisa, Diantha. Student, U. Bonn, Fed. Republic Germany, 1974-75; AB, Oberlin Coll., 1976; MA in Law and Diplomacy, Tufts U., 1979; D of Polit. Sci., U. Geneva, 1981. Economist U.S. Internat. Trade Commn., Washington, 1981; asst. prof. Babson Coll., Wellesley, Mass., 1982-88, assoc. prof., 1988-93, Edward Madden term chair, 1992-97, prof., 1993—; sr. economist U.S. Dept. State, Washington, 1988-89; cons. Internat. Labour Office, Geneva, Switzerland, 1987, NSF, Washington, 1984. Author: Impasse and Crisis in Steel Trade Policy, 1983, Politics vs. Economics in World Steel Trade, 1986, Export Restraint and the New Protectionism, 1994; contbr. articles to profl. jours. Elder Needham Presbyn. Ch., Mass., 1986—. Recipient scholarship, Rotary Internat., 1974, McJannet fellowship, Grad. Inst. U. Geneva, 1979, Cabot Corp. fellowship, Tufts U., Fletcher Sch. of Law and Diplomacy, 1976. Mem. Am. Economic Assn., So. Economic Assn., Western Economic Assn., Phi Beta Kappa. Presbyterian. Office: Babson Coll Econs Dept Babson Park MA 02457

JONES, KRISTIN ANDREA, artist; b. Washington, Aug. 1, 1956; d. Frank W. and Arlene (Swift) Jones; m. Andrew Ginzel, June 14, 1986. Student, St. Martins Sch. Art, London, 1978-79; BFA, R.I. Sch. Design, 1979; MFA, Yale U., 1983. Artistic cons. Hudson River Park Conservancy, N.Y.C., 1997; Executed art works for Oreg. Conv. Ctr., Portland, 1990, Pa. Conv. Ctr., 1994, Battery Park City, N.Y.C., 1992, Olympic Arts Festival, Atlanta, 1996, MTA, N.Y.C., 1997. Executed art works for Oreg. Conv. Ctr., Porltand, 1990, Battery Park City, N.Y.C., 1992, Pa. Conv. Ctr., 1994, Olympic Arts Festival, Atlanta, 1996, MTA, N.Y.C., 1999, Metronome Union Sq. S., N.Y.C., 1999. Recipient Pollack-Krasner Found. award, 1994, Louis Comfort Tiffany Found. award, 1991; Visual Arts fellow Nat. Endowment for the Arts, 1986, 94; Fulbright fellow, 1983-84; Am. Acad. in Rome fellow, 1994-95. Home: 289 Bleecker St New York NY 10014-4106

JONES, L. Q. See MCQUEEN, JUSTUS ELLIS

JONES, LACINDA, assistant principal; b. Baton Rouge, Mar. 1, 1962; d. Carl Lester and Joan (Alford) J. BS, La. State U., 1984; MEd in Guidance/Counseling, Southeastern La. U., 1990; postgrad., Southern U., Baton Rouge, 1990-92. Cert. tchr., elem. sch. prin., adminstr., supr., guidance counselor, resource devel., leadership, supervision of student tchrs. Tchr. grades 1-4 Livingston Parish (La.) Sch. Bd., 1985-89; tchr. grade 5 East Baton Rouge Sch. Bd., 1989-90, guidance counselor, 1990-95, adminstrv. intern, 1993-94, asst. prin., 1995—; lectr. in field; condr. workshops for tchrs./adminstrs., and parents; asst. in implementing Reading Recovery program for at-risk students; assisted other sch. dists. in implementating their guidance programs, diversity trainer; helped implemented La. Bd. Elem. and Secondary Edn./La. Quality Ednl. Support Fund Grant, 1993-94. Featured on WFMF Radio Pub. Affairs program; featured in articles in Baton Rouge Advocate, Ctrl. News newspapers, other pubs.; pub. handbook: Parent-Student Handbook, 1993. Tutor underprivileged children, Baton Rouge, 1986-90; libr. vol. Goodwood Libr., Baton Rouge, 1990; Sunday sch. tchr. Deerford United Meth. Ch., Baton Rouge, 1980-84; vol. fundraiser Acad. Distinction, Baton Rouge, 1990-94; vol. Vols. in P ub. Schs. (VIP), Baton Rouge, 1993. Grantee Exxon Chem. Edn. Involvement Fund, 1996, South Ctrl. Bell, La., 1989, Nat. 4-H Found., 1991, Acad. Distinction Fund, Baton Rouge, 1991, 93. Mem. ASCD, La. Assn. Prins., Am. Sch. Counselor Assn. (membership chair 1990), La. Sch. Counselor Assn. (elem. v.p. 1993-94), East Baton Rouge Counselor Assn. (elem. v.p. 1992-93), Assoc. Prof. Educators (La. membership rep. 1992), East Baton Rouge Counselor Assn. (pres.-elect 1995—), Prins. and Asst. Prins. Adv. Coun. to Supt., Coun. of Asst. Prins. for Instrn., Coun. of Asst. Prins. of Adminstrn., Delta Kappa Gamma (historian 1994), Phi Delta Kappa. Democrat. Avocations: aerobics, exercise, reading, water sports. Home: 17157 Wax Rd Apt D Greenwell Springs LA 70739-5042 Office: Northeast Elem Sch PO Box C Pride LA 70770

JONES, LARRY DARNELL, tax specialist; b. Birmingham, Ala., Feb. 21, 1959; s. Ron Shephard and Londene Jones. Student, Rutgers U., 1980-84, Camden County Coll., 1982. Tax specialist LDJ, Inc., Camden, N.J., 1983-95, AMA, 1993—, GAU, 1995—. Home: 655 Line St Camden NJ 08103-1452 Office: LDJ Inc 655 Line St Camden NJ 08103-1452

JONES, LARRY LEROY, oil company executive; b. Sioux City, Iowa, May 29, 1935; s. Rae Leroy and Margaret Ellen (Acre) J.; m. Phyllis Joan Waggerby, June 18, 1956 (div. Apr. 1969); children: Scott Leroy, Curtis Mark, Wade Kordell, Andrea Lynn; m. Norma Jean Houser, Oct. 25, 1969; 1 child, Todd Bradley. BS, U. Nebr., 1958, MS in Geology, 1961. Geologist, geophysicist Std. Oil Co. Tex. (Chevron), Corpus Christi, Tex., 1958-65; exploration geologist Monsanto Co., Houston, 1965-68, Occidental Petroleum Corp., Houston, 1968-71; area geologist Belco Petroleum Corp., Houston, 1971-72; from exploration mgr. to pres. and COO Dixel Resources Inc., Houston, 1972-78; pres., CEO Spartan Petroleum Corp., Houston, 1978—. Contbr. articles to profl. jours.; spkr. in field. Elder Presbyn. Ch., Houston, 1984—; trustee U. Nebr. Found., Lincoln, 1975—; dir., chmn. adv. bd. dept. geology U. Nebr., 1984—. Capt. UAR, 1958-59. Named Hon. Consul Govt. Belize, 1988-89. Mem. Am. Assn. Petroleum Geologists (cert., del., dir. acad. liaison com., chmn Houston ho. of dels. group 1996-97), Ind. Petroleum Assn. Am., Soc. Ind. Profl. Earth Scientists, Houston Geol. Soc., Houston Energy Fin. Group, Nottingham Club Houston (v.p. 1988-89), Govt. Belize (adv. for trade 1993—), Whitehall Club Houston (pres., dir. 1979—). Republican. Avocations: running, hunting, skiing, tennis. Office: Spartan Petroleum Corp 14027 Memorial Dr # 266 Houston TX 77079-6826

JONES, LARRY WAYNE "CHIPPER", baseball player; b. De Land, Fla., Apr. 24, 1972; m. Karin. Shortstop Jacksonville Jaguars, 1990-95; 3rd baseman Atlanta Braves, 1995—. Office: Turner Field PO Box 4064 Atlanta GA 30302-4064 also: 755 Hank Aaron Dr SE Atlanta GA 30315-1100

JONES, LAUREN EVANS, lawyer; b. Lawrence, Kans., Jan. 10, 1952; s. Kevin Rice and Marcia Jo Ann (Peterson) J.; m. Vivien Craig Long, Mar. 26, 1978; children: Dylan Tyler, Hayden Blake, Carson Reed. BA in History, U. Mich., 1973; JD, Duke U., 1977. Bar: R.I. 1978, U.S. Dist. Ct. R.I. 1978, U.S. Ct. Appeals (1st cir.) 1985, U.S. Ct. Appeals (9th cir.) 1994, U.S. Supreme Ct. 1991. Assoc. Lovett, Morgera, Schefrin & Gallogly, Providence, R.I., 1979-83; ptnr. Jones & Aisenberg, Providence, 1983-89; owner Jones Assocs., Providence, 1990—; mem. Jud. Performance Eval. Commn., 1993—; mem. R.I. Supreme Ct. Com. on Profl. and Civility, 1995-96. Editor R.I. Bar Jour., 1989-95; contbr. articles to profl. jours. Nominee R.I. Supreme Ct., 1993, 95, 96, 97. Mem. R.I. Bar Assn. (exec. com. 1989—, sec. 1995, v.p. 1996, pres. elect 1997, pres. 1998-99). Office: Jones Assocs 72 S Main St Providence RI 02903-2907

JONES, LAURETTA MARIE, artist, graphic designer, computer interface designer; b. Cleve., Mar. 13, 1953; d. Richard Llewellyn and Loretta (Jares) J. BFA, Cleve. Inst. Art, 1975; postgrad., N.Y. Inst. Tech., 1981, 87. Instr. Sch. Visual Arts, N.Y.C., 1984—, dir. undergraduate computer studies, 1988-90; adj. prof. art Manhattanville Coll., Purchase, N.Y., 1985-86; cons. Trintex/Prodigy, White Plains, N.Y., 1986-87, IBM Gallery Sci. and Art, N.Y.C., 1987-88; cons. graphic design IBM T.J. Watson Rsch. Ctr., Yorktown Heights, N.Y., 1988-90, adv. graphic designer, 1990-95, devel. engr., 1995—; rsch. staff mem. and mgr., Network Transaction Systems, 1997—. Exhibited collages, drawings in shows worldwide, 1983—; represented in permanent collection Franklin Inst., Phila., Mus. Sci. and Industry, Chgo. Mem. bus. adv. coun. No. Westchester Ctr. for Arts, 1994-95. Mem. ACLU, Assn. for Computing Machinery-Spl. Interest Group on Computer Human Interfaces, Nat. Computer Graphics Assn. (speaker 1987), Inst. for Ecosystems Studies, Guild of Nat. Sci. Illustrators, Am. Soc. of Bot. Artists, N.Y. Botanical Gardens, Small Computers Arts Network (speaker 1984-89), Computer Arts Discipline Graphic Artists Guild (founding, steering com. 1984-88), ACM-SIGGRAPH (N.Y.C. chpt. editor newsletter, bd. dirs. 1986-92, speaker 1991, nat. courses com. 1991-92, design show jury 1993), Am. Inst. Graphic Arts, Amnesty Internat., Greenpeace, NOW, Nature Conservancy . Avocations: mountain biking, hiking, ballroom dancing, gardening, botanical art. Office: IBM TJ Watson Rsch Ctr PO Box 704 Yorktown Heights NY 10598-0704

JONES, LAURIE GANONG, sales and marketing executive; b. Owatonna, Minn., Feb. 22, 1954; d. Harvey Mathias and Elaine Ione (Mauren) Ganong; m. Daniel Lee Jones, Sept. 6, 1975; 1 child, Jonathon Alexander. AB in Econs., U. Calif., Davis, 1979; MBA, Pepperdine U., Malibu, Calif., 1987. Cert. internal auditor, cert. info. systems auditor. EDP auditor Nat. Blvd. Bank, Chgo., 1980-82; sr. EDP auditor Carnation Co., L.A., 1982-85, Wickes Cos., Santa Monica, Calif., 1985-87; sr. audit mgr. Watt Industries, Santa Monica, 1987-89; dir. audit svcs. Canaudit, Inc., Simi Valley, Calif., 1988-93; prin. Jones & Jones, Sterling, Colo., 1989—; pres. Jones Techs, Inc., Sterling, Colo., 1991-92; dir. support svcs. Sykes Enterprises, Tampa, Fla., 1992-97; dir. market analysis Sykes Enterprises, 1998-99, dir. product planning, 1998-99; guest lectr. Calif. Poly. Inst., Pomona, 1985-87, Calif. State U., Long Beach and Domingez Hills, Calif., 1985-87; conf. spkr. Inst. Internal Auditors, Orlando, Fla., L.A., 1988—; spkr. Software Support Profl. Assn., 1993—; chair Sterling Regional Med. Ctr. Found., 1995—; chmn. adv. bd. Northeastern Jr. Coll., 1994-97. Author: (monograph) Internal Audit Involvement in the Joint Venture Process, 1990, The Successfull In Charge Auditor, 1990, Introduction to Internal Auditing, 1990, 11A Cash Operations Practice Set, 1991, 11A Risk Assessment Tool Kit, 1990. Disaster preparedness coord. Watt Industries, Santa Monica, 1988-89. Named Bus. Person of the Year Logan County C. of C., 1992. Mem. EDP Auditors Assn. (3d pl. rsch. award 1988), Inst. Internal Auditors (bd. govs. L.A. 1987-89, bd. govs. Denver 1990, internat. bd. regents 1988-91, outstanding rsch. paper 1988, Outstanding Mem. 1988, Outstanding Colo. Citizen 1994), Assn. Support Profls. Republican. Methodist. Sterling Country Club. Avocations: farming, cycling, reading, travel, skiing. Office: Sykes Enterprises Inc 777 N 4th St Sterling CO 80751-3244

JONES, LAURIE LYNN, magazine editor; b. Kerrville, Tex., Sept. 2, 1947; d. Charles Clinton and Jean Laurie (Davidson) J.; m. C. Frederick Childs, June 26, 1976; children: Charles Newell (Clancy), Cyrus Trevor; 1 stepchild, Ariel Childs. B.A., U. Tex., 1969. Asst. to dir. coll. admissions Columbia U., N.Y.C., 1969-70; asst. to dir. Office Alumni-Columbia U., N.Y.C., 1970-71; asst. advt. mgr. Book World, 1971-72, Washington Post-Chgo. Tribune, 1971-72; editorial asst. N.Y. Mag., N.Y.C., 1972-74, asst. editor, 1974, sr. editor, 1974-76, mng. editor, 1976-92; mng. editor Vogue Mag., N.Y.C., 1992—. Mem. Am. Soc. Mag. Editors, Women in Coummunication, Advt. Women N.Y. Republican. Methodist. Home: 40 Great Jones St New York NY 10012-1109 Also: 62 Giles Hill Rd Redding Ridge CT 06876 Office: Vogue Magazine 350 Madison Ave New York NY 10017-3704

JONES, LAWRENCE DAVID, insurance and medical consultant; b. Cloquet, Minn., Mar. 4, 1928; s. Ellsworth D. and Opal I. Jones; m. Mary; children: David, Greta, Donald, Christopher, Laura, Sharon. B in Pharmacy, U. Utah, 1954; postgrad., U. N.D., 1960-62; MD, U. Minn., 1964. Bd. cert. ins. medicine. Owner, operator drug ctrs. Kemmerer (Wyo.), Big Piney, Trading Post and Sugar Bowl, 1955-60; intern St. Marys Hosp., Mpls., 1964-65; family practice physician Harlowton, Mont., 1965-69, Arcadia, Calif., 1969-74; med. dir. TransAmerica Occidental Life, 1969-79, Teledyne Life Ins., L.A., 1974-79, Gt. Am. Life, L.A., 1977-79; sr. med. dir. Sentry Ins., A Mut. Co., Stevens Point, Wis., 1979-80; assoc. med. dir. First Colony Life Ins. Co., 1981-83; v.p., assoc. med. dir. First Colony Life Ins. Co., Lynchburg, Va., 1983-85; v.p., med. dir., 1985-90, ind. cons. in ins. medicine/underwriting, 1990—; mem. faculty Bd. Ins. Medicine Triennial Course, 1979, 82, 85, 88, 91; mem. adv. bd. Lab. Corp. Am., Cons. Physicians Network; mem. NIH coordinating com. Nat. Heart Attack Alert Program; chmn. NIH-Nat. Heart Alert Program Task Force on Emergency Access to Med. Care in Managed Care; former mem. bd. dirs. Life and Health Ins. Rsch. Fund; former mem. adv. bd. Lifetime Corp. Am. Svc.Bur.-Meditest, others. Past chmn. utilization rev. com. Santa Teresita Hosp., Duarte, Calif.; past city health officer Harlowton; past county health officer Judith Basin County, Mont; past mem. bd. dirs. Health Sys. Agy., L.A., Deaconess Hosp. Sch. Nursing, Billings, Mont., past asst. scoutmaster, past. asst. dist. scout commr., past dist. scout commr., past scoutmaster. Sgt. U.S. Army, 1952-53, USAR, 1950-53. Mem. AMA, Med. Soc. Va., Calif. State Med. Assn., Am. Acad. Ins. Medicine (chmn. profl. and pub. rels. com.), Am. Coll. Cardiology (co-chmn. liaison com., others), Assn. Life Ins. Med. Dirs. Am. (past pres., past chmn. ethics com., past chmn. profl. and pub. rels. com., past chmn. mortality and morbidity com., others), So. Med. Assn. (chmn. sect. on cardiovascular disease 1994-95), Med. Soc. Va., others. Office: PO Box 6395 Diamondhead MS 39525-6008

JONES, LAWRENCE NEALE, university dean, minister; b. Moundsville, W.Va., Apr. 24, 1921; s. Eugene Wayman and Rosa (Bruce) J.; m. Mary Ellen Cooley, Mar. 29, 1945; children: Mary Lynn, Rodney Bruce. B.Ed., W. Va. State Coll., 1942, LL.D., 1965; M.A., U. Chgo., 1948; B.D., Oberlin Grad. Sch., 1956; Ph.D., Yale U., 1961; LL.D., Jewish Theol. Sem., 1971. Ordained to ministry United Ch. Christ, 1956; student Christian Movement Middle Atlantic Region, 1957-60; dean chapel Fisk U., 1960-65; dean students Union Theol. Sem., N.Y.C., 1965-71; prof. Union Theol. Sem. (Afro-Am. ch. history), 1970; dean Union Theol. Sem., 1971-74, acting pres., 1970; dean Sch. Div. Howard U., Washington, 1975-91, ret., 1991; Pres. Civil Rights Coordinating Council, Nashville, 1963-64. Bd. dirs. Sheltering Arms and Children's Svc., 1970-75, Inst. Social and Religious Studies Jewish Sem., United Ch. Bd. for World Ministries, 1969-75; bd. dirs., sec. exec. com. Assn. Theol. Schs., U.S. and Can.; chmn. exec. com. Fund for Theol. Edn., 1978—. With AUS, 1943-46, 47-53. Rockefeller Doctoral grantee; Lucy Monroe scholar; Rosenwald scholar; Am. Assn. Theol. Schs. Study grantee. Mem. Am. Ch. History Soc., Am. Acad. Religion, Soc. Study Black Religion (pres. 1973-75), Nat. Com. Black Churchmen. *

JONES, LAWRENCE RYMAN, retired research chemist; b. Terre Haute, Ind., Jan. 8, 1921; s. Frank Arthur and Mary Naomi (Ryman) J.; m. Mary Jane Proctor, July 9, 1944; children: Trudi Beth, Lawrence R. II. BS, Ind. State U., 1946. Chemist Comml. Solvents Corp., Terre Haute, 1946-79; chemist, toxicologist St. Anthony Hosp., Terre Haute, 1957-60; mgr. Ryman Farm, Vigo County, Ind., 1957-86; pres. Rymark Labs., Terre Haute, 1970-80; rsch. scientist Internat. Mineral and Chem. Corp., Terre Haute, 1972-86, ret., 1986—. Patentee in field; contbr. over 200 articles to profl. jours. Elder Presbyn. Ch.; active Terre Haute City Coun., 1960-72, pres., 1968; pres. Sr. Citizens Wabash Valley, 1960-64; v.p. Sr. Citizen Housing Devel.; bd. govs. Task Force for Economy; past chmn. Am. chem. Soc., Wabash Valley; past bd. dirs. Am. Inst. Chemists, Exch. Club, Cmty. Theater, Swope Art Gallery; mem. County Zoning Commn.; ch. elder, Sunday sch. tchr. Youth Fellowship. Mem. Am. Chem. Soc. (former chmn. Wabash Valley sect.). Republican. Presbyterian. Avocations: genealogy, gardening, golf. Home: RR 2 Box 2456 Brazoria TX 77422-9630

JONES, LAWRENCE TUNNICLIFFE, lawyer; b. Mineola, N.Y., Jan. 20, 1950; s. Carroll Hudson Tunnicliffe and Florence Virginia (Greene) J. BA, U. Va., 1972; JD, U. Richmond, 1975. Bar: Va. 1975, D.C. 1976, N.Y. 1976, U.S. Dist. Ct. (ea. and so. dist.) N.Y. 1976, U.S. Supreme Ct. 1986. Bus. mgr. law review U. Richmond, Va., 1974-75; ptnr. Carroll Hudson Tunnicliffe Jones and Lawrence Tunnicliffe Jones Attys. at law, Mineola, 1976-91. Trustee Nassau County Hist. Soc., 1976—, pres., 1983-89; bd. dirs. Friends of Hist. St. George's Ch., Hempstead, N.Y., 1982—, v.p., 1990-92, pres., 1992-94; bd. dirs. St. Mary's Devel. Fund, Garden City, N.Y., 1983-89, pres., 1987-89; pres. coun. Cathedral Sch. St. Paul Alumni Fund, Inc., Garden City, 1984—; bd. govs. Cathedral Sch. St. Mary, Garden City, 1983-86. Mem. ABA, Va. State Bar Assn., N.Y. State Bar Assn., Nassau County Bar Assn., Nassau County Tax and Estate Planning Coun., Univ. Club (N.Y.C.), Univ. Club (L.I., pres. 1986-87, 93-94, bd. dirs. 1983-86, 89—), Mineola C. of C. (dir. 1993—), Garden City Golf Club, Mineola-Garden City Rotary (dir. 1991-94), Garden City Fellowship (pres. 1993-94, dir. 1994—), Cathedral Club (Garden City) (pres. 1993-95), Garden City C. of C. Episcopalian. Avocation: historic building preservation. Home: 158 Cathedral Ave Hempstead NY 11550-1140 Office: Jones & Jones 286 Old Country Rd Ste 22 Mineola NY 11501-4106

JONES, LAWRENCE WILLIAM, educator, physicist; b. Evanston, Ill., Nov. 16, 1925; s. Charles Herbert and Fern (Storm) J.; m. Ruth Reavley Drummond, June 24, 1950; children: Douglas Warren, Carol Anne, Ellen Louise. B.S., Northwestern U., 1948, M.S., 1949; Ph.D., U. Calif. at Berkeley, 1952. Research asst. U. Calif. Radiation Lab., Berkeley, 1950-52; mem. faculty U. Mich., Ann Arbor, 1952—; prof. physics U. Mich., 1963—, chmn. dept. physics, 1982-87; physicist Midwestern U. Rsch. Assn., 1956-57; vis. physicist Lawrence Radiation Lab., Berkeley, 1959—, cons., 1964-66; vis. scientist CERN, Geneva, Switzerland, 1961-62, 65, 85—, assoc., 1988—; vis. physicist Brookhaven Nat. Lab., Upton, N.Y., 1963—; vis. physicist Fermi Nat. Accelerator Lab., Batavia, Ill., 1971—; vis. prof. Tata Inst. Fundamental Rsch., Bombay, India, 1979, U. Sydney Australia, 1991; mem. elem. particle physics panel of physics survey com. NRC; cons. ctrl. design group Superconducting Super Collider Nat. Lab., 1985-87, vis. physicist, 1991-94; trustee Univs. Rsch. Assn., 1982-87; disting. vis. scholar U. Adelaide, 1991; vis. scientist U. Auckland, 1991. Mem. adv. panel for Cosmic Rays Jour. of Physics G., 1991-95. Guggenheim fellow, 1965; Sci. Rsch. Coun. fellow, 1977. Fellow Am. Phys. Soc. E-mail LWJones@umich.edu. Home: 2666 Parkridge Dr Ann Arbor MI 48103-1731 Office: U Mich Dept Physics Ann Arbor MI 48109-1120

JONES, LAWRENCE WORTH, poet, editor, performance art producer, songwriter; b. Norman, Okla., Jan. 5, 1950; s. Walter Neil and Jane Elizabeth (McCauley) J. BA in English with deptl. honors, CUNY, 1991. Supr. Fidelity Svc. Co., Boston, 1978-83; compliance dir. Alliance Fund Svcs., N.Y.C., 1985-88; dir. Cafe Nico, artists, writers, photographers collective, N.Y.C., 1991—; advisor ABC No Rio, N.Y.C., 1991—. Author: We Become a Picnic, 1994; contbr. poetry to Downtown Poets, 1999. Coord. Gay Liberation Front, N.Y.C., 1970; plaintiff Gay Cmty. Alliance, Norman, Okla., 1972; campaign coord. Nader NYC '96, 1996. Mem. Poets and Writers, Poetry Project. Avocations: art history, watercolors, collage. E-mail: cafenico@geocities.com. Home: 101 Ave A New York NY 10009

JONES, LEE BENNETT, chemist, educator, university official; b. Memphis, Mar. 14, 1938; s. Harold S. and Martha B. J.; m. Vera Kramar, Feb. 8, 1964; children: David B., Michael B. BA magna cum laude, Wabash Coll, 1960; PhD, M.I.T., 1964; DSC (hon.), Wabash Coll., 1992. Faculty U. Ariz., Tucson, 1964-85; prof. chemistry U. Ariz., 1972-85, asst. head dept. chemistry, 1971-73, head dept., 1973-77, dean Grad. Coll., 1977-79, provost Grad. Studies and Health Scis., 1979-82, v.p. rsch., 1982-85; prof. chemistry, exec. v.p., provost U. Nebr., Lincoln, 1985—; chmn. bd. dirs. Coun. Grad.

Schs., 1986; mem. Grad. Records Exam. Bd., 1986-91; mem. Midwest Higher Edn. Commn., 1995—. Mem. editl. bd. Jour. Chem. Edn, 1975-79; contbr. numerous articles to sci. jours. Mem. Nebr. R&D Authority, 1985—, Midwest Higher Edn. Commn.; vice chmn. Nebr. Ednl. Telecomm. Commn., 1987-88, 91-92. NSF fellow, 1961-63, 64—. Mem. AAAS, AAUP, Am. Chem. Soc., Chem. Soc. (London), N.Y. Acad. Scis., Phi Beta Kappa. Home: 1611 Kingston Rd Lincoln NE 68506-1526 Office: U Nebr 106 Varner Hall 3835 Holdrege St Lincoln NE 68583-0743

JONES, LEON HERBERT, JR. (HERB JONES), artist; b. Norfolk, Va., Mar. 25, 1923; s. Leon Herbert and Edna May (Curling) J.; student William and Mary Coll., 1942-44; m. Barbara Dean, Sept. 14, 1947; children: Robert Clair, Louis Herbert. Marine structural draftsman and designer Norfolk (Va.) Shipbuilding & Dry Dock Co., 1944-46; free-lance comml. artist, 1946-49; prin. Herb Jones Realty, Norfolk, 1949-58; owner, mgr. Herb Jones Art Studio, Norfolk, 1958—; one-man shows: Norfolk Mus., 1968, Potomac Gallery, Alexandria, Va., 1979, Salisbury Gallery, 1979, Walter C. Rawls Mus., Courtland, Va., 1967, Virginia Beach Maritime Mus., 1983 Village Gallery, Virginia Beach, Va., 1984, Va. Mus. Marine Scis., 1986-87, Olde Towne Gallery, 1987, Amoco Oil, 1989, Petersburg Area Art League (affiliate Va. Mus.), 1990, Surrey Borger Lions Club, Surrey, Eng., 1990, Sr. Showcase Creative Living Cen. Libr., Virginia Beach, Va., 1990, Norview Lions Club Sponsored Show for Handicapped, Norfolk, Va., 1991, Surrey (Eng.) Border Lions Club, 1990, Lions Internat., 1991, 93, Cypress Point Lions sponsored show to benefit handicapped, Va. Beach, 1993, Harborfest, 1995, 96, Janaf Art Show, 1997, Jones Art Gallery, Dominion Tower & Waterside, Norfolk, 1998; 45 year retrospective: Louis and Susan Jones Art Gallery, Norfolk, Va., 1994, The Best of Herb Jones, 98; group shows include: Chrysler Mus., Norfolk, 1973, 74, SUNY, Buffalo, 1966, Springfield (Mass.) Mus. Fine Arts, 1966, Mariners Mus., Newport News, Va., 1967-73, Va. Mus., Richmond, 1969, 71, Columbia (S.C.) Mus. Art, 1972, Winston-Salem (N.C.) Gallery Contemporary Art, 1970, 72, Norfolk Mus., 1963-69, Vladimir Arts, Winsbach, West Germany, 1978, 79, Chesapeake Bay Maritime Mus., Md., Mobile Mus. Traveling Show, 1983, Knoxville World's Fair in Fine Arts, 1982, Art Buyers Caravan, Atlanta, 1982, Colonial Wild Fowl Festival, Williamsburg, Va., 1983, Chesapeake Jubilee (Va., Excellence award) 1984, Peninsula Fine Arts Festival, Newport News, 1984, Currituck Wildlife Show, N.C., 1984, Medley of Arts, Hampton (Va.) Coliseum, 1984 (6 awards 1986-87), Easton Nat. Wildfowl and Art Exhibit, Easton, Md., 1984; Mid-Atlantic Art Exhibit, Virginia Beach, Va., 1985, Chincoteague Island Easter Festival, Va., 1985, (2 awards) 1989 (1st and 2d Pl. award), Harborfest Norfolk, Va., 1985-96, Mid-Atlantic Wildfowl Festival, 1986-93 (1st and 3d award), Hampton Wildlife Festival, 1986 (award 1989), Medley of the Arts, 1986, 87, Mid Atlantic Art Exhibits, 1986, 87, Hampton Fall Festival, (award) 1989, Sr. Showcase Creative Living Art Exhibit, Va. Beach, 1990, River Gallery, Chesapeake, Va., 1992, MidAtlantic Waterfowl Festival, Va. Beach, 1993; represented in permanent collections: Chrysler Mus., wardroom USS Skipjack, USS Iwo Jima, USS John F. Kennedy, USS Dwight D. Eisenhower, USS Seattle, USS Raleigh, USS Biddle, USS Whidby Island Commn., 1992, U. Va., Charlottesville, U.S. Treasury Dept., Library of Congress, Washington, Edenton Hist. Commn. (N.C.), USS Whidby Island, 1994, USS Hayler, 1995, also pvt. collections; commd. ltd. edit. print series Ducks Unltd., also Va. Beach Maritime Mus., Boy Scouts Am., Va. Mus. Marine Scis., Wavy TV affiliate of Lin Broadcasting Co., Judy Boone Real Estate, Official Harborfest Poster, 1993—, Harbor Fest Poster, 1993-95, Official Urbanna (Va.) Oyster Festival print, 1993, plaque Chesapeake Bay Bridge and Tunnel Commn., two spl. print edits. Letton Gooch Printers Inc. Recipient diploma di merito Universita delle Arti, 1981, Gold Centaur award 1983, three Awards of Excellence Printing Industries of the Virginias, 1987, 1st and 2d Pl. Awards of Excellence, 1989, Oscar d'Italia, Acad. Italia Calvatore, 1985, award Mid-Atlantic Waterfowl Festival, 1986, 1st and 3d Place awards, 1993, Great Citizen of Hampton Roads award Cox Cable TV, 1991, Best Art Print in Show award Printing Industries Va., 1995; named Cavalier of Arts, Acad. Bedriacense Calvatore, Italy, 1985, Hampton Roads Original, WTAR-AM Radio, 1990, Granby Hall of Fame, 1997; selected as one of 100 leaders to judge "Best of Am.", U.S. News & World Report, 1990. Mem. Nat. Soc. Arts and Lit., Tidewater Artists Assn., Internat. Platform Assn., Virginia Beach Maritime Mus. (charter), Corr. Academie Europeene, Nat. Am. Film Inst., Lion's Internat. (hon., Melvin Jones fellow for dedicated humanitarian svcs. 1994, Disting. Svc. award for dedication to cmty. and Lions, 1997). Methodist. Home and Office: 238 Beck St Norfolk VA 23503-4902

JONES, LEONADE DIANE, media publishing company executive; b. Bethesda, Md., Nov. 27, 1947; d. Leon Adger and Landonia Randolph (Madden) J. BA with distinction, Simmons Coll., 1969; JD, Stanford U., 1973, MBA, 1973. Bar: Calif. 1973, D.C. 1979. Summer assoc. Davis Polk & Wardwell, N.Y.C., summer 1972; securities analyst Capital Rsch. Co., L.A., 1973-75; asst. treas. Washington Post Co., 1975-79, 86-87, treas., 1987-96; dir. fin. services Post-Newsweek Stas., Inc., Washington, 1979-84, v.p. bus. affairs, 1984-86; bd. dirs. Am. Balanced Fund, Inc., Income Fund Am., Inc., Fundamental Investors, Growth Fund Am., Inc., The New Economy Fund, Smallcap World Fund, Inc.; mem. investment mgmt. subcom. of benefit plans com. Am. Stores Co., 1992—; mem. investment adv. com. N.Y. State Tchrs.' Retirement Sys., 1999—. Treas., bd. dirs. Big Sisters Washington Met. Area, 1984-85; bd. dirs. D.C. Contemporary Dance Theatre, 1987-89, Washington Performing Arts Soc., 1990-94, treas., 1992-94; mem. adv. coun. Charlin Jazz Soc., 1988-92; mem. adv. bd. Sta. WHMM-TV, 1989-93; asst. chmn. budget and audit D.C. chpt. Met. Washington, Edges Group, Inc., 1989-93; mem. adv. coun. Bus. Sch., Stanford U., 1991-98, bd. visitors Law Sch., 1982-84, 93-98; trustee Am. Inst. Mng. Diversity, Inc., 1991-96; mem. corp. Simmons Coll., 1992-96; bd. dirs. Yerba Buena Ctr. for Arts, 1999—. Recipient Candace award for bus., 1992, Serwa award, 1993; named to D.C. Women's Hall of Fame, 1992. Mem. ABA, Calif. Bar Assn., D.C. Bar Assn., Stanford U. Bus. Sch. Alumni Assn. (bd. dirs. 1986-88, pres. Washington-Balt. chpts. 1984-85). Avocations: tennis, travel.

JONES, LEWIS ARNOLD, physician, radiologist; b. Detroit, Sept. 16, 1950; s. Lewis Arnold, Sr. and Berlene (Irish) J.; m. Pamela Denise Jennings, Nov. 14, 1992; children: Jennifer Tiffany, Alicia Dawn, Lewis Alexander. *Jones would like to dedicate his entry to the late Lewis A. Jones, Sr., the loving and caring father of four, who instilled the values of academic discipline and achievement.* Student, Highland Park Coll., 1968-69, Wayne State U., 1969-72; MD, U. Mich., 1978. Diplomate Am. Bd. Radiology. Radiology residency Providence Hosp., Southfield, Mich., 1978-82; diagnostic radiologist Tri-County Radiology, P.C., West Bloomfield, Mich., 1983-84; clin. instr. of radiology Wayne State U. Sch. of Medicine, Detroit, 1984-91, clin. asst. prof. radiology, 1991-97; physician cons. Mich. Dept. Cmty. Health, Lansing, 1997—; mem. cmty. adv. com. Karmanas Cancer Inst., Detroit, 1994—; adv. bd. African Am. anti-platelet stroke prevention, Wayne State U., 1996-97; co-investigator Women's Health Initiative, Detroit, 1996-97; co-chmn. 1997 Mich.'s Year of Women's Health, Mich. Dept. Cmty. Health, Lansing, 1997—. Vol. spkr. Am. Cancer Soc., 1986—. Co-creator, co-presenter seminars Ptnrs. for Life, Mich., 1996—; bd. dirs. Oakland County Am. Cancer Soc., 1988—. Recipient Life Saver award Am. Cancer Soc., Southfield, Mich., 1990, Fredrick Douglass award Nat. Assn. Negro Bus. and Profl. Women's Clubs, New Met. Detroit Club, 1996; winner "What a Man" contest, Essence Mag./ Preferred Stock Cologne, N.Y.C., 1995. Mem. AMA, Mich. State Med. Soc., Wayne County Med. Soc., Am. Coll. Radiology, Assn. Univ. Radiologists. Avocations: women's health advocacy spkr., jazz and classical music collector. Home: 4951 Champlain Cir West Bloomfield MI 48323-3529

JONES, LINCOLN, III, army officer; b. Ft. Benning, Ga., Jan. 23, 1933; s. Lincoln and Doris G. (Baltz) J.; m. Alexandra Ann Archbald, June 21, 1958; children: Peter L., Patricia A. BS., U.S. Mil. Acad., 1958; M.S., Auburn U., 1969. Commd. 2d lt. U.S. Army, 1958; advanced through grades to maj. gen.; brigade comdr. 9th Inf. Div., 1978-79; chief staff div. and 9th Inf. Div., Ft. Lewis, 1980; asst. div. comdr. 9th Inf. Div., 1980-82; dep. chief of staff LANDSOUTH, Verona, Italy, 1982-85; dep. comdg. gen. V Corps, Frankfurt, Germany, 1985-87; comdg. gen. USASETAF, Vicenza, Italy, 1987-90; pres., CEO ENRON Power Corp., Houston, 1991-93; pres. ENRON Engring. and Constrn. Co., Houston, 1994-96; vice chmn. ENRON Europe Ltd., London, 1996-98; pres. Lincoln Assocs., Houston, 1999—. Mem. Com. on Fgn. Rels., Houston; bd. dirs. World Coun. Fgn. Affairs. Decorated D.S.M. with oak leaf cluster, Def. Superior Medal, Legion of Merit with oak leaf cluster, D.F.C., Bronze Star, others. Mem. Assn. U.S. Army, Assn. Grads. U.S. Mil. Acad. Episcopalian. Home: 9 Fernglen Dr The Woodlands TX 77380-3957

JONES, LINDA, communications educator. BA in English, U. Mich., 1972; MS in Journalism with distinction, Northwestern U., 1985. Reporter The Chelsea (Mich.) Standard, 1973-75; county govt., police reporter The Marshall (Mich.) Evening Chronicle, 1975-77; edn. reporter The Bay City (Mich.) Times, 1977--79, asst. met. editor, 1979-81, met. editor, 1981-86; vis. asst. prof. dept. journalism Roosevelt (Mich.) U., 1986-88, assoc. prof. journalism, 1992—, interim head, faculty of journalism and comm. studies, 1995-96, dir. sch. comm., 1996; asst. prof. Medill Sch. Journalism Northwestern U., 1988-92; acting dir. Multicultural Journalism Ctr., Urban Journalism Ctr.; pub. com. StreetWise, 1995—; cons. The Times, 1993; adviser advising ctr., 1994-95; tchr. workshop sessions Journalism Edn. Assn./Nat. Scholastic Press Assn. conventions, 1992-96, chair Multicultural Scholarship com., 1996, spkr. com. Ill. host orgn., 1996. Contbr. articles to profl. jours.; judge and lectr. in field. Recipient Parent-Tchr. Assn. Mich. spl. award for edn. coverage, 1977, Mich. AP second place, breaking news, team coverage of major fire, 1980; Regents-Alumni scholarship U. Mich., 1968. Office: Roosevelt Univ 1751-T Robin Hall 600F 430 S Michigan Ave Chicago IL 60605-1301*

JONES, LORETTA LUCEK, chemistry educator, writer; b. Rockford, Ill., Apr. 26, 1943; d. Walter Joseph and Magdalen Mary (Kazunas) Lucek. BS with hons., Loyola U., 1964; MS, U. Chgo., 1968; PhD, D.A., U. Ill., 1979. Sec., treas. Sonicraft, Inc., Chgo., 1968-74; vis. asst. prof. U. Ill., Urbana, 1979-82, asst. dir. gen. chemistry program, lectr., 1982-85, assoc. dir., 1985-92; asst. prof. U. No. Colo., Greeley, 1992-93, assoc. prof., 1993-97, prof., 1997-98; cons. scholar Acad. Info. Syss. IBM Corp., Milford, Conn., 1987-88; mem. adv. bd. Mid-Atlantic Dicovery Project Franklin and Marshall Coll., 1994-98; co-prin. investigator Rocky Mtn. Tchr. Edn. Collaborative, Greeley, Colo., 1994-98; prin. investigator Chemistry for the Info. Age, Greeley, 1995-98. Author: (videotape series) Lecture Demonstrations, 1980 (award Amoco, 1981); co-author: (videotape courses) Chemistry 101, 102, 1980-92, (software) Exploring Chemistry, 1988-94 (Educom award 1987, 89), (textbook) Chemistry: Molecules, Matter and Change, 1997, (textbook) Chemical Principles. Fellow AAAS; mem. AAUW, ACS (councilor 1992—), ACS/Examinations Inst. (bd. trustees), Nat. Assn. Rsch. in Sci. Tchg. Office: U No Colo Dept Chemistry & Biochem 501 20th St Dept & Greeley CO 80639

JONES, LYLE VINCENT, psychology educator; b. Grandview, Wash., Mar. 11, 1924; s. Vincent F. and Matilda M. (Abraham) J.; m. Patricia Edison Powers, Dec. 17, 1949 (div. 1979); children: Christopher V., Susan E., Tad W. Student, Reed Coll., 1942-43; B.S., U. Wash., 1947, M.S., 1948; Ph.D., Stanford U., 1950. Nat. Research fellow, 1950-51; asst. prof. psychology U. Chgo., 1951-57; vis. assoc. prof. U. Tex., 1956-57; assoc. prof. U. N.C., 1957-60, prof., 1960-69, Alumni disting. prof., 1969-92; rsch. prof., 1992—; dir. L.L. Thurstone Psychometric Lab. U. N.C., 1957-74, 79-92, vice chancellor, dean Grad. Sch., 1969-79; pres. Assn. Grad. Schs., 1976-77; cons. in field. Author: (with others) Studies in Aphasia: An Approach to Testing, 1961, The Measurement and Prediction of Judgment and Choice, 1968, (with others) An Assessment of Research-Doctorate Programs in the United States, 5 vols., 1982, Indicators of Precollege Education in Science and Mathematics, 1985; mng. editor: Psychometrika, 1956-61; editorial com. for psychology, Mc-Graw-Hill, 1965-77; contbr. articles to profl. jours. Mng. trustee J. McKeen Cattell Fund, 1974—. With U.S. Army Air Corps, 1943-46. Recipient Thomas Jefferson award U. N.C., 1979; fellow Ctr. Advanced Study in Behavioral Scis., 1964-65, 81-82; grantee NIH, 1957-63, NSF, 1960-63, 71-74, 82-84, 93-97, NIMH, 1963-74, 79-87. Fellow APA (pres. divsn. 1963-64), AAAS, Am. Acad. Arts and Scis., Am. Psychol. Soc., Am. Statis. Assn.; mem. Am. Ednl. Rsch. Assn., Nat. Coun. Measurement Edn., Inst. of Medicine, Psychometric Soc. (pres. 1962-63). Home: 6578 US Highway 15 501 N Pittsboro NC 27312-7793 Office: U NC CB 3270 Davie Hall Chapel Hill NC 27599-3270

JONES, M. DOUGLAS JR., JR., pediatrics educator; b. San Antonio, Apr. 22, 1943. BA, Rice U., 1964; MD, U. Tex., 1968. Diplomate Am. Bd. Pediat. Intern U. Colo. Sch. Medicine, Denver, 1968-69, resident, 1969-71, fellow neonatal-perinatal medicine, 1973-75; pediatrician-in-chief Children's Hosp., U. Hosp., Denver; prof., chmn. pediatrics U. Colo. Sch. Medicine. Mem. Am. Bd. Pediat. (bd. dirs. 1995—), Am. Acad. Pediat., Am. Pediat. Soc., Soc. for Pediat. Rsch. Office: Childrens Hosp 1056 E 19th Ave Denver CO 80218-1088

JONES, MARK LOGAN, educational association executive, educator; b. Provo, Utah, Dec. 16, 1950; s. Edward Evans and Doris (Logan) J. BS, Ea. Mont. Coll., 1975; postgrad. in labor rels., Cornell U.; postgrad., SUNY, Buffalo. Narcotics detective Yellowstone County Sheriff's Dept., Billings, Mont., 1972-74; math tchr. Billings (Mont.) Pub. Schs., 1975-87; rep. Nat. Edn. Assn. of N.Y., Buffalo, Jamestown, 1987-91, Nat. Edn. Assn. Alaska, Anchorage, 1991—. Photographs featured in 1991 N.Y. Art Rev. and Am. Artist. Committeeman Yellowstone Dem. Party, Billings, 1984-87; exec. com. Dem. Cen. Com., Billings, 1985-87; bd. dirs. Billings Community Ctr., 1975-87; concert chmn. Billings Community Concert Assn., 1980-87; bd. dirs. Chautauqua County Arts Coun.; bd. dirs. Big Brothers and Big Sisters Anchorage. With U.S. Army, 1970-72. Recipient Distinguished Svc. award, Billings Edn. Assn., 1985, Mont. Edn. Assn., 1987. Mem. Billings Edn. Assn. (bd. dirs. 1980-82, negotiator 1981-87, pres. 1982-87), Mont. Edn. Assn. (bd. dirs. 1982-87), Ea. Mont. Coll. Tchr. Edn. Project, Accreditation Reviewer Team Mont. Office Pub. Edn., Big Sky Orchard, Masonic, Scottish Rite. Avocations: Bonsai, photography, reading, classical and jazz music, hunting, fishing. Home: PO Box 102904 Anchorage AK 99510-2904 Office: Nat Edn Assn Alaska 1840 S Bragaw St Ste 103 Anchorage AK 99508-3463

JONES, MARK MITCHELL, plastic surgeon; b. Atlanta, Mar. 27, 1951; s. Curtis B. and Julia (Mitchell) J.; m. Regine M.F. Heckel, Jan. 10, 1980; children: Céline Julia Micheline, Cédric André Curtis. Student, Oxford (Ga.) Coll., 1971; BA in Chemistry, Emory U., 1973; DBA, U. Canterbury, Christchurch, New Zealand, 1975; BA, MA, Oxford (Eng.) U., 1977; MD, Med. Coll. Ga., 1979. Surg. intern Med. U. of S.C., Charleston, 1979-80; surg. resident Union Meml. Hosp., Balt., 1980-81; resident in otolaryngology Johns Hopkins Hosp., Balt., 1981-84, mem. staff, instr., 1984-85; resident in plastic surgery Stanford U. Med. Ctr., Palo Alto, Calif., 1985-86; chief resident in plastic surgery, 1987-88; assoc. Calif. Ear Inst., 1988-89; chief surgeon Atlanta Plastic Surgery Specialist, 1989—. Fulbright fellow in plastic surgery, Paris, 1986-87. Home: 985 Foxcroft Rd NW Atlanta GA 30327-2621 Office: Atlanta Plastic Surgery Specialist 2001 Peachtree Rd NE Ste 630 Atlanta GA 30309-1423

JONES, MARK RICHARD, financial advisor; b. Detroit, Apr. 7, 1969; s. John Richard and Jennifer Anita (Stubben) J. BBA, Western Conn. State U., 1992. CFP Coll. Fin. Planning, Denver, 1995. Acct. ColorGraphix, Southbury, Conn., 1988-92; fin. adv. Am. Express Fin. Advs., Inc., West Cornwall, Conn., 1992—, charitable giving and estate planning specialist, 1995—. Mentor Big Brothers/Big Sisters, Torrington, Conn., 1995—. Mem. Nat. Alliance Renaissance Assocs., Internat. Assn. Fin. Planners, Inst. Cert. Fin. Planners, Am. Soc. CLU and ChFC, Nat. Com. of Planned Giving, Planned Giving Group of Conn. Avocations: hiking, tennis, golf, reading, cross county skiing. Office: Am Express Fin Advs Inc PO Box 131 West Cornwall CT 06796-0131

JONES, MARLENE ANN, family and consumer sciences educator; b. Bluffton, Ohio, Nov. 22, 1936; d. Waldo J. and Blanche M. (Criblez) Wilkins; m. Marvin O. Jones, July 3, 1965; children: John O., Dianne M. BS, Bowling Green State U., 1958, EdS, 1978; MA, Ohio State U., 1962. Cert. family and consumer scis. Vocat. home econs. tchr. 7-12 Liberty Ctr. (Ohio) Bd. of Edn., 1958-61; asst. state supr. Ohio Dept. of Edn., Columbus, 1962-65; chairperson of home econs. technologies Owens Cmty. Coll. (formerly Penta Tech. Coll.), Toledo, Ohio, 1965-71; supr. Penta County Vocat. Sch., Perrysburg, Ohio, 1965—. Past pres. United Meth. Women, Colton, Ohio, 1967—. Named 1 of 10 Outstanding Women in Toledo Jaycees, 1971-72; recipient Disting. Centennial Svc. award Ohio Agrl. and Home Econs. Rsch. and Devel. Ctr., 1982, Home Econs. Grad. fellowship award Am. Vocat. Assn., 1990; named Alum of Yr. Coll. of Edn., Bowling Green State U., 1990. Mem. ASCD, Am. Ohio Vocat. Assn., Am. Family and Consumer Svcs. Assn. (past state pres.), Ohio Vocat. Family and Consumer Svcs. Suprs. Assn. (treas.), N.W. Ohio FHA/HERO Alumni Assn. (sec.), Phi Delta Kappa, Phi Upsilon Omicron (past pres. Alumni chpt. 1965—). Methodist. Home: 5-212 US Hwy 24 Liberty Center OH 43532

JONES, MARLENE WISEMAN, elementary education educator, reading specialist; b. Zanesville, Ohio, Oct. 8, 1939; d. Mark Andrew Wiseman and Elizabeth Wiseman (Wilkins) Doughty; m. Herbert Pearce Jones, Sept. 2, 1961. BS in Edn., Muskingum Coll., New Concord, Ohio, 1962; MEd, Ohio U., Zanesville, 1984. Elem. tchr. Zanesville City Schs., 1962-65, reading specialist, 1967-97, ret., 1997; reading instr. Ohio U., Zanesville, 1984, Muskingum Area Tech. Coll., Zanesville, 1991-94; part time with Finley Fine Jewelry Co./Lazarus Dept. Store, 1999. Co-author book Diagnosis for Reading, 1975; creator Games for Reading, 1973. Mem. jr. assembly Bethesda Hosp.; treas. Salvation Army, 1999-2000; 1st v.p. Y-City Women's Club, 1999-2000. Recipient Outstanding Elem. Tchr. award, 1973. Mem. Am. Assn. Ret. Persons, Salvation Army Women's Aux., Y-City Women's Club, Swarovski, Ohio Ret. Tchrs. Assn., Muskingum County Ret. Tchrs. Assn., Zanesville Art Ctr., Order Ea. Star. Democrat. Lutheran. Avocations: golf, reading, crafts, painting, gardening. Home: 2219 Hazel Ave Zanesville OH 43701-2022

JONES, MARSHALL EDWARD, JR., retired environmental educator; b. St. Cloud, Minn., Nov. 13, 1919; m. Stella Jones; children: Susanne, Michael, Marshall III. Student, Pillsbury Mil. Acad., Owatonna, Minn., 1936-38, Breck Sch., 1938, Smiths Welding Sch., St. Paul, 1940. Instr. horsemanship Breck Sch., 1938; owner milk bus., 1939; welder USN Def., 1940-42; welding foreman Ship Yards, San Francisco, 1942; bus driver San Francisco, also Minn., 1942-44, Minn., 1943; driver milk truck, 1944-45; stone carver, foreman, prodn. mgr. Jones Granite Co., 1945-52; rehab. adminstr., founder Green Acres Rehab. Ctr., 1952-59; founder wild life farm Hibbing, Minn., 1959-72; founder Bear Country USA, Black Hills, S.D., 1973; mgr. ranch H. B. P. A., Temecula, Calif., 1974-87; ret., 1987; founder rehab. ctr. for young men convicted of a felony crime for the first time; tchr. edn. of animals to young children; trainer of horses. Avocations: writing, training dogs for the handicapped. Home: 335 N Wateka St San Jacinto CA 92583-2647 *Write out your own obituary, then count up the things you did in your life that made the world a little better for the earth, and all living things.*

JONES, MARY TRENT, endowment fund trustee; b. Durham, N.C., July 15, 1940; d. Josiah Charles Trent and Mary Duke (Biddle) Semans; m. James Parker Jones, June 27, 1964; children: James Trent, Benjamin Parker, Jonathan Edmund. AB, Duke U., 1963. Trustee The Duke Endowment, Charlotte, N.C., 1988—; chmn. Josiah Charles Trent Found., Durham, 1978-83; bd. dirs. Mary Duke Biddle Found., Durham, 1983—, Concert Artists Guild, N.Y.C., 1996—. Mem. Va. Perinatal Svcs. Adv. Bd., Richmond, 1986-91; sec. Va. Arts Commn., Richmond, 1989-92; trustee Va. Intermont Coll., Bristol, Va., 1986-91, 98—; mem. State Coun. Higher Edn. Va., Richmond, 1991-95; trustee Va. Mus. of Fine Arts, Richmond, 1992-97; mem. bd. Washington County Pub. Libr. Found., 1997—; trustee Va. Intermont Coll., 1998—, William King Regional Arts Ctr., 1998—. Recipient outstanding alumni award Durham Acad., 1991. Mem. Va. Highlands Festival Bd. Episcopalian. Avocations: reading, walking, hiking. Home: 107 Hillside Dr NE Abingdon VA 24210-2013

JONES, MERLAKIA, basketball player; b. June 21, 1973. Degree Pub. Recreation, Fla. U., 1995. Guard-forward Santaram (Portugal) Profl. Team, 1996-97, Cleve. Rockers, 1997—. Avocations: softball, tennis, singing. Office: Cleveland Rockers Gund Arena One Center Ct Cleveland OH 44115*

JONES, MICHAEL LYNN, financial consultant, operations manager; b. Tulsa, Okla., Aug. 24, 1967; s. Leonard A. and Loretta F. (Howard) J.; m. Renee D. Carter, Aug. 2, 1986; 1 child, Jonah Jacob. Student, U. Okla., 1985-88, Am. Coll., 1997-98. CFP, Internat. Bd. Cert. Fin. Planners. Retail mgr. The Finish Line, Broken Arrow, Okla., 1985-88; stockbroker Stuart James Co., Tulsa, 1988-89; rep. Am. Bank and Trust, Tulsa, 1989-91; fin. advisor Am. Express Fin. Advisors, Tulsa, 1991-97; fin. cons. PrimeVest Fin. Svcs., Tulsa, 1997-98, Everen Securities, Tulsa, 1998—. Mem. Young Dems., Tulsa, Promise Keepers, Tulsa; vol. Soc. for Prevention of Cruelty to Animals, Salvation Army, Boys Club, Broken Arrow, 1987-92; mem. Jr. C. of C., Tulsa. Mem. Internat. Assn. for Fin. Planning (regional chpt. v.p. 1995—), Inst. of CFP, Okla. U. Alumni Assn., Tulsa Running Club, Green Country Classic Mustangs, Tulsa Optimist Club, Toastmasters Internat. Tulsa, Mensa, Forest Ridge Country Club, Jr. C. of C. Democrat. Avocations: reading, music, physical fitness, family activities. Home: 9226 S Maplewood Ave Tulsa OK 74137-4123 Office: c/o Everen Securities 6120 S Yale Ave Ste 1650 Tulsa OK 74136-4218

JONES, MILTON BENNION, agronomist, educator; b. Cedar City, Utah, Jan. 15, 1926; s. William Lunt and Claire (Bennion) J.; m. Grace Elaine Guymon, Sept. 8, 1951; children: Milton B. Jr., Richard W., Jo Layne, Tamera, Sherilee, Karolyn. BS, Utah State U., 1951; PhD, Ohio State U., 1955. Successively jr. agronomist, asst. agronomist, assoc. agronomist, agronomist, lectr. U. Calif., Hopland, Davis, 1955-91; cons. IRI Rsch. Inst., Campinas, Brazil, 1963-65, CSIRO, Australia, 1974, BLM, Ukiah, Calif., 1970-77, Sulphur Inst., Washington, 1967-88, AID U. Evora, Portugal, 1984, Basque Govt., Bilbao, Spain, 1987, MAF, Invermay, New Zealand, 1990. Contbr. articles to profl. jours. mem. Sch. bd. Ukiah Elem. Sch. Dist., 1962-63; scout leader local chpt. Boy Scouts Am., Ukiah, 1962-70. With USN, 1944-47. Fellow Agronomy Soc., Soil Sci. Soc. Office: U Calif 4070 University Rd Hopland CA 95449-9717 Address: 1140 Hammond Dr NE Ste B2110 Atlanta GA 30328-8104

JONES, MILTON WAKEFIELD, publisher; b. Burbank, Calif., Apr. 18, 1930; s. Franklin M. and Lydia (Sinclair) J.; m. Rita Strong, May 4, 1959; 1 son, Franklin Wayne. Student, Santa Monica City Coll., 1948-50; AA, U. So. Calif., 1950-52. V.p. mktg. Sav-Ink Co., Newport Beach, Calif., 1956-58; account exec. KDES-Radio, Palm Springs, Calif., 1958-60; pres. Milton W. Jones Advt. & Pub. Rels. Agy., Palm Springs, 1960—, Desert Publs., Inc., Palm Springs, 1965—, Riverside Color Press, Inc., Palm Springs, 1976—, Olman Travel Svc., Palm Springs, 1979-84; pres. Franklin Comms. (Sta. KPSL-Radio), 1987-98, Airport Displays Ltd., 1972—; vice chmn. Palm Springs Savings Bank, 1981-96; bd. dirs. Canyon Nat. Bank. Pub. Palm Springs Life Mag., 1965—, Wheeler Bus. Letter, Palm Springs, 1969-77, San Francisco mag., 1973-79, Guest Life, Orange County, Rocky Mountain, N.Mex., Carmel/Monterey, 1978—, Orange County mag., 1987-89, McCallum Theatre Program, 1989—, Ofcl. Guide to Houston, 1993, El Paso Guest Life, 1993, Pub. Record newspaper, 1996. Mem. Desert Press Club (pres. 1965). Home: 422 Farrell Dr Palm Springs CA 92262 also: 206 Abalone Ave Newport Beach CA 92662-1304 Office: 303 N Indian Canyon Dr Palm Springs CA 92262-6015

JONES, MONIAREE PARKER, occupational health nurse; b. Montgomery, Ala., Oct. 20, 1953; d. Jeffie Knod and Amanda Gertrude (Grier) Parker; m. C. Emile Jones, May 24, 1980; 1 child, William Andrew. Assoc. Nursing, Troy State U., 1974; BSN, U. Ala., 1980. Cert. occupational health nurse; cert. Red Cross instr. Nurse emergency rm. Elmore County Hosp., Wetumpka, Ala.; med. auditor State of Ala. Med. Svcs. Adminstrn., Montgomery; instr. women's tng. program State of La., Baton Rouge; occupational health nurse Georgia Gulf Corp., Plaquemine, La., 1984-91; dir. occupational health svcs. River West Med. Ctr., Plaquemine; occupational rehab. cons. Am. Internat. Health and Rehab. Svcs., Birmingham, Ala.; internal coord. CompSolution, Birmingham, Ala., 1992—; client svcs. mgr. Lake Shore Rehab. Ctr.; occupational health nurse State Farm Ins. Co., Birmingham. Mem. La. Assn. Occupational Health Nurses (pres. Baton Rouge chpt.), Ctrl. Ala. Occupational Nurses Assn. (pres.), Am. Assn. Occupational Health Nurses. Home: 505 Highgate Hill Rd Indian Spgs AL 35124-3835 Office: State Farm Ins Co 100 State Farm Pkwy Birmingham AL 35209-7106

JONES, NANCY GALE, retired biology educator; b. Gaffney, S.C., Nov. 12, 1940; d. Louransey Dowell and Sarah Louise (Pettit) J. BA, Winthrop Coll., 1962; MA, Oberlin Coll., 1964; postgrad., Duke U. Marine Biology Lab., 1963, Marine Biol. Lab., Woods Hole, Mass., 1964, N.C. State U., 1965, Stone Lab of Ohio State U., 1966, Ariz. State U., 1970. Lectr. biology Oberlin (Ohio) Coll., 1964-66; from instr. to asst. prof. zoology Ohio U.,

Zanesville, 1966-73; media specialist Muskingum Area Vocat. Sch., Zanesville, 1973-74; salesperson Village Bookstore, Linworth, Ohio, 1975. Vol. hortitherapist for mentally disabled adults Habilitation Svcs., Inc. Gaffney, S.C., 1977-80; vol. dir. emergency assistance to needy PEACHcenter Ministries, Gaffney, 1991-94; mem. planned giving adv. com. Winthrop U.; bd. dirs. Boys and Girls Club of Cherokee County, 1997—. Recipient Winthrop U. Alumni Disting. Svc. award, 1996. Mem. Ohio Retired Tchrs. Assn., Sigma Xi (assoc.). Baptist. Avocations: travel, reading, cats, yard work. Home: 1643 W Rutledge Ave Gaffney SC 29341-1023

JONES, NANCY JANE, English educator; b. Weatherford, Tex., May 30, 1938; d. Hugh and Esther (Brown) Gracy; m. Jesse R. Jones, Aug. 12, 1960; children: Kendall Kaye Jones Nyquist, Jeffery Ryan. BA, Austin Coll., 1960; MS, East Tex. State U., 1986. Cert. tchr., Tex. Tchr. English Dillingham Jr. H.S., Sherman, Tex., 1960-68, Sherman H.S., 1969-79, Sandia H.S., Albuquerque, 1979-80; dist. edn. tchr. Lewisville (Tex.) H.S., 1980-81; tchr. English Marcus H.S., Flower Mound, Tex., 1981—. Mem. Nat. Coun. Tchrs. English, Tex. State Tchrs. Assn. Baptist. Avocations: crafts, reading, choir. Office: Marcus HS 5707 Morriss Rd Flower Mound TX 75028-3730

JONES, NANCY LANGDON, financial planning practitioner; b. Chgo., Mar. 24, 1939; d. Lewis Valentine and Margaret (Seese) Russell; m. Lawrence Elmer Langdon, June 30, 1962 (div. 1970); children: Laura Kimberley, Elizabeth Ann; m. Claude Earl Jones, Jan. 1, 1973. BA, U. Redlands, Calif., 1962; MS, Coll. for Fin. Planning, 1991. CFP; registered investment advisor; accredited tax advisor. Bookkeeper Russell Sales Co., Santa Fe Springs, Calif., 1962-70; office mgr. Reardon, McCallum & Co., Upland, Calif., 1970-77; broker, assoc. ERA Property Ctr., Upland, 1977-84; registered rep. Fin. Network Investment Corp., Pasadena, Calif., 1984-92; pvt. practice fin. planning Upland, 1984—; ptnr. Jones, Graham & Assocs., Registered Investment Advisors, Upland, Calif., 1994; mem. adj. faculty Coll. Fin. Planning, Denver, 1986-94; mem. nat. comprehensive exam. question writing com. CFP Bd. Stds., 1994-98; del. U.S. fin. and investment leaders study mission to China and Hong Kong, 1993; industry spkr. NASA Investment Advisor Workshop, 1999; panelist L.A. Times 3rd Annual Investment Strategies Conf.; featured planner L.A. Times Money Makeover, 1999. Leader Spanish Trails coun. Girl Scouts U.S., 1974-81; mem. exec. com. Corp. 2000 Coun., San Antonio Cmty. Hosp.; mem. planned giving adv. bd. Goodwill Industries of the Inland Counties, 1997-98; mem. planned giving roundtable Inland Empire. Recipient Hon. Svc. award Valencia Elem. Sch., 1978; selected 1 of Top 100 Women Owned Businesses in Inland Empire, Bus. Press, 1996. Mem. SAG, Inland Soc. Tax Cons., Internat. Assn. Fin. Planners (pres. San Gabriel Valley chpt. 1987-88, mem. exec. bd. So. Calif. conf. 1992-98, chmn. So. Calif. Conf., 1996-97), Am. Bus. Women's Assn. (pres. Upland chpt. 1989-90, gen. chmn. 1995, Pacific Spring Conf. Woman of Yr. award 1988), Inst. CFP San Gabriel Valley Soc. (pres. 1992-93, chmn. 1993-94, bd. dirs. 1990-97), Inst. CFPs (nat. practice mgmt. and tech. com. 1996), Nat. Coun. Exchangers (sec. 1986-87), Estate Planning Coun. Pomona Valley (bd. dirs. 1995—, pres. 1998-99), Women's Bus. Network (pres. 1987-88), Registry Fin. Planning Practitioners, Inland Valley Profl. Aux. (charter, bd. dirs. 1991-92), Assistance League Upland, Upland C. of C. Avocation: traveling, acting. Home and Office: 2485 Mesa Ter Upland CA 91784-1078

JONES, NANCY PATRICIA, psychotherapist, consultant; b. Point Pleasant, N.J., May 24, 1961; d. John William and Winona Louise (Johns) J. AA, Martin Coll., Pulaski, Tenn., 1982; BA, Maryville Coll., 1984; MSW summa cum laude, Rutgers U., 1997. Cert. alcohol and drug addictions, internat. cert. alcohol and drug counselor; lic. social worker, N.J. Hospice therapist Blount Meml. Hosp., Maryville, 1982-86; mental health therapist Ridgeview Psychiat. Hosp., Oak Ridge, Tenn., 1985-86; sr. therapist Monmouth Chem. Dependency Treatment Ctr., Long Branch, N.J., 1986-89, clin. supr., 1989-90; sr. therapist Fair Oak Hosp., Summit, N.J., 1990-92; substance abuse therapist Bayshore Community Hosp., Holmdel, N.J., 1989-92; outpatient therapist Carrier Found., Toms River, N.J., 1997—, coord. adult svcs., 1998—; lectr., educator, N.J., 1986—. Author: They That Mourn: A Recovery Guide for the Bereaved, 1984. Recipient various scholarships and fellowships, 1980-90. Mem. NASW. Episcopalian. Avocations: running, swimming, biking, reading. Office: 614 Main St Toms River NJ 08753-7456

JONES, NAPOLEON A., JR., judge; b. 1940. BA, San Diego State U., 1962, MSW, 1967; JD, U. San Diego, 1971. Legal intern, staff atty. Calif. Rural Legal Assistance, Modesto, Calif., 1971-73; staff atty. Defenders, Inc., San Diego, 1973-75; ptnr. Jones, Cazares, Adler & Lopez, San Diego, 1975-77; judge San Diego Mcpl. Ct., 1977-82, San Diego Superior Ct., 1982-94, U.S. Dist. Ct. (so. dist.) Calif., San Diego, 1994—; mem. San Diego County Indigent Def. Policy Bd. Bd. visitors Sch. Social Work San Diego State U.; active Valencia Park Elem. Sch. Mem. San Diego County Bar Assn., Earl B. Gilliam Bar Assn., San Diego Bar Found., Nat. Bar Assn., Calif. Bar Assn., Calif. Black Attys. Assn., Nat. Assn. Women Judges, Masons, Sigma Pi Phi, Kappa Alpha Psi. Office: US Dist Ct So Dist Calif US Courthouse 940 Front St Ste 2125 San Diego CA 92101-8912*

JONES, NATHANIEL, bishop. Bishop Ch. of God in Christ, Barstow, Calif. Office: Ch of God in Christ 1375 Sage Dr Barstow CA 92311*

JONES, NATHANIEL RAPHAEL, federal judge; b. Youngstown, Ohio, May 13, 1926; s. Nathaniel B. and Lillian J. (Rafe) J.; m. Lillian Graham, Mar. 22, 1974; 1 dau., Stephanie Joyce; stepchildren: William Hawthorne, Rickey Hawthorne, Marc Hawthorne, Pamela Haley. A.B., Youngstown State U., 1951, LL.B., 1955, LL.D. (hon.), 1969; LL.D. (hon.), Syracuse U., 1972. Editor Buckeye Rev. newspaper, 1956; exec. dir. FEPC, Youngstown, 1956-59; practiced law, 1959-61; mem. firm Goldberg & Jones, 1968-69; asst. U.S. atty., 1961-67; asst. gen. counsel Nat. Adv. Commn. on Civil Disorders, 1967-68; gen. counsel NAACP, 1969-79; judge U.S. Ct. of Appeals, 6th Circuit, 1979-95, sr. judge, 1995—; adj/ prof. U. Cin. Coll. Law, 1983—; trial observer South Africa, 1985; dir. Buckeye Rev. Pub. Co.; chmn. Con. on Adequate Def. and Incentives in Mil.; mem. Task Force-Vets. Benefits; lectr. South African Judges seminar, Johannesburg. Co-chmn. Cin. Roundtable, Black-Jewish Coalition Cin.; observer Soviet Union Behalf com. on Soviet Jewry; bd. dirs. Interights, USA. Served with USAAF, 1945-47. Mem. Ohio State Bar Assn., Mahoning County Bar Assn., Fed. Bar Assn., Nat. Bar Assn., Am. Arbitration Assn., Youngstown Area Devel. Corp., Urban League, Nat. Conf. Black Lawyers, ABA (co-chmn. com. constl. rights criminal sect. 1971-73), Kappa Alpha Psi. Baptist. Clubs: Houston Law (Youngstown); Elks. Office: US Ct Appeals US Courthouse 100 E 5th St Rm 610 Cincinnati OH 45202-3988*

JONES, NORMA LOUISE, librarian, educator; b. Poplar, Wis.; d. George Elmer and Hilma June (Wiberg) J. BE, U. Wis.; MA, U. Minn., 1952; postgrad, U. Ill., 1957; PhD, U. Mich., 1965; postgrad., NARS, 1978, 79, 80, Nova U., 1983-96. Librarian Grand Rapids (Mich.) Public Schs., 1947-62; with Grand Rapids Public Library, 1948-49; instr. Central Mich. U., Mt. Pleasant, 1954, 55; lectr. U. Mich., Ann Arbor, 1954, 55, 61, 63-65, asst. prof., 1966-68; librarian Benton Harbor (Mich.) Public Schs., 1962-63; asst. prof. library sci. U. Wis., Oshkosh, 1968-70; assoc. prof. U. Wis., 1970-75, prof., 1975—, chmn. dept. library sci., 1980-84, exec. dir. librs. and learning resources, 1987-93; dir. Adult Ctr., 1993-95. Recipient Disting. Teaching award U. Wis.-Oshkosh, 1977. Mem. ALA (chmn. reference cons. 1975), Wis. Libr. Assn., Assn. Libr. and Info. Sci. Educators, Spl. Libr. Assn., Wis. Spl. Libr. Assn., Soc. Am. Archivists, Wis. Assn. Acad. Librs., Phi Beta Kappa, Phi Kappa Phi, Pi Lambda Theta, Beta Phi Mu, Sigma Pi Epsilon. Home: 1220 Maricopa Dr Oshkosh WI 54904-8121

JONES, NORMAN THOMAS, retired agricultural products company executive; b. Herrin, Ill., Feb. 21, 1936; s. Thomas Henry and Mary Frances (Beckner) J.; m. Nevelyn J. Childers, Apr. 11, 1955; children: David, Debra, Deanna. BS in Commerce, U. Ill., 1962. CPA. Auditor Peat Marwick and Mitchell, St. Louis, 1962-63; with mgmt. devel. GE, Bloomington, Ill., 1963-64; various mgmt. positions GROWMARK Inc., Bloomington, 1964-80, exec. dir. human resources, 1980-84, v.p. corp. services, 1984-86, sr. v.p. fin., 1986-87, chief exec. officer, 1987-98; bd. dirs. ADM/Growmark Inc., Decatur, Ill., Nat. coop. Refinery Assn., McPherson, Kans.; bd. dirs., mem. exec. com. Nat. coun. Farmer Coops., Washington, Mut. Svcs. Ins., St. Paul; chmn. CF Industries, Inc., Long Grove, Ill. Chmn. bd. Police and Fire Commrs., Bloomington, 1970-92; mem., pres. Dist. 87 Sch. Bd., Bloomington, 1974-84; mem. Ill. Sch. Bd. Assn., Springfield, 1979-84; mem. bus. adv. coun. coll. commerce and bus. U. Ill., 1994—. Sgt. U.S. Army, 1955-57. Mem. Ill. Soc. CPAs, Ill. Bus. Roundtable, Exch. Club (pres. 1980-81, disting. service award 1980). Republican. Baptist. Avocation: golf. *

JONES, O. T., bishop. Bishop Ch. of God in Christ, Phila. Office: Ch of God in Christ 334-36 N 60th St Philadelphia PA 19139-1206*

JONES, OLIVER HASTINGS, consulting economist; b. Altoona, Pa., Dec. 9, 1922; s. Oliver Hastings and and Mary (Herman) J.; m. Margaret Ann Vogel, July 4, 1942; children: Thomas, William, David, Robert, Richard. BA, St. Francis Coll., Loretto, Pa., 1948; MA, Pa. State U., 1949, PhD, 1961. Analyst, divsn. bank ops., bd. govs. Fed. Res. System, 1951-55; sr. economist, rsch. dept. Fed. Res. Bank, Cleve., 1955-59; assoc. rsch. economist, real estate rsch. program Grad. Sch. Bus. Adminstrn., U. Calif., L.A., 1959-61; economist Stanford Rsch. Inst., 1961-62; dir. rsch. Mortgage Bankers Assn. Am., 1962-67; cons. economist Oliver Jones & Assocs., Washington, 1967-68; exec. v.p. Mortgage Bankers Assn. Am., 1968-77; cons. economist Oliver Jones & Assocs., 1977—; professorial lectr. Am. U., 1967—. Author: (with Leo Grebler) The Secondary Mortgage Market, 1961, Financial Futures Market, 1983. Served with AUS, 1942-45. Mem. Am. Statis. Assn., Am. Econ. Assn., Am. Finance Assn., Nat. Assn. Bus. Economists, Conf. Bus. Economists, Lambda Alpha. (internat. pres. 1976-77). Clubs: Cosmos (Washington), Metropolitan (Washington). Home: 67 Greenfield Dr Carlisle PA 17013-7682

JONES, ORLO DOW, lawyer, drug store executive; b. Logan, Utah, June 10, 1938; s. Orlo Elijah and Joyce (Lewis) J.; m. Ilarene Balls, July 9, 1958; children—Monica, Orlo Courtney. B.S., Utah State U., 1960; LL.B., U. Calif., Berkeley, 1963. Bar: Calif. bar 1964. Atty. Carlson, Collins & Bold, Richmond, Calif., 1968-69, A.T. and T., San Francisco, 1969-71, Longs Drug Stores, Inc., Walnut Creek, Calif., 1971-76; sec., gen. counsel Longs Drug Stores, Inc., 1976—, v.p., 1979-87, sr. v.p., 1987—; lectr. comml. leases Continuing Edn. of Bar Univ. Extension U. Calif., Berkeley. Served to capt. JAGC AUS, 1964-68. Republican. Mormon. Home: 156 Santiago Dr Danville CA 94526-1941 Office: Longs Drug Stores Corp 141 N Civic Dr Walnut Creek CA 94596-3858

JONES, PAMELA SUSAN, middle school educator; b. Abilene, Tex., Mar. 9, 1954; d. Fred Wallace and Elizabeth (Kirkpatrick) J. BS Edn. in Elem. Edn., Abilene Christian U., 1976, MEd in Reading Specialty, 1980. Tchr. 3d grade Killeen (Tex.) Ind. Sch. Dist.-Nolanville Elem., 1976-77; 2d/3d grade tchr. Wingate (Tex.) Ind. Sch. Dist., 1977-80; 7th grade reading tchr. Sweetwater (Tex.) Ind. Sch. Dist., Sweetwater Mid. Sch., 1980-86; 9th grade/10th grade reading tchr. Abilene Ind. Sch. Dist., Abilene H.S., 1986-88; 7th grade lang. arts-gifted talented Grapevine Mid. Sch. Grapevine (Tex.)-Colleyville Ind. Sch. Dist., 1988—; lang. arts dept. chair Heritage Mid. Sch., Colleyville, Tex., 1992—, campus exec. com., 1992-93, 97—, ctrl. curriculum com., 1995—. Recipient Tchr. of Yr. award Region II Tex. Mid.-Sch. Assn. Mem. ASCD, Internat. Reading Assn., Tex. Classroom Tchrs. Assn., Tex. Assn. Gifted and Talented. Mem. Ch. of Christ. Avocations: reading, playing piano, cross stitch, travel. Home: 1809 Maplewood Trl Colleyville TX 76034-3028 Office: Heritage Mid Sch 5300 Heritage Ave Colleyville TX 76034-5911

JONES, PATRICIA LOUISE, elementary counselor; b. Moorhead, Minn., Aug. 20, 1942; d. Harry Wilfred and Myrtle Louise Rosenfeldt; m. Edward L. Marks (div.); m. Curtis C. Jones, July 16, 1973; children: Michon, Andrea, Nathan, Kirsten, Leah. BS, Moorhead State U., 1965; MS, Mankato State U., 1990. Cert. K-12 sch. counselor, Minn. Tchr. Anoka (Minn.) Hennepin Schs., 1966-68; pvt. practice Youth Ctr., Truman, Minn., 1969-72; bookkeeper Fairmont (Minn.) Glass & Sign, 1973, Truman Farmers Elevator, 1973-87; libr. Martin County Libr., Truman, 1988-89; sch. counselor St. James (Minn.) Schs., 1989—; coord. Internat. Fun Fest, St. James, 1992, 96; originator, advisor Armstrong After Sch. Hispanic Club, St. James, 1991—. Coord. Truman Days Parade, 1991, 92, 94—; mem. adv. bd. Watonwan County Big Buddy Program, 1993—; mem. Watonwan County Corrections Adv. Bd., 1998—; foster parent, 1999—. Mem. Am. Counseling Assn., Am. Sch. Counselors Assn., Minn. Sch. Counselors Assn. (bd. dirs. 1997—), S.W. Minn. Counselors Assn. (Elem. Counselor of Yr. 1993, pres. 1997—). Avocations: genealogy, walking, horseback riding, photography. Office: Saint James Sch Dist 1273 10th Ave N Saint James MN 56081-2029

JONES, PAUL, councilman. City councilman City of Indpls., 1998—. Office: City-County Coun Office 200 E Washington St Ste 241 Indianapolis IN 46204-3310*

JONES, PETER D'ALROY, historian, writer, retired educator; b. Hull, Eng., June 9, 1931; came to U.S., 1959, naturalized, 1968; s. Alfred and Madge (Rutter) D'Alroy; m. Johanna Maria Hartinger, Feb. 20, 1987; 1 child, Heather Marie; children from previous marriage: Kathryn Beauchamp Fly Ebert, Barbara Collier Rosenberg. BA, Manchester (Eng.) U., 1952, MA, 1953; PhD, London U. Sch. Econ., 1963; postgrad., U. Brussels, 1954. Freelance editor London, 1953-56; lectr. U.S. history dept. Am. studies Manchester U., 1957-58; vis. asst. prof. econs. Tulane U., 1959-60; from asst. to full prof. Smith Coll., 1960-68; Kennan prof. Am. instns. and values Trinity Coll., Hartford, 1980-81; prof. history U. Ill., Chgo., 1968-98, prof. emeritus, 1998—; vis. prof. Columbia U., U. Mass., U. Hawaii, U. Warsaw, Poland, U. Düsseldorf, Fed. Republic Germany, U. Salzburg, Austria; mem. com. examiners Grad. Record Exams. Ednl. Testing Svc., Princeton, N.J., 1966-70; mem. Am. studies com. Am. Coun. Learned Socs., 1973-75; lectr. U.S. Dept. State, 1973-87; adv. to publs. Author: Economic History of U.S.A. Since 1783, 1956, 2nd edit., 1965, The Story of the Saw, 1961, America's Wealth, 1963, The Consumer Society, 2d edit., 1967, The Christian Socialist Revival, 1968, The Robber Barons Revisited, 1968, Robert Hunter's Poverty: Social Conscience in the Progressive Era, 1965, La Sociedad Consumidora, 1968, Since Columbus: Poverty and Pluralism in the History of the Americas, 1975, The U.S.A.: A History of Its People and Society, 2 vols., 1976, Henry George and British Socialism, 1991; co-editor: Biographical Dictionary of American Mayors, 1820-1980, 1981, Ethnic Chicato, 1981, rev. and enlarged edit., 1984, 4th edit., 1995; contbr. several entries to Ency. World Biography, 1988, 94; contbr. numerous articles and book revs. to profl. jours., popular newspapers. With RAF, 1956-57. Mem. London Sch. Econs. Soc. (life).

JONES, PHILIP HOWARD, broadcast journalist; b. Marion, Ind., Apr. 27, 1937; s. Thomas Howard and Charline (Shugart) J.; m. Paricia Ann Powell, June 4, 1961; children: Pamela Lynn, Paul Howard. BS in Arts and Scis., Ind. U., 1959. Dir. news Sta. WTHI-TV, Terre Haute, Ind., 1960-61; polit. corr. Sta. WCCO-TV, Mpls., 1961-69; White House corr. CBS News, Washington, 1974-76, Capitol Hill corr., 1977-89, nat. corr., 1989-90; corr. 48Hrs. Broadcast, 1990-95; Washington corr., 1995—, Washington polit. corr., 1996—. With USAF, 1961-62. Recipient Internat. News award Radio-TV News Dirs. Assn., 1965, award for Vietnam war reporting, 1966, Emmy award for CBS Indochina air war coverage NATAS, 1971, (6) Emmy awards CBS News 48 Hours Broadcast Coverage, 1992. Mem. Masons. Home: 5105 Westport Rd Chevy Chase MD 20815-3713 Office: CBS News 2020 M St NW Washington DC 20036-3368

JONES, PHILIP KIRKPATRICK, JR., lawyer; b. Baton Rouge, June 26, 1949; s. Philip Kirkpatrick and Mary Jane (Kincade) J.; m. Serena Catherine Cockayne, Apr. 5, 1980; children: Veronica Cockayne, Nicola Kincade, Clare Kirkpatrick, Philip Carruth Elliot. BA in Govt., Dartmouth Coll., 1971; JD, La. State U., 1974; LLB, diploma in legal studies, Cambridge (U.K.) U., 1976. Bar: La. 1974, U.S. Dist. Ct. (ea. and we. dist.) La. 1980, U.S. Ct. Appeals (5th and 11th cirs.) 1981, U.S. Dist. Ct. (mid. dist.) La. 1987, U.S. Supreme Ct. 1992. Law clk. to John A. Dixon Jr. Supreme Ct. La., New Orleans, 1974-75; staff atty. Presdl. Clemency Bd., Washington, 1975; lectr. U. Singapore, 1977-79; from assoc. to ptnr. Liskow & Lewis, New Orleans, 1980—. 1st Lt. USAF, 1975. Republican. Presbyterian. Office: Liskow & Lewis PC 50th Fl One Shell Square New Orleans LA 70139

JONES, PHILIP LINDSEY, librarian; b. Memphis, Feb. 2, 1953; s. Rodney Leo and Velma Marguerite (Brown) J.; m. Alice Marie Worley, July 31, 1982; children: Rachel Elizabeth, Kevin Michael. BA in History, U. Tenn., 1975; MLS, George Peabody Coll., 1979. Libr. lit. dept. Memphis/Shelby County Pub. Libr. & Info. Ctr., 1979-82; reference libr. Ark. State U., Jonesboro, 1983-84, Tulane U., New Orleans, 1984-87; info. svcs. libr. U. Cin. Health Scis. Libr., 1987-89; head reference svcs. dept. Ctrl. Ark. Libr. Sys., Little Rock, 1989—. Mem. ALA, Ark. Libr. Assn. Office: Ctrl Ark Libr Sys Reference Svcs Dept Libr 100 Rock St Little Rock AR 72201-1624

JONES, PHILIP NEWTON, physician, medical educator; b. Billings, Mont., May 27, 1924; s. Robert Newton and Edith (Woodbury) J.; m. Rebecca Ann Means, June 13, 1948; children: Robert Newton II, Rebecca Ann, Margaret Jane. Student, Stanford, 1942-43, U. Wis., 1944; MD, Washington U., St. Louis, 1948. Diplomate Am. Bd. Internal Medicine. Intern St. Luke's Hosp., Chgo., 1948-49; resident in internal medicine St. Luke's Hosp., 1949-51; rssch. fellow internal medicine Northwestern U., Chgo., 1953; clin. asst. medicine Northwestern U., 1954-57; practice medicine, specializing in internal medicine and hepatology Chgo., 1954-94; clin. asst. medicine U. Ill., Chgo., 1957-58; from clin. instr. to clin. assoc. prof. medicine U. Ill., 1958-71; assoc. prof. medicine Rush Coll. Medicine Chgo., 1971-75, prof. medicine, 1975-94, prof. emeritus, 1994—; sr. attending physician Presbyn.-St. Luke's Hosp., Chgo., 1954-94, treas. med. staff, 1960-62, mem. exec. com., med. staff, 1960-62, 72-77, sec. med. staff, 1972-73, pres. med. staff, 1973-75; mem. exec. bd. Rush-Presbyn.-St. Luke's Med. Ctr., Chgo., 1973-75, trustee, 1973-77. Contbr. articles to books and profl. jours. Mem. bd. edn., Kenilworth, Ill., 1962-68, pres., 1965; mem. Welfare Council Met., Chgo., 1965-66; bd. dirs. Presbyn. Home, Evanston, Ill., 1978-88, 93—. Served with AUS, 1943-46, to capt. USAF, 1951-53. Fellow Am. Coll. Physicians, Inst. Medicine Chgo.; mem. Am. Assn. Study Liver Disease, Chgo. Soc. Internal Medicine, Am. Fedn. Clin. Research, AMA, Ill. Med. Assn., Chgo. Med. Soc., Nu Sigma Nu. Republican. Congregationalist (pres. bd. trustees). Clubs: Comml. (Chgo.); Indian Hill. Home: 868 Pembridge Dr Lake Forest IL 60045-4200

JONES, PHYLLIS EDITH, nursing educator; b. Barrie, Ont., Can., Sept. 16, 1924; d. Colston Graham and Edith Luella (Shand) J. BScN, U. Toronto, 1950, MSc, 1969; DNSc (hon.), U. Turku, Finland, 1993. With Victorian Order Nurses, Toronto, 1950-53, asst. dir., 1959-63; supr. Vancouver Dept. Health, 1953-58; prof. nursing U. Toronto, 1963-89, dean Faculty Nursing, 1979-88, prof. emeritus, 1989—; cons. WHO, 1985, 86;. Contbr. articles to profl. jours. Can. Nurses Found. fellow, 1967-69; recipient grants Nat. Health Research and Devel.; recipient grants Ont. Ministry Health. Fellow Am. Public Health Assn.; mem. Coll. Nurses Ont., Registered Nurses Assn. Ont., Can. Public Health Assn., Can. Soc. Study Higher Edn., N.Am. Nursing Diagnosis Assn. (charter), ProNursing Finland (hon.). Home: RR 2, Owen Sound, ON Canada N4K 5N4

JONES, PHYLLIS GENE, judge; b. Fargo, N.D., May 29, 1923; d. Joseph C. and Rosina Belle (Pinkham) Bambusch; m. Dwight Bangs Jones, May 29, 1945 (dec.); children: Stephanie Martineau, Jacqueline Ridge, Kent Carroll; m. David D. Norman, Oct. 9, 1970 (dec.). BA, Macalester Coll., 1944; JD, William Mitchell Coll. Law, 1960. Bar: Minn. 1960. Wirephoto operator AP, St. Paul, 1943-45; reporter St. Paul Pioneer Press, 1945-46; asst. county atty. Ramsey County (Minn.), St. Paul, 1960-71; gen. counsel Minn. Urban County Attys. Bd.-Minn. County Attys. Council, St. Paul, 1971-75; pvt. practice, St. Paul and Cottage Grove, Minn., 1975-84; judge Minn. Dist. Ct. 10th Jud. Dist., Anoka, 1984-93; mem. Minn. Adv. Coun. to State Investment Bd., 1983-84; mem. Washington County Personnel Com., Stillwater, Minn., 1982-84. Supr., Grey Cloud Town Bd. (Minn.), 1971-75. Mem. ABA, Minn. State Bar Assn. (chmn. victimless crimes com. 1974-75, co-chair sr. lawyers com. 1997—), Ramsey County Bar Assn. (exec. com. 1982-83).

JONES, PIRKLE, photographer, educator; b. Shreveport, La., Jan. 2, 1914; s. Alfred Charles and Wilie (Tilton) J.; m. Ruth-Marion Baruch, Jan. 15, 1949. Grad., Calif. Sch. Fine Arts, 1949. Profl. free-lance photographer, 1949—; asst. to Ansel Adams, 1949-52; faculty Calif. Sch. Fine Arts, 1953-58, San Francisco Art Inst., 1971-97; tchr. Ansel Adams Workshops, Yosemite.; Mem. Archtl. Adv. Com., Mill Valley, Calif., 1963-67. Exhibited in leading art mus.; photographic archive established Spl. Collections Libr., U. Calif., Santa Cruz; author: Portfolio One, 1955, (with Dorothea Lange) Death of a Valley, 1960, Portfolio Two, 1968, (with Ruth-Marion Baruch) The Vanguard, A Photographic Essay on the Black Panthers, 1970; author: Berryessa Valley, The Last Year, 1995. Nat. Endowment for Arts photography fellow, 1977; recipient award of honor for exceptional achievement in field of photography Arts Commn. of City and County of San Francisco, 1983. Home: 663 Lovell Ave Mill Valley CA 94941-1086

JONES, RAYFORD SCOTT, surgeon, medical educator; b. Dallas, Aug. 24, 1936. MD, U. Tex., Galveston, 1961. Diplomate Am. Bd. Surgery. Intern U. Tex., 1961-62; resident U. Pa. Hosp., Phila., 1962-67; mem. staff Duke U. and VA Hosp., Durham, N.C.; then prof. surgery Duke U.; now prof., chmn. surgery U. Va., Charlottesville. Mem. Am. Surg. Assn., Am. Coll. Surgeons, Soc. Clin. Surgery, So. Surg. Assn., Soc. Univ. Surgeons. Office: U Va Hosps Dept Surgery Box 181 Jefferson Park Ave Charlottesville VA 22908-0001

JONES, RAYMOND EDWARD, JR., brewing executive; b. New Bern, N.C., Jan. 27, 1927; s. Raymond Edward and Ellen LaVerne (Mallard) J.; children: Leslie Anne, Raymond Edward III. B.S., U. Md., 1953; LL.B., U. Balt., 1962. Bar: Md. 1962. Office mgr. Hopkins Furniture Co., Annapolis, Md., 1953-55; sr. v.p. legal, sec. Nat. Brewing Co., Balt., 1956-75; (merged with Carling Brewing Co. 1975); sr. v.p. legal and indsl. relations, dir. Carling Nat. Breweries, Inc., 1975-78; sec., assoc. gen. counsel Miller Brewing Co., 1978-84, v.p., gen. counsel, sec., 1984-89; house counsel and/or officer Divex, Inc., Laco Products, Inc., Laco Corp., C.W. Abbott, Inc., Pompeian, Inc., Interhost Corp., Solarine Co., Balt. Baseball Club, Inc., 1967-75. Bd. dirs. Soc. Preservation Md. Antiquities, 1969-71. Served with USNR, 1942-45. Mem. ABA, Md. Bar Assn., Balt. Bar Assn., Sigma Chi, Sigma Delta Chi. Presbyterian. Home: 24848 Deepwater Point Dr Saint Michaels MD 21663-2324

JONES, RAYMOND MOYLAN, strategy and public policy educator; b. Phila., Dec. 28, 1942; s. Raymond and Elizabeth (Shaw) J.; m. Barbara Ann Donaghue, May 22, 1965; children: Andrea Marie, Audra Marie. BS, U.S. Mil. Acad., 1964; MBA, Harvard U., 1971; JD, U. Tex., 1973; PhD, U. Md., 1993. Bar: Tex. 1973, U.S. Supreme Ct. 1993. Commd. 2d lt. U.S. Army, 1964, advanced through grades to capt., 1966, ret., 1969; legal asst. to chmn. Occidental Petroleum Corp., L.A., 1973-75; pres. Oxy Metal Industries Internat., Geneva, 1975-77, Occidental Resource Recovery Corp., Irvine, Calif., 1978-81; v.p. Hooker Chem. Corp., Houston, 1977-78; pvt. practice cons. Austin and Irvine, 1981-86; lectr. Calif. State U., Long Beach, 1986, U. Md., College Park, 1986-90, Loyola Coll., Balt., 1990—; cons. to multinational and domestic orgns. Author: Strategic Management in a Hostile Environment: Lessons from the Tobacco Industry, 1998; contbr. articles, book rev. to profl. publs. Mem. Friends of Austin Symphony Orch.; mem. Ludwig Von Mises Inst., Burlingame, Calif., 1987—, Intercoll. Studies Inst., Bryn Mawr, Pa., 1987—; mgmt. con. ARC, Balt., 1988—. Grantee U. Md. 1987, Loyola Coll. 1993. Mem. Am. Econ. Assn., Acad. Internat. Bus., Strategic Mgmt. Soc., Acad. Mgmt., State Bar Tex., Harvard Club. Roman Catholic. Home: 305 Kerneway Baltimore MD 21212-4714 Office: Loyola Coll Sellinger Sch Bus Mgmt Baltimore MD 21210-2699

JONES, REBECCA ALVINA PATRONIS, nurse; b. Quincy, Fla., Sept. 14, 1952; d. Eugene T. Patronis and Ada Lee (Allen) Poole; m. Robert Gerald Jones, Dec. 29, 1979; 1 child, Aislan Hlynn. BS in Nursing, U. Fla., 1974; MS in Nursing, U. S.C., 1988; D in Nursing Sci., Ind. U., Indpls., 1991. RN, Tex.; cert. in nursing adminstrn. advanced. Team leader, teaching staff nurse Shands Teaching Hosp., Gainesville, Fla., 1974-76; commd. 1st Lt. U.S. Army, 1976, advanced through grades to lt. col., held various nursing positions, 1976-83, resigned, 1983; cmty. health nurse Gorgas Army Hosp., Panama City, Panama, 1984-86; nursing rsch. asst. U. S.C., Columbia, 1986-87; asst. dir. nursing Kershaw County Meml. Hosp., Camden, S.C., 1988-89; assoc. instr. Ind. U., Indpls., 1989-91; asst. prof., assoc. dir. nursing La Salle U., Albert Einstein Med. Ctr., Phila., 1991-94; dir., prof. Sch. Nursing and Health Scis., Tex. A&M U., Corpus Christi, 1994—; clin. faculty assoc. U. Tex. Health Sci. Ctr. Sch. Nursing and Grad. Sch. Biomed. Scis. Contbr. articles to profl. jours. Mem. Am. Coll. Healthcare Execs., Nat. League

Nursing, Coun. Nurse Execs., Am. Orgn. Nurse Execs., Am. Assn. Colls. Nursing, Coun. on Grad. Edn. for Adminstrn. in Nursing, Tex. League for Nursing, Tex. Nurses Assn., So. Nursing Rsch. Soc., Tex. Orgn. for Baccalaureate and Grad. Nursing Edn. (chair), Tex. Orgn. NuExecs., Sigma Theta Tau (Eta Omicron chpt.). Republican. Avocations: computers, reading, swimming. Home: 15913 Punta Espada Loop Corpus Christi TX 78418-6626 Office: Tex A&M U Sch Nursing and Health Scis 6300 Ocean Dr Corpus Christi TX 78412-5503

JONES, REES LEE, golf course architect; b. Montclair, N.J., Sept. 16, 1941; s. Robert Trent and Ione (Davis) J.; m. Susan Singleton, Mar. 23, 1968; children: Alden Elizabeth, Amy Singleton. BA, Yale U., 1963; postgrad., Harvard U. Lic. landscape architect, Hawaii, Ky., Mass., N.J., N.C., S.C. V.p. Robert Trent Jones, Inc., Montclair, 1964-74; pres. Rees Jones, Inc., Montclair, 1974—; speaker in field. Author: Golf Course Developments, 1974; contbr. articles to profl. jours.; redesigned golf courses for U.S. Open including The Country Club, Brookline, Mass., 1988, Hazeltine Nat. Golf Club, Chaska, Minn., 1991, Baltusrol Golf Club, Springfield, N.J., 1993. With USAR, 1965-71. Mem. Am. Soc. Golf Course Architects (pres. 1978), Am. Soc. Landscape Architects, Golf Writers Assn. Am., U.S. Golf Assn. (turfgrass com., environ. rsch. com.), Urban Land Inst., Montclair Golf Club, Pine Valley Golf Club, Nat. Golf Links, Royal and Ancient Golf Club of St. Andrews. Home: 10 Belleclaire Pl Verona NJ 07044-5106 Office: Rees Jones Inc PO Box 285 55 S Park St Montclair NJ 07042-2717*

JONES, REGINALD LORRIN, clinical psychologist, consultant; b. St. Petersburg, Fla., Dec. 12, 1951; s. Daniel George Jones and Susie Beatrice (Lewis) W.; divorced; children: Tammy LeVette McKay, Myla Carmel, Regina Yvonne, Deneale Elizabeth Hand. BA, Clark Coll., 1973; MA, U. Cin., 1977, PhD, 1980. Lic. psychologist, Ohio. Statistician Atlanta Pub. Schs., 1973-74; psychology trainee U. Cin., 1974-80; team leader, supr. Social Skills Program, Cin., 1980-81; psychologist, unit dir. Day-Mont West, C.M.H.C., Dayton, Ohio, 1981-83; field psychologist advisor Ohio Indsl. Commn., Dayton, 1983-87; pvt. practice psychology, Dayton, 1983—; clin. asst. prof. Wright State U., Dayton, 1981—; cons. Adapt Inc., Springfield, Ohio, 1986-94; cons. Sickle Cell Awarness Group, Cin., 1986-90, v.p., 1981. Mem. adv. bd. Drew Sickle Cell Ctr., 1989-92; trustee Family Svc. Assn. Dayton, 1989-92. Named One of Outstanding Young Men of Am., 1984. Mem. Nat. Assn. Black Psychologists, Dayton Assn. Black Psychologists (pres. 1983-84, Svc. award 1986). Democrat. Avocations: African history and culture, gardening, basketball, gourmet cooking, travel. Home: 180 Folsom Dr Dayton OH 45405-1108

JONES, RENEE KAUERAUF, health care administrator; b. Duncan, Okla., Nov. 3, 1949; d. Delbert Owen and Betty Jean (Marsh) Kauerauf; m. Dan Elkins Jones, Aug. 3, 1972. BS, Okla. State U., 1972, MS, 1975; PhD, Okla. U., 1989. Diplomate Am. Bd. Sleep Medicine. Statis. analyst Okla. State Dept. Mental Health, Okla. City, 1978-80, divisional chief, 1980-83, adminstr., 1983-84; assoc. dir. HCA Presbyn. Hosp., Okla. City, 1984—; adj. instr. Okla. U. Health Sci. Ctr., 1979—; assoc. staff scientist Okla. Ctr. for Alcohol and Drug-Related Studies, Okla. City, 1979—; cons. in field. Assoc. editor Alcohol Tech. Reports jour., 1979-84; contbr. articles to profl. jours. Mem. assoc. bd. Hist. Preservation, Inc., treas. 1994. Mem. APHA, NAFE, Assn. Health Svcs. Rsch., Alcohol and Drug Problems Assn. N.Am., Am. Sleep Disorders Assn., N.Y. Acad. Scis., So. Sleep Soc. (sec.-treas. 1989-91), Phi Kappa Phi. Democrat. Methodist. Avocations: skiing, scuba diving, racewalking, bicycling, painting. Home: 401 NW 19th St Oklahoma City OK 73103-1911 Office: Columbia Presbyn Hosp NE 13th at Lincoln Blvd Oklahoma City OK 73104

JONES, RICHARD ALLEN, horse breeder, educator; b. Freeport, Pa., Aug. 16, 1931; s. Paul Alfred and Nettie Minerva (Shearer) J.; B.A., Roberts Wesleyan Coll., 1953; MDiv, Asbury Sem., 1956; M.A., SUNY, Buffalo, 1971; M.S., Fredonia State Coll., 1971; m. Ruth B. Kelley, Aug. 1, 1953; children: Jonathan Dwight, Suzanne Ruth, Stephen Kent, Gregory Scott. Tchr., Lower Burrell, Pa., 1957, Rushford, N.Y., 1960, Gowanda, N.Y., 1961, Pine Valley, South Dayton, N.Y., 1962-92; ordained to ministry, Free Meth. Ch., 1957; minister, Salamanca, N.Y., 1957-59, Belfast, N.Y., 1959-61, South Dayton, 1961-66; pres. Eagleview Enterprises, South Dayton, 1980—; owner Eagleview Farm, 1971—. County committeeman Conservative Party, 1982; mem. Hamburg Wesleyan Ch.; founder, chair Chautauqua County Reading Task Force. Mem. Assn. Arabian Horses (dir.), Chautauqua County Reading Assn. (pres., founder), Internat. Platform Assn., Assn. Supervision and Curriculum Devel., N.Y. Reading Assn., Pine Valley Tchrs. Assn. (pres.), Western N.Y. Arabian Assn., Internat. Arabian Assn., U.S. Dressage Assn., Western N.Y. Dressage Assn. Address: Cottage Rd South Dayton NY 14138

JONES, RICHARD JEFFERY, physician, educator; b. Cleve., Apr. 6, 1918; s. Edward Safford and Frances Christine (Jeffery) J.; m. Helen Hart, Oct. 5, 1946; children—Christopher, Ruth, Jeffery, Catherine. A.B., Oberlin Coll., 1938; M.A., U. Buffalo, 1942, M.D., 1943. Diplomate Am. Bd. Internal Medicine. Intern, U. Chgo. Hosps., 1944; resident, 1947-49; assoc. prof. medicine U. Chgo., 1958-76; assoc. prof. clin. medicine Northwestern U., Chgo., 1976-92. Author: Chemistry and Therapy of Chronic Cardiovascular Disease, 1961. Editorial bd. Nutrition Revs., 1964-72. Served to lt. USNR, 1944-46, PTO. Recipient Presl. Letter Commendation, Pres. Truman, 1946, vis. assoc. prof. Rockefeller U., 1965. Fellow Am. Heart Assn.; mem. AMA (dir. scientific activites 1976-83, council sec. 1976-83), Central Soc. Clin. Research, Soc. Experimental Biol. and Med. (editorial bd. 1964-74). Unitarian. Home: 4820 S Kenwood Ave Chicago IL 60615-2016

JONES, RICHARD LAMAR, entomology educator; b. Charleston, Miss., May 31, 1939; s. Raymond Lee and Tyna Louise (Holland) J.; m. Anne Marchman, June 6, 1964 (div. 1995); children: Katherine Mathis, Margaret Holland; m. Joan Marie Wood, Nov. 29, 1997. BS, Miss. State U., 1963, MS, 1965; PhD, U. Calif., Riverside, 1968. Rsch. entomologist Agrl. Rsch. Svc., USDA, Tifton, Ga., 1968-77; assoc. prof. entomology U. Minn., St. Paul, 1977-84, prof., head dept., 1984-91, dean coll. Agr., 1991-95; dean of rsch., dir. Fla. Agrl. Expt. Sta. U. Fla., Gainesville, 1995—. Editor, author: Semiochemicals, 1974; also over 70 articles. With USN, 1958-60. Scholar NIH, 1965-68, Fulbright scholar, Leiden, The Netherlands, 1980. Mem. AAAS, Entomol. Soc. Am. (fin. com. 1989-96), Am. Chem. Soc. Avocations: golf, fishing. Office: U Fla PO Box 110200 Gainesville FL 32611-0200

JONES, RICHARD MELVIN, bank executive, former retail executive; b. Eldon, Mo., Nov. 26, 1926; m. Sylvia A. Richardson, 1950; 3 children. B.S. in Bus. Adminstrn., Olivet Nazarene Coll., 1950, LL.D. (hon.), 1983; grad. Advanced Mgmt. Program, Harvard U., 1973. With Sears, Roebuck & Co., 1950-89, store mgr., 1963-68; gen. mgr. Sears, Roebuck & Co., Washington and Balt., 1974; exec. v.p.-East Sears, Roebuck & Co., 1974-80, corp. v.p., 1980, vice chmn., chief fin. officer, 1980-85, pres., chief fin. officer, 1986-88; chmn., chief exec. officer Guaranty Fed. Savs. Bank, Dallas, 1989-91. Trustee Field Mus. Natural History, Northwestern Univ. Assocs., Chgo.; adv. coun. J.L. Kellogg Grad. Sch. Mgmt. Northwestern U.. Mem. Chicago Club, Commercial Club.

JONES, RICHARD MICHAEL, lawyer; b. Chgo., Jan. 16, 1952; s. Richard Anthony and Shirley Mae (Wilhelm) J.; m. Catherine Leona Ford, May 25, 1974. BS, U. Ill., 1974; JD, Harvard U., 1977. Bar: Colo. 1977, U.S. Dist. Ct. Colo. 1977. Assoc. Davis, Graham & Stubbs, Denver, 1977-81; corp. counsel Tosco Corp., Denver, 1981-82; asst. gen. counsel Anschutz Corp., Denver, 1982-88, gen. counsel, v.p., 1989—. Mem. ABA, Colo. Bar Assn., Denver Bar Assn. Office: Anschutz Corp 555 17th St Ste 2400 Denver CO 80202-3987

JONES, RICHARD NORMAN, physical chemist, researcher; b. Manchester, Eng., Mar. 20, 1913; s. Richard Leonard and Blanche (Mason) J.; m. Magda Kemeny, July 12, 1939; children: Richard Kemeny, David Leonard. B.Sc., Manchester U., 1933, M.Sc., 1934, Ph.D., 1936, D.Sc., 1954; D.Sc. (hon.), U. Poznan, 1972, Tokyo Inst. Tech., 1982. Commonwealth Fund fellow, tutor in biochemistry Harvard U., Cambridge, Mass., 1937-42; asst. prof. Queens U., Kingston, Ont., Can., 1942-46; adj. prof. Queens U., 1984; assoc. research officer in analytical spectroscopy Nat. Research Council Can., Ottawa, 1946-65; prin. research officer Nat. Research Council Can., 1965-78; guest prof. Tokyo Inst. Tech., 1979-82, guest researcher, 1985-86; disting. visitor U. Alta., 1982-83; guest worker Nat. Rsch. Coun. Can., Ottawa, 1986-92; guest scientist U. Alta., 1992—; invested Officer Order of Canada, 1999. Contbr. articles to profl. jours. Decorated officer Order of Can.; recipient Fisher award Chem. Inst. Can., 1971; Herzberg award Spectroscopy Soc. Can., 1979. Fellow Royal Soc. Can., Chem. Soc. (London), Chem. Inst. Can., Spectroscopy Soc. Can. (hon., v.p. 1983); mem. Am. Chem. Soc., Internat. Union Pure and Applied Chemistry (pres. phys. chemistry div. 1973-77), Internat. Council of Sci. Unions (v.p. com. on data for sci. and tech. 1970-74). Home: Ste 1003, 11027 87th Ave, Edmonton, AB Canada T6G 2P9

JONES, RICHARD THEODORE, biochemistry educator; b. Portland, Oreg., Nov. 9, 1929; s. Lester Tallman and Olene (Johnson) J.; m. Marilyn Virginia Beam, June 20, 1953; children: Gary Richard, Alan Donald, Neil William. Student, Calif. Inst. Tech., 1948-51, Ph.D., 1961; B.S., U. Oreg., 1953, M.S., M.D., 1956. Student asst. dept. physiology U. Oreg. Med. Sch., Portland, 1953-56; intern Hosp. U. Pa., 1956-57; asst. prof. Oreg. Health Scis. U. (formerly U. Oreg. Med. Sch.), 1961-64, assoc. prof. exptl. medicine and biochemistry, 1964-67, prof., 1967-95, prof. emeritus, 1996—, chmn. dept. biochemistry and molecular biology, 1967-93; acting pres. U. Oreg. Health Scis. Center, 1977-78; rsch. asst. dept. chemistry Calif. Inst. Tech., 1959-60; mem. biochemistry tng. com. Nat. Inst. Gen. Med. Scis., NIH, 1968-73, med. sci. tng. com., 1971-74; comprehensive sickle cell centers ad hoc rev. com. Nat. Heart, Lung and Blood Inst., 1974-77; biochemistry test com. Nat. Bd. Med. Examiners, 1968-74, FLEX com., 1982-94. Contbr. articles to profl. jours. Mem. Am. Soc. Biochem. and Molecular Biology, AAAS, Sigma Xi, Alpha Omega Alpha, Tau Beta Pi. Home: 2634 SW Fairmount Blvd Portland OR 97201-1433 Office: 3181 SW Sam Jackson Park Rd Portland OR 97201-3011

JONES, RICHARD WALLACE, interior designer; b. Canandaigua, N.Y., Dec. 6, 1929; s. William Wallace and Maybelle Louise (Smith) J.; m. Patricia Hardwick, June 24, 1957 (div. 1973). Student, Hobart Coll., 1946-47; tchr.'s cert., Longy Sch., Cambridge, Mass., 1952; postgrad., Yale U. Sch. Music, 1952-53. Owner, operator Richard W. Jones studios, Boston, Hartford, Conn., 1954-63; designer, mgr. House of Good Taste Pavilion, N.Y. World's Fair, 1963-66; design editor Redbook Mag., N.Y.C., 1967-72; sr. design editor Better Homes & Gardens mag., Des Moines, 1972-76; pres., dir. Circanow Interior Design Firm, Des Moines, N.Y.C., 1974-90; designer, mgr. D.H. Hershel Inc., Nantucket, Mass., 1978-81; ptnr., designer, buyer Portobello, Nantucket, 1981-83; dir. design Laura Ashley Inc., Ridgewood, N.J., 1989-90; interior designer Godfrey & Assocs., Naples, Fla., 1994-97; prin. Richard W. Jones Designs, Naples, Fla., 1997—; curator Hammond Mus., Gloucester, Mass., 1950-60, Hill-Stead Mus., Farmington, Conn., 1962; del. Internat. Fedn. Interior Designers, Amsterdam, The Netherlands, 1975-76. Editor in chief Interiors mag., Residential Interiors, 1976-78. Mem. Pres.' Com. on Barrier Free Design, Washington, 1972-74. Recipient Dorothy Dawe award Sr. Design Editor, 1974. Fellow Am. Soc. Interior Designers (nat. pres. 1976. Disting. Svc. medal 1977); mem. Nat. Soc. Interior Designers (nat. pres. 1972-74), Nantucket C. of C. (bd. dirs. 1980-82, sign approval com. 1982-84). Presbyterian. Avocations: collecting contemporary and African art, travel. Home and office: 292 14th Ave S Naples FL 34102-7244

JONES, RICK H., arts administrator; b. Dayton, Ohio, Jan. 23, 1948; s. Huston Benjamin and Mildred Garnet J.; m. Christine Renee Elliott, Dec. 18, 1971; children: LeAnna, Brandt. BFA, Wright State U., 1970; MFA, Md. Inst. Coll. of Art, 1972. Exec. dir. Wayne Ctr. for the Arts, Wooster, Ohio, 1979-91, Fitton Ctr. for Creative Arts, Hamilton, Ohio, 1991—. Author: An Arts Center In Our Community: How Do We Begin, 1990, The Arts Center Handbook, 1997. Chmn. Vision 2020 Focus Gp., Hamilton, Ohio, 1999—, Main Street Wooster, Wooster, Ohio, 1988-90, Design Commn., Wooster, Ohio, 1989-91. Recipient Governor's award for Arts Adminstrn., Ohio Arts Council, 1991. Mem. ASCD, Nat. Art Edn. Assn., Music Educators Nat. Conf., Ohio Art Edn. Assn., Ohio Mus. Assn., Ams. for the Arts, Ohio Cizitens for the Arts, Ohio Arts Presenters Network, Ohio Alliance Arts Edn., Alliance Ohio Cmty. Arts Agys., World Future Soc., Rotary. Avocations: golf, reading, gardening, 5-string banjo, autographed baseballs. E-mail: rjatfitton@aol.com. Home: 405 Oakwood Dr Hamilton OH 45013

JONES, ROBERT A., equity finance company exeucutive; b. Feb. 11, 1962. With Ford Motor Co., U.K., 1978-87, Paribas Capital Markets, U.K., 1987-89, Morgan Stanley & Co., U.K., 1989-94; equity fin. client exec. Morgan Stanley Dean Witter, San Francisco, 1994—.

JONES, ROBERT ALFRED, retired clergyman; b. Buffalo, July 19, 1930; s. Ralph A. and Edna Mae (Carver) J.; m. Helen T. Webster, July 20, 1957; children: Marc E., Paul R., Nancy L. BA, Houghton Coll., 1953; MA, Alfred U., 1959. Ordained to ministry United Meth. Ch., 1959. Assoc. pastor University United Meth. Ch., Buffalo, 1959-63; campus min. SUNY, Buffalo, 1963-67; pastor Woodside United Meth. Ch., Buffalo, 1967-74; sr. pastor Baker Meml. United Meth. Ch., East Aurora, N.Y., 1974-80; supr. Rochester dist United Meth. Ch., 1980-86; sr. pastor Ctrl. Park United Meth. Ch., 1986-89; asst. to bishop N.Y. west area United Meth. Ch., Syracuse, 1989-91; sr. pastor Williamsville (N.Y.) United Meth. Ch., 1991—. Home: 146 Farber Ln Williamsville NY 14221-5754

JONES, ROBERT ALONZO, economist; b. Evanston, Ill., Mar. 15, 1937; s. Robert Vernon and Elsie Pierce (Brown) J.; m. Ina Turner Jones; children: Lindsay Rae, Robert Pierce, Gregory Alan, William Kenneth. AB, Middlebury Coll., 1959; MBA, Northwestern U., 1961, LLD (hon.) Middlebury (Vt.) Coll., 1992. Economist Hahn, Wise & Assoc., San Carlos, Calif., 1966-69; sr. rsch. officer Bank of Am., San Francisco, 1969-74; v.p., dir. fin. forecasting Chase Econometrics, San Francisco, 1974-76; chmn. bd. Money Market Svcs., Inc., Belmont, Calif., 1974-86; chmn. bd. MMS Internat., Redwood City, Calif., 1986-89, chmn. emeritus, 1989—; chmn. bd. dirs. Market News Svc., N.Y.C.; chmn. emeritus Geonomics Inst., Middlebury, 1995—, chmn. bd., 1986-95; chmn. bd. Jones Internat., 1989—; chmn. bd. Market News Svc., Inc., N.Y.C., 1993—; chmn. bd. Jones Fin. Network, Inc., Incline Village, N.Y., 1991—; dean coun. Harvard U. Div. Sch., Cambridge, Mass., 1991—; mem. Kellogg Alumni Adv. Bd., Northwestern U., 1993—; instr. money and banking, Am. Inst. Banking, San Francisco, 1971, 72; councilman, City of Belmont (Calif.), 1970-77, mayor, 1971, 72, 75, 76; dir. San Mateo County Transit Dist., 1975-77; chmn. San Mateo County Coun. of Mayors, 1975-76; trustee Incline Village Gen. Improvement Dist., Nev., 1984-85,Carlmont United Meth. Ch., 1978-81, Middlebury Coll., 1997—. Author: U.S. Financial System and the Federal Reserve, 1974, Power of Coinage, 1987. 1st lt. USAR, 1961-68. Named Hon. Life Mem. Calif. PTA, ordo honorum Kappa Delta Rho Nat. Fraternity; recipient Ernst & Young Entrepreneur of the Yr. award, 1986; John Harvard fellow Harvard U., 1996, Stanton Recognition award North Shore Country Day Sch., 1996. Mem. Nat. Assn. Bus. Economists, San Francisco Bond Club. Republican. Methodist. Office: Jones Internat Inc PO Box 7498 Incline Village NV 89452-7498 *The entrepreneurial spirit is distinguished by passion, creativity, and the fulfillment of mission through other people.*

JONES, ROBERT BROOKE, microbiologist and immunologist educator; b. Knoxville, Tenn., Sept 14, 1942; s. Robert Melvin and Evaleen (Brooke) J.; m. Barbara Burgess McLawhorn, Sept. 7, 1963; children—Julia Ashley, Jonathan Davis, Quinnette Brooke. A.B. in Chemistry, U. N.C., 1964, M.D., 1970, Ph.D. in Biochemistry, 1970. Diplomate Am. Bd. Internal Medicine. Intern U. Wash., Seattle, 1970-71; resident U. Wash., Seattle, 1974-76; fellow in infectious diseases, 1976-78; asst. prof. Ind. U. Sch. Medicine, Indpls., 1978-83, assoc. prof. medicine, microbiology and immunology, 1983-86, prof., 1986—, assoc. dean, 1997—; dir. Midwest Sexually Transmitted Diseases Research Ctr., Indpls., 1983—; mem. NIH bacteriology rev. group, 1987. Contbr. sci. articles to profl. jours. Served to lt. comdr. U.S. Navy, 1971-74. NIH grantee, 1983. Fellow ACP; mem. Am. Venereal Disease Assn. (bd. dirs. 1983—), Am. Soc. Microbiology, Infectious Disease Soc. Am., Am. Fedn. Clin. Research, Order Golden Fleece, Sigma Xi, Alpha Omega Alpha. Republican. Mem. Society of Friends. Office: Ind U Fisler # 302 Dept Medicine Indianapolis IN 46202-5114*

JONES, ROBERT CLAIR, middle school educator; b. Norfolk, Va., Apr. 9, 1949; s. Leon Herbert and Barbara Dean (Jones) J.; m. Geri Lee Siebels, Feb. 13, 1977; children: Adam, Matthew, Aaron, Lee. BS, Old Dominion U., 1971, MS, 1981. Tchr. Virginia Beach (Va.) Jr. High Sch., 1971-73, Kempsville Jr. High Sch., Virginia Beach, 1973—; adj. faculty Old Dominion U., Norfolk, Va., 1990—; co-chmn. faculty coun. Kempsville Mid. Sch., 1992-93, curriculum coord., grade level chair, 1993—; program devel. com. for mid. schs., Virginia Beach City Schs., 1990-91, chmn. social studies curriculum adv. com., 1990-91, instr. staff devel., 1989-91; speaker in field. Contbr. articles to profl. jours.; featured in Oasis mag. Baseball coach Pony Colt League, Virginia Beach, 1991-92; vol. Make A Wish Found., Virginia Beach, 1990-92. Named Tchr. of Yr., Va. Coun. Social Studies, 1987—. Mem. ASCD, NEA, Nat. Coun. Social Studies, Va. Edn. Assn., Va. Coun. Social Studies, Virginia Beach Edn. Assn. Avocations: profl. musician, collecting records, Beatles memorobilia. Home: 812 Yearling Ct Virginia Beach VA 23464-3214 Office: Kenpsville Mid Sch 260 Churchill Dr Virginia Beach VA 23456

JONES, ROBERT CLIVE, judge; b. Las Vegas, Nev., July 21, 1947; s. Robert E. and Meryl (Dunn) J.; m. Anita Michele Bunker, Mar. 26, 1970; children: JaNae, Justin, Melissa, Kimberly. BS with honors, Brigham Young U., 1971; JD with honors, UCLA, 1975. Bar: Nev. 1976, U.S. Dist. Ct. Nev. 1976, U.S. Tax Ct. 1979; CPA, Nev. Acct. Laventhol & Horwath, Las Vegas, 1971-72, Touche Ross, Los Angeles, 1974-75, Haskins & Sells, Las Vegas, 1976; assoc. Albright & McGimsey, Las Vegas, 1976; ptnr. Jones & Holt, Las Vegas, 1977-83; chief judge U.S. Bankruptcy Ct., Dist. of Nev., Las Vegas, 1983—. Mem. Order of Coif. Office: US Dist Ct 300 Las Vegas Blvd S Ste 4650 Las Vegas NV 89101-5883

JONES, ROBERT EDWARD, federal judge; b. Portland, Oreg., July 5, 1927; s. Howard C. and Leita (Hendricks) J.; m. Pearl F. Jensen, May 29, 1948; children—Jeffrey Scott, Julie Lynn. BA, U. Hawaii, 1949; JD, Lewis and Clark Coll., 1953, LHD (hon.), 1995; LLD (hon.), City U., Seattle, 1984, Lewis and Clark Coll., 1995. Bar: Oreg. Trial atty. Portland, Oreg., 1953-63; judge Oreg. Circuit Ct., Portland, 1963-83; justice Oreg. Supreme Ct., Salem, 1983-90; judge U.S. Dist. Ct. Oreg., Portland, 1990—; mem. faculty Nat. Jud. Coll., Am. Acad. Jud. Edn., ABA Appellate Judges Seminars; former mem. Oreg. Evidence Revision Commn., Oreg. Ho. of Reps.; former chmn. Oreg. Commn. Prison Terms and Parole Stds.; adj. prof. Northwestern Sch. Law, Lewis and Clark Coll., 1963—, Willamette Law Sch., 1988—. Author: Rutter Group Practice Guide Federal Civil Trials and Evidence, 1999. Bd. overseers Lewis and Clark Coll. Served to capt. JAGC, USNR. Recipient merit award Multnomah Bar Assn., 1979; Citizen award NCCJ, Legal Citizen of the Yr. award Law Related Edn. Project, 1988; Service to Mankind award Sertoma Club Oreg.; James Madison award Sigma Delta Chi; named Disting. Grad., Northwestern Sch. Law. Mem. Am. Judicature Soc. (bd. dirs. 1997—), State Bar Oreg. (past chmn. Continuing Legal Edn.), Oregon Circuit Judges Assn. (pres. 1967—), Oreg. Trial Lawyers Assn. (pres. 1959, chair 9th cir. edn. com. 1996-97), Office: US Dist Ct House 1000 SW 3rd Ave Rm 1407 Portland OR 97204-2902

JONES, ROBERT EMMET, French language educator; b. N.Y.C., Sept. 16, 1928; s. Robert Emmet and Lois Kathryn (UpdeGrove) J. A.B., Columbia U., 1948, Ph.D., 1954; certificat de phonetique Sorbonne, Paris, 1949. Vis. instr. French Columbia U., 1953-54; asst. prof. French U. Ga., Athens, 1954-61, U. Pa., 1961-67; asso. prof. French and humanities M.I.T., 1967-71, prof. French and humanities, 1971-92, prof emeritus, 1992—; tchr. French cooking, 1976—. Author: The Alienated Hero in Modern French Drama, 1961, Panorama de la nouvelle critique en France, 1968, Gerard de Nerval, 1974, H.R. Lenormand, 1984; contbr. articles to profl. jours. Mem. MLA, Am. Assn. Tchrs. French, French Library Boston. Episcopalian. Clubs: St. Anthony, St. Botolph. Home: 452 Beacon St Boston MA 02115-1001

JONES, ROBERT GEAN, religion educator; b. Magnolia, Ark., Feb. 17, 1925; s. Emless Bunyan and Eunice (Gean) J.; m. Marian Laverne Alexander, July 23, 1946; 1 dau., Carolyn Ann. B.A. cum laude, Baylor U., 1947; B.D. cum laude, Yale, 1950, M.A., 1957, Ph.D., 1959. Ordained to ministry Bapt. Ch., 1946; minister Deep River (Conn.) Bapt. Ch. and First Bapt. Ch. of, Saybrook, 1950-59; asst. prof. religion George Washington U., Washington, 1959-61; asso. prof. George Washington U., 1961-64, prof., 1964-91, prof. emeritus, 1991—, chmn. dept. religion, 1963-79, univ. marshal, 1969-89; adj. prof. U. Tenn., Chattanooga, 1991-93, Maryville Coll., 1993-95. Author: The Rules for the War of the Sons of Light With the Sons of Darkness, 1957, The Manual of Discipline (1QS), The Old Testament and Persian Religion, 1964. Mem. Soc. Bibl. Lit. and Exegesis, Am. Acad. Religion, Alpha Chi, Omicron Delta Kappa. Home: 307 Amohi Ln Loudon TN 37774-3013

JONES, ROBERT JEFFRIES, lawyer; b. Atlantic City, N.J., Sept. 7, 1939; s. Robert Lewis and Mildred Laura (Jeffries) J.; m. Joan Mary Feichtner, Aug. 17, 1963; children: Christopher, Kendall, Stephen. BA, Colgate U., 1961; LLB with honors, U. Pa., 1964. Bar: Pa. 1965, U.S. Dist. Ct. (ea. dist.) Pa. 1965, U.S. Ct. Appeals (3d cir.) 1965. Assoc. Saul, Ewing, Remick & Saul, Phila., 1964-71, ptnr., 1971—; mem. steering com. Bond Atty.'s Workshop, Chgo., 1980. Mem. Montgomery County Rep. Com., Norristown, Pa., 1967-71; chmn. Whitpain Twp. Park and Recreation Bd., Blue Bell, Pa., 1980-84; bd. dirs. Phila. YMCA Camps, 1970-76. Fellow Am. Coll. Bond Counsel (founder); mem. ABA, Phila. Bar Assn. (chmn. tax exempt fin. com. 1985-86), Pa. Bond Lawyers Assn. (founder Harrisburg, Pa. 1987), Colgate U. Gen. Counsel Alumni Corp. (pres. Phila. chpt. 1980-84), Pa. Economy League (bd. dirs. 1994—). Avocations: skiing, golf, history. Office: Saul Ewing Remick & Saul 3800 Centre Sq W Philadelphia PA 19102

JONES, ROBERT LAWTON, architect, planner, educator; b. McAlester, Okla., May 12, 1925; s. Lawton Henry and Josephine (Troy) J.; m. Lynn Scott, Dec. 2, 1950; children: Jayme, Mark, Paul, Gregory, Laure, Christi, Matthew. BArch cum laude, U. Notre Dame, 1949; MS, Ill. Inst. Tech., 1953; postgrad., Tech. U., Karlsruhe, Fed. Republic Germany, 1954. With Perkins & Will, Chgo., 1949-52; mgr. civic ctr. project Tulsa, 1954-55; arch. David G. Murray & Assocs., Tulsa, 1955-56; dir. planning and design Murray Jones Murray Inc., Tulsa, 1957-88; prof., dir. architecture U. Okla., 1986-88, prof., dir. urban design, 1988-95; campus planner U. Tulsa, 1993-98. prin. works include Chapman Hall Tulsa U., Tulsa Internat. Airport, Okla. U. Coll. Nursing, St. Patrick's Ch., First Nat. Bank, Ctr. Pla., Okla. Coll. Osteol. Medicine and Surgery, Hilti Western Hemisphere Hdqrs., Cities Svc. Tech. Ctr. Chmn. Community Rels. Commn., Tulsa, 1968, Arts Commn., Tulsa, 1970-71, chmn. Tulsa Pollution Control Task Force, 1970; v.p. Arts and Humanities Coun., Tulsa, 1971-74, pres. 1975-76 (Pres.'s award 1986); bd. dirs. Nat. Rsch. Found. on Aging, 1974-78, Tulsa Met. Ministry, 1977-82 (interfaith award 1986). With USNR, 1943-46. Fulbright grantee 1953-54; recipient Tchng. Excellence award Coll. of Arch., U. Okla., 1992-93. Fellow AIA (chmn. nat. jury 1989); mem. NCCJ (chmn. Tulsa chpt., v.p. 1970-73, 90-94, chmn. long-range planning task force 1984, nat. bd. trustees 1984-90, Brotherhood award 1972), Am. Planning Assn., Am. Inst. Cert. Planners, Met. Tulsa C. of C. (dir. 1974-76). Democrat. Roman Catholic. Home: 1916 E 47th St Tulsa OK 74105-4917

JONES, ROBERT LYLE, emergency medical services leader, educator; b. Washington, Feb. 6, 1959; s. Herman Aven and Dorothy Edith J.; m. Cynthia Celia Bogdanowicz, May 15, 1996. B in Gen. Sci., U. Kans., 1982; MA in Adult and Continuing Edn., U. Mo., 1990. Registered paramedic, Kans., Kans. cert. Emergency Med. Svcs. Tng. Officer, 1992—. Paramedic team leader Johnson County (Kans.) Med. Action, 1983-89, dist. supr., 1989-92, edn. supr., 1992—, facilitation cadre, 1997—; BCLS instr., 1979-87, affiliate faculty, 1987—, ACLS instr., 1985-88, affiliate faculty, 1988—, PALS instr., 1993—. Served to Capt. USAR, 1979-94. Mem. Nat. Assn. EMTs (prehosp. trauma life support instr. 1986—), Nat. Soc. EMS Adminstrs., Nat. Soc. EMT Paramedics, Assn. Profls. in Infection Control and Epidemiology, Am. Assn. Individual Investors. Avocations: bicycling, backpacking, running. Office: Johnson County Med Action 111 S Cherry St Ste 300 Olathe KS 66061-3421

JONES, ROBERT MEAD, JR., lawyer; b. Phila., Aug. 13, 1945; s. Robert Mead and Constance (Rommel) J.; m. Bonnie Kay Bushong, Mar. 13, 1968; 1 child: Derek Brandon. BA, Yale U., 1967; student, U. Paris, 1965-66; JD, U. Pa., 1970; MA, 1980. Bar: Pa., 1971, U.S. Dist. Ct. (ea. dist) Pa. 1974,

Beggar's Opera, 1957, The Red Mill, 1958, Maggie Flynn, 1968, On a Clear Day, 1975, Show Boat, 1976, Bitter Suite, 1983; films include role of Laurey in Oklahoma, 1954, later stage tour Paris and Rome, sponsorship U.S. Dept. State, Carousel, 1956, April Love, 1957, Never Steal Anything Small, 1959, Bobbikins, 1959, Elmer Gantry, 1960 (Acad. Best Supporting Actress award 1961), Pepe, 1960, The Two Rode Together, 1961, The Music Man, 1962, The Courtship of Eddie's Father, 1963, A Ticklish Affair, 1963, Bedtime Story, 1964, The Secret of My Success, 1965, Fluffy, 1965, The Happy Ending, 1969, The Cheyenne Social Club, 1970, Beyond the Poseidon Adventure, 1979, Tank, 1984, There Were Times, Dear, 1985; night club tour with husband, 1958, later TV and summer stock; star TV series The Partridge Family, 1970-74, Shirley, 1979; guest star: TV series McMillan, 1976; TV films include: Silent Night, Lonely Night, 1969, But I Don't Want To Get Married!, 1970, The Girls of Huntington House, 1973, The Family Nobody Wanted, 1975, The Lives of Jenny Dolan, 1975, Winner Take All, 1975, Yesterday's Child, 1977, Evening in Byzantium, 1978, Who'll Save Our Children, 1978, A Last Cry for Help, 1979, The Children Of An Lac, 1980, Inmates: A Love Story, 1981, There Were Times Dear, 1987; one-woman concert: TV series Shirley Jones' America 1981; author: Shirley and Marty: An Unlikely Love Story, 1990. Nat. chairwoman Leukemia Found. Named Mother of Yr. by Women's Found., 1978.

JONES, SIDNEY LEWIS, economist, government official; b. Ogden, Utah, Sept. 23, 1933; s. Lewis W. and Anna Vernal (Evans) J.; m. Marlene Stewart, Nov. 24, 1953; children—Randall Sidney, Stanna, Bryan Lewis, Blake Stewart, Allyson. B.S. with honors in Econs, Utah State U., 1954; M.B.A., Stanford, 1958, Ph.D., 1960. Asst. prof. finance Northwestern U., Evanston, Ill., 1960-64; asso. prof. Northwestern U., 1964-65; prof. finance U. Mich., Ann Arbor, 1965-69, 71-72; sr. staff economist Pres.'s Council Econ Advisers, 1969-71, spl. asst. to chmn., 1970-71; minister-counselor for econ. affairs to NATO, Brussels, Belgium, 1972-73; asst. sec. for econ. affairs Dept. Commerce, Washington, 1973-74; dep. asst. to Pres., also; dep. counsellor for econ. policy White House, 1974-75; counselor to sec. Treasury, Washington, 1975; asst. sec. for econ. policy Dept. Treasury, 1975-77; fellow Woodrow Wilson Internat. Center for Scholars, Washington, 1977-78; asst. to bd. govs. FRS, 1978; research scholar Am. Enterprise Inst.; Public Policy Research and lectr. Georgetown U., 1979-84; under sec. for econ. affairs Commerce Dept., Washington, 1984-86; prof. Georgetown U., Washington, 1986-89; assoc. faculty Brookings Inst., Washington, 1986-89; asst. sec. for econ. policy U.S. Dept. of the Treasury, Washington, 1989-93; vis. prof., rsch. assoc. Carleton Coll., 1993—; vis. prof. Cornell U., 1994-95, Dartmouth Coll., 1993, Ariz. State U., 1996. Co-author: The Generalist-Specialist Dichotomy in the Management of Creative Personnel, 1960, Managerial Problems in Finance, 1964, Financial Institutions, 4th edit, 1966, The Development of Economic Policy, 1980. Served to 1st lt. Q.M.C. AUS, 1954-56. Recipient Distinguished Alumni award Utah State U., 1971; Newell scholar; McKinsey fellow; Ford Found. fellow, 1957-60. Home: 8505 Parliament Dr Potomac MD 20854-4001

JONES, SONIA JOSEPHINE, advertising agency executive; b. Belize, Brit., Honduras, Nov. 9, 1945; came to U.S., 1962; naturalized, 1986; d. Frederick Francis and Elsie Adelia (Gomez) Alcoser; m. John Marvin Jones, Mar. 21, 1970; children: Christopher William Edward, Joshua Joseph Paul. Student, Lamar U., 1964-66. With Foley's Federated Dept. Store, Houston, 1965-67; media buyer Vance Advt., Houston, 1967-68; media buyer, planner O'Neill & Assocs., Houston, 1968-75; media supr. Ketchum Houston, 1975-76; v.p., media dir. Rives Smith Bladwin Carlberg/Y&R, Houston, 1976-86; sr. v.p. media dir. Black Gillock & Landberg, Houston, 1986-89; pres. JMM Group, Inc., Houston, 1989—; lectr. U. Houston, 1983—. Vol. Women in Yellow, Houston, 1966; mem. Tom's Moms, St. Thomas H.S., 1992-96, mem. sch. bd. spl. projects, fundraising vol. women's club, 1992—; vol. translator St. Cecilia Clinic, 1993—; mem. sch. bd. spl. projects St. Cecilia Cath. Sch.; head sacristan St. Cecilia Cath. Ch., 1995. Mem. Houston Advt. Fedn., Santana Doston Found. (bd. dirs. 1998—). Republican. Office: JMM Group Inc 2500 City West Blvd Ste 300 Houston TX 77042

JONES, STANLEY, state agency administrator. State rep. Ind. Ho. of Reps., West Lafayette, 1974-90, mem. house ways and means com., 1974-84, mem. state budget com., 1978-84, mem. ho. edn. com., 1990-94, mem. dem. fl. leader, 1989-90; sr. edn. advisor Office of Gov., Ind., 1990-94; dir. of policy Office of Gov., 1994-95; exec. asst. for higher edn. Office of Gov. of Ind., 1992-95, exec. asst. workforce devel., 1992-95. Office: Higher Edn Commn State of Ind Ste 550 101 West Ohio St Indianapolis IN 46204-1971

JONES, STANLEY BOYD, health policy analyst, priest; b. Balt., July 27, 1938; s. Arthur Boyd and Lillian Ailene (Powell) J.; m. Judith K. Miller, Mar. 9, 1981; children—Andrew, Jeffrey, Lisa, Julia. BA, Dartmouth Coll., 1960; postgrad., Yale U., 1960-63. Ordained Episc. priest., 1992. Mem. profl. staff, staff dir. Subcom. on Health, U.S. Senate, Washington, 1970-76; program devel. officer Inst. of Medicine, Nat. Acad. Scis., Washington, 1976-78; v.p. Fullerton, Jones & Wollkstein (Health Policy Alternatives), Washington, 1978-80; v.p. for Washington representation Nat. Assns. Blue Cross and Blue Shield Plans, 1980-83; prin. Health Policy Alternatives, 1983-86; pres. Consol. Healthcare, 1986-89; ind. cons. on health policy Washington, 1989—; clergyman Diocese of W.Va., 1992—; dir. Health Ins. Reform Project George Washington U., 1994—; commr. D.C. Gen. Hosp. Fellow Inst. of Soc., Ethics and the Life Scis.; mem. Inst. of Medicine of Nat. Acad. Scis. Office: 2021 K St NW Washington DC 20006-1003

JONES, STANLEY R., government contracts business consultant; b. Bozeman, Mont., Jan. 13, 1939; s. James Alford and Rose Opal (Bohna) J.; m. Pamela Lynn Ray, Sept. 13, 1980. BS, Mont. State U., 1961; MBA, Ariz. State U., 1970. Cert. profl. contract mgr. Dir. Mid-East Ops. Telemedia, Inc., Chgo., 1974-76; cons. Bellevue, Wash., 1976-80; dir. project mgmt. Tacoma (Wash.) Boat Bldg. Co., 1980-82; pres. Yesterday's Rent-A-Car, Seattle, 1982-88; cons. Price-Waterhouse, Bellevue, 1988-90; principal Stan Jones and Assoc., Renton, Wash., 1990—. Lt. Col. USAF, 1961-89. Fellow Nat. Contract Mgmt. Assn. (chpt. v.p. edn. 1988-90, chpt. pres. 1990-92). Avocations: flying, model airplanes. Office: Stan Jones Assocs 15 S Grady Way Ste 421 Renton WA 98055-3216

JONES, STANTON WILLIAM, management consultant; b. New Orleans, May 24, 1939; s. Albert DeWitt and Clara Arimenta (Stanton) J.; m. Helen Marie Trice, May 23, 1964 (div. Aug. 1972); 1 child, Ellen Marie; m. Gladys Marina Caceres, Aug. 21, 1990; children: Hazel Nathalye, Albert Stanton. BS, Embry-Riddle Aero. U., Daytona Beach, Fla., 1973; MBA, Syracuse (N.Y.) U., 1977. Cert. internal auditor. Commd. 2d lt. U.S. Army, 1963, advanced through grades to lt. col., 1979; fixed wing pilot U.S. Army, Ft. Rucker, Ala., 1965-72, rotary wing pilot, 1972; mgmt. cons. Stanton W. Jones & Assocs., San Francisco, 1987—; joint venture ptnr. Budget Analyst to Bd. Suprs., San Francisco, 1988—. Treas. Hunter's Point Boys & Girls Club, San Francisco, 1987-93. Decorated Meritorious Svc. medal. Mem. Alpha Phi Alpha (pres. 1988-90). Roman Catholic. Avocations: chess, reading, jogging. Home: 1948 Cortereal Ave Oakland CA 94611-2632 Office: Stanton W Jones & Assocs 57 Post St Ste 713 San Francisco CA 94104-5025

JONES, STEPHANIE TUBBS, congresswoman, lawyer. BA, Case Western Res. U., 1971, JD, 1974. Bar: Ohio 1974, U.S. Dist. Ct. (no. dist.) Ohio 1975, U.S. Ct. Appeals (6th cir.) 1981, U.S. Supreme Ct. 1981. Asst. gen. counsel, EEO adminstr. N.E. Ohio Regional Sewer Dist., 1974-76; asst. prosecutor Cuyahoga County Prosecutor's Office, 1976-79; trial atty. Cleve. dist. office EEO, 1979-81; judge Cleve. Mcpl. Ct., 1982-83, Cuyahoga County Ct. of Common Pleas, 1983-91; prosecutor Cuyahoga County, Cleve., 1991-98; mem. U.S. Congress from 11th Ohio dist., 1999—; mem. banking and fin. svcs. com., 1999—, mem. com. on small bus., 1999—; mem. vis. com. bd. overseers Franklin Thomas Backus Sch. Law, Case Western Res. U. Bd. trustees Comty. Re-entry Program; bd. trustees class of 1984 Leadership Cleve. Alumnae; mem. Task Force on Violent Crime, Substance Abuse Initiative; trustee Cleve. Police Hist. Soc.; bd. trustees Bethany Bapt. Ch. Recipient Outstanding Vol. Svcs. in Law and Justice award Urban League Greater Cleve., 1986, Women of Yr. award Cleve. chpt. Nat. Assn. Negro Bus. and Profl. Women's Clubs, Inc., 1987, award in recognition of outstanding svc. to judiciary and black comty. Midwest region Nat. Black Am. Law Student Assn., 1988, Career Women of Achievement award YWCA, 1991, Disting. Svc. award Cleve. chpt. NAACP, 1997; named Black Profl. of Yr., Black Profl. Assn. Cleve., 1995, 1994 Ohio Dem. of Yr., Ohio Dem. Party, 1995; inductee Collinwood H.S. Hall of Fame, 1994, Soc. Benchers of Case Western Res. U. Sch. of Law, 1996. Mem. ABA, Nat. Black Prosecutor's Assn., Nat. Dist. Atty.'s Assn. (met. prosecutor's com.), Nat. Coun. Negro Women, Nat. Coll. Dist. Attys. (bd. regents), Ohio State Bar Assn. (Nettie Cronise Lutes award 1997), Ohio Prosecuting Attys. Assn. (exec. com.), Cleve. Bar Assn. (trustee), Norman S. Miner Bar Assn. (past treas.), Cuyahoga Women's Polit. Caucus, Delta Sigma Theta (Greater Cleve. Alumnae chpt., Althea Simmons award 1993). Office: Ho of Reps 1516 Longworth HOB Washington DC 20515*

JONES, STEPHEN, lawyer; b. Lafayette, La., July 1, 1940; s. Leslie William and Gladys A. (Williams) J.; m. Virginia Hadden (dec.); 1 child, John Chapman; m. Sherrel Alice Stephens, Dec. 27, 1973; children: Stephen Mark, Leslie Rachael, Edward St. Andrew. Student U. Tex. 1960-63; LLB, U. Okla. 1966. Sec. Rep. Minority Conf., Tex. Ho. of Reps., 1963; personal asst. to Richard M. Nixon, N.Y.C., 1964; adminstrv. asst. to Congressman Paul Findley, 1966-69; legal counsel to gov. of Okla., 1967; spl. asst. U.S. Senator Charles H. Percy and U.S. Rep. Donald Rumsfeld, 1968; mem. U.S. del. to North Atlantic Assembly, NATO, 1968; staff counsel censure task force Ho. of Reps. Impeachment Inquiry, 1974; spl. U.S. atty. No. Dist. Okla., 1979; spl. prosecutor, spl. asst. dist. atty. State of Okla., 1977; judge Okla. Ct. Appeals, 1982; civil jury instrn. com. Okla. Supreme Ct., 1979-81; adv. com. ct. rules Okla. Ct. Criminal Appeals, 1980; now mng. ptnr. Jones and Wyatt, Enid, Okla.; adj. prof. U. Okla., 1973-76; instr. Phillips U., 1982-90; bd. dirs. Coun. on the Nat. Interest Found. Author: Oklahoma and Politics in State and Nation, 1907-62, Others Unknown, The Oklahoma City Bombing Case and Conspiracy, 1998, Others Unknown, The Oklahoma City Bombing and Conspiracy (Public Affairs, 1998); co-author: France and China, The First Ten Years, 1964-1974, 1991; contbr. articles to various jours. Bd. dirs. / coun. on Nat. Interest Found.; acting chmn. Rep. State Com., Okla., 1982; Rep. nominee Okla. atty. gen., 1974, U.S. Senate, 1990; spl. counsel to Gov. Okla., 1995; apptd. chief def. counsel by U.S. Dist. Ct., Oklahoma City, U.S. vs. Tim McVeigh, Oklahoma City Bombing Case, 1995-97; mem. vestry, St. Matthews Episc. Ch., 1974, sr. warden 1983-84, 89-90. Mem. ABA, Okla. Bar Assn., Garfield County Bar Assn., Beacon Club, Petroleum Club (Oklahoma City), Oakwood Country Club (Enid). Office: PO Box 472 Enid OK 73702-0472

JONES, STEPHEN WITSELL, lawyer; b. Honolulu, Aug. 12, 1947; s. Allen Newton Jr. and Maude Estelle (Witsell) J.; m. Judy Kaye Mason, Aug. 13, 1977; children: MaryAnn, Adam, Kathleen. Student, Hendrix Coll., 1965-66; AB with high honors, U. Ill., 1969; JD with highest honors, U. Ark., Little Rock, 1978. Bar: Ark. 1978, U.S. Dist. Ct. (ea. and we. dists.) Ark. 1978, U.S. Ct. Appeals (7th and 8th cirs.) 1978, U.S. Supreme Ct. 1984. Rsch. statistician Ark. Dept. Parks and Tourism, Little Rock, 1971-72, dir. tourist info. ctr., 1972-74; affirmative action specialist Office of the Gov., Little Rock, 1974-75; dir. pers. Ark. Social Svcs. Div., Little Rock, 1975-77; mgmt. info. specialist Ark. Health Dept., Little Rock, 1977-78; assoc. House, Holmes & Jewell, Little Rock, 1978-84; ptnr. House, Wallace, Nelson & Jewell, Little Rock, 1984-86; mng. ptnr. Jack, Lyon & Jones, P.A., Little Rock, 1986—; adj. instr. div. lifelong edn. U. Ark., Little Rock, 1992-95. Co-author: Employment Law Deskbook for Arkansas Employers, 1997; editor-in-chief U. Ark. Little Rock Law Rev., 1977; editor Ark. Employment Law Letter, 1996—; contbg. author: Employment Discrimination Law, 2d edit., 1983; editor. Bd. dirs. United Cerebral Palsy of Ctrl. Ark., Little Rock, 1978—; chmn. Ark. Ice Hockey Assn., 1992—; mem. Leadership Greater Little Rock, 1990—. With U.S. Army, 1969-71. Recipient Svc. Recognition award United Cerebral Palsy of Ctrl. Ark., 1986, 95. Fellow Greater Little Rock C. of C.; mem. ABA (labor/litigation law practice mgmt. sect.), Ark. Bar Assn., Def. Rsch. Inst. Episcopalian. Avocations: photography, golf. Home: 1724 S Arch St Little Rock AR 72206-1215 Office: Jack Lyon & Jones PA 3400 TCBY Tower 425 W Capitol Ave Little Rock AR 72201-3405

JONES, STUART CROMER, mechanical engineer; b. Roanoke, Va., Feb. 10, 1959; s. David William and Elizabeth Louise (Cromer) J. BSME, U. Va., 1981, ME in Mech. Engring., 1985. Sr. structures engr. Lockheed Engring. & Sci. Co., Hampton, Va., 1986-92; mech. engr. Gen. Elec. Med. Sys., Florence, S.C., 1992-93, Hankins & Anderson, Richmond, Va., 1993-95; sr. engr. Trax Corp., Lynchburg, Va., 1995-97, Teng Consulting Engrs., Mechanicsville, Va., 1998—. Area coord. Concord Coalition, Charlottesville, 1993. Mem. ASME. Home: PO Box 731 Mechanicsville VA 23111-0731

JONES, SUSAN CHAFIN, management consultant; b. Bryan, Tex., July 14, 1951; d. Othel Viron and Norma Beatrice (Bartley) Chafin; m. Robert Lewis Jones, Apr. 9, 1973 (dec.); children: Karin Lynn Mitchell, Krista Rice, Kyndra Lotspeich, Katrina, Kelli. BS in Edn., Stephen F. Austin State U., 1973; MA, U. Tex., Austin, 1976. Cert. rehab. counselor; lic. marriage and family therapist. Tng. coord. Behavioral Systems Scis. Assoc., Austin, 1973-76; v.p. Jones, Bright Internat., The Woodlands, Tex., 1976-97; CEO Jones, Ragain Internat., Inc., The Woodlands, 1997—; team leader Guatemala Med. Mission, 1999—. Author: Feelings Beneath Words and Messages in Action, 1974, Supervisor's Notes: Guidelines on Employee Counseling, 1977, Youth Ministry: A Manual for Youth Counselors, Leaders and Workers, 1991, 360o Intermetrics, Assessment for Individuals and Organizations, 1993, Therapeutic Approaches to Women's Health: A Program of Exercise and Education, 1995. Active McCullough High Sch. PTA, The Woodlands, 1992-95; v.p. McCullough Highsteppers Parent Club, 1993-95; dir. Stephen Ministry The Woodlands United Meth. Ch., 1992-96, mem. adminstrv. bd., 1993-96; bd. mem. Montgomery County Young Life, 1991-92. Mem. Montgomery County C. of C., Am. Assn. Marriage and Family Therapy (clin.), Am. Assn. Christian Counselors (profl., charter), Christian Counselors Tex. Republican. Avocations: playing piano, skiing, writing. Office: Jones Ragain Internat PO Box 130655 The Woodlands TX 77393-0655

JONES, SUSAN EMILY, fashion educator, administrator, educator; b. N.Y.C., Sept. 9, 1948; d. David and Emily Helen (Welke) J.; m. Henry J. Titone, Jr., Oct. 21, 1974 (div. 1980); m. Douglas S. Robbins, Aug. 21, 1985. B.F.A., Pratt Inst., Bklyn., 1970. Designer Sue Brett, N.Y.C., 1970-74, St. Tropez, 1975; prof. fashion Pratt Inst., Bklyn., 1972-80, prof., 1980—, chairperson fashion dept., 1981-83, chairperson merchandising and design programs fashion dept., 1983—; computer software cons., 1988-89; owner, designer Sej Wearable Artworks, 1992—; internat. observer Jeunes Createurs de Mode, Paris, 1987, judge, 1988; U.S. rep. SAGA Internat. Design Ctr., Copenhagen, 1992. Recipient Young Am. Designer award Internat. Ladies Garment Workers Union, 1970, Ptnr. in Edn. award N.Y.C. Pub. Sch. System Chancellor, 1992-93. Mem. Fashion Group (regional com. 1983-87, mem. com. 1990-93, tech. book reviewer 1994—, ednl. com. 1995-96, co-chair ednl. com. 1996-98), Nat. Retail Fedn., Under Fashion Assn. Home: 220 Willoughby Ave Brooklyn NY 11205-3805 Office: Pratt Inst Dept of Fashion Design 200 Willoughby Ave Brooklyn NY 11205-3899

JONES, SUSAN TAMNY, fundraising executive; b. Annapolis, Md., June 26, 1945; d. Lewis David and Ann Gilmore Tamny; m. Edgar Charles Jones Jr., Apr. 20, 1974; children: Edgar Cooper, Charles Peterson. BS, U. Fla., 1967. Coord. Friends of Art, Lowe Art Mus. U. Miami, Coral Gables, Fla., 1991-92, devel. officer, 1992-94, major gifts officer, 1994-97, dir. sch.-based devel., 1997-98, assoc. dir. major gifts, 1998-99, exec. dir. major gifts, 1999—. Bd. dirs. ARC Ball, Coral Gables, 1996-99, com. chmn., 1998; trustee Ransom Everglades Sch., Coconut Grove, Fla., 1992-98; bd. dirs. Jr. League, 1976-88. Home: 515 Tivoli Ave Coral Gables FL 35143 Office: U Miami PO Box 248073 Coral Gables FL 33124-1210

JONES, SYBLE THORNHILL, dietitian; b. Summit, Miss., July 10, 1932; d. Hurby Lee and Iva Mae (Brown) Thornhill; children: Bruce Clifford, Janice Jones Duvall, Kent Christopher. BS, U. So. Miss., Hattiesburg, 1954; MS, La. Tech. U., Ruston, 1972. Lic. dietitian, La.; registered dietitian. Supr. food svc. U. So. Miss., Hattiesburg, 1954-55; sec. U.S.F. & G. Claims Office, Natchez, Miss., 1955-56; exec. sec. Gen. Agt. Aetna Life, New Orleans, 1956-57; unit mgr. Progressive Cafeterias, Houston, 1959-66; chief dietitian Ctrl. La. State Hosp., Pineville, 1966-68; dir. food and nutrition svc. Rapides Parish Sch. Bd., Alexandria, La., 1968—; trustee Tchrs. Ret. Sys. La., Baton Rouge, 1999—. Mem. adv. bd. Rapides Coun. on Aging, Alexandria, 1973-75. Mem. Am. Dietetic Assn., Am. Food Svc. Assn. (Pres. Gold award 1987, Silver Spirit award 1990), La. Dietetic Assn. (pres. 1971-72, Outstanding Dietitian 1972), La. Sch. Food Svc. Assn. (pres. 1986-87), La. Assn. Sch. Execs. (exec. com. 1980-81), La. Assn. Sch. Bus. Ofcls. (regional dir. 1976-77). Democrat. Methodist. Avocations: motor home travel, reading, dining out, old movies. Home: 138 Ron Mar Dr Pineville LA 71360-4547 Office: Rapides Parish Sch Bd 619 6th St PO Box 1230 Alexandria LA 71309-1230

JONES, SYLVANUS BENSON, adjudicator, consultant; b. Southport, N.C., Nov. 21, 1928; s. Thomas Henry and Katie Mable J.; m. Karen Ann Charbonneau, Aug. 10, 1970 (div. May 1975); 1 child, Donovan. Student, Howard U., 1945-48; AD in Fin., Peter's Bus. Coll., Washington, 1955; postgrad., Fgn. Svc. Inst., Arlington, Va., 1956, George Washington U., 1959-60, Bibliothèque de la Sorbonne U. de Paris, Paris, 1962, Georgetown U., Washington, 1962, Am. U., Washington, 1966-68. Lic. real estate agt.; lic. gen. contractor, Md.; lic. ins. agt., Md., D.C. Enumerator, IBM computer operator U.S. Census Bur., Suitland, Md., 1950-51; clk. typist, claims div. VA, Washington, 1951-52; rsch. clk. Bur. Security and Consular Affairs, U.S. Dept. State, Washington, 1952-53, supr. passport processing sect., 1953-56, from jr. to sr. adjudicator domestic adjudication div., 1956-61, consular affairs officer adv. opinions div., 1961-63, chief pvt. bill staff, office of dep. dir. for ops., 1963-68, chief fraud and investigation unit, 1968-72; adjudicator, gen. cons., 1972—; editor-in-chief The Washington Press, 1957-63; founder, dir. Mut. Fund Investment Program for Govt. Employees, Washingotn, 1969-73; instr. Tennis U. Pubela (Mex.), 1973-75; editor-in-chief The Annapolis (Md.) Press, 1989—; chmn. ad hoc com. to repeal the utilities tax, Annapolis, 1992—. Contbr. articles to profl. jours; grantee hub cap locking device. Treas. Annapolis City Dem. Ctrl. Com., 1992, 97; Dem. candidate for mayor, Annapolis, 1993, 97; chmn. trans. adv. bd., Annapolis, 1992-98. Recipient Cert. of Disting. Citizenship, City of Annapolis, 1987, 97, Gov.'s Citation for Outstanding Svc. to Citizens, State of Md., 1997, Red Cross Citizenship award, Trailblazer award U.S. Dept. State, 1998; numerous meritorious svc. awards; Howard U. scholar. Home: 16 Bausum Dr Annapolis MD 21401-4309

JONES, TAYLOR BURNETT, cartoonist; b. Mineola, N.Y., Dec. 10, 1952; s. Scholten Burnett and Barbara (Heisler) J.; m. Ellen Margaret Palm, Dec. 30, 1986; 1 child, Maya Lin. BA, Cornell Coll., 1974. Intern Delta Dem.-Times, Greenville, Miss., 1974; cartoonist Charleston (W.Va.) Gazette, 1974-81; freelancer N.Y., 1982-89, Augusta, Ga., 1989-98, S.I., N.Y., 1998—; syndicated cartoonist L.A. Times Syndicate, 1977—; cartoonist El Nuevo Dia, San Juan, P.R., 1986—. Author, illustrator: Add-Verse to Presidents, 1982; illustrator, designer: (series) How to Talk Baseball, 1983, 87, How to Talk Football, 1984, 86, How to Talk Golf, 1985, 99; illustrator (weekly polit. column) "Washington Whispers", U.S. News and World Report, 1989-94. Recipient Spl. award The Gong Show, 1977. Mem. Soc. Illustrators, Nat. Cartoonists Soc., Assn. Am. Editl. Cartoonists. Avocations: birdwatching, mapmaking.

JONES, TED C(OOKE), distance learning educator; b. Clarksville, Tenn., Dec. 1, 1947; s. Charles R. and Martha L. (Norris) J. B in Music Edn., Fla. State U., 1969; MA in Comm., Austin Peay State U., 1990; PhD in Mass Comm., U. Ala., 1995. Program coord. Intercampus Interactive Telecom. Sys. U. Ala. Sys., Tuscaloosa, 1992-94; assoc. prof. speech, comm. and theatre Austin Peay State U., Clarksville, Tenn., 1994—; dir. distance learning activities Austin Peay State U., Clarksville, 1995-96; distance edn. com. Tenn. Bd. Regents, Nashville, 1994-96; co-chair Middle Tenn. Telecom. Alliance, 1995-96.

JONES, TERESA A., college official; b. Shreveport, La., July 24, 1962; d. T.J. and Earnestine (Moon) J. BS, Grambling State U., 1980, MPA, 1993. Customer svc. rep. Cablevision of Shreveport, 1981-85; fin. aid adminstr. Grambling (La.) State U., 1985-93; grants acct. Tex. Coll., Tyler, 1995; fin. aid dir. LeMoyne-Owen Coll., Memphis, 1993-95, registrar, 1996—. Mem. So. Assn. Coll. Registrars and Admissions Officers, Tenn. Assn. Coll. Registrars and Admissions Officers, Alpha Kappa Alpha. Democrat. Mem. Disciples of Christ Ch. Avocations: reading, computer games, puzzles. Office: LeMoyne-Owen Coll 807 Walker Ave Memphis TN 38126-6510

JONES, TERRY, film director, author; b. Colwyn Bay, Wales, Feb. 1, 1942; s. Alick George Parry and Dilys Louisa (Newnes) J.; m. Alison Telfer; children: Sally, Bill. Student, St. Edmund Hall, Oxford U. Writer, performer (TV program) Monty Python's Flying Circus; co-author: (TV play) Secrets, Ripping Yarns; co-dir. (film) Monty Python and the Holy Grail; dir. (films) Monty Python's Life of Brian, Monty Python's The Meaning of Life (Cannes Internat. Film Festival Grand Prize), Personal Services, 1986; dir. (TV series) The Chronicles of Young Indiana Jones, 1991; writer, dir. Erik the Viking, 1989, The Wind in the Willows, 1996; author: Chaucer's Knight, 1980, rev. edit., 1994, Fairy Tales, 1981, The Saga of Erik the Viking, 1983, Nicobobinus, 1985, Goblins of the Labyrinth, 1986, The Curse of the Vampire's Socks, 1988, Attacks of Opinion, 1988; presenter, co-author: (book and TV program) Crusades, 1994; co-author: Dr. Fegg's Nasty Book of Knowledge, Ripping Yarns, 1978, More Ripping Yarns, 1980, Fantastic Stories, 1992, Lady Cottington's Pressed Fairy Book, 1994, The Goblin Companion, 1996, The Knight and the Squire, 1997; presenter, co-author (TV program) So This Is Progress, 1991, Ancient Inventions. Offices: Creative Artists Agy c/o Ken Stovitz 9830 Wilshire Blvd Beverly Hills CA 90212-1804*

JONES, THERESE M., special education educator; b. Newport, Vt., Nov. 19, 1950; d. Paul Joseph and Ella H. (Meunier) Messier; m. Wayne Thomas Jones, July 22, 1972; children: Wallace Clifford, Wayne Paul. BS in Elem. Edn., U. Conn., 1972; MS in Elem. Edn., Ctrl. Conn. State U., 1989; MA in Spl. Edn., St. Joseph Coll., 1993; 6th yr. edn. leadership, So. Conn. State U., 1998. Cert. elem. tchr., Conn., spl. edn. tchr., Conn. Substitute Toffolon Sch., Plainville, Conn., 1982-84; tchr. grade 1 St. Dominic Sch., Southington, Conn., 1984-88; spl. edn. classroom tutor Linden St. Sch., Plainville, Conn., 1988-90; spl. edn. resource tchr. Southwest Sch., Torrington, Conn., 1991—; presenter in field. Mem. Coun. Exceptional Children, Assn. Supervision and Curriculum Devel.

JONES, THOMAS F., protective services official; b. Atlantic City, N.J., Dec. 14, 1940. BA, Southeastern U., 1968. From agent to spl. agent in charge FBI, Cleve., 1963-95; ret., 1995; chief of police Cleve. Clinic Found., 1997—. Office: Police Dept Cleve Clinic Found 9500 Euclid Ave Cleveland OH 44195-0001*

JONES, THOMAS OWEN, computer industry executive; b. Phila., Apr. 6, 1932; s. Paul John and Katharine (McCahey) J.; m. Mary Louise Russell, Sept. 19, 1959 (div. Aug. 1979); children: SusanR., Thomas H., Andrew S. BS in Engring., U. Pa., 1954, MBA, 1958. Account mgr. IBM Corp., Phila., 1958-66; asst. to sec. HEW, Washington, 1966-67; v.p. Donaldson, Lufkin & Jenrette, Inc., N.Y.C., 1967-72; pres. Jones/Hosplex Sys., N.Y.C., 1973-84, Carnegie-Madison Inc., N.Y.C., 1984-87, Fifth Generation Computer Corp., N.Y.C., 1987—, Golden Enterprises, Inc., Melbourne, Fla., 1999—; cons. to sec. HEW, Washington, 1967-68; mem. Edn. Commr.'s Adv. Coun. on Copyright Policy, Washington, 1967-70. Mem. N.Y. State Adv. Coun. on Edn., Albany, 1970-75; mem. N.Y.C. #4 Cmty. Planning Bd., 1973-75. With U.S. Army, 1954-56. White House fellow U.S. Commn. on White House Fellows, Washington, 1966-67; named Outstanding Young Man of the Main Line, Jr. C. of C., Bryn Mawr, Pa., 1966. Mem. IEEE, N.Y. Acad. Scis., N.Y. Athletic Club, Union League Club Phila., Wharton Alumni Assocs. (exec. bd. 1993—), Am. Legion. Avocations: tennis, travel. Office: Fifth Generation Computer Corp 232 E 68th St New York NY 10021-6001

JONES, THOMAS RAWLES, JR., federal judge; b. 1948. JD, U. Va., 1973. Law clk. to Hon. Albert V. Bryan, Jr. U.S. Dist. Ct. (ea. dist.) Va., 1973-74; asst. commonwealth atty. Commonwealth of Va., 1974-81; ptnr. Cohen, Dunn & Sinclair; magistrate judge U.S. Dist. Ct. (ea. dist.) Va., Alexandria, 1994—. Office: 401 Courthouse Sq Alexandria VA 22314

JONES, THOMAS ROBERT, social worker; b. Escanaba, Mich., Jan. 3, 1950; s. Gene Milton and Alica Una (Mattson) J.; m. Joy Sedlock. BA, U. Laverne, 1977; MSW, U. Hawaii, 1979. Social work assoc. Continuing Care

Svcs., Camarillo, Calif., 1973-78; psychiat. social worker Camarillo State Hosp., 1980-84; psychotherapist Terkensha Child Treatment Ctr., Sacramento, Calif., 1984-86; psychiat. social worker Napa (Calif.) State Hosp., 1986-87; psychiat. social worker Vets. Home Calif., Yountville, 1987-98, chief of social work svc., 1998—. Mem. Nat. Assn. Social Workers, Soc. Clin. Social Work, Acad. Cert. Social Workers. Avocations: creative writing, reading, meditation, classical music. Home: PO Box 1095 Yountville CA 94599-1095 Office: Vets Home Calif Yountville CA 94599

JONES, THOMAS WALTER, astrophysics educator, researcher; b. Odessa, Tex., June 22, 1945; s. Theodore Sydney and LaVerne Gertrude (Neis) J.; m. Karen Gay Cronquist, June 15, 1968; 1 child, Walter Brian. B.S. in Physics, U. Tex., 1967; M.S. in Physics, U. Minn., 1969, Ph.D. in Physics, 1972. Asst. physicist U. Calif., San Diego, 1972-75; asst. scientist Nat. Radio Astronomy Obs., Charlottesville, Va., 1975-77; asst. prof. dept. astronomy U. Minn., Mpls., 1977-80, assoc. prof., 1980-84, prof., 1984—, chmn. dept. astronomy, 1981-97. Contbr. articles to profl. jours. Mem. Am. Astron. Soc., Royal Astron. Soc., Internat. Astron. Union, Sigma Xi. Home: 1534 Iowa Ave W Saint Paul MN 55108-2127 Office: U Minn Dept Astronomy 116 Church St SE Minneapolis MN 55455-0149

JONES, THOMAS WILLIAM, secondary education educator, consultant; b. Charleroi, Pa., Mar. 13, 1952; s. Frank Jr. and Margaret (Powk) J.; m. Daryl Vernau, Mar. 13, 1975; children: Joshua Thomas, Gwynenn Taylor. BS in Edn., California (Pa.) U., 1974, MS in Earth Sci., 1982, MEd, 1990; postgrad., Indiana U. of Pa., 1996—. Tchr. elem. sch. Rockwood (Pa.) Sch. Dist., 1974-82, tchr. secondary sch., 1982—, acting adminstr., 1989-90; assoc. dir. Bus./Edn. Partnerships, U. Pitts. at Johnstown, 1992—; owner DEC Cons. Svcs., Pa., Highland Computers, Pa.; environ. cons. Allegheny Mountain Rsch., Berlin, 1986-88; instr. Appalachia Intermediate Unit 08, Ebensburg, Pa., 1987-89; edn. cons. ERB Cons., Berlin, 1990—; owner DEC Cons. and Webmaster Svcs. Author curriculum materials, ednl. materials. Officer Rotary Internat., Meyersdale, Pa., 1984-87; organizer Casselman Watershed Assn., Rockwood, 1988, Cen. Pa. Sci. Alliance, Ebensburg, 1989; county organizer, Skywarn vol. NOAA-Nat. Weather Svc., Pitts., 1989—; vol. Pa. Dept. Conservation and Natural Resources, 1998. Recipient Equipment award Spectroscopy Soc. Pitts., 1991, Participant award U.S. Dept. Energy (STRIVE), 1992. Mem. ASCD (internat. network for sci., facilitator 1992-94), NSTA, Nat. Assn. Ptnrs. in Edn., Mid-Atlantic Consortium for Math. and Sci. Edn. (steering com. 1994-95, co-chair 1995-96, chair Pa. Eisenhower state team), Alliance for Tchg. of Sci. (chmn., pres. 1989—, network facilitator 1992-92, PSTA convestion publicity chmn. 1991, tech. chair, internet developer), Nat. Parks Conservancy, Gamma Theta Upsilon, Phi Kappa Theta. Republican. Avocations: martial arts, woodworking. Home: 700 Diamond St Berlin PA 15530-1519 Office: Univ Pitts Johnstown 110 Biddle Hall Johnstown PA 15904

JONES, THORNTON KEITH, research chemist; b. Brawley, Calif., Dec. 17, 1923; s. Alfred George and Madge Jones; m. Evalee Vestal, July 4, 1965; children: Brian Keith, Donna Eileen. BS, U. Calif., Berkeley, 1949, postgrad., 1951-52. Research chemist Griffin Chem. Co., Richmond, Calif., 1949-55; western product devel. and improvement mgr. Nopco Chem. Co., Richmond, Calif., 1955; research chemist Chevron Research Co., Richmond, 1956-65, research chemist in spl. products research and devel., 1965-1982; product quality mgr. Chevron USA, Inc., San Francisco, 1982-87, ret. Patentee in field. Vol. fireman and officer, Terra Linda, Calif., 1957-64; mem. adv. com. Terra Linda Dixie Elem. Sch. Dist., 1960-64. Served with Signal Corps, U.S. Army, 1943-46. Mem. Am. Chem. Soc., Forest Products Research Soc., Am. Wood Preservers Assn., Alpha Chi Sigma. Republican. Presbyterian. Avocations: music, gardening, wine and food.

JONES, TIMOTHY MARK, graphic designer, painter; b. Washington, May 20, 1969; s. William Harry and Susan (Dorfman) J. Student, Brandeis U., 1987-89; BFA, Tufts U./Sch. Mus. Fine Arts, Boston, 1993. Art dir. Inner Tradition Press, Rochester, Vt., 1993-97; prodn. mgr., designer Steerforth Press, South Royalton, Vt., 1997—. Home: RR 1 Box 10 South Royalton VT 05068-9701 Office: 105 Chelsea St # 106 South Royalton VT 05068-9800

JONES, TOM, track and field coach; m. Sandy Jones; children: Sean, Chris. B.Phys. Edn., UCLA, 1969; M.Phys. Edn., U. Wash., 1971. Tchr., coach Metter (Ga.) H.S., 1971-72, Forest Park (Ga.) Sr. H.S., 1972-74, Mainland Sr. H.S., Daytona Beach, Fla., 1974-75, Chamberlain Sr. H.S., Tampa, Fla., 1975-76; asst. coach U. Ala., 1976-78; head coach N.C. State U., 1978-84, U. Tex., El Paso, 1984-88, Ariz. State U., 1988-92; head coach track and field U. fla., Gainesville, 1992—; mem. USA Track & Field's exec. com., bd. dirs., 1988—; U.S. head men's coach 1988 U.S. vs. Gt. Britain meet; head coach U.S. Olympic Festival South team, 1985, 87. With U.S. Army. Named NCAA Men's Coach of the Yr. (Dist. 3), 1984, Indoor Coach of the Yr. (Dist. 7), 1986, Women's Coach of the Yr. (Dist. 8), 1990, Divsn. I Women's Indoor Coach of the Yr., 1997, Divsn. I Women's Outdoor Coach of the Yr., 1997, Dist. 3 Coach of the Yr., 1997, numerous SEC awards; inductee Helms Athletic Hall of Fame. Office: Univ Florida PO Box 14485 Gainesville FL 32604-2485*

JONES, TOMMY LEE, actor; b. San Saba, Tex., Sept. 15, 1946; s. Clyde L. and Lucille Marie (Scott) J.; m. Kimberlea Gayle Cloughley, May 30, 1981. B.A. cum laude in English, Harvard U., 1969. Broadway debut in A Patriot for Me, 1969; other stage appearances include Fortune and Men's Eye's, 1969, Four on a Garden, 1971, Blue Boys, 1972, Ulysses in Nighttown, 1974, True West, 1981; film debut in Love Story, 1970; other film appearances include Eliza's Horoscope, 1972, Life Study, 1972, Jackson County Jail, 1976, Rolling Thunder, 1977, The Betsy, 1978, Eyes of Laura Mars, 1978, Coal Miner's Daughter, 1980, Back Roads, 1981, Nate and Hayes, 1983, River Rat, 1984, Black Moon Rising, 1986, The Big Town, 1987, Stormy Monday, 1988, The Package, 1989, Fire Birds, 1990, JFK, 1991 (Acad. award nominee), Under Siege, 1992, The Fugitive, 1993 (Golden Globe award for best supporting actor 1994, Acad. award for best supporting actor 1993), House of Cards, 1993, Heaven and Earth, 1993, Blown Away, 1994, The Client, 1994, Natural Born Killers, 1994, Blue Sky, 1994, Cobb, 1994, Batman Forever, 1995, Men in Black, 1997, Volcano, 1997, U.S. Marshals, 1997, (voice) Small Soldiers, 1998, Rules of Engagement, 1999, Double Jeopardy, 1999; TV movies include Smash-Up on Interstate 5, 1976, Charlie's Angels, 1976, The Amazing Howard Hughes, 1977, The Rainmaker, 1982, The Executioner's Song (Emmy award), 1982, The Park is Mine, 1985, Yuri Nosenko, KGB, 1986, Broken Vows, 1987, Stranger on My Land, 1988, April Morning, 1988, Gotham, 1988, The Good Old Boys, 1995; appeared in TV miniseries, Lonesome Dove, 1989. *

JONES, TRACEY KIRK, JR., minister, educator; b. Boston, Mar. 16, 1917; s. Tracey Kirk and Marion (Flowers) J.; m. Martha Clayton, Sept. 12, 1942 (dec. June 1975); children: Judith Grace Watson, Tracey Kirk Jones, III, Deborah Anita Jones Breitenbach; m. Junia K. Moss, July 1, 1978. B.A., D.D., Ohio Wesleyan U.; B.D., Yale Div. Sch., 1942. Ordained to ministry Meth. Church, 1945; missionary Meth. Ch., China, 1946-50, Malaya, 1952-55; exec. bd. mission Meth. Ch., 1955; exec. sec. S.E. Asia, 1955-62; assoc. gen. sec. div. world missions, 1962-64, assoc. gen. sec. world div., 1964-68, gen. sec. bd. missions, 1968-72, gen. sec. bd. global ministries, 1972-80; adj. prof. Drew Theol. Sch., Madison, N.J., 1980-89; mem. governing bd. Nat. Coun. Chs., 1st v.p., 1978-80. Author: Our Mission Today, 1963. Home: 700 John Ringling Blvd Apt W308 Sarasota FL 34236-1588

JONES, TREVOR OWEN, biomedical products and automobile supply company executive, management consultant; b. Maidstone, Kent, Eng., Nov. 3, 1930; came to U.S., 1957, naturalized, 1971; s. Richard Owen and Ruby Edith (Martin) J.; m. Jennie Lou Singleton, Sept. 12, 1959; children: Pembroke Robinson (dec.), Bronwyn Elizabeth. Higher Nat. Cert. in Elec. Engring., Aston Tech. Coll., Birmingham, Eng., 1952; Ordinary Nat. Cert. in Mech. Engring., Liverpool (Eng.) Tech. Coll., 1957. Registered profl. engr., Wis.; chartered engr., U.K. Student engr., elec. machine design engr. Brit. Gen. Electric Co., 1950-57; project engr., project mgr. Nuc. Ship Savannah, Allis-Chalmers Mfg. Co., 1957-59; with GM, 1959-78, staff engr. in charge Apollo computers, 1967, dir. electronic control sys., 1970-72, dir. advanced product engring., 1972-74; dir. GM Proving Grounds, 1974-78; v.p. engring., automotive worldwide TRW Inc., Cleve., 1978-80, v.p. transp. electronics group, 1980-87; chmn. bd. dirs. Libbey-Owens-Ford Inc., 1987-94; chmn., CEO Internat. Devel. Corp., 1987—; from vice chmn. to chmn. Echlin Inc., 1995-98, chmn. bd. dirs., interim pres. and CEO, 1997; chmn., CEO Biomec Inc., 1998—; vice chmn. Motor Vehicle Safety Adv. Coun., 1971; chmn. Nat. Hwy. Safety Adv. Com., 1976. Author, patentee automotive safety and electronics. Trustee Lawrence Inst. Tech., 1973-76; mem. exec. bd. Clinton Valley coun. Boy Scouts Am., 1975; mem. bd. govs. Cranbrook Inst. Sci., 1977; mem. Sec. of Def. Def. Sci. Bd. Task Force on Internat. Arms Devel. Cooperation, 1995-98. Officer Brit. Army, 1955-57. Recipient Safety award for engrg. excellence U.S. Dept. Transp., 1978. Fellow Brit. Instn. Elec. Engrs. (Hooper Mem. prize 1950), IEEE (life, exec. com. vehicle tech. soc. 1977-81), Soc. Automotive Engrs. (Arch T. Colwell paper award 1974, 75, Vincent Bendix Automotive Electronics award 1976, Edward N. Cole award 1988), Engring. Soc. Detroit; mem. NAE, Engring. Soc. Cleve., Union Club, Kirtland Country Club, Bloomfield Hills Country Club. Republican. Episcopalian. Home: Two Bratenahl Pl Bratenahl OH 44108 also: 3971 Gulf Shore Blvd N Apt 1501 Naples FL 34103-2105 *Innovation and the acceptance of change are fundamental seeds of progress, and only hard work and an open mind will permit you to harvest its fruits.*

JONES, TRINA WOOD, special education educator; b. Murfreesboro, N.C.; d. James Elton I and Sarah Virginia (Bishop) Wood; 1 child, Ashleigh Erin. BA in Early Childhood Edn., N.C. Cen. U., 1977, MEd in Mental Retardation, 1978. Educator Granville County Pub. Schs., Stovall, N.C., 1978-81, Norfolk (Va.) Pub. Schs., 1981-84, Chgo. Pub. Schs., 1984—. Mem. Coun. for Exceptional Children. Avocations: coin and stamp collector, writing, reading, travel. Home: 5230 S Cornell Ave Chicago IL 60615-4200 Office: Jackie Robinson Elem Sch 4225 S Lake Park Ave Chicago IL 60653-3017

JONES, VERNON DALE, educator; b. Dec. 5, 1955. BS in Aero. Engring., USAF Acad., 1979; MBA in Mgmt., Wright State U., 1982; MA in Internat. Affairs, George Washington U., 1990; PhD in Pub. Adminstrn., Syracuse U., 1995. Engr., def. analyst Pentagon, Washington, 1980-87; aide to Pres. Reagan White House, Washington, 1987-88; pub. policy rschr. Syracuse (N.Y.) U., 1992-95; assoc. prof. USAF Acad., Colorado Springs, Colo., 1995—. Home: 15919 Longmeadow Ln Colorado Springs CO 80921

JONES, VIRGINIA MCCLURKIN, social worker; b. Anniston, Ala., Mar. 13, 1935; d. Louie Walter and Virginia Keith (Beaver) McClurkin; m. Charles Miller Jones Jr., Mar. 16, 1957; children: Charles Miller III, V. Grace. BA, Agnes Scott Coll., 1957; M.A., U. Tenn., 1965, MS in Social Work, 1979. Instr. English, U. Tenn., Knoxville, 1967-71; religious edn. dir. Oak Ridge Unitarian Ch., 1972-73, 76-78; co-owner, mgr. The Bookstore, 1973-76; instr. English, Roane State Community Coll., 1975-80; pvt. practice clin. social work, Oak Ridge, 1980—; cons. Mountain Community Health Ctr., Coalfield, Tenn., 1980-83, Valley Ridge Hospice, 1987-89. Mem. Nat. Assn. Social Workers, Oak Ridge Ministerial Assn., Knoxville Area Agnes Scott Alumnae (pres.), Univ. Club, Concord Yacht Club, Rotary. Democrat. Episcopalia. Contbr. articles to newspapers. Office: 1345 Oak Ridge Tpke # 358 Oak Ridge TN 37830-6446

JONES, WALTER BEAMAN, JR., congressman; b. Pitt County, N.C., Feb. 10, 1943; m. Joe Anne Jones; 1 child. BA in History, Atlantic Christian Coll., 1967. Mgr. Walter B. Jones Office Supply Co., 1967-73; salesman Dunn Assoc., 1973-82; pres. Benefit Reserves, Inc., 1989-94, Judson Co., 1990-94; rep. N.C. Ho. of Reps., 1983-92; mem. 104th Congress from 3d N.C. dist., 1995—. Republican. Office: US House Reps 422 Cannon Bldg Ofc Bldg Washington DC 20515-3303

JONES, WALTER DEAN, community program director; b. Rockport, Ind., May 14, 1938; s. Kenneth Walter and Marjorie Lucille (Leonard) J.; m. Alice Dorothy Boger, May 21, 1966; 1 child, Julie Dean. BS in Agr., Purdue U., 1961; MS in Community Devel., U. Louisville, 1970. Farmer with Jones Feed Svc., Grandview, Ind., 1955-65; exec. dir. Lincoln Hills Devel. Corp., Tell City, 1965-73; county extension dir. Purdue U., LaGrange, 1973-76, Vincennes, 1976-80; area community devel. agt. Purdue U., Ft. Wayne, 1980-83; county extension dir. Purdue U., Lake County, Ind., 1983—; treas. Lake County Econ. Devel. Authority, Highland, 1984-92; pres. Lake County Parks and Recreation Bd., Crown Point, 1990-91, 97-98; coord. Lake County Community Devel., Crown Point, 1983—. Editorial adv. com.: The Times (Hammond, Ind.); contbr. articles to profl. jours. Mem. Lake County Libr. Found., Merrillville, 1986, pres., 1988, 89; pres. Lake County Planning Commn., 1992, 99; bd. dirs. Leadership Northwest Ind., sec. 1992, treas., 1996—; mem. Borman Beautification Task Force; bd. dirs. Drifting Dunes coun. Girl Scouts U.S.A., 1998—. With U.S. Army, 1961-63. Recipient Achievement award Nat. Assn. County Agrl. Agts., 1981. Mem. Ind. Extension Agts. Assn. (pres. 1989), Ind. Agrl. and CD Agts. (pres. 1988), Ind. Community Devel. Soc., Crown Point Rotary Club (pres. 1995-96), Epsilon Sigma Phi, Gamma Sigma Delta. Office: Lake County Coop Ext 2293 N Main St Crown Point IN 46307-1885

JONES, WALTER EDWARD, communications executive; b. Atlanta, Apr. 8, 1951; s. Walter B. and Jean S. (Sumner) J.; m. Luann Bailey, Sept. 21, 1974; children: Anna Christine, Abigail Louise. BBA in Econs., Oglethorpe U., 1977; MBA in Fin., Mercer U., 1983. With So. Bell Telephone, Atlanta, 1972-79, sales, coord. mktg. and sales edn. and tng., 1979-82; divestiture transition staff AT&T, Atlanta, 1982-83; program dir. AT&T Ctr. for Exec. Edn., Columbus, Ga., 1983-85; sales, tech. and customer svc. mgr. AT&T, Nashville, 1985-86; pres. Exec. Edn. and Mgmt., Atlanta, 1987-97; v.p. strategic comms. Caribiner Internat., Inc., Atlanta, 1997-98; sr. v.p. consulting rsch. and measurement svcs. Right Source, Inc. divsn. Caribiner Internat., Atlanta, 1998—; owner, v.p. Clock Svcs., Inc., Atlanta, 1977—. Mem. adv. bd. Ctr. Info. Comm. Scis. Ball State U., Muncie, Ind., 1986—, Fellow of Yr., 1987; mem. sch. bd. Mt. Carmel Christian Sch., Atlanta, 1992-96, chmn., 1995. Mem. Nat. Assn. Watch and Clock Collectors, U.S. Distance Learning Assn., Ga. Motortrucking Assn. (bd. dirs. 1981). Avocations: antique automobiles, clocks, boats. Office: Cabiner Internat Inc 763 Trabert Ave NW Atlanta GA 30318-4231

JONES, WALTER HARRISON, chemist, educator; b. Griffin, Sask., Can., Sept. 21, 1922; s. Arthur Frederick and Mildred Tracy (Walter) J.; BS with honors, UCLA, 1944, PhD in Chemistry, 1948; m. Marion Claire Twomey, Oct. 25, 1959 (dec. Jan. 1976); m. Dorothy-Lynne Byrne, 1979 (div. 1981, remarried 1994). Rsch. chemist Dept. Agr., 1948-51, Los Alamos Sci. Lab., 1951-54; sr. rsch. engr. N.Am. Aviation, 1954-56; mgr. chemistry dept. Ford Motor Co., 1956-60; sr. staff and program mgr., chmn. JANAF-ARPA-NASA Thermochem. panel Inst. Def. Analyses, 1960-63; head propulsion dept. Aerospace Corp., 1963-64; sr. scientist, head advanced tech. Hughes Aircraft Co., 1964-68; prof. aero. systems, dir. Corpus Christi Center, U. West Fla., Pensacola, 1969-75, prof. chemistry, 1975-95; vis. rsch. chemist UCLA, 1994—; vis. prof. U. Toronto, 1979, 92, U. Queensland 1998; cons. pvt., fed. and state agys. Mem. Gov.'s Task Force on Energy, Regional Energy Action Com., Fla. State Energy Office, adv. com. Tampa Bay Regional Planning Coun.; judge regional and state sci. fairs. Fed. and state grantee; rsch. corp. grantee; Fellow ASEE/ONR, NATO, Am. Inst. Chemists; mem. AIAA, AAUP, AAAS, Am. Astron. Soc. (propulsion com.), Am. Chem. Soc. (chmn. Pensacola sect.), N.Y. Acad. Scis., Am. Phys. Soc., Internat. Solar Energy Soc., Combustion Inst. World Assn. Theoretical Organic Chemists, Am. Ordnance Assn., Air Force Assn., Philos. Soc. Washington, Pensacola C. of C., Phi Beta Kappa, Sigma Xi (pres. local chpt.), Pi Mu Epsilon, Phi Lambda Upsilon (sec. local chpt.), Alpha Mu Gamma, Alpha Chi Sigma (pres. local chpt.). Author: (fiction) Prisms in the Pentagon, 1971; contbr. numerous articles tech. jours., chpts. in books. Patentee in field. Home and office: 355 Calle Loma Norte Santa Fe NM 87501-1256

JONES, WALTON LINTON, internist, former government official; b. McCaysville, Ga., Dec. 4, 1918; s. Walton Linton and Pearl Josephine (Gilliam) J.; m. Caroline Wells Schachte, June 5, 1943; children—Walton Linton III, Francis Stephen, Kathleen Caroline. B.S., Emory U., 1939, M.D., 1942. Diplomate Am. Bd. Preventive Medicine. Commd. lt. (j.g.) U.S. Navy, 1942, advanced through grades to capt., 1956; rotating intern U.S. Naval Hosp., Charleston, S.C., 1942-43, aerospace medicine, 1944; flight surgeon USMC Aircraft Squadrons, 1944-47; head aero. med. safety Navy Dept., 1947-53; sr. med. officer U.S.S. Randolph, 1953-55; dir. aero. med. ops. and equipment Bur. Medicine and Surgery, Navy Dept., 1955-64; dir. biotech. and human research div. NASA, 1964-66; ret. U.S. Navy, 1966; civilian dir. biotech and human research div. NASA, Washington, 1966-70, dep., dir. life scis., 1970-75, dir. occupational medicine, 1975-82, dir. occupational health, 1982-85; cons. aerospace medicine, 1985—; mem. exec. com. hearing and bioacoustics Nat. Acad. Scis., 1964-85, chmn., 1970, mem. exec. com. on vision, 1964-85; Kober lectr. Georgetown U., 1968. Leader, mem. com. Nat. Capital Area council Boy Scouts Am., Falls Church, Va., 1956-64. Decorated Legion of Merit; recipient Exceptional Service medal NASA, 1979, Outstanding Leadership medal NASA, 1985. Fellow Aerospace Medicine Assn. (Bauer award 1970, pres. 1980), AIAA (assoc., recipient John Jeffries award 1970), Royal Soc. Health; mem. Internat. Astronautics Acad., Assn. Mil. Surgeons (Founders award 1956), Internat. Acad. Aerospace Medicine.

JONES, WAYNE ROSS, agronomist; b. Chenoa, Ill., July 14, 1925; g. Everett Elmer and Martha Elizabeth (Falkingham) J.; m. Myrtle (Dolly) Geissler, Apr. 26, 1947; children: Kathy, Keith, Connie. Grad., Arrowsmith (Ill.) H.S., 1944. Supt. tool design ITT Canon Electric, Santa Ana, Calif., 1959-68; mgr. ops. RDS Labs., Exeter, Calif., 1970-73; engring. and mfg. cons. Upright Harvester, Selma, Calif., 1974-75; owner, operator Sci. Agrl. Svcs., Inc., Napa, Calif., 1975—. Mem. NRA, Am. Soc. Agronomy, Am. Quarter Horse Assn., Crop Sci. Soc. Am., Soil Sci. Soc. Am. Republican. Avocation: hunting. Office: Sci Agrl Svcs Inc 3393 Atlas Peak Rd Napa CA 94558-9667

JONES, WILLIAM ALLEN, lawyer, entertainment company executive; b. Phila., Dec. 13, 1941; s. Roland Emmett and Gloria (Miller) J.; m. Margaret Smith, Sept. 24, 1965 (div. 1972); m. Dorothea S. Whitson, June 15, 1973; children—Darlene, Rebecca, Gloria, David. BA, Temple U., 1967; MBA, JD, Harvard U., 1972. Bar: Calif. 1974. Atty. Walt Disney Prodns., Burbank, Calif., 1973-77, treas., 1977-81; atty. Wyman Bautzer et al, L.A., 1981-83; atty. MGM/UA Entertainment Co., Culver City, 1983, v.p., gen. counsel, 1983-86; sr. v.p., corp. gen. counsel, sec. MGM/UA Communications Co., Culver City, Calif., 1986-91; exec. v.p., gen. counsel, sec. Metro-Goldwyn-Mayer Inc., Santa Monica, Calif., 1991-95, exec. v.p. corp. affairs, 1995-97, sr. exec. v.p., 1997—; bus. mgr. L.A. Bar Jour., 1974-75; bd. dirs. The Nostalgia Network Inc.; mem. bd. of govs. Inst. for Corp. Counsel, 1990-93. Charter mem. L.A. Philharm. Men's Com., 1974-80; trustee Marlborough Sch., 1988-93, Flintridge Preparatory Sch., 1993-96. With USAF, 1960-64. President's scholar Temple U., 1972. Mem. Harvard Bus. Sch. Assn. So. Calif. (bd. dirs. 1985-88). Home: 1557 Colina Dr Glendale CA 91208-2412 Office: Metro-Goldwyn-Mayer Inc 2500 Broadway Santa Monica CA 90404-3065

JONES, WILLIAM ANTHONY, artist, educator, illustrator; b. Raleigh, N.C., Feb. 12, 1958; s. Charles William and Elizabeth (Kennedy) J.; m. Deborah Grant, May 23, 1987; children: Lydia Lee, Samuel Allen, William Thomas. BA in Painting/Printmaking, St. Andrews Coll., 1980; MFA in Painting/Printmaking, La. Tech. U., 1982. Artist, designer Ingraham Time Products, Toastmaster, Inc., Laurinburg, N.C., 1982-86; illustrator, tchr. N.C., Fla., Conn., 1987-91; art instr. Ea. Conn. State U., Willimantic, 1991-97. Group shows include Fayetteville (N.C.) Mus. Art, 1980, 81, 82, Barnwell Art Ctr., Shreveport, La., 1981, 82, Masur Mus., Monroe, La., 1981, 82, Broussard Gallery, Baton Rouge, La., 1981, Ball State U. Art Gallery, Muncie, Ind., 1981, St. Tammany Art Assn., Covington, La., 1981, S.W. Tex. State U., San Marcos, 1981, La. Tech. Art Gallery, Ruston, 1982, Tom Peyton Meml., Alexandria, La., 1982, Nat. Acad. Galleries, N.Y.C., 1982, Pembroke (N.C.) State U. Gallery, 1982, Vardell Gallery, Laurinburg, N.C., 1982; group exhbns. include Silvermine Galleries, New Canaan, Conn., 1989, Slater Meml. Mus., Norwich, Conn., 1989, 90, Mus. Art, Sci. and Industry, Bridgeport, Conn., 1989, Artspace, New Haven, Conn., 1989, Mattatuck Mus., Waterbury, Conn., 1989, Art Space New Haven, Conn., 1989, Old State House, Hartford, 1991, Artworks Gallery, Hartford, 1992, Silvermine Galleries, 1992, Akus Gallery Willimantic, Conn., 1992, 93, 94, U. Maine, Presque Isle, 1993, 94, 95, 96, Conn. Commn. on Arts, Rocky Hill, 1995, Oklahoma Meml. Internat. Design, 1997; designer Conn./U.S. Quarter for U.S. Mint Edit., 1999. Avocations: tennis, maple sugaring, basketball. Home: 350 E Old Route 6 Hampton CT 06247-1423

JONES, WILL(IAM) (ARNOLD), writer, former newspaper columnist; b. Dover, Ohio, Jan. 29, 1924; s. Vinton W. and Eva M. (Ringheimer) J.; m. Ruth Hines Johnson, May 4, 1968; children by previous marriage—Judson D., Jeffrey B., Brinley W., Megan A., Snake C. Student, Ohio State U., 1942-45, U. Minn. Law Sch., 1945-46. Movie reviewer Tuscarawas County Republican News, Ohio, 1938-39; reporter Dover Daily Reporter, 1939-42, Columbus Citizen, Ohio, 1942-45; reporter Mpls. Tribune, 1945-47, entertainment and food columnist, 1947-84; creative cons., freelance writer advt. agencies 1962—. Author: cook book Wild in the Kitchen, 1961; also numerous articles. Founder S.H.A.M.E. Smokers, anti-smoking group, 1964. Served with USAAF, 1943. Home and Office: 2102 Cedar Lake Pky Minneapolis MN 55416-3616

JONES, WILLIAM AUGUSTUS, JR., retired bishop; b. Memphis, Jan. 24, 1927; s. William Augustus and Martha (Jones) J.; m. Margaret Loaring-Clark, Aug. 26, 1949; 4 children. B.A., Southwestern at Memphis, 1948; B.D., Yale U., 1951. Ordained priest Episcopal Ch., 1952; priest in charge Messiah Ch., Pulaski, Tenn., 1952-57; curate Christ Ch., Nashville, 1957-58; rector St. Mark Ch., LaGrange, Ga., 1958-65; asso. rector St. Luke Ch., Mountainbrook, Ala., 1965-66; dir. research So. region Assn. Christian Tng. and Service, Memphis, 1966-67; exec. dir. Assn. Christian Tng. and Service, 1968-72; rector St. John's, Johnson City, Tenn., 1972-75; bishop of Mo. St. Louis, 1975-93.

JONES, WILLIAM BENJAMIN, JR., electrical engineering educator; b. Fairburn, Ga., Sept. 17, 1924; s. William Benjamin and Katherine (Davenport) J.; m. Mary Pierce Hammond, Sept. 8, 1948; children: William Benjamin III, Katherine P., Joseph L. B.S., Ga. Inst. Tech., 1945, M.S., 1948, Ph.D., 1953. Mem. tech. staff Hughes Aircraft Co., Culver City, Calif., 1954-58; prof. elec. engring. Ga. Inst. Tech., 1958-67; prof. Tex. A&M U., 1967-90, head dept. elec. engring., 1967-84; vis. prof. U. Fla., 1984-85. Author: Introduction to Optical Fiber Communication Systems, 1987. Served with USNR, 1943-46. Mem. IEEE (sr. mem., editor transactions on communication systems 1960-61, chmn. communication tech. group 1966-67, mem. tech. activities bd. 1966-69, v.p. communications soc. 1972-73, chmn. elec. engring. dept. heads assn. 1983-84), Sigma Xi, Tau Beta Pi, Eta Kappa Nu. Home: 43 Hyalite Rd W Dahlonega GA 30533-3925

JONES, WILLIAM BOWDOIN, political scientist, retired diplomat, lawyer; b. L.A., May 2, 1928; s. William T. and LaValle (Bowdoin) J.; m. Joanne Fairchild Garland, June 27, 1953; children: Lisa, Stephanie, Walter. AB in Polit. Sci., UCLA, 1949; JD, U. So. Calif., 1952; postgrad., U. Southampton, Eng., 1949, Sch. Internat. Rels., U. So. Calif., 1955-60. Bar: Calif. 1953, U.S. Supreme Ct. 1964, D.C. 1968, U.S. Ct. Internat. Trade 1988. Pvt. practice law L.A., 1953-62; joined Fgn. Svc., Dept. State, Res., 1962-68, active svc., 1968-84; dep. dir. Office African Programs, 1964-67; dir. program analysis staff, 1967-68; dir. Office Program Devel. and Evaluation, 1968; dep. asst. sec. state for edn. and cultural affairs, 1969-73; chmn. U.S. del. to 17th Gen. Conf. UNESCO, Paris, 1972; permanent rep. minister Dept. State, 1973-77; mem. U.S. del. to European Ministers Edn. Conf., Bucharest, Rumania, 1973, Internat. Oceanographic Commn. Gen. Conf., Paris, 1973, 18th Gen. Conf. UNESCO, 1974; head U.S. del. Conf. on Cultural Policies, Africa, Accra, Ghana, 1975; mem. U.S. del., chmn. legal com. 19th Gen. Conf. UNESCO, Nairobi, Kenya, 1976; chmn. performance standards bds. U.S. Fgn. Svc., 1976; amb. to Haiti Port-au-Prince, 1977-80; diplomat-in-residence Hampton (Va.) Inst., 1980-81; with law of sea mgmt. ops. Dept. State, Washington, 1981-84, ret., 1984; Amb.-in-residence prof. U. Va., 1984-85; fellow Woodrow Wilson Found., Princeton (N.J.) U., 1986—; ptnr. law firm, 1989—; bd. dirs. Nat. Cap. Assn. UN, U.S. Coun. UN U.; disting. vis. prof. Pepperdine U., 1993-95, vis. prof., 1995; adj. prof. Hamden Sydney Coll., 1991-94, 97, amb.-in-residence, 1996-98; staff dir. subcom. on Western hemisphere affairs, fgn. affairs com. Ho. of Reps., 1987; White House del. to observe elections in Suriname, 1987; cons. internat. affairs, Washington, 1989. Chmn. exec. com. Am. Soc. African Culture, 1961-62; mem. L.A. World Affairs Coun., 1945-62; mem. pres.'s adv. coun. St. Mary's Coll., Md., 1988-94, mem. pres.' coun., 1989—, trustee Hampden-Sydney Coll., Va., 1992-95; bd. dirs. Ctr. for Excellence in Pub. Affairs, Hampden-Sydney Coll., 1998. Recipient Alumni Profl. Achievement award UCLA,

1978, Alumni Merit award U. So. Calif., 1980. Mem. ABA, Am. Acad. Polit. and Social Sci., Academia de Derecho Internacional, Am. Fgn. Svc. Assn., Assn. Black Am. Ambs. (bd. dirs. 1995), Internat. Club, Am. Club (Paris), Kappa Alpha Psi, Pi Sigma Alpha, Sigma Pi Phi Boule. Home and Office: 4807 17th St NW Washington DC 20011-3705 *As a Black American, I have always strongly resisted being stereotyped. My family for generations was well educated, with a tradition of excellence, pride and achievement. I have always felt I could compete with anyone and that I had a right to expect to achieve positions of highest authority. My advice is to stand on your own two feet. Work with determination to suceed.*

JONES, WILLIAM ERNEST, chemistry educator; b. Sackville, N.B., Can.; s. Frederick W. and Jennie E. (Tuttle) J.; m. Norma Florence McKinney Reid, Aug. 9, 1958; children: Mary Ellen E., Jennifer A.J., Sarah A.L., K. Martha M. B.Sc., Mt. Allison U., 1958, M.Sc., 1959; Ph.D., McGill U., 1963. Asst. prof. Dalhousie U., Halifax, N.S., 1962-68, assoc. prof., 1968-73; prof. chemistry Dalhousie U., Halifax, 1973-91, chmn. dept. chemistry, 1974-83; chmn. univ. senate Dalhousie U., Halifax, N.S., Can., 1983-89; prof. chemistry, dean of sci. Saint Mary's U., Halifax, N.S., Can., 1989-91; prof. chemistry, v.p. acad. affairs U. Windsor, Ont., Can., 1991-98, prof. chemistry, 1991—. Contbr. articles to profl. jours. Fellow Chem. Inst. Can.; mem. Can. Assn. Physicists, Spectroscopy Soc. Can., Sigma Xi. Home: 2555 St Patrick's Ave, Windsor, ON Canada N9E 3G5 Office: U Windsor, 401 Sunset Ave, Windsor, ON Canada N9B 3P4

JONES, WILLIAM KINZY, materials engineering educator; b. Miami, Fla., July 23, 1946; s. Harold Grover and Josephine (Kinzy) Jones; m. Sharon Mattingly, June 6, 1981; children: Kelli, Kinzy, Brent. BS, Fla. State U., 1967, MS, 1968; PhD, MIT, 1972. Mgr. engring. Cordis Corp., Miami, 1977-87; group head C.S. Draper Lab., Cambridge, Mass., 1972-77; assoc. prof. engring. Fla. Internat. U., Miami, 1987-91; prof., assoc. dean for rsch. Fla. Internat. U., Miami, 1991—; adv. bd. Nat. Elec. Packaging and Product Conf., Des Plaines, Ill., 1988—; cons. in field; chmn. advanced rsch. workshop NATO, 1994-95; gen. chair Internat. Microelectronics Conf., 1992, Multi-Chip Module Conf., 1995; tech. co-chair Electronic Packaging Conf., China, 1996, 98. Contbr. articles to profl. jours.; patentee in field. Recipient Rsch. award Fla. Internat. U., 1991. Fellow Internat. Soc. Hybrid Microelectronics (chmn. materials divsn. 1990, pres. 1992-93, v.p. membership 1998, Tech. Achievement Wagnon award 1991, Hughes award 1996); mem. IEEE (sr.). Republican. Home: 75550 Overseas Hwy # 534 Islamorada FL 33036-4005 Office: Fla Internat U University Park Campus Coll of Engring EAS-2441 Miami FL 33199

JONES, WILLIAM MCKENDREY, language professional, educator; b. Dothan, Ala., Sept. 19, 1927; s. William McKendrey and Margaret (Farmer) J.; m. Ruth Ann Roberts, Aug. 14, 1952; children: Margaret, Elizabeth, Bronwen. B.A., U. Ala., 1949, M.A., 1950; Ph.D., Northwestern U., 1953. Asst. prof. English Wis. State U., Eau Claire, 1953-55; asst. prof. U. Mich., Ann Arbor, 1955-59; mem. faculty U. Mo., Columbia, 1959—, prof. English, 1964-89, prof. emeritus, 1989—, assoc. dean Grad. Sch., 1966-68. Author: Stages of Composition, 1964, Form and Experience, 1969, Guide to Living Power, 1975, (with Ruth Ann Jones) Living in Love, 1976, Two Careers—One Marriage, 1980, Speaking Up in Church, 1977, The Present State of Scholarship in 16th Century Literature, 1978, Survival: A Manual on Manipulating, 1979, Protestant Romance, 1980, John Steinbeck, 1982. Served with U.S. Army, 1946-47. Folger Library summer fellow, 1955; U. Mo. distinguished prof., 1972. Home: 209 Russell Blvd Columbia MO 65203-1709 Office: U Mo Dept English Columbia MO 65211

JONES, WILLIAM RANDOLPH, history educator; b. Little Rock, Apr. 6, 1930; s. John Riley Jones and Jewell Esther Spears; m. Anne Steed, Nov. 13, 1960; childen: Anne, Brantley, Mark, Adam. AB in History and Lit., Harvard Coll., 1951; MA in History, Harvard U., 1952, PhD in History, 1958. Prof. Ga. State U., Atlanta, 1956-58, Coll. Charleston, S.C., 1958-59, Ohio Wesleyan U., Delaware, 1959-62, U. N.H., Durham, 1962-95, Armstrong Atlantic State U., Savannah, Ga., 1997—; cons. Testing Svc., Princeton, N.J., 1975-82; cons. in world history and silk road projects UNESCO, Paris, 1978-95; mem. seminar on legal history Columbia Law Sch., 1975-82; founder, co-dir. Internat. Conf. Group on China and Europe in the Middle Ages, 1988-95. Author: Relations of the Two Jurisdictions: Studies in Medieval and Renaissance History, 1970; contbr. articles to profl. jours. With U.S. Army, 1955-58. French Govt. fellow U. Paris, 1951, Fulbright fellow King's Coll., London U., 1958. Democrat. Home: 4 Lanier Rd Jekyll Island GA 31527 Office: History Dept Armstrong Atlantic State U Savannah GA 31419

JONES, WILLIAM REX, law educator; b. Murphysboro, Ill., Oct. 20, 1922; s. Cluade E. and Ivy P. (McCormick) J.; m. Miriam R. Lamy, Mar. 27, 1944; m. Gerri L. Haun, June 30, 1972; children: Michael Kimber, Jeanne Keats, Patricia Combs, Sally Instone, Kevin. B.S., U. Louisville, 1950; J.D., U. Ky., 1968; LL.M., U. Mich., 1970. Bar: Ky. 1969, Fla. 1969, Ind. 1971, U.S. Supreme Ct. 1976. Exec. v.p. Paul Miller Ford, Inc., Lexington, Ky., 1951-64; pres. Bill's Seat Cover Ctr., Inc., Lexington, Ky., 1952-65, Bill Jones Real Estate, Inc., Lexington, Ky., 1965-70; asst. prof. law Ind. U., Indpls., 1970-73, assoc. prof., 1973-75, prof., 1975-80; dean Salmon P. Chase Coll. Law, No. Ky. U., Highland Heights, 1980-85, prof., 1980-93, prof. emeritus, 1993—; vis. prof. Shepard Broad Law Ctr., Nova Southeastern U., Ft. Lauderdale, Fla., 1994-95; mem. Ky. Pub. Advocacy Commn., 1982-93, 97—, chmn., 1986-93. Author: Kentucky Criminal Trial Practice, 2d edit., 1991, Kentucky Criminal Trial Practice Forms, 2d edit., 1993. Served as 1st sgt. U.S. Army, 1940-44. Cook fellow U. Mich., 1969-70; W.G. Hart fellow Queen Mary Coll. U. London, 1985. Mem. ABA, Nat. Legal Aid and Defenders Assn., Nat. Dist. Attys. Assn., Order of Coif. Office: No Ky U Nunn Hall Highland Heights KY 41099-1400

JONES, WILLIAM RICHARD, database administrator; b. Morgantown, Ky., Sept. 27, 1952; s. James Edward Jones and Mahalia Jane (Kuykendall) Bratton; m. Marina del Pilar Lagario, Nov. 20, 1981. AA, Univ. State of N.Y., 1982, BS, 1984; student, U. Tenn., 1987-90. Cert. computer profl. Supr. radar work ctr. USS Midway (CV-41), Yokosuka, Japan, 1980-81; calibration technician Naval Oceanographic Facility, Ford Island, Hawaii, 1981-84; leading petty officer oe divsn. USS Cimarron (AO-177), Pearl Harbor, Hawaii, 1984-85; engring. assoc. Tenn. Valley Authority, Chattanooga, 1986-90, programmer analyst, 1990-92, database administr., 1992-95; open systems product support rep. BMC Software, Inc., Austin, Tex., 1995-98; database adminstr. Acxiom Corp., Little Rock, 1998—; tchg. asst. ZD Net Univ. on Compuserve, 1996. Cert. database adminstr. Team leader web page regional judging team Info. Superhighway Competition sponsored by Blacks in Govt. and The Alliance of Black Tech. Orgns. Recipient Ednl. & Rsch. Found. Essay Scholar Mensa, 1988, Grosswirth-Salny Essay Scholar, Magellan Web Page design award. Mem. Internet Soc., Webmasters Guild, HyperText Markup Lang. Writer's Guild, Nat. Tech. Assn., Assn. for Computing Machinery, Black Data Processing Assocs., Am. Numis. Assn., Intertel, Tenn. State Numis. Soc., Am. Mensa Ltd., Am. Legion. Republican. Avocations: authoring and administering web pages on the Internet, numismatics, reading, authoring and maintaining web pages for non-profit Afro-Centric organizations. Home: 1420 Breckenridge Dr Apt 27 Little Rock AR 72227-4825 Office: Acxiom Corp Bldg E011 301 Industrial Blvd Conway AR 72032

JONES, YVONNE DOLORES, social worker; b. Ft. Knox, Ky., Mar. 13, 1955; d. Earl and Mary Blue (Preston) J.; m. Hezekiah Corppetts, Feb. 1, 1990. AA, U. Md., 1981, BS in Sociology, 1982; MSW, Our Lady of the Lake U., San Antonio, 1984; Diploma in fashion, merchandising, secretarial, Coll. of Hampton Roads, Newport News, Va., 1973,74. Lic. clin. social worker, Tenn., Miss., Ark., Tex., diplomate clin. social work. Enlisted U.S. Army, 1978-84; med. specialist U.S. Army, Ansbach, Fed. Rep. Germany, 1978-81; behavioral sci. specialist, instr. U.S. Army, Ft. Sam Houston, 1981-84; hon. discharge U.S. Army, 1984; commd. 1st lt. USAF, 1984, advanced through grades to major, 1994; clin. social worker USAF, Sheppard AFB, Tex., 1984-86; family advocacy officer USAF, Philippines, 1986-89; chief social work svcs. USAF, Grissom AFB, Ind., 1989-92; chief mental health svcs. USAF, Columbus AFB, Miss., 1992-95; chief mental health svcs., comdr. mental health flight USAF, Little Rock AFB, 1995-98; mem. faculty Acad. Health Scis.; pres., CEO Corppetts & Assocs. Columnist North Miss. Herald Motivational Spkr. Bd. dirs. Grissom Fed. Credit Union, Peru, Ind., House of Grace Women's Shelter, DeSoto County, Miss.; v.p. bd. dirs. Eastside Girls Club, Wichita Falls, Tex.; bd. dirs. DeSoto County Women's Shelter. Decorated 3 Meritirious Svc. medals, Air Force Commendation medal, Nat. Def. Svc. medal, Good Conduct medal; recipient Letter of Appreciation Mayor of Kokomo, Ind., Cert. of Appreciation for Exceptional and Disting. Vol. Svc. Gov. Tex. Mem. NASW, Women Officers Assn. (v.p.), Acad. Cert. Social Workers. Avocations: traveling, ancient history, artifacts, antiques, interior decorating. Home: 6225 Honeysuckle Ln Walls MS 38680-9505

JONES-ATKINS, DEBORAH KAYE, state official; b. Bradenton, Fla., July 2, 1958; d. Ralph and Jewelle Vanessa (Gayle) Jones; m. Larry Bobby Atkins, July 30, 1983; 1 child, Omari Gayle Jones-Atkins. AS with distinction, Monroe C.C., Rochester, N.Y., 1986, cert. in human svcs., 1986; BIS, Va. State U., Petersburg, 1995; postgrad., SUNY, Brockport, 1998. Credit investigator Sears Roebuck & Co., Rochester, N.Y., 1980; customer svc. rep. B. Forman Co., Rochester, 1980-81; youth counselor Brighton Youth Agy., Rochester, 1976-81; staff asst. Makro Inc., Capitol Hts., Md., 1981-82; customer svc. rep. MetroVision Inc., Capitol Hts., 1983-84; teen parent counselor Urban League of Rochester, 1985, program coord., 1988; job developer YWCA of Rochester, 1985-87; prog. support technician, sr. Dept. Med. Assistance Svcs., Commonwealth of Va., Richmond, 1989-96; alt. health care supr. Commonwealth of Va. Med. Assist. Svcs., 1989-96; substitute tchr. Rochester City Sch. Dist., 1996—. Mem. Women's Resource Ctr., Richmond, 1989—; heir link The Links Inc., Rochester, 1982—; vol. United Negro Coll. Fund Telethon, Rochester, 1988, N.Y. State Dept. Labor Career Edn. Expo, 1989, WXXI Auction 21, Rochester, 1989, YMCA Greater Rochester, 1989, Arts Coun., Richmond, Richmond Children's Festival, 1989, Sci. Mus. Va., Richmond, 1989, Arts Coun. Richmond 15th Ann. June Jubilee, 1990, Children's Book Festival, 1990, Maymont Found. Flower Garden Show, 1990, 91, Va. Spl. Olympics, 1990—, Jr. League Richmond 45th Book and Author Dinner, 1990, dinner asst. ticket chairperson 46th Book and Author Dinner, 1991, hostee 45th Dinner, Children's Book Festival Arts Coun. Richmond; mem. agy. svc. com. Friends Assn. for Children, 1990—; mem. student adv. com. Va. Commonwealth U. Health Svcs., 1991, Friends of Art Richmond Mus. Fine Arts, 1991; mem. membership com., audience devel. com. Richmond Profl. Women's Network; placement counselor placement com. Jr. League Richmond, 1991, mem. tng. com., 1991; mem. adv. com. Children's Mus. Richmond; mem. exec. bd. YWCA of Richmond, 1992-95, mem. fin. com., 1996—; mem. policy bd. Jr. League Richmond, 1992-93; mem. bd. dirs. Urban League of Richmond, 1996—. Named one of Outstanding Young Women of Am., 1988. Mem. NAFE, Nat. Coun. Negro Women, Jr. League of Rochester, Nat. Trust Hist. Preservation, Richmond Profl. Women's Network (rec. sec., exec. bd. 1992—), Richmond Jaycees. Democrat. Avocations: jogging, aerobics, tennis, racquetball, the arts, reading, travel. Home: 65 Laurelton Rd Rochester NY 14609-4218

JONES GREGORY, PATRICIA, secondary art educator; b. La Grange, Ga., Apr. 15, 1944; d. Eddie Burrel Jones (dec.), Samuel Lee (stepfather) and Mildred Jones (Johnson) Turrentine; m. Bernard Gregory, Oct. 12, 1985. BFA in Art Edn., Pratt Inst., 1966; MS in Photography, Ill. Inst. Tech., 1970; postgrad. in African Studies and Rsch., Howard U., 1970-74; EdD in Ednl. Adminstrn. and Supervision, Seton Hall U., 1994. Cert. prin./supr., supr., ednl. adminstrn. and supervision, art tchr. grades K-12. Art tchr. Westfield (N.J.) Sch. Dist., 1966-68; art instr. Howard U., Washington, 1970-71; art tchr. Newark (N.J.) Sch. Dist., 1974-79, Irvington (N.J.) Sch. Dist., 1979-80, South Orange (N.J.)-Maplewood (N.J.) Sch. Dist., 1980-81, Montclair (N.J.) Sch. Dist., 1981-82; art instr., docent Newark (N.J.) Mus., 1982-84; art tchr. Weequahic H.S., Newark, 1983-98; mem. com. textbook evaluation curriculum svcs. Bd. Edn., Newark, 1983—; art dir. Ergo-Weequahic H.S., Newark, 1984-93, founder, advisor Kuumba Art Club, 1989-94, PB Graphics Design. Author: Many Moods of the Afro-American Woman, 1971, (catalog) Multicultural Arts Exhibition Catalog, 1992, Pathways to Empowerment, 1997; co-author: (brochure) Multiethnic/Multicultural Women's Initiation Seminar, 1992, Secondary Art Curriculum Guide, 1994, (brochure) Young Women's Seminar Program Brochure, 1996. Rschr. Goldman and Kennedy The New York Urban Athlete, Simon and Schuster, N.Y., 1983. Grace B. Monroe grantee Pratt Inst., Bklyn., 1964; Grad. scholar Ill. Inst. Tech., Chgo., 1968-70; Rsch. fellow Howard U., Washington, 1972-73; recipient Cert. of Recognition, Gov.'s Tchr. Recognition Program, N.J., 1993. Mem. ASCD, Nat. Assn. for Multicultural Edn., Nat. Assn. Art Educators, Newark Mus., Newark Art Coun., Studio Mus. in Harlem, Kappa Delta Pi. Avocations: art, travel, discussion, reading, writing. Home: 78 Woodland Ave East Orange NJ 07017-2006

JONES-MORTON, PAMELA, human resources specialist; b. Balt., Aug. 21, 1947; d. Robert Alfred and Lois Enola (Skilliter) Jones; m. Wayne Daniel Morton, Sept. 7, 1968 (div. Aug. 1990). BS, Frostburg State U., 1970; MA, Mich. State U., 1976; PhD, Ohio State U., 1989. Tchr. Alleghaney High Sch., Cumberland, Md., 1970-72; tchr. Am. Sch. in Japan, Tokyo, 1972-74, dept. head, 1974-77; tchr. The Tatnall Sch., Wilmington, Del., 1977-78; dept. head, athletic dir. Internat. Sch. Dusseldorf, West Germany, 1979-82; athletic dir. Escola Americana De Rio de Janeiro, 1982-85, Am. Cmty. Sch., London, 1985-86; grad. asst. Ohio State U., Columbus, 1986-89; univ. prof. W.Va. U., Morgantown, 1989-91; mgr. human and bus. devel. Honda of Am. Mfg., Inc., Columbus, 1991-95, mgr. expatriate adminstrn. dept., 1995-98, mgr. orgnl. devel. expatriate adminstrn., 1998—; pres. Kanto Plains Athletic Assn., Tokyo, 1973-77; mem accreditation team European Coun., London, 1982; spkr., trustee I Know I Can, Columbus, Ohio; mem. TARGET, The Ohio State U. and Columbus Japanese/Am. Bus. Cmty. Author: (chpt.) Transferring Learning to the Work Place, 1997; contbr. articles to profl. jours. Active Dolphin Rsch. Ctr., Marathon Shores, Fla., 1992—, Marine Conservation, 1994—. Mem. AAUW, Am. Soc. Tng. and Devel. (benchmarking forum 1991-95, spkr. 1993, 94, 95), Soc. Human Resource Mgmt., Inst. Internat. Human Resources, Phi Delta Kappa. Democrat. Avocations: gardening, scuba diving, traveling, photography, puzzles. Office: Honda of Am Mfg Inc 24000 Honda Pkwy Marysville OH 43040-9251

JONES-WILSON, FAUSTINE CLARISSE, education educator emeritus; b. Little Rock, Ark., Dec. 3, 1927; d. James Edward and Perrine Marie (Childress) Thomas; m. James T. Jones, June 20, 1948 (div. 1977); children: Yvonne Dianne, Brian Vincent; m. Edwin L. Wilson, July 10, 1981. A.B., Ark. A.M.&N. Coll., 1948; A.M., U. Ill., 1951, Ed.D., 1967. Tchr., sch. librarian Gary pub. schs. (Ind.), 1955-62, 1964-67; asst. prof. Coll. Edn., U. Ill., Chgo., 1967-69; assoc. prof. adult edn. Fed. City Coll., Washington, 1970-71; prof. edn., grad. prof. Howard U., Washington, 1969-70, 71-93, acting dean Sch. Edn., 1991-92, prof. emeritus, 1993—. author: The Changing Mood in America; Eroding Commitment, 1977, A Traditional Model of Educational Excellence: Dunbar High School of Little Rock, Arkansas, 1981; editor Jour. Negro Edn., 1978-91, 92-93; co-editor: Encyclopedia of African-American Education, 1996. East Coast steering com. chmn. Nat. Conf. on Educating Black Children, 1986-88, 90-92, 3d v.p., 1992-94, mem. bd. dirs. 1994-98. Recipient Frederick Douglass award Nat. Assn. Black Journalists, 1979, Disting. Scholar-Tchr. award Howard U., 1985, Exemplary Leadership award Am. Assn. Higher Edn. Black Caucus, 1988, Gertrude E. Rush award Nat. Bar Assn., 1990, Disting. Career award V.P. for Acad. Affairs, Howard U., 1993, Disting. Alumni award Coll. Edn. U. Ill., 1997; Phelps Stokes Fund sr. fellow, 1993—. Mem. Am. Ednl. Studies Assn. (pres. 1984-85), John Dewey Soc., Soc. Profs. of Edn., Phi Delta Kappa (pres. Howard U. chpt. 1986-87, Svc. key 1990). Democrat. Methodist. Home: 6605 Allview Dr Columbia MD 21046-1005 Office: Howard U Sch Edn 2400 6th St NW Washington DC 20059-0002

JONG, ERICA MANN, writer, poet; b. N.Y.C., Mar. 26, 1942; d. Seymour and Eda (Mirsky) Mann; m. Michael Werthman, 1963 (div. 1965); m. Allan Jong (div. Sept. 1975); m. Jonathan Fast, Dec. 1977 (div. Jan. 1983); 1 child, Molly; m. Kenneth David Burrows, Aug. 5, 1989. BA, Barnard Coll., 1963; MA, Columbia U., 1965. Faculty, English dept. CUNY, 1964-65, 69-70, overseas div. U. Md., 1967-69; mem. lit. panel N.Y. State Council on Arts, 1972-74; faculty Breadloaf Writers Conf. Middlebury, Vt., 1982; mem. faculty Saltzburg Seminar, Saltzburg, Austria, 1993, 98. Author: (poems) Fruits and Vegetables, 1971, reissued edit., 1997, Half Lives, 1973, Loveroot, 1975, At the Edge of the Body, 1979, Ordinary Miracles, 1983, Becoming Light: Poems New and Selected, 1992; (novels) Fear of Flying, 1973, How to Save Your Own Life, 1977, Fanny: Being the True History of the Adventures of Fanny Hackabout-Jones, 1980, Parachutes and Kisses, 1984, Serenissima, 1987 (reissued as Shylock's Daughter, 1995), Any Woman's Blues, 1990, What Do Women Want?, 1998, (poetry and non-fiction) Witches, 1981, reissued edit., 1997, (juvenile) Megan's Book of Divorce, 1984 (reissued as Megan's Two Houses, 1995), (memoir) The Devil at Large, 1993, (autobiography) Fear of Fifty, 1994, Inventing Memory, 1997, (non-fiction) What Do Women Want, 1998; composer lyrics: Zipless: Songs of Abandon from the Erotic Poetry of Erica Jong, 1995, (fiction) Inventing Memory, 1997. Recipient Bess Hokin prize Poetry mag., 1971, Prix Literaire, Deauville Film Festival, 1997; named Mother of Yr., 1982; Woodrow Wilson fellow; Nat. Endowment Arts grantee, 1973. Mem. PEN, Authors Guild U.S.A. (coun. 1975—, pres. 1991-93), Poets and Writers Bd., Writers Guild Am.-West, Poetry Soc. Am. (Alice Faye di Castagnola award 1972), Phi Beta Kappa. Office: Erica Jong Prodns care Kenneth David Burrows 425 Park Ave New York NY 10022-3506

JONG, THERESA ANN, human resource executive; b. Chgo., Aug. 27, 1965; d. Ronald Walter and Marilyn Ruth (Krase) W. BS, San Diego State U., 1989. Dir. personnel and facilities Guild Mortgage Co., San Diego, 1988. Vol. Easter Seals Soc. San Diego, 1988—, Am. Heart Assn., 1989—, Zool. Soc. San Diego, 1986—; coord. (ETC) mgmt. employee transp. San Diego Traffic Demand, 1989—. Mem. Pers. Mgmt. Assn. Roman Catholic. Office: Guild Mortgage Co 9160 Gramercy Dr San Diego CA 92123-4020

JONISH, ARLEY DUANE, retired bibliographer; b. Walker, Minn., June 18, 1927; s. Howard Florian and Mabel Pauline (Rinde) J.; m. Thelma O. Ofstedal, Aug. 13, 1955 (dec. May 1988); children—Eleanor Ann, David Paul. B.S., Bemidji State U., 1949; M.A., U. Minn., 1962. Tchr., librarian Pub. Schs., Red Lake Falls, Minn., 1949-55, Mahnomen, Minn., 1955-60; instr. library sci. U. No. Iowa, Cedar Falls, 1960-62; circulation librarian U. N.Mex., Albuquerque, 1962-63; ref. librarian Western Oreg. Coll., Monmouth, 1963-66; dir. Penrose Meml. Library Whitman Coll., Walla Walla, Wash., 1966-87, bibliographer, 1987-89, ret., 1989; cons. to librs. Walla Walla, 1990—; mem. Wash. Govs. Conf. on Libraries and Info. Sci., Olympia, 1977-80, Wash. State Adv. Council on Libraries, Olympia, 1975-80. Precinct committeeman Republican Party, Walla Walla County, 1980-82. Served with USN, 1945-46, PTO. Mem. ABA, Wash. Library Assn., Pacific Northwest Library Assn., AAUP, NEA, Northwest Assn. Pvt. Colls. and Univs. (chmn. library sect. 1970, 80), Assn. Coll. and Research Libraries (pres. Wash. state chapter 1987), Elks (life). Avocations: gardening; history of printing. Home: 1238 Belle St Walla Walla WA 99362-9401

JONSEN, ALBERT R., retired medical ethics educator; b. San Francisco, Apr. 4, 1931; s. Albert R. and Helen (Sweigert) J. BA, Gonzaga U., 1955, MA, 1956; STM, U. Santa Clara, 1963; PhD, Yale U., 1967. Mem. S.J., 1949-76; ordained priest Roman Catholic Ch.; instr. philosophy Loyola U., Los Angeles, 1956-59; asst. in instrn. Yale Div. Sch., 1966-67; asst. prof. theology and philosophy U. San Francisco, 1967-72, pres., 1969-72; prof. med. ethics Sch. Medicine, U. Calif.-San Francisco, 1972-87; adj. assoc. prof. dept. community medicine and internat. health Sch. Medicine, Georgetown U., 1977; prof. med. ethics, chmn. dept. med. history and ethics Sch. Medicine U. Wash., Seattle, 1987-99; prof. emeritus; mem. artificial heart assessment panel Nat. Heart and Lung Inst., 1972-73, 84-86; mem. Am. Bd. Med. Spltys., 1978-81; cons. Am. Bd. Internal Medicine, 1978-82, Am. Coll. Obstetrics and Gyn., 1983-88; mem. Pres.'s Commn. for Study of Ethical Problems in Medicine, 1979-82, Nat. Commn. for Protection Human Subjects of Biomed. and Behavioral Research, HEW, 1974-78; mem. Nat. Bd. Med. Examiners, 1985-87; mem. Commn. on AIDS Rsch., NRA, 1986-92—, Panel on Social Impact of AIDS (chmn.), 1989-91; chmn. nat. adv. bd. Ethics and Reproduction, 1991-96. Author: Responsibility in Modern Religious Ethics, 1968, Patterns of Moral Responsibility, 1969, Christian Decision and Action, 1970, Ethics of Newborn Intensive Care, 1976, Clinical Ethics, 1982, The Abuse of Casuistry: A History of Moral Reasoning, 1987, The New Medicine and the Old Ethics, 1990, The Social Impact of AIDS in the United States, 1993, Bioethics, 1997, The Birth of Bioethics, 1998, A Short History of Medical Ethics, 1999; mem. editorial bd. Jour. Philosophy and Medicine, Jour. Clin. Ethics. Trustee Inst. Ednl. Mgmt., Harvard U., 1971-74, Ploughshares Found., 1980-84; mem. San Francisco Crime Com., 1969-71; bd. dirs. Found. Critical Care Medicine, 1983-86, Sierra Found., 1987—. Guggenheim fellow, 1995-96. Fellow Inst. for Soc., Ethics and Life Scis.; mem. Soc. Health and Human Values (pres. 1986-87), Am. Soc. Law and Medicine (bd. dirs. 1986-88), Soc. Christian Ethics, Inst. Medicine of NAS (com. human values 1973, coun. 1983-85, 90-92), Instituto de Bioetica (Madrid). Office: Univ Wash Med History and Ethics PO Box 357120 Seattle WA 98195-7120

JONSEN, ERIC R., lawyer; b. San Francisco, June 5, 1958; s. Richard William and Ann Margaret (Parsons) J.; m. Ida-Marie, May 8, 1982; children: Kaitlyn, Jeremy, Michelle. BA, Hartwick Coll., 1980; JD, U. Colo., 1985. Bar: Colo., N.Y., U.S. Dist. Ct. Colo., U.S. Ct. Appeals (10th cir., Fed. cir.). Assoc. William P. DeMoulin, Denver, 1986-88, Fairfield & Woods, Denver, 1988-90; ptnr. Ciancio & Jonsen PC, Denver, 1990—. Mem. ABA, Colo. Bar Assn. E-mail: jonsen@csn.net. Office: Ciancio & Jonsen PC 12000 Pecos St Ste 200 Denver CO 80234-2079

JONSEN, RICHARD WILIAM, educational administrator; b. San Francisco, Mar. 29, 1934; s. Albert Rupert and Helen Catherine (Sweigert) J.; m. Ann Margaret Parsons, Nov. 20, 1955; children: Marie Wood, Eric, Gregory, Stephen, Matthew. BA, U. Santa Clara, 1955; MA, San Jose (Calif.) State U., 1970; PhD, Stanford U., 1973. Pub.'s rep. Hearst Advt. Service, San Francisco, 1955-58; alumni dir. U. Santa Clara, Calif., 1958-70; dir. admissions, asst. dean. Sch. Edn., asst. prof. Syracuse (N.Y.) U., 1972-76; project dir. Edn. Commn. States, Denver, 1976-77; project dir. Western Interstate Commn. Higher Edn., Boulder, Colo., 1977-79, dep. dir., 1979-90; exec. dir., 1990—; vis. prof. U. Tamaulipas, Mex., 1996, 97. Author: State Policy and Independent Higher Education, 1975, Small Liberal Arts Colleges, 1978, Lifelong Learning: State Policies, 1978, The Environmental context for Postsecondary Education, 1986; editor: Higher Education Policies in the Information Age, 1987. Roman Catholic. Office: Western Interstate Commn Higher Edn PO Box 9752 Boulder CO 80301-9752

JONSSON, BJARNI, mathematician, educator; b. Draghals, Iceland, Feb. 15, 1920; came to U.S., 1941, naturalized, 1963; s. Jon and Steinunn (Bjarnadottir) Petursson; m. Amy Sprague, Dec. 16, 1950 (div. 1967); children: Eric M., Meryl S.; m. Harriet Parkes, Jan. 17, 1970; child, M. Kristin. B.A., U. Calif. at Berkeley, 1943, Ph.D., 1946. Faculty Brown U., 1946-56, asst. prof., 1948-56; vis. prof. U. Iceland, 1954-55; vis. asso. prof. U. Calif. at, Berkeley, 1955-56; vis. prof., research mathematician U. Calif., Berkeley, 1962-63; faculty U. Minn., 1956-66, assoc. prof., 1956-59, prof., 1959-66; disting. prof. Vanderbilt U., Nashville, 1966-93, disting. prof. emeritus, 1993—. Mem. Am. Math. Soc., Assn. for Symbolic Logic, AAUP. Research, publs. in lattice theory, universal algebra, founds. of algebra, group theory. Office: Vanderbilt U Dept Math 2305 W End Ave Nashville TN 37203-1700 Address: 5810 Vine Ridge Dr Nashville TN 37205-1326

JONSSON, EGIL SIGURD, artist; b. Mpls., Apr. 15, 1957; s. John Baldwin and Eunice Evenlyn (Erickson) Sigurdson. Student, Luther Coll., 1975-76, U. Minn., 1981-82, U. Iceland, 1984-85. Gallery artist Jack Wold Fine Arts, Mpls., 1994-97, Convergence Gallery, Santa Fe, N.Mex., 1995-96, Firehouse Gallery, Bordertown, N.J., 1997—, Argyle-Zebra Gallery, St. Paul, Minn., 1999—; curator Bohlander Gallery 36, Mpls., 1999. Exhibited in shows at Bloomington (Minn.) Art Ctr. (2d and 4th pl.), Chautauqua (N.Y.) Exhbn. Am. Art, 1996 (Landscape award), Icelandic Festival of Man., Can., 1998 (Best in Show). Jerome Found. very spl. arts grantee Icelandic-Am. Assn. of Minn., 1998. Mem. Studio 125 Focus Group. Avocations: genealogy, opera. Home: PO Box 580902 Minneapolis MN 55458

JONSSON, JENS JOHANNES, electrical engineering educator; b. Mildstedt, Germany, Apr. 4, 1922; came to U.S., 1927, naturalized, 1933; s. John Fredrich and Catharina Maria (Latre) J.; m. Helen Broadbent, Sept. 5, 1945; children: Craig, Diane, Karen, Catherine, Eric. B.S., U. Utah, 1944, B.S. in Elec. Engring., 1947; M.S., Purdue U., 1948, Ph.D., 1951; postgrad., Poly. Inst. Bklyn., 1960-61. Registered profl. engr., Utah. Supr., N.Am. Aviation, 1951-53; prof. elec. engring. Brigham Young U., Provo, Utah, 1953-87; dir. Engring. Analysis Center Brigham Young U., 1964-72, chmn. engring. dept., 1954-55, chmn. elec. engring. sect. dept., 1955-60, 77-83; sr. lectr. Egerton U., Kenya, 1987-88; vis. prof. GE, 1957; mem. sr. staff Conair Astronautics, San

Diego, 1958; mem. sr. rsch. staff Bell Telephone Labs., Whippany, N.J., 1959; field expert UNESCO, Ankara, Turkey, 1967; chief tech. adviser UNESCO-Poly. Inst. Bucharest project, Romania, 1974-76, Qingdao Inst. Chem. Tech., People's Rep. of China, 1990-91. Contbr. to profl. lit. Served with USNR, 1944-46. Recipient award for teaching excellence Western Electric Fund, 1969; certificate of recognition for contbn. to engring. edn. Utah Engring. Council, 1965. Mem. Am. Soc. Engring. Edn. (chmn. Utah relations with industry com. 1963-66), IEEE (pres. Utah sect. 1963, Community Service award 1973), Sigma Xi (pres. Brigham Young U. chpt. 1970-71). Home: 1710 Lambert Ln Provo UT 84604-1852

JONSSON, SKULI, construction company executive; b. 1949. With The Law Co. Inc., Wichita, Kans., 1970-74; v.p. Midwest Drywall Co., Inc., Oklahoma City, 1974—. Office: Midwest Drywall Co Inc 2120 S Prospect Oklahoma City OK 73129*

JONTZ, JEFFRY ROBERT, lawyer; b. Stuart, Iowa, May 28, 1944; s. John Leo Jontz and Leora Burnette (Pittman) Myers; m. Sharyn Sue Kopriva, June 8, 1968; 1 son, Eric Barrett. BA, Drake U., 1966; JD with distinction, U. Iowa, 1969. Bar: Iowa 1969, Fla. 1971, Ohio 1972, U.S. Dist. Ct. (mid. dist.) Fla. 1971, U.S. Ct. Appeals (5th cir.) 1971, fla. 1972, U.S. Ct. Appeals (11th cir.) 1981, U.S. Tax Ct. 1983. Law clk. to Hon. Charles R. Scott U.S. Dist. Ct. (mid. dist.) Fla., Jacksonville, 1969-70; to Hon. Bryan Simpson U.S. Ct. Appeals (5th cir.), Jacksonville, 1970-71; assoc. Jones, Day, Cockley & Reavis, Cleve., 1971-72; asst. U.S. atty. U.S. Dist. Ct. (mid. dist.) Fla., Orlando, 1972-74; pvt. practice Orlando, 1974—; ptnr. Young, Turnbull & Linscott, Orlando, 1974-79, Baker & Hostetler, Orlando, 1979, DeWolf, ward & Morris, Orlando, 1979-84, Jontz, russell & Hull, Orlando, 1985-86, Holland & Knight, 1986-96, Carldon Fields, Orlando, 1996—. Contbr. articles to legal jours.; bd. editors Iowa Law Rev., 1968. past bd. dirs. The Door Drug Rehab. Ctr. of Ctrl. Fla.; past chmn. bd. trustees First Congregational Ch. of Winter Park, Fla., mem. com., long range planning com.; former county committeeman Rep. Party of Orange County, Fla.; bd. dirs. Fla. Symphony Orch., 1985-93, Jr. Achievement Ctrl. Fla., Inc.; mem. Rollins Coll. Tar Boosters; chmn. bankruptcy com. Orange County Bar Assn., 1986-87, chmn. jud. rels. com., 1998—; chmn. bankruptcy com. Code Enforcement Bd. City of Maitland, Fla., 1990-92; chmn. bd. adjustment City of Winter Park, 1995—; mem. parents com. Dartmouth Coll., 1995-99. Recipient Outstanding Individual Cmty. Leadership award Vol. Ctr. Ctrl. Fla., 1991. Mem. Am. Bankruptcy Inst., Ctrl. Fla. Bankruptcy Lawyers Assn., Fla. Bar (ith cir. grievance com. 1979-82, chmn. comml. litigation com. 1981-82, bankruptcy and creditor's rights com. corp. bus. and banking law sect., com. on jud. adminstrn., selection and tenure 1985-86, mem. jud. nominating procedures com. 1995-96, lectr. seminars), Orange County Bar Assn. (chmn. jud. rels. com. 1995—, bankruptcy com.), ABA (mem. comml. transactions litigation com., numerous other coms.), Drake U. Nat. Alumni Assn. (past chmn. ctrl. Fla. chpt., sec., bd. dirs. 1981-93, pres.'s circle coun.), Iowa State Bar Assn., Order of Coif, Winter Park Racquet Club (mem. bd. govs., sec., v.p., pres. 1989-94, 96—), Tiger Bay Club Orlando, Citrus Club, Omicron Delta Kappa, Tau Kappa Epsilon, Phi Delta Phi. Office: Carlton Fields Ward Emmanuel Smith Cutler PA Ste 1600 PO Box 1171 255 South Orange Ave Orlando FL 32802

JOO, MICHAEL, artist, educator; b. Ithaca, N.Y., 1966. BFA, Washington U., 1989; MFA, Yale U., 1991. Adj. instr. The Cooper Union Sch. Art, N.Y.C. One-man shows include Nordanstad--Skarstedt, N.Y., 1992, Thomas Nordanstad Gallery, N.Y., 1994, 95, 96, Stedelijk Mus., Amsterdam, 1995, Galerie Anne de Villepoix, Paris, 1995, Anthony DCOffay Gallery, London, 1995, Anton Kern Gallery, N.Y., 1997; exhibited in group shows at Ctr. Arts at Yerba Buena, San Francisco, 1993, Queens (N.Y.) Mus. Art, 1993, New Mus. Contemporary Art, N.Y., 1993, The Interart Ctr., N.Y., 1994, Kumho Mus., Seoul, 1994, Cohen Gallery, N.Y., 1994, Serpentine Gallery, London, 1994, Inst. Contemporary Art, London, 1995, Randolph Street Gallery, Chgo., 1995, Mus. Contemporary Art, Chgo., 1995, Kwangju Contemporary Mus., Sydkorea, 1995, Bloom Gallery, Amsterdam, 1996, The Post Office, London, 1996, Mus. Africa, Johannesburg, 1997, Anton Kern Gallery, N.Y., 1997, P.S. 1, N.Y., 1998, others. Office: care Cooper Union Sch Art 30 Cooper Sq New York NY 10003*

JOOS, FELIPE MIGUEL, mechanical engineer; b. Montevideo, Uruguay, Sept. 4, 1952; came to U.S., 1973; s. Carlos Jose and Alma Elena Joos; m. Caroline Rose Crocker, Aug. 28, 1982 (div.); children: Carolina Lucia, Catrina Aneliese, Celina Maria. BS in Applied Sci. and Engring., Calif. Inst. Tech., 1976; MSME, MIT, 1978, PhDME, 1982. Cert. engr., Uruguay. Engr. Ingenieros Consultores Latinoamericanos Limitada, Montevideo, Uruguay, 1978-79; mech. engr. research and devel. div. Gen. Electric Corp., Schenectady, N.Y., 1982-85; project engr. Creare, Inc., Hanover, N.H., 1985-87; tech. assoc. Eastman Kodak Co., Rochester, N.Y., 1987—; indsl. fellow Ctr. for Interfacial Engring., U. Minn., Mpls., 1991-92. Contbr. articles to profl. jours.; presenter at internat. symposium and conf. in field; patentee in field. Mem. ASME, Internat. Soc. Coating Sci. and Tech. (tech. session chair 1994, 98), Soc. Hispanic Profl. Engrs. (award 1993, v.p. 1989-90, treas. 1990-92, treas. Ea. Tech. and Career conf. 1991), Tau Beta Pi. Avocation: scuba diving. Home: 75 Wood Creek Dr Pittsford NY 14534-4409 Office: Eastman Kodak Co Kodak Park Rochester NY 14652-3701

JOOS, OLGA MARTÍN-BALLESTERO DE, language educator; b. Zaragoza, Spain, May 2, 1944; came to U.S., 1973; d. Luis and Olga Helena (Hernandez) Martin-Ballestero; m. William Joseph Joos, Oct. 9, 1973; children: Catalina, Louis, Olga, William. Grad., Dames Sacré Coeur Sch., Zaragoza, Spain, 1960; BA, U. Zaragoza, 1969; postgrad., U. North Fla., 1997. Substitute lang. tchr. Assumption Sch., 1989-91, Bolles Sch., 1991-93; h.s. Spanish tchr. Douglas Anderson Sch. of Arts, Jacksonville, Fla., 1993-97; tchr. French and Spanish Episcopal Sch., Jacksonville, Fla., 1997—. Home: 2641 River Rd Jacksonville FL 32207-4020

JOOS, STEVEN LEE, sports editor; b. Peoria, Ill., Feb. 4, 1955; s. Charles Edward and Shirley Ann (Clary) J. AA in English, Ill. Ctrl. Coll., East Peoria, Ill., 1976; BSJ, Bradley U., 1978. Asst. editor Metamora (Ill.) Herald, 1978; corr. Tazewell Pub., Morton, Ill., 1978-79; editor Mason County Dem., Havana, Ill., 1979; staff announcer WDUK-FM Radio, Havana, 1979-88; corr. Pekin (Ill.) Daily Times, 1982-83; reporter Times-Advocate, West Salem, Ill., 1988-89; sports editor Posey County News, Poseyville, Ind., 1989—. Recipient awards for writing. Avocations: writing poetry, historical study. Home: PO Box 372 Poseyville IN 47633-0372 Office: Posey County News 604 Lockwood St Poseyville IN 47633

JOPLIN, JULIAN MIKE, lawyer; b. Littlefield, Tex., Aug. 30, 1936; s. Charles Arbie and Gladys (Douglass) J.; m. Barbara Maye McKinney, Sept. 1, 1957; children: Erin Colleen, Jeffrey Miles. BBA in Fin., Tex. Tech U., 1958; JD, U. Tex., 1963. Bar: Tex. 1963. Ptnr. Strasburger & Price, Dallas, 1963—. Bd. dirs. Notre Dame Spl. Sch., 1986-91, Presbyn. Hosp., Dallas, 1988-93, Ctrl. and Dallas Assn., 1989-98, Children's Hosp., Dallas, 1998—; ruling elder Highland Pk. Presbyn. Ch., Dallas, 1982—. Capt. U.S. Army and Tex. N.G., 1958-63. Mem. State Bar Tex. (bd. dirs. 1989-92), Dallas Bar Assn. (bd. dirs., pres. 1988), Dallas Bar Found. (bd. dirs., chmn. 1997-98), U. Tex. Law Sch. Alumni Assn. (bd. dirs. 1987-90, mem. exec. com. 1998—), Dallas Country Club, City Club, Salesmanship Club. Republican. Avocations: racquet sports, running. Home: 4232 San Carlos St Dallas TX 75205-2050 Office: Strasburger & Price 901 Main St 4300 Nations Bank Plz Dallas TX 75202

JOPPA, ROBERT GLENN, aeronautics educator; b. Orchard, Colo., Aug. 25, 1922; s. Martin and Beatrice Virginia (Winkelseth) J.; m. Dorris Eileen Campbell, Mar. 3, 1944; children—Paul Douglas, Susan Elise. B.S., U. Wash., 1945, M.S., 1951; M.A., Princeton U., 1962, Ph.D., 1972. Wind tunnel operator U. Wash., Seattle, 1942-49; instr. U. Wash., 1949-53, asst. prof., 1953, assoc. prof., 1956, prof. aeronautics, 1970-88, dir. advising Coll. Engring., 1987, prof. emeritus, 1988—; vis. prof. Nat. U. Singapore, 1989-90, 91-92; NSF faculty fellow Princeton U., 1960-62; with Boeing Co., Seattle, summers, 1955, 61; mem. com. NAE, 1984-85; aircraft accident analyst cons. and expert witness in field. Contbr. articles in field to profl. jours. Fellow AIAA (assoc.); mem. Soc. Flight Test Engrs., Sigma Xi. Unitarian. Patentee in field of gliding anchor. Office: U Wash Dept Aero & Astronautics PO Box 352400 Seattle WA 98195-2400

JOPPY, WILLIAM, professional boxer; b. Rockville, Md.. Named WBA Middleweight Champion, 1996, regained WBA Mid. Weight Title, 1998. Achievements include record of 23 wins, no losses, 1 tie, with 19 knock-outs. Office: c/o Consejo Mundial de Boxeo, Genova 33 Despacho # 503, 06600 Mexico City Mexico*

JORAJURIA, ELSIE JEAN, elementary education educator; b. Flagstaff, Ariz., June 28, 1946; d. Frank Y. and Elsie (Barreres) Auza; m. Ramon Jorajuria, June 23, 1973; children: Tonya, Nina. BS in Edn., No. Ariz. U., 1971, MA in Elem. Edn., 1975. Cert. elem. edn., Ariz. First grade tchr. Kinsey Sch., Flagstaff, Ariz., 1971-73; third grade tchr. Mohawk Valley Sch., Roll, Ariz., 1973-77, migrant edn. coord., 1980-83, second lang. English Kindergarten tchr., 1983-84, first grade tchr., 1984—; tchr. ESL Ariz. Wester Coll., Yuma, Ariz., 1987. Cheerleader sponsor, Roll, Ariz., 1984-99; vol. 4-H, Roll, 1986-97, project leader, 1990-97, cmty. leader, 1994-97, sponsor Student Coun., Roll, 1994-95; 4-H supt., 1998-99. Named Tchr. of Yr., Mohawk Valley Sch., 1987-88, 88-89, 95-96, Woman of the Yr., Bus. Profl. Woman, 1994. Mem. NEA, Ariz. Edn. Assn., Mohawk Valley Tchr. Assn. (pres. 1992-94), Ariz. Wool Growers Assn. Democrat. Roman Catholic. Home: PO Box 485 40154 Colorado Ave Tacna AZ 85352 Office: Mohawk Valley Sch PO Box 67 Roll AZ 85347

JORDAHL, KATHLEEN PATRICIA (KATE JORDAHL), photographer, educator; b. Summit, N.J., Aug. 23, 1959; d. Martin Patrick and Marie Pauline (Quinn) O'Grady; m. Geir Arild Jordahl, Sept. 24, 1983. BA in Art & Art History magna cum laude with distinction, U. Del., 1980; MFA in Photography, Ohio U., 1982. Lifetime credential in art and design, Calif. Teaching assoc. Sch. Art Ohio U., Athens, 1980-82; adminstrv. asst. A.D. Coleman, S.I., N.Y., 1981; placement asst. career planning & placement U. Calif., Berkeley, 1983; instr. Coll. for Kids, Hayward, Calif., 1987-88; supr. student/alumni employment office Chabot Coll., Hayward, 1983-87, tchr. photography, 1987-97; assoc. prof. photography and digital imaging Foothill Coll., Los Altos Hills, Calif., 1997—; workshop coord. Friends of Photography, San Francisco, 1990; instr., workshop leader, coord. PhotoCen. Photography Programs, Hayward, 1983—; mem., co-coord., publ. evaluation accreditation com. Chabot Coll., Hayward, 1984, instrnl. skills workshop facilitator, 1994, speaker opening day, 1986, coord. ann. classified staff devel. workshop, 1985; workshop leader Ansel Adams Gallery, Yosemite, Calif., 1991, 92, artist-in-residence Yosemite Nat. Park Mus., 1993; ind. curator numerous exhbns., 1984—; coord., curator Women's Photography Workshop & Exhbn., 1993—. Exhibited in group shows Parts Gallery, Minn., 1992, The Alameda Arts Commn. Gallery, Oakland, 1992, Panoramic Invitational, Tampere, Finland, 1992, Photo Forum, Pitts., 1992, Photo Metro Gallery, San Francisco, 1993, Ansel Adams Gallery, Yosemite, 1994, Yosemite Mus., 1994, 96, Vision Gallery, San Francisco, 1994, 95, San Francisco Mus. Modern Art Rental Gallery, 1994, Photographer's Gallery, Palo Alto, 1997, Hayward Art Coun. Members Show, 1997, Hayward City Hall Gallaria, 1998, Ansel Adams Gallery, Mona Latu, 1999, Yogenji Temple, Tokyo, 1999, Himawarmosato Gallery, Yokahama, Japan, 1999; represented in permanent collections Muse Gallery, Phila., 1982, Ohio U. Libr. Rare Books Collection, Athens, 1982, Yosemite Mus., 1994, Bibliotheque Nationale de France, Paris, 1996; contbr. photos and articles to photography mags. and pubis. Recipient Innovative New Program award Calif. Parks and Recreation Soc., 1990; Sons of Norway scholar U. Oslo, summer 1996. Mem. Internat. Assn. Panoramic Photographers, Soc. Photographic Edn., Friends of Photography, Phi Beta Kappa. Democrat. Avocations: travel, bicycling, reading. E-mail: kate@jordahlphoto.com. Office: PO Box 3998 Hayward CA 94540-3998

JORDAN, ALEXANDER JOSEPH, JR., lawyer; b. New London, Conn., Oct. 11, 1938; s. Alexander Joseph and Alice Elizabeth (Mugovero) J.; m. Mary Carolyn Miller, Aug. 8, 1964; children: Jennifer, Michael, Stephanie. BS, U.S. Naval Acad., 1960; LLB, Harvard U., 1968. Ptnr. Gaston & Snow, Boston, 1968-91, Bingham, Dana & Gould, Boston, 1991-93, Peabody & Brown, Boston, 1994—. Mem., past chmn. adv. com. Town of Hingham, Mass., 1989-95. With USN, 1960-65, capt. USNR, 1965-94, ret. Mem. ABA, Mass. Bar Assn., Boston Bar Assn., U.S. Naval Inst., Naval Res. Assn., Harvard Alumni Assn. (regional dir.), Harvard Club Hingham (trustee, chmn. com. schs. and scholarships, past pres.), Harvard Club of Boston. Office: Peabody & Brown 101 Federal St Fl 13 Boston MA 02110-1832

JORDAN, AMOS AZARIAH, JR., foreign affairs educator, retired army officer; b. Twin Falls, Idaho, Feb. 11, 1922; s. Amos Azariah and Olive (Fisher) J.; m. MarDeane Carver, June 5, 1946; children: Peggy Jordan Hughes, Diana Jordan Paxton, Keith, David, Linda Jordan Mabey, Kent. BS, U.S. Mil. Acad., 1946; BA, Oxford U., Eng., 1950, MA, 1955; PhD, Columbia U., 1961. Commd. 2d lt. U.S. Army, 1946, advanced through grades to brig. gen., 1972; instr. U.S. Mil. Acad., 1950-53, prof. social scis., 1955-72; arty. battery comdr. U.S. Army, Korea, 1954-55; asst. S-3 7th Divsn. Arty. Korea, 1955; adviser econ. and fiscal policy U.S. Econ. Mission to Korea, 1955; ret. U.S. Army, 1972; dir. Aspen Inst., 1972-74; prin. dep. asst. sec. for internat. security affairs Dept. Def., Washington, 1974-76; dep. undersec. and acting undersec. for security assistance Dept. State, Washington, 1976-77; with Ctr. for Strategic and Internat. Studies, Washington, 1977-94, pres, chief exec. officer, 1983-88, vice chmn., 1988-94; pres. Pacific Forum Ctr. for Strategic and Internat. Studies, Honolulu, 1990-94; sr. adviser CSIS, 1994—; counselor Pacific Forum, 1994—; mem. staff Pres.'s Com. to Study Fgn. Assistance Program, 1959; staff dir. Adv. Com. to Sec. Def. on Non-Mil. Instrn., 1962; spl. polit. advisor to U.S. amb. to India, 1963-64; cons. NSC, 1989; mem. Nat. Com. on Security and Econ. Assistance, 1983; Henry Kissinger rsch. chair in nat. security policy CSIS, 1988-92; mem. Pres.'s Intelligence Oversight Bd., 1989-93; internat. co-chmn. Coun. on Sec. Coop. in the Asia Pacific, 1993-96, chmn. U.S. com., 1993-98; co-chmn. Korean-Am. Wisemen Coun., 1991-98; mem. bd. dirs. Pacific Forum, Ctr. for Strategic and Internat. Studies. Author: Foreign Aid and the Defense of Southeast Asia, 1962, Issues of National Security in the 1970's, 1967; co-author: American National Security Policy and Process, 1981, 5th edit., 1999; contbr. chpts. to books and articles to profl. jours. Asia area adminstr. Latter Day Saints Charities, 1998-99. Decorated D.S.M., Legion of Merit with oak leaf cluster, Disting. Civilian Svc. medal Dept. Def. Mem. Coun. Fgn. Rels., Assn. Am. Rhodes Scholars, Pacific Coun. Internat. Policy, Bretton Woods Com. Office: Pacific Forum CSIS Pauahi Tower 1001 Bishop St Ste 1150 Honolulu HI 96813-3429

JORDAN, ANGEL GONI, electrical and computer engineering educator; b. Pamplona, Spain, Sept. 19, 1930; came to U.S., 1956, naturalized, 1966; s. Hilario and Perpetua (Goni) J.; m. Nieves Alfonso Cuartero, July 8, 1956; children: Xavier, Edward, Arthur. M.S., U. Zaragoza, Spain, 1952, Carnegie Inst. Tech., 1959; Ph.D., Carnegie Inst. Tech., 1959; Dr. h.c., Poly. U. Madrid, Spain, 1985. With Naval Ordnance Lab., Madrid, 1952-56; instr. elec. engring. Carnegie-Mellon U., 1956-58, asst. prof. elec. engring., 1959-62, assoc. prof., 1962-65, prof., 1965-90, univ. prof., 1990-97, head dept., 1969-79, U.A. and Helen Whitaker prof., 1972-80, head dept., 1969-79; dean engineering Carnegie-Mellon U. (Carnegie Inst. Tech.), 1979-83; provost Carnegie-Mellon U., 1983-91, J.F and N.P. Keithley univ. prof. elec., computer engring., 1997—; rsch. fellow Mellon Inst. Indsl. Rsch., 1958-59; cons. to industry; bd. dirs. Calif. Micro Devices Corp., Magnascreen Corp., Mirror Sys., Inc., SOCINTEC. Contbr. articles to profl. jours. Dir. Pitts. High Tech. Council, 1983—; bd. dirs. Pa. Sci. and Engring. Found, 1981-83. Recipient Enterprise award Pitts. Bus. Times, 1985; NATO sr. scientist fellow, 1976; Fulbright Disting. scholar, 1988; named Edn. Man of the Yr., Pitts., 1987. Fellow IEEE, AAAS; mem. Am. Phys. Soc., Am. Soc. Engring. Edn., Nat. Acad. Engring., Acad. Engring. Spain, Sigma Xi, Eta Kappa Nu, Phi Kappa Phi, Tau Beta Pi. Home: 5874 Aylesboro Ave Pittsburgh PA 15217-1446 Office: Carnegie-Mellon U Wean Hall # 4618 Pittsburgh PA 15213

JORDAN, ANNE E. DOLLERSCHELL, journalist; b. Golden Valley, Minn., Mar. 30, 1964; d. Allen L. and Marcia G. (Landeen) Dollerschell; m. James Lawrence Jordan, Aug. 16, 1986; children: Davyd, Scott. BA, U. Wis., 1986. From editl. asst. to asst. mng. editor Governing Mag., Washington, 1987—. Mem. Phi Beta Kappa, Phi Kappa Phi, Phi Theta Kappa. Office: Governing Mag Ste 1300 1100 Connecticut Ave NW Washington DC 20036-4109

JORDAN, BERNICE BELL, elementary education educator; b. Calvert, Tex.; d. Ocie Wade and Nannie B. (Westbrook) Bell; m. William B. Jordan, Sept. 28, 1956; children: Beverly, Terrence, Keith Jordan. BA, San Jose State Coll., 1959, MA, 1985; student, Prairie View A and M, Tex. Western Coll. Cert. elem. edn., fine arts, multi-cultural tchr., specially designed acad. instrn. in English. Writer curriculum guide, fine arts Alum Rock Union Elem. Sch. Dist., San Jose, Calif.; writer sch. plan Goss Elem.; elem. tchr. Alum Rock Union Elem. Sch. Dist., San Jose; adv. com., tchr.-cons. San Jose Area Writing Project, San Jose U., 1992—. Mem. ASCD, NEA, Alum Rock Edn. Assn., Calif. Tchrs. Assn., Calif. Reading Assn., Calif. Elem. Edn. Assn., Santa Clara County Reading Coun., Alpha Delta Kappa, Delta Kappa Gamma. Home: 3282 Fronda Dr San Jose CA 95148-2015

JORDAN, BRYCE, retired university president; b. Clovis, N.Mex., Sept. 22, 1924; s. W. Joseph and Kittie (Cole) J.; m. Patricia Jonelle Thornberry, June 10, 1948; children: Julia Cole, Christopher Joseph. Student, Hardin-Simmons U., 1941-42; MusB, U. Tex., 1948, MusM, 1949; PhD, U. N.C., 1956; LLD, Juniata Coll., 1985, Milliken U., 1990. Asst. prof. music Hardin-Simmons U., 1949-51; from asst. prof. to prof. music U. Md., 1954-63; prof. music, chmn. dept. U. Ky., 1963-65, U. Tex., 1965-68; v.p. student affairs U. Tex., Austin, 1968-70, pres. ad interim, 1970-71; pres. U. Tex., Dallas, 1971-81; exec. vice chancellor for acad. affairs U. Tex. System, 1981-83; pres. Pa. State U., 1983-90; mem. faculty Salzburg (Austria) Seminar Am. Studies, 1960, 62, 98; occasional lectr. Fgn. Svc. Inst., Dept. State, 1962-63; mem. Yale Coun. on Music, 1971-73, Nat. Commn. on Higher Edn. Issues, 1982-83. Author: (with Homer Ulrich) Student Manual for Music: A Design for Listening, 1957, Designed for Listening, 1962, also articles, revs.; assoc. editor: Coll. Music Symposium, 1961-66. Bd. dirs. Dallas Grand Opera Assn., 1973-75, Pa. Econ. Devel. Ptnrship, 1987-90; trustee St. Marks Sch. Tex., 1973-81, Dallas Symphony Assn., 1972-81, Presbyn. Hosp., Dallas, 1976-83; v.p. Dallas Civic Music Assn., 1978-79, pres., 1979-80, exec. com. 1980-81; bd. dirs. Dallas County chpt. ARC, 1976-79; div. chmn. United Way of Met. Dallas, 1979; Pa. state chmn. Am. Heart Assn., 1983-84; trustee Com. on Econ. Devel. 1988-90; mem. adv. bd. comml. programs NASA, 1988-90; nat. chmn. higher edn. U.S. Treasury Savs. Bond Programs, 1988-89, 89-90; presiding elder Presbyn. Ch.; chmn. Austin Lyric Opera, 1991-94; mem. vis. com. Eastman Sch. Music U. Rochester, 1991-94; chmn. fine arts adv. coun. U. Tex., Austin, 1994-96; chmn. adv. bd. U. Tex. Press, 1997—. Recipient Hon. Alumni award Pa. State U., 1987, medal, 1990, Doty medal U. Tex., 1996; named Disting. Alumnus, U. N.C., 1985, Hardin-Simmons U., 1987, U. Tex., Austin, 1991. Mem. Coll. Music Soc. (v.p. 1963-65, coun. mem. 1968-70), Am. Musicol. Soc. (chmn. greater Washington chpt. 1958-60), Music Educators Nat. Conf. (pres. Md. br. 1963), Music Tchrs. Nat. Assn., Philos. Soc. Tex., Dallas C. of C. (dir. 1979-82), So. Assn. Colls. and Schs. (commn. on colls. 1981-83), Pa. Assn. Colls. and Univs. (chmn. 1988-89), Phi Kappa Phi, Pi Kappa Lambda, Phi Mu Alpha, Golden Key. Home: # 381 6800 Austin Center Blvd Apt 381 Austin TX 78731-3113 Office: Pa State U Office of Pres University Park PA 16802

JORDAN, CARL DAVID, physical education educator; b. Dallas, Feb. 17, 1944; s. Carl A. and June L. (Turner) J.; m. Roxie L. Ash, Mar. 28, 1970; children: Jennifer, Daniel, Joshua. BA, Baylor U., 1968; MA, Sam Houston State U., 1970; PhD, Tex. A&M U., 1973. From Tex. state rep. to co-dir. U.S. Karate Alliance, Phoenix, Albuquerque, 1976-99; asst. prof., dept. head Le Tourneau U., Longview, Tex., 1973-76; assoc. prof. health & phys. edn. La. Tech. U., Ruston, 1976-99; co-dir. U.S. Karate Alliance, 1989-99; tournament dir. nat. championships, world championships, 1990-99. Named nat. coach of yr. U.S. Karate Alliance 1981, 83-85, 87, 89, 90-91, 93, 96. Mem. La. Assn. Health, Phys. Edn. & Recreation, AAPHERD. Republican. Baptist. Avocations: hunting, fishing. Office: La Tech U PO Box 3028 Ruston LA 71272

JORDAN, CARRIE GRAYSON, writer, poet, drama designer; b. Laurel, Miss.; children: Rickson Vancouver, Corichey Robert. AA in Liberal Arts with honors, Kennedy-King Coll., 1990; student, Bd. Govs. Admissions, fgn. student splst. Kennedy-King Coll.; with modeling group mgmt. Noir Fashions, Chgo., 1976-78. Author: (book) Dear Butterflies; (plays) Grandpa's Stocking, Black Barber Shop; columnist KKC Press. Bd. dirs. S.E. Little League, Chgo., 1986-89; judge Act-SO Contest, NAACP, Chgo., 1996—, annually. Mem. Chrysopoets, Renowned Poetry Club. Avocations: composing songs, writing, designing clothes, clown collecting.

JORDAN, CHARLES MORRELL, retired automotive designer; b. Whittier, Calif., Oct. 21, 1927; s. Charles L. and Bernice May (Letts) J.; m. Sally Irene Mericle, Mar. 8, 1951; children: Debra, Mark, Melissa. BS, MIT, 1949; grad. advanced mgmt. program, Harvard U., 1979; Doctorate (hon.), Art Ctr. Coll. Design, 1992. With GM, Warren, Mich., 1949—, chief designer Cadillac Studio, 1957-61, group chief designer, 1961-62, exec. in charge automotive design, 1962-67, dir. styling Adam Opel A.G., 1967-70, exec. in charge Cadillac, Oldsmobile, Buick Studios, 1970-73, exec. in charge Chevrolet, Pontiac and Comml. Vehicle Studios, 1973-77, dir. design, 1977-86, v.p. design staff, 1986-92; retired, 1992. 1st lt. USAF, 1952-53. Recipient First Nat. award Fisher Body Craftsman's Guild, 1947, disting. svc. citation Automotive Hall of Fame, 1993; named Hon. Judge, Pebble Beach Concours d'Elegance, 1970—. Mem. Calif. Scholastic Fedn. (life), Ferrari Club Am. Address: PO Box 8330 Rancho Santa Fe CA 92067-8330

JORDAN, CHARLES WESLEY, bishop; b. Dayton, Ohio, May 28, 1933; s. David Morris and Naomi Azelia (Harper) J.; m. Margaret May Crawford, Aug. 2, 1959; children: Diana, Susan. BA, Roosevelt U., 1956; MDiv, Garrett Evangel. Theol., Seminary, Evanston, Ill., 1960; LHD (hon.), Morningside Coll., 1994; DD (hon.), Rust Coll., 1995. Ordained to ministry United Meth. Ch., 1960. Pastor Woodlawn United Meth. Ch., Chgo., 1960-66; dir. of urban ministries Rockford, Ill., 1966-71; prog. staff No. Ill. Con./United Meth. Ch., Chgo., 1971-82; dist. supt. Chgo./So. Dist. United Meth. Ch., 1982-87; sr. pastor St. Mark United Meth. Ch., Chgo., 1987-92; bishop Iowa Area United Meth. Ch., Des Moines, 1992—; del. United Meth. Gen. Conf., 1976, 80, 84, 88, 92, Gen. Bd. Global Ministries, 1972-80, Gen. Coun. on Ministries, 1980-88; trustee Garrett Evangel. Theol. Sem., 1982-97. Commnr. Rockford Housing Authority, 1969-71; bd. dirs. Cmty. Mental Health Coun., Chgo., 1989-91, Project Image, Inc., Chgo., 1987-92, Iowa Health System, 1993—; pres. United Meth. Gen. Bd. Ch. & Soc., 1996—, Ecumenical Ministries Iowa, 1999. Named to Hall of Fame Wendell Phillips High Sch., Chgo., 1989. Mem. NAACP (life, chmn. religious affairs 1990-92), Ch. & Soc. (gen. bd.). Home: 3513 Aspen Dr West Des Moines IA 50265-3191 Office: 500 E Court Ave Des Moines IA 50309-2019

JORDAN, CLIFFORD HENRY, management consultant; b. New Orleans, Dec. 27, 1921; s. Clifford Henry and May Rosalie (Duke) J.; m. Clara H. Nordberg, June 1, 1955. Grad. RN, Pa. Hosp. Sch. Nursing, 1949; BS in Nursing Edn., Temple U., 1954, EdD, 1975; MS in Edn., U. Pa., 1957. R.N., Pa. Assoc. dir. Episc. Hosp. Sch. Nursing, Phila., 1958-63, DON, 1963-66; prof. nursing U. Pa., Phila., 1966-82; exec. dir. Assn. Oper. Rm. Nurses, Denver, 1982-90; mgmt. cons. Phila., 1990—; cons. in nursing adminstrn. Pa., N.J., Calif. hosps.; edn. cons. in organizational devel. Pa., Kans., N.J. univs. Mem. Pa. Gov.'s Commn. on Health, 1975-77; bd. govs. Health Systems Agy. So. Pa., 1975-79. Recipient U. Pa. Lindbach award, 1980; named Outstanding alumni U. Pa., 1982. Fellow Am. Acad. Nursing (designated as Living Legend 1996); mem. Am. Nurses Assn. (bd. dirs.), Pa. Nurses Assn. (pres. 1962-66, 72-76), Am. Nurses Found. (v.p. 1980-82). Republican. Roman Catholic. Home and Office: The Wellington # 1610 135 S 19th St Philadelphia PA 19103-4912

JORDAN, DANIEL PORTER, JR., foundation administrator, history educator; b. Philadelphia, Miss., July 22, 1938; s. Daniel Porter and Mildred M. (Dobbs) J.; m. Lewellyn Lee Schmelzer, Dec. 18, 1961; children: Daniel P., Grace Dobbs, Katherine Lewellyn. BA, U. Miss., 1960, MA, 1962; PhD, U. Va., 1970. Various tchg. positions overseas divsn. U. Md., 1962-65, Richmond, Va., 1968-69, U. Va., summers 1970-72; prof. history Va. Commonwealth U., Richmond, 1969-84, Ariz. State, 1995; dir. Stratford Hall Summer Sem., 1981-91; exec. dir. Thomas Jefferson Meml. Found. (Monticello), 1985—, pres., 1994—; scholar in residence U. Va., 1985—. Author: Political Leadership in Jefferson's Virginia, 1983, A Richmond Reader, 1733-1983, 1983, Tobacco Merchant: The Story of Universal Leaf Tobacco Company, 1995. Mem. adv. com. Papers of Thomas Jefferson, Princeton U.; mem. Sec. of Interior's adv. bd. Nat. Pk. Sys., 1984-88, chmn., 1987-88;

mem. Jeffersonian Restoration Adv. Bd., U. Va., 1985—; mem. rev. bd. Va. Hist. Landmarks Commn., 1981-92, chmn., 1989-92; mem. Nat. Pks. and Conservation Bd., 1989-92, Ea. Nat. Bd., 1991—; pres. Richmond Civil War Roundtable, 1983. Served with inf. U.S. Army, 1962-65. Thomas Jefferson Found. fellow, 1965-68; recipient award of merit Am. Assn. for State and Local History, 1977, 88, Pub. Svc. award U.S. Dept. of Interior, 1990, Medal for Va. Svc., AIA, 1993. Mem. Antiquarian Soc., Va. Hist. Soc. (bd. dirs. 1986-91), Mass. Hist. Soc., So. Hist. Assn. (life), Orgn. Am. Historians (life), Walpole Soc., Phi Beta Kappa (pres. Alpha of Va. 1995-98), Omicron Delta Kappa, Sigma Chi. Methodist. Home and Office: Monticello Home of Thomas Jefferson PO Box 316 Charlottesville VA 22902-0316

JORDAN, DAVID FRANCIS, JR., retired judge; b. N.Y.C., Apr. 18, 1928; s. David Francis Jordan and Frances Marion (J.) Edebohls; m. Bess Vukas, Aug. 4, 1956; children: Melissa Marie, David Francis III, Dennis Paul. AB, Princeton U., 1950; JD, NYU, 1953, LLM in Taxation, 1970. Law clk. U.S. Ct. Appeals (2d cir.), 1957-58, chief dep., clk., 1958-59; sole practice, Smithtown, N.Y., 1959-63; ptnr. O'Rourke & Jordan, Central Islip, N.Y., 1963-67; asst. dist. atty. Suffolk County, Riverhead, N.Y., 1969-74; law clk. Supreme Ct., Suffolk County, 1975; investigator N.Y. Supreme Ct. Appellate Div. 2d dept., Bklyn., 1976; corp. counsel City of Newburgh, N.Y., 1976-78; acting city mgr., 1978; U.S. magistrate judge Ea. Dist. N.Y., Bklyn., Uniondale and Hauppauge, N.Y., 1978-94, So. Dist. Calif., San Diego, 1994, So. Dist. Ohio, 1996; mil. judge U.S. Army Judiciary, Washington, 1969-80; legislative analyst Cen. and Ea. European Law Initiative. Served with JAGC, U.S. Army, 1954-57, to col. USAR. Decorated Meritorious Service medal. Mem. ABA (vice chair sr. lawyers divsn. jud. com. 1994-97). Home: 15732 Vista Vicente Dr Ramona CA 92065-4323

JORDAN, DAVID THOMAS, financial analyst, consultant; b. San Antonio, Aug. 31, 1973; s. Thomas David and Linda Susan (Boyanowski) J. BBA, U. Ctrl. Okla., Edmond, 1995; MBA, Oklahoma City U., 1997. Acct. Epworth Villa, Oklahoma City, 1994-97; corp. devel. Svc. Corp. Internat., Houston, 1997-99; fin. analyst Cornell Cos., Houston, 1999—; fin. cons. Jordan Bus. Enterprises, Oklahoma City and Houston, 1995—. Mem. Inst. Mgmt. Accts., Fin. Execs. Inst., Phi Eta Sigma. Republican. Home: 2446 Brandy Mill Rd Houston TX 77067-1217

JORDAN, DAVID WILLIAM, college administrator, faculty dean; b. Wilson, N.C., July 7, 1940; s. William Alexander and Martha Mildred (Ferrell) J.; m. Kay Smith, Nov. 25, 1967; children: Anna, Leah. BA, Davidson Coll., 1962; MA, Princeton U., 1964, PhD, 1966; grad. Inst. Ednl. Mgmt., Harvard U., 1987. From asst. prof. to prof. Grinnell (Iowa) Coll., 1969-85; v.p. acad. affairs, dean faculty Austin Coll., Sherman, Tex., 1985—. Author: Foundations of Representative Government, 1987; co-author: Maryland's Revolution of Government, 1974; co-editor: Biographical Dictionary of the Maryland Legislature, 1635-1789, 1979-85. Bd. dirs., vice chair Habitat for Humanity, Grayson County, Tex., 1995—; bd. dirs. United Way, Grayson County, 1997—. Capt. U.S. Army, 1967-69. Recipient Danforth fellow Danforth Found., 1962, grant NEH, 1974-76. Mem. Am. Conf. Acad. Deans (bd. dirs. 1991-95), Inst. Early Am. History and Culture, Orgn. Am. Historians, Phi Beta Kappa. Democrat. Presbyterian. Home: 809 N Grand Ave Sherman TX 75090-4411 Office: Austin Coll 900 N Grand Ave Sherman TX 75090-4440

JORDAN, DUPREE, JR., management consultant, educator, journalist, publisher, business executive; b. Dec. 14, 1929; s. DuPree and Roslyn (Moncrief) J.; m. Margaret Virginia Malone, Dec. 28, 1948; children: Peggy Jordan DeSear, DuPree III, Lyn Jordan Whitworth, Terri Lee Jordan Chesser. AB, Mercer U., 1947; MEd, Emory U., 1954; LLB, Atlanta Law Sch., 1951, LLD, 1963, DLitt, 1971; postgrad., Crozer Theol. Sem., 1948-49, Nat. Inst. Pub. Affairs, summer 1967; postgrad. Inst. Life-Long Learning, Harvard U., 1979, postgrad. Inst. Ednl. Mgmt., 1981. Ordained to ministry So. Bapt. Conv., 1945;. Pastor Eden Bapt. Ch., Savannah, Ga., 1946-47, Duluth (Ga.) 1st Bapt. Ch., 1953-55; reporter Chester (Pa.) Times, 1948-49; assoc. dir. Radio and TV Commn. So. Bapt. Conv., Atlanta, 1949-52, acting dir., 1952-53; tchr. history, speech Ga. State U., Atlanta, 1952-55; tchr. Bible, English Westminster Schs., Atlanta, 1954-55; editor, pub., owner West End Star, Atlanta, 1955-66, N. DeKalb Record, Chamblee, Ga., 1956-64, TriCounty Graphic, Atlanta, 1962-64, Piedmont Satellite, 1967-68; pres. Jordan Enterprises, Inc., 1957-70, Jordan Internat. Enterprises Inc., 1991—, Jordan & Jordan Advt. and Pub. Rels., 1954—, Fun Products, Inc., 1968-69; pres. Success Publs., Inc., 1969—; pub. Success Orientation, 1969—; ptnr. WE Inc., convenience food stores, 1968-69; dir. pub. affairs and congl. rels. exec. office Pres. U.S., So. region Office Econ. Opportunity, Atlanta, 1965-69; nat. coord. Religious Orgs., OEO, Washington, 1968-69; news reporter, panelist TV stas., Atlanta, 1955-76; exec. dir. Assn. Pvt. Colls. and Univs. in Ga., 1970-81; dir. Successful Selling Seminars; pres. Ga. Coll. for Leadership Devel., 1969—. Mem. Gov.'s Rapid Transit Com., 1963-64, Gov.'s Com. for World's Fair in Atlanta, 1962-64; pres. Christian Coun. Met. Atlanta, 1973; chmn., CEO Jordan Family Found. Svcs., Inc., 1997—; bd. dirs. Atlanta Girls Club, YMCA, Boy Scouts Am. Named Man of Yr. radio stas., Atlanta, 1962, 63, West End Jaycees, 1962; recipient Quill award Sigma Delta Chi, 1962, 63; named Ky. Col., 1967; mem. hon. staff Gov. Ga., 1962-66, 70-74, 74-78; honored with Rev. Dr. DuPree Jordan, Jr. Day in State of Ga., 1973. Mem. AIM, ASTD, Nat. Press Club, West End Bus. Men's Assn. (pres. 1962-63), Chamblee-Doraville Bus. Men's Assn. (pres. 1963-64), Fulton County Grand Jurors Assn. (dir. 1961), Ga. State Chamber/Bus. and Industry Assn., Atlanta, DeKalb County (dir. 1961), World Future Soc., Pub. Rels. Soc. Am., Adminstrv. Mgmt. Soc., Am. Soc. Pub. Adminstrn., Sales and Mktg. Execs. Internat., Soc. Advancement Mgmt., Am. Mgmt. Assn., Am. Mktg. Assn., Am. Soc. Assn. Execs., Soc. Assn. Mgrs., Am. Assn. Coll. and Univ. Execs., So. Assn. Colls. (State Execs. Coun. coordinating chmn. 1980), State Assn. Execs. Coun., Ga., Internat. assn. bus. communicators, Internat. Soc. Ednl. Planners, Am. Acad. Polit. and Social Scis., Meeting Planners Internat., Nat. Spkrs. Assn. (founding mem., profl. awards com. 1980-81, dir. exec. com. 1982-84, sec. bd. 1983-84), Assn. Mgmt. Cons., Internat. Mgmt. Coun., Inst. Mgmt. Cons., Mgmt. Consultants (founding mem.), Internat. Group Agys. and Burs. (gen. program chmn. 1994), Sigma Delta Chi (dir. 1963), Blue Key, Phi Delta, Alpha Chi Omega, Alpha Psi Omega, Kappa Sigma. Home: 965 Oakhaven Dr Roswell GA 30075-1231 Office: Jordan Internat Enterprises PO Box 1400 Roswell GA 30077-1400

JORDAN, EDDIE J., prosecutor; b. Ft. Campbell, Ky., Oct. 6, 1952. BA with honors, Wesleyan U., 1974; JD, Rutgers U., 1977. Bar: Pa. 1977, La. 1982. Law clk. for Hon. Clifford Scott Green U.S. Dist. Ct. (ea. dist.) Pa., Phila.; assoc. Pepper, Hamilton & Scheetz, Phila.; asst. prof. law So. U., Baton Rouge, 1981-83; asst. U.S. atty. U.S. Dept. Justice, New Orleans, 1984-87; assoc. Sessions & Fishman, New Orleans, 1987-91, ptnr., 1991-92; of counsel Bryan Jupiter, New Orleans, 1992-94; U.S. atty. for ea. dist. La. U.S. Dept. Justice, New Orleans, 1994—. Mem. adv. com. on humam rels. City of New Orleans, 1993; mem. various bds. of dirs. Recipient A.P. Tureaud award Louis A. Martinet Legal Soc., 1992. Office: US Atty Ea Dist La Hale Boggs Bldg 501 Magazine St New Orleans LA 70130-3319

JORDAN, EDWARD GEORGE, business investor, former college president, former railroad executive; b. Oakland, Cal., Nov. 13, 1929; s. Edward A. and Alice (Smith) J.; m. Nancy Phyllis Schmidt, June 20, 1954; children: Susan Gail, Kathryn Claire, Jonathan Edward, Christopher Austin. B.A. in Econs. with honors, U. Calif. at Berkeley, 1951; M.B.A., Stanford U., 1953. Pres. Pinehurst Corp. (ins. and pension plans), Los Angeles, 1973-74, U.S. Ry. Assn., Washington, 1974-75; chmn., chief exec. officer Consol. Rail Corp., 1975-80, cons. to chmn., 1981; dean Cornell U. Grad. Sch. Bus. and Public Adminstrn., Ithaca, N.Y., 1981; exec. v.p. U. Pa., 1981-82; pres. Am. Coll., Bryn Mawr, Pa., 1982-87; bd. dirs. Aramark Corp., Global decision Group, Mission Rsch. Corp. Chmn. Hi-Speed Rail Authority. Mem. Merion Golf Club, Monterey Peninsula Country Club, Crosswater Club. Home: 26162 Ladera Dr Carmel CA 93923-9207

JORDAN, ELKE, molecular biologist, government medical research institute executive; b. Gottingen, Germany, Apr. 8, 1937; came to U.S., 1953, naturalized, 1961; d. Peter Friederich and Elisabeth A.K. (Lehmann) J.; m. Thomas H. Edelson, Aug. 21, 1972 (div. 1991). B.A., Goucher Coll., 1957; Ph.D, Johns Hopkins U., 1962. In various rsch. positions Harvard U., 1962-64, U. Cologne, Fed. Republic Germany, 1964-68, U. Wis., Madison, 1968-69, U. Calif., Berkeley, 1969-72; grants assoc. NIH, Bethesda, Md., 1972-73; coord. for collaborative rsch. Nat. Cancer Inst., NIH, Bethesda, Md., 1973-76; health scientist adminstr. Nat. Inst. Gen. Med. Scis., NIH, Bethesda, 1976-82, assoc. dir., 1982-88; dir. Office of Human Genome Rsch., NIH, Bethesda, 1988-89; dep. dir. Nat. Human Genome Rsch. Inst., NIH, Bethesda, 1989—. Contbr. articles on molecular biology of E. coli and bacteriophage lambda to profl. jours. NIH fellow, 1959-65; Helen Hay Whitney Found. fellow, 1965-68. Fellow AAAS; mem. Genetics Soc. Am., Am. Soc. for Human Genetics, Am. Soc. Microbiology. Office: Nat Ctr Human Genome Rsch Inst NIH 9000 Rockville Pike Bethesda MD 20892-0001

JORDAN, FRED, publishing company executive; m. Helen Jordan; children: Lynn, Ken. Sales mgr., advt. mgr., publicity mgr. Grove Press, Inc., N.Y.C., 1956-60, sr. editor, sr. v.p., 1960-71, editor-in-chief, exec. v.p., 1971-79, 85-90, sr. editor, 1983-85; pres., publisher Methuen, Inc., N.Y.C., 1979-81; publisher, editor Fred Jordan Books, N.Y.C., 1981-83; publisher Pantheon Books, N.Y.C., 1990-91, chmn., 1991-93; pub., editor Fred Jordan Books, Croton-on-Hudson, N.Y., 1993—; exec. dir. Fromm Internat. Publ. Co., N.Y.C., 1996—.

JORDAN, GLENN, director; b. San Antonio, Apr. 5, 1936. BA, Harvard U., 1957; postgrad., Yale U. Drama Sch., 1957-58. Dir. regional and stock theatre, including Cafe La Mama, late 1950s; N.Y. directorial debut with Another Evening With Harry Stoones, 1961; other plays include A Taste of Honey, 1968; Rosencrantz and Guildenstern Are Dead, 1969, A Streetcar Named Desire at Cin. Playhouse in the Park, 1973, All My Sons at Huntington Hartford Theatre, 1975; founder, N.Y. TV Theater, 1965, dir. various plays, including Paradise Lost and Hogan's Goat; dir. mini-series Benjamin Franklin, CBS, 1974 (Emmy award 1975, Peabody award); Family, ABC-TV series, 1976-77, including segment Rights of Friendship (Dirs. Guild Am. award); numerous TV plays for public TV, including Eccentricities of a Nightingale, 1976; The Displaced Person, 1976; TV movies including Shell Game, 1975, One Of My Wives Is Missing, 1975, Delta County U.S.A, 1977, In The Matter of Karen Ann Quinlan, 1977, Sunshine Christmas, 1977, Les Miserables, 1978, Son-Rise, A Miracle of Love, 1979, The Family Man, 1979, The Women's Room, 1980, Lois Gibbs and the Love Canal, 1982, Heartsounds, 1984 (Peabody award), Toughlove, 1985, Dress Gray, 1986, Something in Common, 1986, Promise, 1986 (2 Emmy awards for producing, directing, Peabody award, Golden Globe award), Echoes in the Darkness, 1987, Jesse, 1988, Home Fires Burning, 1988, Challenger, 1989, The Boys, 1990, Sarah Plain and Tall, 1990, Aftermath, 1990, O Pioneers!, 1991, Barbarians at the Gate, 1992 (Emmy award Outstanding Made for TV Movie, 1993, Golden Globe award, Best Mini-series or movie made for TV, 1994), To Dance with the White Dog, 1994, Jane's House, 1994, My Brother's Keeper, 1994, A Streetcar Named Desire, 1995, Jake's Women (Neil Simon), 1996, After Jimmy, 1996, Mary and Tim, 1996, A Christmas Memory, 1997, The Long Way Home, 1998, Legalese, 1998, Night Ride Home, 1999; dir: feature film Only When I Laugh (Neil Simon), 1981, The Buddy System, 1983, Mass Appeal, 1984. Recipient Emmy awards for N.Y. TV Theater Plays, 1970, Actors Choice, 1970. Office: Creative Artists Agy 9830 Wilshire Blvd Beverly Hills CA 90212-1825 also: 9401 Wilshire Blvd Ste 700 Beverly Hills CA 90212-2920

JORDAN, HENRY HELLMUT, JR., management consultant; b. Heidelberg, Germany, May 31, 1921; came to U.S., 1934, naturalized, 1940; s. Henry H. and Johanna (Narath) J.; m. Hildegarde C. Dallmeyer, Mar. 11, 1942 (dec. 1987); children: Sandra, Michael, Patric, Henry Hellmut; m. Martha J. McClain Ghafary, Jan. 17, 1995. Student U. Cin., 1938-39. Commd. 2d lt. U.S. Army, 1942, advanced through grades to maj., 1956; staff officer Ordnance Corps; ret., 1961; mgr. prodn. and inventory control Sperry Corp., N.Y.C., 1961-66, dir. quality control and field svc. engring., 1967-68; mgmt. cons. Wright Assos. Inc., N.Y.C., 1969-70; pres. Henry Jordan & Assos., N.Y.C., 1970-74; mng. ptnr. Cons. Svcs., Inc., Atlanta, 1975-88; chmn. Ctr. for Inventory Mgmt., Sugar Hill, Ga., 1975—; chmn. bd. Crugers Svcs. Corp., Atlanta. Editl. bd. Jour. Prodn. and Inventory Mgmt.; editor: Production and Inventory Control Handbook, 1997, System Implementation Handbook, 1982, Cycle Counting for Record Accuracy, 1994. Mem. Sugar Hill United Meth. Ch., vice ch. coun. Mem. Inst. Indsl. Engrs. (sr. life), Inst. Mgmt. Cons. (cert., chmn. Atlanta chpt.), Am. Prodn. & Inventory Control Soc. (chmn. curricula and cert. council; Presdl. award of Merit 1974, 89, hon. life 1989—), Am. Radio Relay League. Methodist. Club: Yacht Hilton Head. Home and Office: 900 Secret Cove Dr Sugar Hill GA 30518-5366

JORDAN, HENRY PRESTON, JR., manufacturer's representative; b. Roanoke, Va., Sept. 3, 1926; s. Henry Preston and Emily Lucille (Luck) J.; m. June Farley Dyson, Sept. 4, 1948; children: Kathryn Jordan Streetman, Rebecca Jordan Lidard, June Jordan Collins. BS in Commerce, U. Va., 1950. Supt. comml. and indsl. constrn. Richardson Way and Elec. Corp., Roanoke, 1952-56; sales engr. H.C. Gundlach Co., Richmond, Va., 1958-64; pres. Jordan Metal Co., Richmond, 1964-76, Jordan Mech. Sales, Richmond, 1976—; chmn. lay adv. sheet metal dept. Richmond Tech. Ctr., 1974. Del. White House Conf. on Sm. Bus., 1986, 95; sec. Jr. Achievement, Roanoke, 1961-62, v.p., Richmond, 1971-73; pres. Beaumont Learning Ctr. Aux., 1979-81, Beaumont Correctional Ctr., 1995; nominating com. Richmond Bapt. Assn., 1993-94; moderator Derbyshire Bapt. Ch., 1982, chmn. bd. deacons, 1967, chmn., 1998; bd. dirs. Justice Fellowship of Va. Task Force; mem. adv. coun. SBA Region III, Richmond, 1978-88, chmn., 1988; bd. dirs. Cmty. Adv. Bd. State Penintentiary; bd. dirs. Douglas S. Freeman H.S., pres. Booster Club, 1972; bus. adv. coun. Henrico County Police, lts. promotion bd., 1996; mem. Nat. Sm. Bus. Attitudes Rsch. Panel; organizing bd. Va. Youth Partnership Found., 1996. Recipient Achievement award Big Bros., Richmond, 1969, Douglas S. Freeman 12th Man award, 1971, Samy Um Meml. award Kmer Mission, 1996. Mem. ASHRAE (treas. Richmond chpt., pres. 1987-88, 2d pl. energy conservation award 1984, '85, 1st pl. 1987), Rotary (pres. West Richmond 1973-74, dist. scholarship com., Paul Harris fellow), Beta Theta Pi, Theta Tau, Lambda Pi. Republican. Home: 10206 Navarre Ct Richmond VA 23233-5539 Office: PO Box 29785 Richmond VA 23242-0785

JORDAN, HOWARD EMERSON, retired engineering executive, consultant; b. State College, N.Mex., May 14, 1926; s. Howard E. and Elizabeth (Bruden) J.; children: Blair, Julie. BSEE, U. Wis., 1946; MS, Case Western Res. U., 1958, PhD, 1966. With Rayovac Co., Madison, Wis., 1946-52; with Reliance Elec., Cleve., 1954-93, dir. corp. R & D, 1993—; pvt. cons. Author: Energy Efficient Electric Motors and Their Application, 1983, 2d edit., 1994; contbg. author: Handbook of Electric Machines, 1987. Served to 1st lt. USAF, 1952-54. Recipient Disting. Svc. citation U. Wis., 1989. Fellow IEEE (sr.); mem. Nat. Electrical Mfrs. Assn. (chmn. motor and generator sect. 1979). Presbyterian.

JORDAN, IRVING KING, university president. Pres. Gallaudet U., Washington, 1988—. Office: Gallaudet U Office of President 800 Florida Ave NE Washington DC 20002-3660

JORDAN, JEFFREY GUY, marketing and marketing research consultant; b. Oshkosh, Wis., May 21, 1950; s. Berwin Russell and Delores Suzanne (Tomlitz) J. BS, U. Wis., Oshkosh, 1973; postgrad., UCLA, 1978. Analyst corp. planning and rsch. May Co. Dept. Store, L.A., 1973-77; dir. mktg. svcs. DJMC Advt., L.A., 1977-80; dir. mktg. Wienerschnitzel, Internat., Newport Beach, Calif., 1980-84, York Steakhouse Restaurants (Gen. Mills), Columbus, Ohio, 1984-85, Paragon Restaurant Group, San Diego, 1985-87; v.p. mktg. Paragon Steakhouse Restaurants, Inc., San Diego, 1987-94; owner, pres. 1-on-One Mktg. Assocs., 1994—; cons., presenter U.S. Internat. U., San Diego, 1989. Mem. Conv. and Visitors Bur., San Diego; vol. Boys' Club of Am., Oshkosh, 1973-74; fundraising coord. Am. Cancer Soc., L.A., 1976. Mem. Am. Mktg. Assn. (treas., bd. dirs. 1996-97), Multi Unit Foodservice Operators Assn., San Diego Advt. Assn. (creative exec. 1986-88), San Diego C. of C. Republican. Lutheran. Avocations: sports, travel, photography.

JORDAN, JOE J., architect; b. Phila., May 5, 1923; s. Edmund F. and Elizabeth N. (Jungkurth) J.; m. Sarah Jeanne Connolly, Nov. 1, 1974. B.S. in Architecture, U. Ill., 1949. Prin. Joe J. Jordan, FAIA, Phila., 1961-81; ptnr. The Delta Group, Phila., 1972-74; prin., pres. Jordan, Mitchell Inc., Phila., 1981-93; UN tech. assistance expert Middle East Tech. U., Ankara, Turkey, 1958-60, acting head dept. architecture, 1959, archtl. advisor to univ. pres., 1960; mem. faculty dept. architecture Drexel U., Phila., 1962, adj. prof., 1964, head dept., 1965-77. Contbr. articles to profl. jours., writer Nat. Coun. Aging. Mem. Citizens Coun. on City Planning, Phila., 1956-70; bd. dirs. Phila. Ctr. for Older People, 1964-70, Reed St. Neighborhood House, Phila., 1968-69; mem. Mayor's Com. on Housing, Phila., 1973-76; mem. Gov. Task Force on Multi-Svc. Sr. Ctrs. in Pa., 1975-78, N.J. Assisted Living Facilities Task Force, 1995-96; pres. Cape May Tennis Club Inc., 1991-93; v.p. Greater Cape May Hist. Soc., 1998—. Recipient numerous archtl. awards including award of excellence Urban Design Mag.; Fulbright fellow, 1954-55. Fellow AIA (Citation for Excellence Phila. Chpt., Honor award, others); mem. Pa. Soc. Architects, Pa. Assn. Non-Profit Homes for the Aging, Nat. Council on Aging. Home: PO 22 Cape May Point PA 08212

JORDAN, JOHN W., II, holding company executive; b. 1948. With The Jordan Co., N.Y.C., 1982—; CEO Jordan Industries, Inc., Deerfield, Ill. Office: The Jordan Co 767 Fifth Ave 45th Fl New York NY 10153 Office: Jordan Industries Inc 875 N Michigan Ave Chicago IL 60611-1803

JORDAN, JOSEPH LOUIS, education educator, government official. Degree in bus. adminstrn. and mktg., St. Lawrence Coll.; MBA, Clarkson U. Prof. bus. St. Lawrence Coll., Brockville, Can., 1984-87, St. Lawrence Coll, Brockville, Can., 1988-93; coord. operational rev. Ministry Colls. and Univs., 1987-88; coord., prof. internat. edn. dept. St. Lawrence Coll, Brockville, Can., 1993—; owner summer retail bus. Brockville, 1990-93; designer, implementor computer tng. courses, Africa; fulltime provincial campaign exec., 1987, 88, 92, 93, 96. Active Parliament for Leeds-Grenville, fed. and provincial liberal assns., nat. policy and leadership convs.

JORDAN, JUDITH VICTORIA, clinical psychologist, educator; b. Milw., July 28, 1943; d. Claus and Charlotte (Backus) J.; m. William M. Redpath, Aug. 11, 1973. AB, Brown U., 1965; MA, Harvard U., 1968, PhD, 1973. Diplomate Am. Bd. Profl. Psychology. Psychologist Human Relations Service, Wellesley, Mass., 1971-73; assoc. psychologist McLean Hosp., Belmont, Mass., 1978-93, psychologist, 1993—, dir. women's studies program, 1988—, dir. tng. in psychology, 1991, dir. Women's Treatment Network, 1992—; vis. scholar Stone Ctr. Wellesley Coll., 1985—; asst. prof. psychiatry Harvard Med. Sch., 1988—; co-dir. Jean Baker Miller Tng. Inst., Wellesley Coll. 1998; adv. bd Fox TV Network, Women First healthcare., 1998; disting. prof. Menninger Clinic, 1999. Author: Empathy and Self Boundries, 1984, Women's Growth in Connection, 1991, (with others) The Self in Relation, 1986; editor, author: Relational Self in Women; editor: Women's Growth in Diversity, 1997. Fellow Am. Psychol. Assn.; mem. Mass. Psychol. Assn. (bd. dirs. 1983-85, Career Achievement award for outstanding contbns. to advancement of psychology as a sci. and a profession), Phi Beta Kappa. Office: McLean Hosp 114 Waltham St Lexington MA 02421-5409

JORDAN, KAREN LEIGH, newspaper travel editor; b. Freeport, Tex., Nov. 20, 1954; d. Matt Culum and Laura Louise (English) Arrington; m. William David Jordan, May 8, 1982; 1 child, Lauren Kathryn. BA in Journalism magna cum laude, Tex. A&M U., 1976. Intern Wall St. Jour., Dallas, summer 1976; asst. news editor Abilene (Tex.) Reporter-News, 1976-77; sports copy editor Dallas Morning News, 1977-79, asst. travel editor, 1979-81, travel editor, 1981—; judge journalism competition Univ. Interscholastic League, Tex., 1976. Contbg. writer (guidebook) Fodor's Tex., 1983—; writer (guidebook) Fodor's Dallas-Fort Worth, 1983—; copy editor Dallas-Ft. Worth Metroplex Football mag., 1978-80. Teaching asst. Garden Ridge Ch. of Christ, Lewisville, Tex., 1988—. Recipient state headline writing award AP Mng. Editors, 1977. Mem. Soc. Am. Travel Writers (writing, editing and photography awards 1981—), Phi Kappa Phi, Sigma Delta Chi, Alpha Lambda Delta. Avocations: travel, snow skiing, photography, reading, sports. Office: Dallas Morning News Comm Ctr PO Box 655237 Dallas TX 75265-5237

JORDAN, KARIN BALTEN-BABKOWSKI, health facility administrator; b. Hannover, Germany, July 26, 1958; came to U.S., 1979; d. Ekkehard and Liselotte (Pache) Babkowski; m. Wayne Donald Jordan, June 13, 1981. BA in Biology cum laude, Colo. Christian Coll., Denver, 1987; MA in Counseling, Rollins Coll., Winter Park, Fla., 1989; PhD in Child and Family Devel., U. Ga., 1992. RN; lic. marriage and family therapist, Colo.; cert. kindergarten tchr., Germany. Intern in counseling Hope and Help Ctr., Orlando, Fla., 1989; intern in marriage and family therapy McPhaul Ctr., Athens, 1990-91; asst. clin. dir. Cross Keys Counseling Ctr., Atlanta, 1991-93; practicum supr. U. Colo., Denver, 1993, clin. dir., faculty, 1994—; bd. dirs. Maria Drost Svcs.; rsch. asst. dept. child and family devel. U. Ga., Athens, 1989-91; bd. dirs., counselor Sun Valley Family Hope Counseling Ctr., Denver, 1996—. Contbr. articles to profl. jours. Mem. mental health com. 9News Health Fair, Denver, 1995—; mem. com. Colo. Okla. Resource Coun., Denver, 1996—; apptd. to augmenting panel Colo. State Grievance Bd., 1997-98. Mem. APA (divsn. 16 com. children, youth, families 1996—), Am. Assn. Marriage Family Therapy (cert. therapist, supr.), Colo. Assn. Marriage Family Therapy (pub. rels. com. 1996—, v.p.), Colo. Counseling Assn., Internat. Assn. Marriage Family Counselors, Nat. Acad. Cert. Family Therapist. Avocations: reading, drawing, traveling. Office: Univ Colo Sch Edn Campus Box 106 PO Box 173364 Denver CO 80217-3364

JORDAN, LARRY R., career officer; b. Feb. 7, 1946. Commd. officer U.S. Army, advanced through grades to lt. gen., 1997—. Office: 1700 Army Pentagon Washington DC 20310-1700

JORDAN, LEO JOHN, lawyer; b. Pittston, Pa., Nov. 24, 1931; s. Joseph Thomas and Agnes (Granahan) J.; children: Leo John, Michael, Paul, Mary Terese; m. Carla Temple. AB in Econ., King's Coll., 1953; JD, U. Md., 1960. Bar: Md. 1960, Tex. 1965, Ill. 1990, N.Y. 1997. Claim supr. Ins. Co. N.AM., Phila., 1956-62; atty. State Farm Ins. Cos., Bloomington, Ill., 1962-96; ret., 1996—. Contbr. articles to profl. jours. Commr. Richardson City Planning Commn., Tex., 1964-68. With USN, 1954-56. Mem. ABA (ho. of dels., chair tort and ins. practice sect. 1992-93), Chgo. Bar Assn., Nat. Com. Property Ins. (chmn. bd. dirs. 1978-79), N.Y. State Bar Assn., Assn. Bar City N.Y., Fedn. Ins. and Corp. Counsel, Def. Rsch. Inst., Md. State Bar Assn., Tex. State Bar Assn., Ill. State Bar Assn. Democrat. Roman Catholic. Avocations: tennis, reading, marathon running. Home: 45 Lilly Rd Wanaque NJ 07465-2419

JORDAN, LINDA SUSAN DARNELL, elementary school educator; b. Greenville, Tex., Sept. 5, 1955; d. Charles Albert and Dorothy Nell (Everheart) Darnell; m. Mark Alan Jordan, Sept. 1, 1979; children: Sarah Tison, Michael Albert. BE, East Tex. State U., 1977. Cert. elem. edn. tchr. 1-8, secondary edn. tchr. 9-12. County ext. agt. Tex. A & M U., Wise County, Tex., 1977-81; tchr. Decatur (Tex.) Ind. Sch. Dist., 1981-87, 91—; tech. planning com. Decatur Ind. Sch. Dist., 1991-95, mem. campus improvement com., 1992-94, 98—. Sun. sch. educator First United Meth. Ch., Decatur, 1992-96, acolyte coord., 1990-91, 95-96, Sun. sch. coord., 1989-90; mem. Decatur Jr. Woman's Club, 1977-79. Recipient Apple of the Month award Twin Lakes Hosp., 1992. Mem. Tex. Classroom Tchrs. Orgn. Avocations: quilting, cake decorating, phys. fitness activities, reading, smocking. Home: 173 PR 4231 Decatur TX 76234-9802 Office: Decatur Elem Sch 1300 Deer Park Rd Decatur TX 76234-4403

JORDAN, LOIS WENGER, university official; b. Madison, Wis., Dec. 28, 1943; d. Alfred and Phyllis Mae (Schaeffer) Wenger; m. William Malcolm Jordan, Dec. 28, 1963; children: William Andre, Christopher Allan. BS, Millersville (Pa.) U., 1969. Tchr. Hempfield Sch. Dist., Lancaster, Pa., 1969-70, Lancaster Sch. Dist., 1975-80; dir. Upward Bound, Millersville U., 1980-82; dir. devel. St. Joseph Hosp., Lancaster, 1982-87; assoc. dir. devel. Pa. State U. Coll. Medicine, Hershey, 1987-97; dir. devel. Pa. State U., Capitol Coll., 1997—. Author: (children's book) What's a Hospital Like?, 1972. Mem. Lancaster Jr. League, 1975—; trustee St. Joseph Hosp., 1979-82, James Buchanan Found., Lancaster, 1982-94, Highland Presbyn. Ch., Lancaster, 1982-85. Recipient Cheston M. Berlin svc. award Pa. State U. Alumni Assn., 1995, Outstanding Cmty. Svc. award Jr. League Assn., 1995. Mem. Assn. Healthcare Philanthropy (bd. dirs. 1990-92), Assn. Am. Med. Colls. Republican. Avocations: travel, hiking, cooking. Home: 1734

Colonial Manor Dr Lancaster PA 17603-6034 Office: Pa State U 777 W Harrisburg Pike Middletown PA 17057-4846

JORDAN, MARK HENRY, consulting civil engineer; b. Lawrence, Mass., Apr. 10, 1915; s. Joseph Augustine and Gertrude (O'Connell) J.; m. Louise Sullivan, June 23, 1939; children: Mary Elizabeth (Mrs. Delio Gianturco), Margaret Michaela. B.S., U.S. Naval Acad., 1937; M. Civil Engring., Rensselaer Poly. Inst., 1942, M.S., 1965, Ph.D., 1968. Registered profl. engr., N.J., N.Y. Commd. ensign U.S. Navy, 1937, advanced through grades to capt., 1955; comdr. 6th Seabee Battalion South Pacific, 1943-44; comdr. 103d Seabee Battalion Central Pacific, 1951-52; comdr. Civil Engr. Corps. Sch. Port Hueneme, Calif., 1960-63; ret., 1963; assoc. prof. civil engring. U. Mo., Columbia, 1966-67; prof. civil engring. Rensselaer Poly. Inst., 1968-77, prof. emeritus, 1977—, dean continuing studies, 1967-72, chmn. civil engring., 1972-73; cons. engr. Smith & Mahoney, Albany, N.Y., 1975-78; individual practice as cons. engr., 1978—. Author: (with others) Saga of the Sixth, 1950, Iron Brigade General, 1993. Mem. Rensselaer County Charter Commn., 1969-71; Bd. dirs. United Community Services, Troy, N.Y., 1969-75. Decorated Bronze Star with V, Presdl. Unit citation. Fellow ASCE (life); mem. NSPE, Am. Arbitration Assn., Am. Soc. Engring. Edn., Soc. Am. Mil. Engrs. (local post pres.), Am. Pub. Works Assn., Sigma Xi, Chi Epsilon. Roman Catholic. Club: Fort Orange (Albany, N.Y.). Home: 46 East Rd Troy NY 12180-6861 Office: 256 Broadway Troy NY 12180-3237

JORDAN, MARVIN EVANS, JR., record company executive; b. Muskogee, Okla., Aug. 13, 1944; s. Marvin Evans and May Elizabeth (Williams) J.; m. Suonja Summirs, Aug. 23, 1969 (div. 1983); m. Kristine Lynn Johnson, Nov. 8, 1984; children: Marvin Edwin, Mary Elizabeth, Michael Evans-Lyman; stepchildren: Daniel Noah Winger, David Paul Winger, Karen LaVohn Winger Van Hofer, Cory Brent Winger, Jay Martin Winger, Aaron Thomas Jones, Benjamin Arthur Jones Jordan, Seth Ailean Jones Jordan, Sara Jean Jones Jordan. BS, City U., Bellevue, Wash., 1981, MBA, 1983. Producer, promoter Natures Green Oratory Presents, Seattle, 1966-67; v.p. North Hollywood Releasing, Seattle, 1967-68; prin. Jordan Assocs., Seattle, 1969-89; chmn. bd. Western-Internat. Artists, Inc., 1976-78; pres. Standard Record Co., Bellingham, Wash., 1989—; mem. agy. mktg. network Star Power, 1991-93; artistic dir. Concerts Nimbus, Seattle, 1981-84; co-dir. Kids Khorus Klub, Olympia, Wash., 1985-87. Composer, lyricist, collaborator (song) Heart Songs, 1994; vocalist (album) After All, 1994; numerous unpub. songs. Asst. dist. commr. Whatcom dist. Mount Baker area coun. Boy Scouts Am., 1987-91, 94-98, chmn. coun. exploring svc. team, 1993-94; steering com. Adult Attention Deficit Disorder Assn., 1993-94. With U.S. Army, 1963-66. Named Disting. Commr. Boy Scouts Am., 1992, recipient Wood Badge, 1990. Mem. Northwest Area Music Assn. Mem. LDS Ch. Avocations: residential design, computer programming, reading. Office: Standard Record Co 3879 Grandview Rd Ferndale WA 98248-8743

JORDAN, MARY LUCILLE, commissioner; m. Ben C. Elliott, Aug. 23, 1980; children: Elizabeth Elliott, Armando Elliott, C. Daniel Elliott. Student, Hull U., 1969-70; BA cum laude, Bonaventure U., 1971; JD, Antioch Law Sch., 1976. Bar: N.Y., 1977, D.C., 1978. Atty. Office of Fed. Register Nat. Archives & Records Adminstrn., Washington, 1976-77; sr. staff atty. United Mine Workers Am., Washington, 1977-94; chmn. Fed. Mine Safety and Health Rev. Commn., Washington, 1994—. Office: Fed Mine Safety Health Rev Commn 1730 K St NW Fl 6 Washington DC 20006-3868*

JORDAN, MATT, professional soccer player; b. Aurora, Colo., Oct. 13, 1975. Student, Clemson U. Goalkeeper Dallas Burn, 1998—. Office: c/o Dallas Burn 2602 McKinney Ste 200 Dallas TX 75204*

JORDAN, MICHAEL HUGH, retired broadcasting and media company executive; b. Kansas City, Mo., June 15, 1936; m. Kathryn Hiett, Apr. 8, 1961; children: Kathryn, Stephen. BSChemE, Yale U., 1957; MSChemE, Princeton U., 1959. Cons., prin. McKinsey & Co., Toronto, London and Cleve., 1964-74; dir. fin. planning PepsiCo, Purchase, N.Y., 1974-76, sr. v.p. planning and devel., 1976-77; sr. v.p. mfg. ops. Frito-Lay div. PepsiCo Internat., Dallas, 1977-82, pres., CEO, 1983-85; pres. PepsiCo Foods Internat., 1982-83; exec. v.p., CFO PepsiCo Inc., Purchase, 1985-86, pres., 1986, also bd. dirs.; pres., CEO PepsiCo Worldwide, Dallas, 1987-92; chmn., CEO Westinghouse Electric Corp., Pitts., 1993—, chmn., bd. dirs.; ptnr. Clayton, Dubilier and Rice, N.Y.C., 1992-93; bd. dirs. Melville Corp., Rhone-Poulenc Rorer, Aetna, Dell Computer Inc. Bd. dirs. United Negro Coll. Fund, 1986—; chmn. Ctr. for Excellence in Edn., Washington, 1988-92. Recipient cert. nuclear engring. Bettis Labs. Atomic Power Labs., Pitts. Office: care CBS Gateway Ctr 51 W 52nd St New York NY 10019-6119*

JORDAN, MICHAEL JEFFREY, retired professional basketball player, retired baseball player; b. Bklyn., Feb. 17, 1963; s. James and Deloris Jordan; m. Juanita Vanoy, Sept., 1989; children: Jeffrey Michael, Marcus James, Jasmine. Student, U. N.C., 1981-84. Basketball player Chicago Bulls, 1984-93, 95-98; ret., 1998; baseball player Chicago White Sox AA Team, 1994-95; mem. NCAA Championship Team, 1982, U.S. Olympic Team (received Gold Medal), 1984, 92; holder record for most points in an NBA playoff game with 63. Author: RareAir: Michael on Michael, 1993. Recipient Naismith award, 1984, Wooden award, 1984, Rookie of Yr. award, NBA, 1985, IBM award, 1985, 89, Schick Pivotal Player award, 1985, 89; named Seagram's NBA Player of Yr., 1987, Slam-Dunk Championship winner, 1987, 88; named to Sporting News All-Am. first team, 1983-84, NBA All-Star team, 1985-93, 96-98, All NBA First Team, 1987-93, 96-98, NBA All-Def. Team, 1988-93, 96-98, NBA All-Star Game Most Valuable Player, 1988, 96, 98, NBA Def. Player of Yr., 1988, NBA Most Valuable Player, 1988, 91, 92, 96-98, NBA Finals MVP 1991-93, 96-98; mem. NBA championship team, 1991-93, 96-98. Mem. NCAA divsn. 1 championship team, 1982; NBA Scoring Leader, 1986-93, 96-98. *

JORDAN, MICHELLE DENISE, lawyer; b. Chgo., Oct. 29, 1954; d. John A. and Margaret (O'Dood) J. BA in Polit. Sci., Loyola U, Chgo., 1974; JD, U. Mich., 1977. Bar. Ill. 1977, U.S. Dist. Ct. (no. dist.) Ill. 1978. Asst. state's atty. State's Attys. Office, Chgo., 1977-82; pvt. practice Chgo., 1983-84; with Ill. Atty. Gen.'s Office, Chgo., 1984-90, chief environ. control div., 1988-90; ptnr. Hopkins & Sutter, Chgo., 1991-93; apptd. dep. regional adminstr. region 5 U.S. EPA, Chgo., 1994—. Active Operation Push, Chgo., 1971—. Recipient Kizzy Image Achievement and Svc. award, 1990; named in Am.'s Top 100 Bus. and Profl. Women, Dollars and SenseMag., Chgo., 1988. Mem. Ill. Bar Assn., Chgo. Bar Assn. (bd. mgrs., chmn. criminal law com. 1987-88, mem. hearing divsn., jud. evaluation com. 1987-88, exec. coun. 1987-88), Cook County Bar Assn., Nat. Bar Assn., Alpha Sigma Nu. Democrat. Baptist. Office: US EPA 19th Fl 77 W Jackson Blvd Ste 19 Chicago IL 60604-3511

JORDAN, MICHELLE HENRIETTA, public relations company executive; b. Sussex, Eng., Sept. 19, 1948; came to U.S., 1975; d. Raymond Cameron and Liliane (Ambar) J.; m. Billy Owens, 1994. Student, Sorbonne, 1966-67. With Coordinated Mktg. Services Ltd., London, 1967-71; dir. Spectrum Public Relations, London, 1971-74; with Rowland Co., N.Y.C., 1975-87, exec. v.p.; sr. v.p., mng. dir. mktg. svcs. div. Hill and Knowlton, N.Y.C., 1987-91; prin. The Dilenschneider Group, N.Y.C., 1991-94; v.p. Digital Pictures, San Mateo, Calif., 1994-96; pres. The GCI Group, L.A., 1996-98; owner Jordan LLC, 1998—. Mem. Mayor N.Y.C. Commn. Status Women, 1980-86; bd. dirs. New Dramatists, Religion in Am. Life, 1992-94. Recipient Matrix award N.Y. Women in Communications, 1990. Office: Jordan LLC Ste 1280 18101 Von Karman Ave Irvine CA 92612

JORDAN, NEIL PATRICK, film director; b. Sligo County, Ireland, Feb. 25, 1950. BA, Univ. Coll., Dublin, Ireland, 1968. Dir. feature films Angel, 1983, Company of Wolves, 1985, Mona Lisa, 1986, High Spirits, 1987, We're No Angels, 1989, The Miracle, 1990, The Crying Game, 1992, Interview with the Vampire, 1994; author: (fiction) The Past, 1979, A Night in Tunisia, 1979 (Guardian Fiction prize 1979), The Dream of a Beast, 1983 (Acad. Award Best Original Screenplay), Sunrise With Sea Monster, 1995. Office: Jenne Casarotto/Casarotto Co Ltd, Nat House 60/66 Wardour St, London WIV 3HP, England*

JORDAN, NEIL ROBERT, government telecommunications consultant; b. Montclair, N.J., Jan. 25, 1951; s. Robert Fredrick and Margaret Louise (Freehauf) J.; m. Susan Holman, Aug. 26, 1983; children: Clinton Robert, Kristen Alexandra, Jessica Anne. Student, U. Ariz., 1979-80, U. Md. Extension, 1978-79, 80-81. Automotive salesman GM, 1970-77; enlisted USN, 1973, telecom., security specialist, 1973-83; telecom., security mgr. Dept. of Def., U.S. Govt., 1985—; cons., CEO, Need To Know Cons., St. Marys, Ga., 1991—; speaker seminars. Author: Auto Buying Power, 1991, Controlling Your Money, 1992, Your Time, Your Freedom, 1992, Positive Thinking, 1993, Free Publicity for Your Business, 1993, Your Business In-House Advertising Agency, 1993, The Wedding Planner, 1994, Total Customer Service, 1995. Mem. Parent Tchrs. Assn. St. Marys, 1991. Mem. St. Marys C. of C. Republican. Methodist. Avocations: water sports, hiking, golf. Home: 306 Westgate Cir Saint Marys GA 31558-4805 Office: Need To Know Cons 555 Charlie Smith Sr Hwy Ste 8 # 142 Saint Marys GA 31558-4805

JORDAN, PAMELA LEE, educator; b. Indpls., Apr. 21, 1956; d. Wilford Lee and Helen Ruth J. MA, Ball State U., 1982, Ind. Wesleyan U., 1992; PhD, Ball State U., 1997. Cert. tchr. Ind. Tchr. Jones Middle Sch., Marion, Ind., 1977-88; res. dir. Ind. Wesleyan U., Marion, Ind., 1988-90; tchr. George Wash. High Sch., Indpls., 1990-91; mem. faculty Taylor U., Fort Wayne, Ind., 1992—. Editor Light and Life Comms., 1998—. Mem. Nat. Coun. Tchrs. English, Conf. Christianity and Lit., Lewis and Friends Soc., George MacDonald Soc. Mem. Free Meth. Ch. E-mail: pmjordan@tayloru.edu. Office: Taylor Univ Fort Wayne 1025 W Rudisill Blvd Fort Wayne IN 46807

JORDAN, PATRICIA JAMES, secondary education educator. Math. tchr. Roslyn (N.Y.) High Sch. Named N.Y. State Tchr. of Yr., 1993, Outstanding Tchr. Math. Disney Am. Tchr. Awards. Office: Roslyn High Sch Round Hill Rd Roslyn Heights NY 11577

JORDAN, PAUL, music director; b. N.Y.C., Mar. 12, 1939; s. Henry Paul and Irene B (Brandt) J.; m. Xilin Feng, Dec. 20, 1993; 1 child, Libai Henry Feng Jordan. State degree in Sacred Music, Staatliche Hochschule für Musik, Frankfurt, Germany, 1963; MusM, Yale U., 1967; D of Mus. Arts in Conducting, Am. Conservatory Music, Chgo., 1998. Music dir. United Church on the Green, New Haven, Conn., 1964-74; music prof. SUNY, Binghamton, 1973-95; music dir. Stratford (Conn.) United Methodist Church, 1996—; instr. Neighborhood Music Sch., New Haven, 1997—. Solo concerts in more than 100 venues on 4 continents including Leipzig Gewandhaus, Berlin State Playhouse, Freiburg and Vienna cathedrals; comml. recs.; composer of 40 works for orchestral, choral and chamber ensembles and for keyboard; contbr. articles to profl. jours. Recipient Deutscher Schallplattenpreis nomination German Phon Acad., 1976; Solo Recitalist's fellow Nat. Endowment for Arts, Washington, 1983. Mem. Conductors Guild, Am. Guild Organists. Home: 16 Hughes Pl New Haven CT 06511-4904

JORDAN, RANDALL WARREN, optometrist; b. Camilla, Ga., May 19, 1952; s. Billie Howard and Sarah Ann (Richards) J.; m. Angela Marie Farmer, May 15, 1982; 1 child, Samantha Marie. BS in Biology, So. Coll. Optometry, 1987, OD, 1989. Supply and distbn. mgr. Phoebe Putney Meml. Hosp., Albany, Ga., 1981-85; ophthalmic technician Omni Eye Svcs., Memphis, 1987; optometrist Albany Retinal-Eye Ctr., Albany, 1989-90, Eyecare Assocs. Ga., Brunswick, 1990-91, Eye Med, Chamblee, 1992-95; optometrist Dougherty County Health Dept., Albany, 1989-90, Dept. Children's Med. Svcs., Albany, 1989-90, Lion's Club Vision Screening, Montezuma, Ga., 1989; mem. Emory Vision Correction Ctr. With U.S. Army, 1972-74. Mem. Am. Optometric Assn., Ga. Optometric Assn., Kiwanis, Beta Sigma Kappa, Omega Delta, Phi Theta Upsilon. Avocations: water skiing, scuba diving, photography, reading, music. Home: 895 1st St NW Cairo GA 31728-1904 Office: PO Box 268 Cairo GA 31728-0268

JORDAN, RICHARD CHARLES, engineering executive; b. Mpls., Apr. 16, 1909; s. A.C. and Estelle R. (Martin) J.; m. Freda M. Laudon, Aug. 10, 1935; children: Mary Ann, Carol Lynn, Linda Lee. B. Aero. Engring., U. Minn., 1931, M.S., 1933, Ph.D., 1940. In charge air conditioning div. Mpls. br. Am. Radiator & Standard San. Corp., 1933-36; instr. petroleum engring. U. Tulsa, 1936-37; instr. engring. expt. sta. U. Minn., Mpls., 1937-41, asst. dir., 1941-44, assoc. prof., 1944-45, prof., asst. head mech. engring. dept., 1946-49, prof., head dept. mech. engring., 1950-77, prof., head Sch. Mech. and Aero. Engring., 1966-77, acting assoc. dean Inst. Tech., 1977-78, assoc. dean, 1978-85; pres. Jordan Assocs., 1985—; dir. Onan Corp. of McGraw-Edison; cons. various refrigeration and air conditioning cos., 1937—; cons. NSF, U.S. Dept. State, Control Data Corp., others.; Mem. engring. sci. adv. panel NSF, 1954-57, chmn., 1957; mem. div. engring. and indsl. research NRC, mem. exec. com., 1957-69, chmn., 1962-65; del. OAS Conf. on Strategy for Tech. Devel. Latin Am., Chile, 1969; chmn. U.S.-Brazil Sci. Coop. Program Com. on Indsl. Research, Rio de Janeiro, 1967, Washington, 1967, Belo Horizonte, 1968, Houston, 1968; del. World Power Conf., Melbourne, 1962; v.p. sci. council Internat. Institut de du Froid, 1967-71; cons. to World Bank on alternative energy for Northeastern Brazil, 1976. Author: (with Priester) Refrigeration and Air Conditioning, 1948, rev. edit., 1956, also more than 300 publs. on mech. engring., environ. control, solar energy, energy resources, engring. edn., tech. transfer.; Contbr. Mech. Engring. Recipient F. Paul Anderson medal ASHRAE, 1966, E.K. Campbell award, 1966, Outstanding Publs. Golden Key award, 1994, Outstanding Achievement award U. Minn., 1979; elected to Solar Energy Hall of Fame, 1980; Richard C. Jordan disting. prof. in mech. engring. established in his honor, 1994. Fellow ASME, AAAS, ASHRAE (presdl. mem.); mem. Nat. Acad. Engring., Assn. Applied Solar Energy (adv. council 1958-61), Am. Soc. Refrigerating Engrs. (1st v.p. 1952, pres. 1953, dir., council mem. 1946-53), Am. Soc. Engring. Edn., AAAS, Nat., Minn. (Engr. of Yr. award 1972), socs. profl. engrs., Internat. Inst. Refrigeration (hon. mem., del. NRC to exec. com. 1957-76, v.p. exec. com. 1959-63, v.p. sci. council 1963-71), Engr. Council Profl. Devel. (chmn. regional edn. and accreditation com.), Sigma Xi, Tau Beta Pi, Pi Tau Sigma, Sigma Chi. Club: Campus. Home and Office: 18418 Horseshoe Circle Rio Verde AZ 85263-7036

JORDAN, ROBERT EARL, business educator; b. Urbana, Ill., Mar. 4, 1937; s. Claude Harold and Imogene Margaret (Jackson) J.; m. Patricia Ann Dunn, Aug. 29, 1959; children: Edwin George, Diana Kay Jordan Westrate. BS, U. Ill., 1966; MBA, Ea. Ill. U., 1985; PhD, U. Miss., 1992. CPA, Ill.; cert. mgmt. acct. Dept. head Ill. Found. Seeds, Tolono, Ill., 1966-68; gen. mgr. Ctrl. Ill. Seed, Inc., Charleston, 1968-85; instr. Ea. Ill. U., Charleston, 1985-87, U. Miss., Oxford, 1987-91; assoc. prof. U. Wis., Superior, 1991—. Contbr. articles to profl. jours. Recipient Faculty achievement award for excellence in rsch U. Wis.-Superior, 1995; Inst. Mgmt. Accts. rsch. grantee, 1991, MBA scholar Ea. Ill. U., 1985. Home: 1348 Trygg Rd Ely MN 55731-8026 Office: Univ of Wisconsin 1800 Grand Ave Superior WI 54880-2873

JORDAN, ROBERT ELIJAH, III, lawyer; b. South Boston, Va., June 20, 1936; s. Robert Elijah and Lucy (Webb) J.; m. Karen Wise Rosenberg, Sept. 14, 1968; children—Janet Elizabeth, Jennifer Anne, Robert Elijah IV. SB, MIT, 1958; JD magna cum laude, Harvard U., 1961. Bar: D.C. bar 1962, Va. bar 1964. Spl. asst. civil rights Office Sec. Def., Washington, 1963-64; asst. U.S. atty. for D.C., 1964-65; exec. asst. for enforcement Office Sec. Treasury, 1965-67; dep. gen. counsel Dept. Army, 1967, acting gen. counsel, 1967-68; gen. counsel of Army, spl. asst. for civil functions to Sec. Army, 1968-71; ptnr. Steptoe & Johnson, Washington, 1971-88, mng. ptnr., 1988-90; mem. Jud. Conf., D.C. Cir., 1973, 86—; mem. bd. cert. U.S. Cir. Cts. of Appeals Cir. Execs., 1987-88; pres. Langley Sch., 1981-82; mem. civil pro bono com. U.S. Dist. Ct., 1991-92. Contbr. articles to profl. jours. Served to 1st lt. AUS, 1961-63. Recipient Karl Taylor Compton award, 1958, Arthur S. Flemming award, 1970, award for exceptional civilian svc. Dept. Army, 1971; Sloan Found. scholar; Edward J. Noble Found. fellow. Mem. ABA, Va. State Bar, D.C. Bar (chmn. ethics com. 1978-83, spl. com. on model rules profl conduct 1983-89, pres. 1987-88), Calif. State Bar, D.C. Bar Found. (pres. 1993-94, 97-98), Atlantic Coun. (bd. dirs. 1993—, exec. com. 1994—, chmn. nominating com. 1997-98), Calif. Club, Tau Beta Pi, Tau Kappa Alpha. Democrat. Home: 6963 Duncraig Ct Mc Lean VA 22101-1568 Office: 1330 Connecticut Ave NW Washington DC 20036-1704

JORDAN, ROBERT LEON, lawyer, educator; b. Reading, Pa., Feb. 27, 1928; s. Anthony and Carmela (Votto) J.; m. Evelyn Allen Willard, Feb. 15, 1958 (dec. Nov. 1996); children: John Willard, David Anthony. BA, Pa. State U., 1948; LLB, Harvard U., 1951. Bar: N.Y. 1952. Assoc. White & Case, N.Y.C., 1953-59; prof. law UCLA, 1959-70, 75-91, prof. law emeritus, 1991—, assoc. dean Sch. Law, 1968-69; vis. prof. law Cornell U., Ithaca, N.Y., 1962-63; co-reporter Uniform Consumer Credit Code, 1964-70, Uniform Comml. Code Articles 3, 4, 4A, 1985-90; Fulbright lectr. U. Pisa, Italy, 1967-68. Co-author: (with W.D. Warren) Commercial Law, 1983, 4th edit., 1997, Bankruptcy, 1985, 5th edit., 1999. Lt. USAF, 1951-53. Office: UCLA Sch Law 405 Hilgard Ave Los Angeles CA 90095-9000

JORDAN, ROBERT LEON, federal judge; b. Woodlawn, Tenn., June 28, 1934; s. James Richard and Josephine (Broadbent) J.; m. Dorothy Rueter, Sept. 8, 1956; children: Robert, Margaret, Daniel. BS in Fin., U. Tenn., 1958, JD, 1960. Atty. Goodpasture, Carpenter, Dale & Woods, Nashville, 1960-61; mgr. Frontier Refining Co., Denver, 1961-64; atty. Green and Green, Johnson City, Tenn., 1964-66; trust officer 1st Peoples Bank, Johnson City, 1966-69; v.p., trust officer Comml. Nat. Bank, Pensacola, Fla., 1969-71; atty. Bryant, Price, Brandt & Jordan, Johnson City, 1971-80; chancellor 1st Jud. Dist., Johnson City, 1980-88; dist. judge U.S. Dist. Ct. (ea. dist.) Tenn., Knoxville, 1988—; mem. adv. com. U. Tenn. Law Alumni, 1978-80; sec. Tenn. Jud. Conf., 1987-88, mem. exec. com., 1988; del. Tenn. State-Fed. Judicial Coun., 1993—. Bd. dirs., v.p. Tri-Cities estate Planning Coun., Johnson City, 1969; bd. dirs. Washington County Tb Assn., Rocky Mount Hist. Assn., High Rock Camp, Johnson City, Jr. Achievement of Pensacola Inc.; bd. dirs., treas. N.W. Fla. Crippled Children's Assn., Pensacola; chancellor's assoc. U. Tenn. With U.S. Army, 1954-56. Named Boss of Yr. Legal Secs. Assn., Washington, Carter County, Tenn., 1982. Mem. Tenn. Bar Assn., Knoxville Bar Assn. (bd. govs.), Washington County Bar Assn. (pres.-elect 1980), Johnson City C. of C., Hamilton Burnett Am. Inn of Ct. (pres. 1993-94), Kiwanis (pres. Met. Johnson City Club 1969, Kiwanian of Yr. award 1986-87). Republican. Mem. Ch. of Christ. Office: Howard H Baker US Courthouse 800 Market St Ste 141 Knoxville TN 37902-2303

JORDAN, ROBERT REED, geologist, educator; b. N.Y.C., June 5, 1937; s. Herbert and Irene (Reed) J.; m. Jane H. Jordan, June 28, 1958; children: Richard P., Judith H. AB, Hunter Coll., 1958; MA, Bryn Mawr Coll., 1962, PhD, 1964. Cert. profl. geologist, Del.; lic. geologist, N.C. Geologist Del. Geol. Survey, Newark, 1958-64, asst. state geologist, 1964-69, state geologist, dir., 1969—; instr. U. Del., Newark, 1962-64, asst. prof., 1964-68, assoc. prof., 1968-88, prof., 1988—; mem. Del. Air and Water Commn., Dover, 1966-73; chmn. Del. State Boundary Commn., Newark, 1971—; mem. Del. State Bd. Registration of Geologists, 1972—; mem. Outer Continental Shelf policy com. U.S. Dept. Interior, 1974-77, 85—, chmn., 1993-94; mem. N.Am. Commn. on Stratigraphic Nomenclature, 1978—, chmn., 1984, 92; mem. U.S. Nat. Com. on Geology, 1990-96. Contbr. numerous articles to profl. jours. Named Hon. Mountaineer, State of W.Va., 1997, Ky. col., 1997. Fellow Geol. Soc. Am.; mem. Am. Inst. Profl. Geologists (hon. mem. award 1996, editor 1989-90, Galey Mem. Pub. Svc. award 1992), Am. Geol. Inst. (fin. com. 1992—, treas., exec. com. 1992-93, Outstanding Svc. award 1992, 93, Ian Campbell award 1996,), Del. Bd. Registration Geologists, Assn. Am. State Geologists (pres. 1983-84, Achievement award), Am. Assn. Petroleum Geologists (hon. mem. award, 1993, Disting. Svc. award 1988, Cohee Pub. Svc. Ea. award 1990, Galey award Ea., 1995, John T. Galey Sr. meml. medal 1998). Office: Del Geol Survey U Delaware Newark DE 19716-7501

JORDAN, ROBERT SMITH, political science educator; b. Los Angeles, June 11, 1929; s. Ralph Burdette and Mary Wright (Smith) J.; m. Sara Jane Hatch, Sept. 19, 1961; children: Sara Jane, Mary Rebecca Wheeler, Robert Hatch, David Thomas. A.B., UCLA, 1951; M.S., U. Utah, 1955; M.A. (E.I. DuBois fellow), Princeton U., 1957, Ph.D., 1960; D.Phil. (Fulbright scholar), Oxford U., Eng., 1960. Asst. to v.p. academic affairs U. Utah, 1954-55; budget examiner internat. div. U.S. Bur. Budget, 1956; instr. dept. politics Princeton U., 1956-57; mem. St. Antony's Coll., Oxford, 1957-59; asst. prof. pub. and internat. affairs, exec. asst. to dean Grad. Sch. Pub. and Internat. Affairs, U. Pitts., 1959-60; asso. professorial lectr. George Washington U., 1960-62; asst. dir. Army War Coll. Center, 1960-61; dir. Air U. Center, 1961-62, assoc. prof. polit. sci. and internat. affairs, 1962-70, asst. to pres., 1962-64; assoc. dir. internat. orgn. and internat. security studies Program of Policy Studies, 1964-65; dir. Fgn. Affairs Intern Program, Sch. Pub. and Internat. Affairs, 1968-70; dean faculty econ. and social studies, head dept. polit. sci. U. Sierra Leone, 1965-67; prof. polit. sci. State U. N.Y. at Binghamton, 1970-76, chmn. dept., 1970-74; dir. research UN Inst. for Tng. and Research, N.Y.C., 1975-79; Dag Hammarskold vis. prof. internat. relations U. S.C., Columbia, 1979-80; prof. polit. sci., rsch. prof. internat. instns., sr. rsch. assoc. Eisenhower Ctr. U. New Orleans, 1980—, dean Grad. Sch., 1980-82; adj. prof. polit. sci. Columbia U., 1978-79; Disting. vis. prof. Naval War Coll., 1984-86; Fulbright prof. Cen. Study of Arms Control and International. Security, U. Lancaster, Eng., Jan.-June, 1988; vis. prof. internat. rels. U.S. Air War Coll., 1992-94. Author/co-author, editor/co-editor: The NATO International Staff/Secretariat, 1967, Problems in International Relations, 1970, Government and Power in West Africa, 1970, rev. edit., 1977, Europe and the Superpowers, 1971, rev. edit., 1990, International Administration, 1971, Multinational Cooperation, 1972, Basic Issues in International Relations, 1974, Political Handbook of the World, 1975, The World Food Conference and Global Problem Solving, 1976, Political Leadership in NATO, 1979, Changing Role and Concepts in the International Civil Service, 1980, Dag Hammarskjold Revisited: The UN Secretary-General as a Force in World Politics, 1983, International Organizations: A Comparative Approach, 1983, 3d rev. edit., 1994, The U.S. and Multilateral Resource Management, 1985, Europe in the Balance: The Changing Context of European International Politics, 1986, Generals in International Politics: NATO's Supreme Allied Commander, Europe, 1987, Maritime Strategy and the Balance of Power: Britain and America in the Twentieth Century, 1989, Alliance Strategy and Navies: The Evolution and Scope of NATO's Maritime Dimension, 1990. Mem. Commn. to Study Orgn. of Peace., Acad. Coun. on the UN System; bd. dirs. Scarsdale-Hartsdale chpt. UN Assn., 1976-79. Served with USAF, 1951-53. Decorated Bronze Star; named Disting. Alumnus Hinckley Inst., U. Utah, 1964; NATO research fellow, 1969-70; fellow African Studies Assn.; Vice Adm. Edwin L. Hooper postdoctoral fellow U.S. Naval Hist. Ctr., 1987; Ctr. Rsch. Assoc. USAF Hist. Rsch. Ctr., 1988, U.S. Army Mil. History Inst., 1990, Consortium for the Study of Intelligence, 1990. Mem. Assn. Princeton Grad. Alumni (pres.), Am. Polit. Sci. Assn., Internat. Studies Assn. (v.p.), Am. Soc. Pub. Adminstrn. (exec. com. sect. on internat. adminstrn.), Am. Soc. Internat. Law, Acad. Coun. UN, Internat. Inst. Strategic Studies, Royal Inst. Internat. Affairs (London), Sigma Chi, Pi Sigma Alpha. Mem. Ch. Jesus Christ of Latter-day Saints. Club: Cosmos (Washington), Plimsoll (New Orleans). Office: U New Orleans Dept Polit Sci New Orleans LA 70148

JORDAN, RUTH ANN, physician; b. Oct. 12, 1928; d. Willard and Esther (Fouts) J.; children: Diane M., Linda J. AB, Ind. U., 1950; MD, Columbia U., 1957. Intern St. Luke's Hosp., N.Y.C., 1957-58, asst. resident, 1958-59; physician Met. Life Ins. Co., N.Y.C., 1960-62, Standard Oil Co. of N.J., N.Y.C., 1962, MIT, Cambridge, Mass., 1963-71; physician New Eng. Mut. Life Ins. Co., Boston, 1963-66, asst. med. dir., 1971-74; fellow internal medicine Mass. Gen. Hosp., Boston, 1974-75; physician Simmons Coll., Boston, 1975-78, Northeastern U., Boston, 1976-78; assoc. med. dir. New Eng. Telephone Co., N.Y.C., 1978, med. dir., 1978-86; dir. occupl. medicine Gen. Med. Assn., N.Y.C., 1986-91; assoc. med. dir. Allmerica, N.Y.C., 1991-97; physician Health Resource, N.Y.C., 1996—; therapeutic dietitian Meth. Hosp., Indpls., 1951-53, Presbyn. Hosp., N.Y.C., part-time 1954-57; nat. coord. com. on cholesterol, 1986—, Mass. Adv. Coun. for Workers Compensation, 1986-89. Fellow Am. Coll. Occupl. and Environ. Medicine (membership com. 1985-88, health edn. com. 1984—, bd. dirs. 1986-92); mem. AMA, DAR, New Eng. Occupl. Med. Assn. (bd. dirs. 1980-89, pres. 1981-84), Mass. Med. Soc. (mem. coun. 1984—, chmn. environ. and occupl. health com. 1985-88), Norfolk County Med. Soc. (v.p., pres 1999—, edn. com., exec. com., alt. to Mass. Med. Soc. nominating com.), Columbia U. Club of New Eng. (v.p. 1981-84, pres. 1989-91), Roxbury Clin. Records Club, The Country Club, Alpha Chi Omega. Home: 105 Rockwood St Brookline MA 02445-7408

JORDAN, SAMANTHA, legislative staff member. Student, Tex. Christian U., 1989-92; BA in History, Tex. A&M U., 1994. Intern U.S. Rep. Joe L.

Barton, Washington, 1995, dist. asst., 1995, dist. asst., caseworker, dist. sys. mgr., 1996, dist. liaison, dep. press sec., 1996-97, dep. press sec., sys. mgr., legis. corr., 1997-98, press sec., 1998, comm. dir., 1998—; mem. Leadership Press Sec. Working Group. Mem. adv. bd., alumnae club Alpha Omega Sorority; vol. Kimbell Art Mus. Mem. Rep. Commn. Assn., Tex. A&M Assn. Former Students, 12th Man Found., Smithsonian Assocs., Libr. Congress Assocs. Fax: 202-225-3052. Home: 1681A S Hayes Arlington VA 22202 Office: Congressman Joe Barton 2264 Rayburn Ho Office Bldg Washington DC 20515

JORDAN, SANDRA, public relations professional; b. Pasadena, Tex., Oct. 10, 1952; d. Royal Wilson and Kathryn Ann (Speck) J.; m. William Anderson Mintz, Aug. 10, 1974 (div. 1980). B of Journalism, U. Tex., 1974. Reporter Austin (Tex.) American Statesman, 1974-76; news dir. KTAE Radio, Taylor, Tex., 1974-76; dir. of news and info. Inst. of Texan Cultures, San Antonio, 1976-82; pub. rels. dir. San Antonio Mus. Assn., 1982-83; dir. news/info. Univ. Tex., San Antonio, 1983-86; sr. publicist Rogers & Cowan, Inc., Washington, 1986-87; communications dir. NARAL, Washington, 1987-88; assoc. Parker, Vogelsingers & Assocs., Washington, 1988-90; pub. rels. and mktg. dir. Girl Scout Coun., Washington, 1990-99; mgr. media rels. Planned Parenthood Fedn. Am., Washington, 1999—; pub. rels. cons. YWCA, Washington; judge, ad contest, Women in Communications, Iowa, 1993; workshop organizer Washington Ind. Writers, 1990; mem. publicity com. CASE Conf., San Antonio, 1986, Smithsonian Nat. Assoc. Prog., San Antonio, 1980; panelist Women in Comms. Roundtable, 1996; workshop presenter in field. Contbg. author: Folk Art in Texas, 1985. Prog. cons. KLRN-TV (pub. TV) San Antonio, 1981, 82; del. Dem. Nat. Conv., Taylor, 1976; docent Kennedy Ctr., Washington, 1989. Recipient Apex '91, '92, '93, '95, '97 and '98 awards, Communications Concepts, 1991, Design honors, Tex. Assn. of Mus., 1993, IABC Silver Inkwell award, 1995, Silver Anvil award, 1996. Mem. Women in Communications (D.C. chpt., mem. literacy project 1992, mentoring program com., v.p. for programs 1998—), Women in Advt. and Mktg., Am. Soc. Assn. Execs., The Writers Ctr., Pub. Rels. Soc. Am. Avocations: fiction writing, quilt making. Home: 6305 E Halbert Rd Bethesda MD 20817-5409 Office: Planned Parenthood Fedn Am Ste 430 1120 Connecticut Ave NW Washington DC 20036

JORDAN, SANDRA DICKERSON, law educator; b. Phila., Dec. 3, 1951; m. Byron Neal Jordan, July 21, 1973; children: Nedra Catherine, Byron Neal II. BS in Edn., Wilberforce U., 1973; JD, U. Pitts., 1979. Bar: Pa. 1979, U.S. Dist. Ct. (we. dist.) Pa. 1979, U.S. Ct. Appeals (3d cir.) 1979. Asst. U.S. atty. U.S. Dept. Justice, Pitts., 1979-88; assoc. ind. counsel Ind. Counsel-Iran/Contra, Washington, 1988-91; prof. U. Pitts. Sch. Law, 1988—, assoc. dean, 1993—; jud. ct. bd. Commonwealth of Pa., 1995—; hearing com. disciplinary bd. Pa. Supreme Ct., PItts., 1989-95; lectr. U.S. Dept. Justice, Pa. Trial Judges Assn., Acad. Trial Lawyers, Pa. Bar Inst. Author tng. video in field, 1982; contbr. articles to profl. jours. Vice pres. Health and Welfare Planning Commn., Pitts., 1986-89; mem. Program to Aid Citizen Enterprise, Pitts., 1983—. Mem. ABA (mem. white collar crimes com. 1988—), Homer S. Brown Law Assn., Allegheny County Bar Assn., Nat. Bar Assn., Urban League (v.p. Pitts. chpt. 1988-90), Alpha Kappa Mu, Alpha Kappa Alpha. Avocation: scuba diving. Office: U Pitts Law Sch 3900 Forbes Ave Pittsburgh PA 15213

JORDAN, STEPHEN M., university president; m. Ruth Kinnie; 3 children. BA in Polit. Sci., U. No. Colo., 1971; MPA in Fin. Adminstrn., U. Colo., Denver, 1979, PhD in Pub. Adminstrn./Policy Analysis, 1990. Fin. ofcl. univs. in Ariz. and Colo., to 1994; exec. dir. Kans. Bd. Regents, 1994—; pres. Eastern Wash. U., Cheney, 1998—. Office: Eastern Wash U Showalter Hall Rm 214 Cheney WA 99005

JORDAN, TERESA MARIE, writer; b. Cheyenne, Wyo., Mar. 5, 1955; d. Lawrence William and Jo (Steele) J.; m. Hal Cannon, Aug. 17, 1991. BA in History, Yale U., 1977. Freelance writer Deeth, Nev., 1977—; instr. writing Lewis & Clark Coll., Portland, Oreg., 1983—; photographer, 1977-85; artistic dir. Great Basin Book Festival, Reno, Nev., 1996-97; nat. adv. bd. mem. Women of the West Mus., Boulder, Colo., 1992—; bd. dirs. Nev. Humanities Commn., Reno. Author: Riding the White Horse Home, 1991, Cowgirls: Women of the West, 1982; editor: Graining the Mare: The Poetry of Ranchwomen, 1994; co-editor: The Stories That Shape Us: Comtemporary Women Write About the West, 1995; essayist, radio documentaries with Hal Cannon, The Open Road feature on The Savvy Traveler, 1998—. Judge Utah Arts Commn., 1996, We. States Book Awards, 1996. Fellow Nat. Endowment for Arts, 1994, Oreg. Inst. of Literary Arts, 1989-90; recipient We. Heritage award Best Documentary Film Cowboy Hall of Fame, 1985. Mem. Pen Ctr. USA West, We. History Assn. Avocations: ranching, riding, restoring old buildings. Home and Office: PO Box 87 Deeth NV 89823-0087

JORDAN, THERESA JOAN, psychologist, educator; b. Irvington, N.J., Sept. 17, 1949; d. Ernest Anthony and Helen Joan (Debski) Balazs; 1 child, Theresa-Helena. BA, NYU, 1971, MA, 1972, PhD, 1979. Lic. psychologist, N.Y., N.J.; diplomate Am. Bd. Forensic Medicine, Am. Bd. Forensic Examiners, Am. Bd. Forensic Psychologists. Grad. fellow Nat. Inst. Occupational Safety and Health, N.Y.C., 1971-74; rsch. asst., rsch. coord. Project City Sci. NYU, 1974-79, assoc. dir. for rsch. Ctr. for Devel. Studies, 1979-82; asst. prof. medicine N.J. Med. Sch., Newark, 1982-92; assoc. prof. applied psychology NYU, 1992—; dir. Ctr. for Med. Info. N.J. Med. Sch., Newark, 1989—; cons. Ctrs. for Disease Control, Atlanta, 1990; spkr. Am. Lung Assn., N.Y., 1990-96, Am. Thoracic Soc., N.Y., 1998-99; spkr. Asia-Pacific Congress on Lung Diseases, Bangkok, Thailand, Bali, Indonesia. Author: Overcoming the Fear of Riding, 1996, Understanding Medical Information, 1999; contbr. articles to profl. jours. Mem. U.S. Icelandic Demonstration Team. Mem. APA, Assn. for the Advancement Ednl. Rsch. (pres.-elect 1998—), Soc. for Med. Decision-Making, Eastern Ednl. Rsch. Assn. (2d v.p. 1985-87), Mem. Internat. Union Against Tuberculosis & Lung Disease. Avocations: rider and trainer of Icelandic horses. Office: NYU Dept Applied Psychology 239 Greene St New York NY 10003-6674

JORDAN, THOMAS FREDRICK, physics educator; b. Duluth, Minn., June 4, 1936; s. Thomas Vincent and Mildred (Nystrom) J. BA, U. Minn., 1958; PhD, U. Rochester, 1962. Rsch. assoc. U. Rochester, 1961-62, instr., 1962-63; NSF postdoctoral fellow U. Bern, Switzerland, 1963-64; asst. prof. U. Pitts., 1964-67, assoc. prof., 1967-70; prof. U. Minn., Duluth, 1970—; vis. prof., workshop participant U. Wis., 1965, Aspen (Colo.) Inst. for Humanistic Studies, 1966, Summer Inst. for Theoretical Physics, U. Colo., 1967, Internat. Ctr. for Theoretical Physics, Trieste, Italy, 1968, U. Rochester, 1976-77, Syracuse U., Nat. Inst. for Nuclear Rsch., Firenze, Italy, U. Geneva., U. Paris 1982, Internat. Ctr. for Theoretical Physics, Trieste, workshop on early universe, Erice, Italy, Geneva, U. Bern, 1986, U. Calif. at Santa Barbara, 1968. Author: Linear Operators for Quantum Mechanics, 1969, Quantum Mechanics in Simple Matrix Form, 1985; contbr. numerous article to profl. jours. Rsch. fellow Alfred P. Sloan Found., 1965-67, Bush Found. fellow U. Tex., Temple U., 1984; Fulbright rsch. grantee U. Gôttingen, Fed. Republic of Germany, 1991-92.

JORDAN, THOMAS HILLMAN, geophysicist, educator; b. Coco Solo, C.Z., Republic of Panama, Oct. 8, 1948; s. Clarence Eugene and Beulah (Greer) J.; m. Margaret Jordan; 1 child, Alexandra Elyse. BS, Calif. Inst. Tech., 1969, MS in Geophysics, 1970, PhD in Geophysics and Applied Math., 1972. Asst. prof. Princeton (N.J.) U., 1972-75; asst. prof. Scripps Instn. of Oceanography, U. Calif. San Diego, La Jolla, 1975-77, assoc. prof., 1977-82, prof., 1982-84; prof. MIT, Cambridge, 1984—, with dept. earth, atmospheric and planetary scis., 1984—. Contbr. over 120 articles to sci. publs. Fellow AAAS, Am. Geophys. Union (James B. Macelwane award 1983, George P. Woolard award 1998); mem. NAS. Office: MIT 54-526 Dept Earth Atmosph/Planet S Cambridge MA 02139

JORDAN, TIMOTHY EDWARD, secondary education educator; b. Knoxville, Iowa, Apr. 16, 1952; s. Richard and Elizabeth Edna (Miller) J. BS, Southwest Mo. State U., 1976, cert., 1982; MS in Edn., U. Tex. Pan Am., 1992, postgrad., 1999—. Cert. secondary tchr., Tex., Mo. Tech. dir. Springfield (Mo.) Civic Ballet, 1977-80; tchr. math. Chadwick (Mo.) Pub. Schs., 1981-82; tchr. math. and physics Marine Mil. Acad., Harlingen, Tex., 1983—, asst. dean acads., 1992-98; math. tchr. Weslaco (Tex.) H.S., 1998-99, tech. coord., 1999—. Mem. Nat. Coun. Tchrs. Math., Nat. Sci. Tchrs. Assn., Tex. Computer Edn. Assn. Avocations: flying, antique cars, piano, sailing, computer programming. Home: 1607 Rio Hondo Rd Harlingen TX 78550-4007 Office: Weslaco HS Math Dept Weslaco TX 78596

JORDAN, VERNON EULION, JR., lawyer, former association official; b. Atlanta, Aug. 15, 1935; s. Vernon Eulion and Mary (Griggs) J.; m. Shirley M. Yarbrough, Dec. 13, 1958 (dec. Dec. 29, 1985); 1 child, Vickee; m. Ann Dibble Cook, Nov. 22, 1986. BA, DePauw U., 1957; JD, Howard U., 1960; hon. degrees, DePauw U., Howard U., Boston Coll., Brandeis U., CUNY, U. Ill. Chgo. Duke U., U. Mass., NYU, Princeton U., Tulane U., Rutgers U., Tuskegee Inst., Yale U., Notre Dame U., Harvard U., plus 50 other instns. higher edn. Bar: Ga. 1960, Ark. 1964. Practice law Atlanta, 1960-61, Pine Bluff, Ark., 1964-65; Ga. field dir. NAACP, 1961-63; dir. Voter Edn. Project So. Regional Council, 1964-68; atty. OEO, Atlanta, 1969; exec. dir. United Negro Coll. Fund, N.Y.C., 1970-71; pres. Nat. Urban League, 1972-81; sr. ptnr. firm Akin, Gump, Strauss, Hauer & Feld, LLP, Washington; dir. Am. Express Co., Bankers Trust Co., Bankers Trust N.Y. Corp., Callaway Golf Co., Chancellor Media Corp., Dow Jones & Co., Union Carbide Corp., J.C. Penney Co., Inc., Xerox Corp., Revlon, Inc., Ryder System, Inc., Sara Lee Corp; frequent guest on maj. nat. TV programs including Meet The Press, Face the Nation; chmn. Clinton Presdl. Transition Bd.; apptd. to Pres.'s adv. com. Points of Light Initiative Found., 1989. Mem. Nat. Adv. Commn. on Selective Svcs., 1966-67, Am. Revolution Bi-Centennial Commn., 1972—, Presdl. Clemency Bd., 1974; adv. coun. Social Security, 1974; trustee Ford Found., LBJ Found., Urban Inst. (life), Howard U.; mem. steering com. Bilderberg Meetings; mem. Coun. on Fgn. Rels.; adv. trustee DePauw U., bd. dirs. NAACP Legal Def. and Ednl. Fund; hon. mem. Ralph Bunche Inst. on the UN. Fellow 2Met. Applied Research Center, 1968; Fellow Harvard Inst. Politics, 1969; recipient Alexis de Tocqueville award United Way Am., 1977. Mem. ABA, D.C. Bar Assn., Nat. Bar Assn., Nat. Conf. Black Lawyers, Am. Law Inst., University Club, Board Room, Council on Fgn. Relations, Century Assn.. Mem. A.M.E. Ch. Office: Akin Gump Strauss Hauer & Feld LLP Ste 400 1333 New Hampshire Ave NW Washington DC 20036-1564

JORDAN, WILLIAM BRYAN, JR., art historian; b. Nashville, May 8, 1940; s. William Bryan and Dixie (Owen) J. BA cum laude, Washington and Lee U., Lexington, Va., 1962; MA, NYU, 1964, PhD, 1967; LHD, So. Meth. U., 1995. Mem. faculty, dir. Meadows Mus. So. Meth. U., 1967-81, chmn. div. fine arts, 1967-73, prof. art history, 1975-81; adj. curator European art Dallas Mus. Fine Arts, 1976-81; dep. dir. Kimbell Art Mus., Ft. Worth, 1981-90; cons., 1990—. Author papers in field, also mus. catalogues. Decorated caballero Orden de Isabel La Católica, Spain, 1985, commander, 1995, officer Orden de Merito Civil, Spain, 1988. Mem. Am. Soc. Hispanic Art Hist. Studies (gen. sec. 1976-78), Hispanic Soc. Am. (corr.). *

JORDAN, WILLIAM CHESTER, history educator; b. Chgo., Apr. 7, 1948; s. Johnnie Parker and Marguerite Jane (Mays) J.; m. Christine Kenyon Hershey, May 30, 1970; children: Victoria Marie, John Mark, Clare Kenyon, Lorna Janice. AB, Ripon Coll., 1969; PhD, Princeton U., 1973. Instr. Princeton U., 1973-74, lectr., 1974-75, asst. to assoc. prof. history, 1975-86, prof. history, 1986—, Behrman sr. fellow in humanities, 1989-94; dir. Shelby Cullom Davis Ctr. for Hist. Studies, 1994—; vis. lectr. U. Pa., Phila., 1981-82; vis. assoc. prof. history Swarthmore (Pa.) Coll., 1985; mem. adv. com. history Grad. Records Exam, 1976-86, chmn., 1980-86; Morgan lectr. Dickinson Coll., Carlisle, Pa., 1985. co-editor: Order and Innovation in the Middle Ages, 1976; author: Louis IX and the Challenge of the Crusade, 1979, From Servitude to Freedom, 1986, The French Monarchy and the Jews, 1989, Women and Credit, 1993, The Great Famine, 1996, The Middle Ages: An Encyclopedia for Students, 1996; contbr. articles on medieval history and medieval law to profl. jours. Fellow Woodrow Wilson Found., Ford Found., Danforth Found, Mellon Found., Rockefeller Found., Annenberg Rsch. Inst. Fellow Medieval Acad. Am.; mem. Am. Hist. Assn. (co-chairperson program com. 1985), Am. Coun. Learned Socs. (sec. 1986-95, bd. dirs. 1982-95), Soc. French Hist. Studies, Soc. Study of the Crusades and Latin East, Haskins Soc. Office: Dept of History Princeton U Princeton NJ 08544

JORDAN, WILLIAM DAVIS, lawyer; b. Palestine, Tex., Aug. 5, 1940; s. Henry Latimer and Evelyn (Davis) J.; m. Toby Stall Feb. 8, 1964; children: Russell Stall Jordan, Stephen Monnig Jordan. BBA with honors, U. Tex., 1963, LLB with honors, 1964. Bar: Tex. 1964. Assoc., then ptnr. Jackson and Walker, Dallas, 1964-97; ptnr. Johnson, Jordan, Nipper & Monk, P.C., 1997—; chmn. U. Tex. Tax Conf., 1977, also planning com.; spkr. in field. Contbr. articles to profl. jours. Mem. Dallas Estate Planning Coun.; chmn. Southwestern Legal Found. Oil and Gas Tax Inst., 1981-86, mem. planning com.; dir., past chmn. Dallas Met. YMCA; past dir. Baylor U. Med. Ctr. Found., YMCA Rockies, Colo.; adv. dir. Comtys. Found. Tex., Dallas Found.; trustee King Found. Presbyterian. Mem. ABA, Tex. Bar Assn. (co-chmn. peer com. 1967-68), Dallas Bar Assn. (chmn. tax sect. 1977), Dallas Estate Planning Coun. (bd. dirs.), Rotary (found. trustee Dallas 1985-91), Dallas Country Club, Beta Theta Pi. Office: Johnson Jordan Nipper & Monk PC 13355 Noel Rd # 8 Dallas TX 75240-6602

JORDAN, WILLIAM REYNIER, SR., therapist, poet; s. Russell Clinger and Lois Eleanor (Van Evera) J.; children: William, Michael, Paul. BS in Journalism cum laude, U. Fla., 1956; South Asia area specialist, U. Pa., 1960-62; grad., Strategic Intelligence Sch., 1962, Gen. Staff Coll., 1968, Def. Lang. Inst., 1970; postgrad., U. So. Fla., 1986-87; PhD in Psychology, Calif. Coast U., 1989. Cpl. U.S. Army, 1947-48, with Mil. Intelligence Res., 1948-51, to 1st lt. inf., 1951-54, re-entered, 1957, advanced through grades to lt. col., 1968; chief of plans and analysis psychol. ops. divsn. Mil. Assistance Command, Vietnam, 1970-71; group ops. officer, later spl. asst. to comdg. officer 902d Mil. Intelligence Group, Washington, 1971-72; ret., 1972; vol. psychotherapist Juvenile Detention, Pensacola, Fla., 1976-77, Colorado Springs (Colo.) Social Svcs. Dept., 1977-78; psychotherapist Med. Clinic, St. Petersburg, Fla., 1980-84, Epilepsy Found., St. Petersburg, 1984-88; vol. VA Mental Health Clinic, Bay Pines, Fla., 1985-99. Author: Darkness and Shadows, 1975, More Than Friends, 1978, Heat Lightning, 1984. Leader Rawalpindi coun. Boy Scouts Am., Pakistan, 1960-62, also troops at Ft. Bragg. N.C., Ft. Leavenworth, Kans., Ft. Holabird, Md., 1964-70; bd. dirs. YMCA, dundalk, Md., 1969-71, Epilepsy Assn., Pensacola, 1975-77. Decorated Legion of Merit with oak leaf cluster, Cross of Gallantry with Palm (Republic of Vietnam); named Vol. of Yr., Colorado Springs Social Svcs. Dept., 1978. Mem. APA (assoc.), DAV, Epilepsy Assn. Am. (pres.'s club), Am. Assn. Counseling and Devel. Democrat. Congregationalist. Avocation: photography. Address: 1051 79th Ave N Apt 111 Saint Petersburg FL 33702-1127

JORDAN, WINTHROP DONALDSON, historian, educator; b. Worcester, Mass., Nov. 11, 1931; s. Henry Donaldson and Lucretia Mott (Churchill) J.; m. Phyllis Henry, Aug. 30, 1952 (div. 1979); children: Joshua H., J. Mott, W. Eliot; m. Cora Miner Reilly, Feb. 27, 1982. AB, Harvard U., 1953; MA, Clark U., 1957; PhD, Brown U., 1960. Instr. history Phillips Exeter (N.H.) Acad., 1955-56; lectr. in history Brown U., Providence, 1959-61; fellow Inst. Early Am. History and Culture, Williamsburg, Va., 1961-63; from asst. prof. to prof. history U. Calif., Berkeley, 1963-82, assoc. dean for minority group affairs Grad. div., 1968-70; vis. prof. history and black studies U. Miss., Oxford, 1981, prof. history and Afro-Am. studies, 1982—; vis. asst. prof. history U. Mich., Ann Arbor, 1966; vis. prof. history U. Calif., Berkeley, 1989; William F. Winter prof. history and prof. Afro-Am. studies, U. Miss., 1993—, F.A.P. Barnard Disting. prof., 1998—; vis. prof. history U. Zimbabwe, 1994. Author: White Over Black, 1968, Tumult and Silence at Second Creek, 1993; co-author: The United States, 1979, The Americans, 1982, The American People, 1986; mem. editorial bd. various scholarly jours. Council mem. Inst. Early Am. History and Culture, 1977-79. Recipient Ralph Waldo Emerson award Phi Beta Kappa, 1968, Parkman prize Soc. Am. Historians, 1969, Nat. Book award for History and Biography Am. Book Pubs., 1969, Bancroft prize Columbia U., 1969, 94, Landry award LSU Press, 1992, Eugene M. Kayden award, 1994, Disting. Alumnus citation Brown U. Grad. Sch., 1993; fellow Charles Warren Ctr. for Study Am. History Harvard U., 1965, Social Sci. Rsch. Coun., 1966, Guggenheim Found., 1967, Ctr. for Advanced Study Behavioral Scis., Palo Alto, 1975-76; grantee NIMH, 1970-73. Mem. Am. Antiquarian Soc. (elected), Am. Hist. Assn., Orgn. Am. Historians, So. Hist. Assn., Mass. Hist. Soc. (elected), Miss. Hist. Soc., Krokodiloes Club. Home: 400 Murray St Oxford MS 38655-2914 Office: Dept History U Miss University MS 38677

JORDAN-BYCHKOV, TERRY GILBERT, geography educator; b. Dallas, Aug. 9, 1938; s. Gilbert John and Vera Belle (Tiller) J.; m. Bella Bychkova; children: Tina, Sonya, Eric. BA, So. Meth. U., 1960; MA, U. Tex., 1961; PhD, U. Wis., 1965. Asst. prof. geography Ariz. State U., Tempe, 1965-69; prof., dept. chmn. U. North Tex., Denton, 1969-82; Walter Prescott Webb prof. geography. U. Tex., Austin, 1982—. Author: German Seed in Texas Soil, 1966, Texas Log Buildings, 1978, Trails to Texas, 1981, Texas Graveyards, 1982, American Log Buildings, 1985, American Backwoods Frontier, 1989, North American Cattle Ranching Frontiers, 1993, The European Culture Area, 1996, The Mountain West: Interpreting the Folk Landscape, 1997, The Human Mosaic, 8th edit., 1999, Siberian Village: Land and Life in the Sakha Republic, 1999; contbr. articles to profl. jours. Fellow Am. Geog. Soc., Tex. State Hist. Assn., Tex. Inst. of Letters, Assn. Am. Geographers (v.p. 1986-87, pres. 1987-88, Honors award 1982). Avocations: travel, genealogy. Fax: 512-471-5049. E-mail: tgjordan@mail.utexas.edu. Office: The U of Tex at Austin Dept Geography Austin TX 78712

JORDANIA, VAKHTANG, conductor, educator; b. Tbilisi, Republic of Georgia, Dec. 9, 1942; came to U.S., 1983; s. Givi and Varvara J.; children: Georgi, Nina, Maria, Dimitri. Student, Tbilisi Conservatory, 1966, Leningrad Conservatory, 1969; MusD, Moscow Conservatory, 1971, People's Artist, 1983. Asst. condr. Leningrad Philharm., 1970-71, assoc. condr., 1971-73; condr., artistic dir. Leningrad Radio Orch., 1973-74; prof. music Saratov (USSR) Conservatory, 1974-77; condr., music dir. Saratov Philharm., 1974-77; condr., artistic dir. Kharkov (USSR) Philharm., 1976-83; guest condr. Shaw Concerts, Inc., N.Y., 1983-85; condr., artistic dir. Chattanooga Symphony and Opera Assn., 1985-92; condr., music dir. Spokane Symphony, 1991-94; prin. guest condr. K.B.S. Sympohony, Seoul, Republic of Korea, 1984—; music dir. St. Petersburg Festival Orch., 1993—, Russian Fed. Orch., 1994—, Kharkov Philharm. and Kharkov Opera, 1993—. Condr. (record) Elmar Olivera-Tchaikovsky competition, 1978, Michaela Martin-Tchaikovsky competition, 1978; (album) Shostakovich Symphonies 6 and 9, USSR State Symphony Orch., Leningrad Chamber orch., 1972; (movie) Dersu Ursula, 1980, (CD) Hovhannes, 1970, 94, Shostakovich, 1994, Tchaikovsky Nutcracker, 1997; other recs. Recipient 1st place USSR Nat. Audition for Internat. Competition, 1971, Herbert Von Karajan prize, 1971. Avocations: horseback riding, dogs, fishing.

JORDEN, ELEANOR HARZ, linguist, educator; b. N.Y.C.; d. William George and Eleanor (Funk) Harz; m. William J. Jorden, Mar. 3, 1944 (div.); children: William Temple, Eleanor Harz, Marion Telva. A.B., Bryn Mawr Coll., 1942; M.A., Yale U., 1943, Ph.D., 1950; D.Litt. (hon.), Williams Coll., 1982; D.H.L. (hon.), Knox Coll., 1985; D. Langs. (hon.), Middlebury Coll., 1991; D. Univ. (hon.), U. Stirling, Scotland, 1993. Instr. Japanese Yale U., 1943-46, 47-48; dir. Japanese lang. program and Fgn. Service Inst. Lang. Sch., Am. Embassy, Tokyo, 1950-55; sci. linguist Fgn. Service Inst., Dept. State, Washington, 1959-69; acting head Far East langs., 1961-64, chmn., 1964-67, 69, chmn. Vietnamese lang. div., 1967-69; vis. prof. linguistics Cornell U., 1969-70, prof., 1970-87, Mary Donlon Alger prof. linguistics, 1974-87, prof. emeritus, 1987—; Bernhard disting. vis. prof. Williams Coll., 1985-86; vis. prof. Williams Coll., 1986-87, adj. prof., 1987-92; dir. Japanese FALCON program, 1972-87; Univ. prof., Disting. fellow Nat. Fgn. Lang. Ctr. Sch. Advanced Internat. Studies Johns Hopkins U., 1987-91; acad. dir. Exchange: Japan's Tchr. Tng. Inst., 1988—; sr. cons. prep. framework Japanese lang. curriculum and Japanese coll. bd. exam, 1991-93; sr. cons. Japanese multi-media project, U. Md., 1995-97; dir. SPENG Program, 1980—; co-dir. Survey on Japanese Lang. Study, 1988-92; guest scholar Wilson Ctr. Smithsonian Instn., 1982; cons., permanent disting. dir. Nat. Assn. Self-Instructional Lang. Programs, pres., 1977-78, 84-85; mem. Fulbright-Hays Com. on Internat. Exchange Scholars, 1972-75; mem. area adv. com. for East Asia, 1972-76; chmn. Social Sci. Research Council Task Force on Japanese Lang. Tng., 1976-78; mem. adv. com. Japan Found., 1979-81; mem. Lang. Attrition Project, 1981-87; advisor Centre for Japanese Studies, Stirling U., Scotland, 1988-92; mem. Yale U. Coun. com. Langs. and Lit., 1990-98. Author: (with Bernard Bloch) Spoken Japanese, 1945, Syntax of Modern Colloquial Japanese, 1955, Gateway to Russian, 1961, Beginning Japanese, Part 1, 1962, Part 2, 1963, (with Sheehan, Quang and others) Basic Vietnamese, vols. I, II, 1965, (with Quang) Vietnamese Familiarization Course, 1969, (with Hamako Chaplin) Reading Japanese, 1976, (with Mari Noda) Japanese: The Spoken Language, part 1, 1987, part 2, 1988, part 3, 1990, (with Richard Lambert) Japanese Language Instruction in the U.S.: Resources, Practice and Investment Strategic, 1992. Decorated Order of Precious Crown Emperor of Japan, 1985; recipient Superior Svc. award Dept. State, 1965, Japan Found. and Social Sci. Rsch. Coun. sr. fellow, 1976, Toyota award Twentieth Anniversary Fund grantee, 1978; Japan Found. award, 1985, Papalia award for Excellence Tchr. Tng., 1993, N.E. Conf. award Disting. Svc. and Leadership in Profession, 1994; honoree Eleanor Harz Jorden Festival, Portland State U., 1995. Mem. Assn. Asian Studies (v.p. 1979-80, pres. 1980-81), Linguistic Soc. Am., Am. Coun. Tchrs. Fgn. Langs., Nat. Assn. Self-Instrnl. Lang. Programs (pres. 1978, 85, permanent disting. dir. 1991—), Assn. Tchrs. Japanese (exec. com., pres. 1978-84), Japan Soc. N.Y. (bd. dirs. 1982-88), Exchange: Japan (bd. dirs., v.p., sec. 1998—). Fax: (610) 658-2563. Office: 3300 Darby Rd Apt 1302 Haverford PA 19041-1067

JORDEN, JAMES ROY, oil company engineering executive, consultant; b. Oklahoma City, Apr. 16, 1934; s. James Roy and Gordon (Peeler) J.; m. Shirley Ann Swan, Nov. 17, 1956; children: Philip Taylor, David Emerson. BS in Petroleum Engring., U. Tulsa, 1957. Engr. Shell Oil Co., various locations, 1957, 1960-81; petrophys. engr. advisor Shell Oil Co., Houston, 1981-85; mgr. petroleum engring. rsch. Shell Devel. Co., Houston, 1985-88, mgr. head office prodn., tech. tng., 1988-93; mgr. CPI tng. Shell Oil Co., Houston, 1993-95; retired, 1995; cons. Quicksilver Resources, Inc., 1998—; mem. industry adv. bd. petroleum engring. U. Tulsa, 1987-92, chmn., 1988; vis. com. petroleum engring. Colo. Sch. Mines, Golden, 1988-95. Co-author: Well Logging I., 1984, Well Logging II, 1986; co-inventor in field. lst lt. USAF, 1957-60. Named to Hall of Fame, Petroleum Engring. Dept. U. Tulsa, 1985. Mem. Am. Inst. Mining, Metall. and Petroleum Engrs., Soc. Petroleum Engrs. (hon., pres. 1984, Disting. Svc. award 1988, DeGolyer Disting. Svc. medal 1991, bd. dirs. 1975-79, dir. svc. corps. 1984-90, life trustee found., treas. found. 1991-92, sr. v.p. found. 1993-95, pres. found. 1995-97), Kappa Alpha. Republican. Presbyterian. Avocations: golf, reading, wine. Home: PO Box 8111 Horseshoe Bay TX 78657-8111

JORDEN, WILLIAM JOHN, writer, retired diplomat; b. Bridger, Mont., May 3, 1923; s. Hugh G. and Jane Ann (Temple) J.; m. Eleanor Harz, 1944 (div.); children: William Temple, Eleanor Harz, Marion Telva; m. V. Mildred Xiarhos, 1972. B.A. with honors, Yale, 1947; M.S., Columbia, 1948. Instr. Japanese Yale, 1945-46; reporter Vineyard Gazette, Edgartown, Mass., 1947; radio news writer N.Y. Herald Tribune, 1948; fgn. corr. A.P., Japan and Korea, 1948-52; fgn. corr. N.Y. Times, Japan and Korea, 1952-55, USSR, 1956-58; diplomatic corr. N.Y. Times (Washington bur.), 1958-6l; mem. Policy Planning Council, State Dept., 1961-62, spl. asst. to under sec. polit. affairs, 1962-65, dep. asst. sec. state pub. affairs, 1965-66; sr. mem. staff NSC, 1966-68, 72-74; mem., spokesman Am. del. Vietnam Peace Talks, Paris, France, 1968-69; asst. to former Pres. Lyndon B. Johnson, 1969-72; U.S. ambassador to Panama, 1974-78; scholar-in-residence LBJ Libr.; adj. prof. LBJ Sch. Pub. Affairs, U. Tex., 1978-80; U.S. chmn. U.S.-Panama Consultative com., 1992-95. Author: Panama Odyssey; co-author: Japan Between East and West. Served with AUS, 1943-45. Shared Pulitzer prize for internat. corr., 1958; Recipient Disting. Honor award Dept. State, 1978; Pulitzer traveling fellow, 1948-49; Council Fgn. Relations fellow, 1955-56; Decorated order of Vasco Nunez de Balboa (Republic of Panama). Mem. Coun. Fgn. Rels., Acad. Polit. Sci., Author's Guild. Clubs: Yale of Washington, Washington Golf and Country, Fgn. Corrs. Japan (pres. 1952-53).

JORDON, ROBERT EARL, physician; b. Buffalo, May 7, 1938; s. James Wallace and Helen Viola (Sampson) J.; m. Mary Ann Michels, July 12, 1969; children: James H., Kathryn L., Marie H. B.A., Hamilton Coll., 1960; M.D., SUNY-Buffalo, 1965; M.S., U. Minn., 1970. Diplomate: Am. Bd. Dermatology, Am. Bd. Dermatological Immunology, Am. Bd. Diagnostic and Laboratory Immunology. Intern straight medicine Buffalo Gen. Hosp., 1965-66; resident, fellow in dermatology Mayo Clinic and Mayo Found., Rochester, Minn., 1966-69, asso. cons., 1971-73, cons. dermatology, 1973-77; instr. pathology U. Minn. Hosps., Mpls., 1971-73; Nat. Inst. Arthritis and Metabolic Diseases spl. research fellow U. Minn., Mpls., 1972-73; asst. prof. dermatology Mayo Grad. Sch. Medicine, Rochester, 1971-73; asst. prof.

dermatology Mayo Sch. Medicine, Rochester, 1973-76, asst. prof. immunology, 1974-77, asso. prof. dermatology, 1976-77; prof. medicine, chmn. dermatology Med. Coll. Wis., Milw., 1977-82; med. career investigator VA, 1978-82; chief dermatology Froedtert Meml. Luth. Hosp., Milw., 1980-82; prof., chmn. dept. dermatology U. Tex. Health Sci. Center, Houston; chief dermatology Hermann Hosp., Houston, 1983—; mem. study sect. NIH, 1983-86; mem. nat. arthritis adv. bd. Nat. Inst. aRthritis and Metabolic Diseases, NIH; mem. nat. adv. bd. Arthritis, Musculoskeletal and Skin Diseases, 1989-91, chmn. 1992-93. Mem. editl. bd. Jour. Investigative Dermatology, 1977-82, Jour. Clin. and Lab. Immunology, 1977—, Archives of Dermatology, 1978-87, sect. editor Am. Jour. Dermatopathology, 1981-83, Clin. Aspects Autoimmunity, 1989-92. Elder Grace Presbyn. Ch., Houston, 1987—; bd. dirs. CAnCare of Houston, 1991—, pres. bd. dirs., 1997—. Lt. comdr. M.C., USN, 1965-71. Recipient Bacelli Research award SUNY, Buffalo, 1965, Med. Spltys. Outstanding Achievement award Mayo Found., 1969, Marion B. Sulzberger award Am. Soc. Dermatologic Allergy and Immunology, 1983. Mem. Soc. Investigative Dermatology (com. nominations 1986—, dir. 1977-82), Am. Acad. Dermatology (co-chmn. com. lab. proficiency and quality control in immunodermatology 1980-83, dir. Immunopathology Symposium 1981-86, bd. dirs. 1993-98), AAAS, Am. Assn. Immunologists, Am. Dermatol. Assn., Am. Fedn. Clin. Research, AMA, Am. Soc. Clin. Investigation, Assn. Profs. Dermatology (bd. dirs. 1987-89), Central Soc. Clin. Research, Dermatology Found. (chmn. med. and sci. com. 1980-81, trustee 1993-98), Soc. Exptl. Biology and Medicine, Lupus Erythematosus Soc. Wis. (mem. med. adv. bd. 1977-83), Wis. Dermatol. Soc. (pres. 1979-80), Wis. State Med. Soc., Chgo. Dermatol. Soc., Tex. Med. Assn., Houston Dermatol. Soc., Lupus Soc. Houston (adv. bd. 1986—), Sigma Xi. Home: 12319 Huntingwick Dr Houston TX 77024-4905 Office: U Tex Health Sci Ctr Houston TX 77030

JORGE, JUAN B., cultural organization administrator, writer; b. Ponce, P.R., Nov. 27, 1945; s. Ernesto-Adela Jorge Rodriguez; children: Juan Enrique, Adelaida, Juan Ernesto, Juan Carlos. Pres. Latino Artists Group, Waterbury, Conn., 1995—. Author: De Amor, Sent. y Patria, 1992, De Ponce Para El Mundo, 1992, Solo Sentimiento, 1995, An Anthology of Writings, 1996. Commr. Office Fin. Assistance, Waterbury, 1997; mem. Mayor's Urban Task Force, Waterbury, 1997. Office: Latino Artists Group Inc 13 Cherry Ave G-322 Waterbury CT 06702

JORGENSEN, ALFRED H., computer software and data communications executive; b. South Gate, Calif., May 1, 1934; s. Peter Hansen and Anna Christine (Nielsen) J.; AA, El Camino Coll., 1958; student UCLA, 1958-60; m. Carole Jean Scott, Sept. 3, 1959; children: Mark Alan, Lora Jean. Assoc. engr. Litton Industries, Beverly Hills, Calif., 1957-60; engr. Daystrom, Inc., 1960-64; with control systems divsn. Foxboro Co., Pitts., 1964-67, dist. and regional mgr., 1967-69; with Interactive Scis., Pitts., 1969-72, v.p., 1970-71; v.p. Computeria Inc., 1971, pres., 1971-72; v.p. Interactive Scis. Corp., Braintree, Mass., 1972-77, pres., 1977-80; exec. v.p. Nat. Data Corp., Atlanta, 1980-83; v.p. Cullinet Software Inc., 1983-85, v.p. Systems and Computer Tech., 1985-87; pres, chief operating officer Infosafe Corp., Atlanta, 1987-88; pres. Corp. Playmakers, 1988-90; dir. bus. alliances Sprint Comm., 1990-95; gen. mgr. Applied Tech. Ctr., 1995—; bd. dirs. Process Corp., Pitts. Bd. dirs. Mass. Assn. Mental Health, 1977-79, v.p., 1978-79. Served with U.S. Army, 1954-56. Mem. Data Processing Mgmt. Assn., Assn. Iron and Steel Engrs., Instrument Soc. Am., IEEE, Cash Mgmt. Assn., Am. Mgmt. Assn., Nat. Platform Assn. Club: Pearson Yacht (commodore 1984). Home: 927 Liberty Church Rd Dawsonville GA 30534-7354

JORGENSEN, ANN, farmer; b. Cedar Rapids, Iowa, Sept. 16, 1940; d. Kenneth Edward and Velma Ann (Baumhoefener) Fry; m. Marlyn L. Jorgensen, Feb. 27, 1961; children: Christopher, Peter, Timothy, Jennifer. BA, U. Iowa, 1962. Lic. commodity broker. Tax acct. Bill Burrell Tax Svc., Urbana, Iowa, 1968-70, Hansen Acctg., Vinton, Iowa, 1970-75; commodity broker First Mid. Am., Cedar Rapids, 1975-85; owner Lakeview Enterprises, Osage Beach, Mo., 1975-85; v.p., treas. Timberlane Hogs, Ltd., Garrison, Iowa, 1971—; mng. ptnr., owner Jorg-Anna Farms, Garrison, 1963—; pres., founder Farm Home Offices, Vinton, 1981—; bd. dirs. Farm Bur. Mut. Funds, Des Moines; commr. Interstate Agrl. Grain Commn. Midwest Compact, 1986-88; mem. Agriculture Products Adv. Bd., Des Moines, 1990—, bd. dirs.; spkr. in field; mem. environ. com. Nat. Pork Producers Coun., 1996—; chair info. tech. com. Am. Farm Bur. Fedn., 1996—. Author: Put PaperWork in its Place, 1982; contbr. articles to profl. jours. Mem., chair Iowa Arts Coun., 1973-79; regent Iowa Bd. Regents, 1979-85; dir., pres. Iowa Alcoholic Beverages Commr., Des Moines, 1985-88; nat. chair Tauke for U.S. Senate, Iowa, 1987-88; bd. dirs. Iowa Dept. Econ. Devel., 1988—; chair bd. Iowa Rural Devel. Coun., 1991-95; mem. Iowa Supreme Ct. Study Com., 1995-96. Named to Iowa Vol. Hall of Fame, 1989. Mem. AACC (bd. dirs. 1995—), Vinton Am. Assn. U. Women (various offices 1980—), Iowa Pub. TV Found. (sec. 1987-95). Avocations: golf, bridge. Home: 1965 64th St Garrison IA 52229-9647 Office: Farm Home Offices PO Box 840 Vinton IA 52349-0840

JORGENSEN, DANIEL FRED, academic executive; b. May 3, 1947; m. Susan Jorgensen, June 20, 1969; children: Kari, Becky. BA in Journalism, S.D. State U., 1969, MS in Journalism, 1974; postgrad., Colo. State U.; grad. with honors, U.S. Army's Def. Info. Sch., 1970. Writer news and sports Sioux Falls (S.D.) Argus-Leader, 1969-70; asst. editor news and sports, part-time instr. S.D. State U. Comm. Office, 1972-74; from publ. editor to asst. dir. Colo. State U., 1974-78; editor news and sports Hot Springs (S.D.) Star, 1978-81; exec. dir. Black Hills (S.D.) Girl Scout Coun., 1981-83; dir. devel. and pub. rels. St. Martin's Acad., Rapid City, S.D., 1983-84; dir. news svc. St. Olaf Coll., Northfield, Minn., 1984-88, dir. pub. rels., 1988-97; v.p. comm. Citizens Scholarship Found. Am., 1997—; bd. dirs. Norwest Bank Northfield. Author and co-author six books; contbr. numerous articles to mags. and jours. Chair bd. Northfield Hosp., 1990—, United Way, 1989-91, chair 1990-91; chair bd. Northfield Rotary, 1987-92, v.p., 1990-91, pres. 1991-92; officer various other cmty. orgns.; mem. coms. Northfield Sch. 1st lt. U.S. Army, 1970-72. Named to first class Leadership Rapid City, 1982-83; honored for community svc. City of Northfield, 1992; recipient Rice County Vol. award, 1992. Mem. Coun. for the Advancement and Support of Edn. (nat. coms. mem. 1991—), Nat. Assn. Sci. Writers, Nat. Edn. Writers Assn., Kappa Tau Alpha, Sigma Delta Chi. Avocations: sports, youth activities, writing, coin collecting, community theater. Home: 505 Wilson Ct Northfield MN 55057-1374 Office: Citizens Scholarship Found 7703 Normandale Rd Minneapolis MN 55435-5311

JORGENSEN, ERIK, forest pathologist, educator, consultant; b. Haderslev, Denmark, Oct. 28, 1921; emigrated to Can., 1955, naturalized, 1960; s. Johannes and Eva Bromberg (Hansen) J.; m. Grete Moller, June 13, 1946; children: Marianne, Birthe. M. Forestry, Royal Vet. and Agrl. Coll., Copenhagen, 1946. Forest pathologist Royal Vet. and Agrl. Coll., Copenhagen, 1948-55; forest pathologist sci. service Agr. Can., 1955-59; asst. prof. U. Toronto, 1959-63, assoc. prof., 1963-67, prof. forest pathology and urban forestry, 1967-73; chief urban forestry program Can. Forestry Service, Environ. Can., 1973-78; arboretum dir., prof. environ. biology U. Guelph, Ont., 1978-87; cons. in field, 1987-89. Author: The Development of an Urban Forestry Concept, 1967; contbr. articles to sci. jours. Served to 2d lt. Danish Army, 1946-48. Recipient Authors citation Internat. Shade Tree Conf., 1970; recipient Maple Leaf award Internat. Shade Tree Conf., 1975, Can. Patents and Devel. Ltd. Inventors cert., 1975, Trees for Tomorrow award Can. Forestry Assn., 1993. Fellow Can. Inst. Forestry; mem. Ont. Profl. Foresters Assn., Internat. Soc. Arboriculture, Ont. Shade Tree Council (life, Jaap Salm Meml. award 1975), Sigma Xi. Lutheran. Home: Apt 507, 172 Metcalfe St Apt 507, Guelph, ON Canada N1E 6T6 *A dedication to the application of forest science to the service of mankind.*

JORGENSEN, ERIK HOLGER, lawyer; b. Copenhagen, July 19, 1916; s. Holger and Karla (Andersen) J.; children: Jette Friis, Lone Olesen, John, Jean Ann. JD, San Francisco Law Sch., 1960. Bar: Calif. 1961. Pvt. practice law, 1961-70; ptnr. Hersh, Hadfield, Jorgensen & Fried, San Francisco, 1970-76, Hadfield & Jorgensen, San Francisco, 1976-88 . Pres. Aldersly, Danish Retirement Home, San Rafael, Calif., 1974-77, Rebild Park Soc. Bay Area chpt., 1974-77. Fellow Scandinavian Am. Found. (hon.); mem. ABA, San Francisco Lawyers Club, Bar Assn. of San Francisco, Calif. Assn. Realtors (hon. life bd. dirs.). Author: Master Forms Guide for Successful Real Estate Agreements, Successful Real Estate Sales Agreements, 1991; contbr. articles on law and real estate law to profl. jours.

JORGENSEN, GARY C., elementary and secondary education educator; b. Yankton, S.D., Sept. 2, 1934; s. Glen Christopher and Carrie Rose (Hansen) J.; m. Ethel Mae Carter, Jan. 27, 1962; children: Steven, Shelly. BS, So. State Tchrs. Coll., Springfield, S.D., 1963; MA, U. S.D., 1968; EdSpec, U. N.Mex., 1994. Sch. rehab. counselor Willmar (Minn.) Pub. Schs., 1968-82; salesman Willmar, 1982-84; spl. edn. tchr. Sioux City (Iowa) Pub. Schs., 1963-68, Albuquerque Pub. Schs., 1984-97; mem. Counsel for Exceptional Citizens, Albuquerque, 1985—, presenter conv., 1995. Bd. dirs. Kandiyohi County Assn. for Retarded Citizens, Willmar, 1970-84. Sgt. USMC, 1954-57. Avocations: antique collecting, crafts. Office: Jorges Enterprises 7120 Wyoming Blvd NE Ste 7 Albuquerque NM 87109

JORGENSEN, GORDON DAVID, engineering company executive; b. Chgo., Apr. 29, 1921; s. Jacob and Marie (Jensen) J.; BS in Elec. Engring., U. Wash., 1948, postgrad. in bus. and mgmt., 1956-59; m. Nadina Anita Peters, Dec. 17, 1948 (div. Aug. 1971); children: Karen Ann, David William, Susan Marie; m. Barbara Noel, Feb. 10, 1972 (div. July 1976); m. Ruth Barnes Chalmers, June 15, 1990. With R.W. Beck & Assos., Cons. Engrs., Phoenix, 1948—, ptnr., 1954-86; pres. Beck Internat., Phoenix, 1971—. Served to lt. (j.g.) U.S. Maritime Service, 1942-45. Recipient Outstanding Service award Phoenix Tennis Assn., 1967; Commendation, Govt. Honduras, 1970. Registered profl. engr., Alaska, Ariz., Calif., Colo., Nev., N.Mex., N.D., Utah, Wash., Wyo. Mem. IEEE (chmn. Wash.-Alaska sect. 1959-60), Nat. Soc. Profl. Engrs., Am. Soc. Appraisers (sr. mem.), Ariz. Cons. Engrs. Assn., Ariz. Soc. Profl. Engrs., Internat. Assn. Assessing Officers, Southwestern Tennis Assn. (past pres.), U.S. Tennis Assn. (pres. 1987-88, chmn. U.S. Open com.); chmn. U.S. Davis Cup com.; chmn. Internat. Tennis Fed., Davis Cup com. Presbyterian (elder). Project mgr. for mgmt., operation studies and reorgn. study Honduras power system, 1969-70. Home: 74-574 Palo Verde Dr Indian Wells CA 92210-7314 Office: RW Beck & Assocs 3003 N Central Ave Phoenix AZ 85012-2902

JORGENSEN, JAMES H., pathologist, educator, microbiologist; b. Dallas, July 11, 1946; m. Jane Drummond, Feb. 18, 1978. BA, North Tex. State U., 1969, MS, 1970, PhD, 1973. cert. microbiologist. Rsch. assoc. Shriners Hosp. for Crippled Children, 1970-73; assoc. dir. Bexar County Hosp., 1973-75; instr. dept. pathology and dept. microbiology, Health Sci. Ctr. U. Tex., San Antonio, 1973-75, asst. prof., 1975-78, assoc. prof., 1978-84; dir. clin. microbiology labs. Univ. Hosp., 1975—; prof. dept. pathology, dept. medicine, dept. microbiology, dept. clin. lab. scis., Health Sci. Ctr. Univ. Ctr. Hosp., 1984—; mem. editorial bd. Antimicrobial Agts. and Chemotherapy, 1982-99, Jour. Clin. Microbiology, 1986—, Clin. Infectious Diseases, 1995-99, Diagnostic Microbiology and Infectious Diseases, 1983-87, reviewer, 1992-93; reviewer of numerous sci. jours.; chairholder Nat. Com. for Clin. Lab. Standards, subcom. on antimicrobial susceptibility testing, 1990-97; chair Nat. Com. for Clin. Lab Stds., Microbiol. Area Com., 1998—. Author: In Vitro Detection of Methicillin-Resistant Staphylococci, 1985, A Clinician's Dictionary of Bacteria and Fungi, 1986, Progress and Pitfalls in Staphylococcus Susceptibility Testing, 1987; editor Automation in Clinical Microbiology, 1987, Manual of Clinical Microbiology, 1995, 2d edit., 1999. Recipient Becton-Dickenson and Co. award in Clin. Microbiology, 1992; James W. McLaughlin Pre-Doctoral fellow in Infection and Immunity, Med. Branch, U. Tex., 1971-73; Pre-Doctoral scholarship, North Tex. State U., 1969-70. Fellow Infectious Diseases Soc. of Am., Am. Acad. Microbiology; mem. Am. Soc. for Microbiology (Tex. branch chmn. clin. divsn. 1987-88), Southwestern Assn. of Clin. Microbiology, Tex. Infectious Diseases Soc. (pres. 1985-86), South Tex. Assn. of Microbiology Profls. (program dir. 1981-86, pres. 1989-90). Office: Univ of Texas Health Sciences Dept of Pathology 7703 Floyd Curl Dr San Antonio TX 78284-6200

JORGENSEN, LELAND HOWARD, aerospace research engineer; b. Rexburg, Idaho, Nov. 1, 1924; s. Leland Maeser and Anne Molyneaux (Howard) J.; m. Lynone Watkins, Mar. 24, 1949; children: Leland Ronald Jorgensen, Paul Victor Jorgensen, Jonathan Arthur Jorgensen, Sara Anne Jorgensen. BS in Mech. Engring. with honors, U. Utah, 1948; MS in Mech. Engring. with honors, Stanford U., 1949; PhD in Mech. Engring. with high honors, Calif. Coast U., 1977. Rsch. engr. NACA-Ames Aero. Lab., Moffett Field, Calif., 1949-59; rsch. scientist NASA-Ames Rsch. Ctr., Moffett Field, Calif., 1959-66, tech. asst. chief thermo and gas dynamics div., 1966-68, tech. asst. chief aeronautics div., 1968-71, aerospace rsch. scientist, 1971-80; aerospace cons. Sandy, Utah, 1980—; mem. aerodyn. panel for space shuttle NASA, 1978-80; cons. on Agile missile USN, 1972; cons. on air-slew missile USAF, 1973. Contbr. over 50 articles on aerodyns. of missiles and aircraft at subsonic, transonic, supersonic and hypersonic speeds to profl. jours. Trustee Saratoga (Calif.) Sch. Dist., 1977-81; v.p., pres. Eagle Scout Assn. Santa Clara (Calif.) coun. Boy Scouts Am., 1962-72; pres. Neighborhood 5 Granite Cmty., Sandy, 1990-93; high priest LDS Ch. Lt. USNR, 1944-46, PTO. Fellow AIAA (assoc.); mem. SAR (pres. Salt Lake City chpt. 1989-90, pres. Utah Soc. 1992-93, chaplain 1994-97, Meritorious Svc. medal 1993, Patriot medal 1997, trustee 1999—), Sons of the Utah Pioneers (life), Tau Beta Pi, Pi Tau Sigma, Sigma Nu, Theta Tau. Achievements include development of analytical method for computing aerodynamics of missile and airplane-life configurations to very high angles of attack; svc. on com. that approved aerodynamics of the space-shuttle orbiter for the first flight. Office: Aerospace Cons 3 La Montagne Ln Sandy UT 84092-6024

JORGENSEN, PAUL ALFRED, English language educator emeritus; b. Lansing, Mich., Feb. 17, 1916; s. Karl and Rose Josephine (Simmons) J.; m. Virginia Frances Elfrink, Jan. 3, 1942; children: Mary Catherine, Elizabeth Ross Jorgensen Howard. A.B., Santa Barbara State Coll., 1938; M.A., U. Calif. at Berkeley, 1940, Ph.D., 1945. Instr. English Bakersfield (Calif.) Jr. Coll., 1945-46, U. Calif., Berkeley, summer 1946, U. Calif., Davis, 1946-47; mem. faculty UCLA, 1947—, prof. English, 1960-81, prof. emeritus, 1981—; vis. prof. U. Wash., summer 1966; mem. editorial com. U. Calif. Press, 1957-60; mem. Humanities Inst. U. Calif., 1967-69; mem. acad. adv. council Shakespeare Globe Ctr. N.Am. Author: Shakespeare's Military World, 1956, (with Frederick B. Shroyer) A College Treasury, rev. edit, 1967, (with Shroyer) The Informal Essay, 1961, Redeeming Shakespeare's Words, 1962; editor: The Comedy of Errors, 1964, Othello: An Outline- Guide to the Play, 1964, (with Shroyer) The Art of Prose, 1965, Lear's Self-Discovery, 1967, Our Naked Frailties: Sensational Art and Meaning in Macbeth, 1971, William Shakespeare: The Tragedies, 1985; mem. bd. editors Film Quar, 1958-65, Huntington Library Quar, 1965-83, Coll. English, 1966-70; mem. adv. com. Publs. of MLA of Am, 1978-82. Guggenheim fellow, 1956-57; Regents' Faculty fellow in humanities, 1973-74. Mem. Modern Lang. Assn., Shakespeare Assn. Am. (bibliographer 1954-59), Renaissance Soc. Am., Philol. Assn., Pacific Coast (exec. com. 1962-63), Internat. Shakespeare Assn. Episcopalian. Home: 234 Tavistock Ave Los Angeles CA 90049-3229

JORGENSEN, PAUL J., research company executive; b. Midway, Utah, Sept. 1, 1930; s. Joseph and Alice P. Jorgensen; m. Ardelle M. Bloom, Sept. 11, 1959; children: Paula, Mark, Janet, LaDell, Brett, Scott. Student, U. Utah, 1948-50, PhD, 1960; BS, Brigham Young U., 1954. Scientist Gen. Electric Co., Schenectady, N.Y., 1960-68; mgr. ceramics group Stanford Research Inst., Menlo Park, Calif., 1968-74, dir. materials research ctr., 1974-76; exec. dir. phys. sci. div. SRI Internat., Menlo Park, 1976-77, v.p. phys. and life sci. div., 1977-80, sr. v.p. scis. group, 1980-88, exec. v.p., COO, 1988-94, also bd. dirs., exec. v.p., 1994—; cons. GTE, 1971-82; mem. com. high temperature chemistry NRC, 1972-75, nat. materials adv. bd., 1982-85; mem. Internat. Panel of Advisors on Tech., Singapore Inst. Stds. & Indsl. Rsch. Contbr. articles to profl. jours.; patentee in field. Served with U.S. Army, 1954-56. Recipient IR-100, Indsl. Research Mag., 1967. Fellow Am. Ceramic Soc. (chmn. basic sci. div. 1975). Republican. Mormon. Office: SRI Internat 333 Ravenswood Ave Menlo Park CA 94025-3453

JORGENSEN, RALPH GUBLER, lawyer, accountant; b. N.Y.C., Mar. 12, 1937; s. Thorvald W. and Florence (Gubler) J.; m. Patricia June Spivey, June 21, 1971 (dec. Oct. 1997); 1 child, Misty. AB, George Washington U., 1960, LLB, 1962. CPA, Md., Nev., N.C. Bar: D.C. 1963, Md. 1963, U.S. Dist. Ct. D.C. 1963, U.S. Ct. Appeals (D.C. cir.) 1963, U.S. Dist. Ct. Md. 1964, U.S. Supreme Ct. 1971, N.C. 1972, U.S. Dist. Ct. (ea. dist.) N.C. 1972, U.S. Ct. Appeals (4th cir.) 1974, U.S. Tax Ct. 1976, U.S. Dist. Ct. (mid. dist.) N.C. 1977, U.S. Ct. Clms. 1979. Sole practice, Washington and Silver Spring, Md., 1963-71, Tabor City, N.C., 1971—. Bd. dirs. Columbus County ARC, N.C., 1974. Mem. ATLA, Am. Assn. Atty.-CPAs, N.C. Bar Assn., N.C. Acad. Trial Lawyers, Alpha Kappa Psi. Democrat. Baptist. Home: 101 Pireway Rd Tabor City NC 28463-2021 Office: 116 W 4th St PO Box 248 Tabor City NC 28463-0248

JORGENSEN, ROBERT WILLIAM, product engineer; b. Allegan, Mich., Jan. 8, 1946; m. Deborah Ann Geiger; children: Linda, Eric, Laura, Lisa. BS in Aerospace Engring., U. Mich., 1969; AS, Radio Electronics Tech. Sch., South Bend, Ind., 1971. Engr. Kawneer Corp., Niles, Mich., 1970-80; tech. dir. Raco, Inc., South Bend, Ind., 1980—; mem. adv. coun. Underwriter's Assn. Holder 36 patents on elec. boxes and fittings. Mem. Underwriters Labs., Nat. Elec. Mfrs. Assn., Nat. Fire Protection Assn., Internat. Assn. Elec. Insps., Can. Stds. Assn. Avocations: private pilot, amateur radio, gardening. Home: 1353 Thompson Rd Niles MI 49120-9332 Office: Raco Inc PO Box 4002 South Bend IN 46634-4002

JORGENSEN, WILLIAM L., chemistry educator; b. N.Y.C., Oct. 5, 1949; s. Axel V. and Alice C. (Lane) J. AB, Princeton U., 1970; PhD, Harvard U., 1975; MA (hon.), Yale U., 1991. Asst. prof. Purdue U., West Lafayette, Ind., 1975-78, assoc. prof., 1979-81, prof. chemistry, 1982-85, H.C. Brown prof., 1985-90; Whitehead prof. Yale U., New Haven, 1990—; sci. advisor Ariad Pharms., Inc., 1991—, Combichem, Inc., 1995—. Contbr. over 200 articles to sci. jours. Recipient ann. medal Internat. Acad. Quantum Molecular Sci., 1986. Mem. FAAAS, Am. chem. Soc. (Cope Scholar 1990). Office: Yale U Dept Chemistry 225 Prospect Ave New Haven CT 06520-8107*

JORGENSON, DALE WELDEAU, economist, educator; b. Bozeman, Mont., May 7, 1933; s. Emmett B. and Jewell (Torkelson) J.; m. Linda Ann Mabus, July 24, 1971; children: Eric Mabus, Kari Ann. BA, Reed Coll., 1955; AM, Harvard U., 1957, PhD, 1959; PhD (hon.), Uppsala U., 1991, Oslo U., 1991. Mem. faculty U. Calif., Berkeley, 1959-69; prof. econs. U. Calif., 1963-69; prof. econs. Harvard U., 1969-80, Frederic Eaton Abbe prof. econs., 1980—, Frank William Taussig rsch. prof. econs., 1992-94; Ford research prof. econs. U. Chgo., 1962-63. Author: (with J.J. McCall and R. Radner) Optimal Replacement Policy, 1967, Econometric Studies of U.S. Energy Policy, 1975, (with R. Landau) Technology and Economic Policy, 1986 (with F.M. Gollop and B.M. Fraumeni) Productivity and U.S. Economic Growth, 1987, (with R. Landau), Technology and Capital Formation, 1989, (with Lars Bergman, Erno Zalai) General Equilibrium Modeling and Economic Policy Analysis, 1990, (with Kun-Young Yun) Tax Reform and the Cost of Capital, 1991, (with Li Jingwen, Zheng Youjing and Masahiro Kuroda) Productivity and Economic Growth in China, USA and Japan, 1993, (with R. Landau) Tax Reform and the Cost of Capital: An International Comparison, 1993, Postwar U.S. Economic Growth, 1995, International Comparisons of Economic Growth, 1995, Capital Theory and Investment Behavior, 1996, Tax Policy and the Cost of Capital, 1996, (with E. Hanushek) Improving America's Schools, 1996, Aggregate Consumer Behavior, 1997, Measuring Social Welfare, 1997, Econometric General Equilibrium Modeling, 1998, Energy, The Environment and Economic Growth, 1998. Fellow AAAS, Am. Phillos. Soc., Econometric Soc. (pres. 1987), Am. Statis. Assn., Am. Acad. Arts and Scis.; mem. Am. Econ. Assn. (John Bates Clark medal 1971, pres.-elect 1999), Nat. Acad. Scis., Royal Swedish Acad. Scis. Home: 1010 Memorial Dr Cambridge MA 02138-4859 Office: Harvard U Littauer 122 Cambridge MA 02138-3001

JORGENSON, MARY ANN, lawyer; b. Gallipolis, Ohio, 1941. BA, Agnes Scott Coll., 1963; MA, Harvard U., 1964; JD, Case Western Res. U., 1975. Bar: Ohio 1975, N.Y. 1982. Ptnr., chair firm's corp. practice Squire, Sanders & Dempsey, 1990—. Office: Squire Sanders & Dempsey LLP 4900 Key Tower 127 Public Sq Ste 4900 Cleveland OH 44114-1284

JORGESON, BRENT WILSON, management executive; b. Atlanta, Aug. 29, 1950; s. Charles Milton and Arleen Irma (Marshall) J.; m. Mary Elizabeth House, June 9, 1973. BS, Ga. Inst. Tech., 1973; MBA, Harvard U., 1975. With Advance Mortgage Corp., Southfield, Mich., 1975-76; v.p. ops. Hosp. Investors, Inc., Atlanta, 1977-80; sr. assoc. Booz, Allen & Hamilton, Inc., Atlanta, 1980-81; v.p. devel. Healthcare Internat., Inc., Austin, Tex., 1981-83, v.p. ops., 1984-88; pres. Regent Health Group, Inc., Austin, 1988-95; chmn. bd. Home Health Care Affiliates Inc., Austin, 1995—. Served 1st lt. U.S. Army, Mil. Intelligence, 1975. Clubs: Harvard Bus. Sch., Harvard. Home: 7705 Baja Cv Austin TX 78759-4541 Office: 4505 Spicewood Springs Rd Austin TX 78759-8584

JORIZZO, JOSEPH L., dermatology educator; b. Rochester, N.Y., Oct. 6, 1951; s. Joseph Lucius and Margaret R. (Volpe) J.; m. Susan MacLeod, Aug. 23, 1975 (div.); children: John Joseph, Michael Wesley; m. Irene Carros, Dec. 30, 1995; 1 child, Melina Margaret. AB, Boston U., 1972, MD magna cum laude, 1975. Diplomate Am. Bd. Dermatology. Intern in internal medicine N.C. Meml. Hosp., Chapel Hill, 1975-76, resident in dermatology, 1976-78, chief resident, 1978-79; overseas registrar Dermatology Inst. St. John's Hosp. for Diseases of the Skin, London, 1979-80; clin. asst. prof. dept. dermatology U. Tex. Med. Br., Galveston, 1979-80, from asst. prof. dept. dermatology to assoc. prof. dept. dermatology, 1980-86; prof., chmn. dept. dermatology Sch. Medicine of Wake Forest U., Winston-Salem, N.C., 1986—; cons. VA Clinic, Winston-Salem, 1986—, Forsyth Meml. Hosp., Winston-Salem, 1989—, VA Hosp., Salisbury, N.C., 1991—; mem. med. adv. bd. Am. Behcet's Disease Assn., 1988—, Winston-Salem/Forsyth County Lupus Found., 1989—; co-chmn. Southeastern Consortium for Dermatology, 1990, steering com., 1987—; mem. internat. steering com. Bechet's Disease, 1989—; mem. adv. com. Nat. Student Rsch. Forum, 1981-86; speaker more than 100 meetings, symposia, U.S. and Europe; vis. prof. Cath. U. Rome Med. Sch., 1981, U. Ark. Med. Scis., Little Rock, 1982, Brooke Army Med. Ctr., San Antonio, 1982, U. Louisville, 1982, U. N.Mex., Albuquerque, 1985, U. Mich., Ann Arbor, 1985, Duke U. Med. Ctr., 1986, U.Va., Charlottesville, 1986, Emory U., Atlanta, 1986, 92, U. South Fla., Tampa, 1987, Brown U. Med. Ctr., Providence, R.I., 1990, U. Ind., Indpls., 1991, NYU Med. Ctr., 1991, Columbia U., N.Y.C., 1993, U. Pitts., 1993, many others; invited speaker numerous meetings including Chapel Hill Alumni Dermatology Conf., 1981, Immunology Club Meeting, Galveston, 1984, Fla. Dermatol. Soc. Ann. Meeting, Ft. Lauderdale, 1984, Stetson lectr. N.Mex. Dermatol. Soc., Albuquerque, 1985, Mich. Dermatological Soc., Shanty Creek, 1985, Charlotte Dermatol. Soc., 1986, Greensboro Dermatopathology/Dermatology Semi-ann. Meeting, 1987, N.C. Med. Soc., 1987, Richmond-Tidewater Dermatologic Soc., Williamsburg, Va., 1988, AARP, Winston-Salem, 1988, No. Calif. Dermatologic Assn., North Lake Tahoe, Calif., 1989, Stiefel Can. Symposium, Key Biscayne, Fla., 1990, Dermatologic Soc. Greater N.Y., 1990, Westwood Conf. Clin. Dermatology, Hilton Head, S.C., 1990, Westwood Conf., Charleston, S.C., 1991, Charlotte Dermatol. Soc. Meeting, 1992, N.C. Med. Soc. Dermatology Sect., 1992, Charlotte Family Practice Soc., 1993. Co-author: Dermatological Signs of Internal Disease, 1988; contbr. chpts. to books, more than 90 articles to profl. jours.; author abstracts in field; reviewer Archives of Dermatology, 1981—, Jour. Am. Acad. Dermatology, 1981—, Pediatric Dermatology, 1986—, Jour. Investigative Dermatology, 1986—, Internat. Jour. Dermatology, 1984—, JAMA, 1988—, others; mem. editorial bd. Clin. and Exptl. Dermatology, 1988—, Jour. Am. Acad. Dermatology, 1988-93, Archives of Dermatology, 1990—, Jour. European Acad. of Dermatology and Venereology, 1992—, Current Problems in Dermatology, 1992—, Practical Cases in Dermatology, 1993—, others. Trustee Forsyth Country Day Sch., Winston-Salem, 1990—, chmn. devel. com., 1991-92, coord. new parent's bldg. fund, 1987-88; participant med bowl fund raiser for Crisis Control, Winston-Salem, 1990. William Reed traveling fellow, 1979, Am. Acad. Dermatology fellow, 1982, 84, Dermatology Found. fellow, 1983, Upjohn Pharm. Co. Spl. grantee, 1982, Ital. Dermatology Soc. grantee, 1981, Italian Found. Rsch. Dermatology grantee, 1981, Wellcome Trust/Royal Soc. Medicine grantee, 1993, Dermatology Found. grantee, 1984, 86, 87, Noah Worcester Dermatologic Soc. grantee, 1986, Nat. Inst. Dental Rsch. grantee, 1985-86, Neutrogena grantee, 1986, Am. Cyanamid Co. grantee, 1987, Hoechst-Roussel grantee, 1988, numerous other grants including Herbert Labs., Genderm, Dermik Labs., R.W. Johnson Pharms., Stiefel Labs., Pfizer Labs., Curatek Pharms., Allergan Herbert, Bristol-Myers Squibb, Hoffman LaRoche Dermatologics, Glaxo Pharm. Co., RJR Nabisco, Ortho-McNeil Pharms. Fellow ACP; mem. AMA, Soc. Investigative Dermatology (sec.-treas. So. sect. 1984-85, v.p. So. sect. 1985-86, pres. So. sect. 1986-87, membership com. 1987-90, chmn. membership com. 1989-90), Am. Acad. Dermatology (mem. numerous coms. including internat. affairs 1981-84, summer session com. 1989—, chmn. clin. studies session 1990, nominating com. 1993—, chmn. various awards coms., media tng. recipient 1984), Am. Coll. Cyrosurgery, Dermatology Found. (dir. membership subcom. 1983-85, devel. com. 1983-86), So. Med. Assn., Forsyth County Med. Soc. (Membership Task Force 1989-90), N.C. Med. Soc., N.C. Dermatology Soc., Am. Fedn. Clin. Rsch., Psoriasis Found., Noah Worcester Dermatologic Soc., N.Am. Clin. Dermatological Soc., Pacific Dermatologic Assn. (hon.), Am. Dermatologic Assn., Am. Bd. Dermatology (Part I test com.), Societe Francaise de Dermatologie et de Venereologie, Am. Skin Assn., Internat. Soc. Tropical Dermatology, St. John's Dermatological Soc. (U.K.), Sir James Saunders Soc., Academia Medicorum Litteratorum (Italy), South Ctrl. Dermatological Soc. (organizing com. 1981-84, program com. 1984-86),Italian Soc. Dermatology and Venereology (corr.), Brit. Assn. Dermatologists (overseas mem.), Assn. Profs. Dermatology (internal medicine com. 1984-86), Dowling Club (U.K.), Phi Beta Kappa, Sigma Chi Rsch. Soc., Alpha Omega Alpha. Home: 150 Stonebrook Ct Winston Salem NC 27104-5137 Office: Wake Forest U Sch Med Dept Dermatology Med Ctr Blvd Winston Salem NC 27157-1071

JORNDT, LOUIS DANIEL, retail drug store chain executive; b. Chgo., Aug. 24, 1941; s. Louis Carl and Margaret Estelle (Teel) J.; m. Patricia McDonnell, Aug. 1, 1964; children—Kristine, Michael, Kara. B.S. in Pharmacy, Drake U., 1963; M.B.A., U. N.Mex., 1974. Various mgmt. positions Walgreen Co., Chgo., 1963-68, dist. mgr., 1968-75; regional dir. Walgreen Co., Deerfield, Ill., 1975-79; regional v.p. Walgreen Co., Deerfield, 1979-82, v.p., treas., 1982-85, sr. v.p., treas., 1985-89, pres., chief oper. officer, 1989-97, CEO, 1997—. Bd. dirs. Better Bus. Bur. Chgo., 1982—, Chgo. Assn. Commerce and Industry; nat. chmn. Drake U. Pharmacy Alumni Fund. Mem. Nat. Assn. Corp. Treas., Fin. Execs. Inst. Clubs: Economic (Chgo.); Glen View (Ill.) Golf. Avocations: golf; swimming; reading. Office: Walgreen Co 200 Wilmot Rd Deerfield IL 60015-4616*

JORNS, DAVID LEE, university president; b. Tulsa, Jan. 10, 1944; s. Victor Lee and Nancy Jane (Pollard) J.; m. Audrey Parkes; children: Molly, Ben. BS in Radio and TV, Okla. State U., 1966, MA in Speech and Drama, 1968; PhD in Theatre History and Criticism, UCLA, 1973. Teaching asst. UCLA, 1970-73; asst. prof. U. Mo., Columbia, 1973-77, assoc. prof., 1977-80, dir. of theatre, 1977-80; chmn. theatre arts Mankato (Minn.) State U., 1980-84; dean fine arts and humanities West Tex. State U., Canyon, 1984-88; v.p. acad. affairs and provost No. Ky. U., Highland Heights, 1988-92; pres. Eastern Ill. U., Charleston, 1992—. Contbr. articles, revs. to profl. publs.; producer 25 plays; editor The Jour. Opinion for the Performing Arts, 1975. Lt. USN, 1967-70. Mem. Ky. Coun. of Chief Acad. Officers, Soc. for Coll. & Univ. Planning, Assn. for Gen. & Liberal Studies, Am. Assn. for Higher Edn. Democrat. Avocations: computers, painting, reading. Office: Eastern Ill U Office of Pres Adminstrn Bldg Charleston IL 61920

JORNS, STEVEN D., hotel executive. Pres. Am. Gen. Hospitality, Inc., Dallas; vice chmn. Meristar Hospitality Corp., Irving, Tex., 1998—. Office: Meristar Hospitality Corp 5605 N Macarthur Blvd Ste 1200 Irving TX 75038-2635*

JORTNER, JOSHUA, physical chemistry scientist, educator; b. Poland, Mar. 14, 1933; s. Arthur and Regina Jortner; m. Ruth Sanger, 1960; 2 children. PhD, Hebrew U. Jerusalem; D (hon.), Tech. U. Munich, 1996. Instr. dept. phys. chemistry Hebrew U. Jerusalem, 1961-62, sr. lectr., 1963-65; assoc. prof. Tel Aviv U., 1965-66, prof., 1966—, Heinemann prof. chemistry, 1973—, head Inst. Chemistry, 1966-72, dep. rector, 1966-69, v.p., 1970-72; rsch. assoc. U. Chgo., 1962-64; vis. prof. U. Chgo., 1965-71, H.C. Orsted Inst., U. Copenhagen, 1974, 78, U. Calif., Berkeley, 1975. Author: (with M. Bixon) Intramolecular Radiationless Transitions, 1968; editor: (with Bernard Pullman) The Jerusalem Symposia on Quantum Chemistry and Biochemistry, 1982-95; contbr. articles to profl. jours. Recipient award Internat. Acad. Quantum Sci., 1972, Weizmann prize, 1973, Rothschild prize, 1976, Kolthof prize, 1976, Israel prize in Chemistry, 1982, Wolf prize, 1988, The Hon. J. Heyrovsky Gold medal, 1993, August-Wilhelm-von-Hofmann medal, 1995. Fellow Indian Sci. Acad. (fgn.), Indian Nat. Scis. Acad. (fgn.); mem. Israel Acad. Scis. and Humanities (v.p. 1980-86, pres. 1986-95), Internat. Acad. Quantum Scis., Am. Philos. Soc., Danish Acad. Scis. and Letters (fgn. mem.), Polish Acad. Scis., Russian Acad. Scis. (fgn.), European Acad. Scis. and Arts, Romanian Acad. Scis., German Acad. Scis. Leopoldina, Internat. Union Pure and Applied Chemistry (v.p. 1996-97, pres. 1998—), U.S. Nat. Acad. Scis. (fgn. assoc.). Avocations: reading, writing. Office: Tel Aviv U Sch Chemistry, Ramat-Aviv, 69978 Tel Aviv Israel also: Israel Acad Scis-Humanities, Einstein Sq PO Box 4040, 91040 Jerusalem Israel

JOSBENO, LARRY JOSEPH, physics educator; b. Elmira, N.Y., Oct. 21, 1938; s. Samuel Joseph and Katherine Lorena (Jessup) J.; m. Cecile Ann Quatrano, Sept. 15, 1962; children: Deborah Ann, John Lawrence. BS in Math., St. Bonaventure U., 1962; MS in Chemistry, U. N.H., 1970. Cert. tchr., N.Y. Tchr. Horseheads (N.Y.) High Sch., 1965-89; prof. Corning (N.Y.) C.C., 1989—; faculty assn. chair, 1995; vis. scientist Cornell U., Ithaca, N.Y., 1986-87; adj. prof. Elmira Coll.; cons. State Edn. Dept., Albany, N.Y., 1987, Math Matrix, Ithaca, 1987—, Corning Inc., 1989. Author: ARCO Physics Review Book, 1983; contbr. articles to profl. jours. Mem. bd. govs. Notre Dame H.S., Elmira, 1977-82; trustee Steele Meml. Lab., Elmira, 1985-94, pres., 1993; obs. presenter Elmira Corning Astron. Soc., Corning, 1968—; trustee So. Tier Libr. Sys., 1995—. Capt. arty. U.S. Army, 1963-65. Recipient N.Y. State Chancellor's award, 1995, Excellence in Tchg. award Bd. Trustees, 1998. Fellow Sci. Tchrs. Assn. N.Y. (pres. 1989-90); mem. Math. Assn. Am., Am. Phys. Soc., Am. Chem. soc., Am. Physics Tchr. Assn. (bd. dirs. 1996—), So. Tier Libr. Assn. (trustee 1995), Alpha Sigma Lambda (Tchr. of Yr. 1985). Democrat. Roman Catholic. Home: 539 W Franklin St Horseheads NY 14845-2356

JOSCELYN, KENT BUCKLEY, lawyer; b. Binghamton, N.Y., Dec. 18, 1936; s. Raymond Miles and Gwen Buckley (Smith) J.; children: Kathryn Anne, Jennifer Sheldon. BS, Union Coll., 1957; JD, Albany (N.Y.) Law Sch., 1960. Bar: N.Y. 1961, U.S. Ct. Mil. Appeals 1962, D.C., 1967, Mich. 1979. Atty. adviser hdqts. USAF, Washington, 1965-67; assoc. prof. forensic studies U. Ind., Bloomington, 1967-76; dir. Inst. Rsch. in Pub. Safety, 1970-75; head policy analysis divsn. Highway Safety Rsch. Inst. U. Mich., Ann Arbor, 1976-81; dir. transp. planning and policy Urban Tech. Environ. Planning Program, Ann Arbor, 1981-84; prin. Joscelyn and Treat P.C., Ann Arbor, 1981-83, Joscelyn, McNair & Jeffrey P.C., Ann Arbor, 1993—; cons. Law Enforcement Assistance Adminstrn., U.S. Dept. Justice, 1969-72; Gov.'s appointee as regional dir. Ind. Criminal Justice Planning Agy., 1969-72; vice chmn. Ind. Organized Crime Prevention Coun., 1969-72; commr. pub. safety City of Bloomington, Ind., 1974-76. Editor Internat. Jour. Criminal Justice. Capt. USAF, 1961-64. Mem. NAS, ABA, NRC, D.C. Bar Assn., N.Y. State Bar Assn., Internat. Bar Assn., Transp. Rsch. Bd. (chmn. motor vehicle and traffic law com. 1979-82), Am. Soc. Criminology (life), Assn. for Advancement Automotive Medicine (life), Soc. Automotive Engrs., Acad. Criminal Justice Scis. (life), Assn. Chiefs Police (assoc.), Nat. Safety Coun., Assn. Former Intelligence Officers (life), Product Liability Adv. Coun., Sigma Xi, Theta Delta Chi. E-mail: jmjpc@msn.com. Office: Joscelyn McNair & Jeffrey PC PO Box 130589 Ann Arbor MI 48113-0589

JOSEFF, JOAN CASTLE, manufacturing executive; b. Alta., Can., Aug. 12, 1922; naturalized U.S. citizen, 1945; d. Edgar W. and Lottie (Coates) Castle; BA in Psychology, UCLA; widowed; 1 son, Jeffrey Rene. With Joseff-Hollywood, jewelry manufacture and rental, Burbank, Calif., 1939—, chmn. bd., pres., sec.-treas. Numerous TV appearances including CBS This Morning, Australia This Morning, Am. Movie Channel. Mem. Burbank Salary Task Force, 1979—, L.A. County Earthquake Fact-Finding Commn., 1981— ; bd. dirs. San Fernando Valley area chpt. Am. Cancer Soc., treas., Genesis Energy Systems, Inc., 1993—; mem. Rep. Cen. Com.; del. Rep. Nat. Conv., 1980, 84, 88, 92, 96; voting mem. Calif. Rep. Party; chmn. Women Legis.; active Beautiful People Award Com. Honoring John Wayne Carcer Clinic; appointed by Gov. Wilson to Barber and Cosmotology Bd; appointed br Pres. Clinton to Selective Svc. System. Recipient Women in Achievement award Soroptomist Internat., 1988. Mem. Women of Motion Picture Industry (hon. life), Nat. Fedn. Rep. Women (bd. dir., Caring for Am. award 1986), Calif. Rep. Women (bd. dir., treas. 1986-90), North Hollywood Rep. Women (pres. 1981-82, parliamentarian), Nat. Fedn. of Rep (voting mem., program chair, 1994—, bylaws chair 1998—), Calif. Fedn. of Rep. Women (chaplain, Americanism chmn. so. div., regent chmn. Women of Achievement award 1988), L.A. County Fedn. of Rep. Women (scholarship chmn.), Home: 10060 Toluca Lake Ave Toluca Lake CA 91602-2924 Office: 129 E Providencia Ave Burbank CA 91502-1922

JOSELYN, JO ANN, space scientist; b. St. Francis, Kans., Oct. 5, 1943; d. James Jacob and Josephine Felzien (Firkins) Cram. BS in Applied Math., U. Colo., 1965, MS in Astro Geophysics, 1967, Ph.D. in Astro Geophysics, 1978. Research asst. NASA-Manned Space Ctr., Houston, 1966; physicist NOAA-Space Environ. Lab., Boulder, Colo., 1967-78; space scientist NOAA-Space Environ. Ctr., Boulder, 1978—; chief Geospace Branch, 1992-95; U.S. del. study group 6 Consultive Com. for Ionospheric Radio, 1981, 83; mem. com. on data mgmt. and computation NASA Space Sci. Bd., 1988. Mem. U. Colo. Grad. Sch. Alumni Coun., 1986-90, U. Colo. Engring. Devel. Coun., 1991-99, U. Colo. Adv. Coun. for the Women in Engring. Program, 1992-98. Recipient unit citation NOAA, 1971, 80, 85, 86, sustained superior performance award 1985, 87-90, 92, 94; group achievement award NASA, 1983, Disting. Engring. Alumnus award U. Colo., 1987, Dir.'s award Space Environ. Lab., 1991, 95, Pacesetter award Boulder County, 1994, Sec. Commerce award for Customer Svc. Excellence, 1994; elected to U. Colo. Disting. Alumni Gallery, 1995; named Woman of Achievement, Zonta Club, Boulder, 1996; fellow Sci. and Tech. Agy. Japan, 1990-91. Mem. AAAS, AAUW, PEO, AIAA (space sci., astronomy tech. com. 1992-96), Am. Women in Sci., Am. Geophys. Union, Union Radio Sci. Internat., Internat. Union Geodesy and Geophysics (commns. G and H, membership chair of commn. H 1993-96), Internat. Assn. Geomagnetism and Aeronomy (co-chair Divsn. V on observatories, instruments, indices and data 1991-95, sec.-gen. 1995—), Internat. Astron. Union (commns. 10 and 49), Rotary Internat., Sigma Xi, Tau Beta Pi, Sigma Tau. Republican. Methodist. Office: NOAA-Space Environ Ctr R/E/SE2 325 Broadway St Boulder CO 80303-3337

JOSEPH, ALLAN JAY, lawyer; b. Chgo., Feb. 4, 1938; s. George S. and Emily (Miller) Cohen; m. Phyllis L. Freedman, Sept. 1, 1958; children—Elizabeth, Susan, Katherine. B.B.A., U. Wis., Madison, 1959; J.D. cum laude, 1962. Bar: Wis. bar 1962, Calif. bar 1964. Ptnr. Pettit & Martin, San Francisco, 1965-80, Rogers, Joseph, O'Donnell & Quinn, San Francisco, 1981—. Served to capt. JACG AUS, 1962-65. Am. Bar Found. fellow, 1978—. Mem.ABA (nat. chmn. pub. contract law sect. 1977-78, ho. of dels. 1980-84, bd. govs. 1995-98, chair fin. com. 1997-98), FBA, Am. Bar Retirement Assn. (trustee 1984-92, pres. 1989-90), State Bar Calif., Nat. Contract Mgmt. Assn., Order of Coif. Home: 2461 Washington St San Francisco CA 94115-1816 Office: 311 California St Fl 10 San Francisco CA 94104-2614

JOSEPH, BURTON M., retired grain merchant; b. Mpls., Apr. 2, 1921; s. I.S. and Anna J.; m. Geri Mack, Apr. 2, 1953; children: Shelley, Scott, Jonathan. B.A., U. Minn., 1942. Vice pres. I.S. Joseph Co., Inc., Mpls., 1945-53; pres. I.S. Joseph Co., Inc., 1953-80, chmn. bd., 1980-85, vice chmn. bd., 1985-97, ret., 1997; vice chmn. Martrade Ltd., 1985; mem. agrl. policy adv. com. for trade U.S. Dept. Agr., 1980—; pres. Joseph Co. Inc. Mpls. (JCI), 1990. Commr. Duluth Port Authority, Mpls. Human Relations Commn.; treas. Nat. Commn. Anti-Defamation League, 1969-76; nat. chmn. Anti-Defamation League of B'nai B'rith, 1976-78, hon. nat. chmn., 1978; trustee Am. Freedom from Hunger Found.; trustee, bd. govs. Hebrew Union Coll.- Jewish Inst. Religion, 1970-75, vice chmn., 1976; commr. Met. Airports Commn., 1985. Home: 1201 Yale Pl Apt 502 Minneapolis MN 55403-1956

JOSEPH, CURTIS SHAYNE, professional hockey player; b. Keswick, Ont., Can., Apr. 29, 1967. Student, U. Wis. Signed as free agt. St. Louis Blues, 1989, goalie, 1989-92; goalie Edmonton Oilers, 1992-98, Toronto (Ont., Can.) Maple Leafs, 1998—; named to NCAA All-Am. West 2d team, 1988-89, WCHA All-Star 1st team, 1988-89; played in NHL All-Star Game, 1994. Named OHA Most Valuable Player, 1986-87, WCHA Most Valuable Player, 1988-89, WCHA Rookie of Yr., 1988-89. Office: care Toronto Maple Leafs, 40 Bay St Ste 300, Toronto, ON Canada M5J 2X2*

JOSEPH, DANIEL DONALD, aeronautical engineer, educator; b. Chgo., Mar. 26, 1929; s. Samuel and Mary (Simon) J.; m. Ellen Broida, Dec. 18, 1949 (div. 1979); children: Karen, Michael, Charles; m. Kay Jaglo, Feb. 9, 1990. M.A. in Sociology, U. Chgo., 1950; B.S. in Mech. Engring, Ill. Inst. Tech., 1959, M.S., 1960, Ph.D., 1963. Asst. prof. mech. engring. Ill. Inst. Tech., 1962-63; mem. faculty U. Minn., 1963—, assoc. prof. fluid mechanics, 1965-69, prof. aerospace engring. and mechanics, 1969-90; Russell J. Penrose prof. U. Minn., Mpls., 1990—. Author 4 books on stability and bifurcation theory and fluid dynamics; editor 3 books; editorial bd. SIAM Jour. Applied Math, Jour. Applied Mechanics, Jour. Non-Newtonian Fluid Mechanics, others; contbr. articles to sci. jours. Guggenheim fellow, 1969-70, Timoshenko medal Am. Soc. of Mechanical Engineers, 1995. Mem. NAS, ASME, NAE, Am. Phys. Soc., Am. Acad. Arts and Scis., Soc. Engring. Sci. (G.I. Taylor medal 1990, Bingham medal Soc. of Rheology). Contbns. to math. theory of hydrodynamic stability; rheology of viscoelastic fluids. Home: 1920 S 1st St Apt 2302 Minneapolis MN 55454-1279 Office: U Minn Dept Aerospace Engring 110 Union St SE Minneapolis MN 55455-0153

JOSEPH, DANIEL MORDECAI, lawyer; b. Paterson, N.J., Aug. 20, 1941; m. Susan Fields, July 30, 1972; 1 child, Nicholas. AB, Columbia U., 1963; LLB, Harvard U., 1966. Bar: N.J. 1967, U.S. Supreme Ct. 1970, D.C. 1974. Law clk. to judge U.S. Ct. Appeals (5th cir.), Dallas, 1966-67; atty. civil div. U.S. Dept. Justice, Washington, 1967-71; asst. gen. counsel EPA, Washington, 1971-72; spl. asst. environ. affairs gen. counsel U.S. Dept. Transp., Washington, 1972-74; ptnr. Akin, Gump, Strauss, Hauer & Feld, Washington, 1974—. Mem. D.C. Bar (rules of conduct rev. com. 1991-96, chmn. 1996—). Office: Akin Gump Strauss Hauer & Feld Ste 400 1333 New Hampshire Ave NW Washington DC 20036-1564

JOSEPH, DAVID B., pediatric urologist; b. Milw., May 1953; s. Arthur and Corraine J.; m. Stephanie R. Fedor, June 6, 1982; 1 child, Hannah Rae. BA, Johns Hopkins U., 1976; MD, U. Wis., 1980. Instr. surgery Children's Hosp., Harvard Med. Sch., Boston, 1985-86; asst. prof. surgery U. Ala., Birmingham, 1986-91, assoc. prof. surgery, 1991-96, assoc. prof. pediatrics, 1992, prof. surgery, 1996—; chief pediatric urology Children's Hosp., Birmingham, 1985—, pres. med. staff, 1998—; urology advisor Spina Bifida Assn. Am., 1998—. Fellow Am. Acad. Pediatrics, Am. Coll. Surgeons, Soc. Pediatric Urology; mem. AMA, Am. Urologic Soc., Am. Assn. Pediatric Urology, Phi Beta Kappa. Avocations: computers, model ship building. Office: Childrens Hosp 1600 7th Ave S Birmingham AL 35233

JOSEPH, DONALD LOUIS, management consultant; b. Chgo., Dec. 29, 1942; s. Herbert H. and Florence (Gaertner) J.; m. Joyce H. Brand, Dec. 20, 1981; children: Richard A., Michael B. BS in Engring. Sci., Washington U., St. Louis, 1964; MBA, harvard U., 1966. Cert. mgmt. cons. Sys. engr. Teletype Corp., Skokie, Ill., 1966-68; sr. assoc. Brandon Applied Sys., Inc., Chgo., 1968-71; sr. cons. Daniel D. Howard Assoc., Inc., Chgo., 1971-72; dir. mgmt. sys. Opelika Mfg. Corp., Chgo., 1972-77; dep. exec. dir. Am. Soc. Clin. Pathologists, Chgo., 1978-80, v.p. fin. and adminstrn., 1980-81; pres. DLJ Assocs., Chgo., 1981—; sr. project cons. Stone Mgmt. Corp., 1982-84; bd. dirs. Inst. Mgmt. Cons., Chgo. chpt., mgmt. adv. svcs. Shepard Schwartz & Harris, C.P.A.s, chgo., 1985-87; dir. Office Automation Sys., Hise, Donahue & Assocs., Inc., 1983-84, controller Meystel, Inc., 1987-92, v.p., 1993-94; v.p., asst. sec. Russell-Field Paper Co., Inc., 1994-97; pres. Northbrook cons. Group, Inc., 1998—; mem. faculty Elmhurst Mgmt. Program Elmhurst Coll., 1982-89. Bd. dirs. Horizon House, Chgo., pres., 1981-82, 89-90; nominating com. Glencoe Sch. Bd., 1994—, vice chmn., 1996—. Mem. Harvard U. Bus. Sch. Assn. Chgo., Am. Soc. Assn. Execs., Inst. Mgmt. Cons. (dir., v.p. membership Midwest chpt.), Tau Beta Pi, Omicron Delta Kappa. Home: 1125 Hohlfelder Rd Glencoe IL 60022-1018

JOSEPH, EDITH HOFFMAN, retired editor; b. Syracuse, N.Y., Jan. 4, 1928; d. Max and Ida (Hodis) Finkelstein; m. Irving Hoffman, Sept. 4, 1949 (dec. Dec. 1965); children: Kenneth R., Maxine E. Neuhauser; m. William Jacob Joseph, May 19, 1968; stepchildren: David E., Harlan L., Saul J., Gail C. BS in Journalism/Bus. Adminstrn., Rider Coll., 1949. Copywriter advt. Swern's-Lit Bros., Trenton, N.J., 1949-51; pub. info. asst. N.J. Div. Pensions, Trenton, 1967-69; pub. rels. asst. N.J. Dept. Labor & Industry, Trenton, 1969-70; mng. editor newsletter N.J. Dept. Environ. Protection, Trenton, 1971-74; environ. news editor N.J. Dept. Environ. Protection-N.J. Outdoors Mag., 1974-84; editor newsletter N.J. Dept. Environ. Protection-Environ. News, 1985-90; editor environ. news sect. N.J. Dept. Environ. Protection-N.J. Outdoors Mag., 1991. Contbr. articles to profl. jours. Avocations: travel, reading, walking, theatre, volunteer work. Home: 8 Llanfair Ln Trenton NJ 08618-1012

JOSEPH, ELLEN R., lawyer. BA, Barnard Coll., 1960; JD, Columbia U., 1976. Bar: N.Y. 1977. Ptnr. Kaye, Scholer, Fierman, Hays & Handler LLP, N.Y.C. Mem. ABA (mem. real property law sect.), N.Y. State Bar Assn. (mem. real property law sect.), Assn. Bar City N.Y., Phi Beta Kappa. Stone Scholar. Office: Kaye Scholer Fierman Hays & Handler LLP 425 Park Ave New York NY 10022-3506

JOSEPH, FREDERICK HAROLD, investment banker; b. Boston, Apr. 22, 1937; s. Edward M. and Sarah (Mostowitz) J.; m. Susan Ferran, Aug. 27, 1960; children: Melissa, Melinda, Amy, Tommi Beth, Mark. BA, Harvard, 1959, MBA, 1963. With E.F. Hutton Co., N.Y.C., 1963-70, Shearson Hamill Co., N.Y.C., 1970-74; with Drexel Burnham Lambert Inc., N.Y.C., 1974-90; vice chmn., CEO Drexel Burnham Lambert Inc., 1985-90; pres. Drexel Burnham Lambert Group, 1987-90; adv. DBL Liquidating Trust, N.Y.C., 1991-93; chmn. Clovebrook Capital Corp., N.Y.C., 1994-98; sr. advt. and mng. dir. ING Baring Furman Selz LLC, N.Y.C., 1998—. With USNR, 1959-61. Office: ING Baring Furman Selz LLC 55 E 52d St New York NY 10055-0003

JOSEPH, GERI MACK (GERALDINE JOSEPH), former ambassador, educator; b. St. Paul, June 19, 1923. BS, U. Minn., 1946; LLD, Bates Coll., 1982; DHL (hon.), Macalester Coll., 1997; LLD, Carleton Coll., 1998; DHL (hon.). Staff writer Mpls. Tribune, 1946-53, contbg. editor, 1972-78; amb. to The Netherlands The Hague, 1978-81; sr. fellow internat. programs Hubert H. Humphrey Inst. Pub. Affairs, U. Minn., 1984-94; chair adv. bd. Hubert Humphrey Inst. Pub. Affairs, U. Minn., 1997—; dir. Mondale Policy Forum, 1990-94; bd. dirs. Nat. Dem. Inst. for Internat. Affairs, George A. Hormel Co.; mem. U.S. President's Commn. on Mental Health, Minn. Supreme Ct. Commn. on Mentally Disabled and the Cts.; mem. com. on Mid. East, Brookings Instn., 1987; mem., bd. dirs. German Marshall Fund, 1987-96. Vice chmn. Gov.'s Commn. on Taxation, 1983-84; trustee Carleton Coll., 1975-94; mem. Democratic Nat. Com., 1960-72, vice chmn., 1968-72; co-chairperson Minn. Women's Campaign Fund, 1982-84; co-chmn. Atty. Gen.'s Com. on Child Abuse within the Family, 1986. Office: U Minn Humphrey Ctr 301 19th Ave S Minneapolis MN 55455-0429

JOSEPH, GREGORY NELSON, media critic, writer; b. Kansas City, Mo., Aug. 25, 1946; s. Theodore Leopold and Marcella Kathryn (Nelson) J.; m. Mary Martha Stahler, July 21, 1973; children: John, Jacqueline, Caroline. AA, Met. C.C., Kansas City, 1967; BA with honors, U. Mo., Kansas City, 1969. Intern, cub reporter Kansas City Star-Times, 1965-67; feature writer, asst. city editor The Pasadena (Calif.) Union, 1971-73; investigative reporter The Pasadena Star-News, 1973-75; bus. writer The Riverside (Calif.) Press Enterprise, 1975-76; reporter, consumer writer, feature writer, TV critic The San Diego Tribune, 1976-90; TV columnist The Ariz. Republic, Phoenix, 1990-94; media critic, writer, 1994—. Recipient various writing awards Copley Newspapers, Pasadena and San Diego, 1971-73, 83, Pub. Awareness award San Diego Psychiat. Physicians, cert. of appreciation Epilepsy Soc. San Diego County, 1989. Mem. SAG, NATAS (bd. govs. 1990-92), TV Critics Assn., Internat. Platform Assn. Roman Catholic. Avocations: scriptwriting, reading, writing about Hollywood, appearing at schools and on radio and TV to discuss TV and film. Home: 4864 W Alice Ave Glendale AZ 85302-5107 Address: Victoria Allen Literary Agy 1489 E Thousand Oaks Blvd Ste 2 Thousand Oaks CA 91362-6207

JOSEPH, GREGORY PAUL, lawyer; b. Mpls., Jan. 18, 1951; s. George Phillip and Josephine Sheha (Nofel) J.; m. Barbara, Jan. 19, 1979. BA summa cum laude, U. Minn., 1972, JD cum laude, 1975. Bar: Minn. 1975, N.Y. 1979, U.S. Dist. Ct. Minn. 1975, U.S. Dist. Ct. (so. and ea. dist.) N.Y. 1979, U.S. Ct. Appeals (8th cir.) 1976, U.S. Ct. Appeals (2d cir.) 1979, U.S. Ct. Appeals (D.C. cir.) 1980, U.S. Supreme Ct. 1983, U.S. Tax Ct. 1987, U.S. Ct. Appeals (7th cir.) 1989, (5th cir.) 1992, (6th cir.) 1999. Pvt. practice Mpls., 1975-79; assoc. Fried, Frank, Harris, Shriver & Jacobson, N.Y.C., 1979-82, ptnr., 1982—; asst. U.S. spl. prosecutor N.Y.C., Washington, 1981-82; mem. U.S. Judicial Conf. adv. com. on fed. rules of evidence, 1993-99; chair Com. of Lawyers to Enhance the Jury Process, N.Y. State Cts., 1998-99, mem. Adv. Com. on Civil Practice, 1999—. Author: Modern Visual Evidence, 1984, Sanctions: The Federal Law of Litigation Abuse, 1989 2d edit., 1994, Civil RICO: A Definitive Guide, 1992; co-author: Evidence in America, 1987; editor: Emerging Problems Under the Federal Rules of Evidence, 1983, reporter 2d edit., 1991; co-editor: Sanctions: Rule 11 and Other Powers, 1986, 2d rev. edit., 1988; editorial bd. Moore's Fed. Practice, 1995—; contbr. articles to profl. jours. Fellow Am. Bar Found., Am. Coll. Trial Lawyers (chair downstate N.Y. com. 1996-98); mem. ABA (chmn. litig. sect. 1997-98), Am. Law Inst., N.Y. Bar Assn. (chair trial evidence com. 1988-94), Minn. Bar Assn., N.Y. County Lawyers Assn., Assn. of Bar of City of N.Y. (chmn. profl. responsibility com. 1993-96, mem. exec. com. 1999—). Home: 188 E 70th St Apt 25A New York NY 10021-5170 Office: Fried Frank Harris Shriver & Jacobson 1 New York Plz Fl 22 New York NY 10004-1980

JOSEPH, J. JONATHAN, interior designer; b. Gloucester, Mass., Jan. 14, 1932; s. George Stephen and Maryann (Lattof) J.; cert. Vesper George Sch. Art, Boston, 1952; student theater design Boston Conservatory Music, 1951. Assoc. designer Reva Lewitt, Boston, 1952-67, Peter Schifando & Co., L.A., 1995—; owner interior design bus., Boston, 1967—; pres. Seraphim Galleries, Inc., L.A., 1998—; cons. in fine arts; spl. research 19th century glass in Am., also Tiffany glass; exhibited Tiffany glass collection Mus. Fine Art, Boston, 1965, Worcester (Mass.) Art Mus., 1968. Important decorating works include: assoc. designer on the restoration of Plaza Hotel, N.Y.C., assoc. designer Ronald Reagan Presdl. Libr., Simi Valley, Calif., 1991. Recipient award Internat. V'Soske Rug Design. Mem. Am. Soc. Interior Designers (chmn. bd. New Eng. chpt. 1965-66, chpt. v.p. 1969-71, pres. 1971-72, bd. dirs. 1986-87), Nat. Early Am. Glass Club (1st v.p. 1967-69), Mus. Fine Arts Boston. Author: Jane Peterson, An American Artist, 1981; co-curator: (exhbn.) Jane Peterson: An Impression, Hickory (N.C.) Mus. of Art, 1987; contbr. revs. and articles to profl. publs. Address: PO Box 1220 Back Bay Annex Boston MA 02117

JOSEPH, JAMES ALFRED, ambassador; b. Opelousas, La., Mar. 12, 1935; s. Adam and Julia Lee (Jones) J.; m. Mary Braxton; children: Jeffrey, Denise. BA, So. U., 1956; MDiv, Yale U., 1963; hon. degree, Loyola U. of Chgo., U. Md., Winthrop Coll., Southeastern U., Fla. Meml. U., Shaw U., Ind. U. Ordained to ministry United Ch. Christ, 1963. Asso. dir. Assn. of Founds., Columbus, Ind., 1967-69; chaplain Claremont (Calif.) Colls., 1969-70; exec. dir. Irwin-Sweeney-Miller Found., Columbus, 1970-72; v.p. Cummins Engine Co., 1972-77, 81-82; also pres. Cummins Found., Columbus, 1972-77, 81-82; ambassador to So. Africa state dept., 1996—; under sec. U.S. Dept. Interior, Washington, 1977-81; chmn. Commn. on No. Mariana Islands, 1980-86; pres., CEO, Coun. on Founds., 1982-95; mem. faculty Stillman Coll., Tuscaloosa, Ala., 1963-64, Pitzer Coll., Claremont, 1966, Claremont Sch. Theology, 1970, Yale U., 1981-82; mem. adv. com. nat. Sci. Acad., Agy. Internat. Devel. Author: The Charitable Impulse, 1990, Remaking America, 1995; co-editor: Three Perspectives on Ethnicity, 1976; contbr. articles to profl. publs. Chmn. Spl. Commn. on Racism and Devel., World Council Chs., Geneva, chmn., U.S. del. to UN Conf. in Kenya, Bilateral Consultation with Mex. Pres. Claremont Intercultural Council, 1965-67; mem. City Park and Recreation Commn., Claremont, 1965-67, apptd. by Pres. Clinton chmn. bd. dirs. Corp. for Nat. Svc., chmn. official U.S. govt. dels. to Mex., Micronesia, Canada; pres. Nat. Black United Fund; bd. dirs. Pitzer Coll., Brookings Inst., Nat. Endowment for Democracy, Points of Light Found., Colonial Williamsburg Found., Africare, Opportunity Funding Corp., Union Theol. Sem., N.Y.C., African-Am. Inst. N.Y., Children's Def. Fund, New Transcentury Found.; bd. visitors Inst. Policy Scis., Duke U. Served to 1st lt., Med. Service Corps U.S. Army, 1956-58.

Fellow Met. Applied Research Center, N.Y.C., 1958; vis. fellow Nuffield Coll., Oxford U. Mem. Assn. Black Found. Execs. (chmn. 1970-76), Council Fgn. Relations, Hague Club, Alpha Phi Alpha. Office: Am Embassy/ Pretoria Dept State Washington DC 20521-9300

JOSEPH, JAMES EDWARD, mechanical engineering technician; b. Napa, Calif., Sept. 24, 1946; s. Wilbur Raymond and Lois Grace (Pouget) J.; m. Deborah Dianne Horvath, June 5, 1971; children: Brian Christopher, Stacy Lynn Joseph Pitts. Diploma, N. Am. Sch. Drafting, 1974, hon. grad. cert., 1977; AA, Napa Valley Coll., 1976; BS, So. Ill. U., 1986. Basic instr. tng. cert., 1993. Naval archtl. aide Mare Island Naval Shipyard, Vallejo, 1967-70; naval archtl. technician Mare Island Naval Shipyard, Vallejo, Calif., 1974-77, 77-89; naval architect tech. supr. Mare Island Naval Shipyard, Vallejo, 1989-91, project leader, 1991-92, material control mgr., 1992-94, engrng. technician, 1994—; refinery operator Union Oil Co. Calif., 1971-74; designer, draftsman Morris Guralnick Assocs., Inc., 1974, propulsion technician, 1977; designer, draftsman, owner, operator Joseph's Drafting & Design Svc., 1984-88; mech. engrng. technician Puget Sound Naval Shipyard, Bremerton, Wash., 1994—; designer, draftsman Napa Babe Ruth Baseball League, 1986. Author: (material control program) Navy-shipydmareinst, 1993, Desk Notes for Ocean Engineering Subsafe Re-Entry Control Group, 1994, Work Control of Critical System Pipe Hangers (Navyshipydmareinst), 1987, Steering & Diving Hydraulic Cylinder Foundation, Inspection, Removal, Repair and Reinstallation (Industrial Process Instruction) 1987. Chair citizen adv. panel Dept. Motor Vehicles, Napa; bd. dirs. Youth Adv. Bd. Oleum Fed. Credit Union, Rodeo, Calif., 1971-74; coach Young Am. Bowling Assn., Napa, 1980-83, 93-94, T-Ball and Babe Ruth Baseball, 1979-80, 85-86; auditor West Park Elem. Sch. PTA, parent vol., outdoor edn. vol. trips; key person for C/124-Puget Sound Naval Shipyard, Combined Fed. Campaign, 1994. With USNR, 1966-72. Mem. AARP, Internat. Platform Assn., Am. Bowling Congress, Olympic Philatelic Soc., Am. Philatelic Soc., Am. Diabetes Assn. Republican. Avocations: golf, bowling, stamp collecting, walking. Home: 12699 Plateau Cir NW Silverdale WA 98383-8006 Office: Puget Sound Naval Shipyard Engring Code 126 Bremerton WA 98314-5000

JOSEPH, JANNAN MARIE, school social worker; b. Evanston, Ill., Jan. 8, 1937; d. Stanley and Kathleen (Murphy) Petkus; m. Peter Ottesen, July 1961 (div. 1985); children: Peter Ottesen, Jr., O. Christian Ottesen, John Richard Ottesen; m. Robert H. Joseph, Nov. 17, 1990. BS, Northwestern U., 1958; MA, Montclair State U., 1986; diploma in Gymnas Fluency, U. Oslo, Norway, 1970. Cert. sch. social worker, pupil personnel svcs., elem. tchr., nursery sch. tchr., N.J., elem. tchr., Ill., nursery sch. tchr., Norway. Tchr. numerous schs., Ill., 1958-65, U.S. Govt. Dept. of Def., 1970-73, Paterson, N.J., 1985-86; founder, dir. Internat. Kindergarten, Oslo, 1973-76; sch. social worker Roxbury (N.J.) Twp. Bd. Edn., 1986—; grant panel reviewer Nat. Ctr. Child Abuse and Neglect, 1997—, U.S. Govt. HHS, ACF, ACYF; council mem. developmental disabilities adv. Rutgers Univ. Deacon Calvary Presbyn. Ch., Florham Park, N.J. Mem. Sch. Social Work Assn. Am. (founding mem.), Coun. for Exceptional Children, N.J. Edn. Assn., N.J. Assn. Sch. Social Workers (cor. sec. 1995—), Morris County Sch. Social Workers Assn. (pres. 1994—), N.E. Coalition of Sch. Social Workers N.J. (founding mem.), Phi Kappa Phi. Home: 83 Tiffany Dr East Hanover NJ 07936-2518

JOSEPH, JOFI JOHN, policy analyst; b. Cologne, Germany, Apr. 1, 1973; s. John Putharampil and Philomena (Kochupural) J. BS in Fgn. Svc., Georgetown U., 1994. Analyst Congl. Budget Office, Washington, 1996—. Mem. benefit com. Sarah's Cir., Washington, 1996—. Harry S. Truman scholar, 1993, Rotary Internat. scholar, 1994-95. Mem. Phi Beta Kappa, Alpha Sigma Nu. Avocations: bicycling, tennis, hiking.

JOSEPH, JULES K., retired public relations executive; b. Cin., Jan. 18, 1927; s. Leslie Bloch and Ellen (Kaufman) J.; m. Elizabeth Levy, Sept. 9, 1948; children—Ellen Beth, Barbara Ann, John Charles. B.A. in Journalism, U. Wis., 1948. Mem. press relations staff Gimbels, Milw., 1948-52; bur. chief Fairchild Publs., Milw., 1952-60; co-founder, chmn. emeritus Zigman-Joseph-Stephenson Assocs. in Pub. Rels., Milw., 1960-94; ret., 1994. Pres. Friends of Art of Milw. Art Ctr., 1961-62; v.p. Milwaukee County Mental Health, 1967; bd. dirs. Milw. Repertory Theatre, Camp Webb, Milw. Pks. Bd., St. John's Home for the Aged, Milw., DePaul Hosp., Charles Allis Art Libr., Wis. Olympics Com.; mem. Frank Lloyd Wright Heritage Tourism Program. Recipient Chancellor's award for outstanding contbn. to mass communication U. Wis., 1988. Mem. Pub. Rels. Soc. Am. (accredited, treas. Wis. 1970-71, bd. dirs. counselors sect. 1991-92), Soc. for Profl. Journalists, Phi Kappa Phi. Episcopalian. Home: 5028 N Lake Dr Milwaukee WI 53217-5748 Office: 111 E Wisconsin Ave Milwaukee WI 53202-4107 *During my first job (summer '47) as a reporter on the Cincinnati Enquirer I was told to leave if I did not get the story. I have translated this to mean there's no excuse for not getting the job done—or reaching your goal.*

JOSEPH, KEVIN MARK, financial services executive; b. Niagara Falls, N.Y., Mar. 4, 1954; s. John Francis and Lorraine Elizabeth (Stearns) J.; m. Debbie Anna Liisa Baren, Aug. 15, 1975; children: Julie Anna Liisa, Liisa Christine, Kristen Nicole. AAS, Niagara County C.C., 1975; BS, Niagara U., 1977. Dir. Whirlpool Fin. Corp., New Castle, Del., 1979-90; v.p., dir. Chrysler First, Inc. (now Nations Credit Corp.), Allentown, Pa., 1990-96; o.v.p. Assocs. Credit Svcs., Inc., Salt Lake City, 1996—. Fellow Consumer Credit Assn.; mem. Nat. Youth Sports Coaches Assn. Roman Catholic. Avocations: exercise, fishing, golf. Office: Assocs Credit Svcs Inc 111 E 300 S Ste 500 Salt Lake City UT 84111-5232

JOSEPH, L. ANTHONY, JR., lawyer; b. Dallas, June 13, 1940; s. Lawrence A. Joseph and Dina (McFarland) Brown; children: Marguerite S., Louisa M., Courtney V., A. Michael, E. Reeves. BA, U. Tex., 1963, LLB, 1968. Bar: Conn. 1971, Calif. 1977, Va. 1980, D.C. 1980. Assoc. Donovan Leisure Newton & Irvine, L.A., 1968-75, cons., 1975-80; ptnr., head tax dept. Hunton & Williams, Richmond, Va., 1980-84; mng. ptnr. Baity & Joseph, Richmond, 1984-86; ptnr., head internat. tax Milbank, Tweed, Hadley & McCloy, N.Y.C., 1986-93; ptnr., head tax dept. Salans Hertzfeld Heilbronn Christy & Viener, N.Y.C., 1993—; chmn. bd. dirs. Program of Acad. Exch., 1995—; lectr. taxation U. Va., Charlottesville, 1980-81; co-dir. Va. Conf. on Fed. Taxation, Charlottesville, 1983-87. Bd. dirs. Richmond Ballet, 1983-86. Lt. USNR, 1963-66. Mem. ABA (taxation sect., mem. regulated pub. utilities com.), N.Y. State Bar Assn., N.Y.C. Bar Assn., Va. Bar Assn., Tax Club N.Y.C. Episcopalian. Office: SHH Christy & Viener 620 Fifth Ave New York NY 10020-2402

JOSEPH, LEONARD, lawyer; b. Phila., June 8, 1919; s. Harry L. and Mary (Pollock) J.; m. Norma Hamberg, 1942; children: Gilbert M., Stuart A., Janet H. Fitzgerald. BA, U. Pa., 1941; LLB, Harvard U., 1947. Bar: N.Y. 1949. Law clk. to chief judge U.S. Ct. Appeals, Boston, 1947-48; since practiced in N.Y.C.; ptnr. Dewey Ballantine, 1957—; bd. dirs., exec. com. Legal Aid Soc. N.Y., 1986-89; mem. panel of disting. neutrals CPR Inst. for Dispute Resolution. Bd. editors Harvard Law Rev., 1946-47. Served with AUS, 1943-46. Fellow Am. Bar Found., Am. Coll. Trial Lawyers; mem. Harvard Club N.Y. Office: Dewey Ballantine 1301 Avenue Of The Americas New York NY 10019-6022

JOSEPH, MICHAEL SARKIES, accountant; b. Peoria, Ill., Dec. 10, 1950; s. Sarkas M. and Theresa I. (Kelch) J.; m. Christine L., June 28, 1975; children: Brian, Christopher, Patrick. BS, No. Ill. U., 1972. CPA. Ptnr. Ernst & Young, Cleve. and Chgo., 1972-89; ptnr. Ernst & Young, N.Y.C., 1989—; profl. acct. fellow Fed. Home Loan Bank Bd., Washington, 1981-83. Roman Catholic. Avocations: golf, swimming, youth athletic programs. Home: 38 Kellogg Hill Rd Weston CT 06883-2620 Office: Ernst & Young LLP 1285 Avenue Of The Americas New York NY 10019-6028

JOSEPH, RAMON RAFAEL, physician, educator; b. N.Y.C., May 17, 1930; s. Felix R. and Helen (Espinet) J.; m. Mary Ann Kowalchik, June 16, 1956; children: Ricardo George, Maria Ann Thompson, Lisa Marie Benson. BS, Manhattan Coll., 1952; MD, Cornell U., 1956. Diplomate Nat. Bd. Med. Examiners, Am. Bd. Internal Medicine. Intern Meadowbrook Hosp., Hempstead, N.Y., 1956-57; resident Meadowbrook Hosp., 1957, Wayne County Gen. Hosp., Westland, Mich., 1959-62; dir. gastroenterology Wayne County Gen. Hosp., 1962-84, asst. dir. internal medicine, 1964-73, dir., chmn., 1973-84, pres. med. staff, 1971-72; cons. internal medicine and gastroenterology Annapolis Hosp., 1962-87; from instr. internal medicine to prof. U. Mich., 1962-85, prof. emeritus, 1998—; asst. dean U. Mich. Med. Sch., 1973-84; 1st v.p., dir. Univ. Med. Affiliates PC, 1981-84; pres. Univ. Med. Affiliates (P.C.), 1985-87; med. dir. Henry Ford Hosp. Westland (Mich.) Ctr., 1987-94; sr. attending physician Henry Ford Hosp., Detroit, 1987——; cons. gastroenterology St. Mary Hosp., Livonia, Mich., 1966—, chmn. divsn. of gastroenterology, 1987-93. Contbr. articles to profl. jours. Mem. Community Commn. on Drug Abuse, Livonia and Westland, Mich., 1970-73; mem. Mich. Dept. Edn. Council on Drug Abuse, cons. on drug abuse public schs., Livonia, 1968-74; pres. Livonia Sch. Bd. Adv. Council, 1970-71. Capt. U.S. Army, 1957-59. Fellow ACP; mem. Am. Fedn. Clin. Research, Am. Gastroent., Assn., AAAS, Assn. Am. Med. Colls., AMA, N.Y. Acad. Sci., Detroit Gastroent. Soc. (pres. 1969-70), Mich., Wayne County Med. Socs., Am. Assn. Lab. Animal Sci., Am. Soc. Gastrointestinal Endoscopy, Am. Soc. Internal Medicine, Mich. Soc. Gastrointestinal Endoscopy (pres. 1982-86), Mich. Soc. Internal Medicine, Assn. Program Dirs. in Internal Medicine. Roman Catholic. Home: 5593 Stratford St West Bloomfield MI 48322-1540 also: 13755 W Via Montoya Sun City W AZ 85375-2054

JOSEPH, RICHARD SAUL, cardiologist; b. N.Y.C., Mar. 27, 1937; s. Charles Irving and Lillian (Horowitz) J.; m. Frances B. Rappaport, Jan. 27, 1963; children: Lauryl, James, Alisa, Jennifer. BA magna cum laude, Hofstra Coll., 1958; MD, Albert Einstein U., 1962. Intern U. Utah Affiliated Hosp., Salt Lake City, 1962-63; resident in chest medicine Bronx Mcpl. Hosp., Bronx, N.Y., 1963-64; resident internal medicine Mt. Sinai Hosp., N.Y.C., 1966-68; fellow in cardiology Nassau County Med. Ctr., East Meadow, N.Y., 1968-69; pvt. practice cardiology Huntington (N.Y.) Hosp., 1969—, chief cardiology, 1981-90, attending cardiology, 1973—; asst. prof. clin. medicine (Ccrdiology) SUNY, Stony Brook, 1973—; cons. in cardiology Kings Park (H.Y.) Hosp., 1971—; electro cardiographer Huntington Hosp., 1971—, co-dir. cardiac stress lab., 1975—; dir. Huntington Cardiac Rehab., 1977-94; adj. attending cardiologist St. Francis Hosp., Roslyn, N.Y., 1993-98. Contbr. articles to profl. jours. Speaker med. adv. bd. Suffolk County Heart Assn., Blue Point, N.Y., 1971-73; speaker med. dir. Huntington (N.Y.) YMCA, 1973-77. Lt. USN, 1964-66. Recipient Pres. prize Hofstra Coll., Uniondale, N.Y., 1954; named Valedictorian Hofstra Coll., Uniondale, N.Y., 1958. Fellow Am. Coll. Cardiology; mem. Alpha Omega Alpha. Hebrew. Avocations: jogging, classical and popular piano. Office: 205 E Main St Huntington NY 11743-2923

JOSEPH, ROBERT DAVID, astronomer, educator; b. New Castle, Pa., June 2, 1939; s. David E. and Helen (Cherry) J.; m. Ruth Elizabeth Fairbanks, June 24, 1961 (div. 1997); 1 child, James Robert Fairbanks; m. Judy Gregory, Dec. 5, 1997. BA, Greenville (Ill.) Coll., 1961; MA, Vanderbilt U., 1964; PhD, Washington U., 1971. Lectr. physics Imperial Coll., U. London, 1973-87, reader astrophysics, 1987-90; astronomer Inst. Astronomy, U. Hawaii, Honolulu, 1989—; divsn. chief NASA Infrared Telescope Facility, 1989—. Bd. editors: Contemporary Physics, 1997—; contbr. over 100 articles to books and profl. jours. Fellow Royal Astron. Soc. (councillor 1988-90); mem. Am. Astron. Soc., Internat. Astron. Union. Anglican. Office: Inst Astronomy 2680 Woodlawn Dr Honolulu HI 96822-1839

JOSEPH, ROBERT THOMAS, lawyer; b. Detroit, June 12, 1946; s. Joseph Alexander and Clara Barbara (Francis) J.; m. Sarah Granger, May 22, 1971; children: Paul, Timothy. AB, Xavier U., 1968; JD, U. Mich., 1971. Bar: Mich. 1971, Ill. 1976, U.S. Dist. Ct. (no. dist.) Ill. 1976, U.S. Ct. Appeals (7th cir.) 1983. Staff atty. FTC Bur. Competition, Washington, 1971-76, asst. to dir., 1972-74; atty. Sonnenschein Nath & Rosenthal, Chgo., 1976—, ptnr., 1978—. Trustee Northbrook (Ill.) Libr. Bd., 1979-89, pres., 1983-85. Recipient Disting. Svc. award FTC, 1976. Mem. ABA (chair franchising com. of antitrust law sect. 1984-87, chair videotapes com. 1987-90, chair publs. com. 1991-94, coun. 1994-97, program officer 1997—, mem. governing bd., forum on franchising). Roman Catholic. Club: Met. (Chgo.). Home: 2836 Shannon Rd Northbrook IL 60062-4333 Office: Sonnenschein Nath Rosenthal 233 S Wacker Dr Ste 8000 Chicago IL 60606-6342

JOSEPH, ROSALINE RESNICK, hematologist and oncologist; b. N.Y.C., Aug. 21, 1929; d. Joseph and Malca (Rosenberg) Resnick; m. Robert J. Joseph, Jan. 2, 1954; children: Joy S., Nina B. AB, Cornell U., 1949; MD, Women's Med. Coll. Pa., Phila., 1953; MS, Temple U., 1958. Intern Kings County Hosp., Bklyn., 1953-54; resident Phila. Gen. Hosp., 1954-55, Temple U. Hosp., 1955-57; instr. dept. medicine Temple U. Med. Ctr., Phila., 1957-60; assoc. in medicine Temple U. Med. Ctr., 1960-63, asst. prof. medicine, 1963-69, assoc. prof. medicine, 1969-77; course co-coordinator Sys. Oncology Interdisciplinary Course, 1968-73; prof. medicine, dir. Med. Coll. Pa., Phila., 1977; course coordinator Med. Coll. Pa., 1978; pres. med. staff Med. Coll. Pa., 1990-91. Contbr. articles to profl. jours. Del. dir. Am. Cancer Soc., 1989—. Recipient Lindback award for disting. teaching, Christian & Mary Lindback Found., 1982, Am. Cancer Soc. Div. Disting. Svc. award, 1987. Fellow ACP; mem. Am. Soc. Hematology, Am. Soc. Clin. Oncology, Alumni Assn. Med. Coll. Pa. (pres. 1988-90). Office: Med Coll Pa Hosp 3300 Henry Ave Philadelphia PA 19129-1121

JOSEPH, SHIRLEY TROYAN, retired executive; b. Buffalo, N.Y., Dec. 13, 1925; d. Louis and Betty (Eisman) Troyan; m. Norman Clifford Joseph, Oct. 20, 1946; children: Todd Michael, Marc Dana, Jonathan L. BA in Polit. Sci., U. Mich., 1947; postgrad., Vanderbilt U., 1973. Instr. SUNY, Buffalo, 1977; area rep. Am. Jewish Com., Buffalo, 1980-82; pub. policy coord. Jewish Fedn., Buffalo, 1984-87; first exec. dir. Erie County Commn. on Status of Women, 1988-92, ex-officio mem., 1997—; accredited non-govtl. rep. UN World Confs. on Women, Copenhagen, Nairobi, Beijing, 1980, 85, 95; mem. Hilary Clinton's Beijing Conf. Circle; mem. steering com. Food for All, Buffalo Area Met. ministries, 1984-88; cmty. adv. bd. Sch. Health Demonstration Project, Buffalo, 1989-92; cmty. advisor Jr. League, Buffalo, 1989-99; founding pres. Women's Taking Action in Politics Fund, Western N.Y. State, 1992—; chair 10 Year Status of Women in Erie County Update. Vice chair U.S. Nat. Commn. for UNESCO, 1973-77, Nat. Jewish Cmty. Rels. Adv. Coun., 1989-93; v.p. Jewish Fedn. Greater Buffalo, 1975-80; del. U.S. Nat. Women's Conf., Houston, 1977; bd. Erie County Mental Health Svcs.-Corp. 2, 1979-80; pres. Jewish Fedn. Housing, Buffalo, 1980-82. Mem. Nat. Coun. Jewish Women (nat. v.p. 1975-83, hon. nat. v.p. 1985—, Buffalo sect. Hannah Solomon Woman of Yr. award 1978), Nat. Women's Conf. Com. (various chairs 1979—). Democrat.

JOSEPH, STEPHEN, nephrology and dialysis nurse; b. Bombay, India, Feb. 1, 1966; came to U.S., 1991; s. Pottoore Chandy and Marykutty Joseph; m. Simi Simon, Jan. 14, 1996. BSN, Coll. Nursing, Trivandrum, India, 1988; MBA in Internat. Bus., Pace U., 1996; grad. in Personal Fin. Planning, CUNY, 1998. RN, India, New Zealand, N.Y. Staff nurse Hinduja Nat. Hosp. and Med. Rsch. Ctr., Bombay, 1989-90; specialist nurse Ministry of Health, Baharain, 1990; nursing instr. Am. Inst., Kottayam, India, 1991; staff nurse/charge nurse Hemodialysis Unit, St. Barnabas Hosp., Bronx, N.Y., 1991—. Mem. Dialysis Patient Assn. (organizer), Servas Internat., Trained Nurses Assn. of India. Roman Catholic. Avocations: training dogs, playing guitar and harmonica, stamp collecting, travel. Home: 2531 Holland Ave 2d Fl Bronx NY 10467-8703 Office: St Barnabas Hosp 183rd St 3rd Ave Bronx NY 10457

JOSEPH, SUSAN B., lawyer; b. N.Y.C., 1958; d. Alfred A. and Bella J. BS in Econ. and Bus. Mgmt., Ramapo Coll. of N.J., 1981; JD cum laude, Seton Hall U., 1985. Bar: N.J. 1985, U.S. Dist. Ct. N.J. 1985, N.Y. 1988, U.S. Dist. Ct. (so. and ea. dist.) N.Y. 1991. Legal asst. Prudential Ins. Co. Am., Newark, 1982-85; assoc. Fox & Fox, Newark, 1985-86, Elkes, Maybruch & Weiss, P.A., Freehold, N.J., 1986-87; asst. counsel N.Am. Reins. Corp., N.Y.C., 1987-90; assoc. Mark D. Lefkowitz, Esq., 1991; mgr. GRE Ins. Group, Princeton, N.J., 1991; atty. GRE Ins. Group, N.Y.C., 1992-95; cons. Fin. Guaranty Ins. Co., N.Y.C., 1996-97, counsel, 1997—. Vol. campaign Bill Bradley for Senate, 1984, 90; vol. Starlight Found., N.Y.C., 1988—, mem. exec. com. Friends of the Maplewood (N.J.) Lib., 1995; mem Transp. Com., Twp. of Maplewood, 1999—. Mem. N.J. State Bar Assn. (sect. on entertainment and arts law, newsletter editor 1992-93, bd. dirs. 1992—; founding sec. ins. law sect. 1996-98, vice chair 1998—). Democrat. Jewish. Avocations: writing, theater, photography. Address: 747 Valley St Maplewood NJ 07040-2664

JOSEPHINE, HELEN BOWDEN, librarian; b. Chgo., Dec. 13, 1948; d. John Newton Bowden and Florence L. (Barker) Hackel; m. Allan J. Dyson, Nov. 28, 1973 (div. Mar. 1979); m. Dale L. Callaway, Dec. 28, 1983; children: Alanna A., Kevin P., Darren E. AB, Monmouth (Ill.) Coll., 1972; MLS, U. Calif., Berkeley, 1974. Ref. libr. Solano County Pub. Libr., Vallejo, Calif., 1976-78; dir. rsch. Info. on Demand, Berkeley, 1978-79; ref. libr. Ariz. State U., Tempe, 1985-87, info. mgr., 1988-93; program dir. U. Hawaii, Honolulu, 1993-96; collections libr. Menlo Coll., Atherton, Calif., 1996-98; account devel. mgr. western region The Gale Group, Foster City, Calif., 1998—. Contbr. articles to profl. jours., chpts. to books. Recipient McKinley Prize in English, Monmouth Coll., 1971, 72; Whitney Fund grantee ALA, 1982. Mem. AAUW, ALA (editor RQ ref. and adult svcs. divsn. 1979-80), Spl. Libr. Assn. Avocations: playing the piano, reading, travel. Home: PO Box 66 Ben Lomond CA 95005-0724 Office: The Gale Group 362 Lakeside Dr Foster City CA 94404

JOSEPHS, ALICE RUTH, retired executive secretary; b. Dvinsk, Latvia, Oct. 19, 1912; came to U.S., 1913; d. Benjamin Solomon and Sarah (Kuritzky) Hodes; m. Ben Gardner, May 10, 1932 (dec. Oct. 1944); 1 child, Steven Robert; m. Fred Josephs, Dec. 8, 1952; children: Susan, Cynthia, David. BA in Journalism, Radio, TV, Film, Calif. State U., Northridge, 1979. Exec. sec. astronomy dept. UCLA, 1965-71; exec. sec. Boy Scouts Am., Van Nuys, Calif., 1988-93. Playwright: Night of Broken Glass. Sec. bd. dirs. Synthaxis Theatre Co., North Hollywood, Calif., 1979-96; bd. dirs. Valley Cities Jewish Comty. Ctr., Van Nuys, 1964, 65, 66, 67-68, pres. women's club, 1967-68; leader Camp Fire Girls, Van Nuys, 1962, 63, 65. Playwright: A Woman's Place, Stars in Her Eyes, Window Panes, Failure Is Impossible—Susan B. Anthony; asst. editor: (mag.) Journalism History, 1977, 78, 79. Mem. AAUW, Am. Assn. Ret. Persons, Nat. Writers Assn., Gold Star Wives Am. (v.p.). Avocations: reading, playing guitar, piano, listening to music, writing. Home: 14341 Chandler Blvd Apt 3 Van Nuys CA 91401-5514

JOSEPHS, RAY, public relations and advertising executive, writer, international relations consultant; b. Phila., Jan. 1, 1912; s. Isaac and Eva (Borsky) J.; m. Juanita Wegner, Feb. 22, 1941. Student, U. Pa., 1927-29. Staff writer Phila. Evening Bull., 1929-40; columnist Buenos Aires Herald, 1940-44, Latin-Am. corr., 1940-55; representing at various times Wash. Post, Christian Sci. Monitor, Pitts. Post-Gazette, Newark Star Ledger, Chgo. Sun, P.M., Variety, Nat. Monthly, others; co-founder, chmn. Internat. Pub. Relations Co., Ltd., N.Y.; chmn. bd. Ray Josephs-David E Levy, Inc.; pub. rels. counsel maj. industries, comml. concerns including Hitachi, Toshiba, Hong Kong Shanghai Bank, Bass Charrington, Fuji Bank, Seiko Time, Nikko Securities, Kubota Ltd., New Otani Hotels, Newhouse Newspapers, House & Garden, Mitsui & Co., Toray Industries, Am. Inst. Imported Steel.; dir. Concorde News Bur., N.Y.C.; Lectr. Columbia Inst. Arts and Scis., Ind. U., Cornell Coll., Sweet Briar, Union Coll., Town Hall of West, San Francisco, Detroit, Indpls., Atlanta, Louisville, Spokane, Los Angeles Town Halls, numerous forums, town meetings from coast to coast; broadcaster NBC, CBS, MBS; cons. on Latin Am. affairs to coordinater Inter-Am. Affairs Brit. Ministry Information, RKO Radio Pictures, Asso. Export Adv. Agys.; cons. Bus. Coun. for Internat. Understanding, others pub. svc. orgns. Author: Argentine Diary, 1944, Spies and Saboteurs in Argentina, 1943, Latin America: Continent in Crisis, 1984, (with James Bruce) Those Perplexing Argentines, 1952, How to Make Money From Your Ideas, 1954, How to Gain an Extra Hour Every Day, 1955, 92; (with David Kemp) Memoirs of a Live Wire, 1956, Streamlining Your Executive Workload, 1958; (with Oscar Steiner) Our Housing Jungle and Your Pocketbook, 1960; (with Stanley Arnold) The Magic Power of Putting Yourself Over With People, 1962 (books pub. in Brit., French, Japanese, Spanish, Italian, German, Korean, Norwegian, Russian, Hungarian, Chinese, other edits.); contbr. to mags. and profl. jours. Mem. Brandeis U. Devel. Council. Mem. Writers Guild Am., Public Relations Soc. Am. (charter, accredited), Soc. Mag. Writers. Clubs: American (Buenos Aires); Overseas Press (N.Y.C.). Home: 860 United Nations Plz New York NY 10017-1810

JOSEPHSON, DIANA HAYWARD, government agency official; b. London, Oct. 17, 1936; came to U.S., 1959; d. Robert Hayward and Barbara (Clark) Bailey. BA with honors, Oxford U., Eng., 1958, MA, 1962; M in Comparative Law, George Washington U., 1962. Bar: Eng. and Wales 1959, D.C. 1963. Assoc. Covington & Burling, Washington, 1959-68; asst. dir. Office of the Mayor, Washington, 1968-74; exec. dir. Nat. Capital Area ACLU, Washington, 1975-78; dep. asst. adminstr. policy and planning, satellites NOAA, U.S. Dept. Commerce, Washington, 1978-82; pres. Am. Sci. and Tech. Corp., Bethesda, Md., 1982-83, Space Am., Bethesda, 1983-85; v.p. mktg. Arianespace, Inc., Washington, 1985-87; v.p. Martin Marietta Comml. Titan Inc., Washington, 1987-89; dir. bus. devel. Martin Marietta Advanced Launch Systems, Denver, 1989-90, Martin Marietta Civil Space and Communications Co., Denver, 1990-93; dep. under sec. commerce oceans and atmosphere, NOAA U.S. Dept. Commerce, Washington, 1993-97; prin. dep. asst. sec. Installations and Environment U.S. Dept. of Navy, 1997—; mem. Space Applications Bd., NRC, 1988-89, Comml. Space Transp. Adv. Commn., U.S. Dept. Transp., Washington, 1984-85; adv. bd. Washington Space Bus. Roundtable, 1985-87. Mem. D.C. Law Revision Commn., Washington, 1975-78, D.C. Internat. Women's Yr. State Coordinating Com., 1977. Recipient Gold medal for Disting. Svc., U.S. Dept. Commerce, 1981. Mem. Am. Astronautical Soc. (bd. dirs. 1985-88), Nat. Space Club (bd. govs.), Women in Aerospace, Washington Space Bus. Roundtable (adv. bd. 1985-87). Avocations: sailing, reading. Office: Dept of Navy 1000 Navy Pentagon Washington DC 20350-1000

JOSEPHSON, KENNETH BRADLEY, artist, retired educator; b. Detroit, July 1, 1932; s. Ernest Gustav and Hilda Christine (Wick) J.; m. Carol A. Compeau, Feb. 1954 (dec. Apr. 1958); m. Sherill A. Petro, Oct. 28, 1960 (div. 1973); children: Matthew W. (dec.), Bradley J., Anissa C.; m. Sally D. Garen, Jan. 30, 1973 (div. 1978); m. Katherine R. Bateman, June 7, 1991 (div. 1998). BFA, Rochester Inst. Tech., 1957; MS, Inst. Design Ill. Inst. Tech., 1960. Photographer Chrysler Corp., Detroit, 1957-58; exch. tchr. Konstfackskolan, Stockholm, 1966-67; assoc. prof. U. Hawaii, Honolulu, 1967-68; vis. prof. Tyler Sch. Art, Temple U., Phila., 1975, UCLA, 1981-82; prof. Sch. Art Inst. Chgo., 1960-97; fellowship panelist Nat. Endowment Arts, Washington, 1975; vis. artist Ecole Régionale des Beaux Arts De Saint-Etienne, France, fall 1995. One-person shows include Art Inst. Chgo., 1971, Visual Studies Workshop, Rochester, N.Y., 1971, U. Iowa Mus. Art, Iowa City, 1974, 291 Gallery, Milan, 1974, Cameraworks Gallery, L.A., 1976, Reicher Gallery Barat Coll., Lake Forest, Ill., 1977, Fotoforum, Kassel, Germany, 1978, Photographer's Gallery, London, 1979, Delpire Galerie, Paris, 1981, Young Hoffman Gallery, Chgo., 1981, Swen Parson Gallery No. Ill. U., 1983, Vision Gallery, Boston, 1983, Retrospective Exhbn. Mus. Contemporary Art, Chgo., 1983, Friends of Photography, Carmel, Calif, 1984, Rhona Hoffman Gallery, Chgo., 1991, La Serre Gallery, Beaux-Arts de Saint Etienne, France, 1996; group shows include Fla. State Mus., Gainesville, 1965, Sheldon Meml. Art Gallery, Lincoln, 1968, Fogg Art Mus., Harvard U., 1967, Eastman House, Rochester and Nat. Gallery of Can., Ottawa, 1967, Mus. Contemporary Crafts, N.Y.C., 1971, Corcoran Gallery, 1972, Art Inst. Chgo., 1973, 93, Walker Art Ctr., Mpls., 1973, Madison Art Ctr., 1973, Mus. Art, Indpls., 1973, Incontri Internazionali d'Arte Precheggio di Villa Borghese, Rome, 1973-74, Atkins Art Gallery, 1974, Kunsthaus, Zurich, 1977, Mus. Contemporary Art, Chgo., 1977, 96, Leslie Tonkonow Art Works and Projects, N.Y.C., 1998, Carol Ehlers Gallery, Chgo., 1999; Mus. Art. R.I. Sch. Design, 1978, Mus. Modern Art, N.Y.C., 1978, Light Gallery, N.Y.C., 1980, Photokina, Koln, Germany, 1980, Seibu Mus. Art, Tokyo, 1982, Barbican Art Gallery, London, 1985, L.A. County Mus. Art, Nat. Mus. Modern Art, 1989, State of Ill. Art Gallery, 1989, U. Hawaii Art Gallery, 1990, Art Inst. Chgo., 1990, Rockford Coll. Art Gallery, 1990, Catherine Edelman Gallery, Chgo., 1991, Davenport Mus. Art, 1992, Seagram Bldg. Gallery, 1992, Renaissance Soc., Chgo., Montreal Mus. of Fine Arts, 1993, Art Inst. Chgo., 1993, Chgo. Cultural Ctr., 1994, U. Ariz., 1994, Mus. Modern Art, 1995, Laurence Miller Gallery, 1995, Ehlers Caudill Gallery, Chgo., 1996, Gallery 312, Chgo., 1996, Mus. Contemporary Photography, Columbia Coll., Chgo., 1996; permanent collections include Mus. Modern Art., N.Y.C., Contemporary Arts Mus., Houston, Addison Gallery Am. Art, Art Inst. Chgo., Bibliothéque Nationale, Paris, Ctr. for Creative Photography, U. Ariz., Fotografiska Museet, Stockholm, Hallmark

Collections, Kansas City, Mo., Mpls. Inst. Arts, Mus. Fine Arts, Boston, Grunwald Ctr. Graphic Arts, UCLA, Nat. Mus. Art Smithsonian Instn., Washington, Nat. Mus. Modern Art, Kyoto, L.A. County Mus. Art, San Francisco Mus. Modern Art, Cartier Internat. Found., Paris, U.S. Trust Co., Art. Inst. of Chgo., Hunter Mus., Chattanooga, Tenn., Deloitte and Louche, Chgo., John D. and Catherine T. MacArthur Found., Seagram Collection, High Mus. Art., Libr. Congress, Internat. Ctr. Photography, N.Y., Cleve. Mus. Art, Tokyo Met. Mus. Photography. Served with U.S. Army, 1953-55. Guggenheim fellow, 1972, Nat. Endowment for Arts fellow, 1975, 79, Ruttenberg Arts Found. grantee, 1983, Ill. Acad. of Fine Arts Photographer award, 1993. Mem. Soc. for Photog. Edn. (founding mem.).

JOSEPHSON, MARVIN, talent and literary agency executive; b. Atlantic City, Mar. 6, 1927; s. Joseph and Eva (Rounick) J.; m. Tina Tann Chen, Apr. 12, 1973; children: Celia M., Claire A., Nancy A., Joseph T. Josephson; YiLing L.T. and YiPei R.T. Chen-Josephson. B.A., Cornell U., 1949; LL.B., N.Y. U., 1952. Atty. CBS, N.Y.C., 1952-55; pres., then chmn. ICM Holdings Inc. (and predecessors), N.Y.C., 1955—; pres., then chmn. exec. com. Internat. Creative Mgmt., Inc. subs. ICM Holdings Inc., N.Y.C., 1975. Served with USN, 1945-46. Office: ICM Holdings Inc 40 W 57th St New York NY 10019-4001

JOSEPHSON, RICHARD CARL, lawyer; b. Washington, Nov. 20, 1947; s. Horace Richard and Margaret Louise (Loeffler) J.; m. Jean Carol Attridge, Aug. 1, 1970; children: Lee Margaret, Amy Dorothy. AB, Case Western Res. U., 1969; JD, Coll. of William and Mary, 1972. Bar: Oreg. 1973. Law clk. Hon. John D. Butzner, Jr., U.S. Ct. Appeals, 4th Cir., Richmond, Va., 1972-73; ptnr. Stoel Rives LLP, Portland, Oreg., 1973—. Bd. dirs. Tucker-Maxon Oral Sch., Portland, 1987—, Vis. Nurse Assn., Portland, 1978-89, Healthlink, Portland, 1984-89, St. Mary's Acad., Portland, 1998—. 1st lt. U.S. Army, 1973-79. Fellow Am. Coll. Bankruptcy, Am. Coll. Comml. Fin. Lawyers; mem. ABA, Am. Bankruptcy Inst., Oreg. Bar Assn. (chmn. debtor-creditor sect. 1980-81). Presbyterian. Avocations: skiing, white water rafting, running, cycling, theatre. Office: Stoel Rives LLP 900 SW 5th Ave Ste 2300 Portland OR 97204-1235

JOSEPHSON, WILLIAM HOWARD, lawyer; b. Newark, Mar. 22, 1934; s. Maurice and Gertrude (Brooks) J.; m. Barbara Beth Haws, June 18, 1995. A.B., U. Chgo., 1952; J.D., Columbia, 1955; commoner, St. Antony's Coll., Oxford (Eng.) U., 1958-59. Bar: N.Y. 1956, D.C. 1966, U.S. Supreme Ct. 1959. Assoc. Paul, Weiss, Rifkind, Wharton & Garrison, N.Y.C., 1955-58, Joseph L. Rauh, Jr., Washington, 1959; Far East regional counsel ICA, 1959-61; spl. asst. to dir. Peace Corps, 1961-62, dep. gen. counsel, 1961-63, gen. counsel, 1963-66; asso. Fried, Frank, Harris, Shriver & Jacobson, N.Y.C., 1966-67; ptnr. Fried, Frank, Harris, Shriver & Jacobson, 1968-94, counsel, 1994-99; asst. atty. gen. in charge charities bur. N.Y. State Law Dept., 1999—; spl. counsel N.Y.C. Human Resources Adminstrn., 1966-67, City Univ. Constrn. Fund, 1967-70; N.Y.C. Bd. Edn., 1968-71, N.Y.C. Employees' Retirement Sys., 1975-86; Nat. Dem. vice presdl. campaign coord., 1972; pres. Peace Corps Inst., 1980—; mem. N.Y. State Gov. Task Force Pension and Investment, 1987-89, N.Y. State His. Records Adv. Bd., 1990-96, N.Y. State Archives Preservation Trust, 1994-96. Bd. editors: Columbia Law Rev, 1953-55. Trustee and treas. St. Antony's Coll. trust, 1994-99. Recipient William A. Jump award exemplary achievement pub. adminstrn., 1965, Disting. Svc. award, Valerie Kantor award, Corp. Social Responsibility award Mex. Am. Legal Def. and Edn. Fund, 1980, 81, 93. Mem. Assn. Bar City N.Y. (spl. com. on Congl. ethics 1968-70), Council on Fgn. Relations. Jewish. Home: 58 S Oxford St Brooklyn NY 11217-1305 Office: Charities Bur NY State Law Dept 120 Broadway Fl 3 New York NY 10271

JOSEY, E(LONNIE) J(UNIUS), librarian, educator, former state administrator; b. Norfolk, Va., Jan. 20, 1924; s. Willie and Frances (Bailey) J.; m. Dorothy Johnson, Sept. 11, 1954 (div. Dec. 1961); 1 dau., Elaine Jacqueline. AB, Howard U., 1949; MA, Columbia U., 1950; MLS, SUNY, Albany, 1953; LHD, Shaw U., 1973; DPS, U. Wis., Milw., 1987; HHD, N.C. Cen. U., 1989; LittD, Clark Atlanta U., 1995. Desk asst. Columbia U. Libraries, 1950-52; libr. tech. asst. central br. N.Y. Pub. Libr., N.Y.C., 1952; libr. I Free Libr., Phila., 1953-54; instr. social scis. Savannah State Coll., 1954-55, libr., assoc. prof., 1959-66; libr., asst. prof. Del. State Coll., 1955-59; assoc. divsn. libr. devel. N.Y. State Edn. Dept., Albany, 1966-68; chief Bur. Acad. and Rsch. Libraries, 1968-76, Bur. Specialist Libr. Svcs., 1976-86; prof. U. Pitts. Sch. Libr. and Info. Scis., 1986-95, prof. emeritus, 1995—; mem. bd. advisors Children's Book Rev. Service, Bklyn., 1972—. Editor, contbg. author: The Black Librarian in America, 1970, What Black Librarians Are Saying, 1972, New Dimensions for Academic Library Service, 1975; co-compiler, co-editor: Handbook of Black Librarianship, 1977; co-editor: A Century of Service: Librarianship in the United States and Canada, 1976, Opportunities for Minorities in Librarianship, 1977, The Information Society: Issues and Answers, 1978, Libraries in the Political Process, 1980, Ethnic Collections in Libraries, 1983, Libraries, Coalitions, And the Public Good, 1987, Politics and the Support of Libraries, 1990, Festchaift E.J. Josey: an Activist Librarian, 1992, The Black Librarian in America Revisited, 1994; mem. editorial bd. Dictionary of Am. Library History, 1974—; mem. editorial adv. bd. ALA Yearbook, 1975-83; spl. advisor: World Ency. Black People, 1974-80; contbr. numerous articles to profl. jours. Mem. Albany Interracial Council, 1972-86; mem. exec. bd. Savannah (Ga.) br. NAACP, 1960-66; state youth advisor Ga. Conf., 1962-66; mem. exec. bd. Albany br., 1968-86, treas., 1970-72, 1st v.p., 1981-82, pres., 1982-86, life mem., 1971—, chmn. program com., 1972-76, also trustee; mem. tech. task force Econ. Opportunity Authority of Savannah, 1964-66; bd. dirs. Correta Scott King Award; trustee Minority Edn. and Devel. Agy., Central Islip, N.Y., 1973; bd. mgrs. Savannah Pub. Library, 1962-66; mem. adv. council Sch. Library Sci., N.C. Central U., Sch. Library and Info. Sci., SUNY-Albany, Sch. Library and Info. Sci., Queen's Coll., CUNY; mem. exec. bd. Albany County Opportunity Authority. Served with AUS, 1943-46.; active Freedom to Read Found. Bd., 1987-91. Recipient cert. of Appreciation Savannah br. NAACP, 1963, NAACP award Savannah State Coll. chpt., 1964, Merit award for work on econ. opportunity task force Savannah Chatham County, 1966, award for disting. service to librarianship Savannah State Coll. Library, 1967, Jour. Library History award, 1970, N.Y. Black Librarians Inc. award, 1979, N.J. Black Librarians Network award, 1984, Joseph W. Lippincott award, 1980, Disting. Alumnus of Yr. award SUNY Albany Sch. Library and Info. Sci. and Policy, 1981, 89, Disting. Service award Library Assn. of CUNY, 1982, Martin Luther King Jr. award for disting. community leadership SUNY, Albany, 1984, award for contbns. to librarianship D.C. Assn. Sch. Librarians, 1984, award Kenyan Library Assn., 1984, Disting. Service award Afro-Caribbean Library Assn., Eng., 1984. Mem. ALA (John Cotton Dana award 1962, 64, founder, chmn. Black Caucus 1970-71, mem. coun. 1970—, exec. bd. 1979-86, v.p./pres.-elect 1983-84, pres. 1984-85, mem. Freedom to Read Found. Bd. 1987—, Black Caucus award 1979, ALA Equality award 1991, Black Caucus of ALA Demco award for disting. svc. to librarianship 1994; ALA Wash. Office award 1996—, Humphrey/OCLC/Forest Press award for contbns. to internat. librarianship 1998), AAUP, ACLU, Pa. Libr. Assn. (Disting. Svc. award 1996), Assn. Study Afro-Am. Life and History, Am. Acad. Polit. and Social Sci., N.Y. Libr. Assn. (Disting. Svc. award 1985), Freedom to Read Found., N.Y. Libr. Club, Internat. Platform Assn., Am. Soc. Info. Scis., Alpha Phi Omega, Kappa Phi Kappa, Sigma Pi Phi. Democrat. Home: Unit 505 5 Bayard Rd Apt 505 Pittsburgh PA 15213-1905 Office: U Pitts Sch Info Scis Bldg Pittsburgh PA 15260

JOSEY, JON RENE, prosecutor; b. Jackson, Miss., Nov. 28, 1960; m. Martha Willis, May 28, 1985; 2 children. BA, Clemson U., 1982; JD, U. S.C., 1985. Bar: S.C. 1985, U.S. Dist. Ct. S.C. 1987, U.S. Ct. Appeals (4th cir.) 1987, U.S. Ct. Appeals (fed. cir.) 1992, U.S. Supreme Ct. 1994. Law clk. to Chief Judge C. Weston Houck U.S. Dist. S.C., 1985-87; assoc. Rogers, McBratney and Josey, Florence, S.C., 1987-91, ptnr., 1991-93; lectr. polit. sci. Francis Marion U., Florence, 1992-93; sole practitioner Florence, 1994-96; interim U.S. atty. U.S. Atty. Dist. S.C., 1996, U.S. atty., 1996—. Contbr. articles to profl. jours. Mem. Florence Area Arts Coun., 1992-96, chair, 1996; mem. choir Ctrl. United Meth. Ch., 1992—, mem. adminstrv. bd., 1995—; 1st v.p. Florence County Dem. Party, 1995—, chair Florence City Dem. party, 1995-96; mem. S.C. Coun. for Mediation and Alternative Dispute Resolution, 1995-96. Fellow S.C. Bar Found.; mem. ABA, ATLA, S.C. Trial Lawyers Assn. Office: US Atty for SC 1441 Main St Ste 500 Columbia SC 29201-2862*

JOSHI, ARAVIND KRISHNA, computer educator, information scientist; b. Poona, India, Aug. 5, 1929; married; two children. B in Engring., U. Poona, 1951; diploma, Indian Inst. Sci., Bangalore, 1952; MS, U. Pa., 1958, PhD, 1960. Rsch. asst. elec. Indian Inst. Sci., Bangalore, 1952-53, Tata Inst. Fundamental Rsch., Bombay, India, 1954; prof. engr. Radio Corp. Am., N.J., 1954-58; from assoc. linguistic analyst to prof. computer sci. U. Pa., 1958—, Henry Salvatori prof. computers & cognitive sci., co-dir. Inst. Rsch. & Cognitive Sci.; assoc. transformations & discourse analysis project NSF, 1958—; cons. Philco Rsch. Lab., Pa., 1962-63, Western Res., 1964—. Guggenheim fellow, 1971-72. Fellow IEEE; mem. Assn. Computing Machinery, Am. Math. Soc., Sigma Xi. Office: U Pa Computer & Info Sci Dept 200 S 33rd St Philadelphia PA 19104-6314*

JOSHI, JAGMOHAN, agronomist, consultant; b. Dhanoa, Panjab, India, Mar. 20, 1933; came to U.S., 1966; s. Gian Chand and Savitri Devi J.; m. Santosh Sharma, Feb. 19, 1961; children: Shallin, Shushen, Shailesh. MS, Panjab U., Chandigarh, India, 1961; PhD, Ohio State U., 1972. Cert. profl. crop scientist. Lectr. Extension Tng. Ctr., Mashobra, India, 1956-61; asst. agrl. officer Ministry Agr., Nairobi, Kenya, 1961-66; rsch. assoc. Ohio State U., Columbus, 1966-73; rsch. assoc. U. Md. Ea. Shore, Princess Anne, 1973-77, rsch. asst. prof., 1977-85, rsch. assoc. prof., 1985-96, prof., 1997—, dir. Soybean Rsch. Inst., 1976—; cons. N.C. Agrl. & Tech. U., Greensboro, 1988, Transkel Washington Bur., 1990; internat. cons. in Zambia, Zimbabwe, Kenya, Nigeria, India, Republic of China, Sri Lanka, the Caribbean Islands, Egypt, Macedonia, and Russia, 1976—; co-team leader China Tech. and Sci. Exch., USDA, Washington, 1990. Co-author: Soybeans for the Tropics, 1987; contbg. editor: Technologies for Sustainable Agriculture in the Tropics, 1993; contbr. articles to profl. jours. Pres. India Assn. Ea. Shore, Salisbury, 1979. Grantee USDA, NASA, 1973—. Mem. Am. Soc. Agronomy, Crop Sci. Soc. Am., Am. Soybean Assn., Assn. Agrl. Scientists of Indian Origin. Achievements include research on host plant resistance, on cultural control of soybean pests, on winged bean, on agronomy of hydrocarbon producing plants and development of high yielding and promiscuous soybean varieties for Zambia; patentee in development of foliar spray for soybeans. Office: Univ Md Ea Shore Trigg Hall Princess Anne MD 21853

JOSHI, JANARDAN SHANTILAL, surgeon; b. Ahmedabad, Gujarat, India, Oct. 19, 1931; came to U.S., 1977; s. Shantilal Jatashanker and Ramlaxmi S. Joshi; m. Hansa Janardan, May 14, 1954; children: Mukesh J., Chetana K. MB BChir, Med. Coll., Baroda, India, 1955; Diploma in Laryngology and Otology, M.S. U., Baroda, 1957. Bd. cert. Am. Bd. Otolaryngology. Prof., head ear, nose and throat dept. NHL Mcpl. Med. Coll. and KM Sch. Postgrad. Medicine/Rsch., Ahmedabad, 1964-76; pvt. practice Ahmedabad, 1966-76, San Jose, Calif., 1983—. Fellow Royal Coll. Surgeons Edinburgh, Am. Acad. Otolaryngology-Head and Neck Surgery Inc.; mem. Am. Acad. Facial Plastic and Reconstructive Surgery. Avocations: foreign travel, photography, wind surfing. Office: 244 N Jackson Ave Ste 201 San Jose CA 95116-1604

JOSHI, PRABHAKAR G., educator; b. Thane, Bombay, India, June 28, 1931; came to U.S., 1963; s. Ganesh Laxman and Saraswatibai G. J.; m. Savita Vijaya Sohoni; 1 child, Chandrashekhar P. BA, U. Bombay, 1954, LLB, 1960; MA, Tex. State U., 1966; ABD, Cath. U., 1976; PhD, Southea. U., 1978. Mem. voluntary faculty dept. Am. govt. and polit. sci. Maharishi U. Mgmt., Fairfield, Iowa; rsch. assoc. Kans. State U., Manhattan, 1980, U.S. Army Depot, Oakland, Calif., Alexandria, Va., Phila.; vis. prof., rsch. assoc. The Pentagon, Washington. Author: India-U.S. Satellite Educational Program, 1978, Problems of Modernization in India, 1978, Problems and Prospects of Economic Development in India, 1977, Boondoggle of Conferences, 1997, An Example for All, 2d edit., 1995, others. Canditate for U.S. Ho. of Reps., 1996. Recipient Hind Rattan Jewel of India, Non-Resident Indians Welfare Soc., 1995, Trophies, Sr. Citizens Sports Sumter County, 1994, 95, 96. Mem. ASPA (life mem., mem. planning com. annual conf.). Avocations: table tennis, travel, learning to transcend. E-mail: PGJoshi@mum.edu. Home: SU 218 MUM Fairfield IA 52557

JOSHI, SATISH DEVDAS, organic chemist; b. Bombay, Maharashtr, India, Sept. 29, 1950; came to U.S., 1982; s. Devdas Ganesh and Premlata (Prabhu) J.; m. Shima Janakimohan Bhadra, May 2, 1974; children: Shruti, Shilpa. BS, Bombay U., 1970, MS, 1972; PhD in Chemistry, Bombay U., Bombay, 1977. Rsch. fellow State U. Gent, Belgium, 1979-81, Louvain Med. Sch., Brussels, Belgium, 1981-82; rsch. assoc. Mt. Sinai Sch. Medicine, N.Y.C., 1982-85; group leader Bachem, Inc., Torrance, Calif., 1985-87; dir. Bachem Biosci. Inc., Phila., 1987-89; pres., chief exec. officer Star Biochems., Torrance, 1989-91; tech. dir. Mallinckrodt Inc., St. Louis, 1991—. Mem. AAAS, ACS, Am. Peptide Soc., Torrance C. of C., Protein Soc. Home: 1928 Via Estudillo Palos Verdes Estates CA 90274

JOSHI, SURESH MEGHASHYAM, research engineer; b. Poona, India; came to U.S., 1969, naturalized 1982. B.S., Banaras U., India, 1967; M.S., Indian Inst. Tech., Kanpur, 1969; Ph.D., Rensselaer Poly. Inst., 1973. Engr., Stone & Webster Corp., Boston, 1972-73; research assoc. NASA, Hampton, Va., 1973-75, sr. scientist, 1983—; rsch. prof. Old Dominion U. Research Found., Norfolk, Va., 1975-83; vis. prof. U. Va., Charlottesville, 1992-93. Author: Control of Large Flexible Space Structures, 1989; co-author: Control of Nonlinear Multibody Flexible Space Structures, 1996; contbr. articles to profl. jours. Recipient Allen B. DuMont prize Rensselaer Poly. Inst., 1973; Group Achievement award NASA, 1977, Cert. of Recognition, 1981, Quality award, 1984, 1988, 90, 91; Spl. Achievement award, 1987, 89, 94, 95; Outstanding Tech. Contributions award, 1989, 90, 92, Floyd Thompson award, 1992, Dual Career Ladder award, 1992. Fellow AIAA, IEEE (control sys. tech. award 1995), ASME. Avocation: amateur cartoonist.st. Office: NASA Langley Research Ctr Mail Stop 132 Hampton VA 23681

JOSHUA, PERCY, English educator; b. Jonesville, Tex., May 5, 1952; s. Clint and Mildred (Lewis) J. BA, U. Dallas, 1974; MEd, Centenary Coll. of La., 1992, postgrad., 1996. Cert. tchr., Tex., La. Tchr. Irving (Tex.) Ind. Sch. Dist., 1975-78, Caddo Parish Schs., Shreveport, La., 1986—; chair English dept. Caddo Parish Schs., Shreveport, 1993-96; mgr. Mr. B's Beauty Supply, Dallas, 1978-85. Fellow NEH, 1993, La. Endowment for Humanities, 1990, 92, 94, 96; Japanese Studies Inst. fellow, 1998. Mem. NEA, Nat. Coun. Tchrs. English (scholarship to Adelaide, Australia conf. 1993), La. Assn. Educators, La. Coun. Tchrs. English, Caddo Assn. Educators (assn. rep. 1987—), Caddo Coun. Tchrs. English (slate rep. 1995—), Shreveport C. of C. (leadership coun. 1996—). Baptist. Avocations: travel, reading, arts, chess, writing. Home: 259 Merrick St Shreveport LA 71104-2433 Office: Caddo Parish Magnet HS 1601 Viking Dr Shreveport LA 71101-5245

JOSKOW, JULES, economic research company executive; b. N.Y.C., July 19, 1922; s. Abraham and Mollie (Neuberg) J.; m. Charlotte Epstein, June 24, 1945; children: Paul, Margaret, Andrew. BS, CCNY, 1941; MA, Columbia U., 1942, PhD, 1953. Mem. faculty dept. econs. CCNY, 1941-60; dir. research Boni, Watkins, Jason & Co., N.Y.C., 1952-61; v.p. Nat. Econ. Research Assocs., N.Y.C., 1961-70, sr. v.p., 1970-76, exec. v.p., 1976-85, pres., 1985-88, chmn. bd., 1988-91, spl. cons., 1991—. Contbr. articles to profl. jours. Mem. nat. governing council Am. Jewish Congress, N.Y., 1968-71; v.p. Temple Emanuel, Gt. Neck, N.Y., 1975-77. Mem. Glen Head Country Club L.I. (pres. 1988-91). Home: 127 Station Rd Great Neck NY 11023-1721

JOSKOW, PAUL LEWIS, economist, educator; b. Bklyn., June 30, 1947; s. Jules and Charlotte Joan (Epstein) J.; m. Barbara Zita Chasen, Sept. 10, 1978; 1 child, Suzanne Zoe. B.A., Cornell U., 1968; M.Phil., Yale U., 1971, Ph.D., 1972. Asst. prof. econs. MIT, Cambridge, 1972-75, assoc. prof. econs., 1975-78, prof. econs., 1978—, Mitsui prof., 1989-96, Elizabeth and James Killian chair, 1996—, head dept. econs., 1994-98, dir. Ctr. for Energy and Environ. Policy Rsch., 1999—; vis. prof. J.F.K. Sch. Govt., Harvard U., Cambridge, Mass., 1979-80; rsch. assoc. Nat. Bur. Econ. Rsch., 1988—; Joel Dean meml. lectr. Oberlin Coll., Ohio, 1983; cons. NERA, White Plains, N.Y., 1972—, The World Bank, 1991-92, Rand Corp., Santa Monica, Calif., 1972-87; pub. mem. Adminstrv. Conf. U.S., Washington, 1980-82; mem. adv. coun. EPRI, Palo Alto, Calif., 1980-84; mem. acid rain adv. com. EPA, 1990-93, mem. sci. adv. bd., 1998—; chmn. rsch. adv. bd. Com. for Econ. Devel., 1991-94, sci. adv. bd. Inst. d'Organization Industrielle, Toulouse, France, 1991—; bd. dirs. New Eng. Electric Sys., Westborough, Mass., State Farm Indemnity Co., Bloomington, Ill., Whitehead Inst. for Biomed. Rsch., Cambridge, Mass.; mem. Presdl. Econ. Policy Adv. Coun., 1994—; trustee Putnam Mutual Funds, Boston, 1997—. Co-author: Electric Power in the U.S., 1979, Markets For Power, 1983; author: Controlling Hospital Costs, 1981; also numerous articles, chpts.; co-editor, then assoc. editor Bell Jour. Econs., 1976-85; co-editor Jour. of Law, Econs. and Orgn., 1992-95; bd. editors Am. Econ. Review, 1993—. Pres. Yale U. Coun., 1993—. Recipient Disting. Svc. award Pub. Utility Rsch. Ctr.-U. Fla., 1993, Ed Hewett award Am. Assn. for the Advancement of Slavic Studies, 1995; fellow Woodrow Wilson Found., 1968, NSF, 1973, Ctr. for Advanced Studies in Behavioral Scis., Palo Alto, Calif., 1985. Fellow Am. Acad. Arts and Scis., Econometric Soc.; mem. ABA (assoc.), Am. Econ. Assn., Econometric Soc., Internat. Assn. for Energy Econs.(Best Paper award, 1994). Home: 7 Chilton St Brookline MA 02446-3902 Office: MIT Dept Econs 50 Memorial Dr Cambridge MA 02142-1347

JOSLIN, DAVID BRUCE, bishop; b. Collingswood, N.J., Jan. 8, 1936; s. Elizabeth (Andrews) J.; m. Kathrine E. Brockett, June 15, 1958; children: Paul Gregory, Suzanne Marie. BA, Drew U., Madison, 1958; M of Divinity (cum laude), Drew U., 1961; Assoc. in Anglican Studies, Episcopal Div. Sch., 1965. Assoc. rector St. Paul's Ch., Montvale, N.J., 1965-67; rector St. David's Ch., Wilmington, Del., 1967-74, Christ Ch., Westerly, R.I., 1974-87, Ch. of St. Stephen the Martyr, Edina, Minn., 1987-91; Episcopal Bishop Ctrl. N.Y. Diocese of Ctrl. N.Y.; keynote spkr. for retreats and confs., cons. liturgies and ch. design, chmn. bd. various state and nat. ch. bds.; mem. Standing Commn. on Ecumenism, 1995—, Coun. for the Devel. of Ministry, 1993—; leader Relationship of Anglican and Old Caths., 1994—. Author: Apostle in Our Midst-the Office of Bishop, 1982. Mem. Downtown Revelopment Task Force, Westerly, 1983-87; Citizen's Adv. Bd. Westerly, 1982-87; deputy gen. conv. Episcopal Ch., 1985. Mem. Fellowship of Sts. Alban and Sergius, Anglican Soc. of the U.S.A. (v.p. 1980-87), Rotary. Avocations: traveling, collector of antique autos. *

JOSLIN, RODNEY DEAN, lawyer; b. Moline, Ill., May 18, 1944; s. Melvin Seth and Dorothy Ruth (Skaggs) J.; m. Ruth Anne Moody, Aug. 21, 1965 (div. July 1985); children: Amy Brooke, Eliot Dean; m. Jeanne Nowaczewski, Nov. 30, 1985; children: Benjamin Case, Cecelia Louise. AB, Augustana Coll., 1966; JD, U. Iowa, 1969. Bar: Iowa 1969, Ill. 1969, U.S. Dist. Ct. (no. dist.) Ill. 1970, U.S. Ct. Appeals (7th cir.) 1970, U.S. Supreme Ct. 1975. Assoc. Jenner & Block, Chgo., 1970-76, ptnr., 1976—. Bd. dirs. United Cerebral Palsy Assn., Chgo., 1988—, pres., 1992—; bd. dirs. Northwestern Libr. Coun., Chgo., 1988—, Augustana Coll., 1996—. Home: 3100 N Sheridan Rd Chicago IL 60657-4954 Office: Jenner & Block The IBM Plz Chicago IL 60611-3603*

JOSLIN, ROGER SCOTT, insurance company executive; b. Bloomington, Ill., June 21, 1936; s. James Clifford Joslin and Doris Virginia (McLaflin) Joslin Browning; m. Stephany Moore, June 14, 1958; children—Scott, Jill, James. BS in Bus., Miami U., 1958; JD, U. Ill., 1961. Bar: Ill. 1961. Assoc. Davis, Morgan & Witherell, Peoria, Ill., 1961-63; controller Union Ins. Group, Bloomington, Ill., 1963-64; asst. v.p. State Farm Mut., Bloomington, 1964-69, v.p., controller, 1969-77, v.p., treas., 1977-87, sr. v.p., treas., 1989-98, vice chmn., treas., 1998—; chmn. bd. State Farm Fire and Casualty Co.; v.p., bd. dirs. State Farm Gen. Ins. Co.; bd. dirs. State Farm Mutual; treas. State Farm County Mut. Co. Tex.; v.p., treas., bd. dirs. State Farm Lloyds, Inc., State Farm Internat. Services, Inc., State Farm Investment Mgmt. Corp., State Farm Growth Fund, Inc., State Farm Balanced Fund, Inc., State Farm Interim Fund, Inc., State Farm Mcpl Bond Fund, Inc.; bd. dirs. State Farm Life Ins. Co., State Farm Life and Accident Assurance Co., State Farm Annuity and Life Ins. Co. Mem. Bloomington Bd. Edn., 1980-91, pres., 1983-84, 85-86; trustee 2d. Presbyn. Ch., 1971-74, pres. bd. trustees, 1973-74; bd. dirs. Brokaw Hosp., 1981-84; pres. BroMenn Healthcare, 1984-86, bd. dirs., 1984-89; bd. dirs. Western Ave. Cmty. Ctr., 1979-85, pres., 1981-83; bd. overseers RAND's Inst. for Civil Justice, 1989-98; chmn. Ins. Info. Inst., 1998—; chmn. bd. trustees Neighborhood Housing Svcs. Am., 1994—, The Social Compact, 1995-98, Natural Disaster Coalition, 1997-98—. Mem. ABA, Ill. State Bar Assn., McLean County Bar Assn., Ill. Soc. C.P.A.s, Miami U. Alumni Assn. (exec. council 1971-74). Presbyterian. Home: 2001 E Cloud St Bloomington IL 61701-5733 Office: State Farm Mut Automobile Ins Co 1 State Farm Plz Bloomington IL 61710-0001

JOSLYN, JAMES, television station executive. V.p., gen. mgr. KSAT-TV, San Antonio. Office: KSAT-TV PO Box 2478 San Antonio TX 78298-2478*

JOSLYN, WALLACE DANFORTH, retired psychologist; b. Cape Girardeau, Mo., Apr. 13, 1939; s. Lewis Danforth and Margaret Bernice (Gallup) J.; m. Annette Andre, Aug. 27, 1966 (div. Feb. 1969); m. Moreen V. Drescher, May 26, 1979; children: Jonathan David, Sarah Analisa Malathi. BA, U. Va., 1961; MS, U. Wis., 1965, PhD, 1967; diplomate, V. Frankl Inst. Logotherapy, 1993. Lic. psychologist, Iowa. Rsch. assoc. Oreg. Regional Primate Rsch. Ctr., Beaverton, 1967-71; clin. psychologist Knoxville divsn. VA Ctrl. Iowa Health Care Sys., Iowa, 1972-97; asst. prof. U. Oreg. Health Scis. U., 1970. Contbr. articles to profl. jours. NIMH fellow. Avocations: photography, running, travel, investing, history. Home: 802 E Competine Knoxville IA 50138-1955

JOSS, PAUL CHRISTOPHER, astrophysicist, atmospheric physicist, educator; b. Bklyn., May 7, 1945; s. Everett Henry and Magda Anna (Hohorst) J.; m. Marjorie Jean Axton, Jan. 24, 1970 (div.); 1 child, Susan Elizabeth; m. Karen Elizabeth Murray, July 3, 1992 (div.); 1 child, Matthew Albert Henry. BA, Cornell U., 1966, PhD, 1971. Mem. Inst. for Advanced Study, Princeton, N.J., 1971-73; asst. prof. MIT, Cambridge, 1973-78, assoc. prof., 1978-83, prof., 1983—, mem. Ctr. for Theoretical Physics, 1973—, mem. Ctr. for Space Rsch., 1973—; assoc. head astrophysics divsn. MIT, Cambridge, 1983-88; vis. scientist Weizmann Inst. Sci., Rehovot, Israel, 1974-75, 78, Inst. Astronomy, Cambridge, Eng., 1977, 93; vis. staff mem. Los Alamos Sci. Lab., 1979-80; cons. Visidyne Inc., Burlington, Mass., 1979-82, 92-93, Los Alamos Nat. Lab., N.Mex., 1980-92; mem. adv. com. Inst. Geophysics and Planetary Physics, Los Alamos Nat. Lab., 1987-92; mem. High Energy Astrophysics Mgmt. Ops. Working Group, NASA, 1988-91, Astronomy and Space Physics Sci. Coun., Universities Space Rsch. Assn., 1988-92; mem. Inst. for Theoretical Physics, U. Calif., Santa Barbara, 1991; spl. asst. to pres. Visidyne Inc., Burlington, Mass., 1993—; pres. Joss Consulting Assocs., 1992—. Contbr. 120 articles to profl. jours. Woodrow Wilson Found. fellow, 1966; NSF fellow, 1970; Alfred P. Sloan Found. fellow, 1976. Mem. Am. Astron. Soc. (Helen B. Warner Prize 1980, exec. com. High Energy Astrophysics div. 1983-85), Am. Phys. Soc., Internat. Astron. Union. Avocations: classical music, chess. Office: MIT Dept Of Physics Rm 6-203 Cambridge MA 02139

JOST, LAWRENCE JOHN, lawyer; b. Alma, Wis., Oct. 9, 1944; s. Lester J. and Hazel L. (Johnson) J.; m. Anne E. Fisher, June 10, 1967; children—Peter, Katherine, Susan. B.S.C.E., U. Wis., 1968, J.D., 1969. Bar: Wis. 1969, U.S. Dist. Ct. (ea. dist.) Wis. 1969, U.S. Ct. Appeals (7th cir.) 1969, U.S. Supreme Ct. 1980. Law clk. to judge U.S. Dist. Ct., Milw., 1969-70; assoc. firm Brady, Tyrrell, Cotter & Cutler, 1970-74; assoc. Quarles & Brady, 1974-76, ptnr., 1976—, coord. real estate group, 1985—; vis. tchr. gen. practice Wis. Law Sch. Bd. dirs., Milwaukee Chamber Theatre, 1998—; Pres. Vis. Nurse Assn. Milw., 1982-85, VNA, Corp., 1982-86; bd. dirs. Wis. Heritage Inc., 1980-82, Vis. Nurse Found., 1986-95, pres., 1993-94; bd. dirs. Milw. Repertory Theater, 1987-95, pres., 1990-92; bd. dirs. United Performing Arts Fund, 1989-93. Mem. ABA, Wis. Bar Assn. (lectr. seminars), Milw. Bar Assn., Am. Coll. Real Estate Lawyers. Mem. Plymouth United Ch. of Christ. Office: Quarles & Brady 411 E Wisconsin Ave Ste 2550 Milwaukee WI 53202-4497

JOST, RICHARD FREDERIC, III, lawyer; b. N.Y.C., Sept. 25, 1947; s. Richard Frederic Jr. and Gertrude (Holoch) J.; m. Sally Ann Galvin, July 29, 1972; children: Jennifer, Richard IV. BA, Dickinson Coll., 1969; JD, Syracuse U., 1975. Bar: N.Y. 1976, Nev. 1978, U.S. Dist. Ct. Nev. 1979, U.S. Supreme Ct. 1984. Dep. dist. atty. Elko (Nev.) County Dist. Atty.'s Office, 1976-80; dep. atty. gen. Nev. Atty. Gen.'s Office, Carson City, 1980-83; ptnr. Jones & Vargas, Las Vegas, Nev., 1983—. Trustee United Meth. Ch., Carson City, Nev., 1982-83; bd. dirs. Ormsby Assn. Retarded Citizens, Carson City, 1982-83. Served to lt. USNR, 1970-74. Mem. ABA (urban, state and local govt. law sect.), Clark County Bar Assn., Nat. Assn. Bond Lawyers. Democrat. Home: 2840 S Monte Cristo Way Las Vegas NV

89117-2951 Office: Jones & Vargas 3773 Howard Hughes Pkwy Las Vegas NV 89109-0949

JOST, WESLEY WILLIAM, automotive executive, mayor; b. Bklyn., Sept. 3, 1930; s. Wesley W. and Virginia Ruth (Holton) J.; m. Barbara J. Herbert, Aug. 29, 1954; children: Polly, Penny, Peggy, Perry, Peter, Philip, Patrick, Pamela, Paul. Grad high sch., Manasquan, N.J. Enlisted U.S. Army, 1951; owner Jost Garage, Inc., Wall, N.J., 1953-90; retired U.S. Army, 1959; owner Ziebart Auto Ctr., Wall, 1970—, Ryder Truck Rental, Inc., Wall, 1980—, Jost Auto Sales, Wall, 1986—; mgr. Sea Coast Chevrolet Truck Ctr., Wall, 1986-89. Editor: Spray Dust Mag., 1964-65. Mem. Cong. Chris Smith Congl. Club, Washington, 1985—, Allaire Airport Adv. Com., Wall, 1985—, Wall Twp. Body, 1987-94, Newark Internat. Airport Adv. Commn.; chmn. Wall Twp. Pub. Works, 1987-89; mayor Twp. of Wall, 1988, 89, 93—, dep. mayor, 1990, 91, 92; mem. N.J. Gen. Aviation Study Commn.; past chmn. Ft. Monmouth, Camp Evans Base Closure Com. Recipient Disting. Achievement award Internat. Franchise Assn., 1975, Award #1, Ziebart Dealer in Nation, 1975. Mem. Wall C. of C. (Golden Osprey award 1985), VFW (Belmar, N.J. chpt., quarter master 1956-60, Plaque 1960), A.O.P.A., 200 Club (Monmouth County, trustee), Elks. Avocations: flying, antique camera collecting. Home: 1448 Ocean Rd Wall NJ 07719-2562 Office: Ziebart 1726 Highway 35 Wall NJ 07719-3440

JOTCHAM, THOMAS DENIS, marketing communications consultant; b. Llandudno, Wales, Feb. 21, 1918; s. George James and Marion (Brand) J.; m. Margaret Jean Thirlwell, Aug. 10, 1940 (dec.); children: Patricia, Douglas, Joy, Candace (dec.). Student, Lower Can. Coll., 1929-36, McGill U., 1937-39. Sales rep. Montreal Lithographing Co., Ltd., Montreal, 1945-47; sales mgr. Wesco Waterpaints Can., Ltd., Montreal, 1947-48; advt. mgr. Pepsi-Cola Co. Can., Ltd., Montreal, 1948-52, mgr., 1952-54; asst. advt. mgr. Reader's Digest Assn., Ltd., Montreal, 1954-56; mgr., v.p. Foster Advt. Ltd., Montreal, 1956-73, exec. v.p., 1973-75, pres., 1977-81, vice chmn., 1981-83; pres. Sherwood Communications Group Ltd., Toronto, 1977-81, vice chmn., 1981-83; mem. coun. Montreal Bd. Trade, 1973-75, v.p., 1977-78, pres., 1979, hon. chmn., 1980-81. Bd. dirs. Grace Dart Hosp., 1973-83, pres., 1979-83; bd. dirs. Can.Coun. Christians and Jews, 1978-81, Les Grands Ballets Canadien, 1976-77; mem. Venetion Condominium, Inc., pres. 1984, 88-92; treas. Freedom Found.-Broward, 1999—. Maj. Can. Army, 1940-45. Recipient ACA Gold medal, 1978; charter recipient McGill Mgmt. Achievement award, 1981. Fellow Inst. Can. Advt. (pres. 1976-77); mem. Can. Advt. and Sales Assn. (pres. 1960-61), Advt. and Sales Execs. Club (pres. 1956-58), Advt. and Sales Assocs. Montreal (pres. 1948-49), Advt. Agy. Coun. Que. (pres. 1975-76), Can.-South African Soc. (bd. dirs. 1980-89, chmn. 1983-86), Internat. Swimming Hall of Fame (bd. dirs., chmn. 1998-99), Mount Stephen Club (pres. 1967-68), St. James Club (com. chmn. 1979-81), Royal Montreal Golf Club, Ont. Club, Thistle Curling Club (pres. 1977-78), Ft. Lauderdale Golf and Country Club (dir. 1990-92), Coral Ridge Yacht Club (gov. 1993-97, commodore 1997), Psi Upsilon. Home and Office: 1 Las Olas Cir Apt 1101 Fort Lauderdale FL 33316-1637

JOUKOWSKY, ARTEMIS A. W., private investor; b. Shanghai, China, Dec. 26, 1930; s. Artemis M.W. and Helen (Skvorzov) J.; m. Martha Content Sharp, June 9, 1956; children: Nina Lydia Koprulu, Artemis W. III, Michael A. AB, Brown U., 1955, LLD (hon.), 1985. Dep. to dir. Am. Internat. Underwriters, Milan, 1960-66, dep. to regional dir. for Europe, 1963-66, dir. Italian div., 1963-65; regional v.p. for Middle East, North Africa Am. Internat. Underwriters, Beirut, 1966-72; pres., regional dir. S.E. Asia Am. Internat. Underwriters, Hong Kong, 1972-74; v.p. Am. Internat. Underwriters, N.Y.C., 1974-77; mng. dir. Middle East Assurance and Reinsurance Co., Beirut, 1966-72; dir. Tam Sigorta, Istanbul, Turkey, 1967-72, Union Atlantique de Reassurance SA, Brussels, 1979-88, European Am. Underwriters, Vienna, Austria, 1979-87; dir., shareholder's rep. AIG Joint Ventures with Govt. Agencies, N.Y.C., 1979-87, pres. socialist countries div. and spl. world markets div., 1977-87. Founder, chmn. Brown U. Sports Found., 1983—; trustee Brown U., Providence, 1985—, vice chancellor 1988-97, chancellor, 1997-98, chancellor emeritus, 1998—; mem. bd. overseers Thomas J. Watson Inst. for Internat. Studies, 1981—, Ctr. for the Study Fin. Markets and Insts., 1987-89, Ctr. for Old World Archaeology and Art, 1981-92; vice chmn. bd. govs. John Carter Brown Libr., 1988—; trustee Lawrenceville Sch., N.J., 1984—, pres. bd. trustees, 1997—; chmn. Lawrenceville Trustees Com., 1994-97, Archaeol Inst. Am., 1992—; pres. bd. trustees Am. Ctr. Oriental Rsch., 1992—; mem. vis. com. Boston Mus. Fine Arts, 1985-92; dir. Clear Pool Camp, 1976-85; co-founder Am. Sch. Milan, 1962, bd. govs., 1961-65, pres. 1963-64, fin. com. 1962-65; trustee St. Croix Landmark Soc., Fredericksted, U.S. V.I., 1995—; trustee Internat. Rsch. and Exchs. Bd., 1998—. Mem. U.S. C. of C. (gov. Hong Kong chpt.), U.S.-USSR Trade and Econ. Coun. (tourist and travel com. 1974-77), Hungarian-Am. Trade and Econ. Coun. (vce chmn. 1984-87), Explorer's Club (N.Y.C.), India House (N.Y.C.), Hong Kong Club (life), Brown Club (N.Y.C.), Larchmont (N.Y.) Yacht Club, St. Croix Yacht Club (U.S. V.I.) Univ. Club (Providence), Hope Club (Providence), Knickerbocker Club (N.Y.C.). Office: Brown U 5 Benevolent St Providence RI 02912-9018

JOURDREN, MARC HENRI, investment banking company executive; b. Paris, Dec. 28, 1960; s. Pierre Auguste Jourdren and Berthe Augustine Dubois. Diploma in econs. and fin., Essec, Paris, 1983; MBA, Harvard U., 1987. Pres., founder Essec Enterprises Internat., Paris, 1982-83; econ. cooperant French Ministry of Economy and Fin., N.Y.C., 1983-85; assoc. Goldman Sachs & Co., N.Y.C. and Tokyo, 1987-88; assoc. Goldman Sachs Internat., London, 1988-91, v.p., exec. dir., 1991—, head Japanese product sales, 1996-99, head global products group, 1999—; fgn. advisor Harvard U., Cambridge, Mass., 1989—. Mem. Harvard Club N.Y., Mensa London. Avocations: piano, Russian art, gastronomy, oenology, skiing. Home: 48 Macready House, Crawford St, London W1H 1HS, England Office: Goldman Sachs Internat, Peterborough Ct 133 Fleet St, London EC4A 2BB, England

JOURNEY, DREXEL DAHLKE, lawyer; b. Westfield, Wis., Feb. 23, 1926; s. Clarence Earl and Verna L. Gilmore (Dahlke) Journey Gilmore; m. Vergene Harriet Sandsmark, Oct. 24, 1952; 1 child, Ann Marie. *Wife Vergene Journey, Registered Nurse St Mary's School of Nursing, 1947 and a member of the National Capitol Harp Ensemble, Holds various concert harp performance credits, including ensemble appearances at the White House and the John F. Kennedy Center for the Performing Arts.* BBA, U. Wis., 1950, LLB, 1952; LLM, George Washington U., 1957. Bar: Wis. 1952, U.S. Dist. Ct. (we. dist.) Wis. 1953, U.S. Supreme Ct. 1955, U.S. Ct. Appeals (4th cir.) 1960, U.S. Ct. Appeals (5th cir.) 1961, U.S. Ct. Appeals (D.C. cir.) 1965, U.S. Ct. Appeals (7th and 9th cirs.) 1967, U.S. Ct. Appeals (1st cir.) 1969, D.C. 1970, U.S. Dist. Ct. D.C. 1970, U.S. Ct. Appeals (2d, 3d, 6th, 8th and 10th cirs.) 1976, U.S. Ct. Appeals (11th cir.) 1981. Counsel FPC, Washington, 1952-66, asst. gen. counsel, 1966-70, dep. gen. counsel, 1970-74, gen. counsel, 1974-77; ptnr. Schiff, Hardin & Waite, Washington, 1977—; mem. mediation program U.S. Dist. Ct. (D.C. cir.), 1989—, early neutral evaluation program, 1989-95; mem. case evaluation program D.C. Superior Ct., 1991—. Author: Corporate Law and Practice, 1975; contbr. articles to profl. jours. Pres. Am. U. Park Citizens Assn., Washington, 1970-72; trustee Lincoln-Wesmoreland Housing Project, Washington, 1978-79. With Mcht. Marine Res., USNR, 1944-46, USNG, 1948-50. Knapp scholar U. Wis., 1952. Mem. ABA, FBA, Fed. Energy Bar Assn., Masons, Army and Navy Club, Phi Kappa Phi, Phi Eta Sigma, Theta Delta Chi. Republican. Congregationalist. Home: 4540 Windom Pl NW Washington DC 20016-2452 Office: Schiff Hardin & Waite 1101 Connecticut Ave NW Ste 600 Washington DC 20036-4390

JOURNIETTE, MELVIN DIAGO, civil engineer; b. Roanoke, Va., May 11, 1973; s. George and Delores Ardelia J. BS in Civil Engring., Va. Tech, 1998, BA in Pub. and Urban Affairs, 1998. Founder, editor, contbr. The Cosmopolitan Jour. Mem. ASCE, Nat. Geog. Soc. Avocations: contemporary urban dance, singing, reading. E-mail: melvinusjt@yahoo.com. Home: 2929 Emissary Dr NW Roanoke VA 24019

JOUSTRA, BARBARA LYNN, nurse; b. Great Lakes, Ill.; d. Stanley and Alice (Strzyzewinski) Abstetar; m. Timothy Joustra; children: Denise, Kimberly. BS in Nursing magna cum laude, Salve Regina Coll., 1984; postgrad., U. Tampa. Staff nurse The Miriam Hosp., Providence, 1984-85, Newport (R.I.) Hosp., 1985-87; charge nurse, asst. nurse mgr. Bayfront Med. Ctr., St. Peterburg, Fla., 1987—, radiology nurse. Mem. Tampa Bay Advance Practice Nurses Coun.

JOVANOVIC, MIODRAG STEVANA, surgeon, educator; b. Tabonovic, Yugoslavia, May 3, 1936; s. Hikola Stevan and Zivina Jelena (Antonic) J.; 3 children. B.A., Coll. Sabac, 1954; M.D., Faculty of Medicine, Belgarde, Yugoslavia, 1963. Intern in France and Can.; resident in surgery in Can., 1965-72. Fellow Am. Coll. Chest Physicians, Med. Council Can., A.C.S., Internat. Coll. Surgeons. Office: 93 Emerson Rd Wellesley MA 02481-3411

JOY, BILL, computer company executive. BSEE, U. Mich., 1975, MSEE and Computer Sci., 1982. Co-founder, v.p. rsch. Sun Microsyss. Inc., Mountain View, Calif., founder, chief scientist, 1998—. Prin. designer U. Calif. (Berkeley) version of UNIX operating sys.; co-designer SPARC microprocessor architecture. Office: Sun Microsyss Inc 901 San Antonio Rd Palo Alto CA 94303-4900*

JOY, CARLA MARIE, history educator; b. Denver, Sept. 5, 1945; d. Carl P. and Theresa M. (Lotito) J. AB cum laude, Loretto Heights Coll., 1967; MA, U. Denver, 1969, postgrad., 1984-87. Instr. history Community Coll. Denver; prof. history Red Rocks Community Coll., Lakewood, Colo., 1970—; cons. for innovative ednl. programs; reviewer fed. grants, 1983-89; mem. adv. panel Colo. Endowment for Humanities, 1985-89. Contbr. articles to profl. publs. Instr. vocat. edn. Mile High United Way, Jefferson County, 1975; participant Jefferson County Sch. System R-1 Dist., 1983-88; active Red Rocks Community Coll. Speakers Bur., 1972-89, strategic planning com., 1992-97; chair history discipline Colo. Gen. Edn. Core Transfer Consortium, 1986-96, faculty transfer curriculum coun., 1997—; mem. history, geography, civics stds. and geography frameworks adv. com. Colo. Dept. Edn., 1995-96; steering com. Ctr. Teaching Excellence, 1991-92, 1996-97; with North Ctrl. Self-Study Process, 1972-73, 80-81, 86-88, 96-98; with K-16 Linkages Colo. Commn. for Higher Ed., 1997-98. Cert. in vocat. edn. Colo. State Bd. Community Colls. and Occupational Edn., 1975; mem. evaluation team for Colo. Awards, edn. and civic achievement for Widefield Sch. Dist. #3, 1989; mem. Red Rocks Community Coll.-Clear Creek Sch. System Articulation Team, 1990-91; mem. Statue of Liberty-Ellis Island Found. Inc., 1987—. Ford Found. fellow, 1969; recipient cert. of appreciation Kiwanis Club, 1981, Cert. of Appreciation Telecommunication Coop. for Colo's. Community Colls., 1990-92; Master Tchr. award U. Tex. at Austin, 1982. Mem. Am. Hist. Assn., Am. Assn. Higher Edn., Nat. Council for Social Studies, Nat. Geog. Soc., Omohundro Inst. Early Am. History and Culture, Nat. Edn. Assn., Colo. Edn. Assn., Colo. Council for Social Studies, World History Assn., Orgn. Am. Historians, The Colo. Hist. Soc., Colo. Geographic Alliance, Soc. History Edn., Phi Alpha Theta. Home: 1849 S Lee St Apt D Lakewood CO 80232-6252 Office: Red Rocks C C 13300 W 6th Ave Lakewood CO 80228-1213

JOY, EDWARD BENNETT, electrical engineer, educator; b. Troy, N.Y., Nov. 15, 1941; s. Herman Johnson and Elizbeth (Bennett) J.; m. Patricia Marie Huddleston, Aug. 27, 1966; children: Frederick Huddleston, Rebecca Elizabeth. BEE, Ga. Inst. Tech., 1963, MSEE, 1967, PhDEE, 1970. Asst. prof. elec. engring. Ga. Inst. Tech., Atlanta, 1970-75, assoc. prof., 1975-80, prof., 1980-98, prof. emeritus, 1998—; pres. Joy Engring. Co., Stone Mountain, Ga., 1981—; cons. to cos., govtl. agys., orgns. Patentee in field; contbr. to profl. publs. Lt. USN, 1963-65, Vietnam. Fellow IEEE; mem. Antenna Measurements Techniques Assn. (past vice-chmn., tech. coord.). Republican. Presbyterian. Avocations: amateur radio, electronics, jogging. Home and Office: 1450 Rembrandt Rd Boulder CO 80302-9478

JOY, HENRY LEE, state legislator; b. Macwohoc, Maine, Nov. 26, 1933. BS in Math. and Sci., Ricker Coll., Houlton, Maine, 1963; MEd, U. Maine, 1976. Mem. from dist. 140 Maine State Ho. of Reps., 1993-95, mem. from dist. 141, 1995-98. Gubernatorial cand., 1998. Address: PO Box 103 Island Falls ME 04747-0103

JOY, ROBERT JOHN THOMAS, medical history educator; b. South Kingstown, R.I., Apr. 5, 1929; s. Angelo Francois and Mary Frances (Egan) J.; m. Beverly June Boxer, July 5, 1952 (div. May 1984); children: Robert L.F., Lisa; m. Janet Lucille Brady, July 12, 1985. BS, U. R.I., 1950; MD, Yale U., 1954; MA, Harvard Coll., 1965; cert., Armed Forces Staff Coll., 1968. Commd. 1st lt. U.S. Army, 1954, advanced through grades to col., 1970; intern, then resident Walter Reed Army Med. Ctr., Washington, 1954-58; asst. dir. environ. medicine U.S.A. Med. Rsch. Lab., Fort Knox, Ky., 1959-61; comdr. U.S.A. Rsch. Inst. for Environ. Medicine, Natick, Mass., 1961-62; chief comdr. U.S.A. Med. Rsch. Team, Saigon, Vietnam, 1965-66; chief med. rsch. div. Office of Surgeon Gen., U.S. Army, Washington, 1968-69; dep. med. and life scis. Office of Dir. Def. Rsch. and Engring., Washington, 1969-71; dep. dir., then dir. Walter Reed Inst. Rsch., Washington, 1971-76; prof., chmn. mil. medicine Uniformed Svcs. U. Health Scis., Washington, 1976-81, prof., chmn. med. history, 1981-96, prof. emeritus, 1996—; ret. U.S. Army, 1981; hon. mem. faculty Indsl. Coll. Armed Forces, Washington, 1990; mem. faculty USAF Sch. Aerospace Medicine, 1992—. Editor Jour. History Medicine and Allied Scis., 1983-87; contbr. articles to jours. in field; editor monographs on mil. medicine. Decorated Disting. Svc. medal, Legion of Merit (4); recipient John Shaw Billings award Am. Mil. Surgeons of U.S., 1986, William P. Clements award Uniformed Svcs. U. Health Scis., 1980. Fellow ACP, AAAS, Coll. Physicians Phila.; mem. Am. Assn. History Medicine (William Osler medal 1954, coun. 1979-81), Am. Physiol. Soc., Osler Soc. (bd. govs. 1986-89). Home: 5821 Highland Dr Bethesda MD 20815-5531 Office: Uniformed Svcs U Dept Med History 4301 Jones Bridge Rd Bethesda MD 20814-4712

JOY, STEPHEN PATRICK, psychology educator, psychotherapist; b. Rochester, N.Y., Mar. 6, 1958; s. John Sanford Joy and Stefanie Patricia (Byrne) Manning; m. Beverly Ann Lawson, July 6, 1984 (div. 1990); m. Deborah Carol Stanger, Oct. 27, 1995; children: Olivia Rhiannon, Julia Rosamond. BA, Bowdoin Coll., 1980; MS, So. Conn. State U., 1988; postgrad., U. Conn., 1990—. Asst. to mgr. Univ. Club, N.Y.C., 1982-86; rsch. assoc. Yale Psychiat. Inst., New Haven, 1986-90; instr. in psychology Albertus Magnus Coll., New Haven, 1989-98; clin. assoc. Norwich Hosp., Preston, Conn., 1992-94; clin. psychology intern Conn. Valley Hosp., Middletown, 1994-95; psychotherapist Student Health Svc. U. Conn., Storrs, 1995-97; asst. prof. Albert Magnus Coll., New Haven, 1998—; presenter in field. Contbr. chpts. to books in field, articles to profl. jours. Mem. APA, AAUP, Am. Psychol. Soc. Office: Albert Magnus Coll Dept Psychology New Haven CT 06511

JOYAUX, ALAIN GEORGES, art museum director; b. East Lansing, Mich., Oct. 28, 1950; s. Georges Jules and Jane (Peckham) J.; 1 child, Daniel Edgar. BFA in Studio Art, Mich. State U., 1973, MFA in Studio Art, 1976, MA in Art History, 1978. Acting dir. Kresge Art Mus., Mich. State U., East Lansing, 1978; asst. dir. Flint Inst. Arts, Mich., 1978-83; dir. Ball State U. Art Gallery (name changed to Mus. of Art), Muncie, Ind., 1983—. Author exhbn. catalogues, 1981—. Mem. Am. Assn. Mus., Intermus, Conservation Assn. (bd. dirs. 1985-93). Office: Ball State U Museum of Art 2000 W University Ave Muncie IN 47306-1022

JOYCE, ANN IANNUZZO, art educator; b. Scranton, Pa., May 23, 1953; d. Albert Joseph and Lucy (Giumento) Iannuzzo; m. Patrick Francis Joyce, July 23, 1977; children: Ryan Patrick, Shawn Patrick. BFA, Maryland Inst., Balt., 1975; MS, U. Scranton, 1988; postgrad., Pa. State U., 1990—. Mech. artist Internat. Corr. Schs., Scranton, Pa., 1975-77; layout artist Lynn Orgn., Wilkes-Barre, Pa., 1977-78; prodn. coord. Jewelcor Merchandising, Wilkes-Barre, 1978-82; adj. lectr. Kings Coll., Wilkes-Barre, 1981-89; art dir. WVIA-TV Pub. Broadcasting, Pittston, Pa., 1985-86; publs. dir. U. Scranton, 1986-89; asst. prof. King's Coll., Wilkes-Barre, 1989—; exec. bd. v.p. Northeastern Pa. Writing Coun., Wilkes-Barre, 1993—; edn. co-chair Northeast Pa. Ad Club, 1994-96. Contbg. author: Handbook of Classroom Assessment: Learning, Achievement, and Adjustment, 1996; group show Everhart Mus., Scranton, Pa., 1997. Cub Scout leader Boy Scouts Am., Moosic, Pa., 1992-95. Mem. ASCD, Nat. Art Edn. Assn., Am. Inst. Graphic Arts (Phila. chpt.), Calligraphers Guild, Artists for Art, Pa. Art Edn. Assn., Nat. Assn. Desktop Pubs., Seminar for Rsch. in Art Edn., Caucus for Social Theory in Art Edn. Democrat. Roman Catholic. Avocations: mixed media art, writing, vegetarian cooking. Home: 148 Joyce Dr Moosic PA 18507-2113 Office: King's Coll 133 N River St Wilkes Barre PA 18711-0852 Address: 148 Joyce Dr Moosic PA 18507-2113

JOYCE, ANNE RAINE, editor, director of publications; b. South Bend, Ind., Oct. 2, 1942; d. James Agee and Marjorie Elizabeth (Gilstrap) Raine; m. Glenn Russell Joyce, Aug. 19, 1962; 1 child, Adam Russell. AB, Cen. Meth. Coll., 1962; MA in French, U. Mo., 1966; MA in Linguistics, U. Iowa, 1979. Cert. tchr., Mo. Tchr. Centralia (Mo.) High Sch., 1962-64; instr. Coe Coll., Cedar Rapids, Iowa, 1978-79, Georgetown U., Washington, 1980-83; asst. editor Am.-Arab Affairs, Washington, 1983-84; editor, dir. publs. Mid. East Policy, Washington, 1984—; gen. sec. Mid. East Policy Coun., Washington, 1991—, v.p., 1993—. Mem. edn. com. Fairfax County (Va.) PTA Bd., 1986-88. U.S. Dept. Def. fellow, 1964-66; recipient Recognition award Am.-Arab Affairs Coun., 1988, Disting. Alumni award Cen. Meth. Coll., 1990. Mem. Middle East Studies Assn., LWV (fin. chair Fairfax county chpt. 1981—). Home: 6916 Tulsa Ct Alexandria VA 22307-1730 Office: Middle East Policy Coun 1730 M St NW Ste 512 Washington DC 20036-4516

JOYCE, BERNITA ANNE, federal government agency administrator; d. Albert A. and Margaret C. Joyce. BA, Duchesne Coll.; MBA, U. Santa Clara, 1968, PhD, 1974; m. Kenneth B. Lucas, Aug. 2, 1975. With Wolfe & Co., CPA's, Washington, 1971-72; fin. dir. Nat. Forest Products Assn., Washington, 1972-74; budget and fiscal officer ICC, Washington, 1974-77, Office Mgmt. and Budget, 1977-80; asst. dir. mgmt. svcs. Bur. Mines, Dept. Interior, 1980-85, asst. dir. Office Policy Analysis Dept. Interior, 1985-96, asst. spl. trustee for Am. Indian., 1996-99. Author: Financial Viability of Private Elementary Schools. Mem. AICPA, Sr. Execs. Assn., Exec. Women in Govt., Assn. Govt. Accts., Beta Gamma Sigma. Home: 6001 Bradley Blvd Bethesda MD 20817-3807

JOYCE, EDWARD ROWEN, retired chemical engineer, educator; b. St. Augustine, Fla., Oct. 20, 1927; s. Edward Rowen and Annie Margaret (Cobb) J.; m. Leland Livingston White, Sept. 11, 1954; children: Leland Ann, Julia, Edward Rowen III, Theo, Adele. BS in Chem. Engring., U. Miss., 1950; M of Engring., U. Fla., 1969; MBA, U. North Fla., 1975. Registered profl. engr., Fla. Petroleum engr. Texaco, Harvey, La., 1953-55; project engr. Freeport Sulphur Co., New Orleans, 1955-59; chem. engr. SCM Corp., Jacksonville, Fla., 1959-81; profl. engr. Jacksonville Electric Authority, 1981-93, ret., 1993; adj. prof. U. North Fla., Jacksonville, 1977—, Jacksonville U., 1989—; newspaper columnist Fla. Times Union, Jacksonville, 1970-87. Co-author: Sulfate Turpentine Recovery, 1971; author booklet; patentee in field. Sci. fair judge Duval County Sch. System, Jacksonville, 1960-92; co-chmn. adv. com. U. North Fla., 1981-85; merit badge advisor Boy Scouts Am., Jacksonville, 1960—; advisor Jr. Achievement, Jacksonville, 1963; vestryman, lay Eucharistic minister, sr. warden local Episcopal ch. Comdr. USN, 1950-53, Korea. Fellow Fla. Engring. Soc. (pres. Jacksonville chpt. 1983); mem. AICE (pres. Peninsular Fla. chpt. 1963-64), Phi Kappa Phi, Alpha Pi Mu, Gamma Sigma Epsilon. Democrat. Avocations: stamp collecting, coin collecting, water sports, camping. Home: 5552 Riverton Rd Jacksonville FL 32277-1361

JOYCE, JAMES A., III (JIM JOYCE), umpire; b. Toledo, Oct. 3, 1955; m. Claudia Kay; children: Jimmy, Keri. BS, Bowling Green State U. Former umpire Midwest League, Tex. League, Internat. League, Dominican Republic Winter League, Pacific Coast League; umpire maj. league baseball Am. League, N.Y.C., 1989—; with Umpires Union, Phila. Avocations: travelling to Oregon coast, golfing, basketball. Office: Am League 350 Park Ave New York NY 10022 also: Umpires Union 1735 Market St Philadelphia PA 19103

JOYCE, JAMES DANIEL, clergyman; b. Spencer, Va., Jan. 12, 1921; s. James Garfield and Mary (Taylor) J.; m. Dorothy Beatrice Campbell, Aug. 2, 1946; 1 son, Kevin Campbell. AB in Religion, Johnson Bible Coll., 1945, Lynchburg Coll., 1946; BD, Butler U., 1949; MA in Biblical Theology, Yale U., 1952, PhD, 1958. Ordained to ministry Disciples of Christ Ch., 1943. Pastor Hanover Ave. Christian Ch., Richmond, Va., 1954-59; sr. student leader ecumenical inst. World Council Chs., Geneva, 1960; prof. New Testament and Bible theology Christian Theol. Sem., Indpls., 1961-62; dean grad. sem. Phillips U., Enid, Okla., 1962-74; pastor Bethany Christian Ch., Houston, 1974-80, Covenant Christian Ch., Houston, 1980—; W.E. Garrison lectr. Disciple students Yale U., 1963; Jesse M. Bader lectr. evangelism Drake U., 1968; columnist Christian Jour., 1962-80; bass soloist rec. Joy-ce Sounds, 1977; pres. World Conv. Chrs. of Christ, 1970-74, mem. exec. com., 1974—; lectr. for armed forces in Far East, 1968; adj. prof. speech and creative writing U. Houston and Houston Community Coll., 1981-82; prof. speech and writing Houston Community Coll., 1982—, also head dept. speech; mem. bd. mgrs. Pension Fund Disciples of Christ. Author: The Living Christ in Our Changing World, 1962, The Place of the Sacraments in Worship, 1967. Recipient cert. of merit Methodist Bishop of Korea, 1972. Mem. Am. Assn. Theol. Schs. (exec. com. 1966-72), Theta Phi. Home: 5211 Carew St Houston TX 77096-1319

JOYCE, JOSEPH M., lawyer. BSBA, U. Minn., 1973; JD, William Mitchell Coll. Law, 1977. Bar: Minn. 1977. Legal counsel Tonka Corp., Minnetonka, Minn., 1977-81, sec., gen. counsel, 1981-87, v.p., sec., gen. counsel, 1987—. Office: Best Buy Co Inc PO Box 9312 7075 Flying Cloud Dr Eden Prairie MN 55344-3538*

JOYCE, LOUIS CYRIL, IV, township administrator, planner; b. Phila., May 27, 1948; s. Louis Cyril III and Rachel Jane (Zimmerman) J.; m. Kory Ann Stuard, Aug. 18, 1979; children: Andrew Russell, Emily Marie. AS, Camden County Coll., 1969; BA, Rowan U. N.J., 1972, MA, 1977. Lic. profl. planner, N.J. Tchr. Salem (N.J.) City Schs., 1972-75, West Deptford Twp. Schs., Thorofare, N.J., 1975-77; environ. planner Cape May County Health Dept., Cape May Court House, N.J., 1977-80; planner, mktg. rep. PQA Engring. Co., Cape May Court House, N.J., 1980-84; chief planner Salem Port Authority, 1984-86; real estate sales and developer Lou Joyce 3rd Agy., Blackwood, N.J., 1986-90; land developer Segal Assocs., Bellmawr, N.J., 1990, Rouse Chamberlain, Inc., Exton, Pa., 1990-91; exec. dir. Gloucester County Improvement Authority, Woodbury, N.J., 1991-96; twp. adminstr. Upper Deerfield Twp., Seabrook, N.J., 1996—; city planner City of Salem, 1992—; twp. planner Upper Deerfield Twp., 1997—. Chmn. Alloway (N.J.) Twp. Planning Bd., 1992—. Mem. Am. Inst. Cert. Planners, Am. Planning Assn., Corinthian Yacht Club Cape May (commodore 1985-86), Rotary Club Brigeton, N.J. Avocations: golf, sailing, skiing, rock climbing. Home: PO Box 225 23 Commissioners Pike Alloway NJ 08001 Office: Upper Deerfield Twp PO Box 5098 Seabrook NJ 08302-5098

JOYCE, MARY ANN, principal; b. Bklyn., May 29, 1935; d. Alfred and Antoinette (Polito) Lo Sasso; m. Michael J. Joyce, Jr., Mar. 2, 1957 (dec. 1982); children: Michael, Debra Grammer, Patricia Sommers. BA in Elem. Edn., Social Scis., Mount St. Mary Coll., 1972; MS in Elem. Edn., Reading, SUNY, New Paltz, 1975, CAS in Ednl. Adminstrn., 1983. Cert. tchr. N-6, N.Y., reading tchr., K-12, N.Y., sch. dist. administr., N.Y., sch. administr./supr., N.Y. Tchr. grades 3 and 4 Temple Hill Sch., Newburgh, N.Y., 1972-74, tchr. reading, 1974-83, tchr. gifted and talented, 1976-83, asst. prin., 1983-85; prin. Horizons-on-the-Hudson Magnet Sch., Newburgh, 1985-98; exec. dir. curriculum and instrn. Newburgh Enlarged City Schs., 1998—; tchr. summer sch. Newburgh (N.Y.) Free Acad., 1976-81; adj. prof. SUNY, New Paltz, 1989-91; nat. review panelist Blue Ribbon Sch. Competition, 1991, 92, FIRST family-sch. partnership program, 1992; speaker numerous confs., seminars. Recipient Elem. Sch. Recognition award U.S. Dept. Edn., 1989-90, 93-94, Excellence in Adminstrn. award Mid-Hudson Sch. Study Coun., 1993, award for Outstanding Leadership, Achievements and Contributions Toward Making the Edn. of our Nation's Youth a Safe and Productive Experience, 1991. Mem. ASCD, Am. Assn. Female Execs., Nat. Assn. Elem. Sch. Prins. (Excellence in Edn. award 1990, 94), State Adminstrs. Assn. N.Y. State (Elem. Schs. Excellence award 1990, 94), Newburgh Suprs. and Adminstrs. Assn., United Univ. Profs., Delta Kappa Gamma. Avocations: reading, sewing, needlework. Office: Newburgh Enlarged City Schs 124 Grand St Newburgh NY 12550-4615

JOYCE, MICHAEL, educator; b. Lackawanna, N.Y., Nov. 9, 1945; s. Thomas Robert and Joanne Hannah Poth J.; m. Martha Jean Petry, Oct. 12, 1975 (div. Nov. 1994); childre; Eamon, Jeremiah; m. Carolyn Jane Guyer, Nov. 2, 1997. BA, Canisius Coll., 1972; MFA, Iowa Writers Workshop,

1974—. Assoc. prof. Ctr. Narrative & Tech., Jackson, Mich., 1975-92, Vassar Coll., Poughkeepsie, N.Y., 1992—. Author: The War outside Ireland, 1982 (GLCA Writers award 1983), Afternoon, A Story, 1987, Twelve Blue, 1997. Biddhist. Home: 43 Point St New Hamburg NY 12590 Office: Vassar Coll 124 Raymond Ave Poughkeepsie NY 12590

JOYCE, MICHAEL DANIEL, personal resource management therapist and consultant, neurolearning therapist; b. St. Cloud, Minn., June 8, 1948; s. Francis Daniel and Bernadette (Ferkinhoff) J.; m. Patricia Mary Boom, July 7, 1969. BA in Psychology and Sociology, St. Cloud State U., 1973, postgrad., 1977; postgrad., Moorhead State U., 1993, Atwood Inst., 1993, Biofeedback Tng. and Treatment Ctr., 1994. Cert. behavior analyst, Minn.; cert. rsch. analyst, Minn.; cert. master practitioner of neuro-linguistic programming, Colo.; cert. hypnotherapist, neurolearning therapist; cert. in hemisphere specific auditory stimulation; cert. to practice hemisphere specific auditory stimulation; cert. in biofeedback; cert in EEG neurofeedback. Resident mgr. Dan J. Brutger, Inc., St. Cloud, 1969-71; rsch. analyst Faribault (Minn.) State Hosp., 1974-75, behavior analyst, 1975-76; therapist/behavior analyst Ctrl. Minn. Mental Health Ctr., St. Cloud, 1977-78; emotional/behavior disabled facilitator, chpt. 1 tutor Perham (Minn.) Dent Schs., 1978-92; tech. cons. Inclusive Edn. Tech. Assistance Team, Region IV, State of Minn., Perham, 1991-93, Personal Resource Strategies, Vergas, Minn., 1994—. Co-author: Life-Threatening Behavior: Analysis and Intervention, 1982. Coord. Youth Assn. for Retarded Citizens, St. Cloud, 1977-78; respite care provider Ctrl. Minn. Mental Health Ctr., St. Cloud and Perham, 1977-78, 79-86; vol. Perham Schs., 1978—, Spl. Olympics - Winter Games, Duluth, Minn., 1980, 81. Named Mem. of Yr. Minn. Sch. Employees Assn., 1989. Mem. Neuro-Linguistic Programming (cert. master level), Internat. Med. and Dental Hypnotherapy Assn. (cert. neurolearning therapist). Avocations: organic gardening and orcharding, tree farming, basketball, computers, psycho-technology hardware and software. Home: RR 1 Box 311A Vergas MN 56587-9760

JOYCE, MICHAEL PATRICK, lawyer; b. Omaha, Oct. 3, 1960; s. Thomas Hunt and Joan Clare (Berigan) J. Student, Miami U., Oxford, Ohio, 1978-79; BSBA, Creighton U., 1982; JD, U. Houston, 1988. Bar: Mo., Kans., U.S. Dist. Ct. (we. dist.) Mo. 1988, U.S. Dist. Ct. Kans. 1989, U.S. Ct. Appeals (8th and 10th cirs.) 1988, U.S. Supreme Ct. 1994. Assoc. mgr. Avco Fin. Svcs. Internat., Inc., Omaha, 1983-85; assoc. Wyrsch, Atwell, Mirakian, Lee & Hobbs, P.C. (formerly Koenigsdorf & Wyrsch, P.C.), Kansas City, Mo., 1988-94; shareholder Wyrsch, Hobbs, Mirakian, & Lee, PC, Kansas City, Mo., 1995-97; pvt. practice, 1997-98; pres. The Joyce Law Firm, LLC, Kansas City, Mo., 1998—; adj. prof. U. Mo. Kansas City Sch. Law, 1997—. Asst. editor (newsletter State Bar Tex.) Caveat Vendor, 1987-88. Grad. NITA, 1992; bd. dirs. Creighton U., 1997-99. Mem. ABA, Nat. Assn. Criminal Def. Lawyers, Am. Health Lawyers Assn., Mo. Bar Assn., Mo. Assn. Criminal Def. Lawyers, Kans. Bar Assn., Kansas City Metro Bar Assn., Johnson County Bar Assn., Creighton U. Alumni Assn. (dir. region IV nat. alumni bd. dirs. 1994-96, pres. 1997-99), Creighton U. Alumni Club (pres. Kansas City area 1992-94). Roman Catholic. Avocations: golf, basketball, community service. E-mail: mpjoyce@worldnet.att.net. Office: 104 W 9th St Ste 303 Kansas City MO 64105-1718

JOYCE, MICHAEL STEWART, foundation executive, political science educator; b. Cleve., July 5, 1942; s. William Michael and Anna Mae (Stewart) J.; m. Mary Jo Olsen, June 2, 1989; children from previous marriage: Mary Therese, Martin Michael. B.A., Cleve. State U., 1967; Ph.D., Walden U., 1974. Intake clk. Cuyahoga County Welfare Dept., Cleve., 1961-64, unit supr., 1964-65; tchr., athletic dir. St. Adelbert Sch., Berea, Ohio, 1965-67; tchr., coach St. Edward High Sch., Lakewood, Ohio, 1965-67; social sci. research assoc. Ednl. Research Council Am., Cleve., 1970-73, asst. dir. social scis., 1973-74, asst. to pres., 1974-75; instr. polit. sci. Baldwin-Wallace Coll., 1972-73; exec. dir. Morris Goldseker Found., Balt., 1975-78, Inst. for Ednl. Affairs, N.Y.C., 1978-79, John M. Olin Found., N.Y.C., 1979-85; pres. Lynde and Harry Bradley Found., Milw., 1985—, also bd. dirs.; trustee John M. Olin Found., N.Y.C., 1982-85, Pinkerton Found., N.Y.C., 1984—, Found. for Cultural Rev., N.Y.C., 1983—, Md. Acad. Scis., Balt., 1976-78, Md. Hist. Soc., Balt., 1977-78; sec. Inst. for Ednl. Affairs, Washington, 1983—; panelist NEH grant rev., Washington, 1983, 84; chmn. Philanthropy Roundtable, 1987—; mem. selection com. Clare Booth Luce Fund, 1988—; bd. dirs. Blue Cross/Blue Shield United of Wis., 1996—. Author: (textbook) Youth and the Law, 1973; contbg. editor: (8 vols. textbook series) The Human Adventure, 1971, (2 vols. textbook series) The American Adventure, 1975; contbr. articles to profl. jours. and chpts. to books. Mem. Nat. Commn. Civic Renewal, Cardinal's Com. on Laity Archdiocese N.Y., 1983—; mem. commn. Catholic Social Teaching and U.S. Economy, 1984-85; nat. co-chmn. Scholars for Reagan-Bush, 1984; mem. exec. com. Pres.'s Pvt. Sector Study Cost Control the Grace Commn., 1983—; exec. com. Caths. for Bush, 1988; mem. adv. bd. USIA for Internat. Ednl. Exchange, 1982—; mem. Eastern Regional Selection Panel on White House Fellowships, 1983—; asst. to chmn. Nat. Productivity Adv. Com., 1982; mem. Presdl. task force on Pvt. Sector Initiatives, 1981; mem. Presdl. transition team, 1980-81; trustee N.Y. Foundling Hosp., 1982-86, Orch. Piccola, Balt., 1976-78; mem. Nat. Commn. on Civil Renewal, 1996—; bd. dirs. Blue Cross Blue Shield, 1996—, United of Wis., 1996—. Mem. Mt. Pelerin Soc., Sovereign Mil. Order Malta, Union League Club (N.Y.C.), Milw. Club., University Club. (Milw.). Republican. Roman Catholic. Address: The Lynde and Harry Bradley Found PO Box 510860 Milwaukee WI 53202-0848*

JOYCE, STEPHEN FRANCIS, human resource executive; b. Pitts., Nov. 24, 1941; s. John F. and Anna May (Boyle) J.; m. Susan; children: Autumn, Shannon. BSBA, Youngstown U., 1964. Asst. employment mgr. Collins div. Rockwell Internat., Newport Beach, Calif., 1967-70; pers. mgr. Hyland div. Baxter Labs., Inc., Costa Mesa, Calif., 1970-76; dir. indsl. rels. Pertec Computer Corp., Irvine, Calif., 1976-83; v.p. human resources Denny's, Inc., La Mirada, Calif., 1983-88; sr. v.p. human resources Ross Stores, Inc., Newark, Calif., 1988-98; ret., 1998. Mem. exec. bd. Pres.'s Com. on Employment of People with Disabilities. With U.S. Army N.G., 1965-71. Mem. Am. Compensation Assn., Coll. Placement Coun., Employment Mgmt. Assn., Soc. Human Resource Mgmt. Republican. Avocations: skiing, sailing. Home: 1018 Bayside Cv Newport Beach CA 92660-7424

JOYCE, STEPHEN THOMAS, occupational and preventive medicine physician; b. Kansas City, Mo., Aug. 23, 1959; s. James Edward and Ruth Hope Joyce; m. Erin Marley Dobson (div.); m. Lee Diane Lister, May 12, 1995; children: Stephan Raphael Seibert, Liam Robert, Evan Alexander. Student, MIT; MPH, U. Mich., 1995; MD, Wash. U., St. Louis, 1984. Diplomate Am. bd. Preventive Medicine, Am. Bd. Occupl. Medicine; ACLS, ATLS. Intern and resident in gen. surgery Cleve. Clinic Found., 1984-86; staff physician emergency medicine Geauga Hosp., Chardon, Ohio, 1986-87; acting med. dir. Rapid Response North, Cuyahoga Falls, Ohio, 1987-88; assoc. med. dir. Med Ctr., Parma, Ohio, 1988-89; staff physician occupl medicine St. Vincent Charity Hosp, Cleve., 1989-90; med. dir. occupl. health Sherman Hosp., Elgin, Ill., 1990-95; med. dir. employee benefit plan Sherman Health Systems, Elgin, 1995—; cons., interim provider Sterling-Rock Falls Clinic, Ltd., 1996; ptnr. Benefit Performance Assocs., L.L.C., 1996—; physician advisor med. dept. Intracorp, Inc. (subsidiary CIGNA Corp.), Itasca, Ill., 1997—; presenter in field. Host CARE 50th Anniversary Commemoration, Chgo., 1995; physician Homeless Health Fair, Elgin, Ill., 1994, Cleve. Free Clinic, 1989-90; field physician Chagrin Valley (Ohio) Hunt Club, 1988-90; mem. Big Bro. Assn., 1978-80; emergency rm. aide Tufts U. Hosp., Boston, 1979; active Back Bay Clean-Up Project, Boston, 1977. Recipient Best Practices Nat. award Am. Soc. Healthcare Human Resources Adminstrn., 1999. Mem. Physicians for Social Responsiblity, Am. Pub. Health Assn., Am. Coll. of Occupl. and Environ. Medicine, Assn. of Occupl. and Environtl. Clinics.

JOYCE, TERI, church organization administrator; b. Oak Park, Ill., May 23, 1962; d. Henry Edward Wierenga and Elaine Joyce Leep. BSBA, Drake U., 1983. Comml. lines underwriter G.P. Assurance Group, Northbrook, Ill., 1984-90; tchr. English English Lang. Inst. of China, San Dimas, Calif., 1990-91; office mgr. South Park ch., Park Ridge, Ill., 1991—, dir. outreach ministries, 1996—, internat. outreach team leader, 1994-96. Mem. Gamma Phi Beta, Alpha Kappa Psi. Avocations: reading, walking, bicycling, scrapbooks, painting ceramics. E-mail:tjsouthpark@compuserve.com. Office: South Park Ch 1330 S Courtland Ave Park Ridge IL 60068

JOYCE, URSULA MARY, psychologist; b. White Plains, N.Y., Oct. 24, 1935; d. William Richard and Beatrice Agnes J. BS, St. Thomas Aquinas Coll., Sparkill, N.Y., 1958, LHD (hon.), 1989; MS, St. John's U., Jamaica, N.Y., 1961; PhD, Fordham U., 1970. Cert. real estate broker, N.Y.; cert. sch. psychologist, N.Y.; lic. psychologist, N.Y. Elem. sch. tchr. Archdiocese of N.Y., N.Y.C., 1954-62; high sch. tchr. Cathedral H.S., N.Y.C., 1962-65; asst. prof. psychology St. Thomas Aquinas Coll., 1965-72; v.p. Dominican Sisters, Sparkill, 1972-76; pvt. practice psychologist N.Y., 1976-81; exec. dir. housing cmty for elderly Thorpe Village, Sparkill, 1981—. Bd. dirs. Stop Orangetown (N.Y.) Stink, 1982—; mem. steering com. Healthy Cmty. 2000, Suffern, N.Y., 1997. Fellow Archdiocese of N.Y., 1965; scholar Fordham U., 1965-70; recipient postdoctoral study award NSF, Ea. Mich. U., 1965, Lehigh U., 1971. Mem. Nat. Leased Housing Assn., United Hospice Rockland (pres. 1989-97), Habitat for Humanity. Democrat. Roman Catholic. Avocations: bird watching, reading, gardening. Home: 175 Route 340 Sparkill NY 10976-1041 Office: Thorpe Village Rte 340 Box 254 Sparkill NY 10976

JOYCE, VICKI MARIE, special education educator; b. Chgo., Sept. 8, 1936; d. Walter and Victoria Juckins; m. Robert Daniel Joyce, Aug., 1956 (div. 1974); children: Jennifer Brining, David. BA, Calif. State U., L.A., 1962; MA, Calif. State U., San Bernadino, 1992. Home econs. tchr. L.A. City Sch. Dist., 1962-65; real estate broker Homes Unltd., Orange County, Calif., 1970-82; tchr. Riverside and San Bernadino County (Calif.) Sch. Dists., 1982-95; resource specialist San Bernadino Unified Sch. Dist., 1995—. Author: A Theoretical Meta-Analysis and Review of Kinesis For Special Education Teachers and Resource Specialists, 1993. Named Outstanding Tchr. Orton Dyslexia Soc., 1993. Mem. Calif. Tchrs. Assn., San Bernadino Tchrs. Assn., Nat. Tchrs. Assn., Nat. Assn. Resource Specialists. Avocations: reading, writing, painting, theater, grandchildren. Home: Unit 37 1965 Coulston St Loma Linda CA 92354-1733

JOYCE, WILLIAM H., chemist; b. 1935. BS, Pa. State U., 1957; MBA, NYU, 1971, PhD, 1984. With Union Carbide Corp., Danbury, Conn., 1957—, past exec. v.p. ops., now chmn., pres., CEO. Recipient Nat. medal of Tech., NSF, 1993, Industry Achievement award Plastics Acad., 1994, Lifetime Achievement award Plastics Acad., 1997. Mem. Nat. Acad. Engrng. Office: Union Carbide Corp 39 Old Ridgebury Rd Danbury CT 06810-5108*

JOYCE, WILLIAM LEONARD, librarian; b. Rockville Centre, N.Y., Mar. 29, 1942; s. John Francis and Mabel Clare (Leonard) J.; m. Carol Gail Bertani, Aug. 13, 1967; children: Susan, Michael. BA, Providence Coll., 1964; MA, St. John's U., 1966; PhD, U. Mich., 1974. Manuscripts libr. William L. Clements Libr. U. Mich., Ann Arbor, 1968-72; curator manuscripts Am. Antiquarian Soc., Worcester, Mass., 1972-81, edn. officer, 1977-81; asst. dir. for rare books and manuscripts N.Y. Pub. Libr., N.Y.C., 1981-86; assoc. univ. libr. for rare books and spl. collections Princeton U., 1986—; numerous cons. assignments including assessment and reporting project Nat. Hist. Publs. and Records Commn., Washington, 1982; lectr. Clark U., 1975-77; adj. faculty Sch. Library Service, Columbia U., N.Y.C., 1984-92; vis. prof. Grad. Sch. Libr. & Info. Sci. UCLA, 1994. Author: Editors and Ethnicity: A History of the Irish-American Press, 1848-1883, 1976; co-author: Documenting America: Assessing the Condition of Historical Records in the States, 1984; booklet Evaluation of Archival Institutions, 1982; co-editor: Printing and Society in Early America, 1983; editor: Catalog of Manuscripts Collections of the American Antiquarian Society, 4 vols., 1979; contbr. articles, revs. to profl. jours. Bd. dirs. Conservation Ctr. for Art and Hist. Artifacts, 1992—, chmn., 1995-98; mem. J.F.K. Assassination Records Rev. Bd., 1994-98; mem. adv. bd. Cannery Row Mus. Found., 1998—. Fellow Soc. Am. Archivists (coun. mem. 1981-85, pres. 1986-87); mem. Am. Hist. Assn. (mem. profl. div. com. 1979-81), Bibliog. Soc. Am. (chmn. fellowship com. 1982-85), Orgn. Am. Historians, Am. Antiquarian Soc., ALA (rare books and manuscripts sect., publs. com. 1985-88, chmn. 1987-88), Grolier Club (coun. 1990-93), Internat. Coun. on Archives (com. on lit. and art, 1993-97), Princeton Club (N.Y.C.). Office: Princeton U Firestone Libr Princeton NJ 08544

JOYCE, WILLIAM ROBERT, textile machinery company executive; b. Springfield, Ohio, Mar. 18, 1936; s. Robert Emmet and Christel Beatrice (Beekman) J.; m. Betty Arlene Provonsha, Aug. 29, 1959; children—Jennifer Lynn, Janet Cathleen. BA in Bus., Calif. Western U., 1982; MBA, Calif. Coast U., 1984. Cert. mfg. engrng. technician Soc. Mfg. Engrs., 1975. Mgr. engrng. Heinicke Instruments, Hollywood, Fla., 1964-68; div. mgr. Jensen Corp., Pompano Beach, Fla., 1969-72; pres. Textiles Supply, Inc., Gerton, N.C., 1972-80; v.p., gen. mgr. Tex-Fab, Inc., Gerton, N.C., 1980-82; pres. Tex-nology Systems, Inc., Gerton, N.C., 1982-90; pres. Corrib Enterprises Ltd., Automation Cons., Fairview, N.C., 1981—; owner The Silver Hammer Jewelry Store Chain, N.C. Mem., co-founder Assoc. Woodland Owners N.C.; Upper Hickory Nut Gorge Vol. Fire Dept., Gerton. Served with USAF, 1958-64. Recipient innovative devel. award, 1985, award Optimist Club, 1953-54. Mem. NSPE, Profl. Engrs. N.C., Guild Master Craftsmen (internat. mem.) Nat. Rifle Assn., Soc. Mfg. Engrs., Am. Inst. Design and Drafting, Mountain Commercial Lending Consortium, Western Carolina Entrepeneurial Council, Handmade in Am. Craft Orgn. Republican. Baptist. Club: Gerton Community Civic. Patentee in field.

JOYNER, CHRISTOPHER CLAYTON, international relations educator; b. Aberdeen, Md., May 16, 1948; s. Houston Clay Joyner and Besse Hyde Sowers; m. Nancy Douglas, Dec. 27, 1972; children: Kristin Elizabeth, Clayton Douglas. BA magna cum laude, Fla. State U., 1970, MA, 1972, 73; PhD, U. Va., 1977. Co-dir. Ctr. for Peace and Environ. Studies Fla. State U., 1971-73, instr. dept. govt., 1972-73; asst. prof. polit. sci. Muhlenberg Coll., 1977-80; vis. prof. dept. govt. and fgn. affairs U. Va., 1980-81; asst. prof. polit. sci. George Washington U., Washington, 1981-85, assoc. prof., 1985-90, prof. dept. polit. sci. and Elliott Sch. Internat. Affairs, 1991-94; prof. dept. govt. Georgetown U., Washington, 1995—; editl. advisor Internat. Legal Materials, 1988-90; vis. prof. government, Dartmouth Coll., 1989, 91, 93, 95, 97; profl. lectr. Sch. Advanced Internat. Studies Johns Hopkins U., 1991, 92; mem. editl. adv. bd. Transnat. Pubs.; mem. editl. adv. coun. U. Tasmania Antarctic and So. Oceans Law and Policy Paper Series. Author: Antarctica and the Law of the Sea, 1992, Eagle Over the Ice: The U.S. in the Antarctic, 1997, Teaching International Law, 1997, Governing the Frozen Commons: The Antarctic Regime and Environmental Protection, 1998; editor: International Law of the Sea and the Future of Deep Seabed Mining, 1975, The Antarctic Legal Regime, 1988, The Persian Gulf War: Lessons for Strategy, Law and Diplomacy, 1990, United Nations Legal Order, 1995, The United Nations and International Law, 1997, Reining in Impunity for International Crimes and Serious Violations of Fundamental Human Rights, 1998; sr. editor Va. Jour. Internat. Law, 1973-77; mem. editl. bd. Mershon Internat. Studies Rev., Va. Jour. Internat. Law, Internat. Studies Notes, Internat. Studies Quarterly, Case Western Res. Jour. Internat. Law, Ocean Devel. and Internat. Law, Terrorism: An Internat. Jour., 1988-92, Internat. Jour. Marine and Coastal Law; contbr. numerous articles to profl. jours. With USAR, 1970-76. Grantee Inst. World Order, Inc., 1971-73, Ford Found., 1989-94, , Nansen Inst./Tinker Found., 1992-94, Fridtjof Nansen Inst., 1995—; rsch. fellow Antarctic Ctr. for Rsch. and Cooperation, U. Tasmania, 1994, sr. rsch. fellow Woods Hole Oceanographic Instn., 1986-87. Mem. Am. Polit. Sci. Assn., Am. Soc. Internat. Law (life, exec. com. 1984-87, 1997-99), Antarctican Soc. (bd. dirs. 1984-87), Internat. Studies Assn. (pres. internat. law sect. 1985-86, 1997-98, mem. governing coun. 1985-86, 96-97), Internat. Law Assn., Law of Sea Inst., Nat. Eagle Scout Assn., UN Assn., Golden Key Hon. Soc., Raven Soc. Hon., Phi Beta Kappa, Omicron Delta Kappa, Phi Kappa Phi, Pi Sigma Alpha, Phi Theta Kappa, Phi Alpha Theta. Democrat. Methodist. Avocations: jogging, autograph seeking, writing. Home: 8102 Chivalry Rd Annandale VA 22003-1334 Office: Georgetown U Dept Govt Washington DC 20057-1034

JOYNER, CLAUDE REUBEN, JR., physician, medical educator; b. Winston-Salem, N.C., Dec. 4, 1925; s. Claude R. and Lytle (Mackie) J.; m. Nina Glenn Michael, Sept. 21, 1950; children: Emily Glenn, Claude Courtney. B.S., U. N.C., 1947; M.D., U. Pa., 1949. Intern Hosp. U. Pa., 1949-50; resident Bowman Grey Med. Sch., 1950; resident U. Pa., 1954-55, fellow in cardiology; Nat. Heart Inst. trainee, 1952-53; asst. instr. medicine Hosp. U. Pa., Phila., 1951-53; instr. Hosp. U. Pa., 1953-56, assoc. medicine, 1956-59, asst. prof., 1959-64, assoc. prof., 1964-72; prof. medicine U. Pitts., 1972-87; prof. medicine Med. Coll. Pa., 1987-96, vice dean, 1989-96; chief medicine Allegheny Gen. Hosp., Pitts., 1972-96. Contbr. articles to profl. jours. Served to lt. M.C. USNR, 1950-52. Fellow Am. Coll. Cardiology, ACP, Councils on Circulation, Arteriosclerosis and Cardiovascular Radiology of Am. Heart Assn.; mem. AAAS, Am. Heart Assn., Am. Clin. and Climatol. Soc. Home: Pulpit Rock 45 Little Sewickley Creek Rd Sewickley PA 15143-8393 Office: Allegheny Gen Hosp Pittsburgh PA 15212

JOYNER, DEE ANN, bank official; b. Alton, Ill., Feb. 26, 1947; d. T. Claxton and Dorothy M. (Troeckler) Burroughs; m. Orville Joyner, Mar. 15, 1973; 1 child, Dawn L. Kotva. BA in Govt., So. Ill. U., 1971, MS in Govt., 1973; MBA, St. Louis U., 1985. Adminstrv. asst. So. Ill. U., Edwardsville, 1970-72; staff assoc. Marshall Kaplan, Gans and Kahn, Washington, 1972-73; dir. community affairs East-West Gateway Coordinating Council, St. Louis, 1973-78; exec. dir. Coro Found., St. Louis, 1978-80, St. Louis County Econ. Council, Clayton, Mo., 1985-89; planning dir. St. Louis County, 1980-84; chief of staff to county exec. St. Louis County, Clayton, Mo., 1989-90; sr. v.p. Commerce Bank St. Louis, 1990—. Bd. dirs. Confluence, St. Louis, 1983-89, Focus St. Louis, 1996—, bd. chmn.; bd. dirs. Civil Svc. Bd., University City, Mo., 1984-93, Better Bus. Bur., 1991-93, Tax Increment Financing Commn./Indsl. Devel. Authority, University City, 1993-97, Alzheimers Assn., 1992—, Girl Scout Coun. of Greater St. Louis, 1993-96, Boys and Girls Town, 1994—, Automobile Club of Mo., 1995—, Delta Dental Mo., 1998—; mem. bd. St. John's Mercy Med. Ctr., 1997—. Recipient Joseph E. Boland Meml. Outstanding Alumnus award St. Louis U., 1992, Spl. Leadership award YWCA, St. Louis, 1987. Mem. Leadership St. Louis, So. Ill. U. Alumni Assn. (Women's Forum, bd. dirs. 1989-90, Alumnus of Yr. 1984), Univ. Club (bd. dirs. 1994-97). Office: 8000 Forsyth Blvd Saint Louis MO 63105-1707

JOYNER, J(AMES) CURTIS, federal judge; b. Newberry, S.C., Apr. 18, 1948; s. George C. and Joan C. (Glenn) J.; m. Mildred Ann Carter, Apr. 5, 1975; children: Jennifer Christine, Nicole Marie, Jacqlyn Ann. Student, Peirce Jr. Coll., Phila., 1967; BS in Acctg., Ctrl. State U., Wilberforce, Ohio, 1971; JD, Howard U., 1974. Bar: Pa. 1975, U.S. Dist. Ct. (ea. dist.) Pa. 1981. Contr. D.C. Project, Washington, 1972-73; legal publ. specialist Fed. Register, Washington, 1974-75; asst. dist. atty. Dist. Atty. Office Chester County, West Chester, Pa., 1975-80, chief dep. dist. atty., 1980-84, 1st asst. dist. atty., 1984-87; judge Ct. of Common Pleas, 15th Jud. Dist., West Chester, 1987-92, U.S. Dist. Ct. (ea. dist.) Pa., Phila., 1992—. Mem. coun. trustees West Chester U., 1983—. Named Trailblazer in Law Enforcement Gov. Thornburgh, 1986; recipient Outstanding Svc. award to law enforcement Pa. Criminal Investigators, 1987, Disting. Law and Justice award County and State Detectives Assn., 1988, Donald K. Anthony Alumni Achievement Hall of Fame Ctrl. State U., 1994. Mem. Fed. Bar Assn. (hon.), Chester County Bar Assn. Avocations: sports, jazz, golf. Office: US Dist Ct 601 Market St Rm 5613 Philadelphia PA 19106-1714

JOYNER, JO ANN, geriatrics nurse; b. Glenwood, Ga., Mar. 9, 1947; d. Roy and Lucille (Mercer) Powell; m. Henry Gene Lamb, Dec. 3, 1965 (div. 1984); children: Henry G. Lamb, Jr., Roy, Melinda, Jody; m. Robert Eugene Joyner, June 14, 1991. Diploma, Swainsboro Vocat./Tech., 1979; student, Ga. So. Coll., 1980. LPN, Ga. Staff nurse Meadows Meml. Hosp., Vidalia, Ga., 1980-82; staff nurse in ICU and critical care unit Toombs Alcohol and Drug Abuse Ctr., Vidalia, 1982-84; charge nurse Conners Nursing Home, Glenwood, Ga., 1984-85; supr. Bethany Nursing Ctr., Vidalia, 1990-92, charge nurse, 1985-92; nurse Claxton (Ga.) Nursing Home, Toombs Nursing and Intermediate Care Home, Lyons, Ga., 1992-93; staff nurse Laurens Convalescent Ctr., Dublin, Ga., 1994, 1994; staff nurse Meadow Brook Manor, 1994—, Dublin, 1994-95; relief house supr. Dublinair Healthcare and Rehab. Ctr., Dublin, 1995-96; staff nurse Telfair State Prison, 1997—; staff charge nurse Bethany Nursing Ctr., Vidalia, Ga., 1999—; mem. ind. nursing registry, Claxton; nurse Meml. Med. Ctr., Savannah, Ga.; office nurse Montgomery County Correctional Inst., Mt. Vernon, Ga., Laurens Convalescent Ctr., 1994-95, Meadowbrook Manor, 1994—; 3-11 relief house supr., supr. medicare spl. unit Gray (Ga.) Nursing Home, 1995-97, 98—, staff nurse. Democrat. Apostolic. Avocations: swimming, walking, singing, dancing. Office: 402 Smith St Vidalia GA 30474

JOYNER, JOHN BROOKS, museum director; b. Balt., Nov. 24, 1944; s. Joseph Brooks and Majel Ethel (Sanichas) J.; m. Marcia Lee Perkins, Apr. 5, 1966 (div. 1979); 1 child, Shelly Lyn; m. Georgina Louise Davis, May 1, 1982; 1 child, Jonathan Burgess. BA, U. Md., 1966, MA, 1969; postgrad., NYU, 1968-71. Teaching asst. U. Md., College Pk., 1966-68, mus. fellow, 1969-70; adj. lectr. Hunter Coll., CUNY, N.Y.C., 1970-71; curator Towson State U. Art Gallery, Towson, MD., 1972-74; dir., curator Nickle Arts Mus./U. Calgary, Alta., Can., 1975-80; lect. U. Alta., Edmonton, Can., 1980-83; exec. dir. South Bend (Ind.) Art Ctr., 1983-87; dir. Montgomery (Ala.) Mus. Fine Arts, 1987-93, Vancouver Art Gallery, 1993-96, The Gilcrease Mus., 1996—; grants reviewer Inst. Mus. Svcs., Washington, 1988-89; project dir. George Rickey in South Bend, 1983-85; founder/dir. Brooks Joyner Art Cons. Ltd., Calgary, Alta., Can., 1980-83. Author: Marion Nicol R.C.A., 1979, (exbn. catalogue) The Drawings of Arshile Gorky, 1969; contbr. articles to art mags. Sec. Cottage Hill Found., Montgomery, 1989; adv. Jr. League of Montgomery, 1988-89. Recipient fellowship NYU, 1969, Smithsonian Instn., Washington, 1972. Mem. Assn. Art Mus. Dirs., Am. Assn. Museums (small mus. adminstrs. com., accreditation reviewer 1989), Can. Art Mus. Dirs. Orgn., Internat. Coun. Museums. Republican. Avocations: gardening, tennis, Jack Russell terriers. Office: Gilcrease Museum 1400 Gilcrease Museum Rd Tulsa OK 74127-2100*

JOYNER, JOHN ERWIN, medical educator, neurological surgeon; b. Grambling, La., Feb. 7, 1935; s. John and Mary (Rist) J.; m. Joyce Nadine Sterling; children: Sheryl, John III, Monica. BS, Albion Coll., 1955; MD, Ind. U., 1959; LHD (hon.), Martin Ctr. Coll., 1988. Pvt. practice Indpls., 1964—; prof. surgery Ind. U. Sch. Meldicine, Indpls., 1969-83, assoc. prof., 1983-91, clin. prof., 1991—; med. dir. RehabCare Inc. Rehab. Ctr. Winona Hosp., Indpls., 1986-89, Maxi Health, 1995—; mem. Congl. Black Caucus Health Braintrust, Washington, 1987-88; bd. dirs. Indpls. Health Inst.; CEO Meridian IPA, 1996—. Mem. med. svcs. com. Indpls. Conv. Assn., 1985-88, Police Athletic League, Indpls., 1985—; trustee Albion Coll., 1991-95. Recipient Disting. Pub. Svc. award HHS, 1988, Dr. Charles Whitten award Sickle Cell Found. Northwest Ind., 1988, Outstanding Svc. award Scott United Meth. Ch., 1988, Disting. Alumnus award Albion Coll., 1990. Fellow ACS; mem. AMA, Nat. Med. Assn. (trustee 1986-87, pres. 1987-88, mem. AIDS info. and edn. adv. com. 1988—, Scroll of Merit award 1988), Congress Neurol. Surgeons, Hoosier State Med. Soc. (pres. 1978-79) , 100 Black Men Am. (chmn. bd. dirs. Indpls. chpt. 1985-87), Alpha Eta Sigma (Indpls. Pi Phi chpt.). Methodist. Avocations: music, fishing, spectator sports, reading. Home: 8860 Alderly Ct Indianapolis IN 46260-1619 Office: 3232 N Meridian St Indianapolis IN 46208-4646

JOYNER, SAM A., federal judge; b. Lawton, Okla., May 21, 1941. BS, George Washington U., 1963; JD with honors, U. Okla., 1966, M of Liberal Studies, 1987. Bar: Okla. 1966, U.S. Dist. Ct. (we. dist.) Okla. Legalpractice lawton, 1966—; formerly asst. judge Lawton Mcpl. Ct.; part-time magistrate judge U.S. Dist. Ct. (no. dist.) Okla., Tulsa, 1976-95, magistrate judge, 1995—; adj. prof. law U. Okla. Law Ctr. Contbr. articles to profl. jours. Past. bd. dirs. and treas. Lawton YMCA; bd. dirs. Lawton Indsl. Found., Wesley Found. of Cameron Coll.; Sunday sch. tchr. youth sponsor First United Meth. Ch. Lt. comdr. USNR. Mem. ABA, Okla. Bar Assn., Comanche County Bar Assn., Lawton C. of C. (past bd. dirs. and v.p.), Order of Coif, Phi Delta Phi. Office: US Courthouse 333 W 4th St Tulsa OK 74103-3839

JOYNER, WALTON KITCHIN, lawyer; b. Raleigh, N.C., Apr. 1, 1933; s. William Thomas and Sue (Kitchin) J.; m. Lucy Holmes Graves, Sept. 23, 1955; children: Sue Carson Clark, Walton K. Jr., James Y. II. AB in Polit. Sci., U. N.C., 1955, JD with honors, 1960. Bar: N.C.; lic. comml. pilot. Ptnr. Joyner & Howison, Raleigh, 1960-80, Hunton & Williams, Raleigh, 1980—; sec., treas. N.C. R.R. Co., Raleigh, 1966; bd. dirs. United Title Ins. Co., Raleigh; bd. mgrs. Wachovia Bank, N.C., 1969-98; bd. govs. U.S. Power Squadrons, 1974-81. Assoc. editor U. N.C. Law Rev. Pres. Rehab. and Cerebral Palsy Ctr. Wake County, Raleigh, 1974; trustee St. Mary's Coll., 1990-91. Mem. ABA, N.C. Bar Assn. (treas. probate sect. 1983), Wake County Bar Assn. (chmn., bd. dirs. 1977), Law Alumni Assn. U. N.C. (bd.

dirs.), Order of Coif, Phi Beta Kappa. Episcopalian. Club: Carolina Country (Raleigh) (pres. 1983-84). Avocation: flying. Home: 620 Marlowe Rd Raleigh NC 27609-7022 Office: Hunton & Williams 1 Hannover Sq PO Box 109 Fl 14 Raleigh NC 27602-0109

JOYNER KERSEE, JACQUELINE, track and field athlete; b. East St. Louis, Ill., Mar. 3, 1962; d. Alfred and Mary Joyner; m. Bob Kersee, Jan. 11, 1986. BA in History, UCLA, 1985; hon. degree, Fontbonne Coll., St. Louis, 1998. Winner 4 consecutive Nat. Jr. Pentathlon Championships; winner heptathlon Goodwill Games, Moscow, 1986, U.S. Olympic Festival, 1986; winner USA/Mobil Outdoor Track and Field Championship, 1987; winner, long jump and heptathlon World Track and Field Championships, 1987; winner Grand Prix Indoor Championships, winner indoor world record 55m hurdlers 7:37 seconds, 1989; winner heptathlon Goodwill Games, St. Petersburg, Russia, 1994; pres., founder JJK & Assocs., Inc. Author: (autobiography) A Kind of Grace, 1997. Founder JJK Cmty. Found. (name now JJK Youth Ctr. Found.); chmn. St. Louis Sports Commn., 1996—. Recipient Silver medal for heptathlon L.A. Summer Olympic Games, 1984, Sullivan award, 1986, Jesse Owens award, Am. Black Achievement award Ebony mag., 1987, Gold medal for long jump at 24 ft. 3 1/2 in. and heptathlon Seoul Summer Olympic Games, 1988, 1st Female Athlete of Yr. award Sporting News, 1988, Gold medal for heptathlon Barcelona Summer Olympic Games, 1992, Bronze medal for long jump Barcelona Summer Olympic Games, 1992, Gold medal for heptathlon World Track and Field Championships, 1993, Bronze medal in long jump in Atlanta, 1996, Jim Thorpe award, 1993, Jackie Robinson "Robie" award, 1994, Grand Prix Outdoor Champion, 1994; named Athlete of Yr., Track & Field News, 1986, Female Athlete of Yr., AP, 1987, Female of Yr. IAAF, 1994, St. Louis Ambassadors Sportswoman of Yr. Set world record of 7161 points at U.S. Olympic Festival, 1986; set world record of 7291 points at Seoul Summer Olympic Games for heptathlon, 1988; holder Am. record in long jump, 1994, 50 meter hurdles, 60 meter hurdles. Office: Elite Internat Sports Mktg Inc 701 Market St Ste 1575 Saint Louis MO 63101-1899*

JOYNT, ROBERT JAMES, academic administrator; b. Le Mars, Iowa, Dec. 22, 1925. MD, 1952, PhD, 1963. Diplomate Am. Bd. Psychiatry and Neurology (past pres.). Intern Royal Victoria Hosp., Montreal, Que., Can., 1952-53; chief neurology Strong Meml. Hosp., Rochester, N.Y., 1966-84; assoc. U. Iowa, Iowa City, 1957-58, asst. prof. neurology, 1958-61, assoc. prof., 1961-66; prof. neurology U. Rochester, 1966—, chmn. dept., 1966-84, dean Sch. Medicine and Dentistry, 1984-89, v.p. and vice provost for health affairs Sch. Medicine & Dentistry, 1989-94. Cambridge U. Fulbright scholar, 1953-54; USPHS neurology fellow, 1954-57; named Disting. Univ. Prof., 1997. Fellow AAAS; mem. AMA (chief editor Arch Neurology 1982-97), Am. Neurol. Assn. (past pres.), Am. Acad. Neurology (past pres.), Am. Electroencephalographic Soc., Royal Soc. Medicine, Inst. Medicine, Nat. Libr. of Medicine (bd. regents 1992-96). Office: U Rochester Sch Medicine and Dentistry Dept Neurology Box 673 Rochester NY 14642

JOZWIK, FRANCIS XAVIER, agricultural business executive; b. El Paso, Tex., July 4, 1940; s. Andrew and Dagmar Elizabeth (Wettermark) J.; m. Phyllis Ann Angevine, Dec. 28, 1974; children: Melissa, John, Monika. Student, Casper Coll., 1958-60, U. Idaho, 1960; BS, U. Wyo., 1962, MS, 1963, PhD, 1966; postgrad., Wash. State U., 1964. Asst. prof. plant physiology Wis. State U., Oshkosh, 1966-67; rangelands scientist Commonwealth Sci. and Indsl. Rsch. Orgn., Canberra, Australia, 1967-69; owner, mgr. Johnny Appleseed, Inc., Casper, Wyo., 1969—; owner Andmar Press, Casper. Author: Plants for Profit, The Greenhouse and Nursery Handbook, How To Make Money Growing Plants, Perennial Plants for Profit or Pleasure, Illustrated Landscape Manual; editor: Nat. Greenhouse Industry mag.; prodr. horticultural videos; contbr. articles in field to profl. jours. NSF fellow, 1963. Mem. U.S. C. of C., Sigma Xi. Roman Catholic. Home and Office: 2941 N Pilot Dr Casper WY 82604-1673

JREISAT, JAMIL ELIAS, public administration and political science educator, consultant; b. Fuheis, Jordan, Apr. 9, 1935; came to U.S., 1960; s. Elias E. and Hanieh J. (Khory) J.; m. Andrea Brunais, July 9, 1977; children: Mark Ramsey, Leila Martine. BA, Am. U., Washington, 1962; MPA, U. Pitts., 1963, PhD, 1968. Sr. ofcl. Govt. Jordan, 1957-60; lectr. pub. adminstrn. U. Pitts., 1967-68; prof. pub. adminstrn. and polit. sci. U. South Fla., Tampa, 1968—, chmn. dept. polit. sci., 1976-80; vis. prof. U. Jordan, 1983, U. Riyad (Saudi Arabia), 1981-82; cons. UN Devel. Program, Internat. Mgmt. Devel. Inst.-U. Pitts., Arab Orgn. Adminstrv. Devel., others. Author: Administration and Development in the Arab World, 1986, Managing Public Organizations, 1992, Politics Without Process, 1997, and others; mem. editorial bd. Internat. Jour. Pub. Adminstrn., 1978, Arab Studies Quar., and others; contbr. articles to profl. jours. and chpts. to books. Mem. ASPA, Am. Polit. Sci. Assn., Arab-Am. Univ. Grads. (bd. dirs., pres. 1991-93), Middle East Club. Home: 6713 Maybole Pl Tampa FL 33617-3131 Office: U South Fla Pub Adminstrn Program Tampa FL 33620

JUAREZ, ANTONIO, psychotherapist, consultant, counselor, educator; b. El Paso, Tex., Nov. 6, 1952; s. Juan Antonio and Amelia (Rivas) J. BS in Psychology, U.Tex.-El Paso, 1976, MA in Clin. Psychology, 1982; postgrad., N.Mex. State U., 1987—, Calif. Coast U., 1990—. Cert. counselor, clin. mental health counselor; cert. diplomate, Am. Psychotherapy Assn., lic. profl. counselor, Tex. Caseworker asst. El Paso Mental Health Ctr., 1978-79, caseworker III, 1982-83; clin. specialist S.W. Mental Health Ctr., Las Cruces, N.Mex., 1979-80; therapist, trainer S.W. Community House, El Paso, 1980-81; psychol. cons. El Paso Guidance Ctr., 1981-82, psychotherapist, 1983—, dir. N.E. svcs.; pvt. practice, El Paso, 1987—; mem. Nat. Bd. for Cert. Counselors; dir. Cross-Cultural Counseling Ctr., 1988—; instr. psychology El Paso C.C., 1988-90, counselor, cons.; cons. Citizens and Students Together, El Paso, 1983—, group facilitator Tai Chi Chuan Instr., Sun Valley Regional Hosp., El Paso, Tex., 1988; psychotherapist El Paso State Ctr., 1997—; adj. prof. counseling Webster U., Ft. Bliss, Tex., 1995—; treatment team coord. El Paso State Ctr., 1997—. Mem. Latin Am. com. N.Mex. State U., 1985. Served with USAF, 1972-76. Fellow N.Mex. State U., 1981. Mem. U.S.-Mex. Border Health Assn., El Paso Psychol. Assn., Tex. Assn. for Counseling and Devel., Tex. Assn. for Children of Alcoholics, Golden Key, Nat. Acad. For Clin. Mental Health Counselors, Eastern U.S.A. Martial Arts Assn. (Black Belt Hall of Fame 1996), Ea. U.S.A. Martial Arts Assn. (Black Belt Hall of Fame 1997). Democrat. Roman Catholic. Avocations: martial arts, playing stringed instruments. Home: PO Box 1493 Santa Teresa NM 88008-1493 Office: Cross-Cultural Counseling Ctr 2112 Trawood Dr # 3B El Paso TX 79935-3318

JUAREZ, MARTIN, priest; b. Kansas City, Kans., Mar. 23, 1946; s. Martin Huerta and Hermelinda (Rocha) J. AS, Colby Community Coll., 1971; BA in sociology, U. Mo., Kansas City, 1974; MDiv, St. Thomas Sem., Denver, 1985; cert. in Hispanic ministry, Oblate Sch. of Theology, San Antonio, 1991, Mexican-Am. Cultural Ctr., 1991. Priest Archdiocese of Kansas City, Kans., 1981—. Bd. dirs. Pioneer Village, Topeka, 1983-88; co-dir. El Centro, Topeka, 1989. Mem. Kans. Registered Animal Hosp. Techs. Assn., N.Am. Veterinary Tech. Assn., U. Mo. Alumni Assn., KC. Office: PO Box 410695 Kansas City MO 64141-0695

JUBINSKA, PATRICIA ANN, ballet instructor, choreographer; b. Norfolk, Va.; d. Joseph John and Lucy (Babey) Topping; children: Vanessa Meredith, Courtney Hilary. Student, Md. State Ballet Sch., Sch. Am. Ballet, N.Y.C.; BA, R.I. Coll.; MA, Wesleyan U.; PhD, Union Inst., 1999. Mem. N.Y.C. Ballet; freelance artist Chamber Ballet of L.A., San Antonio Ballet, Md. State Ballet; artistic dir. Blackstone Valley Ballet, Harrisville, R.I., 1983-84, Am. Ballet, Pascoag, R.I., 1984-92; asst. artistic dir. Odessa Ukrainian Dancers, Woonsocket, R.I., 1991-92; freelance guest artist, 1992—; mem. Mandrivka Dancers of Boston, 1993—. Avocation: equestrian. Home: 1264 Round Top Rd Harrisville RI 02830-1051

JUCEAM, ROBERT E., lawyer; b. N.Y.C., June 16, 1940; s. Benjamin T. and Amelia B. (Spatz) J.; m. Eleanor Pam, May 24, 1970; children: Daniel, Jacquelyn, Gregory. AB cum laude, Columbia U., 1961, LLB, 1964, JD, 1972; LLM, NYU, 1966. Bar: N.Y. 1965, U.S. Dist. Ct. (so. and ea. dists.) N.Y. 1966, U.S. Tax Ct. 1968, U.S. Ct. Appeals (2d cir.) 1967, U.S. Supreme Ct. 1971, U.S. Ct. Appeals (5th cir.) 1978, U.S. Ct. Appeals (D.C. cir.) 1980, U.S. Ct. Appeals (11th cir.) 1987, U.S. Ct. Appeals (7th cir.) 1989. Law clk. U.S. Dist. Ct., N.Y., 1964-66; assoc. Fried, Frank, Harris, Shriver & Jacobson, N.Y.C., 1966-73, ptnr., 1974—; bd. dirs. Nat. Network Def. of the Right to Counsel, Inc., 1985-89, Lawyers Com. for Human Rights, 1986-94, Bar Assurance and Reins. Ltd., 1991—, Am. Immigration Law Found., 1987—, pres., 1991—; gen. counsel U.S. Supreme Ct. Hist. Soc., 1995—, trustee, mem. exec. com., 1999; mem. arbitration panel U.S. Dist. Ct. (ea. dist.) N.Y., 1986—; mem. comml. and constrn. panels Am. Arbitration Assn., 1972-94; dir. civil rights Washington Lawyers Com., 1996-99; mem. bd. advisors D.C. Bar Found., 1996—; treas., bd. dirs. Pro Bono Inst., 1997—. Contbr. articles to legal jours. Trustee Mex.-Am. Legal Def. and Edn. Fund, 1986-90, chmn. program and planning com., 1988-90; adv. com. to task force on racial, gender and minority discrimination U.S. Ct. Appeals for 2d Circuit, 1994-96; bd. dirs. Appleseed Found., Inc., 1997-97, chmn. legal com., 1999—. Recipient Lester Zazuly medal, 1958, Columbia Coll. Alumni Achievement award, 1961, Edward Foxx prize Columbia Coll., 1961, Maldef Corp. Responsibility award, 1993, Valerie J. Kantor award for extraordinary achievement, 1997, Am. Immigration Law Found. hon. fellow and Founder's award, 1989, Lifetime Achievement award Ctr. for Human Rights and Constl. Law, 1993. Fellow Am. Bar. Found. (life), ABA (ho. of dels. 1983—, chmn. com. on immigration sect. litigation 1985-90, immigration pro bono adv. task force, 1992-98, vice chmn., 1995-96, mem. coordinating com. on immigration law 1984-87, chmn. 1989-92, mem. com. environ. controls sect. banking, 1983-86, vice chmn. com. on constrn., sec. gen. practice 1989-90, mem. standing com. lawyers pub. svc. responsibility 1993-96, mem. coun. fund justice & edn. 1994-99, chmn. major gifts com. 1997-98, Pro Bono award 1992); mem. Internat. Bar Assn. (chmn. Sect. Gen. Practice com. bus. migration 1987-88), N.Y. State Bar Assn., Assn. Bar City of N.Y. (com. on trademarks and unfair competition 1983-86, com. immigration 1986-89, com. on profl. and jud. ethics 1989-92, com. Human Rights Law 1994-96), Nat. Assn. Criminal Def. Lawyers (co-chmn. com. on immigration 1988-90), Am. Judicature Soc. (life), Am. Bar Endowment, Nat. Conf. Bar Presidents (assoc.), Am. Immigration Lawyers Assn. (pres. 1982-83, bd. govs. 1971—, chmn. N.Y. chpt. 1971-72, gen. counsel 1986-91, liaison to ABA commn. on nonlawyer practice 1993-94, editor Ann. Symposium Handbook 1985-88, assoc. editor 1989-90, Edith Lowenstein Meml. award 1981, Pro Bono award 1992), Am. Mgmt. Assn., Fed. Bar Assn., Fed. Bar Coun., N.Y. County Lawyers Assn. (reporter N.Y. Equitable Distribution Law Proposals 1968, bd. dirs. 1996-98), Def. Rsch. Inst., N.Y. Criminal Bar Assn., N.Y. State Trial Lawyers Assn., Assn. Profl. Responsibility Lawyers, Cow Neck Peninsula Hist. Soc. (life), Italy and Colonies Philatelic Soc. of Gt. Brit. (life), Jack Knight Soc. (life), L.I. Postal History Soc. (life), Am. Helvetia Philatelic Soc. (life), City Club (Washington), Columbia Club, India House Club, Continental Club, Alpha Epsilon Pi. Home: 106 Hemlock Rd Manhasset NY 11030-1214 Office: Fried Frank Harris Shriver & Jacobson 1 New York Plz Ste 2500 New York NY 10004-1901

JUCHATZ, WAYNE WARREN, lawyer; b. N.Y.C., June 25, 1946; s. Warren Carl and Margaret E. (Trafford) J.; m. Linda K. Wilson, June 21, 1969; children: Bradley T., Scott W. BA, Franklin & Marshall Coll., 1968; JD, U. Va., 1974. Bar: N.Y. 1975, N.C. 1985. Assoc. Cadwalader, Wickersham & Taft, N.Y.C., 1974-77; asst. counsel R.J. Reynolds Industries Inc., Winston-Salem, N.C., 1977-79, assoc. counsel, 1979-80, sr. assoc. counsel, 1980-81; asst. gen. counsel R.J. Reynolds Tobacco Co., Winston-Salem, 1981-84, dep. gen. counsel, 1984-85, v.p., sec., gen. counsel, 1986-87, sr. v.p., sec., gen. counsel, 1987-93, exec. v.p., gen. counsel, 1993-95; exec. v.p., gen. counsel Textron Inc., Providence, 1995—. Served with U.S. Army, 1969-71. Office: Textron Inc 40 Westminster St Providence RI 02903-2525

JUCKEM, WILFRED PHILIP, manufacturing company executive; b. Sheboygan, Wis., Apr. 27, 1915; s. Arvin M. and Martha (Henning) J.; m. Dorothy Iris Dean, Dec. 8, 1941; children—Jean Audrey, Philip Dean. Grad., Sheboygan Bus. Coll., 1934. With Jenkins Machine Co., Sheboygan Falls, Wis., 1933-34, Kohler of Kohler, Wis., 1934-42, Rock Island (Ill.) Arsenal, 1942-45; with Eagle Signal Corp., Moline, Ill., 1947-63; v.p. mfg. Eagle Signal Corp., 1958-63; asst. to pres. E.W. Bliss Co., Canton, Ohio, 1963-64; adminstrv. v.p. E.W. Bliss Co., 1964-66, v.p. press div., 1966-67, v.p. corporate devel., 1967-68; v.p., div. mgr. E.W. Bliss Co. (Eagle Signal div.), 1968-77; chmn. bd. Sears Mfg. Co., Davenport, Iowa, 1977-86; dir. Long Mfg. N.C. Chmn. bd. dirs. Davenport Osteo. Hosp., 1969-80, chmn., 1980-82; bd. dirs. Ridgecrest Retiremenet Village, 1969-87. Chmn. bd. dirs. Davenport Osteo. Hosp., 1979-80, chmn., 1980-82; bd. dirs. Ridgecrest Retirement Village. Recipient Honorary Alumnus award St. Ambrose Coll., Davenport. Mem. Nat. Elec. Mfrs. Assn. (chmn. emeritus traffic control systems sect. 1972-77), Am. Ordnance Assn. (pres. Iowa-Ill. chpt. 1975-76), Asso. Employers Quad Cities (dir., past pres.). Lutheran. Home: Ridgecrest Village C-1 4130 Northwest Blvd Davenport IA 52806-4243

JUDA, RICHARD JOHN, anesthesiologist; b. Glastonbury, Conn., Aug. 12, 1967; s. Richard Joseph and Frances Ann (Urbansky) J. Student, Stonehill Coll., North Easton, Mass., 1985-86; BS in Biology/Health Sci., U. Hartford, 1989; cert. paramedic, Mohegan Cmty. Coll., Norwich, Conn., 1990; postgrad., Ctrl. Conn. State U., 1990-91; MD, St. George's U., Grenada, 1996. Cert. ACLS instr., Advanced Trauma Life Support, Pediatric Advanced Trauma Life Support. Intern U. Conn., 1996-97, resident in surgery, 1997-99, resident in anesthesia, 1999—; asst. faculty dept. EMS edn. Hartford Hosp., 1990—, rsch. asst., 1986-91, 93-94; physician asst. Kingstown Med. Coll.-Kingstown Gen. Hosp., St. Vincent, W.I., 1993, Simon Bolivar Clin.-St. George's U. Sch. Med., 1992-93; presenter in field; med. cons. Glastonbury Fire Dept. Contbr. articles to profl. jours. Polish Nat. Alliance scholar, 1986-89, Geoffrey H. Bourne Meml. scholar, 1991-96. Mem. AMA, Am. Med. Student Assn., Nat. Assn. Grad. and Profl. Students, Internat. Trauma Anesthesia and Critical Care Soc. Roman Catholic. Home: 24 Stony Brook Dr Unit 3A Glastonbury CT 06033-1621

JUDD, BRIAN RAYMOND, physicist, educator; b. Chelmsford, Eng., Feb. 13, 1931; s. Harry and Edith (Saltmarsh) J. B.A., Brasenose Coll., Oxford U., 1952, M.A., 1955, D.Phil., 1955. Fellow Magdalen Coll., Oxford U., 1955-62; instr. U. Chgo., 1957-58; assoc. prof. U. Paris, 1962-64; staff mem. Lawrence Radiation Lab., Berkeley, Calif., 1964-66; prof. physics Johns Hopkins U., Balt., 1966-96, chmn. dept., 1979-84; Gerhard H. Dieke prof. Johns Hopkins U., 1992-96, prof. emeritus, 1997-98, Gerhard H. Dieke prof. emeritus, 1998—; vis. Erskine fellow U. Canterbury, Christchurch, New Zealand, 1968; vis. fellow Australian Nat. U., Canberra, 1975; hon. fellow Brasenose Coll., Oxford U., 1983—. Author: Operator Techniques in Atomic Spectroscopy, 1963, reprinted, 1998, Second Quantization and Atomic Spectroscopy, 1967, (with J.P. Elliott) Topics in Atomic and Nuclear Theory, 1970, Angular Momentum Theory For Diatomic Molecules, 1975. Recipient Spedding award for rare-earth rsch. Rhône-Poulenc, Inc., 1988. Fellow Am. Phys. Soc. Office: Johns Hopkins U Dept Physics and Astronomy Baltimore MD 21218

JUDD, BURKE HAYCOCK, geneticist; b. Kanab, Utah, Sept. 5, 1927; s. Zadok Ray and Elva (Haycock) J.; m. Barbara Ann Gaddy, Mar. 21, 1953; children: Sean Michael, Evan Patrick, Timothy Burke. BS, U. Utah, 1950, MS, 1951; PhD, Calif. Inst. Tech., 1954. Postdoctoral fellow Am. Cancer Soc. U. Tex., Austin, 1954-56; from instr. to prof. U. Tex., 1956-79, dir. Genetics Inst., 1977-79; geneticist Atomic Energy Commn., Germantown, Md., 1968-69; chief lab. genetics Nat. Inst. Environ. Health Sci., Research Triangle Park, N.C., 1979-95; vis. asst. prof. Stanford U., Palo Alto, Calif., 1960; Gosney vis. prof. Calif. Inst. Tech., Pasadena, 1975-76; adj. prof. U. N.C., Chapel Hill, 1979—, Duke U., Durham, 1980—; mem. panel genetic biology NSF, Washington, 1969-73, genetics study sect. NIH, Washington, 1974, 77, 79, 88, com. on germplasm resources NAS, Washington, 1976-77; chmn. human genome initiative rev. panel Dept. of Energy, Washington, 1988. Author: Introduction to Modern Genetics, 1980; editor: Molecular and Gen. Genetics, 1986-95; assoc. editor Genetics, 1973-78; contbr. articles to profl. jours. With U.S. Army, 1946-47. Fellow AAAS; mem. Am. Soc. Naturalists (sec. 1968-70), Genetic Soc. Am. (sec. 1974-76, v.p., pres. 1979-80). Avocations: travel, poetry, fiction. Home: 411 Clayton Rd Chapel Hill NC 27514-7613

JUDD, DENNIS L., lawyer; b. Provo, Utah, June 27, 1954; s. Derrel Wesley and Leila (Lundquist) J.; m. Carol Lynne Chilberg, May 6, 1977; children: Lynne Marie, Amy Jo, Tiffany Ann, Andrew, Jacquelyn Nicole. BA in Polit. Sci. summa cum laude, Brigham Young U., 1978, JD, 1981. Bar: Utah 1981, U.S. Dist. Ct. Utah 1981. Assoc. Nielson & Senior, Salt Lake City and Vernal, Utah, 1981-83; dep. county atty. Uintah County, Vernal, 1982-84; ptnr. Bennett & Judd, Vernal, 1983-88; county atty. Daggett County, Utah, 1985-89, 91-99; pvt. practice Vernal, 1988—; county atty. Daggett County, 1991-99; prosecutor City of Naples, Naples, 1996-99; city atty. City of Naples, 1999—, CIty of Naples, 1999—; legal counsel Uintah County Sch. Dist., 1996—; mem. governing bd. Uintah Basin applied Tech. Ctr., 1991-95, v.p., 1993-94, pres., 1994-95. Chmn. bd. adjustment Zoning and Planning Bd., Naples, 1982-91, 94—; mem. Naples City Coun., 1982-91; mayor pro tem City of Naples, 1983-91; legis. v.p. Naples PTA, 1988-90; v.p. Uintah Dist. PTA Coun., 1990-92; mem. resolution com. Utah League Cities and Towns, 1985-86, small cities com., 1985-86; trustee Uintah Sch. Dist. Found., 1988-97, vice chmn., 1991-93; mem. Uintah County Sch. Dist. Bd. Edn., 1991-95, v.p., 1991-92, pres., 1992-95; chmn. Uintah County Rep. Conv., 1998. Hinkley scholar Brigham Young U., 1977. Mem. Utah Bar Assn., Uintah Basin Bar Assn., Statewide Assn. Prosecutors, Vernal C. of C. Republican. Mormon. Avocations: hunting, photography, lapidary. Home: 460 E 1555 S Naples UT 84078 Office: 461 W 200 S Vernal UT 84078-3049

JUDD, JACQUELINE DEE (JACKIE JUDD), journalist, reporter; b. Johnstown, Pa., Nov. 29, 1952; 2 children. BA in Journalism and Polit. Sci., Am. U., 1973. Reporter WKXL Radio, Concord, N.H., 1974-75, WBAL Radio, Balt., 1975-76; reporter, anchor All Things Considered, Morning Edit., Nat. Pub. Radio, Washington, 1976-82; news anchor, reporter, anchor CBS Radio, N.Y.C., 1982-87; reporter ABC TV, Washington, 1987—. Recipient Overseas Press Club citation Overseas Press Club, N.Y.C., 1989, Emmy award Am. Acad. Arts and Scis., N.Y.C., 1990, 96, Lodestar award Am. U., 1993, Dupont award, 1994, Joan Barone award, Headliner award. Mem. Radio TV Corr. Assocs. of Capital Hill (exec. com. 1993-96), Am. Fedn. Radio and TV Artists. Office: ABC News Washington Bur 1717 Desales St NW Washington DC 20036-4407

JUDD, JAMES, performing company executive. Grad., Trinity Coll. Music, London. Asst. conductor Cleve. Orch.; assoc. music dir. European Cmty. Youth Orch., artistic dir.; conductor Berlin Philharmonic, Israel Philharmonic; music dir. Fla. Philharmonic, 1987—; guest conductor Vienna Symphony, Gewandhaus Orch., Leipzig, Germany, Prague Symphony Orch., Orch. Nat. France, Orch. Suisse Romande, Nat. Arts Ctr. Orch. Ottawa, Cin. Symphony, NHK Symphony Tokyo, Mozarteum Orch., others; co-founder Chamber Orch. Europe. Office: Fla Philharmonic Orch 3401 NW 9th Ave Fort Lauderdale FL 33309-5914

JUDD, LEWIS LUND, psychiatrist, educator; b. L.A., Feb. 10, 1930; s. George E. and Emmeline (Lund) J.; B.S., U. Utah, 1954; M.D. cum laude, UCLA, 1956; m. Patricia Ann Hoffman, Jan. 26, 1974; children by previous marriage: Allison Clark, Catherine Anne, Stephanie. Intern, UCLA Sch. Medicine, 1958-59, resident in psychiatry, 1959-60, 62-64, fellow in child psychiatry, 1964-65, asst. prof. depts. psychiatry and psychology, 1965-70, dir. edn., child and adolescent psychiatry dept. psychiatry, 1968; asso. prof. psychiatry U. Calif. at San Diego, La Jolla, 1970, vice chmn., dir. clin. programs dept. psychiatry, 1970-73, dir. drug abuse programs, 1970-73, prof., from 1973, acting chmn. dept., 1974, co-chmn., 1975-77, chmn., 1977—; dir. NIMH, 1988—; chief psychiat. service San Diego VA Hosp., La Jolla, 1972-77; chief psychiat. service U. Calif. Med. Center, San Diego, from 1982, pres. med. staff, chmn. exec. com., from 1982; mem. adv. com. on evaluation drug abuse programs County of San Diego, 1970-73; chmn. clin. projects rev. com. NIMH, 1975-79; guest faculty San Diego Psychoanalytic Inst. Served to capt., M.C., USAF, 1960-62. Fellow Am. Psychiat. Assn.; mem. Soc. Neuroscis., Psychiat. Research Soc., Assn. Acad. Psychiatry, Soc. Research in Child Devel., Am. Coll. Neuropsychopharmacology, So. Calif., San Diego psychiat. socs., Am. Assn. Chmn. Depts. Psychiatry, Alpha Omega Alpha. Contbr. articles to med. jours. Home: 1367 Via Alta Del Mar CA 92014-2546 Office: Univ Calif San Diego 9500 Gilman Dr La Jolla CA 92093-5003*

JUDD, MARJORIE LOIS, librarian, consultant; b. Presque Isle, Maine, Nov. 5, 1938; d. Mallard L. Nelson and Charlotte Wallin; m. Robert N. Judd, Dec. 27, 1962 (div. June 1980); children: Diana, Jocelyn. BA, Upsala Coll., 1961; MLS, U. Pitts., 1977. Children's libr. Brockton (Mass.) Pub. Libr., 1977-78, Stoughton (Mass.) Pub. Libr., 1978-85; libr. dir. Middleborough (Mass.) Pub. Libr., 1985—. Mem. Downtown Revitalization Com., Middleborough, 1995-97, Sch. Adv. Coun., Middleborough, 1997—; trustee Mass. Archeol. Soc., Middleborough, 1997—. Recipient Cmty Svc. award Middleborough Edn. Assn., 1989, Cmty. Leadership award Cranberry Country Ch. Comm., 1995. Mem. ALA, New Eng. Libr. Assn., Mass. Libr. Assn. (pres. elect 1996-97, pres. 1997-98, past pres. 1998-99), Beta Phi Mu. Democrat. Lutheran. Avocations: hiking, swimming. E-mail: marjorie@tmlp.com. Office: Middleborough Pub Libr 102 N Main St Middleboro MA 02346

JUDD, O'DEAN P., physicist; b. Austin, Minn., May 26, 1937. MS in Physics, UCLA, 1961, PhD in Physics, 1968. Staff physicist and project dir. Hughes Rsch. Lab., Malibu, Calif., 1959-67; postdoctoral fellow UCLA Dept. Physics, 1968-69; researcher Hughes Rsch. Lab., Malibu, Calif., 1969-72; researcher, group leader Los Alamos Nat. Lab., 1972-82, chief scientist for def. rsch. and applications, 1981-87; chief scientist Strategic Def. Initiative Orgn., Washington, 1987-90; energy and environ. chief scientist, lab. fellow Los Alamos (N.Mex.) Nat. Lab., 1990-93; nat. intelligence officer for sci. and tech. Nat. Intelligence Coun., Washington, 1993-94; tech. advisor and cons. Los Alamos, 1994-95, ind. tech. advisor, cons., 1995—; mem. numerous govt. coms. related to sci. and tech., def. and nat. security policy adv. com. to SDIO, 1990-93; adj. prof. of physics U. N.Mex., Albuquerque. Patentee in sci. and tech.; contbr. numerous articles to sci. and def.-related jours. Fellow IEEE, AAAS, Inst. Advanced Engring.; mem. Am. Phys. Soc. Office: Los Alamos Nat Lab MS F650 Los Alamos NM 87544-2648

JUDD, RICHARD LOUIS, academic administrator; b. Bridgeport, Conn., Mar. 22, 1937; s. Wilbur Franklin and Priscilla (Nagy) J.; m. Nancy Ruth Fox, Nov. 30, 1963; children: Sarah, Jonathan. BS with honors, Cen. Conn. State U., 1959; MA, Ohio State U., 1961; PhD, U. Conn., 1971. Prof. emergency med. scis. Ctrl. Conn. State U., New Britain, 1992—, v.p., 1992-96; pres. Ctrl. Conn. State U., New Britain, 1996—; vis. exec. Am. Coun. Edn., USDA, 1981; mem. adv. com. United Tech. Corp., 1994—; chmn. devel. adv. com. Pratt and Whitney, 1994; bd. dirs. New Britain Gen. Hosp. Sr. author: First Responder 3rd edit., 1994, Geriatric Emergencies, 1986. Commr. New Britain Police Dept., 1981-89, 93-95; chmn. Conn. Adv. Bd. EMS, 1992-97; campaign chmn. United Community Svcs., New Britain, 1987-88, pres., 1990-92, Verdienstkreuz, Fed. Republic of Germany, 1990; chmn. New Britain Mus. Am. Art, 1993—. Demi fellow, 1970; named Citizen of Yr., 1990. Home: 119 Ten Acre Rd New Britain CT 06052-1531 Office: Cen Conn State U 1615 Stanley St New Britain CT 06050-2439*

JUDD, THOMAS ELI, electrical engineer; b. Salt Lake City, Apr. 12, 1927; s. Henry Eli Judd and Jennie Meibos; m. Mary Lu Edman, June 21, 1948; children: Shauna, Kirk E., Blake E., Lisa. BSEE, U. Utah, 1950. Registered profl. engr., Utah. Mech. engr. Utah Power & Light Co., Salt Lake City, 1950-55; chief engr. Electronic Motor Car Corp., Salt Lake City, 1955-56, Equi-Tech Corp., Salt Lake City, 1978-79; hydraulic devel. engr. Galigher Co., Salt Lake City, 1956-58; pres. Toran Corp., Salt Lake City, 1958-71, T M Industries, Salt Lake City, 1971-78; chief exec. officer, mgr. Ramos Corp., Salt Lake City, 1979—; project cons. Eimco Corp., Salt Lake City, 1966; design cons. to tech. cos. Patentee in fields in U.S. and fgn. countries; contbr. editor U.S. Rail News, 1982—. Cons. Nat. Fedn. Ind. Bus., 1983—. With USNR, 1945-46, PTO. Mem. Tau Beta Pi. Republican. Mormon. Avocation: flying. Office: Ramos Corp 956 Elm Ave Salt Lake City UT 84106-2330

JUDD, WILLIAM ROBERT, engineering geologist, educator; b. Denver, Aug. 16, 1917; s. Samuel and Lillian (Israelske) J.; m. Rachel Elizabeth Douglas, Apr. 18, 1942; children: Stephanie (Mrs. Chris Wadley), Judith (Mrs. John Soden), Dayna (Mrs. Erick Grandmason), Pamela, Connie. A.B., U. Colo., 1941, postgrad., 1941-50. Registered profl. engr., Colo., engring. geologist, Oreg., Ind. Engring. geologist Colo. Water Conservation Bd., 1941-42; supervisory engring. geologist Denver & Rio Grande Western R.R., Colo. and Utah, 1942-44; head geology sect. No. 1, acting dist. geologist-Alaska U.S. Bur. Reclamation, Office of Chief Engr., Denver, 1945-60; head basing tech. group RAND Corp., Santa Monica, Calif., 1960-65; prof. rock mechanics Purdue U., Lafayette, Ind., 1966-87; head geotech. engring.

Purdue U., 1976-86; tech. dir. Purdue U. Underground Excavation and Rock Properties Info. Center, 1972-79, prof. emeritus civil engring., 1988—; Geotech. cons., U.S., Mexico, Cuba, Honduras, Greece, 1950—; geoscience editor Am. Elsevier Pub. Co., 1967-71; chmn. panel on ocean scis. Com. on Instl. Cooperation, 1971-85; founder and chmn. Nat. Acad. Sci. U.S. Nat. Com. on Rock Mechanics, 1963-69, co-chmn. panel on research requirements, 1977-81, chmn. panel on awards, 1972-82; mem. U.S. Army Adv. Bd. on Mountain and Arctic Warfare, 1956-62, USAF Sci. Adv. Bd. Geophysics Panel Study Group, 1964-67; mem. com. on safety dams NRC, 1977-78, 82-83; Nat. dir. Nat. Ski Patrol System, Inc., 1956-62; Alex du Toit Meml. lectr., S.Africa, 1967; owner Rayanbill Galleries, 1986—. Author: (with E.F. Taylor) Ski Patrol Manual, 1956, (with D. Krynine) Principles of Engineering Geology and Geotechnics, 1957, Sitzmarks or Safety, 1960; editor: Rock Mechanics research, 1966, State of Stress in the Earth's crust, 1964; co-editor: Physical Properties of Rocks and Minerals, 1981; editor-in-chief: Engring. Geology, 1972-92, hon. editor, 1996—. Recipient Spl. Rsch. award NRC, 1982; named to Colo. Ski Hall of Fame, 1983; named hon. life mem. Nat. Ski Patrol System, Inc., 1988. Fellow ASCE, Geol. Soc. Am. (Disting. Practice award engring. geology divsn. 1989), South African Inst. Mining and Metallurgy; mem. Assn. Engring. Geologists (hon. 1990), Internat. Assn. Engring. Geologists (Hans Cloos medal 1994), Ind. Soc. Engring. Geology (life), U.S. Com. on Large Dams (exec. coun. 1977-83, com. on earthquakes 1976-90), U.S. Ski Assn. (hon. life), U.S. Recreational Ski Assn. (hon. life). Home and Office: 10 Elder Ct Lafayette IN 47905-3921 *Are you important? Take your thumb out of a bowl of water, then measure the hole it left.*

JUDD, WYNONNA, vocalist, musician; b. 1964; d. Naomi Judd; children: Elijah, Grace. Mem. country and western mus. duo The Judds; now pursuing solo career; songs include Had a Dream, 1983, Mama, He's Crazy, 1984, Why Not Me, 1984, Love Is Alive, 1985, Have Mercy, 1985, Rockin' with the Rhythm, 1985, Grandpa, 1986, She Is His Only Need, 1992, No One Else on Earth, 1992, Only Love, 1993, To Be Loved By Uou, 1996; albums include The Judds, Why Not Me?, Rockin' with the Rhythm, Christmas Time with the Judds, Heartland, 1987, Greatest Hits, 1988, River of Time, 1989, Love Can Build a Bridge, 1990, Wynonna, 1992, Tell Me Wy, 1993, Revelations, 1996, Collection, 1997, The Other Side, 1997; co-author: (with Naomi Judd) Love Can Build a Bridge, 1993. Recipient Grammy award, 1985, 86, 87, 89, duet award (with Naomi Judd), Acad. Country Music award, 1985-91, Vocal Duo award (with Naomi Judd), Country Music Assn. award, 1984-91, 4 Grammy nominations, Best Country Artist and Best Country Single awards Billboard, 1992, Acad. Country Music award for Top Female Artist, 1994. Address: Mercury Nashville 66 Music Sq W Nashville TN 37203-4322*

JUDELL, CYNTHIA KOLBURNE, craft company executive; b. N.Y.C., Mar. 23, 1924; d. Luma L. and Stella E. (Robins) Kolburne; m. Samuel Judell, Oct. 30, 1949; children: Joy C., Neil H.K. BSEE, Antioch Coll., Yellow Springs, Ohio, 1945; MA, Columbia U., 1948. Cert. secondary tchr. Engr., Jet Propulsion Lab., Pasadena, Calif., 1946-47; tchr. math., sci. Leonard Sch. for Girls, N.Y.C., 1948-49; substitute tchr. Bd. Edn., Ridgefield, Conn., 1964-67; part-time tchr. Bd. Edn., Brookfield, Conn., 1967-73; owner T W M Enterprises, Wilton, Conn., 1976-97, retired, 1997. Dep. registrar of voters Town of Wilton , 1977-93; elected mem. Bd. of Tax Rev., Wilton, 1980-87; treas. Town Assn., Inc., Wilton, 1980-84. Recipient Intergroup scholar Columbia U., 1948. Mem. LWV (budget chair, treas. Conn. chpt. 1978-86, treas. Wilton chpt. 1986-88), Conn. Soc. Women Engrs. (treas. 1971-72).

JUDELL, HAROLD BENN, lawyer; b. Milw., Mar. 9, 1915; s. Philip Fox and Lena Florence (Krause) J.; m. Maria Violeta van Ronzelen, May 5, 1951 (div.); m. Celeste Seymour Grulich, June 24, 1986. BA, U. Wis., 1936, JD, 1938; LLB, Tulane U., 1950. Bar: Wis. 1938, La. 1950. Mem. Scheinfeld Collins Durant & Winter, Milw., 1938; spl. agt., adminstrv. asst. to dir. FBI, 1939-44; legal attache U.S. Embassy Peru Dauphine Orleans Hotel Corp., 1939-44; ptnr. Foley & Judell, LLP, New Orleans, 1950—; v.p., dir. Dauphine Orleans Hotel Corp., 1970—; mem. Tulane U. Bus. Sch. Coun.; trustee Greater New Orleans YMCA, 1981—. Fellow Am. Coll. Bond Counsel (founding); mem. ABA, La. Bar Assn., Nat. Assn. Bond Lawyers (bd. dirs., pres. 1984-85), New Orleans Country Club, Lawn Tennis Club, Met. Club (N.Y.C.). Office: Foley & Judell 365 Canal St New Orleans LA 70130-1112

JUDELSON, DAVID N., company executive; b. Hackensack, N.J., Nov. 22, 1928; s. Oscar I. Judelson; m. Maria Olivia Guerra; children: Paul Allan, Jeaneane Maria, Roy Andrew. BSME, NYU, 1949. Chief engr. Judelson Industries, Randolph, N.J., 1949-51, pres., COO, 1951-55, chmn., CEO, 1955-80; dir. John Dusenbery Co. (formerly Judelson Industries), Randolph, N.J., 1980-98; co-founder Gulf & Western-Paramount Communications, N.Y.C., 1958—, pres., COO, 1967-83; co-founder, vice chmn. Biopure Corp., Boston, 1984—; vice chmn. Horsehead Industries, N.Y.C., 1985—; now dir. Horsehead Industries; bd. dirs. Horsehead Resource and Devel. Co., N.Y.C., 1985—; mem. nat. adv. bd. Chem. Bank, N.Y.C., 1967-96. 1st lt. C.E., U.S. Army Res., 1949-71.

JUDERNATZ, MARY SEEGERS, artist; b. Vero Beach, Fla., Mar. 24, 1939; d. Edward Barnes and Mary Mercedes (Burgner) Seegers; m. Manfred Friedrich Judernatz, April 1, 1978 (div. Jan. 1992). BA in Philosophy, Siena Heights Coll., 1964. Cert. tchr., Fla. Tchr., Dominican nun elem. schs., Ft. Pierce and Melbourne, Fla., 1959-64, Aiken, S.C., 1959-64; commd. USAF, 1966, advanced through grades to capt., 1970, resigned, 1972; asst. adminstrv. svcs. officer Eglin AFB, Fla., 1966-68; WAF tng. officer Officer Tng. Sch. Tex., 1968-69; WAF squadron comdr. Lackland AFB, Tex., 1969-70; chief adminstrv. svcs., 1970-72; draftsperson elec., civil Elec. Power Co., Shreveport, La., 1972-78, Schemmer Assoc., Omaha, 1972-78; calligrapher Miami, 1979-89; artist Franklin, N.C., 1989—; instr. John C. Campbell Folk Sch., Brasstown, N.C., 1992—. One woman shows include Fine Arts Ctr., Ft. Tryon, N.C., 1994; group shows in Highlands, N.C., 1997, Denver, 1989, Asheville, N.C., 1990, Winston-Salem, N.C., 1992, 93, 95, Atlanta, 1996. Delivery person Meals on Wheels, Franklin, N.C., 1989-92; music camp 1st Presbyn. Ch., Franklin, 1997. Named Emerging Artist by Am. Artist mag., 1989. Mem. Southeastern Pastel Soc., Art League of Highland, Franklin Women's Club. Avocations: photography, music, gardening. Home and Office: Judernatz Studio 17 Grandview Dr Franklin NC 28734-2617

JUDGE, BERNARD MARTIN, editor, publisher; b. Chgo., Jan. 6, 1940; s. Bernard A. and Catherine Elizabeth (Halloran) J.; m. Kimbeth A. Wehrli, July 9, 1966; children: Kelly, Bernard R., Jessica. Reporter City News Bur., Chgo., 1965-66; reporter Chgo. Tribune, 1966-72, city editor, 1974-79, asst. mng. editor met. news, 1979-83; editor, gen. mgr. City News Bur. Chgo., 1983-84; assoc. editor Chgo. Sun-Times, 1984-88; editor Chgo. Daily Law Bull., 1988—; pub. Chgo. Lawyer, 1989—; v.p. Law Bull. Pub. Co., Chgo., 1988—. Bd. dirs. Constnl. Rights Found., Chgo., 1992—, chmn. bd. dirs., 1995-97; trustee Fenwick Cath. Prep. H.S., Oak Park, Ill., 1989—. Mem. Sigma Delta Chi. Home: 360 E Randolph St Apt 1905 Chicago IL 60601-7335 Office: Law Bull Pub Co 415 N State St Chicago IL 60610-4631

JUDGE, CHARLES ARTHUR, academic administrator; b. Ames, Iowa, Feb. 19, 1940; s. Frank E. and Florence I. (Ivis) J.; m. Judith Ann Wolf, Aug. 25, 1973; children: Kathryn Elizabeth, Margaret Helen. BBA, U. Mich., 1962, MA, 1964, PhD, 1980. Dir. fin. aid, asst. dean men Lawrence U., Appleton, Wis., 1966-69; asst. dir. admissions Harvard Bus. Sch., Boston, 1969-71; asst. dir. Lit., Sci., Arts acad. advising U. Mich., Ann Arbor, 1972-75, dir. Lit., Sci., Arts acad. advising, 1975-95, dir. Lit., Sci., Arts acad. stds., 1995—. Chair Washtenaw County Cmty. Mental Health Bd., Ann Arbor, 1982-84. Mem. Nat. Acad. Advising Assn. Home: 1500 Barnard Rd Ann Arbor MI 48103-5928 Office: U Mich LSA Advising Ctr 1255 Angell Hall Ann Arbor MI 48109

JUDGE, DOLORES BARBARA, real estate broker; b. Plymouth, Pa.; m. Richard James Judge; children: Susan, Nancy, Richard Jr. Student, North Harris County Coll., 1984-85, U. Tex., 1985, Houston Community Coll., 1988-89. Real estate agt. comml. real estate cos. in area, 1981-84; owner D-J Investment Properties, Conroe, Tex., 1984—; pres. Judge Real Estate, 1996—; pres., ptnr. J&M Mgmt. Co., 1996-97; pres. Judge Mgmt. Co., 1997—; mem. first adv. bd. First Nat. Title Co., Conroe, 1989-90. Chmn. North Houston Econ. Devel. Showcase, 1990; bd. dirs. Montgomery County Crime Stoppers, Inc., 1993—. Mem. Conroe C. of C., Comml. Real Estate Assn. Montgomery County (pres. 1986, 87, bd. dirs. 1988). Avocations: golf, travel, computers, reading. Office: D-J Investment Properties 306 Tara Park Conroe TX 77302-3756

JUDGE, MARTY M., lawyer; b. Neptune, N.J., Mar. 1, 1952; s. Marcel Armond and Vivian Patricia (Sumner) J.; m. Theresa Frances Stroczynski, June 20, 1976. BA with honors, Rutgers Coll., 1975, JD with honors, 1978. Bar: N.J. 1978, Pa. 1984. Law clk. to Hon. Milton B. Conford Asbury Park, N.J., 1978-79; assoc. Smith, Stratton, Wise, Heher & Brennan, Princeton, N.J., 1979-84; dep. atty. gen. State of N.J., Trenton, 1984-88; ptnr. Stryker, Tams & Dill, Newark, 1988-92, Drinker Biddle & Reath LLP, Princeton, 1992—. Co-author: Environmental Dispute Handbook, 1991; contbr. articles to profl. jours. Mem. ABA, N.J. State Bar Assn. Episcopalian. Avocations: tennis, bicycling, French lang. and lit., skiing. Office: Drinker Biddle & Reath LLP 105 College Rd E Princeton NJ 08540-6622

JUDGE, MIKE, animator; b. Guayaquil, Ecuador, Oct. 17, 1962; m. Francesca Morocco, 1989; 2 children. BA in Phys. Sci., U. Calif., San Diego, 1985. Creator (TV series) Beavis and Butt-head, 1993—; (film) Beavis and Butt-head Do America, 1996; co-prodr. (TV series) King of the Hill, 1997—. Office: King of the Hill Watt Plaza 1875 Century Park E Fl 4 Los Angeles CA 90067-2501*

JUDGE, NANCY ELIZABETH, obstetrician, gynecologist; b. Holyoke, Mass., May 21, 1951; d. Martin P. and Barbara Judge; m. David B. Wood, Oct. 30, 1982; children: David, William, Elizabeth, Meredith. AB, Smith Coll., 1973; MD, U. Mass., 1977. Intern Case Western Res. U./MetroHealth Med. Ctr., Cleve., 1977-78, resident, 1978-81; staff physician MetroHealth Med. Ctr. Case Western Res. U. Hosps., Cleve., 1981-90; dir. reproductive imaging ctr. Case Western Res. U. Hosps., 1990—, maternal-fetal medicine cons., 1990—; asst. prof. reproductive biology Case Western Res. U., 1981—; obstetrical advisor Regional Perinatal Network, Cleve., 1990—. Contbr. articles to profl. jours. Active Cleve. Art Mus., Playhouse Sq. Assn., Cleve. Garden Ctr. Fellow Am. Coll. Ob.-Gyn.; mem. Cleve. Ob.-Gyn. Soc. (asst. treas. 1994-95, treas. 1995—). Office: Case Western Res U Hosp Dept Ob-Gyn 1100 Euclid Ave Ste 1200 Cleveland OH 44115-1603

JUDGE, ROSEMARY ANN, oil company executive; b. Jersey City; d. Frank T. and Frances M. (O'Brien) J. A.B., Seton Hall U. Exec. sec. Socony Vacuum, N.Y.C., 1944-56; sec., confidential asst. to v.p. and dir. Socony Mobil, N.Y.C., 1956-59; sec., confidential asst. to pres. Mobil Oil Co. Div., N.Y.C., 1959-61; sec., adminstrv. asst. to pres. Mobil Oil Corp., N.Y.C., 1961-69; adminstrv. asst. to chmn. Mobil Oil Corp., 1969-71, asst. to chmn., sec. exec com., 1971-84, corp. sec., 1975-76; asst. to chmn., sec. bd. and exec. com. Mobil Corp., 1976-84; pres. Mobil Found., N.Y.C., 1973-85. Mem. bd. regents Seton Hall U., 1982-88. Club: Women's Econ. Round Table.

JUDICE, MARC WAYNE, lawyer; b. Lafayette, La., Oct. 22, 1946; s. Marc and Gladys B. Judice; m. Anne Keaty; children: Scott, Renee. BS, U. Southwestern La., 1969; MBA, U. Utah, 1974; JD, La. State U., 1977. Bar: La. 1977; CPA, La.; bd. cert. civil trial law, civil trial advocacy Nat. Bd. Trial Advocacy. Ptnr. Voorhies & Labbe, Lafayette, 1977-85, Juneau, Judice, Hill & Adley, Lafayette, 1985-93, Judice & Adley, Lafayette, 1993-94. Bd. dirs. Univ. Med. Ctr., Lafayette, 1991, Home Savs. Bank, Lafayette, 1996—, Women's & Childrens Hosp., Lafayette, 1992-94; bd. trustees Med. Ctr. Southwest La., 1998—, chmn. bd. dirs., 1999—. Republican. Roman Catholic. Office: Judice & Adley 926 Coolidge Blvd Lafayette LA 70503-2434

JUDSON, ARNOLD SIDNEY, management consultant; b. Brockton, Mass., Mar. 29, 1927; s. Moses Joel and Fanny (Becker) J.; m. June Brenner, June 19, 1949; children: Pamela F., Jill E. BS in Chem. Engring., MIT, 1947, MS in Orgnl. Behavior, 1948. Prodn. foreman U.S. Rubber Co., Providence, 1948-50; personnel mgr., mfg. mgr., then dir. tng. and devel. Polaroid Corp., Cambridge, Mass., 1950-62; gen. mgr., mgmt. cons. The Emerson Cons., Ltd., London, 1962-66; sr. mgmt. cons. Arthur D.Little, Inc., Cambridge, 1966-76; dir., mgmt. cons. The Berwick Group, Inc., Boston, 1976-81; pres., chief exec. officer Gray-Judson-Howard, Inc., Cambridge, 1981-90; chmn. Gray-Judson-Howard, Inc., 1990-94; pres. The Judson Co., Inc., 1994—; cons. Exec. Svc. Corps. Author: A Manager's Guide to Making Changes, 1966, Making Strategy Happen, 1990, 2nd edit., 1996, Changing Behavior in Organizations, 1991; contbr. articles to bus. publs.; composer orchestral and chamber music. Chmn. bd. dirs. Greater Boston Rehab. Svcs., Cambridge, 1984—. With USN, 1945-46. Mem. Univ. Club Boston, Falmouth Yacht Club. Home: 220 Marlborough St Boston MA 02116-1749 Office: The Judson Co Inc 220 Marlborough St Apt 4 Boston MA 02116-1771

JUDSON, C(HARLES) JAMES (JIM JUDSON), lawyer; b. Oregon City, Oreg., Oct. 24, 1944; s. Charles James and Barbara (Busch) J.; m. Diana L. Gerlach, Sept. 7, 1965; children: Kevin, Nicole. BA cum laude, Stanford U., 1966, LLB with honors, 1969. Bar: Wash. 1969, U.S. Tax Ct. 1970, D.C. 1981. Ptnr. Davis Wright Tremaine, Seattle, 1969—; v.p. Eagle River, Inc.; speaker various convs. and seminars. Author: State Taxation of Fin. Instns., 1981; contbr. articles to profl. jours. Chmn. Bus. Tax Coalition, Seattle, 1987; chmn. lawyers div. United Way, Seattle, 1986, 87, commerce and industry div., 1989-91; trustee Wash. State Internat. Trade Fair, Seattle, 1981-86; bd. dirs. Seattle Prep. Sch., 1986-88; bd. dirs. Olympic Park Inst., 1988—, Yosemite Nat. Insts., 1993—; mem. Assn. Wash. Bus. Tax Com., 1978—; tax advisor Wash. State House Reps. Dem. Caucus; advisor Wash. State Dept. Revenue on Tax and Legis. Matters; mem. Seattle Tax Group, 1983—. Fellow Am. Coll Tax Counsel; mem. ABA (chmn. com. on fin. orgns. tax sect. 1978-82, subcom chmn. state and local tax com. tax sect. 1979—, chmn. excise tax com. 1983-90, interorgn. coordination com. 1985—, chmn. environ. tax com. 1991—), Wash. State Bar Assn. (chmn. tax sect. 1984-86, chmn. western region IRS/bar liaison com. 1987-88, mem. rules com. 1991—), Seattle-King County Bar Assn. (mem. tax sect. 1973-86), Seattle C. of C. (tax com. 1982—), Wash. Athletic Club (Seattle), Bear Creek Golf Club (Redmond). Avocation: skiing, basketball, wood working, hiking. Office: Davis Wright Tremaine 2600 Century Sq 1501 4th Ave Ste 2600 Seattle WA 98101-1688

JUDSON, FRANKLYN NEVIN, physician, educator; b. Cleve., Apr. 14, 1942; s. Franklyn S. and Nancy Elizabeth (Nevin) J.; m. Kathleen A. Thompson, June 24, 1972 (div. 1977); m. Marti J. Sachse, Dec. 10, 1981; children: Jennifer, Rachel. BA, Wesleyan U., 1964; MD, U. Pa., 1968. Intern U. Wis. Hosps., Madison, 1968-69, resident, 1969-70; epidemic intelligence svc. officer Ctrs. Disease Control, Atlanta, 1970-72; fellow in infectious diseases U. Colo., Denver, 1972-74, from asst. prof. to assoc. prof. depts. medicine and preventive medicine, 1976-87, prof., 1987—; dir. Denver Disease Control Service, 1976-86; chief infectious disease service Denver Gen. Hosp., 1982—; dir. Dept. Pub. Health City of Denver, 1986—; pres. med. staff Denver Health, 1996—; chmn. anti-infective agts. adv. com. FDA, 1993-95. Editor: Diagnosis of Sexually Transmitted Diseases, 1985; assoc. editor Sexually Transmitted Diseases, 1988—; mem. editorial bd. Genitourinary Medicine, 1984-94; contbr. articles to profl. jours. Pres. met. council Colo. chpt. Am. Lung Assn., Denver, 1988-90, bd. dirs.; pres. Coalition for A Tobacco Free Colo., 1995-96. Mem. Am. Veneral Disease Assn. (bd. dirs. 1981—, pres. 1983-85, Outstanding Investigator 1980), Am. Social Health Assn. (bd. dirs. 1983-90, 97—, v.p. 1987), Group Against Smokers' Pollution (bd. dirs., v.p. Colo. chpt. 1982—), Internat. Soc. Sexually Transmitted Diseases Rsch. (pres. 1997—). Soc. of Friends. Avocations: running, skiing, farming. Home: 662 Josephine St Denver CO 80206-3723

JUDSON, HORACE FREELAND, history of science, writer, educator; b. N.Y.C., Apr. 21, 1931; s. Freeland and Harriet Louise (Babcock) J.; m. Ann Schramm, 1953 (div.); children: Grace Louise Judson, Thomas Alexander; m. Penelope Sylvia Jones, Jan. 11, 1969 (dec. May 1993); children: Olivia Phoebe, Nicholas Matthew Freeland. AB, U. Chgo., 1948, postgrad., 1949-52; postgrad., Columbia U., 1962-63. Reports writer Office of Mil. Gov. U.S., Berlin, 1948-49; various editing, advt., polit. positions N.Y.C., N.J., 1952-62; staff writer, book reviewer Time mag., N.Y.C., 1963-65; arts and scis. corr. Time-Life News Svc., London, 1965-69, Paris, 1969-72; corr. Time-Life News Svc., N.Y.C., 1972-73; free-lance writer Cambridge, Eng., 1973-80, Balt., 1981—; Henry R. Luce prof. writing seminars, prof. history sci. Johns Hopkins U., Balt., 1981-90; vis. prof. Stanford (Calif.) U., 1990-94; rsch. prof. History George Washington U., 1994—; dir. Ctr. for History of Recent Sci., 1995—; cons. Philbrook Mus. Art, Tulsa, 1983-87, PBS Sta. WHYY-TV, Phila., 1985-88, Henry Luce Found., 1988-89, Harvard U. Press, 1990-95; panelist and cons. Office Tech. Assessment, Washington, 1985, 86-87; lectr. U.S. and Europe; keynote spkr. 25th ann. meeting Am. Soc. Cell Biology, Atlanta, Nov. 1985, ann. meeting Pew Scholars, Feb. 1987, symposium on Genetic Experimentation and Evolutionary Change, com. on genetic experimentation Internat. Coun. Sci. Unions, U. Basel, Jan. 1988, DNA Double Helix 40 Yrs. Symposium N.Y. Acad. Scis., 1993, Am. Soc. Human Genetics, 1995; Colin Syme vis. fellow, lectr. Walter and Eliza Hall Inst. Med. Rsch., Royal Melbourne (Australia) Hosp., 1990. Author: The Techniques of Reading, 1954, 3d edit. 1971, Heroin Addiction in Britain, 1974 (Overseas Press Club prize, 1974, Med. Journalists Assn. Great Britain award, 1975), The Eighth Day of Creation, 1979 (transls. in Japanese, German, Spanish, Italian, Chinese, nominated for Nat. Book award 1980), expanded edit. 1996, The Search for Solutions, 1980 (transls. in Japanese, German, Dutch); contbg. editor The Sciences, 1982-89; mem. faculty adv. bd. Johns Hopkins U. Press, 1982-84, editl. bd. The Am. Scholar, 1983-86, bd. editors Science Book Program of N.Y. Acad. Scis., 1985-90; editl. cons. various pubs. including Stanford U. Press, 1981, W.H. Freeman, 1988; author articles in The New Yorker, The Sciences, The New Republic, Harper's, The Atlantic, The N.Y. Times Book Rev., The Spectator (London), Nature, The Lancet, Jour. AMA, Gene, Science 80, 83, 84, 85, Life, Minerva; cons. editor The Eloquent Object, 1987; prodn. cons., scenarist TV films: Plague!, PBS, 1987-88, All My Loving, BBC, 1967. John Simon Guggenheim Meml. Found. fellow, 1979-80, Ctr. for Advanced Study in Behavioral Scis. (fell.), 1980-81, Prize fellow John D. and Catherine T. MacArthur Found., 1987-92, Wissenschaftskolleg zu Berlin fellow, 1987-88. Fellow AAAS; mem. History of Sci. Soc., Lansdowne Club (London), Century Assn., 14 W. Hamilton St. Club. Democrat. Avocation: cooking. Home: 807 W University Pky Baltimore MD 21210-2911

JUDSON, JEANNETTE ALEXANDER, artist; b. N.Y.C., Feb. 23, 1912; d. Philip George and Gertrude (Leichter) Alexander; m. Henry Judson, Sept. 23, 1945; children: S. Robert Weltz Jr., Pauline Raiff; 1 stepson, E. William Judson. Student, Columbia U., 1930-31, N.A.D., 1956-59, Art Student League, N.Y.C., 1959-61. One-man shows Fairleigh Dickinson U., 1965, Bodley Gallery, N.Y.C., 1967, 69, 71, 73, NYU, 1969, Pa. State U., 1969, Laura Musser Mus. Art, Muscatine, Iowa, 1969, Syracuse U. House, N.Y.C., 1975, Ludlow-Hyland Gallery, 1980, Key Gallery, N.Y.C., 1982, Graphic Arts Coun., White Plains, N.Y., 1993, Broome St. Gallery, N.Y.C., 1994, 96, award, 1994; 2 person show, Am. Standard Gallery, 1980; exhibited in group shows including anns. Nat. Assn. Women Artists, N.Y.C., France, Italy, 1965—, Audubon Artists, N.Y.C., 1962, 64, 65-67, Allied Artists, N.Y.C., 1966-67, Graphic Arts Coun. exhibit of collages, 1973, Key Gallery, N.Y.C., 1981; small works exhibits Key Gallery, 1983, NYU, N.Y.C., 1982, Marbella Gallery, N.Y.C., 1989, Graphic Arts Coun., N.Y.; represented in permanent collections Joseph H. Hirshhorn Mus., NYU, Norfolk (Va.) Mus. Arts and Scis., Brandeis U., Peabody Art Mus., Mus. N.Mex., Sheldon Swope Art Mus., Syracuse U., Evansville Mus. Arts and Scis., Rutgers U., Colby Coll., Butler Inst. Am. Art, Laura Musser Mus., Fordham U., Lehigh U., Ga. Mus. Art, U. Ga., Fairleigh Dickinson U., Lowe Mus., U. Miami, Washington County (Md.) Mus. Fine Arts, Miami Mus. Modern Art, Bruce Mus., Greenwich, Conn., Bklyn. Mus., Hudson River Mus., Dartmouth Coll. Mus., Columbia U., Art In Embassies program Dept. State, Am. Embassy, Stockholm, Sweden and Sofia, Bulgaria, also numerous pvt. collections; exhbns. of Nat. Assn. Women Artists, Am. Soc. Contemporary Artists, 1990, 91. Mem. Nat. Assn. Women Artists (Grumbacher award 1967, Lillian Cottan award 1979, Eve Holman award 1997, oil nominating com. 1977-79), Artists Equity N.Y., Art Students League (life), Am. Soc. Contemporary Artists (Dorothy Feigin award 1976, House of Heydenriek award 1977, Ralph Mayer Meml. award 1985, Doris Kreindler award 1994). Home and Studio: 1130 Park Ave New York NY 10128-1255

JUECHTER, JOHN WILLIAM, retired mechanical engineer, consultant; b. Hackensack, N.J., Sept. 21, 1925; s. John William and Mary Irene Juechter; m. Joan Frances Conley, Nov. 2, 1950; m. Jeanne Hale Johnson, Apr. 19, 1975. BS in Bus. and Engring. Adminstrn., MIT, 1948; MBA in Bus. Mgmt., Boston U., 1950; postgrad., Western New Eng. Coll., 1958-59, Rutgers U., 1973. Registered profl. engr., Mass., R.I.; cert. safety profl. Student rschr. Solar Energy Rsch. Lab. MIT, 1946-48; mech. technician Upper Atmosphere Rsch. Lab. Boston U., 1948-50; various positions Package Machinery Co., East Longmeadow, Mass., 1950-55; applications engr. Am. Bosch-Arma Corp., Springfield, Mass., 1955-56; design engr., product engr. R.M. Hallam Co., Springfield, 1956-58, chief mech. engr., 1958-62, engring. mgr., 1962; design project engr. Hamilton Std. divsn. UAC, Windsor Locks, Conn., 1962-70, supr. tech. stds., 1964-67, sys. effectiveness mgr., asst. program mgr., 1967-70; pres. Consultech Inc., East Greenwich, R.I., 1970-92; ret., 1992. Contbr. articles and papers to profl. jours. Mem. fin. com. Town of Wilbraham, 1962, chmn. redistricting com., 1962. Cadet, Naval Air Corp, 1943-45. Mem. NSPE, ASME, Am. Soc. Metals, Am. Soc. Safety Engrs., R.I. Soc. Profl. Engrs., Soc. Automotive Engrs., Boston Computer Soc. Avocations: radio-controlled model airplanes, model railroad, computers. Home: 460 Stoneridge Dr East Greenwich RI 02818-1696

JUENEMANN, SISTER JEAN, hospital executive; b. St. Cloud, Minn., Nov. 19, 1936; d. Leo A. and Teresa M. (Oster) J. Diploma, St. Cloud Sch. Nursing, 1957; student, Coll. St. Benedict, 1957-59; BSN cum laude, Seattle U., 1967; MHA, U. Minn., 1977. Dir. nursing svc. Queen of Peace Hosp., New Prague, Minn., 1963-65, 67-77; asst. adminstr. Queen of Peace Hosp., New Prague, 1967-77, CEO, 1977—; mem. bd. Bush Med. Fellows Program; spkr. at confs. Chmn. Cmty. Com. Prevention Chem. Abuse, New Prague, 1975-80; bd. dirs. St. Cloud (Minn.) Hosp., St. Benedict's Coll., St. Joseph, Minn. Recipient Disting. Svc. award Minn. Hosp. & Health Assn., 1996; Bush Found. Summer fellow Cornell U., U. Calif., Berkeley, 1982. Fellow Am. Coll. Healthcare Execs.; mem. AAUW (past pres. New Prague chpt.), Am. Hosp. Assn. (CEO of Yr. 1989), Soc. Health Care Planning & Mktg., Cath. Hosp. Assn., Women's Health Leadership Trust, New Prague Opportunities, Rotary (pres. New Prague chpt. 1994-95, asst. gov. dist. 1998-99), Sigma Theta Tau.

JUENGER, FRIEDRICH KLAUS, lawyer, educator; b. Frankfurt am Main, Germany, Feb. 18, 1930; came to U.S., 1955, naturalized, 1961; s. Wilhelm and Margarete J.; m. Baerbel Thierfelder, Sept. 15, 1967; children: J. Thomas, John F. Referendarexamen (Studienstiftung des deutschen Volkes scholar), J.W. Goethe-U., 1955; MCL, U. Mich., 1957; JD (Harlan-Fiske-Stone scholar), Columbia U., 1960. Bar: N.Y. 1962, Mich. 1970, U.S. Supreme Ct. 1970. Assoc. Cahill, Gordon & Reindel, N.Y.C., 1960-61, Baker & McKenzie, N.Y.C., Chgo., Madrid,, Frankfurt am Main, 1961-66; assoc. prof. law Wayne State U., Detroit, 1966-68; prof. Wayne State U., 1968-75; prof. U. Calif., Davis, 1975-93, Edward L. Barrett, Jr. prof., 1993—; vis. prof. Max-Planck-Inst. für ausländisches und internationales Privatrecht, Hamburg, Germany, 1981-82, U. Jean Moulin, Lyon, France, 1984; lectr. Hague Acad. Internat. Law, 1983, Uruguayan Fgn. Rels. Inst., 1987; Eason-Weinmann vis. prof. comparative law Tulane U., 1989; vis. prof. J. W. Goethe U., Frankfurt am Main, 1992; Allen Allen and Hemsley fellow U. Sydney, Australia, 1993; vis. prof. U. Française du Pacifique, Tahiti, 1993, U. Mich., 1994, Victoria U., Wellington, N.Z., 1998; sec. State Adv. Commn. Pvt. Internat. Law; advisor U.S. del. 5th Inter-Am. Specialized Conf. on Pvt. Internat. Law, Mexico City, 1994. Author: German Stock Corporation Act, 1967, (with L. Schmidt) Zum Wandel des Internationalen Privatrechts, 1974, Choice of Law and Multistate Justice, 1993; editor Columbia Law Rev., 1959-60; bd. editors Am. Jour. Comparative Law, 1977—, Revue Internat. Droit Comparé, Comité Patronage; contbr. articles on conflict of laws, fgn. and comparative law to legal jours. Recipient Faculty Rsch. award Wayne State U., 1971, Disting. Teaching award U. Calif., Davis, 1985, Gen. Reporter on Judgments Recognition 12th Internat. Congress of Comparative Law, Australia, 1986, Fulbright scholar, 1953-55; Rsch. grantee Volkswagen Found., 1972-73, Humboldt Found. Rsch. grantee Albert-Ludwigs-U. Freiburg, Fed. Republic Germany, 1990; Fulbright sr. rsch. fellow, 1981-82. Mem. ABA, Assn. of Bar of City N.Y., Am. Fgn. Law Assn., Am. Law Inst., Am. Soc. Internat. Law, Am. Soc. Comparative Law (past pres., past hon. pres.), Assn. Can. Law Tchrs., Gesellschaft für Rechtsvergleichung, Internat. Acad. Comparative Law (titular mem., pres. common law group), Internat. Law Assn. (com. on internat. litigation), Soc. Pub. Tchrs. of Law, Academia Mexicana de Derecho Internacional Privado y Comparado (hon.). Office: U Calif Sch Law King Hall Davis CA 95616

JUERGENS, BONNIE KAY, not-for-profit company executive; b. Denver, Sept. 11, 1947; d. Robert and Patricia Elaine (Carnahan) Beckman; adopted d. Donald Frederick Ruschmyer; m. Theodore Louis Juergens, Feb. 2, 1968 (div. 1976); m. Hugh Avery Standifer, Apr. 14, 1979. BA, MacMurray Coll., 1969; MLS, U. Ariz., 1972. Libr. liaison officer SUNY Ctrl. Adminstrn., Albany, 1973-75; spl. project dir. AMIGOS Bibliog. Coun., Inc., Dallas, 1975-77, assoc. dir., 1988-89, exec. dir., 1989-99; exec. dir. Amigos Libr. Svcs. Inc. (formerly Amigos Bibliog. Coun. Inc), Dallas, 1999—; customer rep. C.L. Systems, Inc., Newtonville, Mass., 1977-78; mgr. automation Austin (Tex.) Pub. Libr., 1978-83; ptnr. Justan Enterprises Mgmt. Cons., Austin, 1978-88; vis. assoc. prof. Tex. A&M U., College Station, 1984; mem. users coun. OCLC Inc., Dublin, Ohio, 1979-83, 89-98. Author: Self-Instructional Intro to OCLC Mod 100 Terminal, 1976, revised edit., 1981; contbr. articles to profl. jours. Mem. Ctr. for Nonprofit Mgmt., Dallas, 1990—; bd. advisors U. North Tex. Grad. Libr. Sch., Denton, 1990—. Mem. ALA (mem. coun. 1981-89), Libr. and Info. Tech. Assn. (bd. dirs. 1980-89), Tex. Libr. Assn. Avocations: reading, sewing, travel, literacy-program support activities. Office: Amigos Libr Svcs Inc 14400 Midway Rd Dallas TX 75244-3509

JUERGENS, GEORGE IVAR, history educator; b. Bklyn., Mar. 20, 1932; s. George Odegaard and Magnhild (Julin) J.; m. Bonnie Jeanne Brownlee; children: Steven Erik, Paul Magnus. BA, Columbia Coll., 1953; BA, MA, Oxford U., 1956; PhD, Columbia U., 1965. Instr. Dartmouth Coll., Hanover, N.H., 1962-65; asst. prof. Amherst (Mass.) Coll., 1965-67; assoc. prof. Ind. U., Bloomington, 1967-80, prof. history, 1980—; cons. Nat. Endowment Humanities, Washington, 1971—. Author: Joseph Pulitzer and the New York World, 1966, News From The White House, 1981; assoc. editor: Jour. Am. History, 1968-69. With U.S. Army, 1956-58. Recipient Disting. Teaching award Amoco Found., 1982; Kellett fellow Columbia U., 1954-56; sr. faculty fellow Nat. Endowment Humanities, 1971-72; fellow Rockefeller Found., 1981-82. Mem. AAUP, Orgn. Am. Historians, Phi Beta Kappa. Home: 2111 E Meadow Bluff Ct Bloomington IN 47401-6885 Office: Ind U Dept History Bloomington IN 47405

JUERGENSMEYER, JOHN ELI, lawyer; b. Stewardson, Ill., May 14, 1934; s. Irvin Karl and Clara Augusta (Johannaber) J.; m. Elizabeth Ann Bogart, Sept. 10, 1963; children—Margaret Ann, Frances Elizabeth. B.A., U. Ill., 1955, J.D., 1963; M.A., Princeton U., 1957, Ph.D., 1960. Bar: Ill. 1963, U.S. Supreme Ct. 1968. Mem. faculty extension div. U. Ill., 1961-63, 73-74, U. Hawaii, 1958-60; mem. firm Kirkland, Brady, McQueen, Martin & Schnell, Elgin, Ill., 1963-64; founder, sr. ptnr. Juergensmeyer, Zimmerman, Smith & Leahy, Elgin, 1964-81, Juergensmeyer-Strain & Assocs., Elgin, 1981-95, Juergensmeyer & Assocs., Elgin, 1995—; mgr., owner Tollview Office Complex, 1976-95; asst. pub. defender Kane County, 1964-67, asst. states atty., 1976-78; spl. asst. atty. gen. State of Ill., 1978-85; hearing officer Ill. Pollution Control Bd., 1971-74; commr. U.S. Nat. Commn. on Libraries and Info. Scis., 1982-88; lectr. Inst. for Continuing Legal Edn.; trustee ALA Endowment Fund, 1979-84; assoc. prof. Judson Coll., Elgin, 1963—; bd. dirs. Elgin Nat. Bank. Contbr. articles to profl. jours. Chmn. Hiawatha Dist. Boy Scouts Am.; v.p. Elgin Family Service Assn., 1967-71, Elgin Sister City Comm., 1990—; sec. Lloyd Morey Scholarship Fund, 1967-73; commr. Elgin Econ. Devel. Commn., 1971-75; chmn. Kane County Republican Central Com., 1978-80; adv. bd. Ill. Youth Commn., 1964-68; bd. dirs. Wesley Found. of U. Ill., 1971-75; pres. adv. bd. Elgin Salvation Army, 1973-75. Served to capt. Intelligence Service, USAF, 1958-60. Recipient Anti-Pollution Echo award Defenders of the Fox River, Inc., 1971, Cert. Merit, Heart Fund, 1971, Outstanding Young Man award Jr. C. of C., Elgin, 1967; Princeton U. fellow, 1955-56, Merrill Found. fellow, 1956-58. Mem. Assn. Trial Lawyers Am., ABA (local govt. law sect. spl. taxing dists. com. 1978—), Ill. State Bar Assn. (chmn. local govt. com. 1974-75, editor local govt. law newsletter 1973-74, mem. seminar in USSR 1979), Chgo. Bar Assn. (chmn. local govt. com. 1975-76), Kane County Bar Assn. (chmn. legis. com. 1974, chmn. local govt. com. 1992-93), 7th Cir. Bar Assn. (membership com.), Am. Arbitration Assn. (arbitrator), Am. Polit. Sci. Assn. (panel speaker 1960 convention, mem. African Politics seminar 1966), Fed. Bar Assn., Midwest Polit. Sci. Assn., Ill. Polit. Sci. Assn., Northwest Suburban Bar Assn., Elgin Bar Assn. (chmn. legal aid 1964-67), Rotary (pres. 1977-78, Paul Harris fellow), Jaycees (legal counsel, bd. dirs. 1965-71), Phi Beta Kappa, Phi Alpha Delta, Alpha Kappa Lambda. Author: President, Foundations, and the People-to-People Program, 1965. Contbr. to publs. in field. Methodist. Club: Union League (Chgo.). Lodges: Masons, Shriners, Rotary (pres. 1977-78). Office: Assoc. Prof. Govt. Judson College Elgin IL 60123

JUETTNER, DIANA D'AMICO, lawyer, educator; b. N.Y.C., Jan. 21, 1940; d. Paris T.R. and Dina Adele (Antonucci) D'Amico; m. Paul J. Juettner, June 29, 1963; children: John, Laura. BA, Hunter Coll., 1961; postgrad., Am. U., 1963; JD cum laude, Touro Coll., 1983. Bar: N.Y. 1984, U.S. Dist. Ct. (so. dist.) N.Y. 1984, U.S. Supreme Ct. 1987. Office mgr. Westchester County Dem. Com., White Plains, N.Y., 1976-79; dist. mgr. for Westchester County U.S. Bur. Census, N.Y.C., 1979-80; pvt. practice, Ardsley, N.Y., 1984—; prof. law, program dir. for legal studies Mercy Coll., Dobbs Ferry, N.Y., 1985—, asst. chair dept. law, criminal justice-safety adminstrn., 1994-98, pres. faculty senate, 1996-98; arbitrator small claims matters White Plains City Ct., 1985-89. Co-author booklet: Your Day in Court, How to File a Small Claims Suit in Westchester County, 1976; assoc. editor N.Y. State Probation Officers Assn. Jour., 1990-92; editor-in-chief Jour. Northeast Acad. Legal Studies in Bus., 1996-98; contbr. articles to profl. jours. Councilwoman Town of Greenburgh, N.Y., 1992—; vice chair law com. Westchester County Dem. Com., White Plains, 1987-91; corr. sec. Greenburgh Dem. Town Com., Hartsdale, N.Y., 1986-91; mem. Westchester County Citizens Consumer Adv. Coun., White Plains, 1975-91, chair, 1991; chair Ardsley (N.Y.) Consumer Adv. Commn., 1974-79. Mem. Am. Assn. for Paralegal Edn. (model syllabus task force 1992-95, chair legis. com. 1995-97), N.Y. State Bar Assn. (elder law sect. com. on pub. agy. liaison and legis. 1992-95), Westchester County Bar Assn. (chair paralegal subcom. 1990—, chair bicentennial U.S. Constitution com. 1987-91), Westchester Women's Bar Assn. (v.p. 1989-91, dir. 1994-96, co-chair tech. com. 1996—), Women's Bar Assn. State N.Y. (chair profl. ethics com. 1997-98). Avocation: sailing, walking. Office: Mercy Coll 555 Broadway Dobbs Ferry NY 10522-1134

JUGENHEIMER, DONALD WAYNE, advertising and communications educator, university administrator; b. Manhattan, Kans., Sept. 22, 1943; s. Robert William and Mabel Clara (Hobert) J.; m. Bonnie Jeanne Scamehorn, Aug. 30, 1970 (dec. 1983); 1 child, Beth Carrie; m. Kaleen B. Brown, July 25, 1987. BS in Advt., U. Ill.-Urbana, 1965, MS in Advt., 1968, PhD in Communications, 1972. Advt. copywriter Fillman & Assocs, Champaign, Ill., 1963-64, 66; media buyer Leo Burnett Co., Chgo., 1965-66; asst., assoc. prof. U. Kans., Lawrence, 1971-80, prof. jounralism, dir. grad. studies and rsch., 1980-85; Manship prof. journalism La. State U., Baton Rouge, 1985-87; prof., chmn. dept. communications and speech Fairleigh Dickinson U., Teaneck, N.J., 1987-89, 92-95, dean coll. liberal arts, 1989-92; chair dept. English, lang. and philosphy, 1995; prof., dir. Sch. Journalism So. Ill. U., Carbondale, 1995—; adv. cons. U.S. Army, Fort Sheridan, Ill., Pentagon, Washington, 1981-90, Am. Airlines, 1989-91, IBM Corp., 1989—, U.S. Dept. Def.; cons. editor Grid Publ., Columbus, Ohio, 1974-84; grad. and rsch. dir. U. Kans., 1978-84, adv. chmn., 1974-78; adj. prof. Turku (Finland) Sch. Econs. and Bus. Adminstrn., 1998—. Author: Advertising Media Sourcebook and Workbook, 1975, 3d edit., 1989, 4th edit. 1996, Strategic Advertising Decisions, 1976, Basic Advertising, 1979, 2d edit., 1991, Advertising Media, 1980, Problems and Practices in Advertising Research, 1982, Advertising Media: Strategy and Tactics, 1992; bd. editors Jour. Advt., 1985-89. Subscription mgr. Jour. of Advt., 1971-74, bus. mgr., 1974-79; chmn. U. Div. United Fund, Lawrence, 1971-72; pres. Sch.-Community Relations Council, Lawrence, 1974-75. Recipient Hope Teaching award U. Kans, 1977, 78 Kellogg Nat. fellow W.K. Kellogg Found., 1984-88; named Outstanding Young Men in Am. Nat. Jaycees, 1978. Mem. AAUP, Am. Acad. Advt. (pres. 1984-86), Assn. For Edn. in Journalism (head advertising div. 1977-78), Kappa Tau Alpha, Alpha Delta Sigma. Presbyterian. Avocations: skiing; sailing; writing; travel; reading. Home: 110 Tecumseh Dr Carbondale IL 62901-7113 Office: So Ill U Sch Journalism Carbondale IL 62901-6601

JUGUETA, EDUARDO MALUBAY, mechanical engineer; b. Mauban, Quezon, The Phillipines, July 15, 1943; came to U.S., 1976; s. Felimon Balmeo and Marcella Villamayor (Malubay) J.; m. Aida Marasigan DeGala, July 18, 1969; children: Edgar R., Haidde L., Eduardo A., Regina. BSME, Mapua Inst. Tech., Manilla, The Philippines, 1966. Registered mech. engr. Sr. mech. design engr. Nat. Power Corp., Manila, 1966-76; specifications engr. Sealectro Corp., Mamaronack, N.Y., 1977-81; mech. design engr. ITS, Inc., Islip, N.Y., 1982-83; design/specifications engr. Shaw Aero Devices, Wainscott, N.Y., 1983-84; mech. engr. Ragen Data Sys., Inc., Central Islip, 1984-86; mech. design engr. Automatic Toll Sys., Mt Vernon, N.Y., 1986; gen. sys. engr. Def. Logistics Agency, S.I., N.Y., 1986—. Recipient DCMAO N.Y. Allstars award Def. Logistics Agy., 1995, Svcs. award, 1996. Mem. ASME, KC. Roman Catholic. Avocations: jogging, gardening, fixing cars, bowling, reading. Home: 119 Singingwood Dr Holbrook NY 11741-3009

JUHL, DOROTHY HELEN, social worker, retired; b. Cedar Falls, Iowa, May 3, 1928; d. Henry Karl and Leona Margaret (Wedeking) Brandhorst; m. Eugene Edward Juhl, Feb. 19, 1955; children: Jane Marie, John Karl, Edward Eugene. BA, Capital U., 1949; MSW, Washington U., St. Louis, 1952. Cert. social worker Acad. Cert. Social Work, Nat. Assn. Social Work; lic. ind. social worker, Iowa. Counselor Luth. Children's Home, Waverly, Iowa, 1949-55; dir. Grundy County Dept. Human Svcs., Grundy Center, Iowa, 1968-70; psychiat. social worker Dr. W.G. Stone, Waterloo, Iowa, 1970-76; psychiat. social worker, family and individual therapist Luth. Social Svcs. Iowa, Waterloo, 1976-97; retired, 1997; cons. Bremer-Butler Hospice, Waverly, 1996—. Sec., chair Bremwood Auxiliary, Waverly, 1955-68, Black Hawk-Grundy Mental Health Ctr., Waterloo, 1962-68, 72-77; officer Dike (Iowa) Sch. PTA, 1962-80; bd. dirs., sec. Cedar Falls Luth. Home, 1977-82; bd. dirs., chair Grundy County Farm Bur., Grundy Center, 1982-90; juvenile justice adv. People to People, China, Japan, Taiwan, 1984; bd. dirs. Luth. Rural Econ. Empowerment Com., Des Moines, 1993-98, Christian Crusaders Radio Ministry, Waterloo, 1994-98, N.E. Iowa Synod Women of Evangel. Luth. Ch. in Am., Waverly, 1995—; mental health counselor Self-Help Internat., Ghana, West Africa, 1997—; mem. various bds. and coms. St. Paul's Luth. Ch., Waverly; mem. Amvet Auxiliary, Waverly Cmty. Hosp. Aux.; juvenile justice adv. People to People, China, Japan, Hong Kong, Taiwan, 1984; mental health counselor Self-Help Internat., Ghana, 1997. Recipient Svc. award Luth. Social Svc. Iowa, 1996. Mem. AAUW (pres.), NASW, ACSW. Republican. Avocations: gardening, reading, baking, antiques. Home: 818 6th St NW Waverly IA 50677-1501

JUHL, HAROLD ALEXANDER, retired career officer, construction executive; b. Kearney, Nebr., June 24, 1950; s. Harold Ferdinand and Vivian Lea Louise (Simshauser) J.; m. Becky Sue Adams, July 30, 1971; children: Aaron A., Shane B. Student, Kearney State Coll., 1968-71, Pensacola (Fla.) Jr. Coll., 1977-79; BA, Colo. State U., 1985. Electronic technician GTE Corp., Chgo., 1971-73; enlisted USMC, 1973, advanced through grades to lt. col., 1990; helicopter pilot HML-267, Camp Pendleton, Calif., 1974-76; flight instr. USN VT-3, Milton, Fla., 1976-79; air officer 2d Bn. 4th Marines, Okinawa, Japan, 1979-80; KC-130 pilot, weapons-tactics instr. VMGR 252, Cherry Point, N.C., 1980-83, aviation safety officer, 1986-88; dir. of safety and standardization VMGR-252, 1988-89, Marine Aircraft Group 36, Okinawa, Japan, 1989-90; C-130 class desk officer Navair-Syscom, Washington, N.C., 1990-94; spl. ops. officer Marine Forces Atlantic, Camp LeJuene, N.C., 1994-97; ret., 1997; owner Juhl Designs, Swansboro, N.C., 1997—; cons. Colo. State U. ROTC, Ft. Collins, 1984-85, Aerial Refueling Systems Adv. BGroup, Oxford, Eng., 1987—, KC-130 Aircraft Symposium, El Toro, Calif., 1987-94; presenter to NATO's Partnership for Peace Coordination Cell, Mons, Belgium, 1996; guest lectr. USN Acad., Annapolis, Md., 1983-84; mem. joint US-Japan Battle Studies Program, 1989-90; participant Warfighting Symposium, Okinawa, Japan, 1989, 90; exercise planner for Norway exercises, 1994, 95, 96. Cubmaster Boy Scouts Am., Quantico, Va., 1985-86; coach, referee Quantico Youth Soccer League, 1985; commr. Quantico Little League, 1986; coach Pop Warner Football, Newport, N.C., 1987, 88, 90; coach Ea. Carolina Soccer Assn., 1990-91. Recipient Shield of Service Boy Scouts Am., 1986. Mem. Marine Corps Assn., Marine Corps Aviation Assn., Golden Key, Experimental Aircraft Assn. (charter, bd. dirs. Beafort, N.C. chpt.). Club: Kearney Aero (pres. 1970-71). Avocations: art collecting, metalcrafts, home improvements, travel, airplane constrn. Home: 223 Star Hill Dr Swansboro NC 28584-8935

JUHLIN, DORIS ARLENE, French language educator; b. Atlanta, Dec. 1, 1942; d. Lawrence Alfred and Doris (South) J. BA, Greenville (Ill.) Coll., 1964; MA, Baldwin-Wallace Coll., 1979. Cert. elem. and secondary French and reading tchr., Ohio. Tchr. French Cleve. Bd. Edn., 1965—; chmn. bldg. activities Cleve. Pub. Schs., 1983-93, writer French curriculum, 1980, Acad. Challenge, Cleve., 1995; workshop presenter Ohio Modern Lang. Tchrs. Assn., Columbus, Ohio, 1978; fgn. lang. cons. WV12-TV (PBS), Cleveland, Ohio, 198 0; contbr. CP's Fgn. Lang. Exploratory Program, 1995-96. Cons. and tchr.: Exploring Languages video series, Cleve. Pub. Schs., 1994-95. Dir. jump for heart sch. program Am. Heart Assn., 1986-90; v.p. Womens Ministries Internat.; speaker, editor ann. program resource books Free Meth. Ch., Indpls., 1985-95; sec. Free Meth. Ohio Conf. Bd. Camping Dirs., Mansfield, Ohio, 1990-94; organist, Sunday Sch. tchr. Free Meth. Ch., Westlake, Ohio, 1964—; vol. Nat. Welsh Home for Aged, Rocky River, Ohio, 1970—; mem. task force Edn. 2000, 1992-93. Jennings scholar Martha Holden Jennings Found., 1980. Mem. Ohio Fgn. Lang. Assn., Cleve. Tchrs. Union, Nat. Audubon Soc., MENSA (gifted child coord. 1985-94, columnist Graffiti 1986-94. Democrat. Avocations: reading, walking, piano. Home: 3745 W 213th St Cleveland OH 44126-1216 Office: Wilbur Wright Mid Sch 11005 Parkhurst Dr Cleveland OH 44111-3601

JUHNKE, JAMES CARLTON, humanities educator; b. Newton, Kans., May 14, 1938; s. William Ernest J. and Meta Goering; m. Anna Rachel Kreider, Aug. 31, 1963; children: Joanne Ruth, Carl James. AB, Bethel Coll., 1962; MA, Ind. U., 1966, PhD, 1968. Prof. history Bethel Coll., North Newton, Kans., 1966—; instr. history Sichuan Normal U., Chengdu, China, 1987-88. Author: A People of Mission, 1979, Vision, Doctrine, War, 1989, Creative Crusader: Edmund G. Kaufman, 1994. Country dir. Mennonite Ctrl. Com., Gaborone, Botswana, 1971-73. Rsch. fellow Young Ctr., Elizabethtown, Pa., 1995-96; summer scholar Nat. Found. Humanities, Washington, 1968, Richert Disting. scholar Bethel Coll., 1990. Mem. Am. Hist. Assn., Kans. History Tchrs. Assn. (pres. 1997-98). Home: 104 W 26th St North Newton KS 67117 Office: Bethel Coll 300 E 27th St North Newton KS 67117-8054

JUKES, THOMAS HUGHES, biological chemist, educator; b. Hastings, Eng., Aug. 25, 1906; came to U.S., 1925, naturalized, 1939; s. Edward Hughes and Ann Mary (Barton) J.; m. Marguerite Esposito, July 2, 1942; children: Kenneth Hughes (dec. 1995), Caroline Elizabeth (Mrs. Nicholas Knueppel), Dorothy Mavis (Mrs. Robert Hudson). B.S.A., U. Toronto, 1930, Ph.D., 1933; NRC fellow med. scis., U. Calif. at Berkeley, 1933-34; D.Sc. (honoris causa), U. Guelph, 1972. Instr., asst. prof. U. Calif. at Davis, 1934-42; with pharm. div. Lederle Labs., 1942-45; dir. nutrition and physiology research sect. research div. Am. Cyanamid Co., Pearl River, N.Y., 1945-58; dir. research agrl. div. Am. Cyanamid Co., 1958-59, dir. biochemistry, 1960-62; vis. sr. research fellow in biochemistry Princeton, 1962-63; prof. dept. biophysics and med. physics U. Calif., Berkeley, 1963-91, prof. dept. integrative biology, 1991—, prof. emeritus nutritional scis., 1974—, rsch. biochemist Space Scis. Lab., 1963—, assoc. dir., 1968-70; cons. CWS, AUS, 1944-45, NASA, 1969-70; guest lectr. various univs.; Storer lectr. U. Calif. at Davis, 1973; Fred W. Tanner lectr. Inst. Food Technologists, 1979; vis. prof. U. Wis., River Falls, 1985; plenary lectr. Japanese Molecular Biology and Genetics Socs., Nagoya, 1986; cons. Calif. Cancer Adv. Council, 1981—; invited speaker Internat. Symposium on Evolution of Life, Kyoto, Japan, 1990. Author: B Vitamins for Blood Formation, 1952, Antibiotics in Nutrition, 1955, Molecules and Evolution, 1965; mem. editorial bds., Biochem. Genetics, BioSystems; biog. editor: Jour. Nutrition; assoc. editor: Jour. Molecular Evolution; Contbr. articles to profl. jours. Recipient Gov.-Gen.'s medal, Guelph, Can., 1928, Borden award Poultry Sci. Assn., 1947, Spencer award Am. Chem. Soc., 1976, Agrl. and Food Chemistry award, 1979, Disting. Svc. award Am. Agrl. Editors Assn., 1978, Cain Meml. award Am. Assn. Cancer Rsch., 1987, Klaus Schwartz commemorative medal Internat. Assn. Bioinorganic Scientists, 1988, Disting. Sci. Achievement award Am. Coun. on Sci. and Health, 1993, Disting. Scientist award Ctr. for Study of Evolution and Origin of Life, 1994. Fellow Am. Soc. Animal Sci., Poultry Sci. Assn., Am. Inst. Nutrition (coun. 1941-45, pub. affairs officer 1978-81, chmn. com. on history 1979-83), Calif. Acad. Scis.; mem. Internat. Coun. Sci. Unions (chmn. biology working group COSPAR 1978-80, chmn. interdisciplinary sci. commn. F 1980-84), Human Genome Orgn., Am. Soc. Biol. Chemists, Soc. for Exptl. Biology and Medicine, Trustees for Conservation (San Francisco) (pres. 1970-71), Am. Alpine Club (Golden, Colo.), Explorers Club (N.Y.C.), Chit Chat Club (San Francisco), Sierra Club (San Francisco), Faculty Club (Berkeley, Calif.), Sigma Xi, Delta Tau Delta. Home: 170 Arlington Ave Kensington CA 94707-1135 Office: U Calif Space Scis Lab 6701 San Pablo Ave Spc Scis Oakland CA 94608-1244

JULESZ, BELA, experimental psychologist, educator, electrical engineer; b. Budapest, Hungary, Feb. 19, 1928; came to U.S., 1956; s. Jeno and Klementin (Fleiner) J.; m. Margit Fasy, Aug. 7, 1953. Dipl. Elec. Engring., Tech. U., Budapest, 1950; Dr. Ing., Hungarian Acad. Sci., Budapest, 1956. Asst. prof. dept. communication Tech U. Budapest, Hungary, 1950-51; mem. tech. staff Telecommunication Research Inst., Budapest, 1951-56; mem. tech. staff Bell Labs., Murray Hill, N.J., 1956-64, head sensory and perceptual processes, 1964-83; rsch. head visual perception rsch. AT&T Bell Labs., Murray Hill, N.J., 1984-89; State of N.J. prof. psychology, dir. lab. of vision rsch. Rutgers U., Piscataway, N.J., 1989—; continuing vis. prof. biology dept. Calif. Inst. Tech., Pasadena, 1985-94. Author: Foundations of Cyclopean Perception, 1971, Dialogues on Perception, 1995; author over 200 sci. papers on visual perception; discover computer generated random-dot stereogram technique. Fairchild disting. scholar Calif. Inst. Tech., 1977-79, 87, assoc. Neurosci. Research Progam, 1982; MacArthur Found. fellow, 1983-87; Dr. H.P. Heineken prize Royal Netherlands Acad. Arts and Scis., 1985; Karl Spencer Lashley award Am. Philos. Soc., 1989. Fellow AAAS, Am. Acad. Arts and Scis., Optical Soc. Am.; mem. NAS, Goettingen Acad. Scis. (corr.), Hungarian Acad. Scis. (hon.), Am. Philos. Soc. Home: 30 Valleyview Rd Warren NJ 07059-5229 Office: Rutgers U Lab Vision Rsch Psychology 152 Frelinghuysen Rd Piscataway NJ 08854-8020

JULIAN, JIM LEE, lawyer; b. Osceola, Ark., Dec. 14, 1954; s. John Roland and Lucille Angela (Potts) J.; m. Patricia Lynn Roberts, Jan. 26, 1980; 1 child, Kathryn Elizabeth. BA, Ark. State U., 1976; JD, U. Ark., 1979. Bar: Ark. 1979, U.S. Dist. Ct. (ea. and we. dists.) Ark. 1979, U.S. Ct. Appeals (8th cir.). Assoc. Skillman & Durrett, West Memphis, Ark., 1979-82; staff atty. Ark. Power and Light Co., Little Rock, 1982-84; assoc. House, Wallace & Jewell, Little Rock, 1984-85, ptnr., 1986-89; ptnr. Chisenhall, Nestrud & Julian, Little Rock, 1989—. Pres. Crittenden County (Ark.) Young Dems., 1980-82; chmn. bd. dirs. Northside YMCA, 1992-96. Mem. ABA, Ark. Bar Assn., Pulaski County Bar Assn., Ark. Assn. Def. Counsel, Major Sports Assn., North Hills Country Club. Avocation: golf. Home: 3711 Lochridge Rd North Little Rock AR 72116-8328 Office: Chisenhall Nestrud & Julian 2840 First Commercial Bldg Little Rock AR 72201

JULIAN, LARRY G., education educator; b. Greenville, S.C., July 31, 1948; s. Harold G. and Nelie Edwards J.; m. Tonnie LeAnne Greenwood, Dec. 14, 1996; children; Jason, Amy, Amanda, Andrew, Aaron. BS, Appalachian State U., 1974, MA, 1977; PhD, U. N.C., 1995. Vice chmn. Statesville (N.C.) Airport commn., 1982-91; mem. Iredell County Adolscent Pregnancy Coun., Statesville, 1981-83, Exch. Club, Statesville, 1975-80, Brewton-Parker Chroal Soc., Mt. Vernon, Ga., 1993-99. Maj. USAFR, 1970—. Mem. Nat. Mid. Sch. Assn., Res. Officers Assn. (state v.p. 1982-83), Air Force Assn., Ga. Assn. Tchr. Educators. Republican. Baptist. Avocations: sports officiating, amateur radio, aviation, golf. Office: Brewton-Parker Coll Hwy 280 Mount Vernon GA 30445

JULIAN, MICHAEL, grocery company executive; b. 1950; married. With Human Systems Inc., Florham Pk., N.J., 1975-85, Richfood Inc., Mechanicsville, Va., 1985-87; chief oper. officer, exec. v.p. Farm Fresh Inc., 1987—, chmn., chief exec. officer, 1988—; pres., CEO Jitney Jungle, Jackson, Miss., 1997. Office: Jitney Jungle PO Box 3409 Jackson MS 39207-3409*

JULIANA, JAMES NICHOLAS, ordnance company executive; b. Camden, N.J., Apr. 1, 1922; s. Nicholas and Rosa (de Noti) J.; m. Elizabeth D. Sutton, Nov. 8, 1947; children—James S., Patrick C., Mary E., Thomas E., David J., Richard S., Robert Francis, Ronald Joseph (dec.). B.S., Washington Coll., Md., 1944. Spl. agt. FBI, 1947-53; asst. exec. dir., exec. dir., chief counsel to minority Senate Permanent Sub-com. on Investigations, 1953-58; exec. dir. CAB, 1958-61; pres., dir. Internat. Fact Finding Inst., 1961-62; pres. James N. Juliana Assocs., Washington, 1962-81, 84—; sec., dir. Alaska N.Am. Corp., Washington, 1970-77; v.p. fed. affairs Braniff Internat., 1977-81; prin. dep. asst. sec. for manpower, res. affairs and logistics Dept. Def., Washington, 1981-84; dir. Tround Internat., 1984-97; chmn., CEO, pres., 1993-97; dir. IX Sys., 1985-98. Mem. Pres.'s Com. on Mental Retardation, 1971-77; exec. v.p. Armed Forces Mktg. Council, Washington, 1974-81; bd. visitors, bd. govs. Washington Coll., Chestertown, Md., 1978-84. Served with USNR, 1944-46. Mem. Soc. Former Spl. Agts., FBI, Coalition of Mil. Distributors (exec. dir. 1990—), Capital Hill Club, Kappa Alpha, Omicron Delta Kappa. Home: 11013 Rosemont Dr Rockville MD 20852-3650 also: 66 W 17th St Ocean City NJ 08226-2924 Office: 910 17th St NW # 800 Washington DC 20006-2601

JULIANO, KATHRYN MARIE, artist; b. East Orange, N.J., Feb. 19, 1961; d. Carmine Guetuno and Patricia (Tricoli) J. Art degree, Montclair Art Sch., 1985. Author: the 614, 1997, Tulips, 1998; exhibited in group shows in Essex County, South Orange, Montclair and East Orange, N.J. Bd. dirs. Hon. Patricia Juliano Civic Assn., Orange, 1976—. Avocations: riding, steam locomotives, drawing, 19 century figuratives. Home: 390 Hon Patricia Juliano Wy Orange NJ 07050

JULIANO, ROBERT F., bureau chief. Various positions Conn. Dept. Transp., airport ops. mgr., 1974-82; adminstr. Conn. Dept. Transp., 19982; bur. chief, aviation and ports Conn. Dept. Transp. Fax: 860594-2574. Office: Bur Chief 2800 Berlin Turnpike PO Box 317546 Newington CT 06131-7546

JULIANO, RUDOLPH L., medical educator; b. July 18, 1941. BS in Physics, Cornell U., 1963; PhD in Biophysics, U. Rochester, 1971; post grad. dept. experimental pathology, Roswell Park Mem. Inst., 1971-72. Investigator Hosp. for Sick Children, Ont., Can., 1972-78; asst. prof. dept. med. biophysics U. Toronto, Can., 1973-78; assoc. prof. dept. pharmacology U. Tex. Med. Sch., Houston, 1978-82, prof., 1982-86; prof., chair dept. pharmacology U. N.C., Chapel Hill, 1986—; part-time asst. prof. dept. biology SUNY, 1971-72. Author: Drug Delivery Systems: Characteristics and Biomedical Applications, 1981, Biological Approaches to the Controlled Delivery of Drugs, 1987, Targeted Drug Delivery, 1991; co-author: Cell Surface Glycoproteins: Structure, Biosynthesis and Biological Functions, 1979; mem. editl. bd. Jour. Cell Biology, Antisense Rsch. and Devel., Cell Adhesion and Communication, Pharmaceutical Rsch.; editor Advanced Drug Delivery Reviews; assoc. editor Cancer Rsch.; contbr. over 100 articles to profl. pubs. including Life Sci., Biochemistry, Experimental Cell Rsch., others.; contbr. chpts. to books including Adhesion Receptors as Therapeutic Targets, Delivery of Protein Drugs, Prolonged Arrest of Cancer, also others; patentee in field. Tchr., cmty. devel. organizer U.S. Peace Corps, Philippines, 1964-66. NIH fellow in biophysics, 1966-70, Internat. Union Against Cancer Travel fellow, 1978, Fogarty Sr. Internat. fellow Cambridge U., England, 1993; ACS grantee, 1992-95, NIH grantee, 1992-96, 89-94, 92-97, 94-97. Mem. Am. Soc. Cell Biology, Am. Soc. Pharmacology and Experimental Therapeutics, Am. Assn. Cancer Rsch., Assn. Med. Sch. Pharmacology. Home: 408 Lyons Rd Chapel Hill NC 27514-7631 Office: Univ NC Dept Pharmacology CB 7365 Chapel Hill NC 27599*

JULIBER, LOIS, manufacturing executive; b. 1949; m. John Adams. BA, Wellesley Coll.; MBA, Harvard U. Former v.p. Gen. Foods Corp.; from gen. mgr. to pres. Far East/Can. divsn. Colgate-Palmolive Co., N.Y.C., 1988-92, chief tech. officer, 1992-94, pres. Colgate—N.Am. divsn., 1994—; bd. dirs. DuPont Corp. Trustee Brookdale Found., Wellesley Coll. Mem. Harvard Bus. Sch. Club N.Y. (bd. dirs.). Avocations: tennis, gardening, cooking. Office: Colgate Palmolive Co 300 Park Ave Fl 8 New York NY 10022-7499*

JULIEN, GAIL LESLIE, model, public relations professional; b. L.I., N.Y., Apr. 13, 1940; d. David William Syme and Virginia Martha (Burth) Miller; m. Michael Louis Woodman, Sept. 12, 1958 (div.); children: Jho'meyr Renei, Sabrina Michelle; m. Francis Dana Julien, Dec. 24, 1977. Diploma in modeling, Coronet of Calif., 1960; grad., Am. Beauty Finishing Sch., 1961. Playboy bunny Playboy Club, Kansas City, Mo., 1970-72; Gremlin girl AMC, Kansas City, 1972; Dodge girl Dodge, Kansas City, 1972-73; owner, pres. Gail Woodman Enterprises Inc., Overland Park, Kans., 1972-76; sales rep. Kansas City Brit. Motors, Lenexa, Kans., 1976-78; dir. pub. rels., mktg. Downtown Air Ctr., Kansas City, 1978-80; dir. pub. rels., media rels. Bretney Corp., Kansas City, 1980-82; v.p. Nuwalters Co., Overland Park, 1983-84; regional mgr. aviation Multi Svc. Corp., Overland Park, 1984—; rep. Nat. Bus. Aircraft Assn., 1984—, Can. Bus. Aircraft Assn., 1984—, Nat. Aircraft Transp. Assn., 1984—, Abbotsford Internat. Airshow, 1991, 93, 95, 98, Schedulars & Dispatchers Conv., 1994-99, Internat. Operators Conf., 1998, Women in Aviation, 1997-99, Helicopter Assn. Internat., 1994-99; sec. Women in Corp. Aviation, 1999. Author: Physician's Nutritional Guide, 1984; author numerous poems, self improvement and modeling course. Vol. Live On Stage '88 (AIDS), Santa Ana, Calif., 1988, St. Joseph Hosp., Kansas City, 1986-88; v.p. Young Dems., Midland, Mich., 1960; active Northshore Animal League, Christian Children's Fund, City of Hope, L.A., 1991; bd. dirs., fundraiser Make A Wish of Tri Counties. Recipient Outstanding Sales Achievement award Brit. Leyland, 1976-77. Mem. Am. Bus. Women's Assn. Avocations: art, writing, swimming, acting. Home: 28129 Peacock Ridge Dr Apt 312 Palos Verdes Peninsula CA 90275-7121 Office: Multi Svc Corp 8650 College Blvd Shawnee Mission KS 66210-1886

JULIEN, JEFFREY P., investment company executive. V.p. fin., CFO Raymond James Fin. Inc., St. Petersburg, Fla. Office: Raymond James Fin Inc 880 Carillon Pkwy Saint Petersburg FL 33716-1100*

JULIEN, ROBERT MICHAEL, anesthesiologist, author; b. Port Townsend, Wash., Mar. 24, 1942; s. Frank Felton and Mary Grace (Powers) J.; m. Judith Dianne DeChenne, Feb. 26, 1963; children: Robert Michael, Scott M. BS in Pharmacy, U. Wash., 1965, MS in Pharmacology, 1968, PhD, 1970; MD, U. Calif.-Irvine, 1977. Intern, Good Samaritan Hosp., Portland, Oreg., 1977-78; resident Oreg. Health Scis. U., 1978-80; asst. prof. pharmacology U. Calif.-Irvine, 1970-74, asst. clin. prof., 1974-77; assoc. prof. anesthesiology and pharmacology U. Oreg., Portland, 1980-83; staff anesthesiologist St. Vincent Hosp., Portland, 1983—. Author: Primer of Drug Action, 1975, 8th edit., 1998, Understanding Anesthesiology, 1984., Drugs and the Body, 1987. Recipient Service award Am. Epilepsy Soc., 1975. Mem. Am. Soc. Anesthesiologists, Am. Assn. Pharmacology and Exptl. Therapeutics, Soc. Neurosci., Oreg. Med. Assn., Western Pharmacology Soc., Oswego Lake (Lake Oswego, Oreg.) Club. Roman Catholic. Home: 1212 SW Hessler Dr Portland OR 97201-2807 Office: St Vincent Hosp Dept Anesthesia 9205 SW Barnes Rd Portland OR 97225-6603

JULIEN, THOMAS THEODORE, religious denomination administrator; b. Arcanum, Ohio, June 27, 1931; s. Russel Ray and Clara (Cassel) J.; m. Doris Mardella Briner, Aug. 21, 1953; children: Becky Jean, Terry Lee, Jacqueline Sue. BA, Bob Jones U., 1953; MDiv, Grace Theol. Sem., Winona Lake, Ind., 1957, DD (hon.), 1996; cert. French lang., U. Grenoble, France, 1960. Ordained to ministry Fellowship of Grace Brethren Chs., 1956. Pastor Grace Brethren Ch., Ft. Wayne, Ind., 1955-58; missionary Grace Brethren Fgn. Missions, Grenoble, 1959-64; field supt. Grace Brethren Fgn. Missions, Macon, France, 1964-78, dir. for Europe, 1964-86; exec. dir. Grace Brethren Fgn. Missions, Winona Lake, 1986—. Author: Handbook for Young Christians, 1959, Inherited Wealth, 1976, Spiritual Greatness, 1979. Decorated chevalier de Republique (Ctrl. African Republic). Home: 545 S Circle Dr Warsaw IN 46580 Office: Grace Brethren Foreign Missions PO Box 588 Winona Lake IN 46590-0588

JULIFS, SANDRA JEAN, community action agency executive; b. Jersey City, July 12, 1939; d. Roy Howard and Irma Margrete (Barkhausen) Walters; m. Harold William Julifs, July 22, 1961; children: David Howard, Steven William. BA, U. Va., 1961; postgrad., U. Minn., 1962-63, Mankato State Coll., 1963. Cert. comty. action profl. Tchr. St. James (Minn.) Pub. Schs., 1961-62; substitute tchr. Sleepy Eye (Minn.) Pub. Schs., 1963-67, home bound tutor, 1967; lay reader, rater U. Wis., Stevens Point, 1968; co-founder Family Planning Service Portage County, Stevens Point, 1970-72; family planning dir. Tri-County Opportunities Coun., Rock Falls, Ill., 1971-77; energy programs coord. Tri-County Opportunities Coun., Rock Falls, 1977-78, planner, EEO officer, 1978-83, pres., chief exec. officer, 1983—; sec. Ill. Ventures for Comty. Action Springfield, 1983-91, bd. dirs. 1991-94, 96—. Mem. Nat. Cmty. Action Found., Washington, 1987—; bd. dirs. Twin Cities Homeless Coalition, 1989-96; mem. adv. coun. Sauk Valley Coll. Human Svcs., 1990-99; mem. Sauk Valley Coll. Workforce Devel. Coun., 1999—; mem. Whiteside County Overall Econ. Devel. Coun., 1990—; mem. adv. coun. Inst. for Social and Econ. Devel., 1992-95; cons. com. No. Ill. Synod, Evang. Luth. Ch. Am., 1993-99, churchwide assembly del., 1995; mem. Statewide Rural Poverty Conf. Com., 1996-97; mem. Ill. State Microenterprise Initiative; mem. cmty. svcs. adv. com. Ill. Dept. Commerce and Cmty., 1998—. Recipient Appreciation award Western Ill. Agy. on Aging, 1980, 81, Spl. Recognition award Ill. Head Start and Day Care Assn., Recognition award Ill. Community Action Fund, 1984, Recognition award Ill. Ventures for Cmty. Action, 1996. Mem. AAUW, NAFE, Am. Soc. Pub. Adminstrn., Whiteside County Welfare Assn., Lee County Welfare Assn. (sec.-treas. 1983-84), Nat. Cmty. Action Assn., Ill. Cmty. Action Assn. (com. chair 1985-88, dir. exec. com. 1986-95, treas. 1988, 89, sec. 1989, 90, v.p. 1991-93, pres. 1993-95, Recognition award 1985-95). Lutheran. Avocations: travel, reading. Office: Tri-County Opportunities Coun PO Box 610 Rock Falls IL 61071-0610

JULIUS, DANIEL J., university administrator, educator; b. N.Y.C., July 29, 1950; s. Jacob and Arline (Kahn) J.; m. Elyse C. Oppenheim, June 11, 1972; children: Illana, Micah, Rachel. BA, Ohio State U., 1972; postgrad., Cornell U., 1975-76; EdD, MA, Columbia U., 1978. Dir. Ctr. for Higher Edn. Tchrs. Coll., Columbia U., 1975-77; sr. mgmt., cons. Boone, Young and Assocs., Washington, Phila., N.Y.C, 1978-79; dir. pers. svcs. faculty and staff rels. Vt. State Coll. System, 1979-81; asst. vice chancellor, dir. faculty and staff rels. Calif. State U. System, 1981-85; assoc. v.p. acad. affairs, dir. ctr. strategic leadership U. San Francisco, 1985—; vis. scholar Ctr. for Orgns. Rsch., Grad. Sch. of Bus., 1990-91, others; vis. lectr. Continuing Profl. Edn., U. Toronto, 1997—, Mgmt. Program, City U., U.K., 1997, Sch. of Pub. Adminstrn., U. Hawaii, 1995; vis. prof. Sup de Co. Grad. Sch. of Mgmt., Montpellier, France, 1996, Internat. Sch. of Bus., U. Shanghai, People's Republic of China, 1994, Whittemore Sch. of Bus. and Econs., U. N.H., 1992, Sch. of Bus., San Diego State U., 1984-85; vis. faculty Ctr. for Higher Edn. R&D, U. Manitoba, 1993—; sr. lectr. Grad. Sch. of Edn., Stanford U., 1992, 97—; instr. Tchr. Coll., Columbia U., 1976-78; adj. prof. Sch. of Bus., Nursing, Coll. of Liberal Arts and Scis., U. San Francisco, 1985—; spkr. in field. Author nine books; editl. bd. Jour. of Higher Edn., 1998—, Prescott Pubs., 1995—, Aspen Pubs., 1994—, indsl. Rels. Rsch. Assn., 1985, 88, Small Coll. Creativity, 1987-89, Am. Coun. on Edn., 1980, Am. Ednl. Rsch. Assn., 1979, Assn. for the Study of Higher Edn., 1978; editor Jour. fo the Coll. and Univ. Pers. Assn. Dir. Big Bro./Big Sister Program, Ohio State U., 1971-72; dir. Ctr. for Higher Edn., Tchrs. Coll., Columbia U., 1975-77. Sr. fellow Grad. Sch. Edn., Stanford U., 1997, Kellogg fellow Tchrs. Coll., Columbia U., 1976-77, Internat. fellow Sch. Internat. Affairs, 1975-76; recipient numerous grants. Democrat. Jewish. Avocations: skiing, wine tasting, travel. Home: 91 Mountain Muir Ct San Rafael CA 94903 Office: U San Francisco Lone Mountain #304 2130 Fulton St San Francisco CA 94117-1080

JULL, EDWARD V., electrical engineer, radio scientist, educator; b. Calgary, Alta., Can., Aug. 8, 1934; s. Walter Kingsley and Rebecca Olive (Hamilton) J.; m. Anne Eva Kjellberg, Sept. 18, 1965; children: Victoria, Charlotta, Walter, Philip. BSc, Queens U., Kingston, Ont., 1956; PhD in electrical engring., Univ. Coll, London, 1960; DSc, U. London, 1979. Registered profl. engr. Province of B.C. Jr. rsch. officer divsn. radio and elec. engring. Nat. Rsch. Coun., Ottawa, Ont., 1956-57, from asst. to assoc. rsch. officer divsn. radio and elec. engring., 1961-72; asst. prof. dept. elec. engring. U. Alberta, Edmonton, 1960-61; from assoc. prof. to prof. U. Brit. Columbia, Vancouver, 1972—; guest researcher Tech. U. Denmark, Lyngby, 1963-65; vis. prof. Royal Inst. Tech., Stockholm, 1991-92; lectr., researcher in electromagnetic fields. Author: Aperture Antennas and Diffraction Theory, 1981; contbr. articles to profl. jours. Fellow IEEE (life, Antennas and Propagation Soc. adcom. 1986-89, J.T. Bolljahn Meml. award 1965, awards bd. 1995-97); mem. Internat. Union Radio Sci. (v.p. 1987-90, pres. 1990-93, past pres. 1993-96), Internat. Coun. Sci. Unions (mem. gen. com. 1991-93). Office: Univ of BC, U BC, Dept Elec/Computer Engring, Vancouver, BC Canada V6T 1Z4*

JUMISKO, MARCI KAY, economics educator; b. Zion, Ill., Nov. 21, 1970; d. Raymond H. and Kathleen M. Jumisko. BA in Econs., Rockford Coll., 1992; MA in Econs., No. Ill. U., 1994. Rsch. intern instnl. rsch. Coll. of Lake County, Grayslake, Ill., 1994-95, rsch. assoc., 1995-99, acting dir., 1998-99, adj. instr. econs., 1994—; rsch. analyst County Adminstr.'s Office, Lake County, Waukegan, Ill., 1999—. Contbr. articles to profl. jours. Vol. Lake County Mus., Wauconda, 1996—. Mem. Ill. Assn. for Instnl. Rsch., Rockford Coll. Alumni Assn. (bd. dirs., chmn. alumni admissions 1997—). Office: Lake County Courthouse 18 N County St 9th Fl Waukegan IL 60085-4334

JUMONVILLE, FELIX JOSEPH, JR., physical education educator, realtor; b. Crowley, La., Nov. 20, 1920; s. Felix Joseph and Mabel (Rogers) J.; m. Mary Louise Hoke, Jan. 11, 1952; children: Carol, Susan. BS, La. State U., 1942; MS, U. So. Calif., 1948, EdD, 1952. Assoc. prof. phys. edn. Los Angeles State Coll., 1948-60; prof. phys. edn. Calif. State U., Northridge, 1960-87, emeritus prof. phys. edn., 1987—; owner Felix Jumonville Realty, Northridge, 1974-82, Big Valley Realty, Inc., 1982-83, Century 21 Lamb Realtors, 1983-86, Cardinal Realtors, 1986-87; varsity track and cross-country head coach L.A. State Coll., 1952-60, Calif. State U., Northridge, 1960-71. Served with USCGR, 1942-46. Mem. Assn. Calif. State Univ. Profs., AAHPER, Pi Tau Pi, Phi Epsilon Kappa. Home: 2001 E Camino Parocela UniN Palm Springs CA 92264-8283

JUMP, BERNARD, JR., economics educator; b. Dayton, Ohio, Mar. 9, 1938; s. Bernard and Elin S. (Peterson) J.; m. Elizabeth Gay Ferguson, Aug. 22, 1959; children: Eric Christopher, Edie. BBA, U. Cin., 1960; MA in Econs., Ohio State U., 1962, PhD in Econs., 1964. Asst. prof. econs. Ball State U., Muncie, Ind., 1964-65; economist Esso Standard Eastern Inc., N.Y.C., 1965-66; assoc. prof., chmn. dept. econs. Hollins Coll., 1966-74; NSF postdoctoral fellow in urban econs. Maxwell Sch., Syracuse U., N.Y., 1970-71, vis. prof. in pub. adminstrn. and econs., 1974-76, prof. pub. adminstrn., 1976—, sr. research assoc., met. studies program, 1976—, dir. master pub. adminstrn. program, 1976-79; chmn. dept. pub. adminstrn. Maxwell Sch., Syracuse U., 1979-95, assoc. dean, 1984-95, dir. environ. fin. ctr., 1994-97; fellow in systems analysis NASA, 1969; fellow Acad. for Contemporary Problems, 1975-79; cons. in field. Co-editor Public Employment and State and Local Government Finances, 1980; contbr. articles to profl. publs., chpts. to books, monographs. NDEA fellow, 1961-64. Mem. Nat. Tax Assn. (mem. intergovtl. fiscal relations com. 1975—, mem. property taxation com. 1971-74, bd. dirs. 1986-89), Am. Soc. Pub. Adminstrn., Govt. Fin. Officers Assn., Assn. for Pub. Policy Analysis and Mgmt., Am. Econs. Assn., N.Y. State Govt. Fin. Officers Assn. (gov.), Beta Gamma Sigma. Home: 8300 Salt Springs Rd Manlius NY 13104-8774 Office: Syracuse U Maxwell Sch Dept Pub Adminstrn 215 Eggers Hall Syracuse NY 13244-1090*

JUMP, CHESTER JACKSON, JR., clergyman, church official; b. Covington, Ky., Mar. 31, 1918; s. Chester Jackson and Inez (Moore) J.; m. Margaret Elizabeth Savidge, Sept. 5, 1942; children—Karen Jane, Richard Alan, Catherine Louise, Robert Jon. AB, Albright Coll., 1938; MA, Columbia U., 1940; BD, Union Theol. Sem. N.Y.C., 1943; postgrad., Ecole Coloniale, Brussels, Belgium, 1950-51; DD, Eastern Bapt. Theol. Sem., 1965. Ordained to ministry Bapt. Ch., 1943. Pastor N.E. Larger Parish, Lyndon Center, Vt., 1943-44; missionary Belgian Congo, Republic of Congo, 1945-62; regional rep. Am. Bapt. Fgn. Mission Socs., Valley Forge, Pa., 1961-64; exec. dir. Am. Bapt. Fgn. Mission Socs., 1965-83; assoc. gen. sec. Am. Bapt. Chs., 1965-83, dir. world relief, 1983-88, interim gen. sec., 1987-88; mem. gen. bd. Nat. Council Chs., 1965-75, mem. program bd., exec. com. div. overseas ministries, 1965-83, mem. gov. bd., 1965-75, 87-88; mem. exec. com. Bapt. World Alliance, 1965-85, 87-88, v.p., 1980-85; bd. dirs., exec. com. Am. Bapt. Chs., Pa., Del., 1989-97; chmn., budget commn. Commn. on New Ch. Planting and Adminstrv. Svcs., 1989-99; Trustee Eastern Bapt. Theol. Sem.; mem. Ch. World Service Commn., 1983-88, fin. com., 1983-88; mem. Bapt. World Aid, 1970-85; mem. bd. personnel com. IMPACT. Author: (with wife) Congo Diary, 1950, Coming, Ready or Not, 1959. Mem. Pi Gamma Mu. Home and Office: # K2 Delta Pl Lewisburg PA 17837

JUMPER, JOHN PHILLIP, career officer; b. Paris, Tex., Feb. 4, 1945; s. Jimmy Jefferson and Maree Loretta (Nowell) J.; m. Ellen Elizabeth McGhee, Mar. 29, 1969; children: Catherine, Janet, Melissa. BSEE, Va. Mil. Inst., 1966; MBA, Golden Gate U., 1978; postgrad., Air Command and Staff Coll., Maxwell AFB, Ala., 1977-78, Nat. War Coll., Washington, 1981-82. Commd. 2d lt. USAF, 1966, advanced through grades to gen., 1997; instr. pilot 414th Fighter Weapons Squadron, Nellis AFB, Nev., 1974-77; action officer Directorate for Ops. and Tng., Washington, 1978-81; comdr. 430th Tactical Fighter Squadron, Nellis AFB, Nev., 1982-83; exec. officer to comdr. Hdqrs. Tactical Air Command, Langley AFB, Va., 1983-86; vice comdr. 33d Tactical Fighter Wing, Egling AFB, Fla., 1986-87, comdr., 1987-88; comdr. 57th Fighter Weapons Wing, Nellis AFB, 1988-90; dep. dir. politico-mil. affairs Joint Staff, Washington, 1990-92; sr. mil. asst. for sec. def. Office Sec. Def., Washington, 1992—; comdr. 9th AFB, Shaw AFB, 1994-96; Deputy Chief of Staff, Air and Space HAF, Washington, 1996-97; commdr. USF in Europe, 1997—, Allied Air Forces Ctrl. Europe, Ramstein AB, Germany, 1997—. Contbr. articles to mil. pub. Decorated Def. DSM with oak leaf cluster, Legion of Merit DSM with oak leaf cluster, DFC with 2 oak leaf clusters, Air medal with 17 oak leaf clusters. Mem. Air Force Assn. Roman Catholic. Avocations: racquet ball, jogging, piano, guitar, computers.

JUN, JONG SUP, public administration educator; b. Sunsan, Korea, July 26, 1936; s. Myung D. and Jeum S. (Pai) J.; m. Soon Y. Jun, Sept. 16, 1964; children: Eugene, Amy. LLB, Yeungnam U., Taegu, Korea, 1960; MA, U. Oreg., 1964; PhD, U. So. Calif., 1969. Prof. Calif. State U., Hayward, 1968—; vis. prof. Hosei U., Tokyo, 1992-93; coord. Pub. Adminstrn.Theory Network, 1993—; coord. The Pub. Adminstrn. Theory Network. Author: Public Administration: Design and Problem Solving, 1986, Philosophy of Administration, 1994; editor: Development in the Asia Pacific, 1994, Jour. Adminstrn. Theory and Praxis, 1993—; editl. mem. Internat. Rev. Adminstrv. Sci., 1991; co-editor Globalization and Decentralization, 1996. Recipient Rsch. Grant award Social Rsch.Coun., N.Y., 1979, Outstanding Acad. Achievement award Am. Soc. Pub. Adminstrn., San Francisco, 1982; Fulbright scholar Yonsei U., Korea. Fellow Nat. Acad. Public Adminstrn. Avocation: Japanese gardening. Home: 18698 Mount Lassen Ct Castro Valley CA 94552-1955 Office: Calif State U Hayward CA 94552

JUNCK, MARY, newspaper publishing executive. Pub., pres. St. Paul Pioneer Press, St. Paul, until 1993; pub., CEO The Baltimore Sun, 1993-97; pres. ea. newspapers The Times Mirror Co., Balt., 1997—. Office: The Times Mirror Co 501 N Calvert St Baltimore MD 21202-3604

JUNE, ROY ETHIEL, lawyer; b. Forsyth, Mont., Aug. 12, 1922; s. Charles E. and Elizabeth F. (Newnes) J.; m. Laura Brautigam, June 20, 1949; children: Patricia June, Richard Tyler. BA, U. Mont., 1948, BA in Law, 1951, LLB, 1952. Bar: Mont. 1952, Calif. 1961. Sole practice Billings, Mont., 1952-57; atty. Sanders and June, 1953-57; real estate developer Orange County, Calif., 1957-61; ptnr. Dugan, Tobias, Tornay & June, Costa Mesa, Calif., 1961-62; city prosecutor Costa Mesa, 1962-63, asst. city atty., 1963-67, city atty., 1967-78, sole practice, 1962—; Atty., founder, dir. Citizens Bank of Costa Mesa, 1972-92; atty. Costa Mesa Hist. Soc., Costa Mesa Playhouse Patron's Assn., Red Barons Orange County, Costa Mesa Meml. Hosp. Aux., Harbor Key, Child Guidance Ctr. Orange County, Fairview State Hosp. Therapeutic Pool Vols., Inc. Active Eagle Scout evaluation team Harbor Area Boy Scouts Am., YMCA; atty. United Fund/Cmty. Chest Costa Mesa and Newport Beach; bd. dirs. Boys' Club Harbor Area, Mardan Ctr. Ednl. Therapy, United Cerebral Palsy Found., Orange County; docent Palm Springs Mus., 1996—. With USAF, WWII. Decorated Air medal with oak leaf cluster, DFC. Mem. Calif. Bar Assn., Costa Mesa C. of C. (bd. dirs.), Masons, Scottish Rite, Shriners, Santa Ana Country, Amigos Viejos, Los Fiestadores, Palm Springs Calif. Air Mus. (docent).

JUNEAU, PIERRE, broadcasting company executive; b. Verdun, Que., Can., Oct. 17, 1922; s. Laurent Edmond and Marguerite (Angrignon) J.; m. Fernande Martin, Mar. 17, 1947; children: Andre, Martin, Isabelle. BA, College Sainte-Marie, Montreal, 1944; postgrad. in philosophy, Sorbonne, Paris, 1949; lic. in philosophy, Inst. Cath., Paris, 1949; PhD (hon.), York U., Toronto, 1972, LLD (hon.), 1973; PhD (hon.), Trent U., Peterborough, Ont., 1981, LLD (hon.), 1987; PhD (hon.), Moncton (New Brunswick, Can.) U., 1988, Ryerson Poly. U., Toronto. With Nat. Film Bd. Can., 1949-66; dist. rep., asst. regional supr. of Que., chief internat. distbn. Nat. Film Bd. Can., Montreal, 1951; asst. head European office Nat. Film Bd. Can., London, 1952-54; sec. Nat. Film Bd. Can., Montreal, 1954-64, sr. asst. to commr. and dir. French Lang. prodn., 1964-66; vice chmn. Bd. Broadcast Govs., Ottawa, 1966-68; chmn. Can. Radio-TV Commn., Ottawa, 1968-75; minister communications Govt. Can., Ottawa, 1975, adviser to Prime Min., 1975; chmn. Nat. Capital Commn., 1976-78; under sec. state Govt. Can., 1978-80, dep. min. communications, 1980-82; pres. CBC, Ottawa, 1982-89; vis. prof. U. Montreal, 1989—; co-founder Cité libre, periodical, 1949; co-founder, 1st pres. La Fedn. des Mouvements de Jeunesse au Que., early 1950's; bd. dirs. Electromome Ltd., Sta. CISM Radio. Co-founder Montreal Internat. Film Festival, 1950's, pres., 1959-68; former sec., former bd. dirs. Albert-Prevost Psychiat. Inst., Montreal, 1960s; former chmn. bd. Ecole nouvelle St.-Germain; co-founder, bd. dirs. Institut Canadien d'Education des Adultes; bd. dirs. Nat. Arts Centre. Decorated officer Order Can. Mem. Royal Soc. Can., Club of Rome. Office: U Montreal, Dept Communications, Montreal, PQ Canada R3C 2H1

JUNEWICZ, JAMES J., lawyer; b. Oct. 1, 1950; s. John and Genevieve J.; m. Virginia Bornyas. BS, Georgetown U., 1972; JD, Duquesne U., 1976; LLM, NYU, 1978. Bar: Pa. 1977, D.C. 1978, Ill. 1984. Asst. gen. counsel SEC, Washington, 1982-84; ptnr. Mayer, Brown & Platt, Chgo., 1987—. Office: Mayer Brown & Platt 190 S La Salle St Ste 3900 Chicago IL 60603-3410

JUNG, BETTY CHIN, health program associate, epidemiologist, educator; b. Bklyn., Nov. 28, 1948; d. Han You and Bo Ngan (Moy) C.; m. Lee Jung, Oct. 1, 1972; children: Daniel, Stephanie. AA, Kings Coll., 1968; BS, Columbia U., 1971; MPH, So. Conn. State U., 1993. RN, Conn., Miss., N.Y.; cert. health edn. specialist. Adminstrv. asst. Columbia U., N.Y.C., 1968-69; practical nurse Babies Hosp., N.Y.C., 1969-70, charge nurse, 1974-76; staff nurse Columbia-Presbyn. Hosp., N.Y.C., 1971-73; sch. nurse Nassau County Sch. System, Long Island, N.Y., 1984-85; grad. asst. So. Conn. State U., New Haven, 1991-92; coop. edn. intern Conn. Dept. Health Svcs., Hartford, 1991-92; intern North Ctrl. Dist. Health Dept., Enfield, Conn., 1992; epidemiologist Conn. Dept. Pub. Health, Hartford, Conn., 1992-98; health program assoc. Conn. Dept. Pub. Health, Hartford, 1998—; staff nurse Quinnipiac Coll. Student Health Svcs., 1998; health promotion cons. So. Conn. State U. Dept. Pub. Health, New Haven, 1991, lectr., adj. faculty 1998—; tchg. asst. So. Conn. State U., New Haven, 1992, curriculum developer, 1992, vol. rsch. analyst, 1993, founder grad. alumni mentor program, 1993-94, mem. adv. coun., 1997—; instr. Albertus Magnus Coll., 1995-96; computer cons., course dir. continuing edn. program, Dept. Pub. Health, So. Conn. State U., 1998—; health columnist Baldwin (N.Y.) Newcomers Club, 1977-78; coord. Dept. Pub. Health and Svcs./Conn. EPI Info. Network, Hartford, 1994—; mem. Nat. Lead Info. Ctr. Spkrs. Bur., 1997-98; vol. scientist Sci.-By-Mail, 1997-98; mem. Nat. Safety Coun. Environ. Health Ctr. Spkrs. Referral Bur., 1998—; apptd. mem. Conn. Dept. of Pub. Health's Affirmative Action Employee Adv. Com., 1998—. Mem. editl. bd. Data Quality, 1994-98; mem. manuscript rev. bd. Jour. Clin. Outcomes Mgmt., 1995—, Pub. Health Reports, 1997, Women's Health in Primary Care, 1998—; contbg. editor Episource, A Guide to Resources in Epidemiology, 1998—; contbr. articles to profl. jours. Vol. nurse health educator, coord. Chinatown's First Ann. Health Fair, 1971-72; treas. Tenant Assn., Bronx, N.Y., 1976-77; pre-confirmation tchr. Bethlehem Luth. Ch., Baldwin, N.Y., 1981-85. Merit scholar Kings Coll., 1968, Columbia U. scholar, 1968-69, Bessie Lee Gambrill scholar So. Alumni Assn., 1992; grantee USPHS, 1992-98, Fed. HUD, 1995-98, U.S. Preventive Health and Health Svcs., 1998, block grant Maternal Child Health, 1998—. Fellow Soc. for Pub. Health Edn.; mem. APHA (health care reform activist network, peer assistance the model stds. project), Am. Med. Writers Assn., Am. Statis. Assn. (OSPA media experts list 1997—), Coun. State and Territorial Epidemiologists (alternate cons. environ. health, HIV/AIDS and surveillance, occpl. health, managed care, pub. health tng. 1996—, occpl. health, managed care, pub. health svcs.), Nat. Lead Info. Ctr. Spkrs. Bur., Conn. Pub. Health Assn., So. Conn. State U. Alumni Assn. (founder pub. health chpt. 1994, interim pres. 1994, pres. 1994-98, chair exec. com. 1994—, chair MPH accreditation com. 1994—, chair svc. com. 1994, svc. com. survey rschr. 1994—, coord. pub. health alumni mentor program 1994—, founder, dir., coord. pub. health alumni spkrs. bur. 1997—, editor MPH Alumni Record 1995—, database cons. 1994—, data mgr. 1994—, rsch. analyst 1994—, mem. scholarship com. 1998—, Alumni Appreciation award 1998), Conn. Women in Healthcare Mgmt., Inc., Columbia U. Sch. Nursing Alumni Assn. (survey cons. 1994—), Nat. Acad. Sci. (mentor Career Planning Ctr. for Beginning Scientists and Engrs. 1997—), Boston Mus. Sci. (vol. scientist, 1997-98). Avocations: reading, writing, research, bicycling. Home: 25 Driftwood Ln Guilford CT 06437-1929 Office: Conn Dept Pub Health PO Box 340308 Hartford CT 06134-0308

JUNG, CHARLENE, city treasurer; b. Maoui, Hawaii. BA, Univ. S.C., 1977; postgrad., Calif. State Univ. City treas. Anaheim, Calif., 1992—. Office: City Hall 200 S Anaheim Blvd Anaheim CA 92805-3820*

JUNG, DAVID JOSEPH, law educator; b. St. Louis, Aug. 19, 1953; s. Joseph Henry and Leona Louise Jung; m. Jennifer Beryl Hammett, Oct. 15, 1951; 1 child, David O'Grady Hammett. BA, Harvard U., 1975; JD, U Calif., Berkeley, 1980. Lectr. in law U. Calif., Berkeley, 1980-82; from asst prof. to assoc. prof. Hastings Coll. Law U. Calif., San Francisco, 1982-88, prof., 1988—; vis. prof. U. Hamburg, Germany, 1992, U. Iowa, Iowa City, 1993—; dir. Pub. Law Rsch. Inst., 1994—. Co-author: Remedies: Public and Private, 2d edit., 1996; contbr. articles to profl. jours. Bd. dirs. San Francisco Neighborhood Legal Aid, 1983, North of Market Child Car Ctr., 1984-86; sec. El Cerrito Youth Baseball, 1997—. Recipient U.S. Law Week award U.S. Law Week, 1980, 1066 Found. award 1066 Found., 1986. Mem. Am. Assn. Law Schs. (remedies section, exec. com. 1991-92). Office: U Calif Hastings Coll Law 200 Mcallister St San Francisco CA 94102-4707

JUNG, DIANA LYNN, graphic designer; b. Toledo, May 23, 1969; d. Wan J. and Jin J. BS, Ohio State U., 1991. Graphic designer Dusseau Design, Columbus, 1992-96; graphic designer BancOne Svcs. Corp., Columbus, 1996-97; pres./owner MESH Design and Comm., 1997—. Mem. Columbus Soc. Communicating Arts, Digital Designers Club. Office: MESH Design and Comm 3701 1/2 N High Commons Columbus OH 43214

JUNG, DORIS, dramatic soprano; b. Centralia, Ill., Jan. 5, 1924; d. John Jay and May (Middleton) Crittenden; m. Felix Popper, Nov. 3, 1951; 1 son, Richard Dorian. Ed., U. Ill., Mannes Coll. Music, Vienna Acad. Performing Arts; student of, Julius Cohen, Emma Zador, Luise Helletsgruber, Winifred Cecil. Debut as Vitellia in: Clemenza di Tito, Zurich (Switzerland) Opera, 1955, other appearances with, Hamburg State Opera, Munich State Opera, Vienna State Opera, Royal Opera Copenhagen, Royal Opera Stockholm, Marseille and Strasbourg, France, Naples (Italy) Opera Co., Catania (Italy) Opera Co., N.Y.C. Opera, Met. Opera, also in Mpls., Portland, Oreg., Washington and Aspen, Colo.; soloist: Wagner concert conducted by Leopold Stokowski, 1971; with, Syracuse (N.Y.) Symphony, 1981, voice tchr., N.Y.C., 1970—. Home: 40 W 84th St New York NY 10024-4749 *Whether performing as a singer or teaching, attempting to understand the voice is tremendously daunting. As with life itself, the human voice defies understanding with its day to day differences and one's everchanging points of view. The secret of unflagging devotion to this life's work lies in accepting its elusiveness.*

JUNG, HENRY HUNG, mechanical engineer; b. Hong Kong, Aug. 3, 1957; s. Cheuk-Sun and Siu-Kuen (Ma) J.; m. Mi-Ying Miranda, Mar. 28, 1986. BS MechE, Ariz. State U., 1980; MS MechE, U. Ill., 1983; MBA, Santa Clara U., 1994. Engr. Lockheed Aircraft, Burbank, Calif., 1981-82; researcher U. Ill., Champaign-Urbana, 1982-83; engr. Pratt & Whitney Aircraft, West Palm Beach, Fla., 1983-84; sr. scientist Lockheed Missiles & Space Co., Palo Alto, Calif., 1984-94; sr. mfg. engr. Sun Microsystems Co., Mountain View, Calif., 1994-96; sr. supplies engr. Apple Computer, Cupertino, Calif., 1996-97; sr. mech. project engr. Intel, Santa Clara, Calif., 1997—. Mem. ASME, AIAA, N.Y. Acad. Scis., Sigma Xi, Tau Beta Pi, Pi Tau Sigma. Avocations: tennis, swimming. Home: 21486 Holly Oak Dr Cupertino CA 95014-4928 Office: Intel Corp Mail Stop SC12-201 2200 Mission College Blvd Santa Clara CA 95054-1549

JUNG, RICHARD KIETH, headmaster; b. St. Louis, Mar. 16, 1949; s. Donald and Anne (Hegykozi) J.; m. Carol Murray, Feb. 11, 1976; m. Janice K. Anderson, Feb. 6, 1982; children: Sarah, Andy. BA in English, U. Mo., St. Louis, 1971; MA in Linguistics, Ball State U., 1972; MA in Ednl. Adminstrn., Stanford U., 1981, EdD in Ednl Adminstrn. and Policy Analysis, 1983. Cert. tchr. English, Mo., secondary sch. adminstrn., Calif. Tchr. English University City (Mo.) High Sch., 1972-77; chair dept. English University City Pub. Schs., 1973-77; analyst Ctr. for Rsch. on Pvt. Edn., San Francisco, 1977-78; asst. prin. San Jose (Calif.) Unified Sch. Dist., 1979-80; dir. rsch. Nat. Adv. Coun. for Edn. of Disadvantaged Children, Washington, 1980-81; dir. divsn. edn. and human svcs. rsch. Advanced Tech., Inc., Reston, Va., 1981-84; sr. analyst Nat. Inst. Edn., Washington, 1984-87; prin. grades 9 and 10 John Burroughs Sch., St. Louis, 1987-91; headmaster Bullis Sch., Potomac, Md., 1991—; master tchr. Washington U. Tchr. Preparation Program, 1976-77; adj. prof. Washington U., St. Louis, Maryville Coll., St. Louis, 1988-91; mem. nat. review panel on progam effectiveness U.S. Dept Edn., 1988-97; mem. rev. panel D.C. Pub. Charter Sch. Bd., 1997—; mem. planning group D.C. Math Sci. and Tech. Pub. Charter Sch.; bd. dirs. Brown Acad.; cons. and presenter in field. Author: Educational Leaders, Society and Institutions, 1988, (handbook) Handbook of Research and Educational Administration, 1988; reviewer Jour. Ednl. Evaluation and Policy Analysis, 1988—; contbr. articles to profl. jours. Recipient Merit citation U.S. Dept. Edn., 1986; Rsch. fellow Ford Found., 1978-79. Mem. Am. Ednl. Rsch. Assn., Nat. Assn. of Prins. of Schs. for Girls (sec. of bd.), Assn. Ind. Sch. Greater Washington (bd. dirs.), Assn. Ind. Md. Schs., Cosmos Club. Avocations: jogging, cycling, theatre, golfing. Home: 2908 Cortland Pl NW Washington DC 20008-3429 Office: Bullis Sch 10601 Falls Rd Potomac MD 20854-4404

JUNG, RODNEY C., internist, academic administrator; b. New Orleans, Oct. 9, 1920; s. Frederick Charles and Clara (Cuevas) J. B.S. in Zoology with honors, Tulane U., 1941, M.D., 1945, M.S. in Parasitology and Microbiology, 1950, Ph.D., 1953. Diplomate: Am. Bd. Internal Medicine. Intern Charity Hosp. La., New Orleans, 1945-46; dir. Hutchinson Meml. Clinic, 1948; asst. parasitology Tulane U., 1948-50, instr. tropical medicine, 1950-53, asst. prof., 1953-57, assoc. prof. tropical medicine, 1957-63, prof. tropical medicine, 1963-73, clin. prof. internal medicine, 1973-91, clin. prof. tropical medicine, 1983-92, prof. emeritus tropical medicine, 1992—, head div. tropical medicine, 1960-63; health dir. City of New Orleans, 1963-70, 79-82; internist in charge Ill. Central Hosp., New Orleans, 1956-70; sr. vis. physician Charity Hosp., 1959—; mem. study sect. on tropical medicine and parasitology Nat. Inst. Allergy and Infectious Disease, 1963-67; mem. Commn. on Parasitic Diseases Armed Forces Epidemiol. Bd., 1967-73; chief communicable disease control, City of New Orleans, 1978; sr. in internal medicine Touro Infirmary. Co-author: Animal Agents and Vectors of Disease and Clinical Parasitology; editl. bd. Am. Jour. Tropical Medicine and Hygiene, 1972-94; contbr. articles to profl. jours. Pres. Irish Cultural Soc. New Orleans, 1980-92, pres. emeritus 1992—; officer res. div. New Orleans Police Dept., 1977-84; chmn. New Orleans Mosquito Control Bd. Served as lt. (j.g.) M.C. USNR, 1946-48. John and Mary Markle Scholar in med. sci. Fellow ACP; hon. fellow Brazilian Soc. Tropical Medicine; mem. Am., Royal socs. tropical medicine and hygiene, Am. Soc. Parasitologists, La. State Med. Soc., Orleans Parish Med. Soc., Nat. Rifle Assn., Irish Georgian Soc., La. Mosquito Control Assn., La. Soc. Internal Medicine, Am. Soc. Internal Medicine, New Orleans Acad. Internal Medicine, Am. Def. Preparedness Assn., Irish-Am. Cultural Inst., Nat. Trust. Historic Preservation, La. Landmarks Soc., Naval Inst., New Orleans Mus. Art, New Orleans Opera Assn., La. Wildlife Fedn., Phi Beta Kappa, Sigma Xi, Delta Omega, Alpha Omega Alpha. Presbyterian. Office: 3434 Prytania St Ste 460 New Orleans LA 70115-3579

JUNG, TIMOTHY TAE KUN, otolaryngologist; b. Seoul, Korea, Dec. 1, 1943; came to U.S., 1969; s. Yoon Yong and Helen Chung-Hyuk (Im) J.; m. Lucy Moon Young, Sept. 10, 1972; children: David, Michael, Karen. BS, Seoul Nat. U., 1966, Loma Linda U., 1971; MD, Loma Linda U., 1974; PhD, U. Minn., 1980. Diplomate, Am. Bd. Otolaryngology. Med. intern Loma Linda (Calif.) U. Med. Ctr., 1974-75; resident in surgery U. Minn. Med. Sch., Mpls., 1975-76; resident in otolaryngology U. Minn. Med. Sch., 1976-80, asst. prof. otolaryngology, 1980-84, clin. asst. prof., dir. prostaglandin lab., 1984-85; assoc. prof., dir. otolaryngology rsch. Loma Linda U., 1985-90, prof., dir. otolaryngology rsch., 1990-92, clin. prof., assoc. dir. otolaryngology rsch., 1992—; mem. deafness and communications disorders rev. com. Nat. Inst. Deafness and Communications, NIH, 1989-92. Bd. editors Annals of Otology, Rhinology & Laryngology, 1994—; contbr. numerous chpts. to med. books, over 100 articles and abstracts to med. jours. Sgt. Korean army, 1966-69. Recipient Edmund Price Fowler award. Fellow ACS, Triological Soc., Am. Acad. Otolaryngology (honor award 1990); mem. AMA, Am. Otol. Soc., Am. Neurotol. Soc., Soc. Univ. Otolaryngologists, Assn. Rsch. in Otolaryngology, Centurions, Collegium Otorhinolaryngologicum Amicetiae Sacrum, N.Am. Skull Base Soc., Alpha Omega Alpha. Seventh-day Adventist. Avocations: horticulture, photography, hiking. Home: 11790 Pecan Way Loma Linda CA 92354-3452 Office: 3975 Jackson St Ste 202 Riverside CA 92503-3947

JUNGBLUTH, CONNIE CARLSON, accountant, tax professional; b. Cheyenne, Wyo., June 20, 1955; d. Charles Marion and Janice Yvonne (Keldsen) Carlson; m. Kirk E. Jungbluth, Feb. 5, 1977; children: Tyler, Ryan. BS, Colo. State U., 1976. CPA, Colo., Ariz. Sr. acct. Rhode Scripter & Assoc., Boulder, Colo., 1977-81; mng. acct. Arthur Young, Denver, 1981-85; asst. v.p. Dain Bosworth, Denver, 1985-87; v.p. George K. Baum & Co., Denver, 1987-91; acct. Ariz. Luth. Acad., 1994-95; sr. tax acct. Ernst & Young, LLP, Phoenix, 1995-96; nat. tax mgr. McGladrey & Pullen, LLP, 1996—. Active Denver Estate Planning Coun., 1981-85, Ctrl. Ariz. Estate Planning Coun., 1997-98; organizer Little People Am., Rocky Mountain Med. Clinic and Symposium, Denver, 1986; adv. bd. Children's Home Health, Denver, 1986-89; fin. adv. bd. Gail Shoettler for State Treas., Denver, 1986; campaign chmn. Kathi Williams for Colo. State Legislature, 1986; mem. Sch. dist. 12 Colo. Edn. Found. Bd., 1991, Napa Sch. Dist. Elem. Site com., 1992-94; apptd. Ariz. Gov.'s Coun. Develpmental Disabilities, 1998-99, chmn. planning com., 1998-99. Named one of 50 to watch, Denver mag., 1988. Mem. AICPA, Internat. Assn. Fin. Planners, Colo. Soc. CPAs (strategic planning com. 1987-89, instr. bank 1983, trustee 1984-87, pres. bd. trustees 1986-87, bd. dirs. 1987-89, chmn. career edn. com. 1982-83, pub. svc. award 1985-87), Little People of Am., Colo. Mcpl. Bond Dealers, Ariz. Herb Assn., Metro North C. of C. (bd. dirs. 1987-90), Denver City Club (bd. dirs. 1987-88), Phi Beta Phi. Avocations: faith, family, horticulture, philanthropy, gourmet cooking. Office: McGladrey & Pullen LLP 2231 E Camelback Rd Ste 315 Phoenix AZ 85016-3447

JUNGBLUTH, KIRK E., real estate appraiser, mortgage banking executive; b. Lima, Ohio, Apr. 5, 1949; s. Harold A. and Marjorie J. (Brown) J.; m. Connie Carlson, Feb. 5, 1977; children: Tyler, Ryan. Student, Mesa Coll., Grand Junction, Colo., Regis Coll., Denver. Cert. Gen. real estate appraiser, Calif., Ariz. Loan officer, real estate appraiser Home Fed. Savs. & Loan, Ft. Collins, Colo., 1973-76; real estate appraiser Jungbluth & Assocs., Ft. Collins, 1976-83; pres., bd. dirs. Security Diamond Corp., Denver, 1982-90; nat. sales dir. InfoAm. Computers, Denver, 1982-90; chmn. bd. dirs., CEO U.S. Capital Lending Corp., Denver, 1987-91; ct.-appointed receiver Dist. Ct. State of Colo., 1990; mgr. real estate appraisal World Savs. & Loan Assn., Walnut Creek, 1992-93, Pleasanton, Calif., 1993-94. Sgt. USMC, 1969-71. Republican. Avocations: golf, snow skiing, scuba diving.

JUNGEBERG, THOMAS DONALD, lawyer; b. Berea, Ohio, June 12, 1950; s. Wilbert Donald and Carolyn Francis (Gaube) J.; m. Kathleen Ann Killmer, Oct. 5, 1973; children: Kimberlee Ann, Allison Lynn, Zebulun Thomas, Nathan Aaron. BA, Kent State U., 1972; JD, Cleve. State U., 1976. Bar: Ohio 1976, U.S. Dist. Ct. (no. dist.) Ohio 1977, U.S. Tax Ct. 1980, U.S. Supreme Ct. 1980. Tchr., Berea City Schs., Ohio, 1972-75; staff atty. Palmquist & Palmquist, Medina, Ohio, 1977-80, Gibbs & Craze, Parma Heights, Ohio, 1980-81; sole practice, Medina, 1981-87; v.p., gen. counsel, corp. sec. Shelby (Ohio) Ins. Co., 1987-95; prin. Lexington (Ohio) Ins. Cons., 1995-96; sole practice, Lexington, 1995-96; v.p. legal Reliance Nat., Cleve., 1996-98. Tchr., First Baptist Christian Sch., Medina, 1981-84; elder, sec. First Bapt. Ch. of Medina, 1979-86, chmn. First Bapt. Christian Sch., Medina, 1984; bd. govs. Ohio Med. Profl. Liability Underwriting Assn., 1993-95; dir. Ins. Inst. Ind., 1994-95. Mem. Ohio State Bar Assn., Am. Corp. Counsel Assn., Gideons Internat. (v.p. S.W. Camp). Republican. Avocations: piano; golf; archery. Home: 10236 Foxwood Dr North Royalton OH 44133

JUNGER, MIGUEL CHAPERO, acoustics researcher; b. Dresden, Germany, Jan. 29, 1923; came to U.S., 1941, naturalized, 1946; s. José and Adrienne (Junger) Chapiro; m. Ellen Sinclair, 1960; children: M. Sebastian, A. Carlotta. BS, MIT, 1944, SM, 1946; ScD (Gordon McKay scholar), Harvard U., 1951. Postdoctoral rsch. fellow in acoustics Harvard U., 1951-55; partner Cambridge Acoustical Assocs., Inc., 1955-59, pres., 1959-89, chmn. bd. dirs., 1989-97; sr. vis. lectr. ocean engring. dept. MIT, Cambridge, 1968-78; vis. prof. U. Technologie de Compiègne, 1975, 77-82. Author: Sound, Structures and Their Interaction, 1972, 2d edit., 1986, rev. edit., 1993, Eléments d'Acoustique Physique, 1978, Handbook of Acoustic Characteristics of Turbomachinery Cavities, 1997; guest editor, author: Structural Acoustics, 1997; contbr. articles to profl. jours. Fellow ASME (Rayleigh lectr., Per Bruel Noise Control and Acoustics Gold medal 1992), Acoustical Soc. Am. (Trent-Crede medal). Achievements include patents in field. Home: 90 Fletcher Rd Belmont MA 02478-2017

JUNGERMAN, JOHN ALBERT, physics educator; b. Modesto, Calif., Dec. 28, 1921; s. Albert Augustus and Freda (Durst) J.; m. Nancy Lee Kidwell, Oct. 23, 1948; children: Mark, Eric, Roger, Anne. AB, U. Calif., Berkeley, 1943, PhD, 1949. Research physicist Manhattan Project, Oak Ridge, Tenn. and Berkeley, 1944-45, Los Alamos, N.Mex., 1945-46, Lawrence Berkeley Lab., Berkeley, 1946-49, 50-51; asst. prof. physics U. Calif., Davis, 1951, prof. physics, 1960-91, prof. emeritus, 1991, founding dir. Crocker Nuclear Lab., 1965-80, chmn. physics dept., 1981-82, 83-87; assoc. mem. faculty Starr King Sch. for Ministry, Berkeley, Calif., 1992-93; vis. prof. U. Grenoble, France, 1972; prin. investigator nuclear physics Atomic Energy Commn., U. Calif., Davis, 1956-71; cons. OAS U. Chile, Santiago, 1982, OAS, 1971, Internat. Atomic Energy Agy., 1982. Author: Nuclear Arms Race: Technology and Society, 1986, 2d edit., 1990. Organizer, instr. Davis Summer Insts. on Nuclear Age Edn. for Secondary Sch. Instrs., 1986-93. NSF Nuclear Physics grantee, 1971-73, NSF Sci. Edn. grantee, 1990-93. Fellow Am. Physical Soc.; mem. Am. Solar Soc., Sigma Xi. Democrat. Avocations: piano, sailing, bicycling, painting. Office: Univ of Calif Davis Dept Physics Davis CA 95616

JUNGERS, FRANCIS, oil consultant; b. July 12, 1926; s. Frank Nicholas and Elizabeth (Becker) J.; children—Gary M., Randall O. BSME, U. Wash., 1947; student, Advanced Mgmt. Program, Harvard U., 1967. With Arabian Am. Oil Co., 1947-78, chmn. bd., chief exec. officer, 1973-78; bd. dirs. Donaldson Lufkin & Jenrette, Ga. Pacific Co., Thermo Quest Corp., Thermo Electron, The AES Corp., Esco, Thermo Ekotek Corp., Statia. Trustee Am. U., Cairo; bd. overseers Oreg. Health Scis. With USN, 1944-46. Mem. Waverly Golf Club, Multnomah Athletic Club, Athletic Club of Bend. Republican. Roman Catholic. Office: 822 NW Murray Blvd Ste 242 Portland OR 97229-5868*

JUNG HO, PAK, artistic director. Artistic dir. San Diego Symphony; condr. U. Southern Calif.; music dir. NEXT Chamber Orch., Phila., 1987; prin. condr. Disney Young Musicians Symphony Orch.; condr. Debut Orch., L.A.; guest condr. including L.A. Philharmonic, L.A. Chamber Orch., New Haven Symphony, Louisville Orch.; spkr. in field. Office: New Haven Symphony Orch 70 Audubon St New Haven CT 06510

JUNGKIND, WALTER, design educator, writer, consultant; b. Zurich, Switzerland, Mar. 9, 1923; came to Can., 1968; s. Oskar and Frieda (Leuthold) J.; m. Jenny Voskamp, 1953; children—Christine, Stefan, Brigit. Nat diploma, Kunstgewerbeschule, Zurich, 1943; nat diploma, Regent Street Poly tech., London, 1953. Freelance designer London, 1955-68; lectr. London Coll. Printing and Graphic Arts, 1960-65, sr. lectr., 1965-68; assoc. prof. dept. art and design U. Alta., Edmonton, Can., 1968-72, prof., 1972-90, prof. emeritus, 1990—; Design cons. pub. works Province of Alta., 1972-75; chmn. Canadian Adv. Com. Standards Council Can., 1978—. Initiator and curator internat. exhbn. Graphic Design for Pub. Service, 1972, Language Made Visible, 1973. Recipient Design Can. award Nat. Design Council Can., 1979, 1984; Chmns. award Nat. Design Council Can., 1982. Fellow Soc. Chartered Designers Gt. Britain, Soc. Graphic Designers Can. (pres. 1978-82); mem. Internat Coun. Graphic Design Assns. (pres. 1974-76, Design for Edn. award 1972.). Home: 6304-109th Ave, Edmonton, AB Canada T6A 1S2

JUNKER, BOBBY RAY, research and development executive, physicist; b. San Antonio, Tex., Aug. 29, 1943; s. Richard Eugene and Alice Emma (Gruetzmacher) J.; m. Judith Lynne Combs, Sept. 12, 1968 (div. Aug. 1974); 1 child, Bryce Allyn; m. Sheryl Ann Watson, Oct. 8, 1976 (div. July 1995); children: Melissa Sheryl, Evan Ryan; m. Virginia C. Katt, July 13, 1996. BS, U. Southwestern La., 1965; MA, U. Tex., 1967, PhD in Chemistry, 1969. Instr. chemistry U. Tex., Austin, 1969-70; rsch. assoc. physics U. Pitts., 1970-72; asst. prof. physics U. Ga., Athens, 1972-76; sci. officer Office Naval Rsch., Arlington, Va., 1977-84, dir. physics. divsn., 1983-86, dir. math. and phys. scis. dept., 1986-93, head electronics, info. and surveillance dept., 1993—. Contbr. chpts. to books. Treas. PTA, Fairfax, Va., 1988-89, county rep., 1990-92; treas. Fairfax Christian Ch., 1982-87, 92-95. Recipient Presdl. Meritorious Rank award U.S. Govt., 1989. Mem. AAAS, Am. Phys. Soc., Sigma Xi. Rsch. theoretical atomic physics, including electron-atom and ion-atom collisions. Avocations: woodworking, computers, remodeling. Office: Office Naval Rsch Sci and Tech Directorate 800 N Quincy St Arlington VA 22203-1906

JUNKER, EDWARD P., III, retired diversified financial services company executive. BS, Pa. State U., 1959; postgrad., Rutgers U. With Marine Bank, 1964-84, exec. v.p., 1972-74, pres., 1974-83, CEO, 1983-84; with PNC Bank (Marine Bank merger), 1984-97; chmn., CEO, vice chmn. PNC Bank Corp. PNC Bank N.W. Pa., 1985-97. Vice chair campaign steering com., mem. exec. bd., mem. Nat. Devel. Coun., pres. bd. trustees Pa. State U., 1998—; mem. exec. com. The Campaign for Pa. State; bd. dirs., mem. exec. com. Pa. State Geisinger Health Sys.; former chmn., mem. Coun. of Fellows Pa. State Erie, The Behrend Coll.; mem., treas. Erie-Western Pa. Port Authority; pres. Erie Zool. Soc.; immediate past pres., bd. dirs., mem. exec. com. Erie Conf. on Cmty. Devel.; trustee, treas. Erie Cmty. Found.; former chmn. bd. trustees, hon. life mem. bd. corporators Hamot Health Found.; mem. bd. incorporators St. Vincent Health Ctr.; pres. Pa. Bankers Assn., 1988-89. Recipient Philip Philip Mitchell Alumni Svc. award Pa. State U., 1984, Outstanding Citizen award Ams. for Competetive Enterprise Sys., 1992, Alexis de Tocqueville Soc. award United Way of Erie County, 1994, Disting. Pennsylvanian award Gannon U., 1995; named Man of Yr., Erie and Chautauqua Mag., 1997; Alumni fellow Coll. Health and Human Devel., Pa. State Erie, The Behrend Coll., 1987. Office: Pa State U Bd Trustees 205 Old Main University Park PA 16802*

JUNKER, HOWARD HENRY, periodical editor; b. Port Washington, N.Y., Oct. 8, 1940; s. Howard Ralph Junker and Evelyn Pott; m. Rozanne Enerson, Nov. 23, 1985; 1 child, Madison. BA, Amherst Coll., 1961; MA, U. San Francisco, 1978. Editor ZYZZYVA, San Francisco, 1985—. Editor: (anthologies) Roots and Branches, 1991, The Writer's Notebook, 1995, Strange Attraction, 1995, Lucky Break: How I Became a Writer, 1999. With U.S. Naval Air Res., 1964-66. Office: ZYZZYVA 41 Sutter St Ste 1400 San Francisco CA 94104-4903

JUNKINS, JOHN LEE, aerospace engineering educator; b. Oakman, Ga., 1943; s. N. Elouise Click; children: J. Stephen, Kathryn L. B in Aerospace Engring., Auburn U., 1965; MS in Engring., UCLA, 1967, PhD in Engring. with distinction, 1969. Registered profl. engr., Tex. Engring. aide NASA-Marshall Space Flight Ctr., Huntsville, Ala., 1962-64; aerospace engr. NASA-Marshall Space Flight Ctr., Huntsville, 1965-66; engr., scientist specialist McDonnell Douglas Astronautics Co., Santa Monica, Calif., 1966-70; asst. prof. aerospace engring. U. Va., Charlottesville, 1970-74, assoc. prof. aerospace engring., 1974-78; prof. engring. sci. and mechanics Va. Poly. Inst. and State U., Blacksburg, 1978-85; prof. aerospace engring. Tex. A&M U., College Station, 1985—, Tex. Engring. Experiment Sta. Disting. chair prof., 1985-89, George J. Eppright chair prof., 1989—, dir. Ctr. for Mechanics and Control, 1991—; vis. scientist AFOSR's Univ. Rsch. Resident Program, Wright-Patterson Flight Dynamics Lab., Dayton, Ohio, 1981-82; vis. prof. Naval Postgrad. Sch., Monterey, Calif., 1992-93; v.p., bd. dirs. Digital Scanning Sys., Inc., Santa Rosa, Calif., 1992—; assoc. dir. Tex. Space Grant Consortium, Austin, 1995—; cons. in field to numerous orgns. including Analytical Dynamics Assocs., College Station, 1988-92, SPARTA, Laguna Hills, Calif., 1990-91, ACTA, Inc., Downey, Calif., 1993, GM Design Ctr., Warren, Mich., 1994—; presenter in field. Author: Optimal Spacecraft Rotational Maneuvers, 1978, Optimal Estimation of Dynamical Systems, 1986, Mechanics and Control of Flexible Structures, 1993; mem. editl. bds. 6 jours.; contbr. chpts. to books and articles to profl. jours. Recipient John Leland Atwood award AIAA and Am. Soc. Engring. Edn., 1988; named Outstanding Alumnus, Auburn U., 1991. Fellow AIAA (assoc. editor Jour. Guidance, Control and Dynamics 1986-88, Mechanics and Control of Flight award 1983, Disting. Svc. citation 1989, G. Edward Pendray Aerospace Lit. award 1990, Paper Citation award 1994, Theodore Von Karman Lectureship award 1997), Am. Astronautical Soc. (assoc. editor Jour. Astronautical Scis. 1977-83, Disting. Svc. award for 1983, Dirk Brouwer award 1987); mem. Nat. Acad. Engring., Internat. Acad. Astronautics, Celestial Mechanics Inst. (assoc. editor Jour. Celestial Mechanics, Disting. Svc. award 1983), Sigma Xi (Disting. Scientist award 1992), Phi Kappa phi, Sigma Gamma Tau. Office: Tex A&M U Aerospace Engring Dept 701 HR Bright Bldg College Station TX 77843-3141*

JUNN, ELLEN N., psychology educator; b. Champaign, Ill., Apr. 11, 1958; d. Robert Sungjook and Sue Lee J.; m. Mark Tobin Murphy, July 28, 1984 (div. Jan. 1999); 1 child, Anna Junn Murphy. BS in Psychology cum laude, U. Mich., 1979; MA in Cognitive and Devel. Psychology, Princeton U., 1982, PhD in Cognitive and Devel. Psychology, 1984; cert., Calif. State U., San Jose, 1996, U. Pa., 1998, Harvard U., 1998. Vis. lectr. dept. psychology Ind. U., 1984-86; asst. prof. Calif. State U., San Bernardino, 1986-91; prof. dept. child and adolescent studies Calif. State U., Fullerton, 1991-97, ednl. equity coord. Sch. Human Devel. and Cmty. Svc., 1992-94, dir. office ednl. equity, 1994-97, acting head dept. child devel., 1995, with Office V.p. Acad. Affairs, 1996-98, adminstrv. fellow Office V.p. Acad. Affairs, 1996-97, dir. Faculty Devel. Ctr., 1998—; keynote spkr. Author: Child Growth and Devel., 1994, 95, 96, 97, 98, 99; guest expert Leeza TV, 1996; peer reviewer numerous publs.; presenter in field; contbr. articles to profl. jours. Edn. expert panelist Orange County Register, 1997; mem. Orange County Together Living Room Dialogue Program, 1994-95; vol. Thanksgiving Dinner for Homeless, Placentia, 1993—; mem. Med. Aid Sta. Incident Command Sys. Cmty. Task Force and Office Emergency Svcs. Vol. Disaster Svc., Anaheim Hills, Calif., 1993; participant AIDS Walk Orange County 10-K, Irvine, 1993. Grad. fellow Princeton U., 1980. Mem. AAUW, APA (mem. Asian Women's Task Force div.), Am. Assn. Higher Edn., Am. Edn. Rsch. Assn., Am. Psychol. Soc. (charter mem., liaison 1992—), Nat. Assn. Edn. Young Children, Calif. Assn. Edn. Young Children (pub. policy chair 1996-97), Orange County Assn. Edn. Young Children, Soc. Rsch. Child Devel., We. Psychol. Assn., Phi Eta Sigma. Democrat. Avocations: reading, traveling, art, gourmet cooking, fashion. Fax: 714-278-5805. E-mail: ejunn@fullerton.edu. Office: Calif State U Fullerton Faculty Devel Ctr PO Box 6850 Fullerton CA 92834-6850

JUNOD, DANIEL AUGUST, podiatrist; b. Vandalia, Ill., Sept. 12, 1928; s. Louis August and Nettie Louise (Martin) J.; m. Joanne Alice Denton, Mar. 29, 1952; children: Paul, John, Timothy, David, Stephen. Student, Greenville (Ill.) Coll., 1946-48; DPM, Scholl Coll. Podiatric Med., Chgo., 1952. Lic. podiatric physician, Ill. Pvt. practice podiatrist Greenville, 1952—; staff podiatrist Fair Oaks Nursing Home, Greenville, 1970—, Brauns Terrace, Greenville, 1989—, Faith Countryside Homes Nursing Ctr., Highland, Ill., 1992—, Highland (Ill.) Health Care Ctr., 1993—; staff podiatrist 25 different nursing homes in several south ctrl. Ill. cities, many yrs. Contbr. articles to profl. jours. Avocations: photography, volksmarching, video photography, photography and artwork. Home: 511 S 2nd St Greenville IL 62246-1742 Office: 309 W College Ave PO Box 697 Greenville IL 62246-0697

JUNZ, HELEN B., economist; d. Samson and Dobra Bachner. B.A., U. Amsterdam; M.A., New Sch. Social Research, 1956. Acting chief consumer price sect. Nat. Indsl. Conf. Bd., N.Y.C., 1953-58; research officer Nat. Inst. Econ. and Social Research, London, 1958-60; economist Bur. Econ. Analysis, Dept. Commerce, Washington, 1960-62; adviser div. internat. fin. bd. govs. Fed. Res. System, Washington, 1962-77; dep. asst. sec. Office of Asst. Sec. for Internat. Affairs, Dept. Treasury, Washington, 1977-79; v.p., sr. advisor 1st Nat. Bank Chgo., 1979-80; v.p. Townsend Greenspan & Co., Inc., N.Y.C., 1980-82; sr. advisor European dept. IMF, 1982-87, dep. dir. exch. and trade rels. dept., 1987-89, spl. trade rep., dir. Geneva office, 1989-94; dir. gold econs. svc. World Gold Coun., Geneva, Switzerland, 1994-96; pres. HBJ Internat., London, 1996—; adviser OECD, Paris, 1967-69; sr. internat. economist Council of Econ. Advisers, The White House, Washington, 1975-77. Contbr. articles to profl. jours. Mem. Am. Econ. Assn., Nat. Women's Forum, Coun. Fgn. Rels., Cosmos Club, Reform Club. Office: HBJ Internat, 23 Warwick Sq, London SW1V 2AB, England

JUODVALKIS, EGLE, writer; b. E. Chicago, Ind., Jan. 28, 1950; d. Antanas and Ona (Norkus) J.; m. Henryk Skwarczynski, Sept. 2, 1989. BA, U. Chgo., 1973. Sr. editor Radio Free Europe/Radio Liberty, Inc., Munich, 1976-95. Author: (poetry) If You Touch Me, 1972, Who Has the Ring?, 1983, The Necklace of Mnemosine, 1996. Mem. Lithuanian Writers' Union, Santara-Sviesa, Korp! Neo-Lithuania. Avocation: touring Greece. Home: 8608 Sayre Ave Burbank IL 60459-2260

JURA, JAMES J., electric utility executive; b. Creston, Nebr., Dec. 9, 1942; s. Joseph James and Edna Helena (Mackenstadt) J.; m. Fredericka Lee Benton, Sept. 5, 1972; children: Joseph, James, John, Fredericka. BA, U. Wash., Seattle, 1967; MBA, Seattle U., 1971; postgrad., Harvard U., 1985. With indsl. rels. staff Boeing Co., Seattle, 1968-71; with policy devel. staff OSHA, Washington, 1971-73; legis. and budget analyst Office Mgmt. and Budget, Washington, 1973-78; asst. adminstr. Bonneville Power Adminstrn., U.S. Dept. Energy, Washington, 1978-80; from exec. asst. adminstr. to adminstr. Bonneville Power Adminstrn., U.S. Dept. Energy, Portland, Oreg., 1980-91; CEO, gen. mgr. Assoc. Electric Coop. Inc., Springfield, Mo., 1991—; bd. dirs. N.Am. Electric Reliability Coun., Springfield C. of C. Bd. dirs. Assn. Mo. Elec. Coops., Mo. Employees Mut. Ins. Co. With U.S. Army, 1963-65. Republican. Office: Associated Electric Coop PO Box 754 Springfield MO 65801-0754

JURAN, JOSEPH MOSES, engineer; b. Braila, Rumania, Dec. 24, 1904; came to U.S., 1912, naturalized, 1917; s. Jakob and Gitel (Goldenberg) J.; m. Sadie Shapiro, June 5, 1926; children: Robert, Sylvia, Charles, Donald. BS in Elec. Engring., U. Minn., 1924; JD, Loyola U., 1935; DEng (hon.), Stevens Inst. Tech., 1988; DSc (hon.), U. Minn., 1992, Rochester Inst. Tech., 1992; LLD (hon.), U. New Haven, 1992. Bar: Ill. 1935; registered profl. engr., N.Y., N.J. With Western Electric Co., Inc., 1924-41; asst. adminstr. Office Lend-Lease Adminstrn., 1941-43, Fgn. Econ. Adminstrn., 1943-45; prof., chmn. dept. adminstrv. engring. NYU, 1945-51, prof. ind. engr., 1951; pvt. cons. N.Y.C., 1951-79; chmn. emeritus Juran Inst., Inc., Wilton, Conn., 1979—; cons. numerous indsl. cos. and govt. agys., 1945—, vis. lectr. numerous Am. and Fgn. univs.; founder, chmn. Juran Inst., Inc., 1979-87, emeritus, 1987—; founder, chmn. Juran Found., Inc., 1986—. Editor: Quality Control Handbook, 4th edit., 1988 (translated into Japanese, Spanish, Russian, Hungarian, Chinese, Portuguese); author numerous books including: (with N.N. Barish) Case Studies in Industrial Management, 1955, Managerial Breakthrough, 1964, (with J.K. Louden) The Corporate Director, 1966, (with F.M. Gryna, Jr.) Quality Planning and Analysis, 1970, 2d edit.,

1980, (video cassette series) Juran on Quality Improvement, 1981, Juran on Planning for Quality, 1988, Juran on Leadership for Quality, 1989, Juran on Quality by Design, 1992; lectr., author numerous papers on mgmt. Decorated Order of Sacred Treasure (Japan), 1981; recipient alumni medal U. Minn., 1954, Scroll of Appreciation Japanese Union Scientists and Engrs., 1961, 250th Anniversary medal Czech Higher Inst. Tech., 1965, Wallace Clark medal, 1967, ann. medal Technikhaza Esztergom, Hungary, 1968, medal Fedn. Tech. and Sci. Industries, Hungary, 1968, medal of honor camera Official de la Industria, Madrid, 1970, Plaque Appreciation Republic Korea, 1978, Stevens medal Stevens Inst. Tech., 1984, Chairman's award Am. Assn. Engring. Socs., 1988, Nat. medal Tech. U.S., 1992, Mng. Automation award Automation Hall of Fame, 1995. Fellow AAAS, ASME (hon., Warner medal 1945, Eli Whitney award 1995, Soichior Honda medal 1995), Internat. Acad. Mgmt., Am. Soc. for Quality Control (hon., Brumbaugh award 1958, Edwards medal 1962, Eugene L. Grant medal 1967), Am. Inst. Indsl. Engrs. (Gilbreth medal 1981), Am. Mgmt. Assn.; mem. NAE, European Orgn. Quality Control (hon., medal 1993), Romanian Acad. (academician 1992, established Juran award 1992), Australian Orgn. for Quality Control (Juran medal named in his honor 1975), Argentine Orgn. for Quality Control, Philippine Soc. for Quality Control, Spanish Assn. for Quality Control, Brit. Inst. Quality Assurance, Spanish Soc. for Quality Control, Sigma Xi, Tau Beta Pi, Alpha Pi Mu; mem., sometime officer many profl. assns. Office: Juran Inst Inc 11 River Rd Wilton CT 06897-4025

JURAN, SYLVIA LOUISE, editor; b. Chgo.; d. Joseph Moses and Sadie (Shapiro) J. BA, U. Minn.; MA, Columbia U., 1960; PhD, Harvard U., 1975. Project editor Macmillan Pub. Co., N.Y.C., 1981-91; editor Ralph Appelbaum Assocs. Inc., N.Y.C., 1991—; faculty The New Sch., N.Y.C., 1980-82. Project editor: Ency. of the Holocaust, 1990 (Dartmouth medal ALA, 1990), Ency. of the Third Reich, 1991; editor scripts for mus. exhbns.; contbr. articles to profl. jours. Nat. def. fgn. lang. fellowship, 1960-61, 62-63. Mem. Harvard Club of N.Y.C., Harvard Grad. Sch. Alumni Assn. (N.Y. exec. com. 1984—), James Beard Found. Office: Ralph Appelbaum Assocs Inc 133 Spring St New York NY 10012-3802

JURAND, JERRY GEORGE, periodontology educator, researcher; b. Gostyn, Piaski, Poland, Apr. 23, 1923; came to U.S., 1956; s. Piotr and Maria (Mizerska) J.; m. Ruth Edith I. Kujus, 1950; children: Lydia U., Robert B., Darlene S. Diploma, Polish Humanistic Lyceum, Ingolstad, Germany, 1947; Dr.Med.Dent., Friedrich Alexander U., Erlangen, Germany, 1956; DDS, U. Tenn., Memphis, 1965. Cancer rsch. scientist in biochemistry Roswell Park Meml. Inst., Buffalo, 1957-62; rsch. assoc. in immunology St. Jude Children's Rsch. Hosp., Memphis, 1962-65; assoc. prof. periodontology U. Tenn., Memphis, 1965-70, prof. periodontology, 1970—, rsch. dir. in periodontology, 1965-75, clinic dir. in periodontology, 1975-80; cons. in periodontics St. Jude Children's Rsch. Hosp., 1965—. Contbr. to book: Surface Chemistry and Dental Integuments, 1973; contbr. articles to profl. jours. Advisor Boy Scouts Am., Memphis, 1965-75; discussion panelist Amnesty Internat., Memphis, 1982. Capt. Dental Corps U.S. Army, 1953-56. NIH rsch. grantee, 1965-75. Mem. ADA (life), AAAS, Am. Assn. Dental Rsch. (life), Internat. Assn. Dental Rsch. (life), N.Y. Acad. Scis. Avocations: camping, scouting, nature preservation, canoeing, painting. Office: U Tenn Coll Dentistry 875 Union Ave Memphis TN 38103-3513

JURASEK, JOHN PAUL, mathematics educator, counselor; b. Flushing, N.Y., June 23, 1959; s. John Steven and Eleanor Rita Jurasek; m. Gale Marie Abrahamsen, May 22, 1993; 1 child, John IV. BS, Fairleigh Dickinson U., 1982; BA, SUNY, New Paltz, 1991; MS, Iona Coll., 1995. Cert. pub. sch. math. tchr., N.Y., N.J. Acct. Sony Corp., Park Ridge, N.J., 1982-85; learning ctr. coord. Rockland Community Coll., Suffern, N.Y., 1985-91; math. instr. Collegiate Sch., Passaic, N.J., 1991-92, Ridgefield Park (N.J.) Schs., 1992—. Contbr. articles to profl. jours. Mem. Town Dem. Com., Piermont, N.Y., 1980. Recipient Above and Beyond award RAMAQUOIS, Pomona, 1990, Counselor of Yr. award 1990. Mem. Internat. Soc. Technology in Edn., Math. Assn. Am., Nat. Coun. Tchrs. of Math., N.J. Edn. Assn., Northvale Rifle and Pistol Club, Am. Mensa, British Mensa. Democrat. Roman Catholic. Avocations: model rocketry, target shooting, computer programming. Home: 193 Howard Ave Orangeburg NY 10962-2314 Office: Ridgefield Park Schs 1 Ozzie Nelson Ct Ridgefield Park NJ 07660

JURASEK, RANDALL JOHN, project manager, educational consultant; b. Rockford, Ill., Nov. 19, 1954; s. Walter John and Florence (Misuraca) J.; m. Elizabeth Leigh Lichter, Sept. 22, 1979; children: Nicholas John, Alex Joseph. BS in Edn., Western Ill. U., 1977; MEd, Nat. Louis U., 1986; Cert. Advanced Studies, Nat. Louis U., 1997. Tchr. spl. edn. Kankakee Area Spl. Edn. Coop., 1977-78, Harlem Consol. Dist. 122, Loves Park, Ill., 1978-79, Rockford (Ill.) Sch. Dist. 205, 1980-88; systems engr. IBM, Rockford, 1988-91, edn. specialist, 1991-93; networking specialist, trainer Byron (Ill.) Comm. Unit Sch. Dist. 226, 1993-95, staff developer, 1995-97; project mgr. IBM K-12 Cons. Svcs., Indpls., 1997—; cons., presenter in field. Mem. parish coun. St. Mary's Ch., Byron, 1995—; mem. regional adv. bd. Discovery Ctr. Rockford, 1992—, Coun. Exceptional Children, Rockford, 1984-88, pres., 1987-88; mem. bus. adv. coun. Goodwill Industries; mem. N. Ill. Ctr. Adaptive Techs. Mem. ASCD, Phi Delta Kappa (newsletter editor 1986-88). Roman Catholic. Avocations: model railroading, O-guage, gardening, technology.

JURCYK, JOHN JOSEPH, JR., lawyer; b. Kansas City, Kans., Apr. 15, 1930; s. John Joseph Sr. and Ann (Kordash) J.; m. Rita Menghini, July 13, 1957; children: Jeff, John David, Amy L., Alison C., Ann E. AB in History, Rockhurst Coll., 1952; JD, U. Kans., 1957. Bar. Kans. 1957, U.S. Dist. Ct. Kans. 1957, U.S. Ct. Appeals (10th cir.) 1957, U.S. Ct. Appeals (8th cir.) 1984, U.S. Supreme Ct. 1970. Law clk. to chief judge U.S. Dist. Ct. Kans., Kansas City, 1957; assoc. McAnany, Van Cleave & Phillips, Kansas City, Kans., 1958-63, ptnr., 1963—, sr. trial lawyer, pres. corp., 1978-89; mem. nominating commn. 29th Jud. Dist., 1978-79; mem. merit selection panel for magistrate U.S. Dist. Ct. Kans., 1986-89, mem. adv. group Civil Justice Reform Act, 1991-94, mem. 10th Cir. Adv. Com., 1998—. Editor-in-chief Kans. Law Rev., 1957. Chmn. Civic Arts Council Kansas City (Kans.), 1965-69, Citizens Commn. on Local Govt. Wyandotte County (Kans.), 1969-70, United Way of Wyandotte County, 1995, 96; chmn. bd. edn. Bishop Ward High Sch., 1968-71; pres. St. Patrick Sch. Bd., Kansas City, Kans., 1979-80; bd. dirs. Kansas City region NCCJ, 1964-72, Kansas City, Kans., YMCA, 1971-76, Cath. Housing Svcs., 1978—, pres., 1985—; hon. dir. Rockhurst Coll., Kansas City, Mo.; mem. Kans. Citizen Justice Commn., 1997-99. Recipient Exceptional Performance citation Def. Rsch. and Trial Lawyers Assn., 1985. Fellow Am. Coll. Trial Lawyers, Am. Bar Found., Kans. Bar Found. (pres. 1995-96); mem. ABA, Kans. Bar Assn. (numerous coms., Outstanding Svc. award 1986), Johnson County Bar Assn., Wyandotte County Bar Assn. (pres. 1970-71, editor Advocate 1968-74), Internat. Assn. Def. Counsel, Kans. Assn. Def. Counsel (pres. 1984-85), U. Kans. Law Soc. (bd. govs. 1985-88), U. Kans. Law Alumni Assn. Greater Kansas City (pres. 1966), Kansas City Area C. of C. (sec. 1971-72, bd. dirs., chmn. 1991-92), Cursillo Movement Kansas City (lay dir. 1980-83), Serra Club, Rotary (bd. dirs. Kansas City 1979). Democrat. Roman Catholic. Office: McAnany Van Cleave & Phillips PO Box 1300 707 Minnesota Ave Fl 4 Kansas City KS 66101-2703

JUREDINE, DAVID GRAYDON, insurance company executive; b. Rahway, N.J., Aug. 26, 1937; s. Gordon Mounier and Ruby Fern (Thomas) J.; m. Carol Marie Nemec, Feb. 7, 1970; children: Adam, Jason. BS, Bowling Green State U., 1960; postgrad., Cleve.-Marshall Law Sch., 1963-66. Sales rep. Sperry Rand Corp., Cleve., 1960-62; claims rep. CNA Ins. Co., Cleve., 1962-66; div. mgr. Progressive Corp., Cleve., 1966-73; with Ohio Indemnity Co. (subs. of Bancins. Corp.), Columbus, Ohio, 1973-95, exec. v.p., 1987-95, also bd. dirs.; exec. v.p. Bancinsurance Corp., Columbus, 1980-95; ins. cons., 1995; mng. dir. RLI Ins. Co., Worthington, Ohio, 1995-98; pres. Am. Lenders Ins. Agy., Worthington, Ohio, 1998—. Avocations: charities, sports.

JURGENSEN, KAREN, newspaper editor. BA in Eng., U. N.C., 1971. Editorial and feature writer, columnist, editorial page layout editor Charlotte (N.C.) News, 1972-75; writer, editor Sea Grant Coll. Program U. N.C., Raleigh, 1976-79; from asst. lifestyle editor to lifestyle editor Miami News, 1979-82, asst. city editor, 1982; topics editor, life dept. USA Today, Arlington, Va., 1982; spl. projects editor, life dept. USA Today, 1983-85, dep. mng. editor, life dept., 1985-86, mng. editor, cover stories dept., 1986-87, sr. editor, days/spl. projects, 1987-91, editor of editorial page, 1991—, now editor of newspaper; participant Penney-Mo. Workshop, Columbia, Mo., 1981, Am. Press Inst. Workshops, 1981, 84, newspaper execs. mktg. sem. Am. Newspaper Pubs. Assn., 1986. Chair bd. vis. Chapel Hill Sch. Journalism and Mass Comm., U. N.C. Exchange scholar U. P.R., 1969-70. Mem. Am. Soc. Newspaper Editors (chair/vice chair press bar com. 1993-95, convention com. 1991-94, vice chair convention com. 1995-96, vice chair, chair literacy com. 1989-91, future of newspapers com. 1988-90, 91, writing awards bd. 1989-91), Nat. Conf. Editorial Writers. Office: USA Today 1000 Wilson Blvd Ste 600 Arlington VA 22209-3905*

JURIGA, RAYMOND MICHAEL, dentist; b. Uniontown, Pa., May 29, 1949; s. John Martin and Elizabeth Ann (Vanek) S.; m. Barbara Diane Menni, Aug. 13, 1972; children: Vanessa Rae, Max Nicholas. BS, Calif. State Coll., 1971; DMD, U. Pitts., 1975. Diplomate Am. Bd. Forensic Dentistry. Dentist Office of Patrick Piovesan, White Oak, Pa., 1975-76; dentist Westmore Dental Arts Group, Mt. Pleasant, Pa., 1976-78, dentist, ptnr., 1980—; dentist Office of Robert Sepp DDS, Connellsville, Pa., 1978-80; staff dentist Health South Outpatient Surg. Ctr., Mt. Pleasant, 1990—; cons. staff Harmon House, Mt. Pleasant, 1990—; part-time clin. instr. dental hygiene Westmoreland C.C., Youngwood, Pa., 1994—. Fellow Acad. Gen. Dentistry, Am. Endodonic Soc., Acad. Dentistry Internat.; mem. Pa. Dental Assn. (10th dist. rep. 1997—, forensic odontology com.), Pa. Dental Assn. (dental identification team), Am. Acad. Forensic Scis., Am. Soc. Forensic Odontology. Democrat. Roman Catholic. Avocations: photography, model railroading, stamp collecting, racquetball, bicycling. Office: Westmore Dental Arts Group 220 Bessemer Rd Ste 301 Mount Pleasant PA 15666-9141

JURKA, EDITH MILA, psychiatrist, researcher; b. N.Y.C., Dec. 4, 1915; d. Charles Anton and Edith Dorothy (Schevcik) J. BA, Smith Coll., 1936; postgrad., Charles U., Prague, Czechoslovakia, 1936-38; MD, Yale U., 1944. Diplomate Am. Bd. Psychiatry and Neurology. Intern in children's med. svc. Bellevue Hosp., N.Y.C., 1944-45, asst. alienist, 1947-49; rotating intern Gallinger Hosp., Washington, 1945-46; intern N.Y. State Psychiat. Inst., N.Y.C., 1946-47; asst. psychiatrist Mt. Sinai Hosp., N.Y.C., 1949-51; pvt. practice N.Y.C., 1949—; asst. psychiatrist Roosevelt Hosp., N.Y.C., 1954-57; chief psychiatrist Pleasantville (N.Y.) Cottage Sch., 1961-74; bd. dirs. intuition network Inst. Noetic Scis.; dir. Wind Song Programs. Fellow Am. Orthopsychiat. Assn.; mem. Am. Psychiat. Assn., N.Y. Coun. Child and Adolescent Psychiatry, N.Y. County Med. Soc., N.Y. State Med. Soc. (psychiat. medicine com.), Westchester Psychiat. Soc. Avocations: architecture, parapsychology, travel, gardening, theater. Home: 16 Applebee Farm Ln Croton On Hudson NY 10520 Office: 116 E 66th St New York NY 10021-6504

JURKAT, MARTIN PETER, management educator; b. Berlin, July 23, 1935; came to U.S., 1946, naturalized, 1951; s. Ernest Herman and Dorothy (Bergas) J.; m. Mayme Porter, May 31, 1958; children: Martin Alexander, Susanna, Maria. B.A. in Math. and Stats. with honors, Swarthmore (Pa.) Coll., 1957; M.A., U. N.C., 1961; Ph.D., Stevens Inst. Tech., Hoboken, N.J., 1972. Programmer Burroughs Corp. Research Lab., Paoli, Pa., 1960-61; sr. program analyst ITT Corp., Paramus, N.J., 1961-64; dir. Center Mcpl. Studies and Services Stevens Inst. Tech., 1975-77, chief transp. analysis div. Davidson Lab., 1964-75, Alexander Crombie Humphreys prof. mgmt. sci., 1979—; cons. Tank-Automotive Devel. Command, U.S. Army, 1975-88, AT&T, 1995—, Lucent, 1996—; dir. Cause project NSF, 1978-81. Co-author: The NATO Reference Mobility Model, 1980; author studies, reports on mobility, transp., human factors, math. edn. Mem. Assn. Computing Machinery, Soc. for Info. Mgmt., Artificial Intelligence Assn. Am. Democrat. Mem. Soc. of Friends. Home: 706 Hudson St Hoboken NJ 07030-5914 Office: Stevens Inst Tech Howe Sch Tech Mgmt Castle Point Sta Hoboken NJ 07030

JURKIEWICZ, MARGARET JOY GOMMEL, secondary education educator; b. Indpls., Sept. 5, 1920; d. Dewey Ezra and Joy Agnes (Edie) Gommel; m. Walter Stephen Jurkiewicz, Jan. 1, 1942; children: Mary Margaret, Dewey John, Walter Stephen Jr., Hugh Louis. BS, Ind. U., 1941; postgrad., U. Minn., 1942-43, Butler U., 1950-51, U. Cin., 1958-60, Ind. U., 1971-72, Ball State U., 1974-75. Cert. secondary tchr., Ind., Ohio. Tchr. home econs. Plymouth (Ind.) H.S., 1941-42, Indpls. Pub. Schs., 1949-57, Mt. Confort-Hancock Co. Schs., Mt. Comfort, Ind., 1957-58, Cin. Pub. schs., 1958-61; tchr. 6th grade Plymouth (Ind.) Sch. corp., 1961-63; tchr. home econs. and art Argos (Ind.) Cmty. Schs., 1963-67; thcr. home econs. Penn-Harris-Madison Schs., Mishawaka, Ind., 1967-83; tchr. chapt. I South Bend (Ind.) Sch. Corp., 1983-85; vol. teacher art various schs., Ind., 1985—, Mich., 1985-96, Ill., 1985-96. Author newsletter and booklet Polish Cultural Soc., 1979—, Ind. Home Econ. Assn., 1975—; editor newsletter Marshall County Chpt. Am. Assn. Ret. Persons, Plymouth, Ind., 1993—. Bd. dirs. Area Agy. on Aging Coun., Plymouth, Ind., 1987-94, Garden Cts. Sr. Housing, Plymouth, 1989-96; vol. tchr. schs. and librs. Mem. AAUW (pres., chair various coms.), Am. Home Econs. Assn., Am. Assn. Ret. Persons, Ind. Home Econ. Assn., Ind. Polish Cultural Soc. (v.p., chair various coms.), Marshall County Ret. Tchrs. (pres. 1993-95), Plymouth Pub. Libr. Friends (pres., chair various coms.), Tippecanoe Audubon Soc., PEO Sisterhood. United Methodist. Avocations: gardening, camping, travel, football games, sewing. Home: 11570 9A Rd Plymouth IN 46563-9581

JURKIEWICZ, MAURICE JOHN, surgeon, educator; b. Claremont, N.H., Sept. 24, 1923; s. Charles B. and Mary (Ostrowska) J.; m. Mary de Forest Freeman, July 7, 1951; children—Elizabeth de Forest, John Christopher. D.D.S. magna cum laude, U. Md., 1946; M.D., Harvard U., 1952. Diplomate: Am. Bd. Surgery, Am. Bd. Plastic Surgery (mem. bd. 1971-77, chmn. 1977-78). Intern Barnes Hosp., Washington U., St. Louis, 1952-53; resident Barnes Hosp., Washington U., 1953-58, clin. fellow, 1958-59, instr. surgery, 1957-59; mem. staff U. Fla. Hosp., Gainesville; asst. prof. surgery U. Fla., 1959-64, assoc. prof., 1964-67, prof., 1967-71, chief div. plastic and reconstructive surgery, 1959-71; chief of surgery VA Hosp., Gainesville, 1968-71; prof. surgery, chief of plastic and reconstructive surgery Emory Affiliated Hosps., Atlanta, 1971-92; chief surg. services Grady Meml. Hosp., Atlanta, 1972-77; chief of surgery VAMC, Atlanta, 1989-93; cons. in plastic surgery Walter Reed Gen. Hosp., Washington, 1971-91; sci. counselor Nat. Inst. Dental Rsch., 1966-71; chmn. com. on study of evaluation procedures Am. Bd. Med. Spltys., 1979-81; mem. at large Nat. Bd. Med. Exams., 1985-93; commr. Joint Commn. on Accreditation of Health Care Orgns., 1985-94 (sec. 1989-90, treas. 1990-91, vice chmn. 1991-92), Nat. Cons. in Plastic Surgery to the Shriners Hosp., 1995—. Editor: Operative Techniques in Plastic Surgery, 1994—; assoc. editor: Plastic and Reconstructive Surgery, 1972-78, 79-83, co-editor, 1985-89; assoc. editor Am. Surgeon, 1977-87. Served to lt. (j.g.) USNR, 1946-48. Fellow Royal Australasian Coll. Surgeons (hon.); mem. AMA, Am. Cancer Soc., Am. Cleft Palate Assn., ACS (bd. regents 1979-88, vice chmn. 1985-88, pres.-elect 1988, pres. 1989-90), Am. Soc. Plastic and Reconstructive Surgeons, Southeastern Soc. Plastic and Reconstructive Surgeons, Ga. Soc. Plastic and Reconstructive Surgeons, Southeastern Surg. Congress, Am. Soc. Head and NEck Surgeons (pres. 1989), Ednl. Founds. Plastic Surgery Coun., Am. Assn. Plastic Surgeons (pres. 1989-81), Am. So. surg assns. (1st v.p. 1993-94), Med. Assn. Ga. Home: 715 Old Post Rd NW Atlanta GA 30328-4758 Office: Emory U Clinic 25 Prescott St NE Atlanta GA 30308-2209

JURKOWSKI, ORION LECH, librarian; b. June 1, 1971. BA, DePaul U., Chgo., 1993; M Libr. and Info. Sci., Dominican U., River Forest, Ill., 1997. Libr. dir. River Grove (Ill.) Pub. Libr., 1997—. E-mail: rgs@sls.lib.il.us. Office: 8638 W Grand Ave River Grove IL 60171

JURMAN, ELISABETH ANTONIE, economist; b. Gnadenfeld, Germany, Aug. 3, 1938; came to U.S., 1961, naturalized, 1979; d. Alois and Margarete Koschella. MBA in Econs. with honors, U. Bridgeport, 1979; PhD, Fordham U., 1996. Market rsch. analyst Richardson-Merrell, Wilton, Conn., 1977-79; bus. analyst Am. Chain & Cable Co., Trumbull, Conn., 1979-81; corp. economist So. Conn. Gas Co., Bridgeport, 1982-94; sr. economist Am. Soc. Composers, Authors & Pubs., N.Y.C., 1994—; staff economist, energy rev. team State of Conn., spring 1978. Mem. Blue Ribbon Commn. on Revaluation for City of Bridgeport, 1983-84; mem. adv. com. Advanced Workshop in Regulation and Pub. Utility Econs., Rutgers U., 1985-95; mem. economists' forum adv. group Commr. Dept. Econ. Devel. for State Conn., 1989-95. Asst. editor Thrust, The Jour. for Employment and Tng. Profls., 1978. Recipient Disting. Alumni award U. Bridgeport, 1986. Mem. Am. Econ. Assn., Nat. Assn. Bus. Economists (bd. dirs., past pres., mem. exec. com. Conn. chpt.), MBA Assn. U. Bridgeport, Beta Gamma Sigma, Phi Kappa Phi. Home: 20 Arrowhead Ln Fairfield CT 06430-7201 Office: 1 Lincoln Plz New York NY 10023-7129

JURTSHUK, PETER, JR., microbiologist; b. N.Y.C., July 28, 1929; s. Peter and Mary (Ferens) J.; m. Rebecca Jones, Jan. 2, 1971; children: Peter, Larissa. A.B., NYU, 1951; M.S., Creighton U., 1953; Ph.D., U. Md., 1957. Asst. prof. pharmacology Bklyn. Coll. Pharmacy, L.I. U., 1957-59; asst. prof. enzyme chemistry U. Wis.-Madison, 1962-63; asst. prof. microbiology U. Tex., Austin, 1963-69; assoc. prof. biology and biochemistry U. Houston, 1970-76, prof., 1976—, dir. program in microbiology, 1990—; mem. vis. biol. program Am. Inst. Biol. Scis., 1969-72. Contbr. chpts. to books. Recipient Disting. Service award Am. Soc. Microbiology, 1982; NIH grantee, 1964-75; NSF grantee, 1986-89. Fellow Am. Acad. Microbiology; mem. Am. Soc. Microbiology (pres. Tex. br. 1972-74), N.Y. Acad. Scis., Am. Soc. Biochemistry and Molecular Biology, Am. Chem. Soc., Sigma Xi (pres. U. Houston chpt. 1979-80). Russian Orthodox. Home: 879 Ramada Dr Houston TX 77062-5607 Office: U Houston Biology Dept Houston TX 77204-5513

JURY, MEREDITH A., federal judge. Apptd. bankruptcy judge cen. dist. U.S. Dist. Ct. Calif., 1997. Office: 3420 12th St Riverside CA 92501-3801

JUSKOWIAK, TERRY EUGENE, career military officer; b. Danville, Pa., May 29, 1951; s. Joseph Leon and Betty Lorraine (Dilliplane) J.; m. Susan Kay Renn, Sept. 15, 1974; children: John, Christopher, Jennifer. BA, The Citadel, Charleston, S.C., 1973; MS, Fla. Inst. Technology, Melbourne, 1981. Commd. 2d lt. U.S. Army, 1973, advanced through ranks to brig. gen.; contract cost mgmt. analyst Army Mat. Ctr. U.S. Army, Alexandria, Va., 1980-84; aide-de-camp Sec. Army U.S. Army, Washington, 1984-85; dep. V Corps logistics officer U.S. Army, Frankfurt, Germany, 1986-88; exec. officer 122 Main 3d Armored Divsn. U.S. Army, Hanau, Germany, 1988-89; from divsn. staff to battalion cmdr. 82d Airborne Divsn. U.S. Army, Ft. Bragg, N.C., 1989-92; spl. asst. to chief of Staff U.S. Army, Washington, 1992-94; brigade cmdr. 10th Mtn. Divsn. U.S. Army, Ft. Drum, N.Y., 1994-96, asst. divsn. cmdr. support 10th Mtn. Divsn., 1996—; dep. comdg. gen. NATO SFOR Spt Cmd, 1996-98; dir. logistics I4 U.S. Atlantic comd. Norfolk, Va., 1997-98; comdr. 1st Corps Support Command (Airborne), Ft. Bragg, N.C., 1998—. Decorated Legion of Merit, Bronze Star, Def. Meritorious Svc. medal. Mem. Assn. Citadel Men, Assn. U.S. Army, Quartermaster Assn., 82d Airborne Assn., 10th Mtn. Divsn. Assn. Presbyn. Avocations: reading, running, skiing. Home: 4 Adams St Fort Bragg NC 28307-2002 Office: 1st Corps Support Command Quartermaster St Fort Bragg NC 28307-5000

JUST, GEMMA RIVOLI, retired advertising executive; b. N.Y.C., Nov. 29, 1921; d. Philip and Brigida (Consolo) Rivoli; B.A., Hunter Coll., N.Y.C., 1943; m. Victor Just, Jan. 29, 1955. Copy group head McCann Erickson, N.Y.C., 1958-62; copy. supr. Morse Internat., N.Y.C., 1962-67; v.p., dir. creative svcs. Deltakos div. J. Walter Thompson, N.Y.C., 1967-75; v.p., copy dir. Sudler & Hennessey, div. Young & Rubicam, N.Y.C., 1980-87; sr. v.p., assoc. creative dir. copy, 1987-88, ret., 1989. Mem. Episcopal Ch. Women of Incarnation, N.Y.C., also ch. altar guild pres. and acolyte. Named Best Writer, Art Dirs. Club N.Y., 1979, Best Writer Young & Rubicam, 1981; recipient Aesulapius awards Modern Medicine mag., 1980-88. Mem. Coun. Communications Socs., Pharm. Advt. Coun., Am. Med. Writers Assn. (exec. com. 1973). Mem. Episcopal Women's Club of Ch. of the Incarnation, also altar guild. Home: 155 E 38th St Apt 5D New York NY 10016-2663

JUST, JENNIE MARTHA, mental health nurse; b. Glasgow, Mont., Apr. 22, 1936; d. Nels Peter and Cecilia G. (Damman) Larsen; m. Robert E. Just, Aug. 30, 1958; children: Daniel Richard, Mark William. Diploma, Hamline U. Sch. Nursing, St. Paul, 1957. Cert. psychiat. and mental health nurse. Staff nurse med.-surg. Mounds Park Hosp., St. Paul, 1958-64, Loretto Hosp., New Ulm, Minn., 1964-72; instr. Sch. Practical Nursing New Ulm Sch. System, 1973-74; staff nurse acute psychiatry Knoxville (Iowa) VA Med. Ctr., 1975-86, coord., case mgr. psychiat. teaching program, 1986-97, fed. women's program mgr., 1992-95. Bd. dirs. Iowa divsn. Am. Cancer Soc., 1990-95, chmn. pub. edn. local unit, 1990. Home: 1472 N Shore Dr Knoxville IA 50138-8445

JUST, RICHARD EUGENE, agricultural and resource economics educator consultant; b. Tulsa, Feb. 18, 1948; s. William and Leah (Flaming) J.; m. Janet Lee Humphries, Aug. 26, 1989; children: Angela K. Eisinger, David R., Ronald L. Mower. BS, Okla. State U., 1969; MA, U. Calif., Berkeley, 1971, PhD, 1972. Prof. agrl. econs. and stats. Okla. State U., Stillwater, 1972-75; prof. agrl. and resource econs. U. Calif., Berkeley, 1975-85; prof. agrl. and resource econs. U. Md., College Park, 1985-92, chmn. dept., 1992-95, disting. univ. prof., 1995—; cons. The World Bank, Washington, 1976—, Oak Ridge Nat. Lab., 1976-81, Winrock Internat., 1979-81, Electric Power Rsch. Inst., 1981-83, Stanford Rsch. Inst., 1981, Safeway Stores, Inc., Oakland, Calif., 1983-86, Price Waterhouse, 1987-91, The Pillsbury Co., Mpls., 1988-89, U.S. Gen. Acctg. Office, Washington, 1978-79, 90-95, others; prin. Law and Econs. Consulting Group, 1996—; vis. prof. Ben Gurion U. Negev, 1977, Brigham Young U., 1977, 79-80, 94; sr. rsch. fellow The Inst. for Policy Reform, 1991—. Author: Applied Welfare Economics and Public Policy, 1982, Commodity and Resource Policies in Agricultural Systems, 1991, Conflict and Cooperation on Trans-Boundary Water Resources, 1998, (monographs) Econometric Analysis of Production Decisions, 1975, Econometric Analysis of Processing Tomatoes, 1978; editor Am. Jour. Agrl. Econs., 1984-86, editorial com., 1978-80; mem. editorial bd. Jour. Devel. Planning Lit., 1985—, Springer-Verlag, 1989—; mem. editorial coun. Western Jour. Agrl. Econs., 1982-84; also articles to jours. Mem. task force on economy Calif. Dem. Com., 1981-83; mem. agrl. policy task force for speaker Calif. Assembly, 1983-84; bishop LDS Ch., 1993-97, state pres., 1997—. Internat. Inst. Ecol. Econs. fellow, 1991—. Fellow Am. Agrl. Econs. Assn. (dissertation awards com. 1976-78, selected papers com. 1981-93, com. on jour. pub. 1986, fellows election com. 1991-96, mem. pub. enduring quality com. 1998—, Quality of Rsch. Discovery award 1977, 80, 83, 89, 90, 96, Outstanding Jour. Article award 1981, 93, Enduring Quality award 1992, 94, 98); mem. Western Agrl. Econs. Assn. (editorial coun. 1982-84, Outstanding Pub. Rsch. award 1974, 83, 96), Am. Econ. Assn., Royal Econ. Soc., Econometric Soc., Atlantic Econ. Soc., Alpha Zeta. Office: Agrl/Resource Econs U Md College Park MD 20742-5535

JUST, WARD SWIFT, author; b. Michigan City, Ind., Sept. 5, 1935; s. F. Ward and Elizabeth (Swift) J. Student, Lake Forest (Ill.) Acad., 1949-51, Cranbrook (Mich.) Sch., 1951-53, Trinity Coll., Hartford, Conn., 1953-57. Reporter Waukegan (Ill.) News-Sun, 1957-59, Newsweek, 1959-61, Reporter mag., 1962-63; corr. Newsweek, 1963-65, Washington Post, 1965-70; writer Vineyard Haven, Mass., 1970—. Author: To What End, 1968, A Soldier of the Revolution, 1970, Military Men, 1970, The Congressman Who Loved Flaubert and Other Washington Stories, 1973, Stringer, 1974, Nicholson at Large, 1975, A Family Trust, 1978, Honor, Power, Riches, Fame, and the Love of Women, 1979, In the City of Fear, 1982, The American Blues, 1984, The American Ambassador, 1987, Jack Gance, 1989, Twenty-One Selected Stories, 1990, The Translator, 1991, Ambition & Love, 1994, Echo House, 1997, A Dangerous Friend, 1999; contbr. to Best Am. Short Stories, 1972, 73, 76. Recipient O. Henry award, 1985, 86, 93.

JUSTEN, RALPH, museum director; b. Milw., Mar. 10, 1952. Exec. dir. Nat. R.R. Mus., Green Bay, Wis., 1997—. Office: Nat RR Mus 2285 S Broadway Green Bay WI 54304-4832

JUSTESEN, DON ROBERT, psychologist; b. Salt Lake City, Mar. 8, 1930; s. Richard Carvel and Elizabeth Agnes (Gustafson) J.; m. Patricia Ann Larson, Feb. 14, 1957; children: Lyle Richard, Jonille Jacelyn, Tracy Ann, Anthony Ray. BA in Psychology and Philosophy, U. Utah, 1955, MA, 1957, Ph.D., 1960. Asst. prof., chmn. dept. psychology Westminster Coll., Salt Lake City, 1959-62; lectr. to prof. dept. psychology U. Mo.-Kansas City, 1963-75; vis. prof. U. Colo., Boulder, 1965; asst. prof. to prof. dept. psychiatry U. Kans. Sch. Medicine, Kansas City, 1963-96; dir. behavioral radiology labs. VA Med. Ctr., Kansas City, 1962-95; cons. Nat. Coun. on Radiation Protection and Measurements, Washington, 1977—, EPA, NAS, NIH, NSF, USN, 1972-95, to assocs. programs NRC/NAS, 1988-94. Contbr. articles to profl. jours.; assoc. editor Jour. Microwave Power and Electromagnetic Energy, 1975-88; editor Spl. Supplements to Radio Sci., Washington, 1977-79; editor in chief Bioelectromagnetics, 1988-93; mem. editorial bd. Bioelectromagnetics Soc., 1979-83, 88-93. Pres. Fountains Homes Assn., Grandview, Mo., 1974-75. Served with USN, 1948-52, ATO; served to lt. USNR, 1962-65. Recipient First Cash prize in psychopharmacology Am. Psychol. Assn., 1968; VA Research Career Scientist, 1980; USPHS grantee, 1971-86. Fellow AAAS, APA, Am. Psychol. Soc.; mem. IEEE (sr.), Soc. for Neurosci., Bioelectromagnetics Soc. (pres. 1984-85), Brit. Soc. Philosophy of Sci., Nat. Acad. Sci., Internat. Union Radio Sci. (U.S. nat. com., commn. on metrology). Home: 12416 Ewing Circle Grandview MO 64030-1834 *My father, the late Richard Carvel Justesen, was an inventor who never sought a patent or a penny for his inventions. When I asked why he invented, he said his reward was a complex ecstacy that bloomed at the moment of creation, a rapture of elation tinged with sadness. I failed to understand this paradox of affect until experiencing it myself. The elation derives from making or thinking something significant that's never been made or thought before. The sadness inheres in the utter inability to share the emotional joy. One is confined, to paraphrase Hume, to the solipsism of the creative moment.*

JUSTICE, (DAVID) BLAIR, psychology educator, author; b. Dallas, July 2, 1927; s. Sam Hugh and Lou-Reine (Hunter) J.; m. Rita Norwood, July 26, 1972; children: Cynthia, David, Elizabeth. BA, U. Tex., Austin, 1948; MS, Columbia U., 1949; MA, Tex. Christian U., 1963; PhD, Rice U., 1966. Diplomate Am. Bd. Med. Psychotherapists. Reporter Ft. Worth Star-Telegram, 1952-55; sci. writer N.Y. Daily News, 1955-56, Ft. Worth Star-Telegram, 1956-64; sci. editor, columnist Houston Post, 1964-73; exec. asst. to Mayor Houston, 1966-72; prof. psychology Sch. Pub. Health, U. Tex., Houston, 1968—; assoc. dean for acad. affairs U. Tex., Sch. Pub. Health, Houston, 1994—; dir. Project Support, Imagery & Immune Function in Breast Cancer, 1993—; co-investigator Alt. Medicine Ctr. for Cancer Rsch. U. Tex. Sch. Pub. Health, Houston, 1995—; co-investigator U. Tex. Ctr. for Alternative Med. Cancer Rsch.; sr. psychologist, group therapist, psychiat. residency faculty Tex. Rsch. Inst. Mental Scis., 1973-85; cmty. assoc. Rice U., Lovett Coll.; cons. child abuse Tex. Dept. Human Resources; faculty assoc. Ctr. for Health Promotion, R & D, U. Tex. Health Sci. Ctr., mem. inter-faculty coun., 1991-92; dir. Ctr. for Prevention of Violence and Injury, 1987-89, chmn. faculty Sch. of Pub. Health, 1990-91, chmn. faculty policy com., 1989-90, faculty marshal, 1990, mem. exec. com., 1991-93, vice chair interfaculty coun., 1992-93; vis. scholar U. Colo., 1990—; founding assoc. Blaffer Gallery U. Houston. Author: Violence in the City, 1969, Detection of Potential Community Violence, 1967, (with Rita Justice) The Abusing Family, 1976, The Broken Taboo: Sex in the Family, 1979, Perspectives in Public Mental Health, 1982, Who Gets Sick: Thinking and Health, 1987, Who Gets Sick: How Beliefs, Moods and Thoughts Affect Your Health, 1988, The Abusing Family, rev. edit., 1990, A Different Kind of Health: Finding Well-Being Despite Illness, 1998; Visits with Violet: Lessons on How to Be Happy 100 Years, 1999; editor: Your Child's Behavior, 1972; editorial bd.: Internat. Jour Mental Health, 1980—. Gen. chmn. Houston Job Fair, 1967-73; chmn. Houston Manpower Area Planning Council, 1972-74; mem. Tex. Urban Devel. Commn., 1970-72; bd. dirs. Houston Housing Devel. Corp., Tex. Citizens Human Devel., 1979-84, Greater Houston Com. Prevention of Child Abuse, 1982-88; sec. bd. mgrs. Tarrant County Hosp., Dist., 1961-64; pres. Greater Houston Youth Council, 1978-79, Houston Area Council on Sudden Infant Death Syndrome, 1977-78; mem. nat. adv. com. Marine Biomed. Inst., U. Tex. Med. Br., 1971-84; mem. Office of Minority Affairs, Resource Persons Network, HHS, 1988—; mem. community bd. Tex. Youth Council; vestry, chmn. adult edn. St. John The Divine Episc. Ch., 1984-88. Served with USNR, 1945-46. Recipient most outstanding book award Tex. Writers Roundup, 1970, award of recognition City of Houston, 1973, Benjamin Franklin Book award Pubs. Mktg. Assn. Am., 1988, Excellence in Media award Am. Psychol. Assn., 1988, Friends of Fondren Libr. book award Rice U., 1989, 91, Heritage award for child abuse rsch. Child Abuse Prevention Coun., 1989; named One of Five Outstanding Young Men of Tex., 1962; recipient numerous awards for sci. writing; grantee NIH. Fellow Am. Coll. Psychology, Am. Inst. Stress; mem. Nat. Assn. Sci. Writers (life; exec. com. 1965-67), Houston Psychol. Assn. (pres. 1975), Am. Public Health Assn. (chmn. mental health sect. 1980-81, governing council 1983-85, action bd. 1985-87, mental health sect. award 1989), Coun. on Behavioral and Social Scis., Am. Assn. Schs. Pub. Health, Phi Beta Kappa (dir. Houston chpt. 1979-89, pres. Houston chpt. 1982-83), Phi Beta Kappa Assocs. Clubs: Dr.'s of Houston, Knights of the Vine. Home: 6416 Sewanee St Houston TX 77005-3760 Office: 1200 Hermann Pressler Dr Houston TX 77030-3900

JUSTICE, BOB JOE, corporate development executive b. Ardmore, Okla., Dec. 14, 1946; s. Jesse William and Nora Estell (Boston) J.; BBA, U. Okla., 1970; MBA, Coll. William and Mary, 1973; m. Patricia Ann Thorpe, Dec. 26, 1970; children: Chad Andrew, Melanie Katherine, Kimberly Ann. Landman, Mobil Oil Co., Oklahoma City, 1970-71; planning analyst DuPont Corp., Wilmington, Del., 1973-75; planning specialist Houston Oil & Minerals Corp., Houston, 1976-79; mgr. planning and econs. Dome Petroleum Corp., Denver, 1979-82; mgr. investment and bus. analysis Union Pacific Resources, Ft. Worth, 1982-89; mgr. fin. Lasmo Energy, Tulsa, 1989-90; mgr. corp. devel Aquila Energy Corp., Omaha, 1990-94; cons., 1994—. Served with U.S. Army, 1971-73. Am. Assn. Petroleum Landmen scholar, 1968-70. Mem. Planning Forum, Assn. Corp. Growth, Am. Petroleum Inst. Republican. Mem. Reformed Ch. Am. Home: 15818 Howard St Omaha NE 68118-2108 Office: 14536 W Center Rd Ste 153 Omaha NE 68144-3218

JUSTICE, BRADY RICHMOND, JR., medical services executive; b. Albertville, Ala., Dec. 26, 1930; s. Brady R. and Kate (McEachern) J.; m. Sandra Gearner, Dec. 29, 1956; children: David, Michael, Lori Blankenship, Kathryn Baker. BBA, Baylor U., 1953. CPA, Ind. Ptnr. Arthur Andersen & Co., Dallas, 1953-64, Indpls., 1964-72; exec. v.p. Basic Am. Industries, Inc., Indpls., 1972-83; pres. Basic Am. Med., Inc., Indpls., 1983-92; sr. v.p. Columbia Hosp. Corp., 1992-93; chmn. Heritage Capital Corp., Indpls., 1993—. Mem. Columbia Club, Lions (pres. Indpls. chpt.). Republican. Baptist. Home: 5435 Hedgerow Dr Indianapolis IN 46226-1625 Office: Heritage Capital Corp 6900 Gray Rd Indianapolis IN 46237-3209

JUSTICE, DAVID CHRISTOPHER, baseball player; b. Cin., Apr. 14, 1966; m. Halle Berry, Jan. 1, 1993 (div. 1997). Student, Thomas More Coll. With Atlanta Braves, 1989-96, Cleve. Indians, 1997—. Named Rookie of Yr. Baseball Writers' Assn. Am., 1990, Sporting News, 1990; mem. Nat. League All-Star Team, 1993, 94; named to Sporting News Silver Slugger Team, 1993. Player World Series, 1991, 92. Office: Cleve Indians Jacobs Field 2401 Ontario St Cleveland OH 44115-4003*

JUSTICE, DONALD RODNEY, poet, educator; b. Miami, Fla., Aug. 12, 1925; s. Vascoe J. and Mary Ethel (Cook) J.; m. Jean Catherine Ross, Aug. 22, 1947; 1 son, Nathaniel Ross. BA, U. Miami, 1945; MA, U. N.C., 1947; postgrad., Stanford U., 1948-49; PhD, U. Iowa, 1954. Instr. English U. Miami, 1947-51; asst. prof. Hamline U., St. Paul, Minn., 1956-57; lectr. U. Iowa, 1957-60, asst. prof., 1960-63, assoc. prof., 1963-66, prof., 1971-82; prof. Syracuse U., 1966-70, U. Fla., Gainesville, 1982-92. Author: The Summer Anniversaries, 1960, Night Light, 1967, Departures, 1973, Selected Poems, 1979, Platonic Scripts, 1984, The Sunset Maker, 1987, A Donald Justice Reader, 1992, New and Selected Poems, 1995, Oblivion: On Writers and WRiting, 1998, Orpheus Hesitated beside the Black River, 1998; editor: The Collected Poems of Weldon Kees, 1962. Rockefeller Found. fellow in poetry, 1954, Ford Found. fellow, 1964, Guggenheim Found. fellow in poetry, 1976, Acad. Am. Poets fellow, 1988; Nat. Endowment for the Arts grantee, 1967, 73, 80, 89; recipient Pulitzer Prize in poetry for Selected Poems, 1980, Bollingen prize for poems, 1991, Lannan Literary award, 1996. Mem. Am. Acad. Arts and Letters, Acad. Am. Poets (chancellor 1997). Home: 338 Rocky Shore Dr Iowa City IA 52246-3836*

JUSTICE, EUNICE MCGHEE, missionary, evangelist; b. Fairchance, Pa., Feb. 13, 1922; d. Felix McGhee and Clara May Chavous; divorced; children: Rebecca L. Brothers, William Wood. Leader, youth dir. Avalon Zion Foursquare Ch., L.A., 1969-71; missionary, prayer warrior Pentecostal Faith Ch. for All Nations, N.Y.C., 1971-77, missionary, evangelist(ordained), 1979—; trainer missionaries, 1977—; prophetess, pres. Missionary Evang. Tng. Ctr., Inc., Tampa, Fla., AKA, Dorcas House Ministries, Tampa, 1986-93; producer Dorcas House childrens Workshop, Jones Intercable Pub. Access TV. Editor: Untitled, 1970; paintings exhibited Fla. and Ga., 1980—. Advocate for the poor, 1980—. Recipient Nat. Achievement award Nat. Assn. Negro Bus. and Profl. Womens Clubs, N.Y.C., 1956, Excellence in Gov. Publs. award Nat. Advt. Coun. Cols., Ohio, 1962, VIC award, Fruit of the Spirit award for Committed Christian Svc., 1997, Joseph award Nat. Neighborhood Enterprise Coun., Inc., 1998. Mem. Browns Meml., Cogic. Home: 101 E Amelia Ave Tampa FL 33602-2235 Office: Dorcas House Ministries PO Box 664 Tampa FL 33601-0664 *The greatest challenge to humanity today is to get hold of the abundant life that Jesus came and showed us is within.*

JUSTICE, FRANKLIN PIERCE, JR., oil company executive; b. Wanego, W.Va., May 5, 1938; s. Franklin Pierce and Jeneta Ruth (Cooley) J.; m. Eva Mae Hartley, June 8, 1960; children: Kerry, Kelly, Kevin. BSBA, W.Va. State Coll., 1967; MBA in Fin., Marshall U., 1977; postgrad., U. Louisville, 1971-72. Reporter Dun & Bradstreet, Inc., Charleston, W.Va., 1960-63, reporting mgr., 1963-65, office mgr., Huntington, W.Va., 1966-68; domestic trade specialist U.S. Dept. Commerce, Charleston, 1968-70; pres., investment mgr. Equal Opportunity Fin., Inc., Ashland, Ky., 1970-93; adminstrv. asst. to v.p. personnel Ashland Oil, Inc., 1973-74, adminstrv. asst. to v.p. external affairs, 1974-75, mgr. spl. projects, 1975-76, dir. pub. affairs, 1976-78, v.p. pub. rels., 1978-82, v.p., 1985-93; v.p. ops. support Ashland Services Co., 1982-85; ret., 1993; exec. dir. Rsch. and Econ. Devel. Ctr. Marshall U., Huntington, W.Va., 1993-95; v.p. devel. Marshall U., 1995—; pres. Marshall U. Rsch. Corp., 1993—; bd. dirs., exec. com. Econ. Devel. Corp., Ashland, Ky.; dir. W.Va. Roundtable; pres. Roundtable Venture Fund; exec. com. East Ky. Corp.; cons. in field. Vice chmn. Ky. Ctr. for Arts, Louisville, 1982-92; bd. dirs. Ky. Coun. Econ. Edn., 1978-90, chmn. bd., 1980-83; dir. Marshall U. Bus. Adv. Bd., 1982—; exec. com. bd. dirs. W.Va. State Coll. Found., Inc., 1988-95; bd. dirs. LEadership W.Va., Delta Dental of Ky., Ram Technologies, Inc., HAdco Inc., 1992—. Mem. W.Va. C. of C. (chmn. bd. dirs. 1992-94, exec. com.), Ashland Area C. of C. (1st v.p. 1978-79, pres. 1980, bd. dirs. 1978-98), Ky. C. of C. (chmn. bd. dirs. 1983). Republican. Home: 226 Governors Landing Murrells Inlet SC 29576 Office: Marshall U 400 Hal Greer Blvd 107 Corbly Hall Huntington WV 25755

JUSTICE, JACK BURTON, retired lawyer; b. Hardy, Ky., Aug. 2, 1931; s. George Edward and Goldia (Alley) J.; m. Martha Monser, Dec. 28, 1957 (dec. Feb. 1974); m. Judith Farquhar Lang, Apr. 26, 1975; children—Jonathan Burton, George Lewis, Paul Williamson. A.B. in Polit. Sci, W.Va. U., 1952, postgrad. in law, 1954-55; B.A. in Jurisprudence, Oxford (Eng.) U., 1954, M.A., 1960. Bar: Pa. bar 1956. Assoc. firm Drinker Biddle & Reath, Phila., 1956-62; ptnr. Drinker Biddle & Reath, 1962-82, White & Williams, Phila., 1982-96; bus. mgr. Am. Oxonian, 1967-86; lectr. in field. Contbr. articles t profl. jours. Pres. Youth Svc., Phila., 1962-65; chmn. Phila. Com. on City Policy, 1966-67, Southeastern Pa. chpt. Ams. for Democratic Action, 1968-70; bd. overseers William Penn Charter Sch., Phila., 1978-91, clk., 1986-89. Rhodes scholar, 1952-54. Mem. Assn. Am. Rhodes Scholars (sec. 1967-86, pres. 1986-94), Franklin Inn (pres. 1991-94). Democrat. Home: The Kenilworth at Alden Pk Apt 903K 2979 W Schoolhouse Ln Philadelphia PA 19144

JUSTICE, MELISSA MORRIS, family nurse practitioner; b. Jellico, Tenn., June 3, 1953; d. Amos and Mabel Ruth (York) Morris; m. Leon Justice, July 5, 1974; children: Heather Renee, Thomas Leon. Diploma, St. Mary's Sch. Nursing, 1973; BSN with honors, Lincoln Meml. U., 1989; MSN, U. Tenn. Cert. coronary care, infection control Ctr. for Disease Control Atlanta. Supr. ICU and critical care unit LaFollette (Ind.) Med. Ctr.; DON svc. Laurel Manor, New Tazewell, Tenn.; dir. of nursing Meadowbrook Manor, La Follette, Tenn.; nurse CCU, infection control, quality assurance, coord. Jellico (Tenn.) Community Hosp.; family nurse practitioner Area Health Ctr., Huntsville, Tenn., Cmty. Health Clinic, LaFollette, Tenn., LaFollette Med. Ctr. Clin., 1994—. Recipient Most Outstanding Student Nurse award, Acad. Achievement award. Mem. ANA, Tenn. Nurses Assn, Sigma Theta Tau. Home: 1219 Middlesboro Hwy La Follette TN 37766-2835

JUSTICE, WILLIAM WAYNE, United States district judge; b. Athens, Tex., Feb. 25, 1920; s. William Davis and Jackie May (Hanson) J.; m. Sue Tom Ellen Rowan, Mar. 16, 1947; 1 dau., Ellen Rowan. LL.B., U. Tex., 1942. Bar: Tex. 1942. Ptnr. firm Justice & Justice, Athens, 1946-61; part-time city atty. Athens, 1948-50, 52-58; U.S. atty. U.S. Dist. Ct. (ea. dist.) Tex., Tyler, 1961-68, U.S. dist. judge, 1968—, chief judge, 1980-90, sr. judge, 1998—. Subject of book William Wayne Justice, A Judicial Biography (Frank R. Kemerer), 1991. Vice pres. Young Democrats Tex., 1948; adv. council Dem. Nat. Com., 1954; alternate del. Dem. Nat. Conv., 1956, presdl. elector, 1960. Served to 1st lt. F.A. AUS, 1942-46, CBI. Recipient Nat. Outstanding Fed. Judge award ATLA, 1982, Outstanding Civil Libertarian award Tex. Civil Liberties Union, 1986, Lifetime Achievement award NACDL, 1996. Episcopalian. Office: 903 San Jacinto Blvd Ste 310 Austin TX 78701

JUSTICE-MALLOY, RHONA JEAN, educator, theatrical artist; b. Boston, May 22, 1954; d. Joseph Miller and Regina Lucille (Burge) J.; m. James Kevin Malloy, Apr. 21, 1979; 1 child, Amanda Katherine. BS, U. Evansville, 1974; MFA, U. Ga., 1979, PhD, 1994. Profl. performer free-lance, 1979-89; instr. Truman Coll., Chgo., 1986-89, South Suburban Coll., South Holland, Ill., 1989-90, Ind. Univ. N.W., Gary, Ind., 1989-90, U. Ga., Athens, 1994-95; co-producer, dir. Highlands (N.C.) Playhouse, 1996—; asst. prof. Ctrl. Mich. U., Mt. Pleasant, 1995—; adjudicator Am. Coll. Theatre Festival, Region III, 1995—; mem. U. Ga. Alumni Network, Athens, 1995—, U. Evansville Alumni Network, 1996—; v.p. Mid-Am. Theatre Conf., 1997—; adv. coun. to the Sch. Classical Studies Am. Acad. Rome. Contbr. articles to profl. jours. and chpts. to books. Mem. Highlands Assn. for Religious Thought, N.C., 1996—, Highlands Women's Discussion Group, 1996—, PTA, Mt. Pleasant, Mich., 1996—. Recipient Mortar Bd., U. Evansville, 1976. Mem. Actor's Equity Assn., Screen Actor's Guild, Am. Fedn. Radio and Television Artists, Congress of European Theatre, Internat. Fedn. for Theatre Rsch., Soc. for Sci. and Lit., Am. Soc. for Theatre Rsch., Mid-Am. Theatre Conf. (coord. 1996—), Popular Culture Assn., Performance Studies Internat., Phi Beta Kappa. Home: 301 W Broomfield St Apt 201 Mount Pleasant MI 48858-4534 Office: Central Mich. U. 333 Moore Hall Mount Pleasant MI 48859

JUSTUS, ADALU, writer, designer; b. Lawrenceville, Ill., Aug. 5, 1928; d. Edward G. and Zerma E. (Ike) Johnston; m. Gary Hunt; children: Brett Justus, Richard Lee, Sheryl Marlene, Ira James, Jeffrey Lynn, Melinda Sue. Diploma in child psychology, San Fernando (Calif.) U., 1957. Free-lance writer (first novel pub.) Calif., 1960—, owner child care ctr., 1968-73; mastecomy advisor Orange County Physicians, Victor Valley, Calif., 1976-87; owner The Elegant Lady Boutique, Calif., 1974-89; lectr. Ariz., Ill., Calif., Tex., Nev., 1975-90; instr. tng. seminars Custom Undergarment Com., Calif., Ariz., Nev., Tex., 1974-89; instr. breast clinic, breats exam. classes Victor Valley Hosp., 1973-87; owner Calif. Silo Pub., Calif., 1985-92; designer doll clothes, wardrobes, Calif., Ariz., Tenn., 1987-94; designer custom undergarments Bjene, Calif., 1976-82, Bejene, Calif., 1985; designer, instr., cons. Command Performance, Waco, Tex., 1985-89. Author: In The Shadow of Death, 1960, Dorit's Soft Sculpture Doll Techniques, 1988, Dorit Schendzielorz, Justus Ike Family Cookbook, 1989, Please Don't Say Good-Bye, 1998, So You're Married to One of Those, 1998, Wanta See My Attic, 1998, (screenplay) Body & Soul, 1963, Mommy Please Don't Kill Me, 1983, (with Ira S. Marlin) My Son, My Mother, 1985, Bipity-Bop, 1999, The StoryTeller House, 1999. Pres., founder Friends for Life, Victor Valley. Mem. Friends of Libr. (sponsor), Christian Found. Children & Aging (sponsor), Women St. Anne Parish. Republican. Roman Catholic. Avocations: reading, embroidery, quilting. Home: 32 Bland Ave Sumter SC 29150-3816 Office: J Ike Books PO Box 8028 Sumter SC 29150

JUSZCZAK, NICHOLAS MAURO, psychology educator; b. Chorely, Lancashire, Eng., May 19, 1955; came to U.S. 1956; s. Adam and Augusta (Lugnan); 1 child, Amanda; m. Margie Nina Malkin, Oct. 9, 1988; children: Kimberly, Melissa, Nina, Nicole. BA cum laude, Baruch Coll., N.Y.C., 1980; MS, Hunter Coll., N.Y.C., 1984. Rschr. psychophysiology lab Baruch Coll., N.Y.C., 1980-88, instr. psychology, 1984—; cons. statistics BOE/CUNY Student Mentor Program, 1987-91; creator, pres. world wide web Homeroom Dot Net, 1997—. Contbr. articles to profl. jours. Cons. Office of Instructional Tech., N.Y. State Bd. Edn., 1999—. Mem. N.Y. Acad. Sci. E-mail: nmj@homeroom.net. Home: 12-22 149th St Whitestone NY 11357-1742

JUSZCZYK, JAMES JOSEPH, artist; b. Chgo., Jan. 30, 1943; s. Joseph Peter and Pauline (Polak) J.; m. Phyllis Ann Pozar, May 30, 1965 (dec. Jan. 1992). BFA, Cleve. Inst. of Art, 1966; MFA, U. Pa., 1969. Artist pvt. practice, Zurich, 1986-92; lectr., cons. Binney & Smith Liquitex Paints, Easton, Pa., 1992-94, Lascaux Colours & Restauro, Alois Diethelm AG, Zürich, Switzerland, 1995-98; lectr. Daler-Rowney USA, Cranbury, N.J., 1998—; adj. prof. art CCNY, 1996—; presented master class workshops in acrylic techniques in the Benelux countries (Amsterdam, DeHaag, Antwerp, Brussels), 1996-97, 98. Artist: solo exhibitions include Phila. Coll. of Textiles and Sci., 1970, Rosa Esman Gallery, N.Y.C., 1974, 76, 1978-79, Gimpel-Hanover Galerie, Zurich, 1975, 82, Galerie Christel, Stockholm, 1980, Jan Cicero Gallery, Chgo., 1980, 83, 92, Galerij S65, Aalst, Belgium, 1981, Andre Emmerich Galerie, Zurich, 1982, Galerie Konstructiv Tendens, Stockholm, 1982, Galerie Storrer, Zurich, 1987, Galerie Meissner Edition, Hamburg, 1987, Merril Lynch Internat., Zurich, 1987, ACP Viviane Ehrli Galerie, Zurich, 1988, 93, 94, 97, Galerie Bruno Bucher, Poitiers, France, 1992, Galerie Vromans, Amsterdam, 1995, Fine Arts Gallery L.I. U., Southampton, 1997, Found. for Concrete and Constructivist Art, Zurich, 1991, Galerie Albergo Giardino, Ascona, Switzerland, Ann Reid Art Gallery, Princeton, N.J., 1998; group exhibitions include 16 Young Artists, Inst. Contemporary Art, Phila., 1969, Eight Abstract Painters, 1978, Andre Zarre Gallery, N.Y., The Geometry of Color, 1977, Cleve. Mus. Art, Centenary Exhibition, 1982, Bronx Mus. of the Arts, 50th Anniversary Exhibition of The American Abstract Artists, Editions Fanal, Basel, Paris, Saga '93, '96, 97, ACP Viviane Ehrli Gallerie Art-Frankfurt, 1994-96, The Noyes Mus., Oceanville, N.J. Am. Abstract Artists Persistence of Abstraction, 1994, Mus. Coopmanhus, Franeker, Netherlands, 1995, DePaul U. Art Gallery, Chgo., 1997; Forum Konkrete Kunst, Erfurt, Germany, 1998, represented in corp. and pub. collections, AT&T, N.Y.C., Arco. Internat.-Anaconda Aluminum, Chgo., Art Inst. Chgo., Chase Manhattan Bank, N.Y.C., Citicorp, N.Y.C., Lehman Bros, N.Y.C., Madison (Wis.) Art Ctr., Merrill Lynch Internat., Zurich, Prudential Life Ins., Newark, Shearson Am. Express, N.Y.C., Svenska Handelsbanken, Stockholm, Swiss Bank Corp., N.Y.C., N.J. State Mus., Whitney Mus. of Am. Art. Recipient Student Work scholarship Cleve. Inst. Art, Angel Fund award U. Pa.; Ford Found. Undergrad. grantee Cleve. Inst. Art, 1965, Pollock-Kranser Found., 1995. Mem. Am. Abstract Artists (treas.), Zen Studies Soc. Home and Studio: 74 Grand St New York NY 10013-2253

JUVET, RICHARD SPALDING, JR., chemistry educator; b. L.A., Aug. 8, 1930; s. Richard Spalding and Marion Elizabeth (Dalton) J.; m. Martha Joy Myers, Jan. 29, 1955 (div. Nov. 1978); children: Victoria, David, Stephen, Richard P.; m. Evelyn Raeburn Elthon, July 1, 1984. BS, UCLA, 1952, PhD, 1955. Research chemist Dupont, 1955; instr. U. Ill., 1955-57, asst. prof., 1957-61, assoc. prof., 1961-70; prof. analytical chemistry Ariz. State U., Tempe, 1970-95, prof. emeritus, 1995—; vis. prof. UCLA, 1960, U. Cambridge, Eng., 1964-65, Nat. Taiwan U., 1968, Ecole Polytechnique, France, 1976-77, U. Vienna, Austria, 1989-90; mem. air pollution chemistry and physics adv. com. EPA, HEW, 1969-72; mem. adv. panel on advanced chem. alarm tech., devel. and engring. directorate, def. sys. divsn. Edgewood Arsenal, 1975; mem. adv. panel on postdoctoral associateships NAS-NRC, 1991-94; mem. George C. Marshall Inst., 1998—. Author: Gas-Liquid Chromatography, Theory and Practice, 1962, Russian edit., 1966; editl. advisor Jour. Chromatographic Sci., 1969-85, Jour. Gas Chromatography, 1963-68, Analytica Chimica Acta, 1972-74, Analytical Chemistry, 1974-77; biennial reviewer for gas chromatography lit. Analytical Chemistry, 1962-76. Deacon Presbyn. Ch., 1960—, ruling elder, 1972—, commr. Grand Canyon Presbytery, 1974-76; moderator, communion com. Valley Presbyn. Ch., Scottsdale, Ariz., 1999—. NSF sr. postdoctoral fellow, 1964-65; recipient Sci. Exch. Agreement award to Czechoslovakia, Hungary, Romania and Yugoslavia, 1977. Fellow Am. Inst. Chemists; mem. AAAS, Am. Chem. Soc. (nat. chmn. divsn. analytical chemistry 1972-73, nat. sec.-treas. 1969-71, divsn. com. on chem. edn., subcom. on grad. edn. 1988—, councilor 1978-89, coun. com. analytical reagents 1985-95, co-author Reagent Chemicals, 7th edit. 1986, 8th edit. 1993, chmn. U. Ill. sect. 1968-69, sec. 1962-63, directorate divsn. officers' caucus 1987-90), Internat. Union Pure and Applied Chemistry, Internat. Platform Assn., Am. Radio Relay League (Amateur-Extra lic.), Sigma Xi, Phi Lambda Upsilon, Alpha Chi Sigma (faculty adv. U. Ill. 1958-64, Ariz. State U. 1975-95, profl. rep.-at-large 1989-94, chmn. expansion com. 1990-92, nat. v.p. grand collegiate alchemist 1994-96). Rsch. on gas and liquid chromatography, instrumental analysis, computer interfacing, plasma desorption mass spectroscopy. Home: 4821 E Calle Tuberia Phoenix AZ 85018-2932 Office: Ariz State U Dept Chem and Biochem Tempe AZ 85287-1604

JUVILER, PETER HENRY, political scientist, educator; b. London, Mar. 26, 1926; s. Adolphe Adam and Katie (Henry) J.; m. Anne C. Stephens, June 20, 1982; children: Gregory, Geoffry. BE, Yale U., 1948, ME, 1949; PhD, Columbia U., 1960. Project engr. Sperry Gyroscope Co., 1949-52; taught polit. sci. Princeton U., 1957-58, Columbia U., 1959-60, Hunter Coll., CUNY, 1960-64; prof. Barnard Coll., 1974—; co-dir. Columbia U. Ctr. for Study Human Rights, 1986—. Author: Revolutionary Law and Order, 1976, Freedom's Ordeal: The Struggle for Human Rights and Democracy in Post-Soviet States, 1998; co-editor, contbr. Gorbachev's Reforms: U.S. and Japanese Assessments, 1988, Human Rights for the 21st Century, 1993, Religion and Human Rights: Competing Claims?, 1999; contbr. numerous articles. With USN, 1944-46.

KAAS, JON H., psychology educator. BA, Northland Coll., 1959; PhD, Duke U., 1965. With Vanderbilt U., 1973—, now Centennial prof. psychology. Office: Vanderbilt U Dept of Psychology 301 Wilson Hall Nashville TN 37240

KAATZ, LYNN ROBERT, artist, graphic designer; b. Elyria, Ohio, Apr. 28, 1945; s. Herbert and Mildred K.; m. Linda Lee Sarnovsky. Aug. 8, 1945; children: Stephanie Lyn, Tiffaney Lyn Lambert. Student, Ohio State U., 1964-65, Cooper Sch. Art, Cleve., 1965-68. Designer, art dir. Evans Type Art, Elyria, 1964-68; designer, art dir. photography, packaging, advt. Buzza Cardosa Greeting Cards, Anaheim, Calif., 1968-71; artist/prin. Calif. Graphics, Anaheim, 1972-74, Great Lakes Graphics, Elyria, 1974-81, Sportsman's Collection, Inc., Lagrange, Ohio, 1978—; spkr. Elyria Art Coun., 1994—. Designer Ducks Unltd. 50th-yr. logo, 1985, Ohio wetlands habitat stamp/print, 1986, 89, 99, Ky. duck stamp/print, 1987; illustrations in book The Labrador Retriever; designer various corp. logs; participant in many fine art shows and exhibits. Recipient award of merit for packaging design Soc. Illustrators, 1969, Nat. Paper Box, 1971, Pacific Paper Box, 1971, Best of Show award for waterfowl Ducks Unltd., 1979, Advt. Excellence award Graphex Art Dir. Club, 1980, Plate of Yr. award Bradford Exch., 1991; named Artist of Yr. Genesse du Artist of Yr., 1994. Mem. Ohio Watercolor Soc. (bronze medal 1987), Watercolor U.S.A. (hon., Purchase award 1994), Fretted Instrument Guild Am., Ducks Unltd. (sponsor, Pallet and Chisel award 1987, Nat. Artist Yr. 1999). Republican. Office: Sportsmans Collection Inc 14309 Meadow Creek Ln LaGrange OH 44050

KABABIK, DANA LYNNE, health communications executive; b. Newark, Nov. 12, 1960; d. Stephen Earl and Lila Muriel (Seletsky) A. BS, Boston U., 1982. Asst. acct. exec. Doremus & Co., N.Y.C., 1982-84; sr. acct. exec. Manning Selvage & Lee, N.Y.C., 1984-85; mgr. pub. rels. United Media, N.Y.C., 1985-91; v.p. pub. rels. Am. Diabetes Assn., Somerset, N.J., 1991-94, v.p. programs, 1994-98; dir. health comm. Doctors & Designers, Westfield, N.J., 1998—. Recipient Silver Anvil award Pub. Rels. Soc., 1988. Avocations: quilting, ice skating, gardening, hiking, birding. Office: Doctors and Designers 53 Cardinal Dr Westfield NJ 07090-1020

KABACINSKI, STANLEY JOSEPH, health and physical education educator, consultant, speaker; b. Duryea, Pa., May 23, 1949; s. Bernard Merlyn and Anna (Polaski) K.; m. Mary Claire Finnerty, June 26, 1971; children: Ryan Michael, Michael Joseph. BS in Health, Phys. Edn. and Dance, East Stroudsburg State Coll., 1971, MEd in Health, Phys. Edn. and Dance, 1975;

postgrad., Millersville U., 1981. Tchr., coach basketball, softball, soccer, volleyball Washington (N.J.) Boro Elem., 1971-78; asst. football coach, head coach offense, scouting coord. East Stroudsburg (Pa.) State Coll., 1971-78, cooperating tchr. for student tchrs., 1974-78; asst. prof. Millersville (Pa.) U., 1978—, offensive coord., adminstrv. asst., recruiting coord., strength coach, 1978-88, coord., minor in athletic coaching, 1989—, grad. program coord. MEd in sport mgmt., 1999—, chair health and phys. edn. dept., 1999—; chair dept. health and phys. edn.; cons. Sch. Dist. of Lancaster, 1991—, Clarion (Pa.) U., 1991—, Gov's. Coun. on Phys. Fitness and Sports, Harrisburg, Pa., 1991—, East Stroudsburg U., 1994—, Mansfield U., 1998—; rschr. U.S. Mil. Acad. Performance Enhancement Ctr., West Point, N.Y., 1989, Am. Coaching Effectiveness Program and Coaching Minor Nat. Survey, Millersville, 1989; motivational cons., 1991—; ASEP instr. coaching principles, sport 1st aid, sport psychology; clinician various tng. programs and spkr. in field; also TV appearances. Dir., instr. activities in field Warren County Elem., Washington, N.J., Willow St. (Pa.) Elem., Ch. of Apostles Pre-Sch., Rohrerstown, Pa., Hans Herr Elem., Lampeter, Pa., Willow St. Family Festival, Fulton Elem. Sch., Lancaster, Pa.; head coach, cons. Willow St. Youth Baseball, 1987-91; cons. Willow St. PTO, 1983-87; coord. Elks Hoop Shoot, Washington, N.J., 1971-78. Mem. AAHPERD, Am. Football Coaches Assn., Pa. State Assn. Health, Phys. Edn., Recreation and Dance, Assn. Pa. State Coll. and Univ. Profs., Pa. Scholastic Football Coaches Assn., N.J. State Football Coaches Assn., Lancaster County Quarterback Club, Phi Epsilon Kappa. Avocations: coaching, baseball and football card collecting, model railroading, landscaping. Office: Millersville U Pucillo Gymnasium Millersville PA 17551

KABACK, ELAINE, career counselor, consultant; b. Phila., Feb. 22, 1939; d. Sol and Evelyn Zitman; children: Douglas, Stephen, Michelle. Student Pa. State U., 1956-58; BA, Temple U., 1960; MS, Calif. State U., 1977; PhD, Calif. Grad. Inst., 1998. Nat. cert. career counselor; cmty. coll. counselor credential. Tchr. English Sayre Jr. High Sch., Phila. Public Schs., 1960-62; tchr. English and history Beth Tfiloh Pvt. Day Sch., Balt., 1968-72; mgmt. cons., trainer SWA, Palos Verdes, Calif., 1975-85; counselor Career Planning Ctr. and Mid-Life Ctr., Long Beach City Coll., 1977-78; dir. program devel. Univance Career Ctrs., Inc., Los Angeles, 1978-80; pvt. practice career counseling, 1980—, outplacement cons. Exec. Horizons, Inc., Newport Beach, Calif., 1985-96; coord. career transition program, trainer, instr. UCLA Extension, 1980—; cons. in career systems, outplacement and orgnl. devel. Pres. Palos Verdes chpt. NOW, 1974-76; treas. S.W. chpt. Nat. Women's Polit. Caucus, 1973, 78; bd. dirs. STEP Adult Edn. Programs, Palos Verdes, 1974—. Mem. Calif. Counseling and Devel., Am. Counseling Assn., Calif. Assn. Marriage and Family Therapy, Orgn. Devel. Network, Phi Kappa Phi. Office: 11340 W Olympic Blvd Ste 255 Los Angeles CA 90064-1697

KABACK, MICHAEL, medical educator; b. Phila., Sept. 1, 1938. MD, U. Pa., 1963. Diplomate Am. Bd. Med. Genetics, Am. Bd. Pediatrics. Intern Johns Hopkins Hosp., Balt., 1963-64, resident pediatrics, 1966-68; fellow molecular biology and genetics NIH, Bethesda, Md., 1964-66; mem. staff Children's Hosp., San Diego; prof. pediatrics and reproductive medicine U. Calif., San Diego. Recipient William Allan Meml. award Am. Soc. Human Genetics, 1993. Fellow AAAS; mem. AMA, NAS, Inst. Medicine, Am. Acad. Pediatrics, Am. Pediatric Soc., Am. Soc. Human Genetics, Soc. for Pediatric Rsch. Office: Children's Hosp San Diego 8110 Birmingham Way San Diego CA 92123-2758

KABAK, DOUGLAS THOMAS, lawyer; b. Elizabeth, N.J., Nov. 19, 1957; s. Aaron and Marilyn Virginia (Johnson) K.; m. Elisabeth Wiggin McDuffie, Oct. 21, 1989; 1 child, Matthew Thomas McDuffie Kabak. BA, Rutgers U., 1979, MBA, 1990; JD, Seton Hall U., 1982; postgrad., U. Exeter, Eng., 1980. Bar. N.J. 1982, U.S. Dist. Ct. N.J. 1982. Law clk. Superior Ct. N.J., Elizabeth, 1982-83; assoc. Z. Lance Samay, Morristown, N.J., 1983-86; asst. dep. pub. defender Office Pub. Defender, Elizabeth, 1986—; legal rep. St. Joseph's the Carpenter Bd. Edn., Roselle, N.J., 1985-87. Dir. St. Joseph the Carpenter Cath. Youth Orgn., Roselle, 1986-88, coach, 1981-86. Mem. ABA, N.J. Bar Assn., Union County Bar Assn., KC. Roman Catholic. Home: 16 Indian Spring Rd Cranford NJ 07016-1616 Office: Pub Defender Office 65 Jefferson Ave Ste 3 Elizabeth NJ 07201-2441

KABAKOFF, JACOB, retired religious studies educator; b. N.Y.C., Mar. 20, 1918; s. Solomon and Rose (Katzman) K.; m. Dorothy Arian, June 18, 1950; children: David, Daniel, Joel. BA, Yeshiva U., 1938; D in Hebrew Letters, Jewish Theol. Sem., N.Y.C., 1958; D in Humane Letters, Hebrew Union Coll., 1988; DDiv, Jewish Theol. Sem., 1972. Editl. staff Ency. Hebraica, Jerusalem, 1950-52; dean Cleve. Coll. Jewish Studies, 1952-68; prof. Lehman Coll., Bronx, N.Y., 1968-86. Author: Pioneers of American Hebrew Literature, 1966, Naphtali Herz Imber: Selected Writings, 1985, Seekers and Stalwarts, 1978; editor: Jewish Book Annual, vols. 34-53, 1977-95. Mem. Nat. Assn. Profs. Hebrew, Assn. Jewish Studies, Nat. Coun. Jewish Edn. Home: 40 Winslow Rd White Plains NY 10606-3519

KABALIN, JOHN NICHOLAS, urologist; b. L.A., Dec. 23, 1958; s. Nicholas Augustin and Mary Jane (Engleman) K.; m. Pamela Grace White, July 11, 1981. BS, Stanford U., 1980; MD, Johns Hopkins U., 1984. Diplomate Am. Bd. Urology. Intern in surgery Stanford U. Med. Ctr., 1984-85, resident in surgery, 1985-86, resident in urology, 1986-90, chief resident in urology, 1989-90; chief urology sect. Va Med. Ctr., Palo Alto, Calif., 1990-97; asst. prof. urology Stanford (Calif.) U., 1990-97; asst. prof. surgery U. Nebr. Coll. Medicine, 1999—. Contbr. over 100 articles to profl. jours., 15 chpts. in books. Fellow ACS; mem. AMA, AAAS, Am. Urol. Assn., Am. Soc. for Laser Medicine and Surgery, Am. Soc. Clin. Oncology, Soc. Urologic Oncology, Soc. Univ. Urologists, N.Y. Acad. Scis., Phi Beta Kappa, Alpha Omega Alpha. Roman Catholic. Achievments include adaptation and clinical development of Holmium laser sources for soft tissue prostatic surgery. Office: 2 W 42nd St Ste 2200 Scottsbluff NE 69361-4669

KABARA, JON JOSEPH, biochemical pharmacology educator; b. Chgo., Nov. 26, 1926; s. John Stanley and Mary Elizabeth (Wielgus) K.; m. Virginia Christie (dec. 1974); children: Christie Anne, Mary K., Sheila Jon, Pat Lee; m. Annette Elser Sproull (dec. 1986), children: Timothy, Steven; m. Betty Z. Tabor, 1992. B.S., St. Mary's Coll., Minn., 1948; M.S., U. Miami, 1950; Ph.D. (Univ. scholar), U. Chgo., 1959. Prof. chemistry U. Detroit, 1957-68; prof., assoc. dean Mich. Coll. Osteo. Medicine, Pontiac, 1967-70; prof. assoc. dean pharmacology Mich. State U., E. Lansing, 1970-71; prof. biomechanics Mich. State U., 1971-89, prof. emeritus, 1989; dir. research and devel. Med.-Chem. Labs., Galena, Ill., 1950—, Kabe Realtor, 1986—; pres. div. research and devel. Galena's Kitchen Chemist, 1989—, Tech. Exch. Inc., 1989; co-owner, pres., dir. R&D Lil Gen. Miniature Golf Course, Galena, Ill., 1996—; cons. in neurochemistry and microbiology. Contbr. over 200 articles to profl. jours.; editor: Cosmetic Preservation Preservative-Free Cosmetic & Drug Formulations and Korkies Cookbook, other books on lipid pharmacology; U.S. and fgn. patentee in field. Pres. Mich. NE PTA, 1959; active Little League, 1973-75. Damon Runyon Cancer fellow, 1949-50; Mt. Sinai fellow, 1949-51; Bishop Heffron awardee St. Mary's Coll., 1970; named Man of Year St. George High Sch. Alumni Club, 1970; recipient Disting. Alumni award 50th Anniversary, St. Mary's U., Minn., 1998. Fellow Am. Inst. Chemists; mem. Am. Oil Chem. Soc., N.Y. Acad. Sci., Detroit Physiology Soc., Assn. Analytical Chemists, AAAS, Am. Soc. Clin. Pathologists, Sigma Xi, other orgns. Address (winter): 4350 Chatham Dr Longboat Key FL 34228-2342 *One of the more important rules in life is good communication. Communication (speaking and listening) is the keystone to understanding.*

KABAT, ELVIN ABRAHAM, immunologist; b. N.Y.C., Sept. 1, 1914; s. Harris and Doreen (Otis) K.; m. Sally Lennick, Nov. 28, 1942; children: Jonathan, Geoffrey, David. PhD (hon.), Northwestern U., 1994; M.A., Columbia U., 1934, Ph.D., 1937; LL.D. (hon.), U. Glasgow, 1976; Doctoral degree (hon.), U. Orleans (France); Ph.D. (hon.), Weizmann Inst. Sci., Rehovot, Israel; DSc honoris causa, Columbia U., 1987. Lab. asst. immunochemistry Presbyn. Hosp., 1933-37; Rockefeller Found. fellow Inst. Phys. Chemistry, Upsala, Sweden, 1937-38; instr. pathology Cornell U., 1938-41; mem. faculty Columbia U., N.Y.C., 1941—; asst. prof. bacteriology Columbia U., 1946-48, assoc. prof., 1948-52, prof. microbiology, 1952-85, prof. human genetics and devel., 1969-85, Higgins prof. microbiology, 1984-85, Higgins prof. emeritus microbiology, 1985—; lectr. 15th Ann. Louis Weinstein lecture Tufts U. Sch. Medicine. Author: (with M.M. Mayer) Experimental Immunochemistry, 1948, 2d edition, 1961, Blood Group Substances, Their Chemistry and Immunochemistry, 1956, Structural Concepts in Immunology and Immunochemistry, 1968, 2d edit., 1976, (with T.T. Wu and H. Bilofsky) Variable Regions of Immunoglobulin Chains, 1976, Sequences of Immunoglobulin Chains, (with others) Sequences of Proteins of Immunological Interest, 1983, 4th edit., 1987, 5th edit., 1991 (with T.T. Wu, M. Reid-Miller, H.M. Perry and K.S. Gottesman).; mem. editorial bd.: Jour. Immunology, 1961-76, Transplantation Bull, 1957-60. Recipient numerous awards including: Am. Research award City of Hope, 1974, award Center for Immunology, State U. N.Y., Buffalo, 1976, Louisa Gross Horwitz award Columbia U., 1977, R.E. Dyer lectr. award NIH, 1979, Townsend Harris medal CCNY, 1980, Philip Levine award Am. Soc. Clin. Pathology, 1982, award for excellence Grad. Faculties Alumni Columbia U., 1982, Disting. Svc. award Columbia U. Coll. Physicians and Surgeons, 1988, Dickson Prize for Medicine U. Pitts, 1986, Academy medal, N.Y. Acad. Medicine, 1989, Nat. Medal of Sci. 1991; named Pierre Grabar Lectr. Societe Francaise d'Immunologie and German Soc. of Immunology; Fogarty scholar NIH, 1974-75. Mem. Am. Assn. Immunologists (Lifetime award 1995), Am. Acad. Microbiology. Fax: 212-854-1754. Office: Columbia U Coll Physicians and Surgeons Dept Microbiology 701 W 168th St Rm 1212 New York NY 10032-2704*

KABAT, LINDA GEORGETTE, civic leader; b. Cleve., Nov. 26, 1951; d. Michael G. and Georgette (deVos) Paul; m. John Edward Kabat Jr., Apr. 23, 1977; 1 child, Susan Marie. Student, Cleve. Inst. Music, 1969-72. With sales dept. Higbee Co., Fairview Park, Ohio, 1972; customer svc. rep. Ashland Chem. Co., Cleve., 1972-74, Celanese Corp., Lakewood, Ohio, 1974-76; with sales dept. May Co., North Olmsted, Ohio, 1979; customer svc. rep. Diamond Shamrock Corp., Cleve., 1979-82; in sales May Co., North Olmsted, 1989-97. Chpt. pres. Cath. War Vets. Aux., Cleve., 1973-75, pres. Ohio, 1975-77, nat. sec., 1977-79, state sec., 1991-92. Mem. Mu Phi Epsilon (pres. 1971-72, historian 1970-71). Republican. Avocations: camping, traveling, needlework, music.

KABEL, ROBERT JAMES, lawyer; b. Burbank, Calif., Nov. 30, 1946; s. Herman James and Margaret Elizabeth (Doyle) K. B.A., Denison U., 1969; J.D., Vanderbilt U., 1972; LL.M. in Taxation, Georgetown U., 1979. Bar: D.C., Tenn., Ohio, U.S. Supreme Ct. Adminstrv. asst. to Gov. Winfield Dunn of Tenn., Nashville, 1972-75; legis. asst. to Senator Paul Fannin, Washington, 1975-77; legis. dir. Senator Richard G. Lugar of Ind., Washington, 1977-82; spl. asst. to pres. White House, Washington, 1982-84; ptnr. Manatt, Phelps & Phillips and precedessor firm, Washington, 1985—; part-time mem. Fgn. Claims Settlement Commn., 1987-91; chair Greater Washington Bd. Trade Task Force Internat. Trade & Intellectual Property, 1996-97. Mem. Bretton Woods Commn.; Vanderbilt Law Sch. Alumni Bd., 1997—; bd. trustees Denison U., 1999—; chmn. bd. dirs. Log Cabin Reps., 1994-99; chmn. Liberty Edn. Fund, 1999—; mem. D.C. Rep. Com. Recipient citation Denison U. Alumni. Mem. ABA, Ohio Bar Assn., D.C. Bar Assn., Tenn. Bar Assn., Rep. Lawyers Assn., Denison U. Alumni Soc. (pres. 1994-96), Met. Club Washington, Capitol Hill Club, The Federalist Soc. Republican. Presbyterian. Office: Manatt Phelps & Phillips 1501 M St NW Ste 700 Washington DC 20005-1737

KABEL, ROBERT LYNN, chemical engineering educator; b. Champaign, Ill., Apr. 3, 1932; s. Myron Charles and Marietta Louise (Lynn) K.; m. Barbara Jean Robb, June 8, 1958; children: Joseph Robb, Douglas Alan. BS, U. Ill., 1955; PhD, U. Wash., 1961. Registered profl. engr., Pa., Calif. Engr. Conoco, Ponca City, Okla., 1954, Sun Oil Co., Marcus Hook, Pa., 1955, Chevron Rsch. Co., LaHabra and Richmond, Calif., 1967, 68; rsch. scientist NASA Ames Rsch. Ctr., Palo Alto, Calif., 1969; engr. Exxon, Linden, N.J., 1976, 77, 89; prof. chem. engring. Pa. State U., University Park, 1963—; invitational prof. chem. and bioengring. Ariz. State U., Tempe, 1984-85; vis. prof. Tech. U. Norway, Trondheim, 1971-72, Pahlavi U., Shiraz, Iran, 1978, U. N.S.W., Sydney, Australia, 1988, 89, U. Canterbury, Christchurch, New Zealand, 1989, Chulalongkorn U., Bangkok, 1989; co-editor/author: Scaleup of Chemical Processes, 1985; cons. in field. Co-author: Sources and Control of Air Pollution, 1998. With USAF, 1961-63. Decorated Air Force Commendation medal; recipient Outstanding Tchg. award Amoco Found., 1983, award for Excellence in Instrn., Western Electric, 1983, Nat. Catalyst award for Excellence in Chem. Tchg., Chem. Mfrs. Assn., 1984, Disting. Achievement award Ariz. State U., 1985; ASEE faculty fellow, 1969, Royal Norwegian Coun. for Sci. and Indsl. Rsch. fellow, 1971-72, NATO fellow, 1974, Erskine fellow, 1989. Fellow AIChE (editorial bd. 1980-85); mem. AAUP, ASEE (Corcoran award 1989), Am. Chem. Soc., Sigma Xi, Phi Lambda Upsilon, Alpha Chi Sigma, Tau Beta Pi, Phi Eta Sigma. Republican. Presbyterian. Office: 130 Fenske Lab University Park PA 16802-4400

KABELA, FRANK, JR., broadcast executive; b. Hackensack, N.J., July 31, 1938; s. Frank Sr. and Margaret Louise (Erlinger) K.; m. Patricia Ann Bors, Apr. 22, 1961; children: Elisabeth Ann, David John. AB, Rutgers U., 1960. Reporter Bergen Evening Record, Hackensack, N.J., 1960-61; editor Johnson & Johnson, New Brunswick, N.J., 1962-63; pub., gen. mgr. Sentinel Pub. Co., East Brunswick, N.J., 1963-66; pres. Kabela & Dragoset, Inc., Princeton, N.J., 1966-69; exec. v.p. Greater Media, Inc., New Brunswick, 1969-71; pres., COO Greater Media, Inc., East Brunswick, N.J., 1981—; co-owner Princeton Ptnrs., 1971; pres. The Kabela Co., Phoenix, Ariz., 1974-81. With U.S. Army, 1961, USAR, 1961-67. Avocations: jogging, windsurfing, tennis, reading. Office: 2 Kennedy Blvd East Brunswick NJ 08816-1248

KABRIEL, MARCIA GAIL, psychotherapist; b. El Reno, Okla., Jan. 8, 1938; d. Gail Frederick and Katherine (Marsh) Slaughter; m. J. Ronald Kabriel, May 25, 1957; children: Joseph Charles, Jeffrey Gail, Jae B. BA, U. Okla., 1965, MSW, 1968; postgrad., Am. U. Psychiat. social worker Dept. Mental Hygiene, N.Y.C., 1968-69; psychiat. social worker Washington Hosp. Ctr., 1970-72, assoc. mem. dept. psychiatry, 1972-75, sr. psychotherapist Counseling Ctr., 1972-75, chief dept. social svcs., 1976-82, cons. spl. projects, 1974-82; psychotherapist Md. Inst. Pastoral Counseling, Annapolis, Md., 1972-97; supr. continuing protective svcs. State Md., 1983-91; supr. rsch. project on child sexual abuse AACO, 1991-93; forensic social worker Anne Arundel Cir. Ct., 1991-97; exec. v.p. Kent Island Transport, Inc., 1985-97; pvt. practice Woodstock, Va., 1998—; program dir. Shenandoah Meml. Hosp., Life Ctr. of Galax, Woodstock, 1997-98; field instr. Cath. U., Washington, 1973-75, U. Md., 1976-91; adjunct prof. U. Md. 1992-97. Mem. NASW, Acad. Cert. Social Workers (bd. cert. diplomate). Democrat. Presbyterian. Home: 547 Zepp Rd Star Tannery VA 22654 Office: 122 N Main St Woodstock VA 22664-1417

KAC, VICTOR G., mathematician, educator; b. Buguruslan, USSR, Dec. 19, 1943; came to U.S., 1977; s. Gersh and Clara (Landman) K.; m. Elena Bourdenko; children: Luba, Marianne. Diploma, Moscow State U., 1965, cand. of sci., 1968. Asst. Moscow Inst. Electronic Machine Bldg., 1968-71; sr. tchr. MIEM, Moscow, 1971-76; assoc. prof. MIT, Cambridge, Mass., 1977-81; prof. MIT, Cambridge, 1981—. Author two books on infinite-dimensional Lie algebras and a book on vertex algebra; contbr. numerous articles to profl. jours. Recipient Medal Coll. de France, 1981, Wigner medal Group Theory Found., 1994; Guggenheim fellow, 1985, Sloan fellow, 1981. Mem. Am. Math. Soc., Moscow Math. Soc. (hon.). Achievements include structure and representation theory of infinite-dimensional groups and algebras that arise in mathematics and physics. Home: 10 Kilsyth Rd Brookline MA 02445-2002 Office: MIT Math Dept 77 Massachusetts Ave Cambridge MA 02139-4307

KACEK, DON J., management consultant, business owner; b. Berwyn, Ill., May 4, 1936; s. George J. and Rose (Krizik) K.m. Carolyn K. Hiner, July 22, 1961; children: Scott M., Stacey M, BSME, Ill. Inst. Tech., 1958. Engring. sect. mgr. Sunstrand Corp., Rockford, Ill., 1958-72; group v.p. Kysor Indsl. Corp., Cadillac, Mich., 1972-76; dir. product devel. Ransburg Corp., Indpls., 1976-77, pres., 1977-88, CEO, chmn. bd. dirs., 1978-88; mgmt. cons. Indpls., 1988—; owner, pres., chmn. bd. dirs. Advanced Automation Techs., Inc. (formerly S & J Automation, Inc.), Indpls., 1989—; bd. dirs. Arvin Industries, Inc., Columbus, Ind. Inventor Burn Rate Control Valve, 1966. With AUS, 1960. Recipient Sagamore of the Wabash award Gov. Ind., 1985. Office: Advanced Automation Tech 6880 Hillsdale Ct Indianapolis IN 46250-2001

KACHADOORIAN, ZUBEL, artist, educator; b. Detroit, Feb. 7, 1924; s. Simpat and Queen (Kegulian) K.; m. Deena Morguloff, Aug. 17, 1974; children: Karina, Nika. Student, Meinzinger Art Sch., Detroit, 1953-44, Ox-Bow Summer Sch. Painting, Saugatuck, Mich., 1944-45, Skowhegan (Maine) Sch. Painting-Sculpture, 1946, Colo. Fine Arts Center, Colorado Springs, 1947. Artist-in-residence Art Inst. Chgo. Sch., 1960-61, Norton Gallery Sch., West Palm Beach, Fla., 1961, Mich. Council of Arts, 1981—; instr. Ox-Bow Summer Sch. Painting, 1960-61, 68-69, Skowhegan Sch. Painting-Sculpture, 1964; asst. prof. art Wayne State U., 1967-73; art dir. Detroit Repertory Theatre, 1970-75; mem. adv. panel Detroit Council of Arts, 1979-81. Exhibited in one-man shows, Art Inst. Chgo., 1961, Nordness Gallery, N.Y.C., 1960, 62, 64, Main St. Gallery, Chgo., 1957-61, Detroit Artists Market, 1949, 50, 53, 66, 76, 89, 91, Forsythe Gallery, Ann Arbor, Mich., 1953-57, 61, 65, 76, Battle Creek Art Ctr. (Mich.), 1983, U. Mich., Dearborn, 1986; exhibited in group shows, Johnson Wax Collection, 1962, 66, N.Y. World's Fair, 1963, 64, Ball State Ann., Muncie, Ind., 1973, 74, 77, 78, 79, 80, 81, Am. Drawing III Touring Exhibit, 1980-83, Butler Inst. Am. Art, Youngstown, Ohio, 1985, Mich. Vintage Artists Touring Exhibit, 1987—, Mich. Arts Coun. Grantee Exhbn.-Detroit Artst Market, 1991; represented in permanent collections, Detroit Inst. Art, Hist. Trinity Ch., Detroit, Art Inst. Chgo., Smithsonian Instn., Worcester (Mass.) Art Mus., Tate Gallery, London, Ball State U., Muncie, Ind., Oakland U., Rochester Hills, Mich., U. Mich. Ann Arbor, William Rockhill Nelson Gallery Art, Kansas City, Mo., Norton Gallery Art, West Palm Beach, Fla., Jesse Besser Mus., Alpena, Mich., 1967, Wayne State U. Detroit, Henry ford C.C., Mich., Porthmouth (Va.) Cmty. Arts Ctr.; works include gold leaf and oil Altar painting, St. John's Armenian Ch. Greater Detroit, 1966-67, Annunciation and Baptism, 1997; sculptured silver medallion, Henry Ford Community Coll., 1978 (Eleanor Heth Art award 1976), Five Artists: Post Industrial Romanticism (Detroit Artists' Mkt. Sculpture), 1990, Art for Life-Ind. Artis, 400 Galleria Offcentre, Southfield, Mich., 1990, Concordia Coll., Ann Arbor, Mich., 1992-94, Center Galleries, Detroit, 1994, New Millennium, Detroit Artists Market, Detroit, 1996, Patrimonio Legacy of Italian Art in Mich., Wayne State U. Recipient Richard-Linda Rosenthal award Nat. Inst. Arts and Letters, 1961; Midwest Pepsi-Cola fellow, 1946, Prix de Rome fellow, 1956-59; Mich. Arts Coun. grantee, 1983-84, 90-91. Home and Office: 1214 Beaubien St Detroit MI 48226-2342

KACHUBA, JOHN BARRIE, writer, editor; b. Astoria, N.Y., Jan. 11, 1950; m. Mary Anne Newman, June 8, 1991; children: Amy, Kristen, Jeff, Sarah, Matt. BA in English, Sacred Heart U., 1972; MA in Creative Writing, Antioch U., 1996. Sales mgr. Beiersdorf, Inc., Norwalk, Conn., 1981-89; v.p. Structural Graphics, Essex, Conn., 1989-90; pres. Med. Constrns., Milford, Conn., 1990-92; freelance writer Loveland, Ohio; cons. editor DaScribe Lit. Mktg. Svcs., Cin., 1997; bd. dirs. Lisle Inc., Leander, Tex. Author: An Asbestos Abatement Program for Healthcare Institutions, 1990, Monitoring Chemical Exposures in Healthcare Institutions, 1994, Why is This Job Killing Me?, 1999; editor: (novel) The Journals, 1997. Program coord. Writers' Voice project N.E. YMCA, Loveland, 1997; founder, chmn. Arts and Cultural Coun. Greater Loveland, 1996—; vol. Loveland Greenbelt Cmty. Coun., 1996—; event organizer Share Our Strength Writers' Harvest, Yellow Springs, Ohio, 1995. Recipient Profl. Devel. Assistance award Ohio Arts Coun., 1994. E-mail: jkachuba@aol.com.

KACHUR, BETTY RAE, elementary education educator; b. Lorain, Ohio, June 12, 1930; d. John and Elizabeth (Stanko) K. BS in Edn., Kent State U., 1963; MEd, U. Ariz., 1971. Cert. tchr.; cert. in reading. Tchr. Lorain City Schs., 1961-94. Bd. dirs. Habitat for Humanity Lorain County, Lorain Pub. Libr., Ohio Friends Librs. Mem. AAUW (social com., scholarship com. 1999), Internat. Reading Assn. (by-laws com. Ohio Coun.), Daniel T. Gardner Reading Assn. (pres. 1978-79, treas. 1988-94). Mem. United Ch. of Christ. Avocations: reading, writing, quilting, travel.

KACIR, BARBARA BRATTIN, lawyer; b. Buffalo, Ohio, July 19, 1941; d. William James and Jean (Harrington) Brattin; m. Charles Stephen Kacir, June 3, 1973 (div. Aug. 1977). BA, Wellesley Coll., 1963; JD, U. Mich., 1967. Bar: Ohio 1967, D.C. 1980. Assoc. Arter & Hadden, Cleve., 1967-74, ptnr., 1974-79; ptnr. Jones, Day, Reavis & Pogue, Washington, 1980-83, Cleve., 1983-95; dep. gen. counsel-litigation Textron Inc., Providence, 1995—; instr. trial tactics Case-Western Res. U., Cleve., 1976-79. Mem. nat. com. visitors, nat. fund raising com. U. Mich. Mem. ABA, Ohio Bar Assn., D.C. Bar Assn., Cleve. Bar Assn. (trustee 1973-76, treas. 1978-79), Am. Law Inst., Def. Rsch. Inst. Republican. Office: Textron Inc 40 Westminster St Ste 2 Providence RI 02903

KACMARCIK, THOMAS, manufacturing company executive; b. Ironwood, Mich., Sept. 28, 1925; s. Mathew T. and Mary (Murra) K.; m. Josephine Tody, June 19, 1948; children—Sharon, Karen, Thomas, Shirley, James. EE, U. Ga., 1944. Pres. F.W. Busch Co., Grafton, Wis., 1960-68; treas., dir. Cargo Ties Co., Cedarburg, Wis., 1968—; pres., dir. Milsted Products Co., Cedarburg, 1964—, Ataco Steel Products Co., Grafton, 1964—; chief exec. officer Continental Mfg. Co., Kapco Inc. (both Grafton); v.p. prodn. Stamping Corp., Milw.; dir. Snow Mobile Accessories, Inc. Mem. adv. com. Cedarsburg Sch., 1968—. Served as pilot USNR, 1943-48. Mem. Personal Mgmt. Assn., Grafton C. of C. (dir. 1982). Clubs: Lions (pres. 1969), Kiwanis (dir.). Home: 1536 Fielding Rd Cedarburg WI 53012-9707 Office: 1046 Hickory St Grafton WI 53024-1128 also: 1000 Badger Circle Grafton WI 53024

KACPROWICZ, DONNA MARIE (LEONETTI), staff nurse; b. Lower Merion, Pa., Feb. 1, 1965; d. Rosemary G. (Noone) Anastasia; m. Kenneth Kacprowicz. AS, C.C. of Phila., 1988. Cert. IV. Staff nurse Grad. Hosp., Phila., N.J., 1997—.

KACUR, LOIS MARIE, obstetric and pediatric nurse; b. Perry, Ohio, Nov. 19, 1915; d. Mark Benjamin and Floy Vivian (Penhollow) Johnson; m. Michael Kacur, Aug. 31, 1947; children: Michael Brian, Barton Winslow, David Lyle, Ellen Marie. Diploma, Cleve. City Hosp., 1939. RN. Ret. Mem. Cleve. Met. Gen. Hosp. Nurses' Alumni Assn. (life).

KACZANOWSKA, LAURIE HYSON SMITH, lawyer; b. Palmerton, Pa., July 7, 1953; d. James Donaldson and Mary Ann (Hyson) Smith; m. Donald James Gerber, Aug. 1976 (div. May 1981); m. Witold-K, Dec. 11, 1993; 1 child, Wit Thomas Kaczanowski. BS, Pa. State U., 1975; MSW, U. Denver, 1981; JD, Northeastern U., 1989. Adminstrv. staff, resource coord., vol. coord., counselor Women in Crisis, Lakewood, Colo., 1977-79; program adminstr. Big Sis. of Colo., Life Choices Program, Denver, 1979-80; legis. coord., lobbyist Common Cause, Denver, 1980-81; social work advocate Denver Legal Aid Soc., 1982-86; legis. analyst Nat. Conf. State Legis., Denver, 1987; mediator, intake coord. Harvard Law Sch., Cambridge, Mass., 1988; law clk. Supreme Jud. Ct. State Mass., Boston, 1988-89; legis. staff Rep. Patricia Schroeder, U.S. Congress, Washington, 1989; dir., ptnr. Pfaff & Smith Family Law Clinic, Denver, 1990-91; asst. city atty., sr. atty. unit leader, dir. alternative resolution program Denver City Attys. Office, Denver, 1991—; Co-owner, Arte Gallery, Inc.; pres., Apollon, Inc. Mem. Colo. Women's Bar Assn., Colo. Bar Assn., Colo. Lawyers for the Arts, Denver Bar Assn. Presbyterian. Avocations: daydreaming. Home: 3216 East 6th Ave Denver CO 80206 Office: Denver City Attys Office 303 W Colfax Ave Ste 500 Denver CO 80204-2623

KACZMARCZYK, JEFFREY ALLEN, journalist, classical music critic; b. Patuxent River Naval Air Base, Md., Jan. 7, 1963; s. Frank Joseph and Diane Catherine Kaczmarczyk; m. Cynthia L. Shimmel, Aug. 13, 1988; children: Jessica, Michael, David. BA, Western Mich. U., 1986; postgrad., Calif. State U. Editor-in-chief Western Herald, Kalamazoo, Mich., 1986-87; staff writer, acting editor Albion (Mich.) Recorder, 1987; staff writer, columnist Hastings (Mich.) Banner, 1987-92; arts writer, classical music critic The Grand Rapids (Mich.) Press, 1992—; freelance arts writer, critic Kalamazoo (Mich.) Gazette, 1990-93; editor The Weekender, Hastings, 1991-93. Dir., sec. Thornapple Arts Coun., Hastings, 1992-97; dir. Grand Rapids Area Coun. for Humanities, 1995—; vestryman Emmanuel Episcopal Ch., Hastings, 1997—, sr. warden, 1999. Episcopalian. Home: 314 S Park St Hastings MI 49058-1635 Office: The Grand Rapids Press 155 Michigan St NW Grand Rapids MI 49503-2353

KACZOROWSKI, GREGORY JOHN, biochemist, researcher, science administrator; b. South Bend, Ind., Nov. 20, 1949; s. John Walter and Jean (Bankowski) K.; m. Maria L. Garcia, June 21, 1982. BS in Chemistry summa cum laude, U. Notre Dame, 1972; PhD in Biochemistry, MIT, 1977. Helen Hay Whitney postdoctoral rsch. fellow Roche Inst. Molecular Biology, 1977-80; sr. rsch. biochemist Merck Inst. for Therapeutic Rsch., Rahway, N.J., 1980-84, assoc. dir. dept. membrane biochemistry and biophysics, 1986-88, dir., 1988-96, sr. dir., 1996—; rsch. fellow Biochemistry, Fundamental and Exploratory Rsch., Rahway, 1984-86; reviewer NIH, NSF, U.S.-Israel Binational Sci. Found.; invited speaker, presenter papers at various profl. meetings; adj. prof. dept. pharmacology and physiology UMDNJ, 1995—. Contbr. numerous articles, revs. to profl. jours.; patentee in field. Hoosier scholar, 1968-72, Notre Dame scholar, 1968-72. Mem. AAAS, Am. Chem. Soc., Am. Soc. Biol. Chemists, Am. Physiol. Soc., Biophys. Soc., N.Y. Acad. Sci., Phi Beta Kappa. Home: 5 Ashbrook Dr Edison NJ 08820-4318 Office: Merck Sharp & Dohme Rsch Labs PO Box 2000 Rahway NJ 07065-0900

KADAMUS, JAMES ALEXANDER, educational administrator; b. Syracuse, N.Y., Oct. 26, 1949; s. Alexander J. and Alice M. Kadamus; m. Carol Ann Wierzchowski, June 26, 1971; children: Christopher James, Benjamin Andrew. BA in Polit. Sci., Union Coll., Schenectady, 1971; M Regional Planning, U. N.C., 1973. Planner, rschr. Syracuse-Onondaga County Planning Agy., 1968-71; asst., then assoc. planner Office Long Range Planning N.Y. State Edn. Dept., Albany, 1974-78; exec. asst. to dep. commr. elem., secondary-continuing edn. N.Y. State Edn. Dept., Albany, 1978-79, chief Bur. Proprietary Sch. Supervision, 1979-82, asst. commr. Office Elem., Secondary and Continuing Edn., 1982-88, asst. commr. Office Higher and Continuing Edn., 1988-93, assoc. commr. Office Fin., Mgmt. and Info. Svcs., 1992-95, dep. commr. elem., mid., secondary-continuing edn., 1995-97; mem. Nat. Skill Standards Group, Washington, 1992-94; mem. Congl. Commn. on Tech. and Literacy, Washington, 1991-92; mem. Nat. Commn. to Assess Vocat. Edn., Washington, 1989-90; mem. Nat. Rsch. Coun. Forum on Edn1. Excellence and Testing Equity, 1999—. Author: New Directions for Vocational Edn. at the Secondary Level, 1987; also articles. Bd. dirs. Jr. Achievement, Albany, 1993-96, Capital Dist. YMCA, Albany, 1995—; v.p. Guilderland (N.Y.) Cmty. Ctr. YMCA, 1993-98; coach Guilderland Soccer Club, 1983-93; chief Guilderland YMCA Indian Guides. Mem. Am. Edn. Fin. Assn., Nat. Assn. State Dirs. Vocat. Edn. (pres. 1990-91). Avocations: soccer, golf, boating. Office: NY State Edn Dept Washington Ave Albany NY 12234

KADANE, JOSEPH B., statistics educator; b. Washington, Jan. 10, 1941; s. David Kurzman and Helene Margret (Born) K.; m. Kathleen Coleman, 1969 (div. 1975); m. Caroline Mitchell, 1992. B.A. cum laude in Math., Harvard Coll., 1962; Ph.D. in Stats., Stanford U., 1966. Asst. prof. Yale U., New Haven, 1966-68; staff analyst Ctr. for Naval Analysis, Arlington, VA., 1968-71; prof. stats. Carnegie-Mellon U., Pitts., 1971-86, L.J. Savage prof., 1986—; mem. Commn. on Behavioral and Social Scis. and Edn., NRC, 1986-92, 1996-98; mem. Bd. on Math Scis., 1988-91. Assoc. editor Jour. Am. Statis. Assn., 1968-73, dep. editor, 1976-78, editor, 1983-85; assoc. editor Annals of Stats., 1974-76; contbr. articles to profl. jours. NSF grantee; Office Naval Research grantee; Japan Soc. for Promotion of Sci. fellow, 1978. Fellow Am. Statis. Assn. (Pitts. statistician of yr. 1980), Inst. Math. Stats., AAAS; mem. Internat. Statis. Inst. Democrat. Jewish. Home: 2 Darlington Ct Pittsburgh PA 15217-1502 Office: Carnegie-Mellon U Dept Stats Pittsburgh PA 15213

KADAR, AVRAHAM, immunologist; b. Rishon Le Zion, Israel, Nov. 13, 1950; s. Yosef and Amalia (Hayon) K.; m. Naomi Carol Prawer, Sept. 2, 1976; children: Maya, Nadav, Einat. BS in Physics, Hebrew U., Jerusalem, 1972; MD, Sackler Sch. Medicine, Tel Aviv, Israel, 1983. Diplomate Am. Bd. Pediatrics, Am. Bd. Diagnostic Lab. Immunology, Am. B. Allergy and Immunology, Am. Bd. Medicine. Intern Tel-Hashomer, Ramat Gan, Israel, 1982; intern Albert Einstein Coll. of Medicine, N.Y.C., 1983, resident, 1984-86, asst. prof., 1989-92, asst. clin. prof., 1992—; fellow NIH, Bethesda, Md., 1986-89; immunology cons. Pediatric HIV Primary Care, N.Y.C., 1989—. Mem. AAAS, N.Y. Acad. Scis. Avocations: classical music, literature. Home: 5 Woodland Ct Bedford NY 10506-2034 Office: 530 Park Ave New York NY 10021-8015 also: 666 Lexington Ave Mount Kisco NY 10549-3632

KADAR, KARIN PATRICIA, librarian; b. Oil City, Pa., May 30, 1951; d. Michael Joseph and Bette Lee (Painter) Kadar; divorced; 1 child, Michael L. BS, Clarion U., 1973; MLS, U. Pitts., 1975. Lic. instrnl. II in libr. sci. and elem. edn. Substitute tchr. McKeesport (Pa.) Area Schs., 1973, elem. sch. libr., 1973-75, 3d grade tchr., 1975-78, elem. sch. libr., 1978-81; adj. prof. Pa. State U., McKeesport, 1988; periodicals libr. Seton Hill Coll., Greensburg, Pa., 1986-89; dir. Penn Twp. Pub. Libr., Level Green, Pa., 1989-90; grade sch. libr. substitute St. Agnes Sch., North Huntington, Pa., 1992; mid. sch. libr. substitute Belle Vernon (Pa.) Area Sch. Dist., 1993-95; dir. West Newton (Pa.) Pub. Libr., 1993-95, Highland Cmty. Libr., Richland, Pa., 1996; libr. Ridgeland (S.C.) Elem. Sch., 1996-98; spl. orders coord. Barnes and Noble, Hilton Head Island, SC, 1998—; mgr. Bluffton (S.C.) Cmty. Libr., 1998-99; mem. consumer appeals bd. Ford Motor Co., 1989-92. Author: (booklet) Sammy the Smokeless Dragon, 1976; mem. adv. panel Pa. Mag., 1992-94. Panelist Scan Trak Shoppers, 1984—, Nat. Family Opinion, 1984—; vol. Am. Cancer Soc., 1969-94, pub. edn. chmn., 1974-80, cancer prevention study II chmn., 1982-88, pub. affairs chmn., 1984-86, residential area crusade chmn., 1984-85. Named Vol. of Yr. Am. Cancer Soc. Mon Youch Unit, 1983-84; recipient Crusade award Am. Cancer Soc., Mon Yough unit, 1985-86. Mem. ALA, Pa. Libr. Assn., Parent-Tchr. Guild, Pa. State Edn. Assn., Low Country Reading Assn., Westmoreland County Hist. Soc., McKeesport Coll. Club. Avocations: freelance writing, collecting books, genealogical research. Office: Barnes and Noble 20 Hatton Pl Hilton Head Island SC 29910

KADEN, ELLEN ORAN, lawyer, consumer products company executive; b. N.Y.C., Oct. 1, 1951. AB, Cornell U., 1972; MA, U. Chgo., 1973; JD, Columbia U., 1977. Bar: N.Y., 1978. Law clerk U.S. Dist. Ct. (so. dist.) N.Y., 1977-78; asst. prof. Columbia U. Sch. Law, 1978-82, assoc. prof., 1982-84; exec. v.p., gen. counsel, sec. CBS Inc., N.Y.C., 1991-98; sr. v.p. law and govt. affairs Campbell Soup Co., Camden, N.J., 1998—; reporter jud. coun. 2nd Cir. Adv. Comm. on Planning for Dist. Cts., 1979-81; assoc. Cravath, Swaine & Moore, 1981-86. Trustee Columbia U. Mem. Nat. Legal Aid and Defender Assn. (corp. adv. com.), Inst. Jud. Adminstrn. (trustee), Lawyers' Com. for Civil Rights (internat. rule of law coun.). Office: Campbell Soup Co One Campbell Pl Camden NJ 08103

KADEN, LEWIS B., law educator, lawyer; b. 1942. AB, Harvard U., 1963, LLB, 1967. Bar: N.Y. 1970, N.J. 1974. Harvard scholar Emmanuel Coll. Cambridge U., 1963-64; law clk. U.S. Ct. Appeals, 1967; legis. asst. Senator Robert F. Kennedy, 1968; ptnr. Battle, Fowler, Stokes & Kheel, 1969-73; chief counsel to gov. State of N.J., 1974-76; assoc. prof. Columbia U., 1976-79, prof., 1979-84, adj. prof., 1984—, dir. Ctr. for Law and Econ. Studies, 1979-83; ptnr. Davis, Polk & Wardwell, N.Y.C., 1984—; bd. dirs. Bethlehem Steel Corp. Chmn. N.Y. State Indsl. Coop. Council, 1986-92. Office: Davis Polk & Wardwell 450 Lexington Ave New York NY 10017-3911

KADEN, LORI JILL, school counselor; b. Hoboken, N.J., Sept. 29, 1955; d. Jack and Rosanna (Rosenberg) Weiss; m. Henry Jude Kaden, Oct. 4, 1981; 1 child, Chelsea Nicole. BA in Edn., Jersey City State Coll., 1978, MA in Guidance and Counseling, 1989. Cert. elem. edn.; cert. student pers. svcs. Elem. sch. tchr. Union City (N.J.) Sch. Sys., 1978-92, sch. counselor, 1992—; pupil assistance com. coord. Union City Bd. Edn., 1989—, sch. improvement team adv. bd. mem., 1992-98, sch. support svcs. facilitator, 1996—, sch. mgmt. team adv. bd. mem., 1998—. Mem. Mensa. Avocations: hot air ballooning, games and puzzles, travel, theater, para-sailing. Office: Guidance Robert Waters Sch 2800 Summit Ave Union City NJ 07087-2323

KADER, NANCY STOWE, nurse, consultant, bioethicist; b. Ogden, Utah, May 29, 1945; d. William Hessel and Mildred (Madsen) Stowe; m. Omar Kader, Jan. 25, 1967; children: Tarik, Gabriel, Aron, Jacob. BSN, Brigham Young U., 1967; postgrad., U. Md. RN ICU Glendale (Calif.) Adventist Hosp., 1970-75, Utah Valley Hosp., Provo, 1975-83; campaign coord. Matheson for Gov., Salt Lake City, 1976-85, Wilson for Senate, Salt Lake City, 1980; RN cons. MESA Corp., Reston, Va., 1984-85; mgr. cost containment Health Mgmt. Strategies, Washington, 1985-88; nurse cons. Birch & Davis, Washington, 1988-90; cons. Inst. Medicine NAS, Washington, 1990-92; cons. Pal-Tech Inc., Arlington, Va., 1992—; vice chmn. Utah State Bd. Nursing, Salt Lake City, 1977-83; cons. in field. Dem. county chmn., Utah, 1977-79; del. Dem. Nat. Conv., 1980; del. Va. State Dem. Conv., 1984-95; vice chmn. Gov.'s Commn. on Status of Women, Salt Lake City, 1975-78. Democrat. Home: 11401 Tanbark Dr Reston VA 20191-4121

KADI, OSAMA, ; b. Aleppo, Syria, June 27, 1968; came to U.S., 1994; s. Mohammad Kadi and Hamida Aswad. B in Econs., Aleppo U., 1989, diploma in econs. and planning, 1992; MA in Econs., Ea. Mich. U., 1999. Pres. Thought and Edn. Club, Farmington, Mich., 1996—; grad. asst. econs. dept. Ea. Mich. U., Ypsilanti, 1997-98, rsch. asst. sociology dept., 1997-98; presenter in field. Author, editor: Anticipated Role of Islam, 1997, For Better Morality in the Next Century, 1998; contbr. articles to profl. jours.; corr. Al-Ahram Internat. Newspaper, Cairo, 1997-98; host, co-dir. E.O.F. (Educate Our Families WNZK) Radio Sta., Southfield, Mich., 1997—. Recipient the award of sci. invention Dar-Sauad Al-Sabah, Kuwait, 1994. Mem. Am. Econ. Assn., Middle East Econs. Assn., Middle East Studies Assn., Arabic Heritage Inst., Acad. Polit. Sci., Ctr. for Presidency Studies, Mich. Assn. Broadcasters (ofcl. Arab Am. mem.). Avocations: acting, basketball. E-mail: OKadi@aol.com. Fax: 248-262-9254. Office: TEC PO Box 2772 Farmington MI 48333

KADISH, ANNA STEIN, pathologist, educator, researcher; b. Mexico City, Feb. 27, 1942; came to U.S., 1942; d. Emanuel and Rose (Herzig) Stein; m. Lawrence J. Kadish, July 1, 1965; children: Deborah, Rachel, Sam. BA, Barnard Coll., 1963; MD, Harvard U., 1967. Diplomate Am. Bd. Pathology. Resident in pathology Alber Einstein Coll. Medicine, Bronx, N.Y., 1967-69, 71-72, Roosevelt Hosp., N.Y.C., 1970-71; from asst. to assoc. prof. pathology Albert Einstein Coll. Medicine, 1972-84, prof., 1984—; attending pathologist Jacobi Med. Ctr., 1972—. Contbr. articles to profl. jours. Grantee NIH. Office: Albert Einstein Coll Medicine 1300 Morris Park Ave Rm G705 Bronx NY 10461-1926*

KADISH, LORI GAIL, clinical psychologist; b. Newark, Mar. 6, 1962; d. Gerald Bernard and Marlene (Brodsky) K. BA in Psychology, Emory U., 1984; MS in Clin. Psychology, Fla. Inst. Tech., 1987, PsyD in Clin. Psychology, 1988. Lic. psychologist, N.J., N.Y., Fla.; cert. addiction specialist. Tutor Dekalb County Juvenile Detention Ctr., Atlanta, 1982-83; edn. counselor, interviewer Planned Parenthood, Atlanta, 1983; crisis intervention counselor Helpline, Atlanta, 1982-84; therapist Brevard Community Mental Health Ctr., Melbourne, Fla., 1984-86; therapist adolescent-adult psychiat. unit Wuesthoff Meml. Hosp., Rockledge, Fla., 1986-87; psychology intern South Oaks Hosp., Amityville, N.Y., 1987-88; staff clin. psychologist, team leader Fair Oaks Hosp., Summit, N.J., 1988-92; clin. dir. Outpatient Substance Abuse Ctr., Paramus, N.J., 1993-94; pvt. practice clin. psychology, Summit, 1990-94, Livingston, N.J., 1992-93, Ft. Lee, N.J., 1992—; presenter in field. Vol. recreational and occupational therapist asst. St. Barnabas Hosp., Livingston, 1983; vol. psychiat. nurse asst. Muhlenberg Hosp., Plainfield, N.J., 1983. Mem. APA, N.Y. State Psychol. Assn., N.J. Psychol. Assn., Fla. Psychol. Assn., Soc. Psychologists in Addictive Behaviors, Assn. for Advancement Behavior Therapy, Bergen County Assn. Lic. Psychologists. Avocations: travel, photography, music, beach. Office: 2083 Center Ave Ste G Fort Lee NJ 07024-4999

KADISH, RICHARD L., lawyer; b. Newark, Dec. 1, 1943; s. Irving Jerome and Henrietta (Appleblatt) K.; m. Bethany Tortis, Aug. 6, 1972; children: Jennifer, Andrew, Jill. BA, U. Pa., 1965; MA, Rutgers U., 1968, JD, 1970. Deputy atty. gen. N.J. Atty Gen., Trenton, N.J., 1971-74; deputy exec. dir. N.J. Housing Fin. Agy., Trenton, N.J., 1974-77; sr. v.p. CRI Inc., Rockville, Md., 1978-87, exec. v.p., 1987-94; pres. Capital Apt. Properties, Inc., Rockville, Md., 1994-97, Capreit, Inc., Rockville, Md., 1998—; dir. Nat. Multifamily Housing Coun. Mem. ABA, N.J. Bar Assn. Office: CAPREIT 11200 Rockville Pike Rockville MD 20852-3154

KADISH, SANFORD HAROLD, law educator; b. N.Y.C., Sept. 7, 1921; s. Samuel J. and Frances R. (Klein) K.; m. June Kurtin, Sept. 29, 1942; children: Joshua, Peter. B Social Scis, CCNY, 1942; LLB, Columbia U., 1948; JD (hon.), U. Cologne, 1983; LLD (hon.), CUNY, 1985, Southwestern U., 1993. Bar: N.Y. 1948, Utah 1954. Pvt. practice law N.Y.C., 1948-51; prof. law U. Utah, 1951-60, U. Mich., 1961-64; prof. law U. Calif., Berkeley, 1964-91, dean Law Sch., 1975-82, Morrison prof., 1973-91, prof. emeritus, 1991—; Fulbright lectr. Melbourne (Australia) U., 1956; vis. prof. Harvard U., 1960-61, Freiburg U., 1967, Stanford U., 1970; lectr. Salzburg Seminar Am. Studies, 1965; Fulbright vis. lectr. Kyoto (Japan) U., 1975; vis. fellow Inst. Criminology, Cambridge (Eng.) U., 1968. Author: (with M.R. Kadish) Discretion to Disobey—A Study of Lawful Departures from Legal Rules, 1973, (with Schulhofer) Criminal Law and Its Processes, 6th edit., 1995, Blame and Punishment—Essays in the Criminal Law, 1987; editor-in-chief Ency. Crime and Justice, 1983; contbr. articles to profl. jours. Reporter Calif. Legis. Penal Code Project, 1964-68; pub. mem. Wage Stblzn. Bd., region XII, 1951-53; cons. Pres.'s Commn. Adminstrn. of Justice, 1966; mem. Calif. Coun. Criminal Justice, 1968-69. Lt. USNR, 1943-46. Fellow Ctr. Advanced Study Behavioral Scis., 1967-68; Guggenheim fellow Oxford U., 1974-75; vis. fellow All Souls Coll. Oxford U. Fellow AAAS (v.p. 1984-86), Brit. Acad. (corr.); mem. AAUP (nat. pres. 1970-72), Am. Assn. Law Schs. (exec. com. 1960, pres. 1982), Order of Coif (exec. com. 1966-67, 74-75), Phi Beta Kappa. Home: 774 Hilldale Ave Berkeley CA 94708-1318

KADISON, RICHARD VINCENT, mathematician, educator; b. N.Y.C., July 25, 1925; married, 1956; 1 child. MS, U. Chgo., 1947, PhD, 1950; hon. doctorate, U. d'Aix-Marseille, 1986, U. Copenhagen, 1987. NRC fellow math. Inst. Advanced Study, 1950-52; from asst. prof. to prof. Columbia U., 1952-64; Kuemmerle prof. math. U. Pa., 1964—. Fulbright rsch. grantee, Denmark, 1954-55; Sloan fellow, 1958-62; Guggenheim fellow, 1969-70. Mem. NAS, Am. Math. Soc. (Steele prize for lifetime achievement 1999), Royal Danish Acad. Sci. and Letters (fgn. mem.), Norwegian Acad. Sci. and Letters (fgn. mem.), Sigma Xi. Office: U Pa Dept Math Philadelphia PA 19104-6395

KADISON, STUART, lawyer and educator; b. Richmond, Va., Nov. 17, 1923; s. Elliot Theodore and Rebecca (Lesser) K.; m. Carita Silverman, June 23, 1946; children: Dana, Brian, Warne. Student, NYU, 1938-40; A.B., U. Md., 1942; LL.B., Stanford U., 1948. Bar: Calif. 1948. Practiced law Los Angeles; now ret. ptnr. Sidley & Austin, Los Angeles; lectr. Southwestern U. Sch. Law, L.A., 1948-52, Stanford U. Sch. Law, 1977-82; Herman Phleger vis. prof. Stanford Law Sch., 1994; vis. prof. Brigham Young U. Law Sch., 1995—; co-chmn. ABA-Am. Newspaper Pubs. Assn. Task Force, 1977-83. Bd. visitors Stanford Law Sch., 1964-72, chmn., 1969-70; bd. dirs. Friends of Huntington Libr., v.p. and treas., 1977-82, pres., 1983-85, bd. overseers, 1978-91; chmn. lawyers adv. com. Constl. Rights Found., 1978-81; trustee Santa Barbara Mus. Art, 1991-97. Lt. USNR, 1942-46. Elected to Townsend Harris Hall of Fame, 1994. Fellow Am. Coll. Trial Lawyers, Am. Bar Found.; mem. ABA (chmn. spl. com. on delivery of legal svcs. 1973-75, chmn. resource devel. coun. 1983-84), Am. Law Inst. (life), L.A. County Bar Assn. (pres. 1971-72, chmn. com. on judiciary 1976-77, Shattuck-Price Meml. award 1986), State Bar Calif. (gov. 1973-76), Destroyer Escort Commanding Officers WWII. Home: 4853 Glencairn Rd Los Angeles CA 90027-1135

KADNER, CARL GEORGE, biology educator emeritus; b. Oakland, Calif., May 23, 1911; s. Adolph L. and Otilia (Pecht) K.; m. Mary Elizabeth Moran, June 24, 1939; children: Robert, Grace Wickersham, Carl L. BS, U. San Francisco, 1933; MS, U. Calif., Berkeley, 1936, PhD, 1941. Prof. biology Loyola Marymount U., Los Angeles, 1936-78, prof. emeritus, 1978—; trustee Loyola U., Los Angeles, 1970-73. Served to maj. U.S. Army, 1943-46. Mem. Entomol. Soc. Am. (emeritus), Sigma Xi, Alpha Sigma Nu. Republican. Roman Catholic. Avocation: insect photography. Home: 8100 Loyola Blvd Los Angeles CA 90045-2639

KADNER, ROBERT JOSEPH, microbiology educator; b. L.A., Mar. 19, 1942; s. Carl George and Mary Elizabeth Kadner; m. Carole F. Mashburn, July 29, 1967; children: Kristen Elizabeth, Robert James. BS, Loyola U., L.A., 1963; PhD, UCLA, 1967. Rschr. NYU, N.Y.C., 1967-69; asst. prof. microbiology U. Va., Charlottesville, 1969-75, assoc. prof., 1975-80, prof., 1980—; mem. microbial physiology and genetics study sect. NIH, 1980-84, 91-95; mem. pers. for rsch. C rev. panel Am. Cancer Soc., 1989-93. Editor Jur. Bacteriol., 1998—. NIH grant, 1972—. Mem. Am. Soc. for Microbiology (Grad. Microbiology Tchg. award 1998), Am. Soc. Biol. Chemists, Genetics Soc. Am. Roman Catholic. Home: 104 Bennington Ct Charlottesville VA 22901-2407 Office: U Va Dept Microbiol Charlottesville VA 22908

KADO, CLARENCE ISAO, molecular biologist; b. Santa Rosa, Calif., June 10, 1936; s. James Y. and Chiyoko K.; m. Barbara M. Kawahara, June 30, 1963; children—Deborah, Diana M. B.Sc., U. Calif., Berkeley, 1959, Ph.D., 1964. Rsch. asst. Virus Lab., U. Calif., Berkeley, 1960-64, NIH postdoctoral fellow, 1964-67, asst. rsch. biochemist, 1967-68; asst. prof. plant pathology U. Calif., Davis, 1968-72, assoc. prof., 1972-76, prof., 1976—; dir. Fallen Leaf Lake Confs., 1985—. Author: Principles and Techniques in Plant Virology, 1972; editor: Molecular Mechanisms of Bacterial Virulence, 1994, Horizontal Gene Transfer, 1998; assoc. editor Virology, 1970-73, Jour. Bacteriology, 1987-93, Molecular Microbiology, 1989—. Recipient Bronze medal for virus research WHO, 1968; NATO sr. fellow, 1974-75; NIH grantee, 1968—; Am. Cancer Soc. grantee, 1969-73, 1980-82; SEA grantee, 1979-85; CRGO grantee, 1985—. Fellow Am. Phytopath. Soc., Am. Acad. Microbiology; mem. AAAS, N.Y. Acad. Scis., Am. Soc. Microbiology, Am. Soc. Biochemistry and Molecular Biology, Internat. Soc. Molecular Plant-Microbe Interactions, Fedn. Fly Fishers, Fly Fishers Davis (dir., past pres.), Sigma Xi. Office: U Calif Davis Crown Gall Group One Shields Ave Davis CA 95616

KADOHIRO, JANE KAY, educator, nurse, diabetes consultant; b. Lima, Ohio, July 20, 1947; d. Howard M. and Betty J. (Joboske) Keller; m. Howard M. Kadohiro, Dec. 27, 1969; children: Christopher, Jennifer. BA in Sociology and Edn., U. Hawaii, Manoa, 1969; BS in Nursing, U. Hawaii, Honolulu, 1977, MPH, 1990; MS, U. Hawaii, 1994, DrPHC, 1996, DrPH, 1998. Staff nurse Children's Hosp., Honolulu, 1977-78; staff pub. health nurse Hawaii State Dept. Health, Honolulu, 1978-80, coord. hypertension and diabetes, 1980-85, projects adminstr., 1985-89, chief chronic diseases, 1989-91; office mgr. Hanalei Trends, Honolulu, 1985-89; clin. nurse specialist Queen's Med. Ctr., Honolulu, 1991-94; cons. Aiea, Hawaii, 1991—; nurse investigator Honolulu Heart Program, 1991-95; faculty U. Hawaii at Manoa, Honolulu, 1991—; mem. diabetes project Office Hawaiian Affairs, Honolulu, 1993-95. Leader, advisor, life mem. Girl Scouts U.S., Honolulu, 1978—; mem. diabetes project Office of Hawaiian Affairs, 1993-95. Named Disting. Alumni U. Hawaii Sch. Nursing, 1987; one of Hawaii's Unsung Heroes, Honolulu Star Bull., 1993. Mem. ANA (polit. action com. 1994—), APHA, Hawaii Nurses Assn. (Excellence in Clin. Practice award 1995), Am. Diabetes Assn. (nat. del. yearly, nat. programs com. nat. youth congress 1993-95, nat. youth task force and design team 1996-97, nat. profl. edn. com. 1997—, Pacific N.W. regional pres.-elect 1998—, outstanding contbns. to diabetes and camping nat. award 1994, Hawaii affiliate founding bd. dirs. 1978—, camp nurse and camp dir. 1982, past pres. 1986, chair mem. coms. 1978—), Hawaii Pub. Health Assn., Am. Assn. Diabetes Educators (nat. bd. dirs. 1997—), Hawaii Assn. Diabetes Educators (founding mem., bd. dirs. 1989—, pres. 1996—, state legis. coord. 1996—, treas. 1994-95, pub. affairs chair 1996—, diabetes camp edn. nat. award 1995), Diabetes Advocacy Alliance Hawaii (convener and chair 1997—), Internat. Diabetes Fedn., Internat. Soc. Pediat. and Adolescent Diabetes (steering com. Internat. Diabetes camping program 1989—), Am. Heart Assn. (cardiovasc. nursing coun. 1985-97), Sigma Theta Tau (founding mem., chair nominating com. 1995-97 Gamma Psi chpt. and chpt.-at-large, chmn. recognition com. 1986-89). Avocations: travel, people, community and organization work, lifelong learning. Home: 98-1773 Kaahumanu St Apt C Aiea HI 96701-1846 Office: Univ Hawaii at Manoa 2528 The Mall/Webster Honolulu HI 96822

KADONAGA, JAMES TAKURO, biochemist; b. Ft. Bragg, N.C., Aug. 24, 1958; s. Tadashi and Alice Ayako K.; m. Anne Kadonaga, Sept. 15, 1984; children: William, Natalie. SB, MIT, 1980; AM, Harvard U., 1982, PhD, 1984. Fellow U. Calif., Berkeley, 1984-88; asst. prof. biology U. Calif., San Diego, 1988-92, assoc. prof., 1992-94, prof., 1994—. Mem. editl. bd. Molecular Cell Jour., 1997—, Genes and Devel. Jour., 1994—, Molecular and Cellular Biology, 1993—, Protein Expression and Purification, 1990—; contbr. articles to profl. jours. Recipient Biochemistry award Eli Lilly, 1989-91, Am. Inst. of Chemists/MIT award, 1980, prize Alpha Chi Sigma/MIT, 1980; named to Hall of Fame, East Side Union H.S. Dist., San Jose, Calif., 1991; DuPont fellow Harvard U., 1983-84, Miller fellow, 1984-86, sr. fellow Am. Cancer Soc. (Calif. div.), 1986-87, Presdl. Faculty fellow Pres. George Bush, 1992-97; Lucille P. Markey scholar, 1987-93. Fellow AAAS, Am. Acad. Microbiology; mem. Am. Chem. Soc., Am. Soc. Microbiology, Am. Soc. Biochemistry and Molecular Biology. Office: U Calif San Diego 9500 Gilman Dr La Jolla CA 92093-5003

KADOTA, TAKASHI THEODORE, mathematician, electrical engineer; b. Omogo, Ehime-Ken, Japan, Nov. 14, 1930; s. Shigeru and Kikuko (Tominaga) K.; m. Helena Littau, Dec. 21, 1956 (div.); children: Mari, Amy, Kimberley; m. Charlie Frances Hampton. BSEE, Yokohama (Japan) Nat. U., 1953; MSEE, U. Calif., Berkeley, 1956, PhDEE, 1960. Mem. tech. staff AT&T Bell Labs., Whippany, N.J., 1960-66, Murray Hill, N.J., 1966-94; ret., 1994; vis. prof. U. Hawaii, Honolulu, 1978, U. Calif., Berkeley, 1975, Stanford U., 1974. Fellow IEEE (assoc. editor 1977-80).

KADOW, CATHI, academic counselor; b. Chgo.. AA, South Suburban Coll., South Holland, Ill., 1987, AS, 1988; BA in Writing, Purdue U. Calumet, Hammond, Ind., 1990, MA in English Lit., 1992; postgrad., Loyola U., Chgo., 1998—. Sec. South Suburban Coll., 1984-90; adj. instr. prep. writing Prairie State Coll., Chicago Heights, Ill., 1991, Lewis U., Romeoville, Ill., 1994; grad. asst. Purdue U. Calumet, 1990-92, vis. instr. English, 1992-94, acad. counselor, 1995—, editor univ. catalog, 1991-93. Contbr. poetry to lit. jours., including Skylark, Crossroads Poetry Jour., World of Poetry (hon. mention 1988, Silver Poet awrd 1989), Chasing Rainbows, Midwest Poetry Anthology, Interior Lighting, Impressions, Writer II, Am. Poetry Anthology. Recipient 3d place award writing contest Woman's Day, 1985; scholar South Suburban Coll., 1986, President's scholar, 1988-89. Mem. Nat. Acad. Advising Assn., Ind. Acad. Advising Network, Phi Theta Kappa, Alpha Chi. Avocations: travel, photography. Office: Purdue U Calumet 2200 169th St Hammond IN 46323-2068

KAEL, PAULINE, film critic, author; b. Petaluma, Calif., June 19, 1919; d. Isaac Paul and Judith (Friedman) K.; 1 child, Gina James. Student, U. Calif., Berkeley, 1936-40; LLD (hon.), Georgetown U., 1972; D. Arts and Letters (hon.), Columbia Coll., Chgo., 1972; LittD (hon.), Smith Coll., 1973, Allegheny Coll., 1979; LHD (hon.), Kalamazoo Coll., 1973, Reed Coll., 1975, Haverford Coll., 1975; DFA (hon.), Sch. Visual Arts, N.Y.C., 1980. Movie critic New Yorker mag., 1968-91. Author: I Lost it at the Movies, 1965, Kiss Kiss Bang Bang, 1968, Going Steady, 1970, Deeper into Movies, 1973 (Nat. Book award 1974), Reeling, 1976, When the Lights Go Down, 1980, 5001 Nights at the Movies, 1982, enlarged edit., 1991, Taking It All In, 1984, State of the Art, 1985, Hooked, 1989, Movie Love, 1991, For Keeps, 1994, Conversations with Pauline Kael, 1996; contbg. author: The Citizen Kane Book, 1971; contbr. to numerous other mags. Recipient George Polk Meml. award, 1970, Front Page award Newswomen's Club N.Y., 1974, 83; Guggenheim fellow, 1964. Mem. Phi Beta Kappa (hon.). Office: New Yorker Mag 20 W 43rd St New York NY 10036-7400

KAESBERG, PAUL JOSEPH, virology researcher; b. Engers, Germany, Sept. 26, 1923; came to U.S., 1926, naturalized, 1933; s. Peter Ernst and Gertrude (Mueller) K.; m. Marian Lavon Hanneman, June 13, 1953; children—Paul Richard, James Kevin, Peter Roy. B.S. in Engring, U. Wis., Madison, 1945, Ph.D. in Physics, 1949; D. Natural Scis. (hon.), U. Leiden, The Netherlands, 1975. Instr. biometry and physics U. Wis., 1949-51, asst. prof. biochemistry, 1956-58, assoc. prof., 1958-60, prof., 1960-63, prof. biophysics and biochemistry, 1963—, Beeman prof. biophysics and biochemistry, 1983-87, chmn. Biophysics Lab., 1970-88, Wis. Alumni Research Found. prof., 1981—, Beeman prof. molecular virology and biochemistry, 1987-90, prof. emeritus, 1990; cons. in field. Contbr. chapts. to books and articles to profl. jours. Mem. NAS, Am. Soc. Virology (pres. 1987-88). Home: 5002 Bayfield Ter Madison WI 53705-4811 Office: U Wis Inst Molecular Virology 1525 Linden Dr Madison WI 53706-1534

KAESTNER, JOHN THOMAS, beverage company executive; b. St. Louis, Nov. 25, 1950; s. Albert Theodore Jr. and Dolores Marion (Zulpo) K.; m. Linda Sue Kincaid, Feb. 16, 1973 (div. Sept. 1991); children: Jennifer, John Jr.; m. JoAnn M. Rhodus Breheny, Dec. 19, 1992; stepchildren: Patrick Breheny, Julie Breheny, Kathleen Breheny. BA in Elem. Edn., Harris Tchrs. Coll., 1973; MA in Edn., St. Louis U., 1977. Cert. tchr., prin., Mo. Tchr. Parkway Sch. Dist., Chesterfield, Mo., 1973-78; sales tng. instr. Anheuser-Busch Cos., Inc., St. Louis, 1978-80, mgr. beer mktg. mgmt. devel., 1980-86, mgr. mktg. planning and analysis, 1986-89, sr. mgr. consumer awareness and edn., 1989-94, sr. group, dir. consumer awareness and edn., 1994—. Bd. trustees, BACCHUS, 1999, bd. dirs. Provident Counseling, St. Louis, 1995—, Family and Relationship Ctr., LaJolla, 1997—, Nat. Bus. Alliance of the Am. Sch. Counselor Assn., Alexandria, 1995—, Nat. Acad. League, Salt Lake City, 1997—; planning and adv. com. Personal Responsibility Edn. Process, St. Louis, 1995—; com. mem. 2004, St. Louis, 1997—. Recipient Disting. Alumni award Harris Tchrs. Coll., 1997. Roman Catholic. Avocations: golf, snow skiing, softball. Home: 777 Carman Meadows Dr Manchester MO 63021-7174 Office: Anheuser-Busch Cos Inc One Busch Place Saint Louis MO 63118

KAFARSKI, MITCHELL I., chemical processing company executive; b. Detroit, Dec. 15, 1917; s. Ignacy A. and Anastasia (Drzazgowski) K.; m. Zofia Drozdowska, July 11, 1967; children: Erik Michael, Konrad Christian. Student, U. Detroit, 1939-41, Shrivenham (Eng.) Am. U., 1946. Process engr. Packard Motor Car Co., Detroit, 1941-44; organizer, dir. Artist and Craftsman Sch., Esslingen, Germany, 1945-46; with Nat. Bank of Detroit, 1946-50; founder, pres. Chem. Processing Inc., Detroit, 1950-65, also bd. dirs.; chmn. bd., pres., treas. Aactron Inc., Madison Heights, Mich., 1965—; chmn. bd., pres. Imtech of Mich., Inc., 1988-92; treas. Detroit Magnetic Insp. Co., 1960-65; also dir.; v.p. KMH Inc., Detroit, 1960-64; also dir.; treas. Packard Plating Inc., Detroit, 1962-67, also dir. Commr. Mich. State Fair, 1965-72; mem. com. devel. and planning to build Municipal Stadium State of Mich., 1965-88; benefactor, mem. Founders Soc., Detroit Inst. Arts, 1965—; trustee Founders' Soc., Detroit Inst. Arts, 1982-90; sponsor, host world celebrity for World Preview Mich., 1965-66; mem. dist. adv. council SBA, 1971-73; del. White House Conf. on Aging, 1971; organizer, treas. Mich. Reagan for Pres. Com., 1980; treas. Straith Meml. Hosp., Southfield, Mich., 1972—, chmn. bd., 1976; trustee Mich. Opera Theater, 1982—; bd. dirs. Gilbert and Sullivan Light Opera Soc., Palm Beach, Fla., 1985—; White House rep. to opening of first U.S. Trade Center, Warsaw, Poland, 1972; chmn. fund-raising Bloomfield Arts Assn., Birmingham, Mich., 1973-74; mem. Space Theatre Consortium, Inc., Seattle, 1981-83; bd. regents Orchard Lake (Mich.) Schs., 1981-83; Vice chmn. Republican State Nationalities Council Mich., 1969-73; bd. dirs. Bloomfield Arts Assn., 1973-84, Friends of Kresge Library, Oakland U., 1973-86; presdl. appointee bd. dirs. U.S.A. Pennsylvania Ave. Devel. Corp., Washington, 1973-81; chmn. bd. Straith Meml. Hosp., Detroit, 1971—, Detroit Sci. Center, 1972—, corp. dir.; mem. Internat. Soc. Palm Beach; trustee Greater Palm Beach Symphony, 1986; mem. Citizen's Commn. to Improve Mich. Cts., 1986-88; contbr. Kravis Ctr. for Performing Arts, West Palm Beach, 1989; mem. Bus. Com. for the Arts, Palm Beacvh, 1991—. Served with AUS, 1944-46, ETO. Recipient Nat. award for war prodn. invention War Prodn. Bd., 1943; decorated knight's Cross Order of Poland's Rebirth Restituta, 1975, chevalier Chaine des Rotisseurs, 1982, Knight of Malta Order of St. John. Mem. Nat. Assn. Metal Finishers, Mich. Assn. Metal Finishers (dir., chmn. bd. 1976), N.A.M., Am. Electroplaters Soc., Cranbrook Acad. Arts, Am.-Polish Action Coun. (chmn. 1971-76), Am. Assn. Mus. (treas. Detroit), Poinciana Club, Village Club. Clubs: Capitol Hill (Washington); Detroit Athletic. Home: 240 Chesterfield Rd Bloomfield Hills MI 48304-3520 Office: Aactron Inc 29306 Stephenson Hwy Madison Heights MI 48071-2394 *A basic ingredient to success usually is determined by special events in one's life. In the course of my experiences, a sprinkling of tribulations were a must. From these were gleaned the principles, goals and conduct in attaining success. During the course of my life's pursuit, the ability to help others ensured a complete fulfillment of my goals.*

KAFENTZIS, JOHN CHARLES, journalist, educator; b. Butte, Mont., Aug. 18, 1953; s. Christian and Betty Ann (Gaston) K.; m. Teresa Marie Nokleby, June 5, 1976; children: Kathryn Anne, Christian John. BA in Journalism, U. Mont., 1975. Reporter The Missoulian, Missoula, Mont., 1974-76, The Hardin (Mont.) Herald, 1976; reporter The Spokesman-Rev., Spokane, Wash., 1976-80, copy editor, 1980-83, chief copy desk, 1983-89, news editor, 1989-94, news designer, 1994—; adj. faculty Ea. Wash. U., Cheney, 1982—, Whitworth Coll., 1998. Greek Orthodox. Avocation: competitive swimming. Office: The Spokesman-Rev 999 W Riverside Ave Spokane WA 99201-1098

KAFF, ALBERT ERNEST, journalist, author; b. Atchison, Kans., June 14, 1920; s. John and Ethel Mae (Worley) K.; m. Lee Chuan Diana Fong, Oct. 15, 1960; children: Arthur Fong, Alban Fong. B.A. in Econs., U. Colo., 1942. Reporter Atchison Globe, summers 1939-41, Ponca City (Okla.) News, 1946-48, Daily Oklahoman, Oklahoma City, 1948-50; fgn. corr. U.P.I., Korea and Japan, 1952-56; bur. mgr. U.P.I., Vietnam, 1956-58, Taiwan, 1958-61, The Philippines, 1961-63; news editor U.P.I., Japan, 1963-72; dir. Asian svcs. U.P.I., Hong Kong, 1972-75; asst. dir., dir. pers. rels. U.P.I., N.Y.C., 1975-78; v.p., gen. mgr. Asia-Pacific U.P.I., Hong Kong, 1978-84; v.p., mgr. N.Y. U.P.I., 1984-85; media cons., 1985; bus. internat. editor Cornell U. News Svc., 1986-93; freelance journalist Stamford, Conn., Alexandria, Va., Fairfield, Conn., 1993—; columnist Overseas Press Club Bull. Contbg. author: How I Got That Story, 1967, Eyewitness on Asia, 1997, Foreign Correspondents in Japan: From 1945 to the Present, 1998, Foreign Correspondents in Japan: Covering a Half Century of Upheavals from 1945 to the Present, 1998; author: (with Avner Arbel) Crash: Ten Days in October. . . Will It Strike Again?, 1989. Served with AUS, 1943-46, 50-52. Decorated Bronze Star. Mem. Fgn. Corrs. Club Japan (pres. 1967-68), Fgn. Corrs. Club Hong Kong (pres. 1974-75), Overseas Press Club Am. (v.p. 1984-86, bd. dirs. 1988-92, trustee Found. 1992—), Ithaca Press Club (vice chmn. 1987-88) Sigma Chi. Episcopalian. Home and Office: 393 Unquowa Rd Fairfield CT 06430-5028 *During 52 years of reporting, writing and editing the news, I missed several opportunities because I ignored a basic rule: If you can accomplish the assignment today or tomorrow, do it today. Tomorrow will bring new demands.*

KAFFER, ROGER LOUIS, bishop; b. Joliet, Ill., Aug. 14, 1927; s. Earl Louis and Helen Ruth (McManus) K. BA, St. Mary of the Lake, Mundelein, Ill., 1950, STB, 1952, MA, 1953, licentiate in sacred theology, 1954; licentiate of canon law, Pontifical Gregorian U., Rome, 1958; D of Pastoral Ministry, St. Mary of the Lake, Mundelein, Ill., 1983; MEd, DePaul U., 1965; LHD (hon.), Felician Coll., 1986; hon. doctorate, Coll. of St. Francis, 1990, Lewis U., 1990. Ordained priest Roman Cath. Ch., 1954; cert. K-14 supr., Ill. Eccles. notary Roman Cath. Diocese of Joliet, 1954-56; asst. chancellor Roman Cath. Diocese Joliet, 1958-65; aux. bishop Roman Cath. Diocese of Joliet, 1985—, vicar gen., vicar for clergy, 1985—; rector St. Charles Borromeo Sem., Lockport, Ill., 1965-70; prin. Providence High Sch., New Lenox, Ill., 1970-85; rector Cathedral of St. Raymond, Joliet, 1985; consecrated bishop, 1985; past. mem. Marriage Tribunal, Diocesan Sem. Bd., Diocesan Bd. Religious Edn. Recipient DeLa Salle medallion, Lewis U., 1984; named Cleric of Yr., KC, 1973, Citizen of Yr., New Lenox Assn. Commerce, 1976, Man of Yr. Joliet Cath. High Alumni Assn., 1978. Mem. Nat. Conf. Cath. Bishops Conf. Ill., KC (Ill. state chaplain 1993—). Avocations: youth work, retreat work. Address: 425 Summit St Joliet IL 60435-7155*

KAFKA, BARBARA POSES, author; b. N.Y.C., Aug. 6, 1933; d. Jack and Lillian (Shapiro) Poses; m. Ernest Kafka, June 19, 1959; children: Nicole, Michael. AB cum laude, Radcliffe Coll., 1954. cons. in field. Author: American Food California Wine, 1981, 94, (Tastemaker award), Microwave Gourmet, 1987 (N.Y. Times Best Seller), Food for Friends, 1987, 93, Microwave Gourmet Healthstyle Cookbook, 1989, (Tastemaker award), Party Food, 1992, Roasting A Simple Art, 1995 (Julia Child Cookbook award), Soup, A Way of Life, 1998; compiler, editor pro bono: The James Beard Celebration Cookbook, 1990; editor: The Four Seasons, 1980, The Cook's Catalogue, (mags.) Cooking, The Pleasures of Cooking; contbg. editor Vogue, 1981-89, Gourmet, 1988-96; contbg. columnist N.Y. Times, 1987—; contbr. articles to profl. jours. Mem. Internat. Assn. Culinary Profls., Am. Inst. Wine and Food, Culinary Historians Boston, James Beard. Home and Office: 23 E 92nd St New York NY 10128-0607

KAFKA, GERALD ANDREW, lawyer; b. Martins Ferry, Ohio, Sept. 9, 1951; s. Andrew and Mary (Spustek) K.; children: Andrea, Sarah, Justin. BA, Wheeling Jesuit Coll., 1972; JD, U. Cin., 1975; LLM in Taxation, Georgetown U., 1979. Bar: Ohio 1975, D.C. 1982, Md. 1984, U.S. Tax Ct. 1977, U.S. Claims Ct. 1978, U.S. Supreme Ct. 1979, D.C. 1982, U.S. Dist. Ct. (D.C. dist.) 1983, U.S. Ct. Appeals (D.C. cir.) 1983. Trial atty. honors program tax div. U.S. Dept. Justice, Washington, 1975-79; ptnr. Scribner, Hall & Thompson, Washington, 1979-84, Steptoe & Johnson, Washington, 1984-92, Dewey Ballantine, Washington, 1992—; mem. adj. faculty Georgetown U. Law Ctr., Washington, 1979—; master J. Edgar Murdoch Am. Inn of Ct., U.S. Tax Ct., 1989—. Author: Litigation of Federal Tax Civil Controversies, 1996; editor procedure dept. Jour. Taxation; contbr. articles to profl. jours. Named Outstanding Atty., Tax Divsn. U.S. Dept. Justice, Washington, 1977. Fellow Am. Coll. Tax Counsel; mem. ABA (chair ct. procedure com. tax sect. 1993-95, chmn. task force civil tax litigation process 1989-90, task force on large case audits and litigation 1990-91, ad hoc joint com. tax ct. jurisdiction 1987, task force on taxpayer bill of rights legis 1987-88), D.C. Bar Assn. (steering com. tax sect. 1986-91, chmn. com. audits and litigation tax sect. 1987). Office: 1775 Pennsylvania Ave NW Washington DC 20006-4605

KAFKA, MARIAN STERN, neuroscientist; b. Richmond, Va., Mar. 30, 1927; d. Henry Sycle and Adele (Lewit) Stern; m. John S. Kafka, Oct. 3, 1952; children: David Egon, Paul Henry, Alexander Charles. AB in Zoology, Conn. Coll., 1948; PhD in Physiology, U. Chgo., 1952. Rsch. asst. dept. physiol. chemistry Emory U. Sch. Medicine, Atlanta, 1952-53; rsch. assoc. Ill. Neuropsychiat. Inst., U. Ill. Sch. Medicine, Chgo., 1953-54; rsch. asst. dept. internal medicine Yale U. Sch. Medicine, New Haven, 1954-57; USPHS postdoctoral fellow endocrinology br. Nat. Heart, Lung and Blood Inst. NIH, Bethesda, Md., 1965-68, physiologist hypertention-endocrine br., 1968-74; physiologist sect. biochemistry and pharmacology Biol. Psychiatry Br. NIH, Bethesda, 1974-82; physiologist Clin. Neurosci. Br. NIMH, Bethesda, 1982-86; exec. sec. neurobehavioral rsch. rev. subcom., neurosci. rsch. rev. com. NIMH, Rockville, Md., 1986, exec. sec. cellular neurobiology & psychopharmacology com., 1986-90; chief clin. rev. br. divsn. extramural activities NIMH, Rockville, 1990. Contbr. articles, revs. to sci. publs. Recipient Adminstr.'s award for Meritorious Achievement, ADAMHA, 1989; Marie J. Mergler fellow in physiology, 1950. Mem. AAAS, Am. Physiol. Soc. (mem. pub. affairs and pub. info. com. 1974-79, chair pub. info. com. 1980-84, centennial com. 1979-85), Soc. for Neurosci., Endocrine Soc., Biophys. Soc., Internat. Soc. Chronobiology, Fedn. Am. Soc. for Exptl. Biology (pub. info. com. 1977-82), Phi Beta Kappa, Sigma Xi. Achievements include research in neurotransmitter receptors in animals and humans, molecular interactions between neurotransmitters, receptors and cell membranes, central nervous system control of circadian rhythms. Home: 7834 Aberdeen Rd Bethesda MD 20814-1102 Office: NIMH Parklawn Bldg 5600 Fishers Ln Rm 902C Rockville MD 20852-1750

KAFKER, FRANK A., historian, educator; b. N.Y.C., Dec. 18, 1931; s. Robert and Ida (Schear) K.; m. Serena Lipton, Dec. 20, 1953; children: Scott, Roger. BA, Columbia Coll., 1953, MA, 1954, PhD, 1961. From instr. to assoc. prof. Corning (N.Y.) C.C., 1958-62; from asst. prof. to prof. U. Cin., 1962-98, emeritus prof., 1998—. Author: The Encyclopedists as a Group, 1996; co-author: The Encyclopedists as Individuals, 1988; editor: Notable Encyclopedias of the 17th & 18th Centuries, 1981, Notable Encyclopedias of Late 18th Century, 1994; co-editor: The French Revolution, 1968, 4th edit., 1989, Napoleon and His Times, 1989. Fulbright fellow, 1954-55, Camargo Found fellow, 1993, Am. Philosophical Soc. fellow, 1978. Mem. Soc. French Hist. Studies (co-editor 1985-92), Soc. 18th Century French Studies (pres. 1995-97), Am. Soc. 18th Century Studies, Soc. Diderot, Br. Soc. 18th Century Studies, 18th Century Scottish Studies Soc. E-mail: fkafker@msn.com. Home: 31 Brimmer St Apt 4 Boston MA 02108-1014

KAFOURY, MARGE, city official. BA, Wash. State U., 1963. Dir. govt. rels. City of Portland, Oreg., 1986—. Office: City of Portland Dept Govt Rels 1221 SW 4th Ave STe 410 Portland OR 97204-1909*

KAGAN, CONSTANCE HENDERSON, philosopher, educator, consultant; b. Houston, Sept. 16, 1940; d. Bessie Earle (Henderson) Davis; m. Morris Kagan, May 27, 1967. BA, Baylor U., 1962; MSSW, U. Tex. Austin, 1966; PhD, U. Okla., 1979. congl. fellow, 1981-82. Mem. NASW, Am. Philos. Assn.

KAGAN, DONALD, historian, educator; b. Kurshan, Lithuania, May 1, 1932; came to U.S., 1934, naturalized, 1940; s. Max and Leah (Benjamin) K.; m. Myrna Dabrusky, Jan. 13, 1955; children: Robert William, Frederick Walter. A.B., Bklyn. Coll., 1954; M.A., Brown U., 1955; Ph.D., Ohio State U., 1958. Instr. history Pa. State U., University Park, 1959-60; asst. prof. ancient history Cornell U., 1960-64, asso. prof., 1964-67, prof., 1967; prof. history and classics Yale U., 1969—, master Timothy Dwight Coll., 1976-78, acting dir. athletics, 1987-88, dean Yale Coll., 1989-92. Author: The Great Dialogue, 1965, The Outbreak of the Peloponnesian War, 1969, The Archidamian War, 1974, The Western Heritage, 1979, (with Frank Turner and Steven Ozment) The Peace of Nicias and the Sicilian Expedition, 1981, The Fall of the Athenian Empire, 1987, Pericles of Athens and the Birth of Democracy, 1991, On the Origins of War and the Perservation of Peace, 1995. Home: 37 Woodstock Rd Hamden CT 06517-2949 Office: Yale Univ Hall of Grad Studies 215 New Haven CT 06502

KAGAN, JEROME, psychologist, educator; b. Newark, Feb. 25, 1929; s. Joseph and Myrtle (Liebermann) K. B.S., Rutgers U., 1950; Ph.D., Yale, 1954. Instr. psychology Ohio State U., 1954-55; research asso. Fels Research Inst., Yellow Springs, Ohio, 1957-59; chmn. dept. psychology Fels Research Inst., 1959-64; asso. prof. psychology Antioch Coll., 1959-64; prof. psychology Harvard U., 1964—, dir. Mind Brain Behavior Initiative, 1996—; Adv. com. Nat. Inst. Child Health and Devel. Author: (with G.S. Lesser) Contemporary Issues in Thematic Apperceptive Methods, 1961, (with Moss) Birth to Maturity, 1962, (with Mussen, Conger and Huston) Child Development and Personality, 7th edit., 1990, (with Segal) Psychology, 7th edit., 1991, (with Janis, Mahl and Holt) Personality, 1969, Understanding Children, 1971, Change and Continuity in Infancy, 1971, (with Kearsley and Zelazo) Infancy, 1978, (with Brim) Constancy and Change, 1980, The Second Year, 1981, The Nature of the Child, 1984, Unstable Ideas, 1989, Galen's Prophecy, 1994, Three Seductive Ideas, 1998. Served with AUS, 1955-57. Recipient Lucius Cross medal Yale U., 1981; Phi Beta Kappa scholar, 1988-89. Fellow AAAS, APA (Disting. Sci. Contbn. award 1987, G. Stanley Hall award 1995), Am. Acad. Arts and Scis., Soc. Rsch. Child Devel. (Disting. Sci. Contbn. award 1989); mem. NAS, Inst. Medicine, Ea. Psychol. Assn. Home: 210 Clifton St Belmont MA 02478-2605 Office: Harvard U Dept Psychology William James Hall 33 Kirkland Hl Cambridge MA 02138 *My success has been aided by a combination of hard work, openess to new ideas, a readiness to discard beliefs that are proven invalid; a desire to nurture the growth of others; and belief in the beauty of ideas and the perfectibility of man.*

KAGAN, JULIA LEE, magazine editor; b. Nurnberg, Fed. Republic Germany, Nov. 25, 1948; d. Saul and Elizabeth J. Kagan. A.B., Bryn Mawr Coll., 1970. Researcher Look Mag., N.Y.C., 1970-71; editorial asst., asst. editor McCall's Mag., N.Y.C., 1971-74, assoc. editor, 1974-78, sr. editor, 1978-79; articles editor Working Woman mag., N.Y.C., 1979-85, exec. editor, 1985-88; editor Psychology Today, 1988-90; sr. editor McCalls, 1990-91; contbg. editor Working Woman, 1991-93; editor-in-chief Lamaze Parents' Mag., 1992-93, Lamaze Baby Mag., 1993; spl. projects dir. Child Mag., 1993-94; sr. v.p. EDK Assocs., N.Y.C., 1994; psychology/health dir. Fitness Mag., N.Y.C., 1995-96; dep. editor Consumer Reports, Yonkers, N.Y., 1996—, editor, 1996—; vis. J. Stewart Riley prof. journalism Ind. U., 1991-93. Co-author: Manworks: A Guide to Style, 1980; contbg. author: The Working Woman Success Book, 1981, The Working Woman Report, 1984. Pres. Appleby Found., N.Y.C., 1982-84. Recipient 2d Ann. Advt. Journalism award Compton Advt., 1983. Mem. Am. Soc. Mag. Editors, Womens Media Group (bd. dirs.), Journalism and Women Symposium (treas. 1993-94, pres. 1995-96). Club: Princeton (N.Y.C.). *

KAGAN, SIOMA, economics educator; b. Riga, Russia, Sept. 29, 1907; came to U.S., 1941, naturalized, 1950; s. Jacques and Berta (Kaplan) K.; m. Jean Batt, Apr. 5, 1947 (div. 1969). Diplom Ingenieur, Technische Hochschule, Berlin, 1931; M.A., Am. U., 1949; Ph.D. in Econs, Columbia U., 1954. Sci. asst. Heinrich Hertz Inst., Berlin, 1931-33; partner Laboratoire Electro-Acoustique, Neuilly-sur-Seine, France, 1933-48; chief French Mission Telecom. French Supply Council in N.Am., Washington, 1943-45; mem. telecom. bd. UN, 1946-47, econ. affairs officer, 1947-48; econs. cons. to govt. and industry; asso. prof. econs. Washington U., St. Louis, 1956-59; staff economist Joint Council Econ. Edn., N.Y.C., 1959-60; prof. internat. bus. U. Oreg., Eugene, 1960- 67; prof. internat. bus. U. Mo., St. Louis, 1967-87, prof. emeritus, 1987—; faculty leader exec. devel. programs Columbia, Northwestern U., NATO Def. Coll., Rome, others. Contbr. numerous articles profl. publs. Served with Free French Army, 1941-43. Decorated Legion of Honor (France). Recipient Thomas Jefferson award U. Mo., 1984. Fellow Latin Am. Studies Assn.; mem. Am. Econ. Assn., Acad. Polit. Sci., Assn. Asian Studies. Clubs: University (St. Louis); Conanicut Yacht (Jamestown, R.I.). Home: 8132 Roxburgh Dr Saint Louis MO 63105-2436 Office: U Mo Sch Business Saint Louis MO 63121

KAGAN, STEPHEN BRUCE (SANDY KAGAN), network marketing executive; b. Elizabeth, N.J., Apr. 27, 1944; s. Herman and Ida (Nadel) K.; m. Susan D. Kaltman, July 3, 1966; children—Sheryl, Rachel. BS in Econs., U. Pa., 1966; MBA in Fin., Bernard Baruch Coll., 1969. Chartered fin. analyst. Security analyst Merrill Lynch Pierce Fenner & Smith, N.Y.C., 1966-68; dir. rsch. Deutschmann & Co., N.Y.C., 1968-70; v.p. Equity Sponsors, Inc., N.Y.C., 1970-72; v.p., investment counselor Daniel H. Renberg & Assocs., Inc., Los Angeles, 1972-78; regional v.p. Carlson Travel Network, Van Nuys, Calif., 1978-95; rep. Excel Telecomms., Van Nuys, Calif., 1995—. Vice pres. bd. Temple Beth Hillel, North Hollywood, Calif., 1976-83. Mem. Inst. Cert. Fin. Analysts, Beta Gamma Sigma. Avocations: golf; skiing; poker; travel. Home and Office: 13952 Weddington St Van Nuys CA 91401-5751

KAGAN, STUART MICHAEL, pediatrician; b. Milw., June 22, 1944; s. Harry and Bertha (Pittleman) K.; m. Gloria Jean Glass, Aug. 1, 1971; children: Jennifer Anne, Abigail Elizabeth. BS, U. Wis., 1966; MD, U. Utah, 1969; MPH, U. Kans., 1997. Diplomate Am. Bd. Pediat. Intern in pediats. Kans. U. Med. Ctr., Kansas City, 1969-70, resident in pediats., 1970-71, fellow in pediat. cardiology, 1971-73; pvt. practice Overland Park, Kans., 1975-88; occupational medicine physician Employer Health Svc., Kansas City, Mo., 1988—, med. rev. officer, 1994—, acting med. dir., 1994—. Lt. comdr. USN, 1973-75. RecipientKans. Cardiology fellowship Kans. U. Med. ctr., 1972. Mem. Am. Coll. Occupational and Environ. Medicine, Am. Soc. Addiction Medicine, Great Plains Occupational and Environ. Medicine. Avocations: conservation, jogging, computers, astronomy. Office: Employer Health Svcs 8511 Hillcrest Rd Ste 100 Kansas City MO 64138-2776

KAGAN, VAL ALEXANDER, engineer, researcher, educator; b. Odessa, Ukraine, Aug. 24, 1940; came to U.S., 1991; m. Rina V. Kaplan, July 5, 1969; children: Atalia, Anna. BS, MS in Mech. Engring., Tech. U. Kaunas, Lithuania, 1964, PhD in Engring., 1970; DSc, Acad. Scis., Moscow, 1985. Design engr. R&D Co. Priekalas, Kaunas, 1965-66; postgrad. course scientist Tech. U. Kaunas, 1967-69, postdoctoral fellow, 1970-71, asst. prof., 1971-72; assoc. prof. Tech. U., Vilnius, Lithuania, 1972-84, prof., rsch. fellow, head ctr., 1984-91; engr., sr. engr. Allied Signal, Inc., Morristown, N.J., 1992-95, sr. prin. scientist, 1996-98, applied technology leader, 1998—; sr. cons. Acad. Sci., Vilnius, 1984-91; mem. sci. coun. Russian Acad. Sci., Moscow, 1986-91; mem. adv. bd. Vilnius U., 1983-91. Editor Applied Mechanics, 1986-91; author 4 monographs; contbr. more than 200 articles to profl. jours. Mem. ASTM, AIAA, ASME, Soc. Plastics Engrs. Achievements include 11 U.S., Russian and Lithuanian patents. Home: 122 Edgefield Dr Morris Plains NJ 07950-1960 Office: Allied Signal Inc 101 Columbia Rd Morristown NJ 07960-4658

KÅGE, JONAS, ballet company artistic director; b. Stockholm; m. Deborah Dobson; 1 child, Isabelle. Student, Royal Swedish Ballet Sch. Mem. Royal Swedish Ballet, mem. Am. Ballet Theatre, 1971-75, soloist, 1972-75, prin. dancer, 1973-75; prin. dancer Stuttgart (Germany) Ballet, 1975-76, Geneva (Switzerland) Ballet, 1976-78, Zürich (Switzerland) Ballet, 1978-88; artistic dir. Malmo (Sweden) Opera Ballet, 1988-95; freelance guest artist, master tchr., 1995-97; artistic dir. Ballet West, Salt Lake City, 1997-98; Guest artist Am. Ballet Theatre, 1977—, Frankfort (Germany) Ballet, Basel (Switzerland) Ballet, Royal Swedish Ballet, 1980-81, Deutsche Opera Berlin, 1982, Pitts. Ballet, 1984-85, Nat. Ballet of Can., 1984-85, 85-86, Milw. Ballet, 1984-85, NAPAC Dance Co., 1985-86, Munich Opera Ballet, 1985-86, Nat. Ballet of Portugal, 1986-87, Ariz. Ballet, 1987-88,. Prin. dancer Swan Lake, Coppélia, La Bayadere, Tales of Hoffmann, Lander's Etudes, Shadowplay, Leaves are Fading, Balanchine's Theme and Variations, Gemini, Some Times, Intermezzo, Les Noces, Am. Ballet Theatre, 1971-75, Swan Lake, Don Quixote, Sphinx, Voluntaries, 1977; prin. dancer The Taming of the Shrew, Romeo & Juliet, Onegin, Gemini, La Sacre de Printemps, Greening, Stuttgart Ballet, 1975-76, Apollo, The Four Temperaments, Agon Symphony in C, Who Cares?, Geneva Ballet, 1976-77, Romeo & Juliet, The Sleeping Beauty, Sphinx, Rosalinda, London Festival Ballet (now English Nat. Ballet), 1977, La Sylphide, Cinderella, Swan Lake, Giselle, Romeo & Juliet, 1982-83; prin. dancer Swan Lake, Frankfort Ballet, Giselle, Basel Ballet, Don Quixote, Vienna Ballet, The Taming of the Shrew, Manon, Royal Swedish Ballet, 1980-81, La Sylphide, Deutsche Opera Berlin, 1982, Coppélia, Giselle, Greening, Apollo, Spoleto and Naples, 1982, Swan Lake, Pitts. Ballet Theatre, 1984-85, Romeo & Juliet, Nat. Ballet of Can., 1984-85, Swan Lake, 1985-86; prin. dancer The Merry Widow, Milw. Ballet, 1984-85, Apollo, NAPAC Dance Co., 1985-86, Romeo & Juliet, Munich Opera Ballet, 1985-86, Apollo, Nat. Ballet of Portugal, 1986-87, The Nutcracker, Ariz. Ballet, 1987-88; creator prin. role Chopin Pas de Deux, Malmo Opera Ballet, 1993-94; choreographer Swedish TV, 1983, Simple Symphony, Zurich Ballet, 1984, Baroque Variations, Malmo Opera Ballet, 1988, Swan Lake, 1992-93 (Thalia prize 1993); master of ceremonies dance competition, Swedish TV, 1997. Bd. dirs. Swedish Dance U., Stockholm, Dalhalla amphitheater, Rattvik, Sweden. Recipient Carina Ari Found. for Dance medal, 1994. Avocations: photography, skiing, mountain climbing, horseback riding, wilderness guide training. Office: Ballet West Capitol Theatre 50 W 200 S Ste 100 Salt Lake City UT 84101-1663

KAGGEN, ELIAS, physician; b. Bklyn., Dec. 27, 1915; s. Joseph and Lena (Zalbowitz) K.; student NYU, 1932-34; DO, Phila. Coll. Osteo. Medicine, 1938; MD, Chgo. Coll. Medicine, 1947; m. Sylvia Muntner, May 15, 1941 (dec.); children: Lois S., Marilyn D.; m. Rissel Karlins. Trustee, Temple Beth Emeth N'ohr Progressive Shaari Zedek of Flatbush. Diplomate Am. Osteo. Bd. Gen. practice. osteopathic medicine, Bklyn., 1947—. Mem. N.Y. State Osteo. Med. Soc., Am. Osteopath. Assn., N.Y.C. Soc. Osteo. Physicians and Surgeons (trustee, chmn. public relations, past dir., v.p. 1959-60, pres. 1961-62, chmn. bd. dirs. 1962-63; chmn. com. health and edn. 1963-64), Am. Coll. Gen. Practitioners in Osteo. Medicine and Surgery (sec. N.Y. chpt. 1983-88), Am. Coll. Osteo. Family Physicians (sec. N.Y. chpt. 1983-93), Lambda Omicron Gamma (life). Home: 1655 Flatbush Ave Apt B1505 Brooklyn NY 11210-3282 Office: 917 8th Ave Brooklyn NY 11215-4309

KAGGEN, LOIS SHEILA, non-profit organization executive; b. N.Y.C., Jan. 2, 1944; d. Elias and Sylvia (Muntner) K.; m. Harold Jay Burns, June 29, 1969 (dec. June 1975); 1 child, David Henry (dec.); m. Michael Francis McCann, Sept. 26, 1984. BS in Fine Arts, Skidmore Coll., 1964; postgrad., Cooper Union, 1967-70; MA in Art Edn., CCNY, 1973; PhD in Art Edn., NYU, 1997. Tchr. fine arts grades 7-9 Jr. H.S. 149, Bronx, N.Y., 1967-74; founder, pres. Resources for Artists With Disabilities, N.Y.C., 1987—; Traumatic Brain Injury Consumer Adv., 1977—; mem. adv. bd. com. Art in Edn. Project, N.Y. State Coun. on the Arts, Ctr. for Safety in the Arts, N.Y.C., 1987; cons. Ea. Paralyzed Vets. Assn., Guggenheim Mus. Art, N.Y.C., 1990; mem. bd. advisors Ind. Arts Gallery, Queens Ind. Living Ctr., Jamaica, N.Y., 1987-97, 98; mem. steering com. Ann. Disability Independence Day March, 1992-93, mem. Media Outreach, 1992; provider written and oral testimony in field to orgns. including N.Y. City Coun., 1992, 93, Nat. Coun. on Disability, N.Y.C., 1994, Washington, 1995, N.Y. State Assembly mems. and N.Y. State senators, 1994, N.Y. State Standing Com., 1996, mem. citizens adv. coun. Andrew Heiskell Libr. for the Blind and Physically Handicapped, N.Y.C., 1997—; bd. dirs. Ctr. for Independence of the Disabled of N.Y., Inc., N.Y.C., 1996—, Gov.'s appt. to Traumatic Brain Injury Svcs. Coordinating Coun., Albany, 1997-98, 98—, others; presenter NIH Consensus Devel. Conf. on Rehab. of Persons with Traumatic Brain Injury, Bethesda, Md., 1998, 5th Ann. Conf., Traumatic Brain Injury Program, N.Y. State Dept. Health, Albany, 1998; originator, conf. com. co-organizer, consumer panelist NYU Moses Ctr. for Students with Disabilities and Ctr. for Independence of Disabled of N.Y., Loeb Student Ctr., NYU, N.Y.C., 1998; panel organizer, moderator, presenter Inst. for Rsch. on Women's 16th Ann. Celebration of Our Work Conf., Douglass Coll., Rutgers U., New Brunswick, N.J., 1998; art presenter in field. Photography exhbns. include 80 Washington Sq. East Galleries, N.Y.C., 1977, Soho Photo Gallery, N.Y.C., 1978, 4th St. Photo Gallery, N.Y.C., 1979, Womanart Gallery, N.Y.C., 1979, Leslie-Lohman Gallery, N.Y.C., 1980, 81, Window Gallery, Met. Savs. Bank, N.Y.C., 1980, Cathedral St. John-the-Devine Gallery, N.Y.C., 1980, Donnell Libr. Gallery, 1981; originator, organizer various exhbns. African-Am. Artists with Disabilities, Artists with Phys. Disabilities; contbr. articles, photographs to profl. jours. Mem. disability rights steering com. 504 Dem. Club for Persons with Disabilities, 1987-88, mem. exec. com., 1990—; active Disabled in Action of Greater N.Y., 1989—, Manhattan Borough Pres. Adv. Com. on Disabled, 1988-98, 99—, Mayor's Adv. Com. on People with Disabilities, N.Y.C., 1991-93, Citywide Coalition on Disability, N.Y.C., 1994-95, Nat. Inst. on Disability and Rehab. Rsch., Office Spl. Edn. and Rehab. Svcs., U.S. Dept. Edn., Washington, mem. peer rev. registry, 1995—; mem. New York County Dem. Com., 1995—. Grantee Whitney Mus. Am. Art and the Smithsonian Instn., summer 1967, summer film inst. Stanford U., 1968; Cooper Union scholar, 1967-70; recipient Appreciation cert. Manhattan Borough Pres., 1991, Dean's Disting. Alumni Achievement award NYU, N.Y.C., 1998. Mem. Coll. Art Assn. (com. mems. with disabilities for accessible programs and places 1990—). Office: Resources for Artists with Disabilities 77 7th Ave Ste Ph-h New York NY 10011-6645

KAGIWADA, REYNOLD SHIGERU, advanced technology manager; b. L.A., July 8, 1938; s. Harry Yoshifusa and Helen Kinue (Imura) K.; children: Julia, Conan. BS in Physics, UCLA, 1960, MS in Physics, 1962, PhD in Physics, 1966. Asst. prof. in residence physics UCLA, 1966-69; asst. prof. physics U. So. Calif., 1969-72; mem. tech. staff TRW, Redondo Beach, Calif., 1972-75, scientist, sect. head, 1975-77, sr. scientist, dept. mgr., 1977-83, lab. mgr., 1984-87, project mgr., 1987-88, MIMIC chief scientist, 1988-89, asst. program mgr., 1989-90; advanced technology mgr. TRW, Redondo Beach, 1990—. Presenter papers at numerous profl. meetings, co-author more than 41 articles; patentee eight solid state devices. Recipient Gold Medal award TRW, 1985, Ramo Tech. award, 1985, Transfer award, IEEE MTT-S N. Walter Cox award, 1997. Fellow IEEE (v.p. IEEE MTT-S Adminstrn. Com. 1991, IEEE MTT-S N. Walter Cox 1997, pres. 1992); mem. Assn. Old Crows, Sigma Pi Sigma, Sigma Xi. Home: 3117 Malcolm Ave Los Angeles CA 90034-3406 Office: TRW-SEG Bldg M5 Rm 1470 One Space Park Bldg Redondo Beach CA 90278

KAGLE, JOSEPH LOUIS, JR., artist, arts administrator; b. Pitts., May 2, 1932; s. Joseph Louis and Edith (Marcellus) K.; m. Anne Cornelia Schiller, Jan. 19, 1957; children: Samantha Anne, Christopher Yung Wook. Student, Carnegie Mus. Sch. Art, 1938-51; BA in English, Dartmouth Coll., 1955; MFA in Art and Art History, U. Colo., 1958; MEd in Gifted and Talented Edn., U. Ark., Little Rock, 1984. Instr. Wis. State U., Whitewater, 1958-60; head dept. art, asst. prof. Washington and Jefferson Coll., Pa., 1960-64; head dept. art, assoc. prof. Keuka Coll., 1964-68; artist in residence Chapman Coll., World Campus Afloat, 1968-69; prof., head dept. fine arts, visual arts, dance, music and theatre U. Guam, 1970-76; prof. art Community Coll. Finger Lakes, 1976-78; exec. dir. S.E. Ark. Arts and Sci. Center, Pine Bluff, 1978-84; dir. Brockton (Mass.) Art Mus., 1984-86, The Art Ctr., Waco, Tex., 1987—, Bridgewater State Coll., 1986-87; artist in residence Wash. State U., Spokane, 1965-66, Naples Mill Sch., 1976-78; bd. contbrs. Wald Tribune-Herald Opinion Editorials; lectr. USIS, Taiwan, 1970-76; critic Pine Bluff (Ark.) News. Work exhibited in over 400 nat. and internat. exhbns. including Nat. Gallery, Washington; dir. 50 TV shows on art; muralist, Hafa Adai Theatre, Bank of Guam, Fine Arts Bldg. U. Guam; author: Death Is All the Time, 1976. Mem. planning bd. Pine Bluff Com. Gifted and Talented, 1979-80; mem. adv. bd. Sta. KCTF, 1989-92; bd. dirs. Greater Waco Coun. on the Arts, 1989—; bd. dirs. Assn. for Retarded Citizens., chmn., 1990-92, 93-94. Fulbright scholar; Smithsonian Instn. Kellog Found. Project scholar, 1983, 84; named artist of year Pacific chpt. A.I.A., 1976-77. Mem. Am. Mus. Assn., Coll. Art Assn., Tex. Assn. Mus., Coll. Art Assn., Am. Assn. Mus., Waco Assn. Mus. (chmn. bd. dirs. 1995-97), Waco C. of C. (bd. dirs. 1994-97). Fax no. 254-752-3506. Home: 3400 Obrien Cir Waco TX 76708-1747 Office: The Art Ctr 1300 College Dr Waco TX 76708-1497

KAHALAS, HARVEY, business educator; b. Boston, Dec. 3, 1941; s. James and Betty (Bonfeld) K.; m. Dianne Barbara Levine, Sept. 2, 1963; children: Wendy Elizabeth, Stacy Michele. BS, Boston U., 1965; MBA, U. Mich., 1966; PhD, U. Mass., 1971. Data processing coord. Ford Motor Co., Wayne, Mich., 1963-66; lectr. Salem (Mass.) State Coll., 1966-68; asst. prof. bus. Worcester (Mass.) Poly. Inst., 1970-72; asst. prof. Va. Poly. Inst. and State U., Blacksburg, 1972-75, assoc. prof., 1975-77; assoc. prof. SUNY, Albany, 1977-79, assoc. dean, 1979-81, prof., 1979-89, dean, 1981-87; pres. HKE Inc., 1987-97; prof. U. Mass., Lowell, 1989-94, dean, 1989-94, exec. dir. Ctr. Indsl. Competitiveness, 1990-94; Commonwealth disting. prof. U. Mass., 1994-97; dir. Ctr. for Bus. Rsch. and Competitiveness, U. Mass., Dartmouth, 1994-97; prof., dean Wayne State U., 1997—; program dir. Aspen Inst., 1994-97; cons. Aspen Inst./Fund for Corp. Initiatives, N.Y.C., 1980-94, GE, Schenectady, N.Y., 1981-85, GM, Tarrytown, N.Y., 1987-89; bd. dirs. Lumigen Inc., Southfield, Mich. Contbr. articles to profl. jours. Bd. dirs. Fund for Corp. Initiatives, N.Y.C., 1980—, Nat. Found. Ileitis and Colitis, Albany, 1982-89, Blue Cross Northeastern N.Y., Albany, 1983-89, Capital Dist. Bus. Rev., Albany, 1984—, Greater Detroit Area Health Coun., 1998—. Named Disting. Alumni, U. Mass., 1982, Disting. Lectr. USIA, 1985, Am. Participant USIA, 1989; Fulbright scholar, 1987, 88, Aspen Inst. scholar, 1997. Mem. Fulbright Assn. (life), Acad. Mgmt. (treas. 1971-73, mem. exec. com.), Human Resource Planning Soc. (hon.), Human Resource Systems Profls. (hon.), Pers. Accreditation Inst. (life), Beta Gamma Sigma, Sigma Iota Epsilon, Delta Tau Kappa. Office: Wayne State Univ Sch Bus Adm 226 Prentis Bld 5201 Cass Ave Detroit MI 48202-3930

KAHAN, BARRY DONALD, surgeon, educator; b. Cleve., July 25, 1939; s. Jacob Marvin and Pearl (Schultz) K.; m. Rochelle Liebling, Sept. 22, 1963, 1 child, Kara. B.S., U. Chgo., 1960, Ph.D., 1964, M.D., 1965. Intern Mass. Gen. Hosp., Boston, 1965-66; resident in surgery Mass. Gen. Hosp., 1968-72; staff asso. in immunology NIH, 1966-68; asst. prof. surgery and physiology Northwestern U. Sch. Medicine, Chgo., 1972-74; asso. prof. Northwestern U. Sch. Medicine, 1975-76; prof. surgery U. Tex. Med. Sch., Houston, 1977—; also dir. divs. organ transplantation dept. surgery, dir. program immunology, grad. sch. U. Tex. Med. Sch. Bd. dirs. Ill. Kidney Found., 1974-76. Mem. ACS, AAAS, Soc. Univ. Surgeons, Am. Soc. Clin. Investigation, Am. Soc. Transplant Surgeons (pres. 1989—), Am. Surg. Assn., Internat. Transplantation Soc. (charter, treas. 1990—), Am. Surg. Assn., Am. Assn. Immunologists, Am. Assn. Cancer Rsch., Am. Physiol. Soc. Office: U Tex Houston 6431 Fannin St MSB 6.240 Houston TX 77030

KAHAN, MARLENE, professional association executive; b. Bronx, N.Y., June 10, 1952; d. Meyer and Ruth (Baroth) Schmulewitz. BA in Psychology, CUNY, 1973. Tchr. elem. sch., Bronx, 1974-75; asst. to pres. Mag. Pubs. Am., N.Y.C., 1976-83; asst. dir. Am. Soc. Mag. Editors, N.Y.C., 1983-90, exec. dir., 1990—. Recipient Gold Key award PR News, 1991. Mem. Am. Soc. Assn. Execs., N.Y. Soc. Assn. Execs., Women in Comms. (program com. N.Y.C. 1991-93, bd. dirs. 1993-95, v.p. programs 1993-95). Avocations: ballet, jazz dance and music, tennis. Office: Am Soc Mag Editors 919 3rd Ave New York NY 10022-3902*

KAHAN, MITCHELL DOUGLAS, art museum director. BA, U. Va., 1973; MA, Columbia U., 1975; M of Philosophy, CUNY, 1978, PhD, 1983. Mus. aide Nat. Mus. Am. Art, Washington, 1978; curator Montgomery (Ala.) Mus. Fine Art, 1978-82, N.C. Mus. Art, Raleigh, 1982-86; dir. Akron (Ohio) Art Mus., 1986—; cons. La. World's Exposition, New Orleans, 1983-84. Author: Art Inc.: American Paintings in Corporate Collections, 1979, Roger Brown, 1981, Minnie Evans, 1986. Columbia U. fellow, 1973, Smithsonian Inst. fellow, 1976-78, CUNY grad. research fellow, 1978, Nat. Endowment for Arts fellow, 1987. Mem. Coll. Art Assn., Intermus Conservation Assn. (trustee 1986-95, pres. 1990-92, 95), Assn. Art Mus. Dirs. Home: 529 Bastogne Dr Akron OH 44303-1606 Office: Akron Art Mus 70 E Market St Akron OH 44308-2084

KAHAN, ROCHELLE LIEBLING, lawyer, concert pianist; b. Chgo., Sept. 5, 1939; d. Arnold Leo and Helly (Ichilson) Liebling; m. Barry D. Kahan, Sept. 22, 1962; 1 child, Kara. BA, Northwestern U., 1960, JD, 1963. Bar: Ill. 1963, Tex. 1977. Atty. Treasury Dept., Chgo., 1964-65, Boston, 1965-66, 68-72, Washington, 1966-67; atty. pvt. practice, Chgo. and Houston, 1972—. Mem. ABA, Tex. Bar Assn. Houston Bar Assn., Tuesday Musical Club (1st v.p.), Treble Clef Club (pres.), Kappa Beta Pi (past pres.), Mu Phi Epsilon. Avocation: early music.

KAHAN, SHELDON JEREMIAH (CHRISTOPHER REED), musician, singer; b. Honolulu, Mar. 5, 1948; s. Aaron Kahan and Marianne (Royjiczek) Sann. Student, Tel Aviv U., 1967-69, Merritt Coll., 1972-74. Guitarist The Grim Reapers, Miami Beach, Fla., 1965-66; bassist The Electric Stage, Jerusalem, 1969-71; music dir., musician Fanfare, L.A., 1974-75, Jean Paul Vignon & 1st Love, L.A., 1975-76; musician Jenny Jones & Co., L.A., 1976; musician, vocalist Fantasy, L.A., 1977-79; leader, musician, vocalist Fortune, L.A., 1980-83; bassist Johnny Tillotson Show, Nev., 1983; ptnr., musician, vocalist Heartlight, L.A., 1983-84; leader, musician, vocalist The Boogie Bros., L.A., 1984—; arranger, conductor L.A. Rock Chorus, 1988; musician, vocalist Jeremiah Kahan, L.A., 1988; bass player LIX, L.A., 1990—; solo act Sheldon Kahan, L.A., 1990—; spokesman Moore Oldsmobile & Cadillac, Valencia, Calif., 1987. Compiled musical work copyrighted in Libr. Congress: Sheldon Jeremiah Kahan The Early Years-Vol. I; prodr., disk jockey Kaleidoscope Radio Mag., Am. Radio Ntwork; one-man show El Caapitan, Irvine, Calif., 1990, Sagebrush Cantina, Calabassas, Calif., 1990, Don Jose, Artesia, Calif., Pineapple Hill, Tustin, Calif., 1991, The Fling, Tustin, 1992, Beverly Garland, North Hollywood, Calif., Brian Patch, Garden Grove, Calif., Sugar Suite, Granada Hills, Calif., 1993, The Blarney Stone, Fountain Valley, Calif., 1994, Sunset Lounge, Fullerton, Calif., Rembrandts, Placentia, Calif., 1995, Chez Lynn, Orange, Calif., 1996, Maxwells, Anaheim Hills, Calif., Royal Crown, Fullerton, Calif., 1997, The Oasis, Garden Grove, Calif., 1997, Azar's Red Robin, Newbury Park, Calif., The Stovepiper, Northridge, Calif., Volare, Northridge, 1998, Oh Grady's, Granada Hills, Calif., 1998, Sportsage, Placentia, Calif., 1998, Mary White & Christopher Reed (duo) The Odyssey, Granada Hills, Calif., 1999. Mem. AFTRA, Am. Fedn. Musicians. Democrat. Jewish. Avocations: chess, aerobics, weight training, comparative religions. Home: 3915 1/2 Fredonia Dr Los Angeles CA 90068-1213

KAHANA, EVA FROST, sociology educator; b. Budapest, Hungary, Mar. 21, 1941; came to U.S., 1957; d. Jacob and Sari Frost; m. Boaz Kahana, Apr. 15, 1962; children: Jeffrey, Michael. BA, Stern Coll., Yeshiva U., 1962; MA, CCNY, CUNY, 1965; PhD, U. Chgo., 1968; HLD (hon.), Yeshiva U., 1991. Nat. Inst. on Aging predoctoral fellow U. Chgo. Com. on Human Devel., 1963-66; postdoctoral fellow Midwest Council Social Research, 1968; with dept. sociology Washington U., St. Louis, 1967-71, successively research asst., research assoc., asst. prof.; with dept. sociology Wayne State U., Detroit, 1971-84, from assoc. prof. to prof., dir. Elderly Care Research Ctr., 1971-84; prof. Case Western Res. U., Cleve., 1984—, Armington Prof., 1989-90, chmn. dept. sociology, 1985—, dir. Elderly Care Research Ctr., 1984—, Pierce and Elizabeth Robson prof. humanities, 1990—; cons. Nat. Inst. on Aging, Washington, 1976-80, NIMH, Washington, 1971-75. Author: (with E. Midlarsky) Altruism in Later Life, 1994; editor: (with others) Family Caregiving Across the Lifespan, 1994; mem. editl. bd. Gerontologist, 1975-79, Psychology of Aging, 1984-90, Jour. Gerontology, 1990-94, Applied Behavioral Sci. Rev., 1992—; contbr. articles to profl. jours., chpts. to books (recipient Pub.'s prize 1969). Bd. dirs. com. on aging Jewish Community Fedn., Cleve.; vol. cons. Alzheimer's Disease and Related Disorders Assn., Cleve. NIMH Career Devel. grantee, 1974-79, Nat. Inst. Aging Merit award grantee, 1989—; Mary E. Switzer Disting. fellow Nat. Inst. Rehab., 1992-93; recipient Arnold Heller award excellence in geriatrics and gerontology Menorah Park Ctr. for Aged, 1992; named Disting. Geontological Rschr. in Ohio, 1993. Fellow Gerontol. Soc. Am. (chair behavioral social sci. com. 1984-85, Disting. Mentorship award 1987, Polisher award 1997); mem. Am. Sociol. Assn. (coun. sect. on aging 1985-87, Disting. Scholar award sect. on aging and life course 1997), Am. Psychol. Assn., Soc. for Traumatic Stress, Wayne State U. Acad. Scholars (life), Sigma Xi. Avocations: reading, antiques, travel.

KAHANA, MICHAEL JACOB, cognitive neuroscientist; b. St. Louis, May 7, 1969; s. Boaz and Eva (Frost) K. BA, Case Western Res. U., 1989; PhD, U. Toronto, 1993. Postdoctoral fellow Harvard U., Cambridge, Mass., 1993-94; asst. prof. Brandeis U., Waltham, Mass., 1994—. Mem. editl. bd.: Memory and Cognition, 1997—. Recipient 1st award NIH, 1997-2002. Mem. APA. Office: Brandeis U Ctr for Complex Sys Waltham MA 02254

KAHANE, JEFFREY, music director; b. L.A., Sept. 12, 1956. Music dir. L.A. Chamber Orch., 1996—. Office: 611 W 6th St Ste 2710 Los Angeles CA 90017*

KAHARICK, JEROME JOHN, lawyer; b. Johnstown, Pa., Apr. 15, 1955; s. Stanley Joseph and Emily (Solic) K.; m. Carolyn Marie Safko, Aug. 7, 1977; children: Natalie, Allison. BA summa cum laude, U. Pitts., 1977; JD, Duquesne U., 1991. Bar: Pa. 1991, U.S. Dist. Ct. (we. dist.) Pa. 1991, U.S. Ct. Appeals (3d cir.) 1992, U.S. Supreme Ct., 1997. Sales rep. Met. Life, Johnstown, Pa., 1977-84; owner, stockholder Planned Fin. Svcs., Johnstown, Pa., 1984-88; law clk. Wayman, Irvin & McAuley, Pitts., 1988-89; legal analyst Elliott Co., Jeannette, Pa., 1989-92; pvt. practice Johnstown, 1992-95, 97—; asst. pub. defender Cambria County, Pa., 1993-99; ptnr. Weaver and Kaharick, 1995-97; atty. in pvt. practice Johnstown, Pa., 1997—. Exec. production editor Duquesne Law Rev., 1990-91. Mem. ABA, Assn. Trial Lawyers Am., Nat. Assn. Criminal Def. Lawyers, Pa. Bar Assn., Order of Barristers. Republican. Roman Catholic. Office: Lincoln Center 1st Flr 419 Lincoln St Ste 103 Johnstown PA 15901-1906

KAHIKINA, MICHAEL PUAMAMO, social services administrator, state legislator; b. Honolulu, Jan. 16, 1950; m. Naomi Abigail Barros; children: Puamamo, Kealoha, Kaua'i, Kanoe. AA, Leeward C.C., Pearl City, Hawaii, 1988; BS in Pub. Adminstrn., U. Hawaii-West Oahu, 1990. Utility electrician U.S. Navy Exch., Pearl Harbor, Hawaii, 1972-74; electrician City & County of Honolulu, 1974-75; outreach counselor Waianae Rap Ctr., 1975-79; social worker II Queen Liliuokalani Ctr., Nanakuli, Hawaii, 1979-85; agrl. specialist Honolulu Cmty. Action Program, Waianae, 1985-87; cmty. outreach . Hale Ola Ho'opakolea, Nanakuli, 1987-90; unit dir. Boys & Girls Club-Waianae, 1990—. Mem. State Ho. Reps. (Dist. 43), 1994—; bd. dirs. Neighborhood Bd.-Waianae, 1988-92; mem. Tchr. Retention Task Force, Waianae, 1987, Sch. Cmty. Based Mgmt. Task Force, Honolulu, 1988. Sgt. USAF, 1968-72. Democrat. Avocations: songwriting, music. Home: 89-416 Nanakuli Ave Waianae HI 96792-4037 Office: Ho Reps State Capitol 435 S Beretania St Honolulu HI 96813-2410

KAHIN, GEORGE MCTURNAN, political science and history educator; b. Balt., Jan. 25, 1918; s. George Stanley and Helen Agnew (Andrews) K.; m. Margaret Baker, July 4, 1942 (div.); children: Brian, Sharon; m. Audrey Richey, Mar. 8, 1967. B.A., Harvard U., 1940; M.A., Stanford U., 1946; Ph.D., Johns Hopkins U., 1951. Instr. Johns Hopkins U., Balt., 1949-51; asst. prof. Cornell U., Ithaca, N.Y., 1951-54, assoc. prof., 1954-59, prof., 1959-68, Aaron L. Binenkorb prof. internat. studies, 1968-88; exec. dir. Cornell South East Asia Program, Ithaca, 1951-60, dir., 1961-70; dir. Cornell Modern Indonesia Project, Ithaca, 1954-88; vis. prof. U. London, 1962-63; cons. Rockefeller Found., N.Y.C., 1964-65; hon. fellow Sch. Oriental and African Studies U. London, 1992. Author: Nationalism and Revolution in Indonesia, 1952, (with John Lewis) The United States in Vietnam, 1967, Intervention: How America Became Involved in Vietnam, 1986, (with Audrey Kahin) Subversion as Foreign Policy: The Secret Eisenhower and Dulles Debacle in Indonesia, 1995; editor: Major Governments of Asia, 1958, Governments and Politics of Southeast Asia, 1959. Served to sgt. U.S. Army, 1942-45, ETO. Recipient Fulbright S.E. Asia Regional Rsch. Program award, 1990-91; Social Sci. Rsch. Coun. fellow, Indonesia, 1948-49; John Simon Guggenheim fellow, 1975; Henry Luce Found. fellow, 1977; NEH fellow, 1981-82. Fellow Am. Acad. of Arts and Scis., Ctr. Study Democratic Instns.; mem. Council Fgn. Relations, Asia Soc. (chmn. Indonesia council 1962-66), Assn. Asian Studies (pres. 1973-74). Home: 1017 Cayuga Heights Rd Ithaca NY 14850-1021 Office: Cornell U Ctr for Adv Rsch on SE Asia 640 Stewart Ave Ithaca NY 14850-3857*

KAHL, DAVID BURR, artist; b. Glendale, Calif., Apr. 16, 1965; s. William Carl and Dorothy Beth (Adams) K.; m. Stephanie Garcia, June 6, 1992. BA, Calif. State U., Northridge, 1988; BFA, Art Ctr. Coll. Design, 1991. Freelance digital artist Hoboken, N.J., 1991—; imaging cons., Hoboken, 1991—. Officer Hoboken Evangel. Free Ch., 1994—. Republican.

KAHL, WILLIAM FREDERICK, retired college president; b. May 23, 1922; s. William Frederick and Bessie (Glading) K.; m. Mary Carson, Jan. 25, 1964; children: Frederick Glading, Sarah Hartwell. BA, Brown U., 1945; MA, Harvard U., 1947, PhD, 1955, LHD, 1993. Lectr. history Boston U., 1947-48, 50; from instr. to prof. Simmons Coll., Boston, 1948-76; provost Simmons Coll., 1965-76; pres. Russell Sage Coll., Troy, N.Y., 1976-88; bd. dir. Norstar. Author: The London Livery Companies: An essay and bibliography, 1960; contbr. articles to profl. jours. Vice-chmn. Hudson River Valley Assn.; bd. dirs. Albany Symphony Orch., Lower East Side Conservancy; chmn. bd. Tenement Mus., N.Y. State Nature Conservancy, Albany Inst. History and Art, Friends of the Hudson River Valley, Hudson River Valley Coordinating Coun., Russell Sage Pres. Adv. Coun.; pres., trustee, Albany Acad. for Girls, Wildwood Sch., Albany C. of C. Found. Social Sci. Coun. rsch. grantee, 1957-58. Mem. Am. Hist. Assn., Anglo-Am. Hist. Conf. Episcopalian. Home: 29 Old Niskayuna Rd Albany NY 12211-1349 Office: Russell Sage Coll Troy NY 12180

KAHLE, BREWSTER, communications executive; m. Mary Austin; 1 child, Caslon. Grad., MIT. Founder Wide Area Info. Servers Inc.; pres. Internet Achives, San Francisco, Calif.; CEO Alexa Internet, San Francisco. Office: Internet Archives PO Box 29141 San Francisco CA 94129-0141*

KAHLENBECK, HOWARD, JR., lawyer; b. Fort Wayne, Ind., Dec. 7, 1929; s. Howard and Clara Elizabeth (Wegman) K.; m. Sally A. Horrell, Aug. 14, 1954; children: Kathryn Sue, Douglas H. BS with distinction, Ind. U., 1952, LLB, U. Mich., 1957. Bar: Ind. 1957. Ptnr. Krieg, DeVault, Alexander & Capehart, Indpls., 1957—; sec., bd. dirs. Maul Tech. Corp. (formerly Buehler Corp.), Indpls., 1971-81, Am. Monitor Corp., Indpls., 1971-86, Am. Interstate Ins. Corp. Wis., Milw., 1973-84, Am. Interstate Ins. Co. Ga., Am. Underwriters Group, Inc., Indpls., 1973-86, Pafco Gen. Ins. Co., 1987-88. Served with USAF, 1952-54. Mem. ABA, Ind. Bar Assn., Indpls. Bar Assn., Alpha Kappa Psi, Delta Theta Phi, Beta Gamma Sigma, Delta Upsilon Internat. (sec., bd. dirs. 1971-83, chmn. 1983-86, trustee found. 1983-98). Lutheran. Home: 6320 Old Orchard Rd Indianapolis IN 46226-1041 Office: Krieg DeVault Alexander & Capehart 2800 Indiana National Bank Tower One Indiana Sq Ste 2800 Indianapolis IN 46204

KAHLENBERG, JEANNETTE DAWSON, retired civic organization executive; b. Chgo., May 22, 1931; d. Horace and Frances Jeannette (Ledlie) Dawson; m. Richard Walter Kahlenberg, Sept. 3, 1955; children: Joy Kahlenberg Fallon, Trudi Kahlenberg Picciano, Richard Dawson. BA, Wellesley Coll., Wellesley, Mass., 1953; MA, Union Theol. Sem.-Columbia U., 1956. Dir. Christian edn. The Presbyterian Ch., Madison, N.J., 1955-56; dir. fin. devel. LWV of Minn., St. Paul, 1978-80; cons. fin. devel. Nat. Bd. YWCA of U.S.A., N.Y.C., 1981-84; v.p. adminstrn. China Inst. in Am., N.Y.C., 1984-86; exec. dir. Citizens Union of City of N.Y., 1986-98. Author: A History of Citizens Union, 1897-1997; co-author: What's the Score in Minnesota, Equal Opportunity for Girls in Athletics, 1979; editor (newsletter) Citizens Union Reports, 1986-98. Mem. sch. bd. White Bear Lake (Minn.) Area Schs., 1975-80, Spl. Vocat. Tech. Sch. Dist., NE Suburban St. Paul, 1978-80; trustee United Theol. Sem. of the Twin Cities, New Brighton, Minn., 1975-80; local pres. state bd. dirs. LWV, Minn., 1973-79; pres. Ch. Women United of Ridgewood and Vicinity, 1990-93. Presbyterian. Home: 480 Fairway Rd Ridgewood NJ 07450-3412 also: 10 Scott Ave Chautauqua NY 14722

KAHLENBERG, SUSAN GALE, communications educator; b. Trenton, N.J., June 13, 1971; d. Michael Alan and Patricia Joy Kahlenberg; m. Wayne Francis McWilliams, Sept. 7, 1997. BA in Comm., Muhlenberg Coll., 1993; MA in Comm., U. Del., 1995; postgrad., Temple U. Grad. asst. U. Del., Newark, 1993-95; grad. asst. Temple U., Phila., 1995-98, instr., 1998; vis. instr. Muhlenberg Coll., Allentown, Pa., 1998—; data analyst Pub. Rels. Soc. Am., Phila., 1996; presenter in field. Contbr. chpt. to book. Mem. Internat. Comm. Assn., Broadcast Edn. Assn., Assn. Edn. in Journalism and Mass Comm. (grad. interest group 1992—), Omicron Delta Kappa. Avocation: art history. E-mail: skahlenb#astro.ocis.temple.edu.

KAHLER, HERBERT FREDERICK, diversified business executive; b. St. Augustine, Fla., Sept. 20, 1936; s. Herbert E. and Marie (Strieter) K.; m. Erika Rozsypal, May 16, 1964; children: Erik, Stephen, Christopher, Michael, Craig. AB, Johns Hopkins, 1958; LLB, Harvard U., 1961. Bar: N.Y. bar 1962. With Simpson, Thacher & Bartlett, N.Y.C., 1961-65; sec., gen. counsel Insilco Corp., Meriden, Conn., 1965-70; pres., chief exec. officer W.H. Hutchinson & Son, Inc., Chgo., 1970-73, Miles Homes Co., Mpls., 1973-86; v.p., dir. Insilco Corp., 1979-88; pres. Kahler & Assocs., 1988—; pres., chief exec. officer Crown Fixtures, Inc., Plymouth, Minn., 1990—, Power Generation Svc., Inc., 1990—. Bd. corporators Meriden Hosp., 1965-70, Harvard, 1970; bd. govs. Meriden/Wallingford Hosp., 1987; bd. dirs. St. Paul Chamber Orch., 1974-87, St. Paul Opera Assn., 1975-77, Minn. Opera Co., 1977-87. Lt., arty. AUS, 1962-64. Mem. ABA, Newcomen Soc., Mpls. Club, Phi Beta Kappa. Office: Crown Fixtures Inc 10700 Highway 55 Ste 160 Plymouth MN 55441-6134

KAHLOW, BARBARA FENVESSY, statistician; b. Chgo., June 26, 1946; d. Stanley John and Doris (Goodman) Fenvessy; m. Lloyd Fitch Reese, Dec. 6, 1969 (div. 1977); m. Allan Howard Young, Mar. 31, 1979 (div. 1982); m. Ronald Arthur Kahlow, Sept. 28, 1985 (div. 1990). BA, Vassar Coll., 1968. Statistician U.S. Govt./Dept. HEW, Nat. Ctr. Health Statistics, 1968-70, Nat. Ctr. for Ednl. Statistics, 1970-72, Exec. Office of Pres. Office Mgmt. and Budget, Washington, 1972-98; mem. profl. staff House Govt. Reform Com., 1998—. Author: Motor Vehicle Accident Deaths in the U.S.: 1950-69, 1970; contbr. articles to profl. jours. N.Y. State Regents scholar, 1964-68. Mem. Am. Statis. Assn., Foggy Bottom Assn., League of Rep. Women of D.C., Friends of the Kennedy Ctr., Friends of the Corcoran, Smithsonian Assocs., Washington Vassar Club. Republican. Episcopalian. Home: #404 2555 Pennsylvania Ave NW Washington DC 20037-1640 Office: House Govt Reform Com B-377 Rayburn House Office Bldg Washington DC 20515

KAHN, A. DAVID, federal judge. BA, Tulane U.; JD, Emory U. Gen. law practice Atlanta, 1959-68; bankruptcy judge U.S. Dist. Ct. (no. dist.) Ga., Atlanta, 1968—. Office: 1492 US Courthouse 75 Spring St SW Atlanta GA 30303-3309

KAHN, ALAN EDWIN, lawyer; b. N.Y.C., Aug. 9, 1929; s. Joseph and Harriet Rose (Rubel) K.; m. Regina Wolf, Aug. 7, 1960 (div. Jan. 1978); 1 child, Jolie Galen; m. Patricia Ann Dugan, June 4, 1978. BBA, CCNY, 1950; JD, Bklyn. Law Sch., 1956. Bar: N.Y. 1956, U.S. Dist. Ct. (so. and ea. dists.) N.Y. 1978, U.S. Tax Ct. 1978; CPA, N.Y. Staff asst.-acct. Feinberg, Jacobs & Furman, N.Y.C., 1956-57; pvt. practice, N.Y.C., 1957-96; sr. ptnr. Kahn & Kahn, LLC, N.Y.C., 1996-98, Kahn, Boyd, Levychin CPAs, N.Y.C., 1993; pvt. practice, 1998—; tax cons. to various nonprofit orgns., N.Y.C., 1977—. Cons. Vol. Lawyers for the Arts, N.Y.C., 1978—. Sgt. U.S. Army, 1951-52. Mem. ATLA (mem. com. 1990—), N.Y. State Bar Assn. (elder law com.), N.Y. State Trial Lawyers Assn. (chmn. subcom. on legis. estate and trusts 1979, spkr. bd. 1990—, mem. com. 1991—), N.Y. County Lawyers Assn. (taxation com. 1988—, sec. com. on taxation 1996—), Spkr.'s Bur., Assn. Trial Lawyers City N.Y., Jewish Lawyers Guild, N.Y. State Soc. CPAs, Nat. Sculpture Soc. (patron mem.), Odd Fellows (grand adv. bd. N.Y. chpt. 1979-80, gen. counsel grand lodge 1989—), Mchts. Club (bd. govs., asst. treas., treas. and gov. 1992—, award chmn. legal com. 1995—). Democrat. Avocation: collecting prints, paintings and oriental ceramics. Home: 370 1st Ave New York NY 10010-4923 Office: 67 Wall St New York NY 10005-3101

KAHN, ALAN HARVEY, therapist, administrator, consultant; b. Bklyn., Aug. 8, 1950; s. Murray and Dorothy Maxine (Nally) K. Student, Western

Mich. U., 1968-69; BA in Psychology, Memphis State U., 1969-73, MEd in Rehab. Counseling, 1973-75, MS in Therapeutic Recreation Adminstrn., 1974-76. Cert. Rehab. Counsleor, Therapy Recreation Specialist. Instr. Northwest Jr. Coll., Senatobia, Miss., 1976-77; program coord. Muscular Dystrophy Assn., Memphis, 1977-78; dist. dir. Muscular Dystrophy Assn., Columbus, Ga., 1978-81; vocat. cons. Crawford Rehab. Svcs., Macon, Ga., 1982; recreation therapist VA, Waco, Tex., 1982-85; asst. chief recreation therapy Dept. Vetrans Affairs, Waco, 1985—. Author: (poetry) Many Voices, Many Lands, 1987, The Speed Bag Bible, 1995; contbr. articles to profl. publs. Bd. mem. City of Woodway (Tex.) Park Commn., 1990-93. Mem. Nat. Assn. Rehab. Profls. in Pvt. Sector, Tex. Assn. Rehab. Profls. in Pvt. Sector. Avocations: martial artist, scuba diving, videography, writing, computers. Home: 432 Elmwood Rd Waco TX 76712-3830 Office: VA Med Ctr 4800 Memorial Dr Dept 11 K Waco TX 76711-1329

KAHN, ALFRED EDWARD, economist, educator, government official; b. Paterson, N.J., Oct. 17, 1917; s. Jacob and Bertha (Orlean) K.; m. Mary Simmons, Oct. 10, 1943; children: Joel, Rachel, Hannah. AB, NYU, 1936, MA, 1937; postgrad., U. Mo., 1937-38; PhD, Yale U., 1942; LLD (hon.), Colby Coll., 1978, U. Mass., 1979, Ripon Coll., 1980, Northwestern U., 1982, Colgate U., 1983; DHL (hon.), SUNY, Albany, 1985. Mem. staff Brookings Inst., 1940, 51-52; with anti-trust div. Dept. Justice, 1941-42, Dept. Commerce, 1942, WPB, 1943; economist on Palestine surveys, 1943-44, Twentieth Century Fund, 1944-45; asst. prof., chmn. dept. econs. Ripon Coll., 1945-47; asst. prof. Cornell U., 1947-50, assoc. prof., 1950-55, prof., 1955-89, chmn. dept. econs., 1958-63, Robert Julius Thorne prof. econs., 1967-89, emeritus, 1989—, dean Coll. Arts and Scis., 1969-74; chmn. N.Y. State Pub. Service Commn., 1974-77, CAB, 1977-78, Council on Wage and Price Stability (adviser to Pres. on inflation), 1978-80; mem. atty. gen's nat. com. to study anti-trust laws, 1953-55; sr. staff U.S. Coun. Econ. Advisers, 1955-57; spl. cons. Boni, Watkins, Jason & Co., N.Y.C., 1957-61, Nat. Econ. Rsch. Assocs., 1961-74, 80—, U.S. Fgn. Agrl. Svc., Israel, 1960-61, Dept. Justice, 1963-64, FTC, 1965, Ford Found., 1967; econ. adv. coun. AT&T, 1968-74; econ. adv. com. U.S. C. of C., 1964-66; mem. environ. adv. com. Fed. Energy Adminstrn., 1974-77; mem. rev. com. sulfur emissions from power plants Nat. Acad. Scis., 1974-75; adv. bd. Electric Power Rsch. Inst., 1974-77; mem. Nat. Antitrust Law Rev. Com., 1978-79; adv. to N.Y. gov. on comm. regulation, 1980-81; mem. usage panel Am. Heritage Dictionary, 1982—; mem. N.Y. Gov.'s Adv. Com. on Pub. Power for L.I., 1986, N.Y. Gov.'s Fact-Finding Panel on Shoreham Nuclear Plant, 1983, N.Y. State Coun. on Fiscal and Econ. Priorities, 1983-89; chmn. adv. com. on price reform and competition in the USSR Internat. Inst. for Applied Systems Analysis, 1990-92; econ. commentator Nightly Bus. Report (pub. TV), 1981-97; mem. Ohio Blue Ribbon Panel Telecomm. Regulation, 1992-93; mem. N.Y. State Telecomm. Exch., 1992-94; Ct.-apptd. expert U.S. Dist. Ct., 1993-94; com. study of competition U.S. airline industry Nat. Rsch. Coun., 1999—. Author: Great Britain in the World Economy, 1946, (with J.B. Diriam) Fair Competition, The Law and Economics of Anti-Trust Policy, 1954, (with M.G. de Chazeau) Integration and Competition in the Petroleum Industry, 1959, The Economics of Regulation, 2 vols., 1970, 71, reprinted, new intro., 1988, Letting Go: Deregulating The Process of Deregulation, 1998; bd. editors Am. Econ. Rev., 1961-64, Rev. Indsl. Econs., 1992—. Trustee Cornell U., 1964-69; mem. nat. governing bd. Common Cause, 1982-85. Fulbright Rsch. fellow Italy, 1954-55; recipient Wilbur Cross medal for outstanding achievement Yale U., 1995, L. Welch Pogue award for Lifetime Contbn. to Aviation, 1997, Soverign Fund award 1997, J. Rhoads Foster award, 1999. Mem. Am. Econ. Assn. (v.p. 1981-82), Nat. Assn. Regulatory Utility Commrs. (exec. com., chmn. com. on electricity 1975-77), Am. Acad. Arts and Scis., Phi Beta Kappa. Home: 221 Savage Farm Dr Ithaca NY 14850-6501 Office: 308 N Cayuga St Ithaca NY 14850-4209

KAHN, ALFRED JOSEPH, social worker and policy scholar, educator; b. N.Y.C., Feb. 8, 1919; s. Meyer and Sophie (Levine) K.; m. Miriam Kadin, Sept. 3, 1949 (div. 1980); 1 child, Nancy Valerie. B in Social Sci., CCNY, 1939; B in Hebrew Lit., Sem. Coll. Jewish Studies, N.Y.C., 1940; MS, Columbia U., 1946, D in Social Welfare, 1952; DHL (hon.), Adelphi U., 1984; DSc (hon.), U Md., 1989; Dr. (hon.), York U., Eng., 1998. Psychiat. social worker Jewish Bd. Guardians, N.Y.C., 1946-47; mem. faculty Sch. Social Work Columbia U., 1947-89, prof. Sch. Social Work, 1954-89, prof. emeritus, 1989; co-dir. Cross Nat. Studies Rsch. Program, 1973—; Disting. vis. prof. Grad. Sch. Social Svc., Fordham U., 1990—; staff cons. Citizens Com. for Children, N.Y.C., 1948-72; mem. summer faculty Smith Coll. Sch. Social Work, 1949-54; cons. govts., founds., vol. agys., 1949—; mem. numerous adv. coms.; mem. adv. com. child devel. NRC-Nat. Acad. Scis., 1971-76, mem. com. child devel. rsch. and pub. policy, Acad. Scis., 1977-83, chmn., 1980-83; mem. adv. bd. Inst. Rsch. Poverty, U. Wis., 1967—. Author: A Court for Children, 1953, Planning Community Services for Children in Trouble, 1963, Neighborhood Information Centers, 1966, (with Anna Mayer) Day Care as a Social Instrument, 1966, Theory and Practice of Social Planning, 1969, Studies in Social Policy and Planning, 1969, Social Policy and Social Services, 1973; co-author: Not for the Poor Alone, 1975, Social Service in the U.S., 1976, Social Services in International Perspective, 1977, Child Care, Family Benefits and Working Parents, 1981, Helping America's Families, 1982, Maternity Policies and Working Women, 1983, Income Transfers for Families With Children, 1983, Child Care: Facing the Hard Choices, 1987, The Responsive Workplace, 1987, Mothers Alone, 1988, Social Services for Children, Youth and Families in the United States, 1989, Social Services for Children, Youth and Families: The New York City Study, 1990, A Welcome for Every Child, 1994, Social Policy and the Under 3s, 1994, Starting Right, 1995, Big Cities in the Welfare Transition, 1998; contbr. monographs, articles to profl. jours., chpts. to books; editor: Issues in American Social Work, 1959, Shaping The New Social Work, 1973; co-editor: Family Policy: Government and Famlies in Fourteen Countries, 1978, Child Support, From Debt Collection to Social Policy, 1988, Privatization and the Welfare State, 1989, Child Care, Parental Leaves and The Under 3s: Policy Innovation in Europe, 1991, Children and Their Families in Big Cities, 1996, Family Change and Family Policies in Great Britain, Canada, New Zealand, and the United States, 1997. With USAAF, 1942-46. Mem. AAUP, Nat. Assn. Social Workers (chmn. div. practice and knowledge 1963-66, bd. dirs. 1967-70), Council Social Work Edn., Assn. for Policy Analysis and Mgmt. Home: 250 Gorge Rd Cliffside Park NJ 07010-1301 Office: Columbia U Sch Social Work New York NY 10025

KAHN, ANTHONY F., lawyer; b. Washington, Apr. 29, 1954; s. Henry and Claudia F.; m. Cynthia Marie Farhart, Aug. 11, 1979; children: Brian, Andrew, Stephen. BA, Wake Forest U., 1976; MBA summa cum laude, U. Notre Dame, 1980, JD magna cum laude, 1980. Bar: N.Y. 1981. Ptnr. White & Case LLP, N.Y.C., 1980—. Office: White & Case LLP 1155 Avenue of the Americas New York NY 10036-2711

KAHN, ARLENE JUDY MILLER, nurse, educator; b. Chgo., Dec. 16, 1940; d. Fred and Sophie (Schilbe) Miller; RN, AB, U. Ill., Chgo., 1963, MSN, 1970; EdD, U. San Francisco, 1986; m. Roy M. Kahn PhD, Oct. 25, 1968; 1 child, Jennifer M. Head nurse psychiat. unit Grant Hosp., Chgo., 1966; supervising nurse Ill. Psychiat. Inst., Chgo., 1967; instr. psychiat. nursing Calif. State U., San Francisco, 1968-70; mem. faculty Calif. State U., Hayward, 1974—, assoc. prof. nursing, 1980-86, prof., 1986—, chair dept. nursing and health scis. Sch. Sci., 1992—; cons. in field. Research grantee Calif. State U., Hayward, 1980-81. Fellow Am. Assn. Psychiat. Nursing; mem. Calif. Assn. Colls. of Nursing (treas. 1996—), Calif. Nursing Assn., Bay Area Nursing Diagnosis Assn. (officer 1986—), Sigma Theta Tau. Author articles in field. Home: 95 Sonia St Oakland CA 94618-2548 Office: Hayward State U School of Science Hayward CA 94542

KAHN, BERND, radiochemist, educator; b. Pforzheim, Baden, Germany, Aug. 16, 1928; came to U.S., 1938; s. Eric Herman and Alice Dora (Meyer) K.; m. Gail Pressman, Aug. 6, 1961; children: Jennifer, Elizabeth. B-SChemE, N.J. Inst. Tech., 1950; MS in Physics, Vanderbilt U., 1952; PhD in Chemistry, MIT, 1960. Commd. officer USPHS, 1954, advanced through grades to capt., 1970, health physicist, radiochemist, Oak Ridge (Tenn.) Nat. Lab., 1951-54; engr. various facilities USPHS, Tenn., Mass., Ala., Ohio, 1954-74, ret., 1974; prof. nuc. engring. and health physics Ga. Inst. Tech., Atlanta, 1974-96, prof. emeritus, 1996—, dir. Environ. Resources Ctr., 1974—. Co-editor: Management of Low-Level Radioactive Waste, 1979; co-inventor recovery of magnesium salts from sea water. Mem. Nat. Coun. Radiation Protection and Measurments (hon.), Am. Chem. Soc., Am. Phys. Soc., Health Physics Soc. Research specialization: radiochemistry and environmental radioactivity. Office: Ga Inst Tech Nuclear Engring Health Physics Atlanta GA 30332

KAHN, CARL RONALD, research laboratory administrator; b. Louisville, Jan. 14, 1944; s. David L. and Reva W. (Waldman) K.; m. Susan Becker; children: Stacy, Jeffrey. BA, U. Louisville, 1964, MD, 1968, MS, 1984; MA (hon.), Harvard U., 1984; DSc (honoris causa), U. Louisville, 1984, U. Paris-Pierre and Marie Curie, 1990. Diplomate Am. Bd. Internal Medicine, Am. Bd. Endocrinology and Metabolism. Intern and resident in ward medicine Barnes Hosp., St. Louis, 1968-70; clin. assoc., sr. clin. assoc., clin. endocrinology br. Nat. Inst. Arthritis, Metabolism and Digestive Diseases, NIH, Bethesda, Md., 1970-73; sr. investigator Diabetes Br. NIH, Bethesda, Md., 1973-78, chief diabetes br., 1979-81; rsch. dir Joslin Diabetes Ctr., Boston, 1981—, dir., 1997—; exec. v.p., dir. Joslin Diabetes Ctr., 1997—; assoc. prof. Harvard Med. Sch., Boston, 1981-84, prof. medicine, 1984—, Mary K. Iacocca prof. medicine, 1986—; lectr. symposia, meetings, thesis supr., course dir. and devel. numerous med. instns.; admitting and attending physician NIH Clin. Ctr., 1972-81; physician Brigham and Women's Hosp., Boston, 1981, chief div. Diabetes and Metabolism, 1981-92; assoc. staff Endocrinology/Internal Medicine, New Eng. Deaconess Hospital, Boston, 1982, active staff, 1986; clin. assoc. prof. medicine, Uniformed Svcs. U. Health Scis, Bethesda, Md., 1979-81; vis. scientist Centre de Moleculaire, Centre National de la Recherche Scientifique, Gif-sur-Yvette, France, 1979-80; adj. prof. genetics George Washington U., 1980-81; overseas vis. prof. Royal Melbourne Hosp., Australia, 1985; vis. prof. Royal Postgrad. Hosp., London, 1985; Rosemary Sarver vis. prof. in endocrinology and metabolism, The Hosp. of the Good Samaritan, L.A., 1985. Author or co-author over 430 publs. in field; mem. editl. bds. Jour. Clin. Endocrinology and Metabolism, 1977-80, Diabetes, 1977-84, Am. Jour. Medicine, 1979-84, Jour. Clin. Investigation, 1979-84, Jour. Receptor Rsch., 1980-83, Hormone and Metabolic Rsch., 1980-83, Endocrinology, 1981-85, Jour. Biol. Chemistry, 1983-88, Diabetes and Metabolism Revs., 1984, Receptor, 1989—; exec. editor Trends in Endocrinology and Metabolism, 1989-90; cons. editor Jour. Clin. Investigation; assoc. editor Diabetes, 1996—. Mem. Nat. Diabetes Adv. Bd., 1981-85, co-chmn. rsch. com., 1982-85. Recipient David Rumbough Meml award for Sci. Achievement Juvenile Diabetes Found., 1977, CIBA-Geigy Drew award for biochem. rsch., 1981, Mary Jane Kugel award Juvenile Diabetes Found., 1982, AFCR award for Outstanding Clin. Rsch. under Age 40, 1983, Sol Berson Meml. lectureship NIH, 1983, Hehnemann Lectr. in Pharmacology U. Calif.,1984, Pfizer Biomed. Rsch. award, Pfizer inc., 1986, Cristobal Diaz award Internat. Diabetes Fedn., 1988, Banting award Am. Diabetes Assn., 1993, others. Fellow AAAS; mem. Am. Acad. Arts & Scis., Am. Fedn. Clin. Rsch., The Endocrine Soc. (Edwin B. Astwood lectr. 1987), Am. Diabetes Assn. (Eli Lilly award for rsch. 1980, Otto Brandman award N.J. affiliate 1989, Elliott P. Joslin medal Mass. affiliate, Albert Renold award 1998), Am. Soc. Clin. Investigation (nat. coun. 1986—, pres. elect 1987-88, pres. 1988-89), Am. Soc. Biol. Chemistry, Assn. Am. Physicians, Sigma Xi, Alpha Epsilon Delta, Phi Kappa Phi, Alpha Omega Alpha. Rsch. interests include insulin receptors and insulin action, insulin-like growth factors, diabetes mellitus, hypoglycemia, immunity, autoimmunity and viruses in endocrine disorders. Office: Joslin Diabetes Ctr One Joslin Pl Boston MA 02215*

KAHN, CHARLES HOWARD, architect, educator; b. Birmingham, Ala., Feb. 10, 1926; s. Benjamin Arthur and Dorothy (Goldman) K.; m. Annette Lee, May 12, 1956; children: Kathryn Lauren, Sarah Elizabeth, Benjamin Arthur. A.B., U. N.C., 1946; B.C.E., N.C. State U., 1948; B. Arch., 1956; M.S., M.I.T., 1949; Fulbright grantee, Inst. di Urbanistico, Rome, 1957-58; postgrad., U. N.C., 1991. With Robert & Co. (architects and engr.), Atlanta, 1949-51, Frederick Snare Corp., N.Y.C., 1951-52, F. Carter Williams (AIA), Raleigh, N.C., 1952-54; propr. Charles Howard Kahn & Assocs. Architects and Engrs., Raleigh, N.C., 1954-68, Lawrence, Kans., 1968-91; dean Sch. Architecture and Urban Design, U. Kans., Lawrence, 1968-81, prof. emeritus, 1991—; pvt. practice Charles H. Kahn, FAIA & Assoc., Chapel Hill, N.C., 1991—; vis. prof. Sch of Design, N.C. State U., 1992—. Works include Carter Stadium, N.C. State U., 1966, Minges Auditorium, E Carolina Coll., 1967, Poliedro, Caracus, Venezuela, 1973; mem. editorial bd.: Jour. Archtl. and Planning Research. Bd. dirs. Cmty. Devel. Ctr., 1968-75; bd. dirs. Environ. R&D Found., 1968-91, v.p., 1975-87, pres. 1987-91; mem. Kans. Bldg. Commn., 1978-80. Recipient Hon. Alumnus and Disting. Alumnus awards U. Kans., 1989; Fulbright vis. rsch. scholar Gt. Brit., 1977-78. Fellow AIA; Mem. Assn. Collegiate Schs. of Architecture, Kans. Soc. Architects (pres. elect 1986, pres. 1987), Phi Beta Kappa, Phi Kappa Phi, Sigma Xi, Tau Beta Pi. Democrat. Jewish.

KAHN, DAVID, editor, author; b. N.Y.C., Feb. 7, 1930; s. Jesse and Florence (Abraham) K.; m. Susanne Monika Fiedler, Oct. 22, 1969 (div. Jan. 1995); children: Oliver, Michael. AB, Bucknell U., 1951; DPhil, Oxford (Eng.) U., 1974. Reporter Jersey Jour., Jersey City, 1952-53; copyboy N.Y. Daily News, 1953-55; reporter Newsday, Garden City, N.Y., 1955-63; freelance writer, 1963-65, 67-74; news desk editor Internat. Herald Tribune, Paris, 1965-67; prof. journalism NYU, 1974-79; asst. viewpoints editor Newsday, Melville, N.Y., 1979-94, mem. editorial bd., 1988-94; scholar in residence Nat. Security Agy., 1995; asst. editor features Newsday, Melville, N.Y., 1996-98; ret., 1999, freelance author, 1999—; adj. prof. modern polit. and mil. intelligence Yale U., New Haven, 1985, Columbia U., N.Y.C., 1986-88; founding co-editor Cryptologia mag., 1977—; mem. editorial bd. Intelligence and Nat. Security, 1986—, Internat. Jour. Intelligence and Counterintelligence, 1986—, Jour. Cryptology, 1991—; witness Congl. coms.; adj. prof. journalism, State U. of New York, Stony Brook, 1991-94. Author: Two Soviet Spy Ciphers, 1960, Plaintext in the New Unabridged, 1963; The Codebreakers, 1967, Hitler's Spies, 1978, Seizing the Enigma, 1991 (named Notable Naval Book of 1991 U.S. Naval Inst.); editor: Kahn on Codes, 1983; editor, translator: Clandestine Operations, 1983; cons. on cryptology to Oxford English Dictionary; contbr. articles to profl. jours. and encys. Bd. trustees St. Antony's Coll. Trust; bd. dirs. Nat. Cryptologic Mus. Found.; sr. assoc. mem. St. Antony's Coll., Oxford U., 1972-74. Recipient spl. award Nat. Security Agy., 1991, Nat. Intelligence Study Ctr., 1992. Mem. Am. Cryptogram Assn. (pres. 1965-67), World War II Studies Assn. (bd. dirs. 1987—), Arbeitskreis Geschichte der Nachrichtendienste, Internat. Assn. for Cryptologic Rsch. (bd. dirs. 1980-90), Century Assn., Phi Beta Kappa. Democrat. Jewish. Avocation: tennis. Home and Office: 120 Wooleys Ln Great Neck NY 11023-2301

KAHN, DAVID MILLER, lawyer; b. Port Chester, N.Y., Apr. 21, 1925; m. Barbara Heller, May 9, 1952; children: William, James, Caroline. BA, U. Ky., 1947; LLB cum laude, N.Y. Law Sch., 1950. Bar: N.Y. 1951, U.S. Dist. Ct. (ea. and so. dists.) N.Y. 1953, U.S. Supreme Ct. 1950. Sole practice White Plains, N.Y., 1951-60; ptnr. Kahn & Rubin, White Plains, 1960-66, Kahn & Goldman, White Plains, 1967-80; sr. ptnr. Kahn & Landau, White Plains, Palm Beach, Fla., 1980-88, Kahn and Kahn, Fla. and N.Y., 1988-95, Kahn, Kahn & Scutieri Esq., Palm Beach Gardens, 1995—; lectr. N.Y. Law Sch., 1982—; spl. counsel Village Port Chester, N.Y., 1960-63; commr. of appraisal Westchester County Supreme Ct., 1973-77; counsel Chemplex Industries, Inc., BIS Communications Corp., Bilbar Realty Co. Chmn. Westchester County Citizens for Eisenhower, 1950-52; pres. Westchester County Young Reps. Clubs, 1958-60; founder, chmn. bd. dirs. Port Chester-Rye Town Vol. Ambulance Corps, 1968-77; pres. Driftwood Corp., Amagansette, L.I., N.Y., 1984-91. Served with Counter Intelligence Corps USAF, 1942-46. Recipient John Marshall Harlan fellow N.Y. Law Sch., 1990-93. Fellow Am. Acad. Matrimonial Lawyers (bd. govs. N.Y. chpt. 1976-79); mem. ABA, N.Y. State Bar Assn., Westchester County Bar Assn., White Plains Bar Assn., N.Y. Law Sch. Alumni Assn. (bd. dirs. 1970-80), Elmwood C.C. (legal counsel), Eastpointe Country Club. Home and Office: 6419 Eastpointe Pines St Palm Beach Gardens FL 33418-6906 also: 175 Main St White Plains NY 10601-3105

KAHN, DONALD WILLIAM, mathematics educator; b. N.Y.C., Nov. 21, 1935; s. Irving and Ruth (Perl) K.; m. Phyllis Lubbert, June 10, 1956; children: Tamar, Jeremy. BA, Cornell U., 1957; PhD, Yale U., 1961. J.F. Ritt instr. Columbia U., N.Y.C., 1961-64; from asst. prof. to assoc. prof. U. Minn., Mpls., 1964-84, prof., 1984—; dir. grad. studies U. Minn., Mpls., 1992-95, 96—; vis. prof. U. Heidelberg, Germany, 1965, U. Mexico City, 1966, U. Toulouse, France, 1988, 89. Author: Topology, Global Analysis, (TV prodn.) Calculus. Mem. Am. Math. Soc., Soc. Math. France, European Math. Union. Avocations: music, photography. Office: U Minn VH 127 Minneapolis MN 55455

KAHN, DOUGLAS ALLEN, legal educator; b. Spartanburg, S.C., Nov. 7, 1934; s. Max Leonard and Julia (Rich) K.; m. Judith Bleich, Sept. 24, 1959; m. Mary Briscoe, June 12, 1970; children—Margery Ellen, Jeffrey Hodges. B.A., U. N.C., 1955; J.D. with disting., George Washington U., 1958. Bar: D.C. 1958, Mich. 1965, U.S. Ct. Appeals (D.C. cir.) 1958, U.S. Ct. Appeals (5th and 9th cirs.) 1959, U.S. Ct. Appeals (3d, 4th and 6th cirs.) 1960, U.S. Supreme Ct. 1963. Atty. Civil and Tax div. U.S. Dept. Justice, 1958-62; assoc. Sachs and Jacobs, Washington, 1962-64; prof. law U. Mich., Ann Arbor, 1964—, Paul G. Kauper Disting. prof., 1984—; vis. prof. Stanford Law Sch., 1973, Duke Law Sch., 1977, Fordham Law Sch., 1980-81, U. Cambridge, 1996. Author: (with Gann) Corporate Taxation, 1989, (with Lehman) Corporate Income Taxation, 1994, (with Waggoner and Pennell) Federal Taxation of Gifts, Trusts and Estates, 1997, Federal Income Tax, 1999; comment editor George Washington U. Law Rev., 1956-58; contbr. articles to profl. jours. Recipient Emil Brown Found. prize, 1969. Mem. ABA, Order of Coif. Republican. Jewish. Office: U Mich Law Sch 625 S State St Ann Arbor MI 48109-1215

KAHN, DOUGLAS MARC, osteopath; b. Hackensack, N.J., Aug. 27, 1965; s. Irwin and Caryl Joy (Blumenfeld) K.; m. Rachelle Rose Lombardi, Sept. 15, 1995, BS, N.Y. Inst. Tech., 1987; DO, N.Y. Coll. Osteo. Medicine, 1990. Diplomate Am. Bd. Internal Medicine. Intern Coney Island Hosp., Bklyn., 1990-91; intern, then resident in internal medicine Beth Israel Med. Ctr., N.Y.C., 1991-95, chief resident in internal medicine, 1995-96; fellow in pulmonary critical care medicine Sch. Medicine Brown U., Providence, 1996—. Mem. ACP, AMA, Am. Osteo. Assn., Am. Thoracic Soc., Am. Coll. Chest Physicians, Am. Sleep Disorders Assn., Soc. Critical Care Medicine. Office: Brown U Sch Medicine RI Hosp 593 Eddy St Providence RI 02903-4923

KAHN, EDWIN LEONARD, lawyer; b. N.Y.C., Aug. 1, 1918; s. Max L. and Julia (Rich) K.; m. Myra J. Green, Oct. 20, 1946 (dec. 1994); children: Martha L., Deborah K. Spiliotopoulos. AB, U. N.C., 1937; LLB cum laude, Harvard U., 1940. Bar: N.C. 1940, D.C. 1949. Atty., asst. head legislation and regulations div. Office Chief Counsel IRS, 1940-52, dir. tech. planning div., 1952-55; ptnr. Arent, Fox, Kintner, Plotkin & Kahn, Washington, 1955-86, of counsel, ret., 1986—; lectr. NYU Tax Inst., mem. adv. bd., 1959-70; lectr. tax insts. Coll. William and Mary, U. Chgo., U. Tex. Editor: Harvard Law Rev, 1939-40; editorial adv. bd. Tax Advisor of Am. Inst. CPA's, 1974-86. Bd. dirs. Jewish Community Ctr. Greater Washington, 1972-78; trustee Cosmos Club Found., 1989-93, chmn., 1989-91. With U.S. Army, 1943-46, ETO. Decorated Bronze Star. Fellow Am. Bar Found. (life); mem. ABA (coun. 1963-66, vice chmn. sect. taxation 1965-66), Fed. Bar Assn. (chmn. taxation com. 1967-68), D.C. Bar Assn., Nat. Tax Assn.-Tax Inst. Am. (adv. coun. 1967-69, bd. dirs. 1969-73), Am. Law Inst. (life), Am. Coll. Tax Counsel, J. Edgar Murdock Am. Inn Ct. (master bencher 1988-91), Phi Beta Kappa (life mem. assocs.). Jewish. Home: 4104 40th St N Arlington VA 22207-4805 Office: 1050 Connecticut Ave NW Washington DC 20036-5303

KAHN, ELLIS IRVIN, lawyer; b. Charleston, S.C., Jan. 18, 1936; s. Robert and Estelle Harriet (Kaminski) K.; m. Janice Weinstein, Aug. 11, 1963; children: Justin Simon, David Israel, Cynthia Kahn Nirenblatt. AB in Polit. Sci., The Citadel, 1958; JD, U. S.C., 1961. Bar: S.C. 1961, U.S. Ct. Appeals (5th cir.) 1963, U.S. Ct. Appeals (4th cir.) 1964, U.S. Supreme Ct. 1970, D.C. 1978, U.S. Claims Ct. 1988; diplomate Nat. Bd. Trial Advocacy, Am. Bd. Profl. Liability Attys. (trustee 1989—). Law clk. U.S. Dist. Ct. S.C., 1964-66; prin. Kahn Law Firm, Charleston; adj. prof. med.-legal jurisprudence Med. U. S.C., 1978-87; mem. rules com. U.S. Dist. Ct., 1984-96. Chmn. campaign Charleston Jewish Fedn., 1986-87, pres., 1988-90, S.C. Organ Procurment Agy., 1987-94, chmn. bd. 1989-94, mem. nat. coun. Am. Israel Pub. Affairs Com., 1982-88, Hebrew Benevolent Soc., pres., 1994-96; mem. Hebrew Orphan Soc. Capt. USAF, 1961-64. Fellow Internat. Soc. Barristers; mem. S.C. Bar, ABA, ATLA (state committeeman 1970-74), S.C. Trial Lawyers Assn. (pres. 1976-77), 4th Cir. Jud. Conf. (permanent mem.). Home: 316 Confederate Cir Charleston SC 29407-7431 Office: PO Box 898 Charleston SC 29402-0898

KAHN, GEORGE ARNETT, economist; b. Oak Ridge, Tenn., July 8, 1956; s. Jack Henry and Martha Sue (Upchurch) K. BA in Econs. and Math., U. N.C., 1978; MA in Econs., Northwestern U., 1980, PhD in Econs., 1983. Economist Fed. Res. Bank Kansas City, Mo., 1982-85, sr. economist, 1986-92; asst. v.p., economist Fed. Res. Bank Kansas City, 1993-96, asst. v.p., economist, asst. sec., 1994-95, v.p., economist, 1997—; vis. asst. prof. U. B.C., Vancouver, Can., 1985-86. Contbr. numerous articles to profl. jours. Northwestern U. fellow, 1978-80; rsch. grantee Social Sci. Rsch. Coun., Washington, 1981-82, U. B.C., 1985-86. Mem. Am. Econ. Assn., Nat. Assn. Bus. Economists. Home: 1249 W 64th Ter Kansas City MO 64113-1516 Office: Fed Res Bank Kansas City 925 Grand Blvd Kansas City MO 64198-0001

KAHN, GORDON BARRY, retired federal bankruptcy judge; b. Mobile, Ala., Dec. 3, 1931; s. Al and Molly (Prince) K.; 1 son, Andrew Fortier. BS, U. Ala., 1953, LLB, 1958; LLM, NYU, 1959; postgrad., U. London, 1957—. Bar: Ala. 1958. Practice in Mobile, 1959; mem. firm Lyons, Pipes & Cook, 1959-74; bankruptcy judge U.S. Dist. Ct. for So. Ala., 1974-95, ret., 1995. Chmn. Mobile United Jewish Appeal, 1963-64; pres. Friends of Mobile Pub. Library, Jewish Community Center of Mobile, 1974; Trustee Mobile Pub. Library, 1973-74; bd. dirs. Salvation Army Mobile, 1973-74, B'nai B'rith Home for Aged, Memphis, 1973-74. Served to 1st lt. U.S. Army, 1953-55. Mem. Ala., Mobile County bar assns. Jewish. Lodge: Masons. Home: 2558 S Delwood Dr Mobile AL 36606-1726

KAHN, HERMAN L. (BUD KAHN), financial advisor; b. Pitts., Dec. 14, 1954; s. Joseph Carl and Sylvia (Herman) K.; m. Jane Beth Resnick, June 10, 1984; children: Aaron H., Elliot C. BA cum laude, U. Pitts., 1975, MBA, 1976; MS in Taxation, Robert Morris Coll., 1985. CPA, Pa., CFP. Staff acct. Coopers & Lybrand, Pitts., 1976-77, sr. acct., 1977-79; tax mgr. Horovitz, Rudoy and Roteman, Pitts., 1979-85, Arthur Young, Pitts., 1985-88; sr. v.p. Mid Atlantic Capital Group, Pitts., 1988-91; pres. Wealth Mgmt. Strategies, Inc., Pitts., 1991—. Bd. dirs. Jewish Chronicle, Pitts.; mem. Leadership Pitts. XIV. Mem. AICPA (accredited pers. fin. specialist), IMCA, Estate Planning Coun. of Pitts., Allegheny Tax Soc., Inst. Cert. Fin. Planners. Democrat. Jewish. Office: Wealth Mgmt Strategies Inc 147 Delta Dr Ste 200 Pittsburgh PA 15238-2805

KAHN, HERTA HESS (MRS. HOWARD KAHN), retired stockbroker; b. Wuerzburg, Germany; came to U.S., 1939, naturalized, 1944; d. Ferdinand and Lilly (Suesser) Hess; m. Herbert Levy, Jan. 4, 1947 (dec. 1966); 1 dau., Linda; m. Howard Kahn, 1970 (dec. 1997). Student, Northwestern U. Sch. Commerce, 1947-49, 51-56. Joined Paine, Webber, Jackson & Curtis, Inc., Chgo., 1941; registered rep. Paine, Webber Inc., 1955-94; acct. v.p., 1955-86; v.p. investments Paine, Webber Inc., 1986-94, ret., 1994; mktg. cons., 1995—. Author: What Every Woman Should Know About Investing Her Money, 1968. Hon. life mem. nat. commn., hon. life mem. Chgo. exec. com. Anti-Defamation League B'nai B'rith; dir. Found. Hearing and Speech Rehab. Mem. N.Y. Soc. Security Analysts, Investment Analysts Soc. Chgo., Chgo. Fin. Exch. Chgo Crime Commission. Clubs: Northmoor Country (Highland Park, Ill.); Standard, Economic, Execs. (Chgo.); Tamarisk Country (Palm Springs, Calif.).

KAHN, JAMES ROBERT, lawyer; b. Indpls., Apr. 11, 1953; s. Robert D. and Rose Doris (Hyman) K.; m. Debra Amper, Oct. 21, 1984; children: Adam Joshua, Aliza Toby. BA, U. Pa., 1974; JD, Harvard U., 1978. Bar: Pa. 1978, U.S. Dist. Ct. (ea. dist.) Pa. 1978, U.S. Ct. Appeals (3d cir.) 1982, N.J. 1985, U.S. Dist. Ct. N.J. 1985, U.S. Dist. Ct. (ea. and so. dists.) N.Y. 1988. Jud. clk. U.S. Dist. Ct. Dist. N.J., Camden, 1978-79; assoc. Blank, Rome, Comisky & McCauley, Phila., 1979-88, ptnr., 1988-95; ptnr. Margolis Edelstein, 1995—; chair Phila. Bar state civil cts. com., 1994. Bd. dirs., v.p. Jewish Family and Children's Svcs., Phila., 1988—; bd. dirs. Phila. Pride, Inc., 1994-97; bd. dirs., sec. Schylkill River Devel. Coun., Inc., 1993—; trustee Jewish Fedn. Greater Phila., 1993—; mem. United Jewish Appeal Young Leadership Cabinet, 1992-96. Recipient Young Leadership award Jewish Fedn. of Greater Phila., 1993, Stella Moore award for contbns. to dance in Phila., 1994. Mem. Pa. Bar Assn., Phila. Bar Assn., Assn. Trial Lawyers Am., Pa. Trial Lawyers Assn., Phila. Trial Lawyers Assn., Phila.

Bicycle Club. Avocation: biking. Home: 2420 Fitlers Walk Philadelphia PA 19103-5562 Office: Margolis Edelstein Curtis Ctr 4th Fl Independence Sq W Philadelphia PA 19106-3304

KAHN, JAMES STEVEN, retired museum director; b. N.Y.C., Oct. 14, 1931; 3 children. BS in Geology, CCNY, 1952; MS in Minerology, Pa. State U., 1954; PhD in Geol. Sci., U. Chgo., 1956. Instr. U. R.I., Kingston, 1957, asst. prof., 1958-60, research assoc. Narragansett Marine Lab., 1957-60; group leader U. Calif., Livermore, 1960-70; dept. head Physics Internat. Co., San Leandro, Calif., 1970-71; div. head geophysics U. Calif., Livermore, 1971-75; dep. assoc. dir. human resources U. Calif., 1975-78, assoc. dir. nuclear testing, 1978-80, dep. dir. lab., 1980-87; pres., chief exec. officer, dir. Mus. Sci. and Industry, Chgo., 1987-97; retired, emeritus; trustee Mus. Sci. and Industry; strategic planning com. Econ. Devel. Commn. of City of Chgo., 1988-91; mem. math. scis. edn. bd. NAS, 1991-94; chmn. sci. adv. com. Gov. Ill., 1994-98; mem. vis. com. divsn. phys. scis. U. Chgo., 1996—; mem. adv. bd. dirs. Bank of Am., Ill.; IMAX Corp. Co-author: Statistical Analysis in Geological Sciences, 1962, Microstructure, 1968; contbr. articles to scientific jours. Bd. dirs. Franklin and Eleanor Roosevelt Inst.; rector sci. and medicine Lincoln Acad. of Ill.; mem., vice-chmn. Bd. Natural Resources and Conservation, State of Ill. Centennial fellow Pa. State U. Coll. Earth and Mineral Scis., 1996. Fellow Geol. Soc. Am.; mem. Quadrangle Club, Sigma Xi. Unitarian.

KAHN, JAN EDWARD, manufacturing company executive; b. Dayton, Ohio, Aug. 29, 1948; s. Sigmund Lawrence and Betty Jane K.; m. Deborah Ann Deckinga, Nov. 28, 1975; children: Jason Edward, Justin Allen, Julie Ann. BS in Metall. Engring., U. Cin., 1971. Mgmt. trainee U.S. Steel Corp., Gary, Ind., 1971-72; plant metallurgist Regal Tube Co., Chgo., 1972-74, gen. foreman, 1974-76, supt., 1976-77, mgr. tech. svc., 1978-80, materials mgr., 1980-81; mgr. quality contrl Std. Tube Co., Detroit, 1977-78; dir. ops. Boye Needle Co., Chgo., 1981-82, v.p. ops., 1982-83, v.p., gen. mgr., 1984-85, pres., 1985-88; v.p. sales and mktg. Caron Internat., Washington, N.C., 1988—. Mem. Am. Soc. Metals, AIME, ASTM, Ravenswood Indsl. Coun. (bd. dirs. 1983-84, pres. 1985), hand Knitting Assn. (chmn. 1986-88), Triangle Club. Republican. Mem. Christian Reformed Ch. Home: 13909 Teakwood Dr Lockport IL 60441-8697 Office: Caron Internat PO Box 3000 Orland Park IL 60462

KAHN, JIM, magazine publisher; m. Cyd Kahn; 1 child, Miranda. BS in Bus. Mgmt., SUNY, Binghamton, 1980. Account exec. Golf Mag. Properties, N.Y.C., 1986; west coast mgr. Golf Mag. Properties, L.A.; assoc. pub. Golf Mag. Properties, N.Y.C., 1990-96, pub., sr. v.p., 1996—. Office: Golf Mag Times Mirror Mags Inc 2 Park Ave New York NY 10016-5675*

KAHN, KATHLEEN PICA, photojournalist, journalist, mediator, arbitrator; b. Houston, Feb. 21, 1951; d. Adrien and Sarah Retha (McGuffey) K. A, Delgado Coll., New Orleans, 1985; cert., U. De L'Etat A Mons, Belgium, 1986, U. Cath. de L'Ouest, Angers, France, 1987; BA, Nichols State U., 1988; MH, U. Houston, 1989, postgrad., 1997—. Video editor Cox Cable TV, New Orleans, 1984-85; film editor French Consulate, New Orleans, 1984-87; journalist, corr. Daily Shipping Guide, New Orleans, 1990; journalist, corr. spl. sects. Houston Chronicle, 1990—; Pres. Bay Area Mediators Assn., Houston, 1996; interviewer Steven Spielberg's Shoah Found., L.A., 1996—. Bd. dirs. Congregation B'Nai Israel, 1996. Grantee City New Orleans, 1985; scholar Coun. Devel. French Lang., Quebec, Can., 1986, Mons, Belgium, 1987, Angers, France, 1988. Mem. Nat. Fedn. Press Women, Nat. Coun. Jewish Women, Soc. Profl. Journalists, Tex. Accts. Arts, Hadassah. Avocations: sculpting, jewelry design. Home: 1419 Lotus Rt 2 Tiki Island TX 77554

KAHN, LAURENCE, communications executive; b. N.Y.C., May 17, 1959; s. Paul and Anita (Winograd) K. BA, Rollins Coll., 1982. Prodr.-talk radio Sta. WKIS Radio, Orlando, Fla., 1982-85, Sta. WRKO Radio, Boston, 1985-87; prodr.-talk radio Sta. WOR Radio, N.Y.C., 1987-88, exec. prodr.-talk radio, 1988-94; dir. talk programming Westwood One Entertainment, N.Y.C., L.A., 1994—; mem. adv. bd. Radio & Records Talk Radio Seminar, Washington, 1996—; bd. dirs. Nat. Assn. Radio Talk Show Hosts, Boston, 1995—. Avocations: marathon running, skiing. Office: Westwood One Entertainment 1675 Broadway New York NY 10019-5820

KAHN, LAWRENCE E., judge. BA, Union Coll., 1959; JD, Harvard U., 1962; postgrad., Oxford (Eng.) U., 1962-63. Judge U.S. Dist. Ct. (no. dist.) N.Y., 1996—. Office: James T Foley US Courthouse Rm 424 445 Broadway Albany NY 12207

KAHN, LAWRENCE EDWIN, judge; b. Troy, N.Y., Dec. 8, 1937; s. Moe and Ann (Coplon) K.; m. Michele Kagan, Sept. 15, 1968; three children. AB, Union Coll., Schenectady, N.Y., 1959; JD, Harvard U., 1962; cert., Oxford U., Eng., 1963. Bar: N.Y. 1963, U.S. Dist. Ct. (no. dist.) N.Y. 1964. Asst. corp. counsel City of Albany, N.Y., 1963-69; surrogate Albany County, 1974-79; justice N.Y. Supreme Ct., Albany, 1979—. Author: Divorce Lawyer's Casebook, 1972, When Couples Part, 1982. Served with N.Y. N.G., 1955-65. Recipient Bailey Cup Union Coll., 1959; named one of 10 Outstanding Young Men N.Y., N.Y. State Jaycees, 1967. Mem. N.Y. State Trial Lawyers Assn. (outstanding jurist 1982). Republican. Office: Albany County Courthouse Supreme Ct Chambers Rm 310 Albany NY 12207

KAHN, LEONARD RICHARD, communications and electronics company executive; b. N.Y.C., June 16, 1926; s. Robert and Hattie (Grossman) K.; m. Ruth M. Repetti, Jan. 26, 1963. BEE, Poly. U., Bklyn.; student, Syracuse U. Registered profl. engr., N.Y. Rsch. engr. RCA Communications, N.Y.C., 1947-50, Crosby Labs., Syosset, N.Y., 1950-52; pres. Kahn Rsch. Labs., Garden City, N.Y., 1957-74, Kahn Communications, Inc., Westbury, N.Y., 1974—; adj. prof. elec. engring. Poly. U.; patent agt.; cons. Willys Motors, Grumman Aircraft & Electronics, Fairchild, FAA, USIA. Contbr. articles to profl. jours. Holder 80 U.S. patents, also fgn. patents. 2d lt. U.S. Army. Fellow IEEE (Regional Wheeler award), Radio Club Am. (Armstrong medal 1980), Coun. for Competitive Economy (bd. dirs.), Tau Beta Pi, Eta Kappa Nu, Sigma Xi. Republican. Jewish. Home: 137 E 36th St Apt 6A New York NY 10016-3528 Office: Kahn Communications Inc 320 E 42nd St New York NY 10017-5900

KAHN, LINDA MCCLURE, actuary, consultant; b. Jacksonville, Fla.; d. George Calvin and Myrtice Louise (Boggs) McClure; m. Paul Markham Kahn, May 20, 1968. BS with honors, U. Fla.; MS, U. Mich., 1964. Actuarial trainee N.Y. Life Ins. Co., N.Y.C., 1964-66, actuarial asst., 1966-69, asst. actuary, 1969-71; v.p., actuary US Life Ins., Pasadena, Calif., 1972-74; mgr. Coopers & Lybrand, L.A., 1974-76, sr. cons., San Francisco, 1976-82; dir. program mgmt. Pacific Maritime Assn., San Francisco, 1982-97; pres., CEO, P.M. Kahn & Assocs., 1997—. Chmn., CEO, Paul and Linda Kahn Found., 1998—; bd. dirs. Pacific Heights Residents Assn., sec.-treas., 1981; trustee ILWU-PMA Welfare Plan, 1982-97, SIU-PD-PMA Pension and Supplemental Benefits Plans, 1982-90, Seafarers Med. Ctr., 1982-90, others. Fellow Soc. Actuaries (chmn. com. on minority recruiting 1988-91, chmn. actuary of future sect. 1993-95), Conf. Cons. Actuaries; mem. Internat. Actuarial Assn., Internat. Assn. Cons. Actuaries, Actuarial Studies Non-Life Ins., Am. Acad. Actuaries (enrolled actuary), Western Pension and Benefits Conf. (newsletter editor 1983-85, sec. 1985-88, treas. 1989-90), Actuarial Club Pacific States, San Francisco Actuarial Club (pres. 1981), Met. Club, Commonwealth Club, Soroptimists (v.p. 1973-74), Concordia-Argonaut Club, Pacific Club (Honolulu). Home and Office: 2430 Pacific Ave San Francisco CA 94115-1238

KAHN, MADELINE GAIL, actress; b. Boston; d. Bernard B. Wolfson and Paula Kahn. BA, Hofstra U.; trained as opera singer; ArtsD (hon.), Boston Conservatory. Appeared in: satirical revue Upstairs at the Downstairs, N.Y.C., 1966-67, New Faces of 1968, New Faces, Booth Theatre, N.Y.C., Candide, Philharmonic Hall, 1968, Two by Two, Imperial Theatre, N.Y.C., 1970-71, Broadway mus. Two by Two; motion picture appearances include What's Up Doc?, 1972, Paper Moon, 1973 (Academy award nomination 1973, Golden Globe award nomination), From the Mixed-up Files of Mrs. Basil E. Frankweiler, 1973, Blazing Saddles, 1974 (Academy award nomination 1974, First Ann. Acad. of Humor award 1975), Young Frankenstein, 1974 (Golden Globe award nomination), At Long Last Love, 1975, The Adventure of Sherlock Holmes' Smarter Brother, 1975, Won-Ton-Ton, the Dog Who Saved Hollywood, 1976, High Anxiety, 1977, The Cheap Detective, 1978, The Muppet Movie, 1979, Simon, 1980, Happy Birthday Gemini, 1980, Wholly Moses!, 1980, First Family, 1980, History of the World, Part I, 1981, Yellowbeard, 1983, Slapstick of Another Kind, 1984, City Heat, 1984, Clue, 1985, (voice) My Little Pony, 1986, (voice) An American Tail, 1986, Betsy's Wedding, 1990, Shadows and Fog, 1992, Mixed Nuts, 1994, Nixon, 1995, (voice) A Bug's Life, 1998; stage appearances in Boom Boom Room, Vivian Beaumont Theater, 1973 (Tony nominee, Drama Desk award), Broadway prodn. On the 20th Century, 1978 (Tony nominee), Born Yesterday, 1989 (Tony nominee), Broadway prodn. The Sisters Rosensweig (Tony Award Best Actress in a Play), 1992-93; in ABC-TV afterschool special, 1986-87 (Emmy award); star TV series Oh, Madeline, ABC, from 1983 (People's Choice award), Mr. President, FOX-TV, 1987, New York News, 1995, Cosby, 1996; TV movie London Suite, 1996, Danny Kaye: A Legacy of Laughter, 1996; appeared as Madame Arcati in Blithe Spirit, Santa Fe Festival Theater, 1983; New York News (tv series), 1995. Recipient Disting. Service award Hofstra Alumni Assn., 1975. Office: William Morris Agency c/o Marc Schwartz 151 S El Camino Dr Beverly Hills CA 90212-2775*

KAHN, MARC LESLIE, orthopedic surgeon; b. Phila., Mar. 12, 1956; s. Sigmund and Joanne (Pokras) K.; divorced; two children. AB, Lafayette Coll., 1978; MD, Hahnemann Med. Coll., 1982. Resident in orthopedics Monmouth Med. Ctr., Long Branch, N.J., 1987; surgeon, maj. U.S. Army, Ft. Dix, N.J., 1987-91; orthopedic surgeon Garden State Orthopedics, Pennsauken, N.J., 1991—. Fellow Am. Acad. Orthopedic Surgeons; mem. AMA, N.J. Med. Soc., Camden County Med. Soc., N.J. Orthopedic Soc. Home: 40 Meetinghouse Ct Shamong NJ 08088

KAHN, MARIO SANTAMARIA, international marketing executive; b. Manila, Jan. 16, 1956; came to U.S., 1980; s. Rene L. and Dolores (Santamaria) K.; m. Maria Victoria Legaspi, Dec. 28, 1987; 1 child, Marc Daniel. AB in Mktg. & Comm., De La Salle U., Manila, 1977; MA in Comm. Mgmt. cum laude, U. So. Calif., 1982; postgrad., Stanford U., 1989. Account mgr. McCann-Erickson, Manila, 1977-80; teaching asst. U. So. Calif., L.A., 1980-82; ops. mgr. Dayton-Hudson Corp., Mpls., 1982-85; sr. mgr. Asia Sunkist Growers, Ontario, Calif., 1986—; bd. dirs. Sunkist Soft Drink Internat. Mem. Am. Mktg. Assn., Am. Mgmt. Assn., Stanford Alumni Assn., Annenberg Alumni Assn., De La Salle Alumni Assn. Office: Sunkist Growers Inc 720 E Sunkist St Ontario CA 91761-1861

KAHN, MARK LEO, arbitrator, educator; b. N.Y.C., Dec. 16, 1921; s. Augustus and Manya (Fertig) K.; m. Ruth Elizabeth Wecker, Dec. 21, 1947 (div. Jan. 1972); children: Ann Mariam, Peter David, James Allan, Jean Sarah; m. Elaine Johnson Morris, Feb. 12, 1988. BA, Columbia U., 1942; MA, Harvard U., 1948, PhD in Econs., 1950. Asst. economist U.S. OSS, Washington, 1942-43; tchg. fellow Harvard U., 1947-49; dir. case analysis U.S. WSB, Region 6-B Mich., 1952-53; mem. faculty Wayne State U., Detroit, 1949-85, prof. econs., 1960-85, prof. emeritus, 1985—, dept. chmn., 1961-68, dir. indsl. rels. M.A. program, 1978-85; arbitrator union-mgmt. disputes. Co-author: Collective Bargaining and Technological Change in American Transportation, 1971; mem. editl. bd. Employee Responsibilities and Rights Jour., 1988-96; contbr. articles to profl. jours. Bd. govs. Jewish Welfare Fedn. Detroit, 1976-82; bd. dirs. Jewish Home for Aged, Detroit, 1978-93, Lyric Chamber Ensemble, Southfield, Mich., 1995-97, Detroit Empowerment Zone Devel. Corp., 1996-99. Capt. AUS, 1943-46. Decorated Bronze Star; recipient Disting. Svc. award U.S. Nat. Mediation Bd., 1987, Am. Arbitration Assn., 1992. Mem. AAUP (past chpt. pres.), Nat. Acad. Arbitrators (bd. govs. 1960-62, v.p. 1976-78, chmn. membership com. 1979-82, pres. 1983-84, chmn. nominating com. 1995-96), Indsl. Rels. Rsch. Assn. (pres. Detroit chpt. 1956, exec. sec. 1979-89, nat. exec. bd. 1985-88), Soc. Profls. in Dispute Resolution (v.p. 1982-83, pres. 1986-87). Home and Office: 15151 Ford Rd # 321 Dearborn MI 48126

KAHN, MARTIN JEROME, art gallery owner; b. Paterson, N.J., July 11, 1946; s. Macwell C. and Doris (Altman) K.; m. Carole Magagnoli, Nov. 7, 1976; children: Lisa, Maya, Sol. BA in Art History, Rutgers U., 1968. Tchr., 1968-72; owner Kahn Sandals, St. Croix, U.S. V.I., Kauai Leather, Hawaii, 1975-79, Kauai Gold Ltd., Hawaii, 1979-84; pres. Kahn Galleries, Hawaii, 1984—. Past pres. Jewish Cmty. Kauai, Rotary of Kapaa. Mem. Kaiola Canoe Club. Avocations: marathon running, karate. Office: Kahn Galleries 4569 Kukui St Kapaa HI 96746-1718

KAHN, MICHAEL, stage director; b. N.Y.C.; s. Frederick J. and Adele (Gaberman) K. BA, Columbia U.; hon. degree, U. S.C., 1994, Kean Coll., 1974. Artistic dir. Am. Shakespeare Theatre, Stratford, Conn., 1969-77, The Acting Co., 1978-88, Chautauqua Conservatory Theatre Co., 1985-88, Shakespeare Theatre, Washington, 1986—; dir. Chautauqua Inst. Theatre Sch., 1983-88; dir. drama divsn. Juilliard Sch., N.Y.C., 1992—; acad. chmn. Brit. Am. Drama Acad., Oxford, Eng., 1992-96; mem. faculty Circle in the Square, N.Y.C., Princeton U.; mem. faculty grad. program Sch. Arts, NYU; mem. panel League of Profl. Theatre Tng. Programs; bd. dirs. Theatre Comm. Group, Theatre Panel, N.Y. State Coun. of Arts; mem. theatre panel Nat. Endowment for Arts; panel mem. D.C. Commn. on Humanities and the Arts. Dir. Romeo and Juliet (Helen Hayes nomination), The Winter's Tale, Macbeth (Helen Hayes nomination), All's Well that Ends Well (Helen Hayes nomination), Anthony and Cleopatra, As You Like It, Twelfth Night (Helen Hayes award 1989), Merry Wives of Windsor (Helen Hayes nomination), Richard III, 1990 (Helen Hayes nomination), King Lear, 1991, Much Ado About Nothing, 1992, Measure for Measure, 1992, Hamlet, 1993 (Helen Hayes award 1993), Mother Courage (Helen Hayes award), 1993, Richard II, 1993, The Doctor's Dilemma, 1994, Henry IV, 1994 (Helen Hayes award), Henry V (Helen Hayes nomination), Volpone, 1996, Henry VI (Helen Hayes award), 1996, Mourning Becomes Electra, (Helen Hayes Award) 1997; Peer Gynt (1997); Sweet Bird of Youth, 1998, A Woman of No Importance, 1998, King John, 1999, The Merchant of Venice, 1999; producing dir. McCarter Theater, Princeton, N.J.; plays including Beyond The Horizon, Mother Courage, Grave Undertaking, The Heiress, Angel City, The Torchbearers, A Month in the Country, Put Them All Together, 1974—; dir. Broadway prodns. The Death of Bessie Smith, 1967, Here's Where I Belong, 1968, Cat On A Hot Tin Roof, 1974, Night of the Tribades, 1977, Whodunnit, 1983, Showboat, 1983 (Tony nomination); off-Broadway prodns. Funnyhouse of A Negro, 1966, Rimers of Eldritch, 1967, Thorton Wilder plays, 1967, N.Y. Shakespeare Festival's Measure for Measure, 1966, Grand Magic, Manhattan Theatre Club, 1978, A Month in the Country, Roundabout, 1980, Hedda Gabler, Roundabout, 1981, Flux, 1982, Something Different, 1983, Ten By Tennessee, 1986, Sleep Deprivation Chamber, 1996, Goodman Theatre, Chgo., Old Times, 1972, Tooth of Crime, 1973, Tis Pity She's a Whore, 1974, Showboat, Cairo, Egypt, 1987, Five By Tennessee, 1989, Moscow, Leningrad, Vilmius Warsaw, Belgrade, 1990, Signature Theatre Otabenga, Va., 1994; TV prodn. Beyond the Horizon, WNET, 1975; San Francisco Opera Julio Cesare, 1978, The Acting Co., 1978—, A New Way to Pay Old Debts, 1984, The White Devil, 1979, Carmen, Houston Grand Opera, 1981, Carmen, Washington Opera, 1982, The Glass Menagerie, Chautauqua Conservatory Theatre, 1985, Tis Pity She's a Whore (Am. Repertory Theatre), 1988, Much Ado About Nothing, McCarter Theatre, 1993, Vanessa, Dallas Opera, 1994, Washington Opera, 1995. Recipient Best Dir. Revival award Saturday Rev., 1966; Charles MacArthur award for best dir. Old Times, 1973, Joseph Jefferson award, 1974, Washington Post award, 1989; named Best Dir. N.J. Drama Critics, 1974, 76, Washingtonian of Yr. Washingtonian mag., 1989; nominated for 4 Vernon Rice awards, 1967, John Houseman award, Globe Theater award, Bravo award Opera Music Theatre Internat., 1997, D.C. Mayor's Art award, 1997. Home: 1 W 72nd St New York NY 10023-3486 Office: The Shakespeare Theatre 301 E Capitol St SE Washington DC 20003-3808

KAHN, NANCY VALERIE, publishing and entertainment executive, consultant; b. N.Y.C., Dec. 15, 1952; d. Alfred Joseph and Miriam (Kadin) K. BA magna cum laude, Princeton U., 1974. Dir. prodn. and devel. Bus. Rsch. Publs., Inc.-MacRAE'S Directories, N.Y.C., 1984-86; assoc. pub., exec. editor Leadership Directories Inc., N.Y.C., 1987-88; dir. new product devel. Gale Rsch. Inc., N.Y.C., 1988-89; pub., editorial dir. directories and info. devel. Adweek/BPI Comm., N.Y.C., 1989-93; v.p. Everlink Corp., N.Y.C., 1993-94; prin. NVK Comm., N.Y.C., 1994—. Univ. scholar Princeton U., 1974. Mem. Directory Pubs. Forum N.Am., Manhattan Assn. Cabarets, Theater Resources Unltd. Avocations: musical theatre, foreign travel, walking, cabaret. Office: NVK Comm PO Box 826 New York NY 10021-0008

KAHN, NORMAN, pharmacology and dentistry educator; b. N.Y.C., Dec. 28, 1932; s. Louis Meyer and Dorothy (Simon) Kohn; m. Dale Krasnow, Mar. 30, 1958. A.B., Columbia U., 1954, D.D.S., 1958, Ph.D., 1964. Lic. dentist, N.Y. State. Dental intern Montefiore Hosp., Bronx, N.Y., 1958-59; instr. Coll. Physicians and Surgeons, Columbia U., N.Y.C., 1962-65, asst. prof., 1965-72, assoc. prof., 1972-80, prof. pharmacology, 1980-99, prof. dentistry, 1980-92, Edwin S. Robinson prof. dentistry, 1992-99; assoc. dean acad. affairs Sch. Dental and Oral Surgery, Columbia U., 1989-94, acting dean, 1994-95; attending dentist Presbyn. Hosp., N.Y.C., 1985-99, Robinson prof. dentistry & pharm. emeritus, spl. lectr., 1999—, cons. dentist, 1999—; vis. assoc. prof. UCLA, 1978; chair instl. rev. bd. Columbia-Presbyn. Med. Ctr., N.Y.C., 1981-91; cons. pharmcologist Harlem Hosp., N.Y.C., 1966-80; vis. scientist U. Pisa, Italy, 1965-66. Contbr. chpts. to books, articles to profl. jours. NIH grantee, 1969-75, Nat. Fund Med. Edn. grantee, 1973; recipient Outstanding Contbn. to Teaching award Columbia U. Coll. Physicians and Surgeons, 1980; hon. research fellow Univ. Coll., London, 1986. Mem. Am. Physiol. Soc., ADA, Am. Assn. Dental Schs., Confrerie des Chevaliers du Tastevin, Alpha Omega Alpha, Omicron Kappa Upsilon. Jewish. Avocation: oenology. Office: Columbia U 630 W 168th St New York NY 10032-3795

KAHN, PAUL FREDERICK, executive search company executive; b. Indpls., Oct. 10, 1935; s. Paul L. and Florence (Copeland) K.; m. Helen Gail Bass, Dec. 27, 1961; children—Hartley, Meredith. B.S., Purdue U., 1957; M.B.A., Harvard U., 1963. Brand mgr. Procter and Gamble, Cin., 1963-69; v.p. Foote, Cone & Belding, N.Y.C., 1969-70; sr. v.p. Wilson Sporting Goods, Chgo., 1970-78, Sara Lee Corp., Chgo., 1978-87; pres., chief exec. officer Kayser-Roth Hosiery Co., 1988; mng. ptnr. Heidrick & Struggles, Chgo., 1989—. Served with USMC, 1957-60. Presbyterian. Clubs: Indian Hill Country, University, Harvard Club N.Y. Home: 100 Low Rd Sharon CT 06069 also: 177 Scott Ave Winnetka IL 60093

KAHN, PAULINE GITMAN, volunteer; b. Dayton, Ohio, Oct. 8, 1921; d. Samuel and Rose (Getz) Gitman; m. Raymond Kahn, Sept. 24, 1939 (dec. Aug. 1995); children: Norma Kahn Katcher, Shepard, Herbert, Shelly Kahn Reiner. Diploma, Steele H.S., Dayton, Ohio, 1939. Bd. dirs., charter pres. Columbus WaZoo, B'Nai B'rith Women, Franklin County Heart-Women's Spl. Gifts, Kidney Found., Temple Israel Sisterhood (pres. 1968-70 life), Temple Israel Found., Ohio Valley Fedn. Temple Sisterhoods (sec. 1966-67), Nat. Women's United Jewish Appeal (v.p. 1968-71), Coun. Jewish Fedns. and Nat. Welfare Funds, Jewish Family Svc., Jewish Ctr. Pre-Sch., Heritage House, Nat. Coun. Jewish Women, Women's Am. Ort, Am. Women Panel, Franklin County Zoo. Assn.; bd. dirs. Project HOPE, 1965—, pres., 1971-72; Sustainer Goodwill, chater pres. Marburn Acad. Sch. for Retarded Children, 1987-88; trustee United Jewish Fedn., 1966-80, mem. found. bd. trustees, 1975-84; founder Renaissance Fund, Temple Israel, 1995. Recipient Living Legacy award Children's Hosp., Columbus, 1999. Mem. Brandeis Women (life), Nat. Coun. Jewish Women (life), Pres.'s Club OSU, Benefactor Cols. Mus. Art. Republican. Jewish.

KAHN, PETER B., physics educator; b. N.Y.C., Mar. 18, 1935; s. Morton E. and Lillian E. (Miller) K.; m. Lois Gibbs, Sept. 16, 1956 (div. 1986); children: Miriam, David, Jeffrey; m. Victoria McLane, Jan. 8, 1989. BS, Union Coll., 1956; PhD, Northwestern U., 1960. Research assoc. U. Iowa, Iowa City, 1960-61; from asst. to assoc. prof. physics SUNY, Stony Brook, 1961-71, prof. physics, 1971—, chmn. dept. physics, 1974-85. Fellow Am. Physics Soc. Office: SUNY Dept Physics Stony Brook NY 11794

KAHN, PETER R., secondary school educator; b. N.Y.C., July 24, 1967; s. Herb J. and Bonnie P. Kahn. BA, Tufts U., 1989; MA, Ohio State U., 1993. Cert. English and social studies tchr., Ill. Job readiness workshop coord., GED tchr. Jobs for Youth, Chgo., 1990-91; caseworker, counselor, edn. coord. Neon St. Ctr. for Youth, Chgo., 1991-92; English tchr. Young Scholars program Ohio State U., Columbus, 1993-94; English tchr. Oak Park (Ill.) River Forest H.S., 1994—; adj. instr., tutor Columbus State C.C., 1993-94. Vol. Godman Guild Head Start, Columbus, 1992-94. Mem. Phi Kappa Phi. Avocations: basketball, travel, reading multicultural literature. Office: Oak Park/River Forest HS 201 N Scoville Ave Oak Park IL 60302-2264

KAHN, RICHARD DREYFUS, lawyer; b. N.Y.C., Apr. 25, 1931; s. David Effrian and Lucille (Kahn) K.; m. Judith Raff, Sept. 10, 1961 (div. 1977); children—Jason, Adam, Alexander; m. Elaine H. Peterson, July 21, 1983. A.B., Harvard U., 1952, J.D., 1955. Bar: N.Y. 1955. Assoc. Debevoise & Plimpton, N.Y.C., 1955-62, ptnr., 1963-90; of counsel Debevoise & Plimpton, 1991-93. Editor Harvard Law Rev., 1953-55. Trustee Am. Soc. Psychical Rsch., N.Y.C., 1966-73; bd. dirs. The Emerson Sch., N.Y.C., 1968-71, J. M.R. Barker Found., N.Y.C., 1968—, C. G. Jung Found. Analytical Psychology, 1984-90, Concerned Citizens of Montauk, 1991—, Group for the South Fork, 1993—; bd. dirs. Found. Child Devel, N.Y.C., 1970-88, coun. vice chmn., 1996—; mem. Montauk Citizens Adv. Com., 1992—. Mem. Assn. of Bar of City N.Y. (chmn. com. atomic energy 1965-68), Harvard Club N.Y.C. (bd. mgrs. 1991-93), Phi Beta Kappa. Home: 224 W Lake Dr Montauk NY 11954-5235 Office: Debevoise & Plimpton 875 3rd Ave Fl 23 New York NY 10022-6256

KAHN, ROBERT IRVING, management consultant; b. Oakland, Calif., May 17, 1918; s. Irving Herman and Francesca (Lowenthal) K.; m. Patricia E. Glenn, Feb. 14, 1946; children: Christopher, Roberta Anne. BA cum laude, Stanford U., 1938; MBA, Harvard U., 1940; LLD (hon.), Franklin Pierce Coll., 1977. Exec. rschr. R.H. Macy's, Inc., N.Y.C., 1940-41; contr. Smith's, Oakland, 1946-51; v.p., treas. Sherwood Swan & Co., Oakland, 1952-56; prin. Robert Kahn & Assocs. (mgmt. cons.), Lafayette, Calif., 1956—; pres. Kahn & Harris Inc. (investment bankers), San Francisco, 1974-90; v.p. Hambrecht & Quist, investment bankers, San Francisco, 1977-80; cons. to comdg. gen. U.S. Army and Air Force Exch. Svc., 1987-91; bd. dirs. Components Corp.; bd. dirs. Marc Paul Inc.; bd. dirs., sec. Piedmont Grocery Co.; cons. to sr. mgmt. Wal-Mart Stores. Pub. newsletter Retailing Today, 1965—; author: weekly newspaper column Pro and Kahn, 1963-77, 86-89; mem. editl. bd. Jour. Retailing; editor ethics dept. Jour. Mgmt. Cons. Mem. Nat. Eagle Scout Assn., Boy Scouts Am., past dir. Oakland Coun.; past bd. dirs. Oakland Area ARC; past bd. dirs., officer San Francisco Bay Girl Scout Coun., Fannie Wall Day Home and Nursery; bd. dirs., officer, mem. exec. com. United Way Bay Area, 1946-81, chmn. allocations, membership, fin., by-laws, and pers. coms.; trustee Kahn Found.; past sec. League to Save Lake Tahoe; founder Lafayette Forward, 1970, sec., 1976-98; mem. adv. com. Retail Mgmt. Inst. Santa Clara U., 1983—. With USAAF, 1941-46; with USAF, 1951-52; lt. col. Res. ret. First recipient Mortimer Fleishhacker award as outstanding vol. United Way Bay Area, 1980, Best Article award Jour. Mgmt. Cons., 1985; founding mem. Baker Scholar Harvard Bus. Sch., 1939. Fellow Inst. Mgmt. Cons.; mem. Assn. Mgmt. Cons. (pres. 1977), Inst. Mgmt. Cons. (founder, Lifetime Contbn. to Profession award 1996), Nat. Retail Fedn., Nat. Eagle Scout Assn., Baker Scholars (founding), Mensa, Phi Beta Kappa. Fax: 925-284-5612. Home: 3684 Happy Valley Rd Lafayette CA 94549-3040 Office: PO Box 249 Lafayette CA 94549-0249 *Each night as I put my head on my pillow I think back over the day. I hope I can say "I spent this day the way I should have spent it."*

KAHN, SANDRA S., psychotherapist; b. Chgo., June 24, 1942; d. Chester and Ruth Sutker; m. Jack Murry Kahn, June 1, 1965; children: Erick, Jennifer. BA, U. Miami, 1964; MA, Roosevelt U., 1976. Tchr. Chgo. Pub. Schs., 1965-67; pvt. practice psychotherapy, Northbrook, Ill., 1976—. Host Shared Feelings, Sta. WEEF-AM, Highland Park, Ill., 1983—; author: The Kahn Report on Sexual Preferences, 1981, The Ex Wife Syndrome Cutting The Cord and Breaking Free After The Marriage Is Over, 1990; columnist Single Again mag. Mem. Ill. Psychol. Assn., Chgo. Psychol. Assn. (past pres. 1990). Jewish. Office: 801 Skokie Blvd Northbrook IL 60062-4039

KAHN, SIGMUND BENHAM, retired internist and dean; b. Phila., May 18, 1933; s. Maxwell Louis and Clara (Parris) K.; m. Joanne Pokras, June 11, 1955; children: Marc L., Elissa Kahn Petrosky, Hillary Kahn Roth, Lauren B. BA, U. Pa., 1954, MD, 1958. Diplomate Am. Bd. Internal Medicine;

cert. hematology and med. oncology. Rotating intern Albert Einstein Med. Ctr., Phila., 1958-59; resident in internal medicine Hosp. of U. Pa., Phila., 1959-61; fellow in hematology Hosp. of U. Pa., 1961-62, USPHS rsch. fellow dept. hematology, 1962-63; assoc. in hematology medicine Hahnemann U. Hosp., Phila., 1963-66; asst., assoc., then prof. medicine Hahnemann U. Hosp., 1966-94; prof. dept. neoplastic disease Hahnemann Univ. Hosp., Phila., 1978-94; dir. edn., vice chmn. dept. Hahnemann Univ. Hosp., 1978-94; assoc. dean Hahnemann U., Phila., 1986-94; prof. dept. medicine divsn. hematology/ med. oncology Med. Coll. Pa./Hahnemann U., Phila., 1992-94, assoc. dean edn., 1992-94; cons., chmn. dean's com. Wilkes-Barre (Pa.) VA Hosp., 1987-92. Mem. editl. bd. Jour. Cancer Edn., 1985-95, Am. Jour. Clin. Oncology; contbr. articles to profl. jours. Instl. rep. Boy Scouts Am., 1970-75; pres. Temple Beth Sholom, Cherry Hill, N.J., 1977-80; mem. med. bd. Lupus Found., Delaware Valley, 1977-79. Mem. AMA, ACP, Phila. County Med. Soc., Phila. Hematology Soc., Pa. Med. Soc., Am. Fedn. Clin. Rsch., Am. Hematology Soc., Am. Assn. Cancer Rsch., Am. Soc. Clin. Oncology, Am. Assn. Cancer Edn., Am. Cancer Soc. (chmn. patient svc. com. Phila. divsn. 1981-83, chmn. med. subcom. profl. edn. com. 1979-81, fin. com. 1981), Phi beta Kappa, Alpha Omega Alpha. Jewish. Home: 324 Surrey Rd Cherry Hill NJ 08002-1540

KAHN, STEVEN EMANUEL, medical educator; b. Durban, South Africa, July 28, 1955; m. Stephanie Berk; 2 children. MB, ChB, U. Cape Town, South Africa, 1978. Diplomate Am. Bd. Internal Medicine. Intern depts. ob./gyn. and medicine Somerset Hosp., Cape Town, South Africa, 1979; resident dept. ob./gyn. 2 Mil. Hosp., Wynberg, South Africa, 1980, resident and coord. dept. ob./gyn., 1981; resident dept. medicine divsn. endocrinology Groote Schuur Hosp., Cape Town, 1982; rsch. fellow diabetes and endocrine rsch. group U. Cape Town, 1983; resident dept. medicine Albert Einstein Med. Ctr., Phila., 1983-86; sr. rsch. fellow divsn. metabolism, endocrinology and nutrition Dept. Medicine U. Wash. Sch. of Medicine, VA Med. Ctr., Seattle, 1986-88; assoc. investigator, staff physician divsn. endocrinology and metabolism Dept. Medicine VA Med. Ctr., Seattle, 1988-91, rsch. assoc., staff physician divsn. endocrinology and metabolism Dept. Medicine, 1991-95; acting instr. divsn. metabolism, endocrinology and nutrition Dept. Medicine U. Wash. Sch. of Medicine, Seattle, 1988-92, asst. prof. divsn. metabolism, endocrinology and nutrition Dept. Medicine, 1992-95, assoc. prof. divsn. metabolism, endocrinology and nutrition Dept. Medicine, 1995—. Mem. editl. bd. Jour. Clin. Endocrinology and Metabolism, 1995-98, Diabetes Care, 1997—; contbr. articles to profl. jours. Amelia Schenkman scholar, 1973-75; named Assoc. Investigator, Dept. VA, 1988, Rsch. Assoc., 1991; recipient Career Devel. award Juvenile Diabetes Found., 1988, Feasibility award Dana Found., 1989, Clin. Investigator award NIH, 1991, New Investigator award Diabetes Rsch. Coun., 1992-94, Rsch. award Am. Diabetes Assn., 1996. Mem. ACP, Am. Diabetes Assn. (bd. dirs. Wash. affiliate 1993-94, exec. bd. dirs. 1994-98, rsch. grant rev. panel 1994-97), Am. Fedn. Clin. Rsch. (chair program com. for metabolism 1994, 96, councillor western sect. 1994-96, pres.-elect western sect. 1996, pres. western sect. 1997, nat. councillor 1996), Western Soc. Clin. Investigation (councillor 1998—), Gen. Med. Coun. (U.K.), Endocrine Soc. Office: VA Puget Health Care Sys Dept Medicine 151 1660 S Columbian Way Seattle WA 98108-1532

KAHN, SUSAN BETH, artist; b. N.Y.C., Aug. 26, 1924; d. Jesse B. and Jenny Carol (Peshkin) Cohen; m. Joseph Kahn, Sept. 15, 1946 (dec.); m. Richard Rosenkranz, Feb. 1, 1981. Grad., Parsons Sch. Design, 1945; student, Moses Soyer, 1950-57. Subject of: book Susan Kahn, with an essay by Lincoln Rothschild, 1980; One-woman shows include Sagittarius Gallery, 1960, A.C.A., Galleries, 1964, 68, 71, 76, 80, Charles B. Goddard Art Center, Ardmore, Okla., 1973, Albrecht Gallery Mus. Art, St. Joseph, Mo., 1974, N.Y. Cultural Center, N.Y.C., 1974, St. Peter's Coll., Jersey City, 1978, Heidi Neuhoff Gallery, N.Y.C., 1989, Sindin Galleries, 1996; exhibited in group shows Audubon Artists, N.Y.C., Nat. Acad., N.Y.C., Springfield (Mass.) Mus., City Center, N.Y.C., A.C.A., Galleries, N.Y.C., Nat. Arts Club, N.Y.C., Butler Inst., Youngstown, Ohio, Islip Art Mus., East Islip, N.Y., 1989, Fine Arts Mus. of S., Mobile, Ala., 1989, Chatanooga Regional History Mus, 1989, Longview (Tex.) Mus. Art, 1990; represented in permanent collections, Tyler (Tex.) Mus., St. Lawrence U. Mus., Canton, N.Y., Fairleigh Dickinson U. Mus., Rutherford, N.J., Syracuse U. Mus., Sheldon Swope Gallery, Terre Haute, Ind., Montclair (N.J.) Mus. Fine Arts, Butler Inst. Am. Art, Youngstown, Ohio, Reading (Pa.) Mus., Albrecht Gallery Mus. Art, St. Joseph(Mo.), Cedar Rapids (Iowa) Art Center, N.Y. Cultural Center, N.Y.C., Edwin A. Ulrich Mus., Wichita, Kans., Wichita State U., Johns Hopkins Sch. Advanced Internat. Studies, Washington, Joslyn Mus., Omaha, U. Wyo., Laramie. Recipient Knickerbocker prize for best religious painting, 1956; Edith Lehman award Nat. Assn. Women Artists, 1958; Simmons award, 1961; Knickerbocker Artists award, 1961; Nat. Arts Club award, 1967; Knickerbocker Medal of Honor, 1964; Famous Artists Sch. award, 1967. Mem. Nat. Assn. Women Artists (Anne Barnett Meml. prize 1981, Solveig Stromsoe Palmer Meml. award 1987, Dorothy Schweitzer award 1990), Artists Equity, Met. Mus., Mus. Modern Art, Nat. Assn. Women Artists (meml. award 1987). *I choose to be a realist and humanist in my work. The most important objects of my concern are people, their lives and times. I believe that art is a way of communicating, subject matter translated into color, form and line, so that the work will express the idea convincingly.*

KAHN, THOMAS, medical educator; b. Offenburg, Germany, June 23, 1938; s. Ludwig and Ellen (Kaufman) K.; m. Si Mi Pak, Nov. 7, 1968; children: Diana, David, Philip. BA, NYU, 1958, MD, 1962. Intern medicine Balt. City Hosps., 1962-63, U. Pitts. Hosps., 1963-64; intern medicine Mt. Sinai, N.Y.C., 1964-65, resident in nephrology, 1965-67; chief renal sect. Bronx VA Med. Ctr., 1979-96; prof. medicine Mt. Sinai Sch. Medicine, N.Y.C., 1988—. Maj. U.S. Army, 1967-69. Office: VA Med Ctr 130 W Kingsbridge Rd Bronx NY 10468-3992

KAHN, WALTER KURT, engineering and applied science educator; b. Mannheim, Baden, Germany, Mar. 24, 1929; came to U.S., 1938; s. Simon and Hilde (Ullmann) K.; m. Barbara Fairberg, Mar. 25, 1962; children: Hilde Elisabeth, Jonathan Daniel. BEE, Cooper Union, 1951; MEE, Poly. Inst. Bklyn., 1954, DEE, 1960. Engr. Wheeler Labs., Inc., 1951-54; rsch. assoc. Microwave Rsch. Inst. Poly. Inst. Bklyn., 1954-60, asst. prof. elec. engring., asst. to dir. Microwave Rsch. Inst., 1960-62, assoc. prof. electrophysics, 1962-68, prof. electrophysics, 1968-69; mem. tech. staff Bell Telephone Labs., Murray Hill, N.J., summer 1963; liaison scientist U.S. Office Naval Rsch.-London Br., 1967-68; mem. tech. staff IBM Thomas J. Watson Rsch. Ctr., summer 1969; prof. engring. and applied sci. dept. elec. engring. and computer sci. The George Washington U., 1969—, chmn. dept., 1970-74, dir. Inst. for Info. Sci. and Tech., 1982-91, past mem. faculty senate, univ. com. on sponsored rsch., faculty advisor TBII chpt., mem. faculty senate grievance com.; vis. rsch. scientist MIT, spring 1984; bd. dirs. ANRO Engring., Inc., Sarasota, Fla.; cons. Eaton Corp., Radio Corp. Am., Sperry Rand, Maxson Electronics Corp., Inst. for Def. Analyses, Naval Rsch. Lab., Washington;. Contbr. sci. papers to profl. publs. Recipient Cert. of Achievement Group on Antennas and Propagation IEEE, Rsch. Publs. award Naval Rsch. Lab, 1976; NATO sr. fellow in sci., 1973. Fellow IEEE (adv. bd. Jour. Quantum Electronics, mem. com. for tech. forecasting and assesssment, chmn. tech. program com. 1978 AP-S, mem. editorial bd. Proceedings 1986-93, assoc. editor 1989-92), AAAS, Optical Soc. Am.; mem. Antennas and Propagation Standards of IEEE (adminstrv. com., microwave theory and techniques standards com., basic. sci. com., assoc. editor Trans. on Microwave Theory and Techniques, 1964-65, editor Trans. Antenna and Propagation, 1977-80, cert. of achievement 1970), Internat. Sci. Radio Union (Commns. B and C), Philos. Soc. of Washington, Soc. Photo-Optical Instrumentation Engrs., Cosmos Club, Sigma Xi, Eta Kappa Nu, Tau Beta Pi. Office: George Washington U Dept Elec & ComputerEngring Washington DC 20052

KAHN, WOLF, artist; b. Stuttgart, Germany, Oct. 4, 1927; came to U.S., 1940, naturalized, 1946; s. Emil and Nellie (Budge) K.; m. Emily Mason, Mar. 2, 1957; children: Cecily, Melany. Student, Hans Hofmann Sch., 1948-49; BA, U. Chgo., 1951. vis. prof. painting U. Calif., Berkeley, 1960; adj. assoc. prof. Cooper Union Art Sch., 1961-77; jury mem. numerous regional art shows; artist-in-residenceDartmouth Coll., 1984. One-man shows include Borgenicht Gallery, N.Y.C., 1957-95, Beadleston Gallery, N.Y.C., 1998, Thomas Segal Gallery, Balt., 1997, Jerald Melberg Gallery, Charlotte, N.C., 1993-98, Ft. Lauderdale Mus. Art, 1991, Boca Raton Mus. of Art, 1997; group shows include Whitney Mus., N.Y.C., 1960, 77, Met. Mus., N.Y.C., 1975-76; represented in permanent collections Mus. Modern Art, N.Y.C., Whitney Mus., Houston Mus. Fine Arts, Chase Manhattan Coll., Va. Mus., Met. Mus., N.Y.C., L.A. County Mus., Hirschhorn Mus., Washington; author: Pastel Light, 1983; contbr. articles to profl. jours. Trustee Brattleboro Mus. Vt., 1979—, Vt. Studio Sch.,1988—; apptd. N.Y.C. Art Commn., 1993-95. With USNR, 1945-46. Recipient award for art Am. Acad. Arts and Letters, 1979; Fulbright fellow Italy, 1964-65; Guggenheim fellow, 1967-68; Ford Found. grantee, 1969. Mem. Nat. Acad. Design (coun. mem. 1982-96), Nat. Arts Club, Am. Acad. Arts and Letters. Democrat. Jewish. Office: care Beadleston Gallery 724 5th Ave New York NY 10019-4106

KAHNE, STEPHEN JAMES, systems engineer, educator, academic administrator, engineering executive; b. N.Y.C., Apr. 5, 1937; s. Arnold W. and Janet (Weatherlow) K.; m. Irena Nowacka, Dec. 11, 1970; children: Christopher, Kasia. BEE, Cornell U., 1960; MS, U. Ill., 1961, PhD, 1963. Asst. prof. elec. engring. U. Minn., Mpls., 1966-69; assoc. prof. U. Minn., 1969-76; dir. Hybrid Computer Lab., 1968-76; founder, dir., cons. InterDesign Inc., Mpls., 1968-76; prof. dept. sys. engring. Case Western Res. U., Cleve., 1976-83, chmn. dept., 1976-80; dir. divsn. elec., computer and sys. engring. NSF, Washington, 1980-82; prof. Poly Inst. N.Y., 1983-85, dean engring., 1983-84; pres. Oreg. Grad. Ctr., Beaverton, 1985-86, prof. dept. applied physics and elec. engring., 1985-89; chief engr. civil systems divsn. MITRE Corp., McLean, Va., 1989-90, chief scientist Washington Group, 1990-91, cons. engr. Ctr. for Advanced Aviation Sys. Devel., 1991-94; exec. dir., CEO Triangle Coalition for Sci. and Tech. Edn., 1994; chancellor, v.p. Embry-Riddle Aeronautical U., Prescott, Ariz., 1995—; cons. in field; exchange scientist NAS, 1968, 75. Editor: IEEE Transactions on Automatic Control, 1975-79; hon. editor: Internat. Fedn. of Automatic Control, 1975-81, dep. chmn. mng. bd. publs., 1976-87, chmn., 1999—, v.p., 1987-90, pres.-elect, 1990-93, pres., 1993-96, advisor, 1999—; assoc. editor: Automatica, dep. chmn. editl. bd., 1976-82; mem. editl. bd. IEEE Spectrum, 1979-82; contbr. articles to sci. jours. Active Mpls. Citizens League, 1968-75; regent L.I. Coll. Hosp., Bklyn., 1984-85; trustee Yavapi Regional Med. Ctr., 1999—; chmn. Beaverton Sister Cities Found., 1986-87. Served with USAF, 1963-66. Recipient Amicus Poloniae award POLAND Mag., 1975, John A. Curtis award Am. Soc. Engring. Edn., Outstanding Svc. award Internat. Fedn. Automatic Control, 1990; Case Centennial scholar, 1980. Fellow AAAS, IEEE (pres. Control Sys. Soc. 1981, bd. dirs. 1982-86, v.p. tech. activities 1984-85, Centennial medal 1984, Disting. Mem. award 1983, Richard Emberson award 1991, Disting. Lectr. 1998—), Am. Soc. Engring. Edn., Air Traffic Control Assn., Eta Kappa Nu. Office: Embry Riddle Aero U 3200 Willow Creek Rd Prescott AZ 86301-3721

KAHNG, SUN MYONG, economics educator; b. Cheju, Republic of Korea, Apr. 29, 1926; came to U.S., 1955; s. Yoosup and Ki-ah Kahng; m. Patricia K. Oh, Dec. 17, 1959; children: Margaret, Robert, Grace, Samuel, Diane. BA, Seoul Nat. U., Rep. of Korea, 1952; MA, Ind. U., 1957, PhD, 1975. Staff economist Rsch. dept. Bank of Korea, Seoul, 1952-53, sect. chief Rsch. dept., 1954-55; resident lectr. Ind. U., Ft. Wayne, 1960-61; instr. Northwest Mo. State U., Maryville, 1961-62; asst. prof. Austin Peay State U., Clarksville, Tenn., 1962-65; from asst. prof. to prof. econs. U. Minn., Morris, 1965—, head regional rsch. ctr. for community devel., 1969—; vis. prof. Seoul Nat. U., 1985-86, Gadjah Mada U., Yogyakarta, Indonesia, 1984-85, Cheju Nat. U., 1993; cons. in field. Co-author: Trade in Services and Foreign Direct Investment of Asia-Pacific Countries, 1991; contbr. articles to profl. jours. Fellow NEH, 1979, 84, 88, 92, GE Found., 1981; Higher Edn. Act grantee, 1971-72. Mem. Internat. Soc. Korean Studies (chair acad. coun. 1992-94), Minn. Econ. Assn. (pres. 1979-80), Kiwanis (bd. dirs. 1987-89, 92-93). Avocations: fishing, music, traveling. Office: Univ Minn 145 Social Sci Morris MN 56267

KAHRILAS, PETER JAMES, medical educator, researcher; b. Culver City, Calif., June 9, 1953; s. Peter Jerome and Leticia (Llorett) K.; m. Elyse Anne Lambiase, Mar. 30, 1984; children: Genevieve Anne, Ian James, Miranda Elyse. Student, Yale U., 1971-75, U. Rochester, N.Y., 1975-79. Resident in medicine U. Hosp. of Cleve., 1979-82; fellow in gastroenterology Northwestern U., Chgo., 1982-84; rsch. fellow Med. Coll. of Wis., Milw., 1984-86, asst. prof. medicine, 1986-90, assoc. prof. medicine, 1990-95, prof. medicine, 1995-99; chief gastroenterology and hepatology Northwestrn U. Med. Sch., Chgo., 1999—; dir. lab. Northwesterm Meml. Hosp., Chgo. Contbr. articles to profl. jours. NIH grantee, 1990—. Fellow ACP, Ctrl. Soc. for Clin. Rsch., Am. Coll. Gastroenterology; mem. Am. Gastroenterol. Assn., Am. Fedn. for Clin. Rsch., Am. Soc. for Clin. Investigation, Am. Motility Soc. Democrat. Home: 203 Columbia Ave Park Ridge IL 60068-4923 Office: Northwestern U 746 Passavant 303 E Superior St Chicago IL 60611-4804

KAHRL, ROBERT CONLEY, lawyer; b. Mt. Vernon, Ohio, June 2, 1946; s. K. Allin and Evelyn Sperry (Conley) K.; m. LaVonne Elaine Rutherford, July 12, 1969; children: Kurt Freeland, Eric Allin, Heidi Elizabeth. AB, Princeton U., 1968; MBA, JD, Ohio State U., 1975. Bar: Ohio 1975, U.S. Ct. Appeals (6th cir.) 1976, U.S. Dist. Ct. (no. dist.) Ohio 1977, U.S. Ct. Appeals (9th cir.) 1979, U.S. Ct. Appeals (fed. cir.) 1984, U.S. Ct. Appeals (D.C. cir.) 1986. Law clk. to presiding judge U.S. Ct. Appeals (6th cir.), Cleve., 1975-76; assoc. Jones, Day, Reavis & Pogue, Cleve., 1976-84, ptnr., 1985—, chair intellectual property sect., 1991—. Served to lt. USN, 1968-72. Mem. Ohio State Bar Assn. (chmn. intellectual property sect.), Am. Intellectual Property Law Assn., Order of Coif, Am. Guild Organists. Republican. Congregationalist. Home: 7624 Red Fox Trl Hudson OH 44236-1926 Office: Jones Day Reavis & Pogue 901 Lakeside Ave E Cleveland OH 44114-1116

KAHRMANN, LINDA IRENE, child care supervisor; b. Newark, Feb. 25, 1949; d. Mitchell Augustus and Irene Constance (Banta) Bradshaw; m. Robert George Kahrmann, Aug. 22, 1993; children: Jeannette Regan, Kellie Ann, Jeffrey Robert. Student, Mansfield State Coll., 1967, Middlesex County Coll., 1968-70. Tchr. K-2d grade Holy Spirit Sch., Perth Amboy, N.J., 1970-75; child care supr. North Brunswick (N.J.) Bd. Edn., 1985—; mathworks aide Parsons Sch., North Brunswick, 1991-93; ESL child care coord. megaskills child care coord. North Brunswick Bd. Edn., 1990—. Tchr. summer elem. enrichment program North Brunswick Bd. Edn., 1988—; v.p. North Brunswick Band Parents, 1989, 92. Named to Band Parent Hall of Fame Band Parents Assn. North Brunswick, 1992. Episcopalian. Avocations: needlework, reading, travel, gourmet cooking. Home: 21 Allison Ct Monmouth Junction NJ 08852-2624 Office: North Brunswick Bd Edn Old Georges Rd North Brunswick NJ 08902

KAHRMANN, ROBERT GEORGE, educational administrator; b. New Brunswick, N.J., Dec. 12, 1940; s. Robert George and Susan Rose (Budish) K.; m. Linda Irene Bradshaw, Aug. 22, 1993; children: Kellie, Jeffrey, Jeannette. BS, Monmouth Coll., West Long Branch, N.J., 1963; MA in Edn., Seton Hall U., 1964; EdD, NYU, 1970. Tchr. social studies Middletown Twp. (N.J.) H.S., 1964-66; asst. dir. Jersey City State Coll., 1968-71; dir. continuing edn. Somerset County Coll., Somerville, N.J., 1971-77; dir. continuing edn. Seton Hall U., South Orange, N.J., 1977-78, dean, 1978-84; mgr. continuing engring. edn. IEEE, Piscataway, N.J., 1984-95; dean Pa. Inst. of Tech., Media, 1995-98; v.p. acad. affairs Berkeley Coll., West Paterson, N.J., 1998-99; pvt. practice Monmouth Junction, N.J., 1999—; assoc. dean Hudson County C.C., 1999—; adj. prof. Seton Hall U., 1977-83; cons. N.J. Funeral Dirs. Assn., 1978-84, Westmoreland County (Pa.) C.C., 1975, N.Y.C. Fire Lts. Assn., 1974-75. Editor: Fire Problems in Modern Building, 1971; contbr. articles to profl. jours. Pres., treas. H.S. Band Parents, North Brunswick, N.J., 1985-93; chmn. Charter Study Commn., North Brunswick, 1981-82; chmn. and mem. Parks and Recreation Com., North Brunswick, 1984-92, Devel. Com., 1977-83. Recipient TAB Pioneer award IEEE Computer Soc., 1988, Edn. award N.J. Ind. Ins. Agts., 1982, Founder's Day award NYU, 1971. Mem. Internat. TV Assn., Phi Delta Kappa. Avocations: travel, stamp collecting. Office: Hudson County CC 26 Journal Sq Jersey City NJ 07306

KAID, LYNDA LEE, communications educator; b. Harrisburg, Ill., Aug. 22, 1948; d. Billy Cameron and Leona Elizabeth (Oglesby) K.; m. Clifford Alan Jones. BA, So. Ill. U., 1970, MS, 1972, PhD, 1974. Prof. dept. comm. U. Okla., Norman, 1974—, dir. Polit. Comm. Ctr., 1984—; mem. adv. bd. Mus. of Broadcast Comm., Chgo., 1990—. Co-author: Political Campaign Communication: A Bibliography and Guide to the Literature, 1974 (Outstanding Reference Book of 1974, Choice mag.); co-editor Political Communication Yearbook 1984, 1985, Political Campaign Communication: A Bibliography and Guide to the Literature, Vol. 2, 1973-1982, 1985, New Perspectives on Political Advertising, 1986, The Political Commercial Archive: A Catalog and Guide to the Collection, 1991, Mediated Politics in Two Cultures: Presidential Campaigning in the United States and France, 1991, Die Massenmedien im Wahlkampf, 1993, The Lynching of Language: Gender, Politics and Power in the Hill-Thomas Hearings, 1996, Political Advertising in Western Democracies: Parties and Candidates on Television, 1995; contbr. numerous articles to profl. jours. Recipient Rsch. award on Polit. Advt., NSF & Nat. Endowment for Humanities, 1992—; Fulbright scholar USIA-Fulbright Commn., Western Europe, 1987-88, 1997. Mem. Am. Film Inst., League of Women Voters, Internat. Comm. Assn. (pres. polit. comm. divsn. 1979-81). Avocation: internat. travel. Office: U Okla Polit Comm Ctr 610 Elm Ave Norman OK 73019-2080

KAIDA, TAMARRA, art and photography educator; b. Lienz, Austria, July 6, 1946; came to U.S., 1950; d. Ivan and Matrona (Bratasuk) K.; m. Paul S. Knapp; 1 child, Krister. BA, Goddard Coll., 1974; MFA, SUNY, Buffalo, 1979. Tutor photography Empire State Coll., 1977-79; asst. dir. dept. edn. Internat. Mus. Photography, George Eastman House, 1976-79; vis. lectr. Ariz. State U., Tempe, 1979-80, asst. prof., 1980-85, assoc. prof., 1985-92, prof., 1992—; represented by Etherton Gallery, Tucson, Califia Books, San Francisco; mem. faculty Internat. Sommerakademie fur Bildende Kunst, Salzburg, Austria, 1985, Friends of Photography Summer Workshop, Carmel, Calif., 1989, vis. photographers program R.I. Sch. Design, 1989, guest artist lecture and lazer print transfer demonstration Photography Studies in France, Paris, 1991; panelist NEA S.W. Regional Photography Task Force, 1980; juror nat. photography competition Calif. Inst. Arts, Valencia, 1981; curator, lectr., cons. in field. Author: (with Rita Dove) The Other Side of the House, 1988; Tremors from the Faultline, 1989; contbr. articles to profl. jours.; author short stories; many one-woman shows including Scottsdale (Ariz.) Ctr. Arts, 1987, Fine Arts Gallery RISD, 1989, OPSIS Found. Gallery, N.Y.C., 1990, Fyerweather Gallery U. Va., Charlottesville, 1991, Photography Gallery, Fine Art Ctr., U. R.I., Kingston, R.I., 1992, Kharkov (Ukraine) Regional Mus. Art, 1993, Sky Harbor Airport, Phoenix, Ariz., 1994; numerous nat. and internat. group shows including Coconino Ctr. Arts, Flagstaff, Ariz., 1985, Frankfurt Art Soc., Germany, 1985, Mus. Art and Trade, Hamburg, Germany, 1985, Boulder (Colo.) Ctr. Visual Arts, 1985, Art Inst. Chgo., Mpls. Coll. Art & Design, 1986, Hood Mus. Art Dartmouth Coll., Hanover, N.H., 1987, Lawrence (Kans.) Art Ctr., 1987, Miller's Studio, Zurich, Switzerland, 1987, Palazzo Braschi, Rome, 1987, Sante Fe Ctr. Photography, 1987, Dinnerware Gallery, Tucson, 1987, Sante Fe Ctr. Arts (purchase award), 1987, Rockwell Mus., Corning, N.Y., 1987, Grand Canyon Coll., Phoenix, 1987, Tucson Mus. Art, 1988, Halsey Gallery Coll. of Charleston, S.C., 1988, Long Beach (Calif.) Coll. Fine Arts, 1988, Atrium Gallery U. Conn. Storrs, 1988, Gallery of Kans. City (Mo.) Artists Coalition (1st prize, fellowship award) 1989, Lieberman and Saul Gallery, N.Y.C., 1989, Downey (Calif.) Mus. Art, 1989, Anderson Ranch Arts Ctr., Aspen, Colo., 1989, San Francisco Camerawork, 1990, Phoenix Mus. Art, 1990, Ctr. for Photography, Cin., 1991, Mus. Art U. Okla., 1991, Rockford (Ill.) Coll., 1991, Ctr. for Creative Photography, Tucson, 1991-92; Huntington Gallery, Mass. Coll. Art, Boston, 1992, Ariz. State Capital, Phoenix, 1992, Barbara Zusman Art and Antiques Gallery, Santa Fe, N.Mex., 1992; internat. traveling exhbns.; represented in permanent collections Union Russian Art Photography, Moscow, U. Calif. Santa Cruz, Kennedy Ctr. Performing Arts, Washington, L.A. County Mus. Art, Internat. Mus. Photography George Eastman House, Rochester, N.Y., N.Y. Pub. Libr., SUNY Buffalo, Libr. Congress, Polaroid Corp., Cambridge, Mass., Sante Fe Mus. Fine Arts, Scottsdale Ctr. Art, Snell and Wilmer, Phoenix, Valley Nat. Bank, Phoenix, others; photographs featured various works. Judge spring art show Scottsdale C.C., 1980; organizer Artist Against Hunger money and food drive Ariz. State U. Sch. Art, 1984; juror New Times Newspaper, 1985, Tempe Fine Arts Ctr., 1989, Yavapai Coll., Prescott, Ariz., 1989. Recipient Faculty Grant-in-Aid, 1982, 85, 93, Current Works 1989 Excellence award Soc. Contemporary Photography, Visual Artists fellowship grant Nat. Endowment for Arts, 1986, rsch. grant Coll. Fine Arts, 1987, 93, grant Arts/Social Svcs./Humanities, 1989, Sch. Art Assistance to Faculty, 1990, Visual Arts fellowship grant Ariz. Commn. Arts, 1989-90, Inst. for Studies in Arts, 1992, materials grant Polaroid Corp., 1992, Gov.'s Arts award, 1992, Women's Studies Summer Rsch. award., 1992. Mem. Coll. Arts Assn., Soc. Photographic Edn. (co-chair, organizer West/S.W. Regional Conf. 1983), Friends of Photography (Ferguson award 1983). Democrat. Russian Orthodox. Home: 534 N Orange Mesa AZ 85201-5609

KAIDANOV, EMMANUIL GREGORY, coach; came to U.S., 1979; MS in Phys. Edn., M Sport of Fencing, State Coll. Phys. Edn., Kharkov, Russia, 1962. Fencing master, head coach men's and women's fencing teams Pa. State U., University Park, 1982—; coach U.S. World Championship teams, 1985, 86, 87, World U. Games, 1985, 89, 91, 93, Maccabiah Games, Pan Am. Jr. Championships, World Under-20 Championships. Named to NCAA Championship Team, 1990, 91, 95, 96, 97, 98; Coach of Yr. awards Nat. Coll. Athletic Assn., 1990, 91, U.S. Fencing Coaches Assn., 1996. Office: Pa State U 111C Bryce Jordan Ctr University Park PA 16802-7101

KAIER, EDWARD JOHN, lawyer; b. Sewickley, Pa., Sept. 23, 1945; s. Edward Anthony and Mary Patricia (Crimmins) K.; m. Annette Thomas, July 31, 1976; children: Elizabeth Anne, Charles Crimmins, Thomas Edward. AB, Harvard U., 1967; JD, U. Pa., 1970. Bar: D.C. 1970, Pa. 1970, U.S. Dist. Ct. (ea. dist.) Pa. 1971, U.S. Ct. Appeals (3rd and D.C. cirs.) 1971, U.S. Dist. Ct. D.C., 1971. Law clk. to presiding justice U.S. Dist. Ct. for D.C., Washington, 1970-71; assoc. Dechert Price & Rhoads, Phila., 1971-74; ptnr. Kaier and Kaier, Phila., 1974-77, Hepburn Willcox Hamilton & Putnam, Phila., 1977—; pres. Savoy Co., Phila., 1978-80; bd. dirs. Mgrs. Funds, Norwalk, Conn. Vice chmn. Rosemont (Pa.) Sch. of Holy Child, 1981-90. Mem. ABA, Phila. Bar Assn. (chmn. office practice com. probate sect. 1987-90, exec. com. 1990-92), Merion Cricket Club, Phila. Club, Phila. Country Club, Avalon Yacht Club (trustee 1987-90, 92-93, treas. 1990-92), Harvard-Radcliffe Club (Phila., sec. 1989—). Republican. Roman Catholic. Avocations: sailing, golf. Home: 111 N Lowrys Ln Rosemont PA 19010-1408 Office: Hepburn Willcox Hamilton & Putnam 1100 One Penn Ctr Philadelphia PA 19103

KAIGE, ALICE TUBB, retired librarian; b. Obion, Tenn., Jan. 27, 1922; d. George Easley and Lucile (Merryman) Tubb; m. Richard H. Kaige, Aug. 1952; children: Robert H., Richard C. (dec.), John S. (dec.). BA, Vanderbilt U., 1944; BS in Libr. Sci., Geo. Peabody Coll., 1947. Libr. Martin (Tenn.) High Sch., 1946-47, Demonstration Sch. Geo. Peabody Coll. Joint U. Librs., Nashville, Tenn., 1947-52; acquisitions libr. Lincoln Libr., Springfield, Ill., 1967-70; office coord. Springfield (Ill.) Chpt. ACLU, 1974; staff rep. Am. Fed. State, County & Mcpl. Employees, Springfield, 1975; libr. Ill. Dept. of Commerce and Community Affairs, Springfield, 1976-89. Vice chmn. Women's Internat. League for Peace and Freedom, 1969-70, various coms., 1970—; treas. Cen. Ill. Women's Lobby, 1971-72; com. on local govt. League of Women Voters, 1973-76; career day com. Urban League Guild, 1970-71; mem. NAACP,steering com. Springfield chpt. ACLU, 1974-75; co-founder West Side Neighborhood Assn., Springfield, 1977. Recipient Elizabeth Cady Stanton award, Springfield Women's Political Caucus, 1982. Mem. Sangamon County Hist. Soc., NOW, Women's Internat. League for Peace and Freedom, War Resisters League, LWV, Springfield Women's Polit. Caucus. Avocations: reading, walking. Home: 701 S State St Springfield IL 62704-2445

KAIL, KONRAD, physician; b. Iowa City, July 7, 1949; s. Joseph Andrew Kail and Jean Lucille (Peterson) Tienan; m. Jane Marie Petersen, Jan. 5, 1973. BS in Biology, U. Houston, 1974; BS in Medicine, Baylor Coll. Medicine, 1976; ND, Nat. Coll. Naturopathic, Medicine, 1983; DACNFM, Am. Coll. Naturopathic Family, Medicine, 1995. Lic. naturopathic physician. Cardiac-catherization technician St. Luke's/Tex. Children's Hosp., Houston, 1972-75; physician's asst. various clinics, Silver City, N.Mex., 1976-80; dir. Naturopathic Wheeling and Healing Around Country Bike Tour, 1983-84; chmn. bd. dirs. U.S. Complementary Health, Inc., Phoenix, 1995—; bd. dirs., co-founder, mem. faculty S.W. Coll. of Naturopathic Medicine, Phoenix, 1996—; owner, operator Naturopathic Family Care, Inc., Phoenix, 1990—; cons. Ins. Cos., Nutrient Supplement Cos., Govt. Agys., 1985—. Editor: Alternative Medicine, 1994; contbr.

articles to profl. jours. Mem. adv. bd. Inst. for Natural Medicine. With USN Res., 1971-76. Fellow Am. Assn. Naturopathic Physicians (chmn. scientific affil. 1986-97, pres. 1992-94, Physician of Yr. 1997), Am. Coll. Naturopathic Family Practice (chmn., pres. 1995—). Green Party. Avocations: ultimate frisbee, bicycling, skiing, golf. Office: Naturopathic Family Care 13832 N 32nd St Ste C2-4 Phoenix AZ 85032-5616

KAILAS, LEO GEORGE, lawyer; b. N.Y.C., May 28, 1949; s. George and Evanthia (Skoulikas) K.; AB, Columbia U., 1970, JD, 1973; m. Merle S. Duskin; children: Arianne, George, Shirley. Bar: N.Y. 1974. Assoc. firm Olwine, Connelly, Chase, O'Donnell and Weyher, N.Y.C., 1973-77; partner specializing in internat., comml. and admiralty litigation, firm Milgrim Thomajan Jacobs & Lee, P.C., (now Piper & Marbury L.L.P.) N.Y.C., 1977—, mem. internat. trade and litigation group. Mem. ABA, Assn. of Bar of City of N.Y. (chmn. admiralty com. 1985-88). Office: Piper & Marbury LLP 1251 Avenue Of The Americas New York NY 10020-1104

KAILATH, THOMAS, electrical engineer, educator; b. Poona, India, June 7, 1935; came to U.S., 1957, naturalized, 1976; s. Mamman and Kunjamma (George) K.; m. Sarah Jacob, June 11, 1962; children—Ann, Paul, Priya, Ryan. BE, U. Poona, 1956; SM, MIT, 1959, ScD, 1961; hon. degree, Linkoping U., Sweden, 1990, Strathclyde U., Scotland, 1992, U. Madrid, 1999. Comm. rschr. Jet Propulsion Labs., Pasadena, Calif., 1961-62; faculty Stanford (Calif.) U., 1963—, prof. elec. engring., 1968—, Hitachi Am. prof. engring., 1988—; dir. Info. Systems Lab., 1971-81, assoc. chmn. dept., 1981-87; vis. prof., cons. univs., industry, govt. Author: Linear Systems, 1980, Least-Squares Estimation, 2d edit, 1981, State-Space Estimation Theory, 1999; edit. bd. various jours.; contbr. articles to profl. jours. Recipient Edn. award Am. Control Coun., 1986, Tech. Achievement and Soc. awards Signal Processing Soc. IEEE, 1989, 91, Donald G. Fink Prize award, 1996; Sr. Vinton Hayes fellow MIT, 1992, Guggenheim fellow, 1970, Churchill fellow, 1977, Michael fellow Weizmann Inst., Israel, 1984, Royal Soc. guest rsch. fellow, 1989. Fellow IEEE (Edn. medal 1995), Inst. Math. Stats., Am. Acad. Arts and Scis.; mem. Indian Nat. Acad. Engring., Nat. Acad. Engring., Am. Math. Soc., Soc. Indsl. and Applied Math., Third World Acad. Scis., Sigma Xi. Home: 1024 Cathcart Way Palo Alto CA 94305-1047 Office: Stanford U Dept Elec Engring Stanford CA 94305-9510

KAILIAN, ARAM HARRY, architect; b. Phila., Oct. 23, 1949; s. Harry G. and Louise (Haledjian) Caily; m. Kathryn I. Zakian, May 27, 1973; children: Arsine K., Aram E. BS, Temple U., 1973; student, Tyler Sch. Fine Art, Phila., 1967-69, Drexel U., 1970-71. Project architect Kuljian Corp., Phila., 1970-73, Urban Engrs. Inc., Phila., 1973-76; project designer Wm. F. Lotz Designers, Horsham, Pa., 1976-78; prin./architect Clyde H. Goff & Assocs./A.H. Kailian, Architects, Interior Design, Constrn. Mgmt., Bala Cynwyd, Pa., 1982-94, Kailian Assocs., Bryn Mawr, Pa., 1978-94; spl. asst. to the commr. Pub. Bldgs. Svc./Gen. Svcs. Adminstrn., Washington, 1994-96, sr. adviser to commr., 1997—; interagency coord. Pres. Cmty. Empowerment Bd., 1997—; bd.dirs. NIBS CADD Coun., 1994—. Contbr. articles to profl. jours. Mem. Dem. Nationalities Coun., Washington, 1976—, Nat. Rep. Heritage Groups Coun., 1976—; bd. dirs. Armenian Nat. Com. Am., 1983-89. Mem. AIA, D.C. Soc. Architects, Am. Arbitration Assn., Nat. Acad. Conciliators, Nat. Trust for Historic Preservation, Acad. Polit. Sci. Democrat. Armenian Orthodox. Office: GSA PBS Office of Commr Ste 6344 18th and F Sts Washington DC 20405

KAIMOWITZ, GABE HILLEL, civil rights lawyer; b. N.Y.C., May 5, 1935; s. Abraham and Esther (Bialogursky) K.; children: David, Beth. BS, U. Wis., 1955; MA, U. Cen. Fla., 1988; LLB, NYU, 1967. Bar: N.Y. 1969, Mich. 1971, Fla., 1987, U.S. Dist. Ct. (mid. dist.) Fla., 1987, U.S. Ct. Appeals (6th cir.) 1971, U.S. Ct. Appeals (3d cir.) 1982, U.S. Ct. Appeals (2d cir.) 1983, U.S. Ct. Appeals (11th cir.), 1989 U.S. Ct. Appeals (7th cir.) 1990, U.S. Ct. Appeals (D.C. cir.) 1998. Atty. Ctr. Social Welfare, Politics and Law, N.Y.C., 1967-70; sr. atty. Mich. Legal Services, Detroit, 1971-79; assoc. P.R. Legal Def., N.Y.C., 1980-84; exec. dir. Greater Orlando (Fla.) A. Legal Services, 1985-86; atty. Attys. Against Am. Apartheid, Fla. and various other civil rights orgns., Orlando, 1969—; lectr., adj. prof. numerous univs. Contbr. articles to profl. jours.; author poems. Served with U.S. Army, 1956-57, with Res. 1958-60. Smith fellow, 1970-71, Legal Services Corp. fellow, 1979-80. Mem. N.Y. State Bar Assn., Fla. Bar Assn. Jewish. Avocations: writing and editing. Home: 4411 SW 34th St Gainesville FL 32608-2562 Office: PO Box 140119 Gainesville FL 32614-0119

KAIMOWITZ, JEFFREY HUGH, librarian; b. N.Y.C., Nov. 3, 1942. A.B., Johns Hopkins U., 1964; Ph.D. in Classics, U. Cin., 1970; M.S. in Library Service, Columbia U., 1976. Asst. prof. Miami U., Oxford, Ohio, 1969-73; librarian trainee N.Y. Pub. Library, N.Y.C., 1973-77; curator Watkinson Library Trinity Coll., Hartford, Conn., 1977—; bd. dirs. Capitol Region Library Council, Windsor, Conn., 1982-85. Contbr. articles to profl. jours. Fulbright fellow 1966; Woodrow Wilson Found. fellow, 1964. Mem. ALA, Am. Philol. Assn., Bibliog. Soc. Am., Am. Printing History Assn. (v.p. for publs., 1988-89), Conn. Acad. Arts and Scis., Conn. Hist. Soc., Classical Assn. New Eng., Jewish Hist. Soc. Hartford (bd. dirs. 1981-92), Phi Beta Kappa, Beta Phi Mu. Clubs: Grolier, Appalachian Mountain (Boston), Columbiad (Meriden, Conn.). Avocations: hiking; cross country skiing; reading; book collecting. Home: 50 Silo Way Bloomfield CT 06002-1653 Office: Trinity College Watkinson Library 300 Summit St Hartford CT 06106-3186

KAIN, RICHARD YERKES, electrical engineer, researcher, educator; b. Chgo., Jan. 20, 1936; s. Richard Morgan and Louise Kinsey (Yerkes) K.; m. Helen Buchanan, Dec. 16, 1961 (div. 1980); children—Helen, Karen, Susan; m. Katherine Simon Frank, Aug. 4, 1981. BS, MIT, 1957, MS, 1959, ScD, 1962. Asst. prof. elec. engring. MIT, Cambridge, 1962-66; assoc. prof. elec. engring. U. Minn., Mpls., 1966-77, prof., 1977-98; cons. in field. Author: Automata Theory, 1972 (transl. to Japanese 1978), Computer Architecture, 2 vols., 1989, Advanced Computer Architecture, 1996. Recipient Goodwin medal MIT, 1961. Mem. IEEE (sr.), Assn. Computing Machinery, AAAS, Sigma Xi, Eta Kappa Nu. Office: U Minn Dept Elec Engring/Computer 200 Union St Minneapolis MN 55455

KAIN, RIKKI FLOYD, investment company executive; b. Plymouth, Ind., Aug. 26, 1958; s. Floyd Dale and Marjean Ann (Winter) K.; m. Katherine Rhoades, July 30, 1983; children: Matthew, Benjamin, Austin. BS, Ball State U., 1981. CPA, Ind. Sr. acct. McGladrey & Pullen, Elkhart, Ind., 1981-86; v.p. fin. Rockwood, Inc., Goshen, Ind., 1986-91; sr. v.p. corp. devel., treas., sec. Starcraft Automotive Corp., Goshen, 1991-96; founder, CEO, Emmanuel Investments, Inc., Elkhart, 1996—. Treas. Riverview Adult Day Ctr., Elkhart, 1991—. Mem. AICPA, Ind. CPA Soc. Republican. Methodist.

KAINEN, JACOB, artist, former museum curator; b. Waterbury, Conn., Dec. 7, 1909; s. Joseph and Fannie (Levin) K.; m. Bertha Friedman, Aug. 28, 1938; children: Paul Chester, Daniel Bernard; m. Ruth Priscilla Cole, Feb. 19, 1969. Grad., Pratt Inst., 1930; postgrad., N.Y.U., 1936-38, George Washington U., 1944-46; DFA (hon.), Corcoran Sch Art, 1992. Aide div. graphic arts U.S. Nat. Mus., Smithsonian Instn., Washington, 1942-44; asst. curator U.S. Nat. Mus., Smithsonian Instn., 1944-46, curator, 1946-66; curator Nat. Collection Fine Arts, 1966-70, spl. cons., 1970-82; lectr. painting and history graphic arts U. Md., 1970-71. Work represented in permanent collections, Met. Mus. Art, Corcoran Gallery of Art, Phillips Collection, Carnegie Inst., Balt. Mus. Art, Art Inst. Chgo., Kunsthalle, Hamburg, Germany, Brit. Mus., Hirshhorn Mus. and Sculpture Garden, Yale U. Mus. Art, Phila. Mus. Art, N.Y.U., Newark Mus., U. Neb., Bezalel Nat. Mus., Jerusalem, Nat. Gallery of Art, Mus. Modern Art, Whitney Mus. Am. Art, Bklyn. Mus. Art, Portland (Ore.) Mus. Art, Achenbach Found. Graphic Arts, Grunwald Ctr. Graphic Arts, San Francisco Mus. Art, Cleve. Mus. Art, Nat. Mus. Am. Art, Addison Gallery Am. Art, others.; author: George Clymer and the Columbian Press, 1950, The Half Tone Screen, 1951, Why Bewick Succeeded, 1959, John Baptist Jackson: 18th Century Master of the Color Woodcut, 1962, The Etchings of Canaletto, 1967; painting retrospective Nat. Mus. Am. Art, 1993, Mixed Media color print Smithsonian Assocs., 1989, Cleveland Print Club, 1977, Floor Medallion Nat. Airport, Washington, 1994-97; also articles. Research grantee Am. Philos. Soc., 1956. Mem. Print Council Am. (dir.). Home: 27 W Irving St Chevy Chase MD 20815-4263

KAINLAURI, EINO OLAVI, architect; b. Lahti, Finland, June 13, 1922; came to U.S., 1947, naturalized, 1954; s. William and Eva K.; m. Genevieve Marjorie Mobley, Aug. 20, 1949; children: John Stanford, William Eino, Mary Ann. Student, Finland Inst. Tech., 1945-47; B.Arch., U. Mich., 1950, M.Arch., 1959, Ph.D., 1975. Draftsman U. Mich. Architect's Office, Ann Arbor, 1951-55; dealer systems planner Ford div. Ford Motor Co., Livonia, Mich., 1955-56; ptnr., gen. mgr. Davis, Kainlauri & MacMullan (architects, engrs., planners), Ann Arbor, 1956-59; pres. KMM Assocs. (architects, engrs., planners), Ann Arbor, 1959-75; prof. architecture Iowa State U., Ames, 1975-92, prof. emeritus, 1992—. Works include Finnish Cultural Ctr., Farmington, Mich., also schs. and chs.; author: Multinational Cooperation in Regional Planning for Lapland, 1976; editor proc. internat. symposia and confs.; contbr. numerous articles to profl. jours. Served to 1st lt. Finnish Army, World War II. Decorated cross and medal of Liberty; Fulbright Hayes sr. scholar, 1973-74; Fulbright rsch. scholar, 1983-84; recipient Knighthood of the Order of White Rose, 1st Class, Finland, 1993. Fellow AIA (design com., Architects in Edn.); mem. ASTM, ASHRAE (disting. svc. awrad 1995), Soc. Bldg. Sci. Educators, Nat. Trust Historic Preservation, Am. Solar Energy Soc., Internat. Solar Energy Soc., Am.-Scandinavian Found., Finnish-Am. Soc., Intelligent Bldgs. Inst., Finland Soc. Lutheran. Clubs: Optimist (life), Lions. Home: 3604 Ross Rd Ames IA 50014-3964 Office: Iowa State U Dept of Architecture Coll of Design Ames IA 50011 *As an advocate of life-long learning, I feel that what really counts is what you learn after you "know it all." Too often, we limit our opportunities by what we learn at a university or during the first years in a profession. We need to continue and expand our knowledge for wider opportunites in the world.*

KAINTHLA, RAMESH CHAND, manufacturing company executive; b. Shimla, India, Feb. 18, 1954; came to U.S., 1983; s. Hira Nand and Belku (Devi) K.; m. Neetu Dua, Aug. 9, 1981; children: Priyanka, Radhika. BS, HP Univ., Shimla, 1973, MS in Physics, 1975; PhD in Physics, IIT Delhi, India, 1980. Rsch. assoc. IIT Delhi, 1980-81, U. NSW, Sydney, Australia, 1981-83; rsch. assoc. Tex. A&M U., College Station, 1984-86, sr. rsch. assoc., 1986-88, rsch. scientist, 1988-89; v.p. Rechargeable Battery Corp., College Station, 1989—; dir. Rechargeable Battery Corp., 1990—. Contbr. articles to profl. jours.; patentee in field. Mem. Electrochem. Soc. Avocations: music, movies, gardening, Web creation. E-mail: kainthla@tca.net. Office: Rechargeable Battery Corp 809 University Dr # 100E College Station TX 77840

KAISCH, KENNETH BURTON, psychologist, priest; b. Detroit, Aug. 29, 1948; s. Kenneth R. Kaisch and Marjorie F. (Howe) Bourke; m. Suzanne Carol LePrevost, Aug. 31, 1969; 1 child, Samuel. BA, San Francisco State U., 1972; MDiv, Ch. Divinity Sch. Pacific, 1976; MS, Utah State U., 1983, PhD in Clin. Psychology, 1986. Ordained deacon Episcopal Ch., 1976, priest, 1977; lic. clin. psychologist, Calif. Intern local parish, 1973-76; ordinand tng. program Ch. of the Good Shepherd, Ogden, Utah, 1976-77; pastor St. Francis' Episc. Ch., Moab, Utah, 1977-80, St. John's Episc. Ch., Logan, Utah, 1980-84; psychol. asst. Peter Ebersole, Ph.D., Fullerton, Calif., 1984-86; intern in clin. psychology Patton State Hosp., Calif., 1985-86; psychol. asst. Ronald Wong Jue, Ph.D., Fullerton and Newport Beach, Calif., 1986-88; pvt. practice clin. psychologist Calif., 1988—; clin. dir. Anxiety Clinic, Fullerton, 1993—; exec. dir. Contemplative Congress, Fullerton, 1988-91, Inner Peace Conf., 1995-97; founder, pres. OneHeart, 1986-98, Contemplative Visions, Fullerton, 1990—; supply priest Episc. Diocese of L.A.; invited lectr. Acad. Sch. Profl. Psychology, Moscow, 1992, 93, Moscow Med. Acad., 1998. Co-author: Fundamentals of Psychotherapy, 1984, Developing Your Feel for Golf, 1998; author: Finding God: A Handbook of Christian Meditation, 1994, The Mental Golf Inventory, 1998; co-editor: God in Russia: The Challenge of Freedom, 1999; contbr. numerous articles to profl. jours. Mem. St. Andrew's Episc. Ch., Fullerton. Mem. APA, Calif. Psychol. Assn., Anxiety Disorders Assn. Am., Nat. Register of Health Svc. Providers in Psychology, Phi Kappa Phi, Rotary (past bd. dirs., past officer). Episcopalian. Office: 2555 E Chapman Ave Ste 617 Fullerton CA 92831-3621

KAISER, ALBERT FARR, diversified corporation executive; b. N.Y.C., May 14, 1933; s. Albert Louis and Lucille (Daggett) K.; m. Joy E. White, Sept. 16, 1961; children—Elizabeth Ann, Albert Farr. BA, Hamilton Coll., Clinton, N.Y., 1955; MBA, Harvard U., 1960. With acquisitons dept. AMF Inc., 1960-61; with data processing div. IBM Corp., 1961-84; with Sperry and Hutchinson Co., 1974-82; pres. The Gunlocke Co., Inc., 1977-79, pres. promotional services div., also chmn. motivation and travel div., 1979-80; corp. exec. v.p. Sperry and Hutchinson, Inc., N.Y.C., 1980-82; investment banker J.J. Lowrey & Co., N.Y.C., 1983-84; pres. ABB Power Distbn. Inc., 1984-92; ret., 1992—. Served to lt. (j.g.) USNR, 1955-58. Mem. Hamilton Coll. Aumni Assn. (former pres. Westchester County chpt.), Fox Meadow Tennis Club (Scarsdale), Bradenton Country Club. Republican. Mem. Reformed Ch. Am. Home: PO Box 2205 105 Sunset Ln Anna Maria FL 34216

KAISER, ANN, municipal agency administrator; b. Watertown, N.Y., 1946. BA, St. Lawrence U., 1970; MA in Pub. Adminstrn., Pace U., 1984. Sr. case worker Westchester County Dept., White Plains, N.Y., 1970-78; program dir. Hastings (N.Y.) Youth Project, 1978-84; asst. exec. dir. Cage Teen Ctr., White Plains, 1984-89; dir. bur. youth svcs. City of Yonkers, N.Y., 1989—. Office: City of Yonkers Bur Youth Svcs 285 Nepperhan Ave Yonkers NY 10701-3425*

KAISER, ANN CHRISTINE, magazine editor; b. Milw., Apr. 7, 1947; d. Herbert Walter and Annette G. (Werych) Gohlke; m. Louis Dan Kaiser; children: Richard L., Michael D. BS in Journalism, Northwestern U., 1969. Reporter Waco (Tex.) Tribune-Herald, 1969-71; editor Country Woman, Greendale, Wis., 1971—; mng. editor Taste of Home, Greendale, 1993—. Named among People of the Yr., Milw. Mag., 1998. Lutheran. Avocations: sailing, tennis, golf, travel. Office: Reiman Publs 5400 S 60th St Greendale WI 53129

KAISER, DANIEL HUGH, historian, educator; b. Phila., July 20, 1945; s. Walter Christian and Estelle Evelyn (Jaworsky) K.; m. Jonelle Marie Marwin, Aug. 10, 1968; children: Nina Marie, Andrew Eliot. AB, Wheaton Coll., 1967; AM, U. Chgo., 1970, PhD, 1977. Asst. prof. history U. Chgo., 1977-78; asst. prof. history Grinnell (Iowa) Coll., 1979-84, assoc. prof., 1984-86, prof. history, 1986—, Joseph F. Rosenfield prof. social studies, 1984—, chair dept. history, 1988-90, 96-98; mem. adv. bd. Soviet Studies in History, 1979-85; rsch. assoc. dept. Slavonic studies, vis. mem. Darwin Coll., Cambridge (Eng.) U., 1992-93; vis. prof. dept. Slavic langs. and lits. Ctr. for Medieval and Renaissance Studies, UCLA, 1996. Author: The Growth of the Law in Medieval Russia, 1980; editor: The Workers' Revolution in Russia, 1917, 1987; translator, editor: The Laws of Rus' Tenth to Fifteenth Centuries, 1992; co-editor: (with Gary Marker) Reinterpreting Russian History 860-1860s, 1994; editl. bd. Slavic Rev., 1996—. Elder 1st Presbyn. Ch., Grinnell, 1985, 87-89. FEllow Nat. Endowment Humanities, 1979, 92-93, John Simon Guggenheim Meml. Found., 1986, Fulbright-Hays Faculty Rsch. Abroad Found., 1986, Woodrow Wilson Internat. Ctr. Scholars, 1986, Internat. Rsch. Exchs. Bd. fellow to USSR/Russia, 1974-75, 78-79, 86, 93. Mem. Am. Assn. for Advancement Slavic Studies, Am. Hist. Assn., Early Slavic Studies Assn. (v.p., pres. 1997-99), Slavonic and East European Medieval Studies Group (U.K.), Study Group on 18th Century Russia (U.K.), 18th Century Russian Studies Assn. Office: Grinnell Coll Dept History PO Box 805 Grinnell IA 50112-0805

KAISER, DON, media trainer; b. St. Louis, Apr. 25, 1961; s. Donald L. and Shirley Lois K. B of Journalism, U. Mo., 1990; MA, U. Ill., 1994. Political reporter KIMU-TV, Jefferson City, Mo., 1988-92; state capitol bur. chief WCIA-TV/WMBD-TV, Champaign, Peoria, Ill., 1992-96; Santa Fe bur. chief KRQE-TV, Albuquerque, 1996-98; pres. Media Synergy, Inc., Santa Fe, N.Mex., 1998—. Author: Guerilla Public Relations, 1998. Recipient NATAS Emmy award, 1994. Mem. Pub. Rels. Soc. Am., Ill. News Broadcasters Assn. (com. chair 1993—), Women in Comm., Soc. Profl. Journalists. Republican. Roman Catholic. Avocations: travel, history, biographies. Office: Media Synergy Inc 369 Montezuma Ave #202 Santa Fe NM 87501

KAISER, GLEN DAVID, construction company executive; b. David and Margaret Jane (Frye) K.; m. Pamela Blyo Barris, Sept. 7, 1972 (div. 1974); m. Pamela Blyo Barris, Nov. 7, 1976; children: Barris David, Katrina Tara. BS in Civil Engring., Stanford U., 1974, MS in Constrn. Mgmt., 1975. Registered profl. engr., Nev., Calif. Constrn. engr. Kaiser Engrs., Oakland, Calif., 1975-79; project coord. Corrao Constrn., Reno, 1979-81; chief estimator Marnell Corrao Assocs., Las Vegas, Nev., 1981-82, exec. v.p., 1982-91, pres., 1991—. Bd. dirs. Pop Warner, Las Vegas, 1991-93, Las Vegas Symphony, 1992-93. Mem. Associated Gen. Contractors (2d v.p. 1992, sec.-treas. 1993), Sigma Chi Alumni Assn., Stanford U. Alumni Assn. Roman Catholic. Avocations: snow skiing, horseback riding, golf. Office: Marnell Corraeo Assocs 4495 S Polaris Ave Las Vegas NV 89103-4119*

KAISER, GREG CHRISTOPHER, pediatric gastroenterologist; b. Tampa, Fla., Mar. 24, 1966; s. Alexander and Elinor (Blackwell) K. BS, Furman U., 1988; MD, U. Fla., 1992. Diplomate Am. Bd. Pediatrics, Am. Bd. Pediatric Gastroenterology. Intern Orlando (Fla.) Regional Healthcare Sys., 1992-93, resident in pediats., 1993-95; chief resident in pediats. Orlando Regional Hosp., 1994-95; fellow in pediat. gastroenterology Vanderbilt U. Med. Ctr., Nashville, 1995-98; pediat. gastroenterologist All Children's Hosp., St. Petersburg, Fla., 1998—. Contbr. articles to profl. jours. Football referee Fla. H.S. Athletic Assn., Tampa, 1996—. Recipient Elliot V. Newman Rsch. award Vanderbilt U., 1998. Mem. AMA (polit. action com. 1992—), Am. Acad. Pediats., Am. Gastroenterology Assn., N.Am. Soc. for Pediat. Gastroenterology and Nutrition (Rsch. award 1997, 98), Phi Beta Kappa. Republican. Office: All Childrens Hosp Dept Pediat Gastroent 480 7th Ave S Saint Petersburg FL 33701-4839

KAISER, KENNETH J., umpire; b. Rochester, N.Y., July 6, 1945; 2 children. Student, Al Somers Sch. Former umpire Carolina League, Ea. League, Internat. League; umpire maj. league baseball Am. League, N.Y.C., 1977—; with Umpires Union, Phila.; organizer Ken Kaiser Celebrity Dinner; spkr. in field. Office: Am League 350 Park Ave New York NY 10022 also: Umpires Union 1735 Market St Philadelphia PA 19103

KAISER, MARTIN, newspaper editor; b. Milw., Oct. 11, 1950. Editor Milw. Jour.- Sentinel, 1997—. Office: Milwaukee Journal PO Box 661 333 W State St Milwaukee WI 53203-1309*

KAISER, MICHAEL, performing company, foundation administrator. BA in Econs. magna cum laude, Brandeis U., 1975; MS in Mgmt. and Fin., MIT, 1977. Rsch. assoc. Harvard Econ. Rsch. Project, 1974-75; sr. assoc. Data Resources, Inc., 1975-77, Goldman Sachs & Co., 1977-78; v.p. Strategic Planning Assocs., 1978-81; pres., founder Michael M. Kaiser Assocs., Inc., 1981-85; exec. dir. State Ballet Mo., 1985-87; assoc. dir. Pierpont Morgan Libr., 1987-89; exec. dir. Alvin Ailey Dance Theater Found., 1991-93; pres., founder Kaiser Planning Group, known as Kaiser/Engler Group, 1989-90, 94-95; exec. dir. Am. Ballet Theatre, 1995—; cons. to chmn. Ernst & Young, 1994—; adj. prof. bus. adminstrn. Rockhurst Coll., Kansas City, Mo., 1985-86; adj. prof. arts adminstrn. NYU, N.Y.C., 1992—, U. Witwatersrand, Johannesburg, South Africa, 1995; guest lectr. instns. including Bus. Sch. Harvard U., U. Mich., Stanford U., Wharton Sch. Bus., U. Pa., 1978-85; developer video series on arts mgmt. for distbn. in South Africa, USIA; overseer confs. and publs. regarding strategic planning in the arts Dance U.S.A. Contbr. articles to profl. publs. Bd. dirs. N.Y. Found. for Arts; past bd. dirs. Alvin Ailey Dance Theater Found., Washington Opera, State Ballet Mo., Ensemble Studio Theater, PS 122. Office: Ballet Theatre Found 890 Broadway New York NY 10003-1211

KAISER, MICHAEL BRUCE, elementary education educator; b. New Albany, Ind., Mar. 6, 1949; s. Bobby Bruce and Maxine Delores (Roberts) K.; m. Patricia Gibson, Aug. 15, 1970; children: Lesa, Kevin, Todd. BS in Elem. Edn., Ind. U., Jeffersonville, 1971; MS in Elem. Edn., Ind. U., New Albany, 1977, MS, 1989. Reading tutor S. Ellen Jones Sch., New Albany, 1968-69; summer sch. aide Hazelwood Jr. High, New Albany, 1969-70; elem. tchr. Pine View Elem. Sch., New Albany, 1971—; gifted and talented coord. Project AHEAD, Ind. U. Southeast, New Albany, 1987—; tchr. creativity fellow Lilly Found., Ind., 1988. Recipient Profl. Best Leadership award Learning Mag., Oldsmobile Corp., Mich. State U., 1990, State Tchr. of Yr. award, Ind., Coun. of Chief State School Offices, 1992, Burger King Nat. Edn. award, 1992; inducted into Nat. Tchrs. Hall of Fame, 1995; Christa McAuliffe fellow, 1994. Mem. NEA, Ind. State Tchrs. Assn., New Albany-Floyd County Edn. Assn. Avocations: bubbleology, volleyball, camping. Office: Pine View Sch 2524 Corydon Pike New Albany IN 47150-6126

KAISER, PHILIP MAYER, diplomat; b. Bklyn., July 12, 1913; s. Morris and Temma (Sloven) K.; m. Hannah Greeley, June 16, 1939; children: Robert Greeley, David Elmore, Charles Roger. A.B., U. Wis., 1935; B.A., M.A. (Rhodes scholar), Balliol Coll., Oxford (Eng.) U., 1939. Economist, bd. govs. Fed. Res. System, 1939-42; chief project ops. staff, also chief planning staff enemy br. Bd. Econ. Warfare and Fgn. Econ. Adminstrn., 1942-46; expert on internat. orgn. affairs State Dept., 1946; exec. asst. to asst. sec. labor in charge internat. labor affairs, 1946-47; dir. Office Internat. Labor Affairs, Dept. Labor, 1947-49, asst. sec. labor for internat. labor affairs, 1949-53; labor adviser to Com. for Free Europe, 1954; spl. asst. to Gov. W. Averell Harriman of N.Y., 1955-58; prof. internat. rels. Sch. Internat. Svc. Am. U., 1958-61; U.S. ambassador to Republic Senegal, Islamic Republic Mauritania, 1961-64; minister Am. Embassy, London, Eng., 1964-69; chmn. Ency. Brit. Internat. Ltd., London, 1969-75; dir. Guinness Mahon Holdings, Ltd., 1975-77; ambassador to People's Republic of Hungary, 1977-80, Austria, 1980-81; professorial lectr. Johns Hopkins Sch. Advanced Internat. Studies, 1983-85, Woodrow Wilson vis. fellow, 1984; sr. cons. SRI Internat., 1981-97; mem. interdept. com. to develop programs under Marshall Plan, 1947-48, interdept. com. to develop programs for Greek-Turkish aid and Point 4 Tech. Assistance, 1947-49, Internat. del. to Hungary's Parliamentary elections, 1990. Author: Journeying Far and Wide: A Political and Diplomatic Memoir, 1993. Bd. dirs. Am. Ditchley Found., Ptnrs. for Dem. Change, Soros Hungarian Found., Coun. Am. Ambs., Assn. Diplomatic Studies, Am. Acad. Diplomacy. Decorated knight comdr. Austrian Govt., Cross of Order of Merit of Republic of Hungary. Mem. Am. Assn. Rhodes Scholars, Coun. Fgn. Rels., Washington Inst. for Fgn. Affairs, Phi Beta Kappa. Fax: 202-332-6124. Home: 2101 Connecticut Ave NW Washington DC 20008-1728

KAISER, ROBERT BLAIR, journalist; b. Detroit, Dec. 3, 1930; s. Robert Pisar and Olive Grace (Blair) Hungate; m. Susan Ann Mulcahey, Nov. 26, 1959 (div. July 7, 1964); m. Karen McCaffery, June 7, 1966 (div. Feb. 7, 1972); children: Margaret Anne, John Gustave, William Grant. BA, Gonzaga U., 1954, MA, 1955. Reporter Arizona Republic, Phoenix, 1958-61; corr. Time mag., N.Y.C., 1961-66; reporter New York Times, N.Y.C., 1979-81; prof., chmn. dept. journalism U. Nev., Reno, 1981-84; columnist The Tribune, San Diego, 1984-86; freelance journalist Phoenix, 1966—. Author: Pope, Council and World, 1963, R.F.K. Must Die!, 1970, Melvin Belli: My Life on Trial, 1976, Pat Haden: My Rookie Season with the Los Angeles Rams, 1977, The Politics of Sex and Religion, 1985, Life Is Too Short, 1991, Just Farr Fun, 1994, The Search for Sonny Skies, 1994, Jubilee 2000, 1998. Bd. dirs. Assn. for Rights of Caths. in the Ch., 1996—, Kino Inst., 1998—, Jesuit Alumni in AZ, 1997—. Mem. Overseas Press Club (Best Mag. Reporting of Fgn. Affairs 1963), Soc. of Profl. Journalists. Avocations: skiing, tennis, fly fishing. E-mail: rùkaiser@speedchoice.com. Office: PO Box 33698 Phoenix AZ 85067-3698

KAISER, ROBERT GREELEY, newspaper editor; b. Washington, Apr. 7, 1943; s. Philip Mayer and Hannah (Greeley) K.; m. Hannah Jopling, July 14, 1965; children: Charlotte Jerome, Emily Eli. B.A., Yale U., 1964; M.Sc., London Sch. Econs., 1967; postgrad., Columbia U., 1970-71. Reporter met. staff Washington Post, 1967-69, corr. Saigon Bur., 1969-70, bur. chief Moscow Bur., 1971-74, nat. corr., 1975-82, assoc. editor, columnist, 1982-85, asst. mng. editor for nat. news, 1985-90, dep. mng. editor, 1990-91, mng. editor, 1991-98, assoc. editor, sr. corr., 1998—; Vis. prof. Duke U., 1974-75, adj. prof., 1980-90. Author: Cold Winter, Cold War, 1974, Russia, The People and The Power, 1976, (with Jon Lowell) Great American Dreams, 1979, (with Hannah Jopling Kaiser) Russia From the Inside, 1980, Why Gorbachev Happened, 1991. Recipient Overseas Press Club award for best reporting from abroad, 1975. Mem. Coun. Fgn. Rels., Elihu Club. Office: Washington Post Co 1150 15th St NW Washington DC 20071-0002

KAISER, ROY, artistic director; b. Perth Amboy, N.J.. Studied ballet with, Karen Irvin; student, San Francisco Ballet Sch., Sch. Pa. Ballet. With Pa.

Ballet, 1979, prin. dancer, 1980-92, asst. ballet master, 1987-92, ballet master, 1992, assoc. artistic dir., 1993, interim artistic dir., 1994-95, artistic dir., 1995—; featured artists (with brothers) N.Y. World's Fair and throughout the U.S.; performer on TV with Wayne Newton, Music Carnival, Cleve., NBC-TV's Kraft Music Hall. Leading classical roles include Siegfried in Swan Lake, Franz in Coppelia, the Cavalier in The Nutcracker, Bolero, Symphonic Etudes, A Musical Offering; other prin. roles include George Balanchine's Symphony in C, Western Symphony, Symphony in Three Movements, Iago in The Moor's Pavane, Franklin Ct. Office: Pennsylvania Ballet 1101 S Broad St Philadelphia PA 19147-4410*

KAISER, SUZANNE BILLO, investment banker; b. Bronxville, N.Y., Apr. 9, 1948; d. Otto Emile and Barbara (Leggett) Billo; divorced; 1 child, Kate. Student, U. Lausanne, Switzerland, 1968, U. Paris, 1969; BA in Politics with honors, Hollins Coll., 1971; MBA, Georgetown U., 1997; MS, Columbia U. Sch Journalism, 1999. Staff mem. U.S. Congresswoman Margaret Heckler, Washington, 1971-72; adminstrv. officer internat. divsn. Kidder, Peabody & Co., Inc., N.Y.C., 1980-86; v.p., corp. sec. Concord Internat. Investments, N.Y.C., 1986—. Bd. dirs. Coun. Jr. Leagues Westchester, 1976-77, Bronxville (N.Y.) Mid. Sch. Coun., 1989-90, Bronxville Pub. Libr., 1990-95; mem. H.S. Coun., Bronxville Sch., 1992-93. Mem. Soc. Profl. Journalists, Bronxville Field Club, Hollins Club of N.Y., Georgetown U. Club (N.Y.C.). Office: Concord Internat Investment 667 Madison Ave New York NY 10021-8029

KAISER, WALTER, English language educator; b. Bellevue, Ohio, May 31, 1931. AB magna cum laude, Harvard Coll., 1954; PhD, Harvard U., 1960. Allston Burr sr. tutor Eliot House Harvard U., 1957-58; from instr. to assoc. prof. English, comparative lit. Harvard U., Cambridge, Mass., 1960-62, prof. English, comparative lit., 1969—, chmn. dept., 1969-75, 82-85; mem. coms. degrees in history and lit. Harvard U., 1960—, Faculty coun., 1971-74, libr. com., 1971-74; dep. dir. Villa I Tatti, Florence, 1971-86, dir. 1988—. Author: Praisers of Folly: Erasmus, Rabelais, Shakespeare, 1964, Essays of Montaigne, 1964; co-author Program in Literature and the Arts for the Core Curriculum, 1977; transl.: (with intro.) Three Secret Poems, (George Seferis), 1969, Alexis (Marguerite Yourcenar), 1984, Two Lives and a Dream (Marguerite Yourcenar), That Mighty Sculptor, Time (Marguerite Yourcenar), 1992, (with M. Mallon) On Artists and Art Historians: Selected Book Reviews of John Pope-Hennessy, 1994; edit. bd. Studies in English Lit., 1977-88; editor-in-chief I Tatti Studies: Essays in the Renaissance, 1988—; editor (with M. Mallon) On Artists and Art Historians: Selected Book Reviews of John Pope Hennessy, 1994; contbr. numerous articles, reviews, poems to profl. jours. Chair ad hoc vis. com. to Addison Gallery Am. Art, 1978; trustee Michael Rockefeller Meml. Fellowship, 1965-68, 69-70, Rockefeller Family Fund, 1973-79, Mus. Fine Arts, Boston, 1978-88; bd. dirs. Philip H. Rosenbach Found., 1974-78. Fulbright fellow U. Paris, 1954-55; Tower fellow Ecole Normale Supérieure Paris, 1955-56; fellow to Rome Am. Coun. Learned Socs., 1964-65; Walter Channing Cabot fellow Fac. Arts. and Scis., 1977-78. Mem. PEN, Boston Athenaeum, Am. Comparative Lit. Assn., Renaissance Soc. Am., Signet Soc. (assoc.), Modern Greek Studies Assn., Shakespeare Assn. Am., Coun. Fgn. Rels., Knickerbocker Club, Somerset Club, Harvard Club, Old Salopian, Boston Libr. Soc., Century Assn., Phi Beta Kappa. Home and Office: Villa I Tatti, via di Vincigliata 26, Florence 50135, Italy

KAISERLIAN, PENELOPE JANE, publishing company executive; b. Paisley, Scotland, Oct. 19, 1943; came to U.S., 1956; d. W. Norman and Magdalene Jeanette (Houlder) Hewson; m. Arthur Kaiserlian, June 29, 1968; 1 child, Christian. BA, U. Exeter, Eng., 1965. Copywriter, sales rep. Pergamon Press, Elmsford, N.Y., 1965-68; exhibits mgr. Plenum Pub., N.Y.C., 1968-69; asst. mktg. mgr. U. Chgo. Press, 1969-76, mktg. mgr., 1976-83, assoc. dir., 1983—. Mem. Soc. for Scholarly Pub., Am. Geog. Assn., Quadrangle Club. Office: U Chgo Press 5801 S Ellis Ave Chicago IL 60637-5418

KAISH, LUISE CLAYBORN, sculptor, former educator; b. Atlanta, Sept. 8, 1925; d. Harry and Elsa (Brown) Meyers; m. Morton Kaish, Aug. 15, 1948; 1 child, Melissa. BFA magna cum laude, Syracuse U., 1946, MFA, 1951; student, Escuela de Pintura y Escultura, Escuela de las Artes del Libro, Taller Grafico, Mexico, 1946-47. artist-in-residence Dartmouth Coll., 1974; prof. sculpture and painting, 1980-93, chmn. div. painting and sculpture Columbia U., 1980-86, prof. emerita, 1993; vis. artist U. Wash., Seattle, Battelle seminars and study program, Seattle, 1979; artist-in-residence U. Haifa, Israel, 1985. One-man shows Meml. Art Gallery, Rochester, N.Y., 1954, Sculpture Ctr., N.Y.C., 1955, 58, Staempfli Gallery, N.Y.C., 1968, 81, 84, 87, 88, Minn. Mus. Art, St. Paul, 1969, Jewish Mus., N.Y.C., 1973, U. Ark., 1990, The Century Assn., 1998; exhibited (with Morton Kaish), Rochester Meml. Art Gallery, 1958, USIS, Rome, 1973, Dartmouth Coll., 1974, Oxford Gallery, Rochester, 1988; represented in permanent collections Whitney Mus. Am. Art, N.Y.C., Met. Mus. Art, N.Y.C., Jewish Mus., N.Y.C., Export Khleb, Moscow, Minn. Mus. Art, Gen. Mills Corp., Minn., Rochester Meml. Art Gallery, Smithsonian Instn., Nat. Mus. Am. Art, Washington, also numerous pvt. collections, commns., Syracuse U., Temple B'rith Kodesh, Rochester, Temple Israel, Westport, Conn., Holy Trinity Mission Sem., Silver Springs, Md., Temple Beth Shalom, Wilmington, Del., Beth-El Synagogue Ctr., New Rochelle, N.Y., Temple B'nai Abraham, Essex City, N.J., Continental Grain Co., N.Y. Trustee Am. Acad. in Rome, 1973-81, mem. exec. com., 1975-81, trustee emerita, 1994; trustee St. Gaudens Found., 1978-90, mem. exec. com., 1980-90. Recipient awards Everson Mus., Syracuse, 1947, awards Rochester Meml. Art Gallery, 1951, awards Ball State U., 1963, awards Ch. World Service, 1960, awards Council for Arts in Westchester, 1974, Emily Lowe award, 1956, Audubon Artists gold medal, 1963, Honor award AIA, 1975, Arents Pioneer medal, Syracuse U., 1989; Louis Comfort Tiffany grantee, 1951; Guggenheim fellow, 1959; Rome prize fellow Am. Acad. in Rome, 1970-72. Mem. The Century Assn., NAD (elect), Eta Pi Upsilon. Home and Office: 610 W End Ave # 9-a New York NY 10024-1605

KAISH, MORTON, artist, educator; b. Newark, Jan. 8, 1927; s. Morris and Sophie (Furman) K.; m. Luise H. Meyers, Aug. 15, 1948; 1 dau., Melissa. BFA, Syracuse U., 1949; postgrad., Academie de la Grande Chaumiere, Paris, 1951, Istituto d' Arte, Florence, Italy, 1952, Accademia delle Belle Arti, Rome, 1957. Vis. critic Parsons Sch. Design, N.Y.C., 1966-70, Phila. Coll. Art, 1983; mem. faculty Art Students League, N.Y.C., 1974—; guest critic Sch. Visual Arts, N.Y.C., 1967; vis. prof. Queens Coll., Flushing, N.Y., 1979; vis. artist U. Wash., Seattle, 1979; fellow MacDowell Colony, 1976; artist-in-residence Dartmouth Coll., 1974, U. Haifa, Israel, 1985; prof. Fashion Inst. Tech., SUNY, N.Y.C., 1973—; vis. artist Susquehanna U., 1985; dir. Carl Fischer Mus. Instrument Co., 1964-70; vis. artist Columbia U., N.Y.C., 1986, Boston U., 1987. One-man shows include Manhattanville Coll., Purchase, N.Y., 1955, Rochester (N.Y.) Meml. Art Gallery, 1955, Guild Hall, Easthampton, L.I., 1969, U.S. Info. Service, Rome, 1973, Dartmouth ,Coll., Hanover, N.H., 1974, Staempfli Gallery, N.Y.C., 1964, 67, 71, 73, 79, 83, 86, 89, Oxford Gallery, Rochester, N.Y., 1989, Century Assn., N.Y., 1989, Hollis Taggart Galleries, Washington, 1993, N.Y.C., 1996; group shows Mus. Galleria 11 Torcoliere, Rome, 1957, Barone Gallery, N.Y.C., 1959, Art Inst. Chgo., 1964, Sheldon Meml. Art Gallery, Lincoln, Nebr., 1964, U. Nebr., Lincoln, 1964, Krannert Art Mus., U. Ill., Urbana, 1965, 68, Herron Mus. Art, Indpls., 1965, Mary Washington Coll., Fredericksburg, Va., 1965, Am. Acad. Arts and Letters, N.Y.C., 1966, Pa. Acad. Fine Arts, Phila., 1966, Ark. Art Ctr., Little Rock, 1966, Whitney Mus. Am. Art, N.Y.C., 1966, Finch Coll. Mus. Art, N.Y.C., 1966, N.J. State Mus., Trenton, 1966, Krannert Art Mus., 1968, Kent (Ohio) State U., 1970, U.S. Info. Service, Rome, 1972, New Sch. Social Research, N.Y.C., 1973, Child Hassam Purchase Fund Exhbn., N.Y.C., 1973; invitational exhbns. Child Hassam Purchase Fund, 1975, Am. Acad. Arts and Letters, 1975, Drawings U.S.A., 1975, Minn. Mus. Art, St. Paul, 1975, Springfield Art Mus., 1975, Springfield Mus. Art, Mo., 1975, Galerie Brusberg, Berlin, W.Ger., 1980, Taft Mus., Cin., 1981, NAD, N.Y.C., 1983, 85, 89, 91; represented in permanent collections Met. Mus. Art, N.Y.C., Whitney Mus. Am. Art, N.Y.C., Bklyn. Mus., Nat. Mus. Art, Smithsonian Instn., Washington, Brit. Mus., London, The Fitzwilliam Mus., Cambridge, Guild Hall, Easthampton, N.Y., Williams Coll., Williamstown. Mass., Syracuse U., N.Y., Swarthmore Coll., Indpls. Mus. Art, U. Mich. Mus. Art., Guilford Coll., Greensboro, N.C., Rochester (N.Y.) Meml. Art Gallery. Recipient SUNY Rsch. Found. award, 1983, Gervasi award, 1985, William Ward Ranger Fund purchase award, 1983, 85, Benjamin Altman prize, 1989, Andrew Carnegie prize, 1992, Disting. Alumni award for Achievement in the Visual Arts Syracuse U., 1989; faculty exch. scholar SUNY, 1987. Mem. NAD (corr. sec., William A. Paton prize 1983), Century Assn., Artists' Choice Mus. (bd. artists), Artists' Fellowship (trustee, v.p.). Address: 610 W End Ave New York NY 10024-1605

KAJI, HIDEKO KATAYAMA, pharmacology educator; b. Tokyo, Jan. 1, 1932; came to U.S., 1954; d. Sakae and Tsuneko (Matsuda) Katayama; m. Akira Kaji, Aug. 23, 1958; children: Kenneth, Eugene, Naomi, Amy. BS, Tokyo U. Pharm. Scis., 1954; MS, U. Nebr., 1956; PhD, Purdue U., 1958. Vis. scientist Oak Ridge (Tenn.) Nat. Lab., 1962-63; assoc. U. Pa., Phila., 1963-64; rsch. assoc. The Inst. Cancer Rsch., Phila., 1965-66, asst. mem., 1966-76; vis. mem. Max Planck Inst. Molek. Gen., Berlin, 1972-73, Nat. Inst. Med. Rsch., London, 1973; assoc. prof. Jefferson Med. Coll., Phila., 1976-82; vis. prof. Wistar Inst., Phila., 1984-85; prof. biochemistry and molecular pharmacology Jefferson Med. Coll., Phila., 1983—; cons. Nippon Paint Co., Ltd., Tokyo, 1990—, Coatesville (Pa.) VA Hosp., 1982-84. Contbr. articles to profl. jours. Fellow NIH (bd. dirs. 1986-89); mem. Am. Soc. Biochemistry and Molecular Biology, Am. Soc. Pharmacol. and Exptl. Therapeutics, Am. Soc. Microbiology, Sigma Xi. Home: 334 Fillmore St Jenkintown PA 19046-4328 Office: Jefferson Med Coll 1020 Locust St Philadelphia PA 19107-6731

KAK, NEERAJ, public health specialist; b. Kashmir, India, July 4, 1954; came to U.S., 1979; s. Ram Nath and Sarojini (Kaul) K.; m. Lily Patir, Jan. 22, 1981; children: Rahul, Manisha. PGDBM, U. Jammu, India, 1975; PhD, SUNY, Stony Brook, 1984; postgrad., Johns Hopkins U., 1985. Mem. rsch. staff Johns Hopkins U., Balt., 1985-86; sr. scientist Univ. Rsch. Corp., Bethesda, Md., 1987-93; sr. assoc. Futures Group Internat., Washington, 1993—; resident advisor Nat. Population Coun., Egypt, 1994-95, Nat. Family Planning Coordinating Bd., Indonesia, 1987-91. Population Coun. fellow, 1983. Mem. APHA, Am. Soc. for Quality. Home: 28 Hollyberry Ct Rockville MD 20852-4222 Office: Futures Group Internat 1050 17th St NW Washington DC 20036-5503

KAKOS, GERARD STEPHEN, thoracic and cardiovascular surgeon; b. N.Y.C., Mar. 15, 1943; s. Stephen George Kakos and Margaret Misouic; m. Diana Toon, Dec. 19, 1964; children: Stephanie Lynn, Anna Katherine, Kristin Margaret. BA, Ohio State U., 1963, MD, 1967. Bd. cert. Am. Bd. Surgery, Am. Bd. Thoracic Surgery; lic., Ohio. NIH rsch. fellow in cardiovasc. surgery Duke U. Med. Ctr., Durham, N.C., 1970-71; intern in surgery Coll. Medicine Ohio State U., Columbus, 1967-68, asst. resident in surgery Coll. Medicine, 1969-73, sr. resident in surgery Coll. Medicine, 1971-72, adminstrv. chief resident in surgery Coll. Medicine, 1971-72, chief resident thoracic & cardiovasc. surgery Coll. Medicine, 1972-73, from asst. prof. to assoc. prof. surgery Coll. Medicine, 1970-85, assoc. clin. prof. surgery Coll. Medicine, 1985—; chief divsn. thoracic surgery dept. surgery Ohio State U., Columbus, 1984-86, assoc. dir. working party for therapy of lung cancer (Nat. Cancer Inst.), 1973-76. Contbr. numerous articles to med. jours. Bd. dirs. Franklin County chpt. Cen. Ohio Heart Assn., 1978, Columbus Sch. for Girls, 1993-95. Capt. U.S. Army, 1968-76. Fellow ACS; mem. AMA, Internat. Soc. for Surgery, Am. Assn. Thoracic Surgery, Soc. for Vascular Surgery, Soc. Thoracic Surgery, Assn. for Acad. Surgery, Ohio State Med. Assn., Ohio State U. Hosps. Med. Soc., Columbus Surg. Soc., Acad. Medicine of Columbus and Franklin County, R. M. Zollinger Club, Alpha Epsilon Delta, Alpha Omega Alpha, Sigma Xi (Ohio state chpt.). Republican. Roman Catholic. Avocations: hunting, scuba diving. Office: Cardiothoracic Surgeons Inc 300 E Town St Fl 12 Columbus OH 43215-4632*

KAKU, MICHIO, theoretical nuclear physicist, educator; b. San Jose, Calif., Jan. 24, 1947; s. Toshio and Hideko (Maruyama) K. BA, Harvard U., 1968; PhD, U. Calif., Berkeley, 1972; PhD (hon.) Hofstra U., 1997, SUNY, Old Westbury, 1997. Rsch. assoc. Princeton U., N.J., 1972-73; assoc. prof. CCNY and Grad. Ctr., 1973-83, prof., 1983—; vis. prof. NYU, 1988, Inst. for Advanced Studies at Princeton U., 1990. Author: Nuclear Power: Both Sides, 1983; Beyond Einstein, the Cosmic Quest for the Theory of the Universe, 1986, Introduction to Superstrings, 1988, Strings, Conformal Fields, and Topology, 1991, Quarks, Symmetries, and Strings, 1991, Quantum Field Theory: A Modern Introduction, 1993, Hyperspace: A Scientific Odyssey Through Parallel Universes, Time Warps, and the 10th Dimension, 1994, Frontiers in Quantum Field Theory, 1996, Visions: How Science Will Revolutionize the 21st Century, 1997; contbr. 70 articles to profl. jours. Fellow Am. Phys. Soc. Avocations: nuclear arms control, nuclear power. Office: CCNY Physics Dept 138th St at Convent Ave New York NY 10031

KAKUGAWA, TERRI ETSUMI, osteopath; b. Honolulu, Sept. 16, 1965; d. Paul Katsumi and Ruby Yetsuko (Oshiro) K.; m. Colin Tamashiro. BA, U. Hawaii, 1987; DO, Kirksville Coll. Osteo. Medicine, 1992. Diplomate Am. Bd. Osteo. Family Physicians. Intern Cmty. Health Ctr., Branch County, Coldwater, Mich., 1992-93, resident in family medicine, 1993-95; group practice Waianae, Hawaii, 1995—. Mem. Am. Osteo. Assn., Am. Coll. Osteo. Family Physicians, Hawaii Assn. Osteo. Physicians and Surgeons. Democrat. Avocations: reading, cooking, travel. Office: Waianae Coast Comprehensive Health Ctr 87-2070 Farrington Hwy Waianae HI 96792-3757

KAKUTANI, MICHIKO, critic. Chief book critic N.Y. Times, N.Y.C. Recipient Pulitzer prize for criticism, 1998. Office: c/o NY Times 229 W 43d St New York NY 10036*

KALABA, ROBERT EDWIN, applied mathematician; b. Mt. Vernon, N.Y., Sept. 21, 1926; s. Edwin Albert and Leona Margaret (Winkler) K.; m. Wilma Joy Becker, Dec. 23, 1950; children: Robert John, Darlene Day, Kathy Lynn, Richard William. B.A., NYU, 1948, Ph.D., 1958. Mathematician Rand Corp., Santa Monica, Calif., 1951-70; prof. econs., elec. and biomed. engring U. So. Calif., Los Angeles, Calif., 1969—. Author: Quasilinearization and Nonlinear Boundary-Value Problems, 1965, Imbedding Methods in Applied Mathematics, 1973, Integral Equations via Embedding Methods, 1974, Control, Identification and Input Optimization, 1982, Numerical Derivatives and Nonlinear Analysis, 1986, A New Analytical Dynamics, 1995; founding editor Jour. Applied Math. and Computation, 1975; contbr. articles to profl. jours. Served with USN, 1945-46. Mem. IEEE (life), Assn. Computing Machinery, Math. Assn. Am., Phi Beta Kappa. Home: 370 Aderno Way Pacific Palisades CA 90272-3344 Office: U So Calif Los Angeles CA 90089

KALAFSKY, KURT M., architect; b. East Orange, N.J., June 1, 1965; s. Frank M. Jr. and Paula Ruth (Kratzke) K.; m. Joy Risner, Dec. 1, 1990; children: Connor, Courtney, Austin. Student, Syracuse U., 1983-87; BArch, N.Y. Inst. Tech., Old Westbury, 1990. Draftsman Samuel P. Abate &Assocs., Ocean, N.J., 1984-90, Bach & Rodetsky, Freehold, N.J., 1990; dir. CADD/CAP/CAPM Brenner, Newark, 1990-93; prin. The Aztec Corp./Aztec Architects, P.C., Iselin, N.J., 1993—. Pres., coach Ocean Twp. Pop Warner Football, 1987—. Mem. AIA, Constrn. Specification Inst. Office: The Aztec Corp 517 Route One South Iselin NJ 08830

KALAFUT, GEORGE WENDELL, distribution company executive, retired naval officer; b. Chgo., Feb. 21, 1934; s. George Andrew and Ann Catherine (Panak) K.; m. Alice Quinn, Nov. 9, 1957; children: Katherine, Tracy. AB in Econs., St. Joseph's Coll., Rensselaer, Ind., 1955; MBA, Harvard U., 1969. Commd. USN, 1956, advanced through grades to capt., 1976; asst dir. air equipment purchasing divsn. Naval Air Systems Command, Washington, 1969-71; dep. dir. F14/Grumman rev. team Naval Air Systems Command, Washington and Bethpage, N.Y., 1971; dir. airframes purchasing div. Naval Air Systems Command, Washington, 1972-73; supply officer USS Ranger CV61, San Francisco, 1973-75; dir. plans and budget Naval Supply Systems Command, Washington, 1976-78; retired USN, 1978; dir. inventories Motion Industries, Birmingham, Ala., 1979, v.p., 1980-83, v.p. fin., chief fin. officer, 1983-85, sr. v.p., 1985-89, also bd. dirs.; sr. v.p. fin. and adminstrn. Genuine Parts Co., Atlanta, 1989-91, exec. v.p. fin. and adminstrn., chief fin. officer, 1991—. Baker scholar Harvard Bus. Sch., 1969. Home: 1755 Spalding Dr Atlanta GA 30350-4321 Office: Genuine Parts Co 2999 Circle 75 Pky NW Atlanta GA 30339-3050

KALAHER, RICHARD A., company executive; b. Milw., Apr. 4, 1940; s. Williard Michael and May (Koch) K.; m. Ann Hoogland, Aug. 8, 1970; children: Richard Alan Jr., Kathleen Marie, Kimberly Ann, Alison Helene. AB, Union Coll., 1962; JD, Northwestern U., 1965. Bar: N.Y. 1966. Assoc. Shearman & Sterling, N.Y.C., 1965-66, 69-74; sr. atty. AMAX Inc., N.Y.C., 1974-75; v.p., gen. counsel AMAX Coal Co., Indpls., 1975-77; assoc. gen. counsel AMAX Inc., N.Y.C., 1977-85, v.p., assoc. gen. counsel, 1985-91, v.p., gen. counsel, 1991-94; acting gen. counsel, sec. Am. Stds. Inc., Piscataway, N.J., 1994-95; v.p., gen. counsel, sec. Am. Std. Cos. Inc., 1995—. Chmn. The Conf. Bd., Coun. Chief Legal Offices, 1996—. Capt. USAF, 1966-69. Office: American Standard Cos Inc One Centennial Ave Piscataway NJ 08855-6820

KALAI, EHUD, decision sciences educator, researcher in economics and decision sciences; b. Tel Aviv, Dec. 7, 1942; came to U.S., 1963; s. Meir and Elisheva (Rabinovitch) K.; m. Marilyn Lott, Aug. 24, 1967; children: Kerren, Adam. AB with distinction, U. Calif. at Berkeley, 1967; MS, Cornell U., 1971, PhD in Applied Math., 1972. Asst. prof. dept. statistics Tel Aviv U., 1972-75; vis. asst. prof. decision scis. J.L. Kellogg Grad. Sch. Mgmt. Northwestern U., Evanston, Ill., 1975-76, assoc. prof. decision scis., 1976-78, prof. managerial econs. and decision scis., 1978-82, The Charles E. Morrison Chair prof. decision scis., 1982—; prof. math. Northwestern U., Evanston, 1990—; IBM rsch. chair managerial econs. Northwestern U., Evanston, Ill., 1980-81, J.L. Kellogg rsch. chair in decision theory, 1981-82, chmn. meds. dept., 1983-85; dir. Ctr. for Strategic Decision-Making Kellogg Sch. Mgmt., Northwestern U., 1995—; Oskar Morgenstern rsch. prof. game theory NYU, 1991; expert testimony in ct. cases, 1982—; cons. Israeli Def. Forces, 1974-75, 1st Nat. Bank Chgo., 1987, ARthur Anderson, 1990, Kaiser Permanente, 1995. Founder, editor Games and Econ. Behavior Jour., 1988—; editl. bd. Math. Social Scis., 1980-90, Jour. Econ. Theory, 1980-88, Internat. Jour. Game Theory, 1984—; contbr. numerous articles on game theory and econs. to profl. jours. Sgt. Israeli Def. Forces, 1960-63. NSF grantee, 1979—; Sherman Fairchild Disting. scholar, Calif. Inst. Tech., 1994-95. Fellow Econometrics Soc.; mem. Am. Math. Soc., Pub. Choice Soc., Game Theory Soc. (founder, exec. v.p. 1998—), Beta Gamma Sigma. Home: 507 Greenleaf Ave Wilmette IL 60091-1913 Office: Kellogg Grad Sch of Mgmt Northwestern Univ Evanston IL 60208

KALAINOV, SAM CHARLES, insurance company executive; b. Steele, N.D., May 11, 1930; s. George and Celia Mae (Makedonsky) K.; m. Delores L. Holm., Aug. 10, 1957; children: John Charles, David Mark. B.S., N.D. State U., 1956. CLU. Life ins. agt. Am. Mut. Life Ins. Co., Fargo, N.D., 1956-60; supt. agys. Am. Mut. Life Ins. Co., Des Moines, 1960-70, sr. v.p. mktg., 1972-80, pres., chmn., CEO, 1980-95; v.p. agy. Western States Life Ins. Co., Fargo, 1970-72; chmn. bd. dirs. Am. Mut. Holding Corp., Amerus Life, 1995—; bd. dirs. Am. Coun. Life Ins., Washington, Bankers Trust, Des Moines; past chmn. Des Moines Devel. Corp. Bd. dirs. Luth. Health Sys., Fargo, 1974-91, City Corp., Des Moines, 1981-95, Civic Ctr. Ct., 1981-95, Iowa Luth. Hosp., 1982-91; trustee Drake U.; past chmn. Des Moines Conv. and Visitors Bur.; civilian aide to Sec. Army at Large, 1991; past state dir. Selective Svc. Sys. With inf. AUS, 1947-49, lt., 1952-55. Decorated Bronze Star; recipient Alumni Achievement award N.D. State U., 1983, Patrick Henry award Army Nat. Guard, 1998. Mem. Nat. Assn. Life Underwriters, Greater Des Moines C. of C. (past chmn., Nat. Leadership award 1978), Corp. for Internat. Trade (chmn.), Am. Legion, Rotary (past pres. Des Moines chpt.). Home: 681 50th St Des Moines IA 50312-1807 Office: AmerUs Group 699 Walnut St Des Moines IA 50309-3929

KALAJIAN-LAGANI, DONNA, publishing executive; b. Mountainside, N.J., Feb. 8, 1955; d. Jack and Analid Kalajian; m. Ron Galotti, Oct. 14, 1981. BS, Penn State U., 1975. Internat. credit analyst Irving Trust Co., N.Y.C., 1976-77; ad sales rep. BMT Pub., N.Y.C., 1977-79; ad sales rep. Woman's Day Mag., N.Y.C., 1979-81, cosmetics mgr., 1981-83, ea. mgr., 1984-87; v.p., advt. dir. Ladies' Home Jour., N.Y.C., 1987-89, v.p., pub., 1989—; pub./sr. v.p. Cosmopolitan Mag. Home: 100 Park Ave New York NY 10017-5516 Office: Cosmopolitan Hearst Magazines 224 W 57th St New York NY 10019-3299*

KALAMOTOUSAKIS, GEORGE JOHN, economist; b. Chios, Greece, July 26, 1936; came to U.S., 1953; s. John S. and Marika (Nikolaides) K.; 1 child, Yannis. B.A., CUNY, 1956, M.A., 1958; Ph.D., NYU, 1966. Instr. Fairleigh Dickinson, U., Teaneck, N.J., 1958-59; asst. prof. Ithaca (N.Y.) Coll., 1959-62; chief economist Brown Engr., N.Y.C., 1963-64; instr. Washington Sq. Coll., NYU, 1963-65; econ. cons. N.Y. State Office Regional Devel., Albany, 1964-66; adv. economist IBM, Armonk, N.Y., 1969-73; internat. economist Am. Standard, Inc., N.Y.C., 1973-76; prof. finance Grad. Sch. Bus., NYU, 1971-77; external dir. Rank-Xerox, Hellas, Greece, Atlantic Union Ins. Co., Athens, Greece; vis. prof. U. Md. European divsn. USAF, 1960, 67-68; head dept. pub. fin. Ctr. of Planning and Econ. Rsch., Athens, Greece; dir. econ. rsch. Bank of Greece, 1977-79; chief exec. officer, vice-chmn. bd. Bank of Crete, Athens, 1979-84; exec. dir., country head, gen. mgr. Greece, head Middle Ea. region Am. Express Bank Ltd., N.Y.C., 1985-94, fin. svcs. cons., 1995—; mem. William J. Fulbright Scholarship com., Athens; bd. dirs. Egyptian Am. Bank, Cairo, 1989-94. Contbr. articles to profl. jours.; Author books on internat. fin., Cyprus and self determination, common market and econ. devel. Greece. Bd. dirs., trustee Hellenic Theatre Found., bd. dirs. Aegian U., Greece. Am. Ford Found. Faculty Research fellow, 1962. Mem. Am. Econ. Assn., AAUP (v.p. chpt. 1961), Omicron Delta Epsilon. Home: 124 Lakeview Ave Lynbrook NY 11563-1755 Office: 43 Diamantidou Ave, Paleo Psychico 15452 Athens Greece

KALANT, HAROLD, pharmacology educator, physician; b. Toronto, Nov. 15, 1923; s. Max Isaac and Sophia (Shankman) K.; m. Oriana Josseau, July 22, 1948. M.D., U. Toronto, 1945, B.S. in Medicine, 1948, Ph.D., 1955. Intern. Toronto Gen. Hosp., 1945-46; resident in medicine Saskatoon Dept. Vets. Affairs Hosp., 1947, Toronto Gen. Hosp., 1948-49, Hospital del Salvador, Santiago, Chile, 1949-50; attending physician Bell Clinic, Toronto, 1952-55; Med. Research Council postdoctoral fellow in biochemistry Cambridge, Eng., 1955-56; biochemistry sect. head Def. Research Med. Labs., Toronto, 1956-59; assoc. prof., prof. pharmacology U. Toronto, 1959-89, prof. emeritus, 1989—; assoc. research dir. Addiction Research Found., Toronto, 1959-89; dir. emeritus Addiction Research Found., 1989—. Author: Experimental Approaches to the Study of Drug Dependence, 1969, Drugs, Society and Personal Choice, 1971, Alcoholic Liver Pathology, 1975; editor (Kalant & Roschlau) Principles of Medical Pharmacology. Chmn. bd. sci. counselors Nat. Inst. Alcohol Abuse and Alcoholism, Bethesda, Md., 1984-87; extramural sci. adv. bd. Nat. Inst. Drug Abuse, Rockville, Md., 1990-92; bd. dirs. Can. Centre on Substance Abuse, 1989-94. Served with M.C. Royal Can. Army, 1943-47. Recipient Nathan B. Eddy medal Coll. on Problems of Drug Dependence, 1986, Jellinek Meml. award for alcoholism rsch., 1972. Mem. Acad. Scis. Can., Pharm. Soc. Can. (Upjohn award 1985), Internat. Soc. Biomed. Rsch. on Alcoholism (pres. elect 1989, pres. 1990-94), Soc. Biol. Paris (fgn. corr. 1993—). Office: U Toronto, Dept Pharmacology, Toronto, ON Canada M5S 1A8

KALANTARI, BEHROOZ, political science educator; b. Dec. 12, 1952. BA in Bus. Adminstrn., Tehran (Iran) Bus. Coll., 1974; BA in Pub. Adminstrn., Avila Coll., Kansas City, Mo., 1981; MPA, So. Ill. U., 1984, PhD in Polit. sci., 1990. Asst. prof. No. State U., Aberdeen, S.D., 1990-93, N.C. Ctrl. U., Durham, 1993-97; assoc. prof. polit. sci. Savannah (Ga.) State U., 1997—. Office: Savannah State U PO Box 20385 Savannah GA 31404

KALAYJIAN, ANIE, psychotherapist, nurse, educator, consultant; b. Aleppa, Syria; came to U.S., 1971; d. Kevork and Zabelle (Mardikian) K.; m. Shahé Navasart Sanentz, Dec. 16, 1984. BS, L.I. U., 1979; MEd, Columbia U., 1981, EdD, 1985, profl. nursing tng. course, 1984; cert. photography, Pratt Inst., 1979. RN, N.Y., N.J., Conn.; cert. psychiat. mental health specialist; Dutch diplomate in logotherapy; advanced cert. in Eye Movement Desensitization and Reprocessing, advanced cert. in disaster mgmt. ARC; bd. cert. expert in traumatic stress. Psychiat. nurse Met. Hosp., N.Y.C., 1979-84; staff psychiat. mental health nurse Project Renewal, N.Y.C., 1978—; instr. Hunter Coll., N.Y.C., 1980-82; prof. Bloomfield Coll., N.J., 1984-85; lectr. Jersey City Coll., N.J., 1985; prof. Seton Hall U., South Orange, N.J., 1985-87; assoc. prof. grad. program St. Joseph Coll., 1987-91; prof. John Jay Coll. Criminal Justice Fairleigh Dickinson U., 1991-92, vis. prof., 1991-92; vis. prof. Pace U., N.Y.C., 1994-95; adj. prof. Coll. Mt. St.

Vincent, Riverdale, N.Y., 1995-97, Fordham U., 1998—, Coll. New Rochelle, 1998—, disting. lectr. Columbia U. N.Y.C., 1995; spkr. in field; keynote spkr. Mid Am. Logotherapy Inst., 1995, Coll. Mt. St. Vincent, 1995, Hollins Coll., Va., 1995, UN. Author: Disaster and Mass Trauma: Global Perspectives on Post Disaster Mental Health Management, 1995; contbr. articles to profl. jours., chpts. to books; reviewer: Readings: A Journal of Reviews and Commentary in Mental Health, 1990—. Active com. for presdl. task force on nursing curriculum Soc. for Traumatic Stress Studies; co-founder, East coast coord. Mental Health Outreach to Earthquake Survivors in Armenia; dir. Julia Richman-Pace U.-N.Y. State Bd. Edn.-Visiting Nurse Svc.-Partnership program, 1991-92; UN rep. World Fedn. for Mental Health, mem. mental health/human rights com., 1996—. Recipient Clark Found. scholarship award, 1985, Outstanding Rsch. award Columbia U., 1993, ABSA Outstanding Achievement award APA, 1995; rsch. grantee Pace U., 1992; Endowed Nursing Edn. Columbia U., scholar, 1984; Armenian Relief Soc. scholar, 1976-77, Armenian Students Assn. Am. scholar, 1976-78, Columbia U. Tchrs. Coll. Outstanding Rsch. award, 1993. Fellow Am. Orthopsychiat. Assn., N.Y. State Nursing Assn. (planning com. nursing edn.), APA (outstanding achievement award 1995); mem. Coun. on Continuing Edn., Psychiat. and Mental Health Nursing, Am. Psychol. Soc., Am. Psychiat. Nurses Assn., Am. Acad. Experts in Traumatic Stress, Internat. Coun. Psychologists, Internat. Trauma Counselors, Inst. for Psychodynamics and Origins of Mind, Armenian Students Assn. (treas. 1980-81, pres. 1981-83, scholarship chairperson 1983-85, v.p. Ctrl. Exec. com. 1987-88, pres. 1988-89, elected nat. pres. 1988-90), Armenian Info. Profls. (corr. sec. 1992—), Armenian-Am. Soc. for Studies on Stress and Genocide (founder, pres. 1988—), N.Y. Registered Nurses' Assn. (chairperson edn. com. 1989—), World Fedn. for Mental Health (UN rep. 1994—, treas., sec., UN com. on human rights 1994—, chair human rights com. 1996—), Univ. for Peace (corr. sec. UN com.), Internat. Soc. Traumatic Stress Studies (v.p. N.Y. chpt. 1993-95, pres. 1995—), N.Y. State Nurses Assn. (coun. Human Rights 1996—), N.Y. Counties RN Assn. (Jane Delano Disting. Svc. award 1994), Kappa Delta Pi (advisor 1989-90), Sigma Theta Tau (Alpha Zeta chpt. 1981—). Avocations: aerobics, photography, acting, hiking. E-mail: kalayjiana@aol.com. Office: 130 W 79th St New York NY 10024-6477

KALB, BENJAMIN STUART, television producer, director; b. L.A., Mar. 17, 1948; s. Marcus and Charlotte K. BS in Journalism, U. Oreg., 1969. Sportswriter, Honolulu Advertiser, 1971-76; traveled with tennis profl. Ilie Nastase; contbr. articles N.Y. Times, Sport Mag. and Tennis U.S.A., 1976; editor Racquetball Illustrated, 1978-82; segment producer PM Mag. and Hollywood Close-Up, 1983-86; exec. producer Ben Kalb Prodns., 1986—; instr. sports in soc. U. Hawaii, 1974-75. Producer (video) The Natural Way to Meet the Right Person, 1987; producer, dir. (video) Casting Call: Director's Choice, 1987, The Natural Way to Meet The Right Person (Best Home Videos of Yr. L.A. Times), (TV pilot and home video) Bizarro, 1988, (infomercial) How To Start Your Own Million Dollar Business, 1990, The Nucelle Promise, 1993-94, Koolatron Companion, 1997; prodr.-dir. (infomercials) Banamex USA Credit Card, 1995, Slimaster Exerciser, 1996, Koolatron Companion, 1997, Yonex Golf, 1998 (short feature film) Against the Ropes, 1996; segment dir. (home video) Movie Magic, 1990, (TV show) Totally Hidden Video; writer-segment dir. (home video) Making of The American Dream Calendar Girl, 1991; producer, host (cable TV show) Delicious Sports, 1987-88; segment dir. Totally Hidden Video (Fox TV Network), 1991-92; prodr., dir. short feature film Love Match, 1995. Served with Hawaii Army N.G., 1970-75. Named Outstanding Male Grad. in Journalism, U. Oreg., 1969. Mem. Sigma Delta Chi (chpt. pres. 1968). Democrat. Jewish. Contbr. articles to mags. and newspapers. Home: 3392 Brookfield Dr Las Vegas NV 89120-1964 Office: 3840 S Jones Blvd Las Vegas NV 89103-2228

KALB, JOHN W., manufacturing engineer; b. Columbus, Ohio, June 6, 1918. BS, Swarthmore Coll., 1940. Sr. devel. engr. Ohio Brass Co., 1940-63, dir. rsch., 1963-81; prin. Low Country Candles, 1981—. Mem. Nat. Acad. Engrs.; fellow Inst. Electric & Electronics Engrs. Home: 101 Pier Pont Condos 100 Floyd St Saint Simons GA 31522*

KALB, MARVIN, public policy and government educator. Diploma, CCNY; MA, Harvard U., postgrad. in Russian History. Prof. press and pub. policy John F. Kennedy Sch. Govt. Harvard U., dir. Joan Shorenstein Ctr. on Press, Politics, & Pub. Policy, 1987—; Edward R. Murrow prof. press and pub. policy JFK Sch. Govt., 1987—; host PBS series: Candidates '88; chief diplomatic corrs. CBS News, NBC News; moderator Meet The Press; sr. rsch. assoc. Ctr. for Sci. and Internat. Affairs; exec. com. Harvard's Russian Rsch. Ctr. Co-author: (with Hendrik Hertzberg) Candidates '88; author or co-author 7 non-fiction books, including: The Nixon Memo, Kissinger, Roots of Involvement: The U.S. and Asia, and 2 best-selling novels. Recipient numerous awards for excellence in diplomatic reporting including two Peabody prizes, U. Ga., DuPont prize, Columbia U., and numerous Overseas Press Club awards. Mem. Coun. on Fgn. Rels. Avocations: rsch. of ethical/polit. legacy of the Ten Commandments; Washington Redskins football. Office: Harvard U 79 Jfk St Cambridge MA 02138-5801*

KALBA, KAS, international telecommunications consultant; b. Wangen, Germany, Apr. 13, 1945; came to U.S., 1950; s. Simon J. and Sophia Kalba; m. Patricia A. Carvalho, June 18, 1966; children: Simon Michael, Sontine. BA, Yale U., 1966; MA in Communications, U. Pa., 1967, PhD, 1974. Staff asst. Sloan Commn. on Cable Communications, N.Y.C., 1970-71; lectr., instr. communications planning Harvard U., Cambridge, Mass., 1971-76; vis. lectr. mass media MIT, Cambridge, 1976-77; pres. Kalba Internat. Inc., Lincoln, Mass., 1973—. Mem. adv. com. Cable World (China). Trustee Cambridge Ctr. for Adult Edn., 1984-85, Pacific Telecomms. Coun., trustee, 1997—; mem. satellite comms. adv. com. U.S. Info. Agy., 1989-93. Mem. Internat. Inst. Comms., Mass. Telecomms. Coun., Internat. House of Japan. Office: Kalba Internat Inc Reservoir Pl 1601 Trapelo Rd Waltham MA 02451-7333

KALBFLEISCH, JOHN MCDOWELL, cardiologist, educator; b. Lawton, Okla., Nov. 15, 1930; s. George and Etta Lillian (McDowell) K.; m. Jolie Harper, Dec. 30, 1961. AS, Cameron A&M U., Lawton, 1950; BS, U. Okla., 1952, MD, 1957. Diplomate Am. Bd. Internal Medicine, Am. Bd. Cardiovascular Disease. Intern U. Va. Hosp., 1957-58; resident and fellow U. Okla. Med. Ctr., 1958-62, instr. medicine, 1964-66, asst. prof., 1966-69, assoc. clin. prof., 1970-78, clin. prof. Tulsa br., 1978—; pvt. practice Tulsa, 1969—; founder, chmn. bd., CEO Cardiology of Tulsa, Inc., 1969—; dir. cardiovascular svcs. St. Francis Hosp., Tulsa, 1975—; physician adv. bd. City of Tulsa, 1978-81; bd. dirs. St. Francis Hosp., exec. com., 1987-97; exec. v.p., chief med. officer St. Francis Health Sys., 1998—; treas. Tulsa Med. Edn. Found., 1988-89, v.p., 1990-92, pres., 1992-94; med. dir., chmn. bd. Warren Clinics, 1990-97; mem. Okla. Ctr. for Advancement of Sci. and Tech., 1989-95; mem. adv. com. Ctr. for Lasser Devel. and Applications, Okla. State U. Contbr. articles to profl. jours. With USPHS, 1962-64. Fellow ACP (gov.-elect Okla. 1990-91, gov. 1991-95, Okla. Laureate award 1995), Am. Coll. Cardiology (gov. Okla. 1978-81); mem. AMA, AAAS, Tulsa County Med. Soc., Okla. State Med. Assn., Am. Heart Assn. (Fellow coun. on clin. cardiology), tchg. scholar 1967-69), Okla. Soc. Internal Medicine v.p., pres.-elect 1983-84, pres. 1985-86), Am. Soc. Internal Medicine, Am. Fedn. Clin. Rsch., Am. Inst. Nutrition, U. Okla. Med. Alumni Assn. (Physician of Yr. in Pvt. Practice 1999), Delta Upsilon. Republican. Presbyterian. Office: 6151 S Yale Ave Ste 400 Tulsa OK 74136-8321

KALCEVIC, TIMOTHY FRANCIS, airline pilot, educator; b. Glenwood Springs, Colo., May 11, 1950; s. Victor and Marjorie Ann (Golden) K. BA in Acctg., Mich. State U., 1972; MBA cum laude, Roosevelt U., 1982; MA in Econs., U. Ill., Chgo., 1986; postgrad, U. Ill. CPA, Ill.; lic. airline transport pilot. Officer, pilot USN, various, 1972-79; pilot Am. Airlines, Chgo., 1979-81, 1984—; acct. Morton Mfg., Libertyville, Ill., 1981-82; acctg. mgr. Dexter Corp., Midland div., Waukegan, Ill., 1982-84; instr. McHenry County (Ill.) Coll., 1983; ind. cons. acctg. Waukegan, 1984-85. Lt. USN, 1972-79. Mem. Am. Econ. Assn., Allied Pilots Assn. (chmn. scheduling com. Chgo. chpt. 1989-91, chmn. chgo. chpt. 1991-93), Am. Ind. Cockpit Alliance (chmn. fin. 1994). Avocation: fishing. Office: Pilot-Am Airlines O'Hare Internat Airport PO Box 66065 AMF Ohare IL 60666

KALECH, MARC, newspaper editor. Managing editor New York Post, N.Y.C., 1993—. Office: NY Post 1211 Avenue Of The Americas New York NY 10036-8790*

KALELKAR, ASHOK SATISH, consulting company executive; b. Ahmedabad, India, June 10, 1943; came to U.S., 1960; s. Satish Dattatrey and Chandan (Parekh) K.; m. Joanne Bottiglieri, June 21, 1969 (div. Sept. 1983); children: Dorian, Jessie, Milan. BS in Math., George Wash. U., 1963; SBME, SMME, MIT, 1964, postgrad., 1966; PhD in Engring., Brown U., 1969. Sr. scientist Factory Mut. Rsch. Co., Norwood, Mass., 1969-71; staff Arthur D. Little Inc., Cambridge, Mass., 1971-76, sr. staff, 1976-80, v.p., 1980-85, sr. v.p., 1985; also bd. dirs. Arthur D. Little Inc., Cambridge, Mass., worldwide; chmn. bd. dirs. Program Sys. Mgmt. Co., Cambridge; bd. dirs. ADL Enterprises, Cambridge Cons. Ltd; chmn., pres. Arthur D. Little Internat.; dir. Arthur D. Little Ltd. Contbr. articles to profl. jours. Mem. Soc. for Risk Mgmt., Combustion Inst., Ops. Research Soc. Am. Unitarian. Avocations: fishing, boating, stamp collecting, bridge. Office: Arthur D Little Inc 25 Acorn Park Cambridge MA 02140-2301

KALER, ROBERT JOSEPH, lawyer; b. Boston, July 20, 1956; s. Robert Joseph and Joanne (Bowen) K. BA, Dartmouth Coll., 1978; JD, Am. U., 1981. Bar: D.C. 1981, Mass. 1983, U.S. Dist. Ct. D.C. 1982, U.S. Dist. Ct. Mass. 1984, U.S. Ct. Appeals (D.C. cir.) 1983, U.S. Dist. Ct. Appeals (1st cir.) 1984, U.S. Supreme Ct. 1986. Law clk. Sullivan & Cromwell, Washington, 1979-80, U.S. Dept. Justice, Washington, 1980-81; assoc. McKenna, Connor & Cuneo, Washington, 1981-83; ptnr. Gadsby & Hannah, Boston, 1983—. Contbr. articles to profl. jours. Mem. ABA, Internat. Bar Assn., Mass Bar Assn. Office: Gadsby & Hannah 225 Franklin St Boston MA 02110-2804

KALICK, LAURA JOY, lawyer, exempt organization tax speciality; b. N.Y.C., Mar. 1, 1949; d. Murray Gordon and Selma B. (Suekoff) Lowenthal; m. Theodore Kent Kalick, Oct. 22, 1972; children: Sara, Daniel, Lila. BA, U. Mich., 1970; JD, George Washington U., 1973; LLM in Taxation, Georgetown U., 1977. Bar: Pa. 1973, D.C. 1976. Tax law specialist Internal Review Svc., Washington, 1973-77; tax legis. counsel U.S. Senator Haskell, Washington, 1977-79; tax mgr. Laventhol & Horwath, Washington, 1979-85; tax dir. Coopers & Lybrand, Washington, 1985-97; tax sr. mgr. Ernst & Young LLP, 1997-99; pvt. practice Chevy Chase, Md., 1999—; adv. bd. Exempt Orgn. Tax Rev., Washington, 1990—. Primary author: Hospital Tax Management, 1983, NACUBO Guide to IRS Audits: A Manual for Colleges and Universities, 1994. Incorporator, former treas., Bethesda-Chevy Chase Ednl. H.S. Found., 1995-97, tax officer, 1997-98; subcom. chair of compensation and benefits, ABA exempt orgn. com. Chgo., 1995-97; subcom. co-chair Unrelated Bus. Income Tax., 1997—. Mem. ABA, Nat. Healthcare Fin. Mgmt. Assn., Am. Soc. of Assn. Execs., D.C. Bar Assn. Democrat. Jewish. Avocations: painting, swimming, gardening. E-mail: KalickEOTC@aol.com.

KALIHER, MICHAEL DENNIS, librarian, historian; b. Santa Monica, Calif., Nov. 7, 1947; s. Eugene Charles and Phyllis Joan (McCrary) K. BA, U. Ariz., 1990. Pres. Klamath County (Oreg.) Hist. Soc., 1985; founder Native Am. History Week, Klamath County Mus., 1985-86. Contbr. articles to various hist. jours. Mem. Ariz. Libr. Assn., Pi Lambda Theta, Phi Alpha Theta. Roman Catholic. Avocations: backpacking, trout fishing. Home: PO Box 634 Winslow AZ 86047-0634

KALIKOW, PETER STEPHEN, real estate developer, former newspaper owner, publisher; b. N.Y.C., Dec. 1, 1942; s. Harold J. and Juliet K.; m. Mary T. Jacobatos; children: Nicholas, Kathryn. BSBA, Hofstra U., 1965, LLD (hon.), 1986. With H.J. Kalikow & Co., N.Y.C., 1966—, pres., 1973—; owner N.Y. Post, 1988-93; bd. dirs. N.Y. State Mortgage Agy., 1981-86, chmn. ins. com. Gov. N.Y. Hosp. and Presbyn. Hosp.; trustee Hofstra U., Mus. Jewish Heritage; gen. chmn. real estate and constrn. divsn. Israel Bonds; apptd. to Met. Transit Authority, 1994, Port Authority of N.Y. and N.J., 1995. Recipient Israel Peace medal, Israeli Govt. 1982; named Alumnus of Yr., Hofstra U., 1988. Mem. N.Y. Athletic Club, Palm Beach Country Club, Fenway Club (Scarsdale, N.Y.), Royal Automobile Club (London). Office: H J Kalikow & Co LLC 101 Park Ave Fl 25 New York NY 10178-0002*

KALIKOW, THEODORA JUNE, university president; b. Lynn, Mass., June 6, 1941; d. Irving and Rose Kalikow. AB, Wellesley Coll., 1962; ScM, MIT, 1970; PhD, Boston U., 1974. From instr. to prof. Southeastern Mass. U., North Dartmouth, 1968-84; dean Coll. Arts and Scis., U. No. Colo., Greeley, 1984-87; dean of the coll. Plymouth (N.H.) State Coll., 1987-94, interim pres., 1992-93; pres. U. Maine, Farmington, 1994—. Contbr. articles to profl. jours., 1975—. Chair steering com. Maine ACE/NIP, 1995—; chair Coun. Pub. Liberal Arts Colls., 1997-99. NSF grantee, 1978; Am. Council on Edn. fellow Brown U., Providence, 1983-84. Mem. Am. Philos. Assn., Soc. Values in Higher Edn. (bd. dirs. 1991-94), Am. Coun. on Edn. (commn. on women 1994-97). Office: U Maine at Farmington Office of the Pres 86 Main St Farmington ME 04938-1911

KALIL, JAMES, SR., investment executive; b. Buffalo, Oct. 22, 1919; s. Harry and Nazira (Owens) Rossi; m. Claire Homsey, May 5, 1947; children: Donald, Janice, Laura, James Jr. BSChemE, CCNY, 1941; M in ChemE, Poly. U., Bklyn., 1947, PhDChemE, 1951. Rsch. engr. DuPont Co., Wilmington, Del., 1951-80; investment mgr., chmn. bd. dirs. Compu-Val Investments, Inc., Wilmington, 1974—; Contbr. articles to newspapers; patentee chem products and processes. Fellow Poly. U., 1989. Avocations: reading, travelling, writing. Office: Compu-Val Investments Inc 1702 Lovering Ave Wilmington DE 19806-2120

KALIN, D(OROTHY) JEAN, artist, educator; b. Kansas City, Mo., Feb. 11, 1932; d. William Warner and Esther Dorothy (Peterson) Johnson; m. John Baptist Kalin, Jr., Jan. 5, 1952; children: Jean Loraine, Debra Ann, Diana Yvonne. AA, St. Joseph (Mo.) Jr. Coll., 1951. Artist Hallmark Cards, Inc., Kansas City, Mo., 1952-53, 73-93; freelance artist Kansas City, 1953-72; owner Portraits of Life, Kansas City, 1986—, art tchr., 1988—. Illustrator article for Directory of Am. Portrait Artists, 1985; featured in Rockport Pubs. Best of Watercolor 2 and Painting Light and Shadow, 1997, Am. Artist Mag., 1998, Splash 5, 1998. Kansas City Art Inst. scholar, 1951-52. Mem. Nat. Oil and Acrylic Painters Soc. (signature mem.), Nat. Acrylic Painters Assn. (signature mem.), Kans. Watercolor Soc. (signature mem.), Women Artists of the West (signature mem.), Am. Watercolor Soc. (assoc.), Nat. Watercolor Soc. (assoc.), Midwest Watercolor Soc. (assoc.), Nat. Mus. Women in the Arts (charter mem.), Internat. Platform Assn. Avocations: gardening, traveling.

KALIN, ROBERT, retired mathematics educator; b. Everett, Mass., Dec. 11, 1921; s. Benjamin and Celia (Kraff) K.; m. Shirley Sharney, Oct. 22, 1944; children: Susan Leslie, John Benjamin; m. 2d Madelyn Pildish, Aug. 17, 1962; children: Sandra Kim, Richard Dean. Student, Northeastern U., 1940-43; BS, U. Chgo., 1947; MAT, Harvard U., 1948; PhD, Fla. State U., 1961. Tchr. math. Holten H.S., Danvers, Mass., 1948-49, Beaumont H.S., Hadley Tech. Sch., Soldan-Blewitt H.S., St. Louis, 1949-52; ednl. statistician Naval Air Tech. Tng. Ctr., Norman, Okla., 1952-53; test specialist, assoc. in research Ednl. Testing Svc., Princeton, N.J., 1953-55; exec. asst. Commn. on Math. of Coll. Entrance Exam. Bd., 1955-56; instr. dept. math. edn. Fla. State U., Tallahassee, 1956-61; asst. prof. Fla. State U., 1961-63, assoc. prof., 1963-65, prof., 1965-90; prof. emeritus Fla. State U., Tallahassee, 1990; assoc. dept. head Fla. State U., 1968-73, program chmn., 1975-78. Co-author: Elementary Mathematics, Patterns and Structure, 11 vols., 1966, (with George Green) Modern Mathematics for the Elementary School Teacher, 1966, (with E.D. Nichols) Analytic Geometry, 1973, Holt School Mathematics, 9 vols., 1974, rev. 1978, Holt Mathematics, 9 vols., 1981, rev., 1985, (with M.K. Corbitt) Prentice Hall Geometry, 1990, rev. edit., 1993. Mem., treas. Brownsville-Haywood County Libr. Bd., 1991-95, chmn., 1995-97; bd. dirs. Friends of Tenn. Librs., 1995—, sec., 1996-97, pres.-elect, 1997-99; pres. Temple Adas Israel, 1992-94, treas., 1994—; bd. dirs. Jewish Hist. Soc. of Memphis and the Mid-South, 1998—. Mem. Math. Assn. Am. (sec.-treas. Fla. sect. 1985-91, Svc. award Fla. sect. 1991), Fla. Coun. Tchrs. Math. (pres. 1960-61), Fla. Assn. Math. Educators (pres. 1984-86), Nat. Coun. Tchrs. Math. (chmn. external affairs com. 1972-73), Nat. High Sch. and Jr. Coll. Math. Clubs (gov. 1972-75, pres. 1978-80). Home: 7 Stoneleigh Pl Brownsville TN 38012-2463

KALINA, RICHARD, artist; b. N.Y.C., May 21, 1946; s. Jacob Wilbert and Helen Ruth (Weinberg) K.; m. Valerie Jaudon, Oct. 23, 1979. B.A., U. Pa., 1966. Assoc. prof. studio art, art history Fordham U., N.Y.C. One-man shows include Jack Glenn Gallery, L.A., 1970, OK Harris Gallery, 1970, Tibor de Nagy Gallery, 1979, 80, 82, 84, Piezo Electric Gallery, N.Y.C., 1986, 87, L.A., 1986, Elizabeth McDonald Gallery, 1988, 89, Diane Brown Gallery, N.Y.C., 1992, Ledisflam Gallery, N.Y.C., 1992, Lennon, Weinberg Gallery, N.Y.C., 1993, 95, Lennon, Weinberg Gallery, NYC, 1998; group shows include Morris Gallery, Toronto, 1970, Lunn Gallery, Washington, 1970, Inst. Contemporary Arts, Boston, 1970, U. Ala., 1971, Jack Glenn Gallery, 1970, 71, NYU, 1972, Indpls. Mus. Art, 1971, 74, Walker Art Ctr., Mpls., 1974, Cas Thomas Jefferson, Brasilia, Brazil, 1975, Lehigh U., 1975, Norton Gallery, Palm Beach, Fla., 1975, Mus. Am. Found. for Arts, Miami, 1977, Sewall Gallery, 1978, 80, Nobe Gallery, 1978, Rutgers U., 1978, Weatherspoon Art Gallery, Greensboro, N.C., 1978, Ill. Wesleyan U., 1980, Aldrich Mus., Ridgefield, Conn., 1970, 80, Sidney Janis Gallery, N.Y.C., 1981, McIntosh-Drysdale Gallery, Washington, 1981, Ericson Gallery, N.Y.C., 1982, Mus. Art, Ft. Lauderdale, Fla., 1982, Okla. Mus. Art, Oklahoma City, 1982, Santa Barbara Mus. Art, (Calif.), 1982, Grand Rapids Art Mus., (Mich.), 1982, Hudson River Mus., Yonkers, N.Y., 1983, U. Tex., Austin, 1983, Kalamazoo Inst. Art, 1983, Madison (Wis.) Art Ctr., U. Chgo., 1983, Loch Haven Art Ctr., (Fla.), 1983, Jacksonville (Fla.) Art Mus., 1983, Haber-Theodore Gallery, N.Y.C., 1983, Tibor de Nagy Gallery, 1984, Monmouth Mus., N.J., 1984, Steinbaum Gallery, N.Y.C., 1985, Bass Mus., Miami Beach, Fla., 1985, New Orleans Mus. Contemporary Art, 1985, Anchorage Mus. Fine Arts, 1985, Piezo Electric Gallery, L.A., 1986, N.Y.C., 1987, Barbara Mathes Gallery, 1987, R.C. ERPF Gallery, N.Y.C., 1987, Elizabeth McDonald Gallery, 1987, 89, Tower Gallery, N.Y.C., 1988, White Columns, N.Y., 1988, Hunter Coll. Gallery, 1988, John Good Gallery, N.Y.C., 1988, 91, John Davis Gallery, N.Y.C., 1988, Gallerie Rahmel, Cologne, Fed. Republic Germany, 1989, J.B. Speed Art Mus., Louisville, 1989, Shea Beker Gallery, N.Y.C., 1989, Scott Hanson Gallery, N.Y.C., 1990, Fay Gold Gallery, Atlanta, 1991, Trenkmann Gallery, N.Y.C., 1991, Bennington Coll., Vt., 1991, Pamela Auchincloss Gallery, N.Y.C., 1991, 92, Sidney Janis Gallery, N.Y.C., 1991, Diane Brown Gallery, 1992, Lennon, Weinberg Gallery, N.Y., 1992, 93, 95, Max Protetch Gallery, N.Y.C., 1992, Sergio Tossi Arte Contemporaneo, Prato, Italy, 1992, Stark Gallery, N.Y., 1993, 95, Addison Ripley Fine Art Mus., Washington D.C., 1993, Guild Hall Mus., East Hampton, N.Y., 1993, Arco Gallery, Turin, Italy, 1994, USF Contemporary Art Mus., Tampa, Fla., 1995, The Century Assn., N.Y., 1996, McNay Art Mus., San Antonio, Lennon Weinberg, Inc., 1998others; represented in permanent collections Indpls. Mus. Art, Norton Gallery Art, Palm Beach, NYU Aldrich Mus., Nat. Mus. Am. Art, Washington, Ind. U. Mus., Rutgers U. Mus., assoc. prof. Fordham U., N.Y., art history and studio art; also numerous pvt. collections. Nat. Endowment for Arts grantee. Mem. bd. dirs. and sec., Internatl. Assn. of Art Critics, USA Sect.; chair, Dept. Theatre and Vis. Arts, Fordham U.

KALINA, ROBERT EDWARD, physician, educator; b. New Prague, Minn., Nov. 13, 1936; s. Edward Robert and Grace Susan (Hess) K.; m. Janet Jessie Larsen, July 18, 1959; children: Paul Edward, Lynne Janet. B.A. magna cum laude, U. Minn., 1957, B.S., 1960, M.D., 1960. Diplomate Am. Bd. Ophthalmology (dir. 1981-89). Intern U. Oreg. Med. Sch. Hosp., Portland, 1960-61; resident in ophthalmology U. Oreg. Med. Sch. Hosp., 1961-62, 63-66; asst. in retina surgery Children's Hosp., San Francisco, 1966-67; Nat. Inst. Neurol. Diseases and Blindness Spl. fellow Mass. Eye and Ear Infirmary, Boston, 1967; instr. ophthalmology U. Wash., 1967-69, asst. prof., 1969-71, acting chmn. dept. ophthalmology, 1970-71, asso. prof., 1971-72, chmn. dept. ophthalmology, 1971-96, prof., 1972—; mem. staffs Univ. Hosp., Harborview Hosp., Children's Hosp., Seattle; cons. VA Hosp., Seattle, Pacific Med. Ctr., Seattle, Madigan Hosp., Tacoma; assoc. head divsn. ophthalmology dept. surgery Children's Hosp., Seattle, 1975-86; pres. U. Wash. Physicians, 1990-93. Contbr. author: Introduction to Clinical Pediatrics, 1972, Ophthalmology Study Guide for Medical Students, 1975; contbr. numerous articles to profl. publs. Served to capt., M.C. USAF, 1962-63. Fellow ACS, Am. Acad. Ophthalmology (Sr. Honor award 1989); mem. AMA, Assn. Univ. Profs. Ophthalmology (pres. 1983-84, exec. v.p. 1989-94), Assn. Rsch. in Vision and Ophthalmology, Pacific Coast Oto-Ophthalmol. Soc. (councilor 1972-74), King County Med. Soc., Wash. State Acad. Ophthalmology, Phi Beta Kappa. Home: 2627 96th Ave NE Bellevue WA 98004-2107 Office: U Wash Dept Ophthalmology Box 356485 1959 NE Pacific St Seattle WA 98195-0001

KALIPOLITES, JUNE ELEANOR TURNER, rehabilitation professional; b. Grasmere, N.H.; d. Louis O. and Edith Mae (Allen) Turner; m. Nicholas G. Kalipolites, Feb. 12, 1955; children: George, Stephanie, Athena. AA, Hesser Coll., Manchester, N.H., 1977; B of Gen. Studies, U. N.H., 1980; MS in Rehab. Adminstrn. and Svcs., So. Ill. U., Carbondale, 1982; EdD in Ednl. Adminstrn., Vanderbilt U., 1992. Cert. rehab. counselor. Office mgr. Harris Upham and Co., Inc., Manchester; mgr. Amoskeag Bank & Trust Co.; rehab. counselor Div. Vocat. Rehab., Nashua, N.H.; rehab. cons. N.H. Divsn. Vocat. Rehab., Concord, 1986-94, tng. coord., 1993-94; rehab. cons. spl. svcs. N.H. Divsn. Adult Learning and Rehab., Concord, 1995—. Author: Profile of Women in Rehabilitation Administration: A Common Theme, 1992, Projects with Industry: A Unique Concept for Providing Rehabilitation Services to Persons with Severe Disabilities, 1982. LaVerne Noyes scholar. Mem. ACA, ASTD, AAUW, ASTD, Am. Rehab. Counseling Assn., Nat. Rehab. Assn. (nat. bd. dirs. 1994-97), Nat. Rehab. Counseling Assn. (bd. dirs. 1986-87), Nat. Rehab. Adminstrn. Assn. (nat. bd. dirs. 1983-87, 92-94), N.E. Rehab. Counseling Assn. (bd. dirs. 1977-81, 82-98, pres. 1999), N.E. Rehab. Assn. (bd. dirs. 1999—), N.H. Rehab. Assn. (bd. dirs. 1977—, treas. 1978, 89-92, sec. 1977-78, 98—), Rho Sigma Chi, Chi Sigma Iota. Democrat. Greek Orthodox. Avocations: swimming, travel, research, genealogy. Home: 668 Lake Ave Manchester NH 03103-3538 Office: NH Divsn Adult Learning and Rehab 78 Regional Dr Concord NH 03301-8530

KALISCH, BEATRICE JEAN, nursing educator, consultant; b. Tellahoma, Tenn., Oct. 15, 1943; d. Peter and Margaret Ruth Petersen; m. Philip A. Kalisch, Apr. 17, 1965; children—Philip P., Melanie J. BS, U. Nebr., 1965; MS, U. Md., 1967, PhD, 1970. Pediatric staff nurse Centre County Hosp., Bellefonte, Pa., 1965-66; instr. nursing Philipsburg (Pa.) Gen. Hosp. Sch. Nursing, 1966; pediatric staff nurse Greater Balt. Med. Center, Towson, Md., 1967; asst. prof. maternal-child nursing Am. U., 1967-68; clin. nurse specialist N.W. Tex. Hosp., Amarillo, 1970; assoc. prof. maternal-child nursing, curriculum coordinator nursing Amarillo Coll., 1970-71; chmn. baccalaureate nursing program, asso. prof. nursing U. So. Miss., 1971-74; prof. nursing, chmn. dept. parent-child nursing U. Mich. Sch. Nursing, Ann Arbor, 1974-86; Shirley C. Titus Disting. prof. U. Mich. Sch. Nursing, 1977—, Titus Disting. prof. nursing mgmt., 1989—; prin., dir. nursing consultation svcs. Ernst & Young, Detroit, 1986-89; prin. investigator USPH grant to study image of nurses in mass media and the informational quality nursing news, U. Mich., 1977-86, prin. investigator to study intrahosp. transport of critically ill patients, 1991—; prin. investigator to study use of HIA nurse in N.Y.C. labor market, U. Mich.; prin. investigator to study the impact of managed care on critical care, U. Mich.; vis. Disting. prof. U. Ala., 1979, U. Tex., 1981, Tex. Christian U., 1983. Author: Child Abuse and Neglect: An Annotated Bibliography, 1978; co-author: Nursing Involvement in Health Planning, 1978, Politics of Nursing, 1982, Images of Nurses on Television, 1983, The Advance of American Nursing, 1986, revised, 1994, The Changing Image of the Nurse, 1987; co-editor: Studies in Nursing Mgmt.; contbr. articles to profl. jours. Recipient Joseph L. Andrews Bibliog. award Am. Assn. Law Libraries, 1979; Book of Yr. award Am. Jour. Nursing, 1978, 83, 86, 87, Outstanding Achievement award U. Md., 1987, Distinguished Alumni award U. Nebr., 1985, Shaw medal Boston Coll., 1986; USPHS fellow. Fellow Am. Acad. Nursing; mem. Am. Coll. Healthcare Execs., ANA, APHA, Am. Orgn. Nurse Execs., Sigma Theta Tau, Phi Kappa Phi. Presbyterian. Home: 27675 Chatsworth St Farmington MI 48334-1821 Office: U Mich Sch Nursing 400 N Ingalls St Ann Arbor MI 48109-2003

KALISCHER, CLEMENS, photographer; b. Hoyren, Bavaria, Germany, Mar. 30, 1921; came to U.S., 1942; s. Haus John and Ella (Norden) K.; children: Angela, Cornelia, Tanya. Student, New Sch., N.Y.C., Cooper

Union, N.Y.C. Photographer France Press, N.Y.C., 1946-48, Coronet Mag., 1949-50; free-lance photographer Stockbridge, Mass., 1951—. Contbr. photography to profl. jours. and textbooks; one-man shows include Carnegie Hall, N.Y., Spiral Gallery, Nexus Gallery, Boston 200, Berkshire Mus., Pittsfield, Mass., Welles Gallery, Lenox, Mass., Black Mountain Coll., N.C., U. N.C., Chapel Hill, Durham Arts Ctr., Sharon Arts Ctr., N.H., Bennington (Vt.) Coll., Williams Coll., Mass., Emma Willard Sch., Troy, N.Y., Photographers Gallery, Litchfield, Conn., Fla. State U., Tallahassee, Park McCullough Mansion, North Bennington, Vt., Cary Meml. Gallery, Lexington, Mass., Forbes Libr., Northampton, Mass., Washington (Conn.) Art Assn., Harvard U., Music Theatre Group, Stockbridge, Mass., Brattleboro (Vt.) Mus., Bertha Urdang Gallery, N.Y.C.; exhibited in group shows at Mus. Modern Art, Met. Mus., C.S. Exhibit, Eng., Expo '67, Montreal, DeCordova Mus., Lincoln, Mass., Conn. Arts Festival, Rochester Internat. Salon, mus. Fine Arts, Carl Siembab Gallery, Smithsonian Instn.; represented in permanent collections at: Bklyn. Mus., Libr. Congress, Lawrence Art Mus., Williams Coll., Met. Mus., Bavarian Mus., Munich, Internat. Ctr. Photography, Mpls. Inst. Art, Museo Nat. del la Montagna, Torino; also pvt. collections. Pres. Laurel Hill Assn., Stockbridge; mem. sch. com., South Berkshire; mem. planning bd., Stockbridge; mem. Food & Land Coun., Berkshire. POW, 1939-42, France. Mem. Am. Soc. Picture Profls. Jewish. Home and Office: Image Photos 34 Main St Stockbridge MA 01262

KALISH, ARTHUR, lawyer; b. Bklyn., Mar. 6, 1930; s. Jack and Rebecca (Biniamofsky) K.; m. Janet J. Wiener, Mar. 7, 1953; children: Philip, Pamela. BA, Cornell U., 1951; JD, Columbia U., 1956. Bar: N.Y. 1956, D.C. 1970. Assoc. Paul, Weiss, Rifkind, Wharton & Garrison, N.Y.C., 1956-64, ptnr., 1965-95, of counsel, 1996—; lectr. NYU Inst. Fed. Taxation, Hawaii Tax Inst., Law Jour. Seminars. Contbr. articles to legal jours. Assoc. trustee L.I. Jewish Med. Ctr., New Hyde Park, N.Y., 1978-82, trustee, 1982-95, hon. trustee, 1995-97; trustee emeritus North Shore - L.I. Jewish Health Sys., 1997-98, life trustee, 1998—; bd. dirs. Cmty. Health Program of Queens Nassau Inc., New Hyde Park, 1978-94, pres., 1981-89, chmn. emeritus, 1994-97; bd. dirs. Managed Health, Inc., New Hyde Park, 1990-98, chmn., 1994-95. Fellow Am. Coll. Tax Counsel; mem. ABA, N.Y. State Bar Assn., Assn. Bar City N.Y., Columbia Law Sch. Assn. (bd. dirs. 1990-94). Home: 2 Bass Pond Dr Old Westbury NY 11568-1307 Office: Paul Weiss Rifkind Wharton & Garrison Ste 4200 1285 Avenue Of The Americas Fl 21 New York NY 10019-6065

KALISH, MYRON, lawyer; b. N.Y.C., Dec. 3, 1919; s. Louis and Bertha (Nacht) K.; m. Evelyn J. Zobler, Apr. 1, 1944; children—Nita Jane, Pamela Sue. BS in Social Sci., CCNY, 1940; LLB cum laude, Harvard U., 1943. Bar: N.Y. bar 1944. Since practiced in N.Y.C.; sr. ptnr. Arthur, Dry & Kalish P.C. (and predecessors), 1961-84; gen. counsel UNIROYAL, Inc., 1961-84; spl. ptnr. Shea & Gould, N.Y.C., 1985-91, of counsel, 1992-94; of counsel Parker Duryee Rosoff & Haft, N.Y.C., 1994—. Editor: Harvard Law Rev., 1942-43. Adv. bd. Southwestern Legal Found. Lt. USNR, 1943-46. Mem. ABA, N.Y. State Bar Assn., Assn. Bar City N.Y., NAM (mem. lawyers adv. com. to gen. cousnel), Harvard Club, Bellport Country Club, Rockefeller Ctr. Luncheon Club, Westhampton Yacht Squadron. Home: 50 E 79th St New York NY 10021-0232 Office: Parker Duryee Rosoff & Haft 529 5th Ave New York NY 10017-4608

KALISKI, STEPHAN FELIX, economics educator; b. Warsaw, Poland, Nov. 4, 1928; emigrated to Can., 1941, naturalized, 1947; s. Jacob and Ludwika (Romanus) K.; m. Marian Ieleen Nelson, Oct. 6, 1960; 1 dau., Susan Maria. B.A., U. B.C., 1951; M.A., U. Toronto, 1953, postgrad., 1953-54; Ph.D., U. Cambridge, Eng., 1959. Statistician I Dominion Bur. Statistics, 1951-52; Alexander Mackenzie Research fellow U. Toronto, 1953-54; lectr. Queen's U., Kingston, Ont., 1954-56; prof. econs. Queen's U., 1969-94; chmn. div II Queen's U. (Grad. Sch.), 1971-73; prof. emeritus, 1994—; research fellow in econ. statistics Manchester (Eng.) U., 1958-59; asst. prof. Carleton U., Ottawa, Ont., 1959-62; asso. prof. Carleton U., 1962-65, prof., 1965-69, cmn. dept. econs., 1962-63, 64-66; research supr. Royal Commn. Taxation, 1963-64; Can. Council Sr. fellow, Dept. Labour-Univs. Research Com. research grantee, research asso. U. Calif., Berkeley, 1966-67; Can. Council leave fellow, 1973-74; hon. research asso. in econs. Harvard U., 1973-74; Social Sci. and Humanities Research Council Can. leave fellow, 1980-81, research grantee, 1978, 81; bd. dirs. Nat. Bur. Econ. Research, 1978-84; cons. Royal Commn. on Econ. Union, 1984-85, Commn. of Inquiry on Unemployment Ins., 1985-86. Author: Adjustment Assistance under the U.S. Trade Expansion Act, 1963, The Tradeoff Between Inflation and Unemployment, Some Explorations of Recent Evidence for Canada, 1972; editor, author: Canadian Economic Policy since the War, a Series of Six Public Lectures in Commemoration of the Twentieth Anniversary of the White Paper on Employment and Income of 1945, 1966; mng. editor: Can. Jour. Econs, 1976-79; contbr. articles to profl. publs. Can. Council research grantee, 1969, 77-81; Social Sci. Research Council research fellow, 1956-57. Fellow Royal Soc. Can.; mem. Am. Econ. Assn., Can. Econs. Assn. (v.p. 1984-85, pres.-elect 1985-86, pres. 1986-87, past pres. 1987-88), Queen's Univ. Club. Home: 649 Fernmoor Dr, Kingston, ON Canada K7M 8K5 Office: Queen's U, Dept Econs, Kingston, ON Canada K7L 3N6

KALISZEK, ANDREW WOJCIECH, mechanical engineer; b. Zlotow, Poland, Apr. 8, 1946; s. Jan Wojciech and Wiera (Labenska) K.; m. Anna D. Makosa, Dec. 26, 1974 (div. Dec. 1979); 1 child, Agata Karina; m. Barbara Nickles, Apr. 16, 1983; 1 stepchild, Mark Robert. MME, Warsaw U. of Tech., 1969, PhD, 1979. Registered profl. engr., Ariz. Rsch. engr. Warsaw U. of Tech., 1972-75, mgr. rsch. lab., 1975-78, acad. lectr., 1978-81; project engr. Universal Rsch. Lab., Elk Grove Village, Ill., 1981-83; sr. project engr. Wico Corp., Niles, Ill., 1983-84; sect. mgr. Zenith Electronics Corp., Glenview, Ill., 1984-87; staff engr. Honeywell Inc., Phoenix, 1987-95; staff rsch. scientist fiber optic sensors Honeywell Technology Ctr., Phoenix, 1995—. Contbr. articles to profl. jours. Mem. Sufact Mount Tech. Assn., Western Chopin Soc. (exec. officer 1989—). Republican. Roman Catholic. Achievements include patents in field. Avocations: bridge, hiking, travels. Home: 1156 E Beverly Ln Phoenix AZ 85022-2668 Office: Honeywell Technology Ctr 21111 N 19th Ave Phoenix AZ 85027-2700

KALKHOF, THOMAS CORRIGAN, physician; b. Wellsville, N.Y., Aug. 12, 1919; s. Arthur Albert and Evelyn (Corrigan) K.; m. Mary E. Jones, Mar. 3, 1946 (dec. 1955); children: Thomas E., Susan A., Mark A., Patricia D.; m. 2d Constance N. McCarthy, Apr. 19, 1958 (dec. 1998); children: Christopher J., Constance M., Craig Alan. B.S., Gannon U., 1943; M.D., Marquette U., 1946. Intern, resident St. Vincent's Hosp., Erie, Pa., 1946-47; pvt. practice in holistic medicine, nutritional problems, continued breast cancer rehab. and thermography, gen. geriatrics and psychosomatic, Erie, 1947—; pvt. practice holistic medicine Erie, 1947—; med. dir. Twinbrook Med. Ctr., 1960-84; dir. Iroquois Med. Centre, Erie; staff mem. St. Vincent's Health Ctr., Hamot Med. Ctr., Erie; pres., dir. Small Hosp. Cons., Inc., Erie, 1954—. Past chmn. Pa. Bd. Accreditation Nursing Homes and Related Facilities; past pres. Cath. Social Svcs., Erie; past pres. Erie County Ind. Coun. on Aging.; bd. dirs. Cath. Charities USA Commn. on Aging. With M.C., AUS, 1943-44. Fellow Am. Coll. Health Care Adminstrs., Am. Geriatric Soc., Am. Acad. Family Physicians, Acad. Psychosomatic Medicine (past pres.); mem. AMA, Pa. Health Care Assn. (past pres.), Acad. Psychomatic Medicine (past pres.), Pa. Acad. Family Physicians (past pres. Erie chpt.), Assn. Physicians in Chronic Disease Facilities (past pres.), Am. Soc. Clin. Hypnosis, Pa., Erie County Med. Socs., Nat. Geriatric Soc. (pres.), Soc. Prospective Medicine, Ind. Coun. on Aging (past pres.), KC (4 deg.), Internat. Transactional Analysis Assn. Republican. Roman Catholic. Home: 3749 E Lake Rd Erie PA 16511-1346 Office: PO Box 7265 4401 Iroquois Ave Erie PA 16511-2219

KALKSTEIN, JOSHUA ADAM, lawyer; b. Phila., Oct. 1, 1943; s. Abraham and Helen (Ponemone) K.; children: Aleta K., Trevor W., Maxim J. AB, Brown U., 1965; JD, U. Pa., 1968. Bar: N.Y. 1968, N.J. 1971, Mass. 1978, U.S. Dist. Ct. N.Y. 1968, U.S. Dist. Ct., N.J. 1971, U.S. Dist. Ct., Mass. 1978, U.S. Ct. of Appeals (3d cir.) 1973, U.S. Ct. Mil. Appeals 1969. Sr. corp. counsel rsch. Pfizer Inc., Groton, Conn., 1978—; assoc. Hellring, Lindeman & Landau, Newark, 1972-75; corp. counsel Hooper Holmes Inc., Basking Ridge, N.J., 1975-78; vis. counsel Harvard U., MIT Ctr. for Exptl. Pharmacology and Therapeutics, Cambridge, 1995—. Bd. dirs. Howland Art Ctr., Beacon, N.Y., 1987-91, Congregation Beth El, New London, Conn., 1995-96; commr. Waterfront Redevel. Commn., Beacon, 1990-91. Lt. USNR, 1969-72. Mem. N.Y. State Bar Assn., N.J. Bar Assn., Mass. Bar Assn. Jewish. Avocations: art collecting, book collecting, golf. Home: 76 Library St Mystic CT 06355-2420 Office: Pfizer Inc Eastern Point Rd Groton CT 06340

KALKUS, STANLEY, librarian, administrator, consultant; b. Prague, Czechoslovakia, Apr. 27, 1931; came to U.S., 1952; s. Frank and Zdenka (Hynkova) K.; m. Marta J. Pokorna, Jan. 12, 1952; children: Michaela Z., Olen A., Hynek P. Abitur, Classical Gymnasium, Prague, 1950; Cert. in Germanistics, Charles U., Prague, 1951; MA, U. Chgo., 1959. Librarian, audio-visual coordinator Chgo. Bd. Edn., 1960-62; base librarian U.S. Air Force, Sidi Slimane, Morocco, 1962-63, Hahn AFB, Fed. Republic Germany, 1963-68; slavic bibliographer U. N.C., Chapel Hill, 1968-69; head library dept. Naval Underwater Systems Ctr., Newport, R.I., 1969-77; dir. U.S. Dept. Navy Library, Washington, 1977-86, coord., 1986-89, libr. of Navy, 1990-92; lectr. U. N.C., Chapel Hill, 1968-69; participant tech. info. panel AGARD (NATO), Brussels, 1974, Copenhagen, 1975, Washington, 1976, Oslo, 1977; mem. adv. com. Intergovtl. Libr. Cooperation, 1981-82; mem. exec. adv. com. Fedlink, 1986-88; vis. prof. charles U., Prague, Czechoslovakia, 1992—; rep. Dept. of Navy on Fed. Libr. and Info. Ctrs. com., 1991-92; chmn. libr. com. Ctrl. European Rsch. and Grad. Edn./Econ. Inst., Acad. Scis., Prague, 1994—; mem. libr. com. Parliament of Czech Republic, 1997—; mem. adv. bd. U. Koblenz (Germany) Exernal LS Studies, 1998—. Editor Navy Libraries in 1980s, 1976; contbr. articles to profl. jours. Mem. core com. R.I. Gov.'s Conf. on Libraries, 1976-77. Served with U.S. Army, 1953-55. Recipient cost reduction award Naval Underwater Systems Ctr., Newport, R.I., 1972, 84; fellow U. Chgo., 1957-58. Mem. ALA (pres. Armed Forces sect. 1974), Spl. Libr. Assn. (chmn. mil. librs. div. 1978-79), Internat. Fedn. Libr. Assns. (mem. standing com. on social librs. 1986-96, mem. standing com. edn. and tng. 1996—), Am. Translators Assn., Czech Libr. and Info. Profl. Assn. Roman Catholic. Clubs: Newport Ski, Friends of Newport Pub. Library. Avocations: skiing; tennis. Office: Charles U Prague, FF UISL Celetna 20, 11000 Prague Czech Republic also: 18 Shields St Newport RI 02840-4317

KALKWARF, KENNETH LEE, academic dean; b. Lincoln, Nebr., Apr. 12, 1946; s. Robert G. and Grace L. (Beck) K.; m. Sharon R. Moore, July 6, 1974; children: Kyle J., Kevin J. Student, U. Nebr., 1964-66, DDS, 1970, MS, 1973. Diplomate Am. Bd. Periodontology. Asst. prof. Univ. Nebr., Lincoln, 1973-78; prof. U. Nebr., Lincoln, 1980-87; assoc. prof. U. Okla., Oklahoma City, 1978-80; prof./assoc. dean U. Tex. Health Sci. Ctr., San Antonio, 1987-88, prof./dean, 1988—; cons. Cen. Regional Dental Testing, Topeka, Kans., 1980-87, VA, Nebr., 1981-87, ADA, Chgo., 1982—; vis. prof. Svc. U. Autonoma de Guadalajara/Mexico, 1980-82. Contbg. author textbooks, 1978—; contbr. articles to profl. jours., rsch. abstracts. Bd. dirs. McAllister Park Little League, San Antonio, 1990-94, mem. Leadership San Antonio, 1989-90. Recipient Alumni Achievement award U. Nebr., 1990, Outstanding Tchr. award U. Okla., 1980. Fellow Internat. Coll. Dentists, Am. Coll. Dentists; mem. ADA, San Antonio Dist. Dental Soc. (bd. dirs. 1988-93), Am. Acad. Periodontology, S.W. Soc. Periodontology (bd. dirs. 1984-97, pres. 1993-94), Tex. Soc. Periodontists (bd. dirs. 1988-95), Internat. Assn. for Dental Rsch. Republican. Methodist. Avocations: spectator sports, jogging, reading. Office: Univ Tex Health Sci Ctr 7703 Floyd Curl Dr San Antonio TX 78284-6200

KALKWARF, LEONARD V., minister; b. Parkersburg, Iowa, Mar. 17, 1928; s. John Jr. and Helen (Haats) K.; m. Beverly Jane Hardy, May 22, 1954; children—Deborah Joy, Cynthia Sue, Scott Craig. BA, Central Coll., Pella, Iowa, 1950; BD, New Brunswick Sem., 1953; MA, NYU, 1957; STM, Luth. Sem., Phila., 1973; DMin, Princeton Sem., 1980; DD (hon.), Central Coll., 1983. Ordained to ministry Ref. Ch. in Am., 1953. Assoc. pastor Bellevue Ref. Ch., Schenectady, N.Y., 1953-55; assoc. pastor Levittown (N.Y.) Community Ch., 1955-57; pastor Ref. Ch., Willow Grove, Pa., 1957-64, 65-91, Nat. Evang. Ch., Kuwait, Kuwait, 1964-65; pres. Particular Synod of N.J., 1969-70, 70-71, Gen. Synod of Ref. Ch. in Am., 1983-84. Author: History, 1st Reformed Church of Philadelphia, 1960, God Loves His World, Book I, 1963, Book II, 1964; contbr. articles to religious jours. Pastoral asst. Abington, Pa. Presbyn. Ch., 1998—. Served as Chaplain CAP, 1960-62. Republican. Lodge: Rotary.

KALLA, ALEC KARL, writer, rancher; b. Pitts., Feb. 7, 1950; s. Milton Miklos and Marion Dorothy Kalla. Attended, Boston U., 1968-72. Rancher Conifer, Colo., 1977—; v.p. Health Care Assocs., Evergreen, Colo., 1989; freelance writer Conifer, 1990—; guest author, panelist Rocky Mountain Book Fesitval, Denver, 1993-95. Author: Velvet, 1993; patentee in field, 1984. Mem. Mystery Writers Am. Avocations: folk guitar and banjo, archery, shooting sports. Home and Office: PO Box 85 Conifer CO 80433-0085

KALLAHER, MICHAEL JOSEPH, mathematics educator; b. Cin., Sept. 4, 1940; s. Martin Henry and Lou Will (Huff) K.; m. Donalyn May Laraway, Aug. 17, 1963; children: Jay, Michael, Christopher, Daniel, Raymond. BS, Xavier U., 1961; MS, Syracuse U., 1963, PhD, 1967. Postdoctoral fellow U. Man., Winnipeg, Can., 1967-69; from asst. prof. prof. math. Wash. State U., Pullman, 1969—, assoc. dean scis., 1979-84, acting dean scis., 1982, chmn. math dept., 1984-92; vis. prof. Auckland U., New Zealand, 1988. Author: Affine Planes with Transitive Collineation Groups; contbg. editor Finite Geometries, 1982; contbr. articles to profl. jours. Grantee NSF; Fulbright Research scholar, Kaiserslautern, Fed. Republic Germany, 1975-76. Fellow Inst. Combinatories and Its Application (founding); mem. Am. Math. Soc., Math. Assn. Am., N.Y. Acad. of Scis., Assn. of Research Profs. (pres. 1986-87), Sigma Xi. Home: 235 NW Joe St Pullman WA 99163-3410 Office: Wash State U Dept Of Math Pullman WA 99163

KALLAKIS, ACHILLEAS MICHALIS S., shipping company executive; b. London, Sept. 3, 1968; s. Michalis and Erinoula (Angelinakis) K.; m. Pamela Anne Stachowsky, Sept. 1995; children: Erinoula, Michalis and Aristotelis (twins). BSc in Econs. with honors, Buckingham (Eng.) U., 1989. Dir. Global Transport, Del., N.Y., 1989-91; chmn., CEO The Pacific Group of Cos., London, N.Y.C., 1991—; dir. U.S. C. of C., London, 1997—, Ocean Group USA, 1989—, Pacific Maritime, N.Y., 1991—, Bernouli Trust Corp., N.Y., 1994—, South Pacific Adv. Bd., Sydney, Australia, 1994—; chmn., CEO Pacific Coffee Corp.; chmn. Pacific Vending Group. *Achilleas Kallakis is involved in a number of children's, Royal and cancer-related charities, taking an active role wherever he can. He sits on the boards of a wide variety of companies, world-wide, which enjoy benefiting from his valuable knowledge and experience of the transportation industry (air and shipping) and international diplomatic relations. Currently, he is working on a new paper entitled "Modern-day diplomatic strategies", which is now nearing completion after two years of research. Achilleas Kallakis is also highly active in promoting Trans-Atlantic relations via the American Chamber of Commerce.* Author: Maritime Registers of the World, 1994, Transport Economics, 1996; co-editor: The Wonders of Italy, 1996. Pres. Youth Anglo-Hellenic Soc. U.K., London, 1986-88; dir. Friends of Florence, Italy, 1997—; mem. com. Youth Enterprise Initiative, London, 1989-92; mem. Royal Opera, London, Met. Opera Guild, N.Y., Navy League. Recipient Churchill award for Excellence Churchill Enterprise Found., 1993, Pres.'s Golden Honor award South Pacific Action, Foru, 1995, Prime Min.'s award South Pacific Action Forum, 1996, Outstanding Emerging Leader award Office of Maritime Affairs, 1997. Fellow Inst. Dirs., Inst. Transport and Tourism; mem. Friends of Conservation, Cliveden Club, Queen's Club, U.S. C. of C. Japan, Met. Opera Guild (N.Y.C.), Met. Club (N.Y.C.), Nat. Trust (London), Soc. for the Protection of Ancient Bldgs. (London), The Landmark Tust (Eng.). Greek Orthodox. Avocations: travel, Italian studies, Back-gammon, fencing, tennis. Office: Pacific Group Cos 67 Wall St Fl 24 New York NY 10005-3101 also: 1st Fl 50 Hans Crescent, Knightsbridge, London SW1X 0NA, England

KALLAND, LLOYD AUSTIN, minister; b. Superior, Wis., Aug. 8, 1914; m. Jean Williams, July 20, 1945; children—Doris Jean Kalland McDowell. A.B., Gordon Coll., 1942; B.D., Phila. Theol. Sem., 1945; M.A., U. Pa., 1945; M.Th., Westminster Theol. Sem., 1946; Th.D., No. Bapt. Theol. Sem., 1955. Ordained to ministry Am. Bapt. Chs. in U.S.A., 1947. Pastor 1st Bapt. Ch., Slatington, Pa., 1946-49, Calvary Bapt. Ch., Chgo., 1949-55; lectr. N.T., No. Bapt. Theol. Sem., Chgo., 1949-51; exec. v.p. Gordon-Conwell Theol. Sem., South Hamilton, Mass., 1973-81, prof. contemporary theology, 1955-70, prof. Christian ethics, 1971-86; ret., 1986, interim min. in chs., 1955—. Cons. editor The Bible Newsletter; book rev. editor Christian Life mag., 1949-61; contbr. articles to religious jours. Mem. Evang. Theol. Soc., Dietrich Bonhoeffer Soc. (Eng.). Home: 102 Chebacco Rd South Hamilton MA 01982-2718

KALLAY, MICHAEL FRANK, II, medical devices company official; b. Painesville, Ohio, Aug. 24, 1944; s. Michael Frank and Marie Francis (Sage) K.; BBA, Ohio U., 1967; m. Irma Yolanda Corona, Aug. 30, 1975; 1 son, William Albert. Salesman, Howmedica, Inc., Rutherford, N.J., 1972-75, Biochem. Procedures/Metpath, North Hollywood, Calif., 1975-76; surg. specialist USCI div. C. R. Bard, Inc., Billerica, Mass., 1976-78; western and central regional mgr. ARCO Med. Products Co., Phila., 1978-80; Midwest regional mgr. Intermedics, Inc., Freeport, Tex., 1980-82; Western U.S. mgr. Renal Systems, Inc., Mpls., 1982—; pres. Kall-Med, Inc., Anaheim Hills, Calif., 1982—. Mem. Am. Mgmt. Assn., Phi Kappa Sigma. Home and Office: PO Box 17248 7539 E Bridgewood Dr Anaheim CA 92808-1407

KALLENBERG, JOHN KENNETH, librarian; b. Anderson, Ind., June 10, 1942; s. Herbert A. and Helen S. K.; m. Ruth Barrett, Aug. 19, 1965; children: Jennifer Anne, Gregory John. A.B., Ind. U., 1964, M.L.S., 1969. With Fresno County Library, Fresno, Calif., 1965-70, dir., 1976—; librarian Fig Garden Pub. Library br., 1968-70; asst. dir. Santa Barbara (Calif.) Pub. Library, 1970-76; mem. Calif. Libr. Svcs. bd., 1990—, v.p., 1992-95, pres., 1996-98; Beth Ann Harnish lectr. com., 1988-91, chmn., 1989-90. Mem. Calif. Libr. Assn. (councilor 1976-77, v.p., pres. 1987), Calif. County Librs. Assn. (pres. 1977), Calif. Libr. Authority for Sys. and Svcs. (chmn. authority adv. coun. 1978-80), Kiwanis (pres. Fresno 1981-82, lt. gov. divsn. 5 1991-92, co-editor Cal-Nev-Ha News 1993-94, 95-96). Presbyterian. Office: Fresno County Free Libr 2420 Mariposa St Fresno CA 93721-2204

KALLENDORF, CRAIG WILLIAM, English, speech and classical languages educator; b. Cin., June 23, 1954; s. Earl Roy and Hazel Greene (Griffith) K.; m. Hilaire Richey, Oct. 16, 1993. BA, Valparaiso U., 1975; MA, U. N.C., 1977, PhD, 1982. Asst. prof. dept. English Tex. A&M U., College Station, 1982-88, assoc. prof. English and classics, 1988-93, prof. English, classics and speech, 1993—; cons. NEH, Washington, 1987—. Author: Bibliography of Latin Influences..., 1982, Petrarch: Selected Letters, 1987, In Praise of Aeneas, 1989, Epistle of St. Paul to the Romans, 1991, A Bibliography of Venetian Editions of Virgil, 1470-1599, 1991, Vergil: The Classical Heritage, 1993, A Bibliography of Renaissance Italian Translations of Virgil, 1994, Aldine Press Books, 1999, The Myth of Venice, 1999, Landmark Essays on Rhetoric and Literature, 1999; editor Jour. Allegorica, 1989—, Rhetorica, 1993-96; co-editor: Neo-Latin News, 1992—; contbr. articles to profl. jours. Grantee Tex. A&M U., 1983—, South Ctrl. MLA, 1984, NEH, 1985, 90-92, Delmas Found., 1987, 92, ACLS, 1992, Humanities Rsch. Ctr., U. Tex., 1994. Lutheran. Office: Tex A&M U Dept English College Station TX 77843

KALLFELZ, FRANCIS A., veterinary medicine educator; b. Syracuse, N.Y., July 17, 1938; s. Alois Joseph and Josephine Marie (Honold) K.; m. Leonie Heidi Gantner, June 26, 1965; children: Andrew F., Susan E., Douglas P. Student, Lemoyne Coll., 1956-58; DVM, Cornell U., 1962, PhD, 1966. Diplomate Am. Coll. Vet. Nutrition (charter). Asst. prof. vet. medicine Cornell U., Ithaca, N.Y., 1966-73, assoc. prof., 1973-80, prof., 1980—; dir. Vet. Med. Tchg. Hosp., 1990-98, James Law prof. medicine (nutrition), 1997—; sr. Fulbright lectr., Zagreb, Yugoslavia, 1978; cons. FAO/IAEA, Vienna, 1977-78, Indonesia, 1980-83; vis. prof. Johns Hopkins U. Sch. Medicine, 1999. Contbr. articles to profl. jours. Mem. Am. Inst. Nutrition, Soc. Nuclear Medicine, AVMA (coun. on rsch. 1983-89, Am. Bd. Vet. Specialties 1989—), Soc. Exptl. Biology and Medicine. Republican. Roman Catholic. Avocations: handball, philately, camping. Home: 11 Bean Hill Ln Ithaca NY 14850-9775 Office: Cornell Univ Coll Vet Medicine Dept Clin Sci Ithaca NY 14853

KALLGREN, EDWARD EUGENE, lawyer; b. San Francisco, May 22, 1928; s. Edward H. and Florence E. (Campbell) K.; m. Joyce Elaine Kislitzin, Feb. 8, 1953; children: Virginia K. Pegley, Charles Edward. AB, U. Calif., Berkeley, 1951, JD, 1954. Bar: Calif. Assoc., ptnr. Brobeck, Phleger & Harrison, San Francisco, 1954-93, of counsel, 1993—. Bd. dirs. Olivet Meml. Park, Colma, Calif., 1970-98, pres., 1991-98; chair, pres. Five Bridges Found., 1998—; mem. Berkeley City Council, 1971-75; bd. dirs., v.p./treas. Planned Parenthood Alameda/San Francisco, 1984-89. Served to sgt. USMC, 1945-48. Mem. ABA (ho. of dels. 1985—, state del. 1997-98, coun. sr. law divsn. 1996—, chair 1999—), State Bar of Calif. (bd. govs. 1989-92, v.p. 1991-92), Found. of State Bar Calif. (bd. dirs. 1993-98, v.p., 1994-96, chair fellows soc. 1996-98), Bar Assn. San Francisco (pres. 1988, bd. dirs.), San Francisco Lawyers Com. Urban Affairs (co-chair 1983-85), Lawyers Com. Civil Rights Under Law (trustee 1985—), The TenBroek Soc. (chair bd. dirs. 1992-95). Democrat. Office: Brobeck Phleger & Harrison Spear St Tower 1 Market Plz Ste 341 San Francisco CA 94105-1193

KALLGREN, JOYCE KISLITZIN, political science educator; b. San Francisco, Apr. 17, 1930; d. Alexander and Dorothea (Willett) K.; m. Edward E. Kallgren, Feb. 8, 1953; children: Virginia, Charles. BA, U. Calif., Berkeley, 1953, MA, 1955; PhD, Harvard U., 1968. Jr. researcher to asst. researcher Ctr. Chinese Studies U. Calif., Berkeley, 1961-65, research assoc., 1965—, chair, 1983-88; assoc. dir. Inst. of East Asian Studies, Berkeley, 1987-95; from lectr. to prof. polit. sci. emeritus U. Calif., Davis, 1965—; cons. in field. Contbg. editor: Asean and China: An Evolving Relationship, 1988, Academic Exchanges: Essays on the Sino-American Experience, 1987, Developing a Nation State: China After Forty Years, 1990; editor: Jour. Asian Studies, 1980-83, Asian Survey, 1991—; contbr. articles to profl. jours. and chpts. to books. Ford Found. awardee, 1978-79. Mem. Am. Polit. Sci. Assn., Assn. Asian Studies, Nat. Com. U.S./China Rels., U.S. Com. on Security and Coop. in Asia Pacific. Home: 28 Hillcrest Rd Berkeley CA 94705-2807 Office: U Calif Inst East Asian Studies Berkeley CA 94720

KALLICK, DAVID A., lawyer; b. Chgo., Nov. 7, 1945; s. Joseph N. and Elizabeth A. (Just) K.; m. Arline E. Chizewer, Nov. 26, 1972; children: Michelle, Robert. AB in History, Princeton U., 1967; JD, Northwestern U., 1971. Bar: Ill. 1971, Calif. 1972. Law clk. to presiding justice Ill. Appellate Ct., Chgo., 1971-72; assoc. McCutchen, Doyle, Brown & Enersen, San Francisco, 1972-74; asst. dean U. So. Calif. Law Ctr., L.A., 1974-76, Ill. Inst. Tech.-Kent Coll. Law, Chgo., 1976-79; ptnr. Hurley Kallick & Schiller, Ltd., Deerfield, Ill., 1979-92, Tishler & Wald, Ltd., Chgo., 1992—; bd. dirs. Capitol Bank and Trust, Chgo., Capitol Bank of Westmont, Ill. Bd. dirs. Congregation Solel, Highland Park, Ill., Birchwood Club, Highland Park; past bd. mem., pres. Sch. Dist. 107, Highland Park; former trustee Legacy 107 Edn. Found., Highland Park. With USAR, 1968-74. Mem. ABA, Calif. Bar Assn., Ill. Bar Assn., Chgo. Bar Assn., Princeton Univ. Club. Home: 1887 Spruce Ave Highland Park IL 60035-2150 Office: 200 S Wacker Dr Ste 2600 Chicago IL 60606-5802

KALLINA, EMANUEL JOHN, II, lawyer; b. Balt., Dec. 18, 1948; s. Robert Wooding and Elanor Lee (Stinson) K.; m. Anne M. Vik, Jan. 16, 1982; children: James E. (dec.), Deborah A., Kristine L., Abigail M. BA in English, Bowdoin Coll., Brunswick, Maine, 1970; JD, U. Md., 1973; LLM in Taxation, NYU, 1974. Bar: Md. 1974, D.C. 1977. Law clk. Hon. R. Dorsey Watkins, U.S. Dist. Judge, Balt., 1974-75; assoc. McKenney, Thomsen & Burke, Balt., 1975-77; pvt. practice Balt., 1977-78; ptnr. Niles, Barton & Wilmer, Balt., 1978-82; pres., atty. Kallina, Levinson & Burns, Balt., 1982-85, Kallina & Assocs., Balt., 1985-92; pres., mng. ptnr. Kallina & Ackerman, Balt., 1993—; real estate broker Kallina Realty Assocs., Balt., 1985—; life ins. agt., Balt., 1990—. Contbr. articles to profl. jours.; frequent speaker in field. Bd. dirs. Nat. Com. on Planned Giving, 1993-95, chmn. govt. rel. com., 1994-98; co-founder Chesapeake Planned Giving Coun.; mem. The Working Group; chmn. bd., pres. The James Found., 1995—. Mem. ABA, Md. Bar Assn., Balt. Assn. Tax Counsel (pres. 1981-82), D.C. Bar Assn. Republican. Office: Kallina & Ackerman LLP 6507 York Rd Baltimore MD 21212-2115

KALLIR, JANE KATHERINE, art gallery director, author; b. N.Y.C.; d. John Otto and Joyce (Ruben) K. BA, Brown U., 1976. Asst. to dir. Lefebre Gallery, N.Y.C., 1977; asst. to dir. Galerie St. Etienne, N.Y.C., 1977-78, co-dir., 1979—; guest curator N.Y. State Mus., Albany, 1983, Internat. Exhbns.

Found., Washington, 1984-85, Mus. of City of Vienna, 1986, Austrian Nat. Gallery, 1990, Nat. Gallery Art, Washington, 1994, Indpls. Mus. Art, 1994, San Diego Mus. Art, 1994; guest lectr. Mus. Am. Folk Art, N.Y.C., 1982-85, NYU, 1982-85, Nat. Gallery Art, 1994, Ft. Lauderdale Mus. Art, 1996, Mus. Modern Art, 1997, Internat. Found. for Art Rsch., 1998. Author: Gustav Klimt-Egon Schiele, 1980, Austria's Expressionism, 1981, The Folk Art Tradition, 1981, Grandma Moses, The Artist Behind the Myth, 1982, Arnold Schoenberg's Vienna, 1984, Viennese Design and the Wiener Werkstaette, 1986, Gustav Klimt: 25 Masterworks, 1989, Egon Schiele: The Complete Works, 1990, rev., 1998, Richard Gerstl/Oskar Kokoschka, 1992, Egon Schiele, 1994, Egon Schiele: 27 Masterworks, 1996, Gramdma Moses, 25 Masterworks, 1997. Mem. Art Dealers' Assn. Am. (bd. dirs. 1994-97). Democrat. Office: Galerie St Etienne 24 W 57th St New York NY 10019-3918

KALLMAN, BURTON JAY, foods association director; b. N.Y.C., Nov. 1, 1927; s. Leo Melville and Muriel Kallman; m. Ellis Katherine Hachikian, Dec. 12, 1958; children: Lisa, David. BS, Bethany Coll., 1947; MS, U. So. Calif., 1951, PhD, 1958. Research biochemist U.S. Govt., Denver, Los Angeles, 1959-67; mem. profl. staff TRW Systems, Redondo Beach, Calif., 1967-76; sr. scientist Sci. Applications Inc., La Jolla, Calif., 1976-80; prin. Interdisciplinary Sci. Assocs., Torrance, Calif., 1980-82; lab. dir. Applied Biol. Scis., Glendale, Calif., 1982-85; dir. sci. and tech. Nat. Nutritional Foods Assn., Newport Beach, Calif., 1985-96; cons. Nat. Nutritional Foods Assn.; cons. Children's Asthma Research Inst., Denver, 1961-63, Behavioral Health Services, Redondo Beach, 1973-77, Centinela Child Guidance, Inglewood, Calif., 1984-86. Mem. editl. bd. Jour. Applied Nutrition, 1991—, Jour. Optimal Nutrition, 1992—; reviewer sci. books and films, 1978—; contbr. articles to profl. jours. Recipient Merit award NASA, 1976, Burton Kallman Scientific Achievement award, Nat. Nutritional Foods Assn., 1997. Mem. Am. Chem. Soc., Sigma Xi. Democrat. Jewish. Home: 23214 Robert Rd Torrance CA 90505-3244 Office: Nat Nutritional Foods Assn 3931 Macarthur Blvd Ste 101 Newport Beach CA 92660-3013

KALLMAN, KATHLEEN BARBARA, marketing and business development professional; b. Aurora, Ill., Mar. 23, 1952; d. Kenneth Wesley and Germaine Barbara (May) Eby. Legal sec. Sidley & Austin, Chgo., 1973-76, Winston & Strawn, Chgo., 1976-78; exec. sec. Beatrice Cos., Inc., Chgo., 1978-81, adminstrv. asst., 1981-83, asst. to chmn. bd. dirs., 1983-84, asst. v.p., 1984-85; pres., mng. dir. Stratxx Ltd., Charlotte, N.C., 1985—. Mem. Chgo. Coun. on Fgn. Rels., 1986—. Mem. Am. Soc. Profl. and Exec. Women, Nat. Assn. Women Bus. Owners, Charlotte Women Bus. Owners Assn., Charlotte Assn. Profl. Saleswomen, Chgo. Assn. Profl. Saleswomen, Internat. Assn. Bus. Communicators. Avocation: photography. Office: Stratxx Ltd PO Box 470008 Charlotte NC 28247-0008

KALLMANN, HELMUT MAX, music historian, retired music librarian; b. Berlin, Aug. 7, 1922; emigrated to Can., 1940, naturalized, 1946; s. Arthur and Fanny (Paradies) K.; m. Ruth Singer, Dec. 31, 1955 (dec. July 1993); 1 stepdaughter, Lynn Salter. MusB, U. Toronto, Ont., Can., 1949, LLD, 1971. With CBC Music Libr., Toronto, 1950-70; supr. CBC Music Libr., 1962-70; chief music divsn. Nat. Libr. Can., Ottawa, Ont., 1970-87, ret., 1987; Can. del. Internat. Assn. Music Librs., 1959-71. Author: A History of Music in Canada, 1534-1914, 1960; editor; Catalogue of Canadian Composers, 1952, Music for Orchestra I, Vol. 8, 1990, (with Gilles Potvin and Kenneth Winters) Ency. of Music in Canada, 1981, French edit., 1983, (with Potvin) 2nd edit., 1992, French 2nd edit., 1993, Music for Piano III, vol. 22, 1998; contbr. articles to profl. publs. Decorated Order of Can., 1986; dedicatee Musical Canada, Words and Music Honouring Helmut Kallmann, 1988; recipient Award of Merit Assn. for Can. Studies, 1998. Mem. Can. Music Coun. (v.p. 1971-76, medal 1977), Can. Assn. Music Librs. (cofounder 1956, past chmn.), Bibliog. Soc. Can., Can. Mus. Heritage Soc. (chmn. 1982—), Faculty Music Alumni Assn. U. Toronto (pres. 1963-64), Order of Can. Home: 38 Foothills Dr, Nepean, ON Canada K2H 6K3

KALLNER, NORMAN GUST, management information systems manager; b. Rockford, Ill., Apr. 28, 1950; s. Gust and Vera May (Brinkmeyer) K.; m. Mary Ann Wikoff, July 30, 1976; 1 child, Stephanie Ann. Student, U. Ill., 1968-70, No. Ill. U., 1975-79; BS in Bus. Adminstrn./Computer Info. Sys. summa cum laude, Culver-Stockton Coll., 1994. Programmer Woodward Gov. Co., Rockford, 1970-73, Rock Valley Coll., Rockford, 1973-74; programmer, analyst Kysor of Byron, Ill., 1974-76; systems programmer Rockford Bd. Edn., 1976-80; systems programmer Harris Corp., Quincy, Ill., 1980-84, mgmt. info. systems tech. support mgr., 1984-86, prin. software, data base analyst, 1986-92, prin. sys. analyst, 1992—; cons. Outboard Marine Corp., Beloit, Wis., 1979-80. Treas. Our Redeemer Luth Ch., Quincy, 1986-87, vice-chmn., 1992-93, pres. 1995-96, 98-99; asst. leader Girl Scouts Am., Quincy, 1986-96, trainer scout leaders, 1989—. Avocation: woodworking. Home: 1520 S 28th St Quincy IL 62301-6302 Office: Harris Corp PO Box 4290 Quincy IL 62305-4290

KALLSTROM, CHARLES CLARK, dentist; b. Chgo., Jan. 15, 1943; s. Charles Edward and Margaret Jane (Clark) K.; m. Roberta Lou Easterday, June 19, 1965; children: Cynthia Ann, Heidi Lynn, Karen Kristine. BS in Chem. Engring., Purdue U., 1965; DDS, Northwestern U., Chgo., 1971. Project engr. Chgo. Bridge & Iron Co., Oakbrook, Ill., 1965-67; pvt. practice dentistry Geneva, Ill., 1973—; mem. dental staff Cmty. Hosp., Geneva, 1974—, chmn., 1980-81; chmn. Elgin C.C. Dental Assisting Adv. Bd., 1994—. Author, editor: Dental Assisting for the Red Cross Aide, 1971. Bd. dirs. Tri City Family Svcs., Geneva, 1983-90, v.p., 1985-87, pres., 1988-90, chmn. capitol gifts campaign, 1992-93; bd. dirs. Men's Found. Delnor Cmty. Hosp., Geneva, 1979—; pres. Geneva chpt. Am. Cancer Soc., 1986-88. Lt. USN, 1971-73. Fellow Am. Coll. Dentists, Internat. Coll. Dentists, Acad. Gen. Dentistry (master); mem. ADA, Ill. State Dental Soc. (dental edn. com.1989-92, bd. trustees 1992—, access to care com. 1992-93, fin. and planning com. 1992-95, chmn. annual planning com. 1993-94, dental benefits com. 1994-95, ins. com. 1995—, chmn. 1999), Fox River Valley Dental Soc. (sec. 1986, treas. 1987, v.p. 1988, bd. dirs. 1988-91, pres. 1989), Ill. Acad. Dental Practice Adminstrn., Geneva Golf Club (sec. 1988, bd. dirs. 1986-88, 92-96, v.p. 1995, pres. 1996). Republican. Presbyterian. Avocations: traveling, golf, paddle tennis. Home: 615 Carriage Dr Batavia IL 60510-1159 Office: 302 Randall Rd Ste 105 Geneva IL 60134-4209

KALM, ARNE, investment banker; b. Tallinn, Estonia, Apr. 4, 1936; came to U.S., 1945; s. Juri and Aino (Kalm) Sammul; m. Celia Riddle, June 14, 1975; children: Michael, Linda, Peter. BS, Calif. Inst. Tech., 1956, MS, 1957; MBA, Harvard, 1961. V.p. Shareholders Mgmt. Co., L.A., 1970-72, Hollywood Turf Club, Inglewood, Calif., 1972-73; pres. Berry Enterprises, Long Beach, Calif., 1973-82, Berry Industries Corp., Santa Fe Springs, Calif., 1975-84, First Arcadia Corp., L.A., 1984—; bd. dirs. Baltic Cresco Investment Group, Estonia, So. Calif. Healthcare Systems; mem. employment tng. panel State of Calif., 1990-92. Bd. dirs. Meth. Hosp. So. Calif., 1995—, chmn. 1999—; v.p. Estonian League West Coast, 1961-63, pres. 1997—; v.p. Americans for Congl. Action to Free the Baltic States, 1961-71; West Coast dir. Estonian/Am. Nat. Coun., 1966-74; pres. Calif. Rep. Heritage Groups Coun., 1971-73; nat. chmn. Calif. Inst. Tech. Alumni Fund, 1979-80. Mem. Calif. Inst. Tech. Alumni Assn. (pres. 1982-83). Lutheran. Office: First Arcadia Corp 444 E Huntington Dr Arcadia CA 91006-6203

KALMAN, ANDREW, manufacturing company executive; b. Hungary, Aug. 14, 1919; came to U.S., 1922, naturalized, 1935; s. Louis and Julia (Bognar) K.; m. Violet Margaret Kish, June 11, 1949; children: Andrew Joseph, Richard Louis, Laurie Ann. With Detroit Engring. & Machine Co., 1947-66, exec. v.p., gen. mgr., 1952-66; exec. v.p. and dir. Indian Head, Inc., 1966-75, also dir.; dir. Acme Precision Products, 1959-80, Reef Energy Corp., 1980-84. Trustee emeritus Alma (Mich.) Coll.; bd. dirs. Am. Hungarian Found., New Brunswick, N.J.; mem. adv. coun., mem. exec. com., U. Mich. Ctr. for Communication Disorders. Home: 708 S Military St Dearborn MI 48124-2108 Office: 600 Woodbridge St Detroit MI 48226-4302

KALMAN, MARC, radio station executive; b. Appleton, Wis.; m. Gail Thoen; children: Robert, Todd, Stacie. Student, Am. U. Disc jockey Sta. WJPD, Ishpeming, Mich., 1967, Sta. WMBD, Peoria, Ill., 1967; account exec. Sta. WMIN, 1968, Sta. KRSI, 1968-69; account exec. Sta. WDGY, 1969-74, gen. sales mgr., 1974-81; v.p./gen. mgr. Blair Radio, 1981-88; gen. sales mgr. Sta. WCCO, 1988-92; v.p./gen. mgr. Sta. WRQC/KDWB/KTCZ, Mpls. Bd. dirs. Variety Children's Hosp. Mem. Minn. Broadcasters Assn. (bd. dirs.). Avocation: spectator sports. Office: WRQC/KDWB/KTCZ 60 S 6th St Ste 930 Minneapolis MN 55402-4409

KALMAN, RUDOLF EMIL, research mathematician, system scientist; b. Budapest, Hungary, May 19, 1930; s. Otto and Ursula (Grundmann) K.; m. Constantina Stavrou, Sept. 12, 1959; children: Andrew E.F.C., Elisabeth K. SB, MIT, 1953, SM, 1954; DSc, Columbia U., 1957; DEng (hon.), U. Bologna, 1988; DSc (hon.), U. Kyoto, Japan, 1990; PhD (hon.), Heriot Watt U., Edinburgh, Scotland, 1990, Tech. U. Crete, 1993. Staff engr. IBM Research Lab., Poughkeepsie, N.Y., 1957-58; research mathematician Research Inst. Advanced Studies, Balt., 1958-64; prof. engring. mech. and elec. engring. Stanford U., 1964-67, prof. math. system theory, 1967-71; grad. rsch. prof. Ctr. for Math. System Theory U. Fla., 1971-92; dir. Center for Math. System Theory, U. Fla., 1971-92, prof. emeritus, 1992—; prof. math. sys. theory Swiss Fed. Inst. Tech., Zurich, 1973-97; sci. adviser Ecole Nationale Superieure des Mines de Paris, 1968—; mem. sci. adv. bd. Laboratorio di Cibernetica, Naples, 1970-73. Author: Topics in Mathematical System Theory, 1969, over 150 sci. and tech. papers.; editorial bd. Internat. Jour. Math. Modelling, Jour. Computer and Systems Scis., Jour. Nonlinear Analysis, Jour. Optimization Theory and Applications, Applied Math. Letters, Math. of Control, Signals and Systems, Jour. Forecasting, Revue Internationale de Systemique. Named outstanding young scientist Md. Acad. Sci., 1962; recipient IEEE medal of honor, 1974, Rufus Oldenburger medal ASME, 1976, Centennial medal IEEE, 1984, 1st Kyoto prize Inamori Found., 1985, Steele prize Am. Math. Soc., 1987; Guggenheim fellow IHES Bures-sur-Yvette, 1971. Fellow Am. Acad. Arts and Scis.; mem. NAE (U.S.), NAS (U.S.), Hungarian Acad. Scis. (fgn.), Académie des Scis., Inst. de France (fgn.), Russian Acad. Scis. (fgn.). Office: ETH Zentrum, Weinbergstrasse 94, CH-8006 Zurich Switzerland *It is good to do everything as it was done yesterday, but it is better to examine all accepted assumptions. This is the key to scientific progress as well as to happier interpersonal relations.*

KALMANOFF, MARTIN, composer; b. Bklyn., May 24, 1920; s. Joseph and Anna (Mirin) K.; m. Margaret E. Tharaldsen, Sept. 21, 1974. BA cum laude, Harvard U., 1941, MA, 1942. Composer numerous works for musical theatre, 17 operas, including collaborations with William Saroyan, Eugene Ionesco, Eric Bentley and the Gertrude Stein opera Photograph 1920 (finalist in 3 Film-Video competitions); works performed on NBC, CBS and ABC Radio and TV networks, also Carnegie Hall, Town Hall, Avery Fisher Hall, Kennedy Ctr., Toronto Arts Ctr.; composer-lyricist original musical version of Fourposter, 1963, Young Tom Edison, 1962-85; composer children's musical Give Me Liberty, Edison Theatre, N.Y.C., 1975; on tour, 1975-76, 84-85; provided music for movie Puccini: Portrait of a Bohemian (winner Robert Merrill contest for best opera 1950); composer The Joy of Prayer (Sacred Svc. recorded by Sherrill Milnes and Am. Symphony Orch. and Chorus), Empty Bottle (3-act opera), Insect Comedy (3-act opera, performed by Ctr. for Contemporary Opera), 1993, Bald Soprano (Danny Kaye Playhouse), 1997, The Audition, Radford U., Va., 1999; works recorded by Elvis Presley, Mario Lanza, Vic Damone, Robert Goulet, Engelbert Humperdinck, Pat Boone, Tony Bennett, Dean Martin, others; The Amato Opera Co. did 6 performances of Empty Bottle, 1991; opera The Harmfulness of Tobacco, St. Peter's Ch., N.Y.C.; condr. 50 musicals for summer stock theater; contbr. articles to profl. jours. Mem. ASCAP, Nat. Opera Assn., Central Opera Service. Home and Office: 392 Central Park W Apt 14P New York NY 10025-5868

KALMUS, ELLIN, art historian, educator; b. N.Y.C.; d. Victor and Mata (Heineman) Roudin; m. Murray L. Silberstein, Oct. 6, 1949 (dec. 1968); children: James, Barbara Silberstein Keezell, John; m. Allan H. Kalmus, May 16, 1969 (dec. 1997). BA cum laude, Vassar Coll., 1946. Asst. dept. publs. and exhbns., asst. tchr. Mus. Modern Art, N.Y.C., 1946-50; lectr. Riverdale Country Sch., N.Y.C., 1970-90, Dalton, Trinity, Columbia Grammar, Birch Wathen Schs., N.Y.C., 1971-83, Fifth Ave. Presbyn. Ch., St. James Episcopal Ch., N.Y.C., 1982-83; vis. com. photograph and slide libr. Met. Mus. Art, N.Y.C., 1978—, lectr., 1986, 87; mem. tchg. staff Ethical Culture Sch. for Adult Edn., New Sch. for Social Rsch., 1980-81; Paris lectr. Friends of Vielles Maisons Francaises, 1988; series lectr. Darien Cmty. Assn., 1988—; London lectr. Arts Club of London, 1990; lectr. Albert Einstein Coll. Medicine, 1993-97, Christie's, London, 1994, Old Westbury Gardens, 1994-95, Cosmopolitan Club, 1988, 97, others. Trustee, head edn. com. Riverdale Country Sch., N.Y.C., 1978-84. Pierpont Morgan Libr. fellow, 1986, Frick Collection fellow, 1992. Mem. Cosmopolitan Club, Sunningdale Club (Scarsdale, N.Y.), Phi Beta Kappa. Home: 125 E 72d St New York NY 10021-4250

KALNAY, EUGENIA, university administrator, meteorologist; b. Buenos Aires, Oct. 1, 1942; came to U.S., 1971; d. Jorge and Susana (Zwicky) K.; m. Alberto Mario Rivas, July 24, 1965 (div. 1981); 1 child, Jorge Rodrigo; m. Malise Cooper Dick, July 13, 1981. Lic. in meteorology, U. Buenos Aires, 1965; PhD in Meteorology, MIT, 1971. Asst. prof. U. Uruguay, Montevideo, 1971-73; rsch. assoc. MIT, Cambridge, 1973-75, asst. prof. meteorology, 1975-76, assoc. prof., 1977-78; sect. head NASA Goddard Space Flight Ctr., Greenbelt, Md., 1979-82, br. head, 1983-86; chief devel. div. Nat. Weather Svc., NOAA Nat. Meteorology Ctr., Washington, 1987-99; univ. chair dept. meteorology U. Md., 1999—; mem. several coms. NRC, NAS, Washington; prin. investigator NASA, 1973—; adj. prof. meteorology U. Md., 1980-83. Editor several jours.; contbr. over 100 articles to sci. jours. Recipient gold medal for exceptional sci. achievement NASA, 1981, silver medal Dept. Commerce, 1990, Gold medal Dept. Commerce, 1993, 97. Mem. NAE, Am. Meteorl. Soc. (Charney award 1995). Home: 56 Lakeside Dr Greenbelt MD 20770*

KALOGREDIS, VASILIOS J., lawyer, health care management consultant; b. New Bedford, Mass., Mar. 3, 1949; s. John V. and Rose (Simeonidis) K.; m. Stephanie Pahides, May 26, 1974; children: Maria, John. BS in Acctg., Providence Coll., 1971; JD, Villanova U., 1974. Bar: Pa. 1974. Assoc. Beck & Kalogredis, Bala Cynwyd, Pa., 1974-81; ptnr. Kalogredis Law Assocs., Wayne, Pa., 1981-95; founder, pres. Kalogredis Tsoules and Sweeney Ltd., Wayne, 1996—; speaker in field. Contbg. author: The Physician's Practice, 1980. Contbr. articles to profl. jours. Pres. St. George Greek Orthodox Ch., Media, Pa., 1980, 86, chmn. bldg. com., 1984-87. Dougherty fellow Villanova U., 1971-74. Mem. ABA, Pa. Bar Assn., Soc. Med.-Dental Cons., Soc. Profl. Bus. Cons., Nat. Health Lawyers Assn. Republican. Office: 995 Old Eagle School Rd Ste 315 Wayne PA 19087-1709

KALOW, WERNER, pharmacologist, toxicologist; b. Cottbus, Germany, Feb. 15, 1917; emigrated to Can., 1951, naturalized, 1957; s. Johannes Bernhard and Maria Elisabeth (Heyde) K.; m. Patricia M. Arnold, May 3, 1991; children from earlier marriage: Peter Bernard, Barbara Irene. Student in medicine, U. Greifswald, Ger., 1935-36, U. Graz, Austria, 1936-37, U. Gottingen, Ger., 1939-40; M.D., U. Konigsberg, Ger., 1941. Research asst. Berlin U., 1947-49; research fellow, instr. U. Pa., 1949-51; lectr. U. Toronto, Ont., Can., 1951-53; asst. prof. pharmacology U. Toronto, 1953-55, assoc. prof., 1955-62, prof., 1962—, chmn. dept. pharmacology, 1966-77; dir. biol. research C.H. Boehringer Sohn, Ingelheim, Ger., 1965-66. Author: Pharmacogenetics, Heredity and the Response to Drugs, 1962; editor: (with B.N. La Du) Pharmacogenetics, 1968, (with R.A. Gordon and B.A. Britt) International Symposium on Malignant Hyperthermia, 1973, (with H.W. Goedde and D.P. Agarwal) Ethnic Differences in Reactions to Drugs and Xenobiotics, 1986, Pharmacogenetics of Drug Metabolism, 1992. Recipient Drug Info. Assn. Disting. Career award, 1997. Fellow Royal Soc. Can.; mem. Pharm. Soc. Can. (pres. 1963-64, Upjohn award 1982), Can. Physiol. Soc., Am. Soc. Pharmacology and Exptl. Therapeutics (Oscar B. Hunter Meml. award 1993), Can. Anaesthetist Soc. (hon., Rsch. Recognition award 1993), Deutsche Pharmakologische Gesellschaft. Discovered pharmacogenetic variants of cholinesterase, 1956; devel. pharmaco-diagnosis of malignant hyperthermia, 1970; promoted studies of pharmacoanthropology (interethnic drug comparisons), 1983-84; used caffein metabolism as a tool of biochemical epidemiology, 1986. Home: 130 McGill St, Toronto, ON Canada M5B 1H6 Office: U Toronto, Med Scis Bldg, Toronto, ON Canada M5S 1A8 *It is good to be curious. It is better if being curious is one's work.*

KALSOW, KATHRYN ELLEN, library clerk; b. Stevens Point, Wis., Dec. 31, 1938; d. Wilbert Otto and Vivian Frances (Peterson) K. BA, Luther Coll., 1961. Libr. clk. Luther Coll. Libr., Decorah, Iowa, 1961-97. Del. county conv. Rep. com., Decorah, Iowa, 1970-84, state conv., Des Moines, 1970-84; del. Nat. Fedn. Rep. Women, Washington, 1971. Mem. AAUW (treas. 1966-68, 79-81, internat. rels. area rep. 1975-77, 85-87, 90-92, named Gift Honoree, 1982), UN Assn. of USA, Iowa Libr. Assn. Lutheran. Avocations: collecting political buttons, collecting Scandinavian dolls. Home: 307 View St Decorah IA 52101-1262

KALTENBACH, C(ARL) COLIN, dean, educator; b. Buffalo, Wyo., Mar. 22, 1939; s. Carl H. and Mary Colleen (McKeag) K.; m. Ruth Helene Johnson, Aug. 22, 1964; children: James Earl, John Edward. BSc, U. Wyo., 1961; MSc, U. Nebr., 1963; PhD, U. Ill., 1967. Postdoctoral fellow U. Melbourne, Australia, 1967-69; from asst. prof. to prof. U. Wyo., Laramie, 1969-89, assoc. dean, dir. Agrl. Expt. Sta., 1980-89; vice dean, dir. Agrl. Expt. Sta. U. Ariz., Tucson, 1989—. Contbr. 200 articles to prof. publs. Named Outstanding Alumnus Coll. Agriculture U. Wyo., 1991. Mem. Nat. Assn. State Univs. and Land Grant Colls. (chmn. expt. sta. sect. 1997), Soc. for Study Reprodn. (treas. 1979-82), Am. Soc. Animal Sci., Civitan (officer 1972-85), Agrl. Experiment State Dirs. (chair 1996-97). Office: Univ of Arizona Coll Agriculture Tucson AZ 85721

KALTENBACHER, PHILIP D(AVID), industrialist, former public official; b. Orange, N.J., Nov. 7, 1937; s. Joseph C. and Helen (Lowy) K.; m. Unni Hovde, Sept. 7, 1976; children: Laura Jean, Gail Ellen, Mark Eric. BA, Yale U., 1959, LLB, 1963. Bar: Conn. 1963, N.J. 1964. With Seton Co., Newark, N.J., 1964—, chmn., chief exec. officer, 1974—; commr. Port Authority of N.Y. and N.J., 1983-93, chmn., 1985-90; dir. Chelsea GCA Realty, Inc. (NYSE), 1993; chmn. internat. conf. and gen. assembly World Trade Ctrs. Assn., 1992; chmn. bd. govs. The Club at World Trade Ctr., 1993. Rep. N.J. Gen. Assembly, Trenton, 1968-73; chmn. N.J. Rep. State Com., 1981-83. With U.S. Army, 1961. Recipient Alumni Achievement award Newark Acad., 1987, Humanitarian award Cath. Community Svcs., 1987, Svc. to Humanity award, Greater N.Y. March of Dimes Birth Defects Found., 1988. Mem. Yale Club (Ctrl. N.J. and N.Y.C.), Mountain Ridge Country Club (West Caldwell, N.J.), Longboat Key Club (Fla.), Tournament Players Club (Prestancia) Bird Key Yacht Club (Fla.), Gator Creek Golf Club (Fla.). Home: 614 S Owl Dr Bird Key Sarasota FL 34236 Office: Seton Co 849 Broadway Newark NJ 07104-4300

KALTER, ALAN, advertising agency executive; m. Chris Lezotte. With W.B. Doner & Co., Southfield, Mich., 1967—, exec. v.p., dir. retail divsn., 1990, vice chmn. account mgmt., 1990-92, pres., COO, 1992-95; CEO, chmn. W. B. Doner & Co., Southfield, Mich., 1995—. Office: W B Doner & Co 25900 Northwestern Hwy Southfield MI 48075*

KALTER, SEYMOUR SANFORD, virologist, educator; b. N.Y.C., Mar. 19, 1918; s. Aaron H. and Jessie (Schulman) K.; m. Gloria V. Verstein, Mar. 3, 1946 (dec.); children: Susan P., Steven P., Debra I. (dec.); m. Yvette L. Levine, Apr. 15, 1982. B.S., St. Joseph's Coll., Phila., 1940; M.A., U. Kans., 1943; postgrad., U. Pa., 1943-45; Ph.D., Syracuse U., 1947. Diplomate: Am. Bd. Microbiology. Asst. instr. microbiology U. Kans., 1941-43; research asst. dept. med. bacteriology U. Pa., 1943-45; asst. and asso. prof. med. microbiology Upstate Med. Center, N.Y. State U., Syracuse, 1945-56; cons. virology Pan Am. San. Bur., 1959-62, Cologne (Germany) U.; adj. prof. dept. biology Trinity U., San Antonio, 1967-98; dept. pediatrics U. Tex. Health Sci. Center, San Antonio, 1971—; dept. life scis. (microbiology) U. Tex., San Antonio, 1976-98; dental br. Dental Sci. Inst., U. Tex. Health Sci. Center, Houston, 1976-98; adj. prof. dept. microbiology U. Tex. Health Sci. Ctr., San Antonio, 1973-75; chief virus diagnostic methodology unit Communicable Disease Center, USPHS, Atlanta, 1956-61; chief virology sect. Sch. Aerospace Medicine, Brooks AFB, Tex., 1961-63; chmn. dept. microbiology S.W. Found. Rsch. and Edn., 1963-86, dir. dept. microbiology and infectious diseases, 1966-88; dir. NIH and WHO Collaborating Ctr. Reference and Rsch. in Simian Viruses, 1988—, dir. reference lab.; cons. M.D. Anderson Hosp. and Tumor Inst., Houston, 1974-98; cons. study zoonoses of primates WHO, also WHO Smallpox Eradication Unit, 1976-98 ; cons. biohazards control and containment sect. Nat. Cancer Inst., 1968-74; chmn. com. simian viruses WHO/FAO; cons. Office Pesticide Programs, EPA, 1973-75, Diagnostic Products Adv. Com., FDA, 1975-83; rsch. adv. Alamo chpt. Nat. Multiple Sclerosis Soc., San Antonio, 1970-98; pres. Virus Reference Lab., Inc., 1989-98. Fellow AAAS, Am. Pub. Health Assn., Tex. Pub. Health Assn.; mem. Am. Assn. Lab. Animal Sci., Am. Inst. Biol. Scis., Am. Soc. Primatologists, Assn. Gnotobiotics, Internat. Assn. Biol. Standardization, Internat. Assn. Comparative Research on Leukemia and Related Diseases, Tissue Culture Assn., U.S. Fedn. Culture Collection, Internat. Primatol. Soc., Am. Acad. Microbiology, Am. Soc. Virology, Am. Assn. Immunologists, Am. Assn. Lab. Animal Sci., Soc. Exptl. Biology and Medicine, N.Y., Tex. acads. scis., Am., Tex. socs. microbiologists, Am. Soc. Tropical Medicine and Hygiene, Royal Soc. Health (Eng.), Tex. Soc. Electron Microscopy, Am. Soc. Cryobiology, Wildlife Diseases Assn., Sigma Xi. Home: 206 Wood Shadow St San Antonio TX 78216-1629 Office: Ste 202-20 7540 Louis Pasteur Dr San Antonio TX 78229-4018

KALTON, GRAHAM, survey statistician; b. Bromley, Kent, Eng., Mar. 5, 1936; came to U.S., 1979; s. Gordon and Stella (Vickery) K.; m. Francis Helen Johnson, Mar. 31, 1962; children: Alan Gordon, Alison Frances. BS in Econs., London Sch. Econs., 1958, MS, 1960; PhD, U. Southampton (Eng.), 1979. Grade B tchr. The Polytechnic, Regent St, London, 1959-60; asst. lectr. London Sch. Econs., 1961-64, lectr., 1964-68, sr. lectr., 1968-70, reader, 1970-71; prof. U. Southampton, 1971-79; prof. dept biostats., rsch. scientist U. Mich., Ann Arbor, 1979-91, prof. dept. stats., 1989-91; sr. statistician, sr. v.p. Westat Inc., 1992—; rsch. prof. joint program in survey methodology U. Md., 1995—; vis. rsch. fellow Social and Community Planning Rsch. Inst., London, 1972-86. Author: The Public Schools: A Factual Survey, 1966, (with C.A. Moser) Survey Methods in Social Investigation, 1971, Introduction to Survey Sampling, 1983, Compensating for Missing Survey Data, 1983. Fellow AAAS, Royal Stats. Soc. U.K. (chmn. social stats. sect. com. 1976-78), Internat. Statis. Inst. (chmn. nominations com. 1987), Am. Statis. Assn. (chmn. survey rsch. methods sect. 1986), Internat. Assn. Survey Statisticians (pres. 1991-93), Am. Assn. for Pub. Opinion Rsch., Wash. Stats. Soc. (pres. 1997-98). Office: Westat 1650 Rsch Blvd Rockville MD 20850

KALTSOS, ANGELO JOHN, electronics executive, educator, photographer; b. Boston, Aug. 19, 1930; s. John Angelo and Rita Thomas (Goudas) K.; m. Verna Kay Wilson, June 30, 1952 (dec. Jan. 1973); children: Pamela, Elaine, Gregory, Stephanie, Lenora, Demetra, Dana. Student, Mass. Radio and TV Sch., Boston, 1955-57, Harvard Coll. Extension, 1964, Boston State Coll., 1965-67, U. N.M., 1976, Fitchburg State Coll., 1977. Clk. U.S. Postal Svc., Boston, 1954-57; electronic rsch. technician Crosley div. Avco, Cin., 1957; electronic technician Raytheon Mfg. Co., Waltham, Mass., 1957-63; educator Cambridge (Mass.) Sch. Dept., 1961-81; ind. ethnology rsch. N.Mex., 1969—; mgr. Pampas, Inc., Boston, 1987-90; bd. dirs. Expansion Dance Co., Boston; cons. 5 P.I.E., Albuquerque, 1976—, Indian Tribal Group, N.Mex.; lectr. S.W. Indian Culture in Boston, Cambridge area, 1990—; pres., treas. Spartan Enterprises, Inc., 1965-69. Author: Southwest Indian, 1986; one-man photo exhibits: Christmas Tree Gallery, Manteo, N.C., 1977, The 4th St. Photo Gallery, N.Y.C., 1980, Cambridge Rindge and Latin Sch., Mass., 1981, Jay's, Cambridge, Mass., 1983, Here Today Gallery, Boston, 1984, Andover (Maine) Town Hall, 1984, 86, Piedmont Art Assn., Martinsville, Va., 1985-86, Cambalache Gallery, Boston, 1986-87, The 4th St. Gallery, N.Y.C., 1990, Andover (Maine) Pub. Libr., 1997, 98; contbg. journalist in field. Chmn. No Thank Q Hydro Quebec, Andover, Maine, 1988-91, coord., Dryden, Maine, 1991—; regional and media coord. N.E. Alliance to Protect James Bay, 1990-91, mem. exec. bd., mem. adv. bd., treas., 1991—, project dir., 1995; mem. senate faculty Cambridge Sch. Dept., 1980-81; sec. New Eng. Model Car Assn. of Raceways, 1966-69; educator Cambridge Adult Ctr., 1990-97, Paulist Ctr., Boston, 1991-92. Recipient Robert Sweeney award Rindge Alumni Assn., 1996. Mem. Appalachian Mountain Club. Greek Orthodox. Avocations: ethnography, entomology, cooking, gardening, hiking. Home: PO Box 33 Andover ME 04216-0033

KALUDIS, GEORGE, management consultant, book company executive, educator; b. Balt., Oct. 7, 1938; s. Steven George and Theresa (Topal) K.; m. Eugenia Lione Mihalakis, July 21, 1962; children: Stephen George, Michele

Maria, William Michael, Kirk Jamie. BA, U. Md., 1960, MEd, 1965; PhD, Fla. State U., 1968. Asst. dean student life U. Md., 1960-65; resident instr. U. S. Fla., 1965-66; dir. div. planning and evaluation State Univ. Sys. Fla., 1966-70; vice chancellor ops. and fin. planning, assoc. prof. mgmt. Vanderbilt U., 1970-76, adj. assoc. prof. mgmt., 1976-78; exec. v.p. Ingram Book Co., 1976-78; chmn., pres. Kaludis Consulting Group, Washington, 1978—; mem. tech. coun. Nat. Ctr. Higher Edn. Mgmt. Sys., 1970-72, chmn. bd., 1975-76; pres., bd. dirs. Frat. Advisors Group, Inc., Tallahassee, 1968-70; mem., com. chmn. Nat. Com. on Financing Postsecondaary Edn., 1972-74. Editor: Strategies for Budgeting, New Directions in Higher Education, 1973; mem. editl. bd. On the Horizen, 1996—. Bd. dirs. NCCJ, Nashville, St. Photios Nat. Shrine, 1986-87; 1st v.p. Family and Children's Svcs., Inc., 1978-80; chmn. Spl. Com. on Cable TV, Nashville, 1982-95; mem. parish coun. Holy Trinity Greek Orthodox Ch., 1971-94, pres., 1972-78, 81-83, 92-94, Stewardship Commn., Greek Orthodox Archdiocese, 1993-95, archdiocesan coun., 1994-98, co-chmn. com. on strategic and long range planning, 1994-97, parish coun. St. George Greek Orthodox Ch., Bethesda, 1998, sec., chair stewardship com. With U.S. Army, 1962-64. Recipient Medal of St. Paul award Greek Orthodox Archdiocese, 1992, Disting. Alumnus award U. Md. Coll. Edn., 1995. Mem. Am. Assn. Higher Edn., Assn. Instnl. Rsch., Nat. Assn. Coll. and Univ. Bus. Officers, Fin. Execs. Inst. (pres. Nashville chpt. 1975), Nashville Area C. of C. (gov.), Am. Hellenic Ednl. Progressive Assn., U. Md. alumni ctr. cabinet, U. Md. arena seating planning com., Exchange Club, Omicron Delta Kappa, Pi Sigma Alpha, Sigma Phi Epsilon (chmn. commn. on univ. rels. 1992-93). Office: Ste 400 1055 Thomas Jefferson St NW Washington DC 20007-5259

KALUGER, GEORGE, clinical psychologist, educator; b. Tataria, Alba Iulia, Romania, Sept. 20, 1921; s. Niculae and Valeria (Suteu) K.; m. O. Meriem Fair, June 11, 1947. BS in Edn., Slippery Rock (Pa.) U., 1946; MEd, U. Pitts., 1948, PhD, 1950; postdoctoral, Pa. State U., Univ. Park, 1955. Lic psychologist, Pa., tchr., Pa. Tchr. science and math. Butler (Pa.) City Schs., 1946-49, guidance counselor, 1949-53; prof. edn. and psychology Shippensburg (Pa.) U., 1953-72, prof. psychology, 1972-89, chair dept. psychology, 1972-76; part time pvt. practice in clin. psychology, 1954-93; cons. rsch. learning disabilities Capital Area Inter. Unit, Camp Hill, Pa., 1960-74, Lincoln Intermediate Unit, Cross Keys, Pa., 1970-76; psychol. cons. Bur. Vocat. Rehab., Harrisburg, Pa., 1954-64; cons. perceptual devel. ctr. Shippensburg Area Schs., 1970-74. Co-author: (books) Clinical Aspects of Remedial Reading, 1963, 5th printing; Psychology and Sociology, 1969, Profiles in Human Development, 1976, Reading and Learning Disabilities, 1969, 78 (2 edits.), Human Development: Span of Life, 1974, 79, 84 (3 edits.). Pres. Tuesday Club, Shippensburg, 1958, Shippensburg Hist. Soc., 1961, Rotary Club, Shippensburg, 1963; nat. co-chmn. Shippensburg Univ. Found., 1987. 1st Lt. USAAF, 1942-45. Recipient Commonwealth Disting. Chair award Commonwealth of Pa., 1978-79, Commonwealth Disting. Tchg. Fellow award, 1978-79, Citation for Humanitarian Svc. Pa. Cerebral Palsy, 1964, Shippensburg U. Alumni Exceptional Svc. award, 1996. Fellow Pa. Psychol. Assn. (pres. acad. divsn. 1972); mem. Am. Psychol. Assn., Cumberland Valley Masonic Lodge, Ancient Order of Scottish Rites, Phi Delta Kappa (Educator of the Yr. award 1990). Avocations: travelling, cultural photography, workshops in neuropsychology, writing. Home: 625 Brenton St Shippensburg PA 17257-2113

KALWARA, JOSEPH JOHN, engineer; b. Syracuse, N.Y., June 4, 1953; s. Stanley W. and M. Bonita (Caraglin) K; m. Edith Ann Doust, 1980; children: John C., Joseph S., James V. BS in Forestry, Syracuse U., 1977; BS in Wood Products Engring., SUNY, Syracuse, 1977; AAAS in Archtl. Tech., Onondaga County C.C., 1980. Asst. engr. Firestone Bldg. Products, Carmel, Ind., 1983-84; regional tech. coord. Firestone Bldg. Products, Carmel, 1984-86, product assurance engr., 1986-88, sr. engr., 1988—. Contbr. articles to profl. jours. Mem. Single-Ply Roofing Inst., Riviera Club (Indpls.). Achievements include research in the development and engineering of building products, insulations and adhesives, sealants, and tapes relative to single-ply roofing membranes and systems; patentee in field. Avocations: Olympic style competitive weightlifting, photography, astronomy, Rolleiflex twin lens cameras. Home: 6050 N Broadway Indianapolis IN 46220 Office: Firestone Bldg Products 525 Congressional Blvd Carmel IN 46032-5647

KAM, MITCHELL M.T., international career specialist; b. Honolulu. BA in Psychology, UCLA, 1986; JD, U. San Diego, 1991; MBA, U. Tex., 1993. Bar: Tex. 1993, D.C. 1996. Project coord. Hawaii Transfer Co., Ltd., Honolulu, 1987-88; legal rsch. specialist U. San Diego Sch. Law, 1989-91; cons./group mgr. Novotel Hotel, Venlo, The Netherlands, 1992; dir. bus. devel. and mktg. Pia Piasecki Hurt i Detal, Kielce, Poland, 1994-95; cons. MBA Enterprise Corps, San Francisco, 1996-97; asst. program coord. Ctr. Internat. Bus. Edn. and Rsch., Austin, Tex., 1997; internat. career specialist U. Tex. Ford Career Ctr., Coll. and Grad. Sch. Bus., Austin, 1998—; bd. dirs. MBA Enterprise Corps, 1999—. Sr. editor Jour. Contemporary Legal Issues, U. San Diego Sch. Law, 1989-91; assoc. editor: Motions Newspaper, U. San Diego Sch. Law, 1989-91. Mem. ABA, Am. Mgmt. Assn., Am. Mktg. Assn., Soc. Competitive Intelligence Profls., State Bar of Tex., D.C. Bar, Phi Kappa Tau. Republican. Roman Catholic. Office: U Tex Ford Career Ctr Coll and Grad Sch Bus CBA 2.116 2100 Speedway Austin TX 78712-1170 Mailing Address: PO Box 7453 Austin TX 78713-7453

KAMADA-COLE, MIKA M., allergist, immunologist, medical educator; b. Denver, Dec. 9, 1957; m. Joe Lyn Cole, Dec. 7, 1991. BA in Biology, U. Mo., 1980, BA in Chemistry, 1980, MD, 1982. Diplomate: Am. Bd. Allergy and Immunology, Am. Bd. Internal Medicine, Nat. Bd. Med. Examiners. Intern in medicine Barnes Hosp., St. Louis, 1982-83, jr. resident in medicine, 1983-84; rsch./clin. fellow in allergy and immunology Dept. of Rheumatology and Immunology Brigham and Women's Hosp., Boston, 1985-88; assoc. in medicine Washington U., 1982-85; rsch. fellow in medicine Harvard Med. Sch., 1985-88, instr. in pediatrics, 1988-90; instr. Southwestern Med. Sch., 1991-92, U. Tex. Health Sci., 1992—; staff Santa Rosa Healthcare, San Antonio, 1992—, Southwest Gen. Hosp., San Antonio, 1992—, Methodist Hosp., San Antonio, 1992—. Contbr. munerous articles to med. jours. Recipient Vice Chancellor for Student Affairs Honor, 1982, Honor Grad. award Am. Med. Women's Assn., Schering Rsch. award. Fellow Am. Coll. Allergy; mem. Am. Acad. Allergy and Immunology (mem. com. asthma mortality 1987—), Tex. Med. Assn., Bexar County Med. Soc. Office: 5323 Broadway San Antonio TX 78209

KAMALI, NORMA, fashion designer; b. N.Y.C., June 27, 1945; d. Sam and Estelle (Mariategui) Arraez. Grad., Fashion Inst. of Tech., 1965. Established Kamali Ltd., N.Y.C., 1967-78; owner, designer On My Own Norma Kamali, N.Y.C., 1978—. Designer costumes for Emerald City in The Wiz, 1977; for Twyla Tharp dance In the Upper Room, 1986; Parachute Designs displayed Met. Mus. of Art, N.Y.C., 1977; prodr., dir. (video) Fall Fantasy; dir. (video) Fashion Aid, 1985. Recipient CFDA award for Outstanding Women's Fashion, 1982, Cotay Return award, 1982, Coty Hall of Fam award, 1983, Ernie awards Earnshaw Rev., 1983, Fashion Inst. Design and Merchandising award, 1984, Salute to Women award N.Y. Fashion Group, 1986, Disting. Arch. award N.Y. chpt. AIA, 1986, Outstanding Grad. award Pub. Edn. Assn. N.Y., 1988, Award of Merit, Internat. Video Culture Competition, 1988, Am. Success award Fashion Inst. Tech., 1989. Office: 11 W 56th St New York NY 10019-3902*

KAMAN, CHARLES HURON, diversified technologies corporation executive; b. Washington, June 15, 1919; s. Charles W. and Mabel (Davis) K.; m. Helen Sylvander, Oct. 20, 1945 (div.); children: Charles William II, Cathleen, Steven Wardner; m. Roberta C. Hallock, Sept. 1, 1971. BS in Aero. Engring. magna cum laude, Cath. U. Am., 1940; DSc (hon.), U. Colo., 1984, U. Hartford, 1985; LLD (hon.), U. Conn., 1985. With Hamilton Standard Propellers div. United Aircraft Corp., East Hartford, Conn., 1940-45; pres. Kaman Corp., Bloomfield, Conn., 1945-90, chmn. bd., 1945—; chief exec. officer, 1986—, pres., 1995—; chmn. Vertical Lift Aircraft council of Aerospace Industries Assn., 1964, Helicopter council, 1954; former mem. The World Affairs Ctr. Honors adv. bd. Bd. govs. Cath. U. Am.; bd. dirs. Inst. of Living; founder, pres., bd. dirs. Fidelco Guide Dog Found., Inc.; founder, Am. Leadership Forum, U. Hartford; former trustee Western New England Coll.; former mem. Catholic U. bd. govs.; past corporator Health Care Facilities Planning Council of Greater Hartford; past indsl. com. mem. Greater Hartford YMCA. Recipient Outstanding Young Man of Yr. award Hartford Jr. C. of C., 1948, Disting. Svc. award Conn. Jr. C. of C., 1953, Alumni Achievement award Cath. U. Am., 1961, The Fleet Adm. Chester W. Nimitz award Navy League of the U.S., 1986, Nat. Human Rels. award NCCJ, 1987, Vocat. Svc. award Rotary Club of Hartford, 1988, Oliver Filley Cmty. Svc. awrad Bloomfield C. of C., 1989, Nat. award for Entrepreneurial Excellence , Entrepreneurship Inst., 1990, Paul Harris Fellow award Rotary Internat., 1991, Father Michael J. McGivney award Conn. State Coun. K.C., 1991, Kim Abbot award Bloomfield Com. Svcs. to the Handicapped, 1992, Cert. of Honor, Nat. Aero. Assn., 1992, Pioneer award Assn. Unmanned Vehicle Systems 1993, Industry Leadership award Music Distributors Assn., 1993, Thomas Hooker award Antient Burying Ground Assn., 1993, Dept. of Def. award Disting. Pub. Svc., 1995, Nat. Medal of Tech., 1996; named for Outstanding Achievement in Vocat. Edn., Nat. Coun. Vocat. Edn., 1990, So. New England Socially Responsible Entrepreneur of Yr., 1991, Conn. Night Honoree, Univ. Club of Hartford, 1992. Fellow Am. Helicopter Soc. (pres. 1958, dir. 1959-61, Dr. Alexander Klemin award 1981, Disting. Svc. award 1995), AIAA, Royal Aeronautical Soc. (hon., London); mem. Helicopter Assn. Internat. (Disting. Svc. award 1995), Conn. Bus. and Industry Assn. (dir., exec. com.), Nat. Acad. Engring., Conn. Soc. Profl. Engrs. (Engr. of Yr. award 1961), Aviation Hall of Fame (charter), Nat. Mus. of Naval Aviation (Hall of Honor 1996), Navy Helicopter Assn. (hon. Assoc. award 1975), Newcomen Soc. Am., Navy League of U.S. (nat. adv. coun.), Pi Tau Sigma (hon.), Conn. Acad. Sci. and Engring., Conn. Aero. Hist. Assn., Beta Gamma Sigma. Office: Kaman Corp 1332 Blue Hills Ave Bloomfield CT 06002-1303*

KAMANAROFF, CHARLENE, elementary education educator; b. Gary, Ind., Oct. 18, 1948; d. Charles and Sue (Petrovich) Markovich; m. Mike P. Kamanaroff, July 24, 1971; 1 child, Christie Michelle. BS in Elem. Edn., Ball State U., 1970; MS in Elem. Edn., Purdue U., 1974. Elem. tchr. Merrillville (Ind.) Community Schs. Corp., 1970—, developer lang. arts curriculum, 1981—. Dir. pre-sch. program St. Joan of Arc Ch., Merrillville, 1987—. Mem. Delta Kappa Gamma (v.p. 1980-82, pres. 1990-92), Pi Beta Phi (pres. Southlake Alumnae club 1973-75, 86-88, 96—). Roman Catholic. Avocations: reading, downhill and cross country skiing. Home: 7728 Delaware Pl Merrillville IN 46410-5635 Office: Homer Iddings Sch 7249 Van Buren St Merrillville IN 46410

KAMARCK, MARTIN ALEXANDER, financial services executive; b. Rome, May 15, 1949; came to U.S., 1950; s. Andrew Martin and Margaret Ellen (Goldenweiser) K.; m. Elaine Frances Ciulla, June 17, 1972; children: Abraham Andrew, Benjamin Alexander, Chloe Margaret. BA, Haverford Coll., 1971; JD, Stanford U., 1975. Bar: Calif. 1975, U.S. Dist. Ct. (no. dist.) Calif. 1975, D.C. 1976, U.S. Ct. Appeals (D.C. cir.) 1982. Assoc. Morrison & Foerster, San Francisco, 1975-76; assoc. Morrison & Foerster, Washington, 1980-81, ptnr., 1981-86; assoc. Fried, Frank, Harris, Shriver & Kampelman, Washington, 1976-80; 1st v.p., assoc. gen. counsel Fin. Guaranty Ins. Co., N.Y.C., 1987-88, sr. v.p., gen counsel, 1988-89, dir. real estate fin., 1990-91, co-dir. structured fin., 1992-93; vice chair, COO Export-Import Bank, Washington, 1993-95, pres., chmn., 1996-97; pres., COO AEW Capital Mgmt., Boston, 1997-98; pres. fin. svcs. divsn. The Related Cos., N.Y.C., 1999—. Mem. Transp. Commn., Arlington, Va., 1981-85, chmn. 1985-87; trustee Berkeley Carroll Sch., 1989-93, emeritus, 1998—. Democrat. Unitarian. Home: 9 Griggs Ter Brookline MA 02446-4702 Office: The Related Cos 625 Madison Ave New York NY 10022-1801

KAMBER, VICTOR SAMUEL, political consultant; b. Chgo., May 7, 1944; s. Samuel J. and Cordelia A. Kamber. BA, U. Ill., 1965; MA, U. N.Mex., 1966; JD, Am. U., 1969; LLM, George Washington U., 1971. Adminstrv. asst. Congressman Seymour Halpern, Washington, 1969-72; asst. to pres. Bldg. & Constrn. Trades Dept., Washington, 1974-78; dir. AFL-CIO Labor Law Reform Task Force, Washington, 1978-80; pres., chief exec. officer The Kamber Group, Washington, 1980—; nat. v.p. Ams. for Dem. Action, Washington; bd. dirs. BB&T Bank, Washington, Whitman-Walker Clinic, Washington; sr. adv. bd. Am. League Lobbyists, Washington; bd. trustees The Nat. Theatre. Mem. Nat. Dem. Club. With U.S. Army, 1972-74. Mem. ACLU, NOW, Internat. Assn. Polit. Cons., Am. Assn. Polit. Cons. (bd. dirs. 1987-92, treas. 1991-92), Coalition Labor Union Women, Indsl. Rels. Rsch. Assn., Nat. Press Club, Local 35 Newspaper Guild, Phi Gamma Delta. Democrat. Presbyterian. Home: 129 11th St NE Washington DC 20002-6243 Office: Kamber Group 1920 L St NW Ste 700 Washington DC 20036-5018

KAMBERG, MARY-LANE, writer, journalist; b. Kansas City, Mo., Jan. 3, 1948; d. Frederick Kenneth and Jessie Marie (Lorenz) Ladewig; m. Kenneth Dee Kamberg, June 22, 1968; children: Rebekka Dyan, Johanna Lynne. BS in Journalism, U. Kans., 1981. Freelance writer Olathe, Kans., 1985—; creative writing tchr. Johnson County C.C., Overland Park, Kans., 1987—, Avila Coll., Kansas City, 1987-90; corr. Kansas City Star, 1990-96; presenter workshops in field; pres. bd. dirs. Whispering Prairie Press, Prairie Village, Kans., 1996-98, adv. bd. 1998—; mem. adv. bd. Potpourri Publs., Prairie Village, 1994-97; contbg. editor Hydro Rev. Mag., Kansas City, 1991—. Author: From Patient to Payment, 1993, Tips From Tina, 1995, Cabin Fever Relievers, 1997; project leader, editor, author anthology: Handprint in the Woods, 1997, Alzheimer's Legal Survival Guide, 1999; contbr. to nat. mags., including Better Homes and Gardens, TeenAge, Marriage and Family Living, numerous others, poetry and fiction to profl. publs. Recipient Hon. Mention award Writers Digest Mag., 1987, 88, 89, 4th pl. award Writers Digest Mag., 1990, 3d pl. award Kans. State Poetry Soc., 1992, James P. Immroth Meml. award ALA, 1996. Mem. Kansas City Writers Group (co-leader 1991-97), The Writers Place. Republican. Presbyterian. Avocations: coaching swimming, reading, youth sports. Home and Office: 2128 E 144th St Olathe KS 66062-2355

KAMBOUR, ROGER PEABODY, polymer physical chemist, researcher; b. Wilmington, Mass., Apr. 1, 1932; s. George Constantine and Ada Grace (Mattraw) K.; m. Virginia L. Dyer, Oct. 4, 1958 (div. Dec. 1982); children—Annaliese S., Christian R.; m. Barbara Jean Vivier, June 23, 1984; 1 child, Joshua V. B.A. cum laude, Amherst Coll., 1954; Ph.D. in Chemistry, U. N.H., 1960. Rschr. GE R & D Ctr., Schenectady, N.Y., 1960-94, U. Mass. rsch. prof., 1994—; vis. prof. MIT, 1991; vis. scientist Nat. Inst. Standards & Tech., Washington, 1993. Mem. editl. bd. Polymer Engring. and Sci., 1968-87, Ann. Revs. of Materials Sci., 1985-89; contbr. articles on polymer physics and phys. chemistry to profl. pubs.; patentee in field. Supr. 1st ward Schenectady County Bd. Suprs., N.Y., 1964-65; mem. Schenectady County Charter Commn., 1964-65; mem. Schenectady City Hist. Dist. Commn., 1975-81; mem. art com. Schenectady Mus., 1975-82; mem. Nat. Ski Patrol, 1988-93; chmn. Freedom Forum, 1975-76. Fellow Am. Phys. Soc. (Ford High Polymer Physics prize 1985); mem. NAE, Am. Chem. Soc. (Union Carbide Chems. award 1968). Democrat. Unitarian. Avocations: choral singing; skiing; sailing. Home: 2572 Rosendale Rd Niskayuna NY 12309-1312 Office: GE Rsch & Devel Ctr PO Box 8 Schenectady NY 12301-0008

KAMEEN, JOHN PAUL, newspaper publisher; b. Carbondale, Pa., June 2, 1941; s. Joseph Charles and Mary Veronica (O'Neill) K.; m. Carole Helen McCusker, Nov. 8, 1969; 1 child, Patricia. BS in Electronics, U. Scranton, 1963, postgrad., 1964-65. Publisher The Forest City (Pa.) News, Inc., 1967—; sec. Greater Forest City (Pa.) Industry, Inc., 1968-98; bd. dirs. Community Bancorp, Inc., Forest City, 1978—. Contbr. numerous articles on hunting to mags. and pubs. Mem. Forest City Rep. Com., 1968-78; councilman Forest City Borough, 1974-78; vice chmn. Susquehanna County Rep. Party, 1994-96, chmn. 1996—; pres. Susquehanna County Rep. Club, 1991-92. Recipient Community Betterment award, Pa. C. of C., Harrisburg, 1970, Cert. of Nat. Merit, US Dept. HUD, Washington, 1982. Mem. Pa. Newspaper Pubs. Assn. (bd. dirs. 1980-84), Nat. Newspaper Assn., Susquehanna County C. of C. (dir. 1994—). Roman Catholic. Avocations: big game hunting, fishing, golf. E-mail: bcnews@nep.net. Office: The Forest City News 636 Main St Forest City PA 18421-1430

KAMEMOTO, FRED ISAMU, zoologist; b. Honolulu, Mar. 8, 1928; s. Shuichi and Matsu (Murase) K.; m. Alice Takeyo Asayama, July 20, 1963; children: Kenneth, Garett, Janice. Student, U. Hawaii, 1946-48; A.B., George Washington U., 1950, M.S., 1951; Ph.D., Purdue U., 1954. Research assoc., acting instr. Wash. State U., 1957-59; asst. prof. zoology U. Mo., 1959-62; asst. prof. U. Hawaii, Honolulu, 1962-64; assoc. prof. U. Hawaii, 1964-69, prof. zoology, 1969-94, prof. emeritus, 1995—, chmn. dept., 1964-65, 71-80, 81-90, dir. biology program, 1992-94; vis. rsch. scholar Ocean Rsch. Inst., U. Tokyo, Biol. Lab., Fukuoka U., 1968-69; vis. prof. Coll. Agr. and Vet. Medicine, Nihon U., Tokyo, summer 1973, 1979; vis. scholar dept. biology Conn. Wesleyan U., 1975-76; sr. scientist dept. fisheries Nihon U., Tokyo, 1986; vis. fgn. rschr. Tropical Biosphere Rsch. Ctr. U. of Ryukyus Okinawa, Japan, 1994. Contbr. articles to profl. jours. Chmn. Hawaii State Natural Areas Reserve System Commn., 1985-88. Served with AUS, 1954-57. NSF grantee, 1960-79; National Oceanic and Atmospheric Administration grantee, 1985-89. Fellow AAAS; mem. Hawaii Acad. Sci., Sigma Xi. Buddhist. Home: 3664 Waaloa Way Honolulu HI 96822-1151 Office: U Hawaii Dept Zoology Honolulu HI 96822

KAMEMOTO, GARETT HIROSHI, reporter; b. Honolulu, Oct. 30, 1966; s. Fred I. and Alice T. (Asayama) K. BA, U. Hawaii, 1989. Reporter Sta. KHVH, Honolulu, 1989-92, 93-94; Sta. KGMB-TV, Honolulu, 1992-93, 94—. Home: 3664 Waaloa Way Honolulu HI 96822-1151 Office: Sta KGMB-TV 1534 Kapiolani Blvd Honolulu HI 96814-3715

KAMEN, MARTIN DAVID, physical biochemist; b. Toronto, Aug. 27, 1913. BS with honors, U. Chgo., 1933, PhD, 1936, ScD (hon.), 1969; PhD (hon.), U. Paris, 1969; ScD (hon.), Washington U., St. Louis, 1977, U. Ill., Chgo., 1978, U. Freiburg, Germany, 1979, Weizmann Inst., Rehovot, Israel, 1987, Brandeis U., 1988. Fellow nuc. chemistry Radiation Lab. U. Calif., 1937-39, rsch. assoc., 1939-41; marine test engr. Kaiser Cargo., Calif., 1944-45; assoc. prof. biochemistry Wash. U., 1945-46; assoc. prof. chemistry and chemist Mallinckrodt Inst., 1945-57; prof. biochemistry Brandeis U., 1957-61; prof. chemistry U. Calif., San Diego, 1961-74, chmn. dept., 1971-73, prof. biol. scis., 1974-78, prof. emeritus biol. scis., 1978—; prof. emeritus chem. scis. U. So. Calif., Los Angeles, 1978—. NSF sr. fellow, 1956, Guggenheim fellow, 1956, 72; recipient C.F. Kettering Award Am. Soc. Plant Physiologists, 1969. Fellow Am. Inst. Chemists, Am. Philos. Soc.; mem. Nat. Acad. Sci., Am. Chem. Soc. (award 1963), Am. Soc. Biol. Chemists (Merck award 1982), Am. Acad. Arts and Scis. (John Scott award Phila., 1989, Einstein award, Fermi award 1996). *

KAMEN, MICHAEL ANDREW, lawyer; b. N.Y.C., May 13, 1952; s. Milton and Renée (Weiss) K. AB, Columbia Coll., 1974; JD, U. Miami, Fla., 1978. Bar: Fla. 1978, U.S. Dist. Ct. (so. dist.) Fla. 1979, U.S. Ct. Appeals (11th cir.) 1987, U.S. Supreme Ct. 1988. Assoc. Fine & Burton, P.A., Ft. Lauderdale, Fla., 1979-84; of counsel Tworoger & Sader, P.A., Ft. Lauderdale, 1984-88; founding ptnr. Kamen & Orlovsky, P.A., West Palm Beach, Fla., 1988—. Author: (with others) Civil Trial Practice, 1994. Recipient Probate Law award Palm Beach County Bar Assn., 1993. Mem. ABA, Assn. Trial Lawyers Am., Acad. Fla. Trial Lawyers. Office: Kamen & Orlovsky PA 1601 Belvedere Rd West Palm Beach FL 33406-1541

KAMENAR, ELIZABETH, neurologist, neuropathologist; d. Frank Edward and Goldie (Racz) K. BA, Case Western Reserve U., 1971; MD, Ohio State U., 1975. Diplomate Am. Bd. Pathology, Am. Bd. Psychiatry and Neurology. Resident in anatomic pathology and neuropathology Duke U. Med. Ctr., Durham, N.C., 1975-79; asst. prof. neuropathology U. Tex. Med. Sch., Houston, 1979-80; resident in neurology Cleve. Clinic, 1980-84; staff neurologist Kaiser Permanente Med. Ctr., Cleve., 1984-85, 90-95; lt. comd. M.C. U.S. Navy, 1987; staff neurologist Naval Hosp., Bethesda, Md., 1987-90; pvt. practice neurology, 1995—; asst. prof. Uniformed Svcs. U. Health Scis., Bethesda, 1987-90. Contbr. articles to med. jours. Mem. Am. Acad. Neurology, Phi Beta Kappa.

KAMENSKY, JOHN MICHAEL, federal agency administrator; b. Washington, Jan. 13, 1953; s. John Thomas and Margaret Kamensky; m. Jeanne Marie Berrang, Oct. 8, 1983; children: John Andrei, David Michael. BA, Angelo State U., 1975; MPA, U. Tex., 1977. Asst. dir. U.S. Gen. Acctg. Office, Washington, 1977-93; deputy dir. Nat. Partnership for Reinventing Govt., Washington, 1993—; asst. to deputy dir. for mgmt. U.S. Office Mgmt. & Budget, Washington, 1996—. Contbr. articles to profl. jours. Capt. USAFR, 1975-81. Recipient Pub. Innovator Leadership award Alliance Redesigning Govt., Washington, 1997. Mem. Am. Soc. Pub. Adminstrn. (sect. chair 1988). Democrat. Roman Catholic. Office: Nat Partnership for Reinventing Govt 750 17th St NW Ste 200 Washington DC 20006-4607

KAMENTSKY, LOUIS AARON, biophysicist; b. Newark, July 28, 1930; s. Harry and Etta (Brodsky) K.; m. Marcia Alpern, Aug. 28, 1955; children: Lee, Howard, Ellen. B.S.E.E., N.J. Inst. Tech., 1952; Ph.D., Cornell U., 1956. Mem. staff Columbia U. ERL, N.Y.C., 1954-55, Bell Telephone Labs., Murray Hill, N.J., 1956-60, IBM Research, N.Y.C., 1960-68; pres. Biophysics Systems, Mahopac, N.Y., 1968-76; v.p. rsch. Ortho Diagnostics Systems, Cambridge, Mass., 1976-88; chmn. CompuCyte Corp., Cambridge, Mass., 1988—; vis. scientist Karolinska Inst., Stockholm, 1966; sr. rsch. scientist MIT, Cambridge, 1981-88. Patentee in field; contbr. articles to profl. jours. Home: 180 Beacon St Boston MA 02116-1401 Office: Compucyte Corp 12 Emily St Cambridge MA 02139-4507

KAMER, JOEL VICTOR, insurance company executive, actuary; b. N.Y.C., Nov. 2, 1942; s. Archie Harry and Helen Lillian (Unick) K.; m. Jane Edith Casdin, Aug. 20, 1967; children—Wendy Lynn, Allen Samuel. BS, CCNY, 1963; MA, Pa. State U., 1964; MS, Northeastern U., 1967. Actuarial asst. John Hancock Mut. Life Ins. Co., Boston, 1964-69, actuarial assoc., 1969-71, asst. controller, 1971-75, assoc. contr., 1975-79, gen. dir., 1979-82, 2d v.p., 1982-85, v.p., group ins. actuary 1985-87, sr. v.p., group ins. actuary, 1988-89, sr. v.p. retail mktg. and distbn., 1989—; dir. John Hancock Health Plans Inc. Recipient Goldman Meml. award CCNY, 1963. Fellow Soc. Actuaries, mem. Am. Acad. Actuaries. Jewish. Office: John Hancock Mut Life Ins Co PO Box 111 Boston MA 02117-0111

KAMER, LARRY, public relations executive. MA, Northwestern U. Prin. Kamer-Singer & Assocs., Inc., San Francisco, 1990—. Mem. Pub. Rels. Soc. Am. Office: Kamer-Singer & Assocs Inc Ste 450 74 New Montgomery St San Francisco CA 94105

KAMERICK, EILEEN ANN, financial executive, lawyer; b. Ravenna, Ohio, July 22, 1958; d. John Joseph and Elaine Elizabeth (Lenney) K.; m. Victor J. Heckler, Sept. 1, 1990; 1 child, Connor Joseph Heckler. AB in English summa cum laude, Boston Coll., 1980; postgrad., Exeter Coll., Oxford, Eng., 1980; JD, U. Chgo., 1984, MBA in Finance and Internat. Bus. with honors, 1993. Bar: Ill. 1984, U.S. Dist. Ct. (no. dist.) Ill. 1985, Mass. 1986, U.S. Ct. Appeals (7th cir.) 1988, U.S. Supreme Ct. 1993. Assoc. Reuben & Proctor, Chgo., 1984-86, Skadden, Arps et al, Chgo., 1986-89; atty. internat. Amoco Corp., Chgo., 1989-93, sr. fin. mgr. corp. fin., 1993-95, sr. fin. cons., 1995-96, dir. banking and fin. svcs., 1996-97; v.p., treas. IMC Global Inc., Northbrook, Ill., 1997—, Whirlpool Corp., Benton Harbor, Mich., 1997; v.p., gen. counsel GE Capital Auto Fin. Svcs., Barrington, Ill., 1997-98; v.p., treas. Amoco Corp., Chgo., 1998-99; v.p. fin. BP Amoco plc, Chgo., 1999—; CFO BP Am., 1999—; advisor fin. com. Am. Petroleum Inst., 1992; bd. dirs. Century Place Devel. Corp. Vol. adv. 7th Cir. Bar Assn., Chgo., 1987—. Mem. ABA, Phi Beta Kappa. Roman Catholic. Home: 2658D N Southport Ave Chicago IL 60614-1228 Office: BP Amoco PLC 200 E Randolph Dr MC 3206A Chicago IL 60601

KAMERMAN, SHEILA BRODY, educator, social worker; b. Jan. 7, 1928; d. S. Lawrence and Helen (Golding) Brody; m. Morton Kamerman, Sept. 11, 1947; children: Nathan Brody, Elliot Herbert, Laura Kamerman-Katz. BA, NYU, 1946; MSW, Hunter Coll., 1966; D in Social Welfare, Columbia U., 1973; Doctorate (hon.), York U., Eng., 1998. Social worker N.Y.C. Dept. Social Svcs., 1966-68; social work supr. Bellevue Psychiat. Hosp., 1968-69; assoc. prof. social work Hunter Coll., 1977-79; from rsch. assoc. to sr. rsch. assoc. Columbia U. Sch. Social Work, 1971-79, assoc. prof. social policy and planning, 1979-81; prof. Sch. Social Work Columbia U., 1981—, Compton Found. Centennial prof., 1996—; chmn. NAS-NRC panel on work, family and community, 1980-82; mem. Com. Child Devel. Rsch. and Pub. Policy, 1983-88; mem. com. on prenatal care Inst. Medicine, 1986-88; cons. in field; mem. numerous social welfare coms. and adv. bds.; mem. Gov. Cuomo's Task Force on Poverty and Welfare Reform, 1986-87, adv. com. on Work and Family, 1987-88, UN Expert groups on social welfare and family policies; mem. Inst. Medicine/Nat. Rsch. Coun. bd. on children and families, 1998—. Author: (with Alfred J. Kahn) Not for the Poor Alone, 1975, Social

Services in the United States, 1976, Social Services in International Perspective, 1977, Family Policy: Government and Families in Fourteen Countries, 1978, Child Care, Family Benefits and Working Parents, 1981, Parenting in an Unresponsive Society, 1980, Maternity and Parental Benefits and Leaves, 1980, Helping America's Families, 1982, Maternity Policies and Working Women, 1983, Income Transfers for Families with Children, 1983, Child Care: Facing the Hard Choices, 1987, The Responsive Work Place, 1987, Child Support: From Debt Collection to Social Policy, 1988, Mothers Alone: Strategies for a Time of Change, 1988, Privatization and the Welfare State, 1989, Social Services for Children, Youth and Families in the United States, 1990, Child Care, Parental Leave, and the Under 3's, 1991, A Welcome for Every Child, 1994, Starting Right: How America Neglects Its Youngest Children and What We Can Do About It, 1995, Children in big Cities, 1996, Confronting the New Politics of Child and Family Policies, (series of 6 reports), 1997, Family Change and Family Policies in Britain, Canada, New Zealand and the United States, 1998, Big Cities in the Welfare Transition, 1998; contbr. more than 200 articles to profl. jours. Recipient Hexter award Hunter Coll. Sch. Social Work, 1977, Nat. Leadership award in Social Policy, Heller Sch. Brandeis U., 1989; named to Hunt Coll. Hall of Fame, 1981; fellow Ctr. Advanced Study in Behavioral Scis., 1983-84. Mem. NASW, Am. Pub. Human Svcs. Assn., Assn. Policy Analysis and Mgmt., Phi Beta Kappa. Home: 1125 Park Ave New York NY 10128-1243 Office: Columbia U Sch Social Work 622 W 113th St New York NY 10025-7982

KAMEROW, DOUGLAS BIRON, epidemiologist, family physician, assistant surgeon general; b. Washington, Mar. 26, 1950; s. Allan Lee and Betty Jean (Clayman) K.; m. Celia Dean Shapiro, May 25, 1986; children; Anna Malka, Eli Joseph, Simon David. AB, Harvard Coll., 1972; MD, U. Rochester, 1978; MPH, Johns Hopkins U., 1984. Cert. Am. Bd. Family Practice, Am. Bd. Preventive Medicine. Intern Harbor-UCLA Med. Ctr., Torrance, 1978-79; gen. practitioner USPHS, Rochester, N.Y., 1979-81; resident Highland Hosp., Rochester, N.Y., 1981-83; chief primary care rsch. program NIMH, Rockville, Md., 1986-88; dir. clin. preventive svcs. staff USPHS Office of Disease Prevention & Health Promotion, Washington, 1988-94; dir. Ctr. for Practice and Tech. Assessment USPHS Agy. for Health Care Policy and Rsch., 1994—, asst. surgeon gen., 1997—; clin. prof. Georgetown U. Dept. Family Medicine, Washington, 1997—. Editor: Guide to Clinical Preventive Services, 1989, 2nd edit., 1995, Clinician's Handbook of Preventive Services, 1994; assoc. editor Am. Family Physician, 1989-94. Epidemiology fellow NIMH, 1983-85. Fellow Am. Acad. Family Physicians, Am. Coll. Preventive Medicine; mem. Am. Pub. Health Assn., Soc. Tchrs. of Family Medicine, Assn. Tchrs. of Preventive Medicine. Jewish. Home: 5403 Center St Chevy Chase MD 20815-7123 Office: Ctr for Practice and Tech Assessment 6010 Executive Blvd Ste 300 Rockville MD 20852-3803

KAMEROW, NORMAN WARREN, business owner, financial services executive; b. Balt., Aug. 27, 1927; s. Jacob A. and Anna M. (Adler) K.; m. Helen Adele Rosenthal, Dec. 5, 1948; children: Susan K. Meyers, Brenda K. Cohen, Julie K. Skalkos. Cert. CLU, Am. Coll., 1965, cert. in chartered fin. cons., 1982, MS in Fin. Svcs., 1984. Pres. J.A. Kamerow & Co., Washington, 1956-61; prin. Norman W. Kamerow & Assoc., Washington, 1961-79; co-owner Kamerow & Meyers, Bethesda, Md., 1979—; chmn. bd. KHHM Chartered, Silver Spring, Md., 1980-84, Capital Fin. Group, Bethesda, 1986—; chmn. bd. Capital Fin. Group, Bethesda, 1986—; bd. dirs. H. Beck, Inc., Bethesda. With U.S. Army, 1946-47. Fellow Life Underwriter Tng. Coun. (trustee 1987—); mem. Assn. for Advanced Life Underwriting, Am. Soc. CLUs/Chartered Fin. Cons., Internat. Assn. Fin. Planners, D.C. Estate Planning Coun., Million Dollar Round Table. Avocations: tennis, travel, family. Office: Capital Fin Group 11140 Rockville Pike Fl 4 Rockville MD 20852-3144

KAMERSCHEN, DAVID ROY, economist, educator; b. Chgo., Dec. 8, 1937; s. Robert R. and Elsie D. Kamerschen Barkell; m. Gena Faye Hampton, Apr. 27, 1985; children: Christine, Steven, Laura, Robert, David, Caroline. Student, Ind. U., 1959-60; B.S. in Econs., Miami U., Oxford, Ohio, 1959, M.A., 1960; Ph.D. in Econs., Mich. State U., 1964. Instr. dept. econs. Miami U., Oxford, Ohio, 1960-61; asst. instr. Mich. State U., summer 1962, 64; asst. prof. econs. U. Washington, St. Louis, 1964-65 65-66; assoc. prof. econs. U. Mo.-Columbia, 1966-68, prof., 1968-74; prof., head dept. econs. U. Ga., Athens, 1974-80, Disting. prof., Jasper N. Dorsey chair, 1980—; cons. numerous cases or hearings in antitrust, pub. utilities and personal injury fields; guest appearance Mac Neil-Lehrer Report; host TV show Kamerschen Report. Author: Readings in Microeconomics, 1969, (with Walter L. Johnson) Macroeconomics: Selected Readings, 1970, Readings in Economic Development, 1972, (with George M. Vredeveld) Economics, 1975, (with Lloyd Valentine) Intermediate Microeconomic Theory, 1981, (with Albert L. Danielsen) Current Issues in Public-Utility Economics, 1983, (with Albert L. Danielsen) Telecommunications in the Post-Divestiture Era, 1986, (with James C. Bonbright and Albert L. Danielsen) Principles of Public Utility Rates, 2nd edit., 1988, (with Richard McKenzie and Clark Nardinelli) Economics, 1989, Money and Banking, 10th edit., 1992; editor Rev. Social Theory, 1973-74; mem. editorial bds.: Bus. and Govt. Rev., 1968-72, Internat. Behavioral Scientist, 1970—, Indsl. Orgn. Rev., 1974-80, Rev. Indsl. Orgn., 1982-91, Rev. Fin. Econ., So. Econ. Jour., 1978-82, Mgmt. and Decision Econs., 1980-94; contbr. approximately 190 articles to profl. jours. Recipient Outstanding Grad. Tchr. award U. Ga., 1978; Swift Outstanding Tchr. of Yr. award, 1985; Amy Hayden scholar, 1959; Mich. State U. fellow, 1964; Disting. Research award U. Ga. Coll. Bus. Adminstrn., 1984; Swift Outstanding Teaching award, 1985. Mem. Am. Econ. Assn., So. Econ. Assn., Nat. Assn. Forensic Economists, ABA, (assoc), Phi Kappa Phi, Delta Sigma Pi, Beta Gamma Sigma, Omicron Delta Kappa, Sigma Alpha Epsilon. Fax #: (770) 542-8774. E-mail: drkaml@juno.com. Home: 3818 Sweet Bottom Dr Duluth GA 30096-1416 Office: U Ga Dept Econs Terry Coll Bus 536 Brooks Hall Athens GA 30602-6254

KAMERSCHEN, ROBERT JEROME, consumer products executive; b. Laurium, Mich., Feb. 16, 1936; s. Robert Raymond Kamerschen and Elsie D. (Barsanti) K. Barkell; m. Judith A. Campbell, July 26, 1958; children: Kathryn, Carol, Jean. B.S., Miami U., Oxford, Ohio, 1957, M.B.A., 1958. Exec. sales trainee Nat. Cash Register, Gary, Ind., 1958-59; mgmt. trainee Foote Cone & Belding, Chgo., 1959-60; dir. consumer mktg. Scott Paper Co., Phila., 1960-71; v.p. mktg. Revlon Inc., N.Y.C., 1971-73; sr. v.p. mktg. ops. Dunkin Donuts Inc., Randolph, Mass., 1973-77; pres., chief operating officer Chanel Inc. and Christian Dior Parfums Inc., N.Y.C., 1977-79; sr. v.p. Norton Simon Inc., N.Y.C., 1979-80; pres., chief exec. officer Max Factor & Co., Hollywood, Calif., 1979-83; exec. v.p., office of chmn. sector exec. Norton Simon Inc., 1980-84; pres., chief operating officer Mktg. Corp. of Am., 1984-87; pres., chief exec. officer RKO Six Flags Entertainment, Inc. div. Wesray Capital Corp., N.Y.C., 1987-88; chmn. ADVO Inc., Windsor, Conn., 1988—, ADVO, Inc., Windsor, 1999—; also bd. dirs. ADVO, Inc., Windsor, Conn.; disting. practitioner, lectr. U. Ga. Coll. Bus. Adminstrn., 1979-81; guest lectr. various univs. and trade assns.; bd. dirs. Micrografx, Inc., IMS Health Inc., R.H. Donnelley Corp.; mem. bus. adv. coun., exec.-in-residence Miami U., 1979-82. Trustee, 1st vice chmn. Emerson Coll., 1984-89; trustee Columbia Coll., 1993-96, Bushnell Hall, 1995—; exec. com. Wadsworth Atheneum, 1993—; regent U. Hartford, 1999—. Mem. N.Y. Athletic Club, Met. Club, Hartford Club, Beta Gamma Sigma, Delta Sigma Pi, Sigma Alpha Epsilon. Home: 204 Parade Hill Rd New Canaan CT 06840-4132 Office: ADVO Inc 1 Univac Ln Ste 3 Windsor CT 06095-2614

KAMES, KENNETH F., manufacturing company executive; b. Winthrop, Mass., Apr. 2, 1935; m. Edythe I. Eisenberg, June 13, 1954; children: Linda, Karen, Steven. Cert. in acctg., Bentley Coll., 1955; BSBA, Suffolk U., 1965, postgrad., 1968-70. Mgr. br. adminstrn. EDP div. Honeywell, Wellesley Hills, Mass., 1955-68; asst. contr. toiletries div. Gillette Co., Boston, 1968-70; gen. mgr. Japan Gillette Co., Tokyo, 1970-73; dir. spl. projects Gillette Co., Boston, 1973-78, fin. dir. new bus. devel., 1979-89, corp. v.p., 1989—; trustee, treas. Broadview Condo Assn., Gilford, N.H., 1994; pres. Boston chpt. Assn. Corp. Growth, 1995-97; dir. Dynamics Rsch. Corp. Mem. Mfrs. Alliance Strategic Planning and Devel. Coun.; mem. bus. adv. coun. Bentley Coll. Grad. Sch. Bus. Mem. Fin. Execs. Inst. Avocations: water sports, fishing, reading. Office: Gillette Co Prudential Tower Bldg Boston MA 02199

KAMHI, MICHELLE MARDER, editor, writer; b. N.Y.C., June 9, 1937; d. Maurice (Macy) and Ida (Michaelson) M.; m. Samuel R. Kamhi, Dec. 27, 1959 (div. Mar. 5, 1982); 1 child, Max; m. Louis Torres, Aug. 28, 1987. BA, Barnard Coll., 1958; postgrad., U. Paris, 1958-59; MA in Art History, CUNY, 1970. Asst. editor Ednl. Divsn. Houghton Mifflin Co., Boston, 1960-64; editor Columbia Univ. Press, N.Y.C., 1966-70; freelance editor, writer N.Y.C., 1970-84; assoc. editor Aristos, N.Y.C., 1984-91, co-editor, 1992—; co-founder, vice chmn. Aristos Found., N.Y.C., 1986—. Producer/dir.: (documentary film) Books Our Children Read, 1984; contbr. articles to profl. jours. Bd. dirs. Maternity Ctr. Assn., N.Y.C., 1976-81. Fulbright scholar U. Paris, 1958-59; recipient Gold award for Disting. Health Journalism, Am. Chiropractic Assn., 1980. Mem. Am. Philos. Assn., Am. Soc. for Aesthetics, Ayn Rand Soc., Assn. for Art History, Assn. Lit. Scholars and Critics. Office: Aristos Found 147 W 94th St New York NY 10025-7016

KAMIENSKA-CARTER, EVA HANNA, designer, artist; b. Warsaw, Feb. 19, 1960; came to U.S., 1987; d. Witold and Kamilla (Karwowska) K.; m. Bernard Owen Carter, July 25, 1992; children: Lisa Camille, Maya Lee. MArch, Warsaw Tech. U., 1983; grad. with honors, Art Inst. Pitts., 1991. Certificate to practice art Ministry of Culture. Freelance artist, design cons. Warsaw, 1983-87, N.Y.C., Detroit, Boston, Pitts., 1987-92; design cons., ptnr. Carter-Kamienska Design, Pitts., 1992—; freelance set designer in motion picture prodn., Pitts., 1994—; art tchr. Carnegie Mus. Art, Pitts., 1991-92, Pitts. Ctr. Arts, 1991-92. Storyboard illustrator: (software) The Ripper, 1995; one woman shows include Zdzisiaj Gallery, Warsaw, Poland, 1981, Na Brechta Gallery, Warsaw, 1984. At 700 PArker, Detroit, 1988; group exbhns. include Manfred Schuller Gallery, Zurich, 1985, Zdzisiaj Gallery, 1985, Tripoli Gallery, Phila., 1987, Pitts. Ctr. Arts, 1989. Birmingham Loft, Pitts., 1989, Mendelson Gallery, Pitts., 1989, Monroeville (Pa.) Libr. Gallery, 1989, IUP Gallery, Indiana, Pa., 19981, Carnegie (Pa.) Libr., 1992, Associated Artists Pitts. Gallery, 1993. Mem. Assoc. Artists Pitts., Pitts. Soc. Artists, Pitts. Ctr. Arts. Avocations: attending cultural and social events, hiking, canoeing, computers. Home: 853 Phineas St Pittsburgh PA 15212-8026 Office: Carter-Kamienska Design 853 Phineas St Pittsburgh PA 15212-8026

KAMIL, ELAINE SCHEINER, physician, educator; b. Cleve., Jan. 26, 1947; d. James Frank and Maud Lily (Severn) Scheiner; m. Ivan Jeffery Kamil, Aug. 29, 1970; children: Jeremy, Adam, Megan. BS magna cum laude, U. Pitts., 1969, MD, 1973. Diplomate Am. Bd. Pediats., Am. Bd. Pediat. Nephrology. Intern in pediats. Children's Hosp. Pitts., 1973-74, resident in pediats., 1974-76; clin. fellow in pediat. nephrology Sch. Medicine, UCLA, 1976-79, acting asst. prof. pediats., 1979-80; rsch. fellow in nephrology Harbor-UCLA Med. Ctr., Torrance, Calif., 1980-82; med. dir. The Children's Clinic of Long Beach, Calif., 1984-87; med. dir. pediat. nurse practitioner program Calif. State U., Long Beach, 1984-87; asst. clin. prof. pediats. Sch. Medicine, UCLA, 1988-90, assoc. clin. prof. pediats., 1991-97; assoc. dir. pediat. nephrology and transplant immunology Cedars-Sinai Med. Ctr., L.A., 1990—; clin. prof. pediats. Sch. Medicine, UCLA, 1997—; adj. asst. prof. pediats. Harbor-UCLA, Torrance, Calif., 1983-87, UCLA, 1987-88; cons. in pediat. nephrology Hawthorne (Calif.) Cmty. Med. Group, 1981—. Author chpts. to books; contbr. articles to profl. jours. Mem. AAUW, Am. Soc. Nephrology, Am. Soc. Pediat. Nephrology, Am. Fedn. Clin. Rsch., Internat. Soc. Nephrology, Internat. Soc. Pediat. Nephrology, Internat. Soc. Peritoneal Dialysis, Renal Pathology Soc., So. Calif. Pediatric Nephrology Assn. (chair steering com. 1998—), Nat. Kidney Found. So. Calif. (mem. med. adv. bd. 1987-96, rsch. com. 1987-90, chmn. pub. info. med. adv. bd. 1988-92, mem. handbook com. 1988, co-chair med. adv. bd. cmty. svcs. com. 1992-93, chair-elect patience svcs. and cmty. edn. com. 1993-94, chair patients svcs. and cmty. edn. com. 1994-95, kidney camp summer vol. physician 1988-91, 93, 94, 97, Arthur Gordon award 1991, Exceptional Svc. award 1992, Exceptional Leadership and Support award 1995, bd. dirs. 1995-96), Alpha Omega Alpha, Phi Beta Kappa. Office: Cedars-Sinai Med Ctr 8700 Beverly Blvd Los Angeles CA 90048-1865*

KAMIN, BLAIR DOUGLASS, newspaper critic; b. Red Bank, N.J., Aug. 6, 1957; s. Arthur Z. and Virginia P. Kamin. BA, Amherst Coll., 1979; M in Environ. Design, Yale U., 1984. Reporter Des Moines Register, 1984-87; reporter Chgo. Tribune, 1987-88, suburban affairs writer, 1988-92; culture news reporter, 1992, architecture critic, 1992—. Contbr. articles to profl. jours. Recipient Nat. Edn. Reporting award Edn. Writers Assn., 1985, Edward Scott Beck award Chgo. Tribune, 1990, Pulitzer Prize for Criticism, Chicago Tribune, 1999. Jewish. *

KAMIN, CHESTER THOMAS, lawyer; b. Chgo., July 30, 1940; s. Alfred and Sara (Liebenson) K.; m. Nancy Schaefer, Sept. 8, 1962; children—Stacey Allison, Scott Thomas. A.B. magna cum laude, Harvard Coll., 1962; J.D., U. Chgo., 1965. Bar: Ill. 1965, U.S. Dist. Ct. (no. dist.) Ill. 1965, U.S. Dist. Ct. D.C. 1994, U.S. Ct. Appeals (7th cir.) 1970, U.S. Supreme Ct. 1971, U.S. Ct. Appeals (5th cir.) 1975, U.S. Ct. Appeals (2d cir.) 1987, U.S. Ct. Appeals (6th cir.) 1996. Law clk. Ill. Appellate Ct., 1965-66; assoc. Jenner & Block, Chgo., 1966-72, ptnr., 1975—; spl. counsel to Gov. Ill., Springfield, 1973-74; mem. steering com. Com. on Cts. and Justice, 1971—; mem. Ill. Law Enforcement Commn., 1975-77. Contbr. articles to profl. jours. Fellow Am. Bar Found., Am. Coll. Trial Lawyers; mem. ABA, Ill. State Bar Assn., Chgo. Bar Assn., Chgo. Council Lawyers, Law Club, Quadrangle Club. Office: Jenner & Block 1 E Ibm Plz Fl 4700 Chicago IL 60611-3599

KAMIN, KAY HODES, financial planner, lawyer, entrepreneur, educator; b. Chgo., July 3, 1940; d. Barnet and Eleanor (Cramer) H.; m. Malcolm S. Kamin, June 12, 1963; children; Kim Alison, Kyle Barret. BA, Vassar Coll., 1961; MA, U. Chgo., 1962, PhD, 1970; JD cum laude, Northwestern U., 1981. Bar: Ill. 1981, U.S. Dist. Ct. (no. dist.) Ill. 1981; registered investment advisor, Ill. History tchr. Lincoln Park H.S., Chgo., 1963-67; social studies coord. U. Chgo., 1968-69; assoc. prof. edn. Rosary Coll., River Forest, Ill., 1970-76; jud. law clk. Ill. Appellate Ct., Chgo., 1981-83; assoc. Mayer, Brown & Platt, Chgo., 1983-85; v.p., gen. counsel Glencorp, Inc. dba Benetton, Chgo., 1985-93; also bd. dirs. Glencorp, Inc., Chgo., 1985-93; pres. Sutton Pl. Fin., Inc., Chgo., 1993—. Co-author Contract Law, 1983; fin. editor, columnist Today's Chgo. Woman, 1998—; frequent guest on Making Money, CLTV; contbr. articles to profl. jours. Pres. Chgo. Coun. for Social Studies, 1967-69; bd. govs., life mem. Chgo. Art Inst., 1974—; pres. Soc. for Contemporary Art, 1974-76; pres. Sedoh Found., 1986—;v.p., bd. dirs. Women's Bd., Northwestern U., 1998-99; mem. exec. com., treas. collectors' forum Chgo. Mus. Contemporary Art. Fellow U. Chgo. Grad. Sch., 1967-70. Mem. Chgo. Bar Assn. (vice chair fin. svcs. com. 1995-96), Arts Club, John Evans Club (Northwestern U.), Chgo. Capital Club (founder 1995, pres. 1995—). Avocations: golf, jogging, art collecting. Office: Sutton Place Financial Inc 1305 N Sutton Pl Chicago IL 60610-2007

KAMIN, SHERWIN, lawyer; b. N.Y.C., Feb. 5, 1927; s. Theodore and Esther K.; children: Lawrence O., Samuel N., Janet C., David W., Julia E.; m. S. Jeanne Hall, Oct. 1, 1993. BBA, CCNY, 1948; LLB, Harvard U., 1951. Bar: N.Y. 1953. Asst. to reporter Fed. Income Tax Project, Am. Law Inst., Cambridge, Mass., 1951-52; assoc. Botein, Hays, Sklar & Herzberg, N.Y.C., 1952-62, ptnr., 1962-68; ptnr. Kramer, Levin, Naftalis, Nessen, Kamin & Frankel, N.Y.C., 1968-93; of counsel Kramer, Levin, Naftalis & Frankel, N.Y.C., 1993—. Served with USN, 1945-46. Mem. ABA, Assn. of Bar of City of N.Y., N.Y. State Bar Assn., Am. Law Inst., Am. Coll. Tax Counsel. Home: 163 W 76th St New York NY 10023-8325 Office: Kramer Levin Naftalis & Frankel 919 3rd Ave New York NY 10022-3902

KAMINE, BERNARD SAMUEL, lawyer; b. Dec. 5, 1943; m. Marcia Phyllis Haber; children: Jorge H., Benjamin H., Tovy H. BA, U. Denver, 1965; JD, Harvard U., 1968. Bar: Calif. 1969, Colo. 1969. Dep. atty. gen. Calif. Dept. Justice, L.A., 1969-72; asst. atty. gen. Colo. Dept. Law, Denver, 1972-74; assoc. Shapiro & Maguire, Beverly Hills, Calif., 1974-76; ptnr. Kamine, Steiner & Ungerer (and predecessor firms), L.A., 1976—; judge pro tem Mcpl. Ct., 1974—, Superior Ct., 1989—; bd. dirs., sec. Pub. Works Stds., Inc., 1996—; arbitrator Calif. Pub. Works Contract Arbitration Com., 1990—, Am. Arbitration Assn., 1976—; mem. adv. com. legal forms Calif. Jud. Coun., 1978-82. Author: Public Works Construction Manual: A Legal Guide for California, 1996; contbr. chpts. to legal texts and articles to profl. jours. Mem. L.A. County Dem. Ctrl. Com., 1982-85; mem. Pacific S.W. regional bd. Anti-Defamation League, 1982—, pres. bd., 1998—, nat. commr., 1998—. Col. USAR, 1969—. Mem. ABA, Calif. State Bar Assn. (chair conf. dels. calendar coordinating com. 1991-92), L.A. County Bar Assn. (chair Superior Cts. com. 1977-79, chair constrn. law subsect. of real property sect. 1981-83), Engring. Contractors' Assn. (bd. dirs. 1985—, affiliate chair 1992-93, affiliate DIG award 1996), Assoc. Gen. Contractors Calif. (L.A. dist. bd. dirs. 1995—), Am. Constrn. Insps. Assn. (bd. registered constrn. inspectors 1990-97), Beavers, Res. Officers Assn. (pres. chpt. 1977-78), Omicron Delta Kappa. Office: 350 S Figueroa St Ste 250 Los Angeles CA 90071-1201

KAMINER, BENJAMIN, physician, educator; b. Slonim, Poland, May 1, 1924; came to U.S., 1959, naturalized, 1973; s. Idel and Bluma (Zayoncik) K.; m. Freda Shnitke, Aug. 22, 1948; children—Brian, Lauren. M.B., B.Ch., U. Witwatersrand, South Africa, 1946; diploma child health, Royal Coll. Physicians and Surgeons, Eng. House physician, surgeon Johannesburg (South Africa) Gen. Hosp., 1947-48; registrar Edgeware Hosp., London, 1949-50; lectr. physiology Med. Sch. Johannesburg, 1951-54, sr. lectr., 1955-59; investigator Marine Biol. Lab., Woods Hole, Mass., 1959-69; lectr. Harvard Med. Sch., Boston, 1968-69; prof., chmn. dept. physiology Boston U. Sch. Medicine, 1970—. Rockefeller fellow, 1959-60. Mem. Marine Biol. Lab., Soc. Gen. Physiology, Am. Physiol. Soc., Soc. Cell Biology, Biophys. Soc. Office: Boston Univ Sch medicine 715 Albany St Boston MA 02118-2526

KAMINOW, IVAN PAUL, physicist; b. Union City, N.J., Mar. 3, 1930; s. Benjamin and Belle (Glazer) K.; m. Florence Fischer, Nov. 26, 1952; children: Paula, Leonard, Ellen. BSEE, Union Coll., Albany, N.Y., 1952; MS, UCLA, 1954; AM, Harvard U., 1957, PhD, 1960. Diplomate Am. Bd. Laser Surgery. Physicist Hughes Aircraft Co., Culver City, Calif., 1952-54, AT&T Bell Labs., Holmdel, N.J., 1954-96, Lucent Bell Labs., Holmdel, 1996—; vis. lectr. Princeton U., 1968, U. Calif., Berkeley, 1977, Columbia U., 1986; vis. prof. Tokyo U., 1990-91; cons. Kaminow Lightwave Tech., 1997—. Author: Introduction to Electrooptic Devices, 1974; assoc. editor: Jour. Quantum Electronics, 1978-83; co-editor: Optical Fiber Telecommunications II, 1988, III, 1997; contbr. articles to profl. jours. Mem. Tinton Falls Bd. Edn., 1966-74; mem. sci. com. U.S. House of Reps. Hughes fellow UCLA, 1954, Bell Labs. fellow Harvard U., 1957-60. Fellow IEEE (life, Quantum Electronics award 1983, Congl. fellow 1996), Am. Phys. Soc., Optical Soc. Am. (Charles Hard Townes award 1995, Tyndall award 1997); mem. NAE. Patentee in field. Office: Lucent Techns/Bell Labs 791 Holmdel Rd Holmdel NJ 07733-1661

KAMINS, BARRY MICHAEL, lawyer; b. Oct. 3, 1943; s. Abe and Evelyn Bertha (Goffen) K.; m. Fern Louise Kamins, Mar. 30, 1968; 1 child, Allyson. BA, Columbia U., 1965; JD, Rutgers U., 1968. Bar: N.Y. 1969, U.S. Dist. Ct. (ea. and so. dists.) N.Y. 1973, U.S. Supreme Ct. 1974. Asst. dist. atty., 1969-73; dep. chief Criminal Ct. Bur., 1971-73; ptnr. flamhaft, Levy Kamins & Hirsch, 1973—; chmn. grievance com. 2d and 11th Jud. Dist., 1994-98; adj. assoc. prof. Fordham Law Sch.; adj. asst. prof. in criminal law N.Y. Tech. Coll.; apptd. spl. prosecutor, Kings County, 1990-92; adj. assoc. prof. N.Y. criminal procedure, law sch. Fordham U., 1994—. Author: The Social Studies Student Investigates the Criminal Justice System, 1978, New York Search and Seizure, 1991; contbr. numerous articles on criminal law to profl. jours. Mem. ABA, N.Y. State Bar Assn. (mem. ho. dels., co-chair com. on justice and the cmty. 1994—), Bklyn. Bar Assn. (past pres., chair jud. com. 1994—), Kings County Criminal Bar Assn. (past pres.), Nat. Dist. Attys. Assn., Assn. of Bar of City of N.Y. (chair jud. com. 1998—, chairperson oversight com. for criminal def. orgns., 2d appellate divsn. 1997—). Office: 16 Court St Brooklyn NY 11241-0102

KAMINS, PHILIP E., diversified manufacturing company executive; b. 1936. Salesman H. Muehlstein, 1957-62; founder Kamco Plastics Inc., Sun Valley, Calif., 1965-71; pres., CEO PMC Inc., Sun Valley, Calif., also bd. dirs. Office: PMC Inc 12243 Branford St Sun Valley CA 91352-1010

KAMINSKI, DONALD LEON, medical educator, surgeon, gastrointestinal physiologist; b. Elba, Nebr., Nov. 9, 1940; s. Edwin and Irene (Syntek) K.; m. Maureen M. Cudmore, Nov. 28, 1964; children: Christian, Julie, Jane, Kathryn. B.S., Creighton U., 1962, M.D., 1966. Diplomate: Am. Bd. Surgery. Intern. St. Louis U., 1966-67, resident in surgery, 1967-71; attending surgeon St. Louis U. Hosp., 1972—, dir. gen. surgery, 1982—. Mem. Soc. Univ. Surgeons, Am. Physiol. Soc., Am. Gastroent. Assn., Am. Surg. Assn., Central Surg. Soc., Alpha Omega Alpha. Republican. Roman Catholic. Home: 1025 Joanna Ave Saint Louis MO 63122-1821 Office: St Louis U 3635 Vista at Grand PO Box 15250 Saint Louis MO 63110-0250

KAMINSKI, JANUSZ ZYGMUNI, cinematographer; b. Ziembice, Poland, June 27, 1959; came to U.S., 1981; s. Marian Kaminski and Jadwiga Celner; m. Holly Hunter, May 20, 1995. BA in Film, Columbia Coll., 1987. Dir. photography film Lisa, 1988 (Line Eagel award Ill. Film Festival), Absence, 1988, Selling Short, 1988, Grim Prairie Tales, 1989, All The Love in The World, 1989, Rain Killer, 1990, The Terror Within II, 1991, The Adventures of Huck Finn, 1992, Cool As Ice, 1992, Mad Dog Coll, 1992, Trouble Bound, 1993, Schindler's List, 1993 (Academy Award, Best Cinematography), How to Make an American Quilt, 1995, Jerry Maguire, 1996, Lost World, 1997, Amistad, 1997, Saving Private Ryan, 1998 (Academy Award, Best Cinematography). Office: 1223 Wilshire Blvd # 645 Santa Monica CA 90403-5400*

KAMINSKI, PAUL GARRETT, federal agency administrator, investment banker; b. Cleve., Sept. 16, 1942; s. Theodore Albert and Eleanor Marie (Dobranski) K.; m. Julia Kent Crafts, Oct. 8, 1966; children: Laura Denise, Garrett Kent. BS, USAF Acad., 1964; MS in Aerospace and Astronautics, MIT, 1966, MSEE, 1966; PhD in Aeronautics and Astronautics, Stanford U., 1971. Commd. 2d lt. USAF, 1964, advanced through grades to col., 1979; spl. asst. to under sec. of def. USAF, Washington, 1977-81; dir. low observables tech. Office Dep. Chief Staff for R&D, Dept. Air Force, 1981-84; ret., 1984; pres., COO, Tech. Strategies & Alliances, Burke, Va., 1985-93, chmn., CEO, 1993-94; under sec. of def. for acquisition and tech. Dept. Def., Washington, 1994-97; chmn., CEO Technovation, Inc., 1997—; sr. ptnr. Global Tech. Ptnrs. LLC, 1998—; chmn. Def. Sci. Bd., Washington, 1993-94. Contbr. articles to sci. jours. Dir. Spl. Olympics, Palos Verdes (Calif.) H.S., 1971-73. Decorated Legion of Merit; recipient D.S.M., Office Sec. Def., 1981, Disting. Pub. Svc. medal, 1966, 97; Medal of Merit in gold Netherlands Ministry Def., 1997. Mem. IEEE, NAE, AIAA, AAAS, Sigma Xi, Tau Beta Pi, Sigma Gamma Tau. Avocations: golf, tennis, jogging, cross-country skiing. Office: Technovation Inc 6691 Rutledge Dr Fairfax Station VA 22039-1753

KAMINSKY, ALICE RICHKIN, English language educator; b. N.Y.C.; d. Morris and Ida (Spivak) Richkin; m. Jack Kaminsky; 1 son, Eric (dec.). B.A., NYU, 1946, M.A., 1947, Ph.D., 1952. Mem. faculty dept. English NYU, 1947-49, Hunter Coll., 1952-53, Cornell U., 1954-57, Broome Community Coll., 1958-59, Cornell U., 1959-63; mem. faculty dept. English SUNY, Cortland, 1963—, prof., 1968-91, prof. emeritus, 1991—, faculty exchange scholar. Author: George Henry Lewes as Critic, 1968, Logic: A Philosophical Introduction, 1974; editor: Literary Criticism of George Henry Lewes, 1964, Chaucer's Troilus and Criseyde and the Critics, 1980, The Victim's Song, 1985; contbr. more than 70 articles and revs. to numerous jours. Mem. MLA, Chaucer Soc. Office: SUNY Coll Dept English Cortland NY 13045 *At a very early age I learned that life is fragile, that many loved and lovely things die or disappear. My way of coping with that knowledge was to latch on to the work ethic. This meant working to achieve some end.*

KAMINSKY, ANATOL, educator, writer; b. Ukraine, May 17, 1925; came to U.S., 1960; s. Gregory and Eudokia Kaminsly; m. Tatjana Kaminsky; 1 child, Taras. Magister juris, Ukrainian Free U., Munich, 1954, JD, 1990; cert. in internat. rels., London Sch. Econs./Polit. Sci., 1958. Editor Ukrainian Ind., Munich, 1953-58; v.p. rsch. Prolog Assocs., N.Y.C., 1960-81; sr. editor Suchsnist, N.Y.C., 1962-83; dir., chief editor Urkainian svc. Radio Free Europe/Radio Liberty, N.Y.C., 1983-89; prof. internat. rels. Ukrainian Free U., 1993—, dean faculty of law and socio-econ. scis., 1996-98; guest prof. Lviv (Ukraine) State U., 1993—. Author; 12 books in Ukrainian. Chmn. polit. coun. Rep. of Ukrainian Supreme Liberation Coun., N.Y.C. and Munich, 1996—; assoc. mem. nat. coun. Dem. Party of Ukraine, 1996—.

Recipient Internat. Orlyk prize Dem. Party of Ukraine, 1994. Mem. Orgn. Ukrainian Nationalists (chmn. 1991—). Home: 68 The Rise Warwick NY 10990-4232

KAMINSKY, ARTHUR CHARLES, lawyer; b. Bronx, N.Y., Dec. 29, 1946; s. Daniel and Claire (Sternberg) K.; m. Andrea Lynn Polin, Dec. 28, 1969; children: Alexis Kate, Thomas Suradet, Eric Vorapong. BA cum laude with distinction, Cornell U., 1968; JD, Yale U., 1971. Bar: N.Y. 1974, U.S. Dist. Ct. (so. dist.) N.Y. 1975, U.S. Tax Ct. 1977, U.S. Supreme Ct. 1984. Assoc. Paul Weiss Rifkind Wharton & Garrison, 1973-74; ptnr. Taft & Kaminsky, N.Y.C., 1974—; pres. A.C.K. Sports, Inc. (now The Marquee Group, Inc.), N.Y.C., 1977—, Profl. Sports Investors, Inc., N.Y.C., 1982—; mem. selection com. U.S. Olympic Hockey Team, Mpls., 1980. Co-author: One Goal; A Chronicle of the 1980 U.S. Olympic Hockey Team, 1984; weekly columnist N.Y. Times, 1973-77; intern for 3d congl. dist. N.Y. Adlai E. Stevenson Meml., 1967. Dep. campaign mgr. Lindsay for Pres., N.Y.C., 1972; del. credentials com. Dem. Nat. Conv., Miami, 1972; adminstrv. asst. Rep. Michael Harrington, Washington, 1972-73; pres. Plandome Civic Assn., 1981-82; trustee African-Am. Athletic Assn., 1992—. Recipient Outstanding Sr. award Cornell U., 1968, Friends of Edn. award N.Y. State Teachers Union, 1988; named one of the 100 Most Powerful Poeple in Sports, The Sporting News, 1991-92; finalist Thurman Arnold Moot Ct. competition, 1970; inducted charter mem. Jericho H.S. Hall of Fame, 1991. Mem. N.Y. State Bar Assn., Assn. of Bar of City of N.Y., Com. Entertainment and Sports, ABA, New Sch. Soc. Research (lectr.), Sports Lawyers Assn. (lectr.), Quill and Dagger, Friars Club, Plandome Country Club, Phi Beta Kappa (hon.). Democrat. Jewish. Home: 25 Middle Dr Manhasset NY 11030-1414 Office: The Marquee Group 888 7th Ave Fl 37 New York NY 10019-5841

KAMINSKY, GLENN FRANCIS, deputy chief of police retired, business owner, teacher; b. Passaic, N.J., Apr. 29, 1934; s. Francis Gustave and Leona Regina (Tubach) K.; m. Janet Lindesay Strachan (div. June 1985); childrenn: Lindesay Anne, Jon Francis; m. Melanie Sue Rhamey, Mar. 11, 1989. BS in Police Sci., San Jose (Calif.) State Coll., 1958; MS in Adminstrn., San Jose State U., 1975. Cert. tchr., Alaska, N.Y., Calif., Colo., Fla., N.Mex., Oreg., Wyo., Va., Oreg., also others. Police officer San Jose Police Dept., 1957-65, sgt., 1965-75, lt., 1975-81; dep. chief Boulder (Colo.) Police Dept., 1981-92; ret.; pres. Kaminsky & Assocs., Inc., Longmont, Colo. 1981—. Author, editor: textbook Implementing the FTO Program, 1981—; contbr. articles to profl. jours. Exec. dir. Nat. Assn. Field Tng. Officers Assn. Sgt. U.S. Army, 1957-61, Korea. Mem. Police Mgmt. Assn. (sec. 1983-88), Calif. Assn. Police Tng. Officers, Internat. Assn. Women Police, Calif. Assn. Adminstrn. of Justice Educators, Internat. Assn. Chiefs of Police (use of deadly force com.). Republican. Episcopalian. Avocations: bowling, softball, art collecting. Home and Office: 8965 Sage Valley Rd Longmont CO 80503-8885

KAMINSKY, MANFRED STEPHAN, physicist; b. Koenigsberg, Germany, June 4, 1929; came to U.S., 1958; s. Stephan and Kaethe (Gieger) K.; m. Elisabeth Moellering, May 1, 1957; children: Cornelia B., Mark-Peter. First diploma in physics, U. Rostock, Germany, 1951; Ph.D. in Physics magna cum laude, U. Marburg, Germany, 1957. German Research Soc. fellow and grad. asst. in physics U. Rostock, 1950-52; lectr. Rostock Med. Tech. Sch., 1952; German Research Soc. fellow and research asst. Phys. Inst., U. Marburg, 1953-57, sr. asst., 1957-58; research asso. Argonne (Ill.) Nat. Lab., 1958-59, asst. physicist, 1959-62, assoc., 1962-70, sr. physicist, 1970-86, dir. Surface Sci. Center-CTR Program, 1974-80, dir. Tribology Program, 1984-86; sole propr. Surface Treatment Sci. Internat., Hinsdale, Ill., 1986—; cons. Office Tech. Assessment U.S. Congress, 1986, NRC com. on tribology, 1986-88; guest prof. Inst. Energy, U. Que., Montreal-Varennes, 1976-82; E.W. Mueller lectr. U. Wis., Milw., 1978; symposium chmn. Internat. Conf. Metall. Coatings, 1985-93. Author: Atomic and Ionic Impact Phenomena on Metal Surfaces, 1965; contbr. articles to profl. jours.; editor: Radiation Effects on Solid Surfaces, 1976; co-editor: Surface Effects on Controlled Fusion, 1974, Surface Effects in Controlled Fusion Devices, 1976, Dictionary of Terms for Vacuum Science and Technology, 1980. Bd. dirs. Com. 100, Hinsdale, 1970-75, 90-92, pres., 1973-74; pres. St. Vincent de Paul Soc., Hinsdale, 1972-73. Named Outstanding New Citizen of Year Citizenship Council Chgo., 1968; Japanese Soc. Promotion of Sci. fellow, 1982. Fellow Am. Phys. Soc.; mem. Am. Chem. Soc., Scientific Research Soc., Research Soc. Am., AAAS, Union German Phys. Socs., Am. Vacuum Soc. (sr., trustee 1982-84, chmn. Midwest sect. 1967-68, co-founder Gt. Lakes chpt., dir. 1968-70, chmn. fusion tech. div. 1980-81, editorial bd. jour. 1978-83, hon. 1986), Internat. Union Vacuum Sci., Techs. and Applications (chmn. fusion div. 1984-86), Sigma Xi. Patentee in field. Home: 906 S Park Ave Hinsdale IL 60521-4519 also: 300 Galen Dr Apt 506 Key Biscayne FL 33149-2177 Office: Surface Treatment Sci Internat PO Box 175 Hinsdale IL 60522-0175

KAMINSKY, PHYLLIS, international consulting executive; b. Montreal, Que., Can., Dec. 1, 1936; came to U.S., 1945, naturalized, 1958; d. Julius and Betty (Shapiro) Levitt; m. Samuel Kaminsky, June 24, 1971; children: David, Glenn. BA in Polit. Sci., U. Mich., 1957; postgrad., Columbia U., 1957-58. Sec. spkrs. bur. Fgn. Policy Assn., N.Y.C., 1957-58; editor disarmament procs. UN, Geneva, 1958; secretarial supr. McKinsey and Co., Geneva, 1963-64; adminstrv. asst. Chrysler Internat. S.A., also Internat. Rsch. Cons. S.A., Geneva, 1959-63, Grey Advt. Internat., N.Y.C., 1965-67; exec. asst. Lee Burdick Advt., Inc., N.Y.C., 1967-68; bilingual press attache S.B.M. Resort Complex, Monte Carlo, 1968-69; pub. rels. asst. Mayor's Com. for 25th Anniversary of UN, N.Y.C., 1970-71; consular corps liaison officer N.Y.C. Dept. Pub. Events, 1967-68; media cons., pub. rels. adv. United Jewish Appeal, N.Y.C., 1971-80; media cons. Bush for Pres. Campaign, Pa., Ill., 1980; dep. dir. comm. Coalition for Reagan-Bush, 1980; press sec. to sr. fgn. policy adv. Office of Pres.-Elect, 1980-81; press liaison White House, Nat. Security Coun., 1981; dir. Office of Pub. Liaison, USIA, 1981-83; dir. UN Info. Ctr., Washington, 1983-88; pres. Kaminsky Assocs., 1989—; mem. U.S. ofcl. del. 29th session UN Commn. on Status of Women, 1982. Co-founder Jerusalem Women's Seminar, 1979—; mem. adv. com. trade policy Dept. Commerce and U.S. Trade Rep., 1989-93. Recipient Gold Key award PR News, 1984. Mem. AAUW, Pub. Rels. Soc. Am., Internat. Pub. Rels. Soc., Women in Comm. (chmn. pub. affairs adv. bd. 1984-85), Exec. Women in Govt., Internat. Women's Forum (bd. dirs. 1986-89), Internat. Women's Media Found. (pres. 1989), Internat. Inst. Women's Polit. Leadership (bd. dirs. 1989-94), The European Inst. (exec. com. 1989), Internat. Rep. Inst. (bd. dirs. 1989-94), USAF Acad. (pres. apptd. bd. visitors 1990-92), Assn. Univs. for Rsch. in Astronomy (bd. dirs. 1992-96), U.S. Commn. for Preservation Ams. Heritage Abroad (presdl. appointee), Nat. Def. U. Found. (bd. dirs. 1995-98), Kids Votings USA (bd. dirs. 1995-98).

KAMINSKY, RICHARD ALAN, lawyer; b. Toledo, Nov. 15, 1951; s. Jack and Sally (Kale) K. BA, Johns Hopkins U., 1973; JD, U. Mich., 1975. Bar: Ill. 1976, U.S. Dist. Ct. (no. dist.) Ill. 1976. Assoc. Vedder, Price, Kaufman & Kammholz, Chgo., 1976-83; atty. Borg-Warner Corp., Chgo., 1983-89; v.p., assoc. gen. counsel CNA Ins. Cos., Chgo., 1989—. Contbr. chpt. to book. Mem. ABA, Chgo. Bar Assn., Ill. State C. of C. Home: 47 Williamsburg Rd Evanston IL 60203-1813 Office: CNA Ins Cos CNA Pla Chicago IL 60685

KAMLOT, ROBERT, performing arts executive; b. Vienna, Austria, Nov. 28, 1926; came to U.S., 1938, naturalized, 1943; s. Paul and Elsa (Wilhelm) K.; m. Jayne Bullard, Sept. 18, 1948. Student, CCNY, Syracuse U., Hunter Coll., N.Y.C. Freelance mgr. Broadway prodns., 1964-71; prodn. exec. Zev Bufman Prodns., N.Y.C., 1969-71; co.-mgr. Much Ado About Nothing, N.Y.C., 1972, Two Gentlemen From Verona (nat. co.), Los Angeles, 1973. Gen. mgr. N.Y. Shakespeare Festival, 1973-83; gen. mgr. The Real Thing, Sunday in the Park With George, Biloxi Blues, The Odd Couple, Moon for the Misbegotten, Whoopi Goldberg, Social Security, Long Day's Journey Into Night, 1983-86, (nat. tour) Catskills on Broadway, Fool Moon, Wrong Turn at Lungfish; prodr. Hayfever, 1986; gen. mgr. Carole Shorenstein Hays Enterprises; prodr. Fences, 1987; gen. mgr. Martin Starger/The Really Useful Co. Lend Me a Tenor, 1988, Cates Films-Elmer Gantry, 1991-92, Martin Starger The Red Shoes, 1992, Fool Moon (European prodn.), 1994, BIG The Musical, 1995. Served with AUS, 1944-47. Mem. League N.Y. Theatres and Producers (gov.), Assn. Theatrical Press Agts. and Mgrs. Home: 175 W 93rd St New York NY 10025-9313

KAMM, CHRISTIAN PHILIP, manufacturing company executive; b. Lakewood, Ohio, Oct. 30, 1967; s. Jacob and Judith (Steinbrenner) K. BA cum laude, Ohio Wesleyan U., 1990; MBA, Baldwin Wallace Coll., 1992. Chief fin. analyst, asst. treas. Electric Furnace Co., Salem, Ohio, 1992-93; v.p., treas. Wilkinson Co., Inc., Stow, Ohio, 1993-94; pres. Ostalden Corp., Cleve., 1994—; pres., COO Wilkinson Co., Inc., Stow, Ohio, 1994-97; vice chmn., CFO EFCO Inc., Salem, Ohio, 1995—; pres. Kamm Investment Co., Cleve., 1995—; chief, rep. office Kamm Investment, Inc., Ho ch'i Minh City, Vietnam; bd. dirs., exec. com. Electric Furnance Co., Inc., Salem; bd. dirs. Canefco, Ltd., Toronto, Can., Turner Machine Co., Kamm Investment Co. Inventor recycle bin system, home recycle chute system. Mem. Cleve. Athletic Club, Akron City Club. Office: Kamm Investment Co 526 Superior Ave # 730 Cleveland OH 44114-1900

KAMM, HERBERT, journalist; b. Long Branch, N.J., Apr. 1, 1917; s. Louis and Rose (Cohen) K.; m. Phyllis I. Silberblatt, Dec. 6, 1936; children: Laurence R., Lewis R., Robert H. Reporter, sports editor Asbury Park (N.J.) Press, 1935-42; with AP, 1942-43; with N.Y. World-Telegram and Sun, 1943-66, successively rewrite man, picture editor, asst. city editor, feature editor, mag. editor, 1943-63, asst. mng. editor, 1963, mng. editor, 1963-66; exec. editor N.Y. World Jour. Tribune, 1966-67; editorial cons. Scripps Howard Newspapers, 1967-69; assoc. editor Cleve. Press, 1969-80, editor, 1980-82, editor emeritus, 1982; edit. dir. Sta. WJW-TV, Cleve., 1982-85; instr. journalism Case Western Res. U., 1972-75, Calif. Poly., San Luis Obispo, 1991—. Radio and TV news commentator and panelist, 1950-85, TV talk show host, 1974-85; freelance writer, 1985—; author: A Candle for Popsy, 1953; editor: Junior Illustrated Encyclopedia of Sports, 1960. Bd. overseers Case Western Res. U., 1974-78. Herb Kamm scholarship in journalism established Kent State U., 1983, Calif. Poly., 1995; inducted Cleve. Journalism Hall of Fame, 1986. Mem. AFTRA, Soc. Profl. Journalists (pres. Calif. Missions chpt. 1986-87), Calif. Ambassadors for Higher Edn. Clubs: City of Cleve. (pres. 1982), Silurians. Home: 147 River View Dr Avila Beach CA 93424-2307 *Journalism lifted a poor boy with a limited formal education into a world of learning, excitement and fulfillment. But none of this could have been possible without a devoted wife of more than 60 years.*

KAMM, LAURENCE RICHARD, television producer, director; b. Long Branch, N.J., Oct. 10, 1939; s. Herbert and Phyllis Irene (Silberblatt) K.; m. Claire Louise Cadieux, Oct. 5, 1977; children: Lauren Michelle, Kristin Marie. B.S. in Speech, Northwestern U., 1961. Prodn. asst. ABC-TV, N.Y.C., 1962-64; assoc. dir. ABC Sports, N.Y.C., 1964-70, dir., prodr., 1970-95; coord. dir. Turner Sports, Atlanta, 1995—. Dir. numerous major sports events including: Super Bowl XXII, Super Bowl XXV Pre-Game, Half-Time and Post Game Shows, Super Bowl XXX Super Bowl TV spls., Coll. Football Scoreboard Show, Monday Night Football Half-Time Show, Summer Olympic Games, 1972, 76, 84 (Emmy award 1984), world dir. gymnastics Summer Olympic Game4s, 1996, Winter Olympic Games, 1976-88 (Emmy award 1976), Nagano Olympic Winter Games, 1998, Goodwill Games, 1998, Great Am. Bike Race, 1983 (2 Emmy awards), Indianapolis 500, 1980-87 (Emmy award 1982), Western States 100 Mile Endurance Race, 1985, 86, 20th anniversary spl. for Wide World of Sports (Emmy award 1981), New York Marathon, 1985, 86, Monday Night Football, 1987 (Emmy award), CFA Big 10 and Pac 10 Coll. Football, Major League Baseball, Tour de France Bicycle Race, Profl. Bowler Tours, Grand Prix of Monaco, Indy and NASCAR Racing, Coll. and NBA Basketball, Amateur and Profl. Figure Skating Championships; mem. directing team 25th Anniversary Spl. for Wide World of Sports (Emmy award 1986); directing team ABC News Coverage Election Night, 1972, 76, 80, 84, 88, 92., Reagan, Bush and Clinton Inaugurations, numerous ABC News Specials; dir. team 1994 World Cup Soccer Championships; coord. dir. Goodwill Games, 1994. Recipient Emmy award for Wide World of Sports, 1986, 88, 90, Individual Achievement Emmy award for Winter Olympics spl. camera mount project, 1988, Lifetime Achievement award in sports Dirs. Guild Am., 1997, Emmy award for tech. achievement TNT Virtual Studio, 1997. Mem. NATAS, Dir.'s Guild Am. (Lifetime Achievement in Sports award 1996), Am. Film Inst. Office: Turner Sports 1 Cnn Ctr NW 13th Fl S Atlanta GA 30303-2762

KAMM, LINDA HELLER, lawyer; b. N.Y.C., Aug. 25, 1939; d. Seymour A. and Mary Heller; children: Lisa, Oliver. BA in History, Brandeis U., 1961; LLB, Boston Coll., 1967. Bar: Mass. 1967, D.C. 1978, U.S. Supreme Ct. 1985. Counsel Dem. Study Group, Washington, 1968-71; counsel select com. on coms. U.S. Ho. of Reps., Washington, 1973-75, gen. counsel budget com., 1975-77; gen. counsel U.S. Dept. Transp., Washington, 1977-80; ptnr. Foley and Lardner, Washington, 1980-84, of counsel, 1984-95; pvt. practice Boies and Lazarus, 1995—. Office: 230 Park Ave New York NY 10169-0005

KAMM, ROGER DALE, biomedical engineer, educator; b. Ashland, Wis., Oct. 10, 1950; s. Rudolph Wilhelm and Betty Jane (White) K.; m. Judith Mary Brown, Sept. 1, 1974; 1 child, Peter Martin. BS, Northwestern U., 1972; SM, MIT, 1973, PhD, 1977. Lectr. MIT, Cambridge, 1977-78, asst. prof., 1978-81, assoc. prof., 1981-87, prof. mech. engring., 1987—, assoc. dir. Ctr. for Biomed. Engring., 1995—. Contbr. more than 80 articles to profl. jours. Fellow Am. Inst. Med. and Biol. Engring. (founding); mem. ASME, Am. Physiol. Soc., Biomed. Engring. Soc. (sr., chmn. awards com. 1989-91, bd. dirs. 1994-97). Home: 31 Nonesuch Rd Weston MA 02493-1021 Office: MIT 77 Massachusetts Ave Rm 3-260 Cambridge MA 02139-4307

KAMM, THOMAS ALLEN, air transportation company executive; b. Lynden, Wash., June 10, 1925; s. Charles J. and Teena I. (Kampen) K.; m. Geraldine V. Leek, Sept. 4, 1948; children—Kristine E., Thomas A. Jr. B.S., U. Wash., 1947; J.D., U. Detroit, 1957; LL.M., George Washington U., 1973. Bar: Mich. 1957, Calif. 1980, D.C. 1981. Commd. ensign U.S. Navy, 1945, advanced through grades to rear adm., 1975; various assignments antisubmarine warfare, transport squadrons, res. units, 1947-62; assigned (Transport Squadron 21), Japan; in support (7th Fleet), 1962-65; mgr. antisubmarine program, officer flight tng. (Naval Air Res. Unit), Alameda, Calif., 1965-67; mem. staff (Chief of Naval Air Reserve Tng.), Glenview, Ill., 1967-69; asst. naval air reserve coordinator (Office of Dep. Chief Naval Ops.), 1969-71; asst. dir. (Office of Dep. Asst. Sec. Def.), 1971-72; comdg. officer (Naval Air Res. Unit), Alameda, 1972-75; asst. dep. to dir. (Naval Res., Office Chief of Naval Ops.), Washington, 1975-76; dep. chief (Naval Res.), New Orleans, 1976-78; dep. dir. (Naval Res.), Washington, 1978-80; pvt. practice, Calif., 1980-95; pres. Kamm Air, Inc., Santa Rosa, Calif., 1991—; v.p. Ralph C. Wilson Agy., Detroit, 1952-59; gen. assoc. John M. Grubb Co., Oakland, Calif., 1959-61; adj. asst. prof. internat. law Golden Gate U. Law Sch., San Francisco. Decorated Legion of Merit, Meritorious Service medal. Mem. ABA, Naval Res. Assn., Res. Officers Assn., Assn. Naval Aviation, Phi Delta Theta, Delta Theta Phi, Bohemian Club, N.Y. Yacht Club, Army-Navy Country Club, Ironwood Country Club. Home: 11000 Chalk Hill Rd Healdsburg CA 95448-9649

KAMMAN, CURTIS WARREN, ambassador; b. Chgo., Jan. 15, 1939; s. Glenn Forrest and Mildred Isabel (Merry) K.; m. Mary Glasgow Curtis, Feb. 10, 1962; children: Edward, John, W. Stephen. BA, Yale U., 1959; postgrad., U. Washington, 1964-65. Joined Fgn. Service, U.S. Dept. State, 1960; various diplomatic positions Am. embassies, Washington, Mexico City, Hong Kong, Moscow, Nairobi, 1960-80; dir. East African Affairs, Washington, 1980-82; polit. counselor Am. embassy, Moscow, 1982-84, minister, counselor, 1984-85; prin. officer U.S. Interests sect. Swiss embassy, Havana, Cuba, 1985-87; dep. asst. sec. U.S. Dept. State, Washington, 1987-91; amb. to Chile Santiago, 1991-94; amb. to Bolivia, 1994-97, amb. to Colombia, 1997—. Bd. dirs. Fgn. Students Sch., Havana, 1985-87. Mem. Phi Beta Kappa. Episcopalian. Avocation: choral singing. Address: Apartado Aereo 3831, Bogota Colombia also: 5102 US Embassy APO AA 34038

KAMMAN, WILLIAM, historian, educator; b. Geneva, Ind., Mar. 23, 1930; s. Harry August and Ruth Lois (Shoemaker) K.; m. Nancy Ellen Prichard, Apr. 19, 1957; children: Frederick William, Elizabeth Ellen, David Paul. A.B., Ind. U., 1952, Ph.D., 1962; M.A., Yale U., 1958. Tchr. pub. schs. Bloomington, Ind., 1955-57, 58-59; asst. prof. history U. North Tex. (formerly North Tex. State U.), Denton, 1962-66, assoc. prof., 1966-69, prof., 1969—, chmn. dept. history, 1977-89, 93-94, assoc. dean arts and scis., 1996-97, 98—, interim dean arts and scis., 1997-98. Author: A Search for Stability: United States Diplomacy Toward Nicaragua, 1968; contbg. author: Makers of American Diplomacy, 1974, Ency. World Biography, 1973, 87—, Ency. Am. Fgn. Policy, 1978, The War of 1898 and U.S. Interventions, 1898-34: An Ency., 1994. Mem. Denton Planning and Zoning Commn., 1976-79, 86-92. Served with U.S. Army, 1952-54. Mem. Am. Hist. Assn., Orgn. Am. Historians, Soc. Historians Am. Fgn. Relations (exec. sec.-treas. 1985-89), Phi Alpha Theta. Methodist. Home: 2225 Scripture St Denton TX 76201-3707 Office: U North Tex History Dept Denton TX 76203

KAMMEN, CAROL KOYEN, historian, educator; b. Plainfield, N.J., Nov. 14, 1937; d. Elmer Albert and Helen Edith (Kingberry) Koyen; m. Michael Kammen, Feb. 26, 1961; children: Daniel Merson, Douglas Anton. BA, George Washington U., Washington, 1959. Tchr. Am. history Ithaca (N.Y.) H.S., 1971-73; lectr. history Tompkins Cortland C.C., Dryden, N.Y., 1973-84; lectr. history Cornell U., Ithaca, 1983-85, lectr., 1986-92, sr. lectr., 1992—; cons. Nat. Humanities Faculty, Atlanta, 1981—; project dir. Nat. Youth Grant, Ithaca H.S., 1972-74; arts coun. dir. Tompkins County Arts Coun., Ithaca, 1984; cons., historian Empire State Partnership on Arts in Edn. Program, Hangar Theater, 1998-99. Author: Simeon DeWitt Proprietor of Ithaca, 1969; author: What They Wrote, 1978, Lives Passed, 1984, Peopling of Tompkins County, 1986 (RCHA award of Merit 1987), On Doing Local History, 1986, repub., 1996 (Merit award 1987), Plain as a Pipestem, 1989; editor: One Day in Ithaca, 1989 (Spl. award 1989), The Finger Lakes of New York, 1996, Pursuit of Local History, 1997; author plays, including: Central New York (video script) 1978, Between the Lines, 1985, Testimony for Black Voices, 1986, Counting Wheat Street, 1986, Jazz a la Mode, 1987, A Chamber Entertainment with Clowns, 1988, Flight to Ithaca, 1995, Womens' Proper Place, 1997, Peaces and Bird, 1998, Ain't I a Man, Too?, 1998, Escape to the North, 1999; columnist The Ithaca Jour., 1978—; ednl. writer History News; contbr. articles to profl. jours. Recipient award of excellence Tompkins County Trust Co., Ithaca, 1995. Mem. Am. Assn. State and Local History (editl. writer History News 1995—). Democrat. E-mail: CKK6@cornell.edu. Home: 16 Sun Path Rd Ithaca NY 14850-9781 Office: Cornell U Dept History McGraw Hall Ithaca NY 14853

KAMMER, RAYMOND GERARD, JR., government official; b. Arlington, Va., Jan. 5, 1947; s. Raymond Gerard and Kathleen Elizabeth (Nahow) K.; m. Mauna Kathleen Vogan, Mar. 23, 1967 (div. Aug. 1981); 1 child, Kathleen J.; m. Wilma Norma McMasters, May 15, 1985. BA, U. Md., 1969. Budget analyst Nat. Bur. Standards, Gaithersburg, Md., 1974-75, program analyst, 1975-76, sr. program analyst, 1976-78, assoc. dir. programs, budget and finance, 1978-80, dep. dir., 1980-91; dep. under sec. for oceans and atmosphere NOAA, 1991-93; dep. dir. Nat. Inst. Standards and Tech., 1993-96; acting chief fin. officer, acting asst. sec. for adminstrn. Dept. of Commerce, 1996-97; dir. Mat. Inst. Standards and Tech., 1997—. Recipient Silver medal Dept. Commerce, 1977, Gold medal Dept. Commerce, 1983, William J. Jump Meml. award William A. Jump Found., 1984, Meritorious Exec. award Dept. Commerce, 1980, 86, Roger W. Jones Exec. Leadership award, Am. U., 1988. Home: PO Box 246 Olney MD 20830-0246 Office: Nat Inst Standards & Tech Gaithersburg MD 20899

KAMMERER, JOSEPH T., government official. BS in Engring., U. Md., 1961, MS in Engring., 1964; postgrad., Cath. U., Washington, 1965-68; MS in Bus. Adminstrn., U. Rochester, 1969. Registered profl. engr., Va. Naval architect, structural rsch. engr. Dept. Navy, 1961-70; advisor resource analysis Chief Naval Ops. and Asst. Sec. Navy, 1970-76; assoc. asst. adminstr. Fed. Energy Adminstrn., Dept. Energy, 1976-77; dir. manpower, logistics and support forces Systems Analysis Divsn., Office Chief Naval Ops., Dept. Navy, 1977-78; dir. contracts, cost estimating and analysis Office Chief Naval Material, Dept. Navy, 1978-81; dep. asst. sec. def. U.S. Dept. Def., 1981-85; v.p. fiscal mgmt., CFO McDonnell Douglas Astronautics Co., 1985-89; v.p. bus. mgmt., CFO McDonnell Douglas Electronic Systems Co., 1989-93; tech. advisor, assoc. dir. Nat. Security Analysis Gen. Acctg. Office, 1993; intelligence cmty. comptr., dep. dir. resource mgmt. Cmty. Mgmt. Staff, Office Dir. Ctrl. Intelligence, 1993-94; dir. planning Nat. Security and Internat. Affairs divsn. U.S. Gen. Acctg. Office, 1994-96; CFO, chief adminstrv. officer NOAA, Washington, 1996—; mem. chief fin. officers task force Pvt. Sector Coun.; past vice chmn. McDonnell Douglas Employee Charity and Cmty. Svcs. Contbr. articles to profl. jours. Past treas. Ecumenical Housing Prodn. Corp.; past pres. Tamarack Triangle Civic Assn. Mem. Nat. Jr. Acad. Scis., Ops. Rsch. Soc. Am., Mil. Ops. Rsch. Soc., inst. Cost Analysis, Soc. Naval Architects and Marine Engrs., Am. Soc. Naval Engrs., Twin Farms Swim and Tennis Club (past pres.), Chi Epsilon. Office: NOAA Office Fin & Adminstrn HCHB Rm 6811 14th & Constitution Ave NW Washington DC 20230*

KAMMERER, KELLY CHRISTIAN, lawyer; b. N.Y.C., Nov. 29, 1941; s. William Henry and Edith (Langley) K. BA, U. Notre Dame, 1963; LLB, U. Va., 1968. Bar: Va. 1968, N.Y. 1969, D.C. 1969, Fla. 1969. Peace Corps vol. Colombia, 1963-65; Reginald Heber Smith atty./fellow U. Pa., Washington, 1968-70; atty.-advisor, dep. gen. counsel Peace Corps, Washington, 1970-74; atty.-advisor AID, Dept. State, Washington, 1975-76, asst. gen. counsel, 1976-78, sr. dep. gen. counsel, 1978-82, legal counselor, 1981-82, dir. congl. rels., 1983-89; mission dir. Kathmandu, Nepal, 1989-93, counselor to the agy., 1994-99; vice chmn., U.S. rep. OECD/DAC, Paris, 1999—. Recipient Disting. Honor award AID, 1979, 83, Equal Opportunity award, 1982; presdl. rank of Disting. Sr. Execs., 1984, 89. Mem. Inter-Am. Bar Assn., Soc. Internat. Law. Address: 11 bis Jules Sandeau, 75016 Paris France

KAMMEYER, SONIA MARGARETHA, real estate agent; b. Stockholm, June 21, 1942; came to U.S., 1964; d. Bengt Henrik and Margot Elsa M. (Hodin) Sjoberg; m. Whitman Ridgway, June 13, 1964 (div. 1978); children: Sean, Siobhan; m. Kenneth C.W. Kammeyer, Dec. 28, 1982. Student, Fleisher's Art Meml. Sch., Phila., 1966-69. With Ben Bell Real Estate, Lanham, Md., 1972-73, Robert L. Gruen Real Estate, Silver Spring, Md., 1973-81, Panarama Real Estate, Silver Spring, 1981-82, Long & Foster Real Estate, Inc., Silver Spring, 1982—. Named to Montgomery County Bd. Realtors Hall of Fame, 1994; recipient Nat. Sales Award, Realty Alliance, 1997. Mem. Montgomery County Bd. Realtors (life), Howard County Bd. Realtors, Swedish Profl. Women. Avocations: sculpture, painting, jewelry making, gardening, guitar playing. Home: 14600 Triadelphia Mill Rd Dayton MD 21036-1217 Office: Long & Foster Real Estate 3901 National Dr Burtonsville MD 20866-1141

KAMP, ARTHUR JOSEPH, JR., lawyer; b. Rochester, N.Y., July 22, 1945; s. Arthur Joseph and Irene Catherine (Ehrstein) K.; m. Barbara Hays, Aug. 24, 1968; children: Sara, Nathaniel. BA, SUNY, 1968, JD, 1970. Bar: N.Y. 1971, U.S. Dist. Ct. (we. dist.) N.Y. 1971, Va. 1973, U.S. Dist. Ct. (ea. dist.) Va. 1973. Atty. Neighborhood Legal Svcs., Buffalo, 1971; assoc. Diamonstein & Drucker, Newport News, Va., 1972-77; ptnr. Diamonstien, Drucker & Kamp, Newport News, 1977-84, Kamp & Kamp, Newport News, 1984-87, Kaufman & Canoles, 1987-96, David, Kamp & Frank L.L.C., 1996—; v.p., Peninsula Legal Aid Ctr., Inc., 1978-92. Chmn. Newport News Planning Commn., 1994-95, commr., 1990-97; bd. vis. Med. Coll. Hampton Rds. Lt. USAF, 1971-72. Mem. ABA, Va. State Bar Assn., Newport News Bar Assn. (past bd. dirs., chmn. legal aid com.), Va. Bar Assn., Va. Peninsula C. of C. (bd. dirs., exec. com., chmn. 1997). Democrat. Office: David & Kamp LLC 301 Hiden Blvd Ste 200 Newport News VA 23606-2939

KAMP, CYNTHIA LEA, elementary education educator; b. Johnstown, Pa., June 29, 1956; d. Charles Jr. and Helen Lois (Paff) Lane; m. Robert Thomas Kamp, June 9, 1979; children: Jason, Meghan, Jordan. BFA, Miami U., Oxford, Ohio, 1978, MA, 1984. Cert. fine arts tchr., Ohio. Tchr. art Mt. Healthy City Schs., Cin. Mem. ASCD, Ohio Arts Edn. Assn., Ohio Edn. Assn. Home: 25 Brompton Ln Cincinnati OH 45218-1314

KAMPE, CAROLYN JEAN, elementary art and special education educator; b. Chicago Heights, Ill., July 8, 1943; d. Fred H. and Harriet (Bobrowski) K. Student, Mt. St. Clare Jr. Coll., Clinton, Iowa, 1966-68; BA in Art, St. Ambrose U., 1970; MA in Cultural Studies, Gov. State U., 1974; EdD in Art Edn., Ill. State U., 1990. Cert. art tchr.; cert. spl. edn.; cert. K-12 specialist. Art supr., coord., and elem. art tchr. Dist. 170, Chicago Heights, 1970-87; grad. asst. art dept. Ill. State U., Normal, 1987-90; spl. edn. tchr. Hugh Jr. H.S., Matteson, Ill., 1990-91, Burr Oak, Calumet Park, Ill., 1991-92; homebound tchr. Dist. 162, Matteson, 1991-98; art edn. for spl. edn. Dist. 170, Chicago Heights, 1992—; art tchr. Field Sch. Dist. 152, Harvey, Ill., 1994-96, Vogt Visual Art Ctr., Tinley Park, Ill., 1996-99; spl. edn. tchr. Hufford Jr. H.S., Joliet, Ill., 1996-98; vis. faculty and adaptive art specialist

St. Norbert Coll., DePere, Wis., 1990-92; active in Put Your Heart Illinois Youth Art Month, 1985-86 and 1993-94, spl. edn. "Earth Day" Art Exhbn. (200 works on display); homebound tchr. Dist. 162 and 227, 1991-98; bd. dirs. Very Spl. Arts, Ill. State U., Normal, 1992-96. Group exhbns. include Chicago Heights Libr., Chicago Heights Mcpl. Bldg., 1993-94, Wash. Jr. H.S., Chicago Heights, 1994; contbr. articles to profl. jours. Bd. dirs. Very Spl. Arts Ill., Ill. State U., Normal, 1992-94; Ill. Coalition for Disabilities, Normal, 1985-86; pres. Self Help for Hard of Hearing, Ill., 1984-86; mem. White House Exhbn. Com., Chgo., 1992-93; vol. Chgo. Pub. Libr., 1993; mem. Put Your Heart in Month, Ill. Youth Art Month, 1985-86; art judge Girl Scout Art Contest, 1982, Chicago Heights Jaycees, 1982-83. Named One of 5 Best and Brightest Outstanding Disabled Coll. Grads., Mainstream Mag. and Am. Bus. Women's Assn., 1990, to Hall of Fame for Outstanding Achievement, Mt. St. Clare Coll., 1996, to Hall of Fame for Fine Art, Marian Cath. H.S. Alumni Assn., 1997; recipient Kohl Internat. Tchg. award 1993. Mem. Nat. Assn. Art Edn., Ill. Art Edn. Assn. (Best Art Tchr. award 1984). Roman Catholic. Achievements include: first deaf female doctoral graduate from Ill. State Univ. Avocations: fishing, sports, visiting museums, oil painting, reading.

KAMPF, MARILYN JEANNE, medical analyst; b. Kenton, Ohio, Apr. 6, 1940; d. Earl Eugene and Vivian Ruth (Linke) Brown; m. Robert C. Kampf, June 27, 1964 (dec. 1999); 1 child, Robert W. (dec. 1998). Diploma, Lima (Ohio) Meml. Sch. Nursing, 1962, Ohio No. U., 1960. Head nurse pediatrics Lima Meml. Hosp., 1962-77; supr. med. fl. Van Wert (Ohio) County Hosp., 1977-82; sr. med. analyst Cen. Ins. Co., Van Wert, Ohio, 1982—; utilization rev. agt. Workers Compensation Claims, Mass., N.J., Conn. Mem. Am. Bus. Women's Assn., Nat. Assn. Ins. Women (pres.), County RN Assn., Twigs, Nat. Managed Care Cert. (cert. manged care 1998—).

KAMPFE, DORIS ELAINE, storyteller, folk artist, poet; b. Monona, Iowa, Feb. 2, 1926; d. Frederick Conrad and Alvina Ulrika (Hass) Daugs; m. LaVern Arthur Kampfe, June 1, 1945; children: Lanny, Elisa Kay. Student, U. No. Iowa, 1965-68. Sec. Singr Sewing Machine Co., Denver, 1943, Interstate Power Co., Dubuque, Iowa, 1944, Ill. Supreme Ct., Chgo., 1979; tchr., mem. adv. bd. Headstart, Waterloo, Iowa, 1965-68; sec., tutor Japan Trade Ctr., Chgo., 1979—; feature writer Shopping News, Cedar Falls, Iowa, 1981-85, writer column Personalities and Wandering Around Waverly, 1981; folk artist Iowa Arts Coun., Des Moines, 1986—; storyteller Very Spl. Arts Iowa, Des Moines, 1992—; cruise storyteller Delta Steamboat Line, New Orleans, 1990—; storyteller at folk and art festivals, mus., librs., chs., schs., colls., retirement ctrs., Spl. Olympics, theatre, Old Opera House, restaurants, nature ctrs. and parks, banquets and confs., reunions, parties, county homes and country clubs, civic ctrs. Author: (play) Caramella, The Curious Camel, 1982; contbr. poetry to various publs., anthologies. Advisor N.W. opportunity bd. Headstart, Hoffman Estates, Ill., 1979; mem. social concerns bd. St. Paul's Luth. Ch., Waverly, Iowa, 1981, mem. cable TV cmty. bd., 1990; dinner vol. Waverly Dem. Com., 1995. Recipient award for poetry Pen Women, Inc., 1995, 96, 98; grantee Iowa Arts Coun., 1992, 95, 97, 98. Mem. AAUW, Nat. League Am. Pen Women, Internat. Platform Assn., Soc. Children's Book Writers, Nat. Assn. Storytellers, Iowa Poetry Assn., Northlands Storytellers, Haiku Club, Children's Reading Round Table, Short Story Writers Assn., Women in Arts, ACTS, Friends of Ctr., Print Club, Walt Whitman Guild. Avocations: watercolors, ballroom dancing, gourmet cooking, reading, gardening. Home: 1508 Circle Dr Waverly IA 50677-1001

KAMPINE, JOHN P., anesthesiologist. MD, PhD, U. Wis. Prof., chair dept. anesthesiology Froedtert Meml. Luth. Hosp., Milw., 1979—. Mem. Inst. Medicine-NAS. Office: Froedtert Meml Hosp PO Box 26099 9200 W Wisconsin Ave Milwaukee WI 53226-3596*

KAMPMEIER, CURT, management consultant; b. Evanston, Ill., Aug. 15, 1941; s. Carlos Otto and Neva Lou (Brown) K.; m. Susan Brooks, Dec. 30, 1961; children: Rand, Elizabeth, Paul, John. BA with honors, Coll. of Wooster (Ohio), 1964; cert. bus. program, Alexander Hamilton Inst., N.Y.C., 1967. Cert. mgmt. cons. Sales rep. Westminster Press, Phila., 1964-67, Random House, Inc., N.Y.C., 1967-73; owner The Kampmeier Group, Columbus, Ohio, 1973—. Author numerous articles and The Bus. Skills Inventory, 6 editions, 1993; book rev. editor, columnist Jour. Mgmt. Cons. Trustee Ohio Presbyn. Retirement Svcs., Columbus, 1984-87, Westminster Thurber Community, Columbus, 1984-87; commencement speaker Shawnee State Coll., Portsmouth, Ohio. Mem. Inst. Mgmt. Cons., Columbus C. of C.

KAMPMEIER, JACK AUGUST CARLOS, chemist, educator; b. Cedar Rapids, Iowa, June 11, 1935; s. Carlos and Nevalou (Brown) K.; m. Anne Margaret Derk, June 14, 1958; children—Scott, Margaret, Stephen. A.B., Amherst Coll., 1957; Ph.D. (NSF fellow), U. Ill., 1960. From instr. to prof. chemistry U. Rochester, N.Y., 1960-71; prof. U. Rochester, 1971—, chmn. dept. chemistry, 1975-79, assoc. dean grad. studies Coll. Arts and Sci., 1982-88, dean Coll. Arts and Sci., 1988-91; assoc. dir. NSF Sci. and Tech. Ctr. for Photoinduced Charge Transfer, 1991—. Contbr. sci. and pedagogical articles to profl. jours. Recipient Nat. Catalyst award Chem. Mfrs. Assn., 1999; NSF sci. faculty fellow U. Calif., Berkeley, 1971-72; Fulbright Hays sr. rsch. scholar U. Freiburg, Germany, 1979-80; NATO sr. scientist, 1979-80. Mem. Am. Chem. Soc., Sigma Xi. E-mail: kamp@chem.rochester.edu. Home: 86 Reservoir Ave Rochester NY 14620-2754 Office: U Rochester Dept Chemistry Rochester NY 14627

KAMPOURIS, EMMANUEL ANDREW, corporate executive; b. Alexandria, Egypt, Dec. 14, 1934; came to U.S., 1979; s. Andrew George and Euridice Anne (Caralli) K.; m. Myrto Stellatos, July 4, 1959 (dec.); children: Andrew, Alexander. Student, King's Sch., Bruton, Somerset, U.K., 1953; M.A. in Law, Oxford U., 1957; cert. in ceramic tech., North Staffordshire Coll. of Tech., U.K., 1962. Plant mgr., dir. "KEREM", Athens, Greece, 1962-64; dir. "HELLENIT", Athens, Greece, 1962-65; mng. dir. Ideal Standard, Athens, 1966-79; v.p., group exec. internat. and export Am. Standard Inc., New Brunswick, N.J., 1979-84, sr. v.p. bldg. products, 1984-89; pres., chief exec. officer Am. Standard Inc., Am. Standard Cos. Inc., N.Y.C., 1989—, now chmn.; bd. dirs. Ideal Refractories SAI, Athens, Ideal Standard Mexico, Am. Standard Sanitaryware (Thailand) Ltd., INCESA, San Jose, Costa Rica, Hoxan Corp., Sapporo, Japan. Bd. dirs. Greek Mgmt. Assn., Athens, 1975-77, Fedn. of Greek Industries, Athens. Mem. Young Pres. Orgn., Chief Execs. Orgn., Econ. Club of N.Y., Oxford Union, Oxford Law Soc., Am. Hellenic C. of C. (gen. sec. 1975-79), Chemists Club, Laurel Valley Golf Club. Greek Orthodox. Clubs: Spring Brook Country (Morristown, N.J.); Quogue Field, Quogue Beach (L.I., N.Y.). Avocations: golf; tennis; classical music. Office: Am Standard Cos Inc 1 Centennial Ave Piscataway NJ 08854-3921*

KAMPS, CHARLES Q., lawyer; b. Milw., Mar. 21, 1932; s. John G. and Mary (Quarles) K.; m. Mary B. Stehling, Sept. 28, 1963; children: Charles Jr., Louisa. LLB, Marquette U., 1959. Bar: Wis. 1959. Ptnr. Quarles & Brady, Milw., 1959—. Mem. U.S. Sailing Assn. (mem. sailing team, Olympic yachting com. of U.S.), Milwaukee Yacht Club (past commodore, 1971-72). Office: Quarles & Brady 411 E Wisconsin Ave Ste 2550 Milwaukee WI 53202-4497

KAMRIN, MICHAEL ARNOLD, toxicology educator; b. Bklyn., Aug. 5, 1940; s. Benjamin Barnett and Bessie (Bloom) K.; m. Ritva Anneli Nieminen, July 19, 1964; children: Kari and Edward (twins). BA in Chemistry, Cornell U., 1960; MS in Biophys. Chemistry, Yale, 1962, PhD in Biophys. Chemistry, 1965. Teaching asst. then rsch. asst. dept. chemistry Yale U., New Haven, 1960-63; rsch. assoc. biology div. Oak Ridge (Tenn.) Nat. Lab., 1963-66; NIH postdoctoral trainee Hopkins Marine Sta. Stanford (Calif.) U., 1966-67; asst. prof. natural sci. Mich. State U., East Lansing, 1967-72, assoc. prof., 1972-79, prof., 1979-89, prof. Inst. for Environ. Toxicology, 1982—, prof. resource devel., 1990—; vis. lectr. dept. zoology U. Turku, Finland, 1973-74, docent, 1996—; vis. scientist Legis. Office Sci. Advisor, State of Mich., 1980-81; participant numerous confs. and workshops, 1965—; mem. internat. evaluation team on environ. toxicology Acad. Finland, Helsinki, 1988; expert Media Resource Ctr., Scientists' Inst. for Pub. Info.; mem. risk comm. project planning group, grant reviewer USDA; peer reviewer for agy.-sponsored rsch. projects Agy. for Toxic Substances and Disease Registry, HHS; numerous others. Author: Toxicology: A Primer on Toxicology Principles and Applications, 1988, (with D.J. Katz and M.L. Walter) Reporting on Risk: A Journalist's Handbook, 1995; also other; editor: (with F.M. D'Itri) PCBs: Human and Environmental Hazards, 1983, (with P. Rodgers) Dioxins inthe Environment, 1985; editor: Pesticide Profiles, 1997, Environmental Risk Harmonization, 1997; contbr. numerous articles and abstracts to sci. jours. Numerous presentations to Rotary, Consumers Coun., LWV, county commrs., Ch. Women United, sch. dists., Mich. Med. Soc.; participant in news broadcasts, radio call-in shows and interview programs. Recipient Meml. medal U. Turku, 1974; grantee USDA, 1983-84, 86-87, 88-89, 91-98, All-Univ. Rsch. Initation grantee, 1989, All-Univ. Outreach grantee, 1995-96, EPA, 1992-95, Agy. for Toxic Substances and Disease Registry, 1992-98, Nat. Food Safety and Toxicology Ctr., 1993-94, grantee Nat. Inst. Environ. Health Scis., 1995-2000. Fellow AAAS; mem. Am. Chem. Soc., Soc. Toxicology (editor newsletter Mich. chpt. 1984-87, chmn. nominating com. 1986, pres.-elect 1992-93, pres. 1993-94; nat. pub. comm. com. 1987-90, Nat. Pub. Comm. award 1994), Soc. Environ. Toxicology and Chemistry (bd. dirs. Ctrl. Gt. Lakes chpt. 1985-87, v.p. 1988, pres. 1989-90, Disting. Svc. award 1993; nat. govt. affairs com. 1986—), Soc. for Risk Analysis, Sigma Xi. Office: Mich State U Inst Environ Toxicology C-231 Holden Hall East Lansing MI 48824

KAMROWSKI, GEROME, artist; b. Warren, Minn., Jan. 29, 1914; s. Felix and Mary (Rizke) K.; m. Mary Jane Dodman, Sept. 12, 1965; children: Felix, Kirby Jay. Student, St. Paul Sch. Art, 1933-36, Art Students League, N.Y.C., 1933-34, New Bau Haus, Chgo., 1937, Hans Hofmann Sch., N.Y.C., 1938—. One-man shows Washburn Gallery, 1987; group shows Mus. Modern Art, N.Y.C., 1978, Hayward Gallery, London, 1981, Met. Mus. Art, N.Y.C., 1993. Solomon R. Guggenheim fellow, 1938; Horace H. Rachkam fellow, 1982. Home: 1501 Beechwood Dr Ann Arbor MI 48103-2941

KAMSTRA, BETTYE MAURICE, secondary education educator; b. Merkel, Tex., June 26, 1941; d. Eldon Maurice and Susie Grace (Burk) Reeves; m. L. Duane Kamstra, Aug. 25, 1966. BS, Hardin-Simmon U., 1965; MS, Calif. State U., Northridge, 1979; postgrad., Ariz. State U., U. Calif., Santa Barbara. Tchr. South Kern Unified Schs., Rosamond, Calif. Mem. NEA, Nat. Bus. Edn. Assn., Nat. Coun. Tchrs. of English (assembly lit. for adolescents), Calif. Assn. Tchrs. of English, Southland Coun. Tchrs. of English, Western Bus. Edn. Assn.

KAMUF, RACHAEL L., reporter. Degree in Journalism, U. Ky. Reporter Bus. First, Louisville, AP, Louisville.

KAMYSZEW, CHRISTOPHER D., museum curator, executive educator, art consultant; b. Warsaw, Poland, May 7, 1958; came to U.S., 1982; s. Mieczyslaw and Zofia (Kubik) K.; children: Oliver G., Samuel. BA, U. Warsaw, 1982, MA in Polish Lit. and Lang., 1984. Freelance writer and translator Poland, 1977-81; freelance theatre dir. Dearborn Theatre Co., Chgo., 1982-83, Ossetynski Actors Lab., L.A., 1982-83; head lit. sect. Krag-Underground Publishers, Warsaw, 1980-83; head archives dept. Polish Mus. Am., Chgo., 1985-88, dir., curator, 1988-93; exec. dir. Soc. for the Arts, Chgo., 1993—; bd. dirs. Gallery 58, Chgo.; pres. Inst. Symbological Rsch., Chgo., 1986-95, Internat. Ind. Theatre Found., Washington, 1985-86; exec. dir. Polish TV-USA, 1994-97. Co-author, editor: Collective Works of L.-F Celine, 1983, Literary Essays by L. Tyrmand, 1983; curated over 50 exhbts. in U.S. Dir., CEO Polish Film Festival, 1988—, Europe Film Festival, 1996—. Recipient Zycie Warszawy award, 1977, Audience award Edinburgh Theatre Festival, 1980, award for disting. translation Assn. Polish Translators, 1990, award Found. of Friends of Polish Mus., 1991, award of the Ministry of Fgn. Affairs of Poland, 1993, Laterna Magica award for disting. achievements in film, 1994; Wiehmann Found. scholar, 1982. Avocations: reading, classical music, map collecting, cross-country skiing. Office: Society for Arts 1112 N Milwaukee Ave Chicago IL 60622-4017

KAN, DIANA ARTEMIS MANN SHU, artist; b. Hong Kong, Mar. 3, 1926; came to U.S., 1949, naturalized, 1964; d. Kam Shek and Sing-Ying (Hong) K.; m. Paul Schwartz, May 24, 1952; 1 son, Kan Martin Meyer Sing-Si. Student, Art Students League, 1949-51, Beaux Arts, Paris, 1951-52, Grande Chaumiere, Paris, 1951-52. Fgn. corr., city editor Cosmorama Pictorial Mag., Hong Kong, 1968; art reviewer Villager, N.Y.C., 1960-69; lectr. Birmingham So. U., N.Y. U., Mills Coll., St. Joseph's Coll., Phila. Mus., Smithsonian Instn. Author: White Cloud, 1938, The How and Why of Chinese Painting, 1974; One-man shows, London, 1949, 63, 64, Paris, 1949, Hong Kong, 1937, 39, 41, 47, 48, 52, Shanghai, 1935, 37, 39, Nanking, 1936, 38, Macao, 1947, 48, Bankok, 1947, Casablanca, 1951, 52, San Francisco, 1950, 67, N.Y.C., 1950, 54, 59, 67, 71, 72, 74, 78, Naples, 1971, Elliot Mus., Stuart, Fla., 1967, 73, Bruce Mus., Greenwich, Conn., 1969, Nat. Hist. Mus., Taipei, Taiwan, 1971, N.Y. Cultural Center Mus., 1972, Galerie Barbarella, Palm Beach, Fla., 1972, Hobe Sound (Fla.) Galleries, 1976, 81, Nat. Arts Club, 1979, Dyansen Galleries, 1987-90 others; exhibited in group shows Allied Artists of Am., 1957-90, Royal Acad. Fine Arts, London, 1963-64, Royal Soc. Painters, London, 1964, Nat. Arts Club, N.Y.C., 1964-90, Am. Water Color Soc., N.Y.C., 1966-90, Nat. Acad., N.Y.C., 1967-90, Charles and Emma Frye Mus., Seattle, 1968, Willamette U., Salem, Oreg., 1968, Columbia (S.C.) Mus. Art, 1969, Audubon Artist, 1974-90, Evansville (Ind.) Mus., 1991, Dyansen Gallery, Boston, 1991; represented permanent collections, Met. Mus. Art, Phila. Mus. Art, Nelson Gallery, Elliot Mus., Fla., Bruce Mus., Dalhousie U., Atkin Mus., Kansas City, Nat. Hist. Mus., Taipei; subject of film Eastern Spirit, Western World—A Profile of Diana Kan. Recipient Summer Festival award N.Y.C., 1959, 1st Prize Nat. Art Club, 1982; named most Outstanding Profl. Woman of the Yr., Washington Sq. chpt. N.Y. League Bus. and Profl. Women's Club, 1971, 79, Gold medal of honor Knickerbocker Artists, 1990, Gold medal of honor Audubon Artists, 1991; Diana Kan Appreciation Day proclaimed by Mayor of Boston, 1991; offl. citation proclaimed by Pres. Senate of Mass., 1991. Fellow Royal Soc. Arts; mem. Pen and Brush Club (dir. 1968, Brush Fund award 1968, Alice S. Buell Meml. award 1969, Margaret Sussman award 1991), Nat. Acad. Design (assoc., John Pike Meml. award 1987, cert. of merit 1991), Am. Watercolor Soc. (traveling award 1968, Marthe T. McKinnon award 1978, dir. 1975-77), Art Students League, Nat. League Pen Women, Audubon Artists (v.p. 1983), Allied Artists Am. (Barbara Vassilieff Meml. award 1969, Ralph Fabri Meml. award 1975, corr. sec. 1975-78), Catharine Lorillard Wolf Art Club (Anna Hyatt Huntington bronze medal 1970, 74, Gold medal of honor 1982). Clubs: Overseas Press Am., Lotos, The Nat. Arts (N.Y.C.). Home: 15 Gramercy Park S New York NY 10003-1705 *Failure is the mother of success.*

KAN, YUET WAI, physician, investigator; b. Hong Kong, June 11, 1936; came to U.S., 1960; s. Tong-Po and Lai-Wai (Li) K.; m. Alvera Lorraine Limauro, May 10, 1964; children—Susan Jennifer, Deborah Ann. BS, MB, U. Hong Kong, 1958, DSc, 1980, DSc (hon.), 1987; DSc (hon.), Chinese U., Hong Kong, 1981; MD (hon.), U. Cagliari, Sardinia, Italy, 1981. Investigator Howard Hughes Med. Inst., San Francisco, 1976—; prof. lab. medicine U. Calif., San Francisco, 1977—, Louis K. Diamond prof. hematology, 1991-95; mem. NIDDK adv. coun. NIH, 1991-95; trustee Croucher Found., Hong Kong, 1992—, chmn., 1997—. Contbr. over 233 articles to med. jours., chpts. to books. Recipient Dameshek award Am. Soc. Hematology, 1980, George Thorn award Howard Hughes Med. Inst., 1980, Gairdner Found. Internat. award, 1984, Allan award Am. Soc. Human Genetics, 1984, Lita Annenberg Hazen award for Excellence in Clin. Rsch., 1984, Waterford award, 1987, ACP's award, 1988, Genetic Rsch. award Sanremo Internat., 1989, Warren Alpert Found. prize, 1989, Albert Lasker Clin. Med. Rsch. award, 1991, Christopher Columbus Discovery award, 1992, City of Medicine award, 1992, Excellence 2000 award, 1993, Helmut Horten Rsch. award, 1995. Fellow Royal Coll. Physicians (London), Royal Soc. (London), Third World Acad. Scis., AAAS, Am. Acad. Arts and Scis.; mem. Nat. Acad. Scis. USA, Acad. Sinica (Taiwan), Chinese Acad. Scis. (fgn. mem.), Assn. Am. Physicians, Am. Soc. Hematology (pres. 1990), Soc. Chinese Bioscientists in Am. (pres. 1998-99). Avocations: tennis; skiing. Office: U Calif 3D Parnassus Ave # U426 San Francisco CA 94117-4342

KANABY, ROBERT F., sports association administrator. BA in English, Social Studies, Jersey City State Coll., 1961, MA Secondary Sch. Reading Specialist, 1968; postgrad. studies of 50 credits, Rutgers and Lehigh Univs., Montclair State Coll. Tchr. health St. Anthony's H.S., Jersey City, 1959-60; tchr. social studies, English Union Hill H.S., Union City, N.J., 1961-66; reading cons. Bridgewater (N.J.) -Raritan H.S., 1966-68, vice prin., 1968-72; prin. South Hunterdon (N.J.) Regional H.S., 1972-78; — Hunterdon Ctrl. H.S., 1978-80; exec. dir. N.J. State Interscholastic Athletic Assn., 1980-93, Nat. Fedn. State H.S. Assns., Kansas City, Mo., 1993—; mem. football com. Nat. Fedn. State H.S. Assns., telecomm. com.; chmn. selection com., dreamers and doers; past mem. All Am. Student Com.; particpant task force on steroids, on catstrophic injuries; v.p. TARGET, rep. of Nat. Fedn. in Ind. U. Study which contbr. to document The Case for Student Activities, Ad Hoc Ins. Com. to define participant; speaker at Fedn. confs., mem. Athletic Bus. Mag. Edtl. Bd.; mem. U.S. Olympic Com. task force to strengthen relationships with NCAA; bd. dirs. U.S. Olympic Com., U.S.A. Basketball; bd. trustees Naismith Basketball Hall of Fame. Mem. N.J. Coun. on Phys. Fitness and Sports, Nominating Com. for N.J. Sports Hall of Fame, Gov.'s Task Force on Drug Edn.; past pres. Hunterdon County Heart Assn.; bd. dirs. N.J. Special Olympics; mem. 1995 Kansas City Star Selection Com. for Scholar Athlete, James W. Bunn Award Com. Recipient N.J. State Interscholastic Athletic Assn. award of honor, Ohio Athletic Assn. Ethics and Integrity award. Mem. Nat. Assn. Secondary Sch. Principals, N.J. Assn. Principals, Suprs. (bd. govs.), N.J. Assn. Sch. Adminstrs., N.J. Coun. Edn., Dirs. of Athletics Assn. N.J., N.J. Interscholastic Coaches Assn., Hunterdon County Adminstrs. Assn. (past pres.), Hunterdon County Career Coord. Coun. (past pres.), NFICA/NFIOA, Phi Delta Kappa. Office: Nat Fed of St HS Assoc 11724 NW Plaza Cir Kansas City MO 64153-1158 Office: PO Box 20626 Kansas City MO 64195-0626*

KANADE, TAKEO, science educator, institute administrator; b. Hyogo, Japan, Oct. 24, 1945; came to U.S., 1980; s. Kumaichi and Harue (Yamauchi) K.; m. Yukiko Kubo, Mar. 23, 1974; children: Shinichi, Sayaka. BE, Kyoto (Japan) U., 1968, ME, 1970, PhD in Elec. Engring., 1973. Asst. prof. Kyoto U., 1973-76, assoc. prof., 1976-80; sr. rsch. scientist Carnegie Mellon U., Pitts., 1980-82, assoc. prof., 1982-85, prof. computer sci. and robotics, 1985-94, dir. robotics inst., 1992—, U.A. & Helen Whitaker prof. computer sci. and robotics, 1994—; cons. NASA Advanced Tech. Adv. Com., Washington, 1988-90, Martin Marietta, Denver, 1991—. Author: Computer Recognition of Human Faces, 1977; editor: Three-Dimensional Machine Vision, 1987; founding editor Internat. Jour. Computer Vision, 1987—; contbr. articles to profl. jours.; patentee in field. Pres. Japan-Am. Soc. Greater Pitts., 1991-92. Recipient Best Presentation award Audio Visual Info. Rsch. Group, 1980. Fellow IEEE (Marr award 1988), Am. Assn. Artificial Intelligence; mem. Aeronautics and Space Engring. Bd. of NRC. Office: Carnegie Mellon U Robotics Inst 5000 Forbes Ave Pittsburgh PA 15213-3890*

KANAGY, STEVEN ALBERT, foundation administrator; b. Chgo., Sept. 26, 1956; s. John West and Hazel Elizibeth (Montgomery) K. *Great Great Grandfather was the explorer Henry Hudson, the discoverer of Hudson Bay in Canada. Father John Kanagy was at Iwo Jima during World War II to raise the U.S. flag on Mount Suribachi.* Student, Kendall Coll., Evanston, Ill., 1974-76, W. Carey Coll., Hatiesburg, Miss., 1980, U. Southern Miss. Staff worker Longbeach Pub. Libr., Miss., 1978; mgr. Kanagy Art Found., Inc., Longbeach, Miss., 1982—, lead dir., 1997—; distbr. Amway Corp., Ada, Mich., 1984—; cmty. devel. explorer Harbour Dist., Gulfport, Miss., 1985-89, mng. ptnr., 1989—; mng. ptnr. Archival Restorations, 1992—; lead dir. Kanagy Art Found., Inc., 1997. Contbr. article to mag. Kendall Coll. scholar. Mem. Am. Mgmt. Assn., Nat. Trust for Hist. Preservation, Internat. Platform Assn., N.Am. Hunting Club. Republican. Roman Catholic. Avocations: building restoration, archery, photography. Home: PO Box 1014 Long Beach MS 39560-1014

KANCELBAUM, JOSHUA JACOB, lawyer; b. Cleve., May 9, 1936; s. Charles P. and Bertha (Wigotsky) K.; m. Pamela Scotty, Nov. 21, 1973; 1 child, Barbara R. BA, Case Western Res. U., 1958, LLB, 1960. Bar: Ohio 1960, U.S. Ct. Mil. Appeals 1963, U.S. Supreme Ct. 1966, U.S. Tax Ct. 1976. Assoc. Ulmer, Berne, Laronge, Glickman & Curtis, Cleve., 1961-63, Berkman & Gordon, 1963-65; ptnr. Berkman, Gordon, Kancelbaum, Levy & Murray, 1966-79; pvt. practice Ohio, 1979—; adj. prof. law Cleve. State U., 1979-80; spl. ch.-state counsel ACLU of Ohio, 1965-85. Pres. Am. Jewish Congress of No. Ohio, 1979-81, mem. nat. governing coun., chmn. commn. on law and social action, 1982-84. With U.S. Army, 1961. Mem. Greater Cleve. Bar Assn., Ohio Bar Assn., Geauga County Bar Assn., Geauga County Law Libr. Assn. (trustee 1995—). Home: PO Box 657 Newbury OH 44065-0657 Office: 8228 Mayfield Rd Chesterland OH 44026-2542

KANDAL, TERRY R., sociology educator, consultant; b. Chgo., Sept. 17, 1940; s. Terry Olaf and Gertrude Linda Kandal; m. Nancy Jean Fried, 1965 (div. 1973); 1 child, Joshua Terry; m. Anita Aurora Acosta, Feb. 13, 1998. AA, City Coll. San Francisco, 1963; BA, U. Calif., Berkeley, 1965, MA, 1967, PhD, 1974. Rsch. asst. U. Calif., Berkeley, 1965, tchg. asst., 1966-67; tchg. asst. U. Calif., Davis, 1965-66; from asst. prof. to assoc. prof. Calif. State U., L.A., 1968-83, prof. dept. sociology, 1983—; cons. Mex.-Am. Edn. Commn., L.A., 1969-70, others. Author: The Woman Question in Classical Sociological Theory, 1988; editor: Studies of Development and Change in the Modern world, 1989; editor spl. issue Calif. Sociologist, 1992; reviewer for numerous publs. V.p. cmty. adv. coun. Glassell Park elem. sch., L.A., 1981-82. Mem. Am. Sociol. Assn., Pacific Sociol. Assn., Calif. Sociol. Assn., S.W. Labor Studies Assn., Internat. Soc. for Comparative Study of Civilizations, Golden Key (hon.), Phi Beta Kappa. Achievements include writing of first history of the way founding fathers of sociology in the 19th and early 20th centuries responded to the feminist movements of their times. Avocations: photography, pocket billiards, listening to world music. Home: 440 W Ave 46 Los Angeles CA 90065-5006 Office: Calif State U Dept Sociology Los Angeles CA 90032

KANDARIAN, SUSAN CHRISTINE, medical educator; b. Apr. 10, 1959. BS in Biology cum laude, Albion (Mich.) Coll., 1981; MS in Edn., U. Mich., 1983, PhD in Kinesiology, 1988. Asst. prof. health scis. Boston U., 1988-94, postdoctoral, 1989-91, rsch. asst. prof. physiology, 1991-96, rsch. asst. prof. neuromuscular rsch. ctr., 1993-96, assoc. prof. health scis., 1994—, rsch. assoc. prof. neuromuscular rsch. ctr., 1996-97. Reviewer profl. jours.; contbr. numerous articles to profl. jours. Grantee Boston U., 1989-92, Am. Coll. Sports Medicine Found., 1989-90, Am. Heart Assn. 1992—, NIH, 1992—, Nat. Aero. and Space Adminstrn., 1995-96. Fellow Am. Coll. Sports Medicine; mem. AAAS, Am. Physiol. Soc. Office: Boston U 635 Commonwealth Ave Boston MA 02215-1605

KANDEL, DONALD HARRY, financial analyst; b. Phila., Jan. 20, 1956; s. Lawrence Harold and Carol Ethel (Dettelbach) K.; m. Bonnie Susan Daduk, Aug. 1, 1982; children: Ian Alexander, Michael Andrew. BA, Franklin and Marshall U., 1978; MBA, LaSalle U. Fin. affairs adminstr. United Cerebral Palsy Assn., Phila., 1979-84; contr., data processing Dow Jones and Co., Princeton, N.J., 1984-87; v.p. ops. Pvt. Industry Coun., Phila., 1987-95; assoc. exec. dir., CFO Crime Prevention Assn., Phila., 1995—. Bd. dirs. Valley Athletic Assn. Avocations: coaching baseball, soccer, basketball. Home: 9 Auburn Dr Richboro PA 18954-1269 Office: Crime Prevention Assn 230 S Broad St Philadelphia PA 19102-4121

KANDEL, ERIC RICHARD, neuroscience educator; b. Vienna, Austria, Nov. 7, 1929; arrived in U.S., 1939; married, 1956; two children. BA, Harvard Coll., 1952; MD, NYU, 1956. Intern Montefiore Hosp., N.Y.C., 1956-57; rsch. assoc. neurophysiology lab. NIH, Washington, 1957-60; rsch. psychiatrist NIH, 1960-62, 63-64; dir. Mass. Mental Health Ctr., Boston, 1960-65; assoc. prof. physiology, psychiatry to prof. NYU Sch. Medicine, 1965-74; prof. physiology and psychiatry Howard Hughes Med. Inst. Columbia U. Coll. Physicians and Surgeons, N.Y.C., 1974-83, Univ. prof. Howard Hughes Med. Inst., 1983—. Recipient Harvey Prize, Technion, 1993. Fellow AAAS; mem. NAS, Am. Acad. Arts and Scis., Soc. Neurosci. (pres. 1980-81), Internat. Brain Rsch. Orgn, NY Acad. of Scis. (Mayor Awd. Excellence in Sci. & Tech., 1994). Office: Columbia U Coll Physicians & Surgeons Howard Hughes Med Inst 722 W 168th St New York NY 10032-2603*

KANDEL, NELSON ROBERT, lawyer; b. Balt., Sept. 15, 1929; m. Brigitte Kleemaier, Feb. 28, 1957; children: Katrin, Christopher, Peter. BA, U. Md., 1951, LLB, 1954. Bar: Md. 1954, U.S. Supreme Ct. 1964, D.C. 1980. Prin. law firm, Kandel & Assocs. P.A., Balt., 1957—. With U.S. Army. Mem. Md. Bar Assn., Balt. Bar Assn. Democrat. Lutheran. Office: Kandel & Assocs PA Legg Mason Tower 100 Light St Ste 1010 Baltimore MD 21202-1184

KANDEL, PETER THOMAS, lawyer; b. Balt.; s. Nelson Robert and Brigitte (Kleemaier) K.; m. Marion Hoogstraten, Nov. 18, 1989; children: Andrew, Margaret, James. Student, Johns Hopkins U., 1980-81; BA magna cum laude, Williams Coll., 1984; JD, Yale U., 1987. Bar: N.Y. 1988, Md. 1989, D.C., 1989. Assoc. Jones Day Reavis & Pogue, N.Y.C., 1987-89, Piper & Marbury, Balt., 1990-93; stockholder Kandel & Assocs. P.A., Balt., 1993—. Vol. New Haven Legal Assistance, 1985-87. Horace F. Clark prize Williams Coll., 1984. Mem. ABA, Md. Bar Assn., Williams Coll. Alumni Assn. Md. (pres., mem. exec. com.), Phi Beta Kappa, Phi Delta Phi, Delta Phi. Democrat. Lutheran. Office: Kandel & Assocs PA Legg Mason Tower 100 Light St Ste 1010 Baltimore MD 21202-1184

KANDEL, WILLIAM LLOYD, lawyer, lecturer, author; b. N.Y.C., Apr. 25, 1939; s. Morton H. and Lottie S. (Smith) K.; m. Joyce Roland, Jan. 27, 1974; 1 child, Aron Daniel (Ari). AB cum laude, Dartmouth Coll., 1961; JD, Yale U., 1964; LLM in Labor Law, NYU, 1967. Bar: N.Y. 1965, U.S. Dist. Ct. (ea., so. and no. dists.) N.Y., U.S. Ct. Appeals (2d cir.), U.S. Dist. Ct. (no. dist.) Calif. 1988, U.S. Ct. Appeals (3rd cir.). Assoc. Lorenz, Finn & Giardino, N.Y.C., 1964-66; labor atty. NAM, N.Y.C., 1966-68; with Singer Co., N.Y.C., 1968-79, asst. v.p. pers. dept., 1973-76, mng. counsel pers. office of gen. counsel, 1976-79; assoc. Skadden, Arps, Slate, Meagher & Flom, N.Y.C., 1979-85; ptnr. Finley, Kumble, Wagner, Heine, Underberg, Manley, Myerson & Casey, N.Y.C., 1985-87, Myerson & Kuhn, N.Y.C., 1987-89, McDermott Will & Emery, 1989-97, Orrick, Herrington & Sutcliffe, 1997—; lectr. to Law and bus. groups, 1974—; adj. prof. employment law Fordham U., 1983-86; lectr. Practising Law Inst.'s Ann. Inst. on Employment Law, 1980—, co-chair, 1995, chair, 1996—; mem. adv. panel Am. Arbitration Assn., 1996—; mem. adv. com. employment law City Coun. N.Y., 1996—. *William L. Kandel, a litigator and counselor in employment law, brings more than 30 years' experience to his specialty of representing employers. His nation-widetrial practice is before courts, administrative agencies, and arbitration/mediation bodies at the federal, state, and city levels. He defends local and multi-national employers in individual and class actions involving discrimination, wrongful discharge, benefits, unions, and contract or tort claims. He is also active in alternate dispute resolution and non-competition/trade secret and employment-related government contract and defamation cases. His counseling role includes advising employers, adoption and application of policies, work force reductions, affirmative action programs, cost-effective compliance with statutes and regulations, internal investigations and low-risk resolution of employment disputes.* Contbg. editor Employee Rels. Law Jour., 1975—; contbr. articles to profl. jours. V.p., bd. dirs. Assn. for Integration Mgmt., 1979-85; bd. dirs. N.Y. chpt. Am. Jewish Com., 1980-82; mem. human resources com. N.Y. YMCA, 1994—. Recipient award of Merit, Nat. Urban Coalition, 1979. Democrat. Jewish. Office: Orrick Herrington & Sutcliffe 666 5th Ave New York NY 10103-0001

KANDELL, HOWARD NOEL, pediatrician. BS, U. Miami, 1956; MD, Tulane U., 1959. Diplomate Am. Bd. Pediatrics. Intern Phila. Gen. Hosp., 1959-60; resident N.Y. Hosp. Cornell Med. Ctr., N.Y.C., 1960-62; pediatrician Phoenix, 1965—; chief pediatrics Health Maintenance Assocs., Ltd., Phoenix, 1977-82; assoc. chmn. dept. pediatrics, Maricopa County Hosp., Phoenix, 1965-71, svc. chief dept. pediatrics, 1972-77; assoc. in pediatrics U. Ariz. Coll. Medicine, 1970-82, clin. instr. 1982-83; asst. prof., 1983-87; chmn. pediatric dept. CIGNA Healthplan of Ariz., Phoenix, 1984-87; adj. faculty mem. Ariz. State U. Coll. Nursing, 1986—; med. dir. INA Healthplan (CIGNA) South Fla., 1982-83. Capt. MC USAF, 1962-64. Recipient Tchr. of Yr. award dept. pediatrics Maricopa County Gen. Hosp., 1972. Fellow Am. Acad. Pediatrics; mem. Am. Coll. Phys. Exec., Ariz. Pediatric Soc. (treas., exec. com. 1970-76), Phoenix Pediatric Soc. (v.p. 1970-72). Office: 12635 N 42nd St Phoenix AZ 85032-7601 Home: 7257 E Echo Ln Scottsdale AZ 85258-2768

KANDER, JOHN HAROLD, composer; b. Kansas City, Mo., Mar. 18, 1927; s. Harold S. and Bernice (Aaron) K. BA, Oberlin Coll., 1951, D (hon.), 1988; MA, Columbia U., 1953. Composer for theatrical prodns. (with James and William Goldman) A Family Affair, 1961, (with Fred Ebb) Flora, the Red Menace, 1964, Cabaret, 1966 (Tony award, N.Y. Drama Critic's Circle award), The Happy Time, 1967, Zorba, 1968, 70 Girls 70, 1971, Chicago, 1975, rev., 1996, The Act, 1977, Woman of the Year, 1981 (Tony award), The Rink, 1984, Kiss of the Spider Woman, 1990 (Best Mus. Score Tony award 1993, N.Y. Drama Critics Circle award 1993), And the World Goes Round, 1991, Steel Pier, 1997, Over and Over, 1999, (films) Something for Everyone, 1969, Cabaret, 1972, Funny Lady, 1975, A Matter of Time, French Postcards, Lucky Lady, 1976, New York, New York, 1977, Kramer vs. Kramer, 1980, Still of the Night, 1982, Blue Skies Again, 1982, Places in the Heart, 1984; composer for Liza Minnelli TV spl. Liza with a Z, 1974 (Emmy award), for Shirley MacLaine in Gypsy in My Soul, for Goldie Hawn and Liza Minnelli in Goldie and Liza Together, Baryshnikov on Broadway, An Early Frost, 1985, for Liza Minnelli in London, Steppin'Out, 1993 (Emmy award), Breathing Lessons, 1994, The Boys Next Door, 1995. Recipient Kennedy Ctr. Honoree. Mem. Dramatists Guild., Nat. Inst. Music Theatre, Songwriters Hall of Fame.

KANDRAC, JO ANN MARIE, school administrator; b. Warren, Ohio, May 5, 1943; d. Clyde Joseph and Micheline (Vescera) Battista; m. Thomas Michael Kandrac, Sept. 25, 1965; children: Michael, Richard, David. B Music in Edn., Youngstown U., 1965, MS in Edn., 1983. Cert. tchr., administrator, Ohio. Tchr. St. Mary Sch., Warren, 1965-66, Blessed Sacrament Sch., Warren, 1967-68, 70-86, Plew Elem. Sch., Niceville, Fla., 1968-70; prin. Saints Mary and Joseph Sch., Newton Falls, Ohio, 1986-91, Blessed Sacrament Sch., Warren, 1991-97, St. Thomas Aquinas Sch., St. Cloud, Fla., 1997—. Area chair United Way, Warren, 1986-97. Tchr. of Yr. award Diocese of Youngstown, 1981. Mem. Trumbull Assn. Reading Coun., Delta Kappa Gamma. Roman Catholic. Avocations: travel, reading, cross-stitch, knitting, ceramics. Office: St Thomas Aquinas Sch 800 Brown Chapel Rd Saint Cloud FL 34769-2001

KANDRAVY, JOHN, lawyer; b. Passaic, N.J., May 9, 1935; s. Frank and Anna (Chan) K.; m. Alice E. Sullivan, Feb. 17, 1962; children: Elizabeth Ann, Katherine Ann. BA, Wesleyan U., Middletown, Conn., 1957; JD, Columbia U., 1960. Bar: N.J. 1960, D.C. 1969, U.S. Supreme Ct. 1973, N.Y. 1982. From assoc. to ptnr. Shanley & Fisher, Newark, 1961-80; ptnr. Shanley & Fisher, Morristown, N.J., 1980—, mng. ptnr., 1983-85, 89—; bd. dirs. Tingue, Brown & Co., G.A.R. Internat. Corp., Ridgewood Savs. Bank of N.J., Ridgewood Fin., Inc. Mem. Gov.'s Mgmt. Commn., State of N.J., 1970; chmn. Planning Bd., Ridgewood, N.J., 1981-85, Zoning Bd. Adjustment, 1979-81; mem. bd. advisors Coll. Bus. Adminstrn., Fairleigh Dickinson U., 1983-87, chmn. bd. advisors, 1985-86; mem. Soc. of Valley Hosp., Ridgewood, 1971—, chmn. bd. trustees Cen. Bergen Comty. Mental Health Ctr., N.J., 1970-73; trustee Palisades Counseling Ctr., Rutherford, 1968-81, The Forum Sch., Waldwick, N.J., 1987—, The Forum Sch. Found., Waldwick, 1978—, The Valley Hosp., Ridgewood, 1992—, Peer Found. for Plastic Surgery and Rehab., Florham Park, 1996—, Valley Health Sys., Inc., Ridgewood, 1997—, Children's Aid and Family Svcs., Inc., Paramus, N.J., 1998—; mem. lawyers' adv. coun. Rutgers Law Sch., Newark, 1994-98, mem. vis. com., 1994-98. Edward John Noble Found.grantee, 1957-60. Mem. ABA, N.J. Bar Assn., Essex County Bar Assn., D.C. Bar Assn., Morris County Bar Assn., Essex Club (gov. 1976-85), Wesleyan U. Alumni Assn. (chmn. 1981-83), Indian Trail Club (Franklin Lakes, N.J.), Ridgewood Country Club, Park Ave. Club (gov. 1992—). Republican. Presbyterian. Home: 56 Monte Vista Ave Ridgewood NJ 07450-2428 Office: Shanley & Fisher 131 Madison Ave Morristown NJ 07960-6097

KANDT, RAYMOND S., neurologist; b. Rochester, N.Y., July 8, 1950; m. Irene; children: Melanie, Lauren. AB cum laude, U. Va., 1972; MD, U. Va. Sch. Medicine, 1976. Diplomate Am. Bd. Med. Examiners, Am. Bd. Pediatrics, Am. Bd. Psychiatry & Neurology with spl. competence in child neurology and with added qualifications in clin. neurophysiology; cert. neurovascular & pediat. neurosonologist. Intern, resident in pediatrics Johns Hopkins Hosp., Balt., 1976-78; resident in pediatric neurology, fellow in devel. pediatrics Johns Hopkins Hosp., 1978-81; instr. depts. neurology, pediatrics U. Mich., Ann Arbor, 1981-82, asst. prof. depts. neurology & pediatrics, 1982-84; asst. prof. pediatrics div. pediatric neurology Duke U. Med. Ctr., Durham, N.C., 1984-89; assoc. prof. pediatrics div. pediatric neurology Duke U. Med. Ctr., 1989-92, asst. prof. medicine div. neurology, 1990-92; assoc. prof. neurology, pediatrics Bowman Gray Sch. Medicine, Winston-Salem, N.C., 1992-97; clin. assoc. prof. pediatrics Wake Forest U./Bapt. Med. Ctr., Winston-Salem, 1997—; chief sect. child neurology Bowman Gray Sch. Medicine, 1992-97, grad. med. edn. com. 1993-97, clin. faculty adv. coun., 1993-97; faculty advisor pediatric house staff U. Mich., 1981-84, faculty advisor med. students, 1983-84, com. on edn., 1982-84; pediatric rep. continuing med. edn. com. Duke U. Med. Ctr., 1985-92; mem. gen. clin. rsch. ctrs. com. nat. ctr. for rsch. resources NIH, 1991-95; cons. in field. Reviewer Am. Jour. Human Genetics, 1992, Jour. Neurol. Scis., 1993—, Nature Genetics, 1993, Annals of Neurology, 1998; cons. editor Annals of Behavioral Medicine, 1991-93. Adv. bd. My Father's House Group Homes, 1993; med. adv. com. Children's Ctr. for the Physically Handicapped, Winston-Salem, N.C., 1993—. Grantee NIH, 1986-91, 89-92, Nat. Tuberous Sclerosis Assn., 1992-93, grantee Glaxo, 1995-96; recipient Merck award, 1976. Mem. Am. Neurol. Assn., N.C. Pediatric Soc., Child Neurology Soc., Alpha Omega Alpha, Nat. Tuberous Sclerosis Assn. (mem. profl. adv. bd. 1990—, scientific adv. bd. 1995—, chmn. clin. care adv. bd. 1995-97, scientific grant rev. com. 1995—, chmn. med. adv. com. N.C. chpt. 1988—), Phi Sigma. Home: 3428 Jameson Ln Winston Salem NC 27106-4771 Office: Johnson Neurologic Clinic 606 N Elm St High Point NC 27262-4336

KANDUS, RICHARD JAY, adult education educator; b. L.A., May 25, 1952; s. Irving and Anita June Cohen; m. Colleen Nagel Kandus, June 11, 1988; 1 child, Julia Tenaya. BA, UCLA, 1974; MA, Humboldt State U., 1979. Instr. Humboldt State U., Arcata, Calif., 1979-97, Coll. Redwoods, Eureka, Calif., 1980-98, Mt. San Jacinto Coll., Menifee, Calif., 1998—; dir. Biofeedback Ctr., Arcata, 1980-98; libr. liason Coll. Redwoods, Eureka, 1995-97, rep. Acad. Senate, 1989-92. Author: Daily Health and Stress Scale, 1986, 1995; (with others) Personal Growth, 1994. Docent Audubon Soc., Arcata, 1996. Mem. AAUP, APA. Office: Mt San Jacinto Coll Menifee CA 92584

KANE, AGNES BREZAK, pathologist, educator; b. Danbury, Conn., Nov. 3, 1946; d. John Edward and Mary Elizabeth (Hatfield) Brezak; m. David E. Kane, June 22, 1970. BA, Swarthmore Coll., 1968; MD, Temple U., 1974, PhD, 1976. Diplomate Am. Bd. Pathology. Resident Temple U. Hosp., Phila., 1975-76, 77-78; postdoctoral fellow Karolinska Inst., Stockholm, 1976-77; asst. prof. Temple U. Sch. Medicine, Phila., 1977-82; asst. prof. Brown U., Providence, 1982-87, assoc. prof. pathology, 1987-95, prof. pathology, 1995-96, chair dept. pathology and lab. medicine, 1996—; mem. merit rev. bd. for basic scis. VA, Washington, 1984-86; cons. R.I. Commn. for Safety and Occupational Health, Providence, 1986—; commr. Commn. to Identify Occupational Diseases, Providence, 1987-88; mem. rev. com. Nat. Inst. Environ. Health Scis., Research Triangle Park, N.C., 1988—. Assoc. editor Am. Jour. of Pathology, 1992—; contbr. articles on exptl. pathology to sci. publs. Lucretia Mott fellow Swarthmore Coll., 1969-71; recipient Rsch. Career Devel. award NIH, 1981-86. Mem. Am. Assn. Pathologists (women's com. 1987—, program com. 1990—), Assn. Women Med. Faculty Brown U. (founder, coord.), Women in Medicine (faculty advisor Brown U. chpt.; Mary Putnam Jacobi award 1986), Phi Kappa, Sigma Xi. Avocation: gardening. Office: Brown Univ Box G Providence RI 02912

KANE, ALAN HENRY, lawyer; b. Seattle, Nov. 7, 1940; s. Henry and Alice (Harbak) K.; m. Martha Dressler, June 25, 1966; children: Karen, Graham, AMy. BA in Law, U. Wash., 1963, JD, 1965. Bar: Wash. 1965. Ptnr. Sax & Maciver, Seattle, 1966-84, Preston Gales & Ellis, LLP, Seattle, 1985—. Fellow Am. Coll. Trusts and Estates Counsel (Wash. State chair 1985-88). Avocations: boating, water and snow skiing, fishing. Office: Preston Gates & Ellis LLP 701 5th Ave Ste 5000 Seattle WA 98104-7078

KANE, ALICE THERESA, lawyer; b. N.Y.C., Jan. 16, 1948. AB, Manhattanville Coll., 1969; JD, NYU, 1972; grad., Harvard U. Sch. Bus. Program Mgmt. Devel., 1985. Bar: N.Y. 1973, U.S. Dist. Ct. (so. dist.) N.Y. 1974. Atty. N.Y. Life Ins. Co., N.Y.C., 1972-83, v.p., assoc. gen. counsel, 1983-85, v.p. dept. personnel, 1985, sr. v.p., gen. counsel, 1986-89, corp. sec., 1989-92, exec. v.p., gen. counsel, sec., 1992-95, exec. v.p. corp. mktg., 1995-98; exec. v.p. Am. Gen. Investment Mgmt. Corp., N.Y.C., 1998—. Mem. ABA (chmn. employee benefits com., tort and ins. practice sect. 1984-85, mem. corp., banking and bus. law sects., tort and ins. practice sects.), Assn. of Life Ins. Counsel (deps. solvency com.). Office: Am Gen Investment Mgmt Corp 125 Maiden Ln 7th Fl New York NY 10038*

KANE, ALLEN, postal service executive; b. Bklyn., Apr. 23, 1945; m. Sylvia Kane; 2 children. Bachelor, CUNY, MBA; grad. Advanced Mgmt. Program, Harvard U. Mgmt. assoc. dept. ops. U.S. Postal Svc., Jamaica, N.Y., 1971; mgr. distbn. U.S. Postal Svc., Queens, N.Y.; dist. dir. mail processing U.S. Postal Svc., L.I., N.Y.; gen. mgr. air mail John F. Kennedy Airport, U.S. Postal Svc., N.Y.C.; dir. ops. N.E. region U.S. Postal Svc., v.p. ops. support, 1994, sr. v.p., chief mktg. officer, 1996—. FAX: 202-268-6057. Office: US Postal Svc Chief Mktg Officer 475 Lenfant Plz SW Rm 2340 Washington DC 20260-1531

KANE, ANNETTE PIESLAK, religious organization executive; b. Trenton, N.J., May 2, 1933; d. Theodore P. and Stella (Mackiewicz) Pieslak; m. Joseph P. Kane, Sept. 6, 1958; children: Paula M., Stephen J., Brian P., Christine A. BA, Trinity Coll., Washington, 1954; MA, U. Pa., 1956. Asst. prof. Rosemont (Pa.) Coll., 1955-58; asst. prof. Trinity Coll., Washington, 1958-61, editor alumni jour., 1973-79; program dir. Nat. Coun. Cath. Women, Washington, 1979-86, exec. dir., 1986—. Bd. dirs. Nat. Coun. Aging, Washington, 1985-87, CARA-Ctr. for Applied Rsch. in Apostolate, Washington, 1989—, Nat. Relig. Partnership for Environ., 1993—. Office: Nat Coun Cath Women 1275 K St NW Ste 975 Washington DC 20005-4006*

KANE, CAROL, actress; b. Cleve., June 18, 1952. Stage debut in The Prime of Miss Jean Brodie, 1966; other N.Y.C. theatre appearances include Ring 'Round the Bath Tub, 1972, The Tempest, 1974, 80, The Effect of Gamma Ray on Man-in-the-Moon Marigolds, 1978, Are You Now or Have You Ever Been?, 1978, Benefit of a Doubt, 1978, Tales from Vienna Woods, 1979, Sunday Runners in the Rain, 1980, Macbeth, 1980, The Fairy Garden, 1984, The Debutante Ball, 1988, Frankie and Johnny in the Clair de Lune, 1988; film appearances include Carnal Knowledge, 1971, Desperate Characters, 1971, Wedding in White, 1972, The Last Detail, 1974, Dog Day Afternoon, 1975, Hester Street, 1975 (Acad. award nomination for Best Actress), Harry and Walter Go to New York, 1976, Annie Hall, 1977, Valentino, 1977, The World's Greatest Lover, 1977, The Mafu Cage, 1978, When a Stranger Calls, 1979, The Muppet Movie, 1979, The Sabiana, 1979, Les Jeux, 1980, Pandemonium, 1982, Norman Loves Rose, 1982, Can She Bake A Cherry Pie?, 1983, Over the Brooklyn Bridge, 1984, Racing With the Moon, 1984, The Secret Diary of Sigmund Freud, 1984, Transylvania 6-5000, 1985, Jumpin' Jack Flash, 1986, The Princess Bride, 1987, Ishtar, 1987, License to Drive, 1988, Scrooged, 1988, Sticky Fingers, 1988, Flashback, 1990, Joe Versus the Volcano, 1990, The Lemon Sisters, 1990, My Blue Heaven, 1990, Ted and Venus, 1991, In the Soup, 1992, Adams Family Values, 1993, When a Stranger Calls Back, 1993, Even Cowgirls Get the Blues, 1993, Baby on Board, 1993, Addams Family Values, 1993, The Crazysitter, 1995, Trees Lounge, 1996, Sunset Park, 1996, The Pallbearer, 1996, Big Bully, 1996, American Strays, 1996, Office Killer, 1997, Gone Fishin', 1997, The Tic Code, 1998, Jawbreaker, 1999, Man on the Moon, 1999; TV series Taxi, 1981-83, All is Forgiven, 1986, American Dreamer, 1990, (voice) Alladin, 1994, Pearl, 1996, Noah's Ark, 1999; TV films An Invasion of Privacy, 1983, Burning Rage, 1984, All is Forgiven, 1986, Drop Out Mother, 1988, Dad, the Angel & Me, 1995, Freaky Friday, 1995; TV spls. Shelly Duvall's Tall Tales and Legends: Case at the Bat, 1985, Bob Goldthwait-Don't Watch This Show, 1986, Paul Reiser: Out on a Whim, 1987, Rap Master Ronnie-A Report Card, 1988, Tales from the Crypt, 1992, Merry Christmas George Bailey, 1997. Recipient Emmy award for outstanding supporting actress in a comedy series, 1981. Office: Krost/Chapin Mgmt 9465 Wilshire Blvd Ste 430 Beverly Hills CA 90212-2612*

KANE, CHRISTOPHER, lawyer; b. L.A., Aug. 4, 1944; s. William Jerome and Mary Katherine (Galvin) K.; m. Kathryn Ann Lalley, June 27, 1970; children: Kevin Jerome, Ryan Robert, Matthew Christopher, Molly Kathryn. BA in Polit. Sci., Seattle U., 1966; JD, Georgetown U., 1969. Bar: Wash. 1969, U.S. Ct. Mil. Appeals 1969, U.S. Dist. Ct. (we. dist.) Wash. 1973, U.S. Dist. Ct. (ea. dist.) Wash. 1975, U.S. Ct. Appeals (9th cir.) 1976, U.S. Ct. Appeals (10th cir.) 1977; cert. internat. arbitrator. Legis. aide to Henry M. Jackson U.S. Senate, Washington, 1968-69; assoc. Ferguson & Burdell, Seattle, 1973-79, ptnr., 1979-95; prin. Law Offices Christopher Kane, Seattle, 1995-96; chmn. bd., pres. Lawyer Selection Advisors, Seattle, 1996-97; of counsel Foster, Pepper & Shelfelman, Seattle, 1998—; adj. prof. European single market law and bus. Seattle U., 1994-95. Contbr. articles to profl. jours. Capt. USAR, 1969-73. Mem. ABA (sects. of corp. law, internat. law and practice, antitrust), Wash. State Bar Assn. (chmn. antitrust sect. 1986-87), Rotary (vice chmn. internat. students com. 1992), Wash. Athletic Club, Seattle Tennis Club. Roman Catholic. Avocations: skiing, tennis, jogging, writing. Office: Foster Pepper & Shefelman Ste 3400 1111 Third Ave Bldg Seattle WA 98101

KANE, DANIEL HIPWELL, lawyer; b. Far Rockaway, N.Y., Aug. 18, 1908; s. David and Bertha (Schilling) K.; m. Helen Shirkey, July 30, 1932 (dec. Feb. 1985); children: Ailene Kane Rogers, Daniel Hipwell, Patricia Kane Hennin, Kevin Kane. B.S., NYU, 1929; J.D., 1931. Bar: N.Y. 1932. Since practiced in N.Y.C.; specializing in patents; sr. partner Kane, Dalsimer, Sullivan, Kurucz, Levy, Eisele & Richard, N.Y.C., 1946-89; mem. faculty N.Y.U. Sch. Law, 1947-85, adj. prof., 1964-85; lectr. Practising Law Inst., 1951—; v.p., bd. dirs. Dzus Fastener Co., Inc., West Islip, N.Y., 1941-88; bd. dirs. Pickering & Co., Inc., Plainview, N.Y., 1965—. Contbr. articles to profl. jours. Pres. bd. edn. Union Free Sch. Dist. 6, Huntington, N.Y., 1954-55; Trustee William Dzus Fund; bd. dirs. Ukrainian Inst. Am. Mem. ABA, Assn. of Bar of City of N.Y., Am., N.Y. patent law assns., Am. Judicature Soc., Phi Delta Phi. Clubs: NYU (N.Y.C.); Centerport Yacht; Hibernian United Service (Dublin). Home: 22 Spring Hollow Rd Centerport NY 11721-1123 Office: 711 3rd Ave New York NY 10017-4014 *Like many others who grew up during the early part of this century, I simply assumed that America offered boundless opportunities. Free from doubts, hang ups, or inhibitions, I simply seized a very small portion of the opportunities which were offered.*

KANE, DAVID SHERIDAN, insurance company executive; b. Deadwood, S.D., July 12, 1940; s. Arthur Sheridan and Grace Marie K.; m. Oline; children: Jennifer Marie Bergstrom, Brenna Marie, Mackenzie Sheridan. Ph.B., U. N.D., 1964. CFP, CLU. Agt., Fidelity Union Life Ins. Co., Grand Forks, N.D., 1963-65, gen. agt., 1965; pres., founder D.S. Kane & Assocs., Inc., Fargo, N.D., 1968—; pres. Heritage Mktg. Group Inc., 1991—, Fin. Benefits Co., 1988—; nat. dir. sales ITT Life, 1980-81. Mem. Nat. Assn. Life Underwriters, Fargo-Moorhead Life Underwriters Assn. (pres. 1980), Am. Soc. C.L.U., Sigma Nu (pres. ednl. found.). Lutheran. Office: Financial Benefits Co. PO Box 5676 University Sta Fargo ND 58105

KANE, EDWARD K., lawyer. LLB, Fordham U., 1959; BBA, Manhattan Coll., 1951. Bar: N.Y. 1959. With Gardian Life Ins. Co. Am., N.Y.C., 1951—; exec. v.p. Guardian Life Ins. Co. Am., N.Y.C., 1971—. Office: Guardian Life Ins Co Am 7 Hanover Sq New York NY 10004-1699*

KANE, EDWARD RYNEX, retired chemical company executive, corporate director; b. Schenectady, N.Y., Sept. 13, 1918; s. Edward Marion and Elva (Rynex) K.; m. Doris Norma Peterson, Apr. 3, 1948; children: Christine K. Plant, Susan K. Booth. BS in Chemistry, Union Coll., 1940; PhD in Phys. Chemistry, MIT, 1943. Instr. chem. MIT, Cambridge, 1942-43; from rsch. chemist to pres. DuPont, Wilmington, Del., 1943-79; various positions textile fibers dept. DuPont, 1943-66; dept. head indsl. and biochemicals DuPont, Wilmington, 1967-69, v.p., mem. exec. com., 1969-73, pres., vice chmn., exec. com., mem. fin. com., 1973-79, also bd. dirs., 1969-89; mem. dir.'s adv. coun. JP Morgan, 1989—; hon. dir. INCO Ltd., 1989—. Trustee, Com. Economic Devel., N.Y.C., 1970-79, Union Coll., Schenectady, 1972-77; bd. dirs. Coun. for Fin. Aid to Edn., N.Y.C., 1976-79; chmn. Nat. Adv. Coun. on Minorities in Engring., Washington, 1977-78; mem. corp. MIT, Cambridge, 1979-89; mem. bd. govs. Nat. Rsch. Coun., 1990-93. Recipient Bus. Leader of Year award Drexel U., 1977, Internat. Palladium medal Societe de Chimie Industrielle, 1979. Mem. Am. Chem. Soc., Am. Inst. Chem. Engrs., Mfg. Chemists Assn. (chmn. 1975), NAE (treas. 1986-93, coun. 1986-93), Soc. Chem. Industry (chmn. Am. sect. 1974, pres. London 1979-80), Wilmington Country Club, Greenville Country Club (Del.), Sigma Xi. Republican. Episcopalian. Avocations: travel, tennis. Address: Old Kennett Rd Wilmington DE 19807

KANE, GEORGE FRANCIS, systems analyst; b. Palo Alto, Calif., Aug. 11, 1948; s. John Francis and Dorothy Desdemona (De Leito) K.; m. Tandy Jo Warnow, July 20, 1974 (div. Feb. 1981); 1 child, Kristin Aviva. BA in Philosopy, U. Calif., Berkeley, 1970. With Unisys Corp., 1979; engring. documentation specialist Unisys Corp., Santa Clara, Calif., 1985-90; product info. specialist Unisys Corp., Rancho Bernardo, Calif., 1990-94; product info. analyst Unisys Corp., Roseville, Minn., 1994—. Author: (chess instructions books) Chess and Children, 1974, What's My Next Move, 1974; contbr. New Unionist Monthly Newsletter, 1984—. Active New Union Party, Mpls., 1984—. Mem. Unisys Toastmasters Club (various offices). Home: 3540 Hennepin Ave Minneapolis MN 55408-3848 Office: Unisys Corp 2276 Highcrest Rd Roseville MN 55113-2529

KANE, JACK ALLISON, physician, county administrator; b. Meadville, Pa., Feb. 28, 1921; s. Thomas Emery and Mildred (McMahon) K.; m. Virginia Joanne (Gasque), Sept. 28, 1946; children: Jeffrey, Marsha, Sharman, Cheryl. BS, Allegheny Coll., Meadville, Pa., 1943; MD, Case Western Res. U., 1949. Diplomate Am. Bd. Preventive Medicine. Intern U.S. Naval Hosp., 1949-50; fellow Sch. of Pub. Health U. Mich., 1950-51; med. dir. power train div. GM, Defiance, Ohio, 1954—; med. dir. Defiance County Health Dept., 1975-96; pres. J. Kane MD, Inc., Defiance, 1977—; pres. Defiance County Bd. Health, 1962-82, Defiance County Lung Assn., 1968-78. Lt. USNR, 1952-54. With USN, 1942-45. Fellow Am. Coll. Occupl. and Environ. Medicine; mem. AMA, Ohio State Med. Assn., Ohio Thoracic Soc. Avocations: photography, biking, travel. Home: PO Box 501 Defiance OH 43512-0501 Office: GM Powertrain Div PO Box 70 Defiance OH 43512-0070

KANE, JAMES ROBERT, financial executive; b. Pitts., Mar. 22, 1959; s. John William Sr. and Helen Mary (Neimeier) K. AS, Allegheny County Community Coll., 1979; BBA, Robert Morris Coll., 1981; MBA, So. Meth. U., 1993. CPA, Ind.; cert. mgmt. acct.; cert. fin. mgmt. Staff acct. UCCEL Corp., Dallas, 1982-83, fin. reports analyst, 1983-85, fin. systems analyst, 1985-86, fin. reporting, analysis supr., 1986; acct. Zoecon Corp., Dallas, 1986, sr. acct., 1987-90, mgr. acctg., 1990-93; mgr. corp. acctg. Kimball Internat., Inc., Jasper, Ind., 1994-96, dir. acctg., 1996-98, dir. treasury, 1998—; cons. in field. Recipient Achievement award UCCEL Corp., 1985. Mem. AICPAs. Republican. Methodist. Home: PO Box 797 Santa Claus IN 47579-0797 Office: Kimball Internat Inc Corp Annex 1600 Royal St Jasper IN 47549-1022

KANE, JAY BRASSLER, banker; b. Bklyn., June 4, 1931; s. Arthur Ferris and Margaret (Brassler) K.; grad. Poly. Prep. Sch., 1949; m. Marian Albertson, Oct. 15, 1960 (dec. 1993); children: Lisa Kane Brown, James Brassler. AB; Columbia, 1953, postgrad. Sch. Bus., 1954; MBA, NYU, 1961. With Met. Life Ins. Co., N.Y.C., 1954-55; with Bankers Trust Co., N.Y.C., 1955—, asst. v.p., 1965-68, v.p., 1968-88; v.p. BT Brokerage Corp., 1988-90; regional dir. Frank Russell Trust Co., N.Y.C., 1990-97; assoc. P.P.I. Internat., 1997—; also mgr. corp. pension funds, mktg. dir. trust svcs.; spkr. Am. Bankers Assn.; lectr. New Sch. for Social Rsch., Attach bd. dirs. Contbr. articles to profl. jours. Mem. N.Y. Soc. Security Analysts, Fin. Analysts Fedn., Am. Pension Conf., Riverside (Conn.) Yacht Club. N.Y. Yacht Club. Home and Office: Hilton Heath Cos Cob CT 06807

KANE, JOHN LAWRENCE, JR., federal judge; b. Tucumcari, N.Mex., Feb. 14, 1937; s. John Lawrence and Dorothy Helen (Bottler) K.; m. Stephanie Jane Shafer, Oct. 5, 1993; children: Molly Francis, Meghan, Sally, John Pattison. B.A., U. Colo., 1958; J.D., U. Denver, 1961, LL.D. (hon), 1997. Bar: Colo. 1961. Dep. dist. atty. Adams County, Colo., 1961-62; assoc. firm Gaunt, Byrne & Dirrim, 1961-63; ptnr. firm Andrews and Kane, Denver, 1964; pub. defender Adams County, 1965-67; dep. dir. eastern region of India Peace Corps, 1967-69; with firm Holme Roberts & Owen, 1970-77, ptnr., 1972-77; judge U.S. Dist. Ct. Colo., Denver, 1978-88, U.S. sr. dist. judge, 1988—; adj. prof. law U. Denver, U. Colo., 1996—; vis. lectr.

Trinity Coll., Dublin, Ireland, winter 1989; adj. prof. U. Colo., 1996. Contbr. articles to profl. jours. Recipient St. Thomas More award Cath. Lawyers Guild, 1983, U.S. Info. Agy. Outstanding Svc. award, 1985, Outstanding Alumnus award U. Denver, 1987, Lifetime Jud. Achievement award Nat. Assn. Criminal Def. Lawyers, 1987, Civil Rights award B'nai B'rith, 1988. Fellow Internat. Acad. Trial Lawyers, Am. Bd. Trial Advs. (hon.). Roman Catholic. Office: US Dist Ct C-428 US Courthouse 1929 Stout St Denver CO 80294-0001 *There is a tendency to gild the past with uncritical generosity but an even more pronounced one to forget Santayana's dictum that one who forgets history is bound to repeat it. Law is that indispensable mechanism by which we may survive as a free people if we use it to apply a critical understanding of history to a confusing and dynamic present.*

KANE, LOANA, foreign language educator; b. Sarzana, Liguria, Italy, Dec. 15, 1940; d. Leonardo and Maria (Colombini) Fumagalli; m. William D. Kane, July 10, 1964; children: David C., Jonathan A. BA, U. Messina, Italy, 1967; MA, Tufts U., 1971; PhD, U. Messina, 1985. Cert. china painter; qualified lang. specialist Italian/Sicilian FBI, 1987; Italian lang. proficiency tester CIA Lang. Sch., 1985; qualified courtroom interpreter U.S. Fed. Cts., 1996. Teaching asst. Tufts U., Medford, Mass., 1969-72; instr. French Fairfax County (Va.) Pub. Schs., 1980-81; instr. ESL Am. Embassy, Caracas, Venezuela, 1981-82; instr. Italian C.I.A. Lang. Sch., Arlington, Va., 1985-86; lectr. French George Mason U., Fairfax, Va., 1986-88, coord. Italian studies, 1988-90; asst. prof. Latin and Romance lang. Gallaudet U., Washington, 1990-95; Romance langs. prof. U.S. Dept. Agr. Grad. Sch., Washington, 1995—; Italian lang. proficiency examiner John Hopkins U., Washington, 1995—; Spanish lang. interpreter Fairfax County Dist. Ct. for Juvenile and Domestic Rels., Fairfax, Va., 1996—; dir. Italian cultural activities Tufts U., 1969-72; guest spkr. Italian Cultural Soc., Washington, 1989, Order Sons of Italy in Am. Heritage Lodge, 1990, Greater Washington Area Tchrs. Fgn. Langs. Conf., 1994; keynote spkr. Italian Festival, Alexandria, Va., 1993; organizer confs. in field including Pride in Our Heritage, Sons of Italy Heritage Lodge, Fairfax, Va., 1989, The Panare Indians, Am. Embassy, Caracas, Venezuela, 1983, others. Author: Everyday Italian, 3 vols., 1988, Signs of Italy, 1992; co-author: Theodor Billroth, 1994; co-author Inaugural Conf. Soc. Sicilian Surgeons, 1989, 90, 91; china painting exhbns., 1982, 84, 86, 90; co-host (cable TV show) Our Place, Fairfax, Va., 1992-93; translator monograph Italian Gestures and Am. Sign Langs. TV program Communicating Today, Fairfax County Cable TV, 1995. Sec. exec. bd. Am. Nursery Sch., Bonn, Germany, 1976-77; pres. Am. Embassy Women Assn., Caracas, Venezuela, 1982-83. Faculty Devel. Fund. Study grantee Gallaudet U., 1991, Italian Govt. study grantee, 1990; recipient Disting. Mem. award Order Sons of Italy, 1989, Gold Medal award C. of C. Italy, 1991. Mem. MLA, AAUP, China Painters Assn., Tufts U. Alumni Assn., Tufts Washington Alliance, Order Sons of Italy in Am., Italian Cultural Soc. Washington, Am. Assn. Tchrs. Italian (pres. Washington chpt.). Roman Catholic. Avocations: china painting, oil painting.

KANE, LORIE, professional golfer; b. Prince Edward Island, Can., Dec. 19, 1964; d. Jack Kane. Student, Acadia U. Mem. Can. Internat. Team, 1989-92, Can. World Amateur Team, 1992; golfer LPGA, 1993—; du Maurier Ltd. Series champion, 1994, 95, series event winner, 1993-95; 2d place Toray Japan Queens Cup, 1997. Recipient Heather Farr award, 1998. 1 LPGA career hole-in-one. Office: c/o LPGA 100 International Golf Dr Daytona Beach FL 32124-1082*

KANE, LOUIS ISAAC, merchant; b. Boston, Mar. 25, 1931; s. George Ernest and Sally Charlotte (Smith) K.; m. Katharine Fitzhugh Daniels, Sept. 21, 1957; children—Elizabeth Holliday, Jennifer Johnston, Joseph Daniels. AB, Harvard U., 1953. Pres., CEO, dir. Kane Financial Corp., Boston, 1958-72; CEO, dir., chmn. bd. dirs. Healthco, Inc., Boston, 1967-71; gen. ptnr. Boston Ptnrs., 1972-83; chmn., CEO, dir. Au Bon Pain Co., Inc., 1978-88, co-chmn., co-CEO, dir., 1988-94, co-chmn., 1994—. Dem. com. chmn. McGovern Fin. Com., Mass., 1972; councilor Harvard Coll. Fund, 1971-73, 75-85, vice chmn., 1978-85, 91-98, co-chmn. 1998—; mem. exec. com. on univ. resources Harvard U., co-chmn. gift com. Class of 1953; co-chmn. Harvard Campaign for Faculty of Arts and Scis.; hon. trustee Inst. Contemporary Art, Boston, 1990, pres., 1967-75; trustee West End House, Inc., 1970—, v.p., 1975-89, pres., 1989-98, chmn., 1998—; trustee DU Club Harvard, pres., 1987; trustee Bentley Coll., Waltham, Mass., 1992—, Fly Club, Harvard U., 1996; bd. dirs. Harvard-Radcliffe Hillel, 1976—, Harvard Alumni Assn., 1981-85, 91-93, 98—, Boston Mcpl. Rsch. Bur., 1990—; mem. corp. Mass. Gen. Hosp., Ogunquit Mus. of Am. Art, Maine; past bd. dirs. or trustee Eaglebrook Sch., Deerfield, Mass., Cambridge Sch., Weston, Mass., Boston Zool. Soc., Artists Found. Boston, Charles Playhouse, Boston. Capt. USMC, 1953-58. Mem. Union Boat Club, Somerset Club, Harvard Club of Boston (bd. dirs. 1977-82), Harvard Club of N.Y.C. Home: 10 Chestnut St Boston MA 02108-3602 Office: Au Bon Pain Co Inc 19 Fid Kennedy Ave Boston MA 02210-2497

KANE, LUCILE MARIE, retired archivist, historian; b. Maiden Rock, Wis., Mar. 17, 1920; d. Emery John and Ruth (Coty) Kane. BS, River Falls State Tchrs. Coll., 1942; MA, U. Minn., 1946. Tchr. Osceola (Wis.) High Sch., 1942-44; asst. publicity dept. U. Minn. Press, Mpls., 1945-46; rsch. fellow, editor Forest Products History Found., St. Paul, 1946-48; curator manuscripts Minn. Hist. Soc., St. Paul, 1948-75; sr. rsch. fellow Minn. Hist. Soc., 1979-85, sr. rsch. assoc. emeritus, 1985—, mem. hon. coun., 1988—; state archivist, 1975-79. Author, compiler: A Guide to the Care and Administration of Manuscripts, 2d edit., 1966, (with Kathryn A. Johnson) Manuscripts Collections of the Minnesota Historical Society, Guide No.2, 1955, The Waterfall That Built a City, 1966 (updated edit. pub. as The Falls of St. Anthony, 1987), Guide to the Public Affairs Collection Minn. Historical Society, (with Alan Ominsky) Twin Cities: A Pictorial History of Saint Paul and Minneapolis, 1983; transl., editor, Military Life in Dakota, The Jour. of Philippe Regis de Trobriand, 1951; editor: (with others) The Northern Expeditions of Major Stephen H. Long, 1978; contbr. articles to profl. jours. Recipient award of Merit Western History Assn., 1982, Disting. Svc. award Minn. Humanities Commn., 1983, award of Distinction Am. Assn. State and Local History, 1987; co-recipient Theodore C. Blegen award Minn. Hist. Soc., 1996. Fellow Soc. Am. Archivists. Home: 1298 Fairmount Ave Saint Paul MN 55105-2703 Office: 345 Kellogg Blvd W Saint Paul MN 55102-1903

KANE, MARGARET BRASSLER, sculptor; b. East Orange, N.J., May 25, 1909; d. Hans and Mathilde (Trumpler) Brassler; m. Arthur Ferris Kane, June 11, 1930; children: Jay Brassler, Gregory Ferris. Student, Packer Collegiate Inst., 1920-26, Syracuse U., 1927, Art Students League, 1927-29, N.Y. Coll. Music, 1928-29, John Hovannes Studio, 1932-34; PhD (hon.), Colo. State Christian Coll., 1973. head craftsman sculpture, arts and skills unit ARC, Halloran Gen. Hosp., N.Y., 1942-43; jury mem. Bklyn. Mus., 1948, Am. Machine & Foundry Co., 1957; com. mem. An Am. Group, Inc. Work exhibited at Jacques Seligmann Gallery, N.Y., Whitney Ann. Exhbns., all Sculptors Guild Mus. and Outdoor Shows, Nat. Sculpture Soc. Ann. Bas-Relief Exhbn., 1938, Whitney Mus. Sculpture Festival, 1940, Bklyn. Mus. Sculptors Guild, 1938, Bklyn. Soc. Artists, 1942, Lawrence (Mass.) Art Mus., 1938, N.Y. World's Fair, 1939, Sculptors Guild World's Fair Exhbn., 1940, Robinson Gallery, N.Y., 1939, Traveling Mus. and Instns., 1938, Lyman Allyn Mus., 1939, Met. Mus., Internat. Exhbns., 1940, 1949, Roosevelt Field Art Ctr., N.Y.C., 1957, Phila. Mus., N.Y. Archtl. League, Nat. Acad., Penn. Acad., Chgo. Art Inst., Am. Fedn. Arts, Riverside Mus., Montclair Mus., Grand Cen. Art Galleries, Lever House, N.Y.C., 1959-81, Rye (N.Y.) Library, 1962, Lever House Sculptors Guild Ann. Exhbn., 1973-81, N.Y. Bot. Garden, 1981, 60th Anniversary Exhbn. Lever House, 1987-98, Sculptors Guild 50th Anniversary Exhbn., Lever House, 1987-96, 1st Bi-Coastal exhibits San Francisco, Collection Donald Trump, 1988, Collection Rene Anselmo, 1991, Shidoni Galleries, Santa Fe, N.Mex., 1989, Am. Sculpture, Hofstra Mus., 1990, Stamford Mus. and Nature Ctr., 1996; permanent collections Zimmerli Art Mus., Rutgers U., N.J., 1992, 99—, Nat. Mus. Am. Art, Smithsonian Instn., Washington, 1993, (CD-ROM) Nat. Mus. Am. Art, Smithsonian Instn., Washington, 1995, Bruce Mus., Greenwich, Conn., 1996; nat. tour. Am. sculpture by EducArt Projects Inc., 1992; also exhbns. of nat. scope, 1938—; solo sculpture exhbn., Friends Greenwich (Conn.) Library, 1962; executed plaque for Burro Monument, Fairplay, Colo.; exhibited N.Y. Bank for Savs., 1968, Mattatuck Mus., Con., 1967, Lamont Gallery, N.H., 1967, Phila. Art Alliance Exhibition Sculpture of the American Scene, 1987, Am. References (Artists) Chicago, 1989—; executed: 18 foot carving in limewood depicting History of Man, additional 6 foot square carving Dinosaur Age, 1996-99; reprodns. in Contemporary Stone Sculpture, 1970, Contemporary American Sculptures, Am. References, Chgo., 1989—; contbr. articles to mags.; feature article in Greenwich (Conn.) Time, 1990, 93. Recipient Anna Hyatt Huntington award, 1942; Am. Artists Profl. League and Montclair Art Assn. Awards, 1943; 1st Henry O. Avery Prize, 1944; Sculpture Prize Bklyn. Soc. Artists, Bklyn. Mus., 1946; John Rogers Award, 1951; Lawrence Hyder Prize, 1952, 54; David H. Zell Meml. Award, 1954, 63; hon. mention U.S. Maritime Commn., 1941 and; A.C.A. Gallery Competition, 1944; Med. of honor for sculpture Nat. Assn. Women Artists, 1951; Med. of honor for sculpture Nat. Acad. Galleries, N.Y.; prize for carved sculpture, 1955; animal sculpture, 1956; 1st award for sculpture Greenwich Art Soc., 1958, 60; 1st award for sculpture Annual New Eng. Exhbns., Silvermine, Conn. Fellow Internat. Inst. Arts and Letters (life); mem. Nat. Assn. Women Artists (2nd v.p. 1943-44), Nat. League Am. Pen Women, Inc. (OWL award for the Arts 1991), The Pen and Brush (emeritus 1992), Artists Coun. U.S.A., Bklyn. Soc. Artists, Greenwich Soc. Artists (mem. coun.), Internat. Sculpture Ctr., Internat. Soc. Artists (charter), Sculptors Guild, Inc. (lifetime mem., 1993—, sec. to exec. bd. 1942-45, chmn. exhbn. com. 1942, 44), Silvermine Guild Artists, Nat. Trust for Hist. Preservation. Home and Studio: 30 Strickland Rd Cos Cob CT 06807-2729 *It is not possible to overestimate the deep satisfaction experienced in having created countless direct carvings in marble, stone, wood and models for bronze. I strongly believe mankind needs to express itself in some meaningful way. My recent mahogany woodcarvings are dedicated to Peace, Love and an end to Violence. If these goals should inspire the many thousands of viewers of my art form, then I am content that my sculpture is a worthwhile contribution to American culture.*

KANE, MARY KAY, law educator, college dean; b. Detroit, Nov. 14, 1946; d. John Francis and Frances (Roberts) K.; m. Ronan Eugene Degnan, Feb. 3, 1987 (dec. Oct. 1987). BA cum laude, U. Mich., 1968, JD cum laude, 1971. Bar: Mich., N.Y., Calif. Rsch. assoc., co-dir. NSF project on privacy, confidentiality and social sci. rsch. data sch. law U. Mich., 1971-72, Harvard U., 1972-74; asst. prof. law SUNY, Buffalo, 1974-77; mem. faculty Hastings Coll. Law U. Calif., San Francisco, 1977—, prof. law, 1979—, assoc. acad. dean Hastings Coll. Law, 1981-83, acting acad. dean Hastings Coll. Law, 1987-88, acad. dean. Hastings Coll. Law, 1990-93, dean Hastings Coll. Law, 1993—; vis. prof. law U. Mich., 1981, U. Utah, 1983, U. Calif., Berkeley, 1983-84, sch. law U. Tex., 1989; cons. Mead Data Control, Inc., 1971, 74, Inst. on Consumer Justice, U. Mich. Sch. Law, 1972, U.S. Privacy Protection Study Commn., 1975-76; lectr. pretrial mgmt. devices U.S. magistrates for 6th and 11th cirs. Fed. Jud. Ctr., 1983; Siebenthaler lectr. Samuel P. Chase Coll. Law, U. North Ky., 1987; reporter ad hoc com. on asbestos litigation U.S. Jud. Conf., 1990-91; mem. 9th Cir. Adv. Com. on Rules Practice and Internal Oper. Procedures, 1993-96; spkr. in field. Author: Civil Procedure in a Nutshell, 1979, 4th edit., 1996, Sum and Substance on Remedies, 1981; co-author: (with C. Wright and A. Miller) Pocket Supplements to Federal Practice and Procedure, 1975—, Federal Practice and Procedure, vols. 10, 10A and 10B, 3d edit., 1998, vols. 7-7C, 2d edit., 1986, vols. 6-6A, 2d edit., 1990, vols. 11-11A, 2d edit., 1995, (with J. Friedenthal and A. Miller) Hornbook on Civil Procedure, 3d edit., 1999, (with D. Levine) Civil Procedure in California, 6th edit., 1998; mem. law sch. divsn. West. Adv. Editl. Bd., 1986—; contbr. articles to profl. jours. Mem. ABA (mem. bar admissions com. 1995—), Assn. Am. Law Schs. (com. on prelegal edn. statement 1982, chair sect. remedies 1982, panelist sect. on prelegal edn. 1983, exec. com. sect. on civil procedure 1983, 86, panelist sect. on tchg. methods 1984, spkr. new tchrs. conf. 1986, 89, 90, chair sect. on civil procedure 1987, spkr. sects. civil procedure and conflicts 1987, 91, chair planning com. for 1988 Tchg. Conf. in Civil Procedure 1987-88, nominating com. 1988, profl. devel. com. 1988-91, planning com. for workshop in conflicts 1988, planning com. for 1990 Conf. on Clin. Legal Edn. 1989, chair profl. devel. com. 1989-91, exec. com. 1991-93), Am. Law Inst. (assoc. reporter complex litigation project 1988-93, coun. 1998—), ABA/Assn. Am. Law Schs. Commn. on Financing Legal Edn., State Bar Mich. Home: 8 Admiral Dr Ste 421 Emeryville CA 94608-1567 Office: U Calif Hastings Coll Law 200 Mcallister St San Francisco CA 94102-4707

KANE, MICHAEL JOEL, physician; b. Erie, Pa., July 2, 1951. BS, U.S. Naval Acad., 1973; MD, N.J. Med. Sch., 1983. Diplomate Am. Bd. Internal Medicine. Med. intern Thomas Jefferson U. Hosp., Phila., 1983-84, resident in medicine, 1984-86; fellow in neoplastic diseases Mt. Sinai Med. Ctr., N.Y.C., 1986-88; attending physician Jefferson Med. Coll., Phila., 1988-91, Med. Ctr. at Princeton, N.J., 1991-96, Cancer Inst. N.J., Hamilton, 1996—. Served to lt. U.S. Navy, 1969-79. Decorated Navy Achievement medal. Fellow ACP, Acad. Medicine of N.J., Am. Soc. Clin. Oncology, Am. Assn. Cancer Rsch., Am. Soc. Hematology, Oncology Soc. N.J., Med. Soc. N.J. Office: Cancer Inst NJ at Hamilton 5 Hamilton Health Pl Ste 120 Hamilton NJ 08690-3542

KANE, PATRICIA LANEGRAN, language professional, educator; b. St. Paul, June 23, 1926; d. Walter B. and Lita E. (Wilson) Lanegran; m. Donald Patrick Kane, Apr. 1, 1947; children: Laura Kane Gustafson, Maura L. B.A. cum laude, Macalester Coll., St. Paul, 1947; M.A., U. Minn., 1950, Ph.D., 1961. Mem. faculty Macalester Coll., 1950-91, prof. English, 1971-91, DeWitt Wallace prof., 1978-91, prof. emeritus, 1992—, chmn. dept., 1977-86, faculty assoc., office of v.p. acad. affairs, 1979-83; mem. Minn. planning com. nat. identification project advancement women in acad. adminstrn. Nat. Council Edn., 1979-81. Co-author: A St. Paul Omnibus, 1979; Contbr. articles to profl. jours. Recipient Jefferson prize for teaching excellence, 1980, Disting. Alumni citation Macalester Coll., 1992; Danforth grantee, 1957-58. Mem. MLA, Soc. Study So. Lit.

KANE, PAUL, English language educator, poet; b. Cobleskill, N.Y., Mar. 23, 1950; s. T. Paul and Jeanne (Meagher) K.; m. Christine Reynolds, June 21, 1980. BA, Yale U., 1973, MA, 1987, MPhil, 1988, PhD, 1990; MA, U. Melbourne, 1985. Owner Warwick (N.Y.) Bookstore, 1977-79; constrn. worker Merritt Constrn., Warwick, 1980-81; pub. affairs assoc. Inst. for World Policy, N.Y.C., 1981; dir. admissions, tchr. Wooster Sh., Danbury, Conn., 1982-83; prof. English Vassar Coll., Poughkeepsie, N.Y., 1990—; adj. lectr., poet-in-residence Briarcliff Coll., Briarcliff Manor, N.Y., 1975-77. Author: The Farther Shore, 1989,Australian Poetry, 1996; editor: Poetry of the American Renaissance, 1995; co-editor: Collected Poems of Ralph Waldo Emerson, 1994. Fellow NEH, 1998, Guggenheim Meml. Found., 1998-99; grantee Fulbright Found., 1984. Mem. PEN, Ralph Waldo Emerson Soc., Am. Assn. of Australian Literary Studies (exec. bd., pres. 1991-96), Elizabethan Club of Yale U. Home: 8 Big Island Warwick NY 10990 Office: Vassar Coll 124 Raymond Ave Poughkeepsie NY 12604

KANE, ROBERT BARRY, career officer; b. Astoria, N.Y., Aug. 13, 1951; s. Murray K. and Virginia Bolin; m. Anita Louise Van Deursen, Aug. 25, 1984; children: Virginia Marie, David Matthew. BA with high honors, Clemson U., 1973; MA, U. S.C., 1975; Edn. Splst., George Washington U., 1979; PhD, UCLA, 1997. Commd. 2d lt. USAF, 1973, advanced through grades to lt. col., 1991; sq. sect. comdr. 1st component repair Sq. USAF, Langley AFB, Va., 1976-79; chief base adminstr. 5072nd Air Base Sq. USAF, Galena Airport, Alaska, 1979-80; sq. sect. comdr. 401st Supply Sq. USAF, Torrejon AFB, Spain, 1980-83; exec. officer Navstar Global Positioning Sys. Program Office USAF, L.A. AFB, 1983-85; exec. officer/hqrs. sq. sect. comdr. 340th Air Refuel Wing USAF, Altus AFB, Okla., 1985-87; DET 9 comdr., chief aerial mail term 7025th Air Post Sq. USAF, Frankfurt, Germany, 1987-90; dir. resource mgmt. Directorate of Prog. Mgmt. USAF, L.A. AFB, 1990-94, chief edn./tng. flight 61st Mission Spt. Sq., 1994-96; nonresident studies faculty Air War Coll. USAF, Maxwell AFB, 1996—; ajd. faculty St. Leo's Coll., Langley AFB, Va., 1977-79, U. Alaska, Galena, 1979-80, Troy State U., Torrejon Air Base, Spain, 1980-83, We. Okla. State Coll., Altus, 1987, City Coll. Chgo., Wiesbaden, Germany, 1990, Chapman U., El Segundo, Calif., 1990, Troy State U., Montgomery, Ala., 1998—. Deacon, tchr. Hawthorne (Calif.) Seventh Day Adventist Ch., 1994-96, Montgomery (Ala.) First Seventh Day Adventist Ch., 1996—; usher, tchr. base chapel, various locations, 1976-94. Strom Thurmond scholar Clemson U., 1969. Avocations: military history, sightseeing, amateur photography. Office: AWC Nonresident Studies 325 Chennault Cir Maxwell AFB AL 36112-6427

KANE, ROBERT LEWIS, public health educator; b. N.Y.C., Jan. 18, 1940; m. Rosalie Smolkin, June 17, 1962; children: Miranda, Ingrid, Kate. AB, Columbia Coll., N.Y.C., 1961; MD, Harvard U., 1965. Acting coordinator sr. clerkship program dept. community medicine U. Ky., Lexington, 1968-69; svc. unit dir. USPHS Indian Hosp., Shiprock, N.Mex., 1969-70; spl. asst. to regional health dir. USPHS HEW Region VIII, Denver, 1970-71; from asst. to assoc. prof. family and community medicine U. Utah Sch. Medicine, Salt Lake City, 1970-77; sr. researcher The Rand Corp., Santa Monica, Calif., 1977-85; from assoc. prof. to prof. medicine UCLA Sch. Medicine, 1978-85; prof. Sch. Pub. Health UCLA, 1980-85; prof. Sch. Pub. Health U. Minn., 1985—, dean, 1985-90; intern U. Ky. Med. Ctr., Lexington, 1965-66, resident in community medicine, 1966-69; adj. prof. Leonard Davis Sch. Gerontology, U. So. Calif., 1982-85; mem. expert com. on aging WHO, 1986—; Minn. endowed chair in long-term care and aging, 1989—; mem. adv. com. on Alzheimer's Disease, Washington, 1988-96; mem. com. on quality Inst. Medicine, 1988-90. Co-author: A Will and A Way, 1985, Long-term Care: Principles, Programs, and Policies, 1987, Essentials of Clinical Geriatrics, 3d edit., 1984, Understanding Health Care Outcomes Research, 1997, The Heart of Long Term Care, 1998. With USPHS, 1969-70. Home: 2715 E Lake Of The Isles Pky Minneapolis MN 55408-1053 Office: U Minn Sch Pub Health 420 Delaware St SE PO Box 197 Minneapolis MN 55440-0197

KANE, RYAN THOMAS, corporate executive; b. New Brunswick, N.J., Feb. 12, 1973; s. Charles Robert and Cathy Jayne (Jones) Jaeger; m. Barbara Anne Renk, July 29, 1995; 1 child, Madelyn Anne. AS, Mercer County Coll., 1994; postgrad., Rutgers U., 1995—. Treas. N.J. Aux. Police Officers Assn., Monmouth Junction, 1992—, exec. dir., 1994—; project mgr. SimStar Digital Media, Inc., 1997-99; pres. Fourth Degree Media Group, Inc., 1998—; account mgr. I-Frontier, Inc., 1999—; aux. officer South Brunswick Twp. Police Dept., Monmouth Junction, 1991-94; dep. sheriff Essex County Sheriff's Office, Newark, 1993-96; cons. Ctr. for Res. Law Enforcement, Santa Fe, N. Mex., 1992-96. Editor: Reserve Law Enforcement in the U.S., 1993. Vol. Stony Brook Millstone Watershed Assn., Pennington, N.J., 1994—, Kateri Environ. Ctr., Wickatunk, N.J., 1995—. Methodist. Avocations: golf, tennis, computers.

KANE, SAM, meat company executive; b. Spisske Podhradie, Czechoslovakia, June 23, 1919; s. Leopold and Bertha (Narcisenfeld) Kannengiesser; grad. Rabbinical Coll. Galanta, 1939; m. Aranka Feldbrand, Jan. 15, 1946; children—Jerry, Harold Ira, Esther Barbara. Came to U.S., 1948, naturalized, 1953. Pres., Sam Kane Wholesale Meat, Inc., Corpus Christi, Tex., 1956—, Sam Kane Meat, Inc., Corpus Christi, 1956—, Sam Kane Packing Co., Corpus Christi, 1962—, Kane Enterprises, Inc., Corpus Christi, 1956—; pres., chmn. bd., CEO Sam Kane Beef Processors, Inc., 1956—. Pres., Jewish Welfare Appeal, 1962—; pres. Combined Jewish Appeal, 1968, chmn. bd., 1962-64; mem. nat. cabinet United Jewish Appeal; bd. dirs. Tex. Council on Econ. Edn. mem. Gov. Tex. 2000 Commn.; Recipient award chmn. bd. edn. B'nai Israel Synagogue, 1965; Israel Service award, 1966; Koach award State of Israel, 1976; Prime Minister of Israel Peace Medal, 1980; Brotherhood award Corpus Christi chpt. NCCJ, 1984, Torch of Liberty award Anti Defamation League, 1984; named Outstanding Jewish Citizen of Corpus Christi, 1969. Mem. Tex. Council on Econ. Edn. (bd. dirs.), Tex. Taxpayers Assn. Jewish (pres. synagogue 1964-65; Mem. Tex. Taxpayers Assn. Lodge: B'nai B'rith. Home: 27 Hewitt Dr Corpus Christi TX 78404-1662 Office: San Kane Beef Processors 9001 Leopard St Corpus Christi TX 78409-2502

KANE, SIEGRUN DINKLAGE, lawyer; b. N.Y.C., Sept. 21, 1938; d. Ralph Dieter and Lisbeth (Adam) Dinklage; m. David H.T. Kane, Jan. 24, 1964; children: David D., Brendon T. BA cum laude, Mt. Holyoke Coll., 1960; LLB, Harvard U., 1963. Bar: N.Y. 1963, U.S. Ct. Appeals (2d cir.) 1964, U.S. Ct Appeals (5th cir.) 1978, U.S. Ct. Appeals (7th cir.) 1984. Ptnr. Kane, Dalsimer, Sullivan, Kurucz, Levy, Eisele & Richard, N.Y.C., 1963—; bd. mem. Bur. Nat. Affairs Adv. Com., Washington, 1988—; mem. U.S. Patent and Trademark Office Pub. Adv. Com., Washington, 1989-95; lectr. trademarks Practicing Law Inst., N.Y.C., 1980—. Author: Trademark Law: A Practitioner's Guide, 1987, 3d edit., 1997; contbr. articles on trademark law to profl. jours. Mem. Briarcliff Zoning Bd. Appeals, Briarcliff Manor, N.Y., 1978-90, Briarcliff Hist. Soc. Bd., Briarcliff Manor, 1986-90. Mem. ABA, Internat. Trademark Assn., N.Y. Patent Law Assn. Avocations: aerobics, tennis, travel. Office: Kane Dalsimer Sullivan Kurucz Levy Eisele & Richard 711 3rd Ave Fl 20 New York NY 10017-4014

KANE, STANLEY BRUCE, food products executive; b. N.Y.C., June 5, 1920; s. Jacob and Anna (Epstein) K.; m. Janet Marilyn Haas, May 23, 1948; children: Katherine, Betsy, Priscilla. Student, NYU, 1938-39. With Kane-Miller Corp., N.Y.C., 1938—, chmn. bd., 1959-77, pres., chief exec. officer, 1977—, also bd. dirs. Served with USAAF, 1942-45. Home: 539 Norsota Way Sarasota FL 34242-1029 Office: Kane-Miller Corp 555 White Plains Rd Tarrytown NY 10591-5109

KANE, STANLEY PHILLIP, insurance company executive; b. St. Paul, Oct. 3, 1930; s. Bernard J. and Bertha (Pusin) K.; m. Judith Zaikaner, July 1, 1952; children: Brian, Debra, Elizabeth, David. Student, Beck Radio Sch., Mpls., 1948-49. V.p. Arlan Agys., Inc., Mpls., 1950-57; pres. BOMA Inc., Mpls., 1957-68, North Central Life, St. Paul, 1972-76; exec. v.p. North Central Cos., St. Paul, 1968-76; chmn. bd., pres., chief exec. officer Early Am. Life Ins. Co., St. Paul, 1976-90; cons., 1990—, cons. ins. asset mgmt. Radio announcer, writer, WJMC, Rice Lake, Wis., 1949-50. Scoutmaster Boy Scouts Am., 1967-69, dist. chmn., 1971-74; Bd. dirs., v.p. Jewish Family Service, 1975-81; chmn. bd. Alfred Adler Inst. of Minn., 1980-84; pres.-elect Mt. Zion Temple, St. Paul, 1987-89, pres., 1989-91. With M.C. AUS, 1952-54. Mem. Life Underwriters Assn., Presidents Assn. Jewish (bd. dir. temple 1960-64, 75-79, pres. men's club 1960-64), Am. Council Life Ins. (chmn. exec. roundtable 1985-87, bd. dirs. 1989-91). Home: 1575 Dodd Rd Saint Paul MN 55118-2823

KANE, STEVEN MICHAEL, psychotherapist, educator; b. Boston, July 25, 1947; s. Harry and Annette (Oranburg) K. AB, Boston U., 1971; MA, U. N.C., 1973; PhD, Princeton U., 1979. Staff psychotherapist Mass. Treatment Ctr., Bridgewater, Mass., 1985-86; staff psychologist Bridgewater State Hosp., 1986-89; pvt. practice psychotherapy Providence, R.I., 1990—; psychologist R.I. Sex Offender Treatment Program, 1995—; dir. Sr. Empowerment Prgm. Westminster Sr. Ctr., Providence, 1998—; dir. clin. edn. Interfaith Counseling Ctr., Providence, 1988—; part-time faculty RISD, Providence, 1989—, U. R.I., Providence, 1992—; spl. lectr. Providence Coll., 1990-94; cons. and spkr. in field. Reviewer Internat. Assn. of Jazz Record Collectors Jour.; contbr. articles to profl. jours. Bd. dirs. The Music Sch., Providence, 1993-95. Recipient Outstanding Faculty award U. R.I./Providence Ctr., 1997; Nat. Def. Edn. Act Title IV fellow Fed. Govt.-U. N.C., 1971-73, Postdoctoral Social Sci. Rsch. fellow NIMH, 1979-81; Doctoral Dissertation Rsch. grantee NSF, 1975-76. Fellow Am. Anthropol. Assn.; mem. Soc. for Psychol. Anthropology, Soc. for the Anthropology of Consciousness, Am. Assn. of Pastoral Counselors, Psi Chi. Avocations: jazz pianist, writer on jazz, jazz educator. Home: 64 Bluff Ave Cranston RI 02905-5108

KANE, SYDELL, elementary school principal; b. N.Y.C., Jan. 13; d. Harry and Ruth (Albert) Friedman; m. Howard E. Kane; children: Bradford, Marcia Kane Hittner. BA, NYU, 1951; MA, Queen's Coll., 1968. Cert. guidance counselor, adminstr., supr., prin., N.Y. Tchr. N.Y.C. Pub. Schs., 1972; asst. prin. P.S. 220, N.Y.C., 1973-88; prin. P.S. 144, N.Y.C., 1988-99; ednl. cons., 1999—. Author skills books. Named Supr. of Yr., Dist. 28, 1995, Outstanding Sch. Supr., St. John's U. Sch. Edn. and Human Svcs., 1997. Mem. ASCD, Queensboro Coun. on Reading, Phi Delta Kappa (pres. 1989, del.). Office: PS 144 93-02 69th Ave Forest Hills NY 11375

KANE, THOMAS JAY, III, orthopaedic surgeon, educator; b. Merced, Calif., Sept. 2, 1951; s. Thomas J. Jr. and Kathryn (Hassler) K.; m. Marie Rose Van Emmerik, Oct. 10, 1987; children: Thomas Keola, Travis Reid, Samantha Marie. BA in History, U. Santa Clara, 1973; MD, U. Calif., Davis, 1977. Diplomate Am. Bd. Orthopaedic Surgery. Intern U. Calif. Davis Sacramento Med. Ctr., 1977-78, resident in surgery, 1978-81; resident in orthopaedic surgery U. Hawaii, 1987-91; fellowship adult joint reconstruction Rancho Los Amigos Med. Ctr., 1991-92; ptnr. Orthop. Assocs. of Hawaii, Inc., Honolulu, 1992—; asst. prof. surgery U. Hawaii, Honolulu, 1993—, chief divsn. implant surgery, 1993—. Contbr. articles to profl. jours. Mem. AMA, Am. Assn. Hip and Knee Surgeons, Hawaii Med. Assn., Hawaii Orthop. Assn., Am. Acad. Orthop. Surgery, Western Orthopedic Assn., Alpha Omega Alpha, Phi Kappa Phi. Avocations: tennis, golf, skiing, music, surfing. Office: Orthopaedic Assocs Hawaii 1380 Lusitana St Ste 608 Honolulu HI 96813-2442

KANE, THOMAS PATRICK, broadcast executive; b. N.Y.C., Aug. 28, 1945; s. Thomas Patrick and Rosemary Ann (Tenanty) K.; m. Judith Ann Riccardo, m. Feb. 7, 1970; children: Thomas, Colby, F. Todd. Account exec. Edward Petry and Co., N.Y.C., 1971-72, Peters Griffin and Woodward, N.Y.C., 1972-74, Storer Broadcasting, N.Y.C., 1974-75; account exec. nat. TV sales ABC, Detroit, 1977-78, N.Y.C., 1978; ea. sales mgr. nat. TV sales ABC, N.Y.C., 1978-82; account exec. Sta. WABC-TV, N.Y.C., 1975-77, nat. sales mgr., 1982-86, gen. sales mgr., 1986-93, pres., gen. mgr., 1997—; pres., gen. mgr. WPVI-TV, Phila., 1993-97. Served to sgt. U.S. Army, 1966-68, Vietnam. Roman Catholic. Office: Sta WABC-TV 7 Lincoln Square New York NY 10023-7101*

KANE, THOMAS REIF, engineering educator; b. Vienna, Austria, Mar. 23, 1924; came to U.S., 1938, naturalized, 1943; Ernest Kanitz and Gertrude (Reif) K.; m. Ann Elizabeth Andrews, June 4, 1951; children: Linda Ann, Jeffrey Thomas. BS, Columbia U., 1950, MS, 1952, PhD, 1953; D Tech. Scis. (hon.), Tech. U. Vienna, Austria, 1990. Asst. prof., assoc. prof. U. Pa., Phila., 1953-61; prof. Sch. Engring. Stanford U., Calif., 1961-93, prof. emeritus, 1993—; cons. NASA, Harley-Davidson Motor Co., AMF, Lockheed Missiles and Space Co., Vertol Aircraft Corp., Martin Marietta Co., Kellet Aircraft Co. Author: (vol. 1) Analytical Elements of Mechanics, 1959, (vol. 2), 1961, Dynamics, 1972, Spacecraft Dynamics, 1983; Dynamics: Theory and Applications, 1985; contbr. over 150 articles to profl. jours. Served with U.S. Army, 1943-45, PTO. Recipient Alexander von Humboldt prize, 1988. Fellow Am. Astron. Soc. (Dirk Brouwer award 1983); mem. ASME (hon.), Sigma Xi, Tau Beta Pi. Office: Stanford University Dept Mechanical Engring Stanford CA 94305

KANE, YVETTE, lawyer, federal judge; b. Donaldsonville, La., Oct. 11, 1953; d. Thomas R. Pregeant and Julia Tucker; m. Michael Kane; children: Kathleen, Madeline. BA, Nicholls State U., Thibodeaux, La., 1973; JD, Tulane U., 1976. Bar: Pa. Dep. atty. gen. rev. and advice sect. Pa. Office Atty. Gen., 1986-91; chief counsel Pa. Ind. Regulatory Rev. Commn., 1991-92; sr. assoc. Wolf, Block, Schorr & Solis-Cohen, Harrisburg, Pa., 1993-95; sec. state Commonwealth of Pa., 1995-98; U.S. dist. judge U.S. Dist. Ct. (mid. dist.) Pa., Harrisburg, 1998—. Mem. Parents Anonymous of Ctrl. Pa. Office: Office Sec of State North Office Bldg Rm 302 Harrisburg PA 17120 Office: US Dist Ct Box 11817 North Office Bldg Rm 302 Harrisburg PA 17108*

KANEB, GARY, oil industry executive; b. 1961. Grad., U. Notre Dame, 1983. Chase Manhattan Bank, N.Y.C., 1984-86; Pres. Catamount Mgmt. Corp., Chelsea, Mass., 1988—; gen. ptnr., pres. Gulf Oil LP, Chelsea, Mass., 1986—, CEO, 1997—. Office: Gulf Oil LP 90 Everett Ave Chelsea MA 02150-2337*

KANEDA, DAVID KEN, electrical engineering company executive; b. Norristown, Pa., May 13, 1958; s. Ben and Sumako Florence Kaneda; m. Stephania Kareda, Nov. 16, 1993. B Archtl. Engring., Pa. State U., 1981; MBA, U. London Bus. Sch., 1993. Registered profl. engr., Ill., Calif.; registered architect, Wis.; chartered engr., U.K., European Engr. Tech. instr. Internat. Edn. Svcs., Tokyo, 1981-82; assoc. Skidmore, Owings & Merrill, Chgo., 1982-87, London, 1987-91, L.A., 1991; regional mgr. Elliptipar Inc., New Haven, 1993-95; prin. Am. Cons. Engrs. Inc., Santa Clara, Calif., 1995-99; pres., ceo Integrated Design Assoc., Inc., Santa Clara, CA, 1999—; cons. Pinniger & Ptnr./Franz Sill, Gmbh, London and Berlin, 1992, ECS Lighting Controls Ltd., London, 1993. Recipient Edison award GE, 1987, achievement award Pa. Electric Assn., 1981, award of merit Chgo. Lighting Inst., 1987, design award Santa Clara Valley AIA, 1996, 98. Mem. AIA (bd. dirs., Santa Clara Valley Chapt., 1998-99) Chartered Inst. Bldg. Svcs. Engrs. U.K., Engring. Coun. U.K., European Fedn. Nat. Engring. Assns., Illuminating Engring. Soc. N.Am. (E.F. Guth award of merit 1987, design award 1987), Nat. Coun. Examiners for Engring. and Surveying, Nat. Assn. Asian Am. Profls. (bd. dirs. 1986-87), Alpha Phi Omega (pres. Alpha Beta chpt. 1979-80). Avocations: karate, skiing, international travel. Office: Integrated Des Assoc Inc Ste 110 3140 De La Crue Blvd Santa Clara CA 95054

KANE HITTNER, MARCIA SUSAN, bank executive; b. N.Y.C., June 4, 1959; d. Howard Eugene and Sydell (Friedman) Kane; m. Ellis Hittner, May 23, 1993. Cert. fin. planning, NYU, 1980, BA in Communications, 1986. Cert. Nat. Ret. Plans Tgn. Ctr., 1987; software capability maturity model cert. interim profile adminstr. Carnegie Mellon U., 1998. Pension specialist Union Dime Savs. Bank, N.Y.C., 1978-81; money market specialist Goldome (formerly Union Dime Savs. Bank), N.Y.C., 1981-82; customer svc. unit mgr. Citibank, N.A., N.Y.C., 1982-85, keogh product mgr., 1986-87, shareholder communications mgr., 1988-89, asst. v.p., tax shelter conversion mgr., 1990-93, asst. v.p. tech. client interface, 1993-95; asst. v.p. U.S., Europe Consumer Bank, N.Y.C., 1995-98; with product design and devel. Software Engring. Process Group, 1995—; asst. v.p. tng. N.Am. Consumer Bank, 1999—. Author: (with others) Critical Reading-Level G, 1980. Bd. dirs. Forest Hills Owners Corp., N.Y.C., 1991-92. Mem. N.Y. Bus. and Profl. Women's Club. Office: Citibank NA Product Design & Devel 1 Court Sq Fl 35 Long Island City NY 11120-0001

KANEKO, HISASHI, engineering executive; b. Tokyo, Nov. 19, 1933; came to U.S., 1989; s. Shozo and Toshi K.; m. Motoko Washino; children: Satoshi, Makoto, Hajime. BSEE, U. Tokyo, 1956, PhD in Engring., 1967; MSEE, U. Calif., 1962. Rsch. staff NEC Corp., Japan, 1956-60, rsch. mgr., 1962-68, gen. mgr. transmission div., 1970-85, v.p., 1985-89, sr. v.p., 1989-93; pres., CEO NEC America, N.Y.C., 1991-93; exec. v.p. NEC Corp., Tokyo, 1993-94, pres., 1994—; rsch. asst. U. Calif., Berkeley, 1960-62; mem. tech. staff Bell Telephone Labs., Holmdel, N.J., 1968-70; Now CEO NEC Corp. Author 4 books in communications; contbr. 100 articles to profl. jours. Holder 70 patents in Japan, 5 in U.S.A. Recipient Kajii Meml. prize Elec. Comm. Assn., Japan, 1979. Fellow IEEE (E.H. Armstrong award 1992); mem. Nat. Acad. Engring. (fgn. assoc.), Inst. Electronics, Info. and Communications Engrs. (Achievement award 1985), Engring. Acad. Japan. Office: NEC Corp, 5-7-1 Shiba Minatoku, 108-01 Tokyo Japan

KANEKO, YOSHIHIRO, cardiologist, researcher; b. Shizuoka, Japan, Jan. 22, 1922; s. Rokurohei and Yoshino (Momochi) K.; m. Toyo Nozaki, Apr. 8, 1962; children: Kyoko, Eriko, Hiroko. MD, Tokyo U. Med. Sch., Japan, 1945, DMS, 1951. Clin. assoc. dept. internal medicine Tokyo U. Hosp., Japan, 1945-53, instr., 1953-70; rsch. fellow Cleve. Clinic Found., 1958-61, 1962-63; asst. prof. 2d dept. internal medicine Tokyo U. Med. Sch., 1971-73; prof. medicine, chmn. dept internal medicine Yokohama City (Japan) U. Med. Sch., Japan, 1973-87, emeritus prof., 1987—; dir. Yokohama Hypertension Rsch. Ctr., 1987—; prof. emeritus Yokohama City U., 1987—; hon. dir. Nishi-Yokohama Internat. Hosp., 1987-93. Contbr. articles to profl. jours. Com. mem. Pharm. Bur. Japan Ministry Health & Welfare, Tokyo, 1974-87, Med. Affairs Bur., Tokyo, 1976-79. Grantee NIH, 1965-67; recipient award Japanese Kidney Found., 1986, Internat. Soc. Hypertension, 1988. Fellow High Blood Pressure Coun.; mem. Japanese Soc. Hypertension (1st pres. 1978-79, dir. 1978-89), Japanese Soc. Internal Medicine (councilor), Japan Circulation Soc., Japan Soc. Nephrology (dir. 1974-87), Am. Heart Assn. (coun. mem.), Internat. Soc. Hypertension, (coun. 1982-90, chmn. 1988). Avocations: reading, gardening. Home: 2-27-14 Nishishiba, Kanazawa-ku, Yokohama 236-0017, Japan Office: Yokohama Hypertension Rsch Ctr, Yokohama Hypertension Rsch, Deiki 2-8-19-402 Kanazawa-k, Yokohama 236-0021, Japan

KANENAKA, REBECCA YAE, microbiologist; b. Wailuku, Hawaii, Jan. 9, 1958; d. Masakazu Robert and Takako (Oka) Fujimoto; m. Brian Ken Kanenaka, Nov. 10, 1989; children: Kent Masakazu, Kym Sachiko. Student, U. Hawaii, Manoa, 1976-77; BS, Colo. State U., 1980. Lab. asst. Colo. State U., Ft. Collins, 1979-80; microbiologist Foster Farms, Livingston, Calif., 1980-81; microbiologist Hawaii Dept. Health, Lihue, 1981-86, Honolulu, 1986—. Mem. Am. Soc. Microbiology (Hawaii chpt.), Nat. Registry of Microbiologists, Am. Soc. Microbiology, Brown Bag Club (Lihue, pres. 1985-86), Golden Ripples (4-H leader), Clover Kids (4-H leader). Avocations: tennis, fishing, golf, jogging. Home: 485 Luakini St Honolulu HI 96817-1449 Office: Hawaii Dept Health Lab 2725 Waimano Home Rd Pearl City HI 96782-1401

KANER, CEM, lawyer, computer software consultant; b. Detroit, July 8, 1953; s. Harry and Wilma Kaner; 1 child, Virginia Rose. Student, U. Windsor (Ont., Can.), 1971-72; BA, Brock U., St. Catharines, Ont., 1974; postgrad., York U., Toronto, Ont., 1975-76; PhD, McMaster U., Hamilton, Ont., 1984; JD, Golden Gate U., 1993. Cert. quality engr.; Bar: Calif., 1993. Asst. mgr. Gallenkamp Shoes, Toronto, 1975; systems analyst Kaners and 1 plus 1, Windsor, 1981-83; lectr. McMaster U., 1981-83; software testing supr. MicroPro (WordStar), San Rafael, Calif., 1983-84; human factors analyst, software engr. Telenova, Los Gatos, Calif., 1984-88; software testing mgr. creativity div. Electronic Arts, San Mateo, Calif., 1988; software devel. mgr., documentation group mgr., dir. of documentation and software testing Power Up Software, San Mateo, 1989-94; pvt. practice Calif., 1994—; sr. assoc. Psylomar Orgn. Devel., San Francisco, 1983-85; lectr. U. Calif., Berkeley Ext., 1995—, U. Calif., Santa Cruz Ext., 1998—; spkr. in field. Author: Testing Computer Software, 1988, (with Jack Falk and Hung Q Nguyen) Testing Computer Software, 2d edit., 1993 (award for excellence No. Calif. Tech. Publ. Competition 1993), (with David Pels) Bad Software: What to do when Software Fails, 1998; (video course) Testing Computer Software, 1995; columnist Software QA; contbr. articles to profl. publs. Cons. Dundas (Ont.) Pub. Library, 1982-83; vol. Santa Clara County Dept. Consumer Affairs, San Jose, 1987-88; alt. mem. San Mateo County Dem. Central Com., 1988-89; chmn. Foster City Dem Club, 1989; vol. dep. dist. atty. County of Santa Clara, Calif., 1994; grievance handler, intellectual property, book contract advisor Nat. Writers Union, San Francisco, Calif., 1994—; bd. dir. No. Calif. Hemophilia Found., Oakland, Calif., 1995-97; participating observer NCCUSL drafting com. for UCC article 2B, NCCUSL com. for uniform electronic transaction act. Scholar, Can. Nat. Rsch. Coun., 1977-78, Can. Natural Scis. and Engring. Rsch. Coun., 1979, Golden Gate U. Tuition scholar, 1989-93. Mem. IEEE (Computer Soc.), ABA, ATLA, APA, Assn. for Computing Machinery, Assn. Support Profls., Am. Soc. Quality (sr.), Human Factors and Ergonomics Soc., Soc. for Tech. Comm. (sr.), Software Support Profls. Assn., Software Pubs. Assn. Jewish. Avocation: development of the law of software products liability. E-mail: kaner@kaner.com. Office: PO Box 580 Santa Clara CA 95052-0580

KANER, HARVEY SHELDON, lawyer, executive; b. June 26, 1930; s. Rueben and Lillian Kaner; m. Caren Lee Gross, June 5, 1960; children: Amy B., Daniel E., Jason M. (dec.), Joshua A. B.B.A., U. Minn., 1952, LL.B., 1955. Bar: Minn. Sole practice Mpls., 1956-58; asst. corp. counsel Farmers Union GTA (now Harvest States Cooperatives), St. Paul, 1958-59, corp. counsel, 1959-77, v.p. law, 1977-82, sr. v.p., corp. counsel, 1982-93; sr. v.p. and exec. counsel Harvest States Cooperatives, St. Paul, 1993-94; ret., 1994; past sec. St. Louis Grain Corp.; lectr. extension program U. Wis., Madison; past dir. Farmers Export Co.; trustee Corp. Pension Funds. Author publs. Products Liability, 1977. Served with USNG, 1947-49. Mem. ABA, Minn. State Bar Assn., Hennepin County Bar Assn., Nat. Council Farmer Coops. (mem. legal, tax and acctg. com.). Jewish. Home: 4000 Royal Marco Way Apt 622 Marco Island FL 34145-7812 Office: Cenex Harvest States Coop 500 Cenex Dr Inver Grove Heights MN 55077

KANES, WILLIAM HENRY, geology educator, research center administrator; b. N.Y.C., Oct. 15, 1934; married. BS in Geol. Engring., CCNY, 1956; MS in Geology, W.Va. U., 1958, PhD in Geology, 1965. Sr. rsch. geologist Esso Prodn. Co., Houston Rsch. Co., 1964-65; sr. exploration geologist, head New Concepts Group Esso Stds., Libya, 1966-67, frontier exploration geologist, administr. Frontier Area Group, 1967-69; asst. prof. geology W.Va. U., Morgantown, 1970-71; assoc. prof. geology U. S.C., Columbia, 1971-74, prof. geology, dir. Earth Scis. and Resources Inst., 1975-95, Disting. prof. earth resources, chair Rsch. and Devel. Found., 1984-97, disting. prof. emeritus, 1998; prof. civil amd environ. engring. U. Utah, 1994-96, dir. Earth Scis. and Resources Inst., 1994-96, dir. Energy and Geoscis. Inst., rsch. prof., civil and environ. engr., 1996—; NSF Resident Rsch. prof. Acad. Sci. Rsch. and Tech., Cairo, 1976-77; hon. professorial fellow Univ. Coll. Aberystyth U. Wales, 1979-83, Univ. Coll. Swansea U. Wales, 1985-88, U. Bristol, U.K., 1986-89; hon. mem. Acad. Engring., Republic of Kazakhstan, 1994; academician Internat. Acad. Mineral Resources, Russia; vis. professorial fellow Univ. Coll. Swansea, 1977-83; vis. prof. Postgrad. Rsch. Inst. Sedimentology, U. Reading, U.K., 1989-92; co-dir. Earth Resources Inst. Univ. Coll. Swansea, U. Wales, U.K., 1980-86; advisor Atomic Energy Establishment, Egypt, 1974-77, Nat. Oil Co., Libya, 1975-78, U.S. Pres., exec. br. Energy Problems and Controls, 1977-78, Nuclear Materials Corp., Egypt, 1977-81; mem. tech. adv. task force Fed. Power Commn. Contbr. numerous articles, papers to profl. publs. 1st lt. C.E., U.S. Army, 1955, 58-59. Recipient Disting. Svc. award U. S.C. Ednl. Found., 1985; grantee NSF, 1971-81, U.S. Dept. Interior, 1972-74, others. Fellow AAAS, Geol. Soc. Am.; mem. Am. Assn. Petroleum Geologists (cert., chmn. rsch. symposium 1976, acad. affairs com. 1973-76, acad. liaison com. 1976—, rsch. com. on pub. affairs 1975—), Am. Geophys. Union, Sigma Xi. Office: Univ Utah Energy & Geoscis Inst 423 Wakara Way Salt Lake City UT 84108-1242

KANESTA, NELLIE ROSE, chemical dependency counselor; b. Zuni, N.Mex., Aug. 8, 1939; d. Paxton E. and Bessie (Thompson) Boone; m. Patrick Tsethlikia, Apr. 10, 1959 (div. Mar. 1973); children: Nina, Frederick William, Pamela, Judson, Marie Christine, Paxton, Clifford. AA in Human Svcs., U. N.Mex., Gallup, 1996. Lic. alcohol and drug abuse counselor, N.Mex. Alcoholism counselor Zuni (N.Mex.) Indian Hosp., 1985-86; counselor Friendship Svcs., Inc., Gallup, N.Mex., 1986-87; trainer Hazelden Found., Center City, Minn., 1987-88; intense residential guidance counselor Ramah (N.Mex.) Navajo Dormitory, 1988-89; Title V counselor, dir. Pine Hills (N.Mex.) Schs., 1989-91, phys. ednl. aide, 1992-93, group home life skills counselor, 1993—; substance abuse counselor Cibola County Correctional Ctr., Milan, N.Mex., Western Correctional Facility, Grants, N.Mex., 1997; adult counselor Zuni Recovery Ctr., N.Mex., 1996-97; counselor Zuni Pub. Health Svc. Indian Hosp., 1985, Regional Conf. on Children of Alcoholics, Albuquerque, 1985; insvc. tng. confs. Western N.Mex. U., 1986, Native Am. Cultural Issues in Substance Abuse, Coll. of Santa Fe, 1986, Chem. Dependency and Intervention, The N.Mex. Alcoholism and Drug Abuse Counselors, 1986, In-Svc. Tng. on Battered Families and Its Relation to Alcohol/Drug Abuse, 1987, N.Mex. Alcoholism and Drug Abuse Counselors Assn., 1986-88, Hazelden Chem. Dependency Counselor Tng. Program, 1988; family advocate for mentally ill Zuni Pub. Health Svc., 1993-95; court offender case worker Teen Health Ctr., 1997-99. Avocations: reading, fishing, pottery making, basketball, listening to music. Home: PO Box 1479 Zuni NM 87327-1479 Office: Cibola County Correctional Ctr Milan NM 87021

KANET, ROGER EDWARD, political science educator, university administrator; b. Cin., Sept. 1, 1936; s. Robert George and Edith Mary (Weaver) K.; m. Joan Alice Edwards, Feb. 16, 1963; children: Suzanne Elise, Laurie Alice. PhB, Berchmanskolleg, Pullach-bei-Muenchen, Ger., 1960; AB, Xavier U., Cin., 1961; MA, Lehigh U., 1963; AM, Princeton U., 1965, PhD, 1966. Asst. prof. polit. sci. U. Kans., Lawrence, 1966-69, assoc. prof., 1969-74; joint sr. fellow Russian Inst. and Rsch. Inst. Communist Affairs, Columbia U., N.Y.C., 1972-73; vis. assoc. prof. U. Ill., Champaign, 1973-74; assoc. prof. U. Ill., Urbana-Champaign, 1974-78; prof. polit. sci. U. Ill., Urbana, 1978-97; prof. emeritus U. Ill., Urbana, $Da., 1997—; head dept. polit. sci. U. Ill., Urbana, 1984-87, assoc. vice chancellor for acad. affairs, dir. internat. progs. and studies, 1989-97; prof., dean Sch. Internat. Studies U. Miami, Fla., 1997—; partipant exch. with Hungary and Poland, Internat. Rsch. and Exchs. Bd., 1976; cons. Inst. Pub. Policy Devel., Washington, 1977-79; assoc. Ctr. Advanced Study, U. Ill., 1981-82; mem. Coun. on Fgn. Rels., N.Y., 1991—; mem. Chgo. com. Chgo. Coun. on Fgn. Rels.; chair internat. edn. panel Com. Instl. Coop. (Big 10 & Chgo., 1993-96); co-founder Ill. Consortium for Internat. Edn. Editor: The Behavioral Revolution and Communist Studies, 1971, On the Road to Communism, 1972, The Soviet Union and the Developing Countries, 1974, Soviet and East European Policy, 1974, Soviet Economic and Political Relations with the Developing World, 1975, Background to Crisis: Policy and Politics in Gierek's Poland, 1981, Soviet Foreign Policy and East-West Relations, 1982, Soviet Foreign Policy in the 1980s, 1982, The Soviet Union, Eastern Europe and the Third World, 1987, Asia in Soviet Global Strategy, 1987, The Limits of Soviet Power in the Developing World: Thermidor in the Revolutionary Struggle, 1989, The Cold War as Cooperation: Superpower Cooperation in Regional Conflict Management, 1991, Soviet Foreign Policy in Transition, 1992, Regional Conflicts and Conflict Resolution, 1995, Coping with Conflict After the Cold War, 1996, Foreign Policy of the Russian Fed., 1997, Resolving Regional Conflicts, 1998; contbr. numerous articles to scholarly jours. and books. Co-founder, pres. Kans. Parents Assn. Hearing-Handicapped Children, 1968-70. Recipient U.S. Dept. State Rsch. award, 1976, Excellence in Undergrad. Teaching award U. Ill., 1981, 84, Faculty Achievement award Burlington No. Found., 1989,U.S. Inst. Peace award, 1991; fellow NDEA, 1963-66, NATO, 1976, Internat. fellow Fed. Inst. for East European and Internat. Studies, Cologne, Fed. Republic of Germany, 1988; Am. Coun. Learned Socs. grantee, 1972-73, 78. Mem. Am. Assn. Advancement of Slavic Studies, Am. Polit. Sci. Assn., Assn. Internat. Edn. Adminstrs. (bd. dirs.), Internat. Polit. Sci. Assn., Internat. Studies Assn. (chairperson Am.-Soviet rels. sect. 1990-92), Midwest Slavic Conf. (program chmn. 1980-81), Internat. Coun. for Ctrl. and Ea. European Studies (program chmn. 1st World Congress 1974), Ctrl. Slavic Conf. (pres., program chmn. 1966-67), Midwest Polit. Sci. Assn., Assn. Internat. Edn. Adminstrs., Midwest Univ. Consortium Internat. Activities (bd. dirs. 1989-97), Nat. Assn. State Univ. and Land Grant Colls. (internat. commn. 1992-97), Ill. Consortium for Internat. Edn. (co-founder 1993). Roman Catholic. Home: 9225 SW 142d St Miami FL 33176 Office: U Miami Sch Internat Studies PO Box 248123 Miami FL 33124-8123*

KANE-VANNI, PATRICIA RUTH, lawyer, production consultant, educator; b. Phila., Jan. 12, 1954; d. Joseph James and Ruth Marina (Ramirez) Kane; m. Francis William Vanni, Feb. 14, 1980; 1 child, Christian Michael. AB, Chestnut Hill Coll., 1975; JD, Temple U., 1985. Bar: Pa. 1985, U.S. Ct. Appeals (3d cir.) 1988. Freelance art illustrator Phila., 1972-80; secondary edn. instr. Archdiocese of Phila., 1980-83; contract analyst CIGNA Corp., Phila., 1983-84; jud. aide Phila. Ct. of Common Pleas, 1984; assoc. atty. Anderson and Dougherty, Wayne, Pa., 1985-86; atty. cons. Bell Telephone Co. of Pa., 1986-87; sr. assoc. corp. counsel Independence Blue Cross, Phila., 1987-96; pvt. practice law, 1996-97; dinosaur educator Acad. Natural Scis., Phila., 1997—; atty. cons., 1996-99; counsel Reliance Ins. Co., Phila., 1998—; cons. Coll. Consortium on Drug and Alcohol Abuse, Chester, Pa., 1986-89; speaker in field; paleo-sci. educator Pa. Acad. Natural Scis., 1997—. Contbr. articles and illustrations to profl. mags. Judge Del. Valley Sci. Fairs, Phila., 1986, 87, 98, 99; Dem. committeewomen, Lower Merion, Pa., 1983-87; ch. cantor, soloist, mem. choir Roman Cath. Ch.; mem. Phila. Assn. Ch. Musicians, also bd. dirs. Recipient Legion of Honor award Chapel of the Four Chaplins, 1983. Mem. ABA, Pa. Bar Assn., Phila. Bar Assn. (Theatre Wing), Phila. Assn. Def. Counsel, Phila. Vol. Lawyers for Arts (bd. dirs.), Nat. Health Lawyers Assn. (spkr. 1994 ann. conv.), Hispanic Bar Assn., vice pres. Delaware Valley Paleontological Soc., Pa. Acad. Nat. Scis. (vol.), Delaware Valley Paleontological Soc. (v.p. 1998—). Democrat. Avocations: choral and solo vocal music, portrait painting and illustrating, paleontology. E-mail: pkv1@erols.com. Home: 119 Bryn Mawr Ave Bala Cynwyd PA 19004-3012

KANE-VILLELA, GRACE MCNELLY, maternal, women's health and pediatrics nurse; b. Auburn, Ill., Mar. 31, 1939; d. Irving Benjamin and Ruby Louise (Stinnett) McNelly; m. Robert John Kane, July 23, 1960 (dec. 1994); children: Scott Robert, Timothy Phillip, Pamela Collette, Glenn Randall, Andrew Keith, Bruce Ryan; m. Carlos Albert Villela, Mar. 21, 1998. Diploma, Mem. Hosp. Sch. Nursing, Springfield, Ill., 1960; BS in Profl. Arts, St. Joseph's Coll., North Windham, Maine, 1985. RN, Ill.; cert. in occupational hearing conservation, fetal monitoring I and II; cert. ACLS. Staff nurse nursery-newborn units Walther Meml. Hosp., Chgo., 1962-67; staff nurse rooming-in nursery Luth. Gen. Hosp., Park Ridge, Ill., 1977-85; staff nurse med.-surg. unit Swedish Covenant Hosp., Chgo., 1989; staff nurse occupational clinic Rush-Presbyn-St. Luke's, Elk Grove Village, Ill., 1988; nurse various hosps., Arlington Heights, Ill., 1989-93; staff nurse couplet care St. Joseph's Hosp., Phoenix, 1997—. Address: 5821 E ACOMA DR Scottsdale AZ 85254

KANEYOSHI, TAKAHITO, physicist; b. Otaru, Hokkaido, Japan, Aug. 24, 1940; s. Chukichi and Ine (Yoshikawa) K.; m. Yoshiko Yamashina, Mar. 24, 1968; children: Yoshitaka, Akihiro, Yukako. B Tech., Waseda U., Tokyo, 1963; MS, Kyoto (Japan) U., 1965, DSc, 1969. Rsch. assoc. Nagoya (Japan) U., 1968-92, assoc. prof., 1992-93, prof. physics, 1993—. Author: Amorphous Magnetism, 1984, Introduction to Surface Magnetism, 1991, Introduction to Amorphous Magnets, 1992. Mem. Phys. Soc. Japan, Applied Magnetic Soc. Japan, Am. Phys. Soc. Office: Nagoya U, Furoucho, Chikusaku, Nagoya Aichi 464-8601, Japan

KANFER, FREDERICK H., psychologist, educator; Married; 2 children. Student, Cooper Union Sch. Tech., Sch. Engring., 1942-44; BS cum laude, L.I. U., 1948; MA, Ind. U., 1952, PhD, 1953. Lic. psychologist, Oreg. Rsch. asst. Ind. U., 1949-52; asst. Psychol. Clinic, 1952-53, tchg. fellow in abnormal psychology, 1953; trainee VA Hosp., Indpls., 1951-52; asst. prof. psychology, dir. Psychoednl. Clinic, Washington U., St. Louis, 1953-57; cons. and asso. E.H. Parsons, M.D. and Assocs., St. Louis, 1955-57; assoc. prof. Purdue U., 1957-62; vis. prof. med. psychology U. Oreg. Med. Sch., summers 1958, 60, prof. psychiatry, 1962-69; vis. prof. psychology U. Oreg., Eugene, summers and winters 1967, 79; prof. psychology U. Cin., 1969-73; prof. U. Ill., Champaign, 1973-95, prof. emeritus, 1995—; sr. fellow, prof. U. Minn., Mpls., 1995-98; Fulbright lectr. Ruhr U., Bochum, Germany, 1968; guest prof. U. Salzburg, Austria, 1987; cons., spkr. in field; lectr., vis. prof. including univs. Oxford, Madrid, Heidelberg, Amsterdam, Berlin, Oslo, Cologne, Munich, Graz, Rome, Verona, Munster, Marburg, Wurzburg, London, Nijmegen, Copenhagen, Basel, Stockholm, Trondheim, Salzburg, Fribourg, Bern, Athens, Budapest; organizer, supr. postdoctoral tng. program for European psychologists univs. Cin. and Ill., 1969-87; vis. lectr. Inst. Environ. Health, U. Cin. Med. Sch., 1970-73, vis. prof. psychiatry, 1973-79; Morton vis. prof. Ohio U., 1976; sr. lectr. U. Bern, 1980-92; Disting. vis. prof. Dept. Air Force, 1983; adv. bd. Cambridge Ctr. for behavioral Studies, 1982—; bd. advisors Internat. Alliance Health Edn., Stockholm, 1983—; mem. internat. adv. bd. Max-Planck Inst. Psychiatry, 1985-90. Author: (with J.S. Phillips) Learning Foundations of Behavior Therapy, 1970, (with others) Premier Symposium Sobre Apprendizaje y Modificacion de Conducta en Ambientes educativos, 1975, (with Bruck K. Schefft) Guiding the Therapeutic Change Process, 1988, (with H. Reinecker and D. Schmelzer) Selbstmanagement-Therapie, 1991, 2d rev. edit., 1996; contbr. numerous articles to profl. publs.; editor: (with A.P. Goldstein) Helping People Change: A Textbook of Methods, 1975, 3d rev. edit., 1980, 4th rev. edit., 1991, Maximizing Treatment Gains: Transfer Enhancement in Psychotherapy, 1979, (with P. Karoly) The Psychology of Self-Management, 1982; (with S. Englund, C. Lenhoff and J. Rhodes) A Mentor Manual: For Adults Who Work With Pregnant and Parenting Teens, 1995; assoc. editor: Psychol. Reports, 1961—, Jour. Addictive Behaviors, 1974-80; editl. bd. Behavior Therapy, 1969-74, Behavior Modification, 1975-84, Cognitive Therapy and Research, 1976-80, 83-92, Behavioral Assessment, 1979-81, Clin. Psychology Rev., 1980-85, 87-92, Revista de Psicologia Generaly Aplicada, 1980—, Jour. Social and Clin. Psychology, 1982-98, Jour. Clin. Psychology and Psychosomatics, 1982—; internat. editl. bd. Verhaltens Therapie (Behavior Therapy), study and editl. reviewer; adv. editor: Research Press, 1978-96. With U.S. Army, 1944-46. Recipient Alexander von Humboldt Sr. Scientist award, 1987-88; U. Ill. Rsch. Bd. grantee, 1973-78; U. Ill. Rsch. Bd. univ. scholar, 1990-93. Fellow Am. Psychol. Assn. (exec. council div. 12); mem. Midwestern Psychol. Assn., AAAS, Assn. Advancement Behavioral Therapies (dir. 1972-74), Am. Bd. Examiners Profl. Psychology (diplomate), Sigma Xi; hon. life mem. Italian Soc. Behavior Therapy, German Assn. Clin. Behavior Therapy, Orgn. Behavior Therapy Uruguay. Office: U Ill Dept Psychology 603 E Daniel St Champaign IL 61820-6232

KANFER, JULIAN NORMAN, biochemist, educator; b. Bklyn., May 23, 1930; s. Benjamin N. and Clara (Lichtenberger) K.; m. Beverly Kanfer; children—Brian, Rachel. BSc, Bklyn. Coll., 1954; MSc, George Washington U., 1958, PhD, 1961. Biochemist Mass. Gen. Hosp., Boston, 1969-75; dir. biochem. research E.K. Shriver Center, Waltham, Mass.; also dir. research W.E. Fernald State Sch., Waltham, 1969-75; adj. asso. prof. biochemistry Brandeis U., Waltham, 1969-75; asso. prof. neuropathology Harvard, 1969-75, prin. research assoc., 1974-75; prof. U. Man., Winnipeg, Can., 1975—; head dept. biochemistry U. Man., 1975—; cons. Health Scis. Centre, Winnipeg, 1976—; mem. med. adv. bd. Nat. Tay-Sachs Found., N.Y.C., 1970—; mem. study sect. on pathobiol. chemistry NIH, 1974—; postdoctoral fellowship com. NRC, 1983—; mem. Grant Commn. Nutrition and Metabolism Med. Rsch. Coun., Can., 1992—; vis. prof. dept. psychiatry U. Pitts. Med. Ctr., 1993-94; vis. prof. Stetson U., Deland, Fla., 1998—. Contbr. articles to profl. jours. Bd. dirs. Winnipeg chpt. Multiple Sclerosis Soc. Can., 1976.

Named Hon. Citizen of New Orleans, 1997,. Fellow Inst. de la Sante et de la Recherche Medicale (France); mem. Am. Soc. Biol. Chemistry, Am., Internat. neurochemistry socs., Am. Chem. Soc., AAAS, Soc. for Complex Carbohydrates, Fedn. Am. Socs. for Exptl. Biology, Can. Fedn. Biol. Socs., Canadian Biochem. Soc. Office: 770 Bannatyne St, 1415 Ocean Shore Blvd, Ormond Beach, FL Canada R3E 0W3

KANG, BANN C., immunologist; b. Kyungnam, Korea, Mar. 4, 1939; d. Daeryong and Buni (Chung) K.; came to U.S., 1964, naturalized, 1976; A.B., Kyungpook Nat. U., 1959, M.D., 1963; m. U. Yun Ryo, Mar. 30, 1963. Intern, L.I. Jewish Hosp.-Queens Hosp. Center, Jamaica, N.Y., 1964-65, resident in medicine, 1965-67; teaching assoc. Kyungpook U. Hosp., Taegu, Korea, 1967-70; fellow in allergy and chest Creighton U., Omaha, 1970-71; fellow in allergy Henry Ford Hosp., Detroit, 1971-72; clin. instr. medicine U. Mich. Hosp., Ann Arbor, 1972-73; asst. prof. Chgo. Med. Sch., 1973-74; chief allergy-immunology Mt. Sinai Hosp., Chgo., 1975—; asst. prof. Rush Med. Sch., Chgo. 1975-84, assoc. prof., 1984-86; assoc. prof. U. Ky. Coll. Medicine, 1987-92, prof., 1992—; cons., 1976—, Nat. Heart, Lung, Blood Inst., 1979—; mem. Exptl. Transplantation Adv. Bd., Ill., 1985-86, Diagnostic and Therapeutic Tech. Assessment (AMA), 1987—, Gen. Clin. Rsch. Com. (NIH), 1989-93; adv. com. Ctr. for Biologics and Rsch., FDA, 1993-96; counselor Chgo. Med. Soc., 1984-86, mem. policy com., adv. com. to health dept. Chgo. and Cook County, 1984-86. Recipient NIH award U. Mich., 1972-73. Diplomate Am. Bd. Internal Medicine, Am. Bd. Allergy-Immunology. Fellow ACP, Am. Acad. Allergy; mem. Am. Fedn. Clin. Research, AMA, Inter-Asthma Assn. Contbr. over 50 articles to profl. jours. Home: 2716 Martinique Ln Lexington KY 40509-9509 Office: U Ky Coll Medicine K528 Albert B Chandler Med Ctr 800 Rose St Lexington KY 40536-0001

KANG, BENJAMIN TOYEONG, writer, clergyman; b. Republic of Korea, Mar. 30, 1931; came to U.S., 1963; naturalized, 1979; s. Tae-Un and Kumjoo (Lee) K.; m. Katherine Chungcha Chung, Apr. 29, 1955; children: Jennifer, Mira, Gregory. BA, Yonsei U., Republic of Korea, 1954; MA, Kyungbuk U., Republic of Korea, 1959; BD, Temple U., 1967; ThD, Internat. Sem., 1981. Ordained to ministry Christian Ch., 1970. Instr. Yonsei U., Republic of Korea, 1956-58; exec. dir. Kyungju YMCA, Republic of Korea, 1958-59; asst. prof. Keimyoung U., Republic of Korea, 1959-61; pastor Korean Ch. of Lower Bucks, Levittown, Pa., 1974-84; pres. Korean Sch. of Lower Bucks, 1980-82; pastor Korean Gloria Ch., Phila., 1984-89; parish assoc. 1st Presbyn. Ch. Levittown, Pa., 1990—; freelance writer, 1992—; columnist Dong-A Daily News, 1992-94. Trustee Presbytery of Phila., Presbyn. Ch. (USA), 1982-88, Met. Christian Coun. Phila., 1984-88, Coun. Korean Chs. in Phila., 1985-89; comdr. Vol. Student Army Kyungju, Republic of Korea, 1950-51. Author: (hymn) In a Strange Land, 1992. Home: 3128 Benjamin Rush Ct Bensalem PA 19020-1903

KANG, ISAMU YONG, nuclear medicine physician; b. Osaka, Japan, Aug. 27, 1939; came to U.S., 1966; s. Chi-Chieh and Ichi (Morita) K.; m. Midori Ishibashi, Mar. 15, 1971; children: Rika Florence, Hiroshi Frederick. MD, Kyushu U., Fukuoka, Japan, 1965. Diplomate Am. Bd. Pathology, Am. Bd. Nuc. Medicine. Intern Grad. Hosp. U. Pa., Phila., 1967-68; resident in pathology U. Calif., San Diego, 1972-74, Letterman Army Med. Ctr., San Francisco, 1974-76; resident in nuclear medicine Walter Reed Army Med Ctr., Washington, 1976-78; asst. chief nuclear medicine Walter Reed Army Med. Ctr., Washington, 1978-80; co-dir. clin. lab., nuclear med. staff physician Kaiser Permanente Med. Ctr., Oakland, Calif., 1980-86; chief nuclear medicine Kaiser Permanente Med. Ctr., Walnut Creek, Calif., 1986—, radiation safety officer, 1986—. Lt. col. U.S. Army, 1969-80, Vietnam; col. USAR, 1980-97. Mem. Soc. Nuc. Medicine, Calif. Med. Assn. Buddhist. Avocations: jogging, golf, tennis, carpentry, reading. Home: 3554 Via Los Colorados Lafayette CA 94549-5332 Office: Kaiser Permanente Med Ctr 1425 S Main St Walnut Creek CA 94596-5318

KANG, JUAN, pathologist; b. Chang-Young, Kyung-Nam, Republic of Korea, Aug. 10, 1935; came to U.S., 1965; s. Bugon and Umchun (Chung) K.; children: Angie, Alex, Erik. PreMed, Kyung-Pook U., Taegu, Republic of Korea, 1955; MD, Kyung-Pook U., 1959. Diplomate Am. Bd. Pathology, Am. Bd. Radioisotopic Pathology, Am. Bd. Hematology, Am. Bd. Dermatopathology. Capt. Med. Corps Republic of Korea Army, 1959-65; intern Watts Hosp., Durham, N.C., 1965-66; resident St. Louis U. Hosp., 1968-70; pathologist Allen Pathology Group, St. Louis, 1971—; clin. asst. prof. St. Louis U. Med. Sch., 1979-. Mem. AMA, Am. Soc. Clin. Pathologists, Coll. Am. Pathologists, Internat. Acad. of Pathologists, Am. Soc. Dermatopathology, Soc. for Hematopathology. Home: 12939 Banyan Town Dr Saint Louis MO 63146-4300 Office: Christian Hosp NE 11133 Dunn Rd Saint Louis MO 63136-6192

KANG, JULIANA HAENG-CHA, anesthesiologist; b. Mokpo, Cheonnam, People's Republic of Korea, July 1, 1941; came to U.S., 1965; d. Johan and E-E-Suk (Lee) Kang; m. Chang-Song Choi; children: Mee-Kyung, Mee-Ae, Han-Bae. MD, Yonsei U., Seoul, People's Republic of Korea, 1965. Diplomate Am. Bd. Anesthesiology. Intern Pittsfield (Mass.) Gen. Hosp., 1965-66; asst. prof. biology Yonsei U., 1965; resident in anesthesiology D.C. Gen. Hosp., 1966-67, Yale-New Haven (Conn.) Hosp., 1967-69; asst. prof. anesthesiology U. Conn., Farmington, 1970-75, 82-85; vice chairperson anesthesia dept. Conn. Surgery Ctr., Hartford, Conn., 1985-86; med. dir., chairperson anesthesia dept. Conn. Surgery Ctr., Hartford, 1986—. Fellow Am. Coll. Anesthesiologists; mem. Am. Med. Women's Assn., Am. Soc. Ambulatory Surgery Anesthesia, Am. Soc. Anesthesiologists, Conn. Soc. Anesthesiology, Nat. Abortion Rights Action League, Naral Polit. Arm of Pro-Choice. Office: Conn Surgery Ctr 81 Gillett St Hartford CT 06105-2630

KANG, SUNG-MO (STEVE KANG), electrical engineering educator; b. Seoul, Korea, Feb. 25, 1945; came to U.S., 1969; s. Chang-Shik and Kyung-Ja (Lee) K.; m. Myoung-A Cha, June 10, 1972; children: Jennifer, Jeffrey. BSEE, Fairleigh Dickinson U., 1970; MSEE, SUNY, Buffalo, 1972; PhD in Elec. Engring., U. Calif., Berkeley, 1975. Asst. prof. Rutgers U., Piscataway, N.J., 1975-77; mem. tech. staff AT&T Bell Labs., Murray Hill, N.J., 1977-82; supr. AT&T Bell Labs., Murray Hill, 1982-85; prof. U. Ill., Urbana, 1985—, head dept. electrical and computer engring., 1995—, assoc. Ctr. for Advanced Study, 1991-92, assoc. dir. microelectronics lab., 1988-95; univ. scholar U. Ill., Urbana, 1995-96; dir. Ctr. for ASIC R&D. Author 6 books; contbr. over 250 papers to internat. jours. and confs. Recipient Meritorious Svc. award Cirs. and Sys. Soc., 1994, Humboldt Rsch. award for Sr. U.S. Scientists, 1996, Grad. Teaching award IEEE, 1996, IEEE CAS Soc. Tech. Achievement award, 1997, KBS award in Sci. and Tech., 1998, SRC Tech. Excellence award, 1999. Fellow AAAS, IEEE (various offices in Circuits and Systems Soc. including pres. 1991, founding editor-in-chief Trans. on VSLI systems, Disting. lectr. 1994-97, Darlington award, SRC Inventor Recognition award 1993, 96, Meritorious Svc. award Compuer Soc. 1990), Nat. Acad. Engring. of Korea (fgn. mem.). Presbyterian. Avocations: tennis, travel. Home: 1909 Trout Valley Rd Champaign IL 61821-9783 Office: Univ Ill Everitt Lab 1406 W Green St Urbana IL 61801-2918

KANG, YOUNG WOO, special education educator; b. Kyonggi, Korea, Jan. 16, 1944; came to U.S., 1972; naturalized; s. Myung Ki Kang and Lin Hee Lim; m. Kyoung Sook Suk, Feb. 26, 1972; children: Paul, Christopher. BA, Yonsei U., Seoul, Korea, 1972; MEd, U. Pitts., 1973, PhD, 1976. Cert. tchr. ESL, spl. edn.; cert. rehab. counselor. Spl. edn. cons. Gary (Ind.) Sch. Corp., 1976—; adj. prof. Northeastern Ill. U., Chgo., 1979—; prof., dean Taegu (Korea) U., 1978—; pres. EREF (Edn. Rehab. Exch. Found.) Internat., 1993—; vice-chmn. World Com. on Disability, 1995—; dir. Nat. Orgn. on Disability, 1995—, Goodwill Industries Internat., 1998—. Author: A Light in My Heart, 1987, Love, Light, Liberty, 1989, (with Kyoung Sook Kang) Two Candles Shining in the Darkness of the World, 1990, Secrecy to Success Through Education, 1995, Dreams of a father and his sons, 1998. First blind Korean to earn a PhD. Mem. Internat. Coun. for Exceptional Children, Edn. Rehab. Exch. Found. Internat. (founding pres. 1992—), Rotary (bd. dirs., trustee Munster, Ind. chpt. 1982—, chmn. internat. svc. and youth svc. coms. dist. 6540 1983-85, presenter confs. 1983, 87, 88, one of 75 candles in 75th anniversary celebration 1992, Meritorious Svc. citation 1982, Paul Harris fellow 1987, scholar 1973). Presbyterian. Avocations: public speaking, writing, reading, travel, advocating rights of disabled. Home: 8912 Chestnut Ln Munster IN 46321-3224 Office: Gary Community Sch Corp 1988 Polk St Gary IN 46407-2443

KANGAS, EDWARD A., accounting firm executive; b. 1944; m. Catherine Elizabeth Stephens, Sept. 17, 1994. Student, Univ. of Kansas, 1967. CPA, staff acct. Touche Ross & Co., Kansas City, 1967-74, ptnr., 1975-76, dir. mgmt. consulting ops., 1976-81, nat. dir. mgmt. consulting, 1981-85; mng. ptnr., CEO Touche Ross & Co., N.Y.C., 1985-89; also CEO Touche Ross Internat.; mng. ptnr. Deloitte and Touche, N.Y.C., 1989-94; also chmn, chief exec. Deloitte Touche Tohmatsu Internat., 1989—, CEO. Bd. dirs., mem. fin. com., mem. and chmn. fund raising com. Nat. Multiple Sclerosis Soc.; trustee Com. Econ. Devel.; bd. overseers The Wharton Sch.; bd. advisors U. Kans. Sch. of Bus. Office: Deloitte & Touche PO Box 820 10 Westport Rd Wilton CT 06897-0820*

KANICK, VIRGINIA, radiologist; b. Coaldale, Pa., Nov. 10, 1925; d. Martin and Anna (Pisklak) K. BA, Barnard Coll., 1947; MD, Columbia U., 1951. Diplomate Am. Bd. Radiology. Intern Western Reserve U. Hosps., Cleve., 1951-52; resident in radiology St. Luke's Hosp., N.Y.C., 1952-55, attending radiologist, 1955-74; acting dir. radiology St. Luke's Roosevelt Hosp., N.Y.C., 1981-84, dep. dir. of radiology, 1984-89; ptnr. West Side Radiology, N.Y.C., 1989—; clin. prof. radiology Coll. Physicians and Surgeons Columbia U., N.Y.C., 1975—; pres. Med. Bd. St. Luke's Roosevelt Hosp., 1980-82. Contbr. articles to profl. jours. Bd. dirs. Health System Agy. of N.Y.C., 1978-81. Fellow Am. Cancer Soc., 1955. Fellow Am. Coll. Radiology; mem. Am. Roentgen Ray Soc., Radiol. Soc. N.Am., N.Y. County Med. Soc. (sec., dir. 1978—), N.Y. State Radiol. Soc. (bd. dirs. 1975—). Republican. Roman Catholic. Avocations: skiing, travel, archeology. Home: 560 Riverside Dr Apt 17B New York NY 10027-3215

KANIECKI, MICHAEL JOSEPH, bishop; b. Detroit, Apr. 13, 1935; s. Stanley Joseph and Julia Marie (Konjora) K. BA, Gonzaga U., 1958, MA in Philosophy, 1960; MA in Theology, St. Mary's, Halifax, Can., 1966. Ordained priest, 1965; consecrated bishop, 1984. Missionary Alaska, 1960-83; coadjutor bishop Diocese of Fairbanks, Alaska, 1984-85, bishop, 1985—. Address: Bishop of Fairbanks 1316 Peger Rd Fairbanks AK 99709-5199

KANIN, DENNIS ROY, lawyer; b. Boston, Feb. 22, 1946; s. Irving Lynwood and Doris May (Small) K.; m. Carol Ann Licht, July 9, 1978; children: Zachary Joshua, Jonah Louis, Franklin Jacob. AB, Harvard U., 1968, JD, 1971. Bar: Mass. 1971, D.C. 1978. Assoc. Mahoney Atwood & Goldings, Boston, 1971-73; legis. asst. to congressman Frank Evans U.S. Ho. Reps., Washington, 1973-74, adminstrn. asst. to congressman Paul Tsongas, 1975-78; adminstrv. asst. to senator Paul Tsongas U.S. Senate, Washington, 1979-84; ptnr. Foley, Hoag & Eliot, Boston, 1985—. Mgr. campaign Tsongas for U.S. Senate, Boston, 1978; mem. Nat. Dem. Charter Commn., Washington, 1973-74, Nat. Commn. Dem. Platform Accountability, Washington, 1983-84; mem. exec. com. Mass. Ams. for Dem. Action, Boston, 1985-87; campaign mgr. Tsongas for pres.; mem., treas. New England Bd. of Anti-Defamation League, 1985—; mem. bd. dirs. New England Coun., 1993—; bd. dirs. Concord Coalition Citizens Coun., 1995—, Epiphany Sch., 1999—; bd. overseers Children's Hosp., Boston, 1996—. Jewish. Home: 65 Stuart Rd Newton MA 02459-1210 Office: Foley Hoag & Eliot One Post Office Sq Boston MA 02109

KANIN, DORIS MAY, political scientist, consultant; b. Somerville, Mass., Mar. 28, 1928; d. Sidney J. and Ida Gail (Gelbsman) Small; m. Irving L. Kanin, June 11, 1944; children: Dennis, Erik, Lisa Hochheiser. BA in Govt., Boston U., 1966; MA in Govt., 1970; postgrad., Boston U., 1970-74. Dir. cultural activities Staff of George McGovern, 1972; legis. dir. to congressman Joe Moakley, 1972-74; nat. polit. dir. Frank Church for Pres., 1975-76; spl. asst. Paul Tsongas U.S. Senate campaign, Boston, 1977-78; dir. Human Svcs. Dept. Fed. State Rels., Mass., 1979-81; nat. dir. pub. affairs Physicians for Social Responsibility, 1981-82; exec. of Pub. Rels. and Comms. Lynwood Labs. Inc., 1982—; polit. adv. Paul Tsongas for pres. campaign, Mass., 991-92. Inventor, creator: Spray-n-Starch aerosol, 1968; editor: Quincy Mass. Cmty. Ctr. Newsletter, 1956-58, Mass. Liberal Citizens of Mass. Bulletin; journalist Boston Daily Record, 1944; reporter Boston Daily Record-Am. Pres. LWV, Norwood, Mass., 1956-59; Mass. Citizens for Participation in Politics, Boston, 1973-74; chair, bd. mem., mem. state bd. Mass. Civil Liberties Union, Boston, 1976-81; elected del. to all Nat. Nominating Conventions, 1972-92; dir. Mass. Cultural Affairs for Pres. Campaign, George McGovern; elected Dem. Nat. Committeewoman, Mass., 1972-76, mem. women's caucus, 1972-76; mem. steering com. Capitol Hill Women's Polit. Caucus; mem. edn. and tng. coun. Dem. Nat. Com., 1976-80; chair Mass. Citizens for Participation in Politics, 1973-74; bd. dirs. Mass. Ams. for Dem. Action, 1978-80, Mass. Pax; del. Dem. Nat. Conv., 1972, 76, 80, 82; chair divsn. cultural affairs Mass. Presdl. Staff for George McGovern, 1992. Named: Woodrow Wilson Semi-Finalist, 1972-76, Mass. Spelling Bee Champion, Boston Herald Traveler, 1939. Mem. Internat. Aerosol Congress. Democrat. Avocations: travel, painting, poetry writing, opera, ballet. Home: 511 Boylston St Brookline MA 02445-5701 also: 1289 Breakers West Blvd West Palm Beach FL 33411-1881

KANIN, FAY, screenwriter; b. N.Y.C.; d. David and Bessie Mitchell; m. Michael Kanin (dec.); children: Joel (dec.), Josh. Student, Elmira Coll., LHD (hon.), 1981; BA, U. So. Calif. mem. Western regional exec. bd., judge Am. Coll. Theatre Festival, 1975-76. Writer: (with Michael Kanin) screenplays including The Opposite Sex, Teacher's Pet; Broadway plays including Goodbye My Fancy, His and Hers, Rashomon, Grind (Tony nomination 1985); writer, co-prodr. TV spls. including Friendly Fire, ABC-TV (Emmy award for best TV film, San Francisco Film Festival award, Peabody award), Hustling (Writers Guild award for best original drama), Tell Me Where It Hurts (Emmy award, Christopher award); Heartsounds (Peabody award). Mem. Writers guild Am. West (pres. screen br. 1971-73, Val Davies award 1975, Morgan Cox award 1976), Am. Film Inst. (trustee), Acad. Motion Picture Arts and Scis. (pres. 1979-82), Nat. Ctr. Film and Video Preservation (co-chmn.), Am. Film Preservation Bd. (chmn.).

KANJORSKI, PAUL EDMUND, congressman, lawyer; b. Nanticoke, Pa., Apr. 2, 1937; s. A. Peter and Wanda (Nedbalski) K.; m. Nancy Marie Hickerson, Nov. 22, 1962; 1 child, Nancy Marie. Student, Temple U., 1961, Dickinson Sch. Law, 1965. Bar: Pa. Ptnr. Kanjorski & Kanjorski, Wilkes-Barre, Pa., 1966-84; mem. 99th-106th Congresses from 11th Pa. dist., Washington, D.C., 1985—; mem. banking and fin. svcs., govt. reform coms. 99th-106th Congresses from 11th Pa. dist., Washington. Acting solicitor City of Nanticoke, 1969-81; Pa. Workmen's Compensation referee, 1972-80; bd. dirs. Wyoming Valley Sanitary Authority, Wilkes-Barre, 1972-84; former trustee Wilkes U. Mem. Wilkes-Barre Law Library Assn. Democrat. Roman Catholic. Avocation: fishing. Office: 2353 Rayburn Bldg Washington DC 20515-3811

KANKEY, ROLAND DOYLE, academic administrator; b. Batesville, Ark., Nov. 17, 1946; s. William Jasper Jr. and Verline Violet (Dockins) K.; m. Linda Grace Johnson, July 6, 1974; children: Jason, Andrew, Adam. *Linda Kankey has dispatched for the Enon Emergency Medical Service (EMS) since 1978, and is currently the head fire and EMS dispatcher and EMS Treasurer. A member of the Greenon Band Boosters since 1989, she served on their board as treasurer 1997-1999. Jason completed a Bachelor of Science degree in chemical engineering at the University of Dayton in 1999 and works for U.S. Gypsum. Andy started working toward a degree in engineering at Ohio State University in 1998. Adam has been in drama, marching band, pep band, concert band, and lab band as a 1998 freshman at Greenon High School.* BS in Math, Wichita State U., 1968; MS in Math, Oklahoma State U., Stillwater, 1970; MA in Bus. Adminstrn., Ohio State U., Columbus, 1985, PhD in Bus. Adminstrn., 1988. Tech. mgr. Rome Air Devel. Ctr., Rome, N.Y., 1970-72; chief, mgmt. analysis 51st Air Base Wing, Osan, Korea, 1972-73; mgmt./cost analysis Headquarters USAF, Pentagon, 1973-77; faculty mem. AFIT, Wright-Patterson, 1977-90, dir. grad. cost analysis program, 1988-90, head dept. quantitative mgmt., 1990-93; sr. IMA to the commdr. Aerospace Guidance & Meteorology Ctr., Newark AFB, 1995-96; sr. IMA to the comptr. Aero. Systems Ctr., Wright Patterson, 1996-99; head grad. acquisition mgmt. dept. AFIT, Wright Patterson, 1993-98; mem. nat. bd. dirs. Soc. Cost Estimating & Analysis, Alexandria, Va., 1993-97, chmn. 1994 nat. conf., 1990-94, editor Jour. Cost Analysis, 1992-98; editor National Estimator Nat. Estimating Soc., Alexandria, 1989-92. Editor: (book) Cost Analysis & Estimating, 1991; contbr. articles to profl. jours. Mem. Greenon H.S. Band Boosters, Enon, 1995—, sec. 1995-97. Capt. USAF, 1968-80. Mem. Am. Soc. Military Comptrollers (chpt. pres. 1997-98), Wright-Patterson Air Force Base Officers Club, Soc. Cost Estimating & Analysis, Beta Gamma Sigma Honor Soc., Phi Kappa Phi. Avocations: genealogy, golf, moderate running, military and air force memorabilia, family history. Home: 115 Cimmaron Trl Enon OH 45323-1653 Office: AFIT/LS 2950 P St Dayton OH 45433-7765

KANN, PETER R., publishing executive; b. Princeton, N.J.. B in Govt., Harvard U. Reporter Dow Jones Publs., Pitts., L.A., 1964-67, Hong Kong, 1967-75; editor Asian Wall St. Jour., Hong Kong, 1976-79; from assoc. pub. to editl. dir. Dow Jones Publs., N.Y.C., 1979-91, chmn., CEO and pub., 1991—. Mem. bd. trustees The Asia Soc., Inst. Advanced Study Princeton, Atlanta, The Aspen Inst. Office: Dow Jones & Co Inc 200 Liberty St Fl 12 New York NY 10281-1099

KANN, PETER ROBERT, journalist, newspaper publishing executive; b. N.Y.C., Dec. 13, 1942; s. Robert A. and Marie (Breuer) K.; m. Francesca Mayer, Apr. 12, 1969 (dec. 1983); m. Karen Elliott House, 1984; children: Hillary Francesca, Petra Elliott, Jason Elliott, Jade Elliott. BA, Harvard U., 1964. With The Wall St. Jour., 1964—; journalist N.Y.C., 1964-67, Vietnam, 1967-68, Hong Kong, 1968-75; pub., editor Asian edit., 1976-79, assoc. pub., 1979-88; formerly asst. to chmn. and mem. exec. com. Dow Jones & Co., 1986-89, pres. internat. and mag. groups, 1986-89, also chmn. bd. dirs.; chmn. CEO, pub. Wall St. Jour., 1989—; pres. Dow Jones & Co., N.Y.C., 1989-91, chmn., CEO, 1991—; chmn. bd. Far Ea. Econ. Rev., 1987-89; mem. Pulitzer Prize Bd., 1987-96. Trustee Asia Soc., 1989-94, Inst. for Advanced Study, Princeton, N.J., 1990—, Aspen Inst., 1994—, Spelman Coll., 1994-97. Recipient Pulitzer prize for internat. reporting, 1972. Mem. Spee Club (Cambridge, Mass.). Office: Wall Street Journal 200 Liberty St New York NY 10281-0083

KANNAN, SRIMATHI, environmental and occupational health educator; b. Sept. 12, 1966. MS, Bharathiar U., Coimbatore, India, 1988; PhD, U. Tenn., 1995. Grad. rsch. asst. U. Tenn., Knoxville, 1991-92, grad. tchg. asst., 1992-95; postdoctoral rsch. fellow Purdue U., West Lafayette, Ind., 1995-97; asst. prof. environ. and occupational health U. Mich., Ann Arbor, 1997—. E-mail: kannans@umich.edu. Home: 1141 Nielsen Ct Apt 4 Ann Arbor MI 48105-1959 Office: U Mich Dept Dept Env & Indsl Health 109 Observatory St Ann Arbor MI 48109-2029

KANNATEY-ASIBU, ELIJAH, engineering educator; b. Senya Beraku, Ghana; came to U.S., 1975; s. Elijah and Grace (Afful) Kannatey-Asibu; divorced; children: Bianca, Araba. BSc, U.S.T., Kumasi, Ghana, 1974; MS, U. Calif., Berkeley, 1977, PhD, 1980. Asst. prof. Gen. Motors Inst., Flint, Mich., 1980-82; asst. prof. U. Mich., Ann Arbor, 1983-88, assoc. prof., 1988-94, prof., 1994—, assoc. chair dept. mech. engring., 1997—. Contbr. articles to profl. jours. Fellow ASME (chair mfg. engring. divsn. 1996-97, assoc. editor jour. 1991-94), Am. Soc. for Metals, Soc. Mfg. Engrs. Office: U Mich 2250 GG Brown Ann Arbor MI 48109-2125

KANNE, MARVIN GEORGE, newspaper publishing executive; b. St. Louis, 1937. Student, St. Louis U. V.p., dir. ops. St. Louis Post-Dispatch. Mem. Am. Assn. Indsl. Mgmt., Am. Mgmt. Assn., IRRA Indsl. Rels. Rsch. Assn. Office: Saint Louis Post-Dispatch 900 N Tucker Blvd Saint Louis MO 63101-1099*

KANNE, MICHAEL STEPHEN, federal judge; b. Rensselaer, Ind., Dec. 21, 1938; s. Allen Raymond and Jane (Robinson) K.; m. Judith Ann Stevens, June 22, 1963; children: Anne, Katherine. Student, St. Joseph's Coll., Rensselaer, 1957-58; BS, Ind. U., 1962, JD, 1968; postgrad., Boston U., 1963, U. Birmingham, Eng., 1975. Bar: Ind. 1968. Assoc. Nesbitt and Fisher, Rensselaer, 1968-71; sole practice Rensselaer, 1971-72; atty. City of Rensselaer, 1972; judge 30th Jud. Cir. of Ind., 1972-82, U.S. Dist. Ct. (no. dist.) Ind., Hammond, 1982-87, U.S. Ct. Appeals, Chgo., 1987—; chmn. U.S. Cts. Design Guide, 1988-95; lectr. law St. Joseph's Coll., 1975-89, St. Frances Coll., 1990-91; faculty Nat. Inst. for Trial Advocacy, South Bend, Ind., 1978-88. Bd. visitors Ind. U. Sch. Law, 1987—, Ind. U. Sch. Pub. and Environ. Affairs, 1991—; trustee St. Joseph's Coll., 1984—. Served to 1st lt. USAF, 1962-65. Recipient Disting. Service award St. Joseph's Coll., 1973, Disting. Grad. award Nat Cath. Ednl. Assn.; named Outstanding Alumnus Today's Catholic Teacher, 1991. Mem. Fed. Bar Assn., Ind. State Bar Assn. (bd. dirs. 1977-79, Presdl. citation 1979), Jasper County Bar Assn. (pres. 1972-76), Tippecanoe County Bar Assn., Law Alumni Assn. Ind. U. (pres. 1980). Roman Catholic. Avocations, horseback riding, weightlifting. Home: PO Box 1340 Lafayette IN 47902-1340 Office: US Ct Appeals 219 S Dearborn St Chicago IL 60604-1702

KANNENSTINE, MARGARET LAMPE, artist; b. St. Louis, Apr. 1, 1938; d. John Avery and Elizabeth (Phillips) Lampe; m. Louis Fabian Kannenstine, Oct. 3, 1959; children: David Edward, Emily Ann. BFA, Washington U. St. Louis, 1959; postgrad., Art Students League, N.Y.C., 1959-61. bd. trustees Pentangle Coun. Arts, 1982-88, 93-96, chair, 1984-87, 94, 95, hon. bd., 1997—; bd. trustees Vt. Studio Ctr., 1989-94, chair, 1990, 91, 92, 93; workshop tchr. Fleming Mus., Burlington, 1991, Kimball Union Acad. Enfield, N.H., 1993; bd. trustees Vt. Coun. Arts, 1994—, chair, 1994-98. One-woman shows include Vt. Artisans, Strafford, 1976, Gallery Two, Woodstock, Vt., 1974, 77, 85, Red Mill Gallery, Johnson, Vt., 1990, Green Mountain Power Corp., South Burlington, Vt., 1991, Vt. Coun. on Arts, Montpelier, Vt., 1991, Woodstock Gallery Art, 1991, 94, Beside Myself Gallery, Arlington, Vt., 1992, Taylor Gallery, Meriden, N.H., 1993, Dartmouth Coll., Hanover, N.H., 1993, 99, Kent (Conn.) Sch., 1993, Chittenden Bank, Burlington, Vt., 1994, Windy Bush Gallery, New Hope, Pa., 1995, N.H. Coll., Manchester, 1996, The Flynn Theater Gallery, Burlington, 1996, Nat. Wildlife Fedn. Gallery, Vienna, Va., 1996, McGowan Fine Art, Concord, N.H., 1997, Grayson Gallery, Woodstock, 1997, Spheris Gallery, Walpole, N.H., 1997, The Gallery at Johnny D's, Somerville, Mass., 1997, AVA Gallery, Hanover, Lebanon, 1998, Flynn Theater Gallery, Burlington, Vt., 1998, Main Street Mus. Art, Hartford, Vt., 1999, Collis Ctr., Dartmouth coll., 1999, Gallery of Graphic Arts, New york, N.Y., 1999; group shows include Gallery Two, 1973-88, Carl Battaglia Gallery, N.Y.C., 1979-80, The Gallery, Williamstown, Mass., 1981-84, Vt. Coun. Arts, 1988, 96, AVA Gallery, Hanover, 1989, 90, 96, 98, Woodstock Gallery Art, 1989, Beside Myself Gallery, 1990, Fleming Mus., U. Vt., Burlington, 1991, Arts Festival for AIDS, Bennington Coll., 1992, Windy Bush Gallery, 1994, VCA, Woodstock, 1994, Riverfest, White River Junction, Vt., 1995, Firehouse Gallery, Burlington, 1995, McGowan Fine Art, Concord, N.H., 1995, Chaffee Gallery, Rutland, Vt., 1997, Helen Day Art Ctr., Stowe, Vt., 1997, Champion Internat., Stamford, Conn., 1997, New Art New England, Newport, N.H., 1997, AVA Gallery, Lebanon, N.H., 1998, Gallery Graphic Art, N.Y.C., 1998, 99, Grayson Gallery, Woodstock, Vt., 1999 Ute Stebich Gallery, Lenox Mt., 1999; represented in permanent collections at The Hood Mus., Hanover, Robert Hull Fleming Mus., Burlington, Vt. Employees Credit Union, Montpelier, Vt., Champion Internat. Corp., Stamford, Conn., Union Mut. Ins. Co., Montpelier, Vt. Law Sch., South Royalton, Fletcher Allen Hosp., Burlington, Vt., others. Trustee New Eng. Found. for the Arts, 1996—; incorporator Upper Valley Cmty. Found., 1996—, trustee, 1999—; founding dir. Woodstock Comty. Trust, v.p. 1998, 99. Washington U. scholar, 1955. Mem. Nat. Women's Caucus Art, Cosmopolitan Club. Avocations: music, gardening, hiking.

KANNER, EDWIN BENJAMIN, electrical manufacturing company executive; b. N.Y.C., July 2, 1922; s. Charles and Grace (Edelson) K.; m. S. Barbara Penenberg, Aug. 3, 1944; children: Jaimie Sue, Richard, Keith. BBA, CCNY, 1943; MBA, Harvard U., 1947. Asst. West Coast mgr. Fairchild Publs., N.Y.C. and L.A., 1948-50; gen. mgr. Dible Enterprises, L.A., 1951-53; sales mgr., gen. mgr., prs. Western Insulated Wire Co. div. Teledyne, L.A., 1954-68; pres. Carol Cable Co. West div. Avnet, L.A., 1969-79; exec. v.p., COO Avnet Inc., N.Y.C., 1980-83; pres. Pacific Electricord and Am. Ins. Wire Co., L.A., also Providence, 1948—. Lt. comdr. USNR, 1943-47, PTO. Office: Pacific Electricord 747 W Redondo Beach Blvd Gardena CA 90247-4203*

KANNER, FREDERICK W., lawyer; b. N.Y.C., Apr. 25, 1943. BA, U. Va., 1965; JD, Georgetown U., 1968. Bar: N.Y. 1969. Ptnr. Dewey Ballantine LLP, N.Y.C., 1976—. Editor: Georgetown Law Jour., 1967-68. Mem. ABA, N.Y. State Bar Assn., Assn. Bar City N.Y. (former mem. securities regulation com.). Office: Dewey Ballantine LLP 1301 Avenue Of The Americas New York NY 10019-6022*

KANNER, GIDEON, lawyer; b. Lwów, Poland, Apr. 15, 1930; came to U.S., 1947; s. Stanley and Claire Kanner; children: Jonathan, Jesse. B of Mech. Engring., The Cooper Union, 1954; JD, U. So. Calif., 1961. Bar: Calif. 1962, U.S. Supreme Ct. 1967. Rocket engr. USN, N.J., 1954-55, Rocketdyne, Calif., 1955-64; assoc. Fadem & Kanner, L.S., 1964-74; prof. law Loyola U., L.A., 1974-90; assoc. Crosby, Heafey, Roach & May, L.A., 1990-95; lawyer Berger & Norton, Santa Monica, Calif., 1995—; cons. Calif. Law Revision Commn., 1968-77, 97—. Co-editor: Nichols on Eminent Domain, Compensation for Expropriation-A Comparative Study, Vol. II, 1990, After Lucas: Land Use Regulation and the Taking of Property Without Compensation, 1993; editor, pub. Just Compensation, 1974—; contbr. articles and revs. to profl. law jours. Recipient Shattuck prize Am. Inst. Real Estate Appraisers, Harrison Tweed Spl. Merit award for continuing legal edn. Am. Law Inst.-ABA. Home: PO Box 1741 Burbank CA 91507-1741 Office: Berger & Norton 1620 26th St Ste 200 Santa Monica CA 90404-4059

KANOF, NORMAN B., dermatologist; b. N.Y.C., May 31, 1920. AB, George Washington U., 1941, MD, 1941; D in Med. Sci., Columbia U., 1949. Diplomate Am. Bd. Dermatology. Clin. prof. dermatology NYU Sch. of Medicine, N.Y.C. Home: 737 Park Ave New York NY 10021-4256 Office: 10 E 70th St New York NY 10021-4913

KANOFSKY, JACOB DANIEL, psychiatrist, educator; b. Phila., Apr. 16, 1948; s. Philip and Mollie (Edelstein) K. BA in Physics, Temple U., 1965-69; MD, Thomas Jefferson Med. Coll., Phila., 1974; MPH in Epidemiology, Johns Hopkins U., 1978. Diplomate Am. Bd. Psychiatry and Neurology. Intern Met. Hosp., N.Y.C., 1974-75; resident in psychiatry St. Luke's-Roosevelt Hosp. Ctr., Columbia U., N.Y.C., 1978-80, fellow in psychiat. epidemiology, 1980-82; asst. editor-in-chief Med. Tribune, N.Y.C., 1984-85; ward chief rsch. unit Bronx (N.Y.) Psychiat. Ctr., 1986, assoc. clin. dir., 1986-87, acting clin. dir., 1987, pres. med. staff orgn., 1987-89; assoc. dir. schizophrenia rsch. Albert Einstein Coll. Med./Bronx Psychiat. Ctr., 1989-90, sr. rsch. psychiatrist, 1989—, asst. prof. psychiatry, 1986—; asst. prof. epidemiology and social medicine Albert Einstein Coll. Med., 1993—; lectr. in psychiatry Columbia U., N.Y.C., 1980—; attending psychiatrist St. Luke's-Roosevelt Hosp. Ctr., 1980—; contbg. editor Med. Tribune, 1986—; nutrition cons. Office of Alternative Medicine, NIH, 1992, Time Life Books, 1994—. Consulting editor Jour. of the Am. Coll. of Nutrition, 1990—; contbr. over 50 articles to profl. jours. Fellow Am. Coll. Nutrition; mem. Am. Psychiat. Assn. Jewish. Avocations: swimming, hiking, piano. Office: Bronx Psychiat Ctr 1500 Waters Pl Bronx NY 10461-2723

KANOUSE, DONALD LEE, wastewater treatment executive; b. Kankakee, Ill., Mar. 11, 1935; s. Rueben Thomas and Ethel Lee (Small) K.; m. Delourese Mae Welch, May 9, 1967; children: Roseanna, Michael, Karen, Kristine. Student, LaSalle U., 1970, Mich. U., 1991. Gen. foreman Kroehler Furniture Mfg., Kankakee, 1963-80; ops. supr. Met. Wastewater Utility, Kankakee, 1980-98. Mem., environ. del. to China, People to People Citizen Amb. Program divsn. Internat. Amb. Programs, Inc., 1994. With USN, 1951-52, U.S. Army, 1954-57, 60-63, USAR, 1957-60. Named Parent of Yr. Eureka Coll., 1989-90. Mem. Nat. Platform Assn., Ill. Assn. Wastewater Opers., Water Environ. Fedn., Am. Legion (post 85). Avocations: woodworking, cabinet making, wood toys and models, fishing, hunting. Home: 47 Iroquois Mobile Est Chebanse IL 60922-9512 Office: Kankakee Met Wastewater Util PO Box 588 1600 W Brookmont Blvd Kankakee IL 60901-2023

KANOV, MARK, radio station executive; married; 3 children. BS in Advt., U. Fla., 1967. With retail advt. sales divsn. Atlanta Jour. and Constitution, 1967-68; with sales staff Sta. WQXI-FM, 1968-70, Sta. WQXI-AM and WQXI-FM, 1970-80; local sales mgr. Sta. WQXI, Atlanta, 1980-85; gen. sales mgr. Sta. WSTR-FM, WQXI, Atlanta, 1985-90, station mgr., 1990-93, sr. v.p./gen. mgr., 1993—. Office: WSTR 3350 Peachtree Rd NE Atlanta GA 30326-1040*

KANOVITZ, HOWARD, artist; b. Fall River, Mass., Feb. 9, 1929; s. Meyer Julius and Dora (Rems) K. BS, Providence Coll., 1949; postgrad., R.I. Sch. Design, 1949-51, NYU, 1959-61. Instr. Bklyn. Coll., 1962-64, Pratt Inst., 1964-66; prof. Southhampton Coll., 1977-78, Sch. Visual Arts, N.Y.C., 1981-85. Artist, painter exhibited Tibor de Nagy Gallery, 1956, Stable Gallery, 1962, Jewish Mus., 1966, Waddell Gallery, 1969; one-man shows include U.S. and Europe, Stefanotty Gallery, N.Y.C., 1975, Galerie Jöllenbeck, Cologne, 1977, Benson Gallery, Bridgehampton, L.I., N.Y., 1977, Akademie der Kunste, Berlin, 1979, Kestner Gesellschaft, Hannover, 1979, Alex Rosenberg Gallery, 1982, Inge Baecker Gallery, 1987, 88, 91, Cologne, 1987, Marlborough Gallery, 1988, 90, Hokin-Kaufman Gallery, Chgo., 1989, Gana Art Gallery, Seoul, 1990, Ulrich Gering Gallery, Frankfurt, 1997, Nabi Gallery, Sag Harbor, L.I., 1998; group exhibits include Whitney Mus., N.Y.C., 1972, Dokumenta 5, Kassel, 1972, Berlin Nat. Gallery, 1976, Guild Hall, East Hampton, L.I., 1976, Dokumenta 6, Kassel, 1977, Alex Rosenberg Gallery, 1978, Louise Himmelfarb Gallery, Watermill, L.I., 1979, L.A. Mus. Contemporary Art, 1984, Indpls. Mus. Art, 1985, Ludwig Mus., Cologne, 1988, Parrish Art Mus., Southampton, L.I., 1988, Fla. Internat. U., Miami, 1989, Met. Mus., N.Y.C., 1991, Weatherspoon Art Gallery, Greensboro, N.C., 1991. Studio: 361 N Sea Mecox Rd Southampton NY 11968

KANSFIELD, NORMAN J., seminary president; b. East Chgo., Ind., Mar. 24, 1940; s. Orval Russell and Margaret Jeannette (Norman) K.; m. Mary L. Klein, June 25, 1965; children: Ann Margaret, John Livingston. BA, Hope Coll., 1962; BD, Western Theol. Seminary, 1965; M of sacred theology, Union Theol. Seminary, 1968; MA, U. Chgo., 1970, PhD, 1981. Pastor Second Reformed Ch., Astoria, Queens, 1965-68; interim pastor First Reformed Ch., Berwin, Ill., 1968-69; assoc. pastor Ivanhoe Reformed Ch., Riverdale, Ill., 1969-70; libr., prof. theology Western Theol. Seminary, Holland, Mich., 1970-83; dir. libr. svcs., assoc. prof. ch. history Colgate Rochester (N.Y.) Divinty Sch., 1983-92; dir. libr. svcs. St. Bernard's Inst., Rochester, 1983-92; pres. New Brunswick (N.J.) Theol. Seminary, 1993—; commn. on history, mem. Reformed Ch. in Am., 1969-74. Co-author: Evangelism: The Church's Proclamation, 1988; editor, contbr. (hymnbook) Rejoice in the Lord, 1985; mem. editl. bd. Perspectives, 1997—; contbr. articles to profl. jours. Chair Hist. Adv. Com., Holland, 1970-83; dir. New Brunswick Tomorrow, 1994—. Sealantic fellow Rockefeller Bros. Found., 1968-70, Conant fellow Episc. Ch. in USA, 1989-90; Rabbi Nathan Keller Meml. lectr. Temple Anshe Emeth, New Brunswick, 1995. Mem. Am. Theol. Libr. Assn. (dir. 1978-89, dir., chair Index Bd. 1983-89). Democrat. Avocations: book collecting, carpentry, fishing, gardening. Home: 25 Seminary Pl New Brunswick NJ 08901-1107 Office: New Brunswick Theol Seminary 17 Seminary Pl New Brunswick NJ 08901-1107

KANSTEINER, BEAU KENT, city official; b. St. Charles, Mo., Mar. 15, 1934; s. Herbert Henry and Coramery (Wallenbrock) K. BS in Mech. Engring., U. Kans., 1957. Engr. The Boeing Co., Seattle, New Orleans and Wichita, Kans., 1961-68, 69, 71, Beech Aircraft Corp., Wichita, 1970; mgr. prodn. distbn. Leavenworth (Kans.) Water Works Bd., 1971—. Lt. comdr. USN, 1957-61, USN ret. Mem. NRA, Am. Water Works Assn. (chmn. Kans. sect. 1984-85, dir. 1991-94), Naval Res. Assn., U. Kans. Alumni ASsn. Office: Leavenworth Water Dept 601 Cherokee St Leavenworth KS 66048-2627

KANT, GLORIA JEAN, neuroscientist, researcher; b. Chgo., June 6, 1944; d. Hans Georg and Jo Sefa Kant; m. Philip Herbert Balcom, July 1, 1967 (div. 1976). BS in Chemistry, Mich. State U., 1965; PhD in Physiol. Chemistry, U. Wis., 1969. Chemist dept. psychiatry Walter Reed Army Inst. Rsch., Washington, 1970-71, neurochemist dept. microwave rsch., 1971-77, neurochemist dept. med. neuroscis., 1977-87, chief dept. med. neuroscis., 1987-95, dir. divsn. neuroscis., 1995—. Mem. editl. bd. Pharmacology, Biochemistry and Behavior, 1991—; contbr. over 80 articles to sci. jours. Mem. AAAS, Soc. for Neurosci., Internat. Behavioral Neurosci. Soc., Women in Neurosci. Avocations: golf. Home: 1124 Dennis Ave Silver Spring MD 20901-2171 Office: Walter Reed Army Inst Rsch Divsn Neurosciences Washington DC 20307

KANTER, ARNOLD LEE, international businesss consultant, policy analyst; b. Chgo., Feb. 27, 1945; s. Norton and Mary Kanter; m. Anne Strassman, June 28, 1969; children: Clare Megan, Noah Charles. AB, U. Mich., 1966; MPhil in Polit. Sci., Yale U., 1969, PhD in Polit. Sci., 1975. Rsch. fellow, asst. Brookings Instn., Washington, 1969-71; instr. Ohio State U., Columbus, 1971-72; asst. prof., rsch. assoc. U. Mich., Ann Arbor, 1972-77; spl. asst. to dir. Bur. Politico-Mil. Affairs, Dept. State, Washington, 1977-78, dep. dir. Office Systems Analysis, 1978-81, dir. Office Policy Analysis, 1981-83, prin. dep. asst. sec., 1984-85; dep. to undersec. for polit. affairs Dept. State, 1983-84; assoc. program dir. internat. security and def. policy RAND Corp., Santa Monica, Calif., 1985-86, program dir. nat. security strategies, 1986-87, sr. rsch. staff, 1987-89; spl. asst. to Pres. of U.S., sr. dir. for arms control and def. policy NSC, Washington, 1989-91; under Sec. of State Pol. Affairs, 1991-93; sr. fellow the RAND Corp., Washington, 1993—, The Forum for Internat. Policy, 1993—; prin. The Scowcroft Group. Author: Defense Politics: A Budgetary Perspective, 1979; co-author: Bureaucratic Politics and Foreign Policy, 1974; co-editor: Readings in American Foreign Policy, 1973; contbr. numerous articles to profl. jours. Mem. Coun. on Fgn. Rels., Internat. Inst. Strategic Studies, Phi Beta Kappa. Office: The Scowcroft Group 900 17th St NW Ste 500 Washington DC 20006-2507

KANTER, BURTON WALLACE, lawyer; b. Jersey City, Aug. 12, 1930; s. Morris and Beatrice (Wilsker) K.; m. Naomi R. Krakow, June 17, 1927; children: Joel, Janis, Joshua. BA, U. Chgo., 1951, JD, 1952. Bar: Ill. 1952. Cons. U.S. Treasury Dept., 1959-61; atty.-advisor Tax Ct. U.S., 1954-56; mem. Law Offices of David Altman, Chgo., 1956-60; ptnr. Altman, Levenfeld & Kanter, Chgo., 1961-64, Levenfeld & Kanter, Chgo. and San Francisco, 1964-80, Kanter & Eisenberg, Chgo., 1980-87, of counsel Neal, Gerber, Eisenberg, 1987—; bd. dirs. Sci. Measurement Systems, Inc., Logic Devices, Inc., First Health Group, Inc.; chmn. Walnut Fin. Svcs. Inc.; faculty U. Chgo. Law Sch. Mem. adv. bd. Wharton Real Estate Ctr. U. Pa.; bd. dirs. Chgo. Internat. Film Festival, Midwest Film Ctr. of Sch. Art Inst.; mem. U. Chgo. Tax Policy Council; trustee Mus. Contemporary Art. Mem. ABA, Ill. Bar Assn., Chgo. Bar Assn., Urban Land Inst. Editor Jour. Taxation; contbr. articles to profl. jours. Office: 22nd Fl 2 N La Salle St Fl 22 Chicago IL 60602-3702

KANTER, CARL IRWIN, lawyer; b. Jersey City, Feb. 17, 1932; s. Morris and Beatrice (Wilson) K.; m. Gail Herman, Nov. 27, 1963; children—Deborah, David, Andrew, Aaron. A.B., Harvard U., 1953, LL.B., 1956. Bar: Calif. 1956, N.Y. 1959. Assoc. Stroock & Stroock & Lavan, N.Y.C., 1959-67, ptnr., 1967-92; sr. v.p., co-gen. counsel Merck-Medco Managed Care L.L.C., Montvale, N.J., 1992-97, spl. counsel, 1997-99. Served with U.S. Army, 1957-58. Home: 19 Tompkins Rd Scarsdale NY 10583-2839

KANTER, DONALD RICHARD, pharmaceutical executive; b. Detroit, Jan. 22, 1951; s. Harry Richard and Dorothy May (Kelch) K.; m. Diane Lynn Fickert, July 9, 1971 (div. Sept. 1993); children: Sean Richard, Donald Mathew, Lauren Marie. BA, Oakland U., Rochester, Mich., 1976; MS, Eastern Mich. U., 1979; PhD, U. Cin., 1983. Instr., lectr. U. Cin., 1978-84; health scis. officer VA med. Ctr., Cin., 1980-85; supr. med. affairs Genetic Systems, Seattle, 1985-88; dir. stats. and clin. rsch. Solvay Pharm.; pres. PharmData, Inc.; cons. in field. Author: (with Karoly et al) Child Health Psychology, 1982; (with Daniel B. Berch) Sustained Attention in Human Performance, 1983; contbr. med. articles to profl. jours. Oakland U. grantee, 1976, NIMH grantee, 1984, VA merit grantee, 1984, Outstanding Contbn. award, 1985. Mem. AAAS, Sigma Xi. Roman Catholic. Home: 2034 Kinridge Trl Marietta GA 30062-1828 Office: Bldg E 205 1000 Johnson Ferry Rd Ste E205 Marietta GA 30068-2175

KANTER, IRVING, mathematical physicist; b. N.Y.C., Oct. 30, 1924; s. Samuel and Sarah (Goodman) K.; m. Gladys Veronica Ruth, Aug. 12, 1951; children: Lisa, Joan, Susan, Madge, Natalie. AB in Physics, Bklyn. Coll., 1944; postgrad., Oak Ridge Inst. Nuclear Studies, 1947; PhD in Applied Math., Brown U., 1953. Physicist Kellex Corp., 1944-45, Union Carbide Corp., 1945-47, U.S. Army Corps Engrs., Oak Ridge, Tenn., 1944-46; design specialist Lockheed Aircraft Co., Burbank, Calif., 1951-54; systems engr. Radio Corp. Am., Moorestown, N.J., 1954-66; consulting scientist Raytheon Co., Tewksbury, Mass., 1966-92; cons. Army Rsch. Orgn., Durham, N.C. Inventor, monopulse, ground mapping, detection, classification. Rockefeller fellow Brown U., 1948-51. Fellow IEEE (author detection, estimation papers 1974-91). Jewish. Avocation: ancient history. Home: 9 Bushnell Dr Lexington MA 02421-4901

KANTER, JEROME JACOB, insurance company executive; b. Detroit, May 30, 1957; s. Austin A. and Harriet (Egrin) K.; m. Sherry Lynn Grossinger, Aug. 9, 1980; children: Jason Aaron, Joshua Samuel. BA, U. Mich., 1979; JD, Wayne State U., 1982. Agent Nat. Life of Vt., Detroit, 1980—, middle mgr., 1985-89, asst. gen. agent, 1990—; gen. agent, 1991—; chief oper. officer Kanter & Assocs., ABG, Detroit, 1989-91; gen. agt. Nat. Life of Vt., Detroit, 1991—. Mem. Mich. Gen. Agts. and Mgrs. Assn. (pres. S.E. chpt. 1996-97), Greater Detroit Assn. Life Underwriters, Gen. Agts. and Mrs. Assn., Southeast Mich. Agts. and Mgrs. Assn. (bd. dirs. 1991), Nat. Assn. Life Underwriters. Avocations: sailing, horseback riding, sports.

KANTER, L. ERICK, public relations executive; b. New Ulm, Tex., Dec. 15, 1942; s. Lawrence and Wilma A. (Kellner) K.; m. Mary Anne Meadows, Feb. 28, 1970. Staff reporter, Newsweek Mag., Boston, 1965-66, Newsweek Mag., Boston, 1970-71. Dir. media rels. U.S. Pay Bd. and Cost of Living Coun., Washington, 1971-74; dep. dir. pub. affairs NOAA, Washington, 1974-77; dir. pub. affairs White House Conf. on Econ. Devel., Washington, 1977-78, Presdl. Commn. on Coal Industry, Washington, 1978-80; cons. Energy Concepts, Inc., Washington, 1980-84; v.p. pub. info. and mktg. Investment Co. Inst., Washington, 1984-95; with Kanter & Assocs., Arlington, Va., 1995—. Co-author: Four Days, Forty Hours, 1970; editor: Final Report, White House Conference, 1978, Final Report, President's Commission on Coal, 1979. Lt. (j.g.) USN, 1967-69, Vietnam, the Pentagon. Mem. Nat. Press Club, Soc. Profl. Journalists. Avocations: photography, fishing. Office: Kanter & Assocs 5313 Lee Hwy 2d Fl Arlington VA 22207-1607

KANTER, LYNN, writer; b. Chgo., June 10, 1954; d. Lois W. and Julian Paul K. BA, Kirkland Coll., 1976. Proposal writer Ctr. Cmty. Change, Washington, 1992—. Author: On Lill Street, 1992, The Mayor of Heaven, 1997; writer (documentary) Fighting for the Obvious, 1982. E-mail: Lynnkanter@aol.com.

KANTER, ROSABETH MOSS, management educator, consultant, writer; b. Cleve., Mar. 15, 1943; d. Nelson Nathan and Helen (Smolen) Moss; m. Stuart Alan Kanter, June 20, 1963 (dec. Mar. 1969); m. Barry Alan Stein, July 2, 1972; 1 child, Matthew Moss Kanter Stein. BA in Sociology magna cum laude, Bryn Mawr Coll., 1964; MA, U. Mich., 1965, PhD, 1967; postgrad., Harvard U. Law Sh., 1975-76; MA (hon.), Yale U., 1978, Harvard U., 1986; DSc (hon.), Bucknell U., 1980, Babson Coll., 1984, Bryant Coll., 1986, Bentley Coll., 1990, U. Mass., Boston, 1996; LHD (hon.), Antioch U., Westminster Coll., 1984, Suffolk U., N. Adams State Coll., 1987, Colby-Sawyer Coll., 1988, U. New Haven, 1989; DCL (hon.), Union Coll., 1987; LLD (hon.), Regis Coll., 1987; DSS (hon.), Fla. Internat. U., 1990; DHL (hon.), SUNY Inst. Tech., 1991, Dowling Coll., 1991, Claremont Coll., 1992, Monmouth Coll., 1994, U. Mass., Boston, 1996. Vis. prof. mgmt. Harvard U., 1973-74, MIT, 1979-80; from assoc. to asst. prof. Brandeis U., 1967-77; prof. Yale U., 1977-86; Class of 1960 prof. bus. adminstrn. Harvard U. Bus. Sch., 1986—; chmn. bd. Goodmeasure, Inc., 1977—; trustee Coll. Retirement Equities Fund, N.Y., 1985-89, Am. Leadership Forum, Houston, 1982-86; mem. work group on entrepreneurship Pres.'s Commn. Indsl. Competitiveness, 1984; Govs.'s innovation adv. com. Commonwealth of Mass, chair subcom., 1986; mem. Spl. Commn. on Employee Involvement and Ownership, Mass., 1986-87; mem. Gov.'s Commn. Rev. Anti-Takeover Laws, Mass. 1988; mem. Gov.'s Counc. Econ. Growth, Mass., 1994—, co-chair internat. trade task force, 1995—; Katz-Newcomb lectr. in social psychology U. Mich., 1986; Disting. speaker Orgn., Theory, Careers and Women in Mgmt. divs. Nat. Acad. Mgmt., 1987, Eastern Acad. Mgmt., 1993; Centenniel lectr. APA, 1992; Lilly Found. Disting. lectr. Nat. Assn. Community Leadership Orgns., 1985; Leavey Disting. lectr. U. Santa Clara, 1984; vis. scholar Newberry Libr. Program in Humanities, Chgo., 1973, Norwegian Rsch. Coun. on Sci., and Humanities, Oslo, 1980; Kellogg Found. 50th Anniv. lectr. Am. Assn. Higher Edn., 1979, Blazer lectr. U. Ky., 1974, Davidson lectr. U. N.H., 1975; Sigma Chi scholar-in-residence Miami U., Oxford, Ohio, 1978; bd. dirs. Am. Productivity and Quality Ctr., Houston. Author: Work and Family in the U.S., 1977, Men and Women of the Corporation, 1977 (C. Wright Mills award 1977), 93, The Change Masters, 1983, (with M.S. Dukakis) Creating The Future: The Massachussetts Comeback and Its Promise for America, 1988, When Giants Learn to Dance, 1989 (Johnson Smith Knisely Exec. Leadership award 1990), (with B.A. Stein and T.F. Jick) The Challenge of Organizational Change: How Companies Experience It and Leaders Guide It, 1992, World Class: Thriving Locally in the Global Economy, 1995, Rosabeth Moss Kanter on the Frontiers of Management, 1997; 6 other books, also monographs; mem. editorial bd. Human Resource Mgmt. jour., 1982-89, Orgn. Dynamics jour., 1983-85, 89, Jour. Bus. Venturing, 1985-89, Jour. Contemporary Bus., 2987-89, others; adv. bd. Society jour., 1987-89; editor Harvard Bus. Rev., 1989-92; contbr. over 150 articles to profl. jours., books, mags. (articles Harvard Bus. Rev. McKinsey award). Bd. dirs. Alliance for the Commonwealth, 1995—, City Yr., 1995—, NOW Legal Def. and Edn. Fund, N.Y.C., 1979-86, 93-95, Ctr. New Democracy, Washington, 1985-88, Am. Prodn. and Quality Ctr., Houston, 1989—, Econ. Policy Inst., 1994—; incorporator Babson Coll., 1984-87, Boston Children's Mus., 1984—, Mt. Auburn Hosp., 1991—; bd. overseers Malcolm Baldridge Nat. Quality Award U.S. Dept. Commerce, 1994—. Guggenheim fellow; numerous rsch. grants; named Woman of Yr. New Eng. Women's Bus. Owners, 1981, Internat. Assn. Personnel Women, 1981, MS Mag., 1985; named to Cleve. Heights H.S. Hall of Fame, 1986, Working Woman Hall of Fame AT&T/Working Women Mag., 1986, Ohio Women's Hall of Fame, 1990; recipient Athena award Intercollegiate Assn. Women Students, 1980, Gold medal award Big Sister Assn. Greater Boston, 1985, Women Who Make a Difference award Internat. Women's Forum, 1988, Richard M. Cyert award Profl. Excellence Carnegie-Mellon U. Grad. Sch. Indsl. Adminstrn., 1989, Project Equality award, 1990, Crohn's and Colitis Found. award, 1993, 1994, McFeely award YMCA, 1995, Leadership award New Eng. Coun., 1995. Fellow Acad. Mgmt. (Disting. speaker mgmt. cons. divsn. 1985, women in mgmt. divsn. 1987, orgn. mgmt. theory divsn. 1994, Disting. Scholar award OMT divsn. 1994), Am. Soc. Quality & Participation, World Productivity Cong. (Ams. divsn.), World Econ. Forum; mem. Am. Sociol. Assn. (exec. coun. 1982-85), Eastern Sociol. Soc. (exec. com. 1975-78, Gellman award 1978), Soc. for Advancement of Socio-Econs., Com. of 200 (founder), Internat. Women's Forum, Coun. on Fgn. Rels. Avocations: tennis, swimming. Office: Harvard Bus Sch Grad Sch Bus Adminstrn Soldiers Field Rd Boston MA 02163*

KANTNER, HELEN JOHNSON, church education administrator; b. Chgo., Oct. 22, 1936; d. Wilbert E. and Edna M. (Benson) Johnson; m. Robert O. Kantner, Aug. 22, 1959; children: Robert O. Jr., Sheryl Jackson. BA, Wheaton Coll., 1958; MS in Education, Youngstown State U., 1987. Asst. to prin. 1st Bapt. Day Sch., West Palm Beach, Fla., 1970-72; elem. tchr. Am. Heritage Schs., Ft. Lauderdale, Fla., 1973-76; social studies tchr. Champion High Sch., Warren, Ohio, 1977-88; edn. dir. Ocean Dr. Presbyn. Ch., North Myrtle Beach, S.C., 1988—. Vice pres. bd. dirs. Horry County (S.C.) Arts Coun.; bd. dirs. Christian Acad. of Myrtle Beach. Youngstown State U. scholar. Mem. NEA, Ohio Edn. Assn., Champion Classroom Tchrs. Home: 3610 Golf Ave Little River SC 29566-6049 Office: 410 6th Ave S North Myrtle Beach SC 29582-3306

KANTOR, MEL LEWIS, dental educator, researcher; b. N.Y.C., 1956; s. Irving and Sarah Kantor. BA in Chemistry and Math., CUNY, 1977; DDS, U. N.C., 1981; MPH, U. Medicine and Dentistry N.J., Rutgers U., 1999. Diplomate Am. Bd. Oral and Maxillofacial Radiology. Resident Hennepin County Med. Ctr., Mpls., 1981-82, U. Conn. Health Ctr., Farmington, 1982-84; asst. prof. U. N.C. Sch. Dentistry, Chapel Hill, 1984-88, U. Conn. Sch. of Dental Medicine, Farmington, 1988-92; assoc. prof. N.J. Dental Sch., U. Medicine and Dentistry N.J., Newark, 1993—, clin. assoc. prof. N.J. Med. Sch., 1993—; health svcs. rsch. fellow Robert Wood Johnson Med. Sch., 1997-99; cons. dental selection criteria panel FDA, 1985-87; test constructor Nat. Bd. Dental Examinations, 1989-93, 96—. Assoc. editor Jour. Dental Edn., 1986—; mem. editl. bd. Dentomaxillofacial Radiology, 1997—; contbr. articles to Jour. Chem. Physics, Jour. ADA, Jour. Dental Rsch., Oral Surgery, Oral Medicine and Oral Pathology, Jour. Dental Edn., Dentomaxillofacial Radiology. Mem. Internat. Assn. Dental Rsch. (founding mem. diagnostic sys. group, group program chmn. 1993-97), Am. Acad. Oral and Maxillofacial Radiology (constitution and bylaws com., splty. recognition com., nominating com.), Am. Assn. Dental Schs. (steering com. competency-based predoctoral edn. initiative), Internat. Assn. Dentomaxillofacial Radiology, Radiol. Soc. N.Am., Soc. for Med. Decision Making, Soc. for Health Svcs. Rsch. in Radiology, Phi Beta Kappa, Sigma Xi, Omicron Kappa Upsilon. Office: UMDNJ-NJ Dental Sch 110 Bergen St Rm C827 Newark NJ 07103-2400

KANTOR, SIMON WILLIAM, chemistry educator; b. Brussels, Belgium, Mar. 23, 1925; came to U.S., 1939, naturalized, 1946; s. Joseph Uszer and Josephine (Perez) K.; m. Karen Christine Eisenbeiser, 1989; children from previous marriage: Michael Bruce, Sharon Inez; stepchildren: Michael John Eisenbeiser, Jason James Eisenbeiser, Justin Ryan Eisenbeiser. B.S., City Coll. N.Y., 1945; Ph.D., Duke U., 1949. Postdoctoral fellow Duke U., 1949-51; research asso. Gen. Electric Co. Research and Devel. Center, Schenectady, 1951-60; sect. mgr. Gen. Electric Co. Research and Devel. Center, 1960-65, br. mgr., 1965-72; v.p. research and devel. GAF Corp., Wayne, N.J., 1972-82; prof. U. Mass., Amherst, 1982—. Contbr. articles to chem. jours. Mem. Am. Chem. Soc., AAAS, Soc. Chem. Industry, Indsl. Research Inst., Phi Beta Kappa, Phi Lambda Upsilon. Patentee in field. Home: 153 Silver Lake Dr Agawam MA 01001-2351 Office: U Mass Dept Polymer Sci & Engring 629 Conte Amherst MA 01003

KANTROWITZ, ADRIAN, surgeon, educator; b. N.Y.C., Oct. 4, 1918; s. Bernard Abraham and Rose (Esserman) K.; m. Jean Rosensaft, Nov. 25, 1948; children: Niki, Lisa, Allen. AB, NYU, 1940; MD, L.I. Coll. Medicine, 1943; postgrad. physiology, Western Res. U., 1950. Diplomate: Am. Bd. Surgery, Am. Bd. Thoracic Surgery. Gen. rotating intern Jewish Hosp. Bklyn., 1944; asst. resident, then resident surgery Mt. Sinai Hosp., N.Y.C., 1947; asst. resident Montefiore Hosp., N.Y.C., 1948; asst. resident pathology Montefiore Hosp., 1949, fellow cardiovascular rsch. group, 1949, chief resident surgery, 1950, adj. surg. svc., 1951-55; USPHS fellow cardiovascular rsch., dept. physiology Western Res. U., 1951-52; asst. prof. surgery SUNY Coll. Medicine, 1955-56, assoc. prof. surgery, 1957-64, prof., 1964-70; dir. cardiovascular surgery Maimonides Med. Ctr., Bklyn., 1955-64; dir. surgery Maimonides Med. Ctr., 1964-70; chmn. dept. surgery Sinai Hosp. Detroit, 1970-75, chmn. dept. cardiovascular surgery, 1975-85; prof. surgery Wayne State U. Sch. Medicine, 1970—. Contbr. articles profl. jours. 1st lt. to capt., M.C. AUS, 1944-46. Recipient H.L. Moses prize to Montefiore Alumnus for outstanding rsch. accomplishment, 1949; 1st prize sci. exhibit Conv. N.Y. State Med. Soc., 1952; Gold Plate award Am. Acad. Achievement, 1966; Max Berg award for outstanding achievement in prolonging human life, 1966; Theodore and Susan B. Cummings humanitarian award Am. Coll. Cardiology, 1967. Fellow ACS, N.Y. Acad. Sci.; mem. Internat. Soc. Angiology, Am. Soc. Artificial Internal Organs (pres. 1968-69, Barney Clark award 1993), N.Y. County Med. Soc., Harvey Soc., N.Y. Soc. Thoracic Surgery, N.Y. Soc. Cardiovascular Surgery, Am. Heart Assn., Am. Physiol. Soc., Am. Coll. Cardiology, Am. Coll. Chest Physicians, Bklyn. Thoracic Surgery Soc. (pres. 1967-68), Pan Am. Med. Assn., Soaring Soc. Am., Am. Ski Assn. Pub. pioneer motion pictures taken inside living heart, 1950; contbr. to devel. pump- oxygenators for human heart surgey; pioneer devel. mech., artificial hearts; performed 1st permanent partial mech. heart surgery in humans, 1966; 1st use phase-shift intra-aortic balloon pump in patient in cardiogenic shock; 1st human heart transplant in U.S., Dec. 1967. Home: 70 Gallogly Rd Auburn Hills MI 48326-1227 Office: 300 River Place Dr Detroit MI 48207-4225

KANTROWITZ, ARTHUR, physicist, educator; b. N.Y.C., N.Y., Oct. 20, 1913; s. Bernard A. and Rose (Esserman) K.; m. Rosalind Joseph, Sept. 12, 1943 (div.); children: Barbara, Lore, Andrea; m. Lee Stuart, Dec. 25, 1980. B.S., Columbia U., 1934, M.A., 1936, Ph.D., 1947; DEng (hon.), Mont. Coll. Mineral Sci. and Tech., 1975; D.Sc. (hon.), N.J. Inst. Tech., 1981. Physicist NACA, 1935-46; prof. aero. engring. and engring. physics Cornell U., 1946-56; founder, dir., chmn., chief exec. officer Avco-Everett

Research Lab., Everett, Mass., 1955-78; sr. v.p., dir. Avco Corp., 1956-79; prof. Thayer Sch. Engring., Dartmouth Coll., 1978—; vis. lectr. Harvard U., 1952; Fulbright and Guggenheim fellow Cambridge and Manchester univs., 1954; fellow Sch. Advanced Study, MIT, 1957, vis. inst. prof., 1957—; Joseph Wunsch lectr. Technion, Haifa, Israel, 1968; mem., fellow lectr. Am. Inst. Chemists, 1977; Messenger lectr. Cornell U., 1978; 1st Hastings lectr. NIH, 1977; hon. prof. Huazhong Inst. Tech., Wuhan, China, 1980; mem. Presdl. Adv. Group on Anticipated Advances in Sci. and Tech., head task force on sci. ct., 1975-76; mem. tech. adv. bd. U.S. Dept. Commerce, 1974-77; mem. adv. panel NOVA, Sta. WGBH-TV, 1975—; bd. overseers Center for Naval Analyses, 1973-83; mem. adv. council Israel-U.S. Binational Indsl. Research and Devel. Found., 1978-81; bd. govs. The Technion (hon. life); mem. adv. council NASA, 1979, 80; life trustee U. Rochester; past mem. sci. and engring. adv. com. U. Rochester, Princeton U., Stanford U. and Rensselaer Poly Inst.; vis. prof. U. Calif., Berkeley, 1983. Contbr. articles to profl. jours.; patentee in field. Bd. dirs. Hertz Found., 1972—. Recipient award Am. Acad. Achievement, 1966, Theodore Roosevelt medal, 1967, Kayan medal Columbia U., 1973, MHD Faraday Meml. medal UNESCO, 1983. Fellow AAAS, AIAA (1st Von Kármán lectr. 1964, Fluid and Plasmadynamics medal 1981, Aerospace Contbn. to Soc. award 1990, hon. fellow 1998), Am. Acad. Arts and Scis., Am. Phys. Soc., Am. Astronautical Soc., Am. Inst. for Med. and Biol. Engring.; mem. NAS, NAE, Internat. Acad. Astronautics, Am. Inst. Physics, Sigma Xi. Achievements include high-energy lasers, heart assist devices, MHD generators, re-entry from space; early work in fusion and molecular beams noteable. Email address: ark@dartmouth.edu. Home: 4 Downing Rd Hanover NH 03755-1902

KANTROWITZ, JEAN ROSENSAFT, research program administrator medical products; b. Passaic, N.J., May 27, 1922; d. Nathan and Yetta (Applebaum) Rosensaft; m. Adrian Kantrowitz, Nov. 25, 1948; children: Niki, Lisa, Allen. BS, Rider Coll., 1942; MS, U. N.C., 1945; MPH, U. Mich., 1975. Adminstrv. asst. Maimonides Med. Ctr., Bklyn., 1961-70, Sinai Hosp., Detroit, 1970-78, '80-83; program coord., sr. clin. instr. child psycíatry divsn. Case Western Res. U. Sch. Medicine, Cleve., 1978-80; v.p., adminstrv. mgr. L.VAD Tech., Inc., Detroit, 1983—; mgmt. cons. NIH, Washington, 1974—. Mem. Am. Soc. Artificial Internal Organs (co-chairperson history work group). Home: 70 Gallogly Rd Auburn Hills MI 48326-1227 Office: LVAD Tech Inc 300 River Place # 6850 Detroit MI 48207-4225*

KANTROWITZ, MELANIE KAYE, writer; b. Sept. 9, 1945. BA, CCNY-CUNY, 1966; MA, U. Calif., Berkeley, 1968; PhD, U. Calif., 1975. Exec. dir. Jews for Racial and Econ. Justice, N.Y.C., 1992-95; Jane Watson Irwin Disting. prof. Hamilton Coll., Clinton, N.Y., 1995-97; Belle Zeller Disting. prof. Bklyn. Coll.-CUNY, 1997—. E-mail: mkk@netstep.net.

KANTROWITZ, SUSAN LEE, lawyer; b. Queens, N.Y., Jan. 15, 1955; d. Theodore and Dinah (Kotick) Kantrowitz; m. Mark R. Halperin; 1 child, Jacob Joseph Kantrowitz-Sirotkin. BS summa cum laude, Boston U., 1977; JD, Boston Coll., 1980. Bar: Mass. 1982. Assoc. producer Sta. KOCE-TV, Huntington Beach, Calif., 1980-81; acct. exec. Bozell & Jacobs, Newport Beach, Calif., 1981; atty. WGBH Ednl. Found., Boston, 1981-84, dir. legal affairs, 1984-86, gen. counsel, dir. legal affairs, 1986—, v.p., gen. counsel, 1993. Co-author: Legal and Business Aspects of the Entertainment, Publishing and Sports Industries, 1984. Mem. ABA, Mass. Bar Assn., Boston Bar Assn.

KANUK, LESLIE LAZAR, management consultant, educator; b. N.Y.C.; d. Charles and Sylvia Lazar; m. Jack Lawrence Kanuk; children: Randi Kanuk Dauler, Alan Robert. MBA, Baruch Coll., 1964; PhD, CUNY, 1974; PhD (hon.), Mass. Maritime Acad., 1981, Maine Maritime Acad., 1988. Pres. Leslie Kanuk Assocs., mgmt. cons., 1965-78, 81—; Lippert chair, prof. mktg. Baruch Coll., N.Y.C., 1981—; bd. dirs. Cleve. Cliffs Inc.; mem. maritime transp. research bd. Nat. Acad. Scis., 1975-78; commr., vice chmn., chmn. Fed. Maritime Commn., 1978-81; chmn., pres., dir. Containerization and Intermodal Inst., 1981-93; panelist NRC-NAS, 1975-78, 91; vis. prof. grad. studies program Maine Maritime Acad., 1984-93. Author: Mail Questionnaire Response Behavior, 1974, Toward an Expanding U.S.M.M., 1976, Consumer Behavior, 1978, rev. edits., 1983, 87, 89, 94, 97; mem. editorial bd. Intermodal Forum, 1984-92. Trustee United Seamen's Svc., 1988—; bd. visitors Maine Maritime Acad., 1989-97. Recipient Connie award Containerization and Intermodal Inst., 1980, Diamond Superwoman award Harpers Bazaar mag., 1980, Person of Yr. award N.Y. Fgn. Freight Forwarders and Brokers Assn., 1981, Person of Yr. award Baruch Fgn. Trade Soc., 1981, Disting. Alumnus award CCNY, 1984, Disting. PhD Alumni award CUNY, 1988, Townsend Harris medal, 1986. Mem. Beta Gamma Sigma. Office: 700 New Hampshire Ave NW Washington DC 20037

KANUSHER, LAWRENCE ALLEN, lawyer; b. Suffern, N.Y., Apr. 6, 1962; s. Joseph Morris and Carole Leona (Epstein) K.; m. Cindy J. Washor, Mar. 9, 1991; children: Samuel Jason, Alyson Dale. BA in Polit. Sci., Union Coll., Schenectady, N.Y., 1984; JD, Bklyn. Law Sch., 1988. Law clk. Judge Mitchell H. Cohen U.S. Dist. Ct. N.J., Camden, N.J., 1988-89; atty. Gold, Farrell & Marks, N.Y.C., 1989-90; atty. bus. affairs EMI Records, N.Y.C., 1990-92; dir. bus. affairs Sony Music Internat., N.Y.C., 1992-95; sr. counsel law dept. Sony Music Entertainment Inc., N.Y.C., 1995-98; v.p. bus. affairs Island Records, Inc., N.Y.C., 1998—. Contbr. chpt./article to Entertainment Industry Contracts. Mem. NARAS, Assn. Bar of City of N.Y. Fax: (212) 333-1069. E-mail: kanusher@us.polygram.com. Office: Island Records Inc 825 Eighth Ave New York NY 10019

KANWAR, ANJU, English educator; b. Delhi, India, Sept. 18, 1962; d. Lachhman Dass and Updesh Kujan (Mehta) K. BA in English with honors, U. Delhi, 1983, MA in English, 1986; PhD in English, No. Ill. U., 1995. Lectr. U. Delhi, 1986-88; instr. Triton Coll., River Grove, Ill., 1993, Coll. DuPage, Glen Ellyn, Ill., 1993-94, Waubonsee Cmty. Coll., Sugar Grove, Ill., 1993, 96—; temporary asst. prof. dept. English No. Ill. U., DeKalb, 1993-94; vis. lectr. North Cen. Coll., Naperville, Ill., 1998, 99. Author: The Sound of Silence, 1999; contbr. articles to profl. jours. Recipient Outstanding Svc. award Children's World Learning Ctr., 1996. Mem. MLA. Avocations: music, reading, theatre. Home: 30w049 Granada Ct Apt 104 Naperville IL 60563-1926 Office: Waubonsee Cmty Coll Route 47 at Harter Rd Sugar Grove IL 60554

KANWAR, DEEPAK VINEET, telecommunications company executive; b. Lucknow, India, Nov. 10, 1959; s. Shiv N. and Sunila (Chaudhri) K.; m. Cindy C. Collins, Sept. 6, 1987; children: Ishan A., Anjali S. BSEE, Indian Inst. of Tech., 1980; MS in Computer Sci., Ohio State U., 1983. Software engr. Advanced Programming Resolutions, Columbus, 1983-84, group leader, 1984-86; mem. tech. staff AT&T Bell Labs., Columbus, 1986-88, supr. software devel., 1988-90, tech. mgr., 1990-94, mgr., 1994-95; dir. Lucent Techs., Brussels, 1995-96; dir. Lucent Techs., Columbus, 1996-98, group dir. network surveillance unit, 1998—; chief architect AT&T Network Systems (TNM), Columbus, 1990-92, project mgr., 1992-94; chair OS Unix Users Group, U.S., 1987. Pres. Asian Americans for Affirmative Action, AT&T Columbus, 1986-87. Avocations: certified scuba diver, squash, travel. Home: 6331 Little Deer Ln Columbus OH 43213-3488 Office: Lucent Techs 6200 E Broad St Rm 3q233 Columbus OH 43213-1530

KANY, JUDY C(ASPERSON), health policy analyst, former state senator; b. June 29, 1937; d. Helmer C. and Florence P. Casperson; m. Robert Kany, Aug. 16, 1958; children: Kristin, Geoffrey, Daniel. BBA, U. Mich., 1959; MPA, U. Maine-Orono, 1976. Mem. Maine Ho. Reps., 1975-82, Maine Senate, 1982-92; project dir. for health professions regulation Med. Care Devel., Augusta, Maine, 1993-97; mem. Pew Health Professions Commn. task force on health workforce regulation, 1994-97; chmn. Maine's Adv. Commn. on Radioactive Waste, 1981-87, Joint Standing Com. Legal Affairs, 1987-88, Joint Standing Com. on State Govt., 1979-82, Joint Standing Com. Energy and Natural Resources, 1983-84, 89-90, Joint Standing Com. Banking and Ins., 1991-92, com. Maine Lakes, 1990-92, adv. com. on accountability to the Maine Health Care Reform Commn., 1994-95; mem. Commn. on Maine's Future, 1976, 87-89; mayor Waterville, Maine, 1988-89; mem. issues and policy adv. com. Citizens Advocacy Ctr., Washington, 1994—. Democrat. Home: 36832 S Stoney Flower Dr Tucson AZ 85739-1672 also: PO Box 508 Belgrade Lakes ME 04918-0508

KANZEG, DAVID GEORGE, radio programming director; b. Cleve., Apr. 9, 1948; s. George and Ida Marie Ada (Hienz) K. BA, Coll. Wooster (Ohio), 1970; MS, Syracuse (N.Y.) U., 1971; postgrad., SUNY, 1972. Cert. ESL lang. instr. Instr. English Meyer Lang. Ctr., Bogota, Colombia, 1969; grad. teaching asst. Syracuse U., 1971; instr. speech State U. Coll. at Buffalo, N.Y., 1971-73; exec. producer Sta. WCMU-FM Cen. Mich. U., Mt. Pleasant, 1973-76; radio program mgr. Sta. WLRH/Madison County Pub. Libr., Huntsville, Ala., 1976-77; radio program dir. Sta. WOUB-AM-FM Ohio U. Telecommunications, Athens, 1977-83; mgr. programming Sta. WNYC/N.Y. Pub. Radio, N.Y.C., 1983-86; sta. advisor Corp. for Pub. Broadcasting, Cleve., 1978-87; dir. programming Sta. WCPN/Cleve. Pub. Radio, 1987—; cons. Corp. for Pub. Broadcasting Mgmt. Consulting Svc., 1993—; participant seminars on future pub. radio, San Francisco and Washington, 1984-85; panel mem. Airlie IV Seminar on Art of Radio, N.Y.C., 1983; radio organizer Nat. Assn. Ednl. Broadcasters, Washington, 1976-78; exec. producer Future Forward Nat. Radio Series, 1985. Author: Transit Revisions, 1988, Ever Young: Douglas Moore and the Persistence of Legend, 1993; contbr. articles to publs; author, co-creator website. Mem. Isabella County sub-com. on transp., Mt. Pleasant, Mich., 1975; incorporator Mid-Mich. Opera Assn., Mt. Pleasant, 1975, Tenn. Valley Opera Assn., Hunstville, 1976; mem. media panel Ohio Arts Coun., Columbus, Ohio, 1979-80; active Airlie II Seminar on Art of Radio, 1979. Recipient Tech. Prodn. award Ohio Ednl. Broadcasting, 1980, Ohio State award, 1986. Mem. Ohio Pub. Radio Programming (group chmn. 1978-80), Assn. Inds. in Radio, No. Ohio Bibliophilic Soc., Sigma Delta Pi. Avocations: roller coasters, opera, traction, bicycling, travel. Home: 16253 Shurmer Rd Cleveland OH 44136-6115 Office: Sta WCPN/Cleve Pub Radio 3100 Chester Ave Ste 300 Cleveland OH 44114-4604

KANZER, LARRY, small business owner, food service director; b. Albany, N.Y., June 13, 1942; s. Sanford and Beatrice Helen (Strick) K.; m. Ginger Sherman, July 13, 1966 (div. 1983); 1 child, Glen Harris; m. Lynn Karen Trost, June 2, 1985. AAS in Culinary Arts, N.Y.C. Community Coll., 1962; Cert. Food Service supr. Auburn U., 1982-83; Master Locksmith, Foley Belsaw Inst., 1985. Food beverage controller Longchamps Restaurants, N.Y.C., 1962-65; dir. food service Laurelcrest Prep Sch., Bristol, Conn., 1965-69; owner, operator Anze's Place Restaurant, Nashua, N.H., 1969-73; dir. food service Servend-Seilers, Waltham, Mass., 1973-76, Service Systems, Cambridge, Mass., 1976-78, ARA Services, White Plains, N.Y., 1978-88; owner Lots of Lock, Etc., 1988—. Com. chmn. Cub Scouts Am., Nashua, 1977-80; umpire Little League, Nashua, 1978-81. Served to sgt. USMCR, 1963-69. Recipient Otto Klitgord Meml. award N.Y.C. Community Coll., Bklyn., 1962, Student Govt. Service award, 1962; Cert. of Merit Jewish War Vets. of U.S., Bronx, N.Y., 1982, Cert. and Publ. Locksmith Ledger, Nat. Locksmith, Cert. Cmty. Svc., Pike County Sheriff's Office. Mem. Pike County C. of C. Democrat. Avocations: gunsmithing, clock repair, woodworking, antiques, gardening. Office: Lots of Lock Etc Locksmith Shop Hemlock Plz Rt 739 Hawley PA 18428

KANZLER, GEORGE, journalist, critic; b. Elizabeth, N.J., Mar. 30, 1939; s. George and Helen (Yorkunas) K.; m. Margaret A. Dudas, Dec. 31, 1978; children; Sarah Ella Dudas-Kanzler. BA, Seton Hall U., 1960; postgrad. Bread Loaf Sch. of English, Middlebury Coll., 1960; MA, NYU, 1969; postgrad., U. Wis., 1972. Reporter, editor Linden (N.J.) Leader, 1961-63; instr., asst. prof. Ibadan (Nigeria) Polytech., 1966-68; writer, pop and jazz critic Star Ledger, Newark, 1968-90, writer, jazz critic, 1990—; writer, jazz critic Newhouse News Svc., Washington, 1975—; jazz disc jockey We. Nigeria Radio, Ibadan, 1966-68; instr. Essex C.C., Newark, 1970-73; elector Am. Jazz Hall of Fame, 1989—. Author: (TV show) One Way to Heaven, 1967. V.p. bd. dirs. Newark Jazz Festival, 1991-93; vol. U.S. Peace Corps. With U.S. Army, 1963-65, Congo. Fellow Newspaper Fund, 1972, Music Critics Assn./Smithsonian Inst., 1974. Mem. Nat. Acad. Recording Arts and Scis., Friends of Nigeria, Mbari Artists and Writers Club (sec. pro-tem. 1966-68), Jazz Journalists Assn., N.Y. Jazz Critics Cir. Avocations: hiking, unicycling. Home: 124 Reynolds Pl South Orange NJ 07079-2622 Office: Newark Morning Ledger Co One Star Ledger Plz Newark NJ 07102-1200

KAO, CHARLES KUEN, electrical engineer, educator; b. Shanghai, China, Nov. 4, 1933; s. Chun-Hsien and Tisung Fong K.; m. May Wan Wong, Sept. 19, 1959; children—Simon M.T., Amanda M.C. B.Sc. in Elec. Engring., U. London, 1957, Ph.D. in Elec. Engring., 1965. Devel. engr. Standard Telephones & Cables Ltd., London, 1957-60; prin. research engr. Standard Telecommunications Lab. Ltd., Harlow, Eng., 1960-70; prof. electronics, chmn. dept. Chinese U. Hong Kong, 1970-74, vice chancellor, 1987-96; chief scientist Electro Optical Products div./ITT, Roanoke, Va., 1974-81; v.p., dir. engring. Electro Optical Products div./ITT, Roanoke, VA, 1981-83; exec. scientist, dir. research ITT Advanced Tech. Ctr., Shelton, Conn., 1983-87; chmn., CEO Transtech Svcs. Ltd., Hong Kong, 1996—. Author: Optical Fiber Technology II, 1981, Optical Fibers Systems: Technology, Design and Applications, 1982, Optical Fibre, 1988, A Choice Fulfilled--The Business of High Technology, 1991; contbr. articles to profl. jours.; patentee in field. Decorated Commdr. Brit. Empire, 1993; recipient Morey award Am. Ceramic Soc., 1976, Stewart Ballantine medal Franklin Inst., 1977, Rank prize Rank Trust Funds, 1978, LM Ericsson Internat. prize, 1979, gold medal Armed Forces Comm. and Electronics Assn., 1980, Internat. C & C prize Found. for C & C Promotion, Japan, 1987, New Materials prize Am. Phys. Soc., 1989, Gold medal Internat. Soc. for Optical Engring., 1992, Japan prize The Sci. and Tech. Found. Japan, 1996; Marconi Internat. fellow, 1985. Fellow IEEE (Morris Liebmann Meml. award 1978, Alexander Graham Bell medal 1985, Faraday medal 1989), Inst. Elec. Engring. (U.K.), Chinese Acad. Scis., Royal Soc. (U.K.), Royal Acad. Engring. (U.K.), Royal Swedish Acad. Engring. Scis. (fgn. mem.), Academia Sinica (Taiwan); mem. NAE (U.S.). Office: Telecom House Rm 1641, 3 Gloucester Rd, Wan Chai Hong Kong

KAO, WILLIAM CHISHON, dentist; b. Santiago, Chile, July 10, 1952; s. John S. and Mary Kao; m. Susie M. Moy, June 3, 1978; children: Jonathan, Kristen. BS with high honors, U. Ill., Chgo., 1974, BS in Dentistry with honors, 1976, DDS with honors, 1978. Comprehensive inst. U. Ill. Coll. Dentistry, Chgo., 1978-80; dentist, assoc. Dental Bldg., Oak Lawn, Ill., 1978-83; pvt. practice Carol Stream, Ill., 1978-82; dentist Preventive Dental Group, Glendale Heights, Ill., 1982-86; pvt. practice Roselle, Ill., 1986—. Mem. ADA (presiding chmn. ltd. attendance clinic at midwinter conv. 1980), Am. Acad. Implant Dentistry, U.S. Dental Inst., Ill. State Dental Soc., Chgo. Dental Soc., Ill. Dental Soc., Roselle C. of C., Bloomingdale Study Club, Bloomingdale Study Club (pres.). Avocation: tennis. Office: 1150 Lake St Roselle IL 60172-3350

KAPANKA, HEIDI, emergency physician; b. Bronxville, N.Y., Dec. 29, 1953; d. Louis John Kapanka and Orla M. Smith. BA cum laude, Boston U., 1976, MD, 1980; MPH, U. Tex., Houston, 1987. Diplomate Am. Bd. Emergency Physicians. Intern Naval Regional Med. Ctr., San Diego, 1980-81; resident in emergency medicine U. Fla. Health Svcs., Jacksonville, 1987-89, U. Ala., Birmingham, 1989-90; attending staff, physician Life Saver Helicopter, Carraway Meth. Med. Ctr., Birmingham, 1992—, dir. med. control, 1992—; flight surgeon USN, 1982-85, NASA Space Shuttle Program, 1985-86; organizer, spkr. EMT Day, 1994-96; inst. ACL; reviewer quality assurance. Vol. emergency physician 1996 Olympic Games, Birmingham, Ala., 1996, PGA Golf Tournament, 1996, NASCAR Races, Talladega Speedway, 1996, 99, Rolling Stones concert, U. Ala. football games, BDCTA Horse Show; guest spkr. on flight medicine local schs., colls., U. Ala., Boy Scouts, Civic Leaders Breakfast Club, 1990-96; violinist, bd. dirs. Red Mountain Chamber Orch., 1990—. Fellow Am. Coll. Emergency Physicians; mem. AMA, Soc. NASA Flight Surgeons, Jefferson County Med. Soc. Mem. LDS Ch. Office: Carraway Meth Med Ctr 1600 Carraway Blvd Birmingham AL 35234-1913

KAPCSANDY, LOUIS ENDRE, building construction and manufacturing executive, chemical engineering consultant; b. Budapest, Hungary, June 5, 1936; came to U.S., 1957; s. Lajos Endre and Margit (Toth) K.; m. Roberta Marie Henson, Jan. 25, 1964; 1 son, Louis. B.S. in Chem. Engring., Tech. U. Hungary, 1956; postgrad. in law, U. San Francisco, 1963-64; M.S. in Petroleum Tech., U. Calif.-Berkeley, 1969. Freedom fighter Hungarian Revolution, Budapest, 1956; profl. football player San Diego Chargers, 1963-65; western regional mgr. Norton Co., San Francisco, 1965-72; product mgr. Koch Industries, Wichita, Kans., 1972-74; v.p., gen. mgr. Flow Systems, Inc., Seattle, 1974-78; pres. Fentron Bldg. Products, Inc., Seattle, 1978-85; CEO Baugh Enterprises Inc., Seattle, 1985—; chem. engring. cons. HK Assocs., Seattle, 1974—. Contbr. articles to profl. jours.; patentee vacuum fraction of crude oil, purification of hydrogen. Bd. dirs. Boy Scouts Chief Seattle, Seattle C. of C., Virginia Mason Med. Ctr.; active United for Wash., Seattle, 1982. With U.S. Army, 1959-62. Fellow AIChE; mem. Constrn. Specifications Inst., TAPPI, Columbia Tower Club, Washington Athletic Club, Rainier Club, Glendale Country Club, Seattle Rotary Lodge, PGA West. Republican. Roman Catholic.

KAPELMAN, BARBARA ANN, physician, educator; b. N.Y.C., Apr. 30, 1949; d. Leonard A. and Helen (Hass) K.; m. Lawrence William Koblenz, Mar. 24, 1979; 1 child, Adam. BA, Barnard Coll., 1970; MS in Microbiology, Yale U., 1972; MD, Albert Einstein Coll. Medicine, 1975. Diplomate Am. Bd. Internal Medicine, Am. Bd. Gastroenterology. Intern Roosevelt Hosp.-Columbia U., N.Y.C., 1975-76, resident, 1976-78, fellow gastroenterology, 1978-80; fellow liver diseases Mt. Sinai Sch. Medicine-CUNY, N.Y.C., 1980-81; asst. attending physician in gastroenterology Beth Israel Hosp., N.Y.C., 1982-88, assoc. attending physician in medicine and gastroenterology, 1988-96, attending physician in medicine and gastroenterology, 1996—; clin. instr. in medicine Mt. Sinai Sch. of Medicine, N.Y.C., 1981-87, asst. clin. prof. medicine, 1987-94; bd. dirs. Beth Israel Med. Ctr., N.Y.C., 1984—; asst. clin. prof. medicine Albert Einstein Coll. Medicine, N.Y.C., 1994—; attending physician Beth Israel North, Beth Israel Med. Ctr., N.Y.C., 1982—, Hosp. for Joint Diseases-Orthopedic Inst., N.Y.C., 1982—; vis. clin. fellow Columbia U. Coll. Physicians and Surgeons, N.Y.C., 1975-80. Co-author: Gastroenterology for the House Officer, 1989; contbr. articles to profl. jours. Fellow ACP, Am. Coll. Gastroenterology; mem. Am. Women's Med. Assn., Women's Med. Assn. N.Y.C. (officer), Am. Gastroent. Assn., Am. Assn. for Study of Liver Diseases, Am. Soc. for Gastrointestinal Endoscopy, Am. Med. Informatics Assn., N.Y. Acad. Gastroenterology, N.Y. Soc. for Gastrointestinal Endoscopy. Avocations: computers, culinary arts, educational activities. Office: 944 Park Ave New York NY 10028-0319

KAPETANAKOS, CHRISTOS ANASTASIOS, science administrator, physics educator; b. Xirokabi, Lakonia, Greece, Jan. 2, 1936; s. Anastasios and Alexandra (Doukas) K.; m. Ioanna Plafoutzi, June 23, 1962 (div. 1993); children: Anastasios, Yula. Diploma, Nat. U. Greece, Athens, 1960; M in Nuclear Engring., MIT, 1964; PhD, U. Md., 1970. Rschr. U. Tex., Austin, 1970-71; br. head, sect. head, rschr. Naval Rsch. Lab., Washington, 1971-92; acting dir. Inst. Plasma Physics, U. Crete, Iraklion, Crete, Greece, 1993-95; prof. of physics U. Crete, Iraklion, 1993-96; pres. Leading Egde Tech. Corp., Washington, 1995—; cons. Fuel and Mineral Resources, Reston, Va., Icarus Rsch. Inc. Bethesa MD., Naval Rsch. Lab., Washington, SFA. Inc., Largo, Md., FERMI Nat. Accelerator Lab. Patentee in field; contbr. over 100 articles to profl. publs. 2d lt. Artillery, 1960-62, Greece. Grantee Dept. Def., Washington, Dept. Energy, Washington, Office of Naval Rsch. Def. Advanced Project Agy., Washington, ELINOIL, Athens. Fellow Am. Phys. Soc., Washington Soc. Scis. Home: 4431 Macarthur Blvd NW Washington DC 20007-2564

KAPITAN, MARY L., retired nursing administrator, educator; b. Lawrence, Mass., July 9, 1920; d. Vincent and Concetta (Tomaselli) Zazzo; m. John A. Kapitan, Sept. 6, 1947. Diploma, Somerville (Mass.) Hosp., 1944; BS in Nursing Edn., DePaul U., Chgo., 1960, MS in Nursing Adminstrn., 1962. RN; lic. health facility adminstr., Ind. Occupational health nurse E. I. duPont de Nemours & Co., Lincolnwood, Ill., Senco Corp., Newtown, Ohio; asst. prof. psychiat. and med. nursing No. Ky. U., Highland Heights; nursing coord. VA Hosp., Butler, Pa.; instr. psychiat. nursing Ohio Valley Community Hosp., McKees Rocks, Pa.; dir. nursing svc. Presbyn. Home, Evanston, Ill., Edgewater Hosp., Chgo., Franklin Blvd Hosp., Chgo. 1st lt. U.S. Army Nurse Corps, 1944-47. Mem. ANA, Am. Assn. Occupational Health Nurses, Am. Coll. Health Facility Adminstrs., Ohio Nurses Assn., Ill. Nurses Assn., Ind. Nurses Assn., Mass. Nurses Assn., Southwestern Ohio Assn. Occupational Health Nurses (chmn. legislation and edn. com.), Women in Mil. Svc. for Am., Women's Meml. Found.

KAPLAN, ALAN LESLIE, gynecology educator, oncologist; b. Atlanta, Sept. 10, 1930; m. Susan Ann Kaplan, (div.); children: John, Robert. AB, Washington and Lee U., 1951; MD, Columbia U., 1955. Diplomate Am. Bd. Ob-Gyn. Intern Jackson Meml. Hosp., Miami, Fla., 1955-56; resident in ob-gyn Columbia-Presbyn. Med. Ctr., N.Y.C., 1956-59, 61-63; prof. dept. ob-gyn, dir. divsn. oncology Baylor Coll. Medicine, Houston, 1963—; med. dir. gynecologic oncology program Meth. Hosp., Houston, 1989—. Capt. M.C., U.S. Army, 1959-61. Mem. ACS, AMA, Am. Coll. Obstetricians and Gynecologists, Am. Cancer Soc., Am. Soc. Clin. Oncology, Soc. Gynecol. Oncology, Houston Gynecol. and Obstet. Soc. Office: Baylor Coll Medicine 6550 Fannin St Ste 701 Houston TX 77030-2738

KAPLAN, ALLEN P., physician, educator, researcher; b. West New York, N.J., Oct. 27, 1940; m. Lee Kaplan, Aug. 22, 1965; children: Rachel, Seth. AB, Columbia U., 1961; MD, Downstate Med. Coll. Diplomate Am. Bd. Internal Medicine, Am. Bd. Rheumatology, Am. Bd. Allergy and Clin. Immunology; cert. in diagnostic lab. immunology. Head allergic disease sect. NIH, Bethesda, Md., 1972-78; prof. medicine, head divsn. allergy rheumatology & clin. immunology SUNY, Stony Brook, 1978-87, chmn. dept. medicine, 1987-94. Assoc. editor Allergy Clin. Immunol. Internat.; contbr. over some 225 articles to profl. jours. Lt. comdr. USPHS, 1972-78. Recipient Commendation medal USPHS, 1976. Mem. Am. Acad. Allergy & Immunology (pres. 1989-90), Clin. Immunology Soc. (pres. 1992-93), Internat. Assn. Allergology and Clin. Immunology (sec. gen. 1991-97, pres. elect 1997—). Office: Med U SC Dept Medicine Divsn Pulmonary-Allergy 171 Ashley Ave Charleston SC 29425-0001

KAPLAN, ALVIN IRVING, lawyer, adjudicator, investigator; b. Providence, Apr. 19, 1925; s. David J. and Pauline (Rosenberg) K.; m. Eleanor Ruth Apt, Apr. 7, 1957; 1 son, Laurence J. A.B., Cornell U., 1948; LL.B., N.Y. U., 1963. Bar: N.Y. bar 1964, U.S. Supreme Ct 1970. Internat. rep., staff engr. Internat. Ladies Garment Workers Union, AFL-CIO, St. Louis and N.Y.C., 1950-56; asst. personnel dir. Lightolier, Inc., Jersey City, 1956-59; dir. indsl. relations Climatic, Inc., Yonkers, N.Y., 1959-67; mgr. indsl. relations Koracorp Industries Inc., San Francisco, 1967-70, dir. indsl. relations, asst. sec., 1971-74, sec., 1974—, v.p., 1978-79; v.p. legal affairs, indsl. relations Diversified Apparel Enterprises, Inc., 1979-80; asst. gen. counsel Levi Strauss & Co., 1980-83; asst. v.p., sr. trust officer Cen. Banking Systems, Inc., Walnut Creek, Calif., 1984-90; asylum officer polit. asylum unit, Immigration and Naturalization Svc. U.S. Dept. Justice, San Francisco, 1992—; equal opportunity specialist Office of Fair Housing HUD, San Francisco, 1993-95; compliance officer U.S. Dept. of Labor, 1995-97; ind. cons. civil rights investigations, 1997—; mem. wage bd. 1 Calif. Indsl. Welfare Commn., 1976, 79; cons. Bank Trust Svcs., 1990-91. Trustee Homewood Terrace, San Francisco, 1971-73, Internat. Ladies Garment Workers Nat. Retirement Fund, Nat. Retirement Fund United Hatters, Cap and Millinery Workers Union. Served with C.E. AUS, 1943-46. Mem. ABA, N.Y. State Bar Assn., Fed. Bar Assn., Indsl. Relations Research Assn., Am. Arbitration Assn. (mem. comml. panel arbitrators), Internat. Soc. Labor Law and Social Security, Am. Soc. Corp. Secs. Democrat. Jewish. Club: Cornell No. Calif. Office: AZK Assocs 151 Edgewood Ave San Francisco CA 94117-3712

KAPLAN, ANDY, broadcast executive. Exec v.p. Columbia Tristar TV Group, Culver City, Calif. Office: Columbia Tristar Television Group 9336 W Washington Blvd Culver City CA 90232*

KAPLAN, BARBARA BEIGUN, university official, educator; b. Chgo., Aug. 7, 1943; d. Jack L. and Mollie (Schulman) Beigun; m. Howard T. Kaplan, June 20, 1965; children: Jeffrey Mark, Eric Michael, Brian Robert, Robyn Stacie. BA, U. Chgo., 1965, MA, 1966; PhD, U. Md., College Park, 1979. Sr. instrnl. designer U. Md. Univ. Coll., College Park, 1985-90, program developer, dir. program in sci., tech., soc. studies, 1988-90, dir. Office Faculty Devel., 1993-98, exec. dir. Ctr. for Tchg., Learning and Assessment, 1998—; adj. instr. history of tech., women's studies, intellectual history Grad. Sch. at NIH, Bethesda, Md., 1981; adj. instr. history sci. and medicine U. Md. Univ. Coll., College Park, 1981—, part-time adj. prof. history, 1983-90; adj. instr. U. Md. Baltimore County, Catonsville, 1981-83;

adj. instr. humanities Hood Coll., Frederick, Md., 1989; instrnl. technologist Applied Sci. Assocs., McLean, Va., 1990-91; cons. on faculty devel. Johns Hopkins U., Balt., 1998; peer reviewer To Improve the Acad. jour., 1998-99; presenter workshops on faculty devel. U. Richmond, Johns Hopkins U., Montgomery Coll., Charles County C.C.; presenter, guest lectr. in field. Author: Divulging Useful Truths of Physics: The Medical Agenda of Robert Boyle, 1993, Land and Heritage in the Virginia Tidewater: A History of King and Queen County, 1993; contbr. articles and book revs. to profl. jours., chpt. to book on tchg. in higher edn. Pres. Potomac Commons Garden Club, 1978, Fox Hills Green Cmty. Assn., 1988, Quince Orchard H.S. Parents, Tchrs. and Students Assn., 1990; mem. exec. bd. Com. for Upcounty Montgomery County, Md., 1984. Predoctoral fellow Smithsonian Instn., 1979-72, U. Md. fellow, 1979-72. Mem. History of Sci. Soc., Am. Assn. Higher Edn., Am. Hist. Soc., Profl. and Orgnl. Devel. Network in Higher Edn., Nat. Assn. Sci., Tech. and Society (charter mem.), Univ. Continuing Edn. Assn., Washington Soc. for History Medicine (pres. 1985-86), Nu Pi Sigma. E-mail: bkaplan@umuc.edu. Office: U Md Univ Coll Ctr for Tchg Learning and Assessment Univ Blvd at Adelphi Rd College Park MD 20742

KAPLAN, BARRY HUBERT, physician; b. Bklyn., Nov. 16, 1938; s. Samuel and Mildred (Rabiner) K.; m. Rosalind Perlow Kaplan, June 23, 1962; children: Andrew, Scott. BA summa cum laude, NYU, 1958; MD, Johns Hopkins U., 1962, PhD, 1967. Diplomate Am. Bd. Internal Medicine, Am. Bd. Hematology, Am. Bd. Med. Oncology. Intern in medicine Johns Hopkins Hosp., 1962-63; fellow dept. physiol. chem. Johns Hopkins Sch. of Medicine, 1963-64; rsch. assoc. NIH, 1964-66; resident in medicine Bronx Mcpl. Hosp. Ctr., 1966-67; assoc. in medicine Albert Einstein Coll. Medicine, 1967-70, asst. prof. medicine, 1970-75, asst. prof. biochemistry, 1973-82, acting dir., divsn. med. oncology, 1974-81, acting assoc. dir. clin. rsch., Cancer Ctr. to assoc. dir., 1975-82, assoc. prof. medicine, 1975-82, assoc. clin. prof. medicine, 1982-93, vis. clin. assoc. prof. of medicine, 1993-95; clin. assoc. prof. of medicine Cornell Med. Coll., 1995—; dir. divsn. of med. oncology Albert Einstein Coll. of Medicine, 1981-82, vis. asst. prof. biochemistry, 1982-87; physician in charge med. oncology Booth Meml. Med. Ctr., 1985-91, physician in charge med. oncology/hematology N.Y. Hosp. Med. Ctr. of Queens, 1991—; asst. attending physician Bronx Mcpl. Hosp. Ctr., 1967-71; attending physician The Weiler Hosp. of the Albert Einstein Coll. of Medicine, 1972-93, Bronx Mcpl. Hosp. Ctr., 1972-93, Westchester Square Hosp., Bronx, 1982-93, Union Hosp., 1983-91, N.Y. Hosp. Med. Ctr. of Queens, 1983—. Contbr. articles to profl. jours. Mem. Am. Assn. for Cancer Rsch., Am. Soc. for Clin. Oncology, Am. Soc. Hematology, N.Y. Cancer Soc. (pres. 1981-82), Am. Cancer Soc. (N.Y.C. divsn. bd. dirs. 1981-84, steering com. profl. ednl. and grants com. 1981-83), Queens County Med. Soc., Phi Beta Kappa (Edward J. Noble Found. fellowship student leadership 1958-62). Home: 165 E 72nd St Ph D New York NY 10021-4351 Office: 59-16 174th St Fresh Meadows NY 11365

KAPLAN, BARRY MARTIN, lawyer; b. N.Y.C., Nov. 9, 1950; s. Stanley Seymour and Lillian (Schner) K.; m. Erica Green, July 26, 1981; children: Matthew Aaron, Elizabeth Rose, Andrew Nathan. BA, Colgate U., 1973; JD cum laude, U. Mich., 1976. Bar: Mich. 1976, Wash., 1978, U.S. Dist. (ea. dist.) Mich. 1976, U.S. Dist. Ct. (we. dist.) Wash. 1978, U.S. Dist. Ct. (ea. dist.) Wash. 1986, U.S. Tax Ct. 1983, U.S. Ct. Appeals (9th cir.) 1990. Law clk. to Hon. Charles W. Joiner U.S. Dist. Ct. (ea. dist.) Mich., Detroit, 1976-78; assoc. Perkins Coie, Seattle, 1978-85, ptnr., 1985—; spkr. in field. Author: Washington Corporation Law and Practice, 1991; contbr. articles to legal jours. and procs. Mem. ABA (litigation sect., securities litigation com., bus. law sect., bus. and corp. litigation com., subcom. chmn. on control transactions 1993), Wash. State Bar Assn. (CLE spkr., bus. law sect., securities com., subcom. chair on dir.'s liability 1993), Wash. Athletic Club. Office: Perkins Coie 1201 3rd Ave Fl 40 Seattle WA 98101-3000

KAPLAN, BEN AUGUSTUS, financial services executive; b. Toronto, Nov. 15, 1952; came to U.S., 1974; s. Sidney and Eva Kaplan. BA, Fla. Internat. U., 1976; MBA, NYU, 1981. Budget analyst Consol. Edison Co., N.Y.C., 1979-81; fin. analyst Becton Dickinson Co., Paramus, N.J., 1981-85; fin. mgr. IMNET (joint venture Merrill Lynch/IBM), Princeton, N.J., 1986; asst. contr. Merrill Lynch, N.Y.C., 1987, contr., asst. v.p., 1989-92; v.p., contr. Global Ops. and Systems Merrill Lynch, Jersey City, 1992-93; v.p., mgr. futures fin. systems Merrill Lynch Futures, Jersey City, 1993-94; bus. unit controller for Europe, Middle East Merrill Lynch, London, 1994; v.p. sr. fin. officer global ops. svcs. Internat. Merrill Lynch, Jersey City, 1995-96; v.p. fin. systems ops., svc. and tech. Merrill Lynch, Jersey City, 1996—, v.p., sr. fin. officer, fin. reporting and analysis, 1997-99, v.p., sr. fin. officer for fin. and operational oversight, 1999—. Mem. NYU Fin. Club. Home: 1786 Lilbet Rd Teaneck NJ 07666-2267 Office: Merrill Lynch 101 Hudson St 6th Fl Jersey City NJ 07302-3997

KAPLAN, BENJAMIN, judge; b. N.Y.C., Apr. 9, 1911; s. Morris and Mary (Berman) K.; m. Felicia Lamport, Apr. 16, 1942; children: James L., Nancy L. Mansbach. A.B., CCNY, 1929; LL.B., Columbia, 1933; LL.D., Suffolk U., 1974, Harvard U., 1981, Northeastern U., 1981. Bar: N.Y. 1934, Mass. 1950. Assoc., then mem. firm Greenbaum, Wolff & Ernst, N.Y.C., 1933-42, 46; vis. prof. law Harvard, 1947, prof. law, 1948—, Royall prof. law, 1961-72, emeritus, 1972—; assoc. justice Supreme Jud. Ct. Mass., 1972-81; recalled to serve as judge Appeals Ct. Mass., 1983—; Reporter to adv. com. on civil rules Jud. Conf. U.S., 1960-66, mem., 1966-70; co-reporter restatement (2d) of judgments to Am. Law Inst., 1970-73. Served to lt. col. AUS, 1942-46. Mem. Am. Law Inst., Assn. Bar City of N.Y., Phi Beta Kappa. Assisted Justice Jackson on Nuremberg Trial, 1945. Home: 2 Bond St Cambridge MA 02138-2308 Office: Harvard Law Sch Cambridge MA 02138

KAPLAN, BERNICE ANTOVILLE, anthropologist, educator; b. N.Y.C., Apr. 21, 1923; d. Meyer and Marie (Antoville) K.; m. Gabriel Ward Lasker, July 31, 1949; children: Robert Alexander, Edward Meyer, Anne Titiani. B.A., Hunter Coll., N.Y.C., 1943; M.A. (Univ. fellow 1944-45, Univ. and Field Mus. fellow 1945-46), U. Chgo., 1947, Ph.D., 1953. Asso. in anthropology Am. Mus. Natural History, 1941-44, Field Mus. Natural History, 1947-48; instr. anthropology and sociology U. Wis., 1946-47, Hobart and William Smith Colls., 1948-49; instr. to asso. prof. anthropology Wayne State U., Detroit, 1949-67; asso. prof. Wayne State U., 1967-79, prof., 1979—; lectr. U. Mich., Ann Arbor and Grand Rapids, summers 1955, 59, U. Calif., Berkeley, 1960-61; field work, Michoacán, Mex., 1948, 52, 53, 59, 61, 65, and Province of Lambayeque, Peru, 1957-58, London, 1977. Contbr. articles to profl. jours. Rep., Birmingham (Mich.) PTA Council to Birmingham Bd. Edn., 1971-76; bd. dirs. Southfield Jr. Symphony, 1972-75. Fulbright scholar, 1957-58; fellow-commonorship Churchill Coll., Cambridge U. (Eng.), 1983-84; named to Hunter Coll. Hall of Fame, 1988. Fellow Am. Anthrop. Assn., AAAS (chmn. sect. H 1973-74), Am. Assn. Phys. Anthropologists, Soc. for Applied Anthropology (mem. exec. bd. 1976-79); mem. Am. Ethnological Soc. (sec. 1978-82), Central State Anthrop. Soc. (pres. 1972-73, co-editor Central Issues in Anthropology 1978-89), Sigma Xi. Office: Wayne State U Dept Anthropology Manoogian Hall Detroit MI 48202

KAPLAN, BRUCE MICHAEL, oncologist; b. Miami Beach., Fla., Feb. 28, 1954; s. Ralph Roy Kaplan and Gladys Sparber-Kaplan; m. Merle Kaplan, May 31, 1987; children: Michael and Hannah (twins). BA, Emory U., 1975; MD, U. South Fla., 1979. Intern U. Tenn., Memphis, 1979-80; resident Med. Coll. Wis., Milw., 1980-83; dir. radiation oncology St. Francis Hosp., Hartford, Conn., 1983—. Head med. affairs com. Am. Cancer Soc., Hartford, 1990, bd. dirs., 1991—. Mem. Am. Soc. Therapeutic Radiologists (human resources com. 1997-98), Am. Soc. Clin. Oncologists, Am. Coll. Radiology, Conn. State Med. Soc., Hartford County Med. Soc. Avocations: winter skiing, water skiing, tennis, golf. E-mail: bkaplan@stfranciscare.org. Office: St Francis Hosp Cancer Ctr 114 Woodland St Hartford CT 06105

KAPLAN, CANDIA POST, psychologist; b. Amityville, N.Y.; d. John E.H. and Marie (Calhoun) Post; m. Paul E. Kaplan, June 18, 1966; children: Steven, Heather, Danielle, Colby. BA, Adelphi U., 1965; MA, UCLA, 1966, U. Mo., 1989; PhD Psychology Dept., Ohio State U., Columbus, 1993; postgrad. Palo Alto UAMC, U. of Washington Col. of Med. Contbr. articles to profl. jours. Mem. APA, Congress Rehab. Medicine, Nat. Academy of Neuropsychology, Kappa Delta Pi, Phi Alpha Theta.

KAPLAN, CARL ELIOT, lawyer; b. N.Y.C., Apr. 17, 1939; s. Lawrence S. and Pearl (Eisenberg) K.; m. Diane L. Garvin, Dec. 16, 1965; children: Lynn, Jonathan. BA, Columbia Coll., 1959; LLB, 1962. Bar: U.S. Dist. Ct. (so. and ea. dists.) N.Y. 1964, U.S. Ct. Appeals (2nd cir.) 1966, U.S. Supreme Ct. 1970. Assoc. Fulbright & Jaworski L.L.P., N.Y.C., 1963-69; ptnr., 1969—; sec. Data Gen. Corp., Westboro, Mass. Bd. dirs. Columbia Law Rev., 1961-62. Mem. ABA, N.Y. Bar Assn., Assn. of Bar City of N.Y., Am. Soc. Corp. Secs., Columbia Club (N.Y.C.), Univ. Club (N.Y.C.), Phi Beta Kappa. Avocations: skiing, jogging, tennis. Office: Fulbright & Jaworski LLP 666 5th Ave New York NY 10103

KAPLAN, (CLAUDIA) CLAUDETTE S., volunteer, professional leader, philanthropist; b. Chgo., June 4, 1931; d. Jacob and Celia (Lopaty) Mirotsnic; m. Saul M. Kaplan, Nov. 28, 1953 (div. Mar. 1980); children: Allan, Laurie K., David. Grad., Chgo. City Coll., 1951; student, Coll. Jewish Studies, 1951-53. Pres. Hadassah, Memphis, 1970-72, So. region, 1978-81, nat. svc. com., 1981-83, mem. nat. pres.'s coun., 1984—, founder major & big gifts event, 1974, area founders chair nat. major gifts dept. Nat. Israel Edn. Svcs. Com.; bd. dirs. NCCJ, Memphis Jewish Cmty. Rels. Coun., Memphis Jewish Fedn./Unite Jewish Appeal, 1972-80; mem. So. Poverty Law Ctr. Recipient 25th Anniversary prize State of Israel Bonds, 1973, Guardian of the Dream Founder award Hadassah, 1995, donor award, 1974. Mem. AIPAC (leadership com.), Nat. Coun. Jewish Women, World Jewish Congress, Hadassah Women's Zionist Orgn. of Am., City Hope (life), Memphis & Mid-South Jewish Hist. Soc., B'nai B'rith (Baron Hirsch Synagogue). Home: 408 River Oaks Pl Memphis TN 38120-2538

KAPLAN, DONNA ELAINE, artist, educator; b. South Amboy, N.J., Dec. 30, 1942; d. Oscar Ivan and Otta Theora (Hamilton) Olsen; m. Barnett Morris Kaplan, Sept. 20, 1975; children: William, Ivan, Benjamin. Diploma in profl. nursing, Chaffey Coll., Alta Loma, Calif., 1964; BS in Occupl. Therapy, U. Puget Sound, Tacoma, 1972; student, Factory of Visual Arts, Seattle, 1977-79. RN, Wash.; cert. psychiat. nurse, Calif.; registered occupl. therapist. Shift charge nurse rsch. unit Langley Porter Neuropsychiat. Inst., San Francisco, 1967-70; supr. nursing Western State Hosp., Steilacoom, Wash., 1972-73; instr. in-svc. edn. Inst. Pa. Hosp., Phila., 1974-75; owner DK Design Studio, North Bend, Wash., 1984—; juror No. Calif. Reg. Fiber Show, Sacramento, Calif., 1993; guest curator Northwest Gallery, 1994; nat. touring guest arts instr. 1987—. Co-author: Beads as Warp and Weft, 1996; contbr. articles to art jours.; exhibitions include: Tacoma Art Mus., Wash., 1980, Window Gallery of Fine Art, Alaska, 1989, Craft Alliance Gallery, St. Louis, 1989, Tohomo Chul Park Gallery, Ariz., 1995, Whatcom Mus. History and Art, Wash., 1995, Bellevue Art Mus., Wash., 1982, 89, 96, Contemporary Crafts Ctr., Seattle, 1996, Raindance Gallery, Oreg., 1996, La. State U., Baton Rouge, 1997. Recipient Best Creative Use of Materials award Absolutely Beads Show/Beads and Beyond, Bellevue, Wash., 1994, Mus. Purchase award Edmonds (Wash.) Art Festival Mus., 1994, 1st pl. award Art Splash, City of Redmond, Wash., 1995. Mem. Seattle Weavers' Guild (corr. sec. 1982-83, Peoples Choice award 1986, Art 3D award 1995), N.W. Designer Craftsmen, N.W. Craft Alliance (v.p., bd. dirs. 1994-96), N.W. Bead Soc., Fiber Art Profls., Friends of Fiber Art Internat. Studio: DK Design Studio 43406 SE 88th St North Bend WA 98045-9455

KAPLAN, DOUGLAS ALLEN, county official; b. L.A., Aug. 14, 1956; s. Martin and Sally Kaplan. BA in Pub. Svc./Polit. Sci., U. Calif., Davis, 1978; cert., Solano (Calif.) Fire Acad., 1979. Cert. Calif. Pub. Guardians Assn., Nat. Guardianship Assn. Fire safety supr. Davis & Winter Fire Dept., 1979-80; asst. manpower analyst Yolo County, Woodland, Calif., 1980, voter outreach coord., 1980-82, pub. guardian, adminstr., 1983—; tchr. U. Calif. Ext., 1992—; chair conservatorship adv. com. Am. River Coll., Sacramento, 1989-90. Mem. exec. bd. Calif. Dem. Party, Sacramento, 1987-88, 93-94, state ctrl. com., 1985—; bd. mem. N.C.A. Ombudsman Adv. Bd., Sacramento, 1996—. Recipient Grassroots Activism award Nat. Jewish Dem. Coun., Washington, 1993. Mem. Nat. Guardianship Assn. (legis. chair, bd. mem. 1988—, pres. 1994-96), Calif. Pub. Guardian Assn. (pres. 1988-89), Calif. State Bar (planning, probate and trust sect. com. 1995—). Jewish. Avocations: scuba diving, white water rafting. Office: Yolo County Pub Guardian/Adminstr 640 Bluebird Pl Davis CA 95616-0175

KAPLAN, ELISSA, social worker, children's counselor, consultant; b. Queens, N.Y., Jan. 6, 1969; d. Warren and Judith Kaplan. BS, U. Tampa, 1990; M Sports Sci., U.S. Sports Acad., Daphne, Ala., 1991; MSW, Fla. Internat. U., 1996. Registered social worker, Fla. Mgr. pub. and investor rels. Action Products Internat. Inc., Ocala, Fla., 1991-94; wellness counselor, exercise physiologist Jewish Cmty. Ctr., North Miami Beach, Fla., 1994-95; state atty.'s victim adv. State Atty.'s Office, Ft. Lauderdale, Fla., 1995; children and families counselor Broward Family Svcs. Agy., Ft. Lauderdale, 1996, Dept. Children and Families, Lauderdale, Fla., 1995-97; keeping families together social worker Children's Home Soc., Ft. Lauderdale, 1997—; mem. treatment plan com. Fla. Dept. Children and Families, Ft. Lauderdale, 1997-98; personal trainer; pub. rels. cons. Co-author: Case Planning Guidelines for Caseworkers, 1997. Mem. spkrs. bur. Broward County Prevention Child Abuse Com., 1997—. Mem. NASW, Toastmasters. Avocations: marathon running, bicycling, rollerblading, horseback riding, skiing. Home: 400 E 77th St Apt 4L New York NY 10021-2348 Office: Children's Home Soc 401 NE 4th St Fort Lauderdale FL 33301-1151

KAPLAN, ERICA LYNN, typing and word processing service company executive, pianist; b. Aug. 6, 1955; d. George William and Raylia (Eagle) Kaplan; m. James Laurence Kellermann, Feb. 26, 1982. B in Mus., Manhattan Sch. Music, N.Y.C., 1976, M in Mus., 1979. Clk. dept. edn. 92d St Y, N.Y.C., 1972-76, assoc. dept. pub. rels., 1977-78, catalogue coord., sec. to exec. dir., 1978, assoc. dept. performing arts, 1978-79, assoc. dir. dept. publs., 1979-80; pres. Eric Kaplan Typing/Word Processing/Music Svcs., N.Y.C., 1980—; piano soloist Huntington (N.Y.) Philharmonia, 1975; rehearsal pianist, performance accompanist The Mikado, Playwrights Horizons, N.Y.C., 1975, Fiona in Swan Song, N.Y.C., 1986; mus. dir., accompanist A Salute to Vaudeville/A Tribute to Fred Astaire, N.Y.C., 1980-95; mus. dir., pianist Portrait of a Man, Hyde Pk. (N.Y.) Festival Theatre, 1981, Am. Renaissance Theater, N.Y.C., 1982, 86, The Fantasticks, Dalton Sch., N.Y.C., 1983; performance accompanist Okla. Theatreworks, Bklyn., 1984; resident pianist Am. Renaissance Theater, N.Y.C., 1981—; audition accompanist Interboro Repertory Theater, N.Y.C., 1986—; accompanist, tchr. vocal lessons class Stuyvesant Adult Ctr., N.Y.C., 1988-97; tchr. performance singing, 1997—; accompanist The Singing Experience, 1990-91; mus. dir. Gift of the Magi, 1991. Transl., annotator with additional mus. examples: L'Anacrouse dans la Musique Moderne, 1978; composer: (songs) Four by Feiffer, 1978, Hey Boys, 1984, Unborn Child, 1988, Neighbor, 1991; arranger Postcards from the Apple, 1993, Isn't It Romantic, 1996. Mem. New Eng. Anti-Vivisection Soc., Boston, 1982—, Nat. Anti-Vivisection Soc., 1988—, Common Cause, Washington, 1983—, SANE/FREEZE, 1988—. Mem. Am. Fedn. Musicians, Union Concerned Scientists, Mensa. Democrat. Jewish.

KAPLAN, GARY, executive recruiter; b. Phila., Aug. 14, 1939; s. Morris and Minnie (Leve) K.; m. Linda Ann Wilson, May 30, 1968; children: Michael Warren, Marc Jonathan, Jeffrey Russell Wilson. BA in Polit. Sci., Pa. State U., 1961. Tchr. biology N.E. High Sch., Phila., 1962-63; coll. employment rep. Bell Telephone Labs., Murray Hill, N.J., 1966-67; supr. recruitment and placement Unisys, Blue Bell, Pa., 1967-69; pres. Electronic Systems Personnel, Phila., 1969-70; staff selection rep. Booz, Allen & Hamilton, N.Y.C., 1970-72; mgr. exec. recruitment M&T Chems., Rahway, N.J., 1972-74; dir. exec. recruitment IU Internat. Mgmt. Corp., Phila., 1974-78; v.p. personnel Crocker Bank, Los Angeles, 1978-79; mng. v.p. ptnr. western region Korn-Ferry Internat., Los Angeles, 1979-85; pres. Gary Kaplan & Assocs., Pasadena, Calif., 1985—; bd. dirs. Vis. Nurse Found., Home Pharmacy of Calif.; bd. trustees Greater L.A. Zoo Assn.; Pa. State U. Alumni Coun. Mgmt. columnist, Radio and Records newspaper, 1984-85. Chmn. bd. dirs. Vis. Nurse Assn., L.A., 1985-87; former bd. dirs. The Wellness Cmty.-Nat., Pa. State U. Indsl./Orgnl. Psychology Adv. Bd.; Capt. Adj. Gen. Corps., U.S. Army, 1963-66. Alumni fellow Pa. State U., 1998. Mem. Am. Compensation Assn., Soc. Human Resources Mgmt., Big Ten Club of So. Calif. Home: 1735 Fairmount Ave La Canada Flintridge CA 91011-1632 Office: Gary Kaplan & Assocs 201 S Lake Ave Ste 600 Pasadena CA 91101-3018

KAPLAN, GEORGE WILLARD, urologist; b. Brownsville, Tex., Aug. 24, 1935; s. Hyman J. and Lillian (Bennett) K.; m. Susan Gail Solof, Dec. 17, 1961; children: Paula, Elizabeth, Julie, Alan. BA, U. Tex., 1955; MD, Northwestern U., 1959, MS, 1966. Diplomate Am. Bd. Urology. Intern Charity Hosp. of La. at New Orleans, 1959-60; resident Northwestern U., 1963-68; instr. Med. Sch. Northwestern U., Chgo., 1968-69; clin. prof., chief pediatric urology Sch. Medicine U. Calif., San Diego, 1970—; trustee Children's Hosp. and Health Ctr., San Diego, 1978-90, Am. Bd. Urology, Bingham Farms, Mich., 1991-96; del. Am. Bd. Med. Specialties, Evanston, Ill., 1992-96. Author: Genitourinary Problems in Pediatrics; asst. editor Jour. Urology, Balt., 1982-89, 98—; assoc. editor Child Nephrology and Urology, Milan, Italy, 1988—; contbr. articles to profl. publs. Pres. med. staff Children's Hosp., San Diego, 1980-82. Lt. USN, 1960-63. Recipient Joseph Capps prize Inst. of Medicine, 1967. Fellow ACS (pres. San Diego chpt. 1980-82), Am. Acad. Pediatrics (chmn. sect. on urology 1986); mem. AMA, Soc. for Pediatric Urology (pres. 1993), Am. Urol. Assn., Soc. Internat. Urologie, Soc. Univ. Urologists, Am. Assn. Genito-Urol. Surgery. Republican. Jewish. Avocations: history of medicine, rare books. Office: Pediatric Urology Assocs 7930 Frost St Ste 407 San Diego CA 92123-4286

KAPLAN, HARLEY LANCE, financial planner; b. Far Rockaway, N.Y., Sept. 26, 1961; s. Norman and Evelyn (Goz) K. BBA, Boston U., 1983. Cert. fin. planner. Interior designer United Electric Co., Boston, 1979-82; internat. cons. Etibank, Ankara, Turkey, 1982-83; fin. planner Cigna Corp., Boston, 1983-89; registered investment advisor, prin. Beta Industries, Inc., Boston, 1989—. Bd. dirs. Jewish Meml. Hosp., Roxbury, Mass. Recipient Citizenship award Sch. Dist. Town of Woodmere, N.Y., 1979, Top Coll. Fighter award N.Am. Karate Fedn., 1981. Mem. Internat. Assn. Fin. Planning, Coll. Fin. Planning (registry lic. practitioners), Boston U. Downtown Alumni (bd. dirs. 1987-97), Mensa, Sambo-Karate Club (instr. 1984—). Democrat. Jewish. Avocations: karate, polo, art, music, travel. Home: 68 Maple St Sherborn MA 01770-1023

KAPLAN, HAROLD PAUL, physician, health science facility administrator; b. N.Y.C., Jan. 22, 1939; s. David Benjamin and Sophie (Cohen) K.; m. Barbara Anne Sundstrom, Mar. 28, 1962; children: Todd, Jonathan, Robin, Scott. BS, Tufts U., 1959; MD, Yale U., 1963. Diplomate Am. Bd. Internal Medicine. Physician Internal Medicine Assocs., Meriden, Conn., 1970—; v.p. Internal Medicine Assocs., Meriden, 1974—, med. dir., mng. ptnr., 1985-93; clin. asst. prof. internal medicine Yale U. Sch. Medicine, 1994—; chief of gastroenterology Meriden-Wallingford (Conn.) Hosp., 1976-91, chief of medicine, 1980-82, corporator, 1984—; chief of medicine WWII Vets. Meml. Hosp., 1977-79; corporator Vets. Meml. Med. Ctr., 1991—, gov., 1990—; chief of staff-elect Mid State Med. Ctr., 1997-99, chief of staff, 1999—; bd. dirs. Healthworks, Ltd., Wallingford. Contbr. articles to profl. jours. Pres. Alliance for Edn. of North Haven, Conn., 1974-86, So. Conn. Swim League, 1978-83; chmn. ofcls. tech. com. Conn. Swimming, 1981-85; mem. parents coun. exec. com. Bowdoin Coll., 1988-91. Fellow ACP; mem. Am. Gastroent. Assn., Am. Soc. Gastrointestinal Endoscopy, Am. Soc. Internal Medicine, Farms Country Club of Wallingford (bd. govs. 1981-86). Republican. Avocation: swimming official, video, photography. Office: Internal Medicine Assocs 97 Barnes Rd Wallingford CT 06492

KAPLAN, HARVEY L., lawyer; b. Kansas City, Mo., Nov. 11, 1942. BS in Pharmacy, U. Mich., 1965; JD, U. Mo., 1968. Bar: Mo. 1968, U.S. Tax Ct. 1971, U.S. Supreme Ct. 1971. Ptnr. Shook, Hardy & Bacon LLP, Kansas City; faculty mem. NITA Advanced Advocacy Program, 1988-89; mem. Kansas City-St. Louis Panel, Ctr. Pub. Resources Inst. Dispute Resolution, 1989—. Bd. editors Mo. Law Rev., 1967-68, Mo. Lawyers Weekly, 1989—; mem. editorial adv. bd. Drug Product Liability Reporter, 1987-92. Fellow Internat. Acad. Trial Lawyers (bd. dirs. 1991-97), Internat. Soc. Barristers, Am. Bar Found.; mem. Am. Soc. Pharmacy Law, Mo. Orgn. Def. Lawyers (bd. dirs. 1985-93), Internat. Assn. Def. Counsel (mem. exec. com. 1991-94, mem. def. counsel trial acad. 1989, dir.-elect 1992, dir. 1993), Def. Rsch. Inst. (chmn. drug and med. device litigation com. 1991-94, bd. dirs. 1995-98), Nat. Judicial Coll. (mem. coun. for the future), Law Inst., Phi Delta Phi. Office: Shook Hardy & Bacon LLP 1 Kansas City Pl 1200 Main St Ste 2700 Kansas City MO 64105-2118

KAPLAN, HELENE LOIS, lawyer; b. N.Y.C., June 19, 1933; d. Jack and Shirley (Jacobs) Finkelstein; m. Mark N. Kaplan, Sept. 7, 1952; children: Marjorie Ellen, Sue Anne. AB cum laude, Barnard Coll., 1953; JD, NYU, 1967; LLD (hon.), Columbia U., 1990. Bar: N.Y. 1967. Pvt. practice N.Y.C., 1967-78; ptnr. Webster & Sheffield, N.Y.C., 1978-86, counsel, 1986-90; of counsel Skadden, Arps, Slate, Meagher & Flom, N.Y.C., 1990—; bd. dirs. The May Dept. Stores Co., Met. Life Ins. Co., The Chase Manhattan Corp., Mobil Corp., Bell Atlantic Corp. Trustee N.Y. Coun. for Humanities, 1976-82, chmn., 1978-82; trustee Barnard Coll., 1973—, chair bd. trustees, 1984-94; trustee Columbia U. Press, 1977-80, MITRE Corp., 1978-95, N.Y. Found., 1976-86, John Simon Guggenheim Meml. Found., 1981-98, NYU Law Ctr. Found., 1985-87, Inst. for Advanced Study, 1986—, Neuroscis. Rsch. Found., 1986-92, Am. Mus. Natural History, 1989—, vice chair, 1993—; trustee Am. Trust for Brit. Libr., 1991-93, Com. for Econ. Devel., 1993-96, Commonwealth Fund, 1990—, vice chair, 1996—; trustee J. Paul Getty Trust, 1992—, vice chair 1997—; trustee Olive Free Libr.; trustee Carnegie Corp. N.Y., 1979—, vice-chair bd. trustees, 1981-84, 98—, chair bd. trustees, 1984-91; trustee Mt. Sinai Hosp. Med. Ctr. and Med. Sch., 1977—, vice-chair bd. trustees, 1993-99; trustee N.Y.C. Pub. Devel. Corp., 1978-83, vice-chair bd. trustees, 1978-82; adv. com. on South Africa, U.S. Sec. of State, 1986-88; mem. N.Y. State Gov.'s Task Force on Life and the Law, 1985-90, Women's Forum, Inc., 1982—, Rockefeller U. Coun., 1984-94, Bretton Woods Com., 1985-96, Carnegie Coun. on Adolescent Devel., 1986-96; chairperson task force on sci. and tech. and jud. decision making Carnegie Commn. on Sci., Tech. and Govt., 1988-93; ptnr. N.Y.C. Partnership, 1987-92; bd. dirs. Am. Arbitration Assn., 1978-82. Mem. ABA, AAAS, Am. Philos. Soc., N.Y. State Bar Assn., N.Y.C. Bar Assn. (treas. 1991-93, mem. com. on philanthropic orgns. 1975-81, mem. com. on recruitment of lawyers 1978-82, mem. com. on profl. responsibility 1980-83), Century Assn., Cosmopolitan Club.

KAPLAN, HENRY JERROLD, ophthalmologist, educator; b. N.Y.C., Dec. 29, 1942; s. Ralph and Henrietta (Davis) K.; m. Adele Lotner, June 26, 1966; children: Wendi Suzanne, Todd Daniel, Ariane Dev. AB, Columbia U., 1964; MD, Cornell U., 1968. Diplomate Am. Bd. Ophthalmology. Intern in medicine Lakeside Hosp., Univ. Hosps. Cleve., Case-Western Res. U., 1968-69; surg. resident Bellevue Hosp., NYU Med. Ctr., 1969-70; NIH rsch. fellow in immunology U. Tex. (Southwestern) Med. Sch., Dallas, 1972-74; asst. prof. dept. cell biology U. Tex. (Southwestern) Med. Sch., 1974-75; resident in ophthalmology U. Iowa Hosps. and Clinics, Iowa City, 1975-78; retina-vitreous fellow dept. ophthalmology Med. Coll. Wis., Milw., 1978-79; assoc. prof. dept. ophthalmology Emory U. Sch. Medicine, Atlanta, 1979-84, prof., dir. rsch., 1984-88, assoc. prof. dept. microbiology, 1985-88; prof. dept. ophthalmology and visual scis. Washington U. Sch. Medicine, St. Louis, 1988—, chmn. dept. ophthalmology and visual scis., 1988-98; ophthalmologist in chief Barnes-Jewish Hosp., Washington U. Med. Ctr., 1988-98; affiliate scientist in pathology and immunology Yerkes Regional Primate Rsch. Ctr., Atlanta, 1981—; adj. prof. dept. small animal medicine U. Ga., Athens, 1985—; assoc. chief ophthalmology Emory U. Hosp., 1985-88; mem. visual scis. study sect. A-1 NIH, Bethesda, Md., 1985-89, chmn., 1987-89; pres. Barnes Eye Care Network, 1994-98. Author, co-author or editor, co-editor more than 175 med. textbooks, chpts. and articles on uveitis and macular degeneration and retinal degeneration pub. in refereed sci. and med. jours., 1974—; mem. sci. jour. rev. bds. Archives Ophthalmology, 1978—, Retina, 1982—, Am. Jour. Ophthalmology, 1983—, Ophthalmology, 1983—, Current Eye Rsch., 1986—, Exptl. Eye Rsch., 1986—; mem. sci. rev. bd. Investigative Ophthalmology and Visual Sci., 1983—, mem. editorial bd., 1990-92; co-editor Ocular Immunology and Inflammation, 1994-98; editor: Ocular Immunology and Inflammation, 1999—. Maj. M.C., USAF, 1970-72. Recipient sci. award Alcon Rsch. Inst., 1987; Olga Keith Weiss rsch. scholar to Prevent Blindness, Inc., N.Y.C., 1984. Fellow ACS, Am. Acad. Ophthalmology (Honor award 1984, Sr. Honor award 1994); mem. AMA, Assn. for Rsch. in Vision and Ophthalmology, Am. Assn. Immunologists, Macula Soc., Am. Uveitis Soc. (pres. 1997—), Retina Soc., St. Louis Ophthal. Soc., St. Louis Met. Med. Soc., Mo. Ophthal. Soc. Jewish. Office: Washington U Sch Medicine Dept Ophthalmology and Visual Scis 660 S Euclid Ave # 8096 Saint Louis MO 63110-1010 ***Faith in pursuit of one's own ideas and persistence in the face of adversity will bring success, but more importantly - personal satisfaction.***

KAPLAN, HUETTE MYRA, business educator, training consultant; b. Chgo., July 11, 1933; d. Max and Jeannette (Smith) Lazan; m. Jerrold M. Kaplan, Feb. 14, 1954 (dec.); children: Lawrence, Jeffrey. BS in Bus. Edn., DePaul U., 1971. Instr. Pub. Svc. Careers Program State of Ill., Chgo., 1971-72; instr., dir. Patricia Stevens Bus. Sch., Chgo., 1972; relocation mgr., tng. specialist, dir. tng. and devel. Zurich-Am. Ins. Cos., Chgo. and Schaumburg, Ill., 1972-80; pres., tng. cons. H.K. & Assocs., Lansing, Ill., 1980—; tng. dir. Calumet Area Lit. Coun., Hammond, Ind., 1985—; trainer Chgo. Literacy Coordinating Ctr., 1988-93; instr. Purdue U.-Calumet, Hammond, 1976—; substitute tchr. Sch. Dist. 171, Lansing, 1995—. Bd. dirs. Temple Beth El, Hammond, 1986-88, Calumet Area Literacy Coun., 1990-92, 94-95, pres. 1995—; mem. task force Chgo. Coalition for Edn. and Tng. for Employment, 1984-86; literacy vol. tutor.; cand. Dist. 215 Sch. Bd. Mem. ASTD, Nat. Bus. Edn. Assn., Kappa Gamma Pi. Jewish. Avocations: reading, pet therapy programs, travel. Home and Office: HK & Assocs 2843 192nd St Lansing IL 60438-3717

KAPLAN, ISAAC RAYMOND, chemistry educator, corporate executive; b. Baranowicze, Poland, July 10, 1929; came to U.S., 1957; s. Morris and Anny (Chait) K.; m. Helen Fagot, Sept. 4, 1955; children: Debora, David Joel. BS, Canterbury U., Christchurch, New Zealand, 1951, MS, 1953; PhD, U. So. Calif., 1961. Rsch. scientist Commonwealth Sci. and Indsl. Rsch. Orgn., Sydney, Australia, 1953-57; postdoctoral fellow Calif. Inst. Tech., Pasadena, 1961-62; guest lectr. Hebrew U., Jerusalem, 1962-65; assoc. prof. UCLA, 1965-69, prof., 1969-93, prof. emeritus, 1993—; pres. Global Geochemistry Corp., Canoga Park, Calif., 1977—; cons. city, county, state and fed. regulatory agys., L.A. Contbr. and co-contbr. over 300 sci. rsch. articles to profl. jours. Guggenheim Found. fellow, Sydney, 1970-71. Fellow AAAS, Am. Inst. Chemists, Geol. Soc. Am.; mem. Russian Acad. Natural Sci. (fgn., Kapitsa medal 1998), Am. Chem. Soc., Geophys. Union, Geochem. Soc. (Alfred Treibs medal for organic geochm. 1993). Office: U Calif ESS Dept Plaza Circle Dr Los Angeles CA 90024

KAPLAN, JAMES LAMPORT, writer, editor, publisher; b. Washington, Mar. 6, 1944; s. Benjamin and Felicia (Lamport) K.; m. Jeanette Marie Muñoz, Mar. 25, 1967 (div. Aug. 1985); children: Benjamin, Matthew; m. Brooks Robards, June 25, 1988. BA, Yale U., 1966; MS in Journalism, Northwestern U., 1967. Staff writer Mpls. Star, 1967-70; reporter, writer Sports Illustrated, N.Y.C., 1970-86; editor Baseball Rsch. Jour., 1987-90; bridge columnist Daily Hampshire Gazette, Vineyard Gazette, Mass., 1990—; editor, polisher China Daily, Beijing, 1993-94; co-pub. Summerset Press, Northampton, Mass., 1995—; freelance writer, 1986—. Author: Pine-Tarred and Feathered: A Year on the Baseball Beat, 1985, Playing the Field: Why Defense Is the Most Fascinating Art in Major League Baseball, 1987, The Fielders, 1989, The Official Baseball Hall of Fame Book of Superstars, 1989, The Second Official Baseball Hall of Fame Book of Superstars, 1991, The Giants, 1991, Golden Years of Baseball, 1992, (with Ira Berkow) The Gospel According to Casey: Casey Stengel's Inimitable, Instructional, Historical Baseball Book, 1992, Raising Your Bridge: Valuable Tips for Improving Players, 1993, (with Brooks Robards) Sweet & Sour: One Woman's Chinese Adventure, One Man's Chinese Torture, 1995; contbr. articles to numerous mags., newspapers. Mem. Conservation Commn., Northampton, 1997—. Mem. Nat. Writers Union, Rotary Internat. Democrat. Jewish. Avocations: golf, bridge. Home and Office: 20 Langworthy Rd Northampton MA 01060-2122

KAPLAN, JARED, lawyer; b. Chgo., Dec. 28, 1938; s. Jerome and Phyllis Enid (Rieber) K.; m. Rosellen Engstrom, Dec. 28, 1964 (div. 1978); children: Brian F., Philip B.; m. Maridee Quanbeck, June 2, 1990. AB, UCLA, 1960; LLB, Harvard, 1963. Bar: Ill. 1963, U.S. Dist. Ct. (no. dist.) Ill. 1969, U.S. Tax Ct. 1978. Assoc. Ross & Hardies, Chgo., 1963-69, ptnr., 1970; ptnr. Roan & Grossman, Chgo., 1970-83, Keck, Mahin & Cate, Chgo., 1983-94, McDermott, Will & Emery, Chgo., 1994—; bd. dirs. ESOP (Employee Stock Ownership Plan) Assn., Washington, 1987-90, Family Firm Inst., Boston, 1996—; adv. coun. Ill. Employee-Owned Enterprise, Chgo., 1984—; chmn. Ill. Adv. Task Force on Ownership Succession and Employee Ownership, 1994-95. Editor in chief: Callaghan's Fed. Tax Guide, 1988; author: Employee Stock Ownership Plans, 1999. Nat. pres. Ripon Soc., Washington, 1975-76; adv. council mem. Rep. Nat. Com., Washington, 1978-80; alt. delegate Rep. Nat. Conv., Detroit, 1980; bd. dirs. Family Firm Inst., 1996—. Fellow Ill. Bar Found.; mem. ABA (chmn. section of taxation, administrv. practice com. 1978-80), City Club, Chgo. (bd. govs. 1982-92), Univ. Club, Met. Club. Republican. Jewish. Home: 105 W Delaware Pl Chicago IL 60610-3200 Office: McDermott Will & Emery 227 W Monroe St Fl 44 Chicago IL 60606-5018

KAPLAN, JAY, cultural organization administrator, editor; b. Newark, Mar. 2, 1946; s. Jacob and Sadie (Ziegler) K.; m. Marion Weinberg, Aug. 27, 1967 (div. 1985); 1 child, Ruth Anna. BA, Rutgers U., 1966; MA, Johns Hopkins U., 1968; PhD, Columbia U., 1974. Policy rsch. specialist N.Y. State Divsn. Budget, Albany, 1973-74, 1977-78; asst. prof. SUNY, Geneseo, 1974-77; rsch. assoc. Project on Cmty. Alternatives, N.Y.C., 1978-79; asst. v.p. Criminal Justice Inst., N.Y.C., 1979-80; exec. dir. N.Y. Coun. Humanities, N.Y.C., 1980—; reviewer Elie Wiesel Found., N.Y.C., 1993—. Editor Syracuse Univ. Press, 1996—, Culturefront Magazine, 1992—. Office: NY Coun Humanities 150 Broadway Ste 1700 New York NY 10038-2515

KAPLAN, JEFFREY A., federal judge; b. 1956. BA, Vanderbilt U., 1978; JD, So. Meth. U., 1981. Law clk. Tex. Ct. Appeals 5th Jud. Cir., 1981-82; pvt. practice, 1982-92; justice Tex. Ct. Appeals (5th dist.), Dallas, 1992-93; assoc. Johnston & Budner, 1993-94; magistrate judge U.S. Dist. Ct. (no. dist.) Tex., Dallas, 1994—. Fax: (214) 767-3366. Office: US Dist Ct No Dist Tex 1100 Commerce St Rm 16F41 Dallas TX 75242

KAPLAN, JERRY, magazine publisher. Publisher, Country Home magazine, WOOD magzine Meredith Corp., Des Moines, Iowa, until 1989; v.p., group publisher Meredith Integrated Mktg., Better Homes and Gardens, Des Moines, Iowa, 1989—, Meredith Group Sales, New Media, N.Y.C., Iowa, 1989—. Office: Better Homes & Gardens 750 3d Ave New York NY 10017*

KAPLAN, JOCELYN RAE, financial planning firm executive; b. Apr. 23, 1952; d. Eugene S. and Adeline (Dembo) K. BS, Northwestern U., 1975. CFP. Ins. agt. Fidelity Union Life Ins. Co., College Park, Md., 1976-77, Bankers Life Ins. Co., Rockville, Md., 1977-80; fin. planner Reutemann & Wagner, McLean, Va., 1980-82; fin. planning casewriter McLean Fin. Group, 1982-83; dir. fin. planning DeSanto Naftal Co., Vienna, Va., 1983-85; pres. Advisors Fin., Inc., Falls Church, Va., 1985—. Founding mem., treas. Congregation Bet Mischpachah, Washington, 1981, v.p., 1982, pres., 1983. Recipient Nat. Quality award Nat. Assn. Life Underwriters, 1978, Agent of Yr. award Gen. Agent and Mgrs. Assn., 1978; named among Top 300 Fin. Planners in U.S.A., Worth Mag., 1998. Mem. Internat. Assn. Fin. Planners, Inst. CFPs. Home: 1029 N Stuart St Apt 308 Arlington VA 22201-4752 Office: Advisors Fin Inc 510 N Washington St # 300 Falls Church VA 22046-3537

KAPLAN, JOEL STUART, lawyer; b. Bklyn., Feb. 1, 1937; s. Abraham Larry and Phayne (Moses) K.; m. Joan Ruth Katz, June 19, 1960; children: Andrea Beth, Pamela Jill. BA, Bklyn. Coll., 1958; LLB, NYU, 1961. Bar: N.Y. 1962, U.S. Dist. Cts. (ea. and so. dists.) N.Y. 1964, U.S. Ct. Appeals (2d cir.) 1966, U.S. Supreme Ct. 1979, Fla. 1982, D.C. 1987. Asst. town atty. Town of Hempstead, Nassau County, N.Y., 1962-67; ptnr. Jaspan, Kaplan, Levin & Daniels and predecessors, Garden City, N.Y., 1970-83; sole practice Garden City, 1983-95; counsel Levin Belsky Ross and Daniels, Garden City, 1995—. Chmn. Hempstead Town Pub. Employment Rels. Bd., 1973-81; pres. dist. #1 B'nai B'rith, 1986-87, internat. bd. govs., 1987—; chmn. Nat. Ctr. Cmty. Action, 1996—, B'nai B'rith Found. U.S., 1989-90; rep. candidate N.Y. State Senate, 1974. Mem. ABA, N.Y. State Bar Assn., Nassau County Bar Assn. Home: 973 E End Woodmere NY 11598-1005 Office: 585 Stewart Ave Ste 700 Garden City NY 11530-4785

KAPLAN, JOHN, photojournalist, consultant, educator; b. Wilmington, Del., Aug. 21, 1959; s. Ralph Benjamin and Ruth Jillya (Denkin) K. BJ cum laude, Ohio U., Athens, 1982; MS in Journalism, Ohio U., 1998. Photojournalist, designer Spokesman Rev./Chronicle, Spokane, Wash., 1983-84; photojournalist, picture editor Pitts. Press, 1984-90; photojournalist Pitts. Post-Gazette, 1990-92; spl. corr. Block Newspapers, 1992-94; dir. Media Alliance, con., Pitts., 1990—; vis. lectr. Bradley U., Peoria, Ill., 1989; tchr., lectr. numerous univs., seminars, profl. groups, U.S., Can., 1984—; adj. prof. Syracuse U., London campus, 1993; mem. Pulitzer Prize jury, 1994, 95; Knight fellow U. Ohio, 1997—; mem. photojournalism mem. Ball State Univ., Muncie, 1998-99; assoc. prof. U. Fla., Gainesville, 1999—. Author: Mom and Me, 1996; contbr. to book series The Best of Photojournalism, Vols. 6, 7, 9, 10, 11, 14, 18, 1981-93. Recipient Golden Quill Journalism award Pitts. Press Club, 1986, 89, Pitts. Photographer of Yr. News Photographers Assn. Greater Pitts., 1986, 89, 92, Robert F. Kennedy Journalism award Kennedy Found., 1989, Pulitzer Prize for feature photography, 1992, Matrix Mag. award Women in Comm., 1992, Ohio U. Disting. Grad. award, 1993; named Photographer of Yr. Pa. Press Photographers Assn., 1989, No. Photographer of Yr., 1992, Ohio U. Coll. Comm. Hall of Fame, 1993; work in permanent collection Carnegie Mus. of Art, Pitts.; named Knight fellow Ohio U., 1997-98. Mem. Nat. Press Photographers Assn. (contest chmn. Region 3, 1987-89, Regional Photographer of Yr. awards 1985, 86, 87, 89, Nat. Newspaper Photographer of Yr. award 1989, Nikon Documentary Sabbatical award 1990, other awards), Soc. Newspaper Design (Gold award 1989), Amnesty Internat. Avocations: racquet sports, furniture design, wines. Address: 3067 Weimer Hall Gainesville FL 32611-8400

KAPLAN, JONATHAN HARRIS, healthcare business transformation and information technology specialist; b. N.Y.C., Apr. 29, 1957; s. Bernard and Arlene (Lavender) K.; m. Lorraine Caryl Weiss, Aug. 6, 1983; children: Alexandra Lindsay, Elizabeth Sydney. AB, Cornell U., 1979; MPH, U. Pitts., 1980; grad. Exec. Program, Northwestern U. Cert. data processor, mgmt. cons., systems profl. Statistician Nat. Ctr. Health Stats., Hyattsville, Md., 1980; assoc. installation dir. Shared Med. Systems, N.Y.C., 1981, installation dir., 1981-82; cons. Ernst & Young, N.Y.C., 1982-83, sr. cons., 1984, supr., 1985, mgr., 1985-86, sr. mgr., 1986-90, ptnr., 1990—, regional dir. healthcare info. tech./performance improvement, 1991-95, Great Lakes area dir., 1996—; adj. prof. health care adminstrn. Baruch Coll., CUNY. Speaker in field. Bd. govs. Arthritis Found., Larchmont Manor Park Soc.; bd. dirs. Juvenile Diabetes Found. Recipient Westinghouse Sci. award, Shared Med. Systems Field Svc. award; grantee USPHS, 1979, 80. Mem. Am. Coll. Healthcare Execs., Am. Assn. Healthcare Cons., Am. Med. Informatics Assn., Am. Hosp. Assn., Inst. Mgmt. Cons., Healthcare Info. and Mgmt. Sys. Soc., Healthcare Fin. Mgmt. Assn., N.Y. Acad. Scis., Inst. Cert. Computer Profls., Cornell U. Alumni Assn., U. Pitts. Alumni Assn., N.Y. Athletic Club, U.S. Rowing Assn., Lacrosse Found.. Met. Club, Econs. Club of Chgo., Execs. Club of Chgo., The Chgo. Club. Office: Ernst & Young LLP Sears Tower 233 S Wacker Dr Chicago IL 60606-6306

KAPLAN, JONATHAN STEWART, film director, writer; b. Paris, Nov. 25, 1947; s. Sol and Mary Frances (Heflin) K. Student, U. Chgo., 1965-67; BFA, NYU, 1969; postgrad., New World Pictures Roger Corman Post-Grad. Sch. Film Making, Hollywood, Calif., 1971-73. Mem. tech. staff Bill Graham's Fillmore East, N.Y.C., 1969-71. Actor: Broadway prodn. The Dark at the Top of the Stairs, 1956-57; dir. films: Night Call Nurses, 1972, Student Teachers, 1973, The Slams, 1973, Truck Turner, 1974, White Line Fever, 1975, Mr. Billion, 1976, Over the Edge, 1978, 11th Victim, 1979, Gentleman Bandid, 1981, White Orchid, 1982, Heart Like a Wheel, 1983, Project X, 1986, The Accused, 1987, Immediate Family, 1989, Love Field, 1990, Unlawful Entry, 1992, Bad Girls, 1994; dir. Showtime anthology series: Fallen Angels, 1994, Rebel Highway, 1994, Picture Windows, 1995; student film Stanley Stanley, 1970 (1st prize Schlitz Nat. Student Film Festival); dir. miniseries In Cold Blood, 1997, Brokedown Palace, 1999. Address: Industry Entertainment 953 S Carrillo Dr Ste 300 Los Angeles CA 90048*

KAPLAN, JOSEPH, pediatrician; b. Boston, Mar. 7, 1941. Student, Dartmouth U., 1958-60; BA, NYU, 1962; MD, Johns Hopkins U., 1966. Intern, resident in pediatrics Johns Hopkins Hosp., Balt., 1969-72; mem. staff Children's Hosp. Mich., Detroit, 1972—; prof. pediat., medicine and immunology-microbiology Wayne State U. Sch. Medicine, Detroit, 1972—. Contbr. article to profl. publ. Maj. U.S. Army, 1969-72. Recipient Rsch. Career Devel. award NIH, 1975-80. Office: Children's Hosp 3901 Beaubien St Detroit MI 48201-2119*

KAPLAN, JOSEPH SOLTE, lawyer; b. Paterson, N.J., Mar. 14, 1935; s. Sidney C. and Estelle (Solte) K.; m. Lily Chariton, Dec. 28, 1958; children: Michele Kaplan Green, Andrew Ezra, David Baruch. BA, Yeshiva U., 1956; LLB, Harvard U., 1959. Bar: N.J. 1960, N.Y. 1966, U.S. Dist. Ct. N.J. 1960, U.S. Dist. Ct. (ea. and so. dists.) N.Y. 1967, U.S. Ct. Internat. Trade 1966, U.S. Ct. Appeals (fed. cir.) 1975. Assoc. Baker, Garber & Chazen, Hoboken, N.J., 1960-65; gen. atty. U.S. Dept. Treasury, N.Y.C., 1965-66; assoc. Siegel Mandel & Davidson, N.Y.C., 1966-70; assoc. Busby, Rivkin, Sherman, Levy & Rehm, N.Y.C., 1970-71, ptnr., 1971-77; ptnr. Rivkin, Sherman & Levy, N.Y.C., 1977-81, Kaplan & Pellegrini, N.Y.C., 1981-83, Baskin & Steingut, N.Y.C., 1984-85; ptnr. Ross & Hardies, N.Y.C., 1985—, exec. com., 1992-95; mem. U.S. Ct. Internat. Trade Adv. Com., N.Y.C., 1989-97, chair 9th jud. conf. planning com. Articles editor Internat. Law Practicum, 1995—; contbr. articles to profl. jours. and publs. Bd. dirs. Jewish Bd. Family and Children's Svcs., N.Y.C., 1985-93, v.p., 1996-97, pres.-elect, 1996-97, pres., 1998—, chmn. ct. and legal svc. com., 1976-84, chmn. cmty. edn. divsn. com., 1985-92, chmn. human resources com. 1989—, chmn. exec. com., 1993—. With U.S. Army N.G., 1959-65. Mem. ABA (standing com. on customs law 1979-85), Am. Assn. Importers and Exporters (chmn. harmonized systems com. 1980-90, bd. dirs. 1993—), Customs and Internat. Trade Bar Assn. (chmn. trial and appellate practice com. 1988-92, sec. 1992-94, bd. dirs. 1988-94), N.Y. State Bar Assn. (editor Internat. Trade Newsletter 1986-87), N.J. Bar Assn., D.C. Bar Assn. Office: Ross & Hardies Park Ave Tower 65 E 55th St New York NY 10022-3219

KAPLAN, JUSTIN, author; b. N.Y.C., Sept. 5, 1925; s. Tobias D. and Anna (Rudman) K.; m. Anne F. Bernays, July 29, 1954; children: Susanna Bernays, Hester Margaret, Polly Anne. BS, Harvard U., 1944, postgrad., 1944-46; D Humane Letters (hon.), Marlboro Coll., 1984. Free-lance editing, writing N.Y.C., 1946-54; sr. editor Simon & Schuster, Inc., N.Y.C., 1954-59; lectr. English Harvard U., 1969, 73, 76, 78; prose writer in residence Emerson Coll., Boston, 1977-78; vis. lectr. Griffith U., Brisbane, Australia, 1983; lectr. in field; judge Nat. Book Awards, 1968, 73, 78, 87, 93, Pulitzer prizes, 1989, 94, 97; resident Bellagio Study and Conf. Ctr., Italy, spring, 1990; Jenks prof. contemporary letters Coll. of Holy Cross, Worcester, Mass., 1992-95. Author: Mr. Clemens and Mark Twain, 1966, Lincoln Steffens, A Biography, 1974, Mark Twain and His World, 1974, Walt Whitman: A Life, 1980, (with Anne Bernays) The Language of Names, 1997; editor: Dialogues of Plato, 1948, With Malice Toward Women, 1949, The Pocket Aristotle, 1956, The Gilded Age, 1964, Great Short Works of Mark Twain, 1967, Mark Twain, A Profile, 1967, Walt Whitman: Complete Poetry and Collected Prose, 1982, The Harper American Literature, 1987, 94, Best American Essays, 1990; gen. editor: Bartlett's Familiar Quotations, 16th edit., 1992; contbr. to N.Y. Times, New Republic, Am. Scholar, Newsweek, Ploughshares, Yale Rev., others. Participant cultural programs USIA, Israel, Dominican Republic, Mex., 1985; mem. Mass. Hist. Soc. Recipient Pulitzer prize for biography, 1967, Nat. Book award in arts and letters, 1967, Am. Book award for biography, 1981; Guggenheim fellow, 1975-76. Fellow Am. Acad. Arts and Scis., Soc. Am. Historians; mem. Am. Acad. Arts and Letters, Harvard Club (N.Y.), Phi Beta Kappa. Home: 16 Francis Ave Cambridge MA 02138-2010

KAPLAN, KALMAN JOEL, psychologist, educator; b. Chgo.; s. Lewis C. and Edith (Saposnik) K.; 1 child, Daniel Lewis. BA in Mathematics, Northwestern U., 1963; MA in Psych., U. Ill., 1966, PhD in Psych., 1968. Lic. clin. psychologist. Tech. staff Bell Labs., 1971-73; prof. dept. psychology Wayne State U., Detroit, 1968—; dir. Suicide Rsch. and Prevention Ctr. Michael Reese Hosp. and Med. Ctr., Chgo., 1995—; adj. prof. U. Psychology and Psychiatry-U. Ill., Chgo., 1996—; vis. lectr. Harvard U., 1977-78, Bar Ilan U., 1994; vis. prof. Northwestern U. Med. Sch., 1984-85, Spertus Inst. for Jewish Studies, 1995-96. Author: (with others) The Family: Biblical and Psychological Foundations, 1984, A Psychology of Hope, 1993, Living with Schizophrenia, 1997, Jewish Approaches to Suicide, Martyrdom and Euthanasia, 1998, TILT-Teaching Individuals to Live Together, 1998. Home: 1360 N Lake Shore Dr Chicago IL 60610-2181 Office: Michael Reese Hosp Dept Psych 2959 S Cottage Grove Ave Chicago IL 60616

KAPLAN, KEITH EUGENE, insurance company executive, lawyer; b. Rahway, N.J., Apr. 6, 1960; s. Eugene Aloysius and Barbara Ann (Dempski) K.; m. Rita Maria Baker, Aug. 8, 1987; children: Matthew Joseph Kaplan, William Alexander Kaplan (dec.). BS, U. Pa., 1982; JD, Temple U., 1992. Bar: Pa. 1992. Underwriter Home Ins. Co., Phila., 1982-85, underwriting supr., 1985-86; product line mgr. Home Ins. Co., N.Y.C., 1987; underwriting dir. Reliance Ins. Co., Phila., 1987-88; asst. v.p. Reliance Nat., Phila., 1988-90; asst. v.p. Reliance Nat., N.Y.C., 1990-92, v.p., 1992-96, mng. v.p., 1996—. Mem. ABA, Phila. Bar Assn., Soc. CPCU, Wharton Club. Home: 1240 Pickering Ln Chester Springs PA 19425-1423 Office: Reliance National 77 Water St New York NY 10005-4499 also: Reliance Ins Co Three Parkway Philadelphia PA 19102

KAPLAN, KEITH JACOB, physician; b. Chgo., Oct. 5, 1970; s. Martin and Adrienne Kaplan; m. Stephanie Jo Schul, Apr. 20, 1996. BS with honors, Mich. State U., 1992; MD, Northwestern U., 1996. Intern Walter Reed Army Med. Ctr., Washington, 1996-97, resident in pathology, 1997—. Capt. M.C., U.S. Army, 1996. Mem. AMA, Am. Soc. Clin. Pathologists, Coll. Am. Pathologists, Ill. State Med. Soc., Chgo. Med. Assn. Democrat. Avocations: fishing, boating, golf, running. Home: 15106 Alpine Valley Ct Silver Spring MD 20906 Office: Walter Reed Army Med ctr 6825 16th St NW Washington DC 20307

KAPLAN, KENNETH BARRY, psychologist; b. Boston, Mar. 15, 1947; s. Harold Irving and Eleanor (Miller) K.; m. Rhonda I. Sherer; children: David B., Rachel L., Howard D., Amy M. BA, U. Mass., Boston, 1969; EdM in Ednl. Counseling Psychology, Suffolk U., 1972; postgrad., Boston State Coll., 1974-76, Emmanuel Coll., 1974-76, Bridgewater State Coll., 1982-83, Fitchburg State Coll., 1989-90. Lic. cert. social worker, ednl. psychologist, sch. psychologist, tchr., secondary sch. prin. Asst. mgr. S.S. Pierce Co., 1970-71; tchr. Boston Pub. Schs., 1972-82; cons. svc. specialist for retarded individuals Wrentham State Sch., 1972-79; secondary sch. psychologist Bridgewater/Raynham (Mass.) Pub. Schs., 1982—. Chair edn. sector United Way of Greater Taunton, Mass., 1991—, bd. dirs., 1991—; bd. dirs. Taunton Family. Named Horace Mann Tchr., Mass. Dept. Edn., 1986-87; Alliance Against Drugs grantee, 1993. Mem. NEA, NASW, NASP, Mass. Soc. Psychol. Assn., Mass. Sch. Counselors Assn., Mass. Assn. Social Workers, Mass. Tchrs. Assn., Raynham Edn. Assn. (pres. 1988-94), Bristol County Educators Assn., Bridgewater Raynham Edn. Assn., Plymouth County Educators Assn., Rotary. Home: 2 Sherwood Cir Sharon MA 02067-2262 Office: Bridgewater Raynham Schs 777 Pleasant St Raynham MA 02767-1561

KAPLAN, KENNETH FRANKLIN, manufacturing company financial executive; b. N.Y.C., July 14, 1945; s. Harold and Jeannette (Rubin) K.; m. Judith Zacharias, Aug. 26, 1967; children: Teri, Joshua. BS in Math., U. Mich., 1967; MBA in Mgmt., UCLA, 1969. Fin. analyst Northrop Corp., L.A., 1969-71; sr. fin. analyst Dart Industries, L.A., 1971-74; asst. controller consumer products group West Bend (Wis) Co., 1974-76, dir. fin. planning and analysis, 1976-77; controller Graham Co., Milw., 1977-81, v.p. fin. and adminstr., 1981-85; treas. Gehl Co., West Bend, 1986-96, corp. controller, 1985-87, v.p. fin., 1988-96; v.p., CFO Regal-Beloit Corp., Beloit, Wis., 1996—; sec. Regal-Beloit Corp., Beloit, 1997—. Bd. dirs., chmn. fin. com. Kettle Moraine YMCA, West Bend, 1981-96; bd. dirs. West Bend C. of C., 1988-94. Mem. Fin. Execs. Inst., Greater Beloit C. of C. (bd. dirs. 1999—). Office: Regal-Beloit Corp 200 State St Beloit WI 53511-6254

KAPLAN, LAWRENCE EDWARD, lawyer; b. Brookline, Mass., Nov. 6, 1943; s. Sidney Stanley and Estelle Irene (Shapiro) K.; m. Elizabeth Ann Joseph, Apr. 26, 1987; children: Rachel Elizabeth, Joanna Elizabeth. BS, Boston U., 1965, LLB cum laude, 1968. Bar: Mass 1969, U.S. Supreme Ct. 1986. Ptnr. Rackemann, Sawyer & Brewster, Boston, 1968-88, Goodwin, Procter & Hoar, Boston, 1988—. Contbr. article to profl. jour. Zoning bd. Appeals Brookline, Mass., 1988—. Mem. ABA, Internat. Coun. Shopping Ctrs., Boston Bar Assn., Mass. Bar Assn. (chmn. Real Property Coun. 1983), Boston U. Law Alumni Assn. (pres. 1990), Masonic Freedom Lodge. Avocations: family, biking, golf. Office: Goodwin Procter & Hoar LLP Exchange Pl Boston MA 02109-2881

KAPLAN, LAWRENCE RICE, psychologist; b. Long Island City, N.Y., Dec. 27, 1948; s. Meyer I. and Jeanette (Rice) K. BA, Columbia Coll., 1970; MA, Fordham U., 1973, PhD, 1993. Lic. psychologist, N.Y. Fellow in clin. psychology Westchester divsn. N.Y. Hosp.-Cornell Med. Ctr., White Plains, N.Y., 1975-77; staff psychologist South Beach Psychiat. Ctr., S.I., N.Y., 1977-82, Mount Kisco Mental Health Svc., Harlem Valley Psychiat. Ctr., N.Y., 1982-90, Huguenot Ctr. of Rockland Psychiat. Ctr., New Rochelle, N.Y., 1990-93; sr. psychologist Queens Family Ct. Mental Health Svc., Jamaica, N.Y., 1993-97; chief psychologist, clinic dir. Bklyn. Family Ct. Mental Health Svc., 1997—. Mem. APA, Soc. for Personality Assessment. Office: Bklyn Family Ct Mental Health Svc 283 Adams St Fl 5 Brooklyn NY 11201-2804

KAPLAN, LEE LANDA, lawyer; b. Houston, Jan. 26, 1952; s. Charles Irving and Ara Celine (Seligman) K.; m. Diana Morton Hudson, Feb. 6, 1982. AB, Princeton U., 1973; JD, U. Tex., 1976. Bar: Tex., U.S. Dist. Ct. (no., we., ea. and so. dists.) Tex., U.S. Ct. Appeals (5th, 11th and Fed. cirs.), U.S Supreme Ct. Law clk. to sr. cir. judge U.S. Ct. Appeals (5th cir.), Houston, 1976-77; assoc. Baker & Botts, L.L.P., Houston, 1977-84, ptnr., 1985-94; ptnr. Smyser Kaplan & Veselka, L.L.P., Houston, 1995—. Mem. Tex. Aerospace Commn., 1994-99. Mem. ABA, State Bar Tex., Houston Bar Assn., Am. Bd. Trial Advs. (assoc.), Am. Intellectual Property Law Assn., Houston Intellectual Property Law Assn. Democrat. Jewish. Avocation: history. Office: Smyser Kaplan & Veselka LLP 700 Louisiana St Ste 2300 Houston TX 77002-2728

KAPLAN, LEO SYLVAN, social scientist, former college administrator; b. N.Y.C., Feb. 14, 1924; s. Max and Frieda (Kuritzky) K.; m. Matilda Correa, Dec. 28, 1946; children: Michael, Harry, Hannah. B.A., CCNY, 1946; M.A., Columbia U., 1949. Mem. faculty econs. dept. Queens Coll., N.Y.C., 1952-54; research dir. Lic. Beverage Industries Inc., N.Y.C., 1955-58; mem. faculty Cooper Union, N.Y.C., 1958—, v.p., provost, 1972-84. Author book reviews and articles for profl. jours.; editor: Internat. Jour. Sociology, 1972-78. Served with AUS, 1943-45, PTO. Decorated Purple Heart. Office: Cooper Union Cooper Square New York NY 10003

KAPLAN, LEONARD EUGENE, accountant; b. Chgo., Mar. 3, 1940; s. David Solomon and Faye Gertrude (Grossman) K.; m. Myrna Dee Shellist, Dec. 20, 1959; children: Sheri Kaplan Hall, Jodi Kaplan Hoffman, Jeffrey. Student, U. Ill., Chgo., 1958-59; BSC in Acctg., De Paul U., 1961. CPA, Tex., Ill.; cert. ins. counselor. Staff acct. Goldstein, Engerman & Shane, Chgo., 1960-63; staff acct. BDO Seidman, Chgo., 1963-72, ptnr., 1972-79; ptnr. BDO Seidman, Houston, 1979-95, regional tech. dir. region III, 1982-84, mng. ptnr., 1984-89, nat. dir. industry specialization, 1990-92; also bd. dirs.; exec. v.p., sec., CFO Delta Ins. Group Corp., Houston, 1995—; mem. adv. coun. dept. acctg. U. Tex., 1989-95. Contbr. articles to various publs. Bd. dirs. Chocolate Bayou Theater Co. Ill. State scholar, 1958-61, Jack Claitor Meml. scholar Tex. Surplus Lines Assn., 1998. Mem. AICPA, Tex. Soc. CPAs (vice chmn. com. on rels. with attys. Houston chpt. 1984-85), Ill. CPA Soc., Bus. and Profl. Soc. of Jewish Fedn., Meyerland Cmty. Improvement Assn., Tex. Surplus Lines Assn. (mem. regulatory liaison com.), Westwood Country Club (pres. 1985-86), B'nai B'rith (newsletter editor 1971-72). Jewish. Avocations: golf, tennis, crossword puzzles. *Concern for what might have been is never productive. Yesterday is what it is. Today and the rest of your life are what you make them. Focus on the future and never look back.*

KAPLAN, LEWIS A., judge; b. S.I., N.Y., Dec. 23, 1944; s. Alfred H. and Dorothy A. K.; m. Nancy Gelberg, Aug. 29, 1968; 1 child, Merrill. AB, U. Rochester, 1966; JD, Harvard U., 1969. Bar: N.Y. 1970, U.S. Ct. Appeals (1st and 2d cirs.) 1970, U.S. Dist. Ct. (so. and ea. dists.) N.Y. 1971, U.S. Ct. Appeals (3d cir.) 1973, U.S. Supreme Ct. 1973, U.S. Dist. Ct. (we. dist.) N.Y. 1975, U.S. Ct. Appeals (D.C. cir.) 1976, U.S. Ct. Appeals (4th and 5th cirs.) 1979, U.S. Dist. Ct. (no. dist.) Calif. 1980, U.S. Ct. Appeals (9th cir.) 1980, U.S. Dist. Ct. (ea. dist.) Mich. 1983, U.S. Ct. Appeals (6th cir.) 1983, D.C. 1985, U.S. Ct. Appeals (Fed. and 11th cirs.) 1987, U.S. Dist. Ct. D.C. 1988. Law clk. to judge U.S. Ct. Appeals (1st cir.), 1969-70; assoc. Paul, Weiss, Rifkind, Wharton & Garrison, N.Y.C., 1970-77, ptnr., 1977-94; judge U.S. Dist. Ct. (so. dist.) N.Y., N.Y.C., 1994—; spl. master Westway litigation U.S. Dist. Ct. (so. dist.) N.Y., 1982; trustee Lawyers Com. for Civil Rights Under Law, 1992-94; mem. Comm. on Automation and Tech., Jud. Conf. U.S., 1997—. Mem. trustees' coun. U. Rochester, 1982-88; mem.

trustees' vis. com. William E. Simon Grad. Sch. Bus. Adminstrn., 1986-88; village trustee N.Y., 1988-91. Fellow Am. Coll. Trial Lawyers (jud.); mem. ABA, N.Y. State Bar Assn., Fed. Bar Coun., Am. Law Inst., Fed. Judges' Assn. (dir. 1997—). Office: US Courthouse 500 Pearl St New York NY 10007-1316

KAPLAN, MANUEL E., physician, educator; b. N.Y.C., Nov. 6, 1928; s. Morris Jacob and Sylvia (Schiff) K.; m. Rita Goldman, May 22, 1955; children—Anne J., Eve D., Joshua M. BSc. Diplomate Am. Bd. Internal Medicine, Am. Bd. Hematology. Intern Boston City Hosp., 1954-55, resident, 1955-56, 58-59; fellow in hematology Thorndike Lab., 1959-62; attending hematologist Mt. Sinai Hosp., N.Y.C., 1962-65, asst. chief hematology, 1963-65; asst. prof. medicine Washington U. Sch. Medicine, St. Louis, 1965-69; asso. prof. medicine U. Minn. Sch. Medicine, Mpls., 1969-72, prof. medicine, 1972-97, prof. emeritus, 1997—; chief hematology and oncology Mpls. VA Med Ctr., 1969-93; med. dir. physician asst. program Augsburg Coll., Mpls., 1995—. Contbr. numerous articles to profl. jours. Served with USPHS, 1956-58. Mem. Am. Fedn. Clin. Research, Am. Soc. Clin. Investigation, Am. Soc. Hematology, Am. Assn. Immunology, AAAS, others. Jewish. Home: 2950 Dean Pky Apt 1201 Minneapolis MN 55416-4427 Office: Augsburg Coll Physician Asst Program Minneapolis MN 55454

KAPLAN, MARJORIE ANN PASHKOW, school district administrator; b. Bronx, N.Y., Apr. 10, 1940; d. William B. and Laura (Libov) Pashkow; m. Marvin R. Kaplan, Aug. 16, 1962 (dec. 1980); children: Eliot, Mara; m. Timothy Sweeney, 1985 (div. 1986). BA, Smith Coll., 1962; MA, Ariz. State U., 1974, PhD, 1979. Presch. dir., tchr. Temple Beth Israel, Phoenix, 1967-72; tchr. Washington Sch. Dist., Phoenix, 1972-74, coord., 1974-75, prin., 1975-81; asst. supt. Paradise Valley Unified Sch. Dist., Phoenix, 1981-83, supt., 1984-92; supt. Shawnee Mission Unified Sch. Dist., Overland Park, Kans., 1992—. Named Ariz. Supt. of Yr., 1992, Ariz. Sch. Bd. Assn. Supt. of Yr., 1987-88; named to Top 100 Educators, Exec. Educator mag., 1986. Mem. Am. Assn. Sch. Adminstrs. Office: Shawnee Mission Unified Sch Dist 512 7235 Antioch Rd Shawnee Mission KS 66204-1758*

KAPLAN, MARTIN P., allergist, immunologist, pediatrician; b. Bklyn., Oct. 28, 1928. MD, SUNY Downstate. Diplomate Am. Bd. Allergy & Immunology, Am. Bd. Pediatrics. Resident Jewish Hosp., Bklyn., 1954-55, SUNY Upstate Med. Ctr., Syracuse, 1957-58; fellow Children's Hosp., Washington, 1958-59; active staff mem. dept. medicine St. Joseph Hosp., Lexington, Ky., 1959—; clin. assoc. prof. pediatrics and medicine U. Ky. Coll. Medicine, 1982-97. Mem. AAACI, ACAI, AMA, Ky. Med. Assn. Office: 2370 Nicholasville Rd Ste 102 Lexington KY 40503-3014

KAPLAN, MARTIN PAUL, pediatrician, educator; b. N.Y.C., Sept. 30, 1946; s. Abraham I. and Shirley (Bercovici) K.; m. Cynthia Gordon, June 21, 1970; children—Benjamin Mark, Dara Beth, Rachel Eve. B.A., U. Pa., 1968; M.D., N.Y. U. 1972; Intern, N.Y. U. Bellevue, N.Y.C., 1972-73, resident, 1973-74; sr. resident in pediatrics Duke Hosp., Durham, N.C., 1974-75; practice medicine specializing in pediatrics, Port Jefferson, N.Y., 1978—; mem. staff St. Charles Hosp.; chief pediatrics , 1994—, John T. Mather Hosp., (both Port Jefferson); bd. dirs. L.I. Physicians Holding Corp; clin. asst. prof. SUNY Stony Brook, 1981—. Mem. Brookhaven Youth Bd., Patchogue, N.Y., 1981-88. Served to lt. comdr. USNR, 1975-78. Fellow Am. Acad. Pediatrcis; mem. AMA, N.Y. State Med. Soc., Sufolk Pediatric Soc. (treas. 1984, sec. 1985, v.p. 1986, pres. 1987), Suffolk County Med. Soc. Democrat. Jewish. Office: 12 Medical Dr Port Jefferson Station NY 11776-1588

KAPLAN, MELVIN HYMAN, immunology, rheumatology, medical educator; b. Malden, Mass., Dec. 23, 1920; s. Harry and Rena (Chernoff) K. A.B., Harvard U., 1942, M.D., 1952. Intern Boston City Hosp., 1952; research fellow medicine House of Good Samaritan, Boston; also asst. bacteriology and immunology Harvard Med. Sch., 1953; research assoc. medicine, instr., also established investigator Am. Heart Assn., 1954-57, assoc. bacteriology and immunology, 1957-58; practice medicine, specializing in rheumatology and clin. immunology Cleve., 1958—; asst. prof. medicine Sch. Medicine Western Res. U., 1958-60, assoc. prof., 1960-65, prof., 1965-74; prof. medicine U. Mass., 1974-91, prof. emeritus, 1991—, dir. div. immunology and rheumatology, 1974-82, acting chmn. lab. medicine, 1974-79; assoc. physician Cleve. Met. Gen. Hosp., 1958-62, physician, 1962-74; Cons. allergy and immunology study sect. USPHS, 1964-69; asso. mem. com. streptococcal diseases Armed Forces Epidemiological Bd., 1956-70; temp. adviser WHO Study Cardiomyopathies in Africa, 1965; mem. merit review bd. VA, 1972—; mem. med. adv. bd. Arthritis Found., New Eng. Lupus Found. Assoc. editor: Jour. Lab. and Clin. Medicine, 1963-68, Jour. Clin. and Exptl. Immunology, 1965-71; Contbr. articles to profl. jours. Served with AUS, 1942-46. Recipient Research Career award USPHS, 1964. Mem. Am. Soc. Clin. Investigation, Am. Rheumatism Assn., Am. Assn. Immunologists. Home: 1550 Worcester Rd Apt 519 Framingham MA 01702-8988 Office: 55 Lake Ave N Worcester MA 01655-0002

KAPLAN, MICHAEL DANIEL, physics and chemistry researcher, educator; b. Kishinev, Moldova, USSR, June 29, 1946; came to U.S., 1991; s. Daniel Michael and Bluma Daniel (Portugeise) K.; m. Pauline Boris Rosenhaupt, Apr. 5, 1968; 1 child, Daniel. MS in Physics, Kishinev U., 1969; PhD in Solid State Physics, Leningrad (Russia) U., 1976; Dr Sci in Solid State Physics, Moscow U., 1985. Rsch. assoc. All-Union Inst. Non-Destructive Evaluation, Kishinev, 1970-76, sr. rschr., 1976-80; sr. rschr. Inst. Chemistry Acad. Scis. Moldova, Kishinev, 1980-85, leading rschr., 1985-91; vis. prof. phyics dept. Boston U., 1992-93; lectr. chemistry dept. U. Mass., Lowell, 1992-93; lectr. physics dept. Boston U., 1993, vis. rsch. prof., 1993—; adj. assoc. prof. chemistry dept. Simmons Coll., Boston, 1993-97, assoc. prof. dept. chemistry, 1997—; invited lectr.; cons. Aspen Licensing Corp., West Palm Beach, Fla., 1992, The BOC (Brit. Oxygen Corp.) Group, Murray Hill, N.J., 1996. Author: (with B. Vekhter) Cooperative Phenomena in Jahn-Teller Crystals, 1995; contbr. numerous articles to profl. jours.; patentee in field. Recipient Inventor of USSR medal Ministry Instrumentation Design and Automation, 1988; grantee MIDA, Inst. Electronics Wave Rsch. and Mfg. Corp. Mem. AAUP, Am. Chem. Soc. Jewish. Avocations: music, table tennis. Home: 44 Upton Rd Waltham MA 02452-8020 Office: Simmons Coll Chemistry Dept 300 Fenway Boston MA 02115-5820

KAPLAN, MICHAEL J., federal judge; b. 1947. BA, Columbia U., 1968; JD, Boston U., 1971. Bar: N.Y. Pvt. practice, Rochester, N.Y., 1974-81; clk. of ct. U.S. Dist. Ct. for Western Dist. N.Y., Buffalo, 1988-91; bankruptcy clk. U.S. Bankruptcy Ct., Buffalo, 1981-88, chief bankruptcy judge for western N.Y., 1991—; adj. asst. prof. Monroe C.C., Rochester, 1973-79; mem. adj. faculty bus. law Rochester Inst. Tech., 1979-81. Office: US Bankruptcy Ct 310 US Courthouse 68 Court St Buffalo NY 14202-3405

KAPLAN, MIKE, film and video producer, director, and distributor, marketing executive; b. Providence, Mar. 16, 1943; s. Julius and Ida (Rabinovitz) k. BA, U. R.I., 1964. Assoc. editor Ind. Film Jour., N.Y.C., 1964-65; publicist MGM, N.Y.C., 1965-68, publicity coord., 1968, nat. publicity dir., 1968-71; v.p. Polaris Prodns. (Stanley Kubrick), London, 1971-73; internat mkgt. exec. Warner Bros., L.A., London, 1973-74; pres. Circle Assocs. Ltd., U.S., London, 1973—, Lion's Gate Distbn., 1975-80; mktg. v.p. Lion's Gate Films (Robert Altman), 1975-80; producer, pres. Circle Assoc. Ltd., L.A., 1978—; v.p. mktg. Northstar Internat., Hal Ashby, L.A., 1981-83; pres. mktg. Alive Films, L.A., 1985-87. Producer: (Film) The Whales of August, 1987; (video) Oak Grove Sch., 1988; assoc. prodr.; (film) Short Cuts, 1992; prodr., dir. (documentary) Luck, Trust and Ketchup: Robert Altman in Carver Country, 1994, (documentary) Ann Sothern: The Sharpest Girl In Town, 1999; actor: Buffalo Bill and The Indians, Welcome To L.A., Choose Me, The Player. Recipient Best Film award Nat. Media Awards, Retirement Rsch. Found., 1987, Key Art award Hollywood Reporter, 1976, 87. Mem. Acad. Motion Picture Arts and Scis., Screen Actors Guild, Publicists Guild. Avocations: songwriting, vintage paper collectibles. Fax: (310) 574-1950. Office: Circle Assocs PO Box 5730 Santa Monica CA 90409-5730

KAPLAN, MITCHELL ALAN, sociologist, researcher; b. Bklyn., Jan. 26, 1954; s. Murray Robert and Claire (Meshnick) K. BA in Sociology and Psychology cum laude, L.I. U., 1976; MA in Sociology, New Sch. for Social Rsch., 1979; PhD in Sociology, CUNY, 1987. Cert. social rsch. specialist; cert. profl. sociol. practitioner Am. Acad. Profl. Sociol. Practitioners. Rsch. fellow Narcotic and Drug Rsch. Inc., N.Y.C., 1986-89, cons., 1989-90; cons. Am. Found. for AIDS Rsch., N.Y.C., 1989-90; rsch. scientist Rsch. & Tng. Inst. Nat. Ctr. for Disability Svcs., Albertson, N.Y., 1991-92; acad. rsch. cons. Acad. Rsch. Consulting Svcs., Bklyn., 1993—; evaluations cons. office rsch. and ednl. assessment Bklyn. divsn. N.Y.C. Bd. Edn., 1992-93; acad. rsch. cons. Acad. Rsch. Consulting Svcs., Inc., 1993—; devel. rschr. Am. Heart Assn. N.Y.C. Affiliate, 1994; sr. rsch. assoc., program evaluator Office Acad. Affairs, CUNY, Kennedy Fellows Program, 1994-95; evaluation cons. Mayor's Office on AIDS Policy Coordination, 1996. Co-author: (chpt.) Days with Drug Distribution Which Drugs? How Many Transactions? With What Returns? 1990; contbr. articles to profl. jours. Nat. Inst. on Drug Abuse fellow, 1986-89. Mem. APHA, Nat. Rehab. Assn., Soc. for Disability Studies, N.Y. Acad. Scis., Am. Sociol. Assn. (cert. med. sociologist, social policy & evaluation rschr. law & social control rschr.), N.Y. State Sociol. Assn., Am. World Health Assn., Am. Assn. Sex Educators, Counselors and Therapists, Am. Assn. for Pub. Opinion Rsch., Nat. Rehab. Counseling Assn., Nat. Rehab. Assn. (job placement div. 1991), Pi Gamma Mu, Psi Chi, Phi Theta Kappa. Democrat. Jewish. Achievements include research in the areas of Aids and intravenous drug use, the relationship between drug use and criminal behavior, drug treatment methods, and vocational rehabilitation and the physically and emotionally disabled. Home and Office: 2560 Batchelder St Apt 8K Brooklyn NY 11235-1558

KAPLAN, MORTON A., political science and philosophy educator; b. Phila., May 9, 1921; s. Lewis J. and Anthea (Ginsberg) K.; m. Azie Mortimer, 1967. BS, Temple U., 1943; PhD, Columbia, 1951. Instr. Ohio State U., 1951-52; asst. prof. polit. sci. Haverford Coll., 1953-54; mem. staff Brookings Instn., Washington, 1954-55; asst. prof. polit. sci. U. Chgo., 1956-61, asso. prof., 1961-65, chmn. com. internat. relations, 1959-85, prof. polit. sci., 1965-89, Disting. Svc. prof., 1989-91, Disting. Svc. prof. emeritus, 1991—; editor, pub. The World & I, 1985—; dir. Ford. workshop program in internat. relations, 1961-76, dir. faculty arms control and fgn. policy seminar, 1970-75; dir. Ctr. for Strategic and Fgn. Policy Studies, 1976-85; cons. Japan War Coll. and Defense Agy., 1979; rsch. assoc. Ctr. of Internat. Studies, Princeton, 1958-62; vis. assoc. prof. polit. sci. Yale U., 1961-62; mem. staff Hudson Inst., 1961-78, cons., 1978-80; lectr. Command and Gen. Staff Sch., 1965-67, Fgn. Svc. Inst., 1967, Air War Coll., 1967-69, NAt. Def. Coll. Can., 1970-72; bd. assocs. Fgn. Policy Rsch. Inst., 1967-90; Gabrielson Disting. lectr. Bowdoin Coll., 1968; Nulton Disting. lectr. Goucher Coll., 1969; cons. NEH, 1972-74; pres. Cetra Music Corp., 1962—, Moraz Prodns., Inc., 1963—; cons. Com. Econ. Devel., 1965, Braddock, Dunn and McDonald, 1969, 72; cons. USIA, 1972; sect. chmn. Internat. Confs. in Unity Scis., 1975, 76, 78, 79, chmn., 1980-83; bd. dirs. Univ. Ctrs. for Rational Alternatives, 1969-96; bd. govs., rsch. com. Stratis, Israeli Inst. Strategic Studies and Policy Analysis, 1974-79; trustee U. Bridgeport, 1992—. Author: System and Process in International Politics, 1957, Some Problems in the Strategic Analysis of International Politics, 1959, The Communist Coup in Czechoslovakia, 1960, (with Nicholas de B. Katzenbach) The Political Foundations of International Law, 1961, (with Reitzel and Coblenz) United States Foreign Policy, 1945-55, 1956, Macropolitics: Essays on the Philosophy and Science of Politics, 1969, On Historical and Political Knowing: An Inquiry into Some Problems of Universal Law and Human Freedom, 1971, Dissent and the State in Peace and War: An Essai on the Grounds of Public Morality, 1970, On Freedom and Human Dignity: The Importance of the Sacred in Politics, 1973, The Rationale for NATO; Past and Future, 1973, (with others) Vietnam Settlement: Why 1973, Not 1969?, 1973, Alienation and Identification, 1976, Towards Professionalism in International Theory: Macrosystem Analysis, 1979, Science, Language and the Human Condition, 1984, rev. edit., 1989, Law in A Democratic Society, 1993; editor: The Revolution in World Politics, 1962, The New Approaches to International Relations, 1968, SALT: Problems and Prospects, 1973, Strategic Thinking and Its Moral Implications, 1973; editor, contbg. author: Great Issues of International Politics, 1970, 74, Isolation or Interdependence? - Today's Choices for Tomorrow's World, 1975, NATO and Dissuasion, 1974, Global Policy: Challenge of the 80s, 1983, Character and Identity vol. 1: Philosophical Foundations of Political and Sociological Perspectives, 1998, vol 2: Historical and Literary Perspectives, 1999; coauthor: The Life and Death of the Cold War: Selected Studies in Post-War Statecraft, 1976; co-editor, contbg. author: Japan, America, and the Future World Order, 1976, Justice, Human Nature, and Political Obligation, 1976; co-editor: The Soviet Union and the Challenge of the Future, 4 vols., 1988-89; mem. editl. bd. Jour. Conflict Resolution, 1961-79; mem. editorial bd. World Politics, 1961-71, ORBIS, 1967-90; editor, contbr. The Many Faces of Communism, 1978; editor, Consolidating Piece in Europe, 1987; co-editor: Morality and Religion, 1992, The World of 2044: Technological Development and The Future of Society, 1994. Bd. trustees U. Bridgeport, 1994—; pres. Profs. World Peace Acad., 1983—. With AUS, 1943-46. Fellow Center Internat. Studies Princeton, 1952-53; Center Advanced Study in Behavioral Scis., 1955-56; Carnegie fellow, 1959-60. Mem. AAAS, Am. Polit. Sci. Assn., Inst. Strategic Studies London, Instituto Mexicano de Cultura (corr.), Internat. Cultural Soc. Korea (hon.), Profs. World Peace Acad. Internat. (pres. 1983—). Address: 5446 S Ridgewood Ct Chicago IL 60615-5315 *Constantly to seek new ideas, not for their newness, but for their ability to illuminate the condition of man.*

KAPLAN, NADIA, writer; b. Chgo., Feb. 28, 1921; d. Peter and Aniela (Buchynska) Charydchak; m. Norman Kaplan, July 25, 1942 (dec. July 1989); children: Fawn Marie Stom, Norma Jean Martinez. BEd, Pestalozzi Froebel Tchrs. Coll, Chgo., 1948; postgrad., UCLA, 1947, L.A. City Coll., U. Hawaii, Pepperdine U., 1970, Santa Monica Coll., 1981-87. Cert. tchr., Calif. Photographer, mgr. Great Lakes (Ill.) Naval Tng. Sta., 1942-45; primary/kindergarten tchr. L.A. Unified Sch. Dist., 1946-81. Contbr. articles to profl. jours.; creator puzzles various mags. Vol. recreational tchr. Found. for Jr. Blind, L.A., 1956-75, vol. camp counselor Camp Bloomfield, Calif., camp dir., 1956-61, leader cross-country study tour for blind teenagers, 1962; mem. dem. Nat. Com., 1985—. Pestalozzi Froebel Tchrs. Coll. scholar, 1938-41. Mem. AAUW, Women Writers West (membership chair 1982-84), United Tchrs. L.A., Calif. Ret. Tchrs. Assn., Assn. Ret. Tchrs. Ukrainian Orthodox. Avocations: writing, bonsai cultivation, doll collecting, travel, golf. Home: 1827 Fanning St Los Angeles CA 90026-1439

KAPLAN, NORMAN CHARLES, industrialist, philanthropist; b. Cleveland, OH, Nov. 11, 1952; s. Sydney and Doris R. Kaplan. Student, Calif. Inst. Arts, L.A., 1970-71; BA in Poetry, U. Calif., San Diego, 1975, postgrad., cancer rsch., Biology Dept., 1977-79; postgrad., Harvard U., 1975-76, 79-81, MA in Edn., 1977; postgrad., Salk Inst. Biol. Studies, 1978-79. Chmn., pres. Calcol Inc., 1981—; chmn. Calcol Changbaishan Pharm. Co. Ltd., Shenzhen, China, 1994—, Sanhe Meile Soft Drinks Co. Ltd., Beijing, 1995—. Exhibited paintings and sculptures at various shows; contbr. articles to profl. jours.; author of poetry; patentee in field. Active Temple Emanuel N.Y.C.; bd. mem. Nat. Jewish Dem. Coun., 1995-96, Inst. for Social and Econ. Policy in the Middle East, John F. Kennedy Sch. Govt., Harvard U., 1996-98, dean's com. internat. devel., 1999—; hon. dep. dir. Beijing Ctr. Jewish Studies, 1994—; founder Norman C. Kaplan Fund in Water Resource Mgmt., Hebrew U., Jerusalem, 1988. Recipient Sixtieth Anniversary medal Hebrew U., Cleve. Ohio Br. of Am. Friends of the Hebrew U., 1988. Mem. Harvard U. Club N.Y. (former mem. athletic subcom., house and program coms.). E-mail: CALCOL@aol.com. Address: 23425 Bryden Rd Shaker Heights OH 44122

KAPLAN, OZER BENJAMIN, environmental health specialist, consultant; b. Santiago, Chile, Jan. 3, 1940; naturalized U.S. citizen, 1969; s. David and Raquel (Klorman) K.; m. Adele M. Brandt, Jan. 12, 1974 (div. 1993);m. Janna Mirkh, Nov. 20, 1994. Student, U. Chile, 1958-59; BS, Calif. Polytech. U., 1964; MS, U. Calif., Davis, 1966, PhD, 1969; MPH, UCLA, 1973. Teaching and rsch. asst. U. Calif., Davis, 1968-69; assoc. prof. soil sci. N.C. A & T State U., Greensboro, 1969-70; assoc. prof. biology Morris Coll., Sumter, S.C., 1970-71; ind. cost/benefit cons. L.A., 1971-72; mem. environ. health task force Inland Counties Health Systems Agy., San Bernardino, Calif., 1974-76; environ. health planning coord. San Bernardino County, Calif., 1974-80; ind. cons. environ. health San Bernardino, 1987—. Author: Septic Systems Handbook, 1986, 2d edit. 1990. V.p. Citizens Against Pass Area Prisons, Riverside County, Calif., 1982-86, Pass Citizens for Sound Planning, Riverside County, 1986-91. Mem. Soil Sci. Soc. Am. (emeritus), Am. Botanical Coun./Herb Rsch. Found., Calif. Environ. Health Assn. (chmn. land use com., chmn. environ. health sect., Cert. of Appreciation, 1976, 77), Sigma Xi. Achievements include collection and development of data which helped persuade state of California to relocate planned prison from Beaumont to isolated desert location in Blythe; research on solving septic systems problems.

KAPLAN, PETER JAMES, lawyer; b. Cambridge, Mass., Jan. 27, 1943; s. George I. and Ethel B. K.; m. Sally Grueskin; children—Benjamin D., Theodore B., Emily A. B.S., Wharton Sch. Fin. and Commerce, U. Pa., 1964; J.D., Georgetown U., 1967; postgrad. in labor law, N.Y. U., 1976—. Bar: Mass. 1967, N.Y. 1976. Investment banker Hallgarten & Co., N.Y.C., 1968-72; dir. ops. Wildcat Service Corp—Vera Inst. Justice, N.Y.C., 1972-74; sec., gen. counsel Wildcat Svc. Corp Vera Inst. Justice, 1974-77, Seligman & Latz, Inc., N.Y.C., 1977-81; pres. Nat. Media Group Inc., N.Y.C., 1981—; bd. dirs. Indonesia Fund, Inc. Home: 310 W 86th St New York NY 10024-3142 Office: Nat Media Group Inc 1790 Broadway New York NY 10019-1412

KAPLAN, PETER ROBERT, cardiologist; b. Peterson, N.J., June 10, 1939. BA, Princeton U., 1960; MD cum laude, U. Pa., 1964. Diplomate Nat. Bd. Med. Examiners, Am. Bd. Internal Medicine. Intern U. Va. Hosp., 1964-65, jr. asst. resident medicine, 1967-68, sr. asst. resident medicine, 1968-69, clin. fellow cardiovascular disease, 1969-71, chief resident, asst. attending physician, 1971-72; cardiologist St. Thomas Cardiology Group, Nashville, 1972—; chief cardiology St. Thomas Hosp., Nashville, 1995—, pres. med. staff, 1995-97. Capt. Med. Corps U.S. Army, 1965-67. Mem. Tenn. Med. Assn., Albermarle County Med. Soc., Davidson Med. Soc., Seton Soc., Phi Beta Kappa. Office: St Thomas Cardiology Group 4230 Harding Rd Ste 805 Nashville TN 37205-4900*

KAPLAN, PHYLLIS, computer artist, painter; b. Bklyn., July 4, 1950; d. Abraham and Ida (Heller) K. BFA, Cooper Union, 1972; postgrad., Domus Acad., Milan, 1985. Computer artist; curator art exhibit Orgn. Ind. Artists, N.Y.C., 1995-96, Westside Arts Coalition, N.Y.C., 1997; lectr., presenter in field. Exhibited paintings at Lever House, N.Y.C., 1968, Berkshire Mus., Pittsfield, Mass., 1970, L.I. U., N.Y.C., 1975, Biola U., La Mirada, Calif., Nat. Mus. Women in the Arts, Beijing, China, 1995, Three Rivers Arts Festival, Carnegie Mus., Pitts., 1995-96, Fine Arts Mus. L.I., Hempstead, 1996-97, Halpert Biennial, Boone, N.C., 1997, Cork Gallery, Lincoln Center, N.Y., 1997, Blue Mountain Gallery Invitationals, N.Y.C., 1996-98, World Artists for Tibet at Blue Mountain, 1998, Trevi Flash Art Mus., Italy, 1998; contbr. paintings to various publs. including Kings Courier, 1974, The Villager, N.Y.C., 1994, CPM News, 1994, Bklyn. Graphic, 1996. Recipient award for patriotism U.S. Savs. Bond Dr., 1987, hon. mention award Internat. Female Artist's Art Biennial, Stockholm, 1994; grantee Artists Space/Ind. Project, 1999. Mem. Orgn. Ind. Artists (contbr. to ann. calendar), Nat. Mus. Women in the Arts, Greene County Coun. on Arts. Avocations: travel, collecting antique tin toys, classical music. Home: 98 Park Ter E New York NY 10034-1417

KAPLAN, RANDY KAYE, podiatrist; b. Detroit, Sept. 18, 1954; s. Earl Gene and Renee Joy (Sheftel) K. D of Podiatric Medicine, Ohio Coll., Cleve., 1979. Diplomate Am. Bd. Podiatric Surgery. Resident Kern Hosp., Warren, Mich., 1979-80; pvt. practice specializing in podiatric medicine, surgery Detroit, 1980—; clin. instr., mem. staff Kern Hosp., Warren, 1980—; adj. prof. Ohio Coll. Podiatric Medicine, 1986—, Pa. Coll. Podiatric Medicine, 1986—; mem. staff Providence Hosp., 1995; lectr. in field. Contbr. articles to profl. jours. Co-founder The Great Lakes Conf., 1988. Recipient Earl G. Kaplan award for polit. action excellence, 1994; Inspector Gen's. Integrity award U.S. HHS, 1995. Fellow Am. Coll. Foot Surgeons; mem. Am. Diabetes Assn., Am. Podiatric Med. Assn. (mem. continuing edn. com. 1988-94, mem. labor rels. com. 1990-94), Mich. Podiatric Med. Assn. (bd. dirs. 1985—, 2nd v.p. 1988-90, pres. 1990-91, 92-93, Podiatrist of Yr. Southeastern divsn. 1987-88, Shining Star award for excellence 1992), Kern Hosp. Resident Alumni Assn., Mich. Pub. Health Assn., Phi Alpha Pi (Man of Yr. 1979). Jewish. Office: 25725 Coolidge Hwy Oak Park MI 48237-1307

KAPLAN, RICHARD JAMES, producer, director, writer, educator, consultant; b. N.Y.C., Jan. 3, 1925; s. Benjamin David and Nathalie (Blaustein) K.; m. Blanche Beatrice Aanesen, Nov. 15, 1957 (div. 1981); children: Kjeld, Kirsti, Eve, Erica. BA in Polit. Sci., Antioch Coll., 1949; Diploma Cinema, U. So. Calif., 1951. Pres. Richard Kaplan Prodns., N.Y.C., 1957—; dir., promotional films Am. Film Theater, N.Y.C., 1973; media dir. Alternative Conf. on Environ., Stockholm, 1972; media cons. CUNY, 1974-75; dir. pub. programing Astoria Motion Picture and TV Studios, N.Y.C., 1979-80; assoc. dean Pratt Inst. Sch Art and Design, N.Y.C., 1984-85; producer ABC News, N.Y.C., 1986; pres., exec. producer The Exiles Project, Inc., N.Y.C., 1987-90; cons. Harvard U., Cambridge, Mass., 1986-90; instr. NYU, CUNY, Parsons, Hunter Coll., U. Soc. Calif., U. Md., 1970-87; lectr., workshop dir. U.S. Info Svc., Arts Am., 1980, Israel, Egypt, India, Pakistan, Sri Lanka, Bangladesh, 1985; prof. Columbia U. Sch. of the Arts, 1991—; founder, dep. dir. Documentary Ctr. at Columbia U.; panelist NEH Pub. Media Program. Dir. documentary The Eleanor Roosevelt Story, 1965 (oscar 1966); producer documentary King: Montgomery to Memphis, 1970 (numerous awards 1970-71); writer, dir., producer TV film A Look at Liv, 1976, and others; dir., producer The Exiles, 1989 (Emmy award 1991), Assignment Rescue..The Story of Varian Fry and the Emergency Rescue Committee, 1997. Trustee Antioch Coll., Yellow Springs, Ohio, 1975-78; vice chmn. Rockland County Human Rights Commn., Rockland County, N.Y., 1968-71, Town of Ramapo (N.Y.) Housing Authority, 1972-76. Cpl. U.S. Army, 1943-46, ETO. Grantee NEH, Washington, 1987. Mem. Acad. Motion Picture Arts and Sci., Writers Guild of Am., Assn. Ind. Film and Video, N.Y. Film Video Council (bd. dirs.).

KAPLAN, RICHARD N., broadcast executive, cable; married; 2 children. Prodr. The CBS Evening News with Walter Cronkite, N.Y.C.; sr. prodr. World News Tonight, ABC, N.Y.C., 1979; exec. prodr. World News This Morning, Good Morning Am., Nightline, ABC, N.Y.C., 1984-89, Viewpoint, The Koppel Report; creator, exec. prodr. Capitol to Capitol; coord. ABC News; exec. prodr. PrimeTime Live, 1989-94, World News Tonight with Peter Jennings, 1994-96; exec. prodr. spl. projects ABC Television Network, 1996-97; pres. Cable News Network, Atlanta, 1997-. Recipient 32 Emmy awards, 4 Overseas Press Club awards, 3 George Foster Peabody awards, 2 George Polk awards, 4 Alfred I. du Pont-Columbia U. awards, 2 Gold Batons. Office: Cable News Network One CNN Ctr PO Box 105366 Atlanta GA 30348-5366*

KAPLAN, ROBERT B., linguistics educator, consultant, researcher; b. N.Y.C., Sept. 20, 1929; s. Emanuel B. and Natalie K.; m. Audrey A. Lien, Apr. 21, 1951; children—Robin Ann Kaplan Gibson, Lisa Kaplan Morris, Robert Allen. Student, Champlain Coll., 1947-48, Syracuse U., 1948-49; B.A., Willamette U., 1952; M.A., U. So. Calif., 1957, Ph.D., 1962. Teaching asst. U. So. Calif., Los Angeles, 1955-57, instr. coordinator, asst. prof. English communication program for fgn. students, 1965-72, assoc. prof., dir. English communication program for fgn. students, 1972-76, assoc. dean continuing edn., 1973-76, prof. applied linguistics, 1976-95, prof. emeritus, 1995—, dir. Am. Lang. Inst., 1986-91; instr. U. Oreg., 1957-60; cons. field service program Nat. Assn. Fgn. Student Affairs, 1964-84; pres.-elect faculty senate U. So. Calif., 1988-89, pres., 1989-90; adv. bd. internat. comparability study of standardized lang. exams. U. Cambridge Local Exams. Syndicate; vis. sr. prof. grad. sch. applied lang. studies Meikai U., Urayasu City, Chiba, Japan, 1998—. Author: Reading and Rhetoric: A Reader, 1963; (with V. Tufte, P. Cook and J. Aurbach) Transformational Grammar: A Guide for Teachers, 1968; (with R.D. Schoesler) Learning English Through Typewriting, 1969; The Anatomy of Rhetoric: Prolegomena to a Functional Theory of Rhetoric, 1971; On the Scope of Applied Linguistics, 1980; The Language Needs of Migrant Workers, 1980; (with P. Shaw) Exploring Academic English, 1984; (with U. Connor) Writing Across Languages: Analysis of L2 Text, 1987; (with W. Grabe) Introduction To Applied Linguistics, 1991, Writing Around the Pacific Rim, 1995, (with W. Grabe) Theory and Practice of Writing: An Applied Linguistics Perspective, 1996—, (with R.B. Baldauf) Language Policy from Practice to Theory, 1997; coeditor: (with R.B. Baldauf) series The Language Situation in Malawi, Mozambique, The Philippines, 1998—; editl. bd. Jour. Asian Pacific Comm., Internat. Educator, BBC English Dictionary, Second Lang. Instruction/Acquisition Abstracts, Jour. of Second Lang. Writing, Forensic Linguistics, Jour. Multilingual and Multicultural Devels., Asian Jour. of English Lang. Tchg.; contbr. articles to profl. jours., U.S. Australia, Brazil, Can., Chile,

Germany, Holland, Japan, Mexico, N.Z., Philippines and Singapore; mem. editorial bd. Oxford Internat. Encyclopedia Linguistics; editor in chief Ann. Rev. Applied Linguistics, 1980-91, editorial bd., 1991—; contbr. notes, revs. to profl. jours. U.S. and abroad. Bd. dirs. Internat. Bilingual Sch. L.A., 1986-91, Internat. Edn. Rsch. Found., 1986-94. Served with inf. U.S. Army, Korea. Fulbright sr. scholar, Australia, 1978, Hong Kong, 1986, New Zealand, 1992. Mem. Am. Anthrop. Assn., AAAS, Am. Assn. Applied Linguistics (v.p., pres. 1992-94), AAUP, Assn. Internationale de Linguistique Applique, Assn. Internationale Pour La Researche et La Diffusion Des Methodes Audio-Visuelles et Structuro-Globales, Assn. Tchrs. English as Second Lang. (chmn. 1968-69), Calif. Assn. Tchrs. English to Speakers Other Langs. (pres. 1970-71), Can. Council Tchrs. English, Nat. Assn. Fgn. Student Affairs (nat. pres. 1983-84), Linguistics Soc. Am., Tchrs. English to Speakers of Other Langs. (1st v.p., pres. 1989-91).

KAPLAN, ROBERT SAMUEL, educator; b. N.Y.C., May 2, 1940; s. Bernard R. and Jeanette (Lieman) K.; m. Ellen F. Lasher, Dec. 25, 1965; children: Jennifer Beth, Dina Rebecca. BSEE, MIT, 1961, MSEE, 1962; PhD, Cornell U., 1968; DPhil, U. Stuttgart, Germany, 1995. Prof. Carnegie-Mellon U., Pitts., 1968-84, dean bus. sch., 1977-83; prof. Harvard Bus. Sch., Boston, 1984—; dir. Pitts. Fed. Res. Bank, 1980-85, J.I. Kislak, Miami, Fla., 1986-97, Renaissance Solns, Lincoln, Mass., 1995-97; trustee Technion Inst. Tech., Haifa, Israel, 1995—. Author: Relevance Lost, 1986, Measures for Manufacturing Excellence, 1989, The Balanced Scorecard, 1996, Cost and Effect, 1998. Mem. Am. Acctg. Assn. (v.p. 1986-88), Am. Soc. Tech. (bd. trustees 1994—). Jewish. Office: Harvard Bus Sch Soldiers Fld Boston MA 02163-1317

KAPLAN, SAMUEL, pediatric cardiologist; b. Johannesburg, South Africa, Mar. 28, 1922; came to U.S., 1950, naturalized, 1958; s. Aron Leib and Tema K.; m. Molly Eileen McKenzie, Oct. 17, 1952. MB, BcH., U. Witwatersrand, Johannesburg, 1944, MD, 1949. Diplomate: Am. Bd. Pediatrics. Intern Johannesburg, 1945; registrar in medicine, 1946; lectr. physiology and medicine U. Witwatersrand, 1946-49; registrar in medicine U. London, 1949-50; fellow in cardiology, research assoc. U. Cin., 1950-54, asst. prof. pediatrics, 1954-61, assoc. prof. pediatrics, 1961-66, prof. pediatrics, 1967-87, asst. prof. medicine, 1954-67, assoc. prof. medicine, 1967-82, prof. medicine, 1982-87; prof. pediatrics UCLA, 1987—; cons. NIH; hon. prof. U. Santa Tomas, Manila. Mem. editl. bd. Circulation, 1974-80, Am. Jour. Cardiology, 1976-81, Am. Heart Jour., 1981-96, Jour. Electrocardiology, 1977-94, Clin. Cardiology, 1979—, Jour. Am. Coll. Cardiology, 1983-87, Progress Pediat. Cardiology, 1990—. Cecil John Adams fellow, 1949-50; grantee Heart, Lung and Blood Inst. of NIH, 1960—. Mem. Am. Pediatric Soc., Am. Soc. Pediatric Rsch., Am. Heart Assn. (med. adv. bd. sect. circulation), Am. Fedn. Clin. Rsch., Am. Coll. Cardiology, Internat. Carviovascular Soc., Am. Acad. Pediatrics, Midwest Soc. Pediatric Rsch. (past pres.), Sigma Xi. Alpha Omega Alpha; hon. mem. Peruvian Soc. Cardiology, Peruvian Soc. Angiology, Chilean Soc. Cardiology, Burma MEd. Assn. Achievements include research and publications on cardiovascular physiology, diagnostic methods, cardiovascular complications of pediatric AIDS and heart disease in infants, children and adolescents. Office: UCLA Sch Medicine Dept Pediatric Cardiology Los Angeles CA 90095

KAPLAN, SANFORD ALLEN, internist, allergist; b. Elizabeth, N.J., Feb. 27, 1929; s. Theodore and Rose (Fisher) K.; m. Maxine Jewel Schoenfeld, July 4, 1954; children: Lloyd Austin, Dean Ian, Keith Wayne. BS in Chemistry, Ind. U., 1950; MD, Chgo. Med. Sch./Finch U., 1954. Diplomate Nat. Bd.; charter diplomate Am. Bd. Family Practice, recert.; cert. diplomate Am. Bd. Allergy and Immunology; lic. medicine and surgery, N.Y.; lic. medicine and surgery, Fla.; cert. sch. health inspector N.Y.C. Bd. Edn.; cert. compensation rating CIM; cert. local health officer grade 2, N.Y. Rotating intern Kings County Hosp., Bklyn., 1954-55; pvt. practice specializing in internal medicine and allergy Bronxville, N.Y., 1958—; fellow in allergy Misericordia Hosp. Allergy Clinic, 1963-68; attending in medicine Mt. Vernon (N.Y.) Hosp., 1970—, Lawrence Hosp., Bronxville, 1975—; assoc. attending allergy sect. dept. medicine Westchester County Med. Ctr., 1978—; clin. assoc. prof. medicine N.Y. Med. Coll., 1986—; chmn. utilization com. Cross County Hosp., 1965-75; proctor family practice St. Joseph Hosp. Family Practice Residency Program, 1974-78; mem. med. bd. Mt. Vernon Hosp., 1977-81; clin. cons. for programs administered by N.Y. State Dept. Health; vis. clin. asst. prof. medicine N.Y. Coll. Osteopathic Medicine, 1978—; mem. hosp. bd. Westchester County Med. Ctr., 1974-76, 84-97, mem. exec. com., 1986-94, sec., 1989-94. Contbr. numerous articles to profl. jours. and confs. Dir. Big Bros.-Big Sister Program, Yonkers, N.Y., 1963-74, dir. adv. bd., 1975-95; v.p. Big Bros.-Big Sister, Inc., 1972-74; former mem. Yonkers Econ. Devel. Bd.; dir. Milton Budnick Found., 1966—, Tax Payers of N.E. Yonkers, 1964-86, Mark Brent Dolinsky Found., 1981—; chmn. Westchester Coord. Com. for Handicapped, 1977-79; apptd. advisor on narcotics to Mayor of Yonkers 1970; chmn. Narcotics Guidance Coun. 1972-75; mem. drug abuse com. Yonkers Bd. Edn., 1979-86. Maj. USAF, 1955-57, res., ret. Recipient Hon. Award of Yr., Big Bros.-Big Sister of Yonkers, 1974, Proclamation for svc. to handicapped Westchester County Exec., 1980, Cert. of Award-Winning for original writing Med. Econs., 1972. Fellow Am. Acad. Family Physicians (charter, Recognition award for active family practice tchg. 1975, 76), Am. Acad. of Allergy, Asthma and Immunology, Am. Assn. Clin. Immunology and Allergy, Am. Coll. Allergy, Asthma and Immunology; mem. AMA, Am. Geriatric Soc. (chmn. drug abuse and alcoholism com. Lawrence Hosp. 1977-80, chmn. med.-nursing liaison com. Mt. Vernon Hosp. 1984-86, mem. disaster com. Lawrence Hosp. 1981—), N.Y. State Allergy Soc., Med. Soc. of State of N.Y. (exec. com. hosp. med. staff sect., legis. com., drug abuse com., geriatric com., councilor 9th dist. 1992-95, 95-98, Presdl. Citation for comty. svc. 1975), Westchester County Med. Soc. (pub. rels. 1966-68, editl. bd. Bull. 1982—, vice chmn. legis. com. 1974-76, chmn. legis. com. 1981-86, pres.-elect 1990, pres. 1991). Home: 6 Greenwood Ct Briarcliff NY 10510-2529 Office: 821 Bronx River Rd Bronxville NY 10708-8008

KAPLAN, SHEILA, academic administrator; b. Bklyn.. BA in European History, CUNY, PhD in Modern European History; MA, Johns Hopkins U. Instr. history CUNY System; dir. spl. baccalaureate program CUNY; v.p. acad. affairs Winona (Minn.) State U.; vice-chancellor for acad. affairs Minn. State U. System; chancellor U. Wis.-Parkside, Kenosha, 1986-93; pres. Met State Coll., Denver, CO, 1993—. Bd. dirs. Kenosha Area Devel. Corp., Racine County Econ. Devel. Corp.; chmn. bd. Council for Adult and Experiential Learning. Office: Metropolitan State Coll Office of President PO Box 173362 Denver CO 80217-3362*

KAPLAN, SHELDON, lawyer; b. Mpls., Feb. 16, 1915; s. Max Julius and Harriet (Wolfson) K.; m. Helene Bamberger, Dec. 7, 1941; children—Jay Michael, Mary Jo, Jean Burton, Jeffrey Lee. BA summa cum laude, U. Minn., 1935; LLB, Columbia U., 1939. Bar: N.Y. 1940, Minn. 1946. Pvt. practice N.Y.C., 1940-42, Mpls., 1946—; mem. firm Lauterstein, Spiller, Bergerman & Dannett, N.Y.C., 1939-42; ptnr. Maslon, Kaplan, Edelman, Borman, Brand & McNulty, Mpls., 1946-80; chmn. Kaplan, Strangis and Kaplan, Mpls., 1980—; bd. dirs. Stewart Enterprises Inc., Creative Ventures Inc., Bank Windsor. Decisions editor Columbia Law Review, 1939. Served to capt. AUS, 1942-46. Mem. Minn. Bar Assn., Hazeltime Nat. Golf Club, Mpls. Club, Phi Beta Kappa. Home: 2950 Dean Pkwy Minneapolis MN 55416-4446 Office: Kaplan Strangis & Kaplan 5500 Norwest Ctr Minneapolis MN 55402

KAPLAN, SIDNEY MOUNTBATTEN, lawyer; b. Bombay, Jan. 31, 1939; s. Charles von Pickens Kaplan and Jennie (Churchill) Goldberg; m. Donna Darrow, Feb. 14, 1989; children: Gary, Michael, Rory Patel. BA cum laude, Roosevelt U., 1960; JD, Ill. Inst. Tech., 1964. Bar: Ill., 1964, Minn., 1977, Colo., 1982, U.S. Dist. Ct. Ill. (no. dist.) 1964. Ptnr. Hess & Kaplan, Chgo., 1975-89, Baker & McKenzie, Chgo., 1989—; bd. dirs. Jerome Gerson Meml. Found. Mem. Ill. Bar Assn., DuPage County Bar Assn. Office: Baker & McKenzie 130 E Randolph Dr 1 Prudential Plz Chicago IL 60601*

KAPLAN, STEVEN F., business management executive; b. Bklyn., Feb. 10, 1956; s. Allen J. and Hilda K.; m. Erica Cohen; children: David, Michael. BSEE, MIT, 1977, BS in Mgmt. Sci., 1977, MS in Mgmt., 1979. Engr. Data Gen. Corp., Southboro, Mass., 1975-77; mgr., officer Strategic Planning Assocs., Washington, 1979-83; v.p., dir. The Boston Consulting Group, 1983-87; pres. Harris Graphics Web Press Group div. AM Internat., Dover, N.H.., 1987-89; pres. AM ventures and chief strategic officer AM Internat., Chgo., 1989-93, exec. v.p., chief fin. officer, chief strategic officer, 1989-93, bd. dirs.; CFO Marcam Corp., Newton, Mass., 1994-95; exec. v.p., CFO The Coleman Co., Inc., 1996-98; pres., COO, CFO Favorite Brands Internat., Inc.; dir. Kurzweil Applied Intelligence, Inc., Healthcare Data Corp.; ptnr. CAF/Tex. Pacific Group; pres., COO, CFO Favorite Brands Internat., Inc., Bannockburn, Ill.

KAPLAN, STEVEN MARK, accountant; b. Bklyn., June 22, 1952; s. Irwin and Ruth (Lieberman) K.; m. Susan Lynn Rosenberg, Nov. 19, 1972; children: Eric, Corey, Shannon. BS in Acctg., Bklyn. Coll., 1973. CPA, N.Y. Staff acct. Morris Sherwood & May, N.Y.C., 1973-74; sr. acct. Slater & Slater, Rockville Centre, N.Y., 1974-75; ptnr. Kaplan and Roberts CPA, East Rockaway, N.Y., 1975-95; prin. Steven M. Kaplan, CPA, P.C., Merrick, N.Y., 1995—. Treas. Temple Beth Am., Merrick, N.Y., 1989-94, Merrick-North Merrick Little League, 1984-97, v.p., 1989, treas., 1990-92, pres. 1993-97; bd. dirs. Merrick-North Merrick Police Athletic League, 1984-88. Mem. AICPA, N.Y. State Soc. CPA's, Nat. Soc. Pub. Accts. Avocations: baseball, photography. Office: 28 Merrick Ave Ste 8 Merrick NY 11566-3433

KAPLAN, THEODORE NORMAN, insurance company executive; b. Newburgh, N.Y., July 23, 1935; s. Edward and Bella (Kesten) K.; m. Madeline Kahn, Nov. 14, 1982; children: Garrett, Judith. BS in Acctg., Syracuse U., 1957. CLU. Ins. sales Aetna Life, N.Y.C., 1959-67, Bankers Life, N.Y.C., 1967-73, Conn. Mut., N.Y.C., 1973-77; benefits cons. Theodore N. Kaplan Assoc., Inc., N.Y.C., 1977—. Mem. Life Underwriters Assn., Million Dollar Round Table (life and qualifying mem.). Office: Theodore N Kaplan Assoc Inc 515 Madison Ave New York NY 10022-5403

KAPLANSKY, IRVING, mathematician, educator, research institute director; b. Toronto, Ont., Can., Mar. 22, 1917; came to U.S., 1940, naturalized, 1955; s. Samuel and Anna (Zuckerman) K.; m. Rachelle Brenner, Mar. 16, 1951; children—Steven, Daniel, Lucille. B.A., U. Toronto, 1938, M.A., 1939; Ph.D., Harvard, 1941; LL.D. (hon.), Queen's U., 1969. Instr. math. Harvard, 1941-44; mem. faculty U. Chgo., 1945-84, prof. math., 1956-84, chmn. dept., 1962-67, George Herbert Mead Distinguished Service prof. math., 1969-84; dir. Math. Scis. Research Inst., Berkeley, Calif., 1984-92; dir. emeritus, 1992; Mem. exec. com. div. math. NRC, 1959-62. Author books, tech. papers. Mem. Nat. Acad. Scis., Am. Math. Soc. (pres. 1985-86). Office: Math Scis Rsch Inst 1000 Centennial Dr Berkeley CA 94720-5070

KAPLOW, HERBERT ELIAS, journalist; b. N.Y.C., Feb. 2, 1927; s. Solomon and Belle (Bernstein) K.; m. Betty Koplow, Aug. 10, 1952; children—Steven, Robert, Lawrence. B.A., Queens Coll., N.Y.C., 1948; M.S., Northwestern U., 1951. News corr. NBC, Washington, 1951-72, ABC, Washington, 1972-94. Served with AUS, 1945-46. Recipient Alumni awards Queens Coll., 1963, Alumni awards Northwestern U., 1959. Mem. Sigma Delta Chi. Jewish. Home: 211 N Van Buren St Falls Church VA 22046-3654 *Curiosity and an open, receptive mind are essential characteristics of good journalism. So too is a certain humility growing from the realization that peoples' lives can be affected by a journalist's work. It is a sobering responsibility.*

KAPLOW, LEONARD SAMUEL, pathologist, educator; b. N.Y.C., Feb. 11, 1920; s. Max and Rose (Augenstreich) Kaplowitz; m. Sheila Maureen Briscoe, July 10, 1955; children: Roberta Kit, David Ross. B.S., Rutgers U., 1941; M.S., U. Vt., 1955, M.D., 1959; M.A. hon., Yale U., 1975. Diplomate: Am. Bd. Pathology. Asst. prof. pathology Med. Coll. Va., Richmond, 1963-64; asst. clin. prof., then assoc. prof. pathology and lab. medicine Yale U., New Haven, 1964-75, prof., 1975-88, prof. emeritus, 1988; chief clin. pathology VA Med. Ctr., West Haven, Conn., 1966-74, acting assoc. chief of staff research, 1974-77, chief lab service, 1974-87; lab. dir. Community Health Care Program, New Haven, 1987-88; med. dir. med. lab. technician program Housatonic Community Coll., Bridgeport, Conn., 1977-87; mem. assoc. clin. faculty Quinnipiac Coll., Hamden, Conn., 1968-75; chmn. med. adv. com. New Haven chpt. ARC, 1967-74; mem. com. lab. regulation Conn. Health Dept., Hartford, 1977-84; del. Internat. Com. Standardization in Hematology, 1974-76; program specialist pathology reserach VA Med. Research Service, Washington, 1974-78; mem. com. cytology automation Nat. Cancer Inst., NIH, 1977-81, acting chmn., 1979-81. Mem. editorial bd. Jour. Histochemistry and Cytochemistry, 1979-87; assoc. editor Jour. Soc. Analytical Cytology, 1983-87. Served to capt. AUS, 1942-46, PTO. Cited in Citation Classics Inst. Sci. Info., 1982. Mem. Histochem. Soc. (councilor 1975-80, pres. 1985), Assn. VA Chiefs of Lab. Services (pres. 1978-80), Sigma Xi, Alpha Omega Alpha. Home: PO Box 929 Mink Hill Bradford VT 05033

KAPLOW, LOUIS, law educator; b. Chgo., June 17, 1956; s. Mortimer and Irene (Horwich) K.; m. Jody Ellen Forchheimer, July 11, 1982; children: Irene Miriam, Leah Rayna. BA, Northwestern U., 1977; AM, Harvard U., 1981, JD, 1981, PhD, 1987. Bar: Mass. 1983. Prof. law Harvard U., Cambridge, Mass., 1982—, assoc. dean for rsch. and spl. programs, 1989-91. Contbr. articles to profl. jours.; co-author: Antitrust Analysis, 1988; editorial bd. Jour. of Law, Econs. and Orgn., 1989—, Internat. Rev. of Law and Econs., 1988—. Faculty rsch. assoc. Nat. Bur. Economic Rsch., Cambridge, Mass., 1985—. Mem. Am. Econ. Assn., Nat. Tax Assn. Jewish. Office: Harvard U Law Sch Cambridge MA 02138

KAPLOW, ROBERT DAVID, lawyer; b. Bklyn., Feb. 6, 1947; s. Herbert and Geraldine Rhoda K.; m. Lois Susan Silverman, May 22, 1971; children: Julie, Jeffrey. BS, Cornell U., 1968; JD, U. Mich., 1971; LLM, Wayne State U., 1978. Bar: Mich. 1972, U.S. Dist. Ct. (ea. dist.) Mich. 1972, U.S. Tax Ct. 1976, U.S. Ct. Appeals (6th cir.) 1991. Assoc. Milton Y. Zussman, Birmingham, Mich., 1972-75, Rubenstein, Isaacs, Lax & Bordman, Southfield, Mich., 1975-89; ptnr. Maddin, Hauser, Wartell, Roth, Heller & Pesses P.C., Southfield, 1989—. Bd. dirs. Jewish Assn. Retarded Citizens; mem. Fin. and Estate Planning Coun. of Detroit, Inc., Oakland County Fin. and Estate Planning Coun., Inc. Mem. ABA, Mich. Bar Assn., Oakland County Bar Assn., Cornell Club of Mich. Office: Maddin Hauser Wartell Roth Heller & Pesses PC 28400 Northwestern Hwy Fl 3 Southfield MI 48034-1839 also: PO Box 215 Southfield MI 48037-0215

KAPLOWITZ, LISA GLAUSER, physician, educator; b. Phila., Apr. 18, 1951; d. Felix E. and Charlotte (Gordy) Glauser; m. Paul Bernard Kaplowitz, Dec. 28, 1970; children: Joshua Michael, Daniel Steven. BS, U. Mich., 1970; MD, U. Chgo., 1975. Diplomate Am. Bd. Internal Medicine, Am. Bd. Infectious Diseases. Resident U. N.C., Chapel Hill, 1976-78; post-grad. fellow U. N.C., 1978-80, inst. Dept. Medicine, 1980-82; asst. prof. Dept. Medicine Med. Coll. Va., Richmond, 1982-89; assoc. prof. Dept. Medicine Med. Coll. Va., 1989—; dir. HIV/AIDS Ctr. Va. Commonwealth U., Richmond, 1993—; asst. v.p. fed. health policy Va. Commonwealth U.; bd. dirs. AIDS Action Coun., Washington, 1995-96. Contbr. (book chpt.) Conn's Current Therapy, 1985, 2d rev. edit., 1988, 3d edit., 1998, Principles of Critical Care Medicine, 1992. Mem. adv. bd. Va. League for Planned Parenthood, Richmond, 1993—, Richmond AIDS Ministry, 1988-92, Leadership Metro Richmond, 1992-93. Named Woman of Year Va. Commonwealth U., 1995, mem. Va. Women's Hall of Fame Va. Coun. on Status of Women, 1992; health policy fellow Inst. Medicine, 1996-97, fellow Office of Senator Jay Rockefeller, 1997. Fellow ACP, Infectious Disease Soc. Am.; mem. APHA, Am. Soc. Microbiology. Avocation: piano. Office: HIV AIDS Ctr Va Commonwealth U 1001 E Broad St Ste 125 Richmond VA 23219-1928

KAPNICK, HARVEY EDWARD, JR., retired corporate executive; b. Palmyra, Mich., June 16, 1925; s. Harvey E. and Beatrice (Bancroft) K.; m. Jean Bradshaw, Apr. 5, 1947 (dec. 1962); m. Mary Redus Johnson, Aug. 5, 1963; children—David Johnson, Richard Bradshaw, Scott Bancroft. Student, James Miliken U., 1942-44; B.S., Cleary Coll., 1947, D.Sc. in Bus. Adminstrn. (hon.), 1971; MBA, U. Mich., 1948; D.H.L. (hon.), DePauw U., 1979. C.P.A., Ill. Mem. staff, mgr. Arthur Andersen & Co. (CPAs), Chgo., 1948-56, partner, 1956-62; mng. ptnr. Arthur Andersen & Co. (CPAs), Cleve., 1962-70; chmn., chief exec. Arthur Andersen & Co. (CPAs), 1970-79; dep. chmn. 1st Chgo. Corp., 1st Nat. Bank Chgo., 1979-80; pres. Kapnick Investment Co., 1980-84, 89—; chmn., pres., CEO Chgo. Pacific Corp., 1984-89; vice chmn. Gen. Dynamics, 1991-94, retired, 1994; past mem. Adv. Com. on Internat. Investment, TEch. and Devel., Adv. Com. for Trade Negotiations. Mem. Pres.'s Commn. on Pension Policy, Ill. Fiscal Commn., 1977; mem. Adv. Com. Fed. Consol. Fin. Statements, 1976-78; life trustee Mus. Sci. and Industry, Northwestern U., Meninger Found., Orchestral Assn., Lyric Opera Chgo.; trustee Cmty. Found. of Collier County, Fla. 2d lt. USAAF, 1943-46. Clubs: Met. (Washington); Mid-America (gov. 1971-76, treas. 1974-76), Chgo., Univ., Indian Hill, Comml. (Chgo.), Naples Yacht, Hole-in-Wall, Port Royal. Home: 4000 Rum Row Naples FL 34102-7863 Office: 1300 3rd St S Naples FL 34102-7239

KAPNICK, RICHARD BRADSHAW, lawyer; b. Chgo., Aug. 21, 1955; s. Harvey E. and Jean (Bradshaw) K.; m. Claudia Norris, Dec. 30, 1978; children: Sarah Bancroft, John Norris. BA with distinction, Stanford U., 1977; MPhil in Internat. Rels., U. Oxford, 1980; JD with honors, U. Chgo., 1982. Bar: Ill. 1982, N.Y. 1993. Law clk. to justice Ill. Supreme Ct., Chgo., 1982-84; law clk. to Justice John Paul Stevens U.S. Supreme Ct., Washington, 1984-85; assoc. Sidley & Austin, Chgo., 1985-89, ptnr., 1989—. Mng. editor U. Chgo. Law Rev., 1981-82. Trustee Chgo. Symphony Orch., 1995—, governing mem., 1988-95; bd. dirs. Cabrini Green Legal Aid Clinic, 1990-94, chmn. bd., 1991-93. Marshall scholar, 1978-80; fellow Leadership Greater Chgo., 1989-90. Mem. Order of Coif, Chgo. Club, Econ. Club Chgo., Law Club Chgo., Phi Beta Kappa. Republican. Episcopalian.

KAPNICK, S. JASON, oncologist; b. Providence, Mar. 28, 1949; s. I.H. and Martha (Shaulson) K.; children: Senta Marie-Rose, Isrel Berndt-Stefan, Besselja Edda. BLS summa cum laude, boston U., 1974; MD, Harvard Med. Sch., 1981. Surg. rsch. assoc. Harvard Med. Sch., Boston, 1976-77, assoc. in ob/gyn., lectr., 1981-85, instr. in gynecology, 1985-87; cons. in gynecologic oncology Dana Farber Cancer Inst., Boston, 1985-87; clin. fellow Am. Cancer Soc., Boston, 1985-87; attending gynecologic oncologist West Palm Beach, Fla., 1989—; asst. cons. prof. gynecol. oncology Duke U. Med. Ctr., Durham, N.C., 1994—; reviewer of rsch. submissions Cancer med. jour., Bethesda, Md., 1995—; invited lectr., 1995, Palm Beach County Hosps., 1990—, Am. Cancer Soc., Bethesda, 1995, also Switzerland, Germany, France and Eng., 1990—. Contbr. articles on colon, breast, and female pelvic cancers to profl. jours. Vol., contbr. Ctr. for Family Svcs., West Palm Beach, 1992—; active Cath. Diocese children's programs, 1998—; mem., religious edn. tchr. First Unitarian Ch., North Palm Beach, Fla., Bullfinch Soc., Mass. Gen Hosp.; mem. dean's coun. Med. Sch. Harvard U.; bd. dirs. Palm Beach Opera, 1992—. Mem. Harvard Club of Palm Beach. Avocations: philosophy, music. Office: Farris Bldg Gynecol Oncology 1411 N Flagler Dr Ste 5000 West Palm Beach FL 33401-3410

KAPNICK, STEWART, investment banker; b. N.Y.C., Mar. 10, 1956; s. Charles and Ruth Kapnick; m. Alison Sue Cherry, 1988; children: Jordan Leigh, Michael Taylor. BA with honors, George Washington U., 1978; MBA, Baruch Coll., 1986. Summer internship IBM Corp., White Plains, N.Y., 1977-78; acct. exec. L & C Pub. Inc., Los Angeles, 1979-82, 3M Corp., N.Y.C., 1982-83; pres., fin. ops. prin. Ulysses Capital, N.Y.C., 1983-87; lease fin. cons. SK Capital, N.Y.C., 1987—; assoc. dir. product devel. and lease fin. Continental Info. Systems Corp., N.Y.C., 1987-89; dir. equity fin. Info. Processing Systems Inc. subs. USF&G Fin. Svcs. Corp., Hackensack, N.J., 1989-92; v.p. lease acquisitions The CIT Group, Livingston, N.J., 1992-94; 1st v.p. corp. banking-lease fin. Republic Nat. Bank of N.Y., N.Y.C., 1994—. Mem. Equipment Lessors Assn., Computer Dealers and Lessors Assn. Avocations: basketball, tennis, golf, playing options and foreign currency. Home: 145A Camp Hill Rd N Pomona NY 10970-2832

KAPOR, MITCHELL DAVID, venture capitalist; b. Bklyn., Nov. 1, 1950; s. Jesse and Phoebe L. (Wagner) K.; m. Judith M. Vecchione, June 4, 1972 (div. 1979); m. Ellen M. Poss, Aug. 7, 1983 (div. 1998). BA, Yale U., 1971; MA, Beacon Coll., 1978; postgrad., Sloan Sch. Mgmt., MIT, 1979; DHL (hon.), Boston U., 1985, Mass. Sch. Profl. Psychology, 1990; DSc (hon.), Suffolk U., 1988, U. Mass., 1996. Freelance cons. Cambridge, Mass., 1978-80; product mgr. Personal Software, Sunnyvale, Calif., 1980; pres. Lotus Devel. Corp., Cambridge, Mass., 1982-84, chmn., 1984-86; chmn. ON Tech. Inc., Cambridge, Mass., 1987-90; chmn. Electronic Frontier Found., Inc., Cambridge, 1990-94, chmn., pres., 1994—; chmn. Mass. Commn. on Computer Tech. and Law, 1992; tchr. Mass. Inst. Tech. Author: (with others) (software program) Lotus 1-2-3, 1983. Trustee Kapor Family Found., 1986—,. Jewish. *

KAPP, C. TERRENCE, lawyer; b. Pine Bluff, Ark., Oct. 1, 1944; s. Robert Amos and Guenevere Patricia (DeVinne) K.; m. Betsy Langer, May 2, 1987. BA, Colgate U., 1966; JD, Cleve. State U., 1971; MA summa cum laude, Holy Apostles Coll., 1984. Bar: Ohio 1971, U.S. Dist. Ct. (no. dist.) Ohio 1973, U.S. Supreme Ct. 1980, U.S. Tax Ct. 1996. Ptnr. Kapp & Kapp, East Liverpool, Ohio, 1971-84; pvt. practice Cleve., 1984—; ptnr. Marshman, Snyder & Kapp, Cleve., 1991-93, Kapp Law Offices, Cleve., 1994—. Contbr. articles to profl. jours. Pres., bd. dirs. Lake Erie Nature & Sci. Ctr., Bay Village, Ohio, 1991-92; chair St. John's Cathedral Endowment Trust, Cleve., 1992-94. Mem. ABA (commr. presdl. commn. on non-lawyer practice 1992-96; judge finals nat. appellate adv. competition 1987, nat. chmn. divorce laws and procedures com. Family law sect. 1989-93, vice-chmn. step families com. 1991-93, chmn. alternative funding com. 1992—, taxation com. exec. 1988—, task force on client edn. 1991—, chair nat. symposium on Image of Family law Atty.-Fact or Myth 1993, cert. Outstanding Svc. 1988, 89, 93, 95, domestic rels. taxation problems com. exec. Tax sect., Litigation sect.), Ohio State Bar Assn. (family law com. exec. 1987—, family law curriculum com. Ohio CLE Inst. 1992—), Cuyahoga County Bar Assn. (chair family law sect. 1991-92, bar admissions com. exec. 1986—, cert. grievance com. 1990—, jud. selection com. 1991—, unauthorized practice of law com. 1992—, cert. Outstanding Leadership 1992), Cleve. Athletic Club (pres., bd. dirs.), Bay Men's Club. Roman Catholic. Avocations: sailing, handball, racquet sports. Office: Kapp Law Offices 1370 Ontario St Cleveland OH 44113-1701

KAPP, JOHN PAUL, lawyer, physician, educator; b. Galax, Va., Feb. 22, 1938; s. Paul Homer and Jesse Katherine (Vass) K.; m. Emily Lureese Evans, June 23, 1961; children: Paul Hardin, Emily Camille. MD, Duke U., 1963, BS, 1966, PhD in Anatomy, 1967; JD, Wake Forest U., 1990. Bar: N.C. 1990, Va. 1991, Fla. 1991. Intern Med. Coll. Va., Richmond, 1963; resident in surgery Duke U., Durham, N.C., 1964, resident in neurosurgery, 1964-69; asst. prof. neurosurgery U. Tenn., Memphis, 1971-72; attending neurosurgeon Bay Meml. Med. Ctr., Panama City, Fla., 1972-80, Gulf Coast Cmty. Hosp., 1977-80; assoc. prof. neurosurgery U. Miss., Jackson, 1980-83, prof., 1983-85; prof., chmn. dept. neurosurgery SUNY, Buffalo, 1985-87; pvt. practice as lawyer Galax, 1990—. Editor: The Cerebral Venous System and Its Disorders, 1984; contbr. articles to profl. jours. and chpts. to books; patentee arterial pressure control system, prosthetic vertebral body, cranial sensor attaching device. Major U.S. Army, 1969-71. USPHS Neurosurgy fellow, 1965-67; recipient Rsch. award Am. Acad. Neurol. Surgery, 1967. Mem. N.C. Acad. Trial Lawyers, N.C. Bar Assn., Va. State Bar Assn. Democrat. Methodist. Avocations: hunting, dog training. Office: 2433 Thomas Dr # 104 P C Beach FL 32408-5808

KAPP, MICHAEL KEITH, lawyer; b. Winston-Salem, N.C., Nov. 28, 1953; s. William Henry and Betty Jean (Minton) K.; m. Mary Jo Chancy McLean, Aug. 13, 1977; 1 child, Mary Katherine. AB with honors, U. N.C., 1976, JD with honors, 1979. Bar: N.C. 1979, U.S. Dist. Ct. (ea. dist.) N.C. 1980, U.S. Ct. Appeals (4th cir.) 1982, U.S. Dist. Ct. (mid. dist.) N.C. 1986, U.S. Supreme Ct. 1988. Law clk. to presiding justice N.C. Ct. Appeals, Raleigh, 1979-80, N.C. Supreme Ct., Raleigh, 1980-81; assoc. Maupin, Taylor & Ellis, Raleigh, 1981-85; ptnr. Maupin, Taylor & Ellis, P.A., Raleigh, 1985—. Research editor U. N.C. Jour. Internat. Law and Comml. Regulation, 1978-79; editor Survey of Significant Decisions of North Carolina Court of Appeals and North Carolina Supreme Court, 1979-81, 2d vol., 1981-82. N.C. teen Dem. advisor, 1983-85; mem. exec. council N.C. Dem. Party, 1983-85; founding dir. N.C. Vol. Lawyers for Arts, Raleigh, 1982-85; counsel Moravian Music Found., Winston-Salem, 1982-85, trustee, 1985-90, pres., 1990-92; counsel Raleigh Little Theatre, 1996—; bd. dirs. Moravian Ch. Archives, Wiston-Salem, 1984-89, Soc. for Preservation of Historic Oakwood, Raleigh, 1981-83, Carolina Charter Corp., 1990—, dir. 1995—. Morehead scholar U. N.C., 1972. Mem. ABA, N.C. Bar Assn. (chmn. young lawyer div. continuing legal edn. 1980-82, membership 1984-86, bd.

govs. 1983-86), N.C. State Bar (ethics com. 1981-91, com. on professionalism 1986-87), Wake County Bar Assn. (bd. dirs. 1988-90, pres.-elect 1995, pres. 1996), Kiwanis (Raleigh Kiwanis Found. dir., 1996-98), Raleigh Execs. Club (pres. 1998-99), Phi Beta Kappa, Phi Delta Phi, Pi Lambda Phi. Avocation: historic preservation, hiking, gardening. Home: 1615 Craig St Raleigh NC 27608-2201 Office: Maupin Taylor & Ellis Highwoods Tower One 3200 Beech Leaf Ct Ste 500 Raleigh NC 27604-1063

KAPP, RICHARD P., conductor, arts administrator; b. Chgo., Oct. 9, 1936; s. Paul and June Tamara (Raff) K.; m. Nancy Walz, Mar. 24, 1964 (div. Dec. 1979); children: Joanna E. de Seyne, Alexandra D. Horner; m. Barbara A. Borders, Sept. 9, 1981; 1 child, Madeline W. BA, The Johns Hopkins U., 1957; student, Staatl. Hochschule für Musik, Stuttgart, Germany, 1957-59; JD, NYU, 1966. Korrepetitor, Kapellmeister Stadttheater, Basel, Switzerland, 1960-62; nat. music dir. Young Audiences, Inc., N.Y.C., 1965-67; dir. Ctr. for Regional Arts Devel., Manchester, N.H., 1967-68; program officer The Ford Found., N.Y.C., 1969-78; v.p. Gen. Music Publ. Co. Inc., Dobbs Ferry, N.Y., 1978-82; music dir. Philharmonia Virtuosi, N.Y.C., 1974—; pres., owner Essay Recordings, Dobbs Ferry, N.Y., 1988—; guest condr. orchs. U.S., Euro pe, 1972—. Composer musicals Bibi, 1960, Teddy and Alice, 1988. Home: 20 Oakdale Dr Hastings Hdsn NY 10706-1208 Office: Essay Recordings 145 Palisade St Dobbs Ferry NY 10522-1617*

KAPP, ROBERT HARRIS, lawyer; b. Chgo., Mar. 9, 1934; s. Ben and Gladys (Harris) K.; m. Jean Schlusberg, June 22, 1958; children: Stephen, Lisa, Jonathan, Diana. BS in Econs., U. Pa., 1955; JD, U. Mich., 1958. Bar: Ill. 1958, D.C. 1961. Trial atty. U.S. Dept. Justice, Washington, 1958-61; ptnr. Hogan & Hartson, Washington, 1961—; mem. adv. bd. Transnational Arbitration Assn., 1994-97. Bd. dirs. Internat. Human Rights Law Group, 1978—, chmn., 1986-89; bd. dirs. Lawyers' Com. for Civil Rights Under Law, 1976—, chmn., 1983-85; bd. dirs. Washington Lawyers' Com. for Civil Rights and Urban Affairs, 1974—, chmn., 1980-82; bd. dirs. ACLU of Nat. Capitol Area, 1983-95, chmn., 1992-94; bd. dirs. Washington Sch. Psychiatry, 1980-86, Higher Achievement Program, 1991-94; mem. area I planning com. Montgomery County Pub. Schs., 1970; mem. adv. bd. Internat. Legal Studies Program, Am. U. Law Sch., Ctr. for Human Rights and Humanitarian Law; mem. bd. visitors U. Mich. Law Sch.; commr. Commn. on Independence for Nambia. Fellow Am. Bar Found.; mem. ABA (chmn. taxation com., sect. individual rights and responsibilities 1987-92, Wiley A. Branton Sr. award 1994, Alan Barth Svc. award 1996), C. Anthony Friedrich Meml. award, 1999, Wiley A. Branton Sr. award Wash. Lawyers Com. for Civil Rights and Urban Affairs, Alan Burth Svc. award ACLU of Nat. Capitol Area, C. Anthony Friedrich Meml. award Internat. Human Rights Law Group. Office: Hogan & Hartson 555 13th St NW Ste 800E Washington DC 20004-1161

KAPPAN, SANDRA JEAN, elementary education educator; b. Buffalo, N.Y., Sept. 25, 1961; d. Joseph Albert Sr. and Margaret Alice (Krupa) Savash; 1 child, Jason T. Cert. in dental assisting, Bd. of Coop. Ednl. Svcs., 1979; AAS in Secretarial Sci., Erie C.C., 1982; BS, Daemen Coll., 1997; MS in Edn. and Reading, St. Bonaventure U., 1998. Cert. spl. edn., pre-kindergarten, kindergarten, grades 1-6. Acctg. clk. Children's Hosp. of Buffalo, 1984-87; legal sec., receptionist Lofton, Savage, & Cain, Esqs., Charleston, S.C., 1987-88; sec., transciptionist Trident Regional Med. Ctr., Charleston, S.C., 1988-90; adminstrv. asst. Children's Hosp. of Buffalo, 1990-93; substitute tchr. Erie 1 Bd. Coop. Ednl. Svcs., Erie County, N.Y., 1996-97; resource room tchr. Lancaster (N.Y.) Ctrl. Sch. Dist., 1997; spl. edn. tchr. Erie I Bd. Ednl. Ednl. Svcs., Erie County, N.Y., 1997-98; elem. tchr. St. James Sch., Depew, N.Y., 1998-99, Amherst Ctrl. Sch. Dist., 1999—; spl. edn. tchr. Erie I BOCES, summer 1999; presenter in field. Vol., PTA mem. Lancaster Ctrl. Sch. Dist., 1994—; vol., mem. St. John's Luth. Ch., Sunday Ch. Sch. and Choir, Lancaster, 1993—; vol. BOCES/Head Start Collaborative Presch. Program, Lancaster, 1993-94. Scholarship Lancaster Assn. of Svc. Pers., 1996. Mem. Coun. for Exceptional Children, Internat. Reading Assn., Daemen Coll. Alumni Assn., Phi Delta Kappa. Democrat. Lutheran. Home: 479 Lake Ave Lancaster NY 14086-9666

KAPPAS, ATTALLAH, physician, medical scientist; b. Union City, N.J., Nov. 4, 1926; s. Attie and Sofia (Kozam) K.; m. Oct. 26, 1963; children: Peter, Michael, Nicholas. AB, Columbia U., 1947; MD with honors, U. Chgo., 1950; ScD, N.Y. Med. Coll., 1978. Diplomate: Am. Bd. Internal Medicine. Med. intern Univ. Service, Kings County Hosp., N.Y.C., 1950-51; ACS rsch. fellow divsn. steroid biochemistry and metabolism Sloan Kettering Inst., N.Y.C., 1951-54; asst. resident physician and sr. asst. resident physician Peter Bent Brigham Hosp. Harvard Med. Sch., Boston, 1954-56; assoc. div. steroid biochemistry and metabolism Sloan Kettering Inst., 1956-57; from asst. prof. to assoc. prof. dept. medicine, head div. metabolism and arthritis U. Chgo. Med. Sch., 1957-67; Guggenheim fellow, guest investigator Rockefeller U., N.Y.C., 1966-67; assoc. prof., physician Rockefeller U., 1967-71, sr. physician, 1971-74, prof., 1971-81, Sherman Fairchild prof., 1981—, v.p., 1983-91, physician-in-chief, 1974-91, physician-in-chief emeritus, 1991—; Vincent Astor chair clin. sci. Meml. Sloan-Kettering Cancer Ctr. and Cornell U. Med. Coll., 1980-81, prof. medicine, 1972—, prof. pharmacology, 1972-87; bd. dirs. Russell Sage Inst. Pathology Cornell U., 1977-87; vis. com. div. biol. scis. Pritzker Sch. Medicine, U. Chgo., 1977-86; attending physician N.Y. Hosp., 1972—, Meml. Hosp. Cancer and Allied Diseases, 1977-91; mem. selection com. John A. Hartford Found. Fellowship program in clin. scis., N.Y.C., 1979-83; co-dir. Rockefeller U.-Cornell U. combined MD-PhD program, 1980-85; mem. com. pyrene and selected analogs NRC-Nat. Acad. Sci., Washington, 1981-83, cons. Merck Sharp & Dohme Rsch. Labs., 1974-79, 82-84, Abbot-Ross Labs., 1985-90, Hoffman LaRoche Labs., 1985-87, Glaxo Rsch. Labs., 1988-90; mem. sci. adv. bd. Environ. Scis. Lab. Mt. Sinai Med. Ctr., 1983-87; prof. adj. faculty dept. pediat. Karolinska Inst., Stockholm, 1987-90; vis. prof. dept. pediatrics U. Vt. Coll. Medicine, Burlington, 1993—; mem. coun. SUNY Health Sci. Ctr., Bklyn., 1998—. Contbr. articles to profl. jours. Bd. dirs. Vis. Nurse Service N.Y., 1982-86, 98—; mem. gov.'s com. on rev. sci. studies and devel. pub. policy on problems resulting from hazardous wastes N.Y. State, 1980. Served with U.S. Army, 1945-46. Commonwealth Fund fellow, 1961-62, Guggenheim fellow, 1966-67; recipient Spl. award in clin. pharmacology Burroghs Wellcome Fund, 1973, Disting. Svc. award in med. scis. U. Chgo. Sch. Medicine, 1975, Citation for profl. achievement U. Chgo. Alumni Assn., 1995, 1st Ann. award for excellence in clin. rsch. NIH, 1989; named Sr. Henry Hallet Dale Meml. lectr. and vis. prof. Johns Hopkins Hosp., 1975, Pfizer lectr. clin. pharmacology Peter Bent Brigham Hosp., Harvard Med. Sch., 1977, Pfizer lectr. Pa. State U., 1980, first Rolf Blomstrand lectr. Karolinska Inst., 1988, first Glaxo lectr. Cornell U. Med. Sch., 1984; Gunner and Lillian Nicholson Found. exch. prof. Karolinska Inst., Stockholm, 1985-86; Barowsky Meml. lectr., N.Y. Med. Coll., 1986; Lang scholar in medicine N.Y. Hosp. Med. Ctr., Queens, N.Y., 1998—. Fellow ACP; mem. Assn. Am. Physicians, Am. Soc. Clin. Investigation, Am. Clin. and Climatol. Assn., Am. Soc. Pharmacology and Exptl. Therapeutics (pub. affairs com., award for exptl. therapeutics 1978), Practitioners Soc. N.Y., Harvey Soc., Endocrine Soc., Interurban Clin. Club, Cosmos Club (Washington), N.Y. Athletic Club, Lotos Club, Univ. Club. Office: Rockefeller U Hosp 1230 York Ave New York NY 10021-6307

KAPPAZ, MICHAEL H., engineering company executive; b. Cartagena, Colombia, May 14, 1942; came to the U.S., 1963; s. George and Elena (Hegel) K.; m. Chafica Maria Dau; children: George, Nur-Helene, Christine, Karen, William, Patricia. BA, La Salle Coll., Cartagena, 1961; BS in Indsl. Engring. & Ops. Rsch., Poly. Inst. N.Y., 1970; MBA in Fin. Mgmt., Golden Gate U., 1976; cert. in Global Strategic Mgmt., U. Pa., 1984; cert. in exec. mgmt., Stanford U., 1986. Indsl. engr. for iron and steel Ramseyer and Miller, Inc., N.Y., 1964-71; v.p., gen. mgr. internat. ops. Bechtel Power Corp., Bechtel Group, Gaithersburg, Md. and San Francisco, 1971-86; v.p., mgr. Overseas Bechtel, Inc., Cairo, 1982-84; v.p., project mgr. Internat. Bechtel Corp., Inc., Venezuela, 1979-82; chmn., CEO K&M Engring. and Consulting Corp., Washington, 1987—; chmn. bd. dirs. KMR Power Corp., Arlington, Va., 1993—; chmn. K&M Interamerican Investment Corp., Arlington, 1993, K&M Interamerican Energy Leasing, Arlington, 1993, K&M Ventures, L.P., Arlington, 1993, KMtel LLC, 1995—. Contbr. articles to various publs., papers to confs. and seminars. Mem. adv. bd. Rep. Nat. Com., 1993—; mem. Am. Rsch. Ctr. (Egyptology and Archeology), 1982-86; mem. engring. adv. com. Am. U., Cairo, 1982-86; co-chmn. coun. Latin Am. studies Johns Hopkins U., 1987-89, mem. adv. coun. 1987—, mem. devel. com. 1993—; bd. dirs. Bus. Coun. for Internat. Understanding; vice-chmn. U.S.-Colombia Bus. Partnership; bd. dirs. Washington Opera. Recipient Deal of Yr. award Project Fin. Internat. Yearbook, 1993, Infrastructure Fin. Mag., 1993, Blue Chip Enterprise award, 1995, Fast Track award, 1995, Inc 500 award, Nat. Tech. Fast 500 award, 1995, Fast 50 award 1996. Mem. U.S. Energy Assn., Am. Soc. Macro Engring., Am. C. of C. (charter, Cairo), Am. Assn. Cost Engrs. (past v.p., dir. Capital chpt.), Egyptian-Am. C. of C., Washington Internat. Trade Assn., Hispanic Am. C. of C., Greater Washington Bd. Trade, D.C. C. of C., Royal Automobile Club, Univ. Club, Georgetown Club, Avenel Country Club, Damascus Lodge. Republican. Roman Catholic. Avocations: opera, baseball, golf, bridge. Office: K & M Engring & Consulting Corp 2001 L St NW Ste 500 Washington DC 20036-4944

KAPPEL, DAVID A., lawyer; b. Pitts., May 5, 1964. BA, U. Pitts., 1982; JD, U. Houston, 1986. Bar: Tex. 1986, Pa. 1987. Atty. Southern Alleghenies Legal Aid, Inc., Somerset, Pa., 1996—; advocate Women's Help Ctr., Johnstown, Pa., 1996—. Mem. ABA (advocate), Somerset County Bar Assn., Cambria County Bar Assn. Presbyterian. Avocations: pro bono legal services to poor, antiques, stamp collecting. Office: So Alleghenies Legal Aid Inc 147 East Union St Somerset PA 15501

KAPPENBERG, MARILYN LORRIN, library director; b. Hicksville, N.Y., July 19, 1948; d. Adolf A. and Mary T. Kascius; m. Richard L. Kappenberg, Apr. 5, 1975; children: Neal, Glenn. BA, Molloy Coll., 1970; MLS, L.I. U., 1972. Children's libr. Hicksville (N.Y.) Pub. Libr., 1972-90; head ref. Hicksville Pub. Libr., 1990-95, asst. libr. dir., 1992-95; libr. dir. Wantagh (N.Y.) Pub. Libr., 1995—. Sec. Hicksville Lions Club, 1990-95. Mem. ALA, Nassau County Libr. Assn., Wantagh C. of C. (mem.-at-large 1995—). Avocations: writing, volunteering. Home: 2873 Janet Ave North Bellmore NY 11710 Office: Wantagh Pub Libr 3285 Park Ave Wantagh NY 11793

KAPPES, PHILIP SPANGLER, lawyer; b. Detroit, Dec. 24, 1925; s. Philip Alexander and Wilma Fern (Spangler) K.; m. Glendora Galena Miles, Nov. 27, 1948; children: Susan Lea, Philip Miles, Mark William. Bar: Ind. 1948. Assoc. Armstrong and Gause, 1948-49, C.B. Dutton, 1950-51; ptnr. Dutton, Kappes & Overman, 1952-85, of counsel, 1983-85; ptnr. Lewis Kappes Fuller & Eads, Indpls., 1985-89, Lewis & Kappes, Indpls., 1989-92, Lewis & Kappes PC, Indpls., 1993—, Labeco Properties, Creston Group, Indpls.; pres., dir. K&K Realty, Inc., Indpls.; sec., dir., mem. exec. com. Lab. Equipment Corp., Mooresville, Ind.; instr. bus. law Butler U., 1948-49, chmn. bd. govs., 1965-66, bd. trustees, 1987-90; chmn. Ovid Butler Soc., 1982-83. Life bd. dirs. Crossroads Am. coun. Boy Scouts Am., 1965—, v.p. fin., mem. exec. com., pres., 1977-79, chmn. trustees endowment fund, 1987-92, trustee, 1987—; bd. dirs. Fairbanks Hosp., Indpls., 1986-94, chmn. bd., 1988-91, exec. com., 1987-94, mem. audit and fin. com., 1992-94, life dir. emeritus, 1994—, chmn. nominating com., 1991; trustee Butler U., 1987-90, Children's Mus., Indpls., 1969-88, pres. bd. trustees, 1984-85, bd. disting. advisors, 1990—; mem. First Meridian Heights Presbyn. Ch., 1933—, chmn. bd. trustees, 1958-61, 69-72, 1996— ruling elder 1982-85, 94—, deacon, 1950-58; mem. planning com. and dir. 32-Degree Scottish rite Children's Learning ctr., 1997—. Recipient Paul H. Buchanan award of excellence Indpls. Bar Found. Mem. ABA (ho. of dels. 1970-71), Ind. State Bar Assn. (ho. dels. 1959—, chmn. pub. rels. exec. com. 1966-69, sec. 1973-74, bd. mgrs. 1975-77, chmn. law practice mgmt. com. 1991-92), Indpls. Bar Assn. (treas., 1st v.p. 1965, pres. 1970, bd. mgrs. 1968-71, 75-77, chmn. law day com. 1991-92, settlement week com. 1989-95, co-chair Family Law Study Commn., co-chair ct. liaison com. 1992-93, family law implementation com. 1993-97, mem. exec. com. bd. mgrs. 1994-96, counsel bd. mgrs. 1994, chmn. sr. lawyers divsn. 1999—), Am. Judicature Soc., Indpls. Legal Aid Soc., Indpls. Jr. C. of C. (past 1st v.p., dir. ct. unification implementation com., chmn. 1995—), Butler U. Alumni Assn. (past pres.), Mich. Alumni Assn., Meridian Hills Country Club, Lawyers Club, Gyro Club (pres. 1966), Masons (worshipful master 1975), Valley Scottish Rite Found. (33d degree, most wise master 1982-84, trustee 1987-97, chmn. bd. trustees 1998-99, bd. govs. 32nd rite learning ctr1997—, pres. Indpls. Scottish Rite Cathedral Found., trustee 1997—, chmn. 1998-99), Shriners, Phi Delta Theta (chpt. advisor 1950-82), Tau Kappa Alpha. Republican. Presbyterian. Home: 624 Somerset Dr W Indianapolis IN 46260-2924 Office: 1 American Square PO Box 82053 Indianapolis IN 46282-0003

KAPPNER, AUGUSTA SOUZA, academic administrator; b. Bronx, June 25, 1944; d. Augusto and Monica Thomasina (Fraser) Souza; m. Thomas Kappner, Aug. 14, 1965; children: Tania, Diana. AB, Barnard Coll., 1966; MSW, Hunter Coll., N.Y.C., 1968; DSW, Columbia U., 1984. Cert. social worker, N.Y. Lectr., community affairs specialist Dept. Urban Affairs, Grad. Div., Hunter Coll., 1968-70; adj. instr., field supr. N.Y.C. C.C., 1970-71; instr., coord. urban leadership unit Columbia U. Sch. Social Wk., 1970-72; asst. prof., dir. admissions and student svcs. SUNY, Stony Brook, 1973-74; assoc. prof., chmn. human svcs. divsn. LaGuardia C.C., 1974-78, prof., dean continuing edn., 1978-84; dean acad. affairs Adult & Continuing Edn., CUNY, 1984, dean acad. affairs, instructional rsch., adult learning, 1984-86; pres. Borough of Manhattan C.C./CUNY, 1986-92; asst. sec. of vocat. and adult edn. Dept. of Edn., Washington, 1993-95; pres. Bank Street Coll., N.Y.C., 1995—; cons. in field; lectr. in field; chmn. adv. bd. Fund for the Improvement of Post Secondary Edn., U.S. Dept. of Edn, Adult Literacy Media Alliance; commr. Mid. States Assn., Commn. on Higher Edn., Commn. for a Nation of Lifelong Learners; bd. dirs. Markle Found., Nat. Writing Project, Tchg. Matters, Inc.; mem. N.Y.C. Bd. Edn. Adv. Bd. for Universal Pre-Kindergarten. Trustees Marymount Manhattan Coll.; mem. N.Y. State Edn. Commr.'s Task Force for the Edn. of Children and Youth at Risk, N.Y. State Gov.'s Coun. on Literacy, N.Y.C. Bd. Edn. Chancellor's U./Schs. Collaborative steering com.; appointed by Mayor of City of N.Y. to Joint Commn. on Integrity in Pub. Schs.; bd. dirs. N.Y. Urban Coalition; mem. N.Y.C. Coun. on Econ. Edn. Whitney M. Young Jr. fellow, 1982, USPHS awardee, 1981, Ford Found. fellow, 1973, Silverman Fund awardee, 1968, NIMH fellow, 1967, others; recipient Harlem Sch. Arts Humanitarian award, 1990, Am. Assn. Women in Community and Jr. Colls. Presdl. award, 1989, Asian Ams. for Equality Community Svc. award, 1989, Columbia U. Medal of Excellence, 1988, Barnard Coll. medal of distinction, 1988, others. Mem. Am. Coun. on Edn. (commn. on women in higher edn.), Nat. Coun. on Black Am. Affairs (bd. dirs.), Assn. Black Women in Higher Edn. (adv. bd.). *

KAPR, JOHN ROBERT, operations executive; b. Dumont, N.J., Dec. 15, 1954; s. Charles Frank and Gertrude (Baird) K.; m. Karen Marie Hansen, May 22, 1976 (div. July 1996); children: Kristin, Jennifer, Jon; m. Diane Bongiovanni, July 26, 1998; stepchild, Neil. AAS, Bergen Community Coll., 1976. Parts specifier Volvo of Am., Rockleigh, N.J., 1976-77; parts technical specialist BMW of N.Am., Inc., Montvale, N.J., 1977-78, dist. parts mgr., 1978-81, depot mgr., 1981-84; parts distbn. mgr. BMW of N.Am., Inc., Mount Olive, N.J., 1984-90; v.p. ops. Transeuro Group Inc., Edison, N.J., 1990-91; pres. Ka-Pro Builders, Midland Park, N.J., 1991-93; ops. mgr. Car Quest BWP Distributors, Bronx, N.Y., 1993-98; site leader Mercedes-Benz, USA, Inc., Hanover, Md., 1998—. Mem. Coun. of Logistics Mgmt., Internat. Material Mgmt. Soc., Mount Olive C. of C., Morris County C. of C., NRA, Am. Motorcyclist Assn., Sports Car Club Am., Internat. Motor Sports Assn., BMW Car Club Am., 200 Club of Warren County, 200 Club of Bergen County. Presbyterian. Avocations: automobiles, motorcycles, autoracing. Home: 219 Cedar St Franklin Lakes NJ 07417-1402

KAPRAL, FRANK ALBERT, medical microbiology and immunology educator; b. Phila., Mar. 12, 1928; s. John and Erna Louise (Melching) K.; m. Marina Garay, Nov. 22, 1951; children: Frederick, Gloria, Robert. BS, U. of the Scis. in Phila., 1952; Ph.D, U. Pa., 1956. With U. Pa., Phila., 1952-66, assoc. in microbiology, 1958-66; assoc. microbiologist Phila Gen. Hosp., 1962-64, chief microbiology research, 1964-66, chief microbiology, 1965-66; asst. chief microbiol. research VA Hosp., Phila, 1962-66; assoc. prof. med. microbiology Ohio State U., Columbus, 1966-69, prof. med. microbiology and immunology, 1969—; cons. Ctr. Disease Control, Atlanta, 1980, Proctor and Gamble Co., 1981-87. Contbr. articles to profl. jours.; patentee implant chamber. Active Ctrl. Ohio Diabetes Assn., 1992-93. With AUS, 1946-47. NIH rsch. grantee, 1959—; Ctrl. Ohio Diabetes Assn. grantee, 1992-93. Fellow Am. Acad. Microbiology, Infectious Diseases Soc. Am.; mem. AAAS, Am. Soc. for Microbiology, Am. Assn. for Immunologists, Sigma Xi. Democrat. Roman Catholic. Home: 873 Clubview Blvd S Columbus OH 43235-1771 Office: Ohio State U Dept Med Micro and Immunol 2166A Graves Hall Columbus OH 43210

KAPRANOV, MIKHAIL M., mathematician, educator; b. June 26, 1962. PhD, Steklov Inst., Moscow, Russia, 1987. Prof. math. Northwestern U., Evanston, Ill., 1997—. Home: 707 E Green St Urbana IL 61802-3409 Office: Northwestern U Dept Math Lunt Bldg 218B Evanston IL 60208

KAPRIELIAN, VICTORIA SUSAN, medical educator; b. The Bronx, N.Y., June 30, 1959; d. Walter and Julia (Hachigian) K. BA, Brown U., 1981; MD, UCLA, 1985. Diplomate Am. Bd. Family Practice. Resident Duke-Watts Family Practice, Durham, N.C., 1985-88; fellow UCLA Family Medicine, L.A., 1988-89; asst. clin. prof. Duke U. Med. Ctr., Durham, N.C., 1989-98, assoc. clin. prof., 1998—; chief, divsn. predoctoral edn. and faculty devel., dept cmty and family medicine Duke U., Durham, N.C., 1994-96, fellowship dir., dept. cmty. and family medicine, 1994—, dir. predoctoral edn. and faculty devel., 1996—; dir. inpatient svc. divsn. cmty. medicine Duke U., 1989-90, dir. sports medicine, 1989-94, dir. arts medicine, 1989-95, dir. predoctoral edn., 1990—; dir. quality improvement Dept. Cmty. & Family Med., 1996—, dir. continuing med. edn., 1994—. Fellow Am. Acad. Family Physicians (pub. com. 1985, mental health com. 1986-88); mem. N.C. Acad. Family Physicians (edn. com. 1989-90, med. sch. affairs 1990—, chair of com. 1991-97), Soc. Tchrs. Family Medicine (steering com., predoc. dir. working group 1995—, chair 1998). Avocations: physical fitness, singing, science fiction, ethnic cooking. Office: Duke U Div Family Medicine PO Box 3886 Durham NC 27710-0001

KAPRIELIAN, WALTER, advertising executive; b. N.Y.C., June 2, 1934; s. Vartan and Shoushan (DerBargamian) K.; m. Julia Hachigian, July 7, 1957 (dec. Nov. 1983); children: Victoria Susan, Siran Marion, John Vartan; m. Dinaz Boga, May 20, 1988. AAS, SUNY, 1953. Licensed charterboat capt. Art dir. BBD&O, N.Y.C., 1953-64; group head, art dir. Grey Advt., N.Y.C., 1964-65; sr. art dir. Ketchum MacLeod & Grove, N.Y.C., 1965-66; v.p., head art dir., 1966-67, v.p., assoc. creative dir., 1967-71, sr. v.p., creative dir., 1971-77, exec. v.p., asst. gen. mgr., 1977-80, gen. mgr., 1980-81; pres., chief exec. officer Ketchum New York, 1981-82; ptnr., co-creative dir., vice chmn. Fearon O'Leary Kaprielian, Inc., 1983-84; chmn., creative dir. Kaprielian O'Leary Advt., 1984-95; pres. Walter Kaprielian & Co., East Hampton, N.Y., 1995—; instr. N.Y.C. Tech. Coll., 1971-79, Sch. Visual Arts, 1982-88; mem. adv. bd. N.Y.C. Tech. Coll., 1980—; lectr. Graphic Arts Tech. Found., 1970-81; v.p. ADC Pub. Co., N.Y.C., 1986-88. Author/illustrator: The Captain's Cookbook, 1976, rev. edit., 1979; designer: Bliss in Chrysalis, 1968; designer/editor: The Consecration of a Cathedral, 1968; contbr. articles to profl. jours. V.p. Visual Communicators Scholarship Fund, 1986-88, pres., 1988-90; chmn. parish coun. Holy Cross Ch. of Armenia, 1965-66, Armenian Ch. of Holy Martyrs, 1968-69; bd. dirs. N.Y.C. Tech. Coll. Found., Fish Unlimited. Recipient awards Art Dirs. Club N.Y., awards Art Dirs. Club N.J., awards Soc. Illustrators, awards Am. Inst. Graphic Arts, awards Type Dirs. Club, awards Clio, awards Graphis, awards Advt. Club N.Y., awards Am. Advt. Fedn.; Theodore Rossevelt Meml. medal; St. Gauden's medal. Mem. Am. Inst. Graphic Arts, Art Dirs. Club (bd. dirs. 1974-76, 78-81, 91-93, pres. 1981-83, chmn. adv. bd. 1983-85, mem. adv. bd. 1984—, 1st v.p. 1993, pres. visual communicators scholarship fund 1988-90), U.S. Power Squadron, Nat. Party Boat Owners Alliance, Internat. Game Fish Assn., Knights of Vartan. Republican. Avocation: seafood cooking, fishing.

KAPSON, JORDAN, automotive executive; b. 1923. Chmn. Jordan Motors, Inc. dba Jordan Ford, Mishawaka, Ind., 1947—, Jordan Toyota dba Jordan Volvo, Jordan Mitsubishi, 1981—, Jordan Toyota dba Jordan Lincoln-Mercury. Office: Jordan Motors 609 E Jefferson Blvd Mishawaka IN 46545-6524*

KAPTEYN, HENRY CORNELIUS, physics and engineering educator; b. Oak Lawn, Ill., Jan. 21, 1963; m. Margaret Mary Murnane, 1988. BS, Harvey Mudd Coll., 1982; MA, Princeton U., 1984; PhD, U. Calif., Berkeley, 1989. Rsch. asst. U. Calif., 1985-89, postdoctoral rschr., 1989-90; asst. prof. physics Wash. State U., Pullman, 1990—, assoc. prof., 1995; assoc. prof. U. Mich., Ann Arbor, 1996-99; prof. JILA, U. Colo., Boulder, 1999—. Contbr. articles to profl. jours. Regents fellow U. Calif., 1985, Sloan rsch. fellow, 1995. Fellow Optical Soc. Am. (Adolph Lomb medal 1993); mem. Am. Phys. Soc., Soc. Photo-Optical Instrumentation Engrs. (scholar 1988). Office: JILA Univ Colo Boulder CO 80309-0440

KAPTOPODIS, LOUIS, supermarket chain executive. CEO, pres. Fiesta Mart, Houston. Office: Fiesta Mart 5235 Katy Fwy Houston TX 77007-2210*

KAPTUR, MARCIA CAROLYN, congresswoman; b. Toledo, Ohio, June 17, 1946. B.A., U. Wis., 1968; M. Urban Planning, U. Mich., 1974; postgrad., U. Manchester, (Eng.), 1974, MIT; LLD (hon.), U. Toledo. Urban planner; asst. dir. urban affairs domestic policy staff White House, 1977-79; mem. 98th-106th Congresses from 9th Ohio dist., Washington, D.C., 1983—; mem. Appropriations com., subcom. Agrl., D.C., Veterans, HUD, indep. agys. Bd. dirs. Nat. Ctr. Urban Ethnic Affairs; adv. com. Gund Found.; exec. com. Lucas County Democratic Com.; mem. Dem. Women's Campaign Assn. Mem. Am. Planning Assn., Am. Inst. Cert. Planners, NAACP, Urban League, Polish Mus., U. Mich. Urban Planning Alumni Assn. (bd. dirs.), Polish Am. Hist. Assn. Roman Catholic. Clubs: Lucas County Dem. Bus. and Profl. Women's, Fulton County Dem. Women's. Office: US House of Reps 2311 Rayburn Bldg Washington DC 20515-3509*

KAPUCU, NAIM, researcher; b. Nov. 4, 1969. MPM, Carnegie Mellon U., 1997; PhD, U. Pitts., 1999. Cons. Dept. Health and Human Svcs., Trenton, N.J., 1996-97; rsch. assoc. Nat. Ctr. Pub. Productivity, Newark, 1997, U. Pitts., Phila., 1998—. Address: 5826 Fifth Ave # 3-12 Pittsburgh PA 15232

KAPUR, KAILASH CHANDER, industrial engineering educator; b. Rawalpindi, Pakistan, Aug. 17, 1941; s. Gobind Ram and Vidya Vanti (Khanna) K.; m. Geraldine Palmer, May 15, 1969; children: Anjali Joy, Jay Palmer. BS, Delhi U., India, 1963; M of Tech., Indian Inst. Tech., Kharagpur, 1965; MS, U. Calif., Berkeley, 1968, PhD, 1969. Registered profl. engr., Mich. Sr. rsch. engr. Gen. Motors Rsch. Labs., Mich., 1969-70; sr. reliability engr. TACOM, U.S. Army, Mich., 1978-79; mem. faculty Wayne State U., Detroit, 1970-89, assoc. prof. indsl. engring. and ops., 1973-79, prof., 1979-89; prof., dir. Sch. Indsl. Engring. U. Okla., Norman, 1989-92; dir., indsl. engring. U. Wash., Seattle, 1992—; vis. prof. U. Waterloo, Can., 1977-78; vis. scholar Ford Motor Co., Mich., summer 1973. Author: Reliability in Engineering Design, 1977; contbr. articles to profl. jours. Grantee GM, 1974-77, U.S. Army, 1978-79, U.S. Dept. Transp., 1980-82. Fellow Am. Soc. Quality Control; mem. Ops. Rsch. Soc. Am. (sr.), Inst. Indsl. Engrs. (assoc. editor 1980—). Home: 4484 E Mercer Way Mercer Island WA 98040-3828 Office: U Wash PO Box 352650 Seattle WA 98195-2650

KARA, PAUL MARK, lawyer; b. Valparaiso, Ind., Mar. 7, 1954; s. Charles J. and June F. (Williams) K.; m. Elizabeth Louise Smith, Aug. 18, 1979; children: Adeline M., Emily L., Charles J., Phillip H. BA, Ind. U., 1977, JD, 1980. Bar: Mich. 1980, U.S. Dist. Ct. (we. dist.) Mich. 1980, U.S. Ct. Appeals (6th cir.) 1985. Assoc. Landman, Luyendyk, Latimer Clink & Robb, Muskegon, Mich., 1980-84, ptnr., 1984-86; ptnr. Varnum, Riddering, Schmidt & Howlett, Grand Rapids, Mich., 1986—. Pres., bd. dirs. Sr. Services of Muskegon, Inc., 1985-86, Cath. Social Services of Muskegon, 1985-86. Glenn Peters fellow, Ind. U., 1977-79, Louden Meml. fellow Ind. U., 1977-79. Mem. ABA (labor law sect., litig. sect., com. on devels. under NLRA), Mich. Bar Assn. (labor rels. law sect. coun. 1985-96, chairperson 1995-96), Muskegon County Bar Assn. (pres. 1985-86), Grand Rapids Bar Assn., Univ. Club Chgo. Republican. Home: 3905 Norton Hills Rd Muskegon MI 49441-4456 Office: Varnum Riddering Schmidt & Howlett Bridgewater Place PO Box 352 Grand Rapids MI 49501-0352

KARABASZ, FELIX FRANCOIS "SAM", engineering and manufacturing company executive; b. Phila., June 3, 1939; s. Victor Stanislaus and Mary Audry (Pie) K.; m. Norma Christine Goss, June 8, 1963; children: Michael J., Douglas N. BS in Naval Sci., U.S. Naval Acad., 1963. Commd. ensign USN, 1963, advanced through grades to lt. comdr., 1971, resigned, 1967; lt.

comdr. USNR, 1972—; with Container Corp. Am., Phila., 1967-72, Masonite Corp., 1972-80; plant mgr. Sun Electric Corp., Crystal Lake, Ill., 1981; v.p., dir. mfg. Hart & Cooley, Holland, Mich., 1982-86; sr. v.p. ops. Lau div. Philips Industries, Dayton, Ohio, 1986; v.p., gen. mgr. Indsl. Air div. Philips Industries, Amelia, Ohio, 1987-91; gen. mgr. Quickdraft div. C.A. Litzler Co., Inc., Canton, Ohio, 1992—. Home: 5536 Armistice Ave NW Canton OH 44718-1300 Office: Quickdraft PO Box 80659 1525 Perry Dr SW Canton OH 44710-1098

KARADY, GEORGE GYORGY, electrical engineering educator, consultant; b. Budapest, Hungary, Aug. 17, 1930; came to U.S., 1976; s. Gyozo and Anna (Szamek) K.; 1 child, Gyuri. MSEE, Tech. U. Budapest, 1952, DEng, 1960, D (hon.), 1996. Registered profl. engr., N.Y., N.J., Que. From instr. to assoc. prof., docent Tech. U. Budapest, Hungary, 1952-66; lectr. U. Baghdad, Iraq, 1966-68, U. Salford, Eng., 1968-69; program mgr. Hydro Quebec Inst. of Rsch., Can., 1969-76; chief elec. cons. engr. Ebasco Svcs., N.Y.C., 1976-86; Salt River Project Chair prof. Ariz. State U., Tempe, 1986—; adj. prof. McGill U., Montreal, 1972-76, Poly. Inst. N.Y., 1980-86; lectr. (part time) U. Montreal, 1970-76. Author: Operation of Electric Appliances and Network (in Hungarian), 1964; (with others) Advances in Electronics and Electron Physics, 1976; co-author: Electric Power Systems, Vol. V (in Hungarian), 1963, Electrical Power Systems and Networks (in Hungarian), 1964; contbr. more than 150 papers to tech. jours. Fellow IEEE (paper award 1982, working group achievement award 1986); mem. U.S. Nat. Com. of Internat. Conf. of Large Elec. Network (sec.-treas. 1978-94), Princeton Ski Club (bd. dirs. 1977-86). Avocations: skiing, sailing, tennis, opera. Home: 9755 N 93rd Way Unit 255 Scottsdale AZ 85258-9118 Office: Ariz State U Coll Engring and Applied Sci Dept Elec Engring Tempe AZ 85287-5706

KARAFOTIAS, NICHOLAS CHARLES, finance professional; b. Boston, Aug. 18, 1969; s. Charles Nicholas and Pauline (Pechilis) K. BSBA, Stonehill Coll., 1991; MBA, Babson Coll., 1997. Sr. pricing analyst Boston Co., 1991-93; dir. pricing svcs. First Data Investor Svcs., Boston, 1993-96; mgr. market data svcs. Fidelity Mgmt. and Rsch. Co., Boston, 1996—. Mem. Nat. Assn. Securities Dealers, Inst. Internat. Rsch., Greek Orthodox Youth Am., Info. Industry Assn., Hellenic Bus. Network, Gold Key Soc. Avocations: running, skiing, reading, investing. Office: Fidelity Investments 82 Devonshire St # E31B Boston MA 02109-3614

KARAIM, BETTY JUNE, librarian, retired; b. Devils Lake, N.D., May 27, 1936; d. Erick Henry and Anna Caroline (Steen) Keck; m. William James Karaim, Dec. 7, 1955 (dec. 1983); children: Reed, Lisa, Ryan, Lynn, Rachel, Lee, Lara. BS in Edn., Mayville (N.D.) State U., 1958; postgrad., U. N.D., summer 1961; MLS, U. Okla., 1972; postgrad., No. Mont. Coll., 1979, 81. Libr. Cando (N.D.) High Sch., 1960-62; asst. libr., tchr. Mayville State Coll., 1962-79; libr. Havre (Mont.) Pub. Schs., 1979-82; libr. dir. Mayville State U., 1982-99, ret., prof. emerita, 1999. Bd. dirs. Mayville (N.D.) Pub. Libr., 1991-97, pres., 1994-97. Recipient Orville Johnson Meritorious Svc. award, 1992, Disting. Alumni award Mayville State U. Alumni Found., 1997. Mem. ALA, NEA, Assn. of Coll. and Rsch. Librs. (nat. adv. coun. 1990-94), Mountain Plains Libr. Assn., N.D. Libr. Assn. (chair acad. sect. 1987-88), N.D. Edn. Assn. (chpt. pres. 1985-89), N.D. Pub. Employees Assn. (chpt. sec.-treas. 1998-99). Democrat. Avocations: reading, travel. Home: 320 1st St NW Mayville ND 58257-1107 Office: Mayville State U 330 3rd St NE Mayville ND 58257-1299

KARAKASH, JOHN J., engineering educator; b. Istanbul, Turkey, June 14, 1914; came to U.S., 1936, naturalized, 1948; s. Joachim Theodore and Irene (Georges) K.; m. Marjorie Rutherford, June 21, 1945; 1 child, John Thomas. Student, Robert Coll., Istanbul, 1932-35; BS, Duke U., 1937; MS (Moore fellow), U. Pa., 1938; D Engring. (hon.), Lehigh U., 1971. Registered profl. engr., Pa. Instr. U. Pa., 1938-40; project engr. Moore Sch. Elec. Engring., 1944-46; rsch. engr. Am. TV Labs., Chgo., 1940-42; edn. dir. 6th Svc. Command Signal Corps Radar Sch., Chgo., 1942-44; from asst. prof. to assoc. prof. elec. engring. Lehigh U., 1946-55, prof., head dept., 1955-58, disting. prof., 1962-81; dean Lehigh U. Coll. Engring., 1965-81; project engr. UHF filters Lehigh U., 1950-54; project dir. active networks Signal Corps., 1954-60; cons. Bell Telephone Labs., Murray Hill, N.J., 1950-56, Dept. Edn. Commonwealth P.R., 1972, IBM, 1980-93; bd. dirs. Komline & Sanderson Engring. Corp. Author: Transmission Line and Filter Networks, 1950, also articles. Mem. Gen. State Authority Commonwealth of Pa., 1974-81. Recipient Alfred Nobel Robinson award for svc. to univ., 1948, Hillman award for disting. svc. Lehigh, 1962, 81, Outstanding Tchr. award, 1968, Outstanding Prof. award Lehigh U. Alumni Assn., 1990, Pa. Profl. Engring. award for distinction, 1965; rebuilt north wing Packard Lab. dedicated in his honor, 1981. Fellow IEEE (life, co-founder Lehigh Valley chpt. 1963, Centennial medal award 1984); mem. Am. Soc. Engring. Edn. (life), Engring. Coun. for Profl. Devel. (nat. accreditation com. for engring.), Franklin Inst., Pergamon Inst. (hon. adv. bd.), Phi Beta Kappa, Sigma Xi, Phi Beta Delta, Tau Beta Pi, Omicron Delta Kappa, Eta Kappa Nu, Iota Gamma Pi. Home: 2112 Kirkland Village Cir Bethlehem PA 18017-4713 *In free societies, whenever rules and regulations, because of changing times, are in conflict with principles—it is the principles that need be conserved, and the conflicting rules and regulations summarily discarded.*

KARAKEY, SHERRY JOANNE, financial and real estate investment company executive, interior designer; b. Wendall, Idaho, Apr. 16, 1942; d. John Donald and Vera Ella (Frost) Kingery; children: Artist Roxanne, Buddy (George II), Kami JoAnne, Launi JoElla. Student, Ariz. State U., 1960. Corp. sec., treas. Karbel Metals Co., Phoenix, 1963-67; sec. to pub. Scottsdale (Ariz.) Daily Progress, 1969-72; with D-Velco Mfg. of Ariz., Phoenix, 1959-62, dir., exec. v.p., sec., treas., 1972-87; mng. ptnr. Karitage, Ltd., Scottsdale, 1987—.

KARALEKAS, ANNE, media executive; b. Boston, Nov. 6, 1946; d. Christus and Helen (Vogiantzis) K. AB, Wheaton Coll., Norton, Mass., 1968; AM, Harvard U., 1969, PhD, 1974. Chief project mgr. def. and arms control project Commn. on Orgn. of Govt. for Conduct of Fgn. Policy, Washington, 1974-75; sr. staff mem. Senate Select Com. on Intelligence, Washington, 1975-78; sr. assoc. McKinsey & Co., Washington, 1978-85; mktg. mgr. The Washington Post, 1985-87, dir. mktg., 1987-89; pub. Washington Post Mag., 1989-96, dir. specialty products group, 1993-96; gen. mgr. Washington Sidewalk, Microsoft Corp., Washington, 1996—. Author: History of the CIA, 1976; contbr. articles and book revs. to profl. publs. Advisor fgn. policy Mondale-Ferraro Presdl. Campaign, Washington, 1984; trustee Wheaton Coll., Norton, 1985-88. Mem. Council on Fgn. Relations, The Phillips Collection (corp. adv. com.), Phi Beta Kappa. Greek Orthodox. Avocation: twentieth century art and lit.

KARALEKAS, GEORGE STEVEN, advertising agency executive, political consultant; b. Boston, Nov. 26, 1939; s. Steven George and Sotiria (Sarris) K. B.S., Boston U., 1962. Vice pres., assoc. media dir. Grey Advt., Inc., N.Y.C., 1962-70; dir. advt. services Can. Dry Corp., N.Y.C., 1970-72, dir. mktg. N.Y. ops., 1972-74; exec. v.p., dir. media and mktg., mgmt. account dir. deGarmo Advt., Inc., N.Y.C., 1974-80; sr. v.p., exec. dir. media, mgmt. dir. D'Arcy-MacManus & Masius, N.Y.C., 1980-85; pres. Karalekas & Co., N.Y.C. and Washington, 1985—; sr. v.p., exec. dir. media November Group, Pres. Nixon, N.Y.C., Washington, 1971-72; sr. v.p., spl. advt. cons. Campaign 76, Pres. Ford, N.Y.C., Washington, 1975-76; sr. v.p., exec. dir. media Campaign 80, Pres. Reagan, N.Y.C., Washington, 1979-80; spl. advt. cons. Nov. Co., President Bush, N.Y.C., Washington, 1992. Mem. Republican Nat. Com., 1970—. Mem. Internat. Radio and TV Soc., Am. Mgmt. Assn. Republican. Greek Orthodox. Home: Holiday Point 8 Circle Dr Sherman CT 06784-1643 Office: Karalekas & Co 360 E 72nd St New York NY 10021-4753 also: 1211 Connecticut Ave NW Washington DC 20036-2701

KARALIS, JOHN PETER, computer company executive, lawyer; b. Mpls., July 6, 1938; s. Peter John and Vivian (Deckas) K.; m. Mary Curtis, Sept. 7, 1963; children: Amy Curtis, Theodore Curtis. BA, U. Minn., 1960, JD, 1963. Bar: Minn. 1963, Mass. 1972, Ariz. 1983, N.Y. 1986, Pa. 1986. Pvt. practice Mpls., 1963-70; assoc. gen. counsel Honeywell Inc., Mpls., 1970-83, v.p., 1982-83; pvt. practice Phoenix, 1983-85; sr. v.p., gen. counsel Sperry Corp., N.Y.C., 1985-87; v.p. gen. counsel Apple Computer Inc., Cupertino, Calif., 1987-89; of counsel Brown and Bain, Phoenix, 1989-92; sr. v.p. corp. devel. Tektronix, Inc., Portland, 1992-98; pres. Corp. Alliance Consulting, LLC, Scottsdale, Ariz., 1998—; mem. bd. advisors Ctr. for Study of Law, Sci. and Tech., Ariz. State U. Coll. Law, Tempe, 1983-89, adj. prof., 1990-91. Author: International Joint Ventures, A Practical Guide, 1992. Recipient Disting. Achievement award Ariz. State U., Tempe, 1985. Mem. Met. Club (N.Y.C.), Gainey Ranch Golf Club.

KARAM, NAJI E., cardiologist; b. Brummana, Lebanon, May 29, 1966; s. Emile Karam and Mona Ashkar; m. Courtney Shadid, May 25, 1996; 1 child, Emile. MD, Am. U. Beirut, 1991. Intern GSH/John Hopkins U., Balt., 1991-92; resident in internal medicine U. Tex., Houston, 1992-94; fellow in cardiology U. Tex. Med. Br., Galveston, 1994-97; asst. prof. medicine U. Okla. Health Sci. Ctr., Oklahoma City, 1997—; invasive cardiologist & echocardiographer, dir. coronary intensive care unit Univ. Hosp., Oklahoma City. Fellow Am. Coll. Cardiology.

KARAN, DONNA (DONNA FASKE), fashion designer; b. Forest Hills, N.Y., Oct. 2, 1948; m. Mark Karan; 1 child, Gabrielle. BFA, Parsons Sch. Design, 1987. With Addenda Co., to 1968; with Anne Klein & Co., N.Y.C., 1968-84; co-designer Anne Klein & Co., 1971-74, designer, 1974-84; owner, designer, ptnr. Donna Karan Co., N.Y.C., 1984-96, chmn. bd., head designer, 1996—. Showed first complete collection for Anne Klein & Co. in 1974; collaborator on Anne Klein collections with Louis dell'Olio. Recipient Coty award, 1977, Awards Coun. of Fashion Designers of Am., 1985, 86, 92, Frontrunner award Sara Lee Corp., 1992; co-recipient (with Louis dell'Olio) Coty Return award, 1981, Coty Hall of Fame citation, 1982, Coty award, 1984. Office: Donna Karan Co 550 7th Ave New York NY 10018-3203*

KARAN, PAUL RICHARD, lawyer; b. Providence, June 12, 1936; s. Aaron Arnold and Sadye (Persky) K.; m. Susan Clare Brody, Jan. 3, 1964 (dec. Apr. 1986); children: Jennifer Hilary, Steven Lee; m. Linda Doris Adler, July 2, 1987. BA, Brown U., 1957; JD, Columbia U., 1960. Bar: NY 1961, U.S. Dist. Ct. (so. dist.) N.Y. 1962, U.S. Supreme Ct. 1967, U.S. Tax Ct. 1975, U.S. Claims Ct. 1976. Assoc. Demov & Morris, N.Y.C., 1960-65, ptnr., 1966-85; ptnr. Gordon Altman Weitzen Shalov & Wein, N.Y.C., 1985—. Contbr. articles to profl. jours. Chmn. Bd. Assessment Rev., Greenburgh, N.Y., 1978-86; mem. Planning Bd., Greenburgh, 1975-78, Bd. Edn., Greenburgh, 1980-83. Fellow Am. Bar Found., Am. Coll. Trust and Estate Counsel (chmn. downstate N.Y. 1996—), N.Y. Bar Found.; mem. ABA, N.Y. State Bar Assn. (chmn. trusts and estates law sect. 1990-91), Assn. of Bar of City of N.Y. Avocation: golf. Office: Gordon Altman Weitzen Shalov & Wein 114 W 47th St New York NY 10036-1510

KARANIKAS, ALEXANDER, English language educator, author, actor; b. Manchester, N.H., Oct. 5, 1916; s. Stephen and Vaia (Olgas) K.; m. Helen J. Karagianes, Jan. 2, 1949; children: Marianthe Vaia, Diana Christine, Cynthia Maria. Student, U. N.H., 1934-36; A.B. cum laude, Harvard, 1939; M.A., Northwestern U., 1950, Ph.D. in English, 1953. With N.H. Writers Project, 1940-41; editor Allegheny-Kiski Valley Edit. The CIO News, 1941-42; radio news commentator Sta. WMUR, Manchester, 1946; grad. asst. Northwestern U., Evanston, Ill., 1950-52; instr. Kendall Coll., Evanston, Ill., 1952-53, Northwestern U., Evanston, 1953-54, 57-58; mem. faculty U. Ill. at Chgo., 1954—, prof. English, 1974-82, prof. emeritus, 1982—; owner Deerhaven Orchard, 1974-96; cons. in field. Author: When a Youth Gets Poetic, 1934, In Praise of Heroes, 1945, Tillers of a Myth: The Southern Agrarians as Social and Literary Critics, 1966 (Friends of Lit. award 1967), (with Helen Karanikas) Elias Venezis, 1969, Hellenes and Hellions: Modern Greek Characters in American Literature, 1981, Nashville Dreams (mus. comedy with songs by Larry Nestor), 1991, Stepping Stones (poems), 1994. Mem. nat. cabinet Am. Youth Congress, 1937-39; exec. sec. Mass. Youth Coun., 1939-40; co-chmn. Nat. Bicentennial Symposium on the Greek Experience in Am., 1976; Publicity dir. N.H. Ind. Voters, 1946; sec. Manchester Vets. Council, 1946; Candidate for Congress, 1948; mem. exec. com. United Hellenic Am. Congress, 1983—; exec. sec. Am. Coun. for Dem. Greece, 1947. Served with USAAF, 1942-45, Alaska corr. YANK, 1943-45. Mem. Hellenic Profl. Soc. Ill., Modern Greek Studies Assn., Screen Actors Guild, Friends of Lit., Phi Eta Sigma, Order Ahepa (dist. sec. 1946). Mem. Greek Orthodox Ch. Home: 618 N Harvey Ave Oak Park IL 60302-1740 Office: Univ of Ill at Chicago English Dept Chicago IL 60680

KARASA, NORMAN LUKAS, home builder, developer, geologist; b. Balt., June 10, 1951; s. Norman and Ona K.; m. Lois J. Hansen, Jan. 4, 1974; children: Andrew, Jane. AB in Geology, Rutgers Coll., 1973; MS in Geophysics, U. Wyo., 1976; MBA in Fin., U. Colo., Colorado Springs, 1990. Systems mgr. Brit. Petroleum, N.Y.C., 1973-74; seismic processing leader Phillips Petroleum, Bartlesville, Okla., 1976-79; geophysicist Phillips Petroleum, Houston, 1979-80; internat. spl. project geophysicist Marathon Oil, Findlay, Ohio, 1980-82; internat. exploration geophysicist Marathon Oil, Houston, 1982-85, internat. reservoir geologist/geophysicist, 1985-86; home builder, designer, owner D'signer Inc., Monument Homes, Colo., 1986—, developer, hydrologist, 1992—; owner Tri-Lakes Montessori Sch.; lic. stock broker, ins. advisor Prin. Group, Colo., 1987—; realtor ReMax. Active Boy Scouts Am., Colo., 1987—. Mem. Home Builder Assocs. Presbyterian. Office: Monument Homes PO Box 1423 Monument CO 80132-1423

KARASU, T(OKSOZ) BYRAM, psychiatry educator; b. Feb. 11, 1935. MD, U. Istanbul, Turkey, 1959. Jr. intern St. Jeanne D'Arc Hosp., Montreal, Can., 1963-64; sr. intern St. John Gen. Hosp., New Brunswick, Can., 1964-65; resident in psychiatry Yale-New Haven Med. Ctr., 1967-68, Conn. Mental Health Ctr., 1968-69; fellow in psychiatry Yale U., New Haven, 1969; dir. dept. psychiatry Jacobi Med. Ctr., N.Y., 1975-93; prof. psychiatry Albert Einstein Coll. Medicine, Bronx, N.Y., 1981—; Silverman prof. psychiatry Albert Einstein Coll. Medicine, Bronx, 1993—; chmn. Albert Einstein Coll. Medicine, 1993—; psychiatrist-in-chief Montefiore Med. Ctr., 1993—. Author: Wisdom in the Practice of Psychotherapy, 1992, Deconstruction of Psychotherapy, 1996; editor: Psychotherapy Research, 1982, The Psychiatric Therapies, 1984, Treatments of Psychiatric Disorders, 1989, other books and numerous articles; editor-in-chief Am. Jour. Psychotherapy, 1994, Psychotherapist's Interventions: Integrating Psychodynamic Perspectives in Clinical Practice, 1998. Fellow Am. Psychiat. Assn. (chmn. commn. 1979-83, task force 1981-90, practice guidelines in major depression 1991-98, Disting. Svc. award 1983, Spl. Presdl. award 1988, recipient Sigmund Freud Laureate Award Am. Soc. Psychoanalytic Physicians, 1997. Home: 2 E 88th St New York NY 10128-0555 Office: Albert Einstein Coll Medicine 1300 Morris Park Ave Bronx NY 10461-1975

KARATHANASIS, SOTIRIOS KONSTANTINOU, biochemist; b. Corinth, Greece, Feb. 13, 1951. BSc, U. Patras, Greece, 1975; MSc, U. Ga., 1978, PhD, 1980. Instr. dept. pediatrics Harvard Medical Sch., Boston, 1982-84; rsch. assoc. dept. cardiology Children's Hosp. Medical Ctr., 1984-90; asst. prof. dept. pediatrics Harvard Medical Sch., Boston, 1984-90; rsch. assoc. div. metabolism Children's Hosp. Medical Ctr., 1982-84; assoc. prof. dept. pediatrics and dept. physiology Harvard Medical Sch., Boston, 1990-92; sr. rsch. assoc. dept. cardiology Children's Hosp, Medical Ctr., 1990-92; dept. head cardiovascular molecular biology Lederle Labs., Pearl River, N.Y., 1992-96; Disting. rsch. scientist Wyeth-Ayerst/Women's Health, Phila., 1996—; editorial bds. Jour. Lipid Rsch., 1987-95; tchg. rsch. fellows dept. cardiology Children's Hosp., Harvard Med. Sch., 1984-92. Author reviews, book chpts.; contbr. articles to profl. jours. Recipient Established Investigator award Am. Heart Assn., 1985, Irvine H. Page Arteriosclerosis Rsch. award, 1983, fellow Greek Nat. Inst. Fellowships, 1969. E-mail: karaths@bellatlantic.net. Home: 862 Old State Rd Berwyn PA 19312-1443 Office: Wyeth-Ayerst Rsch Bldg 145 Rm 2099 PO Box 8299 Philadelphia PA 19101-8299

KARATZ, BRUCE E., business executive; b. Chgo., Oct. 10, 1945; s. Robert Harry and Naomi Rae (Goldstein) K.; m. Janet Louise Dreisen, July 28, 1968; children: Elizabeth, Matthew, Theodore. BA, Boston U., 1967; JD, U. So. Calif., 1970. Bar: Calif. 1971. Assoc. Keatinge & Sterling, Los Angeles, 1970-72; assoc. corp. counsel Kaufman and Broad, Inc., Los Angeles, 1972-73; dir. forward planning Kaufman and Broad, Inc., Irvine, Calif., 1973-74; pres. Kaufman and Broad Provence, Aix-en-Provence, France, 1974-76, Kaufman and Broad France, Paris, 1976-80, Kaufman and Broad Devel. Group, Los Angeles, 1980-86; chmn., pres., CEO Kaufman and Broad Home Corp., Los Angeles, 1985—, also bd. dirs., also chmn. bd. dirs., 1993; bd. dirs. Nat. Golf Properties, Inc., Honeywell Inc., Fred Meyer, Inc.; trustee Rand Corp. Founder Mus. Contemporary Art, L.A., 1981; trustee Pitzer Coll., Claremont, Calif., 1983—; bd. councilors U. So. Calif. Law Ctr. Mem. Calif. Bus. Roundtable, Coun. on Fgn. Rels., Pacific Coun. on Internat. Policy, L.A. World Affairs Coun. Democrat. Avocations: modern art, skiing, travel, golf. Office: Kaufman & Broad Home Corp 10990 Wilshire Blvd Fl 7 Los Angeles CA 90024-3913*

KARATZ, WILLIAM WARREN, lawyer; b. Benton Harbor, Mich., Aug. 9, 1926; s. Harry E. and Grace M. (Campbell) K.; m. Barbara Lansburgh Low, May 25, 1989. Ph.B. (La Verne Noyes scholar), U. Chgo., 1948; postgrad., Sch. Pol. Sci., 1949; LL.B. (Harlan Fiske Stone scholar), Columbia U., 1952. Bar: N.Y. State 1953, U.S. Supreme Ct. 1960. Assoc. in law Columbia U. Sch. Law, N.Y.C., 1952-53; assoc. firm Winthrop, Stimson, Putnam & Roberts, N.Y.C., 1953-62; partner Winthrop, Stimson, Putnam & Roberts, 1963-86, sr. counsel, 1987—; bd. dirs. Burnham Fund., Inc. Bd. editors: Columbia Law Rev, 1950-52. Served with USN, 1944-46. Fellow Am. Bar Found. (life); mem. ABA, Am. Law Inst. (life), Bar Assn. City of N.Y. (mem. exec. com. 1969-73, chmn. 1972-73, v.p. 1973-74), N.Y. State Bar Assn., (mem. ho. of dels. 1972-77), Am. Coll. Trial Lawyers, Am. Judicature Soc., Century Assn., India House Club (N.Y.C.), Confrerie des Chevaliers du Tastevin (grand officer). Home: 100 E 50th St New York NY 10022 Office: Winthrop Stimson Putnam & Roberts 1 Battery Park Plz Fl 29 Apt 34R New York NY 10004-1490

KARAU, JON OLIN, judge; b. Shelby, Mich., Sept. 15, 1918; s. Edward Karl and Pearl Margaret (Ackerman) K.; m. Luella Gay Nichols, Feb. 14, 1945 (dec. 1982); m. Lana Lee Lovelace, Jan. 15, 1983 (div. 1992); 1 child, Larry Jon (dec.); 1 adopted child, John F. Nicholson-Karau; m. Louise Rogers, Sept. 17, 1995; 1 child, Bruce. BSIE, Can. Inst., Windsor, 1947; LLD, Detroit Coll. Law, 1956. Payroll auditor Fisher Body div., Flint, Mich., 1940-47; with Avery Corp., Detroit, 1947-49; supr. blueprint rm. Detroit Arsenal, 1949-59; specs. writer U.S. Govt.-Navy, Port Hueneme, 1959-63; specs. supr. U.S. Govt.-DSA, Detroit/Washington, 1963-68; sr. mgmt. officer USAF, Washington, 1968-73; stockbroker EGT-J.O. Karau Assocs., Sherman, Tex., 1973-78; mcpl. judge City of Pottsboro, Tex., 1978-91; ret., 1991; cons. Grayson C.C., Denison, 1981; with Reiki Wellness Ctr., Denison, 1993-97. Contbr. articles to profl. jours. Bd. dirs. ARC, Sherman, 1974-77, Campfire Denison; chmn. Grayson County Housing Authority, Sherman, 1986-97. With U.S. Army, 1943-45, ETO; lt. col. USAR and Guards, 1947-85. Mem. Internat. Assn. Fin. Planning, Am. Inst. Mgmt., Am. Inst. Fin., Am. Inst. Indsl. Engrs., U.S. Def. Forces Assn., Tex. Mcpl. Cts. Assn., Tex. Judges Assn. (cons.), Mensa, Elks, Lions (regional chmn.), MAsons, Epsilon Delta Chi. Democrat. Avocations: flying, driving, camping, swimming, Reiki healing. Home: 5048 Ridgeview Dr Las Vegas NV 89120-1259

KARAWINA, ERICA, artist, stained glass designer; b. Germany, 1904; came to U.S., 1923, naturalized, 1937; d. Paul Wilhelm and Meta (Jaenecke) K.; m. Sidney C. Hsiao, June 21, 1938. Studied under, Charles J. Connick. Invited artist 25th anniversary of Hawaii Craftsmen, Honolulu Acad. Arts., 1992. One-woman shows include Grace Horne Gallery, Boston, 1933, U. N.H., 1936, Art Club, Lancaster, Pa., 1937, Wadsworth Atheneum, 1938, Colby Coll., Maine, 1938, U. Dayton, Ohio, 1939, Okla. Art Center, 1939, Grand Rapids Mich., 1940, Ferargil Galleries, N.Y.C., 1947, Fitchburg Art Mus., 1949, Currier Gallery, 1949, Beaux Arts Gallery, Honolulu, 1952, Gima's, 1953, China. Inst., Taipei, 1956, The Gallery, Honolulu, 1957, Contemporary Arts Center, 1977, Queen Emma Gallery, Honolulu; numerous stained glass commns. including glass mural for Kapiolani Coll., Hawaii commissioned by State Found Culture and Arts, and retrospective exhbn., 1988, stained glass mural for St. Francis Med. Ctr. West, Waipaho, 1990, Stained Glass in Hawaii 1950-92, Honolulu; represented in permanent collections Libr. of Congress, Washington, Boston Mus. Fine Arts, Fine Arts Mus., Mobile, Ala., Met. Mus., Worcester (Mass.) Fine Arts Mus., Colorado Springs Art Ctr., Addison Gallery, Mus. Modern Art, N.Y.C., Honolulu Acad. Arts, Tennent Art Found., Contemporary Mus., Honolulu. Recipient John Poole Meml. Prize, James C. Castle award Narcissus Festival of Arts, 1961. Fellow Internat. Inst. Arts; mem. Arts Council Hawaii, Stained Glass Assn. Hawaii.

KARAYANIS, PLATO STEVEN, opera company executive; b. Pitts., Dec. 24, 1928. BFA, Carnegie Mellon U., 1952; artist's diploma in performance, Curtis Inst. Singer, stage dir. Luzern and Zürich, Switzerland, 1958-65, Met. Opera Nat. Co., 1965-67; exec. v.p., treas. Affiliate Artists Inc., 1967-77; mgr. rehearsal dept. San Francisco Opera; gen. dir. The Dallas Opera, 1977—. Performing scholar Berkshire Music Festival, 1952, Curtis Inst., 1952-56; recipient creative arts award Dallas Hist. Soc., TACA award for Excellence in Performing Arts, 1998. Mem. Opera Am. (chmn. bd. dirs. 1993-97), Dallas Assembly, Sigma Alpha Iota. Office: The Dallas Opera 3102 Oak Lawn Ave Dallas TX 75219-4241

KARBEN, RYAN SCOTT, county legislator; b. Bronx, N.Y., Sept. 29, 1974; s. Barry Richard and Shelley Valerie (Gross) K.; m. Lauren Cheryl Bekritsky, June 23, 1996. BA in English, Yeshiva U., 1996; JD, Columbia U., 1999. Mem. planning bd. Town of Ramapo, Suffern, N.Y., 1992-97; county legislator County of Rockland, New City, N.Y., 1997—; assoc. Simpson Thacher and Bartlett, N.Y.C., 1999—; dir. Tomorrow's Leaders Today, N.Y.C., 1996—. Bd. trustees United Jewish Appeal Fedn., New Hempstead, N.Y., 1996—; adv. bd. Martin Luther King Ctr., Spring Valley, N.Y., 1993—, Big Bros./Big Sisters, New City, 1996—; treas. N.Y. State Young Dems., Albany, 1994—; mem. Arts Coun. Rockland. Mem. Spring Valley NAACP. Jewish. Avocations: reading, jogging. Office: Rockland County Legislature 11 New Hempstead Rd New City NY 10956-3636

KARBEN, SHELLEY VALERIE, elementary and special education school educator; b. Mt. Vernon, N.Y., Dec. 1, 1944; d. Sidney and Helen (Minskoff) Gross; children: Ryan Scott, Lori Jennifer. BS, 1966; MA, NYU, 1971. Cert. tchr. spl. edn., N.Y. Tchr. kindergarten and elem. East Ramapo Ctrl. Sch. Dist., Spring Valley, N.Y., 1966—, tchr. learning disabilities, emotionally handicapped, mentally handicapped, resource room; chairperson Child Study Team E. Ramapo Ctrl. Sch. Dist., 1989; mem. pub. rels. panel, supt.'s adv. panel, 1992; cons. Jewish Day Schs, Yeshivas Schs., Hebrew Schs. for Spl Edn., 1969—; dir. summer spl. edn. program Yeshiva. Mem. Profl. Cons. Staff, N.Y. State Sen. Commn. on Child Abuse, Albany, 1974; mem. Commn. of Ethnic Studies, Westchester County, 1975-76; exec. com. Dem. Party, Town of Ramapo, N.Y., 1985—, mem. task force affordable housing, 1991, mem. bd. assessment rev., 1988—; mem. Hebrew Programs for the Disabled, Nat. Commn. on Torah Edn., Yeshiva U., 1974-76, Fleetwood Synagogue Sisterhood, Mt. Vernon, N.Y., pres., 1976-77; pres. Hillcrest Civic Assn., 1990-98; dir. Club ARC Rockland County, 1994; facilitator site-based mgmt. team, 1998—; v.p. Yehillat and Kehillat, New Hempstead, 1997—. Mem. Assn. for Children with Learning Disabilities, Coun. for Exceptional Children, Assn. for Supervision and Curriculum Devel., B'nai Brith (pres. Mt. Vernon 1975-77). Jewish.

KARBER, JOHNNIE FAYE, elementary education educator; b. Enid, Okla., June 24, 1949; d. William Harvard Sr. and Marilyn Faye (Morehead) Benton; m. Jerry Lynn Karber, June 7, 1969; children: Jason Kelly, Jennifer Lyn, Julee Dawn. BS, Okla. Panhandle State U., 1972; postgrad., Wichita State U. and West. Tex. State U. Tchr., kindergarten and music Goodland (Kans.) Unified Sch. Dist.; tchr., music Perryton (Tex.) Ind. Sch. Dist. Active church and community orgns. Mem. Tex. Music Educators Assn., ATPE, Kodaly Educators of Tex. Avocation: pianist.

KARCH, GEORGE FREDERICK, JR., lawyer; b. Cleve., Apr. 24, 1933; s. George Frederick, Sr. and Mary (Sargent) K.; m. Carolyn Biggar, Aug. 26, 1958; children—Geoffrey, George III, Margaret Ruth. A.B. cum laude, Amherst Coll.; L.L.B., U. Mich. Ptnr. Thompson, Hine and Flory, Cleve., 1959-98, ret., 1998; sr. counsel Berick Pearlman & Mills, Cleve., 1999—; adj. prof. litigation & trial tactics Case Western Reserve U. Sch. Law, 1993—. Mem. bd. trustees Geauga County Met. Housing Authority, Chardon, Ohio, 1960-84, chmn., 1981-83. Mem. ABA (life), Sixth Circuit Judi. Conf. Presbyterian. Clubs: Kirtland Country (Willoughby); Tavern (Cleve.). Avocations: reading history, golf, politics. Home: 12112 Kile Rd Chardon OH 44024-9594

KARCH, KAREN BROOKE, principal; b. Greensburg, Pa., Feb. 17, 1944; d. John Daniel and Louise Fluke (Reinfried) Karle; m. Robert Charles Karch, Apr. 2, 1966; children: Kara Brooke, Krista Kimberly. BA, Ohio Wesleyan U., 1965; MEd, Am. U., 1973, EdD, 1981. Tchr. Prince George County schs., Md., 1965-70; instr. English Montgomery Coll., Rockville, Md., 1976-79, No. Va. C.C., Alexandria, 1977-79; reading specialist Frederick (Md.) County Bd. Edn., 1979-81, media specialist, 1981-82, vice-prin., 1982-83; prin. Mid. sch., Walkersville, Md., 1983-88, Gaithersburg (Md.) Elem. Sch., 1988-94, Potomoc (Md.) Elem Sch., 1994—; instr. Bowie State U.; presenter in field. Leader Capital coun. Girl Scouts U.S.A., 1977-80. Mem. ASCD, Md. Mid. Sch. Assn., Nat. Mid. Sch. Assn., Nat. Assn. Secondary Sch. Prin., Montgomery County Elem. Sch. Adminstrs. Assn. (pres. 1989-90), Phi Kappa Phi, Phi Delta Kappa, Delta Kappa Gamma. Republican. Methodist. Avocations: running, skiing, sailing, tennis. Home: 13001 Glen Rd North Potomac MD 20878-8851 Office: Potomac Elem Sch 10311 River Rd Potomac MD 20854-4971*

KARCH, ROBERT E., real estate company executive; b. Bklyn., May 30, 1933; s. Charles H. and Etta R. (Becker) K.; m. Brenda Schechter, Sept. 7, 1958; children: Barry S., Karen D., Brian D. AB, Syracuse U., 1953, MBA, 1958; student in Russian, Army Lang. Sch., Monterey, Calif., 1953-54. Lic. real estate broker, Tex., N.Mex., Colo.; lic. comml. pilot. With Nationwide Beauty & Barber Supply Co., Syracuse, N.Y., 1956-87, pres., 1966-74, chmn., 1974-87; also dir. Nationwide Beauty & Barber Supply Co.; sales mgr. Helen of Troy Corp., El Paso, Tex., 1974-76, v.p. sales and mktg., 1976-79, also dir.; v.p., dir. Bormex Constrn. Inc., 1980-81; pres. BKB Properties, 1978—, The Prudential BKB Realtors, Inc. (formerly BKB Properties), 1994—, Southwest Rental Svcs., 1992—, Best Mortgage Svcs., 1997—; ptnr. BKB Ins. Agy., 1987-89; instr. investment real estate Acad. Real Estate, 1984-88. Author: Data Processing for Beauty/Barber Dealers, 1968; pub. Real Estate Investor's Newsletter, 1982-87, Property Mgmt. Newsletter, 1985—. Pres. Syracuse Hebrew Day Sch., 1972-73. Served with U.S. Army, 1953-56. Mem. Beauty and Barber Supply Inst., Direct Mail/Mktg. Assn., Aircraft Owners and Pilots Assn., Real Estate Securities and Syndication Inst., El Paso Real Estate Investment Club (pres. 1985), Jewish War Vets., El Paso Aviation Assn., El Paso Bd. Realtors (comml. investment div., mem. Exchangers Club, Top Vol. Producer award 1984, 85, 86, Real Estate Exchange award 1986), El Paso Apt. Assn., Coronado Country Club, Lancer's Club, Vista Hills Country Club. Home: 6016 Torrey Pines Dr El Paso TX 79912-2030 Office: Prudential BKB, Realtors 10622 Montwood Dr Ste A El Paso TX 79935-2753 also: 400 Shadow Mountain Dr El Paso TX 79912-4030 also: 1300 Country Club Rd Santa Teresa NM 88008-1748

KARCHER, DONALD STEVEN, medical educator; b. New Orleans, Aug. 23, 1948. BS, U. New Orleans, 1970; MD, La. State U., 1974. Diplomate Am. Bd. Pathology in hematopathology and anatomic and clin. pathology; lic. physician, D.C. Rotating intern Brooke Army Med.Ctr., Ft. Sam Houston, Tex., 1974-75, resident anatomic and clin. pathology, 1974-78; med. dir. hematopathology sect. dept. pathology/faculty mem. Walter Reed Army Med. Ctr., Washington, 1978-81; asst. prof. pathology La. State U. Med. Ctr., New Orleans, 1981-82, clin. asst. prof., 1982-84; staff pathologist Hotel Dieu Hosp., New Orleans, 1982-84; assoc. med. dir. Am. Bio-Sci. Labs., 1983-84; asst. prof. pathology George Washington U. Med. Ctr., 1984-92, assoc. prof., 1992-97, prof., 1997—, chief hematopathology svc., 1984-93, interim dir. divsn. clin. pathology, 1992-93, dir., 1993-96, dir. labs., 1996—; vis. pathologist Charity Hosp. La., New Orleans, 1981-82; faculty mem. New Orleans Combined Med. Tech. Course, 1981-84; cons. pathologist St. Tammany Parish Hosp., Covington, La., 1982-84, Riverside Med. Ctr., Franklinton, La., 1982-84; lectr. various meetings, orgns., hosps., univs., confs. Mem. editl. rev. panel Human Pathology, 1989—; contbr. articles to profl. jours., chpts. to books. Maj. M.C., U.S. Army, 1974-81. Grantee George Washington U., 1986-87, NIH, 1997—. Fellow Am. Soc. Cln. Pathologists, U.S. and Can. Acad. Pathology; mem. Soc. Hematopathology, Phi Eta Sigma,Alpha Theta Epsilon, Alpha Omega Alpha. Office: U Hosp Dept Pathology 901 23rd St NW Washington DC 20037-2327

KARCHER, JOHN DRAKE, textile and apparel company executive; b. Washington, Sept. 10, 1939; s. Raymond Edward and Mary Frances (Drake) K.; B.B.A., Wake Forest U., 1961; M.B.A., Wharton Sch., U. Pa., 1964; m. Lois Allison Lynch, Apr. 3, 1965; children: Kimberly P. Karcher-Nelson, John Drake, II, Christopher Brett. Pres. Wamsutta Decorative Fabrics, N.Y.C., 1972-77, Baxter/Kelly, Inc., N.Y.C., 1977-80; pres., dir. Scorpio Ventures, Inc., cons. and investment firm, Darien Conn., 1981-83; v.p. mktg. home fashions div. Dan River Inc., N.Y.C., 1983-84; pres., mktg. dir. Soc. Brand Industries, Inc., N.Y.C., 1985-87; chmn. bd., pres., chief exec. officer, dir. P.L. Industries, Inc., N.Y.C., 1987—, P.L. Mex., LLC, N.Y.C., 1995—. Co-chmn. Ox Ridge Sch. PTA, Darien, 1977-78; mem. bldg. fund drive Darian YMCA, 1977; head coach Darien Youth Hockey, 1977-79, Darien Little League, 1977-79, Darien Babe Ruth League, 1981-83; active fund raising Wake Forest U., New Canaan Country Sch.; bd. dirs. Bucknell U. Parents Assn., 1990-93, chmn. devel. com., mem. exec. com., 1991-93, chairperson fund raising com., 1992-93. Named Darien Little League Coach of Yr., 1977. Office: PL Industries Inc 500 5th Ave New York NY 10110

KARCHIN, LOUIS SAMUEL, composer, educator; b. Sept. 8, 1951; s. Isadore David and Ida (Kessler) K. MusB, U. Rochester, 1973; MA, Harvard U., 1975, PhD, 1978. Asst. prof. music NYU, N.Y.C., 1979-85, assoc. prof. music, 1985—; pres. U.S. sect. Internat. Soc. for Contemporary Music, 1981-83, chmn., 1983-85; pub. C. F. Peters Corp. Composer: Capriccio for Violin and Seven Instruments, 1978, Duo for Violin and Cello, 1981, Viola Variations, 1982, Songs of John Keats, 1985, Canonic Mosaics, 1986, Sonata for Piano, 1987, Songs of Distance and Light, 1988, Sonata for Cello and Piano, 1989, Romulus, an Opera in One Act, 1990, String Quartet, 1991, Galactic Folds for chamber ensemble, 1993, Sonata da Camera, 1994, Summer Song, 1994, Rustic Dances, 1995, Rhapsody for Orchestra, 1996, Cascades, 1997, American Visions: Two Songs on Poems of Yevgeny Yevtushenky, 1998; commd. by Koussevitzky Found., 1998; recs. on CRI and New World Records. Recipient Walter Hinrichsen award AAAL, 1985, NEA Composer awards, 1982, 83, Joseph H. Bearns prize Columbia U., 1972, Koussevitsky Composition prize Tanglewood, 1971. Office: NYU 24 Waverly Pl Rm 268 New York NY 10003-6757

KARCZMAR, MIECZYSLAW, economist; b. Lodz, Poland, Jan. 22, 1923; came to u.S., 1973; s. Henryk and Franciszka (Lubicz) K.; m. Gabriela Bogucka, Dec. 22, 1947; children: Thomas, Peter. MS in Econs. and Commerce, Acad. Commerce, Poznan, Poland, 1948; PhD in Econs., Main Sch. Planning Stats, Warsaw, Poland, 1960; postgrad., London Sch. Econs., 1958. With Nat. Bank Poland, Warsaw, 1949-62, dep. dir. planning dept., 1955-58, dep. dir. internat. dept., 1958-62; dir. fin. dept. Polish Ministry Fgn. Trade, Warsaw, 1962-69; trade commr., comml. counselor to Can. Polish Ministry Fgn. Trade, Montreal, 1969-73; sr. v.p., chief economist European Am. Bank & Trust Co., European Am. Banking Corp., N.Y.C., 1974-86; econ. advisor Deutsche Bank, N.Y.C., 1986—; mem. supervisory bd. Warta-Ins. Reins. Co., Warsaw, 1962-69; lectr., asst. prof. Main Sch. Planning Stats., Warsaw, 1951-68; lectr. vocat. courses in fin. planning and credit sys., 1950-56. Author: (with W. Pruss) Credit in Trade, 1956; (with others) Accountant's Guidebook, 1956, Money and Credit, 1960; contbr. articles to newspapers, mags., profl. jours.; rschr. in money, credit theory, internat. monetary system, banking.

KARDON, BRIAN, publishing company executive; m. Kara Silver, Mar. 23, 1991; children: Max, Elliot, Isabel. BS, U. Pa., 1979, MBA, 1987. V.p. corp. mktg. Cahners Pub. Co., Newton, Mass.; sr. v.p. mktg. Cahners Bus. Info., Newton. Office: Cahners Business Info 275 Washington St Newton MA 02458-1646

KARDON, DENNIS, artist,, educator. BA cum laude, Yale U., 1973. Mem. faculty Sch. Fine Arts, N.Y.C. One-man shows Barbara Toll Fine Arts, N.Y.C., 1981, 84, 86, 89, Studio Space, N.Y.C., 1990, Richard Anderson Fine Arts, N.Y.C., 1996; exhibited in numerous group shows, 1983—, including Mus. Modern Art, N.Y.C., 1983, 86, List Art Ctr., MIT, Cambridge, 1985, Wellesley (Mass.) Coll. Mus., 1986, Indpls. Mus. Art, 1986, Blkyn. Mus., 1986, Barbara Toll Fine Arts, 1987, Lorence-Monk Gallery, N.Y.C., 1988, Nat. Gallery Art, Washington, 1989, Fernando Alcolea Gallery, Barcelona Spaing, 1989, Althea Viafora Gallery, N.Y.C., 1990, Marc Richards Gallery, L.A., 1990rts and Letters, N.Y.C., 1994, Aldrich Mus. Contemporary Art, Ridgefield, Conn., 1995, Albright Gallery, Reading, Pa., 1995, 96, Mus. Fine Arts, Boston, 1996, Jewish Mus., N.Y.C., 1996 (travelled to San Francisco, L.A., Balt.); represented in permanent collections Jewish Mus., J.V. Speed Mus., Los Angeles County Mus. Art, Boston Mus. Fine Art, Walker Art mus., New Mus., Mus. Modern Art, Met. Mus., Des Moines Art Ctr., Ind. U. Art Mus., U. Iowa Mus. Art, Bklyn. Mus., Nat. Mus. Am. Art, Fogg Art Mus., N.Y. Pub. Libr., also pvt. and corp. collections; work review and represented in newspapers and mags. Grantee N.Y. Found. on Arts, Louis Comford Tiffany Found., 1991; Guggenheim fellow, 1998. Office: Sch Visual Arts 209 E 23d St New York NY 10010*

KARDON, JANET, museum director, curator, educator; b. Phila.; d. Robert and Shirley (Drasin) Stolker; m. Robert Kardon, Nov. 19, 1955; children: Ross, Nina, Roy. BS in Edn., Temple U.; MA in Art History, U. Pa. Lectr. Phila. Coll. Art, 1968-75, dir. exhbns., 1975-78; dir. Inst. Contemporary Art, Phila., 1978-89, Am. Craft Mus., N.Y.C., 1989-95; ind. curator, 1996—; adj. prof. Fashion Inst. of Tech., N.Y.C., Pratt Inst., Bklyn.; cons., panel mem. Nat. Endowment for Arts, 1975—; mus. panel mem. Pa. Coun. on Arts, Phila., 1988—; U.S. commr. Venice Biennale, Venice, 1980. Curated and created essays for 30 exhbns., including Labyrinths, Time, Artists Sets and Costumes, Laurie Anderson, Robert Mapplethorpe, David Salle, Gertrude and Otto Natzler; editor: Twentieth Century Americian Craft: A Centenary Project, 1900-1920, Revivals/Diverse Traditions, 1920-45, Craft in the Machine Age, 1920-45. Grantee Nat. Endowment for Arts, 1978. Home and Office: 150 E 69th St Apt 21J New York NY 10021-5704

KARDON, PETER FRANKLIN, foundation administrator; b. N.Y.C., May 5, 1949; s. Leonard and Annette (Rappaport) K. AB, Dartmouth Coll., 1970; MA, U. Chgo., 1975, PhD, 1984. Asst. to exec. dir. MLA of Am., N.Y.C., 1980-84; acad. affairs assoc. Office of Chancellor, NYU, N.Y.C., 1984-86, dir. acad. projects, 1986-88; dir. planning John Simon Guggenheim Meml. Found., N.Y.C., 1988-98, dir. L.Am. program, 1991—, dir. info., 1998—; adj. prof. medieval and Renaissance studies NYU, N.Y.C., 1986—. Reynolds scholar Dartmouth Coll., 1970-71; Fulbright-Hayes fellow, 1973-74, Georges Lurcy fellow, 1976-77, Whiting fellow U. Chgo., 1978-79; NYU Golden Dozen Disting. Tchg. award, 1996. Office: JS Guggenheim Meml Found 90 Park Ave New York NY 10016-1301

KARDON, RANDY H., ophthalmologist; b. Des Moines, Feb. 17, 1954; s. Fred and Thelma (Sherman) K. BS, U. Iowa, 1975, MD, PhD, 1982. Diplomate Am. Bd. Ophthalmology; lic. physician, Iowa. Neuro-ophthalmology fellow U. Iowa Hosps., Iowa City, 1987-89, assoc. prof., 1989—; clin. scientist VA Hosp., Iowa City, 1995—; dir. neuro-ophthalmology svc. U. Iowa, Iowa City, 1997; examiner Am. Bd. Opthalmology, Phila., 1997—; coord. com. Clin. Rsch. Ctr., 1997; grant review com. Fight for Sight Sci. Program, 1995. Co-author: Walsh & Hoyt Clinical Neuro-Ophthalmology, 1997, Atlas of Neuro-Ophthalmology, 1997; mem. editl. bd. Jour. Clin. Neuro-Ophthalmology, 1997. Recipient Lew Wasserman award Rsch. to Prevent Blindness, 1997, Career Devel. award VA, 1995-98, Merit Review award 1993-98. Jewish. Office: Univ Iowa Hosps and Clinics 200 Hawkins Dr Iowa City IA 52242-1009

KARDON, ROBERT, mortgage company executive; b. Phila., Mar. 8, 1922; s. Morris and Sophie (Winkleman) K.; m. Janet Stolker, Nov. 19, 1949; children—Roy, Nina, Ross. Student, U. Miami (Fla.), 1940-42, Shrivenham Am. U., Swindon, Eng., 1945-46. Chmn. bd. B.T. Babbitt Co., Inc., 1964-66, Pitts. Mortgage Corp., 1964-72, Murphree Mortgage Co., Nashville, 1966-72, Kardon Investment Co., 1945-75, Peoples Bond & Mortgage Co., Phila., 1950-72; chmn. bd., v.p. United Container Co., Phila., 1938-75; pres., chief exec. officer Kardon Industries, Inc., 1974—, also chmn.; dir. Continental Bank Phila. Trustee Phila. Mus. Art. Served with AUS, 1942-46. Mem. Young Pres. Orgn., World Bus. Council. Home: 150 E 69th St # 21J New York NY 10021-5704 Office: Kardon Industries Inc 1201 Chestnut St Ste 6 Philadelphia PA 19107-4176

KARELITZ, RICHARD ALAN, financial executive, lawyer; b. Elizabeth, N.J., Nov. 1, 1949; s. David Karelitz and Doris Frances (Tuck) Kahn; m. Virginia Lee Harris, Aug. 18, 1974; children: David Benjamin, Daniel Seth. AB, Coll. William and Mary, 1971; JD, Boston U. Sch. Law, 1974; LLM, 1977. Bar: Mass. 1974, U.S. Supreme Ct. 1979. Tax atty. Coopers & Lybrand, Boston, 1974-75; comptroller Internat. Forest Products Corp., Boston, 1975-79, treas., 1979-91, sr. v.p., 1991—; treas. New England TV Corp., 1987-91, Sta. WHDH-TV, Inc., 1987-91; gen. coun., New Eng. Patriots (NFL) Football Club, 1994—, Foxboro Stadium Assocs. L.P., Foxboro, Mass., 1989—, New England Revolution (Major League Soccer Team), Foxboro, 1996—; dir., Carmel Container Sys. Ltd., Tel Aviv, Israel, 1988—, chmn. Audit Com., 1992—; treas., Chestnut Hill Mgmt. Corp., Boston, 1991—. Trustee, Kraft Found., Boston, 1979—; Notary pub. Commonwealth of Mass., 1981—; dir. Temple Sinai, Sharon, Mass., 1995—. Mem. ABA, Mass. Bar Assn. Jewish. Avocations: travel, family activities. Home: 31 Sunset Dr Sharon MA 02067-1738 Office: Internat Forest Products Corp One Boston Pl Boston MA 02108

KAREN, LINDA TRICARICO, fashion designer; b. Bklyn., June 8, 1961; d. John William and Phyllis Jean (D'Addario) T. Student, Bucks County Community Coll., 1978-79; AAS, Fashion Inst. Tech., 1992. Retail mgr. Canadians, Brooks, Casual Corner, 1980-83; coord. sales and design Sure Snap Corp., N.Y.C., 1983-84; asst. designer E.S. Sutton Inc., N.Y.C., 1984-86; designer Good 'N Plenty Inc., N.Y.C., 1986-90; sr. designer, merchandiser Leonard A. Feinberg, Inc., N.Y.C., 1991-98; freelance designer, ind. contractor, 1998—; free-lance illustrator, designer. Contbr. fashion trend reports, Milan, Italy, 1984, Rome, 1985, Milan and Florence, Italy, 1986, London and Paris, 1987, Montreal, 1988, 94, 95, L.A., 1993, 95, 96. Mem. Fashion Soc., NAFE. Republican. Roman Catholic. Avocations: fashion design, illustration, travel. Home: 166 Berry Rd Monroe NY 10950-5237

KARES, ROBIN LEE, English educator; b. Indpls., Mar. 14, 1955; d. Robert Franklin and Virginia Lee (Dixon) K. BA in Secondary Edn., U. Evansville, Ind., 1977; MA in English, So. Ill. U., Carbondale, 1980; postgrad., So. Ill. U., 1982. Adminstrv. asst., fundraiser Big Sisters of Ctrl. Ind., Indpls., 1986-89; lectr. in English Ind. U. Purdue U., Columbus, Ind., 1990-98; devel. officer Goodwill Industries of Ctrl. Ind., Inc., 1998—; faculty advisor Literalines Mag. of the Arts, Columbus, 1993—. Named to Hall of Fame, ARC, Indpls., 1987.

KARESH, JANICE LEHRER, special education consultant; b. N.Y.C., May 22, 1924; d. Maxwell and lillian (Cohen) Lehrer; m. Irwin Karesh, June 15, 1947 (dec. 1959); children: Sara, Hyman, Ann, Charles. BS in Pre-Medicine, Rutgers U., 1945; MA in Psychol. Counseling, NYU, 1946. Tchr. algebra Chicora H.S., Charleston, S.C., 1946-47; tchr. math. Charleston H.S., 1963; tchr. gifted Addleston Hebrew Acad., Charleston, 1963-64; tchr. physics, biology Rivers H.S., Charleston, 1964-65; cons. spl. edn. S.C Dept. Mental Retardation, Charleston, 1966-69; dir. spl. svcs. Beaufort (S.C.) Sch. Dist., 1969-89; ind. cons. spl. edn. Charleston, 1989—. Vol. advocate guardian at litem, Family Ct., S.C., 1990—; mem. exec. com. Charleston Democratic Party, 1994—. Mem. LWV (past bd. dirs.), Nat. Coun. Jewish Women (pres. 1951, past bd. dirs.), Coun. for Exceptional Children, Poetry Soc. of S.C., Douglass Alumnae Assn. (v.p. 1995—). Democrat. Jewish. Avocations: needlepoint, writing poetry and essays, child advocacy issues. E-mail: j.karesh@bellsouth.net. Home: 150 Wappoo Creek Dr Apt 9 Charleston SC 29412-2140

KARFF, SAMUEL EGAL, rabbi; b. Phila., Sept. 19, 1931; s. Louis and Reba (Margalit) K.; m. Joan Mag, June 29, 1959; children: Rachel Karff Weissenstein, Amy Karff Halevy, Elizabeth Karff Kampf. AB magna cum laude, Harvard U., 1953; MAHL, DHL, Hebrew Union Coll., 1956. Rabbi Congregation Beth Israel, Hartford, Conn., 1958-60, Temple Beth El, Flint, Mich., 1960-62, Chgo. Sinai Congregation, 1962-74; sr. rabbi Congregation Beth Israel, Houston, 1975—; lectr. U. Chgo. Divinity Sch., 1968-75; vis. assoc. prof. U. Notre Dame, 1966-67; adj. prof. religious studies Rice U., Houston, 1976—. Author: Agada: The Language of Jewish Faith, 1970; editor Centennial Vol. Hebrew Union Coll.-Jewish Inst. of Religion, 1981-84; contbr. chpts. Judaism Religions of the World, 1982. Bd. dirs. United Way, Houston, 1991—, Inst. Religion, Houston, 1990—. Recipient Homiletics award HUC-JIR, Cin., 1956; John Harvard scholar Harvard U., 1951-52. Mem. Cen. Conf. Am. Rabbis (pres. 1989-91), Houston Philos. Soc., Phi Beta Kappa, Kiwanis. Avocations: tennis, walking, movies, reading. Office: Congregation Beth Israel 5600 N Braeswood Blvd Houston TX 77096-2901

KARI, DAVEN MICHAEL, religion educator; b. Hot Springs, S.D., Sept. 24, 1953; s. John Nelson and Corinna Nicolls (Morse) K.; m. Priya Perianayakam, Apr. 4, 1988; children: David Prem, Daniel Michael, Dante Gabriel. BA in English, Bibl. Studies, History, Fresno Pacific Coll., 1975, BA in Music, 1977; MA in English, Baylor U., 1983; MA, PhD in English, Purdue U., 1985, 86; MDiv, PhD, So. Bapt. Theol. Sem., 1988, 91. Lic. to ministry So. Bapt. Ch., 1971, ordained to ministry, 1996. Photography studio technician Johnson's Studio, Manteca, Calif., 1975-77; grad. teaching asst. Baylor U., Waco, Tex., 1978-79; minister of music Calvary Bapt. Ch., West Lafayette, Ind., 1984-85; grad. teaching asst. Purdue U., West Lafayette, Ind., 1979-85; lectr. in English Jefferson C.C., Louisville, 1987-90, Spalding U., Louisville, 1986-90, U. Louisville, 1986-90; asst. prof. English Mo. Bapt. Coll., St. Louis, 1991; assoc. prof. English Calif. Bapt. Coll., Riverside, 1991-93; assoc. prof., dir., Christian Ministry and Fine Arts Christian Ministry Ctr., 1994-98; prof. Christian Studies and English Calif. Baptist U., 1998; acad. dean Washington Bible Coll., Lanham, Md., 1998—. Author: T. S. Eliot's Dramatic Pilgrimage, 1990, Bibliography of Sources in Christianity and the Arts, 1995; co-editor: Baptist Reflections on Christianity and the Arts: Learning from Beauty, 1997, Contemporary Authors, 1997. Founder, co-dir. local Boys Brigade, Linden, Calif., 1969-71; asst. pastor Linden (Calif.) First Bapt. Ch., 1971; chair transp. com. Calvary Bapt. Ch., West Lafayette, 1982-83, dir. singles ministry, 1983-85; moderator Scholar's Bowl Quiz Contest, Riverside, 1993-94. Recipient Lit. Criticism award Purdue U., 1983; named to Outstanding Young Men Am., 1985; named Faculty Mem. of Yr., Calif. Bapt. Coll., 1993; named to Contemporary Authors, 1997. Mem. Am. Acad. Religion, Conf. on Christianity and Lit. Democrat. Baptist. Avocations: poetry, stained glass windows, sculpture, photography, painting, composing music. Home: Collamore Residence # 4 6511 Princess Garden Pkwy Lanham Seabrook MD 20706-3538

KARIBO, JOHN MICHAEL, allergist, immunologist, pediatrician; b. Louisville, Ky., 1930. MD, U. Louisville. Diplomate Am. Bd. Allergy and Immunology, Am. Bd. Pediatrics. Intern St. Joseph Infirmary, 1963-64, resident, 1964-65; resident Children's Hosp., Louisville, 1965-66; fellow Cin., 1966-67; pvt. practice Allergy Care and Immunology, Louisville. Office: Allergy Care 1261 Goss Ave Louisville KY 40217-1239*

KARIN, MARDI ROSS, surgeon; b. Endicott, N.Y., Nov. 13, 1960; d. Albert and Joan Hunt (Ross) Dornfest; m. Rom Rodney Karin, July 5, 1981; children: Todd, Benjamin, Evelyn. MD, UCLA, 1985. Diplomate Am. Bd. Surgery, Am. Bd. Med. Examiners. From intern to resident in surgery U. Iowa, 1985-90; staff surgeon Santa Teresa Cmty. Hosp., San Jose, Calif., 1990—, The Permanente Med. Group, San Jose, 1990—. Recipient U. Calif. Regent Scholar. Fellow ACS; mem. Santa Clara County Med. Assn. (mem. coun. 1996-97), Phi Beta Kappa, Alpha Omega Alpha. Office: Santa Teresa Cmty Hosp 280 Hospital Pkwy San Jose CA 95119-1103

KARIYA, PAUL, professional hockey player; b. Vancouver, Oct. 16, 1974. Forward/hockey player Anaheim (Calif.) Mighty Ducks, 1994—. Winner Lady Byng Meml. Trophy for sportsmanship and gentlemanly conduct, 1995-96; mem. silver-medal-winning Can. Olympic team, 1994. Office: Anaheim Mighty Ducks PO Box 61077 2695 E Katella Ave Anaheim CA 92803-6177

KARKANIAS, GEORGE B., neurologist, educator. BS in Biology, Rutgers U., 1983-87; MS with honors, Albert Einstein Coll. Medicine, 1991, PhD, 1993. Postdoctoral fellow dept. neurosci. Albert Einstein Coll. Medicine, 1993-94, instr., 1994-95, asst. prof., 1995—. Contbr. articles to profl. jours. Rsch. grantee Juvenile Diabetes Found. Mem. AAAS, Am. Diabetes Assn. (rsch. grantee 1995—), N.Y. Acad. Scis., Internat. Brian Rsch. Orgn., Soc. Neurosci. Office: Albert Einstein Coll Medicine 1300 Morris Park Ave U103A Bronx NY 10461-1926*

KARKHANIS, SHARAD, librarian, political science educator; b. Khopoli, India, Mar. 8, 1935; came to U.S., 1959; s. Dwarkanath D. and Indira (D.) K. BA in Econs., U. Bombay, 1958; MLS, Rutgers U., 1962; MA in Polit. Sci., CUNY, 1967; PhD in Polit. Sci., NYU, 1978. Libr. U.S. Info. Svc., Bombay, 1955-58; libr. trainee Leyton Pub. Libr., Layton, Eng., 1958-59, Montclair (N.J.) Pub. Libr., 1959-60; libr. East Orange (N.J.) Pub. Libr., 1960-63, CUNY, Bklyn., 1963-64; prof. libr. and polit. sci. depts. Kingsborough Community Coll., Bklyn., 1964--. Author: Indian Politics and the Role of the Press,1981, Jewish Heritage in America, 1988; editor How to Avoid Dead End in Your Career, 1988; Educational Excellence of Asian Americans, 1989. Mem. Ethnic Task Force borough pres., Bklyn., 1987--. Mem. ALA, Asian/Pacific Am. Librs. Assn. (pres. 1980-82), Libr. Assn. CUNY pres. 1967-69). Republican. Hindu. Avocations: political biographies, movies. Office: Kingsborough Community Coll Oriental Blvd Brooklyn NY 11235

KARKHECK, JOHN PETER, physics educator, researcher; b. N.Y.C., Apr. 26, 1945; s. John Henry and Dorothy Cecilia (Riebling) K.; m. Kathleen Mary Shiels, Nov. 8, 1969; children: Lorraine, Michelle, Eric. BS, LeMoyne Coll., 1966; MA, SUNY, Buffalo, 1972; PhD, SUNY, Stony Brook, 1978. Various positions Grumman Corp., Bethpage, N.Y., 1964-68; grad. asst. SUNY, Buffalo, 1968-70; tchr. secondary schs. Mattituck (N.Y.) Sch. Dist., 1970-71, Shelter Island (N.Y.) Sch. Dist., 1971-73; grad. asst. SUNY, Stony Brook, 1973-78, postdoctoral fellow, 1978-79; rsch. assoc. SUNY, Stony Brook, N.Y., 1979-81; asst. prof. physics GMI Engring. and Mgmt. Inst., Flint, Mich., 1981-84, assoc. prof., 1984, prof., dir. physics, 1988-89, head. dept. sci. and math., 1989-93; prof., chmn. dept. physics Marquette U., Milw., 1993—; physics assoc. Brookhaven Nat. Lab., Upton, N.Y., 1975-79, cons., 1979-85, STS, Hauppauge, N.Y., 1983, BID Ctr., Flint, 1985-90; acad. assoc. Mich. State U., 1988, 90, vis. scholar, 1989, vis. scientist, 1991; reviewer Addison-Wesley Pub., 1990, 93; regional dir. Mich. Sci. Olympiad, 1991-92, 92-93. Contbr. numerous articles to profl. jours. Den leader Cub Scouts Am., Flint, 1987-91; leader Boy Scouts Am., 1991—; bd. dirs. Flint Area Sci. Fair, 1991-93; judge local sci. fairs. Dept. Energy rsch. grantee, 1977-79, NATO travel grantee, 1983-86, 89, NATO ASI grantee, 1998. Mem. Am. Phys. Soc., AAAS, AAPT (pres. 1999—), Sigma Xi (v.p. Marquette U. chpt. 1998-99). Roman Catholic. Avocations: swimming, reading, travel, learning German. Home: 6592 N Bethmaur Ln Glendale WI 53209-3320 Office: Marquette Univ Dept Physics PO Box 1881 Milwaukee WI 53201-1881

KARKOSCHKA, ERICH, planetary science researcher, writer; b. Stuttgart, Federal Republic of Germany, Nov. 6, 1955; came to U.S., 1983; s. Erhard Karkoschka and Rothraut Leiter. Diploma in math., U. Stuttgart, 1981; PhD, U. Ariz., 1990. Wissenschaftlicher Mitarbeiter U. Stuttgart, 1982; rsch. assoc. U. Ariz., Tucson, 1992—; group leader Internat. Workshop Astronomy, Europe, 1981-89. Author: The Observer's Sky Atlas, 1990, German edit., 1988, Japanese edit., 1991, Czech edit., 1995, Drehbare Welt-Sternkarte, 1990; co-author: Das Himmelsjahr, 1982—. Recipient 2d European prize European Philips Contest for Young Scientists and Inventors, 1973. Mem. Am. Meteorol. Soc. Avocations: playing violin in symphony orchestra, playing organ, amateur astronomy, worldwide travel. Office: Univ Ariz Lunar & Planetary Lab Tucson AZ 85721-0092

KARKUT, RICHARD THEODORE, clinical psychologist; b. Derby, Conn., Apr. 28, 1948; s. Harry Chester and Mary (Katz) K. AB, William Jewell Coll., 1971; MA, U. Mo., Kansas City, 1976; D Psychology, Forest Inst. Profl. Psychology, 1988. Lic. psychologist, Ohio, Ind.; cert. in biofeedback. Psychology intern Burrell Mental Health Ctr., Springfield, Mo., 1987-88; clin. psychologist Wabash Valley Hosp., Lafayette, Ind., 1989-91, Quinco Cons., North Vernon, Ind., 1991-93; CEO Adkar Assocs., Inc., Bloomington, Ind., 1993—; cons. Div. Family Svcs., Lafayette, 1989-90. Guest editor jour. Ind. Psychologist; contbr. articles to profl. jours. Mem. Am. Psychol. Assn., Soc. Behavioral Medicine, Assn. Applied Psychophysiology and Biofeedback, Am. Pain Soc., Am. Soc. Clin. Hypnosis, Am. Orthopsychiat. Assn., Am. Assn. Counseling and Devel., Am. Mental Health Counselor's Assn., Ind. Psychol. Assn., Ill. Psychol. Assn., Ind. Biofeedback Soc. Anglican. Home: PO Box 1396 Bloomington IN 47402-1396

KARL, BARRY DEAN, historian, educator; b. Louisville, July 24, 1927; s. Aaron and Anne (Simons) K.; m. Alice Hideko Woodard, June 14, 1957; children: Elisabeth Mead, Sarah Anne. BA, U. Louisville, 1949; MA, U. Chgo., 1951; PhD, Harvard U., 1961. Assoc. editor for humanities and history U. Chgo. Press, 1951-55; exec. sec. to com. on gen. edn. Harvard U., 1959-61; asst. prof. history Washington U., St. Louis, 1962-63, prof., 1963-68; prof. Brown U., Providence, 1968-71; prof. Am. history U. Chgo., 1971—, Norman and Edna Freehling prof., 1977-96, Norman and Edna Freehling prof. emeritus, 1996—; William Henry Bloomberg prof. philanthropy Harvard U., 1998—; chmn. dept. history U. Chgo., 1976-79; lectr. Jefferson Meml., U. Calif., Berkeley, 1991. Author: Executive Reorganization and Reform in the New Deal, 1963, Presiential Planning and Social Science Research, 1969, Charles E. Merriam and the Study of Politics, 1974, Public Administration and American History, 1976 (Frederick Mosher award), Executive Reorganization and Presidential Power, 1978, (with Stanley N. Katz) The American Private Philantrophic Foundation and the Public Sphere 1890-1930, 1981, The Citizen and the Scholar: Ships That Crash in the Night, 1982, Corporate Philantrophy: Historical Background, 1982, The Uneasy State: The U.S. from 1915-1945, 1983, Lo, The Poor Volunteer, 1984 (with Stanley Katz) Foundations and Ruling Class Elites, 1987, The American Bureaucrat, 1987, Constitution and Central Planning, 1989, Legislatures and Bureaucracy, 1994, Foundations and Public Policy, 1995, Volunteers and Professionals, 1996, Foundations and the Federal Government, 1998, Foundations and Government, 1999. Co-recipient Faculty prize Harvard U. Press, 1962-63; Charles Warren Ctr. fellow Harvard U., 1965. Mem. Orgn. Am. Historians. Office: Harvard Hauser Ctr Kennedy Sch Govt 79 JFK Strnell Ave Cambridge MA 02138 Also: U Chgo Dept History 1126 E 59th St Chicago IL 60637-1580

KARL, GABRIEL, physics educator; b. Cluj, Romania, Apr. 30, 1937; came to Can., 1960; s. Alexander and Frida (Izsak) K.; m. Dorothy Rose Searle, Apr. 10, 1965; 1 child, Alexandra. Ph.D., U. Toronto, Ont., Can., 1964. Research assoc. Oxford U., Eng., 1966-69; prof. physics U. Guelph, Ont., Can., 1969—. Contbr. articles to profl. jours. German-Canadian Research Prize (Deutsch-Kanadischer Forschungspreis), 1992. Fellow Royal Soc. Can.; mem. Am. Phys. Soc., Can. Assn. Physicists (CAP medal 1991). Office: Univ Guelph, U Guelph Macnaughton Bldg, 50 Stone Rd E, Guelph, ON Canada N1G 2W1*

KARL, GEORGE, professional basketball coach; b. Penn Hills, Pa., May 12, 1951; m. Cathy Karl; children—Kelci Ryanne, Coby Joseph. Grad., U. N.C., 1973. Guard San Antonio Spurs, NBA, 1973-78, asst. coach, head scout, 1978-80; coach Mont. Golden Nuggets, Continental Basketball Assn., 1980-83; dir. player acquisition Cleve. Cavaliers, 1983-84, coach, 1984-86; head coach Golden State Warriors, Oakland, Calif., from 1986, Albany (N.Y.) Patrons, 1988-89, 90-91, Real Madrid, Spain, 1991-92, Seattle Supersonics, 1992-98, Milwaukee Bucks, 1998—. Named Coach of Yr., Continental Basketball Assn., 1981, 83. Mem. Continental Basketball Assn. *

KARL, JONATHAN DAVID, television journalist; b. Stamford, Conn., Jan. 19, 1968. BA, Vassar Coll., 1990. Reporter, rschr. New Rep., Washington, 1990-91; editor Freedom House, N.Y.C., 1991-93; reporter N.Y. Post, N.Y.C., 1993-95; corr. CNN, N.Y.C. and Washington, 1996—; lectr. in field; co-founder European Journalism Networ, 1992. Author: The Right to Bear Arms, 1995; co-author: Third Millennium Declaration, 1993; gen. editor: Freedom onthe World, 1991-93; contbr. articles to profl. publs. Mem. Phi Beta Kappa. Avocations: writing, skiing, wine collecting, chess. Office: CNN 820 1st St NE Washington DC 20002

KARL, MICHAEL M., endocrinology professor; b. Milw., Jan. 30, 1915. BS, U. Wis., 1936; MD, U. Louisville, 1938. Am. Bd. Internal Med., 1946. Intern St. Louis City Hosp., 1938-42, resident Internal Med., 1940-42; pvt. practive St. Louis, 1942-87; dir. clinical affairs, dept. Medicine St. Louis City Hosp., 1987-93; prof. Clinical Medicine Wash. U. Sch. Med., St. Louis, 1972—; dir. third yr. medicine clerkship St. Louis City Hosp., 1942-44 and Dept. Med. Jewish Hosp., St. Louis, 1963-64; med. dir. Red Cross Mobile Blood Unit, 1942-44; bd. dirs. Munic Nursing Bd., St. Louis; cons. USAF, 1962-64; co-organizer Jeff-Vander-Lou Med. Clinic, 1967-72; pres. Faculty Ctr., Wash. U., 1969; exec. faculty mem. Sch. Med., 1975-76, 85-86; chmn. Com. Svc. to Elderly, Nat. Coun. Jewish Fedns., 1976-81; mem. White House conf. Families, 1978-80; mem. Accreditation Coun. Continuing Med. Edn., 1987—, chmn. 1991; mem. prog. com. Inst. Med. Nat. Acad. Sci., 1988-90; Irene & Michael Karl prof. endocrinology. Recipient Laureate award Am. Col. Physicians, 1988, Ralph O. Claypoole Sr. Meml. award Am. Col. Physicians, 1990. Mem. AMA, Inst. Med. Nat. Acad. Sci., Am. Col. Physicians (fellow and master), Ctr. Soc. Clin. Rsch., Am. Assn. Study Liver Disease, Am. Soc. Internal Med.. Office: Dept Med Wash U Sch Med 660 S Euclid Ave # Saint Louis MO 63110-1010

KARL, ROBERT HARRY, cardiologist; b. Milw., Sept. 4, 1947; s. Max Henry and Anita Rene (Davis) K.; m. Nilza Maria Secomandi, Jan. 14, 1979; children: Daniel, Lara, Kevin. BA, Northwestern U., Evanston, Ill., 1969; MD, Washington U., St. Louis, 1973. Diplomate cardiovascular disease subsplty. Am. Bd. Internal Medicine. Intern internal medicine U. Miami (Fla.), 1973-74, resident internal medicine, 1974-76, cardiology fellow, 1976-78; pvt. practice cardiology Miami, 1978—; asst. clin. prof. U. Miami Med. Sch., 1978—; chief cardiology Bapt. Hosp. Miami, 1986-88; asst. chief of medicine Bapt. Hosp., 1992-94, chief of medicine, 1994-97; pres. Medicard Am., Inc., Miami, 1992-97, Biocard Corp., Miami; v.p. Schoolink, Inc., Miami, 1996-97. Mem. exec. com. South Dade Jewish Fedn., Miami, 1986-89; bd. dirs. Beth David Congregation, Miami, 1985-87, Bet Shira Synagogue, Miami, 1987-88, Child Abuse Prevention Project, 1986—, Aish Hatorah, Miami, 1991—, David and Mary Alper JCC, 1997—, Hebrew Acad. of Miami Beach, 1997—. Fellow Am. Coll. Cardiology (dist. councillor Fla. chpt. 1995—), Coun. Clin. Cardiology of Am. Heart Assn.; mem. ACP, Fla. Med. Assn., Dade County Med. Assn. (peer rev. com. 1980-82), Young Israel of Kendall (v.p. 1995—). Avocations: piano, karate, golf, horseback riding, skiing. Office: 8950 N Kendall Dr Ste 601 Miami FL 33176-2139

KARLAN, SANDY ELLEN, judge; b. N.Y.C.; d. Bernard and Muriel (Richter) K. BA, U. Miami, 1971; JD cum laude, Nova Southeastern U., 1978. Bar: Fla. 1978, U.S. Ct. Appeals (5th and 11th cirs.) 1981, U.S. Bankruptcy Ct. 1985, U.S. Dist. Ct. (so. dist.) Fla. 1988; cert. in matrimonial law, Fla. Law clk. to Hon. Alan R. Schwartz Third Dist. Ct. Appeals, Miami, Fla., 1978-80; assoc. Gars, Dixon & Shapiro, Miami, 1980-82; ptnr. Chaykin, Karlan & Jacobs, Coral Gables, Fla., 1982-85; sr. ptnr. Sandy Karlan, P.A., Miami, 1985-95; judge 11th Jud. Cir. Ct., Miami, 1995—; chair steering com. gender bias commn. Fla. Supreme Ct., 1987, mem. family ct. steering com., 1994, Conf. Cir. Ct. Judges, 1995—. Author: (with others) Florida Family Law, 1986; contbr. articles to profl. jours. Bd. govs. Shepard Broad Sch. Law Nova Southeastern U., Ft. Lauderdale, Fla.; trustee Dade Marine Inst., Miami, 1993—. Recipient Sojourner Truth award NOW, 1989. Fellow ABA; mem. Nat. Assn. Women Judges, Fla. Bar (mem. legislation com. 184-88, grievance com. 11J 1985-87, vice chair disciplinary rev. com. 1987-89, vice chair access com. 1988-89, bd. govs. 1988-92, chair pub. rels. com. 1989-92, mem. gender equality com. 1994), Fla. Assn. Women Lawyers (pres. Dade County chpt. 1984-85), Dade County Bar Assn. (bd. dirs. 1986-89), Bankruptcy Bar Assn. (bd. dirs. 1991-94), Leadership Miami Alumni Assn. Address: 73 W Flagler St Ste 1015 Miami FL 33130-4763

KARLE, ISABELLA L., chemist; b. Detroit, Dec. 2, 1921; d. Zygmunt Apolonaris and Elizabeth (Graczyk) Lugoski; m. Jerome Karle, June 4, 1942; children: Louise Hanson, Jean Marianne, Madeleine Tawney. BS in Chemistry, U. Mich., 1941, MS in Chemistry, 1942, PhD, 1944; DSc (hon.), U. Mich., 1976, Wayne State U., 1979, U. Md., 1986, Athens (Greece) U., 1997, U. Pa., 1999; LHD (hon.), Georgetown U., 1984. Assoc. chemist U. Chgo., 1944; instr. chemistry U. Mich., Ann Arbor, 1944-46; physicist Naval Rsch. Lab., Washington, 1946—; Paul Ehrlich lectr. NIH, 1991; mem. exec. com. Am. Peptide Symposium, 1975-81, adv. bd. Chem. and Engring. News, 1986-89. Mem. editorial bd. Biopolymers Jour., 1975—, Internat. Jour. Peptide Rsch., 1981—; contbr. articles to profl. jours. Recipient Superior Civilian Service award USN, 1965, Fed. Women's award U.S. Govt., 1973, Annual Achievement award Soc. Women Engrs., 1968, Annual Achievement award U. Mich., 1987, Dexter Conrad award Office Naval Rsch., 1980, WISE Lifetime Achievement award Women in Sci. and Engring., 1986, award for disting. achievement in sci. Sec. of Navy, 1987, Gregori Aminoff prize Swedish Royal Acad. Scis., 1988, Adm. Parsons award Navy League U.S., 1988, Ann. Achievement award CCNY, 1989; Bijvoet medal U. Utrecht, The Netherlands, 1990, Vincent du Vigneaud award Gordon Conf. (Peptides), 1992, Bower Sci. award Franklin Inst., 1993, Nat. medal of Sci. Pres. of the U.S., 1995; named to Michigan Women's Hall of Fame, 1989, Chem. Scis. award Nat. Acad. Scis., 1995. Fellow Am. Acad. Arts Scis., Am. Inst. Chemists. (Chem. Pioneer award 1984); mem. NAS (Chem. Scis. award, 1995), Am. Crystallographic Assn. (pres. 1976), Am. Chem. Soc. (Garvan award 1976, Hillebrand award 1970, Ralph Hirschmann award in Peptide chemistry 1998), Am. Phys. Soc., Am. Philos. Soc., Biophys. Soc. Home: 6304 Lakeview Dr Falls Church VA 22041-1309 Office: Naval Rsch Lab Code 6030 Washington DC 20375-5341

KARLE, JEROME, physicist, researcher; b. N.Y.C., June 18, 1918; married, 1942; 3 children. B.S., CCNY, 1937; A.M., Harvard U., 1938; M.S., U. Mich., 1942, Ph.D. in Phys. Chemistry, 1943. Rsch. assoc. Manhattan project, Chgo., 1943-44, U.S. Navy Project, Mich., 1944-46; head electron diffraction sect. Naval Rsch. Lab., Washington, 1946-58, head diffraction br., 1958-68, now head lab. for structure matter, 1968—; mem. NRC, 1954-56, 67-75, 78-87; chmn. U.S. Nat. Com. for Crystallography, 1973-75. Recipient Nobel prize in chemistry, 1985. Fellow Am. Phys. Soc.; mem. NAS (chairperson chemistry sect. 1988-91), AAAS, Am. Chem. Soc., Am. Math. Soc., Crystallograph Assn. (treas. 1950-52, pres. 1972), Internat. Union Crystallography (mem. exec. com. 1978-87, pres. 1981-84). Office: US Naval Rsch Lab Lab for Structure of Matter Code # 6030 Washington DC 20375-5341 *There is too much administration of everything creative. It distorts our society and its character. The solution is to select competent, well-qualified people and give them freedom and support to pursue their creative gifts.*

KARLEN, DOUGLAS LAWRENCE, soil scientist; b. Monroe, Wis., Aug. 28, 1951; s. Lawrence Herman and Marian Bertha (Trumpy) K.; m. Linda Sue Bender, June 9, 1973; children: Sarah Jean, Steven Douglas, Holly Lin. BS, U. Wis., 1973; MS, Mich. State U., 1975; PhD, Kans. State U., 1978. Rsch. soil scientist Coastal Plains Soil, Water Conservation Rsch. Ctr., USDA-ARS, Florence, S.C., 1978-88, Nat. Soil Tilth Lab. USDA-ARS, Ames, Iowa, 1988—; team leader Leopold Ctr. for Sustainable Agr., Ames, 1989-94. Asst. scoutmaster, com. chmn. Boy Scouts Am., Ankeny, Iowa, 1991—. Fellow Am. Soc. Agronomy (bd. rep. Ag sys. 1997—), Crop Sci. Soc. Am. (assoc. editor 1988-93, tech. editor 1994—), Soil Sci. Soc. Am. (Agronomic Achievement awrad-soils 1996); mem. Coun. Agrl. Sci. and Tech., Soil and Water Conservation Soc. Am. Episcopalian. Office: USDA-ARS-MWA-NSTL 2150 Pammel Dr Ames IA 50010-4420

KARLIN, GARY LEE, insurance executive; b. Chgo., Jan. 18, 1934; s. Jack and Pearl (Malin-Weiss) K.; children: David, Paige; m. Cheryl Daneman; stepchildren: Chad, Brooke. Student U. Ill., 1951-52, Roosevelt U., 1952. With Mut. of N.Y., 1956-62, sales mgr., Chgo., 1958-62, regional trainer, 1962-63; pres. Exec. Motivation, Inc., Chgo., 1964—; fin. planner, 1980—; chmn. field underwriters benefits/contracts com. MONY, 1974-85; v.p. Exec. Planning Svcs. div. Alexander & Alexander, Inc., 1990-96; dir., chmn. audit com. Vasocor, Inc., Miami, Fla., 1990—, Perception, Inc., Miami, 1993-98; v.p., treas. Exec. Fin. Group divsn. F.P.I.S., Inc., 1993-99; cons. in field; speaker numerous ins. seminars. Contbg. editor Profl. Mgmt. mag., 1965-67; subject (poem) There are No Hero's Anymore; contbr. articles to profl. jours; subject of ins. film Impressions of Life (award). Mem. Internat. Assn. Fin. Planners, Chgo. Assn. Life Underwriters (past. bd. dirs.), Nat. Assn. Life Underwriters (life), Million Dollar Round Table (Top of Table), Ill. Leaders Round Table (past pres.). Home: 110 E Delaware Pl Chicago IL 60611-1481 also: 55230 Broughton Govs Club Chapel Hill NC 27514

KARLIN, JOEL MARVIN, allergist; b. N.Y.C., Oct. 5, 1944; s. Louis and Frances (Weisenberg) K.; m. Caroline McInerney, July 7, 1977; children: Scott, Bradley, Bethany, Becky. BA, NYU, 1964; MD, Washington U., St. Louis, 1968; MS, U. Colo. Med. Sch., 1972. Bd. Cert. Am. Bd. Pediatrics and Am. Bd. Allergy and Immunology. Intern, residency pediatric Cornell U. Med. Ctr., N.Y.C., 1968-70; fellow pediatric allergy and immunology U. Colo. Med. Ctr., Denver, 1970-72; pres., CEO Denver Allergy & Asthma Assocs., Lakewood, 1972—; bd. dirs. Colo. Physicians' Network; CEO Allergy and Asthma Assocs. Colo., Inc. Maj. USAF, 1970-72. Fellow Am. Acad. Allergy & Immunology, Am. Coll. Allergy & Immunology; mem. AMA (coun. on legis. 1995—), Colo. Med. Soc. (pres. 1995-96), Phi Beta Kappa. Avocations: golf, skiing. Office: 8805 W 14th Ave Lakewood CO 80215-4848

KARLINS, M(ARTIN) WILLIAM, composer, educator; b. N.Y.C., Feb. 25, 1932; s. Theodore and Gertrude Bertha (Leifer) K.; m. Mickey Cutler, Apr. 6, 1952; children: Wayne, Laura. MusB, MusM, Manhattan Sch. Music, 1961; PhD in Composition, U. Iowa, Iowa City, 1965; studied with, Frederick Piket, Vittorio Giannini, Stefan Wolpe, Philip Bezanson, Richard Hervig. Asst. prof. music Western Ill. U., 1965-67; assoc. prof. theory and composition Northwestern U. Sch. Music, Evanston, Ill., 1967-73, prof., 1973—, dir., co-dir. Contemporary Music Ensemble, 1967—, apptd. Harry N./Ruth F. Wyatt prof. music theory/composition, 1998—; vis. guest composer Ariz. State U., 1978, Ill. Wesleyan U., 1978; guest composer Nazareth Coll., Rochester, N.Y., 1978, Bowling Green State U., 1982, 89, Navy Band, Washington, 1988, Nat. Conf. for Condrs., Chgo., Ball State U., Bloomington, Composer's Symposium U. N.Mex., Albuquerque, 1991, Alta. (Can.) Coll. Conservatory Music, 1991, Sigma Alpha Iota Internat. Am. Music Awards Competition, 1993; featured guest composer We. Ill. U., Macomb, 1994; participant Coll. Band Dirs. Nat. Assn. Nat. Conf., Northwestern U., 1987; coord. composers workshops Internat. World Congress Saxophones, London; lectr., composer-in-residence World Saxophone Congress, Bordeaux, France, 1974, 6th summer festival Nat. Saxophone Tng. Course, Duras, France, 6th Stage de Saxophone, Duras, France, 1991; panelist 43d Nat. Conf. Am. Symphony Orch. League; lectr., guest composer Franz Liszt Acad. Music, Budapest Spring Festival, Franz Liszt Musical Coll., Györ, Hungary, 1995; panelist, guest composer Stefan Wolpe Festival, Temple U., Phila.; honored composer, Sofia, Bulgaria, 1997; guest lectr., composer Vienna, Austria, 1999, Bowdoin Coll., Maine, 1999. Composer: Concert Music 1 through 5, Lamentations-In Memoriam, Elegy for Orchestra, Reflux (concerto for double bass), Symphony No. 1, Concerto Grosso 1 and II, Woodwind Quintet I and II, Saxophone Quartet I and II, Night Light Quartet No. 3 for Saxophones, 3 Piano Sonatas, Outgrowths-Variations for piano, Suite of Preludes for piano, Catena I, (clarinet and chamber orchestra), Catena II (soprano saxophone and brass quintet), Catena III (concerto for horn and orch.), Birthday Music I (flute, bass clarinet/clarinet and double bass) and II (flute and double bass), Under and Over (flute and double bass), Variations on Obiter Dictum, (cello, piano and percussion), Music for Cello Alone I and II, Music for Oboe, Bass Clarinet, and Piano, Music for Tenor Saxophone and Piano, Music for Alto Saxophone and Piano, Music for English Horn and Piano, Four Inventions and a Fugue for Bassoon, Piano and Female Voice, Infinity for oboe d'amore, clarinet, viola and female voice, Song for Soprano, with Alto Flute, Cello, for soprano, flute, and piano, Chameleon for harpsichord, Drei Kleine Cembalostücke (harpsichord), Celebration, for Flute, Oboe, and Harpsichord, Kindred Spirits, for mandolin, guitar and harp, Impromptu for saxophone and organ, Nostalgie for 12 saxophones ensemble, Introduction and Passacaglia for 2 Saxophones and Piano, Saxtuper for Saxophone, Tuba and Percussion, Seasons for solo saxophonist, Concerto for Alto Saxophone and Orch., String Quartet with soprano in the last movement, Children's Bedtime Songs for mixed chorus, Three Love Songs for male chorus, Three Poems for mixed chorus, Looking Out My Window for Treble Chorus and Viola; recs. include Music for Tenor Saxophone and Piano, music for alto, saxophone, and piano, Variations on Obiter Dictum for cello, piano and percussion, introduction and passacaglia for 2 saxophones and piano. Solo Piece with Passacaglia for clarinet, Sonata No. 2 and Outgrowth Variations for piano, Saxophone Quartets Nos. 1 and 2, Night Light (Quartet No. 3 for saxophones), Woodwind Quintets Nos. 1 and 2. Grantee MacDowell Colony, Nat. Endowment for Arts, 1979, 85, Meet the Composer, 1980, 84, 85, 90, 95, Ill. Arts Coun., 1985, 87, 90, 96, 98. Mem. Am. Music Ctr., Broadcast Music, Inc., Am. Woman Composers (trustee Chgo. chpt.), Pi Kappa Lambda, Sigma Alpha Iota (nat. arts. assoc.). Office: Northwestern U Sch Music Evanston IL 60208

KARLINSKY, SIMON, language educator, author; b. Harbin, Manchuria, Sept. 22, 1924; came to U.S., 1938, naturalized, 1944; s. Aron and Sophie (Levitin) K. BA, U. Calif., Berkeley, 1960, PhD, 1964; MA, Harvard U., 1961. Conf. interpreter, music student Europe, 1947-57; teaching fellow Harvard U., Cambridge, Mass., 1960-61; asst. prof. Slavic langs. and lits. U. Calif., Berkeley, 1963-65, prof., 1967-91, prof. emeritus, 1991—, chmn. dept., 1967-69; vis. asso. prof. Harvard, 1966. Author: Marina Cvetaeva: Her Life and Her Art, 1966, The Sexual Labyrinth of Nikolai Gogol, 1976, 2d edit., 1992, Russian Drama from Its Beginnings to the Age of Pushkin, 1985, Marina Tsvetaeva: The Woman, Her World and Her Poetry, 1986, 2nd edit., 1988, Italian edit., 1989, Spanish edit., 1990, Japanese edit., 1991; editor: The Bitter Air of Exile, 1977; editor, annotator: Anton Chekhov's Life and Thought, 1974, 2d edit. 1997, The Nabokov-Wilson Letters, 1979, 2nd edit., 1980, French edit., 1988, German edit., 1995; co-editor: Language, Literature, Linguistics, 1987, O RUS! Studia literaria slavica in honorem Hugh McLean, 1995; contbr. articles to profl. jours. Served with AUS, 1944-46. Woodrow Wilson fellow, 1960-61; Guggenheim fellow, 1969-70, 77-78. Mem. Phi Beta Kappa. Office: U Calif Dept Slavic Lang & Lit Berkeley CA 94720

KARLL, JO ANN, state agency administrator, lawyer; b. St. Louis, Nov. 16, 1948; d. Joseph H. and Dorothy Olga (Pyle) K.; m. William Austin Hernlund, Sept. 9, 1990. Bar: Mo. 1993. Ins. claims adjuster, 1967-88; mem. Mo. Gen. Assembly dist. 104, 1991-93; dir. Mo. State Divsn. Worker's Compensation, Jefferson City, 1993—. Founder, 1st pres. scholarship fund Mo. Kids' Chance, Inc., 1995-96, bd. dirs., 1995—. Mem. Internat. Assn. of Indsl. Accident Bds. and Commns. (pres., mem. exec. bd.). Office: Mo St Divsn Worker's Compensation 3515 W Truman Blvd Jefferson City MO 65109-5715

KARLS, NICHOLAS JAMES, engineering executive; b. Mandan, N.D., Nov. 19, 1951; s. Clarence Joseph and Irene (Kallberg) K. Student, U. Minn., 1982—. Inventory contr. Brown Boveri Turbomachinery, St. Cloud, Minn., 1972-78, mfg. engr., 1978-82; engring. documentation coord. Check Tech. Corp., Minnetonka, Minn., 1982—. Mem. Engring. Reprographic Soc. (v.p. 1987-88, exec. v.p. 1988-89, pres. 1989-91, planning dir. 1991-92, Disting. Svc. award 1990, Appreciation award 1989, Honor award 1991), KC (Grand Knight). Roman Catholic. Avocations: fishing, golf, downhill and cross country skiing, trapshooting, vocal music. Home: 26065 Wildrose Ln Shorewood MN 55331-7936 Office: 12500 Whitewater Dr Hopkins MN 55343-9420

KARLSON, ESKIL LEANNART, biophysicist; b. Johnkoping, Sweden, Jan. 5, 1920; came to U.S., 1925, naturalized, 1933; s. John Benjamin and Matilda Johann (Green) K.; children: John B., Paul L., Judith O.; m. Betty Ore, Dec. 1982. M.S., U. Pitts., 1949, D.Sc., 1977; D.Sc., Occidental U., St. Louis, 1977. V.p. research and devel. Pollution Control Industries Inc., Stamford, 1967-71; pres. Life Support Sys., Inc., Stamford, 1971-72, Erie, Pa., 1972—; exec. v.p. research and devel. Iconex Systems, Inc., Stamford, 1976-77; chmn. bd. Iconex Systems, Inc., 1968—, pres., 1983—; cons. N.B.S., Northeast Utilities Co., Hartford, Conn.; pres. Karlson's Industries. Author. Served with USCGR, 1941-44. Research fellow U. Gannon, Erie, Pa. Mem. Optical Soc. Am., Instrument Soc. Am., Health Physics Soc., Am. Nuclear Soc., Internat. Ozone Inst., Sigma Xi. Club: Circumnavigators. Achievements include patents in medicine, radiation, pollution control, space science, computers, continuous ion exchange system, ozone sterilization systems, efficient heat exchanges. Home: 4634 State St Erie PA 16509-3666 Office: Life Support Inc 2926 State St Erie PA 16508-1832

KARLSTROM, PAUL JOHNSON, art historian; b. Seattle, Jan. 22, 1941; s. Paul Isadore and Eleanor (Johnson) K.; m. Ann Heath, Dec. 29, 1964; 1 dau., Clea Heath. BA in English Lit, Stanford U., 1964; MA, UCLA, 1969, PhD (Samuel H. Kress fellow), 1973. Asst. curator Grunwald Center for Graphic Arts, UCLA, 1967-70; Samuel H. Kress fellow Nat. Gallery Art, Washington, 1970-71; instr. Calif. State U., Northridge, 1972-73; West Coast regional dir. Archives Am. Art, Smithsonian Instn. at De Young Mus., San Francisco, 1973-91, Huntington Libr., San Marino, Calif., 1991—; guest curator Hirshhorn Mus., Washington, 1977. Author: Louis M. Eilshemius, 1978, Los Angeles in the 1940s Post Modernism and the Visual Arts, 1987, The Visionary Art of James M. Washington, Jr., 1989, Turning the Tide: Early Los Angeles Modernists, 1920-56, 1990; editor: On the Edge of America: California Modernist Art, 1900-1950, 1996, (with others) Diego Rivera: Art and Revolution, 1999; video prodr. David Hockney, 1984, 93, George Tsutakawa in Japan, 1988, Richard Shaw, 1998; prin. advisor, editor Calif. Asian Am. Artist Biog. Dir.; contbr. articles to profl. jours. Mem. adv. bd. Humanities West, Jacob Lawrence Catalogue Raisonné Project; former bd. dirs. S.W. Art History Coun., Bay Area Video Coalition; sec. Va. Steele Scott Found, Hans and Thordis Burkhardt Found., Noah Purifoy Found., Light Bringer Project. E-mail: pkarlstrom@earthlink.net. Office: Archives Am Art Huntington Libr 1151 Oxford Rd San Marino CA 91108-1218

KARLTON, LAWRENCE K., federal judge; b. Bklyn., May 28, 1935; s. Aaron Katz and Sylvia (Meltzer) K.; m. Mychelle Stiebel, Sept. 7, 1958 (dec.). Student, Washington Sq. Coll., 1952-54; LL.B., Columbia U., 1958. Bar: Fla. 1958, Calif. 1962. Acting legal officer Sacramento Army Depot, Dept. Army, Sacramento, 1958-60; civilian legal officer Sacramento Army Depot, Dept. Army, 1960-62; individual practice law Sacramento, 1962-64; mem. firm Abbott, Karlton & White, 1964, Karlton & Blease, 1964-71, Karlton, Blease & Vanderlaan, 1971-76; judge Calif. Superior Ct. for Sacramento County, 1976-79, U.S. Dist. Ct. (ea. dist.) Calif., Sacramento, 1979-83; formerly chief judge U.S. Dist. Ct., Sacramento, 1983-90, chief judge emeritus, 1990—. Co-chmn. Central Calif. council B'nai B'rith Anit-Defamation League Commn., 1964-65; treas. Sacramento Jewish Community Relations Council, chmn., 1967-68; chmn. Vol. Lawyers Commn. Sun Valley ACLU, 1964-76. Mem. Am. Bar Assn., Sacramento County Bar Assn., Calif. Bar Assn., Fed. Bar Assn., Fed. Judges Assn., 9th Cir. Judges Assn. Club: B'nai B'rith (past pres.). Office: US Dist Ct 501 I St 15th Fl Ste 230 Sacramento CA 95814

KARLUK, LORI JEAN, craft designer, copy editor; b. Scranton, Pa., Aug. 29, 1958; d. Edward Julius and Josephine Anne (Cuozzo) K. Grad., high sch., 1976. Consignor, designer various shops, Pa., 1982-85; owner mail order bus. Loveables, 1983-85; staff designer Tradition Today, Roselle, Ill., 1985-86; designer All Occasion Crafts, Sparks, Nev., 1986-88; copy editor McCalls, N.Y.C., 1987-90; copy editor, product designer Herrschners, Inc., Schaumburg, Ill., 1988-92; designer Banar Designs, Fallbrook, Calif., 1991-92, Yarn Kits, Inc., N.Y.C., 1992-94; freelance designer, 1984—, teddy bear artist, 1994—. Author: Safari Friends, 1987, Bear-E-Tale Bears, 1991. Sec. MADD, Lackawanna County, 1991. Recipient numerous spl. awards for designs. Mem. NOW, Soc. Craft Designers, People for the Ethical Treatment of Animals, United Friends of the Children, Internat. Soc. for Animal Rights, Teddy Bear Artists Assn., Good Bears of the World. Avocations: travel, reading, art. E-mail: ljkbears@aol.com. Office: PO Box 68 Jessup PA 18434-0068

KARMALI, RASHIDA ALIMAHOMED, lawyer; b. Uganda, May 12, 1948; came to U.S., 1978; d. Alimahomed and Sakina (Govani) K. BSc, MakerereU., 1971; MSc, Aberdeen U., 1973; PhD, U. Newcastle Upon Tyne, 1976; JD, Rutgers U., 1993. Bar: N.Y. 1994; registered to practice U.S. Patent Office. Fellow Clin. Rsch. Inst., Montreal, 1976-78; rsch. assoc. E. Carolina U., Greenville, N.C., 1978-80, Meml. Sloan-Kettering Inst., N.Y.C., 1980-84; adj. assoc. prof. Cook Coll., New Brunswick, N.J., 1984-90; law clk., assoc. Hopgood, Calimafde, Kalil, N.Y.C., 1992-94; assoc. Pennie & Edmonds, N.Y.C., 1994-95, Bryan Cave LLP, N.Y.C., 1995-97, Stroock & Stroock & Lavan LLP, N.Y.C., 1997—; bd. dirs. Skin Rsch. Found., N.Y.C. Grantee NIH, Am. Cancer Soc. Mem. ABA, Assn. Bar City N.Y. (com. on patents), Am. Intellectual Property Law Assn. (internat. and fgn. law com.). Office: 180 Maiden Ln New York NY 10038-4925

KARMANOS, PETER, JR., professional sports team executive; m. Debra Karmanos; children: Peter III, Nick, Jason. Grad., Wayne State U. CEO/gov. Hartford Whalers, 1994-96; co-chmn., CEO Compuware, Detroit, 1973—; CEO, gov. Carolina Hurricane, 1996—. Sponsor youth hockey programs, Conn., Mich., also New Eng. Jr. Whalers, Detroit Jr. Whalers. Named Entrepreneur of Yr., Inst. Am. Entrepreneurs, 1989. Office: Carolina Hurricanes 5000 Aerial Center Ste 100 Morrisville NC 27560-8418*

KARMAZIN, MEL, broadcast executive; b. 1944. Past sta. mgr. CBS radio, N.Y.C., 1960-70; v.p., gen. mgr. Metromedia Inc., N.Y.C., 1970-81; pres. Infinity Broadcasting Corp., N.Y.C., 1981-96; CEO Infinity Broadcasting Corp. Md, 1988-96; pres., CEO CBS Station Group, 1996—. Office: CBS Corp 51 W 52d St New York NY 10019-4001*

KARMAZIN, SHARON ELYSE, library director; b. Bklyn., Aug. 31, 1946; d. Abram and Doris (Tabachnick) Matlofsky; children: Dina Elkins, Craig. BA, Douglass Coll., 1967; MLS, Rutgers U., 1969. Cert. secondary sch. tchr., N.J.; cert. libr., N.J. Tchr. East Brunswick (N.J.) Pub. Schs., 1967-68; libr. East Brunswick Pub. Libr., 1968-79, asst. dir., 1979-88, dir., 1988—; pres. Libr. Pub. Rels. Coun., 1990-92. Bd. dirs. George St. Playhouse, New Brunswick, N.J., 1995—, Assoc. Alumnae Douglass Coll., 1996—; pres. The Karma Found. Recipient Librs. of Middlesex Disting. Cmty. Svc. award, 1993; named Citizen of Yr. East Brunswick Elks Club, 1997. Mem. ALA, Pub. Libr. Assn., N.J. Libr. Assn. (Pres.'s award 1997), Alumni Rutgers Sch. Comm. Info. & Libr. Sci. (sch. fund agt. 1988—), Libr. Adminstrn. and Mgmt. Assn. (sec. pub. rels. sect. 1996—). Jewish. Office: East Brunswick Pub Libr 2 Jean Walling Civic Ctr East Brunswick NJ 08816-3549*

KARMEIER, DELBERT FRED, consulting engineer, realtor; b. Okawville, Ill., Apr. 2, 1935; s. Wilbert and Ida (Harre) K.; m. Naomi Firnhaber, Oct. 18, 1958; children: Kenton Howard, Dianne Jill. BSCE, U. Ill., 1957, MS in Transp. Engring., 1959. Research assoc. U. Ill., 1958-59; traffic engr. St. Louis County, Mo., 1959-65; traffic commr. St. Louis County, 1965-69; dir. transp. City of Kansas City, Mo., 1969-74; dir. aviation and transp. City of Kansas City, 1974-90; dir. pub. works City of Hartford, Conn., 1990-92; assoc. exec. dir. Am. Pub. Works Assn., Chgo., 1992-94; cons. Torres Cons. Engrs., Kansas City, Mo., 1994-95; assoc. J.D. Reece, Leawood, Kans., 1995—; mem. Nat. Com. on Uniform Traffic Control Devices, 1971-85. Automotive Safety Found. fellow U. Ill., 1959. Mem. Inst. Transp. Engrs. (pres. Missouri Valley sect. 1965-66), Airport Operator's Coun. Internat., Am. Rd. and Transp. Builder's Assn. (dir. 1973-83, chmn. pub. transit adv. coun. 1980-83), Transp. Rsch. Bd., Am. Pub. Works Assn., U. Ill. Alumni Club Kansas City (pres. 1996—), Beta Sigma Psi (nat. editor 1963-69, pres. Kansas City alumni 1981-82, Disting. Alumnus award 1971, nat pres. 1986-88, nat. treas. 1996—). Lutheran. Home: 12206 Avila Dr Kansas City MO 64145-1750 Office: JD Reece 13002 State Line Rd Leawood KS 66209-1756

KARMEL, ROBERTA SEGAL, lawyer, educator; b. Chgo., May 4, 1937; d. J. Herzl and Eva E. (Elin) Segal; m. Paul R. Karmel, June 9, 1957 (dec. Aug. 1994); children: Philip, Solomon, Jonathan, Miriam; m. S. David Harrison, Oct. 29, 1995. BA, Radcliffe Coll.; LLB, NYU, 1962. Bar: N.Y. 1962, U.S. Dist. Ct. (so. and ea. dists.) N.Y. 1964, U.S. Ct. Appeals (2d cir.) 1968, U.S. Supreme Ct. 1968, U.S. Ct. Appeals (3d cir.) 1987. With SEC, 1962-69, 77-80, asst. regional adminstr., until 1969; commr. SEC, Washington, 1977-80; assoc. Willkie Farr & Gallagher, N.Y.C., 1969-72; ptnr. Rogers & Wells, N.Y.C., 1972-77, of counsel, 1980-85; ptnr. Kelley Drye & Warren, N.Y.C., 1987-94, of counsel, 1995—; adj. prof. law Bklyn. Law Sch., 1973-77, 82-85, prof., 1985—, co-dir. Ctr. for Study of Internat. Bus. Law; bd. dirs. Mallinckrodt, Inc., Kemper Ins Cos.; trustee Practicing Law Inst.; mem. nat. adjudicatory coun. NASDR, 1998—. Author: Regulation by Prosecution, 1982; contbr. articles to legal publs. Fellow Am. Bar Found.; mem. ABA, Assn. Bar City N.Y., Am. Law Inst., Fin. Women's Assn. Home: 66 Summit Dr Hastings On Hudson NY 10706-1215 Office: Bklyn Law Sch 250 Joralemon St Brooklyn NY 11201-3700

KARMELIN, MICHAEL ALLEN, financial executive; b. Bronx, N.Y., Feb. 26, 1947; s. Samuel and Fannie (Levine) K.; m. Risa G. Kaplan, Apr. 2, 1966. BBA, Baruch Coll. CUNY, 1972; MBA, NYU, 1979. CPA, N.Y. Staff acct. Allied Chem. Corp., N.Y.C., 1965-69; consol. acct. Avco Corp., Greenwich, Conn., 1969-72, supr. consol. acctg., 1972-73, subs. asst. controller, 1973, mgr. consol. plans and forecasts, 1973-75, mgr. planning, 1975-78, dir. fin. planning and analysis, 1979-85, sr. dir. long-range fin. planning and auditing Avco Systems div., Wilmington, Mass., 1985, v.p., corp. staff, GRP mgr. corp. real estate Merrill Lynch & Co., N.Y.C., 1985—, v.p., CFO Merrill Lynch Hubbard, 1994—; v.p., CFO Merrill Lynch Investment Ptnrs., 1997-98; v.p., treas. Ocwen Fin. Corp., West Palm Beach, Fla., 1998-99; CFO, dir. Touch Tone Techs., Inc., Boca Raton, Fla., 1999—. Mem. Treasury Mgmt. Assn., Inst. Mgmt. Accts., Strategic Leadership Forum. Home: 132 Banyan Isle Dr Palm Beach Gardens FL 33418 Office: Touch Tone Techs Inc 1900 Glades Rd Ste 200 Boca Raton FL 33431

KARN, RICHARD WILSON, actor; b. Seattle, Feb. 17, 1956; s. Gene and Louise Karn; m. Tudi Roche. Actor starring as Al Borland in TV series Home Improvement, 1991-99; tv movies include: Picture Perfect, 1995; movies include: Legend of the Mummy, 1997, Pooch and the Pauper, 1999; creative cons. Picture Perfect, 1995; tv guest appearances include: Boy Meets World, 1993, Burke's Law, 1994. Office: Wind Dancer Prodn Group Prodn Bldg 3rd Flr 500 S Buena Vista Burbank CA 91521-2215*

KARNAS, FRED G., JR., government agency administrator; b. Olean, N.Y., Sept. 9, 1948. BCP, U. Va., 1971; MSW, Va. Commonwealth U., 1980; PhD, Va. Tech. U., 1984. Gen. program dir. Cmty. Coun., Phoenix, 1983-87; exec. dir. Cmty. Housing Partnership, Phoenix, 1987-89, Ctrl. Fla. Coalition for the Homeless, Orlando, Fla., 1989-91, Nat. Coalition for the Homeless, Washington, 1991-95; with HUD, Washington, 1995—, dep. asst. sec., 1997—. Office: Dept HUD 451 7th St SW Washington DC 20410-0001

KARNATH, LORIE MARY LORRAINE, bank officer, consultant; b. Chgo.; d. Albert Welch and Carole Margaret (Bohrer) K. m. Robert Emil Roethenmund, Jan. 8, 1994. BA, Fordham U., 1981; MBA, Inst. Superior des Etudes Adminstrv., Fontainebleau, France, 1990. Loan officer Chem. Bank, N.Y.C., 1981-84; team leader Credit Suisse, N.Y.C., 1984-86; assoc. Kidder, Peabody, N.Y.C. and Madrid, 1986-91; cons. E.M.C. Group, Hamburg, Germany, 1991-95; v.p. licensing, strategic planning, mergers and acquisitions The Stride Rite Corp., Lexington, Mass., 1995-98; sr. v.p. U.S. Region IIC, N.Y.C., 1998—; mem. adv. bd. Arthur Treacher's Inc. Contbg. author: Adventure Challenge, 1988; contbg. editor Next Mag., 1984-85. Mem. N.Y. Acad. Scis., Explorers Club (internat.), Royal Geog. Soc. (com.). Avocations: skiing, fine arts, travel and exploration, writing, photography. Home: 6 Passage Chesnard, 27750 La Couture Boussey France

KARNAUGH, MAURICE, computer scientist, educator; b. N.Y.C., Oct. 4, 1924; s. George Victor and Fannie (Weinstein) K.; m. Linn Blank; children: Robert Victor, Paul Joseph. BS, CCNY, 1948; MS, Yale U., 1950, PhD, 1952. Mem. tech. staff Bell Telephone Labs., Murray Hill, N.J., 1952-56, mgr. digital techs., 1956-66; chief scientist exploratory systems ctr., fed. system ctr. IBM, Gaithersberg, Md., 1966-70; mem. rsch. staff IBM Watson Rsch. Ctr., Yorktown Heights, N.Y., 1970-93; disting. adj. prof. Poly. U., Bklyn., 1981—. Contbr. articles on digital switching and artificial intelligence to profl. jours.; patentee in field. With U.S. Army, 1943-46, ETO. Fellow IEEE; mem. Internat. Coun. Computer Communications (gov. emeritus 1988—). Office: Poly U 36 Saw Mill River Rd Hawthorne NY 10532-1507

KARNES, DANIEL ELMO, clinical social worker; b. Roanoke, Va., June 2, 1946; s. Elmo Morgan and Vivian (Ballard) K.; m. Nancy Walters, Jdec. 8, 1973. BS, Radford U., 1975; MSW, Va. Commonwealth U., 1979; MPA, Va. Poly. Inst. and State U., 1998. Lic. clin. social worker, Va. Clin. social worker VA, Salem, Va., 1979-97; clin. social worker readjustment counseling svcs. VA, Roanoke, 1997—. Chmn. bd. trustees VA Vets. Care Ctr., Roanoke, 1995-98; chmn. bd. dirs. Blue Ridge Cmty. Svcs., Roanoke, 1990-92. Officer U.S. Army, from 1963; lt. col. USAR, 1965-68. Fellow Am. Orthopsychiat. Assn.; mem. NASW, ASPA, Assn. U.S. Army, Nat. DDay Meml. Found. (bd. dirs.). Office: 350 Albemarle Ave Roanoke VA 24016

KARNI, EDI, economics educator; b. Tel Aviv, Israel, Mar. 20, 1944; s. Eliezer and Sara (Vitis) K.; m. Barbara Shapiro, Mar. 16, 1980; children: Anat, Anna. B.A. in Econs., Hebrew U., 1965, M.A. in Econs., 1970; M.A. in Econs., U. Chgo., 1970, Ph.D. in Econs., 1971. Asst. prof. Ohio State U., Columbus, 1971-72; fellow Inst. for Advanced Studies/Hebrew U., Jerusalem, Israel, 1976-77; vis. prof. U. Chgo., 1977-79; assoc. prof. Tel Aviv U., 1972-81; prof. econs. Johns Hopkins U., Balt., 1981—; disting. vis. prof. Vanderbilt U., 1987. Author: Decision Making Under Uncertainty, 1985; contbr. articles to profl. jours. Mem. Am. Econ. Assn. Jewish. Home: 6208 Sareva Dr Baltimore MD 21209-3530 Office: Johns Hopkins U Dept Econs Baltimore MD 21218

KARNI, SHLOMO, engineering and religious studies educator; b. Lódz, Poland, June 23, 1932; came to U.S., 1956; BSEE cum laude, Technion, Israel, 1956; MEngring., Yale U., 1957; PhD, U. Ill., 1960. Asst. prof. U. Ill., Urbana, 1960-61; assoc. prof. U. N.Mex., Albuquerque, 1961-64, prof., 1967—, the Gardner-Zemke prof., 1993—; vis. prof. U. Hawaii, 1969, Tel Aviv U., 1970, Technion, 1977; cons. Dept. Energy, Westinghouse Corp., USAF, Los Alamos Nat. Labs., Burnell Electronics, DOE, major pub. houses, 1962—; vis. mem. Acad. Hebrew Lang., Jerusalem, 1970-71. Author 7 engring. and Hebrew lang. textbooks, more than 90 papers in profl. jours.; editor or assoc. editor several IEEE publs. Fellow IEEE (life). Office: U New Mex Dept Elect & Computer Engring Albuquerque NM 87131-2436

KARNILOVA, MARIA, actress; b. Hartford, Conn., Aug. 3, 1920; d. Phillip Dovgolenko and Stefanida (Shlonskaya) K.; m. George S. Irving, Oct. 17, 1948; children: Alexander, Katherine. Student, Met. Opera Sch., 1927-34. Performed Children's Corps de Ballet, 1927, Dandria Opera Co., Caracas, Venezuela, 1935; soloist Ballet Theatre, 1939-48, 1955-56, 59; ballerina Met. Opera Co., 1952-53, St. Louis Mcpl. Opera, 1953, N.Y.C. Ctr., 1957, State Fair Music Hall, Dallas, 1953, 63, Imperial, N.Y.C., Fiddler on the Roof, 1964 (Tony award, Antoinette Perry award), 68, N.Y.C. Opera, 1994; films include Unsinkable Molly Brown, 1964. Avocations: gardening, needlepoint.

KARNIOTIS, STEPHEN PAUL, computer scientist; b. Detroit, July 27, 1963; s. Christ Emmanuel and Mary (Zangkas) K. BA in Computer Sci., Wayne State U., 1985, MBA in Mgmt. Info. Systems, 1994. Cert. Oracle database adminstr., cert. Oracle 7 database adminstr. Computer lab. mgr. Wayne State U., Detroit, 1982-85; programmer, analyst A.J. Foland & Co., Dearborn and Livonia, Mich., 1984-85; ednl. cons. Compuware Corp., Farmington Hills, Mich., 1985-88; programmer, analyst Compuware Copr., Farmington Hills, Mich., 1989-92, oracle database adminstr., 1990—, mgr. oracle tech., 1993—; assoc. prof. Walsh Coll., Troy, Mich., 1997—; v.p. Detroit Oracle Users Group, 1994-96; tech. advisor Oracle VMS Spl. Interest Group, 1991-96, Midwest Oracle User Group, 1992—; v.p., advisor Oracle for MVS Spl. Interest Group, Redwood Shores, Calif., 1990-93; tech. judge Ednl. Testing Svc., Princeton, N.J., 1995; adj. prof. Walsh Coll., Troy, Mich., 1997—. Contbr. articles to jours. and newsletters. Treas., bd. dirs. Greek Orthodox Young Adult League Detroit Diocese, 1991-96. Recipient Peer Recognition award Ford Motor Co. Powertrain Ops., 1994. Mem. Alpha Kappa Psi (life, pres. Wayne State U. chpt. 1984-85). Avocations: fine dining, international travel, racquetball, rollerblading. Office: Compuware Corp 31440 Northwestern Hwy Farmington Hills MI 48334

KARNOFSKY, MOLLYNE, artist, poet, art educator; b. New Orleans, July 19, 1932; d. Nick Samuel and Lena (Gaethe) Finegold; m. Dave E. Winston, Sept. 17, 1952 (div. Sept. 1975); children: Craig T. Winston, Janelle R. Winston Lewis. BBS in Bus. Adminstrn., Tulane U., New Orleans, 1966; student in Art Studio Courses, Tulane, Newcomb Coll., New Orleans, 1966-70; MAT in Painting and Teaching, Tulane U., New Orleans, 1972. Lic. teaching La., 1972, N.Y.C. Bd. Edn., 1986. Dir., owner La. Lic. Art Sch., New Orleans, 1972-77; art tchr., art workshops, 1977—; subject of art videotape Vesteras Mus., Sweden, 1981; film, interview Fuji TV Network, Japan, 1981; artist Coll. Art Assn., N.Y.C., 1980; artist, panelist Soho Photo Gallery, N.Y.C., 1993, Fulcrum Gallery, N.Y.C., 1994; host artist, spkr. Mid. Am. Arts Alliance, Kansas City., 1994. Artist: Spirit of New Orleans, 1975, Contemporary Art Ctr., New Orleans, 1977, Paper Environment March 1978, Galerie Leger, Galerie Forum, Sweden, 1980; collages: Found Spaces and Other Places, N.Y.C., 1977-85, Bronx Mus. Satellite Gallery, 1980, Testing-One-Two WPA Gallery, Wash., 1983, Art Parade, 1983, N.Y.C. Mail Art Franklin Furnace Gallery, N.Y.C., 1984, Mixed-media, World Congress on Arts and Medicine, N.Y.C., 1992; painting and sculpture: Hands on Hands, Leonard Stern Bldg. Gallery, N.Y. U., 1994, Painting-Yes!, Chuck Levitan Gallery, N.Y.C., 1998, Multi-Arts Collide A Scope, Chuck Levitan Gallery, N.Y.C., 1998; poet: Judson Poets Theater, N.Y.C., 1977 Contemporary Art Ctr., New Orleans, 1978, Emily Harvey Gallery, N.Y.C.; represented in permanent collections Ins. Co. N.Am. (INA), Cigna, postcrypt Columbia U., N.Y.C., 1983, N.Y. Pub. Libr., 1988, Anthology Film Archives, N.Y.C., 1996, Chuck Levitan Gallery, N.Y.C., 1998; editor Tulane Assn. Bus. Alumni Rev., 1971. Pres. Tulane Commerce Women's Club, New Orleans, 1951; publicity dir. Chevra Thilim Congregation, New Orleans, 1960-63; com. mem. Coun. of Jewish Women, New Orleans, 1960-70; tour dir. Spring Fiesta Assn., New Orleans, 1960-70. Grantee for performance poetry, Poets and Writers, N.Y.C., 1982—; named Artist in Residence Avenue B. Gallery, N.Y.C., 1985, honorarium, spl. project, Coal Bin PSI Inst. for Arts and Urban Resources, Queens, N.Y., 1978, Contemporary Art Ctr., New Orleans, 1978. Mem. Tulane Alumni Assn., Artists Equity, Mcpl. Art Soc. Avocations: genealogy, music, urban archaeology.

KARNOVSKY, MORRIS JOHN, pathologist, biologist; b. Johannesburg, South Africa, June 28, 1926; came to U.S., 1955; s. Herman Louis and Florence (Rosenberg) K.; m. Shirley Esther Katz, Aug. 26, 1952; children: David Mark, Nina Jane. BS, U. Witwatersrand, Johannesburg, 1946, MB, BCh, 1950, DSc, 1984; diploma clin. pathology, U. London, 1954; M.A. (hon.), Harvard U., 1965. Prof. pathology Harvard U. Med. Sch., Boston, 1968-72, Shattuck prof., 1972—, chmn. program in cell and devel. biology, 1975-90, chmn. pathology dept., 1991-93. Recipient E.B. Wilson award The Am. Soc. for Cell Biology, Gold Head Care award Am. Soc. for Investgative Pathology, 1994, Maude Abbott award U.S. and Can. Acad. of Pathology, 1994; hon. mem. German Soc. for Cell Biology. Fellow Royal Microscopic Soc.; mem. NAS Inst. Medicine, Am. Soc. Cell Biology (pres. 1983-84), Am. Assn. Pathologists (co-pres. 1978-79, Rous-Whipple award), Am. Soc. for Investigative Pathology (Gold-Headed Cane award 1994), U.S. and Can. Acad. Pathology (Maude-Abbott award 1994). Office: Harvard Med Sch 200 Longwood Ave Boston MA 02115-5701

KARNOW, STANLEY, journalist, writer; b. N.Y.C., Feb. 4, 1925; s. Harry and Henriette (Koeppel) K.; m. Claude Sarraute, July 15, 1948 (div. 1955); m. Annette Kline, Apr. 21, 1959; children: Curtis Edward, Catherine Anne, Michael Franklin. B.A., Harvard U., 1947; student, U. Paris, France, 1948-49; Inst. d'Etudes politiques, U. Paris, Paris, 1949-50. Corr. Time mag., Paris, 1950-57; bur. chief North Africa Time-Life, 1958-59, Hong Kong, 1959-62; spl. corr. London Observer, 1961-65, Time, Inc., 1962-63; Far East corr. Sat. Eve. Post, 1963-65; Far East corr. Washington Post, 1965-71, diplomatic corr., 1971-72; spl. corr. NBC News, 1973-75; assoc. editor The New Republic, 1973-75; columnist King Features, 1975-88, Le Point, Paris, 1976-83, Newsweek Internat., 1977-81; editor Internat. Writers Service, 1976-86; chief corr. PBS series Vietnam: A Television History, 1983; chief corr., narrator PBS Series The U.S. and the Philippines: In Our Image, 1989. Author: Southeast Asia, 1963, Mao and China: From Revolution to Revolution, 1972, Vietnam: A History, 1983 (Emmy, Dupont, Polk Peabody awards 1984), In Our Image: America's Empire in the Philippines, 1989 (Pulitzer Prize for history 1990), Paris in the Fifties, 1997; co-author: Asian Americans in Transition, 1992; contbg. author: Passage to Vietnam, 1994, Mekong, 1995, Historical Atlas of the Vietnam War, 1995, Past Imperfect: History According to the Movies, 1995. Served with USAAF, 1943-46. Recipient citation Overseas Press Club, 1966, Ann. award for best newspaper interpretation of fgn. affairs, 1968; fellow Inst. Politics John F. Kennedy Sch. Govt.; Neiman fellow Harvard U., 1957-58, East Asian-Research Ctr. fellow, 1970-71. Mem. Coun. Fgn. Rels., Asia Soc., Soc. Am. Historians, Signet Soc., Century Assn., PEN Am. Ctr. Club, Shek-O Club (Hong Kong). Home: 10850 Spring Knolls Dr Potomac MD 20854-1550

KARNS, BARRY WAYNE, lawyer; b. Baton Rouge, Aug. 28, 1946; s. William G. and Margery N. (Lanehart) K.; children: David Adam, Julie Shannon, Shelby Allison. BSBA, La. State U., 1968, JD, 1971. Bar: La. 1971; CPA, La. Asst. dir. La. State Bond Commn., 1973-78, dir., 1978-80; 1st asst. state treas. State of La., Baton Rouge, 1980-85; sr. v.p. Donaldson, Lufkin & Jenrette Securities Corp., Baton Rouge, 1985-88; atty. Brooks and McCollister Joint Venture, 1989-91, sr. atty. dept. ins., 1991-92, dep. gen. counsel, 1992-99, dep. commr. ins., 1998—; treas. La Capitol Fed. Credit Union, 1979-86; lectr. Chmn. Dept. Sheriff's Supplemental Pay Bd., 1980-85; chmn. investment commn. La. Employees Retirement System, 1982-85; chmn. Kiwanis Found. Baton Rouge, Inc., 1980-84. La. State scholar, 1964-66. Mem. Phi Alpha Delta, Delta Sigma Pi. Democrat. Baptist. Office: PO Box 94214 Baton Rouge LA 70804-9214

KAROL, CECILIA KALIJMAN, psychiatrist, psychoanalyst; b. Mohilof, Ukraine, Jan. 28, 1926; came to U.S., 1958; d. Mendel and Ethel (Sterenthal) Kalijman; m. Morris T. Karol; 1 child, Peter Douglas. B of Pre-Medicine, Instituto Vasquez Acevendo, 1942; MD in Medicine and Surgery, Facultad Medicina, Montevideo, Uruguay, 1953. Diplomate Am. Bd. Psychiatry and Neurology; bd. cert. child-adolescent and adult psychoanalysis. Trainee in child, adolescent, and adult psychoanalysis N.Y. Downstate Med. Sch.; trainee in forensic psychiatry Albert Einstein Sch. Medicine; dir. child and adolescent psychiatry Hackensack Hosp. U. Med. Ctr.; pres. N.J. Coun. Child and Adolescent Psychiatry; clin. instr. psychiatry NYU Med. Ctr., 1980. Author: (with others) Psychosomatic Symptoms, 1989; contbr. articles to profl. jours. Fellow Am. Psychiat. Assn. (life), AMA (life); mem. N.J. Psychiat. Assn. (mem. coms.), N.J. Psychoanalytic Assn. (pres.), Psychoanalytic Assn. of N.Y. Avocations: travel, cinematography, reading, sailing. Home: 1055 River Rd Apt 511S Edgewater NJ 07020-1360

KAROL, EUGENE MICHAEL, school system administrator; b. Mifflinville, Pa., Nov. 28, 1933; s. Michael F. and Catherine R. K.; m. Victoria Diane Karol, Aug. 9, 1996; children: Paul Eugene, Eugene Michael, Theodore Lee. BS, U. Md., 1955; MEd, Western Md. Coll., 1964; EdD, Nova U., EdD, 1975; postgrad., Vanderbilt U. Cert. elem. and secondary tchr., Md. Tchr., bldg. level. adminstr. Balt. County Pub. Schs., Towson, Md.; exec. asst. to state supt. Md. State Dept. Edn., Balt.; supt. Somerset County Pub. Sch., Princess Anne, Md., Calvert County Pub. Schs., Prince Frederick, Md., 1980-93; dir. So. Md. Higher Edn. Ctr., 1994-96; campus dean Strayev U., 1996—; coord. nat. EdD program for ednl. leaders Nova U., 1970—. Contbr. articles to profl. jours. Recipient Meritorious Svc. award Md. Tchrs. Assn., 1970, Disting. Svc. award NEA, 1971, Golden Apple award Md. PTA. Mem. NAESP, ASCD, Am. Assn. Sch. Adminstrs. (Supt. of Yr. award 1991), Assn. Sch. Bus. Ofcls., Coun. for Exceptional Children, Coun. Ednl. Adminstrv. and Supervisory Orgns. Md. (past pres.), Nat. Assn. Elem. Sch. Adminstrs., Balt. Coun. on Fgn. Affairs. Home: 2410 Vern Rd Port Republic MD 20676

KAROL, FREDERICK JOHN, industrial chemist; b. Norton, Mass., Feb. 28, 1933; s. John and Valeria (Bzdula) K.; m. Ruth Helen Lindbom, May 31, 1958; children: Mark, Donald, Cynthia. BA, Boston U., 1954; PhD in Chemistry, MIT, 1962. With Union Carbide Corp., Bound Brook, N.J., 1956—, chemist, 1956-59, 62-65, project scientist, 1965-67, rsch. scientist, 1967-72, sr. rsch. scientist, 1972-76, rsch. assoc., 1976-80, corp. fellow, 1980-84, sr. corp. fellow, 1984—. Contbr. numerous articles to profl. jours. With U.S. Army, 1954-56. Recipient Thomas Edison award R & D Coun. N.J., 1982, Excellence in Catalysis award Met. N.Y. Catalysis Soc., 1987, Chem. Pioneer award Am. Inst. Chemists, 1988, Perkin Medal Soc. Chem. Industry, N.Y., 1989, S.P.E. Conley award Soc. Plastics Engrs., 1989, Internat. Gold medal, 1990, ACS award for Creative Invention, 1991; named to Nat. Plastics Hall of Fame, 1997. Fellow Soc. of Plastics Engrs.; mem. NAE, Am. Chem. Soc., Am. Inst. Chemists, Sigma Xi. Achievements include 90 U.S. patents. Home: 18 Hiland Dr Belle Mead NJ 08502-3225 Office: Union Carbide Corp PO Box 670 Bound Brook NJ 08805-0670

KAROL, JOHN J., JR., producer, filmmaker; b. Mt. Kisco, N.Y., Apr. 1, 1935; s. John J. and Ann (Hale) K.; m. Georgina P. Forbes, Oct. 1963 (div. 1977); children: Angelisse F., Christopher H.; m. Portia L. Fitzhugh, June 21, 1980; 1 child, Fitzhugh B. BA, Williams Coll., 1958; LLB, Yale U., 1962. Assoc. Lord, Day & Lord, N.Y.C., 1962-64; parliamentary draftsman Atty. Gens. Chambers, Zomba, Malawi, Africa, 1964-67; dep. commr., gen. counsel State of Vt. Dept. Taxes, Montpelier, Vt., 1967-69; prodr., filmmaker Apertura, Orford, N.H., 1969—. Prodns. include (films) Brush Dance, 1985, Ben's Mill, 1982 (Acad. award nomination 1982, Golden Eagle award 1982), Main Street, 1979, A Place in Time, 1977 (Golden Eagle award 1977), Settling In, 1974, (video) Photographing with Fred Picker, 1991 (Telly award 1992), Printing with Fred Picker, 1990 (Golden Eagle award 1990, Telly award 1990), Ben's Water Tub, 1990. Dir. Inherit N.H., Concord, 1984-90; trustee Upper Valley Land Trust, Norwich, Vt., 1987-90, mem. exec. bd. St. Martin's Ch., Fairlee, Vt., 1976-79, jr. warden, 1978. Mem. Soc. Motion Picture and TV Engrs., Century Assn. (N.Y.C.), Tavern Club (Boston). Home and Office: Apertura Main St Orford NH 03777

KAROL, MERYL HELENE, immunotoxicology educator; b. N.Y.C., Aug. 10, 1940; m. Paul Jason; children: Darcie, Deverin, Meredith. BS, Cornell U., 1961; PhD, Columbia U., 1967. NIH fellow SUNY-Stony Brook, 1967-68; research assoc. U. Pitts., 1974-76, research asst. prof., 1976-79, assoc. prof., 1979-85, prof. environ. and indsl. health, 1985—, assoc. dept. chair, 1993—; sec.-gen. Internat. Union Toxicologists; advisor numerous govt. health adv. bds., agys.; lectr. in field. Assoc. editor Toxicology Sci.; editl. bd. Inhalation Toxicology, Environ. Health, Toxicology and Ecotoxicology News, Biomed and Environ. Scis.; bd. dirs. Internat. Union of Toxicologists; contbr. articles to profl. jours. Recipient Women in Sci. award U. Mich., 1986, Rachel Carson award, 1993, Outstanding Contbns. to Pub. Health, 1999. Mem. AAAS, Am. Chem. Soc., Am. Thoracic Soc., Am. Conf. Govt. Indsl. Hygienists, Soc. Toxicology (v.p. 1993, pres. 1994, Frank R. Blood award), N.Y. Acad. Scis., Am. Assn. Immunologists. Avocations: sports, decorating, design, travel. Office: U Pitts Dept Environ Occupational Health 260 Kappa Dr Pittsburgh PA 15238-2818

KAROL, MICHAEL ALAN, editor; b. New Brunswick, N.J., Mar. 1, 1953; s. Reuben Hirsch and Sylvia (Gross) K. BA in Sociology and Comm., U. Pa., 1975; MS in Comm./TV Broadcasting, Boston U., 1977. Rhythm and blues editor Pop Top Mag. Little Face, Inc., Boston, 1976-78; staff photographer, prodn. editor Nat. Jewel Mag., N.Y.C., 1978-79; assoc. editor Gift and Stationery Bus. Gralla Publs., N.Y.C., 1979; mng. editor Modern Floor Coverings Charleson Pub. Co., N.Y.C., 1979-82; editor-in-chief Floor Covering Bus. Thomson Retail Press, N.Y.C., 1982-89; mng. editor Graphic Arts Monthly Cahners Pub.Co., N.Y.C., 1990-96; copy chief Computer Shopper, Ziff-Davis, Inc., N.Y.C., 1996-98; freelance writer, editor, copy editor, 1998—. Recipient Silver awards for graphic excellence Modern Floor Coverings, MFC Mkt. Report, 1981, 84, Regional Design awards for Modern Floor Coverings covers Print Mag., 1985, 88, 65th Ann. Exhbn. Merit award Art Dirs. Club, 1986, Cert. of Distinction in editl. design for Elvis Lives!, Art Direction mag., 1992, Cert. of Merit, Cmty. Action Network, 1992, Bronze Editl. Medal of Excellence for How'd They Print That?, Cahners Pub. Co., 1995. Democrat. Avocations: travel, biking, reading, writing.

KAROL, NATHANIEL H., lawyer, consultant; b. N.Y.C., Feb. 16, 1929; s. Isidore and Lillian (Orlow) K.; m. Liliane Leser, July 20, 1967; children: David, Jordan. B.S. in Social Sci, CCNY, 1949; M.A. (fellow), Yale U., 1950, LL.B., N.Y. U., 1957, LL.M., 1959, J.D., 1966. Bar: N.Y. 1957. Mgmt. trainee Curtiss Wright Corp., Wood-Ridge, N.J., 1956-57; practiced in N.Y.C., 1957-58; contracting officer USAF, N.Y.C., 1958-62; chief contract mgmt. survey and cost adminstrn. Office of Procurement, NASA, Washington, 1962-64; asst. dir. cost reduction, 1964-66; dep. asst. sec. Grants Adminstrn., HEW, Washington, 1966-69; univ. dean City U. N.Y.; exec. dir. Research Found., 1969-73; v.p. Hebrew Union Coll., Cin., 1973-75; partner, nat. chmn. cons. services for edn. Coopers & Lybrand (C.P.A.s), Chgo., 1975-81; pres. Nathaniel H. Karol & Assocs. Ltd., 1981—; cons. to govt. agys. and ednl. instns., 1969—. Author: Managing the Higher Education Enterprise. Served with U.S. Army, 1953-56. Recipient Outstanding Performance award HEW, 1968, Superior Performance award, 1969. Mem. N.Y. Bar, Nat. Assn. Coll. and Univ. Bus. Officers, Nat. Assn. Coll. and Univ. Attys. Home and Office: 1228 Cambridge Ct Highland Park IL 60035-1014 *What one is, is as important as what one does. I regard as successful the man who is able to establish a set of values and to observe them consistently. If there is a single thing for which I would wish to be remembered, it is that I was a man whose word was his bond.*

KAROL, REUBEN HIRSH, civil engineer, sculptor; b. Toms River, N.J., Aug. 25, 1922; s. Joel Benjamin and Molly Karol; m. Sylvia Gross, Sept. 3, 1943 (dec. Oct. 1991); children: Diane, Leslee, Michael; m. Joan B. Baker,

Feb. 6, 1993. B.S. in Civil Engring., Rutgers U., 1947, M.S., 1949. Lic. profl. engr., N.J. Asst. prof. civil engring. Rutgers U., New Brunswick, N.J., 1947-51, dir. Rutgers Ctr. Continung Engring. Studies, 1967-85, prof. civil engring., 1980-85; prof. emeritus Rutgers U., 1985—; cons. engr. chem. grouting, design engr. Standard Oil Devel. Co., Linden, 1951-56; dir. Engring. Chem. Research Ctr. Am. Cyanamic Co., Princeton, 1956-67; pres. Karol-Warner, Inc., mfr. sci. instruments, 1952-85. Author 4 coll. textbooks, including Chemical Grouting, 2d edit., 1990; contbr. numerous articles to profl. jours.; U.S. and fgn. patentee in field; exhibited wood sculptures in 12 one-man shows, 9 group shows; commd. wood sculpture Busch Student Ctr., outdoor concrete sculpture Civil Engring. Lab., Rutgers U.; represented in permanent collections in galleries, N.J., Fla., Pa., Chgo. Served to 1st lt. Signal Corps U.S. Army, 1943-46. Mem. ASCE (chmn. grouting com. 1976-82 Robert Ridgway award), ASTM (chmn. grouting com. 1979—, Outstanding Achievement award), Am. Soc. Engring. Edn., Nat. Soc. Profl. Engrs. Office: Rutgers U Dept Civil Eng New Brunswick NJ 08901

KAROL, VICTORIA DIANE, educational administrator; b. Bremerhaven, Germany, Sept. 22, 1956; d. Arthur Lee and Esther Marie Stephens; married; 1 child, Theodore L. BS in Elem. Edn. magna cum laude, Towson State U., 1978; M Adminstrn. and Supervision, Bowie State U., 1992; EdD in Ednl. Leadership, Nova Southeastern U., Fla., 1996. Cert. tchr., Md. Tchr. Calvert County Pub. Schs., Prince Frederick, Md., 1978-89, supr. staff devel. and art and dance Title IV, Tchr. Ctr., student tchrs., media svcs., 1989—; cons. coop. learning strategies, adult learners, team-building strategies tech., dimensions of learning, supervision, sch. to work, internet, multicultural edn., 1990—; adv. com. Bowie (Md.) State U., 1990-91. Bd. dirs. St. Mary's Elem. Sch., sec., 1990—; mem. adv. coun. on Multicultural Edn. Md. State Dept. of Edn. Mem. Calvert Assn. Suprs. and Adminstrs. (pres.), Calvert County Pub. Sch. Ctrl. Office Social Com. (chairperson), So. Md. Tri-County Staff Devel. Consortium. Roman Catholic. Avocations: dance, sports, baton twirling, gardening. Office: Calvert County Pub Schs 1305 Dares Beach Rd Prince Frederick MD 20678-4208

KAROL, ZACHARY R., judge; b. NYC, July 31, 1946; m. Joy S. Kaufman, Aug. 25, 1968; 2 children. BA, Amherst (Mass.) Coll., 1968; JD, Harvard U., 1973. Bar: Mass. 1973, U.S. Dist. Ct. Mass., U.S. Ct. Appeals (1st cir.), U.S. Supreme Ct. Assoc. Bingham, Dana & Gould, Boston, 1973-80, ptnr., 1980-93; U.S. magistrate judge U.S. Dist. Ct., Boston, 1993—. Office: US Dist Ct Ste 6400 1 Courthouse Way Boston MA 02210

KAROLAK, DALE WALTER, aerospace company executive; b. Detroit, Sept. 18, 1959; s. Walter Joseph and Betty Jane (Bugala) K.; m. Lorraine Kay Theunissen; children: Jessica Ann, Ryan Walter, Christine Marie. BS, Cen. Mich. U., 1981; MBA, U. Phoenix, 1985; PhD, Union Inst., 1994. Computer programmer Lowry and Assocs., Brighton, Mich., 1980-81; engr. GTE Comm. Systems, Phoenix, 1981-85; engring. mgr. optical divsn. ITT Aerospace, Ft. Wayne, Ind., 1985-94; engring. dir. TRW Automotive Electronics, Farmington Hills, Mich., 1994—. Author Software Engring. Risk Mgmt., 1995, Finding Your Path Through the Jungle, 1998, Global Software Development, 1998. Mem. IEEE, Assn. Computing Machinery, Assn. MBA Execs., Soc. Automotive Engrs. Achievements include patent for communications management system architecture. Office: TRW Automotive Electronics 24175 Research Dr Farmington Hills MI 48335

KAROLEVITZ, ROBERT FRANCIS, writer; b. Yankton, S.D., Apr. 26, 1922; s. Frank Bernard and Martha Anne (Rathjen) K.; m. Phyllis Jane Gunderson, Jan. 4, 1951; children: Jan Marie, Martha Jill. BS, S.D. State Coll., 1947; MS, U. Oreg., 1950; LHD (hon.), Mt. Marty Coll., 1999. Author: Newspapering in the Old West, 1965, Doctors of the Old West, 1967, Where Your Heart Is, 1970 (Best Art Book of Yr. 1970), Flight of Eagles, 1974, Challenge: The South Dakota Story, 1975, From Quill to Computer, 1985, Yesterday's Motorcycles, 1986, They Always Called Him Coach, 1993, Commitment to Care, 1997, 25 others; contbr. over 1000 articles to newspapers and mags. Bd. trustee S.D. State Hist. Soc., Pierre, S.D. Art Mus., Brookings, S.D. Hall of Fame, Chamberlain, S.D. State U., Brookings. Capt. U.S. Army, 1943-46, 51-52, Korea. Named to S.D. Hall of Fame, 1978, S.D. Newspaper Hall of Fame, 1997, Disting. Alumnus S.D. State U.; recipient Wrangler Statuette Nat. Cowboy Hall of Fame and Heritage Ctr., Okla. City. Mem. K.C., VFW (life), Am. Legion (life), Elks (life), Soc. of Profl. Journalists (life), S.D. State Hist. Soc. Roman Catholic. Avocations: golfing, fishing, 1940s music. Home: 44342 307th St Mission Hill SD 57046-6011

KAROLIDES, NICHOLAS J., English educator; b. Albany, N.Y., Aug. 5, 1928; s. James and Katherine (Kaplanides) K.; m. Inga Schaumann, Nov. 24, 1962; children: Melissa, Alexis. BS, NYU, 1950, MA, 1951, PhD, 1963. Tchr. English Pierre Van Cortlandt Sch., Croton-on-Hudson, N.Y., 1954-59; tchg. fellow NYU, 1959-60; guidance counselor Pierre Van Cortlandt Sch., 1960-64; from asst. prof. to prof. English, assoc. dean arts & scis. U. Wis., River Falls, 1964—. Author: The Pioneer in the American Novel, 1900-1950, 1967, Focus on Physical Impairments, 1990, Banned Books: Literature Suppressed on Political Grounds, 1998; co-author (with daughter, Melissa) Focus on Fitness, 1993, Banned Books: Literature Suppressed on Political, Religions, Sexual and Social Grounds, 1999; editor: Reader Response in the Classroom: Evoking and Interpreting Meaning in Literature, 1992, rev. edit., 1999, Reader Response in Elementary Classrooms: Quest and Discovery, 1996; co-editor: Celebrating Censored Books, 1985, Censored Books: Critical Viewpoints, 1994. Mem. Nat. Coun. Tchrs. English, Conf. on English Edn., Wis. Coun. Tchrs. English, Assembly Adolescent Lit. Office: U Wis River Falls 410 S 3rd St River Falls WI 54022-5013

KAROW, CHARLES STANLEY, computer consultant; b. Detroit, Aug. 9, 1954; s. Stanley Eugene and Juliette (Seelye) K.; m. Pornwadee Yenbutr, May 27, 1996. BSEE magna cum laude, Vanderbilt U., 1975. Registered profl. engr., Md.; cert. computing prof. Project engr. IIT Rsch. Inst., Annapolis, Md., 1976-79; electronic engr. dept. commerce Nat. Telecom. and Info. Adminstr., Washington, 1979-87; pres. Karow Assocs., Inc., Balt., 1987—; v.p. devel. NetFanatics, Inc., 1998—. Contbr. articles to profl. jours. Mem. IEEE, Ind. Computer Cons. Assn. Achievements include development of software applications for national and international use. Home and Office: 2208 E Baltimore St Baltimore MD 21231-2001

KARP, ALLEN, motion picture company executive; b. Toronto, Ont., Can., Sept. 18, 1940; s. David and Mollie (Newman) K.; m. Sharon Silver, May 23, 1961; children: Debra Anne, Amy Lynn, Melanie Claire. LLB, U. Toronto, 1964; LLM, York U., Can., 1975. Bar: Ont. 1966. With Goodman and Carr, 1966-70, sr. ptnr., 1970-86; with Cineplex Odeon Corp., Toronto, 1986-90, pres., CEO, 1990-98, chmn., CEO, 1998—, also bd. dirs.; bd. dirs. Loews Cineplex Entertainment Corp., Speedy Muffler King, Teknion Corp., Alliance Comm. Corp.; former head of corp. and comml. law sect., bar admission course Ont.; chmn., lectr. legal edn. programs. Contbr. legal articles and papers regarding corp. matters. Co-chmn. Laskin Chair Endowment; bd. dirs. Coun. for Can. Unity; former co-chair arts and entertainment divsn. United Jewish Appeal. Mem. Motion Picture Pioneers (v.p., dir.), Can. Film Ctr. (dir.), Toronto Internat. Film Festival (dir.), N.Y.C. Partnership CEOs. Avocation: sailing. Office: Cineplex Odeon Corp, 1303 Yonge St, Toronto, ON Canada M4T 2Y9*

KARP, BARRIE, artist; b. Laredo, Tex., Feb. 10, 1945; d. Leonard and Ethel (Weiss) K. BS, Columbia U., 1967; MPhil, CUNY, 1978, MA, 1979, PhD, 1980. Lectr. philosophy CCNY, Bklyn. Coll., Hunter Coll., Manhattan C.C., 1970-94; instr. humanities Sch. of Visual Arts, N.Y.C., 1982—; instr. liberal studies Parsons Sch. of Design, New Sch. for Social Rsch., N.Y.C., 1982—; instr. Eugene Lang. Coll./New Sch. for Social Rsch., N.Y.C., 1988—; participant Sexuality, Gender and Consumer Soc. and Sexual Difference and Psychoanalysis Seminar, N.Y. Inst. for Humanities at NYU, 1988-97; lectr. in field. Group exhibits include Bklyn. Mus., Provincetown Art Assn. Mus., Kunstlerhaus, Vienna, Vassar Coll., Bard Coll., Parsons Sch. of Design, Gasworks, London, The Corner House, Manchester, Eng., Pierogi 2000, A.I.R. Gallery, N.Y.C., 1984-98, Provincetown Mus., 1984, Women's Studio Workshop, Rosendale, N.Y., 1986, Jus de Pomme Gallery, N.Y.C., Civilian Warfare Gallery, N.Y.C., 1984; one-person shows include Everhart Mus., Scranton, Pa., 1987, Rastovski Gallery, N.Y.C., 1986, 87; two-person shows include A.I.R. Gallery, 1988, Rastovski Gallery, N.Y.C., 1987, Women's Studio Workshop, Rosendale, N.Y., 1986. Recipient Ford Found. Diversity grant, Eugene Lang. Coll., 1991, 92; grantee New Sch. Faculty Devel., 1989, 92, 94, 95, Artists Space, Ind. Artist grant, 1986, 88. Jewish. Avocation: jazz. Office: New Sch for Social Rsch Eugene Lang Coll 66 W 12th St New York NY 10011-8603

KARP, DAVID, communications executive, writer; b. N.Y.C., May 5, 1922; s. Abraham and Rebecca (Levin) K.; m. Lillian Klass, Dec. 25, 1944 (dec. Sept. 1987); children: Ethan Ross, Andrew Gabriel; m. Claire Leighton, June 23, 1988. BS, CCNY, 1948. Continuity dir. Sta. WNYC, N.Y.C., 1948-49; freelance writer N.Y.C., Los Angeles, 1950—; producer, writer Cinema Ctr. Films, North Hollywood, Calif., 1969-70, MGM TV, Culver City, Calif., 1973-74, Paramount Pictures TV, Hollywood, Calif., 1974-75, 20th Century Fox Films, Los Angeles, 1970-71; pres. Leda Prodns., Inc., Los Angeles, 1968-87; trustee Producer-Writers Guild Pension Plan, Burbank, Calif., 1969—, Writers Guild Industry Health Fund, 1973—, chmn., Pension Fund, 1974, 88, 96; chmn. Health Fund, 1974, 88, 96. Author: (novels) One, 1953, The Day of the Monkey, 1955, All Honorable Men, 1956, Leave Me Alone, 1957, Enter, Sleeping, 1960, The Last Believers, (with M. D. Lincoln) Vice President in Charge of Revolution, 1960, (feature films) Sol Madrid, Che!, Cervantes the Young Rebel, Tender Loving Care, others, (TV movies) The Brotherhood Of the Bell, The Brothers Rico, The Girl Who Saved Our America, Death And the Maiden, Crime And Commitment, Arthur the King, others, (TV series) The Defenders, Playhouse 90, The Goodyear Playhouse, Profiles in Courage, The Untouchables, others; creator: (TV series) Garrison's Gorillas, Storefront Lawyers, Hawkins (exec. producer), Archer (exec. producer), W.E.B. (story cons.); contbr. numerous publs. including Saturday Evening Post, Esquire, New York Times Book Review, Collier's. Served to cpl. U.S. Army, 1942-46, PTO. Recipient 1st award Look mag., 1958, Edgar award Mystery Writers Am., 1959, Gavel award ABA, 1964, Emmy award, 1965; Guggenheim fellow, 1956. Mem. PEN, Writers Guild Am. (bd. dirs. East chpt. 1962-66, West chpt. 1967-74, pres. TV-radio br. 1969-71, chmn. bd. trustees Industry Health Fund and Pension Plan 1974, 88, sec., 1995, chmn. 1996), Acad. Motion Picture Arts and Scis. (writers br.), Pen Club. Jewish.

KARP, DONALD MATHEW, lawyer, banker; b. Newark, N.J., Jan. 15, 1937; s. Michael N. and Beatrice (Laufer) K.; m. Margery Paula Lesnik, June 28, 1962; children: Jonathan David, Kathryn Jill. BA, U. Vt., 1958; JD, Cornell U., 1961. Bar: N.J. 1961, N.Y. 1981. With Broad Nat. Bank and Broad Nat. Bancorp., Newark, N.J., chmn. bd., 1985—, CEO, 1991; regional counsel SBA, N.J., 1966. Coun. trustees N.J. Performing Arts Ctr.; trustee United Way of Essex and West Hudson; bd. govs. N.J. Hist. Soc., Am. Jewish Com.; bd. dirs. Friends of Newark Pub. Libr., Newark Preservation and Landmarks Commn., Regional Bus. Partnership, Local Initiatives Support Corp., Newark Mus.; mem. adv. com. SBA; mem. exec. com. United Way Essex and West Hudson, Regional Bus. Partnership. Recipient CEO of the Yr. Bronze award Fin. World mag., 1994; named City News 100 Most Influential, Newark, Rotary Club Person of the Yr., St. Philip's Acad. Role Model, 1998. Mem. ABA, N.J. Bar Assn., N.Y. State Bar Assn., Fed. Bar Assn., Assn. Bar City of N.Y., Essex County Bar Assn. Club: Mountain Ridge Country (West Caldwell). Office: Broad Nat Bank 905 Broad St Ste 2 Newark NJ 07102-2695

KARP, GARY, marketing and public relations executive. V.p. mktg. and pub. rels. Alliant Foodsvc., Deerfield, Ill., 1992-96, v.p. catagory mgmt., 1996—. Office: Alliant Foodsvc 1 Parkway N Deerfield IL 60015-2532*

KARP, HARVEY LAWRENCE, metal products manufacturing company executive; b. N.Y.C., Nov. 26, 1927; s. Harry and Sadie (Zimmerman) K.; children: David, Nicholas. BA, Coll. City N.Y., 1949; LLB, Yale U., 1952. Bar: N.Y. 1952, Calif. 1954. Lawyer Chesapeake Industries, Inc., N.Y.C., 1952-54; gen. counsel, v.p. Houston Fearless Corp., Los Angeles, 1955-60; founder, vice-chmn. bd. dirs., pres. Monogram Industries, N.Y.C., 1960-83; chmn. bd. Mueller Industries, Inc., 1991—. Bd. dirs. Neuroscis. Rsch. Found. Served with USNR, 1945. Mem. Harmonie Club, Explorers Club, Atlantic Golf Club, Fenway Golf Club, Bel Air Country Club. Home: PO Box 30 East Hampton NY 11937-0030 also: 888 7th Ave New York NY 10106-0001

KARP, HERBERT RUBIN, neurologist, educator; b. Atlanta, Apr. 13, 1921; s. Louis and Sadie (Fischer) K.; m. Hazel Berman, June 16, 1948; children—Eleanor Beth, Miriam Sarah, Benjamin Chaim. B.A., Emory U., 1943, M.D., 1951. Diplomate Am. Bd. Psychiatry and Neurology. Intern then resident in internal medicine Grady Meml. Hosp., 1951-54; resident in neurology Duke U. Med. Center, 1954-56; clin. and research fellow in neurology and neuropathology Harvard U.-Mass. Gen. Hosp., 1956-58; asst. prof. neurology Emory U., Atlanta, 1958-63, prof., 1963-91, prof. emeritus, 1991—, prof. medicine, 1983-91, prof. emeritus, 1991—, chmn. dept. neurology, 1974-83, dir. geriatrics program dept. medicine, 1983-90; dir. med. services Wesley Woods Geriatric Ctr., 1983-91, med. dir. emeritus, 1991—. Assoc. med. dir., prin. clin. coord. Ga. Med. Care Found.; trustee Atlanta Symphony Orch., 1975-95, bd. counselors 1996—, sec., 1979-80; pres. Ahavath Achim Synagogue, 1980-82; trustee Nat. Found. Jewish Culture, 1976-84, mem. bd. overseers, 1984-90. Served with USNR, 1943-46. Recipient Thomas Jefferson award Emory U., 1984, Outstanding Med. Alumnus award, 1986; Eternal Light award Jewish Theol. Sem. Am., 1985, Civic Endeavor award Med. Assn. Atlanta, 1989, Myrtle Wreath award Hadassah, 1990, Wakeman award Duke U., 1990; spl. fellow Nat. Inst. Neurol. Diseases, 1956-58; Herbert R. Karp Leadership award established in his name Dept. of Neurology, Emory U., 1999. Fellow Am. Acad. Neurology; mem. Am. Neurol. Assn. (mem. coun.), Assn. Univ. Profs. Neurology, Atlanta Interfaith Broadcasters (bd. dirs. 1991—, sec. 1997—), Alpha Omega Alpha. Democrat. Home: 880 Somerset Dr NW Atlanta GA 30327-3732 Office: Ste 200 57 Executive Park South NE Atlanta GA 30329-2208

KARP, JUDITH ESTHER, oncologist, science administrator; b. San Diego, July 15, 1946; d. Louis Moses and Bella Sarah (Perlman) K.; m. Stanley Howard Freedman, Sept. 21, 1975. BA in Chemistry, Mills Coll., Oakland, Calif., 1966; MD, Stanford U., 1971. Diplomate Am. Bd. Internal Medicine. Intern in medicine, jr. resident in medicine Stanford Hosps., 1971-72; asst. resident in medicine Johns Hopkins Hosp., 1972-73; clin. and rsch. fellow oncology Johns Hopkins Med. Sch., 1973-75, instr. oncology and medicine, 1975-78, asst. prof., 1978-85, assoc. prof., 1985-92; spl. asst. to dir. Nat. Cancer Inst., NIH, 1990-94, asst. dir. applied sci., 1995-96; prof. medicine and oncology U. Md. Cancer Ctr. Dept. Medicine, U. Md. Sch. Medicine, 1996—; dir. hematology-oncology fellowship program U. Md. Cancer Ctr., 1997—; mem. consensus com. Immuno-compromised Host Soc., 1987-88. Mem. editl. bd. Exptl. Hematology, 1998—. Mem. med. and sci. affairs com. Leukemia Soc. Am., 1995—, trustee, 1998—, vice chair clin. rsch., med. and sci. affairs com., 1998—. Am. Cancer Soc. Jr. clin. faculty fellow, 1976-79; San Diego Heart Assn. grantee, 1965-67; recipient Aurelia Henry Reinhardt prize Mills Coll., 1966, Cancer Rsch. award Washington chpt. Awards for Rsch. Coll. Scientists, 1975, Resolution of Commendation award State of Md., 1982, Recognition award City of Balt., 1984, NIH Dirs. award, 1995. Mem. Am. Soc. Hematology, Am. Soc. Clin. Oncology, Cell Kinetics Soc. (clin. counsellor governing council 1985-87), Am. Soc. Microbiology, Immunocompromised Host Soc., Internat. Soc. Exptl. Hematology, Nat. Bd. Med. Examiners, Phi Beta Kappa. Democrat. Jewish. Home: 3422 Manor Hill Rd Baltimore MD 21208-1824 Office: U Md Cancer Ctr 22 S Greene St Rm S9d15 Baltimore MD 21201-1544

KARP, MARTIN EVERETT, management consultant; b. N.Y.C., Apr. 30, 1922; s. Albert and Bessie (Orenstein) K.; m. Naomi Joslyn Kaplan, Mar. 14, 1948; children: Betsy, Leslie Karp Goldenberg, Jonathan. B.M.E., CCNY, 1942; student, Harvard U., 1944, MIT, 1945, Northeastern U., 1951-52. Lab. engr. Gen. Electric Co., Lynn, Mass., 1942-44; mgr. research and devel. Nat. Pneumatic Co., Boston, 1946-52; dir. product planning, engring. Remington Office Machine div. Sperry Rand Co., 1953-66, dir. mfg., 1966-68; staff asst. to office of pres. ITT, 1968-69, v.p., group gen. mgr., 1969-82, group exec., 1977-82, dir. product and mktg. strategy, 1980-82; mgmt. cons.; adj. prof. Stevens Inst. Grad. Sch. Mgmt., 1984—. Contbr. articles to tech. jours. Dir. Coun. N.Y. Coops. Served as lt. (j.g.) USNR, 1944-46. Mem. ASME, Tau Beta Pi. Jewish (pres. congregation 1961-63). Patentee control systems. Home and Office: 250 E 87th St New York NY 10128-3115

KARP, NATHAN, political activist; b. Bklyn., Apr. 25, 1915; s. Daniel and Sarah (Goldenzweig) K.; m. Anne Werthamer, June 19, 1937; children: Alan, Diane, Stanley. Student pub. schs., Vineland, N.J. Garment worker; mem. nat. exec. subcom. Socialist Labor Party, 1943-63, asst. to nat. sec., 1964-68, nat. sec., 1969-80, fin. sec., 1980-82; mem. hdqrts. staff Socialist Labor Party, N.Y.C., 1963-74, Palo Alto, Calif., 1974-85. Author: Unionism, Fraudulent or Genuine, 1958, Crises in America: A Revolution Overdue, 1970; contbr. numerous articles to Weekly People (ofcl. jour. Socialist Labor Party). Candidate for lt. gov. State of N.Y., 1946, 50, U.S. senator from N.Y., 1952, mayor City of N.Y., 1953, for gov. State of N.Y., 1954. Home: 2250 Homestead Ct Apt 308 Los Altos CA 94024-7332 Office: 156 E Dana St Mountain View CA 94041-1508

KARP, PETER SIMON, marketing executive; b. New City, N.Y., Dec. 9, 1935; s. Joseph Bernard and Esther (Wexler) K.; m. Mona Leea Pecheux; children: Matthew Henry, Mark Andrew. BA, Hobart Coll., 1954; MFA, Columbia U., 1957. Rschr. Bur. Advt., Am. Newspaper Pubs. Assn., N.Y.C., 1954-56; media dir. Smith, Hagl & Knudsen, Inc., N.Y.C., 1957-59; media and rsch. dir. CAG Advt., Inc., N.Y.C., 1960-62; exec. v.p. Bennett-Chaiken, Inc., N.Y.C., 1963-66; founder, CEO BSI/Bus. Sci. Internat., N.Y.C., 1967—; mng. dir. The Concept Testing Inst., N.Y.C., 1972—; chairperson, CEO Pimi. Inc., N.Y.C., 1986—; dir. Office of the Future Panel, N.Y.C., 1976—; co-dir. The Genesis Group, N.Y.C., 1983—. Co-author: Customer Satisfaction: How to Maximize, Measure and Market your Company's Ultimate Product, 1989, Competing on Value, 1991; creator BSI Tech. Value Assessments, 1989-90; editor BSI Newsletter, 1976—. Pollster Ken Keating Campaign, State of New York, 1964; vol. Grand Cen. YMCA, N.Y.C., 1964-82. Fellow Inst. Dirs. (London); mem. Am. Mktg. Assn., Advt. Rsch. Found., Artificial Intelligence Assn., N.Y. Acad. Scis., Palisades Tennis Club. Jewish. Avocations: art, sculpture, travel, music. Home: 159 Tweed Blvd Nyack NY 10960-4913

KARP, RICHARD M., advertising and communication executive; b. N.Y.C., Aug. 17, 1929; s. Harry and Jo Golden (Bosk) K.; m. Jane Hausman, Nov. 26, 1978; 1 son, David. BS, BA, N.Y. U., 1950; postgrad., Boston U. Publicist 20th Century Fox Film Corp., 1954-56; sr. writer Donahue & Coe Advt., N.Y.C., 1956-58; asso. creative dir., account supr. Reach, McClinton Advt., N.Y.C., 1958-63; exec. v.p., creative dir. Grey Advt. Inc., N.Y.C., 1963-93, ret., 1993—; guest lectr. Baruch U., 1977-79; chmn. bd. dirs. L.A. Weekly, 1993-95; chmn. bd., CEO Hitthebeach.com., Inc., 1999—. Author: monograph The Films of Buster Keaton, 1949. Bd. dirs. United Cerebral Palsy; exec. v.p. K.D.C., 1993—; coun. of trustees Am. Friends of the Hebrew U., 1998. With AUS, 1950-51, USAF, 1951-54. Recipient Clio award, Internat. Advt. award, Screen Advt. award, Copywriters Club award. Mem. Brit. Inst. Practitioners in Advt. Office: 4600 S Ocean Blvd Highland Beach FL 33487

KARP, ROBERTA S., wholesale apparel and accessories executive; married; 2 children. BA, SUNY, Binghampton; JD, Hofstra U. Atty. Kramer, Levin et al., N.Y.C.; from legal counsel to v.p. corp. affairs and gen. coun. Liz Claiborne, Inc., N.Y.C., 1986—. Office: Liz Claiborne Inc 1 Claibourne Ave North Bergen NJ 07047-6499*

KARP, ROSANNE, medical/surgical nurse; b. Lynn, Mass., Oct. 8, 1946; d. Max and Dorothy (Cohen) Sidman; children: Stacy, Matthew. ADN, Northeastern U., 1967; postgrad., Lesley Coll., 1990—. RN, Mass. Staff nurse Holy Family Hosp., Methuen, Mass., 1969-90; staff nurse Mass. Gen. Hosp., Boston, 1990-96, case mgr. gynecology svc., 1996—; chair, prof. edn. Greater Lawrence unit Am. Cancer Soc., bd. dirs. Mass. div., 1990-92. Recipient Excellence in Med./Surg. Nursing award Merrimack Valley Area Health Edn. Ctr., 1988, Award for Disting. Vol. Leadership Greater Lawrence unit ACS, 1995, nat. leadership award Hadassah, 1997.

KARP, STEVE, producing director; b. Mt. Vernon, N.Y., Apr. 5, 1943; s. Mortimer Lester and Pearl Marion (Radding) K. BA, Tufts U., 1965; postgrad., Boston U., 1965-66, Am. Acad. Dramatic Arts, 1968. Actor Light Opera Manhattan, N.Y.C., 1969-70, Am. Shakespeare Festival, Stratford, Conn., 1972, Long Wharf Theatre, New Haven, Conn., 1972-74, N.Y. Shakespeare Festival, N.Y.C., 1974-75; founder, pres. Perk Prodns. Ltd., N.Y.C., 1974-88; artistic dir. Maxwell Anderson Playwrights Series, Stamford, Conn., 1986-87; founder, artistic dir. Stamford Theatre Works, 1988—; tchr. playwriting Westport (Conn.) Playhouse Theatre Sch., 1986-87; tchr. screenwriting Fairfield (Conn.) U., 1986-87; cons. Perk Prodns. Ltd., N.Y.C., 1988—. Appeared in Broadway plays The Changing Room, 1973, Hertzl, 1975-76; writer, dir., prodr. (dramatic short films) The Tennis Lesson, 1976 (Silver medallion Va. Islands Film Festival 1976-77, Achievement award Am. Film Festival 1976-77, Achievement award Chgo. Film Festival 1976-77), Inside The Jogger, 1977 (Nat. Film Collection Libr. Congress 1979, Gold medallion Va. Islands Film Festival 1977-78, Excellent Achievement award Melbourne Film Festival 1977-78), The Tennis Match, 1978 (Nat. Film Collection Libr. Congress 1979, Achievement award Am. Film Festival 1978); playwright, dir. The Warehouse, 1991. Recipient Best Dir. Theatre award Conn. Critics Cir., 1991-92, Outstanding Contribution to Conn. Theatre award, 1996-97; Film Prodn. grantee Am. Film Inst.-Nat. Endowment, 1976. Mem. Theatre Artists Workshop Westport. Avocations: jogging, tennis. Office: Stamford Theatre Works 95 Atlantic St Stamford CT 06901-2403

KARPAN, KATHLEEN MARIE, former state official, lawyer, journalist; b. Rock Springs, Wyo., Sept. 1, 1942; d. Thomas Michael and Pauline Ann (Taucher) K. B.S. in Journalism, U. Wyo., 1964, M.A. in Am. Studies, 1975; J.D., U. Oreg., 1978. Bar: D.C. 1979, Wyo. 1983, U.S. Dist. Ct. Wyo., U.S. Ct. Appeals (D.C. and 10th cirs.). Asst. news editor Cody Enterprise, Wyo., 1964; press sec. to U.S. Congressman Teno Roncalio U.S. Ho. of Reps., Washington, 1965-67, 71-72, adminstrv. asst., 1973-75; asst. news editor Wyo. Eagle, Cheyenne, 1967; free-lance writer, 1968; tchg. asst. dept. history U. Wyo., 1969-70; desk editor Canberra Times, Australia, 1970; dep. dir. Office Congl. Relations, Econ. Devel. Adminstrn. U.S. Dept. Commerce, Washington, 1978-80, atty. advisor Office of Chief Counsel, Econ. Devel. Adminstrn., 1980-81; campaign mgr. Rodger McDaniel for U.S. Senator, Wyo., 1981-82; asst. atty. gen. State of Wyo., Cheyenne, 1983-84, dir. Dept. Health and Social Services, 1984-86, sec. of state, 1987-95; dir. surface mining reclamation Dept. of the Interior, 1997—. Del. Dem. Nat. Conv., San Francisco, 1984, Atlanta, 1988, N.Y.C., 1992; mem. bd. govs. Nat. Dem. Leadership Coun., drafting com. Dem. Nat. Platform, Santa Fe, 1992. W.R. Coe fellow, 1969. Mem. Wyo. Bar Assn., Bus. and Profl. Women, Rotary, Zonta. Roman Catholic. Home: 1300 Crystal Dr # 1101 Arlington VA 22202-3234 Office: Dept of the Interior 1951 Constn Ave NW Washington DC 20240

KARPATI, GEORGE, neurologist, neuroscientist; m. Shira Tannor, July 31, 1966; children: Adam, Joshua. MD, Dalhousie U., Halifax, N.S., 1960; Doctorate (hon.), U. Marseille, 1995. Postdoctoral tng. Mont. Neurol. Inst., Can., 1960-64, neuroscientist; rsch. tng. NIH, Bethesda, Md., 1965-67; staff neurologist Mont. Neurol. Hosp., 1967—; prof. neurology and pediat. McGill U., Mont., 1978—, Isaac Walton Killam chmn. neurology, 1984; assoc. dir. Mont. Neurol. Inst., 1984-92. Co-author: Pathology of Skeletal Muscle, 1984; contbr. over 260 articles to sci. jours. Recipient 125th Commemorative medal of Can., Gov. Gen. of Can., 1993; recipient Disting. Scientist award Can. Soc. Clin. Investigation, 1997. Fellow Royal Coll. Physicians and Surgeons Can., Am. Acad. Neurology, Royal Soc. Can.; mem. Am. Neurol. Assn., Can. Acad. Medicine (elected 1992). Achievements include research in neuromuscular diseases, nerve-muscle biology, and qeue therapy. Office: Mont Neurol Inst, 3801 University St, Montreal, PQ Canada H3A 2B4

KARPATKIN, RHODA HENDRICK, consumer information organization executive, lawyer; b. N.Y.C., June 7, 1930; d. Charles and Augusta (Arkin) Hendrick; m. Marvin Karpatkin, June 16, 1951 (dec.); children: Deborah Hendrick, Herbert Isaac, Jeremy Charles. BA, Bklyn. Coll., 1951; LLB, Yale U., 1953. Bar: N.Y. 1954. Pvt. practice law, 1954-74; ptnr. Karpatkin & Karpatkin, 1958-61, Karpatkin, Ohrenstein & Karpatkin, N.Y.C., 1961-74; pres. Consumers Union of U.S. Inc., Yonkers, N.Y., 1974—; pres. Internat. Orgn. Consumers Unions (name changed to Consumers Internat.), 1984-91, v.p., 1994-97; pres. Consumers Union U.S., Inc., 1994—; hon. sec. Consumers Internat., 1997—; Spl. counsel for decentralization N.Y.C. Bd.

Edn., 1969-70; adj. prof. dept. urban studies Queens Coll., 1972-74; commr. Nat. Commn. on New Tech. Uses of Copyrighted Works, 1975-78; mem. Pres.'s Com. Trade Policy and Negotiation, 1993—; mem. Pres.'s Trade and Environ. Policy Adv. Com., 1995—. Contbg. author: Current School Problems, 1971, Consumer Education in the Human Services; contbr. articles to profl. publs. Mem. Local Sch. Bd. 5, N.Y.C., 1966-70, chmn., 1967-69; mem. Community Sch. Bd. 3, N.Y.C., 1970-71; mem. com. acad. freedom ACLU, 1973-84; mem. Pres.'s Commn. for Nat. Agenda for the Eighties., 1979-80; trustee Pub. Edn. Assn., 1972-85. Mem. ABA (commn. on law and the economy 1976-79, commn. to reduce costs and delay 1978-84, commn. access to justice 2000 1993—), Assn. of Bar of City of N.Y. (com. consumer affairs 1969-80, chmn. 1974-79, com. on internat. human rights 1987-90, audit com. 1982-83, com. Ea. European affairs), Nat. Inst. for Dispute Resolution (bd. dirs. 1982-89), Helsinki Watch (mem. adv. bd.), Assn. Yale Alumni (rep.-at-large 1982-85). Office: Consumers Union US Inc 101 Truman Ave Yonkers NY 10703-1057*

KARPEL, CRAIG S., journalist, editor; b. Midland, Tex., 1944; married. AB, Columbia U., 1965. Contbg. editor Harper's mag., N.Y.C., 1985-92; editor Strategic Weekly Briefings, N.Y.C., 1996—. Author: The Rite of Exorcism, 1974, The Retirement Myth, 1995; contbr. numerous articles to mags. and newspapers, U.S., S.Am., Europe, Africa, Asia. E-mail: karpel@aol.com. Office: Don Congdon Assocs 156 Fifth Ave Ste 625 New York NY 10010-7002

KARPELES, DAVID, museum director; b. Santa Barbara, Calif., Jan. 26, 1936; s. Leon and Betty (Friedman) K.; m. Marsha Mirsky, June 29, 1958; children: Mark, Leslie, Cheryl, Jason. BS, U. Minn., 1956, postgrad., 1956-59; MA, San Diego State U., 1962; postgrad., U. Calif., Santa Barbara, 1965-69. Founder Karpeles Manuscript Libr. Mus., Montecito, Calif., 1983—; dir., founder Karpeles Manuscript Libr. Mus., Santa Barbara, Calif., 1988—, N.Y.C., 1990—, Tacoma, Wash., 1991—, Jacksonville, Fla., 1992—, Duluth, Minn., 1993—, Charleston, S.C., 1995—, Buffalo, 1995—; founder, dir. 102 mini-museums throughout U.S. and Can.; established the 1st cultural literacy program, presented to schs. by respective mus. staffs, 1993—. Creator program to provide ownership of homes to low-income families, 1981. Recipient Affordable Housing Competition award Gov. Edmund G. Brown Jr., State of Calif., Dept. Housing and Community Devel., 1981; invited to present Commencement Address to graduating class, U. Minn., Duluth, 1996, also recipient Disting. Alulmni award. Jewish. Home: 465 Hot Springs Rd Santa Barbara CA 93108-2029

KARPILOW, CRAIG, physician; b. Oct. 23, 1947; s. David and Babette (David) K. BSc, U. Alta., CAn., 1967; MA, U. So. Calif., 1970; MD, Dalhousie U., Halifax, N.S., Can., 1974. Diplomate Can. Coll. of Family Practice; licentiate Med. Coll. Can. Intern Dalhousie U., 1974-75; resident in family practice medicine Meml. U. Nfld., St. John's, 1975-77; practice medicine specializing in family & occupl. medicine Snohomish, Wash., 1981-83; pres. Internat. Profl. Assocs. Ltd., 1978—; med. dir./clin. N.W. Occupl. Health Ctrs., Seattle, 1983-84; ptnr. physician, co-dir. CHEC Med. Ctr., Seattle, 1984-85; head dept. occupl. and diagnostic medicine St. Cabrini Hosp., Seattle, 1984-86; med. dir. N.W. Indsl. Health Svcs., 1985-86, Queen Anne Md. Ctr., Seattle, 1985-95, Travel Med. Clinic of Seattle, 1986-94; ptnr. Clin. Assocs., 1990-95; prof. Sch. Pub. Health U. Alta., 1996—; cons. Unum Provident Co. Inc., Worcester, Mass., 1997-99. Author: Occupational Medicine in the International Workplace, 1991, Handbook of Occupational Medicine, 1994. Fellow Am. Acad. Family Practice, Am. Coll. Occupl. & Environ. Medicine, Royal Soc. Tropical Medicine, Am. Coll. Occupl. Medicine (recorder Ho. of Dels./bd. dirs. 1990-91); mem. AMA, Am. Soc. Tropical Medicine and Hygiene, Wash. State Med. Assn. King County Med. Soc., Wash. Acad. Family Physicians (rsch. collaborative, Com. on Rsch.), Am. Coll. Occupl. and Environ. Medicine (chmn. internat. occupl. medicine sect.), N.W. Occupl. Med. Assn. (bd. dirs. 1985-92, 95—, pres. 1990-91), Can. Soc. for Internat. Health, Can. Pub. Health Assn., Am. Com. Clin., Tropical and Travel Medicine, Can. Soc. N.W., Marimed Found. Pacific N.W. (adv. bd.), Finnish Soc., Corinthian Yacht Club, Nature Conservancy, Rotary (bd. dirs., chmn. internat. rels. com., chmn. Hepatitis Project, chmn. Malaria Project), U. So. Calif. Alumni Assn., Kappa Sigma.

KARPINOS, ROBERT DOUGLAS, anesthesiologist; b. Oscoda, Mich., July 8, 1965; s. Stewart Harvey and Karyl Mae (Schatz) K.; m. Deborah Sue Haizen, Aug. 13, 1989; children: Marc, Brett, Rebecca. BA, U. Mich., 1987; MD, Sackler Sch. Medicine, Tel Aviv, 1991. Diplomate Am. Bd. Anesthesiologists; cert. Basic Life Support, Neonatal ACLS, ACLS, ATLS. Intern in internal medicine Northshore Univ. Hosp.-Meml. Sloan-Kettering Cancer Ctr., Manhassett, N.Y., 1991-92; resident in anesthesia NYU Med. Ctr., N.Y.C., 1992-95; attending anesthesiologist Hackensack (N.J.) U. Med. Ctr., 1995—, dir. divsn. critical care anesthesia, 1995—. Contbr. articles to profl. jours. Mem. AMA, Am. Soc. Critical Care Anesthesiologists, Am. Soc. Anesthesiologists, N.J. State Med. Soc., N.J. State Soc. Anesthesiologists, Bergan County Med. Soc.

KARPINSKI, GENE BRIEN, non-profit group administrator, think tank executive; b. Bridgeport, Conn., Jan. 14, 1952; s. Eugene Daniel and Madlyn Ann (Capasso) K.; m. Elizabeth Collaton, Sept. 28, 1991; children: Andrew Hunter., Lauren Gayl. BA, Brown U., 1974; JD, Georgetown U., 1977. Field dir. Pub. Citizen's Congress Watch, Washington, 1977-81; exec. dir. Colo. Pub. Interest Rsch. Group, Boulder, 1981; field dir. People for the Am. Way, Washington, 1982-84; exec. dir. U.S. Pub. Interest Rsch. Group, Washington, 1984—; bd. dirs. League of Conservation Voters, Washington, 1993—, Nat. Assn. for Pub. Interest Law, Washington, 1987—, Earthshare, Washington, 1992-95. Contbr. chpts. to books, articles to profl. jours.; appeared on four maj. TV news networks. Home: 807 N Irving St Arlington VA 22201-2007 Office: US Pub Interest Rsch Group 218 D St SE Washington DC 20003-1900*

KARPINSKI, HUBERTA ELAINE, library trustee; b. Cato, N.Y., Jan. 4, 1925; d. Alfred Raymond and Lena Margaret (Fuller) Tuxill; m. Edward Karpinski, Nov. 17, 1956; children: Susan Tanielian, Rebecca Hitch, Amy Jaward. Student, U. Mich., 1943-45, Wayne U., 1949-50; grad., N.Y. Art Acad. Design, 1972. Operator to svc. observer supr. Mich. Bell Telephone Co., Detroit, 1946-57; tchr. art Birmingham (Mich.) Pub. Sch., 1977-87; libr. trustee Redford (Mich.) Twp. Dist. Libr., 1971—. Chmn. Lola Valley Civic Assn., Redford, 1960-70; vice chmn. Redford Twp. Coun. Civic Assn., 1967-71; bd. dirs. 17th Dist. Mich. Dem. Party, Redford, 1968-71. Mem. Nat. Mus. Women in arts (charter), Mich. Porcelain Artists, Internat. Porcelain Art Tchrs. Avocations: portrait painting in pastel, oil or on porcelain. Home: 17418 Macarthur Redford MI 48240-2241

KARPISCAK, LINDA SUE, pediatrics nurse; b. Elizabeth, N.J., Mar. 10, 1958; d. Elof Folke and Margaret Florence (Cummings) Anderson; m. John Karpiscak III, June 11, 1983. BSN, Trenton State Coll., 1980. RN, Mo., Va., Tex.; cert. BCLS, NALS. Charge nurse postpartum/antepartum St. Elizabeth Hosp., Elizabeth, N.J., 1981-84; staff nurse pediatrics surg. unit Children's Hosp. Newark, 1980; staff nurse neonatal ICU, pediatrics ICU Providence Meml. Hosp., El Paso, Tex., 1984-85; staff nurse nursery Vista Hills Med. Ctr., El Paso, Tex., 1985-87; staff nurse mother-baby unit Alexandria (Va.) Hosp., 1987; home health nurse Mo. Home Care, Rolla, Mo., 1988-92; charge nurse nursery U.S. Army, Ft. Leonard Wood, Mo., 1989-92; staff nurse NICU Mary Washington Hosp., Fredericksburg, Va., 1992-94; supr. personal care aide Competent Health Care, Manassas, Va., 1995-97, home health nurse, 1995-97; clin. nurse NICU, NSY Potomic Hosp., Woodbridge, Va., 1997-99. Home: 1802 Genther Ln Fredericksburg VA 22401-5207

KARPLUS, MARTIN, chemistry educator; b. Vienna, Austria, Mar. 15, 1930; came to U.S., 1938; s. Hans and Isabella (Goldstern) K.; m. Marci Anne Hazard. BA, Harvard U., 1950; PhD, Calif. Inst. of Tech., 1953; DSc (hon.), U. Sherbrooke, 1998. NSF fellow Oxford (Eng.) U., 1953-55; asst. prof. chemistry U. Ill., 1957-60, assoc. prof., 1960; prof. Columbia U., N.Y.C., 1960-66; prof. Harvard U., Cambridge, Mass., 1966—, Theodore William Richard prof. chemistry, 1979—; prof. U. Paris VII, 1974-75, Coll. de france, Paris, 1980; prof. associè U. Paris-Sud, 1980-81, U. Louis Pasteur, Strasbourg, France, spring 1992, 94-95, prof. conventionné, 1995—. Author: (with R.N. Porter) Atoms and Molecules: An Introduction for Students of Physical Chemistry, 1970, (with C.L. Brooks III and B.M. Pettitt) Proteins: A Theoretical Perspective of Dynamics, Structure and Thermodynamics, 1988; also articles. Westinghouse scholar, 1947; recipient Fresenius award Phi Lambda Epsilon, 1965, Harrison Howe award Am. Chem. Soc., 1967, Outstanding Contbn. award Internat. Soc. Quantum Biology, 1979, Disting. Alumni award Calif. Inst. Tech., 1986, Irving Langmuir award Am. Phys. Soc., 1987, Theoretical Chemistry award Am. Chem. Soc., 1993, Joseph O. Hirschfelder prize in theoretical chemistry U. Wis. Theoretical Chemistry Inst., 1995; nat. lectr. Biophys. Soc., 1991. Mem. NAS, Am. Acad. Arts and Scis., Internat. Acad. Quantum Molecular Sci., Netherlands Acad. Art and Scis. (fgn.). Office: Harvard U Dept Chemistry 12 Oxford St Cambridge MA 02138-2902

KARPLUS, WALTER J., engineering educator; b. Vienna, Austria, Apr. 23, 1927; came to U.S., 1938; s. Robert and Garda K.; m. Takako Kohda, Feb. 8, 1969; children—Maya, Anthony. B.E.E., Cornell U., 1949; M.S., U. Calif. at Berkeley, 1951; Ph.D., U. Calif. at Los Angeles, 1955. Field engr. Sun Oil Co., 1949-50; research engr. Internat. Geophysics, Inc., Los Angeles, 1951-52; prof. enging. and applied sci. UCLA, 1955—, chmn. computer sci. dept., 1972-79, 94-95; Co-founder, chmn. bd. Torr Labs., Inc. Author or co-author: Analog Simulation, 1958, Analog Methods, 1959, High-Speed Analog Computers, 1961, On-Line Computing, 1967, Solution Des Equations Differentielles, 1968, Hybrid Computation, 1968, Digital Computer Treatment of Partial Differential Equations, 1981, The Heavens are Falling: The Scientific Prediction of Catastrophes in our Time, 1992; contbr. articles to profl. jours. Served with USNR, 1945-46. Fulbright research fellow, 1961-62; Guggenheim fellow, 1968-69. Fellow IEEE; mem. Assn. Computing Machinery, Soc. Computer Simulation, Sigma Xi. Patentee in field. Home: PO Box 24673 Los Angeles CA 90024-0673 Office: U Calif 3732 Boelter Hall Los Angeles CA 90095-1596

KARPMAN, HAROLD LEW, cardiologist, educator, author; b. Belvedere, Calif., Aug. 23, 1927; s. Samuel and Dora (Kastleman) K.; m. Molinda Karpman. Student, UCLA, 1945-46; BA, U. Calif., Berkeley, 1950; MD, U. Calif., San Francisco, 1954. Diplomate Am. Bd. Internal Medicine. Rotating intern L.A. County Gen. Hosp., L.A., 1954-55; cardiovascular trainee Nat. Heart Inst., L.A., 1957-58; asst. resident Beth Israel Hosp., Boston, 1955-57; fellow Wyley Winsor Rsch. Found., L.A., 1958-59; pvt. practice Beverly Hills, Calif., 1958—; clin. instr. medicine U. So. Calif., L.A., 1958-64, asst. clin. prof., 1964-71, assoc. clin. prof., 1971-72; assoc. clin. prof. medicine UCLA Sch. Medicine, 1972-92, clin. prof. medicine, 1992—; attending physician, bd. govs. Cedars-Sinai Med. Ctr., L.A.; attending physician UCLA Med. Ctr., Westside Hosp., L.A., Brotman Med. Ctr., Culver City, Calif.; examiner in cardiovascular diseases Calif. Indsl. Accident Commn., Calif. Dept. Vocat. Rehab.; founder, bd. dirs., chmn. bd. Cardio-Dynamics Labs., Inc., 1969-82; gen. ptnr. Camden Med. Bldg., L.A., 1970-86; bd. dirs. Mcht. Bank Calif.; bd. dirs. med. rsch. Faberge, Inc., N.Y.C., 1980-84; cardiovascular cons. Delta Air Lines, 1992-94; founder, bd. dirs., chmn. bd., chief med. officer CORDA Med. Care, Inc., 1995—. Author: Your Second Life, 1979, Preventing Silent Heart Disease, 1989; assoc. editor Internat. Medicine Alert, 1992—; contbr. numerous articles to med. jours. Fellow ACP, Am. Coll. Cardiology, Am. Coll. Chest Physicians, Internat. Cardiovascular Soc., Am. Coll. Angiology, Internat. Coll. Angiology, Am. Thermographic Soc. (charter, pres. 1971-72), Am. Acad. Thermology; mem. AMA, Calif. Med. Assn., L.A. Med. Assn., Nat. Cardiovascular Network (exec. com., bd. dirs. 1994—), Western Cardiovascular Network (chmn., med. dir. 1993—), Am. Soc. Internal Medicine, Am. Heart Assn., Calif. Heart Assn., L.A. County Heart Assn., CORDA Med. Care, Inc. (chmn., founder, med. dir.). Office: 414 N Camden Dr Beverly Hills CA 90210-4532

KARR, BEVERLY ANN, counselor; b. Birmingham, Ala., Jan. 24, 1967; d. Ollis Graham and Betty Lou (Simmons) Karr; m. Judson Barber. BS in English/Spanish/Secondary Edn., U. Ala., Birmingham, 1990, MA in Agy. Counseling, 1993, MA in Sch. Counseling, 1994, Ednl. Specialist in Sch. Counseling, 1999. Cert. secondary edn. tchr., sch. counselor. Tchr. Birmingham Bd. Edn., 1990-91; acad. counselor Bradford Adolescent, Pelham, Ala., 1991-93; counselor Jefferson County Bd. Edn., 1994—. Mem. ACA, U. Ala. Birmingham Alumni Assn. (bd. dirs.), Sigma Delta Pi, Chi Sigma Iota, Kappa Delta Pi, Delta Kappa Gamma. Democrat. Office: 225 16th St S Irondale AL 35210-1647

KARR, DAVID DEAN, lawyer; b. Denver, Sept. 3, 1953; s. Dean Speece and Jean (Ransbottom) K.; m. Laura A. Foster, Apr. 10, 1982; children: Emily Ann, Bradley Foster. BA, U. Puget Sound, 1975; JD, Loyola U., 1979. Bar: Colo. 1979, U.S. Dist. Ct. 1979, U.S. Ct. Appeals (10th cir.) 1981, U.S. Supreme Ct. 1983. Assoc. Pryor Carney & Johnson, P.C., Englewood, Colo., 1979-84, ptnr., 1984-95; ptnr. Pryor, Johnson, Montoya, Carney and Karr, P.C., Englewood, Colo., 1995—. Mem. ABA (lead atty. pro bono team death penalty project Tex. chpt. 1988—), Colo. Bar Assn. (interprofl. com. 1990—), Arapahoe County Bar Assn., Denver Bar Assn. Home: 5474 E Hinsdale Cir Littleton CO 80122-2538 Office: Pryor Johnson Montoya Carney and Karr PC Ste 1313 6400 S Fiddlers Green Cir Englewood CO 80111-4939

KARR, GERALD LEE, agricultural economist, state senator; b. Emporia, Kans., Oct. 15, 1936; s. Orren L. and Kathleen M. (Keller) K.; B.S., Kans. State U., 1959; M.S. in Agrl. Econs., So. Ill. U., 1962, Ph.D. in Econs., 1966; m. Sharon Kay Studer, Oct. 18, 1959; children: Kevin Lee, Kelly Jolleen. Livestock mgr. Eckert Orchards Inc., Belleville, Ill., 1959-64; grad. asst. So. Ill. U., Carbondale, 1960-64; asst. prof. econs. Central Mo. State U., Warrensburg, 1964-67; asst. prof. agrl. econs., head dept. Njala U., Sierra Leone, West Africa, 1967-70; asst. prof. agrl. econs. U. Ill., Urbana, 1970-72; asso. prof. agrl. econs., chmn. dept., mgr. coll. farms Wilmington (Ohio) Coll., 1972-76; farmer, Emporia, Kans., 1976—; mem. Kans. Senate, 1981-98, minority leader, 1991-96; rsch. advisor Bank of Sierra Leone, Freetown, summer 1967; agrl. sector cons. Econ. Mission to Sierra Leone, IBRD, 1973. Mem. Lyon County Farmer Union, Lyon County Livestock Assn., Omicron Delta Epsilon, Farm House. Contbr. articles to profl. jours. Democrat. Methodist. Club: Kiwanis.

KARR, JAMES RICHARD, ecologist, educator, research director; b. Shelby, Ohio, Dec. 26, 1943; s. Rodney Joll and Marjorie Ladonna (Copeland) K.; m. Kathleen Ann Reynolds, Mar. 23, 1963 (div. Nov. 1982); children: Elizabeth Ann, Eric Leigh; m. Helen Marie Herbst Serrano, Dec. 22, 1984. BS, Iowa State U., 1965; MS, U. Ill., 1967, PhD, 1970. Postdoctoral fellow in biology Princeton (N.J.) U., 1970-71; postdoctoral fellow in biology Smithsonian Tropical Rsch. Inst., Balboa, Panama, 1971-72, dep. dir., 1984-87; acting dir. Smithsonian Tropical Rsch. Inst., Balboa, 1987-88; asst. prof. biology Purdue U., Lafayette, Ind., 1972-75; assoc. prof. U. Ill., Urbana, 1975-80, prof., 1980-84; Harold H. Bailey prof. biology Va. Poly. Inst. and State U., Blacksburg, 1988-91; prof. zoology, fisheries, environ. health, civil enging. and pub. affairs U. Wash., Seattle, 1991—, dir. Inst. Environ. Studies, 1991-95; cons. on water resources EPA, 1978—, OAS, Washington, 1980, South Fla. Water Mgmt. Dist., West Palm Beach, 1989—. Grantee EPA, 1972-85, 93—, U.S. Forest Svc., 1980-81, 90-91, U.S. Fish and Wildlife Svc., 1979-82, NSF, 1982-84, 1997—, TVA, 1990-93, Dept. Energy, 1995—. Fellow AAAS, Am. Ornithologists Union; mem. Ecol. Soc. Am., Am. Soc. Naturalists. Achievements include development of Index of Biotic Integrity, now used in North and South America, Asia, Australia, and Europe to assess directly the quality of water resources. Office: U Wash PO Box 357980 Seattle WA 98195-7980

KARR, MARIE ALINE CHRISTENSEN, executive; b. L.A., Oct. 28, 1952; d. William Doane and Lois Aline (Christensen) K. BA, Sonoma State U., 1975; MA, San Francisco State U., 1982. Editor city desk L.A. Times, 1975-78; free-lance journalist San Francisco & L.A., 1978—; tchr. L.A. Unified Sch. Dist., 1985-88, San Bernardino (Calif.) SanCLASS, 1989-93; dir. ComputED LearningLabs, Cardiff, Calif., 1993—; pres. San Diego Ctr. for Ednl. Tech., Cardiff, 1996—; chair lang. arts com. SanCLASS, San Bernardino, 1989-93, chair tech. com., 1990-93, mentor tchr., 1991-93; cons. in field. Contbr. articles to profl. jours. Chair Learning Labs. Avocations: music, golf, landscaping. Office: Computed/San Diego Ctr Ednl Tech 2611 S Highway 101 Ste 103 Cardiff By The Sea CA 92007

KARR, NORMAN, trade association executive; b. N.Y.C., July 30, 1927; s. Arnold and Hilda (Horowitz) K.; m. Selma Butter, June 17, 1951; children: Arnold J., Joanne Karr Skop. BA, CCNY, 1950. Textile reporter, editor Jour. of Commerce, 1950-55; editor Driver's Digest, 1955-56; pub. rels. dir., asst. to pres. Am. Inst. Men's and Boy's Wear (renamed Men's Fashion Assn. of Am., then The Fashion Assn. Am.), N.Y.C., 1956-66, exec. dir., 1966-95; exec. dir. Internat. Assn. Clothing Designers and Execs., 1986-98, Jeanswear Comm., 1991—. Contbr. editor MR Mag. Bd. dirs. menswear divsn. UJA/Fedn., NCCJ; appointed nat. office vols. March of Dimes, 1997. With U.S. Army, 1945-46. Office: 475 Park Ave S Fl 17 New York NY 10016-6901

KARRAKER, LOUIS RENDLEMAN, retired corporate executive; b. Jonesboro, Ill., Aug. 2, 1927; s. Ira Oliver and Helen Elsie (Rendleman) K.; m. Patricia Grace Stahlheber, June 20, 1952; children: Alan Louis, Sharon Elaine Cohen. BA, So. Ill. U., 1949, MA, 1952; postgrad., U. Wis., 1951-52, Washington U., St. Louis, 1954-56. V.p. personnel Am. Appraisal Assocs., Inc., Milw., 1969-73, v.p. adminstrn., 1973-74, group v.p., dir., 1974-77, exec. v.p., dir., 1977-79, pres., dir., 1979-82; bus. mgr. Concordia Coll., Ann Arbor, Mich., 1986-91; cons. in field, 1982-86; asst. to chmn. Parker Pen Co., Janesville, Wis., 1967-69, personnel mgr., 1964-67; asst. to pres. Augustana Coll., Sioux Falls, S.D., 1962-64, acting chmn., dept. social scis., 1960-61, asst. prof. history, 1956-60. Columnist The Jour. Times, Racine, Wis., 1993—; speaker Rep. and civic groups, Wis., 1993—. Trustee Better Bus. Bur., Milw., 1979-82, Citizens Govtl. Rsch. Bur., Milw., 1979-82; speaker, canvasser Rep. Party, S.D., 1956-60. With USNR, 1952-53, Korea. Mem. The Heritage Found., Hoover Presdl. Libr. Assn., Am. Legion. Lutheran. Avocation: church activities, travel, family activities, fishing. Home: 217 S 7th St Apt 11 Waterford WI 53185-4500

KARRAS, ALEX, actor, former professional football player; b. Gary, Ind., July 15, 1935; m. Susan Clark. Player Detroit Lions, 1958-71; host NFL Monday Night Football Preview WLS-TV, Chgo.; co-owner Georgian Bay Prodns. Former commentator Monday Night Football, ABC-TV; numerous TV appearances including Tonight Show, TV movies: Paper Lion, The 500 lb. Jerk, Mad Bull, Mighty Moose & The Quarterback Kid, Babe, 1975, Mulligan's Stew, 1977, Centennial, 1978, Jimmy B. and Andre, 1979, Alcatraz: The Whole Shocking Story, When Fame Ran Out, 1980, Maid in America, 1982, Fudge-A-Mania, 1994; star TV series Webster, ABC-TV, 1983-86; films include: Blazing Saddles, 1974, Win, Place or Steal, 1977, FM, 1978, Nobody's Perfect, 1981, Victor, Victoria, 1982, Porky's, 1982, Against All Odds, 1984; author: (with Herb Gluck) Even Big Guys Cry, 1977, Alex Karras: My Life in Football, 1979, Tuesday Night Football, 1991. Named All-Pro, 1960, 61, 63, 65; recipient Outland Trophy, 1957, 79. Office: Georgian Bay Prodns 13400 Riverside Dr Ste 308 Sherman Oaks CA 91423

KARRH, BRUCE WAKEFIELD, retired industrial company executive; b. Carbon Hill, Ala., Aug. 29, 1936; s. Barney Bruce and Lorene Elizabeth (Wakefield) K.; m. Betty Cook, Nov. 11, 1956; children: Kathryn E., Bruce W., Lee P. BS in Chemistry, U. Ala., 1958; MD, Med. Coll. Ala., 1962. Diplomate Am. Bd. Preventive Medicine in Occupl. Medicine. Gen. practice medicine Athens, Ala., 1965-70; from med. supr. to mgr. rsch. E.I. du Pont de Nemours & Co., Richmond, Va., 1970-74; from asst. med. dir. to med. dir. E.I. du Pont de Nemours & Co., Wilmington, Del., 1974-83, gen. dir. med. safety and fire protection, 1983-84, v.p., 1984-96; ret., 1996. Contbr. articles to profl. jours. Former trustee Thomas Jefferson U., Phila., 1983-97. Fellow Am. Coll. Occpl. and Environ. Medicine (Health Achievement award 1979, William S. Knudsen award 1986); mem. AMA, The Landings Club (Savannah, Ga.). Avocations: tennis, reading.

KARROS, ERIC PETER, baseball player; b. Hackensack, N.J., Nov. 4, 1967. BA in Econs., UCLA, 1993. 1st baseman L.A. Dodgers, 1988—. Named Nat. League Rookie of the Year, 1992, The Sporting News, N.L. Silva Slugger Team, 1995. Office: Dodger Stadium 1000 Elysian Park Ave Los Angeles CA 90012-1199*

KARSEN, SONJA PETRA, retired American-Spanish literature educator; b. Berlin, Apr. 11, 1919; came to U.S., 1938, naturalized, 1945; d. Fritz and Erna (Heidermann) K. Titulo de Bachiller, 1937; BA, Carleton Coll., 1939; MA (scholar in French), Bryn Mawr Coll., 1941; PhD, Columbia U., 1950. Instr. Spanish Lake Erie Coll., Painesville, Ohio, 1943-45; instr. modern langs. U. P.R., 1945-46; instr. Spanish Syracuse U., 1947-50, Bklyn. Coll., 1950-51; asst. to dep. dir. gen. UNESCO, 1951-52, Latin Am. Desk, tech. assistance dept., 1952-53, mem. tech. assistance mission Costa Rica, 1954; asst. prof. Spanish Sweet Briar Coll., Va., 1955-57; assoc. prof., chmn. dept. Romance langs. Skidmore Coll., Saratoga Springs, N.Y., 1957-61, chmn. dept. modern langs. and lits., 1961-79, prof. Spanish, 1961-87, prof. emerita, 1987; cons. Hudson-Mohawk Assn. Colls. and Univs., 1990; faculty rsch. lectr. Skidmore Coll., 1963; mem. adv. and nominating com. Books Abroad, 1965-67; Fulbright lectr. Free U. Berlin, 1968; lectr. U. Gesamthochschule, Paderborn, Germany, 1995. Author: Guillermo Valencia, Colombian Poet, 1951, Educational Development in Costa Rica with UNESCO's Technical Assistance, 1951-54, 1954, Jaime Torres Bodet: A Poet in a Changing World, 1963, Selected Poems of Jaime Torres Bodet, 1964, Versos y prosas de Jaime Torres Bodet, 1966, Jaime Torres Bodet, 1971, Ensayos de Literatura E Historia Iberoamericana/Essays on Iberoamerican Literature and History, 1988, Papers on Foreign Languages, Literature and Culture, 1982-87, 88, Bericht Über Den Vater: Fritz Karsen 1885-1951, 1993; translator: The Role of the Americas in History (Leopoldo Zea), 1992; editor Lang. Assn. Bull., 1980-83; mem. editl. adv. bd. Modern Lang. Studies, 1977-93; contbr. articles to profl. jours. Decorated Chevalier dans l'Ordre des Palmes Académiques, 1964; recipient Leadership award N.Y. State Assn. Fgn. Lang. Tchrs., 1973, 76, 78, Nat. Disting. Leadership award, 1979, Disting. Service award, 1983, 86, Capital Dist. Fgn. Language Disting. Service award, 1987; recipient Spanish Heritage award, 1981, Alumni Achievement award Carleton Coll., 1982; exchange student auspices Inst. Internat. Ednl. at Carleton Coll., 1938-39; Buenos Aires Conv. grantee for research in Colombia, 1946-47; faculty research grantee Skidmore Coll., summer 1959, 61, 63, 64, 67, 69, 70, 73, ad hoc faculty grantee, 71, 78, 85. Mem. Am. Assn. Tchrs. Spanish and Portuguese, Nat. Assn. Self-Instructional Lang. Programs (v.p. 1981-82,pres. 1982-83), AAUW, AAUP, MLA (del. assembly 1976-78, Mildenberger medal selection com 1984-86), El Ateneo Doctor Jaime Torres Bodet (founding mem.), Nat. Geog. Soc., Asociación Internacional de Hispanistas, UN Assn. U.S.A., Am. Soc. French Acad. Palms, Fulbright Alumni, Phi Sigma Iota, Sigma Delta Pi. Home: 1755 York Ave Apt 37A New York NY 10128-6875 *Perseverance, hard work and high ethical standards coupled with the opportunities for fulfilling one's potential, available in the United States to a greater extent than anywhere else in the world, have made my life what it is today.*

KARSH, PHILIP HOWARD, advertising executive; b. Salt Lake City, Sept. 19, 1935; s. Sol and Ruth (Marks) K.; m. Carol Hyman, July 3, 1962 (div. Sept. 1973); children: Michael David, Jill Ann; m. Linda Love, Sept. 7, 1984. BA, U. Colo., 1957. Account exec. Ted Levy/Richard Lane & Co., Denver, 1957-59; v.p. Jerome/Philip Advt., Denver, 1959-62, pres., 1962-65; v.p. Frye Sills Advt., Denver, 1966-77; pres. Karsh & Hagan Advt. Inc., Denver, 1977-85, chmn., 1985-97. Trustee Nat. Jewish Ctr. Immunology and Respiratory Medicine, Denver, 1963—, chmn. 1991-95, Kern Rsch. Found., Denver, 1984—, Mile High United Way, Denver, 1986-92; mem. Denver Metro Conv. and Visitors Bur., 1994—, chmn., 1997. Mem. Worldwide Ptnrs. (internat. chmn. 1986-87), Denver Advt. Fedn. (bd. dirs. 1968-69, 87-88), Rotary (pres. S.E. Denver club 1989-90). Republican. Jewish. Avocations: skiing, traveling, reading. Home: 6235 S Iola Ct Englewood CO 80111-6825 Office: Karsh & Hagan Comm Inc 707 17th St Denver CO 80202-3404

KARSH, YOUSUF, photographer; b. Mardin, Armenia, Dec. 23, 1908; emigrated to Can., 1924; s. Amsih and Bahia K.; m. Estrellita Nachbar, Aug. 28, 1962. Pupil, John H. Garo; numerous hon. degrees including; LL.D., Queen's U., Kingston, Ont., Carleton U.; D.H.L., Dartmouth Coll., Ohio U., Mt. Allison U.; D.C.L., Bishop's U., Lennoxville, Que.; D.H.L., Emerson Coll.; B in Profl. Arts, Brooks Inst.; D.F.A., U. Mass., 1979; DFA, U. Hartford, 1980; MFA, Tufts U., 1981, Dawson Coll., Montreal, Can., 1981; DFA (hon. degree), Syracuse U., 1986, Yeshiva U., N.Y.C., 1989, Columbia Coll., Chgo., 1990, U. Victoria, B.C., Can., 1990, U. B.C., Can., 1991, Salisbury Coll., 1998. Opened photog. studio Ottawa, Ont., Can., 1932; vis. prof. photography Ohio U., Emerson Coll.; lectr in field. Author: Faces of Destiny, 1946, Portraits of Greatness, 1959, This Is the Mass, 1958, This Is Rome, 1959, This Is the Holy Land, 1960, These are the Sacraments,

1962, In Search of Greatness (autobiography), 1962, The Warren Court, 1965, Karsh Portfolio, 1967, Faces of Our Time, 1971, Karsh Portraits, 1976, Karsh Canadians, 1978, Karsh: A Fifty-Year Retrospective, 1983, paperback edit., 1986, Karsh: American Legends, 1992, Karsh: A Sixty-Year Retrospective, 1996; portrait photographer leading nat. and internat. statesmen, corporate execs., polit. and govtl. ofcls., religious leaders including royal families of, Eng., Monaco, Norway, Greece, Pope John Paul II, also leading intellectual and entertainment figures; first one-man show, Nat. Gallery Can., 1959, one man shows Men Who Make Our World, Expo 67, Internat. Ctr. Photography, N.Y.C., 1983, Mus. Photography, Bradford, Eng., 1983, Nat. Portrait Gallery, London, 1984, Edinburgh, Scotland, 1984, People's Republic China, 1985, Helsinki, 1985, Muscarelle Mus. Art, 1987, William and Mary Coll., Williamsburg, Va., 1987, Barbican Ctr., London, 1988, Palais de Tokyo, Paris, 1988, Geneva Inst. Photography, Mus. für Gestahlung, Zürich, Switzerland, 1988, Huntington Library and Art Gallery, San Marino, Calif., 1988, 1988—, Frankfurter Kunstverein, Frankfurt, 1989, Internat. Ctr. Photography, 1992, Nat. Gallery, Copenhagen, Buda Castle Palace, Budapest, Hungary, Gulbenkian Found., Lisbon, Portugal; retrospective Nat. Gallery Ottawa, Karsh: The Art of the Portrait, 1989; one-man retrospective exhbn. Vancouver (B.C.) Art Gallery, 1990, Glenbow Mus., Calgary, 1990, Art Gallery N.C., 1992, Montreal Mus. Fine Arts, 1992, Halifax, Nova Scotia, 1992, Toronto, Ont., Can., 1992; exhbn. of gift of portraits Nat. Portrait Gallery, London, 1991, one man retrospective Nat. Gallery, Nova Scotia, 1992, Montreal Mus. Fine Arts, 1992, McMichael Mus., Toronto, 1992, exhbn. Am. Legends Internat. Ctr. of Photography, 1992, Corcoran Gallery, Washington, 1993, Mint Mus. Charlotte, 1993, 10th anniversary inaugural retrospective, 85th birthday tribute exhibition Mus. Photography Film and TV, Bradford, Eng., 1993, Art Gallery Can. Embassy, Washington, 1994, Mus. Fine Arts, Boston, 1996, Mus. of Fine Arts, Montgomery, Ala., 1996, Detroit Art Inst., 1996—, Tower Gallery, Yokahama, Japan, 1997, Canada House, London, 1998, Charlottetown (Canada) Festival, June-Sept. 1998, Nat. Portrait Gallery of Australia, Canberra, 1999; exhibited throughout Can., U.S., Europe, Australia, TV appearances; works represented in permanent collections: Mus. Modern Art, N.U.C., Met. Mus. Art, N.Y.C., Detroit Inst. of Arts; Internat. Ctr. of Photography, N.Y., Montgomery Mus. of Art. Montgomery, Art Inst. Chgo., St. Louis Art Mus., George Eastman House, Rochester, N.Y., Nat. Portrait Gallery, London, Nat. Gallery Can., Mus. Fine Arts, Boston, Can. House, London numerous others; photographer ann. poster child: Muscular Dystrophy Assn. Am; 20 photographs used on postage stamps in 15 countries. Decorated Order of Can., Companion of Can., 1990; recipient Centennial medal, Can. Council medal, U.S. Presdl. citation for service to handicapped, 1971, Achievement in Life award Ency. Brit., Silver Shingle award Boston U. Sch. Law, 1983, America's Soc. medal, 1989, Creative Edge award Time Inc. and NYU, 1989, 90, Gold medal of merit Nat. Soc. Arts and Letters, 1991, Jerusalem prize in the arts, Bezalel Acad., Israel, 1997, Fox Talbot award, Eng., 1998; named Master Photog. Arts Profl. Photographers Assn. Can. (Infinity award), Master Photographer Internat. Ctr. Photography, Person of the Week, World News Tonight-ABC, 1997, 60 Minutes update on 1977 segment, 1999-2000; annual Karsh Lectureship, Karsh prize in photography established Mus. Fine Arts, Boston, 1998; portraits of med. and scientific luminaries gift Harvard Med. Sch., 1998. Fellow Royal Photog. Soc. Gt. Britain; mem. Royal Can. Acad. Arts, Dutch Treast Club (N.Y.C.), Century Club (N.Y.C.), Rideau Club (Ottawa). E-mail: karshphoto@aol.com. Office: c/o Jerry Fielder PO Box 430 Monterey CA 93942

KARSON, BURTON LEWIS, musician; b. Los Angeles, Nov. 10, 1934; s. Harry L. and Cecilia K. B.A., U. So. Calif., 1956, M.A., 1959, D.M.A., 1964. Instr. music Univ. Coll., U. So. Calif., Los Angeles, 1958-59; univ. chapel organist U. So. Calif., 1960-61; instr. music Glendale (Calif.) Coll., 1960-65; asst. prof. music Calif. State U., Fullerton, 1965-69; assoc. prof. Calif. State U., 1969-74, prof., 1974-97, prof. emeritus, 1997—; writer, critic Los Angeles Times, 1966-71. Founder, condr., artistic dir., Baroque Music Festival, Corona del Mar, Calif., 1980—; concert preview lectr. Los Angeles Philharm. Orch., Carmel Bach Festival, Pacific Symphony and Pacific Chorale, Orange County Phil. Soc., others; editor: Festival Essays for Pauline Alderman, Brigham Young Univ. Press, 1976; contbr. articles to profl. jours. including Mus. Quar. Pianist, harpsichordist, organist, choirmaster St. Joachim Ch., Costa Mesa, Calif., 1974-82, St. Michael and All Angels Episc. Ch., Corona del Mar, Calif., 1982—; choral condr. Luth. Chorale L.A., 1979-83. Mem. Am. Musicol. Soc., Am. Guild Organists, Phi Mu Alpha Sinfonia (province gov. 1976-81, chair nat. com.), Pi Kappa Lambda. Profl. rsch. on music history and criticism in early Calif., German, Czech and English Baroque, cantatas and concertos; conductor first American performances. Home: 404 De Sola Ter Corona Del Mar CA 92625-2650 Office: Calif State U Dept Music PO Box 6850 Fullerton CA 92834-6850

KARSON, CATHERINE JUNE, computer programmer, consultant; b. Salt Lake City, Jan. 26, 1956; d. Gary George and Sylvia June (Naylor) Anderson; m. Mitchell Reed Karson, June 14, 1987; 1 child, Rhonda. A in Gen. Studies, Pima C.C., Tucson, 1989, AAS in Computer Sci., 1990. Night supr. F.G. Ferre & Son, Inc., Salt Lake City, 1973-76, exec. sec., 1977-79; operating room technician Cottonwood Hosp., Salt Lake City, 1976-77; customer svc. rep., System One rep. Ea. Airlines, Inc., Salt Lake City and Tucson, 1979-88; edn. specialist Radio Shack Computer Ctr., Tucson, 1988-89; programmer/analyst Pinal County DPIS, Florence, Ariz., 1989-90; systems analyst Carondelet Health Svcs., Tucson, 1990; programmer/analyst Sunquest Info. Sys., Tucson, 1990-94, sr. tech. proposal specialist, 1994-95, software developer, 1995-97, sr. sys. software specialist/dba, 1997—; cons. Pinal County Pub. Fiduciary, Florence, 1990, UBET, Barbados, W.I., 1990-96, numerous clients, Tucson, 1990-93. Mem. bus. adv. coun. Portable Practical Ednl. Preparation, Inc., Tucson, 1990-91. Mem. Nat. Sys. Programmer Assn. Republican. Jewish. Avocations: reading, painting, music, light opera performance, dance classes. Home: 5413 N Ventana Vista Rd Tucson AZ 85750-7203

KARSON, EMILE, international business executive; b. Berlin, Sept. 10, 1921; came to U.S., 1948, naturalized, 1955; s. Bogdan and Zorka (Natowa) Karastoyanoff; m. Lilia Usunowa, Dec. 31, 1944; 1 child, Danielle. LLB, U. Sofia, 1946, U. PAris, 1946; Docteur-en-Droit, U. PAris, 1948; LLM, Yale U., 1951, JD, 1953; postgrad., U. So. Calif., 1953-54, U. Pa., 1978, Harvard U., 1978, Cornell U., 1991. Internat. atty. World Bank, Washington, 1951-55; gen. counsel Coast Fed. Savs., Great West Savs., L.A., 1955-58; F-104 exec. Lockheed Aircraft Internat., L.A., 1958-63; treas. Europe, Zurich, Switzerland Litton Industries, Inc., 1964-69; corp. treas. Continental Grain Co., N.Y.C., 1969-72; v.p. fin. & adminstrn. Loctite Corp., Newington, Conn., 1972-81; founder, CEO INTECH (internat. high tech. venture capital), Washington, 1981-85; internat. atty., 1998—; vis. prof. law U. P.R., 1957; organizer 1st symposium on atomic energy and law for L.Am.; lectr. Naval War Coll., Fgn. Svc. Inst., U. So. Calif., Ind. U., U. Pitts.; mem. Rep. Assocs., 1954-56; Bus. Internat. Round Table, 1960-65; cons. Dept. State, 1983, U.S. Dept. Labor intern programs, 1991, 92. Dir. 2 documentary films shown at Cannes and Venice Film Festivals, 1947. Mem. adv. bd. Genetics Unique Fund, 1985-87; broadcaster Voice of Am., 1949-51; pres. Ea. European Orphans, Washington; steering com. Am. U. in Bulgaria, 1992-96; chmn., pres. Bulgarian-Am. Charitable and Ednl. Ctr., 1989-98. Fellow French Govt., 1946-48. Mem. ABA, State Bar Calif., Bar U.S. Supreme Ct., World Affairs Coun., Harvard Club, Harvard Bus. Club, Yale Club (Calif.), Yale Law Sch. Club (Calif.).

KARSON, SAMUEL, psychologist, educator; b. Baltimore, Md., Jan. 3, 1924; s. Norman Jacobson and Annie (Raskin) K.; m. Dorothy Faye Libert, Sept. 6, 1946; children: Linda Catherine, Michael Craig. B.S., L.I. U., 1948; Ph.D., Washington U., St. Louis, 1952. Diplomate Clin. Psychology Am. Bd. Profl. Psychology. With psychiatric unit U.S. Naval Tng. Ctr., San Diego, 1952-55; asst. prof. dept. psychology U. N.H., 1957-58; chief psychologist, dir. rsch. Dade County Child Guidance Clinic, Miami, Fla., 1958-62; rsch. asst. prof. dept. nursing U. Miami, Fla., 1959-62; chief clin. psychologist, office aviation medicine FAA, Washington, 1962-66; prof., head dept. psychology Ea. Mich. U., Ypsilanti, 1966-77; chief psychologist, adminstr. overseas mental health program Dept. State, Washington, 1977-81; regional psychologist Southeast Asia Am. Embassy, Bangkok, Thailand, 1981-83; prof. clin. psychology Sch. Psychology Fla. Inst. Tech., Melbourne, 1983-85, prof., dir. grad. clin. tng., 1985-89; prin. investigator Second Genesis, Inc., Bethesda, Md., 1990-95; cons. clin. psychology to office aviation medicine FAA, Washington, 1966-75. Author: (with J. O'Dell and M. Karson) 16PF Interpretation in Clinical Practice, 1997, The Karson Clinical Report; editl. cons. Psychotherapy in Private Practice, 1988; contbr. articles to profl. jours. Served with USAAF, 1942-45, with USAF, 1955-57. Recipient Appreciation certificate Sec. State Alexander Haig, 1981, Personality Assessment award Thai Psychol. Assn., 1983, Disting. Profl. Contbns. award Md. Psychol. Assn., 1987. Fellow APA, Am. Orthopsychiat. Assn. (life), Soc. Personality Assessment (life); mem. Soc. Multivariate Exptl. Psychology, Assn. Aviation Psychologists (pres. 1973-74).

KARST, GARY GENE, architect; b. Barton County, Kans., Sept. 2, 1936; s. Emil and Clara (Nuss) K.; m. Loretta Marie Staub, Nov. 30, 1957; children: Kevin Gene, Sheri Lynn, Stacey Marie. BArch, Kans. State U., 1960. Registered profl. architect., Kans., Mo. Staff architect Horst & Terrill Architects, Topeka, 1960-64; ptnr. Horst, Terrill & Karst Architects, Topeka, 1965—, dir. design, 1965—, sec., 1973-78, v.p., treas., 1978-92, v.p., 1992—; design architect Ruhnau, Evans, Brown & Steinman Architects, Riverside, Calif., 1964-65; mem. Capital City Redevel. Agy., Topeka, 1978-86; mem. adv. bd. dept. architecture Kans. State U., Manhattan, 1986-87. Prin. works include Emporia (Kans.) H.S., 1972, (Kans. Soc. Architects award 1975), S.W. Bell Telephone Co. Equipment Bldg., 1974 (Bell Sys. award 1976), Durland Hall-Univ. Engrng. Bldg., 1981 (Kans. Soc. Architects award 1983), Kans. State Prison Medium Security Facility, 1983 (Kans. Soc. Architects award 1985), Lansing H.S., 1988 (William W. Caudill citation Am. Sch. and Univ. Mag.), Leavenworth H.S., 1990 (citation Am. Sch. and Univ. Mag.), Plant Scis. Bldg., Kans. State U., 1994, Tomanek Hall, Ft. Hays State U., 1995; featured in publs. including Archtl. Record Mag. Recipient citation Am. Sch. and Univ. Mag.; Weigel scholar Kans. State U., 1958-60; Bales Organ Recital Hall U. Kans., 1995. Mem. AIA, Kans. Soc. Architects (pres. 1981-82), Coun. Edn. Facilities Planners Internat. (recognized edn. facility profl.), Future Heritage Topeka, Optimists (pres. Topeka breakfast club 1970-71, lt. gov. Kans. dist. 1981-82). Avocations: woodworking, photography, sculpting. Home: 3535 SW Macvicar Ave Topeka KS 66611-1841 Office: Horst Terrill & Karst Archs 2900 SW Macvicar Ave Topeka KS 66611-1790

KARST, KENNETH LESLIE, legal educator; b. Los Angeles, June 26, 1929; s. Harry Everett and Sydnie Pauline (Bush) K.; m. Smiley Cook, Aug. 12, 1950; children—Kenneth Robert, Richard Eugene, Leslie Jeanne, Laura Smiley. A.B., UCLA, 1950; LL.B., Harvard U., 1953. Bar: Calif. 1954, U.S. Dist. Ct. (cen. dist.) Calif. 1954, U.S. Ct. Appeals (9th cir.) 1954, U.S. Supreme Ct. 1970. Assoc. Latham & Watkins, Los Angeles, 1954, 56-57; teaching fellow law Harvard U. Law Sch., 1957-58; asst. prof. Ohio State U. Coll. Law, Columbus, 1958-60, assoc. prof., 1960-62, prof., 1962-65; prof. law UCLA, 1965-90, David G. Price and Dallas P. Price prof. law, 1990—. Author: (with Harold W. Horowitz) Law, Lawyers and Social Change, 1969, (with Keith S. Rosenn) Law and Development in Latin America, 1975, Belonging to America: Equal Citizenship and the Constitution, 1989, Law's Promise, Law's Expression: Visions of Power in the Politics of Gender, Race, and Religion, 1993; assoc. editor Ency. of Am. Constn., 1986; contbr. articles to profl. jours. Served to 1st lt. JAGC, USAF, 1954-56. Law faculty fellow Ford Found., 1962-63. Fellow Am. Acad. Arts and Scis.; mem. State Bar Calif. E-mail: karst@law.ucla.edu. Office: UCLA Law Sch PO Box 951476 Los Angeles CA 90095-1476

KARSTEN, ALBERT, religious organization administrator. Dir. Christian Ref World Missions Can., Burlington, Ont., 1992—. Office: Christian Ref World Missions Can, Station LCD 1, 3475 Mainway PO Box 5070, Burlington, ON Canada L7R 3Y8*

KARTIGANER, JOSEPH, lawyer; b. Berlin, June 5, 1935; came to U.S., 1939; s. Harold and Lilly (Wolkowitz) K.; children: Deborah Lynn, Alison Beth. A.B., CCNY, 1955; LL.B., Columbia U., 1958. Bar: N.Y. 1960, Fla. 1978, D.C. 1979. Assoc. White & Case, N.Y.C., 1960-69, ptnr., 1969-88; ptnr. Simpson Thacher & Bartlett, N.Y.C., 1988—; lectr. law Columbia Law Sch., N.Y.C., 1973-80; vis. lectr. Sch. Law Yale U., 1997—; mem. adv. com. N.Y. EPTL-SCPA, 1997—. Fellow Am. Bar Found., Am. Coll. Trust and Estate Counsel (regent 1978-84), Am. Coll. Tax Counsel, N.Y. State Bar Found.; mem. ABA (chmn. real property, probate and trust law sect. 1986-87), N.Y. State Bar Assn., Assn. of Bar of City of N.Y. (chmn. com. on trusts, estates and surrogate's cts. 1990-92), Nat. Conf. Lawyers and Corp. Fiduciaries (co-chair 1991-93), Am. Law Inst., Internat. Acad. Estate and Trust Law (academician), The Yale Club N.Y.C., Scarsdale Golf Club (Hartsdale, N.Y.). E-mail: joekart@yahoo.com. Home: 179 E 79th St New York NY 10021-0421 Office: Simpson Thacher & Bartlett 425 Lexington Ave Fl 15 New York NY 10017-3954

KARU, GILDA M(ALL), lawyer, government official; b. Oceanport, N.J., Dec. 1, 1951; d. Harold and Ilvy (Meriloo) K.; m. Frederick F. Foy, May 23, 1981. AB, Vassar Coll., 1974; JD, Ill. Inst. Tech., 1987. Bar: Ill. 1987, U.S. Dist. Ct. (no. dist.) Ill. 1987. Quality control reviewer Food and Nutrition Svc. USDA, Robbinsville, N.J., 1974-77, team leader, 1977-78, supr., 1978-81; sect. chief Food and Nutrition Svc. USDA, Chgo., 1991—, acting dir. field ops., 1998; employer adviser Ctr. for Rehab. and Tng. Disabled Persons, Chgo., 1986-93; chief mgmt. negotiator for collective bargaining agreement Nat. Treasury Employees Union, 1990. Bd. dirs., legal counsel, regional dir. North Ctrl. Estonian Am. Nat. Coun., N.Y.C.; v.p. 1st Estonian Evang. Luth. Ch., Chgo., treas., 1994—; mem. Chgo. Vol. Legal Svcs., Friends of Arlington Heights Meml. Libr.; vol. dep. voter registration officer Cook County, Ill.; exec. bd. Arlington Heights-Mt. Prospect-Buffalo Grove area LWV. Recipient cert. of recognition William A. Jump Meml. Found., 1987, Arthur S. Flemming award Washington Downtown Jaycees, 1987, Ill. Dem. Ethnic Heritage award, 1989, cert. of appreciation Assn. for Persons with Disabilities in Agr., 1992, Group Honor award for work on 1993 Miss. River Flood Disaster Relief, Sec. of USDA, 1994. Mem. ABA, AAUW, NAFE, LWV (bd. dirs. 1992—), Ill. Bar Assn., Chgo. Bar Assn., Baltic Bar Assn., United Coun. on Welfare Fraud, Internat. Platform Assn., Nat. Audubon Soc., Chgo. Area Seven Sisters Coll. Consortium (sec. 1995—), Mensa, Vassar Club (chpt. treas. 1988-90, v.p. 1990-91, coord. pub. rels. 1991—). Avocations: photography, reading, travel, crafts. Office: USDA Food and Nutrition Svc 20th Fl 77 W Jackson Blvd Fl 20 Chicago IL 60604-3591

KARWA, GATTU LAL, urologist; b. Karimnagar, India, Aug. 19, 1935; came to U.S., 1974; s. Devikishan and Kamala Bai Karwa; widowed; children: Neeta, Manoj, Sangeeta. MD, Osmania Med. Coll., Hyderabad, India, 1957. Intern Osmania Gen. Hosp., Hyderabad, 1957-58; resident in urology Boston City Hosp., 1968-71; resident in surgery Lancaster (Eng.) Royal Infirmary, 1959-60, Montefiore Hosp., Pitts., 1966-67, Columbia (S.C.) Hosp., 1967-68; assoc. prof. urology Einstein Med. Sch., Bronx, N.Y.; attending urologist Montefiore Hosp., Bronx. Fellow Royal Coll. Surgeons Edinburgh, Royal Coll. Surgeons Urology Can. Office: Montefiore Hosp 111 E 210th St Bronx NY 10467

KARWACKI, JEROME JOHN, physician; b. Balt., Dec. 24, 1948. BS in Biology, Loyola Coll., 1970; MD, U. Md., 1980; MPH, Johns Hopkins U., 1982. Commd. 2d lt. U.S. Army, 1970, advanced through grades to col. Contbr. articles to profl. jours. Mem. VFW. Avocations: travel, reading.

KARWACKI, ROBERT LEE, judge; b. Balt., Aug. 2, 1933; s. Lee Daniel and Marie Ann (Budzynski) K.; m. Patricia Ann Deal, Nov. 3, 1956 (dec. May 1972); children: Ann Elizabeth, Lee Daniel, John Robert; m. Marion Elizabeth Harper, June 16, 1973. AB, U. Md., 1954; LLB, U. Md., Balt., 1956. Bar: Md. 1956, U.S. Supreme Ct. 1963, U.S. Dist. Ct. Md. 1957, U.S. Ct. Appeals (4th cir.) 1960. Law clk. to Hon. Stephen R. Collins Ct. Appeals Md., Annapolis, 1956-57; assoc. Miles & Stockbridge, Balt., 1957-63, ptnr., 1965-73; asst. atty. gen. State of Md., Balt., 1963-65; assoc. judge Cir. Ct. Balt. City, 1973-84, Ct. Spl. Appeals Md., Annapolis, 1984-90, Ct. Appeals Md., Annapolis, 1990-97. Pres. Balt. City Sch. Bd., 1970-72. Sgt. USAR, 1956-62. Recipient Man for All Seasons award St. Thomas More Soc., 1977. Fellow Md. Bar Found.; mem. Lawyer's Roundtable, Wednesday Law Club (pres. 1984). Democrat. Roman Catholic. Avocations: golfing, boating, fishing, hunting.

KARWAN, MARK HENRY, engineering educator, dean; b. Cleve., Nov. 16, 1951. B in Engring. Scis. with full honors, MS in Engring., Johns Hopkins U., 1974; PhD, Ga. Inst. Tech., 1976. From asst. prof. to assoc. prof. dept. indsl. engring. SUNY, Buffalo, 1976-86, prof. dept. indsl. engring., 1986—, prof., chair dept. indsl. engring., 1987-92, prof., assoc. dean grad. edn. Sch. Engring. & Applied Scis., 1992-94, prof., acting dean Sch. Engring. & Applied Scis., 1994-95, dean Sch. Engring. & Applied Scis., 1996—; CEO U. at Buffalo Bus. Alliance, 1998—; cons. Mgmt. Adv. Svcs., Inc., Columbia, Md., 1974, Health Care Plan, Inc., Buffalo, 1984-87, Praxair, Inc., Tonawanda, N.Y., 1987—; faculty advisor student chpt. Inst. Indsl. Engrs. 849, 1977-83; proposal reviewer NSF-Sys. Theory and Ops. Rsch., NSF-Applied Math.; cluster chmn. ORSA/TIMS joint nat. meeting, 1986, chmn. numerous sessions, 1977—; mem. grad. sch. fellowship com. SUNY, Buffalo, 1980-82, grad. sch. exec. com., 1982-85, 92-94, grad. sch. polyc rev. com., 1984-91, chmn., 1984-88, honors coun., 1992-98, mem. Sch. Engring. and Applied Scis. divisional com. of grad. sch., 1976-79, Sch. Engring. and Applied Scis. acad. programs com., 1981-87, chmn. Sch. Engring. and Applied Scis. acad. programs com., 1982-85, 89-90, 93-95, dir. Ctr. for Indsl. Effectiveness, 1993—, undergrad. affairs com., 1976-78, grad. affairs com., 1979-87, dir. grad. studies, 1982-87. Assoc. editor: Naval Research Logistics, 1987—, IEE Transactions, 1991-93; co-editor spl. issue Naval Rsch. Logistics, 1988; mem. editl. adv. bd. Computers & Ops. Rsch., 1984—; contbr. refereed papers to profl. jours. including Annals of Discrete Math., European Jour. Operational Rsch., IEEE Transactions on Automatic Control, Jour. Mechanics Design, Mgmt. Sci., Math. Programming, Networks, Ops. Rsch., Water Resources Rsch.; contbr. over 70 articles to profl. publs.; patentee two-phase method for real time process control. Pres.'s fellow Ga. Tech. U., 1974-75. Mem. Alpha Pi Mu, Omega Rho (regional dir. N.E. U.S. chpt. 1982-84). Office: SUNY Sch Engring and Appld Scis Buffalo NY 14260-1900

KARWIC, RICHARD A., management consultant, educator; b. Hartford, Conn., Dec. 16, 1946; s. Adam A. and Isabella L. (Festa) K.; m. Kathleen A. Bassell, Aug. 14, 1967; children: Robert, Michael, Glenn, Jeffrey. BS in Accounting, Ctrl. Conn. State U., 1970; MBA, Western New England Coll., 1995. Staff acct. Soc. for Savings, Hartford, Conn., 1971-72; contr. The Stanley Works, New Britain, Conn., 1972-80; cost control analyst Emhart Corp., Farmington, Conn., 1980-84; divsn. contr., CFO EIS Brake Parts, Berlin, Conn., 1984-90; v.p. Linatex Corp. of Am., Stafford Springs, Conn., 1990-93; priv. practice Wethersfield, Conn., 1993—; v.p. Technicarbon Co. LP., Springfield, Mass., 1996-97; prof. Western New England Coll., Springfield, Mass., 1996-98. Mem. Berlin (Conn.) C. of C., dir. 1984-90, treas. 1988-90. Mem. Inst. Mgmt. Accts. Avocations: jogging, tennis, chess, reading, travel. Home: 100 Lantern Ln Wethersfield CT 06109-4047 Office: Indepco Inc 100 Lantern Ln Wethersfield CT 06109-4047

KASAKOVE, SUSAN, interior designer; b. Newark, N.J., Nov. 11, 1938. BFA, U. Buffalo, 1958, Hunter Coll., 1960; postgrad., N.Y. Sch. of Interior Design, 1960-64, New Sch. for Social Rsch., 1967-68, Pratt Inst., 1968-69. Asst. interior designer Rodgers Assocs., N.Y.C., 1964-66; interior designer Walter Dorwin Teague Assocs., N.Y.C., 1966-70; sr. interior designer N.Y. State Facilities Devel. Corp., N.Y.C., 1970-95; Dormitory Authority for the State of N.Y., 1995—. Reading tutor Vols. for Children's Svcs., N.Y.C., 1976-82; chair Friends of White Plains (N.Y.) Symphony, 1981-83; vol. dept. Asian Dept. Work Endod, 1995, vol. guide edn. dept., 1978—; Rep. treas. 11th Ward, Yonkers, N.Y., 1979-81. Recipient Outstanding Svc. to Sch. award Rockland County (N.Y.) Lions Club, 1955. Mem. Environ. Design Rsch. Assn. Avocations: photography, history of art and architecture, golf, swimming. Home: 793 Palmer Rd Apt 3F Bronxville NY 10708-3337 Office: 1 Penn Plz Fl 52 New York NY 10119-5299

KASAMA, HIDETO PETER, accountant, business advisor, real estate consultant; b. Tokyo, Nov. 21, 1946; came to U.S., 1969; s. Toshiyoshi and Hamako (Yoshioka) K.; m. Evelyn Patricia Cruz (div. Apr. 1990); children: Jennifer, Nicole, Leona; m. Heidi W. Snare, June 29, 1991; 1 child, Serena. BABA, Seattle U., 1971, MBA, 1973. CPA. Mgmt. trainee Seafirst Bank, Seattle, 1972-74; audit supr. Ernst & Young, Seattle, 1974-79; pres. KASPAC Corp., Seattle, 1979-89; mng. ptnr. Kasama & Co., Seattle, 1980-98; shareholder Von Harten & Co., Seattle, 1998—. Contbr. articles to newspapers. Mem. AICPA, Wash. Soc. CPA's, Columbia Tower Club (founder). Avocations: golf, classical guitar, gardening. Home: 725 9th Ave S Edmonds WA 98020-3311 Office: Von Harten & Co 1809 7th Ave Ste 1400 Seattle WA 98101-1313

KASAMI, TADAO, information science educator; b. Kobe, Hyōgo, Japan, Apr. 12, 1930; m. Fumiko Okada, May 9, 1964; children: Yuuko, Ryuichi. B in Engring., Osaka (Japan) U., 1958, M in Engring., 1960, D in Engring., 1963. Assoc. prof. engring. Osaka (Japan) U., 1963-66, prof. engring., 1966-94, dean engring. sci., 1990-92, prof. emeritus, 1994—; prof., Grad. Sch. Info. Sci. Nara (Japan) Inst. Sci. and Tech., 1992-98, dean, Grad. Sch. Info. Sci., 1992-94, dir. libr., 1994-98, prof. emeritus, 1998—; prof. Hiroshima (Japan) City U. Sch. Info. Sci., 1998—; adj. prof. Grad. Sch., U. Hawaii, Honolulu, 1992-97. Author: Coding Theory, 1978, Discrete Structure II, 1983, Formal Language Theory, 1988, Introduction to Information and Coding Theory, 1989, Trellises and Trellis-based Decoding Algorithms for Linear Block Codes, 1998. Fellow IEEE; mem. Inst. Electronics, Info. and Comms. Engrs. (Achievement award 1987), Soc. Info. and it's Applications (pres. 1993), IEEE Info. Theory Soc. (Claude E. Shannon award 1999). Office: Hiroshima City U, Ozukahigashi 3-4-1, Hiroshima 731-3194, Japan

KASANIN, MARK OWEN, lawyer; b. Boston, June 28, 1929; s. Jacob Sergei and Elizabeth Owen (Knight) K.; m. Anne Camilla Wimbish, Dec. 18, 1960; children: Marc S., James W. B.A., Stanford U., 1951; LL.B., Yale U., 1954. Bar: Calif. Assoc. McCutchen, Doyle, Brown & Enersen, San Francisco, 1957-62, 63-67; ptnr. McCutchen, Doyle, Brown & Enersen, 1967—. Mem. planning commn. City of Belvedere, Calif., 1974-76. Served with USNR, 1955-57. Named among Best Lawyers in Am., 1997-98. Fellow Am. Coll. Trial Lawyers; mem. Maritime Law Assn. U.S. (exec. com. 1984-87, trustee Product Liability Adv. Coun. Found. 1990—, mem. fed. civil rules adv. com. 1992—). Fax: 415-393-2286. Home: PO Box 698 Belvedere Tiburon CA 94920-0698 Office: McCutchen Doyle Brown & Enersen 3 Embarcadero Ctr San Francisco CA 94111-4003

KASARI, LEONARD SAMUEL, quality control professional, concrete consultant; b. Los Angeles, Sept. 22, 1924; s. Kustaa Adolph and Impi (Sikio) K.; m. Elizabeth P. Keplinger, Aug. 25, 1956; children: Lorraine Carol, Lance Eric. Student, Compton Coll., 1942-43, UCLA, 1964-70. Registered profl. engr., Calif. Gen. construction Los Angeles, 1946-61; supr. inspection service Osborne Labs., Los Angeles, 1961-64; mgr. customer service Lightweight Processing, Los Angeles, 1965-77; dir. tech. service Crestlite Aggregates, San Clemente, Calif., 1977-78; quality control mgr. Standard Concrete, Santa Ana, Calif., 1978-92. Camp dir. Torrance YMCA, High Sierras, Calif., 1969-80, mem. bd. mgrs., 1970—. Served with USN, 1943-46. Recipient Sam Hobbs Svc. award ACI-So. Calif., 1992; named Hon. Life Mem. Calif. PTA, 1983. Mem. Am. Concrete Inst. Democrat. Lutheran. Avocations: skiing, hunting, fishing, backpacking. Office: 2450 W 233rd St Torrance CA 90501-5730

KASBERGER-MAHONEY, ELVERA A., educational administrator; b. Oak Park, Ill., July 2, 1952; d. Lawrence and Aura Louise (Rutledge) Petrongelli; m. Daniel Mahoney, July 14, 1988. BA, Northeastern Ill. U., 1974, MA, 1978; grad., Calif. Sch. Leadership Acad., 1990. Tchr. Social Emotionally Disturbed Children Warren Twp. High Sch., Gurnee, Ill.; dean of students Adlai Stevenson High Sch., Prairie View, Ill.; asst. prin. Hesperia (Calif.) Unified Sch. Dist.; prin., supt. schs. San Bernardino County, 1988-90; asst. prin. Elsinore High Sch., Lake Elsinore, Calif., 1990-95, Temescal Canyon H.S., Elsinore, 1995-96; asst. prin. of student svcs. Jurupa Valley H.S., Jurupa Unified Sch. Dist., Mira Loma, Calif., 1996—. Chpt. I grantee; Job Tng. Partnership grantee. Mem. ASCD, Assn. Calif. Sch. Adminstrs., Coun. for Exceptional Children.

KASCHAK, DAVID JAMES, accountant; b. South Weymouth, Mass., Nov. 8, 1960; s. Thomas John and Joan Marie (Holahan) K. Student, Rider U., 1979-81; BS in Acctg., Pa. State U., 1983. CPA, N.J. Prin. auditor Office of State Auditor, Trenton, N.J., 1984—. Baseball coach Lawrence Twp. (N.J.) Babe Ruth, 1992-94. Mem. AICPA, Assn. Govt. Accts. (officer 1995-99, scholar 1982, Chpt. Svc. award 1997, exec. bd. 1998—), Alpha Chi Rho (nat. treas. 1989-95). Avocations: jogging, softball, ice hockey, collectibles. Home: 980 Bear Tavern Rd Trenton NJ 08628-1017

KASCHAK, VIRGINIA RUTH, elementary education educator; b. Pitts., Dec. 10, 1929; d. Walter O. and Theresa (Debes) Billingsley; m. Joseph Robert Kaschak, Apr. 19, 1952; children: Ruth Ann, Robert G. BS in Elem. Edn. with honors, Carlow Coll., 1978. Tchr. religion Diocese Pitts., 1964-75; primary tchr. St. Elizabeth Elem. Sch., Pitts., 1975-89; ret., 1989; coord. dept. Ch. Coun. Spl. Minister, 1979-90, spokesperson primary dept., 1980-86. Mem. Pa. State Edn. Assn., Am. Legion Aux. (historian 1970—, scholarship com. 1990-95).

KASDAN, LAWRENCE EDWARD, film director, screenwriter; b. Miami Beach, Fla., Jan. 14, 1949; s. Clarence Norman and Sylvia Sarah (Landau) K.; m. Meg Goldman, Nov. 28, 1971; children: Jacob, Jonathan. B.A., U. Mich., 1970, M.A. in Edn., 1972. Copywriter W.B. Doner & Co. (Advt.), Detroit, 1972-75, Doyle, Dane Bernbach, Los Angeles, 1975-77; freelance screenwriter, 1977-80; motion picture dir., screenwriter Los Angeles, 1980—. Co-screenwirter: The Empire Strikes Back, 1980, Return of the Jedi, 1982; screenwriter: Continental Divide, 1981, Raiders of the Lost Ark, 1981; writer, dir.: Body Heat, 1981, Grand Canyon, 1992; co-screenwriter, dir., exec. prodr.: The Big Chill, 1983; co-screenwriter, dir., prodr.: Silverado, 1985, The Accidental Tourist, 1988; prodr. Cross My Heart, 1987; dir. I Love You to Death, 1989; co-screenwriter with dir. Wyatt Earp, 1994; screenwriter, co-prodr. The Bodyguard, 1992; exec. prodr. Jumpin at the Boneyard, 1992; dir. French Kiss, 1995. Recipient Clio awards for advt., Writers Guild Am. award for the Big Chill, 1983; nominated 4 Acad. Awards. Mem. Writers Guild Am. West, Dirs. Guild Am. West. Address: United Talent Agy 9560 Wilshire Blvd Fl 5 Beverly Hills CA 90212-2401

KASER, DAVID, retired librarian, educator, consultant; b. Mishawaka, Ind., Mar. 12, 1924; s. Arthur Leroy and Loah (Steele) K.; m. Jane Jewell, Sept. 1, 1950; children: John Andrew, Kathleen Jewell. A.B., Houghton Coll., 1949; M.A., U. Notre Dame, 1950; A.M. in L.S, U. Mich., 1952, Ph.D., 1956. Serials librarian, instr. library sci. Ball State U., 1952-54; asst. in exchanges U. Mich. Library, 1954-56; chief acquisitions Washington U. Libraries, St. Louis, 1956-59; asst. dir. Washington U. Libraries, 1959-60; prof. library sci. Peabody Coll. and dir. libraries Vanderbilt U., 1960-68; dir. libraries Cornell U., 1968-73; prof. library sci. Ind. U., Bloomington, 1973-86, Disting. prof., 1986-91, Disting. prof. emeritus, 1991—; pres. Kaser Assocs., Inc., libr. bldg. cons., Bloomington, 1988-95; fgn. assignments in Ireland, 1960, Korea, 1965, 81, 93, Laos, 1966, Taiwan, 1967, 79, 81, 88, 89, 93, S.E. Asia, 1969, Eng., 1971, France, 1972, Saudi Arabia, 1975-76, 83, Nigeria, 1978, Indonesia, 1978, Malaysia, 1992. Author: Messrs. Carey & Lea of Philadelphia, 1957, Washington University Manuscripts, 1958, Cost Book of Carey & Lea, 1825-1838, 1963, Joseph Charless, Printer in the Western Country, 1963, Books in America's Past, 1966, Book Pirating in Taiwan, 1969, Library Development in Eight Asian Countries, 1969, Book for a Sixpence, 1980, Books and Libraries in Camp and Battle, 1984, The Evolution of the American Academic Library Building, 1997; editor Mo. Libr. Assn. Quar., 1958-60, Coll. and Rsch. Librs., 1963-69. Guggenheim fellow, 1967. Mem. ALA (councilor 1965-69, 75-79), Assn. Coll. and Research Libraries (pres. 1968-69), Assn. Southeastern Research Libraries (chmn. 1966-68), Tenn. Library Assn. (pres. 1968-69), Am. Antiquarian Soc., Phi Beta Kappa, Beta Phi Mu (internat. pres. 1975).

KASER, RICHARD TODD, communications executive; b. Dover, Ohio, Aug. 29, 1952; s. Richard I. and Mary (Miller) K.; m. Victoria Cox, June 29, 1974; 1 child, Adaline. BS in Journalism summa cum laude, Ohio U., 1974; MA in Internat. Communications, Ohio State U., 1976. Public info. officer State of Ohio, Columbus, 1974-75; mgr. sales promotion Columbia Nat. Corp., Columbus, 1976-77; sales promotional specialist Chem. Abstracts Svc., Columbus, 1977-79, advt. mgr., 1979-83, corp. communications mgr., 1983-87, planning and communications mgr., 1987-90; group v.p., spl. asst. planning and communication Maxwell Macmillan, McLean, Va., 1990-94; exec. dir. The Nat. Fedn. Abstracting and Info. Svcs., Phila., 1994—. Mem. fin. com. Cen. Ohio Council Internat. Visitors, Columbus, 1985-86. Mem. Nat. Fedn. Abstracting and Info. Svcs. (chmn., newsletter editor adv. bd. 1985—), Phi Kappa Phi. Democrat. Episcopalian. Avocations: jogging, swimming, antiques, books, writing. Office: Nat Fedn Abstracting & Info Svcs 1518 Walnut St Ste 307 Philadelphia PA 19102-3419*

KASH, DON ELDON, political science educator; b. Macedonia, Iowa, May 29, 1934; s. Albert W. and Blanche Opal (Smith) K.; m. Elizabeth Gunn; children: Kelli Denise, Jeffrey Paul. BA, U. Iowa, 1959, MA, 1960, PhD, 1963. Instr. Tex. Tech. U., 1960-61; asst. prof. Ariz. State U., 1963-65, U. Mo., Kansas City, 1965-66; assoc. prof. Purdue U., West Lafayette, Ind., 1966-70; prof. polit. sci. U. Okla., Norman, 1970-91, George Lynn Cross rsch. prof. polit. sci., 1975-91, dir. Sci. and Pub. Policy Program, 1970-78; John T. Hazel Sr. and Ruth D. Hazel chair in pub. policy George Mason U., Fairfax, Va., 1991—; vis. assoc. prof. Ind. U., 1969-70; chief conservation div. U.S. Geol. Survey, 1978-81; mem. Assembly Engring., Marine Bd. NRC; prof. Tsinghua U., Beijing. Author: The Politics of Space Cooperation, 1967, Energy Under the Oceans: A Technology Assessment of Outer Continental Shelf Oil and Gas Operations, 1973, North Sea Oil and Gas: Implication for Future U.S. Development, 1973, Energy Alternatives: A Comparative Analysis, 1975, Our Energy Future, 1976, U.S. Energy Policy: Crisis and Complacency, 1983, Perpetual Innovation: The New World of Competition, 1989, The Complexity Challenge: Technological Innovation in the 21st Century, 1999; contbr. articles to profl. jours. With AUS, 1952-54. Recipient Disting. Alumni award U. Iowa, 1988. Fellow AAAS. Office: George Mason U Inst Public Policy 4400 University Dr Fairfax VA 22030-4444

KASH, WYATT KEITH, publishing executive; b. Chgo., Mar. 26, 1955; s. Edward E. and Doris (Glenn) K.; m. Ellen Raymond, Oct. 12, 1986. BS cum laude, Syracuse U., 1979; student, U. Vt., 1974-75. Supr. material control Parson's Corp., Prudhoe Bay, Alaska, 1975-77; field editor Nat. Home Ctr. News/Lebhar-Friedman, N.Y.C., 1980-81; assoc. editor Nat. Home Ctr. News/Lebhar-Friedman, 1981, exec. editor, 1981-82, editor-in-chief, 1983-87, pub., 1987—.

KASHA, KENNETH JOHN, agriculturist, educator; b. Lacombe, Alta., Can., May 6, 1933; s. John Clarence and Mary Jennette (Proudfoot) K.; m. Marion Eileen Lenz, Aug. 14, 1958, children: Lorelei Marion, David John. BSc in Agr., U. Alta., Edmonton, 1957, MSc, 1958; PhD, U. Minn., 1962; LLD (hon.), U. Calgary, Alta., 1986. Rsch. asst. U. Minn., Mpls., 1958-61, fellow rsch. agronomy and plant genetics, 1961-62; rsch. scientist forages Agr. Can. Rsch. Sta., Ottawa, Ont., 1962-66; asst. prof. crop sci. dept. U. Guelph, Ont., 1966-69, assoc. prof. crop sci. dept., 1969-74, prof. crop sci. dept., 1974-98—, prof. emeritus, 1998—; cons. Ciba Geigy Seeds Ltd., Ailsa Craig, Ont., 1974-81; organizing chair and editor 1st Internat. Symposium on Haploids in Plants, Guelph, 1974; dir. Plant Biotech Centre, Guelph Waterloo Biotech, 1984-87; program chmn. XVI Internat. Congress Genetics, Toronto, 1988. Editor: Haploids in Higher Plants, 1974, Plant Cell Culture in Agriculture and Forestry, 1980; contbr. articles to profl. jours.; mem. numerous jour. editorial bds. Recipient Agrl. Inst. Can. Grindley medal, 1977; Can. Award of Excellence EC Manning Found., 1983, Disting. Rsch. award Ont. Agr. Coll. Alumni, 1984, decorated officer of the Order of Can., 1994. Fellow Royal Soc. Can.; mem. Sigma Xi (Disting. Researcher award Guelph chpt. 1974), Genetics Soc. Can. (pres. 1976-77, sec. 1966-69, award of Excellence 1994), Internat. Assn. Plant Tissue Culture (nat. corr. 1990-94), Can. Soc. Plant Molecular Biology (founding mem.), Genetics Soc. Am., Am. Soc. Agronomy, Sigma Xi. Home: 28 Halesmanor Ct, Guelph, ON Canada N1G 4E2 Office: U Guelph, Dept Crop Sci, Guelph, ON Canada N1G 2W1

KASHANI, JAVAD HASSAN-NEJAD, physician; b. Meshed, Iran, Aug. 30, 1937; came to U.S., 1971; s. Ali-Akbar and Kobra F. Kashani; m. Soraya Rezvani, Mar. 23, 1962; children: Fred, Donna. BS, Meshed Med. Coll., 1960; MD, Meshed Med. Sch., 1969. Diplomate Am. Bd. Psychiatry and Neurology, Can. Bd. Psychiatry. Intern St. Ann's Hosp., Chgo., 1972; resident Northwestern U., Chgo., 1972-75; fellow U. Mo., Columbia, 1976-77, prof. psychiatry, psychology and pediat., 1985-99; prof. psychiatry Case Western Rsch. U., Cleve., 1999—; dir. children's svcs. Mid-Mo. Mental Health Ctr., Columbia, 1981—; dir. edn. dept. psychiatry and neurology U. Mo., Columbia, 1996—. Avocation: oil painting. *

KASHDIN, GLADYS SHAFRAN, painter, educator; b. Dec. 15, 1921; d. Edward M. and Miriam P. Shafran; m. Manville E. Kashdin, Oct. 11, 1942 (dec.). BA magna cum laude, U. Miami, 1960; MA, Fla. State U., 1962, PhD, 1965. Photographer N.Y.C. and Fla., 1938-60; tchr. art Fla. and Ga., 1956-63; from asst. prof. humanities to assoc. prof. to prof. U. South Fla., Tampa, 1965-87, prof. emerita, 1987—; lectr.; adv. bd. Hillsborough County Mus., 1975-83. Works exhibited in 65 one-woman shows, 43 group exhbns.; maj. touring exhibits include: The Everglades, 1972-75, Aspects of the River, 1975-80, Processes of Time, 1981-91, Retrospective 1941-96, Tampa Mus. Art, 1996, Appleton Mus. Art, Ocala, 1999; represented in permanent collections, Taiwan, China, Columbus Mus. Arts, LeMoyne Art Found., Tampa Internat. Airport, TAmpa Mus. Art, Appleton Mus. Art, Ocala, Mus. Sci. and Industry, Tampa, Miss. Mus. Art, Jackson. Mem. U.S. Fla. Status of Women Com., 1971-76, chmn., 1975-76. Recipient Women Helping Women in Art award Soroptimist Internat., 1979, Citizens Hon. award Hillsborough Bd. County Commrs., 1984, Mortar Bd. award for tchg. excellence, 1986. Mem. AAUW (1st v.p. Tampa br. 1971-72), Phi Kappa Phi (chpt.-pres. 1981-83, artist/scholar award 1987). Home: 441 Biltmore Ave Temple Terrace FL 33617

KASHGARIAN, MICHAEL, pathologist, physician; b. N.Y.C., Sept. 20, 1933; s. Toros and Arax (Almasian) K.; m. Jean Gaylor Caldwell, July 2, 1960; children: Michaele, Thea. A.B., N.Y. U., 1954; M.D., Yale U., 1958. Diplomate: Am. Bd. Pathology. Intern Barnes Hosp., St. Louis, 1958-59; asst. in medicine Washington U., St. Louis, 1958-59; asst. resident in pathology Yale New Haven Med. Center, 1959-61, resident in pathology, 1962-63; research fellow in renal physiology (U. Goettingen), Germany, 1961-62; practice medicine specializing in pathology New Haven, 1962—; instr. Yale U., 1962-64, asst. prof., 1964-67, asso. prof., 1967-74, prof., 1974—, vice chmn. dept., 1976-89, chmn., 1990— assoc. pathologist Yale New Haven Hosp., 1964-66, asst. attending pathologist, 1966-69, attending pathologist, 1969—, pres. med. staff, 1983-84; cons. in pathology, 1962—. Author: (with J.P. Hayslett, B.H. Spargo) Renal Disease, 1974, (with G.N. Burrow) The Endocrine Glands; editor: Yearbook of Nephrology, Yale Medicine, Current Opinion in Nephrology; mem. editorial bd. Nephron, 1970—, Am. Jour. Pathology, 1975—, Am. Jour. Kidney Diseases; contbr. articles to med. jours. Chmn. edni. adv. council North Haven Bd. Edn., 1971; chmn. Christian edn. com. Ch. of Christ, Yale, 1970; bd. dirs. New Haven Symphony Orch.; v.p. Conn. Fund for Environ. 1st lt., M.C. USAR, 1954-65. USPHS fellow, 1963-65; research career devel. awardee, 1965-75. Fellow AAAS, Am. Soc. Clin. Pathologists, Coll. Am. Pathologists; mem. AMA, Am. Soc. Nephrology, Internat. Acad. Pathology, Conn. State Med. Soc. (chmn. com. on organ and tissue transfer), New Haven County Med. Assn. (pres. bd. govs.), Am. Soc. Investigative Pathologists, Conn. Soc. Pathologists (pres. 1975), Am. Heart Assn., Am. Physiol. Soc., Gesellshaft Nephrologie (hon.), Sigma Xi, Alpha Omega Alpha, Alpha Kappa Kappa. Home: 22 Old Orchard Rd North Haven CT 06473-3022 Office: 310 Cedar St PO Box 208023 New Haven CT 06520-8023

KASHYAP, SATCHITANAND, research scientist; b. Bangalore, Karnataka, India, May 17, 1970; came to U.S., 1992; s. Krishna Swamy and Sundari Iyer. BSMechE, Bangalore U., 1991; MSMechE, Rensselaer Poly. Inst., 1994, PhD in Mech., Aeronautics & Mechanics, 1996. Rsch. asst. Indian Inst. Sci., Bangalore, 1990-92; instr., rsch. assoc. Rensselaer Poly., Troy, N.Y., 1992-96; mem. tech. staff Bell Labs., Holmdel, N.J., 1997—. Author: (book) Integrated Methodology for Fixture Design Analysis and Optimization, 1996 (award 1998); contbr. papers to sci. jours. (Best Paper award 1998). NSF rsch. fellow, 1996. Mem. ASME (assoc., conf. chair 1996-98, editl. staff design divsn. 1996-98, editl. staff Jour. Mfg. Sci. and Engring. 1996-98), Internat. Instn. Elec. and Electronics Engrs., Soc. Mfng. Engrs. (assoc., conf. chair 1996-98). Avocations: soccer, tennis, swimming, photography, outdoor activities. E-mail: satchitukashyap@worldnet.att.net. Office: Bell Labs/Lucent Techs 101 Crawfords Lorner Rd Holmdel NJ 07733

KASICH, JOHN R., congressman; b. McKees Rocks, Pa., May 13, 1952. B.A., Ohio State U., 1974. Administrv. asst. Ohio State Senate, 1975-77; mem. Ohio Legislature, 1979-82, 98th-106th Congressses from 12th Ohio dist., Washington, D.C., 1983—; mem. nat. security com., mem. house budget com., chmn. Office: House of Reps 1111 Longworth Bldg Washington DC 20515-3512*

KASIMOS, JOHN NICHOLAS, pathologist; b. Chgo., Jan. 26, 1955; s. Nicholas John and Mia (Panos) K.; m. Helen Papadakis, July 10, 1994. BS in Biology, Loyola U., Chgo., 1978; MS in Biology, Ill. Inst. Tech., 1980; DO, Chgo. Coll. Osteopathic Med., 1984. Diplomate Nat. Bd. Examiners for Osteo. Physicians and Surgeons, Am. Osteo. Bd. Pathologists, Anatomic Pathology and Lab. Medicine. Intern Chgo. Osteo. Health Systems, 1984-85, resident pathology, 1985-89, pathologist, 1989—, resident in family medicine, 1997—; asst. prof. pathology Chgo. Coll. Osteo. Medicine, 1989-93; assoc. prof. pathology Midwestern U., 1993-98, prof. pathology, 1998—; acad. mentor, advisor Chgo. Coll. Osteo. Medicine, 1989—, dir. residence tng. dept. pathology, dir. deptl. edn./rsch., vice chmn. dept. pathology, 1993-96, acting chmn. dept. pathology, 1996-97, chmn. dept. pathology, 1997—; resident family medicine Chgo. Osteo. Health Systems, 1997—. Fellow Coll. Am. Pathologists, Am. Soc. Clin. Pathologists, Am. Osteo. Coll. Pathologists; mem. Am. Osteo. Assn., U.S. and Can. Acad. Pathologists, Ill. Assn. Osteo. Physicans and Surgeons, Ill. Pathology Soc., Chgo. Pathology Soc., Am. Acad. of Osteopathy. Greek Orthodox. Achievements include research in nuclear magnetic resonance spectroscopy of tumors and pathophysiologic development of disease. Office: Columbia Olympia Fields Osteo Hosp & Med Ctr Dept Pathology 20201 Crawford Ave Olympia Fields IL 60461-1010

KASINEC, EDWARD JOSEPH, library administrator; b. N.Y.C., Oct. 10, 1945; s. Ignac A. and Justina I. (Kundrik) K. BA cum laude, St. John's U., Jamaica, N.Y., 1963; MA, Columbia U., 1966, M in Philology, 1979; MLS, Simmons Coll., 1976. Rsch. bibliographer, libr. Harvard U. Libr., Cambridge, Mass., 1973-80; libr. Slavic collection U. Calif., Berkeley, 1980-84; chief Slavic and Baltic div. N.Y. Pub. Libr., N.Y.C., 1984—; cons. Nat. Library Can., Ottawa, Soviet and E. European Ctr., U. Pa., U. Tex. Author: Slavic Books and Bookmen: Papers and Essays, 1984. Russian Inst. fellow Columbia U., 1972-73, Astor fellow N.Y. Pub. Libr., 1989—; Can. Inst. Ukrainian Studies grantee U. Alta, 1979; vis. fellow grantee Newberry Libr., Chgo., 1980, Kennan Inst., Washington, 1980, Aitken fellow, 1991-92; rsch. grantee Libr.'s Assembly, U. Calif., 1981-83. Mem. Am. Assn. for Advancement Slavic Studies (co-chmn. bibliography and documentation com. 1983-89). Office: NY Pub Libr Slavic & Baltic Div Central Bldg Rm 217 Fifth Ave and 42d St New York NY 10018-2788

KASINITZ, PHILIP, sociologist; b. Chgo., Sept. 18, 1957; s. Julius and Margaret (Van Gorp) K.; m. Lisa Jane Gibbs, Aug. 16, 1987; 1 child, Basya X. BA magna cum laude, Boston U., 1979; MA, NYU, 1982, PhD, 1987. Asst. prof. sociology Williams Coll., Williamstown, Mass., 1987-93; assoc. prof. sociology Hunter Coll., CUNY, N.Y.C., 1993-98, prof. sociology, 1999—; cons. in field. Author: Caribbean New York, 1992; editor: Metropolis, 1995. Vis. scholar Wagner Sch., NYU, 1990-91; NEH fellow, 1990-91. Mem. Am. Sociol. Assn. (chair internat. migration sect. 1998-99, Thomas and Zmaniecki award 1996), Families Children from China. Democrat. Jewish. Home: 821A Union St Apt 4 Brooklyn NY 11215-1337 Office: Hunter Coll 695 Park Ave New York NY 10021-5024

KASISCHKE, LOUIS WALTER, lawyer; b. Bay City, Mich., July 18, 1942; s. Emil Ernst and Gladys Ann (Stuady) K.; m. Sandra Ann Colosimo, Sept. 30, 1967; children: Douglas, Gregg. BA, Mich. State U., 1964; JD, Detroit Coll. Law, 1967; LLM, Wayne State U., 1971. Bar: Mich. 1968, U.S. Dist. Ct. (southeastern dist.) Mich. 1968; CPA. Acct. Touche Ross & Co., Detroit, 1967-71; atty. Dykema Gossett, Detroit, 1971—; pres. Pella Window and Door Co., West Bloomfield, Mich., 1990—; bd. dirs. Barton Malow Co., Southfield. Author: Michigan Closely Held Corporations, 1986; contbr. articles to profl. jours. Mem. ABA, AICPA, State Bar Mich. (editor column Mich. Bar Jour. 1971-83), Mich. Assn. CPAs, Am. Coll. Tax Counsel. Republican. Lutheran. Avocations: mountaineering, skiing, running, squash, golf. Home: 810 Hidden Pine Rd Bloomfield Hills MI 48304-2409 Office: Dykema Gossett 1577 N Woodward Ave Ste 300 Bloomfield Hills MI 48304-2840

KASKA, CHARLES POWERS, psychologist; b. Orange, N.J., Apr. 26, 1943; s. Charles Basil and Florence May (Powers) K.; m. Barbara Perreault, Apr. 4, 1968 (div. June 1986); 1 child, Juliet. AA in Psychology, Monmouth Coll., 1965, BA in Psychology, 1969; MA in Psychology, Newark State Coll., 1972; PsyD, Rutgers U., 1978. Diplomate Am. Bd. Disability Analysts, Am. Bd. Forensic Examiners, Profl. Acad. Custody Evaluators, Prescribing Psychologists Register; lic. psychologist, Pa., N.J.; cert. sch. psychologist, Pa., N.J. Sch. psychologist Trenton (N.J.) Pub. Schs., 1971-75, 85—, Alexandria Twp. (N.J.) Schs., 1979-84; clin. psychologist Devereux Found., Devon, Pa., 1984-85; dir. Northover Coop. Sch., Boundbrook, N.J., 1975-76; pvt. practice psychologist Yardley, Pa., 1976-79; child custody expert ATLA, Tech. Adv. Svc. for Attys., TASA, 1994—; child welfare cons. Divsn. Youth and Family Svcs., N.J., 1987—; pres. Delaware Valley Forensic Psychology, P.C., 1997—. Editor, pub. The Hawker mag., 1965-66. Prin. organizer Christmas Project, Jackson, Miss., 1965. Vol. Peace Corps, 1966-68. Mem. Assn. Family and Conciliation Cts., Profl. Soc. on the Abuse of Children, Assn. Children N.J., Nat. Children's Advocacy Ctr. Avocations: natural environment and sustainable energy. Office: 55 Lookover Ln Yardley PA 19067-1520

KASKELL, PETER HOWARD, association executive, lawyer; b. Berlin, Germany, Mar. 29, 1924; s. Joseph and Lilo (Schaeffer) K.; m. Joan Folsom Macy, Nov. 30, 1968; stepchildren: Bryn, Alison. Grad., Horace Mann Sch., N.Y.C., 1940; BA, Columbia U., 1943, LLB, 1948. Bar: N.Y. 1948. Assoc. White & Case, N.Y.C., 1948-51; atty. Nat. Prodn. Authority, Washington, 1951-52, W.R. Grace & Co., N.Y.C., 1952-54; div. counsel Curtiss-Wright Corp., Buffalo, 1954-56; with Olin Corp., Stamford, Conn., 1956-83; v.p. legal affairs Olin Corp., 1971-83; sr. v.p. CPR Inst. for Dispute Resolution, N.Y.C., 1983—; overseer, mem. program com. CARE; trustee CARE Found.; mem. adv. com. U.S. Dist. Ct. (ea. dist.) N.Y. Former trustee Aldrich Mus. Contemporary Art, Ridgefield, Conn., Boys' Athletic League, N.Y.C.; vice chmn. Conn. Humanities Coun.; organizer, chmn. Lawyers Com. for Conv. on Contracts for Internat. Sale of Goods. With Intelligence Svc., AUS, 1943-45, ETO. Decorated Bronze Star. Mem. Assn. of Bar of City of N.Y., Am. Arbitration Assn. (comml. arbitration panel), Wilton Riding club (past gov.), Century Assn. (mem. admissions com.). Home: 226 Nod Hill Rd Wilton CT 06897-1717 Office: 366 Madison Ave New York NY 10017-3122

KASKEY, BAYLEN, communications corporation executive; b. Phila., Apr. 1, 1929; s. Sydney S. and Selma (Silver) K.; m. Marjorie Ann Updegrove, June 27, 1954; children—Jeffrey Allen, Cynthia Louise, Michael Andrew. B.S. in Mech. Engring., U. Pa., 1950; cert. communications and electronics, Bell Labs. Community Devel., N.Y.C., 1953. Faculty, Kans. State Coll., Manhattan, 1950-51; mem. tech. staff Bell Labs., Whippany, N.J., 1951-58, supr., 1958-62, dept. head Bellcomm, Inc., Washington, 1962-67, Columbus, Ohio, 1967-80, dir. Bell Labs., Naperville, Ill., 1980-89. Author: (with others) Telecommunications, An Interdisciplinary Survey, 1979; Innovations in Telecommunications, 1982. Contbr. articles to profl. jours. Chmn., PTA, Worthington, Ohio, 1974, council rep., 1977; founder, v.p. Citizens for Union Sta. Architecture, Columbus, 1977-80; founder, bd. dirs. Columbus Landmark Found., 1978-80; bd. dirs., v.p. Friends of Danada, Inc., DuPage County, Ill., 1986-89, chmn. hist. com., 1993-95, chmn. planning com., East Marlborough Twp. Pa., 1995—; pres. East Marlborough Land Trust, 1999—; chmn. adv. bd. Pa. Hist. and Mus. Com., 1995—. Served with AUS, 1954-56. Mem. AIAA, ASME, Am. Mgmt. Assn., Tau Beta Pi, Sigma Tau. Avocations: orchid culture; historic preservation.

KASKOWITZ, EDWIN, social services executive; b. St. Louis, May 15, 1936; s. Nathan and Fannie K.; children: Joy, Sara, Naomi. B.A., Washington U., St. Louis, 1958, M.S.W. (grad. scholar), 1961. Lic. clin. social worker. Sr. social worker St. Louis County Health Dept., 1965-67; exec. dir. Gerontol. Soc. Am., 1967-80; pres. Business Radio Corp., Atlanta, Ga., 1981-82; pres., chief exec. officer The Association Mgmt. Group, Chevy Chase, Md., 1982-86; dir. JCCA Sr. Adult Services, Creve Coeur, Mo., 1986-89, The Forum on Aging Consumers and Employees, St. Louis U., 1989-90; pres. Gerontology Svcs. of Mo., 1991—. Pres. B'nai-Brith-Habirah, Washington, 1974-75; adv. bd. Over Easy program Sta. KQED-TV, 1977-81. With USAR, 1954-62. Fellow Royal Soc. Health; mem. Gerontol. Soc. Am., Am. Soc. Assn. Execs. (cert. assn. exec.), Nat. Assn. Social Workers, Acad. Cert. Social Workers.

KASLICK, RALPH SIDNEY, dentist, educator; b. Bklyn., Oct. 17, 1935; s. John J. and Dorothy K.; m. Jessica Hellinger, Oct. 24, 1976; 1 child, Andrew. A.B., Columbia U., 1956, D.D.S., 1959, cert. in periodontology, 1962. Instr. Fairleigh Dickinson U., Coll. Dental Medicine, Hackensack, N.J., 1965-67, asst. prof., 1967-70, assoc. prof., 1970-74, prof., 1974-88, asst. dean for acad. affairs, 1973-75, acting dean, 1975-76, dean, 1976-88, acting provost, Teaneck-Hackensack campus, 1983-85, sr. dean Teaneck-Hackensack campus, 1985-88; dir. dentistry Coler-Goldwater Meml. Hosp., Roosevelt Island, N.Y., 1988—, pres. med. staff, 1992-94, 97—, dir. consultative svcs., 1995—; clin. prof. periodontics Coll. Dentistry, NYU, 1988—; cons. in field. Contbr. chpts. to textbooks, articles to profl. jours. Served to capt. U.S. Army, 1962-64. Recipient Journalism award of the Internat. Coll. of Dentists, 1972, medal of Japan Stomatological Soc., 1977, Stanley S. Bergen award for contbn. to dental edn. Seton Hall U., 1982, Disting. Alumnus award Columbia U. Periodontal Alumni Assn., 1984, Achievement award Fairleigh Dickinson U. Periodontal Alumni Assn., 1984, Hirschfeld Meml. medal and cert. Northeastern Soc. Periodontists, 1987, Disting. Practitioner medallion Nat. Acad. Practice, 1999. Fellow Am. Coll. Dentists, N.Y. Acad. Dentistry; mem. ADA, Am. Assn. Dental Schs., Internat. Assn. Dental Rsch. (past pres. N.J. sect.), Am. Acad. Periodontology, Fedn. Spl. Care Orgns. in Dentistry, Sigma Xi, Omicron Kappa Upsilon. Office: Coler-Goldwater Meml Hosp New York NY 10044

KASLOW, FLORENCE WHITEMAN, psychologist, educator; b. Phila., Jan. 6; d. Irving and Rose (Tarin) Whiteman; m. Solis Kaslow; children: Nadine Joy, Howard Ian. AB in Sociology with distinction, Temple U., 1952; MA, Ohio State U., 1954; PhD, Bryn Mawr Coll., 1969. Lic. psychologist, lic. marriage and family therapist, Fla., diplomate Am. Bd. Clin. Psychology, Am. Bd. Forensic Psychology, Am. Bd. Family Psychology, pres., 1996-98. Pvt. prac., 1964—; dir. Fla. Couples and Family Inst., Palm Beach Gardens, 1982—; adj. prof. med. psychology Duke U. Med. Ctr., Durham, N.C., 1982—; vis. prof. psychology Fla. Inst. Tech., Melbourne, 1985—; disting. vis. prof. Calif. Grad. Sch. Family Psychology, 1989-92; cons. USN Dept. Psychiatry Residency Tng. Programs, San Diego, Portsmouth, Va., Phila., 1976-88, Palm Beach Inst., 1983-90; weekly radio guest Voice of Am., Focus on Families, 1993—. Editor: Voices in Family Psychology, 1990; author: (with L.L. Schwartz) Dynamics of Divorce: A Life Cycle Perspective, 1987, The Military Family in Peace and War, 1993, Handbook of Relational Diagnoses and Dysfunctional Family Patterns, 1996, Painful Partings, 1997; contbr. articles to profl. jours., chpts. to books; mem. editl. bd. Jour. Marital and Family Therapy, 1976—, Marriage and Family Rev., 1977-92, Jour. Sex and Marital Therapy, 1984—, Jour. Clin. Child Psychology, 1986—. Recipient Disting. Psychology Contbn. award Am. Bd. Profl. Psychology, 1994, Outstanding Family Therapy Contbn. award Am. Assn. Marriage and Family Therapy, 1991; Ohio State U. Grad. Sch. fellow, 1954; NIMH trainee, 1969. Mem. APA (divsn. family psychology pres. 1987, sec. 1983-85, com. mem. 1987—, pres. divsn. media psychology 1993), Am. Bd. Forensic Psychology (pres. 1978-80, bd. dirs. 1978-81), Am. Assn. Marital and Family Therapy, Am. Family Therapy Acad., Coalition Family Diagnosis (chmn. 1989-93), Am. Psychology Law Soc., Am. Assn. Sex Educators, Counselors and Therapists, Internat. Family Therapy Assn. (pres. 1987-90), Acad. Family Mediators (bd. dirs. 1982—, treas. 1985-87), Fla. Assn. Profl. Family Mediators (pres. 1984-86).

KASNOWSKI, CHESTER NELSON, artist, educator; b. Perth Amboy, N.J., Jan. 23, 1944. BFA, Dayton Art Inst., 1971; MFA, Tulane U., 1973. Curator New Orleans Mus. Art, 1971-74; tchr. So. Vt. Art Ctr., Manchester, 1981—. One-man show includes Bertha Udang Gallery, N.Y.C., 1984, 85, 87, 91, 93, Carmen Llewellyn Gallery, New Orleans, 1996; group exhbns. at Dartmouth Coll., 1978, Robert Hall Fleming Mus., 1981, Franklin Furnace, 1982, 84, Bertha Udang Gallery, 1983, Hand Gallery, 1985; permanent collections include Bklyn. Mus., Franklin Furnace, Solomon R. Guggenheim Mus., Stedelijk Mus., Tate Gallery, Whitney Mus. of Am. Art. Grantee Nat.

Endowment Arts, 1974, 78. Mem. Coll. Art Assn. Home and Studio: PO Box 1 Weston VT 05161-0001

KASOUF, JOSEPH CHICKERY, lawyer; b. Syracuse, N.Y., July 3, 1954; s. Herbert Chickery and Helen (Hawa) K.; m. Nancy A. Middleton, Sept. 10, 1977; children: Jennifer C., Lauren E., Joseph P. A, Onondaga C.C., 1976; BA, Syracuse U., 1987, MS, 1990, JD, 1990. Police officer, detective Syracuse Polic Dept., 1977-87; asst. gen. counsel The Pyramid Co., 1988-91; mgr. claims counsel Nationwide Mutual Ins. Co., 1991—; adj. prof. Syracuse Univ., 1991—. Contbr. articles to profl. jour. Mem. Civic Action Program, Syracuse, 1991—. Mem. N.Y. State Bar Assn. sect. torts, ins. and compensation law), Def. Assn. N.Y., Onondaga County Bar Assn., Def. Rsch. Inst. Avocations: golf, skiing. Office: Nationwide Mutual Ins Co 110 Elwood Davis Rd North Syracuse NY 13212

KASOWITZ, MARC ELLIOT, lawyer; b. New Haven, June 28, 1952; s. Robert and Felice Beverly (Molaver) K. BA, Yale U., 1974; JD, Cornell U., 1977. Bar: N.Y. 1978, U.S. Dist. Ct. (so. and ea. dists.) N.Y. 1978. Assoc. Rosenman & Colin, N.Y.C., 1977-86, ptnr., 1986-88; ptnr. Mayer, Brown & Platt, N.Y.C., 1988-93, Kasowitz, Benson, Torres & Friedman LLP, N.Y.C., 1993—. Home: 1160 Park Ave Apt 4B New York NY 10128-1212 Office: Kasowitz Benson Torres & Friedman LLP 1301 Ave of Ams New York NY 10019-6022

KASPER, HORST MANFRED, lawyer; b. Dusseldorf, Germany, June 3, 1939; s. Rudolf Ferdinand and Lilli Helene (Krieger) K.; 1 child, Olaf Jan. Diploma in chemistry, U. Bonn, 1963, D. in Natural Scis., 1965; JD, Seton Hall U., 1978. Bar: N.J. 1978, U.S. Patent Office 1977. Mem. staff Lincoln Lab., MIT, Lexington, 1967-69; mem. tech. staff Bell Tel. Labs., Murray Hill, N.J., 1970-76; assoc. Kirschstein, Kirschstein, Ottinger & Frank, N.Y.C., 1976-77; patent atty. Allied Chem. Corp., Morristown, N.J., 1977-79; pvt. practice Warren, N.J., 1980-83; with Kasper and Weick, Warren, 1983-85, Kasper and Laughlin, 1985—. Contbr. numerous articles to profl. jours.; patentee semicondr. field. Mem. ABA, AAAS, N.J. Bar Assn., Internat. Patent and Trademark Assn., Am. Patent Law Assn., N.J. Patent Law Assn., Am. Chem. Soc., Electrochem. Soc., Am. Phys. Soc., N.Y. Acad. Scis. Home and Office: 13 Forest Dr Warren NJ 07059-5832 Office: ul Na Grzgdkach 9, 30421 Cracow Poland

KASPER, LARRY JOHN, accountant, litigation support consultant; b. Springfield, Ohio, Apr. 17, 1947; s. Billy D. and Phyllis M. (McCauley) K.; m. Helen L. Harrison, Dec. 22, 1976. BSBA, Ohio State U., 1969, M in Acctg., 1975; MBA in Ops. Rsch., U. Mich., 1971. CPA, Ohio. Econometrician Dean Witter, N.Y.C., 1971; economist Battelle Meml. Inst., Columbus, Ohio, 1971-75; acct. Touche Ross, Columbus, Ohio, 1975-76; pvt. practice Larry J. Kasper, CPA, Columbus, Ohio, 1976—; treas. Inst. Mgmt. Accts., Columbus, 1981-82. Author: Business Valuations: Advanced Topics, 1997; contbr. articles to profl. jours. Mem. Ohio Child Support Guidelines Adv. Commn., Columbus, 1991-93. Featured in Acctg. Today, 1992. Mem. Ohio Soc. CPAs (litigation support com. 1976—, seminar writer 1990—), Inst. Bus. Appraisers, Nat. Assn. Cert. Valuation Analysts (cert. value analyst). Avocation: weight training. Office: Larry J Kasper CPA 773 Dennison Ave Columbus OH 43215-1364

KASPER, VICTOR, JR., economics educator; b. Rochester, N.Y., Apr. 12, 1947. BS in Agrl. Econs., Rutgers U., 1969, MS in Agrl. Econs., 1972, PhD in Econs., 1983. Instr. dept. agrl. econs. and mktg. Rutgers U., 1980-84; asst. prof. econs. St. John Fisher Coll., Rochester, N.Y., 1985-86; asst. prof. Rochester (N.Y.) Inst. Tech., 1986-90; asst. prof. econs. Elmira (N.Y.) Coll., 1990-97, Buffalo State Coll., 1997-98, Ramapo Coll., Mahwah, N.J., 1998—. Contbr. articles to profl. jours. Mem. AAUP, Am. Econs. Assn., Eastern Econs. Assn., Assn. for Econ. and Social Analysis, Sci. Soc. E-mail: vkaster@ramapo.edu.

KASPERBAUER, MICHAEL JOHN, plant physiology educator, researcher; b. Manning, Iowa, Oct. 8, 1929; s. John Sixtus and Clara Mary (Balk) K.; m. Isabel Maria Giles, June 3, 1962; children: Maria, John, Paul, Sandra. BS, Iowa State Coll., 1954; PhD, Iowa State U., 1961. NSF postdoctoral fellow botany dept. U. Md., College Park, 1961-62; NRC/NAS rsch. assoc, rsch. plant physiologist USDA Pioneering Rsch. Lab., Beltsville, Md., 1962-63; rsch. plant physiologist USDA-Agrl. Rsch. Svc., Lexington, Ky., 1963-83, Florence, S.C., 1983—; mem. grad. faculty U. Ky., Lexington, 1965-83, adj. prof., 1965-83, Clemson (S.C.) U., 1983—. Editor, author: Biotechnology in Fescue Improvement, 1990; assoc. editor Agronomy Jour., 1975-83; contbr. over 200 articles to profl. jours. Bd. dirs. Gardenside Little League Baseball, Lexington, 1975-78; v.p. Turfland Babe Ruth Baseball League, Lexington, 1979-82. 1st lt. U.S. Army, 1954-56. Recipient L.M. Ware Rsch. award Am. Soc. Hort. Sci., 1990. Fellow Am. Soc. Agronomy (Agronomic Rsch. award 1994), Crop Sci. Soc. Am. (Crop Sci. Rsch. award 1990, Fed. Lab. Consortium award 1998); mem. Am. Soc. Plant Physiologists, Am. Soc. Photobiology, Scandinavian Soc. Plant Physiology, Sigma Xi, Phi Delta Kappa, Gamma Sigma Delta, Phi Kappa Phi. Achievements include research in botany, photobiology, forage grasses, tissue and cell culture and molecular biology. Home: 1717 Williamsburg Ct Lexington KY 40504-2010 *Awards and professional recognitions are nice, but family is the only thing that is really important to me.*

KASPERCZYK, JÜRGEN, business executive, government official, educator; b. Pitschen, Germany, Mar. 4, 1941; arrived in Luxembourg, 1980; s. Gerhard Max and Edith Clara (Utta) K.; m. Katrin Schimbke, Apr. 25, 1968 (div.); children: Martin, Kristina; m. Le Ngoc Nguyen, Jan 30, 1997. MSc in Mining Engring., Tech. U., Berlin, 1968, PhD in Chem. Engring., 1970. Rsch. scientist Bergbauforschung GmbH., Essen, Germany, 1968-72; mgr. coking plant Rhodesian Iron and Steel Co., Ltd., Redcliff, Rhodesia, 1972-74; project mgr. Exploration und Bergbau GmbH., Düsseldorf, Germany, 1974-76; tech. mgr. Hansen Neuerburg GmbH., Essen, Germany, 1976-78; mng. dir. CARBOMINA Rohstoffhandel GmbH., Essen, Germany, 1978-82; pres., CEO ENSCH Internat. S.A., Luxembourg, 1980-90, ENSCH Internatls. A., Luxembourg, 1990-96; dir. Entec Computer Taiwan Ltd., Taipei, 1985—; hon. prof. Institut des Hautes Etudes Economiques et Sociales, Brussels; pres. Entex Intl. S.A., Luxembourg, 1996—; vice chmn. S.P. Otema, Moscow, 1988-92, Implus Internat., Vinnitsa, Ukraine, 1989—; pres. Entex Ltd., Sofia, Bulgaria, 1994—. Contbr. papers on coal and cokemaking rsch. to tech. mags., internat. confs. Dep. Internat. Parliament for Safety and Peace, 1993—. Mem. Inst. Mining and Metallurgy, Verein Deutscher Eisenhüttenleute, Deutsche Wissenschaftliche Gesellschaft für Erdöl, Erdgas and Kohle, Gesellschaft Deutscher Metallhütten-und Bergleute, Am. Iron and Steel Soc., Golf Grand-Ducal Club, Cercle Munster Club, Old Tablers Club (Essen), Order of the Knight Templars of Jerusalem (Great Prior). Office: Entex Internat SA, 66 Bd Napoleon 1er, L-2210 Luxembourg Luxembourg

KASPIN, JEFFREY MARC, floor covering professional; b. Bklyn., May 30, 1948; s. Seymour and Frances (Babad) K.; m. Susan Jane Engel, Apr. 17, 1977; children: Jodi-Anne, Stacey, Melanie. BA, Am. U., 1970. Cert. tchr., Va.; cert. archtl. carpet rep.; cert. tech. carpet rep. Tchr. Fairfax (Va.) Sch. System, 1970-72; exec. v.p. sales and mktg. Atlantic Distbrs., S.I., 1972-88; sales and ter. mgr. Norman D. Lifton Co., Mt. Vernon, N.Y., 1988-89; mgr. customer svc. Norman D. Lifton Co., Yonkers, N.Y., 1990-92, gen. adminstrv. mgr., 1992-93; gen. mgr. Western Carpet Distbrs., Bklyn., 1989-90; sales and ter. mgr. Columbus (Ga.) Carpet Mills, 1990; gen. mgr. Norman D. Lifton Co., Yonkers, N.Y., 1992—; territory mgr. Aladdin Carpet Mills divsn. Mohawk Industries, 1997—; floor convering cons. to architects, contractors, builders, retailers, publs.; floor convering profl. speaker, 1984-90. Vol. Spl. Olympics, Washington, 1968-69; bd. dirs. Country Swim Club, East Brunswick, N.J., 1982—; fundraising chmn. Am. Cancer Soc., Middlesex County, N.J., 1984-96, 93-94; trustee Temple B'nai Shalom, East Brunswick, 1986-89; v.p. U.S. Jaycees, 1978-85. Mem. L.I. Carpet Club, Nat. Assn. Floor Covering Distbrs., N.J. Carpet Club. Avocations: running, swimming, reading, camping, swim coaching.

KASPIN, SUSAN JANE, child care specialist; b. Bklyn., May 28, 1950; d. Stanley Engel and Thelma Rosenblum; m. Jeffrey Marc Kaspin, Apr. 17, 1977; children: Jodi-Anne, Stacey, Melanie. BA, Bklyn. Coll., 1972. Cert. tchr. N.J. Adminstrv. asst. Stone & Webster Mgmt. Cons., N.Y.C., 1972-74, Am. Electric Power Co. (formerly in N.Y.C.), Columbus, Ohio, 1974-78; program dir. Office for Youth/Sch. Age Child Care Twp. of E. Brunswick, N.J., 1989—; staff liaison E. Brunswick Alliance for the Prevention of Alcoholism and Drug Abuse, 1990—. Mem. twp. ad-hoc com., N.J. tpk. expansion, East Brunswick, 1985-90; mem. adv. bd. Local Law Enforcement Block Grant Program. Mem. N.J. Sch. Age Child Care Coalition, Middlesex County Sch. Age Child Care Coalition, Assn. for Children of N.J. (John Alexander Outstanding Project award 1992), N.J. Recreation and Parks Assn., Middlesex County Mcpl. Alliance Network.

KASPRICK, LYLE CLINTON, volunteer, financial executive; b. Angus, Minn., Aug. 23, 1932; s. Max Peter and Mary (Taus) K.; m. Harriet Susan Lydick, July 14, 1953; children: Susan, Michael, John; m. Kathleen M. Westby, June 4, 1977; 1 stepchild, Kristin. BSBA magna cum laude, U. N.D., 1959. CPA, Minn., N.D. Tax mgr. Arthur Andersen & Co., Mpls., 1959-69; v.p. Search Investments Corp., Mpls., 1969-77; fin. v.p., treas. Tropicana Hotel and country club, Las Vegas, 1970-72; COO Key Pharms. Inc., Miami, Fla., 1972-76; v.p. MEI Corp., Mpls., 1977-86, MEI Diversified Inc., Mpls., 1986-88; bd. dirs. N.Am. Vaccine Inc., Montreal, Que., Can. and Columbia, Md., chmn. bd. 1991-95; speaker in field of finance. Del. Rep. Com., 1964, 66, 68, 70; bd. dirs. U. N.D. Found., 1993—. With USN, 1951-55. Mem. AICPA, Minn. Soc. CPAs, Am. Legion, U. N.D. alumni Assn. (bd. dirs. 1993—), U. N.D. Nat. Alumni Leadership Coun., Beta Gamma Sigma. Republican. Roman Catholic. Home: 1067 Linden Ln Orono MN 55364-9754 Office: N Am Vaccine Inc 10150 Old Columbia Rd Columbia MD 21046

KASPROW, BARBARA ANNE, biomedical scientist, writer; b. Hartford, Conn., Apr. 23, 1936; d. Stephen G. and Anna M. Kasprow. AB cum laude, Albertus Magnus Coll., 1958; postgrad., Laval U., 1958, Yale U., 1958-61; PhD, Loyola U., Chgo., 1969. Staff microbiology dept. Conn. State Dept. Health, 1957; lab. asst. dept. microbiology Yale U., New Haven, 1958-59; tng. scholar USPHS, 1959-60; asst. rsch. and editl. dept. anatomy Yale U., New Haven, 1961; rsch. assoc. N.Y. Med. Coll., 1961-62; from rsch. assoc. to sr. rsch. and adminstrv. assoc., asst. to dir. grad. med. edn., asst. dir. adminstrn. grad. rsch. endocrinology Inst. for Study Human Reprodn. St. Ann Ob-Gyn. Hosp., Cleve., 1962-67; sr. rsch. assoc. dept. anatomy Stritch Sch. Medicine, Chgo., Hines, Ill., 1967-69; asst. prof. anatomy Loyola U., Chgo., 1969-75; asst. to v.p. University Rsch. Sys., 1975-79, v.p. med. topics, 1979—; asst. to pres. Internat. Basic and Biol.-Biomed. Curricula, Lombard, Ill., 1979—; lectr. in field; invited U.S. del. on reprodn. to Vatican, 1964; round table leader Brazil-Israel Congress on Fertility and Sterility, Brazil Soc. Human Reprodn., São Paulo, 1972. Editl. asst. vol. VIII/3 Handbuch der Histochemie, Gustav Fischer Verlag, 1963; prodn. aide ednl. med. film The Soft Anvil, 1965-66; co-editor: Biology of Reproduction, Basic and Clinical Studies, 1973; contbr. articles to profl. jours. Recipient Certificate of Outstanding Achievement and Scholarship award Am. Assn. German Tchrs. and New Britain German Assn., 1954; named Honorary Citizen São Paulo, 1972. Mem. AAAS (life), Am. Assn. Anatomists, Am. Soc. Zoologists, The Soc. Integrative and Comparative Biology, Pan Am. Assn. Anatomy (co-organizer symposium on reproduction New Orleans 1972), Midwest Anatomists Assn. (program officer ann. meeting Chgo. 1974), Sigma Xi (life). Roman Catholic. Achievements include biological elucidation of growth horizons in uterine development, growth, and maturity; perfection of a hormonal model-system in highly controlled (surgerized) animals to ascertain quantitative relationships of purified estradiol-17beta and progesterone required for promotion of and duplication of these uterine growth horizons; development of experimental paradigms for the biomorphological elucidation of hormonally stimulated growth responses in endocrine target organs, and cyto- and histochemical elucidation of growth stimulants. Home: 243 E View St PO Box 385 Lombard IL 60148-0385 Office: 607 E Wilson Ave Lombard IL 60148-4062

KASPRZAK, LUCIAN ALEXANDER, physicist, researcher, technical manager; b. Scranton, Pa., July 22, 1943; s. Alexander Lucian and Helen Frances (Skubic) K.; m. Carole Anne Nowakowski, July 22, 1967; children: Brian, Dawn. BS in Physics, Stevens Inst. Tech., 1965, PhD in Materials, 1972; MS in Physics, Syracuse U., 1970. Engr. failure analysis IBM East Fishkill, Hopewell Junction, N.Y., 1965-69, engr. reliability Large Scale Integration, 1972-77, mgr. Very Large Scale Integration devel., 1977-81; mgr. vendor memory IBM Gen. Tech. Div. Assurance, Poughkeepsie, N.Y., 1981-82; tech. asst. to corp. v.p. IBM Corp. Hdqrs., White Plains, N.Y., 1982-83, mgr. memory tech., Gen. Tech. Div., 1983-84; program mgr., tech. support IBM Data Systems Div. Assurance, Poughkeepsie, 1984-85; program mgr. tech. profl. relations IBM Corp. Hdqrs., Thornwood, N.Y., 1985-92; assoc. prof. physics and engrng. sci. Franciscan U. Steubenville, Ohio, 1992-96; reliability mgr. direct radiography Sterling Diagnostic Imaging, Newark, Del., 1996-97, dir. reliability direct radiography, 1997—; bd. dirs. Internat. Reliability Physics Symposium, 1985—, chmn. 1986-87. Contbr. articles to profl. jours.; co-discoverer hot electron effect in Metal Oxide Semiconductor Field Effect Transistor; patentee in field. Mem. Environ. Bd., Wappingers Falls, N.Y., 1973; coach East Fishkill Youth Soccer League, 1974-82; coun. mem. St. Columba Parish, Hopewell Junction, 1985-91. Recipient Benefactors award Franciscan U. of Steubenville, 1989; IBM resident fellow, Yorktown and Hoboken, N.J., 1969-72. Fellow IEEE; mem. Electron Devices Soc. of IEEE (adminstrv. com. 1986—, treas. 1988—, adv. bd. Circuits and Devices mag. 1987-98, treas. trans. of semiconductor mfg. 1992—, chmn. device reliability com. 1983-97, treas. Device Rsch. Conf. 1989-92, chmn. device reliability physics com. 1997—), Am. Phys. Soc. Roman Catholic. Avocations: music, astronomy, philosophy, theology, art. Office: PO Box 6020 Newark DE 19714-6020

KASPUTYS, JOSEPH EDWARD, corporate executive, economist; b. Jamaica, N.Y., Aug. 12, 1936; s. Joseph John and Henrietta Viola (Derenthall) K.; m. Marilyn Patricia Kennedy, Oct. 29, 1953; children: Clare Victoria, Patricia Jeanne, Jacqueline Ann, Veronica Joy. BA magna cum laude, Bklyn. Coll., 1959; MBA with high distinction, Harvard U., 1967, DBA, 1972. U.S. Dept. Def., Washington, 1967-70; Asst. adminstr. U.S. Maritime Adminstrn., Washington, 1972-75; asst. sec. U.S. Dept. Commerce, Washington, 1975-77; exec. v.p., COO Data Resources, Inc., Lexington, Mass., 1977-81, pres., CEO, 1981-84; exec. v.p. McGraw-Hill, Inc., N.Y.C., 1984-87; pres., COO Primark Corp. Inc., Waltham, Mass., 1987-88; chmn., CEO Primark Corp. Inc., Waltham, 1988—; lectr. Am. U., Washington, 1967-68, Bentley Coll., Boston, 1971-72; assoc. prof., lectr. George Washington U., Washington, 1967-77; bd. dirs. Lifeline Systems, Inc., Boston, New Era of Networks, Denver. Chmn. Hitachi Found., Washington, Coun. for Excellence in Govt., Washington; mem. Com. for Econ. Devel., Washington. Comdr. USN, 1956-76. Decorated Legion of Merit; Warren G. Harding Aerospace fellow, 1971. mem. Phi Beta Kappa. Republican. Roman Catholic. Clubs: Harvard Bus. Sch. (Boston); Capitol Hill (Washington). Home: 398 Simon Willard Rd Concord MA 01742-1624 Office: Primark Corp Ste 4100 1000 Winter St Waltham MA 02451-1241

KASS, BENNY LEE, lawyer; b. Chgo., Aug. 20, 1936; s. Herman and Ethel (Lome) K.; m. Salme Lundstrom, Aug. 30, 1963; children: Gale, Brian. BS, Northwestern U., 1957; LLB, U. Mich., 1960; LLM, George Washington U., 1967. Bar: D.C. 1960. Atty. Maritime Adminstrn., 1960-61; counsel House Info. Subcom., 1962-65; asst. counsel Senate Adminstrv. Practice Subcom., Washington, 1965-69; pvt. practice law Washington, 1969—; mem. Kass & Skalet, P.L.L.C., 1995—; prof. communication law Am. U.; pub. mem. Nat. Advt. Rev. Bd., 1971-74; life mem. Conf. on Uniform State Laws. Columnist Washington Post, L.A. Times; contbr. articles to profl. jours. Chmn. consumer affairs subcom. Mayors Econ. Devel. Com., 1968-70; chmn. Ad Hoc Com. on Consumer Protection, 1965—. With USAF, 1961-62. Am. Polit. Sci. Assn. Congl. fellow, 1966. Mem. ABA, FBA, Am. Polit. Sci. Assn., Sigma Delta Chi. Office: Kass & Skalet PLLC 1050 17th St NW Ste 1100 Washington DC 20036-5596

KASS, EMILY, art museum administrator. Director Tampa (Fla.) Mus. of Art. Office: Tampa Mus Art 600 N Ashley Dr Tampa FL 33602-4305*

KASS, EVAN J., pediatric urologist; b. N.Y.C., Oct. 26, 1943; s. Sol Kass and Florence Gilbert.; children: Jordan, Bryce, Sloan. BS, CCNY, 1964; MD, SUNY, Bklyn., 1968. Diplomate Am. Bd. Urology. Intern Montefiore/Einstein, N.Y., 1968-69, resident in surgery, 1969-70; resident in surgery U. Mich., 1972-73, resident in urology, 1973-76; fellow in pediatric urology Hosp. For Sick Children, Toronto, Can., 1978; asst. prof. U. Mich., Ann Arbor, 1978-80; assoc. prof. Children's Hosp., Washington, 1980-85; chief pediat. urology Beaumont Hosp., Royal Oak, Mich., 1985—; assoc. prof. urology Wayne State U., Detroit, Can., 1978; asst. prof. U. Mich., Ann Arbor, 1978-80; assoc. prof. Children's Hosp., Washington, 1980-85; chief pediat. urology Beaumont Hosp., Royal Oak, Mich., 1985—; assoc. prof. urology Wayne State U., Detroit; past vis. prof., lectr. U.S. and internationally. Contbr. articles to sci. and profl. jours. Med. volulnteer Saving the Children, Lithuania. Maj. USAF, 1970-72. Fellow ACS, Am. Acad. Pediats. (chmn. urology sect. 1998, exec. com. 1985-89, 93-99, sec.-treas. 1993-96), Soc. Pediat. Urology, European Pediat. Urolog. Soc.; mem. Am. Urolog. Assn. (bd. dirs. north ctrl. sect. 1992-95), Mich. Urol. Assn. (sec.-treas. 1986-89, pres. 1989-92). E-mail ekass@beaumont.edu. Office: Birmingham Urolog Assocs 1915 E 14 Mile Rd Birmingham MI 48009

KASS, HOWARD R., information systems consultant; b. Bklyn.; m. Ilana; children: Stephanie, Stuart. BA, NYU. Mgr. sys. & programs Sterling Drug, Montvale, N.J., 1974-77; dir. MIS Gen. Mills Crystal Brands Women's Apparel Divsn., Aston, Pa., 1978-86; gen. mgr. MIS Diamond-Bathurst Corp., Malvern, Pa., 1986-87; v.p. MIS SMH Inc., Lancaster, Pa., 1987-96; chief info. officer Conestoga Wood Specialty Corp., East Earl, Pa., 1996—. Office: Conestoga Wood Specialty Corp PO Box 158 East Earl PA 17519-0158

KASS, JEROME ALLAN, writer; b. Chgo., Apr. 21, 1937; s. Sidney J. and Celia (Gorman) K.; children from previous marriage: Julie, Adam; m. Delia Ephron, May 21, 1982. BA, NYU, 1958, MA, 1959. Playwright: Monopoly, 1965, Saturday Night, 1968, (mus.) Ballroom, 1978 (Tony nomination), (TV) A Brand New Life, 1973, Queen of the Stardust Ballroom, 1975 (Writers Guild Am. award, Emmy nomination), My Old Man, 1979, The Fighter, 1982, Scorned and Swindled, 1984, Crossing to Freedom (aka Pied Piper), 1989, Last Wish, 1991, The Only Way Out, 1993, Secrets, 1995; screenwriter: The Black Stallion Returns, 1981, (miniseries) Evergreen, 1985; author: Four Short Plays by Jerome Kass, 1966, Saturday Night, 1969; adapted to concert form Finian's Rainbow, L.A., 1997, Pajama Game, L.A., 1998; musical version Queen of the Stardust Ballroom, Chgo., 1998. Mem. Dramatists Guild, Writers Guild Am., Phi Beta Kappa.

KASS, LAWRENCE, hematologist, oncologist, hematopathologist; b. Toledo, Ohio, Sept. 30, 1938. AB magna cum laude, U. Mich., 1960; MD with hons., U. Chgo., 1964, MS Anatomy, 1964. Diplomate Nat. Bd. Med. Examiners, Am. Bd. Internal Medicine/Internal Medicine and Hematology, Med. Oncology, Am. Bd. Pathology/Hematology. Intern Peter Bent Brigham Hosp., Boston, 1964-65, asst. resident internal medicine, 1965-66; sr. asst. resident internal medicine U. Hosps. of Cleve., 1966-68; Elliott Hoyt fellow in hematology Univ. Hosps. of Cleve., 1967-68; various to rsch. assoc. U. Chgo., 1968-70; asst. prof. internal medicine U. Mich. Med. Sch., Ann Arbor, 1970-73, assoc. prof. internal medicine, 1973-78; prof. path., medicine Case Western Res. U. Sch. Medicine, Cleve., 1978—; head hematopathology MetroHealth Med. Ctr., Cleve., 1978—; cons. in medicine, VA Hosp., Ann Arbor; editorial cons. Williams and Wilkins Pubs., Balt., 1974—, Archives of Pathology and Lab. Medicine Blood, The Jour. of Hematology, The Jour. of Histochemistry and Cytochemistry, Western Jour. of Medicine, Am. Jour. of Hematology, Biotechnic & Histochemistry, 1975—, Rsch. Career Selection Rev. Com., VA, Washington, 1976—; active numerous coms. in field. Contbr. articles to profl. jours. Maj. med corps. U.S. Army, 1968-70. Recipient Internat. Giovanni DiGuglielmo prize, Giovanni DiGuglielmo Found., Accademia Nazionale Die Lincei, Rome, 1976, Diamond Cover award Nat. Soc. Histotechnologists and Jour. of Histotechnology, 1988, C.V. Mosby award, 1964, Merck award 1964. Fellow Am. Coll. Phys., Coll. Am. Pathologists; mem. AAAS, Am. Soc. Hematology, Am. Fedn. Clin. Rsch., Am. Soc. Clin. Oncology, Soc. Exptl. Biology and Medicine, Cen. Soc. Clin. Rsch., Histochem. Soc., Biol. Stain Commn., Am. Soc. Clin. Path., Phi Eta Sigma, Phi Beta Kappa, Alpha Omega Alpha. Office: Metro Health Med Ctr 2500 Metro Health Dr Cleveland OH 44109-1957

KASS, LEON RICHARD, educator; b. Chgo., Feb. 12, 1939; s. Samuel and Anna (Shoichet) K.; m. Amy Judith Apfel, June 22, 1961; children—Sarah, Miriam. B.S., U. Chgo., 1958, M.D., 1962; Ph.D. in Biochemistry, Harvard U., 1967. Intern Beth Israel Hosp., Boston, 1962-63; staff assoc. Lab. Molecular Biology, Nat. Inst. Arthritis and Metabolic Diseases, NIH, Bethesda, Md., 1967-69; staff fellow Lab. Molecular Biology, Nat. Inst. Arthritis and Metabolic Diseases, NIH, 1969-70, sr. staff fellow, 1970; exec. sec. com. on life scis. and social policy NRC-NAS, Washington, 1970-72; tutor St. John's Coll., Annapolis, Md., 1972-76; Joseph P. Kennedy Sr. research prof. in bioethics Kennedy Inst., Georgetown U., 1974-76; Henry R. Luce prof. liberal arts of human biology in coll. U. Chgo., 1976-84, prof. com. on social thought, 1984-90, Addie Clark Harding prof. in coll. and com. on social thought, 1990—; founding fellow, bd. dirs. Hastings Ctr., 1969-96; bd. govs. U.S.-Israel Binat. Sci. Found., 1982-88; mem. coun. Nat. Humanities Coun., 1984-91, vice chmn. 1987-89. Author: Toward a More Natural Science: Biology and Human Affairs, 1985, The Hungry Soul: Eating and the Perfecting of Our Nature, 1994, (James Q. Wilson) The Ethics of Human Cloning, 1998; contbr. articles to profl. jours. Served with USPHS, 1967-69. NIH postdoctoral fellow, 1963-67, John Simon Guggenheim Meml. Found. fellow, 1972-73, Nat. Humanities Ctr. fellow, 1984-85, W.H. Brady, Jr. Disting. fellow Am. Enterprise Inst., 1991-92, 98-99; NEH grantee, 1973-74. Mem. Phi Beta Kappa, Alpha Omega Alpha. Jewish. Office: 1116 E 59th St Chicago IL 60637-1578

KASSAKIAN, JOHN GABRIEL, research electrical engineer, engineering director; b. Mar. 27, 1943; m. Wilma Riemenschneider, 1968; 2 children. SB, MIT, 1965, SM, 1967, EE, 1967, ScD in Electrical Engring., 1973. Tech. rep. to Univac naval data sys. USN, 1969-71; from asst. prof. to assoc. prof. electrical engring. MIT, 1973-84, dir. electrical power sys. engring. lab., 1979-83, prof. electrical engring., 1984—, dir. electromagnetic & electronic sys. lab., 1991—; sr. staff scientist Gould Labs., Gould, Inc., 1975; bd. dirs. Ault, Inc., Sheldahl, Inc., ISO New Eng. Inc. Fellow IEEE (Centennial medal, 1984); mem. Nat. Acad. Eng., European Power Electronics Assn., Sigma Xi, Tau Beta Pi, Eta Kappa Nu. Research simulation, analysis, synthesis of electronic energy conversion systems; power semiconductor devices; manufacturing technologies for electronic apparatus, automotive electrical and electronic systems. Office: Lab for Electromagnetic & Electronic Sys Bldg 10-172 77 Massachusetts Ave Cambridge MA 02139-4301*

KASSAPOGLOU, CHRISTOS, aeronautical engineer; b. Athens, Nov. 27, 1959; came to U.S., 1978; s. George and Dia (Alexis) K. BS, MIT, 1982, MS in Aeros. and Astronautics, MSME, 1984. Stress analyst Beech Aircraft Corp., Wichita, Kans., 1984-87; sr. structures researcher Sikorsky Aircraft, Stratford, Conn., 1987—; seminar speaker on cert. of civil composite aircraft in Milan (Italy), Toronto, and Ottawa (Can.); seminar spkr. applicatiohs of compsites Aristotle U. of Thessaloniki, Greece, Advance Tech. Svcs. Internat., Wichita, 1987—. Recipient Salisbury Webb award MIT, 1982, R. DuPont fellow, 1983. Mem. AIAA, Am. Helicopter Soc., Soc. for Advancement of Material and Process Engring., Phi Beta Kappa, Tau Beta Pi, Sigma Gamma Tau. Avocations: snow skiing, tennis. Office: Sikorsky Aircraft MS S314A2 6900 Main St Stratford CT 06614-1385

KASSEBAUM, NANCY See BAKER, NANCY KASSEBAUM

KASSEL, CATHERINE M., community and maternal-women's health nurse; b. Bklyn., Dec. 18, 1953; d. Christopher Frank and Ana Rosa (Sousa) Pannone; m. David L. Kassel, Dec. 27, 1979. Diploma in nursing, Kings County Hosp., Bklyn., 1974; BA in Cmty. Health, CUNY, 1979; BSN, Columbia U., 1989. RN, N.Y. V.p. Kassel Mgmt. Co., N.Y.C., 1985—. Documentary writer Radio Sta. WBAI. Bd. dirs., co-chair legis. com. N.Y. Counties of RNs, Dist. 13, trustee, treas. polit. action com.; past bd. dirs. Nat. Abortion Rights Action League; bd. dirs., treas., chmn. fundraising, nominating com. Global Kids Inc.; pres. Not-for-Profit Issues, N.Y.C. Mem. ANA (polit. action com.), ANA Found. (founding mem.), N.Y. State Nurses Assn., PAC. Home: 61 W 62nd St Apt 21L New York NY 10023-7022

KASSEL, VIRGINIA WELTMER, television producer, writer; b. Omaha; d. Tyler and Inez (Willard) Weltmer. B.A., Bryn Mawr Coll. Producer Sta. WGBH-TV, Boston; producer NET, N.Y.C.; coordinator nat. programs NET; mgr. spl. projects, exec. prodr. humanities programs WNET, N.Y.C.;

exec. producer humanities programs; sr. producer CBS Cable, N.Y.C., 1981-83; dir. devel. and prodn. East Coast Primetime Entertainment, Inc., 1983-87; v.p. East Coast Primetime Entertainment, Inc., 1987-89; assoc. dir. performance programs, prodn. exec. Great Performances Sta. WNET-TV, N.Y.C., 1989-91; producer, dir., writer Potter Prodns., 1991-92; dir. devel. Internat. Cultural Programming, 1992-94. Creator, prodr.: The Adams Chronicles, Sta. WNET, N.Y.C.; prodr.: The Soong Connection, 1995; contbr. articles to profl. publs. Recipient George Foster Peabody award, 1977, 2 Ohio State awards, 1977, Spl. Achievement award Nat. Assn. Ednl. Broadcasters, 1977, Triangle award, 1986, NEH, Mellon Found. grants. Mem. NATAS (4 Emmy awards), Writers Guild Am. East, Am. Acad. TV Arts and Scis., Brit. Acad. Film and TV Arts, N.Y. and London Women in Film, Univ. Women's Univ. Club London, Princeton Club N.Y.C., N.Y. Women in TV and Film, Women's City Club N.Y. (bd. dirs.). Home: 4 E 89th St New York NY 10128-0636

KASSELL, NEAL FREDERIC, neurosurgery educator; b. Phila., Mar. 17, 1946; s. Martin Buddy and Evelyn Abigail (Block) K.; m. Nancy Coffin, Dec. 14, 1967 (div.); children: Natasha Lynn, Lauren Tamara, Nicole Tristan; m. Denise Etheridge, Aug. 30, 1986 (div. 1987); m. Lynn Haire, Mar. 12, 1994. MD, U. Pa., 1972. Diplomate Am. Bd. Neurol. Surgery. Intern Pa. Hosp., Phila., 1972-73, resident in neurology, 1973-74, resident in neurosurgery, 1974-75; resident in neurosurgery U. Western Ont., London, 1975-77; asst. prof. neurosurgery U. Iowa, Iowa City, 1977-81, assoc. prof. neurosurgery, 1981-82, prof. neurosurgery, 1982-84; prof. and vice chmn. neurosurgery U. Va. Sch. Medicine, Charlottesville, 1984-97, prof., co-chmn. neurosurgery, 1997—; pres. Va. Neurol. Inst., 1993—; mem. staff U. Va. Hosp., Charlottesville; chmn. bd., founder Multimedia Med. Sys., Inc., 1995—; bd. dirs. CapCure, Va. Nat. Bank, INC Rsch; dir. Coop. Aneurysm Study, 1977—, also other various NIH-Nat. Inst. Neurol. Disorders and Stroke study sects., 1984—. Reviewer Neurosurgery, Jour. Cerebral Blood Flow and Metabolism, 1977—; mem. editl. bd. Stroke, Surg. Neurology; contbr. over 450 papers to profl. jours. Recipient numerous rsch. grants and contracts; recipient McKenzie Meml. award, 1977, Gross award. Republican. Avocations: riding, squash, classical music, hiking. E-mail: nfk8g@virginia.edu. Home: Wingate 2154 Garth Rd Charlottesvle VA 22901-5412 Office: U Va Hosps Dept Neurosurgery Box 212 Charlottesville VA 22908-0212

KASSELL, PAULA SALLY, editor, publisher; b. N.Y.C., Dec. 5, 1917; d. Daniel Herman and Bertha Blanche (Jaret) K.; m. Gerson Gustav Friedman, Aug. 16, 1941 (dec.); children: Daniel, Claire Florence Friedman. BA, Barnard Coll., 1939. Tech. editor Bell Labs., Whippany, N.J., 1955-65; methods analyst Bell Labs., Murray Hill, N.J., 1965-70; founder, editor, pub. New Directions for Women, Dover, N.J., 1971-77; assoc. editor New Directions for Women, Englewood, N.J., 1977-87; sr. editor New Directions for Women, Englewood, 1987-93; index editor New Directions for Women, Dover, 1993-98; v.p., UN rep. Women's Inst. for Freedom of Press, Washington, 1990—; convenor, mem. media task force Com. on Status of Women, UN, 1990-98. *Contrubutor chapters to books: "Planning an International Communications System for Women" in Communications at the Crossroads: The Gender Gap Connection (Ablex Publishing Corporation, 1989). "The Birth, Success, Death and Lasting Influence of a Feminist Periodical: New Directions for Women (1972-1993-?)" in Women Transforming Communications: Global Intersections (Sage Publications, 1996). "New Directions for Women" in Women's Periodicals in the United States: Social and Political Issues (Greenwood Press, 1996).* Co-convenor Lakeland chpt. NOW, Dover, 1970; v.p. Dover (N.J.) Child Care Ctr., 1979-91; bd. dirs. Nat. Woman's Party, Washington, 1991-98; mem. media com. Forum 95, UN, N.Y.C., 1994-95; mem. adv. bd. Vet. Feminists Am., Lafayette, La., 1995—; mem. TV task force Morris County NOW, Morristown, N.J., 1995—; trustee Women's Media Initiative, 1997. Recipient First Feminist Action award NOW N.J., 1985, Women Making Herstory award, 1995, Elizabeth Cady Stanton award Women's Rights Info. Ctr., 1993, Woman of Achievement award Douglass Coll., 1994, Medal of Honor, Vet. Feminists Am., 1998. Mem. Am. Journalism Historians Assn., Internat. Women's Media Found., Journalism & Women Symposium. Avocations: attending opera, concerts, ballet performances, visiting museums, travelling. Home: 25 W Fairview Ave Dover NJ 07801-3417

KASSER, JOHN, athletic director; b. 1937; m. Carol Kasser; children: Karen, Sharon. BS, Pepperdine U. Asst. athletic dir. U. Calif., Irvine, 1977-81; asst. athletic dir. U. Houston, 1981-82, athletic dir., 1982-84; athletic dir. Long Beach (Calif.) State U., 1984-87; athletic dir. U. Calif., Santa Barbara, 1989-91, Berkeley, 1992—; assoc. exec. dir. Coll. Football Assn., 1987-89; mem. nat. com. NCAA Women's Volleyball, Women's Basketball, Men's Water Polo, NCAA Coun.; v.p. Pacific 10 Conf. Office: U Calif 210 Memorial Stadium Berkeley CA 94720-4426*

KASSER, JOSEPH E., educational administrator; b. London, May 1, 1946; came to U.S., 1970; s. Moses Jacob and Paula Kasser; m. Fay Kasser, Dec. 20, 1970; children: Susan, Elisabeth, Michael. MS in Telecomm Ops, George Washington U., 1978, DSc in Engring. Mgmt., 1997. Cert. mgr.; chartered engr., U.K., Europe. Mem. tech. staff Comsat Labs., Clarksburg, Md., 1974-81; mgr. control and electronics dept. LuZ Industries Inc., Jerusalem, 1981-85; v.p. engring. Israel Strategic Computers Ltd., Jerusalem, 1985-87; engring. specialist Loral AeroSys, Seabrook, Md., 1988-94; v.p. engring., owner Anticipatory Testing Corp., Silver Spring, Md., 1994—; assoc. dir. info. and telecomm. studies U. Md. Univ. Coll., College Park, 1997—. Author: Microcomputers in Amateur Radio, 1981, Software for Amateur Radio, 1984, Basic Packet Radio, 1992, Applying Total Quality Management to Systems Engineering, 1995; contbr. articles to profl. jours. Recipient Silver Snoopy award NASA, 1991. Mem. Inst. Elec. Engrs., Inst. Cert. Profl. Mgrs. Avocation: amateur radio. Home: PO Box 3419 Silver Spring MD 20918-3419 Office: U Md U Coll Grad Sch Univ Blvd at Adelphi Rd College Park MD 20742-1614

KASSEWITZ, RUTH EILEEN BLOWER, retired hospital executive; b. Columbus, Ohio, May 15, 1928; d. E. Wallett and Helen (Daub) Blower; m. Jack Kassewitz, July 28, 1962 (dec.); 1 stepchild, Jack. BS in Journalism-Mgmt., Ohio State U., 1951. Copywriter Ohio Fuel Gas Co., Columbus, 1951-55, Merritt Owens Advtsg. Agy., Kansas City, 1955-56; acct. exec. Grant Advtsg., Inc., Miami, 1956-59; acct. supr. Venn/Cole & Assocs., Miami, 1959-67; dir. comms. Ferendino/Grafton/Candela/Spillis Archs. & Engrs., Miami, 1967-69, Dade County dept. Housing and Urban Devel., Miami, 1969-72, Met. Dade Conty Govt., 1972-78; adminstr. pub. rels. U. Miami/Jackson Meml. Med. Ctr., 1978-90, ret., 1990. Bd. dirs. Girl Scouts USA Tropical Fla., 1974-76, 81-83, Lung Assn. Dade-Monroe Counties, 1976-87, Met. YMCA, 1996—; mem. exec. com. Miami-Dade C. C. Found., 1984—; pres. Mental Health Assn. Dade County, 1982; mem. City of Miami Ecol. and Beautification Com. (now TREEmendous Miami, Inc.), 1978—, first vice-chmn., 1996-98; bd. govs. Barry U., Miami, 1981-83; trustee Nat. Humanities Faculty, 1981-83; trustee emeritus United Protestant Appeal, 1992-99; treas., past chmn. Health, Edn., Promotion Coun., Inc.; mem. adv. bd. Miami's For Me, 1987-88; mem. Coral Gables Cable TV Bd., 1983-86; ch. moderator Plymouth Congl. Ch., 1986-88, trustee, 1995-99; mem. cmty. adv. bd. Jr. League Gtr. Miami, Inc., 1989-92; founding mem. Nat. Honor Roll Women in Pub. Rels, No. Ill. U., 1993. Recipient Disting. Svc. award Plymouth Congl. Ch., Miami, 1979; Ann Stover award, 1983; Golden Image award Fla. Pub. Rels. Assn., 1987; named Woman of Yr. Plymouth Congl. Ch., U. Miami Med. Sch., 1991, Humanitarian of Yr. YMCA of Gtr. Miami, 1998. Fellow Pub. Rels. Soc. Am. (pres. South Fla. chpt. 1969-70, nat. chmn. govt. sect. 1973-74, nat. dir. 1974-76; cont. edn. coun. 1981-83; Silver anvil award 1973, del Assembly 1970-73, 86-89, Paul M. Lund Pub. Svc. award 1993, Miami chpt. Lifetime Achievement award 1995); mem. Women in Comms. (pres. Gtr. Miami chpt. 1962-63; Clarion awards 1973, 75, Cmty. Headliner 1985), Miami Internat. Press Club (bd. dirs. 1986-87, treas. 1992), Rotary Club of Miami (bd. dirs. 1988-97, pres. 1993-94, Disting. Rotarian of Yr. 1996), Delta Delta Delta (pres. Miami alumnae chpt. 1997-99). Home: 1136 Aduana Ave Miami FL 33146-3206

KASSEY, JACQUELYN MARIE BONAFONTE, pediatrics nurse; b. Middletown, Conn., May 11, 1960; d. Benjamin John Bonafonte and Carol Ann (Amato) Woodmancy; m. Mark George Kassey, Sept. 11, 1986. Diploma, Ona M. Wilcox Sch. Nursing, 1981; AA, Middlesex Community Coll., 1984; BSN, St. Joseph's Coll., West Hartford, Conn., 1996; postgrad., U. Hartford, 1997—. RN, Conn.; cert. med.-surg. nurse, pediatric nurse, pediatric advanced life support. Staff nurse med./surg. unit Middlesex Meml. Hosp., Middletown, 1981-82, 83-84; staff nurse SICU Hartford (Conn.) Hosp., 1982-83, Newington (Conn.) VA Med. Ctr., 1984-86; staff nurse respiratory care New Britain (Conn.) Meml. Hosp. (now Hosp. for Special Care), 1987-90; staff nurse pediatrics, medically complex children Hosp. for Special Care, 1990-99, Interim Health Care, 1997—. Mem ANA, Soc. Pediatric Nurses. Home: 168 Royal Oak Dr Southington CT 06489-2158

KASSIDAY, JOEL DAVID, legislative staff member; b. Chgo., Sept. 1, 1952; m. Zmira Alfie. BA with high distinction, Colo. State U., 1973. Staff writer, assoc. editor, mng. editor Ft. Collins Rev. newspaper, 1974-79; legis. asst., press sec. U.S. Rep. James P. Johnson, 1979-81; adminstrv. asst., press sec. U.S. Rep. then U.S. Senator Hank Brown, 1982-94; chief of staff U.S. Rep. Rick Lazio, 1994-97; press sec. U.S. Senator Kay Bailey Hutchinson, 1997-98; chief of staff Congressman Elton Gallegley, Washington, 1998—. Mem. Phi Beta Kappa, Phi Kappa Phi. Office: Hon Elton Gallegly US Ho Reps 2427 Rayburn HOB Washington DC 20515

KASSIN, SAUL, psychology educator; b. N.Y.C., Apr. 25, 1953; s. Mordy and Betty (Ashear) K.; m. Carol Beth Goldner, Sept. 19, 1952; children: Briana Rachel, Marc Joseph. BS, Bklyn. Coll., 1974; MA, U. Conn., 1976, PhD, 1978. NIH postdoctoral fellow U. Kans., Lawrence, 1978-79; asst. prof. Purdue U., West Lafayette, Ind., 1979-81, Williams Coll., Williamstown, Mass., 1981-84; rsch. assoc. Fed. Jud. Ctr., Washington, 1984-85; NIH postdoctoral fellow Stanford (Calif.) U., 1985-86; from assoc. to full prof. Williams Coll., Williamstown, 1986—; jury cons., expert witness. Author: Psychology, 1995, 2d edit., 1998; co-author: The American Jury on Trial, 1988, Confessions in the Courtroom, 1993, Social Psychology, 1990, 4th edit., 1999; co-editor: Developmental Social Psychology: Theory and Research, 1981, The Psychology of Evidence and Trial Procedure, 1985, On The Witness Stand: Controversies in the Courtroom, 1987, In the Jury Box: Controversies in the Courtroom, 1987; cons. editor Jour. Exptl. Social Psychology, 1982-87, Jour. Personality and Social Psychology: Attitudes and Social Cognition, 1992-94; editl. cons. Law and Human Behavior, 1986—; ad hoc reviewer in field; contbr. articles to profl. jours. Rsch. grantee Found. Child Devel., 1984-85; Jud. fellow U.S. Supreme Ct., Washington, 1984-85. Mem. APA, Am. Psychol. Soc., Am. Psychology-Law Soc., Soc. for Exptl. Social Psychology, Phi Beta Kappa. Office: Williams Coll Bronfman Sci Ctr Williamstown MA 01267

KASSIRER, JEROME PAUL, medical educator, editor-in-chief; b. Buffalo, Dec. 19, 1932; s. Irvin D. Kassirer and Belle Fried; m. Geraldine Weinger, June 20, 1957 (div. 1979; children: Amy, Richard, Wendy, Elizabeth; m. Sheridan L. Kassirer, Mar. 25, 1979; children: Winston, Samuel. Grad., U. Buffalo, 1953, MD magna cum laude, 1957; DS (hon.), U. Mass., 1992; D honoris causa, L'Universite Rene Descartes, Paris, 1992; DS (hon.), Thomas Jefferson U., 1994, SUNY, 1995. Diplomate Am. Bd. Internal Medicine (mem. certifying examination com. 1987-89, bd. dirs. 1989-96, mem. exec. com. 1993-96, chmn. 1995-96). Intern, asst. resident in medicine Buffalo Gen. Hosp., 1957-59; fellow in nephrology New Eng. Med. Ctr., Boston, 1959-61, sr. resident in medicine, 1961-62, asst. physician, 1961-65, physician renal svc., 1969-74, assoc. physician-in-chief, 1971-91, acting physician-in-chief, 1976-77; instr. medicine Sch. Medicine, Tufts U., Medford, Mass., 1961-65, asst. prof. medicine, 1965-69, assoc. prof., 1969-74, vice chmn. dept. medicine, 1971-91, acting chmn. dept. medicine, 1974-75, prof. medicine, 1974—, Sara Murray Jordan Prof. Medicine, 1987-91; editor-in-chief New Eng. Jour. Medicine, Boston, 1991—; lectr. in medicine Harvard U., 1991—; bd. dirs. Postgrad. Med. Inst. Mass. Med. Soc., 1988-91. Editor-in-chief Current Therapy in Internal Medicine, 1990; co-editor Clin. Problem Solving, Hosp. Practice, 1985-91; consultant editor Am. Jour. Medicine, 1976-86; mem. editorial bd. New Eng. Jour. Medicine, 1972-75; co-editor Nephrology Forum, Kidney Internat., 1978-91, Med. Decision Making, 1987-89; editorial advisor Outline of Knowledge, Part 4: Human Life, The New Encyclopaedia Britannica, 1989. Recipient Ednl. Rsch. Found. award AMA, 1993. Master Am. Coll. Physicians (chmn. sci., chmn. 1985-88, gov. Mass. 1985-89, mem. exec. com. bd. govs. 1988-89, mem. health and pub. policy com. 1989-91, bd. regents 1990-91); fellow AAAS; mem. Am. Soc. Nephrology, Am. Fedn. Clin. Rsch., Inst. Medicine NAS, Assn of Am. Physicians, Nat. Libr. Medicine (chmn. bd. sci. counselors 1989-90, mem. biomed. journalism award com. 1992—), Mass. Med. Soc., Buffalo Acad. Medicine (hon. life), Soc. Clin. Decision Making (charter mem.). Jewish. Avocation: photography. Office: New Eng Jour Medicine 10 Shattuck St Boston MA 02115-6011

KASSMAN, DEBORAH NEWMAN, university administrator, writer, editor; b. Elizabeth, N.J, Feb. 22, 1927; d. Arthur Hersh and Cecelia (Ginsberg) Newman; m. Herbert S. Kassman, Aug. 22, 1948 (div. Dec. 1996); 1 child, Judith K. Wexler. BA, Wellesley Coll., 1948. Editor The Writer, Inc., Boston, 1948-68; asst. to pres. Brandeis U., Waltham, Mass., 1968-70, univ. editor, 1970-75; dir. of stewardship Harvard U., Cambridge, Mass., 1976—; mem. adv. bd. Alice James Books, Boston; cons. on stewardship. Author: Holiday Plays for Little Players, 1956, also plays for U.S. Treasury Dept.; editor, writer Harvard Mag., 1968-69; editor The Parents Newsletter, Harvard Coll., 1969-97; contbr. articles to popular mags. Dir. Five Fields, Inc., Lexington, Mass., 1995—. Home: 5 Stonewall Rd Lexington MA 02421-8018 Office: Harvard U Cambridge MA 02138

KASSNER, HERBERT SEYMORE, lawyer; b. N.Y.C., Dec. 3, 1931; s. Abraham and Rose (Rosenblatt) K.; m. Sheilah Goodwin, 1957 (div. 1965); children: Andrew, Kenneth; m. Marjorie Fern Golding, 1974 (div. 1992); children: Robin, Jeffrey; m. Linda Rubinstein Finder, 1993. BA (hon.), Franklin and Marshall U., 1952; cert., Hague (Netherlands) Acad. of Internat. Law, 1953; MA, NYU, 1955; LLB (hon.), Harvard U., 1955. Bar: N.Y. 1955, Conn. 1986. Atty. Gallap, Climenko & Gould, N.Y.C., 1955, Otterbourg, Steindler, Huston & Rosen, N.Y.C., 1956; pvt. practice law N.Y.C., 1957-65, 1969; atty. Dryer & Traub, N.Y.C., 1966-68, Kassner & Detsky, N.Y.C., 1970-80, Kassner & Haigney, N.Y.C., 1981-90; instr. Ohio State U., Columbus, 1956-57; asst. prof. Ark. State U., Pine Bluff, 1965. Contbr. articles to profl. jours. on 1st amendment law. Mem. Phi Beta Kappa. Home: 7221 Montrico Dr Boca Raton FL 33433-6931

KASSNER, MICHAEL ERNEST, materials science educator, researcher; b. Osaka, Japan, Nov. 22, 1950; (parents Am. citizens); s. Ernest and Clara (Christa) K.; m. Marcia J. Wright, Aug. 19, 1972 (div. Dec. 1976). BS, Northwestern U., 1972; MS, Stanford U., 1979, PhD, 1981. Metallurgist Sargent and Lundy Engrs., Chgo., 1977; metallurgist Lawrence Livermore (Calif.) Nat. Lab., 1981-90, head phys. metallurgy and joining sect., 1988-90; lectr. San Francisco State U., 1983; prof. Naval Postgrad. Sch., Monterey, Calif., 1984-86; prof., dir. grad. program in materials sci. Oreg. State U., Corvallis, 1990—, Chevron endowed prof., 1996, Northwest Aluminuim prof., 1997—; temporary assignment as project mgr. Office Basic Energy Scis., U.S. Dept. Energy, 1991-96; vis. scholar dept. physics U. Groningen, Netherlands, 1985-87; vis. scholar dept. materials, sci. and engring. Stanford U., 1981-83; vis. prof. U. Calif., San Diego, 1997—. Author over 120 articles; author book on binary phase diagrams; editor various sci. jours. Lt. USN, 1972-76; lt. comdr. USNR, 1976-81. Fulbright scholar, The Netherlands; fellow ASM Internat., 1998. Mem. ASME, Am. Soc. Metals, The Metall. Soc., Materials Research Soc., Sigma Xi. Home: PO Box 269 Otter Rock OR 97369-0269

KASSOF, ALLEN H., foundation administrator; b. N.Y.C., Dec. 17, 1930; s. Morris and Sophia B. Kassof; m. Arianne Scholz, 1953; children: Andrea, Arlen, Anita. BA, Rutgers U., 1952; AM, Harvard U., 1954, PhD, 1960. Asst. prof. Smith Coll., Northampton, Mass., 1957-60; asst. prof. Princeton (N.J.) U., 1961-65, assoc. prof., asst. dean coll., 1965-68; exec. dir. Internat. Rsch. and Exchs. Bd., N.Y.C. and Princeton, 1968-92; pres. Project on Ethnic Rels. in Ea. Europe, Carnegie Corp. N.Y., Princeton, 1991—; cons. conf. security and cooperation Europe, Hamburg, Germany, Budapest, Hungary, 1980, 85, Warsaw, Poland, 1993; mem. pres. com. fgn. lang., Washington, 1978-79; mem. U.S. task force Romania, Bucharest, 1990-92; prin. mediator between Govt. of Romania and Democratic Union Hungarians in Romania, 1993—; mem. Coun. for Ethnic Accord, 1992—; chair roundtable talks between Slovak and Ethnic Hungarian parliamentary parties of Slovakia, 1995—, Serb-Albanian Roundtable on Future of Kosovo, N.Y.C., 1997; co-chmn. Euro-Atlantic group on interethnic conflicts NATO, Brussels, 1998. Mem. Am. Assn. Advancement Slavic Studies, Coun. Fgn. Rels. Avocation: photography. E-mail: kassof@compuserve.com. Home: 949 Mercer Rd Princeton NJ 08540-4823 Office: Project on Ethnic Rels 15 Chambers St Princeton NJ 08542-3707

KASSOUF, ESTHER KAY, middle school education educator; b. Kinston, N.C., Apr. 19, 1950; d. William Gid and Josephine (Smith) Holland; m. John Michael Kassouf Jr., May 8, 1976. AS, Mt. Olive (N.C.) Jr. Coll., 1970; BS, Atlantic Christian Coll., 1972; MEd, U. Nev., 1990. Tchr. 6th grade Kinston City Pub. Schs., 1972-76; tchr. 5th, 7th, 8th grades Clark County Sch. Dist., Las Vegas, Nev., 1976—. Avocations: reading, shopping, crafts. Office: Clark County Sch Dist Silvestri Jr High Las Vegas NV 89121

KASSOY, HORTENSE (HONEY KASSOY), artist, sculptor, painter, printmaker; b. N.Y.C., Feb. 14, 1917; d. Adolph and Mary (Apfel) Blumenkranz; m. Bernard Kassoy, June 30, 1946; children: Meredith, Sheila. Diploma, Pratt Inst., 1936; BS, Columbia U., 1938, MA, 1939; student, Parsons Sch. Design, Paris, U. Colo., 1966, NYU, 1966-67; studied sculpture with Sahl Swarz, Chaim Gross & Oronzio Maldarelli. Solo exhbns. include Caravan House Gallery, 1974, Women in the Arts Gallery, 1978, Ward-Nasse Gallery, 1986, Pioneer Gallery, Cooperstown, N.Y., 1987, 91, 97, 80th Birthday Retrospective Solo of Wood Sculpture Prints and Watercolors, Vladeck Hall Gallery, N.Y., 1997, Pioneer Gallery, Cooperstown, 1997; group exhbns. include Bronx (N.Y.) Mus., 1971, 75, 85-86, Toledo Mus. Art, Toronto Mus. Art, Hudson River Mus., Bklyn. Mus., New Age Gallery, Lever House, Bklyn. Coll., Fordham U., Lehman Coll., Cork Gallery, Nat. Acad. Design; permanent collections include Slater Meml. Mus. Co-chair visual arts Bronx (N.Y.) Coun. on Arts, 1973-76. Fellow Va. Ctr. for Creative Arts, 1986, 88, 89, 92, 95, 97; recipient 1st prize in watercolor Painters Day at N.Y. World's Fair, 1940. Mem. Am. Soc. Contemporary Artists (v.p. 1989-94, awards in sculpture 1979, 80, 83, 90, 92, 96), N.Y. Artists Equity Assn. (v.p., bd. dirs. 1971-83), Internation Assn. Art (corr. sec. 1979-93, del. to 10th Congress 1983), Contemporary Arts Guild (rec. sec.). Home: 130 Gale Pl Apt 6B Bronx NY 10463-2853 Also: Butternut Hill Studio 1577 County Rt 16 Burlington Flats NY 13315-9728

KASSULKE, NATASHA MARIE, reporter; b. Milw., July 8, 1969; d. Russell Owen and Deborah (Iglinski) K. BS in English, Edgewood Coll., Madison, Wis., 1991; M.Journalism, U. Wis., 1993. Tech. writer Wis. Dept. Natural Resources, Madison, 1989—; reporter Wis. State Jour., Madison, 1992—; mentor Partnership in Journalism, Madison, 1994—. Day of Caring vol. United Way, Madison, 1997. Named Disting. Alumni Edgewood Coll., 1997. Avocation: tennis.

KASTAN, DAVID SCOTT, university educator, writer; b. New York, N.Y., Jan. 4, 1946; s. Peter Lewis and Audrey Brown (Kastan); m. Susan Elise, March 20, 1983; children: Marina Claire. A.B., Princeton U., Princeton, N.J., 1967; M.A., U. Chgo., 1968, Ph.D., 1974. Asst. prof. Dartmouth Coll., 1973-79; assoc. prof. Dartmouth Coll., 1979-86; visiting prof. University College of London, 1980-81, 1983-84; prof. Columbia U., 1987—; disting. vis. prof. Am. U., Cairo, 1995, Copenhagen U., 1998. General editor: Arden Shakespeare, 1995; assoc. ed., Bantam Shakespeare 1988; author, (book) Shakespeare and the Shapes of Time, 1982, Shakespeare after Theory, 1999; editor: Staging the Renaissance, 1991, New History of Early English Drama, 1997, A Companion to Shakepeare, 1999. Woodrow Wilson Fellowship, 1968, Folger Library Fellowship, 1994, Huntington Libr. Mellon Fellowship, 1995. Mem. MLA (divisional exec. com.), Renaissance English Text Soc. (coun. mem.), Shakespeare Assn. Am., Renaissance Soc. Am., Phi Beta Kappa. Office: Columbia Univ Dept English 116th St & Broadway New York NY 10027

KASTANTIN, JOSEPH THOMAS, accounting educator; b. Ottumwa, Iowa, Aug. 30, 1947; s. Brony Frank and Virginia Mae (Smith) K.; m. Jane A. Mondanaro, Sept. 16, 1966 (div. Jan. 1971); children: Anthony Joseph, Leilani Michelle; m. Linda Krause, Sept. 21, 1974; 1 child, Andrew Thomas. AA, El Paso C.C., 1974; BS, Marian Coll., 1976; MBA, Butler u., 1979; faculty devel. in internat. bus. & fin., U. S.C., 1992. CPA, cert. mgmt. acct. Enlisted U.S. Army, 1966, advanced through grades to sgt. 1st class, 1975, resigned, 1978; controller Top Value Fabrics, Carmel, Ind., 1978-79; bus. mgr. Ray Hutson Chevrolet, La Crosse, Wis., 1979-80; mgr. Frank Uhler Assocs. CPAs, La Crosse, 1980-82; pres. Horizon Designs, Inc., Kearney, Nebr., 1982-83; asst. prof. acctg. U. Wis., La Crosse, 1983—; cons. Small Bus. Devel. Ctr., La Crosse, 1984—; tchr. internat. acctg. and internat. bus. specializing in internat. acctg. stds. KPMG, Dalkeith, Scotland, 1991, Caen, France, 1993, 94; tng. mgr. Bratislava, Slovakia, 1997-98; chmn. bd. dirs. La Crosse Funds, Inc., 1998—. Author: Professional Accounting Practice Management, 1988, (novel) God Gave Teeth; co-author: The Management Accountants Guide to Fraud Discovery and Control, 1991; contbr. articles to profl. jours. Pres., bd. dirs. Vis. Nurses Assn., 1988-89; pres. Western Wis. Regional Arts, La Crosse, 1986-87. Decorated Bronze Star, 1972; recipient Lybrand Cert. Merit for Literary Excellence, 1986; named Disting. Alumnus Marian Coll., 1988; Fulbright Fgn. scholar Slovak Republic, Mates Bel U., Banska Bystrica, Slovak Republic, 1995-96. Mem. Vietnam Vet. Assn., AICPA, Wis. Inst. CPAs (treas. West Ctrl. chpt. 1989-90), Nat. Assn. Accts. (pres. LaCrosse/Winona chpt. 1990-91). Republican. Congregationalist. Avocations: writing, jogging, studying Charles Dickens. Home: N1702 Paris Angel Dr La Crosse WI 54601-8444 Office: U Wis 1725 State St La Crosse WI 54601-3742

KASTEL, HOWARD L., lawyer, business executive; b. Chgo., June 11, 1932; s. William A. and Beatrice (Seltzer) K.; m. Joan Herron, Dec. 20, 1953; children: Mark Alan, Jeffrey Lawrence. BA, Harvard U., 1954; JD cum laude, Loyola U., Chgo., 1960. Bar: Ill. 1960, U.S. Dist. Ct. (no. dist.) Ill. 1960, U.S. Ct. Appeals (7th cir.) 1965, U.S. Ct. Appeals (2d, 3d, 4th, 5th, 8th and 9th cirs.), U.S. Supreme Ct. Assoc. Aaron, Aaron, Schimberg & Hess, Chgo., 1960-62; ptnr. Altheimer & Gray, Chgo., 1962-80, Kastel & Rutkoff, Chgo., 1980-83, Holleb & Coff, Chgo., 1983-84; ptnr. McDermott, Will & Emery, Chgo., 1984-97, of counsel, 1997—; pres., CEO Wanger Asset Mgmt. Ltd., Chgo., 1998-99; ptnr. Wanger Asset Mgmt. LP, Chgo., 1998-99; mem. Fin. Acctg. Standards Bd. Task Force on Non-Bus. Orgns., 1981-83, mem. Labor Law Com., 1961-72, Civil Practice Com., 1971-88, Securities Law Com., 1981-88, Jud. Com., 1983—. Sgt. USMC, 1954-56. Mem. ABA (law and acctg. com. 1977—, chmn. subcom. internat. acctg., fed. regulations of securities subcom. on SEC practice and enforcement matters 1979—), Am. Arbitration Assn. (nat. panel arbitrators). Avocations: yacht racing, treking, cross country skiing, running. Home: 1501 N State Pkwy Chicago IL 60610-1676 Office: McDermott Will & Emery 227 W Monroe St Chicago IL 60606-5096*

KASTELIC, ROBERT FRANK, aerospace company executive; b. Granite City, Ill., July 17, 1934; s. Joseph and Anna Marie (Kries) K.; m. Patricia Ann Dalton, Apr. 8, 1961; children: Michael J., Constance A., Robert J., Kirsten S. B.S. in Acctg., U. Ill., 1956. Sr. acct. Price Waterhouse & Co., St. Louis, 1956-63; v.p., chief fin. officer, comptroller Merc. Bancorp., St. Louis, 1963-72; exec. v.p., chief fin. officer Equimark Corp. and Equibank, Pitts., 1972-83; vice-chmn. bd. Equimark Corp. and Equibank, 1983-84; pres., chief operating officer Astrotech Internat. Corp., Pitts., 1985-86, 86—; chmn., chief exec. officer X-Mark Industries, Washington, Pa., 1988—; bd. dirs. Glenshaw (Pa.) Glass Co., Quasitronics, Inc., X-Mark Industries, Astrotech Internat., Pitts., Fidelity Savs. Bank; chmn. St. Francis Fin. Corp. Mem. rev. com. United Way, Pitts., 1977-78; bd. dirs. St. Francis Hosp., Civic Light Opera. Served with U.S. Army, 1956-58. Mem. AICPA, Am. Mgmt. Assn., Am. Soc. Corp. Secs., Mo., Pa. insts. CPAs, Bank Adminstrn. Inst., Fin. Execs. Inst., Nat. Investor Relations Inst. Club: Duquesne. Home: 825 Fox Chapel Rd Pittsburgh PA 15238-2003 Office: X-Mark Industries 2001 N Main St Washington PA 15301-6180

KASTELIC, ROBERT L., education educator; b. July 2, 1949. BA in Edn., Ariz. State U., MEd; EdD, Columbia U. Tchrs. Coll., 1993. Educator Scottsdale, Ariz.; asst. prof. Pacific U., Oreg.; dir. rsch. & devel. Southwest Ednl. Rsch. Svcs., Scottsdale, Ariz. Home: 5936 E Chukwalla Tr Cave Creek AZ 85331

KASTELY, JAMES LOUIS, English language educator; b. Nov. 6, 1947. AB, U. Mich., 1969; MA, U. Chgo., 1972, PhD, 1980. Asst. prof.

dept. English U. Hawaii, Honolulu, 1980-93; vis. prof. St. Mary's U. Law Sch., San Antonio, 1993-94; assoc. prof. English, U. Houston, 1994—. E-mail: jkastely@jetson.uh.edu. Office: U Houston Dept English Houston TX 77204-3012

KASTEN, G. FREDERICK, JR., investment company executive. Pres. Baird Fin. Corp., Milw., CEO. Office: Baird Fin Corp 777 E Wisconsin Ave Milwaukee WI 53202-5300*

KASTEN, KARL ALBERT, painter, printmaker, educator; b. San Francisco, Mar. 5, 1916; s. Ferdin and Barbara Anna Kasten; m. Georgette Gautier, Mar. 29, 1958; children: Ross, Lee, Beatrix, Joellen, Cho-An. MA, U. Calif., 1939; postgrad., U. Iowa, 1949; student, Hans Hofmann Sch. Fine Arts, 1951; PhD in Art History, Yale U., 1992. Instr. Calif. Sch. Fine Arts, 1941, U. Mich., 1946-47; asst. prof. art San Francisco State U., 1947-50; prof. U. Calif., Berkeley, 1950-83. Bibliography appears in Etching (Edmondson), 1973, Collage and Assemblage (Meilach and Ten Hoor), 1973, Modern Woodcut Techniques (Kuroski), 1977, California Style (McClelland and Last), 1985, Art in the San Francisco Bay Area (Albright), 1985; group shows include San Francisco Mus. Art, 1939, Chgo. Art Inst., 1946, Whitney Mus., 1952, Sao Paolo Internat. Biennials, 1955, 61, Achenbach Found., 1976, World Print III Traveling Exhbn., 1980-83, Gallery Sho, Tokyo, 1994, Inst. Franco-Americain, Rennes, 1995; patentee etching press. Capt. U.S. Army, 1942-46. Decorated 4 battle stars; fellow Creative Arts Inst., 1964, 71, Tamarind Lithography Artist Fellowship, 1968, Regents Humanities, 1977. Mem. Berkeley Art Ctr. Assn. (bd. dirs. 1987-92), Calif. Soc. Printmakers (Disting. Artist award 1997), Univ. Faculty Club, Univ. Arts Club. Home: 1884 San Lorenzo Ave Berkeley CA 94707-1841 Office: Univ Calif Berkeley Art Dept Berkeley CA 94720

KASTEN, PAUL RUDOLPH, nuclear engineer, educator; b. Jackson, Mo., Dec. 10, 1923; s. Arthur John and Hattie L. (Krueger) K.; m. Eileen Alma Kiehne, Dec. 28, 1947; children: Susan (Mrs. Robert M. Goebbert), Kim Patrick, Jennifer. BSChemE, U. Mo., Rolla, 1944, M.S., 1947; Ph.D. in Chem. Engring., U. Minn., 1950. Staff mem. Oak Ridge Nat. Lab., 1950-88, dir. gas-cooled reactor and thorium utilization programs, 1970-78, dir. HTGR and GCFR programs, 1978-86, tech. dir. gas cooled reactor programs, 1986-88; cons., 1988—; guest dir. Inst. Reactor Devel., Nuclear Research Center, Jülich, Fed. Republic Germany, 1963-64; mem. faculty U. Tenn., Knoxville, 1953—, part-time prof. nuclear engring., 1965-95, hon. adj. prof. nuclear engring., 1995—. Fellow AAAS, Am. Nuclear Soc.; mem. Sigma Xi, Tau Beta Pi, Phi Lambda Upsilon. Lutheran. Research and publications in role of thorium in power reactor development, high temperature gas-cooled reactors and modular gas reactors for gas-turbine and process-heat application, fuel performance modeling of gas-cooled reactors, and reactor evaluations. Office: 341 Louisiana Ave Oak Ridge TN 37830-8514 also: U Tenn Dept Nuclear Engring Knoxville TN 37996

KASTEN, ROBERT W., JR., former senator; b. Milw., June 19, 1942; s. Robert W. and Mary (Ogden) K.; m. Eva Jean. BA, U. Ariz., 1964; MBA, Columbia U., 1966. With Genesco, Inc., Nashville, 1966-68; dir., v.p. Gilbert Shoe Co., Thiensville, Wis., 1968-75; mem. Wis. Senate, Madison, 1972-75; mem. joint fin. com., 1973-75, chmn. joint survey com. on tax exemptions, 1973-75; mem. 94th-95th congresses from 9th Wis. Dist.; U.S. Senator from Wis., 1980-93; founder Kasten & Co., Thiensville, Wis., 1993—; sr. assoc. Strategic and Internat. Studies Ctr., Washington, 1993—; mem. 100th Congress Com., appropriations com., budget com., commerce, sci. and transp. com., small bus. com. Regional dir. Milw. Coalition for Clean Water; active Milw. Soc. for Prevention of Blindness; founder Legis. Studies Inst. 1st lt. Wis. Air N.G., 1967-72. Named Jaycee of Yr., 1972; named Legis. Conservationist of Yr. Wis. Wildlife Fedn., 1973, 86; One of Best Legislators Senate Rep. Class of 1980 Nat. Jour., 1985. Mem. Nat. Audubon Soc., Ducks Unltd., Sigma Nu, Alpha Kappa Psi. Office: Kasten & Co # 700 888 16th St NW Washington DC 20006-4004

KASTEN, STANLEY HARVEY, sports association executive; b. Lakewood, N.J., Feb. 1, 1952; s. Nathan and Sylvia (Saltztreger) K.; m. Helen Weisz, Aug. 14, 1977; children: Alana Marie, Corey Richard, Sherry Leigh, Jay Bradley. AB, NYU, 1973; JD, Columbia U., 1976. Exec. asst. Turner Broadcasting Co., Atlanta, 1976-77; v.p. for sports TBS, Atlanta, 1986—; in-house counsel Atlanta Braves, 1976-77, pres., 1986—; v.p., asst. gen. mgr. Atlanta Hawks, 1978-79, v.p., gen. mgr., 1980-86, pres., gen. mgr., 1986—, dir., 1986-90, pres., 1990—, also bd. dirs.; bd. govs. Nat. Basketball Assn., N.Y.C., 1978—. Named NBA Exec. of Yr., 1985-86, 86-87. Mem. ABA, N.J. Bar Assn. Office: Atlanta Hawks South Tower 1 Cnn Ctr NW Ste 405 Atlanta GA 30303-2762 also: Atlanta Braves PO Box 4064 Atlanta GA 30302-4064*

KASTENBERG, WILLIAM EDWARD, engineering and applied science educator; b. N.Y.C., June 25, 1939; s. Murray and Lillian Kastenberg; m. Berna R. Miller, Aug. 18, 1963; children: Andrew, Joshua, Lillian; m. Gloria Hauser, May 3, 1992. BS, UCLA, 1962, MS, 1963; PhD, U. Calif., Berkeley, 1966. Asst. prof. Sch. Engring. and Applied Sci. UCLA, 1966-71, assoc. prof. Sch. Engring. and Applied Sci., 1971-75; guest scientist Karlsruhe (Fed. Republic Germany) Nuclear Rsch., 1972-73; sr. fellow U.S. NRC, Washington, 1979-80; assoc. dean Sch. Engring. and Applied Sci. UCLA, 1981-85, chmn. mech. aerospace and nuclear engring., 1985-88, prof. mech., aerospace and nuclear engring. dept., 1975-94; prof. nuclear engring. dept. U. Calif., Berkeley, 1995—, chmn. nuclear engring. dept., 1995—; chmn. nuclear reactor safety Am. Nuclear Soc., 1984-85; chmn. peer rev. com. USNRC, Washington, 1987-88; mem. Nat. Rsch. Com. on Reactor Safety, 1985-86, mem. adv. com. nuclear facility safet DOE, 1988-92; mem. adv. com. Diablo Canyon Nuclear Power Plant, 1990—; dir. Risk and Sys. Analysis Control Toxics Program, UCLA, 1989-95; chmn. Ctr. for Clean Tech., UCLA, 1992-94; project dir. Ctr. for Nuclear and Toxic Waste Mgmt., U. Calif., Berkeley, 1995—. Contbr. articles to Jour. Hazardous Materials, Nuclear Sci. & Engring., Am. Jour. Pub. Health, Nuclear Engring. and Design, Jour. for Risk Analysis, Nuclear Tech. Recipient Disting. Teaching award Am. Soc. Engring. Edn., 1973. Fellow AAAS, Am. Nuclear Soc.; mem. NAE (elected). Office: Nuclear Engring Dept U Calif Berkeley 4155 Etcheverry Hall Berkeley CA 94720-1731

KASTER, LAURA A., lawyer; b. N.Y.C., May 24, 1948. BA, Tufts U., 1970; JD magna cum laude, Boston U., 1973. Bar: Mass. 1973, Ill. 1975. Law clk. to Hon. Frank M. Coffin, U.S. Ct. Appeals for 1st circuit, Boston, 1973-75; assoc. Jenner & Block, Chgo., 1975-81, ptnr., 1981-97; gen. atty. law and govt. affairs AT&T Corp., Liberty Corner, N.J., 1997—. Co-author: Sanctions in Federal Litigation, 1991; co-editor: The Attorneys' Guide to the Seventh Circuit Court of Appeals, 1987; note editor Law Rev. Boston U., 1973-72; contbr. chpt. to book and articles to profl. jours. Fellow Am. Bar Found. (life); mem. ABA, Ill. Bar Assn., 7th Circuit Bar Assn.

KASTING, JAMES FRASER, research meteorologist, physicist; b. Schenectady, N.Y., Jan. 2, 1953; married; 3 children. AB, Harvard U., 1975; MS in Physics and Atmospheric Sci., U. Mich., 1978, PhD in Atmospheric Sci., 1979. Rsch. fellow Nat. Ctr. Atmospheric Rsch., 1979-81; rsch. fellow Ames Rsch. Ctr., NASA, 1981-83, rsch. scientist, 1983-88; prof. geosci., meteorology Pa. State U., State College, 1988—. Fellow AAAS; mem. Am. Geophys. Union, Internat. Soc. Study of Origin of Life. Achievements include research on evolution of planetary atmospheres; history of the earth and why it is different from that of Mars and Venus. Office: Pa State U Dept Geo Scis 443 Deike Bldg University Park PA 16802-2713*

KASTNER, CHRISTINE KRIHA, newspaper correspondent; b. Cleve., Aug. 27, 1951; d. Joseph Calvin and Grace (Weber) Kriha; m. Donald William Kastner, June 30, 1979; 1 child, Paul Donald. Assoc., Lakeland C.C., 1976; BA in Comms., Cleve. State U., 1983. Asst. editor, comms. specialist TRW, Inc., Cleve., 1978-85; editor Kaiser Permanente, Cleve., 1985-87; dir. pub. rels. Northeastern Ohio chpt. Arthritis Found., Cleve., 1991-92; newspaper corr. The Plain Dealer, Cleve., 1992—. Contbg. author: Encyclopedia of Cleveland History, 1988. Recipient Gold Addy award Am. Advt. Fedn., 1986, Award of Excellence Women in Comms., Inc., 1987, Bronze Quill award Internat. Assn. Bus. Communicators, 1987. Mem. Soc. Profl. Journalists. Roman Catholic. Avocations: bicycling, reading. Home and Office: 5003 Clubside Rd Lyndhurst OH 44124-2540

KASTNER, CYNTHIA, lawyer; b. Woonsocket, R.I., July 22, 1948; d. Everett Lathrop and Edith Stark; m. Robert W. Kastner, June 26, 1971. BA, Rutgers U., Newark, 1970; postgrad., Cornell U., 1970-71; JD, Seton Hall U., 1973. Bar: N.J. 1973, U.S. Dist. Ct. N.J. 1973, U.S. Supreme Ct. 1984. Assoc. Wharton, Stewart & Davis, Somerville, N.J., 1973-76; v.p., gen. counsel AT&T Consumer Products, Parsippany, N.J., 1992-96; corp. counsel Lucent Techs.-Global Real Estate & Procurement, 1996—. Adminstrv. coun., pres. Women's Circle, pres. bd. trustees New Providence (N.J.) Meth. Ch. Mem. ABA, N.J. Bar Assn., N.J. Assn. Corp. Counsel. Avocations: gardening, travel. Home: 70 Lacey Ave Gillette NJ 07933-1407 Office: Lucent Techs Inc 475 South St Morristown NJ 07960-6459

KASTNER, MARC AARON, physics educator; b. Toronto, Ont., Can., Nov. 20, 1945; came to U.S., 1952; s. Jacob and Ida Pearl (Shidlowsky) K.; m. Marcia Jill Paul, Aug. 27, 1967; 2 children. BS in Chemistry, U. Chgo., 1967, MS, 1969, PhD in Physics, 1972. Rsch. fellow Harvard U., Cambridge, Mass., 1972-73; asst. prof. physics MIT, Cambridge, 1973-77, assoc. prof., 1977-83, prof., 1983-89, Donner prof. of physics, 1989—; dir. Consortium for Superconducting Electronics, 1989-91, Ctr. for Materials Sci. and Engring, 1993-98; head MIT Dept. Physics, 1998—. Recipient David Adler Lectureship award Am. Physical Society, 1995. Fellow AAAS, Am. Phys. Soc. (councillor at large 1991-94). Research in electronic, optical and magnetic properties of condensed matter, including semiconductors and high temperature superconductors.

KASTNER, MICHAEL JAMES, dentist; b. Huntington, Ind., Oct. 20, 1954; s. James H. and Barbara A. (Bartrom) K.; m. Kimberly A. Ricke, June 18, 1983; children: Kevin Michael, Ryan James, Derek Edward. BS in Biology and Chemistry, Manchester Coll., 1977; DDS, Ind. U., Indpls., 1981. Gen. practice dentistry Toledo, 1981—; asst. dentist Toledo Zoo, 1991—; mem. Ohio Mass Disaster Team, 1995—; asst. Lucas County Coroner's Office, 1987—. Bd. trustees Dental Ctr. Northwest Ohio, 1995—. Recipent Alumni Honor award Manchester Coll., 1997, Recognition for Honor award Ohio State Senate Resolution, 1997. Mem. ADA (Recognition for Vol. Svc. Fgn. Country award in Dominican Republic 1987, in Costa Rica 1990, in Nepal 1994), Ohio Dental Assn. (Humanitarian of Yr. 1995), Toledo Dental Soc. (bd. dirs. 1996—), Am. Acad. Cosmetic Dentistry, Am. Soc. Forensic Odontology, Am. Coll. Oral Implantology, Am. Soc. Osseointegration Internat. Congress Oral Implantologists, Mensa. Roman Catholic. Avocations: photography, basketball, tennis, travel, outdoor activities. Home: 4616 Waterford Ct Toledo OH 43623-2988

KASTOR, FRANK SULLIVAN, English language educator; b. Evanston, Ill., Aug. 19, 1933; s. Herman Walker and Rebecca (Sullivan) K.; m. Tina Bennett, Oct. 28, 1979; children: Jeffrey, Mark, Harlan, Kristina, Patrick, Liam, Mary Elisabeth, Caroline. BA, U. Ill., 1955, MA, 1956; PhD, U. Calif., Berkeley, 1963. Teaching asst. U. Ill., 1955-56, U. Calif., Berkeley, 1960-63; asst. prof. English U. So. Calif., 1964-66, 67-68; assoc. prof. English No. Ill. U., 1968-69; prof. English, Wichita State U., 1969—, chmn. dept., 1969-75, prof. emeritus, 1998. Contbr. to: The Milton Ency., The Dictionary of Literary Biography; author books, articles, revs., TV documentaries, C.S. Lewis study guides. Served with USAF, 1956-59. Rsch. grantee U. Calif., Berkeley, 1962, U. So. Calif., 1964, No. Ill. U., 1969, Wichita State U., 1970, 72, 73, 74, 84, 86, 92; Fulbright lectr., Spain, 1966-67; Kans. Com. for Humanities grantee, 1973, 74, 94; recipient NEH award, 1971, 84. Mem. MLA, Milton Soc. Am., Conf. on Christianity and Lit., AAUP, N.Y. C.S. Lewis Soc., C.S. Lewis Soc. of Kans. (founder, pres.), Phi Kappa Phi. Christian Ch. E-mail: kastor@wsuhub.uc.twsu.edu.

KASTOR, JOHN ALFRED, cardiologist, educator; b. N.Y.C., Sept. 15, 1931; s. Alfred Bernard and Ellen Voigt Bentley; m. Mae Belle Eisenberg, July 4, 1954; children: Elizabeth Mae, Anne Sarah, Peter John. BA, U. Pa., 1953; MD, NYU, 1962. With NBC, N.Y.C., 1956-58; intern, asst. resident in medicine Bellevue Hosp., N.Y.C., 1962-64; chief resident physician N.Y. U. Hosp., N.Y.C., 1964-65; clin. and research fellow in medicine Mass. Gen. Hosp., Boston, 1965-68; clin. asst. and asst. in medicine Mass. Gen. Hosp., 1968-69; instr. in medicine Harvard Med. Sch., 1968-69; dir. med. intensive care unit Hosp. U. Pa., Phila., 1969-72; assoc. chief cardiovascular sect. Hosp. U. Pa., 1972-77, chief, 1977-81; physician-in-chief U. Md. Hosp., 1984-97; prof. medicine U. Pa. Sch. Medicine, Phila., 1976-83; Theodore E. Woodward prof. medicine U. Md. Sch. Medicine, 1984-97, chmn. dept. medicine, 1984-97, prof. medicine, 1997—; vis. prin. fellow Nat. Heart and Lung Inst., London, 1995. Author: Arrhythmias, 1994; founding editor Internat. Jour. Cardiology, 1981-84; contbr. numerous articles on cardiac electrophysiology and gen. cardiology to med. jours. Served with U.S. Army, 1953-55. Fellow ACP, Am. Coll. Cardiology, Coun. Clin. Cardiology Am. Heart Assn.; mem. Am. Fedn. Clin. Rsch., Am. Heart Assn. (bd. govs. Southeastern Pa. chpt. 1975-81, bd. govs. Md. affiliate 1990-93), Assn. Am. Physicians, Assn. Univ. Cardiologists, Assn. Profs. Medicine (bd. govs. 1992-95), Venezuelan Soc. Internal Medicine, Paul Dudley White Soc. (dir. 1977-86), Alpha Omega Alpha. Home: 2415 Boston St Baltimore MD 21224-4733 Office: U Md Hosp 22 S Greene St Baltimore MD 21201-1544

KASTRUP, DIETER, United Nations official. Mem. German permanent mission to UN, N.Y.C. Office: Permanent Mission to UN 871 UN Plaza New York NY 10017*

KASULIS, THOMAS PATRICK, humanities educator; b. Bridgeport, Conn., Mar. 5, 1948; s. Joseph John and Albina Anna (Checkanouskas) K.; m. Ellen Elizabeth Sponheimer, June 5, 1970; children: Telemachus, Matthias, Benedict. BA, Yale U., 1970, MPh, 1972, PhD, 1975; MA, U. Hawaii, 1973. Asst. prof. philosophy U. Hawaii, Honolulu, 1975-80; from asst. prof. to prof. philosophy and religion Northland Coll., Ashland, Wis., 1981-91; prof. comparative studies The Ohio State U., Columbus, 1991—, chair East Asian langs. and lit., 1993-95, chair comparative studies, 1995-98; Mellon faculty fellow in humanities Harvard U., Cambridge, Mass., 1979-80; vis. facility rschr. Osaka (Japan) U., 1982-83; Numata vis. prof. U. Chgo., Ill., 1988. Author: Zen Action/Zen Person, 1981; editor, co-translator: The Body: Toward an Eastern Mind-Body Theory, 1987; co-editor: Self as Body in Asian Theory and Practice, 1993, Self as Person in Asian Theory and Practice, 1994; contbr. chpts. to books and articles to profl. jours. Fellow Japan Found., 1982-83; NEH fellow for Coll. Tchrs., NEH, 1986-87; Sr. Rsch. fellow East West Ctr., Honolulu, 1988. Mem. Soc. for Asian and Comparative Philosophy (pres. 1988-91), Am. Soc. for the Study of Religion (v.p.), Soc. for Values in Higher Edn. Home: 1465 Montcalm Rd Upper Arlington OH 43221 Office: Comparative Studies Ohio State Univ 230 W 17th Ave Columbus OH 43210-1361*

KATAI, ANDREW ANDRAS, chemical company executive; b. Gyor, Hungary, Sept. 17, 1937; came to U.S., 1956; s. Ivan and Clara (Szel) K.; m. Debbie Judwin, May 12, 1963 (div. 1970); children: Alisa, Gregory; m. Joan Eleanor Klein, July 30, 1972; children: Peter, Daniel. BS, Juniata Coll., 1960; MS, PhD, Syracuse U., 1965; MS, PhD in Chemistry, SUNY, Syracuse, 1965. Internat. mktg. asst. Esso chem. Co., N.Y.C., 1965-66; asst. prof. Hunter-Lehman Coll. N.Y.C., 1965-70; research chemist Union Carbide Corp., Tarrytown, N.Y., 1966-67; internat. assoc. prodn. mgr. Union Carbide Corp., N.Y.C., 1967-69, internat. product mgr., 1969-71; new bus. devel. mgr. W.R. Grace Constrn. Co., Cambridge, Mass., 1971-73; bus. mgr. internat. div. Inolex Corp., Chgo., 1973-77; Far East devel mgr. Eschem (Swift) Inc., Chgo., 1977, gen. mgr. internat. div., 1977-81, dir. internat. div., 1981-82, v.p. internat. div., 1982-83; pres. Swift Adhesives subs. Reichhold Chem. Co., Downers Grove, Ill., 1983-93; sr. Corridor fellow, assoc. prof. internat. bus. North Ctrl. Coll., Naperville, Ill., 1994—. Contbr. articles to profl. jours. Chmn. coll. fundraising dr., Westchester County, N.Y., 1969; co-chmn. Homeowners' Assn., Flossmoor, Ill., 1981-82. Mem. Adhesive Mfrs. Assn. (treas. 1986-88, pres.-elect 1988, pres. 1990), East West Corp. Corridor Assn. (v.p. 1992—), Am. Chem. Soc., Sigma Xi, Phi Lambda Upsilon. Avocations: bridge, classical music, kayaking, photography, travel. Home: 1105 E Johnson Dr Naperville IL 60540-8245

KATAKKAR, SURESH BALAJI, hematologist, oncologist; b. Poona, India, Feb. 9, 1944; s. Balaji Vasudeo Katakkar and Padmavati (Gangadhar) Varavandkar; m. Sunila Moghe; children: Smita, Sucheta, Swati. MB, BS, Poona U., India, 1969; grad., Ednl. Coun. Fgn. Med., 1970. Diplomate Am. Bd. Internal Medicine, Am. Bd. Oncology, Am. Bd. Quality Assurance and Utilization Rev., Am. Bd. Forensic Med.; lic. Med. Coun. Calif. Intern, then resident St. Paul's Hosp., Saskatoon, 1969-71; resident U. Hosp., Saskatoon, 1971-72; resident clin. hematology Gen. Hosp., Ottawa, 1973-74; fellow in med. oncology W.W. Cross Cancer Inst., Edmonton, Can., 1974-75; sr. cancer clin. assoc. Sasketchewan Cancer Commn., 1975-78; clin. investigator NCI, USA, 1975—; med. oncologist Madigan Army Med. Ctr., 1978-80; pvt. practice Tucson, Ariz., 1980—; med. dir., chmn. cancer com. N.W. Cancer Ctr., 1991—; chmn. tumor bd. St. Mary's Hosp., Tucson, 1981-83, chmn. transfusion com., 1982—; chmn. dept. med. Northwest Hosp., 1983-84, chief of staff, 1984-86, bd. trustees, 1984—, clin. lectr. Univ. Med. Ctr., Ariz. Cancer Ctr., 1989—. Contbr. articles to profl. jours.; spkr, presenter, abstracts in field. W.W. Cross Cancer Inst. fellow, 1974-75. Fellow ACP, Royal Coll. Physicians Can., Internat. Acad. Thrombosis/Hemostasis; mem. AMA, Am. Soc. Clin. Oncology, Internat. Soc. Preventative Oncology, Am. Geriatrics Soc., Am. Hosp. Assn., Am. Assn. Blood Banks, Am. Bd. Med. Dirs., Am. Coll. Med. Quality, N.Y. Acad. Scis., European Soc. Med. Oncology, European Assn. Cancer Rsch. Home: 1391 E Placita Mapache Tucson AZ 85718-3929 Office: NW Cancer Ctr 1845 W Orange Grove Rd Bldg 2 Tucson AZ 85704-1144

KATAYAMA, ARTHUR SHOJI, lawyer; b. Los Angeles, June 10, 1927; s. Asaji and Teru (Mori) K.; m. Mie Nakamura, Dec. 23, 1976. A.B., Morningside Coll., 1951; LL.B., Pacific Coast U., 1956. Bar: Calif. 1959, U.S. Dist. Ct. (cen. dist.) Calif. 1959, U.S. Ct. Appeals (9th cir.) 1959, U.S. Tax Ct. 1971, U.S. Supreme Ct. 1971. With intelligence div. U.S. Treasury Dept., Los Angeles, 1953-58; with N. Am. Aviation, Los Angeles, 1958-59; practiced in Los Angeles, 1959-60; mem. firm Mori & Katayama, Los Angeles, 1960-77; prin. Nagata, Masuda & Katayama, 1980-83, Katayama & Nagata, 1983-84; pvt. practice Arthur S. Katayama, P.C., Newport Beach, Calif., 1984—; Mem. adv. bd. Sumitomo Bank of Calif., Los Angeles.; Mem. Calif. Democratic State Ctrl. Com., 1958-60. Served with AUS, 1945-47. Mem. ABA, Los Angeles County, Orange County bar assns. Clubs: Mesa Verde/Costa Mesa Country; Big Canyon Country (Newport Beach). Home: 2233 Martin Apt 402 Irvine CA 92612-1452 Office: 4400 Macarthur Blvd Ste 700 Newport Beach CA 92660-2038

KATAYAMA, ROBERT NOBUICHI, lawyer; b. Honolulu, Oct. 11, 1924; s. Sanji K.; widowed; children: Alyce A. Katayama Jenkins, Robert Nobuichi, Kent J. BA, U. Hawaii, 1950; LLB, Yale U., 1955; grad., Command and Gen. Staff Coll., 1964; LLM, George Washington U., 1967; grad., Indsl. Coll. Armed Forces, 1971. Bar: Calif. 1956, Ill. 1973, Hawaii 1989. Commd. 1st lt. JAGC U.S. Army, 1958, advanced through grades to col., 1973, ret., 1973; gen. counsel Overseas Mdse. Inspection Co., San Francisco, 1956-58, Army Contract Adjustment Bd., Washington, 1964-68; prof. law JAG Sch. U. Va., 1968-70; from assoc. to ptnr. Baker & McKenzie, Chgo., Tokyo and San Francisco, 1973-85; ptnr. Seki & Jarvis, San Francisco and San Jose, 1985-86, Nutter, McClennen & Fish, San Francisco, 1986-88; spl. counsel, sr. advisor Crosby, Heafey, Roach & May, Oakland, Calif., 1988; ptnr. Carlsmith Ball, Honolulu, 1988-95, counsel, 1995—; bd. dirs. BIC Bridal Hawaii Inc., Honolulu; chmn., CEO Kapolei People's Inc. dba Kapolei Golf Course, Honolulu, 1996—; pres. Kapolei Holding Corp. Trustee Nat. Japanese Am. Meml. Found., 1995-97, gov., 1997—; bd. dirs. Japanese Cultural Ctr. Hawaii, 1997-98. Named Real Dean U. Hawaii, Honolulu, 1950; Community Chest scholar Honolulu Community Chest, 1950. Mem. ABA, Calif. Bar Assn., Hawaii Bar Assn., Japan Am. Soc. Hawaii, Nat. Japanese Am. Hist. Soc. (legal officer 1984-89), Japanese Am. Soc. Legal Studies, Ret. Officers Assn., 442d Regimental Combat Team Found. (trustee 1993—), 442d Vets. Club (legal advisor 1994-95, pres.-elect 1996, pres. 1997-98), Japanese C. of C. of No. Calif. (bd. dirs. 1978-89), Japan Am., Oahu AJA Vets. Coun. (pres. 1997). Democrat. Buddhist. Office: Carlsmith Ball 1001 Bishop St Ste 2200 Honolulu HI 96813-3405

KATAYAMA, TOSHIHIRO, artist, educator; b. Osaka, Japan, July 17, 1928; s. Hiromu and Hatsuko (Ito) K.; m. Atsumi Fukui, Mar. 20, 1960. Prof. dept. visual and environ. studies Harvard U., Cambridge, Mass., 1966-95; dir. Carpenter Ctr. Visual Arts, Harvard U., Cambridge, Mass., 1990-93. Exhibited in over 25 one-man shows, 1964—, including Herman Miller, Basel and Zurich, Switzerland, 1964-65, Am. Inst. Graphic Arts, N.Y.C., 1968, Gallery Plaza DIC, Tokyo, 1970, Grad. Sch. Design, Harvard U., 1971, Rose Art Mus., Boston, 1971, Kunstlerhaus, Vienna, Austria, 1977; retrospective shows at Sogetsu Kaikan, Tokyo, 1981, Nantenshi Gallery, Tokyo, 1978, 80, 83, 86, 89; works include large wall scultpure, Akasaka Prince Hotel, Tokyo, 1983, theatre curtain (tapestry), Ohmiya Cultural Ctr., Japan, 1985; various environ. graphics and signage design, Boston Subway; granite wall sculpture, Ohara Art Mus., Kurashiki, Japan, 1991; grand flr. landscape design, including steel sculpture and waterfall, Panasonic Head Office, Tokyo, 1992, stone sculpture and 2 wall lerief, Mitsui Kaijo Co., Chiba, 1994, wall lerief by copper, corridor and foyer J.T. Main Office, Tokyo, 1995, monumental sculpture W.H.O. Bldg., Kobe, 1998; subject of book: The Work of Toshihiro Katayama - Visual Construction/Square, Movement/Topology: Homage to a Cube, 1981, Toshi Katayama's Class Graphic Design Work at Harvard U., 1993; Three Notations-Rotations, 1974, Visual Poetry with Octavio Paz, 1974.

KATCHER, RICHARD, lawyer; b. N.Y.C., Dec. 17, 1918; s. Samuel and Gussie (Applebaum) K.; m. Shirley Ruth Rifkin, Sept. 24, 1944; children: Douglas P., Robert A., Patti L. BA, U. Mich., 1941, JD, 1943. Bar: Mich. 1943, N.Y. 1944, Ohio 1946. Assoc. Noonan, Kaufman & Eagan, N.Y.C., 1943-46; from assoc. to ptnr. Ulmer, Berne & Laronge, Cleve., 1946-72; ptnr. Baker & Hostetler, Cleve., 1972-95; lectr. in fed. income taxation Case Western Res. U. Sch. Law, Cleve., 1953-69, 71-72. Contbr. articles on fed. tax to profl. jours. Recipient Disting. Alumni Service award U. Mich., 1987, Leadership medal Pres.' Soc. of U. Mich., 1991. Fellow ABA (coun. sect. taxation 1973-76), Am. Coll. Tax Counsel (regent); mem. Am. Bar Retirement Assn. (bd. dirs., v.p. 1986-87, pres. 1987-88), U. Mich. Pres. Soc. (chmn. exec. com. 1987-90), U. Mich. Cleve. Club (pres. 1959, Outstanding Alumnus award 1987), U. Mich. Alumni Assn. (dir. 1994-98, sec. 1997-98). Avocation: tennis. Home: 26150 Village Ln Apt 104 Beachwood OH 44122-7527 Office: Baker & Hostetler 3200 National City Ctr 1900 E 9th St Ste 3200 Cleveland OH 44114-3475

KATEB, GEORGE ANTHONY, political science educator; b. Bklyn., Feb. 27, 1931; s. Anthony Francis and Victoria Anna (Mesnooh) K. A.B., Columbia U., 1952, A.M., 1953, Ph.D., 1960; D.H.L. (hon.), Amherst, 1989. Mem. faculty Amherst Coll., 1957, prof., 1967-87, Kenan prof. polit. sci., 1974-78, Joseph B. Eastman prof. polit. sci., 1980-87; prof. politics Princeton U., 1987—; vis. lectr. Mt. Holyoke Coll., 1958, Yale U., 1973, Harvard U., 1986; cons. NEH. Author: Utopia and Its Enemies, 2d edit., 1972, Political Theory: Its Nature and Uses, 1968, Utopia, 1971, Hannah Arendt: Politics, Conscience, Evil, 1984, The Inner Ocean: Individualism and Democratic Culture, 1992 (Spitz prize Conf. for Study Polit. Thought 1994), Emerson and Self-Reliance, 1994; mem. editorial bd. Mass. Rev., 1961-70, Polit. Theory,1972—, Am. Polit. Sci. Rev., 1976-81, Jour. History Ideas, 1976—, Jour. Utopian Studies, 1977-80, Raritan, 1980—; cons. editor: Polit. Theory, 1983—. Univ. fellow Columbia U., 1953-54; fellow Soc. Fellows, Harvard U., 1954-57; Guggenheim fellow, 1971-72. Mem. AAUP, Am. Acad. Arts and Scis., Am. Polit. Sci. Assn., New Eng. Polit. Sci. Assn. (exec. com. 1965-66, pres. 1978-79), Am. Soc. Polit. and Legal Philosophy (v.p. 1972-74), Conf. for Study of Polit. Thought, ACLU, Phi Beta Kappa. Office: Princeton U Dept Politics Princeton NJ 08544

KATEMOPOULOS, MILDRED JOSEPHINE, executive secretary; b. Shanghai, China, Apr. 29, 1925; came to the U.S., 1977; d. James Jeremiah and Camille Helmana (Barradas) O'Leary; m. Theodore Demetrius Katemopoulos, Apr. 29, 1946; children: Maureen, Eileen, Kathryn, Paul, Anne-Marie. Grad., Loretto H.S., Shanghai. Pvt. sec. Royal Netherlands Embassy, Shanghai, 1946-49; sec. to mng. dir. Dairy Farm Co., Hong Kong, 1949-58; confidential sec. H.K. Land Co., Hong Kong, 1958-66; writer Children's Page H.K. Sunday Std., Hong Kong, 1966-71; pub. rels. staff Mandarin Hotel, Hong Kong, 1970-73; asst. to CEO Regent Internat. Hotels, Hong Kong, 1974-77; sr. sec. Stanford Rsch. Inst., Menlo Park, Calif., 1977-79; asst. to CEO Cath. Charities, San Jose, Calif., 1981-89, Econ. and Social Opportunities, San Jose, 1989-94; adminstrv. asst. Christ United Presbyn. Ch., San Jose, 1995—; Author: Loretto School, 1990, Born in Shanghai, 1996, (book of poems) When Silver Turns to Gold, 1996. Chmn. Loretto Internat. in the Far East, Hong Kong, 1966-77; founder, pres. Tuesday Club of Hong Kong, 1970-77; pres. Little Flower Club, Hong

Kong, 1972-77. Recipient resolution for decade of svc. to Cath. Charities, Bishop of San Jose, 1989. Roman Catholic. Avocations: writing, editing, gardening, crafts and doll collecting. Home: 6330 Blackberry Ct Gilroy CA 95020

KATER, KATHRYN M., critical care nurse; b. Scranton, Pa., Sept. 22, 1948; d. C. Judd and Gertrude T. (Engel) Holt; m. Victor Kater, Oct. 4, 1975; 1 child, Andrew. Diploma, Barnes Sch. Nursing, St. Louis, 1969; BSN, St. Louis U., 1977, MS in Nursing, 1985; ARNP, U. Fla., 1994. Instr. Forest Park Community Coll., St. Louis; asst. head nurse Barnes Hosp., St. Louis, nurse specialist; clin. nurse specialist Washington U.-Barnes Hosp., 1994; advanced registered nurse practitioner U. Fla. Shands Hosp.; adj. clin. instr. St. Louis U., U. Mo. Translator, researcher, computer expert; contbr. articles to profl. jours. Mem. nat. nurses adv. bd. Nat. Myasthenia Gravis Found. Named Woman of Yr., Myasthenia Gravis Found., 1982. Mem. AACCN. Home: 13309 NW 16th St Pembroke Pines FL 33028

KATES, GERALD SAUL, printing executive; b. Phila., May 7, 1932; s. Millard M. and Beatrice (Soifer) K.; m. Barbara Sue Engelbach, Oct., 1958; children: Lauren Beth, Susan Ellen. BA, Pa. State U., 1954. Pres. The Advertisers Press, Inc., Phila., 1955—, Nelsonian Press Inc., Phila., 1996—; chmn. printing adv. bd. East Montgomery City Vocat. Tech. Sch., Willow Grove, Pa., 1989. Editor Alumni Bulletin Crtl. High Sch., 1994—. Mem. bd. of mgr. Ctrl. High Sch., 1993-95, mem. exec. com., 1994—, v.p. Alumni Assn., 1995-99, hon. life mem. bd. mgrs., 1999—. Decorated Four Chaplains Legion of Honor. Mem. Phil. Table Tennis Club (v.p. and dir. 1970-79, bd. dirs. Liberty Bell chpt. 1990—), U.S. Power Squadron (lt. comdr. 1976-84), Golden Slipper Club, Cardozo Lodge (selectman 1979—, exec. bd. 1961—, Man of Yr. 1988), Nat. Assn. Watch and Clock Collectors, Graphic Arts Assn. Greater Tri-State Area (bd. dirs.). Avocations: table tennis, celestial navigation. Home: 716 Harvard Rd Bala Cynwyd PA 19004-2108

KATES, MORRIS, biochemist, educator; b. Galati, Romania, Sept. 30, 1923; emigrated to Can., 1924, naturalized, 1944; s. Samuel and Toby (Cohen) K.; m. Pirkko Helena Sofia Makinen, June 14, 1957; children: Anna-Lisa, Marja Helena, Ilona Sylvia. Student, Parkdale Coll., 1936-41; B.A., U. Toronto, Ont., Can., 1945, M.A., 1946, Ph.D., 1948. Research asst. Banting Inst., U. Toronto, 1948-49; postdoctoral fellow Nat. Research Council Can., Ottawa, Ont., 1949-51; research officer bioscis. div. Nat. Research Council Can., 1951-68; prof. chemistry U. Ottawa, 1968-69, prof. biochemistry, 1969-89, prof. emeritus, 1989—, vice-dean research Faculty Sci. and Engring., 1978-82, staff research lectr., 1981, chmn. dept. biochemistry, 1982-85. Author: Techniques of Lipidology, 1972, 2d edit., 1986; co-editor: Metabolic Inhibitors vols. II and IV, 1972, 73, Biomembranes vol. 12, 1984, Handbook of Lipid Rsch., vol. 6, 1990, Biochemistry of Archaea (Archaebacteria), 1993; co-editor: Can. Jour. Biochemistry, 1974-84; contbr. numerous articles on lipid rsch. to profl. jours. Fellow Chem. Inst. Can., Royal Soc. Can.; mem. Can. Biochem. Soc. (pres. 1987-88), Am. Chem. Soc., Am. Soc. Biol. Chemists, Biochem. Soc. (London, Morton lectr. 1995), Am. Oil Chemists Soc. (Supelco rsch. award 1984), Ottawa Biol. and Biochem. Soc. (Sci. prize 1977, pres. 1974-75). Rsch. on lipid biochemistry. Home: 1723 Rhodes Crescent, Ottawa, ON Canada K1H 5T1 Office: U Ottawa Dept Biochemistry, 40 Marie Curie, Ottawa, ON Canada KIN 6N5

KATES, ROBERT WILLIAM, geographer, educator, independent scholar; b. Bklyn., N.Y., Jan. 31, 1929; m. Eleanor Hackman, Feb. 9, 1948. Student, NYU, 1946-48, U. Ind., 1957; A.M., U. Chgo., 1960, Ph.D., 1962; Doctorate (hon.), Clark U. Mem. faculty grad. sch. geography Clark U., Worcester, Mass., 1962—, prof., 1968-92, univ. prof., 1974-88; univ. prof., dir. Alan Shawn Feinstein World Hunger Program, Brown U., Providence, 1986-92, univ. prof. emeritus, 1992—; dir. Bur. Resource Assessment and Land Use Planning, U. Coll., Dar es Salaam, Tanzania, 1967-69; hon. research prof. U. Dar es Salaam, 1970-71. Author: Risk Assessment of environmental Hazard, 1978, (with Ian Burton and Gilbert F. White) The Environment as Hazard, 1978; co-editor: Climact Impact Assessment, 1985, Hunger in History, 1990, The Earth as Transformed by Human Action, 1990; also author, editor or co-editor 15 other books, monographs; exec. editor: Environment; contbr. numerous articles to profl. jours. Prize fellow MacArthur Found; recipient Nat. Medal of Sci. President Bush NSF, 1991. Mem. NAS, AAAS, Assn. Am. Geographers (pres. 1993-94), Academia Europaea, Tanzania Soc., Am. Acad. Arts and Scis.

KATHAN, JOYCE C., social worker, administrator; b. Middletown, Conn., Oct. 28, 1931; d. Herbert G. and Mabel Elizabeth (Lee) Clark; m. Boardman W. Kathan, Aug. 17, 1952; children: Nancy Lee, David Wardell, Robert Boardman. BSW magna cum laude, So. Conn. State U., 1976. Dist. dir. Coun. Greater Boston Camp Fire Girls, 1969-73; dir. sr. citizen programs Town of Woodbury, Conn., 1976-97; info. officer Conn. Coalition of Aging, 1998—; participant Global Assembly of Women and Environ., 1991; mem. adv. bd. VNA health Care, 1985-95. Co-author: Youth Where the Action Is, 1970; (with others) Management of Hazardous Agents, Vol. 2: Social and Political Aspects, 1992. Bd. dirs. E. Irene Boardman Found., 1996—, Waterbury YWCA, 1977-83, rec. sec.; mem. Prospect Commn. on Aging, Prospect, Conn., 1979-89, chair 1979-87; apptd. mem. Congl. Dist. 5 adv. coun. Conn. Permanent Commnon Status of Women, 1996—; bd .dirs. Western Conn. Area Agy. on Aging, 1986-92, pres., 1990-92, adv. coun., 1994—. Recipient Outstanding Conn. Women award, 1987. Mem. NASW, AAUW (pub. policy chmn. Conn. chpt. 1996—, com. mem. Assn. Pub. Policy Com. 1985-89, mem. local and state coms. 1978—, Named Gift award Conn. chpt. 1981, 85, 97, Outstanding Cmty. Svc. award Conn. chpt. 1994), LWV (pres. Cheshire chpt. 1989-93), Conn. LWV (pub. policy com. 1988—), Conn. Assn. Sr. Ctr. Pers. (charter mem., rec. sec. 1995-97, Svc. award 1986), Womens Environ. and Devel. Orgn.

KATHER, GERHARD, retired air force base administrator; b. Allenstein, Germany, Jan. 30, 1939; came to the U.S., 1952, naturalized, 1959; s. Ernst and Maria (Kempa) K.; m. Carol Anne Knutsen, Aug. 18, 1962; children: Scott T., Cynthia M., Tracey S., Chris A.; m. Mary Elsie Frank, Oct. 25, 1980. BA in Govt., U. Ariz., 1964; MPA, U. So. Calif., 1971; cert. in pers. adminstrn., U. N.Mex., 1987. Tchr. social studies Covina, Calif., 1965-67; tng. officer Civil Pers., Ft. MacArthur, Calif., 1967-70; chief employee tng. and devel. Corps Engrs., L.A., 1970-72, Frankfurt Area Army Pers. Office, 1972-73; chief employee rels. and tng. brs. Corps Engrs., L.A., 1973-74; chief employee devel. and tng. Kirtland AFB, N.Mex., 1974-87; labor rels. officer Kirtland AFB and detachments in 13 U.S. cities, 1987-90; project coord., adv. Protection and Advocacy Sys., 1991-96; ret., 1996. Mem. adv. com. Albuquerque Tech.-Vocat. Inst., 1982-92, U. N.Mex. Valencia Campus, 1985-92; mem. Coalition for Disability Rights, 1988-96; chmn. Comprehensive Accessibility Network, 1990-96; adv. coun. N.Mex. Disability Prevention, 1992-96; rec. sec. N.Mex. Commn. Blind State Rehab. Adv. Coun., 1993-96. With USAF, 1958-64. Named Prominent Tng. and Devel. Profl., H. Whitney McMillan Co., 1984. Mem. ASTD (treas. chpt. 1984-85), Paralyzed Vets. Am. (bd. dirs. 1986-87, pres. local chpt. 1986-87, 90-92), Toastmasters Internat. (chpt. treas., v.p., pres. 1967-70), Vietnam Vets. Am. (chpt. newsletter editor 1994-95), Phi Delta Kappa. Democrat. Roman Catholic.

KATHERINE, ROBERT ANDREW, chemical company executive; b. Phila., May 26, 1941; s. John and Winifred Irene (Smith) K.; m. Lynda Ann Ketchell, Dec. 27, 1988. B.S.Ch.E., Drexel Inst. Tech., 1964, M.B.A., 1968; P.M.D., Harvard U. Grad. Sch. Bus., 1977. Plant mgr. synthetic phenol plastics div. Allied Chem. Corp., 1964-66; asst. to dir. Far East sales Air Products & Chems., Phila., 1966-70; product group mgr. corp. devel. P.Q. Corp., 1970-72, div. sales mgr. splty. chems., 1972-74; bus. dir. polymers Hooker Chem. & Plastics div. Occidental Petroleum Corp., Burlington, N.J., 1974-78; v.p., gen. mgr. Ruco div. Hooker Chem. & Plastics div. Occidental Petroleum Corp., 1978-80, v.p., gen. mgr. fabricated products div., 1980-81; pres. The McCloskey Corp., 1981-83, chmn. bd., chief exec. officer, 1983—; chmn. bd. McCloskey Corp. (Calif.), McCloskey Corp. (Oreg.); instr. Villanova U., 1973-75; asst. prof. Phila. Coll. Textiles and Sci., 1969-75. Mem. adv. bd. Modern Paint & Coatings Mag.; contbr. numerous articles to profl. jours. and newspapers. Bd. dirs. Inter-Sci. Found., UCLA Med. Sch., 1983-86; bd. dirs., chmn. fin. com., exec. compensation com., mem. exec. com. Hahnemann U.; corp. adv. bd. Huntington's Disease of Am. Mem. Soc. Plastics Industry (chmn. vinyl film group, exec. com. plastic bottle inst.), Nat. Paint and Coatings Assn. (bd. dirs., indsl. coatings steering com.), Young Pres. Orgn., Am. Chem. Soc., Am. Mgmt. Assn. (pres.' assn.), Pa. Soc. Republican. Baptist. Clubs: Harvard Bus. Sch. (Phila., N.Y.C.); Union League (Phila.); Aronimink. Home: 4102 Battles Ln Newtown Square PA 19073-1602 Office: 7600 State Rd Philadelphia PA 19136-3404

KATHKA, DAVID ARLIN, director educational services; b. Columbus, Nebr.; s. Arlin Arthur and Edith Ferne (Wilcox) K.; m. Anne Condon Butler, Aug. 15, 1965. BA, Wayne (Nebr.) State Coll., 1964, MA, 1966; PhD in History, U. Mo., 1976. Tchr. Ravenna (Nebr.) Pub. Schs., 1964-65; instr. Midwestern Coll., Denison, Iowa, 1966-68; prof. history Western Wyo. Coll., Rock Springs, 1972-87, dean acad. affairs, 1980-84, interim pres., 1984-85, v.p. acad. affairs, 1985-87; dir. State Pks. and Cultural Resources Divsn., State of Wyo., Cheyenne, 1987-94, Sweetwater Bd. Coop. Ednl. Svcs., Wyo., 1994—; adj. prof. U. Wyo., Laramie, 1976—, adj. prof. history Western Wyo. Coll., 1996—; vis. instr. U. Mo., St. Louis, 1971-72; cons. various Wyo. govt. agys.; mem. gov.'s Blue ribbon Task Force on Cultural Resources, Wyo. Trails adv. com. Author hist. papers; contbr. hist. articles to mags. Bd. dirs. Sweetwater Mus. Found., Wyo. Territorial Park, 1987-94, Tracks Across Wyo., Wyo. Hist. Found., Rock Springs Area Cmty. Found.; mem. Wyo. Centennial Commn., 1986-87, Rock Springs Libr. Bd.,1 984-87, Gov.'s Com. on Hist. Preservation, 1982; v.p. Rocky Mountain Region Kidney Found., Denver, 1976-77. Recipient Wyo. Humanities award for exemplary svc., 1990. Mem. Orgn. Am. Historians, Wyo. State Hist. Soc. (pres. 1984-85), Wyo. Assn. Profl. Historians (v.p. 1994-96, pres. 1996-97). Democrat. Office: Sweetwater Bd Coop Ednl Svcs PO Box 428 Rock Springs WY 82902-0428*

KATHLENE, LYN, political science edcuator; b. Ft. Wayne, Ind., Feb. 28, 1957; d. Keith Renee and Martha Ann Barker. BA magna cum laude, U. Colo., 1985, MA, 1988, PhD, 1991. Asst. prof. dept. Polit. Sci. Purdue U., West Lafayette, Ind., 1990-96, assoc. prof., 1996-98; dir. masters program pub, policy analysis U. Nebr., Lincoln, 1998—, assoc. prof. dept. polit. sci., 1998—; vis. prof. U. Colo., Boulder, 1991, U. Minn., Mpls., 1996-97; adj. prof. Women's Studies Purdue U., 1990-98. Contbr. articles to profl. jours.; mem. editl. bd. Politics Rsch. Quar., 1991-94, Argumentation and Advocacy, 1997—, SUNY Univ. Press, 1997—. Vol. Cmty. Actin Program, Boulder, 1984-85; com. mem. United Way, Boulder, 1987; coach Odyssey of the Mind Auzora-7 Sch., Boulder, 1989. Rsch. grantee Ctr. Am. Women & Politics, Rutgers U., 1989-90; Gallup Rsch. professorship, 1999—. Mem. AAUW, Am. Polit. Sci. Assn., Western Polit. Sci. Assn., Midwest Polit. Sci. Assn. (women's caucus pres. 1998-99). Democrat. Avocations: running, yoga, weaving, gardening. E-mail: lkathlene@unl.edu. Office: U Nebr Dept Polit Sci 511 Old Father Hall Lincoln NE 68588-0328

KATHOL, ANTHONY LOUIS, finance executive; b. San Diego, June 12, 1964; s. Cletus Louis and Regina Antoinette (Ellrott) K.; m. Kathleen Marie Moore, Jan. 23, 1988; children: Nicole Kathleen, Natalie Antoinette, Holly Rose. BS, U. So. Calif., 1986; MBA, U. San Diego, 1988. Fin. aid analyst U. San Diego, 1986-87; bookkeeper Golden Lion Tavern, San Diego, 1987-88; fin. and budget coord. Santa Fe Pacific Realty Corp. (name now Catellus Devel. Corp.), Brea, Calif., 1988-91; mgr. fin. analysis SW U.S. Catellus Devel. Corp., Anaheim, Calif., 1992-93; mgr. leasing Pacific Design Ctr., West Hollywood, Calif., 1994-95, dir. fin. and policy, 1995-96, v.p. asset mgmt., 1996-97; project mgr. Spieker Properties, Orange, Calif., 1997—. Calif. Bldg. Industry Assn. fellow, 1986, U. San Diego fellow, 1987. Mem. U. San Diego Grad. Bus. Students Assn., K.C. (fin. sec. 1990-91), Tau Kappa Epsilon. Republican. Roman Catholic. Avocations: Civil War history, collecting commerative plates and coins, reading, basketball, golf. Home: 3805 Maxon Ln Chino CA 91710-2073 Office: Spieker Properties Ste 165 600 City Pkwy West Orange CA 92868

KATHREIN, MICHAEL LEE, leasing company executive, real estate company executive; b. Chgo., Nov. 26, 1953; s. Joseph A. and Mildred M. Kathrein; children: Jane Emily, Joseph Andrew, Theodore Michael, Elizabeth Grace. BS in Acctg., U. Nebr., 1978; M in Mgmt., Northwestern U., 1985. CPA, Ill.; lic. real estate broker, pilot. Tax mgr. Touche Ross & Co., Chgo., 1978-84; corp. contr., v.p. Lettuce Entertain You Enterprises, Chgo., 1984-86; pres., CEO Kathrein Leasing Co., Chgo., 1983—; also bd. dirs.; pres., chief exec. officer Empire Real Estate Investment Co., Chgo., 1986—; bd. dirs., speaker Nat. Speakers Bur., N.Y.C., 1985-94; cons. Fla. Investor, Inc., Cocoa, 1986—. Author: (how-to book) Real Estate Comparative Analysis, 1986. Bd. dirs. Revenue Crusade of Mercy, United Way, Chgo., 1980. Mem. AICPA, Cert. Mgmt. Accts. Assn. (cert.), Cert. Internal Auditors Assn. (cert.), Nat. Assn. Realtors, Young Pres.'s Orgn., Northwestern U. Alumni Assn., Mensa. Avocations: aviation, lecturing. Home: 7618 N Eastlake Ter # G Chicago IL 60626-1422

KATINSKY, STEVEN, communications company executive; b. Phila., Feb. 6, 1959. BS, Rutgers Coll., 1981. CEO, pres. Media and Transactions, Inc., Santa Monica, Calif.; co-founder, former CEO Hollywood Online, Santa Monica. Office: Media and Transactions Inc 3015 Main St Ste 400 Santa Monica CA 90405-6401

KATKIN, EDWARD SAMUEL, psychology educator; b. N.Y.C., Aug. 15, 1937; s. Nathan and Rosalind (Davis) K.; m. Felice Lapin, Aug. 10, 1958 (dec. 1961); m. 2d Wendy Sue Freedman, Feb. 3, 1963; children: Kenneth, Elizabeth. B.A., CCNY, 1958; Ph.D., Duke U., 1963. Asst. prof. SUNY, Buffalo, 1963-66, assoc. prof., 1966-70, prof. dept. psychology, 1970-86 (chmn. 1980-86); prof. dept. psychology SUNY, Stony Brook, 1986—, chmn. dept. psychology, 1986-92, dean divsn. social and behavioral scis., 1993-96. Fellow Am. Psychol. Soc.; mem. Soc. Psychophysiol. Rsch. (pres. 1983-84), Am. Psychosomatic Soc., N.Y. Acad. Sci. Home: 11 Bayview Ave East Setauket NY 11733-3903 Office: SUNY Dept Psychology Stony Brook NY 11794-2500

KATLEMAN, HARRIS L., television executive; b. Omaha; m. Helen Breitweiser, Aug., 1997; children: Steven, Lisa, Michael. Sr. exec. v.p., dir. Goodson-Todman Broadcasting, 1961-80; pres. Four Star Entertainment; sr. v.p. MGM, Inc.; pres. MGM-TV, 1972-77; exec. producer Bennett, Katleman Prodns., 1977-80; chmn. bd. 20th Century Fox TV, 1980-92; pres., CEO Shadowhill Prodns., 1992-93; COO Mark Goodson Prodns., L.A., 1993-95; COO, ptnr. Jonathan Goodson Ptnrs., L.A., 1996—; exec. prodr. Forgive or Forget, 1998—. Mem. bd. govs. Mcpl. League of Beverly Hills, Calif.; bd. govs. Cedar Sinai Med. Ctr. Recipient Emmy nomination Richard Boone Repertory Theatre. Mem. Acad. TV Arts and Scis., Hollywood Radio and TV Soc. (bd. dirs., sec., pres.). Office: Jonathan Goodson Partners care Paramount Pictures 4500 Wilshire Blvd2nd Fl Los Angeles CA 90010

KATLIC, JOHN EDWARD, management consultant; b. Washington, Pa., Nov. 3, 1928; s. Frederick John and Dorothy Ann (Gideon) K.; m. Nancy Jean Nicely, Aug. 26, 1950; children: Mark Richard, Kerry Leigh, Kevin Edward, Kathleen Diane, Nancy Ellen. BS in Engring. of Mines, W.Va. U., 1955, MS in Engring. of Mines, 1961. Mine surveyor Rochester & Pittsburgh Coal Co., Indiana, Pa., 1948-49; mine supt. Consolidation Coal Co., Morgantown, W.Va., 1959-62, gen. supt., 1962-66; v.p. Consolidation Coal Co., Pitts., 1973-75; sr. mining engr. Ea. Assn. Coal, Pitts., 1967-68, divsn. mgr., 1969, v.p. pers. safety and indsl. rels., 1970; v.p., gen. mgr. Semet-Solvay divsn. Allied Chem. Ea. Assn. Coal, Pitts., N.J., 1970-73; exec.v.p. adminstrn. engring. and govt. rels. Island Creek Coal Co., Lexington, Ky., 1975-83; sr. v.p. fuel supply Am. Electric Power Svc. Corp., 1983-93; pres. So. Ohio Coal, Cen. Ohio Coal, Windsor Coal, Conesville Coal (all subs.), 1983-93; mem. negotiating team Nat. Bituminous Coal Wage Agreement, Joint Industry Devel. Com., 1978; cons. projects in Russia, Siberia, Kazakhstan, S. Africa. Patentee mining machine indicator, dust control in longwall mining. Mem. Morgantown City Coun., 1964-66, Marshall U. Found., 1979; bd. dirs. W.Va. Edn. Found., 1983-90, Inland Waterways Users Bd., 1992-93, Fairfield County Found.; mem. Steering com. W.Va. U.; chmn. bd. trustees Lancaster Fairfield Community Hosp., 1990-91. With inf. U.S. Army, 1946-47, C.E., 1950-52. Named Man of Yr., Coal Age Mag., 1987, Ohio Mining and Reclamation Assn., 1988; recipient Erskine Ramsay medal AIME, 1995, Kingery Safety award Pa. Coal Mining Inst. Am., 1995. Mem. AIME, VFW, Soc. Mining Engrs., Nat. Mine Rescue Assn., Nat. Mining Assn. (chmn. 1990-92), Mine Rescue Vets. of Pitts. Dist., Lancaster Fairfield C. of C. (pres. 1989), Symposiarchs, King Coal Club, Ky. Cols., Cherry River Navy Club, Buckeye Lake Yacht Club, Masons, Shriners. Republican. Presbyterian. Home: 1233 Ridgewood Way Lancaster OH 43130-1154

KATO, BRUCE, curator. Chief curator Alaska State Mus., Juneau, 1987—. Office: Alaska State Mus 395 Whittier St Juneau AK 99801-1718

KATO, MASANOBU, lawyer, educator; b. Nagasaki, Japan, Sept. 9, 1946; s. Nobutaro and Miyoko (Inoue) K.; m. Machiko Kawashima, Sept. 30, 1973; children: Masayuki, Mitsumasa. LLB, U. Tokyo, 1969, D of Juridical Sci., 1986. Bar: Japan 1968. Assoc. prof. law Nagoya (Japan) U., 1973-82, prof. law, 1982—, vice dean, 1989—; rsch. fellow Tokyo U., 1969-73; vis. fellow Harvard U., Boston, 1980-81; vis. scholar Columbia U., N.Y.C., 1981-82, London U. SOAS (Sch. of Oriental and African Studies), 1996-97; vis. prof. law Hawaii U., Honolulu, 1985, Columbia U., N.Y.C., 1986-87, Beijing U., China, 1991; vice rep. of Japan for treaty for unification of lease Dept. Fgn. Affairs, Ottawa, Ont., Can., 1988; examiner Nat. Bar Exam., 1992-96. Author: The Civil Law System and Law of Unjust Enrichment, 1986, (with others) A Textbook on Torts, 1977, Contemporary Tort Law Study, 1991, Contemporary Civil Code Study, 1993, The Emperor System of Japan, 1994, (with others) Japan Business Law Guide, 1988; editor: From Torts to Social Welfare, 1989, Law of Product Liability, 1994, Law and Politics in Contemporary Japan, 1994; co-editor: Law of International Transaction, 1988; contbr. articles to profl. jours. Commr. Environ. Protection Agy., Nagoya, 1986-87; family ct. arbitrator Nagoya Family Ct., 1988—. Mem. Comparative Law Soc. Tokyo, Pvt. Law Soc. Tokyo (commr. mng. com. 1985). Avocations: essay writing, tennis. Office: Nagoya U Sch Law, Furacho, Chikusa-ku, Nagoya 464, Japan

KATO, PAMELA KIYOMI, lawyer; b. Mountain View, Calif., Oct. 24, 1964; d. George Mas and Satsuki May Kato. BA, U. Calif., Santa Barbara, 1987; JD, Santa Clara U., 1990. Bar: U.S. Dist. Ct. (no. dist.) Calif., 1991, U.S. Ct. Appeals 1991. Asst. dist. atty. Santa Cruz County, Santa Cruz, Calif., 1991—. Office: 701 Ocean St Santa Cruz CA 95060-4003

KATO, TERRI EMI, elementary school and gifted and talented educator; b. Gardena, Calif., Sept. 1, 1953; d. Shunji James and Ruby Miyo (Sumi) K. BA, Calif. State U., Long Beach, 1976; MA, U.S. Internat. U., 1987. Cert. tchr. multiple subjects, learning handicapped, severely handicapped, resource specialist, lang. devel. specialist, c.c.'s, Calif. Learning disabled group specialist Montebello (Calif.) Unified Sch. Dist., 1979-81; resource specialist ABC Unified Sch. Dist., Cerritos, Calif., 1981-82; spl. day class tchr. Santa Ana (Calif.) Unified Sch. Dist., 1982—; math. resource tchr., 1990—; 1st and 2nd grade tchr. Santa Anna (Calif.) Unified Sch. Dist., 1996—. Mem. NEA, Calif. Tchrs. Assn., Santa Ana Educators Assn. (mem. spl. edn. task force rules and election com., bldg. rep. 1992—, mem. supt.'s cabinet 1995—), Coun. for Exceptional Children, Orange County Math. Coun. Avocations: travel, reading, hiking, dog grooming, golf. Office: James Monroe Elem 417 E Central Ave Santa Ana CA 92707-3501

KATO, WALTER YONEO, physicist; b. Chgo., Aug. 19, 1924; s. Naotaro and Hideko (Kondo) K.; m. Anna Chieko Kurata, June 26, 1953; children—Norman, Cathryn, Barbara. BS, Haverford (Pa.) Coll., 1946; MS, U. Ill., 1949; PhD, Pa. State U., University Park, 1954. Rsch. assoc. Ordnance Research Lab., Pa. State U., 1949-52, Brookhaven Nat. Lab., Upton, N.Y., 1952-53; sr. nuclear engr., asso. chmn. dept. applied sci. Brookhaven Nat. Lab., 1975-77, assoc. chmn. dept. nuclear energy, 1977-80, dep. chmn., 1980-88, chmn., 1988-91, sr. nuclear engr., 1991-97, cons., 1997—; rsch. affiliate dept. nuclear engring. MIT, Cambridge, 1999—; sr. physicist Argonne (Ill.) Nat. Lab., 1953-75; vis. prof. dept. nuclear engring. U. Mich., Ann Arbor, 1974-75; cons. Office Nuclear Regulatory Research, U.S. Nuclear Regulatory Commn., 1974-76. Contbr. articles to profl. jours. Bd. dirs. Naperville (Ill.) YMCA, 1966-74; mem. Order of Sacred Treasure Japanese Govt., 1992. Served with Ordnance Corps AUS, 1946-47. Fulbright Research fellow, 1958-59, STA (Japan) fellow, 1998. Fellow Am. Nuclear Soc. (dir.), Argonne Univ. Assn. (Distinguished Appt. award 1974); mem. Am. Phys. Soc., AAAS, Sigma Xi. Methodist. Home: 324 Washington St Apt 309 Wellesley MA 02481-4941

KATONA, BRUCE RICHARD, real estate company executive; b. Perth Amboy, N.J., Aug. 16, 1960; s. Julius Richard and Carol Arlene (Jugan) K.; m. Wing-Ming Wu, Jan. 4, 1991; 1 child, Morgan Alexandra. BS in Environ. Sci., Stockton State Coll., Pomona, N.J., 1982; BS in Environ. Design, Rutgers U., New Brunswick, N.J., 1986. Cert. profl. planner, landscape architect, N.J. Project mgr. Bradgate Assocs., East Brunswick, N.J., 1985-88; project coord. Hills Devel. Co., Bedminster, N.J., 1988-91; landscape architect, planner Storch Engrs., Florham Park, N.J., 1991-92; v.p. Gale, Wentworth & Dillon, Bedminster, N.J., 1992—. Mentor Renaissance Newark, 1995—; fundraiser N.J. Spl. Olympics, 1994—; bd. dirs. Morris Habitat for Humanity, 1998—. Mem. Am. Soc. Landscape Architects, Urban Land Inst., Am. Planning Assn. Avocations: golf, tennis, skiing. Office: Ste 105 100 Campus Dr Florham Park NJ 07932

KATONA, PETER GEZA, biomedical engineer, educator; b. Budapest, Hungary, June 25, 1937; came to U.S., 1956, naturalized, 1962; s. Stephan and Irene (Renner) K.; m. Jaroslava Blanar, Aug. 27, 1966; children—Catherine Iris, Andrew George. B.S. in Elec. Engring, U. Mich., 1960; S.M. in Elec. Engring. (Sloan fellow, 1960-62), M.I.T., 1962, Sc.D. in Elec. Engring, 1965. Asst. prof. elec. engring. M.I.T., 1965-69; assoc. prof. biomed. engring. Case Western Res. U., Cleve., 1969-78; prof. Case Western Res. U., 1978-92, chmn. dept., 1980-87; program dir. biomed. engring. and aiding the disabled NSF, 1989-91; v.p. biomed. engring. The Whitaker Found., 1991-95, exec. v.p. biomed. engring., 1995—, pres. biomed. engring., 1998—. Editorial bd.: American Jour. Physiology, 1975-81; contbr. articles on cardio-respiratory control and automated drug delivery to profl. jours. Recipient Alexander von Humboldt award, 1987-88. Fellow AAAS, Am. Inst. Med. & Biol. Engring. (founding); sr. mem. IEEE, Am. Physiol. Soc., Biomed. Engring. Soc. (bd. dirs. 1977-80, pres. 1984-85), Am. Soc. Engring. Edn. Office: The Whitaker Found 1700 N Moore St Ste 2200 Arlington VA 22209-1923

KATOPE, CHRISTOPHER GEORGE, English language educator; b. Lowell, Mass., Apr. 1, 1918; s. George and Bessie (Savas) K.; m. Marjorie Spencer King, June 6, 1942; children: Theodora Katope Rowland, Christopher Lawrence. Student, U. Louisville, 1939-41; M.A., U. Chgo., 1947; Ph.D., Vanderbilt U., 1954. Instr. English Westminster Coll., 1947-50; instr. English Allegheny Coll., 1952-54, asst. prof., 1954-62, asso. prof., 1962-69, prof. English, 1969-83, prof. emeritus, 1983—; Fulbright prof. Athens Coll., 1959-60, Anatolia Coll., Greece, 1960-61. Author, editor: (with P. Zolbrod) Beyond Berkeley, 1966, Rhetoric of Revolution, 1970; Contbr. articles to profl. jours. Served with USNR, 1941-45. Home: 705 Alden St Meadville PA 16335-2352

KATRITZKY, ALAN ROY, chemistry educator, consultant; b. London, Eng., Aug. 18, 1928; s. Frederick Charles and Emily Gertrude (Lane) K.; m. Agnes Juliane Dietlinde Kilian, Aug. 5, 1952; children: Margaret, Erika, Rupert, Freda. B.A., Oxford U., 1951, B.Sc., 1952, M.A., 1954, D.Phil., 1954; Ph.D., Cambridge U., 1958, Sc.D., 1963; Sc.D. (hon.), U. Nac. Madrid, 1986, U. Poznan, Poland, 1990, U. Gdansk, Poland, 1994, U. East Anglia, U.K., 1995, Beijing Inst. Tech., 1995, U. Toulouse, France, 1996; Hon. Prof., Xian Modern U., 1995. ICI fellow U. Oxford, 1956-58; lectr. chemistry U. Cambridge, 1958-63; fellow Churchill Coll.; prof. chemistry U. East Anglia, 1963-80; dean U. East Anglia (Sch. Chem. Scis.), 1963-70, 76-80; Kenan prof. organic chemistry U. Fla., Gainesville, 1980—; dir. Fla. Inst. Het. Cpds., 1986—. Editor: Advances in Heterocyclic Chemistry, vols. 1-68, 1963—; regional editor: Tetrahedron, 1980—; chmn. editl. bd. Comprehensive Heterocyclic Chemistry, 1st edit., 9 vols., 1985, 2d edit., 10 vols., 1996, Comprehensive Organic Functional Group Transformations, 7 vols., 1995. Named Cavaliere Ufficiale. Fellow Royal Soc.; mem. Am., Brit., Japanese, Swiss, Italian (hon. mem.), Polish (hon. mem.) Chem. Socs., Internat. Soc. Het. Chem., Polish Acad. Sci. (fgn. mem.), Real Catalan Acad. Home: 1221 SW 21st Ave Gainesville FL 32601-8417 Office: U Fla Dept Chemistry Gainesville FL 32611

KATSAKIORES, GEORGE NICHOLAS, state legislator, retired restauranteur; b. Derry, N.H., Dec. 11, 1924; s. Nicholas G. and Agorista

(Siatravinos) K.; m. Lucille Brunelle, Nov. 11, 1963 (div. July 1980); children: Sheila, Glen, Greg, Karen, Gary; m. Phyllis M. Harrie, Oct. 9, 1983. Student, U. N.H., 1946-48. Owner White's Restaurant, Derry, 1948-88, ret.; mem. N.H. Ho. of Reps., 1982—, chair transp. com., chmn. emeritus; dir. Derry Devel. and Preservation Corp.; vice chmn. Airport Access Hwy. Task Force, Manchester, N.H.; mem. transp. task force Am. Legis. Exch. Coun., Washington. Dir. Northeast Corridor Initiative, Boston; mem. Rockingham County Com., Brentwood, N.H., vice chmn. Rock City Del., Rep. Nat. Party, N.H. Rep. Com. Cpl. Med. Corps. U.S. Army, 1943-45, ETO. Mem. Am. Legion #9, VFW (Post 1617), AARP, N.H. Transp. and Hwy. Users Coalition, N.H. R.R. Revitalization Assn., Hoodkroft County Club (Derry). Greek Orthodox. Avocations: golf, politics. Home: 1 Bradford St Derry NH 03038-4258

KATSH, M. ETHAN, law educator; b. N.Y.C., Sept. 3, 1945; s. Abraham Isaac and Estelle (Wachtell) K.; m. Beverly Schwartz; children: Rebecca, Gabriel, Gideon. BA, NYU, 1967; JD, Yale U., 1970. Bar: N.Y. 1970. Asst. prof. legal studies U. Mass., Amherst, 1970-76, assoc. prof., 1977-88, prof., 1988—, chair legal studies dept., 1993-94; dir. Ctr. Info. Tech. and Dispute Resolution, 1997—. Author: The Electronic Media and the Transformation of Law, 1989, Law in a Digital World, 1995; co-author: Before the Law, 6th edit., 1998; editor: Taking Sides: Clashing Views on Controversial Legal Issues, 1982, 8th edit., 1998; bd. of editors: Cyberspace Law Abstracts; contbr. articles on law, media and computers to profl. jours. and mags. Co-founder U. Mass. Mediation Project, 1980; founder, dir. Online Ombuds Office, 1996—. Mem. Am. Legal Studies Assn. (pres. 1978-80). E-mail: katsh@legal.umass.edu. Office: U Mass Dept Legal Studies Dept Legal Studies Amherst MA 01003

KATSH, SALEM MICHAEL, lawyer; b. N.Y.C., May 5, 1948; s. Abraham Isaac and Estelle (Wachtell) K.; m. Jennette Williams, Sept. 4, 1983; children: Halley Rachel, Emmet Walker. BA, NYU, 1970, JD cum laude, 1972. Bar: N.Y. 1973, U.S. Dist. Ct. (so., ea., no. dists. N.Y.) 1975, U.S. Ct. of Appeals (2d cir.) 1975, U.S. Ct. of Appeals (9th cir.) 1977, U.S. Supreme Ct. 1983, U.S. Ct. Appeals (fed. cir.) 1990, U.S. Dist. Ct. (no. dist.) Calif. 1993. Assoc. Weil, Gotshal & Manges, N.Y.C., 1972-80, ptnr., 1980-97; ptnr. Shearman & Sterling, N.Y.C., 1997—; adj. prof. New York Law Sch., 1980-84. Author: (monograph) Industrial Policy and the Law, 1982; (with others) The Limits of Corporate Power, 1981; founder Jour. Proprietary Rights; contbr. articles to profl. jours. Mem. ABA (chmn. nat. inst. com., antitrust law sect. 1986-88), N.Y. State Bar Assn., Order of Coif. Office: 599 Lexington Ave New York NY 10022-6030

KATSIANIS, JOHN NICK, financial executive; b. Chgo., Oct. 27, 1960; s. John Nick and Rosalie A. (Kitzberger) K. BS in Acctg. and Fin., U. Ill., Chgo., 1982. CPA, Ill. Staff acct. gen. acctg. Svc. Master Industries, Inc., Downers Grove, Ill., 1983-84, staff acct. spl. projects, 1984-85; staff acct. Svc. Master Home Health Care Svcs., Downers Grove, 1985, controller, 1985-89; dir. fin., asst. treas. Rush-Presbyn.-St. Luke's Med. Ctr., Chgo., 1989-93; sr. v.p., CFO NYLCare Health Plans of the Midwest, Oak Brook, Ill., 1993-98; regional pres. Avanti Health Sys. Ill., Inc., Oak Brook, 1995-96; dir. fin. Elmhurst (Ill.) Meml. Health Sys., 1998—. Vice pres. Countryside (Ill.) Police Pension Bd., 1987—. Mem. AICPA, Ill. CPA Soc., Healthcare Fin. Mgmt. Assn., Chgo. Healthcare Exec. Forum. Baptist. Avocations: golf, snow skiing, swimming, softball. Home: 860 Tam Oshanter Bolingbrook IL 60440

KATSIFF, BRUCE, artist; b. Phila., Dec. 10, 1945; s. Myer and Rose (August) K.; m. Joane Mitnick, Dec. 30, 1965; 1 child, Timothy. BFA, Rochester Inst. Tech., 1968; MFA, Pratt Inst., 1973; postgrad., Oxford (Eng.) U., 1987. Film producer Eastman Kodak Co., Rochester, N.Y., 1968; adj. prof. Thomas Edison Coll., Trenton, N.J., 1970-74; chmn. fine art Bucks County Coll., Newtown, Pa., 1973-84, prof., 1984-88; chmn. art and music Bucks Coll., Newtown, 1988-89; dir. James A. Michener Art Mus., 1990—; mng. bd. dirs. Photography Sesquicentennial, Phila., 1988-90. Exhibited at Mus. Modern Art, N.Y.C., 1968, Internat. Mus. Photography, Rochester, N.Y., 1969, Phila. Art Mus., 1970, Am. Arts Ctr., Exeter, Eng., 1970, Tainjan Inst., China, 1987, Pa. Acad. Fine Arts, 1990, Washington Photography Ctr., 1993. Grantee NEA, 1973; fellowship Pa. Arts Coun., 1990. Fellow Soc. Photographic Educators; mem. Pa. Coun. on Arts (mus. panel 1982-85, visual arts panel 1987-90). Home: PO Box 28 Lumberville PA 18933-0028

KATSON, ROBERTA MARINA, economist; b. Albuquerque, Oct. 5, 1947; d. Robert V. and Penelope (Papafrangos) Katson; student Emory U., 1966-67, Ga. State U., 1967-69; children: Justin Cyrus, Renee Alexis. BA, U. N.Mex., 1974, MA, 1977. Gen. mgr. Window Rock (Ariz.) Motor Inn, Navajo Reservation, 1972-73; research asst. dept. econs. U. N.Mex., Albuquerque, 1974-75, research asso. Resource Econ. Group, 1975-77; economist program analysis Econ. Devel. Adminstrn., Dept. Commerce, Washington, 1977-79; economist Dept. Energy, Washington, 1979-84; cons. Calligraphic Design, Fairfax, Va., 1986-88, owner, 1989-91; fin. analyst Adminstrn. for Children and Families, Dept. of HHS, Washington, 1991—. Mem. Phi Kappa Phi, Omicron Delta Epsilon. Democrat. Contbr. articles to profl. jours. Home: 11125 Watermans Dr Reston VA 20191-4310 Office: HHS/ACF 370 L'Enfant Promenade SW Washington DC 20447-0001

KATSORIS, CONSTANTINE NICHOLAS, lawyer, consultant; b. Bklyn., Dec. 5, 1932; s. Nicholas C. and Nafsika (Klonis) K.; m. Ann Kanganis, Feb. 19; children: Nancy, Nicholas, Louis. BS in Acctg., Fordham U., 1953; JD cum laude, 1957; LLM, NYU, 1963. Bar: N.Y. 1957, U.S. Dist. Ct. (so. and ea. dist.) N.Y. 1959, U.S. Tax. Ct. 1959, U.S. Ct. Appeals (2nd cir.) 1959, U.S. Supreme Ct. 1961. Assoc. Cahill, Gordon, Reindel & Ohl, N.Y.C., 1958-64; asst. prof. Law Sch. Fordham U., N.Y.C., 1964-66; assoc. prof. Fordham U., 1966-69; prof., 1969—, apptd. Wilkinson prof. law, 1991; cons. N.Y. State Temporary Commn. on Estates, 1964-67; arbitration panelist N.Y. Stock Exchange, 1971—, Nat. Assn. Securities Dealers, 1968—, 1st Jud. Dept., 1972—; pub. mem. Securities Industry Conf. on Arbitration, 1977-97, emeritus pub. mem., 1997—; pvt. judge adjudication ctr. Duke U. Law Sch., 1989—. Contbr. articles to profl. jours. Mem. sch. bd. Greek Orthodox Parochial Sch. St. Spyridon, 1975-89, chmn. sch. bd., 1983-89. With U.S. Army, 1963. Recipient Cert. Appreciation Nat. Assn. Securities Dealers, 1982, Ellis Is. Medal of Honor award, 1999. Mem. ABA (fed. estate and gift tax com. 1966-68), N.Y. State Bar Assn. (sect. on trust and estates 1969—), Assn. Bar City of N.Y. (trusts, estates and surrogates' cts. com. 1968-70, legal assistance com. 1965-67), Fordham U. Law Alumni Assn. (bd. dirs. 1972—), Fordham U. Law Ref. Alumni Assn. (pres. 1968-64). Republican. Greek Orthodox. Office: 140 W 62nd St New York NY 10023-7407

KATSOYANNIS, PANAYOTIS GEORGE, biochemist, educator; b. Greece, Jan. 7, 1924; came to U.S., 1952; naturalized U.S. citizen, 1961.; MS in Organic Chemistry, U. Athens, Greece, 1948, PhD in Organic Chemistry, 1952. Rsch. asst. Lab. Organic Chemistry U. Athens, 1947-50, vis. scientist Lab. Organic Chemistry, 1957-58; rsch. assoc. dept. biochemistry Cornell U. Med. Coll., 1952-56, asst. prof. biochemistry, 1956-57; assoc. prof. biochemistry U. Pitts. Sch. Medicine, 1958-64; head divsn. biochemistry Med. Rsch. Ctr. Brookhaven Nat. Lab., Upton, N.Y., 1964-68; Dorothy H. and Lewis Rosenstiel prof. biochemistry Mt. Sinai Sch. Medicine, CUNY, 1968-98, prof. biochemistry and molecular biology, 1998—, head chmn. dept. biochemistry, 1968—; Edwin J. Meml. lectr. Harvard U., 1963. Patentee in field; contbr. over 130 articles to profl. jours., chpts. to books. Fellow State Scholarship Found. of Greece, 1952-54, sr. rsch. fellow USPHS, 1958-63; recipient Commemorative medallion Am. Diabetes Assn., 1972, Jacobi Medallion Mt. Sinai Alumni, 1995, Rsch. Career Devel. award USPHS, 1963. Fellow N.Y. Acad. Scis.; mem. AAAS, Am. Chem. Soc., Royal Soc. Chemistry., Nat. Acad. Greece (corr.), Biochem. Soc., Am. Soc. Biochemistry and Molecular Biology, Pharm. Soc. Japan. Office: Mt Sinai Sch Medicine CUNY Box 1020 One Gustave L Levy Pl New York NY 10029 Home: 69 Drake Ln Manhasset NY 11030-1229*

KATTAMIS, THEODORE ZENON, metallurgy educator, material engineering; b. Kythrea, Cyprus, May 7, 1936; came to U.S., 1962; s. Zenon Nicholas and Maria (Zachariades) K.; m. Jessica Ann Firme, Dec. 11, 1976 (div. Aug. 1987); children: Alexis, Nicholas. Mining Engr., Liege (Belgium) U., 1960, Geol. Engr., 1961, MetE, 1962; MS, MIT, 1963, ScD, 1965. Registered profl. engr., Mass., Conn. Lectr. Liege U., 1960-62; rsch. assoc. MIT, Cambridge, 1965-69; asst. prof. metallurgy U. Conn., Storrs, 1969-70, assoc. prof., 1970-75, prof., 1975—; vis. prof. Centre des Matériaux, Ecole Nationale Supérieure des Mines de Paris, 1977, Nat. Bur. Standards, Gaithersburg, Md., 1983; cons. in field to Ctr. for Composite Materials, MIT, 1985-88, U.S. Army Materials Rsch. Lab., Watertown, Mass., 1988—. Contbr. numerous articles to profl. jours. Recipient Cert. Recognition, NASA, Marshall Space Flight Ctr., 1980; Rsch. grantee NASA, 1973, 75, NSF, 1972-75, Air Force Office Sci. Rsch., Washington, 1977-81. Mem. ASM Internat., Metall. Soc. :Home: 74 Church St Watertown MA 02472-3837 Office: U Conn 97 S Eagleville Road Ext Storrs Mansfield CT 06268-2224

KATTWINKEL, JOHN, physician, pediatrics educator; b. Newton, Mass., June 24, 1941; s. Egon Emil and Dorothy Lucile (Fish) K.; m. Phyllis Ann Denton, Sept. 14, 1963; children: Susan, Linda. BS, Rensselaer Poly. Inst., 1964; B in Med. Sci., Dartmouth Coll., 1966; MD, Harvard U., 1968. Diplomate Am. Bd. Pediatrics, Am. Bd. Neonatology (bd. dirs. 1981-86). Resident in pediatrics Duke Med. Ctr., Durham, N.C., 1968-70; clin. assoc. NIH, Bethesda, Md., 1970-72; neonatology fellow Case Western Res. U., Cleve., 1972-74; asst. prof. pediatrics U. Va., Charlottesville, 1974-78, assoc. prof., 1978-84, prof., 1984—, dir. neonatology, 1974—, Charles Fuller chair in neonatology, 1998—; founder Perinatal Edn. Ctr., Charlottesville, 1976—; Poland and China cons. Project HOPE, Milwood, Va., 1979-92; hon. prof. Zhejiang Med. U., Hangzhou, People's Republic of China, 1985. Mem. editl. bd. Pediatrics, 1999—; contbr. articles on newborn respiration and med. edn. to profl. jours.; inventor device for nasal ventilation of infants. Lt. comdr. USPHS, 1970-72. Fellow Am. Acad. Pediatrics (fetus and newborn com. 1983-89), Ross Profl. Edn. award 1989, neonatal resuscitation program steering com. 1989-98, chair 1994-98, SIDS task force chair 1992—); mem. Am. Pediatric Soc., Soc. for Pediatric Rsch. Avocation: tennis. Home: 920 Charter Oaks Dr Charlottesville VA 22901-0629 Office: U Va Dept Pediatrics Charlottesville VA 22908

KATZ, ABRAHAM, retired foreign service officer; b. Bklyn., Dec. 4, 1926; s. Alexander and Zina (Rabinowitz) K.; children: Tamar, Jonathan, Naomi; m. Marion Scheinberger, July 29, 1996. B.A. cum laude, Bklyn. Coll., 1948; M.I.A., Columbia U., 1950; Ph.D., Harvard U., 1968. Commd. fgn. service officer Dept. State, 1951; 1st sec. U.S. missions to NATO, OECD, Paris, 1959-64; counselor Am. Embassy, Moscow, 1964-66; dir. office of OECD European Communities and Atlantic Polit. Econ. Affairs, Washington, 1967-74; dep. chief of mission OECD, Paris, 1974-78; dep. asst. sec. for internat. econ. policy and research Dept. Commerce, Washington, 1978-80; asst. sec. internat. econ. policy Dept. Commerce, 1980-81; U.S. rep., ambassador OECD, Paris, 1981-84; pres. U.S. Coun. Internat. Bus., 1984-99, pres. emeritus, 1999—; employer mem. gov. body Internat. Labor Orgn., 1984-99. Author: The Politics of Economic Reform in the Soviet Union, 1972. Decorated grand officier Ordre National du Merite (France); recipient U.S. Coun. Internat. Bus. Internat. Leadership award. Mem. Am. Polit. Sci. Assn., Assn. Advancement Slavic Studies, Am. Fgn. Svc. Assn., Am. Assn. Comparative Econ. Studies, Coun. of Fgn. Rels., Cosmos Club, Harvard Club, B'nai Brith, Century Assn. Office: US Coun Internat Bus 1212 Avenue Of The Americas New York NY 10036-1602

KATZ, ADRIAN IZHACK, physician, educator; b. Bucharest, Romania, Aug. 3, 1932; came to U.S., 1965, naturalized, 1976; s. Ferdinand and Helen (Lustig) K.; m. Miriam Lesser, Mar. 31, 1965; children—Ron, Iris. M.D., Hebrew U., 1961. Research fellow Yale U., 1965-67, Harvard U., 1967-68; intern Belinson Med. Center, Israel, 1961; resident Belinson Med. Center, 1962-65; practice medicine specializing in internal medicine and nephrology New Haven, 1966-67, Boston, 1967-68, Chgo., 1968—; attending physician U. Chgo. Hosps., 1968—, head nephrology sect., 1973-82; asst. prof. medicine U. Chgo., 1968-71, assoc. prof., 1971-74, prof., 1975—; Fogarty sr. internat. fellow, vis. scientist Lab Cell Physiology, Coll. de France, Paris, 1977-78; vis. prof. cellular and molecular physiology Yale U., 1988; vis. scientist dept. molecular medicine Karolinska Inst., Stockholm, 1994—. Co-author: Kidney Function and Disease in Pregnancy; contbr. chpts. to books, articles to profl. jours. Fellow A.C.P.; mem. Am. Physiol. Soc., Am. Soc. Clin. Investigation, Assn. Am. Physicians, Am. Soc. Nephrology, Internat. Soc. Nephrology, Central Soc. Clin. Research, N.Y. Acad. Scis. Home: 1125 E 53rd St Chicago IL 60615-4410 Office: U Chgo 5841 S Maryland Ave Chicago IL 60637-1463

KATZ, ALAN CHARLES, toxicologist; b. Kearny, N.J., Nov. 10, 1946; s. Edward Myron and Margaret Ellen Katz; m. Marcia Anne Ellenwood, July 26, 1974; children: Bryan Jeffrey, Jeffrey Alan. BS in Biology, Fairleigh Dickinson U., 1970, MS in Human Physiology, 1977; CIM, Ctrl. Conn. State U., 1981. Diplomate Am. Bd. Toxicology, Am. Bd. Forensic Examiners. Chemist Union Carbide Corp., Bound Brook, N.J., 1965-70; toxicologist Ortho Pharm. Corp., Raritan, N.J., 1971-74; sr. ophthalmic pharmacologist Cooper Labs., Cedar Knolls, N.J., 1974-76; sr. assoc. toxicologist J&J Rsch. Found., North Brunswick, N.J., 1976-79; study dir. Stauffer Chem. Co., Farmington, Conn., 1979-84; sr. toxicologist EPA, Washington, 1984-87; exec. dir. TAS, Inc., Washington, 1987-97; mgr. tech. affairs Sanachem USA, Inc., 1997-98; pres. TOXCEL, 1999—; prin. Katz Assocs., 1985—. Contbg. editor Acute Toxicity, 1991-97. Mem. Am. Coll. Forensic Examiners, N.Y. Acad. Scis., Soc. Comparative Ophthalmology (past pres.), Soc. Toxicology, Am. Coll. Toxicology, Am. Chem. Soc., Soc. Toxicologie du Can. Home: 16090 Simon Kenton Rd Haymarket VA 20169-2109

KATZ, ALAN ROY, public health educator; b. Pitts., Aug. 21, 1954; s. Leon B. and Bernice Sonia (Glass) K.; m. Donna Marie Crandall, Jan. 19, 1986; 1 child, Sarah Elizabeth. BA, U. Calif., San Diego, 1976; MD, U. Calif., Irvine, 1980; MPH, U. Hawaii, 1987; postgrad., U. So. Calif., 1980-81, U. Hawaii, 1982-83. Staff physician emergency medicine L.A. County U. So. Calif. Med. Ctr., 1981-82; staff physician, med. dir. Waikiki Health Ctr., Honolulu, 1983-87; dir. AIDS/STD prevention program Hawaii State Dept. of Health, Honolulu, 1987-88; asst. prof. dept. pub. health scis. U. Hawaii, Honolulu, 1988-94, assoc. prof., 1994—, dir. preventive medicine residency program, 1994—; bd. dirs. Hawaii AIDS Task Group; mem. Chlamydia control workgroup USPHS, 1985-87, sci. adv. bd. Hawaii AIDS Clin. Trials Rsch. Program; staff physician, lab. dir. Diamond Head STD Clinic, Hawaii State Dept. Health, 1998—. Contbr. articles to profl. jours. Me. Leptospirosis ad hoc com. Hawaii State Dept. Health, Honolulu, 1988—, mem. prenatal screening adv. com., 1992—; mem. com. human subjects U. Hawaii, 1989—. USPHS Chlamydia Prevalence Survey grantee, Hawaii, 1986, Tuberculosis Survey grantee U. Hawaii, 1991; recipient presdl. citation for meritorious teaching, U. Hawaii, 1989, regents medal excellence in teaching U. Hawaii, 1992. Fellow Am. Coll. Preventive Medicine; mem. Am. Pub. Health Assn., Soc. Epidemiologic Rsch., Delta Omega. Office: U Hawaii Sch Pub Health Dept Pub Health Sci 1960 E West Rd Honolulu HI 96822-2319

KATZ, ALEX, artist; b. Bklyn., July 24, 1927; s. Isaac and Ella (Marion) K.; m. Ada Del Moro, Feb. 1, 1958; 1 child, Vincent. Degree in fine arts, Cooper Union, 1949; DFA (hon.), Colby Coll., 1984; PhD (hon.), 1986. One-man exhbns. include Roko Gallery, N.Y.C., 1954, 57, Fischbach Gallery, N.Y.C., 1964, 65, 67, 68, 70, 71, Stable Gallery, N.Y.C., 1960-61, Tanager Gallery, N.Y.C., 1959, 62, Martha Jackson Gallery, N.Y.C., 1962, Grinnell Gallery, Detroit, 1964, Sun Gallery, Provincetown, Mass., 1958, 59, Pa. State Coll., 1957, David Stuart Gallery, L.A., 1966, Bertha Eccles Art Center, Ogden, Utah, 1968, Towson State Coll., Balt., 1968, Phyllis Kind Gallery, Chgo., 1969, 71, W.Va. U., 1969, Galerie Dieter Brusberg, Hanover, Germany, 1971, Thelen Galerie, Cologne, Germany, 1971, Reed Coll., Portland, 1972, Sloan-O'Sickey Gallery, Cleve., 1972, Carlton Gallery, N.Y.C., 1973, Marlborough Gallery, N.Y.C., 1973, 75, 76, Whitney Mus. Am. Art, N.Y.C., 1974-75, Va. Mus. Fine Arts, Richmond, 1974-75, Santa Barbara (Calif.) Mus. Art, 1974-75, U. Minn., 1974-75, Indpls. Mus. Art, 1975, Marlborough Fine Art, London, 1975, Galerie Marguerite Lamy, Paris, 1975, Galerie Roger d'Amé court, Paris, 1977, traveling show Fresno Arts Center, Art Galleries Calif. State U., Seattle Art Mus., Vancouver Art Gallery, 1977-78, Marlborough Galerie, A.G., Zurich, 1977, Rose Art Mus., Brandeis U., Waltham, Mass., Balt. Art Mus., 1978, Brooke Alexander Gallery, N.Y.C., 1979, Robert Miller Gallery, N.Y.C., 1987, Inge Baecker Galerie, Cologne, Germany, 1987, Hokin Gallery, Chgo., 1987, Bklyn. Mus., 1988, Galerie Daniel Templon, Paris Marlborough Gallery, N.Y., 1988, Seibu Mus., Tokyo and Osaka, 1988, Cleve. Mus. Art, 1988, Bernd Kluser, Munich, 1989, Mario Diacono, Boston, 1989, Michael Kohn, L.A., Moscow-USSR CAT, 1989, Palma de Malorca, Spain, 1989, I.C.A., London, 1991, Turin, Italy, 1992, Marlborough Gallery N.Y. CAT, 1992, Munson-Williams-Proctor Inst., 1992, Colby Coll. Art Mus., 1992, Robert Miller Gallery, N.Y.C., 1993, Betsy Senior Gallery, N.Y.C., 1993, Rubenstein/Diacono Gallery, 1993, Marlborough Gallery, N.Y.C., 1993, 95, Ark. Art Mus., 1993, 94, Robert Mullen Gallery, 1994, Staatliche Kunsthalle, Baden-Baden, Germany, 1995, Peter Blum, N.Y.C., 1996, Balt. Mus. Fine Arts, 1996, Inst. Valencia de Arte Moderna Mus., Valencia, Spain, 1996, Fred Hoffman, L.A., 1996, Galerie Jablonka, Cologne, Germany, 1997, Saatchi Gallery, London, 1998, The Cultural Found., Germany, 1998, Galerie Thaddaeus Ropac, Paris, 1998, Galerie Barbara Thumm, Berlin, 1998, P.S.I. Contemporary Art Ctr., N.Y., 1998, Centro Cultural Recoleta, Buenos Aires, 1998, others; retrospective exhbn. at Utah Mus. Fine Arts, Salt Lake City, U. Calif. at San Diego, Mpls. Mus. Art, Wadsworth Atheneum, Hartford, Conn., 1971, Am. Found. Arts, Miami, Fla., 1976, Whitney Mus. Am. Art, N.Y.C., 1986 (paintings), Bklyn. Mus., 1980 (prints), 1986, 88, Galerie Templon, Paris (paintings), Marlborough Gallery, N.Y.C., Massimo Audiello, N.Y.C., Seibu Mus. at Tokyo, Osaka, Japan, 1988 (paintings, cutouts); group shows include Pa. Acad. Fine Arts, 1960, Va. Mus., Richmond, 1960, Whitney Mus. Am. Art, N.Y.C., 1960, 67-68, 72 (Ann.), 73 (Biennial), 79, 86 (traveling show), 88 (Philip Morris), 91 (Biennial), Art Inst. Chgo., 1961, 62, 64, 72, Yale Mus., 1962, Colby Coll., 1961, 63, 64, 70, 85, Am. Fedn. Art., 1964-65, Mus. Modern Art, N.Y.C., 1964, 65, 66, 68, 69, 91, 93 (Pfizer), Milw. Arts Center, 1966, 69, 75, R.I. Sch. Design, 1966, Cin. Art Mus., 1968, Am. Acad. Design, 1968, U. Calif. at LaJolla, 1969, N.Y. Acad. Design, N.Y.C., 1973, Marlborough Gallery, N.Y.C., 1976, Cleve. Mus. Art, 1974, DeCordova Mus., Mass., 1975, Mus. Fine Arts, St. Petersburg, 1975-76, U. Mo., 1979, Bowdoin Coll., Maine, 1985, Wichita State Mus., Kans., 1985, Found. Daniel Templon, 1989, France Madison (Wis.) Art Ctr., 1989, Walker Art Ctr, Mpls., 1989, Whitney Mus. at Equitable Ctr., N.Y.C., P.S. 1 Mus., Kuznetsky Most Exhibition, Moscow, 1990, Nassau County Art Mus., 1991, Art Contemporaire, Lyon, France, 1993, Mus. Contemporary Art, São Paulo, Brazil, 1993, Nat. Gallery Art, Washington, 1993, Nat. Portrait Gallery, Washington, 1993, Whitney Mus., N.Y.C., 1994, Mus. Modern Art, N.Y.C., 1994, 1995, travelling exhibitions solo, 1996—; Krusthalle, Baden-Baden, Germany; Alex Katz, American Landscape, 1996; Alex Katz Under the Stars: American Landscapes, 1951-1995, 1998, numerous others; exhibited in group shows at Mus. fur Moderne Kuust, Frankfurt, Germany, 1996, Deichtorhallen, Hamburg, Germany, 1996, Kunsthaus, Zurich, Switzerland, 1997; represented in permanent collections Whitney Mus., Mus. Modern Art, Met. Mus. Art, Brandeis U., N.Y.U., Bowdoin Coll., Detroit Mus., Allentown (Pa.) Art Mus., Weatherspoon Gallery of Art, Greensboro, N.C., Tokyo (Japan) Gallery, Allen Meml. Art Mus., Oberlin, Ohio, Houston Mus., Tate Gallery, London, The Israel Mus., Jerusalem, Iwaki City Mus., Japan, Hiroshima Mus., Museo Rufino Tamayo, Mex., Honolulu Acad. Art, Reina Sofia, Madrid, Valencia Mus., numerous others; vis. critic Yale U., 1960-63; Marshall Crogan vis. artist Harvard U., 1991-92. Subject of books: Alex Katz (Irving Sandler), 1979, Alex Katz: The Complete Prints (Nick Maravell), 1983, Alex Katz (Marshall and Rosenblum), 1986; also contbr. prints to Give Me Tomorrow (Ratcliff), 1984, A Tremor in the Morning (Vincent Katz), 1986, Alex Katz (Ann Beattie), Alex Katz Night Paintings (Donald Kuspit), Alex Katz (Sam Hunter), 1992; represented in permanent wing for Alex Katz Colby (Me.) Coll. Mus. Art. Recipient award New Eng. Art, Provincetown, Mass., 1971, Art in Pub. Places award, Harlem Station, Chgo., 1985, Profl. Achievement citation Cooper Union, 1974, alumni medal for achievement, 1980, Augustus St. Gaudens award for professionalism in art, 1980, medal for achievement in painting Skowhegan Sch., 1980; Guggenheim fellow, 1972; U.S.-USSR cultural exch. gurantee 1978; resident Am. Acad. in Rome, 1983; inducted into Am. Acad. and Inst. of Arts and Letters; opening of Paul J. Schupf wing for the Alex Katz collection Colby Coll. Mus., 1996. Address: 435 W Broadway New York NY 10012-5902

KATZ, ALIX MARTHA, respiratory care practitioner; b. Newark, Dec. 7, 1948; d. Leo F. and Anne (Chase) K. AS, Passaic County Community Coll., Paterson, N.J., 1982. Cert. respiratory therapy technician. Staff respiratory therapist Hosp. Ctr. at Orange, N.J., 1979-82; home care respiratory practitioner Homed Convalescent Equipment, Mountain Lakes, N.J., 1982-85; clin. respiratory supr. Elizabeth (N.J.) Gen. Med. Ctr., 1985-86; dir. respiratory therapy Paramed. Specialities, Inc., Fairfield, N.J., 1986-88; respiratory therapist Ultra-Care Health Care Svcs., West Orange, N.J., 1988-94, Rahway (N.J.) Hosp., 1994—. Drug and Hosp. Union scholar, 1980. Mem. Am. Assn. for Respiratory Care, Nat. Soc. Cardio-Pulmonary Technologists, Respiratory Therapy Hist. Soc., Methaphys. Ctr. N.J. Democrat. Jewish. Avocations: science, medicine, language, religion, philosophy. Home: 230 Clarken Dr West Orange NJ 07052-3400

KATZ, ANNE HARRIS, biologist, educator, writer, aviator; b. Long Branch, N.J. BS, Ursinus Coll., Collegeville, Pa., 1966; MS, U. Mass., 1974, PhD, 1976. Cert. pvt. pilot. Tchr. biology Middletown (N.J.) Twp. High Sch., 1966-69; instr. biology Holyoke (Mass.) Community Coll., 1969; teaching and research assoc. U. Mass., 1969-76; asst. prof. biology Fordham U., N.Y.C., 1977-83; assoc. prof. biology, asst. dean Coll. St. Elizabeth, Convent Station, N.J., 1983-86; assoc. dean Coll. Natural Scis. and Math. Ind. U. Pa., 1987-91, interim dean Coll. Natural Scis. and Math., 1988-89; dean of the coll., prof. biology Lycoming Coll., Williamsport, Pa., 1991-93; founding editor Aviation Mus. and Event News, 1993-97; Cert. pvt. pilot; cert. ecologist. Founder, editor, pub. Aviation Mus. & Event News, 1993; contbr. abstracts and articles to profl. jours. Aerospace educator Ninety-Nines. Vis. scholar Drew U., Madison, N.J., 1984-87; grantee Ctr. Field Rsch., Watertown, Mass., 1981-82, Geraldine R. Dodge Found., Morristown, N.J., 1981-83, N.J. DEP, 1983, Pa. Dept. Edn., 1989, GTE, 1990, CDC, 1991. Mem. AAAS, Ecol. Soc. Am., Aircraft Owners and Pilots Assn., Ninety Nines (aerospace edn.), Civil Air Patrol (aerospace edn. officer, pub. affairs officer), Soc. Study Reprodn., Am. Inst. Biol. Scis., N.Y. Acad. Sci., N.J. Acad. Sci., Pa. Acad. Sci. Avocations: hiking, traveling, writing, flying small airplanes.

KATZ, ARNOLD MARTIN, medical educator; b. Chgo., July 30, 1932; s. Louis Nelson and Aline (Grossner) K.; m. Phyllis Beck, Apr. 18, 1959; children: Paul, Sarah, Amy, Laura. BA with honors, U. Chgo., 1952; MD cum laude, Harvard U., 1956; D.Med. (hon.), Carol Davila U., 1994. Diplomate Nat. Bd. Med. Examiners. Intern Mass. Gen. Hosp., Boston, 1956-57, asst. res., 1959-60; rsch. assoc. NIH, Bethesda, Md., 1957-59; asst. registrar Inst. Cardiology, London, 1960-61; rsch. fellow dept. medicine UCLA, 1961-64; asst. prof. physiology Columbia U., N.Y.C., 1963-67; assoc. prof. medicine and physiology U. Chgo., 1967-69; Philip J. and Harriet L. Goodhart prof. cardiology Mt. Sinai Sch. Medicine, N.Y.C., 1969-77; prof. medicine, head cardiology divsn. U. Conn., Farmington, 1977-95, prof. medicine/divsn. chief emeritus, 1995—; cons. VA, 1970; coord. Problem Area #3, US-USSR Collaboration in Cardiovascular Rsch., 1983-86; mem. adv. com. Chinese Acad. med. Sci., 1982-89; R.T. Hall lectr. Cardiac Soc., Australia and New Zealand, 1991; chair sci. bd. Stanley J. Sarnoff Endowment Cardiovascular Sci. Inc., 1992-93; chair, sci. adv. bd. Patrick, Catherine, Weldon, Donaghue Med. Rsch. Found., 1994-97; mem. bd. sci. counsellors Nat. Heart Lung Inst., 1989-92. Author: Physiology of the Heart, 1977, 2d edit., 1992; editor: The Heart and Cardiovascular System, 1986, 91; mem. editorial bd.: Am. Jour. Cardiology, 1970-75, Am. Jour. Medicine, 1971-77, Am. Jour. Physiology, 1966-72, Can. Jour. Cardiology, 1988-91, Cardiology, 1980-85, Cardioscience, 1988-95, Cardiovascular Pharmacol., 1979-88, Circulation, 1992—, Circulation Rsch., 1974-80, Jour. Am. Coll. Cardiology, 1983-87, Jour. Clin. Investigation, 1971-76, Jour. Mechanochemistry and Cell Motility, 1970-72, Jour. Molecular and Cellular Cardiology, 1970-92, also editor-in-chief, 1986-92, Life Sciences, 1979-88, Physiol. Rev. 1976-80; reviewer several profl. jours.; contbr. articles to profl. jours. Served with USPHS, 1957-59. Humboldt fellow Alexander von Humboldt Found., 1975-76, Moseley traveling fellow Harvard U., 1960-61. Fellow ACP, Am. Coll. Cardiology (gov. Conn. 1984-87); mem. Am. Heart assn. (advanced rsch. fellow 1961-63, established investigator 1963-68, v.p. couns. 1992-94, bd. dirs. 1992-94, chmn. coun. affairs com. 1992-94, chmn. exec. com. basic sci. coun. 1990-92, Conn. affiliate bd. dirs. 1986-94, Greater Hartford chpt. bd. dirs. 1977-84, sec. 1982-84, v.p. 1984-86, pres. 1986-88, Rsch. Achievement award 1989, Disting. Achievement award Basic Sci. Coun. 1991, award of Meritorious Achievement 1995, Honoree Louis N. and Arnold M. Katz prize Basic Sci. Coun. 1995), N.Y. Heart Assn. (bd. dirs. 1971-74, 75-77), Am. Physiol. Soc., Cardiac Muscle Soc. (pres. 1969-71),

Assn. Am. Physicians, Internat. Soc. Heart Rsch. (pres. Am. sect. 1985), Assn. Univ. Cardiologists, Alpha Omega Alpha. Home: PO Box 1048 1592 New Boston Rd Norwich VT 05055-1048 Office: U Conn Health Ctr Divsn Cardiology Dept Farmington CT 06030-2249

KATZ, ARNOLD MARTIN, insurance brokerage firm executive; b. Schenectady, N.Y., Mar. 22, 1940; s. David and Minna Katz; 1 child, Sharon. BS in Pub. Relations, Boston U., 1962. Cert. life underwriter, Pa. Sales rep. Mass. Gen. Life Ins. Co., Hartford, Conn., 1964-66, sr. sales rep., 1966-67, asst. mgr., 1967; mgr. Phila., 1967-72; v.p. Boston, 1972-76; pres. Brokerage Concepts, Inc., Phila., 1977—; chmn. bd. dirs. Brokers Svc. Inc., N.Y.; pres. BCI Holdings Inc., Atlantic Adminstrs., Waltham, Mass., Group Source, Phila., Am. Ind. Life Ins. Co. Contbr. articles to profl. jours. Bd. dirs. Moss Rehab. Hosp., Phila., 1985-93, Police Athletic League, Phila., 1986—; exec. com. Einstein Hosp., Phila., 1987—; active Belmont Hosp. 1987—. Served to maj. U.S. Army, 1962-73. Mem. Life Underwriter Assn., CLU (bd. dirs. Phila. chpt.). Jewish. Office: Brokerage Concepts Inc 651 Allendale Rd King Of Prussia PA 19406

KATZ, SIR BERNARD, physiologist; b. Leipzig, Germany, Mar. 26, 1911; s. Max and Eugenie (Rabinowitz) K.; m. Marguerite Penly, Oct. 27, 1945; children: David, Jonathan. MD, U. Leipzig, Germany, 1934; MD (hon.), U. Leipzig, German Dem. Republic, 1990; PhD, U. London, 1938, DSc, 1943; DSc (hon.), U. Southampton, 1971, U. Melbourne, 1971, Cambridge U., 1980; PhD (hon.), Weizmann Inst. Sci., 1979. Beit Meml. Research fellow, 1938-39; Carnegie Research fellow Sydney, Australia, 1939-42; asst. dir. biophys. research U. Coll., London, 1946-50, reader, 1950, prof., head biophysics dept., 1952-78, prof. emeritus, 1978—; lectr. univs., socs. Author: Electric Excitation of Nerve, 1939; Nerve, Muscle and Synapse, 1966; The Release of Neural Transmitter Substances, 1969; also articles. Mem. Agrl. Research Council, 1967-77. Recipient Feldberg award, 1965, Copley medal Royal Soc., 1967, Nobel prize in medicine-physiology, 1970, Cothenius medal Deutsche Akademie der Naturforscher Leopoldina, 1989; created knight, 1969. Fellow Royal Soc. (council 1964-65, v.p. 1965, biol. sec. 1968-76), Royal Coll. Physicians (Baly medal 1967); fgn. mem. Royal Danish Acad. Scis. and Letters, Acad. Nat. Lincei, Am. Acad. Arts and Sci., Nat. Acad. Scis. U.S. (fgn. assoc.), Order Pour le Mérite für Wissenschaften und Künste (fgn.). Research on nerve and muscle function especially transmission of impulses from nerve to muscle fibers. Office: U Coll Dept Physiology, Gower St, London WC1E 6BT, England

KATZ, BRUCE R., company executive; b. Newton, Mass., Feb. 17, 1947; s. Saul T. and Dorothy (Golden) K. Student, Cornell U., 1965-69. Founder, chief exec. officer Rockport Shoe Co., Marlboro, Mass., 1970-86; founder, chief exec. officer Rosewood Stone Group, San Francisco, 1986—, chmn., 1986—. Trustee, Pacific Crest Outward Bound Sch. Recipient Cross-Cultural award EdVenture Holdings, Inc., 1989. Mem. Social Venture Network, Global Bus. Network. Office: 2320 Marine Shipway Sausalito CA 94965-1966*

KATZ, CARLOS, electrical engineer; b. Nentershausen, Hessen, Germany, Aug. 18, 1934; came to U.S., 1962; s. Willy and Martha (Hamburger) K.; m. Sandra P. Rodin, Aug. 18, 1963; children: Joseph, David. Student, Technishe Hochshule, Darmstadt, Federal Republic of Germany, 1958-59; BSEE, Poly. Inst., Quito, Ecuador, 1961; M in Mgmt. Sci., Stevens Inst. Tech., 1970. Rsch. engr. Gen. Cable Corp. R&D Ctr., Bayonne, N.J., 1962-69, mgr. cable component lab., 1969-71; asst. dir. R&D power and control cables Gen. Cable Corp. R&D Ctr., Union, N.J., 1974-80; chief rsch. engr. Cable Tech. Labs. Inc., New Brunswick, N.J., 1978—, pres., 1997—; cons. power cables Gen. Cable Internat., Greenwich, Conn., 1981-87; asst. dir. R&D high voltage cables Phelps Dodge Cable & Wire Co., Yonkers, N.Y., 1971-74; mem. internat. sci. and tech. com. JICABLE, France; mem. Conf. Internationale. Grands Reseaux Electriques. Contbr. articles to profl. jours.; patentee in field of high and extra high voltage power cables. Fellow IEEE (mem. insulated condr. com.). Home: 15 Eagle Rd Edison NJ 08820-2763 Office: Cable Tech Labs Inc 690 Jersey Ave New Brunswick NJ 08901-3661

KATZ, CHARLES J., JR., lawyer; b. San Antonio, Mar. 25, 1948. AB, Stanford U., 1969; MA, N.Y.U., 1973; JD, U. Tex., 1976. Book review editor Tex. Law Review, 1975-76; mem. Perkins Coie, Seattle, 1982. Mem. Order of the Coif. Office: Perkins Coie 1201 3rd Ave Fl 40 Seattle WA 98101-3099

KATZ, COLLEEN, publisher; b. Newark. BA in Math., Montclair (N.J.) Coll.; cert., Ctr. Linguistique Etrangers, Tours, France. Assoc. editor Fawcett Publs., N.Y.C., 1972-73, editor, 1973-76; editorial dir. Butterick Fashion Mktg. Co., N.Y.C., 1976-77; editor Ency. of Textiles, N.Y.C., 1979; editor in chief N.J. Monthly, Morristown, 1982-85; dir. publs. Ins. Info. Inst., N.Y.C., 1985-88; editor Journal of Accountancy, N.Y.C., 1988—. Editor Ins. REv., 1985-88; pub. mags. and newsletters AICPA, 1997—. Vol. tchr. Elizabeth (N.J.) Sch. System, 1965; vol. editor Nat. Council Jewish Women, N.J., 1967-71; vol. pub. relations worker Essex County Mental Health Assn., N.J., 1980-81. Named Woman of Yr., Cen. N.J. March of Dimes, 1984, Outstanding Alumnus, Montclair Coll., 1984; recipient Gold Cir. award Am. Soc. Assn. Execs., 1989, award for pub. excellence Communication Concepts, 1990, pub. excellence award Mag. Week, 1990, gen. excellence award Soc. Nat. Assn. Publs., 1991. Mem. Soc. Profl. Journalists, Am. Soc. Mag. Editors, Nat. Arts Club, Soc. Nat. Assn. Publs. (Silver medal for gen. excellence 1997). Avocation: foreign languages. Office: Jour of Accountancy Harborside III Jersey City NJ 07311

KATZ, DAVID ALLAN, judge, former lawyer, business consultant; b. Nov. 1, 1933; s. Samuel and Ruth (Adelman) K.; m. Joan G. Siegel, Sept. 4, 1955; children: Linda, Michael S., Debra K. BBA, Ohio State U., 1955, JD summa cum laude, 19757. Bar: Ohio 1957. Ptnr. Spengler Nathanson, Attys., Toledo, 1957-86, mng. ptnr., 1986-93; judge U.S. Dist. Ct. (no. dist.) Ohio, Toledo, 1994—; dir., corp. sec. Seaway Food Town, Inc., Maumee, Ohio, 1980-94; trustee St. Vincent Med. Ctr., 1987-96, sec., 1988-90, vice chmn.-treas., 1990-94, chmn., 1994-96, St. Vincent Med. Ctr. Found., chmn., 1990-92, The Toledo Symphony, v.p. Jewish Edn. Service N.Am., 1985-91, Mercy Health Sys. NW Ohio, 1996—. Pres. Temple B'nai Israel, Toledo, 1970-73, Jewish Welfare Fedn., Toledo, 1977-79, Toledo Bar Assn. Found., 1983-94. Fellow Ohio Bar Found., Toledo Bar Found.; mem. ABA, Toledo Bar Assn. (sec., trustee 1972-78), Ohio State Bar Assn., Rotary. Office: US Court House 1716 Spielbusch Ave Ste 210 Toledo OH 43624-1347

KATZ, DAVID M., airport administrator. Dir. Detroit WCM Airport, 1998—. Office: Detroit WCM Airport Mezzanine Level Smith Terminal Detroit MI 48412*

KATZ, DOUGLAS JEFFREY, naval officer, retired, consultant; b. Madison, Wis., May 1, 1942; s. Harold Leroy and Lois Wayne (Hoops) K.; m. Sharon Lynne Mustard, June 11, 1965; children: Robert Douglas, Erica Lynne. BS in Engring., U.S. Naval Acad., 1965; MS in Material Mgmt., Naval Postgrad. Sch., 1973. Commd. ensign USN, 1965, advanced through grades to vice adm.; mil. advisor Fleet Adv. Unit USN, Vietnam, 1971-72; exec. officer USS Mahan USN, Charleston, S.C., 1977-79, surface ops. office Cruiser-Destroyer Group 2, 1979-80; plans/budget officer Chief of Naval Ops. USN, Washington, 1980-83; comdg. officer USS Deyo USN, Charleston, S.C., 1983-85; dir. prof. devel. U.S. Naval Acad. USN, Annapolis, Md., 1985-87; comdg. officer USS New Jersey USN, Long Beach, Calif., 1987-89; dir. surface warfare Chief of Naval Ops. USN, Washington, 1989-90; comdr. Cruiser-Destroyer Group 2 USN, Charleston, S.C., 1990-92; comdr. forces ctrl. command USN, 1992-94; cmdr. Naval Surface Forces Atlantic, 1994-97, ret., 1997, cons., 1997—. Decorated Disting. Svc. medal with two gold stars, Legion of Merit with three gold stars, Bronze Star with combat V, Meritorious Svc. medal with two gold stars, Navy commendation medal with one gold star. Mem. U.S. Naval Inst., U.S. Naval Acad. Alumni Assn. Avocation: athletics. Home and Office: 1530 Gordon Cove Dr Annapolis MD 21403-5004

KATZ, EDWARD MORRIS, banker; b. Passaic, N.J., Apr. 18, 1921; s. David and Badane (Gubersky) K.; m. Phyllis Kushner, June 20, 1948; children—David, Alan, Michael. B.A., Bklyn. Coll., 1947; M.A., NYU, 1948. Auditor Amalgamated Bank N.Y., N.Y.C., 1951-55; cashier Amalgamated Bank N.Y., 1955-73, v.p., 1957-61, sr. v.p., 1961-71, exec. v.p., 1971-78, pres., chief exec. officer, 1978-89, dir., 1966-89, ret., 1989. Bd. dirs. N.Y. Tech. Coll., Bklyn., 1984-89. Home: 48 Windsor Rd Great Neck NY 11021-2740

KATZ, ERWIN I., federal judge; b. 1935. BA, Yeshiva U.; JD, Ill. Inst. Tech., 1962. Atty. Canel & Canel, Hoffman & Davis; asst. U.S. atty. U.S. Dist. Ct. (no. dist.), Ill., 1962-66; bankruptcy judge U.S. Bankruptcy Ct. (no. dist.), Ill., 1987—. FAX: 312-408-7750. Office: US Bankruptcy Ct 219 S Dearborn St Rm 668 Chicago IL 60604-1702

KATZ, GREGORY, lawyer; b. Suresnes, Seine, France, Sept. 4, 1950; came to U.S., 1960; s. Joseph and Ida (Stein) K.; m. Evelyn Katz, 1972; children: Daniel, Philip. AB, U. Pa., 1970; JD, Harvard U., 1973. Bar: N.Y. 1974, U.S. Dist. Ct. (so. dist.) N.Y. 1974. Assoc. Roth, Carlson & Spengler, N.Y.C., 1973-80; ptnr. Spengler, Carlson & Gubar, N.Y.C., 1980-92, Reid & Priest, N.Y.C., 1992-97, Thelen, Reid & Priest, N.Y.C., 1997—. Mem. Internat. ABA, Am. Arbitration Assn. (arbitrator), N.Y. Bar Assn. (com. fgn. investment in U.S.). Home: 60 East End Ave New York NY 10028-7907 Office: Thelen Reid & Priest 40 W 57th St New York NY 10019-4001*

KATZ, HILLIARD JOEL, physician; b. Stockton, Calif., May 26, 1918; s. Nelson and Pauline (Landman) K.; m. Jeanette Lillian Gordon, Aug. 18, 1946; children: Stephanie, Steven Nelson, Hilary. A.B., U. Calif. at Berkeley, 1939; M.D., U. Calif. at San Francisco, 1942. Diplomate: Am. Bd. Internal Medicine. Intern U. Calif. Hosps., San Francisco, 1942-43; asst. resident internal medicine U. Calif. Hosps., 1943-44, attending physician, electrocardiographer, 1948—, chief staff, 1964-66, physician charge CCU, 1966-73; resident, sr. resident in internal medicine San Francisco VA Hosp., 1946-48; practice medicine specializing in cardiology San Francisco, 1948—; clin. instr. medicine U. Calif. Sch. Medicine, San Francisco, 1948-53; asst. clin. prof. U. Calif. Sch. Medicine, 1953-61, asso. clin. prof., 1961-70, clin. prof. cardiovascular div., 1970—; asst. to chancellor for spl. events U. Calif. Sch. Medicine, San Francisco; chmn. Nat. Com. Emergency Coronary Care, 1974-76; mem. rsch. coun., Am. Wine Alliance for Rsch. and Edn. Served to capt. M.C. AUS, 1944-46. Fellow ACP, Am. Coll. Cardiology, Am. Heart Assn. (coun. clin. cardiology 1963, Disting. Svc. award 1963, Svc. Recognition award 1964); mem. Calif. Heart Assn. (dir. 1956-71), San Francisco Heart Assn. (pres. 1955-57, Disting. Svc. cert. 1959), Calif. Acad. Medicine (pres. 1965), U. Calif. Sch. Medicine Alumni-Faculty Assn. (pres. 1961-62), Soc. Med. Friends Wine (pres. 1968, bd. govs.), Wine and Food Soc., San Francisco (chmn.), Club Culinaire Francais de Californie, Commanderie du Bontemps de Medoc et des graves, Commanderie de Bordeaux de San Francisco, Cercle de l'Union, Phi Beta Kappa, Alpha Omega Alpha. Home: 223 Cherry St San Francisco CA 94118-1606

KATZ, IRWIN, marketing executive; b. N.Y.C., Oct. 6, 1942; s. Sam and Ethel (Weinstein) K.; m. Beatrice Eva Kraus, July 11, 1965; children: Ivan Todd, Andrew Craig. BBA, Ohio U., 1964. Sales analyst J.B. Williams Co., N.Y.C., 1964-67; product mgr. Thayer Knomark div. Revlon Co., N.Y.C., 1967-69; supr. accounts Rumrill-Hoyt Advt. Agy., N.Y.C., 1969-71; exec. v.p., ptnr. Popofsky Advt. Agy., N.Y.C., 1971-78; v.p. mktg. Commerce Drug Co. div. Del Labs. Inc., Plainview, N.Y., 1979-81; v.p. strategic planning Del Labs Inc., Farmingdale, N.Y., 1981-83; sr. v.p. Ansell-Ams. Inc., Tinton Falls, N.J., 1983-89, Eatontown, N.J., 1989; pres. Irwin Katz and Assocs., Marlboro, N.J., 1989—. Jewish. Lodge: Free Sons. Avocation: karate. E-mail: irkatz@concentric.net. Office: Ste 1 746 Highway 34 Matawan NJ 07747

KATZ, JACK, audiology educator; b. N.Y.C., Mar. 25, 1934; s. Morris L. and Anna (Stratievsky) K.; m. Irma H. Laufer, June 24, 1956; children—Mark David, Miriam Beth. BA, Bklyn. Coll., 1956; MS, Syracuse U., 1957; PhD, U. Pitts., 1961. Lic. audiologist, N.Y. Asst. prof. speech No. Ill. U., DeKalb, 1961-62; asst. prof. otolaryngology Tulane Sch. Med., New Orleans, 1962-65; dir. speech and hearing dept. Menorah Med. Ctr., Kansas City, Mo., 1965-74; prof. audiology, communicative disorders and scis. SUNY, Buffalo, 1974—, chmn. dept., 1982-87; Fulbright-Hays sr. lectr., Ankara, Turkey, 1972-73; vis. prof. Kans. U. Med. Ctr., 1987-88; cons. NASA, 1964-65, Leavenworth Penitentiary, Kans., 1973-74, Roswell Park Meml. Inst., Buffalo, 1975-98, Chedoke-McMaster Hosps., Hamilton, Ont., Can., 1981-83, Buffalo VA Med. Ctr., 1984-94, Riverside Pub. Co., 1998—; adj. prof. dept. otolaryngology SUNY, Buffalo, 1994—. Author: (with others) Site of Lesion: Audiometric Interpretation, 1984; (test and therapy program) Phonemic Synthesis, 1982; (diagnostic test) SSW Test, 1964, CES Test, 1976; (computer software with others) SSW C*I*R*: Calculations, Interpretations, Recommendations, 1988, SSW-Plus, 1999; editor, contbr. (with others) The SSW Test: Development and Procedures, 1982, Central Auditory Processing Disorders, 1983; Handbook of Clinical Audiology, 1972, 4th edit., 1994, Central Auditory Processing: A Transdisciplinary View, 1993, Central Auditory Processing: Mostly Management, 1998; editor SSW Reports, 1978—, Central Test Battery CD, 1997. Mem. Jewish Community Relations Bur., Kansas City, 1973-74. Recipient Disting. Alumnus award Bklyn. Coll. Hearing and Speech Ctr., 1983, Chancellor's award for excellence in tchg. SUNY, Central, 1991. Fellow Am. Speech, Lang. and Hearing Assn. (book rev. editor 1967-72, cert. clin. competence in audiology 1962, speech-lang. pathology 1969, Continuing Edn. award 1983, 87); mem. N.Y. State Speech, Lang. and Hearing Assn. (v.p. univs. and labs. 1981-83, Disting. Achievement award 1987), Orton Dyslexia Soc. (bd. dirs. western N.Y. chpt. 1987-90), N.Y. Acad. Scis., Am. Acad. Audiology (Profl. Achievement award 1999, Jewish Geneal. Soc. of Buffalo (pres. 1996-98). Office: SUNY 122 Cary Hall Buffalo NY 14214-3005

KATZ, JANE, swimming educator; b. Sharon, Pa., Apr. 16, 1943; d. Leon and Dorothea (Oberkewitz) Katz; B.S. in Edn., CCNY, 1963; M.A., NYU, 1966; M.Ed., Columbia Tchrs. Coll., 1972, Ed.D., 1978. Mem. faculty Bronx C.C., CUNY, 1964—, prof. phys. edn., 1972—; mem. U.S. Round-the-World Synchronized Swim Team, 1964; synchronized swimming solo tour of Eng., 1969; founding co-organizer, coach 1st Internat. Israeli Youth Festival Games, 1970; mem. winning U.S. Maccabiah Swim Team, 1957; vice chmn. Metro Master AAU Swim Team, 1974—; mem. AAU Nat. Masters All-Am. Swimming Team, 1974—, synchronized swimming solo champion, 1975; speaker, judge in field. Trainee Fed. Adminstrn. Aging, 1971-72; mem. Internat. Hall. of Fame, Ft. Lauderdale, Fla. Named Healthy Am. Fitness Leader U.S. Jaycees and the Pres's. Coun. on Phys. Fitness, 1987, Outstanding Masters Synchroured Swimming, 1987; winner CCNY Towsend Harris Acad. medal, 1989. Mem. AAHPER, U.S. Com. Sports for Israel (dir., co-chmn. women's swimming com. 1970—), Nat. Jewish Welfare Bd., Internat. Aquatics. Author: Swimming for Total Fitness, A Progressive Aerobic Program, 1981, rev. ed. 1993, Swimming Through Your Pregnancy, 1983, W.E.T. Workouts: Water Exercises and Techniques to Help You and Tone Up Aerobically, 1985, Fitness Works: Blueprint for Lifelong Fitness, 1988, Swim 30 Laps in 30 Days, 1991, The Workstation Workout, 1994, Aquatic Handbook for Lifetime Fitness, 1996; author: (video) The W.E.T. Workout, 1994, The All-American Aquatic Handbook: Your Passport to Lifetime Fitness, 1996, The New W.E.T. Workout, 1996; contbr. Encyclopedia Britannica Med. and Health Ann., 1997; papers in field. Address: 400 2nd Ave Apt 23B New York NY 10010-4052

KATZ, JAY, psychiatry and law educator; b. Zwickau, Fed. Republic Germany, Oct. 20, 1922; came to U.S., 1940, naturalized, 1945; s. Paul and Dora (Ungar) K.; m. Marilyn B. Arthur, June 18, 1989; children from previous marriage: Sally Jean, Daniel Franklin, Amy Susan. BA, U. Vt., 1944, DS (hon.), 1995; MD, Harvard U., 1949; DS (hon.), Northeastern Ohio U., 1994. Intern Mt. Sinai Hosp., N.Y.C., 1949-50; resident Northport (N.Y.) VA Hosp., 1950-51, Yale U., 1953-55; instr. psychiatry Yale U., New Haven, 1955-57, asst. prof., 1957-58, asst. prof. psychiatry and law, 1958-60, asso. prof. law, asso. clin. prof. psychiatry, 1960-67, adj. prof. law and psychiatry, 1967-79, prof., 1979-81, John A. Garver prof. law and psychoanalysis, 1981-90, Elizabeth K. Dollard prof. law, medicine and psychiatry, 1990-93, Elizabeth K. Dollard prof. law, medicine and psychiatry emeritus, Harvey L. Karp Profl. lectr. in law and psychoanalysis, 1993—; tng. and supervising psychiatrist Western New Eng. Inst. for Psychoanalysis, 1972—; cons. to asst. sec. health and sci. affairs HEW, 1972-73, mem. artificial heart assessment panel, 1972-73; active Presdl. Adv. Com. on Ho. Radiation Experiments, 1994-95. Author: (with Joseph Goldstein) The Family and the Law, 1964, (with Joseph Goldstein and Alan M. Dershowitz) Psychoanalysis, Psychiatry and Law, 1967, Experimentation with Human Beings, 1972, (with Alexander M. Capron) Catastrophic Diseases—Who Decides What?, 1975; The Silent World of Doctor and Patient, 1984. Bd. dirs. Family Service of New Haven. Served to capt. M.C. USAF, 1951-53. Recipient Henry K. Beecher award Hastings Ctr. for Ethics and Life Scis., 1993; John Simon Guggenheim Meml. Found. fellow, 1981. Fellow ACP (William C. Menninger award 1983), Am. Psychiat. Assn. (Isaac Ray award 1975), Am. Orthopsychiat. Assn., Am. Coll. Psychiatry, Center for Advanced Psychoanalytic Studies; mem. Inst. Medicine, Nat. Acad. of Scis., Group for Advancement of Psychiatry, Am. Psychoanalytic Assn. Jewish. Home: 81 Alston Ave New Haven CT 06515-2702 Office: Yale Law Sch PO Box 208215 127 Wall St New Haven CT 06511-6636

KATZ, JEFFREY HARVEY, lawyer, mayor; b. Newark, Apr. 16, 1947; s. Jack and Beatrice (Weinstock) K.; m. Sharon R. Davis, Nov. 7, 1971; children: Stacey, Justin. B of Engring, Stevens Inst. Tech., 1970; JD, Seton Hall U., 1981. Bar: N.J. 1981, U.S. Dist. Ct. N.J. 1981, U.S. Ct. Appeals (3d cir.) 1984, U.S. Supreme Ct. 1985. Engr. RKO Gen., Sta. WOR-AM-FM-TV, N.Y.C., 1967-70; mgr., engr. Pub. Svc. Electric & Gas Co., Newark, 1970—, mgr. telecomm. sys., 1977-90; mgr. telecomm. advanced tech. Pub. Svc. Electric & Gas Co., 1990-93, sr. info. technologies cons., 1993-98; prosecutor Twp. of Springfield, N.J., 1982-85, governing body, 1985-95; cons. Enterprise IT, 1998—; mem. Downtown Redevel. Com., Springfield, 1990-94, Springfield Bicentennial Com., logistics chmn., 1993-94; chmn. adv. com. Mcpl. Cable TV, Springfield, 1974-76; mem. Union County Rep. Com., Springfield Rep. Mcpl. Com., 1986-98. Mem. bd. health Twp. of Springfield, 1986-87, 1990-93, mayor, 1988-89, planning bd., local assistance bd., commr. pub. safety, 1988-93, dep. mayor, 1992; trustee Stevens Inst. Tech., Hoboken, N.J., 1971-74, mem. pres. sch. and sel. com., fin. com., lower campus lounge project; trustee Union County Coll., Cranford, N.J., 1995—, mem. ednl. planning and policy com., bldgs. and grounds com., vice-chair audit com.; lt. Aux. Police, Springfield, 1968—; mem. Gov.'s Mgmt. Improvement Program, Trenton, N.J., 1982-83; local govt. affairs adv. com. N.J. Assembly, 1989-91, mem. recreation com., 1990-92, 94; logistics chief People for Whitman campaign, 1993. Named One of Outstanding Young Men of Am., U.S. Jaycees, 1971-73, Citizen of Yr. Springfield B'nai B'rith, 1976, Citizen of Yr. Policemen's Benevolent Assn. Local, 1976, Springfield, 1985; recipient award for 25 continuous yrs. of pub. svc. N.J. Bldrs. Assn., 1989, Silver Life Card award Policemen's Benevolent Assn. Local 76, 1991. Mem. ABA, IEEE, Soc. Cable TV Engrs., N.J. State Bar Assn., Union County Bar Assn., Internat. Platform Assn., Jewish War Vets. of U.S., Fed. Comms. Bar Assn. Republican. Jewish. Avocations: amateur radio, running, photography. Office: 182 Meisel Ave Springfield NJ 07081-1830

KATZ, JERI BETH, lawyer; b. Washington, Nov. 6, 1964; d. Stanley J. and Paula (Goldberg) K.; m. Daniel Alan Ezra, June 19, 1988 (div. Dec. 1990). BA, U. Md., 1987; JD, Cath. U., Washington, 1990. Bar: Md. 1990, D.C. 1991, U.S. Ct. Appeals (6th cir.) 1991, U.S. Ct. Internat. Trade 1992, Colo. 1994. Assoc. Winston & Strawn, Washington, 1990; ptnr. Law Offices Royal Daniel, Washington, 1990-94, Daniel & Katz, L.L.C., Breckenridge, Colo., 1994-98; pvt. practice, Breckenridge, 1998—; mem. jud. performance commn. 5th Jud. Dist., 1998—. Bd. dirs. Snowmass Ski Acad., 1995-98, Breckenridge Resort Chamber, 1998—; mem. Breckenridge Town Coun., 1998—; chairperson Summit County Transfer of Devel. Rights Commn. Mem. Continental Divide Bar Assn. (v.p. (1997-98), Colo. Criminal Def. Bar (rap sheet com. 1998). Home: PO Box 6602 Breckenridge CO 80424-6602 Office: PO Box 6602 130 Ski Hill Rd Ste 210 Breckenridge CO 80424-6602

KATZ, JEROME CHARLES, lawyer; b. Boston, Sept. 25, 1950; s. Ralph and Thelma M. (Clark) K.; m. Nancy M. Green, Aug. 29, 1976; children: Jonathan Green, Elizabeth Rachel. AB, Duke U., 1972; JD, Columbia U., 1975. Bar: N.Y. 1976, U.S. Dist. Ct. (so. and ea. dists.) N.Y. 1976, U.S. Supreme Ct. 1979, U.S. Ct. Appeals (2d cir.) 1981, U.S. Dist. Ct. (we. dist.) N.Y. 1990. Assoc. Chadbourne & Parke, N.Y.C., 1975-83, ptnr., 1983—. Assoc. editor Columbia Jour. Transnat. Law, 1974-75. Harlan Fiske Stone scholar Columbia U., 1974. Mem. ABA, Assn. of the Bar of the City of N.Y., Phi Beta Kappa. Home: 77 E 12th St New York NY 10003-5002 Office: Chadbourne & Parke 30 Rockefeller Plz New York NY 10112-0002

KATZ, JERRY PAUL, corporate executive; b. L.A., Jan. 24, 1944; s. Samuel and Dorothy Rose (Solovay) K.; m. Judy Simmering, Sept. 10, 1985 (div. 1988); m. Julie Stacey, Aug. 26, 1990; 1 child, Brandon Louis. AA, East L.A. Coll., 1964; BS, BA, Calif. State U., 1970. Registered sanitarian, Calif. Sanitarian L.A. County Health Dept., L.A., 1971-73; dir. Compton (Calif.) Model Cities Vector Control, 1973-74; health officer Lynwood (Calif.) City, 1974-76; pres., chief exec. officer Associated Industries, L.A., 1976—; cons., bd. dirs. All Am. Fire Protection, L.A., 1987—. Founding mem. Moore St. Homeowners Assn., Monterey Park, Calif., 1989—; mem. Nature Conservancy, World Wildlife Fund. Recipient World Record (2) hang gliding Nat. Assn. Aeronautics, 1977; named for Distance-Altitude Gain, Guinness Book of World Records, London, 1977. Mem. Native Am. Rights Fund, Green Peace, Surfrider Found., U.S. Hangliding Assn., Sea Shepard Soc. Avocations: surfing, skiing, flying, mountain bike riding, sailing. Office: Associated Industries 5140 Via Corona St Los Angeles CA 90022-2007

KATZ, JOEL ABRAHAM, lawyer, music consultant; b. Bronx, N.Y., May 27, 1944; s. Harry and Hilda (Wiesenthal) K.; Kane Swims, 1994; children from previous marriage: Leslie Helaine, Jeni Michelle. BA in Econs., Hunter Coll., 1966; JD, U. Tenn., 1969. Bar: Tenn. 1969, D.C. 1970, Ga. 1971, U.S. Dist. Ct. (ea. dist.) Tenn. 1970, U.S. Dist. Ct. Appeals (11th cir.) 1971. Owner, sr. ptnr. Greenberg Traurig, Atlanta; gen. coun., bd. dirs. Farm Aid Inc., T.J. Martell Found.; bd. contbg. editors Entertainment Law & Finance. Mem. exec. coun. T.J. Martell Found. for Leukemia Rsch., N.Y.C.; mem. adv. bd. Atlanta Com. for Olympic Games; mem. Ga. Music Hall of Fame Authority; bd. dirs. Very Special Arts. Mem. NARAS (past v.p., past nat. trustee, dir. found. bd., nat. chmn. bd. trustees, trustee Atlanta chpt., chmn. emeritus), ABA, Fed. Bar Assn., Ga. Bar Assn., Tenn. Bar Assn., Atlanta C. of C. (bd. advisors), D.C. Bar Assn., Atlanta Bar Assn. Home: 3234 W Andrews Ct NW Atlanta GA 30305-2015 Office: Greenberg Traurig 3423 Piedmont Rd NE Ste 200 Atlanta GA 30305-1742*

KATZ, JOETTE, state supreme court justice; b. Bklyn., Feb. 3, 1953. BA, Brandeis U., 1974; JD, U. Conn., 1977. Bar: Conn. 1977. Pvt. practice, 1977-78; asst. pub. defender Office Chief Pub. Defender, 1978-83; chief legal svcs. Pub. Defender Svcs., 1983-89; judge Superior Ct., 1989-92; assoc. judge Conn. Supreme Ct., Hartford, 1992—; instr. U. Conn. Sch. law, 1981-84; tchr. ethics and criminal law Quinnipiac Coll. Mem. Am. Law Inst. (chairperson evidence code drafting com.), Am. Inns Ct. (past pres. Fairfield County br.). Office: Conn Supreme Ct Drawer N Sta A Hartford CT 06106-1548*

KATZ, JOHN, investment banker; b. Washington, Aug. 2, 1938; s. Milton and Vivian (Greenberg) K.; divorced; children: Ellen, Allison; m. Laura Cherkis, May 29, 1988; stepchildren: Ann Cherkis, Nancy Cherkis. AB, Harvard U., 1960, JD, 1963. Bar: N.Y. 1964. With Hall, Casey, Dickler & Howley, 1963-67; asst. corp. counsel City of N.Y., 1967-69; spl. asst. to Congressman Richard L. Ottinger, 1969; with Poletti, Freidin, Prashker, Feldman & Gartner, 1969-75; atty. Equitable Life Assurance Soc. of U.S., 1975-79, v.p., counsel, 1979-82, v.p. Office of Chief Investment Officer, 1982-86; sr. v.p. Equitable Investment Corp., 1986-88, exec. v.p., 1989-91; chmn., CEO Sam's Restaurant Group, Inc., N.Y.C., 1991-92, investment banker, 1992—; bd. dirs. The Legends Fund, Inc., Nations Flooring, Inc. Mem. Greater N.Y.C. Com. of Harvard Law Sch. Fund; chmn. admissions com. Harvard Club N.Y.C., 1988-89; bd. dirs. Resources for Children with Spl. Needs, Inc., 1985-98; bd. dirs. My Sisters' Place, 1995—, co-chmn., 1996—. Home and Office: 10 Hemlock Rd Hartsdale NY 10530-2951

KATZ, JOHN W., lawyer, state official; b. Balt., June 3, 1943; s. Leonard Wallach and Jean W. (Kane) K.; m. Joan Katz, June 11, 1969 (div. 1982); 1 child, Kimberly Erin. BA, Johns Hopkins U., 1965; JD, U. Calif., Berkeley, 1969; DDL (hon.) U. Alaska, 1994. Bar: Alaska, Pa., U.S. Dist. Ct. D.C. 1971, U.S. Ct. Appeals (D.C. cir.), U.S. Tax Ct., U.S. Ct. Claims, U.S. Ct. Mil. Justice, U.S. Supreme Ct. Legis. and adminstrv. asst. to Congressman Howard W. Pollock of Alaska, Washington, 1969-70; legis. asst. to U.S. Senator Ted Stevens of Alaska, Washington, 1971; assoc. McGrath and

Flint, Anchorage, 1972; gen. counsel Joint Fed. State Land Use Planning Commn. for Alaska, Anchorage, 1972-79; spl. counsel to Gov. Jay S. Hammond of Alaska, Anchorage and Washington, 1979-81; commr. Alaska Dept. Natural Resources, Juneau, 1981-83; dir. state fed. relations and spl. counsel to Gov. Bill Sheffield of Alaska, Washington and Juneau, 1983-86; dir. state-fed. relations, spl. counsel to Gov. Steve Cowper of Alaska, Washington, 1986-90, Gov. Walter J. Hickel of Alaska, Washington, 1990-94, Gov. Tony Knowles, 1994—; mem. Alaska Power Survey Exec. Adv. Com. of FPC, Anchorage, 1972-74; mem. spl. com. hard rock minerals Govs. Council of Sci. and Tech., Anchorage, 1979-80; guest lectr. on natural resources U. Alaska, U. Denver. Contbr. articles to profl. jours.; columnist Anchorage Times until 1991. Acad. supr. Alaska Externship Program, U. Denver Coll. Law, 1976-79; mem. Reagan-Bush transition team for U.S. Dept. Justice, 1980. Recipient Superior Sustained Performance award Joint Fed. State Land Use Planning Commn. for Alaska, 1978, Resolution of Commendation award Alaska Legis., 1988. Republican. Office: State of Alaska Office of Gov 444 N Capitol St NW Ste 336 Washington DC 20001-1529

KATZ, JOSEPH JACOB, chemist, educator; b. Apr. 19, 1912; s. Abraham and Stella (Asnin) K.; m. Celia S. Weiner, Oct. 1, 1944; children: Anna, Elizabeth, Mary, Abram. BSc, Wayne U., 1932; PhD, U. Chgo., 1942. Research asso. chemistry U. Chgo., 1942-43, asso. chemist metall. lab., 1943-45; sr. chemist Argonne Nat. Lab., Ill., 1945—; Tech. adviser U.S. delegation UN Conf. on Peaceful Uses Atomic Energy, Geneva, Switzerland, 1955; chmn. AAAS Gordon Research Conf. on Inorganic Chemistry, 1953-54. Am. editor Jour. Inorganic and Nuclear Chemistry, 1955-82. Recipient Distinguished Alumnus award Wayne U., 1955, Profl. Achievement award U. Chgo. Alumni Assn., 1983, Rumford Premium Am. Acad. Arts & Scis., 1992; Guggenheim fellow, 1956-57. Mem. Am. Chem. Soc. (award for nuclear applications in chemistry 1961, sec.-treas. div. phys. chemistry 1966-76), Nat. Acad. Scis., Phi Beta Kappa, Sigma Xi. Home: 1700 E 56th St Apt 1901 Chicago IL 60637-1970 Office: Argonne Nat Lab 9700 Cass Ave Argonne IL 60439-4803

KATZ, JOSEPH LOUIS, chemical engineer, educator; b. Colon, Panama, Aug. 4, 1938; naturalized, 1970; s. Adolfo and Margarita (Eisen) K.; m. Liliane Capelluto, Apr. 10, 1965; children: Daniel P., Alan R. BS, U. Chgo., 1960, PhD, 1963. Amanuensis U. Copenhagen Chem. Lab. III, 1963-64; mem. tech. staff N.Am. Aviation Sci. Ctr., Thousand Oaks, Calif., 1964-70; assoc. prof. chem. engring. Clarkson Coll. Tech., Potsdam, N.Y., 1970-75, prof., 1975-79; prof. Johns Hopkins U., Balt., 1979—, chmn. dept. chem. engring., 1981-84; dir. Energy Rsch. Inst., 1981-83; prof. U. Aix-Marseille, France, 1976; vis. prof. MIT, Cambridge, 1977. Recipient John W. Graham Rsch. prize, Clarkson U., 1975; John Simon Guggenheim Meml. Found. fellow, 1976-77. Fellow AAAS, Am. Phys. Soc.; mem. AIChE, Am. Chem. Soc. (Md. sect. Chemist of Yr. 1982), Combustion Inst., Material Rsch. Soc., Sigma Xi. Home: 5600 Greenspring Ave Baltimore MD 21209-4308 Office: Johns Hopkins U Dept Chem Engring Baltimore MD 21218-2689

KATZ, LARRY, writer, columnist; b. Bklyn., Nov. 30, 1948; s. Samuel and Ruth (Greger) K.; m. Kelly Richards, Aug. 23, 1985; children: Samantha, Alexander, Cora Della. BA, CCNY, 1971; MusB, Manhattan Sch. Music, 1975. Arts writer The Real Paper, Cambridge, Mass., 1980-81; arts critic Boston Herald, 1983-87, music columnist, 1987—; radio commentator Sta. WFNX-FM, Lynn, Mass., 1987-93, columnist Boston Mag., 1989-91; syndicated by Reuters and L.A. Times Entertainment News, 1993—. Musician, bassist, N.Y.C., 1970-80. Office: Boston Herald 1 Herald St Boston MA 02118-2200*

KATZ, LAWRENCE FRANCIS, economics educator; b. Ann Arbor, Mich., Apr. 21, 1959; s. Robert and Vera (Reichenfeld) Gantz. AB, U. Calif., Berkeley, 1981; PhD, MIT, 1986; MA (hon.), Harvard U., 1991. Asst. prof. U. Calif., Berkeley, 1985-86; asst. prof. econs. Harvard U., Cambridge, 1986-90, prof. econs., 1991—; chief economist U.S. Dept. Labor, Washington, 1993-94; rsch. assoc. Nat. Bur. of Econ. Rsch., Cambridge, 1985—; project dir., Project on the Well-Being of Children and Econs. of the Family, Nat. Bur. Econ. Rsch., 1994-96. Co-editor: Differences and Changes in Wage Structures, 1995; editor Quar. Jour. of Econs., 1991—; contbr. numerous articles to profl. jours. Named Global Leader for Tomorrow World Econ. Forum, 1993; grantee NSF, 1988-90, 90-92, 96-99, Russell Sage Found. grantee, 1988-90; Olin fellow in econs., 1988-89, NSF fellow, 1981-84. Fellow Econometric Soc.; mem. Am. Econs. Assn. Avocations: hiking, bird watching. Home: 14 Scott St Cambridge MA 02138-2016 Office: Harvard Univ Dept of Econs Cambridge MA 02138

KATZ, LAWRENCE SHELDON, lawyer; b. Newark, N.J., Jan. 30, 1943; s. Edward and Pearl (Weiss) K.; divorced; 1 child, Scott. BBA in Govt., U. Miami, 1965, JD, 1968. Assoc. Hoffman & St. Jean, Miami Beach, Fla., 1968-70, Jack R. Nageley Law Office, Miami Beach, Fla., 1970-72, Swickle, Katz & Brotman, Miami Beach, Fla., 1972-77; pvt. practice, Miami Beach, 1977—; gen. counsel Fraternal Order of Police, Hialeah, Fla., 1972-89, U.S. Shooting Team, Colorado Springs, 1978-95. 2d lt. U.S. Army, 1965-69. Recipient Pres.'s award Nat. Assn. Criminal Def. Atty.'s, 1977. Mem. ABA, NRA (bd. dirs. 1957), Fla. Sportshooting Assn. (pres. 1985), The Fla. Bar, Safari Club Internat. (v.p. 1995, pres. 1992). Jewish. Avocations: flying, photography, scuba, skiing, hunting. Office: 3225 Aviation Ave Coconut Grove FL 33133-4741

KATZ, LEANDRO, artist, filmmaker; b. Buenos Aires, June 6, 1938; came to U.S., 1965; s. Mauricio and Elisa (Boklin) K.; m. Eve Berge, (div. 1972); 1 child, Vanessa. BFA, U. Nacional, Buenos Aires, 1961; student, Pratt Graphic Arts Inst., N.Y.C., 1967. Faculty Sch. Visual Arts, N.Y.C., 1971—; asst. prof. Brown U., Providence, 1980-84; assoc. prof. William Paterson U., Wayne, N.J., 1987—. One person shows include Nina Menocal Gallery, Mexico, 1994, Museo del Barrio, 1996, Betty Rymer Gallery/Sch. Art Inst. Chgo., 1998; exhibited in group shows Whitney Mus. Am. Art, 1982, R.I. Sch. Design Mus., 1984, Bronx Mus. Art, 1988, New Mus. Contemporary Art, 1990; author: Es Una Ola, 1965, others; filmmaker numerous titles. Recipient Coral prize for The Day You'll Love Me, Havana L.Am. Film Festival, 1997; Meml. fellow Guggenheim Found., 1979-80, fellow NEA, 1979, 91, 94, N.Y. State Coun. on Arts, 1990, 98, Rockefeller Found., 1993; grantee Jerome Found., 1982, 90, N.Y. Found. for Arts, 1989. Home: 25 E 4th St New York NY 10003-7061 Office: William Paterson Univ Wayne NJ 07470

KATZ, LEONARD, psychology educator; b. Boston, Mar. 6, 1938; s. William and Ruth K.; m. Barbara A. Mahoney, May 28, 1962; children: Nicholas, Stephen, Alexis. BS, U. Mass., 1959, PhD, 1963. Postdoctoral fellow Stanford (Calif.) U., 1963-65; prof. psychology U. Conn., Storrs, 1965—; researcher Haskins Labs., New Haven, 1974—. Contbr. articles to profl. jours. Fulbright fellow, Yugoslavia, 1986. Fellow Am. Psychol. Soc., Am. Assn. Advancement of Sci. Office: U Conn Dept Psychology WAB U-20 Storrs Mansfield CT 06269

KATZ, LEW, advertising executive. Dir. finance Team One Advertising, El Segundo, Calif. Office: Team One Advertising 1960 E Grand Ave Ste 700 El Segundo CA 90245-5059

KATZ, LEWIS ROBERT, law educator; b. N.Y.C., Nov. 15, 1938; s. Samuel and Rose (Turoff) K.; m. Jan Karen Daugherty, Jan. 14, 1964; children: Brett Elizabeth, Adam Kenneth, Tyler Jessica. AB, Queens Coll., 1959; JD, Ind. U., 1963. Bar: Ind 1963, Ohio 1971. Assoc. Snyder, Bunger, Cotner & Harrell, Bloomington, Ind., 1963-65; instr. U. Mich. Law Sch., Ann Arbor, 1965-66; asst. prof. Case Western Res. U. Law Sch., Cleve., 1966-68, assoc. prof., 1968-71, prof., 1971—, John C. Hutchins prof. law, 1973—; dir. Ctr. for Criminal Justice, Case Western Res. U., 1973-91, dir. fgn. grad. studies, 1992—; cons. criminal justice agys. Author: Justice is the Crime, 1972, The Justice Imperative: Introduction to Criminal Justice, 1979, Ohio Arrest Search and Seizure,ann. publ. 1998, New York Suppression Manual, 1991, Know Your Rights, 1994, (with P.C. Giannelli) Ohio Criminal Law, 1996, (with B.W. Griffin) Ohio Felony Sentencing Law, ann. publ., 1999, (with P.C. Giannelli) Ohio Criminal Justice, ann. publ., 1998. Mem. regional bd. Anti-Defamation League; trustee Women's Law Fund. Recipient Disting. Tchr. award Case West Res. U. Law Alumni Assn.; Nat. Defender Project of Nat. Legal Aid and Defender Assn. fellow, 1968. Mem. ABA. Home: 2873 N Park Blvd Cleveland OH 44118-4030 Office: Case Western Res U Law Sch Cleveland OH 44106

KATZ, LOIS ANNE, internist, nephrologist; b. Rockville Centre, N.Y., Dec. 1, 1941; d. Irvin Martin and Frances (Berenstein) Fradkin; m. Arthur A. Katz, Aug. 18, 1962; children: David, Brian. BA, Wellesley Coll., 1962; MD, NYU, 1966. Diplomate Am. Bd. Internal Medicine, Am. Bd. Nephrology. Intern medicine Bellevue Hosp., NYU, N.Y.C., 1966-67, resident medicine, 1967-68; sr. resident medicine N.Y. Hosp., N.Y.C., 1968-69; chief resident medicine N.Y. VA Med. Ctr., N.Y.C., 1969-70, fellow nephrology, 1970-71, staff physician, 1970-74, assoc. chief nephrology, 1974—, assoc. chief of staff ambulatory care, 1980—; asst. prof. clin. medicine NYU Sch. Medicine, N.Y.C., 1974-79, assoc. prof., 1979-94, prof. clin. medicine, 1994—. Alumna admission rep. Wellesley-in-Westchester, N.Y.; bd. mem. Women's Med. Assn., N.Y.C., 1986—. Fellow ACP; mem. Am. Soc. Nephrology, Am. Med. Women's Assn., Soc. Gen. Internal Medicine, Women in Nephrology (treas. 1985-89), Am. Soc. Hypertension, Sigma Xi, Alpha Omega Alpha. Jewish. Avocations: reading, swimming, cooking, music. Office: Dept Vets Affairs Med Ctr 423 E 23rd St New York NY 10010-5050*

KATZ, MARCIA, public relations company executive; b. N.Y.C., Mar. 20, 1950; d. Alexander and Dorothy Harriet (Frank) K.; m. R. Glenn Brode, Oct. 3, 1982; 1 child, Richard Gregory. BS magna cum laude, CUNY, 1972, MS, 1975. Tchr. N.Y.C. Bd. Edn., 1972-76; exec. v.p. worldwide Burson-Marsteller, N.Y.C., 1976-91; exec. v.p. U.S.A. Hill and Knowlton, N.Y.C., 1991-92; pres., CEO InterScience, N.Y.C., 1993—; cons. Nat. Coun. on Patient Inf. and Edn., Washington, 1985—, Am. Health Found., N.Y.C., 1991—. Editor: Perspectives on Aging Worldwide, 1989; contbr. articles to profl. jours. Cons. Nat. Neurofibromatosis Soc., 1988-90; mktg. counselor Nat. Multiple Sclerosis Soc., 1990—. Named to Acad. Women Achievers, YWCA, N.Y.C., 1985. Mem. Healthcare Bus. Women's Assn., Healthcare Comms. Council (pub. rels. chair 1985), Phi Beta Kappa. Office: InterScience 1675 Broadway New York NY 10019-5820

KATZ, MARTHA LESSMAN, lawyer; b. Chgo., Oct. 28, 1952; d. Julius Abraham and Ida (Oiring) Lessman; m. Richard M. Katz, June 27, 1976; children: Julia Erin, Meredith Evin. AB, Washington U., St. Louis, 1974; JD, Loyola U., Chgo., 1977. Bar: Ill. 1977, U.S. Dist. Ct. (no. dist.) Ill. 1977, Calif. 1981, U.S. Dist. Ct. (so. dist.) Calif. 1981, U.S. Dist. Ct. (no. dist.) Calif. 1982, Md. 1993, U.S. Supreme Ct. 1993, D.C. 1994. Assoc. Fein & Hanfling, Chgo., 1977-80, Rudick, Platt & Victor, San Diego, 1981-82, 84-91; asst. sec., counsel Itel Corp., San Francisco, 1982-84; ptnr. Katz & Mann, Attys. at Law, 1991-95; with legal dept. U.S. Fidelity and Guaranty Co., 1995-99; chair tech. practice group Miles & Stockbridge PC, Balt., Md., 1999—. Mem. Calif. State Bar Assn., Md. Bar Assn., Ill. State Bar Assn., Bar Assn. Balt. City, Bar Assn. D.C., Phi Beta Kappa. Jewish. Fax: 410-385-3700. E-mail: mkatz@milesstockbridge.com. Office: 10 Light St Baltimore MD 21202

KATZ, MARTIN HOWARD, lawyer; b. Bklyn., Jan. 21, 1931; s. Nathan and Sally K.; m. Theresa Victory, June 22, 1975; 1 son, Norman. B.A., Bklyn. Coll., 1952; J.D., Bklyn. Law Sch., 1955, LL.M., 1957. Sr. ptnr. firm Katz, Lubkin & Katz, Bklyn., 1955-68; gen. counsel AAMCO Industries, Inc., Bridgeport, Pa., 1968-74; sr. assoc. Blank, Rome, Comisky & McCauley, Phila., 1974-76; dep. atty. gen., chief antitrust div. Pa. Dept. Justice, 1978; v.p., corp. counsel Jewelcor Inc., Wilkes-Barre, Pa., 1978-82; gen. counsel U.S. Consumer Product Safety Commn., Washington, 1982-85; lectr. bus. orgns. and mgmt. Pres. Long Beach (N.Y.) Civic Assn., 1965-68, Stonybrook Condominium Council, Norristown, Pa., 1976-78, Timber Green Homeowners Assn., New Port Richey, Fla., 1995-96; trustee Temple B'nai B'rith, Kingston, Pa.; bd. dirs. Congregation B'nai Emmanuh, Tarpon Springs, Fla., 1997. Recipient Pres.'s award Long Beach chpt. Nat. Cystic Fiborsis Found., 1967; Hero award United Way, 1978; Angel award, 1979. Mem. ABA, Fed. Bar Assn., U.S. Consumer Product Safety Commn. (10th ann. and chmn. award).

KATZ, MARVIN, federal judge; b. 1930. B.A., U. Pa., 1951; LL.B., Yale U., 1954. Pvt. practice law, 1954-77; asst. commnr. IRS, 1977-81; assoc. Mesirov, Gelman, Jaffe, Cramer & Jamieson, Phila., 1981-83; judge U.S. Dist. Ct. (ea. dist.) Pa., Phila., 1983-97, sr. judge, 1997—. Office: US Courthouse 13613 US Courthouse Ind Mall W 601 Market St Philadelphia PA 19106-1713*

KATZ, MARYANNE, artist, educator; b. Buffalo, Feb. 5, 1931; d. Samuel Sulim and Elma Burns (Aitken) Vineberg; m. David Robert Katz, Feb. 7, 1953; children: Avery Myron, Regina, Samuel Ellis, Sarah Beth Gonta. Student, SUNY, Buffalo, 1948-51, Academie Julien, Paris, 1951-53; BS in Art, Daemen Coll., Amherst, N.Y., 1973; MS in Art Edn., State U. Coll., Buffalo, 1983. Cert. tchr., N.Y., N.J., Va. Art dir. Herald Plastics, Tonawanda, N.Y., 1979-80; substitute tchr. Williamsville (N.Y.) Ctrl. Sch., 1981-86; substitute art tchr. Warren County Vocat.-Tech. Sch., Washington, N.J., 1987-88, Hackettstown (N.J.) H.S., 1994; substitute tchr. Mt. Olive (N.J.) Schs., 1986-94, Chesapeake (Va.) Ctrl. Sch. Sys., 1996—; adj. prof. State U. Coll., Buffalo, 1982-85; art demo, lectr. Associated Art Orgn., Buffalo, 1975-85, art show judge, 1980; art show judge Sr. Citizens Coun., Chesapeake, Va., 1996; tchr. watercolor painting Chesapeake Parks & Recreation Dept. 6 one-woman shows pub. and pvt. galleries, N.Y., N.J., Va., 1976-97; author: Fezants and Other Bird Wirds, 1983; artist paintings, drawings, lithographs, miniatures, illustrations, 1950—. Docent Chrysler Mus. Art, Norfolk, Va., 1996—. Recipient artist-in-sch. award Allentown Art Soc., Buffalo, 1983; featured artist Watercolor mag., N.Y.C., 1996. Mem. Tidewater Artists Assn., Va. Watercolor Soc. Avocations: indoor gardening, floral design. Home: 828 Fallcreek Run Chesapeake VA 23322-2147

KATZ, MICHAEL, pediatrician, educator; b. Lwow, Poland, Feb. 13, 1928; came to U.S., 1946, naturalized, 1951; s. Edward and Rita (Gluzman) K.; m. Robin J. Roy, July 19, 1986; 1 child, Edward Alexander. AB, U. Pa., 1949, postgrad. (Harrison fellow), 1950-51; MD, SUNY, Bklyn., 1956; MS, Columbia U. Sch. Public Health, 1968. Intern UCLA Med. Ctr., 1956-57; resident Presbyn. Hosp. (Babies Hosp.), N.Y.C., 1960-62; dir. pediatric svc. Presbyn. Hosp. (Babies Hosp.), 1977-92, cons., 1992—; hon. lectr. pediatrics Makerere U. Coll., Kampala, Uganda, 1963-64; instr. in pediatrics Columbia U., 1964-65, prof. tropical medicine Sch. Pub. Health, 1971-92, prof. pub. health emeritus, 1992—, prof. pediatrics Coll. Physicians and Surgeons, 1972-77, prof. pub. health, 1977-92, Reuben S. Carpentier prof., 1977-92, Reuben S. Carpentier prof. emeritus, 1992—; v.p. rsch. March of Dimes Birth Defects Found., White Plains, N.Y., 1992—; assoc. mem. Wistar Inst., Phila., 1965-71; asst. prof. pediats. U. Pa., 1966-77; cons. WHO, Guatemala, Venezuela, Egypt, Yemen; mem. U.S. del. 32d World Health Assembly, Geneva, 1979; cons. UNICEF, N.Y.C. and Tokyo, USAID, Egypt, 1982, Poland, 1987; mem. bd. sci. councillors Nat. Inst. Dental Rsch., 1986-90, chmn., 1990-92; vis. prof. U. Würzburg, Fed. Republic Germany, 1988; vis. prof. pediats. U. Negev, Beer Sheva, Israel, 1996. Author: (with others) Parasitic Diseases, 1982, 2d edit., 1989; editor: (with Volker ter Meulen) Slow Virus Infections of the Central Nervous System, 1977; mem. editorial bd. Med. Microbiology and Immunology, 1975-90, Pediatric Infectious Diseases Jour., 1981-92, Vaccines, 1983-94; co-editor: Manuals in Pediatrics; contbr. articles to profl. jours. Pres. World Alliance of Orgns. for the Prevention of Birth Defects, Inc., 1995—. Lt. M.C., USNR, 1957-59. NIH grantee, 1968-76; WHO grantee, 1972-76; recipient Jurzykowski Found. award in Medicine, 1983, Alexander von Humboldt Sr. U.S. Scientist award, 1988. Fellow AAAS, Infectious Diseases Soc. Am., Am. Acad. Pediat.; mem. SOc. Pediatric Rsch., Am. Pediatric Soc., Harvey Soc., Am. Soc. Microbiology, Deutsche Gesellschaft für Neuropathologie und Neuroanatomie E.V. (corr.), Am. Soc. Tropical Medicine and Hygiene, N.Y. Soc. Tropical Medicine (pres. 1976-77), Royal Soc. Tropical Medicine and Hygiene (London), Pediatric Infectious Disease Soc., World Alliance of Orgns. for the Prevention of Birth Defects (pres. 1995—), Inst. Medicine of Nat. Acad. Scis., Ea. Soc. for Pediatric Rsch., Sigma Xi. Home: 1 Griggs Ln Chappaqua NY 10514 Office: March of Dimes Birth Defects Fdn 1275 Mamaroneck Ave White Plains NY 10605-5298

KATZ, MICHAEL JEFFERY, lawyer; b. Detroit, May 11, 1950; s. Wilfred Lester and Bernice (Ackerman) K. BE with honors, U. Mich., 1972; JD, U. Colo., 1976; cert. mgmt., U. Denver, 1985, cert. fin. mgmt., 1990. Bar: Colo. 1978. Rsch. atty., immigration specialist Colo. Rural Legal Svcs., Denver, 1976-77, supervising atty. migrant farm lab., 1977-78; ind. contractor Colo. Sch. Fin., Denver, 1978-79; sole practice Denver, 1978-86; assoc. Levine and Pitler, P.C., Denver, 1986-88; gen. counsel, sec. Grease Monkey Internat., Inc., Denver, 1988-92; prin. Katz & Co., Denver, 1992—; exec. v.p. Nat. Network Exchange, Inc., Denver, 1992—; lectr. on incorporating small bus. and real estate purchase agreements Front Range Coll., 1986—, condr. various seminars on real estate and landlord/tenant law, 1980—; of counsel Levine and Pitler, P.C., Englewood, Colo., 1985—. Contbr. Action Line column Rocky Mountain News; contbr. articles to profl. jours. Mem. Assn. Trial Lawyers Am., Am. Arbitration Assn. (mem. panel of arbitrators 1989), Denver Bar Assn. (mem. law day com. 1985—, mem. real estate com. 1980—, mem. pro bono svcs. com. 1984—), U.S. Yacht Racing Assn., Dillon Yacht Club. Avocations: sailing, bicycling, swimming, art collecting, reading. Fax: 303-790-0927. Office: Tower One 12835 E Arapahoe Rd Ste 400 Englewood CO 80112-3940

KATZ, MICHAEL RAY, Slavic languages educator; b. N.Y.C., Dec. 9, 1944; s. Louis M. and Alice (Gordon) K.; m. Mary K. Dodge, Nov. 19, 1978; 1 child, Rebecca Marie Dodge-Katz. BA, Williams Coll., 1966; MA, Oxford U., 1968, PhD, 1972. From asst. to assoc. prof. Williams Coll., Williamstown, Mass., 1972-83; prof., chmn. dept. Slavic langs. U. Tex., Austin, 1984-97, dir. Russian, East European and Eurasian studies; dean langs. and internat. studies Middlebury (Vt.) Coll., 1998—. Author: The Literary Ballad in Early 19th Century Russian Literature, 1976, Dreams and the Unconscious in Russian Literature, 1984; translator: Who Is To Blame? (A. Herzen), 1984, Notes from Underground (Dostoevsky), 1989, What Is To Be Done: (Chernyshevsky), 1989, Tolstoy's Short Fiction, 1991, Devils (Dostoevsky), 1992, Polina Saks (Druzhinin), 1992, Fathers and Sons (Turgenev), 1994, Antonina (Turgenev), 1997, Prologue (Chernyshevsky), 1995, Antonina (Tur), 1997. NEH grant, 1981-82; recipient Max Haywood Translation prize, 1982. Mem. Am. Assn. Advancement Slavic Studies, Am. Assn. Tchrs. Slavic and East European Langs. (v.p. 1989-92, pres.-elect 1995-96, pres. 1997-98), Am. Coun. Tchrs. of Russian (bd. dirs. 1984—). Avocations: flute; jogging. Home: 1712 Sperry Rd Middlebury VT 05753-9442 Office: Middlebury Coll 209 Sunderland Middlebury VT 05753

KATZ, MITCHELL JAY, public affairs specialist; b. Washington, May 2, 1966; s. Lester Allen and Rayna Paula Katz. BA, U. Vt., 1988; MS in Journalism, Northwestern U., 1989. Capitol Hill corr. The Concord (N.H.) Monitor, Washington, 1989; writer, editor NOAA, Silver Spring, Md., 1990-96; pub. affairs specialist Dept. Justice Immigration and Naturalization Svc., Washington, 1996—; cons. mem. Nat. Ocean Svc. Mktg. Com., 1994-96; team mem. Office Ocean Resources Conservation and Assessment Mktg. Com., 1994-96. Editor, designer The Communicator, 1994—; corr. writer Nat. Assn. Zool. Parks and Aquariums, 1993; sr. editor, contbg. writer Fla. Keys Nat. Marine Sanctuary Mgmt. Plan, 1993-96; news analysis editor White House Office Comms., 1993-95; mng. editor Nat. Assn. Newspapers Pubs. News, 1989. Sr. literacy counselor Montgomery County Literacy Coun., 1993. Recipient Cert. Achievement, Computer Cons. and Tng., Inc., 1992. Mem. Pub. Rels. Soc. Am., Nat. Assn. Govt. Communicators, Fed. Communicators Network (Most Improved Periodical 3d pl. award 1997). Office: INS Office Pub Affairs 425 I St NW Washington DC 20536

KATZ, PHYLLIS ALBERTS, developmental research psychologist; married; 2 children. AB in Psychology summa cum laude, Syracuse U., 1957; PhD in Devel. Clin. Psychology, Yale U., 1961. Assoc. prof. psychology CUNY, 1969-72, chairperson devel. psychology sect. PhD program in edn., 1969-75, acting exec. officer PhD program in edn., 1974-75, prof., 1973-76; dir. Inst. Rsch. on Social Problems, Boulder, 1975—; adj. prof. U. Colo., Boulder, 1980—. Author: The Feminist Dollar, 1997; editor: Towards the Elimination of Racism, 1976; co-editor: Eliminating Racism: Profiles in Controversy, 1988, Health Issues for Minority Adolescents, 1995; founding editor: Sex Roles: Jour. Rsch., 1976-91; editor: Jour. Social Issues, 1996-2000; mem. editl. bd. Devel. Psychology, 1992; contbr. chpts. on racism, gender-role rsch., and only-child rsch. to books; also numerous articles. Trustee Colo. Music Festival, 1982-84, pres. bd. trustees, 1984-85; mem. Colo. Women's Forum, 1992—; bd. dirs. Women's Found., Colo., 1986-92. USPHS trainee Yale U., 1956-59; grantee NYU Arts and Sci. Rsch., 1963-66, CUNY Faculty Rsch., 1973, Nat. Inst. Child Health Human Devel., 1966-68, 68-72, 79-81, 81-83, 87-91, 92-97, Office of Child Devel., 1972-75, NIMH, 1977-79, Carnegie Found., 1996-98. Mem. APA (editor jour. 1974-77, chmn. child advocacy com. 1973, mem. fin. com. 1990-93, coun. rep. 1983-86, 89-92, divsn. pres. 1986-87, fellow divsns. 7, 8, 9, 35 and 45, pres.-elect divsn. 35, editor 1996—), Soc. Rsch. in Child Devel., Assn. Women in Sci.

KATZ, RANDY H., electrical engineering, computer sciences educator. AB, Cornell U., 1976; MS, U. Calif., Berkeley, 1978, PhD, 1980. With U. Wis., Madison; program mgr. Computing Sys. Tech. Office Def. Advanced Rsch. Projects Agy., office dep. dir.; with U. Calif., Berkeley, 1983-93, 94—, prof., chairperson dept. elec. engring. and computer sci., 1996—; participant U.S. V.p. Al Gore's Nat. Performance Rev.; presenter sci. confs. Author: Contemporary Logic Design, 1993; contbr. articles to profl. publs. Office: Univ Calif Adminstrv Office Rm 231 Cory Hall # 1770 Berkeley CA 94720-1770 also: Univ Calif Rsch Office Rm 637 Soda Hall # 1776 Berkeley CA 94720-1776*

KATZ, RICHARD JON, marketing and advertising company executive; b. Bklyn., Feb. 26, 1932; s. Irving Paul and Lillian Katz; AAS, Bklyn. Coll., 1960; m. Helene Borow, June 7, 1953; children: Robin Lee, Juli Beth, Jennifer Sue. Pres., creative dir. Katz, Jacobs & Douglas Advt., N.Y.C., 1960-75; pres., creative dir., KNL Advt., N.Y.C., 1975-78, Ric Katz & Assos. Inc., N.Y.C., 1978—; pres., chief exec. officer Rams Mktg. Inc., N.Y.C., 1978-90; pres., creative dir. The Ramstar Group Advt., 1986-95; cons. Pinnacle Mktg. & Resources, Inc., 1990; COB Fitness Clinic for Ageless Dynamics; CEO World Digital Deliverance Techs., LLC, 1997; lectr. Fashion Inst. Tech., NYU. Trustee inst. geriatric care New Sch. for Research, Hunter, N.Y, The Parker Jew. Inst. geriatric care. Served with USAF, 1951-55. Recipient awards for creativity, graphics, design and mktg. Mem. Am. Mgmt. Assn., President's Club. Author: Professional Guidelines for Effective Advertising.

KATZ, ROBERT DAVID, architecture educator; b. N.Y.C., June 27, 1929; s. Harry and Irene (Rubin) K. B in Architecture, Cornell U., 1952; M in City Planning, MIT, 1954. Planner Santa Clara Planning Dept., San Jose, Calif., 1956-58; asst. prof. coll. architecture Cornell U., Ithaca, N.Y., 1958-59; asst. and assoc. prof. dept. urban and regional planning U. Ill., Urbana-Champaign, 1959-69, prof. dept. architecture, 1969-94, prof. inst. govt. and pub. affairs, 1993-94, prof. emeritus, 1994—, dir. housing rsch. and devel. program, office vice chancellor rsch., 1969-93, dir. grad. coll. office gerontology and aging studies, 1979-87; vis. prof. South Bank U., London, 1996—; cons. U.S. Pub. Housing Adminstrn., Chgo., U.S. HUD, Washington, Friendship Village, Milw.; speaker in field. Author: Intensity of Development and Livability of Multifamily Housing Projects-Design Qualities of European and American Housing Projects, 1965, Design of the Housing Site: A Critique of American Practice, 1967, Housing in the 90s: Common Issues, 1990, Jobs and Housing in the Chicago Metropolitan Region, 1993, Developing and Planning a Demonstration Program to Provide Care and Repair Services to Older Homeowners, 1995; contbr. articles to profl. jours. Chmn. Bd. Zoning Appeals, Urbana, 1976-94; bd. dirs., v.p. Midwest Ctr. Housing and Cmty. Devel., 1989-91, Met. Housing Devel. Corp., 1993-94. Skidmore, Owings and Merrill Archtl. scholar Cornell U., 1951-52, Grad. scholar MIT, 1952-53, 53-54, fellow Graham Found., 1966, vis. fellow Age Concern Inst. Gerontology Kings Coll., 1987. Mem. AIA (housing com., Waid fellow 1961, rsch. fellow 1966), Am. Planning Assn., Am. Inst. Cert. Planners, Nat. Assn. Housing and Redevel. Ofcls. (mem. various coms., John D. Lange Internat. award 1989), Can. Housing and Renewal Assn. (hon.), Brit. Chartered Inst. Housing (affiliate), Internat. Fedn. Housing and Planning (mem. U.S. delegation seminar housing Ea. Europe 1990), Gargoyle Soc., Tau Beta Pi, Phi Kappa Phi.

KATZ, ROBERT LANGDON, human relations educator, rabbi; b. Ft. Dodge, Iowa, Sept. 18, 1917; s. Raphael Mordecai and Rebecca Genendel (Rebbe) K.; m. Miriam Katz, May 9, 1948; children: Amy Jean, Michael S.

(dec.), Jonathan R. BA, Lake Forest Coll., 1938; MA, Hebrew Union Coll., 1943, DHL, 1952. Ordained rabbi, 1943. Rabbi Temple Beth El, Steubenville, Ohio, 1943-44; dir. admissions and field work Hebrew Union Coll., Cin., 1947-57, coordinator dept. human relations, 1950-57, prof. human relations, 1957—; lectr. sociology U. Cin., 1965—. Author: Empathy, 1963, Pastoral Care and the Jewish Tradition, 1985 (transl. Dutch 1987). Served to capt. U.S. Army, 1944-46, ETO. Mem. Cen. Conf. Am. Rabbis. Democrat. Avocations: tennis, jogging, boating. Home: 4187 Rose Hill Ave Cincinnati OH 45229-1422 Office: Hebrew Union Coll 3101 Clifton Ave Cincinnati OH 45220-2404

KATZ, ROBERT NATHAN, ceramic engineer; b. Williamsport, Pa., Sept. 2, 1939; s. Louis and Rose Bernice (Golbitz) K.; S.B., M.I.T., 1961, Ph.D., 1969; M.S., U. Mich., 1963; children—Pamela Lynn, Jonathan Adam; m. Barbara Kurn Rubin, June 15, 1986. Research asst. U. Mich., 1961-62; metallurgist Army Materials Research Agy., Watertown, Mass., 1962-65; ceramic engr. Army Materials Tech. Lab., Watertown, 1965-70, chief ceramics research div., 1970-87, chief materials technologist, 1987-95; Norton assoc. prof. mech. engring. Worcester (Mass.) Poly. Inst., 1990-91, Norton rsch. prof., 1991—; prin. R. Nathan Katz Assocs., 1995—; liaison mem. various coms. Nat. Materials Adv. Bd.; participant Nat. Acad. Sci. Naval Studies Bd., Future Carreir Tech. Study, 1990-91; external examiner Bd. Grad. Studies, U. Cambridge (Eng.), 1979; cons. Dept. Def., Dept. Energy, Congl. Office of Tech. Assessment; mem. U.S. del. NATO Com. on Challenges of Modern Soc., 1974; mem. organizing com., lectr. NATO Advanced Study Inst. Nitrogen Ceramics, 1976, 81. Columnist Ceramic Industry Mag., 1999—. Trustee, Temple Israel of Natick, 1979-80, Temple Beth Zion, Brookline, 1998—. Recipient tech. writing award Dept. Army, 1981. Fellow Am. Ceramic Soc.; mem. Nat. Inst. Ceramic Engrs., New Eng. Ceramic Soc. (F.H. Norton award 1978), Am. Soc. Metals, Sigma Xi. Editor: Ceramics for High Performance Applications, 1974, Vol. II, 1978, Vol. III, 1983. Mem. editorial bd. Internat. Jour. High Tech. Ceramics, 1984-89, Jour. European Ceramic Soc., 1989—. Contbr. articles to tech. publs. Home: 1731 Beacon St Apt 1403 Brookline MA 02445-4329 Office: Dept Mech Engring Worcester Polytechnic Inst Worcester MA 01609

KATZ, ROBERTA R., lawyer; b. Denver, Dec. 12, 1947; m. Charles J. Katz Jr.; children: Sarah, Sydney. BA, Stanford U., 1969; PhD, Columbia U., 1977; JD, U. Wash., 1980. Bar: Wash. 1980, U.S. Dist. Ct. (we. dist.) Wash. 1980. Assoc. Preston, Thorgrimson, Ellis & Holman, Seattle, 1981-83, Sirianni & Youtz, Seattle, 1983-85; assoc. then ptnr. Heller Ehrman White & McAuliffe, Seattle, 1986-92; gen. counsel, sr. v.p. LIN Broadcasting Corp., Kirkland, Wash., 1992-95, McCaw Cellular Comm., Inc., Kirkland, Wash., 1993-95; gen. counsel, sr. v.p., sec. Netscape Comms. Corp., Mountain View, Calif., 1995—. Mem. vis. com. sociology dept. U. Wash., Seattle, 1991—; co-founder, chair Seattle Art Fair, 1992-93; bd. dirs. Seattle Children's Theatre, 1990-93, Lakeside Sch., 1994-97. Fellow Discovery Inst., 1992—. *

KATZ, ROGER, pediatrician, educator; b. Menominee, Mich., Feb. 23, 1938; s. Peter W. and Mae C. (Chudacoff) K.; m. Barbara Morguelan, Feb. 6, 1966; children: Carl, Gary, Robyn. BS, U. Wis., 1960; MD, U. Louisville, 1965. Diplomate Am. Bd. Allergy and Immunology, Am. Bd. Pediatric Allergy, Am. Bd. Pediatrics. Clin. prof. pediatrics UCLA, 1978—; spkr. in field; expert legal evaluator. Author and editor sci. books and manuscripts. Maj. U.S. Army, 1970-72. Named 1 of Best Drs. in Am., 1996, 97. Fellow Am. Acad. Allergy, Asthma and Immunology, Am. Coll. Allergy, Asthma and Immunology (bd. regents 1990-93), Am. Acad. Pediat., Am. Coll. Chest Physicians, Joint Coun. Allergy, Asthma and Immunology (pres. 1986-90). Office: UCLA Med Ctr 100 Ucla Medical Plz Ste 550 Los Angeles CA 90024-6990

KATZ, RONALD LEWIS, physician, educator; b. Bklyn., Apr. 22, 1932; s. Joseph and Belle (Charnis) K.; children: Richard Ian, Laura Susan, Margaret Karen. B.A., U. Wis.-Madison, 1952; M.D., Boston U., 1956; postgrad. in Pharmacology (NIH fellow), Coll. Physicians and Surgeons, Columbia U., 1959-60; postgrad. (John Simon Guggenheim fellow), Royal Postgrad. Med. Sch., U. London, 1968-69. Intern USPHS Hosp., S.I., 1956-57; resident Columbia-Presbyn. Med. Center, 1957-60; asst. prof. anesthesiology Coll. Physicians and Surgeons, Columbia U., 1960-66, assoc. prof., 1966-70, prof., 1970-73; prof., chmn. dept. anesthesiology UCLA, 1973-90, prof. anesthesiology, 1990-94, chief staff Med. Ctr., 1984-86; prof., chmn. dept. anesthesiology U. So. Calif., L.A., 1995—; Cons. NIH, FDA, numerous state agys. Author, editor: Muscle Relaxants, 1975; Contbr. numerous articles to profl. jours.; Mem. editorial bd.: Handbook of Anesthesiology, 1972—, Progress in Anesthesiology, 1973—; editor in chief Seminars in Anesthesia, 1982—. Mem. Am. Soc. Anesthesiologists, Am. Physiol. Soc., Am. Soc. Pharmacology and Exptl. Therapeutics, N.Y. Acad. Medicine; Faculty Anaesthetists of Royal Coll. Surgeons of Eng. Inventor peripheral nerve stimulator. Home: 2910 Neilson Way Apt 407 Santa Monica CA 90405-5323 Office: U So Calif Dept Anesthesiology Health Sci Campus 1200 N State St Rm 14901 Los Angeles CA 90033-1029

KATZ, RONALD SCOTT, lawyer; b. Norwich, Conn., Dec. 14, 1946; s. Irving David and Joan (Lebovitz) K.; m. Ann Lisa Mark, Dec. 27, 1969; children: Benjamin, Cynthia. BA, Johns Hopkins U., 1968; JD, Columbia U., 1972. Bar: N.Y. 1972, U.S. Ct. Appeals (2d cir.) 1974, U.S. Ct. Appeals (4th cir.) 1993. Assoc. Golenbock & Barell, N.Y.C., 1972-80, ptnr., 1981-89; ptnr. Whitman & Ransom, N.Y.C., 1990-93; shareholder, dir. Shack & Siegel, PC, N.Y.C., 1993—. Mem. ABA, N.Y. State Bar Assn. Avocation: tennis. Home: 16 Paxford Ln Scarsdale NY 10583-3318 Office: Shack & Siegel PC 530 5th Ave New York NY 10036-5101

KATZ, S. SHELDON, neurolosurgeon; b. N.Y.C., Mar. 12, 1929. AB cum laude, NYU, 1949; MD, State Med. Ctr. N.Y., 1953. Diplomate Am. Bd. Neurosurgery. Intern Kings County Hosp., N.Y.C., 1953-54; resident Bklyn. Jewish Hosp., N.Y.C., 1954-55; resident in neurosurgery Albert Einstein Coll. Med., N.Y.C., 1957-61; asst. attending neurosurgery Montefiore Hosp., N.Y.C., 1961—; sr. attending, chief neurosurgery Good Samaritan Hosp., Suffern, N.Y., 1973-82; sr. attending, chief neurosurgery Nyack (N.Y.) Hosp., 1975-80, dir. surgery, 1979-82; clin. assoc. prof. neurosurgery emeritus N.Y. Med. Coll., Valhalla, N.Y.; cons. Rockland State Hosp., Orangeburg, N.Y., Helen Hayes Rehab. Hosp., West Haverstraw, N.Y., Letchworth Village Hosp., Thiells, N.Y. Capt. USAF, 1955-57. Mem. ACS, AMA (physicians recognition award), Internat. Coll. Surgeons, Acad. Medicine, Congress Neurol. Surgeons, Am. Assn. Neurol. Surgeons, Soc. Neurosurgeons N.Y.C., Med. Soc. State N.Y. (pres.), Rockland County Med. Soc. (pres. 1981), Phi Beta Kappa, Beta Lambda Sigma. Home: 15 Elrod Dr West Nyack NY 10994

KATZ, SAMUEL, geophysics educator; b. Berlin, Germany, Feb. 13, 1923; came to U.S., 1934, naturalized, 1940; s. Herman and Bertha (Low) K.; m. Jean Barbara Parker, July 10, 1953; children—David R., Daniel M., Miriam E. B.S., U. Mich., 1943; A.M., Columbia, 1947, Ph.D., 1955. With radiation lab. Mass. Inst. Tech., 1943-46; mem. sci. staff Lamont Geol. Obs., Columbia, 1948-53; sr. physicist Stanford Research Inst., 1953-57; mem. faculty Rensselaer Poly Inst., 1957—, prof. geophysics, 1962-86, prof. emeritus, 1986—, chmn. dept. geology, 1964-69. Contbr. articles in field to profl. jours. Mem. Am. Geophys. Union, AAAS, Sigma Xi. Home: 908 Karenwald Ln Niskayuna NY 12309-6416

KATZ, SAMUEL LAWRENCE, pediatrician, scientist; b. Manchester, N.H., May 29, 1927; s. Morris and Ethel (Lawrence) K.; m. Betsy Jane Cohan, June 27, 1950; children: Samuel Lawrence Jr. (dec.), John S.L., David L., Deborah Susan, William L., Susan Johanna, Penelope Jennifer; m. Catherine Minock Wilfert, July 23, 1971; stepchildren: Rachel Ann, Katie Claiborne. AB magna cum laude, Dartmouth Coll., 1948; MD cum laude, Harvard U., 1952; DSc (hon.), Georgetown U., 1996, Dartmouth Coll., 1998. Intern Beth Israel Hosp., Boston, 1952-53; resident Children's Hosp., Boston, 1953-54, 55-56, Mass. Gen. Hosp., 1954-55; from rsch. fellow to asst. prof. Harvard Med. Sch., 1956-68; prof., chmn. dept. pediat. Duke Med. Sch., 1968-90, Wilburt C. Davison prof., 1972-97; mem. sci. adv. bd. Hasbro Children's Found., St. Jude's Children's Rsch. Hosp.; chmn. bd. Burroughs Wellcome Fund, Albert Sabin Vaccine Found., Pediat. AIDS Found.; rschr. on virology, virus vaccines and immunization coms. and study sects. WHO, Children's Vaccine Initiative; chmn. adv. com. immunization practice Ctrs. for Disease Control, Atlanta, 1985-93. Developer (with John F. Enders) attenuated live measles-virus vaccine; contbr. to books, articles to profl. jours. With USNR, 1945-46. Nat. Found. fellow, 1956-58; NIH Rsch. Career Devel. awardee, 1965-68; recipient Presdl. medal of achievement Dartmouth Coll., 1991. Mem. APHA (Needleman medal and award 1997), Am Fedn. Clin. Rsch., Am. Soc. Clin. Investigation, Soc. Pediat. Rsch., Am. Pediat. Soc. (pres. 1986-87, St. Geme award 1988), New England Pediat. Soc., Infectious Diseases Soc. Am. (co-chmn. vaccine initiative 1998—, Bristol award 1988, Soc. citation 1993), Am. Assn. Immunologists, Am. Acad. Pediat. (Grulee award 1975, Jacobi award 1986), Assn. Med. Sch. Pediat. Dept. Chmn. (pres. 1977-79), Pediat. Infectious Diseases Soc. (Disting. Physician award 1991), Inst. Medicine of NAS. Home: 1917 Wildcat Creek Rd Chapel Hill NC 27516-9786 Office: Duke U Med Ctr PO Box 2925 Durham NC 27710-2925

KATZ, SANFORD NOAH, lawyer, educator; b. Holyoke, Mass., Dec. 23, 1933; m. Joan Raphael; children: Daniel, Andrew. BA in History with distinction, Boston U., 1955; JD, U. Chgo., 1958; postgrad., Yale U., 1963-64. Bar: D.C. 1959, U.S. Supreme Ct. 1963, Mass. 1970. Law clk. to chief judge U.S Ct. Claims, Washington, 1958-59; instr. Sch. of Law Cath. U., 1959-60; asst. prof. law Am. Sch. Law, Cath. U., 1960-62, assoc. prof., 1962-64; assoc. prof. U. Fla., 1964-66, prof., 1966-68; prof. Boston Coll., 1968—; vis. prof. U. Mich., summer 1967; lectr. in law and social work Smith Coll., summers 1965-69; assoc. Clare Hall, Cambridge (Eng.) U., 1973; mem. Faculty of Laws, 1973; vis. fellow Hampstead Child Therapy Clinic, London, 1973, All Souls Coll., Oxford U., 1997, Pembroke Coll., Oxford U., 1999; del. White House Conf. on Children, 1970; mem. Spl. Adv. Com. Atty. Gen. Mass., 1974; Joint Mass. House and Senate Commn. on Family, 1977, Mass. Jud. Nominating Commn., 1977-79. Author: When Parents Fail, 1971, Adoptions Without Agencies: A Study of Independent Adoptions, 1978, Child Snatching-The Legal Response to the Abduction of Children, 1981, (with Weyrauch) American Family Law in Transition, 1983, (with Weyrauch) Cases and Materials on Family Law-Legal Concepts and Changing Human Relationships, 1994, others; also monographs, book introductions; editor: The Youngest Minority: Lawyers in Defense of Children, vols. I and II, 1974, (with John Eekelaar) Family Violence: An International and Interdisciplinary Study, 1978, Marriage and Cohabitation in Contemporary Societies, 1980; editor-in-chief Family Law Quar., 1970-83; mem. editl. bd. Mass. Family Law Jour.; contbr. articles, revs. to profl. publs. Chmn. Lydia Rapoport Endowment Fund Smith Coll. Grantee Field Found., 1968-69, Grant Found., 1971-75, HEW, 1973-78. Mem. Internat. Soc. Family Law (pres. 1981-84), Mass. Bar Assn., ABA (chmn. family law sect. 1980-81). Chief drafter HEW model acts; research on child abuse and neglect, marriage, child custody in divorce, model legislation, contract law.

KATZ, SHERMAN E., lawyer; b. Pitts., July 13, 1943; s. Saul H. Katz and Ann (Sklov) Cohen; m. Maureen Murphy, Jan. 26, 1980; 1 child, Barnaby Simon. Student, U. Stockholm, 1963-64; BA cum laude, Amherst Coll., 1965; JD, Columbia U., 1969, MA in Internat. Affairs, 1969; diploma in European Law, Oxford U., 1992. Bar: N.Y. 1969, D.C. 1969, U.S. Ct. Appeals D.C. 1970, U.S. Supreme Ct. 1973, U.S. Ct. Internat. Trade 1984. Ptnr. Coudert Bros., Washington, 1977-94, Squire, Sanders & Dempsey, Washington, 1994-98, Kelley, Drye & Warren, Washington, 1998—. Contbr. numerous articles to profl. jours. regarding internat. trade and investment. Commr. D.C. Commn. on Arts & Humanities, Washington, 1987—; chmn. exec. com., hon. dir. Washington Performing Arts Soc., 1981—; bd. dirs. The Washington Opera, 1988—, The Source Theatre, Folger Poetry Series. Named Knight of the Royal Polar Star by King of Sweden, 1989. Mem. ABA (chmn. svcs. trade com. 1987-89), N.Y. State Bar Assn., Assn. of Bar of City of N.Y., D.C. Bar Assn., Am. Soc. Internat. Law (chmn. publs. com. 1984-87), Nat. Fgn. Trade Coun. (chmn. internat. trade com. 1986), Washington Fgn. Law Soc., Cosmos Club. Office: Kelley Drye & Warren 1201 Pennsylvania Ave NW Washington DC 20004-2491

KATZ, SIDNEY, medical educator; b. Cleve., Feb. 4, 1924; m. 1946; 4 children. MD, Case Western Res. U., 1948; MA, Brown U., 1984. Intern and resident in internal medicine Univ. Hosp.-Case Western Res. U., Cleve., 1948-50, Am. Cancer Soc. fellow in pathology, 1950-51, from instr. to prof. Sch. Medicine, 1952-71; prof. medicine, dir. Office Health Svc. Edn. and Rsch.-Mich. State U., 1971-77, prof. cmty. health, chmn. dept., 1978-82; assoc. dean medicine, prof. cmty. health and medicine Brown U., 1982-87; prof. architectonics and medicine Case Western Res. U., 1987-89; emeritus prof. geriatrics Columbia U., N.Y.C., 1989—; spl. advisor White House Conf. on Aging, 1980-81; cons. Health Care Fin. Adminstrn., Nat. Ctr. Health Stats., Nat. Ctr. Health Svc. Rsch., Rand Corp., others. Author 4 books; contbr. over 50 articles to med. jours. Fellow Gerontological Soc.; mem. AMA, Inst. Medicine-NAS, Am. Geriatrics Soc., Soc. Epidemiology Rsch., Internat. Epidemiology Assn. Office: Columbia U 100 Haven Ave New York NY 10032*

KATZ, SIDNEY FRANKLIN, obstetrician, gynecologist; b. Detroit, Sept. 5, 1928; m. Sally R. Katz. BS, Wayne State U., 1949; MD, U. Mich., Ann Arbor, 1953. Diplomate Am. Bd. Ob-Gyn. Intern Wayne County Gen. Hosp., Detroit; resident Grace Hosp., Detroit, 1956-57; pvt. practice Dearborn, Mich., 1959—. Served as capt. USAF, 1954-56. Fellow Am. Coll. Ob-gyn., ACS, Mich. Soc. Gynecologists, So. Mich. Surgical Soc. Office: 4407 Roemer St Dearborn MI 48126-3405

KATZ, STANLEY NIDER, law history educator; b. Chgo., Apr. 23, 1934; s. William Stephen and Florence (Nider) K.; m. Adria Holmes, Jan. 16, 1960; children: Derek Holmes, Marion Holmes. AB, Harvard U., 1955, MA, 1959, PhD, 1961; LLD (hon.), Stockton State Coll., 1981; DHL (hon.), U. Puget Sound, 1994, C.W. Post/L.I. U., 1997, Sacred Heart U., 1997; LLD, Ohio State U., 1998, U. Hartford, 1998. Asst. prof. history Harvard U., 1961-65, U. Wis., Madison, 1965-71; prof. legal history Law Sch. U. Chgo., 1971-78; Class of 1921 Bicentennial prof. history Am. law and liberty Princeton U., 1978-86, sr. fellow Woodrow Wilson Sch., 1986-97, lectr. with rank of prof. Woodrow Wilson Sch., 1997—; pres. Am. Council Learned Socs., N.Y.C., 1986-97; dir. Ctr. for Arts and Cultural Policy Rsch./Woodrow Wilson Sch., 1998—; vis. prof. law U. Pa., 1978-86; mem. Oliver Wendell Holmes Devise, Washington, 1976-84; bd. govs. Inst. European Studies, Chgo., 1976—; chmn. Coun. on Internat. Exchange Scholars, Washington, 1981-85; adj. prof. Cardozo Law Sch., 1999. Author: Newcastle's New York, 1968; editor: The Case and Tryal of John Peter Zenger, 1963, rev. edit., 1972, Oliver Wendell Holmes Devise History of U.S. Supreme Court, 1984—, Colonial America, 1971, 76, 83, 92, American History: Promise and Progress, 1983, Constitutionalism and Democracy, 1993, The Life of Learning, 1994, Philanthropy in the World's Traditions, 1998. Active N.J. Com. for Humanities, 1978-84, 96—; trustee So. Meth. U., 1988—, Nat. Cultural Alliance, 1990—, chmn., 1997—; trustee Rsch. Librs. Group, 1991-93, 1997-99, Brit.-Am. Arts. Assn., 1991—, Newberry Libr., Chgo., ind. sector, 1990-95, chmn. rsch. com. ind. sector, 1989-92, Toynbee Prize Found., 1994-97, pres. 1995-97; Nat. Faculty, 1995, Fulbright Internat. Ctr., 1995—, Copyright Clearance Ctr., 1997—, civic edn. project, 1997—; v.p. Friends of the Law Libr., Libr. of Congress, 1991—, Supreme Ct. N.J., disciplinary oversight com., 1994—, N.J. Ethics Commn., 1991-94, com. model rules of profl. conduct, 1982-83, com. sale of law practices, 1983-84, 89. Fellow Am. Soc. Legal History (pres. 1978-81); mem. AAAS, Papers of the Founding Fathers (chair 1985—), Inst. Early Am. History and Culture (coun. 1974-76, 90-93, 97—), Am. Hist. Assn. (v.p. rsch. 1997—), Orgn. Am. Historians (exec. com. 1976-79, pres. elect 1986-87, pres. 1987-88), Am. Antiquarian Soc., Mass. Hist. Soc., Am. Philos. Soc., Soc. Am. Historians, Coun. Fgn. Rels., Phi Beta Kappa. Democrat. Jewish. Clubs: Princeton (N.Y.C.). Office: Princeton U Woodrow Wilson Sch Princeton NJ 08544

KATZ, STEPHEN I., dermatologist; b. Bklyn., Jan. 26, 1941. BA with honors, U. Md., 1962; MD with honors, Tulane U., 1966; PhD in Immunology, U. London, 1974. Diplomate Am. Bd. Dermatology. Chief dermatologist Nat. Cancer Inst./NIH, Bethesda, Md., 1974-95; v.p., rschr. March of Dimes, Fla., 1995—; asst. dermatology Walter Reed Gen. Hosp., Washington, 1970-72; rsch. fellow dept. pathology Royal Coll. Surgeons Eng., London, 1972-74; sr. investigator dermatology Nat. Cancer Inst./NIH, Bethesda, Md., 1974-77, acting chief dermatology br., 1977-80, chief dermatology br., 1980—; Marion B. Sulzberger prof. dermatology Uniformed Svcs. U. Health Scis., Bethesda, 1989-95, acting chmn. dermatology dept., 1993-95; dir. Nat. Inst. Arthritis and Musculoskelatal and Skin Diseases; cons. Georgetown U., 1970-72, Walter Reed Army Hosp., 1975-79, Nat. Naval Med. Ctr., 1976-95, Washington Dermatol. Soc., 1980-81. Editl. bd. Internat. Jour. Dermatology, 1977-81, Jour. Investigative Dermatology, 1979-82, Jour. Am. Acad. Dermatology, 1979-83, Jour. Immunology, 1981-85, Am. Jour. Dermatopathology, Epithelia, 1986-88, Regional Immunology, 1988-95, Medicine, 1992—, Am. Jour. Contact Dermatitis, 1992—, Dermatology Internat., 1992—, Proceedings Assn. Am. Physicians, 1995—, others. Goldberger Summer fellow AMA, 1965, Advanced Tng. fellow Dermatology Found., 1972-74. Mem. Inst. Med.-Nat. Acad. Sci. Office: Nat Cancer Inst 9000 Rockville Pike 10 Ctr Dr MSC 1908 Bethesda MD 20892-1908*

KATZ, STEPHEN IRA, dermatologist; b. Bklyn., 1941. MD, Tulane U., 1966. Cert. dermatology. Intern La. County Hosp., 1966-67; resident U. Miami, 1967-70; fellow rsch. London, 1972-74; mem. staff Nat. Cancer Inst., Bethesda, Md., 1974—; dir. Natl. Inst. Arthritis & Musculoskeletal & Skin Dis. Dept. Hlth. & Human Svcs., Bethesda, Md., 1995—. Fellow Royal Soc. Medicine; mem. Am. Assn. Dermatology, Soc. Investigative Dermatology. Office: Nat Inst Arthritis Musculoskeletal Skin Diseases Bldg 31 Rm 4C32 31 Center Dr Bethesda MD 20892-2350

KATZ, STEVEN BARRY, English educator, writer; b. Albuquerque, Oct. 27, 1953; s. Elliot Saul and Leona Katz; m. Alison Gaylord Burns, Sept. 27, 1980; 1 child, Jason Michael. BA, Mich. State U., 1977; MA, U. R.I., 1980; PhD, Rensselaer Poly. Inst., 1988. Tchg. asst. U. R.I., Kingston, 1978-81; tchg. asst. Rensselaer Poly. Inst., Troy, N.Y., 1981, 82-83, writing instr. Ctr. for Urban and Environ. Studies, 1982, instr. lang., lit. and comm., 1983-85; instr. English N.C. State U., Raleigh, 1986-87, asst. prof., 1988-94, assoc. prof., 1994—; dir. MS program in tech. comm. N.C. State U., 1995-98, dir. profl. writing cert. program, 1995-97, cons. Ctr. for Comm. in Sci., Tech. and Mgmt., 1998; manuscript reviewer Tech. Comm. Quar., 1991—, others. Author: The Epistemic Music of Rhetoric, 1996; co-author: Writing in the Sciences, 1998; contbr. articles to profl. jours., poetry to mags. and lit. jours.; asst. editor, poetry editor The Center Design, 1977-78; contbg. editor Group Creation, 1976-77; poetry editor Suffolk Jour., 1973-75; recordings include (CD) Insigth and Vision, 1999; mem. jewish musical group Mishpacha. Vol. Against End of World benefit; panelist, lectr. in field; judge various poetry competitions. Grantee N.C. State U., 1992-93, Am. Coun. Learned Socs., 1995. Mem. MLA, N.C. MLA, Internat. Soc. for History of Rhetoric (grantee 1999), Rhetoric Soc. Am., Nat. Coun. Tchrs. English (award 1992), Assn. for Expanded Perspectives in Learning, Sci. Fiction Poetry Assn., Assn. for Tchrs. of Tech. Writing, Soc. for Literature and Sci., Assn. Tchrs. Tech. Writing, Nat. Comm. Assn., Popular/Am. Culture Assn. Jewish. Avocations: classical guitar, songwriting, performing, Jewish studies, languages. E-mail: sbkeg@unity.ncsu.edu. Office: NC State U Dept English Box 8105 Raleigh NC 27695

KATZ, STEVEN MARTIN, lawyer, accountant; b. Washington, Feb. 8, 1941; s. Joseph and Pauline (Weinberg) K.; m. Lauri Gail Berman, Aug. 23, 1964; children: Benjamin, Aaron, Rebecca, Joshua. BS, U. Md., College Park, 1962; JD, George Washington U., 1965. Bar: D.C. 1966, Md. 1971; CPA, Md. Ptnr. Euzent, Katz & Katz, Washington, 1969-72; sr. ptnr. Katz, Frome & Bleecker, P.A., and predecessors, Rockville, Md., 1972-95; pvt. practice Rockville, 1995—; mem. Md. State Grievance Commn., 1991—. Mem. Am. Soc. Atty.-CPAs, Md. Bar Assn., Md. Assn. CPAs, D.C. Bar, Montgomery County Bar Assn., Md. Soc. Accts., Md. State Bar Found. Jewish. Fax: 301-294-9484. Office: 401 E Jefferson St Ste 208 Rockville MD 20850-2617

KATZ, STEVEN THEODORE, religious studies educator; b. Jersey City, Aug. 24, 1944; s. Abraham and Mary (Bell) K.; m. Rebecca Anne Horwich, Jan. 5, 1969; children: Shira, Tamar, Yehuda. BA, Rutgers U., 1966; MA, NYU, 1967; PhD, Cambridge U., 1972; DHL, Gratz Coll., 1987; BD, Cambridge U., Eng., 1991. From asst. to assoc. to full prof. Dartmouth Coll., Hanover, N.H., 1972-84; prof. Near Ea. studies Cornell U., Ithaca, N.Y., 1985-96, chmn. dept., 1985-88; dir. program in Judaic Studies, prof. religion Boston U., 1996—; vis. prof. Hebrew U., Jerusalem, 1971, U. Lancaster, Eng., 1974, U. Toronto, Ont., Can., 1978, 80, U. Calif., Santa Barbara, 1981, Harvard U., Cambridge, Mass., 1982-84, Brandeis U., Waltham, Mass., 1983, Yale U., New Haven, 1983, Yeshiva U., 1995-96; Mason prof. Coll. William and Mary, 1983; Meyerhoff prof. U. Pa., 1989. Author: Jewish Philosophers, 1975, Jewish Ideas and Concepts, 1977, Mysticism and Philosophical Analysis, 1978, Mysticism and Religious Traditions, 1983, Post-Holocaust Dialogues, 1984 (Nat. Jewish Book award 1984), Historicism, The Holocaust and Zionism, 1992, Mysticism and Language, 1992, Frontiers of Jewish Thought, 1992, Interpreters of Judaism, 1993, The Holocaust in Historical Context, 3 vols., 1994 (Outstanding Book in Philosophy and Religion, Am. Assn. Pubs. 1994), American Rabbi, 1997, The Essential Agus, 1997; editor: Modern Jewish Masters Series, 1984—, Johns Hopkins Studies in Judaica Series, 1987—; editor Modern Judaism, 1981; mem. editl. bd. Ency. of Holocaust, 1986—, Ency. of Spirituality, 1986—. Recipient Lakrits prize Hebrew U., 1978, Leopold Lucas prize U. Tübingen, 1999; NEH fellow, 1981, David Baumgardt fellow Am. Philos. Assn., 1984. Fellow Am. Soc. Study Religion, Am. Acad. Jewish Philos., Assn. Jewish Studies (v.p. 1980-86), Am. Acad. Religion; mem. Internat. Metaphysical Soc. Avocations: book collecting, travel, photography. Home: 842 Commonwealth Ave Newton MA 02459-1043 Office: Boston Univ Dept Religion Boston MA 02215

KATZ, STUART CHARLES, lawyer, concert jazz musician; b. Chgo., June 9, 1937; s. Jerome H. and Sylvia L. (Singer) K.; m. Penny Schatz, Jan. 23, 1959; children: Steven, Lauren. BA, Roosevelt U., Chgo., 1959; JD with distinction John Marshall Law Sch., 1964. Bar: Ill. 1964, U.S. Dist. Ct. (no. dist.) Ill. 1965, U.S. Supreme Ct. 1967; lic. real estate broker, Conn., Ill., Minn., Nebr., Pa., Va., Wis., D.C. Assoc. Raymond I. Suekoff, Chgo., 1964-67; ptnr. Yacker & Katz, Chgo., 1967-70; spl. in-house counsel Salk, Ward & Salk, Inc., Chgo., 1970-72; exec. v.p. Heitman Fin. Ltd., Chgo., 1972—; mem. program com. Internat. Council Shopping Ctrs., U.S. Law Conf.; lectr. World Trade Inst. seminars on Fgn. Investment in U.S. Real Estate, Minn. Inst. Continuing Edn., Louisville Bar Assn.; jazz pianist and vibraphonist, appeared in concerts with Benny Goodman, Gene Krupa, Bud Freeman. Mem. ABA, Chgo. Bar Assn., Ill. Bar Assn., Mortgage Bankers Am., Chgo. Assn. Realtors, Minn. Real Estate Bd. Jewish. Office: 180 N La Salle St Ste 3600 Chicago IL 60601-2805

KATZ, THEODORE H., federal judge; b. 1947. BA magna cum laude, Brandeis U., 1968; JD, Columbia U., 1973. Bar: N.Y. Law clk. to Hon. Robert L. Carter, U.S. Dist. Ct. for So. Dist. N.Y., N.Y.C., 1973-74; dir. prisoners' rights project Legal Aid Soc., N.Y.C., 1981-91; magistrate judge for so. dist. N.Y., U.S. Magistrate Ct., N.Y.C., 1991—. Editor Columbia Law Rev., 1972-73. Harlan Fiske Stone scholar. Mem. Assn. Bar City N.Y. Office: 1600 US Courthouse 500 Pearl St New York NY 10007-1316

KATZ, THOMAS J., chemistry educator; b. Prague, Czechoslovakia, Mar. 21, 1936; m. Meta Oehmsen, 1963; 1 child, Joshua. BA, U. Wis., 1956; MA, Harvard U., 1957, PhD in Chemistry, 1959. Instr. Columbia U., 1959-61, from asst. prof. to assoc. prof., 1961-68, prof. chemistry, 1968—; Sloan fellow, 1962-66, Guggenheim fellow, 1967-68. Recipient Arthur C. Cope Scholar award Am. Chemical Soc., 1995. Fellow AAAS; mem. Am. Chem. Soc., Royal Soc. Chem. Office: Columbia U 3000 Broadway New York NY 10027*

KATZ, TONNIE, newspaper editor. BA, Barnard Coll., 1966; MSc, Columbia U., 1967. Editor, reporter newspapers including The Quincy Patriot Ledger, Boston Herald Am., Boston Globe; Sunday/projects editor Newsday; mng. editor Balt. News Am., 1983-86, The Sun, San Bernardino, Calif., 1986-88; asst. mng. editor for news The Orange County Register, Santa Ana, Calif., 1988-89, mng. editor, 1989-92, editor, v.p., 1992-98, editor, sr. v.p., 1998—. Office: Freedom Newspapers Inc Orange County Register 625 N Grand Ave Santa Ana CA 92701-4347*

KATZ, VERA, mayor, former college administrator, state legislator; b. Dusseldorf, Germany, Aug. 3, 1933; came to U.S., 1940; d. Lazar Pistrak and Raissa Goodman; m. Mel Katz (div. 1985); 1 child, Jesse. BA, Bklyn. Coll., 1955, postgrad., 1955-57. Market research analyst TIMEX, B.T. Babbitt, N.Y.C., 1957-62; mem. Oreg. Ho. of Reps., Salem; former dir. devel. Portland Community Coll., from 1982; mayor City of Portland, Oreg., 1993—;

mem. Gov.'s Council on Alcohol and Drug Abuse Programs, Oreg. Legis., Salem, 1985—; mem. adv. com. Gov.'s Council on Health, Fitness and Sports, Oreg. Legis., 1985—; mem. Gov.'s Commn. on Sch. Funding Reform; mem. Carnegie task Force on Teaching as Profession, Washington, 1985-87; vice-chair assembly Nat. Conf. State Legis., Denver, 1986—. Recipient Abigail Scott Duniway award Women in Communications, Inc., Portland, 1985, Jeanette Rankin First Woman award Oreg. Women's Polit. Caucus, Portland, 1985, Leadership award The Neighborhood newspaper Portland, 1985, Woman of Achievement award Commn. for Women, 1985, Outstanding Legis. Advocacy award Oreg. Primary Care Assn., 1985, Service to Portland Pub. Sch. Children award Portland Pub. Schs., 1985. Fellow Am. Leadership Forum (founder Oreg. chpt.); mem. Dem. Legis. Leaders Assn., Nat. Bd. for Profl. Teaching Standards. Democrat. Jewish. Avocations: camping, jogging, dancing. Office: Office of the Mayor City Hall 1220 SW 4th Ave Rm 303 Portland OR 97204-1909*

KATZ, VICTORIA MANUELA, public relations executive, educator, consultant; b. N.Y.C., Mar. 12, 1941; d. Isaac William and Sylvia (Katz) Penner; m. Ronald Mark Katz, Sept. 8, 1974 (dec. Dec. 1996). BA in Journalism, Hofstra Coll., 1962. Sr. editor real estate, fin. Long Island (N.Y.) Comml. Review, 1962-72; freelance writer, publicist N.Y., 1972-74; managing editor North Shore News Group, Smithtown, N.Y., 1974-88; dir. u. news svcs. SUNY, Stony Brook, 1988—; dir. Long Island Bus. Inc., Ronkonkoma, N.Y., 1965-98; adj. journalism prof. C.W. Post, Greenvale, N.Y., 1986-88, Hofstra Coll., Hempstead, N.Y., 1987. Author: (study) Smithtown Minorities, 1983. Trustee Harbor County Day Sch., St. James, N.Y., 1977-93, mktg. and pub. rels. com. mem. United Way, L.I., 1988—; program com. mem. Mus. at Stony Brook, 1990-93. Recipient Media award for govtl. reporting Press Club L.I., 1987, 88. Mem. AAUW (past v.p.), Pub. Rels. Soc. Am. (chair steering com. L.I. chpt. 1996-97), Soc. Profl. Journalists (nat. com. mem., co-chair chpt. health and welfare com., regional dir. 1994-98), Press Club L.I. Chpt. Soc. Profl. Journalists (pres. 1974, treas. 1985-93, 98-99, Deadline Club bd. 1994, program co-chair 1993, v.p. 1995-99). Home: 19 Millbrook Dr Stony Brook NY 11790-2930 Office: SUNY at Stony Brook Adminstrn Bldg 144 Stony Brook NY 11794

KATZ, WILLIAM A., library science educator; b. Seattle, July 6, 1932; m. Linda Sternberg, Dec. 11, 1970; children: Randy, Janet. BA, U. Wash., 1953, MA, 1955; PhD, U. Chgo., 1965. Librarian King County Pub. Library, Seattle, 1955-60; asst. to dir. publishing dept. ALA, 1960-63; asso. prof. U. Ky., 1963-66; prof. Sch. Library and Info. Sci., State U. N.Y., Albany, 1966—; cons. in field. Author: Introduction to Reference Work, 2 vols., 7th edit., 1997, Magazines for Libraries, 9th edit., 1997, Writer's Choice, 1983, The Columbia Granger's Guide to Poetry Anthologies, 1990, Magazines for Young People, 1991, Community Colleges Reference Services., 1993, A History of Book Illustration, 1994, Dahl's History of the Book, 1995, Cuneiform to Computer, 1998; editor: Jour. Edn. for Librarianship, 1964-72, Reference Quar., 1963-73, Best of Libr. Lit., 1970-91, The Reference Libr., 1981, The Acquistions Libr., 1987; contbr. to Ency. Brit. Yearbook, 1970—. Recipient award of merit Seattle Hist. Soc., 1965, Shores-Oryx Press award, 1993. Mem. ALA (Isadore G. Mudge citation 1973). Address: SUNY Sch Info Sci and Policy 135 Western Ave Albany NY 12203-1011

KATZ, WILLIAM EMANUEL, chemical engineer; b. Honesdale, Pa., June 12, 1924; s. Edward David and Aimee Helen (Rosenfelder) K.; m. Martha Elizabeth Legg, Feb. 13, 1960; children: Susan Katz Miller, Martha Katz Laserson, E. David II, James A.L. BSChE, MIT, 1948, MSChE, 1949. With Ionics Inc., Watertown, Mass., 1949—, chem. engr., 1949-51, asst. treas., 1951-53, treas., 1953-58, v.p. and dir., 1958-81, exec. v.p. and dir., 1981—; dir. Ionics Ultrapure Water Corp., San Jose, Calif., 1984—, Ionics Asia Pacific, Singapore, Ionics Enersave Engring. Sys., Kuala Lumpur, Malaysia, Ionics Watertec, Brisbane, Australia, 1997. Author chapter in AWWA Manual of Water Quality and Treatment, 1964, and 30 articles on water and waste treatment; patentee in field. With U.S. Army, 1942-46, PTO. Mem. Am. Inst. Chem. Engrs., Am. Water Works Assn., Am. Desalting Assn. (Water Quality Person of Yr. 1992), Internat. Desalting Assn. Avocations: piano, composing. Home: 11 Sunset Rd Weston MA 02493-1623 Office: Ionics Inc 65 Grove St Watertown MA 02472-2882

KATZ, WILLIAM LOREN, author; b. Bklyn., June 2, 1927; s. Bernard and Madeline (Simon) K.; m. Laurie Lehman, Sept. 10, 1994. BA, Syracuse U., 1950; MA, NYU, 1952. Tchr. Am. history N.Y.C., 1954-60, Hartsdale, N.Y., 1960-67; author, 1967—; cons. N.Y. State Edn. Dept., 1967-68, 83-84, USAF Sch. in Eng., Belgium and Holland, 1974-75; scholar in residence Tchrs. Coll. Columbia, 1971-73, NYU, 1987-91; tchr. Black history Tombs Prison, N.Y.C., 1973, N.Y. U. Afro-Am. Inst., 1973; faculty Inst. Urban and Minority Edn., Gen. Assistance Ctr., Tchrs. Coll. Columbia U., 1976; tchr. Am. history New Sch. for Social Rsch., N.Y.C., 1977-83; pres. Ethrac Publs., 1971—. Author: Eyewitness: The Negro in American History, 1967 (Gold Medal award for non-fiction NCCJ), 4th edit., 1996, Teachers' Guide to American Negro History, 1968, (with Warren J. Halliburton) American Majorities and Minorities: A Syllabus of United States History for Secondary Schools, 1970, The Black West: A Documentary and Pictorial History, 1971, 3rd edit., 1988, 4th edit., 1996, (with Warren J. Halliburton) A History of Black Americans, 1973, The Constitutional Amendments, 1974, Making Our Way: America at the Turn of the Century, 1975, Black People Who Made the Old West, 1977, 2nd edit., 1993, Teaching Approaches to Black History in the Classroom, 1973, An Album of the Civil War, 1974, An Album of Reconstruction, 1974, Minorities in American History, Vols. I-VI, 1974-75, An Album of the Great Depression, 1978, An Album of Nazism, 1979, Black Indians: A Hidden Heritage, 1986, 2nd edti., 1997, The Invisible Empire: The Ku Klux Klan Impact on History, 1986, The Lincoln Brigade, 1989, Breaking The Chains: African American Slave Resistance, 1990, 2d edit, 1998, A History of Multicultural America, 1993, 8 vols., Proudly Red and Black, 1993, Black Women of the Old West, 1995, Black Legacy: A History of New York's African Americans, 1997, Black Pioneers: An Untold Story, 1999; editor: The American Negro: History and Literature, 147 Vols., 1968-71, (with James M. McPherson) The Anti-Slavery Crusade in America, 69 Vols., 1969, Minorities in America: Picture Histories, 1972-76, Pamphlets in American History, 1977-82, Flight From the Devil: Six Slave Narratives, 1996; editorial bd. jour.: Black Studies, 1971-73; editorial dir.: (with Henry Steele Commager and Arthur Schlesinger, Jr.) Vital Sources in American History for High School Students, 168 vols, 1980; columnist N.Y. Daily Challenge, 1986—, Interrace Mag., 1993-97, The Black Child, 1995-97; contbr. articles to Sat. Rev., Jour. Negro History, N.Y. Times, Jour. Negro Edn., Jour. Black Studies, African Commentary, Reader's Digest, Am. Legacy, Congl. Record, Amsterdam News, others; radio commentator Pacifica Network, 1996—. Mem. exec. bd. Art Against Apartheid, 1984; mem. nat. council Nat. Emergency Civil Liberties Com., 1983-85; curator Black West Exhibit, Schomburg Ctr. for Research in Black Culture, N.Y.C., 1985-86. Served with USNR, 1945-46. *If you believe that people have no history worth mentioning, it's easy to assume they have no humanity worth defending.*

KATZANEK, ROBIN JEAN, physical therapy educator; b. N.Y.C., Jan. 19, 1957; d. Reynold and Gertrude (Kupetzky) K. BS in Phys. Therapy, Boston U., 1979; MA in Sport Scis., U. Denver, 1987, postgrad., 1989—. Lic. phys. therapist, R.I., Colo. Phys. therapist Rose Med. Ctr., Denver, 1979-86; lab. asst. Sport Sci. Lab. U. Denver, 1987-90; phys. therapist III, Nat. Jewish Ctr. for Immunology and Respiratory Medicine, Denver, 1989-93; phys. therapist Colo. Easter Seal Soc., Lakewood, 1989-93, dir. phys. therapy, 1993-96; clin. asst. prof. U. R.I., Kingston, 1996—, acad. coord. clin. edn. phys. therapy program, 1996—; clin. instr. phys. therapy program U. Colo. Health Scis. Ctr., Denver, 1987-88; phys. therapist Gaylord Street Phys. Therapy, Denver, 1988-89. Contbr. articles and abstracts to sci. jours. Alumni mentor U. Denver, 1988—; asst. leader Brownie troop Mile Hi coun. Girl Scouts U.S.A., 1994-96. Mem. Am. Phys. Therapy Assn. (Advocates for the Disabled and Access spl. interest group, health policy, legis. and regulation sect., chmn. nominating com. 1994—), Am. Coll. Sports Medicine, Am. Coll. Rheumatology, Assn.-Assn. Rheumatology Health Profls. Avocations: needlepoint, baseball, photography. Office: U RI Phys Therapy Program 25 W Independence Way Kingston RI 02881-1124

KATZBERG, JANE MICHAELS, health care administrator, consultant, educator; b. Bklyn., Apr. 17, 1940; d. David Donn and Shirley (Ingram) Michaels; m. Mitchell Ronald Katzberg, Jan. 19, 1959; children: L. Michael, Todd Alexander. BS, Adelphi U., 1961; M of Profl. Studies in Health Care Adminstrn., L.I. U., 1975. Cert. home economist, tchr., N.Y. Mgr. quality assurance Suffolk Physicians Rev. Orgn., Central Islip, N.Y., 1979-81; dir. quality assurance and utilization rev. Cmty. Hosp. of Glen Cove, N.Y., 1982-84; dir. intermediate care facilities program United Cerebral Palsy, Commack, N.Y., 1985-86; dir. svcs. for handicapped Town of Huntington, L.I., N.Y., 1986-95; tchr. DayCare Town of Smithtown, L.I., 1995-96; pres., cons. Images, Dix Hills, N.Y., 1985-88; cons. JMK Cons., pres., 1994—; lectr. in field. Mem. Citizen's Adv. Com. for Handicapped, Town of Huntington, 1985-86; mem. selection and steering com. C. of C. Found., 1993-97, Leadership Round Table, Huntington Health and Human Svcs. steering com., 1992-97, Huntington Hosp. Dolan Cmty. Health Ctr. Bd., 1992-97; mem. adv. bd. Dept. Social Svcs., Huntington, L.I., 1986-97, Devel. Ctr., Melville Estates, 1989-97; facilitator Nat. Orgn. Disability award N.Y. State Eleanor Roosevelt award for Town Huntington; pres. Howell Rd. Sch. PTA, North Valley Stream, N.Y., 1973; meeting rep. N.Y. State Advocate for Disabled, 1986-95; mem. divsn. dirs. Cmty. Resource Dept., 1986-89, divsn. dirs. human svcs., 1989-95. Acad. scholar C.W. Post Coll., Greenvale, N.Y., 1974. Mem. Assn. Local Govt. Advocates for Disabled. Republican. Jewish. Avocations: reading, stock market, oil painting, clothing design, jewelry design and manufacturing. Home: 81 Buttonwood Dr Dix Hills NY 11746-4804

KATZEN, MOLLIE, writer, artist; b. Rochester, N.Y., Oct. 13, 1950; d. Leon and Betty (Heller) K.; m. Jeffrey David Black, June 26, 1983 (div. Oct. 1985); 1 child, Samuel Katzen Black; m. Carl Shames, Dec. 12, 1986. BFA, San Francisco Art Inst., 1972. Author, illustrator: Mossewood Cookbook, 1977, Enchanted Broccoli Forest, 1982, Still Life with Menu, 1988, Molly Katzen's Still Life Sampler, 1993, Pretend Soup & Other Real Recipes: A Cookbook for Preschoolers & Up, 1994, Enchanted Broccoli Forest, 1995, Moosewood Cookbook Classics: Miniature Edition, 1996. Recipient Graphic Arts award Arnot Art Gallery, 1976, Cert. of Commendation, Calif. State Assembly, 1989. Jewish. Avocations: classical pianist, painter. Office: care Ten Speed Press PO Box 7123 Berkeley CA 94707-0123*

KATZEN, RAPHAEL, consulting chemical engineer; b. Balt., July 28, 1915; s. Isidor and Esther (Stein) K.; m. Selma M. Siegel, June 19, 1938; 1 child, Nancy Katzen Riedel. B.Chem. Engring., Poly. U. Bklyn., 1936, M.Chem. Engring., 1938, D.Chem. Engring., 1942. Registered profl. engr. in 12 states. Tech. dir. Northwood Chem. Co., Phelps, Wis., 1938-42; project mgr. Diamond Alkali Co., Painesville, Ohio, 1942-44; mgr. engring. divsn. Vulcan, Cin., 1944-53; mng. partner Raphael Katzen Assos., Cin., 1953-80; chmn. Raphael Katzen Assos. Internat., Inc., 1956—. Contbr. articles to profl. jours; patentee in field. Mem. Cin. Air Pollution Bd., 1972-75. Recipient Disting. Alumnus award Poly. Inst. Bklyn., 1970, Dedicated Alumnus award, 1977; Disting. cons. award Ohio Assn. Cons. Engrs., 1978; Profl. Accomplishment, Disting. Engr. award Tech. and Sci. Socs. Coun., 1978, 79, Personal Achievement in Chem. Engring. award Chem. Engring., McGraw Hill, 1988; Poly. U. fellow, 1981. Fellow AIChE (Chem. Engring. Practice award 1986, Robert L. Jacks Meml. award 1990), Am. Inst. Chemists; mem. NAE (elected), TAPPI, PPTAC, Am. Chem. Soc., Chemists Club N.Y.C., Am. Club Miami, Fla., Sigma Xi, Tau Beta Pi, Phi Lambda Upsilon. E-mail: rkatzenpe@aol.com. Home: 27901 Riverwalk Way Bonita Springs FL 34134 Office: 9220 Bonita Beach Rd #200 Bonita Springs FL 34135 *We are put on this earth to produce to the best of our ability to improve the lot of mankind, and our talents should not be wasted through lack of effort or misguided direction.*

KATZEN, SALLY, lawyer, government official; b. Pitts., Nov. 22, 1942; d. Nathan and Hilda (Schwartz) K.; m. Timothy B. Dyk, Oct. 31, 1981; 1 child, Abraham Benjamin. BA magna cum laude, Smith Coll., 1964; JD magna cum laude, U. Mich., 1967. Bar: D.C. 1968, U.S. Supreme Ct. 1971. Congl. intern Sente Subcom. on Constl. Rights, Washington, 1963; legal rsch. asst. civil rights div. Dept. Justice, Washington, 1965; law clk. to Judge J. Skelly Wright U.S. Ct. Appeals (D.C. cir.), 1967-68; assoc. Wilmer, Cutler & Pickering, Washington, 1968-75, ptnr., 1975-79, 81-93; gen. counsel Coun. on Wage and Price Stability, 1979-80; dep. dir. for policy, 1980-81; adminstr. Office of Info. and Regulatory Affairs, Office of Mgmt. and Budget, Washington, 1993-98; dep. dir. Nat. Econ. Coun., The White House, Washington, 1998—; pub. mem. Adminstrv. Conf. U.S., 1988-93, govt. mem. and vice chair, 1993-95; mem. exec. com. Prettyman-Leventhal Inn of Ct., 1988-90, counselor, 1990-91; mem. Jud. Conf. for D.C. Cir., 1972-91; adj. prof. Georgetown U. Law Ctr., 1988, 90-92. Editor-in-chief U. Mich. Law Rev., 1966-67. Mem. com. visitors U. Mich. Law Sch., 1972—. Fellow ABA (ho. of dels. 1978-80, 89-91, coun. adminstrv. law sect. 1979-82, chmn. adminstrv. law and regulatory practice sect. 1988-89, governing com. forum com. communications law 1979-82, chmn. standing com. Nat. Conf. Groups 1989-92); mem. D.C. Bar Assn., Women's Bar Assn., FCC Bar Assn. (exec. com. 1984-87, pres. 1990-91), Women's Legal Def. Fund (pres. 1977, v.p. 1978), Order of Coif. Home: 4638 30th St NW Washington DC 20008-2127 Office: Nat Econ Coun Old Exec Office Bldg Rm 231 Washington DC 20502

KATZENBACH, JOHN STRONG MINER, author; b. Princeton, N.J., June 23, 1950; s. Nicholas deB. and Lydia Phelps (Stokes) K.; m. Madeleine Helena Blais, May 10, 1980; children: Nicholas, Justine. BA, Bard Coll., 1972. Author: In the Heat of the Summer, 1982, First Born, 1984, The Traveler, 1987, Day of Reckoning, 1989, Just Cause, 1992, The Shadow Man, 1995, State of Mind, 1997. Mem. Internat. Assn. Crimewriters, Mystery Writer's of Am., PEN Internat. Avocation: fly fishing. *

KATZENBACH, NICHOLAS DEBELLEVILLE, lawyer; b. Phila., Jan. 17, 1922; s. Edward Lawrence and Marie Louise (Hilson) K.; m. Lydia King Phelps Stokes, June 8, 1946; children—Christopher Wolcott, John Strong Minor, Maria Stokes, Anne deBelleville. B.A., Princeton U., 1945; LL.B., Yale U., 1947; Rhodes scholar, Balliol Coll., Oxford (Eng.) U., 1947-49. Bar: N.J. 1950, Conn. 1955, N.Y. 1972. With firm Katzenbach, Gildea & Rudner, Trenton, N.J., 1950; atty.-adviser Office Gen. Counsel Air Force, 1950-52, part-time cons., 1952-56; asso. prof. law Yale Law Sch., 1952-56; prof. law U. Chgo. Law Sch., 1956-60; asst. atty. gen. Dept. Justice, 1961-62, dep. atty. gen., 1962-64, acting atty. gen., 1964, atty. gen., 1965-66, under sec. state, 1966-69; sr. v.p., gen. counsel IBM Corp., 1969-84, sr. v.p. law and external relations, 1984-86, also bd. dirs.; ptnr. Riker, Danzig, Scherer, Hyland & Perretti, Morristown, N.J., 1986-91. Author: (with Morton A. Kaplan) The Political Foundations of International Law, 1961; editor-in-chief: Yale Law Jour, 1947; contbr. articles to profl. jours. Served to 1st lt. USAAF, 1941-45. Decorated Air medal with three clusters; Ford Found. fellow, 1960-61. Mem. AAAS, Am. Law Inst. (mem. coun.), Am. Bar Assn., Am. Judicature Soc., Am. Philos. Soc. Democrat. Episcopalian. Home: 33 Greenhouse Dr Princeton NJ 08540-4802

KATZENBERG, JEFFREY, motion picture studio executive; b. 1950; m. Marilyn Siegel; children: Laura, David. Asst. to chmn., chief exec. officer Paramount Pictures, N.Y.C, 1975-77, exec. dir. mktg., 1977; then v.p. programming Paramount TV, Calif., 1977-78; v.p., feature prodn. Paramount Pictures, 1978-80, sr. v.p., prodn. motion picture div., 1980-82, pres. prodn., motion pictures & TV, 1982-94; chmn. Walt Disney Studios, Burbank, Calif., 1994; chmn., founding ptnr. DreamWorks SKG, 1994—. Office: Dreamworks SKG 100 Universal Plz # 477 Universal City CA 91608-1001*

KATZEN-GUTHRIE, JOY, performance artist, engineering services executive; b. Memphis, Nov. 11, 1958; d. Eli and Bess (Bloomfield) Katzen; m. Mark C. Guthrie, Aug. 7, 1983. BFA in Music cum laude, Stephens Coll., Columbia, Mo., 1980, BA in Comms. magna cum laude, 1980. Traffic dir. WPLP News/Talk Radio, Pinellas Park, Fla., 1981-83; ops. mgr. WPLP News/Talk Radio, Pinellas Park, 1982-83; traffic reporter WUSA-FM and WDAE-AM, Tampa, Fla., 1985-86; announcer, programmer, pub. rels. mgr. WXCR-FM Classics 92, Safety Harbor, Fla., 1983-87; v.p., dir. Katzen and Guthrie Assocs., Inc., Palm Harbor, Fla., 1987—; pres. Tune-of-the-Century Music, 1989—; creator, designer, owner website www.JoyfulNoise.net, 1998—. Co-author, composer musical comedy Once Around Manhattan, 1985; author: (one-act play) A Murder in Pine County, 1987; composer, lyricist some 600 songs; performance artist CD/Cassette albums Seasons of Joy, 1989, Heart of Ancient Promise, 1993, New State of Mind, 1993, How Good and Pleasant, 1996, Passages, 1998; studio vocalist Jeff Arthur Prodns., St. Petersburg, Fla., 1985, 86, Studio C. Prodns., Tampa, 1991-92; studio vocalist, jingle writer West End Rec., Tampa, 1989, 90; session musician Hurricane Pass Studios, Clearwater, Fla., 1993—. Music dir. religious sch. Temple B'nai Israel, Clearwater, 1988-89; music dir. Perry-Mansfield Performing Arts Camp, Steamboat Springs, Colo., 1987; cantorial soloist B'nai B'rith Hillel Found., Tampa, 1990-93, Temple Shir Shalom, Gainesville, 1994—, Congregation B'nai Emunah, Tarpon Springs, 1996—. Recipient 1st and 3d place awards Memphis Songwriters Assn. Competition, 1988, others; Pinellas County Arts Coun. grantee, 1997. Mem. AAUW (dir. pub. rels. 1985-97), ASCAP, Songwriters Guild Am., Dramatists Guild, Nat. Acad. Songwriters, Nashville Songwriters Assn. Internat., Guild of Temple Musicians, Fla. Music Assn., Women's Musicians' Alliance (bd. dirs. 1998—), Hadassah (life). Democrat. Jewish. Avocations: photography, travel, music, theatre, film, books. Home and Office: 2487 Indian Trl E Palm Harbor FL 34683-2806

KATZENSTEIN, THEA, retail executive, jewelry designer; b. N.Y.C., Mar. 30, 1927; d. Carl E. and Lillian (Rosenblatt) Schustak; m. William Katzenstein, Sept. 10, 1950; children: Leo, Ranee. Student, Sarah Lawrence Coll., 1948-50; BS, Columbia U., 1962, MA, 1967. Pres. Gallery A., N.Y.C., 1967-71, Melita, N.Y.C., 1972-77, TK Studio, Miami Beach, Fla., 1977—; adj. prof. of jewelry Fla. Internat. U., 1989-90; enamelling instr. U. Miami, 1991. Author: Early Chinese Art and The Pacific Basin, 1967; painting, graphics and jewelry represented in numerous pvt. collections. Trustee Miami Metro Zoo, 1994—. Mem. Soc. N.Am. Goldsmiths, Enamel Guild South, Nat. Enamelist Guild, Fla. Soc. Goldsmiths (pres. S.E. chpt.), Fla. Craftsmen, Zonta (sec. Coral Gables chpt. 1989-90). Democrat. Jewish. Home: Apt 1501 9 Island Ave Miami Beach FL 33139-1360

KATZMAN, HERBERT HENRY, artist; b. Chgo., Jan. 8, 1923; s. Louis and Fay (Horowitz) K.; m. Judith Baker, Nov. 25, 1949; children: Nicholas, Steven, Ann; m. Laurel Carroll, Oct. 25, 1982. Certificate, Sch. Art Inst. Chgo., 1946. Tchr. painting and drawing Sch. Visual Arts, N.Y.C., 1959—. One-man shows include Butler Inst. Am. Art, 1993; exhibited in group shows at Mus. Modern Art, N.Y.C., 1952, Whitney Mus., N.Y.C., 1954, Venice (Italy) Biennial, 1957, Pa. Acad. Fine Arts; represented in permanent collections Art Inst. Chgo., Mus. Modern Art, Whitney Mus., Hirschorn Mus., Washington, U. Mass., U. Minn., W.Va., Wright State U., Dayton, Ohio, Butler Art Inst., Youngstown, Ohio, Retrospective Artists Choice Mus., 1985. Served with USN, 1942-44. Nat. Acad. Arts and Letters grantee, 1958; Nat. Acad. Arts and Letters grantee Nat. Council Humanities, 1966; Guggenheim fellow, 1968; Gottlieb Found. grantee; NY Council on the Arts grantee. Mem. Coll. Nat. Gallery Am. Art, NAD. Home: 463 West St Apt 919C New York NY 10014-2038

KATZMAN, IRWIN, lawyer; b. Windsor, Ont., Can., June 29, 1931; s. Aaron and Rose (Tarnow) K.; m. Helen Frances Blecher, Dec. 20, 1952; children: Barry, Harriet, Kenneth, Rhonda, Aaron. BS, Wayne State U., 1953, MBA, 1963; JD cum laude, Loyola U., L.A., 1974. Bar: CAlfi. 1974, U.S. Dist. Ct. (cen. dist.) Calif. 1974, U.S. Ct. Appeals (9th cir.) 1980, U.S. Supreme Ct. 1980, U.S. Tax Ct. 1988. Chemist E.I. Dupont de Nemours, Phila., 1953-54; asst. quality mgr. Chrysler Corp., Detroit, 1956-63; mfg. plans mgr. Ford Motor Co., Newport Beach, Calif., 1963-70; prodn. control mgr. Dresser Industries, Huntington Park, Calif., 1970-73; purchasing mgr. Hughes Aircraft Co., Inglewood, Calif., 1973-74; v.p. First Alliance Mortgage Co., Santa Ana, Calif., 1976-77; pvt. practice Anaheim, Calif., 1975-94, San Jose, Calif., 1995—. Pres. Temple Beth Emet, Anaheim, 1988-90. With U.S. Army, 1953-56. Mem. State Bar of Calif., Orange County Bar Assn., Santa Clara County Bar Assn., Alpha Epsilon Pi (life). Avocations: sailing, golf, amateur radio. Office: 8346 Riesling Way San Jose CA 95135-1435

KATZMAN, MERLE HERSHEL, orthopaedic surgeon; b. Hartford, Conn., Aug. 28, 1928; s. Samuel Sidney and Bertha (Hirshberg) K.; m. Charna Lytell, June 26, 1955; children: Beth, Amy, Sam, Robert. BS, Trinity Coll., 1950; MD, Jefferson Med. Coll., 1954. Diplomate Am. Bd. Orthop. Surgery. Intern Hartford (Conn.) Hosp., 1954-55, resident in surgery, 1957-58; surgeon N.Y. Orthop. Hosp., 1958-61; attending orthop. surgeon, chief orthop. dept. Englewood Hosp., 1965-94, attending orthop. surgeon, 1980-94; pres. Katzman, Tarsney & Feldman, Tenafly, N.J., 1994; ret., 1994; mem. credentials com., exec. com., chmn. future devel. com., Englewood Hosp. Lt. USNR, 1955-57. Fellow ACS, Am. Acad. Orthopaedic Surgeons, Bergen County Med. Soc. (del., health ins. review com. mem.), N.J. State Med. Soc., N.J. Orthopaedic Soc. (exec. com. pres. 1977-78), Stannard Beach Assn. (exec. com. mem., pres. 1996-98). Office: Katzman Tarsney & Feldman 111 Dean Dr Tenafly NJ 07670-2708

KATZMAN, RICHARD A., cardiologist, consultant; b. Cleve., Mar. 22, 1931; s. Abraham N. and Anne Ruth (Kustin) K.; m. Roberta Brown, July 28, 1962; children: Audrey, Sharon, Naomi, Noah. BS, Case Western Reserve U., 1952; MD, U. Chgo., 1955. Diplomate Am. Bd. Internal Medicine. Prin. Richard A. Katzman M.D., Cleve., 1963—; dir. electrocardiography, dept. cardiology Metro Health Med. Ctr., 1992-97; staff cardiologist Mt. Sinai Hosp., Cleve., 1992—; assoc. clin. prof. medicine Case Western Reserve U. V.p. Cleve. Coll. Jewish Studies, 1985-88. Capt. U.S. Army Med. Corps., 1956-58. Fellow Am. Coll. Physicians, Am. Coll. Chest Physicians. Home: 28950 Gates Mills Blvd Pepper Pike OH 44124-4744 Office: Mt Sinai Hosp Dept Cardiology 1 Mount Sinai Dr Cleveland OH 44106-4199

KATZMAN, ROBERT, medical educator, neurologist; b. Denver, Nov. 29, 1925; s. Maurice and Leah K. (Schnitt) K.; m. Nancy Bernstein, Sept. 2, 1947; children: David Jonathan, Daniel Mark. BS, U. Chgo., 1949, MS, 1951; MD cum laude, Harvard U., 1953. Diplomate Am. Bd. Psychiatry and Neurology. Intern Boston City Hosp., 1953-54; chief resident Neurol. Inst. Columbia Presbyn. Hosp., N.Y.C., 1956-57; faculty mem. Albert Einstein Coll. Medicine, N.Y.C., 1957-84, prof., chmn. neurology dept., 1964-84, dir. Resnick Gerontology Ctr., 1979-84; chmn. dept. neuroscis. U. Calif., San Diego, 1984-90, Florence Riford prof. neuroscis. and rsch. in Alzheimer's disease, 1984-94, rsch. prof. neuroscis., 1994—; mem. clin. rsch. adv. com. Nat. Found. March of Dimes, 1975-76; mem. adv. coun. Nat. Inst. on Aging, 1982-85; chmn. med. and sci. bd. Alzheimer Disease and Related Disorders Assn., Chgo., 1979-85; mem. adv. panel on Alzheimer's disease HHS, 1987-93. Co-author: Brain Electrolytes and Fluid Metabolism, 1973, Neurology of Aging, 1983; co-editor: Basic Neurochemistry, 1972-81, Principles of Geriatric Neurology, 1992, Alzheimers Disease, 1994, Alzheimers Disease, second edit., 1999. Served with USN, 1944-46, PTO. Recipient Humanitarian Award Alzheimer's Disease and Related Disorders Assn., 1985, Disting. Svc. award, 1989, Allied Achievement in Aging award Allied Signal Corp., 1985, Henderson Meml. award Am. Geriatric Soc., 1986, 7th Ann. Chgo. Rita Hayworth Gala award recipient, Alzheimer's Assn., 1994. Fellow Am. Acad. Neurology (S. Weir Mitchell award 1960, George W. Jacoby award 1989, co-recipient Potamkin prize for Alzheimer's disease rsch. 1992); mem. Assn. for Rsch. in Nervous and Mental Disorders (pres. 1977), Am. Physiol. Soc. (cons.) Inst. Medicine, Am. Neurol. Assn. (pres. 1985-86), Internat. Soc. for Alzheimer's Disease Rsch. (pres. 1996—), Alpha Omega Alpha. Office: U Calif Sch Medicine Dept Neurosci Alzheimers Disease Rsch 9500 Gilman Dr Dept 949 La Jolla CA 92093-0949

KATZMANN, GARY STEPHEN, lawyer; b. N.Y.C., Apr. 22, 1953; s. John and Sylvia (Butner) K. AB summa cum laude, Columbia U., 1973; MLitt, Oxford U., 1976; MPPM, JD, Yale U., 1979. Bar: Mass. 1982, U.S. Dist. Ct. Mass. 1983, U.S. Ct. Appeals (1st cir.) 1983, D.C.. 1984, U.S. Ct. Appeals (2d cir.) 1987, N.Y. 1990, U.S. Ct. Appeals (fed. cir.) 1991. Law clk. to judge U.S. Dist. Ct. (so. dist.) N.Y., N.Y.C., 1979-80; law clk. to Hon. Stephen Breyer U.S. Ct. Appeals (1st cir.), Boston, 1980-81; rsch. assoc. ctr. criminal justice Law Sch. Harvard U., Cambridge, Mass., 1981-83; asst. U.S. atty., chief appellate atty., dep. chief criminal div., chief legal counsel U.S. Atty.'s Office, Mass., 1983—; assoc. dep. atty. gen. U.S. Dept. Justice, Washington, 1993-94; lectr. Harvard U. Law Sch., 1989—; rsch. fellow J.F. Kennedy Sch. Govt., Harvard U., 1997—; participant Yale Law Sch. Sentencing Seminar, 1999—. Author: Inside the Criminal Process, 1991; editor Yale U. Law Jour. Recipient Dir's. Superior Performance award U.S. Dept. Justice, 1993. Mem. ABA, Phi Beta Kappa. Office: US Attys Offcie US Courthouse Ste 9200 1 Courthouse Way Boston MA 02210

KATZMANN, ROBERT ALLEN, law educator, non-profit association executive, political scientist; b. N.Y.C., Apr. 22, 1953; s. John and Sylvia Edith (Butner) K. AB summa cum laude, Columbia U., 1973; MA in Govt.,

Harvard U., 1975, PhD in Govt., 1978; JD, Yale U., 1980. Bar: Mass. 1982, U.S. Ct. Appeals (1st cir.) 1983, D.C. 1984, U.S. Dist. Ct. Mass. 1984. Law clk. to judge U.S. Ct. Appeals (1st cir.), Concord, N.H., 1980-81; rsch. assoc. Brookings Instn., Washington, 1981-85, fellow, 1985—; adj. prof. law, pub. policy Georgetown U., Washington, 1984-92; William J. Walsh prof. govt., prof. law Georgetown U., 1992—; pres. Governance Inst., Washington, 1986—; acting dir. govt. studies Brookings Instn., Washington, 1998; vis. prof. polit. sci. UCLA, Washington program, 1990-92; vis. chair, Wayne Morse prof. law and politics U. Oreg., 1992; cons. Fed. Cts. Study Com., 1990. Author: Regulatory Bureaucracy: The Federal Trade Commission and Antitrust Policy, 1980, Institutional Disability, 1986, Courts and Congress, 1997; co-editor: Managing Appeals in Federal Courts, 1988; editor: Judges and Legislators, 1988, The Law Firm and the Public Good, 1995; article and book editor Yale U. Law Jour., 1979-80. Mem. ABA (adminstrv. law sect. vice chair com. on govt. ops. and separation of powers 1991-94, pub. mem. adminstrn. conf., 1992-95), Am. Judicature Soc. (bd. dirs. 1992-98), Am. Polit. Sci. Assn., Assn. Pub. Policy Analysis and Mgmt., Phi Beta Kappa. Office: Brookings Instn Govtl Studies Program 1775 Massachusetts Ave NW Washington DC 20036-2188

KATZNELSON, IRA ISAAC, social sciences educator, writer; b. N.Y.C., July 3, 1944; s. Ephraim and Sylvia (Rosenbaum) K.; m. Deborah Ruth Socolow, Jan. 14, 1967; children: Jessica, Zachary, Emma, Leah. BA summa cum laude, Columbia U., 1966; PhD, Cambridge U., 1969. Asst. prof. Polit. Sci. Columbia U., N.Y.C., 1969-73; assoc. prof. Columbia U., 1973-74, Ruggles prof. Polit. Sci., History, 1994—; assoc. prof., prof. Polit. Sci. U. Chgo., 1974-82; dean grad. faculty New Sch. for Social Rsch., N.Y.C., 1983-89; Loeb prof. Polit. and Social Sci. New Sch. for Social Rsch., 1983-94, co-dir. Ctr. for Politics, Theory and Policy, 1989-94; trustee Russell Sage Found., N.Y.C., 1992—; mem. acad. adv. bd. Inst. for Human Scis., Vienna, 1997—, chair selection com. Rsch. and Policy Reform Program on the Social Costs of Economic Transformation in Central Europe, 1996—. Author: Liberalism's Crooked Circle: Letters to Adam Michnik, 1996 (Lionel Trilling book award, 1997, Michael Harrington award, 1997), Paths of Emancipation: Jews, States and Citizenship, 1995, Marxism and the City, 1993, Working Class Formation: Nineteenth Century Patterns in Western Europe and North America, 1986 (Socialist Rev. book award, 1986), Schooling for All: Class, Race and the Decline of the Democratic Ideal, 1985, City Trenches: Urban Politics and the Patterning of Class in the United States, 1983, The Politics of Power: A Critical Introduction to American Government, 1987, The Politics and Society Reader, 1974, Black Men, White Cities: Race, Politics, and Migration in the United States, 1900-1930, and Britain, 1948-1968, 1973, rev. edit., 1976; editl. bd. Jour. Policy History, 1993—, U. Chgo. Wilder House Series in Politics, History, and Culture, 1988-94, Politics and Soc., 1969— (founding editor 1969-75); co-editor: (with Martin Shefter and Theda Skocpol) (book series) Princeton Studies in American Politics: Historical, International, and Comparative Perspectives, 1991—; adv. bd. Social Policy, 1989—; editl. adv. bd. Polit. Sci. Quarterly, 1977—. Recipient German Marshall Fund fellowship, 1978, 79, Danforth Found. fellowship, 1966-69, Euretta J. Kellett fellowship, 1966-68; Phi Beta Kappa vis. scholar, 1990-91; Disting. Polit. Scientist U. Vermont, 1989-90. Mem. Social Sci. History Assn. (pres. 1997-98), Am. Polit. Sci. Assn. (pres. politics and history sect. 1992-93), Phi Beta Kappa.

KAUCHER, JAMES WILLIAM, lawyer; b. Belleville, Ill., Oct. 20, 1958; s. Robert Frederick and Mary Ellen (Shepard) K.; m. Janine Kaucher, Oct. 24, 1993. BA, U. Colo., 1980; JD, U. Ill., 1983. Bar: Ariz. 1983, U.S. Dist. Ct. Ariz. 1983. Assoc. Evans, Kitchel & Jenckes, Phoenix, 1983-85, Teilborg, Sanders & Parks, Phoenix, 1985-92; ptnr. Cavett and Kaucher, Tucson, 1992-98; of counsel Goodwin Raup PC, Tucson, 1998—; chmn. human rsch. rev. bd. Humana Hosp., Phoenix, 1989-94. Mem. Maricopa Bar Assn., Def. Rsch. Inst., Forum on Health Law, Ariz. Soc. Health Care Risk Mgrs. (bd. dirs. 1989-91), Ariz. Assn. Def. Counsel, Ariz. Mountaineering Club, Am. Alpine Club. Avocations: mountaineering, flying, bicycle racing. Office: Goodwin Raup PC Ste 2130 One S Church Ave Tucson AZ 85701

KAUDERER, BERNARD MARVIN, retired naval officer; b. Phila., July 21, 1931; s. Harry Thau and Anne Mae (Mandell) K.; m. Myra Frances Weissman, Mar. 21, 1954; children: Howard Todd, Heidi Susanne, Robin Beth. BS, U.S. Naval Acad., 1953. Commd. ensign U.S. Navy, 1953, advanced through grades to vice adm., 1983; comdr. Submarine Group Five, 1977-79; dep. dir. research, devel., test and evaluation Office Chief Naval Ops., Navy Dept., Washington, 1979-81; comdr. submarine forces U.S. Pacific Fleet, 1981-83; comdr. submarine force 2d U.S. Atlantic Fleet, 1983-86; ret. U.S. Navy, 1986. Decorated D.S.M., Legion of Merit, Meritorious Service medal, Navy Commendation medal, Navy Expeditionary medal. Mem. Naval Submarine League (dir.), Masons, Shriners. Home: 7025 Ibis Pl Carlsbad CA 92009-5011

KAUFER, VIRGINIA GROSS, family therapist, mental health program, manager; b. Middletown, N.Y., Apr. 8, 1937; d. Bernard and Estelle (Singer) Gross; divorced; children: Michael, Jill, Jonathan, Wendy, Elizabeth, Amy, Abigail. BS with honors, Carnegie Inst. Tech., 1959; MA summa cum laude, U. Pitts., 1982, postgrad., 1980-85. Case worker Allegheny County Children and Youth, Pitts., 1988-89, 92-93; therapist chem. dependency St. Francis Med. Ctr., Pitts., 1989-91; mental health case mgr. Charters Mental Health/Mental Retardation, Pitts., 1991-92; therapist chem. dependency Ligonier Outpatient, Pitts., 1992-93; family therapist Alternative Program Assn., Pitts., 1993-97; mgr. Auberle, residential treatment facility, McKeesport, Pa., 1997—; bd. dirs. Recovery Ctr., Pitts.; rschr. in field. Mem. Integrated Delivery Network. Republican. Jewish. Avocations: dogs and cats, designing, making and creating needlepoint canvases, acrylic painting, fashion design. Home: 1722 Wharton St Pittsburgh PA 15203-1736 Office: Auberle 1101 Hartman St McKeesport PA 15132-1500

KAUFFMAN, ALAN CHARLES, lawyer; b. Atlantic City, Aug. 12, 1939; s. Joseph Bernard and Lilyan (Abraham) K.; children: Julie Beth, Debra Amy, Paige Tyler. AB, Rutgers U., 1961; JD, Villanova U., 1964. Bar: Pa. 1964, U.S. Ct. Appeals (3d cir.) 1965, U.S. Dist. Ct. (ea. dist.) Pa. 1965, U.S. Supreme Ct. 1968, Fla. 1985. Pres. Alan C. Kauffann & Assocs., P.A., Boca Raton, Fla.; Mem., bd. dirs. Am. Diabetic Assn., Fla. Philharmonic Orch., Caldwell Theater; vice chmn. Fla. Victory Com.; founding chmn. Gold Coast Forum; bd. mem. Fla. Elections Commn. Cmty. Rels. bd. City of Boca Raton; mem. Greater Boca Raton Senate, Palm Beach County Film & TV Bd.; mem. Jewish Adv. Coun. U.S. Senator Connie Mack; Mem. Internat Bd. Weizmann Inst., Rep. Senatorial Inner Circle. Mem. ABA, ATLA, Pa. Bar Assn. (former mem. bd. govs., former trustee), Palm Beach County Bar Assn., Acad. Fla. Trial Lawyers, Phila. Trial Lawyers Assn. Office: The Plaza Ste #1102 5355 Town Center Rd Boca Raton FL 33486

KAUFFMAN, BRUCE W., judge. BA, U. Pa., 1956; LLB, Yale U., 1958. Judge U.S. Dist. Ct. (ea. dist.) Pa., 1998—. Office: US Courthose Rm 5918 601 Market St Philadelphia PA 19106

KAUFFMAN, DAGMAR ELISABETH, writer, researcher; b. Hamburg, Fed. Republic of Germany, Feb. 24, 1961; came to U.S., 1983; d. Gustav Ewald and Margot Hildegard (Holz) Franke; m. Bruce Alan Kauffman, July 25, 1986; children: Philip Uwe, Patrick Axel. BA, U. Hamburg, 1984; MA, U. Md., 1987, postgrad., 1987-90. Rschr., teaching asst. U. Hamburg, 1982-83; editorial/mktg. asst. Ednl. Svcs. USA Today, Arlington, Va., 1983-84; adminstrv. asst. U. Md., College Park, 1985-86; rschr., info. program assoc. Am. Assn. Colls. for Tchr. Edn., Washington, 1986-89; freelance rschr., edn. writer Columbia, Md., 1989-97; PTA pres., substitute tchr. Internat. Sch. Hamburg, Germany, 1998—; freelance writer/rschr. Hamburg, Germany, 1997—; editl. cons. Morgan Fin. Group, Balt., 1993-95. Author, rschr.: A Practical Guide to Recruiting Minority Teachers, 1989, Comprehensive Services Guide, 1995; editor: Minority Teacher Recruitment and Retention: A Public Policy Issue, 1987; contbr. articles to profl. jours. Pres. PTA, Internat. Sch. of Hamburg. German Acad. Exch. Svc. scholar, 1983-84. Mem. AAUW, Am. Studies Assn. (regional Chesapeake chpt.), Formerly Employed Mothers at Leading Edge, Balt. Coun. on Fgn. Affairs, Am. Women's Club Hamburg. Democrat. Lutheran. Avocations: travel, literature, sports, politics.

KAUFFMAN, GEORGE, financial administrator; b. Harrisburg, Pa., May 13, 1950. BA, Temple U., 1972; MA, Pa. State U., 1980. Dir. fin. City Harrisburg, 1978-80, city treas., 1980-82; budget & fin. dir. Dauphin City, Pa., 1982-85; mgr. acctg. & fin. Dallas Water Utilities, 1986-94; mng. dir. Fin. Svcs. Dept. City Garland, Tex., 1994—. Mem. Govt. Fin. Officers Assn. Am., Nat. Pub. Power Assn., Govt. Fin. Officers Assn. Tex., Tex. Pub. Power Assn. Office: Fin Svcs Dept City Garland PO Box 469002 Garland TX 75046-9002*

KAUFFMAN, GEORGE BERNARD, chemistry educator; b. Phila., Sept. 4, 1930; s. Philip Joseph and Laura (Fisher) K.; m. Ingeborg Salomon, June 5, 1952 (div. Dec. 1969); children: Ruth Deborah (Mrs. Martin H. Bryskier), Judith Miriam (Mrs. Mario L. Reposo); m. Laurie Marks Papazian, Dec. 21, 1969; stepchildren: Stanley Robert Papazian, Teresa Lynn Papazian Baron, Mary Ellen Papazian Yoder. BA with honors, U. Pa., 1951; PhD, U. Fla., 1956. Grad. asst. U. Fla., 1951-55; rsch. participant Oak Ridge Nat. Lab., 1955; instr. U. Tex., Austin, 1955-56; rsch. chemist Humble Oil & Refining Co., Baytown, Tex., 1956, GE, Cin., 1957, 59; asst. prof. chemistry Calif. State U., Fresno, 1956-61; assoc. prof. Calif. State U., 1961-66, prof., 1966—; guest lectr. coop. lecture tours Am. Chem. Soc., 1971; vis. scholar U. Calif., Berkeley, 1976, U. Puget Sound, 1978; dir. undergrad. rsch. participation program NSF, 1972. Author: Alfred Werner—Founder of Coordination Chemistry, 1966, Classics in Coordination Chemistry, Part I, 1968, Part II, 1976, Part III, 1978, Werner Centennial, 1967, Teaching the History of Chemistry, 1971, Coordination Chemistry: Its History through the Time of Werner, 1977, Inorganic Coordination Compounds, 1981, The Central Science: Essays on the Uses of Chemistry, 1984, Frederick Soddy (1877-1956): Early Pioneer in Radiochemistry, 1986, Aleksandr Porfirevich Borodin: A Chemist's Biography, 1988, Coordination Chemistry: A Century of Progress, 1994, Classics in Coordination Chemistry, 1995, Metal and Nonmetal Biguanide Complexes, 1999; contbr. numerous articles to profl. publs.; contbg. editor: Jour. Coll. Sci. Teaching, 1973—, The Hexagon, 1980—, Polyhedron, 1983-85, Industrial Chemist, 1985-88, Jour. Chem. Edn., 1987—, Today's Chemist, 1989-91, The Chemical Intelligencer, 1994—, Today's Chemist at Work, 1995—, Chemical Heritage, 1996—, The Chemical Educator, 1998—; guest editor: Coodination Chemistry Centennial Symposium (C3S) issue, Polyhedron, 1994; editor tape lecture series: Am. Chem. Soc, 1975-81. Named Outstanding Prof., Calif. State U. and Colls. Sys., 1973; recipient Exceptional Merit Svc. award, 1984, Meritorious Performance and Profl. Promise award, 1986-87, 88-89, Coll. Chemistry Tchr. Excellence award Mfg. Chemists Assn., 1976, Chugaev medal, 1976, Kurnakov medal, 1990, Chernyaev medal, 1991, USSR Acad. Sci., George C. Pimentel award in chem. edn. Am. Chem. Soc., 1993, Dexter award in history of chemistry, 1978, Marc-Auguste Pictet medal Soc. Physique et Histoire Naturelle de Genéve, 1992, Pres.'s medal of Distinction, Calif. State U., Fresno, 1994; Rsch. Corp. grantee, 1956-57, 57-59, 59-61, Am. Chem. Soc. Petroleum Rsch. Fund grantee, 1963-64, 69-70, NSF grantee, 1960-61, 63-64, 67-69, 76-77, NEH grantee, 1982-83; John Simon Guggenheim Meml. Found. fellow, 1972-73, grantee, 1975; Strindberg fellow Swedish Inst., Stockholm, 1983. Mem. AAAS, AAUP, Assn. Univ. Pa. Chemists, History of Sci. Soc., Soc. History Alchemy and Chemistry, Am. Chem. Soc. (chmn. divsn. history of chemistry 1969, mem. exec. com. 1970, councilor 1976-78, George C. Pimentel award in Chem. Edn., 1993), Mensa, Sigma Xi, Phi Lambda Upsilon, Phi Kappa Phi, Alpha Chi Sigma, Gamma Sigma Epsilon. Home: 1609 E Quincy Ave Fresno CA 93720-2309 Office: Calif State U Dept Chemistry Fresno CA 93740-8034

KAUFFMAN, GODFREY, newspaper publishing executive. V.p. circulation Globe Newspaper Co, Boston. Office: Globe Newspaper Co 135 Morrissey Blvd Boston MA 02125-3310*

KAUFFMAN, GORDON LEE, JR., surgeon, educator; b. Grand Rapids, Mich., Mar. 30, 1946; s. Gordon Lee Sr. and Jeanne (Klunder) K.; m. Christie Lyn VanSweden, June 28, 1969; children: Gordon Lee III, Christian Anthony. BS, Wheaton Coll., 1968; MD, U. Mich., 1972. Diplomate Nat. Bd. Med. Examiners, Am. Bd. Surgery. Resident in surgery U. Mich., Ann Arbor, 1972-77; rsch. assoc. VA Wadsworth, L.A., 1977-80, staff surgeon, 1977-85; asst. prof. surgery UCLA Sch. Medicine, 1979-83, assoc. prof., 1983-85; prof. surgery and physiology, chief div. gen. surgery Pa. State U., Hershey, 1985—, vice chmn. dept. surgery, 1994—; investigator Ctr. for Ulcer Rsch. and Edn., L.A., 1979-81, key investigator, 1981-85; cons. City of Hope Nat. Med. Ctr., Duarte, Calif., 1982-85, Harbor Gen. Hosp., Torrance, Calif., 1983-85; mem. surgery and bioengring. study sect. NIH, 1990-94, mem. consensus devel. panel on helicobacterpylori, 1994. Mem. editl. bd. Surgery, 1988—, Jour. Gastrointestinal Surg., 1997—, Jour. Surg. Rsch., 1990-97, Am. Jour. Surgery, 1994-97; contbr. chpts. to books, numerous articles to profl. jours. Grantee Coun. Tobacco Rsch., 1969, VA, 1980-85; Galens Fgn. fellow, 1971, Med. Assistance Program Fgn. fellow, 1971, Frederick Coller resident fellow, 1976, James IV fellow, 1991. Mem. ACS (sec.-treas. cen. Pa. chpt. 1990-96), Assn. Acad. Surgery (chmn. edn. com. 1985-87), Am. Fedn. for Clin. Rsch., Soc. for Exptl. Biology and Medicine, Am. Gastroenterol. Assn. (chmn. abstract rev. com. 1986-87, 95-96), Soc. Univ. Surgeons (chmn. com. on publs.), Soc. Surgery of Alimentary Tract (nominating com. 1990, publ. com. 1991-93, chmn. 1994, recorder 1994-97), Frederick A. Coller Surg. Soc., Collegium Internat. Chirurgiae Digestivae, Surg. Biology Club I, Soc. Clin. Surgery (membership com. 1992-95, chmn. 1995-96), Cent. Surg. Soc. (councilman at large 1995-96), Am. Surg. Assn. (membership adv. com. 1993-97). Office: Milton S Hershey Med Ctr H149 500 University Dr # H149 Hershey PA 17033-2391

KAUFFMAN, KAETHE COVENTON, art educator, artist, author; b. Washington, Aug. 12, 1948; d. Richard G. and Kathleen B. (Coventon) K.; m. James William Hite, Oct. 23, 1983; children: James Haydn, Kauffman Hite. BA, U. Wash., 1970, U. Nev., 1975; MFA, U. Calif., Irvine, 1978; PhD, Union Inst. Cin., 1989. Art dept. faculty U. Nev., Las Vegas, Mount St. Mary's Coll., L.A.; chmn. art dept. Sierra Nevada Coll., Incline Village, 1989-91, assoc. prof., 1991—; mem. faculty dept. art U. Calif., Irvine; mem. editorial adv. bd. Collegiate Press. Author: Sex and the Avant-Garde: A Gender Revolution in the Visual Arts 1830-1993, Female Forms of Originality and the New, Women Artists in the Avant-Garde, How Art Professors Teach Avant-Garde Values, Women Artists Deconstruct the Male Avant-Garde, A Modern Renaissance of the Arts; columnist: Lake Tahoe World newspapers; art exhibited at Utrecht, Holland, 1977, Inst. Modern Art, Brisbane, Australia, 1978, George Patton Gallery U. Melbourne, Australia, 1979, Newport Harbor Art Mus., Calif., 1980, Fiberworks Gallery, Berkeley, Calif., 1981, Galerie Triangle, Washington, 1982, Nev. Mus., Reno, 1983, Schoharie Nat., Cobleskill, N.Y., 1984, Pinnacle Gallery, N.Y., 1986, Space Gallery, Las Vegas, Nev., 1988, Manville Gallery, U. Nev., Reno, 1989, Galerie Art-Jeunesse, Montreal, Que., 1990, Kleinert Gallery, N.Y., 1991, West Gallery, Claremont Grad. Sch., 1992, Sierra Nev. Coll. Art Gallery, Lake Tahoe, Nev., 1995, Exhbn. Hall U. Prague, Czech Republic, CERES Gallery, N.Y., 4th Women's UN Conf., Beijing, Nat. Mus. Women in Arts, Washington, Gallery of the Pali, Honolulu, Czech Mus. of Fine Arts, Prague; represented in permanent collections Women's Studio Workshop, N.Y.C., Calif. Mus. Photography, L.A., Fluor Corp., L.A., Harris Found., Las Vegas, Nev., Computer Scis. Corp., L.A., Sheraton Plaza Inn, L.A., Glendale Fed. Bank, L.A. Juror 3d biennial Nev. Craft Show. Recipient Max H. Block award for Humanism, Juror's award Am. Pen Women Bienniale, Dr. Wu and Elsie Ject-Key meml. award for photography Nat. Assn. Women Artists, N.Y.; Laguna Beach Festival of the Arts fellow; TOSCO Corp. grantee; Artists grantee Sierra Arts Found. Mem. Nat. Mus. Women in Arts, Women's Caucus for Art, Nat. Assn. for Women Artists (medal of honor for works on paper, Elizabeth Morse Genius Found. award), Ceres Gallery, Am. Pen Women (3 awards for non-fiction writing nat. competition), Arts and Letters, Natl. Assn. for Women Artists.

KAUFFMAN, KRISTINA MARIE, political science educator; b. Oct. 3, 1955. Student, Pasadena City Coll., 1975; BA in Polit. Sci., Whittier Coll., 1976; MA in Govt., Claremont Grad. Sch., 1978, postgrad., 1978-79. Lectr. polit. sci. Whittier (Calif.) Coll., 1979, 83-84; adj. prof. polit. sci. Riverside (Calif.) C.C., 1978-79, assoc. prof., 1979—, dir. student affairs, 1980-82, evening and Saturday adj. dean, 1990-93, dir. Title III acad. activity, 1998—; cons., text reviewer D.C. Heath, McGraw Hill, Brooks Cole, St. Martin's Press, Houghton Mifflin Co., Prentice Hall, Wadsworth, West Pub. Co., 1984—; cons. incorporation com. Jurupa C. of C., 1986; founding mem. bd. dirs., dir. rsch. Ctr. for Polit. Rsch., 1983-85; moderator Town Meeting sponsored by U.S. Dept. State and World Affairs Coun., 1987; spkr., panelist on internat. econs. U. Calif., Riverside Ext., 1991, 95, 96; spkr. on online edn. TechEd99, NISOD. Author: Instructor's Guide to Accompany American Politics by William Lasser, 1996; contbg. editor : Study Guide for The American Democracy, 2d edit., 1993. Judge Riverside County's History Day Competition, 1987; bd. dirs. World Affairs Coun. Inland So. Calif., 1978-82, mem., 1978—; bd. dirs. Citrus Belt chpt. UN Assn., 1988-91, v.p., 1990, acting pres., 1990-91; bd. dirs. Model UN of Far West, Inc., 1989-91; v.p. for media and pub. rels. So. Calif. divsn. UN Assn., 1990-91; mem. nat. membership com. UN Assn/U.S.A., 1991-93, spkr. ann. meeting Citrus Belt chpt., 1994; mem. Riverside Seventh Day Bapt. Ch.; spkr. on history of Mid. East and Gulf Crisis to various cmty. groups, 1991; also others. Recipient New Leader award So. Calif. divsn. UN Assn., 1990; fellow Claremont Grad. Sch., 1977. Mem. Calif. Tchrs. Assn., Model UN Alumni Assn. E-mail: kristina@rccd.cc.ca.us. Office: 4800 Magnolia Ave Riverside CA 92506-1293

KAUFFMAN, LEON A., internist, educator; b. Phila., July 26, 1934; s. Isadore and Clara (Kenig) K.; B.A., Temple U., 1957, M.D., 1961; m. Rita A. Young, Apr. 2, 1969; children—Christopher I., Chandler S. Intern, Einstein Med. Center, Phila., 1961-62, resident in pathology, 1962-63; resident in internal medicine Hahnemann U. Hosp., Phila., 1963-65, fellow in pulmonary physiology and chest diseases, 1965-66; sr. instr. medicine Hahnemann U. Med. Sch., 1966-70, asst. prof., 1970-77, assoc. prof., 1977—, dir. pulmonary function lab., 1968-70, dir. respiratory intensive care unit, 1969-73, pulmonary cons. to shock and trauma unit, 1970-80; asst. dir. div. pulmonary medicine, 1970-73; pulmonary cons. U.S. Naval Hosp., 1973-77; med. dir. respiratory therapy St. Agnes Med. Center, Phila., 1973-78, assoc. attending in medicine; chmn. div. pulmonary medicine Met. Hosp., Phila., 1974-83, dir. Sch. Respiratory Therapy Tech., 1978-83; chmn. sub com. on sterilization of respiratory therapy equipment Am. Lung Assn. of Phila., 1975-81. Past mem. adv. com. Sch. Respiratory Therapy, Community Coll. Phila. Diplomate Am. Bd. Internal Medicine, subsplty. Bd. Pulmonary Disease. Fellow Am. Coll. Chest Physicians, Phila. Coll. Physicians; mem. Laennec Soc. Phila. (pres. 1975-76, exec. com. 1972-78), AMA, Pa. Med. Soc., Am. Thoracic Soc., A.C.P., Phila. Drinker Soc. Critical Care Medicine, N.Y. Acad. Scis. Contbr. articles to profl. jours. Office: 1930 Pine St Philadelphia PA 19103-6626

KAUFFMAN, MARTA, producer. With Bright-Kauffman-Crane Prodns., Burbank, Calif. Creator, prodr. Dream On, 1990—; creator, exec. prodr. Friends, 1994— (Emmy nominee 1995, 96), Veronica's Closet, 1997—, Jesse, 1998. Office: Bright Kauffman Crane Prodns Bldg 160 Ste 750 4000 Warner Blvd Burbank CA 91522*

KAUFFMAN, MARVIN EARL, geoscience consultant; b. Lancaster, Pa., Aug. 31, 1933; s. D. Ivan and Leah Kauffman; m. Sue Cox (Pilgrim); children: Dorinda, Barbara, Douglas, Betsy, Ruth, Peter, Philip. BS, Franklin and Marshall Coll., 1955; MS, Northwestern U., 1957; PhD, Princeton U., 1960. Prof. and past chmn. dept. geology Franklin & Marshall Coll., Lancaster, Pa., 1959-84; exec. dir. Am. Geol. Inst., Alexandria, Va., 1985-90; program dir. Nat. Sci. Found., Washington, 1990-94; cons., 1994—; cons. Martin Marietta Corp., Balt., 1964-65, R.E. Wright Assocs., Middletown, Pa., 1978-81, 1990-91, Meiser & Earl Assocs., State Coll., Pa., 1981-84; vis. prof. U. Christchurch & Dunedin, New Zealand, 1994-95; adj. prof. geoscis. Mont. State U., Western Mont. Coll., Dillon, U. Mont., Billings. Author: (with others) Physical Geology, 1978, 5th, 6th edit., 1982, 7th edit., 1987, 8th edit., 1990. NSF Grad. fellow, 1955-59, sci. faculty fellow 1965-66. Fellow Geol. Soc. Am.; mem. Nat. Assn. Geology Tchrs. (pres. 1983-84), Am. Inst. Profl. Geologists. Methodist. Home and Office: PO Box 833 540 Upper Continental Dr Red Lodge MT 59068-0833

KAUFFMAN, ROBERT JOSEPH, magistrate; b. Springfield, Ill., Feb. 17, 1935; s. William V. and Elizabeth M. (Malone) K.; m. Elizabeth Patterson, Sept. 12, 1959; children—Thomas J., Jean Marie, Susan Lynn, Carol Ann. Student Marquette U. Coll. Liberal Arts, 1956, LL.B., Law Sch., 1959. Bar: Wis. 1959, Ill. 1975, U.S. Dist. Ct. (so. dist.) Ill. 1975, U.S. Ct. Mil. Appeals 1962, U.S. Ct. Appeals (7th cir.) 1975, U.S. Supreme Ct. 1962. Sole practice, West Bend, Wis., 1965-67; asst. dist. atty., West Bend, 1965-67; dist. atty. Washington County (Wis.), West Bend, 1967-73; trial atty. Dept. Justice Criminal Div., Washington, 1973-75; asst. U.S. atty., Peoria, Ill., 1975-76; clk. U.S. Dist. Ct. (so. then cen. dist.) Ill., Peoria, 1977-84; magistrate U.S. Dist. Ct. (cen. dist.) Ill., Peoria, 1978—. Served to capt. JAGC, USAF, 1960-65. Mem. Fed. Ct. Clks. Assn., Nat. Council U.S. Magistrates. Club: Rotary (dir. 1979-83, v.p. 1984) (Peoria). Office: US Dist Ct 271 Federal Bldg 100 NE Monroe St Peoria IL 61602-1003

KAUFFMAN, TERRY, broadcast and creative arts communication educator, artist; b. San Francisco, Aug. 24, 1951; d. Raymond Roger and Patricia Virginia Kauffman. BA in Journalism summa cum laude, U. Calif., Berkeley, 1974; MA in Comm. summa cum laude, U. Tex., 1980; PhD in Psychology with distinction, Union Inst., 1996. With Alta. Ednl. TV, 1970; sr. writer, prodr. and dir. Ampex Corp., Calif., 1980; writer, news prodr., reporter, anchor ABC, Tex., 1974-75; mem. faculty dept. radio, TV and motion pictures U. N.C., Chapel Hill, 1985; mem. faculty dept. comm. N.C. State U., Raleigh, 1986—; pvt. practice expressive arts, Raleigh, 1995—; adj. prof. music, theatre and comm. dept. Meredith Coll., Raleigh, 1990—; mem. adv. bd., chmn. publicity Raleigh Conservatory Music; v.p. Wake Visual Arts Assn. and Gallery; tchr. art Meredith Coll., 1995—; founder, owner Creative Spaces; owner Expressive Arts and Comm., 1994—; therapist at psychit. hosps. and pvt., 1994—. Author: I'm Clueless, Confessions of a College Teacher, The Script as Blueprint, 1994, 8 vol. set poetry including Psalms of Teresa, Secret Place, Just Visiting, others; contbr. poetry to various publs.; composer, prodr., dir., composer for TV programs, including When the Wind Blows, The Rainbow, The Seasons of Change, PBS, Women Today, Profiles in Leadership; commd. and exhibited in solo art shows (1st place painting), San Francisco, Raleigh; artist for documentary series, rschr., writer, Alta., Can., 1976; prodr., dir., writer, composer I'm One Person...Or The Other, Thanksgiving (PBS), 1980—; writer, prodr. Consumer Hotline, PBS, Customs Operations at the Border; main character, vocalist, composer live and radio tape Little Miss Puppet Talks to the Angels; exptl. arts and comm. shows; numerous others; interviewd on TV and radio about arts, media, comm., psychology; pub. music book: Songs by Terry Kauffman. Singer/composer for chs. and retirement homes; past bd. dirs. Tex. Consumer Assn., Wake visual Arts. Recipient Emmy nomination for documentary Otters from Oiled Waters, 1991, more than 15 1st place nat. awards in TV, including writing, producing, directing, music composition, acting, art, and photography, various art and music shows; named Outstanding Lectr. of Yr. Coll. of Humanities and Social Scis., 1999, finalist Outstanding Tchr. N.C. State U. Mem. APA, NATAS, Internat. TV Assn. (judge nat. contests), Nat. Broadcasting Soc. (8 1st place nat. awards 1973—, named Outstanding Mem., 1993-94, Profl. Mem. of Yr. 1994), Assn. Humanistic Psychologists, Calif. Scholastic Fedn. (life), Calif. Scholastic Assn., Berkeley Honor Soc., Am. Psychol. Assn., Phi Kappa Phi. Achievements include created first frame by frame animated computer art in world for video at Ampex Corp. Calif. Home: 407 Furches St Raleigh NC 27607-4017

KAUFFMAN, WILLIAM JOSEPH, editor, writer; b. Batavia, N.Y., Nov. 15, 1959; s. Edward Joseph and Sandra Jean (Baker) K.; m. Lucine Margaret Andonian, May 22, 1987; 1 child, Gretel. BA, U. Rochester, 1981. Rsch. asst. Senator D.P. Moynihan, Washington, 1981-82, legis. asst., 1982-83; asst. editor Reason, Santa Barbara, Calif., 1985-86, Washington, 1986-87; assoc. editor The Am. Enterprise, Washington, 1994—. Author: Every Man a King, 1989, Country Towns of New York, 1994, America First! Its History, Culture and Politics, 1995, With Good Intentions? Reflections on the Myth of Progress in America, 1998; corr. editor Chronicles, 1993—; contbg. editor Liberty, 1992—. Dir. Genesee Landmark Soc., 1993—, Holland Purchase Hist. Soc., 1993—, Friends of the Richmond Meml. Libr., 1995—. Mem. John Randolph Club. Roman Catholic. Avocations: astronomy, music, collecting coins and political campaign items. Home: 28 Chapel St PO Box 266 Elba NY 14058-0266 also: 257 Bank St Batavia NY 14020-1540

KAUFFMANN, ROBERT FREDRICK, software engineer; b. Willingboro, N.J., Dec. 13, 1963; s. Robert Albert and Lori Kathleen (Mastroni) K. AS in Computer Sci., Burlington County Coll., Pemberton, N.J., 1984; BA in Computer Sci., Rutgers U., 1987; postgrad., N.J. Inst. Tech., 1995. Engr. software Computer Scis. Corp., Moorestown, N.J., 1989—. Illustrator Robert's Rhymes, 1988; filmmaker Animated Shorts, 1995, Masque of Olock, 1999. Recipient Silver award Artist's Guild of Delaware Valley, 1997,

Bronze award Worldfest Houston, 1997. Mem. Assn. Computing Machinery. Avocations: karate, poetry. Home: 2401 Arden Rd Cinnaminson NJ 08077-3601

KAUFFMANN, STANLEY JULES, author; b. N.Y.C., Apr. 24, 1916; s. Joseph H. and Jeannette (Steiner) K.; m. Laura Cohen, Feb. 5, 1943. B.F.A., NYU, 1935. Mem. Washington Sq. Players, 1931-41; asso. editor Bantam Books, 1949-52; editor-in-chief Ballantine Books, 1952-56, consulting editor, 1957-59; editor Alfred A. Knopf, 1959-60; film critic New Republic, N.Y.C., 1958-65, 67—, assoc. lit. editor, 1966-67; theater critic New York Times, 1966, New Republic, N.Y.C., 1969-79, Saturday Rev., 1979-85; condr. program The Art of Film, Channel 13, N.Y.C., 1963-67; vis. prof. Sch. of Drama, Yale U., 1967-86, 95, 97; vis. prof. CUNY, 1973-76, 77-92, Hunter Coll, 1993-99; Disting. vis. prof. Adelphi U., 1992-94, profl. performing arts, 1994-96. Author: The Hidden Hero, 1949, The Tightrope, 1952, A Change of Climate, 1954, Man of the World, 1956, A World on Film, 1966, Figures of Light, 1971; editor: (with Bruce Henstell) American Film Criticism: from the Beginnings to Citizen Kane, 1973, Living Images, 1975, Persons of The Drama, 1976, Before My Eyes, 1980, Albums of Early Life, 1980, Theater Criticisms, 1983, Field of View, 1986, Distinguishing Features, 1994. Recipient George Jean Nathan award for dramatic criticism, 1972-73, George Polk award for criticism, 1982, Outstanding Tchr. award Assn. for Theater in Higher Edn., 1995, Telluride Film Festival medal, 1998; Ford Found. fellow for study abroad, 1964, 71, hon. fellow Morse Coll., Yale U., 1964, Guggenheim fellow, 1979-80. Address: 10 W 15th St New York NY 10011-6838

KAUFMAN, ALEX, chemicals executive; b. Lemburg, Poland, Sept. 9, 1924; came to U.S., 1950; naturalized, 1955; s. Isadore and Bronislava (Halpern) K.; children: Bernice, Irene, Mark. Grad. in chemistry, Stuttgart Poly. Inst., Fed. Republic Germany, 1950. With Hatco Chem. div. W.R. Grace & Co., Fords, N.J., 1961—, pres. parent co., N.Y.C., 1962-78, corp. v.p., 1967, exec. v.p., 1968-78, also bd. dirs., group exec., Hatco Group, 1968-78; pres. Grace Petrochems., Inc., P.R., 1969-78, Kalex Chem. Products, Inc., 1978—, Hatco Chem. Corp., 1978—; bd. dirs. Raritan Bay Health Svcs. Corp. Mem. nat. adv. bd. Multiple Sclerosis Soc. Named Ernst & Young Entrepreneur of Yr., 1998. Mem. Soc. Plastics Industry, Chem. Mfrs. Assn., Soc. Chem. Industry, Woodbridge C. of C., Chemist's Club. Office: 1020 King George Post Rd Fords NJ 08863-2329

KAUFMAN, ANDREW LEE, law educator; b. Newark, Feb. 1, 1931; s. Samuel and Sylvia (Meltzer) K.; m. Linda P. Sonnenschein, June 14, 1959; children: Anne, David, Elizabeth, Daniel. A.B., Harvard U., 1951, LL.B., 1954. Bar: D.C. 1954, Mass. 1979, U.S. Supreme Ct. 1961. Assoc. Bilder, Bilder & Kaufman, Newark, 1954-55; law clk. to Justice Felix Frankfurter U.S Supreme Ct., 1955-57; ptnr. Kaufman, Kaufman & Kaufman, Newark, 1957-65; lectr. in law Harvard U., Cambridge, Mass., 1965-66, prof., 1966-81, Charles Stebbins Fairchild prof. law, 1981—, assoc. dean, 1986-89. Author: (with others) Commercial Law, 1971, 82, Problems in Professional Responsibility, 1976, 84, 89, Cardozo, 1998. Treas. Shady Hill Sch., 1969-76; treas. Hillel Found. Cambridge, Inc., 1977-86. Mem. Mass. Bar Assn. (chmn. com. profl. ethics 1982—). Office: Harvard U Law Sch Cambridge MA 02138

KAUFMAN, ANTOINETTE D., business services company executive; b. Phila., Mar. 10, 1939; d. Joseph and Maria Falcone; m. John R. Kaufman, Apr. 30, 1988. Ed., St. Joseph's U., 1968. With N.W. Ayer & Son, Inc., N.Y.C., 1956-81; adminstrv. asst. N.W. Ayer ABH Internat., 1960, asst. corp. sec., 1977, corp. sec., 1978-79, stock transfer agt., 1969-79, info. specialist, 1979-81; exec. v.p., sec., creative dir., chief oper. officer Help Bus. Svcs., Inc., Swarthmore, Pa., 1981—. Office: Help Bus Svcs Inc 110 Park Ave HBS Bldg Swarthmore PA 19081

KAUFMAN, ARTHUR STEPHEN, lawyer; b. N.Y.C., July 27, 1946; s. Jacob and Helen (Chalphin) K.; m. Susan Werner, Jan. 31, 1971; children: Lewis Scott, Jonathan Charles. AB, Columbia Coll., 1968, JD, 1971. Bar: N.Y. 1972. Assoc. Dewey, Ballantine, Bushby, Palmer & Wood, N.Y.C., 1971-79; ptnr. Shea & Gould, N.Y.C., 1980-85, Fried, Frank, Harris, Shriver & Jacobson, N.Y.C., 1985—. Home: 17 Withington Rd Scarsdale NY 10583-3305 Office: Fried Frank Harris Shriver & Jacobson 1 New York Plz Fl 22 New York NY 10004-1980

KAUFMAN, BARBARA, municipal official. Mem. indsl. expert panel Contractor's State Lic. Bd., 1986-87; mem. consumer adv. coun. Fed. Res. Bd., 1989-91; mem. bd. suprs. City of San Francisco, 1992-97, pres. bd. suprs., 1997-98, mem. bd. suprs., 1998—; chairwoman Budget Com., 1992—, Fin. Com., 1997; mem. Econ. and Develop and Social Policy Com., 1992—; chmn. Select Com. on Charter Reform, 1992—; vice chmn. San Francisco County Transp. Authority, chmn., 1997—; vice chairwoman Econ. Vitality and Social Policy Com., 1995-96; bd. dirs. Golden Gate Bridge Hwy. and Transp. Dist., 1996-97. Author: Barbara Kaufman's Consumer Action Guide: Your Rights from A to Z, 1991, Nolo's Pocket Guide to Consumer Rights, 1994. Founding dir. Call for Action KCBS radio, 1981-93, host, 1984-90; bd. dirs. Jewish Family and Children's Svc., 1982-89, Coro Found., 1983-88, United Way, 1994. Recipient Pres.'s award U. San Francisco, 1996, Dean's Outstanding Alumnus award, 1996, 1996 Domestic Violence Awareness awards San Francisco Commn. on Status of Women, 1996. Mem. Assn. Bay Area Govts. (bd. dirs. 1994). E-mail: barbaraukaufman@ci.sf.ca.us. Address: City of San Francisco Bd of Suprs 1 Dr Carlton B Grodlett Pl San Francisco CA 94102-4524*

KAUFMAN, BEL, author, educator; b. Berlin; d. Michael J. and Lala (Rabinowitz) K.; divorced; children: Jonathan Goldstine, Thea Goldstine. BA magna cum laude, Hunter Coll., 1934; MA with highest honors, Columbia U., 1936; LLD (hon.), Nasson Coll., Maine, 1965. Adj. prof. English CUNY; lectr. throughout country, also appearances on TV and radio.; Mem. Commn. Performing Arts. Editorial bd., Phi Delta Kappan.; Author: Up the Down Staircase, 1965, Love, etc, 1979; also short stories, articles, TV play, translations from Russian, lyrics for musicals. Bd. dirs. Shalom Aleichem Found.; adv. council Town Hall Found. Recipient plaque Anti-Defamation League, award and plaque United Jewish Appeal, Paperback of Year award, Ky. Col. award, Bell Movie award; also ednl. journalism awards; named to Hall of Fame Hunter Coll., winner short story contest sponsored by NEA and PEN, 1983. Mem. Author's Guild, Dramatists Guild, P.E.N., English Grad. Union, Phi Beta Kappa. Address: 1020 Park Ave New York NY 10028-0913

KAUFMAN, CHARLES DAVID, controller; b. N.Y.C., Apr. 17, 1931; s. M. Laurence and Anna (Goldberg) K.; m. Elvira Sampere Camps, Mar. 1, 1955; children: John, Janet. BS, Northwestern U., 1952; MBA, NYU, 1958. CPA, N.Y. Fin. analyst Nestle Co., Stamford, Conn., 1958-61; area contr. IBM World Trade Corp., Mexico City, 1967-69; dir. fin. controls ITT Corp., Brussels and N.Y.C., 1974-85, controller's dept., 1985-94; ret., 1994. Bd. dirs. Scottsdale League for The Arts, Valley Acad.; vol. cons. Exec. Svc. Corps Ariz., Svc. Corps Ret. Execs. Cpl. U.S. Army, 1952-54. Mem. AICPAs, N.Y. Soc. CPAs, Ariz. Soc. CPAs.

KAUFMAN, CHARLOTTE KING, artist, retired educational administrator; b. Balt., Dec. 5, 1920; d. Ben and Belle (Turow) King; A.B., Goucher Coll., 1969; M.P.H., Johns Hopkins U., 1972, M.Ed., 1976; m. Albert Kaufman, July 22, 1945; children—Matthew King, Ezra King. Dir. public relations Balt. Jewish Community Center, 1962-67; research and editor Johns Hopkins U. Sch. Hygiene and Public Health, Balt., 1969-72, admissions officer, 1972-74, dir. admissions and registrar, 1974-86, dir. study cons. program undergraduates, 1986-89, pub. health acad. adviser, 1989-95. Mem. Am. Pub. Health Assn., Am. Assn. for Higher Edn., Am. Assn. Collegiate Registrars and Admissions Officers, Artists Equity Assn. (v.p. Md. chpt. 1988-90), Md. Printmakers (exec. bd. 1989-94), Palm Springs Desert Mus. Artists Coun. (exec. bd. 1997—), Delta Omega. Democrat. Jewish. Home: Monterey Country Club 159 Las Lomas Palm Desert CA 92260-2153

KAUFMAN, CHARLOTTE S., communications executive; b. Bridgeport, Conn., Mar. 8, 1918; d. Samuel N. and S. Elizabeth (Cohen) Schnee; m. William Kaufman, May 9, 1940. BA, U. Mich., 1938. Med. office assoc., 1941-63; dir. pub. rels. Parents and Friends of Retarded Children, Bridgeport, 1965-66; founder, exec. dir. Family Life Film Ctr. of Conn., Fairfield, Conn., 1967-74; exec. producer Topic '69/WNHC-TV, New Haven, Conn., 1969; project dir. pilot project with Social/Rehab. Svc. U.S. Dept. HEW, 1969-70; pub. rels. chmn. Friendship Fair of Aux./Bridgeport Regional Ctr. Retarded, 1979; founder CAT-TV, pub. access channel, Winston-Salem and Forsyth County, 1994; coord. five annual Film Day Workshops, Fairfield U., 1967-71; coord. coms. of jurors for Am. Film Festival, N.Y.C., 1968-74; chmn./mem. planning and adv. bd. Bridgeport Regional Ctr. for the Retarded; exec. bd. Bd. of Assocs., U. Bridgeport, others; film use cons. to many local and state orgns. Author: Film Discussion: A Technique to Communicate Information About Rehabilitation, 1970; exec. producer: A Day in the Life of P.T. Barnum, 1971; author publs. in field. Vol. patient advocate for nursing homes, Southwestern Conn. Area Agy. on Aging, 1976-78; v.p. Oronoque Village Improvement Assn., 1986-88. Home: 3180 Grady St Winston Salem NC 27104-4008

KAUFMAN, CHRISTOPHER LEE, lawyer; b. Chgo., Mar. 17, 1945; s. Charles R. and Violet-Page (Koteen) K.; m. Carlyn A. Clement, Jan. 25, 1986; children: Charles Alexander, Caroline Clement. BA, Amherst Coll., 1967; JD, Harvard U., 1970. Bar: Ill. 1970, Calif. 1972. Law clk. to judge U.S. Ct. Appeals (2d cir.), N.Y.C., 1970-71; from assoc. to ptnr. Heller, Ehrman, White and McAuliffe, San Francisco, Palo Alto, Calif., 1974-90; ptnr. Latham & Watkins, Menlo Park, Calif., 1990—. Editor: Harvard Law Review., 1968-70. Mem. ABA (com. on negotiated acquisitions, com. on fed. regulation of securities). Office: Latham & Watkins 135 Commonwealth Menlo Park CA 94025-3656

KAUFMAN, DAVID GRAHAM, construction company executive; b. North Canton, Ohio, Mar. 20, 1937; s. DeVere and Josephine Grace (Graham) K.; student Kent State U., 1956; grad. Internat. Corr. Schs., 1965; grad. N.Y. Inst. Photography, 1983; postgrad. Calif. Coast U.; m. Carol Jean Monzione, Oct. 5, 1957 (div. Aug. 1980); children—Gregory Allan, Christopher Patrick. Cert. constrn. insp.; cert. constrn. project mgr.; cert. asbestos insp.; cert. lead insp.; cert. asbestos project designer; cert. lock-out/tag-out. Machinist apprentice Hoover Co., North Canton, Ohio, 1955-57; draftsman-designer Goodyear Aircraft Corp., Akron, Ohio, 1957-60, Boeing Co., Seattle, 1960-61; designer Berger Industries, Seattle, 1961-62, Puget Sound Bridge & Drydock, Seattle, 1963, C.M. Lovsted, Seattle, 1963-64, Tracy, Brunstrom & Dudley, Seattle, 1964, Rubens & Pratt Engrs., Seattle, 1965-66; founder, owner, Profl. Drafting Svcs., Seattle, 1965, Profl. Take-Off Svcs., Seattle, 1966, Profl. Representation Svcs., Seattle, 1967, pres. Kaufman Inc., Seattle, 1967-83, Kaufman-Alaska Inc., Juneau, 1975-83 , Kaufman-Alaska Constructors, Inc., Juneau, 1975-83. Trustee, advisor Kaufman Internat., The Kaufman Group, Kaufman Enterprises; constrn. mgr. U. Alaska, 1979-84; constrn. cons. Alaskan native and Eskimo village corps., 1984—; prin. Kaufman S.W. Assocs., N. Mex., 1984—, Graham Internat., 1992—. Mem. Constrn. Specifications Inst., Assn. Constrn. Insps., Associated Gen. Contractors Seattle Constrn. Coun., Producers Coun. Oreg., Wash., Idaho, Hawaii, Alaska, Portland C. of C., Nat. Eagle Scout Assn., Toastmasters (past gov.), Lions. Republican. Roman Catholic. Home: PO Box 1781 Santa Fe NM 87504-1781 Office: PO Box 458 Haines AK 99827-0458 also: PO Box 915 Crown Point NM 87313-0915

KAUFMAN, DAVID JOSEPH, lawyer; b. Harrisburg, Pa., Apr. 7, 1931; s. S. Herbert and Bessie (Claster) K.; m. Virginia Stern, Aug. 30, 1959; children: David J. Jr., James H. BS in Econs. cum laude, Franklin and Marshall Coll., 1952; JD cum laude, U. Pa., 1955. Bar: Pa. 1955. First assoc., to ptnr., then of counsel Wolf, Block, Schorr & Solis-Cohen, Phila., 1957—; chmn., exec. com., 1979, 83. Trustee Abington (Pa.) Meml. Hosp., 1981—, chmn. bd. trustees, 1992-94; pres. Congregation Rodeph Shalom, Phila., 1983-86. Fellow Am. Coll. Trust and Estate Counsel; mem. ABA, Pa. Bar Assn. (chmn. real property, probate and trust sect. 1986-87), Phila. Bar Assn. (chmn. probate sect. 1977). Republican. Home: 2191 Paper Mill Rd Huntingdon Valley PA 19006-5817 Office: Wolf Block Schorr & Solis-Cohen LLP 1650 Arch St Philadelphia PA 19103

KAUFMAN, DAVID MARC, pediatric neurologist; b. Bronx, N.Y., July 10, 1945; s. Harold M. and Edna M. (Markowtiz) K.; m. Harriet B. Kaufman, June 30, 1968; 1 child, Jill R. BS, Union Coll., 1967; MD, Boston U. Sch. of Medicine, 1975. Diplomate Am. Bd. Pediatrics. Intern-resident N.Y. Hosp., N.Y.C., 1975-77; resident-fellow Mt. Sinai Med. Ctr., N.Y.C., 1977-80; pvt. practice in pediatric neurology N.Y.C., 1980—; mem. admissions com. Mt. Sinai Sch. of Medicine, N.Y.C., 1992—, ethics com. Child Neurology Soc., Mpls., 1995—; adv. bd. Winston Prep Sch. Spl. Edn. Sch., N.Y.C., 1990, Young Adult Inst., N.Y.C., 1995—. Author: (with others) The Founders of Child Neurology, 1990. Fellow Am. Acad. Pediatrics; mem. Am. Acad. Neurology, Child Neurology Soc. Office: 3 E 83d St New York NY 10028*

KAUFMAN, DONALD LEROY, building products executive; b. Erie, Pa., May 9, 1931; s. Isadore H. and Lena (Sandler) K.; m. Estelle Friedman, Aug. 15, 1954; children: Craig Ivan, Susan Beth, Carrie Ellen. B.S. in Bus. Adminstrn, Ohio State U., 1953, LL.B., 1955. Bar: Ohio 1955. Pres. Alside, Inc., Akron, Ohio, 1974—, chief exec. officer, 1982—; v.p., bd. dirs. Assoc. Materials Inc. Mem. adv. com. U. Akron; trustee Jewish Welfare Fund, Akron, 1958-65, young leaders div., 1961-65; trustee Akron City Hosp. Found., 1984-91, Menorah Park Home for Aged, Akron Children's Hosp. Found. Mem. Akron Bar Assn., Sigma Alpha Mu, Tau Epsilon Rho. Home: 2825 Roundhill Rd Akron OH 44333-2273 Office: PO Box 2010 Akron OH 44309-2010

KAUFMAN, DONALD WAYNE, research ecologist; b. Abilene, Tex., June 7, 1943; s. Leo Fred and Marcella Genevieve (Hobbie) K.; m. Glennis Ann Schroeder, Aug. 5, 1967; 1 child, Dawn. BS, Ft. Hays Kans. State Coll., 1965, MS, 1967; PhD, U. Ga., 1972. Postdoctoral fellow U. Tex., Austin, 1971-73; asst. prof. U. Ark., Fayetteville, 1974-75, SUNY, Binghamton, 1975-77; assoc. program dir. Population Biology, NSF, Washington, 1977-80; asst. prof. biology Kans. State U., Manhattan, 1980-84, assoc. prof. biology, 1984-91, prof. biology, 1991—; adj. prof. biology U. N.Mex., 1998; vis. scientist Savannah River Ecology Lab., Aiken, S.C., 1973-74; acting dir. Konza Prairie Rsch. Natural Area, 1986-87, coord., 1990-91; dir. Konza Prairie Long-Term Ecol. Rsch. Program, 1985-90; grant rev. panelist EPA, 1981-85, USDA, 1995-96; cons. NSF, 1984. Contbr. articles to profl. jours. NDEA fellow, 1967-69; NSF grantee, 1981—. Mem. AAAS, Am. Soc. Mammalogists (award 1972, bd. dirs. 1989-92), Ecol. Soc. Am., Am. Inst. Biol. Scis., Soc. for the Study Evolution. Office: Kans State U Div Biology Ackert Hall Manhattan KS 66506

KAUFMAN, EDWARD PHILLIP, psychotherapist; b. Bronx, N.Y., Aug. 8, 1939; s. Harry Oscar and Terry Rose (Saeperstein) K.; m. Adele Mae Weltman, June 24, 1962; children: Elizabeth Ann, Daniel Mark. BA, U. Ill., 1962, MSW, 1964. LCSW, BCD, cert. social worker, child psychotherapist. Acting dir. admissions children's svcs. Chigo. Read Mental Health Hosp., 1964-66; adminstr., clin. supr. Jewish Children's Bur., Chgo., 1966-85; pvt. practice psychotherapy Chgo. and Highland Park, Ill., 1969—; clin. supr., adminstrv. cons. St. Mary's Svcs., Chgo., 1977-84, cons. spl. edn. dept. Glenbrook H.S., Northbrook, Ill., 1978-81; cons. various child welfare agys. and schs., Chgo., 1977—; mem. CAPT faculty Inst. Psychoanalysis, Chgo., 1982—; lectr. in field. Co-editor: Emotions and Learning Reconsidered, 1993. Mem. Mayor's Commn. on Vandalism, city of Highland Park, Ill., 1978-79; bd. dirs. Highland Park Youth Comm., 1980-86. Mem. Assn. Child Psychotherapists (treas. 1977-79, exec. com. 1983-85, pres. 1997-98), Ill. Soc. Clin. Social Work, Nat. Assn. Social Workers, Nat. Registry Clin. Social Workers (cert.). Avocations: photography, scuba diving, tennis. Home: 825 Edgewood Rd Highland Park IL 60035-4621 Office: 111 N Wabash Ave Ste 1804 Chicago IL 60602-1903 also: Ste 212 508 Central Highland Pk Highland Park IL 60035-2628

KAUFMAN, GLEN FRANK, art educator, artist; b. Fort Atkinson, Wis., Oct. 28, 1932; s. Eli J. and Elynor B. (Jensik) K. BS with honors, U. Wis., 1954; MFA, Cranbrook Acad. Art, 1959; cert., State Sch. Arts and Crafts, Copenhagen, 1960. Head fibers dept. Cranbrook Acad. Art, Bloomfield Hills, Mich., 1961-67; assoc. prof. art U. Ga., Athens, 1967-72, prof. art, 1972—, prof. in charge, fabric design, 1967—, grad. faculty, 1969—; staff designer Dorothy Liebes Design Studio, N.Y.C., 1960-61; designer Regal Rugs, Inc., North Vernon, Ind., 1966-82; vis. artist Sch. Textiles, Royal Coll. Art, London, 1976; juror The Albuquerque (N.Mex.) Mus., 1981, Midland (Mich.) Art Coun., 1985, Itami Craft Ctr., Osaka, Japan, 1991, others; panelist Visual Artists Fellowship/Crafts, Nat. Endowment for the Arts, Washington, 1992—; cons. in field; lectr. and workshop presenter in field. one-man shows include Gallery Maronie, Kyoto, Japan, 1984, Sembikiya Gallery, Tokyo, 1985, Arrowmont Sch. Arts and Crafts, Gatlinburg, Tenn., 1986, Fiberworks, Berkeley, Calif., 1987, Madison (Ga.)-Morgan Cultural Ctr., 1988, Fuji Gallery, Osaka, Japan, 1988, Wacoal Ginza Art Space, Tokyo, 1989, Allrich Gallery, San Francisco, 1990, Azabu Mus. of Arts and Crafts, Tokyo, 1991, Lamar Dodd Art Ctr., LaGrange (Ga.) Coll., 1992, Gallery Gallery, Japan, 1992, Wacoal Ginza Art Space, Tokyo, 1994, Gallery Nouveau, Pusan, Korea, 1994, Ba Tang Gol Arts Ctr., Seoul, korea, 1994, Wacoal Ginza Art Space, Tokyo, 1996, Gallery Gallery, Kyoto, Japan, 1996, many others; exhibited in group shows at Columbia Mus. Art, S.C., 1980, No. Ill. U., DeKalb, 1981, Visual Arts Ctr. Alaska, Anchorage, 1982, Robert L. Kidd Gallery, Birmingham, 1983, Am. Craft Mus., N.Y., 1986, Denki Kaikan Gallery, Nagoya, Japan, 1987, Gayle Wilson Gallery, Southampton, N.Y., 1988, Sch. Visual Arts, N.Y., 1989, Itami Craft Ctr., Osaka, 1989 (Silver prize), Farrell Collection, Washington, 1991, Allrich Gallery, San Francisco, 1991, Nagoya Trade and Industry Ctr., 1991, New Visions Gallery Contemporary Art, Atlanta, 1992, Mus. Kyoto, 1992, Smithsonian Instn., Washington, 1992-93, Atlanta (Ga.) Fin. Ctr., 1993, The Nat. Mus. Modern Art, Kyoto, Japan, 1993, Art Inst. Chgo., Ill., 1993, Brenau U. Gallery, Gainesville, Ga., 1993, Mus. Kyoto, 1994, Asian Arts Ctr. Towson (Md.) State U., 1994, Am. Craft Museum, N.Y., 1995, Nogaya and Trade Industry Ctr., Japan, 1995, Gallery, Gallery, Kyota, Japan, 1995, Harbourfront Ctr., Toronto Can., 1995, Musee Marsil, Montreal, Can., 1995, The Brown/Grotta Gallery, Wilton, Conn., 1995, New Jersey Ctr. for Visual Arts, Summit, 1997, Georgia State U. Gallery, Atlanta, 1997, Brown/Grotta Gallery, Wilton, Conn. 12997, Vanderbilt U. Sarratt Gallery, Nashville, 1997, Georgia Museum of Art, Athens, 1997, others; represented in permanent collections Am. Craft Mus., N.Y.C., Juraku Mus, Kyoto, Cleve. Mus. Art, Art Inst. Chgo., U. Wis., Madison, Itami City Craft Ctr., Hyogo Prefecture, Japan, Ithaca (N.Y.) Coll. Mus. Art, Long House Found., L.I., N.Y., Nat. Mus. Modern Art, Kyoto, Smithsonian Instn., Rockford Art Assn., Ill., S.C. Johnson Collection, U.S.A. Collection Contemporary Crafts, SUNY, Oneonta, Wichita Art Assn., Kans., pvt. collections; works illustrated in many books; contbr. articles to jours. Recipient Fulbright grant to Denmark, 1959-60, Grant for rsch. and travel to Europe, U. Ga., Dept. Art, 1973, Nat. Endowment for the Arts Craftsmen's Fellowship grant, 1976, Nat. Endowment for the Arts Svcs. to the Field grant, 1980-81, 81-82, Faculty Rsch. grant U. Ga. Athens Office of V.P. for Rsch., 1983-96, Nat. Endowment for the Arts Visual Artist's Fellowship grant, 1990, Ga. Coun. for the Arts Individual Artist grant, 1991, Sr. Faculty Rsch. grant U. Ga. Athens Rsch. Found., 1992, others. Fellow Am. Craft Coun.; mem. World Craft Coun., Surface Design Assn. (S.E. regional rep. 1977-80, pres. 1980-82, named hon. life mem. 1983), Phi Beta Delta. Office: Sch of Art Univ Ga Athens GA 30602

KAUFMAN, GORDON DESTER, theology educator; b. Newton, Kans., June 22, 1925; s. Edmund George and Hazel (Dester) K.; m. Dorothy Wedel, June 11, 1947; children: David W., Gretchen E., Anne Louisa, Edmund G. AB with highest distinction, Bethel (Kans.) Coll., 1947, LHD (hon.), 1973; MA in Sociology, Northwestern U., 1948; BD magna cum laude, Yale U., 1951, PhD in Philos. Theology, 1955. Ordained to ministry Mennonite Ch., 1953. Asst. prof. religion Pomona Coll., 1953-58; asso. prof. theology Vanderbilt U., 1958-63; prof. theology Harvard U. Div. Sch., Cambridge, Mass., 1963-95, Edward MallincKrodt Jr. prof. div., 1969-95, prof. emeritus, 1995—; vis. prof. United Theol. Coll., Bangalore, India, 1976-77, Doshisha U., Kyoto, Japan, 1983, U. South Africa, Pretoria, 1984; vis. lectr. Oxford U., 1986, Chinese U. Hong Kong, 1991. Author: Relativism, Knowledge and Faith, 1960, The Context of Decision, 1961, Systematic Theology: a Historicist Perspective, 1968, God the Problem, 1972, An Essay on Theological Method, 1975, 3d edit., 1995, Nonresistance and Responsibility and other Mennonite Essays, 1979, The Theological Imagination: Constructing the Concept of God, 1981, Theology for a Nuclear Age, 1985, In Face of Mystery: A Constructive Theology, 1993, God—Mystery—Diversity: Christian Theology in a Pluralistic World, 1996. Mem. Am. Acad. Religion (pres. 1981-82), Am. Theol. Soc. (pres. 1979-80). Democrat. Home: 6 Longfellow Rd Cambridge MA 02138-4736 Office: 45 Francis Ave Cambridge MA 02138-1911

KAUFMAN, HAROLD RICHARD, mechanical engineer and physics educator; b. Audubon, Iowa, Nov. 24, 1926; s. Walter Richard and Hazel (Steere) K.; m. Elinor Mae Wheat, June 25, 1948; children: Brian, Karin, Bruce, Cynthia. Student, Evanston Community Coll., 1947-49; B.S.M.E., Northwestern U., 1951; Ph.D., Colo. State U., 1971. Researcher in aerospace propulsion NACA, Cleve., 1951-58; mgr. space propulsion research NASA, Cleve., 1958-74; prof. physics and mech. engring. Colo. State U., Ft. Collins, 1974-84; prof. emeritus Colo. State U., 1984—, chmn. dept. physics, 1979-84; pres. Front Range Research, Ft. Collins, 1984—; v.p. R&D Commonwealth Sci. Corp., Alexandria, Va., 1984-96; pioneer in field of electron bombardment ion thruster, 1960; cons. ion source design and applications. Contbr. over 140 publs. and 30 patents in field. Served with USNR, 1944-46. Recipient NASA medal for exceptional sci. achievement, 1971. Fellow Am. Vacuum Soc. (Albert Nerken award 1991), AIAA (assoc. fellow, James H. Wyld Propulsion award 1969); mem. Tau Beta Pi, Pi Tau Sigma. Office: Front Range Rsch 1306 Blue Spruce Dr Ste 2A Fort Collins CO 80524-2067

KAUFMAN, HARRY, retail executive; b. Altoona, Pa., July 16, 1937; s. Nathan and Ethel (Ritchin) K.; m. Margaret Anne Weiss; children: Ira, David. BBA, U. Pitts., 1959, M.Bus. Retailing, 1960. Owner, chief exec. officer Kaufman's & Sons Stores and Wedding World Stores, Altoona, Pa., 1970—, Kaufman's Real Estate & Devel., Altoona, 1980—; developer The Kaufman Gallery, Altoona, 1987. Chmn. Pa. Retailers Polit. Action Com., 1987—; nat. bd. dirs. Union Am. Hebrew Congregations-N.Am., 1987—, regional pres., 1993-97; pres. Temple Beth Israel, Altoona, 1977-79; bd. dirs. Jewish Meml. Ctr., Altoona, 1989—; pres. Greater Altoona Econ. Devel. Corp., 1991-93, chmn. bd. dirs., 1993-95; mem. Sesquicentennial Com., Altoona, 1989; vice chmn. Altoona Redevel. Authority, 1989-94, chmn., 1996—; bd. dirs. Am. Heart Assn., Altoona, 1992—. Named Retailer of Yr., Pa. Retailers Assn., 1987. Mem. Pa. Retailers Assn. (v.p. 1986—), Kiwanis. Home: 3509 Baker Blvd Altoona PA 16602-1827 Office: Kaufman's & Sons Stores 1301 11th Ave Altoona PA 16601-3301

KAUFMAN, HARVEY ISIDORE, neuropsychology consultant; b. Virginia, Minn., May 13, 1937; s. Carl and Marcia (Borkon) K.; m. Glenda Kaufman, Oct. 16, 1971; children: Jason Alexis, Justin Bram. BA, U. Minn., Duluth, 1959, BS cum laude, 1960; MA, U. Minn., Mpls., 1961; PhD, Marquette U., 1967, Southwest U., 1992. Fellow and diplomate Am. Bd. Neuropsychology, Am. Bd. Med. Psychotherapists; Diplomate Internat. Acad. of Behavioral Medicine; cert. in clin. hypnosis. Psychology supr. Winnebago (Wis.) Mental Health Inst., 1971-75; dir. outpatient svcs. Health Care Ctr., Fond du Lac, Wis., 1975-81; neuropsychologist Sharpe Clinic, Fond du Lac, 1983-89, St. Mary's Hosp., Milw., 1986-89; cons. Fond du Lac, 1990—; cons. in neurology Racine, 1992—. Fellow dept. neurology med. sch. U. Wis., 1981-82. Mem. Am. Psychol. Assn., Wis. Psychol. Assn., Nat. Acad. Neuropsychologists, Am. Soc. Clin. Hypnosis, Internat. Soc. Clin. Hypnosis, Internat. Neuropsychol. Soc. Home and Office: 409 Berkley Pl Fond Du Lac WI 54935-5205

KAUFMAN, HERBERT MARK, finance educator; b. Bronx, N.Y., Nov. 1, 1946; s. Henry and Betty (Fried) K.; m. Helen Laurie Fox, July 23, 1967; 1 child, Jonathan Hart. BA, SUNY, Binghamton, 1967; PhD, Pa. State U., 1972. Economist Fed. Nat. Mortgage Assn., Washington, 1972-73; asst. prof. Ariz. State U., Tempe, 1973-76; econs. prof. Ariz. State U., 1980-88; fin. prof. Ariz. State U., Tempe, 1988—, chair dept. fin., 1991—; exec. dir. Ctr. for Fin. System Ariz. State U., 1988—; cons. World Bank, Washington, 1985-86, Gen. Acctg. Office, Washington, 1985, Congl. Budget Office, Washington, 1980, N.Y. Stock Exch., 1995—. Author: Financial Markets, Financial Institutions and Money, 1983, (with others) The Political Economy of Policy Making, 1979, Money and Banking, 1991; contbr. articles to profl. jours. Mem. Am. Econ. Assn., Am. Fin. Assn., Nat. Assn. of Bus. Economists. Avocations: tennis, piano. Home: 1847 E Calle De Caballos Tempe AZ 85284-2505 Office: Ariz State U Dept Fin Tempe AZ 85287

KAUFMAN, IRA GLADSTONE, judge; b. N.Y.C., Dec. 13, 1909; s. Joseph and Esther K.; m. Margaret Kaufman, Sept., 1988; children: Harvey David, Sylvia Kaufman Delin. BS, NYU, 1933, JD, 1936; DSc in Bus. Adminstrn. (hon.), Cleary Coll., Ypsilanti, Mich., 1976. Bar: Mich. 1939. Pvt. practice law, Detroit, 1939-59; judge of brobate Wayne County Probate Ct., Detroit, 1958-84, presiding judge, 1962-63, 66-67, 72-73, 77-85; chief judge pro tem Wayne County Probate and Juvenile Ct., 1981-85; Moot Ct. judge U. Detroit, 1966-72; lectr. Trustee Children's Hosp. of Detroit, chmn. devel., 1980-83, hon. chmn. ann. concert 1983, chmn. ad hoc com. alcoholism Detroit United Cmtys. Svcs., 1967-68; chmn. Detroit Com. Fgn. Rels., 1974-76; trustee Mich. Cancer Found., 1973, hon. life trustee emeritus, 1985; trustee Detroit Inst. Tech., 1962-72, Park Cmty. Hosp., 1962-73; pres. Inter-Agy. Council on Alcoholism, 1967; pres., chmn. bd. Met. Soc. for Blind, 1966-70, bd. dirs., 1960—; mem. Gov.'s Com. Mental Health Statute Rev. Commn., 1970-72, Mich. Soc. Mental Health, 1960—; hon. life mem. Children's Charter Mich., 1965-75; exec. bd. League Handicapped-Goodwill 1949-60; bd. overseers Dropsie Coll., 1973-75; bd. dirs. Hebrew Free Loan Soc., Detroit, 1979-84, Jewish Nat. Fund Bd.; v.p. United Hebrew Schs. Detroit, 1947-58; founding sec. Midrasha Coll. Hebrew Studies, 1948-58; pres. Adat Shalom Synagogue, 1945-51, founder cemetary, 1948, hon. life pres. 1953; founding chmn. Einstein Luncheon Forum, 1986—. Fellow Mich. State Bar Found. (life mem.); mem. ABA, Mich. Probate and Juvenile Ct. Assn. (exec. bd. 1969-72, pres. 1970-71), Mich. Bar Assn., Detroit Bar Assn., Supreme Ct. Hist. Soc., Mental Health Assn. Mich. (Advocacy award 1989), U.S. Air Force Assn. (ann. installing officer 1983-84), B'nai B'rith (hon. pres. Tikvah Lodge 1974), Valley of Detroit, Masons (33 degree, sovereign prince), Shriners, Jesters. Contbr. biog. sketches of Mich. judges to Jewish Hist. Soc. publ., 1983-84. Home: 4224 Wabeek Lake Dr S Bloomfield Hills MI 48302-1663

KAUFMAN, IRVING, retired engineering educator; b. Geinsheim, Germany, Jan. 11, 1925; came to US., 1938, naturalized, 1945; s. Albert and Hedwig Kaufmann; m. Ruby Lee Dordek, Sept. 10, 1950; children—Eve Deborah, Sharon Anne, Julie Ellen. BE, Vanderbilt U., 1945; MS, U. Ill., 1949, PhD, 1957. Engr. RCA Victor, Indpls., Ind. and Camden, N.J., 1945-48; instr., research assoc. U. Ill., Urbana, 1949-56; sr. mem. tech. staff Ramo-Wooldridge & Space Tech. Labs., Calif., 1957-64; prof. engring. Ariz. State U., 1965-94, ret., 1994; founder, dir. Solid State Research Lab., 1968-78; collaborator Los Alamos Nat. Lab., 1989, 91; vis. scientist Consiglio Nazionale delle Ricerche, Italy, 1973-74; vis. prof. U. Auckland, N.Z., 1974; liaison scientist U.S. Office Naval Rsch., London, 1978-80; lectr. and cons. elec. engring. Contbr. articles to profl. jours. and encys. Recipient Disting. Research award Ariz. State U. Grad. Coll., 1986-87; Sr. Fulbright research fellow Italy, 1964-65, 73-74, Am. Soc. for Engring. Edn./Naval Rsch. Lab. fellow, 1988. Fellow IEEE (life, Phoenix sect. leadership award 1994); mem. Electromagnetics Acad., Gold Key (hon.), Sigma Xi, Tau Beta Pi, Eta Kappa Nu, Pi Mu Epsilon. Jewish. Patentee in field. E-mail: irving.kaufman@asu.edu. Office: Ariz State U Dept Elec Engring Tempe AZ 85287-5706

KAUFMAN, JAMES JAY, lawyer; b. Newark, N.Y., Jan. 23, 1939; s. Joseph Julius and Ann Gertrude (Quick) K.; m. Patricia Ann Patterson, Sept. 3, 1966; children: Kristine, Jeffrey. BA, Bucknell U., 1960; LLB, JD, Union Coll., Albany, 1964. Bar: N.Y. 1965, U.S. Ct. Appeals (2nd cir.) 1966, U.S. Dist. Ct. (we. and no. dists.) N.Y. 1968, N.C. 1985, Pa. 1985, U.S. Supreme Ct. 1985, U.S. Dist. Ct. (ea. dist.) N.C. 1991, U.S. Ct. Appeals (4th cir.) 1991, U.S. Ct. Appeals (7th cir.) 1992, U.S. Dist. Ct. (mid. dist.) N.C. 1993. Legal counsel, legis. and adminstrv. asst. Rep. Theodore R. Kupferman, U.S. Congress, Washington, 1965-67; assoc. Houghton, Pappas & Fink, Rochester, N.Y., 1967-70; ptnr. Culley, Marks, Rochester, 1970-75; sr. ptnr. James J. Kaufman, P.C., Newark, 1975-84, Kaufman & Forsyth, Rochester, 1984-91, Barefoot & Kaufman, Wilmington, N.C., 1991-93, Kaufman, Barefoot & Green, Wilmington, 1993-94; of counsel Hancock & Estabrook, Syracuse, N.Y., 1994-96; sr. ptnr. Kaufman & Green, L.L.P., Wilmington, 1994—; V.p. Fed. Bar Coun., 1968; mem. 7th Jud. Dist. Grievance Com., 1983-89; del. U.S./China Joint Session on Trade, Investment and Econ. Law, Beijing, 1987; strategic planning cons., counsel Hometown Funding, Inc., Rochester, 1994-95; panel mem. Commerce Tech. Adv. Bd. on Noise Abatement, Washington, 1968; chmn. noise task force Genesee Region Health Planning, Rochester, 1970-71, mem./counsel noise task force, mem./counsel environ. health planning com., 1972-73. Author: What to Do Before the Money Runs Out—A Road Map for America's Automobile Dealers, 1993; contbr. articles to profl. publs. Justice Town of Arcadia, Newark, 1976-89. Mem. N.Y. State Bar Assn. (mem. spl. com. on environ. law 1974-77, mem. com. on profl. discipline, mem. com. on ct. in cmty. banking com. 1986—), Wayne County Bar Assn. (pres. 1986-87, v.p. 1985-86, chmn. family law sect. 1975-80, chmn. com. on profl. discipline 1975-89), N.C. Bar Assn., Pa. Bar Assn., New Hanover County Bar Assn., Monroe County Bar Assn., Wilmington Inns of Ct. (pres. 1994-97). Republican. Presbyterian. Avocations: boating, scuba diving, fishing. Office: Kaufman & Green LLP 1985 Eastwood Rd Ste 200 Wilmington NC 28403-7208

KAUFMAN, JEROME BENZION, neurosurgeon; b. Waterloo, Iowa, July 22, 1934; s. Louis and Dorothy (Rosenbloom) K.; m. Judith Ellen Lasker, June 29, 1967; children: David, Jonathan, Jefferey. BA, Wayne State U., 1955, MD, 1961; postgrad., U. Madrid. Diplomate Am. Bd. Neurol. Surgery, 1975. Rotating intern Michael Reese Hosp. and Med. Ctr., Chgo., 1961-62; resident in internal med. Michael Reese Hosp. and Med. Ctr., Chgo., 1962-63; resident in gen. surgery VA Hosp., Bronx, 1965-66, resident in neurology, 1966, resident in neurosurgery, 1967, from sr. to chief resident neurosurgery, 1969-70; resident neurosurgery Neurol. Inst. N.Y., Columbia Presbyn. Hosp., 1968; resident neuropathology Mt. Sinai Hosp. and Med. Sch., N.Y.C., 1968; chief resident neurosurgery City Hosp., Elmhurst, N.Y., 1969; chmn. dept. neurosurgery Carle Clinic Assn. and Found. Hosp., Urbana, Ill., 1972—; cons. neurosurgery McKinley Hosp., Urbana, Covenant Hosp., Urbana; asst. instr. internal medicine Chgo. Med. Sch., 1963; clin. assoc. prof. neurosurgery U. Ill. Coll. Medicine, Urbana, 1982—. Contbr. articles to profl. jours. Served to capt. USAF, 1963-65. Named one of Best Drs. in Am.- Midwest (Ill.). Fellow ACS, Am. Assn. Neurol. Surgeons (Continuing Edn. award in neurosurgery 1980, 83, 85, 87, 89, 93, 96), Internat. Coll. Surgeons (vice regent) N.Y. Acad. Scis.; mem. AMA (Physicians Recognition award 1980, 82, 85, 89, 93), Ill. Med. Soc., Champaign County Med. Soc., Congress Neurol. Surgeons, Ctrl. Neurosurg. Soc., Assn. Mil. Surgeons U.S., Chgo. Neurol. Soc. (Best Doctors in Am. Midwest). Home: 2104 Zuppke Dr Urbana IL 61801-6706 Office: 602 W University Ave Carle Clinic Assn Urbana IL 61801

KAUFMAN, JEROME SEYMOUR, retired ophthalmologist; b. Detroit, June 13, 1929; s. Sam and Libby Friedman K.; m. Suzanne Heller (div.); four children. DO, Kans. City Coll. Osteopathy, 1954. Pvt. practice ophthalmology Garden City, Mich., 1957-90. Pres. Zionist Orgn. Am., State of Mich. nat. sec. 20A, 1996—. Fellow Am. Coll. Ophthalmology. Jewish. Avocations: politics, golf, tennis, tournament bridge. Home: 1728 Saint Johns Ct Bloomfield Hills MI 48302-1776

KAUFMAN, JESS, communication, financial and marketing consultant; b. Bklyn., June 12, 1920; s. Samuel and Alice (Simon) K.; m. Selma Helen Bruckner, June 20, 1948; children: Steven, David, Susan. BS, NYU, 1949, also postgrad. Staff tax dept. G.A. Saxton & Co., N.Y.C., 1938-41; chief acct. 3d Naval Dist., 1943-46; comptroller, ast. treas. Hytron divsn. CBS, N.Y.C., 1946-48; v.p. mktg. Contel, Jericho, N.Y., 1948-81; cons. Weinrich-Zitzmann-Whitehead Inc. Fin. Svcs., 1981-84; pres. Kaufman Assocs. Internat., 1981-94; chmn. bd., CEO Express Telecom Inc., 1983-84; fin. cons. Stratford, Conn., 1985-88; dir. sr. observer program Nass Am. C.C., Garden City, N.Y., 1989-94; cons. exec. info. sys. Conn., 1991-96; cons. telecom., electronics, computer data transmission Rubbins Eye Ctrs. and Ambulatory Surg. Ctrs., Monroe, Ansonia, Bridgept, Conn.; surrogate for Pres. Clinton's Health Reform Act, N.Y.; guest lectr. Grad. Sch. Pub. Health, NYU, Grad. Sch. Pub. Health Columbia U., N.Y.C., Grad. Sch. Pub. Health, Yale U., New Haven, Army Surgeon Gen. Inst. for Rsch., Washington, Sch. of Architecture, Stanford (Calif.) U., Am. Hosp. Assn. Inst. on Elec. and Mech. Engring. Design for Hosps., Chgo.; cons. comms. and med. electronics AID, industry interface Exec. Br. of U.S. Govt.; participant in confs.; vis. lectr. hosp. comm. systems andhealth care to various hosp. assns. Contbr. articles on hosp. comms. to profl. publs. Participant Gov.'s Conf. on Aging, State of N.Y.; bd. dirs. Producers Coun., Inc., Washington. Served with USN, 1941-43. Decorated Purple Heart; elected to Student Hall of Fame, NYU. Fellow APHA, AAAS, Royal Soc. Health; mem. AMA, Assn. Mil. Surgeons U.S., Internat. Hosp. Fedn., Am. Hosp. Assn., Fgn. Policy Assn., Am. Mgmt. Assn., Pub. Health Assn. N.Y., NYU Alumni Assn. (mem. fund campaign com.), Alpha Phi Sigma. Home: Oronoque Village 314B South Trl Stratford CT 06614-8108

KAUFMAN, JOEL M., physician executive, neurologist; b. Boston, Sept. 2, 1951; m. Carol Goodman, 1977. AB, Boston U., 1973, MD, 1977. Diplomate Am. Bd. Psychiatry and Neurology. Neurologist Fallor Clinic, Inc., Worcester, Mass., 1981-96; med. dir. Fallon Cmty. Health Plan, Worcester, 1988-96; pres., CEO Lifespan/Physicians Profl. Svc. Orgn., Providence, 1997—. Bd. chair, Congregation Beth Israel, Worcester, 1982—; com. mem. Boy Scouts Am., Worcester, 1990-98; bd. dirs. Jewish Healthcare Ctr., Worcester, 1991—. Recipient Young Leader award Worcester Jaycees, 1990. Mem. AMA, Am. Acad. Neurology, Am. Coll. Physician Execs., Mass. Med. Soc., R.I. Med. Soc., Worcester Dist. Med. Soc. E-mail: jkaufman@lifespan.org. Office: Lifespan/Physicians Profl Svc Orgn 55 Claverick St Providence RI 02903

KAUFMAN, JOHN ROBERT, marketing and information management consultant; b. New Cumberland, Pa., Dec. 13, 1931; s. Jean Coulsen and Mercedes Katherine (Beshore) K.; m. Antoinette Anna Dolores Falcone, Apr. 30, 1988. AB, Pa. State U., 1953; MBA, U. Pa., 1955. V.p. N.W. Ayer & Son, Inc., Phila., 1965-80; pres. HBS, Inc. (Help Bus. Services, Inc.), Swarthmore, Pa., 1980—, Swarthmore Bus. Dist. Authority, 1991—. Pres. Swarthmore Bus. Dist. Authority, 1991—. Capt. USNR, ret. Mem. Am. Mktg. Assn. (nat. v.p., publisher 1975-80), Am. Mktg. Assn. (pres. Phila. chpt. 1968), Parlin Bd. Govs. (chmn. 1982-84), Soc. Competitor Intelligence Profls. Club: University (N.Y.C.), Penn Club (N.Y.C.). Lodge: Rotary (local pres. 1985). Avocations: reading, gourmet cooking, tennis, outdoor landscape design. Home: 112 Park Ave Swarthmore PA 19081-1724 Office: HBS Inc Hbs Bldg 110 Swarthmore PA 19081

KAUFMAN, JONATHAN ALLAN (JON), public relations executive; b. N.Y.C., May 31, 1943; s. Stephen Allan (dec.) and Jean (Friedman) K.; m. Jill J. Horowitz, July 17, 1983. BA, Carleton Coll., 1966; MA, Syracuse U., 1967. Vol. VISTA, N.Y.C., 1967-69; rsch. dir. Nat. Welfare Rights Orgn., Washington, 1969-71; polit. campaign mgr. various, San Francisco, 1971-77; exec. dir. Calif. Tax Reform Assn., San Francisco, 1972-77; asst. mgr. Household Fin. Corp., San Francisco, 1977-79; account exec. Solem & Assocs., San Francisco, 1979-84, v.p., 1984-86, exec. v.p., 1986—. Contbr. articles to profl. jours. Bd. dirs. Ann Martin Children's Ctr., Oakland, Calif., Am. Israel Pub. Affairs Com. of No. Calif., San Francisco; chmn. com. mktg. Jewish Fedn. Greater East Bay. Andrew W. Mellon Fellow, Syracuse U., 1966, Max Bondy Citizenship award Windsor Mt. Sch., Lenox, Mass., 1962. Mem. Am. Assn. Polit. Cons., Am. Mktg. Assn. Jewish. Avocations: hiking, travel, food. E-mail: jonúkaufman@solem.com. Home: 107 Alvarado Rd Berkeley CA 94705-1510 Office: Solem & Assocs 550 Kearny St Ste 1010 San Francisco CA 94108-2527

KAUFMAN, JULIAN MORTIMER, broadcasting company executive, consultant; b. Detroit, Apr. 3, 1918; s. Anton and Fannie (Newman) K.; m. Katherine LaVerne Likins, May 6, 1942; children: Nikki, Keith Anthony. Grad. high sch., Newark. Pub. Elizabeth (N.J.) Sunday Sun, Inc., 1937-39; account exec. Tolle Advt. Agy., San Diego, 1947-49; pub. Tucson Shopper, 1948-50; account exec. ABC, San Francisco, 1949-50; mgr. Sta. KPHO-TV, Phoenix, 1950-52; gen. mgr., v.p. Bay City TV Corp., San Diego, 1952-85; v.p. Jai Alai Films, Inc., San Diego, 1961—; TV cons. Julian Kaufman, Inc., San Diego, 1985—; dir. Spanish Internat. Broadcasting, Inc., L.A.; chmn. bd. dirs. Bay City TV Inc. Contbr. articles to profl. jours.; producer (TV show) Pick a Winner. Mem. Gov.'s adv. bd., Mental Health Assn., 1958—; bd. dirs. Francis Parker Sch., San Diego Better Bus. Bur., 1979-84, San Diego Conv. and Visitors Bur., World Affairs Coun., Pala Indian Mission. Served with USAAF, 1942-46. Recipient Peabody award, 1975, Emmy award, 1980. Mem. San Diego C. of C., Advt. and Sales Club, Sigma Delta Chi. Republican. Clubs: San Diego Press, University (San Diego). Home: 3125 Montesano Rd Escondido CA 92029-7302 Office: 7677 Ronson Rd Ste 210 San Diego CA 92111-1538

KAUFMAN, LLOYD, film director, producer; b. Dec. 30, 1945. BA, Yale U., 1968. Co-founder film studio Troma Entertainment, Inc., N.Y.C., 1974—. Dir., prodr., writer Sgt. Kabukiman N.Y.P.D., Tromeo and Juliet, The Toxic Avenger I, II, III, Troma's War, Class of Nuke 'Em High, Terror Firmer, others; prodr. Fortress of Amerikka; writer, prodr. Class of Nuke 'Em High II and III, others; writer: All I need to know about filmmaking I learned from the Toxic Avenger; writer, dir. Terror Firmer, 1998. Office: Troma Entertainment Inc 733 9th Ave Fl 2 New York NY 10019-7297

KAUFMAN, MICHELE BETH, clinical pharmacist, educator; b. Perth Amboy, N.J., May 13, 1963; d. Harold Alexander and Elaine Sue (Sommers) K. BS in Pharmacy, U. R.I., 1986; PharmD, Mass. Coll. Pharmacy, 1991. RPh, Mass., N.J., N.Y. Staff pharmacist Robert Wood Johnson U. Hosp., New Brunswick, N.J., 1986-91; product devel. pharmacist Reed & Carnrick Pharm. Co., Piscataway, N.J., 1987-89; poison info. specialist Mass. Poison Control System Children's Hosp., Boston, 1990-92; drug info. specialist U. R.I. Drug Info. Ctr., Providence, 1991-92; asst. clin. prof. pharmacy St. John's U., Jamaica, N.Y., 1992-96; clin. coord. internal medicine, drug info. specialist L.I. Jewish Med. Ctr., New Hyde Park, N.Y., 1992-96; clin. pharmacy coord. HIP of N.Y., N.Y.C., 1996—, Drug Info. Cons., 1996—; reviewer Micromedex Info. Sys. Contbg. editor The Pharmacist jour.; mem. editl. bd. The Formulary; contbr. articles and revs. to profl. jours.; patent pending for pineapple colon electrolyte lavage solution. Player tenor sax St. John's Univ. Jazz Ensemble, 1992-97. Fellow Drug Info., 1992; recipient Indsl. Pharm. Tech. award Am. Pharm. Assn., 1986. Mem. Acad. Managed Care Pharmacy, Am. Soc. Health Sys. Pharmacists, New Eng. Coun. Health Sys. Pharmacists, Am. Coll. Clin. Pharmacy, N.Y. State Coun. Health Sys. Pharmacists, Lambda Kappa Sigma (pres. Xi chpt. 1985-86, v.p. 1984-85, fund raiser 1983-84). Avocations: travel, cultural events, racquet sports, postcard collecting, playing tenor sax. Home: 97 Preusser Rd Craryville NY 12521-5218 Address: 445 W 23rd St # 14E New York NY 10011

KAUFMAN, MICHELLE STARK, lawyer; b. N.Y.C., June 11, 1954; d. Maurice E. and Mary (Murray) Stark; m. Daniel M. Kaufman, Oct. 6, 1984; children: Jane Stark, David Stark, Carolyn Stark. BA, Iowa State U., Ames, 1976; JD, U. Mo., Kansas City, 1983. Bar: Mo. 1983, U.S. Dist. Ct. (we. dist.) Mo. 1983. Graphic artist Douglas Stone & Assocs., Newport Beach, Calif., 1976-78; chief news bur. Midwest Records, Kansas City, Mo., 1978-80; ptnr. Stinson, Mag and Fizzell, P.C., Kansas City, 1983-95, Sonnenschein Nath & Rosenthal, Kansas City, 1995—; lectr. in law U. Mo. Sch. Law, Kansas City, 1984-85; trustee U. Mo.-Kansas City Law Sch. Found., 1992—, exec. com., 1996—, sec., 1998—. Bd. dirs. Heart of Am. Family Svcs., Kansas City, 1989-98, vice-chmn., 1991-93, chmn., 1994-95, bd. mem. of the year award, 1995; bd. dirs., sec. Countryside Homes Assn., Kansas City, 1985. Mem. ABA (forum on franchising), Am. Health Lawyers Assn., Mo. Bar Assn., Greater Kansas City C. of C. (chmn. club 1990-96, vice chmn. 1991-92, chmn. 1992-93, Mo. state affairs com. 1995—, Chmn.'s Club Hall of Fame, 1996), U. Mo. Kansas City Law Alumni Assn. (bd. dirs. 1992-96, pres. 1994-95), Kansas City Tomorrow Alumni Assn. (bd. dirs., pres.-elect 1997-98, pres. 1998-99), Delta Delta Delta (exec.bd. 1979). Office: Sonnenschein Nath & Rosenthal 4520 Main St Ste 1100 Kansas City MO 64111-7700

KAUFMAN, NATHAN, pathology educator, physician; b. Lachine, Que., Can., Aug. 3, 1915; s. Solomon and Anna (Sabesinsky) K.; m. Rita Friendly, Sept. 10, 1946; children: Naomi, Michael, Miriam, Hannah, Judith. B.Sc., McGil U., Montreal, 1937, M.D., C.M., 1941. Mem. faculty Western Res. U. Med. Sch., 1948-60, asst. prof., 1952-54, asso. prof., 1954-60; pathologist-in-charge Cleve. Met. Gen. Hosp., 1952-60; prof. pathology Duke Sch. Medicine, 1960-67; prof. dept. pathology Queen's U. Med. Sch., Kingston, Ont., Can., 1967-81; prof. emeritus Queen's U. Med. Sch., 1981—, head dept., 1967-79; clin. prof. office of humanities Med. Coll. Ga., Augusta, 1980-85; pathologist-in-chief Kingston Gen. Hosp., 1967-79; past cons. Hotel Dieu Hosp., St. Mary's of the Lake Hosp., Kingston Clinic, Ont. Cancer Treatment and Research Found.; asso. editor Lab. Investigation Jour., 1952-66, editor, 1972-75, mem. editorial bd., 1975—; asso. editor Am. Jour. Pathology, 1967, mem. editorial bd., 1967-71; Mem. grants panel Med. Research Council Can., 1970-74, mem. council, 1971-77, exec. com., 1971-74; active coms. Ont. Council Health, 1968-79, chmn. provincial rev. ednl. sub-com., 1972-75. Editor Modern Pathology, 1988, mem. editl. bd., 1989-95. Served to capt. M.C., Royal Can. Army, 1942-46. Decorated Order Brit. Empire; recipient Disting. Alumni award Duke U., 1975, Internat. Acad. Pathology Gold medal, 1996. Mem. Internat. Acad. Pathology (v.p. 1972-74, pres. elect 1974, pres. 1976-78, pres. U.S.-Can. div. 1973-75, sec.-treas. 1979-91, F.K. Mostofi Disting. Svc. award U.S.-Can. div. 1990), U.S. and Can. Acad. Pathology, Royal Coll. Physicians and Surgeons Can. (com. on exams. 1972), Cleve. Soc. Pathologists (past pres.), Am. Assn. Pathologists (editor Symposium series 1970-71), Am. Soc. for Investigative Pathology, Am. Soc. Clin. Pathologists, Am. Assn. Cancer Research, Am. Soc. Cytology, Coll. Am. Pathologists, Canadian Med. Assn., Can., Ont. assns. pathologists, Ont. Med. Assn., Can. Soc. Cytology. Home: 185 Ontario St # 704, Kingston, ON Canada K7L 2Y7

KAUFMAN, PAULA T., librarian; b. Perth Amboy, N.J., July 26, 1946; d. Harry and Clara (Katz) K.; m. L. Ratner, 1989. AB, Smith Coll., 1968; MS, Columbia U., 1969; MBA, U. New Haven, 1979. Reference libr. Columbia U., N.Y.C., 1969-70, bus. libr., 1979-82, dir. libr. svcs., 1982-86, dir. acad. info. svcs., 1986-87, acting v.p., univ. libr., 1987-88; dean of librs. U. Tenn., Knoxville, 1988-99; univ. libr. U. Ill., Champaign Urbana, 1999—; reference coord. McKinsey & Co., N.Y.C., 1970-73; founder, ptnr. Info. for Bus., N.Y.C., 1973-76; prin. reference libr. Yale U., New Haven, 1976-79; bd. dirs. Ctr. Rsch. Librs., 1994—, chmn., 1996-97; bd. dirs. CAUSE, 1996-98; bd. dirs. Assn. Rsch. Librs., 1997—. Contbr. articles to mags., 1983—. Bd. dirs. Cmty. Shares, Knoxville, 1993-97. Mem. ALA, Soc. for Scholarly Pub., Solinet (bd. dirs., chmn. 1992-93).

KAUFMAN, PETER BISHOP, biological sciences educator; b. San Francisco, Feb. 25, 1928; s. Earle Francis and Gwendolyn Bishop (Morris) K.; m. Hazel Elizabeth Snyder, Apr. 5, 1958; children—Linda Myrl, Laura Irene. B.S., Cornell U., 1949; Ph.D. in Botany, U. Calif.-Davis, 1954. Instr. botany U. Mich., Ann Arbor, 1956-58, asst. prof., 1958-62, assoc. prof., 1962-72, prof. botany, cellular and molecular biology and bioengring. program, 1972-97, emeritus prof. dept. biology, 1998—, instr. seminar Residential Coll., 1997—; cons. NASA Space Biology Program; vis. prof. U. Lund, Sweden, 1964-65, U. Colo., Boulder, 1973-74; mem. faculty agr. Nagoya U., Japan, 1981. Author: Laboratory Experiments in Plant Physiology, 1975, Plants, People and Environment, 1979, Botany Illustrated, 1983, Practical Botany, 1983, Plants: Their Biology and Importance, 1989; co-author: Handbook of Molecular and Cellular Methods in Biology and Medicine, 1995, Methods in Gene Biotechnology, 1997, Natural Products from Plants, 1998. Mem. Mich. Natural Areas Coun.; mem. exec. com. U. Mich. Program in Scholarly Rsch. for Urban Minority Students. Grantee NSF, NASA. Fellow AAAS; mem. Am. Inst. Biol. Scis., Am. Soc. Plant Physiologists, Am. Soc. for Gravitational and Space Biology (sec.-treas.), Internat. Soc. Plant Molecular Biologists, Bot. Soc. Am., Mich. Bot. Club (pres. 1985-89), Sigma Xi. Democrat. Presbyterian. Home: 8040 Huron River Dr Dexter MI 48130-9322 Office: U Mich 1063 Natural Sci Bldg 830 N University Ave Ann Arbor MI 48109-1048

KAUFMAN, PHILIP, film director; b. Chgo., Oct. 23, 1936. Ed., U. Chgo., Harvard U. Law Sch. Dir., screenwriter: Fearless Frank, 1966, The Great Northfield Minnesota Raid, 1972, The Right Stuff, 1983; dir.: The White Dawn, 1974, Invasion of the Body Snatchers, 1978; co-screenwriter: Outlaw Josey Wales; dir., co-screenwriter: The Wanderers, 1979, The Unbearable Lightness of Being, 1987, Henry and June, 1990, Rising Sun, 1993; co-dir., co-screenwriter, co-prodr.: Goldstein, 1964; co-story Raiders of the Lost Ark; narrator, exec. prodr. China: The Wild East, 1995. Mem. Dirs. Guild Am., Writers Guild Am. Office: William Morris Agy 151 S El Camino Dr Beverly Hills CA 90212-2775*

KAUFMAN, RAYMOND HENRY, physician; b. Bklyn., Nov. 24, 1925; s. Morris and Anne (Markewich) K.; m. Patricia Ann Judson, June 23, 1946; children: Susan Jo (Mrs. Edward B. Kahn), Wendy Beth (Mrs. Seth Katzman), Murri Ellen (Mrs. Raymond Simonetti), Elisabeth Ann. Student, Coll. William and Mary, 1942-43, U. N.C., 1943-44; M.D., U. Md., 1948. Diplomate: Am. Bd. Obstetrics and Gynecology. Intern Beth Israel Hosp., N.Y.C., 1948-49; resident obstetrics and gynecology Beth Israel Hosp., 1949-53; fellow pathology Meth. Hosp., Houston, 1955-58; asst. prof. obstetrics, gynecology, pathology Baylor Coll. Medicine, Houston, 1959-65; assoc. prof. Baylor Coll. Medicine, 1965-72, acting chmn. dept., 1968-72, prof., chmn. dept. ob-gyn, 1973-93, prof. pathology, 1973—, prof. dept. ob-gyn, 1973—. Author: (with H.L. Gardner) Benign Diseases of Vulva and Vagina, 1969, 4th edit. (with S. Faro, E. Friedrich and Gardner), 1994; contbr. over 200 articles to profl. jours. Served with USNR, 1943-45; to capt. USAF, 1953-55. Mem. Am. Coll. Obstetrics and Gynecology, ACS, Cen. Assn. Obstetrics and Gynecology (chmn. com. for cons. gynecol. pathology 1968-87, pres. 1976), Tex. Assn. Obstetrics and Gynecology (v.p. 1971, 81, pres. 1983), Am. Gynecol. and Obstet. Soc. (v.p. 1985-86), Houston Obstet. and Gynecol. Soc. (pres. 1971-72), Soc. Gynecol. Oncology (v.p. 1983-84), Am. Cytology Soc., Am. Fertility Soc., Am. Soc. Colposcopy, Internat. Soc. Vulvar Disease (pres. 1978-79), Phi Delta Epsilon (nat. sec. 1970-75). Office: Baylor Coll Med 1 Baylor Plz Houston TX 77030-3411

KAUFMAN, RAYMOND L., energy company executive; b. Cleve., Mar. 9, 1940; s. Eugene and Elizabeth T. Kaufman; m. Janet Spangler, Sept. 1, 1962; 1 child, Jason. Student, Kent State U., 1958. Personnel dir. NESCO, Cleve., 1965-71; owner, pres., founder Advancement Corp., Cleve., 1971—; pres., owner Art Healan. Served with U.S. Army, 1961-63. Mem. AIC, Cleve. C. of C. Lodge: Rotary. *

KAUFMAN, RICHARD C., federal lawyer; b. June 4, 1949. BS, Ind. State U., 1972; JD, Emory U., 1976. Ptnr. Ball, Easley & Kaufman, Loveland, Colo., 1977-80; legis. asst. U.S. Rep. Hank Brown, Washington, 1981; dep. atty. gen. Colo. Atty. Gens. Office, Denver, 1982-88, 90-91; legis. affairs Texaco, USA, Denver, 1988-90. Office: 1961 Stout St # 1100 PO Drawer 3608 Denver CO 80294

KAUFMAN, ROBERT JULES, communications consultant, lawyer; b. N.Y.C., Jan. 21, 1921; s. Ernst B. and Gertrude S. (Popper) K.; m. Susan H. Sanger, Feb. 22, 1951; children—Peter S., James H. Student, Columbia Coll., 1942, Yale U. Law Sch., 1948. Bar: N.Y. bar 1949. Assoc. Gale, Bernays, Falk & Eisner, N.Y.C., 1948-53; ptnr. Gale & Falk, 1953-55; asst. gen. counsel DuMont TV Network, 1953-55; with ABC, N.Y.C., 1955-86; v.p., gen. atty. network govtl. regulation ABC, 1968-86; comm. cons. Scarsdale, N.Y., 1986—; mem. internat. copyright panel Dept. State; guest speaker on radio and television matters at Practicing Law Inst. and N.Y. U. Law Sch. Served to lt. USN, 1942-46. Mem. Bar Assn. City N.Y. (communications com.), Copyright Soc. U.S.A., Nat. Acad. TV Arts and Scis. (mem. U.S. Olympic job opportunity program com.), Phi Beta Kappa. Home and Office: 33 Clarendon Rd Scarsdale NY 10583-2452

KAUFMAN, ROBERT MAX, lawyer; b. Vienna, Austria, Nov. 17, 1929; came to U.S., 1939, naturalized, 1945; s. Paul M. and Bertha (Hirsch) K.; m. Sheila Seymour Kelley. BA with honors, Bklyn. Coll., 1951; MA, NYU, 1954; JD magna cum laude, Bklyn. Law Sch., 1957. Bar: N.Y. 1957, U.S. Supreme Ct. 1961. Successively jr. economist, economist, sr. economist N.Y. State Div. Housing, 1953-57; atty. antitrust div. U.S. Dept. Justice, 1957-58; legis. asst. to U.S. Senator Jacob K. Javits, 1958-61; assoc. Proskauer Rose LLP, N.Y.C., 1961-69, ptnr., 1969—; chmn. bd. Pirelli Cables & Systems, LLC, Pirelli Tires LLC, Old Westbury Funds, Inc.; bd. dirs. Roytex Inc., Meadowbrook Equity Fund, L.L.C.; mem. N.Y. State Legis. Adv. Com. on Election Law, 1973-74; chmn. adv. com. N.Y. State Bd. Elections, 1974-78; chmn. N.Y. State Bd. Pub. Disclosure, 1981-82, U.S. Army Chief of Staff's Spl. Commn. on Honor System, 1988-89, N.Y. Chief Judge's Com. on Availability of Legal Svcs., 1988-90; referee Commn. on Jud. Conduct; spl. master N.Y. Supreme Ct. Appellate Divsn., 1999—; mem. Adminstrv. Conf. U.S. (chair com. regulations), 1988-95; chmn. Fund for Modern Cts., 1990-95; mem. Def. Adv. Com. on Women in the Svcs., 1997-99, vice chair com. on equality mgmt., mem. exec. com. 1998—. Co-author: Congress and the Public Trust, 1970, Disorder in the Court, 1973; co-gen. editor: Matthew Bender Treatise on Health Care Law, 4 vols., 1992—. Bd. dirs., mem. exec. com. Lawrence M. Gelb Found., Inc., Lawyers in the Public Interest, 1986-

95, Am. Judicature Soc., pres. 1995-97, Citizens Union of N.Y.C., vice chair, 1997—, Citizen's Union Found., 1993—; bd. dirs., chmn. exec. com. Cmty. Action for Legal Svcs., Inc., 1976-78; dir., mem. exec. com. Legal Aid Soc., 1985-90, mem. exec. com. Vols. of Legal Svc., 1986-94; mem. platform com. N.Y. Rep. State Com., 1974; mem. jud. selection adv. coms. Senator Javits, 1972-80, and Senator Moynahan, 1977—; compensation elected ofcl. N.Y.C. Quadrennial Comm., 1995, 99; mem. distbn. com. N.Y. Cmty. Trust; bd. dirs. N.Y. Cmty. Funds, James Found.; bd. vis. U.S. Mil. Acad., 1976-79; dir., mem. exec. com., chmn. bd. Times Square Bus. Improvement Dist.; trustee Bklyn. Law Sch. With U.S. Army, 1957-58. Fellow Am. Bar Found., N.Y. State Bar Found.; mem. ABA, Assn. of Bar of City N.Y. (pres. 1986-88, chmn. com. on bldg. cons., co-chmn. com. on campaign fin. reform 1997—, past chmn. com. on 2d Century; past chmn. exec. com., past chmn. com. profl. responsibility, past chmn. spl. com. on campaign expenditures, past chmn. com. civil rights, com. on past vice chmn. com. grievances, chmn. delegation to state bar ho. dels.), N.Y. State Bar Assn. (ho. of dels. 1978, 86-90), N.Y. County Lawyers Assn. (past chmn. com. on civil rights), Am. Law Inst. Office: Proskauer Rose LLP 1585 Broadway New York NY 10036-8200

KAUFMAN, ROGER WAYNE, state judge; b. Elizabeth, N.J., Aug. 27, 1938; s. Albert Henry and Selma Bernice (Cloner) K.; m. Lou Jan Erwin, Apr. 20, 1968; children: David Michael, Erin Anne. BA, Cornell U., 1960; JD, Harvard U., 1963. Bar: Ariz. 1964, U.S. Dist. Ct. Ariz. 1964, U.S. Ct. Appeals (9th cir.) 1965, U.S. Supreme Ct. 1971. Assoc. Lewis and Roca, Phoenix, 1963-68, ptnr., 1968-93; judge pro tem Superior Ct. State of Ariz. for Maricopa County, Phoenix, 1977-80; judge Maricopa County Superior Ct., Phoenix, 1993—; also chmn. alternative dispute resolution com. Maricopa County Superior Ct., 1993-95, presiding judge Civil Dept., 1995-98, presiding judge Criminal Dept., 1998—; chmn. Civil Jury Instrns. Com., 1993-96. Author: Arizona Courtroom Handbook, 1967, 70, Consent Manual, 1979. Mem. bd. visitors Ariz. State U. Law Sch., Tempe, 1979-85; bd. dirs. Bapt. Hosp. Found., Phoenix, 1980-83, Am. Cancer Soc., Phoenix, 1985-90. Mem. ABA, Ariz. Bar Assn. (bd. govs. 1979-81), Am. Judicature Soc., Ariz. Judges Assn. (sec., v.p., pres. 1995-96). Democrat. Home: 6112 N 31st Pl Phoenix AZ 85016-2322

KAUFMAN, RONALD PAUL, physician, school official; b. Hartford, Conn., Nov. 30, 1929; s. Louis Elliot and Sarah K.; m. Beth Winkler, Dec. 28, 1968; children: Ronald Paul, Michael, Karyn, Leesa, Jennifer. BS, Trinity Coll., 1951; MD, U. Pa., 1955. Intern Hartford Hosp., 1955-56, resident in internal medicine, 1956-58, chief resident, 1960-61, Asst. dir. dept. medicine, 1966-70, dir. med. edn. dept., 1967-70; med. dir. George Washington U. Hosp., Washington, 1970-75; asso. dean clin. affairs. Univ. Med. Ctr., 1972-73, dean, 1973-77, acting v.p. for med. affairs, 1975-76, v.p. for med. affairs, 1976-87; v.p. for health scis. Health Scis. Ctr. U. So. Fla., 1987-94, prof. medicine, dir. divsn. med. practice mgmt., 1994—; exec. dir. USF Physicians Group, 1996—; chmn. bd. dirs. Dow Sherwood Corp. Contbr. articles to profl. publs. Mem. D.C. Med. Community com. Mayor's Panel on Human Resources Orgn. and Mgmt. of D.C., 1977. Served to capt. M.C. USAF, 1958-60. Mem. Am. Acad. Med. Dirs., Am. Bd. Med. Mgmt. (treas. 1990, sec. 1991-93, pres.-elect 1993, pres. 1994-95, immediate past pres. 1995-96), ACP, AMA, Am. Soc. Internal Medicine, Assn. Acad. Health Ctrs. (chmn. 1986-87), Assn. Am. Med. Colls., Assn. for Hosp. Med. Edn., D.C. Med. Soc., Nat. Bd. Med. Examiners, Am. Coll. Physician Execs. (pres. 1986), Nat. Acad. Med. Examiners (editl. adv. bd. 1991—), World Access Inc., D.C. Consortium Univ. Health Sci. Ctrs., Soc. Med. Adminstrs. (treas. 1992-97), Soc. Med. Assn., D.C. Hosp. Assn., Nat. Assn. Biomed. Rsch. Office: U South Fla Divsn Med Practice Mgmt 3500 E Fletcher Ave Ste 530 Tampa FL 33613-4708

KAUFMAN, RUSSELL EUGENE, hematologist, oncologist; b. Kenton, Ohio, Mar. 7, 1946; s. George W. and Eileen M. (Risner) K.; m. Jane Ann Steinman, Sept. 25, 1948; children: Jonathon R., Emily J. BS, Ohio State U., 1968, MD cum laude, 1973. Diplomate Am. Bd. Internal Medicine. Resident medicine Duke U. Med. Ctr., Durham, N.C., 1973-77, chief resident medicine, 1977; rsch. hematologist NIH, Bethesda, Md., 1978-80; asst. prof. medicine Duke U. Med. Ctr., Durham, 1980-86, from asst. prof. to assoc. prof. biochemistry, 1985—, from assoc. prof. to prof. medicine, 1986—, chief divsn. hematology and oncology, 1989-96, chief divsn. med. oncology & transplantation, 1996-98, vice chair dept. medicine, 1995—, assoc. dean Sch. of Medicine,, 1998—; mem. sci. adv. com. Am. Cancer Soc., Atlanta, N.Y.C., 1987—; mem. com. Nat. Acad. Sci., Washington, 1983-86; mem. sci. rev. coms. NIH, Bethesda, Md., 1985—; assoc. chief of staff edn. Durham VA Med. Ctr. Contbr. articles to profl. jours., chpts. to books. Searle Found. scholar, 1983-86, Leukemia Soc. scholar, N.Y.C., 1986-90. Mem. AAAS, Am. Soc. Biochemistry, Am. Soc. Hematology (head subcom. on red cell 1985-88, chmn. com. on tng. programs 1995-98), Assn. Subspity. Profs. (exec. coun. 1994, treas. 1997-98, pres.-elect 1998-99, pres. 1999—), Assn. Hematology/Oncology Program Dirs. (chair 1997-98). Presbyterian. Avocations: golf, tennis. Office: Duke U Med Ctr PO Box 3250 Durham NC 27715-3250

KAUFMAN, SANDERS, computer programmer; b. Indpls., Aug. 3, 1965; m. Sanders Seymore and Judith Ann (Allen) K. Columnist The Jersey Voice, Jersey City, N.J., 1990-91; full-charge bookkeeper DeMaria, Ellis, Hunt, Newark, 1991-92; CTI developer IDCI/Fax 2 Fax, Inc., Dallas, 1994-95; ActiveX programmer The Kaufman Network, Dallas, 1988—. Author: Teach Yourself ActiveX Programming, 1997. With USN, 1985-88. Jewish. Avocations: guitar, history. Home and Office: 844 Mary Lee Cir Irving TX 75060-2854

KAUFMAN, SANFORD PAUL, lawyer; b. N.Y.C., Jan. 4, 1928; s. Max and Rose (Kornitzky) K.; m. Bernice R. Sulkis, June 17, 1956; children—Leslie Keith, Brad Leigh, Rona Sheryl, Jeffrey Scott, Adam Ira. B.B.A. in Accounting, Coll. City N.Y., 1948; LL.B., N.Y. U., 1952, LL.M. in Taxation, 1957. Bar: N.Y. bar 1953, Calif. bar 1962. With firm Garey & Garey, N.Y.C., 1953-55; asst. gen. counsel Olympic Radio & TV, L.I. City, 1961-63; sec., gen. counsel Tel-Autograph Corp., L.A., 1961-63; asst. gen. counsel Nat. Gen. Corp., L.A., 1963-74; sec., gen. counsel Familian Corp., L.A., 1974-77; pvt. practice Torrance, Calif., 1977—. Bd. dirs. Temple Ner Tamid, S. Bay, Calif. Mem. Am. Soc. Corporate Secs., Los Angeles County Bar Assn., Beverly Hills Bus. Men's Assn. Club: K.P. (past chancellor). Home: 28412 Golden Meadow Dr Palos Verdes Peninsula CA 90275-2926 Office: 23505 Crenshaw Blvd Ste 246 Torrance CA 90505-5221 *A person's finest attributes: honesty, integrity, loyalty, dependability and reliability, and the fear of God.*

KAUFMAN, SARAH HALL, legal assistant; b. Danville, Va., Mar. 5, 1964; d. Wallace Vann and Mary Lou (Cooke) Hall; m. Robert Gene Kaufman II, Oct. 25, 1997. BA in Polit. Sci., East Carolina U., 1985; Legal Asst. Cert., Meredith Coll., Raleigh, N.C., 1985. Cert. legal asst., 1987. Legal rschr. N.C. Housing Fin. Agy., Raleigh, 1984-85; legal asst. Moore & Van Allen PLLC, Raleigh, 1985—; adj. prof. legal assts. program Meredith Coll., 1988—; instr. CLA rev. course N.C. Paralegal Assn., Inc., Raleigh, 1996—; instr. notary pub. instr. cert. and re-cert. courses N.C. Sec. of State, 1997. Mem., social chair Chapel Hill (N.C.) Village Band, 1997—. Mem. ABA (assoc.), Raleigh Wake Paralegal Assn. (past v.p., past sec.), N.C. Paralegal Assn., Nat. Assn. Legal Assts. Democrat. Methodist. Home: 3 Kandes Ct Durham NC 27713-8315 Office: Moore & Van Allen PLLC PO Box 26507 Raleigh NC 27611-6507

KAUFMAN, SEYMOUR, biochemist; b. Bklyn., Mar. 13, 1924; s. Charles and Anna Kaufman; m. Elaine Elkins, Feb. 6, 1948; children: Allan, Emily, Leslie. BS, U. Ill., 1945, MS, 1946; PhD, Duke U., 1949. Fellow Dept. Pharmacology, NYU Med. Sch., 1949-50, instr., 1950-53, asst. prof., 1953-54; biochemist Lab. Cellular Pharmacology NIMH, Bethesda, Md., 1954-56, chief sect. on cellular regulatory mechanisms Lab. of Gen. and Comparative Biochemistry, 1956-68, acting chief Lab. Neurochemistry, 1968-71, chief Lab. Neurochemistry, 1971—. Contbr. articles to profl. jours. U.S. Pub. Health fellow Duke U., 1949. Mem. Am. Soc. Biol. Chemists, Am. Chem. Soc., Am. Acad. Arts and Scis., Internat. Soc. for Neurochemistry, Am. Soc. for Neurochemistry, Nat. Acad. Sci. Home: 10300 Rossmore Ct Bethesda MD 20814-2226

KAUFMAN, STEPHEN P., electronics company executive; b. Cambridge, Mass., Nov. 19, 1941; s. Arthur Samuel and Dorothy Ethel (Birman) K.; m. Sharon Kay Malin, Sept. 28, 1969; 1 child, Jeremy Scott. BS, MIT, 1963; MBA, Harvard U., 1965. Asst. to pres. Grand Steel & Mfg. Co., Clawson, Mich., 1965-67; group controller Chase, Brass & Copper Co., Cleve., 1967-69; assoc. McKinsey & Co., Cleve., 1969-75, ptnr., 1976-80; group v.p. Midland Ross Corp., Cleve., 1980-82; exec. v.p. Arrow Electronics, Inc., Melville, N.Y., 1982-84, pres., 1984—, chief operating officer, 1984-86, chief exec. officer, 1986—, chmn., 1994—; also bd. dirs. Arrow Electronics, Inc. Bd. dirs. L.I. Philharm., Melville, 1984—; trustee L.I. U., Brookville, 1985—. Recipient Corp. Leadership award MIT, 1987. Clubs: Mill River (Oyster Bay, N.Y.); Lloyd Neck Bath (N.Y.). Avocations: sailing, tennis. Office: Arrow Electronics Inc 25 Hub Dr Melville NY 11747-3509*

KAUFMAN, SUSAN JANE, journalist, educator; b. Hubbell, Mich., Feb. 13, 1944; d. Joseph R. Kaufman; partner Marlaine L. Francis, Dec. 20, 1977. Student, Marquette U., 1961-65; BA, Mich. Technol. U., 1976; MS, Ind. State U., 1981, PhD, 1992. Reporter Milw. Sentinel, 1965-66, Rockford (Ill.) Morning Star, 1966-68; news editor The Spirit, Green Bay, Wis., 1968-71; employment counselor Milw. Agys., 1971-74; dir. sports info. U. Wis. Green Bay, 1974; asst. dir. news WMPL-AM/FM, Hancock, Mich., 1976-77; coord. ops. WGGL-FM, Houghton, Mich., 1977-79; asst. gen. mgr. WAAC-AM, Terre Haute, Ind., 1980-81; city editor, columnist Terre Haute Tribune-Star, 1981-86; prof. journalism Ea. Ill. U., Charleston, 1986—. Co-editor: Women Transforming Communication: Global Intersections, 1996; contbr. chpts. in books. Mem. Not In Our Town Task Force, Charleston; bd. trustees Lakeview Coll. Nursing, Danville, Ill. Mem. AAUW, NOW, Soc. Profl. Journalists, Women in Comms., Assn. Edn. in Journalism and Mass Comm. (head commn. Status of Women 1994-95), Univ. Profls. Ill. (pres. Ea. Ill. U. chpt., Disting. Prof. award 1999), Rotary. Office: Eastern Ill Univ Dept Journalism 2546 Buzzard Hall Charleston IL 61920

KAUFMAN, VICTOR A., broadcast executive, former film company executive; b. 1943. Various sr. positions Columbia, 1974-87; founding chmn., CEO Tri-Star Pictures, 1987-89; pres. CEO Columbia Pictures Entertainment, Inc., 1987-89; chmn. Savoy Pictures Entertainment, N.Y.C., 1990-96; CFO, chmn. HSN, Inc., 1996-98, USA Networks, Inc., N.Y.C., 1998—. Office: USA Networks Inc 42d Fl 152 W 57th St New York NY 10019-3310*

KAUFMAN, WILLIAM, internist; b. Dec. 31, 1910; s. Leo and Marie Kaufman; m. Charlotte R. Schnee, May 9, 1940. BA, U. Pa., 1931; MA in Chemistry, U. Mich., 1932, PhD in Physiology, 1937, MD cum laude, 1938. Diplomate Am. Bd. Internal Medicine. Intern Barnes Hosp., Washington U. Sch. Medicine, St. Louis, 1938-39; asst. resident, then resident Mt. Sinai Hosp., N.Y.C., 1939-40; Emanuel Libman fellow Yale U. Sch. Medicine, New Haven, 1940-41, Dazian Found. fellow, clin. asst., 1940-42; pvt. practice Bridgeport, Conn., 1940-65; courtesy staff mem. Bridgeport Hosp., 1941-65; courtesy staff St. Vincent's Hosp., Bridgeport, 1941-65; assoc. med. dir. L.W. Frohlich and Co./Intercon Internat. Inc., N.Y.C., 1964-65, med. dir., 1965-67, dir. med. affairs, 1967-68; assoc. med. dir. Klemtner Casey, Inc., N.Y.C., 1969-70, dir. med. affairs, 1970-71; v.p., dir. med. affairs Klemtner Advt., Inc., N.Y.C., 1971, sr. v.p., dir. sci. and med. affairs, 1971-81; pres., chmn. program and pub. edn. coms. Acad. Psychosomatic Medicine, 1953-55; founder fellow, mem. governing coun. Collegium Internationale Allergologicum, 1955-62; chmn. psychosomatic sect. 3d Internat. Congress Allergology, 1958; D. C. Y. Moore Meml. lectr. Manchester (Conn.) Med. Soc., 1967; cons. Family Life Film Ctr. Conn. Inc., 1967-74; mem. screening jury med. edn. sect. Am. Film Festival, 1975. Author: The Common Form of Niacinamide Deficiency Disease (Aniacinamidosis), 1943, The Common Form of Joint Dysfunction: Its Incidence and Treatment, 1949; (drawings) Kaufman's Kritters, 1990; (play) People Like Us, A Bad Day for Spiders, The Waiting Room; contbg. editor Internat. Archives Allergy and Applied Immunology, 1952-54, 67-69, Am. editor in chief, 1954-67; mem. bd. editorial collaborators Psychotherapeutica, Psychosomatica et Orthopaedagogica, 1955-62; contbg. editor Quar. Rev. Allergy and Applied Immunology, 1955; contbr. numerous articles to profl. and popular jours.; exhibited drawings and paintings at Housatonic Community Coll., New Canaan Art Show, others. Mem. adv. bd. Huxley Inst. So. Conn. for Biosocial Rsch., 1980-84. Recipient citation Internat. Assn. Gerontology, 1983, 1st Pl. award Faculty of Fine Arts, Housatonic Community Coll., 1983, Sci. and Math. medal Rensselaer Poly. Inst., 1928, Sternberg Meml. Gold medal, 1938. Hon. fellow Internat. Acad. Preventive Medicine (Tom Spies Meml. award and lectr. 1978); fellow AAAS, Am. Coll. Allergy, Asthma and Immunology (emeritus, chmn. pub. edn. com. 1951-55, chmn. com. on allergy of nervous system 1962, Award of Merit 1981), Am. Coll. Nutrition, ACP (life), Gerontol. Soc. Am. (mem. various sects.), N.Y. Acad. Medicine, Royal Soc. Medicine (life; London); mem. AMA (life), Am Psychosomatic Soc. (emeritus), Conn. State Med. Soc. (life), Fairfield County Med. Assn. (life), Nat. Assn. Sci. Writers, N.Y. Acad. Scis., Dramatists Guild, Sigma Xi, Alpha Omega Alpha, Phi Sigma, Phi Lambda Upsilon, Phi Kappa Phi. Achievements include clin. rsch. using niacinamide (alone or with other vitamins) to reverse certain concomitants of aging, with resultant improvement in osteoarthritis and rheumatoid arthritis, muscle strength, muscle working capacity and balance sense. Home: 3180 Grady St Winston Salem NC 27104-4008

KAUFMAN, WILLIAM MORRIS, engineer consultant; b. Pitts., Dec. 31, 1931; s. Nathan and Sarah M. (Paper) K.; m. Iris F. Picovsky, June 21, 1953; children: Nathan E., Marjorie L., Emily M. BSEE, Carnegie Inst. Tech., 1953, MSEE, PhD in EE. Registered profl. engr. Supr. Westinghouse Electric Corp., Pitts., 1955-62; dir. rsch. Gen. Instrument Corp., Newark, 1962-65; cons. engr. GE, Valley Forge, Pa., 1965-66; mgr. med. engr. dept. Hittman Assocs. Inc., Columbia, Md., 1966-71; v.p. engring. ENSCO, Springfield, Va., 1971-83; v.p. Ocean Data Systems Inc., Rockville, Md., 1984-85; v.p. applied rsch., dir. Carnegie Mellon Rsch. Inst. Carnegie Mellon U., Pitts., 1985-97, mem. tech. transfer bd., 1989-94, mem. employee retirement and welfare benefit plan com., 1988-97; chmn. tech. adv. group Fostin Capital, Pitts., 1986-95; mem. adv. bd. Pitts. Seed Fund, 1986-97; bd. dirs. Mellon Pitt Carnegie Corp., Maglev, Inc., Tech. Devel. and Edn. Corp.; treas. Ben Franklin Tech. Ctr. of Western Pa. Patentee in field. Mem. adv coun. on regional devel. U. Pitts., 1986; bd. dirs. Ben Franklin Tech. Ctr. of Western Pa., 1988-94, treas. Fellow IEEE (life); mem. Sigma Xi, Tau Beta Pi, Eta Kappa Nu. Home and Office: 38 Sheridan Rd Swampscott MA 01907-2045

KAUFMANN, CAROLINE ELIZABETH, surgical technologist, critical care nurse; b. N.Y., Jan. 28, 1961; d. Joseph and Karolina (Donaubauer) Meszaros; m. Albert Kaufmann, June 6, 1981; children: Christine, Matthew, Colleen. AAS in Surg. Tech. cum laude, Nassau C.C., Garden City, N.Y., 1981; BSN magna cum laude, Adelphi U., Garden City, 1986. RN, N.Y.; CNOR; cert. surg. technologist. Surg. technologist, nurse Booth Meml. Med. Ctr., Flushing, N.Y., 1981-89; prof. surg. tech. Nassau C.C., 1989—. Mem. Assn. Oper. Rm. Nurses (chair nominating com. 1991-92, bd. dirs. 1994-96, 98—, trends and issues com.), Assn. Surg. Technologists.

KAUFMANN, CHARLES ARTHUR, psychiatrist, educator; b. N.Y.C., Mar. 10, 1951; s. Harold Joseph and Martha Marcia (Martel) K.;m. Joan Ruth Zoldessy, Apr. 25, 1980; children: Sasha Zoldessy, Amelia Maude, Samuel Aslan. SB, MIT, 1971; MD, Columbia U., 1977. Lic. physician medicine and surgery, N.Y., D.C.; diplomate Am. Bd. Psychiatry and Neurology. Intern dept. medicine Meml. Sloan Ketterin Cancer Ctr., 1977; intern N.Y. Hosp., N.Y.C., 1977-78; resident psychiatry Payne Whitney Psychiat. Clinic, N.Y. Hosp., N.Y.C., 1977-81; sr. staff fellow adult psychiatry br. NIMH, Washington, 1981-85; postdoctoral fellow Lab. Molecular Neurobiology Ctr. Neurobiology and Behavior, Columbia U., N.Y.C., 1986-88; ward adminstr. William A. White divsn. St. Elizabeths Hosp., Washington, 1981-82, attending psychiatrist, 1981-85; attending psychiatrist George Washington U. Hosp., Washington, 1982-85; asst. attending psychiatrist Presbyn. Hosp., N.Y.C., 1986-90, assoc. attending psychiatrist, 1990—; psychiatrist II N.Y. State Psychiat. Inst., N.Y.C., 1986—, head Lab. Molecular Neurobiology, dept. med. genetics, 1988—, sci. dir. Schizophrenia Rsch. Unit, 1989—; guest investigator neuropsychiatry br. NIMH, Washington, 1986—; dir. Diagnostic Ctr. for Schizophrenia Linkage Studies Columbia U., N.Y.C., 1989-97; rsch. asst. Neal E. Miller Lab. Physiol. Psychology, The Rockefeller U., N.Y.C., 1977, guest investigator Mary Jeanne Kreek Lab. Biology of Addictive Diseases, 1979-81, D. Carleton Gajdusek Lab. Ctrl. Nervous Sys. Studies, Nat. Inst. Neurol. and Communicative Disorders and Stroke, Bethesda, Md., 1982-85; vis. assoc. physician Rockefeller U. Hosp., N.Y.C., 1981; instr. clin. psychiatry Cornell U. Med. Coll., N.Y.C., 1980-81; asst. clin. prof. psychiatry and behavioral scis. George Washington U., Washington, 1982-85; asst. prof. clin. psychiatry Columbia U., N.Y.C., 1986-90, assoc. prof., 1990—; vis. lectr. Cornell U. Med. Coll., N.Y.C., 1992—; examiner Am. Bd. Psychiatry and Neurology, 1985—; pvt. practice psychiatry Columbia Presbyn. Med. Ctr., N.Y.C., 1986—; spl. reviewer psychopathology and clin. biology rsch. rev. com. NIMH, Washington, 1987—; spl. reviewer Ont. Mental Health Found., 1992—; mem. epidemiology and genetics rev. com. NIMH, 1992-96; mem. residency selection com. dept. psychiatry Columbia U., N.Y.C., 1994—, qualifying examiner dept. genetics and devel., 1995; mem. mental health task force Coalition for the Homeless, Washington, 1982-85, chair, 1982-83; mem. Task Froce on Homeless Mentally Ill, Am. Psychiat. Assn., 1983-84; cons. Sarah House Women's Shelter, Washington, 1983-85; mem. Working Group on Mental Health Svcs. to Homeless, D.C. Mental Health Sys. Reorgn. Project, Washington, 1985. Mem. editl. bd. Neuropsychiat. Genetics, Schizophrenia Bull.; editor: (with others) The American Psychiatric Press Review of Psychiatry Volume 9, 1990, Schizophrenia: New Directions for Clnical Research and Treatment, 1996; contbr. articles to profl. jours., chpts. to book. MIT nat. scholar, Cambridge, 1967; recipient Physician Scientist award NIMH, 1987-92, Judith Silver Meml. Young Scientist award Nat. Alliance for Mentally Ill, 1990, Scientist Devel. award NIMH, 1992-97, Disting. Investigator award NARSAD, 1997; grantee NIMH, 1989—, G. Harold and Leila Y. Mathers Charitable Trust, 1994-96, Scottish Rite Schizophrenia Rsch. Program, 1995-97, NARSAD, 1997—. Fellow Am. Psychiat. Assn. (Falk fellow 1979-81), Am. Psychopath. Assn., N.Y. Acad. Medicine; mem. AAAS, Soc. Biol. Psychiatry (membership com. 1993—), Am. Soc. Clin. Psychopharmacology, Am. Soc. Human Genetics, Assn. Rsch. in Nervous and Mental Disease, Internat. Brain Rsch. Orgn., Internat. Soc. Psychiat. Genetics, N.Y. Acad. Scis., Physicians for Social Responsibility, Soc. Neurosci., Psychiat. Soc. Westchester County, Phi Beta Kappa, Sigma Xi, Alpha Omega Alpha. Jewish. Avocations: hiking, sea kayaking. Office: NY State Psychiat Inst 1051 Riverside Dr New York NY 10032-1001

KAUFMANN, ED, lawyer; b. Davenport, Iowa, May 17, 1938. AB, Cornell U., 1960; LLB cum laude, Harvard U., 1966. Bar: N.Y. 1967. Mem. Hughes Hubbard & Reed, N.Y.C. Mem. Phi Beta Kappa. Office: Hughes Hubbard & Reed 1 Battery Park Plz New York NY 10004-1482

KAUFMANN, HORACIO CARLOS, neurologist, educator; b. Buenos Aires, Nov. 23, 1954; came to u.S., 1982; s. Mateo and Becky (Schapira) K. BA, Colegio Nacional Buenos Aires, 1972; MD, U. Buenos Aires, 1978. Diplomate Am. Bd. Psychiatry and Neurology; lic. physician, N.Y. Resident Centro de Educacion Medica e Investigaciones Clinicas, Buenos Aires, 1979-82; resident in neurology Mt. Sinai Sch. Medicine, N.Y.C., 1982-85, fellow in neurology, 1985-86, asst. prof. neurology, 1986—, asst. atending, 1986—, dir. autonomic nervous system lab., 1987—; assoc. prof. of neurology, assoc. attending, 1996—. Contbr. articles to profl. jours. Mem. Am. Acad. Neurology (chmn. sect. autonomic nervous system), Am. Autonomic Soc., World Fedn. Neurology (sec.-treas., rsch. group autonomic nervous system), Soc. Neurosci., Clin. Autonomic Rsch. Soc. (London). Home: 41 Central Park W New York NY 10023-6002 Office: Mt Sinai Med Ctr New York NY 10029

KAUFMANN, JACK, lawyer; b. Davenport, Iowa, May 14, 1942; s. Ed Kaufmann Jr. and Jean Gilchrist (Ploehn) Wernentin; m. Elizabeth Amanda Phillips, Jan. 27, 1973; children: Suzanne Cathryn, John Frederick, Christine Elizabeth, Amanda Jean. AB, Dartmouth Coll., 1964; JD, Columbia U., 1971. Bar: N.Y. 1972. Assoc. Dewey Ballantine, N.Y.C., 1971-79, ptnr., 1980—. Atty. Village of Pelham Manor, N.Y., 1977-83, trustee, 1983-87, mayor, 1987-89; councilman Town of Pelham, N.Y., 1990-91. Lt. (j.g.) USNR, 1964-68. Mem. ABA, N.Y. State Bar Assn., Assn. of Bar of City of N.Y., Delta Kappa Epsilon, Pelham Country Club (pres. 1994-96). Republican. Episcopalian. Home: 649 Ely Ave Pelham NY 10803-2401 Office: Dewey Ballantine 1301 Avenue Of The Americas New York NY 10019-6022*

KAUFMANN, MARK STEINER, banker; b. N.Y.C., Dec. 3, 1932; s. Milton L. and Elsa S. (Steiner) K.; B.S. cum laude in Bus. Adminstrn., Lehigh U., 1953; m. Carole Richard, June 16, 1957; children—Jon Richard, Susan Helen. Vice pres., dir. mktg. Standard Fin. Corp., N.Y.C., 1958-64; sr. v.p., dir. Milberg Factors, Inc., N.Y.C., 1964-73; dir. corp. devel. Chase Manhattan Bank, N.Y.C., 1973-87, sr. v.p., 1987-96, chmn. Kaufmann and Ptnrs., LLC, N.Y.C., 1996—; ret. chmn. banking div. UJA/Fedn. Hon. trustee Calhoun Sch., N.Y.C.; hon. dir. Lower Manhattan Cultural Coun.; chmn. bd. Temple Israel, N.Y.C.; mem. bus. adv. coun. Lehigh U. Served as 1st lt. USAF, 1953-55. Recipient Human Relations award Anti-Defamation League, 1973, Human Relations award Am. Jewish Com., 1987. Mem. Am. Arbitration Assn., Harmonie Club, Old Oaks Country Club, Beta Gamma Sigma, Lambda Mu Sigma, Pi Gamma Mu, Omicron Delta Kappa. Home: 124 W 79th St New York NY 10024-6446 Office: Kaufmann and Ptnrs LLC 712 5th Ave Fl 22D New York NY 10019-4108

KAUFMANN, RACHEL NORSWORTHY, educator; b. Los Angeles, Feb. 12, 1964; d. Ralph Henry and Audely (Gutierrez) N.; m. Karl Alexander Kaufmann, May 28, 1988. BA, Scripps Coll., 1988; MA, Webster U., 1997. Pharmacy tech. Torrance (Calif.) Meml. Hosp., 1982-88, St. Mary Med. Ctr., Long Beach, Calif., 1987-88; asst. area mgr. AutoFuel Co., Abilene, Tex., 1989-90; adminstrv. asst. McMurry U., Abilene, 1990-92; 911 tech. asst. West Cen. Tex. Coun. of Govts., Abilene, 1992-94; adminstrv. asst. Piedmont Natural Gas, Greenville, S.C., 1995-97; gen. psychology and devel. psychology tchr. Sandhills C.C., Pine Hurst, N.C., 1998—; marriage and family counselor pvt. practice, 1999—. Auction com. Am. Cancer Soc., Abilene, 1994; bd. dirs. West Tex. Girl Scout Coun., Abilene, 1992-94. Mem. AAUW (bd. dirs. 1989-94). Presbyterian. Avocations: sewing, cooking, travel, music. Home: 565 S Bethesda Rd Southern Pines NC 28387-6401

KAUFMANN, URLIN MILO, English literature educator; b. Cleve., Aug. 27, 1934; s. Albert Walter and Alda Winona (Aiken) K.; m. Helen Elizabeth Olson, Sept. 1, 1956; children: Felice, Laurie, Andrew. BA, Greenville (Ill.) Coll., 1956; MA, U. Ill., 1957; PhD, Yale U., 1960. Instr. North Park Coll., Chgo., 1961-62; instr. U. Ill., Urbana, 1962-63, asst. prof., 1963-67, assoc. prof. English, 1967-94, prof. emeritus, 1994—. Author: The Pilgrim's Progress and Traditions in Puritan Meditation, 1967, Paradise in the Age of Milton, 1978, Heaven: A Future Finer Than Dreams, 1981; Contbg. author, editor: Households Under God, 1996. Pres. Light and Life men's aux. Free Meth. Ch. N.Am., Indpls., 1985-95; bd. dirs. Empty Tomb, Inc., Urbana-Champaign, 1980—. Mem. Conf. on Christianity and Lit. (treas. 1962-64). Democrat. Home: 1807 N Concord Ln Urbana IL 61802-7725

KAUGER, YVONNE, state supreme court chief justice; b. Cordell, Okla., Aug. 3, 1937; d. John and Alice (Bottom) K.; m. Ned Bastow, May 8, 1982; 1 child, Jonna Kauger Kirschner. BS magna cum laude, Southwestern State U., Weatherford, Okla., 1958; cert. med. technologist, St. Anthony's Hosp., 1959; J.D., Oklahoma City U., 1969, LLD (hon.), 1992. Med. technologist Med. Arts Lab., 1959-68; assoc. Rogers, Travis & Jordan, 1970-72; jud. asst. Okla. Supreme Ct., Oklahoma City, 1972-84, justice, 1984-94; vice chief justice Okla. Supreme Ct., 1994-96, Chief Justice, 1997—; mem. appellate div. Ct. on Judiciary; mem. State Capitol Preservation Commn., 1983-84; mem. dean's adv. com. Oklahoma City U. Sch. Law; lectr. William O. Douglas Lecture Series Gonzaga U., 1990. Founder Gallery of Plains Indian, Colony, Okla., Red Earth (Down Towner award 1990), 1987; active Jud. Day, Girl's State, 1976-80; keynote speaker Girl's State Hall of Fame Banquet, 1984; bd. dirs. Lyric Theatre, Inc., 1966—, pres. bd. dirs., 1981; past mem. bd. dirs. Civic Music Soc., Okla. Theatre Ctr., Canterbury Choral Soc.; mem. First Lady of Okla.'s Artisans' Alliance Com. Named Panhellenic Woman of Yr., 1990, Woman of Yr. Red Lands Coun. Girl Scouts, 1990, Washita County Hall of Fame, 1992. Mem. ABA (law sch. accreditation com.), Okla. Bar Assn. (law schs. com. 1977—), Washita County Bar Assn., Washita County Hist. Soc. (life), St. Paul's Music Soc., Iota Tau Tau, Delta Zeta (Disting. Alumna award 1988, State Delta Zeta of Yr. 1987, Nat. Woman of Yr. 1988). Episcopalian.

KAUL, DHANANJAYA KUMAR, physiologist; b. Etawah, India, July 23, 1943; came to U.S., 1974; s. Gopal K. and Kamla (Devi) K. MS, Agra U., Nainital, India, 1963; PhD, Rajasthan U., Jaipur, India, 1969. Lectr. Rajasihan U., Jaipur, 1966-74; staff assoc. Columbia U., N.Y.C., 1974-77; assoc. Albert Einstein Coll. Medicine, Bronx, N.Y., 1978-81, asst. prof. medicine, 1981-88, assoc. prof., 1988-94, prof., 1994—. Fellow WHO, Lyon, France, 1974; rsch. grantee Am. Heart Assn., 1986-93, NIH, Bethesda, Md., 1990—. Mem. Am. Soc. Hematology, Microcirculatory Soc. USA, N.Am. Soc. Biorheologists. Achievements include elucidation of microcirculatory and hemodynamic behavior of pathologic human red cells in situ and ex vivo microvascular preparations; mechanisms of cell adhesion and vascular obstruction in cerebral malaria and sickle cell anemia. Office: Albert Einstein Coll Med Dept Medicine Rm U-917 1300 Morris Park Ave Bronx NY 10461-1926

KAULA, WILLIAM MASON, geophysicist, educator; b. Sydney, Australia, May 19, 1926; s. Edgar Louis and Edna (Mason) K.; m. Denise Bouche, June 11, 1949; children: Anne, Jacqueline, Charles, Marie; m. Gene Hurley, July 22, 1978. B.S., U.S. Mil. Acad., 1948; M.S. in Geodesy, Ohio State U., 1953; D.Sc. (hon.), 1975. Commd. 2d lt. C.E. U.S. Army, 1948; advanced through grades to capt., 1953, resigned, 1957; geodesist U.S. Army Map Service, 1957-60; researcher orbital dynamics and planetary structure NASA, 1960-63; prof. geophysics UCLA, 1963-93; ret., 1993; on leave as chief Nat. Geodetic Survey, 1984-87. Author: Theory of Satellite Geodesy, 1966, Introduction to Planetary Physics, 1968; Contbr. papers to profl. lit. Fellow Am. Geophys. Union; mem. NAS. Achievements include research in geophysics and planetary physics. Home: 710 S Westgate Ave Los Angeles CA 90049-4219 Office: UCLA Dept Earth and Space Scis Los Angeles CA 90095-1567

KAULAKIS, ARNOLD FRANCIS, management consultant; b. Lewiston, Maine, Oct. 6, 1916; s. Frank Kaulakis and Amelia (Vilaniskis) K.; m. Marguerite Marie Adams, Oct. 18, 1940; children: Bernadette, Robert, Michael, Marguerite. B.S. in Chem. Engring., MIT, 1938. V.p., dir. Exxon Research & Engring. co., Linden, N.J., 1961-66; dep. refining coordinator Exxon Corp., N.Y.C., 1966-68; exec. chmn., chief exec. officer BOC-Airco Cryogenic Plant Ltd., London, 1968-71; mng. dir. Cryoplants Ltd., London, 1971-72; v.p. energy devel. The Pittston Co., Greenwich, Conn., 1972-81; chmn. bd., chief exec. officer Pittston Petroleum Inc., Montvale, N.J., 1977-83; pres. Afkay Assocs., Rye, N.Y., 1983—. Patentee in field; contbr. articles to profl. jours. Mem. Welding Research Council (vice chmn. exec. com. 1964-68), Jr. Engring. Tech. Soc. (dir. 1962-68), Am. Petroleum Inst., Am. Mining Congress (synthetic fuels com.). Address: 5005 Theall Rd Rye NY 10580-1445

KAUNE, JAMES EDWARD, ship repair company executive, former naval officer; b. Santa Fe, N.Mex., Mar. 4, 1927; s. Henry Eugene and Lucile (Carter) K.; B.S., U.S. Naval Acad., 1950; Naval Engr. degree Mass. Inst. Tech., 1955; B.S. in Metallurgy, Carnegie-Mellon U., 1960; m. Pauline Stamatos, June 24, 1956; children: Bradford Scott, Audrey Lynn, Jason Douglas. Commd. ensign U.S. Navy, 1950, advanced through grades to capt., 1970; asst. gunnery officer U.S.S. Floyd B. Parks, 1950-52; project officer U.S.S. Gyatt, Boston Naval Shipyard, 1955-57; main propulsion officer U.S.S. Tarawa, 1957-58; asst. planning officer Her Majesty's Canadian Dockyard, Halifax, N.S., Can., 1960-62; repair officer U.S.S. Cadmus, 1962-64; fleet maintenance officer Naval Boiler and Turbine Lab., 1964-68; various shipyard assignments, 1968-70, material staff officer U.S. Naval Air Forces Atlantic Fleet, 1971-74; production officer Phila. Naval Shipyard, 1974-79; comdr. Long Beach Naval Shipyard, Calif.; exec. v.p. Am. Metal Bearing Co., Garden Grove, Calif., from 1979; gen. mgr. San Francisco div. Topp Shipyards, Alameda, Calif., v.p. engring. Point Richmond Shipyard, Calif., 1983-84; v.p. engring., mktg. Svc. Engring. Corp, San Francisco, 1984-92; CEO Am. Modular Power Sys., Walnut Creek, Calif., 1992—; pres., CEO BioLumber, Inc. Mem. Am. Soc. Naval Engrs., Am. Soc. Quality Control, Soc. Naval Architects and Marine Engrs., U.S. Naval Inst., Am. Soc. Metals. Episcopalian. Club: Masons. Contbr. articles to profl. jours. Home: 403 Camino Sobrante Orinda CA 94563-1844 Office: BioLumber Inc 1200 Hensley Street Richmond CA 94801

KAUP, DAVID EARLE, law enforcement officer; b. Pitts., May 10, 1952; s. Paul Edwin and Patricia Elizabeth (Kaelin) K.; m. Pak Tu-Im, Nov. 24, 1979 (div. 1999); children: Paul Marshall, Steven Lyle. BS in Criminal Justice Mgmt., Ctrl. Mo. State U., 1975; MS in Criminal Justice Mgmt., Sam Houston State U., 1988; MPA, U. Houston, 1994. Cert. master peace officer, Tex., profl. in criminal justice, U.S. Patrolman Clinton (Mo.) Police Dept., 1973-74, Lake Lotawana (Mo.) Police Dept., 1974-75; security guard Burns Internat. Security Service, Pitts., 1975-76; dep. Harris County Sheriff's Dept., Houston, 1980-81, detective, 1981-84, sgt., 1984-98; CEO, Union Stron LLC, 1998—; instr. Calif. C.Cs., extension svc., 1977-79; security coord. Westminster Village Apts., Houston, 1981-84, com. chmn. Fairmont Park Crimewatch, LaPorte, Tex., 1987-98; owner Keystone Rsch. & Cons. Svcs.; CEO Union Star LLC; dir. Tex. Pole Inst., 1995—. Editor Union Star newspaper, 1993-95; editor/pub. The Texas Street Beat newspaper, 1995—. Trustee Shin Hae Won Orphanage, Pusan, Korea, 1978; bd. dirs. Fairmont Park East Homeowners Assn., 1990-92, pres., 1993-98; sec.-treas. Harris County Dep. Sheriff's Union, 1991. Mem. Harris County Dep. Sheriff's Assn., Citizens Adv. Coun., LaPorte Plant Mgmt. Assn., Masons. Mem. FOP, Harris County Dep. Sheriff's Assn., Tex. Police Inst. (dir. 1994—), Masons. Avocations: gardening, firearms, reading, personal computers. Home: 4542 Holmes Rd Houston TX 77033-2502

KAUSER, FAZAL BAKHSH, aerospace engineer, educator; b. Multan, Panjab, Pakistan, Nov. 15, 1943; came to U.S., 1980; s. Haji Khuda Bakhsh and Bagh Begum; m. Qamar, May 29, 1969; children: Hina Kauser, Shella Kauser. BSc in Physics and Math., Panjab U., 1961; BSc (hons.) in aero engring., Loughborough U., 1966, diploma in indsl. studies, 1966; MS in Aero. Engring., Air Force Inst. Tech., Wright-Patterson AFB, Ohio, 1976. Registered profl. engr., aerospace engr., Fla., mech. engr., Calif. Dir. wind tunnels labs. Pakistan Air Force Engring. Acad., Karachi, 1966-76, head aerodynamic divs., 1977-80; rsch. asst. Pa. State U., College Park, Pa., 1980-82; asst. prof. Embry Riddle Aeronautical U., Daytona Beach, Fla., 1982-86; assoc. prof. Calif. State Polytechnic U., Pomona, 1986—; car Calif. Poly. State U., Pomona, 1986-96; prof. airbreathing propulsion and advanced aerodyns. Calif. Poly. Inst., Pomona, 1995; cons. Lockheed Aeronautical Systems Co., Burbank, Calif., 1988, NASA Jet Propulsion Lab, Pasadena; prin. investigator rsch. projects in field, 1978-90. Contbr. articles to profl. jours. Squadron leader Pakistan Air Force, 1966-80. Fellow NASA/ASEE Summer Faculty Program, 1996, 97, USAF OSR, 1998. Fellow AIAA (assoc., mem. airbreathing propulsion com., reviewer Jour. Propulsion and Power); mem. ASME, Am. Soc. Engring. Edn., Tau Alpha Pi, Tau Beta Pi. Achievements include establishment of dept. aerospace engring. and setting up subsonic/supersonic wind tunnel test facilities at Engring. Acad., Pakistan Air Force, Karachi; designer of low turbulence level annular wind tunnel for grad. research in turbulence at department of aerospace engineering of Pa. State Univeristy. Office: Calif State Poly Tech U 3801 W Temple Ave Pomona CA 91768-2557

KAUSHIK, SURENDRA KUMAR, economist; b. Malsisar, India, June 21, 1944; came to U.S., 1970; naturalized, 1980; s. Lakminarain Sharma and Rathi Chaturvedy; m. Helena Pokornicki, Sept. 12, 1973. BS in Commerce, U. Rajasthan, India, 1965, MA in Econs., 1967; PhD in Econs., Boston U., 1976. Rsch. asst., instr. Inst. Econ. Growth, Delhi, India, 1968-70; tchg. fellow, rsch. asst., then sr. tchg. fellow and lect. Boston U., 1971-75; lectr. Lowell Tech. Inst. Boston State Coll., 1973-74; asst. prof. Babson Coll., Wellesley, Mass., 1976-81; dir. Inst. Internat. Banking Lubin Grad. Sch. Bus., 1981—; prof. Pace U., White Plains, 1984—; instr. Northeastern U., Bosron, 1972-73; cons. UN, 1976-77. Condr. rsch. internat. banking and fin.; editor: Banking, Money Markets and Monetary Policy, 1980, International Banking and Global Financing, 1983, Debt Crisis and Financial Stability: The Future, 1985, Internal Banking and World Economic Growth, 1987, The Practical Financial Manager, 1988; co-author: The Practical Financial Manager, 1988, Multinational Financial Management, 1989. Mem. AAUP, Am. Econ. Assn., Am. Fin. Assn., Western Econ. Assn., Ea. Econ. Assn., Atlantic Econ. Soc. Office: Pace U Lubin Grad Sch Bus 1 Martine Ave White Plains NY 10606-1932

KAUTH, BENJAMIN, podiatrist consultant; b. N.Y.C., Oct. 20, 1913; m. Bertha Locke. Student, CCNY, 1936-39; D in Podiatric Medicine, N.Y. Coll. Podiatric Medicine, 1939, postgrad., 1944-45, HHD (hon.), 1981. Pvt. practice N.Y.C., 1939-78; podiatric cons., 1960—; co-chief podiatry staff St. Clare's Hosp., N.Y.C.; chief of staff podiatry Jewish Home and Hosp. for Aged, Village Nursing Home of St. Vincents Hosp.; mem. staff French Polyclinic; chief podiatry panel 1199 Nat. Fund; coord. podiatry panel 32 B-J Health Ctr.; mem. med. panel Med. Malpractice Bronx County; trustee, mem. exec. coun. N.Y. Coll. Podiatric Medicine; cons. Podiatrist Local 1199 Health Fund, Equitable Life Assurance Co., various other third-party insurers, pub. rels. firms. Editorial asst. N.Y. Podiatrist Del. to Nat. Conv.; contbr. articles to profl. jours. Bd. dirs. Adams Sch. for Retarded Children, Am. Jewish Distbn. Com. Fellow Nat. Assn. of Professions; mem. Am. Coll. Foot Surgeons (assoc.), Am. Podiatric Med. Assn. (pub. affairs com., editorial asst.), Podiatry soc. of the State N.Y. (spl. asst. to pres., editorial asst. ann. meeting), N.Y. County Podiatry Soc. (sec., exec. bd.), Fair Harbor Yacht Club (sec.), Friars. Home and Office: 302 W 12th St New York NY 10014-6025

KAUTSCH, M(IKE) A., law educator; b. Omaha, Feb. 16, 1945; s. C.O. and A. K.; m. Elaine M.G., Aug. 5, 1945; children: M.E., K.E. BA, U. Iowa, 1968, JD, 1971. Reporter Iowa City Press-Citizen, Iowa City, 1968-71, Atlanta Jour., Augusta, Ga., 1972-79; asst. to prof. U. Kans., Lawrence, 1979—, acad. dean, 1987-97, prof. of law, 1997—; lectr. U. Kans., 1979. Contbr. chpts. to book. Exec. com. Lawrence C. of C., 1992-95; dir. William Allen White Found., Lawrence, 1987-97. 2d lt. Signal Corps, 1972. Recipient Excellence in Tchg. award Poynter Inst. and Am. Soc. News Editors, 1981, recipient of the Kansas Bar Assn. Outstanding Svc. award, 1997. Mem. Kans. Bar Assn. Media Bar Com., Kansas City Metro. Bar Assn. Media Law Com. Office: U Kans Sch Law Lawrence KS 66045

KAUTT, GLENN GREGORY, financial planner; b. Arlington, Va., Jan. 25, 1948; s. Elmer Curtis and Phyllis Ruth (Schmalz) K.; m. Elisabeth B. Emerson, Aug. 19, 1973 (div. 1975); 1 child, Christopher Curtis; m. Elizabeth M. Dansereau, Dec. 22, 1989. BS, Purdue U., 1973; MBA, Harvard U., 1979. Cert. fin. planner; enrolled agt., admitted to practice before IRS. Commd. lt. USN, 1969, resigned, 1977; sr. assoc. ICF, Inc., Washington, 1979-81; mng. dir. The Challenger Group, Silver Spring, Md., 1981-85; sr. planner Fin. Svc. Group, Vienna, Va., 1985-87; prin., dir. Capitol Fin. Cons., Inc., Vienna, 1987-91; pres. Kautt Fin. Svcs., Inc., Vienna, 1991-99, The Monitor Group, Inc., Fairfax, Va., 1999—; lectr. ADA, Am. Mgmt. Assn., US SBA, also maj. corps. Co-author, editor Inside the Real Estate Business, 1981; contbr. articles to profl. mags. Mem. Registry Fin. Planning Practitioners, Inst. Cert. Fin. Planners, No. Va. Soc. Cert. Fin. Planners (bd. dirs., pres. 1999—). Republican. Avocations: flying, skiing, scuba diving, singing. Office: 12450 Fair Lakes Cir Fairfax VA 22033-3810

KAUTZ, BONNIE MITCHELL, school nurse; b. Millboro, Va., May 28, 1934; d. Terry Glenn and Roasamond Virginia (Loan) Mitchell; m. John Lewis Kautz, June 15, 1957; children: Rosamond Amelia Kautz Learn, John Mitchell, Rachel Ann Kautz Lambert. BS, Alderson-Broaddus Coll., 1957; M. in Litt. in Nursing Svc. Adminstrn., U. Pitts., 1961; postgrad., Carlow Coll., 1988-89. RN, W.Va., Pa., Va., Ga.; cert. ednl. specialist II, Pa. Charge nurse Presbyn. Hosp., Pitts., 1957; head nurse Magee Hosp., Pitts., 1957-62; adminstrv. asst. dental office Office John L. Kautz, DDS, Apollo, Pa., 1964—; substitute sch. nurse Apollo-Ridge, Kiski Area, New Kinsington-Arnold, Highlands sch. dists., Pa., 1987-93; long term substitute sch. nurse Kiski Area Sch. Dist., Vandergrift, Pa., 1990-91, 92, sch. nurse, 1993—. Ch. organist, treas. First United Ch. of Christ, Apollo, nurse for ch. camp, 1983—, past mem. ch. consistory, past Sunday sch. supt., past. music dir. and past fin. sec. community vacation bible sch., past youth advisor; mem. past sec., past. pres., past treas. Apollo Area Ch. Women United; treas. for elem. and jr. high PTA; vol. ARC Blood Bank; chmn. Well Baby Clinic; mem. Community Chorus, Sweet Harmony's female barbershop quartet. Mem. ANA, NEA, Pa. State Edn. Assn., Pa. State Nurses Assn., Armstrong County Nurses Assn., Nat. Assn. Sch. Nurses, Pa. Assn. Sch. Nurses , Vis. Nurses Assn.-Home Health Svcs. Found. Inc. (bd. dirs.,chmn. profl. adv. com., sec.), Alderson-Broaddus Coll. Alumni Coun. (chairperson gifts com., sec., pres. 1982-84, 96-97, v.p. 1993-94, 94-95, pres. 1995-97), Alumni Assn. of Sch. Home: 309 S 3rd St Apollo PA 15613-1131

KAUTZ, JAMES CHARLES, investment banker; b. Cin., Mar. 3, 1931; s. Paul Daniel and Marie M. (Fisher) K.; m. Caroline Miller, June 15, 1957; children: Leslie Barnes, Daniel Paul. A.B., U. Cin., 1953; M.B.A., U. Pa., 1957; LLD (hon.), U. Cin., 1995. With food advt. dept. Procter & Gamble Co., Cin., 1957-59; corp. sec. Main Supply, Cin., 1959-66; with Goldman, Sachs & Co., N.Y.C., 1966—, gen. ptnr., 1978-87, ltd. ptnr., 1987—. Trustee Vassar Coll., 1983-95, chmn. bd. trustees, 1989-95; trustee Greater N.Y. coun. Boy Scouts Am., 1983—, Nat. Geog. Soc. Edn. Found., 1988-94, Deer Creek Found., 1989—, U. Cin. McMicken Found., 1990—, Nat. Geog. Soc., 1994—; gov. Fgn. Policy Assn., 1991—, Brookings Inst. Coun., 1992—. With U.S. Army, 1953-55. Mem. Beacon Hill Club (Summit, N.J.), Phi Delta Theta. Home: 251 Oak Ridge Ave Summit NJ 07901-3258 Office: Goldman Sachs & Co 85 Broad St New York NY 10004-2456*

KAUTZ, RICHARD CARL, chemical and feed company executive; b. Muscatine, Iowa, Aug. 1, 1916; s. Carl and Leah (Amlong) K.; m. Mary Elda Stein, Dec. 24, 1939; children: Linda Kautz Osterkamp, Judith, John Terry, Thomas R., Susan E. Kautz Spencer, Sarah J. Kautz Aavang, Mary Catherine Kautz Huff, Jennifer W. Kautz-McKee. Student, U. Ariz., 1936-37; BS with high distinction, U. Iowa, 1939; DHL, George Williams Coll., 1973. Supr. in fin. dept. Gen. Electric Co., 1939-43; with Grain Processing Corp. and Kent Feeds, Inc., Muscatine, 1943-88, chmn. bd. dirs., mem. exec. com., 1966-88; with Varied Investments, Inc., 1988—; chmn., dir., mem. exec. com., chmn. fin. com., 1988—; mem. adv. com. Export-Import Bank U.S., 1984—. Mem. citizens com. Rock Island dist. U.S. Army Engrs.; bd. trustees, mem. Herbert Hoover Presdl. Library Assn., 1976—; chmn. nat. bd. dirs. YMCA, 1970-73, mem. exec. com. and bd. dirs.; mem. exec. com. World Alliance YMCA's, 1973—, mem. pres.'s com., exec. com.; mem. Bd. Trustees YMCA's; trustee YMCA Retirement Fund, Ctr. for Study of Presidency, 1977—; bd. dirs., mem. exec. com., chmn. Bus.-Industry Polit. Action Com., 1977—. Named to Iowa Bus. Hall of Fame, 1987. Mem. NAM (bd. dirs., chmn. exec. com. 1977, chmn. fin. com. 1978, vice chmn. 1975, chmn. 1976), Iowa Mfrs. Assn. (bd. dirs.), Muscatine C. of C., DeMolay Legion of Honor, Beta Gamma Sigma (dirs. table), Sigma Chi (named Significant Sig.). Presbyterian. Clubs: Union League (Chgo.); Met., Capitol Hill (Washington); Marco Polo, U. Iowa Pres.'s, Univ. Athletic (Iowa City); Des Moines, Lincoln (Des Moines). Lodges: Masons, Shriners, Elks, Rotary. Home: 2355 200th St Muscatine IA 52761-8441 Office: Varied Investments Inc 1600 Oregon St Muscatine IA 52761-1404*

KAUTZMAN, DWIGHT C.H., federal judge; b. 1945. BA, N.D. State U., 1968; JD, U. N.D., 1971. Pvt. practice Mandan, N.D., 1971-73; judge Mandan Mcpl. Ct., 1973-76; chmn. Legal Svcs. Com. N.D., 1976-79; magistrate judge U.S. Dist. Ct. N.D., Bismark, 1978—. Fax: 701-250-4259. Office: US Courthouse 220 E Rosser Ave Bismarck ND 58502

KAUTZMAN, JOHN FREDRICK, lawyer; b. Indpls., Aug. 23, 1959; s. Fred L. and Barbara J. (Seeger) K. BA, Ind. U., 1981; JD, Ind. U., Indpls., 1984. Bar: Ind. 1985, U.S. Dist. Ct. (no. and so. dists.) Ind. 1985, U.S. Ct. Appeals (7th cir.) 1992. Law clk. Marion County Pros. Office, Indpls., 1981; bailiff Marion County Cir. Ct., Indpls., 1981-84, commr., judge pro tempore, 1985-89; assoc. Ruckelshaus, Roland, Hasbrook & O'Conner, Indpls., 1985-89, ptnr., 1990-98; ptnr. Ruckelshaus, Roland, Kautzman & Hasbrook, Indpls., 1998—; mem. faculty Ind. Trial Advocacy Coll., 1998—. Contbg. author The Indiana Lawyer newspaper, 1991—. Mem. bd. assocs. Ind. U. Found., Bloomington, 1993—, v.p. 1997—; precinct committeeman Marion County Rep. Party, Indpls., 1994-96. Mem. ABA, Indpls. Bar Assn. (v.p. 1998, bd. mgrs. 1994-96, young lawyers divsn. chmn. 1988-89, Disting. fellow 1993), Ind. State Bar Assn., Phi Delta Phi. Methodist. Avocations: professional piano, golf. Office: Ruckelshaus Roland Kautzman & Hasbrook Ste 900 107 N Pennsylvania St Indianapolis IN 46204-2424

KAUVAR, ABRAHAM J., gastroenterologist, medical administrator; b. Denver, May 8, 1915; s. Charles Hillel and Belle Gertrude (Bluestone) K.; m. Jean Bayer, Aug. 22, 1943; children: Kenneth B., Jane Kauvar Athens, Lawrence, David. B.A., U. Denver, 1935; M.D., U. Chgo., 1939; Sc.D. (hon.), Hawthorne Coll., 1981. Diplomate: Am. Bd. Internal Medicine. Intern Billings Hosp., U. Chgo., 1939-40; resident Peter Bent Brigham Hosp., Boston, 1940-41, Mayo Clinic, Rochester, Minn., 1941-42; practice medicine specializing in gastroenterology Denver, 1946-74; mgr., chief exec. officer Health and Hosps. Agy., City and County of Denver, 1974-80; pres. Health and Hosp. Corp., N.Y.C., 1980-81; spl. cons. med. Care and Rsch. Found., Denver; Goodstein Disting. prof. emeritus medicine and geriatrics U. Colo. Med. Sch.; adj. prof. Health Policy Univ. Colo. at Denver; health cons. govts., Ireland, Israel; mem. Social Security Appeals Coun., Dept. Health and Human Svcs.; pres. med. staffs Colo. Gen. Hosp., 1954-55, Rose Meml. Hosp., 1955-56; dir. Nat. Jewish Hosp., 1957—; pres. Tchrs. Award Found., 1957. Contbr. articles to profl. jours.; lectr.: hypoglycemia Am. Lecture Series, 1954. Bd. dirs. Salvation Army, 1957—. Served to maj. U.S. Army, 1942-46. Recipient Disting. award Denver Med. Soc., 1975, Disting. Humanitarian award U. Chgo. Alumni Assn., 1981, Disting. Svc. award U. Colo., 1987, award for profl. achievement U. Denver, 1994, Lifetime Achievement award Denver Med. Soc., 1996. Mem. Am. Fedn. Clin. Research, ACP, Am. Gastroent. Assn., Am. Endoscopic Soc., Am. Geriatric Soc., Soc. Med. Adminstrs., Am. Coll. Gastroenterology (v.p. 1976-77). Jewish. Clubs: Denver, Denver Tennis, Rotary. Home: 70 S Ash St Denver CO 80246-1004 Office: Univ Colo Health Scis Ctr 4545 E 9th Ave #330 Denver CO 80220-3700 *Seize the opportunities that are presented whether it be in terms of work, family, friends.*

KAUZLARICH, RICHARD DALE, ambassador, foreign service officer; b. Moline, Ill., Aug. 18, 1944; s. Victor and Eva Marie (Kronfeld) K.; m. Anne Elizabeth Bregstone, Aug. 26, 1967; children—Richard Dale Jr., Terri Lynne. AA, Black Hawk Coll., Moline, Ill., 1964; BA, Valparaiso U., 1966; MA, Ind. U., 1967, U. Mich., 1976. 2d sec. U.S. Embassy, Addis Ababa, Ethiopia, 1973-75; fin. economist Office Devel. Fin. Dept. State, Washington, 1976-77; dep. office dir. Office Investment Affairs Dept. State, Washington, 1977-80; counselor for econ. affairs U.S. Embassy, Tel Aviv, Israel, 1980-83; office dir. ops. ctr. Dept. State, Washington, 1983-84, dep. asst. sec. Internat. Orgn. Affairs, 1984-86, dep. dir. policy planning staff, 1986-89, office dir. Regional Polit.-Econ.. Affairs, 1989-91, dep. asst. sec. Bur. European Affairs, 1991-93; prin. dep. to the amb.-at-large and spl. adviser Dept State, S/NIS; U.S. amb. Republic of Azerbaijan, 1994-97, Bosnia and Herzegovina, 1997—. Mem. Am. Internat. Sch. Bd., Tel Aviv, Israel, 1981-83. Recipient Presl. Meritorious Svc. award, 1993, Hall of Fame award Black Hawk Coll. Alumni Assn., 1993, Valparaiso U. Disting. Alumnus award, 1999; named Internat. Person of Yr. Dnevi Avaz, 1997. Lutheran. Office: US Embassy Sarajevo Dept State Washington DC 20521-7130

KAUZMANN, WALTER JOSEPH, chemistry educator; b. Mt. Vernon, N.Y., Aug. 18, 1916; s. Albert and Julia Maria (Kahle) K.; m. Elizabeth Alice Flagler, Apr. 1, 1951; children: Charles Peter, Eric Flagler, Katherine Elizabeth Julia Kauzmann Pacala. B.A., Cornell U., 1937; Ph.D., Princeton U., 1940; PhD (hon.), U. Stockholm, 1992. Westinghouse research fellow Westinghouse Mfg. Co., E. Pittsburgh, Pa., 1940-42; mem. staff Explosives Research Lab., Bruceton, Pa., 1942-44, Los Alamos Lab., 1944-46; asst. prof. Princeton U., 1946-51, asso. prof., 1951-60, prof. chemistry, 1960-82, chmn. dept., 1964-68, David B. Jones prof. chemistry, 1963-82, chmn. biochem. sci. dept., 1980-81; vis. scientist Atlantic Research Lab., NRC Can., 1983; vis. lectr. Kyoto U., 1974; vis. prof. U. Ibadan, 1975. Author: Quantum Chemistry, 1957, Kinetic Theory of Gases, 1966, Thermal Properties of Matter, 1967, (with D. Eisenberg) Structure and Properties of Water, 1969. Recipient Linderstrom-Lang medal, 1966, Stein and Moore award, 1993; Jr. fellow Soc. Fellows, Harvard U., 1942. Fellow AAAS, Am. Acad. Arts and Scis., Am. Phys. Soc.; mem. NAS, Am. Soc. Biochemistry and Molecular Biology, Protein Soc., Am. Geophys. Union, Am. Chem. Soc., Fedn. Am. Scientists, Royal Astron. Soc. Can., Math. Assn. Am., Soc. of History and Tech., Soc. for History of Sci., Sigma Xi. Office: 301 N Harrison St PMB 152 Princeton NJ 08540-3512

KAVALEK, LUBOMIR, chess expert; b. Prague, Czechoslovakia, Aug. 9, 1943; came to U.S., 1970; s. Lubomir and Stepanka (Kavalkova) K.; m. Irena Koritsanska, Nov. 24, 1971; 1 child, Steven. Student, Faculty of Transp., U. Zilina, 1960-65, Faculty of Journalism, Charles U., Prague, 1967-68, George Washington U., 1970-71. Journalist Voice of Am., USIA, 1971-72; chief editor RHM Chess Pub., Great Neck, N.Y., 1973-89; mem. German chess team, Solingen, 1969-89, U.S. chess team in chess Olympiad, 1972, 74, 76, 78, 82, 84, 86; reporter world chess championship, chess columnist Washington Post, 1986-93; exec. dir. Grandmaster Assn., Brussels, 1987-91, key organizer world cup, 1988-89; coach world championship Challenger, N. Short, 1990-93. Mem. Internat. Assn. Chess Journalists, U.S. Chess Fedn. German chess team champion, 1969, 71, 72, 73, 74, 75, 80, 81, 86, SS Dutch Open champion, 1969, Czechoslovakian champion, 1962, 68, Internat. Grandmaster, 1965—, U.S. co-champion, 1972, 73; U.S. champion, 1978, European Cup team champion, 1976, Olympic champion, 1976, German Internat. champion, 1981.

KAVALER, THOMAS J., lawyer; b. N.Y.C., Dec. 10, 1948. BA, CCNY, 1969; JD, Fordham U., 1972; LLM, NYU, 1975. Bar: N.Y., U.S. Dist. Ct. (so., ea., we. and no. dists.) N.Y., U.S. Ct. Appeals (2d, 4th, 5th, 6th, 8th, 10th, 11th and fed. cirs.), U.S. Supreme Ct. Law clk. to judge U.S. Dist. Ct. N.Y., N.Y.C., 1972-74; assoc. Cravath, Swaine & Moore, N.Y.C., 1974-75; assoc. Cahill Gordon & Reindel, N.Y.C., 1975-80, ptnr., 1980—. Served to capt. USAR, 1969-77. Fellow Am. Bar Found., Internat. Acad. Trial Lawyers. Office: Cahill Gordon & Reindel 80 Pine St Fl 17 New York NY 10005-1790

KAVALER-ALDER, SUSAN, clinical psychologist; b. N.Y.C., Jan. 31, 1950; d. Solomon and Alice (Zelikow) Weiss; m. Thomas Kavaler, July 12, 1970 (div. 1975); m. Saul Michael Adler, Aug. 14, 1983. PhD in Clin. Psychology, Adelphi U., 1974. Psychologist Beth Israel Hosp., N.Y.C., 1974-76, Manhattan Psychiat. Children's Ctr., N.Y.C., 1977-80; pvt. practice psychotherapy-psychoanalysis N.Y.C., 1976—; condr. writing and mourning groups; founding dir., supr. faculty, tng. analyst Object Rels. Inst. for Psychotherapy and Psychoanalysis, 1991—; mem. faculty Postgrad. Ctr. Mental Health, N.Y.C., 1984-86, 90; mem. faculty, supr. Nat. Inst. Psychotherapies, N.Y.C., 1985-91; bd. dirs., supr. Bklyn. Inst. Psychotherapy and Psychoanalysis, ; adj. prof. Fordham U.; founding exec. dir. Object Rels. Inst. Psychotherapy and Psychoanalysis; spkr pvt. seminars, writing groups. Author: The Compulsion to Create, 1993, The Creative Mystique: From Red Shoes Frenzy to Love and Creativity, 1996; contbr. more than 35 articles ro profl. jours. Office: 115 E 9th St 12 P New York NY 10003-5414

KAVANAGH, EILEEN J., librarian. BA, Ladycliff Coll.; MS in Libr. Sci., Columbia U., 1969; MA in Liberal Studies, SUNY, Stonybrook, 1980. Reference libr. Farmingdale (N.Y.) Pub. Libr., 1969-70; from reference libr. to libr. dir. Bay Shore-Brightwaters (N.Y.) Pub. Libr., 1970—. E-mail: ekavanag@suffolk.lib.ny.us. Office: Bay Shore-Brightwaters Pub Libr 1 South Country Rd Brightwaters NY 11718

KAVANAGH, JOHN JOSEPH, medical educator; b. Phila., Aug. 7, 1947; s. John and Christine Kavanagh; m. Teresa Ann Brown. BA, Sch. Internat. Svc., Washington, 1969; MD, Jefferson Med. Coll., 1975. Clin. asst. prof. U. Nebr., Omaha, 1980-81; instr., asst. internist M.D. Anderson Cancer Ctr., Houston, 1981-82; asst. prof., chief sect. gynecologic med. oncology M.D. Anderson Cancer Ctr., 1983-85, assoc. gynecologist, 1987—, assoc. prof., chief sect. gynecologic med. oncology, 1987—; assoc. prof. H. Lee Moffitt Cancer Ctr., Tampa, Fla., 1985-87; assoc. prof. ob-gyn. and reproductive scis. U. Tex. Health Sci. Ctr., Houston, 1991—, prof. dept. clin. investigation, 1996—; cons. S.W. Oncology Group, San Antonio, 1994—; mem. faculty European Sch. Oncology. With USAR, 1969-71. Grantee ASTA Medica, Inc., Hackensack, N.J., 1994, Hoffman-LaRoche, Nutley, N.J., 1994. Fellow ACP, European Soc. Gynecol. Oncology (assoc.); mem. Internat. Gynecologic Cancer Soc. (chmn. membership com., exec. com.), So. Oncology Assn. (pres. 1991-92), So. Med. Assn. (Presdl. com. on endowments 1993—), Tex. Soc. Med. Oncology (founding). Avocations: fishing, boating, reading. Office: M D Anderson Cancer Ctr 1515 Holcombe Blvd # 39 Houston TX 77030-4009

KAVANAUGH, EVERETT EDWARD, JR., trade association executive; b. New Haven, June 9, 1941; s. Everett Edward and Marion (Gallagher) K.; m. Martha Gamble Murphy, Feb. 23, 1963; 1 son, Brett Michael. A.B., Georgetown U., 1963; M.B.A., George Washington U., 1970; J.D., Am. U., 1978. Bar: Md. 1979, D.C. 1990. Sales rep. Northwestern Mut. Ins. Co., Washington, 1963-68; asst. to exec. offices U.S. C. of C., Washington, 1970-72; pres. Cosmetic, Toiletry and Fragrance Assn., Washington, 1972—. Roman Catholic. Clubs: Congressional Country, Burning Tree (Bethesda, Md.). Home: 4915 Jamestown Ct Bethesda MD 20816-2708 Office: Cosmetic Toiletry & Fragrance Assn 1101 17th St NW Ste 300 Washington DC 20036-4702

KAVANAUGH, FRANK JAMES, film producer, educator; b. Chgo., Sept. 12, 1934; s. Kenneth James and Carol Mae (Wilkey) K.; m. Barbara Ann Barrett, Nov. 16, 1957; children: Franklin James Jr., Christopher Barrett, Kenneth Wilkey. BA, Lake Forest Coll., 1956; PhD, Union Inst., 1982. Producer, dir., exec. ABC-TV, Chgo., N.Y.C., 1956-67; pres. Ravens Hollow Ltd., Warrenton, Va., 1967-69; exec. producer Airlie Prodns., Warrenton, 1979-89; prof. comm., prof. med. and pub. affairs, comm. chair George Washington U., Washington, 1983-89; v.p. Airlie Found., 1979—; adj. prof. Union Inst. Grad. Sch., 1987—; pres. Kavanaugh Assocs., Inc., 1989—; mentor Capella U.; v.p. Cooper Inst. for Advanced Studies in Medicine and Humanities, 1989—; pres. Internat. Acad. for Preventive Medicine. Asst. dir. TV Kukla, Fran & Ollie, 1958; producer film The Saving of the President, 1982 (Emmy award 1982); producer dir. films A Moveable Scene, 1968 (Emmy award nominee 1969), Flowers of Darkness, 1969 (Emmy award 1969), Bridge From No Place, 1970 (Emmy award 1970), The Possible Dream, 1970 (Emmy award 1970), More Than a Paycheck, 1978 (Emmy award nominee 1978), others; producer, dir., writer film Each Child Loved, 1972 (Emmy award 1972), others. Bd. dirs. Performing Arts Trust. Recipient Cup of Italy Italian Film Festival, Salerno, 1982, highest award Edinburgh Film Festival, Scotland, 1982, Blue Ribbon Am. Film Festival, N.Y.C., 1983, Gold medal Houston Internat. Film Festival, 1983. Mem. Nat. Acad. TV Arts and Scis. (life), C.I.N.E., Inc. (life), Dirs. Guild Am., Radio and TV Dirs. Guild, Mensa, Nat. Assn. TV Program Execs. (Iris award 1983), Broadcast Pioneers. Avocations: photography, scuba, boating, motorcycling. Office: Kavanaugh Assocs Inc PO Box 713 Punta Gorda FL 33938-0713

KAVESH, ROBERT A., economist, educator; b. N.Y.C., Sept. 12, 1927; s. Samuel and Pearl (Berlin) K.; m. Ruth Freidson, 1951 (div. 1980); children: Richard, Laura, Andrew, Joseph; m. Danielle Nisivoccia, July 11, 1990. BS, NYU, 1949; MA, Harvard U., 1950, PhD, 1954. Asst. prof. econs. Dartmouth Coll., 1953-56; bus. economist Chase Manhattan Bank, N.Y.C., 1956-58; prof. econs. and finance Grad. Sch. Bus. Adminstrn., NYU, 1958-74, Marcus Nadler prof. finance and econs., 1974—, chmn. dept. econs., 1968-83; bd. dirs. Del Labs., Inc., Neuberger and Berman Income Funds; mem. econ. adv. bd. U.S. Dept. Commerce, 1968-70; mem. investment adv. com. N.Y. State Compt., 1976-86; pres. The Money Marketeers, 1983-84. Author: Businessmen in Fiction, 1955, How Business Economists Forecast, 1966, Methods and Techniques of Business Forecasting, 1974; also articles.; Asso. editor: Bus. Economics, 1965—. Bd. dirs. Thomas A. Edison Coll. N.J., 1973-78. Served with U.S. Navy, World War II. Recipient Danforth Found. prize disting. teaching, 1968, Madden Meml. award for profl. achievement NYU, 1979, Gt. Tchr. award NYU, 1983. Fellow Nat. Assn. Bus. Economists (council 1973-76); mem. Am. Fin. Assn. (exec. sec.-treas. 1961-79), Regional Sci. Assn. (past sec.), Am. Econ. Assn. Home: 110 Bleecker St New York NY 10012-2101 Office: 44 W 4th St New York NY 10012-1106

KAVLI, FRED, manufacturing executive; b. Norway, Aug. 20, 1927; came to U.S., 1956; Grad., Norwegian Inst. Tech., 1955. Founder, CEO automotive and aerospace sensor engrng.-mfg. Kavlico Corp., 1958—. Bd. dirs. Surg. Eye Expdns. Internat., The Found. for Santa Barbara City Coll. Avocations: tennis, skiing, travel. Office: Kavlico Corp 14501 E Los Angeles Ave Moorpark CA 93021-9775

KAVOUKJIAN, MICHAEL EDWARD, lawyer; b. Mpls., Apr. 19, 1958; s. Antranik M. and Leikny Dorthea (Oines) K.;. AB with distinction, Stanford U., 1980; JD cum laude, Harvard U., 1984. Bar: Minn. 1984, N.Y. 1986, U.S. Dist. Ct. Minn. 1985, U.S. Dist. Ct. (so. dist.) N.Y. 1988, Fla. 1999. From assoc. to ptnr. White & Case, N.Y.C. and Miami, Fla., 1985—. Mem. ABA (chmn. com. estate planning and drafting 1992-94), Minn. State Bar Assn., The Fla. Bar, Assn. of the Bar City of N.Y., Harvard Club (N.Y.C., Washington), Nat. Press Club (Washington), Lincoln's Inn Soc. Harvard Law Sch. (bd. gov. 1982-84). Republican. Presbyterian. Office: White & Case 1155 Avenue Of The Americas New York NY 10036-2787

KAVULICH, JOHN STEVEN, II, international marketing executive; b. Buffalo, Sept. 2, 1961; s. John Sr. and Emily Helen Anne (Kloc) K. BBA, George Washington U., 1983. Cons. Nat. Voter Contact, Inc., Washington, 1981-82, The Canzeri Co., Inc., Washington, 1982-84; chmn., chief exec. officer Kavulich Internat., Inc., Washington, 1984—. Co-author: (booklet) The Preservation of the Ideas of an Age Old Deerfield, Massachusetts, 1976. Pres. Brooks Sch. chpt. Young Dem. Clubs Mass., 1978-79; pres. U.S.-Cuba Trade and Econ. Coun., Inc., 1994—. Office: Kavulich Internat Inc PO Box 25653 Washington DC 20007-8653

KAW, AUTAR KRISHEN, mechanical engineer, educator; b. Srinagar, India, Feb. 15, 1960; came to U.S., 1982; s. Radha Krishen and Chuni Devi (Mattoo) K.; m. Sherrie Lynn Phillips, May 16, 1986; children: Candace Sandhya, Angelie Kristen. BE with honors, Birla Inst. Tech. & Sci., Pilani, India, 1981; MS, Clemson U., 1984, PhD, 1987. Student trainee Nat. Thermal Power Corp., New Delhi, India, 1980; maintenance engr. Escorts Tractors Ltd., Faridabad, India, 1981-82; grad. rsch. asst. Clemson (S.C.) U., 1982-83, prin. grad. asst., 1984-87; asst. prof. mech. engring. U. South Fla., Tampa, 1987-92, assoc. prof., 1992-96, prof., 1996—, grad. student coord. mech. engring. dept., 1989-90. Author: Mechanics of Composite Materials, 1997; contbr. articles to profl. publs. Recipient Ralph Teetor award Soc. Automotive Engrs., 1991, Tchg. Incentive Program award State of Fla., 1994, 96. Mem. ASME (assoc., chpt. exec. com. 1989-90), Mech. Engring. Assn. India (pres. local chpt. 1982), Am. Soc. Engring. Edn. (recipient New Mechanics Educator award 1992), Soc. Engring. Sci., Am. Acad. Mechanics. Hindu. Avocations: running, racquetball, music. Office: U South Fla Mech Engring ENB 118 4202 E Fowler Ave Tampa FL 33620-9951

KAWACHIKA, JAMES AKIO, lawyer; b. Honolulu, Dec. 5, 1947; s. Shinichi and Tsuyuko (Murashige) K.; m. Karen Keiko Takahashi, Sept. 1, 1973; 1 child, Robyn Mari. BA, U. Hawaii, Honolulu, 1969; JD, U. Calif., Berkeley, 1973. Bar: Hawaii 1973, U.S. Dist. Ct. Hawaii 1973, U.S. Ct. Appeals (9th cir.) 1974, U.S. Supreme Ct. 1992. Dep. atty. gen. Office of Atty. Gen. State of Hawaii, Honolulu, 1973-74; assoc. Padgett, Greeley & Marumoto, Honolulu, 1974-75, Law Office of Frank D. Padgett, Honolulu, 1975-77, Kobayashi, Watanabe, Sugita & Kawashima, Honolulu, 1977-82; ptnr. Carlsmith, Wichman, Case, Mukai & Ichiki, Honolulu, 1982-86, Bays, Deaver, Hiatt, Kawachika & Lezak, Honolulu, 1986-95; propr. Law Offices of James A. Kawachika, Honolulu, 1996-98; ptnr. Kawachika & Ozaki, Honolulu, 1999—; mem. Hawaii Bd. of Bar Examiners, Honolulu; arbitrator Cir. Ct. Arbitration Program State of Hawaii, Honolulu, 1986—. Chmn. Disciplinary Bd. Hawaii Supreme Ct., 1991-97; mem. U.S. dist. Ct. Adv. Com. on the Civil Justice Reform Act of 1990, 1991—. Mem. ABA, ATLA, Hawaii Bar Assn. (bd. dirs. Honolulu chpt. 1975-76, young lawyers sect. 1983-84, 92-93, treas. 1987-88, v.p./pres.-elect 1997-98, pres. 1998-99), 9th Cir. Jud. Conf. (lawyer rep. Honolulu chpt. 1988-90). Avocations: running, tennis, skiing. Office: Grosvenor Ctr Mauka Tower 737 Bishop St Ste 2750 Honolulu HI 96813-3216

KAWACHIKA, JEAN KEIKO, middle school educator; b. Hilo, Hawaii, Nov. 28, 1944; d. Raymond Masato and Shizue (Murai) Atebara; m. Robert Yukichi Kawachika, June 24, 1967; children: Lynn Masako, Bruce Yukio. BA, Whittier (Calif.) Coll., 1966. Cert. tchr. secondary edn., Hawaii. Tchr. Hilo Intermediate Sch., 1971-73; tchr./advisor/program coord. Pahoa (Hawaii) H.S., 1973-86; tchr. Kea'au (Hawaii) Mid. Sch., 1986—, project tchr. Project Bus./Jr. Achievement, 1988—; tchr./advisor Future Flight, NASA, 1992-93. Named to Outstanding Young Women of Am., 1976; grantee Freedoms Found. Valley Forge, 1976, Hawaii Citizenship Inst., 1988-92, Consortium for Tchg. Asia and the Pacific in the Schs., 1989-91, UCLA We the People Inst., 1998; grantee W. Regional Summer Inst., UCLA, 1998. Mem. ASCD, AAUW, Nat. Coun. for the Social Studies, Hawaii Assn. for the Mid. Schs. Buddhist. Avocations: travel, reading historical/mystery novels. Office: Kea'au Middle School 16-565 Keaau Pahoa Rd Keaau HI 96749-8106

KAWAHARA, FRED KATSUMI, research chemist; b. Penngrove, Calif., Feb. 26, 1921; s. Kentaro and Kiku (Seo) K.; m. Sumiko Hayami, May 5, 1952; children: Robert Katsumi, Kiku Seo, Richard Hojo; m. Andrea L. Eary, June 29, 1991. BS with honors, U. Tex., 1944; PhD, U. Wis., 1948. Assoc. chemist USDA, Peoria, Ill., 1948-51; postdoctoral fellow U. Chgo., 1951-53; sr. rsch. scientist Amoco Corp. (formerly Standard Oil of Ind.), Whiting, 1953-65; rsch. chemist EPA, Cin., 1965—; cons., expert witness U.S. Dept. Def., U.S. Dept. Air Force, U.S. Dept. Justice, State of Pa., State of N.J.; mentor EPA, others, 1965—; lectr. in field. Co-author: Fossil Energy Extraction, 1983, Innovative Site Remediation Technology, Chemical Treatment, vol. 2, 1994; contbr. 6 chpts. to books, more than 60 articles to profl. jours. Recipient Five Hundred Gold Medal, Superior Svc. award Bur. Indsl. and Agrl. Chemistry, Internat. Order Merit. Fellow Am. Inst. Chemists. Achievements include 20 U.S. patents and 1 British patent; first to develop mechanism for soybean oil deterioration; first to develop additive for lubrication of ball bearings operating at 600 degrees Fahrenheit and at 10,000 R.P.M. with 50 lbs. axial load for 180 hours to meet requirements for flight and space systems; characterized and identified oil spills with 98% certainty via linear discriminant function analyses and solved 48 oil spills throughout the U.S.; developed a suitable substitute for Freon 113 in order to help curtail ozone deterioration in the stratosphere; involved in hydrodechlorination of organic chlorine compounds which are toxic, carcinogenic to humans and deleterious to the atmosphere; advanced the science of base catalyzed decomposition of polychlorobiphenyls, developed new concept and formulated new hydrogen donors, transfer agents, and new catalyst; involved in research to detoxify organic chemicals used in warfare; discovery that polynuclear aromatic hydrocarbon release from soil during treatment with Fenton's Reagent is due to electron exchange by structural iron in clay material and the swelling of clay layers is proposed as the release mechanism of tightly held polynuclear aromatic hydrocarbon. Development of hydrodechlorination of polychlorobiphenyls at room temperature in ten minutes. Home: 1632 Cumberland St Covington KY 41011-3716 Office: US EPA 26 Martin Luther King Dr W Cincinnati OH 45220-2242

KAWANO, ARNOLD HUBERT, lawyer; b. Phila., Mar. 27, 1948; s. James Tadao and Shigeko (Sakamoto) K.; m. Sandra K. Lee, July 1, 1970; children: Thomas L., Mark L. BS magna cum laude, Columbia U., 1975, JD, 1977. Bar: N.Y. 1978, D.C. 1979, Pa. 1981, U.S. Dist. Ct. (ea. and so. dists.) N.Y. 1978, U.S. Ct. Appeals (fed. cir.) 1992, U.S. Ct. Internat. Trade 1992, U.S. Supreme Ct. 1981. Assoc. Reid & Priest, N.Y.C., 1977-80, Weil, Gotshal & Manges, N.Y.C., 1980-81; counsel Sumitomo Corp. of Am., N.Y.C., 1981-84; pvt. practice N.Y.C., Mineola, N.Y., 1984-87; v.p. J.P. Morgan, N.Y.C., 1987-91; ptnr. Inouye & Ogden, N.Y.C., 1992-93; sr. v.p., gen. counsel ORIX USA Corp., N.Y.C., 1993-98; mng. dir. Harold L. Lee & Sons, Inc., N.Y.C., 1999—; bd. dirs. Harold L. Lee & Sons, Inc., N.Y.C. Bd. dirs. Asian-Am. Legal Def. and Edn. Fund, N.Y.C., 1977-88, N.Y. Civil Liberties Union, 1992-94. Harlan Fiske Stone scholar Columbia Law Sch., 1976, Internat. fellow Columbia U. Sch. Internat. Affairs, 1976. Fellow Am. Coll. Investment Counsel; mem. ABA, NAACP, N.Y. State Bar Assn., D.C. Bar, Assn. of Bar City N.Y., Asian Pacific Am. Bar Assn. N.Y. (bd. dirs. 1992-93), Am. Corp. Counsel Assn., Am. Intellectual Property Law Assn., Computer Law Assn., Fed. Cir. Bar Assn., Assn. for Computing Machinery, Internat. Assn. for Artificial Intelligence and Law, Nat. Press Photographers Assn., Evidence Photographers Internat. Coun., Japanese Am. Citizens League, Phi Beta Kappa. Avocations: camping, canoeing, photography, skiing. Home: 176 Overlook Ave Great Neck NY 11021-3831

KAWANO, JAMES CONRAD, investment analyst. Student, U. Calif., Berkeley, 1972-73; PharmD, U. Calif., San Francisco, 1978; postgrad., U. Pa., 1986—. Registered pharmacist, Calif., Pa. Clin. pharmacist Med. Coll. Pa. and Hosp., Phila., 1978-82; med. devel. coord. E.R. Squibb and Sons, U.S., Princeton, N.J., 1982-84; mktg. rsch. supr. E.R. Squibb and Sons, U.S., Princeton, 1984-85, mktg. rsch. mgr., 1985-86; mgr. strategic planning and bus. analysis Squibb U.S., Princeton, 1986-87, bus. devel. mgr., 1987-88; mgr. product planning worldwide bus. devel. Squibb Pharms. Group, Princeton, 1988-89; mgr. product planning pravastatin, worldwide strategic product planning Bristol-Myers Squibb Pharm. Group, Princeton, 1989-90; sr. product planning mgr., strategic product planning Bristol-Myers Squibb Pharm. Group, 1990-91; cons. mktg. Narberth, Pa., 1991-94, investment analyst, 1991—; pres. Riverfield Investment Rsch., Wynnewood, Pa., 1994—. Pub., editor: The Optimer Report, 1994—; patentee in field. Mem. Japanese Am. Citizens League (bd. dirs. Phila. chpt. 1997-98, treas. Phila. chpt. 1998—, vice-gov. Ea. dist. coun. 1998—), Calif. Pharmacists Assn.

KAWASAKI, GREGORY YUKIO, communications consultant; b. L.A., Feb. 21, 1956; s. George and Satoye Kawasaki; m. Pamela Bock, Oct. 31, 1989; children: Brandon, Alysha. BS in Info. Sys., Calif. Poly. Pomona, 1981. Tech. mktg. dir. Avnet, Inc., Culver City, Calif., 1981-89, v.p. engring., 1989-93; sr. cons. AT&T, Homedale, N.J., 1993-96; sr. cons. info. arch. NCR, Dayton, Ohio, 1996-97, Computer Sci. Corp., Waltham, Mass., 1997—. Vol. Duarte (Calif.) Sch. Dist., 1995—. Office: CSC-CSI 266 2d Ave Waltham MA 02154

KAWCZYNSKI, DIANE MARIE, elementary and middle school educator, composer; b. Milw., Jan. 22, 1959; d. Adalbert Lawrence and Joan (Zernia) K. BMus, Lawrence U., 1981; MMus, U. Wis., 1985. Cert. music tchr., Va. Suzuki violin instr., string methods instr. Brandon (Manitoba, Can.) Univ. Sch. Music, 1982-83; violin/viola instr., univ. prep program U. Wis. Sch. of Music, Madison, 1983-85; elem. and middle sch. string instr. Albuquerque Pub. Schs., 1985-86; middle sch. string and chorus instr. Ft. Morgan (Colo.) Pub. Schs., 1986-87; elem. string instr., middle sch. orchestra instr. Norfolk Pub. Schs., 1987—. Mem. NEA, Am. String Tchr. Assn., Music Educators Nat. Conf. Avocations: knitting, walking, crafts. Home: 860 Gaslight Ln Virginia Beach VA 23462-1232

KAWITT, ALAN, lawyer; b. Chgo., 1937. J.D., Chgo.-Kent Coll. Law, 1965; postgrad. Lawyers Inst. John Marshall Law Sch., 1966-68. Bar: Ill. 1966, U.S. Dist. Ct. (no. dist.) Ill. 1967, U.S. Ct. Appeals (7th cir.) 1971, U.S. Supreme Ct., 1971. Sole practice, 1970—. Mem. Am. Arbitration Assn. (arbitrator). Fax: (773) 472-3556. Office: 226 S Wabash Ave Ste 905 Chicago IL 60604-2319

KAY, ALAN, computer scientist; b. 1940. BS in Math., Molecular Biology, U. Colo., 1966; PhD, U. Utah, 1969. Fellow Xerox Palo Alto (Calif.) Rsch. Ctr.; chief scientist Atari; fellow Apple Computer, Brentwood, Calif., 1984-96, Walt Disney Co., 1996—. Fellow AAAS, NEA, Royal Soc. Arts. Office: Walt Disney Imagineering 1401 Flower St Glendale CA 91221-5020*

KAY, ALAN COOKE, federal judge; b. 1932; s. Harold Thomas and Ann (Cooke) K. BA, Princeton U., 1957; LLB, U. Calif., Berkeley, 1960. Assoc. Case, Kay & Lynch, Honolulu, 1960-64, ptnr., 1965-86; judge U.S. Dist. Ct. Hawaii, Honolulu, 1986-92, chief judge, 1992—; bd. regents Internat. Coll. and Grad. Sch., 1994—. Mem. steering com. Fuller Theol. Sem. Hawaii, 1985-86; pres., trustee Hawaii Mission Children's Soc., Honolulu, 1980-86; bd. dirs. Good News Mission, 1980-86, Econ. Devel. Corp. Honolulu, 1985-86, Legal Aid Soc., Honolulu, 1968-71. Mem. ABA, Hawaii Bar Assn. (exec. com. 1972-73, bd. dirs. real estate sect. 1983-86), Fed. Judges Assn. (9th cir. jud. coun. 1994—, 9th cir. Pacific Islands com. 1994—), Am. Inns of Ct. (counselor Aloha Inn 1987—). Republican. Office: US Dist Ct C-415 Kuhio Federal Bldg 300 Ala Moana Blvd Honolulu HI 96850-5000*

KAY, ALBERT JOSEPH, textile executive; b. Cleve., June 3, 1920; s. Simon and Eszter (Rosenzweig) K.; m. Irene Pramisloff, June 11, 1944; children: Leslie Andrzejewski, Stephen, Adrienne Gallagher. Student, Cuyahoga Community Coll., 1961. Sales rep. The Carnegie Textile Co., Cleve., 1938-68, v.p., gen. mgr., 1968-94, pres., 1994—; mem. citizens adv. com. Centerior Energy, 1991—; adv. bd. ARC, 1988-93. Pres. Mayfield H.S. PTA, 1968-69, Friends Mayfield Regional Libr., 1998-99; former pres. Mayfield Boys Baseball League; past. sect. chmn. United Way; founder Mayfield Heights Bicentennial Com., Mayfield Area Recreation Coun.; mem. Citizens Com. for Edn., 1968; chmn. Citizens for Honest Govt., 1965; past pres. Friends of Hillcrest Libr.; coun. mem. City Mayfield Heights, 1969-97, coun. pres., 1981-85, 1996-97; campaign co-chmn. Aveni for State Rep., Ohio, 1975; chmn. levy renewal com. Cuyahoga County Pub. Libr., 1989; past. mem. exec. com. Hillcrest Dem. Caucus, Mayfield Schs. Acad. Booster's Club; former chmn. planning and zoning commn. City Mayfield Heights; trustee Schnurmann House, 1970—, Assn. Retarded Citizens, 1992-94; cmty. coord. Clinton-Gore campaign, 1992; mem., founder Edn.-Bus. Cmty. Alliance, Mayfield City Schs., 1994—; former pres. Hillcrest Coun. of Couns., 1977; mem. Cuyahoga County Dem. Exec. Com.; mem. Mayfield Heights Planning Commn., 1998—; founder, chmn. Mayfield Dist. Millenium Celebration, 1999—. With U.S. Army, 1943. Recipient Cmty. Svcs. award Hillcrest Cleve. Exch., 1977, Civic Svcs. award Citizens League of Cleve., 1996, Cmty. Svc. award Nat. Exch. Club, 1984, Outstanding Svc. award Mayfield Heights C. of C., 1979, Citizenship award VFW, 1976, Disting. Svc. award Assn. for Retarded Citizens, 1991, Citizen of Yr. award (with wife) Mayfield City Schs., 1995, Award for Disting. Svc., Citizens League of Cleve., 1996, Cert. of Appreciation for Pub. Svc., Gov. Ohio, 1997, Cuyahoga County Commrs., 1997, Ohio Ho. of Reps., 1997, Ohio State Senate, 1997; commendation Ohio State Sen. for Disting. Cmty. Svc., 1997. Mem. Mayfield Heights Planning Commn., 1998, Friends of Mayfield Regional Libr. (pres. 1998—), Internat. Assn. Wiping Cloth Mfrs. (bd.dirs. 1981-85, 89-93, Outstanding and Dedicated Svc. award 1985), Am. Assn. Ret. Persons (bd. dirs. East Suburban Cuyahoga County chpt. 371 1993-95), Secondary/Materials and Recycled Textiles, Jewish Vets Cleve. (comdr. 1946-48), Masons. Democrat. Jewish. Avocations: polit. activity, piano. Home: 1835 Beham Dr Cleveland OH 44124-3121 Office: The Carnegie Textile Co 1734 Ivanhoe Rd Cleveland OH 44112-1623

KAY, CAROL MCGINNIS, literature educator; b. Gadsden, Ala., Jan. 14, 1941; d. Gaston G. and Ruth (Owen) McGinnis; 1 child, David McGinnis Kay. BA, U. Ala., 1962, MA, 1963; PhD, U. Tenn., 1967. Scholar-tchr. U. Ala., 1967-78, chair dept. English, 1978-81, spl. asst. to pres., 1981-82; dean of coll. Randolph-Macon Woman's Coll., 1982-86; dean coll. humanities and social scis. U. S.C., Columbia, 1986-93, prof. English, 1993—. Co-author: "G" Is for Grafton, 1997 (Edgar award for critical work of 1997); co-editor: Shakespeare's Romances Reconsidered, 1978; contbr. articles to profl. jours. Trustee Folger Shakespeare Theatre, Washington, 1986-93, Heathwood Hall Episcopal Sch.; bd. dirs. Coun. Colls. Arts and Scis. Fellow Am. Coun. on Edn., 1981-82; recipient Mortar Bd. Tchg. award, 1994. Mem. Southeastern Renaissance Conf. (past pres.), South Caroliniana Soc. Episcopalian. Avocations: collecting antiques, mystery novels, travel. Home: 359 S Stonehedge Dr Columbia SC 29210-4225 Office: U SC Dept English Welsh Humanities Bldg Columbia SC 29208

KAY, CRAIG, principal. Prin. Dassel (Minn.) Elem. Sch., 1981—. Recipient Elem. Sch. Recognition award U.S. Dept. Edn., 1989-90. Office: Dassel Elem Sch 131 William Ave E Dassel MN 55325-0368*

KAY, CYRIL MAX, biochemist; b. Calgary, Alta., Can., Oct. 3, 1931; s. Louis and Fanny (Pearlmutter) K.; m. Faye Bloomenthal, Dec. 30, 1953; children: Lewis Edward, Lisa Franci. B.Sc. in Biochemistry with honors (J.W. McConnell Meml. scholar), McGill U., 1952; Ph.D. in Biochemistry (Life Ins. Med. Research Fund fellow), Harvard U., 1956; postgrad., Cambridge (Eng.) U., 1956-57. Phys. biochemist Eli Lilly & Co., Indpls., 1957-58; asst. prof. biochemistry U. Alta., Edmonton, 1958-61; assoc. prof. U. Alta., 1961-67, prof., 1967—, co-dir. Med. Rsch. Coun. Group on Protein Structure and Function, 1974-95, mem. protein engring. network Centre of Excellence, 1990—; Med. Rsch. Coun. vis. scientist in biophysics Weizmann Inst., Israel, 1969-70, summer vis. prof. biophysics, 1975, summer vis. prof. chem. physics, 1977, 80; mem. biochemistry grants com. Med. Research Council, 1970-73; mem. Med. Rsch. Coun. Can., 1982-88; Can. rep. Pan Am. Assn. Biochem. Socs., 1971-76; mem. exec. planning com. XI Internat. Congress Biochemistry, Toronto, Ont., Can., 1979; mem. med. adv. bd. Gairdner Found. for Internat. awards in Med. Sci., 1980-89. Contbr. numerous articles to profl. publs.; asso. editor Can. Jour. Biochemistry, 1968-82; editor-in-chief Pan Am. Assn. Biochem. Socs. Revista, 1971-76. Decorated Order of Can.; recipient Ayerst award in biochemistry Can. Biochem. Soc., 1970, Disting. Scientist award U. Alta. Med. Sch., 1988. Fellow N.Y. Acad. Scis., Royal Soc. Can.; mem. Order of Can., Can. Biochem. Soc. (coun. 1971—, v.p. 1976-77, pres. 1978-79). Home: 9408-143d St, Edmonton, AB Canada T5R 0P7 Office: U Alta Dept Biochemistry, Med Scis Bldg, Edmonton, AB Canada T6G 2H7

KAY, DOUGLAS CASEY, leasing consultant; b. Pueblo, Colo., July 2, 1932; s. Cecil Harmon and Nadine (Casey) K.; m. Ann Jeffrey, Dec. 28, 1953; children—Fredrick Charles, Lynn Kay Peters, Balfour Jeffrey. A.B., U. Kans., 1954; M.B.A., Harvard, 1959. Asst. treas. U.S. Leasing Corp., San Francisco, 1959-62; asst. to pres. U.S. Leasing Corp., 1963-66, treas., 1966-67; v.p. U.S. Leasing Corp., Cleve., 1967-69; sr. v.p. U.S. Leasing Internat., Inc., San Francisco, 1969-72; asst. v.p. Laurentide Financial Corp., San Francisco, 1962-63; 1st v.p. leasing White, Weld & Co., San Francisco, 1972-73; chmn. bd. Matrix Leasing Internat., Inc., San Francisco, 1973-74; sr. v.p. GATX Capital Corp., San Francisco, 1974-78, exec. v.p., 1978-84; pres. PLM Fin. Services Inc., San Francisco, 1984-85; pres., also bd. dirs. U.S. Airlease, Inc., 1985-89, Airlease Mgmt. Services, Inc., 1986-89; cons. aircraft leasing, 1989—. Served with USAF, 1954-57. Home: 1878 Heritage Way Yountville CA 94599-9404

KAY, ELIZABETH ALISON, zoology educator; b. Kauai, Hawaii, Sept. 27, 1928; d. Robert Buttercase and Jessie Dowie (McConnachie) K. BA, Mills Coll., 1950, Cambridge U., Eng., 1952; MA, Cambridge U., Eng., 1956; PhD, U. Hawaii, 1957. From asst. prof. to prof. zoology U. Hawaii, Honolulu, 1957-62, assoc. prof., 1962-67, prof., 1967-98, prof. emeritus, 1998—; research assoc. Bishop Mus., Honolulu, 1968—. Author: Hawaiian Marine Mollusks, 1979, Shells of Hawaii, 1991; editor: A Natural History of the Hawaiian Islands, 1972, 94. Chmn. Animal Species Adv. Commn., Honolulu, 1983-87; v.p. Save Diamond Head Assn., Honolulu, 1968-87, pres., 1987—; trustee B.P. Bishop Mus., Honolulu, 1983-88. Fellow Linnean Soc., AAAS; mem. Marine Biol. Assn. (Eng.), Australian Malacol. Soc. Episcopalian. Office: U Hawaii Manoa Dept Zoology 2538 The Mall Honolulu HI 96822-2200

KAY, GEORGE PAUL, environmental engineer; b. McKeesport, Pa., Sept. 25, 1954; s. George and Darlene Ann (Snyder) K.; m. Rosemary Ann Lynam, July 19, 1986; children: Brittany Elaine, Hope Elise. BS in Biology, U. Pitts., 1975, MS in Environ. Health, 1976, MSCE, 1982. Registered profl. engr., Pa., Ohio; cert. sewage treatment plant and waterworks operator, Pa. Rsch. asst. U. Pitts., 1976-79; from asst. aquatic ecologist to sr. environ. engr. Michael Baker Corp., Beaver, Pa., 1979-87; sect. mgr. water and wastewater Michael Baker Corp., Coraopolis, Pa., 1987-89; sr. engr. water and wastewater Armco, Inc., Butler, Pa., 1989—. Contbr. articles to profl. jours. Mem. Am. Soc. Limnology and Oceanography, Pa. Water Environ. Assn. (rsch. com. 1991—), Water Environ. Fedn., West Pa. Water Pollution Control Assn., World Aquaculture Soc. Avocations: traditional archery, bonsai, rock guitar, aquarium science. Home: 4596 Bucktail Dr Allison Park PA 15101-2120 Office: Armco Inc RR 8 Box 832 Butler PA 16001-9808

KAY, HERBERT, retired natural resources company executive; b. Johnsonburg, Pa., Mar. 19, 1924; s. Alexander S. and Carla Z. Racusin; m. Rita Inge Schmidt, May 4, 1956; children: Peter, Darcy, Philip. B.S. in Chem. Engring., Pa. State U., 1944; S.M., MIT, 1947; postgrad., Sloan Sch., 1968. Process engr. Stanolind Oil & Gas Co., Tulsa, 1947-49; group supr. Consolidation Coal Co., Library, Pa., 1949-55; sr. v.p. Climax Molybdenum Co., 1955-77; v.p. Amax Inc., 1977-85; also dir. U.K., Holland, Italy, France, Japan. Served with USNR, 1944-45. Mem. AIChE, Univ. Club (N.Y.), Madison Beach and Country Clubs (Conn.), Audubon Country Club (Fla.). Patentee in field. Home: 2400 Gulf Shore Blvd N Naples FL 34103-4381

KAY, HERMA HILL, dean; b. Orangeburg, S.C., Aug. 18, 1934; d. Charles Esdorn and Herma Lee (Crawford) Hill. BA, So. Meth. U., 1956; JD, U. Chgo., 1959. Bar: Calif. 1960, U.S. Supreme Ct. 1978. Law clk. Justice Roger Traynor, Calif. Supreme Ct., 1959-60; asst. prof. law U. Calif., Berkeley, 1960-62; assoc. prof. U. Calif., 1962, prof., 1963, dir. family law project, 1964-67, Jennings prof., 1987-96, dean, 1992—, Armstrong prof., 1996—; co-reporter uniform marriage and div. act Nat. Conf. Commrs. on Uniform State Laws, 1968-70; vis. prof. U. Manchester, Eng., 1972, Harvard U., 1976; mem. Gov.'s Commn. on Family, 1966. Author: (with Martha S. West) Text Cases and Materials on Sex-based Discrimination, 4th edit., 1996, (with R. Cramton, D. Currie and L. Kramer) Conflict of Laws: Cases, Comments, Questions, 5th edit., 1993; contbr. articles to profl. jours. Trustee Russell Sage Found., N.Y., 1972-87, chmn. bd., 1980-84; trustee, bd. dirs. Equal Rights Advs. Calif., 1976—, chmn., 1976-83; pres. bd. dirs. Rosenberg Found., Calif., 1987-88, bd. dirs. 1978—. Recipient rsch. award Am. Bar Found., 1990, Margaret Brent award ABA Commn. Women in Profession, 1992, Marshall-Wythe medal, 1995; fellow Ctr. Advanced Study in Behavioral Scis., Palo Alto, Calif., 1963. Mem. Calif. Bar Assn., Bar U.S. Supreme Ct., Calif. Women Lawyers (bd. govs. 1975-77), Am. Law Inst. (mem. coun. 1985-), Assn. Am. Law Schs. (exec. com. 1986-87, pres.-elect 1988, pres. 1989, past pres. 1990), Am. Acad. Arts and Scis., Order of Coif (nat. pres. 1983-85). Democrat. Office: U Calif Law Sch Boalt Hall Berkeley CA 94720-7200

KAY, JEREMY H., cartoonist; b. Steubenville, Ohio, July 26, 1942. BFA, Kent State U., 1961; MFA, Calif. State U., Northridge, 1965; grad., Dir.'s Guild Am., 1975. Comml. artist various orgns. L.A., 1965-98; motion picture art dir., prodn. designer L.A., Santa Monica, 1967-83, motion picture and tv writer, dir., 1973-95; dir., curator Am. Mus. Cartoon Art, Inc., Santa Monica, Calif.; prof. art history U. So. Calif., 1980-83. Mem. L.A. Coun. Art. Office: Am Mus Cartoon Art Inc 2930 Colorado Ave #A-8 Santa Monica CA 90404

KAY, JOEL PHILLIP, lawyer; b. Corsicana, Tex., Aug. 27, 1936; m. Marilyn Soltz, July 9, 1961; children: Arthur Hyman, Sarah Anne, Leslie Anette. BS in Econs., Wharton Sch., U. Pa., 1958; LLB, U. Tex., 1961; LL.M., Georgetown U., 1967. Bar: Tex. 1961, U.S. Dist. Ct. (so. and we. dists.) Tex., U.S. Dist. Ct (so. dist.) Ala., U.S. Ct. Appeals (5th cir.), U.S. Supreme Ct. Trial atty. tax div. Dept. Justice, 1963-67; U.S. atty. So. Dist. Tex., 1967-69; ptnr. Sheinfeld, Maley & Kay, P.C., Houston, 1969—; mem. Tex. Bd. Pub. Accountancy, 1984-85, quality rev. oversight bd., 1992-93; speaker at numerous institutes on comml. and bankruptcy law. With AUS, 1961-63. Fellow Am. Bar Found., Am. Coll. Bankruptcy (5th cir. regent); mem. ABA, Tex. Bar Assn. (dir. 1979-81, chmn. bd. 1981-82), Houston Bar Assn., Tex. Bar Found. (trustee 1983-86), Houston Bar Found. (dir. 1995-98), Tex. Supreme Ct. (grievance oversight com. 1987-94). Office: 3700 First City Tower 1001 Fannin St Ste 3700 Houston TX 77002-6707

KAY, KENNETH JEFFREY, entertainment company executive; b. L.A., Apr. 2, 1955; s. Morton M. and Beverly J. Kay; m. Lisa Ellen, July 24, 1982. BS in Acctg., U. So. Calif., 1978, MBA in Fin., 1980. CPA, Calif. Staff acct. in charge Price Waterhouse and Co., Century City, Calif., 1980-82; mgr. acctg. TRW-Fujitsu Co., L.A., 1982-83; corp. controller Ameron, Inc., Pasadena, Calif., 1983-88, sr. v.p. fin. and adminstrn., CFO, 1990-92, group v.p., 1992-94; pres., CEO, dir. Bishop, Inc., Westlake Village, Calif., 1988-90; sr. v.p. fin. and adminstrn., CFO Systemed, Inc., Torrance, Calif., 1994-96; sr. v.p., CFO Playmates Inc., Costa Mesa, Calif., 1997; exec. v.p., CFO Universal Studios Consumer Products Group, Universal City, Calif., 1998—; chmn. supervisory com. Ameron Fed. Credit Union, South Gate, Calif., 1986. Bd. govs. Cedars-Sinai Med. Ctr.; mem. exec. com. Friends for Life, L.A. Mem. AICPA, Am. Mgmt. Assn., Calif. Soc. CPAs, The Strategic Leadership Forum, Fin. Execs. Inst., Commerce Assocs. Office: Universal Studios Consumer Products Group 100 Universal City Plz Universal City CA 91608

KAY, PATRICIA KREMER, business owner; b. Arlington, Va., July 10, 1957; d. George Andrew and Eileen Lois (Ludwig) Kremer; m. Jimmy Lamar Kay, Dec. 4, 1989; children: Sabrina Lea, Kelly Marie. Purchasing agt. Medisorb Techs., Wilmington, Ohio, 1994-96; svc., mktg. purchasing mgr. Medison Techs. Internat.; owner JP Resources Inc, Middletown, OH, 1995—; employment specialist JCS, Dept. VA, 1996—. Avocations: boating, skiing.

KAY, PAUL DE YOUNG, linguist; b. N.Y.C., Nov. 7, 1934; s. William de Young and Alice Sarah Kay; m. Patricia Boehm, Feb. 13, 1934; children: Yvette, Suzanne de Young. BA in Econs., Tulane U., 1955; PhD in Anthropology, Harvard U., 1963. Asst. prof. MIT, Cambridge, Mass., 1964-65; asst prof., prof. dept. anthropology U. Calif., Berkeley, 1966-83, prof. dept. linguistics, 1983—, chmn. dept., 1986-91. Author: Words and the Grammar of Context, 1997; editor: Explorations in Mathematical Anthropology, 1971; co-author: Basic Color Terms, 1969; contbr. articles to Language, Linguistic Inquiry, Foundations of Language, Linguistics and Philosophy, Language and Society, Am. Anthropologist, Current Anthropology, Jour. of Southwestern Anthrop. Assn. Fellow Ctr. Advanced Study in Behavioral Scis., Stanford, Calif., 1965-66, Guggenheim Found., U. Hawaii, Oahu, 1972-73. Mem. NAS, Linguistic Soc. Am., Am. Anthrop. Assn., Soc. for Linguistic Anthropology (pres. 1988-89). Office: U Calif Dept Linguistics Berkeley CA 94720

KAY, RICHARD FREDERICK, paleontology and biological anthropology educator; b. N.Y.C., Oct. 21, 1947; s. G. Marshall and Inez (Clark) K.; m. Blythe Williams, Dec. 22, 1994; children: Elizabeth C., Andrew S., Adam W. BS, U. Mich., 1969; M in Philosophy, Yale U., 1971, PhD, 1973. Asst. prof. anatomy Duke U. Med. Ctr., Durham, N.C., 1973-78, assoc. prof., 1978-83, prof., 1983-88, prof. biol. anthropology and anatomy, chmn. dept., 1988—. Mem. Am. Assn. Phys. Anthropologists (exec. com. 1986-88), Argentine Paleontology Soc., Soc. Vertebrate Paleontology. Democrat. Home: 3 Biddle Ct Durham NC 27705-5499 Office: Duke U Med Ctr PO Box 3170 Dept Biol Anthropology & Anatomy Durham NC 27710

KAY, ROBERT, physician; b. Vallejo, Calif., Dec. 4, 1945; s. Harold and Frances K.; m. Carole Jeanne Ulmer, Oct. 27, 1947; 1 child, Jennifer. BA, U. Calif., L.A., 1967, MD, 1971; MBA, Case Western Res. U., 1990. Intern U. Colo., Denver; resident urology U. Oreg., Portland; head sect. pediatric urology Cleve. Clinic Found., 1980-97, dir. med. ops., 1990—. Contbr. articles to profl. jours. Fellow Am. Coll. Surgeons, Am. Acad. Pediat. Office: Cleve Clinic Found 9500 Euclid Ave Cleveland OH 44195

KAY, THOMAS OLIVER, agricultural consultant; b. Anderson, S.C., Sept. 29, 1929; s. Thomas Crayton and Gertrude (Whitworth) K.; m. Rebecca Moore, Aug. 29, 1954 (div. 1965); children—Michael (dec.), Mitchell; m. Bette Hutto, Oct. 1, 1966 (dec. Nov. 1991); stepchildren—Dallon Weathers, Bruce Weathers. B.A., Furman U., 1950; LL.D. (hon.), John Marshall Law Sch., Atlanta, 1960. Adminstrv. asst. U.S. Congress, Washington, 1966-73; legis. officer USDA, Washington, 1973-77; exec. asst. U.S. Senate, Washington, 1977-79; lobbyist Nat. Assn. Realtors, Washington, 1979-80; asst. to adminstr. Fgn. Agrl. Service USDA, Washington, 1981-82; dir. congl. relations USDA, 1982-83, dep. asst. sec. govtl. and pub. affairs, 1983-85, dep. undersec. internat. affairs and commodity programs, 1985-86, adminstr. fgn. agrl. svc., 1986-90; pres. Kay Assoc., 1989-94. Mem. Litchfield Country Club (Pawleys Island, S.C.). Clubs: Capitol Hill Club, Nat. Dem. Club, Army-Navy Country (Washington). Avocations: golf; swimming. Home: 17 Goodson Loop Pawleys Island SC 29585-8037

KAYE, ALAN DAVID, anesthesiologist, researcher; b. L.I., N.Y., Mar. 21, 1962; s. Joel and Florence Susan (Feldman) K.; m. Kim Sutker, May 26, 1990; children: Aaron, Rachel. BS in Biology, U. Ariz., 1984, BS in Psychology, 1985, MD, 1989; PhD in Pharmacology, Tulane U., 1997. Diplomate Am. Bd. Anesthesiology, Nat. Bd. Med. Examiners; lic. physician, La.; cert. ACLS. Intern Alton Ochsner Med. Found. and Clinic, New Orleans, 1989-90; resident in anesthesiology Mass. Gen. Hosp., Boston, 1990-91; resident in anesthesiology Tulane Med. Ctr., New Orleans, 1991-93, asst. prof. anesthesiology/attending staff, 1993-97, assoc. prof., 1997-99; attending staff/vice med. dir. Greater New Orleans Surg. Ctr., 1995-97, med. dir., 1997-99; prof., chmn., prof. dept. of anesthesia Tex. Tech U. Med. Ctr., Lubbock, 1999—, prof. dept. pharmacology, 1999—; lectr. in field. Contbr. articles and abstracts to profl. jours., chpts. to books; mem. editl. adv. bd. OR Reports, 1997—; co-editor: JASA Mfg. Book, 1986—, JASA Contractor's Book, 1986—; mem. editl. bd. Current Drugs. Capt. U.S. Army Med. Res., 1990—, maj., 1997. Recipient Nat. Student Rsch. Forum 1st place Roche Labs. award for excellence in basic sci. rsch., 1992, Baxter Clin. Rsch. award of Excellence, 1999; Ariz. Med. Assn. scholar, 1987-89, U. Utah Joshua Millbank Scholars Program scholar, 1987, E. Blois du Bois scholar, 1981-89; Tulane Sch. Medicine grantee, 1993-94, 94, 95—, 97—. Fellow N.Y. Acad. Sci., Am. Physiol. Soc.; mem. Bd. Examiners in Anesthesia (nat. assoc.), Am. Soc. Anesthesiology (pres. 1992-93), Am. Heart Assn., Mass. Gen. Hosp. Anesthesia Alumni Assn., Soc. Critical Care Medicine, Soc. Cardiovascular Anesthesiologists, Internat. Anesthesia Rsch. Soc., La. Soc. Anesthesiologists, New Orleans Anesthesia Soc., Tulane Med. Ctr. Anesthesia Alumni Assn., Golden Key, Blue Key, Phi Beta Kappa, Phi Eta Sigma (pres. 1982-83, Baxter award of appreciation 1999). Fax: (806) 743-2984. Office: Tex Tech U Health Sci Ctr Sch Medicine 3601 4th St Rm 1C-282 Lubbock TX 79430

KAYE, BARRY, insurance company executive; b. N.Y.C., May 20, 1928; s. Herbert and Blanche (Sabin) K.; C.L.U., Am. Coll. Life Underwriters, 1966; m. Carole Golison, Mar. 16, 1962; children—Fern L., Alan L., Howard S. Pres., Barry Kaye, Inc., 1960—; owner Barry Kaye Assos., Century City, Calif., 1970—; chmn. Wealth Creation Ctrs. Mem. faculty Practicing Law Inst., 1969—; lectr. U. Calif., Los Angeles, 1970—. Bd. govs. Diamond Circle of Hope; bd. trustees City of Hope. Fellow, Ben Gurion Soc., Ben Gurion U. of the Negev. Founder Wealth Creation Ctrs; co-owner, Carole & Barry Kaye Museum of Miniatures. Author: How To Save a Fortune On Your Life Insurance, 1980, 91, Save a Fortune on Your Estate Taxes, 1990, (tape and audio book) Save a Fortune on Your Estate Taxes, (tape) Wealth Creation and Preservation, Die Rich and Tax Free!, 1995, Live Rich, 1996, The Investment Alternative, 1997. Recipient Founders award Diamond Circle City of Hope, 1972, Lifetime Achievement award Ben-Gurion U. of the Negev, 1987; Man of Year award Gen. Agts. and Mgrs. Conf., 1965, 66, 67. Mem. NCCJ, Am. Soc. C.L.U.s, NCCJ (trustee, bd. dirs.), Senate Advisory Com. on Life and Health Ins. Mem. B'nai B'rith. Presidents Club, Clubs: Uncles of Vista del Mar, Internat. Forum. Office: Wealth Creation Ctrs Barry Kaye Assocs 1901 Avenue Of The Stars Los Angeles CA 90067-6001

KAYE, DANIEL BARNETT, secondary education educator, consultant; b. Phila., Oct. 11, 1948; s. Irving L. and Charlotte B. (Berk) K.; m. Anne E. Schleicher; children: Ethan, Thea. BS in English, East Stroudsburg (Pa.) State, 1970. Secondary tchr. English Wilson Area Sch. Dist., Easton, Pa., 1970—; bus. sales cons. Easton, 1990—. Recipient 1st degree Black Belt, Kosho Ryu Kenpo Ju-Jutsu, 1995, 2nd degree Black Belt, 1996. Mem. NEA, Nat. Coun. Tchrs. English, Pa. Edn. Assn., Pa. Coalition for Arts in Edn. (Excellence in Arts award 1997), Wilson Area Edn. Assn. (pres. 1996—). Avocations: martial arts, bass guitar, drama coaching. Office: Wilson Area HS 424 Warrior Ln Easton PA 18042-4602

KAYE, DONALD, physician, educator; b. N.Y.C., Aug. 12, 1931; s. Morris and Rose (Hirschtritt) K.; m. Janet Miriam Sovitsky, June 26, 1955; children: Kenneth Marc, Karen Lynne, Kendra Beth, Keith Steven. AB, Yale, 1953; MD, NYU, 1957. Diplomate Am. Bd. Internal Medicine, Am. Bd. Infectious Disease. Intern N.Y. Hosp., 1957-58, resident, 1958-60; pvt. practice N.Y.C., 1961-69, Phila., 1969—; asso. attending physician N.Y. Hosp., 1961-69; physician-in-chief Hosp. Med. Coll. Pa., 1969-95; instr. medicine Cornell U. Med. Coll., 1961-63, asst. prof., 1963-66, asso. prof., 1966-69; prof., chmn. dept. medicine Med. Coll. Pa., Phila., 1969-94; prof., chmn. dept. medicine Med. Coll. Pa. and Hahnemann U. Sch. Medicine, 1994-95, prof., 1995-96; prof. Allegheny U. of Health Scis., 1996-98, MCP Hahnemann Sch. Medicine, 1998—; cons. Phila. VA Hosp., 1969-95; CEO, pres. Med. Coll. Hosp., 1991-94, Med. Coll. Pa. and Hahnemann U. Hosp. Sys., 1994-96, Allegheny U. Hosps., 1996-98, Allegheny Integrated Health Group, 1996-97, Allegheny U. Health Scis., 1998; mem. revision com. U.S. Pharmacopeia, 1975-95; mem. VA Merit Rev. Bd. in Infectious Diseases, 1976-78; mem. com. on infectious diseases Am. Bd. Internal Medicine, 1976-84, cons., 1984-86. Author: Urinary Tract Infection and Its Management, 1972, Infective Endocarditis, 1976, Fundamentals of Internal Medicine, 1983, Internal Medicine for Dentists, 1983, 2d edit., 1990, Endocarditis, 1984, Infective Endocarditis, 1992; mem. editorial bd. Aging: Immunology and Infectious Diseases, Gerontology: Med. Sci., 1987-98, Antimicrobial Agts. Chemotherapy, 1972-98; contbr. articles to med. jours. Recipient Disting. Tchg. award Lindback Found., 1972; NIH grantee, 1967-76, 82-96; Pharm. Industry grantee, 1965-96, Emilio Ribas medal for disting svc. Brazilian Soc. of Infectious Diseases, 1994, Disting. Achievement award N.Y. Hosp.-Cornell Med. Ctr. Alumni Coun., 1994, Solomon A. Berson Alumni Achievement award NYU Sch. Medicine, 1996, Strittmatter award Philadelphia County Med. Soc., 1997. Master ACP (gov. Ea. Pa. region 1983-88, pres. Pa. chpt. 1987); fellow Gerontol. Soc. Am., Infectious Disease Soc. Am.; mem. AMA, Pa. Med. Soc. (alt. del to AMA 1991-92), Phila. County Med. Soc. (pres. 1991-92), Am. Soc. for Microbiology, Am. Fedn. for Clin. Rsch., Am. Soc. for Clin. Investigation, Assn. Am. Physicians, Am. Clin. and Climatol. Assn., Phi Beta Kappa, Alpha Omega Alpha, Sigma Xi. Home: 1535 Sweet Briar Rd Gladwyne PA 19035-1216 Office: 3300 Henry Ave Philadelphia PA 19129-1121

KAYE, GAIL LESLIE, healthcare consultant, educator; b. Upland, Pa., Aug. 6, 1955; d. Ronald E. and Doris T. (Welfley) K. BS, W.Va. Welseyan Coll., 1977; MS, Ohio State U., 1982, PhD, 1989. Lic. profl. clin. counselor; registered dietitian. Asst. dir. food svc., chief clin. dietitian Albert Einstein Med. Ctr., Phila., 1983; asst. prof. Ind. State U., Terre Haute, 1983-85; nutrition cons. Ohio State U. Hosp. Clinics, Columbus, 1986-88, grad. rsch. asst., 1986-89; legis. rep. Ohio Assocs. Counseling and Devel., Columbus, 1988-89; rsch. cons. State Dept. Edn., Columbus, 1988-89; lectr. counselor edn. Ohio State U., Columbus, 1989-93, lectr. human nutrition, 1998—; program devel. and clin. rschr. Ross Labs., Columbus, 1990-94; pres. Kaye Consultation Svcs., Inc., 1994—; lectr. dept. human nutrition and food mgmt. Ohio State U., 1998—. Inventor in field; contbr. articles to profl. jours. Recipient Pres. award Ohio Mental Health Counselors Assn., 1990. Mem. Am. Dietetics Assn., Ohio Dietetics Assn. Avocations: swimming, piano, reading, hiking, painting, theatre. Home and Office: 365 Helmbright Dr Gahanna OH 43230-3290

KAYE, GORDON ISRAEL, pathologist, anatomist, educator; b. N.Y.C., Aug. 13, 1935; s. Oscar Swarz and Rebecca (Schachman) K.; m. Nancy Elizabeth Weber, June 4, 1956; children: Jacqueline Elizabeth, Vivienne Rebecca. AB, Columbia U., 1955, AM, 1957, PhD, 1961. Rsch. asst. cytology Columbia U., N.Y.C., 1953-55, asst. zoology, 1954, asst. anatomy, 1958-61, rsch. assoc. dept. anatomy, 1961-63, assoc. surg. pathology, 1963-66, asst. prof. surg. pathology, 1966-70, assoc. prof., 1970-76, dir. F. Higginson Cabot Lab. Electron Microscopy, 1963-76; rsch. and tchg. asst. cytology Rockefeller Inst., N.Y.C., 1957-58; Alden March prof. Albany (N.Y.) Med. Coll., 1976-99, chmn. dept. anatomy, 1976-87, prof. pathology, 1981-99, prof. emeritus pathology, 1999; prof. biomed. sci. SUNY Sch. Pub. Health, 1986—; pres., CEO Waste Reduction by Waste Reduction, Inc., Troy, N.Y., 1993-98, chmn., 1998—; mem. seminar on creative process Wenner-Gren Found., 1964-65; cons. electron microscopy dept. pathology N.Y. VA Hosp., 1965—; Raymond C. Truex Disting. lectr. Hahnemann U., 1987. Co-author: Key Facts in Histology, 1985, Histology: A Text and Atlas, 1995, Atlas der Histologie (in German), 1995, Histology, nat. med. series rev. series, 1997; editor: Current Topics in Cellular Anatomy, 1981; assoc. editor: The Anat. Record, 1972-98; editl. reviewer: Exptl. Eye Rsch., 1964, Cancer, 1972—, Investigative Ophthalmology, 1973—, Gastroenterology, 1969—; patentee (with Dr. Peter B. Weber) Method for Disposal of Radioactively Labeled Animal Carcasses. Trustee Palisades free Libr., 1965-71; mem. Citizens Adv. Com., Sparkill Palisades Fire Dist., 1968-69; pres. Palisades Free Libr., 1969-71; trustee Orangetown Pub. Libr., 1971-73, Friends of Chamber Music, Troy, N.Y., 1988—; mem. citizens adv. com. Title III Program, S. Orangetown Ctrl. Sch. Dist., 1972-75; chmn. N.Y. State Low Level Waste Group, 1986-95; trustee Rockland Country Day Sch., 1974-78. Recipient Charles Huebschman prize in zoology Columbia U., 1954, Career Scientist award Health Rsch. Coun. N.Y.C., 1963-72, Rsch. Career Devel. award Nat. Inst. Arthritis and Metabolic Diseases, NIH, USPHS, 1972-76, Tousimis prize in biology, 1984; Ford Found. scholar, 1951-55; NSF predoctoral fellow, 1955-56, Nat. Inst. Neurol. Diseases and Blindness predoctoral fellow, 1959-61. Mem. Assn. Anatomy Chairmen (pres. 1980-81), Assn. Am. Med. Colls. (rep. council acad. socs. 1979—, mem. adminstrn. bd. CAS 1985-86), Am. Assn. Anatomists, Am. Soc. Cell Biology, Harvey Soc., Assn. Career Scientists Health Research Coun., Internat. Soc. Eye Research, N.Y. Soc. Electron Microscopists (dir. 1964-67), Arthur Purdy Stout Soc. Surg. Pathologists (hon.), Sigma Xi. Club: Waquoit Bay Yacht (Waquoit, Mass.). Office: Waste Reduction by Water Reduction 5711 W Minnesota St Indianapolis IN 46241

KAYE, JHANI, radio station manager, owner production company; b. Maywood, Calif., June 18, 1949; s. Jimmie Eccak and Betty Jo (Holland) Kazaroff. BA, UCLA, 1971. Lic. 1st class radio. Music dir. Sta. KFXM, San Bernardino, Calif., 1969-73; announcer Stas. KUTE-FM/KKDJ-FM, L.A., 1972-74; asst. program dir. Sta. KROQ, L.A., 1973-74, Sta. WCFL, Chgo., 1980-82, Sta. KFI, L.A., 1982; program dir. Sta. KINT-FM, El Paso, Tex., 1975-80; sta. mgr., program dir. Sta. KOST-FM, L.A., 1982—. Appeared in TV series Falcon Crest, 1985, Drew Carey Show, 1998; dir. TV commls., 1986—; voice-over motion picture The Couch Trip, 1987; dir., video editor Dick Clark TV Commls. Recipient Marconi Radio awards Nat. Assn. Broadcasters, 1990, 91. Avocation: video production. Office: Sta KOST FM 610 S Ardmore Ave Los Angeles CA 90005-2322

KAYE, JUDITH SMITH, state supreme court chief justice; b. Monticello, N.Y., Aug. 4, 1938; d. Benjamin and Lena (Cohen) Smith; m. Stephen Rackow Kaye, Feb. 11, 1964; children: Luisa Marian, Jonathan Mackey, Gordon Bernard. BA, Barnard Coll., 1958; LLB cum laude, NYU, 1962; LLD (hon.), St. Lawrence U., 1985, Union U., 1985, Pace U., 1985, Syracuse U., 1988, L.I. U., 1989. Assoc. Sullivan & Cromwell, N.Y.C., 1962-64; staff atty. IBM, Armonk, N.Y., 1964-65; asst. to dean Sch. Law NYU, 1965-68; ptnr. Connelly Chase O'Donnell & Weyher, N.Y.C., 1969-83; judge N.Y. State Ct. Appeals, N.Y.C., 1983-93, chief judge, 1993—; bd. dir. Sterling Nat. Bank. Contbr. articles to profl. jours. Former bd. dirs. Legal Aid Soc. Recipient Vanderbilt medal NYU Sch. of Law, 1983, Medal of Distinction, Barnard Coll, 1987. Fellow Am. Bar Found.; mem. Am. Law Inst., Am. Coll. Trial Lawyers, Am. Judicature Soc. (bd. dirs. 1980-83). Democrat. Office: NY Court of Appeals Court of Appeals Hall 20 Eagle St Albany NY 12207-1009 Office: NY Court of Appeals 230 Park Ave Rm 826 New York NY 10169-0899*

KAYE, KENNETH MARC, physician, educator, scientist; b. N.Y.C., Feb. 5, 1960; s. Donald and Janet Kaye; m. Elaine Tracy, Jul. 4, 1985; 3 children. AB summa cum laude, Harvard U., 1982, MD, 1986. Diplomate Am. Bd. Internal Medicine, also sub-bd. Infectious Disease. Resident in internal medicine Mass. Gen. Hosp., Boston, 1986-89; fellow in infectious disease Dana Farber Cancer Inst. Brigham & Women's Hosp., Beth Israel Hosp., Boston, 1989-91; instr. Med. Sch. Harvard U., Boston, 1991-95; asst. prof. of medicine Boston, 1995—; assoc. physician Brigham & Women's Hosp., Boston, 1991—. Contbr. articles to profl. jours. Recipient Edward H. Kass award for Clin. Excellence, Mass. Infectious Diseases Soc., 1991; Howard Hughes Med. Inst. postdoctoral fellow, 1991-92, Physician Scientist awardee NIH, 1992-97. Fellow ACP; mem. AAAS, IDSA, Phi Beta Kappa. Office: Brigham & Womens Hosp Divsn Infectious Diseases 75 Francis St Boston MA 02115-6106

KAYE, LORI, travel academy executive, consultant; d. Eldin Bert and Katherine Angeline Onsgard. Student, Detroit Inst. Art, 1951, 56, U. N.Mex., 1960. Actress, radio and TV commls., 1951-82, Warner Bros., 1960-64; dir., v.p. John Robert Powers Schs., L.A., 1961-71; v.p. Electron Industries, Torrance, Calif., 1963-65; owner, v.p. Lawrence Leon Photography Studio, L.A., 1964-68; pres. Lori Kaye Cosmetics, Hollywood, Calif., 1964-70; co-woner, v.p. K and S Employment, Calif. Fashion Mart, 1965-67; dir., internat. cons. Airline Schs. Pacific, Van Nuys, Calif., 1972-74; dir. Caroline Leonetti Ltd. Sch., Hollywood, 1976-79; pres. Lori Kaye's Internat. Travel Acad., North Hollywood, Calif., 1980—; internat. cons. Internat. Career Acad., Van Nuys, 1978—; pres. Molori Publs., Studio City, Calif., 1981—; cons. A&T Inst. Travel and Tourism, 1982; lectr. in field, 1969—. Paintings include in UNICEF collection, 1967; hostess TV talk show The New You, Sta. KTTV, Hollywood, 1964-65; hostess TV show Lori Kayes Week-End Escape, Sta. KCBS, 1997—; travel expert, live travel TV show hostess, spl. assignment TV reporter U-Team, Sta. CBS-2, 1997—; instr. travel tourism UCLA, 1997—. Dir. project Camarillo State Hosp., 1963-69; cons. Job Corps; dir., instr., adminstr. Calif. Pvt. Postsecondary Edn. Instns., 1995; instr. travel tourism U. So. Calif., 199798. Recipient Mental Health Achievement award, 1967. Mem. NAFE, Assn. for Promotion of Tourism Africa, AAU, SAG, AFTRA, Smithsonian Assocs., Am. Soc. Travel Agts., Internat. Airline Travel Agts. Network, Internat. Air Transport Assn., Soc. Travel Agts. in Govt., Calif. Assn. Pvt. Postsecondary Schs., U.S. Masters-Internat. Swim Club, Nat. Geog. Soc., Internat. Platform Assn., Better Bus. Bur. (arbitrator), L.A. World Affairs Coun., Universal City-No. Hollywood C. of C. Office: Lori Kayes Internat Travel Ctr 12723 Ventura Blvd Studio City CA 91604-2430

KAYE, MARC MENDELL, lawyer; b. Irvington, N.J., Nov. 25, 1959; s. Aaron Morton and Sandra (Hoch) K. AA, BA, Rutgers U., 1980; JD, U. Toledo, 1983. Bar: N.J. 1984, Fla. 1987, D.C. 1991, N.Y. 1998, U.S. Dist. Ct. N.J. 1984, U.S. Supreme Ct. 1992; cert. civil trial atty. 1991. Trial atty. Shevick, Ravich, Koster et al, Rahway, N.J., 1984-85, Greenberg, Margolis et al, Roseland, N.J., 1985-86, Brian Granstrand, Fairfield, N.J., 1986-90; pvt. practice Livingston, N.J., 1986-94, Short Hills, 1994—; counsel CNA Ins. Co., Fairfield, 1986-90; apptd. arbitrator Union County Arbitrator Program, 1993, Essex County Arbitrator and Mediator Programs, 1995, Millburn Citizen Budget Com., 1998—; adv. coun. mem. Chmn.'s Club Summit Bank, 1989-91. Mem. exec. com. Young Leadership div. United Jewish Appeal, Metrowest, N.J, 1988-91; bd. dirs. Jewish Cmty. Ctr. of MetroWest, 1998—, Opera Music Theatre Internat., 1999—. Mem. N.J. Bar Assn., Essex County Bar Assn. (subcom. chmn. legal med. com. 1993), Union County Bar Assn., Fla. Bar Assn., D.C. Bar Assn., Assn. Trial Lawyers Am., N.J. Trial Lawyers Assn., Lions Club (v.p. 1993-95), Prime Ministers Club, Israel Bonds. Avocations: golf, swimming, scuba diving, travel. Office: One N Brook Dr at S Orange Ave Short Hills NJ 07078-3126

KAYE, NEIL SCOTT, psychiatrist; b. Albany, N.Y., June 1, 1958; s. Jesse J. and Shirley Mae (Poskanzer) K.; m. Susan M. Donnelly, July 2, 1988. BA, Skidmore Coll., 1980; MD, Albany Med. Coll., 1984. Diplomate Nat. Bd. Med. Examiners, Am. Bd. Psychiatry and Neurology; lic. med. practitioner, N.Y., Mass., Del.; bd. cert. geriatric psychiatry, 1991, forensic psychiatry, 1994. Rotating intern Albany (N.Y.) Med. Ctr. Hosp., 1985, resident dept. psychiatry, 1986-87; with crisis unit coverage Capital Dist. Psychiat. Ctr., Albany, 1986-87; forensic fellow dept. psychiatry Syracuse U.-SUNY Upstate, 1987-88; asst. prof. psychiatry sch. medicine U. Mass., Worcester, 1988-90; evening admissions & continuing treatment unit psychiatrist Worcester State Hosp., 1988-90; dir. consultation and liaison psychiatry Med. Ctr. Del., Christiana Hosp., Wilmington, 1990-92; spl. guest instr. Widener U. Sch. Law, 1991—; asst. prof. dept. psychiatry Thomas Jefferson Sch. Medicine, 1991—, asst. prof. family medicine, 1997—; pvt. practice Allied Psychiat. Svcs., 1990—; founding mem. Neurobehavioral Assoc. N.J., 1992-93; dir., sec./treas. Allied Psychiat. Svcs., P.A., 1992-94, pres., 1994-98; pres. Allied Mental Health, 1995-98; pvt. practice, 1999—; chmn. credentials com. Worcester State Hosp., Worcester; cons. psychiatrist State of N.Y., Auburn (N.Y.) Prison, 1987-88; weekend ward coverage VA Hosp., Albany, 1987-88, supr. jail social worker Rensselaer County Jail, Forenic Svc., Rensselaer County Mental Health Dept., 1987-88; supr. social workers, medication mgmt. for the clinic, Social Security and Disability evalutions, child custody Rensselaer County Mental Health Dept., Unified Svcs., Rensselaer, N.Y., 1987-88; lectr., presenter. Contbr. articles to profl. jours. Rowing referee U.S. Rowing Assn., 1987—; founder and co-chmn. Empire State Regatta, Albany, 1984-87; mem. Downtown Redevel. Commn., Albany, 1984-90, Riverfront Devel. Commn., Albany, 1984-90; at-large mem. bd. dirs. Albany Med. Coll. Aluni Assn., 1985—; vol. driver, attendant, EMT, Saratoga Emergency Corps, 1978-80; house counselor Skidmore Coll, 1979, residence asst., 1980; dir. Camp Shelley Day Camp, New Scotland, N.Y., 1977-82; adv. com. Schaffer Libr. Health Scis., 1981-87. Recipient Mayor's Proclamation for Community Svc., Albany, 1985, Tricentennial Proclamation, Albany, 1986; named Rappeport Fellow nominee, 1987. Mem. AMA (Physicians Recognition award for Continuing Med. Edn.), Am. Psychiat. Assn., N.Y. State Med. Soc., Mass. Med. Soc., Nat. Assn. Sports Ofcls., Am. Acad. Forensic Scis. (com. on ethics 1990—, award for best paper by a forensic fellow 1989), Am. Acad. Psychiatry and the Law (com. on AAPL/APA rels. 1988—, com. on ethics 1988—), Assn. Am. Med. Colls. (faculty 1988—), N.Y. Acad. Scis., Internat. Wine and Food Soc., Am. Acad. Psychiat. Adminstrs., Assn. Compulsive Therapy, Am. Assn. Geriatric. Avocations: crew, cooking, music, antiques, boating, hiking. Fax: 302 234

8984. Home: Limestone Hills 3 Hayloft Ct Wilmington DE 19808-1934 also: 5301 Limestone Rd Wilmington DE 19808

KAYE, PETER FREDERIC, television editor; b. Chgo., Mar. 8, 1928; s. Ralph A. and Sara Corson (Philipson) K.; m. Martha Louise Wood, Mar. 20, 1955; children: Loren, Terry, Adam. BA in Govt., Pomona Coll., 1949. Reporter Alhambra (Calif.) Post-Advocate, 1950-53; reporter, editorial writer, polit. writer The San Diego Union, 1953-68; news and pub. affairs dir. KPBS-TV, San Diego State Coll., 1968-72; corr., producer Nat. Pub. Affairs Ctr. for TV, Washington, 1972-74; comm. dir. So. Calif. First Nat. Bank, San Diego, 1974-75; press sec. The Pres. Ford Com., Washington, 1975-76; mgr. Copley Videotex, San Diego, 1982-84; assoc. editor The San Diego Union, 1976-94; editl. dir. KNSD, San Diego, 1996—; freelance TV producer programs KPBS, PBS, BBC; San Diego corr. Newsweek, 1968-71, McGraw-Hill, 1959-67; lectr. comm. U. Calif., San Diego, 1971; copywriter Washburn-Justice Advt., San Diego, 1959-70. Producer 10 TV programs including including Jacob Bronowski: Life and Legacy, Twenty-Five Years of Presidency, The Presidency, The Press and the People. Press asst. Eisenhower-Nixon Campaign, L.A., 1952; asst. press sec. Richard Nixon Presdl. Campaign, Washington, 1960; dir. Pete Wilson for Mayor Campaign, San Diego, 1971; comm. dir. Flournoy for Gov. Campaign, Beverly Hills, Calif., 1974. With U.S. Mcht. Marines, 1945, U.S. Army, 1950-52. Jefferson fellow East-West Ctr., Honolulu, 1987; recipient Golden Mike awards So. Calif. TV News Dirs. Assn., 1969, 70, 71, Best Pub. Affairs Program award Nat. Ednl. TV, 1970, Best Local TV Series award Radio-TV Mirror, 1971, Nat. Emmy award Spl. Events Reporter, Watergate Coverage, 1973-74, Best Editorial awards Copley Newspapers Ring of Truth, 1979, Sigma Delta Chi, 1985, Calif. Newspaper Pubs. Assn., 1985; San Diego Emmy awards, 1985, 87, 91. Mem. NATAS, State Bar Calif. (bd. govs. 1991-97, v.p. 1993-94, 96-97), Sigma Delta Chi. Republican. Home: 240 Ocean View Ave Del Mar CA 92014-3322

KAYE, RICHARD WILLIAM, utility company executive; b. Chgo., May 14, 1939; s. Albert Louis and Helen (Beckman) K.; m. Betty Ann Terry, Aug. 7, 1964; children: Ronald, William, Richard, Timothy. AB, Cornell U., 1960; MBA, Columbia U., 1962. Various fin. positions Inland Steel Co., Chgo., 1964-81; dir. info. svcs. No. Ind. Pub. Svc. Co., Hammond, 1981-86, dir. econ. analysis, 1986-88; vis. dir. Purdue U., 1988; cons., ct. appointed receiver, 1989—; mgmt./fin. cons., 1990—. Advisor Calumet Coll., Whiting, Ind., 1985—; active Village Planning Commn., village trustee. Lt. (j.g.) USNR. Mem. Am. Mgmt. Assn., Cornell U. Alumni Assn., Columbia U. Alumni Assn., Rotary. Avocations: tennis, golf. Home: 2801 Cherrywood Ln Hazel Crest IL 60429-2126 Office: No Ind Pub Svc Co 401 S State St Chicago IL 60605-1225

KAYE, ROBERT, pediatrics educator; b. N.Y.C., July 17, 1917; s. Harry and Anna (Brisk) K.; m. Ellen Eskin, Nov. 16, 1960; children: Elizabeth, Margaret, Hillary, Sanford, Anthony. BA, Johns Hopkins U., 1939, MD, 1943. Intern Johns Hopkins Hosp., Balt., 1943, resident, 1944-45; instr. pediatrics Johns Hopkins Med. Sch., Balt., 1945; assoc. physiology Harvard Sch. Pub. Health, 1946-48; prof. pediatrics U. Pa., 1964-73, 86-88; prof., chmn. Hahnemann Med. Coll. and Hosp., Phila., 1973-86; chmn. dept. pediatrics Med. Coll. Pa., Phila., 1988-92, prof., 1992-95. Contbr. articles to profl. jours. With U.S. Army, 1945-46. Nat. Found. Infantile Paralysis fellow, 1946-48. Mem. AAAS, Am. Pediatric Soc., Soc. Pediatric Rsch., Am. Diabetes Assn., Izaak Walton League, Brodheads Forest and Stream Assn., Pediatric Travel Club, Bala Golf Club. Jewish. Home: 200 Locust St Apt 22bc Philadelphia PA 19106-3914

KAYE, SAMUEL HARVEY, architect, educator; b. Columbia, S.C., Sept. 27, 1940; s. James B. and Mary Louise (Harvey) K.; m. Patsy Cummings, June 27, 1964; children: Kimbelee Cummings, Elizabeth Harvey, Mary Catherine. BArch, Auburn U., 1963. Mem. staff Yeates & Gaskill, Architects, Memphis, 1965-68; mem. staff Walk Jones & Francis Mah, Inc., Memphis, 1968-70, prin., 1970-74; prin. Samuel H. Kaye, Architect, Columbus, Miss., 1974-91, Luke & Kaye, P.A., Columbus, 1991—; instr. architecture Miss. State U., Starkville, 1983-84; instr. interior design Miss. U. for Women, Columbus, 1979-84, asst. prof., 1984-91; mem. Miss. Hist. Preservation Rev. Bd. Contbr. articles on urban design, usage study and historic archeol. research. Mem. St. Paul's Episcopal Ch. Vestry, Columbus, 1975-79, 83-85, bd. mgrs. Gray Ctr., Diocese of Miss., Canton, 1981-86, Salvation Army Adv. Bd., Columbus, 1983—; bd. trustees Miss. Heritage Trust, 1991—, pres. 1991-92. Served to lt. U.S. Army, 1963-65. Recipient preservation honor award Hist. Columbus, 1976, 81, 82, award of merit Miss. Hist. Soc., 1986, 91, 93, 94. Mem. AIA (bd. dirs. Miss. chpt. 1977, v.p. 1978, pres. 1979, state preservation coord. hist. resources com., urban design and planning com., honor award 1976), Nat. Trust Hist. Preservation (bd. advisors 1989-98, emeritus 1998—), Rotary (v.p. Columbus 1985-86, pres. 1986). Avocations: reading, research, photography. Home: 424 7th St S Columbus MS 39701-5752 Office: Luke & Kaye PA 114 5th St S Columbus MS 39701-5728

KAYE, STEPHEN RACKOW, lawyer; b. Nyack, N.Y., May 4, 1931; s. Edward and Florence (Karp) K.; m. Judith Smith, Feb. 11, 1964; children: Luisa Marian, Jonathan Mackey, Gordon Bernard. A.B., Cornell U., 1952, LL.B. with honors, 1956. Bar: N.Y. 1956, U.S. Supreme Ct. 1961. Assoc. Sullivan & Cromwell, N.Y.C., 1956-63; assoc. Proskauer Rose Goetz & Mendelsohn, N.Y.C., 1964-68, ptnr., past chair, co-chmn. lit. dept., 1968—. Author treatise texts on trials and appeals of comml. cases; mng. editor Cornell Law Quar.; contbr. to profl. publs. Served to 1st lt. AUS, 1952-54, Korea. Mem. ABA, N.Y. State Bar Assn., Assn. of Bar of City of N.Y. (past chmn. com. on profl. and jud. ethics, chmn. com. on profl. discipline), N.Y. County Lawyers Assn. (past vice chmn. com. on Supreme Ct.), 1st Dept. Disciplinary Commn. (hearing panel chair, policy com. 1991-96, 99—), Order of Coif, Phi Kappa Phi. Office: Proskauer Rose LLP 1585 Broadway New York NY 10036-8200

KAYE, WALTER, financial executive; b. Bklyn., Aug. 22, 1927; s. Jack and Ida (Shapiro) K.; m. Bernice Glatzer, May 6, 1952; children: Steven Mark, Russell Stuart. Student, CCNY, 1950-53; postgrad. (fellow), N.Y. Inst. Credit, 1956. Credit mgr., treas. A. Steinam Co., Inc., N.Y.C., 1951-68; v.p. Ambassador Factors Corp., N.Y.C., 1968-74; sr. v.p. Congress Factors Corp., N.Y.C., 1974-84; pres., chief exec. officer Mcht. Factors Corp., N.Y.C., 1985—. Bd. dirs. The Crossing Homeowners Assn., Trump Plaza, N.Y.C. Served with U.S. Army, 1944-46. Recipient Yitzak Rabin award B'nai B'rith, 1982; recipient Plaque Manhattan Credit, 1979. Mem. N.Y. Inst. Credit, N.Y. Credit and Fin. Mgmt., Nat. Comml. Fin. Assn., Manhattan Credit (pres. 1978-79) Empire Credit (pres. 1971-74), The Financemen's Group Club, 475 Club, N.Y. Friars Club. Home: 18 The Crossing At Blind Brk Purchase NY 10577-2200 Office: Mcht Factors Corp 1430 Broadway New York NY 10018-3308

KAYE JOHNSON, SUSAN, educational consultant; b. N.Y.C., Jan. 23, 1932; d. Albert and Goldie (Feldman) Sroge; m. Carroll F. Johnson, Jan. 16, 1990; children from previous marriage: Richard M. Kaye, Gillian Kaye Karran. BA in History, Bklyn. Coll., 1953, MS in Counseling, 1958; MEd in Adminstrn., Columbia U., 1976, EdD in Adminstrn., 1978. Cert. adminstr., supr. N.Y., N.J., guidance counselor, history tchr., N.Y. Tchr. 3d grade Ollie Perry Storm Sch., San Antonio, 1954-55; tchr. social studies Jr. High Sch. 214, Bklyn., 1955-57; guidance counselor Jr. High Schs. 214 and 10, Bklyn., 1957-59; evaluation asst., coord. career devel. Great Neck (N.Y.) Pub. Sch., 1966-71, dir. chpt. I, 1971-79; dir. pupil svcs. Bellmore-Merrick High Sch. Dist., Long Island, N.Y., 1979-83; asst. supt. schs. Longwood Sch. Dist., Middle Island, N.Y., 1983-89; supt. schs. Florham Park (N.J.) Pub. Schs., 1989-92; ednl. cons. Longboat Key, Fla., 1992—; adminstr. Sarasota (Fla.) Safe Place and Rape Crisis Ctr., 1996-97; chair women's caucus Am. Assn. Sch. Adminstrs., 1980-82. Co-author: An Analysis of Problems in a School District, 1980, Managing Schools in Hard Times, 1981. Assoc. trustee Dowling Coll., Long Island, 1983-87; trustee Women Svcs. Divsn., Brookhaven, N.Y., 1986, Brookhaven Twp. Youth Bd., 1987, Adult Sch., Florham Park, 1989-92. Mem. AAUW, NOW, Archael. Inst. Am., Phi Delta Kappa. Avocations: archaeology, tennis. Home and Office: 2077 Gulf Of Mexico Dr Longboat Key FL 34228-3202

KAYFETZ, VICTOR JOEL, writer, editor, translator; b. N.Y.C., July 20, 1945; s. Daniel Osler and Selma Harriet (Walowitz) K.; BA, Columbia U., 1966; postgrad. U. Stockholm (Sweden), 1966-67; MA in History, U. Calif.-Berkeley, 1969. Teaching asst. in Swedish, U. Calif., Berkeley, 1969-70; tchr., adminstr. Swedish adult edn. programs, 1970-75; corr. Reuters, Stockholm, 1975-78; sub-editor Reuters World Ser., London, 1978; corr. London Fin. Times, Stockholm, 1979-80; free lance translator Swedish, Danish, Norwegian, 1967—; free lance editor Swedish and Am. mags., 1980—. Henry Evans traveling fellow, 1966-67; Nat. Def. Fgn. Lang. fellow, 1967-69; Thord Gray fellow Am.-Scandinavian Found., 1970. Mem. Swedish Am. C. of C., Soc. Advancement Scandinavian Study, Am. Scandinavian Found., Swedish Assn. Profl. Translators, World Affairs Council No. Calif., Sierra Club, Phi Beta Kappa. Author: Sweden in Brief, 1974, 80; Invest in Sweden, 1984, Skanska, the First Century, 1987; editor, translator numerous books, ann. reports, mags. for Swedish govt. agys. interest orgns., univs., indsl. corps., banks.

KAY-GUELKE, JEANNE, dean, educator; b. Milw., Feb. 11, 1949. BA, Mount Holyoke Coll., 1971; MS, U. Wis., 1973, PhD, 1977. Tchr., asst. prof. to assoc. prof. Dep. Geography, U. Utah, Salt Lake City, 1976-89; prof., chair Dept. Geography, U. Nebr., Lincoln, 1989-92; prof., dean Faculty of Environ. Studies, U. Waterloo, Ont., Can., 1992-97; prof. geography Faculty of Environ. Studies, U. Waterloo, Ont., Can., 1997—. Co-editor The Profl. Geographer, 1988-91; editl. bd. Gender, Place and Culture, 1993-95; contbr. articles to profl. jours. Mem. Assn. of Am. Geographers, Can. Assn. Geographers, Nat. Coun. for Geographic Edn. (exec. bd.). Office: U Waterloo Environ Studies, 200 Univ Ave W, Waterloo, ON Canada N2L 3G1*

KAYLAN, HOWARD LAWRENCE, musical entertainer, composer; b. N.Y.C., June 22, 1947; s. Sidney and Sally Joyce (Berlin) K.; m. Mary Melita Pepper, June 10, 1967 (div. Sept. 1971); 1 child, Emily Anne; m. Susan Karen Olsen, Apr. 18, 1982 (div. June 1996); 1 child, Alexandra Leigh. Student, UCLA, Am. Coll. Metaphys. Theology, St. Paul, Minn., 1998. Lead singer and founder rock group The Turtles, Los Angeles, 1965—; lead singer rock group Mothers of Invention, Los Angeles, 1970-72, Flo and Eddie, 1972-83; radio, TV, recording entertainer various broadcast organizations, Los Angeles, 1972—; screenwriter Larry Gelbart, Carl Gotleib prodns., Los Angeles, 1979-85; producer children's records Kidstuff Records, Hollywood, Fla., 1980-83; singer, producer rock band Flo and Eddie, Los Angeles, 1976-83; singer, producer The Turtles (reunion of original band), Los Angeles, 1980—; actor, TV and film Screen Actors Guild, Los Angeles, 1983—; background vocalist various albums for numerous performers; syndicated talk show host Unistar Radio Network, 1989—; radio personality Sta. WXRK-FM, N.Y.C., 1990-91, KLOU, St. Louis, 1993, WGRR, Cin., 1995-97. Author: Hi Bob, 1995, The Energy Pals, 1995; contbr. articles to Creem mag., L.A. Free Press, Rockit mag., Phonograph Record; screenwriter: (film) Death Masque, 1985; actor: (film) 200 Motels, 1971, Get Crazy, 1985, General Hospital, Suddenly Susan, 1999; performed at the White House, 1970; exec. producer: (radio) Down Eerie Street, 1998. Recipient 10 Gold and Platinum LP album awards while lead singer, 1965—, Fine Arts award, Bank of Am., L.A., 1965, Spl. Billboard Mag. award, 1992; recorded numerous top ten hit songs with Turtles, Bruce Springstein, The Ramones, Duran Duran, T. Rex, John Lennon and others. Mem. AFTRA, Screen Actors Guild, Am. Fedn. Musicians, AGVA.

KAYLOR, ANDREA LYNN, secondary school counselor; b. L.A., May 19, 1946; d. Kenneth D. and Florence R. (Berkman) Cooper; m. Stephan A. Kaylor, Dec. 4, 1983; children: Gavin Chandler, Kiley Chandler. AA, Diablo Valley Coll., Pleasant Hill, Calif., 1971; BS, U. Nev., Reno, 1983, MA in Counseling, 1989. Registered dental hygienist; cert. tchr., sch. counselor. Dental hygienist Davis, Calif., 1971-73, L.A., 1973-78, Reno, 1978-80; elem. tchr. Rita Cannon Sch., Reno, 1984-88, Alice Maxwell Sch., Sparks, Nev., 1989-90; counselor McQueen H.S., Reno, 1990-99; tchr. trainer Math Cadre Washoe County Sch. Dist., Reno, 1987-89; presenter WC Math Assn. Biannual Conf., Reno, 1985-89; rep. Nev. State Edn. Coalition. Del. Democratic County Conv., Reno, 1988; campaign mgr. Mcpl. Judge Race, Reno, 1980; treas., state conv. del. PTA, Reno, 1985-89; tchr. rep. Alice Maxwell PTA, Sparks, 1989-90. Recipient Nat. Sallie Mae Tchr. Award for Outstanding 1st Yr. Tchrs., Sallie Mae Found., 1985; Mary Sartor Meml. scholar for acad. excellence, Dept. Edn. U. Nev. Reno, 1982. Mem. NEA, ACA, Nev. State Edn. Assn., Greater Nev. Sch. Counselors Assn. (past pres., state of Nev. liaison), Am. Sch. Counselor Assn., Assn. for Multicultural Counseling and Devel. Democrat. Avocations: music, woodworking, hiking, travel. Home: PO Box 696 Verdi NV 89439-0696 Office: McQueen High Sch 6055 Lancer St Reno NV 89523-1201

KAYS, ELENA J., interior design educator; b. Phillipsburg, N.J., Nov. 7, 1966; d. Eugene Earl and Karen Jane (Easterly) Hoffman; m. Philip F. Kays Jr., Sept. 16, 1989; 1 child, Lydia Rose. AAS, Chamberlayne Jr. Coll., Boston, 1987; BFA, Centenary Coll., 1992; MA, East Stroudsburg U., 1995. Cert. Nat. Coun. for Interior Design Qualification, N.J. Sr. interior designer Isabel & Co./MACII, Easton, Pa. and N.Y.C., 1986-90; landscape designer, renderer Daniel's Landscaping, Nazareth, Pa., 1986-91; draftsperson Mary Trubek Arch., Alpha, N.J., 1987-88, Tylman Moon Assocs., Flemington, N.J., 1988; design asst. Directions in Design, Hackettstown, N.J., 1990; asst. prof. interior design Centenary Coll., Hackettstown, 1992—; mem. adv. bd. FIDER, Kean U., Union, N.J., 1997-98; task force mem. Nat. Coun. for Interior Design Legis., N.J., 1998. Mem. Internat. Assn. Lighting Designers (educator), Am. Soc. Interior Designers (allied, faculty advisor student chpt. 1992—), Interior Design Educators Coun. (corp., comm. com. 1996—, instrnl. improvement com. 1996—). Office: Centenary Coll 400 Jefferson St Hackettstown NJ 07840-2184

KAYS, WILLIAM MORROW, university administrator, mechanical engineer; b. Norfolk, Va., July 29, 1920; s. Herbert Emery and Margaret (Fechteler) K.; m. Alma Campbell, Sept. 14, 1947 (dec. June 1982); children: Nancy, Leslie, Margaret, Elizabeth.; m. Judith Scholtz, July 17, 1983. A.B., Stanford U., 1942, M.S., 1947, Ph.D. in Mech. Engring., 1951. Asst. prof. mech. engring. Stanford U., 1951-54, assoc. prof., 1954-57, prof., 1957-90, prof. emeritus, 1990—, chmn. dept. mech. engring, 1961-72, dean engring., 1972-84; dir. Acurex Corp., Alcohol Energy Systems; cons. to numerous firms. Author: Compact Heat Exchangers, 1964, 93, Convective Heat and Mass Transfer, 1966, 80. Hon. editorial adv. bd.: Internat. Jour. Heat and Mass Transfer. Served with U.S. Army, 1942-46. Fulbright fellow, 1959-60; NSF sr. postdoctoral fellow, 1966-67. Fellow ASME (Heat Transfer Divsn. Meml. award 1965, Max Jacob award 1992); mem. Am. Soc. Engring. Edn., Nat. Acad. Engring. Office: Stanford U Dept Mech Engring Stanford CA 94305

KAYSEN, CARL, economics educator; b. Phila., Mar. 5, 1920; s. Samuel and Elizabeth (Resnick) K.; m. Annette Neutra, Sept. 13, 1940 (dec. 1990); children: Susanna, Laura; m. Ruth Butler, 1994. A.B., U. Pa., 1940; Ph.D., Harvard U., 1954. Researcher Nat. Bur. Econ. Research, 1940-42; economist OSS, 1942; mem. faculty Harvard U., 1946-66; jr. fellow Harvard U. (Soc. Fellows), 1947-50, asst. prof. econs., 1950-55, assoc. prof., 1955-57, prof., 1957-66, Lucius N. Littauer prof. polit. economy, 1964-66; assoc. dean Harvard U. (Grad. Sch. Public Adminstrn.), 1960-66; dir. Inst. Advanced Study, Princeton, N.J., 1966-76; prof. Inst. Advanced Study, 1966-77; David W. Skinner prof. polit. economy MIT, 1977-90, dir. program in sci., tech. and soc., 1981-87, prof. emeritus, 1990—; clk. to Judge E. E. Wyzanski, U.S. Dist. C., 1950-52; dep. spl. asst. to Pres. Kennedy for nat. security affairs, 1961-63; mem. Carnegie Commn. on Higher Edn.; vice chmn., dir. research Sloan Commn. on Govt. and Higher Edn.; faculty lectr. London Sch. Econs., 1956; Haynes lectr. Calif. Inst. Tech., 1966; Stafford Little lectr. Princeton U., 1968; Oliver W. Holmes lectr. Harvard Law Sch., 1969; Paley lectr. Hebrew U., Jerusalem, 1970; Godkin lectr. Harvard U., 1976; Bernard Brodie lectr., U.C.L.A., 1994; dir. Charles River Assocs. Life trustee U. Pa. Served to capt. air intelligence AUS, 1942-45. Fulbright scholar London Sch. Econs., 1955-56; Guggenheim fellow, 1955-56; Ford Found. fellow Greece, 1959-60. Mem. Am. Philos. Soc., Am. Acad. Arts and Scis., Phi Beta Kappa. Club: Century (N.Y.C.). Office: MIT Security Studies Program E 38-603 Cambridge MA 02139

KAYSER, MARY ELLEN H., nursing consultant and educator; b. Paterson, N.J., July 8, 1938; d. Edward Arthur and Cornelia Jane (Kuyper) Harmon; m. G. Carl Kayser, June 12, 1965; children: Edward Harmon, Janet Cornelia. BS, Syracuse U., 1960; MA, Columbia U., 1965. Mem. faculty Passaic County Community Coll., Paterson, N.J., Felician Coll., Lodi, N.J., Bergen Community Coll., Paramus, N.J., Clara Maass Sch. Nursing, Belleville, N.J.; sch. nurse Essex County (N.Y.) Ednl. Svcs., Cedar Grove. Mem. NLN, AAUW (sec. Essex County br. 1989—), Kappa Delta Pi, Pi Lambda Theta. Home: 656 Grove St Montclair NJ 07043-2019

KAYTON, MYRON, engineering company executive; b. N.Y.C., Apr. 26, 1934; s. Albert Louis and Rae (Danoff) K.; m. Paula Erde, Sept. 5, 1954; children: Elizabeth Kayton Kerns, Susan Kayton Barclay. BS, The Cooper Union, 1955; MS, Harvard U., 1956; PhD, MIT, 1960. Registered engr., Calif. Sect. head Litton Industries, Woodland Hills, Calif., 1960-65; dep. mgr. NASA, Houston, 1965-69; mem. sr. staff TRW, Inc., Redondo Beach, Calif., 1969-81; pres. Kayton Engring. Co., Inc., Santa Monica, Calif., 1981—; chmn. bd. dirs. WINCON Conf., L.A., 1985-92; founding dir. Caltech-MIT Enterprise Forum, Pasadena, Calif., 1984—; tchr. tech. courses UCLA Extension, 1969-88. Author: Avionic Navigation Systems, 1966, 2d edit., 1997, Navigation: Land, Sea, Air and Space, 1990; contbr. numerous articles on engring., econs. and other profl. subjects. Founding dir. UCLA Friends of Humanities, 1971-75; West coast chmn. Cooper Union Fund Campaign, 1989-93. Fellow NSF, Washington, 1956-57, 58-60; recipient Gano Dunn medal The Cooper Union, N.Y.C., 1975. Fellow IEEE (chmn. nominating com. 1999—, corp. bd. dirs. 1996-97, pres. aerospace 1993-94, exec. v.p. aerospace 1991-92, v.p. tech. ops. 1988-90, nat. bd. govs. 1983—, vice-chmn. L.A. coun. 1983-84, M.B. Carlton award 1988, Disting. lectr.); mem. ASME, Harvard Grad. Soc. (coun. mem. chmn. nominating com. 1988-91, Inst. Navigation, Soc. Automotive Engr., Harvard Club So. Calif. (pres. 1979-80), MIT Club (L.A.). Avocations: tennis, history, languages, flying, running. Office: Kayton Engring Co PO Box 802 Santa Monica CA 90406-0802

KAZ, NATHANIEL, sculptor; b. N.Y.C., Mar. 9, 1917; s. I. Rudolph and Ida (Elkan) K.; m. Delfina Nahrgang, 1986; children: Naomi Della, Eric Justin. Student, Art Students League, Samuel Cashwan, 1927, William Zorach; attended, Cooper Union. Tchr. Art Students League, N.Y.C. One-man shows include Downtown Gallery, 1939, Assn. Am. Artists, 1946, Grand Central Moderns, 1954, Joan Avnet Gallery, 1965, Art Students League N.Y., 1991; traveling group exhbn. Bethlehem, Pa., Oshkosh, Wis., Annapolis, Md.; exhbns. include Whitney Mus., Met. Mus. Art, Bklyn. Mus., Art Inst. Chgo., U. Nebr., Phila. Mus. Fine Arts, Mus. Modern Art, N.Y. and San Francisco world's fairs; represented in permanent collections, Bklyn. Mus., Whitney Mus., Met. Mus., Larry Aldrich Mus., N.Y.U., pvt. collections; designed and executed 10 ft. carving in limestone for Vine St. Temple, Nashville, 6 ft. bronze for Pub. Sch. 59, Bklyn.; exhibited 4 ritual works, Grand Central Moderns, 1957, Temple of Beth Emeth, Albany, N.Y., 1965; designed and executed two 7 ft. colored aluminum reliefs of Thespians-Tragedy and Comedy for Jr. High Sch. 164, Queens, New York, 1958. Grantee Nat. Inst. Arts and Letters, 1959; recipient Mich. Sculpture award, 1929, Sect. Fine Arts award, 1940, Artists for Victory award, 1942, Bklyn. Soc. Artists 32d ann. award, 1952, Sculpture prize Bklyn. Mus., 1952, Alfred G. B. Steel prize 148th ann. exhibit Pa. Acad. Fine Arts, 1953; winner nat. competition UN monument design, Nat. Council U.S. Art, 1955; Award for Sculpture Maury Leibovitz Competition, 1986; Nancy Dryfoos Meml. award Allied Artists Am. Exhbn., N.Y.C., 1991, C. Percival Dietsch Sculpture prize Nat. Sculpture Soc., N.Y.C., 1992. Mem. Sculptors Guild, Nat. Sculpture Soc., NAD (academician, Merit award 1976, Agop Agopoff award 1988, Saltus Gold medal 1989), Audubon Artists (Medals of Honor 1960, 1981, 83, 87, 88), Sculpture Soc. Studio: 160 W 73rd St New York NY 10023-3012

KAZA, GREG JOHN, state representative, economist; b. Wyandotte, Mich., Nov. 11, 1960; s. John J. and Mary A. (Lazurek) K. BA in Econs., U. Detroit, 1989; MSF in Internat. Fin., Walsh Coll., Troy, Mich., 1998. Staff A.T. Kearney & Co., Alexandria, Va., 1982-83; journalist Washington and Mich., 1983-89; v.p. policy rsch. The Mackinac Ctr., Midland, Mich., 1989-91; adj. prof. Northwood Inst., Troy, Mich., 1991-93; state rep. State of Mich., 1993—. Author: Michigan: An Agenda for the 90's, 1990, Liberty In the House, 1995, More Liberty in the House, 1996. Named Nat. Legislator of Yr., Rep. Liberty Caucus, 1994, one of Outstanding Young Men of Am., 1992. Fellow Nat. Journalism Ctr.; mem. Highpointers Mountaineering Club, Econ. Club Detroit. Republican. Roman Catholic. Home: 284 Woodside Ct Rochester Hls MI 48307-4159 Office: Ho of Reps State Capitol Lansing MI 48909*

KAZALIA, MARIE ANN, writer; b. Toledo, Feb. 12, 1954; d. Charles and Lois Jean (Gelvin) K.; children: Sarah Jean Richards, Jason Samuel Williams. BFA, Calif. Coll. Arts & Crafts, 1981; MA, Ctr. Mus. Studies, 1983. Mus. register City & County Arts Commn., San Francisco, 1982-83. Author of poems. E-mail: MAKazalia@aol.com. Office: PO Box 422344 San Francisco CA 94142-2344

KAZAM, ABDUL RAOOF, veterinarian; b. Okara, Pakistan; s. Hadayat Ullah Malik and Iqbal Baigum; m. Attia Nusrat Dar, Nov. 25, 1971; children: Imrana G., Irfaan R. BSc in Vet. Sci., Coll. of Animal Husbandry and Vet. Scis., Lahore, Pakistan, 1962; MSc in Vet. Sci. and Parasitology, U. Agr., Faisalabad, Pakistan, 1969. Veterinarian Vineland, N.J., 1976—; supervising vet. med. officer food and safety inspection svcs., USDA, 1977, meat and poultry product inspector. Mem. Vineland Circuit Safety Com., 1982-92, chmn., 1992—. Mem. AVMA, Nat. Assn. Fed. Vets. Muslim. Avocations: gardening, reading, travel, working out, helping others. Home and Office: 1542 Mosswood Dr Vineland NJ 08360-6237

KAZAN, BASIL GIBRAN, religious music composer; b. Jditah-Chtaura, Lebanon, May 16, 1914; came to U.S., 1957; s. Economos Girgeos and Tamam (Shehadey) K.; m. Viola Habeeb, Aug. 16, 1970. BA, Patriarchal Lycee, Damascus, Syria, 1935; diploma in theology, U. Athens, 1956. Prof. St. John's Seminary, Khonchara, Lebanon, 1939-43, Oriental Coll., Zahle, Lebanon, 1943-45, Am. U., Beirut, Lebanon, 1945-47; sec. to Patriarch Alexandros of Antioch, Damascus, 1947-50; pastor, theology student U. Athens, 1950-56; pastor various chs. in U.S.A., 1957-64; bookstore owner, operator Beirut, 1964-67; composer Antiochan Archdiocese N.Am., Englewood, N.J., 1967-95; profl. cantor St. Mary's Orthodox Ch., Bklyn., 1967-92; prof. translator Berlitz Sch. and Translation Svc., N.Y.C., 1970-80; advisor Consulate Gen. of Lebanon, N.Y.C., 1973-80; prof. Byzantine Chant St. Vladimier's Sem., Crestwood, N.Y., 1975-77; asst. examiner Bd. Edn., Bklyn., 1974-84; asked to come from Lebanon in 1966 by Primate of Antiochan Orthodox Christian Archdioces of N.Am. for Byzantine Music Project in English, producing 12 vols. to date with two supplementary vols. to complete the project. Composer music and words Soyo Anthem Syrian Orthodox Youth Orgn., 1986; composed and translated numerous religious verses and svcs. Commd. to melodize The Holy Mass in Spanish Lang., His Grace Bishop A. Shadrawi, The Orthodox Patriarcal Vicar Gen., Mexico City, 1974, melodized abd recorded on two cassette tapes the new text of The Divine Liturgy in Byzantine Way and Western Way for a Group of Western Faithfuls Who Joined the Orthodox Christian Antiochian Archdiocese of North America, 1981. Recipient decoration from Patriarch Alexandros' Golden Jubilee, 1954; presented Highest Antonian Gold Medal of Merit on 25th year of work on Byzantine Music Project, By His Eminence Metropolitan Philip, 1992. Avocations: poetry, writing, composing music. Home: 265 87th St Brooklyn NY 11209-4911

KAZAN, BENJAMIN, research engineer; b. N.Y.C., May 8, 1917; s. Abraham Eli and Esther (Bookbinder) K.; m. Gerda B. Mosse, Nov. 4, 1988; 1 child from previous marriage, David Louis. BS in Physics, Calif. Inst. Tech., 1938; MA in Physics, Columbia U., 1940; PhD in Physics, Tech. U. Munich, 1961. Radio engr. Dept. Def., Ft. Monmouth, N.J., 1940-50; rsch. engr. RCA Labs., Princeton, N.J., 1950-58; head solid state display group Hughes Rsch. Lab., Malibu, Calif., 1958-61; head imaging sect. Electro-Optical Systems, Pasadena, Calif., 1961-68; head exploratory display group T.J. Watson Rsch. Ctr., Yorktown Heights, N.Y., 1968-74; prin. scientist Xerox Rsch. Ctr., Palo Alto, Calif., 1974-85; cons. display and imaging tech., 1985—; cons. Advisory Group Electron Devices, Dept. Def., 1973-82; adj. prof. U. R.I., Kingston, 1970-74. Author: (with others) Storage Tubes, 1952; Electronic Image Storage, 1968. Editor: Advances in Image Pickup and Display series, 1972-84; assoc. editor Advances in Imaging and Electron Physics series, 1984—; contbr. articles to profl. jours.; patentee in field. Recipient Silver medal Am. Roentgen Ray Soc., 1957. Fellow IEEE (assoc.

editor Jour. Electron Devices 1979-83), Soc. Info. Display (editor jour. 1974-78); mem. Am. Phys. Soc., Sigma Xi, Tau Beta Pi. Home: 557 Tyndall St Los Altos CA 94022-3920

KAZAN, ELIA, theatrical, motion picture director and producer, author; b. Constantinople, Turkey, Sept. 7, 1909; s. George and Athena (Sismanoglou) K.; m. Molly Day Thacher, Dec. 2, 1932 (dec.); children: Judy, Chris, Nick, Katharine; m. Barbara Loden, June 5, 1967 (dec.); 1 child, Leo; m. Frances Rudge, June 28, 1982. A.B., Williams Coll., 1930; postgrad., Yale U., 1930-32; M.F.A., Wesleyan U., Middletown, Conn., 1955. Co-founder Actors Studio. Actor with Group Theatre, 1932-39; dir. stage plays, 1940-55, including Skin of Our Teeth, Harriet, Jacobowsky and the Colonel, All My Sons, Deep Are the Roots, A Streetcar Named Desire, Death of a Salesman, Camino Real, Tea and Sympathy, Cat on a Hot Tin Roof, The Dark at the Top of the Stairs, J.B (Antoinette Perry award for direction 1958), Sweet Bird of Youth, After the Fall, But for Whom Charlie, The Changeling; numerous motion pictures, 1944—, including A Tree Grows in Brooklyn, Boomerang, Gentlemen's Agreement (Acad. award for best direction 1947), Pinky, Panic in the Streets, A Streetcar Named Desire, Zapata, Man on a Tight Rope, On the Waterfront, (1954 Acad. Award for best direction), East of Eden, Baby Doll, A Face in the Crowd, Wild River, Splendor in the Grass, America, America, The Arrangement, The Visitors, The Last Tycoon; author: America, America, 1962, The Arrangement, 1967, The Assassins, 1972, The Understudy, 1974, Acts of Love, 1978, The Anatolian, 1982, Elia Kazan-A Life, 1988, Beyond the Aegean, 1994. Recipient D.W. Griffith award Dirs. Guild Am., 1987. *

KAZAN, ROBERT PETER, neurosurgeon; b. Chgo., Mar. 29, 1947; s. Peter Joseph and Genevieve (Pauga) K.; m. Janet Rae Hoiland, June 21, 1975. BS, Loyola U., Chgo., 1969, MD, 1973. Diplomate Am. Bd. Neurol. Surgeons; lic. physician Ill., Minn. Intern Mayo Clinic, Rochester, Minn., 1973-74, resident in neurosurgery, 1974-78; neurosurg. cons. West Suburban Neurosurg. Assocs., Hinsdale, Ill., 1978-92; med. dir. neurosci. dept. Hinsdale Hosp., 1992; clin. asst. prof. neurosurgery U. Ill., Chgo., 1983—; various teaching appointments West Suburban Hosp. Dept. Surgery, Chgo. Med. Soc. Midwest Conf., Northwestern U.; staff neurosurgeon Hinsdale Hosp., vice-chmn. surgery, 1988-90, chmn. dept. surgery, 1990—, med. dir. neurosci., 1992. Contbr. articles to profl. jours. Fellow ACS; mem. AMA, DuPage County Med. Soc., Ill. Med. Soc., Mayo Clin. Neurosurg. Soc., Congress Neurosurg. Surgeons, Am. Assn. Neurol. Surgeons, Cen. Neurosurg. Soc., Soc. Med. Cons. Armed Forces U.S., Am. Assn. Neurol. Surgeons (joint sec. trauma and disorders of spine and peripheal nerves), Congress Neurol. Surgeons (joint sect. trauma and disorders of spine and peripheal nerves), Internat. Skullbase Soc., Ill. State Neurosurg. Soc. (membership chmn. 1995, treas. 1996, sec.-treas. 1997, v.p. 1998). Republican. Roman Catholic. Office: West Suburban Neurosurg Assocs 20 E Ogden Ave Hinsdale IL 60521-3543

KAZANJIAN, JOHN HAROLD, lawyer; b. Newport, R.I., Jan. 25, 1949; s. Powel Harold and Louise T. (Alexander) K.; m. Jane Mitchell Kohlmeyer, Sept. 26, 1981; 1 child, Sara Jane. BA, Providence Coll., 1971; JD, Notre Dame U., 1975. Bar: N.Y. 1976, U.S. Dist. Ct. (so. dist.) N.Y. 1976, U.S. Dist. Ct. (ea. dist.) N.Y. 1977, U.S. Supreme Ct. 1980, U.S. Ct. Appeals (2d crct.) 1986, U.S. Ct. Appeals (fed. crct.) 1991. Assoc. Cadwalader, Wickersham & Taft, N.Y.C., 1975-86; ptnr. Anderson, Kill & Olick, N.Y.C., 1986-98, Beveridge & Diamond, N.Y.C., 1999—. Mem. U.S. Naval War Coll. Found., Newport, 1985—. Mem. ABA (sects. on litigation, tort and ins. practice and internat. law), Assn. Bar City N.Y. (chair com. on product liability), N.Y. County Lawyers Assn. (chair com. on ins. law, tort law sect.), Metro. Club. Episcopalian. Avocations: caricatures, cartoons, long distance running. Office: Beveridge & Diamond 15th Fl 477 Madison Ave New York NY 10022-5802

KAZANJIAN, PHILLIP CARL, lawyer, business executive; b. Visalia, Calif., May 15, 1945; s. John Casey and Sat-ten Arlene K.; m. Wendy Coffelt, Feb. 5, 1972; 1 child, John. B.A. with honors, U. So. Calif., 1967; J.D. with honors, Lincoln U., San Francisco, 1973. Bar: Calif. 1979, U.S. Dist. Ct. (cen. dist.) Calif. 1980, U.S. Tax Ct. 1980, U.S. Ct. Appeals (9th cir.) 1980, U.S. Mil. Ct. Appeals 1980, U.S. Supreme Ct. 1983. Ptnr. Brakefield & Kazanjian, Glendale, Calif., 1981-87; sr. ptnr., Kazanjian & Martinetti, 1987—; judge pro tem L.A. County Superior Ct., 1993—; instr. U.S. Naval Acad., Annapolis, Md., 1981; adj. prof. Glendale Cmty. Coll., 1997—. Mem. Calif. Atty. Gen.'s Adv. Commn. on Community-Police Relations, 1973; bd. dirs. L.A. County Naval Meml. Found., Inc., 1981-85; pres. bd. trustees Glendale Community Coll. Dist., 1981-97, L.A. World Affairs Council, Town Hall Calif., Republican Assocs. (dir.), Rep. Lincoln Club; bd. govs. Calif. Maritime Acad., 1986-94. Served to capt. USNR, 1969—. Decorated Navy Commendation medal, Navy Achievement medal, knight Order of Knights Templar, 1990; recipient Patrick Henry medal Am. Legion, 1963, Congressional Record tribute U.S. Ho. of Reps., 1974, Centurion award Chief of Naval Ops., 1978, award Res. Officers Assn. U.S., 1981, commendatory resolutions Mayor of L.A., L.A. City Council, L.A. County Bd. Suprs., Calif. State Assembly and Senate, and Govt. of Calif., 1982, Justice award Calif. Law Student Assn., 1973. Mem. ABA (Gold Key 1972), Calif. Bar Assn., Los Angeles County Bar Assn., Am. Judicature Soc., Assn. Trial Lawyers Am., Glendale C. of C. (bd. dirs., Patriot Yr. 1986), Res. Officers Assn. (nat. judg adv.), Naval Res. Assn. (nat. adv. com.), U.S. Naval Inst., Interallied Confedn. Res. Officers (internat. chmn. 1987-94), Explorers Club. Republican. Episcopalian. Club: Commonwealth of Calif. Author: The Circuit Governor, 1972; editor in chief Lincoln Law Rev., 1973. Office: Kazanjian & Martinetti 520 E Wilson Ave Ste 250 Glendale CA 91206-4346

KAZANJIAN, SHANT, religious organization administrator. Exec. coord. Armenian Religious Edn. Coun., N.Y.C., 1990—. Office: Armenian Religious Edn Coun 138 E 39th St New York NY 10016-0914*

KAZAZIAN, HAIG HAGOP, JR., medical scientist, physician, educator; b. Toledo, July 30, 1937; s. Haig Hagop and Hermine Adriene (Papelian) K.; m. Lillian Agnes Cleaver, Oct. 13, 1962; children: Haig Hagop III, Sonya Elizabeth. AB, Dartmouth Coll., 1959; MD, Johns Hopkins U., 1962. Asst. prof. pediatrics Johns Hopkins U., Balt., 1969-74, assoc. prof. pediatrics, 1974-77, prof. pediats., 1977-94, prof. biology, 1978-94, prof. ob-gyn., 1985-94, prof. medicine, 1989-94, dir. Ctr. Med. Genetics, 1989-94, Sutland prof. pediat. genetics, 1991-94; chmn. dept. genetics U. Pa. Sch. Medicine, Phila., 1994—; mem. mammalian genetics study sect. NIH, Bethesda, Md., 1981-85; pres. bd. dirs. Citizens for Good Govt., Balt., 1973-75. Author more than 250 sci. papers; editor jour. Human Mutation, 1992. Sr. surgeon USPHS, 1966-68. Grantee NIH, 1968—; recipient Mead Johnson award Am. Acad. Pediatrics, 1976. Mem. Inst. of Medicine, Am. Pediat. Soc., Am. Soc. Human Genetics (bd. dirs. 1982-85), Am. Soc. Clin. Investigation, Assn. Am. Physicians, Alpha Omega Alpha. Democrat. Episcopalian. Avocations: jogging, tennis, classical music. Home: 1015 Winding Way Baltimore MD 21210-1232 Office: U Pa Sch Medicine 475 Clinical Research Bldg 415 Curie Blvd Philadelphia PA 19104-4218

KAZEM, ISMAIL, radiation oncologist, educator, health science facility administrator; b. Cairo, Feb. 28, 1931; came to U.S., 1966; s. Mohamed and Khadiga A. (Abou-Hadid) K.; m. Barbara Jean Whitelock; children: Farid, Mohamed, Karen, Ramsey. MB, BChir, Ein Shams U., Cairo, 1955; diploma in radiotherapy, Royal Coll. Radiologists, London, 1960. Diplomate Am. Bd. Nuclear Medicine, Am. Bd. Radiology. Intern Demerdach U. Hosp., Cairo, 1955-56; clin. demonstrator radiology dept. Ein Shams U. Faculty Medicine, 1956-59; trainee Meyerstein Inst. Radiotherapy Middlesex Hosp., London, 1959, 60; IAEA fellow Strahlen Klinik, Czerny Krankenhaus U. Heidelberg, Germany, 1959; sr. registrar dept. radiotherapy St. Bartholomew's Hosp., London, 1960-61; lectr., then asst. prof. radiation therapy U. Alexandria, Egypt, 1962-65; sr. rschr. Inst. Nuclear Medicine German Cancer Rsch. Ctr., Heidelberg, 1965-66; from instr. to asst. prof. radiology Hahnemann Med. Coll. and Hosp., Phila., 1966-70; prof., chmn. dept. radiation therapy and nuclear medicine Sint Radboud Acad. Hosp., Cath. U., Nijmegen, The Netherlands, 1970-83; dir. dept. radiation therapy and Regional Cancer Ctr. Mercer Med. Ctr., Trenton, N.J., 1983-92; dir. divsn. radiation oncology U. Medicine Dentistry-NJ Univ. Hosp., Newark, 1992-94; dir. dept. radiation oncology Geisinger Med. Ctr., Danville, Pa., 1994—; clin. prof. radiation oncology Temple U., Phila., 1985-91, Thomas Jefferson U., 1995—; prof. clin. radiology U. Medicine and Dentistry N.J., Newark; presenter in field. Author: (poetry) An Anthology of My Own Thing, 1975, Reflections and Definitions, 1978, Conversations with My Thoughts, 1992, Introduction to Oncology (in Dutch), 1983; mem. editorial bd. N.J. Medicine; editor Mercer County Medicine. Exec. com. Mercer County unit Am. Cancer Soc., pres., 1992-94; mem. pilot project task force for breast cancer screening in Mercer County, N.J. Dept. Health, Trenton, also mem. reaction group licensure reform project; mem. adv. coun. N.J. Office Pub. Guardian for Elderly. WHO fellow, 1963, Disting. fellow Am. Coll. Nuclear Medicine, 1993. Fellow Royal Soc. Medicine (London), Royal Coll. Radiologists (London), Acad. Medicine N.J., Am. Coll. Nuclear Medicine (disting., charter), Am Coll. Radiology; mem. AMA, Soc. Nuclear Medicine, Am. Soc. for Therapeutic Radiology and Oncology, Netherlands Soc. Radiotherapy, European Soc. Therapeutic Radiology and Oncology, Am. Assn. Cancer Edn., Am. Soc. Clin. Oncology, Pan Am. Med. Assn., Am. Endocurietherapy Soc., Pa. Med. Soc., N.J. Med. Soc., N.Y. Acad. Scis., Mercer County Med. Soc. (pres. 1993-94). Office: Geisinger Med Ctr Dept Radiation Oncology 100 N Academy Ave Dept Danville PA 17821-1203 *Because I am alive, I can choose. And I have made my choice: To live my life to completion. (When I am fulfilled, my life shall be completed.) I shall then command: My heart to stand still, my breath to halt, and my brain, through death to achieve perfection!.*

KAZEMI, FARHAD, political science educator; b. Tehran, Iran, Jan. 7, 1943; came to U.S., 1960; s. Parviz and Irandokht (Ehteshami) K.; m. Tina A. Garber, July 9, 1966 (div. 1975); children: Shirin, Sara; m. Jane Opper, Apr. 28, 1977; stepchildren: Lygeia, Maude. BA, Colgate U., 1964; MA, George Washington U., 1966, Harvard U., 1968; PhD, U. Mich., 1973. Teaching fellow U. Mich., Ann Arbor, 1968-70; from instr., asst. prof., assoc. prof. to prof. pol. sci. NYU, 1971-88, acting dean Grad. Sch. Arts and Sci., 1989-91; cons. U.S. Govt., 1980s and 90s; vis. lectr. U. Pa., 1979; dir. Kevorkian Ctr., NYU, 1982-85, chmn. dept. polit. sci., 1985-89, 92-93, 96-97; vis. prof. Princeton Univ., 1996; vis. sr. fellow Oxford (Eng.) U., 1997. Author: Poverty and Revolution in Iran, 1980, Politics and Culture in Iran, 1988; author, editor: Iranian Revolution, 1980, Civil Society in Iran, 1995-96; co-editor: A Way Prepared: Studies on Islamic Culture, 1987, Peasants and Politics in the Modern Middle East, 1991 , other books and articles. Grantee NSF, 1973, Social Sci. Rsch. Coun., 1974-75, 84-85, Kervorkian Fund, 1985, Ford Found., 1992-93, 94-95, Rockefeller Found., 1993, 94. Fellow Middle East Studies Assn. (bd. dirs. 1985-88, pres. 1995-96); mem. Am. Polit. Sci. Assn., Internat. Polit. Sci. Assn., Internat. Studies Assn., Middle East Inst., Soc. Iranian Studies (mem. coun., editor 1982-86, pres. 1998-99), Internat. Soc. Polit. Psychology, Coun. Fgn. Rels., Atlantic Coun. Washington (acad. assoc. 1985—). Democrat. Avocations: tennis, biking, sailing. Office: NYU Dept Politics 715 Broadway New York NY 10003-6860

KAZEMI, HOMAYOUN, physician, medical educator; b. Teheran, Iran, Sept. 28, 1934; came to U.S., 1953, naturalized, 1970; s. Parviz and Irandokht K.; m. Katheryne McNulty, June 7, 1958; children: Paul, Laili. BA, Lafayette Coll., 1954; MD, Columbia U., 1958; MSc (hon.), Harvard U., 1990. Diplomate: Am. Bd. Internal Medicine. Intern M.I. Bassett Hosp., Cooperstown, N.Y., 1958-59; resident in medicine Mass. Gen. Hosp., Boston, 1963; chief pulmonary unit Mass. Gen. Hosp., 1967-89, chief pulmonary and critical care unit, 1989—; assoc. prof. medicine Harvard U., 1971-78, prof., 1979—, prof. medicine Harvard/MIT program in health sci. and tech., 1980—; hon. cons. in intrenal medicine Shanghai 1st People's Hosp., 1992—; vis. scholar dept. medicine, U. Calif., San Diego, 1998-99; bd. dirs. Boston Tb Assn.; vis. prof. U. Ghent, 1975-76, Peking Union Med. Coll., China, 1992; dir. U.S. Beryllium Case Registry, 1968-78; vis. fellow Hammersmith Hosp., London, 1965; cons. Fed. Aviation Agy., 1987. Author: Disorder of the Respiratory System, 1976, (with L.G. Miller) Manual of Pulmonary Medicine, 1982—, Acute Lung Injury, 1986; mem. editorial bd. New Eng. Jour. Medicine, 1981-90, Respiratory Mgmt., 1989-93; mem. editorial bd. Current Opinion in Pulmonary Medicine, 1993—, Current Opinion in Critical Care, 1993—. dir. Am. Lung Assn. Boston; mem. rsch. evaluation subcom. Am. Heart Assn., mem. cardiopulmonary coun., 1979—, v.p. 1985-87, pres. 1987-89, mem. rsch. rev. com.; bd. trustees Dublin (N.H.) Sch., 1987-97. Am. Heart Assn. fellow, 1961-63, Dickinson Richards lectr., 1996; recipient Chadwick medal Mass. Thoracic Soc., 1988. Fellow ACP; mem. Am. Fedn. Clin. Rsch., Am. Thoracic Soc. (pres. Ea. sect. 1974-75), Mass. Med. Soc., Am. Physiol. Soc, Am. Soc. Clin. INvestigation, Soc. Occupl. and Environ. Health, Sigma Xi. Office: Mass Gen Hosp Boston MA 02114

KAZEMI, HOSSEIN, petroleum engineer. BS in Petroleum Engring., U. Tex., 1961, PhD in Petroleum Engring., 1963. Rsch. scientist Sinclair Oil Corp./Atlantic Richfield Co., Tulsa, Dallas, 1963-69; adv. rsch. scientist Petroleum Tech. Ctr., Marathon, Littleton, Colo., 1969-74, sr. rsch. scientist, 1974-79, sr. tech. cons., 1979-81, mgr. engring., 1981-86, mgr. reservoir mgmt., 1986-88, assoc. dir., 1988-94, mgr. product tech., 1994-96, mgr. reservoir tech., 1997—; adj. prof. Colo. Sch. Mines, Golden, 1981—; lectr., speaker in field. Contbr. articles to profl. jours. Mem. Soc. Petroleum Engrs. AIME (hon., disting., Henry Mattson tech. svc. award 1980, John Franklin Carll award 1987, Disting. Svc. award 1991, DeGolyer Disting. Svc. award 1995), Nat. Acad. Engring. Office: Petroleum Tech Ctr Marathon PO Box 269 Littleton CO 80160-0269

KAZEN, GEORGE PHILIP, federal judge; b. Laredo, Tex., Feb. 29, 1940; s. Emil James and Drusilla M. (Perkins) K.; m. Barbara Ann Sanders, Oct. 27, 1962; children: George Douglas, John Andrew, Elizabeth Ann, Gregory Stephen. BBA, U. Tex., 1960, JD with honors, 1961. Bar: Tex. 1961, U.S. Supreme Ct., U.S. Ct. Claims, U.S. Ct. Appeals (5th cir.), U.S. Dist. Ct. (so. dist.) Tex. Briefing atty. Tex. Sup. Ct., 1961-62; founder, first pres. Laredo Legal Aid Soc., 1966-69; assoc. Mann, Freed, Kazen & Hansen, 1965-79; judge U.S. Dist. Ct. (so. dist.) Tex., Laredo, 1979-96; founder, first pres. Laredo Legal Aid Soc., 1966-69; chief judge U.S. Dist. Ct. (so. dist.) Tex., Laredo, 1996—; mem. Jud. Conf. Com. Criminal Law, 1990-96, chair com., 1996—; mem. 5th Cir. Jud. Coun., 1991-94, 96—; adj. prof. law St. Mary's U. Sch. Law, 1990—. Pres. Laredo Civic Music Assn.; chmn. St. Augustine-Ursuline Consol. Sch. Bd.; bd. dirs. Boys' Clubs Laredo; trustee Laredo Jr. Coll., 1972-79; bd. dirs., v.p., pres. Econ. Opportunities Devel. Corp., 1968-70; past bd. dirs. D.D. Hachar Found. With USAF, 1962-65. Decorated Air Force Commendation medal; named Outstanding Young Lawyer, Larado Jaycees, 1970. Mem. ABA, Tex. Bar Found., Tex. Bar Assn., Tex. Criminal Def. Lawyers Assn., Tex. Assn. Bank Counsel, Tex. Assn. Def. Counsel, Laredo C. of C. (bd. dirs. 1975-76), 5th Cir. Dist. Judges Assn. (v.p. 1984-85, pres. 1986-88), U. Tex. Law Sch. Alumni Assn. (bd. dirs. 1976-77). Roman Catholic. Office: US Dist Ct PO Box 1060 Laredo TX 78042-1060

KAZENAS, SUSAN JEAN, consultant; b. Oregon, Ill., Dec. 29, 1956; d. Charles Leroy and Vera Jean (Groenhagen) K. BS, Northwestern U., 1982. CPA, Ill., 1985. Acctg. analyst Allstate Ins. Co., Northbrook, Ill., 1977-80; asst. dir. Steel Tank Inst., Deerfield, Ill., 1980-81; owner, acct. Decker Drug, Oregon, 1981-84; acct., auditor Crone, Kipp & Blomgren, Rockford, Ill., 1984-87; acct., internal auditor Woodward Gov. Co., Rockford, 1987-88; acct., sr. cons. McGladrey & Pullen, Rockford, 1988-90; cons. mgr. BDO Seidman, Rockford, 1990-93, Chgo., 1992-93; acctg. mgr. Danfoss Electronic Drives, Rockford, Ill., 1993-96; sr. prin. cons. Oracle Corp., Chgo., 1996—. Bd. dirs. pub. info. Am. Cancer Soc., Winnebago County, Ill., 1988-92. Mem. AICPA, Ill. CPA Soc. (No. chpt. sec. 1988-89, pres. 1989-90, state bd. dirs. 1993-95)), Inst. Mgmt. Accts. Avocations: cooking, reading, travel, golf, downhill skiing. Home: 154 Millers Xing Itasca IL 60143-2834 Office: Oracle Corp 203 N La Salle St Ste 2000 Chicago IL 60601-1225

KAZHDAN, DAVID, mathematician, educator; b. Moscow, June 20, 1946; came to U.S., 1975; s. Alexander and Rimma (Ivanskaya) K.; m. Helena Slobodkina, Mar. 22, 1968; children: Eli, Dina, Misha, Daniel. MA, Moscow State U., 1967, PhD, 1969; BA (hon), Harvard U., 1977. Researcher Moscow State U., 1969-75, vis. prof., 1975-77; prof. Harvard U., Cambridge, Mass., 1977—. MacArthur fellow. Mem. NAS. Office: Harvard U 1 Oxford St Cambridge MA 02138-2901

KAZIMI, MUJID SULIMAN, nuclear engineer, educator; b. Jerusalem, Nov. 20, 1947; came to U.S., 1969; s. Suliman Ishak Kazimi and Fikrat Nuseibeh; m. Nazik D. Denny, Sept. 1, 1973. B. Engring., Alexandria U., Arab Republic of Egypt, 1969; MS, MIT, 1971, PhD, 1973. Sr. engr. Westinghouse Electric Corp., Madison, Pa., 1973-74; assoc. scientist Brookhaven Nat. Lab., Upton, N.Y., 1974-76; asst. prof. MIT, Cambridge, 1976-79, assoc. prof., 1979-86, prof., 1986—, head dept. nuclear engring., 1989-97; chmn. high-level waste tank safety adv. panel U.S. Dept. Energy, Washington, 1990-95, chmn. new prodn. reactor severe accident group, 1990-91. Co-author: (with Neil Todreas) Nuclear Systems: Volume I: Thermal Hydraulic Fundamentals, 1990, Nuclear Systems: Volume II: Elements of Thermal Hydraulic Design, 1990; editor: Perspectives on Technological Development in the Arab World, 1978. Pres. Assn. Arab-Am. Univ. Grads., Belmont, Mass., 1980, 87. Fellow Am. Nuclear Soc. (bd. dirs. N.E. chpt. 1978, 80, exec. com. thermal hydraulics divsn. 1988-90); mem. ASME, AAAS, AIChE (chmn. nuclear heat transfer com. 19980-83), Am. Soc. for Engring. Edn. (exec. com. nuclear engring. divsn. 1995-97). Office: MIT Dept Nuc Engring 77 Massachusetts Ave Rm 24-205 Cambridge MA 02139-4307

KAZIN, MICHAEL, history educator, writer; b. N.Y.C., June 6, 1948; s. Alfred and Carol Bookman (Salvadori) K.; m. Beth Horowitz, Aug. 24, 1980; children: Daniel, Maia. BA, Harvard U., 1972; PhD, Stanford U., 1983. Instr. history San Francisco State U., 1978-82; asst. prof. history Stanford (Calif.) U., 1983-85; prof. history Am. U., Washington, 1986-99, Georgetown U., 1999—. Author: The Populist Persuasion, 1995, 96, revised editon, 1998, Barons of Labor, 1987, 89 (Gutman award 1988), America Divided, 1999; contbr. articles to profl. hist. jours.; book editor Tikkun, San Francisco/N.Y.C., 1987-96; assoc. editor Socialist Rev., San Francisco, 1978-84; hist. advisor several documentaries, 1982—. Mem. steering com. Com. for a Teach-In with Labor, N.Y.C., 1996-97; spkr., local leader Nuc. Freeze Campaign, San Francisco, 1982-84. John Adams chair Am. Studies, Fulbright program, Utrecht, The Netherlands, 1996; Fulbright lectr. Ritsumeikan U., Tokyo/Kyoto, 1997; sr. fellow William and Mary Coll. Commonwealth Ctr., Williamsburg, Va., 1990-91; postdoctoral fellow Smithsonian Instn., Washington, 1988-89; NEH fellow, 1998-99; Woodrow Wilson Ctr. fellow, 1998-99. Mem. Am. Hist. Assn., Orgn. Am. Historians (chair com. for Ellis Hawley award). Democrat. Jewish. Avocations: baseball, fiction. Office: Georgetown U Dept History Washington DC 20057-1035

KAZLE, ELYNMARIE, producer, performing arts executive; b. St. Paul, June 22, 1958; d. Victor Anton and Marylu (Gardner) K. BFA, U. Minn., Duluth, 1982; MFA, Ohio U., 1984. Prodn. mgr. Great Lakes Shakespeare, Cleve., 1983; prodn. stage mgr. San Diego (Calif.) Opera, 1984, PCPA Theaterfest, Santa Maria, Calif., 1986-87; stage mgr. Bklyn. Acad. Music, 1987; assoc. producer Assn. Am. Theater Actors, N.Y.C., 1988-89; prodn. stage mgr. Time Flies When You're Alive, West Hollywood, Calif., 1988—; asst. advt. display Wall St. Jour., L.A., 1988-89; West Coast adminstr. Soc. Stage Dirs. and Choreographers, 1991-93; assoc. mng. dir. Actors Alley, North Hollywood, Calif., 1993—; mng. ptnr., AIW Prodns., 1997—; founder, stage mgr. mentoring project US ITT, 1991—, project dir., 1991-96; exec. dir. Weathervane Playhouse, Akron, Ohio, 1997—. Editor, pub. The Ohio Network newsletter, 1984-90; prodr. Santa Monica Playhouse, 1988-94; assoc. mng. dir. Actors Alley Repertory Theater, North Hollywood Calif., 1993-96. Trustee Theatre/L.A., 1992-94. Mem. U.S. Inst. Theatre Tech. (bd. dirs. 1990-96, vice commr. 1992—), Stage Mgrs. Assn., Stage Mgrs. Assn. L.A., Actors Equity Assn., North Hollywood/Universal City C. of C. (bd. dirs. 1994-96), Phi Kappa Phi, Delta Chi Omega (past pres. 1978). Avocations: poetry, journalism, flying, rowing. Fax: 330-873-2150. Office: Weathervane Playhouse 1301 Weathervane Ln Akron OH 44313-5186

KAZMAREK, LINDA ADAMS, secondary education educator; b. Crisfield, Md., Jan. 18, 1945; d. Gordon I. Sr. and Annie Ruby (Sommers) Adams; m. Stephen Kazmarek, Jr., Aug. 2, 1981. B of Music Edn., Peabody Conservatory of Music, 1967; postgrad., Morgan U., Towson U. Cert. advanced profl. tchr., K-12, Md.; nat. cert. tchr. Mayron Cole piano method. Organist, choir dir. Halethorpe United Meth. Ch., Balt., min. music, 1978-92, 93—; organist, choir dir. Olive Branch United Meth. Ch., 1973-77; 1978-92, 93—; piano tchr. Modal Cities Program, Balt., Balt. Community Schs; tchr. vocal music Balt. City Schs., 1967—; min. music Halethorpe Meth. Ch., 1993—; pvt. tchr. piano and organ. Composer: A Family of Care (award, 1991, Praise Song, 1992, Thy Way, Lord, 1993, I Asked the Lord, 1993, Peace and Rest, 1994, Sing Praise to Jesus, 1994, Trilogy for piano solo, 1994, Shine Your Light, 1994, Resurrection, 1995, 1-800-Heaven, 1995, God Has A Plan for You, 1995. Concert performer for Meth. Bd. Child Care, 1989, Balt. S.W. Emergency Svcs., 1991, Halethorpe Meth. Ch., 1994; guest performer Balt. City Tchrs. Appreciation Banquet, 1991. Recipient vol. award for music enrichment summer program, 1973, award for voluntarism Fund. for Ednl. Excellence, 1985; Fund for Ednl. Excellence grantee, 1988. Mem. NEA, Md. State Tchrs. Assn., Balt. City Tchrs. Assn., Md. Music Educators Assn. (award for 30 yrs. of svc. in music and music edn. 1997), Music Educators Nat. Conf., Md. State Music Tchrs. Assn., Nat. Music Tchrs. Assn., Washington Songwriters Assn., Gospel Music Assn., Washington Area Music Assn., Peabody Alumni Assn.

KAZMIERCZAK, ELZBIETA TERESA, graphic designer, illustrator, educator, semiotician; b. Lodz, Poland, Dec. 30, 1959; came to U.S., 1990; d. Leon Antoni and Krystyna Irena (Grabowska) K.; (div.). BFA, Acad. Fine Arts, Lodz, 1984; MFA, U. Ill., 1993, MA, 1995. Instr. U. Ill., Urbana-Champaign, 1990-93, Capilano Coll., North Vancouver, B.C., Can., 1995-96; asst. prof. SUNY, Buffalo, 1996—, head illustration program, 1996—; desing cons., U.S., Can. and Poland. Contbr. articles to profl. jours. Creative and Performing Arts fellow, 1991-92; Poland Ministry of Culture and Art scholar, 1987-88. Mem. Semiotic Soc. Am., Inernat. Assn. for Semiotic Studies, Internat. Inst. for Info. Design. Avocations: meditation, reading, movies, classical music, jazz. Home: 22 Claremont Ave # 2 Buffalo NY 14222-1123 Office: SUNY Buffalo Dept Art 202 Ctr for the Arts Buffalo NY 14260-6010

KC, LISA LOUISE, school system administrator, jeweler; b. Peoria, Ill., Nov. 10, 1957; d. Roscoe and Beverly (Dinser) Herget; children: Matthew Krueger, Patricia Krueger. BA in Art Edn., U. No. Iowa, 1980; MEd in Ednl. Adminstrn., Nat.-Louis U., Wheaton, Ill., 1997. Art tchr. Wyoming (Ill.) H.S, LaSalle-Peru H.S., Peru, Ill., Rockford (Ill.) Sch. Dist.; art tchr. Harlem Consol. Schs., Loves Park, Ill., 1991-97, staff developer, 1992—. Mem. spl. activities com. Pub. Health Promotion Coalition, Rockford, 1998. Mem. Nat. Staff Devel. Assn., Phi Delta Kappa (chpt. v.p. programs 1998—). Avocations: gold/silversmithing, canoeing, biking, gardening. Home: 630 Paris Ave Rockford IL 61107-4445

KEA, JONATHAN GUY, instrumental music educator; b. Honolulu, June 2, 1960; s. Gilbert Halemano and Goldie Lee Gum (Chun) K. BMus, cert. teaching, Coe Coll., Cedar Rapids, Iowa, 1982. Band dir. James Campbell High Sch., Ewa Beach, Hawaii, 1982—; asst. condr. Honolulu Cmty. Band, 1988-94; dir. Honolulu Cmty. Jazz Band, 1993—. Mem. NEA, Oahu Band Dirs. Assn., Hawaii Music Educators Assn., Music Educators Nat. Conf., Phi Mu Alpha. Office: James Campbell High Sch 91-980 North Rd Ewa Beach HI 96706-2746

KEACH, JAMES P., actor; b. N.Y.C., Dec. 7, 1950; s. Walter Stacy and Mary Caine (Peckham) K.; m. Jane Seymour; children: John Stacy, Kristopher Steven, Kalen James, Sean, Katie, Jenny. BS, Northwestern U., 1970; MFA, Yale U., 1971. Appeared in over 50 films including The Wright Brothers, The Razor's Edge, Moving Violations, Wildcats, Love Letters, National Lampoon's Vacation; prodr., writer Armed and Dangerous; dir., prodr. (TV series) The Youg Riders; writer, dir., prodr. The Forgotten; prodr. A Winner Never Quits; prodr., dir. (TV series) The Long Riders; performed at Body Politic Theatre, Chgo., N.Y. Shakespeare Festival; dir. The Stars Fell on Henrietta, Camouflage; dir. (TV movies) Sunstroke, False Identity, A Passion for Justice, The Absolute Truth, The New Swiss Family Robinson, A Marriage of Convenience; dir. (TV series) Dr. Quinn Medicine Woman. Recipient Christopher award, N.Y., Ace award, Western Heritage award. Avocations: martial arts, golf, skiing, horseback riding. Office: c/o James Palmer Assocs 1901 Avenue Of The Stars Fl 7 Los Angeles CA 90067-6001

KEACH, STACY, SR., producer, director; b. Chgo., May 29, 1914; s. Walter Edmund and Dora (Stacy) K.; m. Mary Cain Peckham, June 18,

1937; children—Stacy, James. BS, Northwestern U., 1935; MA, 1936; LHD (hon.), Columbia Coll., 1987. Prof. theatrical prodns. Northwestern U., Evanston, Ill., 1935-36, Armstrong Coll., Savannah, Ga., 1936-41, Pasadena (Calif.) Playhouse, 1941-42; pres. Stacy Keach Prodns., Sherman Oaks, Calif., 1948—, Kaydan Record Corp., North Hollywood, 1957-70, Verdict Film Corp., Hollywood, 1972-73. Producer, dir. Universal Studios, Universal City, Calif., 1941-46, RKO Studios, Hollywood, Calif., 1946-48, producer, 1948-50, NBC, Hollywood, 1950-53, Columbia Pictures, Hollywood, 1952-54, appeared as Clarence Birds Eye on Birds Eye Frozen Food comml s., 1981-86; spokesman for Nat. Liberty Ins. TV commls., 1988-91. Recipient Rockefeller Found. award, 1941, Freedom Found. award (2), L.A. City Coun. award, 1973; named Man of Yr. Pasadena Playhouse Alumni Assn., 1995. Mem. Assn. Visual Communicators, Pacific Pioneer Broadcasters (bd. dirs. Twice, Diamond Circle award 1995), Rotary (past pres.), Sigma Alpha Epsilon. *There is nothing in life more precious than the love of one to another. It is the solution for securing happy families, good friends and lasting peace on earth.*

KEADY, GEORGE CREGAN, JR., judge; b. Bklyn., June 16, 1924; s. George Cregan and Marie (Lussier) K.; m. Patricia Drake, Sept. 2, 1950; children: Margaret Keady Goldberg, Marie E., George Cregan, Catherine A. Keady Dunn, Kathleen V. Student, U. Kans., 1943-44; B.S., Fordham U., 1949; J.D., Columbia U., 1950; LL.D., Western New Eng. Coll., 1973. Bar: Mass. 1950. Since practiced in Springfield, Mass.; asso. firm Ganley & Crook, 1950-53; assoc. firm Peter D. Wilson, 1953-57; partner firm Wilson, Keady & Ratner, 1958-79; justice Dist. Ct., Springfield, 1979-82; assoc. justice Superior Ct., Springfield, 1982-93; ret., 1993, freelance mediator and arbitrator, 1993—; dean Western New Eng. Coll. Law Sch., 1970-73; dir. Western Mass. Bar Rev., 1956-63, Western New Eng. Coll. Bar Rev., 1965-72; chmn. Mass. Continuing Legal Edn., Inc., 1977-80; mem. Mass. Commn. on Jud. Conduct, 1988, chmn., 1990-93. Active United Fund, Springfield, 1950-72, Joint Civic Agys.; chmn. fund drive Am. Cancer Soc., 1962, selectman, Longmeadow, Mass., 1958-68, chmn. selectmen, 1960-61, 63-64, 66-68, moderator, 1968-73; vice chmn. Rep. Town Com., Longmeadow, 1956-60; alt. del. Rep. Nat. Conv., 1960, del., 1964; pres. Hampden Dist. Mental Health Clinic, Inc., 1968-71, Child Guidance Clinic, Springfield, 1962-64; corporator, trustee, chmn. bd. Baystate Med. Center, 1985-87, trustee, 1984-92, 94—; chmn. bd. Baystate Health System, 1987-90; trustee Western New Eng. Coll., 1978-84, Baypath Jr. Coll., 1972-87, Baystate Health Systems, 1993-98; dir. BHIC, 1993—. Served with AUS, 1943-46. Decorated Bronze star. Mem. Am. Law Inst., Mass. Bar Assn., Hampden County Bar Assn. (exec. com. 1960-79, pres. 1965-67), Supreme Ct. Hist. Soc., Longmeadow Country Club, Phi Delta Phi. Roman Catholic. Home: 16 Meadowbrook Rd Longmeadow MA 01106-1341

KEAGY, BLAIR ALLEN, surgery educator; b. Altoona, Pa., June 12, 1944; m. Kathleen Elizabeth Salter, Aug. 24, 1968; children: Matthew Blair, Kristin Ann. BA, Duke U., 1966; MD, U. Pitts., 1970. Diplomate Am. Bd. Surgery, Am. Bd. Thoracic Surgery. Intern in surgery N.C. Meml. Hosp., Chapel Hill, 1970-71, resident in surgery, 1971-74, chief resident gen. surgery, 1974-75, asst. res. cardiothoracic surgery, 1975-76, chief. resident cardiothoracic surgery, 1976-77; instr. cardiothoracic surgery U. N.C., Chapel Hill, 1977-78; assoc. in cardiovascular and thoracic surgery Geisinger Med. Ctr., Danville, Pa., 1978-81; asst. prof. cardiothoracic surgery U. N.C., Chapel Hill, 1981-86, assoc. prof. cardiothoracic surgery, 1986-91, prof. surgery, chief sect. vascular surgery, 1991—; fellow in vascular surgery, U. N.C., Chapel Hill, 1978; coord. rsch. seminars dept. surgery, operating room com., disaster com., cardiopulmonary resuscitation com., chmn. pathology adv. com. N.C. Meml. Hosp.; mem. Lineberger Cancer Rsch. Ctr.; mem. faculty coun. U. N.C., 1988-91, mem. clin. cancer program adv. com.; selection com. James W. Woods faculty award; selection com. Jefferson Pilot fellow in medicine; vis. prof. The Bowman-Gray Sch. Medicine, Winston-Salem, N.C., 1986, W. Va. U. Dept. Surgery, Morgantown, 1987; guest faculty mem. U. Tenn. Med. Ctr., 1987. Reviewer numerous jours. in field; Am. Lung Assn. grantee, 1988-89, The Whitaker Found. grantee, 1984-86; contbr. chpts. to books, articles to profl. jours.; presenter in field. Named Attending Surgeon of Yr. 1986. Fellow ACS; mem. So. Thoracic Surgical Assn. (pres.'s award for best scientific paper 1984), Am. Assn. Thoracic Surgery, Am. Coll. Cardiology, Am. Coll. Chest Physicians, Am. Heart Assn. (coun. on basic sci., rsch. rev. subcom. 1984-88), Assn. Academic Surgery, Durham-Orange County Med. Soc., Internat. Soc. Cardiovascular Surgeons, Mid-Atlantic Oncology Program, Nathan A. Womack Surgical Soc., N.C. Surgical Assn., Pa. Assn. Thoracic Surgery, Pa. Med. Soc., Soc. Thoracic Surgeons, So. Assn. Vascular Surgeons. Office: UNC Sch Medicine Vascular Surgery Svc 229 H Clb # 7212 Chapel Hill NC 27599-7212*

KEAGY, DOROTHY (DOTTI KEAGY), copywriter; b. Waltham, Mass., Mar. 3, 1945; d. Albert Stanley and Bertha (Bluestein) Rouffa; m. Neil Woolf, 1996; children: Meredith, Brian. Student, U. Ill., 1963-65, Pratt Inst., N.Y.C., 1965-66. Mgr. depts. Neiman-Marcus, Lou Lattimore, Tex., 1970-75; writer, editor Dallas Morning News, Fashion Showcase, 1975-78; bur. chief, regional editor Women's Wear Daily, Dallas, 1978-84; dir. mktg. communications Dallas Apparel Mart, Trammel Crow Co., 1984-85; sr. editor Women's Wear Daily, N.Y.C., 1985-88; editor fitness N.Y. Times Mag. Group, 1988-90, writer, publicist, 1990-95; copy dir., promotion & design Rowland Co., 1995-97; copy dir. Liz Claiborne Inc., N.Y.C., 1998—; bur. chief, regional editor Women's Wear Daily, Dallas, 1978-84; dir. mktg. communications Dallas Apparel Mart, Trammel Crow Co., 1984-85; copy dir., promotion & design Rowland Co., 1995-97, copy dir. Liz Claiborne Inc. Mem. Tacassociates, Dallas, 1982-83. sr. editor Women's Wear Daily, N.Y.C., 1985-88; editor fitness N.Y. Times Mag. Group, 1988-90; writer, publicist, 1990-95; contbr. mag. articles to publs. Mem. Tacassociates, Dallas. Recipient Editorial award Dallas Apparel Mart, Dallas Fashion awards, 1980. Mem. Fashion Group Internat., Sigma Delta Phi. Home: 6 Wagon Ln East Hampton NY 11937-6410

KEALA, FRANCIS AHLOY, security executive; b. Honolulu, June 1, 1930; s. Samuel Louis and Rose (Ahloy) K.; m. Betty Ann Lyman, Nov. 28, 1952; children—Frances Ann, John Richard, Robert Mark. BA in Sociology, U. Hawaii, 1953. Patrolman Honolulu Police Dept., 1956-62, detective, 1962-65, lt., 1965-68, capt., 1968-69, chief of police, 1969-83; dir. security Hawaiian Telephone Co., 1983-93; bd. dirs. Liliuokalani Trust; trustee St. Louis Sch., 1980-87, S. Keala Trust, 1989—, Kamehameha Schs. Bishop Estate, 1999—. Bd. dirs. Aloha coun. Boy Scouts Am., 200 Club, Sex Abuse Treatment Center, Am. Automobile Assn. of Hawaii, Hawaii Meml. Park Assn., St. Louis Found., ARC-Hawaii chpt., St. Francis Med. Ctr.-West; bd. govs. Boys and Girls Clubs of Honolulu; mem. Civilian Adv. Group U.S. Army; mem. Commn. on Jud. Discipline; v.p., dir. Hawaiian Music Hall of Fame and Mus.; mem. Honolulu City and County Ethics Commn. Served with U.S. Army, 1953-55. Mem. Internat. Assn. Chiefs of Police, Hawaii State Law Enforcement Ofcls. Assn., FBI Nat. Acad. Assocs. Clubs: Oahu Country, Pacific.

KEAN, HAMILTON FISH, lawyer; b. N.Y.C., Mar. 1, 1925; s. Robert Winthrop and Elizabeth Stuyvesant (Howard) K.; m. Ellen Shaw Garrison, Mar. 25, 1950 (div. 1976); children: Leslie K. McKim, Elizabeth Douglas, Lloyd Garrison, Lewis Morris; m. Alice Kay Newcomer, July 6, 1981 (dec. 1986); m. Edith Williamson Bacon, Sept. 23, 1989. A.B. cum laude, Princeton U., 1949; J.D., Columbia U., 1954. Bar: N.Y. 1954, N.J. 1955. Asst. counsel Waterfront Commn. N.Y. Harbor, 1954; law sec. N.J. Supreme Ct., 1954-55; asst. U.S. atty. N.J. Dist., 1955-57; ptnr. Clapp and Eisenberg and predecessors, Newark, 1957-62; trustee various funds, 1963—; lectr. law Rutgers U. Sch. Law, 1960; lectr. environ. law SUNY at Purchase, Westchester Community Coll., 1974-76; supervising atty. clin. program environ. law NYU Sch. Law, 1972-76; chmn. Livingston Nat. Bank, 1984; bd. dirs. Realty Transfer Co. Bd. dirs. Morris County Urban League, 1956-51; mem. Urban Crisis Task Force, 1976; bd. dirs. Youth Counseling League, 1969-93, pres., 1979-83, hon. dir.; bd. dirs. Citizens Com. for Children N.Y., 1971—, pres., 1972-77; chmn. Joint Action for Children, 1976; trustee Natural Resources Def. Coun., 1973—, treas., 1973-76; bd. dirs. Fountain House, 1966—, pres., 1975-78; mem. Adv. Coun. to N.Y. State Office Mental Health, 1979-83; mem. Mental Health Svcs. Coun., 1983-90; trustee Coro Found., 1979-85; mem. N.Y. State Mental Hygiene Planning Coun., 1981-85; trustee Alice Desmond and Hamilton Fish Libr., 1981-98; bd. mgrs. State Cmtys. Aid Assn., 1982—, pres., 1985-92; mem. adminstrv. bd. Lab. Ornithology Cornell U., 1982-87; trustee Hancock Shaker Village, 1986-92; mem. adv. bd. Panel of Ams., 1986—; bd. dirs., sec. Episc. Charities, 1995—. 2d lt. U.S. Army, 1943-46. Decorated Purple Heart. Mem. ABA, N.Y. State Bar Assn. (chmn. conf. on pub. interest law 1975), Assn. Bar City N.Y., Columbia Law Sch. Alumni Assn. (treas. 1958-62). Clubs: Century Assn., Knickerbocker, Princeton, Atrium, Millbrook Golf and Tennis. Office: 120 E 56th St New York NY 10022-3607

KEAN, JOHN VAUGHAN, retired lawyer; b. Providence, Mar. 12, 1917; s. Otho Vaughan and Mary (Duell) K. AB cum laude, Harvard U., 1938, JD, 1941. Bar: R.I. 1942. With Edwards & Angell, Providence, 1941—, ptnr., 1954-87, of counsel, 1987—. Bd. dirs., sec. The Robbins Co., Attleboro, Mass.; chmn. Downtown Providence YMCA, 1964-67; bd. dirs. Greater Providence YMCA, 1964-76. Capt. AUS, 1943-46, 50-52, brig. gen. Decorated Legion of Merit. Mem. ABA, R.I. Bar Assn., N.G. Assn., Res. Officers Assn., Assn. U.S. Army, R.I. Army N.G. (brig. gen. 1964-72), Harvard R.I. Club (pres. 1964-66), Agawan Hunt Club, Hope Club, Providence Art Club, Army and Navy Club (Washington), Sakonnet Golf Club (Little Compton, R.I.). Home: 518 W Main Rd Little Compton RI 02837-1121 Office: Edwards & Angell 2800 Bank Boston Plz Providence RI 02903-2499

KEANE, BIL, cartoonist; b. Phila., Oct. 5, 1922; s. Aloysius William and Florence Rita (Bunn) K.; m. Thelma Carne, Oct. 23, 1948; children: Gayle, Neal, Glen, Christopher, Jeff. Student pvt. schs., Phila. Staff artist, Phila. Bull., 1945-58, syndicated cartoonist, Register & Tribune Syndicate, Des Moines, 1954—; creator, cartoonist: Channel Chuckles, from 1954, Family Circus, 1960—; author numerous books of cartoon collections; cartoonist: Stars and Stripes, 1945. Served with AUS, 1942-45, PTO. Mem. Nat. Cartoonists Soc. (Best Syndicated Panel award 1967, 71, 74, Cartoonist of yr. 1982), Newspaper Features Coun., Cartoonists Guild. Office: care King Features Syndicate 235 E 45th St New York NY 10017-3305

KEANE, CORNELIUS JOHN, fire commissioner; b. Buffalo, N.Y., Nov. 25, 1939. Associates degree in Fire Prevention, Erie Cmty. Coll., 1990. Battalion chief Fire Dept., Buffalo, N.Y., 1976-94, commr., 1994—. Mem. Career Fire Chiefs N.Y. State, Ancient Order of Hibernians, 100 Club (Buffalo chpt.). Office: Fire Dept 195 Court St Buffalo NY 14202-2607

KEANE, GUSTAVE ROBERT, architect, consultant; b. Vienna, Austria, Jan. 7, 1914; s. Robert Kien and Frances (Partl) K.; m. Constance van Lennep, Jan. 30, 1940; children—Robert van Lennep, John Francis. Archtl. engr., State U. Czechoslovakia, 1937. Designer Harvey Wiley Corbett, N.Y.C., 1940-43; with Eggers Partnership, N.Y.C., 1945-73; partner Eggers Partnership, 1963-73; archtl.-engring. cons., tech. adviser to attys. in def. of malpractice litigation against design professions; mgmt. cons. archtl. and engring. firms, 1973—; guest lectr. Bd. dirs. Bldg. Research Inst., Washington, Nat. Bd. Accreditation in Concrete Constrn. Prin. works include Am. Embassy, Ankara, Turkey, U.S. Naval Hosp, P.R., N.J. Coll. Medicine and Dentistry, Lafayette Hosp, N.Y. Times Printing Plant, BASF Corporate Hdqrs. N.J; Contbr. to books, jours. Past chmn. architects com. United Hosp. Fund. Fellow A.I.A., Am. Soc. Testing Materials; mem. Am. Assn. Hosp. Planning. Home and Office: 1012 Pelican Ct Bradenton FL 34209-8209

KEANE, JOHN M., career officer; b. Jan. 2, 1943. Commd. officer U.S. Army, advanced through grades to lt. gen., 1996—. Office: US Atlantic Command Ste 200 1562 Mitscher Ave Norfolk VA 23551-2488

KEANE, JOHN PATRICK, retired secondary education educator; b. N.Y.C., Nov. 28, 1931; s. John and Mary (Walsh) K.; m. Lucille Ann Dunn, Apr. 3, 1976. BA in English, Iona Coll., 1954; JD, Fordham U., 1963, MS in Edn., 1965; EdM, Columbia U., 1973; MA in English, CUNY, 1984. Cert. secondary tchr. (English), adminstr., N.Y.C., N.Y. State. Tchr. area jr. h.s., N.Y.C., 1962-65; tchr. h.s. English N.Y.C. Bd. Edn., Bklyn., 1965-93; dean of boys W.H. Taft H.S., Bronx, 1969-72; reading, writing coord. John F. Kennedy H.S., Bronx, 1985-91; tchr. English advanced placement John F. Kennedy H.S., Manhattan Coll., Bronx, 1991-93, retired, 1993. Editor, compiler: (manual) Handbook for Teachers of Reading and Writing, 1987, Writing Sampler (student's work), 1989-91 biannual. Founder Hamilton Heights Dems., 1965-69; candidate N.Y. State Assembly, 1965; Dem. candidate 1st Selectman, North Stonington, 1997; mem. North Stonington, Conn. Bd. Edn; justice of peace North Stonington; chmn. North Stonington Dem. Town Com. MA thesis placed on permanent display as model, Lehman Coll., CUNY, Bronx, 1984. Mem. NEA (del. local 2), Am. Fedn. Tchrs. (del. local 2), United Fedn. Tchrs. (del N.Y. State, chpt. leader, unity com.), N.Y. State United Tchrs., Delta Kappa Pi, Phi Delta Kappa. Roman Catholic. Avocations: poetry, drama, environmentalist. Home: 6 Wyassup Lake Rd North Stonington CT 06359-1124

KEANE, THOMAS EDWARD, management consultant; b. Jersey City, Oct. 15, 1960; s. Richard T. and Suzanne M. (Duma) K. BS in Civil and Environ. Engring., Cornell U., 1982, M in Engring. and Operations Rsch., 1983, MBA, 1984. Mgmt. cons. Cleve. Consulting Assocs., 1984-89; sr. assoc. Mercer Mgmt. Consulting, Lexington, Mass., 1993-94, Norbridge, Inc., Concord, Mass., 1994—. Co-author: In Line Skating in Greater Boston, 1995; contbr. articles to profl. jours. Mem. Coun. Logistics Mgmt., In Line Club Boston (CFO 1993-96, pres. 1997-98), Chi Epsilon, Tau Beta Pi. Avocations: skating, skiing, writing, reading. Office: Norbridge Inc 30 Monument Sq Concord MA 01742-1858

KEANE, WILLIAM FRANCIS, nephrology educator, research foundation executive; b. N.Y.C., Sept. 21, 1942; s. William F. and Theresa (Crotty) K.; m. Stephanie M. Gaherin, June 10, 1967; children: Alicia Anne, Elizabeth Gaherin. BS, Fordham U., 1964; MD, Yale U., 1968. Diplomate Am. Bd. Internal Medicine, Am. Bd. Nephrology. Intern Cornell N.Y. Hosp. Med. Ctr., 1968-69, resident, internal medicine, 1969-70, 72-73; fellow nephrology U. Minn. Hosps., Mpls., 1973-75; chmn. dept. Hennepin County Med. Ctr., Mpls.; asst. prof. medicine U. Minn., Mpls., 1976-82, assoc. prof., 1982-87, prof., 1987—; pres. Minn. Med. Rsch. Found., Mpls., 1989-95; nephrologist Hennepin County Med. Ctr., Mpls., 1995; chmn. dept. medicine Hennepin County Med. Ctr., 1992—. Mem. Am. Coll. Physicians, Am. Fedn. Clin. Rsch., Am. Soc. Clin. Pharmacology and Therapeutics, Am. Soc. Nephrology. Office: Hennepin County Med Ctr 701 Park Ave Minneapolis MN 55415-1623*

KEANEY, THOMAS ADDIS, strategic studies educator; b. Boston, June 14, 1940; s. James Francis and Anna Catherine (Keefe) K.; m. Mary Beth Martin, June 22, 1963; children: Thomas M., Kathleen P., Maura E., Anna C. BS, USAF Acad., Colo., 1962; MA, U. Mich., 1971, PhD, 1975. Commd. 2d lt. USAF, 1962, advanced through grades to col., 1982; assoc. prof. history USAF Acad., Colo., 1973-77; flight comdr., ops. officer 7th Bomb Wing USAF, Fort Worth, 1977-79; squadron comdr. B-52, 43rd Strategic Wing USAF, Andersen AFB, Guam, 1980-81, dep. base comdr., 1981-82; mil. planner air staff USAF, Washington, 1983-85; base comdr. USAF, Wurtsmith AFB, Mich., 1985-86; chmn. dept. mil. strategy Nat. War Coll., Washington, 1986-91; rschr., author Dept. Air Force, Washington, 1991-92; prof. mil. strategy Nat. War Coll., Washington, 1993-98; exec. dir. Fgn. Policy Inst., Nitze Sch. Advanced Internat. Studies, Johns Hopkins U., Washington, 1998—. Author: Strategic Bombers and Conventional Weapons, 1984, Gulf War Air Power Survey, 2 vols., 1993, Revolution in Warfare?, 1995. Roman Catholic. Home: 3047 Holly St Falls Church VA 22044-2617 Office: Nitze Sch Advanced Intl Studies Fgn Policy Inst 1619 Massachusetts Ave NW Washington DC 20036-2213

KEANINI, RUSSELL GUY, mechanical engineering educator, researcher; b. Denver, June 29, 1959; s. Russell Eldridge and Patricia Ann (Regan) K.; m. Yvette Michelle. BS, Colo. Sch. of Mines, Golden, 1983; MS, U. Colo., Denver, 1987; PhD, U. Calif., Berkeley, 1992. Bldg. specialist Nicor Exploration, Golden, 1984-85; structural designer Commerce City Supply, 1985-86; grad. rsch. asst. U. of Colo., Denver, 1985-87, U. of Calif., Berkeley, Calif., 1987-92; asst. prof. U. N.C., Charlotte, 1992-98, assoc. prof., 1998—. Contbr. articles to profl. jours. Recipient Engring. Found. Rsch. Initiation award Engring. Found. and ASME, 1993-94, Alcoa Found. award, 1995, Jr. Faculty Enhancement award Oak Ridge Assoc. Univs., 1995; Colo. Sch. Mines scholar, 1982-83; NASA grad. rsch. fellow, 1988-89. Mem. AIAA, ASME, Am. Phys. Soc. Home: 405 Morris Dr Harrisburg NC 28075-9489 Office: U NC Charlotte Dept Mech Engring Charlotte NC 28223

KEANY, SUTTON, lawyer; b. Limon, Costa Rica, Feb. 19, 1943; s. Francis Xavier and Winsome (Scoltock) K.; m. Susanne Elvera Andover, June 12, 1965; children: Damian Winsome, Alison Arwen, Courtney Vanessa, Sutton Andover. AB, Yale U., 1963; JD, Harvard U., 1966. Bar: P.R. 1967, N.Y. 1971, U.S. Supreme Ct. 1977. Assoc. McConnell, Valdes, Kelly & Sifre, San Juan, P.R., 1966-70; assoc. Winthrop, Stimson, Putnam & Roberts, N.Y.C., 1970-75, ptnr., 1976—; mediator, early neutral evaluator U.S. Dist. Ct. (ea. dist.) N.Y., 1992—; bd. dirs. Astra Chems., S.A. Author: (with Jay M. Vogelson) Complying with International Antitrust Regulations; contbr. articles to Bklyn. Law Rev. Trustee Aperture Found., N.Y.C., 1988-92; dir. The Fund for Modern Cts., 1992—, The Legal Aid Soc., 1995—. Mem. ABA, Assn. Bar City N.Y., Am. Arbitration Assn. (arbitrator 1990—), Yale Club of N.Y. Avocation: squash. Home: 157 Duane St New York NY 10013-3836 Office: Winthrop Stimson Putnam & Roberts One Battery Park Pla New York NY 10004

KEAR, BERNARD HENRY, materials scientist; b. Port Talbot, South Wales, July 5, 1931; came to U.S., 1959, naturalized, 1965; s. Herbert and Catherine Ann (Rees) K.; m. Jacqueline Margaret Smith, Aug. 22, 1959; children: Andrew, Gareth, Edward, Gwyneth. B.Sc., U. Birmingham, 1954, Ph.D., 1957, D.Sc., 1970. With Tube Investments Ltd., Eng., 1957-59; staff scientist Franklin Inst., Phila., 1959-63; with United Technologies Corp., East Hartford, Conn., 1963-81; sr. cons. scientist United Technologies Corp., 1977-81; sci. adv. Exxon Research and Engring. Co., 1981-86; prof., chmn. dept mechs. and materials sci., dir. ctr. for materials synthesis Rutgers U., N.J., 1986—; John Dorn Meml. lectr., 1980, Henry Krumb lectr., 1983; mem. assessment panel Nat. Inst. Stds. & Tech.-Materials Sci. & Engring. Lab. Program, chmn., 1990; bd. dirs. Acta Metallurgica, Inc., chmn., 1989. Co-editor: (jour.) Nanostructured Materials, 1992—; editor 9 books in field; contbr. 230 articles to profl. jours.; holder 30 patents. Bd. dirs., pres. Interfaith Housing for Elderly Project, Madison, Conn., 1974-79. Recipient Mathewson gold medal Am. Inst. Metall. Engrs., 1971. Fellow Am. Soc. Metals (Howe medal 1970); mem. Nat. Acad. Engring., Nat. Materials Adv. Bd. (chmn. 1986), Metall. Soc., Am. Soc. Metals. Office: Rutgers U Dept Ceramic/Materials Eng PO Box 909 Piscataway NJ 08855-0909*

KEAR, MARIA MARTHA RUSCITELLA, lawyer; b. Phila., May 9, 1954; d. Ulysses Thomas and Joan Marie (Hagner) Ruscitella; m. Daniel John Kear, May 31, 1988; children: Catilin Joan, Daniel John II. BA, Elmira Coll., 1975; JD, Del. Law Sch., 1978. Bar: Pa. 1979, Md. 1985, Va. 1991. Atty. pvt. practice, Wayne, Pa., 1979-80, Paoli, Pa., 1982-83; gen. counsel Theriault's, Inc., Annapolis, Md., 1983-85; corp. counsel Devel. Resources, Inc., Alexandria, Va., 1985-87; st. atty., asst. corp. sec. People's Drug Stores, Inc., Alexandria, Va., 1987-91; gen. counsel Jenco Group, Alexandria, Va., 1991-92; ptnr. Fullerton & Kear, Alexandria, Va., 1992-93; mng. ptnr. Kear & Gilbert, Fairfax, Va., 1993-97; atty. The Kear Law Firm, Fairfax, Va., 1997—. Contbr. monthly newsletter The Dollmasters, 1983; contbr. The Law Forum, 1976—. Mem. Annapolis Law Ctr., 1983—; treas. Women's Law Ctr., Anne Arundel County. Mem. ABA, Pa. Bar Assn., Md. Bar Assn., Va. Bar Assn., Women's Bar Assn. Md., Internat. Conf. Shopping Ctrs., Nat. Retail Tenants Assn., Delta Theta Phi. Republican. Roman Catholic. Home: 6801 Tepper Dr Clifton VA 20124-1639 Office: 10605 Judicial Dr Ste A-2 Fairfax VA 22030-5167

KEARFOTT, JOSEPH CONRAD, lawyer; b. Martinsville, Va., Sept. 24, 1947; s. Clarence P. and Elizabeth (Kelly) K.; m. Mary Jo Veatch, Feb.10, 1969; children: Kelly, David. BA, Davidson Coll., 1969; JD, U. Va., 1972. Bar: Va. 1972, U.S. Dist. Ct. (ea. and we. dists.) Va. 1973, U.S. Ct. Appeals (4th cir.) 1973, U.S. Tax Ct. 1979, U.S. Ct. Appeals (1st cir.) 1981, U.S. Ct. Appeals (5th cir.) 1982. Law clk. to presiding judge U.S. Dist. Ct. (ea. dist.) Va., Richmond, 1972-73; assoc. Hunton & Williams, Richmond, 1973-80, ptnr., 1980—; lectr. NITA program, Washington and Lee U., 1982-83, Va. Com. on Continuing Legal Edn., 1984—; mem. 4th Cir. Jud. conf. Co-author: Virginia Evidentiary Foundation, 1998. Mem. Richmond Bd. Housing, 1977-85, Richmond Dem. Com., 1978-82; trustee Libr. Va. Found., 1994—, William Byrd Cmty. House, 1978-84, chmn., 1982-84; trustee United Way Svcs., Richmond, 1989-95, treas., 1993-95; trustee Libr. Va., 1989-94, vice chmn., 1990-91, chmn., 1991-92; trustee Trinity Episcopal Sch., 1986-94, treas., 1989-92, chmn., 1993-94. Mem. ABA, Va. Bar Assn. (Boyd Graves conf.), Def. Rsch. Inst., Richmond Bar Assn., Order of Coif, Bull and Bear Club. Avocations: golf, skiing. Home: 4436 Custis Rd Richmond VA 23225-1012 Office: Hunton & Williams East Tower Riverfront Pla PO Box 1535 Richmond VA 23218-1535

KEARLEY, F. FURMAN, minister, religious educator, magazine editor; b. Montgomery, Ala., Nov. 7, 1932; s. John Ausban and Zelma Olene (Suggs) K.; m. Helen Joy Bowman, July 18, 1951; children: Janice Gail Kearley Mink, Amelia Lynn Kearley Johnson. BA, Ala. Christian Coll., (now Faulkner U.), 1954; MA, Harding U., 1956; MEd, Auburn U., 1960; MRE, ThM, Harding U., 1965; PhD, Hebrew Union Coll.-Jewish Inst. Religion, 1971; LLD (hon.), Lubbock Christian U., 1985. Min. of the Gospel. Evangelist Chs. of Christ, various cities, 1951—; chmn. Bible dept. Faulkner U., Montgomery, 1956-64; chmn., humanities div. Lubbock (Tex.) Christian Univ., 1970-75; dir., grad. studies in religion Abilene (Tex.) Christian Univ., 1975-85; dean Magnolia Bible Coll., 1993—; sec., treas. S.W. Region Evang. Theol. Soc., 1982-85; adv. bd. Gospel Svcs., Houston, 1985-98; pres.'s coun. Lubbock (Tex.) Christian Univ., 1986-98. Author: (book) God's Indwelling Spirit, 1974; editor: (book) Biblical Interpretation, 1986, (religious periodical) Gospel Advocate, 1985—; contbr. over 500 articles to jours. Recipient Alumnus of Yr. award Harding U., Searcy, Ark., 1985, Harding Grad. Sch. Religion, Memphis, 1986, Outstanding Christian Journalism award Freed-Hardeman U., 1994, Christian Journalism award Harding U., Christian Leadership award Lads to Leaders. Mem. Soc. Bib. Lit., Evang. Theol. Soc., Nat. Assn. Tchrs. and Profs. of Hebrew. Office: Gospel Advocate PO Box 726 Kosciusko MS 39090-0726

KEARNEY, DOUGLAS CHARLES, lawyer, journalist; b. Gloucester, Mass., June 24, 1945; s. Charles Matthew Kearney and Jean (Tarr) Thomas. Student, Brown U., 1963-64; BA, Fla. State U., 1971, JD with high honors, 1973. Bar: Fla. 1974, Calif. 1976, U.S. Ct. Appeals (5th cir.) 1977, U.S. Dist. Ct. (mid. and so. dists.) Fla. 1978, U.S. Ct. Appeals (11th cir.) 1981, U.S. Supreme Ct. 1982, U.S. Dist. Ct. (no. dist.) Tex. 1985, Tex. 1986. Asst. pub. defender Office of Pub. Defender 2d Jud. Cir., Tallahassee, 1973-76; asst. atty. gen. Atty. Gen.'s Office State of Fla., Tallahassee, 1977-78, chief antitrust enforcement unit Atty. Gen.'s Office, 1978-79; prin. Law Offices of Douglas C. Kearney, Tallahassee, 1979-85; assoc. Brice & Mankoff, P.C., Dallas, 1985-87, mem., 1987-89; mem. Choate & Lilly, P.C., Dallas, 1989-92; prin. Kearney & Assocs., Dallas, 1992—. Pres. Legal Aid Found. of Tallahassee, Inc., 1984. With U.S. Army, 1965-68, Vietnam. Mem. Fla. Bar Assn., Tex. Bar Assn., Calif. Bar Assn. Episcopalian. Avocations: sailing, tennis, swimming, gardening. Office: Kearney & Assocs 15105 Cypress Hills Dr Dallas TX 75248-4914

KEARNEY, JOHN FRANCIS, III, lawyer; b. Phila., July 27, 1947; s. John Francis and Adria B. (Linder) K.; m. Roseanne M. McAnally, Feb. 25, 1967 (dec. 1983); children: Jennifer F. Kearney Johnstone, Aileen M. Kearney Jones, John F. IV, Anne L. BBA, Temple U., 1970; JD cum laude, Rutgers U., 1973. Bar: N.J. 1973, U.S. Dist. Ct. N.J. 1973, U.S. Supreme Ct. 1977; cert. criminal trial atty. N.J. Supreme Ct. 1984. Assoc. Tomar, Parks, Seliger, Simonoff & Adourian, Camden, N.J., 1973-74; sr. trial atty. Office of Pub. Defender, Mt. Holly, N.J., 1974-83; pvt. practice Moorestown, N.J., 1983—; judge mcpl. ct. City of Bordentown, Twp. of Delran and Borough of Palmyra, N.J., 1993-97; counsel Burlington County Bd. Social Svcs., Mt. Holly, 1984—; prosecutor Borough of Palmyra, 1992-93; pub. defender Woodland Twp., Chatsworth, N.J., 1990-93, Borough of Riverton, N.J., 1984-93; adj. faculty Burlington County Coll., Pemberton, N.J., 1981; pub. defender Twp. of Mt. Holly and Westampton, 1986-90. Editorial bd. Rutgers Law Jour., 1972-73. Bd. dirs. Camden Regional Legal Svcs., Inc., 1972-74; bd. trustees Burlington County Community Action Program, 1971-74; arbitrator Personal Injury and Comml. Arbitration Programs, Superior Ct. of N.J., Burlington County, 1990—. 1 Lt. U.S. Army, 1973. Recipient Am. Jurisprudence award LCP Pub. Co., 1971. Mem. N.J. Assn. County Welfare Attys., Burlington County Mcpl. Judges Assn., Burlington County

Bar Assn. (sec. 1998-99, treas. 1999—), Trial Attys. of N.J., Assn. Trial Lawyers of Am. Republican. Roman Catholic. Avocations: wildlife and underwater photography, boating, travel, hiking and climbing, collecting Inuit and Native American art. Office: 720 E Main St Ste 2S Moorestown NJ 08057-3058

KEARNEY, JOHN WALTER, sculptor, painter; b. Omaha, Aug. 31, 1924; m. Lynn Haigh, June 2, 1951; children: Daniel Raymond, Jill Ann. Student, Cranbrook Acad. Art, 1946-48. Tchr., 1948—, co-founder, 1949; since co-dir. Contemporary Art Workshop Chgo.; mem. adv. bd. Art Inst. Chgo., A.R.S.G., Fine Arts Work Ctr., Provincetown, Mass., Chgo. Coun. on Fine Arts; vis. artist Am. Acad. in Rome, 1985, 92, 98; mem. summer faculty Fine Arts Work Ctr., Provincetown, 1996. Numerous one-man shows including A.C.A. Gallery, N.Y.C., (5 shows) 1964-79, Ft. Wayne (Ind.) Mus., 1966, Galleria Schneider, Rome, 1969, Ill. Inst. Tech., 1976, 91, Ulrich Mus. Art, Wichita State U., 1976, Dirksen Fed. Bldg., Chgo., 1979, Cherrystone Gallery, Wellfleet, Mass., 1980, 92, Contemporary Art Workshop, 1981, 84, Goldman-Kraft Gallery, Chgo., 1985, others in N.Y.C., 1964-79, Venice, 1964, Rome, 1964, 68, Chgo., 1966-85, Berta Walker Gallery, Provincetown, Mass., 1992, 93, 95, 97, Mitchell Mus., Mt. Vernon, Ill., 1994; sculpture show 1998, Thomas McCormick Fine Art, Chicago, 1998. 2-person show, Art Inst. Chgo., A.R.S.G., 1977; represented in permanent collections, Mus. Contemporary Art, Chgo., Standard Oil Bldg., Chgo., Lawrence U., Appleton, Wis., Interfirst Plaza, Dalla, Mundelein Coll., Chgo., Chrysler Art Mus., Norfolk (Va.) Art Mus., Ulrich Mus. Art of Wichita State U., Canton Art Inst., Capitol Bldg. Complex State Ill., Springfield, 1993, Detroit Children's Mus., Ft. Wayne Art Mus., Minn. Mus., St. Paul, New Sch. Social Research, N.Y.C., City of Chgo. Park Dist., Northwestern U., Roosevelt U., Chgo., U. Wyo. Art Mus., St. Lawrence U., Canton, N.Y., Wichita Art Mus., Peace Mus., Chgo., Chgo. Mus. Sci. and Industry, Lincoln Park Zoo, Chgo., Kans. Coliseum, Wichita, Fourth Fin. Ctr., Wichita, Crown Industries, West Chgo., Ill., Kresge Collection, Troy, Mich., Spertus Mus., Chgo., Ill. State Mus., Ill. Capitol Bldg. Mitchell Mus., Mt. Vernon, Ill., Cranbrook Acad. Art, Bloomfield Hills., Mich., Oakton Coll., Des Plaines, Ill., Oz Park, Chgo.; also pvt. collections including, John D. Rockefeller IV collection, Robert Mayer collection, spl. sculpture in bronze and silver, steel bumpers sculpture, others. Trustee Ill. Com. for Handgun Control. Served with USN, World War II, PTO. Named Man of Year in Arts in Chgo., 1963; Fulbright grantee, 1963-64; Italian Govt. grantee, 1963-64; grantee Nat. Endowment Arts, 1968. Mem. Provincetown Art Assn. (former v.p. and trustee). Home: 830 W Castlewood Ter Chicago IL 60640-4217 Studio: 542 W Grant Pl Chicago IL 60614-3706 also (summer): 830 W Castlewood Ter Chicago IL 60640-4217

KEARNEY, JOSEPH LAURENCE, retired athletic conference administrator; b. Pitts., Apr. 28, 1927; s. Joseph L. and Iva M. (Nikirk) K.; m. Dorothea Hurst, May 13, 1950; children: Jan Marie, Kevin Robert, Erin Lynn, Shawn Alane, Robin James. B.A., Seattle Pacific U., 1952, LL.D., 1979; M.A., San Jose State U., 1964; Ed.D., U. Wash., 1970. Tchr., coach Paradise (Calif.) High Sch., 1952-53; asst. basketball coach U. Wash., 1953-54; coach, tchr. Sunnyside (Wash.) High Sch., 1954-57; prin. high sch., coach Onalaska (Wash.) High Sch., 1957-61; prin. Tumwater (Wash.) High Sch., 1961-63; asst. dir. Wash. High Sch. Activities Assn., 1963-64; athletic dir., assoc. dir. U. Wash., 1964-76; athletic dir. intercollegiate athletics Mich. State U., East Lansing, 1976-80, Ariz. State U., Tempe, 1980; commr. Western Athletic Conf., Denver, 1980-95; hon. chmn. Holiday Bowl, 1994, commr. emeritus, 1994. Pres. Cmty. Devel. Assn., 1957-61; bd. dirs. U.S. Olympic Com., 1985-94, chmn. games preparation com., 1985—. Recipient Disting. Service award Mich. Assn. Professions, 1979, Citation for Disting. Svc., Colo. Sports Hall of Fame, U.S. Olympic Com. Order of Olympic Shield, 1996. Mem. Nat. Football Found. (ct. of honors com.), Nat. Collegiate Athletic Assn., Nat. Assn. Collegiate Dirs. Athletics (Corbett award 1991, Adminstr. Excellence award), Collegiate Commrs. Assn. (pres., award of Merit 1998), Am. Football Assn. (Commrs. award 1996, Athletic Dir.'s award 1998). Home: 2810 W Magee Rd Tucson AZ 85742-1500

KEARNEY, LINDA LEE, secondary education educator; b. Pitts., Sept. 6, 1947; d. Richard Joseph Bracco and Vada Ilene (Conner) Bracco Learn; m. Charles Ray Kearney, June 12, 1971; children: Robert Charles, Richard Leslie, Debra June. BS in Edn., Clarion (Pa.) State U., 1969; MEd Equivalency, Pa. State U., 1975. Tchr. 7th and 8th grade English DuBois (Pa.) Area Sch. Dist., 1969-96, tchr. 9th grade English, 1996—, secondary lead tchr., 1994; lead tchr., mem. profl. devel. and gifted adv. coms., 1991-94; co-founder, adviser Kids Saving Kids Club, DuBois Area Jr. H.S., 1988—; advisor sr. h.s. yearbook, 1996—; coord. Sch. Excellence Program 2000, 1997-98, peer mediation coord., 1996-97. Chair edn. com., Sunday sch. supr. Moorhead Meth. Sch., Brockway, Pa., 1988-90; neighborhood dir. Brockway Girl Scouts, 1993—, coord. Rising Star Girl Scout Area Tng.; coord., mem. coun. splty. and coun. trainer Keystone Tall Tree, Brockway, 1990—; mem. Brockway Recreation Bd., 1996—. Recipient Cross and Flame award Moorhead United Meth. Ch., 1996; mini-grantee or grantee Pa. Acad. for Excellence in Tchg. and Intermediate Unit 6, 1992; Pa. Rivers Writing Project fellow, 1990. Mem. Nat. Coun. Tchrs. English, Delta Kappa Gamma, Alpha Sigma Alpha (chpt. pres. 1967-68). Avocations: reading, camping, gardening, writing, crafts. Home: RR 2 Box 415A Brockway PA 15824-9453 Office: 100 Orient Ave Du Bois PA 15801-2436

KEARNEY, LYNN MARILYN HAIGH, arts administrator, curator; b. Chgo., Nov. 16, 1927; d. Raymond Haigh and Agnes (Dahl Haigh) Thompson; m. John W. Kearney, June 2, 1951; children: Daniel R., Jill Kearney McDonnell. BA, Northwestern U., 1949; cert. in arts adminstrn., Harvard U., 1978. Adminstr. Contemporary Art Workshop, 1951-67; dir. Contemporary Art Workshop, Inc., Chgo., 1967—; juror Sch. Art Inst. Chgo., 1986, So. Ill. Artists Open, Mitchell Mus., Mt. Vernon, Ill., 1991, St. Louis Art Assn. Ann., 1989; lectr. Columbia Coll., Chgo., 1970. Exhibited weaving works Art Inst. Chgo., 1954. Trustee Dedalus Found., Robert Motherwell Found., N.Y.C., 1991—, Francis Parker Sch., Chgo., 1981-84, Provincetown (Mass.) Art Assn. and Mus., 1982-85, Mid-North Assn., Chgo., 1981-84; mem. adv. bd. Oriana Singers, Chgo., 1985—, Lincoln Park Conservation Assn., Chgo., 1994—, Art Rental and Sales Gallery, Art Inst. Chgo., 1984-87; active Ill. Coun. Against Handgun Violence, 1977-97. Grantee Ill. Arts Coun., 1982. Mem. Midwest Designer Craftsmen Orgn. Home: 830 W Castlewood Ter Chicago IL 60640-4217 Office: Contemporary Art Workshop 542 W Grant Pl Chicago IL 60614-3706

KEARNEY, PHILIP CHARLES, biochemist; b. Balt., Dec. 31, 1932; s. Cyrus James and Nola Gertrude (Massengill) K.; m. Rita Anne Rogers, Sept. 4, 1955; children: James Douglas, Kathryn Ellen. BS, U. Md., 1955, MS, 1957; PhD, Cornell U., 1960. NSF postdoctoral fellow dept. biochemistry Mich. State U., East Lansing, 1960-62; rsch. chemist Agrl. Rsch. Svc., USDA, Beltsville, Md., 1962-65, rsch. leader, 1965-88, dir., 1988-95; ret. USDA, 1995; adj. prof. dept. chemistry U. Md., College Park, Md., 1995—; mem. 4 panels NAS; mem. White Ho. Com. on Agt. Orange. Contbr. over 250 articles to profl. jours.; editor 4 vols.: Chemistry of Herbicides, 1975-86. Named Disting. Scientist, Agrl. Rsch. Svc., USDA, 1986; recipient Rsch. award Weed Sci. Soc., 1974. Mem. Am. Chem. Soc. (chmn. divsn. pesticide chemistry 1972, Internat. Award for Rsch. in Pesticide Chemistry 1982), Internat. Union of Pure and Applied Chemistry (pres. applied chemistry divsn. 1985). Achievements include patent for pesticide wastewater destruction unit. Home: 8416 Shears Ct Laurel MD 20723-1016 Office: Water Resources Rsch Ctr Dept Chemistry U Md 2102 Chemistry Bldg College Park MD 20742-5595

KEARNEY, ROBERT EDWARD, biomedical engineering educator; b. Montreal, Que., Can., Jan. 19, 1947. BEng, McGill U., Montreal, 1968, MEng, 1971, PhD, 1976. Computer sys. engr. divsn. neurology Montreal Gen. Hosp., 1974-77; from rsch. asst. to prof. biomed. engrng. and physiology McGill U., 1976—, chair, prof. dept. biomed. engrng.; chmn. dept. biomed. engrng. McGill U., 1990—. Recipient Geddes prize in biomed. engrng., 1972. Mem. IEEE (pres. 1998), Soc. Neurosci., Biomed. Engrng. Soc. Office: McGill Univ Dept BioMed Eng, Lyman Duff Bldg, 3775 University St, Montreal, PQ Canada H3A 2B4*

KEARNEY, STEPHEN MICHAEL, corporate treasurer; b. Washington, Apr. 8, 1956; s. John James and Helen Joan (Gaffney) K.; m. Julie Elizabeth Mosio, June 30, 1984; children: Justin Samuel, Caitlin Elizabeth. BA, McGill U., 1978; MBA, George Washington U., 1985. CFA, cert. cash mgr. Fin. economist U.S. Treasury Dept., Washington, 1978-80; investment officer U.S. Postal Svc., Washington, 1980-81, investment mgr., 1981-90, treas., 1990—. Mem. editl. adv. bd. Treasury Mgmt. Assn. Jour. Mem. sch. bd. of advisors, chmn. endowment com. St. Anselm's Abbey. First class honors, Univ. scholar McGill U., 1978; recipient Alexander Hamilton award for Excellence in Treasury Mgmt., 1996, 98. Mem. Fin. Execs. Inst., Assn. for Investment Mgmt. and Rsch., Washington Assn. Money Mgrs. (pres. 1985-86), Washington Soc. Investment Analysts, Nat. Assn. Corp. Treas., Treasury Mgmt. Assn., Beta Gamma Sigma. Democrat. Roman Catholic. Home: 4339 Clagett Rd Univ Park MD 20782-1140 Office: US Postal Svc 475 Lenfant Plz SW Rm 8118 Washington DC 20260-0004

KEARNS, ALBERT OSBORN, minister; b. Shattuck, Okla., Apr. 15, 1920; s. Arthur Alexander and Grace Mae (Booth) K.; m. Maria Metlova, Oct. 18, 1947; 1 child, Alscot. Student, U. Redlands, 1948-52. Ordained to ministry Lighthouse Gospel Fellowship of Mins. and Chs., 1984. Evangelist L.A., 1971-75, Simi Valley, Calif., 1975-84; pastor Somis (Calif.) Christian Ch., 1984-89, Simi Valley, 1989—; advisor, counselor Women's Aglow Fellowship, Thousand Oaks, Calif., 1987—; pub. A.O.K. Books, 1991. Petty officer 2d class USN, 1940-46, PTO. Republican. Home and Office: 1621 Patricia Ave Simi Valley CA 93065-3403

KEARNS, JAMES JOSEPH, artist; b. Scranton, Pa., Aug. 7, 1924; s. David Joseph and Ann Mary (Keller) K.; m. Betty Ione Hough, June 19, 1948; children: David, Diane, Mark, Aaron, Lisa. B.F.A., Sch. Art Inst. Chgo., 1950. Instr. Sch. Visual Arts, N.Y.C., 1960-90, Skowhegan (Maine) Sch. Painting, summers 1961-64. Illustrator: Can These Bones Live (E. Dahlberg), 1962, The Heart of Beethoven (S. Rodman), 1969; One-man shows include, Grippi Gallery, N.Y.C., 1956, 57, 60, 62, 68, Bloomfield (N.J.) Coll., 1967, 72, Sculpture Center, N.Y.C., 1973, Caldwell (N.J.) Coll., 1976, Trenton (N.J.) State Mus., 1984, group shows include, Whitney Mus. Am. Art, 1959, 60, 61, 80, Am. Fedn. Art, Art Inst. Chgo., 1979, traveling exhbns., Pa. Acad. Fine Arts, Phila., 1964, 65, Butler Inst. Am. Art, Youngstown, Ohio, 1964, Monmouth (N.J.) Mus., 1969, Squibb Gallery, Princeton, N.J., 1974, sculpture, Schenectady Mus., 1976, 35th Audubon Artists, N.Y.C., 1977, Whitney Mus. Am. Art, N.Y.C., 1980; represented in permanent collections, Mus. Modern Art, N.Y.C., Whitney Mus. Am. Art, Newark Mus. Art, Montclair (N.J.) Mus., Topeka Pub. Library, Smithsonian Nat. Collection Fine Arts, Washington, Hirshhorn Mus., Washington, also numerous pvt. collections. Served with U.S. Army, 1943-46. Recipient Ann. Disting. Artist-Tchr. award Sch. Visual Arts, 1990; Nat. Inst. Arts and Letters grantee, 1959.

KEARNS, JANET CATHERINE, corporate secretary; b. Chgo., Oct. 29, 1940; d. Casimir J. and Eleanor (Galus) Kubik; m. Edward P. Kearns, May 4, 1975. Grad., Madonna High Sch., 1958. Legal sec. Seyfarth, Shaw, Fairweather & Geraldson, Chgo., 1960-66; sec. to pres. Bowey's, Inc., Chgo., 1966-69, Sealy, Inc., Chgo., 1969—; corp. sec. Sealy, Inc., 1977-89; adminstrv. sec. RHR Internat. Co., Wood Dale, Ill., 1989—. Address: 921 Dearborn Cir Carol Stream IL 60188-9311

KEARNS, JOHN J., III, lawyer; b. Jersey City, Apr. 24, 1951; s. John J. Jr. and Beverly (Bailey) K.; m. Maria C. DelFemine, May 15, 1976. AB, Columbia U., 1972; JD cum laude, Fordham U., 1976. Bar: N.J. 1976, N.Y. 1977, Pa. 1985. Assoc. firm White and Case, N.Y.C., 1976-84; mem. firm Eckert, Seamans, Cherin and Mellott, LLC, Pitts., 1984—, mem. exec. com., 1989-93, chmn. tax dept., 1994-96, mem. fin. com., 1994—. Contbr. articles to profl. publs. Mem. ABA, Pitts. Tax Club. Avocations: thoroughbred racing, softball, reading. Office: Eckert Seamans Cherin & Mellot 600 Grant St Ste 4400 Pittsburgh PA 15219-2703

KEARNS, JOHN THOMAS, philosophy educator; b. Elgin, Ill., Oct. 28, 1936; s. John Thomas and Catherine Ruth (Cannon) K.; m. Jane Grothaus, Nov. 16, 1963; children: Jane Michelle, Katherine Megan, John Kevin, Jesse O'Sullivan. BA, U. Notre Dame, 1958; MA, Yale U., 1960, PhD, 1962. From asst. prof. to prof. philosophy SUNY, Buffalo, 1964—, chair dept. philosophy, 1994—. Author: Using Language: The Structures of Speech Acts, 1984, The Principles of Deductive Logic, 1988, Reconceiving Experience, 1996. 1st lt. U.S. Army Res., 1962-64. Mem. Am. Philosoph. Assn., Assn. Symbolic Logic, Linguistics Soc. Am. Democrat. Roman Catholic. Home: 159 Highland Ave Buffalo NY 14222-1842 Office: SUNY Dept Philosophy 131 Park Hall Buffalo NY 14260-4150

KEARNS, JOHN WILLIAM (BILL KEARNS), electronics inventor and executive; b. Salem, W.Va., Oct. 30, 1935; s. John D. and Mary Agnes (Nutter) K.; m. Kathleen E. McIntyre, June 10, 1946; children: Mary A., John W. Jr., Chester Paul. BS, St. Mary Coll., Xavier, Kans., 1970; M., U. Mich., Lansing, 1978. Commd. 2d lt. U.S. Army, 1952; advanced through grades to lt. col. U. S. Army, 1973; ret. U.S. Army, various places, 1973; v.p. United Banking Group, W. Palm Beach, Fla., 1973-76; gen. agt. Mass. Mutual Life Ins. Co., Nashville, 1976-79; pres., owner Bill Kearns & Assocs. Inc., Brentwood, Tenn., 1979-88; pres., chief exec. officer Adcom, Paxton, Fla., 1988-91; owner Ed Smith's Antique Old Time Ice Cream Parlor & Fillin Sta., 1992—; co-owner Tri Cities Emporium, Fla., 1998—; bd. dirs. Sister Cities Internat., Washington. Contbr. articles to profl. jours.; inventor T Ball for children, elevator audio machine. Vice mayor City of Brentwood, 1983-85, commr. 1981-85; planning commr. 1981-83. Decorated Vietnamese Cross of Gallantry, Bronze Star, Air medal. Mem. Gideons Internat., Fla. C. of C., Tri-Cities C. of C. (pres.), VFW, Rotary (past pres., lt. gov., zone gov.), Paxton Ruritan Club (pres. lt. gov., zone gov. dist. 27). Republican. Baptist. Avocation: piloting (comml. fixed and rotary wing lic. with instrument rating). Home and Office: PO Box 5240 Paxton FL 32538-5240

KEARNS, KEVIN LAWRENCE, political association executive, lawyer; b. Bklyn., Sept. 5, 1947; s. John C. and Alice C. (Kelleher) K.; m. Judith A. Daly, May 20, 1995; children: Nicole, Leah, Monique, Kathleen, Christopher. BA, Fordham U., 1969; MA, SUNY, Stony Brook, 1970; JD, Bklyn. Law Sch., 1976. Bar: N.Y. 1977, D.C. 1977. Legis. counsel State Senator Sheldon Farber, Queens, N.Y., 1976-77; fgn. svc. officer U.S. Dept. State, Washington, 1977-90; sr. rsch. fellow Econ. Strategy Inst., Washington, 1990-92, Mfg. Policy Project, Washington, 1992-93; pres. U.S. Bus. & Industry Coun., Washington, 1993—. Roman Catholic. Office: US Bus & Industry Coun 910 16th St NW Ste 300 Washington DC 20006-2109

KEARNS, MERLE GRACE, state senator; b. Bellefonte, Pa., May 19, 1938; d. Robert John and Mary Katharine (Fitzgerald) Grace; m. Thomas Raymond Kearns, June 27, 1959; children: Thomas, Michael, Timothy, Matthew. BS, Ohio State U., 1960. Tchr. St. Raphael Elem. Sch., Springfield, Ohio, 1960-62; substitute tchr. Mad River Green Dist., Springfield, 1972-78; instr. Clark Tech. Coll., Springfield, 1978-80; commr. Clark County, Ohio, 1981-91; mem. Ohio Senate, Columbus, 1991—; mem Senate human svcs. and aging com., Senate edn. com., Senate health com., majority whip of Senate; mem. fin. and. instns. com.; co-chair Supreme Ct. domestic violence com.; mem. Joint Com. Agy. Rule Review; pres. bd. county commrs., 1982, 83, 86, 87, 90, v.p., 1985, 88, 89. Bd. dirs. Springfield Symphony, 1980-86, Arts Coun., 1980-85, County Commrs. Assn. Ohio, sec., 1988, 2d v.p., 1989-90, 1st v.p., 1990; mem. exec. com. Springfield Republicans, 1984—; bd. pres. Ohio Children's Trust Fund, 1995-98. Recipient Pub. Policy Leadership award, 1997; named Woman of Yr., Springfield Pilot Club, 1981, Wittenberg Woman of Accomplishment, 1991, Watchdog of Treasury, 1991, 96, Legislator of Yr., Assn. Mental Health and Drug Addiction Svcs. Bds., 1996, Legis. Co-Person of Yr., Assn. Joint Vocat. Sch. Supts., 1996, Ohio Cmty. Colls. Legis. of Yr., 1997; Ohio State U. scholar, 1957-59. Mem. LWV (bd. dirs. 1964-78, pres. 1975-78), Ohio Nurses Assn. (Legislator of Yr. 1995), Rotary, Omicron Nu. Roman Catholic. Avocation: reading. Office: Ohio Senate Senate Bldg Rm 221 Columbus OH 43215

KEARNS, RICHARD P., diversified financial services company executive. Vice chmn. Price Waterhouse L.L.P. - U.S. (now PriceWaterhouse Coopers), N.Y.C. Office: PriceWaterhouse Coopers 1177 Avenue Of The Americas New York NY 10036-2714*

KEARNS, ROBERT WILLIAM, manufacturing inventor; b. Gary, Ind., Mar. 10, 1927; s. Martin William and Mary Ellen (O'Hara) K.; m. Phyllis Joan McElwee, Aug. 1, 1953 (div. Oct. 1980); children: Dennis M., Timothy B., Patrick S., Kathleen A., Maureen M., Robert M. Student, U.S. Army Fin. Sch., Ft. Aiterbury, Ind., 1945-46; BME, U. Detroit, 1952; MS in Engrng. Mechanics, Wayne State U., 1957; cert. Internat. Sch. Nuclear Sci., Argonne Nat. Labs., Chgo., 1958; PhD, Case Inst. Tech., 1964. Registered profl. mech. and elec. engr., Mich.. Rsch. engr. Bendix Rsch. Labs., Detroit, 1952-57; assoc. prof. engrng., faculty advisor SPE student br. Wayne State U., Detroit, 1957-67; commr. Dept. Bldgs. & Safety Engrng., Detroit, 1967-71; prin. investigator for fed. hwy. Nat. Inst. Sci. & Tech., Gaithersburg, Md., 1971-76; trial litigator U.S. Cts.- Auto U.S. Detroit Dist. Ct., 1978—. Inventor intermittent windshield wiper systems; holder numerous patents. Bd. dirs. Vets. of Office of Strategic Svcs. and William J. Donovan Meml. Found., Inc., 1994—, Queen Anne's County (Md.) Hist. Soc., 1995—; cand. Comptroller for State of Md., 1998—. With U.S. Army, 1945-47. Roman Catholic. Avocation: violinist. Office: Kearns Trust 301 Houghton Lab Ln Queenstown MD 21658-2500

KEARNS, WARREN KENNETH, business executive; b. Wilmington, Ohio, July 15, 1929; s. Roy William and Marie (Kay) K. B.S. in Civil Engring., Case Western Res. U., 1951. Registered profl. engr., Ohio, Pa. Supr. Pa. R.R. Co., 1951-56; exec. v.p. Pitts. & W.Va. Rwy. Co., 1956-64; mgr. mfg. services Wheeling Steel Corp., W.Va., 1964-67; v.p. L. B. Foster Co., Pitts., 1967-70, pres., 1979-85; v.p. Sharon Steel Co., Pa., 1970-73; pres. Ogden Steel Co., Cleve., 1973-79, Warren Kearns Assocs., 1985—; bd. dirs. N.W. Pipe & Casing Co., Portland, Oreg., Erie (Pa.) Forge & Steel Co. Mem. Tau Beta Pi, Sigma Xi. Club: Duquesne (Pitts.). Avocation: music. Home: 2 High St Hudson OH 44236-2912 Office: Warren Kearns Assocs 1507 Guenevere St Streetsboro OH 44241-5025

KEARNS, WILLIAM MICHAEL, JR., investment banker; b. Orange, N.J., June 26, 1935; s. William Michael and Doris Mae (Hodgkinson) K.; m. Patricia Anne Wright, Aug. 17, 1957; children: William Michael III, Susan Elizabeth (Mrs. Eric R. Hubbard), Kathleen Anne, Michael Patrick, Elizabeth Anne. AB, U. Maine, 1957; AM, NYU, 1960; postgrad., Boston Coll. Law, 1957-58, NYU, 1960-64; LLD (hon.), Gonzaga U., 1988. With Chase Manhattan Bank, 1958-59; security analyst Hayden, Stone & Co., Inc., N.Y.C., 1960-62; assoc. instl. sales and syndicate dept. Kuhn, Loeb & Co., N.Y.C., 1962-64, asst. v.p., 1964-66, v.p., 1966-68, sales mgr., 1968-69, gen. ptnr., 1970-75; mng. dir. Kuhn, Loeb & Co., Inc., 1976-77, Lehman Bros. Kuhn Loeb Inc., 1977-84, Shearson Lehman Bros. Inc., N.Y.C., 1984-89, Lehman Bros. divsn. Shearson Lehman Bros. Inc., N.Y.C., 1990-92; adv. dir. Lehman Bros., N.Y.C., 1992-93; pres. W. M. Kearns & Co. Inc., Morristown, N.J., 1994—; sr. cons. ING Baring Furman Selz LLC, N.Y.C., 1994-98; vice chmn. Keefe Mgrs., Inc., N.Y.C., 1999—; bd. dirs. Selective Ins. Group, Inc., Branchville, N.J., Transistor Devices, Inc., Cedar Knolls, N.J.; vice chmn. Fundamental Mgmt. Corp., Hollywood, Fla., Malibu Entertainment Holdings, Inc., Dallas, Greenfield Capital Ptnrs., Inc., N.Y.C.; trustee EQ Advisors Trust (Equitable Life Assurance Soc. U.S.), N.Y.C.; dir. Marine Transport Corp., Weehawken, N.J.; adv. dir. Proudfoot Plc, London; investment adv. Young Nichols Gilstrap, Inc., Phoenix; mem. faculty Fairleigh Dickinson U. Coll. Bus. Adminstrn., 1959-68; instr. security analysis N.Y. Inst. Fin., 1961-67; adj. prof. Grad. Sch. Bus. Adminstrn., NYU, 1971-72, chmn. NYU Forum Fin., 1971; lectr. Columbia U., Fairleigh Dickinson U., U. Rochester, NYU. Trustee Drumthwacket Found., Inc., 1985-95, Morristown-Beard Sch., 1982-88, Rider Univ., 1982-88, Morristown Meml. Health Found., 1999—; trustee Morris Mus., 1968-86, mem. adv. bd., 1987—; trustee Tri-County Scholarship Fund, 1982—, v.p., 1985-86, pres., 1987-89, pres. emeritus, 1990—; bd. dirs. Greater N.Y. coun. Boy Scouts Am., 1986—, exec. v.p., 1990—; bd. dirs. The Am. Friends of Covent Garden and the Royal Ballet, London, 1989—; mem. N.J. Rep. Fin. Com., 1978-84; adv. bd. Intrnat. Tennis Hall of Fame, 1984-86, bd. dirs., 1986-95, internat. coun., 1995-97; mem. adv. bd. Templeton Prize, Lyford Cay, Nassau, Bahammas, 1990—; exec. com. William E. Simon Grad. Sch., Bus. Adminstrn., U. Rochester, 1986—; devel. com. U. Maine, 1990-96, diocesan investment com., Diocese of Paterson N.J., 1986—; mem. Cardinal's Com. of Laity, N.Y.C. With USMC, 1955-61. Decorated Am. Assn. Master Knights Sovereign Mil. Order Malta; Pontifical Order of St. Gregory The Great; recipient Silver Beaver award Boy Scouts Am., 1989, Leadership award Tri-County Scholarship Fund, 1990, Leadership award Morristown Meml. Hosp., 1998, Augusta Stone award Morristown Meml. Health Found., 1999. Mem. Nat. Assn. Security Dealers (corp. fin. com. 1976-80), Securities Industry Assn. (minority capital com. 1978-86, exec. com. N.Y. dist. 1970, vice chmn. 1973, chmn. 1974), New Eng. Soc., Soc. Friendly Sons St. Patrick City of N.Y., Univ. Club (N.Y., trustee 1978-81), Bond Club N.Y., Econ. Club (N.Y.), Morris County Golf Club (Convent, N.J. gov. 1976-82, treas. 1978-82), Green Jacket Club (Homestead, Va., founder 1991—), Twin Oaks Club (Morristown, N.J.), Morristown Club, Park Ave. Club (Florham Park, N.J.), Log Cabin Gun Club (Sterling, N.J.), Rolling Rock Club (Ligonier, Pa.), Mid-Ocean Club (Bermuda), Palm Beach (Fla.) Polo and Country Club, Beta Theta Pi, Kappa Phi Kappa. Roman Catholic. Office: W M Kearns & Co Inc 310 South St Morristown NJ 07960-7301

KEARSE, AMALYA LYLE, federal judge; b. Vauxhall, N.J., June 11, 1937; d. Robert Freeman and Myra Lyle (Smith) K. B.A., Wellesley Coll., 1959; J.D. cum laude, U. Mich., 1962. Bar: N.Y. 1963, U.S. Supreme Ct. 1967. Assoc. Hughes, Hubbard & Reed, N.Y.C., 1962-69; ptnr. Hughes, Hubbard & Reed, 1969-79; judge U.S. Ct. Appeals (2d cir.), 1979—; lectr. evidence N.Y. U. Law Sch., 1968-69. Author: Bridge Conventions Complete, 1975, 3d edit., 1990, Bridge at Your Fingertips, 1980; translator, editor: Bridge Analysis, 1979; editor: Ofcl. Ency. of Bridge, 3d edit, 1976; mem. editorial bd. Charles Goren, 1974—. Bd. dirs. NAACP Legal Def. and Endl. Fund, 1977-79; bd. dirs. Nat. Urban League, 1978-79; trustee N.Y.C. YWCA, 1976-79, Am. Contract Bridge League Nat. Laws Commn., 1975—; mem. Pres.'s Com. on Selection of Fed. Jud. Officers, 1977-78. Named Women's Pairs Bridge Champion Nat. div., 1971, 72, World div., 1986, Nat. Women's Teams Bridge Champion, 1987, 9o, 91. Mem. ABA, Assn. of Bar of City of N.Y., Am. Law Inst., Lawyers Com. for Civil Rights Under Law (mem. exec. com. 1970-79). Office: US Ct Appeals US Courthouse 40 Foley Sq New York NY 10007-1502

KEATH, (MARTIN) TRAVIS, business valuation consultant; b. Laredo, Tex., June 5, 1966; s. Adrin Shaw and Saundra (Hunley) K.; m. Patricia Walker, Jan. 26, 1991; 1 child, Matthew Allan Walker. BBA, Tex. A&M U., 1988, MS, 1989. CPA, CFA. Cons. reorganization and litigation svcs. group Price Waterhouse, Dallas, 1989-91; mgr. valuation group Deloitte & Touche, LLP, Dallas, 1991-95; prin. Bus. Valuation Svcs., Inc., Dallas, 1995—. Mem. AICPA, Assn. for Corp. Growth, Assn. Investment Mgmt. and Rsch., Inst. CFAs, Am. Soc. Appraisers, Dallas Assn. Investment Analysts (sec./treas., bd. dirs., chmn. ethics and profl. conduct com., instr. CFA exam. rev. course), Phi Kappa Phi, Beta Gamma Sigma. Baptist. Office: Business Valuation Services Ste 1650 3030 Lyndon B Johnson Fwy Dallas TX 75234-7024

KEATING, BERN, writer, journalist; b. Fassett, Can., May 14, 1915; came to U.S., 1920; s. John Julian Keating and Laure Lalonde; m. Marian West, June 10, 1939; 1 child, John G. BA magna cum laude, U. Ark., 1938. Reporter, relief editor Palm Beach (Fla.) Post Times, 1938-41; news editor Utica N.Y. Radio, 1941; freelance journalist, writer Greenville, Miss., 1945—. Author over 25 books, 800 mag. articles, 1 documentary movie. With U.S. Navy, 1942-45. Recipient Lifetime Achievement award Miss. Inst. Arts Letters, 1995. Mem. Travel Journalists Guild (founder, pres.), Authors Guild, Soc. Am. Travel Writers, Am. Soc. Journalists Authors. Home and Office: 141 Bayou Rd Greenville MS 38701-7732

KEATING, DAVID, photographer; b. Rye, N.Y., Sept. 5, 1962. BA in Philosophy, Yale U., 1985; MA in Studio Art with distinction, U. N.Mex., 1991; student, Calif. Inst. Arts, Santa Clarita, 1992; MFA in Studio Art with distinction, U. N.Mex., 1994. Solo exhbns. include U. N.Mex., 1990 (traveled to Pace U., N.Y.C., Nat. Coun. Alcoholism Conf. of Affiliates, Nashville), 91, Calif. Inst. Arts, 1992, Graham Gallery, Albuquerque, 1994, Univ. Art Mus. Downtown, Albuquerque, 1995-96, George Eastman House, Rochester, N.Y., 1997, others; group exhbns. include Raw Space Gallery, Albuquerque, 1990, Betty Rymer Gallery, Sch. Art Inst. Chgo., 1991, 92, Randolph St. Gallery, Chgo., 1992, Atlanta Gallery Photography, 1992, San

Jose (Calif.) Inst. Contemporary Art, 1992, Univ. Art Mus., Albuquerque, 1993, Ctr. African Am. History and Culture, Smithsonian Instn., Washington, 1994-95, Mus. Photographic Arts, San Diego, 1996-97, SF Camerawork, San Francisco, 1993, 98, others; represented in pub. collections, including Univ. Art Mus., Albuquerque; subject of various articles and catalogs, 1992—. NEA Visual Artists fellow in photography, 1994, Van Deren Coke fellow, U. N.Mex., 1991; recipient award Photographers and Friends United Against AIDS/Art Matters Inc., 1992. Home: 1410 Central Ave SW Apt 38 Albuquerque NM 87104-1166

KEATING, EUGENE KNEELAND, animal scientist, educator; b. Liberal, Kans., Feb. 15, 1928; s. Arthur Hitch and Nilie Charlotte (Kneeland) K.; m. Iris Louise Myers, Aug. 12, 1951; children—Denise Keating Schnagl, Kimberly Alan. BS, Kans. State U., 1953, MS, 1954; PhD, U. Ariz., 1964. Owner, mgr. ranch Kans., 1954-57; instr., farm mgr. Midwestern U., Wichita Falls, Tex., 1957-60; rsch. asst. U. Ariz., Tucson, 1960-64; prof. animal sci. Calif. State Poly. U., Pomona, 1964-98, prof. emeritus, 1998—, chmn. dept., 1971-78. Contbr. articles to profl. jours. Bd. dirs. Los Angeles County Jr. Livestock Fair, 1971-79, chmn., 1975. With USAAF, 1946-49. Fellow Am. Inst. Chemists; mem. NRA (benefactor), NRA Whittington Ctr. Founder's Club, Nat. Intercollegiate Rodeo Assn. (West Coast regional faculty dir. 1972-76), Coun. for Agrl. Sci. and Tech., Calif. Rifle and Pistol Assn. (Gold Eagle), Am. Soc. Animal Sci., Am. Soc. Lab. Animal Sci., Brit. Soc. Animal Prodn., Am. Legion, Block and Bridle Club, Ind. Order Foresters, Santa Fe Trail and Gun Club (life), Western Heritage Ctr., Sigma Xi, Phi Lambda Upsilon, Gamma Sigma Delta, Alpha Zeta. Republican. Presbyterian. Home: 149 W Loretto Ct Claremont CA 91711-1739 Office: 3801 W Temple Ave Pomona CA 91768-2557

KEATING, FRANCIS ANTHONY, II, governor, lawyer; b. St. Louis, Feb. 10, 1944; s. Anthony Francis and Anne (Martin) K.; m. Catherine Dunn Heller, 1972; children: Carissa Herndon, Kelly Martin, Anthony Francis III. A.B., Georgetown U., 1966; J.D., U. Okla., 1969. Bar: Okla. 1969. Spl. agt. FBI, 1969-71; asst. dist. atty. Tulsa County, 1971-72; mem. Okla. Ho. of Reps., 1972-74, Okla. Senate, 1974-81; U.S. atty. No. Dist. Okla., 1981-84; asst. sec. U.S. Treasury Dept., Washington, 1985-88; assoc. atty. gen. Dept. Justice, 1988-89; gen. counsel, acting dep. sec. Dept. Housing and Urban Devel., Washington, 1989-93; gov. State of Okla., 1995—. Mem. Okla. Bar Assn. Office: Office Gov 212 State Capitol Bldg Oklahoma City OK 73105

KEATING, KEITH ANTHONY, English language educator; b. Kingston, Jamaica, Feb. 21, 1924; came to U.S., 1945; s. Joseph Emanuel and Vera Lucille (Lindo) K.; m. Pia Wikstrom, Dec. 26, 1979. AB with honors, Loyola U., 1947; MS summa cum laude, U. Wis., Milw., 1960; MA summa cum laude, L.I. U., 1975; PhD in English, Columbia U., 1992. Editor Spotlight Mag., Kingston, 1947-58, Milw. (Wis.) Pub. Jour., 1958-60; sec., tchr. N.Y.C. (N.Y.) Bd. Edn., 1962-68; prof. English, L.I. U., Garden City, N.Y., 1968—, N.Y. Inst. Tech., Old Westbury, Hofstra U., Hempstead, N.Y., CUNY, Bayside; dir., prodr. SUNY, Garden City, 1977-86, Hofstra U.-PBS-TV, Hempstead; dir., prodr., cons. Wilson Knight Found., London, N.Y., 1980-85; dir. Wilson Knight Interdisciplinary Soc., 1980; founder, dir. Student Arts Club, N.Y. Inst. Tech., Old Westbury; collaborator with nat. and internat. lit. scholars; lectr. in field. *Prophet and practitioner of approaches to his students as the central charactersin the developing classroom drama, to critical thinking, block schedule, metaphor, interdisciplinarity, and interculturalism as modes of thought, and effective teaching itself as cure of apathy and violence, Keating came to the attention of UNESCO and European Academy through his lectures (with tape machine and slide projector) in Europe, Asia, and Canada, and by his circuits in LI. One paper called him "the only significant on college campuses anywhere." Keating attributes his ideals and successes to his study of Shakespeare, his students, and the women in his life, particularly his 2 sisters and his wife, Pia.* Founder, editor: Libido Jour., U. Wis., Milw., 1958-60; experiments in interdisciplinary learning theor and interconnections between arts, scis., humanities, colls., librs. radio, TV, tchr. ctr., etc., 1958-96; contbr. articles to profl. jours. Founder, pres. Interdiscipline Inst. of Arts and Humanities, Lockwood, N.Y., 1993; dir. of seminars for various orgns. including sr. ctrs., librs., schs., temples and chs., 1975—. Recipient Broadcasting award Nat. Dept. for Homebound, Mineola, N.Y., 1983, Tchg. award SUNY, 1983. Fellow UNESCO, Descartes Phil. Soc., Hungarian Acad.; mem. European Acad., Spanish Philos. Soc. Roman Catholic. Avocations: music, art, science, etymology, soccer. Home: 195 Parker Rd Lockwood NY 14859-9763

KEATING, MARGARET MARY, entrepreneur, business consultant; b. Chgo., Feb. 18, 1950; d. Jeremiah Joseph and Margaret Mary (Donnelly) K. Cert. in law, U. Mass., 1993; BS, Emmanuel Coll., 1994; MBA, Simmons Coll., 1996. Sr. merchandiser J.C. Penney Co., Chgo., 1971-73, dist. mgr. fashions, 1973-75, regional mgr., 1976-78; gen. mgr. merchandise J.C. Penney Co., Aurora, Ill., 1978-82; co-founder, exec. v.p., dir. mktg. The Pres. Mgmt. Group, Inc., Hingham, Mass., 1984-88; pres., dir. Keating Konsult, Inc., Scituate, Mass., 1988—; v.p., co-founder Video Tours, Inc., Hartford, Conn., 1986-87. Founder Advocates for Moral and Ethical Treatment by Divorce Attys., Accord, Mass., 1991—. Mem. NAFE, LWV, Nat. Assn. for Women in Careers, Nat. Womens Polit. Caucus, Am. Mgmt. Assn., Ctr. for Entrepreneurial Mgmt. Democrat. Avocations: political and community drives. Home and Office: Keating Konsult 55 Richfield Rd Scituate MA 02066-3425

KEATING, MICHAEL BURNS, lawyer; b. Cambridge, Mass., May 17, 1940; s. John Stuart and Anne Veronica (Burns) K.; m. Martha Harrison McGuire, OCt. 12, 1974; children: Michael Burns, Andrew Wade, Lucy Harrison. BA, Williams Coll., 1962; LLB, Harvard U., 1965. Bar: Mass. 1965, U.S. District Ct. Mass. 1966. Law clk. to presiding justice Superior Ct. Mass., Boston, 1965-66, U.S. Dist. Ct. Mass., Boston, 1966-67; assoc. Foley, Hoag & Eliot, Boston, 1967-74, ptnr., 1974—; adj. prof. trial practice Northeastern Law Sch., Boston, 1985—. Trustee Brooks Sch., North Andover, Mas., 1978—, Foley, Hoag & Eliot Found., Boston, 1981-89, Williams Coll., Williamstown, Mass., 1996—; pres. Crime & Justice Found., Boston, 1985-94; bd. dirs. Navy Meml. Found., 1994—. Lt. (j.g.) USNR, 1967-72. Fellow Am. Coll. Trial Lawyers, Harvard Club; mem. Boston Bar Assn. (treas.). Democrat. Roman Catholic. Avocations: tennis, squash, skiing, sailing. Home: 9 W Cedar St Boston MA 02108-3535 Office: Foley Hoag & Eliot 1 Post Office Sq Ste 1700 Boston MA 02109-2170

KEATING, PATRICIA ANN STACY, retired physical education educator; b. Sewickley, Pa., May 14, 1939; d. Clyde Grant Stacy and Dorothy Rose (Rupnik) Zupancic; m. Arthur J. Keating Jr., Mar. 27, 1998. BS, Slippery Rock (Pa.) U., 1961; MEd, U. Pitts., 1967. Cert. health and phys. edn. tchr., Pa. Tchr. South Hills High Sch., Pitts., 1961-76; tchr. John A. Brashear High Sch., Pitts., 1976-96, instructional chairperson, 1978-87; ret., 1996; swim coach Brashear High Sch., 1971-96. Sponsor, coord. Am. Cancer Soc. Swim-a-Thon, Pitts., Am. Heart Assn. Jump-Rope-for-Heart, community collector, Mt. Lebanon, Pa.; sec. Western chpt. Sports Hall of Fame, Pitts., 1979—. Recipient Profl. Honor award, Pa., 1976, named to Slippery Rock U. Hall of Fame. Mem. Pa. Assn. Health, Phys. Edn., Recreation and Dance (profl., pres. 1985-86, Elmer B. Cottrell award 1991), Allegheny County Assn. for Health, Phys. Edn., Recreation and Dance (pres. 1974-75), Order Ea. Star (worthy matron 1983-84, 89-90, dist. dep. 1987-88), Alpha Delta Kappa (Lambda chpt. pres.-elect 1992-94, pres. 1994-96). Republican. Baptist. Avocations: golf, swimming, reading, puzzles, gardening. Home: 2518 Spring Brook Ave Rockford IL 61107-1556

KEATING, ROBERT B., ambassador; b. Medford, Mass., May 7, 1924; married; 1 child. B.S., U.S. Naval Acad., 1946; M.E.A., George Washington U., 1961. Chmn. com. on transport tech. for developing countries U.S. Dept. State, 1961-62; dir. Chile-Calif. Program for Tech. Coop., 1964-67; sr. adviser Inter-Am. Devel. Bank, 1967-69; dir. gen. Bur. Roads, Ministry Pub. Works, Rep. of Zaire, 1970-73; cons., 1973-79; v.p. Pure Water Systems Inc., 1979-81; cons. on internat. security affairs Office Sec. Def., 1981-82; cons. Office Gen. Counsel, Dept. Navy, 1982-83; ambassador to Madagascar, 1983-86, ambassador to Comoros, 1983-86; U.S. exec. dir. The World Bank and Affiliates, Washington, 1986-89; sr. adviser internat. affairs Pepper, Hamilton & Scheetz, Washington, 1989—; mem. U.S. del. to Law of Sea Conf., Geneva, 1981, N.Y.C., 1982; chmn. Presdl. Study of Third World Hunger, 1984. Author: Food For Progress Initiative. Decorated Nat. Order of Leopard, Republic of Zaire, Nat. Order of Madagascar, Dem. Republic Madagascar, Nat. Order of Star of Anjouan, Fed. Republic of Comoros. Office: Hamilton Square 600 Fourteenth Street NW Washington DC 20005-2004

KEATING, TERRY MICHAEL, commercial banker; b. Seattle, Sept. 30, 1958; s. Donald Joseph and Dorothy Lorraine (DeFur) K.; m. Debbie Wechter, May 28, 1993. BSBA in Econs., Valparaiso U., 1981; MBA in Fin. and Acctg., Keller Grad. Sch. of Mgmt., Chgo., 1987. Loan officer 1st Nat. Bank of Valparaiso, Ind., 1981-84, Unibanc Trust Co., Chgo., 1984-86; loan officer LaSalle Nat. Bank, Chgo., 1986-88, asst. v.p., 1988-90, v.p., 1990-93, 1st v.p., consumer fin. specialist, dep. divsn. head, 1993—, sr. v.p., divsn. head, 1998—. Spkr. Youth Motivation Program, Chgo., 1990-94. Mem. Kaleidoscope (chmn.), Univ. Club Chgo. (past bd. dirs.), Sigma Phi Epsilon (Ill. Mu alumni bd. dirs.). Avocations: soccer, squash, bicycling, philosophy. Office: LaSalle Nat Bank 135 S Lasalle St Fl 5 Chicago IL 60603-4174

KEATING, THOMAS PATRICK, health care administrator, educator; b. Cleve., Jan. 5, 1949; s. Thomas Wilbur and Margaret (Gahllagher) K.; m. Carolyn Elizabeth Kraft, Sept. 4, 1976; children: Jerrod Patrick, Kerri Ann, Zane, Kriste, Marite. BS in Bus., Cleve. State U., 1971; MS in Bus., U. Toledo, 1973. Cert. health care exec. Asst. dir. facilities U. Kans. Med. Ctr., Kansas City, 1977-80; dir. mgmt. svcs. Charleston (S.C.) County Park and Recreation Commn., 1980-84; adminstr. Children's Health Sys., Med. U. of S.C., Charleston, 1984—, instr., 1987—, preceptor adminstrv. residency, master health svcs. adminstrn., 1990-93; adj. instr. Cen. Mich. U., Mt. Pleasant, 1979—, Rockhurst Coll., Kansas City, 1979-80, Kansas City (Kans.) Community Jr. Coll., 1978-80, Fayetteville (N.C.) Tech. Inst., 1974-75; accredited cons. SBA, Charleston, 1980-91; adj. prof. Webster U., St. Louis, 1981—, faculty U. Ala., New Coll., 1974; nursing home cons. Charleston County Mental Retardation Bd., Charleston, 1987-88. Contbr. articles to profl. jours. Vol. Driftwood Health Care Ctr., Charleston, 1981-83. Capt. U.S. Army, 1973-77, lt. col. USAR ret. Fellow Am. Coll. Health Care Execs.; mem. Sigma Phi Epsilon (com. chmn. 1970-71), Alpha Kappa Psi (com. chmn. 1972-73), KC. Roman Catholic. Club: Toastmasters (adminstrv. v.p. 1985-86). Home: 898 Farm Quarter Rd Mount Pleasant SC 29464-9518 Office: Med U SC 171 Ashley Ave Charleston SC 29425-0001

KEATINGE, CORNELIA WYMA, architectural preservationist consultant, lawyer; b. Poughkeepsie, N.Y., July 22, 1952; d. Edwin R. and Josephine B. (Brazis) Wyma; m. Robert Reed Keatinge, Aug. 21, 1982; 1 child, Courtney Elizabeth. BArch, U. Ky., 1974; MA in History and Theory of Architecture, U. Essex, Colchester, Eng., 1976; JD, U. Denver, 1982. Bar: Colo. 1982. Archtl. historian Kans. State Hist. Soc., Topeka, 1975-77; hist. architect Nat. Park Service, Denver, 1977-79; assoc. Richard E. Young, Denver, 1982-84; hist. architect Colo. Hist.Soc., Denver, 1984-86; sole practice, cons. architecture Denver, 1986; hist. preservation specialist Adv. Council Hist. Preservation, Golden, Colo., 1986—. Vol. Denver Art Mus., 1980—, Jr. League Denver, 1983—. Rotary fellow, 1974-75; recipient Spl. Achievement award, Nat. Park Service, 1980. Mem. ABA. Home: 460 S Marion Pky # 1904 Denver CO 80209-2544 Office: 12136 W Bayaud Ave Ste 330 Lakewood CO 80228-2115

KEATINGE, ROBERT REED, lawyer; b. Berkeley, Calif., Apr. 22, 1948; s. Gerald Robert and Elizabeth Jean (Benedict) K.; m. Katherine Lou Carr, Feb. 1, 1969 (div. Dec. 1981); 1 child, Michael Towne; m. Cornelia Elizabeth Wyma, Aug. 21, 1982; 1 child, Courtney Elizabeth. BA, U. Colo., 1970; JD, U. Denver, 1973, LLM, 1982. Bar: Colo. 1974, U.S. Dist. Ct. Colo. 1974, U.S. Ct. Appeals (10th cir.) 1977, U.S. Tax Ct. 1980. Ptnr. Kubie & Keatinge, Denver, 1974-76; pvt. practice Denver, 1976; assoc. Richard Young, Denver, 1977-86; counsel Durham & Assoc. P.C., Denver, 1986-89, Durham & Baron, Denver, 1989-90; project editor taxation Shepard's/McGraw-Hill, Colorado Springs, Colo., 1990-96; of counsel Holland & Hart, LLP, Denver, 1992—; lectr. law U. Denver, 1982-92, adj. prof. grad. tax program, 1983-94. Author, cons. (CD-ROM) Entity Expert, 1996; co-author: Ribstein and Keatinge on Limited Liability Companies, 1992; contbr. articles to profl. jours. and treatises. Spkr. to profl. socs. and univs. including AICPA, ALI-ABA, U. TEx., 1984—. Recipient Law Week award U. Denver Bur. Nat. Affairs, 1974. Mem. ABA (chmn. subcom. ltd. liability cos. of com. on partnerships 1990-95, chmn. com. on taxation 1995—, mem. ho. of dels. 1996—, editl. bd. ABA/BNA Lawyer's Manual on Professional Conduct 1998—, joint editl. bd. ABA/NCCUSL on unincorporated orgns. 1996—), Colo. Bar Assn. (corp. code revision com., co-chmn. ltd. liability co. revision com., taxation sect. exec. coun. 1988-94, sec.-treas. 1991-92, chmn. 1993-94), Denver Bar Assn. Home: 460 S Marion Pky # 1904 Denver CO 80209-2544

KEATON, DIANE, actress; b. Santa Ana, Calif., Jan. 5, 1946. Student, Neighborhood Playhouse, N.Y.C., 1968. Appeared on N.Y. stage in Hair, 1968, Play It Again Sam, 1969, The Primary English Class, 1976; appeared in numerous films including Lovers and Other Strangers, 1970, Play It Again Sam, 1972, The Godfather, 1972, Sleeper, 1973, The Godfather Part II, 1974, Love and Death, 1975, I Will, I Will...For Now, 1975, Harry and Walter Go To New York, 1976, Annie Hall, 1977 (Best Actress Acad. award 1978, Brit. Acad. Best Actress award 1978, N.Y. Film Critics Circle award 1978, Nat. Soc. Film Critics award 1978), Looking for Mr. Goodbar, 1977, Interiors, 1978, Manhattan, 1979, Reds, 1981 (Acad. award nominee), Shoot the Moon, 1982, Little Drummer Girl, 1984, Mrs. Soffel, 1984, Crimes of the Heart, 1986, Radio Days, 1987, Baby Boom, 1987, The Good Mother, 1988, The Lemon Sisters, 1990, The Godfather Part III, 1990, Father of the Bride, 1991, Manhattan Murder Mystery, 1993, Look Who's Talking Now, 1993 (voice), Father of the Bride 2, 1995, Marvin's Room, 1996, First Wives Club, 1996, The Only Thrill, 1997, The Other Sister, 1999, Town and Country, 1999, Hanging Up, 1999; (TV movie) Running Mates, 1992, Amelia Earhart, 1994; dir. film: Heaven, 1987, Wildflower, 1991, Unstrung Heroes, 1995; accomplished artist and singer; author book of photographs: Reservations, 1980; editor: (with Marvin Heiferman) Still Life, 1983, Mr. Salesman, 1994. Recipient Golden Globe award, 1978. Office: John Burnham William Morris Agy 151 S El Camino Dr Beverly Hills CA 90212-2704*

KEATON, LAWRENCE CLUER, safety engineer, consultant; b. Gainesville, Tex., Nov. 24, 1924; s. William Lenard and Lettie (Phipps) K.; m. Emalee Prichard, Feb. 22, 1947; children: Lawrel Larsen, L.C. Jr., T.E. BSME, U. Okla., 1945; MS in Safety Mgmt. (hon.), Western States U., 1989, PhD in Bus. Adminstrn. (hon.), 1989. Registered profl. engr., Tex.; cert. lightning protection inspector; diplomate Coun. of Engring. Specialty Bds. In various engring. positions Phillips Petroleum Co., Borger, Tex., 1946-65; project devel. engr. Phillips Petroleum Co., N.Y.C., 1964-65; mng. dir. Nordisk Philback AB, Malmo, Sweden, 1965-73; dir. carbon black ops. Europe and Africa Phillips Petroleum Co., 1973-74, world-wide dir. carbon black ops., 1974-76; mng. dir. Sevalco Ltd., Bristol, Eng., 1976-81; ind. cons., 1981-85; mng. ptnr. System Engring. and Labs. Northwest Tex., Amarillo, 1985—. 5 patents in petrochem. processes. Lt. (j.g.) USN, 1943-45, PTO. Mem. ASME, Am. Soc. Safety Engrs., Lightning Protection Inst., Nat. Assn. Corrosion Engrs., Nat. Acad. Forensic Engrs., Nat. Assn. Fire Investigators, Nat. Assn. Profl. Accident Reconstruction Specialists, Nat. Soc. Profl. Engrs., Soc. Am. Mil. Engrs., Tex. Soc. Profl. Engrs., Amarillo Rotary, Shriners, Masons, Amarillo Club, Am. Legion, Tenn. Squires. Methodist. Avocations: gourmet cooking, gardening. Home: 7720 Baughman Dr Amarillo TX 79121-1752 Office: System Engring and Labs NW Tex PO Box 1506 Amarillo TX 79105-1506

KEATON, MICHAEL, actor, comedian; b. Coraopolis, PA, Sept. 9, 1951; m. Caroline MacWilliams (div.); 1 son, Sean. Student, Kent State U. With comedy group Second City, L.A. Appeared in movies Night Shift, 1982, Mr. Mom, 1983, Johnny Dangerously, 1984, Gung Ho, 1985, The Squeeze, 1987, Touch and Go, 1987, Beetlejuice, 1988, Clean and Sober, 1988, The Dream Team, 1989, Batman, 1989, Pacific Heights, 1990, One Good Cop, 1991, Batman Returns, 1992, Much Ado About Nothing, 1993, My Life, 1993,The Paper, 1994, Speechless, 1994, Multiplicity, 1996, Jackie Brown, 1997, Inventing the Abbotts, 1997, Desperate Measures, 1998, Out of Sight, 1998, Jack Frost, 1998; TV appearances include All in the Family, Maude, Mary Tyler Moore Show, Mister Roger's Neighborhood, 1968, The Tony Randall Show; TV series include All's Fair, 1976-77, The Mary Tyler Moore Hour, 1979, Working Stiffs, 1979, Report to Murphy, 1982; TV movie: Roosevelt and Truman; prodr. Body Shots, 1999. *

KEATON, MOLLIE M., elementary school educator; d. Lorenzo and Katie Mae (Thomas) K. BS, Kent State U., 1976; MA, Atlanta U., 1980, EdD, 1985. Counselor DeKalb County Bd. Edn., Decatur, Ga.; rsch. asst. Atlanta U.; tchr. Canton (Ohio) Bd. Edn. Mem. Assn. for Supervision and Curriculum Devel., Phi Delta Kappa. Home: 4076 Chapel Mill Bnd Decatur GA 30034-5335

KEATON, WILLIAM THOMAS, academic administrator, pastor; b. England, Ark., Aug. 29, 1921; m. Theresa Simpson, July 29, 1946; children: Sherrye Ann, William II, Bernard, Denise, Edwin, Karen, Renwick, Zelda, Aloysius. AA, Ark. Bapt. Coll., 1940-42; BA, U. Ark., 1948; MA, Columbia U., 1951. Supt. Howard County Sch. Dist. #38, Mineral Springs, Ark., 1951-56, East Side Sch. Dist., Menifee, Ark., 1956-61; prin. Quachita County High Sch., Bearden, Ark., 1961-68, Peake High Sch., Arkadelphia, Ark., 1968-70; coord. state programs Ark. Dept. Edn., Little Rock, 1970-85; pres. Ark. Baptist Coll., Little Rock, 1985—; vis. prof. Ala. State U., 1972; researcher Office of Edn., Washington, 1973; state insvc. coord. Region VI-AR, staff devel. specialist, Little Rock, 1970-85; staff assoc. adult edn. U. Tex., Austin, 1967-70, Lafayette, La., 1972; pastor Greater Mt. Zion Bapt. Ch., Ashdown, Ark., 1951-72, Greater Pleasant Hill Bapt. Ch., Arkadelphia, Ark., 1972-79, Canaan Missionary Bapt. Ch., Little Rock, 1979—; mem. pres. adv. bd. dirs. Historically Black Colls. and U., 1989. Mem. NCCJ, NEA (life), NAACP (life), Ark. Edn. Assn., Ark. Adult Edn. Assn. (pres. 1969-70), Union Dist. Assn. (dean 1980—), Nat. Assn. Pub. Continuing Edn., Nat. Assn. Equal Opportunity Higher Edn. (sec. 1988-93, bd. dirs. 1989), Masons, Alpha Phi Alpha, Phi Delta Kappa. Democrat. Baptist. Office: Ark Bapt Coll 1600 Bishop St Little Rock AR 72202-6067*

KEATOR, CAROL LYNNE, library director; b. Annapolis, Md., Aug. 9, 1945; d. Lyle H. and Juanita F (Waits) K. BA, Syracuse U., 1967; MS, Simmons Coll., 1968. Librarian Bristol (Conn.) Pub. Sch.s, 1968-69, MIT, Cambridge, 1969-72; librarian Santa Barbara (Calif.) Pub. Library, 1972-77, br. supr., 1977-81, prin. librarian, 1981-88, library dir., 1988—. Mem. ALA, Calif. Libr. Assn., Pub. Libr. Assn. Unitarian. Office: Santa Barbara Pub Libr 40 E Anapamu St Santa Barbara CA 93101-2722

KEATOR, MARGARET WHITLEY, legislative aide; b. Suffolk, Va., Oct. 27, 1945; d. Jacob Jordan and Margaret Mitchell Whitley; m. Philip John Keator, Sept. 2, 1967; 1 child, Jennifer. AB in Govt., Coll. William and Mary, 1968. Tchr. Newport News (Va.) Pub. Sch., 1968-69, M%, 1972-84; rsch. asst. Marine Corps. Ops. Analysis Group, Arlington, Va., 1969-72; v.p. Keator Signs, Inc., Newport News, 1990-93; legis. asst. Congressman Bobby Scott, Newport News, 1993—; polit. cons., Newport News, 1990-93. Mem. Newport News City Coun., 1982-90, Peninsula planning dist. com., 1982-90, Newport News planning com., 1982-87; exec. bd. Va. Peninsula Econ. Devel. Com., Newport News, 1986-90; vice chmn. environ. quality policy com. Va. Mcpl. League, 1988-90; bd. trustees Peninsula Marine Inst., 1992—; citizen adv. bd. Healthy Familites Initiative, 1997—. Mem. AAUW (Newport News br.), Soroptimist Club (pres. 1996-98), Visionaries (recording sec. 1997—), Church Women United (chair citizen action 1994—). Democrat. Methodist. Office: Congressman Bobby Scott 2600 Washington Ave Ste 1010 Newport News VA 23607-4333

KEATS, DONALD HOWARD, composer, educator; b. N.Y.C., May 27, 1929; s. Bernard and Lillian K.; m. Eleanor Steinholz, Dec. 13, 1953; children: Jeremy, Jennifer, Jeffrey, Jocelyn. MusB, Yale U., 1949; MA, Columbia U., 1951; PhD, U. Minn., 1962; student, Staatliche Hochschule fur Musik, Hamburg, Germany, 1954-56. Teaching fellow Yale U. Sch. Music, New Haven, Conn., 1948-49; instr. music theory U.S. Naval Sch. Music, Washington, 1953-54; post music dir. Ft. Dix, N.J., 1956-57; faculty Antioch Coll., Yellow Springs, Ohio, 1957-76; prof. Antioch Coll., 1967-76, chmn. music dept., 1967-71; vis. prof. music U. Wash. Sch. Music, 1969-70, Lamont Sch. Music, U. Denver, 1975-76; composer-in-residence Colo. Music Festival, 1980, Arcosanti, 1986; vis. composer Aspen Music Festival, 1987; prof. music, composer-in-residence Lamont Sch. Music, U. Denver, 1975—, Phipps Prof. in the humanities, 1982-85. Concerts devoted solely to his music often with his participation as pianist, London, 1973, Tel Aviv, 1973, Jerusalem, 1973, N.Y.C., 1975, Denver, 1984, 91; Composer: Divertimento for Winds and Strings, 1949, The Naming of Cats, 1951, The Hollow Men, 1951, String Quartet 1, 1952, Concert Piece for Orchestra, 1952, Variations for Piano, 1955, First Symphony, 1957, Piano Sonata, 1960, An Elegiac Symphony, 1962, Anyone Lived in a Pretty How Town, 1965; ballet New Work, 1966; Polarities for Violin and Piano, 1968-70, String Quartet 2, 1965, A Love Triptych, 1970, Dialogue for Piano, and Winds, 1973, Diptych for Cello and Piano, 1975, Upon the Intimation of Love's Mortality, 1975, Branchings for Orch., 1976, Four Puerto Rican Love Songs: Tierras del Alma for soprano, flute and guitar, 1978, Musica Instrumentalis for chamber group, 1980, Concerto for Piano and Orch., 1990, Revisitations for Violin, Cello and Piano, 1992, Elegy for chamber orch., 1993, Scherzo for String Quartet, 1995, Fanfare for Brass, 1996, String Quartet No. 3, 1999. Served with U.S. Army, 1952-54. Recipient ASCAP awards, 1964—; awards from Ford, Danforth and Lilly founds., Nat. Endowment for Arts; winner Rockefeller Found. Symphonic Competitions, 1965, 66; Guggenheim fellow Europe, 1964-65, 72-73; Nat. Endowment for Arts grantee, fellow, 1975; Fulbright Scholar, 1954-56. Mem. ASCAP, Am. Music Ctr., Soc. of Composers, Phi Beta Kappa. E-mail: dkeats@du.edu. Home: 9261 E Berry Ave Englewood CO 80111-3507 Office: U Denver Lamont Sch Music Denver CO 80208

KEATS, GLENN ARTHUR, manufacturing company executive; b. Chgo., July 1, 1920; s. Herbert J. and Agnes H. (Streich) K.; m. Olga Maria Loor Hurtado, Feb. 13, 1946; children: Maria Susana Keats Eggemeyer, Allwyn Dolores Keats Gustafson. BS in Commerce, Northwestern U., 1941. Sales exec. Keats-Lorenz Spring Co., Chgo., 1947-56; controller, auditor Plantaciones Ecuatorianas, S.A., Guayaquil, Ecuador, 1956-58; co-founder Keats Mfg. Co., Wheeling, Ill., 1958—. Sec. Hispanic Soc. Chgo., 1965—. Lt. comdr. USN, 1941-47. Mem. Spring Mfrs. Inst., Northwestern U. Alumni Assn., Sigma Nu. Republican. Lutheran. Club: Evanston Golf, Amelia Island (Fla.). Home: 368 Woodland Rd Highland Park IL 60035-5055 Office: 350 Holbrook Dr Wheeling IL 60090-5812

KEATS, PATRICIA HART, counselor, educator; b. Boise, Idaho, July 18, 1946; d. Robert James Hart and Joyce Elizabeth (Shroyer) Smith; m. Theodore Eliot Keats, Mar. 30, 1974; 1 child, Ian. AS, Piedmont Coll., 1982; BS, Mary Baldwin Coll., 1983; MEd, U. Va., 1986, EdD, 1992. Cert. Am. Bd. Radiologic Tech.; cert. Nat. Bd. Cert. Counselors; lic. profl. counselor, Va. Rsch. asst. U. Va., Charlottesville, 1982-83, 86-87; counselor Charlottesville, 1986—; mem. faculty, counselor Piedmont Community Coll., Charlottesville, 1987—; Honor lectr. Mary Baldwin Coll., 1988. Pres. Charlottesville Cmty. Children's Theatre, 1974-84, 78; mem. Charlottesville Light Opera Co., 1978—; supr. Albemarle County Fair, 1988—; exec. com. Jefferson Cmty. Theatre, 1991; bd. dirs. Epilepsy Assn. Va., 1993—. Mem. AACD, Am. Soc. Radiologic Tech., Psi Chi, Chi Sigma Iota. Avocations: genealogy, theatre, gardening, travel. Home: 421 Key West Dr Charlottesville VA 22911-8423

KEATS, THEODORE ELIOT, physician, radiology educator; b. New Brunswick, N.J., June 26, 1924; m. Margaret E. McNamara, Aug. 27, 1949 (dec.); children—Matthew Mason, Ian Stuart B.; m. Patricia L. Hart, Mar. 30, 1974. BS, Rutgers U., 1945; MD, U. Pa., 1947. Diplomate: Am. Bd. Radiology (trustee). Intern U. Pa. Hosp., Phila., 1947-48; resident U. Mich. Hosp., Ann Arbor, 1948-51; instr. U. Calif. Sch. Medicine, San Francisco, 1953-54; asst. prof. U. Calif. Sch. Medicine, 1954-56; assoc. prof. U. Mo. Sch. Medicine, Columbia, 1956-59; prof. radiology U. Mo. Sch. Medicine, 1959-63; prof. radiology U. Va. Sch. Medicine, Charlottesville, 1963—, chmn. dept. radiology, 1963-92; vis. prof. Karolinska Hosp., Stockholm, 1963-64; mem. adv. council Greenbrier Clinic. Author: Atlas of Roentgenographic Measurement, 7th edit., 2000, An Atlas of Normal Roentgen Variants That May Simulate Disease, 6th edit., 1995, Self-Assessment of Current Knowledge in Diagnostic Radiology, 2d edit., 1980, An Atlas of Normal Developmental Roentgen Anatomy, 1978, 2d edit., 1988, (with Thomas H. Smith) Radiology of Musculoskeletal Injury, 1990, 2d edit., 2000; editor-in-chief Current Problems in Diagnostic Radiology, 1981,

Emergency Radiology, 1984, 2d edit., 1989, Applied Radiology, 1989—; Am. editor Skeletal Radiology, 1987-97; editor Emergency Radiology, 1993—. Served with AUS, 1943-47; to capt., M.C. AUS, 1951-53. Fellow Am. Coll. Radiology (Gold medal 1995); mem. AMA, Am. Roentgen Ray Soc., Radiol. Soc. N.Am., Soc. Pediatric Radiology (hon.), So. Med. Assn., Internat. Skeletal Soc. (medal 1995), Soc. Emergency Radiology (gold medal 1999), Phi Beta Kappa, Sigma Xi, Alpha Omega Alpha. Home: 421 Key West Dr Charlottesville VA 22901 Office: U Va Hosps Lee St Rm 1831 Charlottesville VA 22911 also: U Va Sch Medicine Dept Radiology Charlottesville VA 22908

KEBABIAN, PAUL BLAKESLEE, librarian; b. Watch Hill, R.I., July 24, 1917; s. John Couzu and Edith Jennie (Blakeslee) K.; m. Justine Richardson, Nov. 21, 1942; children: Jean Edith, Ann Ruth, Helen Jane; m. Johanna Thomas, Jan. 27, 1995. B.A., Yale U., 1938; B.S., Columbia U., 1948. Cataloger, supr. exchanges Yale U. Library, New Haven, 1939-42, 46-47; chief cataloger preparation div. N.Y. Pub. Library, 1949-61, 62-63; Ford Found. program specialist Library of U. Baghdad, Iraq, 1961-62; asso. dir. libraries U. Fla., Gainesville, 1963-66; dir. libraries U. Vt., Burlington, 1966-82; assoc. prof. library sci. U. Fla., 1963-66; cons. in field. Author: American Woodworking Tools, 1978; co-editor, contbr.: Tools and Technologies—America's Wooden Age, 1979; contbr. articles to profl. jours. Served with USAAF, 1942-46. Mem. ALA, Assn. Coll. and Research Libraries, Midwest Tool Collectors Assn., Early Am. Industries Assn. (past pres., dir. 1970-82, editor 1982-84, contbr. Chronicle), Vt. Hist. Soc., Antique Crafts and Tools in Vermont (past pres., editor 1973-88), N.Eng. Tool Collectors Assn. (editor 1988-95). Democrat. Home: 11 Scottsdale Rd South Burlington VT 05403

KEBBLISH, JOHN BASIL, retired coal company executive, consultant; b. Gray, Pa., Jan. 14, 1925; s. Joseph and Catherine (Benya) K.; m. Ruth L. Mueller, Oct. 14, 1955; children: John J., Heather R. BS in Mining Engring., Pa. State U., 1947, BSEE, 1948. With Consol. Coal Co. (and subs. cos.), various locations, 1948-71; pres. Pocahontas Fuel Co. divsn. Consol. Coal Co., Bluefield, W. Va., 1966-70; v.p. Consol. Coal Co., Pitts., 1970-71; exec. v.p. The Pittston Co., N.Y.C., 1971-73; pres., CEO Ashland (Ky.) Coal, Inc. subs. Ashland, Inc., 1974-87, also bd. dirs.; v.p., exec. officer Ashland Oil, Inc., 1976-87; cons. in field. With AUS, 1944-46.

KECHIJIAN, PAUL, dermatologist, educator; b. Providence, Mar. 17, 1940; s. Harry Maderos and Annette (Rhia) Paré; m. Janice Ann Kechijian, July 31, 1976; children: Douglas Paul, Lisa Ann. AB in Psychology, Brown U., 1961, ScM in Biology, 1964; MD, Albany Med. Coll., 1968. Lic. Nat. Bd. Med. Examiners, N.Y. State Med. Lic.; diplomate Am. Bd. Dermatology, diplomate Dermatopathology Am. Bds. of Dermatology and Pathology. Med. intern, med. resident Barnes Hosp., St. Louis, 1968-69, 69-70; dermatology resident Mass. Gen. Hosp., Boston, 1970, Univ. Miami (Fla.) Sch. of Medicine, 1973-75; dermatopathology fellow NYU Med. Ctr., N.Y.C., 1975-76; instr. clin. dermatology NYU Sch. of Medicine, N.Y.C., 1975-78; clin. asst. prof. of dermatology NYU Sch. of Medicine, 1978-84, clin. assoc. prof., 1984—; asst. attending physician to assoc. attending physician Bellevue Hosp., 1976-81, 81—, NYU Med. Ctr., 1976-84, 84—; asst. attending dermatologist to sr. asst. North Shore Univ. Hosp., 1978-87, 87—; chief inpatient dermatology svc. Bellevue Hosp., 1976-86; cons. Holy Martyrs Armenian Day Sch., 1976—; hon. surgeon (dermatology) N.Y.C. Police Dept., 1981—; chief nail sect. NYU Med. Ctr., 1983—; presenter and lectr. in field. Contbg. editor: Jour. Dermatologic Surgery and Oncology, 1983-85; contbr. reports and articles to profl. jours. and chpt. to books. Fellow ACP, Am. Acad. Dermatology (com. on evaluation 1980-84, coun. on govtl. liaison key contact program 1986—), Am. Soc. Dermatopathology; mem. AMA, N.Y. Acad. Scis., Dermatology Found., Soc. for Investigative Dermatology, Nassau County Med. Soc., L.I. Dermatol. Soc., Soc. for Dermatol. Surgery, Internat. Soc. for Tropical Dermatology, Internat. Soc. Dermatol. Surgery, others. Office: 935 Northern Blvd Great Neck NY 11021-5309

KECK, DONALD BRUCE, physicist; b. Lansing, Mich., Jan. 2, 1941; s. William G. and Zelda D. Keck; m. Ruth A. Moilanen, July 10, 1965; children: Lynne Ann, Brian William. BS, Mich. State U., 1962, MS, 1964, PhD, 1967. With Corning (N.Y.) Glass Works, 1968-76, mgr. applied physics, 1976-86; dir. optics and photonics Corning, Inc., 1986-91, v.p., dir. optics and photonics, 1997—; bd. dirs. PCO, Inc., L.A.; lectr. in field. Co-author 4 books on optical fibers; editor Jour. Lightwave Tech., 1989-94; contbr. over 85 articles to profl. jours.; holder 30 patents. Chmn. troop com. Boy Scouts Am., Corning, 1968-71, planning bd. Town of Corning, 1990—; pres. Civic Music Assn., Corning, 1971-75; moderator 1st Congl. Ch., Corning, 1986-87, 91-92; mem. adv. bd. Corning Salvation Army; mem. bd. dirs. Corning chpt.-ARC, 1995—. Recipient Tech. Achievement award Internat. Soc. Optical Engring., 1981, IR-100 award Indsl. Rsch., 1981, Engring. Achievement award Am. Soc. Metals, 1983, Am. Innovator award, 1995, John Tyndall award IEEE/Optical Soc. Am., 1992, Disting. Alumni award Mich. State U., 1996; inductee Nat. Innovators Hall of Fame, 1993; Paul Harris fellow Rotary Internat., 1998. Fellow IEEE, Optical Soc. Am. (bd. dirs. 1994-96), Nat. Acad. Engring., Opto-Electronics Industry Devel. Assn. (bd. chmn. 1999—). Avocations: water and snow skiing, music, woodworking. Home: 2877 Chequer Cir Big Flats NY 14814-9610 Office: Corning Inc Sullivan Pk Corning NY 14831

KECK, JAMES COLLYER, physicist, educator; b. N.Y.C., June 11, 1924; s. Charles and Anne (Collyer) K.; m. Margaret Ramsey, Sept. 6, 1947; children: Robert Lyon, Patricia Anne. B.A., Cornell U., 1947, Ph.D., 1951. Research asst. Cornell U., 1951-52; sr. research fellow Calif. Inst. Tech., 1952-55; prin. scientist Avco-Everett Research Lab., Everett, Mass., 1955-65; dep. dir. Avco-Everett Research Lab., 1960-64; Ford prof. engring. MIT, Cambridge, 1965-89, prof. emeritus, 1989—. Served with AUS, 1944-46. Fellow Am. Acad. Sci.; mem. Am. Phys. Soc., Combustion Inst., Phi Beta Kappa, Sigma Xi, Phi Kappa Phi. Research high energy photonuclear reactions, theory of chem. reaction rates, high temperature gas dynamics, combustion, air pollution, thermodynamics, thermionics. Office: MIT RM-31-168A Cambridge MA 02139

KECK, MICHAEL BRIAN, biologist, educator; b. Ft. Worth, Oct. 11, 1967; s. Jimmie Frisch and Vivian Gayle (Winnett) K.; m. Tricia J. Vickrey, June 5, 1993. BS, Stephen F. Austin State U., 1990; MS, U. Tex., Arlington, 1993, PhD, 1998. From tchg. asst. to rsch. asst. U. Tex., Arlington, 1990-98; asst. prof. Stephen F. Austin State U., 1998—. Mem. Am. Soc. Ichthyologists & Herpetologists, Soc. Study of Amphibians & Reptiles, Soc. Conservation Biology, Soc. Systematic Biologists, Herpetologists' League, Southwestern Assn. Naturalists, Tex. Acad. Sci. Democrat. Avocations: photography, hiking, running. Home: 6312 Greenfield Rd Fort Worth TX 76135-1311

KECK, PHILIP WALTER, transportation executive; b. Wyandotte, Mich., Feb. 6, 1947; s. George and Genevieve (Baranowski) K.; m. Janice Dallas, Aug. 31, 1969; children: Derek James, Lisa Tiffany. BS, USAF Acad., 1969; MBA, U. Colo., 1982; postgrad., U. Tex., 1987—. Commd. 2d lt. USAF, 1969, advanced through grades to capt., 1972; instr. pilot USAF, Beale AFB, 1970-75, DaNang AFB, Vietnam, 1972; instr. USAF Acad. USAF, Colorado Springs, Colo., 1975-77; resigned USAF, 1977; pilot Braniff Internat. Airlines, Dallas, 1977-81; flight data supr. Denver Air Route Traffic Control Ctr., Longmont, Colo., 1981-82; account exec. Merrill Lynch, Denver, 1982-83; pilot Regent Air Corp., L.A., 1983-85; flight mgr., check airman Am. Airlines, Dallas, 1985—; fleet supr. Am. Airlines, 1998—; fin. planner Merrill Lynch, Denver, 1982-83. Co-author (study guide) Windshear Microburst, 1987. Decorated D.F.C., Vietnam. Republican. Lutheran. Avocations: handball (state and regional champion, Colo. 1981, YMCA Nat. Champion, 1992). Home: 786 Windemere Way Keller TX 76248-5210 Office: Am Airlines PO Box 619617 Dallas TX 75261-9617

KECK, VICKI LYNN, special education educator; b. Lancaster, Ohio, Mar. 22, 1961; d. Robert Harvey and Trudy Gay (Fishbaugh) K.; 1 child, Alexandra Joy. BS in Edn., Bowling Green (Ohio) State U., 1983; MEd, Ohio U., 1991. Cert. tchr. of learning disabled, gifted/talented, Ohio, elem. edn. and learning behavior, disorders. Learning disabilities tchr. South Dade Sr. High Sch., Dade County Sch. System, Homestead, Fla., 1983-85; learning disabilities tutor Pickerington (Ohio) High Sch., 1985-86; learning disabilities tchr. Groveport (Ohio)-Madison Mid. Sch. South, 1986—, tchr. regular 6th grade gifted/talented, 1995—; cheerleading advisor Groveport-Madison Mid. Sch. South, 1986-90, student coun. advisor, 1986—; flag corps advisor South Dade Sr. High Sch., 1984-85; workshop speaker student coun. Ohio Assn. Elem. Sch. Adminstrs., Columbus, 1988-92, 98, spkr. Contextual Tchg. and Learning Conf. for Bowling Green State Univ., 1999. Facilitator: (book of student poetry) American Association of Poetry, 1992, 94, 96, 97, 98. Vol. Faith Mission, Long St., Columbus, 1989-92. Named one of All-Ohio Student Coun. Advisors, Ohio Assn. Student Couns., 1989, 1st in State of Ohio, Project Citizen, 7th in the nation, 1998, Ashland Gold Apple Tchr. Awd., 1996. Mem. NEA, Ohio Edn. Assn., Assn. Supervision and Curriculum Devel., Am. Assn. Poetry. Avocations: stained glass, reading, student sports and activities, travel. Office: Groveport-Madison Mid Sch S 4400 Glendenning Dr Groveport OH 43125-9292

KECKEL, PETER J., advertising executive; b. Berlin, Dec. 13, 1942; came to U.S., 1956; s. F. Paul and Frieda G. (Schmidt) K.; m. Katherine Alice Brown, Nov. 27, 1971. BS in Polit. Sci., U. Md., 1966, postgrad., 1966; grad., U.S. Infantry Sch., Ft. Benning, Ga., 1967; grad. advanced officers course, Adjutant Gens. Sch., Ft. Ben Harrison, Ind., 1971. Exec. dir. Med. Personnel Pool, Oklahoma City, 1973-74; regional dir. Medox div. Drake Internat., Oklahoma City, 1974-78; pres., owner Okla. Communities, Inc., Edmond, 1978—, Okla. Gold Jewelry, Inc., Edmond, 1982—; mktg. cons. to various orgns. and groups, 1978—. Bd. dirs. Edmond YMCA, 1980-81, Okla. Disaster Edn. Fund, 1995—. Served to capt. U.S. Army, 1966-73, Vietnam. Decorated Bronze Star; recipient Presdl. Vietnam Veterans Outstanding Community Achievement award Pres. Carter, 1979; received Key to the City of Garland, Tex. Mem. Am. Bus. Clubs (life; bd. dirs. 1979—, pres. 1985-86, chmn. bd. dirs. 1986-87, regional big hat chmn. 1986-87, 2d dist. gov. 1989-90, nat. big hat pres. 1991-92, mem. nat. new club bldg. com., Mr. Ambuc awards 1980-81, 83-84, 87-88, dist. 1987-88, Nat. Ambuc of Yr. 1988-89, top nat. mem. recruiter 1982—, top nat. fundraiser, excellence award 1982-83, #1 club pres. in country 1985-86, chartered New Ambucs chpt., 1988), U. Md. Alumni Assn. (life.), POW-MIA Orgn., Edmond C. of C. (life; officer, awards), Rep. Presdl. Task Force (life) and others. Republican. Lutheran. Club: Edmond Soccer (v.p., bd. dirs. 1977-79, coach, referee 1976-82). Avocations: sports, travel, music, community activities, foreign languages. Home: 908 E 10th St Edmond OK 73034-5451 Office: Okla Communities Inc 222 E 10th St Plz Edmond OK 73034-4737

KEDDERIS, PAMELA JEAN, academic administrator; b. Waterbury, Conn., May 15, 1956; d. Leo George and Evelyn Helen (Fenske) K. Student, U. Nice, 1976-77; BA, Assumption Coll., 1978; MBA, U. New Haven, 1981. Credit analyst, Citytrust Bank, Bridgeport, Conn., 1980-81, sr. credit analyst, 1981-82, fin. analyst, 1982-83, seminar instr., 1981-83; planning analyst Continental Ins. Co., N.Y.C., 1983-84, sr. planning analyst, 1984-85, dir. planning, 1985-87, asst. v.p. 1987-92, v.p., 1992-95, v.p., controller Marine Office of Am., Cranbury, N.J., 1995-97; exec. officer for fin. Conn. State U. Sys., Hartford, 1997-98; chief fin. officer, 1998—. Mem. Am. Coun. on Edn., North Shore Animal League. Democrat. Lutheran. Avocations: music, traveling. Home: 42 Northwoods Rd Farmington CT 06032-1017

KEDDIE, ROLAND THOMAS, physician, hospital administrator, lawyer; b. Altoona, Pa., Oct. 21, 1928; s. John Barkeley and Jessie E. (Keddie) Isenberg; B.S. cum laude, U. Pitts., 1956, M.D., 1957, J.D., 1970; m. Suzanne M. Seno, Feb. 6, 1978; 1 dau., Dawn Michelle; children by previous marriage: Roland, Thomas, Francis, Robert, Michael, Karen, Andrew, Rosemary. Intern St. Josephs Hosp., Pitts., 1958; practice medicine specializing in emergency medicine and family practice; admitted to Pa. bar, 1970; medico legal cons., 1970—; med. dir. Westmoreland Manor, Greensburg, Pa., 1971; dir. emergency dept. Connemaugh Valley Meml. Hosp., Johnston, Pa., 1976-77, Shadyside Hosp., Pitts., 1978-80, chmn. dept. emergency services McKeesport (Pa.) Hosp., 1980-83, also dir. emergency medicine residency program; pres. EmergiCenters Inc., 1983—; chmn. dept. family practice St. Clair Hosp., Pitts., 1990—; pres. Emergency Med. Services Inst., 1982-85; adj. prof. Sch. Nursing, U. Pitts. Served with USN, 1946-47, 50-52. Diplomate Am. Bd. Family Practice. Mem. Am. Coll. Emergency Physicians (life, bd. dirs. Pa. chpt. 1977-81, 83-86, v.p. 1980-81, pres. 1985-86), Pa. Med. Soc., Hosp. Assn. Pa. (mem. profl. practice com. 1981-82), Allegheny County Bar Assn., AMA (Physicians Recognition award 1974, 77, 80), Allegheny County Med. Soc., Pa. Emergency Health Services Council (dir. 1980), Soc. Tchrs. Emergency Medicine, Beta Beta Beta. Roman Catholic. Home: 45 Meadowcrest Dr Cecil PA 15321-1118 Office: Charters Valley Med Ctr Ste 250 1168 Washington Pike Bridgeville PA 15017

KEE, HOWARD CLARK, religion educator; b. Beverly, N.J., July 28, 1920; s. Walter Leslie and Regina (Corcoran) K.; m. Janet Burrell, Dec. 15, 1951; children: Howard Clark III, Christopher Andrew, Sarah Leslie. A.B., Bryan (Tenn.) Coll., 1940; Th.M., Dallas Theol. Sem., 1944; postgrad., Am. Sch. Oriental Research, Jerusalem, 1949-50; Ph.D. (Two Bros. fellow), Yale, 1951. Instr. religion and classics U. Pa., 1951-53; from asst. prof. to prof. N.T. Drew U., 1953-68; Rufus Jones prof. history of religion, chmn. dept. history of religion Bryn Mawr (Pa.) Coll., 1968-77; William Goodwin Aurelio prof. Biblical studies Boston U., 1977-89, chmn. grad. div. religious studies, 1977-86; sr. rsch. fellow U. Pa., 1987—; vis. prof. religion Princeton U., 1954-55, Brown U., 1985; vis. lectr. U. of Durham, 1987, Claremont Sch. of Theology, 1991; Rsch. scholar, Miss. state U., 1992, vis. scholar, Princeton Theological Seminary, 1993; mem. archaeol. teams at Roman Jericho, 1950, Shechem, 1957, Mt. Gerizim, 1966, Pella, Jordan, 1967, Ashdod, Israel, 1968; chmn. Coun. on Grad. Studies in Religion; cons. for transls. Am. Bible Soc., 1989—. Author: Understanding the New Testament, 1957, 4th edit., 1983, 5th edit., 1992, Making Ethical Decisions, 1958, The Renewal of Hope, 1959, Jesus and God's New People, 1959, Jesus in History, 1970, 3d edit., 1995, The Origins of Christianity: Sources and Documents, 1973, The Community of the New Age, 1977, Christianity: An Historical Approach, 1979, Christian Origins in Sociological Perspective, 1980, Miracle in the Early Christian World, 1983, The New Testament in Context: Sources and Documents, 1984, Medicine, Miracle and Magic in New Testament Times, 1986, Knowing the Truth: A Sociological Approach to New Testament Interpretation, 1989, What Can We Know About Jesus?, 1990, Good News to the Ends of the Earth: The Theology of Acts, 1990, Christianity: A Social and Cultural History, 1991, 2d edit., 1998, Who Are the People of God? Early Christian Models of Community, 1995, To Every Nation Under Heaven: The Acts of the Apostles, 1997; editor: Biblical Perspectives on Current Issues, 1976-83, Understanding Jesus Today, 1985—; editor Cambridge UP Annotated Study Bible, 1993, Cambridge Annotated Study Apocrypha, 1994, Cambridge Companion to the Bible, 1997; librettist: New Land, New Covenant (Howard Hanson), 1976; contbr.: Interpreter's Dictionary of the Bible, 1962, supplement, 1976, Harper's Bible Dictionary, Dictionary of Bible and Religion, The Books of the Bible, Anchor Bible Dictionary. Bd. mgrs. Am. Bible Soc., 1956-89, chmn. transls. com., 1985-89; chmn. transls. com. United Bible Socs., 1985-89; bd. dirs. Mohawk Trail Concerts, Inc., Charlemont, Mass.; mem. adv. bd. Yale U. Inst. Sacred Music; exec. bd. Liberty Mus. Am. Assn. Theol. Schs. fellow Germany, 1960; Guggenheim fellow Israel, 1966-67; Nat. Endowment Humanities grantee Eng., 1984. Mem. Soc. Values in Higher Edn., Phila. Seminar on Christian Origins, Am. Acad. Religion, Soc. Bibl. Lit., Bibl. Theologians, Studiorum Novi Testamenti Societas, New Haven Theol. Discussion Group, Assn. for Sociology of Religion (pres.), Am. Interfaith Inst. Presbyterian. Home: 3300 Darby Rd Haverford PA 19041-1061 *Life is a gift from the Creator. It is mediated to us through parents, family, friends, teachers. It is conveyed through love and learning, through challenge and conflict, through accomplishment and disappointment. The gift must be shared, not jealously guarded or proudly prized. By sharing life, we can approach others with candor and honesty, with joy and sympathy, with wonder and understanding. The shared gift brings gratitude and fulfillment.*

KEE, WALTER ANDREW, former government official; b. Phila., July 12, 1914; s. Walter Leslie and Regina Veronica (Corcoran) K.; m. Genevieve O'Hair, Dec. 2, 1943; children: Kathleen, Sheila. B.S., Purdue U., 1949; M.L.S., Columbia U., 1950. Engring. and phys. sci. librarian N.Y. U., N.Y.C., 1950-51; librarian E.I. DuPont de Nemours, Savannah River Lab., Aiken, S.C., 1951-55; head library and documents sect. Martin Co., Balt., 1955-59; chief library br. AEC, Washington, 1959-74; librarian ERDA, Washington, 1975-76; asst. to dir. div. adminstrv. services ERDA, 1976-77, also Freedom of Info. and Privacy Act officer, 1975-77; dir. div. publs. mgmt. Dept. Energy, 1977-78; ret., 1978; chmn. AEC-Dept. of Def. Joint Atomic Weapon Tech. Info. Group, 1962-72. Contbr.: chpt. to Special Librarianship: A New Reader (Eugene Jackson), 1980. Asst. to chief So. Shores Fire Dept.; sec. Dare County Firemen's Assn., 1980-83; historian So. Shores Civic Assn.; legis. officer Alamance County, N.C. fedn. Nat. Assn. Ret. Fed. Employees, 1994-99; bd. dirs. Friends Alamance County Librs. Served with USNR, 1942-45. Mem. Fed. Library Com., Com. on Sci. and Tech. Info., Spl. Libraries Assn. (cons., pres. nuclear sci. divsn. and info. tech. divsn., pres. Balt. chpt.), Am. Soc. Info. Sci. Home: 1652 Wycliff Ct Burlington NC 27215-8739

KEECH, ELOWYN ANN, interior designer; b. Berrien County, Mich., Oct. 5, 1937; d. Earl Docker and Elizabeth Hall (Paullin) Stephenson; 1 child, Robert Eal Stephenson. Cert. contract interior designer. Print designer, copywriter newspaper accounts, dept stores resorts, svc. orgns., industry, 1957-75; freelance interior designer, photoset and video set designer St. Joseph, Mich., 1975—; owner Fog Horn Records & Tapes. Designer interiors 1st Fed. Savs. & Loan Assn., Three Oaks, Mich., 1975, Holland (Mich.) Ctrl. Trade Credit Union, 1978, 1st Fed. Savs. & Loan Assn., Holland, 1978, Yonker Realty Co., Holland, 1979, People's Bank of Holland, 1979, exec. offices Whirlpool Corp., 1980—, human resources St. Joe divsn., 1985, Claeys Residence, 1984, Calley Dental Office, 1985, Sarett Nature Ctr., 1985, Imperial Printing, 1986, Miller Residence, 1986, Schraders Super Market, 1986, Dave's Garage, 1987, Merritt Residence, Kalamazoo, 1987-88, Smith Residence, 1988, Emergency Shelter Svcs., 1991, Butzbach Residence, 1992, Merritt Residence, Del Mar, Calif., 1993-94, Fister Better Homes & Gardens Conf. Room, 1994, Vanderboegh Residence, 1994-96, S.W. Mich. Regional Airport, 1994—, Berrien Hills Country Club, 1995-96, Butzbach Offices, 1995, Merritt Residence, Houston, 1996, Mich. Maritime Mus., 1996, St. Paul Episcopal Ch., 1996, Bacchiocchi Residence, 1996, Internat. Trade Assn. Greater Chgo., 1997, DeVries Residence, 1997-98, others; writer weekly column on design preservation and related subjects Benton Harbor-St. Joseph Herald-Palladium. Bd. dirs., mem. steering and long-range planning coms. United Way Mich., 1980-87; bd. dirs. Blossomland United Way, 1981-86; trustee Mich. Maritime Mus., 1994-97. Mem. AIA (profl. affiliate S.W. Mich. chpt.), Nature Conservancy, Assn. Great Lakes Maritime History, Econ. Club S.W. Mich., Am. Rottweiler Club, Internat. Interior Design Assn., St. Joseph River Yacht Club, Rotary. Home and Office: 375 Ridgeway St Saint Joseph MI 49085-1062

KEECH, PAMELA, artist, curator; b. Elyria, Ohio, Sept. 21, 1947; d. Paul and Mildred Sievert. BFA, Ohio State U., 1978, MFA, 1980. Asst. prof. U. Akron, Ohio, 1989-90; cons. curator Lower E. Side Tenement Mus., N.Y.C., 1994—; sr. exhbn. preparator Am. Mus. Nat. History, N.Y.C., 1997-98; artist-in-residence The John Kohler Arts Ctr., Sheboygan, Wis., 1993, The Muse Machine, Dayton, Ohio, 1995; project dir. centennial block N.Y.C. Dept. Transp., 1998, Lower E. Side Tenement Mus., N.Y.C., 1998. One-woman shows include Broadway Windows, N.Y.C., 1992, Antioch Coll., 1995, Lower E. Side Tenement Mus., 1996, U. Conn., 1996. Recipient Rome prize in sculpture Am. Acad. Rome, 1982; fellow Nat. Endowments Arts, 1982; Rsch. fellow Am. Antiquarian Soc., 1997; Architecture and Design Rsch. grantee N.Y. State Coun. Arts, 1997. Mem. Soc. Fellows Am. Acad. Rome (v.p. 1993—, coun. mem.), Nat. Cambridge Collectors. Office: PKM Studios 451 Greenwich St New York NY 10013

KEEFE, CAROLYN JOAN, tax accountant; b. Huntington Park, Oct. 11, 1926; d. Paul Dewey and Mary Jane (Parmater) K. AA, Pasadena (Calif.) City Coll., 1947; BA, U. So. Calif., 1950. Tax acct. Shell Oil Co., L.A., 1950-71; tax acct. Shell Oil Co., Houston, 1971-91, ret., 1991. Advisor Midwest Mus. of Am. Art, 1993—; vol. Houston Mus. of Fine Arts, 1991—; vol. docent Houston Mus. of Natural Sci., 1991—, Theatre Under the Stars, 1991—, Houston Pub. TV Channel 8, Houston, 1989—; donor 2 ann. coll. scholarships in memory of Paul Dewey and Mary Jane Keefe. Mem. LWV, Inst. Mgmt. Accts. (emeritus life mem.), Desk and Derrick Club (bd. dirs. 1994-95), Houston Alumni Club of Alpha Gamma Delta, USC Houston Alumni Club. Christian Scientist. Avocation: travel. Home: 1814 Auburn Trl Sugar Land TX 77479-6333

KEEFE, DEBORAH LYNN, cardiologist, educator; b. Oklahoma City, Nov. 23, 1950; d. Stanley William and Gloria Jean (Kelsoe) Denton; m. Richard Alan Keefe, May 14, 1971; children: Jennifer, Colin, Corwin. BA, Rice U., 1973; MD, N.Y. Med. Coll., 1976; MPH, Columbia U., 1990. Diplomate Am. Bd. Internal Medicine, Am. Bd. Cardiovascular Disease, Am. Bd. Critical Care, Am. Bd. Clin. Pharmacology. Intern and resident St. Vincent's Hosp., N.Y.C., 1976-79; fellow in cardiology Stanford (Calif.) Univ. Hosp., 1979-81; dir. CCU Bronx (N.Y.) Mcpl. Hosp., 1981-87; assoc. dir. Am. Cyanamid, Pearl River, N.Y., 1987-88; assoc. mem. Sloan-Kettering Meml. Hosp., N.Y.C., 1988-94, mem., 1994—; asst. prof. medicine Albert Einstein Coll. Medicine, Bronx, 1981-87; assoc. prof. medicine Cornell U., N.Y.C., 1988-95, prof. medicine, 1995—; regent Am. Coll. Clin. Pharmacology, 1985-89, 92-96, treas., 1992-94. Assoc. editor Jour. Clin. Pharmacology, 1985-94, editor, 1994—; contbr. articles to Clin. Pharm. Therapeutics, Jour. Cardiovascular Pharmacology, Am. Jour. Cardiology. Fellow Am. Coll. Cardiology, Am. Coll. Chest Physicians, Am. Coll. Angiology; mem. Am. Bd. Clin. Pharmacology, Inc. (sec.-treas. 1994-96). Office: Sloan-Kettering Meml Hosp 1275 York Ave New York NY 10021-6094

KEEFE, JAMES WASHBURN, educational writer, researcher, consultant; b. L.A., Oct. 23, 1931; s. James E. and Leah M. (Washburn) K.; m. Jean Showalter, Dec. 6, 1980. BA Maxima Cum Laude, St. Ambrose Coll., 1953; MusB, Mt. St. Mary's Coll., 1965, MA in Edn., 1966; EdD, U. So. Calif., L.A., 1973. Cert. tchr./adminstr., Calif. Dean of studies Pius X High Sch., Downey, Calif., 1962-67, prin., 1967-75; instr. U. So. Calif., 1972-75; lectr. Loyola Marymount U., L.A., 1975-77, adj. prof. edn., 1977-78; coord. rsch. Nat. Assn. Secondary Sch. Prins., Reston, Va., 1978-80, dir. rsch., 1980-95; mem. various nat. adv. bds. including Dept. of Edn. Ctr. on Orgn. and Restructuring of Schs., NSSE Evaluative Criteria, Sizer Coalition of Essential Schs. Author: Instructional Leadership Handbook, 1984, 91, Learning Style Profile Handbook, 1989, The CASE-IMS School Improvement Process, 1991, Teaching for Thinking, 1992, Leadership in Middle Level Education, 1993, Instruction and the Learning Environment, 1996, Redesigning Schools for the New Century, 1997, A Guide to Personalized Instruction, 1999. Recipient Disting. Achievement award City of Downey, 1975, Award for Outstanding Ednl. Rsch. Calif. State U., Fullerton, 1992-93, Disting. Svc. award Nat. Cath. Edn. Assn., 1981. Mem. Learning Environments Consortium (v.p., forum coord.), Nat. Assn. Secondary Sch. Prins., Nat. Cath. Honor Soc., Phi Delta Kappa. Office: JK Cons Ltd 1419 Belcastle Ct Reston VA 20194-1245

KEEFE, KENNETH M., JR., lawyer; b. Jacksonville, Fla., Nov. 18, 1941; s. Kenneth M. and Lydia (Fleming) K.; m. Vann E. Farnell, Dec. 4, 1982; children: Kenneth M., Fleming Elizabeth. BA, U. Va., 1964, LLB, 1967. Ptnr. McGuire, Woods, Battle & Boothe, Jacksonville. Mem. ABA (real property, probate and trust law sect.), The Fla. Bar (sect. on real property, probate and trust law, Fla. condominium adv. bd. 1979-82), Jacksonville Bar Assn. Office: McGuire Woods Battle & Boothe 3300 Barnett Ctr 50 N Laura St Jacksonville FL 32202-3664*

KEEFE, WILLIAM JOSEPH, political science educator; b. Piper City, Ill., Nov. 28, 1925; s. Joseph and Elfreda (Huxtable) K.; m. Martha Maria Schroeder, Dec. 22, 1948; children: Kathryn, Robert, Nancy, Mary Jo, John. BS, Ill. State U., 1948; MA, Wayne State U., 1949; PhD, Northwestern U., 1951. Asst. prof. polit. sci. U. Ala., 1951-52; mem. faculty Chatham Coll., Pitts., 1952-68; asso. prof. Chatham Coll., 1955-61, prof., 1961-68; prof. dept. polit. sci. U. Pitts., 1968—, chmn. dept., 1968-75; Mem. adv. com. Eagleton Inst. Politics, Rutgers U., 1965—. Author: (with Morris Ogul) The American Legislative Process: Congress and the States, 9th edit., 1996, Parties, Politics and Public Policy in America, 1972, 8th edit., 1998, Congress and the American People, 1980, 3d edit., 1988, American Democracy, 3d edit., 1990; contbr. articles to profl. jours. Del. Democratic Nat. Conv., 1976. Served with USNR, 1944-46. Mem. Am. Polit. Sci. Assn. (chmn. program com. 1975—, chmn. Congl. fellowship program 1968-75, chmn. Woodrow Wilson award com. 1977, treas. 1981, trustee trust and devel. bd. 1981-85, 90-93), Pi Sigma Alpha (pres. 1998—, mem. exec. coun. 1992-96, pres.-elect 1996-98). Home: 838 7th St Oakmont PA 15139-1429 Office: U Pitts Dept Polit Sci Pittsburgh PA 15260

KEEFER, J(AMES) MICHAEL, lawyer; b. Ft. Wayne, Ind., July 16, 1947; s. James Martin and Helen Patricia (Smith) K.; m. Jan Elaine McDonald, June 3, 1972; children: Christopher, Sean, Alison. AB in Hist., U. Notre Dame, 1969, JD, 1972. Bar: Ind. 1972, U.S. Dist. Ct. (no. and so. dists.) Ind. 1972. With legal dept. Lincoln Nat. Corp., Ft. Wayne, 1972—; 2d v.p., assoc. gen. counsel Lincoln Nat. Corp. and Lincoln Nat. Life Ins. Co., Ft. Wayne, 1982-88, v.p., assoc. gen. counsel, 1988—; v.p., gen. counsel Lincoln Investment Mgmt., Inc., Ft. Wayne, 1997—. Bd. dirs. Allen County unit Am. Cancer Soc., Ft. Wayne, 1975-82, Embassy Theatre Found., 1998—, The Lincoln Mus., 1996—, Ft. Wayne-Allen County Hist. Soc., pres., 1993-95; active Ind. Bar Found. Fellow Am. Coll. Investment Counsel; mem. Ind. Bar Assn., Allen County Bar Assn. (bd. dirs., pres. 1996-97), Am. Coun. Life Ins. (various task forces), Am. Corp. Counsel Assn., Assn. Life Ins. Counsel (sec.-treas. 1994—). Roman Catholic. Home: 1130 Woodland Xing Fort Wayne IN 46825-7239 Office: Lincoln Nat Corp 200 E Berry St PO Box 1110 Fort Wayne IN 46801-1110

KEEFFE, JOHN ARTHUR, lawyer, director; b. Bklyn., Apr. 5, 1930; s. Arthur John and Mary Catherine (Daly) K.; m. Frances Elizabeth Rippetoe, July 24, 1952; children: Virginia Frances, Cynthia Louise, Amy Marie. AB, Cornell U., 1950; JD, U. Va., 1953. Bar: Va. 1953, N.Y. 1956. Asst. U.S. atty. so. dist. State of N.Y., 1955-57; assoc. Rogers, Hoge & Hills, N.Y., 1957-63; of counsel Havens, Wandless, Stitt & Tighe, N.Y., 1963-65; ptnr. Keeffe & Costikyan, N.Y.C. and Washington, 1965-74, Keeffe Bros., N.Y.C. and Washington, 1974-77; sec., mng. dir. Saud Al-Farhan Inc., N.Y.C., 1979-80; pres., dir. J.A. Keeffe, P.C., Eastchester, N.Y., 1981—. Bd. dirs., sec. The Street Theater, White Plains, N.Y., 1973—. 1st lt. USAF, 1953-55. Mem. ABA, ATLA, N.Y. State Bar Assn., Va. Bar Assn., Westchester County Bar Assn. (dir. 1989-90, chmn. com. on fed. courthouse plans and procedures 1994—), N.Y. State Trial Lawyers Assn., Eastchester Bar Assn. (v.p. 1988-89, pres. 1989-90, dir. 1990—), Rotary (bd. dirs. 1991—, sec. 1991-92, pres.-elect 1992-93, pres. 1993-94, co-chair Eastchester Rotary Gift of Life 1993-94, co-chair dist. 7230 Gift of Life 1995-97). Republican. Congregationalist. Avocations: golf, reading. Home: 2 Longview Dr Eastchester NY 10709-1425 Office: 700 White Plains Rd Ste 246 Scarsdale NY 10583-5013

KEEGAN, JANE ANN, insurance executive, consultant; b. Watertown, N.Y., Sept. 1, 1950; d. Richard Isidor and Kathleen (McKinley) K. BA cum laude, SUNY-Potsdam, 1972; MBA in Risk Mgmt., Golden Gate U., 1986. CPCU. Comml. lines mgr. Lithgow & Rayhill, San Francisco, 1977-80; risk mgmt. account coordinator Dinner Levison Co., San Francisco, 1980-83; ins. cons., San Francisco, 1983-84; account mgr. Rollins Burdick Hunter, San Francisco, 1984-85; account exec. Jardine Ins. Brokers, San Francisco, 1985-86; ins. cons., San Francisco, 1986-87, ins. adminstr. Port of Oakland, 1987—, risk mgr., 1989—, mgr. accts. payable, 1996—. Vol. San Francisco Ballet vol. orgn., 1981-96, Bay Area Bus., Govt. ARC disaster conf. steering com., 1987-88, 89, 90, 91-92; mem. Nob Hill Neighbors Assn., 1982—, City of Oakland Emergency Mgmt. Bd., 1990—. Mem. Nat. Safety Mgmt. Soc., CPCU Soc. (spl. events chairperson 1982-84, continuing profl. devel. program award 1985, 88, chair loss prevention), Calif. Assn. of Port Authorities (ins. chair 1998—), Risk and Ins. Mgr. Soc. (dep., sec. 1990—, dir. legis. 1993, dir. conf.). Democrat. Roman Catholic. Home: 1065 Las Gallinas Ave San Rafael CA 94903-2464

KEEGAN, JOHN E., lawyer; b. Spokane, Wash., Apr. 29, 1943. BA, Gonzaga U., 1965; LLB, Harvard U., 1968. Bar: Wash. 1968, U.S. Ct. Appeals (9th cir.) 1976, U.S. Supreme Ct. Gen. counsel Dept. Housing and Urban Devel., Washington, 1968-70; instr. in bus. sch. and inst. environ. studies U. Wash., 1973-76, instr. land use and environ. law, 1976-78; now ptnr. Davis, Wright & Tremaine, Seattle. Office: Davis Wright Tremaine 2600 Century Sq 1501 4th Ave Ste 2600 Seattle WA 98101-1688

KEEGAN, KENNETH DONALD, financial consultant, retired oil company executive; b. Buffalo, N.Y., Apr. 29, 1927; s. Walter James and Lillian Frances K.; m. Elizabeth Lillian Peyer, Dec. 17, 1955; children: K. Brian, Karen Lynn. B.S. in Fgn. Service, Georgetown U., 1947; M.B.A., N.Y. U., 1964. Mgr. fin. Texaco Inc., N.Y.C., 1966-68; dir. fin. Texaco Services (Europe) Ltd., Brussels, Belgium, 1968-80; v.p., treas. Texaco Can., Inc., Don Mills, Ont., 1980-87; pvt. practice-internat. trade, mktg. and fin. cons., 1990—; dir. Oilship Ltd., 1980-87. Mem. World Trade Ctr. Assn. Orange County. Republican. Roman Catholic.

KEEGAN, LEO MARTIN, plastic surgeon, educator; b. N.Y.C., Sept. 9, 1959; s. Leo Martin and Joan Agnes (Dillon) K.; m. Nadine Jennifer Mandell, Sept. 9, 1987; children: Dylan, Phoebe, Leo Martin III. BS in Biology, SUNY, Stony Brook, 1981; MD, Mt. Sinai Sch. Medicine, 1986. Diplomate Am. Bd. Plastic Surgery. Pvt. practice, N.Y.C.; asst. clin. prof. plastic surgery Mt. Sinai Sch. Medicine, N.Y.C., 1994—; chief plastic surgery Bronx (N.Y.) VA Med. Ctr., 1994—; attending plastic surgeon Mt. Sinai Med. Ctr., 1994—, Beth Israel Hosp., N.Y.C., 1994—, Englewood (N.J.) Hosp., 1998—. Contbr. articles to med. jours.; patent for wound protection device. Fellow ACS; mem. Am. Soc. Plastic and Reconstructive Surgery, Aesthetic Soc. Plastic Surgeons, Northeastern Soc. Plastic Surgeons, N.Y. RSPS. Avocations: skiing, golf, reading. Office: Fifth Ave Millennium Ptnrs 1125 Fifth Ave New York NY 10128

KEEGAN, LISA GRAHAM, state education agency adminstrator; m. John Keegan; 5 children. BS in Linguistics, Stanford U.; MS in Comm. Disorders, Ariz. State U. Mem. Ariz. Ho. of Reps., 1991-95, chair edn. com., joint legis. budget com., 1993-94; state supt. of pub. instrn. Dept. of Edn., State of Ariz., Phoenix, 1994—; founder Edn. Leaders Coun. Office: Edn Dept Supt of Pub Instrn 1535 W Jefferson Phoenix AZ 85007

KEEGAN, RICHARD JOHN, advertising agency executive; b. New Haven, May 10, 1924; s. Richard Joseph and Katherine Veronica (Shea) K.; m. Joan Elizabeth Noden, Oct. 17, 1953; children—Stephen J., Janet C. Student, Pomona Coll., 1943-44; B.A., Cornell U., 1949; postgrad., Harvard Bus. Sch., 1974. Product mgr. Vick Chem. Co., N.Y.C., 1949-52; account supr. Sherman Marquette Advt. Agy., N.Y.C., 1952-54; sr. v.p. Bryan Houston, Inc., N.Y.C., 1954-60; v.p. Young & Rubicam Inc. Advt. Agy., N.Y.C., 1960-70; sr. v.p., dep. dir. Needham Harper & Steers Inc., N.Y.C., 1970-76; group sr. v.p., dir. Doyle Dane Bernbach Advt. Inc., N.Y.C., 1976-83; exec. v.p. Posey & Quest Inc., 1983-86; pres. Kee Assocs. Inc., 1986—; cons. Magic Mountain, Vt., Pan-Am Satellite, Westminster Bakery Co. Chmn. United Way Drive; rep. Greenwich Town Govt.; trustee, lifetime mem. alumni coun., athletic adv. bd. Cornell U.; pres. Cornell Assn. Class Officer; nat. election pollster. 1st lt. U.S. Army, 1943-46. Decorated Purple Heart, Silver Star. Mem. Am. Assn. Advt. Agys., Proprietary Assn. U.S., Cornell Club (v.p. Fairfield Country), Stanwich Club. Republican. Roman Catholic. Home and Office: 179 N Maple Ave Greenwich CT 06830-4707

KEEGAN, WARREN JOSEPH, business educator, consultant; b. Junction City, Kans., Oct. 19, 1936; s. Donald Rayfield and Edna Segrid (Polson) K.; m. Maryann Bergin, June 17, 1961 (div. July 1975); children: Donald, Mark, Tracy. BS, Kans. State U., 1958, MS, 1959; MBA, Harvard U., 1961, DBA, 1967. Assoc. prof. Columbia Bus. Sch., N.Y.C., 1967-74, Baruch Coll., N.Y.C., 1974-76; prof. George Washington U., Washington, 1976-80, Pace U., N.Y.C., 1982—; vis. prof. NYU, 1980-82; dir. The Cooper Cos., N.Y.C. Author: Global Marketing Management, 6th edit., 1999, Marketing, 2d edit., 1995, Principles in Global Marketing, 1997, Marketing Plans That Work, 1997. Fellow Acad. Internat. Bus.; mem. Am. Mktg. Assn. (v.p.). Presbyterian. Avocations: tennis, running, motorcycle riding, skiing. Home: 210 Stuyvesant Ave Rye NY 10580-3115 Office: Pace U 1 Martine Ave White Plains NY 10606-1932

KEEHN, SILAS, retired bank executive; b. New Rochelle, N.Y., June 30, 1930; s. Grant and Marjorie (Burchard) K.; m. Marcia June Lindquist, Mar. 26, 1955; children: Elisabeth Keehn Lewis, Britta Keehn Scott, Peter. A.B. in Econs, Hamilton Coll., Clinton, N.Y., 1952; M.B.A. in Fin, Harvard U., 1957. With Mellon Bank N.A., Pitts., 1957-80; v.p., then sr. v.p. Mellon Bank N.A., 1967-78, exec. v.p., 1978-79, vice chmn., 1980; v.p. Mellon Nat. Corp., 1979-80, vice chmn., 1980; chmn. bd. Pullman, Inc., Chgo., 1980; pres. Fed. Res. Bank Chgo., 1981-94; ret., 1994; bd. dirs. ABN AMRO Bank, N.V., Amsterdam, ABN AMRO Holding, N.V., Amsterdam, Nat. Futures Assn., CORE Cap, Inc., Chgo. Bd. Options Exch., Inc., mpct Solutions Corp., TEPCO Resources, Inc. Trustee Rush-Presbyn.-St. Luke's Med. Ctr., Hamilton Coll., Clinton, N.Y. With USNR, 1953-56. Mem. Chgo. Club, Comml. Club Chgo., Econ. Club Chgo., Fox Chapel Golf Club, U. Club, Links Club (N.Y.C.), Rolling Rock Club (Ligonier, Pa.), Indian Hill Club. Office: 707 Skokie Blvd Ste 600 Northbrook IL 60062-2841

KEEHNER, MICHAEL ARTHUR MILLER, investment bank executive; b. Cedar Rapids, Iowa, Nov. 15, 1943. BS in Nuclear Physics, MIT, 1965; MBA in Fin. with high distinction, Harvard U., 1971. Registered securities rep. Engring. mgr. Gen. Dynamics Corp., Quincy, Mass., 1965-69; investment banking mgr. Kidder Peabody & Co., 1971-89; exec. mng. dir. individual investor svcs. Kidder Peabody & Co., N.Y.C., 1991-94; pres., chief exec. officer K P Exploration, Inc., N.Y.C., 1982-88; mng. dir., mem. exec. com., bd. mem. Kidder Peabody Group, Inc., N.Y.C., 1987-94; chmn., dir. Internat. Affil. Kidder Peabody Internat. Corp., N.Y.C., 1989-91; mng. ptnr. The Keehner Group, LLC, N.Y.C., 1994—; bd. dirs. Cross Border LLC, Internat. Software Fin. Corp., Inc., LDMI Long Distance, Inc. Trustee Bklyn. Mus. Baker scholar Harvard U.; Loeb Rhodes fellow Harvard U. Mem. Point O'Woods Club (N.Y.), India House (N.Y.C.), Heights Casino, Rembrandt Club (Bklyn.), Long Island Wyandanch Club (N.Y.).

KEEL, ALTON GOLD, JR., ambassador; b. Newport News, Va., Sept. 8, 1943; s. Alton Gold and Ella Clare (Kennedy) K.; 1 child, Kristen Ann. BS in Aerospace Engring., U. Va., 1966, PhD in Engring. Physics, 1970; postdoctoral scholar, U. Calif., Berkeley, 1971. Staff Naval Surface Weapons Ctr., Silver Springs, Md., 1971-77; congl. sci. fellow Senate Armed Services Com., Washington, 1977-79, staff mem., 1977-81; asst. sec. for research, devel. and logistics USAF, Washington, 1981-82; assoc. dir., nat. sec. internat. affairs Office Mgmt. and Budget, Washington, 1982-86; exec. dir. Pres.' Commn. on Challenger Accident, Washington, 1986; acting asst. to pres. for nat. security affairs The White House, Washington, 1986; U.S. permanent rep. NATO, Brussels, 1987-89; dep. chmn. The Riggs Nat. Bank, Washington, 1989-92; pres., mng. dir. Carlyle Internat. The Carlyle Group, Washington, 1992-94; chmn. Carlyle SEAG, 1994-95; chmn., mng. dir. Atlantic Ptnrs., L.L.C., Washington, 1992—; chmn. F-16 fighter aircraft multinat. steering com.; nat. del., bd. dirs. Adv. Group for Aerospace R & D, 1982. Bd. dirs. Fondation pour la Promotion de la Recherche Fundamentale en Cancerologie, Belgium, 1988; mem. dean's adv. bd. U. Va., 1996—. Recipient research award NRC, 1970; Nat. Congl. Sci. fellow AIAA, 1976; recipient Young Engr.-Scientist award AIAA, 1978, Air Force Exceptional Civilian Service award, 1982, NASA Group Achievement award, 1986, Disting. Alumni award U. Va., 1988. Fellow AIAA (assoc., ground testing and simulation tech. com.), Sigma Xi; mem. French Am. C. of C. (mem. sr. adv. group 1990—), Belgian Am. Assn. (bd. dirs. 1990—), Phi Eta Sigma, Tau Beta Pi. Office: Atlantic Ptnrs PO Box 12206 Arlington VA 22219-2206

KEELAN, HUGH, music director; b. London. Grad., Cambridge U. Condr. Essex Youth Orch., Eng.; music dir. Northeastern Pa. Philharmonic; guest condr. St. Louis Symphony, orchs. in Eng., the Netherlands, Venice, Belgium, Can. Condr. recording with New Zealand Symphony Orch. Active Philharmonic's TEAM project. Harkness fellow, coaching and conducting fellow Julliard's Am. Opera Ctr. Office: Northeastern Pa Philharm Warm Bldg PO Box 71 Avoca PA 18641

KEELE, ALAN FRANK, adult education educator; b. Provo, Utah, Nov. 17, 1942; s. Frank Alonzo and Lasca Taft (Smith) K.; m. Linda Kay Sellers, Jan. 29, 1966; children: Kamron, Heather, Kristopher, Brandon, Celeste, Jeremy. Student, U. Utah, 1960-61; BA, Brigham Young U., 1967; PhD, Princeton U., 1971. Prof. Brigham Young U., Provo, 1971—. Author: Paul Schallück, 1972, The Apocalyptic Vision, 1982, Understanding Günter Grass, 1990, When Truth was Treason, 1996. Democrat. Mem. LDS Ch. Avocations: back country skiing, biking, sailing. Office: Brigham Young U 4096 JKHB Provo UT 84602

KEELE, LYNDON ALAN, electronics company executive; b. Clyde, Tex., Nov. 3, 1928; s. Theadore Fannin and Zada (Sikes) K.; B.B.A., U. Tex., 1951; m. Muriel Alice Murphy, June 1, 1968; children—Carolyn Chase, Tiffany Ames. With York div. Borg-Warner Co., York, Pa., 1953-58, asst. gen. plant mgr., 1956-58; program mgr. Sylvania Elec. System div. Gen. Telephone & Electronics Co., Needham, Mass., 1958-62; program mgr. ITT Fed. Labs., Nutley, N.J., 1962-68; exec. v.p. TeleScis., Inc., Moorestown, N.J., 1968-73; chmn. Sci. Dynamics Corp., Cherry Hill, N.J., 1973—. Served with AUS, 1946-47, USAAF, 1951-53. Mem. IEEE. Club: Riverton Country. Office: Sci Dynamics Corp 1919 Springdale Rd Cherry Hill NJ 08003-1603

KEELER, JAMES LEONARD, food products company executive; b. Richmond, Va., Jan. 31, 1935; s. Joseph McCauley and Nora Elizabeth (Thomas) K.; m. Joan Sandra Barnhart, Aug. 14, 1954; children: Mark Leonard, Tracy Ann, Steven James, Gregory Wayne. BS, Bridgewater Coll., 1957; JD, U. Va., 1983. Bar: Va. 1983; CPA, Va. Ptnr., acct. Hueston & Keeler, CPAs, Harrisonburg, Va., 1958-63; mng. ptnr., acct. Keeler, Phibbs & Co., CPAs, Harrisonburg, 1963-80; ptnr., atty. Wharton, Aldhizer & Weaver, Harrisonburg, 1983-88; chief exec. officer WLR Foods, Inc., Broadway, Va., 1988—, pres., 1990—; pres. Wampler Foods, Inc., Broadway, 1997—. Vice chmn. Bridgewater (Va.) Coll., 1974-91, mem. exec. com., trustee, 1974—; exec. adv. coun. James Madison U. Coll. Bus., Harrisonburg, 1989-95; bd. dirs. Valley of Va. Partnership for Edn., James Madison U., Rockingham Meml. Hosp., 1994-98, Va. Econ. Devel. Partnership, 1995—; mem. Va. Bus. Coun., 1995—; mem. Gov.'s Adv. Com. on Va.'s Strategy, 1998. Recipient disting. alumnus award Bridgewater Coll., 1990; named outstanding bus. person award Harrisonburg-Rockingham C. of C., 1995. Fellow Va. Soc. CPAs (pres. 1970-71, Outstanding Mem. 1977); mem. ABA, AICPA (governing coun. 1969-70, 74-75, 76-77), Va. Bar Assn., Va. C. of C. (vice chmn. 1994-96, chmn. 1997-98, exec. com., bd. dirs. 1994-98). Republican. Mem. Brethren Ch. Avocation: boating. Office: WLR Foods Inc PO Box 7000 Broadway VA 22815-7000

KEELER, LYNNE LIVINGSTON MILLS, psychologist, educator, consultant; b. Detroit, Sept. 18, 1934; d. Robert Livingston Mills Staples and Lyda Charlotte (Diehr) Staples; m. Lee Edward Burmeister, July 16, 1955 (div. 1982); children: Benjamin Lee, Lynne Ann; m. Robert Gordon Keeler, Oct. 26, 1986. BS, Ctrl. Mich. U., 1957; MA, U. Mich., 1965; student, Marygrove Coll., Cen. Mich. U., 1971-74. Ltd. lic. psychologist, sch. psychologist; cert. social worker, elem. permanent cons. and tchr. for mentally handicapped. First grade tchr. Shepherd (Mich) Schs., 1957-59; tchr. Kingston (Mich.) Schs., 1959-65; tchr. educationally handicapped Rialto (Calif.) Unified Sch. Dist., 1965-66; tchr., cons. Tuscola Int. Sch. Dist., Caro, Mich., 1966-71; sch. psychologist Huron Int. Sch. Dist., Bad Axe, Mich., 1971-74, Tuscola Int. Sch. Dist., Caro, 1974-89; instr. Delta Coll., University Center, Mich., 1976-88; tchr. spl. day classes Victorville (Calif.) High Sch., 1989; sch. psychologist Bedford (Ind.) Schs., 1990-91; clin. psychologist ACT team and outpatient therapy Sanilac County Mental Health Svcs., Sandusky, Mich., 1991—; cons. sch. psychologist Marlette (Mich.) Schs., 1982-86, Bartholomew Pub. Schs., Columbus, Ind., 1989, Johnson County Schs., Franklin, Ind., 1990; clin. psychologist Thumb Family Counseling, Caro, 1985-88; personnel com. Team One Credit Union, 1993. Conf. presenter in field. Del. NEA-Mich. Edn. Assn. Rep. Assemblies, 1970-89; pres., auction chmn. Altruesa Club, Marlette, 1982-88; style show chmn. Marlette Band Boosters, 1983; mem. exec. bd. Lawrence County Tchrs. Assn., Bedford, 1991; mem. Sanilac Symphonic Band, 1993-94; bd. dirs. Team One Credit Union, 1994-99, Vassar City Band, 1998. Fed. govt. grantee Wayne State U., 1968. Mem. Am. Federated State and Mcpl. Employees (chairperson #219 1993, chairperson #15 chpt. 1993-96), Ind. State Tchrs. Assn. (rep. assembly del. 1991), Mich. Edn. Assn. (sec. exec. bd. 1997—), Ind. Assn. Sch. Psychologists (pub. rels. bd. 1990-91), Lions (bd. dirs. 1996—, 2d v.p. 1999), Emmaus Reunion Group. Democrat. Methodist. Avocations: antiques, swimming, gardening, pets, traveling. Home: 6726 Clothier Rd Clifford MI 48727-9501 Office: Sanilac County Cmty Mental Health 120 E Sanilac Rd Ste #1 Sandusky MI 48471-1009

KEELER, WILLIAM HENRY, cardinal; b. San Antonio, Mar. 4, 1931; s. Thomas Love and Margaret T. (Conway) K. BA, St. Charles Sem., Phila., 1952; STL, Pontifical Gregorian U., Rome, 1956, JCD, 1961; DD (hon.), Lebanon Valley Coll, Pa., 1984, Gettysburg Coll., 1986, Susquehanna U., 1989; LHD (hon.), Mt. St. Mary's Coll., 1985; LLD (hon.), Gannon U., 1993; LHD (hon.), Loyola Coll. Balt., 1995, Shippensburg State U., 1995; DD (hon.), St. Mary's Coll., Winona, Minn., 1995, Elizabeth Coll., 1996, Western Coll., 1996, St. Vincent Sem., 1996, Coll. of Notre Dame of Md., 1997, U. Notre Dame, 1998, Ateneo de Manila U., 1998. Ordained priest Roman Catholic Ch., 1955, consecrated bishop, 1979. Sec. diocesan tribunal Diocese of Harrisburg, Pa., 1956-58, defender of the bond, 1961-66, vice-chancellor, 1965-69, chancellor, 1969-79, aux. bishop and vicar gen., 1979-83, bishop of Harrisburg, 1984-89; archbishop of Balt., 1989-94, cardinal, 1994—; chmn. Md. Cath. Conf., 1989—; co-chmn. Pa. Conf. Inter-Ch. Coop., 1981-89; pres. Pa. Cath. Conf., 1983-89; chmn. com. on ecumenical and inter-religious affairs Nat. Conf. Cath. Bishops, 1984-87, mem., 1987—, Episcopal moderator for Cath.-Jewish Rels., 1988-92, 95—, sec., 1988-89, v.p., 1989-92, pres., 1992-95; mem. Internat. Joint Com. for Cath.-Orthodox Theol. Dialogue, 1986—; apptd. Synod of Bishops Coun., 1997. Mem. Interreligious Forum Greater Harrisburg, 1968-89; mem. exec. bd. Keystone Area coun. Boy Scouts Am., 1979-89; mem. Pontifioal coun. Promoting Christian Unity, 1994—; mem. Congregation for the Oriental Chs., 1994—; mem. Coun. for Assembly of Synod Bishops, 1997—. Recipient Gold medal Pope John XXIII, 1961, John Baum Humanitarian award Dauphin County unit Am. Cancer Soc., 1984, Anti-Defamation League Americanism award, 1985, De Tocqueville Soc. award, 1988, Weil Medallion, Jewish Chataqua soc., 1993, award Salvation Army, 1995, Shaw award Rotary Internat., 1995, Mahmoud Abu Sand Excellence award Am. Muslim Coun., 1995; named papal chamberlain Pope Paul VI, 1965; prelate of honor Pope Paul VI, 1970. Mem. Canon Law Soc. Am., Am. Cath. Hist. Soc.

KEELEY, ETHEL S., secondary education program director; b. Dickinson, N.D., Jan. 2, 1946; d. Clarence and Pauline (Heck) Schmitz; m. Ronald P. Keeley, July 18, 1970; children: Patrick, Ryan, Janine. BEd, Dickinson State U., 1969; MS, No. State U., 1980. Nat. field rep. Alpha Sigma Alpha, Springfield, Mo., 1969-70; instr. English Bismarck (N.D.) Pub. Schs., 1971-94, spl. projects coord., 1994—; prin. Keeley Cons., Bismarck, 1994—; mem. N.D. Tech. Prep. Adv. Coun., Bismarck, 1994—; mem. N.D. Workforce Devel.Coun., 1997—. Author: 10 Steps to Writing a Research Paper, 1990; co-author: Essay Writing, 1995. Active, officer Bismarck Socer Boosters. Recipient Educator award Greater N.D. Assn.; named Tchr. of yr. Bismarck-Mandan C. of C., 1995. Mem. Assn. for Supervision and Curriculum Devel., Am. Vocat. Assn., Phi Delta Kappa. Avocations: reading, music, golf. Home: 97 Country Club Dr Bismarck ND 58501-9374 Office: Bismarack Pub Schs 800 N 8th St Bismarck ND 58501-3929

KEELEY, IRENE PATRICIA MURPHY, federal judge; b. 1944. BA, Coll. Notre Dame, 1965; MA, W.Va. U., 1977, JD, 1980. Bar: W. Va., 1980. Atty. Steptoe & Johnson, Clarksburg, W.Va., 1980-92; dist. judge U.S. Dist. Ct. (no. dist.), W. Va., 1992—; adj. prof. law W.Va. U., 1990-91; bd. dirs. W.Va. U. Alumni Assn., 1995—, 1st v.p., 1997-98; mem. bd. advisors W.Va. U. Vis. com. W.Va. U. Coll. Law, 1987-91, 94-98; chmn. adv. bd. W.Va. U., 1997-98. Mem. ABA, Nat. Conf. Fed. Trial Judges (exec. com. 1996—,), W.Va. State Bar, W.Va. Bar Assn., Harrison County Bar Assn., Clarksburg Country Club, Oral Lake Fishing Club, Immaculate Conception Roman Cath. Ch. Office: US Courthouse PO Box 2808 500 W Pike St Rm 202 Clarksburg WV 26302-2808

KEELEY, ROBERT VOSSLER, retired academic administrator, retired ambassador; b. Beirut, Sept. 4, 1929; s. James Hugh and Mathilde Julia (Vossler) K.; m. Louise Schoonmaker, June 23, 1951; children: Michal M., Christopher J. A.B., Princeton U., 1951, postgrad., 1951-53; postgrad. (Princeton fellow in pub. affairs), 1970-71; postgrad. (Nat. Inst. Pub. Affairs fellow), Stanford U., 1965-66. With Fgn. Service, Dept. State, Washington, 1956-89; officer in charge Congo (Leopoldville) external affairs Washington, 1963-64; officer-in-charge Congo (Brazzaville), Rwanda and Burundi affairs, 1964-65; polit. officer Athens, Greece, 1966-70; detailed Woodrow Wilson fellow Princeton U., 1970; dep. chief mission Kampala, Uganda, 1971-73; alt. dir. E. African affairs Washington, 1974; dep. chief mission Phnom Penh, Khmer Republic, 1974-75; dep. dir. Interagency Task Force for Indochina Refugees, 1975-76; ambassador Mauritius, 1976-78; dep. asst. sec. for African Affairs Dept. State, Washington, 1978-80; ambassador to Zimbabwe, 1980-84; sr. fellow Ctr. for Study Fgn. Affairs, Fgn. Service Inst., Washington, 1984-85; ambassador to Greece, 1985-89; pres. Middle East Inst., Washington, 1990-95; writer, lectr., cons. Pub. Five and Ten Press, 1995—. Bd. mem. Middle East Inst. Lt. (j.g.) USCGR, 1953-55. Mem. Am. Fgn. Svc. Assn., Washington Inst. Fgn. Affairs, Am. Acad. Diplomacy, Cosmos Club. Home: 3814 Livingston St NW Washington DC 20015-2803

KEELING, JOE KEITH, religion educator, college official and dean; b. Muskogee, Okla., Apr. 21, 1936; s. William Lytle and Anna Madge (Watts) K.; m. Marjorie Ann Brotherton, 1957; children: Kara Kay, William Kent. BA in History, Northeastern State U., 1958; BD in Theology, So. Meth. U., 1962; MA in Theology, U. Chgo., 1967, PhD, 1974. Ordained to ministry United Meth. Ch., 1962. Dir. orientation, acad. advisor U. Chgo., 1964-68; asst. prof. religion Augustana Coll., Sioux Falls, S.D., 1968-72; from asst. to assoc. prof. philosophy and religion Rockford (Ill.) Coll., 1972-86, dean of spl. acad. programming, assoc. dean of coll., 1981-86; adj. assoc. prof. dept. medicine U. Ill. Coll of Medicine at Rockford, 1984-86; provost, dean, prof. religion and philosophy Baker U., Baldwin City, Kans., 1986-96; v.p., dean Ctrl. Meth. Coll., Fayette, Mo., 1996—; mem. bd. ordained ministry Kans. Ea. Conf. United Meth. Ch., 1987-96; cons., evaluator, mem. accreditation rev. coun. North Ctrl. Assn. Colls. and Schs., Am. Conf. Acad. Deans, Midwest Bioethics Ctr. Author and lectr. in field. Mem. Kansas City Regional Coun. Higher Edn., 1986-94; mem. instnl. rev. com. Swedish-Am. Hosp., Rockford, 1981-86. Mem. Am. Acad. Religion (v.p., program chmn. Midwest region 1981-82, pres. 1982-83), Rockford C. of C. (bd. dirs. 1983-86), AAUP (Ill. state coun. mem. 1979-81), Archael. Inst. Am. (bd. dirs. Rockford chpt. 1984-86), Rotary. Democrat. Avocations: fishing, camping, canoeing. Home: PO Box 429 878 Highway 5 And 240 Fayette MO 65248-9509 Office: Ctrl Meth Coll Office of Vice Pres 411 Central Methodist Sq Fayette MO 65248-1129

KEELING, KARA KAY, English literature educator; b. Oct. 31, 1961. BA, Carleton Coll., Northfield, Minn., 1983; MA, Purdue U., 1985; PhD, Ind. U., 1993. Assoc. prof. English, Christopher Newport U., Newport News, Va., 1993—. Home: 2 Winder Crescent Newport News VA 23606

KEELING, LARRY DALE, journalist; b. Anderson County, Ky., May 5, 1947; s. Elmer Pascal and Ida Elizabeth (Gregory) K.; m. Cynthia Maria Taylor, Nov. 28, 1987. BA, U. Ky., 1969. Reporter Henry County Jour., Bassett, Va., 1972, Martinsville (Va.) Bull., 1972-74, Bradenton (Fla.) Herald, 1974-75, Lexington (Ky.) Herald, 1975-79; editl. writer Lexington Herald-Leader, 1979—. 1st lt. USAF, 1969-72, Taiwan. Recipient Sigma Delta Chi award for editl. writing, 1993, Nat. Headliner award for editl. writing, 1994, Green Eyeshade award for editl. writing, 1995, 97, spl. citation for opinion Nat. Awards for Edn. Reporting, 1997; fellow Knight Ctr. for Specialized Journalism, 1997. Mem. Soc. Profl. Journalists (Bluegrass chpt.), Nat. Conf. Editorial Writers. Office: Lexington Herald-Leader 100 Midland Ave Lexington KY 40508-1999

KEELY, GEORGE CLAYTON, lawyer; b. Denver, Feb. 28, 1926; s. Thomas and Margaret (Clayton) K.; m. Jane Elisabeth Coffey, Nov. 18, 1950; children: Margaret Clayton, George C. (dec.), Mary Anne, Jane Elisabeth, Edward Francis, Kendall Anne. *Wife, Jane Keely, investor, BA Wellesley, MA Columbia University. Daughter, Margaret Stannard, BA, MA, EdD, CCC-SLP, business/education consultant. Husband, Daniel. Residence, Denver, Colorado. Daughter, Mary Keely, BA, MA, CPA. Children: Elisa, Angelo and Lia Marie. Residence, Austin, Texas. Daughter, Elisabeth Wilson, BA, artist and sculptor. Husband, Gregory. Children: Gregory Jr. and Bradley. Residence, Danville, California. Son, Edward Keely, BA, CFA, vice president and portfolio manager of Janus Funds. Wife, Diane. Daughter, Makenzie. Son, Charles Edward. Residence, Castle Pines, Colorado. Daughter, Kendall Picardi, BA, paralegal/office manager. Husband, Steve. Son, Chris. Residence, Arvada, Colorado.* BS in Bus, U. Colo., 1948; LLB, Columbia U., 1951. Bar: Colo. 1951. Assoc. Fairfield & Woods, Denver, 1951-58, ptnr., 1958-86, sr. dir., 1986-90, of counsel, 1990-91, ret., 1991; v.p. Silver Corp., 1966-86; mem. exec. com. Timpte Industries, Inc., 1970-78, dir., 1980-89. Mem. Colo. Commn. Promotion Uniform State Laws, 1967—; regional planning adv. com. Denver Regional Coun. Govts., 1972-74; bd. dirs. Bow Mar Water and Sanitation Dist., 1970-74; trustee

Town of Bow Mar, 1972-74; trustee, v.p. Silver Found., 1970-90, mem. bd., 1983-90; trustee, v.p. Denver Area coun. Boy Scouts Am., 1985-90; bd. dirs. Pub. Broadcasting of Colo., Inc., 1986-90, Sta. KCFR. With USAF, 1944-47. Fellow Am. Bar Found., Colo. Bar Found.; mem. ABA (ho. of dels. 1977-79), Denver Bar Assn. (award of merit 1980), Colo. Bar Assn., Nat. Conf. Commrs. Uniform State Laws (sec. 1971-75, exec. com. 1971-79, chmn. exec. com. 1975-77, pres. 1977-79, co-chmn. com. U.S.-Can. Transboundary Pollution Reciprocal Access Act 1979-82, chmn. com. Determination of Death Act 1979-80), Am. Law Inst., Cath. Lawyers Guild of Denver (dir. 1965-67), Denver Estate Planning Coun., U. Club of Denver, (dir. 1966-75, pres. 1973-74), Law Club of Denver (pres. 1966-67, Lifetime Achievement award, 1994), Pinehurst Country Club, Hundred Club, Cactus Club, Rotary, Phi Delta Phi, Beta Theta Pi, Beta Gamma Sigma. Home: 5220 W Longhorn St Littleton CO 80123-1408

KEEM, MICHAEL DENNIS, veterinarian; b. Buffalo, July 29, 1950; s. Sanford Joseph and Clara C. (Chmiel) K.; m. Mary Beth Fix, June 1, 1973 (div. 1993); children: Chelsey, Erin, Daniel, Ryan. BS, Niagara U., 1972; MS, U. Wyo., 1974; DVM, Cornell U., 1979. Assoc. veterinarian Spink Vet. Assn., Attica, N.Y., 1979-80; assoc. veterinarian Cheektowaga (N.Y.) Vet. Hosp., 1980-1984, vet., owner, pres., 1985—; vet., owner, pres. Amclare Vet. Hosp., P.C., Williamsville, N.Y., 1987—; ptnr. Greater Buffalo Vet. Emergency Svcs., P.C., 1985—, also bd. dirs. Com. chmn. pack 601 Boy Scouts Am., 1989-91, Webelos den leader, 1991-92, asst. scoutmaster troop 601, 1992-96, com. mem. 1996—. Mem. AVMA, Animal Birth Control Soc. (bd. dirs. 1981—), N.Y. State Vet. Med. Soc., Am. Animal Hosp. Assn., Western N.Y. Vet. Med. Assn. (pres. 1989, bd. dirs. 1991-94), Niagara Frontier Vet. Soc. (bd. dirs. 1986-96), Buffalo Acad. Vet. Medicine (sgt.-at-arms 1995-96, sec./treas. 1996-97, v.p. 1997-98, pres. 1998-99), Phi Kappa Phi, Phi Zeta, Omega Tau Sigma. Republican. Roman Catholic. Office: Cheektowaga Vet Hosp PC 957 Dick Rd Buffalo NY 14225-3554 also: Amclare Vet Hosp PC 895 Hopkins Rd Williamsville NY 14221-1728

KEEN, CHARLOTTE ELIZABETH, marine geophysicist, researcher; b. Halifax, N.S., Can., June 22, 1943; d. Murray Alexander and Elizabeth Randell (Cobb) Davidson; m. Michael J. Keen, May 11, 1963 (div.). B.Sc. with 1st class honors, Dalhousie U., Halifax, 1964, M.Sc. with 1st class honors, 1966; Ph.D., Cambridge U., (Eng.), 1970. Research scientist Atlantic Oceanographic Lab., Energy, Mines, Resources, Dartmouth, N.S., 1970-74, Geol. Survey of Can., Atlantic Geosci. Centre, Dartmouth, 1972—; chmn. Can. Nat. Com. Lithosphere; mem. Can. Nat. Com. Internat. Union Geol. Scis., Geodesy and Geophysics, Iternat. Commn. Marine Geology. Contbr. articles to sci. jours. Recipient Young Scientist medal Atlantic Provinces Inter-Univ. Commn. Sci., 1977. Fellow Royal Soc. Can., Geol. Soc. Can. (Past Pres.'s medal 1979, Keen medal 1993), Geol. Soc. Am. (Woolard award 1994), Can. Soc. Exploration Geophys. (hon.), Am. Geophysics Unions; mem. Can. Geophys. Union (Wilson medal 1995). Anglican. Home: 9 Wenlock Grove, Halifax, NS Canada B3P 1P6 Office: Atlantic Geosci Ctr, Bedford Inst Oceanography, Dartmouth, NS Canada B2Y 4A2

KEEN, CONSTANTINE, retired manufacturing company executive; b. N.Y.C., Jan. 1, 1925; s. Andrew and Sophie (Findani) K.; m. Kally Carajikis, Sept. 23, 1951; children: Katherine, Andrew. BA, NYU, 1952. Asst. treas. Sandz Indsl. Corp., N.Y.C., 1951-55; with Fedders Corp., Edison, N.J., 1955—; asst. credit mgr. Fedders Corp., 1955-57, credit mgr., 1957-60, dir. credit, 1960-68, v.p., dir. credit, 1968-75, v.p., dir. distbr. relations, 1975-77, v.p., treas., 1980-87, v.p. internat., 1984-86; pres. Fedders Internat. Corp., 1987-93, dir., 1996—. With USAAF, 1942-45. Decorated D.F.C., Air medal. Greek Orthodox. Clubs: Ahepa, Masons. Home: 55 Cardinal Rd Manhasset NY 11030-1204

KEEN, DERL WALTER, child development educator; b. Leonard, Tex., July 18, 1932; s. Willard Francis and Ora Edda (Martin) K.; m. Shirley Marie Smith, Nov. 14, 1954; children—Deborha, Gregory, Karen, Cynthia. B.S., U. Calif.-Davis, 1954; M.A., Calif. State U.-Fresno, 1973; Ed.D., U. So. Calif., 1978. Cotton gin mgr. Anderson Clayton & Co., Tulare, Calif., 1956-60, farm mgr., Mendota, Calif., 1960-69; owner, operator Liquor Market Country Store, Chatsworth, Calif., 1969-70; owner, operator Keen's Day Sch., Fresno, Calif., 1970-75; instr. child devel., Fresno City Coll., 1975—; mem. Agr. Adv. Council, U. Calif., Berkeley, 1968-72, West Side Field Sta. Adv. Council, U. Calif., Five Points, 1962-72; dir. Calif. Tomato Growers Assn., Stockton, 1964-70; mem. Calif. State Articulation Council Early Childhood Edn., 1975-85, chmn., 1984-85. Served to 1st lt. U.S. Army, 1955-56.Mem. Calif. Assn. for Edn. Young Children (scholarship chmn. 1981-83), World Orgn. for Edn. Young Children. Republican. Methodist. Office: Fresno City Coll 1101 E University Ave Fresno CA 93704-6219

KEEN, MIKE FORREST, sociologist, educator; b. Tiffin, Ohio, Aug. 14, 1958; s. Tom Clifton and Mary Barbara (Kiss) K. BA, Heidelberg Coll., 1979; MA, U. Notre Dame, 1983, PhD, 1985. Program coord. Ctr. for Social Concerns U. Notre Dame, Ind., 1985-87; vis. prof. Ind. U., South Bend, 1987-89, asst. prof., 1989-95, assoc. prof., 1995—, chair dept. sociology, 1997—; coord. Midwest Student Sociology Conf. Steering Com., South Bend, 1994—. Editor: Eastern Europe in Transformation, 1994; author: Stalking the Sociological Imagination: J. Edgar Hoover's FBI Surveillance of American Sociology, 1999. Bd. dirs. St. Joseph Valley Project, 1998—. Mem. AAUP, Internat. Sociol. Assn., Am. Sociol. Assn. Avocations: cooking, studying foreign languages. Home: 843 Park Ave South Bend IN 46616-1339 Office: Ind U 1700 Mishawaka Ave South Bend IN 46634-7111

KEEN, NOEL THOMAS, plant pathology educator; b. Marshalltown, Iowa, Aug. 13, 1940; s. Walter Thomas and Evelyn Mae (Mayo) K.; m. Diane I. Keen, Nov. 15, 1986. BS, Iowa State U., 1963, MS, 1965; PhD, U. Wis., 1968. Asst. prof. plant pathology U. Calif., Riverside, 1968-72, assoc. prof., 1972-78, prof., 1978—, chmn. dept. plant pathology, 1983-89, chmn. dept. genetics, 1994-97; faculty rsch. lectr. U. Calif., Riverside, 1995-96. Recipient Ruth Allen award, Am. Phytopathological Soc., 1995, Superior Svc. award USDA, 1996. Fellow AAAS, Am. Phytopathol. Soc.; mem. NAS, Internat. Soc. Plant Molecular Biology, Am. Soc. Microbiology, Am. Soc. Plant Physiologists. Office: U Calif Dept Plant Pathology Riverside CA 92521

KEEN, RALPH, religious studies educator; b. Phila., Dec. 21, 1957; m. Mary Szumski; 1 child, MeiLin. BA, Columbia U., 1979; MA, Yale U., 1980; PhD, U. Chgo., 1990. Asst. prof. Alaska Pacific U., Anchorage, 1991-93; asst. prof. U. Iowa, Iowa City, 1993-98, assoc. prof. religion, 1998—. Author: Divine and Human Authority, 1997; editor: Responsio ad Bugenhagium (J. Cochlaeus), 1988, Philippica I-VII (J. Cochlaeus), 1996. Rsch. fellow Calvin Coll., Grand Rapids, Mich., 1991; grantee NEH, 1993, Herzog August Libr., Germany, 1994-95. Mem. Am. Soc. Ch. History (life, mem. coun. 1996-98), Am. Cath. History Assn. (life), Medieval Acad. Am. (life). Jewish. Office: U Iowa Sch Religion 314 Gilmore Hall Iowa City IA 52242-1320

KEENA, J. BRADLEY, political commentator; b. Salina, Kans., Mar. 17, 1955; s. James LeRoy and Janet Lynn (Laybourn) K.; m. Mary Renee Jawish, Apr. 24, 1981 (div.); children: Sallie, Alexander, Mary Anne, Max. BA in Journalism, U. Ga., 1977. News dir. WLBB/WBTR-FM, Carrollton, Ga., 1977-79; afternoon anchor The Ga. Network, Atlanta, 1979; pub. rels. specialist Fed. Emergency Mgmt. Agy., Washington, 1980-81; contr. Mid-Continent Investment Co., Salina, 1981-84; legis. dir. Leadership Found., Bethesda, Md., 1985-87; comm. dir. Dow, Lohnes & Albertson, Washington, 1987-89; spl. asst. to asst. sec. U.S. Dept. Interior, Washington, 1989-93; host, commentator NET-Polit. NewsTalk Network, Washington, 1994—; press sec. Congressman Steve Largent, Oklahoma City, 1999—; corr. The Atlanta Constn., 1978-79; exec. dir. Internat. Policy Forum, Springfield, Va., 1984-85; pres. pers. liaison The White House, 1989; comm. cons., Clifton, Va., 1993-94; mem. U.S. delegation U.S.-Can. Civil Aviation Consultations, 1991-92, U.S.-U.K. Civil Aviation Consultations, 1990-91, U.S.-South Korea Civil Aviation Consultations, 1990; co-host daily talk show Capitol Watch, 1994—; alt. host, commentator Direct Line, 1995—. Town clk. Town of Clifton, 1993-94; ruling elder Presbyn. Ch. Am., 1992—. Recipient awards for excellence in investigative reporting, non-deadline reporting, deadline reporting, criticism/commentary, editorials, feature reporting AP. Avocations: philosophy, theology, oenology, writing. *

KEENAN, BARBARA MILANO, state supreme court justice. Judge Gen. Dist. Ct., Fairfax County, Va., 1980-82, Circuit Ct., Fairfax County, Va., 1982-85, Court of Appeals of Va., 1985-91; justice Supreme Court Va., Richmond, 1991—. Office: Va Supreme Ct 4th Fl 101 N 9th St Richmond VA 23219-2335*

KEENAN, BEVERLY OWEN, entrepreneur; b. Medicine Lodge, Kans., July 29, 1948; d. Neil Harrington and Bertie Geneva (Nurse) Owen; m. Donald Joseph Livingston, Jan. 29, 1963 (div. Mar. 1975); children: Virginia, Rebecca, Wesley, Carrie, Lee; m. Theodore Wayne Keenan, Apr. 23, 1975 (dec. 1991); 1 child, James. Student, Okla. State U., 1978-79. Field rschr. Nat. Analysts, Phila., 1977-79; agt. Daily Oklahoman, Stillwater, Okla., 1979-80; distbr. Rocky Mountain News, Denver, 1980-82, circulation dist. mgr., 1982-88; nat. sales dir. Frame Enterprises, Oklahoma City, 1988; sales and svc. rep. MCI Telecommunications Corp., 1989-92; founder, sr. ptnr. Cowboy Supplier, Cody, Wyo., 1992-93; leader seminars, 1986-90. Spkr. Women in Transitions Groups, Littleton, Colo., 1987-89, seminar leader, 1986-89. Mem. Am. Quarter Horse Assn., Am. Paint Horse Assn., Mensa, AQHA, APHA. Avocations: western and native Am. art collecting. Office: Cowboy Supplier 1137 12th St Cody WY 82414-3611

KEENAN, C. ROBERT, III, lawyer; b. Pitts., July 21, 1954; s. C. Robert Jr. and Catherine (Conley) K.; m. Joann R. Fogle, June 9, 1979; children: Rachel, Rosemary. BA, Bucknell U., 1976; JD, U. Pitts., 1979. Bar: Pa. 1979, U.S. Dist. Ct. (we. dist.) Pa. 1979, U.S. Ct. Appeals (3d cir.) 1981, U.S. Supreme Ct. 1983. Assoc. Shire & Bergstein, Monessen, Pa., 1979-80; ptnr. Jones, Gregg, Creehan & Gerace, Pitts., 1980-89; prin. Keenan and Krug, P.C., Pitts., 1989-92, Grigsby, Gaca & Davies (now Davies, McFarland and Carroll, P.C.), Pitts., 1992—. Editor Real News Jour., 1984-92. Trustee Castle Shannon (Pa.) Cmty. Libr., 1982-84; mem. claims adjudication bd. SSS, Pitts., 1984—, chmn., 1987-90; mem. Def. Rsch. Inst., Pa. Def. Inst.; mem. Allegheny County Rep. Com.; chmn. Mt. Lebanon Rep. Com., 1991-93; mem. bd. sch. dirs. Mt. Lebanon Sch. Dist., 1998—. Mem. ABA (govtl. liability com.), Pa. Bar Assn. (chmn. specialization com. 1990-93), Federalist Soc. Law and Pub. Studies, Allegheny County Bar Assn. (chmn. bd. dirs. real property sect. 1992, jud. com. 1992-95, workers' compensation sect. coun. 1996-98), Christian Bus. Men's Com. (chmn. outreach 1985-88), Dormont-Mt. Lebanon Sportsmen's Club, Rotary (past pres., Disting. Svc. award 1985), Pi Sigma Alpha, Omicron Delta Kappa. Republican. Avocations: marksmanship, music, swimming. Office: Davies McFarland & Carroll 10th Fl One Gateway Ctr Pittsburgh PA 15222

KEENAN, DEBORAH DUANE LEFEVRE, special education educator, student assistance specialist; b. Ventura, Calif., Apr. 20, 1948; d. William George and Edith Louise (Bush) LeFevre; m. Thomas Keenan, Apr. 18, 1969; children: David B. Keenan, T. Kevin Keenan; foster child, Daniel Guandique. BS, U. Tex., Dallas, 1981; postgrad., East Tex. State U., 1990-92. Cert. psychology, generic spl. edn., vocat. home econs., secondary reading tchr., Tex. Asst. mgr. Preston Hollow United Meth. Day Sch., Dallas, 1978-79; tchr. Lake Highlands Jr. High, Dallas, 1981-90; tchr. L.V. Berkner H.S., Richardson, Tex., 1989—, coord. spl. edn., 1996—; team mem. Loving Intervention for Teens, Crisis Intervention Team, Richardson Ind. Sch. Dist., 1987-98, tchr. rep., trainer Tchr. Leadership Collaboration & Instrnl. Strategies for Success - Brain Study, 1997—. Bd. dirs. Sachse (Tex.) Libr. Bd., 1989-93; mem. Rep. Women's Assn., Dallas, Garland, Tex., 1982-92. Named tchr. of month, Berkner H.S., Applebee's Rest., Richardson, Tex., 1995, 96, 98. Mem. Nat. Coun. Tchrs. English, Nat. Assn. Acad. Supervision and Principals, Nat. Assn. Student Asst. Programs (trainer, peer helper, mem. mediation team 1994—), Internat. Read Assn., Learning Disabled Assn. (tchr. of year 1987), Richardson Ednl. Assn. (scholar 1990), Acad. Supervision and Curriculum devel., Phi Delta Kappa, Epsilon Sigma Alpha (pres. 1989). Republican. Roman Catholic. Avocations: needlepoint, reading, travel. Home: 5005 Heritage Cir Sachse TX 75048-4521 Office: L V Berkner High Sch 1600 E Spring Valley Rd Richardson TX 75081-5351

KEENAN, JAMES GEORGE, classics educator; b. N.Y.C., Jan. 19, 1944; s. George F. and Cecilia Ann (Schmidt) K.; m. Ann Frances O'Rourke, Mar. 18, 1967; children: James, Kathleen, Kenneth, Mary, Lisa, Brian, Laura. A.B., Holy Cross Coll., 1965; M.A., Yale U., 1966, Ph.D., 1968. Asst. prof. Classics U. Calif., Berkeley, 1968-73; assoc. to full prof. Classics Loyola U. of Chgo., 1973—, chmn. classics, 1978-84, acting chmn., 1987-88; cons. Petra Scrolls Conservation Project, 1995. Co-editor: edition of Greek papyri: The Tebtunis Papyri, vol. IV, 1976. Fellow Nat. Endowment for Humanities, 1973-74; travel grantee Am. Council Learned Socs., 1974, 83, 86; grant-in-aid Am. Philos. Soc., 1987. Mem. Am. Philol. Assn., Am. Soc. Papyrologists (pres. 1989-93), Classical Assn. Midwest and South, Assn. Internat. des Papyrologues, Egypt Exploration Soc. Roman Catholic. Office: Loyola U Chgo Dept Classical Studies 6525 N Sheridan Rd Chicago IL 60626-5344

KEENAN, JOHN FONTAINE, federal judge; b. N.Y.C., Nov. 23, 1929; s. John Joseph and Veronica (Fontaine) K.; m. Diane R. Nicholson, Oct. 6, 1956; 1 child, Marie Patricia. BBA, Manhattan Coll., N.Y., 1951; LLD (hon.), Manhattan Coll., 1989; LLB, Fordham U., 1954; LLD (hon.), Mt. St. Vincent Coll., 1989. Bar: N.Y. 1954, U.S. Dist. Ct. (so. dist.) N.Y. 1983. From asst. dist. atty. to chief asst. dist. atty. N.Y. County Dist. Atty.'s Office, 1956-76; spl. prosecutor, dep. atty. gen. City of N.Y., 1976-79; chmn. bd., pres. N.Y.C. Off-Track Betting Corp., 1979-82; criminal justice coord. City of N.Y., 1982-83; judge U.S. Dist. Ct. So. Dist. N.Y., N.Y.C., 1983—; chief asst. dist. atty. Queens County Dist. Atty.'s Office, N.Y., 1973; adj. prof. John Jay Coll. Criminal Justice, N.Y.C., 1979-83, Fordham U. Sch. Sch. Law, N.Y.C., 1992, 93; mem. Fgn. Intelligence Svc. Ct., 1994—, Judicial Panel on Multi-Dist. Litigation, 1998—. Contbr. articles to law jours. Chmn. Daytop Village, Inc., N.Y.C., 1981-83. Served with U.S. Army, 1954-56. Recipient Frank S. Hogan award Citizens Com. Control of Crime in N.Y., 1975, Emory R. Buckner award Federal Bar Coun., 1993; cert. of recognition Patrolmen's Benevolent Assn., 1976; 1st Ann. Hogan-Morgenthau Assocs. award N.Y. County Dist. Atty.'s Office, 1976, Medal of Achievement, 1992; Excellence award N.Y. State Bar Assn., 1978, award N.Y. Criminal Bar Assn., 1979, Disting. Faculty award Nat. Coll. Dist. Attys., 1978, Louis J. Lefkowitz award Fordham Urban Law Jour., 1983, Charles Carroll award Guild Cath. Lawyers, 1994, Ellis Island medal of honor, Nat. Ethnic Coalition of Orgns. Found., Inc., 1998. Mem. Amackassin Club, Skytop Club. Republican. Roman Catholic. Office: US Dist Ct US Courthouse 500 Pearl St Rm 1930 New York NY 10007-1316

KEENAN, JOHN PAUL, management educator, consultant, psychologist; b. Boston, Mar. 18, 1944; s. John W. and Claire (Gallagher) K.; m. Kathleen Lennon, Aug. 7, 1976; children: Christopher, Sean Patrick. BA, U. Santa Clara, 1967; MA, San Jose State U., 1969; PhD, U.S. Internat. U., San Diego, 1978. Instr. Chapman Coll., Orange, Calif., 1971-79; asst. prof. mgmt. Coll. of St. Rose, Albany, N.Y., 1979-83; dean C.C. Low County, Beaufort, S.C., 1983-86; assoc. prof. mgmt., dir. leadership devel. programs Mgmt. Inst., U. Wis. Sch. Bus., Madison, 1986-98; dir., assoc. prof. masters in profl. leadership program St. Bonaventure U., Buffalo, 1998—; pres., CEO John Keenan & Assocs., Orchard Park, N.Y., 1986—; exec. v.p. Coun. on Employee Responsibilities and Rights, Norfolk, Va., 1993—; guest spkr. Norwegian Roads Adminstrn., Oslo, 1992, Asia Inc. Sch. Mgmt., Kuala Lampur, Manila, 1996—, Singapore, Malaysia, Philippines, 1997—; keynote spkr. Cairo Internat. Mgmt. Conf., 1993; presenter in field. Co-author: Whistleblowing: Managing Dissent in the Work Place, 1985, Whistleblowing Research, 1985; contbr. articles to profl. jours. Mem. APA, ASTD, Acad. Mgmt., Decision Scis. Inst., Inst. Mgmt. Scis., Soc. for Indsl. and Orgnl. Psychology, Assn. on Employment Practices and Principles (pres.1998—, program chmn. 1993, 97). Avocations: swwimming, hiking, all sports. Home: 2 Hillsboro Dr Orchard Park NY 19127 Office: St Bonaventure Univ 3114 Grainger Hall 5250 S Park Ave Hamburg NY 19075

KEENAN, JOSEPH MICHAEL, military officer; b. Drexel Hill, Pa., Jan. 12, 1969; s. Joseph Michael and Rose Marie Keenan. BA, Villanova U., 1991; MA, Naval Postgrad. Sch., 1998. Commd. ens. USN, 1991, advanced through grades to lt., 1994; comms. officer USS Boulder, Norfolk, Va., 1992-94; damage control asst. USS Ramage, Norfolk, 1995-96; weapons control officer USS Laboon, Norfolk, 1999—. Mem. Surface Navy Assn.

KEENAN, MICHAEL EDGAR, advertising executive; b. Columbus, Ohio, Mar. 15, 1934; s. Edgar Charles and Kathryn Ellen (Dowden) K.; divorced; children: Margaret, Matthew, Emily, Jennifer, Andrew, Martha. AB, Duke U., 1955. Media buyer Compton Advt., N.Y.C., 1957-59; assoc. media dir. Foote, Cone & Belding, N.Y.C., 1959-61; media dir. Lennen & Newell, N.Y.C., 1961-63; sr. v.p., dir., cons. products div. Fuller & Smith & Ross, N.Y.C., 1963-70; chmn. Keenan & McLaughlin Inc., N.Y.C., 1970-82, cons., 1982-85; mng. dir. Western International Media Corp., N.Y.C., 1985-98; pres. Keenan & Co., Inc., N.Y.C., 1998—; lectr. mktg. NYU, 1960-64; cons. FTC, Washington. Served with CIC, AUS, 1955-57. Mem. Am. Assn. Advt. Agys. (chmn. N.Y. coun. 1978), Nat. Agri-Mktg. Assn. (past pres. 1979), Rear Guard (treas., pres.), Thursday Club (chmn. 1960-96). Republican. Roman Catholic. Avocation: sailing. Home: 63 Avenue A Apt 5I New York NY 10009-6539 Office: Keenan & Co Inc 666 5th Ave Ste 281 New York NY 10103

KEENAN, ROBERT ANTHONY, financial services company executive, educator, consultant; b. Jersey City, July 25, 1930; s. Anthony A. and Anne (McCartin) K.; m. Ann Louise Wallenberger, Sept. 12, 1959; children: Jeanne, Robert, Mary, Elizabeth, Paul. BBS in Fin., Pace U., N.Y.C., 1958; postgrad, Pace U., 1959-60; postgrad., NYU, 1967-68. C.P.A., N.Y., N.J. Gen. auditor Johnson & Johnson, New Brunswick, N.J., 1966-68; v.p. ops. and fin. Ortho Pharm., Raritan, N.J., 1968-72; v.p. fin., mem. bd. dirs. Johnson & Johnson Internat., New Brunswick, 1972-76; pres. Fgn. Credit Ins. Assocs., N.Y.C., 1977-84; mng. ptnr. Sigma Ptnrs., 1984—; bd. dirs. Praxis Biologics, Inc., FCS Labs., 1978—; prof. Grad. Sch., Monmouth Coll.; mem. mgmt. com. Internat. Credit Ins. Assn., Berne, Switzerland, 1983; vice chmn. SCORE, Monmouth City, 1996—. Contbg. author: Operational Auditing, 1968-69, International Financial Handbook, 1983. Mem. adv. coun. Middlesex Coll., Raritan, 1978-88; mem. planning commn. Holmdel, N.J.; active Rep. Party. With USN, 1948-52. Recipient Alumnus Achievement award Pace U., 1973. Mem. Fin. Execs. Inst. N.J. (bd. dir. 1970-83, pres. 1980-81), Am. Inst. CPAs, N.Y. State Soc. CPAs, N.J. Soc. CPAs, Internat. C. of C. Roman Catholic. Home: 126 Crawfords Corner Rd Holmdel NJ 07733-1942 Office: Sigma Ptnrs PO Box 111 Lincroft NJ 07738-0111

KEENAN, ROBERT ARTHUR, financial executive; b. Evergreen Park, Ill., Mar. 27, 1965; s. Robert Arthur and Katherine Joanne (Lyne) K.; m. Theresa Lynn Mendick, Oct. 5, 1991; children: Alexis, Lauren, Nicole. BBA in Fin., U. Okla., 1988; MPA, Drake U., 1999. Ops./credit mgr. Sears Credit, Omaha, 1988-92; group asset mgr. Sears Credit, West Des Moines, 1992-94; owner/pres. Movies to Go Video, Des Moines, 1994; v.p. collections Norwest Card Svcs., West Des Moines, 1994-97; mayor/coun. mem. City of West Des Moines, 1994-97; v.p. strategic implementation Chase Manhattan Bank, Matteson, Ill., 1997—; adv. bd. Consumer Credit Coun., Des Moines, 1993-94. Bd. dirs. Visitors Bur., Des Moines, 1996-97, Rep. Mayor's Leaders, Washington, 1995-96. Mem. Inter Credit Assn. (bd. dirs. 1989-91), West Des Moines Chamber (bd. dirs. 1995-97), Lambda Chi Alpha Alumni (pres. 1997). Republican. Roman Catholic. Avocations: family, politics, golf, volleyball, sailing. Home: 7878 Marquette Dr North Tinley Park IL 60477 Office: Chase Manhattan Bank 21780 S Cicero Ave Matteson IL 60443

KEENAN, ROBERT JOSEPH, trade association executive; b. San Francisco, May 25, 1946; s. Lawrence Alexander and Elma Patricia (Frenor) K.; m. Hildegard I. Gerlitz, Aug. 22, 1969; children: Michael Alexander, Patrick Sean. BS in Pub. Rels., Armstrong Coll., Berkeley, Calif., 1971; cert. in orgnl. mgmt., U. Santa Clara, 1975. Asst. mgr. Redwood City (Calif.) C. of C., 1971-73; exec. v.p. Lancaster (Calif.) C. of C., 1973-76, Montclair (Calif.) C. of C., 1976-79, Calif. Electric Sign Assn., Claremont, 1979-91, Bldg. Industry Assn. Tulare/Kings Counties, Visalia, Calif., 1991—; chmn. Lancaster Inc. Com., 1974-76; dir., mktg. chair Workforce Coalition, Visalia, 1995-99; mem. select com. unlicensed contractors Calif. State Assembly, 1987-92. Author city incorp. game, 1974 (Congl. record 1975). Author chpt. 2.5 Calif. Bus. and Profl. Code, 1983-88, Calif. Electric Sign Assn., Claremont, 1989-90; author AB2823 Bldg. Industry Assn., Visalia, 1996. With U.S. Army, 1966-69. Republican. Roman Catholic. Avocations: reading, sailing, billiards, writing. Office: Bldg Industry Assn 315 W Oak Ave Visalia CA 93291-4928

KEENAN, TERRANCE, foundation executive; b. Phila., Feb. 1, 1924; s. Peter Joseph and Marie (Sloupova) K.; m. Joette Kathryn Lehan, Oct. 20, 1979. A.B., Yale U., 1950; J.D. (hon.), Alderson-Broaddus Coll., Philippi, W.Va., 1973. Asst. headmaster Thomas Jefferson Sch., St. Louis, 1950-55; writer Merrill Lynch, N.Y.C., 1955-56; asst. editor office reports Ford Found., N.Y.C., 1956-65; sr. exec. asso. Commonwealth Fund, N.Y.C., 1965-72; v.p. Robert Wood Johnson Found., Princeton, N.J., 1972—. Bd. dirs. Grantmakers in Health, Washington. With USNR, 1943-46. Mem. Pub. Relations Soc. Am., Phi Beta Kappa. Republican. Roman Catholic. Clubs: Yale (N.Y.C.); Nassau (Princeton). Home: 435 Sterling St Newtown PA 18940-2142

KEENAN-ABILAY, GEORGIA ANN, service representative; b. Denver, Oct. 3, 1936; d. Lawrence Edward and Helen Kathleen (Gray) K.; m. Charles Henry Dupree, May 31, 1958 (div. Nov. 1977); children: Phoenix, Therese, Mark, John; m. Joseph D. Abilay, Nov. 26, 1988. BA, Regis Coll., 1968; MA, St. Thomas U., 1978. With reservations United Airlines, Denver, 1956-57; stewardess Trans World Airlines, Chgo., 1957-58; in elem. edn. Notre Dame Sch., Denver, 1969-72; dir. religious edn. Notre Dame Parish, Denver, 1972-77, Archdiocese Denver, 1977-80; v.p., treas. Kilfinane and Cook, Denver, 1980-82; dir. human resources Cosmopolitan Hotel, Denver, 1982-83, Kaanapali Beach Hotel, Lahaina, Hawaii, 1983-85, Royal Lahaina Resort, Hawaii, 1985-90; corp. dir. human resources Hawaiian Hotels and Resorts, Lahaina, 1988; dir. human resources Rock Resorts Lanai Resorts Ptnrs., Island of Lanai, 1990-94; ptnr. Blue Ginger Cafe, Lanai, 1995—; trainer Amfac Hotels and Resorts, Hawaii, 1984-86; vice chmn. Maui Hotel Assn., 1987; bd. dirs. Project 714, Lahaina, 1987. Bd. dirs. Archdiocesan Women's Bd., Denver, 1981-83, Passages, Denver, 1980-83, Maui Econ. Devel. Bd., Kahalui, 1984; chairperson Charity Walk, 1984-86. Named Handicapped Employer of Yr., State of Hawaii, 1987. Mem. Council Hawaii Hotels, Am. Soc. Personnel Assn. Club: Distributive Edn. of Am. (Hawaii) (bd. dirs. 1984—). Avocations: fishing, boating. Home: PO Box 721 Lanai City HI 96763 Office: Blue Ginger Cafe PO Box 1090 Lanai City HI 96763

KEENE, CLIFFORD HENRY, medical administrator; b. Buffalo, Jan. 28, 1910; s. George Samuel and Henrietta Hedwig (Yeager) K.; m. Mildred Jean Kramer (dec.), Mar. 3, 1934; children: Patricia Ann (Mrs. William S. Kneedler), Martha Jane (Mrs. William R. Srpoule), Diane Eve (Mrs. Gordon D. Simonds); m. Mary Oliver Dixon, Dec. 16, 1995. AB, U. Mich., 1931, MD, 1934, MS in Surgery, 1938; DSc, Hahnemann Med. Coll., 1973; LLD, Golden Gate U., 1974. Diplomate Am. Bd. Surgery, Am. Bd. Preventive Medicine (occupl. medicine). Resident surgeon, instr. surgery U. Mich., 1934-39; cons. surgery of cancer Mich. Med. Soc. and Mich. Dept. Health, 1939-40; pvt. practice surgery Wyandotte, Mich., 1940-41; med. dir. Kaiser-Frazer Corp., 1946-53; instr. surgery U. Mich., 1946-54; med. adminstrv. positions with Kaiser Industries and Kaiser Found., 1954-75, v.p., 1960-75; v.p., gen. mgr. Kaiser Found. Hosps. and Kaiser Found. Health Plan, 1960-67; med. dir. Kaiser Found. Sch. Nursing, 1954-67; dir. Kaiser Found. Research Inst., 1958-75; pres. Kaiser Found. Hosps. Health Plan, Sch. Nursing, 1968-75, dir., 1960-80; chmn. editorial bd. Kaiser Found. Med. Bull., 1954-65; lectr. med. econs. U. Calif.-Berkeley, 1956-75; mem. vis. com. Med. Sch., Stanford U., 1966-72, Harvard U., 1967-71, 79-85, U. Mich., 1973-78; Mem. Presdl. Panel Fgn. Med. Grads. (Nat. Manpower Commn.), 1966-69. Contbr. papers to prof. lit. Bd. visitors Harvard Bus. Adv. Council, 1972, Charles R. Drew Postgrad. Med. Sch., 1972-79; trustee Amman Civil Hosp., Jordan, 1973, Community Hosp. of Monterey Peninsula, 1983-92. Lt. col. M.C. AUS, 1942-46. Recipient Disting. Service award Group Health Assn. Am., 1974; Disting. Alumnus award U. Mich. Med. Center, 1976; Disting. Alumnus Service award U. Mich., 1985. Fellow ACS; mem. AMA, Am. Assn. Indsl. Physicians and Surgeons, Inst. Medicine of NAS, Calif. Acad. Medicine, Frederick A. Coller Surg. Soc., Calif. Med. Assn., Alpha Omega Alpha (editl. bd., contbr. to Pharos mag. 1977-97). Home: Unit 322 200 Glenwood Cir Unit Monterey CA 93940-6752

KEENE, DONALD, writer, translator, language educator; b. 1922. Lectr. Cambridge U., 1948-53; guest editor Asahi Shimbun, Tokyo, 1982-92; prof. Columbia U., N.Y.C., 1955-92, prof. emeritus, 1992—. Author: The Battles of Coxinga, 1951, The Japanese Discovery of Europe, 1952, 69, Japanese Literature: An Introduction for Western Readers, 1953, Living Japan, 1957, Bunraku, The Puppet Theatre of Japan, 1965, Nō: The Classical Theatre of Japan, 1966, Landscapes and Portraits, 1971, Some Japanese Portraits, 1978, World Within Walls, 1978, Meeting with Japan, 1978, Travels in Japan, 1981, Dawn to the West, 1984, The Pleasures of Japanese Literature, 1988, Travelers of a Hundred Ages, 1989, Seeds in the Heart, 1993, On Familiar Terms, 1994, Modern Japanese Diaries, 1995, The Blue-Eyed Tarokaja, 1996; editor: Anthology of Japanese Literature, 1955, Modern Japanese Literature, 1956, Twenty Plays of the Nō Theatre, 1970; translator: The Setting Sun, 1956, Five Modern Nō Plays, 1957, No Longer Human, 1958, Sources of Japanese Tradition, 1958, Major Plays of Chikamatsu, 1961, The Old Woman, the Wife and the Archer, 1961, After the Banquet, 1965, Essays in Idleness, 1967, Madame de Sade, 1967, Friends, 1969, Chushingura, 1971, The Man Who Turned into a Stick, 1972, Three Plays by Kobo Abe, 1993, The Narrow Road to Oku, 1996, The Tale of the Bamboo Cutter, 1998. Office: Columbia Univ 407 Kent Hall New York NY 10027

KEENE, JACK DONALD, molecular genetics and microbiology educator; b. Jacksonville, Fla., June 21, 1947; s. Jack Donald and Stella Collene (Ellis) K.; m. Judy May Keene, Sept. 6, 1969; children: Mike, Lisa. AB, U. Calif., Riverside, 1969; PhD, U. Wash., 1974. Staff fellow NINDS/NIH, Bethesda, Md., 1974-78; asst. prof. microbiology and immunology Duke U. Med. Ctr., Durham, N.C., 1979-84, assoc. prof., 1984-88, prof., 1988-92, chmn., 1992—, James B. Duke disting. prof., 1997—; mem. experimental virology study sect. NIH, 1984-88; mem. nat. selection and adv. bd. PEW Scholars in the Biomed Scis., 1991-96; mem. molecular biology study sect. NIH, 1991-95, chmn., 1993-95; co-chmn. Diversity Biotech. Consortium, Santa Fe, 1994—; dir. basic sci. rsch. Duke U. Comprehensive Cancer Ctr., Duke U. Program in Genetics, Program in Molecular and Cellular Biology; dir. combinatorial scis. ctr. Duke U. Med. Ctr., 1994—. Assoc. editor: Virology, 1983—; editorial bd.: Jour. of Virology, 1985-95, Molecular and Cellular Biology, 1991—; editor: Microbiology and Molecular Biology Revs., 1992—, Molecular Diversity, 1995—; primary reviewer Jour. Immunology, 1996—. Mem. fellowship com. Arthritis Found., 1990-92, mem. rsch. com., arthritus found, 1990-92. Recipient Faculty Rsch. award Am. Cancer Soc., Devil's Bag award Arthritis Found.; Nanaline Duke Faculty Scholar, PEW Scholar in the Biomed. Scis. Fellow Am. Acad. Microbiology; mem. Am. Soc. Virology, Am. Soc. Biochemistry and Molecular Biology, Am. Soc. Microbiology, Ribonucleic Acid Soc. Office: Duke Univ Med Ctr Box 3020 Microbiol Dept Research Dr/414 Jones Bldg Durham NC 27710*

KEENE, RHONDA LEIGH, secondary education educator; b. Richlands, Va., Nov. 28, 1972; d. Ronald Lee and Teah Cecilia (Smith) K. BS, U. Va., 1994; MEd, East Tenn. St. U., 1997. Cert. tchr., Va., specific lng. disability, mentally retarded, emotional disturbed, elem. prin. endorsement, secondary prin. endorsement, Va. Learning disabilities resource tchr. Tazewell (Va.) Co. Pub. Schs., 1994, severe and profoundly handicapped tchr., 1994-98, trainable mentally handicapped tchr., 1994-98, adminstrv. intern, 1995-96; adminstrv. intern Fairfax (Va.) Co. Pub. Schs., 1995-96; coord. spl. edn./student svcs. Albemarle County Pub. Schs., Charlottesville, Va. Cheerleading coach Tazewell Co. Pub. Schs., 1994-97, mem. transition team, 1995-98, supt. coun., 1997-98. Mem. Assn. for Supervision and Curriculum Devel., Kappa Delta Pi, Gamma Beta Phi. Home: 69 B Barelay Pl Ct Charlottesville VA 22901

KEENE, SAMUEL JAMES, JR., reliability engineer researcher, educator; b. Washington, Dec. 28, 1939; s. Samuel James and Althea (Dudley) K. BSc in Physics, U. Md., 1962; MSc in Physics, Drexel U., 1966; PhD in Ops. Rsch., U. Colo., 1986. Reliability engr. Bendix, Towson, Md., 1962-64; rsch. scientist NASA Goddard Space Flight Ctr., Greenbelt, Md., 1964-67; adv. engr. IBM, Boulder, Colo., 1967-93; cons. engr. Performance Tech., Boulder, 1993—; adj. prof. Prairie View (Tex.) A&M U., 1973-74; instr. U. Colo., Boulder, 1984-85, Nat. Techs. U., Ft. Collins, Colo., 1992-96; mem. Colo. State U. Quality Improvement Inst., Ft. Collins, 1982—. Contbr. chpts. to books and articles to profl. jours. Scoutmaster Boy Scouts Am., Boulder, 1966-80; Sunday sch. tchr. LDS Ch., Boulder, 1968-83; baseball coach Little League Am., Boulder, 1976-82. Fellow IEEE; mem. IEEE Reliability Soc. (exec. com. 1976-79, 81-83, 84-87, 88-90, 91-93, 96-99, pres. 1991-92, chmn. software reliability tech. com., chmn. reliability prediction tech. com., video tutorial chmn.). Avocations: hiking, fishing, camping, cycling. E-mail: s.keene@ieee.org. Fax: 303-684-1000. Home: 465 Red Gulch Rd Lyons CO 80540 Office: Seagate Storage Products 2505 Trade Center Ave Longmont CO 80503

KEENE, WILLIAM BLAIR, state educaton official; b. Lewisburg, W.Va., July 2, 1933; m. Jean Hayes; children: Linda, Susan, Blair. BA, U. Del., 1956, MEd, 1965; EdD in Ednl. Adminstrn., Nova U., 1975. Marshallton-McKean Sch. Dist., nr. Wilmington, Del., 1960-63, coord. fed. projects, 1963-65, vice prin., 1965-67, prin., 1967-69; supt. Appoquinimink Sch. Dist., Odessa, Del., 1969-78; dep. state supt. State of Del., Dover, 1978-80, state supt. pub. instrn., 1980-90; spl. asst. to dean Coll. Edn. U. Del., 1991—; trustee Goldey-Beacom Coll., 1980—; fellow Harvard U. Sch. Govt., 1981; pres. Coun. of Chief State Sch. Officer, 1990. Mem. Newark (Del.) Bd. Edn., 1965-74. Named Del. Tchr. of Yr., Del. Bd. Edn. 1966. Mem. Del. State Edn. Assn. (pres. 1969), Del. Assn. Sch. Adminstrs., pres. 1978; mem. Del. Chief Sch. Officers Assn., pres. 1972; mem. Del. Assn. Supervision and Curriculum Devel. (pres. 1971), NEA, Am. Assn. Sch. Adminstrs., Vocat. Edn. Assn., Phi Delta Kappa, Kappa Alpha. Republican. Baptist. Lodge: Masons. Author: Community Resources for Delaware Schools, 1967; author curriculum units. Office: U Del Coll Edn 131 Willard Hall Newark DE 19716

KEENE-BURGESS, RUTH FRANCES, army official; b. South Bend, Ind., Oct. 7, 1948; d. Seymour and Sally (Morris) K.; m. Leslie U. Burgess, Jr., Oct. 1, 1983; children: Michael Leslie, David William, Elizabeth Sue, Rachael Lee. BS, Ariz. State U., 1970; MS, Fairleigh Dickinson U., 1978; grad., U.S. Army Command and Gen. Staff Coll., 1986. Inventory mgmt. specialist U.S. Army Electronics Command, Phila., 1970-74, U.S. Army Communications-Electronics Material Readiness Command, Fort Monmouth, N.J., 1974-79; chief inventory mgmt. div. Crane (Ind.) Army Ammunition Activity, 1979-80; supply systems analyst Hdqrs. 60th Ordnance Group, Zweibruecken, Fed. Republic Germany, 1980-83; chief inventory mgmt. div. Crane (Ind.) Army Ammunition Activity, 1983-85, chief control div., 1985; inventory mgmt. specialist 200th Theater Army Material Mgmt. Ctr., Zweibruecken, 1985-88; analyst supply systems U.S. Armament, Munitions and Chem. Command, Rock Island, Ill., 1988-89; specialist logistics mgt. U.S. Army Info. Systems Command, Ft. Huachuca, Ariz., 1989—. Mem. Federally Employed Women (chpt. pres. 1979-80), NAFE, Soc. Logistics Engrs., Assn. Computing Machinery, Am. Soc. Public Adminstrn., Soc. Profl. and Exec. Women, Assn. Info. Systems Profls., AAAS, NOW. Democrat.

KEENER, JOHN WESLEY, management consultant; b. Macedonia, Iowa, Apr. 10, 1927; s. Elza Lee and Florence Evelyn (Rhoades) K.; m. Loucille Clementine Wiedower, Nov. 19, 1949; children: Tonya Florence, Jonellyn Christine. BSEE, La. Tech., 1945; postgrad., St. Mary's Coll., 1945, Air War Coll., 1971. Owner 4K Motors, Medford, Oreg., 1948-51; purchasing agt. White City Lumber, Medford, 1951-52; asst. mgr. Woodbury & Co., Medford, 1952-57, Am. Steel & Supply, Medford, 1957-68; gen. mgr. Am. Steel & Supply, Medford and Redding, Calif., 1968-73, Medford, 1973-85; owner Rogue Pacific, Medford, 1985-91; mgmt. cons. Medford, 1991—; pres., bd. dirs. Jackson C.C. Found., Medford; cons. Oreg. div. Aeronautics, Salem, Oreg. Mem. Medford Planning Commn., 1972-75; chmn. Jackson County Econ. Devel., Medford, 1991; mem. County Airport Adv. Com., Medford, 1983—; chief instr. Oreg. Air Search and Rescue. With USN, 1944-46, col. USAF Aux. CAP, 1972—. Recipient Commendation for Community Svc. Gov. Oreg., 1992, Community Leader Spirit award Broadcasters, 1987. Mem. Loyal Order of Moose, Oreg. Wing Civil Air Patrol (comdr. 1981-82), Pacific Regional Civil Air Patrol (commendation 1981, nat. life saving awards (2)), Jackson County Airport Com. (past chmn., mem.), Rogue Valley Country Club. Republican. Methodist. Avocations: flying, hunting, fishing. Office: PO Box 22 Medford OR 97501-0002

KEENER, POLLY LEONARD, illustrator; b. Akron, Ohio, July 14, 1946; d. George Holman and Alice June (Bolinger) Leonard; m. Robert Lee Keener, Dec. 29, 1967; children: Robert Edward Alan, June Whitney. Student, Kent State U., 1967, Princeton U., 1968, 73; BA, Conn. Coll., 1968. Cert. tchr., Ohio. Illustrator Akron, 1969—; instr. cartooning Northeastern Ohio Univs. Coll. Medicine, 1992-94; instr. cartooning U. Akron, 1979—, instr. soft sculpture, 1979-84; cartoon text writer Prentice Hall Pubs., Englewood Cliffs, N.J., 1985—; pres. Keener Corp., Akron, 1977—; judge arts and crafts competition, Akron, 1982—. Author: Cartooning, 1992; illustrator: Eat Dessert First, 1987, It's Our Serve, 1989, 80 Great Ideas For Making Money At Home, 1992, Writer's Little Instruction Book, 1997; contbr. articles to profl. jours. Trustee Stan Hywet Hall Found., Akron, 1972—; trustee and v.p. Women's History Project, Akron, 1993-96; v.p. Jr. League, Akron, 1988-89, Western Res. Acad. Women's Bd., Hudson, Ohio, 1987-88; active Women's Bd. Blossom Music Ctr., Penninsula, Ohio, 1969—. Named Woman of Yr. Women's History Project Ohio, 1989, Artist of Yr. 1998 Heidelberg Coll. honors program; recipient Unsung Hero award Jr. League Akron, 1988. Mem. AAUP, DAR (trustee, vice-regent Cuyahoga-Portage chpt. 1992—), Nat. Cartoonists Soc. (chmn. Great Lakes chpt. 1996—, nat. rep. and bd. dirs. 1997—), Soc. Illustrators, Portage Country Club. Episcopalian. Avocations: antiques, archaeology, miniatures, science. Home: 400 W Fairlawn Blvd Akron OH 44313-4510

KEENER, WAYNE B., interior designer; b. Windsor, Pa., Feb. 27, 1927; s. Clarence Coleman and Cordia Irene (Brenneman) K. Interior designer Runkle Furniture Co., York, Pa., 1952-53; designer of homes, payroll clk., hardware buyer Smeltzer & Anderson, Inc., Red Lion, Pa., 1953-55; lamp stylist The Lamp Shoppe, Wormleysburg, Pa., 1955-56; interior designer Runkle Furniture Co., York, 1956-59; interior designer, display dir. and buyer Henry J. Koons, Interiors, York, 1959-69; salesperson W&J Sloane, Inc., N.Y.C., 1969-70; interior designer, structural designer, landscape designer Wayne B. Keener, Ambience Design, Red Lion, 1977—; actor, singer, N.Y.C., 1972—; wedding orchestrator Sir Wayne of Windsor Ambience Design, Red Lion, 1995—. Actor feature films, daytime TV dramas, TV movies, commls.; singer Broadway musicals, Cabaret Performances. Sgt. U.S. Army, 1945-46. Mem. Am. Soc. Interior Designers (allied mem.), Internat. Interior Design Assn. (assoc.). Avocations: church choir soloist, model for runway, printwork/corp., concert performer. Home: 132 W Broadway Red Lion PA 17356-2104 Office: Sir Wayne of Windsor & Wayne B Keener Ambience Des 132 W Broadway Red Lion PA 17356-2104

KEENEY, DENNIS RAYMOND, soil science educator; b. Osceola, Iowa, July 2, 1937; s. Paul N. and Evelyn L. (Beck) K.; m. Betty Ann Goodhue, June 20, 1959; children: Marcia, Susan. BS, Iowa State U., 1959; MS, U. Wis., 1961; PhD, Iowa State U., 1965. Postdoctoral research assoc. Iowa State U., Ames, 1965-66; prof. U. Wis., 1966-88, Romnes research prof., 1975—; chmn. dept. soil sci. U. Wis., Madison, 1978-83; chmn. land resources program Inst. Environ. Studies, Madison, 1985-88; prof. dept. agronomy Iowa State U., Ames, 1988—, dir. Leopold Ctr. for Sustainable Agr., 1988—; dir. Iowa State Water Resources Inst., 1991-98; sr. research scientist grasslands Dept. Sci. and Indsl. Research, Palmerston North, N.Z., 1975-76. Fellow Am. Soc. Agronomy (rsch. grantee 1986, pres. 1992-93), Soil Sci. Soc. Am. (pres. 1987-88, rsch. grantee 1981, Profl. Svc. award 1994). Office: Iowa State U 209 Curtiss Hall Ames IA 50011-1050

KEENEY, EDMUND LUDLOW, physician; b. Shelbyville, Ind., Aug. 11, 1908; s. Bayard G. and Ethel (Adams) K.; m. Esther Cox Loney Wight, Mar. 14, 1950; children: Edmund Ludlow, Eleanor Seymour (Mrs. Cameron Leroy Smith). A.B., Ind. U., 1930; M.D., Johns Hopkins U., 1934. Diplomate Am. Bd. Internal Medicine. Intern Johns Hopkins Hosp., 1934-37, vis. physician, instr. internal medicine, 1940-48; practice medicine, specializing internal medicine San Diego, 1948- 55; dir. Scripps Clinic and Research Found., La Jolla, 1955-67; pres. Scripps Clinic and Research Found., 1967-77, pres. emeritus, 1977—; dir. rsch. on fungus infections OSRD, 1942-46. Author: Practical Medical Mycology, 1955, Medical Advice for International Travel; contbr. articles on allergy, immunology and mycology to med. jours. Bd. dirs. U. San Diego, Allergy Found. Am. Fellow A.C.P.; mem. A.M.A., Am. Soc. Clin. Investigation, Am. Acad. Allergy (pres. 1964), Western Assn. Physicians, Calif. Med. Assn., Western Soc. Clin. Research, Phi Beta Kappa, Alpha Omega Alpha, Beta Theta Pi. Republican. Presbyterian. Home: 338 Via Del Norte La Jolla CA 92037-6539 Office: 10666 N Torrey Pines Rd La Jolla CA 92037-1027 *The great use of a lifetime is to spend it for something that outlives it.*

KEENEY, JOHN C., lawyer; b. Wilkes-Barre, Pa., Feb. 19, 1922; s. James M. and Mae M. (Clark) Keeney; widower; children: John C. Jr., Terence, Jean Marie, Joan, Kathleen. BS, U. Scranton, 1947; LLB, Dickinson Sch. of Law, Carlisle, Pa., 1949; LLM, Geo. Washington Law Sch., Washington, 1953. Chief Smith Act Unit, internal security sect. Dept. Justice, Washington, 1957-60, dep. chief organized crime sect. criminal divsn., 1966-69, chief fraud sect. criminal divsn., 1969-73, dep. asst. atty. gen. criminal divsn., 1973—. 1st lt. U.S. Army Air Force, 1943-45 ETO. Recipient Disting. Career award Pres. Reagan, 1983, Disting. Alumnus in Govt. award U. Scranton, 1997, Atty. Gen.'s Disting. Svc. award, 1987, D.C. Bar award for disting. govt. svc., 1996. Roman Catholic. Home: 11101 Lund Pl Kensington MD 20895-1624 Office: US Dept Justice 10th and Pennsylvania NW Washington DC 20530

KEENEY, JOHN CHRISTOPHER, JR., lawyer; b. Washington, Aug. 29, 1951; s. John Christopher and Eugenia M. (Brislin) K.; m. Kathleen V. Gunning. AB summa cum laude, U. Notre Dame, 1973; JD cum laude, Harvard U., 1976. Bar: Md. 1976, D.C. 1977, U.S. Dist. Ct. D.C. 1978, U.S. Dist. Ct. Md. 1977, U.S. Ct. Appeals (4th cir.) 1977, U.S. Ct. Appeals (D.C. cir.) 1978, U.S. Ct. Appeals (7th cir.) 1984, U.S. Supreme Ct. 1980, U.S. Ct. Appeals (10th cir.) 1989, U.S. Ct. Appeals (11th cir.) 1990. Law clk. to presiding judge U.S. Dist. Ct. Md., Balt., 1976-78; assoc. Hogan & Hartson, Washington, 1978-84, ptnr., 1985—; ptnr. in charge pro bono community svcs. dept. Hogan & Hartson, Washington, 1989-93 (rated best in pro bono in U.S. by ABA, 1991). Co-author: Civil and Criminal Remedies for Racially and Religiously Motivated Violence, 1983. Mem. area bus. com. Nat. Symphony Orch., Washington, 1980-81; mem. tech. adv. com. Dem. Nat. Fairness Commn., Washington, 1985-86, small bus. coun., 1987-88; cons. Common Cause Md., Annapolis, 1980-84; counsel for del. selection Babbitt for U.S. Pres. campaign, 1987-88; counsel Dem. credentials com., 1989-91; hearing officer Dem. Nat. Conv., 1992, 96; chmn. Berlage for County Coun. campaign, Montgomery County, Md., 1989-94; dir. Pub. Justice Ctr., Balt., 1990-95, 97—; trustee Washington Lawyers Com. for Civil Rights and Urban Affairs, 1994—; active Dem. Nat. Lawyers Coun., 1993—. Mem. ABA, D.C. Bar Assn. (chmn. subcom. legal needs, pub. svc. activities com., chmn. pro bono subcom. task force on reproductive cancers), Phi Beta Kappa. Roman Catholic. Home: 5516 Lincoln St West Bethesda MD 20817-3724 Office: Hogan & Hartson 555 13th St NW Ste 10W-206 Washington DC 20004-1109

KEENEY, RALPH LYONS, information systems specialist, educator; b. Lewistown, Mont., Jan. 29, 1944; s. Alonzo Stevens and Anna Murel (Lyons) K.; m. Janet L. Beach, Jan. 21, 1984; 1 child, Gregory. BS, UCLA, 1966; MS, MIT, 1967, profl. degree in elec. engring., 1968, PhD in Ops. Rsch., 1969. Engr. Bell Telephone Labs., Holmdel, N.J., 1966-69; asst. prof. civil engring., staff mem. Ops. Rsch. Ctr. MIT, Cambridge, 1969-72; assoc. prof. mgmt. and ops. rsch. MIT, Cambridge, Austria, 1972-74; rsch. scholar Internat. Inst. Applied Sys. Analysis, Laxenburg, Austria, 1974-76; head decision analysis Woodward-Cycle Cons., San Francisco, 1976-83; v.p. Woodward-Cycle Cons., 1980-83; prof. mgmt. and engring. U. So. Calif., 1983—; pvt. cons., 1969—. Author: Siting Energy Facilities, 1980, Value-Focused Thinking, 1992; co-author: (with Howard Raiffa) Decisions with Multiple Objectives, 1976, (with John S. Hammond and Howard Raiffa) Smart Choices, 1998. Recipient Lanchester prize Ops. Rsch. Soc. Am., 1976, Ramsey medal, 1989, Philip McCord Morse lectureship, 1993. Mem. NAE, Inst. Ops. Rsch. & Mgmt. Sci., Soc. Risk Analysis. Achievements include research in decision analysis, risk analysis; probabalistic models. Home: 101 Lombard St Apt 704W San Francisco CA 94111-1150

KEENEY, STEVEN HARRIS, lawyer; b. Phila., Oct. 1, 1949; s. Arthur Hail and Virginia (Tripp) K.; m. Jean Ashburn, May 10, 1974 (div. Oct. 1986); 1 child, Christian Jeffrey. BA, Trinity Coll., Hartford, Conn., 1971; MA, Hartford Sem. Found., 1973; JD, U. Conn., 1980. Bar: Ky. 1980, U.S. Dist. Ct. (we. dist.) Ky. 1981, U.S. Dist. Ct. (ea. dist.) Ky. 1983. Staff reporter/edn. editor The Hartford Courant, 1971-74; asst. to supt. Hartford Pub. Schs., 1974-77; assoc. Igor Sikorsky & Assocs., Hartford, 1979-80, Brown, Todd & Heyburn, Louisville, 1980-82; ptnr. Barnett & Alagia, Louisville, 1982-88, Keeney & Willock, Louisville, 1988-90; prin. Amerilaw, Louisville, 1990-93; pres. LawTech Svcs. Co., Louisville, 1993—; mng. mem. Trautwein & Keeney PLLC, Louisville, 1993—. Co-author/editor: Death Benefit: A Lawyer Uncovers A 20 Year Pattern of Seduction, 1993, 94, Reader's Digest Today's Best Non-Fiction Vol. 24, 1994; contbr. articles to profl. jours. Bd. dirs. Hospice of Louisville, Inc., 1984-86; exec. dir. Juvenile Justice Pub. Edn. Project, West Hartford, Conn., 1978-80; pres. bd. dirs. Stage One: Louisville Children's Theatre, 1982-83; founding bd. dirs. Ky. Citizens for Arts, Frankfort, 1983; mem. Lebanon (Conn.) Bd. Edn., 1975-80; campaign mgr. Mazzoli 3d C.D. Ky., Jefferson County, 1982, 84; elder 2d Presbyn. Ch., Louisville, 1984-86. Recipient Disting. Contbn. award Nat. Com. for Prevention of Child Abuse, Ky. chpt., 1982, Disting. Svc. award Conn. Assn. Bds. of Edn., 1976, Profl. Achievement for Gen. Reporting Series award Soc. Profl. Journalists, Sigma Delta Chi, Conn. chpt. 1974. Mem. ABA (editl. com. The Tax Lawyer 1984-89), Assn. Trial Lawyers of Am., Ky. Acad. Trial Atty's., Ky. Bar Assn., Louisville Bar Assn., Million Dollar Advocates Forum, Jefferson Club. Democrat. Presbyterian. Avocations: bibliophile, marksman, golf. Office: Trautwein and Keeney PLLC 1 Riverfront Plz Ste 510 Louisville KY 40202-2923

KEENUM, MARK E., legislative chief of staff; b. Starkville, Miss., Jan. 28, 1961. AA in Bus. Adminstrn., N.E. Miss. C.C., 1981; BS in Agrl. Econs., Miss. State U., 1983, MAgr in Agrl. Econs., 1984, PhD in Agrl. Econs., 1988. Grad. rsch. asst. Agr. and Forestry Exptl. Sta. Miss. State U., Starkville, 1983-84, ext. mktg. specialist Miss. Co-op Ext. Svc., 1984-86, rsch. assoc. Agr. and Forestry Exptl. Sta., 1986-88, asst. economist, prof. dept. agrl. econs., 1988-89; legis. asst. Office of Senator Thad Cochran, Washington, 1989-96, staff dir., 1995-96, chief of staff, 1997—. Recipient Kiwanian of the Yr. award Starkville Kiwanis Breakfast Club, 1986, Outstanding Pub. Svc. award Coll. Agr. and Life Scis. Alumni Assn., Miss. State U., 1992, Outstanding Contbn. to Delta Agr. award Miss. Delta Coun., 1993, Farm Policy Commendation award Miss. Delta Coun., 1996; Varsity Football scholar N.E. Miss. C.C., 1979-81, Pres. scholar Miss. State U., 1982-83. Mem. Gamma Sigma Delta. Office: 326 Senate Russell Office Washington DC 20510-2402

KEENY, SPURGEON MILTON, JR., association executive; b. N.Y.C., Oct. 24, 1924; s. Spurgeon Milton and Amelia (Smith) K.; m. Sheila Spear, May 3, 1952; children—Christopher Spear, Christy Virginia, Spurgeon Milton III. BA, Columbia U., 1944, MA in Physics, 1946; postgrad., Sch. Internat. Affairs and Russian Inst., 1946-47; LLD (hon.), U. Notre Dame, 1991. With Directorate of Intelligence, Hdqrs. USAF, 1950-55; mem. staff Panel on Peaceful Uses Atomic Energy, Joint Congl. Com. Atomic Energy, Washington, 1955-56; chief atomic energy div. Office of Asst. Sec. Def. for Research and Engring., Washington, 1956-57; mem. Gaither security resources panel Exec. Office of Pres., 1957; tech. asst. to President's Sci. Adviser, Washington, 1958-69; sr. staff mem. Nat. Security Council, 1963-69; asst. dir. for sci. and tech. U.S. Arms Control and Disarmament Agy., Washington, 1969-73; dep. dir. U.S. Arms Control and Disarmament Agy., 1977-81; scholar-in-residence Nat. Acad. Scis., Washington, 1981-85; pres., exec. dir. Arms Control Assn., Washington, 1985—; dir. policy and program devel. Mitre Corp., McLean, Va., 1973-77; mem. U.S. del. to Geneva Conf. Experts on Nuclear Test Detection, 1958; to Geneva Conf. on Discontinuance of Nuclear Weapons Tests, 1958-60; chief U.S. del. U.S./Soviet Talks on Theater Nuclear Forces, 1980; mem. adv. com. Program Sci. and Internat. Affairs, Harvard, 1973-77; dep. chmn. com. environ. decision making Nat. Acad. Scis., 1974-77; chmn. Nuclear Energy Policy Study Ford Found., 1975-77; mem. com. on internat. security and arms control Nat. Acad. Scis., 1981—. Co-author: Nuclear Power Issues and Choices, 1977; Nuclear Arms Control Background and Issues, 1985; Management and Disposition of Excess Weapons Plutonium, 1994, The Future of U.S. Nuclear Weapons Policy, 1997. Served to 1st lt. USAF, 1948-50. Recipient Rockefeller Pub. Service award, 1970; Disting. Honor award U.S. Arms Control and Disarmament Agy., 1981. Fellow Am. Acad. Arts Scis., Am. Phys. Soc. (mem. study group on light-water reactor safety 1974-75, forum award 1986); mem. Council on Fgn. Relations, Phi Beta Kappa. Home: 3600 Albemarle St NW Washington DC 20008-4216 Office: Arms Control Assn 1726 M St NW Washington DC 20036-4502

KEEP, JUDITH N., federal judge; b. Omaha, Mar. 24, 1944. B.A., Scripps Coll., 1966; J.D., U. San Diego, 1970. Bar: Calif. 1971. Atty. Defenders Inc., San Diego, 1971-73; pvt. practice law, 1973-76; asst. U.S. atty. U.S. Dept. Justice, 1976; judge Mcpl. Ct., San Diego, 1976-80; judge U.S. Dist. Ct. (so. dist.) Calif., San Diego, 1980—, chief judge, 1991-98; judge U.S. Office: US Dist Ct Ct Rm 16 940 Front St Ste 5190 San Diego CA 92101-8916

KEEPIN, GEORGE ROBERT, JR., physicist; b. Oak Park, Ill., Dec. 5, 1923; s. George Robert and Erlene Marie (Bennett) K.; m. Madge Mary Twomey, June 13, 1948; children: Robert, William, Ardis, Mavis, Denice. PhB, U. Chgo., 1943; BS, MIT, 1946, MS, 1947; PhD in Physics, Northwestern U., 1949. Tchg. fellow dept. physics MIT, Cambridge, 1947; postdoctoral fellow U. Calif., Berkeley, 1950-52; rsch. physicist Los Alamos (N.Mex.) Sci. Lab., 1952-63, group leader nuclear safeguards rsch., 1966-76, dir. nuclear safeguards program, 1976-80; head physics divsn. IAEA, Vienna, Austria, 1963-65, spl. adviser to dep. dir. gen. nuclear safeguards, 1982-85; fellow Los Alamos Nat. Lab., 1985—; mem. U.S. del. UN Atoms-for-Peace Conf., Geneva, 1955, 71, IAEA tech. adviser, 1964. Author: Progress in Nuclear Energy-Delayed Neutrons, 1956, Physics of Nuclear Kinetics, 1965; Arms Control Verification: The Technologies That Make It Possible, 1986; editor: Nuclear Analysis R and D; patentee in field. Fellow Los Alamos Nat. Lab, Am. Phys. Soc., Am. Nuclear Soc. (exec. com. 1967-69); mem. Inst. Nuclear Materials Mgmt. (nat. chmn. 1978-80, Disting. Service award 1984), N.Y. Acad. Scis., Sigma Xi. Home: 600 La Bajada Way Los Alamos NM 87544-3805

KEER, LEON MORRIS, engineering educator; b. Los Angeles, Sept. 13, 1934; s. William and Sophia (Bookman) K.; m. Barbara Sara Davis, Aug. 18, 1956; children: Patricia Renee, Jacqueline Saundra, Harold Neal, Michael Derek. BS, Calif. Inst. Tech., 1956, MS, 1958; PhD, U. Minn., 1962. Registered Profl. Engr., Calif. Mem. tech. staff Hughes Aircraft Co., Culver City, Calif., 1956-59; research fellow, instr. U. Minn., Mpls., 1959-62; asst. prof. Northwestern U., Evanston, Ill., 1964-66, assoc. prof., 1966-70, prof. engring., 1970—, Walter P. Murphy prof. mech. and civil engring., 1994—; assoc. dean research and grad. studies Northwestern U., 1985-92, chmn. dept. civil engring., 1992-97; preceptor Columbia U., N.Y.C., 1963-64; dept. acad. advisor civil and structural engring. Hong Kong U., 1998—. Co-editor: monograph Solid Contact and Lubrication, 1980; contbr. articles to profl. jours. NATO fellow, 1962; Guggenheim Found. fellow, 1972; JSPS fellow, 1986. Fellow ASCE (chmn. engring. mech. divsn. 1992-93), Am. Acad. Mechanics (sec. 1981-88, pres.-elect 1987-88, pres. 1988-89), ASME (tech. editor Jour. Applied Mechanics 1988-92), Nat. Acad. Engring. (elected 1997); mem. Acoustical Soc. Am., Sigma Xi, Tau Beta Pi. Home: 2601 Marian Ln Wilmette IL 60091-2207 Office: Northwestern U Dept Civil Engring 2145 Sheridan Rd Dept Civil Evanston IL 60208-0834

KEES, MARY ADELE, school psychologist; b. Rice Lake, Wis., Sept. 9, 1948; d. Lloyd Robert and Irene Margaret (Kies) Bushland; m. Lowell Lee Kees, Mar. 9, 1968; children: Erik, Kealynn, Ian. BS in Elem. Edn., U. Wis., River Falls, 1975, MSE in Sch. Psychology, 1990, MSE in Reading, 1991, MSE in Guidance and Counseling, 1995. Lic. sch. psychologist, Wis. Admissions coord. St. Croixdale Hosp., Prescott, Wis., 1980-84; edn. coord. River Hills Hosp., Prescott, 1984-88; sch. psychologist Prescott sch. Dist., 1989—. Mem. Nat. Assn. Sch. Psychologists, Wis. Assn. Sch. Psychologists. Avocation: reading. Home: N8520 1197th St River Falls WI 54022-4716 Office: Prescott Sch Dist 505 Campbell St N Prescott WI 54021-1073

KEESEE, ROGER NEAL, JR., lawyer; b. Lynchburg, Va., Mar. 5, 1963; s. Roger Neal and June B. (Booth) K.; m. Lisa Marie Keesee, Sept. 2, 1989; children: Nicole, Megan. BS in Acctg. magna cum laude, Va. Tech. U., 1985; JD, Wiliam and Mary Coll., 1988. Assoc. Woods, Rogers & Hazelgrove, Roanoke, Va., 1988-95, ptnr., 1996—. Co-chmn. Roanoke pro-bono hotline Legal Aid Soc., 1996-98; bd. dirs Roanoke Valley Trouble Ctr., 1992-98; trustee, mem. Roanoke Tech. Ednl. Coun., roanoke City Schs., 1992—. Mem. ABA, Va. Bar Assn. (young lawyers exec coun. 1992-98), Roanoke Valley Estate Planning Coun., Order of Coif. Office: Woods Rogers & Hazelgrove PO Box 14125 Roanoke VA 24038-4125

KEESEE, THOMAS WOODFIN, JR., financial consultant; b. Helena, Ark., Feb. 11, 1915; s. Thomas Woodfin and Sarah Gladys (Key) K.; m. Patricia Peale, Apr. 6, 1940 (div. Dec. 1951); m. Patricia Hartford, June 26, 1953; children: Allen P.K., Thomas Woodfin, III, Anne H.K. Niemann. BA, Duke U., 1935; JD, Harvard U., 1938. Bar: N.Y. 1939. Assoc. firm Simpson, Thacher & Bartlett, N.Y.C., 1938-42; asst. to pres. Sperry Gyroscope Co., Inc., Gt. Neck, N.Y., 1942-46; with Bessemer Securities Corp., Bessemer Trust Co., N.Y.C., 1946-80; dir., pres., CEO, bd. dirs. Bessemer Securities Corp., N.Y.C., 1970-76; bd. dirs., pres., CEO Bessemer Trust Co., N.Y.C., 1970-76; bd. dirs. emeritus Duke U. Mgmt. Corp.; mem. adv. bd. Nevis Capital Mgmt. Inc.; trustee, chmn. investment com. Nat. Health and Welfare Retirement Assn., 1966-75; chmn. bd., pres. Phipps Houses, 1952-70; bd. govs. Real Estate Bd. N.Y., Inc., 1964-66. Chmn. endowment investment com., trustee Duke U., 1976-85, emeritus trustee, 1985—; trustee Mianus River Gorge Preserve; chmn. Nat. Audubon Soc., 1979-83, bd. dirs., 1972-83, 94-96; pres. The Cisqua Sch., Bedford, N.Y., 1962-67; trustee Allen-Stevenson Sch., N.Y.C., 1950-57; sr. warden St. Matthews Protestant Episc. Ch., 1968-73. Mem. N.Y. State Bar Assn., Harvard Law Sch. Assn., Pilgrims Soc., Phi Beta Kappa, Sigma Chi. Clubs: Harvard, Knickerbocker, Racquet and Tennis, Bedford Golf and Tennis; Clove Valley Rod and Gun (Millbrook, N.Y.); Cosmos (Washington), Ausable (St. Huberts, N.Y.). Home: 140 Sarles St RD 3 Mount Kisco NY 10549-4733

KEESHEN, KATHLEEN KEARNEY, public relations consultant; b. N.Y.C., Dec. 4, 1937; d. James William and Hannah Pauline (Mansfield) Kearney; 1 child (by previous marriage), John Christopher Day; m. Walt Keeshen Jr.; stepchildren: Michael Patrick, Walt John III, Kathleen Marie, William Thomas, Ralph Timothy. BA in English, U. Md., 1959, MA in Journalism, 1973, PhD in Am. Studies, 1983; MLA, Stanford U., 1995. Cert. profl. sec. Congl., legal, med., acad., corp. sec. various orgns., East and Midwest, 1954-63; staff and mgmt. positions IBM, Washington, Md., 1963-73; lab. comm. mgr. Systems Comm. Div. IBM, Manassas, Va., 1974-76; comm. staff corp. hdqrs. IBM, Armonk, N.Y., 1977-83; comm. and community rels. mgr. Almaden Rsch. Ctr. IBM, San Jose, Calif., 1983-92; prin. Keeshen Comm., Coyote (Calif.) Press., 1992—. Contbr. articles to profl. jours.; lectr. in field. Mem. adv. bd. Friends of San Jose Pub. Libr., 1987—, Silicon Valley Info. Ctr., 1986-92, Media Report to Women; mem. corp. task force Stanford U. Inst. for Rsch. on Women and Gender, 1990—, affiliated scholar, 1992-94, assocs. bd., 1994-96; affiliated scholar Beatrice M. Bain Rsch. Group on Gender, U. Calif., Berkeley, 1994-95; libr. commr. City of Morgan Hill, Calif., 1999—. Mem. Am. Journalism Historians Assn., Assn. for Edn. in Journalism and Mass Comm., Women in Comm., Dean's First Edition Club, Coll. of Journalism U. Md., San Jose Rotary Club, San. Jose Profl. Womens Literary Assn., Calif. Writers Club, Sigma Delta Chi, Alpha Xi Delta. Office: Keeshen Comm Coyote Press PO Box 13154 Coyote CA 95013-3154

KEESLING, JAMES EDGAR, mathematics educator; b. Indpls., June 26, 1942; s. Fred Edgar and Martha Belle (Grimes) K.; m. Marian Ellen Calley, Jan. 26, 1963; children: James Jr., Marian Esther, Timothy Carl, Ruth Emily. BS in Indsl. Engring., U. Miami, 1964, MS in Math., 1966, PhD in Math., 1968. Asst. prof. math. U. Fla., Gainesville, 1967-71; assoc. prof. math. U. Fla., 1971-75, prof. math., 1975—; pres. pro-tempore Coll. of Liberal Arts and Scis., U. Fla., 1989-90; vis. faculty U. Ga., 1976-77, U. Utah, 1991-92; vis. lectr. Soc. Indsl. and Applied Math., 1992—; lectr. numerous nat. and internat. conf. in math., 1969—. Contbr. articles to math. jours. Elder, ch. chmn. Creekside Community Ch. (Evangelical Free Ch. of Am.), Gainesville, 1987-90, 94-97. Mem. Am. Math. Soc., Math. Assn. Am., Soc. Indsl. and Applied Math., Tau Beta Pi, Phi Kappa Phi. Home: 710 NE 6th St Gainesville FL 32601-5566 Office: U Fla Dept Math Gainesville FL 32611-8105

KEESLING, KAREN RUTH, lawyer; b. Wichita, Kans., July 9, 1946; d. Paul W. and Ruth (Sharp) K. BA, Ariz. State U., 1968, MA, 1970; JD, Georgetown U., 1981. Bar: Va. 1981, Fla. 1981. Asst. dean of women U. Kans., Lawrence, 1970-72; exec. sec., sec.'s adv. com. on rights and responsibilities of women HEW, Washington, 1972-74; dir. White House Office of Women's Programs, Washington, 1974-77; head civil rights and equal opportunity sect., Gov. Div., Congl. Rsch. Svc. Libr. Congress, Washington, 1977-80; legis. aide Sen. Nancy Kassebaum, Washington, 1979-81; mem. pers. office staff Office of Pres.-elect, Washington, Jan. 1981; pvt. practice Falls Church, Va. and Peoria, Ariz., 1981-88, 90—; dept. for equal opportunity dept. Dept. Air Force, Washington, 1981-82, dep. asst. sec. manpower res. affairs and installations, 1982-83; prin. dep. asst. sec. manpower res. affairs Dept. Air Force, 1983-87; prin. dep. asst. sec. readiness support dept. Dept. Air Force, Washington, 1987-88, prin. dep. asst. sec. manpower and res. affairs, 1988, asst. sec. manpower and res. affairs, 1988-89; acting wage and hour adminstr. U.S. Dept. Labor, Washington, 1992-93; pvt. practice Falls Church, Va., Peoria, Ariz.; bd. advisers Outstanding Young Women Am., 1983-90. Mem. Nat. Fedn. Republican Women's Club, Washington, 1975, Nat. Women's Polit. Caucus, Washington, 1980. Named one of Ten Outstanding Young Women of Am., 1975; recipient Ariz. State U. Alumni Achievement award, 1976, Elizabeth Boyer award Women's Equity Action League, 1986, Meritorious Civilian award USAF, 1987, Woman of Distinction award Nat. Conf. Coll. Women, Student Leaders and Women of Distinction, 1988, Exeptional Civilian Svc. award USAF, 1988. Mem. Va. Bar Assn., Fla. Bar Assn., Va. Fedn. Bus. and Profl. Women's Clubs (2d v.p. 1987-88, 1st v.p. 1988-89, pres.-elect 1989-90, pres. 1990-91), No. Va. Women Atty.'s Assn. (steering com. 1990-95), Va. Bus. and Profl. Women's Found. (trustee 1985-93), The Women's Inst. Inc. (adv. coun. 1985-96), U.S. Com. for the UNIFEM (gen. counsel 1983—), P.E.O., Pi Beta Phi. Avocation: golf (Kans. Women's Golf Champion, 1966, Wichita Women's Champion 1968, 70, Outstanding Woman Golfer in Kans., 1966). Home: 19147 N 84th Dr Peoria AZ 85382-8730

KEETER, LYNN CARPENTER, English educator; b. Charlotte, NC; d. John Franklin and Georgiana (LaVender) Carpenter; children: John Blair, Eric William. BA in English, Gardner-Webb U., 1980, MA in Edn., 1985, MA in English, 1994; devel. educator specialist, Ariz. State U. Instr. Taylor Finishing, Charlotte, 1970-74; instr. Gardner-Webb U., Boiling Springs, N.C., 1980-86, prof. English, 1988—; tchr. Robeson County Schs., Lumberton, N.C., 1986-88; freelance writer for vintage clothing jours.; storyteller Appalachian folklore. Co-author: Fundamentals of Reading and Writing, 1997; writer children's stories. Mem. Internat. Reading Assn. (award 1997), A.C.E.I., pres. local chpt. N.C.R.A., N.C.Reading Assn. (pres. local coun. 1998—), Woman's Club Internat. (v.p., pres., Outstanding Woman 1980), Woman's Prayer Assn. (pres.), Coll. English Assn. (editor newsletter 1993—), Beta Sigma Phi (pres., v.p., sec., Woman of Yr. award 1991, 92, Alpha Omega award 1992), Sigma Tau Delta, Phi Delta Kappa. Avocations: antiques, interior decorating, dancing.

KEETH, BETTY LOUISE, geriatrics nursing director; b. Hayward, Okla., Nov. 15, 1931; d. Harley Enoch and Violet Verona (Space) George; m. Melvin L. Gillham, May 4, 1951 (div. July 1969); children: Melvin L., Dennis Ray, Debra Lynne Gillham; m. William D. Keeth, Nov. 19, 1976 (dec. Aug. 1992). ADN, Carl Albert Jr. Coll., 1984. LPN, Ark. DON MENA Manor, Mena, Ark., 1987-89, Living Ctrs. of Am., Oklahoma City, 1989-90, Westlake Sq. Ctr., Oklahoma City, 1990-91, Bethany Village, 1991-94, East Moore Nursing, Moore, Okla., 1994-95; dir. Ctrl. Okla. Christian Home, Oklahoma City, 1995-98, ret., 1999; with Mariner Health of Bethany, Okla.; cons. Precision Home Health, Oklahoma City. Registrar Lefiore County, Poteau, Okla., 1989; sec. Dem. Women, 1984-90. Avocations: crocheting, bowling, fitness. Home: 2908 Pinto Trl Edmond OK 73003-6667 Office: Mariner Health of Bethany 6900 NW 39th Expressway Bethany OK 73110

KEETON, J. E., retired psychiatrist; b. Brilliant, Ala., Oct. 8, 1925; s. James Willie and Mary Etta (Dodd) K.; m. Mary Ann Trantham, May 31, 1953 (dec. Dec. 1989); children: Jonathan Eric, David Wright, Adam Blake. BS, Birmingham So. U., 1951; MD, U. Ala., 1955. Intern U. Chgo. Clinics, 1955-56; resident psychiatry Inst. Living, Hartford, Conn., 1956-59; dir. day hosp. Vets. Hosp., Washington, 1960-61, asst. chief psychiatry, 1961-64; pvt. practice psychiatry Bethesda, Md., 1964-78; staff psychiatrist Vets. Med. Ctr., Tuscaloosa, Ala., 1978-97; ret., 1998; dir. clozapine rsch. Vets. Hosp., Tuscaloosa, 1991-97. Pharmacist mate USN, 1944-46. Mem. Am. Psychiat. Assn. (life). Home: 4324 Stonehill Ln Tuscaloosa AL 35405-5441

KEETON, ROBERT ERNEST, federal judge; b. Clarksville, Tex., Dec. 16, 1919; s. William Robert and Ernestine (Tuten) K.; m. Betty E. Baker, May 28, 1941; children: Katherine, William Robert. BBA, U. Tex., 1940, LLB, 1941; SJD, Harvard U., 1956; LLD (hon.), William Mitchell Coll., 1983, Lewis and Clark Coll., 1988. Bar: Tex. 1941, Mass. 1955. Assoc. firm Baker, Botts, Andrews & Wharton (and successors), Houston, 1941-42, 45-51; assoc. prof. law So. Meth. U., 1951-54; Thayer teaching fellow Harvard U., 1953-54, asst. prof., 1954-56, prof. law, 1956-73, Langdell prof., 1973-79; assoc. dean Harvard, 1975-79; judge Fed. Dist. Ct., Boston, 1979—; Commr. on Uniform State Laws from Mass., 1971-79; trustee Flaschner Jud. Inst., 1979-86; exec. dir. Nat. Inst. Trial Advocacy, 1973-76; ednl. cons., 1976-79; mem. com. on ct. adminstrn. U.S. Jud. Conf., 1985-87, mem. standing com. on rules, 1987-90, chmn., 1990-93. Author: Trial Tactics and Methods, 1954, 2d edit., 1973, Cases and Materials on the Law of Insurance, 1960, 2d edit., 1977, Legal Cause in the Law of Torts, 1963, Venturing To Do Justice, 1969, (with Jeffrey O'Connell) Basic Protection for the Traffic Victim: A Blueprint for Reforming Automobile Insurance, 1965, After Cars Crash: The Need for Legal and Insurance Reform, 1967, (with Page Keeton) Cases and Materials on the Law of Torts, 1971, 2d edit., 1977, Basic Text on Insurance Law, 1971, (with others) Tort and Accident Law, 1983, 2d edit., 1989, (with others) Prosser & Keeton, Torts, 5th edit., 1984, Pocket Part, 1988, (with Alan Widiss) Insurance Law, 1988, Judging, 1990; also articles. Served to lt. comdr. USNR, 1942-45. Recipient Wm. B. Jones award Nat. Inst. Trial Advocacy, 1980; recipient Leon Green award U. Tex. Law Rev., 1981, Francis Rawle award Am. Law Inst.-ABA, 1983, Samuel E. Gates litigation award Am. Coll. Trial Lawyers, 1984. Fellow Am. Bar Found., mem., Am. Acad. Arts and Scis., Am. Bar Assn., Mass. Bar Assn., State Bar Tex., Am. Law Inst., Am. Risk and Ins. Assn., Chancellors, Friars, Order of Coif, Beta Gamma Sigma, Beta Alpha Psi, Phi Delta Phi, Phi Eta Sigma. Office: US Dist Ct 1 Courthouse Way Ste 3130 Boston MA 02210

KEETS, JOHN DAVID, JR., insurance company executive; b. Atlantic City, N.J., Apr. 1, 1948; s. John D. and Doris F. (Fleiss) Keets; m. Julianne Zellers, Nov. 3, 1973; children: J. David, Brian. BA, High Point Coll., 1970. CLU, cert. fin. planner, chartered fin. cons. Account exec. Mgmt. Recruiters, Phila., 1972-75; sales mgr. Cigna Fin. Svc., Miami (Fla.), Balt., 1975-82; agy. mgr. Fidelty Mut., Balt., 1983-85, Provident Mut. Ins. Co., Phila., 1985-88; regional v.p. Equitable Ins. Co., Mpls., 1988-90; prin. Keets & Assocs., Mpls., 1991-93, 97—; mgr. Prudential Ins. Co., Mpls., 1993-94; v.p. bus. devel. Carlson Mktg. Group, Mpls., 1994—; gen. mgr. Mut. of Omaha Cos., Mpls., 1998—. With U.S. Army, 1970-72, Germany. Mem. Mpls. Assn. Life Underwriter, Gen. Agts. & Mgrs. Assn, Internat. Assn. Fin. Planners, Am. Soc. CLU, Chartered Fin. Cons. Avocations: golf, boating. Home: 2420 Comstock Ln N Minneapolis MN 55447-2303

KEEVE, JACK PHILIP, physician, educator, retired; b. N.Y.C., Jan. 28, 1922; s. Frank and Lillian (Zeitler) K.; m. Grace Celis, June 1, 1972; 1 child, Jonathan. AB, Hobart Coll., 1948; MD, NYU, 1952; MPH, Yale U., 1958. Asst. prof. preventive medicine N.Y. Med. Coll., 1960-68; health programs adminstr. Dept. of State, 1969-79; clin. prof. occupl. medicine George Washington U. Med. Ctr., 1979—; med. dir. Atlantic Richfield Co., 1980-82; clin. prof., assoc. residency dir. U. Calif., Irvine, 1982-83; med. dir. occupl. health Naval Rsch. Lab., 1983-86; dir. civilian employees health svcs. The Pentagon, 1986-89; dir. County Health Dept., Leesburg, Va., 1989-93; med. dir. mid-atlantic region U.S. Postal Svc., 1993-96; ret., 1998; assoc. rsch. prof. U. Pitts., 1966-69; cons. EPA, 1978-80; prof. population planning U. Philippines, 1969-71; lectr. epidemiology Yale Sch. Medicine, 1981-83. Contbr. articles to profl. jours. Fellow ACP, Am. Coll. Occupl. Environ. Medicine, Am. Coll. Preventive Medicine (cert.), Am. Acad. Pediatrics (cert.). Home: 1119A N Utah St Arlington VA 22201-5703

KEEVEY, RICHARD FRANCIS, government official, educator; b. Phila., June 20, 1942; s. Richard Patrick and Eileen (Wright) K.; m. Elizabeth Regina Dwyer, Aug. 5, 1967; children: Richard, Michael, John. BA, La Salle Coll., Phila., 1964; M of Govt. Adminstrn., U. Pa., 1967. Various positions Commonwealth of Pa., City of Phila., State of N.J., 1967-70; dir. adminstrn., fiscal officer dept. community affairs N.J. Dept., Trenton, 1971-75, asst. to dir. div. budget and acctg. Treasury Dept., 1975-81, supr. Bur. Budget, Office Mgmt. and Budget, 1981-83, dep. budget dir., dep. conptr., 1983-89, dir. Office Mgmt. and Budget, 1989-94; dep. under sec. for fin. mgmt. Dept. Def., Washington, 1994-95, dir. defense fin. and acctg. agy., 1995-97; CFO U.S. Dept. Housing and Urban Renewal, 1997-99; dir. budget and fin. practice Arthur Andersen, Washington, 1999—; instr. Rutgers U., New Brunswick, N.J., 1971-75; adj. prof. fin. Rider Coll., Lawrenceville, N.J., 1979-82, mem. adv. com. grad. program in pub. mgmt., 1983-87; adj. prof. Seton Hall U., South Orange, N.J., 1990-93. Contbr. articles to profl. jours.; mem. bd. editors Pub. Adminstrn. Rev., 1979-84. Coach Little League Baseball and Soccer, 1975-82; trustee Police Athletic League Sports, Cinnaminson, N.J., 1978-81; mem. counsle president's adv. bd. La Salle U., 1984-87; bd. dirs. Zurbrugg Meml. Hosp., Willingboro, N.J., 1985-88; mem. Leadership N.J. Class of 1990, 1989—; pres. Cinnaminson Twp. Bd. Edn., 1980-90; mem. N.J. Commn. on Capital Budgeting and Planning, N.J. Bldg. Authority, N.J. Commn. on Health Benefits and Pensions, N.J. Transit Corp., N.J. Capital Joint Mgmt. Commn., N.J. Lease Mgmt.-Planning Bd. Decorated DSM, medal for outstanding svc. U.S. Dept. Def., 1996. Mem. Nat. Assn. State Budget Officers, Nat. Assn. Comptrs., Am. Soc. for Pub. Adminstrn. (N.J. Pub. Adminstr. of Yr. award 1992), Assn. Govtl. Accts. (Disting. Leadership award N.J. chpt. 1991), Govt. Fin. Officers Assn. (tech. group to rev. budgets for nat. award certs.). Home: 1965 Columbia Pike Apt 21 Arlington VA 22204-6172 Office: US Dept Housing & Urban Renewal Washington DC 20301

KEEVIL, NORMAN BELL, mining executive; b. Cambridge, Mass., Feb. 28, 1938; s. Norman Bell and Verna Ruth (Bond) K.; m. Joan E. Macdonald, Dec. 1990; children: Scott, Laura, Jill, Norman Bell III. BA in Sci., U. Toronto, Ont., Can., 1959; PhD, U. Calif., Berkeley, 1964; LLD (hon.), U. B.C., 1993. Registered profl. engr., Ont. V.p. exploration Teck Corp., Vancouver, B.C., Can., 1962-68; exec. v.p. Teck Corp., Vancouver, 1968-81, pres., chief exec. officer, 1981-89, chmn., pres., chief exec. officer, 1989-94, pres., CEO, 1994—; chmn. Cominco Ltd., Vancouver, 1986—. Named Mining Man of Yr. No. Miner, 1979. Mem. Can. Inst. Mining and Metallurgy (Selwyn G. Blaylock medal 1990, Inco medal 1999), Prospectors and Developers Assn. (Disting. Svc. award 1990), Soc. Exploration Geophysicists, Vancouver Club, Shaughnessy Golf and Country Club (Vancouver). Office: Teck Corp, 200 Burrard St # 700, Vancouver, BC Canada V6C 3L9

KEEVIL, PHILIP CLEMENT, investment banker; b. London, Oct. 19, 1946; s. Ambrose Clement Arthur and Olwen Marjorie Enid (Gibbins) K.; m. Augusta Day McGrail, June 10, 1972; children: Adrian Ambrose Clement, Augusta Hall, Peter Larimer. BA, Oxford U., Eng., 1968, MA, 1972; MBA, Harvard U., 1975. Mgr. Unilever plc, Eng., 1968-73; assoc. Morgan Stanley & Co., N.Y.C., 1975-78; assoc. Lazard Freres & Co., N.Y.C., 1979-80, v.p., 1981-82, gen. ptnr., 1983-87; mng. dir., head mergers and acquisitions S.G. Warburg and Co. Inc., N.Y.C., 1987-91, head investment banking, 1991-95; mng. dir. head internat. mergers and acquisitions Salomon Brothers Inc., N.Y.C., 1995-97; head European mergers and acquisitions Salomon Brothers Inc., London, 1997—; bd. dirs. S.G. Warburg & Co., Ltd., London, 1987-95, Am. for Oxford Inc., 1995—. Freeman of City of London, 1968; liveryman Worshipful Co. of Poulters, London, 1968—; mem. of the Court, 1997—, renter warden, 1998-99, upper warden, 1999—; vestryman St. John's Ch., Locust Valley, N.Y., 1986-89; trustee St. Bernard's Sch., N.Y., 1991-97, St. Andrew's Sch., Del., 1993—. Baker scholar Harvard Bus. Sch., Boston, 1975. Mem. British Am. C. of C. (dir. 1993—). Episcopalian. Clubs: Piping Rock (Locust Valley) (gov. 1986-96); Brook, Racquet & Tennis (N.Y.C.), Knickerbocker, Long Island, Wyandanch, Leander (Henley, England). Avocations: choral music, field sports, racquet sports. Office: Salomon Smith Barney, 111 Buckingham Palace Rd, London SW1W 0SB, England

KEFALIDES, NICHOLAS ALEXANDER, physician, educator; b. Alexandroupolis, Greece, Jan. 17, 1927; came to U.S., 1947, naturalized; s. Athanasious and Alexandra (Aematidou) K.; m. Eugenia Georgia Kutsunis, Nov. 24, 1949; children: Alexandra Jane (dec.), Patricia Ann, Paul Thomas. BA, Augustana Coll., Rock Island, Ill., 1951; BS, U. Ill., Chgo., 1953, MS in Biochemistry, 1956, MD, 1956, PhD in Biochemistry, 1965; MS (hon.), U. Pa., 1971; doctorate (hon.), U. Reims, France, 1987. Resident in internal medicine U. Ill. Coll. Medicine, Chgo., 1960-62, NIH fellow in infectious disease, 1962-64, asst. prof. medicine, 1964-65; asst. prof. medicine U. Chgo., 1965-69, assoc. prof. medicine, 1969-70; assoc. prof. medicine and biochemistry U. Pa., Phila., 1970-74, prof. medicine, 1974—, prof. biochemistry and biophysics, 1975—; assoc. dean rsch. U. Pa. Sch. Medicine, 1994-95; mem., chmn. pathobiochemistry study sect. NIH, 1982-86; dir. project on burns NIH, USPHS, Lima, Peru, 1957-60, Connective Tissue Rsch. Inst., Phila., 1977—; exec. chmn. Instn. Rev. Bd. U. Pa., 1998—, chmn., 1995-98; initiator, chair Gordon Rsch. Confs. on Basement Membranes, 1982. Contbr. chpts. to books, articles to profl. jours. Served as surgeon USPHS, 1957-60. Recipient Borden Rsch. Found. award, 1956, award for pioneering rsch. on connective tissue Collagen Gordon Confs. and Collagen Corp., 1997; Guggenheim fellow, 1977. Fellow AAAS; mem. Am. Assn. Pathologists, Am. Soc. Clin. Investigation, Am. Soc. Biochemistry and Molecular Biology, Am. Soc. Cell Biology. Achievements include discovery of Collagen type IV in basement membranes and its role in suppressing tumor cell growth. Office: Connective Tissue Rsch Inst 3624 Market St Ste 500 Philadelphia PA 19104-2681

KEFAUVER, WELDON ADDISON, publisher; b. Canal Winchester, Ohio, Apr. 3, 1927; s. Ross Baker and Virginia Marie (Burtner) K. B.A., Ohio State U., Columbus, 1950. Mem. faculty Columbus Acad., 1956-58; mng. editor Ohio State U. Press, 1958-64, dir., 1964-84, dir. emeritus, 1984—; dir. Am. Univ. Press Services, Inc., 1971-72, 76-79; mem. U.S. del. 2d Asian Pacific Conf. Publs., Taiwan, 1978. Author: Scholars and their Publishers, 1977; editorial adv. bd. Scholarly Publishing. Served with AUS, 1945-46. Recipient Centennial Service award Ohio State U., 1970; citation Ohioana Library Assn., 1974; Disting. Service award Ohio State U., 1986; recognized for service to Ohio State U. by Ohio Senate and Ohio Ho. of Reps., 1986. Mem. Assn. Am. Univ. Presses (v.p. 1971-72, dir. 1971-72, 76-79, pres. 1977-78), Soc. Scholarly Pub., Nathaniel Hawthorne Soc., AAUP, Phi Eta Sigma, Phi Kappa Phi. Clubs: Torch (Columbus), Crichton (Columbus), Ohio State U. Faculty (Columbus). Home: 675 Eastmoor Blvd Columbus OH 43209-2252 Office: 1050 Carmack Rd Columbus OH 43210-1002

KEFFER, CHARLES JOSEPH, consultant; b. Phila., Aug. 7, 1941; s. Raphael Joseph and Clara Emelia (Fefolt) K.; m. Barbara Franke, Aug. 27, 1966; children—Susan Marie, David Charles, Peter John, Dennis Paul. BS, U. Scranton, 1963; AM, Harvard U., 1964, PhD, 1969. From instr. to assoc. prof. physics U. Scranton, Pa., 1967-73; dean coll. U. St. Thomas, St. Paul, 1973-77; v.p. acad. affairs U. St. Thomas, 1973-84, provost, 1977-98; cons.-evaluator N. Central Assn., Chgo., 1980-98. Chmn. Midway Tng. Services, St. Paul, 1977-87. Grad. fellow NSF, Harvard U., 1963-65; summer leadership fellow Bush Found., 1977. Mem. Democratic Farm Labor Party. Roman Catholic. Avocation: soccer.

KEFFER, MARIA JEAN, environmental auditor; b. Sacramento, Dec. 10, 1951; d. George Edwin and Genevieve Nellie (Babuska) Scott; m. Gerry Craig Keffer, Nov. 6, 1971; children: Annemarie, Gregory, Margaret. AA in Liberal Arts, San Bernardino Valley Coll., Calif., 1973; BS in Natural Scis., U. Alaska, 1988, MS in Environ. Quality, 1995. Cert. environ. auditor Nat. Registry of Environ. Profls., prin. environ. auditor/EARA - U.K.; registered environ. health specialist, Nat. Environ. Health Assn. and State of Calif. Rsch. lab. assoc. VA/Loma Linda (Calif.) Hosp., 1988-90; environ. health specialist San Bernardino County, Calif., 1990-91, S&S Engring., Eagle River, Alaska, 1991-92; regulatory specialist ENSR Consulting and Engring., Anchorage, 1992-94; quality assurance environ. specialist Alyeska Pipeline Svc. Co., Anchorage, 1994-98; ISO 14001 project mgr. Hoefler Consulting Group, Anchorage, 1998—. Mem. Environ. Auditing Roundtable, Nat. Environ. Health Assn. Office: Hoefler Consulting Group Ste 200 701 Sesame St Anchorage AK 99503

KEGEL, WILLIAM GEORGE, mining company executive; b. Pitts., Mar. 15, 1922; s. William G. and Gertrude (Holl) K.; m. Jacqueline Treacy, Feb. 17, 1942; children: Kathy, Danyele, Janice, Jacqueline, William, Madeline, Colleen, Lisa, Brian. Student elec. engring, U. Pitts., 1940-43; LLD (hon.), Ind. U. of Pa., 1986. Mgr. mech. and elec. depts. Lee Norse Co., 1941-50; with Jones & Laughlin Steel Corp., Pitts., 1950-76, gen. mgr. raw materials and traffic, 1975-76; pres. Cerro Marmon Coal Group, 1976-79; pres., chief exec. officer Rochester & Pitt. Coal Co., Indiana, Pa., 1979-88, chmn. bd., 1988-98; dir. emeritus Savs. and Trust Co. Pa., Indiana. Mem. Indiana (Pa.) Airport Authority, 1980; bd. dirs. Brownsville Gen. Hosp., 1964-71; mem. Centerville Borough Council, 1952-60. Mem. AIME, Coal Mining Inst. Am., Am. Mining Congress (dir.), Pitts. Coal Mining Inst., Duquesne Club, Ind. Country Club, Laurel Valley Golf Club. Republican. Roman Catholic. Home: 100 Croyhill Dr Indiana PA 15701-1225 Office: Rochester & Pitts Coal Co 655 Church St Indiana PA 15701-2718

KEGERREIS, ROBERT JAMES, management consultant, marketing educator; b. Detroit, Apr. 2, 1921; s. I. G. and A. M. (Merry) K.; m. Katherine L. Falknor, Oct. 30, 1943; children: Merry, Duncan, Melissa. BA, Ohio State U., 1943, BS, 1943, MBA, 1946, PhD, 1968; PhD, U. Dayton, 1982, EdD (hon.), EdD (hon.), U. Dayton; LLD (hon.), U. Akron, Wilberforce U.; ScD (hon.), Cen. State U., Japan, 1992; EconD (hon.), Okayama U., Japan, 1992. Economist Fed. Res. Bank, Cleve., 1946-49; pres. KV Stores, Inc., Woodsfield, Ohio, 1949-69; v.p., sec. KBK Devel. Co., Inc., 1955-62; assoc. prof. Ohio U., Athens, 1967-69; dean Coll. Bus. and Adminstrn. Wright State U., Dayton, Ohio, 1969-71, v.p. adminstrn., 1971-73, pres., 1973-85; cons. RJK Co., Dayton, 1985—; bd. dirs. Robbins & Myers, Dayton, Bank One, Dayton, N.A. Exec. dir. Arts Ctr. Found., Dayton. Lt. (j.g.) USN, 1943-46. Mem. Moraine Country Club, Bicycle Club, Pelican Bay Country Club. Methodist. Avocations: flying, golf. Office: Kettering Tower Ste 1480 Dayton OH 45423-1000

KEGLEY, JACQUELYN ANN, philosophy educator; b. Conneaut, Ohio, July 18, 1938; d. Steven Paul and Gertrude Evelyn (Frank) Kovacevic; m. Charles William Kegley, June 12, 1964; children: Jacquelyn Ann, Stephen Lincoln Luther. BA cum laude, Allegheny Coll., 1960; MA summa cum laude, Rice U., 1964; PhD, Columbia U., 1971. Asst. prof. philosophy Calif. State U., Bakersfield, 1973-77, assoc. prof., 1977-81, prof., 1981—; vis. prof. U. Philippines, Quezon City, 1966-68; grant project dir. Calif. Council Humanities, 1977, project dir. 1980, 82; mem. work group on ethics Am. Colls. of Nursing, Washington, 1984-86; mem. Am. Bd. Forensic Examiners. Author: Introduction to Logic, 1978, Genuine Individuals and Genuine Communities, 1997; editor: Humanistic Delivery of Services to Families, 1982, Education for the Handicaped, 1982; mem. editl. bd. Jour. Philosophy in Lit., 1979-84; contbr. articles to profl. jours. Bd. dirs. Bakersfield Mental Health Assn., 1982-84, Citizens for Betterment of Community. Recipient Outstanding Leadership award Calif. State U., 1997-98, Outstanding Prof. award Calif. State U., 1989-90, Golden Roadrunner award Bakersfield Community, 1991. Mem. Philosophy of Sci. Assn., Soc. Advancement Am. Phil. soc. (chmn. Pacific div. 1979-83, nat. exec. com. 1974-79), Philosophy Soc., Soc. Interdisciplinary Study of Mind, Am. Philosophical Assn., Dorian Soc., Phi Beta Kappa. Democrat. Lutheran. Avocations: music, tennis. Home: 7312 Kroll Way Bakersfield CA 93309-2336 Office: Calif State U Dept Philosophy Bakersfield CA 93311

KEHL, RANDALL HERMAN, executive, consultant, lawyer; b. Furstenfeldbruck, Federal Republic of Germany, May 18, 1954; came to U.S., 1955; s. Raymond Herman and Annabelle (Fair) K.; m. Sharon Kay Barnes; children: Lindsey Elizabeth, Jessica Anne, Austin Randall. BS, USAF Acad., 1976; MBA, U. N.D., 1980; JD, Pepperdine U., 1983. Bar: N.D. 1983, D.C. 1988, U.S. Supreme Ct. 1990. Commd. 2d lt. USAF, 1976, advanced through grades to maj., 1986, chief civil law, 1983-84, chief criminal law, 1984-85; squadron commdr. Alaska Air Command, Anchorage, 1985, chief def. counsel, 1985-86; dep. base atty. Kirtland AFB, Albuquerque, 1986-89; spl. asst. U.S. atty. U.S. Dept. Justice, Albuquerque, 1986-89; chief energy litigation Office of USAF JAG, Washington, 1989-90; White House fellow, 1990-91; chmn., CEO POD Assocs., Inc., 1992-97; cons., counsel to DESA-office of sec. of def. U.S. Dept. Def., Albuquerque, 1993; prin. Randall H. Kehl Consulting, Albuquerque, 1993-98; chmn. RHK Capital Group Internat., San Antonio, 1997—; pres., CEO Safe Zone Sys., Inc., 1998—; mem. staff Pres.'s Coun. on Competiveness, 1990-91; vice chmn. White House Working group on Commercialization of Fed. Lab. Tech., 1991; chmn. Candeli, Ltd., Kerorioni, Ltd., Rep. of Georgia, 1992-96; adj. instr. law U. Alaska, 1985-86; bd. dirs., counsel Kirtland Fed. Credit Union, Albuqueruqe; bd. dirs., sec. Triad Comm., Inc., Albuquerque; chmn. bd. POD Assocs., Inc., 1988-90. Asst. scoutmaster Boy Scouts Am., Minot, N.D., 1977-80; tchr. Officers Christian Fellowship, Minot, 1977-80; civic arbitrator Mediation and Conciliation Svc., 1983-86; mem. pvt. sch. bd. Anchorage, 1984-85; mem. Gov.'s Task Force for Utility Corp. Restructuring, 1987; vice-chmn. N.Mex. Gov.-Elect Transition Team, 1994, Gov.'s Bus. Adv. Coun., 1995—; mem. steering com. Rep. Campaigns, 1995—; co-chmn. N. Mex. Character Counts in the Workplace, 1996—; bd. dirs. Kirtland Partnership Com., 1995—, N.Mex. Ctr. for Civic Values, 1997—; dir. Albuquerque Character Counts, 1998—. Mem. ABA, AMA, Albuquerque Acad. Capital Devel. Com. and Assoc. Trustee, The Forman Sch. (capital devel. com.), Tanoan Country Club, Phi Delta Phi. Republican. Presbyterian. Avocations: swimming, skiing, scuba diving, sailing, golf. Office: Ste 415 5100 John D Ryan Blvd San Antonio TX 78245-3534

KEHLMANN, ROBERT, artist, critic; b. Bklyn., Mar. 9, 1942. BA, Antioch Coll., 1963; MA, U. Calif., Berkeley, 1966. One-man shows include: Richmond Art Ctr., Calif., 1976, William Sawyer Gallery, San Francisco, 1978, 82, 86, Galerie M, Kassel, Fed. Republic Germany, 1985, Anne O'Brien Gallery, Washington, 1988, 90, Dorothy Weiss Gallery, San Francisco, 1993, Hearst Art Gallery, Moraga, 1996; group shows include: Am. Craft Mus., N.Y.C., 1978, 86, Corning (N.Y.) Mus. Glass, 1979, Tucson Mus. of Art, 1983, Kulturhuset, Stockholm, Sweden, 1985; represented in permanent collections at Corning Mus. Glass, Leigh Yawkey Woodson Art Mus., Hessisches Landes Mus., Germany, Bank of Am. World Hdqrs., San Francisco, Toledo Mus. Art, Hokkaido Mus. Modern Art, Sapporo, Japan, Huntington Mus. of Art, W.Va., Am. Craft Mus., N.Y.C., Musée des Arts Décoratifs, Lausanne, Switzerland, Oakland Mus.; instr. glass design Calif. Coll. Arts and Crafts, Oakland, 1978-80, 91, Pilchuck Glass Ctr., Stanwood, Wash., 1978-80. Author: Twentieth Century Stained Glass: A New Definition, 1992; contbg. editor: New Glass Work mag., 1988-89; editor: Glass Art Soc. Jour., 1981-84. NEA grantee, 1977, 78. Chmn. Landmarks Preservation Commn., Berkeley, 1995-98. Mem. Glass Art Soc. (bd. dirs. 1980-84, 89-92, hon. life). Office: Dorothy Weiss Gallery 256 Sutter St San Francisco CA 94108-4409

KEHOE, DORRIE BONNER, museum educator; b. Boston, Nov. 9, 1937; d. Paul Émile and Alice D. (Dardis) Landry; m. William F. Kehoe, Mar. 1, 1997; 1 child from previous marriage, Matthew Emile Bonner. BA, Middlebury Coll., 1959. Tchr. Acton (Mass.) Pub. Schs., 1959-65; coord. cmty. resources Concord (Mass.) Pub. Schs., 1980-87; sch. liaison Tsongas Indsl. History Ctr., Lowell, Mass., 1987-98; ind. mus. cons. Concord, Mass., 1998—. Bd. mem. Middlebury (Vt.) Coll. Alumni Assn., 1986-90, Concord-Carlisle Scholarship Fund, 1991-96, Concord Traffic Com., 1994-96; incorporator Historic Harrisville, N.H., 1991—. Mem. Am. Assn. Mus., Nat. Coun. for the Social Studies (bd. mem. 1991-93), New Eng. Mus. Assn., Boston Mus. Educators Roundtable (bd. mem., treas. 1996-98). Avocations: travel, gardening, cooking, reading, opera appreciation. Home: 1369 Main St Concord MA 01742-2961 Office: Working With Museums 1369 Main St Concord MA 01742

KEHOE, JAMES W., federal judge; b. 1925. A.A., U. Fla., 1947, LL.B., 1950. Bar: Fla. Assoc. firm Worley, Kehoe & Willard, 1952-55; asst. county solicitor Dade County, Fla., 1955-57; assoc. firm Miltor R. Wasman, 1957-61; judge Civil Record Ct., Miami, 1961-63, 11th Jud. Cir. Ct., Fla., 1963-77, U.S. Ct. Appeals (3d cir.), 1977-79; judge U.S. Dist. Ct. (so. dist.) Fla., 1979—, sr. judge, 1993—. Mem. ABA, Fla. Bar Assn. Office: US Dist Ct 8th Fl Tower 301 N Miami Ave Miami FL 33128-7702*

KEHOE, L. PAUL, state judge; b. Carthage, N.Y., May 21, 1938; s. Leo A. and Mildred (Piddock) K.; BA, Syracuse U., 1959, JD, 1962; m. Elizabeth M. Weber, 1963; children: L. Paul, John Michael, Patrick Lewis. Admitted to N.Y. bar, 1962; dist. atty. Wayne County, N.Y., 1967-71; mem. N.Y. Assembly, 1979-80; mem. N.Y. State Senate, 1981-92; justice N.Y. Supreme Ct., 1993—; adminstrv. judge 7th Judicial Dist., 1996—. Served with AUS, 1962-63. Mem. ABA, Wayne County Bar Assn., N.Y. State Bar Assn. Republican. Clubs: Rotary, Elks. Office: 223 Hall Of Justice Rochester NY 14614-2114

KEHOE, PATRICK EMMETT, law librarian, law educator; b. Olympia, Wash., Nov. 12, 1941; s. Adlore Reginald and Elise Josephine (Brophy) K.; m. Carole J. Fitzgerald, Aug. 16, 1969; children: Elisabeth C., Robert P. BCS, Seattle U., 1963; JD, U. Wash., 1966, M in Law Librarianship, 1968. Bar: Wash. 1966, U.S. Supreme Ct. 1976. Law reference libr. U. Wash. Law Sch., 1966-68; asst. prof., asst. law libr. U. Houston, 1968-71; asst. libr. Yale Law Sch., 1971-73; asst. prof. law, law libr. Am. U., 1973-76, assoc. prof. law, law libr., 1976-79, prof. law, dir. law library, 1979—, assoc. dean budgetary matters, 1977-83; cons. in field; bus. mgr. Law Libr. Jour., 1976-92. Editor: Book Appraisals Column, Tex. Bar jour., 1970-71; editor: Law Library Lighrs, 1974-76; (with Heinz Peter Mueller) Law Librarianship: A Handbook, 1983; (with Gary McCann and Louisa Lyman) Law Librarianship: A Handbook for the Electronic Era, 1995; author: Condominiums and Cooperatives, 1974. Mem. Wash. State Bar Assn., Am. Assn. Law Libraries (bd. dirs. 1985-88, 94-97, v.p. 1994-95, pres. 1995-96), Law Librarians' Soc. Washington (pres. 1979-81), Am. U. Employees Fed. Credit Union (sec. 1982-83). Republican. Roman Catholic. Home: 12193 Hidden Brook Ter North Potomac MD 20878-3321

KEHOE, STEPHEN H., lawyer; b. Washington, Sept. 10, 1958; s. William Anthony and Elizabeth (Burlee) K. BA, Duke U., 1980; JD, Case Western Res. U., 1986. Atty. Ewing, Dietz, Turner & Kehoe, P.A., Easton, Md., 1986—. Chmn. Talbot County Dem. Ctrl. Com., 1994—, Ea. Shore Assn. Dem. Ctrl. Coms., 1998—; mem. Md. Dem. Exec. Com., 1994—. Mem. Talbot County Bar Assn. (sec.-treas. 1990-97). Roman Catholic. Home: 603 Winter St Easton MD 21601-3843 Office: Ewing Dietz Turner & Kehoe PA 16 S Washington St Easton MD 21601-3008

KEHOE, VINCENT JEFFRÉ-ROUX, photographer, author, cosmetic company executive; b. Bklyn., Sept. 12, 1921; s. John James and Bertha Florence (Roux) K.; m. Gena Irene Marino, Nov. 2, 1966. Student, MIT, 1940-41, Lowell Technol. Inst., 1941-42, Boston U., 1942; BFA in Motion Picture and TV Prodn., Columbia U., 1957. Dir. make-up dept. CBS-TV, N.Y.C., 1948-49, NBC Hallmark Hall of Fame series, 1951-53; make-up artist in charge of make-up numerous film, tv and stage prodns., 1942—; dir. make-up Turner hall Corp., 1959-61, Internat. Beauty Show, 1962-66; pres., dir. rsch. Rsch. Coun. Make-Up Artists, Inc., 1963—; chief press officer Spanish Pavillion N.Y. World's Fair, 1965; free-lance photographer, 1956—. Author: The Technique of Film and Television Make-Up for Color, 1970, The Make-Up Artist in the Beauty Salon, 1969, We Were There: April 19, 1775, 1974, A Military Guide, 1974, 2nd rev. edit., 1993, 3rd rev. edit., 1998-99, The Re-Created Officer's Guide, 5 vols., 1996-98, The Technique of the Professional Make-Up Artist, 1985, 2nd edit., 1995, Special Make-Up Effects, 1991; author, photographer: (bullfighting book) Aficionado! (N.Y. Art Dirs. Club award 1960), Wine Women and Toros! (N.Y. Art Dirs. award 1962); prodr.: (documentary color film) Matador de Toros, 1959; contbr. photographs to numerous mags. including Time, Life, Sports Illustrated, Argosy, Popular Photography. Served with U.S. Army, WWII, ETO. Decorated Purple Heart, Bronze Star, CIB; recipient Torch award Coun. of 13 Original States, 1979. Fellow Co. Mil. Historians; mem. Tenth Foot Royal Lincolnshire Regimental Assn. (life; hon. col. 1968), Soc. Motion Picture and TV Engrs. (life), Acad. TV Arts and Scis., Soc. Army Hist. Rsch. (Eng., life), Brit. Officers Club New Eng. (life), 10th Mountain Divsn. Assn. (life), NRA (life), Eagle Scout Assn. (life), naval Club (London). Home and Office: PO Box 850 Somis CA 93066-0850

KEHOE, WILLIAM FRANCIS, lawyer; b. Stoneham, Mass., Dec. 3, 1933; s. William Andrew and Josephine Agnes (Crowley) K.; m. Dorothy Landry Kehoe; children by previous marriage: John William, Kathleen Emily. AB summa cum laude, Dartmouth Coll., 1955; MA, Yale U., 1956; LLB, Harvard U., 1963. Bar: Mass. 1963, U.S. Dist. Ct. Mass. 1964. Instr. English Middlebury (Vt.) Coll., 1956-57; ptnr. Gaston & Snow, Boston, 1970-91; counsel Hutchins, Wheeler & Dittmar, Boston, 1991-94, Taylor, Ganson & Perrin, Boston, 1995—; corp. mem. Frederick E. Weber Charities Corp., Boston, 1974—; mem. standing adv. com. on rules of civil procedure Supreme Judicial Ct.; lectr., panelist Mass. Continuing Legal Edn. Program, Boston, 1977—. Author: Enjoying Ireland, 1966; contbr. articles and revs. to profl. jours. Served with U.S. Army, 1957-59. Fulbright scholar, Trinity Coll., Dublin, Ireland, 1959-60. Fellow Am. Coll. Trust and Estate Counsel; mem. Boston Bar Assn., Phi Beta Kappa. Office: Taylor Ganson & Perrin 160 Federal St Fl 20 Boston MA 02110-1722

KEHOE, WILLIAM JOSEPH, business educator, researcher, consultant; b. Cin., Feb. 19, 1941. AB, U. Cin., 1964; MBA, Xavier U., 1969; MA, Marshall U., 1973; D of Bus. Adminstrn., U. Ky., 1976. O'Dell prof. commerce U. Va., Charlottesville, 1975—, assoc. dean, 1982-92, internat. bus. area chair, 1993-99; pres. Albemarle County Police Found., 1993-95; bd. dirs. Fedn. Bus. Honor Socs. Chmn. Charlottesville Airport Authority, 1993, 96, 97, 98, 99, vice chmn., 1992, 95; pres. Jr. Achievement Ctrl. Va., 1985-87; vice chmn. Paramount Theatre and Cultural Ctr., 1990-92; mem. Albermarle County Indsl. Devel. Authority, 1986-94; chmn. Albemarle County Fiscal Resource Com., 1989-91; mem. Regional Econ. Adv. Coun., Commonwealth of Va., 1994-98; chmn. Thomas Jefferson area United Way, 1994. Recipient Leaders' Leader award, 1988, Disting. Leadership award Nat. Assn. Community Leadership, 1989; Doctoral Consortium fellow, fellow George H. Gallup Internat. Inst. Fellow Soc. Mktg. Advances; mem. Am. Acad. Mgmt., Am. Mktg. Assn., Soc. for Bus. Ethics, Acad. Internat. Bus., Charlottesville C. of C. (chmn. 1990), Allied So. Bus. Assn. (pres. 1992), Beta Gamma Sigma (bd. dirs. 1990—). Home: PO Box 4454 Charlottesville VA 22905-4454

KEHR, AUGUST ERNEST, geneticist, researcher; b. Frankfort, Ky., Mar. 2, 1914; s. Carl Frederick August and Anna Esther (Heller) K.; m. Mary Louise Coon, Dec. 26, 1942; 1 child, Janet Marie Kehr Flick. BS, Cornell U., 1937, MS, 1947, PhD, 1950. Assoc. prof. La. State U., Baton Rouge, 1950-54; prof. Iowa State U., Ames, 1954-58; br. chief Agrl. Rsch. Svc. USDA, Beltsville, Md., 1958-72, mem. nat. program staff Agrl. Rsch. Svc., 1972-78. Author: (with others) Encyclopedia of Plant Physiology, 1965; author invitational papers, book chpts.; contbr. articles to profl. jours. Mem. team to study agr. in Egypt, 1975, 80; mem. team sponsored by Acad. Sci. to study vegetable farming in China, 1977. Recipient Gold medal Rhododendron Soc., 1977, Superior Svc. award USDA, 1975, B.Y. Morrison Lectr. award and medal, 1982, Pioneer award Am. Rhododendron Soc., 1994, S.E. chpt. Bronze medal, 1998. Fellow Am. Soc. for Hort. Sci.; mem. Am. Genetics Assn. (pres. 1963-65), Magnolia Soc. (nat. meetings planning com. 1989-91, D. Todd Gresham award 1992), Cosmos Club Washington, Sigma Xi, Phi Kappa Phi, Gamma Sigma Delta. Achievements include development of many varieties of azaleas, rhododendrons and magnolias. Home: 240 Tranquility Pl Hendersonville NC 28739-8314

KEHRET, PEG, writer; b. LaCrosse, Wis., Nov. 11, 1936; d. Arthur Robert and Elizabeth (Showers) Schulze; m. Carl Edward Kehret, July 2, 1955; children: Bob. C., Anne M. Kehret Konen. Student, U. Minn., 1954-55. trustee Pacific Northwest Writers Conf., Seattle, 1983-86. Author: Vows of Love and Marriage, 1979, Refinishing and Restoring Your Piano, 1985, Winning Monologs for Young Actors, 1986, Deadly Stranger, 1987 (Children's Choice award 1988), The Winner, 1988, ENCORE!-More Winning Monologs for Young Actors, 1988, Nightmare Mountain, 1989 (Young Hoosier Book award 1992, Golden Sower award Nebr. Libr. Assn. 1993, Iowa Children's Choice award 1994, Maud Hart Lovelace award 1995), Wedding Vows, 1989, Sisters, Long Ago, 1990, Cages, 1991 (Maud Hart Lovelace award 1996), Acting Natural, 1992, Terror at the Zoo, 1992 (Pacific N.W. Young Reader's Choice award 1995, N.Mex. Land of Enchantment award 1995, Iowa Children's Choice award 1996), Horror at the Haunted House, 1992 (Sequoyah Children's Book award 1995, Young Hoosier award 1995), Night of Fear, 1994, Richest Kids in Town, 1994, Cat Burglar on the Prowl, 1995, Danger at the Fair, 1995, Bone Breath and the Vandals, 1995, Don't Go Near Mrs. Tallie, 1995, Desert Danger, 1995, The Ghost Followed Us Home, 1996, Earthquake Terror, 1996 (W.Va. Children's Book award 1998, Children's Crown award Nat. Christian Sch. Assn. 1998, Utah Children's Book award 1999), Race to Disaster, 1996, Screaming Eagles, 1996, Backstage Fright, 1996, Small Steps: The Year I Got Polio, 1996 (Soc. Childrens Book Writers and Illustrators Golden Kite award nonfiction 1997, PEN Ctr. USA West award 1997, Dorothy Canfield Fisher award 1998, Mark Twain award 1999), Searching for Candlestick Park, 1997, The Volcano Disaster, 1998, The Blizzard Disaster, 1998, The Flood Disaster, 1999, Shelter Dogs, 1999, I'm Not Who You Think I Am, 1999, (plays) Cemeteries are a Grave Matter, 1977, Let Him Sleep 'Till It's Time for His Funeral, 1978, Spirit!, 1979 (Forest Roberts Playwriting award No. Mich. U. 1979, Best New Play award Pioneer Drama Svc. 1980), Dracula, Darling, 1980, Charming Billy, 1981, (musical) Bicycles Built for Two, 1985; contbr. 300 articles and short stories to mags. Vol. Humane Soc., SPCA, Bellevue, Wash., 1975—; bd. dirs. Bellevue Playbarn, 1975-78, Alzheimer's Assn., Bellevue, 1982. Recipient Achievement award Pacific N.W. Writers, Celebrate Lit. award N.W. Reading Coun. of Internat. Reading Assn., 1993; named Artist of Yr., Redmond, Wash., Arts Commn., 1998. Mem. Author's Guild, Soc. Children's Book Writers. Office: Curtis Brown Ltd Ten Astor Pl New York NY 10003

KEHRT, ALLAN WILLIAM, architectural firm executive; m. Michaele Kehrt; children: Matthew, Emily, Kathleen. BA in Econs., Ohio Wesleyan U., 1967; MArch, Va. Polytechnic Inst. and State U., 1978. Registered architect, N.J., Fla. Asst. prof. design Coll. Architecture and Urban Studies Va. Polytechnic Inst. and State U., Blacksburg, 1977-79; mgr. C.D.P. Assocs., Wilmington, Del.; with Geddes Brecher Qualls Cunningham, Princeton, N.J.; founding and design ptnr. Kehrt Shatken Sharon Architects, Princeton, 1983—; vis. critic, lectr. Va. Polytechnic Inst. and State U., U. Pa.; past treas., bd. dirs. Life Industries Corp.; adj. faculty Coll. Arch., Phila. Coll. Textiles and Sci. Vice chmn. N.J. Planning Bd., Cranbury; active N.J. Environ. Commn., Cranbury; past chmn. N.J. Hist. Preservation Commn., Cranbury. With USN, 1967-71. Recipient awards Interfaith Forum Religion, Art and Architecture, 1993. Mem. AIA, N.J. Soc. Architects (awards 1986, 87, 89, 90, 93, 94, 96, 98), Phi Kappa Phi, Tau Sigma Delta. Office: Kehrt Shatken Sharon Architects 337 Witherspoon St Princeton NJ 08542-3470

KEICHER, WILLIAM EUGENE, electrical engineer; b. Pitts., Dec. 28, 1947; s. William John and Gina Rina (Magrini) K.; m. Barbara Marie Gurgacz, Aug. 12, 1972; children: Lisa Anne, Kathy Marie, William Michael. BSEE, Carnegie-Mellon U., 1969, MSEE, 1970, PhD in Elec. Engring., 1974. Sr. elec. engr. CBS Labs., Stamford, Conn., 1974-75; mem. tech. staff Lincoln Lab., MIT, Lexington, Mass., 1975-83, asst. group leader, 1983-85, group leader, 1985-93; assoc. group leader MIT, Lexington, Mass., 1993—; cons. Sci. and Engring. Support Group for Strategic Def. Initiative, Arlington, Va., 1988; co-chair for numerous confs. in field. Editor: Millimeter Wave Technology, 1982, Applied Laser Radar Technology, 1993, Industrial Applications of Laser Radar, 1994; contbr. articles to profl. publs.; patentee spatial filter sys. Capt. U.S. Army, 1974. Mem. IEEE (sr.), Optical Soc. Am., Nat. Rsch. Coun. (Air Force sci. and tech. com. on rev. of Air Force hypersonic tech. program 1997-98), Assn. Old Crows. Roman Catholic. Avocations: history, snorkeling, travel, microcomputers. Home: 6 Winn Valley Dr Burlington MA 01803-4727 Office: MIT Lincoln Lab 244 Wood St Lexington MA 02421-6426

KEIFER, AMY JO, educator; b. East Stroudsburg, Pa., Apr. 6, 1972; d. Joseph H. and Cheryl A. Keifer. BA in Internat. Rels., Am. U., 1994. Cert. secondary tchr., Md. Govt. tchr. Paint Br. H.S., Burtonsville, Md., 1994-98, Gaithersburg (Md.) H.S., 1998—. Office: Gaithersburg High Sch 314 S Frederick Ave Gaithersburg MD 20877

KEIFER, JOHN M., director Norfolk public works department. BS in Civil Engring., Lehigh U., 1970; MS in Civil Engring., U. Pitts., 1977. Registered profl. engr., Va. Commd. ensign USN, 1971, retired, 1991; various assignments Navy Civil Engr. Corps, 1971-91; dir. pub. works dept. City of Norfolk, Va., 1991—. Office: Public Works Dept City Hall 7th Fl 810 Union St Norfolk VA 23510-2717*

KEIGHER, SHARON, physical education educator; b. West Orange, N.J., Sept. 7, 1965; d. James Joseph and Marilyn Lois (Morahan) K. BA, Seton Hall U., 1987; postgrad. in edn., Columbia U. Tchr.'s Coll. Writer, developer Enhanced Comms., Inc., New Providence, N.J., 1987-88; pub. rels. dir. Adtech Advt., Passaic, N.J., 1988-90; unit dir. Boys' & Girls' Clubs Newark, 1988-92; aquatic dir., curriculum designer Asphalt Green, N.Y.C., 1992-94; faculty Trinity Sch., N.Y.C., 1994—. Mem. Eagle Rock Civic Assn., West Orange, N.J., 1993—;. Mem. ARC (instr.), Afterschool Program Dir.'s Network, Am. Swim Coaches Assn., Nat. Swimming Pool Operators Assn., Adventurer's Club, Assn. Athletics in Ind. Schs. (coach 1994—). Avocations: swimming, soccer, writing, reading, hiking. Home: 10 Moore Ter West Orange NJ 07052-5014 Office: Trinity Sch 139 W 91st St New York NY 10024-1399

KEIL, ALFRED ADOLF HEINRICH, marine engineering educator; b. Konradswaldau, Germany, May 1, 1913; came to U.S., 1947, naturalized, 1954; s. Kurt Alfred and Marie (Berger) K.; m. Ursula Leppelt, Oct. 15, 1943; children: Michael G., Juergen G. Dr. nat. sc., U. Breslau, Germany, 1939. Research asst. U. Breslau, 1939-40; research asso. Chem.-Phys. Research Establishment, Kiel, Germany, 1940- 45; chief rsch. scientist underwater explosive rsch. div. Norfolk Naval Shipyard, Portsmouth, Va., 1947-59; tech. dir. structural mech. lab. David Taylor Model Basin, 1959-63, tech. dir. basin, 1963-66; prof., head dept. naval architecture and marine engring. MIT, 1966-71, dean Sch. Engring., 1971-77, Ford prof. engring., 1977-78, prof. emeritus, 1978—; Mem. Nat. Adv. Com. on Oceans and Atmosphere, 1977-79. Contbr. articles profl. jours. Served with German Army, 1939-40. Recipient Civilian Distinguished Service award Navy Dept., 1963; Gibbs Bros. gold medal for naval architecture Nat. Acad. Scis., 1967; Verdienstkreuz 1st Klasse, Fed. Republic Germany, 1985. Mem. NAE, Am. Soc. Naval Engrs. (Gold Medal award 1964), Verein Deutscher Ingenieure (corr. mem.), Marine Tech. Soc. (Lockheed award 1979). Home: 165 Chestnut St Apt 109 Brookline MA 02445-7574*

KEIL, CHARLES EMANUEL, corporation executive; b. N.Y.C., Aug. 27, 1936; s. E. William and Marie Katherine (Diebold) K.; m. Patricia Ann O'Toole, Dec. 21, 1970; children: Brett, Morgan. AB, Bklyn. Coll., 1964, postgrad., 1964-65. Sales mgr. Columbian Bronze Corp., Freeport, N.Y., 1960-66; sr. v.p., pub., mng. dir. Marine Engring.-Log Group Simmons Boardman Pub. Co., N.Y.C., 1966-78; sr. v.p. Thomas Internat. Pub. Co., N.Y.C., 1978-82; gen. mgr. Tech. Pub. Co., Boca Raton, 1983-88; pub. Indsl. Computing, 1989-94; COO Ashlee Pub. Co., N.Y.C , 1995—; v.p. internat. ops. The Maritime Group. With USNR, USMCR, 1956-58. Mem. Internat. Soc. Philos. Enquiry, Soc. Naval Archs. and Marine Engrs., Nat. Propeller Club, Navy League of U.S. Home: 4942 Brandywine Dr Boca Raton FL 33487-2108 Office: Ste 121 4400 N Federal Hwy Boca Raton FL 33431-5187

KEIL, HOLLY MAE, elementary education educator; b. Souix Falls, S.D., Aug. 3, 1954; d. Robert Dean and Alta Mae (Daggett) Brown; m. Randall Keith Keil, Aug. 13, 1977; children: Jason Frederick, Adam Robert. BSE, Chadron (Nebr.) State Coll., 1976; MSE, Wayne (Nebr.) State Coll., 1997. Elem. tchr. Holt County Sch. Dist., O'Neill, Nebr., 1976-78, Holt COunty Sch. Dist. #173, Ewing, Nebr., 1978-80, Inman (Nebr.) Pub. Sch. Dist. #30, 1980—. Pres., mem. Inman Twp. Libr. Bd., 1981—. Mem. Nebr. Edn. Assn., Inman Edn. Assn. (pres., negotiator). Office: Inman Pub Schs PO Box 48 Inman NE 68742-0048

KEIL, JOHN MULLAN, advertising agency executive; b. Rochester, N.Y., Dec. 30, 1922; s. Alvin Richard and Elizabeth (Mullan) K.; m. Barbara Louise Miller, Sept. 16, 1950; children—Peter Mullan, Nicholas John, Elizabeth Jane. B.A., U. Rochester, 1946. Copywriter advt. dept. Armstrong Cork Co., Lancaster, Pa., 1946-48, Wendell P. Colton Advt., N.Y.C., 1948-51, Needham & Grohmann, Inc., N.Y.C., 1951-55; v.p., account exec. Needham & Grohmann, Inc., 1955-60; v.p., creative dir. Dancer, Fitzgerald, Sample, Inc., N.Y.C., 1960-64; copy group head Dancer, Fitzgerald, Sample, Inc., 1964-67, v.p., 1967-70, sr. v.p., creative dir., 1970-75, dir., 1971-87, exec. v.p., 1975-87, chmn. creative planning con., 1973; exec. creative dir. Dancer, Fitzgerald, Sample, 1983-86; dir. creative devel. DFS-Dorland Worldwide, 1986-87; creative cons. Saatchi & Saatchi Adv. Worldwide, 1987—; lectr. Amos Tuck Sch. Dartmouth Coll., Assn. Nat. Advertisers; Phillips Meml. lectr. U. Fla., 1987; painter acrylic on wood Frank J. Miele Gallery, N.Y.C., Toadhall Gallery, N.Y.C., Reed Gallery, Chester, Vt., So. Vt. Art Ctr., Manchester, Vt. Author: The Creative Mystique, How To Manage It, Nurture It, Make It Pay, 1985, How to Zig in a Zagging World, 1987; contbr. articles to Jour. Advt., Air and Space, Smithsonian, Time, N.Y. Times. Vice chmn. Zoning Bd. Appeals, Grandview-on-Hudson, N.Y., 1961-71; pres., trustee Rockland Country Day Sch., 1970-75; mem. trustees coun. U. Rochester, 1979-85, trustee, 1986-91 (life trustee, 1991—), N.Y. State Coun. Governing Bds., 1989-94, Nat. Crime Prevention Coun., 1987—; trustee Tappan Zee Preservation Coalition, 1995—. Served with USAAF, 1943-45. Decorated D.F.C., Air medal with two oak leaf clusters; recipient Silver Bell award Advt. Council, 1981, 84, Carl M. Loeb, Jr.-McGruff award Nat. Crime Prevention Council, 1987. Mem. Alpha Delta Phi. Clubs: Nyack (N.Y.) Field, Upper Nyack Tennis. Home: 251 River Rd Nyack NY 10960-5001

KEIL, KLAUS, geology educator, consultant; b. Hamburg, Germany, Nov. 15, 1934; s. Walter and Elsbeth K.; m. Rosemarie, Mar. 30, 1961; children: Kathrin R., Mark K.; m. Linde, Jan. 28, 1984. M.S., Schiller U., Jena, Germany, 1958; Ph.D., Gutenberg U., Mainz, Fed. Republic Germany, 1961. Rsch. assoc. Mineral. Inst., Jena, 1958-60, Max Planck-Inst. Chemistry, Mainz, 1961, U. Calif., San Diego, 1961-63; rsch. scientist Ames Rsch. Ctr. NASA, Moffett Field, Calif., 1963-68; prof. geology, dir. Inst. Meteoritics, U. N.Mex., Albuquerque, 1968-90; pres., prof. U. N.Mex., 1985-90; chmn. dept. of geology U. N.Mex., Albuquerque, 1986-89; prof. geology U. Hawaii, Honolulu, 1990—, rsch. prof., head planetary geoscis. div., 1990-93, dir. Hawaii Inst. Geophysics and Planetology, 1994—; cons. Sandia Labs., others. Contbr. over 500 articles to sci. jours. Recipient Apollo Achievement award NASA, 1970; recipient George P. Merrill medal Nat. Acad. Scis., 1970, Exceptional Sci. Achievement medal NASA, 1977, Regents Meritorious Service medal U. N.Mex., 1983, Leonard medal Meteoritical Soc., 1988, Zimmerman award U. N.Mex., 1988, numerous others. Fellow Meteoritical Soc., AAAS, Mineral. Soc. Am., Am. Geophys. Union, German Mineral. Soc., others. Office: U Hawaii at Manoa Hawaii Inst Geophys & Planetology Honolulu HI 96822

KEIL, M. DAVID, retired international association executive; b. Hinsdale, Ill., Jan. 22, 1931; s. Milton Derby and Lydia Anne (Landwehr) K.; m. Marilyn Jean Martin, May 15, 1976. BSJ, Northwestern U., Evanston, Ill., 1952. Brand mgr. Armour & Co., Chgo., 1953-60; sr. v.p. Young & Rubicam, Chgo., 1960-74, Sandy Corp., Detroit, 1974-75, D'Arcy-MacManus & Masius, Chgo., 1976-80; pres., mng. dir. Audit Bur. Circulations, Schaumburg, Ill., 1980-96; ret., 1996. Named to Medill Sch. Journalism Hall of Fame, 1997. Mem. Internat. Fedn. Audit Burs., Circulation (sec. gen. 1986-88), Hinsdale Golf Club. Lutheran. Avocations: sports, reading, travel, music.

KEIL, MARILYN MARTIN, artist; b. Balt., Nov. 6, 1932; d. Francis and Mary Blanche (Murphy) Martin; m. Herbert Bruce Keil, Dec. 18, 1954; children: Braden, Mary-Beth, Sue-Ann, Nancy, Bryant. Student, Corcoran Sch. Art, Washington, 1991-94, U. Md., 1995. active art in embassies program U.S. Dept. State; juried Washington area printmakers calendar Balt. Mus. fine Arts, 1995—. One-woman show Ralls Collection, Washington, 1993; exhibited in group shows at Rockville Art League (watercolor award), 1991, Corcoran Sch. Art, 1994, Nat. Cathedral, Washington, 1994, U. Md. Sch. Arts and Sociology, 1995, West Gallery, 1995, Md. Fedn. Art, 1996; contbr. juried Washington Area Printmakers Calendar, Va. Mus. Fine Art, 1997, Calendar Corcoran Gallery, 1998, Nat. Gallery of Art, 1999; represented in permanent collections at Corcoran Gallery Art, Washington, 1996, Nat. Mus. Women in the Arts, 1996, Libr. of Congress, 1996. Bd. dirs. Potomac Glen Civic Assn., Potomac, Md., 1988-94. Mem. AAUW, Rockville Art League, Nat. Mus. Women in the Arts (charter), Washington

Area Printmakers, Golden Key, Alpha Lambda. Avocations: etching, lithography. Home: 11540 S Glen Rd Potomac MD 20854-1852

KEILIN, EUGENE JACOB, investment banker, lawyer; b. Houston, Aug. 21, 1942; s. Charles and Rose (Pone) K.; m. Joanne Witty, Dec. 9, 1977; children: Rachael, Gregory, Charles. Student, Rice U., 1960-65; J.D., Harvard U., 1968. Bar: N.Y. Assoc. Sage Gray Todd & Sims, 1968-71; gen. counsel N.Y.C. Office of Mgmt. and Budget, 1971-76; exec. dir. Mcpl. Assistance Corp. for City N.Y., 1976-78; mem. Lazard Freres & Co., N.Y.C., 1979-89, gen. ptnr., 1984-89; sr. ptnr. Keilin and Co., N.Y.C., 1990—; dir., chmn. fin. com. Mcpl. Assistance Corp. for City N.Y., 1979-95, chmn., 1993-95; lectr. Columbia Law Sch., 1979-81; prin. KPS Spl. Situations Fund, L.P., N.Y.C., 1998—. Trustee Citizens Budget Commn., 1980—, vice-chmn., 1996—, chmn. elect, 1998; trustee Bklyn. Mus., 1991—; mem. N.Y. State Council on Fiscal and Econ. Priorities, 1985-87; mem. Cuomo Commn. on Trade and Competitiveness, 1987-94. Mem. Assn. Bar City N.Y. Office: Keilin and Co 200 Park Ave New York NY 10166*

KEILITZ, GENE MARTIN, retired association administrator; b. Caro, Mich., June 3, 1933; s. Otto Ethlyn and Mildred Ethyl (Horst) K.; m. Marlene Josephine Keihl, Jan. 27, 1968; children: Kelli Ann Hannum Spencer, Kirsten Lynn. D Chiropractic, Nat. Coll. Chiropractic, 1955. Sales rep. Cenco Instruments, Chgo., 1959-66; owner Pewter Bell Restaurant, Traverse City, Mich., 1966-75; exec. v.p. Chateau Grand Traverse, Traverse City, 1975-78; sales mgr. Great Lake Gauge, Bridgeport, Mich., 1977-78; self-employed sales rep. Traverse City, 1978-80; exec. dir. Grand Traverse Area United Way, Traverse City, 1980-91; v.p. United Way of Mich., Lansing, 1991-96; ret., 1996. Bd. dirs. Aspen Inst. Non Profit Sector, Washington, 1994—, Camp Royel, Traverse City , Mich., 1985—, Mich. Restaurant Assn., Detroit, 1968-70; mem. pub. policy com. Untied Way of Am., Alexandria, Va., 1985—; chmn., bd. dirs. Munson Healthcare Regional Found., Traverse City, 1997—; pres., bd. dirs. Traverse Bay Regional Planning Com., 1982-85; sec., mem. Midwest Ski Operators, Pontiac, 1969-71; dist. sec. Rotary, 1988-91, bd. dirs. Rotary Camps and Svcs., 1987-91. Mem. Inland Seas Ednl. Assn. (1st v.p. 1996—). Republican. Lutheran. Avocations: flying, cross-country skiing, gardening. Home: 1073 Garfield Rd N Traverse City MI 49686-8529

KEILL, STUART LANGDON, psychiatrist; b. Binghamton, N.Y., Oct. 5, 1927; s. Kenneth and Dorothy B. (Langdon) K.; m. Joanne Veness, Sept. 2, 1950; children: Elinor Anne Moran, Patricia J., Brian S., Victoria M. Keill Lo Russo. B.A., Princeton U., 1947; M.A., Cornell U., 1948; M.D., Temple U., 1952. Intern Highland Hosp., Rochester, N.Y.; resident in psychiatry N.Y. State Psychiat. Inst., Presbyn. Hosp., Columbia U., N.Y.C., 1955-58; dir. edn., dir. West Side Community Mental Health Ctr., N.Y.C., 1958-71, Roosevelt Hosp., N.Y.C., 1958-71; regional dir. N.Y. State Dept. Mental Health, 1971-75; prof. clin. psychiatry SUNY, Stony Brook, 1975-80; chmn. dept. psychiatry Nassau County Med. Ctr., East Meadow, N.Y., 1975-80; clin. prof. psychiatry SUNY, Buffalo, 1980-86; chief psychiat. service VA Med. Ctr., Buffalo, 1981-86; prof. of psychiatry Sch. of Medicine U. Md., 1986-94, vice chmn. dept. psychiatry, 1986-93, prof. sch. social work, 1993-94, acting chmn., 1991-92; clin. prof. psychiatry Sch. Medicine NYU, 1994—; counselor Advocates Coalition for Psychiat. Patients, 1980-86; med. dir. Inst. for Psychiatry and Human Behavior, 1986-93; mem. adv. com. mental health laws Md. Atty. Gen. Office, 1987-93. Author: (with others) Textbook on Administrative Psychiatry, 1992; also 52 articles; mem. editorial bd. Social Work and Health Care, 1975—, Hosp. and Community Psychiatry; assoc. editor Gen. Hosp. Psychiatry Jour., 1981-94. Chmn. Nassau coun. Health Systems Agy., 1977-80; mem. adv. com. Dr. Glory's Children's Theatre, N.Y.C., 1980—; mental health laws adv. com. State's Atty. Gen., 1987. With USN, 1953-55. Recipient Julius T. Marcus award dept. psychiatry SUNY, Stony Brook, 1980. Fellow Am. Coll. Psychiatrists, Am. Psychiat. Assn. (Distinction in Adminstrn. award 1990); mem. MEDIPP Psychiatry Council (dist. chmn. 1981-86), Am. Assn. Psychiat. Adminstrs. (pres. 1981-82), Am. Hosp. Assn. (chmn. psychiat. services sect. 1985), Am. Assn. Gen. Hosp. Psychiatrists (pres. 1985-87), N.Y. Soc. Clin. Psychiatry (pres. 1974-75, chmn. pub. psychiatry com.), Md. Psychiatric Soc. Office: MPC Ward's Island Dept Psychiatry New York NY 10035

KEILLER, JAMES BRUCE, college dean, clergyman; b. Racine, Wis., Nov. 21, 1938; s. James Allen and Grace (Modder) K.; diploma Beulah Heights Bible Coll., 1957; B.A., William Carter Coll., 1963, Ed.D. (hon.), 1973; LL.B., Blackstone Sch. Law, 1964; M.A., Evang. Theol. Sem., 1965, B.D., 1966, Th.D., 1968; M.A. in Ednl. Adminstrn., Atlanta U., 1977; EdS in Ednl. Adminstrn., Ga. State U., 1987; grad. Nat. Tax Tng. Sch., Monsey, N.Y., 1986; postgrad. Atlanta Law Sch.; m. Darsel Lee Bundy, Feb. 8, 1959; 1 dau., Susanne Elizabeth. Ordained to ministry Internat. Pentecostal Assemblies, 1957; pastor Maranatha Temple, Boston, 1957-58, Midland (Mich.) Full Gospel Ch., 1958-64; v.p. acad. dean Beulah Heights Bible Coll., Atlanta, 1964—, trustee, 1964-92; nat. dir. youth and Sunday sch. dept. Internat. Pentecostal Assemblies, 1958-64, dir. world missions, Atlanta, 1964-76, youth commn., 1958-64, missions com., 1964-76, exec. bd., 1964-76, missionary editor Bridegroom's Messenger, 1964—; dir. global missions Internat. Pentecostal Ch. of Christ, 1976—, mem. exec. com., 1976—; mem. exec. bd. Mt. Paran Christian Sch., 1980-91. Mem. Republican Presdl. Task Force; mem. Nat. Rep. Senatorial Com., Am. Tax Reduction Movement, So. Ctr. Internat. Studies. Named Alumnus of Year, William Carter Coll., 1965. Fellow Coll. of Preceptors; mem. So. Accrediting Assn. Bible Colls. (exec. sec., 1970-93), Ind. Order Foresters, Am. Inst. Parliamentarians, Am. Bd. Master Educators (cert.), Evang. Theol. Soc., Nat. Fedn. for Decency (bd. dirs.), Intercollegiate Studies Inst., Little Mountain Village Condo Assn. (bd. dirs. 1994—), Kiwanis (lt. gov. Ga. dist. 1986-87, chmn. human values state com. Ga. dist. 1989-90). Republican. Fax: (404) 627-0702. E-mail: bhbc@beulah.org. Home: 21A Little Mountain Vlg Ellenwood GA 30294-3150 Office: Beulah Heights Bible Coll 892 Berne St SE Atlanta GA 30316-1873

KEILLOR, GARRISON EDWARD, writer, radio host; b. Anoka, Minn., Aug. 7, 1942; s. John P. and Grace R. (Denham) K.; m. Jenny Lind Nilsson; children: Jason P., Maia Grace. B.A., U. Minn., 1966. Author: Happy to be Here, 1982, Lake Wobegon Days, 1985, Leaving Home, 1987, We Are Still Married: Stories and Letters, 1989, (novel WLT: A Radio Romance, 1991, The Book of Guys, 1993, Cat, You Better Come Home, 1995, The Old Man Who Loved Cheese, 1996, (with J. Nilsson) The Sandy Bottom Orchestra, 1996, Wobegon Boy, 1997, Me, by Jimmy (Big Boy) Valente, 1999; creator, writer and host radio show A Prairie Home Companion; contbr. articles to mags. and newspapers (Harpers, The Atlantic Monthly, The N.Y. Times, others). Recipient Grammy award for best non-mus. recording Lake Wobegon Days, 1987, Ace award, 1988, Best Mus. and Entertainment Host awards, 1988, 89, medal for spoken lang. Am. Acad. and Inst. Arts and Letters, 1990; inducted into Am. Acad. Arts and Scis., 1999. Democrat. Episcopalian. Address: A Prairie Home Companion 45 7th St E Saint Paul MN 55101-2202

KEILLOR, SHARON ANN, electronics company executive; b. St. Thomas, Ont., Can., July 10, 1945; d. Mary Keillor; m. Russel C. Jones; children: Kimberly Nicole, Tamara Melissa. BSChemE, U. Western Ont., 1968; diploma mech. engring., Imperial Coll. Sci. and Tech., London, 1972; PhDME, U. London, 1972; MBA in Bus. Mktg./Fin., Ohio State U., 1976. Asst. prof., faculty engring. and applied sci. Meml. U. Nfld., St. John's, Can., 1972-76; assoc. dir. div. continuing edn., budget planning and fin. U. Mass., Amherst, 1977-78, spl. asst. to provost, 1978-80; corp. mgr. software svcs. tng. Digital Equipment Corp., Stow, Mass., 1980-83, corp. mgr. digital mgmt. edn. and office automation, 1982-83, corp. mgr. software svcs., software engring., 1983-91, v.p. computer spl. systems, 1989-91; v.p. bus. and mktg. mgmt. The Software Group, Stow, Mass., 1991-93, v.p. shared engring. svcs., 1993-95; exec. v.p. CTA Inco., Rockville, Md., 1995-97; v.p. fin. & planning telecom. group Watkins-Johnson Co., Gaithersburg, Md., 1997, chief oper. officer, 1997-98; v.p., mng. dir. Raytheon Marine Co., 1998—; vis. asst. prof. faculty engring. sci. U. Western Ont., London, Can., 1973, 75. Athlone fellow; Nat. Rsch. Coun. Can. scholar. Mem. IEEE, NAFE, AIAA, Soc. Women Engrs., Am. Soc. Engring. Edn. Home: 2001 Mayfair Mclean Ct Falls Church VA 22043-1761 Office: Raytheon Marine Co 676 Island Pond Rd Manchester NH 03109-5420

KEILTY, BRYAN T., government agency administrator. BA, St. Bonaventure U. Supervisory budget analyst U.S. Dept. of Labor, Washington, 1971-82, supervisory manpower devel. specialist, 1982-84, budget officer Office Asst. Sec. for Adminstrn. and Mgmt., 1984-86, dep. contr., 1986-91, dep. adminstr. Office Strategic Planning & Policy Devel., 1991-92, adminstr. Office Fin. and Adminstrn. Mgmt., 1992—. FAX: 908-771-8618. Office: Employment and Tng Adminstrn US Dept of Labor 200 Constitution Ave NW Washington DC 20210-0001

KEIM, BETTY ADELE T., mayor; b. California, Pa., Nov. 14, 1935; d. Glenn L. and F. Edith (Carson) Tinley; m. Richard P. Keim, Mar. 2, 1957 (dec. Sept. 1987); children: Susan Keim Rohrer, Sheila Marie (dec.), Karen Keim Smoot, R. Paul Jr., David C., Katherine Keim Angelides. Grad. nursing, Allegheny Gen. Hosp., Pitts., 1956; student, U. Pitts., 1957-58; BS in Nursing Edn., U. Kans., 1965. RN, Kans., Pa. Nurse biochemistry and nutrition rsch. dept. U. Pitts., St. Margaret's Hosp., 1956-57; pres. Jr. League, Wyandotte, Johnson County, Kans., 1975-76; founding pres. Kans. Action for Children, Topeka, 1978-80; founding mem. Kans. Children's Endowment Fund, Topeka, 1981; pres. Aux. to Kans. Dental Assn., Topeka, 1983-84, United Community Svcs., Johnson County, 1985-87; adv. mem. bd. trustees Bethany Med. Ctr., Kansas City, Kans., 1986-89; dir. Bethany Med. Ctr. Found., Kansas City, Kans., 1989-99; pres. Johnson County C.C. Found., 1990-92; Mem. adv. bd Ctr. on Aging, U. Kans. Med. Ctr., 1999—. Author resource documents. Bd. mem. Community Blood Ctr., Kansas City, Mo., 1988—; mem. Leadership Kans., Topeka, 1991; mem. bd. govs. Am. Royal, Kansas City, 1990—; precinct committeewoman, Mission Hills, Kans., 1988-96; active City Coun., Mission Hills, 1989—, pres., 1991-93, mayor, 1993—; mem. bd. zoning appeals, Mission Hills, 1987-89; chmn. performing arts com. Johnson County C.C. Found., 1993-96, mem. investment com.; mem. nonprofit adv. bd. Park Coll. Graduate Sch. Pub. Affairs, Kansas City, 1995—; mem. celebration steering com. George Brett Baseball Hall of Fame Celebration. Recipient Ann. Child Advocacy award Kans. Action for Children, 1981, Child Abuse Prevention award Kans. Com. for Prevention Child Abuse, 1979, Community Svc. award Jr. League, 1978; named Milton E. Erickson Citizen of Yr. United Community Svcs., Johnson County, 1988, Woman of Yr. Aux. Kans. Dental Assn., 1986. Mem. Allegheny Gen. Hosp. Nurse Alumni Assn., ANA, Kans. State Nurses Assn., Kans. U. Med. Ctr. Nurse Alumni Assn., Jr. League Wyandotte and Johnson Counties Kans., GOP Club, Rep. Elephant Club, Sigma Theta Tau. Presbyterian.

KEIM, DONALD BRUCE, finance educator; b. Bethlehem, Pa., Feb. 7, 1953; s. Elwood Benjamin and Doris Mae (Wanamaker) K.; m. Susan Langshaw, July 10, 1976; children: Sarah Elizabeth, Julia Diane. BSBA, Bucknell U., 1975; MBA, U. Chgo., 1980, PhD, 1983; MS (hon.), U. Pa., 1988. Rsch. assoc. Fed. Deposit Ins. Corp., Washington, 1978; lectr. Loyola U. of Chgo., 1981-82; asst. prof., fin. U. Pa., Phila., 1982-88, assoc. prof. fin., 1988-94, prof. fin., 1994—; vis. prof. INSEAD, Fontainebleau, France, 1994, 96-98; vis. scholar Dimensional Fund Advisors, Santa Monica, Calif., 1990, 1995-96; mem. acad. adv. bd. Brandywine Asset Mgmt., Wilmington, Del., 1993—. Assoc. editor Jour. of Fin. and Quant. Analysis, 1993—; co-editor European Fin. Rev., 1998—; contbr. articles to profl. jours. Rsch. grantee Inst. for Quantitative Rsch., 1984, 92, 99; recipient Graham and Dodd award Fin. Analysts Fedn., 1987, 99, N.Y. Stock Exch. award, 1996. Mem. Am. Fin. Assn., Western Fin. Assn. (program com. 1992-96), European Fin. Assn. (program com. 1996-99). Avocations: music, photography, golf, gardening. Office: Univ Pa The Wharton Sch 2300 Steinberg Hall Philadelphia PA 19104

KEIM, MICHAEL RAY, dentist; b. Sabetha, Kans., June 8, 1951; s. Milton Leroy and Dorothy Juanita (Stover) K.; m. Christine Anne Lorenzen, Nov. 20, 1971; children: Michael Scott, Dawn Marie, Erik Alan. Student, U. Utah, 1969-72; DDS, Creighton U., 1976. Pvt. practice Casper, Wyo., 1976—; vertical math. com. mem. Natrona County Sch. Dist., 1997—. Mem. organizing bd. dirs. Ctrl. Wyo. Soccer Assn., 1976-77; mem. Casper Mountain Ski Patrol, Nat. Ski Patrol Sys., 1980—, avalanche and ski mountaineering advisor No. Divsn. Region III, 1992-96, outdoor emergency care instr. trainer, 1996-99; 1st asst. patrol dir. Nat. Ski Patrol Sys., 1996-98, patrol dir., 1998-99; bd. dirs., dep. commr. for fast pitch Wyo. Amateur Softball Assn., 1980-84; bd. dirs. Ctrl. Wyo. Softball Assn., 1980-84; pres. Wyo. Spl. Smiles Found., 1995-96; mem. organizing com. Prevent Abuse & Neglect thru Dental Awareness Coalition, Wyo., 1996; mem. adv. com. Natrona County Headstart, 1985—. Recipient Purple Merit Star for Saving a Life, 1992. Mem. ADA, Fedn. Dentaire Internat., Pierre Fauchard Acad., Wyo. Acad. Gen. Dentristry (sec.-treas. 1980-82, pres. 1982-87), Wyo. Dental Assn. (bd. dirs 1992-97, chmn. conv. 1993-2000, ADA alt. del. 1994-95, v.p. 1993-94, pres.-elect 1994-95, pres. 1995-96, editor 1997—), Wyo. Dental Polit. Action Com. (sec.-treas. 1985-97), Ctrl. Wyo. Dental Assn. (sec.-treas. 1981-82, pres. 1982-83), Wyo. Dental Hist. Assn. (bd. dirs. 1989-95), Wyo. Donated Dental Svcs. (organizing bd. dirs. 1994, pres. 1995-96), Kiwanis (v.p. Casper club 1988-89, bd. dirs. 1986-96, pres.-elect 1989-90, pres. 1990-91, internat. del. 1989-91, chmn. internat. rels. com. 1992-99, Rocky Mountain dist. lt. gov.-elect divsn. 1 1997-98, lt. gov. divsn. I 1998-99), Creighton Club (pres. 1982-84). Methodist. Avocations: hunting, skiing, sports, woodworking, photography. Home: 58 Jonquil St Casper WY 82604-3863 Office: 1749 S Boxelder St Casper WY 82604-3538

KEIM, ROBERT BRUCE, lawyer; b. Nebraska City, Nebr., Jan. 10, 1946; s. Ernest Jacob and Ruby Rebecca (Mohr) K.; m. Barbara Ann Simmons, Aug. 10, 1968; 1 child, Robert Boyd. BS, U. Nebr., 1968; JD cum laude, Washburn U., 1974. Bar: Mo. 1974, Kans. 1985. Atty. Morris, Larson, King & Stamper, Kansas City, Mo., 1974-89; atty. Shughart, Thomson & Kilroy, P.C., Overland Park, Kans., 1989—, chmn. corp. fin. and transactional law dept.; bd. dirs., mem. audit com. Osborn Labs., Olathe, Kans. Community advisor Jr. League of Johnson & Wyanadotte Counties, Overland Park, 1990—; active fin. com., deacon Rolling Hills Ch., Overland Park, 1990—, Econ. Devel. Coun. Overland Park, 1991—. Lt. U.S. Army, 1968-71. Avocations: running, golf, backpacking. Home: 10021 Juniper Ln Shawnee Mission KS 66207-3446 Office: Shughart Thomson & Kilroy PC 9225 Indian Creek Pkwy Ste 1100 Overland Park KS 66210-2029*

KEIM, ROBERT PHILLIP, retired advertising executive, consultant; b. Ridgewood, N.Y., Jan. 28, 1920; s. William John and Josephine (Becht) K.; m. Gloria Kathleen Smith, Jan. 24, 1943; children: William Gary, Barbara Kathleen. B.A. magna cum laude, Queens Coll.; student, Grad. Sch. Internat. Relations, U. Md., 1950-51. Trainee Compton Advt., N.Y.C., 1942; campaigns mgr. Advt. Council, Inc., N.Y.C., 1954-61; pres. Advt. Council, Inc., 1966-88; also dir.; 2d v.p. marketing service Chase Manhattan Bank, N.Y.C., 1962-66; cons. in field, 1988—; Cons. supt. USAF Acad., 1958; Mem. Air Force Res. Policy Com., 1961-63; del. White House Conf. Edn., 1956, White House Conf. Inflation, 1974; mem. Pres.'s Com. Traffic Safety, 1957-62, Nat. Adv. Council on Minority Bus. Enterprise; mem. exec. com. Air Force Acad. Found. for Falcon Stadium Fund, 1960-61; mem. White House Conf. for a Drug Free Am., 1987-88. Author: Air Force Academy Cadet Procurement Study, 1958, Reserve Forces Utilization Study, 1962; writer, prod.: Air Force Hour, 1946-49, Armed Forces Hour, 1949-50; Adv. bd.: Public Relations News, 1977-81. Bd. visitors Ithaca Coll. Sch. Communications, 1974; bd. dirs. Bus. Council for Internat. Understanding; mem. exec. com. James Webb Young Meml. Fund, U. Ill., 1976-81; mem. Pres.'s Council on Energy Efficiency, 1980, Pres.'s Child Safety Partnership Commn., 1986; mem. bd. Queens Coll. Found. Served to col. USAF, 1942-54. Decorated Legion of Merit, Commendation ribbon; elected fellow R.I. Sch. Design, 1982; scholar Queens Coll., 1941; recipient Dept. English 1st in class award, 1942, Ann. award Internat. Advt. Assn., 1982, Douglas A. Fraser award UAW Internat. Union, 1987, Disting. Alumnus award Queens Coll., 1988. Mem. Madison Winter Club, Clinton Country Club, Phi Beta Kappa. Congregationalist. Address: 17 Longview Ter Madison CT 06443-3409

KEIM, WAYNE FRANKLIN, retired agronomy educator, plant geneticist; b. Ithaca, N.Y., May 14, 1923; s. Franklin David and Alice Mary (Voigt) K.; m. Ellen Joyce Neumann, Sept. 6, 1947; children: Kathryn Louise Keim Logsdon, David Wayne, Julie Anne Keim Hughes. BS with distinction, U. Nebr., 1947; MS, Cornell U., 1949, PhD, 1952. Instr., then asst. prof. Iowa State U., Ames, 1952-56; from asst. prof. to prof. Purdue U., West Lafayette, Ind., 1956-75; vis. prof., NSF sci. faculty fellow U. Lund, (Sweden), 1962-63; vis. prof. Colo. State U., Fort Collins, 1971-72, prof. dept. agronomy, 1975-92; chmn. dept. Colo. State U., 1975-85. Recipient Best Tchr. award Sch. Agr., Purdue U., 1965, 68. Fellow AAAS, Am. Soc. Agronomy (Agronomic Edn. award 1971, Agronomic Svc. award 1991), Crop Sci. Soc. Am. (pres. 1983-84); mem. Am. Inst. Biol. Sci., Council Agrl. Sci. and Tech. (bd. dirs.), Agronomic Sci. Found. (bd. trustees). Home: 1441 Meeker Dr Fort Collins CO 80524-4311 Office: Colo State U Dept Soil and Crop Scis Fort Collins CO 80523

KEINER, CHRISTIAN MARK, lawyer; b. Omaha, Mar. 16, 1953; s. John Frederick Keiner and Geraldine Elizabeth (Smith) Eadie; m. Rosemary Monique White, Nov. 21, 1980; 1 child, Colin MacGregor. BA with high honors, U. Calif., Santa Barbara, 1977; JD with distinction, U. of Pacific, 1980. Bar: Calif. 1980, U.S. Ct. Appeals (9th cir.) 1988, U.S. Supreme Ct. 1991. Assoc. Biddle, Walters, Bukey, Sacramento, 1980-82, Biddle and Hamilton, Sacramento, 1982-92; pvt. practice Sacramento, 1992-98; ptnr. Girard and Vinson, 1998—. Contbr. articles to law jours. Bd. dirs. Calif. Found. for Improvement Employer-Employee Rels., Sacramento, 1994—, Calif. Coun. Sch. Attys., Sacramento, 1996—; instr., mem. labor-mgmt. adv. com. U. Calif. Davis Extension, Sacramento, 1986—. Recipient award for adminstrv. law Am. Jurisprudence, 1979. Mem. ABA (pub. law sect.), Sacramento County Bar (adminstv., pub. and employment law sects.), Sacramento Capitol Club, Harry S. Truman Club (pres. 1992), Order of Coif. Democrat. Catholic. Office: 1006 4th St Ste 701 Sacramento CA 95814-3314

KEINER, R(OBERT) BRUCE, JR., lawyer; b. Washington, July 12, 1942; s. R. Bruce and Alice Miriam (Draeger) K.; m. Suellen Terrill, June 15, 1968; children: Scott, Grant, Terrill. BA, Dickinson Coll., 1964; LLB, U. Va., 1967. Bar: D.C. 1968, U.S. Supreme Ct. 1980. Assoc. to ptnr. Jones, Day, Reavis & Pogue, Washington, 1970-79; ptnr. Crowell & Moring, Washington, 1979—. Capt. U.S. Army, 1968-69. Home: 1730 Crestwood Dr NW Washington DC 20011-5334 Office: Crowell & Moring 1001 Pennsylvania Ave NW Fl 10 Washington DC 20004-2595

KEIR, DUNCAN W., federal judge. JD, U. Md., 1975. Bar: Md. 1975. Assoc., then ptnr. Miles & Stockbridge, 1975-91; gen. counsel Md. Nat. Bank-Am. Security Bank, 1991-93; bankruptcy judge for Md. U.S. Bankruptcy Ct., Greenbelt, 1993—; adj. prof. U. Md. Law Sch., 1989. With USN, 1968-72. Office: US Bankruptcy Ct 6500 Cherrywood Ln Ste 365 Greenbelt MD 20770-1249

KEIR, GERALD JANES, banker; b. Ludlow, Mass., Aug. 22, 1943; s. Alexander J. and Evelyn M. (Buckley) K.; m. Karen Mary Devine, July 22, 1972; children: Matthew J., Katherine B., Megan E. BA, Mich. State U., 1964, MA, 1966. Reporter Honolulu Advertiser, 1968-74, city editor, 1974-86, mng. editor, 1986-89, editor, 1989-95; sr. v.p. corp. comms. First Hawaiian Bank, Honolulu, 1995—. Co-author text: Advanced Reporting: Beyond News Events, 1985, Advanced Reporting: Discovering Patterns in News Events. Bd. govs. Hawaii Comty. Found. Recipient Nat. Reporting award Am. Polit. Sci. Assn., 1971, Benjamin Fine Nat. award Am. Assn. Secondary Sch. Prins., 1981; John Ben Snow fellow, 1983, NEH fellow, 1973. Mem. Soc. Profl. Journalists, Asian-Am. Journalists Assn., Social Sci. Assn., Am. Bankers Assn. (comm. coun.), Pacific Club. Office: First Hawaiian Bank PO Box 3200 Honolulu HI 96847-0001

KEIRN, WENDY GAY, athletic trainer; b. Clearfield, Pa., Sept. 17, 1970; d. Richard L. and Lois J. (Maurer) K. BS, Slippery Rock U., 1992; MS, U. Pitts., 1995. Cert. athletic trainer, Nat. Athletic Trainers' Assn. Athletic trainer Alfred (N.Y.) State Coll., 1995—. Mem. Nat. Athletic Trainers' Assn. Avocations: running, exercise, softball, basketball, reading. Office: Alfred State Coll Orvis Activities Ctr Alfred NY 14802

KEISER, BERNHARD EDWARD, engineering company executive, consulting telecommunications engineer; b. Richmond Heights, Mo., Nov. 14, 1928; s. Bernhard and Helen Barbara Julia (Buerkle) K.; m. Florence Evelyn Keiser, Jan. 22, 1955; children: Sandra, Carol, Nancy, Linda, Paul. BSEE, Washington U., St. Louis, 1950, MSEE, 1951, DScEE, 1953. Registered profl. engr., Va., Md.. Mgr. plans and programs RCA, Cape Canaveral, Fla., 1964-67; adminstr. advanced system planning RCA, Moorestown, N.J., 1967-69; v.p., tech. dir. Page Communication Engring., Washington, 1969-70; dir. advanced engring. Atlantic Rsch. Corp., Alexandria, Va., 1971-72; dir. anaylsis Fairchild Space & Electronics Co., Germantown, Md., 1972-75; pres. Keiser Engring., Inc., Vienna, Va., 1975—. Author: EMI Control in Aerospace Systems, 1979, Principles of Electromagnetic Compatibility, 1979, rev. edit. 1987, Broad band Coding, Modulation and Transmission Engineering, 1989, rev. edit. 1994; co-author: Digital Telephony and Network Integration, 1985, rev. edit. 1995. Fellow IEEE (chmn. No. Va. sect. 1980-81), Washington Acad. Scis., Radio Club Am. Republican. Lutheran. Home and Office: 2046 Carrhill Rd Vienna VA 22181-2917 *I am neither the master of my fate nor the captain of my soul. I owe everything to the Lord Jesus Christ, who is my Savior, my Redeemer.*

KEISER, CAROL JANE, artist; b. Springfield, Mass., Jan. 15, 1945; d. Donald Joseph and Muriel L. (Moulton) K.; m. David Mischke, June 21, 1968 (div. 1980); 1 child, Jude; m. James William Hunt, Oct. 2, 1987. Student, U. N.H., 1963-67, Ohio State U., 1968-69; MEd, Antioch Grad. Sch., Putney, Vt., 1971-72; postgrad., Art Student's League of N.Y., 1982. Self-employed artist working in clay, painting, and tiles, 1970—; owner Studio Tile, Putney, 1985-93, Stoneware Pottery, Putney, 1970-80; work influence includes several years of travel and work in San Miguel de Allende, Mex.; handpainted tiles represented in about 50 galleries throughout the U.S.; painting exhbns. mostly in New Eng. One-woman shows include Interiors, Artisan Gallery, Northampton, Mass., 1993, Remembered Moments, 1991, Paintings from Mexico, River Valley Playhouse, Putney, 1988; group shows include Tile Paintings, Newbury Soc. of Arts and Crafts, Boston, 1993, Woodstock (Vt.) Gallery, 1993, Works from Mexico, Bellows Falls Trust, Putney, 1992, Hands of the Goddess, Michelson Gallery, Amherst, Mass., 1992, Beyond the Borders, Gerard Gallery, Windsor, Vt., 1990, Stratton (Vt.) Arts Festival, 1988, 90-93, more. Mem. Planning Commn., Putney, 1976-78. Recipient Jurors award of Distinction, Stratton Arts Show, 1993; invited to design ornament for White House Christmas tree, 1993; painting selected to appear in Hands of the Goddess calendar, 1992; drawing selected for greeting card design, Frog Hollow Craft Ctr., Middlebury, Vt., 1989; recipient grant to attend bus. seminars at Am. Woman's Devel. Corp., N.Y.C., New Woman mag., 1985. Mem. Newbury Soc. of Arts and Crafts, N.H. League of Arts and Crafts, Vt. State Craft Ctrs. at Middlebury, Burlington, Manchester and Windsor. Democrat. Unity. Avocations: reading, running, tennis, Tai Chi.

KEISER, EDMUND DAVIS, JR., biologist, educator; b. Appalachia, Va., Feb. 18, 1934; s. Edmund Davis and Ora Elizabeth (Wade) K.; m. Alice Sue Tucker, Sept. 10, 1982; children: Mark Edmund, Julie Ann; stepchildren: Louis King III, Jenifer King. B.A., So. Ill. U., 1956, M.S., 1961; Ph.D. in Zoology, La. State U., 1967. Tchr. sci. Kinmundy High Sch., Ill., 1956-57, Mt. Vernon Twp. Sch. Dist., Ill., 1957-58; dist. sci. coordinator Freeburg Sch. Dist. 70, Freeburg, Ill., 1958-62; instr. biology La Salle-Peru-Oglesby Jr. Coll., La Salle, Ill., 1962-64; teaching asst. La. State Univ., Baton Rouge, 1964-66; asst. prof. U. Southwestern La., Lafayette, 1966-70; asso. prof. U. Southwestern La., 1970-75, prof., 1976, mem. council grad. coordinators, 1973-76; prof. biology U. Miss., 1976—; chmn. dept. U. Miss., University, 1976-87; prof. biology U. Miss., 1976—; mem. Atchafalaya River Basin Rsch. Coun., 1972-74; mem. exec. coun., state dir. sci. teaching La. Acad. Scis., 1972-74; rsch. assoc. Gulf South Rsch. Inst., 1972-74; dir. Lafayette Natural History Mus. and Planetarium, 1973, Atchafalaya River Basin herpetofaunal study U.S. Fish and Wildlife Svc., 1973-76; mem. exec. coun. Gopher Tortoise Soc., 1979-81; commr. Miss. Dept. Wildlife Conservation, 1978-79, 80-84, chmn., 1983-84. Mem. Miss. Wildlife Heritage Com., 1980-84, Miss. Gov.'s Select Com. on Radioactivity and Radioactive Waste Depository, 1979-80; environ. cons. NASA/Lockheed Sci. and Engring., 1990-91, 94-95, NASA/Sverdrup Engring., 1994-95; cons. on aquatic ecosys. U.S. Army C.E., 1992-95, 98—; cons. NASA/GBTech, 1998—, Miss. Dept. Wildlife, Fisheries and Parks, 1998—. Recipient numerous grants; Disting. Prof. award U. Southwestern La., 1973; Govs. Meritorious Service award State of Miss., 1979; citation for outstanding sci. teaching Nat. Sci. Tchrs. Assn.-Ill. Supt. Public Instrn., 1962. Fellow Explorers Club; mem. Am. Soc. Ichthyologists and Herpetologists, Soc. for Study Amphibians and Reptiles, Herpetologists League, Nat. Exch. Club, Civitans (exec. com. Lafayette), Sigma Xi (chpt. pres. 1976, 79-80), Beta Beta Beta, Phi Eta Sigma, Phi Kappa Phi. Home: 211 St Andrews Cir Oxford MS 38655-2518 Office: U Miss Dept Biology University MS 38677

KEISER, HARRY ROBERT, physician; b. Chgo., Aug. 9, 1933; s. Harry Rudolph and Anna Mae (Hungerford) K.; m. Linda Lee Hallsten, June 11, 1965 (div. 1989); children: Harry Rudolph, Robert Hungerford; m. Phyllis Swain Bentz, May 9, 1992. B.A., Northwestern U., 1955, M.D., 1958. Diplomate: Nat. Bd. Med. Examiners, Am. Bd. Internal Medicine. Intern Phila. Gen. Hosp., 1958-59; resident in internal medicine VA Research Hosp., Chgo., 1959-60; clin. assoc. Nat. Heart Inst., NIH, Bethesda, Md., 1960-63; resident in internal medicine U. Calif. Hosp., San Francisco, 1963-64; sr. investigator, then acting chief exptl. therapeutics br. Nat. Heart Inst., 1964-73; clin. asst. prof. medicine Georgetown U. Med. Sch., 1965-90, clin. prof. medicine, 1990—; dep. chief hypertension-endocrine br. Nat. Heart, Lung and Blood Inst., 1974-85; chief hypertension-endocrine br., 1985-98, clin. dir. inst., 1976-98; commd. officer USPHS, 1960-98, med. dir., 1972-98; scientist emeritus NIH, 1998—. Author articles on causes of hypertension. Fellow ACP; mem. Am. Fedn. Med. Research, Am. Soc. Pharmacology and Exptl. Therapeutics, Am. Soc. Hypertion, Am. Heart Assn., Sierra Club, Izaak Walton League. E-mail: hkeiser@aol.com. Home: 2367 S Queen St Arlington VA 22202-1550 Office: Nat Heart Lung & Blood Inst Bldg 10 Rm 8C-103 10 Center Dr MSC1754 Bethesda MD 20892-1754

KEISER, JOHN HOWARD, university president; b. Mt. Olive, Ill., Mar. 12, 1936; s. Howard H. and Lorraine G. K.; m. Nancy Peterka, June 27, 1959; children: John, Sam, Joe. B.S. in Edn, Eastern Ill. U., 1958; M.A., Northwestern U., 1960, Ph.D. in History, 1964. Prof. history Westminster Coll., Fulton, Mo., 1963-65, Eastern Ill. U., Charleston, 1965-71; v.p. acad. affairs Sangamon State U., Springfield, Ill., 1971-78; acting pres. Sangamon State U., 1978; pres. Boise (Idaho) State U., 1978-93, S.W. Mo. State U., Springfield, 1993—. Author: Building for the Centuries, Illinois, 1865-1898, 1977, Illinois Vignettes, 1977. Bd. dirs. Abraham Lincoln council Boy Scouts Am., Springfield, Ore-Ida Council, Boise. Recipient Harry E. Pratt Meml. award Jour. Ill. History, 1970, 72; award of merit Ill. State Hist. Soc., 1980; award of merit Am. Assn. State and Local History, 1980. Mem. Orgn. Am. Historians, Am. Hist. Soc., Labor History Soc., Boise C. of C. Roman Catholic. Club: Rotary. Office: SW Missouri St U Off Pres 901 S National Ave Springfield MO 65804-0027*

KEISER, PAUL HAROLD, hospital administrator; b. Dalton, Ohio, June 1, 1927; s. Austin R. and Elrena E. (Tschantz) K.; m. Nancy F. Homan, May 27, 1950; children—James William, Martha Ann Lee, Elizabeth Louise Green, Patricia Elrena Bell. B.S., Mt. Union Coll., 1948; M.S. in Hosp. Adminstrn., Northwestern U., 1952. Adminstr. Community Hosp. Evanston, Ill., 1952-54, Burlington Hosp., Iowa, 1954-67; pres. York Hosp., Pa., 1967-88, ret., 1988, pres. emeritus, 1988—; lectr., seminar leader Northwestern U., Chgo., 1952-54, U. Iowa Hosp., Iowa City, 1955-59; lectr. George Washington U., 1969-86. Contbr. articles to profl. jours. Bd. dirs. United Way, York, Pa., 1970-78, York Habitat for Humanity, 1992—, Nixon County Park Treasury of Wildlife, 1989—, York County Farm and Natural Land Trust, 1992—; dir. adv. bd. Pa. State U., York, 1979—; sec. North Codorus Twp. Plan Commn., 1994-96; mem. North Codorus Twp. Bd. Suprs., 1995—, vice chmn., 1997—; mem. gov. bd. Byrnes Health Edn. Ctr., 1995—. Fellow Am. Coll. Hosp. Adminstrs. (life, regent 1964-67); mem. Iowa Interprofl. Assn. (pres. 1963-64), Iowa Hosp. Assn. (pres. 1961-62), Am. Hosp. Assn. (del. 1975-86), Hosp. Assn. Pa. (chmn. bd. dirs. 1983, bd. dirs. svcs. corp. 1986-89), Northwestern U. Hosp. Adminstrn. Alumni Assn. (pres. 1957-58), Rotary (bd. dirs. 1979-82), Sigma Alpha Epsilon. Republican. Presbyterian. Avocations: tennis; woodworking; handyman. Home: Box 22 RR 8 Box 22 York PA 17403-9617

KEISER, ROBERT LEE, gas and oil industry executive; b. 1942. BSEE, U. Mo., 1965. Engring. trainee Sunray DX, 1965-68; mgr. internat. Sun Co., 1968-87; v.p. planning and devel. Sun Exploration and Prodn. Co., 1987-88; v.p. planning and devel. Oryx Energy Co., Dallas, 1988-91, pres., chief oper. officer, 1991-94; chmn., CEO, pres., 1994—; bd. dirs. U. Tex., Dallas. Mem. Soc. Petroleum Engrs., Dallas Petroleum Club. Office: Oryx Energy Co 13155 Noel Rd Dallas TX 75240-5090

KEISER, TERRY D., biologist, educator; b. Canton, Ohio, Oct. 27, 1942; s. Dean Robert and Neva Juanita K.; m. Patricia D. Peterson, Sept. 1, 1971 (div. Nov. 1976); m. Christine E. Provines, July 14, 1984. BS, Ohio Northern U., 1964; MS, Bowling Green State U., 1966. Instr., prof. Ohio Northern U., Ada, Ohio, 1966—, chair, 1992—; dir. Nature Ctr., Stone Creek, Ohio, 1990—, Midwest Biodiversity Inst., Columbus, 1998—, S. Meyers Auto Sales, Kenton, Ohio, 1996—; chair Ohio Biol. Survey, Columbus, Ohio, 1992—; cons. USGS-NAWQA, Columbus, 1995—. Contbr. articles to profl. jours. Chair Ada/Liberty Ambulance bd., Ohio, 1994—, Ada Area Doctors com., 1995—; pres. Ada City Council, 1984—, Ada CIC, 1993. Fellow Ohio Acad. Sci.; mem. Elks. Avocations: travel, nature study. E-mail: t-keiser@onu.edu. Home: PO Box 262 220 E High Ada OH 45810 Office: Ohio Northern Univ Dept Biol Sciences Ada OH 45810

KEISLING, PHILLIP ANDREW, state official; b. Portland, Oreg., June 23, 1955; s. Les and Ione Keisling; m. Pam Wiley, Sept. 4, 1988. BA, Yale U., 1977. Speech writer Gov. Tom McCall Campaign, Salem, Oreg., 1978; reporter Willamette Week, Portland, 1978-81; editor Washington Monthly mag., 1982-84; sr. legis asst. Oreg. Speakers of the Ho., Salem, 1985-88; mem. Oreg. Ho. of Reps., Salem, 1989-91; sec. of state State of Oreg., Salem, 1991—; mem. State Land Bd., Salem, 1991—. Chmn. Brooklyn Neighborhood Assn., Portland, 1986-88. Office: Office Sec of State State Capitol Rm 136 Salem OR 97310

KEISTER, JEAN CLARE, lawyer; b. Warren, Ohio, Aug. 28, 1931; d. John R. Keister and Anna Helen Brennan. JD, Southwestern U., 1966. Bar: Calif. 1967, U.S. Supreme Ct. 1972, U.S. Dist. Ct. (so. dist.) Calif. 1988. Legal writer Gilbert Law Summaries, L.A., 1967; instr. Glendale (Calif.) Coll. Law, 1968; pvt. practice Glendale, 1967-70, L.A., Calif., 1970-80, Burbank, Calif., 1987-97, Lancaster, Calif., 1992—, Ventura, Calif, 1997—. Mem. Themis Soc., 1989-97. Recipient Golden Poet award World of Poetry. Mem. Burbank Bar Assn. (sec. 1993), Ventura County Bar Assn., Antelope Valley Bar Assn. Avocations: writing prose and poetry, travel, crochet.

KEISTLER, BETTY LOU, accountant, tax consultant; b. St. Louis, Jan. 2, 1935; d. John William and Gertrude Marie (Lewis) Chancellor; m. George E. Keistler, Aug. 3, 1957 (div. Mar. 1981); children: Kathryn M., Deborah J. Birsinger. AS, St. Louis U., 1956; BBA, U. Mo., 1986. Asst. treas. A.G. Edwards & Sons, St. Louis, 1956-57; owner, mgr. B.L. Keistler & Assoc., St. Louis, 1969-82; contr. Family Resource Ctr., Inc., St. Louis, 1982-87; registered rep. Equitable Fin. Svcs., Mo., 1987-88; bus. mgr. Mo. Bapt. Coll., St. Louis, 1987-88, Barnes Hosp. Sch. of Nursing, St. Louis, 1988-91, U. South Fla., St. Petersburg, 1991—; cons. in field, 1982-91; cert. two star sales assoc. Youngevity, Inc., 1995, area assoc. trainer; registered rep. Equitable Fin. Svcs., 1987-88; adminstrv. and profl. coun. mem. U. South Fla., 1994. Treas. Pky. Townhouses at Village Green, Chesterfield, Mo., 1985-87; exec. core United Way Greater St. Louis, 1984-91; mem. Gulfport Hist. Soc., 1996—; mem. bldg. and grounds com. Pasadena Bapt. Ch., Sunday sch. gen. sec., 1994-95, chair trustee com. 1996-97. Scholar Phillip Morris Corp., St. Louis, 1982-84. Mem. Am. Bus. Womens Assn. (v.p. 1978-79, pres. Lewis & Clark chpt. 1979-80, treas. nat. conv. 1981, pres. ADITI chpt. 1988-90, Sand & Sea chpt. 1992—, Woman of Yr. 1979-80, 94-95), U. South Fla. Women's Club, Am. Soc. Women Accts., Ind. Accts. Mo. (sec. 1978-79, v.p. 1980-81, state sec. 1978-79), St. Louis Women's Commerce Assn., 1904 World's Fair Soc., Internat. Platform Assn., Gulfport Hist. Soc., Am. Biog. Inst. (hon. advisor, rsch. bd. advisors nat. divsn. 1991), NAFE, Gulfort Hist. Soc., Alpha Sigma Lambda (life, treas. 1985-87). Republican. Avocations: travel, public speaking, entertaining, reading. Fax: (727) 553-1675. E-mail: bkeistle@stpt.usf.edu. Home: 6060 Shore Blvd S Apt 103 Gulfport FL 33707-5843

KEITEL, HARVEY, actor; b. Bklyn., May 13, 1941; m. Lorraine Bracco (div.); 1 child, Stella. Studied with Lee Strasberg; studied with Frank Corsaro, Actors Studio. Motion picture performances include Who's That Knocking at My Door?, 1968, Mean Streets, 1973, Street Scenes, 1973, Alice Doesn't Live Here Anymore, 1974, That's the Way of the World, 1975, Taxi Driver, 1976, Mother Jugs and Speed, 1976, Buffalo Bill and the Indians or Sitting Bull's History Lesson, 1976, Welcome to L.A, 1977, The Duellists, 1977, Blue Collar, 1978, Fingers, 1978, Eagle's Wing, 1978, La Mort en Direct, 1979, Saturn 3, 1979, Bad Timing: A Sensual Obsession, 1980, The Border, 1982, La Nuit de Varennes, 1982, Copkiller, 1982, Il Mondo Nuovo, 1982, Nemo, 1983, Corrupt, 1983, Exposed, 1983, Une Pierre Dans la Bouche, 1983, Falling in Love, 1984, Knight of the Dragon, 1985, A Complex Plot About Women, Alleys and Crimes, 1985, Comorra, 1985, Off Beat, 1986, Wise Guys, 1986, The Men's Club, 1986, The Pick-Up Artist, 1987, The Inquiry, 1987, L'Inchiesta, 1987, The Last Temptation of Christ, 1988, Caro Gorbaciov, 1988, The January Man, 1988, Blindside, 1988, The Two Jakes, 1990, Grandi Cacciatori, 1990, Two Evil Eyes, 1990, Bugsy, 1991 (Acad. award nominee), Mortal Thoughts, 1991, Thelma and Louise, 1991, Sister Act, 1992, Reservoir Dogs, 1992 (also co-prod.), Bad Lieutenant, 1992, The Piano, 1993, Point of No Return, 1993, Rising Sun, 1993, Snake Eyes, 1993, Dangerous Game, 1993, The Young Americans, 1993, Monkey Trouble, 1994, Pulp Fiction, 1994, Imaginary Crimes, 1994, Smoke, 1995, Clockers, 1995, Blue in the Face, 1995, Ulysses' Gaze, 1995, Get Shorty, 1995, From Dusk Till Dawn, 1995, Blue in the Face, 1995, Somebody to Love, 1996, Copland, 1996; numerous TV appearances including: A Memory of Two Mondays, 1971, This Ain't No Bee-Bop, Down Where The Buffalo Go; TV movies include: The Virginia Hill Story, 1974, Eagle's Way, 1979; appeared on stage in: A Lie in the Mind, Death of a Salesman, 1975, Hurlyburly, 1984. Office: c/o William Morris Agy 151 S El Camino Dr Beverly Hills CA 90212-2704 also: care Susan Culley Assoc 150 S Rodeo Dr Ste 220 Beverly Hills CA 90212-2409

KEITH, ALEXANDER MACDONALD, retired state supreme court chief justice, lawyer; b. Rochester, Minn., Nov. 22, 1928; s. Norman and Edna (Alexander) K.; m. Marion Sanford, April 29, 1955; children: Peter Sanford (dec.), Ian Alexander, Douglas Scott. BA, Amherst Coll., 1950; JD, Yale U., 1953. Assoc. counsel, mem. Mayo Clinic, Rochester, 1955-60; state sen. Olmstead County, St. Paul, 1959-63; lt. gov. State of Minn., St. Paul, 1963-67; pvt. practice, Rochester, 1960-73; ptnr. Dunlap Keith Finseth Berndt and Sandberg, Rochester, 1973-89; assoc. justice Minn. Supreme Ct., St. Paul, 1989-90, chief justice, 1990-98; ret., 1998; of counsel Dunlap & Seeger P.A., Rochester, Minn., 1998—. Sen. del. White House Conf. on Aging, Washington, 1960; U.S. del. UN Delegation for Funding Developing Countries, Geneva, 1966; bd. dirs. Rochester Grad. Edn. Adv. Com., 1988-89, Ability Bldg. Ctr. Inc. 1st lt. USMC, 1953-55, Korea. Named Outstanding Freshman Senator, Minn. Senate, St. Paul. Fax: 507-288-9342. Home: 5225 Meadow Crossing Rd SW Rochester MN 55902-3506 Office: Dunlap & Seeger PA PO Box 549 Rochester MN 55903-0549

KEITH, BARRY ALLEN, clinical social worker; b. Hamilton, Ohio, June 20, 1960; s. Carl Edward and Barbara Ann (Hutson) K.; m. Star Lynn Ramsey, Aug. 14, 1993; children: Kara, Garrett. BA, Otterbein Coll., 1983; MSW, Ohio State U., 1987. Lic. ind. social worker, Ohio. Clin. social worker Charles B. Mills Ctr., Marysville, Ohio, 1984-87, Sawmill Psychol., Worthington, Ohio, 1987-95; clin. social worker, assoc. dir. Ctr. for Cognitive and Behavioral Therapy, Columbus, Ohio, 1995—; dir. Attention Deficit Disorder Diagnostic and Treatment Ctr. Ctrl. Ohio, Columbus, 1997—; cons. mental health specialist Dublin (Ohio) Schs., 1982—. Coach boys baseball Dublin Youth Assn., Dublin Mid. Sch., Upper Arlington (Ohio) Schs., Upper Arlington Baseball Assn. Mem. NASW (qualified, diplomate), Ohio Psychol. Assn. Avocations: weight lifting, coaching. Office: Ctr for Cognitive and Behavioral Therapy 2121 Bethel Rd Columbus OH 43220-1804

KEITH, BARRY HAROLD, environmental scientist; b. Northbridge, Mass., Sept. 16, 1954; s. Harold and Louise Thobia (Hansen) K.; m. Pamela Jean Clemons, May 16, 1981; stepchildren: Shanti, Leif. BS, U. N.H., 1976, MS, 1982. Registered profl. forester, Maine, N.H., profl. Wetland Sci.; cert. wildlife biologist. Wildlife biologist U.S. Army C.E., Franklin, N.H., 1976-77, 78; terrestrial ecologist Wilbur Smith & Assocs., Inc., Concord, N.H., 1977; sr. ecologist BCI Geonetics, Inc., Laconia, N.H., 1977-78; ind. consulting ecologist Laconia, 1978-79; wetlands project mgr. N.H. Extension Svc., Conway, 1979-80; environ. scientist B.H. Keith Assocs., Freedom, N.H., 1980—; cons., U.S. Am. Internat. Devel., Washington, 1987—. Contbr. articles to environ. publs. Mem. Freedom (N.H.) Conservation Commn., 1988—; selectman Town of Freedom, 1999—. Mem. Wildlife Soc. (bull. editorial referee 1983), Soc. Wetland Scientists, Soc. Ecol. Restoratin and Mgmt., Soc. Am. Foresters, N.H. Assn. Wetland Scientists, Ducks Unlimited (chmn. 1985-92, Disting. Svc. award), Soc. for Protection of N.H. Forests, Freedom Club. Republican. Avocations: fishing, hunting, hiking, antiques, wildlife art. Office: BH Keith Assocs Elm St Freedom NH 03836

KEITH, BRIAN THOMAS, automobile executive; b. Houston, Aug. 2, 1951; s. Thomas Ross and Elsie Ann (Carden) K.; m. Anna Lee Rogers, Nov. 17, 1973; children: Kevin Patrick, Lindsay Rogers. BSBA, Samford U., 1973. Educator installation IBM, Birmingham, Ala., 1971-73; salesman Albeco-Ala. Bus. Equipment Co., Birmingham, 1973-74; pres., owner Walter S. White Auto Parts, Inc., Birmingham, 1974—; bd. dirs. Ala. Power Co. Vendor Rels. Bd., Birmingham; trustee Automotive Wholesalers Ins. Trust, Montgomery, 1985—, treas. investment com., 1992—, chmn. trust, 1996—; industry spkr. Automotive Market Rsch. Coun., 1995, Automotive Wholesalers Assn. Ala. and Ga., Automotive Svc. Industry Assn. Pub. mag. Auto Svc. and Repair, 1988—; contbr. articles to publs. and mags. V.p. Park Bd. Patriot Baseball, Homewood, Ala., 1985-89; celebrity fundraiser Am. Cancer Soc., 1993; mem. canvass com. All Sts. Ch., Homewood, 1986-90, youth com., 1992—. Named Outstanding Young Men in Am., U.S. Jaycees, 1983; recipient Tech. Tng. award Arvvin Industries, 1983-88. Mem. Automotive Wholesalers Assn. Ala. (bd. dirs. 1985—, chmn. 1986-91, treas. 1992-95, 98—, polit. action com. 1992—, exec. com. 1991—, Leadership award 1991), Automotive Svc. Industry Assn. (bd. dirs. 1992-98, nat. polit. action com. 1993—, co-chmn. automotive com. 1994-98), Birmingham C. of C., U.S. C. of C., Young Exec. Forum, Assn. Enterprises (pres. 1991-92), Jr. Achievement, Nat. Fedn. Ind. Bus. Episcopalian. Avocations: family, golf, travel.

KEITH, BRUCE EDGAR, political analyst, genealogist; b. Curtis, Nebr., Feb. 17, 1918; s. Edgar L. and Corinne E. (Marsteller) K.; m. Evelyn E. Johnston, Oct. 29, 1944; children: Mona Louise, Kent Marsteller, Melanie Ann. AB with high distinction, Nebr. Wesleyan U., 1940; MA, Stanford U., 1952; grad. Command and Staff, Marine Corps Schs., 1958, Sr. Resident Sch., Naval War Coll., 1962; PhD, U. Calif.-Berkeley, 1982. Commd. 2d lt. U.S. Marine Corps, 1942, advanced through grades to col., 1962, ret., 1971, OinC Marine Corps Nat. Media, N.Y.C., 1946-49, support arms coord. 1st Marines, Seoul, Chosin, Korea, 1950, comdg. officer 3d Bn., 11th Marines, 1958-59, ops. officer, Pres. Dwight D. Eisenhower visit to Okinawa, 1960, G-3 ops. officer Fleet Marine Force, Pacific, Cuban Missile Crisis, 1962, mem. U.S. del. SEATO, Planning Conf., Bangkok, Thailand, 1964, G-3, Fleet Marine Force, Pacific, 1964-65, head Strategic Planning Study Dept., Naval War Coll., 1966-68, genealogist, 1967—, exec. officer Hdqrs. Marine Corps programs, Washington, 1968-71; election analyst Inst. Govtl. Studies, U. Calif.-Berkeley, 1974-86, polit. analyst, 1986—; teaching asst. U. Calif.-Berkeley, 1973-74. Bd. dirs., Bay Area Funeral Soc., 1980-83, v.p., 1981-83. Decorated Bronze Star, Navy Commendation medal, Presdl. Unit citation with 3 bronze stars. Recipient Phi Kappa Phi Silver medal Nebr. Wesleyan U., 1940, Alumni award, 1964. Mem. Am. Polit. Sci. Assn., Acad. Polit. Sci., Am. Acad. Polit. and Social Sci., World Affairs Coun. No. Calif., Marine Corps Assn., Ret. Officers Assn. Phi Kappa Phi, Pi Gamma Mu. Republican. Unitarian. Clubs: Commonwealth of Calif. (San Francisco), Marines' Meml. (San Francisco). Lodge: Masons. Contbg. author: The Descendants of Daniel and Elizabeth (Disbrow) Keith, 1979-81; History of Curtis, Nebraska-The First Hundred Years, 1984; author: A Comparison of the House Armed Services Coms. in the 91st and 94th Congresses: How They Differed and Why, 1982; The Johnstons of Morning Sun, 1979; The Marstellers of Arrellton, 1978; The Morris Family of Brookville, 1977; Japan-the Key to America's Future in the Far East, 1962; A United States General Staff: A Must or a Monster?, 1950; co-author: California Votes, 1960-72, 1974; The Myth of the Independent Voter, 1992; Further Evidence on the Partisan Affinities of Independent " Leaners," 1983. Address: PO Box 2368 Walnut Creek CA 94595

KEITH, CAROL JEAN, writer, regional historian; b. Tarpon Springs, Fla., June 5, 1936; d. Sherrod Raymond and Irene Immoline (Boyd) Skeen; m. Walter Louis Keith,Mar. 16, 1956; 1 child, Barbara Jean. Cert., Am. Banking Inst., 1965; student, Ctrl. Fla. C.C., 1978—. Exec. asst. Nations Banks, Tarpon Springs, 1962-68; adminstrv. asst. to spkr. Fla. Ho. of Reps., Tampa, 1968-69; exec. assn. George Paul Adams, Tampa, 1969-70; coord. med. staff Munroe Regional Hosp., Ocala, Fla., 1974-78; biographer, novelist Bacalou Pub. Co., Crystal River, Fla., 1978—; lectr. history Citrus and Pinellas counties, 1994—. Author: A Watch for Evil, 1990. Mem. Tarpon Springs Hist. Soc., Pinellas County Hist. Soc. (history lectr. 1994—). Democrat. Baptist. Avocations: fishing, hunting, cooking.

KEITH, CAROLYN AUSTIN, secondary school counselor; b. Mobile, Ala., July 15, 1949; d. Lloyd James Jr. and Aletia Delores (Taylor) Austin; m. Carlos Lamar Keith Sr., Aug. 14, 1971; children: Carlos Lamar Jr., Carolyn Bernadette Austin Keith. BA in English and History, Mercer U., 1971; Cert. in Gifted Edn., Valdosta State Coll., 1979, MEd in Counseling, 1982, postgrad., 1987; postgrad., Nova Southeastern U., 1997—. Tchr. English Crisp County High Sch., Cordele, Ga., 1971-77; tchr. gifted Tift County Jr. High Sch., Tifton, Ga., 1977-81, Dooly County Sch. System, Vienna, Ga., 1981-82; counselor Worth County High Sch., Sylvester, Ga., 1982-86, Monroe Comprehensive High Sch., Albany, Ga., 1986-91, Dougherty County Alternative Sch., Albany, 1991-98, Dougherty County Mid. Sch., Albany, 1998—; cons. Ga. State U., Atlanta, 1986-89, Dept. Family and Children Svcs., Albany, 1993, 94; presenter Nat. Dropout Prevention Fall conf., 1997. Mem. West Point Parent's Club, U.S. Mil. Acad., 1992-96, Dougherty County Commn. on Children/Youth, Albany, 1991—; mem. adv. bd. Southwest Ga. Prevention Resource Ctr., Teen Plus Clinic, 1998, S.W. Ga. Area Health Edn. Ctr., 1996—; mem. Nat. Family Life Inst., U. N.C., Charlotte, 1997; presenter Nat. Dropout Prevention Fall Conf., 1997. Named Vol. of Yr., Dougherty County Coun. on Child Abuse, 1993, Student Assistance Program Counselor of Yr. for State of Ga., 1994. Mem. Am. Counseling Assn., Ga. Sch. Counselors Assn. (sec. 2d dist. 1985-91, Counselor of Yr. 1993), Am. Sch. Counselors Assn., Nat. Bd. Cert. Counselors (cert. family life instr.), Ga. Lic. Profl. Counselors, South Ga. Regional Assn. Lic. Profl. Counselors, Delta Sigma Theta. Democrat. Roman Catholic. Avocations: reading, classical music. Office: PO Box 50261 Albany GA 31703-0261

KEITH, DALE MARTIN, management consultant; b. Kansas City, Mo., Oct. 22, 1940; s. Floyd LeRoy and Pauline Constance (Brown) K.; m. Judith Ann Reynolds, May 8, 1964; children: Stephanie Deanna, Kirsten Michelle. BSBA in Indsl. Mgmt., U. Mo., 1965. Cert. mgmt. cons. Staff analyst Black & Veatch, Kansas City, Mo., 1965-68, asst. project mgr., 1968-75, adminstrv. coord., 1975-77, project mgr., 1977-88, mktg. dir., 1988-90, project dir., 1990-92; pres. Cert. Mgt. Cons., 1992—, Keith and Assocs., Ltd., Kansas City, 1993—; prin. The Keith Cos. Interactive Distbn., Stilwell, Kans., 1997—; internat. speaker, trainer, advisor Coun. of Econ. Regulation, Washington, 1988—. Mem. Eggs & Issues Forum, Kansas City, 1988—. Mem. Assn. Energy Engrs., Inst. Mgmt. Cons. (mem. Coll. Firm Prins., bd. dirs., past chmn., pres. Kansas City chpt., founding bd. mem. LAW Spl. Interest Group, IMC Comms. Com. chmn., 1996 IMC Nat. Conv. chpt. leadership and mgmt. com.), Assn. Mgmt. Cons., Nat. Trust for Scotland, St. Andrews Soc., Menninger Soc., U.S. Energy Assn. (tech. collaboration com.), Inst. of Ams., Internat. Platform Assn., Internet Soc., Optimists Internat. (bd. dirs. Kans. dist., pres. Blue Valley chpt., Optimist Youth Homes). Republican. Presbyterian. Avocations: Jaguar motor cars, photography, golf, reading, computers/elecric on-line world. Home: 17101 Canterbury Dr Stilwell KS 66085-9035

KEITH, DAMON JEROME, federal judge; b. Detroit, Mich., July 4, 1922; s. Perry A. and Annie L. (Williams) K.; m. Rachel Boone, Oct. 18, 1953; children: Cecile Keith, Debbie, Gilda. BA, W.Va. State Coll., 1943; JD, Howard U., 1949; LLM, Wayne State U., 1956; PhD (hon.), U. Mich., Howard U., Wayne State U., Mich. State U., N.Y. Law Sch., Detroit Coll. Law, W.Va. State Coll., U. Detroit, Atlanta U., Lincoln U., Marygrove Coll., Detroit Inst. Tech., Shaw Coll., Ctrl. State U., Yale U., Loyola Law Sch., L.A., Ea. Mich. U., Va. Union U., Ctrl. Mich. U., Morehouse Coll., Western Mich. U., Tuskegee U., Georgetown U., Hofstra U., DePaul U. Bar: Mich. 1949. Atty. Office Friend of Ct., Detroit, 1952-56; sr. ptnr. firm Keith, Conyers Anderson, Brown & Wahls, Detroit, 1964-67; mem. Wayne County Bd. Suprs., 1958-63; dist. judge U.S. Dist. Ct. (ea. dist.) Mich., 1967-77, chief judge, 1975-77; judge U.S. Ct. Appeals (6th cir.), Detroit, 1977-95, sr. judge, 1995—; mem. Wayne County (Mich.) Bd. Suprs., 1958-63; chmn. Mich. Civil Rights Commn., 1964-67; pres. Detroit Housing Commn., 1958-67; commr. State Bar Mich., 1960-67; mem. Mich. Com. Manpower Devel. and Vocat. Tng., 1964, Detroit Mayor's Health Adv. Com., 1969; rep. dist. judges 6th Cir. Jud. Conf., 1975-77; adv. com. on codes of conduct Jud. Conf. U.S., 1979-86; subcom. on supporting pers. Jud. Conf. Com. on Ct. Adminstrn., 1983-87; chmn. Com. on the Bicentennial of Constn. of Sixth Cir., 1985—; nat. chmn. Jud. Conf. Com. on the Bicentennial of Constn., 1987—; mem. Commn. on the Bicentennial of U.S. Constn., 1990; lectr. Howard U., 1972, Ohio State U. Law Sch., 1992, N.Y. Law Sch., 1992; guest lectr. Howard U. Law Sch., 1981; Bicentennial of Constn. lectr. W.Va. State Coll., 1987; keynote speaker Black Law Students Assn., Harvard Law Sch., 1987. Contbr. articles to profl. jours. Trustee Med. Corp. Detroit; trustee Interlochen Arts Acad., Cranbrook Sch., U. Detroit, Mich. chpt. Leukemia Soc. Am.; mem. Citizen's Adv. Com. Equal Ednl. Opportunity Detroit Bd. Edn.; gen. co-chmn. United Negro Coll. Fund Detroit; 1st v.p. emeritus Detroit chpt. NAACP; mem. com. mgmt. Detroit YMCA, Detroit coun. Boy Scouts Am., Detroit Arts Commn; vice chmn. Detroit Symphony Orch.; vis. com. Wayne State U. Law Sch.; adv. coun. U. Notre Dame Law Sch.; bd. dirs. Detroit Bd. Table, NCCJ; deacon Tabernacle Missionary Bapt. Ch.; chmn. Citizen's Coun. for Mich. Pub. Univs. With AUS, World War II. Recipient Mich. Chronicle outstanding Citizen award, 1960. 64. 74, Alumni citation Wayne State U., 1968, Ann. Jud. award, 1971, Citizen award Mich. State U., Disting. Svc. award Howard U., 1972, Jud. Independence award, 1973, Spingarn medal NAACP, 1974, Fed. Judge of Yr. award, Black Law Students Assn., 1974, award for Outstanding Contbns. to Black Community, Nat. Assn. Black Social Workers, 1974, Judge of Yr. award Nat. Conf. Black Lawyers, 1974, Bill of Rights award Jewish Community Coun., 1977, A. Philip Randolph award Detroit Coalition Black Trade Unionists, 1981, Human Rights Day award B'nai B'rith Women's Coun. Met. Detroit, Robert L. Millender award So. Christian Leadership Conf. Mich. chpt., 1982, Afro-Asian Inst. award Histadrut in Israel, 1982, civil rights lectr. award, Creighton U. Ahmanson Law Ctr., 1983, Nat. Human Rels. award Greater Detroit Roundtable of NCCJ, 1984, Knights of Charity award Pontifical Inst. for Mission Extension, 1986, Disting. Pub. Svc. award Mich. Anti-Defamation League of B'nai B'rith, 1987, Nat. Chpt. award, 1988, Black Achievement award Equitable Fin. Cos., 1987, Menorah award Afro-Asian Inst. Histadrut of Israel, 1988, Dr. George Derry award Marygrove Coll. Detroit, One Nation award The Patriots Found./GM, 1989, 1st Ann. Move Detroit Forward award City of Detroit, 1990, Gov's. Minuteman award Rotary Club Lansing, 1991; named 1 of 100 Most Influential Black Ams. Ebony Mag., 1971-92; Damon J. Keith Elementary Sch. named in his honor Detroit Bd. Edn., 1974; Damon J. Keith Ann. Civic and Humanitarian award established in his honor Highland Park YMCA, 1984; 15th Mich. Legal Milestone The Uninvited Ear presented in honor of The Keith Decision, 1991. Mem. ABA (coun. sect. legal edn. and admission to bar), Nat. Bar Assn. (William H. Hastie award Jud. Coun., 8th Ann. equal Justice award), Mich. Bar Assn. (champion of justice award), Detroit Bar Assn. (pres'. award), Nat. Lawyers Guild, Am. Judicature Soc., Alpha Phi Alpha. Baptist (deacon). Club: Detroit Cotillion. Office: US Ct Appeals US Courthouse 231 W Lafayette St Rm 240 Detroit MI 48226-2702*

KEITH, DAVID LEMUEL, actor; b. Knoxville, Tenn., May 8, 1954; s. Lemuel Grady Jr. and Hilda Earle (Coulter) K. BA, U. Tenn., 1985. Actor: (stage prodns.) Red Bluegrass Western Flyer Show, 1977, Harvey, 1985, Greater Tuna, 1986, Bus Stop, 1986, (feature films) The Great Santini, 1979, The Rose, 1980, Brubaker, 1980, Back Roads, 1981, Take This Job and Shove it, 1982, An Officer and a Gentleman, 1982 (Golden Globe award nomination 1982), Independence Day, 1982, The Lords of Discipline, 1983, Firestarter, 1984, Deadly Sins, 1995, Red Blooded American Girl II, 1995, Judge and Jury, 1996, A Family Thing, 1996, Invasion of Privacy, 1996, Secret of the Andes, 1998, Running with Scissors, 1998, Ambushed, 1998, U-571, 1999, If...Dog...Rabbit, 1999, Question of Privilege, 1999, others; (TV movies) Are You in the House Alone?, 1978, Friendly Fire, 1978, The Golden Moment, 1980, Gulag, 1985, If Tomorrow Comes, 1985, Heartbreak Hotel, 1988, The Two Jakes, 1990 ; TV series: Happy Days, 1978, Co-Ed Fever, 1979, Flesh 'N' Blood, 1991; dir. (film) The Farm (also rec. artist for soundtrack). Mem. Screen Actors Guild, AFTRA, Dirs. Guild. Methodist. Office: care John Fagelman William Morris Agy 151 S El Camino Dr Beverly Hills CA 90212-2704 Office: Peluce Accts 449 S Beverly Dr Beverly Hills CA 90212-4428*

KEITH, EVERETT EARNEST, educator, education administrator; b. Buffalo, Mo., Sept. 1, 1906; s. William Anderson and Nora Jelina (Woods) K.; m. Anna Catherine Blanchard, June 1, 1933 (dec. 1994); 1 child, Katherine Anne. BS in Edn., Southwest Mo. State U., 1929; Ma, U. Mo., 1932, Gregory scholar, 1933-35; LLD (hon.), Lindenwood Coll., St. Charles, Mo., 1957; EdD (hon.), U. Mo., 1998. Cert. sch. adminstrn. Tchr. pub. schs. (elem.), Buffalo, Mo., 1926-27, pub. high sch., Buffalo, 1928-29; sch. supt. pub. schs., Buffalo, 1930-32; instr. U. Mo., Columbia, 1934; asst. state supt. Mo. Dept. Edn., Jefferson City, 1935-37; dir. pub. relations Mo. State Tchrs. Assn., Columbia, 1938-40, exec. sec., 1941-72, exec. sec. emeritus, 1972—. Author: In Retrospect, 1991, A Primer for Legislative Activity, 1973; contbr. articles to profl. jours. Pres., mem. Mo. State Bd. of Edn., 1946-53; v.p. Mo. Congress of Parents and Tchrs.; treas. Mo. Assn. Sch. Adminstrs., 1941-73; del. White House Conf. on Edn., White House Conf. on Aging, 1995; pres. Ret. Tchrs. Assn. Mo., 1986-87. Recipient Citation of Merit, Coll. of Edn. and Alumni Assn. U. Mo., Disting. Svc. award Ctrl. Mo. State, Northeastern Mo. State, Southwestern Mo. State Univs.; Everett Keith Week proclaimed by Gov. of Mo., 1972; Recognition Day named in his honor Mayor of Columbia, 1992. Mem. AARP (mem. legis. coun. 1976-81), Internat. Reading Assn. (Svc. award), Am. Assn. Sch. Adminstrs. (Disting. Svc. award 1982), Mo. Acad. of Squires, Columbia Kiwanis, Masons, Shriners, Phi Delta Kappa (Outstanding Contbr. to Edn. award), Alpha Pi Zeta, Pi Gamma Mu, numerous ednl. orgns. Methodist. Avocations: reading, yardwork, walking. Home: 23 Bingham Rd Columbia MO 65203-3504

KEITH, GARNETT LEE, JR., investment executive; b. Atlanta, Nov. 27, 1935; s. Garnett Lee and Agnes (Roark) K.; m. Martha Holmes, Oct. 12, 1957; children: Suzanne, Geoffrey. B.Indsl. Engring., Ga. Inst. Tech., 1957; M.B.A., Harvard U., 1962. Asst. sec. Irving Trust Co., 1962-64; v.p. Irwin Mgmt. Co., 1964-75; pres. Irwin Union Corp., 1975-76; vice chmn. Prudential Ins. Co., Newark, 1977-96; chmn., CEO Seabridge Investment Advisors, Summit, 1996—; bd. dirs. Super Valu Stores, Minn. Trustee Drew U., Madison, N.J. Mem. Inst. Chartered Fin. Analysts. Republican. Club: Harvard (N.Y.C.). Office: Seabridge Investment Advisors 450 Springfield Ave Ste 301 Summit NJ 07901-2610

KEITH, HOWARD BARTON, surgeon; b. Enid, Okla., Aug. 23, 1932; s. John A. and Dorothy O. (Murphy) K.; m. Joanne Lee Norman, Mar. 12, 1954; children: Preston Jonathan, Kim Keith Glazier, Shaun Howard, Spencer Norman. Degree, U. Okla., 1953, MD, 1957. Diplomate Am. Bd. Surgery, Am. Bd. Thoracic Surgery. Intern in surgery U. Okla. Med. Ctr., 1957-58, resident in gen. surgery, thoracic, cardiovascular surgery, 1958-63; gen. and thoracic surgeon Newman Meml. Hosp., Shattuck, Okla., 1963-87, chief of staff, bd. dirs., 1963-83; gen. and thoracic surgeon Woodward (Okla.) Hosp. and Health Ctr., 1988—; pres. N.W. Okla. Specialty Clinic, Woodward, 1988-92; assoc. preceptor U. Okla. Med. Ctr., Shattuck, 1963-79, preceptor, 1979-87; preceptor U. Okla. Med. Ctr., Woodward, 1988—; pvt. practice MedWest Physicians Network, Inc., Woodward; clin. asst., prof. surgery U. Okla., 1980—; pres. Newman Med. Ctr., Inc., 1977, 85-87; cons. utilization and peer rev. Region VI Dept. Human Health Svc., 1973—; bd. dirs. Okla. Regional Med. Program, 1964-70; med. dir., bd. dirs. Shattuck Convalescent Ctr., 1964-78; aviation med. examiner FAA, 1967-92; cancer liaison physician Woodward Hosp. and Health Ctr., 1988; gen. surgery cons. Dept. Human Health Svcs., 1979—; presenter in field. Contbr. articles to profl. publs. Trustee Shattuck Hosp. Authority, 1964-76; mem. exec. bd. dirs. Great Salt Plains coun. Boy Scouts Am., 1969-82, mem. fin. com., 1970-82; med. advisor N.W. Okla. chpt. Okla. State TB Assn., 1964-80; bd. edn. Shattuck Pub. Sch. Sys., 1964-71; pres. Lions Club, Shattuck, 1967; bd. dirs. Big Bros-Big Sisters, N.W. Okla., 1986, Woodward Indsl. Found., 1988—, Okla. Found. for Peer Rev., 1981-91, K-101 Classic Bowl, 1989, Grand Nat. Quail Found., 1991, Okla. U. Club of N.W. Okla., 1989-92, Woodward Rotary Club, 1989-92; med. advisor Angel Fire Ski Patrol, 1981-84; mem. adv. bd. Blue Cross Blue Shiels, 1984—; chmn. Shattuck Bus. Devel. Com., 1987; trustee Alumni Assn. Sch. Medicine U. Okla., 1987; advisor to tech. med. direction com. Okla. State Health Dept., 1979-93; bd. govs. Angel Fire Corp., 1980-84; mem. ad hoc adv. com., High Plains adv. com. High Plains Vo-Tech. Sch., Woodward, 1984, mem. supt.'s bd., 1989; chmn. EMS, tech. med. direction com. Okla. State Dept. Health, 1984-93; v.p. Okla. Trauma Soc., 1990; chmn. med. direction subcom. Okla. EMS Adv. Coun., 1990; bd. EMS-C consortum sect. gen. pediatrics U. Okla. Health Sci. Ctr., 1990. Mem. AMA, ACS (liaison fellow commn. on cancer 1968—, mem. coun. 1977—, mem. Okla. cancer com. 1971-77, mem. Okla. trauma com. 1972—, chmn. 1979-89, Okla. adv. com. 1975—, v.p. Okla. chpt. 1980-81, pres.-elect 1982, pres. 1982-83, nat. com. on trauma 1989-95), Nat. Assn. EMS Physicians, Okla. Thoracic Soc. (pres. 1972), Okla. State Med. Assn. (med. advisor N.W. Okla. 1964-80, chmn. peer rev. com. 1965-74), N.W. Counties Med. Soc. (pres. 1965, 82-83), Okla. Surg. Soc. (pres.-elect 1976, pres. 1977), Aerospace Med. Assn., Am. Nuclear Soc., Pan Am. Med. Assn., Am. Soc. for Laser Medicine and Surgery, Soc. Am. Gastrointestinal Endoscopic Surgeons. Avocation: hunting. Home: 2402 Brentford Pl Woodward OK 73801-6378

KEITH, JENNIE, anthropology educator and administrator, writer; b. Carmel, Calif., Nov. 15, 1942; d. Paul K. and Romayne Louise (Fuller) Hill; m. Marc Howard Ross, Aug. 25, 1968 (div. 1978); 1 child, Aaron Elliot Keith Ross; m. Roy Gerald Fitzgerald, June 21, 1980; 1 child, Kate Romayne Keith-Fitzgerald. BA, Pomona Coll., 1964; MA, Northwestern U., 1966, PhD, 1968. NIMH fellow Paris, 1968-70; asst. prof. anthropology Swarthmore Coll., 1970-76, assoc. prof., 1976-82, prof., 1982—, Centennial prof. anthropology, 1990—, chmn. sociology and anthropology, 1987-92, provost, 1992—; mem. rsch. edn. rev. com. NIMH, Washington, 1979-82; co-dir. workshop on age and anthropology Nat. Inst. Aging, Washington, 1980-81, task group leader nat. rsch. plan on aging, 1981; mem. human devel. rev. bd. NIH, 1985-89; mem. adv. coun. Brookdale Found., 1990-93. Author: Old People, New Lives, 1977, 2d paperback edit., 1982 (Am. Jour. Nursing Book of Yr. 1978), Old People as People, 1982; co-author: The Aging Experience, 1994 (Richard Kalish award Gerontol. Soc. Am. 1994); co-editor: New Methods for Old-Age Research, 1980, 2d edit., 1986, Age in Anthropological Theory, 1984; mem. editorial bd. Gerontologist, 1981-89, Jour. Gerontology, 1987-91, Jour. Aging Studies, 1989-98; assoc. editor Rsch. on Aging, 1981-88. Bd. dirs. Cmty. Svcs., Folsom, Pa., 1980-82, Inst. Outdoor Awareness, Swarthmore, 1980—; bd. dirs. Kendal-Crosslands, 1987-92, chmn., 1989-92, Kendal Corp., 1992-95. Conf. grantee Nat. Inst. Aging, 1980, rsch. grantee, 1982-90. Fellow Am. Anthrop. Assn., Gerontol. Soc. Am. (exec. bd. behavioral and social scis. sect. 1985-87, program chmn. 1989, chair 1989-90, publs. com. 1993-95); mem. Assn. Anthropology and Gerontology (founder, sec. 1980-81). Office: Swarthmore Coll Office of the Provost Swarthmore PA 19081

KEITH, JOHN PIRIE, urban planner; b. Windsor, Ont., Can., May 17, 1921; came to U.S., 1930; s. Alexander Clarence and Jean Booth (Pirie) K.; m. Doris Jean Clark, May 17, 1948; childen: Janet Hamilton, Alexander Clark. BA, U. Ariz., 1945; MPA, Wayne State U., 1946; D in Pub. Adminstrn., Inst. Pub. Adminstrn., 1952; D Engring. (hon.), Poly. U., 1989; LLD (hon.), Sacred Heart U., 1990. Asst. to dir. Providence Govtl. Rsch. Bur., 1945-46; dean lower sch. So. Ariz. Sch. for Boys, Tucson, 1947-48; rsch. assoc. Inst. Pub. Affairs, U. Tex., Austin, 1948-51, Citizens Rsch. Coun. Mich., Detroit, 1951-53; sr. rsch. assoc. Nat. Civic League, N.Y.C., 1953-56; asst. dir. ASPA, Chgo., 1956-59; exec. v.p. Regional Plan Assn., 1959-69, pres., 1969-89, pres. emeritus, 1989—; sr. assoc. Inst. Pub. Adminstrn., N.Y.C., 1989—; N.Y. dir. The Four World Ctrs. Transport Study, The Stationery Office, 1998. Author: City and County Home Rule in Texas, Methods of Constitutional Revision, Public Relations Program for a Citizen Committee, contbr., The Four World Cities Study of Urban Transport; contbr. articles to profl. publs. Mem. Greater Jamaica (Queens, N.Y.) Devel. Corp., 1989—; mem. City Innovation, Mpls., 1989—; mem. exec. bd. Ency. of Environment, N.Y.C., 1991-94. Named Hon. Park Ranger, Nat. Park Svc. Fellow Nat. Acad. Pub. Adminstrn.; mem. ASPA (Outstanding Adminstrs. award 1971), Am. Planning Assn. (Orton award 1989), Am. Polit. Sci. Assn., Am. Inst. Cert. Planners, Acad. Polit. Sci., Nat. Civic League, Assn. Mondiale des Grandes Metropoles (hon., founder), Counc. on Transportation, NYU, 1996—, Delta Sigma Rho, Phi Gamma Delta, Pi Alpha Alpha. Democrat. Presbyterian. Avocations: travel, hiking, farming. Fax: (212) 995-4876. E-mail: johnkeith@nyu.edu. Home: 5 E 22nd St Apt 11F New York NY 10010-5323 Office: Inst Pub Adminstrn 411 Lafayette St New York NY 10003

KEITH, KENT MARSTELLER, academic administrator, corporate executive, government official, lawyer; b. N.Y.C., May 22, 1948; s. Bruce Edgar and Evelyn E. (Johnston) K.; m. Elizabeth Misao Carlson, Aug. 22, 1976. BA in Govt., Harvard U., 1970; BA in Politics and Philosophy, Oxford (Eng.) U., 1972, MA, 1977; JD, U. Hawaii, 1977; EdD, U. So. Calif., 1996. Bar: Hawaii 1977, D.C. 1979. Assoc. Cades, Schutte, Fleming & Wright, Honolulu, 1977-79; coord. Hawaii Dept. Planning and Econ. Devel., Honolulu, 1979-81, dep. dir., 1981-83, dir., 1983-86; energy resources coord. State of Hawaii, Honolulu, 1983-86, chmn. State Policy Coun., 1983-86; chmn. Aloha Tower Devel. Corp., 1983-86; project mgr. Mililani Tech. Park Castle and Cooke Properties, Inc., 1986-88, v.p. pub. rels. and bus. devel., 1988-89; pres. Chaminade U., Honolulu, 1989-95; v.p. devel. and comm. YMCA Honolulu, 1998—; bd. dirs. Grove Farm Co., Inc., 1990-93. Author: Jobs for Hawaii's People: Fundamental Issues in Economic Development, 1985, Hawaii: Looking Back from the Year 2050, 1987, For the Love of Students, 1992; contbr. articles on ocean law to law jours. Pres. Manoa Valley Ch., Honolulu, 1976-78; mem. platform com. Hawaii Dem. Conv., 1982, 84, 86; trustee Hawaii Loa Coll., 1986-89, vice chmn., 1987-89; mem. Diocesan Bd. Edn., 1990-95, chmn., 1990-93; bd. dirs. St. Louis Sch., 1990-95, Hanahauoli Sch., 1990—; chmn. Manoa Neighborhood Bd., 1989-91; v.p. YMCA, Honolulu, 1998—. Rhodes scholar, 1970; named one of 10 Outstanding Young Men of Am., U.S. Jaycees, 1984; recipient Disting. Alumni award U. Hawaii, 1993. Mem. Am. Assn. Rhodes Scholars, Internat. House of Japan, Nature Conservancy, Pla. Club, Pacific Club, Harvard Club Hawaii (Honolulu, bd. dirs. 1974-78, sec. 1974-76), Rotary (Honolulu Sunrise). Home: 2626 Hillside Ave Honolulu HI 96822-1716

KEITH, LEROY ALLEN, aviation safety executive. BS in Aeronautics and Astronautics, U. Wash., 1964. V.p., gen. mgr. quality McDonnell Douglas Aircraft Co.; with FAA, aero. engr., aviation stds. program mgr.; flt. test engr. USAF, Edwards AFB, Calif., 1964-68; rsch. engr. The Boeing Co., Seattle, Wash., 1968-71; engr., program mgr. FAA, 1971-81, mgr. transport airplane directorate, 1978-92; dir. aviaiton safety Civil Aviation Safety Authority, Canberra, ACT, Australia, 1995-98; v.p., gen. mgr. quality McDonnell Douglas Aircraft Co., 1992-95; aviation cons., 1998—. Address: 3 Haynes Pl, Stirling, ACT 2611, Australia

KEITH, NORMAN THOMAS, aerospace company administrator; b. Antioch, Calif., Jan. 12, 1936; s. Dean Theodore and Edna Margaret (Doty) K.; m. Marla Mildred Osten, Sept. 9, 1962. B of Tech., Tex. State Tech. Inst. Cert. profl. mgr. Field service engr. Gen. Dynamics Corp., San Diego, 1955-66, supr. Data Ctr., 1966-76, chief data systems, 1976-81, chief property adminstrn., 1981-83, motivational mgr., 1983-86, sr. program adminstr., 1986-90, mgr. total quality mgmt.Convair divsn., 1990—. Contbr. articles to profl. jours. Mem. mil. adv. bd. congressman Ron Packard, 1983-86; sgt. Res. Dep. Sheriff's Office, San Diego County; bd. dirs. San Dieguito Boys/Girls Clubs, Encinitas, 1966-69; loaned exec. United Way, San Diego, 1980-81; security lt. 22nd Dist. AG Assn. State of Calif. Del Mar Fairgrounds, 1992—. Mem. Nat. Mgmt. Assn. (bd. dirs., pres.), Nat. U. Alumni Assn. (life), Woodbury Coll. Alumni Assn., San Diego State U. Alumni Assn., Hon. Dep. Sheriff's Assn. (bd. dirs.). Republican. Lutheran. Lodges: Lions (sec. 1962-63), Elks. Home: 620 Cole Ranch Rd Encinitas CA 92024-6522 Office: Gen Dynamics Convair Div 5001 Kearny Villa Rd San Diego CA 92123-1407

KEITH, PAULINE MARY, artist, illustrator, writer; b. Fairfield, Nebr., July 21, 1924; d. Siebelt Ralph and Pauline Alethia (Garrison) Goldenstein; m. Everett B. Keith, Feb. 14, 1957; 1 child, Nathan Ralph. Student, George Fox Coll., 1947-48, Oreg. State U., 1955. Illustrator Merlin Press, San Jose, Calif., 1980-81; artist, illustrator, watercolorist Corvallis, Oreg., 1980—. Author 5 chapbooks, 1980-85; editor: Four Generations of Verse, 1979; contbr. poems to anthologies and mags. and articles to mags.; one-woman shows include Roger's Meml. Libr., Forest Grove, Oreg., 1959, Corvallis Art Ctr., 1960, 98-99, Human Resources Bldg., Corvallis, 1959-61, Chintimini Sr. Ctr., 1994—, Corvallis Parteral Counseling Ctr., 1992-94, 96, Hall Gallery, Sr. Ctr., 1993, 94, 95-96, 97, 98, 99, Consumer Power, Philomath, Oreg., 1994, Art, Etc., Newburg, Oreg., 1995, 96, 97, 98,; exhibited in group shows at Hewlett-Packard Co., 1984-85, Corvallis Art Ctr., 1992, Chintimini Sr. Ctr., 1992. Co-elder First Christian Ch. (Disciples of Christ), Corvallis, 1988-89, co-deacon, 1980-83, elder, 1991-93; sec. Hostess Club of Chintimini Sr. Ctr., Corvallis, 1987, pres., 1988-89, v.p., 1992-94. Recipient Watercolor 1st price Benton County Fair, 1982, 83, 88, 89, 91, 2d prize, 1987, 91, 3d prize, 1984, 90, 92. Mem. Oreg. Assn. Christian Writers, Internat. Assn. Women Mins., Am. Legion Aux. (elected poet post II Covallis chpt. 1989-90, elected sec. 1991-92, chaplain 1992-93, 94-95, v.p. 1994-95), Chintimine Artists. Republican. Avocations: nature walks, singing in church choir. Office: 304 S College St Newberg OR 97132-3114

KEITH, SUSAN, kinesiology educator; b. Wichita Falls, Tex., Mar. 26, 1961. BS, U. Ctrl. Okla., 1986; MS in Edn., Baylor U., 1988; PhD, Tex. Woman's U., 1996. Instr. Kilgore (Tex.) Coll., 1988-97, dir. fitness programs, 1991-93; asst. prof. kinesiology Angelo State U., San Angelo, Tex., 1997—. Mem. editl. bd. (textbook) Perspectives: Health, 1998, Perspectives: Community Health, 1999; contbr. articles to profl. jours. Bd. dirs., mem. recreation adv. bd. City of San Angelo, 1999—. Mem. AAHPER, Tex. Assn. Health, Phys. Edn., Recreation and Dance, Tex. Sch. Health Assn. Office: Angelo State U Box 10803 ASU Sta San Angelo TX 76909

KEITH, THOMAS WARREN, JR., marketing executive; b. Evanston, Ill., Sept. 27, 1951; s. Thomas and Patricia (Ogden) K. BA, Colgate U., Hamilton, NY, 1973; MBA, Columbia U., N.Y.C., 1975. Acct. exec. Leo Burnett Co., Chgo, 1975-80, Needham Harper & Steers, Chgo, 1980-81; acct. supr. Tatham-Laird & Kudner, Chgo, 1981-85; mktg. dir. Dean Foods Co., Franklin Park, IL, 1986-90; pres. Thomas Keith & Assoc., Mktg. Svcs., Evanston, Ill.; dir. Dairy Nutrition Coun., Ill., 1989-90; dir. Dairy Coun. of Wis., Ill., 1987-90. Home and Office: 1005 Dempster St Evanston IL 60201-4210

KEITH, TIMOTHY ZOOK, psychology educator; b. Providence, R.I., May 7, 1952; s. Charles Herbert and Julia Mercer (Zook) K.; m. Mary Anne Forbes, Aug. 16, 1975 (dec. Mar. 1989); children: Davis Henry, Scott Forbes, William Howe; m. Patricia Josephine Berg, Sept. 15, 1990. BA, U. N.C., 1974; MA, East Carolina U., 1978; PhD, Duke U., 1982. Licensed psychologist, N.C. Lead psychologist Montgomery County Schs., Troy, N.C., 1978-80; sch. psychologist Durham (N.C.) City Schs., 1981-82; asst. prof. U. Iowa, Iowa City, 1982-85, assoc. prof., 1985-87; assoc. prof. Va. Poly. Inst. and State U., Blacksburg, Va., 1987-91, prof., 1991-93; prof. Alfred (N.Y.) U., 1993-97, Powell prof. of psychology and schooling, 1997—; rsch. cons. Iowa Dept. Corrections, 1985-86, Iowa Dept. Edn., Des Moines, 1983-87; nat. adv. com. mem. Buros Inst. Mental Measurements, 1992—. Contbr. articles to profl. jours.; author: (videotape) Sch. Psychologist's Applications of Computers in Edn., 1984; mem. editl. bd. Sch. Psychology Rev., 1985-98, assoc. editor, 1987-90, Jour. Sch. Psychology, 1987—, Jour. Psychoednl. Assessment, 1994; assoc. editor Sch. Psychology Quarterly, 1996—. Iowa Measurement Rsch. Found. grantee, 1984-85; U. Iowa grantee, 1983-84, 85-86; Va. Dept. Edn. grantee, 1991-93; sr. rsch. fellow Office Ednl. Rsch. and Improvement, U.S. Dept. Edn., 1987-88; recipient N.C. Sch. Psychology Assn. award, 1981, Disting. Rsch. award N.C. Assn. Rsch. in Edn., 1981, 93, , Ea. Ednl. Rsch. Assn., 1993, Rsch. Excellence award Iowa Ednl. Rsch. and Evaluation Assn., 1985, Women's Rsch. award Iowa Psychol. Assn., 1987, Presdl. award Iowa Sch. Psychologists Assn., 1987, Outstanding Article award Sch. Psychology Quarterly, 1993, Outstanding Article award Jour. Sch. Psychology, 1999. Fellow APA (mem. membership com. sch. psychology divsn. 1985, program co-chmn. 1993-95, Lightner Witmer award 1988); mem. AAAS, NASP, Am. Ednl. Rsch. Assn., Am. Psychol. Soc., Sigma Xi. Episcopalian. Home: 17 Sayles St Alfred NY 14802-1314 Office: Alfred U Divsn of Sch Psychology Saxon Dr Alfred NY 14802-1222

KEITHLEY, BRADFORD GENE, lawyer; b. Nov. 23, 1951; s. Sanderson Irish and Joan G. (Kenneday) K.; m. Ginger W. Wilhelmi, Mar. 26, 1994; children: Paul Michael, Rachel Austin Bernstein. BS, U. Tulsa, 1973; JD, U. Va., 1976. Bar: Va. 1976, Okla. 1978, D.C. 1979. Atty. Office of Gen. Counsel to Sec. USAF, Washington, 1976-78; ptnr. Hall, Estill, Hardwick, Gable, Collingsworth and Nelson, Tulsa, 1978-84; sr. v.p. gen. counsel Arkla, Inc. (now NorAm Energy Corp. divsn. Reliant Energy, Inc.), Shreveport, La., 1984-90; ptnr. head oil and gas practice team Jones, Day, Reavis and Pogue, Dallas, 1990—. Mem. ABA, Fed. Energy Bar Assn., Va. State Bar, Okla. Bar Assn., D.C. Bar Assn., Am. Gas Assn. (mem. legal sect.), Dallas Petroleum Club, Prestonwood Country Club. Home: 12652 Sunlight Dr Dallas TX 75230-1856 Office: Jones Day Reavis & Pogue 2300 Trammell Crow Ctr 2001 Ross Ave Dallas TX 75201-2958

KEIZER, JOEL EDWARD, theoretical scientist, educator; b. North Bend, Oreg., Aug. 31, 1942; s. John Phil and Julia Elaine (Robinson) K.; m. Susan Jane Swank, Dec. 8, 1964; children: Sidney Jacob, Sarah Rebecca. BA, Reed Coll., 1964; PhD, U. Oreg., 1969. Fellow Battelle Inst., Columbus, Ohio, 1969-71; asst. prof. chemistry U. Calif., Davis, 1971-75, assoc. prof., 1975-78, prof., 1978-93, prof. biol. sci., 1993—; dir. Inst. Theoretical Dynamics, Davis, 1986—; vis. scientist Frei Univ., Berlin, 1972, NIH, Bethesda, Md., 1978-79, 86-87, 88-98. Author: Statistical Thermodynamics of Nonequilibrium Processes, 1987; assoc. editor Accounts of Chem. Rsch., 1977-86, Am. Jour. of Physiology, 1995-97; contbr. numerous articles to profl. jours.; editl. bd. Am. Jour. Physiology: Cell, 1998—. Fellow NSF, 1964, J.S. Guggenheim Meml. Found., 1986-87. Fellow AAAS; mem. Am. Diabetes Assn., Biophys. Soc. Office: U Calif Inst Theoretical Dynamics One Shields Ave Davis CA 95616

KEKATOS, DEPPIE-TINNY Z., microbiologist, researcher, lab technologist; b. Buffalo, Oct. 16, 1960; d. Soter Spyros and Mary Soter (Kassimis) Zarifopoulos; m. Dion Kekatos; 1 child, Mary. BS, CUNY, 1983; MS, St. John's U., Jamaica, N.Y., 1986; grad. pharmacy technician program, ICS, 1999. Lic. lab. technologist, N.Y. Clin. lab. technologist trainee Booth Meml. Hosp., Flushing, N.Y., 1986-87; clin. lab. technologist L.I. Jewish Hosp., New Hyde Park, N.Y., 1988-89, Elmhurst (N.Y.) Hosp., 1990-95; asst. supr. microbiology United Health Labs., Woodside, N.Y., 1995-96. Mem. Am. Pharm. Assn., St. John's U. Alumni Fedn. Home: 25-34 Crescent St Apt 5K Long Island City NY 11102-2928 Office: United Health Labs 72-34 Calamus Ave Woodside NY 11377

KEKES, JOHN, philosopher, educator; b. Budapest, Hungary, Nov. 22, 1936; came to U.S., 1965, naturalized, 1977; s. Eugene and Anna (Borsodi) K.; m. Jean Justilliano, May 20, 1968. BA, Queen's U., Kingston, Ont., Can., 1961, MA, 1962; PhD, Australian Nat. U., 1967. Instr. to assoc. prof. philosophy Calif. State U., Northridge, 1965-71; prof. U. Sask., Regina, Can., 1971-74; prof. SUNY, Albany, 1974—, chmn. dept. philosophy, 1974-77, prof. philosophy and pub. policy, 1981—; sr. rsch. fellow Ctr. for Philosophy of Sci., U. Pitts., 1984-85; vis. prof. U.S. Mil. Acad., West Point, N.Y., 1985-86, Nat. U. Singapore, 1989. Author: A Justification of Rationality, 1976, The Nature of Philosophy, 1980, Dimensions of Ethical Thought, 1987, The Examined Life, 1988, Moral Tradition and Individuality, 1989, Facing Evil, 1990, The Morality of Pluralism, 1993, Moral Wisdom and Good Lives, 1995, Against Liberalism, 1997, A Case for Conservatism, 1998; gen. editor: Studies in Moral Philosophy, 1986-91; editor Pub. Affairs Quarterly, 1999—. Recipient Comdrs. Pub. Svc. award U.S. Army, 1986; Rockefeller Found. humanities fellow, 1980-81, fellow Earhart Found., 1983, 88, 89, 98; resident scholar Rockefeller Found. Study Ctr., Bellagio, Italy, 1982, 89. Mem. Am. Philos. Assn., Royal Inst. Philosophy. Home: 2041 Cook Rd Charlton NY 12019-2909 Office: SUNY Dept Philosophy Albany NY 12222

KELAHER, JAMES PEIRCE, lawyer; b. Orlando, Fla., Oct. 28, 1951; s. Philip James and Neva Cecelia (Peirce) K. BA, U. Cen. Fla., 1973; JD, Fla. State U., 1981. Bar: Fla. 1981, U.S. Dist. Ct. (mid. dist.) Fla. 1982, U.S. Ct. Appeals (11th cir.) 1983, U.S. Supreme Ct.; cert. civil trial law. Assoc. Law Office of Nolan Carter, P.A., Orlando, 1981-83, Law Office of James Kelaher, P.A., Orlando, 1983-87; ptnr. Kelaher & Wieland, P.A., Orlando, 1987—, Kelaher, Wieland and Hilado, P.A., Orlando, 1996-98, Kelaher Law Offices, P.A., Orlando, 1998—. Contbr. articles to profl. jours. Eagle benefactor Rep. Party. Mem. ABA, ATLA (sustaining), Orange County Bar Assn., Acad. Fla. Trial Lawyers (sec. 1994-95, treas. 1995-96, pres. 1997-98, bd. dirs. coll. diplomates, membership exec. com. bd. trustees Fla. lawyers action group), Ctrl. Fla. Trial Lawyers Assn. (pres. 1992-94). Roman Catholic. Avocations: tennis, golf, snow skiing, fishing. E-mail: jim@kelaherlaw.com. Office: Kelaher Law Offices 800 N Magnolia Ave Ste 1301 Orlando FL 32803

KELALIS, PANAYOTIS, pediatric urologist; b. Nicosia, Cyprus, Jan. 17, 1932; came to U.S., 1960, naturalized, 1969; s. Peter and Julia (Petrides) K.; m. Barbara Wilson, Apr. 8, 1970. Student, U. Edinburgh, 1950-51; MB, BChir, U. Dublin, 1957; MS in Urology, Mayo Grad. Sch. Medicine, 1964. Resident in urology Mayo Grad. Sch. Medicine, Rochester, Minn., 1960-64; asst. to staff Mayo Clinic, 1964, cons. urology, 1965—, head sect. pediatric urology, 1975-91, chmn. dept. urology, 1982-91; chmn. dept. urology Mayo Clinic, Jacksonville, Fla., 1991, chair internat. activities, 1991—; prof. urology Mayo Med. Sch., 1975—, Anson L. Clark prof. pediatric urology, 1985—; assoc. dir. surgery and subspecialities Mayo Grad. Sch. Medicine, 1994—. Editor: Clinical Pediatric Urology, 2 vols., 1976, 3rd edit., 1992; contbr. numerous sci. articles to profl. jours., chpts. in books. Hon. consul Republic of Cyprus. Recipient Edward J. Noble Found. award, 1964, Pediatric Urology medal, 1996; decorated knight Order of St. Andrew. Fellow ACS; mem. Am. Assn. Genito-Urinary Surgeons, Internat. Soc. Urology, Am. Urol. Assn., Soc. Pediatric Urology (pres.), Am. Acad. Pediatrics (pres., chmn. urology sect., Urology medal 1996), Sociedad Latino Americana de Urologia Infantile (hon.), Assn. Francaise d'Urologie (hon.), Hellenic Urol. Soc. (hon.), Sociedad Argentine de Urologia (corr.), Venezuelan Urol. Soc. (corr.). Office: Mayo Clinic 4500 San Pablo Rd S Jacksonville FL 32224-3899

KELBER, WERNER HEINZ, religious educator; b. Burghausen, Fed. Republic of Germany, Sept. 13, 1935; came to U.S., 1962; s. Karl and Mathilde (Bucher) K.; m. Mary Ann Long, Mar. 24, 1962. BD, U. Erlangen, 1962; ThM, Princeton Theol. Seminary, 1963; MA, U. Chgo., 1967, PhD, 1970. Asst. prof. religious studies U. Dayton, Ohio, 1970-73; from asst. to assoc. prof. religious studies Rice U., Houston, 1973-81, Turner chair in Bibl. studies, 1981—, chmn. dept. religious studies, 1989-95; vis. prof. U. des Scis. Humaines, Strasbourg, France, 1985-86; editorial bd. Oral Tradition, 1986—, Mercer Univ. Press, 1987—; reader Fortress Press, Mpls., 1975—. Author: The Kingdom in Mark, 1974, Mark's Story of Jesus, 1987, The Oral and the Written Gospel, 1983, reprint 1997; editor: The Passion in Mark, 1976; contbr. articles to profl. jours. Mem. Soc. Bibl. Lit. (editorial bd. monograph series 1980-83, editorial bd. jour. 1988-91, chmn. nat. seminar gospel Mark 1977-80, pres. Southwest region 1978-79, coun. 1990—), Cath. Bibl. Assn. Am., Studiorum Novi Testamenti Societas, Ctr. for Study Religion in Greco-Roman World (assoc.). Lutheran. Office: Rice U Dept Religious Studies Houston TX 77251

KELBLE, WILLIAM FRANCIS, information services editor; b. Abington, Pa., Dec. 6, 1953; s. J. Richard and Mary Dolores (Bedesem) K.; m. Catharine Louise McGurk, Nov. 18, 1978. BA in Journalism, Pa. State U., 1975; MBA, Rutgers U., 1991. News reporter Montgomery Newspapers, Ft. Washington, Pa., 1976-78; night editor Montgomery Newspapers, 1978-79; copy editor Herald-Jour., Syracuse, N.Y., 1979-81; wire editor Herald-Jour., 1981-82; database writer, editor Dow Jones & Co., Princeton, N.J., 1982-84, asst. news editor, 1984-86, news editor, project mgr., 1986-94, assoc. dir., 1994-96, dep. editorial dir., 1996-97; mng. editor Dow Jones & Co., Princeton, 1997—. Judge writing awards Syracuse Press Club, 1990. Recipient Keystone Press award Pa. Newspaper Pubs. Assn., 1979. Mem. Soc. Profl. Journalists. Home: 17 Neshanic Dr Ringoes NJ 08551-1845 Office: Dow Jones & Co Interactive Pub PO Box 300 Princeton NJ 08543-0300

KELCH, ROBERT PAUL, pediatric endocrinologist; b. Detroit, Dec. 3, 1942; s. Paul and Iona Bertha (Schmitt) K.; m. Jeri Anne Parker, Aug. 17, 1963; children: Randall Paul, Julie Marie. PhB, Wayne State U., Detroit, 1964; MD, U. Mich., Ann Arbor, 1967. Intern then Wyeth pediatric residency fellow U. Mich. Med. Center, 1967-70, research fellow, 1969-70, mem. faculty, 1972-94, prof. pediatrics, 1977-94, acting chmn. dept., 1979-80, chmn. dept., 1981-94; physician-in-chief C.S. Mott Children's Hosp. U. Mich., 1983-94; chief clin. affairs U. Mich. Hosps., 1989-92; NIH trainee pediatric endocrinology U. Calif. Med. Center, San Francisco, 1970-72; prof. pediatrics, dean U. Iowa Coll. Medicine, Iowa City, 1994—. Co-author: A Practical Approach to Pediatric Endocrinology, 1975; contbr. articles med. jours. Served with USNR. Fellow Am. Acad. Pediatrics; mem. Inst. of Medicine/Nat. Acad. Scis., Soc. Pediatrics Rsch. (pres. 1988), Am. Bd. Pediatrics (sec.-treas. 1992, chmn. 1995), Endocrine Soc., Am. Fedn. Clin. Rsch., Am. Soc. Clin. Investigation, Assn. Med. Sch. Pediatric Dept. Chmn. (pres. 1989), Ctrl. Soc. Clin. Rsch., Lawson Wilkins Pediatric Endocrine Soc., Midwest Soc. Pediatric Rsch. (pres. 1983-84). Methodist. Home: 620 Larch Ln Iowa City IA 52245-3435 Office: U Iowa 212 CMAB Iowa City IA 52242-1101

KELEHER, JAMES P., bishop; b. July 31, 1931. BA, St. Mary of the Lake Sem., Mundelein, Ill., 1954; DST, St. Mary of the Lake Sem., 1961, Licentiate in Sacred Theology, 1968; MA in Ednl. administrn., Loyola U., Chgo., 1967; PhD, Gregorian U., Rome. Ordained priest, Roman Catholic ch., 1958. Rector Quigley Sem. South, Chgo., 1976-78; pres., rector St. Mary of the Lake Sem., Mundelein, Ill., 1978-84; bishop Belleville, Ill., 1984-93, Kansas City, 1993—; Mem. Papal Visitation Com. for Sems.; chmn. bishop's com. on priestly formation, mem. com. migration, mem. com. econ. concerns of the Holy See Nat. Conf. Cath. Bishops. Mem. Nat. Cath. Edn. Assn. (sem. dept.), Midwest Assn. Theol. Schs. Office: Archdiocese of Kansas City Chancery Office 12615 Parallel Kansas City KS 66109*

KELEMEN, CHARLES F., computer science educator; b. Mt. Vernon, N.Y., Jan. 7, 1943; s. Frank K. and Eleanor E. (Scott) K.; m. Sylvia J. Brown, July 26, 1975; children—Rebecca, Colin, Elizabeth. BA, Valparaiso U., 1964; MA, Pa. State U., 1966, PhD, 1969. Asst. then assoc. prof. Ithaca Coll., N.Y., 1969-80; prof. LeMoyne Coll., Syracuse, N.Y., 1980-84, Swarthmore Coll., Pa., 1984—; cons. in field; dir. computer sci. program Swarthmore Coll., 1984—; vis. assoc. prof. Cornell U., Ithaca, N.Y., 1978, summers 1979-81. Co-author: (with others) Fundamentals of Computing II Abstraction Data Structures, and Large Software Systems, 1995, Fundamentals of Computing II C Laboratory Manual, 1995. Grantee NSF, 1977-81. Mem. Assn. Computing Machinery, IEEE, Computer Soc., Math. Assn. Am. Home: 2105 N Providence Rd Media PA 19063-1841 Office: Swarthmore Coll Dept Computer Sci Swarthmore PA 19081

KELEMEN, JOHN, neurologist, educator; b. Nyíregyháza, Hungary, Apr. 28, 1948; s. Ignac and Anna (Hartman) K. BA, SUNY, Binghamton, 1970; MD, Georgetown U., 1974. Cert. Am. Bd. Psychiatry and Neurology-Neurology, Am. Bd. Electrodiagnostic Medicine. Med. intern Nassau County Med. Ctr., East Meadow, N.Y., 1974-75; neurology resident Nassau County Med. Ctr., East Meadow, 1975-78, staff neurologist, 1980-85, dir. MDA clinic, 1980-85, chief neuromuscular program, 1981-85; neuromuscular fellow Tufts U.-New Eng. Med. Ctr., Boston, 1978-80; pntr. Island Neurol. P.C., Plainview, N.Y., 1985—; clin. asst. prof. neurology NYU Sch. of Medicine, 1996—; clin. asst. prof. neurology Cornell U. Med. Coll., N.Y.C., 1986-95; tchg. residents and med. students Stony Brook U., Cornell U., NYU, Manhasset, East Meadow, 1980—; lectr. in field. Contbr. chpts. to books and articles to profl. jours. Rsch. grantee Muscular Dystrophy Assn., Boston, 1979, Nassau Heart Assn., East Meadow, 1984. Fellow Am. Acad. Neurology. Avocations: tennis, sailing, skiing, computers, cinema. Office: Island Neurol PC 824 Old Country Rd Plainview NY 11803-4935

KELEN, JOYCE ARLENE, social worker; b. N.Y.C., Dec. 5, 1949; d. Samuel and Rebecca (Rochman) Green; m. Leslie George Kelen, Jan. 31, 1971; children: David, Jonathan. BA, Lehman Coll., 1970; MSW, Univ. Utah, 1974, DSW, 1980. Recreation dir. N.Y.C. Housing Authority, Bronx, 1970-72; cottage supr. Kennedy Home, Bronx, 1974; sch. social worker Davis County Sch. Dist., Farmington, Utah, 1976-86; clin. asst. prof. U. Utah., Salt Lake City, 1976—; sch. social worker Salt Lake City Sch. Dist., 1986—; cons. in field, Salt Lake City, 1981—. Editor: To Whom Are We Beautiful As We Go?, 1979; contbr. articles to profl. jours. Utah Coll. of Nursing grantee, 1985. Mem. Nat. Assn. Social Workers (chairperson Gerontology Council, 1983-84, Utah Sch. Social Worker of Yr., 1977), NEA, Utah Edn. Assn., Davis Edn. Assn. Democrat. Jewish. Avocations: tennis, camping, guitar. Home: 128 M St Salt Lake City UT 84103-3854 Office: Franklin Elem Sch 1100 W 400 S Salt Lake City UT 84104-2334

KELER, MARIANNE MARTHA, lawyer; b. Budapest, Hungary, Oct. 2, 1954; d. Tibor and Margaret (Feja) K.; m. Michael Richmond Kershow, Aug. 21, 1981; children: Stefan, Madeleine. BS, Georgetown U., 1976, JD, 1980. Bar: D.C. 1980. Law clk. to Assoc. Judge U.S. Ct. Appeals (D.C. cir.), Washington, 1980-81; staff atty. Office of Gen. Counsel, SEC, Washington, 1981-83; counsel to chmn. Office of Gen. Counsel, IRS, Washington, 1983-84; sr. atty. Student Loan Mktg. Assn., Washington, 1985-86, asst. gen. counsel, 1986-88, sr. asst. gen. counsel, 1988-90, v.p., assoc. gen. counsel, 1990—. Mem. ABA (corp. and securities div.), Women's Bar Assn. D.C. Office: SLM Holding Corp 11600 Sallie Mae Dr Reston VA 20193*

KELETI, GEORG, retired microbiologist, researcher; b. Michalovce, East Slovakia, Czechoslovakia, May 30, 1925; s. Louis and Lilly (Silberstein) K.; m. Martha Helene Maxian, July 28, 1956; children: Eva, Daniel. Degree in pharmacy, Comenius U., Bratislava, Czechoslovakia, 1950, PhD in Microbiology, 1952; candidate of sci. in biology, Acad. Scis., Bratislava, 1961; cert., Continuing Edn. Physicians, Bratislava, 1963. Asst. prof. microbiology Comenius U., 1950-53, prof.'s asst., 1953-63, assoc. prof., 1963-68; sr. fellow Max-Planck Inst., Freiburg, Fed. Republic of Germany, 1968-70; asst. rsch. prof., then assoc. prof. U. Pitts., 1970-96; sr. scientist Bactex Pitts., 1979-81; cons. in field, 1986—; adj. prof. occupational environ. health Grad. Sch. Pub. Health, U. Pitts., 1986-96, ret., 1996; adj. assoc. prof., U. Pitts. Author: Handbook of Micromethods for the Biological Sciences, 1974; contbr. articles to profl. jours. Patentee Anti-tumor process using a Brucella Abortus preparation, 1989. Served to 1st lt. Czech. Army, 1951-54. Mem. Am. Soc. Microbiology, Allegheny Soc. Microbiology. Avocation: swimming. Home: 5831 Nicholson St Pittsburgh PA 15217-2309

KELL, DEBORAH ELLEN HARVEY, mathematics educator; b. Newark, June 15, 1954. BA in Edn., Glassboro State Coll., 1976; MEd, Trenton State Coll., 1981, counseling cert., 1981. Coord., instr. N.J. Dept. Corrections, Trenton, 1978-83; asst. prof. Mercer County C.C., West Windsor, N.J., 1984—; coord. basic math program Mercer County C.C., West Windsor, 1984—; presenter Coll. Bd., Balt., 1994; chair Mercer County C.C. Assembly, 1996-98. Editl. rev. various pub. cos.; designer, creator on-line math learning ctr. website, 1998. Mem. math curriculum task force Ewing Twp., N.J., 1990. State of N.J. grantee, 1990. Mem. Am. Math. Assn. Two Yr. Colls., Nat. Coun. Tchrs. of Math., Edn. Network, N.J. Edn. Assn., Kappa Delta Pi. Office: Mercer County CC PO Box B Old Trenton Rd Trenton NJ 08610

KELLAM, BECKY, business educator, consultant; b. Austin, Tex., Sept. 7, 1938; d. Carruth Brisco and Madge Lee (Swindell) K.; m. June 20, 1958 (div. 1979); m. Thomas G. Dougherty, June 21, 1987. BA, Calif. State U., Hayward, 1973; postgrad., U. San Diego, 1978-79, U. So. Calif., L.A., 1979; MBA, Nat. U., 1982. Legal sec. Neil Strain, San Mateo, Calif., 1967-69, Hrusoff & Graham, Attys., La Mesa, Calif., 1975-77; owner, mgr. DataText, San Diego, 1976-80; paralegal Miller, Boyko and Bell, San Diego, 1976-77; legal adminstr. Gade & Hayne, Attys., San Diego, 1977-79, Thacher & Hurst, P.C., San Diego, 1979-80; mgmt. cons. Profl. Bus. Svcs., San Diego, 1980-84; instr. Kings River Community Coll., Reedley, Calif., 1984-97, pres. senate, 1992-94; instr. Madera (Calif.) C.C., 1998—; state rep. Calif. Acad. Senate, Sacramento, 1984-87; cons. post secondary edn. Calif. State Dept. of Edn., Sacramento, 1985-88; computer cons. Bus. Solutions, Fresno, Calif., 1988—. Coord. Faculty Assn. of Community Colls., Sacramento, 1985—; bd. dirs. Women's Polit. Inst., L.A., 1982-84, Children Svcs. Network, Fresno, 1990—. Named Outstanding Leader of the Yr., Las Mujeres of Calif., 1982. Mem. Am. Assn. Women of Community and Jr. Colls., Nat. Fedn. Bus. and Profl. Women, Fresno Bus. and Profl. Women (pres. 1989-90, Woman of the Yr. 1990), Office Automation Soc. Internat. (editorial bd. dirs. 1989—), Delta Kappa Gamma, Alpha Psi (pres. 1992-94). Presbyterian. Avocations: travel, antique collector, gardening, quilting. Home: 4974 N Fresno St Fresno CA 93726-0317 Office: Madera Community Coll 30277 Avenue 12 Madera CA 93638-8321

KELLAR, WILLIAM HENRY, university official, history educator; b. Cleve., Feb. 11, 1952; s. William Leo and Mary Jane (Sachrison) K. BA in History Edn., U. Houston, 1983, MA in History, 1990, PhD in History, 1994. Cert. secondary tchr., Tex. History tchr. Houston Ind. Sch. Dist., 1984-93, curriculum writer, 1990-93; adj. instr. history Houston C.C., 1992-98, Kingwood (Tex.) Coll., 1995-97; adj. instr. history U. Houston, 1997—, dir. scholars' cmty., 1997—; pub. historian WHK Hist. Rsch. and Cons., Houston, 1995—; cons. Mus. Fine Arts, Houston, 1989, Rice U., Houston, 1990, Kelsey-Seybold Clinic, Houston, 1998-99. Author: Piping Technology and Products, 1998, Make Haste Slowly, 1999; co-author: Service Corporation International, 1999. Fellow NEH, 1985, Petroleum Inst. for Edn., 1986; grantee Houston Bus. Com. Ednl. Excellence, 1986, 88, 89. Mem. Am. Hist. Assn. (life), Am. Assn. Higher Edn., Assn. for Study of Afro-Am. Life and History (life), Houston Coun. for Social Studies (bd. dirs. 1985-94), So. Hist. Assn. (life), Tex. State Hist. Assn. (life, Commendation 1989). Avocations: theater, symphony, sports, travel, writing. Office: U Houston Scholars Cmty Houston TX 77204-3551

KELLAWAY, PETER, neurophysiologist, researcher; b. Johannesburg, Republic of South Africa, Oct. 20, 1920; s. Cecil John Rhodes and Doreen Elizabeth (Joubert) K.; m. Josephine Anne Barbieri, Apr. 1957; children: David, Judianne, Kevin, Christina, Jaime. BA, Occidental Coll., 1942, MA, 1943; PhD, McGill U., 1947; MD (hon.), U. Gothenberg, Sweden, 1977. Diplomate Am. Bd. Clin. Neurophysiology. Lectr. physiology McGill U., Montreal, Que., Can., 1946-47, asst. prof. physiology, 1947-48; assoc. prof. Baylor U. Coll. Medicine, Houston, 1948-61, prof., 1961-78, prof. neurology, 1978—, prof. div. neurosci., 1990—, dir. lab. clin. electrophysiology, 1948-65; dir. dept. clin. neurophysiology The Meth. Hosp., Houston, 1948-71, mem. attending staff, 1948—, chief, sr. attending Neurophysiology Svc., 1971—; cons., neurophysiologist Hermann Hosp., Houston, 1949-73, dir. dept. electroencephalography, 1955-73; dir. electroencephalography lab. Ben Taub Gen. Hosp., Houston, 1965-79; mem. cons. staff, chief neurophysiology svc. Dept. Medicine Tex. Children's Hosp., Houston, 1972—; mem. cons. staff neurology St. Luke's Episc. Hosp., Houston, 1971-73, mem. cons. staff neurophysiology, chief neurophysiology svc., 1973—; dir. Blue Bird Circle Children's Clinic Neurol. Disorders The Meth. Hosp., 1949-60, dir. Blue Bird Circle Rsch. Labs., 1960-79, chmn. Instnl. Rev. Bd. Human Rsch., 1974-90, dir. Epilepsy Rsch. Ctr., 1975—; chmn. appointment and promotions com. Baylor U. Coll. Medicine, 1968-71, dir. Epilepsy Rsch. Ctr., 1975—, chief sect. neurophysiology Dept. Neurology, 1977—; cons., electrophysiologist VA Hosp., Houston, 1949—; cons. electroencephalography So. Pacific Hosp. Assn., Houston, 1949-57; cons., neurophysiologist M.D. Anderson Hosp. and Tumor Inst., Houston, 1953-62; mem. coun. adminstrs. Tex. Med. Ctr., Houston, 1954-60; cons. electroencephalography sect. NIH, 1961-62; hon. pres. Internat. Congress Clin. Neurophysiology, 1993. Author numerous books; editor Electroencephalography and Clin. Neurophysiology, 1968-71, cons. editor, 1972-75, hon. cons. editor, 1989; mem. editl. bd. Jour. Clin. Neurophysiology, 1995; contbr. over 180 articles to profl. jours. Recipient Sir William Osler medal Am. Assn. History of Medicine, 1946; grantee NIH, NASA; named Grass lectr. Am. Soc. EEG Technologists, 1989; Berger lectr., 1982, 92. Fellow Am. Acad. Pediat. (hon.), Am. Electroencephalographic Soc. (hon., coun. 1954, 64-66, treas. 1956-58, pres.-elect 1962-63, pres. 1963-64, Jasper award 1990); mem. APA, Am. Epilepsy Soc. (sec.-treas. 1955-58, pres.-elect 1959, pres. 1960, Lennox lectr. 1981, Disting. Clin. Investigator award 1989, Lennox award 1996), Am. Physiol. Soc., Am. Acad. Neurology, Am. Neurol. Assn., Can. Physiol. Soc., Internat. Fedn. Clin. Neurophysiology (hon. pres. internat. congress), Internat. League Against Epilepsy (Am. br.), So. Electroencephalographic Soc. (coun. 1953, v.p. 1954, pres. 1955), Ea. Assn. Electroencephalographic Soc., Ctrl. Encephalographic Soc., Houston Neurol. Soc. (v.p. 1957, pres. 1967, chmn. bd. trustees 1970-73), Soc. Neurosci., Child Neurology Soc., Epilepsy Assn. Houston/Gulf Coast (profl. adv. bd. 1985-92). Avocations: scuba diving, photography. Home: 110 Broad Oaks Ct Houston TX 77056-1222 Office: Baylor Coll Medicine 1 Baylor Plz Houston TX 77030-3411

KELLAWAY, RICHARD ALLEN, minister, art association administrator; b. Newton, Mass., July 27, 1934; s. Arthur Kendall and Bertha Allen (Sturtevant) K.; m. Jean Helen Dickinson, July 27, 1967; children: Ronald, Andrea. BA, Antioch Coll., 1956; MA, So. Ill. U., 1957; BTh, Harvard U., 1961. Min. First Unitarian Ch., New Bedford, Mass., 1960-68, 80—, 4th Universalist Soc., N.Y.C., 1968-76; assoc. dir. Unitarian Universalist Svc. Com., Boston, 1976-80; min. Unitarian Universalist Ch., Sarasota, Fla., 1981-86, First Unitarian Ch., New Bedford, 1986—; founding pres. New Bedford Art Mus., 1995—; pres. Tryworks Collection, New Bedford, Mass., 1994—; v.p. Friend of Haffenreffer Mus., Bristol, R.I., 1995—. Author: The Trying Out, 1968; co-curator Mex. Mask 20th Century, 1995—; contbr. articles to profl. jours. Avocations: art collecting, travel. Home and Office: Tryworks Collection 5 Dover St New Bedford MA 02740

KELLEGHAN, KEVIN MICHAEL, writer, trainer; b. Chgo., Sept. 23, 1934; s. James Harold and Angela (Morris) K.; m. Beatriz Monges, Aug. 23, 1956 (div. Feb. 1982); children: Michael Kevin, James Patrick. BA in English, St. Ambrose U., 1956. Gen. mgr. Kelmon S.A., Acapulco, Mex., 1957-61; dir. pub. rels. Televisa S.A., Mexico City, Mex., 1961-65; pres. Comm. Corp., Mexico City, Mex., 1965-72; freelance journalist Mexico City, Mex., 1972-79; founding gen. mgr. Computerworld/Mexico, Mexico City, Mex., 1979-81; editor, bus. & oil industry Daily Iberian, Iberia, La., 1984-85; pres. CED Sems. Internat., Rockford, Ill., 1985—; cons. in field. Author: Business Journalism, 1998, (ghost) Learn How You Can Invest or Retire in Mexico, 1972. Precinct capt. Rep. Party, Chgo., 1957; chmn. bd. dirs. Crusader Ctrl. Clinic Assn., Rockford, 1996—. Mem. Am. Soc. Tng. & Devel. (bd. dirs. 1992—), Authors Guild, Authors League Am., Rockford Area Soc. Human Resource Mgmt. Roman Catholic. Avocations: woodcarving, public speaking, graphic design, computers, reading. Home and office: 504 Fairview Blvd Rockford IL 61107-4861

KELLEHER, HERBERT DAVID, airline executive, lawyer; b. Camden, N.J., Mar. 12, 1931; s. Harry and Ruth (Moore) K.; m. Joan Negley, Sept. 9, 1955; children: Julie, Michael, Ruth, David. BA cum laude, Wesleyan U., 1953; LLB cum laude, NYU, 1956. Bar: N.J. 1957, Tex. 1962. Clk. N.J. Supreme Ct., 1956-59; pres., CEO Southwest Airlines, Dallas; assoc. Lum, Biunno & Tompkins, Newark, 1959-61; ptnr. Matthews, Nowlin, Macfarlane & Barrett, San Antonio, 1961-69; sr. ptnr. Oppenheimer, Rosenberg, Kelleher & Wheatley, Inc., San Antonio, 1969-81; founder, gen. counsel, pres., chmn., dir. Southwest Airlines Co., Dallas, 1967—, now also chief exec. officer. Past chmn. adv. bus. coun. Bus. Sch. U. Tex.; past pres. bd. trustees St. Mary's Hall, San Antonio; past pres. Travelers Aid Soc., San Antonio. Named Chief Exec. Officer of Yr., The Fin. World, 1982, 90, Best Chief Exec. Regional Airline Industry Wall St. Transcript, 1982, Gold award, 1992, Bronze award, 1993, Great Entrepreneur 1992 Southwest CEO Coun.; named to Tex. Bus. Hall Fame, 1988; recipient Fin. Mgmt. award Air Transport World, 1982, Airline Industry Svc. award, 1988, Best Managed Airline, Airline Exec. award, 1990, Master Enterpreneur award Inc. Mag., 1991, Disting. Bus. Leadership award Coll. Bus. Adv. Coun. Univ. Tex., 1992, Bus. Statesman award Harvard Bus. Sch. Club Dallas, 1992, Pro Bono Publico award Dallas Advt. League, 1992, Stewardship of Tex. Values award Tex. Lyceum, 1992, Aircraft Operations Excellence award Am. Inst. Aeronautics and Astronautics, 1994; Olin scholar, Root Tilden scholar. Fellow Tex. Bar Found. (life); mem. ABA, San Antonio Bar Assn., Dallas Bar Assn., State Bar Tex. Home: 144 Thelma Dr San Antonio TX 78212-2516 Office: SW Airlines Co PO Box 36611 Dallas TX 75235-1611*

KELLEHER, JOHN CHARLES, JR., plastic surgeon; b. Bklyn., Oct. 19, 1944; s. John Charles Sr. and Rose Mary Kelleher; m. Cynthia Lane Leiphart, June 24, 1967; children: John III, Kristin, Brian, Brooke. BS, U. Notre Dame, 1966; MD, Northwestern U., 1970. Diplomate Am. Bd. Plastic Surgery. Surgery resident U. Tex. Southwestern, Dallas, 1970-75; plastic surgery resident Med. Coll. Ohio, Toledo, 1975-77; plastic surgeon Amarillo (Tex.) Surg. Group, 1977-82, Panhandle Plastic Surgery P.A., Amarillo, 1982—. Fellow ACS; mem. Am. Soc. Plastic and Reconstructive Surgeons (mem. ethics com. 1990-93, chmn. ethics com. 1992-93), Am. Soc. Aesthetic Plastic Surgery, Tex. Soc. Plastic Surgeons (treas., v.p. 1987-90, pres. 1990-91), Tex. Surg. Soc., Tex. Med. Assn. Avocations: flying, skiing, golfing. E-mail: kelleher@arn.net. Office: Panhandle Plastic Surgery PA 1810 Coulter Rd Amarillo TX 79106

KELLEHER, KEVIN PAUL, journalist; b. Nov. 29, 1962. BA, Reed Coll., 1985; MS, Columbia U., 1991. Reporter Bloomberg Bus. News, Tokyo, Japan, 1991-94; rsch. dir. Trim Tabs Fin. Svcs., Santa Rosa, Calif., 1995-96; exec. editor Wired News, San Francisco, 1996-98; sr. news editor Street.com, San Francisco, 1998—. E-mail: kpk@well.com. Office: 402 Jackson St San Francisco CA 94111

KELLEHER, ROBERT JOSEPH, federal judge; b. N.Y.C., Mar. 5, 1913; s. Frank and Mary (Donovan) K.; m. Gracyn W. Wheeler, Aug. 14, 1940; children: R. Jeffrey, Karen Kathleen Kelleher King. A.B., Williams Coll., 1935; LL.B., Harvard U., 1938. Bar: N.Y. 1939, Calif. 1942, U.S. Supreme Ct 1954. Atty. War Dept., 1941-42; asst. U.S. atty. So. Dist. Calif., 1948-50; pvt. practice Beverly Hills, 1951-71; U.S. dist. judge, 1971-83; sr. judge U.S. Dist. Ct. 9th Cir., 1983—. Mem. So. Calif. Com. Olympic Games, 1964; capt. U.S. Davis Cup Team, 1962-63; treas. Youth Tennis Found. So. Calif., 1961-64. Served to lt. USNR, 1942-45. Mem. So. Calif. Tennis Assn. (v.p. 1958-64, pres. 1983-85), U.S. Lawn Tennis Assn. (pres. 1967-68), Internat. Lawn Tennis Club U.S.A., Gt. Britain, France, Can., Mex., Australia, India, Israel, Japan, All Eng. Lawn Tennis and Croquet (Wimbledon), Harvard Club (N.Y./So. Calif.), Williams Club (N.Y.), L.A. Country Club, Delta Kappa Epsilon. Home: 15 St Malo Bch Oceanside CA 92054-5854 Office: US Dist Ct 255 E Temple St Ste 830 Los Angeles CA 90012-3334

KELLEHER, TIMOTHY JOHN, publishing company executive; b. Massillon, Ohio, Jan. 4, 1940; s. John Joseph and Catherine Isabelle (Quinlan) K.; m. Mary Gray Thornton, Aug. 27, 1966; children—Catherine, Joseph, Sarah. B.S. in Polit. Sci., Xavier U., Cin., 1962; postgrad., Xavier U., 1965, Morehead State U., Ky., 1975-76. Mgr. labor relations Gen. Motors, Norwood, Ohio, 1964-73; personnel mgr. Rockwell Internat., Winchester, Ky., 1973-77; dir. labor relations Rockwell Internat., Troy, Mich., 1977-82; v.p. human resources Detroit Free Press, 1982-89; sr. v.p. labor rels. Detroit Newspaper Agy., 1989—; dir. Detroit Macomb Hosp. Corp. Bd. dirs. Greater Detroit Alliance of Bus., annually 1983-89, Winchester/Clark Hist. Soc., Ky., 1975, pres., 1976-77; bd. dirs. New Detroit Inc., annually 1983-89. Served to sgt. U.S. Army, 1962-64. Mem. Coop. Edn. Assn. Ky. (bd. dirs. 1975-77, Employer of Yr. 1976), Indsl. Rels. Rsch. Assn., Xavier U. Alumni Assn. (pres. Detroit chpt. 1991-93), Forest Lake Country Club (bd. dirs. 1991-94). Republican. Roman Catholic. Avocations: golf; fishing. Home: 4072 Cranbrook Ct Bloomfield Hills MI 48301-1714 Office: Detroit Newspaper Agy 615 W Lafayette Blvd Detroit MI 48226-3124

KELLEHER, WILLIAM EUGENE, JR., lawyer; b. Scranton, Pa., Dec. 7, 1953; s. William E. and Elizabeth Coles (Gates) K.; m. Teresa Marie Iorfido, July 22, 1977. BA in Econs. and Polit. Sci., U. Pitts., 1975; JD, Duquesne U., 1979. Bar: Pa. 1979, U.S. Dist. Ct. (we. dist.) Pa. 1979, U.S. Ct. Appeals (5th cir.) 1989, U.S. Ct. Appeals (3rd cir.) 1990, U.S. Ct. Appeals (11th cir.) 1998, U.S. Supreme Ct. 1992. Assoc. Eckert, Seamans, Cherin & Mellott, Pitts., 1979-86, ptnr., mem., 1987—, adminstr. bankruptcy and creditors rights sect., 1990—; counsel, asst. sec. Brockway (Pa.), Inc., 1984-85; mem. exec. com. Eckert Seamans Cherin & Mellott L.L.C., Pitts., 1995-96. Assoc. editor Duquesne Law Rev., 1978-79. Mem. ABA, ATLA, Pa. Bar Assn., Allegheny County Bar Assn. (bankruptcy and comml. law sect. 1995—, exec. counsel, rules com., ednl. programs com., chmn. 1997), Am. Bankruptcy Inst. (cert.). Avocations: sports, astronomy. Home: 3 Green Brier Dr Allison Park PA 15101-1600 Office: Eckert Seamans Cherin & Mellott LLC 600 Grant St Ste 4400 Pittsburgh PA 15219-2703

KELLER, ALEX JAY, plastic and reconstructive surgeon; b. Nov. 12, 1949. BA, NYU, 1971, MD, 1975. Resident NYU, 1975-78, 80-83, Long Island State, 1978-80; pvt. practice plastic and reconstructive surtery Great Neck, N.Y., 1983—. E-mail: akplastic@worldnet.att.net. Office: 900 Northern Blvd Great Neck NY 10021

KELLER, ARMOR, artist, arts advocate; b. Montgomery, Ala., June 16, 1937; d. Alton Mason and Margaret Elizabeth (Bell) ARmor; m. Ronald Thomas Keller, Nov. 28, 1958; 1 child, Kimberlin Marie. Student, Huntingdon Coll., 1955-56, U. Guam, 1972-74; BA, U. Ala., 1982. mem. planning bd. Nat. Book Makers Conf., Tuscaloosa, Ala., 1995; panelist grant rev. Ala. State Coun. on Arts, Montgomery, 1995, 96, 98; judge high sch. art exhibn. 6th Congl. Dist. Arts Caucus, Birmingham, Ala., 1995, 96; cons. Birmingham Mus. Art, 1996. Shows include Meridian (Miss.) Mus. Art, 1986, Vanderbilt U., Nashville, 1987, Birmingham Mus. Art, 1989, Birmingham So. Coll., 1990, Kennedy-Douglas Ctr. for the Arts, Florence, Ala., 1992, Wiregrass Mus. Art, Dothan, Ala., 1993, Ctr. Cultural Arts, Gadsden, Ala., 1994, Kentuck Mus., Northport, Ala., 1994, Ch. of the Nativity, Huntsville, Ala., 1996, Huntsville Mus. Art, 1999; featured in (film, book, calendar) Wild Wheels, 1992, 93, Smithsonian, Japan Esquire, Spiegel. Artist del. Sister City Commn., Japan, 1994. Fellow Escape to Create Seaside (Fla.) Inst., 1993, 94. Mem. Nat. League Am. Pen Women, Watercolor Soc. Ala. (pres. 1988-89), Birmingham Art Assn. (pres. 1982-83), Montgomery Art Guild (pres. 1976-78), Space One Eleven (pres. 1991-93), Bluff Park Art Assn. (project dir. 1997). Avocations: tai chi, ikebana, travel, music. Home: 1134 Ashbury Square Birmingham AL 35216-5280

KELLER, ARTHUR MICHAEL, computer science researcher; s. David and Luba Keller. BS summa cum laude with honors, Bklyn. Coll., 1977; MS, Stanford U., 1979, PhD, 1985. Instr. computer sci. Stanford (Calif.) U., 1979-81, rsch. asst., 1977-85, acting asst. chmn. dept. computer sci., 1982, rsch. assoc., 1985, 89-91, vis. asst. prof., 1987-89, rsch. scientist, 1991-92, sr. rsch. scientist, 1992—; sr. rsch. scientist Advanced Decision Systems, Mountain View, Calif., 1989-92; chief tech. advisor Persistence Software, San Mateo, Calif., 1991-99; co-founder, COO, CFO Mergent Sys. Inc., Palo Alto, Calif., 1996-99; co-founder, chief tech. officer buyermail.com corp., Los Altos, Calif., 1998—; sys. analyst Bklyn. Coll. Computer Ctr., 1974-77; summer rsch. asst. IBM, Thomas J. Watson Rsch. Ctr., Yorktown Heights, N.Y., 1980; acad. assoc. IBM San Jose Rsch. Lab., 1981; asst. prof. U. Tex., Austin, 1985-88, adj. asst. prof., 1988-89; mem. program com. Internat. Conf. on Data Engring., L.A., 1986, 87, 89, Internat. Conf. on Very Large Data Bases, Amsterdam, The Netherlands, 1989; mem. program com. Internat. Workshop on Advanced Transaction Models & Architectures, Goa, India, 1996, Internat. Conf. on Info. & Knowledge Mgmt., Rockville, Md., 1996. Author: A First Course in Computer Programming Using Pascal, 1982. Bd. dirs. Congregation Kol Emeth, Palo Alto. Mem. IEEE (vice chmn. com. database engring. Computer Soc. 1986-87), Assn. Computing Machinery, TeX Users Group (fin. com. 1983-85, internat. coord. 1985-87), Chai Soc. (communications officer 1987-89, v.p. publicity 1989-90). Avocations: singing, travel. Home: 3881 Corina Way Palo Alto CA 94303-4507 Office: Stanford U Dept Computer Sci Gates Bldg 2A Stanford CA 94305-9020

KELLER, BILL, journalist. Reporter, foreign editor N.Y. Times, -97, mng. editor, 1997—. Recipient Pulitzer prize for coverage of the Soviet Union, 1989. Office: NY Times 229 W 43rd St New York NY 10036-3959*

KELLER, DARLA LYNN, financial manager, organization consultant; b. Lemon, S.D., Jan. 7, 1956; d. Donald Dwight and Bonna Claire (Gilbert) K.; m. Jerry Jerome Eskridge, Aug. 27, 1984 (div. Dec. 1988); children: Lisha Saree, Aram Josias. Diploma, Minn. Sch. Bus., 1975. Sec. Hirschfield's Inc., Mpls., 1974-75, Lionel D. Eide & Co., Mpls., 1975-76; client adminstr. Resource Trust Co., Mpls., 1976-81; family office mgr. Archer & Daniels Families, Mpls., 1981-93; cons. Larry Wilson Enterprises, Mpls., 1987-89, founder, pres. Dellwood Fin. Svcs. Co., Mpls., 1992—; bd. dirs. Summit Acad. O.I.C., 1996-99, mem. exec. com., 1997-99, chair fundraising com., 1997-99. Treas. Como Park Elem. Sch. PTA, St. Paul, 1989-91; treas. St. Croix Valley coun. Girl Scouts U.S.A., 1986-91, mgr. east cen. svc. unit, 1990-91. Mem. Rotary Mpls. #9 Club, Family Firm Inst., U. St. Thomas Inst. Family Bus., Inst. Pvt. Investors, Nat. Assn. Women Bus. Owners. Home: 1315 Dale St N Saint Paul MN 55117-4123 Office: Dellwood Fin Svcs Co 821 Marquette Ave Ste 815 Minneapolis MN 55402-2913

KELLER, DEBORAH KIM, soccer player; b. Winfield, Ill., Mar. 24, 1975. Student in phys. edn., U. N.C. mem. U.S. Nat. Women's Soccer Team, 1995—, inlcuding 3d-place 1995 FIFA Women's World Cup, Sweden; mem. U-20 Nat. Team, Nordic Cup, Germany, 1994; mem. gold-medal North team, 1995 U.S. Olympic Festival, Denver. Named Soccer Am. Player of Yr., 1996; voted Offensive Most Valuable Player, NCAA Tournament, 1996; named U. N.C. Athlete of Yr., 1997. Achievements: led U. N.C. to NCAA Championship, 1996. Office: US Soccer Fedn 1801-1811 S Prairie Ave Chicago IL 60616*

KELLER, DENNIS JAMES, management educator, business executive; b. Chgo., July 6, 1941; s. Ralph and Dorothy (Barckman) K.; m. Constance Bassett Templeton, May 28, 1966; children: Jeffrey Breckenridge, David McDaniel, John Templeton. A.B., Princeton U., 1963; M.B.A., U. Chgo., 1968. Account exec. Motorola Communications, Chgo., 1964-67; v.p. fin. Bell & Howell Comm., Waltham, Mass., 1968-70; v.p. mktg. Bell & Howell Schs., Chgo., 1970-73; pres. Keller Grad. Sch. Mgmt., Chgo., 1973-81, chmn., chief exec. officer, 1981—; chmn. bd., chief exec. officer DeVry Inc., 1987—; cons., evaluator North Central Assn., Chgo., 1979-84; chmn. bd. Precision Plastics, Inc., Columbia City, Ind., 1981—; bd. dirs. Templeton Kenly & Co., Broadview, Ill., Nicor Inc. Trustee Glenwood Sch. for Boys, Ill., 1980—, Chgo. Zool. Soc., Brookfield, Ill., 1979—, Princeton (N.J) U., 1994-98, Lake Forest Acad.-Ferry Hall, Ill., 1980-87, George M. Pullman Found., Chgo., 1987—; bd. trustees U. Chgo., 1998—; bd. dirs. Great Books Found., Chgo., 1986—; chmn. U. Chgo. Grad. Sch. Bus. Coun., 1994—, Princeton (N.J.) U. Sch. Engring. and Applied Scis. Leadership Coun., 1992—; commr. North Cen. Assn.-Commn. on Instns. of Higher Edn., 1985-88. Nat. Merit scholar, 1959-63; U. Chgo. Grad. Sch. Bus. fellow, 1967-68. Mem. Hinsdale Golf Club, Econ. Club, Comml. Club Chgo., Chgo. Club, Nantucket Golf Club, Sankaty Head Golf Club. Republican. Mem. United Ch. of Christ. Office: DeVry Inc 1 Tower Ln Fl 10 Oakbrook Terrace IL 60181

KELLER, EDWARD LOWELL, electrical engineer, educator; b. Rapid City, S.D., Mar. 6, 1939; s. Earl Lowell and E. Blanche (Oldfield) K.; m. Carole Lynne Craig, Sept. 1, 1963; children: Edward Lowell, Craig, Morgan. BS, U.S. Naval Acad., 1961; PhD, Johns Hopkins U., 1971. Mem. faculty U. Calif., Berkeley, 1971—; assoc. prof. elec. engring. U. Calif., 1977-79, prof., 1979-94, prof. emeritus, 1994-99; sr. scientist Smith Kettlewell Eye Rsch. Inst., San Francisco, 1980—; chmn. bioengring. program U. Calif., Berkeley and San Francisco, 1989; assoc. dir., 1999—; chmn. engring. sci. program Coll. of Engring. U. C., Berkeley, 1991-94. Contbr. articles to sci. jours. Served with USN, 1961-65. Sr. Von Humboldt fellow, 1977-78. Fellow IEEE; mem. AAAS, Assn. for Rsch. in Vision and Ophthalmology, Soc. for Neurosci., Internat. Neural Network Soc. Rsch. on primate oculomotor system and math. modelling of nervous system. Office: Smith-Kettlewell Eye Rsch Inst 2232 Webster St San Francisco CA 94115-1821

KELLER, ELIOT AARON, broadcasting executive; b. Davenport, Iowa, June 11, 1947; s. Norman Edward and Millie (Morris) K.; m. Sandra Kay McGrew, July 3, 1970; 1 child, Nicole. BA, U. Iowa, 1970; MS, San Diego State U., 1976. Corr. Sta. WHO-AM-FM-TV, Des Moines, 1969-70; newsman Sta. WSUI, Iowa City, Iowa, 1968-70; newsman, corr. Sta. WHBF-AM-FM-TV, Rock Island, Ill., 1969; newsman Sta. WOC-AM-FM-TV, Davenport, 1970; freelance newsman and photographer Iowa City, 1969-77; pres., dir. KZIA, Inc. (F/K/A KRNA, Inc., Comms., Inc.), Iowa City, 1971-78, KRNA, Inc., Iowa City, 1971-98; gen. mgr. Sta. KRNA, Cedar Rapids, 1974-98, Sta. KQCR, Cedar Rapids, Iowa, 1994-95, Sta. KXMX, Cedar Rapids, Iowa, 1995-98, Sta. KZIA, Cedar Rapids, 1998—; adj. instr. dept. comm. studies U. Iowa, Iowa City, 1983, 84. Mem. Mid-Continent Ry. Hist. Soc., R.R. Passenger Car Alliance, Iowa Assn. RR Passengers (excursion chair). Jewish. Home: 1244 Devon Dr NE Iowa City IA 52240-9628 Office: Sta KZIA 1110 26th Ave SW Cedar Rapids IA 52404-3430 *The chance only comes once.*

KELLER, ERIC TRENT, real estate manager; b. Akron, Ohio, Mar. 10, 1967; s. Kent Eugene and Linda Lee K.; m. Jo Ann Newell, July 6, 1996. BA, U. Calif., Berkeley, 1990. Paralegal Booz Allen Hamilton, San Francisco, 1991-92; project mgr. EMC Planning Group, Inc., Monterey, Calif., 1992-95; planner County of Monterey, Salinas, Calif., 1995-97; devel. specialist Redevel. Agy., San Jose, Calif., 1997-98; devel. mgr. Legacy Ptnrs. Residential, Foster City, Calif., 1998—. Avocations: skiing, golfing, biking, hiking, home improvement. E-mail: ekeller@legacyptr.com. Home: 1904 Hillman Ave Belmont CA 94002

KELLER, EVELYN FOX, history and philosophy educator; b. N.Y.C., Mar. 20, 1936; divorced; children: Jeffrey, Sarah. BA, Brandeis U., 1957; MA, Radcliffe Coll., 1959; PhD, Harvard U., 1963; hon. doctorate, Mt. Holyoke Coll., 1991, U. Amsterdam, 1993; D of Humane Sci. (hon.), Simmons Coll., 1995; LHD (hon.), Rensselaer Polytech. Inst., 1995; D of Tech. (hon.), Tech. U. of Lulea, Sweden, 1996. Prof. math. and humanities Northeastern U., Boston, 1982-88; prof. U. Calif., Berkeley, 1988-92; prof. history and philosophy of sci. MIT, 1992—; vis. fellow MIT Program in Sci., Tech. and Soc., 1979-80, vis. scholar, 1980-84, vis. prof., 1985-86; vis. prof. math. and humanities Northeastern U., 1981-82; Kregerb Wolf Disting. vis. prof. Northwestern U., 1985; sr. fellow Soc. for the Humanities, Cornell U., 1987; mem. Inst. for Advanced Study, Princeton, 1987-88; co-chair U. Calif. Systemwide Coun. on Women's Studies. Editor: A Feeling for the Organism: The Life and Work of Barbara McClintock, 1982, 2d edit., 1993, Reflections on Gender and Science, 1985, 10th edit., 1995, Refiguring Life: Metaphors of Twentieth Century Biology, 1995, Secrets of Life, Secrets of Death, 1992; co-editor Body/Politics: Women and the Discourses of Science, 1990, Conflicts in Feminism, 1990, Keywords in Evolutionary Discourse, 1992, Feminism and Science, 1996; Am. editor Fundamenta Scientiae, Internat. Jour. for Critical Analysis of Sci. and the Responsibility of Scientists; editl. bd. Women's Review of Books, Hypatia, Biology and Philosophy, Literature and Sci. Series, Jour. of the History of Biology; contbr. articles to profl. jours. Numerous grants and fellowships. Mem. History of Sci. Soc. Office: MIT E51-263B 77 Mass Ave Cambridge MA 02139-4307*

KELLER, GEORGE CHARLES, higher education consultant, writer; b. N.J., Mar. 14, 1928; s. Charles and Elizabeth K.; m. Gail Faithfull, 1960 (div. 1973); children: Bayard, Elizabeth; m. Jane Eblen, 1975. AB, Columbia U., 1951, MPhil, 1954. Academic dir. Gt. Books Found., Chgo., 1954-56; instr. polit. sci. Columbia U., N.Y.C., 1957-59; asst. dean Columbia U., 1959-61, editor, 1962-70; asst. to chancellor SUNY, Albany, 1970-78; asst. to pres. U. Md., College Park, 1979-82; sr. v.p. Barton-Gillett Co., Balt., 1983-88; sr. fellow Grad. Sch. Edn. U. Pa., Phila., 1988-94. Author: Academic Strategy, 1983; co-author: Post-Land Grant University, 1981; editor: Planning for Higher Education, 1990—; contbr. numerous articles, revs. to ednl. publs. With USN, 1946-48. Recipient Sibley award, Coun. for Advancement of Edn., 1963, 64, 65, U.S. Steel Found. award, 1965; named Best U.S. Edn. Writer, Atlantic mag., 1968. Mem. Assn. Study Higher Edn., Soc. Coll. and Univ. Planning (Founders award 1988). Office: 4900 Wetheredsville Rd Baltimore MD 21207-6625

KELLER, GLEN ELVEN, JR., lawyer; b. Longmont, Colo., Dec. 21, 1938; s. Glenn Elven and Elsie Mildred (Hogsett) K.; m. Elizabeth Ann Kauffman, Aug. 14, 1960; children—Patricia Carol, Michael Ashby. B.S. in Bus., U. Colo., 1960; J.D., U. Denver, 1964. Bar; Colo. 1964, U.S. Dist. Ct. Colo. 1964, U.S. Ct. Appeals (10th cir.) 1982. Assoc. Phelps, Hall & Keller and predecessor Phelps & Hall, Denver, 1964-67, ptnr., 1967-73; asst. atty. gen. State Colo., Denver, 1973-74; judge U.S. Bankruptcy Ct., Dist. Colo., 1974-82; ptnr. Davis, Graham & Stubbs LLP, Denver, 1982—; lectr. law U. Denver, 1977-87; adj. prof., 1987-98, Frank E. Rickston Jr. adj. prof. law, 1998—; mem. ct. adminstrn. com. Jud. Conf. U.S.; dir/., mem. exec. com. Colo. Lawyers' Com., chmn. task force on sch. discipline; bd. dirs. Western Stock Show Assoc. Mem. Colo. Bd. Health, 1968-74, pres., 1970-74; pres., dir. The Westernaires, Golden, Colo., Jefferson County R-1 Sch. Bd., 1984-89. Fellow Am. Coll. Bankruptcy; mem. ABA, Colo. Bar Assn., Denver Bar Assn., Nat. Conf. Bankruptcy Judges, Law Club. Republican. Office: Davis Graham & Stubbs LLP PO Box 185 370 17th St Denver CO 80201

KELLER, HARRY ALLAN, electronics technician; b. Columbus, Nebr., Dec. 19, 1943; s. Guy and Charlotte (Cameron) K. Degree in electronic technology, Radio Engring. Inst., Omaha, 1965; cert. of tng., Sears Ext. Inst., Dallas, 1969. Lead electronic technician Dale Electronics, Columbus, 1965-70; electronic mech. technician Sears & Roebuck, Columbus, 1969-70; electronic technician Ed's TV, North Bend, Nebr., 1970-73, P&K Electronics, Columbus, 1973-77; electronic mechanic Wards, Columbus, 1977-79; electronic mech. technician Becton Dickinson, Columbus, 1979—. Active State of Nebr. R.A.C.E.S., Civil Def. Nebr. Races Network, Colfax County, 1992. Recipient Speech Craft Cert. Toastmasters Internat., 1970. Mem. Inst. Electronics Engrs. Inc., Am. Radio Relay League (v.p. local club 1976-79). Republican. Methodist. Avocations: amateur radio, car club. Home: 410 Center St Rogers NE 68659-2803 Office: Becton-Dickinson PO Box 987 Columbus NE 68602-0987

KELLER, JACK, agricultural engineering educator, consultant; b. Roanoke, Va., Jan. 5, 1928; s. Eugene and Clara (Lauber) K.; m. Sara Altick, June 4, 1954; children: Andrew A., Jeffery S., Judith. BSCE, U. Colo., 1953; MS in Irrigation Engring., Colo. State U., 1955; PhD in Agrl. Engring., Utah State U., 1967. Registered profl. engr., Utah, Calif. Work unit engr. USDA Soil Conservation Svc., Victor, Colo., 1953; sales engr. So. Irrigation Co., Memphis, 1955-56; chief irrigation engr. W.R. Ames Co., San Jose, Calif., 1956-60; prof. Utah State U., Logan, 1960-88, dept. chmn., 1979-85, project mgr., 1978-88; pres., founder Keller-Bliesner Engring. Co., Logan, 1962—, chief exec. officer, 1989—; co-dir. U.S. AID Water Mgmt. Synthesis Project, Logan, 1978-88, team leader tech. assistance teams, worldwide, 1980-98; chmn. Conservation Verification Cons. for the IID/MWD Conservation Agreement, Imperial, Calif., 1992—; sr. policy advisor to Egyptian Ministry Pub. Works and Water Resources for U.s. AID's WRSR Activity, 1995—; sr. rsch. assoc. Internat. Irrigation Mgmt. Inst., 1995—. Co-author: Trickle Irrigation Design, 1974, Sprinkle and Trickle Irrigation, 1990; contbr. numerous articles to profl. jours.; patentee in field. Mem. Water Need Task Force, Logan, 1989, NRC Com. Soil and Water Rsch. Priorities for Devel. Countries, Washington, 1990-91; Water Resources Rsch., Washington, 1988; chmn. Red River Chloride Control Panel, Tulsa, 1988. With USN, 1945-47, PTO; sgt. USAF, 1951-53. Named Engr. of Yr. Utah Joint Engring. Coun., Salt Lake City, 1988. Fellow Am. Soc. Agrl. Engrs., ASCE; mem. NAE, Internat. Commn. Irrigation and Drainage, The Irrigation Assn. (Man of Yr. 1972). Mem. Bahai Ch. Avocations: bicycling, hiking, gardening, skiing. Home: 35 River Park Dr Logan UT 84321-4345 Office: Keller-Bliesner Engring 78 E Center St Logan UT 84321-4619*

KELLER, JAMES WARREN, college administrator; b. San Francisco, June 28, 1950; s. Ralph Waldo and Jane (Kephart) K.; m. Joan Hardie McIlhiney, June 5, 1976; children: Christina Elizabeth, Kathryn Michelle. AB in Econs., Stanford U., 1972; MBA, Santa Clara U., 1977. Ops. officer Bank of Am., Mt. View, Calif., 1972-73; bus. mgr. Palo Alto (Calif.) Unified Sch. Dist., 1973-89; asst. vice chancellor West Valley-Mission Coll., Saratoga, Calif., 1989-91; vice chancellor Foothill-De Anza Coll., Los Altos Hills, Calif., 1991—. Mem. Assn. Calif. C.C. Bus. Ofcls. (dir. 1993—). Avocations: golf, woodworking, guitar. Home: 12412 Titus Ave Saratoga CA 95070-4030 Office: Foothill-De Anza Coll 12345 El Monte Rd Los Altos CA 94022-4504

KELLER, J(AMES) WESLEY, credit union executive; b. Jonesboro, Ark., Jan. 6, 1958; s. Norman Grady and Norma Lee (Ridgeway) Patrick; m. Patricia Marie Delavan, July 7, 1979. Student, U. Miss., 1976-78; BS in Bus. and Mgmt., Redlands U., 1991, MBA, 1994. Sr. collector Rodkwell Fed. Credit Union, Downey, Calif., 1978-79; acct. Lucky Fed. Credit Union, Buena Park, Calif., 1979-84; pres., chief exec. officer Long Beach (Calif.) State Employees Credit Union, 1984—. Mem. Credit Union Exec. Soc., Calif. Credit Union League (bd. govs. Long Beach chpt., treas. 1985-86), So. Calif. Credit Union Mgrs. Assn., U. Redlands Whitehead Leadership Soc., Nat. Assn. State Charted Credit Unions (chmn. 1995—), Kiwanis. Republican. Baptist. Avocations: photography, skiing, woodworking, biking. Office: Long Beach State Employees Credit Union 3840 N Long Beach Blvd Long Beach CA 90807-3312

KELLER, JAMI ANN, special education educator; b. Hastings, Nebr., Jan. 4, 1961; d. Donald Lee and Gail Angela (England) Stilley; m. Mark Lee Keller, June 19, 1982; children: William England, Robert John Thomas, Alexander James Stilley, Clare Jana Lee, Elyse Markie Ann. BS with distinction, U. Nebr., 1984. Tchr. spl. edn. Grand Island (Nebr.) Pub. Schs., 1985-92, Papillon (Nebr.)/La Vista Pub. Schs., 1992-93. PTA scholar Nebr. PTA, 1983, Beach-Byer scholar, 1983. Mem. NEA, Nebr. Edn. Assn., Pi Lambda Theta, Mu Epsilon Nu.

KELLER, JOHN DAVID, earth science educator; b. Herminie, Pa., Nov. 27, 1940; s. Charles Henry and Goldie Lavinia (Wechtenhiser) K.; m. Virginia Elaine Baldensperger, Aug. 7, 1965; children: Kurt David, Kevin Neil. BA in Sci. Edn., U. Akron, 1965, MS in Earth Sci., 1971; PhD in Sci. Edn., U. Tex., 19783. Cert. tchr., Ohio. Physics, chemistry, biology and earth sci. tchr. Akron Pub. Schs., 1964-74, sci. curriculum specialist, 1974-78, coord. program for gifted and talented in math. and sci., 1978-83, sci. math. and computers curriculum specialist, 1983-90; asst. prof. Kent (Ohio) State U., 1990-98, assoc. prof., 1998—; coord. acad. talented tchr. edn. program Kent (Ohio) Sttae U., 1995-98; sci. curriculum cons. Beaumont, Geauga, Mahoning, Summit, Trumbull, and Tuscarawas County, Ohio, 1990—. Author: Teacher's River Guide, 1994 (1st place Large Market/Cmty. Info. award for Corp. Pub. Broadcasting 1995); contbr. articles to profl. jours. Pres., bd. edn. Coventry Local Sch., Summit County, Ohio, 1978-89; pres., mem. bd. edn. Portage Lakes Joint Vocat. Schs., Summit County, 1979-87. Recipient Excellence in Sci. Tchg. award Am. Mfg. Chemist Assn., 1968; Jennings scholar Martha Holden Jenning Found., 1967. Mem. NSTA (life, talented and gifted adv. bd. 1995-98), Am. Assn. For Tchg. and Curriculum (conf. presentor 1995—), Phi Delta Kappa. Republican. Avocations: woodworking, canoeing. E-mail: dkeller 51@aol.com. Office: Kent State U 401 White Hall Kent OH 44242

KELLER, JOHN FRANCIS, retired wine company executive, mayor; b. Mt. Horeb, Wis., Feb. 5, 1925; s. Frank S. and Elizabeth K. (Meier) K.; m. Barbara D. Mabbott, Feb. 18, 1950; children: Thomas, Patricia, Daniel, David, John. BBA in Acctg., U. Wis., 1949; MBA, U. Chgo., 1963; grad., Exec. Program, Stanford U., 1978. CPA, Wis., Ill. Acct. Bank of Am., 1949-51; mgr. statis. control and gen. accounting Miller Brewing Co., Milw., 1952-58; controller Maremont Corp., 1958-68; with Heublein, Inc., 1968-84; v.p. fin. Hamm's Brewing Co., 1968-70; v.p. finance, dir. United Vintners, Inc., San Francisco, 1970-80; chmn. bd., chief exec. officer, dir. United Vintners, Inc., 1980-84; group v.p. wines Heublein Wines, 1980-84; pres. ISC Wines of Calif., 1983-85; adminstrv. dir. Winegrowers of Calif. (a Calif. state mktg. order for wineries and grape growers), 1985-87; wine industry cons., 1985—; mgmt. cons. for J.F. Keller & Assocs., 1988—; lectr./assoc. prof. Calif. State U. at Hayward Grad. Sch. Bus. and Econs., 1978-82; adj. prof. Golden Gate U. Grad. Sch. Bus., 1983-86, lectr., instr. Coll. San Mateo, 1990; bd. dirs. Servicor, Inc., J.W. Morris Winery, Fife and Horn Vineyards. Councilman City of Hillsborough, Calif., 1982-91, mayor, 1988-90; active Boy Scouts Am., 1952-58, Cmty. Chest; mem. parish coun. St. Lamberts Cath. Ch., 1966-68; pres. parish coun. St. Bartholomew Cath. Ch., 1980; dir. Serra H.S. Bd., 1979-82; bd. dirs. U. Wis. Found., 1986—, Seton Health Scis. Found., 1988—, chmn., 1994-96; bd. dirs. Seton Med. Ctr., 1989-94, sec.-treas., 1992-94; bd. dirs. Big. Bros., San Francisco, 1971-75, Hill High St. St. Paul, 1969-70, Lesley Found., 1983-85, Cath. Health Care West, 1994—, mem. fin. and investment com.; bd. dirs., pres. Alemany Scholarship Found., 1983-95; bd. dirs. Peace and Justic Task Force Commn., 1986-92; mem. Pastoral Planning Commn., 1994-95; trustee St. Patrick's Sem., 1994—, investment advisor, 1990—, Archdiocese of San Francisco. 2d lt. 82d Airborne divsn. AUS, 1944-46, ETO; with USAR, 1946-52. Recipient Disting. Bus. Alumnus award U. Wis. Sch. Bus., 1990; named to Equestrian Order of the Holy Sepulchre of Jerusalem, 1990, Knight of Malta, 1989. Mem. AICPA, Fin. Execs. Inst., Wis. Soc. CPAs, Calif. Soc. CPAs, Nat. Assn. Accts., VFW, American Legion, JUnipero Serra Internat. (pres. 1992-94), Commonwealth Club, World Trade Club, Peninsula Golf and Country Club, Order of Holy Sepulchre KC, Order of Malta (dir., v.p. 1995—), Phi Kappa Alpha (past treas., bd. dirs.). Home and Office: 785 Tournament Dr Hillsborough CA 94010-7423

KELLER, JOHN WARREN, lawyer; b. Niagara Falls, Aug. 6, 1954; s. Joseph and Edith Lillian (Kilvington) K.; m. Sandra D. Hubbard, Dec. 18, 1981; children: Sean, Christopher. BA, Rider U., 1976; JD, Coll. William and Mary, 1979. Bar: Ky. 1980, U.S. Dist. Ct. (ea. dist.) Ky. 1985, U.S. Ct. Appeals (6th cir.) 1988, U.S. Dist. Ct. (we. dist.) Ky. 1988. Staff atty. Appalachian Rsch. & Def. Fund Ky., Inc., Barbourville, 1979-82; assoc. F. Preston Farmer Law Offices, London, Ky., 1982-88; ptnr. Farmer, Keller & Kelley, London, 1988-91, Taylor, Keller & Dunaway, London, 1991—; mem. Fla. Adv. Com. on Arson Prevention, 1990—; chair bd. dirs. Appalachian Rsch. & Def. Fund Ky., 1994-96; founder, chmn. bd. dirs. Ky. Lawyers for Legal Svcs. to the Poor; mem. editl. adv. bd. Ky. West Publ. Group, 1997; bd. mem. Nat. Soc. Ins. Investigators. Contbg. editor: ABA Annotations to Homeowner's Policy, 3rd edit., 1995, ABA Bad Faith Annotations, 2d edit., 1997. Bd. dirs. Christian Ch. in Ky., 1994-98; elder First Christian Ch., London, 1994-97; pres. Access to Justice Found., 1996—. Recipient Access to Justice award Ky. Legal Svcs. Programs, 1995. Mem. ABA (vice chair property ins. law com. 1992-97), Laurel County Bar Assn. (pres. 1992-93), Ky. Bar Assn. (mem. bd. govs. 1996—), The Honorable Order of Ky. Cols. Office: Taylor Keller & Dunaway 1306 W 5th St London KY 40741-1615

KELLER, JOSEPH BISHOP, mathematician, educator; b. Paterson, N.J., July 31, 1923; s. Isaac and Sally (Bishop) K.; m. Evelyn Fox, Aug. 29, 1963 (div. Nov. 17, 1976); children—Jeffrey M., Sarah N. BA, NYU, 1943, MS, 1946, PhD, 1948. Prof. math. Courant Inst. Math. Scis., NYU, 1948-79; chmn. dept. math. Univ. Coll. Arts and Scis. and Grad. Sch. Engring. and Sci., 1967-73; prof. math. and mech. engring. Stanford U., 1979—; hon. prof. math. scis. Cambridge U., 1990—; rsch. assoc. Woods Hole Oceanographic Instn., 1965; Gibbs lectr. Am. Math. Soc., 1977; von Neumann lectr. Soc. Indsl. and Applied Math., 1983; Rouse Ball lectr. U. Cambridge, Eng., 1993. Contbr. articles to profl. jours. Recipient von Karman prize Soc. Indsl. and Applied Math., 1979, Eringen medal Soc. Engring. Scis., 1981, Timoshenko medal ASME, 1984, U.S. Nat. Medal of Sci., 1988, NAS award in Applied Mathematics and Numerical Analysis, 1995, Frederic Esser Nemmers prize in math. Northwestern U., Evanston, Ill., 1996, Wolf prize, Israel, 1997. Mem. NAS, Royal Soc. (fgn.), Am. Acad. Arts and Scis., Am. Math. Soc., Am. Phys. Soc., Soc. Indsl. and Applied Math. Home: 820 Sonoma Ter Stanford CA 94305-1072 Office: Stanford U Dept Math Stanford CA 94305-2125

KELLER, JOYCE, television and radio host, counselor, writer; d. Joseph Michael and Grace Marie ; m. Jack Keller; children: Elaine, Scott. Cert. hypnotherapist, counselor. Host, prodr. Trim & Slim WSNL-TV; host, prodr., creator Joyce Keller Mag. Show Viacom/Joyce Keller Show WGBB; host, prodr. Joyce Keller's Mag. Show Viacom; guest on shows Merv Griffin, Ricky Lake, Regis Philbin, Geraldo, Donahue, Oprah Winfrey, Joan Rivers, Bob Grant, Joan Hamburg, Sally Jessy Raphael, Soupy Sales, A Current Affair, CNBC's Real Personal, Wake Up America, Entertainment Tonight, America's Talking; regular feature on WOR's Joey Reynolds Show, Lifetime TV Online Romance Connection, Relationships, WOR Radio Network, Lifetime TV. Author: Calling All Angels, Heart Hunting; columnist: (monthly mags.) Nightlife Mag., 1981-90, Update Mag., 1990—; host (radio) The Joyce Keller Show, WGBB 1240-AM. Named Best TV Fitness Show, World Body Bldg. Guild. Mem. ASTARA, Inc., Nat. Assn. Talk Show Hosts. Home and Office: 117 Jean Rd West Islip NY 11795-2909

KELLER, JUAN DANE, lawyer; b. Cape Girardeau, Mo., Jan. 30, 1943; s. Irvin A. and Mercedes (Crippen) K.; m. Sandra Anne Solomon; children: Mary, John, Katharine, Robert, Michael, Cassandra. AB in History, U. Mo., 1965, JD, 1967; LLM, Georgetown U., 1971. Bar: Mo. Assoc. Bryan, Cave, St. Louis, 1971-78, ptnr., 1979—. Contbg. author: Missouri Bar Taxation Handbook, 1988-95. Capt. JAGC, U.S. Army, 1967-71. Mem. ABA, Mo. Bar (tax com. 1971—), Met. St. Louis Bar Assn., Order of Coif. Methodist. Office: Bryan Cave 1 Metropolitan Sq Ste 3600 Saint Louis MO 63102-2750

KELLER, KASEY, professional soccer player; b. Olympia, Wash., Nov. 29, 1969; m. Kristin; children: Cameron, Chloe. Student, U. Portland. Goalkeeper Millwall Football Club, Eng., Leicester City Football Club, Eng., 1996—; with U.S. Nat. Team; winner English Cup title; capt. Olympic Team, 1996. Recipient Silver Ball award World Youth Championship, Saudi Arabia, 1989; named to All-Copa Am. Team. Office: Leicester City FC plc, Filbert St, Leicester LE2 7FL, England also: US Soccer Fedn 1801 S Prairie Ave # 1811 Chicago IL 60616-1357*

KELLER, KENNETH CHRISTEN, advertising executive; b. Toledo, Feb. 17, 1939; s. Theodore G. and Edna L. (Christen) K.; m. Mary Carolyn Folsom, Sept. 10, 1960; children: Kathryn Elizabeth Keller Oulevey, David Folsom Keller. Student Ohio State U., 1957-59. Part-time staff announcer Sta. WMNI, Columbus, Ohio, 1958-59, Sta. WTVN, Columbus, 1959, Sta. WBNS-TV, Columbus, 1959; staff announcer Sta. WRFD, Worthington, Ohio, 1959-61; staff announcer, news supr., program dir. Sta. WOSU, Columbus, 1961-65; on-air talent Sta. WBNS, Columbus, 1962-65; copywriter Joe Hill & Assocs., Columbus, 1965-66; creative dir. Myers, Ault & Assocs., Columbus, 1966-70; co-owner, account exec. Angeletti, Wise & Keller, Columbus, 1970-72; co-owner TRIAD, Columbus, 1972-86, owner, 1986—, v.p., dir. creative services, 1972-85, pres., 1985—. Bd. dirs. Friends of WOSU, 1981-88, pres., 1985-87; apptd. by Franklin County Commrs. to bd. dirs. Cen. Ohio Mktg. Council, 1986-89; mem. congregation coun. All Saints Ch., 1995—, v.p., 1999—. Lyricist Best Radio Comml. award Internat. Assn. Fairs and Expns., Ohio State Fair, 1978, 81; pronouncer Scripps-Howard Regional Spelling Bee, 1984—. Mem. AFTRA (chpt. pres. 1978), Kiwanis Club of Columbus. Home: 270 Park Blvd Columbus OH 43085-3660 Office: TRIAD 6525 Busch Blvd Columbus OH 43229-1797

KELLER, KENNETH HARRISON, engineering educator, science policy analyst; b. N.Y.C., Oct. 19, 1934; s. Benjamin and Pearl (Pastor) K.; m. Dorothy Robinson, June 2, 1957 (div.); children: Andrew Robinson, Paul Victor; m. Bonita F. Sindelir, June 19, 1981; children: Jesse Daniel, Alexandra Amelie. AB, Columbia U., 1956, BS, 1957; MS in Engring., Johns Hopkins U., 1963, PhD, 1964. Asst. prof. dept. chem. engring. U. Minn., Mpls., 1964-68, assoc. prof., 1968-71, prof., 1971—, prof. Hubert H. Humphrey Inst. Pub. Affairs, 1996—, Charles M. Denny Jr. prof., assoc. dean Grad. Sch., 1973-74, 99—, acting dean Grad. Sch., 1974-75, head dept. chem. engring. and materials sci., 1978-80, v.p. acad. affairs, 1980-85, pres., 1985-88; Philip D. Reed sr. fellow for sci. and tech. Coun. on Fgn. Rels., 1990-96, sr. v.p., 1993-95; cons. in field; mem. cardiology adv. com. NIH, 1982-86; mem. sci. and tech. adv. panel to dir. CIA, 1995—; mem. commn. on phys. scis., math. and applications NRC, 1996—; bd. dirs. LASPAU: Acad. and Profl. Programs for the Ams., 1996—; bd. trustees Sci. Mus. Minn., 1997—; chmn. Med. Technology Leadership Forum, 1998—. Mem. adv. com. program for Soviet emigré scholars, 1974-82; bd. govs. Argonne Nat. Lab., 1982-85; bd. dirs. Walker Art Ctr., 1982-88, Charles Babbage Found., 1991—. Served from ensign to lt. USNR, 1957-61. NIH Spl. fellow, 1972-73; vis. fellow Woodrow Wilson Sch. of Pub. and Internat. Affairs, Princeton U., 1988-90. Founding fellow Am. Inst. for Med. and Biol. Engring.; mem. Am. Soc. Artificial Internal Organs (pres. 1980-81), AIChE (Food and Bioengring. award 1980), Am. Coun. for Emigrés in the Professions (dir. 1972-80), Mpls. C. of C. (bd. dirs. 1985-88), Coun. Fgn. Rels., Phi Beta Kappa, Sigma Xi (nat. lectr. 1978-80). Office: Hubert H Humphrey Inst U Minn 301 19th Ave S Ste 300 Minneapolis MN 55455-0411

KELLER, KENT EUGENE, advertising and public relations executive; b. Oil City, Pa., Oct. 5, 1941; s. George W. and Lois (Wallace) K.; divorced; children: Eric Trent, Todd Jason. BA, Kent State U., 1963; cert., Chrysler Inst., Detroit, 1968, UCLA, 1973. Editor Oil City (Pa.) Derrick, 1959-60; various mgmt. positions Chrysler Corp., Twinsburg, Ohio, 1960-64, prodn. cont. mgr., 1964-67; group mgr. Chrysler Corp. AMG, Detroit, 1967-69; dir. advt. and pub. rels. Zero Corp., Burbank, Calif., 1969-75; exec. v.p. Basso & Assocs. Inc., Newport Beach, Calif., 1975-80; pres. Jason Trent & Co., Inc., North Tustin, Calif., 1980—; pub. rels. counsel Electronic Convs. Inc., L.A., 1980-85; bd. dirs. Neurosci. Tech. Inc., Tarzana, Calif.; cons. Global Engring., Irvine, Calif., 1989—; co-founder Strategic Concepts, Fountain Valley, Calif., 1990. Editor (industry report) TOLD Report, 1985—, (mag.) Zero Dimensions, 1969-75. Mem. Town Hall of Calif., L.A., 1980—. Mem. Bus. & Profl. Advt. Assn., Pub. Rels. Soc. Am., Back Bay Club. Republican. Presbyterian. Avocations: golf, tennis, collectable art. Home: 18072 Darmel

Pl Santa Ana CA 92705-1916 Office: 1440 S State College Blvd Anaheim CA 92806-5724

KELLER, KENT KYLE, computer technician; b. Bismarck, N.D., Aug. 12, 1964; s. Jacob Edward and Sharon Ann Keller; m. Karen Ann Morrell, Sept. 26, 1986; children: Chadrick, Cameron. Computer technician Fireside Office Plus, Bismarck. SFC U.S. Army Nat. Guard, 1982—. Republican. Roman Catholic. E-mail: k-cubed@gcentral.com and kkeller@firesideop.com. Fax: 701-223-9598. Office: Fireside Office Plus 1713 E Bismarck Expressway Bismarck ND 58504

KELLER, LARRY A., city manager; b. San Pedro, Calif., Mar. 2, 1945; married; 3 children. BA in Anthropology, San Francisco State U. COO Port of L.A., 1996-97, exec. dir., 1997—. Mem. Steamship Assn. So. Calif. (sec.-treas., v.p., pres., chmn.), L.A. C. of C., Danish-Am. C. of C. Office: Harbor Dept Port of Los Angeles 425 S Palos Verdes St San Pedro CA 90731-3309*

KELLER, LEROY, journalist, consultant; b. Longmont, Colo., Aug. 31, 1905; s. Samuel Ashby and Vinnie Alice (Howard) K.; m. Winifred Cora Allen, Mar. 31, 1935; children: John Pierce, Lynn Keller Andrews. A.B., U. Colo., 1929. Joined United Press Assns., 1929, staff writer, 1929-33, syndicate rep., 1933-35, bus. rep., 1936-45, asst. bus. mgr., 1945-48, gen. sales mgr., 1948- 64, v.p., 1952—, dir. client relations, 1959-64, v.p., gen. mgr. internat. divs., 1964-71; newspaper broker, cons., 1971—; v.p. United Features Syndicate, 1958-65; Adv. com. World Press Inst., ANPA-World Press Achievement Awards; established Keller Ctr. for Study of the First Amendment of the Constitution U.S.A. U. Colo., 1992. Mem. Soc. of Profl. Journalists, Inter-Am. Press Assn., Internat. Press Inst., Sigma Alpha Epsilon, Sigma Delta Chi. Clubs: University (N.Y.C.); Scarsdale Golf (N.Y.). Home: 133 Pondfield Rd Bronxville NY 10708-4012 *It is ironic that, having spent most of my life fighting for competition in the news business, the end result is that most daily newspapers in the United States have done away with competition in their markets. Nonetheless, I still believe that competition in all business activities best serves the free enterprise society on which our democracy is founded. A final thought: I believe that large groups should not go public because that forces management to put too much emphasis on the bottom line.*

KELLER, LOUIS, SR., municipal official; b. Vacherie, La., Sept. 25, 1932. Bachelors, Holy Cross Coll., 1987. Registrar Office Registrar Voters, New Orleans, 1988—. Office: Office of the Registrar of Voters City Hall Rm 1W12 1300 Perdido St New Orleans LA 70112-2125*

KELLER, MARTHA ANN, artist, painter; b. N.Y.C., Dec. 8, 1948; d. Charles and Judith (Herman) K.; m. Bradford H. Ensminger, July 12, 1989. Student, Overseas Sch. of Rome, 1961-64, St. Stephen's Sch., Rome, 1964-66, Temple U., 1968, Boston U., 1966-69; BFA, Md. Inst., 1971; postgrad., George Washington U., 1972-73. vis. artist Whitaker Found., Palermo, Italy, 1982, U. Calif., Santa Barbara, 1987, Sch. of the Art Inst. of Chgo., 1990, R.I. Sch. of Design, Providence, 1993, Sarah Lawrence Coll., Bronxville, N.Y., 1991; instr. multi-level painting Sch. of Art Inst. Chgo., 1991, 95; lectr. in visual arts Princeton U., 1991-92, 98-99; instr. N.Y. Studio Sch. of Painting, 1992; adj. instr. Kingsborough Cmty. Coll., Bklyn., 1993, 94; guest lectr. Temple U., Tyler Sch. of Art, Rome, 1994, Parsons' Sch., 1995, 96, 97, Hunter Coll., CUNY, 96, 97, 98, 99, guest artist Ringling Sch., Fla., 1997; chair Coll. Art Assn. Conf., Toronto, 1997-98. One woman shows include Albuquerque Arts Ctr., U. N.Mex., 1978, Whitaker Found. Mus., Palermo, 1982, Stephen Rosenberg Gallery, N.Y., 1986, 87, 89, Conlon Gallery, Santa Fe, N.Mex., 1990, Galleria Plurima, Udine, Italy, 1991, Halsey Gallery, Coll. of Charleston, 1994, Turchetto Gallery, Milan, 1994, Rosenberg & Kaufman Fine Art, N.Y., 1997, 98; exhibited in group shows at Stephen Rosenberg Gallery, 1986, 89, 90, 91, McNay Art Mus., San Antonio, 1986, Gallery 53 Cooperstown, N.Y., 1986, Carlo Lamagna Gallery, N.Y., 1988, Genovese Gallery, Boston, 1988, Dart Gallery, Chgo., 1988, Ill. Ctr. Gallery, Chgo., 1989, 55 Mercer Gallery, N.Y., 1990, Galleria Plurima, Udine and Milan, 1992, Edwin A. Ulrich Mus. of Art, Wichita, 1992, Cummings Art Ctr., Conn. Coll., 1992, 55 Ferris St, Bklyn., 1993, Jessica Berwind Gallery, Phila., 1993, Krasdale Foods Gallery and Lehman Coll., Westchester, N.Y., 1993, Lilian Heidenberg Gallery, N.Y., 1993, Werner Kramarsky, N.Y., 1993, Art in Embassies Program, Vienna, Austria, 1994, Noyes Mus., Oceanville, N.J., 1994, Art Initiatives and Bill Bace, 1995, Rosenberg & Kaufman Fine Art, N.Y., 1995, Mishkin Gallery, Baruch Coll., 1996, Bockenheimer Depot Internat. Exhbn., Frankfurt, Germany, 1996, Islip Art Mus., N.Y.,1997, Condeso/Lawler Gallery, 1997, Snug Harbor Cultural Ctr., 1997, Islip Art Museum., N.Y., 1997; represented in permanent collection Met. Mus. Art, N.Y.C., 1996, Fogg Art Mus., Harvard U., Cambridge, Mass., San Jose Mus. Art, Whitney Mus. Art, Mus. Modern Art N.Y.C., others. Recipient fellowships The Mac Dowell Colony, 1990, Nat. Endowment for the Arts, 1989-90, The Mac Dowell Colony, 1989-90; grantee Ludwig Vogelstein Found., 1987, CETA grantee for costume design Albuquerque Dance Theatre, 1978. Home: 39 Walker St New York NY 10013-6001

KELLER, MARTHA ROCK, artist, educator; b. Youngstown, Ohio, Sept. 25, 1926; d. Louis Henry Rock and Emma Josephine Benson-Rock; m. Robert Brindle Keller, Oct. 18, 1952; children: Ruth Ann, Paul Robert. BA, Ohio Wesleyan U., 1948; MS, Syracuse U., 1951; MFA, U. Mich., 1969. Lab. technician Brookhaven (L.I.) Nat. Lab., 1948-49; lab. technician zoology dept. Syracuse (N.Y.) U., 1949-50; lab. technician UCLA, Long Beach, 1950-51; instr. art Schoolcraft Coll., Livonia, Mich., 1972-84; instr. art dept. Toledo (Ohio) Mus. Sch., U. Toledo, 1984-85; lectr. art dept. Ea. Mich. U., Ypsilanti, 1987-88; adj. prof. Sch. Art and Design, U. Mich., Ann Arbor, 1976-82, 94—; exch. artist City of Ann Arbor/Tübingen, Germany, 1989; lectr. Ann Arbor Dist. Libr., 1997. *Ms. Keller's scientific background allows her to bring an experimental attitude to her art and teaching. Reflecting on the landscape of Tubingen, she began painting international landscapes drawing parallels between Michigan and European scenes. One of her paintings is a landscape that connects views of Lake Michigan's Sleeping Bear Dunes with hills in Tuscany. Her current work relates the terrain of the University of Michigan's arboretum and the terrain of Catalan France and Spain. Writing spurs her artwork and teaching of painting. Her book on public art serves her work as "Commissioner" for public art in Ann Arbor.* Exhibited invitational exhbn. Mich. Theater, 1999; represented in permanent collections Chrysler World Hdqs., Auburn Hills, Mich., Omega Healthcare Investors, Inc., Ann Arbor, Mich.; featured artist TV show Painting the Town, 1997; co-author: (book) Public Art in Ann Arbor and Washtenaw County, 1995; contbr. revs. and articles to profl. publs. Commr. Commn. on Art in Pub. Places, Ann Arbor, 1998-99. Mem. Ann Arbor Art Ctr. (bd. dirs. 1975). United Presbyterian. E-mail: mrkeller@umich.edu. Home: 1603 E Stadium Blvd Ann Arbor MI 48104 Office: Martha Keller Studio 213 S Main St Ann Arbor MI 48104

KELLER, MARY BETH, consumer research consultant; b. N.Y.C., Dec. 18, 1960; d. Thomas Francis and Cynthia Ann (Bez) E. BA in Psychology, U. Rochester, 1982. With Mfrs. Hanover Trust Co., N.Y.C., 1982-88, mgmt. trainee, 1982-85, quality circle facilitator human resources area, 1982-83, fin. planner, 1983-84, account analysis supr. cen. bookkeeping, 1984, communication officer, Communications & Mktg. Ops. div., 1984-86, dir. course adminstrn. corp. profl. devel., 1986-87, tng. analyst, 1987-95; creative rsch. assoc. Saatchi & Saatchi Worldwide Advt., N.Y.C., 1988-95; owner, prin. cons., consumer rsch., new product devel. Creative Waves: Innovations in Qualitative Rsch., Pleasantville, N.Y., 1995—. Editor employee publ., 1985-86, employee devel. course catalog, 1986. Mem. U. Rochester Admissions Network, 1982—. Recipient Productivity awards Ops. div. Mfrs. Hanover Trust, 1983, 84, 85. Mem. Nat. Assn. Bank Women (chmn. edn. and tng. 1987-88, trainer 1987-88, scholarship award 1987), Am. Bus. Women's Assn., Rsch. Cons. Assn., U. Rochester Alumni Assn. (editor newsletter 1983-86, founder, pres. N.Y. chpt. 1982-88), Qualitative Rsch. Cons. Assn. Roman Catholic. Club: Rochester Alumni (pres. 1982-86). Avocations: family, church, creative writing, crafts. Home & Office: 20 Wilton Rd Pleasantville NY 10570-2022

KELLER, MICHAEL ALAN, librarian, educator, musicologist; b. Sterling, Colo., Apr. 5, 1945; s. Ephraim Richard and Mary Patricia (Warren) K.; m. Constance A. Kyle, Sept. 3, 1967 (div. Aug. 1979); children: Kristen J., Paul B.; m. Carol Lawrence, Oct. 6, 1979; children: Laura W., Martha M. BA, Hamilton Coll., 1967; MA, SUNY, Buffalo, 1970, postgrad., 1970-91; MLS, SUNY, Geneseo, 1972. Asst. libr. for reference and cataloging SUNY Music Libr., Buffalo, 1970-73; acting undergrad. libr. Cornell U., Ithaca, N.Y., 1976; music libr., sr. lectr. Cornell U., Ithaca, 1973-81; head music libr. U. Calif., Berkeley, 1981-86; assoc. univ. libr. for collection devel. Yale U., 1986-93; director Stanford (Calif.) U. Librs., 1993-94, univ. libr., dir. acad. info. resources, 1994—; pub. HighWire Press, Stanford, 1995—; cons. Bates Coll., Lewiston, Maine, 1976, Colgate U., Hamilton, N.Y., 1976, Rutgers U., New Brunswick, N.J., 1982, Brown U., Providence, 1983, U. Alta., Edmonton, Can., 1983, NYU, 1984, L.A. Music Ctr. Opera Co., 1985-89, City of Ferrara, Italy, U. Pitts., Villa I Tatti-Biblioteca Berenson, Florence, Italy, Am. Phys. Soc., Princeton U., Newsweek Mag., Hamilton Coll., Clinton, N.Y., Sierra Nev. Coll., Ind. U., Coun. Australian Univ. Librs., U. Tech., Sydney, Griffith U., Brisbane, Ind. U., Occidental Coll., L.A., U. Melbourne; mem. Nat. Digital Libr. Fedn., 1993—; mem. Bibliog Commn., Repertoire Internat. de la Presse Mus. de XIXve Siecle, 1981-84; chmn. music program com. Rsch. Librs. Group, 1982-86; reviewer NEH, 1982-88, panelist, 1979-95; chmn. Assoc. Music Librs. Group, Joint Com. Retrospecive Conversion in Music, 1989-93; mem. collection mgmt. devel. com. Rsch. Librs. Group, 1986-91, chmn., 1989-91, mem. program adv. com., 1991-93; dir. Berkeley Italian Renaissance Project, 1985-95, Digital Libr. Fedr., 1994—; mem. bd. overseers Stanford U., 1997—; mem. gov. com. Stanford-Japan Ctr. Rsch. Author: MSS on Microfilm in Music Libr. at SUNYAB, 1971, (with Duckles) Music Reference and Rsch. Materials; an annotated bibliography, 1988, 94; contbr. articles to profl. jours. Firefighter, rescue squad mem. Cuyuga Heights Vol. Fire Co., N.Y., 1980-81. Recipient spl. commendation Nat. Music Clubs, 1978, Berkeley Bronze medal U. Calif.-Berkeley, 1983; NDEA Title IV fellow SUNY-Buffalo, 1967-70; Cornell Coll. Arts and Scis. rsch. grantee, 1973-81, U. Calif.-Berkeley humanities rsch. grantee, 1983-84, Coun. on Libr. Resources grantee, 1984, 93-99, Libr. Assn. U. Calif. grantee, 1985-86, NEH grantee, 1986, Deems Taylor award ASCAP,, 1988, Stanford U. fellow, 1994-95. Fellow Pierson Coll., Yale U.; mem. ALA, AAUP, Music Libr. Assn. (bd. dirs. 1975-77, mem. fin. com. 1982-83, mem. editl. com. index and bibliography series 1981-85), Internat. Assn. Music Librs., Am. Musicol. Soc. (mem. com. on automated bibliography 1982-83, mem. coun. 1986-88), Conn. Acad. Arts and Scis. (bd. dirs.), Ctr. Rsch. Librs. (mem. adv. com. 1988-90), Conn. Ctr. for Books (bd. dirs.), Book Club of Calif., Roxburghe Club of San Francisco, Bohemian Club, San Francisco. Home: 809 San Francisco Ter Stanford CA 94305-1021 Office: Stanford U Cecil Green Libr Stanford CA 94305-6004

KELLER, PAUL, advertising agency executive; b. Mainz, Germany, Sept. 23, 1921; came to U.S., 1937, naturalized, 1942; s. Bernhard and Johanna (Metzger) K.; m. Ruth Ettinghouse, Dec. 25, 1948; children: Steven A., Richard M., Susan F. B.A., NYU, 1948; M.A., Columbia U., 1949. Research analyst N.W. Ayer, N.Y.C., 1950-55; media research dir. Bryan Houston, N.Y.C., 1955-57; v.p., dir. media and rsch., corp. sec., bd. dirs. Reach McClinton, N.Y.C., 1957-69; v.p., assoc. rsch. dir. Ted Bates Advt., N.Y.C., 1969-80, sr. v.p., rsch. dir., 1980-84; prin. Keller Cons. Co., 1985—; vol. cons. Nat. Exec. Svc. Corps, 1985—. With U.S. Army, 1942-45, PTO. Decorated Bronze Star, Purple Heart. Mem. Phi Beta Kappa, Pi Mu Epsilon.

KELLER, RANDAL JOSEPH, toxicology educator; b. Salem, Ind., Nov. 22, 1957; s. Frank Joseph and Virginia Francis (Barrett) K.; m. Pamela Marie Stroman, Sept. 17, 1994. BA, Eisenhower Coll., Seneca Falls, N.Y., 1979; MS, Utah State U., 1984, PhD, 1988. Cert. indsl. hygienist; cert. safety profl.; diplomate Am. Bd. Toxicology. Postdoctoral fellow Nat. Ctr. Toxicology Rsch., Jefferson, Ark., 1988-90; instr. U. Ark. for Med. Scis., Little Rock, 1990-91, coord. occupl. and environ. health program, 1991-96; asst. prof. dept. occupl. safety and health Murray (Ky.) State U., 1996—; peer reviewer Ctr. for Indoor Air Rsch., 1995—. Contbr. articles to profl. jours. Recipient grad. student fellowship Am. Indsl. Hygiene Found., Fairfax, Va., 1992-96; rsch. grantee U.S. EPA, Washington, 1993-96, NIOSH, Morgantown, W.Va., 1993-95. Fellow Am. Acad. Indsl. Hygiene; mem. Am. Indsl. Hygiene Assn. (pres. elect. Ark. sect. 1993-94, pres. 1994-95), Am. Conf. Govt. Indsl. Hygienists, Am. Soc. Safety Engrs., Am. Soc. Toxicology (1st pl. award metals splty. sect. 1986). Republican. Avocations: racquetball, dog training, running, reading, microbrewing. Home: 411 N 10th St Murray KY 42071-1949 Office: Murray State U Dept Occupl Safety & Health PO Box 9 Murray KY 42071-0009

KELLER, RICHARD LORAN, physician; b. Omaha, Oct. 20, 1954; s. Judith Collins Mathews; m. Deborah Ann Thorson, Oct. 22, 1988; 1 child, Joy Elizabeth; m. Elizabeth Eager, June 17, 1997; 1 child, Hannah Loran. BA in Psychology, U. Nebr., Omaha, 1976, MD, 1980. Diplomate Am. Bd. Emergency Medicine. Staff physician emergency dept. Immanuel Med. Ctr., Omaha, 1982-88; staff physician Hosp. Emergency Physicians, Inc., Kansas City, Mo., 1988-89; staff physician, med. dir. occupl. medicine program No. Ill. Emergency Physicians, LLP, Waukegan, 1989-97; staff physician HIV Med. Mgmt. Clinic Lake County Health Dept., Waukegan, 1993—; staff physician Mercy Walworth Med. Clinic Urgent Care, Walworth, Wis., 1997-98, Provena St. Therese Employee Health Ctr., 1998—; assoc. faculty U. Nebr. Med. Coll., Omaha, 1982-88; med. dir., bd. dirs. HealthReach Clinic for Medically Underserviced, Waukegan, 1992—; bd. dirs., vice chmn. St. Therese Med. Ctr. Found., Waukegan, 1992-97; bd. dirs. St. Therese Physician Assn., 1994-97. Contbg. author: Physician's Book of Home Remedies, 1990, Total Health for Men, 1990; contbg. editor computer data base: Nat. Emergency Medicine Svcs. Physician Assn. Data Base, 1989-92; contbr. articles to profl. jours. Vol. Pub. Action to deliver Shelter, Lake County, Ill., 1989-92; task force participant Waukegan/Lake County Task Force on Street People, 1990, United Way Lake County Cmty. Needs Assessment, Waukegan, 1992, Lake County AIDS Housing Feasibility Study, Waukegan, 1995-97; affiliate faculty Basic Trauma Life Support Internat., 1995. Fellow Am. Coll. Emergency Physicians; mem. AMA, Ill. Coll. Emergency Physicians, Ill. Med. Soc., Lake County Med. Soc., Am. Coll. Occupl. and Environ. Medicine, Am. Pub. Health Assn., Ill. Pub. Health Assn., Internat. Assn. Physicians in AIDS Care. Lutheran. Avocations: reading, boating, fishing, golf. Office: Provena St Therese Employee Health Ctr 1005 Butterfield Rd Vernon Hills IL 60061-1360

KELLER, ROBERT BOUNDS, marketing professional, consultant, inventor; b. Corpus Christi, Tex., June 18, 1957; s. John Leeman (dec.), (stepfather) Berl Dennis Himes and Lell (Edge) K. Himes; m. Karen Lee Himes, Mar. 26, 1983; children: Crystal Lee, Ashley Brooke, Robert Kyle. BBA in Mktg., Tex. A&M U., 1985. Lic. ins. broker, Tex. Sales rep. General Mills, Inc., Corpus Christi, 1985-86, territory mgr., 1986-87; key acct. mgr. General Mills, Inc., San Antonio, 1987-88; regional sales asst. General Mills, Inc., Houston, 1988-89; tech. sales specialist Vanier Graphics Corp., Houston, 1989-90; mktg. and sales mgr. Dr. Pepper Co., Dallas, 1990-95; dir. mktg. Apollo Group, Inc., Phoenix, 1995-96; v.p. mktg. Winterland Prodns., San Francisco, 1997-98; v.p. mktg. and bus. devel. Latent Image Tech., Ltd., Jerusalem, 1998—. Mem. Am. Mktg. Assn., Promotion Mktg. Assn., Point-Of-Purchase Advt. Inst., Tex. A&M Alumni Assn., Tex. A&M 12th Man Found., Tex. A&M Lettermans Assn. Avocations: golf, Internet (web-surfing), travel, water sports, reading. Home: 11803 Moorcreek Dr Houston TX 77070-2417

KELLER, SHIRLEY INEZ, accountant; b. Ferguson, Iowa, Sept. 15, 1930; d. Adelbert Leslie and Inez Marie (Abbey) Hilsabeck; m. Earl Wilson Keller, Feb. 2, 1957 (dec. 1987); children: Earl William, Cynthia Marie, Eric Walter, Kenneth Paul. Student, U. Iowa, 1949-51; AS, Cameron U., 1971, BS, 1973; postgrad., Arapahoe Community Coll., 1986. High speed radio operator U.S. Army Signal Corps, N.Y.C., Japan, 1951-57; auditor U.S. Dept. Justice, Washington, 1973-76, U.S. Dept. Energy, Oklahoma City, 1976-83, U.S. Dept. Interior, Albuquerque, 1983-86; acct. U.S. Dept. Interior, Denver, 1986-95, ret., 1995; seminar instr. U.S. Dept. Interior, Denver, other cities, 1989-94. Author: Oil and Gas Payor Handbook, 1993. Scorekeeper Boy's Baseball, Lawton, Okla., 1964-72; den mother Boy Scouts Am., Lawton, 1965-66. Sgt. U.S. Army, 1951-57. Decorated Merit Unit Commendation, U.N. Commendation, Korean Svc. medal. Mem. Toastmasters Internat. (sec. Buffalo chpt. 1991, sgt.-at-arms Buffalo chpt. 1992, Competent Toastmaster 1993). Democrat. Roman Catholic. Avocations: family activities, gardening, water aerobics, physical fitness, making chocolate truffles. Home: PO Box 280535 Lakewood CO 80228-0535

KELLER, STANLEY, lawyer; b. N.Y.C., Aug. 16, 1938; s. Irving S. and Ceil (Silverstein) K.; m. Sandra Freshman, Dec. 25, 1960; children: Andrew J., Eric L., Matthew A. AB, Columbia U., 1959; LLB, Harvard U., 1962. Bar: Mass. 1962. Assoc. Palmer & Dodge LLP, Boston, 1962-68; ptnr. Palmer & Dodge, Boston, 1969—; lectr. Boston U. Law Sch., 1969-79; treas., trustee Mass. Continuing Legal Edn., Inc., Boston, 1985-91; panelist continuing legal edn. programs for profl. orgns. Chmn. legal sect. United Way of Boston, 1982. Fellow Am. Bar Found., Mass. Bar Found.; mem. ABA (vice chair, federal regulation of securities com.), Nat. Assn. Bond Lawyers (chmn. sec. law and disclosure com. 1989-91), Mass. Bar Assn. (chmn. bus. law sect. 1983-85), Boston Bar Assn. (chmn. corp. law com. 1988-89, chmn. bus. law sect. 1989-91, co-chair legal opinions com. 1992-95). Jewish. Office: Palmer & Dodge LLP 1 Beacon St Ste 2100 Boston MA 02108-3107

KELLER, SUSAN AGNES, insurance executive; b. Moline, Ill., July 12, 1952; d. Kenneth Francis and Ethel Louise (Odendahl) Hulsbrink. Grad. in pub. rels., Patricia Stevens Career Coll., 1971; grad. in gen. ins., Ins. Inst. Am., 1986. CPCU; lic. ins. and real estate agt. Comml. lines rater Bitiminous Casualty Corp., Rock Island, Ill., 1973-78; with Roadway Express, Inc., Rock Island, 1978-81; front line supr. Yellow Freight System, Inc., Denver, 1982-83; supr. plumbing and sheet metal prodn. Bell Plumbing and Heating, Denver, 1983-84; v.p. underwriting farm/ranch dept. Golden Eagle Ins. Co., San Diego, 1985-98; v.p. underwriting Michael E. James Ins. Agy., 1998—; cons. real estate foreclosure County Records Svc., San Diego, 1986-89; tchr. Ins. Inst. of Am., 1991. Vol. DAV, San Diego, 1985—; tchr. IEA and CPCU courses. Mem. Soc. CPCU (pres., bd. dirs.), Profl. Women in Ins., NAFE. Roman Catholic. Avocations: fishing, reading, boating. Home: 500 Anderson Rd Alpine CA 91901 Office: Pub Livery Ins Svc PO Box 1149 Alpine CA 91903-1149

KELLER, THEODORE G., JR., real estate manager; b. Toledo, Ohio, July 22, 1933; s. Theodore George and Edna Louise (Christen) K.; m. Carolyn Mary Lord, Aug. 25, 1956 (dec. May 1985); children: Bradford W., Matthew C., Theodore G. III, Lathrop L.; m. Gayla Claire Rampel, Sept. 20, 1986. BS, Miami U., Oxford, Ohio, 1955; MBA, U. Pa., 1959. Advt. mgr. Procter & Gamble, Cin., 1959-73; v.p. Eastern Airlines, Miami, Fla., 1973-76, Sara Lee Corp., Chgo., 1976-78; corp. officer, exec. v.p. Pet Inc., St. Louis, 1978-92; v.p., gen. mgr. Right Assocs., St. Louis, 1992-96; owner, mgr. 22 Cottage St., LLC, St. Louis, 1986—. Mem. bus. adv. coun. U. Ill.; mem. vestry, mem. vin. commn., chmn. every mem. canvass St. Peter's Episcopal Ch. Lt. USNR, 1951-59. Republican. Avocations: tennis, power boating, sailing. Home: 14 Glenview Rd Saint Louis MO 63124-1308

KELLER, THOMAS CLEMENTS, lawyer; b. New Orleans, Dec. 20, 1938; s. Charles Agustus and Mary (Chisolm) K. BA, Tulane U., 1960, JD, 1963; LLM, NYU, 1964. Bar: La. 1963. Assoc. Jones Walker Waechter Poitevent Carrere & Denegre, New Orleans, 1963-70, ptnr., 1970-98, of counsel, 1998—, exec. dir., 1998—; cons. Hunt Plywood Co., Inc., 1991—; sec. bd. dirs. McIlhenny Co. Bd. dirs. New Orleans Mus. Art, 1982—, pres., 1988-90; bd. dirs. Arts Found., New Orleans. Mem. ABA (sect. on taxation 1970—), La. Bar Assn. (chmn. tax sect. 1978), Metropolitan Club (Washington), Knickerbocker Club (N.Y.C.), Pickwick Club (New Orleans). Democrat. Roman Catholic. Office: Jones Walker Waechter Poitevent Carrere & Denegre 201 Saint Charles Ave Ste 5200 New Orleans LA 70170-5100

KELLER, WILLIAM D., federal judge; b. 1934. BS, U. Calif., Berkeley, 1956; LLB, UCLA, 1960. Asst. U.S. atty. U.S. Dist. Ct. (so. dist.) Calif., 1961-64; assoc. Dryden, Harrington, Horgan & Swartz, Calif., 1964-72; U.S. atty. U.S. Dist. Ct. (cen. dist.) Calif., Los Angeles, 1972-77; ptnr. Rosenfeld, Meyer & Susman, 1977-78; solo practice, 1978-81; ptnr. Mahm & Cazier, 1981-84; judge U.S. Dist. Ct. (cen. dist.) Calif., Los Angeles, 1984—; ptnr. Rosenfeld, Meyer & Susman, Calif., 1977-78; pvt. practice law Calif., 1978-81; ptnr. Hahn & Cazier, Calif., 1981-84. Office: US Dist Ct 312 N Spring St Ste 1653 Los Angeles CA 90012-4718

KELLER, WILLIAM FRANCIS, publishing consultant; b. Meyersdale, Pa., May 22, 1922; s. Lloyd Francis and Dorothy Marie (Shultz) K.; m. Frances Jane Core, Mar. 31, 1944. A.A., Potomac State Coll. of W.Va. U., 1941; B.S., U. Md., 1943, M.S., 1945. Ednl. rep. Blakiston Co., 1945-51, asso. editor, 1951-54; editor coll. div. McGraw Hill Book Co., N.Y.C., 1954-56; editor-in-chief McGraw Hill Book Co. (Blakiston div.), 1956-65, gen. mgr. div., 1965-68; pres. Year Book Med. Publs., Chgo., 1968-81; chmn. bd. Year Book Med. Publs., 1968-82; pub. cons. Crystal Lake, Ill., 1982-95; adminstrv. sec. Am. Med. Pubs. Assn., 1985-91. Served with U.S. Army, 1945-46. Office: 7916 W Hillside Rd Crystal Lake IL 60012-2939

KELLERMAN, FAYE MARDER, novelist, dentist; b. St. Louis, July 31, 1952; d. Oscar and Anne (Steinberg) Marder; m. Jonathan Seth Kellerman, July 23, 1972; children: Jesse Oren, Rachel Diana, Ilana Judith, Aliza Celeste. AB in Math., UCLA, 1974, DDS, 1978. Author: The Ritual Bath, 1986 (Macavity award best 1st novel 1986), Sacred and Profane, 1987, The Quality of Mercy, 1989, Milk and Honey, 1990, Day of Atonement, 1991, False Prophet, 1992, Grievous Sin, 1993, Sanctuary, 1994, Justice, 1995, Prayers for the Dead, 1996, Serpent's Tooth, 1997, Moon Music, 1998, Jupiter's Bone, 1999; contbr. short stories to Sisters in Crime vols. 1 and 3, Ellery Queen Mag., A Woman's Eye, Women of Mystery, the year's 2d finest crime: mystery stories, The Year's 25 Finest Mystery and Crime Stories, A Modern Treasury of Great Detective and Murder Mysteries, Mothers, Murder for Love, Mothers and Daughters. UCLA rsch. fellow, 1978. Mem. Mystery Writers of Am. (So. Calif. bd. dirs.), Womens' Israeli Polit. Action Com., Sisters in Crime. Jewish. Avocations: fencing, gardening, music.

KELLERMAN, JONATHAN SETH, pediatric psychologist, writer; b. N.Y.C., Aug. 9, 1949; s. David Kellerman and Sylvia Fiacre; m. Faye Marilyn Marder, July 23, 1972; children: Jesse, Rachel, Ilana, Aliza. BA in Psychology, UCLA, 1972; MA in Psychology, U. So. Calif., 1973, PhD in Clin. Psychology, 1974. Lic. psychologist, Calif. Intern in psychology Children's Hosp. of Los Angeles, 1973-74, postdoctoral fellow, 1974-75; postdoctoral fellow U. Southern Calif. Sch. Medicine, Los Angeles, 1974-75, staff psychologist, 1975-78, asst. clin. prof. pediatrics, 1978—, clin. assoc. prof. pediatrics, 1979-98; clin. prof. pediats., psychology U. Southern Calif. Sch. Medicine, 1998—; founding dir. Psychosocial Program Children's Hosp., Los Angeles, 1977-81. Author: Psychological Aspects of Childhood Cancer, 1980, Helping the Fearful Child, 1981, When the Bough Breaks, 1985, Blood Test, 1986, Over the Edge, 1987, The Butcher's Theater, 1988, Silent Partner, 1989, Time Bomb, 1990, Private Eyes, 1992, Devil's Waltz, 1993, Bad Love, 1994, Daddy, Daddy Can You Touch the Sky?, 1994, Self-Defense, 1995, Jonathan Kellerman's ABC of Weird Creatures, 1995, The Web, 1996, The Clinic, 1997, Survival of the Fittest, 1997, Billy Straight, 1998, Savage Spawn, 1999, Monster, 1999. Recipient Samuel Goldwyn Creative Writing award UCLA, 1972, Anthony Boucher award Bouchercon, 1986, Disting. Alumnus award dept. psychology UCLA, 1997. Mem. Am. Psychol. Assn. (Media award 1994, Presdl. award 1998), Mystery Writers of Am. (Edgar Allan Poe award 1985), Author's Guild, Internat. Assn. Crime Writers. Jewish. Avocations: painting, guitar playing and collecting, book collecting, art collecting.

KELLERMAN, SALLY CLAIRE, actress; b. Long Beach, Calif., June 2, 1937; d. John Helm and Edith Baine (Vaughn) K.; m. Richard Edelstein, Dec. 19, 1970; 4 step-daughters; m. Jonathan Krane, 1980. Student, Los Angeles City Coll., Actor's Studio, N.Y.C. Stage appearances include Singular Man, N.Y.C., Breakfast at Tiffany's; films include Reform School Girl, 1959, The Third Day, 1965, The Boston Strangler, 1968, The April Fools, 1969, M*A*S*H, 1970 (Acad. award nominee 1970, Golden Globe award 1970), Brewster McCloud, 1970, Last of the Red-Hot Lovers, 1972, Slither, 1973, Reflection of Fear, 1973, Lost Horizon, 1973, Rafferty and the Gold Dust Twins, 1975, The Big Bus, 1976, Welcome to L.A., 1977, The Mouse and His Child, 1977 (voice), Magee and the Lady, 1978, It Rained All Night The Day I Left, 1978, A Little Romance, 1979, Foxes, 1980, Loving Couples, 1980, Serial, 1980, Head On, 1980, September Gun, 1983, Moving Violations, 1985, Lethal, 1985, Back to School, 1986, That's Life, 1986, Meatballs III, 1987, Three for the Road, 1987, Someone to Love, 1987, Paramedics (voice), 1988, You Can't Hurry Love, 1988, All's Fair, 1989, Limit Up, 1989, The Secret of the Ice Cave, 1990, Happily Ever After, 1990 (voice), The Player, 1992, Younger and Younger, 1993, Mirror, Mirror 2: Raven Dance, 1994, Ready to Wear (Prêt-à-Porter), 1994, It's my Party, 1995, She's So Lovely, 1997, The Maze, 1997, The Lay of the Land, 1997, Live Virgin, 1998, Bar Hopping, 1999; also TV roles Chrysler Theatre, Mannix, It Takes a Thief, Columbo: Ashes to Ashes; TV films Verna: USO Girl, 1978, For Lovers Only, 1982, Dempsey, 1983, Secret Weapons, 1985, Elena, 1985, Boris and Natasha, 1992; miniseries Centennial, 1978-79. Recipient nominations Acad. and Golden Globe awards for MASH. Mem. Actor's Equity, AFTRA. Office: Innovative Artists 1999 Ave Of Stars Ste 2850 Los Angeles CA 90067-4612 also: 7944 Woodro Wilson Dr Los Angeles CA 90046*

KELLERMANN, KENNETH IRWIN, astrophysicist; b. N.Y.C., July 1, 1937; s. Alexander Samuel and Rae (Goodstein) K.; m. Michele Kellermann; 1 child, Sarah. SB, MIT, 1959; PhD, Calif. Inst. Tech., 1963. Rsch. scientist CSIRO, Sydney, Australia, 1963-65; asst. scientist Nat. Radio Astronomy Obs., Green Bank, W.Va., 1965-67, assoc. scientist, 1967-69, scientist, 1978; asst. dir. Max Plank Inst. for Radio Astronomy, Bonn, Fed. Republic of Germany, 1978, dir., 1978-79, outside sci. mem., 1980-96; sr. scientist Nat. Radio Astronomy Obs., Charlottesville, W.Va., 1980—, chief scientist, 1996—; adj. prof. U. Ariz, Tucson, 1970-72; rsch. prof. U. Va., Charlottesville, 1985—. NSF fellow, Washington, 1965-66; recipient Rumford prize Am. Acad. Arts Scis., 1970, Warner prize Am. Astron. Soc., 1971, Gould prize NAS, 1973. Mem. NAS (chair astronomy sect. 1995-98, councilor 1999), Am. Philos. Soc., Internat. Astron. Union (pres. com. 40 1982-85, pres. U.S. nat. com. 1990-92, Am. Astron. Soc., Internat. Radio Sci. Union, Am. Acad. Arts and Scis, Russian Astron. Soc., Australian Astron. Soc., Russian Acad. Scis. Avocation: amateur radio. Office: Nat Radio Astron Obs Edgemont Rd Charlottesville VA 22903

KELLERMEYER, ROBERT WILLIAM, physician, educator; b. Wheeling, W.Va., Sept. 4, 1929; s. William F. and Mabel I. (Keller) M.; m. Audrey L. Shanaberger, June 12, 1954; children: Suzanne, Scott, Mark. BA, Washington and Jefferson Coll., 1951; MD, Western Res. U., 1955. Diplomate Am. Bd. Internal Medicine, Am. Bd. Hematology, Am. Bd. Med. Oncology. Intern dept. medicine Univ. Hosps. Cleve., 1955-56, asst. resident, 1956-57, chief resident, 1962-63, co-dir. div. hematology and oncology, 1974-83; sr. instr. dept. medicine Univ. Hosps.-Case Western Res. U., 1963-66, asst. prof. medicine, 1965-68, assoc. prof., 1969-75, prof., 1975-96, emeritus prof., 1996—; David and Inez Myers prof. hematology Case Western Res. U., 1978-96; med. dir. cancer program Aultman Hosp., Canton, Ohio, 1993; prof. medicine N.E. Ohio Univs. Coll. Medicine, 1994—. Author: The Red Cell, 1970. With USPHS, 1957-59. Recipient Career Devel. award USPHS, 1966, Am. Cancer Soc. postdoctoral fellow, 1959-62; John and Mary R. Markle scholar, 1965. Mem. Am. Soc. Hematology, Cen. SOc. Clin. Rsch., Am. Fedn. Clin. Rsch., Am. Assn. Cancer Edn., Ea. Coop. Oncology Group, Am. Soc. Clin. Oncology. Office: Aultman Hosp 2600 6th St SW Canton OH 44710-1702

KELLETT, JOHN M., museum director; b. Albuquerque, July 13, 1963. Grad., Oberlin Coll.; student, Shippensburg U. With Calif. Maritime Heritage Soc., Sea Edn. Assn.; dir. Balt. Maritime Mus. Living Classrooms Found., Balt., 1990—. Co-founder Nat. Hist. Seaport of Balt. Office: Balt. Maritime Mus Pier 3 Pratt St Baltimore MD 21202*

KELLEY, A. BENJAMIN, author, consultant; b. N.Y.C., May 15, 1936; s. Hubert Williams and Anna Alberta (Davis) K.; children: Sumako Chongyol, Hubert Chongsu. Student, Def. Lang. Inst., 1955, Naganuma Inst., Tokyo, 1957-58, Sophia U., Tokyo, 1957, Harvard U. Bus. Sch., 1972. News editor Shipping and Trade News, Japan, 1957-60; Washington transp. corr. N.Y. Jour. Commerce, 1960-63; policy adviser ICC, 1963-65; mgr. transp. and communications dept. U.S. C. of C., 1966-67; dir. pub. affairs Fed. Hwy. Adminstrn., 1967-69; sr. v.p. Ins. Inst. Hwy. Safety, Washington, 1969-85; pres. A.B. Kelley Corp., Crofton, Md., 1985-96, Inst. for Injury Reduction, Crofton, 1988-95; pvt. auto safety cons., 1996—; guest lectr. Johns Hopkins Sch. Pub. Hygiene and Pub. Health, 1974-95, U. So. Calif., 1974, U. Fla., 1972, UCLA, 1970, U. Calif., Davis, 1977; bd. dirs. Center Auto Safety, 1975—, Com. on Non-Theatrical Events, 1984—. Author: The Pavers and The Paved, 1971; author-narrator: Boobytrap!, 1971, Cars That Crash and Burn, 1973, Crashes That Need Not Kill, 1976, Faces in Crashes, 1984; also articles. Served with AUS, 1954-57. Recipient Golden Eagle award Council Internat. Nontheatrical Events, 1971, 73, 76, 1st prize Zagreb (Yugoslavia) Film Festival, 1973, 75, Bronze Venus Medallion Virgin Islands Internat. Film Festival, 1976. Mem. Internat. Transp. Research Forum (past dir.), Nat. Safety Coun. (past dirs.), Am. Assn. Automotive Medicine, Soc. Automotive Engrs., Ctr. for Auto Safety (bd. dirs.).

KELLEY, ALBERT JOSEPH, global management strategy consultant; b. Boston, July 27, 1924; s. Albert Joseph and Josephine Christine (Sullivan) K.; m. Virginia Marie Riley, June 7, 1945 (dec. Aug. 1988); children: Mark, Shaun, David. BS, U.S. Naval Acad., 1945; BSEE, MIT, 1948, ScD, 1956; postgrad., U. Minn., 1954, Carnegie-Mellon U., 1974. Commd. ensign USN, 1945, advanced through grades to comdr., 1961; carrier pilot USN, Korea, 1950-51; exptl. test pilot Naval Air Test Ctr. USN, 1951-53, program engr. F-4 aircraft Bur. Aeros., 1956-58, program mgr. Eagle missile program Bur. Weapons, 1958-60; mgr. Agena program NASA, 1960-61, dir. electronics and control advanced rsch. and technology, 1961-64, dep. dir. Electronics Research Ctr., 1964-67; dean sch. mgmt. Boston Coll., 1967-77; pres. Arthur D. Little Program Systems Mgmt. Co., Cambridge, Mass., 1977-85, chmn., 1985-88; sr. group v.p. Arthur D. Little Inc., Cambridge, Mass., 1985-88; sr. v.p. strategic planning United Tech. Corp., Hartford, Conn., 1988-90; dep. undersec. of def. internat. programs U.S. Dept. Def., Pentagon, Washington, 1990-93; fellow Kennedy Sch. Harvard U., Cambridge, Mass., 1993-94; rsch. group leader MIT, Cambridge, 1994-96, rsch. affiliate, 1994—; chmn. Bd. Econ. Advisors, Commonwealth of Mass., 1970-74; chmn. bd. dirs. Arthur D. Little Valuation Inc., 1985-86; corp. mem. C.S. Draper Lab. Corp., Cambridge, 1975-90; cons. The White House; mem. NRC Space Applications Bd., 1976-82. Author: Venture Capital, 1977, New Dimensions of Project Management, 1982; contbr. articles to profl. jours. Trustee Milton (Mass.) Acad., 1975-83; bd. dirs. Mass. Bus. Devel. Corp., Boston, 1969-78, Am. Assembly Collegiate Schs. Bus., 1970-76, State Street Co., State Street Bank and Trust, 1975-93, Mass. Tech. Devel. Corp., Boston, 1979-82, other mfg. cos. Recipient exceptional svc. medal NASA, 1967, outstanding svc. medal U.S. Sec. Def., 1993. Fellow IEEE, AIAA (assoc.); mem. Internat. Acad. Astronautics, Armed Forces Comms. and Electronics Assn. (v.p. 1962-65), Algonquin Club, Army Navy Country Club, Milton-Hoosic Club, Sigma Xi, Tau Beta Pi, Eta Kappa Nu, Sigma Gamma Tau. Avocations: golf, hiking, travel. Home: 522 Ocean St PO Box 2519 Ocean Bluff MA 02065-2519 Office: MIT Dept Aero & Astro 77 Mass Ave Rm 41-205 Cambridge MA 02139-4307 also: 1401 Park Garden Ln Reston VA 20194-0199

KELLEY, ALLEN CHARLES, economist, educator; b. Everett, Wash., Sept. 5, 1937; s. Charles Edward and Velma L. (Allen) K.; m. Patty Ann Cochran, June 20, 1959; children: Brian Allen, Mark Andrew, Michael Charles. Student, Linfield Coll., 1955-57; A.B., Stanford U., 1959, Ph.D., 1964. Vis. research fellow Australian Nat. U., 1962-63; cons. Rand Corp., 1962-67; acting asst. prof. Stanford U., 1963-64; faculty U. Wis., Madison, 1964-72; prof. U. Wis., 1970-72; prof. econs. Duke U., Durham, N.C., 1972-81, James B. Duke prof., 1981—; chmn. dept. Duke U., 1973-80; asso. dir. Center for Demographic Studies, 1973—; vis. prof. Monash U., Melbourne, Australia, 1970-71; Esmee Fairbairn research prof. Herriot Watt U., Edinburgh, Scotland, 1978; research scholar Internat. Inst. Applied Systems Analysis, Laxenburg, Austria, 1979. Author: (with J.G. Williamson and R.J. Cheetham) Dualistic Economic Development, 1972, (with B.A. Weisbrod et al.) Disease and Economic Development, (with J.G. Williamson) Lessons from Japanese Development - An Analytical Economic History, 1974, The Professor's Guide to TIPS, 1975, (with R.M. Schmidt) The User's Guide to TIPS, 1975, TIPS Program Manual, 1976, (with J.G. Williamson) Modeling Urbanization and Economic Growth, 1980, (with A. Khalifa and M.E. El-Khorazaty) Population and Development in Rural Egypt, 1982; mem. editorial bd. Jour. Econ. Edn, 1973—; Contbr. articles, revs. to profl. jours. Scholar, fellow Weyerhaeuser Co., 1955-59; Scholar, fellow Ford Found., 1961-62; Scholar, fellow Earhart Found., 1959-61; Scholar, fellow Social Sci. Research Council, 1962-63; Richard I. Downing fellow econs. U. Melbourne, 1987-88; grantee Carnegie Found., 1964-65; grantee Exxon Edn. Found., 1965-67, 68-70, 71-74; grantee Ford Found., 1973-79; grantee Nat. Inst. Edn., 1974-75; grantee NSF, 1966-68; grantee Rockefeller Found., 1967-69; grantee Sloan Found., 1969-73, 79—; co-recipient Arthur Cole prize Econ. History Assn., 1972. Mem. Am. Econ. Assn. (chmn. com. econ. edn. 1978—), So. Econ. Assn. (v.p. 1981-82), Internat. Union for Sci. Study Population, Population Assn. Am., Joint Council on Econ. Edn. (trustee 1978—, exec. com. 1978—), Phi Beta Kappa. Home: 4607 Chicopee Trl Durham NC 27707-5208 Office: Duke U Econs Dept Durham NC 27706

KELLEY, ALOYSIUS PAUL, university administrator, priest; b. Carlisle, Pa., Oct. 4, 1929; s. Aloysius Paul and Teresa (Barron) K. AB, St. Louis U., 1955, MA, 1956, PhL, 1956; STL, U. Innsbruck, Austria, 1963; PhD, U. Pa., 1968; LLD (hon.), Sacred Heart U., 1985. Joined S.J., 1949; ordained priest Roman Catholic Ch., 1962; chmn. dept. classics Georgetown U., 1969-71, asst. acad. v.p., 1971-72, acting acad. v.p., 1972-74, exec. v.p. for acad. affairs and provost, 1974-79; pres. Fairfield (Conn.) U., 1979—. Trustee Georgetown Prep. Sch., 1969-72, Loyola Coll., Balt., 1971-75, Scranton U., 1974-80, Bridgeport Area C. of C., 1979-82, St. Joseph's U., Phila., 1980-86, Georgetown U., 1982-88, 89-95, Conn. Grand Opera, 1980-82, John Carroll U., 1987-93, LeMoyne Coll., 1993-99, The Gesu Sch., 1993-97, St. Joseph's Prep. Sch., 1997—, St. Peter's Coll., 1998—, Nat. Assn. Ind. Colls. and Univs., 1997—; mem. D.C. Commn. Postsecondary Edn., 1974-79; vice chmn. Conn. Conf. Ind. Colls., 1980-81, chmn., 1981-83; pres. New Eng. Colls. Fund, 1993-95. Fulbright-Hayes fellow, 1971. Mem. Am. Philol. Assn., Am. Assn. Univ. Adminstrs., Am. Assn. Higher Edn., Patterson Club, Newcomen Soc. Democrat. Home and Office: Fairfield U Office of the Pres 1073 N Benson Rd Fairfield CT 06430-5195

KELLEY, BETTY MARIE, office manager; b. Oil City, Pa., Feb. 23, 1955; d. Robert Charles Miles and Ethel Eleanor (Kelley) Miles. Diploma personal computer specialist, Tri-State Bus. Inst. lectr. Cambridge Grange, 1990—. Owner Betty's Restaurant, Cambridge Springs, Pa., 1980-98; office mgr. Presque Isle Sports Ltd., Erie, Pa.; lectr. Cambridge Grange, 1990—. Mem. Cambridge Pride: Coming Alive, 1992-93; chair Cambridge Springs Cmty. Picnic, 1992—; mem. Cambridge Springs Discover Days Com., 1994—, co-chair baby photo contest, cookie contest; mem. Prison Runathon com. State Correctional Inst., Cambridge Springs, 1993—, others; assoc. mem. Cambridge Area Vol. Ambulance Svc. Mem. Nat. Trust for Historic Preservation, U.S. C. of C., Cambridge Grange (chaplain 1987-90, lectr. 1990—). Republican. Baptist. Avocations: cooking, knitting, reading, embroidery. Office: PO Box 377 Waterford PA 16441-0377

KELLEY, BRUCE DUTTON, pharmacist; b. Hartford, Conn., Jan. 4, 1957; s. Roger Weston and Elizabeth Morrill (Atwood) K.; m. DawnReneé Cinocco, Jan. 19, 1990. Student, U. Hartford, 1975-77; BS in Pharmacy, U. Colo., 1985; diplomas in Russian, Moscow U., Moscow, 1993, 95; BA in Russian, U. Colo., 1995. RPh, Colo. Pharmacist King Soopers, Inc., Boulder, Colo., 1990—; asst. tour leader in Russia U. Tex., El Paso, 1991; Russia asst. guide, U. Ariz., Tucson, 1992 (summer). Vol. Warderburg Student Health Ctr., U. Colo., Boulder, 1981-83, Am. Diabetes Assn. Mem. Elks, Nat. Eagle Scout Assn., Am. Legion. Republican. Avocation: hiking. Home: 6152 Willow Ln Boulder CO 80301-5356 Office: King Soopers Inc 6550 Lookout Rd Boulder CO 80301-3303

KELLEY, BRUCE GUNN, insurance company executive, lawyer; b. Phila., Mar. 17, 1954; s. Robb Beardsley and Winifred Elizabeth (Murray) K.; m. Susan Aldrich Barnes, Oct. 1, 1983; children: Dashle Gunn, Barnes Gunn, Onnalee Kinkaid. AB, Dartmouth Coll., 1976; JD, U. Iowa, 1979. Bar: Iowa 1979; CPCU; CLU. Assoc. Bradshaw, Fowler, Proctor & Fairgrave, Des Moines, 1979-84, ptnr., 1984-85; gen. counsel Employers Mut. Casualty Co., Des Moines, 1985-89, exec. v.p., 1989-91, pres., 1991—, also bd. dirs.; bd. dirs. Alliance Am. Insurers; mem. adv. bd. Iowa Pub. Employees Retirement Sys. Trustee Nat. Com. on Drunk Drivers; pres. Mid-Iowa coun. Boy Scouts Am.; bd. dirs. Salisbury House Found., Greater Des Moines Sports Authority, Des Moines Arts Ctr. Mem. Iowa Bar Assn., Des Moines Club, Rotary, Masons. Republican. Mem. United Church of Christ. Home: 14 Glenview Dr Des Moines IA 50312-2546 Office: EMC Ins Cos PO Box 712 Des Moines IA 50303-0712

KELLEY, DAVID CHRISTOPHER, philosopher; b. Lakewood, Ohio, June 23, 1949; s. Walter Carl and Patricia Hale (von Schmidt) K.; m. Susan McCloskey, Mar 25. 1982. BA, Brown U., 1971, MA, 1971; PhD, Princeton U., 1975. Asst. prof. philosophy Vassar Coll., Poughkeepsie, N.Y., 1975-84; freelance writer, lectr., 1984-89; exec. dir. Inst. for Objectivist Studies, Poughkeepsie, 1990—; vis. lectr. in philosophy Brandeis U., Waltham, Mass., 1989-90. Author: The Evidence of the Senses, 1986, The Art of Reasoning, 1990, Unrugged Individualism, 1996, A Life of One's Own, 1998; co-author: Laissez Parler, 1985. Mem. Am. Philos. Assn. Office: Inst Objectivist Studies 82 Washington St Ste 207 Poughkeepsie NY 12601-2305

KELLEY, DAVID E., producer, writer; b. 1956; m. Michelle Pfeiffer, 1993; children: Claudia Rose, John Henry. BA, Princeton U.; JD, Boston U. Writer (film) From the Hip, 1987; writer, prodr. (film) To Gillian on Her 37th Birthday, 1996; writer, prodr. (film) Lake Placid, 1999, Mystery, Alaska, 1999; writer, story editor, exec. story editor, supervising prodr., exec. prodr. L.A. Law (Emmy award for Outstanding Drama Series 1989, 90, Emmy award for outstanding writing in a dram series 1990); writer, exec. prodr. Picket Fences (Emmy award for outstanding drama series 1993, 94); exec. prodr. Chicago Hope, 1994—, The Practice, 1997— (Golden Globe winner), Ally McBeal, 1997— (Golden Globe winner, Emmy award), Snoops, 1999—. Office: David E Kelly Prodns care 20th Century Fox 10201 W Pico Blvd Bldg 80 Los Angeles CA 90035-2651*

KELLEY, DAVID J., military officer. BS, U.S. Mil. Acad.; MS in Indsl. Engring., U. Mich., MS in Computer Info. & Control Engring.; grad., U.S. Naval War Coll., U.S. Army War Coll. Commd. 2d lt. U.S. Army, 1966, advanced through grades to lt. gen., 1997; ops. officer, chief computer divsn. Office Dep. Chief of Staff for Instrumentation, Ft. Ord, Calif., 1973-77; comdr. 13th Signal Bn. 1st Cavalry Divsn., Ft. Hood, Tex., 1981-84; dir. combat devels. U.S. Army Signal Sch., Ft. Gordon, Ga., 1985-86; comdr. 93d Signal Brigade VII Corps, U.S. Army Europe, Germany, 1986-88; dep. comdg. gen. U.S. Army Signal Ctr. and Ft. Gordon, Ga., 1990-91; dir. sys. mgmt. Office of Sec. of Army, Washington, 1991-93; dep. dir. for def.-wide command, control, comms. & computers J-6, The Joint Staff, Washington, 1993-95; vice dir. Def. Info. Sys. Agy., Arlington, 1995-97. Office: Def Info Sys Agy 701 S Courthouse Rd Arlington VA 22204-2199

KELLEY, DELORES GOODWIN, state legislator; b. Norfolk, Va., May 1, 1936; d. Stephen Cornelius and Helen Elizabeth (Jefferson) Goodwin; m. Russell Victor Kelley, Jr., Dec. 26, 1956; children: Norma Kelley Johnson, Russell III, Brian. BA, Va. State Coll., 1956; MA, NYU, 1958, Purdue U., 1972; PhD, U. Md., 1977. Dir. religious edn. N.Y.C. Protestant Coun., Bronx, 1959-60; tchr. N.Y.C. Pub. Schs., Bklyn., 1962-64, Ctrl. Sch. Dist., Plainview, N.Y., 1965-66; asst. prof. Morgan State U., Balt., 1966-70; prof. speech comms. and English Coppin State Coll., Balt., 1973—; legislator Md. Ho. of Dels., Annapolis, 1991-94, state senator, 1995-98; former chmn. Joint Com. on Fed. Rels./Md. State Senate; vice-chmn. exec. nomination com. Md. State Senate, 1998—; mem. joint com. legis. policy, joint com. legis. ethics.; panelist, reviewer NEH, Washington, 1978-82, Nat. Inst. Justice, 1998—; mem. editorial bd. Md. English Jour., Salisbury, 1980-88; dean Coppin State Coll., Balt., 1979-82; fellow Am. Coun. on Edn., Washington, 1982-83; vice chair bd. dirs. Harbor Bank Md., 1982—; mem. fin. com. Md. State Senate, legis. com., women legislators of Md., 1st v.p., 1995-96, vice chair sen. com. exec. nomination; mem. Gov.'s Commn. on Adoption, 1995, Atty. Gen.'s and Lt. Gov.'s task force on family violence, 1996—, Md. Commn. on Criminal Sentencing Policy, 1996—. Editor (monograph) Concepts of Race, 1981; moderator (TV series) Teaching Writing: Process Approach, 1982. Sec. Md. Dem. Party, Annapolis, 1986-90; bd. dirs. Balt. Urban League, 1986-89; pres. Black Jewish Forum, Balt., 1990-92; commr. Md. Commn. on Values, Annapolis, 1980-85; bd. dirs. Balt. Mental Health Systems, 1991-95; host Internat. Visitors Ctr., 1976—; commn. mem. Md. Commn. Hereditary and Congenital Disorders, Balt., 1992-95; del. White House conf. on Aging, 1995; mem. Md. Medicaid Adv. Com., 1998—. Fellow Purdue U., 1970-72; grantee Md. Com. for Humanities, Balt., 1977-78, NEH, Washington, 1988-89; recipient Racial Justice award YWCA of Met. Balt., 1995; named to Md. Top 100 Women, Warfields Bus. Record, 1995. Mem. Nat. Inst. Justice (panelist, rev. 1997). Inst. for Govtl. Svcs. (bd. dirs. 1993-94), Nat. Polit. Congress Black Women (bd. dirs., Balt. chair 1993-95); Women Legislators Md. (pres. 1998-99), 10th Dist. Dem. Club Md. (founder, pres. 1995—). Baptist. Avocations: travel, public speaking, reading. Office: 315 Senate Office Bldg Annapolis MD 21401 also: 3100 Timanus Ln Ste 101 Baltimore MD 21244

KELLEY, DONALD REED, historian; b. Elgin, Ill., Feb. 17, 1931; s. Walter Louis and Helen Lenore (Davis) K.; m. Bonnie Gene Smith, June 30, 1979; 1 son, John Reed. B.A., Harvard Coll., 1953; M.A., Columbia U., 1956, Ph.D., 1962; postgrad., U. Paris, 1958-59. Instr. Queens Coll., 1960-63; asst. prof. So. Ill. U., 1963-65; asst. prof. SUNY, 1965-68, assoc. prof., 1968-70, prof., 1970-72; vis. prof. Harvard U., 1972-73; prof. U. Rochester, N.Y., 1973—; Marie Curran Wilson and Joseph Chamberlain Wilson prof. history U. Rochester, 1984-91; James Westfall Thompson prof. Rutgers U., New Brunswick, N.J., 1991—. Author: Foundations of Modern Historical Scholarship, 1970, François Hotman, 1973, The Beginning of Ideology, 1981, Historians and the Law in Postrevolutionary France, 1984, History, Law, and the Human Sciences, 1984, The Human Measure, 1990, The Writing of History and the Study of Law, 1997, The Faces of History, 1998; editor: The Monarchy of France (Claude de Seyssel), 1981, History of Ideas, 1990, Versions of History, 1991, The Shapes of Knowledge, 1991, What is Property? (P.-J. Proudhon), 1994, History and the Disciplines, 1997; exec. editor Jour. History of Ideas, 1985—. Served with U.S. Army, 1953-55. Fulbright fellow, 1958-59, Newberry libr. fellow, 1965, Am. Coun. Learned Socs. fellow, 1967-68, Folger Libr. fellow, 1970, 85; mem. Inst. for Advanced Study, 1969-70, 77-78, 96-97; Guggenheim fellow, 1974-75, 81-82, NEH fellow, 1977-78, Nat. Humanities Ctr. fellow, 1984, Shelby Cullom Davis Ctr. fellow, Princeton U., 1987-88, Wilson Ctr. fellow, 1992-93. Fellow Am. Acad. Arts and Scis.; mem. Am. Philos. Soc., Am. Hist. Assn., Renaissance Soc. Am., Medieval Acad. Home: 45 Jefferson Ave New Brunswick NJ 08901-1737 Office: Rutgers U Dept History New Brunswick NJ 08901

KELLEY, EDWARD WATSON, JR., federal agency administrator; b. Eugene, Oreg., Jan. 27, 1932; s. Edward Watson and Allie (Autry) K.; children: Kinsloe K. Queen, James M., Michael; m. Janet H. Kelley. BA, Rice U., 1954; MBA, Harvard U., 1959. Pres., chief exec. officer Kelley Industries, Inc., Houston, 1959-81; chmn. bd. Investment Advisors, Inc., Houston, 1981-87; gov. FRS, Washington, 1987—. Lt. (j.g.) USNR, 1954-56. Mem. Houston Country Club (bd. dirs. 1984-87), Bayou Club. Methodist. Office: FRS Office of Chmn 20th & C Sts NW Washington DC 20551

KELLEY, EUGENE JOHN, business educator; b. N.Y.C., July 8, 1922; s. Eugene Lawrence and Agnes Regina (Meskill) K.; m. Dorothy W. Kane, Aug. 3, 1946; 1 child, Sharon A.; m. Linda S. Phillips, Sept. 30, 1992. B.S., U. Conn., 1945; M.B.A., Boston U., 1949, M.Ed., 1948; Ph.D., N.Y. U., 1955. Instr. mktg. Babson Inst., 1947-49; dir. div. bus. adminstrn. Clark U., 1949-56, asst. prof., 1949-54, assoc. prof., 1954-56; vis. lectr. Harvard U. Bus. Sch., 1956-57; asst. prof. Mich. State U., East Lansing, 1957-58, assoc. prof., 1958-59; prof. mktg., asst. dean Grad. Sch. Bus. Adminstrn. NYU, N.Y.C., 1959-60, prof., assoc. dean, 1960-64; research prof. bus. adminstrn. Coll. Bus. Adminstrn. Pa. State U., 1963-88, dean, 1973-88; Disting. prof. mktg. Fla. Atlantic U., Boca Raton, 1989—, dir. for Svcs. Mktg. and Mgmt., Coll. Bus., 1990—; regional dir. Mellon Bank Central; mem. nat. adv. Council SBA; mem. Commn. on Edn. for Bus. Professions of Nat. Assn. State Univs. and Land Grant Colls.; cons. GAO, N.J. Bd. Higher Edn. Author: Marketing Planning and Competitive Strategy, 1972, Managerial Marketing: Policies, Strategies and Decisions, 1973, Social Marketing: Perspectives and Viewpoints, 1973; Editor: Jour. Mktg, 1967-73. Served with USAAF, 1942-43. Mem. Am. Mktg. Assn. (pres. 1982-83, dir., mem. disting. mktg. educator com.), Acad. Mgmt., Am. Assembly Collegiate Schs. of Bus. Home: 2020 NW Royal Fern Ct Palm City FL 34990-8025 Office: Fla Atlantic U 500 NW 20th St Boca Raton FL 33431-6415

KELLEY, FRANK NICHOLAS, dean; b. Akron, Ohio, Jan. 19, 1935; s. John William Kelley and Rose (Hadinger) Bates; m. Judith Carol Lowe, Jan. 1, 1960; children: Katherine Rose Bruno, Frank Michael, Christopher Patrick. BS, U. Akron, 1958, MS, 1959, PhD, 1961. Br. chief propellant devel. Air Force Rocket Propulsion Lab., Edwards AFB, Calif., 1965-69, chief of plans, 1969-70, chief scientist, 1970-73; chief scientist Air Force Materials Lab., Wright-Patterson AFB, Ohio, 1973-77, dir., 1977-78; dir. Inst. Polymer Sci. U. Akron, 1978-88, dean Coll. Polymer Sci. and Engring., 1988—; bd. dirs. Premix, Inc., North Kingsville, Ohio; cons. USAF, Thiokol Corp., others. Editor: Polymers in Space Research, 1965; contbr. articles to profl. jours. Lt. USAF, 1961-64; capt. USAF Res., 1964. Named Outstanding Alumnus, Tau Kappa Epsilon, 1991. Mem. Am. Chem. Soc. Mem. Disciples of Christ Ch. Avocation: woodworking. Office: U Akron Coll Polymer Sci and Polymer Engring Akron OH 44325-3909*

KELLEY, HAROLD HARDING, psychology educator; b. Boise, Idaho, Feb. 16, 1921; s. Harry H. and Maude M. Kelley; m. Dorothy J. Drumm, Jan. 4, 1942; children: Ann R., Harold S., Laura Megan. AB, U. Calif., Berkeley, 1942, MA, 1943; PhD, MIT, 1948. Study dir. in group dynamics U. Mich., Ann Arbor, 1948-50; asst. prof. psychology Yale U., New Haven, 1950-55; asso. prof., then prof. U. Minn., Mpls., 1955-61; prof. psychology UCLA, 1961-91, prof. emeritus, 1991—. Author: (with C.I. Hovland & I.L. Janis) Communication and Persuasion, 1953, (with J.W. Thibaut) The Social Psychology of Groups, 1959, Interpersonal Relations, 1978, (with others) Attribution: Perceiving the Causes of Behavior, 1972, Personal Relationships, 1979, (with others) Close Relationships, 1983. Served with USAAF, 1943-46. Center for Advanced Study in Behavioral Sci. fellow, 1956-57; Am. Psychol. Soc. William James fellow. Fellow Nat. Acad. Scis., Am. Acad. Arts and Scis., APA (pres. personality and social psychology div. 1965-66, Disting. Sci. Contbn. award 1971, Kurt Lewin Meml. award 1990), Am. Sociol. Assn. (Cooley-Mead award 1999). Home: 21634 Rambla Vista St Malibu CA 90265-5126 Office: U Calif Dept Psychology Los Angeles CA 90095

KELLEY, SISTER HELEN, hospital executive; b. Niagara Falls, N.Y., July 25, 1922; d. Robert Vincent Jr. and Helen Gertrude (O'Neil) K. BSN, Cath. U., 1953; MHA, St. Louis U., 1957; postgrad., Cath. U., Seton Hall, Wayne U., St. Louis U. RN, D.C., N.Y., Mass., Mo. Tchr. elem. and jr. high sch. Endicott, N.Y., 1942-50; faculty divsn. nursing St. Joseph Coll., Emmitsburg, Md., 1953-55; adminstr., pres. bd. dirs. St. Agnes Hosp., Balt., 1958-62; asst. adminstr. Sisters of Charity Hosp., Buffalo, N.Y., 1962-64; adminstr., pres. bd. dirs. Carney Hosp., Boston, 1964-69; provincial councilor Daughters of Charity, Northeast Province, 1969-71; internat. work with Vincentian priests Mex., Rep. Panama, 1971-73; adminstr., pres. Our Lady of Lourdes Hosp., Binghamton, N.Y., 1973-76; pres. Nat. Cath. Health Assn., St. Louis, 1976-78; exec. dir. Laboure Ctr., 1979-82; adminstr. St. Louise House, Albany, N.Y., 1982-83; dir. mktg., plannig Carney Hosp., 1983-85; assoc. dir. Intercounty Home Health Care Agy. Diocese of Albany, 1985-86; dir., coord. health and social svcs. Cath. Worker of Niagara Falls, 1986-88; dir./coord. clin. svcs. Cath. Charities' Programs Adult Mentally Retarded Developmental Disabilities, Bklyn. and Queens, N.Y., 1988-91; v.p. mission svcs. Sisters of Charity Hosp., Buffalo, 1991—; dir. activities St. Louise Retirement Residence and Infirmary, Albany, 1996; docent St. Joseph Provincial House, Emmitsburg, Md., 1997; mem. bd. Filmore Leroy Residents Assn., FLARE, Inc., Buffalo; bd. dirs. St. Mary's Hosp., Rochester; trustee Good Samaritan Hosp., Pottsville, Pa.; participant internat. Commns. Daus. of Charity, 1968; pres. bd. trustees Carney Hosp., Our Lady of Lourdes Hosp., St. Agnes Hosp.; chair, participant profl. religous cmty. studies; cons., spkr. Mercy Hosp., Pitts., St. Mary's Hosp., Amsterdam, N.Y.; mem. couns., coms. nursing, pers., profl. practice, other groups. Docent Nat. Shrine of Elizabeth Ann Seton, Emmitsburg, Md., 1996-97. Recipient Community Svc. award Cedar Grove Civic Assn., Boston, Ladies of Charity, Binghamton, CHA Pres., St. Louis. Fellow Am. Coll. Healthcare Execs.; mem. Am. Acad. Cath. Leadership. Home: 1305 Sausse Ave Troy NY 12180-1636 Office: DePaul Provincial House 27 Webster St Malone NY 12953-1717 also: Pastoral Assoc St John Bosco Parish 57 Rennie St Malone NY 12953-1138

KELLEY, JAMES FRANCIS, lawyer; b. Dec. 30, 1941; s. James O'Connor and Marcella Cecilia (Salb) K.; children: Sarah, Leah, Laurence. AB, Yale U.; JD, U. Chgo. Bars: N.Y. 1967, Tex. 1981. Assoc. Breed, Abbott &

Morgan, N.Y.C., 1967-75; dep. gen. counsel United Tech. Corp., Hartford, Conn., 1975-81; sr. v.p., gen. counsel Diamond Shamrock Corp. (name now Maxus Energy Corp.), Dallas, 1981-88; ptnr. Jones, Day, Reavis & Pogue, Dallas and Paris, 1988-93; sr. v.p. law, gen. counsel Georgia-Pacific Corp., 1993—. Gov. Dallas Symphony Assn., 1985-89; bd. dirs. North Tex. Pub. Broadcasting Found., Dallas, 1983-91, mem. exec. com., 1988-91; bd. dirs. Atlanta Symphony Orch., 1994—, mem. exec. com., 1996—, vice chair fin. com., 1996—; bd. dirs. Ga. Trust Hist. Preservation, 1994—; mem. bd. visitors Emory U., 1999—. Mem. ABA, Assn. Gen. Counsel. Office: Georgia-Pacific Corp 133 Peachtree St NE Atlanta GA 30303-1847

KELLEY, JAMES FRANCIS, civil engineer; b. Boston, Mar. 30, 1920; s. James Aloysius and Rose Frances (Berlo) K.; m. Mary Elizabeth Kelly, June 17, 1946; children: Margaret Coronite, James Francis Jr., Rosemary Doran, Kathleen Clancy. Assoc. Civil and Structural Engring., Northeastern U., Boston, 1950. Registered profl. engr., profl. land surveyor. Sr. engring. aide City of Quincy (Mass.) Engring. Dept., 1942-48; planning engr., design engr. Mass. Dept. Pub. Works, Boston, 1948-64, maintenance engr., dep. chief engr., 1964-77; pvt. cons. J.F. Kelley & Assocs., Quincy, 1977-91; chmn. Quincy Planning Bd., 1990—. Contbr. articles to profl. jours. Mem. NAS (transp. rsch. bd. 1968-88), Am. Pub. Works Assn. (life), Nat. Order Battlefield Commns. (life), VFW (life), Am. Legion, KC (life). Roman Catholic. Home: 63 Vershire St North Quincy MA 02171-2528 Office: Quincy Planning Bd 1305 Hancock St Quincy MA 02169-5119

KELLEY, JANE HOLDEN, archeology educator; b. Abilene, Tex., Aug. 31, 1928; came to Can., 1968, d. Wiliam Curry and Ira Olive (Price) Holden; m. David Humiston Kelley, June 11, 1958; children: Rebecca Ann, Thomas Michael, Dennis W.C., Nancy Megan. B.A., Tex. Tech U., 1949; M.A., U. Tex., 1951; Ph.D., Harvard U., 1966. Instr. Tex. Tech U., Lubbock, 1957-63; assoc. curator Nebr. State Mus., Lincoln, 1964-68; assoc. prof. U. Calgary, Alta., Can., 1968-76, prof., 1976-93, emeritus, 1993, head dept. archeology, 1981-87, dir. Calgary Inst. Humanities, 1993—, assoc. to v.p. rsch., 1995—. Author: The Tall Candle, 1971, Yaqui Women, 1978, (with Marsha Hanen) Archaeology and The Methodology of Science, 1988, Cihuatan, El Salvador: A Preliminary Study in Intra-Site Variability, 1988. Home: 2432 Sovereign Crescent, Calgary, AB Canada T3C 2M2 Office: Dept Archeology, U Calgary, Calgary, AB Canada T2N 1N4

KELLEY, JOHN F., airline executive. Chmn., pres., CEO Alaska Air Group, Seattle. Office: Alaska Air Group PO Box 68900 Seattle WA 98168-0900*

KELLEY, JOHN JOSEPH, JR., lawyer; b. Cleve., June 17, 1936; s. John Joseph and Helen (Meier) K.; m. Gloria Hill, June 20, 1959; children: John Joseph III, Scott MacDonald, Christopher Taft, Megan Meredith. B.S. cum laude in Commerce, Ohio U., 1958; LL.B., Case Western Res. U., 1960. Bar: Ohio bar 1960. Clk. firm Walter & Haverfield, Cleve., 1957-60; assoc. Walter, Haverfield, Buescher & Chockley, Cleve., 1960-66; partner Walter, Haverfield, Buescher & Chockley, 1967-72; chief exec. officer Fleischmann Enterprises, Cin., 1972-77; pvt. practice law Cin., 1977-87; ptnr. Kohnen & Patton, Cin., 1988—; chmn. bd. Basic Packaging Systems, Inc., 1982-87; dir. Orgamac Leasing Ltd; pres. Naples Devel. Inc., 1974-87, Yankee Leasing Co. Mem. Lakewood (Ohio) City Council, 1965-72, pres., 1972; mem. exec. com. Cuyahoga County (Ohio) Republican Central Com., 1965-72; mem. Hamilton County (Ohio) Rep. Policy Com.; Ohio chmn. Robert Taft, Jr. Senate Campaign Com., 1970, 76; bd. govs. Case Western Res. U., 1961, 84-87. Mem. Assn. Ohio Commodores, ABA, Ohio State Bar Assn., Cleve. Bar Assn., Cin. Bar Assn. Clubs: Cin. Country, Queen City (Cin.); Naples Bath and Tennis. Home: 5 Woodcreek Dr Cincinnati OH 45241-3255 Office: Kohnen & Patton Ohio Attorney General # 1400 Cincinnati OH 45202-2800

KELLEY, JOHN PAUL, communications consultant; b. Columbus, Ohio, May 12, 1919; s. John Adrian and Josephine (Nash) K.; m. Dorothy Rose Peters, July 31, 1942; children: John M., Ann P., Daniel O., Peter D. BS in Journalism, Ohio State U., 1941; MBA, Harvard U., 1946. Mgr. sales promotion Seiberling Rubber Co., Akron, Ohio, 1946-48; account supr. Batten, Barton, Durstine & Osborn, Cleve., 1948-51; mgr. consumer advt. Monsanto Chem. Co., St. Louis, 1951-54; pres. Mumm, Mullay & Nichols, Advt. Agy., Columbus, 1954-59; v.p. Goodyear Tire and Rubber Co., Akron, 1959-84; communications consultant, 1984—. Lt. AUS, 1943-46. Mem. Assn. Nat. Advertisers (past chmn.), Advt. Coun. (past chmn. bd. dirs.). Republican. Roman Catholic. Home: 76240 Fairway Dr Indian Wells CA 92210-8822

KELLEY, JOHNNIE L., mental health nurse; b. Jasper, Ala.; 1 child, Grace Kelley-Neal. BSN, Syracuse U., 1975, MS, 1981. RN, N.Y. Staff nurse VA Med. Ctr., Syracuse, N.Y., head nurse, clin. nurse specialist; coord. VA Cmty. Care Ctr. Extended Care Program; clin. nurse splst. mental health Triage VA Med. Ctr., 1997—. Mem. N.Y. State Nurses Assn., Syracuse Area Psychiat. Nurses, Syracuse Area Black Nurses Assn., Sigma Theta Tau (Omicron chpt.). Home: 178 Delray Ave Syracuse NY 13224-1136

KELLEY, JOSEPH E., career officer. BS, USAF Acad., 1974; MD, Rush U., 1977; student, Sch. Aerospace Medicine, Brooks AFB, Tex., 1984, Air Command and Staff Coll., 1986, Air War Coll., 1988, George Washington U., 1992; physician in mgmt. I, ACP Execs., Sheppard AFB, Tex., 1992, physician in mgmt. II, 1994, physician in mgmt. III, 1997. Diplomate Am. Bd. Surgery. Commd. capt. USAF, 1977, advanced through grades to brig. gen., 1997; intern then resident in gen. surgery David Grant Med. Ctr., Travis AFB, Calif., 1977-82; gen. surgeon then chief surgery Nellis USAF Hosp., Nellis AFB, Nev., 1982-84; chief hosp. svcs. Misawa USAF Hosp., Misawa Air Base, Japan, 1984-86; comdr. 90th Strategic Hosp., Francis E. Warren AFB, Wyo., 1986-89, 857th Strategic Hosp., Minot AFB, N.D., 1989-91, Fifth Med. Group, Minot AFB, 1991-92, Ehrling Bergquist Hosp., Offutt AFB, Nebr., 1992-93; chief med. resources, directorate med. programs/resources Office Air Force Surgeon Gen., Bolling AFB, D.C., 1993-95; command surgeon Pacific Air Forces, Hickam AFB, Hawaii, 1995-96; comdr. 74th Med. Group, Wright-Patterson AFB, Ohio, 1996—; lead agt. Dept. Def. Health Svc. Region 5, Wright-Patterson AFB, Ohio, 1996—; Air Force state faculty mem. course ATLS. Decorated Legion of Merit. Mem. ACP Execs., Soc. Med. Cons. Armed Forces. Office: 74 MDG/CC 4881 Sugar Maple Dr Wright Patterson AFB OH 45433-5529

KELLEY, KEVIN H., insurance company executive; b. Boston, Oct. 12, 1950; s. Hugh and Anne Kelley; m. Maryellen Moran; children: Meghan, Maura, Katherine. BS/BA, Boston U., 1972. CPCU. Trainee Fireman's Fund, Boston, 1973-75; exec. underwriter Lexington Ins. Co. (AIG), Boston, 1975-78; casualty mgr. Lexington Ins. Co. (AIG), 1979-83, exec. v.p., 1984-86, pres., 1987-97, chmn., CEO, 1997—. Dir. Mass. Spina Bifida Assn., 1986. Roman Catholic. Office: Lexington Ins Co 200 State St Boston MA 02109-2677*

KELLEY, LISA STONE, public guardian, conservator; b. Sacramento, Calif., Mar. 10, 1947; d. John William and Coral Frances (Roberts) Stone; m. Charles B. Kelley, Oct. 7, 1967 (div. Feb. 1987); children: Brian Christopher, Darren Matthew. Student, Sacramento City Coll., 1965-67, AA in Social Sci., 1978; BA in Social Work with honors, Calif. State U., Sacramento, 1982, MSW with honors, 1985; postgrad. in Psychology, Calif. Coast U., 1994—. Lic. clin. social worker, Calif. Pharmacy clerk S. Sacramento Pharmacy, 1966-68; temp. med. asst. Sacramento, 1978-80; adv., counselor El Dorado Women's Info. Ctr., Placerville, Calif., 1982; dep. patients rights adv. Sacramento County Office Patients Rights, 1983-84; sch. social worker Elk Grove (Calif.) Unified Sch. Dist., 1984-85; mental health counselor Sacramento Mental Health Ctr., 1986; dep. pub. guardian/conservator Sacramento County, 1986—. Mem. NASW, Sacramento County Employees Orgn., Am. Orthopsychiat. Assn., Menninger Found., Calif. Soc. for Clin. Social Work, Am. Rabbit Breeders Assn., Calif. State U. Alumni Assn., Calif. Coast U. Alumni Assn., Holland Lop Rabbit Specialty Club, Phi Kappa Phi. Democrat. Avocations: collecting plates and gnomes, reading, pet rabbits. Office: Sacramento County Pub Guardian/Conservator 4875 Broadway Ste I Sacramento CA 95820-1500

KELLEY, LOUANNA ELAINE, newspaper columnist, researcher; b. Denver, Oct. 17, 1920; d. John Earl and Violet May (Griffin) Richards; m. George Vanstavoren Kelley, Dec. 1942 (dec. Oct. 1975); children: William Richard, John Henry; stepchild, Joan Fenicle; m. Glen Russell Fenicle, Jan. 1984 (dec. Apr. 1996). Student in Dental Tng., Emily Griffith Sch., 1960-61; Student in Bus., Red Rocks Coll., 1976-77. Dental asst. Colo. Dental, Denver, 1961-70; columnist Front Range Jour., Idaho Springs, Colo., 1975-80; reporter Colo. Transcript, Golden, Colo., 1975-82; columnist, reporter Clear Creek Courant, Idaho Springs, Colo., 1980-88, Mountain Messenger, Idaho Springs, Colo., 1988—; researcher Nat. Mining Hall of Fame, Leadville, Colo. 1987—, lectr. Colo. Sch. Mines, Golden, 1977, Jefferson County Schs., Golden, 1975-84; bd. dirs. Vetco Credit Union, Denver. Author: Take Your Pick And Strike It Rich, 1988; contbr. articles to profl. jours. Historian Clear Creek County and Jefferson County, Colo. Mem. Social Ethics (v.p. 1986—), Colo. Fedn. Women's. Republican. Lutheran. Avocations: social and club activities. Home: 12820 Willow Ln Apt 22 Golden CO 80401-6303 Office: Mountain Messenger PO Box 2090 Idaho Springs CO 80452-2090

KELLEY, LYLE ARDELL, insurance company executive; b. Milan, Mo., Aug. 8, 1944; s. Azel Farril and Anne Ellen (King) K.; m. Carol Ann Clark, Nov. 26, 1966; children: Julie Kay, Kristie Lynn. BS in Mgmt. and Acctg., NE Mo. State U., 1967. Acct. Skelly Oil Co., St. Louis, 1967; claims adjuster State Farm Ins., St. Louis, 1967-77; auditor State Farm Ins., Bloomington, Ill., 1977-83, computer systems design analyst, 1983-86; asst. claims supt. State Farm Ins., Madison, Wis., 1986-87; supt. Wis. property State Farm Ins., Milw., 1987—; treas. Crime Stoppers McLean County, Bloomington, Ill., 1984, v.p., 1985, pres., 1986; sec. Madison Area Crime Stoppers, 1987; dist. 10 rep. McLean County Bd., Bloomington, 1985-86; chair auto body curriculum com. Waukesha County Tech. Coll., 1990—. Republican. Roman Catholic. Home: S14w31830 High Meadow Ln Delafield WI 53018-3551 Office: State Farm Ins 2747 Mayfair Rd Milwaukee WI 53222-4403

KELLEY, MARK ALBERT, internal medicine educator, university official; b. Boston, Oct. 31, 1947; s. Albert Joseph and Virginia Marie (Riley) K.; m. Gail Riggs, Aug. 4, 1974; children: Christopher Riggs, Amy Morgan. AB, Harvard U., Cambridge, Mass., 1969; MD, Harvard U., Boston, 1973. Diplomate Am. Bd. Internal Medicine, Am. Bd. Pulmonary Disease, Am. Bd. Critical Care. Intern Hosp. U. Pa., Phila., 1973-74, resident, 1974-76, chief med. resident, 1977-78, fellow in pulmonary diseases, 1976-77, 78-79; dir. pulmonary fellowship U. Pa., Phila., 1979-82, from asst. to assoc. prof. medicine, 1979-92, prof., 1992—; dir. pulmonary fellowship tng. program, 1979-82; vice chmn. med. U. Pa. Sch. Medicine, Phila., 1986-90; dir. pulmonary fellowship tng. program, 1979-82, assoc. chmn. clin. svcs., dir. med. residency tng. program, 1982-86, dir. faculty group practice, 1985-90; vice dean clin. affairs U. Pa. Sch. Medicine, Phila., 1990—; spkr. in field. Mem. editl. bd. Critical Care Clinics, 1989—, Annals Internal Medicine, 1990-93, Critical Care Medicine, 1992—. Fellow ACP, Am. Coll. Chest Physicians; mem. Assn. Program Dirs. Internal Medicine, Am. Thoracic Soc. (chmn. nat. manpower study 1996—), Am. Bd. Internal Medicine (critical care medicine test com. 1988-93, chmn. 1990-93, bd. govs. 1990-98, exec. com. 1993-98, sec.-treas. 1994-96, chmn. 1997-98, foundation bd. 1999—), Soc. Crit. Care Medicine, Am. Bd. Med. Specialties, Alpha Omega Alpha. Office: U Pa Med Ctr 21 Penn Tower Philadelphia PA 19104

KELLEY, MARY ELIZABETH (LAGRONE), computer specialist; b. Temple, Tex., Feb. 12, 1947; d. Harry John and Mary Erma (Windham) LaGrone; m. Roy Earl Kelley, May 10, 1968; children: Roy John, James Lewis, Joanna Marylu. BS, U. Mary Hardin-Baylor, 1968. Cert. tchr., Tex. Math tchr. Killeen (Tex.) High Sch., 1977-78; clk. typist Readiness Region VIII, Aurora, Colo., 1979; statis. clk. Fitzsimons Army Med. Ctr., Aurora, 1980-81, mgmt. asst., 1981-83; clk. typist Corpus Christi (Tex.) Army Depot, 1984; mgmt. asst. Health Care Studies and Clin. Investigation Act, Fort Sam Houston, Tex., 1984-85; computer programmer/analyst Health Care Systems Support Act, Fort Sam Houston, 1985-88, computer systems analyst, 1988-92, computer specialist, 1992-94, data base adminstr., 1994-95, Lotus Notes sys. adminstr., 1995-98; process integrator, asst. comdr. force integration U.S. Army Med. Dept. Ctr. and Sch., Fort Sam Houston, 1998-99, computer specialist, 1999—; tchr. Fitzsimons Army Med. Ctr., 1978-79, cons., 1978-79. Author: (databases) Health Care Management System, 1988-94. Vol. Parents Encouraging Parents, Denver, 1979-83, Friends of Safe House, Denver, 1980-83, Heidi Search Ctr., San Antonio, 1990, Family Assistance Crisis Team, San Antonio Police Dept., 1997-99, Vols. in Policing, San Antonio Police Dept., 1998-99; founder Top of the HIll Residents' Alliance, San Antonio, 1997. Recipient achievement medal for civilian svc. Dept. Army, 1991. Mem. DAR, Daus. of Republic of Tex., United Daus. of Confederacy, Tex. Soc. of Mayflower Descs., Alpha Chi, Delta Psi Theta, Sigma Tau Delta, Alpha Phi. Roman Catholic. Avocations: reading, needlework, geneology, Spl. Olympics, writing poetry.

KELLEY, MICHAEL EUGENE, lawyer; b. Creston, Iowa, June 18, 1941; s. Cletus George and Zelphia Ellen (Billingsley) K.; m. Helen Ann Cox Alger, Apr. 14, 1963 (div. Oct. 1974); 1 child, Kurt Allen; m. Georgia Elyse Lunn Aistrope, Oct. 14, 1974; children: Suzanne Elyse Kelley Porter, Michael Keith. AA, S.W. C.C., 1965; BA, Omaha U., 1968; JD, Creighton U., 1971. Bar: Nebr. 1971, Iowa 1971, U.S. Dist. Ct. Nebr. 1971. Trainman, yardmaster Burlington No., Creston, Council Bluffs, Iowa, 1959-71; assoc. Edgar Cook, Atty., Glenwood, Iowa, 1971-73; pvt. practice, Glenwood, 1973-76; gen. counsel Kearney (Nebr.) Mcpl. Airport Corp., 1976—; atty. Mills County, Glenwood, 1972-74; city atty. City of Kearney, 1976—; spkr. in field. Mem. Kearney cabinet Kearney Gideons, ch. asst. sec., 1988-90. With USN, 1960-64. Mem. Internat. Mpls. Lawyers Assn. (Nebr. state chair 1995—), Nebr. State Bar Assn., Buffalo County Bar Assn., Nebr. Gideons (mem. state cabinet, ch. asst. sec. 1990-93), Full Gospel Businessmen's Fellowship Internat. (v.p. 1987-89). Avocations: ichthyology, model trains and villages, shotgun sports. Home: 1203 E 34th St Kearney NE 68847-3226 Office: City of Kearney PO Box 1180 Kearney NE 68848-1180

KELLEY, MICHAEL JAMES, medical services executive, author; m. Linda. BS, Fla. Atlantic U., 1976, MBA, 1980. Advisor to prime minister Turks and Caicos Islands, Brit. West Indies, 1978-79; chief adminstr. Ft. Lauderdale (Fla.) Eye Inst., 1980-87; v.p. Ambassador Real Estate Equities Corp., Tamarac, Fla., 1984-89, also bd. dirs.; exec. v.p. Ambassador Fin. Group Inc., Tamarac, Fla., 1985-89; exec. dir. Retina Consultants Southwest Fla., Ft. Myers, 1990—; CEO Vision Rehab. Strategies, Ft. Myers, 1994—; CFO, bd.dirs. Lifevision, 1996—. Mem. Med. Group Mgmt. Assn. (AO pres. 1996—), Fla. Atlantic U. Alumni Assn. (bd. dirs. 1989-93), AAO Network for Adminstrs. (chmn.). Avocations: skiing, boating. Office: Retina Cons 2668 Winkler Ave Fort Myers FL 33901-9336

KELLEY, MICHAEL JOHN, newspaper editor; b. Kansas City, Mo., July 5, 1942; s. Robert Francis and Grace Lauretta (Schofield) K.; 1 child, Anne Schofield. BA, Rockhurst Coll., 1964. Reporter, polit. writer Kansas City Star & Times, 1960-69; asst. Sen. Thomas F. Eagleton, Washington, 1969-76; pres. Swensen's Midwest, Inc., Kansas City, 1976-80; exec. asst. Cen. States Pension Fund, Chgo., 1981-83, 85-87; asst. mng. editor Kansas City Times, 1984; editor The Daily Southtown, Chgo., 1987-97; mng. editor Las Vegas (Nev.) Sun, 1997—. Office: Las Vegas Sun 800 S Valley View Blvd Las Vegas NV 89107-4411

KELLEY, PATRICIA AUSTIN, publishing/executive; b. Lynn, Mass.; d. Lorne C. and Margaret M. (Baker) Davis; m. Robert E. Kelley; children: Campbell, Taylor Emily, Loren. BA, Tufts U., 1965; MEd, Salem (Mass.) Coll., 1971; cert. advanced study, Harvard U., 1977. Editorial asst. Saturday Rev., N.Y.C., 1965-67; grant writer Malden (Mass.) Pub. Schs., 1977-85; cons. Austin Assocs., Wenham, Mass., 1985-91; project dir. North Shore C.C., Danvers, Mass., 1991-93; project leader The Network, Andover, Mass., 1993-95; pres., publ. Wright Stuff Press Ariz., Phoenix, 1996—; mem. edn. policies com. Tufts U., Medford, Mass., 1978-82; cons. R.I. Dept. Edn., Providence, 1994-95, Frank Lloyd Wright Found., Scottsdale, Ariz., 1997; mem. faculty Ariz. State U., 1998—. Author: (children's books) Cher Locke: The Case of the Missing Cockatiels, 1996, Cher Locke: The Dragon's Tale, 1997. Bd. dirs. Ariz. Ctr. for the Book, 1998—. Avocations: pianist, tennis, children. Office: Wright Stuff Press Ariz PO Box 32582 Phoenix AZ 85064-2582

KELLEY, PATRICIA COLLEEN, educator, researcher; b. Winchester, Mass., Oct. 14, 1953; d. Joseph Sayward Kelley and Florence Patricia Dougherty; children: Brian, Brandon, Daniel. BA cum laude, U. N.H., 1978; MBA, Boston U., 1985, DBA with honors, 1988. Asst. to pres. dir. Huntington Gen. Hosp., Boston, 1975-76; asst. adminstrv. mgr. Coopers and Lybrand, Boston, 1976-78; adminstrv. mgr. Allyn & Bacon, Inc., Boston, 1978-80; teaching asst. Sch. of Mgmt. Boston U., 1981-83, writing coord. Sch. of Mgmt., 1985-88; asst. prof. Sch. of Bus. U. Wash., Seattle, 1988-90, Western Wash. U., Bellingham, 1990-95; adj. prof. bus. U. Wash., Bothell, Wash., 1995—; cons. various projects relative to ethical decision making and bus.-polit. interaction. Contbr. articles to profl. jours. Coach Lake Hill Soccer Club, King County, Wash., 1989-92; rm. mother Bellevue Schs., 1988-92, Sacred Heart Sch., Bellevue, 1994—; instr. Sacred Heart Ch., Bellevue, 1988-92; treas. Boy Scouts Am., Bellevue, 1989-91; merit badge counselor Boy Scouts of Am., 1994—. Mass. Bd. Higher Edn. scholar, 1972-75, Boston U. scholar, 1985-87. Mem. Acad. of Mgmt. (social issues in mgmt. divsn. 1988—, fin. com. SIM divsn. 1993—, chairperson, 1990-93, sec. editor 1992-95).

KELLEY, PATRICK ALAN, neurologist, educator; b. Hinsdale, Ill., Sept. 24, 1947; s. Joseph John and Carol (Obalil) K.; m. Anne Nancy Trifilo, Feb. 22, 1975 (div. Aug. 1979). BA, Knox Coll., 1969; MD, Loyola U., Maywood, Ill., 1973. Diplomate Am. Bd. Psychiatry and Neurology. Resident in neurology Tufts U., Boston, 1974-77; asst. clin. prof. U. Conn., Farmington, 1977-79, U. Tenn., Chattanooga, 1979-88; staff neurologist Group Health Assn., Washington, 1988-94; chmn. dept. neurology Humana Group Health Plan, Washington, 1994-97; asst. clin. prof. George Washington U., Washington, 1988—; staff neurologist Kaiser Permanente, Kensington, Md., 1997—; neurol. cons., Washington Hosp. Ctr., 1988—, Meml. Hosp., Chattanooga, 1979-88; clin. instr. neurology, Northeastern U., Boston, 1976-77. Author: Clinical Medicine: Selected Problems with Pathophysiologic Correlations, 1988. Candidate for Ho. of Dels., Gen. Assembly of Commonwealth of Va., 1999; mem. Pres.'s club Rep. Nat. Com., Washington, 1996—. Fellow Am. Acad. Neurology; mem. AMA (Physician Recognition award 1998), Am. Epilepsy Soc., Am. Med. EEG Assn., Med. Soc. Va., Phi Beta Kappa. Republican. Roman Catholic. Avocations: collecting original French Impressionist prints, collecting editions of Thomas Jefferson's work. Office: Kaiser Permanente 10810 Connecticut Ave Kensington MD 20895

KELLEY, PATRICK MICHAEL, minister, state legislator; b. Maryville, Mo., Oct. 27, 1948; s. Gilbert B. and Wilma M. K.; m. Nancy E. Schroeder, July 30, 1976; children: Ryan, Shane, Kristen. BS, William Jewell, 1970; MDiv, St. Paul, 1985. V.p. Kelley-Rickman Construction Col, 1970-72, pres., 1972-75; salesman Sequoia Supply Co., North Kansas City, Mo., 1975-77; owner, pres. Energy Expositions, North Kansas City, 1977-83; pastor United Meth. Chs., Bates County, Mo., 1983-87, Aldersgate United Meth. Ch., Lee's Summit, Mo., 1987-90, Glenwood Park United Meth. Ch., Independence, Mo., 1990—; Rep. caucus chmn. Mo. State Ho. Reps., 1991, 92, minority floor leader, 1993, 94. Chmn. Lee's Summit D.A.R.E. task force; adv. bd. Community Mental Health Svcs., Lee's Summit; bd. dirs. Community Svcs. League, Lee's Summit. Mem. Lee's Summit Rep. Club (treas., pres.). Home: 3924 SW Windsong Dr Lees Summit MO 64082-4051 Office: Mo Ho Reps Capitol Bldg Jefferson City MO 65101

KELLEY, PAUL XAVIER, retired marine corps officer; b. Boston, Nov. 11, 1928; s. Albert J. and Josephine C. (Sullivan) K.; m. Barbara Joan Adams, Mar. 4, 1951; 1 child, Christine. B.S. in Econs., Villanova U., 1950, D.Mil. Sci. (hon.), 1982; D.Mil. Sci. (hon.), Norwich U., Vt., 1984, Webster U., 1985; LL.D., Jacksonville U., 1986, Rensselaer Polytechnic Inst., 1996. Dir. edn. U.S. Marine Corps, Quantico, Va., 1976-78; dep. chief staff for requirements and programs U.S. Marine Corps, Washington, 1978-80; comdr. Rapid Deployment Joint Task Force, McDill AFB, Fla., 1980-81; asst. comdt. U.S. Marine Corps, Washington, 1981-83; comdt. U.S. Marine Corps, 1983-87; ret., 1987; ptnr. J.F. Lehman & Co.; bd. dirs. Gencorp Inc., Wackenhut Corp., UST Inc., Sturm, Ruger & Co., Saul Ctrs., Inc. Chmn. bd. Irish Am. Partnership; bd. govs. NFL Alumni; mem. vis. com. U. So. Calif. Sch. Bus. Recipient Maj. Gen. O.A. Anderson award Nat. Geog. Soc., 1969, Nat. Armed Services award VFW, 1984, Golden Eagle award Am. Acad. Achievement, 1984, Admiral John M. Will award Navy League U.S., 1985, Irishman of Yr. for So. Calif., Ireland Fund, 1986, Minuteman Hall of Fame, Res. Officers Assn., 1987. Mem. Council Fgn. Relations, Beta Gamma Sigma, Mil. Order Carabao, Friendly Sons St. Patrick, Alfalfa Club. Home: 1600 N Oak St Apt 1619 Arlington VA 22209-2769

KELLEY, RALPH HOUSTON, judge; b. Chattanooga, Sept. 23, 1928; s. Glenn Blair and Beulah Louise K.; m. Barbara Ann Fahl, June 24, 1960; 3 children. A.B., U. Tenn., Chattanooga, 1952; LL.B., Vanderbilt U., 1954. Bar: Tenn. 1954. Sr. ptnr. Kelly, DiRisio & Shattuck, Chattanooga, 1954-69; judge U.S. Bankruptcy Ct. Ea. Dist. Tenn., Chattanooga, 1969—; mem. com. on budget Jud. Conf. U.S., 1980-90; pres. Nat. Conf. Bankruptcy Judges, 1985-86; active Nat. Conf. Bankruptcy Clks. Mem. Tenn. Ho. of Reps., 1959-61; mayor City of Chattanooga, 1963-69. Served with USAAF, 1946-49. Fellow Am. Coll. Bankruptcy, Tenn. Bar Assn., Chattanooga Bar Assn.; mem. ABA, Am. Bankruptcy Inst., Fed. Bar Assn., Kiwanis (past pres. Chattanooga). Office: US Hist Courthouse 31 E 11th St Chattanooga TN 37402-2722*

KELLEY, RICHARD ROY, hotel executive; b. Honolulu, Dec. 28, 1933; s. Roy Cecil and Estelle Louise (Foote) K.; m. Jane Zieber, June 21, 1955 (dec. 1978); children: Elizabeth, Kathryn, Charles, Linda J., Mary Colleen; m. Linda Van Gilder, June 23, 1979; children: Christopher Van Gilder, Anne Marie. BA, Stanford U., 1955; MD, Harvard U., 1960. Pathologist Queen's Med. Ctr., Honolulu, 1962-70, Kapiolani Maternity Hosp., Honolulu, 1961-70; asst. prof. pathology John A. Burns Med. Sch., U. Hawaii, Honolulu, 1968-70; chmn. bd. Outrigger Enterprises, Honolulu; bd. dirs. First Hawaiian Bank, Outrigger Internat. Travel, Inc. Former trustee, past chmn. Punahou Sch.; dean's adv. bd. Travel Industry Mgmt. Sch., U. Hawaii; former vice-dean Ednl. Inst. AH & MA Pres.'s Acad. Bd. Regents; former chmn. bd. councilors Hawaii Pacific divsn. Am. Cancer Soc., past chmn. commn. on performance stds. State of Hawaii; trustee Kent-Denver Sch. Named Marketer of Yr., Am. Mktg. Assn., 1985, Communicator of Yr., Internat. Bus. Communicators, 1987, Salesperson of Yr., Sales & Mktg. Execs. Honolulu, 1995; named to Hawaii Bus. Hall of Fame, 1993; recipient Hope award Multiple Sclerosis Soc., 1995. Mem. Hawaii Visitors Bur. (bd. dirs., chmn. 1991-92), Waikiki Oahu Visitors Assn., Waikiki Improvement Assn., Chief Execs. Orgn., Japan Assn. Travel Agts., Japan Hawaii Econ. Coun., Pacific Asia Travel Assn., World Pres.'s Orgn., World Travel and Tourism Coun. Office: Outrigger Hotels & Resorts 2375 Kuhio Ave Honolulu HI 96815-2992

KELLEY, ROBERT OTIS, medical science educator; b. Santa Monica, Calif., Apr. 30, 1944; s. David Otis and Onetia May (Nettles) K.; m. Marcia Jean Bell; children: Jennifer Leigh, Karin Michelle, Matthew Philip, Sarah Ann. BS, Abilene Christian U., 1965; MA, U. Calif., Berkeley, 1966, PhD, 1969. Asst. prof. U. N.Mex. Sch. of Medicine, Albuquerque, 1969-74, assoc. prof., 1974-79, prof., 1979—, chmn. dept. anatomy, 1981-97; assoc. vice chancellor rsch., exec. dean grad. coll. U. Ill., Chgo., 1997—; vis. scientist Okazaki (Japan) Nat. Labs., 1984-85; mem. study sect. NIH, Bethesda, Md., 1982-86, U.S. Med. Licensing Exam. Step 1, 1995—; anatomy com. Nat. Bd. mex. Examiners, Phila., 1992—. Author: Basic Histology, 1989; editor Cell and Tissue Rsch., 1970—, Anat. Record, 1970-97; contbr. articles to profl. jours. Patroller Nat. Ski Patrol, 1970—. Recipient Rsch. Career Devel. award NIH, 1972-77, Kaiser award U. Calif., Irvine, 1976; Internat. Exch. Scholar NSF; NIH grantee, 1970—. Mem. Fedn. Am. Socs. for Exptl. Biology (pub. affairs exec. com. 1993—), Am. Soc. Cell Biology, Soc. for Devel. Biology, Electron Microscopy Soc. Am. (bd. dirs. 1987—), Am. Assn. Anatomists (exec. com. 1988—), Assn. Am. Med. Colls. (exec. coun. 1995—, chair assembly 1997-99), Nat. Caucus of Basic Biomed. Sci. Chairs, Nat. Bd. Med. Examiners. Democrat. Protestant. Avocations: sailing, skiing, soaring, SCUBA diving, backpacking. Address: 675 Lake St Apt 324 Oak Park IL 60301-1410 Office: 310 Adminstrv Office Bldg 1737 W Polk St Chicago IL 60612-7224

KELLEY, ROBERT SUMA, systems engineer; b. Chgo., July 2, 1961; s. Jerry Dean and Jean (Laine) K. BA in Philosophy, Western Md. Coll., 1985; MBA in MIS, Ind. U., 1989. Human resource specialist Marriott Corp., Gaithersburg, Md., 1985-86; mgr. in tng. Courtyard by Marriott, Fairfax, Va., 1986-87; sys. analyst Hewlett-Packard, Palo Alto, Calif., 1989-98; network engr. Hewlett-Packard, Sunnyvale, Calif., 1998—; mem. adv. com. for implementation of Calif. Assembly bill for improving edn. opportunities for learning disabled children, 1991-94. counselor Camp Allen for the Physically Handicapped, Manchester, N.H., 1977; track coach for disadvantaged youth Rockville (Md.) Recreation, 1980. Avocation: endurance horseback riding. Home: 408 Grant Ave Apt 306 Palo Alto CA 94306-1813 Office: Hewlett-Packard 3000 Hanover St # 20bj Palo Alto CA 94304-1181

KELLEY, RUTH M., nurse, alcohol, drug abuse services professional; b. Lynn, Mass., Dec. 25, 1941; d. Russell J. Merrick and Ruth R. (Maker) Green; m. Robert P. Nadeau, 1962 (dec. 1974); children: Robert G., Peter J.; m. Raymond W. Kelley, May 2, 1981. LPN, Holy Ghost Hosp., 1960; ADN, RN, Northeastern U., 1980; BSN, Univ. Coll., 1986. RN, cert. addiction RN. LPN Holy Ghost Hosp., Cambridge, Mass., 1960-63; staff nurse Sancta Maria Hosp., Cambridge, 1968-79; staff nurse Sancta Maria Hosp., Cambridge, Mass., 1980-81, acting head nurse, 1985-86, asst. head nurse, 1981-87, nursing quality assurance coord., staffing coord., 1987-89, substabce abuse cons., 1983-89; nurse, counselor New England Meml. Hosp., Stoneham, Mass., 1989-90; coord. pregnant woman program Dimock Cmty. Health Ctr., Roxbury, Mass., 1990-92, dir. detox svcs., 1992-96; dir. transp. Housing for HIV/Substance Abuse Women, 1996-97, dir. residential/inpatient svcs., 1997—; mem. faculty Sancta Maria Hosp. Pastoral Care Group, 1981-87; lectr. Women/Substance Abuse Issues; mem. DPH Women/Substance Abuse Task Force, 1992—; rep. Middlesex County Sheriff, Legislature Issues Women in Prison. Chmn. Cambridge Emergency Shelter Dr., 1986; pres. Arlington Coun. Alcohol Edn.; bd. dirs. Middlesex Human Svc. Agy.; past mem. Archdiocesan Task Force Substance Abuse; past vol. Billerica House of Corrections; co-sponsor 1st Oxford House for Women, Somerville, Mass.; exec. bd. Fed. Healthy Start Initiative to Reduce Infant Mortality. Recipient Human Svc. Needs award, 1992. Mem. ANA (substance abuse task force), Mass. Nurses Assn. (addiction coun., substance abuse subcom., maternal infant substance abuse task force, Human Svc. Needs award 1992), Nat. Nurses Soc. Addictions, Northeastern U. Alumni Assn., Sigma Theta Tau. Democrat. Roman Catholic. Office: Dimock Cmty Health Ctr Sewall Bldg 55 Dimock St Roxbury MA 02119-1029

KELLEY, SHEILA SEYMOUR, public relations executive, crisis consultant; b. Bronxville, N.Y.; d. William Joseph and Jane (Seymour) K.; m. Robert Max Kaufman, 1959. BA magna cum laude, Syracuse U., 1949. Reporter Yonkers Herald Statesman, N.Y.C., 1950; reporter, editor Close Up column Herald Tribune, N.Y.C., 1950-53; writer, producer Sta. WNBC-TV, N.Y.C., 1953-54; media cons. to Senator Jacobs K. Javits, N.Y.C., 1956-74; press sec. Senator Jacobs K. Javits, Washington, 1958-61; account supr., v.p. Harshe Rotman Druck, N.Y.C., 1961-76; founder, pres. VOTES, Inc., N.Y.C., 1973-75; v.p. Doremus Pub. Rels., N.Y.C., 1976-86, sr. v.p., 1987-90, mng. dir., exec. v.p., 1990; exec. v.p. Gavin Anderson & Co., N.Y.C., 1990-96, sr. counselor, 1996-97; prin. The Dilenschneider Group, N.Y.C., 1997—. Mem. Pub. Rels. Soc. Am. (accredited), Women Execs. in Pub. Rels. (pres. 1987-88, sec. 1999—), Phi Beta Kappa. Republican. Avocations: skiing, golf, gardening. Office: The Dilenschneider Group 200 Park Ave Rm 2601 New York NY 10166-0018

KELLEY, SYLVIA JOHNSON, financial services firm executive; b. Butte, Mont., Dec. 29, 1929; d. John O. and Hilja W. (Koski) J.; m. Dan H. Kelley, June 1, 1950 (div. Jan. 1973); children: David D., Bruce J., Sheila K. Miller, Mona K. Nance; m. Richard T. Marshall, June 10, 1979. CLU; ChFC; cert. fin. planner; registered fin. cons.; cert. sr. advisor. Legal sec. various law firms, L.A., 1959-69; registered rep. Met. Life, N.Y.C., 1969-75, SMA Equities, Inc., Worcester, Mass., 1975-89, Multi-Fin. Securities Corp., Denver, Colo., 1989—; pres., chief exec. officer Advance Funding, Inc., El Paso, Tex., 1981—. Contbr. articles to profl. jours. Bd. dirs., chmn. bus. adv. com. Marina Del Rey C. of C., 1974-75; bd. dirs., pub. rels. chmn. Am. Heart Assn., El Paso, 1972-74; charter pres. El Paso Exec. Women's Coun., 1972-73; mem. fin. adv. com. El Paso C.C., 1992—; bd. dirs. El Paso Estate Planning Coun., 1993—. Mem. Am. Soc. CLUs and ChFC (past pres. El Paso chpt., bd. dirs. 1981-85), Registry of CFP Practitioners (cert. sr. advisor). Avocations: contract bridge, ballroom dancing, international travel, photography. Office: Advance Funding Inc 5959 Gateway Blvd W Ste 250 El Paso TX 79925-3316

KELLEY, TIMOTHY EDWARD, state judge; b. Canton, N.Y., Aug. 16, 1954; s. Andrew James and Arlene Ellen (Dishaw) m.; m. Nanette Noland, Mar. 18, 1989. BS, Cornell U., 1976; JD, La. State U., 1983. Bar: La. 1983, Tex. 1991, U.S. Supreme Ct. 1988. Engr. La. Dept. Transp. Devel., Baton Rouge, 1976-78; project engr. Forte & Tablada, Inc., Baton Rouge, 1978-80; cons. engr. Baton Rouge, 1980-83; law clk. to presiding justice La. Supreme Ct., New Orleans, 1983-84; ptnr. Phelps, Dunbar, Marks, Claverie & Sims, Baton Rouge, 1984-93; prin. Timothy E. Kelley, P.L.C., Baton Rouge, 1993-96, Kelley & Guerry L.L.C., Baton Rouge, 1993-96; state dist. ct. judge, 19th judicial dist. ct. State of Louisiana, Baton Rouge, 1997—. Bd. dirs. Greater Baton Rouge YMCA, La. affiliate and Baton Rouge divsn. Am. Heart Assn., pres., 1994-95; mem. Cmty. Fund for Arts, Leadership Baton Rouge Class of 1992. Mem. ABA, Fed. Bar Assn., Baton Rouge Bar Assn., Am. Arbitration Assn. (arbitrator for constrn. industry, cert. mediator), La. Engring. Soc., La. Assn. Def. Counsel, La. Bar Found. (founder), Baton Rouge Area Found., New Orleans Bar Assn., C. of C. La., Greater Baton Rouge C. of C., Baton Rouge Country Club, Baton Rouge City Club, ChamPac (founder). Office: 222 Saint Louis St Rm 623 Baton Rouge LA 70802-5816

KELLEY, VIRGINIA (JUDY) WIARD, dance educator; b. Washington, Nov. 17, 1937; d. David Kyle and Mary Margaret (Barber) Wiard; m. Leo Gilbert Kelley, July 2, 1960; children: Cheryl, Raymond, John, Brenda. Degree in bus. adminstrn., Miller-Motte Bus. Coll., 1958; dance edn. degree, Kent State U., 1986. Grad. Dance Masters of Am. Performer Tony Grant Stars of Tomorrow, Atlantic City, N.J., 1951-53; performer Cressetts Betty Cress Dance Studio, tour of East Coast, 1958, Jacksonville, N.C., 1958-59; instr., performer, choreographer Cuppett's Performing Arts Ctr., Vienna, Va., 1981-99, Vienna Comty. Ctr., 1982-99; actress Wilmington (N.C.) Theatrical Soc., 1957; performer Miss Wilmington Pageant, 1958. Helper Dem. Party, Vienna, 1992. Mem. Dance Masters of Am. (dance educator 1981—), Cameo Club. Democrat. Roman Catholic. Avocations: tap dancing, weight lifting, line dancing, swimming. Home: 22 S Old Globe Rd Unit #1 Arlington VA 22204

KELLEY, WAYNE PLUMBLEY, JR., retired federal official; b. Rochester, N.Y., May 23, 1933; s. Wayne Plumbley and Elspeth Barbour (Moore) K.; m. Margaret Mary Ruikka, June 22, 1964; children: Wayne Plumbley, Richard Daniel. B.A., Vanderbilt U., 1955. City editor, state capitol reporter Chronicle, Augusta, Ga., 1960-65; Washington corr., reporter Atlanta Jour., 1965-69; assoc. editor Congl. Quar. Inc., Washington, 1969-72, mng. editor, 1972-74, exec. editor, 1974-80, pub., 1980-90, exec. v.p., 1984-90; supt. documents Govt. Printing Office, Washington, 1991-97; ret., 1997; mem. adv. com. Am. U. Sch. Comms., 1985-90. Served with U.S. Army, 1956-57. Nieman fellow Harvard U., 1963-64. Mem. Am. Polit. Sci. Assn. (Congl. fellowship adv. com. 1975-90).

KELLEY, WILLIAM, author, screenwriter; b. Staten Island, N.Y., May 27, 1929; s. Edward Thomas and Alethea Waldegrave (Mulligan) K.; m. Cornelia Ann Chamberlin, Sept. 18, 1954; children: Maura Alethea Kelley Deering, Shaun Kelley Jahshan. AB, Brown U., 1955; AM, Harvard U., 1957. West Coast editor Doubleday & Co., N.Y.C., 1958-61; fiction editor McGraw Hill Co., N.Y.C., 1961-62. Author: Gemini, 1959, The God Hunterw, 1965, The Tyree Legend, 1979, (feature film) Witness, 1985 (Academy Award 1986). Sgt. USAF, 1947-50. Recipient Edgar award Mystery Writers Assn., 1986, Best Script award for Witness, W.G.A., 1986, Western Writers, 1972, 77. Home: 864 Rocking K Rd Bishop CA 93514

KELLEY, WILLIAM NIMMONS, physician, educator; b. Atlanta, June 23, 1939; s. Oscar Lee and Will Nimmons (Allen) K.; m. Lois Faville, Aug. 1, 1959; children: Margaret Paige, Virginia Lynn, Lori Ann, William Mark. MD, Emory U., 1963; MA (hon.), U. Pa., 1989. Diplomate Am. Bd. Internal Medicine (chmn. 1985-86). Intern in medicine Parkland Meml. Hosp., Dallas, 1963-64, resident, 1964-65; sr. resident medicine Mass. Gen. Hosp., Boston, 1967-68; clin. asso., sect. on human biochem. genetics NIH, 1965-67; teaching fellow medicine Harvard U. Med. Sch., 1967-68; asst. prof. to prof. medicine, asst. prof. to asso. prof. biochemistry, chief div. rheumatic and genetic diseases Duke U. Sch. Medicine, 1968-75; Macy faculty scholar Oxford U., 1974-75; prof., chmn. dept. internal medicine, prof. dept. biol. chemistry U. Mich. Med. Sch., Ann Arbor, 1975-89; Robert G. Dunlop prof. medicine, biochemistry and biophysics U. Pa., Phila., 1989—, dean Sch. Medicine, 1989—; CEO U. Pa. Med. Ctr. and Health System, Phila., 1989—; mem. human gene therapy subcom. NIH, 1986-92, recombinant DNA com., 1988-92, dirs. adv. com., 1992-95; bd. dirs. Merck & Co., Beckman Instruments, Inc., The Phila. Orch. Assn., Greater Phila. First Corp.; bd. dirs., exec. com. Greater Phila. First Partnership for Econ. Devel., Assn. Acad. Health Ctrs. Author: (with J.B. Wyngaarden) Gout and Hyperuricemia, 1976, (with I.M. Weiner) Uric Acid, 1979, (with Harris, Ruddy and Sledge) Textbook of Rheumatology, 1981, 5th edit., 1997, (with M. Osterweiss and E.R. Rubin) Emerging Policies for Bio-Medical Research (Health Policy Annual III), 1993, (with Harris, Ruddy and Sledge) Arthritis Surgery, 1994; editor-in-chief Textbook of Internal Medicine, 1989, 3d edit., 1997, Essentials of Internal Medicine, 1994; also articles. Trustee Emory U., Woodruff Health Scis. Ctr., Wistar Inst., Leonard Davis Inst., chmn.; chmn. bd. dirs. Inst. Human Gene Therapy. Recipient C.V. Mosby award, 1963, John D. Lane award USPHS, 1969, Geigy Internat. prize rheumatology, 1969, Rsch. Career Devel. award USPHS, 1972-75, Heinz Karger Meml. Found. prize, 1973, John Phillips Meml. award and medal Am. Coll. Phys., 1990, Nat. Med. Rsch. award Nat. Health Coun., 1993, Robert H. Williams award Assn. Profs. of Medicine, 1995, Disting. Med. Achievement award Emory U., 1985; Mead Johnson scholar, 1967; Clin. scholar Am. Rheumatism Assn., 1969-72; Josiah Macy Found. scholar, 1974-75. Master ACP; fellow Am. Acad. Arts and Scis., AAAS, Royal Coll. Physicians Ireland (hon.); mem. Inst. Medicine of NAS (chmn. sect. 4, 1988-90, chmn. membership com. 1990-94, coun. 1996—, exec. com. 1996—), Am. Soc. Clin. Investigation (editorial bd. 1974-79, pres. 1983-84), Central Soc. for Clin. Research (pres. 1986-87), Am. Soc. Biochemistry and Molecular Biology (editorial bd. 1976-81), Am. Fedn. Med. Rsch. (pres. 1979-80), Assn. Am. Physicians, Assn. Profs. Medicine (sec.-treas. 1987-89), Am. Coll. Rheumatology (editl. bd. 1972-77, pres. 1986-87, Gold Medal award 1997), Am. Soc. Human Genetics, Am. Soc. Internal Medicine, Central Rheumatism Soc. (pres. 1978-79), Am. Philos. Soc., Sigma Xi, Alpha Omega Alpha. Home: 768 Woodleave Rd Bryn Mawr PA 19010-1709 Office: Univ of Pa Health Sys 21 Penn Tower 399 S 34th St Philadelphia PA 19104-4385

KELLEY, WILLIAM THOMAS, marketing educator; b. Jersey City, Feb. 4, 1917; s. William Scholes and Elsie (Thomas) K.; m. Barbara Bacher, June 23, 1945; 1 son, Thomas Bacher. B.A., U. Toronto, 1939; M.B.A., Wharton Sch., U. Pa., 1941, Ph.D., 1951. Assoc. economist U. S.C., 1941-42; chief sect. War Shipping Adminstrn., 1942-43; mem. faculty U. Pa., Phila., 1946—, assoc. prof. Annenberg Sch. Comms., 1961-68, prof. bus. adminstrn., 1974-82, emeritus prof. mktg., 1982—; cons. to govt. and industry, 1953—; vis. prof. U. Lancaster, Eng., 1966-67; vis. fellow Ashridge (Eng.) Mgmt. Coll., 1977. Author: Management of Promotion, 1963, Marketing Intelligence, 1968, The New Consumerism, 1973; contbg. author: Handbook of Modern Marketing, 2d edit., 1986; also articles, monographs; editor: Mktg. Abstracts, 1953-61; editorial bd.: Jour. Mktg, 1966-76. Served to 1st lt. AUS, 1943-46. Ford Found. fellow, 1963. Mem. Am. Mktg. Assn. (Impact Marketer of Yr. 1993), Greater Phila. C. of C. (past officer). Quaker. Office: Univ Pa Dept Mktg Dietrich Hall 36th and Locust Walk Philadelphia PA 19104-1999 Address: Insurer Central Scv W Thomas Kelly,President 457 Inveraray Rd Villanova PA 19085-1139

KELLGREN, GEORGE LARS, manufacturing company executive; b. Boras, Sweden, May 23, 1943; came to U.S., 1979; s. Lars Anders and Ann-Marie (Fröberg) Kjellgren; m. Rubi Caridad Godoy, Nov. 6, 1982; children: Adrian Anders, Derek Lars, Viveka Victoria. BS, Umea U., Sweden, 1967. Researcher, developer Husquarna (Sweden) Arms Factory, Husquarna, 1968; tech. officer Council for Sci. and Industrial Research, Pretoria, Republic of South Africa, 1969-74; mng. dir. Interdynamic Forsknings AB, Stockholm, 1975-79; tech. dir. Intratec U.S.A., Inc., Miami, 1979-83; pres. Grendel, Inc., Cocoa, Fla., 1983-95; CEO Kel-Tec CNC Industries, Inc., Cocoa, 1995—. Contbr. articles to profl. jours.; inventor firearms. Republican. Lutheran.

KELLIS, MICHAEL JOHN, osteopathic physician; b. Wheeling, W.Va., Dec. 2, 1958; s. John George and Mary (Moskos) K. BS magna cum laude, Bethany (W.Va.) Coll., 1981; DO, Ohio U., 1985. Resident Brentwood Hosp., Cleve., 1985-86, fellow, 1986-87; pvt. practice, Chardon, Ohio, 1987—; dir. sports medicine Geauga Hosp., 1987—; team physician Berkshire High Sch., Burton, Ohio, 1987—, Notre Dame-Cath. Latin High Sch., Chardon, 1989—. Basketball coach, speaker on drug abuse Sts. Constantine and Helen Green Orthodox Ch., Cleveland Heights, Ohio 1987—; mem. leadership com. Geauga County unit Am. Heart Assn., Chardon, 1990—; ch. bd. mem. Sts. Constantine and Helen Greek Orthodox Ch., 1996-98; founder, pres. Friends of St. Michael non-profit orgn., 1996—; dir. summer camp Monastery of St. Michael, Rhodes, Greece; active Hunger Task Force, Geauga County, 1998-99. Named one of Cleve.'s 50 Most Interesting People, Cleve. Mag., 1997. Fellow Am. Osteopathic Acad. Sports Medicine (bd. dirs. 1996—, dir. nat. conv. 1999); mem. Am. Coll. Osteo. Sports Medicine, Am. Coll. Gen. Practitioners, Am. Osteo. Assn. Republican. Avocations: biking, weightlifting, stamp collecting. Office: 13207 Ravenna Rd Chardon OH 44024-9012

KELLISON, CRAIG M., federal judge; b. 1950. BS, U. Nev., 1972; JD, Gonzaga U., 1976. Law clk. to Hon. Bruce Thompson U.S. Dist. Ct. Nev., 1976; with Office of U.S. Atty., Nev., 1976-78; apptd. magistrate judge ea. dist. U.S. Dist. Ct. Calif., 1988; instr. law Lassen Coll., 1988-94. Mem. Calif. State Bar, Nev. State Bar, Oreg. State Bar, Lassen County Bar Assn., Washoe County Bar Assn. Fax: (916) 257-2021. Office: 60 S Lassen St Susanville CA 96130-4363

KELLISON, DONNA LOUISE GEORGE, accountant, educator; b. Hugoton, Kans., Oct. 16, 1950; d. Donald Richard and Zepha Louise (Lowry) George. BA in Elem. Edn. with honors, Anderson (Ind.) U., 1972; MS in Elem. Edn., Ind. U., 1981. CPA, Ind.; lic. tchr., Ind. Tchr. elem. Maconaquah Sch. Corp., Bunker Hill, Ind., 1972-73; office mgr. Eskew & Gresham, CPA's, Louisville, Ky., 1973-78; para-profl. Blue & Co., Indpls., 1979-83, tax compliance specialist, 1983-84, tax sr., 1984-86, tax supr., 1986-87, tax mgr., 1987-90, tax prin., 1990-92, tax sr. mgr., 1992-94, tax dir., 1995—; pres. Blue Benefits Cons., Inc., 1998—. Vol. Children's Clinic, Indpls., 1985-92; chairperson Most Wanted campaign Am. Cancer Soc., 1995; bd. dirs. Indpls. Estate Planning Coun., 1995—, sec., 1995-96, vice-chair, 1998, chair 1998-99. Mem. AICPA, Ind. CPA Soc. (tax inst. com. 1989-93, govt. rels. com. 1994—), Ind. Tax Inst. (chair 1993). Presbyterian. Home: 382 Pintail Ct Carmel IN 46032-9125 Office: Blue & Co PO Box 80069 Indianapolis IN 46280-0069

KELLISON, JAMES BRUCE, lawyer; b. Richmond, Va., June 18, 1922; s. John Ray and Clara (Cato) K.; m. Audrey Cresswell, May 5, 1962; children: Bruce, Jr., Elizabeth, Julia. B.A., U. Richmond, 1943; J.D., George Washington U., 1948. Bar: D.C. 1948. Ptnr. Hogan & Hartson, Washington, 1954-73, Altmann Kellison & Siegler, Washington, 1973-83; pvt. practice Washington, 1983—; mem. adv. com. on rules of probate procedure Superior Ct., 1972-94. Pres., bd. trustees Louise Home, 1971—; trustee, Columbia Lighthouse for the Blind, 1969-76; trustee Audubon Naturalist Soc., 1968-71. Served with USNR, 1943-45. Fellow Am. Coll. Trust and Estate Counsel; mem. Am., D.C. bar assns., Omicron Delta Kappa, Lambda Chi Alpha, Phi Delta Phi. Republican. Clubs: Metropolitan (Washington), Barristers (Washington), St. Albans Tennis (Washington); Chevy Chase (Md.); Lawyers (Washington). Home: 2801 New Mexico Ave NW Apt 1409 Washington DC 20007-3914 Office: 910 17th St NW Washington DC 20006-2601

KELLISON, STEPHEN GEORGE, insurance executive; b. Ord, Nebr., Mar. 20, 1942; s. Orin Albian and Sarah Viola (Crouch) K.; m. Chery Le Wagner, June 14, 1963 (div. Jan. 1970); m. Erica Elizabeth Bowers, Jan. 27, 1978 (div. June 1985); m. Maureen Antoinette Gage, Nov. 15, 1986. AB, U. Nebr., Lincoln, 1963, MS, 1967. CFP. Actuarial supr. Occidental Life Ins. Co., L.A., 1963-65; actuary Lincoln Liberty Life Ins. Co., Lincoln, Nebr., 1965-66; prof. U. Nebr., 1966-75; consulting actuary G.V. Stennes & Assocs., Dallas, 1975-76; exec. dir. Am. Acad. Actuaries, Washington, 1976-88; chmn. Dept. Risk Mgmt. and Ins. Ga. State U., Atlanta, 1989-93; sr. v.p. instnl. svcs. Am. Gen. Retirement Svcs., Houston, 1994—. Author: The Theory of Interest, 1970, 2d edit., 1991, Fundamentals of Numerical Analysis, 1975. Chmn. tech. panel Social Security Adv. Coun., 1989-91; pub. trustee Social Security and Medicare, 1995—; mem. task force on interest methods Fin. Acctg. Standards Bd., 1989-95; sec. Acturial Edn. and Rsch. Fund, 1989-92. Fellow Soc. Actuaries (bd. dirs. 1973-75, 90-93); mem. Nat. Acad. Social Ins., Am. Acad. Actuaries (bd. dirs. 1975-76), Internat. Actuarial Assn., Actuaries Club of the S.W., Phi Beta Kappa. Home: 3103 W Autumn Run Cir Sugar Land TX 77479-2634 Office: Am General Ret Svcs Houston TX 77019

KELLMAN, BARNET KRAMER, film, stage and television director; b. N.Y.C., Nov. 9, 1947; s. Joseph A.G. and Verona D. (Kramer) K.; m. Nancy Mette, 1982; children: Katherine Mette, Eliza Mette. BA, Colgate U., 1969; postgrad., Yale U., 1970; PhD, Union Grad. Sch., 1972. Dir. plays, TV and film prodns.; tchr., guest dir. N.C. Sch. Arts, 1973-80, CCNY, 1975-76, grad. film div. Columbia U., 1984-87. Dir.: (feature films) Key Exchange, 1985, Straight Talk, 1992, Stinkers, 1997; dir. 6 seasons Eugene O'Neill Theatre Ctr.; assoc. artistic dir. Williamstown Theatre Festival, 1974, 75; dir.: (off-Broadway plays) Key Exchange, 1981, Breakfast with Les and Bess, 1982, The Good Parts, 1982, Danny and the Deep Blue Sea, 1984, The Loman Family Picnic, 1989; dir. (TV series) Gemini Showtime, 1981, All is Forgiven, 1986, My Sister Sam, 1987, Designing Women, 1987, E.R., 1996; prodr., dir.: (TV series) Murphy Brown, 1989-92 (Dir.'s Guild award 1990, Outstanding Dir. in Comedy Series Emmy award 1992); co-exec. prodr., dir.: (TV series) Mad About You, 1992-93, Good Advice, 1992-93, (TV pilot) The Second Half, 1993, Thunder Alley, 1994; exec. prodr., dir.: (TV series) Something Wilder, 1994, (TV pilots) Hope and Gloria, 1995, Bless This House, 1995, If Not For You, 1995, Suddenly Susan, 1996, life with Roger, 1996, For Your Love, 1998. Danforth fellow, 1969-72; Thomas J. Watson fellow, 1969-71. Mem. AEA, SAG, Dirs. Guild Am., Soc. Stage Dirs. and Choreographers (bd. dirs. 1984-86), New Dramatists (bd. dirs.). Jewish. Office: care Marty Adelstein The Endeavor Agy 9701 Wilshire Blvd Fl 10 Beverly Hills CA 90212

KELLNER, IRWIN L., economist; b. N.Y.C., Oct. 4, 1938; s. Philip and Mildred (Isaacson) K.; m. Ann Heimann, Jan. 22, 1961; children: Lori, Shari. BA in Econs., Bklyn. Coll., 1960, MA in Econs., 1964; PhD in Econs., New Sch. for Social Rsch., 1973; LHD (hon.), Hofstra U.; LLD (hon.), St. Joseph's Coll. Asst. bus. outlook editor Bus. Week Mag., prior to 1960, 1966-70; rsch. analyst Philip Morris, Inc., 1960-63; sr. rsch. analyst William Esty Co., Inc., 1963-66; assoc. economist Mfrs. Hanover Trust Co., N.Y.C., 1970-72, v.p., 1972-78, dep. chief economist, 1973-78, sr. v.p., 1978—; chief economist The Chase Regional Bank, N.Y.C., 1980-97; pres. Kellner Econ. advisors, 1997—; Augustus B. Weller Disting. Chair of Econs. Hofstra U., Hempstead, N.Y., 1997—; chief economist, CBS MarketWatch, 1997—; adj. full prof. sch. bus. Adelphi U., 1983-91; adj. faculty Arthur Andersen Consulting, 1997; adj., vis. lectr. colls.; speaker bus. and community groups; mem. bd. economists L.A. Times.; bd. dirs. Columbia Labs, Internat. Bioimmune Systems, Universal Heights, DataTreasury Corp., Austin Travel, Claire's Stores, Inc. Author monthly Econ. Report/Hofstra U.; weekly guest News 12 L.I., Cablevision, CNBC-TV; contbr. articles and commentaries to profl. publs. Mem. village planning bd. Port Washington, N.Y., 1972—; commr. Hist. Landmarks, Village of Port Washington North, 1971-74; former bd. dirs. Juv. Diabetes Found., 1986-92, N.Y. Inst. Tech., sch. bus. Adelphi U.; bd. dirs. Children's AIDS Network, 1986—, Don Monti Found., 1992—; assoc. trustee North Shore U. Hosp., 1992—; chmn. adv. bd. Barry Z. Levine Sch. of Health Scis., Touro Coll., 1991—; mem. L.I. Regional Transp. adv. com. N.Y. State Senate Com. on Transp., 1988—; mem. N.Y. Dist. Adv. Coun. of Sml. Bus. Adminstrn. Region II; mem. N.Y. State Comptroller's Econ. Adv. Com., 1995—; past mem. N.Y.C. Economist's Roundtable, 1991-93; mem. numerous pro bono bds. including North Shore Univ. Hosp., Don Monti Meml. Rsch. Found., Epilepsy Found. of L.I., Nassau County Coun. of Boy Scouts of Am.; mem. adv. bd. C.W. Post's Coll. of Mgmt., 1997; numerous other civic activities. Recipient award for tobacco econs. Tobacco Mchts. Assn., 1978; named Number One Prognosticator, Instl. Investor mag., Most Accurate Forecaster (twice), Bus. Week mag., one of Top 5 Interest Rate Forecasters, Wall St. Jour.; recipient Disting. Leadership award for health edn., Barry Z. Levine Sch., Human Rels. award Am. Jewish Com., Humanitarian award Juv. Diabetes Found., Gary Sherman Humanitarian award North Shore Health System. Mem. Conf. Bd. (mem. Econ. Forum), Forecasters Club N.Y. (past pres.), Money Marketeers (past gov.), N.Y. Assn. Bus. Economists (past pres.), Am. Econ. Assn., Am. Statis. Assn., Bus. Economists Council, Downtown Economists Luncheon Group, Nat. Assn. Bus. Economists, N.Y. Acad. Scis., Met. Econ. Assn., Am. Bankers Assn. (adv. com.). Achievements include the innovation of the Mfrs. Hanover (now Chase) Trade-Weighted Dollar and the Mfrs. Hanover (now Chase) Cost-of-Living Index.

KELLNER, JAMIE, broadcasting executive. With CBS, 1969; former v.p. first-run programming, devel., sales Viacom Enterprises; pres. Orion Entertainment Group, 1979-86; pres., CEO Fox Broadcasting Co., L.A., 1986-93; CEO, pres. WBTV Network, Burbank, Calif. Office: WBTV Network 4000 Warner Blvd Bldg 34R Burbank CA 91522-0001*

KELLNER, RICHARD GEORGE, mathematician, computer scientist; b. Cleve., July 10, 1943; s. George Ernst and Wanda Julia (Lapinski) K.; BS, Case Inst. Tech., 1965; MS, Stanford U., 1968, PhD, 1969; m. Charlene Ann Zajc, June 26, 1965; children: Michael Richard, David George. Staff mem. Los Alamos (N.M.) Scientific Lab., 1969-79, Los Alamos Nat. Lab., 1983-88; co-owner, dir. software devel. KMP Computer Systems, Inc., Los Alamos, 1979-84; mgr. spl. projects KMP Computer Systems div. 1st Data Resources Inc., Los Alamos, 1984-87; with microcomputer div., 1988; owner CompuSpeed, 1986—; co-owner Computer-Aided Communications, 1982-84; v.p. Applied Computing Systems Inc., 1988—; cons., 1979—. Recipient Commendation award for outstanding support of operation Desert Storm. Mem. IEEE, Assn. Computing Machinery, Math. Assn. Am., Soc. Indsl. and Applied Math., Am. Math. Soc. Home: 4496 Ridgeway Dr Los Alamos NM 87544-1960 Office: Applied Computing Systems Inc 120 Longview Dr Los Alamos NM 87544-3728

KELLOGG, C. BURTON, II, financial analyst; b. Plainfield, N.J., June 22, 1934; s. Chester M. and Alice L.; m. Dorothy E. Harasty, July 31, 1954; children: Katharine E., Patricia A., Peter B. BA in Econs., Dartmouth Coll., 1956; MBA in Fin., Columbia U., 1958. With A.M. Best Co., N.Y.C., 1958-68; v.p. A.M. Best Co., Oldwick, N.J., 1968-81, sr. v.p., 1981—, corp. sec. bd. dirs. Editor: Best's Insurance Reports, 1963-94. Sec. Westfield, N.J. YMCA, 1972-76. Mem. Assn. Ins. and Fin. Analysts, Echo Lake Country Club (trustee 1985-90). Office: AM Best Co Ambest Rd Oldwick NJ 08858

KELLOGG, CAL STEWART, II, conductor, composer; b. Long Beach, Calif., July 26, 1947; s. Cal Stewart and Anne Laverne (Yackee) K.; m. Deborah Nelson Wilde, Jan. 25, 1975 (div. Nov. 1983); m. Jean Marie Keister, May 13, 1989 (div. May 1999). Diploma in bassoon, Conservatorio di St. Cecilia, Rome, 1967, Diploma in Composition, 1972, Diploma in Conducting, 1974. Music dir. Va. Chamber Orch., 1993; prin. condr. Austin Lyric Opera, 1996-98, music dir., 1998; prin. condr. Ariz. Opera, 1999. Guest condr. San Francisco Opera, N.Y.C. Opera, Santa Fe Opera, Washington Opera, Spoleto Festival U.S.A. , Wolf Trap Opera, St. Louis Opera Theatre, Houston Grand Opera, Seattle Opera, Balt. Opera, Chautauqua Opera, Cin. Opera, Teatro dell'Opera di Roma, Teatro San Carlo di Napoli, Teatro Comunale di Firenze, Teatro Reggio di Parma, Edinburgh Festival, Israel Festival, Spoleto Festival, Italy, Can. Opera Co., L'Opera de Montreal, Antwerp Philharm., Balt. Symphony, Maggio Florentino, Orchestra of Teatro La Fenice, Venezia, Israel Sinfonietta, New World Symphony, RAI Orchs. of Rome, Naples and Torino, Seattle Symphony, Accademia Nazionale St. Cecilia, Orch. of Monte Carlo, Chautauqua Symphony, Spoleto U.S.A.; bassoonist L'Orchestra Nazionale dell'Accademia di. St. Cecilia, Rome, 1966-72, Il Piccolo Teatro Musicale di Rome, 1967-71; bassoon soloist RAI Orch. of Rome, 1972; vocal coach, prompter, organist I Virtuosi di Roma, Venice, Italy, 1971; composer song cycle Sonnets from the Portuguese, 1986, Shakespeare Sonnets, 1990; orchestral setting Sullivan Ballou's

Letter to His Wife, 1990. Avocation: golf. Office: care John J Miller 801 W 181st St Apt 20 New York NY 10033-4518

KELLOGG, DAVID, publisher; b. N.Y.C., Aug. 26, 1950; s. George Dwight and Wynne (Krementz) K.; m. Sandra Ruffer, Aug. 29, 1976; children: Matthew Dwight, Benjamin William. Student, Groton Sch., Mass., 1968; BA cum laude, Yale U., 1972. Pers. dir. Krementz and Co., Newark, N.J., 1972-74; scriptwriter CBS-TV, N.Y.C., 1974-76; asst. to the pres. Walker and Co., N.Y.C., 1976-79; sr. editor Pergamon Press, Elmsford, N.Y., 1979-83; dir. pubs. Coun. on Fgn. Rels., N.Y.C., 1983—; pub. dir. Fgn. Affairs Mag., N.Y.C., 1987—, pub., 1992—; v.p. Coun. Fgn. Rels., 1997—; chmn. The Leadership Network, N.Y.C., 1991-93; co-dir. the Coming Global Pension Conf., N.Y.C., 1996. Mem. editl. adv. bd. Reform Judaism, 1994-98. Trustee Chappaqua Libr., 1988-93, pres. bd. trustees Chappaqua Libr., 1991-93; v.p. Temple Beth El No. Westchester, 1994-97. Mem. Assn. Am. Pubs., Mag. Pubs. Assn., Smaller Mag. Adv. Coun., Coun. Fgn. Rels. Home: 9 West Pl Chappaqua NY 10514-3614 Office: Coun Fgn Rels 58 E 68th St New York NY 10021-5939

KELLOGG, DAVID WAYNE, agriculture educator, researcher; b. Seymour, Mo., Aug. 19, 1941; s. Martin David and Lula May (Spurlock) K.; m. Mary Sue Powell, June 7, 1964; children: Kirk David, Susan Joann Franz, Kimberley Annelle Van Vacter, Gregory William. BS, U. Mo., 1963, MS, 1964; PhD, U. Nebr., 1968. Profl. animal scientist. Asst. prof. agriculture N.Mex. State U., Las Cruces, 1967-71, assoc. prof., 1971-78, prof., 1978-81; prof., dept. head U. Ark., Fayetteville, 1981-86, prof., 1986—; cons. AID-N.Mex. State U. Mission, Asuncion, Paraguay, 1971; spkr. Ark. Farm Bur., Little Rock, 1981-90, ORFFA Seminar, Rennes, France, 1995, Breda, Holland, 1996; mem. adv. com Ark. Livestock and Poultry Commn., 1989-94; reviewer rsch. proposals USDA, Small Bus. Innovation. Mem. editorial bd. Jour. Dairy Science, 1978-84; contbr. chpts. to book and sci. articles to profl. jours. Mem. Am. Registry Profl. Animal Sci. (bd. dirs. 1989-91, pres.-elect 1993-94, pres. 1994-95, nominating com. 1996-98), Am. Dairy Sci. Assn. (sec. so. sect. 1991, v.p. 1992, pres. 1993, awards com. 1996-98), Am. Soc. Animal Sci. (awards com. 1990-92, spkr. symposium on chelated trace minerals, 1996), Am. Grassland and Forage Coun., So. Assn. Agrl. Sci. (bd. dirs. 1993-94), Ark. Registry Profl. Animal Scientists (charter, sec., treas. 1989-93), Ark. Nutrition Coun., Gideons Internat. (trustee 1975-81), Gamma Sigma Delta. Mem. Life Change Comty. Fellowship. Office: U Ark Dept Animal Sci Fayetteville AR 72701

KELLOGG, FREDERIC HARTWELL, civil engineer, educator; b. Pitts., July 31, 1904; s. Frederic Sherlock and Gertrude (Chew) k.; m. Helen Bishop, Apr. 8, 1937; children: Frederic H., Walter Whitney. Geol. Engr., Colo. Sch. Mines, 1927; AM, Johns Hopkins U., 1929, PhD, 1934. Engring. geologist Panama Canal, 1929-34; engr. soils and founds., constrn. dept. TVA, 1934-45; engr. U.S. Engrs., Mo. Valley Devel., 1945-46; prof. civil engring. U. Miss., 1946-50, chmn. dept. civil engring., 1947-50, dean engring., 1950-64; prof. civil engring., dean Memphis State U., 1964-74, dean, 1965-69, now dean emeritus; cons. engr. found. and earthworks phases of constrn., 1946—; cons. TVA, Govt. of Bombay, Punjab, others. Author: Construction Methods and Machinery, 1954. Mem. Miss. Bd. Engring. Examiners, 1958-64, Miss. River Commn., 1965-74. Fellow ASCE (J. R. Croes medal 1950); mem. Memphis Engrs. Club, Omicron Delta Kappa, Kappa Sigma, Chi Epsilon. Home: 4722 Gwynne Rd Memphis TN 38117-3210

KELLOGG, HERBERT HUMPHREY, metallurgist, educator; b. N.Y.C., Feb. 24, 1920; s. Herbert H. and Gladys (Falding) K.; m. Jeanette Halstead, July 20, 1940; children—Thomas Bartlett, Jane Falding, David Humphrey, Elizabeth Ann. B.S., Columbia, 1941, M.S., 1943. Asst. prof. mineral preparation Pa. State U., State Coll., 1942-46; faculty Columbia U., N.Y.C., 1946—; Stanley-Thompson prof. chem. metallurgy Columbia U., 1968-90, prof. emeritus, 1990—; Chmn. titanium adv. com. Office Def. Mblzn., 1954-58. Research; contbr. numerous articles to publs. Recipient Best Paper award extractive metals div. Am. Inst. Mining., Metall. and Petroleum Engrs.; James Douglas Gold medal Am. Inst. Mining, Metall. and Petroleum Engrs., 1973. Fellow AIME (chmn. extractive metallurgy div. 1958), Metall. Soc., Instn. Mining and Metallurgy (London); mem. NAE, Sigma Xi, Tau Beta Pi. Home: Closter Rd Palisades NY 10964 Office: Dept Metallurgy Columbia U New York NY 10027

KELLOGG, JEFFREY, umpire; b. Coldwater, Mich., Aug. 29, 1961; m. Roxine Tackett, Sept. 14, 1990. BS in Criminal Justice, Ferris State. Former umpire Appalachian League, Midwest League, Ea. League, Triple Alliance, Fla. Instrnl. League, Internat. League; umpire maj. league baseball Nat. League, N.Y.C., 1993—; with Umpires Union, Phila. Avocations: golfing, weight training, aerobics. Office: Nat League 350 Park Ave New York NY 10022 also: Umpires Union 1735 Market St Philadelphia PA 19103

KELLOGG, JOSEPH J., JR., military career officer; b. Dayton, Ohio, May 12, 1944. BA in Polit. Sci., U. Santa Clara; MA in Polit. Sci., U. Kans.; grad., Command and Gen. Staff Coll., U.S. Army War Coll. Commd. 2nd lt. U.S. Army, 1967, advanced through grades to maj. gen., 1996, various positions, 1967-83; comdr. 1st Bn. (airborne), 504th Inf., 82d Airborne Divsn. U.S. Army, Ft. Bragg, N.C., 1983-85; ops. officer Office of the Chief of Staff U.S. Army, Washington, 1985-86; G-3 (ops.), 7th Inf. Divsn. (light) U.S. Army, Ft. Ord, Calif., 1987-88; comdr. 3d Brigade, 7th Inf. Divsn. (light) U.S. Army, Ft. Ord, 1988-90; chief of staff 82d Airborne Divsn. U.S. Army, Saudi Arabia, 1990-91; chief of staff 82d Airborne Divsn. U.S. Army, Ft. Bragg, 1991, asst. divsn. comdr. (ops.) 82d Airborne Divsn., 1991-92; commdg. gen. spl. ops. command Europe U.S. European Command, Germany, 1992-94; asst. dep. chief of staff for combat devel. U.S. Army Tng. and Doctrine Command, Ft. Monroe, Va., 1994-96; dep. chief of staff for combat devel. U.S. Army Tng. and Doctrine Command, Ft. Monroe, 1994-96; commdg. gen. 82nd Airborne Divsn. U.S. Army, Ft. Bragg, 1996-98; asst. dep. chief of staff for ops. and plans U.S. Army, Washington, 1998—. Office: US Army 400 Army Pentagon Washington DC 20310-0400

KELLOGG, JUDITH LILLIAN, English educator; b. May 21, 1945. BA in Comparative Lit., U. Calif., Berkeley, 1968, MA in Comparative Lit., 1970, PhD in Comparative Lit.-Medieval Studies, 1979. Rsch. asst. classical archeology, Corinth, Greece, 1970-71; instr. U. Calif., Berkeley, 1974-77; asst. prof. English U. Hawaii, Honolulu, 1978-88, assoc. prof. English,, 1988—, dir. honors program dept. English, 1998—; co-dir. Conf. on Lit. and Hawaii's Children, 1988, 90, 92, Let's Talk About It, reading and discussion programs throughout Hawaii, 1990-91; founding pres. Children's Lit. Hawaii, Honolulu, 1995. Author: Medieval Artistry and Exchange, 1989; contbr. numerous articles to profl. jours. E-mail: jkellogg@hawaii.edu. Home: 1905 Judd Hillside Rd Honolulu HI 69822 Office: U Hawaii Dept English 1733 Donaghho Rd Honolulu HI 96822-2315

KELLOGG, KENYON P., lawyer; b. Dubuque, Iowa, Aug. 5, 1946; s. Kenyon P. and Maleta (Fleege) K.; m. Carolyn Jo Dick, July 18, 1970; children: Andrew P., Kenyon P., Jonathan P. BSBA summa cum laude, Creighton U., 1968; JD cum laude, U. Mich., 1971. Bar: U.S. Dist. Ct. (we. dist.) Wash. 1971, U.S. Tax Ct. 1980; CPA, Wash. With Arthur Andersen & Co., Omaha and Detroit, 1968-71; assoc. Lane Powell Spears Lubersky, Seattle, 1971-78, ptnr., 1978—. Bd. regents Seattle U., 1989—, dean's coun. Alber's Sch. Bus. and Econs., 1992—; mem. nat. alumni bd. Creighton U., 1995—; trustee Naval Undersea Mus. Found., 1995—; mem. FELES com. USN Acad., 1995—. Capt. USAR, 1968-77. Mem. AICPAs, Wash. Soc. CPAs, Seattle Rotary, Seattle Yacht Club (trustee), Cruising Club of Am., Naval Acad. Sailing Squadron. Avocations: sailing, skiing. Office: Lane Powell Spears Lubersky 1420 5th Ave Ste 4100 Seattle WA 98101-2338

KELLOGG, PETER R., securities dealer; b. 1942; married. Student, Babson Coll., 1963. With Stern Frank Meyer Fox, 1964-67; chief exec. officer, sr. ptnr. Spear Leeds & Kellogg, N.Y.C., 1967—; chmn. Spear Leeds & Kellogg Securities Inc., N.Y.C. Office: Spear Leeds & Kellogg 120 Broadway Lbby 6 New York NY 10271-0094

KELLOGG, ROBERT LELAND, English language educator; b. Ionia County, Mich., Sept. 2, 1928; s. Charles Edwin and Lucille Jeanette (Reasoner) K.; m. Joan Alice Montgomery, Apr. 4, 1951; children: Elizabeth Joan, Jonathan Montgomery, Stephen Robert. BA, U. Md., 1950; MA, Harvard U., 1952, PhD, 1958. Mem. faculty U. Va., 1957—, prof. English, 1967—, chmn. dept., 1974-78, dean Coll. Arts and Scis., 1978-85; prin. Monroe Hill Coll., 1985-88. Author: (with Robert Scholes) The Nature of Narrative, 1966, A Concordance to Eddic Poetry, 1988; translator of works from Icelandic; contbr. to profl. jours. Served with USAR, 1954-56. Am.-Scandinavian Found. fellow, 1956-57; Guggenheim fellow, 1968-69. Mem. Medieval Acad. Am., Modern Lang. Assn., South Atlantic Modern Lang. Assn. (pres. 1974-75), Raven Soc., Phi Beta Kappa (pres. local chpt. 1981). Democrat. Club: Colonnade. Home: 411 N 1st St Charlottesville VA 22902-4610 Office: U Va Bryan Hall Charlottesville VA 22903-3289

KELLOGG, TOMMY NASON, reinsurance corporation executive; b. Ava, Mo., Mar. 29, 1936; s. Charles Roy and Bessie May (Robertson) K.; m. Louise Marie Howard, Dec. 21, 1957 (div. 1960); 1 son, Larry J.; m. Sandra Lee Weydt, Jan. 28, 1965 (div. 1983); children: Todd T., Christopher C.; m. Camille Leone, May 26, 1991. B.A., Drury Coll., 1958; M.S., Mich. State U., 1961; J.D., DePaul U., 1970. Instr. econs. Mich. State U., East Lansing, 1960-61; underwriter Employers Ins. of Wausau, Chgo., 1961-68; with Gen. Reins. Corp., Stamford, Conn., 1968—, v.p., 1974-78, sr. v.p., 1978-91; exec. v.p., chief mktg. officer Gen. Reins. Corp., Stamford, 1992, mem. office of the chmn. for Gen. and Cologne RC, 1995, pres., COO, 1995—; dir. Gen. Reins. Corp., Stamford, Conn., Herbert Clough, Inc., Stamford, Gen. Reins. Corp., Gen. Star Mgmt. Co., Stamford, Gen. Re Services Corp., Genesis Underwriting Mgmt. Co., Stamford; chmn. Holding Co., exec. v.p. Holding Co., Gen. Re Corp., Stamford, Conn., 1995, dir. Gen. Re Fin. Products. Mem. exec. adv. bd. Breech Sch. of Bus.; trustee Drury Coll., Coll. of Ins. With USAR, 1960-68. Edn. research grantee Mich. State U., 1958. Mem. Am. Soc. C.P.C.U.s, Omicron Delta Kappa, Lambda Chi Alpha. Republican. Baptist. Home: 38 Meadowbank Rd Old Greenwich CT 06870-2312 Office: PO Box 10350 Financial Ctr Stamford CT 06904

KELLOGG, WILLIAM S., retail executive; b. 1943. With Federated Dept. Stores, Inc., Cin., 1962-66; with Kohl's Dept. Stores, Inc., Menomonee Falls, Wis., 1966-77, pres., 1977-82, chmn., 1982—. Office: Kohl's Dept Stores N56 W 17000 Ridgewood Dr Menomonee Falls WI 53051-7026*

KELLOGG, WILLIAM WELCH, meteorologist; b. New York Mills, N.Y., Feb. 14, 1917; s. Frederick S. and Elizabeth (Walcott) K.; m. Elizabeth Thorson, Feb. 14, 1942; children: Karl S., Judith K. Liebert, Joseph W., Jane E., Thomas W. BA, Yale U., 1939; MA, UCLA, 1942, PhD, 1949. With Inst. Geophysics UCLA, L.A., 1946-52, asst. prof., 1950-52; scientist Rand Corp., Santa Monica, Calif., 1947-59, head planetary scis. dept., 1959-64; assoc. dir. Nat. Ctr. Atmospheric Research, Boulder, Colo., also dir. lab. atmospheric scis., 1964-73, sr. scientist, 1973-87; sr. rsch. assoc. Nat. Ctr. Atmospheric Rsch., Boulder, Colo., 1994—; mem. earth satellite panel IGY, 1956-59; mem. space sci. bd. Nat. Acad. Scis., 1959-68, mem. com. meteorol. aspects of effects of atomic radiation, 1956-58, mem. com. atmospheric scis., 1966-72, mem. polar research bd., 1972-77; mem. Rocket and Satellite Research Panel, 1957-62; mem. adv. group supporting tech. for operational meteorol. satellites NASA-NOAA, 1964-72; rapporteur meteorology of high atmosphere, commn. aerology World Meteorol. Orgn., 1965-71; chmn. internat. commn. meteorology upper atmosphere Internat. Union Geodesy and Geophysics, 1960-67, mem., 1967-75; mem. internat. com. climate Internat. Assn. Meteorology and Atmospheric Physics, 1978-87; mem. sci. adv. bd. USAF, 1956-65; chmn. meteorol. satellite com. Advanced Research Projects Agy., 1958-59; mem. panel on environment President's Sci. Adv. Com., 1968-72; mem. space program adv. council NASA, 1976-77; chmn. meteorol. adv. com. EPA, 1970-74, mem. nat. air quality criteria adv. com., 1975-76, air pollution transport and transformation adv. com., 1976-78; mem. council on carbon dioxide environ. assessment Dept. Energy, 1976-78; adv. to sec. gen. on World Climate Program, World Meteorol. Orgn., 1978-79; dir. research Naval Environ. Prediction Research Facility, Monterey, Calif., 1983-84; chmn. adv. com. Div. Polar Programs NSF, 1983-86; researcher on meteorology, dynamics and turbulence of upper atmosphere, prediction radioactive fallout and dispersal, applications of infrared techniques, atmospheres of Mars and Venus, theory of climate and causes of climate change. Served as pilot-weather officer USAAF, 1941-46. Co-recipient spl. award pioneering work in planning meteorol. satellite Am. Meteorol. Soc., 1961; recipient Risseca award contbn. human relations in scis. Jewish War Vets. U.S.A., 1962-63, Exceptional Civilian Service award Dept. Air Force, 1966, Spl. award for pioneering meteorol. satellites Dept. Commerce, 1985, Spl. Citation award for atmospheric conservation Garden Club of Am., 1988. Fellow Am. Geophys. Union (pres. meteorol. sect. 1972-74), Am. Meteorol. Soc. (council 1960-63, pres. 1973-74), AAAS (chmn. atmospheric and hydrospheric sect. 1984); mem. Sigma Xi. Home: 445 College Ave Boulder CO 80302-7131 *If there is anything that generally characterizes a gratifying and successful career in science, it is the challenge of diversity. The really important problems of the universe, and especially of society, involve several disciplines, and we are compelled to work at these discipline interfaces. Pigeon holes are for pigeons, not scientists.*

KELLOUGH, RICHARD DEAN, educator; b. Jamestown, Ohio, Oct. 31, 1935; s. Stanley Eugene and Mayme Elizabeth Kellough. BS, Wilmington Coll., 1956; MAT in Botany, Miami U., 1959; EdD, Oreg. State U., 1967. Tchr. Clinton County Schs., Martinsville, Ohio, 1956-59, San Juan Unified Sch. Dist., Carmichael, Calif., 1960-61, Davis (Calif.) Sr. H.S., 1961-69; asst. prof. tchr. edn. Calif. State U., Sacramento, 1969-73, assoc. prof., 1973-77, prof., 1977—; rsch. asst. Kettering Found., Yellow Springs, Ohio, 1957-58; lab. tech. II U. Calif., Davis, 1959-61; NSF rsch. fellow U. Calif., Davis, 1962. Author numerous textbooks including Science for the Elementary and Middle School, 1997, Middle School Teaching: A Guide to Methods and Resources, 1996, A Resource Guide for Teaching: K-12, 1997. Office: Calif State Univ 6000 J St Sacramento CA 95819-2605

KELLOUGH, WILLIAM C., lawyer; b. Tulsa, Dec. 2, 1949; s. Robert B. and Jo M. (Craker) K.; m. Louisa C. Watt, May 22, 1971; children: Sara Louise, Annie Elizabeth, Caroline Alyce. BA, U. Tex., 1972, JD, 1975. Bar: Tex., Okla. Ptnr. Blackstock, Joyce, Blackstock & Montgomery, Tulsa, 1975-80; shareholder Boone, Smith, Davis, Hurst & Dickman, Tulsa, 1980—. Trustee Lorene Cooper Hasbrouck Charitable Trust, Tulsa, 1991—; commr. Tulsa City/County Libr. Sys., 1998—; pres. Gilcrease Mus. Assocs., Tulsa, 1994-95. Recipient Disting. Svc. award Law and You Found., Oklahoma City. Mem. Tex. Bar Assn., Oklahoma Bar Assn., Tulsa County Bar Assn. (named outstanding jr. lawyer 1982). Democrat. Unitarian. Avocations: music, writing. Home: 1965 E 33d Pl Tulsa OK 74105 Office: Boone Smith Davis et al 500 Oneok Plz Tulsa OK 37410-3000

KELLS, ALBERT JOHN, financial consultant; b. Providence, Jan. 20, 1935; s. John S. and Mary M. (Wise) K.; m. Carole P. Coloura, July 6, 1957; children: Karen A., Kathleen M. BS in Fin., Bryant Coll., Providence, 1960; MBA, U. Conn., 1967. Fin. analyst Rexall Drug & Chem., Stamford, Conn., 1960-63; econ. analyst The Fantus Co., N.Y.C., 1963-64; budget mgr. CBS Inc., Stamford, 1964-67; strategic planning mgr. IBM, East Fishkill, N.Y., 1967-90; mergers and acquisitions cons. The Gottesman Co., N.Y.C., 1991, Kells & Co., Stormville, N.Y., 1991—. Chmn. Kells Found., 1981-92; mem. Rep. Nat. Com., 1979. Capt. U.S. Army, 1954-64. Mem. Inst. of Indsl. Engrs. Avocations: tennis, history, computers. Home and Office: 105 Townview Dr Wappingers Falls NY 12590-7017

KELLS, MELVIN RICHARD See ROBERTS, MEL

KELLS, MELVIN RICHARD See ROBERTS, MEL

KELL-SMITH, CARLA SUE, federal agency administrator; b. Highland Park, Mich., Sept. 15, 1952; d. Carl William and Margie May (Cannon) Bodner; m. Joseph Mark Kell, Oct. 10, 1971 (div. Dec. 1980); m. Richard Charles Smith, Jan. 28, 1989; Student, Anderson Coll., 1970-71, Glendale Coll., 1976-77, Ariz. State U., 1978-79, Mesa Coll., 1979-80. Private tutor English, Fed. Republic of Germany, 1971-74; office mgr. Bell & Schore, Rochester, Mich., 1974-75, COL Press, Phoenix, 1978-80; publicity mgr. O'Sullivan Woodside & Col, Phoenix, 1980-81, gen. mgr., 1982-84; pub. relations/promotion cons. GPI Publs., Cupertino, Calif., 1985; pub. cons., 1985-88; project adminstr. FAA, 1986—; account coord. Bernard Hodes Advt., Tempe, Ariz., 1981; cons. freelance mktg., Phoenix, 1983. Vol., Fiesta Bowl Parade Com., Phoenix, 1983, FAA Airport Improvement Project. Office: 1200 Bayhill Dr Ste 224 San Bruno CA 94066-3006

KELLUM, CARMEN KAYE, apparel company executive; b. Greensburg, Pa., Oct. 15, 1952; d. Bruce Lowell and Mildred Louise (Montgomery) Taylor; m. John Douglas Kellum, Aug. 2, 1975 (div. May 1987). Student, MacMurray Coll., 1971-72, Elgin Community Coll.; AA, Coll. DuPage, 1975; BA with honors, Nat. Louis U., 1978. Cert. tchr. Aide occupational therapy Mercy Ctr., Aurora, Ill., 1972-76; tchr. behavior disorders Lake Park High Sch., Roselle, Ill., 1978-80, Salk Pioneer Sch., Roselle, 1980-81; mgr. So-Fro Fabrics Stores, Lombard, Joliet & Chgo., Ill., 1981-84; offshore coord. Florsheim Shoe Co., Chgo., 1984-90; mgr. Linens N Things, Rolling Meadows, Ill., 1990-91; mgr. House of Fabrics, Aurora, Ill., 1992-94, Glen Ellyn, Ill., 1994; store mgr. T.J. Maxx, Naperville and W. Dundee, Ill., 1994-97, W. Dundee, Ill., 1996-97; mgr. Toys R Us, Schaumburg, 1997-98, Kmart, Villa Park, Ill., 1998-99, Kohl's, Downers Grove, Ill., 1999—. Mem. Internat. Dyslexia Assn., Nat. Assn. Female Exec., Kappa Delta Pi. Lutheran. Avocations: dance, swimming, sewing, needlepoint, choir. Home: 30 W 156 Wood Ct and Hwy 59 PO Box 8137 Bartlett IL 60103-8137 Office: Kohl's 2920 S Finley Rd Downers Grove IL 60515

KELLUM, NORMAN BRYANT, JR., lawyer; b. Maysville, N.C., Aug. 12, 1937; s. Norman Bryant and Dollie Mallard Kellum; m. Ruth Taylor, Nov. 24, 1968. BS, Wake Forest U., 1959, JD, 1965. Bar: N.C. 1965, U.S. Dist. Ct. (ea. dist.) N.C. 1965, U.S. Dist. Ct. (mid. dist.) N.C. 1991, U.S. Ct. Appeals (4th cir.) 1968, U.S. Supreme Ct. 1994. Salesman, mgr. The Southwestern Co., Nashville, summers 1962-68; research asst. N.C. Supreme Ct., Raleigh, N.C., 1965-66; atty. Norman Kellum Jr., New Bern, N.C., 1966-68; ptnr. Beaman & Kellum, New Bern, 1968-75; owner Beaman, Kellum, Hollows & Jones, P.A. and predecessor firms, New Bern, 1975-94; shareholder, pres. Kellum & Jones, New Bern, 1994—; bd. dirs. Triangle Bank, New Bern. Deacon, trustee First Bapt. Ch., New Bern. 1st lt. U.S. Army, 1960-62; trustee Meredith Coll., 1988-92, 94-97, 99—, chmn., 1996, 97, 99—; bd. visitors Wake Forest U. Sch. Law, 1992—; mem. Craven Regional Med. Ctr. Found., 1997, pres., 1998, 99. Mem. ATLA, N.C. State Bar, N.C. Acad. Trial Lawyers (bd. govs. 1983-87), N.C. Bar Assn., Ea. N.C. Inn Ct. (pres. 1995), Am. Bd. Trial Advs., Wake Forest U. Law Sch. (Alumni of Yr. award 1993). Avocations: travel, boating, golf, gardening. Office: Kellum & Jones PO Box 866 New Bern NC 28563-0866

KELLY, A. DAVID, lawyer; b. St. Paul, June 8, 1948; s. David and Katherine (Tappins) K.; m. Elizabeth Woehrle, Oct. 25, 1978; children: Charles, George. BA, Carleton Coll., 1970; JD, Harvard U., 1973. Bar: Minn. 1973. Ptnr. Faegre & Benson, Mpls., 1973-90, Oppenheimer, Wolff & Donnelly, Mpls., 1990-95, Kelly, Hannaford & Battles, Mpls., 1995—. Trustee Carleton Coll., Northfield, Minn., 1972-76; chmn. Voyageurs Nat. Pk. Assn., Mpls., 1984-90; treas. Messiah Episc. Ch., St. Paul, 1988-96; pres. St. Paul Boys' and Girls' Club, 1992-95. Office: Kelly Hannaford & Battles 2350 Met Ctr 333 S 7th St Minneapolis MN 55402-2414*

KELLY, ANN TERESE, elementary education educator; b. St. Louis, Jan. 29, 1954; d. Robert Victor and Mary Magdalen (Debrecht) K. BS in Elem. Edn., U. Mo., St. Louis, 1977, postgrad., 1978-79, 86-88, 95; postgrad., Webster U., St. Louis, 1990, U. Mo., Columbia, 1990-92, SUNY, Brockport, 1994, 97. Tchr. 4th grade St. Paul (Mo.) Sch., 1974-75, Assumption Sch., O'Fallon, Mo., 1977-79; tchr. grades 6 to 8 St. Raphael, St. Louis, 1979-86; tchr. grade 7 Our Lady of Sorrows, St. Louis, 1986-88, tchr. grade 5, 1988—; tchr. trainer Sci. Olympiad, St. Louis, 1987—; presenter weather workshops, 1991—; trainer Gr. 5 Developmental Approaches in Sci. and Health, 1993, Archdiocese of St. Louis, 1994—; Am. Meteorol. Soc./Nat. Oceanic and Atmospheric Adminstrn. workshop presenter Maury Project oceanographic studies, 1994—. Mem. Nat. Sci. Tchrs. Assn., Sci. Tchrs. Mo., Cath. Educators Network. Roman Catholic. Avocations: singing, dancing, walking, photography. Home: 10126C Puttington Dr Saint Louis MO 63123-5258 Office: Our Lady of Sorrows 5831 S Kingshighway Blvd Saint Louis MO 63109-3571

KELLY, ANNE CATHERINE, retired city official; b. Buffalo, Mar. 6, 1916; d. John Patrick and Elizabeth Marie (Edwards) Donohue; m. Thomas Edward Kelly, Apr. 19, 1941 (dec. 1993); children: Maureen Anne Kelly, Michael Thomas, Edward John, Kevin Joseph, Theresa Elizabeth Callahan. Student SUNY-Buffalo. Tchr., St. Teresa Sch., Buffalo, 1956-64; clk. City of Buffalo, 1964, sec. to comptroller, 1967-70, coun. clk., 1970-76, sr. coun. clk., 1976-81. Com. woman N.Y. Democratic Com., 1970-87, mem. exec. bd., 1970-87; vice chmn. Erie County Dem. Com., 1985-87; past pres. Mercy League of Buffalo Mercy Hosp., Nash Ladies Guild, South Side Dem. Club. Roman Catholic. Clubs: Daus. of Erin, Nash Ladies. Lodge: KC (past pres. Nash guild). Home: 580 Orchard Park Rd Apt 109 West Seneca NY 14224-2660

KELLY, ANTHONY ODRIAN, flooring manufacturing company executive; b. Dublin, Ireland, June 12, 1935; s. John Peter and Delia Mary (Finnegan) K.; m. Sheila Josephine Clancy, Sept. 4, 1963; children—Barbara Anne, Adrienne Elizabeth, Damian Anthony. Grad., Coll. Commerce, Dublin, 1958; M.B.A., Columbia U., 1965, doctoral degree, 1971. Adj. asst. prof. Columbia U., N.Y.C., 1968-69; dir. econ. studies Sperry & Hutchinson Co., 1969-71, asst. to pres. furnishings div., 1975; dir. mktg. Irish Agrl. Devel. Co., 1971-74; sr. v.p. mktg. Bigelow-Sanford, Inc., Greenville, S.C., 1976-79; exec. v.p., chief operating officer Bigelow-Sanford, Inc., 1979-85, pres., chief exec. officer, 1985-86; pres., chief ops. officer Mannington Mills Inc., 1992, pres., CEO, 1993—. Ford Found. fellow; Samuel Bronfman fellow. Mem. Inst. Cost and Mgmt. Accts., Beta Gamma Sigma, Greenville Country Club, Wilmington Country Club.

KELLY, ARTHUR LLOYD, management and investment company executive; b. Chgo., Nov. 15, 1937; s. Thomas Lloyd and Mildred (Wetten) K.; m. Diane Rex Cain, Nov. 25, 1978; children: Mary Lucinda, Thomas Lloyd, Alison Williams. BS with honors, Yale U., 1959; MBA, U. Chgo., 1964. With A.T. Kearney, Inc., 1959-75, mng. dir., Dusseldorf, Germany, 1964-70, v.p. for Europe, Brussels, 1970-73, internat. v.p., London, 1974-75, ptnr., dir., 1969-75, mem. exec. com., 1972-75; pres., COO, dir. LaSalle Steel Co., Chgo., 1975-81; pres., CEO, dir. Dalta Corp., Chgo., 1982—; mng. ptnr. KEL Enterprises L.P., Chgo., 1983—; chmn., bd. dirs. ARCH Devel. Corp., Chgo.; dir. BMW A.G., Munich, DataCard Corp., Minnetonka, Minn., Deere & Co., Moline, Ill., mpct Solutions Corp., Chgo., Nalco Chem. Co., Naperville, Ill., No. Trust Corp., Chgo., Snap-On, Inc., Kenosha, Wis., Thyssen-Krupp Industrie A.G., Essen, Germany, Bankhaus Trinkaus & Burkhardt KGaA, Dusseldorf, Waccamaw Corp., Myrtle Beach, S.C. Trustee U. Chgo., chmn. vis. com. div. phys. scis.; mem. adv. coun. Ditchley Found., Oxford, Eng.; bd. dirs. Chgo. Coun. Fgn. Rels.; fellow Royal Geog. Soc. (life), London. Mem. World Pres.' Orgn., Econ. Club, Comml. Club, Racquet Club, Casino Club, Brook Club, Yale Club, Beta Gamma Sigma. Office: 20 S Clark St Ste 2222 Chicago IL 60603-1805

KELLY, ARTHUR PAUL, physician; b. Asheville, N.C., Nov. 23, 1938; s. Joseph Paul and Amanda Lee (Walker) K.; m. Beverly Gayle Baker, June 25, 1966; children: Traci Allyce, Kara Gisele. BA, Brown U., 1960; MD, Howard U., 1965. Intern Harper Hosp., Detroit, 1965-66; resident in dermatology Henry Ford Hosp., Detroit, 1968-71; instr. in dermatology Brown U., Providence, 1971-73; asst. prof. internal medicine Charles R. Drew U. Medicine and Sci., Los Angeles, 1973-77; prof. Charles R. Drew U. Medicine and Sci., L.A., 1983; chief div. dermatology King.-Drew Med. Ctr., L.A., 1976—, interim chmn. dept. internal medicine, 1985-86, vice chmn., 1987-91, chmn., 1992-95; assoc. prof. medicine U. So. Calif., L.A., 1977-80; prof. UCLA, 1995—. Contbr. numerous articles to profl. jours., chpts. to books. Served to capt. U.S. Army, 1966-68, Vietnam. Recipient Act So award NAACP, 1983. Fellow Am. Acad. Dermatology; mem. Met. L.A. Dermatology Soc. (v.p. 1986-87, pres. 1987-88), Nat. Med. Assn. (chmn. sect. on dermatology 1978-80, Outstanding Minority Dermatology fellow 1972), Assn. of Profs. of Dermatology (pres.-elect 1996-98, pres. 1998—), Am. Dermatology Assn. (v.p. 1997-98, pres. 1998-99). Democrat. Avocations: travel, tennis. Office: King/Drew Med Ctr 12021 S Wilmington Ave Los Angeles CA 90059-3019

KELLY, AUREL MAXEY, retired judge; b. Cleve., Apr. 24, 1923; d. Chester Collins and Elnora (Campbell) Maxey; m. Thomas F. Kelly, May

29, 1943; children—Shannon, Keven. A.B. cum laude, Whitman Coll., 1943; J.D., Columbia U., 1947. Bar: Wash. State Bar 1949, Colo. bar 1961. Continuity acceptance MBS, N.Y.C., 1947; asst. editor Baker-Voorhis Pub. Co., 1947-48; practiced in Walla Walla, Wash., 1949-60; dep. pros. atty. Walla Walla County, 1955-56; justice of peace Walla Walla precinct, 1956-59; asso. firm Roepnack & Orahood, 1961-62; partner firm Kelly & Kelly, 1962-74; spl. asst. atty. gen. State of Colo., 1963-68; sr. asst. atty. gen., 1968-74, chief criminal div., 1971-74; judge Colo. Ct. Appeals, Denver, 1974-88, chief judge, 1988-90; sr. judge Colo. Ct. Appeals, 1990-91; commr. Colo. Ltd. Gaming Control Commn., 1991-94, chmn., 1991-93; Vice pres. State Fedn. Young Republicans, 1952-54, nat. committeewoman, 1954-56; vice chmn. Walla Walla County Rep. Central Com., 1954-55; mem. Colo. Commn. on Status of Women, 1969-74; bd. overseers Whitman Coll., 1977-87, bd. overseers emeritus, 1987—. Mem. Colo. Bar Assn., Denver Bar Assn., Am. Judicature Soc., Kappa Kappa Gamma.

KELLY, BRIAN, commodities trader; m. Kathleen Kelly; children: Amanda, Brian, Mary Kate. Mem. Coffee, Sugar & Cocoa Exch., Inc., N.Y.C., 1981—, mem. bd. mgrs., 1990—, vice chmn. bd. mgrs., 1993-95, chmn. bd. mgrs., 1995-97; mem. floor com. Coffee, Sugar & Cocoa Exc., Inc., 1986—, vice chmn., 1990-92, chmn., 1992-94, exec. floor com., 1990—, chmn., 1992-94, mem. exec. com., 1992—, chmn., 1993-95; dir. Commodities Exch. Ctr., Inc., 1993—, chmn., 1995-96; dir. Commodity Futures Clearing Corp. of N.Y., 1993-95; sole propr. B. Kelly Trading Co. Office: Coffee Sugar & Cocoa Exch 4 World Trade Ctr New York NY 10048-0204*

KELLY, BRIAN MATTHEW, industrial hygienist; b. Ogdensburg, N.Y., June 16, 1956; s. Lauris F. and Catherine M. (McEvoy) K. BA, SUNY, Oswego, 1978; BS, Clarkson U., 1981; MS in Indsl. Safety, Cen. Mo. State U., 1990. Cert. indsl. hygienist Am. Bd. Indsl. Hygiene; cert. accident investigator U.S. Dept. Energy, NASA and Nuc. Regulatory Commn.; cert. profl. environ. auditor. Maintenance engr. Kelly Sales Corp., Madrid, N.Y., 1978-80, carpenter, 1981-82; hygienist indsl. hygiene and toxicology prin. mem. tech. staff ES&H, quality assessments dept. Sandia Nat. Labs., Albuquerque, 1983—; mem. tech. adv. bd. Albuquerque (N.Mex.) Tech. Vocat. Inst., 1989—. Mem. bd. environ. auditing cert. Mem. Am. Inst. Chemists, Am. Indsl. Hygienists Assn. (mgmt. com. mem., bd. environtl. auditor certs.), N.Y. Acad. Scis., Am. Conf. Govtl. Indls. Hygienists, Am. Soc. Safety Engrs., Am. Acad. Indsl. Hygiene, Gamma Sigma Epsilon, Phi Kappa Phi. Republican. Roman Catholic. Avocations: cycling, fishing, carpentry. Home: 1455 Beall St Bosque Farms NM 87068-9109

KELLY, CAROL WHITE, company executive; b. Shreveport, La., Dec. 23, 1946; d. Verlin Ralph and Mary Louise (Humphries) White; m. James Patrick Kelly, June 6, 1968; children: Mary Louise, Christopher John. BA, Centenary Coll. La., Shreveport, 1968. Corp. sec., treas. Kelly Law Firm P.C., Atlanta, 1986—. Mem. NAFE, Ga. Baptist Med. Guild (life), Atlanta Hist. Soc., Atlanta Ballet Guild (life), Internat. Platform Assn., High Mus. Art, Episcopal Ch. Women (sec.-treas. 1976-80), Chi Omega Alumnae Assn. (pres. 1979-80). Avocations: travel, pub. speaking, collecting teapots. Office: Kelly Law Firm PC 200 Galleria Pkwy SE Ste 1510 Atlanta GA 30339-5946

KELLY, CHARLES ARTHUR, lawyer; b. Evanston, Ill., Mar. 2, 1932; s. Charles Scott and Bess (Loftis) K.; m. Frances Kates, Sept. 9, 1961 (div. 1979); children: Timothy, Elizabeth, Mary; m. Patricia Lynn Francis, June 28, 1979. BA with honors, Amherst Coll., 1953; LLB, Harvard U., 1956. Bar: D.C. 1956, Ill. 1956. Assoc. Hubachek & Kelly, Chgo., 1956-64, ptnr., 1964-82; ptnr. Chapman & Cutler, Chgo., 1982—; sec.l Speedfam Internat., Inc., 1992—, gen. counsel, 1998—. Bd. dirs. Gads Hill Ctr., Chgo., 1960—, pres., 1977-82; bd. dirs. Quetico Superior Found., Mpls., 1960—, v.p., 1964—; bd. dirs. Lakeland Found., Chgo., 1960-96, pres., 1970-85, v.p., 1997—; bd. dirs. Ernest C. Oberholtzer Found., Mpls., 1964—, pres., 1975-85, v.p., treas. 1998—; bd. dirs. Chgo. Hearing Found., 1990-94, Wilderness Rsch. Found., Chgo., 1960-96. Brig. gen. USAFR, 1957-85. Recipient Legion of Merit, USAF, 1982. Fellow Am. Coll. Trust and Estate Counsel; Mem. ABA, Chgo. Bar Assn., Ill. Bar Assn., Fed. Bar Assn., Univ. Club, Mid-Am. Club, Mich. Shores Club (Wilmette, Ill.), Harvard Club (Boston). Republican. Presbyterian. Office: Chapman and Cutler 111 W Monroe St Ste 1800 Chicago IL 60603-4006

KELLY, CHARLES EUGENE, II, gastroenterologist, researcher; b. Salina, Kans., Sept. 4, 1958; s. Charles Eugene and Byrdie Inez (Sowell) K. BA in Chemistry, U. Kans., 1980, MD, 1984; postgrad in internal medicine, U. Mich., 1984-87. Gastroenterology fellow Stanford U. Med. Ctr., 1987—. Recipient Nat. Rsch. Sci. award NIH, 1990. Mem. Am. Coll. Physicians (assoc.), Am. Gastroenterology Assn. (assoc.). Baptist. Avocations: camping, radio controlled cars, jazz, automobiles, languages. Office: Stanford U Med Ctr Gastroenterology Office 300 Pasteur Dr # 069 Palo Alto CA 94304-2203

KELLY, CHRISTOPHER A., brigadier general United States air force; m. Kathy Kelly; children: Nick, Matthew. BS in Mgmt., USAF Acad., 1974; grad., Squadron Officer Sch, Maxwell AFB, Ala., 1979; MS in Mgmt., Webster U., 1984; student, Air Command and Staff Coll., Maxwell AFB, Ala., 1986, Indsl. Coll. of Armed Forces, Ft. McNair, Washington, 1991; nat. securities studies, Johns Hopkins U., 1998. Commd 2d lt. USAF, 1974, advanced through grades to brig. gen., 1998; instr., pilot, evaluator pilot 61st airlift squadron 314th airlift wing USAF, Little Rock AFB, Ark., 1975-81; staff officer Air Staff Tng. Program Hdqs., USAF, Washington, 1981-82; programming officer Hdqs. Mil. Airlift Commmand, Scott AFB, Ill., 1982-85; chief pilot 345th tactical airlift squadron USAF, Yokota Air Base, Japan, 1986-88; dep. exec. asst. chmn. Joint Chiefs of Staff, Washington, 1991-93; comdr. 38th ops. group USAF, Plattsburgh AFB, N.Y., 1993-94; chief spl. air missions Office Vice Chief of Staff Hdqrs. USAF, Washington, 1994-95; exec. officer to vice chief of staff Hdqs. USAF, Washington, 1995-96; comdr. 100th air refueling wing USAF, RAF Base Mildenhall, Eng., 1996-97; comdr. 97th air mobility wing USAF, Altus AFB, Okla., 1997-99. Decorated Legion of Merit, Defense Superior Svcs. medal, Combat Readiness medal with one oak leaf cluster, Meritorious Svc. medal with three oak leaf clusters, Air Force Commendation medal. Office: c/o USAF Pub Affairs Altus AFB OK 73523-5047

KELLY, CHUCK H., singer, writer, trombonist; b. Dallas, Aug. 19, 1930; s. John Richard and Pauline Madrid (Campbell) K.; m. Jaye P. Morgan, Dec. 5, 1959 (div. Dec. 1960); m. Beverly M. Wolfe, July 24, 1961; children: David Gregory, Shawn Charles. BA in Communication Arts, Sierra U., 1983, MA in Communications/Organizational Theory, 1984. Ind. trombonist, singer various big bands, entertainers, nationwide, 1952-80; ind. comml. singer nationwide, 1956-76; ind. motion picture voice-track singer Los Angeles, 1966-70; ind. tech. writer/cons., 1980—. Author: (novelization) High Stakes; tech. writer/editor Alchemy of Intelligence, 1984; tech. editor: Pharmacology, Biology and Clinical Applications of Androgens, 1996; converted articles from rsch. scientists for med. ref./text books; trombonist with various big bands including Glenn Miller (dir. Ray McKinley), 1955, Dizzy Gillespie, 1955-56; singer with various entertainers including Betty Hutton, 1958, Paula Kelly and the Modernaires, 1959-64, Jerry Lewis, 1962-63, Bob Newhart, 1963-64, Ronald Reagan, 1963, Bing Crosby, 1966-71, Andy Griffith, 1968, Dick van Dyke, 1968, Jim Nabors, 1968, Danny Thomas; comml. singer for numerous cos. including Oldsmobile, 1961, Sears, 1972; singer in numerous motion pictures including Hello Dolly, 1968, Sweet Charity, 1969, Peter Gunn, 1969; singer, performer various TV shows including Danny Kaye Show, 1965-67, George Gobel Show, 1962-63, Red Skelton Show, 1964-69; tech. writer for various corps. including Hughes Aircraft Co., Northrop Corp; contbr. articles to profl. jours. Served with USN, 1951. Sierra U. scholar, 1983. Mem. AFTRA, ASCAP, SAG, Soc. of Singers (bd. dirs. 1986-92). Democrat. Avocations: hypnotism, psychology, writing, metaphysics. Home and Office: 248 La Verne Ave Long Beach CA 90803-3515

KELLY, CURTIS HARTT, publishing executive; b. Ft. Atkinson, Wis., May 17, 1935; s. Curtis and Edna (Guenther) K. BA, Yankton Coll., 1957. With fin. divsn. Scott Foresman Co., Glenview, Ill., 1962-86; with info. sys. divsn. Scott Foresman Co., Glenview, 1986-97. Home: 1409 W Farwell Ave Apt G1 Chicago IL 60626-3488

KELLY, DANIEL GRADY, JR., lawyer; b. Yonkers, N.Y., July 15, 1951; s. Daniel Grady and Helene (Coyne) K.; m. Annette Susan Wheeler, May 8, 1976; children—Elizabeth Anne, Brigid Claire, Cynthia Logan. Grad., Choate Sch., Wallingford, Conn., 1969; BA magna cum laude, Yale U., 1973; JD, Columbia U., 1976. Bar: N.Y. 1977, U.S. Dist. Ct. (so. and ea. dists.) N.Y. 1977, Calif. 1986, U.S. Dist. Ct. (cen. dist.) Calif. 1987. Law clk. to judge U.S. Ct. Appeals (2d cir.), N.Y.C., 1976-77; assoc. Davis Polk & Wardwell, N.Y.C., 1977-83; sr. v.p. Lehman Bros., N.Y.C., 1983-85; sr. v.p., gen. counsel Kaufman & Broad, Inc., L.A., 1985-87; ptnr. Manatt, Phelps, Rothenberg & Phillips, L.A., 1987-90, Sidley & Austin, L.A. and N.Y., 1990—. Mem. editl. bd. Columbia Law Rev., 1975-76. Mem. ABA (com. on law firms), L.A. County Bar Assn. (exec. com. bus. and corps. law sect.). Office: Sidley & Austin 875 3rd Ave Fl 14 New York NY 10022-6293

KELLY, DANIEL P., cardiologist, molecular biologist; b. Oct. 6, 1955; m. Therese J. Michelau; 3 children. BS in Biology, U. Ill., 1978, MD, 1982. Diplomate Am. Bd. Internal Medicine, Am. Bd. Cardiovascular Disease. Intern in medicine Barnes Hosp., St. Louis, 1982-83, asst. resident in medicine, 1983-85; chief med. resident John Cochran VA Hosp., Washington U. Svc., 1984-85; rsch. postdoctoral fellow cardiovascular divsn. and dept. biol. chemistry Washington U. Sch. of Medicine, St. Louis, 1985-87, fellow in clin. cardiology, 1987-89, instr. of medicine cardiovascular divsn., 1989-90, asst. prof. medicine cardiovascular divsn., 1990-95, asst. prof. molecular biology and pharmacology, 1993-95, co-dir. Ctr. Adults with Congenital Heart Disease, 1993—, assoc. prof. medicine and molecular biology & pharmacology, 1995—, dir. Ctr. for Cardiovascular Rsch., 1996—; lectr. rsch. and clin. fellowship program Washington U. Sch. of Medicine, 1989, lectr. pharmacology and pathophysiology, 1994; attending physician medicine and cardiology svcs. Barnes and Jewish Hosps., St. Louis, 1989. Contbr. articles to profl. jours., chpts. to books. Recipient Lucille P. Markey Scholar award Markey Found., 1989, Basal O'Connor Scholar award March of Dimes, 1991; Rsch. Tng. grantee NHLBI, 1994—, 96—. Fellow Am. Coll. Cardiology; mem. AAAS, Am. Fedn. Clin. Rsch., Am. Heart Assn. (basic sci. coun., Established Investigator award 1995), Internat. Soc. Heart Rsch., Internat. Soc. Adult Congenital Heart Disease, Am. Soc. for Clin. Investigation, Phi Beta Kappa, Alpha Omega Alpha. Office: Washington U Sch of Medicine Ctr Cardiovasc Rsch 660 S Euclid Ave # 8086 Saint Louis MO 63110-1010*

KELLY, DAVID AUSTIN, investment counselor; b. Mt. Kisco, N.Y., June 24, 1938; s. William Andrew and Katharine Elizabeth (Barrett) K.; m. Judith Boesel, June 18, 1966; children: Carolyn K. Patten, Douglas Austin. BA, Lafayette Coll., 1962; MBA, U. Chgo., 1964. Chartered fin. analyst. Asst. v.p. investment mgmt. group Citibank, N.Y.C., 1964-69; portfolio mgr., v.p. J.M. Hartwell & Co., Inc., N.Y.C., 1969-72; pres., CEO P/H Mgmt. Corp., Pitts., 1972-74; asst. treas. Gulf Oil Corp., Pitts., 1974-80; v.p., treas. Borden, Inc., N.Y.C., 1980-95, treas., prin. fin. officer, dir. BCP Mgmt., Inc., Borden Chemicals and Plastics Ltd. Partnership, 1987-95; pres. Three Lakes Advisors, Inc., 1996—; bd. dirs. BHCF Ednl. Ctr., Inc., Bedford Hills, N.Y. Past councilor N.Y. Soc., Order of Founders and Patriots Am.; mem. fin. policy com. Lafayette Coll., Easton, Pa., 1976-79; trustee, treas. Am. Classical Orch., Norwalk, Conn.; treas. bd. dirs. The Greenwich (Conn.) Land Trust Inc. Served with U.S. Army, 1957-59. Mem. NAM (chmn. auditing com. 1983-92), Assn. for Investment Mgmt. and Rsch., N.Y. Soc. Security Analysts, Stanwich Club (Greenwich, Conn.). Home: 303 Overlook Dr Greenwich CT 06830-6716 Office: Three Lakes Advisors Inc 303 Overlook Dr Greenwich CT 06830-6716

KELLY, DAVID LEE, JR., neurosurgeon, educator; b. Elkin, N.C., Apr. 25, 1935; s. David Lee and Catherine (Church) K.; m. Sarah Brooks Pullen, Aug. 23, 1958; children—Sarah Katherine, David Lee, Mary Brooks, Julia Ann. B.S., U. N.C.-Chapel Hill, 1956, M.D., 1959. Diplomate Am. Bd. Neurol. Surgery; lic. physician, N.C. Instr., Bowman Gray Sch. Medicine, Wake Forest U., Winston-Salem, N.C., 1965-66; asst. prof. Bowman Gray Sch. Medicine, Wake Forest U., 1966-71, assoc. prof., 1971-78, prof. neurosurgery, head sect., 1978—; chmn. com. ednl. requirements Am. Bd. Neurol. Surgery, 1984-86, mem. oral exam. com., 1985-86. Contbr. articles to profl. jours., chpts. to books; editorial bd. Neurosurgery, 1982—, mem. mgmt. com., 1977-82. Bd. dirs. Forsyth County YMCA, Winston-Salem, 1968-75, v.p., 1973, pres., 1974; bd. dirs. Forsyth Country Day Sch., Winston-Salem, 1975-78. Fellow ACS; mem. Am. Acad. Neurol. Surgery (exec. com. 1982-85), Am. Assn. Neurol. Surgeons (fin. com. 1978-83, mem.-at-large bd. dirs. 1980-83, chmn. hon. membership 1982-83, adv. council neurosurgery 1979-83), AMA, Assn. Acad. Surgery, Congress of Neurol. Surgeons (sci. program com. 1967-68, registration com. 1969-70, membership com. 1967-68, 70-71, chmn. residents com. 1971-72, chmn. registration com. 1973-74, sec. 1974-77, pres.-elect 1977-78, pres. 1978-79, chmn. cert. com. 1980—, exec. com. 1982—), Fellowship of Acad. Neurosurgeons, Forsyth-Davie-Stokes County Med. Soc. (chmn. program com. 1970-71), Med. Soc. N.C. (coms.), Neurosurg. Soc. Am. (v.p. 1979-80), N.C. Neurosurg. Soc. (pres. 1976-77, chmn. peer rev. com. 1982-83), So. Neurosurg. Soc. (program com. 1974-76, v.p. 1977-78), Phi Beta Kappa, Alpha Omega Alpha (chpt. counselor 1970-72), Phi Eta Sigma. Presbyterian. Club: Forsyth Country (Winston-Salem). Avocations: tennis; squash; golf; sailing. Office: Bowman Gray Sch Medicine Medical Ctr Blvd Winston Salem NC 27157-1029*

KELLY, DAVID REID, pathologist; b. Morganton, N.C., Nov. 21, 1947; s. Everett Oree and Paris Dereama (Keever) K.; children: Marie Keever, David Reid Jr. AB, U. N.C., 1970; MD, U. Tenn. Ctr. Health Scis., 1974. Diplomate Am. Bd. Pathology, Clin. and Anatomic Pathology, Am. Bd. Pediatric Pathology. Intern, then resident U. Ala., Birmingham, 1974-78; Am. Cancer Soc. fellow dept. pathology and lab. medicine U. Minn., Mpls., 1978-79; pathologist-in-chief, med. dir. labs. Children's Hosp., Birmingham, 1979—; clin. prof. of pathology U. Ala.-Birmingham, 1985—; pathology cons. Pediatric Oncology Group, Chgo., 1979—. Author: Comprehensive Textbook of Oncology, 1986, Clinical Pediatric Oncology, 1991, Pediatric Neoplasia: Morphology and Biology, 1996; contbr. articles to Cancer, Pediat. Pathology, Am. Jour. Clin. Pathology, Med. and Pediat. Oncology, Kidney Internat. Leader Cub Scouts and Boy Scouts Am., Birmingham, 1988-94. Fellow Am. Soc. Clin. Pathologists, Coll. Am. Pathologists; mem. AMA (physician recognition award 1980, 91, 95), Soc. for Pediat. Pathology, Soc. Hematopathology, U.S. and Can. Acad. Pathology, Phi Alpha Theta, Phi Kappa Phi. Baptist. Office: Children's Hosp 1600 7th Ave S Birmingham AL 35233-1785

KELLY, DEBRA ANN, adult education educator; b. Rochester, N.Y., Apr. 26, 1965; d. John William Wooden and Kathaleen Mary O'Shaugnessy; m. Mark Christopher Kelly, Aug. 21, 1993. BSBA, SUNY, Oswego, 1986; MA in Higher Edn. Counseling, U. Cen. Fla., 1998. Social svcs. case mgr. Monroe County Social Svcs., Rochester, N.Y., 1988-92; income tax cons. Sarasota, Fla., 1993-96; employment specialist Talent Tree Staffing, Sarasota, 1994-96; rsch. asst. U. Cen. Fla., Orlando, 1996-98; instr. Manatee C.C., Bradenton, Fla., 1999—. Youth vol. Fellowship of Believers, Sarasota, 1998; events coord. Gateway Chrisitan Ministry, Rochester, 1991-93. Grad. fellow U. Cen. Fla., 1998. Mem. Nat. Assn. for Student Pers. Adminstrs., So. Assn. for Coll. Student Affairs. Republican. Home: 5948 Mirror Lake Rd Sarasota FL 34238-2546

KELLY, DEE J., lawyer; b. Bonham, Tex., Mar. 7, 1929; s. Dee C. and Era L. (Jones) K.; m. Janice LeBlanc, Dec. 30, 1954; children: Cynthia Kelly Barnes, Dee J., Craig LeBlanc. B.A., Tex. Christian U., 1950; LL.B., George Washington U., 1954. Bar: Tex. 1954. Pvt. practice law Ft. Worth, 1956-79; founding, sr. ptnr. Kelly, Hart & Hallman, Ft. Worth, 1979—; bd. dirs. A.M.R., Justin Industries, Inc. The SABRE Group Holdings, Inc. Trustee Tex. Christian U., 1971—; bd. dirs. Tex. Turnpike Authority, 1967-76, chmn., 1969-76; bd. regents Tex. State U. System, 1969-75; trustee U. Tex. Law Sch. Found.; bd. dirs. Southwestern Legal Found.; trustee Scott and White Meml. Hosp. and Scott, Sherwood and Bridley Found., 1998, Moncrief Radiation Ctr.; bd. visitors U. Tex. Cancer Ctr., 1980-87; mem. devel. bd. U. Tex., Arlington, 1975-81, Joint Select Com. on Judiciary, 1988, Task Force on Jud. Selection, 1990; dir. Southwestern Expn. and Livestock Show, 1986—. 1st lt. USAF, 1951-53. Named Disting. Alumni, Tex. Christian U., 1982, Ft. Worth's Outstanding Bus. Exec., 1993, Horatio Alger award, Horatio Alger Assn. Disting. Ams., 1995, Blackstone award, 1998. Mem. Tarrant County Bar Assn. Avocations: golf. Home: 1315 Hillcrest St Fort Worth TX 76107-1577

KELLY, DENNIS MICHAEL, lawyer; b. Cleve., May 6, 1943; s. Thomas Francis and Margaret (Murphy) K.; m. Marilyn Ann Divoky, Dec. 28, 1967; children: Alison, Meredith. BA, John Carroll U., 1961-65; JD, U. Notre Dame, 1968. Bar: Ohio 1968. Law clk. U.S. Ct. Appeals (8th cir.), Cleve., 1968-69; assoc. Jones, Day, Reavis & Pogue, Cleve., 1969-75, ptnr., 1975—. Mem. Ohio Bar Assn., Bar Assn. Greater Cleve. Office: Jones Day Reavis & Pogue North Point 901 Lakeside Ave E Cleveland OH 44114-1116

KELLY, DENNIS RAY, sales executive; b. Olympia, Wash., Aug. 20, 1948; s. William E. and Irene (Lewis) K.; m. Pamela Jo Kresevich, Mar. 16, 1974. BA, Cen. Wash. U., 1972; postgrad., U. Wash., 1977-78. Sales rep. Bumble Bee Sea Foods, Seattle, 1972-74; retail sales mgr. Pacific Pearl Sea Foods, Seattle, 1974-76; regional sales mgr. Castle & Cooke Foods, Seattle, Phila., and N.Y.C., 1976-80; v.p. sales mktg. Frances Andrew Ltd., Seattle, 1980-82; regional sales mgr. Tenneco West, Seattle, 1982-85; sales and mktg. mgr. for western U.S. David Oppenheimer, Seattle, 1985-96; sales mgr. Rogge Co., 1997—. Alumni advisor Ctrl. Wash. U., Ellensburg, 1979-87, alumni bd. dirs., 1986—, fund drive chmn., 1988—, vendor rels.-mktg. com., 1998—, mem. sch. cmty. group bd.; bd. dirs. Bay Vista Tower Assn., v.p., pres., 1998; mem. Statue of Liberty Ellis Island Found.; chmn. ann. fund drive Ctrl. Wash. U., bd. dirs., 1992; pres. Lake Water Dist., 1998; adv. com. United States Senate Seattle. Mem. New Zealand-Am. Soc., Mfrs. Reps. Club Wash. (bd. dirs.). Republican. Avocations: hiking, backpacking, skiing, snowmobiling. Home: 2821 2nd Ave Apt 1204 Seattle WA 98121-1249 Office: 4123 2nd Ave S Seattle WA 98134-2305

KELLY, DONALD PHILIP, entrepreneur; b. Chgo., Feb. 24, 1922; s. Thomas Nicholas and Ethel M. (Healy) K.; m. Byrd M. Sullivan, Oct. 25, 1952; children: Patrick, Laura, Thomas. Student, Loyola U., Chgo., 1953-54, De Paul U., 1954-55, Harvard U., 1965. Mgr. tabulating United Ins. Co. Am., 1946-51; mgr. data processing A.B. Wrisley Co., 1951-53; mgr. data processing Swift & Co., 1953-65, asst. controller, 1965-67, controller, 1967-68, v.p. corporate devel., controller, 1968-70, fin. v.p., dir., 1970-73; fin. v.p., dir. Esmark, Inc., Chgo., 1973, pres., COO, 1973-77, pres., CEO, 1977-82, chmn., pres., CEO, 1982-84; pres. Kelly, Briggs & Assocs., Inc., Chgo., 1984-86; chmn. Beatrice Co., Chgo., 1986-88; chmn., CEO E-II Holdings Inc., Chgo., 1987-88; pres., CEO D.P. Kelly & Assocs., L.P., Oak Brook, 1988—; chmn., pres., CEO Envirodyne Industries Inc., 1989-96. With USNR, 1942-46. Mem. Chgo. Club. Office: DP Kelly and Assocs LP 701 Harger Rd Ste 190 Oak Brook IL 60523-1490

KELLY, SISTER DOROTHY ANN, college chancellor; b. Bronx, N.Y., July 26, 1929; d. Walter David and Sarah (McCauley) K. BA in History, Coll. New Rochelle, 1951; MA in Am. Ch. History, Cath. U., Washington, 1958; PhD in Am. Intellectual History, U. Notre Dame, 1970; LittD (hon.), Mercy Coll., Dobbs Ferry, N.Y., 1976; LLD (hon.), Nazareth Coll. of Rochester, N.Y., 1979; DHL (hon.), Coll. St. Rose, 1981, Manhattan Coll., 1979, LeMoyne Coll., 1990, St. Thomas Aquinas Coll., 1990, St. Joseph Coll., Conn., 1996, Iona Coll., 1997. Joined Order of St. Ursula, Roman Cath. Ch., 1952. Assoc. prof. history Coll. New Rochelle, N.Y., 1957—, chmn. dept. history, 1965-67, acad. dean, 1967-72, acting pres., 1970-71, pres., 1972-97, chancellor, 1997—; mem. Interreligious Coun. New Rochelle, 1974—, exec. com., 1974-79, v.p., 1980-84, pres., 1984-88, mem. Commn. Ind. Colls. and Univs. State of N.Y., 1976-78, chmn. bd. trustees, 1978-80, mem. govt. rels. com., 1980-81; chmn. Com. Higher Edn. Opportunity, 1976-78; mem. commr. of edn. Adv. Coun. on Higher Edn. for N.Y. State, 1975-77, subcom. on postsecondary occupational edn., 1975-77; exec. com. Empire State Found. Ind. Liberal Arts Colls., 1975—, vice chmn., 1977-81, chmn., 1981—; trustee, mem. exec. com. Assn. Colls. and Univs. State of N.Y., 1976-80; mem. com. on purpose and identity Assn. Cath. Colls. and Univs., 1975-80; mem. steering com. Neylan Conf., 1978-81, mem. bishops and pres. com., 1979-84; mem. adv. coun. on fin. aid to students Office Edn., HEW, 1978-86; chmn. Women's Coll. Coalition, 1981-83; chmn. govt. rels. adv. com. Nat. Assn. Ind. Colls. and Univs., 1981-82, chair, 1987-88. Chair City-wide Confs., New Rochelle, 1977-79; bd. dirs. United Way Westchester, 1977-84, mem. planning, allocations, evaluation com., 1977-80, nominating and campaign coms., 1990—; bd. dirs. Westchester County Assn., 1980-90, New Rochelle Community Action Program, 1982-83, New Rochelle Cmty. Fund, 1989-91; mem. steering com. Westchester County Women's Hall of Fame, 1984-85; bd. dirs. Vis. Nurse Svcs. in Westchester, Inc., 1983-86, chair nominating com., 1985-86; trustee LeMoyne Coll., 1982-88, vice chairperson, 1984-87; mem. bd. govs. New Rochelle Hosp. Med. Ctr., 1987—; trustee United Student Aid Funds, 1980-90, Ursuline Sch., New Rochelle, 1988—, Cath. U. Am., 1988—, Am. Coun. on Edn., 1990—, Ind. Coll. Fund Am., 1982-85; mem. ofcl. U.S. del. to UN 4th World Conf. on Women in Beijing, 1995; mem. nat. adv. bd. Nat. Mus. Women in the Arts, 1996—. Recipient Medallion award Westchester C.C., 1978, Leadership award Am. Soc. Pub. Adminstrn., 1986, Sch. Svc. award Thornton-Donovan Sch., 1977, Henry D. Paley award, 1994, Father Theodore M. Hesburgh award, 1998, N.Y. State Gov.'s award for excellence, 1997; inducted into Westchester County/Avon Women's Hall of Fame, 1989; Paul Harris fellow, 1997. Mem. AAUP, AAUW, NCCJ (trustee 1989—), Am. Hist. Assn., Nat. Fedn. Bus. and Profl. Women, Am. Assn. Higher Edn., Nat. Assembly Women Religious, Am. Coun. Edn. (bd. dirs. 1990), Assn. Am. Colls. (bd. dirs. 1983-86), Tchrs. Ins. and Annuity Assn. Am. (trustee 1987—, fin. com. 1987-88, exec. com. 1988—, audit com. 1990—, products and svcs. com. 1990-91, nominating and pers. com. 1991), Assn. Colls. Mid-Hudson Area (pres. 1979-81, exec. com. 1982—). Address: Coll New Rochelle Office of the Chancellor 29 Castle Pl New Rochelle NY 10805-2338*

KELLY, DOUGLAS ELLIOTT, retired biomedical researcher, association administrator; b. Cheyenne, Wyo., Nov. 13, 1932; s. Raymond Douglas and Enid (McCaslin) K.; m. Louise Marie Webster, June 13, 1954 (div. 1984); children: Brian D., Alan D., Erin A., Megan L.; m. Joan Alyce McGreger, July 21, 1984; children: Alison McGreger, Tucker McCaslin. BS in Zoology, Colo. State U., 1954; PhD in Biol. Sci., Stanford U., 1958. Asst. prof. biology U. Colo., Boulder, 1958-62; assoc. prof., vice-chmn. biol. structure U. Wash., Seattle, 1963-70; prof., chmn. biol. structure U. Miami, Fla., 1970-74; prof., chmn. anatomy, cell biology U. So. Calif., L.A., 1974-89; assoc. v.p. biomed. rsch. Assn. Am. Med. Colls., Washington, 1989-97; ret., 1997; human embryology devel. study sec. NIH, Bethesda, Md., 1978-85, chmn. 1983-85; adj. prof. anatomy George Washington U., Washington, 1989-97. Author: (with others) Bailey's Textbook of Histology, 17th edit., 1978, Bailey's Textbook of Microscopic Anatomy, 18th edt., 1984; contbr. articles to profl. jours. Recipient Sigma Xi award Am. Scientist, 1962; Citation medal Japan Assn. Anatomists, Sendai, Japan, 1984; named Honor Alumnus, Colo. State U., 1978. Mem. Am. Assn. Anatomists (pres. 1986-87), Assn. Anatomy Chmn. (pres. 1977-78), Coun. Academic Socs. (chmn. 1987-88).

KELLY, EAMON MICHAEL, university president emeritus; b. N.Y.C., Apr. 25, 1936; s. Michael Joseph and Kathleen Elizabeth (O'Farrell) K.; m. Margaret Whalen, June 22, 1963; children: Martin (dec.), Paul, Andrew, Peter. BS, Fordham U., 1958; MS, Columbia U., 1960, PhD, 1965. Officer in charge Office of Social Devel., Ford Found., N.Y.C., 1969-74; officer in charge program related investments Ford Found., 1974-79; exec. v.p. Tulane U., New Orleans, 1979-81, pres., 1981—; dir. policy formulation div. Econ. Devel. Adminstrn., Dept. Commerce, Washington, 1968; spl. asst. to adminstr. SBA, Washington, 1968-69; spl. cons. to sec. Dept. Labor, 1977; bd. dirs. So. Edn. Found., La. Land and Exploration Co., Nat. Captioning Inst., Assn. Gov. Bds. Colls. and Univ., Econ. Devel. Commn. State of La.; mem. Nat. Sci. Bd., Nat. Security Edn. Bd., Humphrey Fellows Nat. Adv. Bd., Bus. Higher Edn. Forum, com. econ. devel. Gabelli Enterprises Inc., exec. com. Assn. Am. Univs.; pres. Commission NCAA, Found. for Biomed. Rsch., Nat. Sci. Bd., 1996; former chair Presidential Adv. Bd.; chair Nat. Sci. Bd. Pres. city coun., councilman-at-large City of Englewood, N.J., 1974-77; bd. advocates Planned Parenthood of La. Mem. AAUP, La. Conf. Univs. and Colls., La. Assn. Ind. Colls. and Univs., Bus. Coun. New Orleans, City Club, Inc., Met. Area Com., New Orleans Ednl. Telecom. Consortium. Democrat. Roman Catholic. Home: 3122 Octavia St New Orleans LA 70125-4936 Office: Tulane U Payson Ctr 6823 Saint Charles Ave New Orleans LA 70118-5698

KELLY, EDMUND JOSEPH, lawyer, investment banker; b. Mount Vernon, N.Y., May 18, 1937; s. Hugh Joseph and Catherine (Rice) K.; m. Joan Anne Fee, Nov. 18, 1961; children: Kathleen Kelly Broomer, Edmund

Murphy, Thomas More, Mary Kelly Mehr, Michael McNaboe. AB cum laude, Coll. of Holy Cross, 1959; JD (James Kent scholar), Columbia U., 1962. Bar: N.Y. 1962. Sec. of Air Force Office of Gen.Counsel, Washington, 1962-65; assoc. White & Case, N.Y.C., 1965-70; ptnr. White & Case, 1971-84; vice chmn. Dominick & Dominick Co., N.Y.C., 1984-91, Eighteen Seventy Corp., Purchase, N.Y., 1991—; lectr. Practicing Law Inst., Am. Mgmt. Assn.; bd. dirs. Fed. Paper Bd. Co., Inc., Montvale, N.J., 1981-96; bd. dirs., mem. exec. com. Chgo. Pneumatic Tool Co., N.Y.C., 1980-86. Author: The Takeover Dialogues, A Discussion of Hostile Takeovers, 1987; editor Columbia Law Rev., 1961-62; contbr. articles to legal jours. Air Force mem. Armed Services Procurement Regulation Com., 1964-65. Office: Eighteen Seventy Corp Two Manhattanville Rd Purchase NY 10577-2118

KELLY, EDWARD JOHN, V, counselor; b. Saratoga Springs, N.Y., July 10, 1936; s. Edward John IV and Blanch Marie (O'Connor) K.; children: Edward J. VI, Patrick J., Kevin J., Michael J., Kathleen M. Student, Union Coll., Schenectady, N.Y., 1954-56; MEd in Guidance and Counseling, Campbell U., Buies Creek, N.C., 1990; student, U. Dayton, 1967; BA in History, N.C. Wesleyan Coll., 1982. Commd. USAF, 1956, advanced through grades to lt. col., 1975; instr. navigation Strategic Air Command USAF, various locations, 1958-69; scheduler KC-135 USAF, Castle AFB, Calif., 1970-71, chief bomber ops., 1972-73; chief KC-135 planner USAF, Anderson AFB, Guam, 1973-74; 8AF chief of tng. Anderson AFB, Guam, 1974-75; dir. ops. and tng. USAF, Seymour Johnson AFB, N.C., 1977-78; ret. USAF, 1979; job developer, counselor Wayne C.C., Goldsboro, N.C., 1979-80, dir. coop. edn., job placement and apprenticeship, 1980-97; chmn. County Workforce Devel. Coun., Goldsboro, 1980-97; com. chmn. N.C. Internship Coun., 1985-93, N.C. trails com. chmn. 1989-92. Author: Canoeing the Neuse River, 1983, Your Move Into the World of Work, 1988. Chmn. task force Waynesborough State Pk., 1983-86, 90-94, 95—; scoutmaster Boy Scouts Am., Merced., Calif. and Guam, Goldsboro, 1971-86, coun. commr., Goldsboro, 1976-81, 84-88, dist. chmn., 1982-84; cand. Rep. Party, Wayne County, 1982, 84, 86. Recipient Silver Beaver award Boy Scouts Am., 1973. Mem. DAV, VFW, Coop. Edn. Assn., N.C. Coop. Edn. Assn. (bd. dirs. 1985-97, pres. 1994, Outstanding Profl. 1994), N.C. Placement Assn. (program co-chmn. 1990, Outstanding Profl. 1994), Neuse Trails Assn., Air Force Assn. (pres. 1980-82, 90-91, Merit medal 1989), County Pers. Assn. (pres. 1992). Avocations: organic gardening, horticulture, recreational vehicles, canoeing, fishing. E-mail: edphylkelly@earthlink.net. Home: 170 Quail Dr Dudley NC 28333-9518

KELLY, EDWARD JOSEPH, lawyer; b. Scranton, Pa., Oct. 31, 1966; s. Edward Joseph and Jane Elizabeth (Lavelle) K. BA, Duke U., 1988; JD, Boston U., 1991. Bar: N.Y. 1992. Coach Fairfield (Conn.) Preparatory Sch., 1988-91; assoc. Blank Rome Comisky & McCauley, Phila., 1990; ptnr. Kelly Rode & Kelly, LLP, Mineola, N.Y., 1991—; lectr. in field. Cons. Legal Ctr. for Def. of Life, N.Y.C., 1991—. Emery Worldwide Inc. scholar, 1984-88. Mem. N.Y. State Bar Assn., Nassau County Bar Assn., Nassau/Suffolk Trial Lawyers Assn., Nat. Inst. Trial Advocacy, Guild Cath. Lawyers, N.Y. State Trial Lawyers Inst. Republican. Roman Catholic. Avocations: horse raising, golf, hunting, weight training. Home: 312 E 92nd St New York NY 10128-5438 Office: Kelly Rode & Kelly LLP 330 Old Country Rd Ste 305 Mineola NY 11501-4170 also: 218 Griffing Ave Riverhead NY 11901-3009*

KELLY, ELLSWORTH, painter, sculptor; b. Newburgh, N.Y., May 31, 1923. Student, Boston Mus. Fine Arts Sch., Ecole des Beaux-Arts, Paris, 1946-48; DFA (hon.), Pratt Inst., 1993, Bard Coll., 1996; hon. doctorate, Royal Coll. Art, London, 1997. Works exhibited: Salon de Realities Nouvelles, Paris, 1950, 51, Carnegie Inst., 1958, 61, 64, 67, 85, Sao Paulo Biennial, 1961, Tokyo Internat., 1963, Documenta III, Germany, 1964, Documenta IV, 1968, Documenta IX, 1992, Venice Biennale, 1966, Guggenheim Internat., 1967, Corcoran Ann., Washington, 1979, others; one-man shows include Galerie Arnaud, Paris, 1951, Galerie Maeght, Paris, 1958, 64, 65, Sidney Janis Gallery, N.Y.C., 1965, 67, 68, 71, Betty Parsons Gallery, N.Y.C., 1956, 57, 59, 61, 63, Tooth Gallery, London, 1962, Washington Gallery Modern Art, 1964, Inst. Contemporary Art, Boston, 1964, Dayton's Gallery 12, Mpls., 1971, Albright Art Gallery, 1972, Hans Mayer Gallery, Dusseldorf, Germany, 1972, Leo Castelli Gallery, N.Y.C., 1973, 75, 77, 81, 82, 84, 85, 89, 90, 92, Irving Blum Gallery, Los Angeles, 1965-68, 73, Greenberg Gallery, St. Louis, 1973, 89, Whitney Mus. Am. Art, N.Y.C., 1982, St. Louis Mus. Art, 1983, N.Y. Mus. Modern Art, 1973, 78, Pasadena (Calif.) Mus. Modern Art, 1974, Walker Art Mus., Mpls., 1974, 94, Detroit Inst. Fine Arts, 1974, Ace Gallery, Venice, Calif., 1975, Janie Lee Gallery, Houston, 1975, Blum/Helman Gallery, N.Y.C., 1975, 77, 79, 81, 82, 84, 85, 86, 88, 89, 92, Met. Mus., N.Y.C., 1979, Stedelijk Mus., Amsterdam, 1979, Hayward Gallery, London, 1980, Centre Georges Pompidou, Paris, 1980, Staatliche Kunsthalle, Baden Baden, 1980, Margo Leavin Gallery, L.A., 1984, 91, Castelli Graphics, N.Y., 1988, BlumHelman Gallery, L.A., 1988, Daniel Templon, Paris, 1989, 92, Overholland Mus., Amsterdam, 1989, Susan Sheehan Gallery, N.Y.C., 1990, 92, 95, Gallery Kasahara, Osaka, Japan, 1990, Portikus, Frankfurt, Fed. Rep. Germany, 1990, Matthew Marks Gallery, N.Y.C., 1992, 94, Anthony D'Offay, London, 1992, 94, Paula Cooper Gallery, N.Y.C., 1992, Ellsworth Kelly: Works on Paper Modern Art Mus. Ft. Worth, 1987, Mus. Fine Arts, Boston, Art Gallery Ont., Toronto, Balt. Mus. Art, San Francisco Mus. Modern Art, Nelson-Atkins Mus. Art, Kansas City, The Prints of Ellsworth Kelly: A Catalogue Raisonné 1949-85 Detroit Inst. Arts, 1987, Huntsville Mus. Art, Ala., Des Moines Art Ctr., Iowa, Neuberger Art Mus., Purchase, N.Y., Los Angeles County Mus. Art, U. Okla. Mus. Art, Berkshire Mus., Pittsfield, Mass., Univ. Art Mus., Berkeley, Calif., Hood Mus. Art, Hanover, N.H., Ellsworth Kelly, The French Years, 1948-54, Galerie Nationale du Jeu de Paume, Paris, 1992, Westfalishes Landesmus, Munster, Germany, 1992, Nat. Gallery, Washington, 1993, Eli Broad Found., L.A., 1994, Milw. Art Mus., 1994; represented in permanent collections Mus. Modern Art, Met. Mus., Whitney Mus., Carnegie Inst., Albright Art Gallery, Buffalo, Chgo. Art Inst., Worcester Mus., Toronto (Can.) Mus.,Tate Gallery, London, Walker Art Center, Mpls., Guggenheim Mus., N.Y.C., Los Angeles County Mus., Centre Georges Pompidou, Paris,Stedlijk Mus., Amsterdam, Kroller-Mueller Mus., Otterlo, Holland, Munster Mus., Germany, UNESCO, Paris, Centro Reina Sofia, Madrid, Lenbachhaus, Munster, Balt. Mus. Art, Nat. Gallery, Washington, San Francisco Mus. Modern Art. sculpture: lobby, Transp. Bldg., Phila., 1956, Barcelona, Spain, 1985, Balt. Mus. Garden, 1988, Walker Art Ctr. Garden, 1988, Mus. Fine Arts, Houston, 1986, Myerson Symphony Ctr., Dallas, 1989, Nestle S.A., Vevey, Switzerland, 1991, Carre d'Art, Museee d'Art Contemporain, Nimes, France, Holocaust Mus., Washington, 1993. Decorated chevalier Ordre Arts et Lettres, Legion of Honor, comdr. Arts et Lettres (France); recipient Brandeis painting award, 1963, Edn. Min. award Tokyo Internat., 1963, 4th prize Carnegie Inst., 1962, painting prize, 1964; painting prize Art Inst. Chgo., 1964, 74, Showhegan, 1981, medal Pratt Inst., Bklyn., 1993, medal for outstanding achievement Sch. Mus. Fine Arts, Boston, 1996, ann. tribute award Friends Art and Preservation in Embassies, U.S. Dept. State, 1996, Govs. award N.Y. Sate Coun. on Arts, 1998; named Friend of Barcelona and recipient medal Mayor of Barcelona, 1993. Fellow Acad. Arts and Scis.; mem. Nat. Acad. Arts and Letters.

KELLY, ERIC DAMIAN, lawyer, educator; b. Pueblo, Colo., Mar. 16, 1947; s. William Bret and Patricia Ruth (Ducy) K.; children: Damian Charles, Eliza Jane, Valissitie Christina Heeren, Douglas Ray Heeren; m. Sandra Walker, 1996. BA, Williams Coll., 1969; JD, U. Pa., 1975, M of City Planning, 1975; PhD, Union Inst., 1992. Bar: Colo. 1975, U.S. Dist. Ct. 1976, U.S. Tax Ct. 1976, U.S. Ct. Appeals (10th cir.) 1986. Chief citizens' participation unit Region III EPA, Phila., 1971-72; project planner Beckett New Town, N.J., 1972-73; v.p., project mgr. Rahenkamp Sachs Wells & Assocs., Inc., Denver and Phila., 1973-76; sole practice Pueblo, 1976-83; pres. Kelly & Potter, P.C., Pueblo, Albuquerque and Santa Fe, 1983-90; adj. prof. U. Colo. Coll. Architecture and Planning, 1976-90; chmn., prof. Dept. cmty. and regional planning Iowa State U., 1990-95; adj. asst. prof. grad. sch. bus. U. So. Colo., 1986-90; dean coll. architecture and planning Ball State U., 1995-98, prof. urban planning, 1999—; mem. city devel. bd. State of Iowa, 1991-95. Gen. editor Zoning and Land Use Controls, 1995—; author: Enforcing Zoning and Land Use Codes, 1988, Managing Community Growth: Policies, Techniques and Impacts, 1993, Selecting and Retaining Consultants, 1993, Planning, Growth and Public Facilities: A Primer for Public Officials, 1994; editor, prin. author: The Roadtripper, 1969; contbr. articles to profl. planning and legal jours. Mem. adv. bd. Mcpl. Legal Studies Ctr., S.W. Legal Found., 1989—; mem. nat. adv. bd. Rocky Mountain Land Use Inst. Coll. Law U. Denver, 1992—; bd. dirs. Broadway Theatre League, Pueblo, 1976-77, Pueblo Beautiful Assn., 1978-82, Better Bus. Bur., 1988-89; trustee Sangre de Cristo Arts and Conf. Ctr., 1981-87, chmn. 1986; trustee Christ Congl. Ch., 1982-83. With U.S. Army, 1969-71. Named Outstanding Student, Am. Inst. Planners, 1976; recipient Outstanding Faculty award Order of Omega, 1992. Mem. ABA, Am. Inst. Cert. Planners (charter, elected Coll. of Fellows 1999), Am. Planning Assn. (nat. pres., 1997—, chair planning & law divsn. 1996-97, pres. Iowa chpt. 1994-95, amicus curiae com. 1988-94, 95-97, legis. & policy com. 1993-97, Colo. chpt. excellence award 1989), Williams Coll. Alumni Assn. (class sec. 1969-74, regional sec. 1980-82, class agt. 1985-89), Rotary (local dir. 1988-90, dir., pres. Pueblo Rotary Found. 1988-89, v.p. 1988-89, pres. 1989-90, area rep. for dist. gov. 1991-92), Phi Kappa Phi. Democrat. Home: 2312 W Audubon Dr Muncie IN 47304-2003 Office: Ball State U Coll Architecture/Planning Muncie IN 47306

KELLY, FRANCIS DANIEL, retired lawyer; b. Des Moines, Aug. 9, 1909; s. Maximus Vincent and Mary Ellen (Feeney) K.; m. Jane E. Keogh, Dec. 3, 1949; children: Jeremiah F., Mark D., Daniel K., James K. AB, Marquette U., 1931, JD, 1933. Bar: Wis. 1933. With Jour. Co., Milw., 1927-78, sr. v.p., bus. mgr., 1973-77, exec. v.p., 1977-78, ret., 1978; of counsel Miller, Simon and Maier, S.C., Milw., 1978-96. Mem. adv. bd. (jour.) Foundation. Mem. president's exec. senate Marquette U.; emeritus mem., v.p. St. Michael Hosp. Found.; emeritus mem. regional bd. NCCJ; past bd. dirs., formr mem. president's exec. coun. Cardinal Stritch Coll. Lt. comdr. USNR, 1942-45. Named 1 of 3 honorees Regional NCCJ, 1973. Mem. ABA, Wis. Bar Assn., Wis. Newspaper Assn. (Golden mem.). Roman Catholic. Home: 113 W Fox Dale Rd Milwaukee WI 53217-3915

KELLY, FRANCIS J., III, marketing company executive; m. Heather Kelly; children: Whitney, Jay (twins). BA, Amherst Coll.; MBA, Harvard. With Young & Rubicam, N.Y.C., 1978-81; from acct. exec. to sr. v.p., group acct. dir. Humphrey Browning MacDougall, 1983-88; prin., dir. client svcs., COO Leonard Monahan (now Leonard Monahan, Lubars & Kelly), Providence, 1989-94; chief mktg. officer, accts. mgr. Volkswagen, Ocean Spray, Stop & Shop, talbots, Polaroid Arnold, Fortuna, Lawner & Cabot, 1994—; mng. ptnr., chief mktg. officer Arnold Comm., Inc., Boston; spkr. in field. Author: (with Whitney Kelly) What They Really Teach You at the Harvard Business School. Mem. Boston Ad Club (pres.). Avocations: golf, tennis, coaching his children's teams, travel. Office: care Arnold Comm Inc 101 Huntington Ave Boston MA 02199-7603*

KELLY, GEORGE ANTHONY, clergyman, author, educator; b. N.Y.C., Sept. 17, 1916; s. Charles W. and Bridget (Fitzgerald) K. M.A. in Social Sci., Catholic U Am., 1943, Ph.D. in Social Sci., 1946. Ordained priest Roman Cath. Ch., 1942, elevated to monsignor, 1960. Priest St. Monica's Parish, N.Y.C., 1945-56; dir. Family Life Bur., 1955-65, Family Consultation Service, 1955-65; dir. dept. edn. Archdiocese N.Y.C., 1966-70; pastor St. John's Ch., N.Y.C., 1970-74; dir. Inst. Advanced Studies in Cath. doctrine, St. John's U., Jamaica, N.Y., 1975-81; exec. sec. Fellowship of Cath. Scholars, 1976, pres., 1986-88; consultor Archdiocese N.Y., Congregation for the Clergy, Rome, 1984; sec. bd. trustees St. Joseph's Sem.; sec. adv. bd. Pastoral Life Conf.; co-chmn. Archdiocesan Parish Councils, 1966-70. Author: Who Should Run the Catholic Church?, 1976, The Battle for the American Church, 1979, The Crisis of Authority: John Paul II and the American Bishops, 1981, The New Biblical Theorists: Raymond E. Brown and Beyond, 1983, Inside My Father's House, 1989, Keeping the Church Catholic with John Paul II, 1990, The Pastor's Challenge, 1994, The Battle for the American Church Revisited, 1995, others. Recipient 1st Cardinal Wright award Friends of Fellowship of Cath. Scholars, 1979, Faith and Family award Women for Faith and Family, 1988, Pres.'s medal St. John's U., 1992, Courage in Faith award Steubenville U., 1997, Rivs XI award Soc. of Cath. Social Scientists, 1999. Mem. AAUP, Am. Sociol. Assn., Am. Cath. Sociol. Soc., Assn. for Sociology of Religion, Am. Cath. Hist. Soc., Am. Cath. Theol. Soc. Address: 10710 Shore Front Pkwy Far Rockaway NY 11694-2637

KELLY, GERALD WAYNE, chemical coatings company executive; b. Charleston, W.Va., May 21, 1944; s. Wayne Woodside and Sarrah (Myers) K.; m. (div.); children: Scott Wayne, Lauren Melissa (dec.); m. Elizabeth Long, Nov. 18, 1983. BS, W.Va. U., 1966. From sales corr. to regional mgr. duPont Corp., various locations, 1966-83; bus. mgr. Decatur (Ala.) divsn. Whittaker Corp., 1983-85; v.p. Decatur divsn. Morton Internat., 1985-86, pres. Decatur divsn., 1986-93; v.p. Morton Indsl. Coatings, Morton Internat., Chgo., 1993—; pres./owner IRP Inc., Falkville, Ala., 1992—. Bd. dirs. Ind. Cystic Fibrosis Found., Indpls., 1971-73. Mem. Nat. Coil Coaters Assn., Nat. Paint and Coatings Assn., Beta Theta Pi. Republican. Methodist. Avocation: automobiles. Home: 14 Tartan Ridge Rd Burr Ridge IL 60521-8905 Office: Morton Internat 100 N Riverside Plz Chicago IL 60606-1501 also: IRP Inc PO Box 670 Falkville AL 35622-0670

KELLY, GRACE DENTINO, secondary education educator; b. Peoria, Ill., Mar. 30, 1934; d. Michael and Arnita Balagna (Barto) Dentino; cert. med. technology, St. Francis Sch. Med. Tech., 1955; B.S., Bradley U., 1971, M.S., 1973; m. Robert N. Kelly, Aug. 31, 1957; children—Susan, James, Stephen, Patrick. Tchr. sci. St. Mark Sch., Peoria, asst. prin., 1980-83, chmn. jr. high sch. curriculum com. for drug edn.; prin. St. Thomas Sch., Peoria Heights, Ill., 1983-89, tchr. biology and chemistry Woodruff High Sch., Peoria, 1989-90; prin. Blessed Sacrament Sch., Morton, Ill., 1991-92, St. Mark Sch., Peoria, 1992-98; Treywn Middle Sch., 1998—; presenter Ill. Math Tchr. Conv., Peoria, 1992; tchr. Aurora (Ill.) U. Bd. dirs. Spl. People Encounter Christ, 1997. Mem. ednl. adv. bd. Peoria Jour. Star Newspaper, 1973—. Recipient Econs. Educator award Joint Council on Econ. Edn., N.Y.C., 1982—, dedication to excellence in education and to justice and equality award NOW, 1998, Esmark Found. award Ill. Council Econ. Edn., 1984, Those Who Excell award Ill. State Bd., 1989, PARC award, 1989., Today's Cath. Tchr.'s Project: Sharing award, 1992, Adminstr. of Yr. award Today's Cath. Tchr. Mag., 1992, Jean Tucker award Ill. Valley Mental Health Assn., 1994. Mem. AAUW, Nat. Sci. Tchrs. Assn., Am. Soc. Clin. Pathologists, Ill. Sci. Tchrs. Assn. (dir. region III, presenter papers), Ill. Jr. Acad. Sci. (dir. region I), Phi Delta Kappa. Roman Catholic. Home: 1815 W High St Peoria IL 61606-1635 Office: Trewyn Middle Sch 1419 S Folkers Ave Peoria IL 61605

KELLY, HENRY ANSGAR, English language educator; b. Fonda, Iowa, June 6, 1934; s. Harry Francis and Inez Ingeborg (Anderson) K.; m. Marea Tancred, June 18, 1968; children—Sarah Marea, Dominic Tancred. A.B., St. Louis U., 1959, A.M., 1961, Ph.L., 1961; Ph.D., Harvard U., 1965. Asst. prof. English UCLA, 1967-69, assoc. prof. English, 1969-72, prof. English, 1972—, dir. Ctr. for Medieval and Renaissance Studies, 1998—. Author: The Devil, Demonology and Witchcraft, 1968, 74, Divine Providence in the England of Shakespeare's Histories, 1970, Love and Marriage in the Age of Chaucer, 1975, The Matrimonial Trials of Henry VIII, 1976, Canon Law and the Archpriest of Hita, 1984, The Devil at Baptism, 1985, Chaucer and the Cult of St. Valentine, 1986, Tragedy and Comedy from Dante to Pseudo-Dante, 1989, Ideas and Forms of Tragedy from Aristotle to the Middle Ages, 1993, Chaucerian Tragedy, 1997; co-editor Viator 1970-90. Guggenheim felow, 1971-72, Nat. Endowment Humanities fellow, 1980-81, 96-97. Fellow Medieval Acad. Am.; mem. Medieval Assn. of Pacific (pres. 1988-90). Roman Catholic. Home: 1123 Kagawa St Pacific Palisades CA 90272-3838 Office: UCLA Dept English 405 Hilgard Ave Los Angeles CA 90095-9000

KELLY, HUGH RICE, lawyer; b. Austin, Tex., Dec. 16, 1942; s. Thomas Philip and Cecilia Elizabeth (Rice) K.; m. Marguerite Susan McIntosh, Dec. 27, 1971; children: Susan McIntosh, Cecilia Rice. BA, Rice U., 1965; JD, U. Tex., 1972. Bar: Tex. 1972, U.S. Dist. Ct. (so. dist.) Tex. 1974; U.S. Ct. Appeals (5th cir.), U.S. Supreme Ct. 1975. Assoc. Baker & Botts, Houston, 1972-78, ptnr., 1979-84; exec. v.p., gen. counsel Reliant Energy, Inc., Houston Lighting and Power Co. (former, 1984—. 1st lt. U.S. Army, 1966-69. Fellow Tex. Bar Found., Houston Bar Found.; mem. ABA, State Bar Tex., Houston Bar Assn., Coronado Club. Republican. Home: 1936 Rice Blvd Houston TX 77005-1635 Office: Reliant Energy Inc PO Box 1700 1111 Louisiana Houston TX 77251-1700

KELLY, J. MICHAEL, lawyer; b. Hattiesburg, Miss., Dec. 5, 1943. BA, Emory U., 1966; LLB, U. Va., 1969. Bar: Ga. 1969, U.S. Supreme Ct. 1978, D.C. 1980, Utah 1982, Calif. 1988. Law clerk to Judge Griffin B. Bell (5th cir.) U.S. Ct. Appeals, Atlanta, 1969-70; ptnr. Alston & Bird (formerly Alston, Miller & Gaines), Atlanta, 1970-77, 81-82; counselor to atty. gen. U.S. Dept. Justice, Washington, 1977-79; counselor to sec. U.S. Dept. Energy, Washington, 1979-81; ptnr., shareholder, dir. Ray, Quinney & Nebeker, Salt Lake City, 1982-87; ptnr. Cooley Godward LLP, San Francisco, 1987—. Mem. Omicron Delta Kappa, Phi Alpha Delta. Office: Cooley Godward LLP 1 Maritime Plz Fl 20 San Francisco CA 94111-3404

KELLY, JAMES, artist; b. Phila., Dec. 19, 1913; s. James Alphonsus and Mabel (Witzel) K.; m. Sonia Gechtoff, June 23, 1953; children—Susannah, Miles. Student, Pa. Acad. Fine Arts, 1938, Barnes Found., 1941; diploma in painting, Calif. Sch. Fine Arts, 1954. lectr. painting and drawing U. Calif., Berkeley, 1957. One-man shows include San Francisco Art Assn., 1956, Stryke Gallery, N.Y.C., 1963, East Hampton (N.Y.) Gallery, 1965, 69, Albright Coll., Reading, Pa., 1966, L.I. (N.Y.) U., 1968, Westbeth Galleries, N.Y.C., 1971-72, Weigand Gallery, Coll. Notre Dame, Belmont, Calif., 1990; groups shows include Pa. Acad. Fine Arts, Phila., 1951, San Francisco Mus. Art, 1955, 56, 57, 58, 65, Los Angeles County Mus., 1968, Phoenix Art Mus., 1975, Smithsonian Instn., Washington, 1977, Oakland Mus. Art, Calif., 1985, Santa Cruz (Calif.) Art Mus., 1993, Laguna (Calif.) Art Mus., 1996, San Francisco Mus. Modern Art, 1996; represented in permanent collections San Francisco Mus. Modern Art, Los Agneles County Mus., U. Mass., Oakland Mus. Art, Mus. Modern Art, N.Y.C., Westinghouse Corp.; invitational show Gruenebaum Gallery, N.Y.C., 1988; additional collections Richmond (Calif.) Art Ctr., Crocker Art Mus., Sacramento, NYU, Worcester (Mass.) Art Mus. Served with USAF, 1941-45. Recipient painting awards San Francisco Mus. Art, Phoenix Art Mus., Peter and Madeleine Martin Found. for Creative Arts, San Francisco, 1990; Found. grantee Tamarind Lithography Workshop, Los Angeles, 1963; Nat. Endowment for Arts fellow, 1977. Mem. NAD. Home: 463 West St Apt 936 New York NY 10014-2010

KELLY, JAMES ANTHONY, priest; b. Worcester, Mass., Apr. 22, 1949; s. James and Elisabeth (Allen) K. BA in Philosophy and Govt., Harvard Coll., 1971; PhD in Philosophy, CUNY, 1979. ordained priest Roman Cath. Ch., 1982. Dir. Riverside Study Ctr., N.Y.C., 1977-79; procurator Prelature of Opus Dei, Rome, 1984-88; vicar USA region Prelature of Opus Dei, New Rochelle, N.Y., 1988-98. Avocations: philosophy of sci., ethics, basketball, jazz, English lit. Home and Office: 99 Overlook Cir New Rochelle NY 10804-4501

KELLY, JAMES JOSEPH, printing company executive; b. Steubenville, Ohio, Feb. 26, 1941; s. James Geary and Mary Catherine (Maley) K.; m. Judith Ann Miller, June 29, 1963; children: James M., Heather, Sean. BS in Econs., Xavier U., 1963. Acct. exec. Western Pub. Co., Racine, Wis., 1969-79; sales rep. Alden Press/World Color, Chgo., 1979—. 1st lt. U.S. Army, 1963-65. Mem. Direct Mktg. Assn., Mid. Ohi Direct Mktg. Club, St. Louis Direct Mktg., Xavier U. Alumnae Assn. (v.p., then pres. St. Louis chpt.). Republican. Roman Catholic. Avocations: golf, tennis, tournament fishing, running. Home: 216 Greenburn Dr Saint Charles MO 63304-0925 Office: World Color/Alden Press Ste 204 17600 Chesterfield Airport Rd Chesterfield MO 63005-1246

KELLY, JAMES MCGIRR, federal judge; b. 1928. BS, Wharton Sch., 1951; JD, Temple U., 1957. Law clk. to judge U.S. Ct. Common Pleas, Phila., 1957-58; asst. dist. atty. Phila. County, 1958-60; asst. atty. U.S. Dist. Ct. (ea. dist.) Pa., Phila., 1960-62; master jury selection bd. U.S. Ct. Common Pleas, Phila., 1962-64; pvt. practice law Phila., 1962-83; spl. asst. atty. gen. Commonwealth of Pa., 1965; judge U.S. Dist. Ct. (ea. dist.) Pa., Phila., 1983-95, sr. judge, 1995—. Mem. Pa. Pub. Utility Commn., 1966-77. Served with USN, 1951-53. Office: US Courthouse Independence Mall W #8614 601 Market St Philadelphia PA 19106-1713*

KELLY, JAMES MICHAEL, plant and soil scientist; b. Knoxville, Feb. 2, 1944; s. Woodrow Wilson and Thelma Lucille (Miller) K.; m. Susan Kay Morris, Aug. 9, 1969; children: John Kip, Christopher Kenneth. BS, E. Tenn. State U., 1966; MS, U. Tenn., 1968, PhD, 1973. Cert. profl. soil scientist. Assoc. ecologist NUS Corp., Pitts., 1973-74; rsch. assoc. Forestry Dept. Purdue U., West Lafayette, Ind., 1975-76; program mgr. Tenn. Valley Authority, Oak Ridge, 1977-88, sr. rschr., 1990-94; sr. tech. specialist, team leader, 1994-95; prof., chair dept. forestry Iowa State U., Ames, 1995—; vis. prof. agronomy Purdue U., 1988-89; adj. prof. U. Tenn., Knoxville, 1980-95, forestry dept. Purdue U., 1985-95. Author: Carbon Forms and Functions in Forest Soils, 1995; assoc. editor Soil Sci. Soc. Am. Jour., 1989-95, Forest Sci., 1998—; contbr. more than 90 articles to profl. jours. Head referee Ayso Youth Soccer, Oak Ridge, 1985-88; troop com. Boy Scouts Am., Oak Ridge, 1989-95. Oak Ridge Assocs. Univ. fellow, 1970-72; Elec. Power Rsch. Inst. grantee, 1978, 82, 89, 91, 95, NSF grantee, 1995. Fellow Soil Sci. Soc. Am. (chmn. divsn. S7 1986-87, bd. dirs. 1988-89, awards com. 1992-93, fellows com. 1997-99); mem. AAAS, Ecol. Soc. Am., Soc. Am. Foresters, Soil Ecology Soc., Exptl. Aircraft Assn. (chpt. pres. 1991-93), Trees Forever (bd. dirs. 1995—), Sigma Xi, Gamma Sigma Delta, Xi Sigma Pi. Achievements include research and application of environmental science. Office: Iowa State Univ Dept Forestry Ames IA 50011-1021

KELLY, JAMES MICHAEL, lawyer; b. Pitts., May 24, 1947; s. James M. and Catherine C. Kelly; m. Mary J. Armstrong, Dec. 20, 1980; children: Lea Day, Heather Marie. AB, Princeton U., 1969; JD, U. Pitts., 1978. Bar: Mich. 1978, Fla. 1982, U.S. Supreme Ct. 1985, U.S. Ct. Appeals (6th cir.), Ga. 1990. Atty. Chrysler Corp., Highland Park, Mich., 1978-81; corp. counsel Harris Corp., Melbourne, Fla., 1981-87; v.p., gen. counsel, corp. sec. Lanier Worldwide, Inc., Atlanta, 1987—. Editor U. Pitts. Law Rev., 1978. Capt. U.S. Army, 1969-75. Mem. ABA, Am. Assn. Corp. Counsel, Am. Assn. Corp. Secs., Fla. Bar Assn., Ga. Bar Assn., Atlana Bar Assn., DeKalb County Bar Assn., Assn. 82d Airborne Divsn., Cannon Club. Office: Lanier Worldwide Inc 2300 Parklake Dr NE Atlanta GA 30345-2912

KELLY, JAMES P., delivery service executive; b. Jersey City, Apr. 18, 1943. BA, Rutgers U., 1973. With United Parcel Svc. of Am., Inc., Atlanta, 1964—, regional mgr., 1987, sr. v.p., labor rels. mgr., 1988, sr. v.p., COO, 1992-94, exec. v.p., COO, 1994-96, vice chmn., COO, 1996-97, chmn., CEO, 1997—. Office: UPS 55 Glenlake Pkwy NE Atlanta GA 30328-3474

KELLY, JAMES PATRICK, JR., retired engineering and construction executive; b. Bklyn., July 19, 1933; s. James Patrick and Marion Rita (Gleason) K.; children: Kathryn, Mark, Lisa Angelique, Trevor, Lisa, James. BSEngring., U.S. Naval Acad., 1955; postgrad., U. Houston, 1968-69. Registered profl. engr., Calif. Asst. site mgr. Pathfinder reactor Allis Chalmers Mfg. Co., Sioux Falls, S.D., 1963-67; nuclear project mgr. Brown & Root, Houston, 1967-69; from constrn. project mgr. to asst. v.p. Gibbs & Hill, Omaha and N.Y.C., 1969-75; pres. Dravo Lime Co., Pitts., 1975-77; group v.p. natural resources Dravo Corp., Pitts., 1976-81, sr. v.p. engring. and constrn., domestic and internat., 1982-84; pres., dir. C.F. Braun & Co., Alhambra, Calif., 1984-86; pres., CEO Hadson Power Systems, Inc., Irvine, Calif., 1986-91, ret., 1991; bd. dirs. Hadson Corp. Bd. dirs. S.D. Mental Health Assn., 1966-67, Western Pa. Sch. Blind Children, 1978-84; mem. Sioux Falls Bd. Edn., 1965-66, Assn. Retarded Citizens Pitts., 1970—; pres. found. bd. Calif. State U., L.A., 1985-95; pres. Santa Ana Com. for Ednl. and Recreational Redevel. Area, mem. Devel. Disabilities Area Bd.; foreman Orange County Grand Jury, 1997-98. Mem. NSPE, Mensa, Sierra Club. Home: 1413 Franzen Ave Santa Ana CA 92705-6926

KELLY, JANET LANGFORD, lawyer; b. Kansas City, Mo., Nov. 27, 1957. BA, Grinnell Coll., 1979; JD, Yale U., 1983. Bar: N.Y. 1985, Ill. 1989. Law clerk to Hon. James J. Hunter III U.S. Ct. Appeals (3rd cir.), 1983-84; ptnr. Sidley & Austin, Chgo., 1984-89; sr. v.p., sec., gen. counsel Sara Lee Corp., Chgo., 1995—. Sr. editor Yale Law Jour., 1983. Office: Sara Lee Corporation Three First National Plaza 70 W Madison St Ste 4500 Chicago IL 60602-4260*

KELLY, JANICE HELEN, elementary school educator; b. Akron, Ohio, Nov. 28, 1951; d. Joe Ralph and Barbara Ann (Goins) Long; m. W. Gary Kelly, May 10, 1973; children: Benjamin, Chad. BS in Elem. Edn., Akron U., 1984; M in Edn., Kent (Ohio) State U., 1994. Tchr. Suffield United C.C.

Coop., Suffield, Ohio, 1984-86, Mogadore (Ohio) Local Schs., 1986—; cadre mem. Summit County Tech. Acad., Cuyahoga Falls, Ohio, 1994; participant Nat. Bd. Profl. Tech. Stds., 1996. Mem., tchr. Randolph (Ohio) United Meth. Ch., 1973—. Recipient Outstanding Educator award Somers Elem. PTA, Mogadore, 1989; Eisenhower grantee Kent State U., 1990-92, Tech., Industry, Environ. Edn. grantee Gen Corp, 1993. Mem. ASCD, Ohio Edn. Assn., Mogadore Edn. Assn. (sec. 1990-92, v.p. 1995—), Sci. Edn. Coun. Ohio. Avocations: doll-making/collecting, computer technology, golf, swimming. Home: 534 Hartville Rd Atwater OH 44201-9785 Office: Somers Elementary School 3600 Herbert St Mogadore OH 44260-1199

KELLY, JAY THOMAS See KELLY, TOM

KELLY, JEFFREY JENNINGS, mechanical engineer; b. Columbia, S.C., July 28, 1947; s. Jesse Jennings and Mary Katherine (Hawkins) K.; m. Betty Jane Vickers, June 15, 1980 (div. May 1984). BS in Math., Va. Poly. Inst. and State U., 1970, PhD in Engring. Mechanics, 1981. Mathematician Naval Surface Weapons Ctr., Dahlgren, Va., 1970-76; grad. rsch. asst. Va. Poly. Inst. and State U., Blacksburg, 1977-79, rsch. assoc., 1979-81; mech. engr. David Taylor Rsch. Ctr., Bethesda, Md., 1981-82; asst. prof. Old Dominion U., Norfolk, Va., 1983-85; rsch. fellow U. Southampton, Eng., 1985-87; rsch. engr. Northrop Corp., L.A., 1987-90; staff engr. Lockheed Corp., Hampton, Va., 1990—; cons., Southampton, 1986, Hampton, 1991. Referee Jour. of Acoustical Soc. Am., 1981-82. NASA/Am. Soc. Engring. Edn. fellow NASA, Langley, Va., 1983-84. Mem. AIAA (sr.), IEEE, N.Y. Acad. Scis., Inst. Noise Control Engring., Sigma Xi, Pi Mu Epsilon, Phi Kappa Phi. Achievements include development of signal processing schemes and codes for aircraft acoustic signals; performance of basic rsch. in aeroacoustics, duct acoustics, cavitation, structural-acoustic interaction and sound intensity. Home: 260 Marcella Rd Apt 1003 Hampton VA 23666-2591 Office: Lockheed Martin Engring & Scis NASA Langley Rsch Ctr MS303 Hampton VA 23681-0001

KELLY, JERRY BOB, social services administrator; b. Chgo., Feb. 6, 1942; s. Robert Lee and Mildred Florence (Griffin) K.; m. Diane Joyce Wilburn, Nov. 29, 1969; children: Jerold Robert, Joycelyn Reneé. B.S. in Acctg., Roosevelt U., 1968. Lic. real estate salesman and life ins. prodr., Ill. Acct. Weather Bloc Mfg. Co., Chgo., 1967-68; programmer Morton Salt Co., Chgo., 1968-69; br. mgr. Chgo. Econ. Devel. Corp., 1970-77; ptnr. Smith Distbrs., 1977-79; mgr. fin. and adminstrn. Suburban Cook County Area Agy. on Aging, Chgo., 1979-85; exec. dir. Lawndale Bus. and Local Devel. Corp., Chgo., 1985-88; dir. fin. No. Cook County Pvt. Industry Coun., Chgo., 1988-89; contr. Howard Area Cmty. Ctr., Chgo., 1989—; bd. dirs. Northside Cmty. Fed. Credit Union. Treas. Day Care Crisis Coun. Met. Chgo., 1973-76, appreciation award; 1st v.p. West Side Health Planning Orgn., 1974-76, appreciation award; treas. Met. Chgo. chpt. Nat. Caucus and Ctr. on Black Aged, 1992-94; treas. bd. dirs. St. Leonard's House; Cook County State's atty. African-Am. Adv. Coun., 1995—; vol. Ill. CPA. Soc. Served with AUS, 1964-67. Recipient appreciation award Chgo. Black Caucus, Am. Fedn. Tchrs., Chgo. Bd. Election Commrs., Comprehensive Health Planning Orgn. Chgo. Mem. Assoc. Photographers Internat. Baptist. Club: Elks (2d v.p. Ill.-Wis., past grand exalted ruler). Research on redevel. plans for East Garfield. Home: 1415 N Mayfield Ave Chicago IL 60651-1015 Office: Howard Area Community Ctr 7648 N Paulina St Chicago IL 60626-1018 *Personal philosophy: The things that have helped me most in my life is believing in myself, trusting in God and the strength of the Griffin Family.*

KELLY, JOHN FITZGERALD, software developer; b. Denver, June 7, 1961; s. James Delano and Connie Phyllis Kelly; m. Joan Mary Williamson, Sept. 2, 1995. BA in Physics, U. Colo., 1983; MS in Physics, U. Conn., 1990. Rsch. asst. U. Colo., Boulder, 1990-93; mem. tech. staff U.S. West, Boulder, 1993—. Lt. USN, 1984-90. Mem. Toastmasters Internat. (pres. 1992-93). Democrat. Home: 112 Balmora St Lafayette CO 80026

KELLY, JOHN HUBERT, diplomat, business executive; b. Fond du Lac, Wis., July 20, 1939; s. James Daniel and Clarice L. Kelly; m. Helena Marita Ajo; children: David Snowdon, Maria Louise. BA, Emory U., 1961; advanced studies cert., Georgetown U., 1982. Vice consul Am. Consulate, Adana, Turkey, 1965-66; 3rd sec. Am. Embassy, Ankara, Turkey, 1966-67; 2nd sec. Am. Embassy, Bangkok, Thailand, 1968-69; consul Am. Consulate, Songkhla, Thailand, 1969-71; 1st sec. Am. Embassy, Paris, 1976-80; fgn. svc. U.S. Dept. of State, Washington, 1972-76, dep. exec. sec., 1980-81, dep. asst. sec. of state, 1982-85, asst. sec. state for Near East and South Asia, 1989-91; U.S. amb. Am. Embassy, Beirut, 1986-88; amb. Am. Embassy, Helsinki, Finland, 1991-94; mng. dir. Internat. Equity Ptnrs., Atlanta, 1995-99; pres. John Kelly Cons., Conyers, 1999—. Mem. adv. coun. Una Chapman Cox Found., 1982-86. Trustee Lebanese Am. U.; mem. Coun. on Fgn. Rels., Mid. East Inst. Office: John Kelly Cons 1808 Over Lake Dr SE Ste D Conyers GA 30013-6608

KELLY, JOHN J., prosecutor. U.S. atty. for N.Mex. U.S. Dept. Justice, Albuquerque, 1993—. Office: US Atty for Dist NMex PO Box 607 Albuquerque NM 87103-0607*

KELLY, JOHN JAMES, lawyer; b. Rockville Centre, N.Y., July 4, 1949; s. John James Sr. and Eleanor Grace (Vann) K.; m. Clara Sarah Gussin; 1 child, John James III. AB in Govt., Georgetown U., 1971, JD, 1975. Bar: Pa. 1976, D.C. 1979, U.S. Dist. Ct. D.C. 1980, U.S. Claims Ct. 1982, U.S. Ct. Appeals (D.C. cir.) 1980, U.S. Ct. Appeals (fed. cir.) 1982. Law clk. to judge U.S. Dist. Ct., Washington, 1975-77; assoc. Corcoran, Youngman & Rowe, Washington, 1977-80; assoc. Capell, Howard, Knabe & Cobbs, Washington, 1980-83; assoc. Loomis, Owen, Fellman & Howe, Washington, 1983-86; ptnr., 1986-90; v.p., sec., gen. coun. Electronic Industries Alliance, Arlington, VA, 1990-96, exec. v.p., gen. counsel, 1997—; of counsel, Howe, Anderson & Steyer, Washington, 1990—; mem. Jud. Conf., D.C. Cir., Washington, 1983, Jud. Conf. Fed. Cir., Washington, 1988—. Contbr. articles to legal publs. Mem. ABA, D.C. Bar, Pa. Bar Assn., Am. Soc. Assn. Execs. (bd. dirs. legal section 1989-94, chmn. 1992-93), Fed. Bar Assn., Met. Club. Democrat. Roman Catholic. Office: Electronic Industries Alliance 2500 Wilson Blvd Arlington VA 22201-3834

KELLY, JOHN JOSEPH, JR., career officer; b. Paterson, N.J., Dec. 28, 1940; s. John Joseph Sr. and Helen C. (Ebersach) K.; m. Brenda Ruth Miller, July 1, 1966; children: Elizabeth Ann, Kathleen Anne, John J. BS in Chemistry, Seton Hall, 1963; MS, Pa. State U., 1969; MPA, Auburn U., 1976. Commd. 2d lt. USAF, 1963, advanced through grades to brig. gen., 1989; dir. spl. projects, HQ USAF, Scott AFB, Ill., 1978-80; comdr. 15 WEA Squadron USAF, McGuire AFB, N.J., 1980-81; dep. dir. programs/policy Air Force info. systems USAF, Washington, 1981-84; vice comdr. 7th Weather Wing Scott AFB, 1984-85; comdr. 5th Weather Wing Langley AFB, Va., 1985-88; comdr. Air Weather Svc. Scott AFB, 1988-91; dir. weather AF/XOW Washington, 1991-94; dir. Nat. Weather Svc., 1998—; cons. Dept. Commerce, 1991. Fellow Am. Meteorol. Soc., Air Force Assn., Nat. Weather Assn. Roman Catholic. Avocations: golf, reading. Office: NWS 1325 E West Hwy Silver Spring MD 20910-3280

KELLY, JOHN LOVE, public relations executive; b. N.Y.C., Jan. 30, 1924; s. Joseph John McDermott and Mary Florence Keenan (Love) K.; m. Helen M. Griffin Hanrahan, June 28, 1952; children: Janet Ann, J. Scott. BS, St. Peter's Coll., 1951; postgrad., N.C. State U., 1966. Buyer exec. tng. program R.H. Macy's, N.Y.C., 1951-53; mktg. exec. Sanforized divsn. Cluett Peabody Co., N.Y.C., 1953-58; advt. account exec. Batton, Barton, Durstine & Osborn, N.Y.C., 1958-59; advt. mgr. Am. Cyanamid Co., N.Y.C., 1959-64; advt. mgr. Am. fiber divsn. FMC Corp., N.Y.C., 1964-67; v.p., dir. pub. rels. and comm. Avtex Fibers Inc., N.Y.C., 1976-85; pres. Kelhan Ltd., 1985-89; cons. Brazilian Govt. Trade Bur., 1990-93. Cath. co-chmn. Peekskill area NCCJ, 1961-64, bd. dirs. Westchester County, 1969-79, nat. bd. dirs., 1966-69; trustee Mercy Coll., Dobbs Ferry, N.Y., 1965-69; trustee emeritus St. Peter's Coll.; councilman Town of Cortlandt (N.Y.), 1962-66; mem. Simon Wiesenthal Ctr., Am. Conf. for Irish Studies, Zoning Bd., 1971-74, mem. Bd. Ethics, 1975-79; mem. Cardinal's Com. of Laity, 1961-71; mem. Greater N.Y. Area coun. Boy Scouts Am., 1971-79. Mem. Pub. Rels. Club N.Y., Am. Fiber Mfrs. Assn. (chmn. pub. rels. com., edn. and pub. rels. subcoms.), Bd. Trade N.Y. (textile sect., v.p. 1954-60), Am. Israel Friendship League, Am. Irish Hist. Soc., Internat. Platform Assn., St. Peter's Coll. Alumni Assn. (bd. dirs. 1959-65), Hudson Valley Gaelic Soc., Interreligious Affairs Com. and chair Cath./Jewish Spkrs. Bur. Diocese Venice, Fla., Knight Equestrian Order of the Holy Sepulchre of Jerusalem, Mission Balley Golf and Country Club (Nokomis, Fla.), The Univ. Club N.Y.C. Democrat. Roman Catholic. Office: 9000 Midnight Pass Rd Sarasota FL 34242-2927

KELLY, JOHN TERENCE, architect; b. Elyria, Ohio, Jan. 27, 1922; s. Thomas Alo and Coletta Margaret (Conrad) K.; B.Arch., Carnegie Mellon U., 1949; M.Arch., Harvard U., 1951, M.Landscape Architecture (Charles Eliot Norton fellow), 1952. Prin., John Terence Kelly, architect, Cleve., 1954—; vis. critic, lectr. U. Mich., U. Cin., Case Western Res. U., McGill U. Bd. dirs. Nova. Served with inf. AUS, 1943-46. Fulbright fellow, Munich, Germany, 1953. Recipient Cleve. Arts prize in Architecture, 1968, Hist. Bldg. award Architects Society of Ohio, 1986. Mem. AIA (nat. com. on design), Am. Inst. Landscape Architects, Am. Inst. Planners, Am. Soc. Planning Ofcls., Western Res. Hist. Soc. Home: 2646 N Moreland Blvd Cleveland OH 44120-1461 Office: 13125 Shaker Sq Cleveland OH 44120-2399

KELLY, JOHN WILLIAM, JR., university adminstrator; b. Greenville, S.C., Jan. 5, 1955; s. John William and Betty (Kelley) K.; m. Sarah Ellen Moor Kelly, Feb. 8, 1958; children: Christopher, Kimberly. BS, Clemson U., 1977; MS, Ohio State U., 1979, PhD, 1982. Asst. prof. Tex. A&M U., 1982-85; asst. prof. Clemson (S.C.) U., 1985-89, assoc. prof., 1989-91, prof., dept. head, dir. bot. garden, 1991-96, sch. dir., interim v.p. pub. svc. and agr., 1996-97, v.p. pub. svc. and agr., dir. S.C. Bot. Garden, 1997—; cons., Clemson, 1985—. Contbr. articles to 50 profl. jours. Bd. dirs. Discover Upcountry, Greenville, S.C., Am. Distance Edn. Corp., Pate Found. Recipient Outstanding Contbr. award S.C. Nurseryman's Assn., 1991. Fellow Am. Soc. Hort. Sci. (v.p. 1995-99, pres. 1999, Outstanding Rschr. 1994, Outstanding Adminstr. 1995, So. region Outstanding Educator 1989); mem. S.C. Greenhouse Growers Assn. (life, exec. sec. 1991). Avocations: gardening, nature. Office: Pub Svc and Agr Clemson U 130 Lehotsky Hall Clemson SC 29634-5201

KELLY, JOSEPH J., accountant. BS in Acctg., Villanova U., 1977. CPA, 1978. Staff auditor Phila. Nat. Bank; sr. audit mgr. KPMG Peat Marwick; acct. Ewing Cole Cherry Brott, Phila., 1990—. Office: Ewing Cole Cherry Brott Fed Res Bldg 100 N 6th St Philadelphia PA 19106-1590*

KELLY, KATHLEEN ANN, humanities educator; b. Waterloo, Iowa, Oct. 27, 1967; d. John Dale and Phyllis Jean (Woods) K. BA in Spanish and European Studies, U. No. Iowa, 1989, MA in History, 1991. Grad. tchg. asst. Spanish U. No. Iowa, Cedar Falls, 1989-90, grad. rsch. asst. dept. history, 1990-91; history tchr. Acad. Our Lady Guam, Agana, 1992-93; acad. chair humanities dept., instr. Northeast Iowa C.C., Peosta, 1993—; freelance writer, 1996—; mem. scholarship selection com. Never Fear Never Quit Seiferts & Sons, Cedar Rapids, 1997—. Contbr. articles to profl. jours including Calyx Jour., Iris: A Jour. About Women. NEH study grantee, 1995. Mem. NEA (v.p. 1997-98), Phi Delta Kappa. Office: Northeast Iowa CC 10250 Sundown Rd Peosta IA 52068-9776

KELLY, KEVIN, editor; b. Penn State, Pa., Apr. 27, 1952; s. Joseph John and Patricia (Boston) K.; m. Gia-Minn Fuh, Jan. 2, 1987; children: Kaileen, Ting, Tywen. Freelance photographer, 1971-80; editor, pub. Walking! Jour., Athens, Ga., 1982-84, Whole Earth Rev., Sausalito, Calif., 1984-90; exec. editor Wired Mag., San Francisco, 1992—; bd. dirs. Well, Inc., Sausalito. Editor: Signal, 1988; author: Out of Control, 1994, New Rules for the New Economy, 1998. Recipient Gen. Excellence Nat. Mag. Award, 1993, 96. Avocation: beekeeping. Home: 149 Amapola Ave Pacifica CA 94044-3102 Office: Wired 520 3rd St San Francisco CA 94107-1814

KELLY, LARRY E., federal judge. Apptd. chief bankruptcy judge we. dist. U.S. Dist. Ct. Tex., 1986. Office: 903 San Jacinto Blvd Ste 332 Austin TX 78701-2450

KELLY, LINDA L., prosecutor. Atty. U.S. Dept. Justice, Pitts., 1993-99, asst. U.S. atty., 1999—. Office: US Attys Office U.S. Post Office & Courthouse 7th Ave & Grant Street, Room 633 Pittsburgh PA 15219*

KELLY, LUCIE STIRM YOUNG, nursing educator; b. Stuttgart, Germany, May 2, 1925; came to U.S., 1929; d. Hugo Karl and Emilie Rosa (Engel) Stirm; m. J. Austin Young, Aug. 30, 1946 (div. Feb. 1971); m. Thomas Martin Kelly, 1972; 1 child by previous marriage, Gay Aleta (Mrs. Donald Meyer). BS, U. Pitts., 1947, MLitt, 1957, PhD (HEW fellow), 1965; D in Nursing Edn. (hon.), U. R.I., 1977; LHD (hon.), Georgetown U., 1983; DSc (hon.), Widener U., 1984, U. Mass., 1989; D of Pub. Svc. (hon.), Am. U., 1985; DHL (hon.), SUNY, 1996. Instr. nursing McKeesport (Pa.) Hosp., 1953-57, asst. adminstr. nursing, 1966-69; asst. prof. nursing U. Pitts., 1957-64, asst. dean, 1965; prof., chmn. nursing dept. Calif. State U., Los Angeles, 1969-72; co-project dir. curriculum research Nat. League for Nursing, 1973-74; project dir. patient edn., office consumer health edn., also adj. asso. prof. community medicine Coll. Medicine and Dentistry N.J.-Rutgers Med. Sch., 1974-75; prof. pub. health and nursing Sch. Pub. Health and Sch. Nursing Columbia U., N.Y.C., 1975-90, prof. emeritus Sch Pub. Health, Sch. Nursing, 1990—, assoc. dean acad. affairs Sch. Pub. Health, 1988-90, hon. prof. nursing edn. Tchrs. Coll., 1977-93, acting head div. health adminstrn. Sch. Pub. Health, 1980-81, 86-88; on leave as exec. dir. Mid-Atlantic Regional Nursing Assn., 1981-82; cons. U. Nev., Las Vegas, 1970-72, Ball State U., Ind., 1971, Long Beach (Calif.) Naval Hosp., 1971-72, Travis AFB, Calif., 1972, Brentwood VA Hosp., L.A., 1971-72, Ctrl. Nursing Office VA, Washington, 1971-94, N.J. Dept. Higher Edn., 1974-78, John Wiley Pub., 1974-76, Sch. Nursing Am. U. Beirut; mem. spl. med. adv. group VA Dept. Medicine and Surgery, Washington, 1980-84; cons. nursing com. AMA, 1971-74, Citizen's Com. for Children, N.Y.C.; v.p. Pa. Health Coun., 1968-69; mem. adv. com. physicians assts. Calif. Bd. Med. Examiners, adv. com. Cancer Soc. L.A., 1970-72, com. nursing VA, Washington, 1971-74, chair 1975-90, regional med. programs, Pa., 1967-69, Calif. 1970-72; mem. spl. adv. com. on med. licensure and profl. conduct N.Y. State Assembly, 1977-79, mem. nat. adv. com. Encore (nat. YWCA post-mastectomy group rehab. project), 1977-83; assoc. mem. N.Y. Acad. Medicine, 1988-90; mem. ethics com. Palisades Med. Ctr., 1993—, bd. govs., 1995—, mem. profl. and quality rev. com., 1995—, chair, 1995—, exec. com., 1998-99; 2d vice chair N.Y. Presbyn. Healthcare Sys., Palisades Med. Ctr., 1999—; lectr., cons., guest Beijing Med. Coll., China, 1982, Aga Khan U., Pakistan, 1990; bd. visitors U. Pitts. Sch. Nursing, 1986-93; mem. editl. adv. bd. Am. Jour. Pub. Health, 1992, chair, 1993-97; nat. and internat. lectr. in field; chair adv. com. grad. program in pub. health U. Medicine and Dentistry of N.J., 1995—. Author: Dimensions of Profl. Nursing, 8th edit., 1999, The Nursing Experience: Trends, Challenges, Transitions, 3d edit., 1996; contbg. editor Jour. Nursing Adminstrn., 1975-82; mem. editl. bd. Nurse Practitioner, 1976-82; columnist Nursing Outlook, editor-in-chief, 1982-91; mem. bd. advisors Nurses Almanac, 1978, Nurse Manager's Handbook, 1979, Nursing Administration Handbook, 1992; mem. editl. adv. bd. Am. Health, 1981-91, Nursing and Health Care, 1991-95, Internat. Nursing Index, 1997—; contbr. articles to prof. jours. Bd. dirs. ARC, Los Angeles, 1971-72, Vis. Nurse Service N.Y., 1980—, mem. exec. com., chmn. human resources, 1989—; bd. dirs. Concern for Dying, 1983-89; trustee Calif. State Coll. Los Angeles Found., 1971-72, U. Pitts, 1984-90, mem. exec. com. 1988-90; chair bd. visitors U. Pitts. Sch. Pub. Health, 1988-90; bd. visitors U. Miami Sch. Nursing, 1986—; mem. health services com. Children's Aid Soc., N.Y., 1978-84; v.p. Am. Nurses Found., 1980-82; mem. nat. adv. council on nurse tng. HRA, 1981-85; mem. nurses leadership coun. Chlorine Chemistry Coun., 1999—; hon. bd. dirs. NOVA Found. Named Outstanding Alumna U. Pitts. Sch. Nursing, 1966, Pa. Nurse of Yr., 1967, to Roll of Honor N.J. State Nurses Assn., 1990; recipient Disting. Alumna award U. Pitts. Sch. Edn., 1981, Shaw medal Boston Coll., 1985, Bicentennial Medallion of Distinction, U. Pitts., 1987, R. Louise McManus Medallion for Disting. Svc. to Nursing, Tchrs. Coll. Columbia U., 1987, Dean's Disting. Svc. award Columbia Sch. Pub. Health, 1995, Second Century award in health care, Columbia U. Sch. Nursing, 1996. Fellow Am. Acad. Nursing; mem. ANA (dir. 1978-82, Hon. Recognition award 1992), APHA (Ruth Freeman Pub. Health Nursing award 1993), Pa. Nurses Assn. (pres. 1966-69), Nat. League Nursing (bd. govs. 1991-95), Nurses Ednl. Funds Bd., U . Pitts. Sch. Nursing Alumni (pres. 1959), Vis. Nurse assn. Ctrl. Jersey (bd. dirs. 1999—), Am. Hosp. Assn. (com. chmn. 1967-68), Assn. Grad. Faculty Cmty. Health/Pub. Health Nursing (v.p. 1980-81), Sigma Theta Tau (sr. editor Image 1978-81, pres.-elect 1981-83, pres. 1983-85, nat. campaign chair Ctr. for Nursing Scholarship 1987-89, chair devel. com. 1989-95, spl. advisor 1995-97, planned giving task force 1998—, Mentor award 1985, 93, 97, Spirit of Philanthropy award 1997), Pi Lambda Theta, Alpha Tau Delta (Cert. of Merit). Collection papers in Mugar Library, Boston U. Home: 6040 Boulevard E Apt 11G West New York NJ 07093-3825

KELLY, MARGARET ELIZABETH, financial analyst, planner; b. Ridley Park, Pa., Apr. 1, 1960; d. Albert Jeremiah Jr. and Margaret Mae (Claybyn) K. BS, Duke U., 1982; MBA, U. Tex., 1990. CPA, Tex. Staff auditor Deloitte Haskins & Sells, Houston, 1982-84, sr. auditor, 1984-85, sr. tax cons., 1985-88; sr. fin. analyst Pepsi-Cola, Pitts., 1990-91, supr. planning & analysis, 1991-92; bus. planner W.Va. market unit Pepsi-Cola, 1992-93, bus. planner Houston market unit, 1993-95; customer adminstrn. mgr. Landmark Graphics Corp., Houston, 1995; mng. assoc. Continental Airlines, Houston, 1996-97, mgr. revenue analysis, 1998—. Mem. Phi Kappa Phi, Phi Eta Sigma. Avocations: windsurfing, golf, softball, exercising, volleyball. Home: 1238 Muirfield Pl Houston TX 77055-7000 Office: Continental Airlines Inc 1600 Smith HQSGP Houston TX 77002

KELLY, MARGARET FRANCES, English language educator; b. Rockville Centre, N.Y., Mar. 12, 1959; d. William Charles and Dorothy Ann (Noonan) McCulloh; m. Thomas Allen Kelly, Aug. 14, 1992; children: Daniel, Michael, Lisa-Marie. AAS, Nassau C.C., 1980; BS, St. John's U., 1982; MA, C.W. Post Coll., 1989. Cert. tchr. English as 2d lang., spl. edn., elem. edn., N.Y. Adj. prof. ESL Suffolk C.C., Brentwood, N.Y., 1990—; ESL tchr. Smithtown (N.Y.) Adult Edn., 1992-94; cons. Com. Reading & Writing Final Exams, Brentwood, 1997. Author: Best Poems of 1996, 1996. Recipient Outstanding Achievement in Poetry award Nat. Libr. Poetry, Md., 1996. Mem. Tchrs. English Spkrs. Other Langs., PTA. Democrat. Roman Catholic. Avocations: ice skating, bicycling, boating. Home: 82 River Heights Dr Smithtown NY 11787-1742 Office: Suffolk CC ESL Dept Crooked Hill Rd Brentwood NY 11717

KELLY, MARGUERITE STEHLI, fashion executive, consultant; b. N.Y.C., June 9, 1931; d. Henry E. and Grace (Hays) Stehli; m. Charles J. Kelly, Jr., Dec. 23, 1962; children: Marguerite Grace Kelly Walton, Lisa Stehli. BA, Bryn Mawr Coll., 1953. Exec. trainee Macy's, N.Y.C., 1953-54, asst. buyer, 1954-57; buyer Bloomingdale's, N.Y.C., 1957-63; pres. Maggie, Inc., Wayzata, Minn., 1964-86; also brs. Maggie, Inc., Georgetown, D.C., 1964-70, Locust Valley, N.Y., 1970-75; ret., 1986; founder Workshop for Learning, 1987—. Mem. com. for spl. fund Foxcroft Sch., Middleburg, Va., 1974-76, trustee, 1978-87; mem. alumnae coun. Brearley Sch., N.Y.C., 1973-75; trustee Abbott Northwestern Hosp., Mpls., 1984-86; co-founder Citizens for Colin Powell Presdl. Draft Movement, 1994—. Episcopalian. Home: 3018 N St NW Washington DC 20007-3404

KELLY, MARY JOAN, librarian; b. Baton Rouge, Nov. 25, 1947; d. Theodore McKowen Sr. and Patricia Marilyn (Faul) Wilkes; m. Karl Joseph Nix; 1 child, Patricia Lynn. BS, La. State U., 1970, MEd, 1973, EdD, 1980. Cert. English and social studies tchr., city/parish materials and/or media ctr. dir., La. Instr. conversation class La. State U., Baton Rouge, 1979-80; writer, prodr. The Video Co., Baton Rouge, 1983-90; freelance writer DBA-Creative Spl., Baton Rouge; tchr. East Baton Rouge Parish Sch. Bd., ret., 1991; prin. St. Isidore Mid. Sch., 1991-95; libr. Holy Family Sch., Port Allen, La., 1995—; presenter in field. Contbr. numerous articles to profl. jours.; sponsor yearbook and lit. mags. Mem. Non-Pub. Sch. Commn., La. Bd. Elem. and Secondary Edn., 1992-97. Mem. NEA (mem. com.), ASCD, Citizens for Ednl. Freedom, NCEA, La. Mid. Sch. Assn., La. Prin. Assn., La. Assn. Educators (mem. com.), East Baton Rouge Parish Assn. Educators (v.p.), La. Assn. Classroom Tchrs. (mem. com.), East Baton Rouge Parish Assn. Classroom Tchrs. (pres.), Nat. Coun. Tchrs. English, Assn. Ednl. Comm. and Tech., La. Assn. Ednl. Comm. and Tech., Internat. Platform Assn., La. Libr. Assn., Capital Area Reading Coun., Gamma Beta Phi, Phi Lambda Pi, Phi Delta Kappa. Home: 2005 Lee Dr Baton Rouge LA 70808-3932

KELLY, MARY SUSAN, psychologist, educator; b. N.Y.C., July 15, 1954; d. James J. and Veronica (Jacob) Kelly; m. James Houlihan, July 18, 1992. BA, Boston Coll., 1976; MA, Columbia U., 1980, PhD, 1987. Tchr. Kennedy Meml. Hosp., Brighton, Mass., 1976-79; adj. asst. prof. Teachers Coll., Columbia U., N.Y.C., 1987-93; assoc. prof. Western Conn. State U., Danbury, 1993-94; asst. prof. pediatrics Albert Einstein Coll. of Medicine, Bronx, N.Y., 1994—. Contbr. articles to profl. jours., including Jour. Sch. Psychology, Brain & Cognition, Jour. Learning Disabilities, Jour. Am. Bd. Family Practice. Grantee: U.S. Dept. Edn., 1987-89, Fisher-Landau Found., N.Y.C., 1987-91, Bd. Edn. Yonkers, N.Y., 1991-93. Mem. APA, Am. Psychol. Soc. (charter), Am. Ednl. Rsch. Assn., Internat. Reading Assn., Internat. Dyslexia Assn. Office: Rose F Kennedy Ctr Albert Einstein Coll Med 1410 Pelham Pkwy S Bronx NY 10461-1101

KELLY, MATTHEW EDWARD, association executive, retired; b. Parkersburg, W.Va., Apr. 15, 1928; s. Matthew Glenn and Lillian (Schottler) K.; m. Mildred Joan Flasch, June 6, 1953. BA, Marietta Coll., 1952. Asst. mgr. Twin Cities Area C. of C., Benton Harbor, Mich., 1955-62; exec. v.p. Oshkosh (Wis.) C. of C., 1962-69, Springfield (Mo.) Area C. of C., 1969-76, Elgin (Ill.) C. of C., 1977-95. Trustee Northwest Suburban Mass Transit Dist., 1979—; chmn. City of Elgin Metra Task Force. Mem. Am. Chamber Commerce Execs. (past dir.), Inst. for Orgnl. Mgmt. (past dir., mem. nat. bd. regents), Rotary (past pres.). Home: 1955 Powder River Path Elgin IL 60123-2659

KELLY, MAURA ANNE, political reporter; b. Bridgeport, Conn., Apr. 2, 1971; d. Richard Francis and Margaret Mary Kelly. BA, Boston Coll., 1993; MS in Journalism, Northwestern U., 1994. Intern The Patriot Ledger, Quincy, Mass., 1993; corr. Conn. Post, Bridgeport, 1993; reporter Naugatuck bur. Waterbury (Conn.) Rep.-Am., 1994-95, edn. reporter, 1995, city hall reporter, 1995-96, state capitol reporter, 1996—; mem. reporter's roundtable discussion Conn. Jour. on Conn. Pub. TV, Hartford, 1997, 98, 99, WFSB's CT 99, 98, 99, Hartford, 1997. Mem. Soc. Profl. Journalists (Reporting award Conn. chpt. 1998), Investigative Reporters and Editors, Boston Coll. Alumni Assn. Roman Catholic. Avocations: photography, travel, skiing, tennis, swimming. E-mail: maura@cyberbury.net. Home: 34 Koger Rd Trumbull CT 06611 Office: Waterbury Rep-Am 389 Meadow St Waterbury CT 06722

KELLY, MAUREEN ANN, management accountant; b. N.Y.C., July 13, 1965; d. William J. and Frances C. (Scanlon) K. BS, U. Ariz., 1987. Acct. U.S. Govt. Army, Ft. Huachuca, Ariz. Mem. Am. Soc. Mil. Comptrollers (v.p. 1992-93, exec. officer 1993-94, treas. Cochise chpt. 1990-91, 97—, profl. devel. symposium dir. 1991-93, pres. 1995-96), Golden Key, Beta Gamma Sigma. Office: Army Signal Command Attn AFSC-RMA Fort Huachuca AZ 85613-5000

KELLY, MAUREEN H., actress; b. Chgo.; d. Malcolm Francis and Mary Margaret (Hughes) K.; m. Ray Guarna, Aug. 11, 1990. BFA in Music/Theatre, U. Cin., 1982. Actress, writer The Second City, Chgo., 1982-87. Actor, writer: (film) Law of Averages, 1989 (N.Y. Short Film Festival award 1989), Ask Ebbe, (one woman show) Some Women I've Known, 1989; appeared on stage Minamata, 1989, The Inspector General, 1988, on tv Thirty Something, 1990, My Talk Show, 1990; dir., writer, producer (film) I.R.S. Stories, Les Dame qui petént en costume de periode. Contbr. Greenpeace, L.A., 1989-90, The Tree People, L.A., 1989-90. Mem. Nat. Pks. and Conservation Assn. Home: PO Box 461241 Los Angeles CA 90046-9241

KELLY, MAXINE ANN, retired property developer; b. Ft. Wayne, Ind., Aug. 14, 1931; d. Victor J. and Marguerite E. (Biebesheimer) Cramer; m. James Herbert Kelly, Oct. 4, 1968 (dec. Apr. 74). BA, Northwestern U., 1956. Sec., Parry & Barns Law Offices, Ft. Wayne, 1951-52; trust sec. Lincoln Nat. Bank & Trust Co., 1956-58; sr. clk. stenographer div. Mental Health, Alaska Dept. Health, Anchorage, 1958-60; office mgr. Langdon Psychiat. Clinic, 1960-70; propr. A-1 Bookkeeping Svc., 1974-75; ptnr. Gonder-Kelly Enterprises & A-is-A Constrn., Wasilla, Alaska, 1965-92; sales assoc. Yukon Realty/Gallery of Homes, Wasilla, 1989; sec. Rogers Realty, Inc., Wasilla, 1989, MMC Constrn., Inc., 1992-96. Dir. Alaska Mental

Health Assn., Anchorage, 1960-61; pres., treas. Libertarian Party Anchorage, 1968-69, Alaska Libertarian Party, 1969-70. Mem. AAUW (life), Anchorage C. of C., Whittier Boat Owners Assn. (treas. 1980-84). Home: 8653 Augusta Cir Anchorage AK 99504-4202

KELLY, MICHAEL JOSEPH, academic administrator, consultant; b. N.Y.C., July 2, 1931; s. Hugh and Mary Agnes (Harrison) K.; m. Helen Janet Nee, Oct. 4, 1969; children: Joan T., Jean M. BA, Marist Coll., 1955; BEE, Cath. U., 1960, MEE, 1961; DEng, U. Detroit, 1968. Tchr. U. Detroit, 3 yrs., dir. Computer Ctr.; tchr., adminstr. Marist Coll., 4 yrs.; assoc. prof. electrical and mech. engring., dir. engring. case program Stanford U.; mgr. CAD, litho sys. IBM, East Fishkill, N.Y., 1969-79; mgr. Mfg. Tech. Ctr. IBM, Boca Raton, Fla., 1979-84; dir. Quality Inst. IBM, 1984, mgr. quality improvement and profl. devel. programs systems tech. divsn., 1986-87; dir. computer integrated mfg. and tech. transfer N.J. Inst. Tech., 1987-89; dir. def. mfg. office Def. Advanced Rsch. Projects Agy., 1989-91; exec. dir. Nat. Adv. Com. on Semiconductors, 1989-91; dir. Mfg. Rsch. Ctr. Ga. Inst. Tech., 1991-96, prof. technology mgmt., 1995-96; Northrop-Grumman endowed chair mfg. and design Calif. State U., L.A., 1996—. Home: 2107 W Clark Ave Burbank CA 91506-1907

KELLY, MICHAEL JOSEPH, JR., publishing executive; b. Chgo., May 17, 1957; s. Michael Joseph and Mariann Julia (Williams) K.; m. Martha Joann Hall, Oct. 16, 1982; children: Katherine Rose, Mary Elizabeth, Michael Joseph III. Student, U. Wis., 1975-77; BA, U. Ill., 1979; exec. cert., Columbia U., 1995. Sales rep. Chgo. Tribune, 1980-83, Fortune Mag./Time Inc., Chgo., 1983-84; S.E. mgr. Fortune Mag./Time Inc., N.Y.C., 1984-87, N.Y. mgr., 1987-89; ea. sales dir. Entertainment Weekly/Time Inc., N.Y.C., 1989-91, v.p. advt. sales, 1991-93, v.p. advt. sales and mktg., 1993-96, pub., 1996—; bd. mem. Cabin Life Inc., Piermont, N.Y. Bd. mem., com. chair Youth Literacy Vols., Chgo., 1981-85. Mem. Sleepy Hollow Club, Univ. Club N.Y., Alpha Delta Phi (v.p. 1975-79). Avocations: golf, history, Celtic literature. *

KELLY, MICHAEL THOMAS, educator; b. Easton, Pa., Feb. 1, 1961; s. Thomas B. and Marion E. (Beers) K. BA, Westchester U., 1983; EdS, Coll. William & Mary, 1989, EdD, 1991. Dean students Northeastern Ill. U., 1999—. Mem. Nat. Assn. Student Personnel Adminstrs., Assn. Student Jud. Affairs, Coll. William & Mary Alumni Assn., Kappa Delta Pi, Theta Xi. Democrat. Roman Catholic. Avocations: music, civic involvement. Home: 248 S Marion St Apt 5 Oak Park IL 60302-3162 Office: U Ill 1200 W Harrison St Chicago IL 60607-3320

KELLY, NANCY FOLDEN, arts administrator; b. Fredericksburg, Va., Oct. 28, 1951; d. Virgil Alvis Jr. and Frances Virginia (DeShazo) Folden; m. Frank R. Kelly, Aug. 11, 1973; 1 child, Katherine Elizabeth Kelly. BA in Theatre Arts, Va. Poly. Inst. and State U., 1973; MFA in Theatre Directing, So. Meth. U., 1975. Coord. student programs Lincoln Ctr. Inst., N.Y.C., 1976-79; dir. N.Y.C. Opera Nat. Co. and edn. dept. Lincoln Ctr., 1979-93, mem. coun. on ednl. programs, 1979-93; mng. dir. Broadway Arts Theatre for Young Audiences, N.Y.C., 1994-96; dir. family and cmty. programs Ctrl. Park Conservancy, N.Y.C., 1996-98; assoc. dir. devel. Film Soc. Lincoln Ctr., N.Y.C., 1999—.

KELLY, NANCY FRIEDA WOLICKI, lawyer; b. Chgo., Sept. 8, 1953; d. Samuel and Ingrid (Rappel) W.; B.A. in Journalism and Sociology, U. Ariz., 1974, J.D., 1977. Bar: Ariz., 1977; law clk. Ariz. Ct. Appeals, 1977-78; legis. asst. fgn. policy and armed svcs. health, staff atty. Billy Carter investigation to U.S. Sen. Dennis DeConcini, 1979-81; staff dir. Senate Subcom. on Alcoholism and Drug Abuse, Washington, 1981-84; mem. staff Senator Gordon J. Humphrey, Washington, 1984-87; coord. adv. com. Voluntary Fgn. U.S. Aid, 1987; sr. analyst legal and drug related issues President's Commn. on the HIV Epidemic, 1987-88; sr. policy analyst Commn. Exec. Legis. Jud. Salaries, 1988-89; counselor Sec. Energy, 1989-93; v.p. Kelly, Anderson & Assocs., Alexandria, Va., 1993—. Recipient William Spaid Meml. award U. Ariz. Coll. Law, 1977, Senate commendation for Billy Carter investigation, 1980. Mem. Ariz. Bar Assn., Phi Kappa Phi. Jewish. Office: 424 N Washington St Alexandria VA 22314

KELLY, PATRICIA ANN, communication arts educator; b. Kearney, Nebr., Aug. 23, 1949; d. Leonard francis and Mary Pauline (Fordyce) K. BA, U. Mont., 1971, MA, 1981. Cert. tchr., Iowa. Instr. Flathead Valley C.C., Kalispell, Mont., 1971-75, Adult Learning Ctr., Billings, Mont., 1975-77; tchr. Billings West H.S., 1977-81; prof., coord. comm. arts Iowa Western C.C., Council Bluffs, 1981—; CPSA judging bd. graphic arts adv. bd. Columbia U., N.Y.C., 1997. Author poetry: Sinister Wisdom, 1986, Lyrical Iowa, 1987, Nebraska English Councillor, 1989, Iowa Woman, 1990, Dismal River Review, 1991. Recipient Kuphal Worden award Delta Gamma, 1971; Scottish Rite fellow, 1981. Mem. NEA, Nat. Coun. Tchrs. English, Iowa Coun. Tchrs. English/Lang. Arts, C.C. Humanities Assn., S.W. Iowa Writers Assn., Phi Kappa Phi, Phi Beta Kappa. Home: 1426 S 52nd St Omaha NE 68106-2304 Office: Iowa Western Community Coll 2700 College Rd Council Bluffs IA 51503-0567

KELLY, PATRICK FRANKLIN, baseball player; b. Phila., Oct. 14, 1967. Ed., West Chester U. Pa. Second baseman N.Y. Yankees, N.Y.C., 1991-97, Toronto Blue Jays, 1997—. Office: Toronto Blue Jays, One Blue Jays Way Ste 3200, Toronto, ON Canada M5V 1J1*

KELLY, PAUL JOHN, priest; b. Buffalo, N.Y., Sept. 1, 1943; s. John H. and Gertrude A. (Considine) K. Diploma, Syracuse U., 1965; BA, Wadhams Hall, 1970; STM, St. Mary's Sem. and U., Balt., 1974; MA, Fordham U., 1980. Ordained Roman Cath. priest, 1974. Clergy Diocese of Ogdensburg, N.Y., 1974—; dir. Pastoral Inst., Wadhams Hall, Ogdensburg, 1972-75, instr., 1978-81; bd. visitors St. Lawrence Psychiat. Ctr., Ogdensburg, 1979-89, chaplain, 1989-94. Author: Trapezus, Trebizond, Trabzon, 1968, A Teilhard Corrigenda, 1975, A Bibliography for Philosophy, 1980; contbr. articles to profl. jours. Avocations: birding, hiking. Home: PO Box 214 Route 8 Speculator NY 12164

KELLY, PAUL JOSEPH, JR., judge; b. Freeport, N.Y., Dec. 6, 1940; s. Paul J. and Jacqueline M. (Nolan) K.; BBA, U. Notre Dame, 1963; JD, Fordham U., 1967; m. Ruth Ellen Dowling, June 27, 1964; children—Johanna, Paul Edwin, Thomas Martin, Christopher Mark, Heather Marie. Bar: N.Mex. 1967. Law clk. Cravath, Swaine & Moore, N.Y.C., 1964-67; assoc. firm Hinkle, Cox, Eaton, Coffied & Hensley, Roswell, N.Mex., 1967-71, ptnr., 1971-92; judge U.S. Ct. Appeals (10th cir.), Santa Fe, 1992—; mem. N.Mex. Bd. Bar Examiners, 1982-85; mem. N.Mex. Ho. of Reps., 1976-81, chmn. consumer and public affairs com., mem. judiciary com. Mem. N.Mex. Pub. Defender Bd.; bd. of visitors, Fordham U. Sch. of Law, 1992—; pres. Oliver Seth Inn of Ct., 1993—; pres. Roswell Drug Abuse Com., 1970-71; mem. Appellate Judges Nominating Commn., 1989-92. Pres. Chaves County Young Reps., 1971-72; vice chmn. N.Mex. Young Reps., 1969-71, treas., 1968-69; mem. bd. dirs. Zia council Girl Scouts Am., Roswell Girls Club, Chaves County Mental Health Assn., 1974-77; bd. dirs. Santa Fe Orch., 1992-93, Roswell Symphony Orch. Soc., 1969-82, treas., 1970-73, pres., 1973-75; mem. Eastern N.Mex. State Fair Bd., 1978-83. Mem. ABA, Fed. Bar Assn., State Bar N.Mex. (v.p. young lawyers sect. 1969, co-chmn. ins. sub-com. 1972-73, mem. continuing legal edn. com. 1970-73). Roman Catholic (pres. parish council 1971-76). K.C. Office: US Court Appeals 10th Circuit Federal Courthouse PO Box 10113 Santa Fe NM 87504-6113

KELLY, PAUL KNOX, investment banker; b. Boston, Feb. 18, 1940; s. Thomas Joseph and Rita Patricia Kelly; m. Nancy Lee Belden, July 17, 1978; 1 child, 3 stepchildren. A.B. in English, U. Pa., 1962; M.B.A. in Fin, Wharton Sch., 1964. Investment analyst bond dept. Prudential Ins. Co. Am., 1964-65; asst. treas. Comml. Credit Co., 1965-68; v.p. First Boston Corp., N.Y.C., 1968-75; ptnr., mem. mgmt. com., dir. Prescott, Ball & Turben, Cleve., 1975-77; sr. v.p., dir. Butcher & Singer, Inc., 1977-78; exec. v.p., mem. exec. com., dir. Blyth Eastman Dillon & Co., N.Y.C., 1978-80; mng. dir. Merrill Lynch White Weld Capital Markets Group, N.Y.C., 1980-82; exec. v.p., dir. Dean Witter Reynolds, Inc., 1982-84; pres., dir. Quadrex Securities Corp., 1984-85, Peers & Co., N.Y.C., 1985-90, PH II, Inc., Westport, Conn., 1988—, Knox & Co., N.Y.C., 1992—; bd. dirs. THT, Inc. Mem. Union Club (Cleve.), Chagrin Valley Hunt Club, Marco Polo Club, Penn Club N.Y. Office: Knox & Co 33 Riverside Ave Westport CT 06880-4223

KELLY, PHILIP A., bank executive; b. Hagerstown, Md., Nov. 10, 1958; s. James R. and Regina M. Orndorff K.; m. Donna R. Shoemaker, Aug. 9, 1980; children: Sharon, Susan. BSBA, Shippensburg U., 1980, MBA, 1984. Residential conservation specialist Allegheny Power Co., Hagerstown, Md., 1981-83, programmer, analyst, 1983-89, customer svc. supr., 1989-95, asst. to ops. v.p., 1996; mgr. external affairs Citicorp, Hagerstown, Md., 1996—. Campaign chmn. United Way, Hagerstown, 1995, sec., dir., 1995—; pres. Hagerstown-Washington County Chamber, 1997-98; chmn. Bus./Edn. Partnership Commn., Hagerstown, 1993-94; strategic planning com. Washington County Bd. Edn., 1997-98. Mem. Md. C. of C. (bd. dirs. 1998-99), Beta Gamma Sigma. Roman Catholic. Avocations: family, travel, reading, golf. Home: 17907 Garden Spot Dr Hagerstown MD 21740 Office: Citicorp Credit Svcs 14700 Citicorp Dr Hagerstown MD 21742

KELLY, RALPH WHITLEY, emergency physician, health facility administrator; b. Hernando, Miss., Oct. 13, 1949; s. Leslie Athrel and Nina Earline (Christopher) K.; m. Janet Sue Evans Burns, May 15, 1971 (div. May 1991); children: Rochelle, Angela, Melanie, Christopher; m. Virginia Markle Alfson, Mar. 13, 1993. BS, U. Tex., Arlington, 1972; DO, Tex. Coll. Osteo. Medicine, Ft. Worth, 1976. Diplomate Am. Bd. Emergency Medicine, Am. Bd. Pediat. Emergency Medicine, Am. Bd. Pediat., Am. Bd. Quality Assurance and Utilization Rev. Physicians, Nat. Bd. Examiners. Mem. staff pediat. USAF, Wichita Falls, Tex., 1979-82; med. dir. emergency dept. Fischer-Mangold Group, Pleasanton, Calif., 1982-90, EmCare, Inc., Dallas, 1990-91; chmn. emergency dept. Hillcrest Bapt. Med. Ctr., Waco, Tex., 1990-91; dir. EMS tng. programs Vernon Regional Jr. Coll., Wichita Falls, 1991-95; dir. emergency svcs. Wichita Gen. Hosp., Wichita Falls, 1991-95; pres. Texoma Emergency Assn., Wichita Falls, 1991-95; dir. practice mgmt. MEPA, Dallas, 1995-98; chmn. emergency dept. Trinity Med. Ctr., Carrollton, Tex., 1995—, also chmn. QA Ctr.; chmn. emergency dept. RHD Meml. Med. Ctr., 1996—; bd. dirs. Foster Child Advocacy Svcs., Wichita Falls, 1983-85; mem. faculty Tex. affiliate Am. Heart Assn., Austin, 1985—, course dir. ACLS, 1982—; mem. exec. com. Wichita Gen. Hosp., 1991-95; physician advisor for quality Trinity Med. Ctr., 1996—. Rev. editor Tex. Emergency Bulletin of Tex. Coll. Emergency Physicians, 1987-89. Mem. premed. adv. com. Midwestern State U., Wichita Falls, 1987-89; mem. child mortality com. DA's Office, Wichita Falls, 1994-95; EMS med. dir. Lifeline EMS, Wichita Falls, 1992-94, AMT EMS, Waco, 1990-91. Major USAF, 1976-82. Recipient Physician Recognition award AMA, 1985. Fellow Am. Coll. Emergency Physicians, Am. Acad. Pediat.; mem. Tex. Med. Assn., Tex. Osteo. Med. Assn., Group Mgmt. Sect. (charter), Pediat. Emergency Med. Sect. Republican. Avocations: cycling, downhill skiing, numismatics, hiking, computers. Home: 2405 Winding Hollow Ln Plano TX 75093-4108 Office: Trinity Med Ctr 4343 N Josey Ln Carrollton TX 75010-4608

KELLY, RAYMOND W., federal agency administrator; married; two children. LLM, NYU, St. John's U.; grad., Manhattan Coll.; MPA, Harvard U.; Doctorate (hon.), Marist Coll., 1995, Manhattan Coll., 1996, Coll. St. Rose, 1997, St. John's U., 1998. Various positions ending with commr. N.Y.C. Police Dept., ret., 1994; under sec. for enforcement U.S. Treasury Dept., 1996-98; commr. U.S. Customs Svc., Washington, 1998—; v.p. Ams., INTERPOL, 1997. Col. USMCR. Office: US Custom Svc Dept of Treasury 1300 Pennsylvania Ave NW Washington DC 20229

KELLY, REGIS BAKER, biochemistry educator, biophysics educator; b. Edinburgh, Scotland, May 26, 1940; m. Rae L. Burke, 1992; children: Gordon, Alison, Colin. BSc, U. Edinburgh, 1961; PhD, Calif. Inst. Tech., 1967. Instr. neurobiology Harvard Med. Sch., Boston, 1969-71; from asst. prof. to prof. biochem. and biophysics U. Calif., San Francisco, 1971—, chair dept. biochemistry and biophysics, 1995—; dir. cell biology program U. Calif., 1988-95, dir. Hormone Rsch. Inst., 1992—; adv. panelist Nat. Engring. Inst.; mem. study sect. NIH; vis. prof. MIT, Cambridge, 1986—. Helen Hay Whitney Found. fellow, 1967-70, Multiple Sclerosis Soc. fellow, 1970-71. Mem. Soc. Neurosci., Am. Soc. Biol. Chem., Am. Soc. Cell Biology. Office: Univ Calif Dept Biochem & Biophysics Box 0534 San Francisco CA 94143

KELLY, RICHARD DALE, photographer, multimedia producer, filmmaker; b. New Castle, Pa., Apr. 10, 1965; s. Dale George and Glenda Lee (Hennon) K. Grad., Pa. Gov.'s Sch. for the Arts, Lewisburg, 1982. First asst. Art Kane Studio, N.Y.C., 1986-88, Kurt Markus Ltd., Kalispell, Mont., 1988-89; prodr. Richard Kelly Prods., N.Y.C., 1988-90; prin. Richard Kelly Photographer, N.Y.C., 1989-92, Beaver Falls, Pa., 1992-97, Pitts., 1997—. One-man show Center for the Arts, 1998. Mem. Am. Soc. Media Photographers. Democrat. Home and Office: 1942 5th Ave Pittsburgh PA 15219-5544

KELLY, RITA MAE, academic administrator, researcher; b. Waseca, Minn., Dec. 10, 1939; d. John Francis and Agnes Mary (Lorentz) Cawley; m. Vincent Peter Kelly, June 2, 1962; children: Patrick, Kathleen. BA, U. Minn., 1961; MA, Ind. U., 1964, PhD, 1967; doctorate (hon.), U. Umeå, Sweden, 1998. Rsch. scientist Ctr. for Rsch. in Social Systems, 1968-70; sr. rsch. scientist Am. Inst. for Rsch., Inc., Kensington, Md., 1970-72; cons. OEO, 1972-73; pres. Rita Mae Kelly & Assocs., 1973-75; tenured prof. Rutgers U., 1977-79, prof., 1979-82; from tenured to full prof. Sch. Justice Studies Ariz. State U., Tempe, 1982-87, tenured prof. justice studies, pub. affairs, polit. sci. and women's study, 1987-96, chair, dir. Sch. Justice Studies, 1990-95; dean social scis. U. Tex., Dallas, 1996—; mem. credentials com. U.S. Dem. Party, Atlanta, 1988; mem. state com. Ariz. Dem. party, Phoenix, 1988; dist. committeeman Tempe Dist. 27 Dem. Party, 1988; charter mem., hon. bd. dirs. Ariz. Women's Inst., 1988; founding mem. Inst. for Women's Policy Rsch., Washington, 1988, Ariz. Found. for Women, Inc., 1995—; bd. dirs. Ariz. Leadership 2000 Alumni Assn., 1993—; co-dir. Ariz. Leadership 2000 and Beyond, 1993—; co-chair Arizonians for a Healthy Future, 1994-95. Author: (with others) The Making of Political Women: A Study of Socialization and Role Conflict, 1978, Promoting Productivity in the Public Sector: Problems, Strategies, Prospects, 1988, Comparable Worth, Pay Equity, and Public Policy, 1988, (with Mary M. Hale) Gender, Bureaucracy, and Democracy: Careers and Equal Opportunity in the Public Sector, 1989, The Gendered Economy, 1991, Advances in Policy Studies Since 1950, 1992, Gender Power, Leadership and Governance, 1995; editor: book series Women in Politics Series, 1981-88, (with Dennis J. Palumbo) Sage Series in Public Policy, 1989-94, Women & Politics Jour. Dep. gov. Am. Biog. Inst., 1995—; co-chair Airz. Women's Vote Project, 1996—; coord. scientific rsch. com. engendering globalization democratization internat. Social Sci. Coun., 1998—. Internat. Soroptomists of Phoenix, Inc. grantee, 1987, GTE Found. Rsch. grantee, 1988, Ind. U. Rsch. grantee, 1964-65; Ford Found. fellow, 1962-63; recipient Rutgers U. Outstanding Faculty merit award, 1979, All-Am. Women's award, 1985, YWCA Camden County award, 1980; Fulbright award to Brazil, 1991; recipient Aaron Wildovsky award for best book pub. policy, 1992, 93, Outstanding Mentor award Women's Caucus for Polit. Sci., 1991, 97, Miriam Mills award, 1995; U.S. Dept. Labor Step Out grantee, 1993-95. Mem. Am. Polit. Sci. Assn. (chair roundtable 1985, chair B. William Anderson award com. 1983-84, reviewer 1977-78, 83-84, head policy sect. 1989), APA Soc. for Psychol. Study of Social Issues (chair nat. task force on productivity in the pub. sector 1975-80), Am. Soc. for Pub. Adminstrn. (exec. coun. sect. on mgmt. sci. and policy analysis 1986-89, vice chair planning and evaluation com. 1985-86, Achievement award 1981, Disting. Rsch. award for rsch. on women 1991), Internat. Polit. Sci. Assn. (chair com. on status of women 1986-88), Western Polit. Sci. Assn. (pres. 1988-89), Policy Studies Orgn. (pres. 1988-89, Merriam Mills award 1995, Thomas R. Dye Svc. award 1997). Office: U Tex PO Box 830688 Richardson TX 75083-0688

KELLY, ROBERT, airport executive. Gen. mgr. John F. Kennedy Internat. Airport, N.Y.; dir. aviation Port Authority, N.Y. and N.J., 1996—. Office: Port Authority of NY/NJ 1 World Trade Ctr # 65W New York NY 10048-0202*

KELLY, ROBERT EDWARD, JR., lawyer; b. Pitts., Nov. 28, 1950; s. Robert E. Sr. and Adelaide Cecelia (Harris) K.; m. Noreen Theresa Quinn, Oct. 23, 1976; children: Robert E. III, Christopher Patrick, Andrew Clifford. BA, Siena Coll., 1972; JD, Georgetown U., 1975. Bar: Pa. 1975, U.S. Dist. Ct. (we. dist.) Pa. 1975, U.S. Dist. Ct. (ea. and mid. dist.) Pa. 1978, U.S. Ct. Appeals (3d cir.) 1979, U.S. Supreme Ct. 1980, U.S. Dist. Ct. (no. dist.) N.Y. 1992, U.S. Dist. Ct. (no. dist.) Calif. 1994. Assoc. Houston, Harbaugh, Cohen & Lippard, Pitts., 1975-77; assoc., dep. atty. gen. Commonwealth of Pa., Harrisburg, 1977-80; assoc. Duane, Morris & Heckscher, Harrisburg, 1980-86, ptnr., 1986—. Mem. ABA, FBA, Pa. Bar Assn., Pa. Def. Inst., Dauphin County Bar Assn., Pa. Soc., Am. Inns of Ct., St. Thomas More Soc., West Shore Country Club (Camp Hill, Pa.). Republican. Roman Catholic. Home: 3610 Horsham Dr Mechanicsburg PA 17055-2204 Office: Duane Morris & Heckscher 305 N Front St PO Box 1003 Harrisburg PA 17108-1003

KELLY, ROBERT EMMETT, telecommunications company administrator; b. Cambridge, Mass., Feb. 6, 1952; s. Charles Patrick and Patricia Anne (McCormack) K.; m. Ann Marie McDonough, June 1, 1991. Student, St. Michael's Coll., Winooski, Vt., 1969-71. Owner, operator REKording, Everett, Mass., 1976—; asst. staff mgr. New Eng. Telephone Co., Boston, 1985-88, ops. mgr. digital provisioning, 1991-93, staff dir. planning systems support, 1993-95; mem. tech. staff Bell Comm. Rsch., Piscataway, N.J., 1988-91; product mgr. Bell Comm. Rsch. (former Telcordia Techs.), Piscataway, N.J., 1995—. Vol. Cambridge coun. Boy Scouts Am., 1972—. Mem. Audio Engring. Soc. Roman Catholic. Avocations: bicycling, camping, song writing, reading. Home: 335 Old New Ipswich Rd Rindge NH 03461-4016 Office: Bell Comm Rsch PYA 1C269 6 Corporate Pl Piscataway NJ 08854-4120

KELLY, ROBERT F., federal judge; b. 1935. BS, Villanova U., 1957; LLB, Temple U., 1960. Pvt. practice law Media, Pa., 1961-62, 64-76, Chester, Pa., 1962-64; law clk. to Hon. Francis J. Catania Ct. Common Pleas, Delaware County, Pa., 1964-72; prothonotary Delaware County, 1972-76; former judge Ct. Common Pleas 32d Jud. Dist. Pa.; judge U.S. Dist. Ct. (ea. dist.) Pa., Phila., 1987—; lectr. law Villanova U. Law Sch. Voluntary defender Delaware County, 1962; chmn. Delaware County Rep. Exec. Com., 1972-76, Subcom. on Libr. Programs; mem. Judicial Coun. com. on Automation and Tech., 1989—. Mem. ABA, Am. Judicature Soc., Pa. Bar Assn., Pa. Trial Judges Assn., Delaware County Bar Assn. (judicial counsel's com. automation and tech., 1989—, chmn. subcom. libr. programs). Office: US Dist Ct 11613 US Courthouse 601 Market St Philadelphia PA 19106-1713*

KELLY, ROBERT FRANCIS, real estate consultant; b. Parkersburg, W.Va., Sept. 12, 1929; s. Matthew and Lillian (Schottler) K.; m. Audrey Marie Dorstewitz, Apr. 12, 1959 (div. Aug. 23, 1993); children: Michael, Brian, Beth, Bruce. BA, Marietta Coll., 1955. Editor Ohio Valley Jour., Parkersburg, 1951; pub. dir. Marietta (Ohio) Coll., 1953-55; bur. mgr. South Bend (Ind.) Tribune, 1955-60; bus. writer, reporter Chgo. Sun-Times, 1960-65; exec. v.p., gen. mgr. account exec. Carl Byoir & Assocs., Chgo., N.Y.C., 1965-83; pres. Thomas L. Richmond, Inc., N.Y.C., 1984-85; cons., investor Realty Svcs., Inc., Oak Park, Ill., 1986—. Dir. ARC Ill.; acting pres. Proviso Assn. Retarded Citizens, 1994-95. Avocations: cooking, music, biking. Home: 3730 N Lake Shore Dr Chicago IL 60613

KELLY, ROBERT LYNN, advertising agency executive; b. Chgo., Oct. 25, 1939; s. Carl Robert and Annabel Pauline (Lindsay) K.; m. Maria Graciela Gonzalez, Oct. 26, 1963; children: Albert E., Elizabeth A. BA, Gettysburg Coll., 1961. Dir. pub. info. Oxnard AFB, Calif., 1961-64; with Armstrong World Industries, Lancaster, Pa., 1964-67; owner Bob Kelly Advt., Quito, Ecuador, 1967-70; ptnr., writer, acct. exec., mgr. Ibold & Kelly Advt., Lancaster, 1970-72; founder, pres. Kelly Advt., Inc., Lancaster, 1972-84; pres. Kelly Michener, Inc., Lancaster, 1984—; guest lectr. F & M Coll., and Millersville U., 1971—; lectr. Lancaster Community Gallery, 1977. Contbr. articles to profl. jours. Active various civic orgns.; bd. dirs. Lancaster Cmty. Gallery, 1978-89, v.p., 1983-89; mem. campaign coms. Lancaster County Rep. orgns., 1973-75; bd. dirs. Rockford Plantation, 1979-89, v.p., 1988-89; v.p. Let's Lifebelt Lancaster, 1984-85. With USAF, 1961-64. Mem. Nat. Advt. Agy. Network (nat. chmn. 1984), Am. Assn. Advt. Agys. (chmn. regional bd. govs. 1989-90), Lancaster Advt. Agy Coun. (sec. 1987-61, pres. 1992—), N.G. Assn. U.S., Sales and Mktg. Exec., Hamilton Club, Lancaster Tennis and Yacht Club (bd. dirs., v.p. 1986-87, commodore 1988-89), Port Herman Beach Assn. (pres. bd. dirs. 1998-99). Episcopalian. Address: PO Box 959 Lancaster PA 17608

KELLY, ROBERT VINCENT, JR., metal company executive; b. Phila., Sept. 29, 1938; s. Robert Vincent and Catherine Mary (Hanley) K.; m. Margaret Cecilia Taylor, Feb. 11, 1961; children: Robert V. III, Christopher T., Michael J., Tasha Marie. BS in Indsl. Mgmt., St. Joseph's U., Phila., 1960; postgrad., Roosevelt U., 1965-66. Gen. foreman prodn. Republic Steel Corp., Chgo., 1963-68; supt. prodn. Phoenix Steel Corp., Phoenixville, Pa., 1969-73; gen. supt. ops. Continental Steel Corp., Kokomo, Ind., 1973-77; gen. mgr. MACSTEEL div. Quanex Corp., Jackson, Mich., 1977-81; corp. v.p. Quanex Corp., Houston, 1979—; pres. MACSTEEL group Quanex Corp., Jackson, 1982—; pres. La Salle Steel Co., Hammond, Ind., 1985-87, Arbuckle Corp., Jackson, 1984-88. Leader, com. mem. Boy Scouts Am., Jackson. Lt. USN, 1960-63. Mem. Am. Mgmt. Assn. (pres.), Inst. Indsl. Engrs., Assn. Iron and Steel Engrs., Am. Soc. for Metals, USN Inst., Jackson C. of C. Clubs: Jackson Country. Avocations: hiking, camping, sailing, scouting. Home: 1734 Metzmont Dr Jackson MI 49203-5379 Office: Macsteel, Quanex Corp 1 Jackson Sq Jackson MI 49201-1446

KELLY, ROBERT VINCENT, III, transportation executive; b. Sheboygan, Wis., May 22, 1962; s. Robert Vincent Jr. and Margaret Cecilia (Taylor) K. BSE, U. Mich., 1984; MBA, Case Western Res. U., 1986. Ops. analyst Burlington No. R.R., Chgo., 1986-87, mgr. ops. analysis, 1987-88; asst. market mgr. intermodal mktg. Burlington No. R.R., Ft. Worth, 1988, market mgr. intermodal mktg. no. region capacity mgmt., 1989-93, dir. fin. and operational econs., 1993-96; dir. rail contracts, svcs. Sea-Land Svc., Dallas, 1996—. Vol. Habitat for Humanity, Adopt-a-Sch. tutor. Mem. Inst. Indsl. Engrs. (sr. mem.), Transp. Rsch. Forum, Inst. Ops. Rsch. and Mgmt. Sci., Alpha Tau Omega. Home: 4505 Hillside Dr Arlington TX 76013-4103 Office: Sea-Land Svc 4100 Alpha Rd Ste 800 Dallas TX 75244-4368

KELLY, ROBERTO CONRADO (BOBBY KELLY), professional baseball player; b. Panama City, Panama, Oct. 1, 1964. Student, Jose Dolores Moscote Coll., Panama. With N.Y. Yankees, 1982-92, Cin. Reds, 1992-94, Atlanta Braves, 1994, Montreal Expos, 1994-95, L.A. Dodgers, 1995-97, Minn. Twins, 1997-98, Texas Rangers, 98-; mem. Am. League All-Star Team, 1992, Nat. League All-Star Team, 1993. Office: Texas Rangers 1000 Ballpark Way Arlington TX 76011*

KELLY, RODNEY P., military officer. BS in Agr., So. Ill. U., 1966, MBA, 1968; grad., Squadron Officer Sch., 1975, Air Command and Staff Coll., 1978, Air War Coll., 1988. Commd. 2d lt. USAF, 1967, advanced through grades to maj. gen., 1997; standardization and evaluation mem. 12th Flying Tng. Wing, Randolph AFB, Tex., 1975; resource mgr. rated officer assignments Air Force Mil. Pers. Ctr., Randolph AFB, 1975-79; F-15 pilot, A Flight comdr. 525th Tactical Fighter Squadron, Bitburg Air Base, West Germany, 1979-82; chief F-15 standardization and evaluation divsn. 36th Tactical Fighter Wing, Bitburg Air Base, 1982-83; comdr. 527th Aggressor Squadron U.S. Air Forces in Europe, RAF, Alconbury, Eng., 1985-86; dep. comdr. ops. 10th Tactical Reconnaissance Wing, RAF, Alconbury, 1986-87; asst. for air def. NATO policy Office of Sec. of Def., internat. security policy, Washington, 1988-90; vice comdr. 21st Tactical Fighter Wing, Elmendorf AFB, Alaska, 1990-91; comdr. 3d Wing, Elmendorf AFB, 1991-93; Pacific Air Forces asst. dir. ops. Hdqs. Pacific Air Forces, Hickam AFB, Hawaii, 1993-95, dir. plans, 1995-96; dir. plans Hdqs. N.Am. Aerospace Def. Command, Peterson AFB, Colo., 1996-97; dir. ops. Hdqs. U.S. Space Command, Peterson AFB, 1997—. Decorated Def. Superior Svc. medal, Legion of Merit with oak leaf cluster, Meritorious Svc. medal with 3 oak leaf clusters. Office: HQ USSPACECOM/J3 Ste 116 250 S Peterson Blvd Peterson AFB CO 80094-3040

KELLY, SUE W., congresswoman; b. Lima, Ohio, Sept. 26, 1936; m. Edward; 4 children. BA, Denison U., 1958; MA in Health Advocacy, Sarah Lawrence Coll., 1985. Rschr. New England Inst. Med. Rsch., 1958; tchr. John Jay Jr. H.S., 1962-63, Harvey Sch.; real estate rehabilitator, 1963—; campaign coord. Rep. Hamilton Fish, N.Y., 1971-72; intern Ruth Taylor Home, 1973-74; florist, owner Somerstown Flower Shop, 1978-79; patient advocate St. Luke's Hosp., 1984-87; adj. prof. of health advocacy Sarah Lawrence Coll., 1987-92; mem. 105th to 106th Congress from 19th N.Y. dist. U.S. Ho. of Reps., 1995—; mem. Banking & Financial Services subcoms. on fin. instns. and consumer credit and housing, and on cmty. opportunity SBA; chair regulatory reform and paperwork reduction Transp. and Infrastructure subcoms. on surface, water resources, and the environment. Office: US House Reps 1222 Longworth Bldg Washington DC 20515-3219*

KELLY, THADDEUS ELLIOTT, medical geneticist; b. N.Y.C., 1937. MD, Med. Coll. S.C.; PhD, Johns Hopkins U. Diplomate Am. Bd. Genetics (pres. 1993-94), Am. Bd. Pediatrics. Prof. pediatrics U. Va., Charlottesville, dir. med. genetics. Office: U Va Hosp Div Med Genetics Box 386 Charlottesville VA 22908*

KELLY, THOMAS CAJETAN, archbishop; b. Rochester, NY, July 14, 1931; s. Thomas A. Kelly and Katherine Eleanor (Fisher) Conley. A.B., Providence Coll., 1953; S.T.L., Dominican House of Studies, Washington, 1959; D.Canon Law, U. St. Thomas, Rome, 1962; S.T.D. (hon.), Providence Coll, 1979; D.H.L. (hon.), Spalding Coll., 1983. Ordained priest Roman Cath. Ch., 1958. Sec. Dominican Province, N.Y.C., 1962-65; sec. Apostolic Del., Washington, 1965-71; assoc. gen. sec. Nat. Conf. Cath. Bishops-U.S. Cath. Conf., Washington, 1971-77; gen. sec. U.S. Cath. Bishops Conf. Washington, 1977-82, ordained Roman Cath. aux. bishop, 1977; archbishop Archdiocese of Louisville, 1982—; chmn. Cath. Conf. Ky., Louisville, 1982—. Chancellor Bellarmine Coll.; bd. dirs. St. Luke Inst. Recipient Veritas medal St. Catharine Coll., 1984. Mem. Canon Law Soc. Am., Nat. Cath. Edn. Assn. (chmn. bd. dirs. 1991-94). Home and Office: 212 E College St Louisville KY 40203-2334*

KELLY, THOMAS JOSEPH, III, photojournalist; b. Hackensack, N.J., Aug. 8, 1947; s. Thomas J. and Severina (Augenti) K.; m. Patricia Lee Moulder, May 3, 1975; children: Danielle Marie, Devon Lee, Thomas Joseph IV, Taylor Lynn. Student public schs., Woodbury and North Bergen, N.J. Maps and records clk. Phila. Electric Co., Plymouth Meeting, Pa., 1967-71; free lance photographer Norristown, Pa., 1969-71; chief photographer Today's Post, King Of Prussia, Pa., 1971-74; dir. photography The Mercury, Pottstown, Pa., 1974-89; photo dir. St. Louis Sun Ingersoll Publs. Co., 1989; photo dir. The Trentonian, Trenton, N.J., 1990-96; freelance photojournalist and videographer; instr. photography Pa. Press Inst., accident scene photography Pa. State Police Training Ctr.; instr. photojournalism Temple U., Phila.; chmn. photography jury Pulitzer Prize Com., 1983, editorial cartoon juror, 1984; co-founder Northern Short Course in Photojournalism, 1981. Contbr. photographs to Time, Newsweek, Life, Am. Photographer, U.S. News and World Report, USA Today, Sports Illustrated, textbooks, encys., others.; photography exhbn. of Pulitzer Prize, Tokyo, 1998; TV appearances include Hard Copy, Maury Povich, AM Phila., Captain Noah; contbr. VSD, Paris Mag.; news video has appeared on Phila. local news, FOX, NBC Network, Am. Jour., Extra, Inside Edition, Hard Copy, CNN, CBS Network, KR Video, Phila. Online, Time Warner Broadcasting, Tribune Broadcasting. With Pa. N.G., 1966-72. Recipient numerous state, regional and nat. photog. awards including nat. citation AP, 1978, 79, Pulitzer prize for news photography, 1979; Robert F. Kennedy Journalism award, 1980; photog. essay award Am. Cancer Soc., 1984; award Internat. Assn. Fire Fighters, 1984, Silver medal 1st annual photo contest Sports Action Photography Washington Journalism Rev., 1992, Nat. Headliners award Sports Action, 1993. Mem. Nat. Press Photographers Assn. (Region 3 Photographer of Yr. award 1975, 76, 79, bd. dirs. 1981-87), Pa. Press Photographers Assn. (past pres., Pa. Photographer of Yr. 1976), 1st Amendment Coalition of Pa. Roman Catholic. Home: PO Box 2208 Sanatoga Branch Pottstown PA 19464-0208*

KELLY, THOMAS PAINE, JR., lawyer; b. Tampa, Fla., Aug. 29, 1912; s. Thomas Paine and Beatrice (Gent) K.; m. Jean Baughman, July 25, 1940; children: Carla (Mrs. Henry Dee), Thomas Paine III, Margaret Jo (Mrs. Jeffrey Holmes). AB, U. Fla., 1935, JD, 1936. Bar: Fla. 1936, U.S. Dist. Ct. (no. dist.) Fla. 1936, U.S. Ct. Appeals (5th cir.) 1936, U.S. Dist. Ct. (mid. dist.) Fla. 1940, U.S. Dist. Ct. (so. dist.) Fla. 1939, U.S. Ct. Appeals (11th cir.) 1983, U.S. Supreme Ct. 1990. Since practiced in Tampa; assoc. McKay, Macfarlane, Jackson & Ferguson, 1939-40; ptnr. McKay, MacFarlane, Jackson & Ferguson, 1940-48; ptnr. Macfarlane, Ferguson, Allison & Kelly, 1948-83, sr. ptnr., 1983-91; of counsel Shear, Newman, Hahn & Rosenkranz, 1992-95; shareholder MacFarlane Ferguson & McMullen, P.A., Tampa, Fla., 1996—. Chmn. Tampa Com. 100, 1960-61; pres. Tampa Citizens' Safety Coun., 1961-62; Bd. dirs. Tampa chpt. ARC, 1955-62, pres., 1958-59; bd. dirs. Boys Clubs Tampa, 1956-67, pres., 1966-67. Col. F.A. AUS, 1940-45. Decorated Silver Star. Fellow Am. Coll. Trial Lawyers, Internat. Acad. Trial Lawyers; mem. Am. Bar Assn., Bar Assn. Hillsborough County, Fla. Bar (chmn. com. profl. ethics 1953-58, chmn. com. ins. and negligence law 1962-63, chmn. fed. rules com. 1969-70). Republican. Home: 5426 Lykes Ln Tampa FL 33611-4747 Office: McFarlane Ferguson & McMullen PO Box 1531 Tampa FL 33601-1531

KELLY, TIMOTHY MICHAEL, newspaper publisher; b. Ashland, Ky., Nov. 28, 1947; s. Robert John and Pauline Elizabeth (Henneman) K.; m. Carol Ann Knight, Aug. 2, 1969; children: Kimberly, Kevin. BA, U. Miami, Fla., 1970. Sports copy editor, writer The Courier-Jour., Louisville, 1970-71; exec. sports editor The Phila. Inquirer, 1971-75; dep. mng. editor Dallas Times Herald, 1975-81; mng. editor The Denver Post, 1981-84; exec. editor Dallas Times Herald, 1984; editor Daily News, Los Angeles, 1984-87; mng. editor The Orange County Register, Santa Ana, Calif., 1987-89; editor, sr. v.p. Lexington Herald-Leader, Lexington, Ky., 1989-96, pub., 1996—; juror Pulitzer Prize, 1987-88. Recipient Knight-Ridder Excellence award for Cmty. Svc., 1995. Mem. Am. Soc. Newspaper Editors. Roman Catholic. Office: Lexington Herald Leader 100 Midland Ave Lexington KY 40508-1999

KELLY, TIMOTHY T., television station executive. BS in Fin., U. Colo., 1975; postgrad., U. Colo., Denver. Sr. v.p. TV Nat. Geog. TV Inc., Washington, pres., 1995—. Office: Nat Geog TV Inc 1145 17th St NW Washington DC 20036-4701*

KELLY, TIMOTHY WILLIAM, lawyer; b. Chgo., Apr. 27, 1953; s. George Raymond and Mary Therese (Kelly) K.; m. Mary Teresa Harms, May 24, 1980; children: Ryan Timothy, Colin Patrick, Kaitlynn Elizabeth. B.S. in Bus. Adminstrn., U. Dayton, 1975, J.D., 1978. Bar: Ill. 1978, U.S. Dist. Ct. (cen., no. dist.) Ill. 1979. Staff counsel Praire State Legal Aid, Bloomington, Ill., 1978-81; felony asst. McLean County Pub. Defenders, Bloomington, 1981-83; assoc. Jerome Mirza & Assocs., Bloomington, 1983-88; asst. prof. polit. sci. Ill. State U., Normal, 1980-83; faculty mem. Ill. Inst. Continuing Legal Edn. Bd. dirs. Bloomington/Normal Day Care Assn., 1982-83; civil actions arbitrator and mediator McLean County, 1996—; lectr. in field. Contbr. articles to profl. jours. Named one of Top Three Attys. in McLean, Bus. to Bus. Mag., 1997. Fellow Ill. Bar Found.; mem. Ill. State Bar Assn. (mem. civil practice and procedure sect. coun. 1992—, chmn. 1998, Allerton house steering com. 1994, 96, 98, tort law sect. coun. 1995—, assembly mem. 1995—), Ill. Trial Lawyers Assn. (mem. bd. managers 1992—, continuing legal edn. com. 1995-96, exec. com. 1996, chmn. ins. law com. 1996-98), Assn. Trial Lawyers of Am., Chgo. Bar Assn., McLean County Bar Assn. (sec. 1984-85), McLean County Inns of Court. Democrat. Roman Catholic. Office: Allison & Kelly 202 N Prospect Rd Bloomington IL 61704-3555

KELLY, TOM (JAY THOMAS KELLY), major league baseball club manager; b. Graceville, Minn., Aug. 15, 1950; s. Joseph Thomas and Anna Grace (Heisenbottle) K.; children: Sharon Clare, Thomas John. Student, Mesa (Ariz.) Jr. Coll., 1968-69. Profl. baseball player Minn. Twins, Mpls., 1968-77, coach, 1982-86, mgr., 1987—; mgr. minor league team Minn. Twins, Toledo, Ohio, 1978-82. Managed Minn. Twins team to World Series Championship, 1987, 91; named Am. League Mgr. of Yr. Sporting News, 1991. Mem. Assn. Profl. Baseball Players, U.S. Trotting Assn., Nat. Greyhound Assn. Avocation: harness racing. Office: Minn Twins Hubert H Humphrey Metrodome 34 Kirby Puckett Pl Minneapolis MN 55415-1596*

KELLY, WAYNE FRED, journalism educator; b. New Castle, Ind., Apr. 9, 1934; s. James Nolan and Marie Sylvia (Bailey) K.; m. Patricia Anne Moriarity, Nov. 22, 1958; children: Christopher, Timothy, Scott. AA, Valley Coll., 1954; BA, Butler U., 1957; MS, UCLA, 1962. Staff photographer The Indpls. Star, 1954-57; dir. photography/photo editor L.A. Times, 1957-71; bus. owner Kelly Assocs. Photographs, Glendale, Calif., 1971-76; prof. journalism Calif. State U., Long Beach, 1976—; nat. lectr. photographics Dynamic Graphics, Peoria, Ill., 1980-83; adv. bd. U. Nev., Reno, 1969-71, Valley Coll., Van Nuys, Calif., 1971-75. Mem. Parks and Recreation Com., Monterey Park, Calif., 1968-70; pres. Friends of the Libr., Monterey Park, 1968-69; adv. bd. ARC, 1972-74. Mem. Press Photographers Greater L.A. (v.p.), Calif. Press Photographers Assn. (pres.), Nat. Press Photography Assn. (nat. conv. chair), Soc. of Profl. Joursnalists (Best Coll. Feature Article in U.S. 1957). Republican. Avocations: study French language, culture, computer technology, jogging, golf. E-mail: wfkelly@earthlink.net. Home: 24842 Los Gatos Dr Laguna Hills CA 92653 Office: Calif State U Long Beach 1250 Bellflower Blvd Long Beach CA 90840

KELLY, WILLIAM MICHAEL, investment executive; b. Pittsfield, Mass., Feb. 3, 1944; children: Alyssa A., Eileen J. BA in Political Sci., St. Anselm Coll., 1966; MA in Political Sci., Duquesne U., 1968; MBA in Finance, NYU, 1972. Portfolio mngr., v.p. Chase Manhattan Bank, N.Y.C., 1968-77; v.p. Nat. Aviation and Tech., N.Y.C., 1977-80; managing assoc. Lingold Assocs., N.Y.C., 1980—; trustee 1st Eagle Internat. Fund, N.Y.C., 1994—; trustee 1st Eagle Fund Am., N.Y.C., 1998—; ind. gen. ptnr. ML Venture Ptnrs. II, N.Y.C., 1991—; dir., treas., Black Forest Consortium, Inc., Black Forest Preserve, N.Y., 1989—; trustee N.Y. Found., 1985—, chmn., 1992-95; asst. treas. Neuroscis. Rsch. Found., Calif, 1982; v.p., treas. Sergei Zlinkoff Fund Med. Edn.; trustee St. Anselm Coll., N.H. bd. govs. Eugene Lang Coll, 1994—; trustee Pathways for Youth, 1976—, pres. 1981-84. Mem. AAAS, (investment and fin. com. 1985—), N.Y. Acad. Scis., 1987— (fin. affairs com.), India House Club, Sleepy Hollow Country Club. Office: 40 Wall St Rm 4201 New York NY 10005-2301

KELLY, WILLIAM BRET, insurance executive; b. Rocky Ford, Colo., Sept. 28, 1922; s. William Andrew and Florence Gail (Yant) K.; m. Patricia Ruth Ducy, Mar. 25, 1944; children: Eric Damian, Kathryn Gail Kelly Schweitzer. BA cum laude, U. Colo., 1947. CPCU. With Steel City Agys., Inc., and predecessor, Pueblo, Colo., 1946—, pres., 1961-76, chmn. bd., 1977—; dir. United Bank Pueblo, 1963-94, chmn. bd., 1983-88; mem. Pub. Expenditure Coun., 1984—; v.p. Colo. Ins. Edn. Found., 1981, pres., 1982. Mem. Pueblo Area Coun. Govts., 1971-73, Colo. Forum 1985—, trustee Pueblo Bd. Water Works, 1966-80, pres., 1970-71; pres. Pueblo Single Fund Plan, 1960-61, Pueblo Heart Coun., 1962, Family Svc. Soc. Pueblo, 1963; mem. 10th Jud. Dist. Nominating Com., 1967-71; pres. U. So. Colo. Found., 1998-99, v.p., 1991, 92, 93, 94, 95, 96, 97, 98; trustee Jackson Found., 1972—, Farley Found., 1979—, Roselawn Cemetery Assn., 1982—, Kelly-Ducy Found., 1983—; hon. parade marshall Colo. State Fair, 1991. With inf. AUS, 1943-45. Decorated Silver Star, Bronze Star with oak leaf cluster, Purple Heart with oak leaf cluster; recipient Disting. Svc. award U. Colo., 1992; honored for cmty. svc. Parkview Episcopal Med. Ctr., 1992; named to Pueblo Hall of Fame, 1995. Mem. Soc. CPCU's, Pueblo C. of C. (past pres.), Pueblo Kiwanis (past pres.), Pueblo Country Club (treas. 1964-66), So. Colo. Press Club (Outstanding Community Svc. award 1991), Phi Beta Kappa. Democrat. Home: 264 S Sifford Ct Pueblo West CO 81007-2843 Office: 1414 W 4th St Pueblo CO 81004-1205

KELLY, WILLIAM CHARLES, JR., lawyer; b. Mpls., June 9, 1946; s. William Charles and Marian Eileen (Moritz) K.; m. Cynthia Ann Churchill, June 28, 1969; children: Patrick, Brian. AB, Harvard U., 1968; JD, Yale U., 1971. Bar: Maine 1972, D.C. 1973, U.S. Supreme Ct. 1973. Law clk. to Judge Coffin U.S. Ct. Appeals (1st cir.), Portland, Maine, 1971-72; law clk. to Justice Powell U.S. Supreme Ct., Washington, 1972-73; exec. asst. to sec. HUD, Washington, 1975-77; ptnr. Latham & Watkins, Washington, 1978—. Bd. dirs. Nat. Low Income Housing Coalition, Washington, 1983-94, The Governance Inst., 1986—, Washington Legal Clinic for the Homeless, 1999—; trustee Sheridan Sch., 1992-98; mem. Ashoka World Coun., 1997—. Lt. USNR, 1973-75. Mem. ABA, D.C. Bar Assn. Office: Latham & Watkins Ste 1300 1001 Pennsylvania Ave NW Washington DC 20004-2585

KELLY, WILLIAM GARRETT, judge; b. Grand Rapids, Mich., Nov. 30, 1947; s. Joseph Francis and Gertrude Frances (Downes) K.; m. Sharon Ann Diroff, Aug. 11, 1979; children: Colleen, Joseph, Caitlin, Meaghan and Patricia. BA, U. Detroit, 1970, JD, 1975. Bar: Mich. 1975, U.S. Dist. Ct. (we. dist.) Mich. 1975. Tchr. Peace Corps, Ghana, Republic of West Africa, 1970-72; asst. prosecutor Kalamazoo (Mich.) Prosecutor's Office, 1975-77; atty. Office of Defender, Grand Rapids, 1977-78; judge 62d B Dist. Ct., Kentwood, 1979—; mem. faculty Mich. Jud. Inst., Lansing, 1985—, 2d Nat. Conf. on Ct. Tech., Denver, 1988; chmn.-elect Jud. Conf. State Bar Mich., 1990-91, chair, 1991-92; vice chmn. Nat. Conf. Spl. Ct. Judges, 1990-91, chair 1992-93. Bd. dirs. Nat. Ctr. for State Cts., 1994—; pres. Kentwood Jaycees, 1979-80. Named one of Five Outstanding Young Men of Mich., Mich. Jaycees, 1982. Mem. ABA (chair nat. conf. spl. ct. judges 1992-93), State Bar Mich., Grand Rapids Bar Assn., Cath. Lawyers Assn. Western Mich. (pres. 1987), Mich. Dist. Judges Assn. (pres. 1989). Roman Catholic. Office: 62d B Dist Ct PO Box 8848 4900 Breton Rd SE Kentwood MI 49518-8848

KELLY, WILLIAM WATKINS, educational association executive; b. Asheville, N.C., Sept. 21, 1928; s. John Jackson and Trula (Watkins) K.; m. Lura Jane Kelly, Feb. 14, 1953 (div. Jan. 14, 1983); children: William Watkins, Robert Jackson, Blair Massey, Gregory Clark.; m. Catherine Messer Penney, Jan. 22, 1983. B.A., Va. Mil. Inst., 1950; A.M., Duke U., 1955, Ph.D., 1957. Commandant cadets, tchr. English John Marshall High Sch., Richmond, Va., 1950-52; instr. English Va. Mil. Inst., 1952-53; instr. English Air Force Acad., 1957-58, asst. prof., 1958-60; asst. prof. English Va. Mil. Inst., 1960-62; asst. prof. Am. thought and language Mich. State U., 1962-65, assoc. prof., 1965-69; assoc. dir. The Honors Coll., 1965-68, dir., 1968-69; pres. Mary Baldwin Coll., 1969-76, Transylvania U., Lexington, Ky., 1976-81; sr. assoc. Univ. Assos., 1981-82; exec. v.p. L.Q.C. Lamar Soc., 1981-82; pres. Ala. Assn. Ind. Colls. and Univs., 1982-88, Ga. Found. for Ind. Colls. Inc., Atlanta, 1988-96; pres. emeritus, 1996—; pres. Assn. Pvt. Colls. and Univs. in Ga., Atlanta, 1990-96; mem. Va. Commn. on Status of Women, 1973-76, Ky. Commn. on Status of Women, 1977-81; chmn. Ky. Rhodes Scholar Selection Com., 1978-79; pres. Coun. Ind. Ky. Colls. and Univs., 1978-80; bd. dirs. Ala. Humanities Found., 1983-88, chmn. bd. dirs., 1985-87; bd. dirs., exec. com. Ga. Humanities Coun., 1989-96, vice chair, 1991-93, chair, 1994-96. Author: Ellen Glasow: A Bibliography, 1964. Bd. dirs. Ky. State C. of C., 1980-82; trustee Greensboro Coll., 1993—. Served with USAF, 1957-60; lt. col. ret. Res. Ellis L. Phillips Found. intern Rutgers U., 1964-65; Ala. recipient IBM Disting. Performance award Ind. Coll. Funds Am., 1986, Outstanding Ala. Fund Raising Exec. award Nat. Soc. Fund Raising Execs., 1986, Leadership award Brunswich Pub. Charitable Found., 1993; Danforth fellow, 1953-57; Duke scholar, 1954-55; William Watkins Kelly Endowed Scholarship in the Humanities established Ga. Found. Ind. Colls., 1996. Fellow Found. Ind. Higher Edn. (nat. presiding officer 1992-94, Disting. Performance award 1996); sr. assocs. Jon McRae & Assoc., 1996—, mem. MLA, Am. Studies Assn., Soc. Values in Higher Edn., Am. Assn. Higher Edn., Ellen Glasgow Soc. (pres. 1973-75), Newcomen Soc. N.Am., Rotary (Paul Harris fellow), Phi Beta Kappa, Omicron Delta Kappa. Lodge: Rotary. Fax: (404) 325-9610. E-mail: jma@mindspring.com. Home: 4015 Brockton Close Marietta GA 30068-4931 Office: Jon McRae & Assocs Inc Ste 200 1930 N Druid Hills Rd NE Atlanta GA 30319-4120

KELLY-JONES, DENISE MARIE, critical care nurse; b. Staten Island, N.Y., Nov. 16, 1966; d. Edward Augustine and Dorothy Catherine (Ferrante) K. AAS, Coll. of S.I., 1987, BSN, 1989; MS in Adult N.P., SUNY, Stony Brook. Cert. specialist, cardiothoracic surg. nurse practitioner ANCC; CCRN; cert. Nat. Field Archery Assn./Nat. Archery Assn. archery instr., 1997—. From staff nurse to critical care nurse, 1989-94; nurse practitioner Univ. Hosp. at Stony Brook, 1994-96; nurse practitioner cardiac surgery Union Meml. Hosp., 1996—. Mem. AACN (Greater Washington area chpt.). Home: 6 Wellhaven Cir Apt 1334 Owings Mills MD 21117-5269

KELM, BONNIE G., art museum director, educator; b. Bklyn., Mar. 29, 1947; d. Julius and Anita (Baron) Steiman; m. William G. Malis; 1 child, Michael Darren. BS in Art Edn., Buffalo State U., 1968; MA in Art History, Bowling Green (Ohio) State U., 1975; PhD in Arts Adminstrn., Ohio State U., 1987. Art tchr. Toledo Pub. Schs., 1968-71; ednl. cons. Columbus (Ohio) Mus. Art, 1976-81; prof. art Franklin U., Columbus, 1976-88; legis. coord. Ohio Ho. of Reps., Columbus, 1977; pres. bd. trustees Columbus Inst. for Contemporary Art, 1977-81; tech. asst. cons. Ohio Arts Coun., Columbus, 1984-88; dir. Bunte Gallery Franklin U., Columbus, 1978-88; dir. art mus. Miami U., Oxford, Ohio, 1988-96, assoc. prof., 1988-96; dir. Muscarelle Mus. of Art Coll. William and Mary, Williamsburg, Va., 1996—, assoc. prof. art and art history, 1996—; grant panelist Ohio Arts Coun., Columbus, 1985-87, 91-95; art book reviewer William C. Brown Pub., Madison, Wis., 1985-92; mem. acquisitions adv. bd. Martin Luther King Ctr., Columbus, 1987-88; field reviewer Inst. Mus. Svcs., Washington, 1990—; chairperson grant panel Art in Pub. Places, 1992-95; trustee Ohio Mus. Assn., 1993-96; state apptd. mem. adv. com. Ohio Percent for Art, 1994-96; bd. dirs. U.S. Nat. Com. Internat. Coun. Museums, 1998—; bd. dirs., southeast rep. Assn. Univ. & Coll. Mus. Galleries, 1998—. Author, editor (mus. catalogues) Connections, 1985, Into the Mainstream: Contemporary Folk Art, 1991, Testimony of Images: PreColumbian Art, 1992, Collecting by Design: The Allen Collection, 1994, Photographs by Barbara Hershey: A Retrospective, 1995, Modernism Gender & Culture, 1997; contbr. chpt. to book, articles to profl. jours. Founding mem., mem. adv. coun. Columbus Cultural Arts Ctr., 1977-81; coord., curator Cultural Exch. Program, Honolulu-Columbus, 1980; mem. acad. women achievers YWCA, 1991—; guest speaker 1991 Scholastic Arts Award, Cin., 1991; keynote speaker Ohio Mus. Assn., ann. meeting, 1992; speaker Internat. Coun. Mus. Triennial Conf., Quebec City, 1992; session chair Midwest Mus. Assn. ann. meeting, St. Louis, 1993. Recipient Marantz Disting. Scholar award Ohio State U., 1995, Gelpe award YWCA, 1987, Cultural Advancement of City of Columbus award, The Columbus Dispatch, 1984, Disting. Svc. award, Columbus Art League, 1984, Critic's Choice award Found. for Cmty. of Artists, N.Y., 1981; Fulbright scholar USIA, 1988 (The Netherlands); NEH fellow East-West Ctr., Honolulu, 1991. Mem. Am. Assn. Mus. (advocacy task force, surveyor mus. assessment program 1996—), Assn. of Coll. and Univ. Mus. and Galleries, S.E. Mus. Assn., Fulbright Assn., Coll. Arts Assn., Internat. Coun. Mus., Va. Assn. Museums. Office: Muscarelle Mus of Art Coll William & Mary PO Box 8795 Williamsburg VA 23187-8795 *Pay attention to all of the potentials and resources that others overlook in your every day environment. Never let any one convince you that something you're committed to is impossible. Make an art of putting people and possibilities together.*

KELM, LINDA, opera singer; b. Salt Lake City, Dec. 11, 1944; d. Robert Gordon and Hettie Frances Kelm. Studies with Elizabeth Hayes Simpson, Salt Lake City, 1963-75; studies with Jennie Tourel, Aspen, Colo., 1968; studies with Judith Oas, N.Y.C., 1975-84, L.A., 1994-95. Profl. debut in Der Ring des Nibelungen, 1977; performed in Die Walküre and Götterdämmerung, 1977-83; sang title role in Turandot, 1979, Salome, 1984, Fidelio, 1987, Elektra, 1990, Tristan und Isolde, 1991; performed with: Rai Radio Orch. (Rome), Residentie Orkest of Holland, Minn. Orch., Utah Symphony, Opera Orch. N.Y., Chgo. Symphony, San Francisco Symphony, St. Louis Symphony, Pitts. Symphony, Balt. Symphony, Denver Symphony, Detroit Symphony, Seattle Symphony, N.J. Symphony, L.I. Philharm., San Antonio Symphony, Houston Grand Opera, N.Y.C. Opera, San Francisco Opera, Deutsche Oper/Berlin, Associaciones Bilbania de Amigos de Opera-Bilbao, Spain, Hamburgische Staatsoper, Mexico City Opera, Ky. Opera, Utah Opera, Portland Opera, Greater Miami Opera, L.A. Philharm., City of Birmingham Symphony Orch., Eng., Tokyo Symphony Orch., Orchestre de Bordeaux-Aquitaine, Cin. Orch., Phoenix Symphony Orch., Bklyn. Philharm. Orch., Symphony of the New World, Philippine Youth Symphony Orch., Spokane Opera; sang role of Brünnhilde, Seattle Wagner Festival, 1986, 87; appeared in maj. opera houses throughout the world; Met. Opera debut Brünnhilde in Siegfried, 1988; Avery Fisher Hall debut, 1987; Carnegie Hall debut, 1988, Concertgebouw debut, 1983, Royal Festival Hall debut, 1989, May Festival debut, 1986; rec. debut Helmwige in Deutsche Gramophon, Die Walküre Met. Opera, 1988 (Grammy award). Nat. Fedn. of Women's Club scholar, 1968; grantee PEO Sisterhood, 1979, Nat. Inst. of Music Theatre grantee, 1979, 80. Mem. Am. Guild of Musical Artists, Internat. Order of Job's Daughters (past Bethel guardian, majority mem., grand sec.), Daughters of Nile. Methodist. Home: 2744 Grandview Cir Salt Lake City UT 84106-3620

KELMAN, ARTHUR, plant pathologist, educator; b. Providence, Dec. 11, 1918; s. Philip and Minnie (Kollin) K.; m. Helen Moore Parker, June 22, 1949; 1 child, Philip Joseph. BS, U. R.I., 1941, DSc (hon.), 1977; MS, N.C. State U., 1946; PhD, 1949. Faculty N.C. State U., Raleigh, 1948-65, prof., 1957-65, W.N. Reynolds distinguished prof. plant pathology, 1961-65, univ. dist. scholar, 1990—; chmn. dept. plant pathology U. Wis., Madison, 1965-75, L.R. Jones Disting. prof., 1975-89, prof. bacteriology, 1977-89, WARF Sr. Disting. Rsch. prof., 1984-89; chief scientist Competitive Grants Program Nat. Rsch. Initiative, Coop. State Rsch. Svc., USDA, 1991-93; vis. investigator Rockefeller Inst., 1953-54; chmn. div. biol. sci. Assembly Life Sci. NRC, 1980-82, chmn. bd. basic biology, Commn. Life Scis., 1984-85. Author: The Bacterial Wilt Caused by Pseudomonas solanacearum, 1953. Served with AUS, 1942-45. NSF sr. postdoctoral fellow Cambridge (Eng.) U., 1971-72; recipient E.C. Stakman award, 1987. Fellow AAAS, Am. Acad. Arts and Scis., Am. Phytopath. Soc. (chmn. sourcebook com., councilor-at-large, v.p. 1965-66, pres. 1966-67, award of distinction 1983), Am. Acad. Microbiology; mem. NAS (coun. 1986-89, chmn. sect. applied biology 1981-83, chmn. class VI Applied biology and agrl. scis., 1988-91), Internat. Soc. Plant Pathology (v.p. 1968-73, pres. 1973-78), Soc. Gen. Microbiology, Am. Soc. Microbiology, Am. Inst. Biol. Sci., Phytopathol. Soc Japan (hon.), Sigma Xi, Alpha Zeta, Gamma Sigma Delta, Phi Kappa Phi, Phi Sigma, Xi Sigma Pi. E-mail: arthurúkelman@ncsu.edu. Home: 615 Yarmouth Rd Raleigh NC 27607-6650 Office: NC State Univ Dept Plant Pathology Campus Box 7616 Raleigh NC 27695-0716

KELMAN, BRUCE JERRY, toxicologist, consultant; b. Chgo., July 1, 1947; s. LeRoy Rayfield and Louise (Rosen) K.; m. Jacqueline Anne Clark, Feb. 5, 1972; children: Aaron Wayne, Diantha Renee, Coreyanne Louise. BS, U. Ill., 1969, MS, 1971, PhD, 1975. Diplomate Am. Bd. Toxicology. Rsch. assoc. U. Tenn., Oak Ridge, 1974-76, asst. prof., leader prenatal toxicology group, 1976-79; mgr. devel. toxicology sect. Battelle NW, Richland, Wash., 1980-84, assoc. mgr. biology and chemistry dept., 1984-85, mgr., 1985-89, mgr. new products devel. Life Scis. Ctr., 1989-90; mgr. Internat. Toxicology Office Battelle Meml. Inst., Richland, 1986-89; mng. scientist, mgr. toxicology dept. Failure Analysis Assocs., Inc., Menlo Park, Calif., 1990-93; mgr. toxicology and risk assessment Golder Assocs. Inc., Redmond, Wash., 1993, nat. dir. health and environ. scis., 1994-98; pres. GlobalTox, Inc., 1998—; mem. Nation Rsch. Coun. com. on possible effects of electromagnetic fields on biologic sys., 1993-96; adj. prof. N.Mex. State U., Las Cruces, 1983-96. Co-editor: Interactions of Biological Systems with Static and ELF Electric and Magnetic Fields, 1987; mem. editorial bd. Trophoblast Rsch., 1983—, Biological Effects of Heavy Metals, 1990. Adv. coun. Seattle Fire Dept., 1988-90; mem. Wash. Gov.'s Biotech. Targeted Sector Adv. Com., 1989-90. Fellow Am. Acad. Vet. and Comparative Toxicology; mem. Am. Coll. Occupl. and Environ. Medicine, Soc. Toxicology (founding pres. molecular biology splty. sect. 1988-89, pres. metals splty. sect. 1985-86, cert. of recognition 1989), Am. Soc. for Exptl. Pharmacology and Therapeutics, Soc. for Exptl. Biology and Medicine (award of merit 1980), Teratology Soc., Wash. State Biotech. Assn. (bd. dirs. 1989-90). Office: GlobalTox Inc 18372 Redmond-Fall City Rd Redmond WA 98052

KELMAN, CHARLES D., ophthalmologist, educator; b. Bklyn., May 23, 1930; s. David and Eva K.; m. Ann Gur-Arie; children: Evan Ari Kelman, Jason, Seth; children from previoius marriage: David, Lesley, Jennifer. BS, Tufts U., 1950; BMS, U. Geneva, Switzerland, 1952, MD, 1956. Diplomate Am. Bd. Ophthalmology. Intern Kings County Hosp., N.Y.C., 1956-57; resident Wills Eye Hosp., Pa., 1956-60; with Manhattan Eye, Ear, Nose and Throat Hosp., N.Y.C., 1967—, N.Y. Eye and Ear Infirmary, N.Y.C., 1983—; clin. prof. N.Y. Med. Coll., Valhalla, 1980—; Arthur J. Bedell Meml. lectr., 1991; hon. pres.-elect 1994 World Congress on Lens Implant Surgery. Author: Cataracts—What You Must Know About Them, 1982, Atlas of Cryosurgical Techniques in Ophthalmology, 1966; Phacoemulsification Aspiration—The Kelman Technique of Cataract Extraction, 1975; Through My Eyes, 1985; contbr. numerous articles to profl. jours. Recipient Gold Plate award Am. Acad. Achievement, 1969, 1st prize for sci. exhibit, Am. Acad. Ophthalmology, 1970, 1st Outstanding achievement award Am. Soc. Contemporary Ophthalmology, 1981, Physicians Recognition award

AMA, Can. Implant Assn. award, 1982, Congl. Salute, U.S. Senate 97th Congress, 1983, 1st Ann. Innovators award Am. Internat. Intraocular Lens Congress, 1985, Am. Acad. Ophthalmology Sr. Honor award, 1986, Binkhorst medal Am. Soc. Cataract and Refractive Surgery, 1989, Ridley medal Internat. Congress Ophthalmology, 1990, Spl. Rrecognition award Am. Acad. Ophthalmology, Nat. Medal Tech., 1992, Pres. of U.S. Inventor of Yr. award, 1992, Disting. Svc. award Tufts U., 1992, Best Ophthalmologist in Am. award Ophthalmology Times, 1996. Fellow Am. Acad. Ophthalmology;; mem. AMA, Internat. Assn. Ocular Surgeons, Can. Implant Assn. (Ophthalmologist of The Century 1994), N.Y. Implant Soc., Am. Soc. for Contemporary Ophthalmology, Am. Soc. for Cataracts and Refractive Surgery (former pres.; One of Most Influential Ophthalmologists of 20th Century award 1999), N.Y. State Soc. Ophthalmology, N.Y. Acad. Medicine (sec. sect. on ophthalmology), European Phaco-Cataract Soc. (hon. life pres.), Soc. for Phacoemulsification and Related Techniques (hon. life pres.). Jewish. Avocations: golf, saxophone, composing, flying, writing. Office: Eye Center 220 Madison Ave New York NY 10016-3422

KELMAN, EDWARD MICHAEL, lawyer; b. N.Y., Aug. 29, 1943; s. Jack H. and Evelyn (Karp) K.; children: Matthews S., Joshua K. AB, Cornell U., 1965; JD, NYU, 1968. Bar: N.Y. 1969, Conn. 1972. Asst dist. atty. N.Y. County Dist. Atty.'s Office, 1968-71; assoc. Glazer & Wechsler, Stamford, Conn., 1971-72, Squadron, Gartenberg, Elenoff & Plesent, N.Y., 1972-73; sr. atty. CBS Records, CBS, Inc., N.Y., 1973-76; asst. gen. atty. CBS Pub., CBS, Inc., N.Y., 1976-77; v.p. law Chappell Music Co., N.Y., 1977-80; of counsel Law Offices of Michael Sukin, N.Y., 1980-82; v.p. bus. affairs and acquisitions Thorn EMI Video & TV, N.Y., 1982-83; pvt. practice entertainment and media law N.Y., 1983—. Vice chmn. Mayor's TV & Film Commn., Stamford, 1986—; cons. First Night Entertainment Com., Stamford, 1990. Recipient Spl. award Rec. Ind. Assn. Am., 1975. Mem. NARAS, Assn. Bar City N.Y., Conn. Bar Assn., Nat. Acad. Popular Music, Cornell Club of N.Y. Avocations: sports, movies, theatre. Fax: 212-250-1356. Office: 300 Park Ave #1940 New York NY 10022-7402

KELMAN, GARY F., environmental engineer; b. Phila., May 1, 1953; s. Gabriel Morton and Minnie (Meckler) K.; m. Wendy Joan Davidov, May 2, 1982; children: Graham Bennett, Ariel Megan. BS in Life Scis., Phila. Coll. Textiles and Scis., 1974; MS in Civil Engring., U. Md., 1977. Environ. engr. JTC Environ. Cons., Bethesda, Md., 1977-79; water resources engr. State of Md. Dept. Natural Resources, Annapolis, 1979-80; pub. health engr. State of Md. Dept. Environ., Balt., 1980-86, head pretreatment sect., 1986—. Contbg. editor: Environmental Practice, 1999—. Recipient Cert. of Appreciation, Gov. Md., 1993. Mem. ASCE (assoc.), Nat. Assn. Environ. Profls. (co-editor conf. procs. 1991, 93, pres. 1993-94), Am. Chem. Soc., Water Environ. Fedn., Sigma Xi (assoc.). Avocations: piano, computers, antique map collecting. Home: 8398 Windtree Ct Millersville MD 21108-2558 Office: State of Md Dept Environ 2500 Broening Hwy Baltimore MD 21224-6601

KELMAN, HERBERT CHANOCH, psychology educator; b. Vienna, Austria, Mar. 18, 1927; came to U.S., 1940, naturalized, 1950; s. Leo and Lea (Pomeranz) K.; m. Rose Brousman, Aug. 23, 1953. B.A., Bklyn. Coll., 1947, L.H.D. (hon.), 1981; B.H.L., Sem. Coll. Jewish Studies, N.Y.C., 1947; M.S., Yale U., 1949, Ph.D., 1951; A.M. (hon.), Harvard U., 1968; diploma, U. San Martin de Porres, Peru, 1979; L.H.D. (hon.), Hofstra U., 1983. Research asst. Yale U., 1947-51; research fellow Johns Hopkins U., 1 951-54; fellow Center Advanced Study Behavioral Scis., 1954-55, 67; research psychologist NIMH, 1955-57; lectr. social psychology Harvard U., 1957-62; fellow Inst. Social Research, Oslo, Norway, 1960-61; prof. psychology U. Mich., 1962-69, chmn. doctoral program social psychology, 1966-67; research psychologist Center for Research on Conflict Resolution, 1962-69; Richard Clarke Cabot prof. social ethics Harvard U., 1968—; exec. com. Center for Internat. Affairs, 1976—; vis. fellow Battelle Seattle Research Center, 1972-73; disting. vis. prof. Am. U., Cairo, 1977; resident scholar Bellagio Study and Conf. Ctr., 1977, 85; fellow Woodrow Wilson Internat. Center for Scholars, 1980-81; vis. scholar Truman and Davis Insts., Hebrew U. of Jerusalem, 1985; resident scholar Tantur Ecumenical Ctr. for Theol. Research, Jerusalem, 1985; Sterling McMurrin disting. vis. prof. U. Utah, 1985; chmn. internat. conf. social-psychol. research in developing countries U. Ibadan, Nigeria, 1966. Author: A Time to Speak: On Human Values and Social Research, 1968; co-author: Cross-National Encounters, 1970, Crimes of Obedience: Toward a Social Psychology of Authority and Responsibility, 1989; editor, co-author: International Behavior—, A Social-Psychological Analysis, 1965; co-editor: The Ethics of Social Intervention, 1978; contbr. articles to profl. jours. Mem. adv. com. govt. programs behavioral sci. NRC-Nat. Acad. Sci., 1966-68; nat. field rep. CORE, 1954-60; mem. nat. adv. council War Resisters League, 1952-71; mem. exec. com. Fellowship in Israel for Arab-Jewish Youth, 1977—, Jewish Peace Fellowship, 1986—; mem. exec. coun. Nat. Peace Acad. Campaign, 1977-85; trustee Internat. Ctr. for Peace in Middle East, 1982—; mem. adv. council Nat. Peace Inst. Found., 1984—; mem. psychology tng. rev. com. NIMH, 1969-73; mem. acad. coun. Ctr. for Psychol. Studies in the Nuclear Age, 1985—; mem. adv. bd. New Outlook, 1987—. Recipient Socio-Psychol. prize AAAS, 1956, N.Y. Acad. Sci. award, 1983, Mass. Psychol. Assn. award, 1983; Western Behavioral Scis. Inst. fellow, 1964, Guggenheim fellow, 1980-81, Jennings Randolph Disting. fellow U.S. Inst. Peace, 1989-90. Fellow Soc. Psychol. Study Social Issues (pres. 1964-65, Kurt Lewin Meml. award 1973), Am. Psychol. Assn. (com. on sci. and profl. ethics and conduct 1968-71, council 1968-71, dir. 1971-75, pres. div. on personality and social psychology 1970-71, bd. social and ethical responsibility 1972-74, com. on internat. rels. in psychology 1987-90, award for disting. contbn. to psychology in pub. interest 1981), Inst. Soc. Ethics and Life Scis. (dir. 1969-72); mem. Soc. Exptl. Social Psychology, Am. Sociol. Assn. (chmn. social psychology sect. 1977-78), Internat. Studies Assn. (pres. 1977-78), Internat. Peace Research Assn., Internat. Assn. Cross-Cultural Psychology, Internat. Assn. Applied Psychology (pres. div. polit. psychology 1990—), Interam. Soc. Psychology (gov. 1972-73, pres. 1976-79, Interam. Psychology award 1983), Internat. Soc. Polit. Psychology (Sanford award 1983, pres. 1985-86), Peace Sci. Soc. (pres. 1975-76), Internat. Soc. Ednl. Cultural Scientific Interchanges (Fourth Annual award 1976), Psychologists for Scoial Responsibility (pres. 1990—, award for best theoretical rsch. article in peace psychology 1989), Council Fgn. Relations. Home: 984 Memorial Dr Cambridge MA 02138-5741

KELMAN, STEVEN JAY, management educator; b. N.Y.C., May 1, 1948; s. Kurt and Sylvia (Etman) K.; m. Shelley Metzenbaum, July 5, 1980; children: Jody, Leora. AB summa cum laude, Harvard Coll., 1970; PhD, Harvard U., 1978. Asst. prof. pub. policy Harvard U., 1978-80; with Federal Trade Commn., Washington, 1980-81; assoc. prof. and prof. pub. mgmt. Harvard U., 1982-93, 97—; adminstr. Office of Fed. Procurement Policy, Washington, 1993-97. Democrat. Jewish. Office: Harvard Univ JFK Sch of Government Cambridge MA 02138

KELMENSON, LEO-ARTHUR, advertising executive; b. N.Y.C., Jan. 3, 1927; s. Joseph A. and Ruth (Rothberg) K.; m. Gayle Frances Abrams, Sept. 1989; children from previous marriage: Todd-Arthur, Joel Adam. B.S., Columbia U., 1951; postgrad., Grad. Sch. Bus., 1952. From TV prodn. to sr. v.p., asst. to pres. Lennen & Newell, 1951-65; exec. v.p., mem. exec. com. Norman Craig & Kummel, 1965-66; sr. v.p., dir., mem. exec. com. Kenyon & Eckhardt, 1967-68, chmn., chief exec. officer, 1968-86; chmn. Bozell, Jacobs, Kenyon & Eckhardt, 1986-93, chmn. exec. com.; chmn. Bozell Worldwide; chmn. bd. advisors, chmn. devel. com. Tisch Sch of Arts NYU, 1988—; chmn. Bozell de Mexico, 1992; pres. Kelmenson Funds Ltd.; dir. Lorimar, Locations Unltd., On-Line Software Internat.; bd. trustees Am. Cinematheque; lectr. New Sch. Social Rsch.; Adviser communications office U.S. Atty. Gen., 1960-63; spl. project officer Dept. State, 1952-64; co-founder, v.p., dir. African Med. and Rsch. Found., 1957—. Author: (poetry) Epilogue, 1964; also short stories. Mem. pub. rels. com. Nat. Cancer Found., 1958—; adv. com. Nat. Cultural Center, 1962; pres. Shoes for Little Souls, 1960, Remsenburg Assn., 1968; bd. dirs. ASPCA, Stop Cancer Found., 1990, 91; mem. pres.'s adv. coun. Am. Diabetes Assn., 1977-78. Served with USMCR, World War II. Recipient Theodore Roosevelt Man of Year award, 1955; Silver Quill Poetry award, 1955; Res. Officers Assn. award, 1965; Guggenheim World Peace award, 1951; Am. Jewish Com. Humanitarian award; Humanitarian award St. Frances Cabrini. Mem. U.S. Olympic Com., N.Y. Advt. Club, Soc. Am. Businessmen Club, Sigma Phi Epsilon. Clubs: Sands Point, Ocean Reef, Key Largo, Sands Point Yacht, L.I. Polo, U.S. Yacht Racing Assn. (N.Y.). Office: NYU Tisch Sch Arts New York NY 10003*

KELPE, PAUL ROBERT, engineer, consultant; b. St. Louis, July 6, 1948; s. Robert Frederick and Doris Jean (Wood) K.; m. Janice Pauline Frey, Apr. 10, 1971; children: Brian Paul, Mark Robert. BA, Ottawa U., 1970; MS, U. Nebr., 1973; diploma in energy mgmt., Va. Poly. Inst., 1985. Cert. tchr., Nebr. Stationery engr. King Louie Corp., Overland Park, Kans., 1967-70; head tchr. sci. dept. Westside Community Schs., Omaha, 1970-81, energy dir., 1981-92; apptd. mem. Nebr. Energy Coun., 1991-99; sci. instr. Westside Middle Sch. Contbr. articles to profl. jours. Troop com. chmn. Boy Scouts Am., Omaha, 1987-92; bd. trustees Sanitary and Improvement Dist., 1980-84; candidate Sub-Dist. 7 PNRD, Omaha, 1988-89; mem. Gov.'s Energy Policy Coun., 1991-92. Recipient Energy award State of Nebr., 1987; grantee Nebr. Energy Office, 1982-92. Mem. ASHRAE (award 1988), Nebr. Acad. Scis., Nat. Sci. Tchrs. Assn., Nebr. State Tchr. Assn., NEA, Phi Delta Kappa. Republican. Lutheran. Avocations: camping, boating, swimming, water skiing, scuba diving. Office: Westside Community Schs 909 S 76th St Omaha NE 68114-4599

KELSALL, DAVID CHARLES, otologist; b. Denver, May 28, 1957. MD, U. Colo. Sch. Med., 1984. Diplomate Am. Bd. Otolaryngologist. Resident in gen. surgery St. Joseph Hosp., Denver, 1984-89; resident in otolaryngology U. Colo. Health Sci. Ctr., Denver, 1986-90; fellowship in neurotology Denver Ear Inst., 1990-91; surgeon Swedish Hosp., Englewood, Co.; clin. faculty U. Colo. Health Sci. Ctr. Mem. AMA, Am. Neurotology Soc., Am. Acad. Otolaryn. Head and Neck, Colo. Med. Soc., Denver Med. Soc. Office: Denver Ear Assocs 799 E Hampden Ave Ste 510 Englewood CO 80110-2777

KELSAY, BRUCE D., school psychologist; b. Ganado, Ariz., Apr. 17, 1957; s. William Martin and Jeri Diane (Kuester) K.; m. Mary Martha Moran, June 23, 1990; children: Kristen Marie, McKenna Kathleen. BA, Ill. State U., Normal, 1979, MS, 1983; MEd, No. Ill. U., 1997. Nat. cert. sch. psychologist; cert. sch. svcs. pers., Ill. Program ops. specialist U.S. Dept. HHS, Washington, 1980; sch. psychologist Villa Park (Ill.) Elem. Dist. 45, 1984-86, DuPage H.S. Dist. 88, Addison, Ill., 1986—. Mem. Nat. Assn. Sch. Psychologists, Ill. Sch. Psychol. Assn. (dir. Region 1, 1987-91, registration chair 1984—). Avocations: athletic training, computer technology. Office: Addison Trail HS 213 N Lombard Rd Addison IL 60101-1906

KELSAY, DAVID ROLAND, chemist; b. Clinton, Mo., July 25, 1955; s. Ralph Waldo and Mary Fern K.; m. Joyce Elaine Hopkins, Oct. 22, 1983; children: Rebecca Sue, Rachael Anne. BA in Chemistry, William Jewell Coll., 1977. Lab. tech. Upsher Labs., Kansas City, 1978-80; process attendant Kansas City Power & Light, Clinton, Mo., 1980-86; plant chemist, 1986—. State committeeman Mo. Rep. Party, 1992—, congrl. dist. chmn., 1994-98, county com. chmn., 1988-98, county com. sec., 1998—. Baptist. Avocations: sports, reading, geneology, civil war studies. E-mail: jkelsay@earthlink.net. Home: 901 Willow Clinton MO 64735 Office: Kansas City Power & Light 400 Southwest Hwy P Clinton MO 64735

KELSCH, JOAN MARY, elementary education educator; b. Allentown, Pa., Jan. 19, 1953; d. Paul Thomas and Dorothy Mildred (Grim) Reichart; m. William Joseph Kelsch, July 27, 1974; children: Daniel, Dorothy. BS, West Chester (Pa.) State Coll., 1974. Cert. tchr., Pa. Elem. tchr. St. Francis Acad., Bally, Pa., 1974-79, 86—, substitute tchr., 1979-82, establisher, tchr. kindergarten, 1982-86, coord. reading, 1976-79, coord. religion, 1986—, mentor tchr., 1986-87; coord. Rainbows Peer Support Program, 1993-95; mem., chairperson Mid. States Evaluation Coms., 1986-87, 98-99; playground supr. Bally Recreation Com., summer 1990, pool mgr., summer 1991; trained mem. IST, 1995. Mem. ASCD, Nat. Cath. Edn. Assn., Internat. Reading Assn., Home and Sch. Assn. (faculty rep.), Tri-County Reading Assn., Allentown Diocese Assn. Lay Tchrs. Avocations: reading, sewing, travel, collecting, crafts. Home: 331 Main St Bally PA 19503 Office: Saint Francis Acad 7th And Pine Sts Bally PA 19503

KELSEY, ANN LEE, library administrator; b. Kokomo, Ind., June 20, 1946; d. Harry Willard and JoAnn Kelsey. BA in Anthropology and English cum laude, U. Calif., Riverside, 1968; MLS, UCLA, 1969. Adminstrv. libr. U.S. Army Spl. Svcs., Cam Ranh Bay, Vietnam, 1969-70; children's libr. Elmont (N.Y.) Meml. Libr., 1970-71; libr. Queensborough Pub. Libr., Jamaica, N.Y., 1971-73; children's libr. Upper Saddle River (N.J.) Pub. Libr., 1973-75; prin. libr. Morris County Libr., Whippany, N.J., 1975-83; assoc. dir. Learning Resource Ctr., County Coll. Morris, Randolph, N.J., 1983—; networked assoc. fellow 60s workgroup Inst. for Advanced Tech. in Humanities, U. Va., 1994—; ptnr., cons. libr. automation and planning DocuMentors, Rockaway, N.J., 1985—; ind. cons. infosys., Whippany, 1978—. Co-author: Planning for Automation: A How-To-Do-It Manual for Librarians, 1993, 2d edit., 1997; contbr. chpt. to: Insider's Guide to Library Automation, 1993; editor: Resources for Teaching the Vietnam War: An Annotated Guide, rev. edit., 1996; also articles. V.p. Project: Hearts and Minds, Inc., Greenwich, Conn., 1995; bd. dirs. N.J. Vietnam Vets. Oral History Project, Kean U., 1998; mem. edn. adv. com. N.J. Vietnam Vets. Meml. Found., Vietnam Era Ednl. Ctr., 1998; mem. Morris County Dem. com., 1992. Named to honor roll Vietnam Women's Meml. Project, Washington, 1993. Mem. ALA (travel grantee 1988), Am. Soc. Info. Sci., Spl. Librs. Assn. (pres. N.J. chpt. 1989-90, chairperson cataloging com. 1992-93), N.J. Libr. Assn. (chairperson automated libr. svcs. sect. 1992-93, mem. pers. adminstrn. com. 1986-87, mem. pay equity task force 1985-86), Phi Beta Kappa. Avocations: bicycling, Internet, gardening. Office: DocuMentors 7 Valley View Dr Rockaway NJ 07866-1506

KELSEY, CLYDE EASTMAN, JR., philosophy and psychology educator; b. Wadena, Minn., Mar. 30, 1924; s. Clyde Eastman and Lorraine (Lamb) Bagley) K.; m. Betty Jean Williams, Apr. 1, 1949 (dec.); children: Becky Kelsey Marcin, Nancy Kelsey Eargle; m. Jamie Lee Reagan, 1987. B.A., U. Tex., El Paso, 1948; M.A., U. Tulsa, 1951; Ph.D., U. Denver, 1960; hon. degree, U. de Oriente, Venezuela, 1969. Dir. counseling bur. U. Tex., El Paso, 1951-61, prof., head dept. philosophy, psychology, 1961-62, vice chmn. dept. philosophy and psychology, 1951-61; dean students, dir. Inter-Am. Inst., 1962-66; program adv. Venezuela, Ford Found., 1966-69; vice chancellor public affairs U. Denver, 1969-72; v.p. devel. and univ. relations Tex. Tech U., Lubbock, 1972-81, prof. edn., 1981-88, prof. emeritus, 1988—; sr. rsch. fellow Nat. Center Higher Edn. Mgmt., 1983-87; lectr. 4th Army U.S., 1961-65; cons. U.S. Dept. State, Peace Corps, 1961-66; mem. adv. bd. Kans. Wesleyan Coll., 1960-71; vis. scientist NSF, 1962-66; v.p. Colo. Ptnrs. of Alliance, 1971-73; examiner, cons. Tex. State Bd. of Examiners of Psychologists, 1992-98; cons. Agy. for Internat. Devel., Coll. Bd., Civil Svc. Commn., World Bank to India, Saudi Arabia, Turkey, Republic of Mauritius. Contbr. articles to profl. jours. Bd. dirs. El Paso Mental Health Assn., 1951-58, pres. 1953-55; bd. dirs. El Paso Sch. Retarded Children, 1952-57, pres., 1953-55; bd. dirs. Lubbock Goodwill Industries, 1972-85, v.p., 1973-77, pres., 1978-80; bd. dirs. St. Mary's Hosp. Found., 1986—, chmn., 1994-96. With USNR, 1942-45. Decorated Order San Carlos Republic Colombia, 1964; recipient Disting. Alumni Service award U. Denver, 1972; Fulbright scholar Colombia, 1960-61. Fellow Tex. Acad. Sci.; mem. APA, Tex. Psychol. Assn., Phi Beta Delta. Home: 3722 63rd Dr Lubbock TX 79413-5310

KELSEY, EDITH JEANINE, psychotherapist, consultant; b. Freeport, Ill., Oct. 15, 1937; d. John Melvin and Florence Lucille (Ewald) Anderson; divorced; children: Steven Craig, Kevin John. Student, Pasadena Coll., 1955-58; BA in Psychology, Calif. State U., San Jose, 1980; MA in Counseling Psychology, Santa Clara U., 1984. Lic. marriage, family and child counselor. Counselor, cons., cert. trainer Values Tech., Santa Cruz, Calif., 1981—, dir. research, 1982-84; intern in counseling Sr. Residential Services, San Jose, 1983-84; psychotherapist Process Therapy Inst., Los Gatos, Calif., 1983-86, Sexual Abuse Treatment Ctr., San Jose, 1984-87; cons. in field, Santa Clara Valley, 1982-89; trainer, cons. Omega Assoc., 1987-92; teaching asst. Santa Clara U., 1997—, supr. interns counseling high-risk students, 1997-98; pvt. practice psychotherapy, cons., tng., 1987—. Contbr. articles to profl. jours. Vol. Parental Stress Hotline, Palo Alto, Calif., 1980-85. Mem. Am. Assn. Marriage and Family Therapists, Am. Soc. Aging, Calif. Assn. Marriage and Family Therapists (clin.), Palo Alto C. of C. Democrat. Presbyterian. Avocations: skiing, hiking. Home: 431 Casita Ct Los Altos CA 94022-1774 Office: 153 Forest Ave Palo Alto CA 94301-1615

KELSEY, FRANCES OLDHAM (MRS. FREMONT ELLIS KELSEY), government official; b. Cobble Hill, Vancouver Island, Can., July 24, 1914; came to U.S., 1936, naturalized, 1956; d. Frank Trevor and Katherine (Stuart) Oldham; m. Fremont Ellis Kelsey, Dec. 6, 1943; children—Susan Elizabeth, Christine Ann. B.Sc., McGill U., 1934, M.Sc., 1935; Ph.D., U. Chgo., 1938, M.D., 1950. Instr., asst. prof. pharmacology U. Chgo., 1938-50; editorial assoc. AMA, Chgo., 1950-52; assoc. prof. pharmacology U. S.D., 1954-57; med. officer FDA, Washington, 1960-63, chief investigational drug br., 1963-66, dir. divsn. oncology and radiopharm. drug products, 1966-67; dir. divsn. sci. investigations Office of Compliance, FDA, Rockville, Md., 1967-95, dep. for sci. and medicine Office of Compliance, 1995—. Author: (with F.E. Kelsey, E.M.K. Geiling) Essentials of Pharmacology, 1960. Recipient Pres.'s award for Distinguished Fed. Civilian Service (refusal to approve coml. distbn. thalidomide in U.S.), 1962. Mem. Am. Soc. Pharmacology and Exptl. Therapeutics, Am. Med. Writers Assn., Teratology Soc., Sigma Xi, Sigma Delta Epsilon. Office: FDA Office of Compliance 7520 Standish Pl Rockville MD 20855-2730*

KELSEY, STERETT-GITTINGS, sculptor; b. Greenwich, Conn., Dec. 16, 1941; 2 children. BFA in Sculpture, RISD, 1964. crw. Represented in permanent collections Hirschhorn Mus., Nat. Art Mus. of Sport, Royal Porcelain Mus., Hakone Open-air Mus., Stamford Ctr., Westchester Capital Corp., McDonald Corp., Doral Corp, Pegasus Venture Capital, Pepsi Cola Co., Georgetown U. Intercultural Ctr., Choate Rosemary Hall Sch., Garrison Forest Sch., McGhee Libr., Stamford Ctr. Performing Arts, Anne Norton Mus. Home: PO Box 300 Cross River NY 10518-0300

KELSO, DAVID WILLIAM, fine arts publishing executive, artist; b. Van Nuys, Calif., Jan. 29, 1948; s. William Joseph and Elsa Estra (Scipione) K.; m. Christine Barone Mehling, June 19, 1983. BA, U. Calif., Riverside, 1969; postgrad., U. Calif., Berkeley, 1970. Printer El Dorado Press, Berkeley, 1972-78, Crown Point Press, Oakland, Calif., 1978-79; dir., printer Made in California Editions, Oakland, Calif., 1980—. Author: (catalog) Small Wonders, 1997. Recipient purchase award N.W. Internat. Small Format Print Exhbn., Seattle, 1978, juror's award Berkeley (Calif.) Art Ctr., 1991; purchase award L.A. Printmaking Soc., juror's award, 1999; purchase award Portland (Oreg.) Art Mus., 1997, Best of Show award Hand-Pulled Prints VII, Tex., 1999. Mem. Rutgers Archives for Printmaking Studios, Vicente Dance Club. Avocations: social dancing, backpacking, hiking. Office: Made in Calif Intaglio Edits 3246 Ettie St Ste 16 Oakland CA 94608-4016

KELSO, FRANK BENTON, II, naval officer; b. Fayetteville, Tenn., July 11, 1933; s. Thomas Benton and Wista (Muse) K.; m. Landess McCown, June 6, 1956; children: Thomas Benton II, Robert Donald, Mary Kelso Kearns, Kerry Kelso Ward. BS, U.S. Naval Acad., 1956. Commd. ensign USN, 1956, advanced through grades to adm., 1980; with USN/NATO, 1983, Office Sec. of the Navy, 1983; comdr. U.S. Sixth Fleet, 1985-86; comdr.-in-chief U.S. Atlantic Fleet, Norfolk, Va., 1986-88; Supreme Allied comdr., Atlantic comdr.-in-chief Atlantic Command, Norfolk, 1988-90; chief naval ops. Washington, 1990-94; ret., 1994.

KELSO, GWENDOLYN LEE, silver appraiser, consultant; b. Washington, Jan. 5, 1935; d. Leon Hugh and Katherine Estelle (Henderson) K. Mgr. Shaw & Brown Co., Washington, 1967-71, Chas. Schwartz & Son, Washington, 1972-76; silver appraiser Washington, 1976—; ptnr. The Silver Lion, Washington, 1983-85; owner, mgr. The Rampant Lion, Washington, 1985—; cons. FBI and law enforcement agys. and ctrs., 1982—; cataloguer, conservator his. silver belonging to USN and U.S. Naval Acad., 1987—; appraiser presentation silver aboard U.S. Naval vessels and at installations, 1986—; cataloguer, conservator silver Forbes mag. collection, N.Y.C., 1989; mem. USS Alexandria Commissioning Com., 1990, USS Maryland Commissioning Com., 1993; conservator State of Md. for preservation battleship USS Maryland presentation silver, 1990—; instr. USN pers. for care and maintenance preservation silver; guest curator Washington Nat. Cathedral, 1997-98. Author: God's Treasures At Risk?, 1999, United States Navy Presentation Silver-A History and a Manual for its Care and Preservation, 1989, Silver Reflections an American Naval History, 1991 (exhbn. catalogue) Silver for Sacred Spaces—Four centuries of Ecclesiastical Silver from the Judeo-Christian Tradition, Washington Nat. Cathedral, 1998. Mem. NAFE, Internat. Soc. Appraisers (scholar 1989), Am. Soc. Appraisers (sr.), Appraisers Assn. Am., N.Y. Silver Soc., Silver Soc. (London), U.S. Naval Inst., Navy League U.S., Newcomen Soc. U.S. Republican. Episcopalian. Avocations: writing, travel, sewing, volunteering. Home: 3731 39th St NW Washington DC 20016-5522 Office: The Rampant Lion PO Box 5887 Washington DC 20016-1487

KELSO, HAROLD GLEN, family practice physician; b. Newport, Ky., Apr. 1, 1929; s. Harold Glen and Alvina Marie (Hehl) K.; m. Janet Rae Cooper, Aug. 12, 1950; children: Harold Glen III, Susan Annette (Mrs. David Thomas Johnson). BS, U. Dayton, 1951; MD, St. Louis U., 1955. Diplomate Am. Bd. Family Practice. Intern St. Elizabeth Hosp., Dayton, Ohio, 1955-56; pvt. practice Centerville, Ohio, 1956-94; mem. teaching staff St. Elizabeth Hosp., Dayton; mem. staff Kettering (Ohio) Meml. Hosp., chief staff, 1975-76, chief dept. family practice; chief staff Sycamore Med. Ctr., 1978-79; clin. prof. family practice, Wright State U., clin. prof. emeritus, 1994—; mem. faculty Kettering Coll. Med. Arts; med. dir. Kettering Convalescent Ctr. Pres., vice mayor Centerville, 1960-62; pres. Bd. Edn. Centerville City Schs., 1969-72; trustee Western Ohio Found. Med. Care, Kettering Med. Ctr., Sycamore Med. Ctr., Engring. and Sci. Hall of Fame. Named Ohio Family Physician of Yr. Ohio Acad. Family Physicians, 1990. Fellow Am. Acad. Family Practice; mem. AMA, Ohio Med. Assn., Montgomery County Med. Assn. (sec. 1970, pres. 1984), Order Ky. Cols., Dayton Racquet Club, Sugar Valley Country Club, Rotary (local pres. 1974-75, Paul Harris fellow 1979), Masons, Shriners. Republican. Methodist. Avocations: golf, fishing, rose gardening. Home: 2212 E Alex Bellbrook Rd Centerville OH 45459

KELSO, JOHN HODGSON, former government official; b. Iowa City, June 16, 1925; s. Edward Lewis and Eliza (Hodgson) K.; m. Marian Louise Towers, Aug. 22, 1948; 1 child, John T. B.A., State U. Iowa, 1949, M.A., 1950. Occupational research analyst Bur. Naval Personnel, Dept. Navy, Washington, 1951-55; orgn. and methods examiner Agr. Research Services, Dept. Agr., Washington, 1955-57; mgmt. analyst mgmt. adv. br. Bur. State Services, USPHS, HEW, Washington, 1957-58; chief survey group Bur. State Services, USPHS, HEW, 1958-60, chief mgmt. adv. br., 1960-62, asst. exec. officer, 1962-66; exec. officer USPHS, Bethesda, Md., 1966-68; asso. adminstr. mgmt. Health Services and Mental Health Adminstrn., 1968-73; dir. office regional operations USPHS, Office Asst. Sec. for Health, HEW, 1973-76; dep. adminstr. Health Services Adminstrn., 1976-81, acting adminstr., 1981-82; dep. adminstr. Health Resources and Services Adminstrn., 1982-94, acting adminstr., 1985-86, 88-89; cons. United Network for Organ Sharing, Richmond, Va., 1994—. Served with AUS, 1943-46. Recipient Superior Svc. award USPHS, 1969, Disting. Svc. award HEW, 1972, Presdl. Meritorious Rank award 1983, Disting. Presdl. Rank award 1989, Surgeon Gen.'s medallion, 1989. Mem. Sigma Alpha Epsilon. Methodist.

KELSO, LINDA YAYOI, lawyer; b. Boulder, Colo., Mar. 30, 1946; d. Nobutaka and Tai (Inui) Ike; m. William Alton Kelso, June 17, 1968. BA, Stanford U., 1968; MA, U. Wis., 1973; JD, U. Fla., 1979. Bar: Fla. 1980. Assoc. Mahoney, Hadlow & Adams, Jacksonville, Fla., 1979-82; assoc. Commander, Legler, Werber, Dawes, Sadler & Howell, Jacksonville, 1982-86, ptnr., 1986-91; ptnr. Foley & Lardner, Jacksonville, 1992—. Mem. ABA (bus. law sect.), Jacksonville Bar Assn., Phi Beta Kappa, Order of Coif. Avocations: music, gardening, cooking. Office: Foley & Lardner 200 N Laura St Jacksonville FL 32202-3500

KELSO, LYNN A., acute care nurse practitioner; b. Pitts., July 11, 1961; d. Harry Gladden and Colette Louise (Franz) K. BSN, W.Va. U., 1984; MSN, Case Western Res. U., 1991; CRNP, U. Pitts., 1993. RN, Pa., Ky.; cert. CCRN, ACLS; Acute Care Nurse Practitioner cert. specialist. Acute care nurse practitioner liver transplant ICU U. Pitts. Med. Ctr., Pitts., 1993-95; faculty ACNP program Chandler Med. Ctr., U. Ky., 1995—. Mem. AACN,

Soc. Critical Care Medicine, Sigma Theta Tau. Home: 1725 Fox Head Ct Lexington KY 40515-1318

KELSO, MARY JEAN, author; b. Eugene, Oreg., Nov. 27, 1938; d. Thomas Jasper and Eula Ethel (Warren) Williams; m. Byron Eugene Kelso Sr., June 30, 1956; children: Byron Jr., Bryon, Wendy Lynne Whiteman, Byron III. Editorial asst. Aster Pub., Springfield, Oreg., 1983-84; customer svcs. rep. El Jay divsn. Cedarapids Inc., Eugene, Oreg., 1984-95. Author, illustrator: Mystery of Virginia City, 1984, Abducted, 1986, Sierra Summer, 1992, A Virginia City Mystery, 1992; pub. Goodbye, Bodie, 1988. Avocations: travel, photography, painting. Address: PO Box 134 Springfield OR 97477-0022

KELSON, RICHARD B., lawyer; b. Pitts., Nov. 20, 1946. B in Polit. Sci., U. Pa.; JD, U. Pitts. Atty. Alcoa, Pitts., 1974-77, gen. atty., 1977-83, mng. gen. atty., 1983-84, asst. sec., mng. gen. atty., 1984-89, asst. gen. counsel, 1989-91, sr. v.p. environ. health and safety, 1991-94, exec. v.p. environ., health and safety, 1994-97, exec. v.p., CFO, 1997—. Bd. dirs. Alcoa Found., U. Pitts. Law Sch. Bd. Visitors, Conf. Bd. Coun. Fin. Execs., Pa. Bus. Roundtable; mem. Fin. Exec. Inst. the Officers Conf. Group, The Pvt. Sector Coun.'s CFPs. Mem. ABA, Pa. Econ. League (bd. govs.). Office: Alcoa 201 Isabella St Pittsburgh PA 15212-5858

KELTS, DAVID WILLIAM, elementary education educator; b. Loma Linda, Calif., Nov. 21, 1948; s. Donald Romayne and Beverly Oneida (Brandt) K. BA, Claremont McKenna Coll., 1970, cert., 1972. Tchr. grade 4 Carnelian Elem. Sch., Alta Loma, Calif., 1970-73; tchr. elem. grades Dept. Def. Dependents Schs., Sollars Sch., Misawa AFB, Japan, 1973-78, 88-95; tchr. grade 3 Dept. Def. Dependents Schs., Lajes Elem. Sch., Lajes AFB, Azores, 1978-79, Dept. Def. Dependents Schs., M. C. Perry Sch., Iwakuni, Japan, 1979-80; tchr. grade 5 Dept. Def. Dependents Schs., M. C. Perry Sch., Japan, 1980-88. Coach little league, Alta Loma, 1973; scoutmaster Cub Pack 941 Boy Scouts Am., Alta Loma, 1973; active base chapel coun., Iwakuni, 1981-88; lay leader base chapel, Misawa AFB, 1989-95; life mem. Carnelian Elem. Sch. PTA, Alta Loma. Recipient Human Goals award, Misawa AFB, 1976. Mem. Fed. Edn. Assn. (Pacific area dir. 1995—), N.E. Asia Tchrs. Assn. (officer 1981-85, 89-95, rep. 1993-94), Pacific Sci. Tchrs. Assn., Lajes Tchrs. Assn. Republican. Presbyterian. Avocations: travel, reading, cooking, computers, biking.

KELTZ, AMY LYNN, political science organization administrator; b. New Haven, Apr. 11, 1966; d. David Irwin and Sondra Lois (Ofstrock) Marshall; m. Ira Richard Keltz, July 13, 1991; children: Jennifer, Samuel. BA in French Lit., Johns Hopkins U., 1988; Am. Coll. in Paris, Gallaudet U., Y; student, Am. Coll. Paris, 1986, Gallaudet U., 1988. Cert. Fund Raising Exec., Nat. Soc. Fund Raising Execs. Dir. devel. Friendship Ho., Washington, 1990-92; sr. devel. assoc. Econ. Policy Inst., Washington, 1993-95; v.p., dir. devel. Inst. Women's Policy Rsch., Washington, 1996-98; exec. dir. Frederick B. Abramson Meml. Found., Washington, 1998—; fundraising cons. Ben Lomond Manor Ho., Manassas, Va., 1995—; profl. fundraising spkr., AAUW, Prince William, Va., 1997-98. Chair grants panel, Prince William County Arts Coun., 1994—; bd. mem., pub. rels., Prince William Chorale, Manassas, 1993-99; participant Cmty. Leadership Inst., Prince William County, 1994; bd. mem., sec. Prince William Com. of 100, 1995—, bd. mem. Vpstart Crow, Manassas, 1999—; mem. 2d Decade Soc., Johns Hopkins U., 1998—. Mem. Nat. Soc. Fund Raising Execs., Am. Soc. Assn. Execs., Ind. Sector, Washington Regional Assn. Grantmakers, Nat. Ctr. Responsive Philanthropy. Office: The Frederick B Abramson Meml Found 1025 Conn Ave NW Ste 400 Washington DC 20036-5405

KEM, RICHARD SAMUEL, retired army officer; b. Richmond, Ind., Aug. 9, 1934; s. Charles Edward and Janice Allene (Beard) K.; m. Ann Callahan, May 7, 1960; children: Michelle, John Samuel, Steven Edward. B.S., U.S. Mil. Acad., 1956; MS in Civil Engring., U. Ill., 1962; M.S. in Internat. Affairs, George Washington U., 1972; postgrad., Naval War Coll., 1972, Northwestern U., 1979, Harvard U., 1983. Commd. 2d lt. U.S. Army, 1956, advanced through grades to maj. gen., 1984; comdg. officer 577th Engr. Bn. Vietnam, 1968-69; staff, faculty U.S. Mil. Acad., West Point, N.Y., 1969-71; staff officer Mil. Personnel Center, 1972-74, Office Army Chief Staff, 1974-75; chief public affairs Office Chief Engrs., 1975-76; comdg. officer 7th Engr. Brigade, Germany, 1976-78; chief installations and constrn. U.S. Army Europe, 1978-79; dep. asst. chief engrs., 1979-80; dep. dir. civil works Office Chief Engrs., 1980; comdr., div. engr. Ohio River div., 1981-84; bd. engrs. Rivers and Harbors, 1982-84, Mississippi River Commn., 1982-84; comdg. gen. U.S. Army Engr. Sch. and Fort Belvoir, Va., 1984-87; dep. chief of staff, engr. U.S. Army, Europe, 1987-88, chief of staff, 1988-89; dep. chief of engrs. Washington, Washington, 1989-90; ret., 1990; dir. pub. works Arlington (Va.) County, 1990—. Decorated DSM with oak leaf cluster, Legion of Merit with oak leaf cluster, Bronze Star. Mem. ASCE, Soc. Am. Mil. Engrs., Am. Def. Preparedness Assn., Army Engr. Assn. (bd. dirs. 1992—), Am. Pub. Works Assn. (bd. dirs. 1989-90). Episcopalian. Office: Arlington County 2100 Clarendon Blvd Arlington VA 22201-5445

KEMBLE, PENN, government official; m. Marie-Louise Caravatti. BA, U. Colo., 1962. Program dir. League for Indsl. Democracy, 1963-69; chmn. Frontlash, Inc., 1969-72; spl. asst., speech writer Senator Patrick Moynahan of N.Y., 1978-79; producer, writer WETA-TV, Washington, 1979-81; pres. Prodemca, 1981-88; mem. Bd. for Internat. Broadcasting, 1991-93; dep. dir. USIA, 1993-99, acting dir., 1999—; Bd. dirs. Dem. Inst. for Internat. Affairs; mem. radio programs adv. coun. USIA. Contbr. articles to Commentary, The New Republic, N.Y. Times, Washington Post. Office: USIA 301 4th St SW Washington DC 20547-0009*

KEMELHOR, ROBERT E(LIAS), mechanical engineer; b. N.Y.C., May 19, 1919; m. Shirley P. Tennen; children: Judith Ellen, Joel Martin, Barry Alan. Student Pre-Law, Bklyn. Coll., 1936-38; BSME, George Washington U., 1949. Registered profl. engr., Washington. Sr. draftsman Bur. Ships Navy Dept., Washington, 1940-43, design engr. Bur. Ordnance, 1943-46, sr. engr. head weapon launching sect. Bur. Aeros., 1946-53; chief engr. design, devel. prodn. McLean Devel. Labs., Copiague, N.Y., 1953-58; dir. rsch. and devel. Pesco Products div. Borg-Warner Corp., Bedford, Ohio, 1958; with applied physics lab. Johns Hopkins U., Laurel, Md., 1958-91; program mgr. John Hopkins U., Laurel, 1982-85, chief engr. tech. svcs. dept., 1986-91; pvt. practice cons. Bethesda, 1991—; cons. Advanced Tech. and Mfg. Enterpirse Programs, Nat. Inst. Stds. and Tech., U.S. Dept. Commerce, Aeronautics Indsl. Tech. Program, NASA/JPL. Numerous patents in field; contbr. articles to profl. jours. U.S. del. Internat. Standards Orgn. Subcom., Mfg. Automation. Fellow AIAA (assoc.); mem. AAAS (sr. mem.), Soc. Mfg. Engrs. (sr. mem., chmn. Washington chpt. No. 48), Sigma Tau, Tau Beta Pi. Home: 6211 Redwing Ct Bethesda MD 20817-5914

KEMENT, ISABELLA VINICONIS, retired construction company executive; b. Sept. 9, 1923; d. Paul and Mary (Karsokas) Viniconis; married Stanley J. Kement, Feb. 6, 1943; children: Stanley J. Jr., Joan Kement Turbie. Owner, mgr. tobacco farm, 1943-45; bookkeeper, dispatcher, sec., owner Kement Constrn. Co. Inc., Broad Brook, Conn., 1945-70; owner, bookkeeper, mgr., builder E-Z Living Suites, Broad Brook, 1959-84; owner restaurant and hotel, 1959-65; ptnr. Kement Park Landfill and Gravel, Broad Brook, 1947—; sec. Kement Devel. Corp.; mgr., pres., bookkeeper Apt. Complex, Broad Brook, 1959-84; ptnr. Depot St. Gravel Pit; pres. Manor House, Inc., 1959-84, E-Z Living Suite, 1959-84. Mem. bd. North Cen. Health Dist.; mem. ch. coun. and social coms., Broad Brook, 1985-87; Cath. Christian Doctrine tchr. Recipient First Place trophy East Windsor Bicentennial Parade, 1968. Mem. Tobacco Valley Art Assn., Univ. of Third Age. Roman Catholic. Avocations: line dancing, traveling, art, craft design, gardening. Home: 307 North Rd Broad Brook CT 06016-9607

KEMENYFFY, STEVEN, artist, art educator; b. Budapest, Hungary, Aug. 18, 1943; came to U.S., 1951; s. Joseph and Elizabeth (Gosztony) K.; m. Susan Berenice Hale, Oct. 5, 1968; 1 child, Maya. BA, Augustana Coll., Rock Island, Ill., 1965; MA, U. Iowa, 1966, MFA, 1967. Instr. U. Iowa, Iowa City, 1966-67, U. Wis., Whitewater, 1967-69; prof. ceramics Edinboro U. of Pa., 1969—; lectr., workshop presenter; vis. lectr. Nat. Ceramics '88, Wellington, New Zealand, 1988, Internat. Exptl. Ceramic Studio, Kecskemet, Hungary, 1989, Lucia Bittencourt Studio, San Paulo, Brazil, 1989, C.L.A.Y., Phoenix Coll., 1990, Pottersupply Lucky Lambo, Bussum, Holland, 1990, Renwick Gallery of the Nat. Mus. of Am. Art, Smithsonian Instn., Washington, 1991, Fusion, Toronto, Can., 1991, Walnut Creek (Calif.) Civic Arts Edn., 1991, Ea. Ky. U., Richmond, 1992, Touchstone Ctr. for Arts, Pioneer Crafts Coun., Uniontown, Pa., 1993, Clay Factory Inc., Tampa, 1995; co-owner Swift Creek Pottery & Press, McKean, Pa. Exhibited in group shows at Cin. Art Mus., 1987, Craftsmen Potters Assn., London, 1987, New Zealand Soc. Potters, Inc., Wellington, 1988, NCECA, Kansas City, Mo., 1989, John Michael Kohler Art Ctr., Sheboygan, Wis., 1990, Craftsman's Gallery, Cleve., 1991, West Chester (Pa.) U., 1992, Claytrade, Portland, Oreg., 1992., Kipp Gallery-Ind. U. Pa., 1992, Duncan Gallery, Deland, Fla., 1993, Invitational U. Ctrl. Fla., Orlando, 1995, Vigado Galeria, Budapest, 1997, Tolgyfa Galeria, Budapest, 1997, Miller Gallery, Cin., 1997, 5 at the Hungarian Cultural Ctr., Cleve., 1997, Carnegie Mus. Art, Pitts., 1998, San Angelo (Tex.) Mus. Fine Arts, 1998, others; represented in permanent collections at Smithsonian Instn., Washington, Kaiser Permanente Med. Ctr., Irvine, Calif., Everson Mus. Art, Syracuse, N.Y., Ubukata Industries Co., Inc., Nagoya, Japan, Carnegie Mus. Art, others. Avocations: landscape gardening. Home: 4570 Old State Rd Mc Kean PA 16426-2239 Office: U Pa Edinboro Dept Ceramics Edinboro PA 16412

KEMETHER, EILEEN, psychiatrist; b. Staten Island, N.Y., Mar. 25, 1952; d. Fred Martin and Patricia Elizabeth (Hough) K. BA cum laude, East Stroudsburg State U., 1972; MA, The New Sch., 1978; MS, Pace U., 1980; MD, Mt. Sinai Sch. Medicine, 1992. Receptionist to chmn. of bd. IBM, N.Y.C., 1969-70; sec. Pfizer, Inc., N.Y.C., 1970-72; office mgr. Canada Life, N.Y.C., 1974-75; receptionist, sec. Nat. Forge Co., N.Y.C., 1975-78; nurse practitioner Goldwater Meml. Hosp., Roosevelt Island, N.Y., 1980-88; intern in internal medicine Elmhurst Hosp., 1992; intern in neurology Bronx VA, 1992; intern in psychiatry Mt. Sinai Hosp., N.Y.C., 1993, resident in psychiatry, 1993-96; attending psychiatrist (part time) Mt. Sinai Hosp. Psychiat. Emergency Room, 1996-98; assoc. Mt. Sinai Sch. Medicine, N.Y.C., 1996-99; psychiatrist, rschr. Med. Rsch. Network, N.Y.C., 1997; rsch. fellow Pilgrim Psychiat. Ctr., 1998-99; pvt. practice N.Y.C., 1996—; rsc. fellow Pilgrim Psychiat. Ctr., 1998—. Mem. Am. Psychiat. Assn. Office: Ste 2C 903 Park Ave New York NY 10021

KEMME, DAVID MICHAEL, economics educator; b. Cin., Nov. 12, 1950; s. Raymond J. and Velma Mae (Cushing) K.; m. Jan L. Hess, Dec. 17, 1976; children: Sarah Kathryn, Lindsay Rae. BA in Math., Miami U., Oxford, Ohio, 1973; MA in Econs., Ohio State U., 1975, PhD in Econs., 1980. With Wharton E.F. Assocs., 1979-81, SRI Internat., Washington and Arlington, Va., 1979-81, FAO, Rome, 1984, The Rand Corp., Santa Monica, Calif., 1985; asst. prof. econs. Wichita (Kans.) State U., 1986-88, assoc. prof., 1988-89, prof., 1991-94; dir. econs. program Inst. for East-West Studies, N.Y.C., 1989-91; disting. fellow Mitsui Rsch. Inst., Tokyo, 1991; prof. econs., Morris prof. intrnat. econs. U. Memphis, 1994—, interim chmn., 1996-97, dir. Internat. MBAs, 1994-97; cons. IBRD, Washington, 1990-91; vis. prof. U. Warsaw, Poland, 1992; scholar-in-residence Pew Charitable Trusts, Pa., 1989-91. Mem. bd. editors Comparative Econ. Studies, 1994-97, Atlantic Econ. Jour., 1998—; contbr. articles to profl. jours., including Jour. Comparative Econs., Soviet Studies, So. Econs. Jour. Rsch. grantee Nat. Coun. for Soviet and Ea. Europe, 1987-88; Fulbright scholar, 1991-92. Mem. Memphis World Affairs Coun. (bd. dirs. 1995-98), Econ. Club Memphis (exec. dir. 1998—). Home: 1822 Hartwell Mnr N Collierville TN 38017-0827 Office: U Memphis 405 Fogelman College Bus Memphis TN 38152

KEMMERER, DENNIS ALLEN, artist, educator; b. Phila., Nov. 24, 1956; s. Allen Henry and Angelina Marie (Longhi) K.; m. Magdalena Maria Martinez, June 24, 1989. AA, Del Mar Coll., 1977; BA, Corpus Christi State U., 1980; MFA, Stephen F. Austin State U., 1984. Cert. tchr., Tex. Substitute tchr. Corpus Christi Ind. Sch. Dist., 1979-80, paraprofl., 1980-81; grad. asst. Stone Fort Mus. Stephen F. Austin State U., Nacogdoches, Tex., 1981-83, grad. asst. art dept., 1982-84; substitute tchr. Corpus Christi Ind. Sch. Dist., 1985-87; adj. art instr. Del Mar Coll., Corpus Christi, 1986—; art specialist Chula Vista Acad. Fine Arts, Corpus Christi, 1987—, coord. tchr. Russian Art Exch.; adj. art instr. Tex. A&M U., Corpus Christi, 1998—; mem. ad hoc peer panel review com. Mcpl. Art Commn., Corpus Christi, 1998; mem. facility planning com. South Tex. Inst. Arts, 1998; mem. textbook adoption subcom. art: grades 1-5. One person exhbn. drawings and sculpture: Recent Works on Paper and Relief Sculpture, 1996, Recent Work 1993-94, 1994, Sculpture and Works on Board/Paper, 1992, Introductions 85, 1985, (drawings) Scape/Facade Series, 1984, Scape Series 1982, 1983. Mem. art journey's task force Art Mus. South Tex., 1996; mem. mcpl. arts commn. peer-panel rev. com. City of Corpus Christi, 1996; mem. Arts and Cultural Commn., 1999—; subcom. mem. Cultural ARts Devel. Facility, Corpus Christi, 1999. Recipient Program Stds. award Nat. Art Edn. Assn., 1992-93. Mem. Am. Fedn. Tchrs. (bldg. steward 1987—), Tex. Art Edn. Assn. (coun.-at-large 1988). Home: 1001 Meadowbrook Dr Corpus Christi TX 78412-3345 Office: Chula Vista Acad Fine Arts 1761 Hudson St Corpus Christi TX 78416-1826

KEMMERER, PETER REAM, financial executive; b. N.Y.C., Dec. 20, 1942; s. Mahlon Sistie and Colette Noel (Fitch) K.; m. Lillian Reilly, Sept. 15, 1990. BS, Georgetown U., 1966; MBA, Am. U., 1970; MA, New Sch., 1975. Analyst corp. planning Otis Elevator Co., N.Y.C., 1971-74; mgr. fin. and adminstrn. bus. equipment div. SCM Corp., N.Y.C., 1975-80; pres. Mesa Verde, Inc., Cranbury, N.J., 1980—, also bd. dirs.; mng. ptnr. Jezel-Bezel Ptnrs., Cranbury, 1980—. Roman Catholic. Club: Princeton (N.Y.C.). Avocations: sailing, reading, sports. Office: 37 N Main St Cranbury NJ 08512-3203

KEMMERER, SHARON JEAN, computer systems analyst; b. Sellersville, Pa., Apr. 11, 1956; d. John Musselman and Esther Jone (Landis) K. BS, Shippensburg U., 1978; MBA, Marymount U., 1982. Mgmt. analyst Navy Internat. Logistics, Phila., 1978-81; computer systems analyst Navy Supply Sys. Commn., Crystal City, Va., 1981-86, Nat. Inst. Stds. and Tech., Gaithersburg, Md., 1986—; bd. dirs. ComSci, Derwood Sta., 1994-97; adult tutor, 1991-95; mem. diversity bd. Nat. Inst. Stds. and Tech., 1997—. Contbr. articles, poetry to newspapers; author publs. Moderator Lung Assn., Fairfax, Va., 1986; vol. Project Heart, Washington, 1986-87, Montgomery County Health Buddy, 1988—, Stepping Stones Shelter for Homeless, 1989-91, Pets on Wheels, 1994-96; deacon Alexandria (Va.) Ch., 1985-86, v.p. coun., 1985, ch. coun., 1995—. Lutheran. Avocations: renovation, tennis, antiques, volleyball. Office: Nat Inst Stds and Tech/Mfg Engring Lab Gaithersburg MD 20899

KEMMERLY, JACK DALE, retired state official, aviation consultant; b. El Dorado, Kans., Sept. 17, 1936; s. Arthur Allen and Eythel Louise (Throckmorton) K.; m. Frances Cecile Gregorio, June 22, 1958; children: Jack Dale Jr., Kathleen Frances, Grant Lee. BA, San Jose State U., 1962; cert. in real estate, UCLA, 1970; MPA, Golden Gate U., 1973; cert. labor-mgmt. rels., U. Calif., Davis, 1978; cert. orgnl. change, Stanford U., 1985. Right of way agt. Calif. Div. Hwys., Marysville, 1962-71; adminstrv. officer Calif. Dept. Transp., Sacramento, 1971-82; dist. dir. Calif. Dept. Transp., Redding, 1982-83; chief aeros. Calif. Dept. Transp., Sacramento, 1984-94; mgmt. cons. U.S. Dept. Transp., Riyadh, Saudi Arabia, 1983-84; mem. tech. adv. com. on aeronautics Calif. Transp. Commn. Bd. dirs. Yuba-Sutter Campfire Girls, 1972-73. With USN, 1954-57. Recipient superior accomplishment award Calif. Dept. Transp., 1981. Mem. Nat. Assn. State Aviation Ofcls. (nat. pres. 1989—), Am. Assn. State Hwy. and Transp. Ofcls. (aviation com. 1985-94), Calif. Assn. Aerospace Educators (adv. bd. 1984—), Calif. Assn. Airport Execs., Calif. Aviation Coun., Aircraft Owners and Pilots Assn. (Western regional rep.), Elks (exalted ruler Marysville, Calif. 1974-75). Republican. Roman Catholic. Avocations: non-partisan political activities, reading, flying. Office: 1285 Charlotte Ave Yuba City CA 95991-2803

KEMMETT, WILLIAM JOSEPH, poet, educator; b. Boston, Nov. 19, 1936; s. William J. and Mildred K.; m. Jacqueline B. Tompkins, Aug. 2, 1956; children: William III, Kimberley Ann, Christopher, John, Gerald. MFA, Norwich U., 1986; student, Harvard U., 1979-81. Author: Flesh of a New Moon, 1991, The Bradford Poems, 1996. Recipient Mass. Artists Found. award, 1979, 1st prize Yankee Mag. 1986, 2d prize, 1995, 3d prize, 1986, 95. Mem. Poetry Soc. Am., New Eng. Poetry Club (contest dir. 1978-82).

KEMMIS, DANIEL ORRA, cultural organization administrator, author; b. Fairview, Mont., Dec. 5, 1945; s. Orra Raymond and Lilly Samantha (Shidler) K.; m. Jeanne Marie Koester, June 9, 1978; children: Abraham, Samuel; children by previous marriage: Deva, John. BA, Harvard U., 1968; JD, U. Mont., 1978. Bar: Mont. 1978. State rep. Mont. Ho. of Reps., Helena, 1975-84, minority leader, 1981-82, Speaker of House, 1983-84; ptnr. Morrison, Jonkel, Kemmis & Rossbach, Missoula, 1978-80, Jonkel & Kemmis, 1981-84; mayor City of Missoula, Mont., 1990-96; dir. ctr. rocky mountain west Univ. Mont., Missoula, 1996—; cons. No. Lights Inst., Missoula, Mont., 1985-89; Kennedy fellow Inst. Politics Harvard U., 1998. Author: Community and the Politics of Place, 1990, The Good City and the Good life, 1995; contbr. articles to profl. jours. Candidate for chief justice Mont. Supreme Ct.; former mem. adv. bd. and bd. dirs. Nat. Civic League; mem. adv. bd. Pew Partnership for Civic Change, 1991-97, Brookings Instn. Ctr. Urban and Met. Policy, Snake River Inst.; chmn. leadership tng. coun. Nat. League Cities, 1992-94; bd. dirs. Charles F. Kettering Found., Inst. for Environ. & Natural Resources U. Wyo., Bolle Ctr. for People and Forests, U. Mont.; fellow Dallas Inst. for Humanities & Culture, 1991-98. presdl. appt. Am. Heritage Rivers Commn., 1998—. Inst. Politics fellow Kennedy Sch. Govt., Harvard LU., 1998; named Disting. Young Alumnus U. Mont., 1981, 100 Visionaries, Utne Reader, 1995; recipient Charles Frankel prize NEH, 1997, Disting. Achievement award, Soc. for Conservation Biology, 1997, Wallace Stegner award, Ctr. Am. West, 1998. Democrat. Home: 521 Hartman St Apt 10 Missoula MT 59802-4771 Office: U Mont Ctr Rocky Mountain West Missoula MT 59812-1158*

KEMP, ALSON REMINGTON, JR., lawyer, legal educator; b. Rossville, Ga., July 3, 1941; s. Alson R. Dorothy (Walters) K.; m. Martha Gudenrath, Aug. 7, 1967; children—Alson Remington, Colin T. B.S., U. Tenn., 1962; J.D., U. Cin., 1965. Bar: Tenn. 1965, Ohio 1965, Calif. 1970, U.S. Dist. Ct. (no. and cen. dists.) Calif. 1971, U.S. Ct. Appeals (9th cir.) 1971, U.S. Ct. Appeals (D.C. cir.) 1982. Asst. prof. Hancock Coll., Santa Maria, Calif., 1966-68; asst. prof. U. Tenn., Chattanooga, 1969; mem. Morgan & Garner, Chattanooga, 1968-70, Pillsbury, Madison & Sutro, San Francisco, 1970-75; ptnr. Pillsbury, Madison & Sutro, 1975—. Served to capt. USAF, 1965-68. Benwood Found. grantee, 1962-65. Fellow Am. Coll. Trial Lawyers; mem. ABA, Calif. Bar Assn., San Francisco Bar Assn., Bankers Club. Republican. Office: Pillsbury Madison & Sutro 235 Montgomery St # 540 San Francisco CA 94104-2902*

KEMP, ANTHONY MAYNARD, English educator; b. London, Apr. 14, 1956; came to U.S., 1976; s. Frederick George and Margaret (Heald) K. BA in Religious Studies and Philosophy, Northeastern Coll., 1978; MA in English Lit., Drew U., 1981; MPhil in English and Comparative Lit., Columbia U., 1984, PhD in English and Comparative Lit., 1989. Tutor, reader, rsch. asst. Columbia U., N.Y.C., 1981-83; editl. asst. Columbia U. Press, N.Y.C., 1981-82; rsch. assoc. Libr. of Am., N.Y.C., 1983-85; adj. instr. Pace U., N.Y.C., 1994; tchg. asst. Harvard U., Cambridge, Mass., 1984-88; asst. prof. U. So. Calif., L.A., 1988-94, assoc. prof. English, 1994—; lectr. in field. Author: the Estrangement of the Past: A Study in the Origins of Modern Historical Consciousness, 1991; contbr. articles, revs., poems and translations to profl. publs. Mem. MLA, Am. Comparative Lit. Assn. Office: U So Calif Taper Hall Rm 420 Los Angeles CA 90089-0354

KEMP, BARRETT GEORGE, lawyer; b. Dayton, Ohio, Feb. 22, 1932; s. Barrett M. and Gladys M. (Linkhart) K.; children: Becky A., Barrett George II; m. Shirley, 1997. BSC, Ohio U., 1954; JD, Ohio No. U., 1959. Bar: Ohio 1959. With FBI, 1959-61; mem. B.G. Kemp Law Firm, St. Marys, Ohio, 1961—; law dir. City of St. Marys, 1964-80. Sec., treas. Cmty. Improvement Corp., 1967-79; founder St. Marys Sister City, Inc.; founder, organizer sister city with Ho Kudan-cho, Japan, 1985. Recipient Outstanding Citizen award City of St. Marys, 1973, Builder of Bridges award St. Mary's C. of C., 1995. Mem. Ohio Bar Assn., Auglaize County Bar Assn., Rotary (v.p. 1968, pres. 1979, Lifetime achievement 1997, Four Aves. of Cvs. citation 1999), Masons, Shriners, Scottish Rite. Office: Ste 203 Cmty First Bank & Trust Bldg Saint Marys OH 45885

KEMP, BETTY RUTH, librarian; b. Tishomingo, Okla., May 5, 1930; d. Raymond Herrell and Mamie Melvina (Hughes) K. BA in Libr. Sci., U. Okla., 1952; MS, Fla. State U., 1965. Extramural loan libr. U. Tex., Austin, 1952-55; libr. lit. and history dept. Dallas Pub. Libr., 1955-56; head Oaklawn Br., 1956-60, Walnut Hill Br., 1960-64; dir. Cherokee Regional Libr., Lafayette, Ga., 1965-74, Lee County Libr., Tupelo, Miss., 1975-92; bd. libr. commrs. State of Miss., 1979-83, chmn., 1979-80. Chmn. Chickasaw Hist. Soc., 1994-96, bd. dirs., 1994-98; active Native Am. Chickasaw Nation, United Meth. Women. Mem. AAUW, ALA, Nat. Soc. Daus. Am. Colonists, Nat. Soc. U.S. Daus. of 1812, United Daus. of the Confedercy, Nat. Soc. Dames of Ct. of Honor, Am. Indian Cultural Soc., Am. Indian C. of C., First Families Twin Ters, Beta Phi Mu. Democrat. Home: 3313 Winchester Cir Norman OK 73072-2937 Office: Kemp Rsch & Cons Svc PO Box 720531 Norman OK 73070-4388

KEMP, CHARLES E., secondary education educator, history; b. Brunswick, Ga., June 4, 1946; s. Emory Otis and Pauline (Willis) K.; m. Laura Jane Lewis, Apr. 14, 1990; children: Andy, Katie, David. BA in History, N.C. Wesleyan Coll., 1969. Cert. secondary educator, S.C. Tchr. mid. sch. Marietta (N.C.) Elem. Sch., 1969-70; tchr. history Fairmont (N.C.) H.S., 1970—. Columnist: (newspaper) Focus on Fairmont, 1993—. Town councilman Town of Fairmont, 1977—, mayor pro temp, 1995—. Recipient Vol. award Gov. of N.C., Raleigh, 1981, Nat. Home Town Leader award, 1997. Democrat. Methodist. Avocations: swimming, movies, driving. Home: 405 N Main St Fairmont NC 28340-1731

KEMP, EUGENE THOMAS, veterinarian; b. McDonough, N.Y., Mar. 22, 1930; s. Oswald Milton and Almira Dorothy (Allen) K.; m. Ruth Emer Stoll, Sept. 29, 1951 (dec. Sept. 1977); 1 child, William Allen; m. Margaret Atenna Rowland, Dec. 27, 1980. BS, Cornell U., 1951, DVM, 1957. Sr. ptnr. Day Hollow Animal Clinic, Owego, N.Y., 1957—. Contbr. articles to profl. jours. Bd. dirs. First Ch. of Nazarene, Owego, 1991-98; v.p. Tioga County Bd. Health, 1988-97, pres., 1996—; mem. Owego-Apalachin Bd. Edn., 1961-71; mem. Broome-Tioga Bd. Coop. Edn. Svcs., Binghamton, 1969-83, pres., 1971-76; founding pres. Broome-Tioga Coun. Sch. Bd. Pres., 1973. Mem. So. Tier Vet. Med. Assn. (pres. 1992). Republican. Avocations: jazz piano, creative writing. Home and Office: 345 Day Hollow Rd Owego NY 13827-5307

KEMP, GEOFFREY THOMAS HOWARD, international affairs specialist; b. U.K., May 20, 1939; came to U.S., 1967, naturalized, 1974; s. Thomas Howard and Gwendoline (Reeves) K.; m. Vivian Reubens, Sept. 1968 (div. 1979); m. Tamara Levin Weisberg, Nov., 1998. B.A., Oxford U., 1963, M.A., 1967; Ph.D., MIT, 1971. Research assoc. Internat. Inst. Strategic Studies, London, 1965-67; research assoc. Ctr. Internat. Studies, MIT, Cambridge, 1967-71; assoc. prof. internat. politics Fletcher Sch. Law and Diplomacy, Tufts U., 1971-80; spl. asst. to Pres. for nat. security affairs White House, Washington, 1981-85; sr. fellow Ctr. for Strategic and Internat. Studies, Georgetown U., Washington, 1985-86; sr. assoc. Carnegie Endowment for Internat. Peace, 1986-95; dir. regional strategic programs Nixon Ctr., Washington, 1995—. Author: The Control of the Middle East Arms Race, 1991, Forever Enemies? American Policy and the Islamic Republic of Iran, 1994; co-author: Strategic Geography and the Changing Middle East, 1997. Served to lt. Army U.K., 1958-60. Mem. Council on Fgn. Relations (internat. affairs fellow 1976), Internat. Inst. Strategic Studies, Oxford Union Soc. Avocations: tennis, Evelyn Waugh literature, movies, English watercolor paintings. Office: Nixon Ctr 1615 L St NW Washington DC 20036-5610

KEMP, J. ROBERT, beef industry consultant, food company executive; b. Seattle, Nov. 4, 1920; s. S.H. and Bertha (Bankhead) K.; m. Mary M. Filer, Sept. 23, 1942; children: Kandace, Kathy, Karen, Kay. B.S. in Agr, U. Idaho, 1943. With Armour and Co., 1946-62, plant mgr., various locations, 1955-62; v.p., gen. plant mgr. Iowa Beef Processors Inc., Fort Dodge, 1962-63; v.p. sales, mem. exec. com. Iowa Beef Processors Inc., 1963-68; exec. v.p. Iowa Beef Processors Inc., Dakota City, Nebr., 1968-70; co-chmn. bd. Iowa Beef Processors Inc., 1970-75; also dir.; pres. Columbia Foods Inc., 1975-78, Northwest Feeders Inc., 1978—. Served with USAAF, 1943-46, PTO. Phi

Delta Theta. Clubs: Elks, Kiwanis, Arid. Home: 1900 Lake Heron Ln Boise ID 83706-4042

KEMP, JAMES BRADLEY, JR., lawyer; b. New Orleans, Apr. 10, 1932; s. James Bradley and Honora Arlene (Pickren) K.; m. Marguerite Bradburn Freret, Sept. 6, 1952; children: James, Randolph, Ann, Robert. B.B.A., Tulane U., 1953, J.D., 1958. Bar: La. 1958, U.S. Ct. Customs and Patent Appeals 1969, U.S. Supreme Ct. 1970, U.S. Ct. Internat. Trade 1981, U.S. Ct. Appeals (5th, 7th, 11th cirs.), U.S. Dist. Ct. (ea., we. and mid. dists.) La., (so. dist.)Ala., (so. dist.) Tex. Internat. admiralty atty. New Orleans, 1958—; ptnr. Phelps Dunbar, New Orleans, 1964-97, of counsel, 1998—; speaker Southeastern Admiralty Law Inst., 1975, 83, 87, bd. govs., 1977-83, chmn., 1981, adv. coun., 1982—; speaker U. New Orleans Maritime Seminar, 1977; mem. met. area com. Bur. Govtl. Rsch. Mem. bd. editors Tulane Law Rev., 1956-58. Solicitor United Fund, New Orleans, 1963-68; chancellor Greater New Orleans Fedn. Chs., 1981-83; mem. deans coun. Tulane U., 1987-96, speaker Fed. Law Inst., 1988-89, Tulane Admiralty Inst., 1999; mem. religious activities policy com. La. World Expn., 1984. 1st lt. U.S. Army, 1953-55. Mem. ABA (chmn. subcom. maritime financing 1983-90, speaker 1985-87, 90, mem. Ho. Delegates 1996-98), Maritime Law Assn. (mem. various coms., bd. dirs. 1994-97), Fed. Bar Assn., La. Bar Assn. (bar admissions com. 1978-83), Supreme Ct. of La. Hist. Soc., New Orleans Bar Assn., Internat. Bar Assn. (maritime law com.), Def. Rsch. Inst., Propeller Club U.S., New Orleans Def. Counsel Assn., La. Def. Counsel Assn., Internat. Def. Counsel Assn., Am. Counsel Assn. (bd. dirs. 1988-91), Am. Bar Found., La. Bar Found., Fgn. Rels. Assn., Res. Officers Assn. (pres. New Orleans chpt. 1960, Am. Waterways Operators, Am. Legion, Phi Delta Phi. Republican. Presbyterian (elder, clk. of sessions, 1983-84). Clubs: So. Yacht (bd. Govs. 1997—), Plimsoll, World Trade Ctr., Whitehall, Bienville, Mariners of the Port New Orleans. Home: 241 Bellaire Dr New Orleans LA 70124-1010 Office: Phelps Dunbar 30th Fl Texaco Ctr 400 Poydras St New Orleans LA 70130-3245

KEMP, JAMES WILLIAM, graphic artist; b. Alliance, Ohio, Aug. 7, 1950; s. Albert William and Ethel Jean (Bricker) K. BA, U. Pa., Phila., 1972. Project editor Random House, Inc., N.Y.C., 1972-78; prin. designer, ptnr. Compass Projections Design Studio, Bklyn., 1978—; map, lettering designer Random House, N.Y.C., 1978—, Harcourt Brace, San Diego, 1982—, Franklin Libr., N.Y.C., 1978-85, Simon and Schuster, N.Y.C., 1992—, Rolling Stone Mag., N.Y.C., 1980-81, 89-93, N.Y. Times, 1988—, Kirshenbaum & Bond, N.Y.C., 1997, 98, Romann Group, N.Y.C., 1998. exhibited in group shows at Art Dirs. Club, N.Y.C., 1981, 90, 91, 95, Master Eagle Gallery, N.Y.C., 1981, 83-84, 87, 90, Donnell Libr., N.Y.C., 1987, ITC Gallery, N.Y.C., 1987, 90-93, Berthold Type Ctr., Toronto, Ont., Can., 1988, 90, Cooper-Hewitt Mus., N.Y.C., 1996, AIGA Gallery, N.Y.C., 1999; contbr. articles to profl. jours.; artwork appearing in books and anns. Cofounder Summer Mus. Theater for Young Adults, Bennington, Vt., 1985-96. Recipient certs. of excellence Am. Inst. Graphic Arts, N.Y.C., 1987, Type Dirs. Club, N.Y.C., 1989-94, merit award Art Dirs. Club, N.Y.C., 1991, 94. Avocations: writing, drawing. Home and Office: 20 Henry St Apt 5E Brooklyn NY 11201-1348

KEMP, JEANNE FRANCES, office manager; b. L.A., Dec. 8, 1942; d. Damian Thomas and Helen Catherine (Bohin) Hanifee; m. Don H. Kemp, Dec. 16, 1966 (div. 1972). AB, San Francisco State U., 1965. Food svc. technician United Air Lines, San Francisco, 1961-65; clk. N.Y. Life Ins., San Francisco, 1965-66; inventory clk. Ingersoll-Rand, San Francisco, 1966; advt./order clk. Patrick's Stationers, San Francisco, 1966-67; sec. Dartmouth Travel, Hanover, N.H., 1967-68, Olsten Temp. Svcs., N.Y.C., 1968-70; office mgr. Brown U. Devel., N.Y.C., 1970-73; asst. dir. Cen. Opera Svc., N.Y.C., 1974-85; office mgr., sec. Payne, Thompson & Walker, San Francisco, 1986-95; office mgr. Weatherford & Taaffe LLP, San Francisco, 1996—. Editor: Career Guide...Singers, 1985, Operas...for Children, 1985; asst. editor COS Bull., 1976-85; editorial asst.: Who's Who in Opera, 1975. Democrat. Roman Catholic. Avocations: reading, research, writing, theatre, dance. Office: Weatherford & Taaffe LLP Steuart Tower 16th Fl One Market Plz San Francisco CA 94105

KEMP, JOHN D., professional society administrator; b. Waterloo, Iowa, Oct. 10, 1949. AB, Georgetown U., 1971; JD, Washburn U., 1974. With legal dept. Region VII USEPA, Kansas City, Mo., 1974-76; cons. in consumer advocacy Nat. Easter Seal Soc., Chgo., 1976-77, dir. human resources, 1982-84, dir. affiliate rels. and resources, 1984-86, gen. counsel, v.p. devel., 1986-90; pres. Kemp & Young, Inc., Overland Park, Kans., 1977-81, John D. Kemp & Assocs., Inc., Leawood, Kans., 1981-82; exec. dir. United Cerebral Palsy Assns., Inc., Washington, 1990-96; pres., ceo Very Special Arts, Washington, 1996; bd. dirs. Nat. Rehab. Hosp., Washington, Westbridge Condominium, Washington, Rehab Inst. Chgo.; trustee Dole Found. for Employment of People with Disabilities, Washington, 1993—, Commn. on Accreditation of Rehab. Facilities, Tucson, 1978-83, chmn., 1980-82; mem. exec. com. People-to-People Com. for the Handicapped, Washington, 1992—; mem. adv. bd. Amputation Coalition of Am., Rosemont, Ill., 1992—, Am.'s Disability Channel, Houston, 1990—, others; lectr. in field. Contbr. articles to profl. jours. Washburn U. Law Sch. Alumni fellow; named Handicapped Citizen of Yr., Goodwill Industries of Greater Kansas City, Mo., 1976, Person of Yr., New Mobility, 1998; recipient Outstanding Young Citizens award Chgo. Jr. Assn. Commerce and Industry, 1985, Horatio Alger award Horatio Alger Assn. Disting. Ams., 1991; named to Nat. Hall of Fame for Persons with Disabilities, 1988. Mem. ABA, Am. Soc. Assn. Execs. (task force on volunteerism Washington chpt. 1993), Nat. Rehab. Assn. (Switzer scholar Washington chpt. 1990), Nat. Ctr. Non-Profit Bds., Assn. Severely Handicapped, League of Disabled Voters, Ind. Sector (bd. dirs. Washington chpt. 1992—, presdl. search com. 1993). Home: 2555 Pennsylvania Ave NW Washington DC 20037-1613 Office: Very Special Arts 1300 Connecticut Ave NW Ste 700 Washington DC 20036-1715*

KEMP, JOHN DANIEL, biochemist, educator; b. Mpls., Jan. 20, 1940; s. Dean Dudley and Catherine Georgie (Treleven) K.; children: Todd, Christine, Laura. B.A. in chemistry, UCLA, 1962, Ph.D, 1965. NIH postdoctoral fellow U. Wash., Seattle, 1965-68; prof. plant pathology U. Wis., Madison, 1968-81; assoc. dir. Agrigenetics Advanced Research Labs., Madison, 1981-85; prof., dir. plant genetic engring. lab. N.Mex. State U., Las Cruces, 1985—. Author papers on plant molecular genetics. Grantee NSF; grantee Dept. Agr. Mem. Sigma Xi. Office: N Mex State U Plant Genetic Engring Lab PO Box 3GL Las Cruces NM 88004-0003*

KEMP, KAREN, women's basketball coach; b. Chatsworth, Ga., Sept. 12, 1963. BS, Berry Coll., Mount Berry, Ga., 1985. Asst. coach women's basketball U. Tenn., Chattanooga, 1983-90, Miss. State U., Mississippi State, 1990-92; head coach women's basketball East Tenn. State U., Johnson City, 1994—. Named Coach of Yr., So. Conf. Colls., 1995. Mem. Women's Basketball Coaches Am. Office: East Tenn State U Women's Athletic Dept University Dr and State Johnson City TN 37614*

KEMP, KARL THOMAS, insurance company executive; b. Petoskey, Mich., Dec. 16, 1940; s. Vernon L. and Dorothy Jean (Olson) K.; m. Mary Ormston Graham, July 21, 1973; children: Karl Thomas Jr., John Walter, James Edward. BA, Harvard U., 1964. V.p. corp. fin. GEICO Corp., Washington, 1976-81; sr. v.p., pres. Resolute Reins. Co., N.Y.C., 1981-90; pres., CEO Fund Am. Cos., Hanover, N.H., 1997—; bd. dirs., chmn. White Mountains Ins. Co., Hanover, N.H., 1994—; bd. dirs. Folksamerica Holdings, Inc., N.Y.C., chair Human Resources Com., 1996—; bd. dirs. FSA Holdings, N.Y.C., chair human resources com., 1994—; bd. dirs. Eldorado Bancshares, Inc., Calif., chair human resources com., 1996—; bd. dirs. Main St. Am. Holdings, Keane, N.Y., exec. com., 1994—; pres., CEO White Mountain Holdings, Inc., Hanover, 1994—; bd. dirs. Amlin, plc., London. Mem. Am. Bonanza Soc., Aircraft Owners and Pilots Assn., Harvard Club (N.Y.C., Vt., N.H.). Avocation: flying. Home: 6 Goodfellow Rd Hanover NH 03755-4800 Office: White Mountains Holdings Inc 80 S Main St Hanover NH 03755-2053

KEMP, MAE WUNDER, real estate broker, consultant; b. Balt.; d. Edward J. and Helen (Robel) Wunder; m. George C. Segerman, May 17, 1941 (div. 1959); children: Barbara, George C.; m. Robert B. Kemp, July 23, 1960 (dec. 1989). BA, Notre Dame Coll., 1941. Pres. Realty Sales corp., Balt., 1958-60; records mgmt. cons. Boeing Co., Seattle, 1960-65; v.p., real estate broker Satellite Realty, Mercer Island, Wash., 1973-76; real estate broker Washington Properties Real Estate, Seattle, 1970-76; assoc. broker John L. Scott Real Estate, Seattle, 1976-92; tech. adviser of real estate North Seattle C.C., 1973-80. Mem. Seattle Women's Commn., 1973; precinct committeewoman Seattle Rep. Com., 1973; v.p. Freedoms Found., Valley Forge, Pa., 1974; past pres., pres. emeritus Hawthorne Hills Community Club, Inc., Seattle, 1974-90; chmn. Seattle's First Citizen Award. Recipient 5 State Regional Chmn. award, Woman of Yr., Omega Tau Rho medal Nat. Assn. Realtors, Seattle, Sales Assoc. of Yr. award Seattle Real Estate Bd., Outstanding Woman in Real Estate award Past Pres. Club, Woman of Day award Sta. KIXI, CBS. Mem. Wash. Assn. Realtors, Seattle-King County Bd. Realtors (bd. dirs.), Nat. Assn. Real Estate Brokers, Women's Assn. Hilton Head Island, Wash. Athletic Club, Country Club Hilton Head (mem. com., house com.), Navy League of U.S., Hilton Head Island Coun. Republican. Roman Catholic. Avocations: music, tennis, swimming, golf, dancing. Home: The Cypress 99 Birdsong Way Apt D-401 Hilton Head Island SC 29926-1387

KEMP, PATRICIA ANN, principal; b. Wawatosa, Wis., Dec. 24, 1932; d. Lloyd Wolfe and Lydia (Henry) Worden; children: Becky Ann, Barrett George. AB, Albion (Mich.) Coll., 1954; MEd, Wright State U., Dayton, 1979; MRC, Wright State U., 1985. Tchr. St. Marys (Ohio) City Schs., 1961-86; instr. counseling Wright State U., Celina, Ohio, 1985-87; counselor Kinross Correctional Facility, Kinross, Mich., 1985; pvt. counselor Office of Dr. Douglas W. Johnson, PhD, St. Marys, 1985-87; tchr., dir. De Tour Village (Mich.) Day Care, 1987-89; tchr. De Tour (Mich.) Village Pub. Schs., 1989-91, elem. prin., 1991—. Mem. AAUW, Mich. Elem. and Mid. Sch. Prins. Assn., Am. Rehab. Cousneling Assn., Ohio Assn. Counseling and Devel., Ohio Rehab. Counseling Assn., Delta Kappa Gamma, Kappa Delta. Avocations: music, sports, reading. Home: 20441 E Bay St # 493 Spring Bay De Tour Village MI 49725-9718 Office: De Tour Area Schs PO Box 429 De Tour Village MI 49725-0429

KEMP, SHAWN T., professional basketball player; b. Elkhart, Ind., Nov. 26, 1969. Student, U. Ky., Trinity Valley C.C., 1988-89. Basketball player Seattle Supersonics, 1989-97; forward Cleveland Cavaliers, 1997. Named to NBA All-Star team, 1993, Dream Team II, 1994, All-NBA Second Team, 1994. Office: Cleveland Cavaliers 1 Center Court Cleveland OH 44115-4001*

KEMP, STEPHEN FRANK, pediatric endocrinologist, educator, composer; b. Newport, Oreg., Mar. 21, 1947; s. Frank Shirley and Charla Mae (Wait) K. BA, U. Oreg., 1969; PhD in Biochemistry, U. Chgo., 1974, MD, 1976. Diplomate Am. Bd. Pediatrics. Intern Stanford U., 1976-77, resident in pediatrics, 1977-78; postdoctoral fellow in pediatric endocrinology, 1978-80; asst. prof. pediatrics and chief pediatric endocrinology U. South Ala., Mobile, 1980-84; asst. prof. pediatrics U. Ark. for Med Sci., 1984-86, asst. prof. biochemistry, 1985-95, assoc. prof. pediatrics, 1986-95, prof. pediatrics, 1995—, chief pediatric endocrinology, 1987—. Vice pres. Ala. affiliate Am. Diabetes Assn., 1982-84, pres., 1986-88, chmn. youth com. Ark. affiliate, mem. camp com; bd. dirs. Human Growth Found. Recipient NIH postdoctoral nat. research service award, 1978-80. Fellow Am. Coll. Endocrinology; mem. Med. Assn. State Ala., Am. Pediatric Soc., Am. Fedn. Clin. Research, Southern Soc. Pediatric Research, Endocrine Soc. Democrat. Episcopalian. Composer various choir, organ and orchestral works; contbr. articles to profl. jours. Home: 8 Victoria Cir Maumelle AR 72113-6423 Office: U Ark for Med Sci Dept Pediatrics 800 Marshall St Little Rock AR 72202-3510

KEMP, SUZANNE LEPPART, educator, clubwoman; b. N.Y.C., Dec. 28, 1929; d. John Culver and Eleanor (Buxton) Leppart; m. Ralph Clinton Kemp, Apr. 4, 1953; children—Valerie Gale, Sandra Lynn, John Maynard, Renee Alison. Grad. Ogontz Jr. Coll., 1949; B.S., U. Md., 1952. Elem. sch. tchr. Mem. Nat. Soc. Women Descs. of Ancient and Hon. Arty. Co., Nat. Soc. Daus. of Founders and Patriots of Am. (corr. sec.), Nat. Soc. Sons and Daus. of Pilgrims, Nat. Soc. U.S. Daus. of 1812 (chpt. organizing Md. state pres. 1977-79, chpt. v.p. 1979—), Nat. Soc. New Eng. Women (colony pres. 1978-80, Nat. Soc. Colonial Dames XVII Century (state chmn. heraldry and coats of arms 1977-79), Nat. Soc. D.A.R. (chpt. regent 1970-73, chpt. v.p., Md. soc. chmn. transp. 1976-79), Md. State Officers Club, Md. Hist. Soc., Friends of Animals, Defenders of Animal Rights Inc., U. Md. Alumni, English Speaking Union, Star Spangled Banner Flag House Assn., Potter-Balt. Clayworks, Balt. Mus. Art, Walters Art Gallery, Dames of the Court of Honor, Kappa Delta Alumni. Clubs: Baltimore Country; Lago Mar (Ft. Lauderdale, Fla.); Roland Park Women's; Woodbrook-Murray Hill Garden Club, Federation Garden Clubs. Editor; The Spinning Wheel, 1973-76. Home: 7 Ruxton Green Ct Baltimore MD 21204-3548

KEMP, TERENCE P., federal judge; b. 1953. BA, Brown U., 1974; JD, U. Va., 1977. Law clk. to Hon. Malcolm Muir U.S. Dist. Ct. (mid. dist.) Pa., 1977-79; assoc. Baker & Hostetler, Columbus, Ohio, 1980-87; magistrate judge U.S. Dist. Ct. (so. dist.) Ohio, Columbus, 1987—. Mem. Am. Inns of Ct., Fed. Magistrate Judges' Assn., Fed. Bar Assn., Columbus Bar Assn. Fax: (614) 469-5953. Office: US Dist Ct So Dist Ohio 172 US Courthouse 85 Marconi Blvd Columbus OH 43215

KEMP, THOMAS JOSEPH, electronics company executive; b. Holy Cross, Iowa, Aug. 17, 1943; s. Joseph Peter and Margaret Gertrude (Wilgenbusch) K.; m. Ruth Anne Pfohl, Aug. 22, 1964; children: Geoffrey Joseph, Jennifer Anne, Julie Marie, Jack Thomas. BA in Bus. Acctg., Loras Coll., 1964; MS in Sys. Mgmt., St. Mary's U., San Antonio, 1978. Commd. 2d lt. USAF, 1964, advanced through grades to lt. col., 1980, pilot, mgr., 1964-85; ret., 1985; Instructional systems design mgr., dep. program mgr. United Airlines Svcs. Corp., Irving, Tex., 1985-87; divsn. mgr., project mgr. Flight Safety Svcs. Corp., Irving, 1987-90; program mgr. ElectroCom Automation, Arlington, Tex., 1990-97; mgr. integrated logistics support Siemens ElectroCom LP, Arlington, 1997—. Congl. advisor Vets. and Budget Com., Ft. Worth, 1994—; pres. Tarrant County Vets. Coun., Ft. Worth, 1995-96. Mem. ASTD, VFW (life), Internat. Soc. for Performance Instrn., Air Force Assn. (life, state pres. Tex. 1995-97, nat. v.p. 1998-99, Exceptional Svc. award 1990, 91, 94), Am. Legion, KC (dep. grand knight, Knight of Month and Family of Month awards). Republican. Roman Catholic. Avocations: fishing, golf, gardening. Home: 3608 Kimberly Ln Fort Worth TX 76133-2147 Office: Siemens ElectroCom LP 2900 Avenue E Arlington TX 76011-5210

KEMPE, FREDERICK SCHUMANN, newspaper editor, author; b. Salt Lake City, Sept. 5, 1954; s. Fritz Gustav and Johanna Irmgardt (Schumann) K. BA in Comm. magna cum laude, U. Utah, 1976; MA in journalism, Columbia U., 1977; LLD (hon.), U. Md., 1995; HD (hon.), Queen Coll., 1999; LHD (hon.), Queens Coll., 1999. Copy editor Salt Lake Tribune, Salt Lake City, 1974-76; free-lance writer Chgo. Daily News, Christian Sci. Monitor, Rome, 1977-78; Frankfurt corr. AP-Dow Jones, Germany, 1978-79; Bonn corr. Newsweek, Germany, 1979-81; London corr. The Wall St. Jour. (USA), 1981-84; Vienna bureau chief The Wall St. Jour. (USA), Austria, 1984-86; chief diplomatic corr. The Wall St. Jour. (USA), Washington, 1986-89; founder, mng. editor Cen. European Econ. Rev., 1993-94, editor, 1995-96; mng. editor Wall St. Jour. Europe, Brussels, 1992-96; editor, assoc. publ. Wall St. Jour. Europe, 1998—. Author: Divorcing the Dictator: America's Bungled Affair with Noriega, 1990, Siberian Odyssey: A Voyage Into the Russian Soul, 1992, Father/Land: A Personal Search for the New Germany, 1999; contbr. Das Neue Europa, 1992. Recipient Quentus Wilson award U. Utah, 1987; named Top Young Alumnus of Yr. U. Utah, 1987. Mem. Coun. Fgn. Rels., Internat. Inst. Strategic Studies. Avocations: tennis, skiing, basketball. Office: Wall Street Jour Europe, Blvd Brand Whitlock 87, 1200 Brussels Belgium

KEMPE, ROBERT ARON, venture management executive; b. Mpls., Mar. 6, 1922; s. Walter A. and Madge (Stoker) K.; m. Virginia Lou Wiseman, June 21, 1946; children: Mark A., Katherine A. BS in Chem. Engring., U. Minn., 1943; postgrad. metallurgy, bus. adminstrn., Case Western Res. U., 1946-49. Various positions TRW, Inc., Cleve., 1946-53, div. sales mgr., 1953; v.p. Metalphoto Corp., Cleve., 1954-63, pres., 1963-71, Allied Decals, Inc., affiliate, Cleve., 1963-68; v.p., treas. Horizons Rsch. Inc., 1970-71; pres. Reuter-Stokes, Inc. (now subs. of GE Co.), 1971-87; pres. Kempe Everest Ltd., Hudson, Ohio, 1987—; assoc. Paul Williams & Assocs., Medina, Ohio, 1987—; bd. dirs. Bicron Corp., 1987-90, TGM Detectors, Inc., 1988-92, Chagrin Valley Enterprises; mem. adv. com. Manchester Humphreys, Inc., 1992—. Contbr. articles to profl. jours. Lt. (j.g.) USNR, 1944-46, PTO. Mem. Am. Nuclear Soc. (exec. officer, past chmn. No. Ohio sect.), Am. Soc. Metals, Am. Chem. Soc., Ohio Citizens Adv. Coun. on Radiological Safety, Chemists Club (N.Y.C.), Country Club of Hudson, Sigma Chi. Achievements include patents in Method of and Apparatus for Making Poppet Valves, Method of Making Hollow Valves, Method of Making Hollow Castings, Method of Coating of Molybdenum Articles; vitreous coated refractory metals, method for producing the same and vitreous enamel composition, coated refractory body, aluminum plate with plural images and method of making same, process for developing photosensitized anodized aluminum plates. Home: 244 E Streetsboro St Hudson OH 44236-3474 Office: Kempe Everest Ltd 10 W Streetsboro St Hudson OH 44236-2850

KEMPER, DAVID WOODS, II, banker; b. Kansas City, Mo., Nov. 20, 1950; s. James Madison and Mildred (Lane) K.; m. Dorothy Ann Jannarone, Sept. 6, 1975; children: John W., Elizabeth C., Catherine B., William L. B.A. cum laude, Harvard U., 1972; M.A. in English Lit., Oxford, Worcester Coll., 1974; M.B.A., Stanford U., 1976. With Morgan Guaranty Trust Co., N.Y.C., 1975-78; v.p. Commerce Bank of Kansas City, Mo., 1978-79; sr. v.p. Commerce Bank of Kansas City, 1980-81; pres. Commerce Bancshares, Inc., 1982-86, pres., ceo, 1986-91, chmn., pres., ceo, 1991—; also dir. Commerce Bancshares, Inc; chmn. Commerce Bank N.A., St. Louis, 1985—; bd. dirs. Kansas City, Tower Properties, Kansas City, Ralcorp Holdings, Inc., Wave Technologies, Inc. Contbr. articles on banking to profl. jours. Trustee Mo. Bot. Garden, St. Louis Symphony Orch., Washington U. Mem. Acad. Arts and Scis., Bankers Roundtable, Kansas City Country Club, River Club (Kansas City), St. Louis Club, St. Louis Country Club, Racquet Club, Old Warson Country Club (St. Louis). Office: 8000 Forsyth Blvd Saint Louis MO 63105-1707

KEMPER, DONNA MAE, fine art and layoutartist; b. Almont, Mich., Aug. 1, 1954; d. Orville Henry and Josephine (Kramer) Williams; m. John Michael Kemper, June 14, 1986. BS in Fine Art & Psychology, Grand Valley State U., 1982. apprenticeship Larry Blovits PSA, Grand Rapids, Mich., 1984-87. Artist Kemper Art Studio, Grand Rapids, 1983—. Finalist landscape comp. Artist's Mag., 1991, 98; Pastel Soc. Am. scholar. Mem. Am. Artist Profl. League, Oil Painters Am. (assoc.) Soc. Gilders. Avocations: martial arts, tai chi, kung fu, gardening. Office: Kemper Studio PO Box 2045 Grand Rapids MI 49501-2045

KEMPER, JAMES DEE, lawyer; b. Olney, Ill., Feb. 23, 1947; s. Jack O. and Vivian L. Kemper; m. Diana J. Deig, June 1, 1968; children: Judd, Jason. BS, Ind. U., 1969, JD summa cum laude, 1971. Bar: Ind. 1971. Law clk. U.S. Ct. Appeals (7th cir.), Chgo., 1971-72; mng. ptnr. Ice Miller Donadio & Ryan, Indpls., 1972—. Note editor Ind. U. Law Rev., 1970-71; contbr. articles to profl. jours. Past officer, bd. dirs. Marion County Assn. for Retarded Citizens, Inc., Indpls.; past bd. dirs. Cen. Ind. Easter Seal Soc., Indpls., Crossroads Rehab. Ctr., Inc, Indpls.; pres., bd. govs. Orchard Country Day Sch., Indpls.; mem. bd. Eiteljorg Mus. Native Americans. Fellow Ind. Bar Found.; mem. ABA (employee benefit com.), Ind. Bar Assn., Am. Soc. Health Lawyers, The Group, Inc., Midwest Pension Conf., Stanley K. Lacy Leadership Alumni, Corp. Comty. Coun. Office: Ice Miller Donadio & Ryan 1 American Sq Indianapolis IN 46282-0001

KEMPER, JOHN DUSTIN, mechanical engineering educator; b. Portland, Oreg., May 29, 1924; s. Clay Wallace and Leona Bell (Landis) K.; m. Barbara Jeanne Lane, June 28, 1947; 1 dau., Kathleen Lynne. BS, UCLA, 1949, MS, 1959; PhD, U. Colo., 1969. Chief mech. engr. Telecomputing Corp., North Hollywood, Calif., 1949-55, H.A. Wagner Co., Van Nuys, Calif., 1955-56; v.p. engring. Marchant div. SCM Corp., Oakland, Calif., 1956-62; faculty U. Calif., Davis, 1962-91; prof. engring. U. Calif., 1967-91, dean coll. Engring., 1969-83, ret., 1991; panel chmn. Engring. Grad. Edn. and Research, NRC, 1985. Author: Engineers and Their Profession, 1967, 4th edit., 1990, Introduction to the Engineering Profession, 1985, 2d edit., 1993, (with G.C. Andrews) Canadian Professional Engineering Practice and Ethics, 1992, Birding Northern California, 1999. Served with USAF, 1944-46. Fellow ASME (chmn. San Francisco sect. 1962-63), AAAS; mem. Am. Soc. Engring. Edn.

KEMPER, KIRBY WAYNE, physics educator; b. N.Y.C., Apr. 13, 1940; s. Alfred Andrew and Anna (Bobetsky) K.; m. Margaret Ray Thurman, Aug. 24, 1964; children: Margaret, Andrew, Ann. BS, Va. Tech. U., 1962; PhD, Ind. U., 1968. Assoc. prof. Fla. State U., Tallahassee, 1975-79, prof., 1979-94, disting. rsch. prof., 1994—, dir. grad. physics program, 1982-88, assoc. chmn., 1985-88, dir. accelerator lab., 1990-97, chairperson dept. physics, 1997—; vis. fellow Australian Nat. U., Canberra, 1977, 81; trustee SURA, Washington, 1984-88. Recipient Rsch. Support award NSF, 1974—, Coll. Tchg. award Fla. State U., 1990. Fellow Am. Phys. Soc. Democrat. Roman Catholic. Home: 550 Litchfield Rd Tallahassee FL 32312-1857 Office: Fla State U Dept Physics Tallahassee FL 32306

KEMPER, ROBERT VAN, anthropologist, educator; b. San Diego, Nov. 21, 1945; s. Ivan L. and Roberta (King) K.; m. Sandra L. Kraft, Sept. 9, 1967; 1 child, John Kraft. BA, U. Calif., Riverside, 1966; MA, U. Calif., Berkeley, 1969, PhD, 1971; MDiv, So. Meth. U., 1999. Postdoctoral fellow U. Calif., Berkeley, 1971-72; asst. prof. So. Meth. U., Dallas, 1972-77, assoc. prof., 1977-83, prof., 1983—, chmn., 1992-94; visiting rsch. scholar U. Iberoamericana, Mexico City, 1970, 79-80, Ctr. U.S.-Mex. Studies, LaJolla, Calif., 1983, U. Nat. Autónoma Mex., Mexico City, 1990-91, El Colegio de Michoacán, Zamora, Mex., 1991; sec. Inst. Study of Earth and Man, Dallas, 1989-92; Coun. Preservation Anthrop. Records; founding chair Commn. Anthropology Tourism, Internat. Union Anthrop. and Ethnol. Scis., 1993-96. Author: Migration and Adaptation, 1977; co-author: History of Anthropology, 1977; co-editor: Anthropologists in Cities, 1974, Migration Across Frontiers, 1979, (series) Contemporary Urban Studies, 1990—; editor Socio Cultural Anthropology, Am. Anthropologist, 1985-90, Human Orgn., 1995-98; mem. editl. bd. Ency. World Cultures, 1990-96. Elder North Pk. Presbyn. Ch., Dallas, 1987-89, 95-97; mem. Mcpl. Libr. Adv. Bd., Dallas, 1975-79. Fulbright fellow, 1979-80, 91-92, Wenner-Gren fellow, 1974-76, 79-83, Woodrow Wilson fellow, 1966-67. Fellow AAAS, Am. Anthrop. Assn. (bd. dirs. 1990-92), Soc. Applied Anthropology (chmn. Malinowski award com. 1979-80, bd. dirs. 1995-98); mem. Latin Am. Studies Assn. (co-chmn. XI Internat. Congress 1983), Soc. Urban Anthropology (pres. 1988-90), Soc. Latin Am. Anthropology (pres. 1981-82), Phi Beta Kappa (pres. chpt. 1987-88). Home: 10617 Cromwell Dr Dallas TX 75229-5110 Office: So Meth Univ Dept Anthropology 3225 Daniel Ave Dallas TX 75205-1437

KEMPER, VICTOR J., cinematographer; b. Newark, N.J., Apr. 14, 1927; s. Louis and Florence (Freedman) K.; m. Claire Kellermann, May 24, 1953; children: Jan, Steven, Florence. B.S., Seton Hall U. Engr. TV Channel 13, Newark, 1949-54; tech. supr. E.U.E. Screen Gems, N.Y.C., 1954-56; v.p. engring. Gen. TV Network, N.Y.C., 1956-57; pres. V.J.K. Prodns., Studio City, Calif. Cinematographer: (films) Husbands, 1970, The Magic Garden of Stanley Sweetheart, 1970, They Might Be Giants, 1971, Who Is Harry Kellerman and Why Is He Saying Those Terrible Things About Me?, 1971, The Hospital, 1971, The Candidate, 1972, Last of the Red Hot Lovers, 1972, Shamus, 1973, The Friends of Eddie Coyle, 1973, Gordon's War, 1973, The Hideaways, 1973, The Gambler, 1975, The Reincarnation of Peter Proud, 1975, Dog Day Afternoon, 1975, Stay Hungry, 1976, The Last Tycoon, 1976, Mikey and Nicky, 1976, Slapshot, 1977, Audrey Rose, 1977, Oh God!, 1977, The One and Only, 1978, Coma, 1978, Eyes of Laura Mars, 1978, Magic, 1978, ...And Justice for All, 1979, The Jerk, 1979, The Final Countdown, 1980, Night of the Juggler, 1980, Xanadu, 1981, The Four Seasons, 1981, Chu Chu and the Philly Flash, 1981, Partners, 1982, Author! Author!, 1982, National Lampoon's Vacation, 1983, Mr. Mom, 1983, The Lonely Guy, 1984, Cloak and Dagger, 1984, Secret Admirer, 1984, Pee Wee's Big Adventure, 1985, Clue, 1985, BoBo, 1986, Hot to Trot, 1987, Cohen and Tate, 1988, See No Evil, Hear No Evil, 1988, Crazy People, 1990, F/X 2, 1991, Another You, 1991, Beethoven, 1992, Married to It, 1993, Tommy Boy, 1994, Eddie, 1995, Jingle All the Way, 1996. Served with USN, 1944-45. Mem. Am. Soc. Cinematographers (pres.), Acad. Motion Pictures Arts and Scis. Office: The Gersh Agency 232 N Canon Dr Beverly Hills CA 90210-5302*

KEMPER LITTMAN, MARLYN, information scientist, educator; b. Balt., Mar. 26, 1943; d. Louis and Augusta Louise (Jacobs) Janofsky; m. Bennett I. Kemper, Aug. 1, 1965 (dec. June 1987); children: Alex Randall, Gari Hament, Jason Myles; m. Lewis Littman, Apr. 22, 1990. BA, Finch Coll., 1964; MA in Anthropology, Temple U., 1970; MA in LS, U. South Fla., 1983; PhD in Info. Sci., Nova Southeastern U., 1986. Dir., Hist. Broward County Preservation Bd., Hollywood, Fla., 1979-87; automated systems librarian Broward County Main Library, Ft. Lauderdale, Fla., 1983-86; assoc. prof., 1987-94, dir. info. sci. doctoral program Nova U., Ft. Lauderdale, 1987-94; prof. Nova Southeastern U., 1995—. Pub. info. officer Broward County Hist. Commn., 1975-79. Vice chmn. Broward County Libr. Adv. Bd., 1987-92. Bd. dirs. Ctrl. Agy. Jewish Edn., 1992-94. Recipient Judge L. Clayton Nance award, 1977; Broward County Hist. Commn. award, 1979. Mem. ALA, IEEE, Internat. Soc. for Tech. in Edn., Assn. Computing Machinery, Beta Phi Mu, Phi Kappa Phi. Author: A Comprehensive Documented History of the City of Pompano Beach, 1982 A Comprehensive History of Dania 1983, Hallandale, 1984, Deerfield Beach, 1985, Plantation, 1986, Davie, 1987, Networking: Choosing A Lan Path to Interconnection, 1987, (with others) Mosaics of Meaning, New Ways of Learning, 1996; weekly columnist Ft. Lauderdale News, 1975-79; contbg. editor Hyper NEXUS-Jour. Hypermedia and Multimedia Studies, 1996—; assoc. editor Jour. On-line Learning, 1997—; contbr. articles to Microcomputer Environment: Mnagement Issues; also articles to profl. jours. and procs., chpts. to books. Home: 2845 NE 35th St Fort Lauderdale FL 33306-2007 Office: Nova U Sch Computer and Info Sci 3100 SW 9th Ave Fort Lauderdale FL 33315-3025

KEMPERS, ROGER DYKE, obstetrics and gynecology educator; b. Puebla, Mexico, Feb. 29, 1928; (parents Am. citizens); s. John R. and Mable R. (VanDyke) K.; m. Marcia Ann DenHerder, June 17, 1950; children—Mary Christine, Thomas Roger, Steven Edward. A.B. cum laude, Hope Coll., 1949; M.D., Wayne State U., 1954; M.S. in Ob/Gyn., U. Minn., 1960. Diplomate Am. Bd. Ob/Gyn. (examiner 1980-95). Fellow in ob-gyn. Mayo Grad. Sch. Medicine, 1957-60; cons. ob/gyn Mayo Clinic, 1961-95; prof. ob/gyn Mayo Med. Sch., 1977-95, prof. ob-gyn. emeritus, 1995—, dir. edn. dept. ob-gyn, 1970-83, dir. div. reproductive endocrinology, 1985-86, vice chmn. dept. ob/gyn, 1991-95, mem. curriculum com., 1969-80, mem. admissions com., 1973-78; assoc. mem. thesis com. U. Minn., Mpls., 1975-80. Coauthor: (with Edward E. Wallach) Modern Trends in Infertility and Conception Control, vol. I, 1979, vol. II, 1982, vol. III, 1985, vol. IV, 1988 (with J. Cohen, A.C. Haney, J.B. Younger) Fertility and Reproductive Medicine, 1998; editor-in-chief Fertility and Sterility, 1975-97; assoc. editor Ob/Gyn. Survey, 1977-94. Ruling elder First Presbyn. Ch.; bd. dirs. United Way, Children's Home Soc. of Minn., 1967-88. Served to capt. M.C., U.S. Army, 1955-57. Recipient Disting. Alumni award Wayne State U., 1992. Mem. AMA, ACS (Ob/Gyn adv. coun. 1988-95, vice chair 1992-95, liason com. ob-gyn. 1989-95), Ctrl. Assn. Ob/Gyn., Am. Fertility Soc. (program chmn. 1975, pres.-elect 1986-87, pres. 1987-88, exec. coun. 1985-89), Am. Coll. Ob/Gyn (sci. program com. 1980-84, sci. program chmn. 1985, chmn. ann. clin. meeting 1986, chmn. site selection com. 1986-87, internat. affairs com. 1989-95, com. honors and recognitions 1992-95), Am. Soc. Reproductive Medicine (med. dir. 1995—), Fedn. Internat. Ob/Gyn Socs. (N.Am. program chmn. 1989-91, liason com. 1989—, U.S. del. 1994), Internat. Fedn. Fertility Socs. (program com. 1992-95, exec. com. 1995-98, pres.-elect 1998—), Continental Gynecol. Soc., Minn. Ob/Gyn Soc., Am. Gynecol. and Obstet. Soc. (membership com. 1988-90, program com. 1990-92), Am. Gynecol. Club, Minn. State Med. Assn., Zumbro Valley Med. Soc., Rotary (Paul Harris fellow 1987—), Ob-Gyn Travel Club (pres. 1998—), Sigma Xi, Rochester (Minn.) Club. Home: 3971 Gulf Shore Blvd N Apt 602 Naples FL 34103-2102

KEMPF, CECIL JOSEPH, naval officer; b. Maud, Okla., Nov. 20, 1927; s. John Joseph and Sylvia Lorene (Moody) K.; m. Theodosia Ann Suman, Dec. 20, 1950; children: Charles John, David Fuller, Suzanne Ellen. BS Engring., U.S. Naval Acad., 1950; BS Aero. Engring., Naval Postgrad. Sch., 1956; MS Aero. Engring., MIT, 1957. Commd. ensign USN, 1950, advanced through grades to vice admiral, naval aviator, 1951; comdg. officer USS Dubuque, 1972-74, USS Tripoli, 1974-75; dep. mgr. anti-submarine warfare systems project Naval Material Command, 1975-76; comdr. anti-submarine warfare wing U.S. Pacific Fleet, 1976-78; dir. aviation programs div. Office of Chief of Naval Ops., 1978-79; vice comdr. Naval Air Systems Command, 1979-81; asst. dep. chief naval ops. for air warfare, 1981-83; comdr. Naval Res. Force, 1983-87; dir. Naval Res., 1983-87, ret., 1987; cons., 1987-90; dir. maritime warfare systems McDonnell Douglas Aerospace, 1990-96. Decorated Legion of Merit, D.S.M.; recipient Gray Eagle award USN, 1987. Mem. U.S. Naval Acad. Alumni Assn., Assn. Naval Aviation, Navy League U.S., Naval Order U.S. Episcopalian. Avocation: golf. *

KEMPF, DONALD G., JR., lawyer; b. Chgo., July 4, 1937; s. Donald G. and Verginia (Jahnke) K.; m. Nancy Kempf, June 12, 1965; children: Donald G. III, Charles P., Stephen R. AB, Villanova U., 1959; LLB, Harvard U., 1965; MBA, U. Chgo., 1989. Bar: Ill. 1965, U.S. Supreme Ct. 1972, N.Y. 1986, Colo. 1992. Assoc. Kirkland & Ellis, Chgo., 1965-70, ptnr., 1971—. Trustee Chgo. Symphony Orch., 1995—; bd. govs. Chgo. Zool. Soc., 1975—, Art Inst. Chgo., 1984—; bd. dirs. United Charities Chgo., 1985—, chmn. bd., 1991-93; bd. trustees Am. Inns. of Ct. Found., 1997—. Capt. USMC, 1959-62. Fellow Am. Coll. Trial Lawyers; mem. Am. Econ. Assn., ABA, Chgo. Club, Econ. Club, Univ. Club, Mid-Am. Club, Saddle and Cycle Club (Chgo.), Snowmass (Colo.) Club, Quail Ridge (Fla.) Club, Westmoreland Club. Roman Catholic. Office: Kirkland & Ellis 200 E Randolph Dr Fl 54 Chicago IL 60601-6636

KEMPF, KENNETH CHARLES, computer drafting professional; b. Kirkwood, Mo., Jan. 30, 1957; s. Florence Henry and Adele (Lampe) K.; m. Cynthia Marie Meyer, Sept. 26, 1981; children: Stephen Michael, Brian Christopher, Kathleen Allison, Emily Nicole. B in Environ. Design., U. Kans., 1980; Assoc. in Applied Sci., Bus. Adminstrn., St. Louis C.C., 1986; MBA, So. Ill. U., 1993. Computer aided drafting designer St. Louis C.C., 1980—, vice chmn. staff devel. Fund raiser Heritage of the Heart campaign, Valley Park, Mo., 1997; torch lighter United Way, St. Louis, 1996. Mem. Sacred Heart Men's Club. Avocations: coaching baseball. Home: 1030 Remington Oaks Ct Fenton MO 63026-7024 Office: St Louis Cmty Coll 300 S Broadway Saint Louis MO 63102-2800

KEMPF, MARTINE, voice control device manufacturing company executive; b. Strasbourg, France, Dec. 9, 1958; came to U.S., 1985; d. Jean-Pierre and Brigitte Marguerite (Klockenbring) K. Student in Astronomy, Friedrich Wilhelm U., Bonn, Fed. Republic of Germany, 1981-83. Owner, mgr. Kempf, Sunnyvale, Calif., 1985—. Inventor Comeldir Multiplex Handicapped Driving Systems (Goldenes Lenkrad Axel Springer Verlag 1981), Katalavox speech recognition control system (Oscar, World Almanac Inventions 1984, Prix Grand Siecle, Comite Couronne Francaise 1985). Recipient Medal for Service to Humanity Spinal Cord Soc., 1986; street named in honor in Dossenheim-Kochersberg, Alsace, France, 1987; named Citizen of Honor City of Dossenheim-Kochersberg, 1985, Outstanding Businessperson of Yr. City of Sunnyvale, 1990. Avocations: flying, piano, violin, bassoon, studying foreign languages. Office: PO Box 61103 Sunnyvale CA 94088-1103

KEMPIN, FREDERICK GUSTAV, JR., lawyer, educator; b. Phila., Apr. 19, 1922; s. Frederick Gustav and Lydia Edith (Anton) K.; m. Jean Lucille Robb, Jan. 13, 1945 (dec.); children—Frederick Gustav III, Karen Ann Hauckes. BSC, Temple U., Phila., 1942; JD, U. Pa., 1944. Sole practice law Phila., 1945-49; prof. law U. Pa. Wharton Sch., Phila., 1949-87, vice dean, 1964-72, emeritus prof. law, 1987—; ret., 1997. Author: Historical Introduction to Anglo-American Law in a Nutshell, 3d edit., 1990; co-author: Legal Aspects of the Management Process, 4th edit., 1990, Introduction to Law and the Legal Process, 3d edit., 1980, The Legal Environment of Insurance, 4th edit., 1993. Recipient Lindback award for Disting. Teaching, U. Pa., 1963. Mem. Am. Bus. Law Assn., Am. Soc. for Legal History. Republican. Lutheran. Avocations: photography, swimming. Home: 515 Harriet Ln Havertown PA 19083-1817 Office: U Pa Wharton Sch Steinberg Hall-Dietrich Hall Philadelphia PA 19104

KEMPLEY, RITA A., film critic, editor; b. Frankfort, Ky., Sept. 12, 1945; d. Noah and Musaetta (Lathrem) Abrams; m. William Holcomb Kempley, June 31, 1968 (div. 1978); m. Edward Ronald Schneider, Aug. 11, 1986. BJ, U. Mo., 1967. Reporter Copley News Svc., La Jolla, Calif., 1967-68; assoc. editor John F. Holman & Co., Washington, 1968-71; reporter Graphic Arts Mag., Washington, 1972-75; freelance editor-writer Washington, 1975-76; mng. editor Washington Dossier, 1977-79; editor/critic Washington Post, 1979—; commentator Sta. WETA, 1989-96, Sta. WBIG, 1997—. Mem. Kappa Tau Alpha. Office: The Washington Post 1150 15th St NW Washington DC 20071-0002

KEMPNER, ISAAC HERBERT, III, sugar company executive; b. Houston, Aug. 28, 1932; s. Isaac Herbert and Mary (Carroll) K.; m. Helen Hill, July 1, 1967. Grad., Choate Sch., 1951; B.A., Stanford U., 1955, M.B.A., 1959. Asst. v.p. Tex. Nat. Bank, Houston, 1959-64; v.p., sec.-treas., mgr. raw sugar Imperial Holly Corp (formerly Imperial Sugar Co.), Sugarland, Tex., 1964-71, chmn. bd., 1971—; pres. Foster Farms Inc.; bd. dirs., past chmn. Houston br. Dallas Fed. Res. Bank; trustee H. Kempner Trust Assn. Trustee, chmn. planning com. Meth. Health Care Sys., Houston; chmn., Contemporary Arts Mus., Houston. Mem. Coronado Club, Bayou Club, Camden Ale and Quail Club. Office: Imperial Holly Corp PO Box 9 1 Imperial Sq Sugar Land TX 77487

KEMPNER, JONATHAN L., professional society administrator; b. Detroit, Mar. 5, 1951; s. Harold J. Kempner and Helen (Ciesla) Covensky; m. Lise C. Van Susteren, Nov. 28, 1987; children: Aliza, Delaney, Piera. BA with high honors, U. Mich., 1972; JD, Stanford (Calif.) U., 1976. Assoc. Fried, Frank, Harris, Shriver & Kampelman, Washington, 1977-80; asst. gen. counsel Charles E. Smith Cos., Arlington, Va., 1981-82; asst. dir., gen. counsel Pa. Ave. Devel. Corp., Washington, 1982-83; v.p., gen. counsel Oxford Devel. Corp., Bethesda, Md., 1983-87; pres. Nat. Multi Housing Coun., Washington, 1987—; spl. cons. U.S. Dept. Treasury, Washington, 1977-78; bd. dirs., mem. audit com. Advanced Resource Devel. Corp., Columbia, Md., 1983-95. Bd. dirs. D.C. chpt. ARC, 1983-91, treas., bd. dirs., 1986-90, chmn. long range planning com., 1987-89, chmn. budget and fin. com., 1988-90, numerous others. Mem. ABA, D.C. Bar Assn., U.S. Supreme Ct. Bar Assn., Am. Soc. Assn. Execs., Nat. Housing Conf. (bd. dirs.), Urban Land Inst., Ciesla Found. (bd. dirs. 1991—). Jewish. Avocation: squash. Office: Nat Multi Housing Coun 1850 M St NW Ste 540 Washington DC 20036-5816

KEMPNER, JOSEPH, aerospace engineering educator; b. Bklyn., Apr. 25, 1923; s. Arthur and Anna (Richman) K.; m. Carol F. Brown, Jan. 12, 1947; children: Robert M., Marien A. Barker. B.Aero. Engring. summa cum laude, Poly. Inst. Bklyn., 1943, M.Aero. Engring., 1947, Ph.D. in Applied Mechanics, 1950. Registered profl. engr., N.Y. Research fellow Poly. Inst. Bklyn., 1944, mem. faculty, 1947-90, prof. applied mechanics and aerospace engring., 1957-90, prof. emeritus, 1990—, chmn. undergrad. aerospace studies, asst. dir. research, 1962-63, dir. applied mechanics, 1964-76, head dept., 1966-76; aero. engr. NASA, 1944-47; cons. indsl. and govt. research labs; former mem. adv. group II, ship structural design procedure and analysis, ship research com. Maritime Transp. Research Bd., Nat. Acad. Scis.-NRC; also former mem. com. basic research, adv. to Army Research Office, 1973-76, 81-85; prin. investigator research contracts Office Naval Research and Air Force Office Sci. Research. Contbr. articles to profl. jours. Recipient citation disting. research Poly. chpt. Sigma Xi, 1973; named Outstanding Educator Am., 1973, 74-75. Fellow N.Y. Acad. Scis. (I.B. Laskowitz Gold medal 1973), Am. Acad. Mechanics; assoc. fellow AIAA; mem. ASME, Am. Soc. Engring. Edn., Sigma Xi, Tau Beta Pi, Sigma Gamma Tau. Home: 82 Murray Hill Ter Marlboro NJ 07746-1751 Office: 333 Jay St Brooklyn NY 11201-2907

KEMPNER, MAXIMILIAN WALTER, law school dean, lawyer; b. Berlin, Feb. 27, 1929; came to U.S., 1939; s. Paul H. and Marga Marie (von Mendelssohn) K.; m. Barbara Paige Mooney, 1952; children: Paul, Daphne, Emily Mayne. BA, Harvard U., 1951, LLB, 1954; LLM, Columbia U., 1957; LLD, Vt. Law Sch., 1997. Bar: N.Y. bar 1954. With Webster & Sheffield, N.Y.C., 1957-91; dean Vt. Law Sch., South Royalton, 1991-96; adj. prof. Vt. Law Sch., 1997—; dir. Lawyers Com. for Civil Rights under Law; chair Jud. Fellows Commn.; advisor Program on Non-profit Orgns., Yale U. Trustee Marlboro Sch. Music, Inc.; former dir. Legal Aid Soc., Am. Coun. on Germany, Albert Schweitzer Fellowship, Coun. on Libr. Resources; active Coun. Fgn. Rels., Inc. With U.S. Army, 1954-56. Fellow Am. Bar Found.; mem. ABA (past chmn. legal edn. and admissions to bar sect.), Am. Law Inst. (life), Assn. Bar City N.Y., N.Y. State Bar Assn., Harvard Law Sch. Assn. N.Y.C. (past pres.).

KEMPNER, MICHAEL W., public relations executive; b. Chgo., Jan. 31, 1958; s. Lester T. and Lois Kempner; m. Jacqueline Steinberg, Oct. 24, 1987; children: Zachary, Melissa. BS, Am. U., 1981. Spl. asst. to Gov. of N.J. Trenton, 1977-79; state campaign dir. Pres. Jimmy Carter, Washington, 1979-80; dep. fin. chair Dem. Nat. Comm., 1980-82; legis. dir. Congressman Torricelli, Hackensack, N.J., 1983-84; pres. Winter's Chocolates, Emerson, N.J., 1984-86, The MWW Group, East Rutherford, N.J., 1986—; bd. dirs. N.J. Drug Abuse Resistance Edn. Contbr. articles to popular mags. Former fin. vice chair Dem. Nat. Com.; regional chmn. fin. Dem. senatorial campaign, Washington, 1990, chmn. fin. com. Congressman Torriceli, Hackensack, 1984—, committeeman Bergen County Dem. Com., 1991, bd. advisors Ctr. Food Action, Englewood, N.J., 1990-91. Named Entrepreneur of Yr. finalist, 1991, 92, 93, 94. Mem. Pub. Rels. Soc. Am., Young Pres. Orgns., mem. 1992 U.S Olympic Com., regl fin. chmn., mem. Am. Bankruptcy Inst., and Turnaround mgmt. Assn. Office: The MWW Group 1 Meadowlands Plz Fl 6 East Rutherford NJ 07073-2100*

KEMPSKI, RALPH ALOISIUS, bishop; b. Milw., July 16, 1934; s. Sigmund Joseph and Cecilia Josephine (Chojnacki) K.; m. Mary Jane Roth, July 30, 1955; children—Richard, Joan, John. B.A., Augsburg Coll., 1960; M.Div., Northwestern Luth. Theol. Sem., 1963; D.Div., Wittenberg U., Springfield, Ohio, 1980. Pastor Epiphany Luth. Ch., Mpls., 1963-68, St. Stephen Luth. Ch., Louisville, 1968-71, Our Saviour Luth. Ch., West Lafayette, Ind., 1971-79; bishop Ind.-Ky. Synod Luth. Ch. Am., Indpls., 1979-87, Ind.-Ky. Synod Evang. Luth. Ch. Am., 1987-98; bd. dirs. Ind. Coun. Chs., 1979-96, v.p., 1991-94, pres., 1994-96 ; bd. dirs. Ky. Coun. Chs., Luth. Sch. Theology, Chgo., Luth. Sch., Columbia, S.C., Wittenberg U., Springfield, Ohio, Suomi Coll.; governing bd. Nat. Coun. Chs. Christ U.S.A., N.Y.C., 1981-88, Luth. Theol. So. Sem., 1988-96, Trinity Sem., 1996-98. Mem. governing bd. Suomi Coll., Hancock, Mich., 1998—. Avocations: gardening, reading, camping, travelling, flying. Office: Ind-Ky Synod Evang Luth Ch 911 E 86th St Ste 200 Indianapolis IN 46240-1800

KEMPSTER, NORMAN ROY, journalist; b. Sacramento, Jan. 4, 1936; s. Roy Dixon and Viola Alice (Cox) K.; m. Jane Leon, June 30, 1957; children: Jill Suzanne Zemke, David Norman. B.A., Calif. State U., 1957. Reporter U.P.I., 1957-73, Washington Star-News, 1973-76; Reporter Washington Bur. Los Angeles Times, 1976-80, 84—, Reporter Jerusalem Bur., 1981-84; Joe Alex Morris meml. lectr. Harvard U., 1983. Served with AUS, 1959-61. Profl. Journalism fellow, 1967; recipient Gerald Loeb award for disting. journalism, 1980. Mem. Fgn. Press Assn. in Israel (v.p. 1982-83), White House Corrs. Assn. (dir. 1974-75), State Dept. Corrs. Assn. (treas. 1986, v.p. 1987, pres. 1988), Overseas Writers of Washington (pres. 1989-91). Episcopalian. Home: 9503 Midwood Rd Silver Spring MD 20910-1650 Office: 1875 I St NW Washington DC 20006-5409

KEMPTHORNE, DIRK ARTHUR, governor; b. San Diego, Oct. 29, 1951; s. James Henry and Maxine Jesse (Gustason) K.; m. Patricia Jean Merrill, Sept. 18, 1977; children: Heather Patricia, Jeffrey Dirk. BS in Polit. Sci., U. Idaho, 1975. Exec. asst. to dir. Idaho Dept. Lands, Boise, 1975-78; exec. v.p. Idaho Home Builders Assn., Boise, 1978-81; campaign mgr. Batt for Gov., Boise, 1981-82; lic. securities rep. Swanson Investments, Boise, 1983; Idaho pub. affairs mgr. FMC Corp., Boise, 1983-86; mayor Boise, 1986-93; U.S. Senator from Idaho, 1993-98; gov. State of Idaho, 1999—; 1st v.p. Assn. of Idaho Cities, 1990-93; chmn. U.S. Conf. of Mayors Standing Com. on Energy and Environment, 1991-93, mem. adv. bd., 1991-93 ; sec. Nat. Conf. of Rep. Mayors and Mcpl. Elected Officials, 1991-93; mem. Senate Armed Svcs. Com., 1993—, Senate Small Bus. Com., 1993—, Senate Environ. and Pub. Works Com., 1993—, Nat. Rep. Senatorial Com., 1993—; chmn. Senate Drinking Water, Fisheries and Wildlife Subcommittee, 1995—, mem. advisory commn. on Intergovernmental Rels., 1995-96; chmn. Armed Svcs Personnel Subcommittee, 1996—. Pres. Associated Students U. Idaho, Moscow, 1975; chmn. bd. dirs. Wesleyan Presch., Boise, 1982-85; mem. magistrate commn. 4th Jud. Dist., Boise, 1986-93; mem. task force Nat. League of Cities Election, 1988; bd. dirs. Parents and Youth Against Drug Abuse, 1987—; mem. bd. vis. USAF Acad., 1994—; chmn. Idaho Working Ptnrs. Ltd., 1993—; hon. chmn. Idaho Congressional Award, 1994—. Named Idaho Citizen of Yr. The Idaho Statesman, 1988, Legislator of the Year Nat. Assn. Counties, 1995, State Legislator of the Year Nat. Assn. of Towns and Townships, 1995; recipient U.S. Conference of Mayor's Nat. Legis. Leadership award, 1994, Disting. Svc. award Nat. Conf. State Legislatures, 1995, Disting. Congressional award Nat. League of Cities, 1995, Guardian of Freedom award Council of State Governments, 1995. Republican. Methodist. Office: Office of the Governor PO Box 83720 Boise ID 83720-0034

KENAGY, ROBERT COFFMAN, planning consulting company executive; b. Hartford, Conn., July 10, 1931; s. Herbert Glenn and Mary Emily (Hardesty) K.; m. Karen Miriam Emanuelson, June 8, 1957; children: Neil S., Lynn S., Gretchen P. BA, Princeton U., 1953; postgrad., U. Pa., 1953-54. Various mktg. mgmt. positions IBM, N.Y.C., White Plains, Armonk, N.Y., 1957-69; v.p. mktg. Data Dimensions, Inc., Greenwich, Conn., 1969-73; fin. prin. Sidney A. Staunton, Inc., New Canaan, Conn., 1973-78; pres. RCK Mgmt. Co., Ltd., New Canaan, Litchfield, Conn., 1978—. mem. Larchmont-Mamroneck (N.Y.) Bd. Edn., 1968-72; bd. dirs. YMCA, New Canaan, 1975-81, pres., 1980-81, trustee The Aloha Found., Fairlee, Vt., 1976-91, pres., 1983-84, trustee emeritus, 1991—; bd. dirs. United Way, New Canaan, 1979-82, campaign chmn., 1979-80. 1st lt. U.S. Army, 1954-56. Mem. Princeton Club N.Y., Country Club New Canaan, Greenwich Choral Soc. (v.p., dir.). Republican. Avocations: tennis, running, singing, travel. Home and Office: RCK Mgmt Co Ltd 24 Fox Crossing Ln Litchfield CT 06759-2305

KENAN, THOMAS STEPHEN, III, philanthropist; b. Durham, N.C., Apr. 19, 1937; s. Frank Hawkins Kenan and Harriet Gregg (DuBose) Gray. BA in Econ., U. N.C., 1959. Trustee Sarah G. Kenan Found., Durham, 1968-74, N.C. Mus. Art, Raleigh, 1972-91, Randleigh Found. Trust, 1981-95, N.C. Sch. the Arts, Winston-Salem, 1983-91, Mary Duke Biddle Found., Durham, 1984-97, W.R. Kenan Charitable Trust, Chapel Hill, N.C., 1986-97, U. N.C. Arts and Sci. Found., Chapel Hill, 1989-91, The Nat. Tropical Bot. Gardens, Hawaii, The Coun. of Nat. Trust for Hist. Preservation; exec. com. Flagler System, Inc., Palm Beach, Fla., 1968-97; chmn. Kenan Transport Co., Chapel Hill, 1968-97; pres. Westfield Co., Durham, 1971-91. Founder Liberty Hall Restoration Commn., 1966, Duplin Outdoor Drama Soc., 1976; trustee The Duke Endowment. Mem. Hope Valley Country Club, Treyburn Golf and Country Club, Breakers Beach and Golf Club, Univ. Club, Landfall Golf and Tennis Club. Episcopalian. Avocations: music, horseback riding, golfing, reading, gardening. Office: William R Kenan Jr Charitable Trust Kenan Ctr Bowles Dr Chapel Hill NC 27515-3858

KENDALL, CHARLES TERRY, librarian; b. Chambersburg, Pa., Aug. 13, 1949; s. Guy William and Virginia Mae (Naugle) K.; m. Alice Marie Bienz, Aug. 21, 1971; children: Terri, Anita, Kendra. BA, Huntington (Ind.) Coll., 1971; MLS, George Peabody Coll., 1972; postgrad., Asbury Theol. Sem., 1982-83; MA in Religion, Anderson (Ind.) U., 1990. Dir. Byrd Meml. Libr. Anderson Sch. Theology, Anderson U., 1983-89; theol. studies libr. Anderson U. Libr., 1989-98, archivist, 1992-98; dir. Mabee Libr. Sterling (Kans.) Coll., 1998—. Mem. ALA, Kans. Libr. Assn. Office: Mabee Library Sterling Coll Sterling KS 67579

KENDALL, CHRISTOPHER (CHRISTOPHER WOLFF), conductor, lutenist, educator, university official; b. Sept. 8, 1949; s. John Dryden and Catherine (Wolff) K. BA, Antioch Coll., 1972; MusM, U. Cin., 1974. Artistic dir., conductor 20th Century Consort Smithsonian Instn., Washington, 1976—, artistic dir. Romantic Chamber Ensemble, 1979-82; founder, lutenist Folger Consort, Washington, 1977—; artistic dir. Millennium, Inc., Washington, 1980-86; asst. condr. Seattle Symphony Orch., 1987-88, assoc. condr., 1988-92; dir. music divsn., prof. music Boston U. Sch. for Arts, 1993-96; music dir. Boston U. Tanglewood Inst., 1993-96; prof. music, dir. Sch. Music, U. Md., College Park, 1996—; music dir., condr. Washington Sinfonia, 1977-81; artistic dir. Martha's Vineyard Music Festival, 1979-86; guest condr. Da Camara, N.Y. Chamber Symphony, Dayton Philharm., Chamber Music Soc. Lincoln Ctr., N.Y.C., Collage, Annapolis Symphony, Kitchener-Waterloo (Ont.) Symphony, Juilliard Orch., Symphony and Chamber Orch., San Francisco Chamber Symphony, Music Today, N.Y.C., Libr. of Congress, Seattle Symphony, Waterloo Festival, Da Capo Chamber Players, Dinosaur Annex; panelist Nat Endowment for Arts, co-chmn., 1981-82; panelist Smithsonian '85 Conf. on Music in Am., Dance USA Conf. '85; adjudicator Kennedy Ctr. Friedheim Competition, 1991, 92, 94. Performances recorded on ASV, Bard, Delos, Nonesuch, CRI, Centaur, Smithsonian Collection labels.

KENDALL, DAVID E., lawyer; b. Camp Atterbury, Ind., May 2, 1944. BA, Wabash Coll., 1966; MA, Oxford U., England, 1968; JD, Yale U., 1971. Bar: N.Y. 1974, U.S. Ct. Appeals (5th cir.) 1976, D.C. 1978, U.S. Supreme Ct. 1978, Md. 1993. Law clerk to Mr. Justice Byron R. White U.S. Supreme Ct., 1971-72; mem. Williams & Connolly; adj. prof. Columbia U. Law Sch., 1977-78, Georgetown U. Law Ctr., 1985-95. Note and comment editor Yale Law Jour., 1970-71; author (with Leonard Ross) The Lottery and the Draft, 1970. Rhodes scholar. Mem. N.Y. State Bar Assn. Office: Williams & Connolly 725 12th St NW Washington DC 20005-5901*

KENDALL, DOROTHY HELEN, retired art historian; b. Bayonne, N.J., May 27, 1912; d. Frank and Mary Elizabeth (Hart) Hovell; m. Henry John Steinbomer, Dec. 26, 1933 (dec. July 11, 1964); children: Shirley Ann, Richard Henry, Robert Alan; m. James Irving Kendall, Aug. 29, 1972. BA, Our Lady of the Lake U., San Antonio, 1933; MLS, Our Lady of the Lake U., 1968; MFA in Latin Am. Arts, U. Americas, Puebla, Mexico, 1972. Cert. secondary tchr., Tex. Tchr. Covington Park Sch., San Antonio, 1933-34; tchr. St. Mary's Hall H.S., San Antonio, 1941-42; fine arts libr. San Antonio Pub. Libr., 1959-68; dir. Religious Expression in the Arts Hemis-Fair '68, 1967-69; fine arts libr. St. Mary's U., 1968-72; founder, 1st chmn. Urban Studies Dept., St. Mary's U., 1970. Author: Gentilz, Artist of the Old Southwest, 1974; designed stained glass windows for 3 San Antonio chs., 1953-56; developed type of fused glass for decorative use in ch., office, 1956; organizer of exhibit Am. Fedn. Arts, Houston-San Antonio, 1961. Pres. San Antonio Art League, 1958-60 (initiated Artists in Action program, 1958-59); appointed to Fine Arts Adv. Coun., U. Tex., 1959-65; organized Faith into Form nat. exhbn. for Stained Glass Assn. Am., Dallas, 1963; mem. Area Policy Coun., San Antonio, 1969-72. Recipient hon. membership San Antonio Craft Guild, 1962-63; invited with group of artists to visit Mexico's artists by Mexico's Pres. Diaz Ordaz, 1965; included in Best Poets of 1998. Democrat. Episcopalian. Avocations: travel, writing, Maya studies, reading. Home: 2603 Ektom Dr Apt 409 Austin TX 78745-2675

KENDALL, EARNEST JAMES, mental health nurse; b. Kalamazoo, Mar. 4, 1948; s. Earnest Glenn and Mary Eileen (Holcomb) K.; children: Earnest David, Julie Erin. ADN, Penn Valley Community Coll., Kansas City, Mo., 1973; BA in Psychology, U. Mo., Kansas City, 1977, BSN, 1990, MA in Counseling and Guidance, 1981, MSN, 1994. Cert. psychiat./mental health nurse. Staff nurse, head nurse St. Mary's Hosp., Kansas City, Mo., 1973-81; staff nurse St. Luke's Hosp., Kansas City, Mo., 1981-82, Menorah Med. Ctr., Kansas City, Mo., 1982-95, Trinity Lutheran Hosp., Kansas City, Mo., 1995—. With U.S. Army, 1967-70; capt. USAFR. Mem. Sigma Theta Tau, Phi Kappa Phi, Phi Theta Kappa. Home: 6025 Brookside Blvd Kansas City MO 64113-1427

KENDALL, GENE R., military officer, federal agency administrator; b. Newport News, Va.; s. Hugh and Doris Kendall; m. Sandra A. Olivier; children: Jerome Kirk, Christin Scott. Student, Duke U.; BS in Engring. Physics, U. Kans., 1971, M of Engring. Commd. ensign USN, 1968, advanced through grades to rear admiral, gunnery and missile officer, USS Berkeley, 1972, ASW officer, exec. fficer, USS Grasp, chief engr., USS Edward McDonnell, commissioning exec. officer, USS Willamette, founding dir., engring. officer Watch course, dir. engring. splty. tng., spl. asst. to Chief Naval Ops.; dir. divsn. math. and sci. US Naval Acad., Annapolis; comdr. USS Sphinx, USS Fletcher, USS Mt. Whitney USN; dep. dir. for ops., Nat. Mil. Command Ctr. USN, Washington, dir CINC Liaison, 1998—.

Decorated legion of merit (2), meritorious svc. medal (3). Office: USN Dep Dir Ops Nat Mil Command Ctr 2000 Navy Pentagon Washington DC 20350-2000*

KENDALL, GEORGE JASON, accountant, financial planner, computer consultant; b. New Castle, Pa., Aug. 20, 1937; s. George R. and Ester (Belknap) K.; m. Carole J. Stewart, May 5, 1956 (div. Dec. 1985); m. Elaine A. Russell, May 10, 1986; children: Deborah, Penny, Laurie. AA, New Castle Bus. Coll., 1964. CPA, Pa.; CFP; enrolled agt. to practice before the IRS. Payroll clk. Internat. Staple, Butler, Pa., 1964; jr. acct. Bachman, Marsch & Co., Butler, 1964-66; mgr. Lamb, Marsch & Co., Butler, 1967-75; ptnr. Kendall, Marsch & Co., Butler, 1975-84, owner, 1984—; ptnr. Kendall, Metz & Co., Butler, 1988—; cons. in field, 1983—. Mem. Pa. Soc. Pub. Accts., Internat. Assn. Fin. Planning, Inst. CFPs. Republican. Methodist. Avocations: reading, backpacking, hiking. Office: Kendall Metz & Co PO Box 1856 277 Pittsburgh Rd Butler PA 16002-3955

KENDALL, HARRY OVID, internist; b. Eugene, Oreg., Nov. 29, 1929; s. Edward Lee and Jessie Avis (Giem) K.; m. Katherine Alexander, June 20, 1951 (div. 1957); 1 child, Jessica Gail Gress; m. Barbara Ann Matt, Jan. 21, 1961 (div. June 1, 1977); children: David Lee, Brian Padraic; m. Wanda Eve Helmer, July 2, 1993. AB, U. Redlands, 1952; MD, Yale U., 1955. Diplomate Am. Bd. Internal Medicine, Am. Bd. Pulmonary Disease. Intern in internal medicine UCLA Med. Ctr., 1955-57; resident in internal medicine West L.A. VA Med. Ctr., 1957-59; staff physician U.S. Naval Regional Med. Ctr., San Diego, 1959-62, Tulare-Kings Counties Hosp., Springville, Calif., 1962-63; staff physician, ptnr. So. Calif. Permanente Med. Group, Fontana, Calif., 1963-67, Kaiser Hosp. and So. Calif. Permanente Med. Group, San Diego, 1967—; dir. respiratory care Kaiser Hosp., San Diego, 1967—; attending physician San Bernardino County Hosp., 1964-67; asst. clin. prof. medicine U. Calif. San Diego Med. Ctr., 1976—; com. mem. numerous hosps. and med. clinics. Mem. NAACP, Amnesty Internat., ACLU. Lt. USNR, 1954-56, lt. comdr. 1961, comdr. 1973. Mem. Am. Thoracic Soc., cAlif. Thoracic Soc., San Diego Pulmonary Soc. Avocations: western history, paleontology, geneology, book collecting.

KENDALL, JASON DANIEL, professional baseball player; b. San Diego, June 26, 1974; s. Fred Kendall. Selected first-round free-agt. draft Pitts. Pirates, 1992; catcher Gulf Coast League Pirates, 1992, Augusta (South Atlantic League), 1993, Salem (Carolina), 1994, Carolina (So. League), 1994-96, Pitts. Pirates; selected Nat. League All-Star Team, 1996. Named So. League MVP, 1995. Office: c/o Pittsburgh Pirates 600 Stadium Cir Pittsburgh PA 15212-5731*

KENDALL, JILLIAN D., information systems specialist, program developer, educator, consultant; b. Catskill, N.Y., July 27, 1949; d. John S. and Patricia (Murphy) Rogers. Graduated with honors, ITC Tech. Coll., 1972; BA in Bus. and Humanities, Golden Gate U., 1986, Cert. in Info. Systems, 1987; MA with honors in Humanities and Computers, U. San Francisco, 1989; PhD in Humanities, Computers, and Human Factors, U. Tex., 1991. Cert. instructor, Tex. Program developer ITC Tech. Coll., San Francisco, 1968-71; asst. programmer Crown Zellerbach, San Francisco, 1971-72; data processor State of Oreg., Covallis, 1980-82; asst. mgr. inventory control, computer operator Arneson Products, Corte Madera, Calif., 1982-85; with commodities and inventory control Hill Bros. Coffee, San Francisco, 1985-88; computer program developer IBM, Westlake, Tex., 1989-92; mgr. info. sys., dir. rsch. Am. Ch. Lists, Arlington, Tex., 1992-94; founder, dir. Internat. Tech. Inst. and Computer Mus., Arlington, 1992—; cons., documentation specialist edn. devel., tng. Ericsson Radio Systems, Richardson, Tex., 1995—; cons. pub. rels., instr. operating sys., computer literacy, tech. writing, human factors, ethics and tech. U. Tex., Arlington, 1989—; ednl. cons. IBM, 1989—; mentor, founder Student Found., 1990; prof. Dallas C.C., 1991—, Art Inst. Dallas, 1995—; prof. comm., computer based tng., devel. reading, others El Centro C.C., 1991—; cons. CompuTechnologies, Arlington, Tex., 1994—; cons. edn. and tech. writing Ericsson Radio Sys., Plano, Tex. Writer, producer, photographer (videos) The Industrial Revolution in China, 1988, Star Wars, 1989, Computers & Man, 1989; author The Computer is the Prime Symbol of a New Age: The Age of Synthesis; contbr. articles to profl. jours. Charter mem. U. Tex. Student Found., Arlington, 1989-91; vol. ARC, Dallas, Ft. Worth, 1989-91; mem. Kimbel Art Mus., Hist. Soc. Schole U. Calif., San Francisco, 1988, ITC Tech. Coll., 1967, Buck Found., 1988-89; grantee Golden Gate U., 1987. Mem. Computer Profls. for Social Responsibility, Nat. Computer Graphics Assn., Spl. Interest Group for Graphics, Assn. Interdisciplinary Studies, Western Social Sci. Assn., Golden Gate U. Alumni Assn., Toastmasters Internat. (competent toast master, v.p. 1988). Avocations: computer graphics, travel, computers, videos. Home and Office: PO Box 122244 Arlington TX 76012-8244

KENDALL, JOE, federal judge; b. Dallas, 1954; m. Veronica Kendall, 1975; children: Drew, Greg, Alan. BBA, So. Meth. U., 1977; JD, Baylor U., 1980. Bar: Tex. 1980, U.S. Ct. Appeals (5th cir.) 1980, U.S. Supreme Ct. 1980; cert. criminal law specialist. Police officer Dallas Police Dept., 1972-78; asst. dist. atty. Dallas County Dist. Attys. Office, 1980-82; pvt. practice Dallas, 1982-86; judge Tex. State Dist. Ct., Dallas, 1987-92, U.S. Dist. Ct. (no. dist.) Tex., Dallas, 1992—. Office: US Dist Ct 1100 Commerce St 16th Fl Dallas TX 75242-1027*

KENDALL, JOHN WALKER, JR., medical educator, researcher, university dean; b. Bellingham, Wash., Mar. 19, 1929; s. John Walker and Mathilda (Hansen) K.; m. Elizabeth Helen Meece, Mar. 19, 1954; children: John, Katherine, Victoria. BA, Yale Coll., 1952; MD, U. Wash., 1956. Intern, resident in internal medicine Vanderbilt U. Hosp., Nashville, 1956-59, fellow in endocrinology, 1959-60; fellow in endocrinology U. Oreg. Med. Sch., Portland, 1960-62; asst. prof. medicine Oreg. Health Scis. U., Portland, 1962-66, assoc. prof. medicine, 1966-71, prof. medicine, 1971—, head divsn. metabolism, 1971-80, dean Sch. Medicine, 1983-92, dean emeritus Sch. Medicine, 1992—; assoc. chief staff-rsch. VA Med. Ctr., Portland, 1971-83, dep. chief of staff, 1993, VA disting. physician, 1993-96, acad. affiliates officer, 1997—; cons. Med. Rsch. Found. Oreg., Portland, 1975-83; sec., bd. dirs. Oreg. Found. Med. Excellence, Portland, 1984-89, pres., 1989-91. Lt. comdr. M.C., USN, 1962-64. Recipient Outstanding Physician award Found. Med. Excellence, 1995. Mem. AMA (governing coun. med. sch. sect. 1989-93, chair 1991-92, alt. del. 1992-93, Oreg. del. 1994-98, rep. Coun. Grad. Med. Edn. 1993-94), Assn. Am. Physicians, Am. Soc. Clin. Investigation, Am. Fedn. Clin. Rsch., We. Soc. Clin. Rsch. (councillor 1972-75), Endocrine Soc., Multnomah County Med. Soc. (treas. 1989, pres. 1991), Med. Rsch. Found. (Mentor award 1992), Royal Soc. Medicine (endocrinology sect. coun. 1999—). Presbyterian. Home: 3131 SW Evergreen Ln Portland OR 97201-1816 Office: Oreg Health Scis U Sch Medicine 3181 SW Sam Jackson Park Rd Portland OR 97201-3011

KENDALL, JULIUS, consulting engineer; b. Boston, May 14, 1919; m. Edythe Tobias; children: Jane, Richard Tobias. BS in Aero. Engring., Northeastern U., 1941; MS, MIT, 1941. Registered Profl. Engr., N.Y., N.J., Mass., Conn., Maine; cert. fluid power engineer. V.p. Greer Hydraulics, N.Y.C., 1945-56, Arkwin Industries, Inc., Westbury, N.Y., 1956-58; pres. Kenett Corp., Westboro, Mass., 1958-91; cons. engr. Kendall Cons. Group, Weston, Mass., 1991—; v.p. Kenett Hydraulic Distbn. divsn. Entwistle Co., Hudson, Mass., 1993—; cons. in field. Patentee in field. Contbr. many articles to profl. jours. With USN, 1941-46. Mem. Am. Soc. Naval Engrs., ASME, Soc. Automotive Engrs., Fluid Power Soc., Aleppo Yacht Club, Shriners, Masons. Avocations: fishing, boating, golf. Home and Office: 57 Colchester Rd Weston MA 02493-1601

KENDALL, KAY L. ORTH, university official; b. El Dorado, Kans., Feb. 16, 1945; d. William Alva Jr. and Kathryn ELizabeth (Wagner) Orth; m. Richard Tulloss Darville, Apr. 18, 1968 (div. June 1974); 1 child, Herbert William Hugh Darville; m. Bruce George Kendall, July 12, 1975. BA with highest honors, U. Kans., 1967; MA in Russian History, U. B.C., 1972, postgrad. Rsch. publs. officer Dept. Solicitor Gen., Ottawa, Ont., Can., 1976-78; asst. dir. Ottawa Bd. of Trade, 1978-81; mgr. media rels. The Conf. Bd. of Can., Ottawa, 1981-83; dir. pub. rels. Assn. Can. Distillers, Ottawa, 1983-87; v.p. pub. affairs Am. Express Can., Toronto, 1987-89; sr. v.p. Continental-Golin Harris Pub. Rels., Toronto, 1989-90; v.p. Hill & Knowlton Pub. Rels., Houston, 1991-93; chief comm. Inst. Biosci. and Tech., Tex. A&M U., Houston, 1993—; chmn. Tex. Med. Ctr.'s Pub. Rels. Adv. Coun., 1997-98. Contbr. articles to profl. jours. Chmn. pub. rels. Sam Houston area Boy Scout Fair, 1992; charter mem. leadership coun. Greater Houston Partnership Healthcare Congress, 1996—; participant Leadership Tex., 1998. Fellow Woodrow Wilson Found., Harvard U., 1967-68; Watkins scholar U. Kans., 1963-67, Killam Nat. scholar U. B.C., 1972-75. Mem. Pub. Rels. Soc. Am. (chmn. S.W. dist. 1998—), Phi Beta Kappa. Methodist. Avocations: European travel, classical music, 19th Century Russian literature, gourmet cooking. Office: Tex A&M U Sys Health Sci Ctr Inst Biosci and Tech 2121 W Holcombe Blvd Houston TX 77030-3303

KENDALL, KAY LYNN, interior designer, consultant; b. Cadillac, Mich., Aug. 20, 1950; d. Robert Llewellyn and Betty Louise (Powers) K.; 1 child, Anna Renee Easter. BFA, U. Mich., 1973. Draftsman, interior designer store planning dept. Jacobson Stores, Inc., Jackson, Mich., 1974-79; sr. interior designer store planning dept. Jacobson Stores, Inc., Jackson, 1981-98; prin., pres. Kay Kendall Designs, Jackson, 1979—; sr. interior designer Maddalena's Inc., Jackson, 1998—; realtor The Prudential Premier Properties, Inc., Jackson, 1998—; cons. in field. Big sister Big Bros./Big Sisters Jackson County. Mem. Am. Soc. Interior Designers (profl. mem., assoc. Ctrl. Mich. chpt.), Nat. Assn. Realtors, Jackson Area Assn. Realtors, Mich. Assn. Realtors. Avocations: tennis, golf, gardening, skiing. Home: 701 Church St Grass Lake MI 49240-9206 Office: Maddalena's Inc 2418 W Michigan Ave Jackson MI 49202-3920 also: The Prudential Premier Properties Inc 761 W Michigan Ave Jackson MI 49201-1995

KENDALL, LAUREL ANN, geotechnical engineer; b. Detroit, Dec. 4, 1956; d. James McNair and Dorothy Mildred (Frost) K. BSE in Environ. Sci., U. Mich., 1979, MSCE, 1983. Registered profl. engr., Mich., Ill., Ohio. With Bechtel Assocs. P.C., 1979-84; project mgr. NTH Cons., 1984-90; gen. mgr. solid waste ops. Wayne Disposal, Inc. (purchased by Allied Waste Industries), 1990-97, dist. landfill gen. mgr., 1997—; instr. Lawrence Inst. Tech., Southfield, Mich., 1985-91, Wayne State U., 1991-95. Mem. ASCE (past pres. Mich. sect.), Mich. Soc. Profl. Engrs. (past pres. Oakland chpt.), Engring. Soc. Detroit. Congregationalist. Avocations: gardening, jogging, mountain biking, cross-country skiing. Office: Sauk Trail Hills Devel Inc Allied Waste Industries Co 5011 S Lilley Rd Canton MI 48188-2736

KENDALL, LEIGH WAKEFIELD, surgeon; b. Brattleboro, Vt., Mar. 8, 1937; s. Irwin Samuel and Laura Eliza (Walbridge) K.; m. Grace Eleanor Fullarton, July 1, 1961; children: William Leigh, Bradley Edward. AB, U. Pa., Phila., 1959; D of Medicine, U. Vt., 1963; MS, U. Ill., Chgo., 1965. Diplomate Nat. Bd. Med. Examiners, Am. Bd. Surgery; cert. ACLS. Intern then resident surgery U. Ill. Hosp., Chgo., 1963-69; rsch. fellow Am. Cancer Soc., Chgo., 1964-65; clin. fellow Am. Cancer Soc., 1968-69; staff surgeon USN Hosp., Great Lakes, Ill., 1969; surgeon USN Hosp. Ships, Vietnam, 1969-70; pvt. practice Lancaster, Pa., 1971-93; medical dir. St. Joseph P.H.O., Lancaster, Berks, 1995-99, assoc. med. dir., 1999—; instr. surgery U. Ill. Hosp., Chgo., 1968-69; active staff St. Joseph Hosp., Lancaster, 1971—, sect. chief gen. surgery, 1981-88, chmn. dept. surgery, 1989-93; mem. courtesy staff Lancaster Gen. Hosp., 1971—; cons. surgery Franklin & Marshall Coll., Lancaster, Masonic Homes, Elizabethtown, Pa., staff physician, Millersville, U., 1993—; staff physician cardiac rehab., Lancaster Gen. Hosp. Health Campus, 1995—. Lt. comdr. USNR M.C., 1959-71, Vietnam. Decorated 1st Class Mil. Honor medal Republic of Vietnam. Fellow ACS, Internat. Soc. Surgeons; mem. AMA, Pa. Med. Soc., Warren H. Cole Soc. (pres. 1994-95), Royal Soc. Medicine (Eng.), Intrepids Club, Sigma Nu. Republican. Episcopalian. Avocations: photography, travel. Home: 1314 Quarry Ln Lancaster PA 17603-2424 Office: Millersville Univ Witmer Infirmary Millersville PA 17551-0302

KENDALL, LEON THOMAS, finance and real estate educator, retired insurance company executive; b. Elizabeth, N.J., May 20, 1928; m. Nancy O'Donnell; 6 children. BS in Acctg. magna cum laude, St. Vincent Coll., 1949; MBA in Mktg., Ind. U., 1950, DBA in Econs., 1956; LLD (hon.), Cardinal Stritch Coll., 1988. Teaching asso. Ind. U. Sch. Bus., 1950-53; economist Fed. Res. Bd., Atlanta, 1956-58, U.S. Savs. and Loan League, Chgo., 1958-64; v.p., economist N.Y. Stock Exchange, 1964-67; pres. Assn. Stock Exchange Firms, 1967-72, Securities Industry Assn., 1972-74; chmn., dir. Mortgage Guaranty Ins. Corp., Milw., 1974-89; vice chmn. MGIC Investment Corp., 1980-89; prof. of fin. and real estate Kellogg Sch. of Mgmt., Northwestern U., Evanston, Ill., 1988—; bd. dirs. Avatar Corp., Universal Foods Corp., CoreCar, Inc., CBOE; commr. N.J. Mortgage Study, 1971-72; mem. Wis. Expenditures Study Commn., 1985-86. Author: (with Miles Colean) Who Buys the Houses, 1958, The Savings and Loan Business: Its Purposes, Functions and Economic Justification, 1962, Anatomy of the Residential Mortgage, 1964, Readings in Financial Institutions, 1965, The Exchange Community in 1975, 1965; editor: Thrift and Home Ownership: Writings of Fred T. Greene, 1962; contbr.: chpt. to American Enterprise: The Next Ten Years, 1961, The World Capital Shortage, 1977, Securitization Primer, 1996. Mem. deans adv. council Ind. U. Sch. Bus.; mem. adv. bd. Fed. Home Loan Mortgage Corp; vis. com. divsn. social scis. U. Chgo. Served with USAF, 1954-56. Grad. fellow Ind. U., 1950-53; Found. for Econ. Edn. fellow Pitts. Plate Glass Co., 1952. Mem. Acad. Alumni Fellows Ind. U. Sch. Bus., Lambda Alpha, Delta Epsilon Sigma, Beta Gamma Sigma. Office: MGIC Investment Corp MGIC Pla Milwaukee WI 53201

KENDALL, PETER LANDIS, television news executive; b. Toledo, Oct. 8, 1936; s. Roy Cline and Edythe Mae (Kindy) K.; m. Beate Margit Fritz, June 11, 1966; children: Adrian Peter, Stefanie Karin. B.A., U. Cin., 1959; B.S. cum laude, U. Ill., Urbana, 1960. News producer-writer Voice of Am., Washington, 1961-64; corr. Deutsche Welle, Bonn, Fed. Republic Germany, 1964-66; morning news producer CBS News, Washington, 1971-74; producer CBS News, London, 1974-77; bur. chief CBS News, 1977-82; sr. producer-asst. bur. mgr. CBS News, Washington, 1982-86; bur. chief CBS News, Bonn, 1986-88; pvt. practice internat. TV cons. Washington, 1988-90; exec. producer Washington bur. Cable News Network, 1990—; exec. producer CNN Washington Coverage of Gulf War, 1991. Producer: Econ. Summits, London, 1977, 84, Bonn, 1978, Versailles, 1982; Iranian Hostages Return, Frankfurt, West Germany, 1980, Moscow Olympics, 1980, London, The Royal Wedding, 1981; numerous presdl. visits to Europe. Recipient Emmy award for Senate and Watergate coverage Nat. Acad. TV Arts and Scis., 1974. Mem. Am. Corrs. Assn. (exec. bd. London 1977-80), Health Vols. Overseas (bd. dirs. 1996), Sigma Delta Chi. Espiscopalian. Club: Tamesis Sailing (London). Office: CNN 820 1st St NE Washington DC 20002-4243

KENDALL, PHILLIP ALAN, lawyer; b. Lamar, Colo., July 20, 1942; s. Charles Stuart and Katherine (Wilson) K.; m. Margaret Roe Greenfield, May 2, 1970; children: Anne, Timothy. BS in Engring., Stanford U., 1964; JD, U. Colo., Boulder, 1969; postgrad., U. Freiburg (Germany), 1965-66. Engr. Siemens Halske, Munich, 1965; ptnr. Kraemer, Kendall & Benson, Colorado Springs, Colo., 1969—; gen. counsel Peak Health Care, Inc., Colorado Springs, 1979-87; bd. dirs. Norwest Banks Colorado Springs. Pres. bd. Colorado Springs Symphony Orch. Assn., 1977-80; bd. dirs. Penrose Hosps., Colorado Springs, 1982-88; pres. bd. Citizen's Goals, Colorado, 1984-86; bd. dirs. Legal Aid Found., Denver, 1988-94, chmn., 1991-93; bd. dirs. Colo. Nature Conservancy, 1996—. Recipient Medal of Distinction-Fine Arts, Colorado Springs C. of C., 1983. Mem. ABA, Colo. Bar Assn. (bd. govs. 1985-88, outstanding young lawyer 1977), El Paso County Bar Assn. (bd. trustees 1983-85), Nat. Health Lawyers Assn., Colorado Springs Estate Planning Coun. Avocations: triathlons, helicopter skiing, marathon swimming, windsurfing, sailing. Home: 1915 Wood Ave Colorado Springs CO 80907-6714 Office: Kraemer Kendall & Benson PC 430 N Tejon St Ste 300 Colorado Springs CO 80903-1167

KENDALL, ROBERT DANIEL, priest, theology educator; b. Miami, Ariz., Jan. 11, 1939; s. Robert Daniel and Loretto Agnes (Jakle) K. BA, Gonzaga U., 1963, MA, 1964; ThM, Santa Clara U., 1971; SSL, Pontifical Bibl. Inst., Rome, 1973; STD, Gregorian U., Rome, 1975. Tchr. Brophy Coll. Prep., Phoenix, 1964-67; asst. prof. Gonzaga U., Spokane, Wash., 1975-79; from asst. prof. to assoc. prof. U. San Francisco, 1979-90, prof., 1990—. Author: Focus on Jesus, 1996, The Resurrection, 1997, The Bible for Theology, 1997, The Trinity, 1999. Mem. Soc. Jesus, Cath. Bibl. Assn. Avocations: swimming, family genealogy. Home: 650 Parker Ave San Francisco CA 94118-4267

KENDALL, ROBERT LOUIS, JR., lawyer; b. Rochester, N.H., Oct. 13, 1930; s. Robert Louis and Marguerite (Thomas) K.; m. Patricia Ann Palmer, Aug. 13, 1955; children: Linda J., Cynthia J., Janet L. AB cum laude, Harvard U., 1952; JD cum laude, U. Pa., 1955; Diploma in Law, Oxford (Eng.) U., 1956. Bar: Pa. 1957, Ga. 1993. Assoc. Schnader, Harrison, Segal & Lewis, Phila., 1956-65, ptnr., 1966-95; lectr. Temple U. Law Sch., Phila., 1976-77; spl. instr. U. Pa. Law Sch., 1959-62. Contbr. to Antitrust Law Developments, 2d edit. 1984. Bd. dirs. Mann Music Ctr., Inc., Phila., 1971-98, Settlement Music Sch., Phila., Pa., 1984—, Jr. C. of C., Phila., 1962-65; mem. Gladwyne Civic Assn., 1960—, Phila. Orch. Assn., 1983—. Fellow Soc. Values in Higher Edn.; mem. ABA, Pa. Bar Assn., Ga. Bar Assn., Phila. Bar Assn., Atlanta Bar Assn., U. Pa. Law Alumni Assn. (bd. mgrs.), Rotary, Order of Coif (pres. 1979-80), Lawyers Club Atlanta, Harvard Club. Democrat. Episcopalian. Home: 1208 Hartdale Ln Gladwyne PA 19035-1434 Office: Schnader Harrison Segal 1600 Market St Ste 3600 Philadelphia PA 19103-7240

KENDALL, ROBERT STANTON, newspaper editor, journalist; b. Greensburg, Ind., July 30, 1921; s. Wilber Lawrence and Marguerite (Groenier) K.; m. Dorothy Jane Rumbold, Oct. 2, 1943; children: Mark Curtis, Lee Rachel, Amy Robin. BA, Coll. of Wooster, 1946. Asst. pub. Martinsville (Ind.) Daily Reporter, 1946-48, editor, 1948-98; chmn. Reporter-Times Inc., Martinsville, 1983-98, Adkins Inc., Martinsville; editl. columnist Schurz Comms., 1998—. 2d lt. USAAF, 1943-45, ETO. Decorated Air medal; recipient Meritorious Svc. award Am. Legion, Martinsville, 1973, citation Coun. for Def. of Freedom, 1978, Honor medal DAR, 1987. Mem. Kiwanis, Phi Beta Kappa, Phi Alpha Theta. Republican. Lutheran. Home: 460 Park Pl Martinsville IN 46151-1237 Office: Martinsville Daily Reporter 60 S Jefferson St Martinsville IN 46151-1968

KENDE, ANDREW STEVEN, chemistry educator; b. Budapest, Hungary, July 17, 1932; came to U.S., 1941, naturalized, 1951; s. George and Elizabeth Kende; m. Frances Boothe, Sept. 4, 1954; 1 son, Mark. A.B., U. Chgo., 1951; M.S., Harvard, 1954, Ph.D., 1957. Sr. research scientist Lederle Labs., Am. Cyanamid Co., Pearl River, N.Y., 1957-63; cons. Lederle Labs., Am. Cyanamid Co., 1968-94; research asso. Lederle Labs., 1963-66, research fellow, 1966-68; vis. prof. State U. N.Y., Buffalo, 1967, Mich. State U., East Lansing, 1968; prof. chemistry U. Rochester, N.Y., 1968—; chmn. U. Rochester, 1979-83, Charles Frederick Houghton prof. chemistry, 1981—, prof. oncology, 1982—, assoc. chmn., 1989-90; vis. prof. U. Genéve, 1974, U. Amsterdam, 1989; vis. scholar Stanford U., 1975; cons. study sect. NIH, 1972-76, chmn., 1974-76; cons. chem. pathology study sect., 1979-82; cons. Dow Chem. Co., 1975—, Bausch and Lomb Co., 1985-90, Eastman Kodak Co., 1987-94, Procter and Gamble Pharms., 1988—, Dow Agroscis., 1994—; pres. Organic Syntheses Inc., 1992—. Mem. bd. editors: Organic Reactions, 1968-83, editor-in-chief, 1983-88; mem. bd. editors Chem. Revs., 1973-76, Organic Syntheses, 1978-87, Synthetic Comms., 1981-96; mem. editorial adv. bd. Jour. of Am. Chem. Soc., 1995—; assoc. editor Jour. of Organic Chemistry, 1997—. Am. Cancer Soc. fellow Glasgow (Scotland) U., 1956-57; Guggenheim fellow, 1978-79; Bicentenary lectr. Royal Australian Chem. Inst., 1988. Fellow Japan Soc. Promotion of Sci.; mem. Am. Chem. Soc. (exec. bd. Rochester sect. 1970-72, chmn. organic chem. div. 1978-79). Home: 19 Larchwood Dr Pittsford NY 14534-2432 Office: U Rochester River Campus Dept Chemistry Rochester NY 14627-0216

KENDE, CHRISTOPHER BURGESS, lawyer; b. N.Y.C., Apr. 28, 1948; s. Herbert Alexander and Helga Henrietta (Wieselthier) K.; m. Barbara Gonzales, May 22, 1976. BA, MA, Brown U., 1970; JD, NYU, 1973. Bar: N.Y. 1974, U.S. Dist. Ct. (so. and ea. dists.) N.Y. 1974, Mass. 1975, U.S. Supreme Ct. 1978, D.C. 1988, Calif. 1996. Staff atty. Legal Aide Soc., N.Y.C., 1973-76; assoc. Dewey, Ballantine et al., N.Y.C., 1976-78; assoc. Hill Betts & Nash, N.Y.C., 1978-82, ptnr., 1982-89; ptnr. Holtzmann, Wise & Shepard, N.Y.C., 1989-96, Cozer & O'Connor, N.Y.C., 1996—. Contbr. articles to profl. jours. Recipient Silver medal Caisse des Depots, 1984. Mem. ABA, N.Y. County Lawyer's Assn. (chmn. com. on admiralty and maritime law), Maritime Law Assn. (marine ecology com.), French Maritime Law Assn., India House, Edgartown Yacht Club, Order of Coif, Phi Beta Kappa. Democrat. Presbyterian. Avocations: sailing, motorcycling, tennis, fitness, gardening. Home: 545 W End Ave Apt 2B New York NY 10024-2723 Office: Cozen & O'Connor 45 Broadway New York NY 10006-3007

KENDE, HANS JANOS, plant physiology educator; b. Szekesfehervar, Hungary, Jan. 18, 1937; came to U.S., 1965, naturalized, 1970; s. Istvan and Katalin (Grosz) K.; m. Gabriele F. Guggenheim, May 15, 1960; children: Benjamin R., Michael, Judith N. Nat. Ph.D., U. Zurich, Switzerland, 1960; DSc (hon.), U. Fribourg, Switzerland, 1995. Research Council fellow Ottawa, Can., 1960-61; research fellow Calif. Inst. Tech., Pasadena, 1961-63; plant physiologist Negev Inst. of Arid Zone Research, Beersheva, Israel, 1963-65; assoc. prof. Mich. State U.-Dept. Energy Plant Research Lab., East Lansing, 1965-69; prof. Mich. State U.-Dept. Energy Plant Research Lab., 1969—; dir. Dept. Energy Plant Research Lab. Mich. State U., 1985-88; program mgr. for plant growth and devel. USDA, Washington, 1992; vis. prof. Swiss Fed. Inst. Tech., Zurich, 1972-73, 79-80; vis. scientist Friedrich Miescher Institut, Basel, Switzerland, 1991. Mem. editorial bd. Plant Physiology, 1969-84, Biochemie und Physiologie der Pflanzen, 1975-93, Plant Molecular Biology, 1981-84, Planta, 1982-97; (editorial bd.) Jour. Plant Growth Regulation, 1982-84, Sci., 1997—, Plant Jour., 1998—; contbr. articles to profl. jours. Mem. adv. panel for devel. biology NSF, 1974-77. Guggenheim fellow, 1972-73. Fellow AAAS; mem. NAS, Am. Soc. Plant Physiologists (Stephen Hales prize 1998), Leopoldina German Acad. Natural Scis. Home: 805 Virginia Ave East Lansing MI 48823-2835 Office: Mich State U Plant Rsch Lab East Lansing MI 48824

KENDER, WALTER JOHN, horticulturist, educator; b. Camden, N.J., Dec. 20, 1935; s. Walter and Martha K.; m. Carole Holm, May 26, 1957; children—David, Lily. B.S., Del. Valley Coll., 1957, DSc (hon.), 1993; M.S., Rutgers U., 1959, Ph.D., 1962. From asst. prof. to assoc. prof. horticulture U. Maine, Orono, 1962-69; mem. faculty Cornell U., N.Y. State Agrl. Expt. Sta., Geneva, 1969-82; prof. pomology Cornell U., N.Y. State Agrl. Expt. Sta., 1975-82, head dept. pomology and viticulture, 1972-82; chmn. dept. pomology Cornell U., Ithaca, N.Y., 1975-82; prof., dir. citrus research and edn. ctr. U. Fla., Lake Alfred, 1982-96, prof., 1996—; co-chmn. task force fruit rsch. N.E. USDA State Exptl. Stas., 1973-75; sec. Internat. Working Group Juvenility Woody Plants, 1974-82; cons. Winrock Internat. (USAID) Pakistan, 1989, Indonesia, 1992, P.R. Dept. Agr., 1996; disting. scientist Agrl. U., Wageningen, Netherlands, 1974; mem. adv. bd. Archbold Biol. Sta., 1991—. Contbg. author: Blueberry Culture, 1966; contbr. profl. jours. Fellow AAAS, Am. Soc. Hort. Sci. (dir. 1975-85, trustee endowment fund 1982-87); mem. N.Y. State Hort. Soc., Internat. Soc. Hort. Sci., Internat. Citriculture Soc. (corr.), Am. Pomological Soc. (mem. adv. com.), Inst. Food Tech. (Fla.), Coun. Agrl. Sci. and Tech., Fla. State Hort. Soc. (pres. 1996, chmn. of bd. 1997), N.Y. State Fruit Testing Assn. (sec.-treas. 1972-82), Farm Bur. Adv. Com., Haines City Citrus Growers Assn. (bd. dirs. 1991-96), Fla. Citrus Showcase (bd. dirs. 1996—), Sigma Xi (past chpt. pres.). Office: Citrus Rsch & Edn Ctr 700 Experiment Station Rd Lake Alfred FL 33850-2243

KENDERDINE, JOHN MARSHALL, petroleum engineer, retired army officer; b. Ft. Worth, Dec. 6, 1912; s. Robert Leonard and Caroline (Raab) K.; m. Su Anne Carroll, Feb. 26, 1937; children—James Marshall, Su Carroll. B.S. in Petroleum Engring, Tex. A. and M. Coll., 1934; grad., Army War Coll., 1953, Advanced Mgmt. Program, Harvard, 1959, Exec. Decision Inst., 1961. Registered profl. engr., Tex. Petroleum engr. Gulf Oil Corp., 1934-37; br. mgr. Norvell-Wilder Supply Co., Midland, Tex., 1938-41; commd. 1st lt. AUS, 1941, advanced through grades to brig. gen., 1962; mil. logistician in France, Germany and U.S., World War II; spl. asst. to administr. War Assets Adminstrn., 1946; mil. staff and command assignments, 1947-60; joint petroleum officer Europe, 1961; exec. dir. supply operations Def. Supply Agy., 1962-65; comdr. Def. Indsl. Supply Center, Phila., 1965-66, Def. Personnel Support Center, Phila., 1966-67; ret.; v.p. Scott Paper Co., 1967-70; chmn. C.F. Adams, Inc., Ft. Worth, 1970-89, ret., 1989. Contbr. articles to profl. jours. Decorated Legion of Merit, Commendation ribbon with 3 oak leaf clusters, D.S.M. Mem. Am. Logistics Assn., Assn. U.S. Army, Flight Safety Found., Armed Forces Communications and Electronics Assn. (dir. 1965), Commerce and Industry Council Phila., Phila. C. of

C. (dir. 1966), Airline Passengers Assn. (adv. bd.). Clubs: Union League, Petroleum, Century II. Home: 5402 Clover Ct Fort Worth TX 76132-4007

KENDIG, EDWIN LAWRENCE, JR., physician, educator; b. Victoria, Va., Nov. 12, 1911; s. Edwin Lawrence and Mary McGuire (Yates) K.; m. Emily Virginia Parker, Mar. 22, 1941; children: Anne Randolph (Mrs. R.F. Young), Mary Emily Corbin (Mrs. T.T. Rankin). BA magna cum laude, Hampden-Sydney Coll., 1932, BS magna cum laude, 1933, DSc (hon.), 1971; MD, U. Va., 1936. House officer Med. Coll. Va. Hosp., Richmond, Bellevue Hosp., N.Y.C., Babies Hosp., Wilmington, N.C., Johns Hopkins Hosp., Balt., 1936-40; instr. pediatrics Johns Hopkins U., 1944; pvt. practice Richmond, 1940-94; dir. child chest clinic Med. Coll. Va., 1944-94, prof. pediatrics, 1958—; chief of staff St. Mary's Hosp., Richmond, 1966-67; cons. on diseases of chest in children, 1944-94, William P. Buffum orator Brown U., 1978; Abraham Finkelstein Meml. lectr. U. Md., 1983; Derwin Cooper lectr. Duke U., 1984; Renato Ma Guerrero lectr. U. Santo Tomas, Manila, 1984; Bakwin Meml. lectr. NYU-Bellevue Hosp., 1986. Contbr. numerous articles on disease of chest in children to profl. publs.; editor: Disorders of Respiratory Tract in Children, 1967, 72, 77; co-editor: (with V. Chernick) Disorders of Respiratory Tract in Children, 4th edit., 1983, cons. editor to V. Chernick, 5th and 6th edits., pub. as Kendig's Disorders of the Respiratory Tract in Children, 1990, 97; (with C.F. Ferguson) Pediatric Otolaryngology, 1972; contbg. editor: Gellis and Kagan Current Pediatric Therapy, 12 edits., 1993, Burg, Ingelfinger, Wald Current Pediatric Therapy, 14th edit., Antimicrobial Therapy, Kagan, 3 edits., Practice of Pediatrics, Kelley, Practice of Pediatrics, Maurer, Allergic Diseases of Infancy, Childhood and Adolescence, Bierman and Pearlman, Sarcoidosis and Other Granulomatous Diseases, James, 1994; former mem. editl. bd. Pediat. Pulmonology, Pediat. Annals, Pediat., Alumnews U. Va., 1988. Chmn. Richmond Bd. Health, 1961-63; bd. visitors U. Va., 1961-72; former mem. bd. dirs. Va. Hosp. Svc. Assn.; former ofcl. examiner Am. Bd. Pediatrics; mem. White House Conf. on Children and Youth, 1960; pres. alumni adv. com. U. Va. Sch. Medicine, Charlottesville, 1974-75; past bd. dirs. Maymont Found., Richmond; bd. dirs. Children's Hosp., 1997—, Children's Hosp. Found., 1985-97, Sheltering Arms Hosp.; former mem. adv. bd. Ctr. for Study of Mind and Human Interaction, U. Va. Sch. Medicine, 1988; mem. steering com. One Hundred Twenty Fifth Anniversary, Med. Coll. of VA Hosps., 1986; bd. dirs. St. Mary's Health Care Found., 1990. Recipient resolution of recognition Va. Health Commr., 1978, Obici award Louise Obici Hosp., 1979, Bon Secours award St. Mary's Hosp., 1986, Keating award Hampden-Sydney Coll., 1989, Disting. Citizen award Boy Scouts Am., R.E. Lee chpt., 1996; named an Outstanding Alumnus Sch. Medicine U. Va., 1986; The Edwin Lawrence Kendig Jr. Disting Profesorship in Pediatric Pulmonary medicine named in honor Med. Coll. Va. Commonwealth U. Mem. AMA (pediat. residency rev. com.), Am. Acad. Pediat. (past pres. Va. sect., chmn. sect. on diseases of chest, mem. exec. bd. 1971-78, nat. pres. 1978-79, Abraham Jacobi Meml. award with AMA, 1987, cons. com. on internat. child health), Am. Acad. Pediat. for Latin Am. (ofcl. adv. to exec. bd. 1988), Va. Bd. Medicine (former pres.), Richmond Acad. Medicine (pres. 1962, chmn. bd. trustees 1963), Va. Pediat. Soc. (past pres.), Am. Pediat. Soc., So. Med. Assn., So. Soc. Pediat. Rsch., Internat. Pediat. Assn. (cons., standing com., medal 1986), Med. Soc. Va. (editor Va. Med. Quarterly 1982-98, resolution of recognition), Soc. Cin., Raven, Commonwealth, Country Club of Va., Farmington Club, Phi Beta Kappa, Alpha Omega Alpha, Tau Kappa Alpha, Kappa Sigma, Omicron Delta Kappa. Episcopalian. Home: 5008 Cary Street Rd Richmond VA 23226-1643 Office: Laburnum House 1300 Westwood Ave Richmond VA 23227-4624

KENDIG, ELLSWORTH HAROLD, JR., retired corporate lawyer; b. Toledo, Jan. 3, 1922; s. Ellsworth Harold and Ellen Katherine (Owen) K.; m. Donita Rae Porter, Dec. 29, 1972; children by previous marriage: Susan (Mrs. William Willen), Robert E., Richard C., Margaret E. (Mrs. W. Scott Brown). A.B., U. Mich., 1943; postgrad., Wayne State U. Law Sch., 1949. Bar: Calif. 1950. Assoc. Herlihy & Herlihy, L.A., 1950-57; mem. firm Kendig, Stockwell & Gleason, and predecessor firms, L.A., 1957-82, Von Mizener & Kendig, L.A., 1982-87; of counsel Johnson, Rifenbark & Wylie, L.A., 1987-88; resident atty. Liberty Mutual Ins. Co., L.A., 1988-96. Served with USNR, 1943-46, PTO. Mem. Nat. Audubon Soc., Los Angeles Audubon Soc. (officer, bd. dirs. 1983—), Nat. Wildlife Fedn., Nature Conservancy. Methodist. Clubs: Los Angeles Country, Indian Wells Country. Home: 603 S Mccadden Pl Los Angeles CA 90005-3830

KENDIG, JOAN JOHNSTON, neurobiology educator; b. Derby, Conn., May 1, 1939; d. Frank and Agnes (Kerr) Johnston; children: Scott Johnston Kendig, Leslie Anne Kendig. BA, Smith Coll., 1960; PhD, Stanford U., 1966. Rsch. assoc. Stanford U. Med. Sch., 1968-71, asst. prof. biology in anesthesia, 1971-76, assoc. prof., 1976-86, prof., 1986—; mem. physiology study sect. NIH, 1981-85, mem. surgery, anesthesia and trauma study sect., 1996—. NIH neurosci. grantee, 1973—; Javits neurosci. investigator, 1988-95. Mem. Soc. for Neurosci., Assn. U. Anesthesiologists, Am. Pain Soc., Internat. Assn. for Study of Pain. Office: Stanford U Med Sch Dept Anesthesia Stanford CA 94305

KENDIG, WILLIAM LAMAR, retired government official, accountant; b. York, Pa., Apr. 11, 1938; s. Daniel Williamson and Irene Alice Kendig; m. Esther Delores Mostoller, Oct. 14, 1961; 1 child, Marc Daniel. BS, Elizabethtown Coll., 1960; MBA, Am. U., 1965, PhD, 1969. Spl. agt. U.S. Treasury Dept., Washington, 1961-65; staff asst. Procter & Gamble Co., Cin., 1965-66; mgr., cons. Price Waterhouse & Co., Washington, 1968-71; asst. vice chancellor U. Md., College Park, 1971-74, acting vice chancellor, 1974-75; dir., mgmt. cons. U.S. Dept. Interior, Washington, 1975-76, dep. dir. audit and investigations, 1977-78, acting insp. gen., 1978-79, dep. asst. sec., 1979-81, dir. fin. mgmt. and dep. chief fin. officer, 1981-94, acting prin. dep. asst. sec., 1988; mem. Fed. Acctg. Stds. Adv. Bd., 1991-94; ind. cons., 1996—. Contbr. articles to profl. jours. Chmn. ops. com., mem. steering com. 69 Corridor Concerned Citizens, 1996—. Named Meritorious Exec., Pres. of U.S., 1986, Disting. Exec., 1988; recipient Donald Scantlebury award Joint Fin. Mgmt. Improvement Program, 1990. Mem. Fed. Fin. Mgrs. Coun. (chmn. 1982-85, chair mgmt. control coord. com. 1987-92), Assn. Govt. Accts. (nat. exec. com. 1984-87, Chpt. Outstanding Achievement award 1983, 86, Frank Greathouse Disting. Leadership award 1992, Cornelius E. Tierney/Ernst & Young Lifetime Rsch. Achiever award 1996), Pub. Employees Roundtable (bd. dirs. 1987-89, Dir.'s award 1988), Sr. Execs. Assn. (bd. dirs. 1985-91, Ted Kern award 1984), Worldwide Assurance for Employees Pub. Agys. (bd. dirs. 1993-96). Avocations: reading, exercising.

KENDLER, BERNHARD, editor; b. Cin., Jan. 28, 1934; s. Harry Harlan and Mildred (Black) K.; m. Jill Ferguson, Dec. 12, 1975. B.A. in English, NYU, 1955; M.A. in Comparative Lit, U. Mich., 1956. Research asst. Calif. Tchrs. Assn., 1958-60; editor A.S. Barnes & Co., Inc., N.Y.C., 1960-62; copy editor J.B. Lippincott Co., Phila., 1962-63; mng. editor, editor, exec. editor Cornell U. Press, Ithaca, N.Y., 1963—. Mem. Am. Studies Assn., Phi Beta Kappa. Home: 47 Sheraton Dr Ithaca NY 14850-1680 Office:: Cornell U Press PO Box 250 Sage House 512 E State St Ithaca NY 14850-4412

KENDLER, HOWARD H(ARVARD), psychologist, educator; b. N.Y.C., June 9, 1919; s. Harry H. and Sylvia (Rosenberg) K.; m. Tracy Seedman, Sept. 20, 1941; children—Joel Harlan, Kenneth Seedman. A.B., Bklyn. Coll., 1940; M.A., U. Iowa, 1941, Ph.D., 1943. Instr. U. Iowa, 1943; research psychologist OSRD, 1944; asst. prof. U. Colo., 1946-48; assoc. prof. NYU, 1948-51, prof., 1951-63; chmn. dept. Univ. Coll., 1951-61; prof. U. Calif., Santa Barbara, 1963-89, prof. emeritus, 1989—, chmn. dept. psychology, 1965-66; project dir. Office Naval Rsch., 1950-68; prin. investigator NSF, 1953-65, USAAF, 1951-53; mem. adv. panel psychobiology NSF, 1960-62; tng. com. Nat. Inst. Child Health and Human Devel., 1963-66; cons. Dept. Def., Smithsonian Instn., 1959-60, Human Resources Rsch. Office, George Washington U., 1960; vis. prof. U. Calif., Berkeley, 1960-61, Hebrew U., Jerusalem, 1974-75, Tel Aviv U., 1990; chief clin. psychologist Walter Reed Gen. Hosp., 1945-46. Author: Basic Psychology, 1963, 2d edit., 1968, 3d edit., 1974, Basic Psychology: Brief Version, 1977, Psychology: A Science in Conflict, 1981, Historical Foundations of Modern Psychology, 1987; co-author: Basic Psychology: Brief Edition, 1970; co-editor: Essays in Neobehaviorism: A Memorial Volume to Kenneth W. Spence; assoc. editor: Jour. Exptl. Psychology, 1963-65; contbr. to profl. jours., books. Served as 1st lt. AUS. Fellow Center for Advanced Studies in Behaviorial Scis., Stanford, Calif., 1969-70; NSF grantee, 1954-76. Mem. Am. Psychol. Assn. (pres. div. exptl. psychology 1964-65, pres. div. gen. psychology 1967-68), Western Psychol. Assn. (pres. 1970-71), Soc. Exptl. Psychologists (exec. com. 1971-73), Psychonomic Soc. (governing bd. 1963-69, chmn. 1968-69), Sigma Xi. Home and Office: 4596 Camino Molinero Santa Barbara CA 93110-1040

KENDRICK, BUDD LEROY, psychologist; b. Pocatello, Idaho, Apr. 19, 1944; s. Oscar Fredrick Kendrick and Miriam Stuart (Thorn) Stewart; m. Sue Lorraine Allen, Nov. 11, 1966; children: Aaron Matthew and Edgar Seth; m. Beverly Ann Dockter, Dec. 26, 1978; children: Cassandra Rachelle, Angela Priscilla. BA, Idaho State U., 1967, MEd, 1969, EdD, 1974. Lic. psychologist, lic. counselor, Idaho; lic. clin. profl. counselor Mont.; cert. health svc. provider in psychology, nat. cert. counselor; cert. clin. mental health counselor; nat. bd. cert. diplomate hypnotherapist; cert. profl. qualification in psychology. Tchr. psychology Pocatello High Sch., 1967-69; dir. counseling services Midwestern Coll., Denison, Iowa, 1969-70; rehab. counselor Idaho Div. of Vocat. Rehab., Pocatello, 1970-73; counselor (doctoral internship) Counseling Ctr., Idaho State U., Pocatello, 1973-74; rehab. counselor Idaho Div. of Vocat. Rehab., Pocatello, 1974-75; chief of psychology Adult and Child Devel. Ctr., Boise, 1975—; pvt. practice psychology Boise, Idaho, 1977—; vice-chmn. Idaho State Counselor Licensing Bd., 1982-84, chmn. 1984-85, sec. 1985-86; bd. dirs. Nat. Bd. Cert. Counselors Inc., Alexandria, Va., 1986-93, sec., treas., 1987-89; licensure com. Idaho Personnel and Guidance Assn., 1975-78, chmn. 1977-78, rep. Am. Personnel and Guidance Assn. Licensure Network, 1977-78; allied clin. staff Intermountain Hosp., Boise, 1983-93, Northwest Passages Adolescent Hosp., Boise, 1986-93, Saint Alphonsus Regional Med. Ctr., Boise, 1986-93; designated examiner and dispositioner involuntary commitments and guardianships State of Idaho, 1981—; cons. Idaho Personnel Commn., 1982—; grad. sch. lectr. Idaho State U., 1975; grad. sch. faculty affiliate, Coll. of Idaho, Caldwell, 1981-86; presenter concerning counselor credentialing issues, 1981-86; treas. Idaho Mental Health Assn., 1980-81; mem. Idaho Psychology, Social Work reclassification task force, 1990-91; mem. Idaho Assn. Counseling and Devel. Legis. Task Force for Third Party Benefits for Lic. Profl. Counselors, 1990. Editor: Directory of the Idaho Psychol. Assn., 1983; author numerous articles on hypnosis, counseling and profl. credentialing. Mem. adv. bd. Trio (Upward Bound, Talent Search, Head Start), Idaho State U., 1975-76; mem. Human Rights Com., Idaho State Sch. and Hosp., 1977. Recipient Disting. Svc. award Idaho Pers. & Guidance Assn., 1978, Profl. Achievement award Idaho State U., 1987, Spl. Recognition award Idaho Assn. for Counseling and Devel., 1989, Lawrence Schumacher Meml. Employee of Yr. award State of Idaho, 1995. Fellow Am. Coll. Advanced Practice Psychologists (founding), Idaho Psychol. Assn. (sec. 1982-84); mem. Idaho Mental Health Counselors Assn. (charter), Idaho Counseling Assn. (leadership coun. 1977-78), Am. Counseling Assn. (pub. policy and legis. com., mem.-at-large 1992-94, chairperson nat. licensure subcom. 1992-94), Am. Mental Health Counselors Assn., Am. Psychol. Assn. (divsn. 17 counseling psychology, div. 30 psychol. hypnosis), Sons of Confederate Vets., Chi Sigma Iota Internat. Profl. Counseling and Acad. Honor Soc. Avocations: sword collecting, genealogy, collecting limited edits. Civil War pewter sculptures, War Between the States history, collecting autographed celebrity photographs.

KENDRICK, DAVID ANDREW, economist, educator; b. Gatesville, Tex., Nov. 14, 1937; s. Andrew Green and Nina Alice (Murray) K.; m. Gail Tidd, July 4, 1964; children—Ann, Colin. B.A., U. Tex., 1960; Ph.D. (Woodrow Willson fellow 1961-62), MIT, 1965. Asst. prof. Harvard U., Cambridge, Mass., 1966-70; vis. scholar Stanford U., Calif., 1969-70; vis. prof. MIT, Cambridge, 1978-79; prof. econs. U. Tex., Austin, 1970—. Author: (with A. Stoutiesdijk) The Planning of Industrial Investment Programs, 1978, (with P. Dixon and S. Bowles) Notes and Problems in Microeconomic Theory, 1980, Stochastic Control for Economic Models, 1981, Feedback: A New Framework for Macroeconomic Policy, 1988, Models for Analyzing Comparative Advantage, 1990. Served with U.S. Army, 1960-61. Ford faculty fellow, 1969-70. Fellow AAAS; mem. Econometric Soc., Am. Econs. Assn., Soc. Econ. Dynamics and Control. (pres. 1980), Soc. Computational Econs. (pres. 1998). Home: 7209 Lamplight Ln Austin TX 78731-2119 Office: U Tex Dept Econs ECB 3-134E Austin TX 78712

KENDRICK, JAMES EARL, business consultant; b. Indpls., Sept. 12, 1940; s. John William and Mab.e E. (Coleman) K.; m. Carrie L. Fair, July 19, 1969; children: Carrie F., Leslie F., John F. BA, Butler U., 1963; postgrad., Ind. U., 1963-65. Exec. dir. Knox County Econ. Opportunity Coun., Barbourville, Ky., 1965-66; rsch. scientist NYU, 1967-68; mgr. Volt Info. Scis., Washington, 1968-71, Nat. Urban Coalition, 1972-74; pres. Kendrick & Co., Washington, 1974-91; sr. v.p. Kendrick & Co., 1992-93; pres. P2C2 Group, Silver Spring, Md., 1994—; devel. cons. Coppin State Coll., Balt., 1995—. Author: Community Energy Workbook, 1974; National Urban Agenda Survey, 1974; (video) Americans on the Move, 1984; (software) Help for PC DDS, 1985; contbr. articles to profl. jours. and newsletters. Mem. Fellowship Merry Christians. Recipient Rural Svc. award OEO, 1968; citation Washington chpt. Am. Soc. Tng. and Devel., 1971; named one of Outstanding Young Men of Am., 1974, Ranked Among the Best 100 Mgmt. Firms in N.Am. by Consulting News, 1993. Mem. Inst. Mgmt. Consultants, Assn. Proposal Mgmt. Profls., Sigma Delta Chi. Office: P2C2 Group 2402 Darrow St Silver Spring MD 20902-4919*

KENDRICK, JOHN LAWRENCE, software engineer; b. Oak Ridge, Tenn., Oct. 14, 1956; s. Lawrence W. and Ruby Nell (Harper) K.; m. Leslie Lynn Jacobs, Aug. 20, 1988; children: David John, Andrew Robert. BA in Physics, U. Del., 1979; MS in Physics, U. N.C., 1983; MS in Computer Sci., Johns Hopkins U., 1994. Sr. analyst Gen. Physics Corp., Columbia, Md., 1984-89; sr. computer scientist Computer Scis. Corp., Hanover, Md., 1989-97; sr. software engr. Kimmich Software Sys., Inc., Columbia, 1997—. Mem. leadership coun. So. Poverty Law Ctr.; bd. deacons Mt. Hebron Presbyn. Ch. Mem. IEEE, Assn. Computing Machinery, Assn. Preservation of Civil War Sites, Appalachian Trail Conf., Mountain Club Md., Potomac Appalachian Trail Club, Save Historic Antietam Found., Civil War Trust. Presbyterian. Avocations: hiking, tennis, golf. Office: Kimmich Software Sys Inc 7235 Dockside Ln Columbia MD 21045-5049 Office: 8611 Trail View Dr Ellicott City MD 21043-6082

KENDRICK, JOHN WHITEFIELD, economist, educator, consultant; b. N.Y.C., July 27, 1917; s. Benjamin Burks and Elizabeth W.W. (Shields) K.; m. Maxine Fillyaw; children: Bonnie Elizabeth, Karen Johanna, John Burks. AB, U. N.C., 1937, MA, 1939; PhD, George Washington U., 1955. Economist Nat. Resources Planning Bd., Washington, 1941-43; economist U.S. Dept. Commerce, Washington, 1946-53, chief economist, 1976-77; sr. staff mem. Nat. Bur. Econ. Rsch., N.Y.C., 1953-56, part-time, 56-78; prof. econs. George Washington U., Washington, 1956-88, prof. emeritus, 1988—; univ. prof. U. Conn., Storrs, 1964-66; vis. prof. Georgetown U., UCLA, Stanford U., U. Hawaii, Simon Fraser U., v.p. for econ. rsch. The Conf. Bd., N.Y.C., 1972-73, part-time, 1973-76; dir., trustee Pioneer Mut. Funds, Boston, 1961—; bd. dirs. Am. Productivity and Quality Ctr., Houston, 1977—; cons. AT&T, 1964-83, Office Mgmt. and Budget, NSF, GAO, other cos. and govt. agys.; mem. Conf. on Rsch. in Income and Wealth, chmn. 1963-64; adj. scholar Am. Enterprise Inst., 1980-86. Author: Productivity Trends in the United States, 1961 (Pres. Kennedy Libr. award 1962), (with Daniel Creamer) Measuring Company Productivity: Handbook with Case Studies, 1961, rev. edit., 1965, Economic Accounts and Their Uses, 1972, The Formation and Stocks of Total Capital, 1976 (also Russian trans.), Improving Company Productivity, 1977, (with E. Grossman) Productivity in the United States: Trends and Cycles, 1980, (with John B. Kendrick) Personal Productivity, 1988 (trans. in Korean and Japanese), other books; editor 6 conf. vols.; mem. editorial bds. Rev. of Income and Wealth, Bus. Econs.; contbr. over 150 articles to profl. jours. 1st lt. A.C., U.S. Army, 1943-45; served with U.S. Strategic Bombing Survey, 1945-46, ETO. Recipient Graham Dodd award for article Fin. Analysts Jour., 1962, Abramson award for article in Bus. Econs. jour., 1987. Fellow Am. Statis. Assn., Nat. Assn. Bus. Economists; mem. Am. Econ. Assn., So. Econ. Assn. (pres. 1982-83), Nat. Economists Club (pres. 1975-76, chmn. bd. 1976-77), World Acad. Productivity Sci., Atlantic Econ. Soc. (disting. assoc., pres. 1992-93), George Washington U. Club, Phi Beta Kappa. Unitarian-Universalist. Avocations: swimming, walking, reading, TV talk shows. Home: 6363 Waterway Dr Falls Church VA 22044-1323 Office: George Washington U Dept Econ Washington DC 20052*

KENDRICK, JOSEPH TROTWOOD, former foreign service officer, writer, consultant; b. Pryor, Okla., Feb. 5, 1920; s. Joseph Trotwood and Anne (Williams) K.; m. Loreine York, July 18, 1942 (div. 1954); m. Elise Fleager Simpkins, Aug. 20, 1955 (div. 1977); children: Pamela York, Drew Trotwood (dec. 1970), Juliette Simpkins, Katherine Mary. Student, U. Okla., 1938-40; B.S., Georgetown U., 1948; M.A., Columbia, 1951; Ph.D., George Washington U., 1979; postgrad., Cambridge (Eng.) U., 1998. Joined Fgn. Svc., U.S. Dept. State, 1941; assigned Nicaragua, Poland, USSR, Germany, 1941-54; spl. asst. to dir. Office Ea. European Affairs, U.S. Dept. State, Washington, 1954-57, pub. affairs adviser, 1958; 2d sec., consul Am. Embassy, Kabul, Afghanistan, 1959-61; dep. polit. adviser SHAPE, Paris, 1962-64; polit. counselor Am. Embassy, Oslo, 1964-68; dep. dir. Office Atomic Energy and Aerospace, U.S. Dept. State, 1968-70, dir., 1970-71, spl. asst. to dir. Bur. Pol. Mil. Affairs, 1971-72; detailed to Dept. Def., 1972-73; dean, Center for Area and Country Studies, Fgn. Svc. Inst., U.S. Dept. State, 1974-75; writer, cons., 1975—. Author: Executive-Legislative Consultation on Foreign Policy: Strengthening Executive Branch Procedures. Served to lt. (jg.) USNR, 1944-46. Recipient Outstanding Civilian Service medal Dept. Army, 1974. Mem. Am. Assn. Advancement Slavic Studies, Am. Fgn. Service Assn., Am. Polit. Sci. Assn., Inst. Strategic Studies (London), Delta Chi.

KENDRICK, MARK CLEVELAND, real estate executive; b. Augsburg, Germany, Dec. 30, 1957; (parents Am. citizens); s. Chester Delmon and Eva Anna (Mitterndorfer) K.; m. Sharon K. Greenland, 1993. AA in Law Enforcement, Fayetteville (N.C.) C.C., 1982; BA in Social Work, Meth. Coll., Fayetteville, 1983; M in Guidance, Campbell U., Ft. Bragg, N.C., 1986. Cert. internat. employee assistance profl., N.C. Emergency response team Moore Meml. Hosp., Pinehurst, N.C., 1974-76; mgr. Fleishman's, Fayetteville, 1977-78; mgr. furnishings Nowells, Fayetteville, 1978-79; deputy Cumberland Co. Sheriff's Dept., Fayetteville, 1982-83; ptnr. Kendrick Real Estate, Fayetteville, 1983—, KD Graphics, Fayetteville, 1989—; employee assistance profl. Carolina Employee Assistance Svcs., Fayetteville, 1995—. vol. N.C. Dept. of Corrections, 1981-82, intern, 1980; dep. Cumberland County Sheriff's Dept., 1982—, dep. search and recovery team, 1991-97; comptr. Cape Fear Fair Assn., 1985-88; v.p. Cumberland County Heart Assn., 1984-85; sub-sgt. Cumberland County Rescue Squad, 1979-82; adv. commn. Fayetteville Parks and Recreation, 1982-86; bd. dirs. Fayetteville Sr. Citizens Svc. Ctr., 1983-86, Fayetteville Parks and Recreation Five Yr. Study Commn., 1984-86, Cumberland Interfaith Hospitality Network, Inc., 1995-97; pres. Cumberland County Smart Start, 1995-97; Fayetteville City Councilman, 1986—; mem. Fayetteville Revitalization Commn., 1986-89, Fayetteville-Cumberland County Liaison Com., 1986-89, City-County Fire Liaison Com., 1986-89, ARC Disaster Team, 1984-86, Young Dem. Club, N.C. Trnasp. Adv. Com., 1989—; chmn. City Streets-Sidewalks and Transp. Com., 1989—, City County Liaison, 1986-87, PWC Deregulation com., 1998—; mem. comms. and pub. policy com. N.C. League of Municipalities, 1999—; mem. pub. safety and crime prevention com. Nat. League of Cities, 1999—; sec. Myrover-Reese Fellowship Homes, Inc., 1992—; exec. com. Fayetteville Hospitality House, 1992-96; chmn. N.C. Partnership for Children, 1995-97, mem. state strategic planning com., 1996-97; active Fayetteville Once and for All com., 1995—; Sunday Sch. dir. Grace Bapt. Ch., 1996—, deacon, 1997—; bd. dirs. Homeless Coalition, 1997—. Named 1st 10th Degree Jaycee in Nation U.S. Jaycees, 1985, one of Five Outstanding Young Men in N.C. Farm Bur., 1985, Outstanding Young Person in Govt., 1986; recipient Disting. Svc. award, 1985, Charles Kulp Jr. Meml. award U.S. Jaycees, 1985, Thomas Jefferson award Sta. WTVD-TV, 1986. Mem. Fayetteville Jaycees (pres. 1984-85, treas. 1985-87), N.C. Jaycees (regional dir. 1985-86, awards chmn. 1986-87, Freedom Guard award 1984, Linn D. Garibaldi award 1985-86, Larry Bowers Meml. award 1986), Meth. Coll. Alumni Assn. (bd. dirs. 1985-95, v.p. 1993-95), KP, Toastmasters (N.C. state speaker 1984), Lions (v.p., Fayetteville host 1996-97, pres. 1997-98), Lambda Chi Alpha. Democrat. Baptist. Avocations: gun collecting, target shooting, scuba diving, travel, drums. Home and Office: Kendrick Real Estate 2927 Rosecroft Dr Fayetteville NC 28304

KENDRICK, PETER MURRAY, communications executive, investor; b. Winchester, Mass., Oct. 8, 1936; s. Wallace Dolloff and Esther (Burke) K.; m. Grace Terry, June 17, 1967; children: Caroline, Timothy. BSBA, Babson Coll., 1962. Office mgr. Am. Hosp. Supply Corp., Chgo. and Charlotte, N.C., 1962-65; registered rep. Hayden, Stone & Co., 1966-69; gen. mgr. Continental Cablevision, Concord, N.H. and Jackson, Mich., 1969-74; pres. New Eng. Cablevision, Portland, Maine, 1974-79; chmn. bd. New Eng. Cablevision, 1980; pres. Home Theater Network, Portland, 1977-87; chmn. bd. Envirologic Data Corp., Portland, 1984-86; sr. v.p. Watson Techs., Portland, 1994-96; pres., CEO, chmn. Internet Maine, Internet N.E., Inc. (merger Harvard Net, Inc.), Portland, 1997; interim CEO Compass Cablesys., Portland and Marblehead, Mass., 1998; CEO Masterpiece Network, eArt Galleries, Portland, 1999—; founder The Travel Channel, 1981; vice chmn. bd. dirs., pres., treas. Internat. Cablevision, Inc., Bronxville, N.Y., 1987-93; chmn. bd. Kendrick Corp., Portland, Maine, 1986—, Kendrick Tech. Corp., 1992—, Legal Document Systems, Inc., Washington, 1993-94, The Film Channel, Inc., Portland, 1987-90, Yankee Books, Camden, Maine, 1989-91. Trustee North Yarmouth Acad., Yarmouth, Maine, chmn. ann. giving campaign, 1986-87. With USAF, 1956-59. Recipient Highest Programming award Cable TV Nat. Assn., 1973, 86. Mem. New Eng. Cable TV Assn. (v.p. 1972, pres. 1975), Mich. Cable TV Assn. (v.p. 1973), Portland Country Club, Portland Yacht Club, Cable TV Pioneers. Home: Landing Woods Ln Falmouth ME 04105 Office: 565 Congress St Ste 305 Portland ME 04101

KENDRICK, ROBERT WARREN, county administrator, superindendent; b. Houston, July 9, 1946; s. Alford Manuel and Alpha Mae (Carter) K.; m. Margaret Walker, June 9, 1973. BA, U. Houston, 1969, JD, 1977; mgmt. cert., Harvard U., 1989. Cert. security cons., law enforcement and security instr.; tech. mgmt. cert. Tex. A&M U., 1996. Dist. exec. Boy Scouts Am., Monroe, La., 1974; corp. security coord. Foley's Dept. Stores, Houston, 1975-77, staff legal asst., 1978-81; exec. dir. Crimestoppers of Houston, Inc., 1982; coord. criminal justice ct. U. Houston-Downtown, 1983-85, assoc. dir. criminal justice ct., 1985-87, dir. criminal justice ct., 1987-89, exec. dir. divsn. continuing edn., dean's coun., 1989-96, spl. asst., provost, 1996-97; adminstrv. supt. precinct 3 Harris County, 1997—; chair policy com., Dept. Justice Houston Project, 1998—; bd. dirs. Am. Soc. Indsl. Security Found., Washington, 1988—, Internat. Found. Protection Officers, Cochrane, Can., 1988-89, U. Tex. Health Sci. Ctr. Cmty. Adv. Bd., Houston, 1987-89. Mem. editl. adv. bd. Security Jour., 1989-98. Councilman, City of Bellaire, Tex., 1984-86, planning and zoning commr., 1982-84; bd. dirs. Learning Resource Network, 1993-97; mem. regional criminal justice planning com. Houston-Galveston Area Coun. Govts., 1984—; founding bd. dirs. Crime Stoppers Houston, 1981; grand juror Harris County Grand Jury, Houston, 1989; mem. Mayor's Tex. City Action Plan Task Force, 1993; mem. Mayor's Imagine Houston Project, 1994-96; criminal justice com. Leadership Houston, 1989—; chmn. profl. devel. Press Club of Houston, 1996-97; commr. Joint City/County Commn. on Children, 1997—; chair Harris County Internet com., 1998—. Capt. U.S. Army, 1971-73. Recipient Corp. Security award Security World Mag., 1977. Mem. Am. Soc. Indsl. Security (chpt. chmn. 1980, Security Svc. award 1994), Risk and Ins. Mgmt. Soc. (local bd. mem. 1979-81), Tex. Pub. Rels. Assn., Harris County Area Chiefs of Police, Buffalo Bayou Partnership (security com. advisor 1988—), Houston C. of C. (chmn. crime control com. 1988—), Leadership Houston (grad., bd. dirs. 1987—). Avocations: mil. history, Titantic Hist. Soc., swimming. Office: Harris County Precinct 3 16635 Clay Rd Houston TX 77084

KENDRICK, RONALD H., banker; b. San Diego, Sept. 17, 1941; s. Wesley Samuel and Ruth Helen (Hunter) K.; m. Cheryl Donofrio Ayers, June 10, 1989; 1 child by previous marriage, Kirsten Dawn; stepchildren: Joshua Ayers, Benjamin Ayers. AB in Econs., San Diego State U., 1964, MBA in Fin., 1975; grad. investment mgmt. workshop, Harvard U., 1974, grad. strategic mktg. mgmt., 1993; grad., Pacific Coast Banking Sch. U. Wash., 1981. Chartered fin. analyst. Exec. v.p. Union Bank, San Diego, 1959—; lectr. San Diego State U., 1975-81; faculty Pacific Coast Banking Sch., Seattle, 1983-85; regent Fin. Analysts Seminar, Rockford, Ill., 1975-78; bd. dirs. Union Bank Found., Union Bank PAC, Old Globe; bus. and econ. devel. counsel to Mayor of San Diego, 1995. Treas. Boy Scouts Am. San Diego coun., 1984-85, bd. dirs. 1977-94; mem. adv. com. North County Campus San Diego State U., 1984-89; mem. adv. com. Calif. State U., San Marcos, 1989-93; trustee Hall Sci. and Reuben H. Fleet Space Theater, San

Diego, 1984-91, pres., 1988-90; bd. dirs. ARC, SanDiego, 1983-90, chmn., 1985-87; bd. dirs. Symphony Assn., San Diego, 1983-86, San Diegan's Inc., San Diego, 1984-89, United Way San Diego, 1988-94, chmn. United Way San Diego campaign, 1995-96, San Diego County YMCA, 1992—, Old Globe Theatre, 1995; bd. dirs. Lead, Inc., 1985-86, 87-93, pres., 1990-91; bd dirs. Children's Hosp. Found., 1988-98, chmn., 1992-93; bd. dirs. Children's Hosp., 1998—; mem. task force to study indsl. element San Diego gen. plan, 1977; mem. bus. and econ. devel. coun. Mayor of San Diego, 1995. Recipient Disting. Alumnus award Coll. Bus. San Diego State U.,1984, Silver Beaver award, Humanitarian of Yr. Boy Scouts Am., 1991, Disting. Eagle award Boy Scouts Am., 1993; named Alumnus of Yr., Lead Inc., 1992. Mem. Fin. Analysts Soc. (pres. 1978-79), Calif. Bankers Assn. (bd. dirs.), Greater San Diego C. of C. (exec. com. 1989), Zool. Soc. San Francisco, Indian Wells C. of C., La Jolla Country Club (bd. dirs. 1997—), Century Club (bd. dirs. 1996—), Rotary. Republican. Avocations: tennis; golf; woodworking; skiing. Home: 3620 Curtis St San Diego CA 92106-1202 Office: Union Bank 530 B St San Diego CA 92101-4407

KENDRICK, THOMAS RUDOLPH, chemist; b. Muskogee, Okla., Sept. 30, 1933; s. Arthur Lang and Prince Alice (Callins) K. Student, Langston U., 1951-54, U. N.C., Fayetteville, 1961; BS, Northeastern State U., Tahlequah, Okla., 1968; ThM, So. Bible Seminary, Birmingham, Ala., 1971. Ordained to ministry Bapt. Ch. as deacon. Tchr. Carter G. Woodson High Sch., Tullahassee, Okla., 1954-55; various lab. technician positions, 1955-61, mil. pharmacist various locations, 1961-65; lab. technician Fansteel Metals, Muskogee, 1965-68, analytical chemist, 1968-90; analytical chemist Tantalum Prodn. Inc., Muskogee, 1990-92; local cons. chemist Thai Tantalum Inc., Gurnee, Ill., 1993-95; cons. Muskogee, Okla., 1995—; career cons. area schs. and chs., Muskogee, 1969—; judge Regional Sci. Fair, Muskogee, 1970, 95, 98—; instr. sci. and bus., Liberty Bapt. Coll., 1998—. Co-author: (book) Today's Greatest Poems, 1983 (Merit award 1983), Our Western World's Greatest Poems, 1983 (Merit award 1983), Our Western World's Most Beautiful Poems, 1985 (Merit award 1985); inventor in field. 2d rep. congl. dist. committeeman, Muskogee, 1976-83, 93-95; chmn. 3d ward Daxon for Gov. Com., Muskogee County, 1982; chmn., founder Muskogee county Black Rep. Coun., 1977—; Muskogee City bd. Adjustment, 1993-99; kitchen cabinet mem., coord., Gary Richardson for congress, 1978-80; mem. Muskogee County Rep. Exec. Com., 1974—, chmn. resolutions com., 1975; sustaining mem. Rep. Nat. com., 1980—; mem. Nat. Black Rep. Coun.; monitor Okla. Water Resources Bd. Water Watch Program, 1999—. With U.S. Army, 1960-65. Recipient Danforth Leadership award Danforth found., 1951, Appreciation of Commitment award Pres. Ronal Reagan, 1981, 88, Golden Jubilee Bronze plaque Antioch Bapt. ch., Muskogee, 1985, Golden Poet award World of Poetry, 1985-88, 91, Silver Powt award 1989-90, Polit. Leadership Cert. Nat. Black Rep. Coun., 1979-80, Cert. of Appreciation Okla. Reps., 1991; named Muskogee's Artistic Person of Yr. Zeta Phi Beta Sorority, 1998. Mem. Smithsonian Inst. (assoc.), Okla. Black Chemists Guild (founder, pres. 1986—), Am. Legion, Nat. Arbor Day Found., Omega Psi Phi (basileus 1953-54, keeper of records and seal 1975-76, founder Phi Pi chpt. Muskogee 1975). Lodge: Masons (sec., worthy patron). Achievements include invention of special glass stage for micropaleontology microscope; development of method of platinum recovery producing low-oxygen platinum, of various technics involving gasses in refractory metals, of method for producing low-oxygen tantalum powder. Home and Office: PO Box 2635 Muskogee OK 74402-2635

KENDRICK, WILLIAM BRYCE, biology educator, author, publisher; b. Liverpool, Lancashire, Eng., Dec. 3, 1933; arrived in Can., 1958; s. William and Lillian Maud (Latham) K.; m. Laureen Anne Carscadden, Dec. 14, 1978; children: Clinton, Kelly. BSc with honors, U. Liverpool, 1955, PhD, 1958, DSc, 1980. Postdoctoral fellow NRC, Ottawa, Ont., Can., 1958-59; rsch. scientist Agr. Can., Ottawa, 1959-65; asst. prof. U. Waterloo, Ont., 1965-66, assoc. prof., 1966-71, prof., 1971-94, disting. prof. emeritus, 1994—, assoc. dean, 1985-93; adj. prof. U. Victoria, B.C., 1994—; propr. Mycologue Pub. Author: The Fifth Kingdom, 1985, 2d rev. and enlarged edit., 1991, 3rd edit. CD Rom, 1999, A Young Person's Guide To The Fungi, 1986; co-author: Genera of Hyphomycetes, 1980, An Evolutionary Survey of Fungi, Algae and Plants, 1992; editor: Taxonomy of Fungi Imperfecti, The Whole Fungus, Biology of Conidial Fungi; contbr. articles to profl. jours. Guggenheim fellow, 1979-80. Fellow Royal Soc. Can.; mem. Acad. Sci. (hon. sec. 1984-91), Mycological Soc. Am. (Disting. Mycologist award 1995), Br. Mycol. Soc. (centenary fellow 1996). Mem. Green Party. Avocations: reading, music, walking, photography, scuba diving. E-mail: mycolog@pacificcoast.net. Home and Office: 8727 Lochside Dr, Sidney, BC Canada V8L 1M8 *Curiosity is the key to a full life. Keep on asking questions-and keep on trying to answer them-until the day you die.*

KENDZIOR, ROBERT JOSEPH, marketing executive; b. Chgo., Mar. 24, 1952; s. Joseph W. and Josephine R. Kendzior. BArch, Ill. Inst. Tech., 1975. Account supr. Burger King Corp., Rogers Merchandising, Inc., Chgo., 1975-77; account exec. Walgreen Corp., Eisaman, Johns & Laws Advt., Inc., Chgo., 1977-78; v.p./mktg. Dunkin Donuts Am., Inc., Randolph, Mass., 1978-95; v.p., chief mktg. officer Factory Card Outlet Am., Inc., Chgo., 1995-98; v.p. internat. mktg. Allied Domecq Retailing, Glendale, Calif., 1999—. Recipient Most Valuable Promotion award PepsiCo, 1984. Mem. Triangle Fraternity, Merchandising Execs. Club Chgo.

KENEN, PETER BAIN, economist, educator; b. Cleve., Nov. 30, 1932; s. Isaiah Leo and Beatrice (Bain) K.; m. Regina Horowitz, Aug. 21, 1955; children: Joanne Lisa, Marc David, Stephanie Hope, Judith Rebecca. AB, Columbia U., 1954; MA, Harvard U., 1956, PhD, 1958. Mem. faculty Columbia U., 1957-71, prof. econs., 1964-71, chmn. dept., 1967-69, provost univ., 1969-70; prof. econs. and internat. fin. Princeton (N.J.) U., 1971—, dir. internat. fin. sect., 1971-99; Ford rsch. prof. U. Calif., Berkeley, 1979-80; Res. Bank Australia professorial fellow Australian Nat. U., 1983-84; rschr. on internat. monetary theory and policy; cons. Coun. Econ. Advisors, 1961, U.S. Treasury, 1962-68, 77-80, 95-98, Bur. Budget, 1964-68, IMF, 1990, 92. Author: British Monetary Policy and the Balance of Payments (1951-57), 1960, Giant Among Nations, 1960, (with A.G. Hart and A. Entine) Money, Debt and Economic Activity, 4th edit., 1969, (with R. Lubitz) International Economics, 3d edit., 1971, A Model of the U.S. Balance of Payments, 1978, (with P.R. Allen) Asset Markets, Exchange Rates, and Economic Integration, 1980, Essays in International Economics, 1980, Managing Exchange Rates, 1988, Exchange Rates and Policy Coordination, 1989, International Economy, 3d edit., 1994, Exchange Rates and the Monetary System, 1994, Economic and Monetary Union in Europe, 1995; editor: International Trade and Finance, Frontiers for Research, 1975, (with others) The International Monetary System Under Flexible Exchange Rates, 1982, (with R.W. Jones) Handbook of International Economics, 1984, Managing the World Economy, 1994, Understanding Interdependence, 1995; contbr. articles to profl. jours. Recipient David A. Wells prize Harvard U., 1958-59, Univ. medal Columbia U., 1977; Ctr. Advanced Study Behavioral Scis. fellow, 1971-72, John Simon Guggenheim Found. fellow, 1975-76, Royal Inst. Internat. Affairs fellow, 1987-88, German Marshall Fund fellow, 1987-88, Houblon-Norman fellow Bank of Eng., 1991-92. Mem. Am. Econ. Assn., Coun. Fgn. Rels., Royal Econ. Soc., Group of Thirty. Home: 176 Western Way Princeton NJ 08540-7208 Office: Princeton U Dept of Econs Fisher Hall Princeton NJ 08544-1021

KENICK, JOSEPH LOUIS, III, construction executive; b. Nashua, NH, Aug. 1, 1968; s. Joseph Louis Jr. and Betty Jeanne (Kahn) K. AAS in Civil Tech., U. N.H., 1992, AS in Constrn. Mgmt.; 1998; AS in Acctg. and Mgmt., N.H. Cmty. Tech. Coll., Stratham, 1998; BS in Tech. Mgmt., N.H. Coll., Portsmouth, 1998. Merchandiser Maximum Merchandising, N.Y.C., 1988; constrn. contractor Exeter, N.H., 1988-92; machinist 2nd ops. N.H. Machine Products, Exeter, 1991; supr. 2nd ops./shipping receiving Exeter Machine Products, 1991-92; salesman forklift operator Sams Club, Seabrook, N.H., 1992-94; grade foreman, supt. Midway Excavators, South Hampton, N.H., 1994-96; supt. Kendon Corp., Deerfield, N.H., 1997; asst. project mgr. Corcoran Jennison Constrn. Vol., coach, chaperone Exeter Recreation Dept., 1986—; baseball asst. coach Exeter Jr. League, 1988-91; ski coach Spl. Olympics N.H., 1994—; dist. round table commr. historic dist. Boy Scouts Am., So. N.H., 1990—, asst. scoutmaster troop 323, Exeter, 1986—, scoutmaster, 1993-96; mem. student senate N.H. Cmty. Tech. Coll., 1997-98. Recipient Commrs. Arrowhead and Key, Historic Dist., Boy Scouts Am., 1995, Silver Cross award Christ Episcopal Ch., 1986; U.S. All Am. scholar, 1998. Mem. Order of Arrow (brotherhood mem. Passacondway Lodge 1984—), Exeter Sportsman's Club, N.H. Outing Club (trip leader 1986-87), Free Masons. Avocations: community service, outdoor activities, sports, fitness. Home: 3 Charter St Exeter NH 03833-2303

KENIEN, NICHOLAS N., psychologist; b. Binghamton, N.Y., Feb. 16, 1973; s. David Lee and Kathy (Skuse) K. BA in English Lit., Elizabethtown Coll., 1995; MS in Counseling Psychology, Western Md. Coll., 1996; EdS in Sch. Psychology, Millersville U. Pa., 1998. Residential therapist Philhaven Behavioral Healthcare, Mt. Gretna, Pa., 1996—; grad. asst., acad. advisor Millersville U. Pa., Elizabethtown, 1997—. Mem. Nat. Assn. Sch. Psychologists. Avocations: tennis, reading, soccer, fishing. Home: 21 E Walnut St Lancaster PA 17602-4997

KENIN, DAVID S., lawyer; b. N.Y.C., Mar. 26, 1934; s. Louis and Molly Kenin; ;m. Josephine Wien, Oct. 12, 1980; children: Carole Kenin Ganguzza, Marla R. BBA, U. Miami, 1955, LLD cum laude, 1963. Bar: U.S. Dist. Ct. (so. dist.) Fla. 1964, U.S. Ct. Appeals (11th cir.) 1966, U.S. Supreme Ct. 1967. Pres. Kenad Constrn. Co., Miami, Fla., 1955-63; ptnr. Myers, Kenin, Levinson & Richards, Miami, 1963-88; shareholder Greenberg, Traurig, P.A., Miami, 1988—; bd. dirs. Ctrl. Bank, Miami. Trustee Fla. Internat. U. Found., Miami, 1986—. 1st lt. U.S. Army, 1955-56. Mem. Fla. Bar Assn., Fed. Bar Assn., Dade County Bar Assn. Avocation: tennis. Office: Greenberg Traurig PA 1221 Brickell Ave Miami FL 33131-3224

KENISON, LYNN T., chemist; b. Provo, Utah, Feb. 20, 1943; s. John Silves and Grace (Thacker) K.; m. Daralyn Wold, June 10, 1969; children: Marlene, Mark, Evan, Guy, Amy, Suzanne. BS in Chemistry, Brigham Young U., 1968, MS in Chemistry, 1971. Tchr. Weber County Sch. Dist., Ogden, Utah, 1968-69; bench chemist (drugs) Salt Lake City/County Health Dept., 1971-74; chemist U.S. Dept. Labor, OSHA Salt Lake Tech. Ctr., 1974—, bench chemist, 1974-77, supr., br. chief, 1977-84, sr. chemist, 1984—; tech. writer OSHA. Editor: Review Methods and Analytical Papers Before Publication, 1984—; tech. writer, 1984—. Councilman West Bountiful City, Utah, 1980-83, 85-89; scouting coord. Boy Scouts Am., cubmaster local pack, 1990-94, unit commr. scouting, 1995—; full-time missionary LDS Ch., Ark., Mo., Ill., 1962-64; vol. spkr. in local pub. schs., 1988—. Mem. Am. Indsl. Hygiene Assn., Fed. Exec. Assn. (Disting. Svc. award, Jr. Award for Outstanding Fed. and Cmty. Svc. 1980), Toastmasters Internat. (treas. Salt Lake City chpt. 1987-91). Avocations: woodworking, church activities, Boy Scout activities. Home: 1745 N 600 W West Bountiful UT 84087-1150 Office: US Dept of Labor OSHA Salt Lake Tech Ctr 1781 S 300 W Salt Lake City UT 84115-1802

KENISON, RAYMOND ROBERT, fraternal organization administrator, director; b. Mo., Sept. 23, 1932; s. Raymond Roy and Emma Oleta (Holder) K.; m. Marjorie White, Feb. 1, 1955; children: Debra Kenison Brown, Peggy Kenison Crim, Raymond Roger, Robert B. *Wife, Marjorie White Kenison is a interior decorator and a poet. She is currently preparing a book of poetry for publication.* AA, Hannibal LaGrange Coll., 1953; BA, U. Mo., 1961; postgrad., Cen. Bapt. Sem., Kansas City, 1957, Midwestern Bapt. Sem., Kansas City, 1965; cert. fin. planner, Coll. Fin. Planning, Denver; DivD, Hannibal LaGrange Coll., 1994. Cert. instr. Pastor First Bapt.Ch., Bates City, Mo., 1954-56, Friendship Bapt. Ch., Mexico, Mo., 1956-62, Immanuel Bapt. Ch., Hannibal, Mo., 1962-77; dir. devel. Mo. Bapt. Children's Home, Bridgeton, 1977-80, exec. dir., 1980—; pres., 1992—; pres. bd. trustees Hannibal-Lagrange Coll.; co-founder, pres. Viability R & D Group. Mem. Child Welfare League of Am. Inc.; Nat. Soc. of Fund Raising Execs.; pres. Hannibal Coun. Alcohol and Drug Abuse; bd. dirs. Hannibal Cmty. Chest, 1974-79, pres. Hannibal Ministerial Alliance; bd. dirs. Alliance for Children and Families, Mo. Alliance for Children and Families. Kenison Complex named in his honor. Mem. Nat. Foster Parents Assn., So. Bapt. Child Care Execs. (pres.), Nat. Assn. of Homes for Children (sec.), Mo. Child Care Assn. (bd. dirs., pres. 1994—), S.W. Assn. of Child Care Execs., Inst. CFPs, Hannibal Investment Club (pres. 1976-78, 82-83), Viability R&D Group (co-founder, pres.). Home: 193 Lake Apollo Dr Hannibal MO 63401-6218 Office: Mo Bapt Children's Home 11300 Saint Charles Rock Rd Bridgeton MO 63044-2793

KENISTON, KENNETH, psychologist, educator; b. Chgo., Jan. 6, 1930; s. Hayward and Roberta (Cannell) K.; m. Ellen Uviller, June 20, 1960 (div. Aug. 1975); children: Ann Rogers, Sarah Hayward; m. Suzanne Berger, Jan. 10, 1976; 1 child, Daniel Eben. BA, Harvard Coll., 1951; DPhil, Oxford U., 1956; LLD (hon.), Notre Dame U., 1971; DSc (hon.), Colgate U., 1972. From rsch. asst. to rsch. assoc. dept. social rels. Harvard U., Cambridge, Mass., 1955-62; from asst. prof. to assoc. prof. psych. Yale Med. Sch., New Haven, 1962-68; prof. psych. Yale Med. Sch., 1968-75; Andrew W. Mellon prof. human devel. Mass. Inst. Tech., Cambridge, 1975—; lectr. on clin. psychology Harvard U., 1958-62, resident fellow, asst. sr. tutor Eliot House, 1953-59; assoc. dir., acting dir., then dir. Behavior Scis. Study Ctr., Yale Med. Sch., 1965-72; fellow Davenport Coll., Yale U., 1962-75; chmn., exec. dir. Carnegie Coun. on Children, New Haven, 1972-78; dir. program in sci., tech. and soc. Mass. Inst. Tech., 1987-92, dir. grad. studies, 1993-96, dir. projects, 1996—; mem. Carnegie Commn. on Higher Edn., 1968-73, bd. dirs. Overseers Harvard Coll., 1969-75,MacArthur Prize Fellows selection com., 1979-85; com. on selection Guggenheim Found., 1992-94; vis. scholar Ecole de Mines, Paris, 1980-81; vis. prof. U. Paris Sorbonne, 1986-87, Centro de Estudios Avanzados de Ciencias Sociales, Madrid, 1990. Author: The Uncommitted, 1966, Young Radicals, 1968, All Our Children, 1977, The Fragile Contract, 1994, Earth, Air, Fire, Water, 1999; contbr. articles to profl. jours., chpts. to books. Rhodes scholar Balliol Coll., Oxford U., 1951-53; jr. fellow Harvard U., 1953-56; Guggenheim fellow, 1980-81. Fellow AAAS; mem. Coun. Fgn. Rels., Phi Beta Kappa, Sigma Xi. Office: Mass Inst Tech E51-163 77 Massachusetts Ave Cambridge MA 02139

KENLY, GRANGER FARWELL, marketing consultant, college official; b. Portland, Oreg., Feb. 15, 1919; s. F. Corning and Ruth (Farwell) K.; m. Suzanne Warner, Feb. 7, 1948 (div. Nov., 1977); children: Margaret F. Kenly Granger Farwell Jr.; m. Stella S. Angevin, Oct. 8, 1978. AB cum laude, Harvard U., 1941. Adminstrv. asst. to v.p. Poole Bros., Inc., Chgo., 1941-42; asst. advt. mgr. Sunset Mag., San Francisco, 1946-47; pub. relations, sales promotion mgr. Pabco Products, Inc., San Francisco, 1947-51; v.p. mgmt., supr. Needham, Louis & Brorby, Inc., Chgo., 1951-60; mgr. mktg. plans dept. Pure Oil Co., Palatine, Ill., 1961-62; v.p. pub. relations, personnel Pure Oil Co., 1962-66; v.p. pub. affairs Abbott Labs., North Chicago, Ill., 1966-71; v.p. corporate and investor relations IC Industries, Inc., Chgo., 1972-83; career devel. officer Lake Forest Coll., Ill., 1984—; chmn., exec. bd. Keystone-Garrett Properties, Houston, 1984—; Mem. 22d Ann. Global Strategy Conf. U.S. Naval War Coll., 1970; mem. pub. affairs council Am. Productivity Ctr., 1980-85. Bd. dirs. Evanston Hosp., 1963-82; trustee Ill. Soc. Prevention Blindness, 1958-64, Lawson YMCA, Chgo., 1972-83, Off the Street Boys Club, Chgo., 1978—; mem. Exec. Service Corps Chgo., 1984—. Served to maj. USAAF, 1942-46, ETO. Mem. Chgo. Club, Univ. Club (Chgo.), Onwentsia Club (Lake Forest, Ill.), Edgartown (Mass.) Yacht Club, The Reading Room (Edgartown), Hole-in-the-Wall Golf Club (Naples, Fla.), Naples Yacht Club. Republican. Episcopalian. Home: 945 Beverly Pl Lake Forest IL 60045-3903 Office: Lake Forest Coll Career Placement Officer Sheridan and College Rd Lake Forest IL 60045

KENNA, MICHAEL, photographer; b. Widnes, Cheshire, Eng., Nov. 20, 1953. Student, Banbury Sch. Art, Oxfordshire, Eng., 1972-73; HND with distinction, Coll. Printing, London, 1976. Tchr. Friends of Photography, San Francisco. One-man shows Fox Talbot Mus., Lacock, Wiltshire, Eng., 1983, Bampton Arts Ctr., Oxfordshire, 1984, Madison (Wis.) Art Ctr., 1985, Gallery Min, Tokyo, 1987, Fuerte Gallery, Tokyo, 1990, Palace of the Legion of Honor, San Francisco, 1991, Cleve. Art Mus., 1992, Internat. Ctr. for Photography, N.Y., 1993, Galerie Zur Stockeregg, Zurich, 1994, Detroit Inst. of Arts, 1995, Nicephore Niepce Mus., France, 1996; exhibited in group show Georges Pompidou Ctr., Paris, 1982; represented in permanent collections Australian Nat. Gallery, Canberra, Bibliotheque Nationale, Paris, San Francisco Mus. Modern Art, Fox Talbot Mus., Milw. Art Mus., Victoria and Albert Mus., London. Recipient award Friends of Imogene Cunningham, 1981, KQED/Zellerbach award, 1981. Office: care Weston Gallery PO Box 655 Carmel CA 93921-0655*

KENNAMER, LORRIN GARFIELD, JR., retired university dean; b. Abilene, Tex., Dec. 20, 1924; s. Lorrin Garfield and Ruie Lee (Hart) K.; m. Laura Helen Durham, Dec. 22, 1948. A.B., Eastern Ky. State Coll., 1947; M.S., U. Tenn., 1949; Ph.D., Vanderbilt U./George Peabody Coll., 1952. Tchr. Oak Ridge High Sch., 1947-49; from instr. to asso. prof., chmn. dept. geography and geology East Tex. State Coll., Commerce, 1952-56; mem. faculty U. Tex., 1956-67, prof. geography, 1961-67, chmn. dept., 1961-67, assoc. dean arts and scis., 1961-67; dean arts and scis. Tex. Tech. U., 1967-70; dean U. Tex. Coll. Edn., Austin, 1970-87; prof. emeritus geography U. Tex., 1998—; vis. summer prof. U. Vt., 1959, Mich. State U., 1961, U. Wash., 1967; Bd. examiners Tex. Edn. Agy., 1964-71; mem. com. exams. Coll. Entrance Exam. Bd., 1965-71, trustee, 1970—, vice-chmn., 1972-74, chmn., 1974-76; pres. Tex. Council Deans Edn., 1973. Author: (with Bowden, Hoffman) Geography Worktext Series, 4th edit., 1979, (with S. Arbingast) Atlas of Texas, rev. edit., 1976, (with W. Chambers) Texans and Their Land, 1964, (with James Reese) Texas-Land of Contrast, 1972, rev., 1978, (with James Reese) We Texans-Our History and Geography, 1987, (with Reese and Crawford) Texas Lone Star Land, 1993, Classroom Atlas of Texas, 1995; mem. editl. bd. Coll. Bd. Guide to 150 Popular Coll. Majors, 1992. Served to lt. (j.g.) USNR, World War II. Recipient Disting. Service award Nat. Council Geog. Edn., 1972, Ruth Knight Millikan Centennial Professorship, U. Tex., Austin, 1987. Hon. life fellow Tex. Acad. Sci.; mem. Nat. Council Geog. Edn. (exec. bd. 1958-65, sec. 1958-64, pres. 1967), Assn. Am. Geographers (exec. council 1962-64, 68-71), Am. Geog. Soc., Southwestern Social Sci. Assn. (pres. 1972-73), Sigma Xi, Omicron Delta Kappa, Pi Gamma Mu, Phi Delta Kappa, Phi Kappa Phi. Unitarian. Home: 6800 Austin Center Blvd Apt 711 Austin TX 78731-3116

KENNAN, ELIZABETH TOPHAM, former university president and history educator; b. Phila., Feb. 25, 1938. AB summa cum laude, Mt. Holyoke Coll., 1960; MA, Oxford (Eng.) U., 1962; PhD, U. Wash., 1966; LHD (hon.), Trinity Coll., 1978, Amherst Coll., 1980, St. Mary's Coll., 1982, Oberlin Coll., 1983; LLD (hon.), Smith Coll., 1984; LittD (hon.), Cath. U. of Am., 1985, U. Mass., Amherst, 1988. Asst. prof. history Cath. U., Washington, 1966-70, assoc. prof. history, dir. medieval and Byzantine studies, 1970-78, dir. program in early Christian humanism, 1970-78; pres. Five Colls. Inc., 1985-94; pres., prof. history Mt. Holyoke Coll., South Hadley, Mass., 1978-95, pres. emeritus, 1996; bd. dirs. Coun. on Libr. Resources, 1980-95; mem. com. Folger Shakespeare Libr., 1994—; lead dir. N.E. Utilities, Hartford, Conn., 1994-96; bd. dirs. Bell Atlantic, Ky. Home Capital Corp., The Putnam Funds, Boston, Talbots, Hingham, Mass. Contbr. articles to profl. jours. including Georgetown Univ. Press, Univ. of Wash. Press, Cath. Univ. of Am., Cath. Univ. Press, Cistercian Publs.,. Me. Coun. on Econ. Devel., 1991-95; mem. bd. selectors Jefferson awards Am. Inst. for Pub. Svc., 1991-96; trustee U. Notre Dame, 1985-94, Miss Porter's Sch., 1980-85; mem. higher edn. program com. Dana Found., 1986-90; mem. Indo-U.S. Subcommn. on Edn. and Culture, 1986-91; vice chmn. 1000 Friends of Mass., 1989-91; mem. Mass Gov.'s Nominating Coun., 1990-91. Marshall scholar, 1960; Woodrow Wilson fellow (hon.), 1960. Mem. Coun. Fgn. Rels. Home and Office: 197 County Rd Ipswich MA 01938-2570

KENNAN, KENT WHEELER, composer, educator; b. Milw., Apr. 18, 1913; s. Kossuth Kent and Sara Louise (Wheeler) K. Student, U. Mich., 1930-32; B.Mus. in Composition and Theory, Eastman Sch. of Music U. Rochester, 1934, M.Mus. in Composition, 1936; student, Royal Acad. of Santa Cecilia, Rome, 1938. Mem. faculty Kent (Ohio) State U., 1939-40; tchr. composition, orchestration, counterpoint and theory U. Tex., Austin, 1940-42, 45-46, 49-83, prof. emeritus; tchr. theory Ohio State U., 1947-49; tchr. composition, orchestration Eastman Sch. of Music, summers 1954, 56. Orchestral works performed under Toscanini, Ormandy, Hanson, Stokowski, others, by N.Y. Philharm. Symphony, Phila. Orch., Chgo., Houston, Detroit, San Antonio, Boston Symphonies, others; composer: Night Soliloquy, other orch. works, 5 Preludes for Piano, Retrospectives (12 pieces for piano), Sonata for Trumpet and Piano, also vocal, choral and chamber music; author: Counterpoint, 4th edit., 1999, (with D. Grantham) Technique of Orchestration, 5th edit., 1997; numerous recordings of compositions and transcriptions. Served with USAAF, 1942-46. Recipient Prix de Rome in Music, 1936. Mem. ASCAP, Nat. Assn. Composers U.S.A., Delta Tau Delta, Phi Mu Alpha, Pi Kappa Lambda. Address: 1034 Liberty Park Dr Apt 248 Austin TX 78746-6852

KENNAN, STEPHANIE ANN, advisor; b. Frankfurt am Main, Germany, Oct. 25, 1958; d. Ralph Hyde and Loretta (Pumphrey) K. BA in Am. Govt. and Fgn. Affairs, U. Va., Charlottesville, 1980; MA in Creative Writing, Johns Hopkins U., Balt., 1997. Legis. asst. Rep. Larry Smith, Washington, 1983-85; asst. dir. edn. Group Health Assn. Am., Washington, 1985-86; legis. rep. Am. Assn. Ret. Persons, Washington, 1986-89, Am. Coll. Emergency Physicians, Washington, 1989-94; dir. fed. rels. Md. Dept. Health, Balt., 1995-97; sr. policy advisor U.S. Senator Ron Wyden, Washington, 1998—; mem. Montgomery Couty (Md.) Commn. on Aging, 1983-86. Co-author: Health Care Playbook, 1994; contbr. articles to profl. jours. Mem. Women in Govt. Rels., Nat. Press Club. Episcopalian. Office: 717 Hart Senate Ofc. Bldg. Washington DC 20510

KENNARD, JOYCE L., state supreme court justice. Former judge L.A. Mcpl. Ct., Superior Ct., Ct. Appeal, Calif.; assoc. justice Calif. Supreme Ct., San Francisco, 1989—. Office: Calif Supreme Ct 350 McAllister St San Francisco CA 94102-3600

KENNARD, MARY ELIZABETH, lawyer; b. Phila., Dec. 1, 1954; d. Rodman Ramos and Mary Elizabeth Kennard. BAS, Boston U., 1976; JD, Temple U., 1980; LLM, George Washington U., 1982. Bar: Pa. 1980, R.I. 1988, D.C. 1988, U.S. Dist. Ct. (we. dist.) Pa. 1985, U.S. Ct. Appeals (3d cir.) 1985, U.S. Dist. Ct. R.I. 1988, U.S. Ct. Appeals (1st cir.) 1899, U.S. Dist. Ct. D.C. 1996, U.S. Supreme Ct. 1985. Assoc. Obermayer, Rebmannn, Maxwell & Hippel, Phila., 1979-80; asst. exec. dir. Nat. Assn. Coll. and Univ. Attys., Washington, 1981-83; asst. univ. counsel U. Pitts., 1984-85; asst. to v.p. for legal affairs Howard U., Washington, 1985-87; legal counsel U. R.I., R.I. Coll. and C.C. of R.I., Kingston, 1987-94; v.p., univ. counsel, sec. Am. U., Washington, 1995—; mem. The Links, Inc., Reston, Va.; bd. dirs. Washington Trust Bank. Mem. Nat. Assns. Coll. and Univ. Attys., R.I. Black Lawyers Assn. Democrat. Episcopalian. Avocations: golf, antique collecting. Office: Univ Counsel American Univ 4400 Massachusetts Ave NW Washington DC 20016-8165

KENNARD, WILLIAM EARL, federal agency administrator, lawyer; b. L.A., Jan. 19, 1957; s. Robert A. and Helen Z. (King) K.; m. Deborah D. Kennedy, Apr. 9, 1984. BA, Stanford U., 1978; JD, Yale U., 1981. Bar: Calif. 1981, D.C. Ct. Appeals 1985, U.S. Ct. Appeals (D.C. cir.) 1994, U.S. Supreme Ct. 1994. Fellow Nat. Assn. Broadcasters, Washington, 1981-82, asst. gen. counsel, 1983-84; assoc. Verner, Liipfert, Bernhard, McPherson & Hand, Washington, 1984-89, ptnr., 1990-93; gen. counsel FCC, Washington, 1993-97, chmn., 1997—. Office: FCC 445 12th St SW Washington DC 20036-3521*

KENNE, LESLIE F., military officer. B in Aero. Engring., Auburn U., 1970; grad., Squadron Officer Sch., 1975; M in Procurement Mgmt., Webster Coll., 1979; grad., Armed Forces Staff Coll., 1981, Nat. War Coll., 1986, Def. Sys. Mgmt. Coll., 1988; advanced mgmt. program, U. N.H., 1993; nat. and internat. security mgmt., Harvard U., 1995. Cert. level III program mgmt., level III test and evaluation. Commd. 2d lt. USAF, 1971, advanced through grades to maj. gen., 1998; maintenance supr. 474th Orgnl. Maintenance Squadron, Takhli Royal Thai AFB, Thailand, 1973-74; project mgr., dep. test dir. range measurement sys. jt. test Tactical Fighter Weapons Ctr., Nellis AFB, Nev., 1975-78; program mgr. Office of Sec. of Def.-directed joint tests Air Force Test and Evaluation Ctr., Kirtland AFB, N.Mex., 1978-81; chief airborne sys. test br., chief elec. sys. test divsn. 324th Test Wing, Eglin AFB, Fla., 1982-85; dir. ops. and support Airborne Warning and Control Sys. Program Officer, Hanscom AFB, Mass., 1986-88; chief spl. projects divsn. directorate spl. programs Office of Asst. Sec. of Air Force for Acquisitions, Washington, 1988-90; dir. LANTIRN Sys. Program Office Aero. Sys. Divsn., Wright-Patterson AFB, Ohio, 1993-94; dep. dir. fighters and C2 and weapons programs Office of Asst. Sec. of Air Force for Acquisition, Washington, 1992-93; dir. F-16 Sys. Program Office Aero. Sys. Ctr., Wright-Patterson AFB, 1993-94, vice comdr., 1994-95; vice comdr. Sacramento Air Logistics Ctr., McClellan AFB, Calif., 1995-96; dep. dir. Joint Strike Fighter Program, Arlington, Va., 1996-97, dir., 1997—. Decorated Legion of Merit, Bronze Star, Meritorious Svc. medal with 2 oak leaf clusters. Office: JSF Program Office/PD Ste 600 1213 Jefferson Davis Hwy Arlington VA 22202-3402

KENNEDY, ADRIENNE LITA, playwright; b. Pitts., Sept. 13, 1931; d. Cornell Wallace and Etta (Haugabook) Hawkins; m. Joseph C. Kennedy, May 15, 1953 (div. 1966); children: Joseph C., Adam. BS, Ohio State U., 1953; student creative writing, Columbia U., 1954-56; student playwrighting, New Sch. Social Research, Am. Theatre Wing, Circle in the Sq. Theatre Sch., 1957-58, 62. Mem. playwriting unit Actors Studio, N.Y.C., 1962-65; lectr. Yale U., New Haven, 1972-74; CBS fellow Sch. Drama, N.Y.C., 1973; lectr. Princeton (N.J.) U., 1977; vis. assoc. prof. Brown U., 1979-80; rep. to conf. Internat. Theatre Inst., Budapest, 1978; vis. lectr. Harvard U., 1990, 91, vis. prof., 1997—. Author: (plays) Funnyhouse of a Negro, 1964, Cities in Bezique, 1965, A Rat's Mass, 1966, A Lesson in Dead Language, 1966, The Lennon Plays, 1968, Sun, Cities of Bezique, 1969; A Movie Star Has To Star in Black and White, 1976, Ohio State Murders, She Talks to Beethoven, 1990, (with Adam Kennedy) Sleep Deprivation Chamber, 1995; (memoirs) People Who Led to My Plays, 1987 (Manhattan Borough Pres.'s award 1988), Letter to My Students, Lancashire Lad; commd. by Empire State Youth Inst., 1979, Onestes, Electra, Juilliard Sch. Music, 1980, Black Children's Day, Rites and Reason, Brown U., 1980; represented in numerous anthologies Norton Anthology of Am. Lit. Recipient Obie award, 1964, 96, Pierre Lecomte du Novy award Lincoln Ctr., 1994, award Am. Acad. Arts and Letters, 1994; fellow Guggenheim Found., 1968, Rockefeller Found., 1967-68, NEA, 1993, Lila Wallace Readers Digest, 1994, Yale U., 1974-75; grantee Nat. Endowment Arts, 1973, Rockefeller Found., 1974, Creative Artists Pub. Svc., 1974; Disting. lectr. U. Calif., Berkeley, 1980, 86. Mem. PEN (bd. dirs. 1976-77). Address: U Minn Press 111 3rd Ave S Ste 290 Minneapolis MN 55401 *I believe in listening to one's inner voices.*

KENNEDY, ANTHONY MCLEOD, United States supreme court justice; b. Sacramento, July 23, 1936. AB, Stanford U., 1958; student, London Sch. Econs.; LLB, Harvard U., 1961; JD (hon.), U. Pacific, 1988, U. Santa Clara, 1988. Bar: Calif. 1962, U.S. Tax Ct. 1971. Former ptnr. Evans, Jackson & Kennedy; prof. constl. law McGeorge Sch. Law, U. of Pacific, 1965-88; judge U.S. Ct. Appeals (9th cir.), Sacramento, 1976-88; assoc. justice U.S. Supreme Ct., Washington, 1988—; mem. bd. student advisors Harvard Faculty, 1960-61. Fellow Am. Bar Found. (hon.), Am. Coll. Trial Lawyers (hon.); mem. Sacramento County Bar Assn., State Bar Calif., Phi Beta Kappa. Office: US Supreme Ct Supreme Ct Bldg 1 1st St NE Washington DC 20543*

KENNEDY, BARBARA ELLEN PERRY, art therapist; b. Columbus, Ohio, Apr. 22, 1937; d. Donald Earl Perry and Elsie Irene (Strait) Modglin; m. Marvin Roosevelt Kennedy, July 1, 1955 (div. Sept. 1969); children: Sherry Lynn Kennedy Anderson, Michelle Reneé Kennedy Byrd. AS in Mental Health Technology cum laude, Purdue U., 1975, BA in Psychology, 1976; MA in Art Therapy, Wright State U., 1990. Registered art therapist; cert. social worker; cert. marriage and family therapist. Probation officer intern Allen County Juvenile Probation Dept., Ind., 1975; prodn. supr. asst. Allen County Assn. for Retarded, Ft. Wayne, Ind., 1975, relief supr. semi-ind. living, 1975-76; occupational therapist asst. Logansport (Ind.) State Hosp., 1977; rehab. therapist Richmond (Ind.) State Hosp., 1977—, recreation therapy dir. acute intensive treatment unit, 1983-85, dir. art therapy dept., 1986—, art tchr., art therapist with MIDD, adolescent and geriatric, 1995—; pvt. counselor, 1986—; counselor Mental Health Assn., Richmond, 1986; art therapy counselor Battered Women's Shelter, Richmond, 1986; counselor Dayton (Ohio) Pub. Schs., Family Svc. Assn., 1989-90, expressive therapy counselor with Mentally Ill Chemically Addicted population, 1993—; lectr. in field of mental health and art therapy. Author, editor: Mental Stimulation Activities, 1992. Mem. com. LWV, Richmond, 1977-80; publicity officer USCG Aux., Richmond, 1985; chairperson legis. group AAUW, Richmond, 1982-84; bd. dirs. Community Coun. on Disabilities Awareness, Richmond, 1985-86; vol. ARC, Muncie, Ind. and Ft. Wayne, 1969-73; vol. tutor Adult Literacy Resource Ctr., 1991—; pres. Richmond Art Club, 1996-97. Recipient Merit scholarship Purdue U., 1971-76, Gov.'s Showcase award State of Ind., 1990. Mem. Am. Art Therapy Assn., Buckeye Art Therapy Assn., Ind. Art Therapy Assn. (v.p. 1992-95), Mensa. Reorganized Ch. of Jesus Christ of Latter-day Saints. Avocations: sailing, hiking, piano, reading, art. Office: Richmond State Hosp 498 NW 18th St Richmond IN 47374-2898

KENNEDY, BERNARD JOSEPH, utility executive; b. Niagara Falls, N.Y., Aug. 16, 1931; s. Edward J. and Frances (Coyle) K.; m. Geraldine Drexelius, Sept. 20, 1958; children: Mary Kathleen, Maureen Jean, Patricia, Colleen, Joseph B. B.A., Niagara U., 1953; LL.B., U. Mich., 1958. Bar: N.Y. 1960. Legal asst. Nat. Fuel Gas Distbn. Corp., Buffalo, 1958-63, gen. atty., 1963-67, sec., gen. counsel, 1967-75, v.p., gen. counsel, 1975-77, sr. v.p., 1977-87, pres., 1987; chief exec. officer Nat. Fuel Gas Co., Buffalo, 1988—, chmn. bd., 1989—; pres. Nat. Fuel Gas Supply Corp., 1978-89, Penn-York Energy Corp., 1978-89, Seneca Resources Corp., 1983-89, Empire Exploration, 1983-89; chmn. Inst. of Gas Tech., Chgo., 1989—; CEO Nat. Fuel Gas Co., Buffalo, 1989—; bd. dirs. Associated Electric & Gas Ins. Svc. Ltd., Marine Midland Bank Inc. (now HSBC Bank), Mchts. Mut. Ins. Co., Am. Precision Industries Inc., The Bus. Coun. N.Y. State. Past chmn. Greater Buffalo Partnership; past chmn., bd. regents, past chmn. coun. Bus. Sch. of Canisius Coll.; trustee Niagara U.; past chmn. bd. dirs. Erie County chpt. ARC; chmn. Cath. Charities Appeal, 1981; bd. dirs. Nat. Petroleum Coun., 1990—. 1st lt. U.S. Army, 1953-55. Mem. ABA (past vice chmn. gas com.), N.Y. State Bar Assn. (chmn. pub. utilities com. 1973), Fed. Energy Bar Assn., Erie County Bar Assn., Am. Gas Assn., Buffalo Club, Buffalo Canoe Club, Country Club of Buffalo, Sitzmarker Ski Club. Home: 33 Ruskin Rd Buffalo NY 14226-4255 Office: Nat Fuel Gas Co 10 Lafayette Sq Buffalo NY 14203-1824

KENNEDY, BEVERLY (KLEBAN) BURRIS, financial consultant, tv and radio talk show host; b. Pitts., Sept. 23, 1943; d. Jack and Ida (Davis) Kleban; m. Thomas E. Burris, Dec. 31, 1967 (div.); 1 child, Laura Danielle Burris; m. Ed A. Kennedy, Jan 14, 1984; stepchildren: Kathleen, Patricia, Thomas. BS, Pa. State U., 1964; postgrad., Va. Commonwealth U., 1967. Founder, exec. dir. Broward Art Colony, Inc., Broward County, Fla., 1978-80; dir. sales Holiday Inn, Plantation, Fla., 1980-81; agent, registered rep. Equitable Life Assurance Soc., Ft. Lauderdale, Fla., 1982—; pres. Fin. Planning Svcs. Assn., Inc., Ft. Lauderdale, Fla., 1984-86; owner, fin. cons. Beverly B. Kennedy & Assocs., Ft. Lauderdale, Fla., 1982—; republican nominee for U.S. Congress 19th Dist., Fla., 1996; adv. bd. Transflorida Bank, 1983-88; bd. arbitration Nat. Assn. Securities Dealers, Inc., 1992-97. Talk show host Sta. WWNN, 1992-93. Bd. dirs. Community Appearance Bd., 1988-89, Riverwalk, Ft. Lauderdale, 1988-89, First Charter Sch. of Excellence, Ft. Lauderdale, 1997-99; trustee Police and Fireman Fund of Fort Lauderdale, 1990-91; appointed by gov. to Fla. State Bd. Profl. Engrs., 1988-91; cons. Com. on Fin. for Nat. Coun. examiners for Engring and Surveying, 1990-91; Rep. nominee for U.S. Congress 20th dist. Fla., 1992, 94, 19th dist., 1996. Named Woman of the Year (Bus. for Profit), Women in Communications, Broward County, 1986, Bus. & Profl. Women, 1988-89, oustanding alumni, Pa. State Univ. Coll . Edn., 1988-89. Mem. Internat. Assn. Fin. Planning, Nat. Assn. Life Underwriters, East Broward Fed. Women's Rep. Club (pres. 1992-93). Office: 1 Financial Plz Ste 1200 Fort Lauderdale FL 33394-0001

KENNEDY, BRIAN JAMES, marketing executive; b. N.Y.C., Nov. 7, 1941; s. James and Una K.; m. Donna Lee Rugendorf, Dec. 7, 1968; children: Kerry, Kelly. BS in Fgn. Service, Georgetown U., 1963; grad. Japanese lang., Def. Lang. Inst., 1965; postgrad., NYU, Monterey Inst. Fgn. Studies. Various positions, then v.p. advt. and sales TWA, N.Y.C., 1967-83; sr. v.p. mktg. The Hertz Corp., N.Y.C., 1983-87, exec. v.p. mktg and sales, 1987—; pres. Duneview Devel. (real estate) Corp., Wainscott, N.Y. Home: 163 Bay Ln Water Mill NY 11976-3103 Office: Hertz Co 225 Brae Blvd Park Ridge NJ 07656-1888*

KENNEDY, B(YRL) J(AMES), medicine and oncology educator; b. Plainview, Minn., June 24, 1921; s. Arthur Sylvester and Anna Margaret (Fassbender) K.; m. Margaret Bradford Hood, Oct. 21, 1950; children: Sharon Lynn, James Bradford, Scott Douglas, Grant Preston. BA, BS, U. Minn., 1943, MB, 1945, MD, 1946; MS in Exptl. Medicine, McGill U., Montreal, Que., Can., 1951. Diplomate Am. Bd. Internal Medicine, Am. Bd. Med. Oncology. Intern in medicine Mass. Gen. Hosp., Boston, 1945-46, resident in medicine, 1946, 51-52; fellow in medicine Harvard Med. Sch.-Mass. Gen. Hosp., 1947-49; rsch. fellow in medicine McGill U. Med. Sch., 1949-50; fellow in medicine Cornell U. Med. Sch., N.Y.C., 1950-51; asst. prof. medicine U. Minn. Med. Sch., Mpls., 1952-57, assoc. prof., 1957-67, prof., 1967-91, Masonic prof. oncology, 1970-91, prof. emeritus, 1991—, Regents prof. medicine, 1988-91, Regents prof. emeritus, 1991—. Contbr. over 900 articles on cancer to profl. jours. Past chmn. bd. Presbyn. Homes of Minn., St. Paul, bd. dirs., 1964-93. Recipient Nat. Divsn. award Am. Cancer Soc., 1975, Recognition award Assn. Comty. Cancer Ctrs., 1985, Spl. Recognition award Am. Soc. Internal Medicine, 1989, Charles Bolles Bolles-Roger award Hennepin Med. Soc., 1996. Fellow ACP (master 1996, Laureate award Minn. 1992); mem. AMA (Sci. Achievement award 1992), Am. Cancer Soc. (Disting. Svc. award 1991, Medal of Honor-Clin. Rsch. award 1996), Am. Soc. Clin. Oncology (pres. 1987-88), Am. Assn. Cancer Rsch., Am. Assn. Cancer Edn. (pres. 1982-83, Margaret Hay Edwards Achievement medal 1990, Harold S. Diehl award 1999), Minn. Med. Alumni, Town and Country Club (St. Paul). Avocation: photography. Home: 1949 E River Pky Minneapolis MN 55414-3675 Office: U Minn Med Sch and Hosp Box 286 Mayo 420 Delaware St SE Minneapolis MN 55455-0374

KENNEDY, CHARLES, retired medical educator; b. Buffalo, N.Y., Aug. 27, 1920; m. Eulsum Kennedy, Mar. 9, 1946; 3 children from previous marriage. BA in Chemistry cum laude, Princeton U., 1942; MD, U. Rochester, 1945. Diplomate Am. Bd. Pediats., Am. Bd. Psychiatry and Neurology; lic. N.Y., Pa., D.C., Maine, Md. Intern in pathology New Haven (Conn.) Hosp., 1945-46; instr. pathology Sch. Medicine Yale U., New Haven, 1945-46; fellow in child psychiatry Children's Hosp., Buffalo, N.Y., 1948-49; resident pediatrician Children's Hosp., Buffalo, 1949-51; fellow in physiology Grad. Sch. Medicine U. Pa., Phila., 1951-53, assoc. pediats. Sch. Medicine, 1952-55, assoc. in neurology Sch. Medicine, 1955-58, asst. prof. neurology in pediats. Sch. Medicine, 1958-61, assoc. prof. neurology in pediats. Sch. Medicine, 1967-71; prof. pediats., neurology Sch. Medicine Georgetown U., Washington, 1971-90, prof. emeritus, 1990—; chief divsn. neurology, dir. child neurology Children's Hosp., Phila., 1959-67; vis. fellow in neurology Neurol. Inst. Columbia Presbyn. Med. Ctr., 1957-58; guest researcher Lab. Clin. Sci. Nat. Inst. Mental Health, 1967-68, Lab. Cerebral Metabolism, 1968-90;, sr. rsch. scientist, 1979-80, med. officer, spl. expert Lab. Cerebral Metabolism, Bethesda, Md., 1990-96; cons. Pa. Hosp., Phila., 1960-69, Hosp. U. Pa., Phila., 1961-67, Bd. Edn. City of Phila., 1962-64; lectr. U.S. Naval Hosp., Phila., 1962-68, Found. Advanced Edn. in Scis., 1978-87; mem. adv. com. on dyslexia State of Tex., 1965; guest lectr. Nat. Naval Med. Ctr. Uniformed Svcs. U. Health Scis., 1977-87; mem. faculty spl. courses Am. Acad. Neurology, 1978, 80; mem. NIMH AIDS rsch. rev. com., 1988; mem. ad hoc com. evaln. of program project rsch. in learning disabilities NICHHD, 1989, planning com., moderator workshop, Rockville, Md., 1989; researcher in field. Mem. editl. bd. Pediat. Rsch. 1978-84, Brain Rsch., 1980-96, Jour. Cerebral Blood Flow and Metabolism, 1981-88. Lt. jg USNR, 1946-48. Fellow Life Ins. Med. Rsch. Fund, 1951-53. Fellow Coll. Physicians Phila.; mem. Am. Pediat. Soc., Am. Acad. Pediats., Am. Neurol. Assn., Am. Acad. Neurology (chmn. sect. child neurology 1964-66, com. problems of mental retardation 1965-67), Am. Soc. Neurochemistry, Nat. Bd. Med. Examiners (mem. pediat. com. 1960-64), Internat. Soc. Neurochemistry, Internat. Soc. Cerebral Blood Flow and Metabolism (dir. 1989-93, chmn. fin. com. 1992-96), Phila. Pediat. Soc. (pres. 1964), Phila. Neurol. Soc. (v.p. 1967), Assn. Rsch. in Nervous and Mental Disease, Soc. Neurosci., Child Neurology Soc., Profs. of Child Neurology.

KENNEDY, CHARLES ALLEN, lawyer; b. Maysville, Ky., Dec. 11, 1940; s. Elmer Earl and Mary Frances Kennedy; m. Patricia Ann Louderback, Dec. 9, 1961; 1 child, Mimi Mignon. AB, Morehead State Coll., 1965, MA in Edn., 1968; JD, U. Akron, 1969; LLM, George Washington U., 1974. Bar: Ohio 1969. Asst. cashier Citizens Bank, Felicity, Ohio, 1961-63; tchr. Triway Local Sch. Dist., Wooster, Ohio, 1965-67; with office of gen. counsel Fgn. Agr. and Spl. Programs Div., U.S. Dept. Agr., Washington, 1969-71; ptnr. Kauffman, Eberhart, Cicconetti & Kennedy Co., Wooster, 1972-86, Kennedy, Cicconetti & Knowlton, L.P.A., Wooster, 1986—. Mem. ABA, FBA, ATLA, Ohio State Bar Assn., Ohio Acad. Trial Lawyers, Ohio Assn. Criminal Def. Lawyers, Wayne County Bar Assn., Exch. Club, Lions, Elks, Phi Alpha Delta, Phi Delta Kappa. Republican. Home: 1770 Burbank Rd Wooster OH 44691-2240 Office: Kennedy Cicconetti & Know Ken 558 N Market St Wooster OH 44691-3406

KENNEDY, CHARLES G., wholesale distribution executive; b. Thomasville, N.C., Feb. 15, 1954; s. G. Carless and Maye (C.) K.; m. Vickie Houser Kennedy; children: Jason P., Amy M. BS in Acctg., Guilford Coll., 1980. CPA, N.C. Acct. Henley Paper Co., Greensboro, N.C., 1973-78, acctg. supr., controller, 1978-81, treas., 1981-89, exec. v.p. fin., 1989—, also bd. dirs. Fellow N.C. Assn. CPAs; mem. AICPA, Inst. Mgmt. Accts. (bd. dirs. Piedmont High Point chpt.), Fin. Execs. Inst. Office: Henley Paper Co PO Box 20408 Greensboro NC 27420-0408

KENNEDY, CHERYL LYNN, museum director; b. Pekin, Ill., Nov. 25, 1946; d. Paul Louis and Ann Marie (Bingham) Wieburg; children: Kurt Alan, Kimberly Ann. Grad. high sch., Pekin, Ill.; BA, Eastern Ill. U. Prin., and profl. quilter Mahomet, Ill., 1976-81; program coord. Early Am. Mus., Mahomet, 1981-85; dir. Early Am. Mus. Champaign County Forest Preserve, Mahomet, 1986—; chmn. Ill. quilt documentation project Early Am. Mus. and Land of Lincoln Quilt Assn., 1986—. Historian Meth. Local History Com., Mahomet, 1984-86; adv. com. Champaign-Urbana Conv. and Visitors Bur. Mem. Midwest Mus. Coun., Am. Assn. Mus., Am. Assn. State and Local History Mus., Ill. Assn. Mus. (past pres., advocacy chair), Ill. Heritage Assn., Ill. State Hist. Soc., Champaign County Hist. Soc., Nat. Quilt Assn., Am. Quilt Soc., Antique Quilt Study Group, Quilt Conservancy. Avocations: quilting, women's history, walking. Home: 219A S Lake Of The Woods Rd Mahomet IL 61853-9201 Office: Early Am Mus PO Box 1040 Mahomet IL 61853-1040

KENNEDY, CHRISTOPHER ROBIN, ceramist; b. Ottawa, Ont., Can., June 25, 1948; s. Robert Alvin and Ruth Christina (Downie) K.; m. Christine Willa Wayman, Jan. 28, 1978; children: Scott Wayman, Stuart James. BS, Rutgers U., 1969; MS, Pa. State U., 1971, PhD, 1974. Asst. ceramist Argonne Nat. Lab., Ill., 1974-79; ceramist Argonne (Ill.) Nat. Lab., 1979-82; staff engr. Exxon Rsch. and Engring. Co., Florham Park, N.J., 1982-83; group leader materials devel. group Exxon Rsch. and Engring. Co., 1983-84; mgr. materials rsch. sect. Lanxide Corp., Newark, 1984-87, mgr. def. products devel. sect., 1987-92; mgr. composite devel. and engring. sect., 1992-93; v.p. tech. Lanxide Corp., Newark, 1993-98; dir. R & D Ceramco, Burlington, N.J., 1998—. Contbr. numerous articles to profl. jours. Patentee in field. Mem. Am. Ceramic Soc., Nat. Inst. Ceramic Engrs., Keramos. Home: 9 Crocus Ln Newtown PA 18940 Office: 6 Terri Ln Burlington NJ 08016

KENNEDY, CLAUDIA J., military officer. BA in Philosophy, Southwestern U.; grad., U.S. Army Command/Gen. Staff, U.S. Army War Coll. Commd. 2d lt. U.S. Army, 1969, advanced through grades to lt. gen., 1997; strategic intelligence officer 501st military intelligence U.S. Army, Korea, 1977; asst. ops. officer, ops. officer U.S. Army Field Sta., Augsburg, Germany, 1981-84; staff officer, dir. tng. Office of Dep. Chief of Staff for Ops. and Plans, Washington, 1984-86; comdr. San Antonio Recruiting Bn., 5th Recruiting Brigade, Ft. Sam Houston, Tex., 1988-90, 703d Mil. Intelligence Brigade, Kunia, Hawaii, 1991-93; dep. comdr. U.S. Army Intelligence Ctr. and Ft. Huachuca, Ariz., 1994-95; asst. dep. chief of staff for intelligence Office of Dep. Chief of Staff for Intelligence, U.S. Army, Washington, 1995-97. Decorated Legion of Merit with 3 oak leaf clusters, Def. Meritorious Svc. medal, Meritorious Svc. medal with 3 oak leaf clusters. Office: US Army 1000 Army Pentagon Washington DC 20310-1000

KENNEDY, CORNELIA GROEFSEMA, federal judge; b. Detroit, Mich., Aug. 4, 1923; d. Elmer H. and Mary Blanche (Gibbons) Groefsema; m. Charles S. Kennedy, Jr. (dec.); 1 son, Charles S. III. B.A., U. Mich., 1945, J.D. with distinction, 1947; LL.D. (hon.), No. Mich. U., 1971, Eastern Mich. U., 1971, Western Mich. U., 1973, Detroit Coll. Law, 1980, U. Detroit, 1987. Bar: Mich. bar 1947. Law clk. to Chief Judge Harold M. Stephens, U.S. Ct. of Appeals, Washington, 1947-48; assoc. Elmer H. Groefsema, Detroit, 1948-52; partner Markle & Markle, Detroit, 1952-66; judge 3d Judicial Circuit Mich., 1967-70; dist. judge U.S. Dist. Ct., Eastern Dist. Mich., Detroit, 1970-79; chief judge U.S. Dist. Ct., Eastern Dist. Mich., 1977-79; circuit judge U.S. Ct. Appeals, (6th cir.), 1979—. Mem. Commn. on the Bicentennial of the U.S. Constitution (presdl. appointment). Recipient Sesquicentennial award U. Mich. Fellow Am. Bar Found.; mem. ABA, Mich. Bar Assn. (past chmn. negligence law sect.), Detroit Bar Assn. (past dir.), Fed. Bar Assn., Am. Judicature Soc., Nat. Assn. Women Lawyers, Am. Trial Lawyers Assn., Nat. Conf. Fed. Trial Judges (past chmn.), Fed. Jud. Fellows Commn. (bd. dirs.), Fed. Jud. Ctr. (bd. dirs.), Phi Beta Kappa. Office: US Ct of Appeals US Courthouse 231 W Lafayette St Detroit MI 48226-2702*

KENNEDY, CORNELIUS BRYANT, retired lawyer; b. Evanston, Ill., Apr. 13, 1921; s. Millard Bryant and Myrna Estelle (Anderson) K.; m. Anne Martha Reynolds, June 20, 1959; children: Anne Talbot, Lauren K. Mayle. A.B., Yale U., 1943; J.D., Harvard U., 1948. Bar: Ill. 1949, D.C. 1965. Assoc. Mayer Meyer Austrian & Platt, Chgo., 1949-54, 55-59; asst. to U.S. atty. Dept. Justice, Chgo., 1954-55; counsel to minority leader U.S. Senate, 1959-65; sr. ptnr. Kennedy & Webster, Washington, 1965-82; of counsel Armstrong, Teasdale, Schlafly & Davis, Washington, 1983-88; public mem. Adminstrv. Conf. U.S., 1972-82, sr. conf. fellow, 1982-90, chmn. rulemaking com., 1973-82; ret., 1988. Contbr. articles to law jours. Fin. chmn. Lyric Opera Co., Chgo., 1954; chmn. young adults group Chgo. Coun. Fgn. Rels., 1958-59; pres. English Speaking Union Jrs., Chgo., 1957-59; trustee St. John's Child Devel. Ctr., Washington, 1965-67, 75-87, pres., 1983-85 ; exec. dir. Supreme Ct. Hist. Soc., 1984-87. 1st lt., AC U.S. Army, 1942-46. Fellow Am. Bar Found.; mem. Am. Law Inst., ABA (coun. sect. adminstrv. law 1967-70, chmn. sect. 1976-77), Fed. Bar Assn. (chmn. com. adminstrv. law 1963-64). Clubs: Legal Club Chgo., Explorers, N.Y. City, Capitol Hill, Chevy Chase (Md.), Sailing of Chesapeake (Annapolis, Md.), Adventurer's (Chgo.). Home: 8462 Brook Rd Mc Lean VA 22102

KENNEDY, CORTEZ, professional football player; b. Osceola, Ark., Aug. 23, 1968. Student, Northwest Miss. Jr. Coll.; BA, criminal justice, U. Miami, Fla. Defensive tackle Seattle Seahawks, 1990—. Named All-America team defensive tackle, The Sporting News, 1989; AP Defensive Player of Yr., 1992; named to Pro Bowl, 1991-93, NFL All-Pro team defensive tackle, The Sporting News, 1992, 93. Office: Seattle Seahawks 11220 NE 53rd St Kirkland WA 98033-7595*

KENNEDY, CRAIG, foundation administrator. BA, U. Chgo., MA, MBA. Pvt. practice cons. for nonprofit orgns. and govt., 1980-92; pres. German Marshall Fund of U.S., Washington, 1992—; bd. dirs. Van Kampen Am. Capital. Bd. dirs. Sand County Found., LaSalle Adams Fund., Corp. for Enterprise Devel. Office: German Marshall Fund US 11 Dupont Cir NW Ste 750 Washington DC 20036

KENNEDY, DANIEL JOHN, national and international public relations consultant, communications executive. BA in Comm., U. Wis.; MEd in Media/Comm., U. Mass. Pub. rels. and mktg. comm. exec. Kurt Salmon Assocs., 1973-78; sr. comm. mgr. J.C. Penney Co., 1978-88; v.p. mktg. comm. Ruder Finn Pub. Rels., N.Y.C., 1988-90; internat. dir. media rels. Simon & Schuster, 1990-92; mng. dir. Daniel Kennedy Communications Svcs., 1992—; adj. prof. Baruch Coll., CUNY, 1996-97, Fashion Inst. Tech., SUNY, 1996-97, Marymount Manhattan Coll., 1996-99; guest spkr. various colls. and univs.; juror news and pub. affairs categories TV Acad. Emmy awards; cons. in field. Recipient Mercury award for internat. pub. rels. accomplishments, 1997, Gold, Silver and Bronze Bulldog awards for excellence in media rels. and publicity, 1998, Meritorius award Women Execs. Pub. Rels., 1998, ACE award Internat. Assn. Bus. Communicators, 1998. Address: 157 W 79th St New York NY 10024-6413

KENNEDY, DAVID BOYD, foundation executive, lawyer; b. Ann Arbor, Mich., Sept. 2, 1933; s. James Alexander and Elizabeth (Earhart) K.; m. Sally Martin Pyne, 1964; children: Jane Elizabeth, Douglas Earhart. Student, McGill U., 1951-52, U. Mich., 1952-54; AB, Ind. U., 1958; LLB, U. Mich., 1963. Bar: Mich. 1964, Wyo. 1965. Pvt. practive law Sheridan, Wyo., 1964-84; pres., trustee Earhart Found., Ann Arbor, Mich., 1985—; trustee Citizens Rsch. Coun. of Mich.; chmn., bd. dirs. Inst. for Justice, Washington. Mem. Wyo. Ho. Reps., 1967-72; chmn. Wyo. Rep. State Ctrl. Com., 1971-73; Rep. nat. committeeman, 1976-80, vice chmn., 1978-80; atty. gen. State of Wyo., 1974-75; mem. Mont Pelerin Soc.; apptd. mem. Pres.'s Com. on Arts and Humanities, Washington, 1990-93; bd. dirs. Philanthropy Roundtable, Washington; bd. dirs. Univ. Music Soc., 1986-90, pres., 1990. With U.S. Army, 1954-57. Mem. Wyo. Bar Assn., Mich. Bar Assn. Republican. Office: Earhart Found 2200 Green Rd Ste H Ann Arbor MI 48105-1569

KENNEDY, DAVID MICHAEL, historian, educator; b. Seattle, July 22, 1941; s. Albert John and Mary Ellen (Caufield) K.; m. Judith Ann Osborne, Mar. 14, 1970; children: Ben Caufield, Elizabeth Margaret, Thomas Osborne. BA, Stanford U., 1963; MA, Yale U., 1964, Oxford U., 1995; PhD, Yale U., 1968. Asst. prof. history Stanford (Calif.) U., 1967-72, assoc. prof., 1972-80, prof., 1980—, chmn. program in internat. relations, 1977-80, assoc. dean Sch. Humanities and Scis., 1981-85, William Robertson Coe prof. history and Am. studies, 1987-93, Donald J. McLachlan prof. history, 1993—, chair, history dept., 1990-94; vis. prof. U. Florence, Italy, 1976-77; lectr. Internat. Communications Agy., Denmark, Finland, Turkey, Italy, 1976-77, Ireland, 1980; Harmsworth prof. Am. history Oxford U., 1995-96. Author: Birth Control in America: The Career of Margaret Sanger, 1970, Over Here: The First World War and American Society, 1980, (with Thomas A. Bailey and Lizabeth Cohen) The American Pageant: A History of the Republic, 11th edit., 1998, Power and Responsibility: Case Studies in American Leadership, 1986, Freedom From Fear: The American People in Depression & War, 1929-1945, 1999; mem. adv. bd. (TV program) The American Experience, Sta. WGBH, 1986—. Mem. nat. planning group Am. Issues Forum, 1974-75; bd. dirs. CORO Found., 1981-87, Environ. Traveling Companions, 1986—, Stanford U. Bookstore, 1994—. Recipient Bancroft prize, 1971, John Gilmary Shea prize, 1970, Richard W. Lyman award Stanford U. Alumni Assn., 1989; fellow Am. Council Learned Socs., 1971-72, John Simon Guggenheim Meml. Found., 75-76, Ctr. for Advanced Study in Behavioral Scis., 1986-87, Stanford Humanities Ctr., 1989-90. Fellow Am. Acad. Arts and Scis.; mem. Am. Hist. Assn., Orgn. Am. Historians, Soc. Am. Historians. Democrat. Roman Catholic. Office: Stanford U Dept History Stanford CA 94305

KENNEDY, DAVID STEWART, federal judge; b. Reagan, Tenn., Apr. 9, 1944; s. Charles Elco and Ethelyn (Stewart) K.; m. Patricia Kelly, June 18, 1977. B.A., Memphis State U., 1967, J.D., 1970. Bar: Tenn. 1971. "AV"rating with Martindale-Hubbell. Law clk. U.S. Dist. Courts (western dist.) Tenn., 1970-71; sole practice law, mem. pvt. panel bankruptcy trustees, Memphis, 1971-73, 76-80; adminstrv. asst., chief clk. U.S. Bankruptcy Court (western dist.) Tenn., 1974-76; judge, 1980—; adj. prof. Cecil C. Humphreys Sch. Law, Memphis State U. Contbr. articles to profl. publs. Mem. ABA, Tenn. Bar. Assn., Memphis-Shelby County Bar Assn., Nat. Conf. Bankruptcy Judges, Cecil C Humphreys Sch. Law Alumni Nat. Council (pres.). Office: US Bankruptcy Ct US Courthouse 200 Jefferson Ave Ste 645 Memphis TN 38103-2328

KENNEDY, DAVID TINSLEY, retired lawyer, labor arbitrator; b. Richmond, Va., Mar. 6, 1919; s. David Tinsley and Lilian Brady (Butcher) K.; m. Jean Elizabeth Stephenson, Nov. 26, 1949; children: David T. III, Thomas D., Michael F. JD, U. Va., 1948. Bar: Va. 1948, W.Va. 1949, U.S. Dist. Ct. (so. dist.) W.Va. 1949, U.S. Ct. Appeals (4th cir.) 1963. Atty. Dist. 29, United Mine Workers Am., Beckley, W.Va., 1949-61; ptnr. Kennedy & Vaughan, Beckley, 1962-98; arbitrator Coal Arbitration Svc., Washington, 1970—; emeritus dir. Raleigh County Nat. Bank, Beckley. Mem. Raleigh County Dem. exec. com., 1980-86, chmn., 1986-90. Lt. col. U.S. Army, 1942-46, PTO. Mem. ABA, W.Va. State Bar, Va. State Bar, Assn. Trial Lawyers Am. Roman Catholic. Home: 102 Mollohan Dr Beckley WV 25801-2135 Office: Kennedy & Vaughan PO Box 1008 Beckley WV 25802-1008

KENNEDY, DAVID W., law educator; b. 1954. AB, Brown U., 1976; MALD, Fletcher Sch. Law and Diplomacy, 1979, PhD, 1984; JD, Harvard U., 1980. Bar: D.C. 1980. Prof. law Harvard U., Cambridge, Mass., Henry

L. Shattuck prof. Law, dir. European Law Rsch. Ctr. Office: Harvard U Law Sch 79 Jfk St Cambridge MA 02138-5801*

KENNEDY, DAVID WILLIAM, otolaryngologist, educator; b. York, Eng., June 27, 1948; s. Michael Leo and Winifred Pearl (Shepherd) K.; m. Edna Mae Schirmer, Apr. 20, 1978; children: Garrett David, Kirin Suzanne. Ed. pre-med. program, Ampleforth Coll., York, 1962-66; MD, Royal Coll. Surgeons, Ireland, 1972. Diplomate Am. Bd. Otolaryngology, Am. Bd. Head and Neck Surgery; lic. physician Pa., Md. Intern St. Laurence's Hosp., Dublin, Ireland, 1972-73; asst. resident in surgery Johns Hopkins U., Balt., 1973-74, asst. resident in otolaryngology, 1974-77, mem. staff, 1977-91, chief resident in otolaryngology, asst. prof. otolaryngology, 1977-78, asst. prof., 1978-86, assoc. prof. otolaryngology-head and neck surgery, 1986-91, assoc. prof. neurosurgery, 1987-91; mem. staff Loch Raven VA Hosp., Balt., 1980-87, cons. physician, 1987-91; mem. staff Sinai Hosp. Balt., 1981-88; chmn. U. Pa. Med. Ctr., Phila., 1991—; mem. staff VA Hosp., Phila., 1991—; departmental rep. staff conf. com. Johns Hopkins U., 1979-81, chmn. med. student edn. dept. otolaryngology-head and neck surgery, 1980-85, dir. dept. residency tng. program, 1981-91, mem. house staff policy com., 1984-90; chmn. laser com. U. Pa. Med. Ctr., 1991-93, chmn. ambulatory care task force, 1992-94, mem. steering com., 1992-93, 96-97, mem. oversight com., 1992-94, vice chairperson med. bd., 1993-94, chairperson med. bd., 1994-96, prof., chairperson dept. otorhinolaryngology-head and neck surgery, 1991—; chmn. fin. com. Clin. Practices of U. Pa., 1992-95; mem. Md. State Bd. Examiners for Otolaryngologists, 1979-91, Md. State Bd. Examiners for audiologists, 1984-88; cons. Md. State Dept. Health, Balt., 1979-91; vis. prof. ednl. instns., most recently Mayo Clinic, Rochester, Minn., 1993, Duke U. Med. Ctr., Durham, N.C., 1994, U. N.C., Chapel Hill, 1994; vis. Bettinger lectr. U. Minn., Mpls., 1994; John F. Daly vis. prof. NYU Med. Ctr., N.Y.C., 1994; mem. faculty numerous courses at ednl. instns., 1982—; presenter/speaker in field, most recently World Congress Otolaryngology, Sydney, 1997, 75th Ann. Meeting, Finnish Otolaryngology Soc., 1997; mem. 1st World Congress on Endoscopic Surgery, Athens, Greece, 1998, Gulf States Rhinologic Meeting, Kuwait City, Kuwait, 1998; pres. Internat. Symposium Infection & Allergy of the Nose, 1997; bd. dirs. Fessco, 1995-97; bd. dirs. Internat. Symposium Infection and Allergy of the Nose, pres. bd. dirs., 1989-90, pres. VIIIth Internat. Symposium Infection and Allergy of the Nose, 1989; mem. tech. adv. bd. E.M. Warburg Pincus & Co., 1995—; lectr. in field. Contbr. or co-contbr. 13 chpts. to books, including: Rhinitis, 2nd edit., 1991, Diseases of the Nose, Throat, Ear, Head and Neck, 1991, Otolaryngology, 3rd edit., 1991, Surgery for Skull Base Tumors, 1991; contbr. numerous articles to profl. jours.; mem. editl. bd. Ear, Nose and Throat Jour., 1983—, Am. Jour. Rhinology, 1986—, Laryngoscope, 1988—, Auris Nasus Larynx, 1996—, ACTA Oto-Rhino-Laryngologica Belgica, 1995—; editor-in-chief (otolaryngology) Am. Jour. Rhinology, 1984—, Current Opinion in Otolaryngology and Head and Neck Surgery, 1992—, Jour. Otolaryngology, 1993—; editor Auris Nasus Larynx, 1996—, ACTA Oto-Rhino-Larynngologica Belgica, 1995—. Recipient Leonard Abrahamson Meml. Gold medal, 1971, Lyons Meml. medal, 1971, gold medal Coombe Lying-In Hosp., 1971, Reuben-Harvey prize, 1972, Coun.'s prize and gold medal, 1972, Sr. William Wilde medal, 1995; rsch. grantee Schering Corp., 1981, HHS, 1983-88, Norwich-Eaton Corp., 1984-86, Minn. Mining and Mfg. Co., 1984, Healthtek, 1990-91. Fellow Am. Acad. Otolaryngology-Head and Neck Surgery (mem. hearing subcom. 1985-91, mem. rhinology-paranasal sinus com. 1986-93, 97—, mem. CPT com. 1992-97, legis. alt. bd. govs. 1991—, mem. adv. coun. on continuing edn. with TV subcom. 1994, instr. endoscopic sinus surgery 1985), Royal Coll. Surgeons (anatomy demonstrator/lectr. 1972-73, vis. prof. 1980-81, Sir William Wheeler Meml. medal 1972, Fitzsimmons Gold medal for surgery 1972, Bronze medal), Royal Coll. Surgeons (Ireland); mem. ACS, AMA (hon.), Am. Rhinologic Soc. (bd. dirs. 1988-96, v.p. 1989-90, pres. 1992-93, cons. to bd. dirs. 1987-88), Internat. Symposium on Infection of the Nose (bd. dirs., pres. 1989, 97), Internat. Symposium on Infection and Allergy of the Nose (pres. 1997), Internat. Rhinologic Soc. (bd. dirs. 1995—), Phila. Laryngol. Soc., Assn. Acad. Depts. of Otorhinolaryngology (pres. 1996-98), Soc. Univ. Otolaryngologists (mem. nominating com. 1985-86), Pa. Acad. Otolaryngology, John Morgan Soc., Johns Hopkins Med. and Surg. Assn., Danish Otolaryngology Soc. (hon.). Achievements include introduction of endoscopic sinus surgery to U.S.; development of extended applications of endoscopic surgical techniques; clinical development of surgical localizers. Office: Univ Pa Med Ctr 5 Ravdin 3400 Spruce St Philadelphia PA 19104-4204

KENNEDY, DEBBIE A., plastic surgeon; b. Plattsburg, N.Y., Apr. 3, 1958; d. Paul F. and Kathleen A. (Bell) K.; m. Martin F. Moriarty, June 26, 1993. BA in Biology and Chemistry, Coll. of St. Rose, 1980; MD, U. Vt., 1984. Diplomate Am. Bd. Plastic Surgeons, Am. Bd. Surgeons. Intern in gen. surgery St. Elizabeth's Hosp. of Boston, 1984-85, resident in gen. surgery, 1985-89; resident in plastic surgery Albany (N.Y.) Med. Ctr. Hosp., 1989-91, clin. instr. divsn. plastic surgery, 1991-98, clin. assoc. prof. surgery, 1998—; clin. instr. surgery Tufts U., Boston, 1988-89; mem. ad hoc com. on plastic laser surgery Child's Hosp., Albany, 1997, mem. performance improvement com., 1996—, mem. med. records com., 1993—; lectr., spkr., cons. in field. Contbr. articles to profl. jours. Cosmetic fellow, Miami, Fla., 1992. Fellow ACS; mem. Assn. Women Surgeons, Am. Soc. Plastic and Reconstructive Surgeons (mem. women's plastic surgeon's com. 1996-99), Soc. Plastic Surgeons Upstate N.Y., Am. Med. Women's Assn., N.Y. State Med. Soc., Nat. Coalition Physicians Against Family Violence, Delta Epsilon Sigma, Kappa Gamma Pi, Alpha Omega Alpha. Office: Albany Plastic and Reconstructive Surgery Ctr 4 Executive Park Albany NY 12203

KENNEDY, DEBRA JOYCE, marketing professional; b. Covina, Calif., July 9, 1955; d. John Nathan and Drea Hannah (Lancaster) Ward; m. John William Kennedy, Sept. 3, 1977 (div.); children: Drea, Noelle. BS in Communications, Calif. State Poly. U., 1977. Pub. rels. coord. Whittier (Calif.) Hosp., 1978-79, pub. relations mgr., 1980; pub. rels. dir. San Clemente (Calif.) Hosp., 1979-80; dir. pub. rels. Garfield Med. Ctr., Monterey Park, Calif., 1980-82; dir. mktg. and community rels. Charter Oak Hosp., Covina, 1983-85; mktg. dir. CPC Horizon Hosp., Pomona, 1985-89; dir. mktg. Sierra Royale Hosp., Azusa, 1989-90; mktg. rep. PacifiCare, Cypress, 1990-92; regional medicare mgr. Health Net, Woodland Hills, Calif., 1992-95; dist. sales mgr. Kaiser Permanente Health Plan, Pasadena, Calif., 1995—. Mem. Am. Soc. Hosp. Pub. Rels., Healthcare Mktg. Assn., Healthcare Pub. Rels. and Mktg. Assn., Covina and Covina West C. of C., West Covina Jaycees. Republican. Methodist. Club: Soroptimists. Contbr. articles to profl. jours.

KENNEDY, DENNIS L., lawyer; b. Tacoma, Oct. 28, 1950. BA, U. Wash., 1972, JD, 1975. Bar: Nev. 1975. Ptnr. Lionel Sawyer & Collins, Las Vegas, Nev., 1979—. Bd. editors Washington Law Review, 1974-75. Fellow Am. Coll. Trial Lawyers; mem. ABA (administrv. law sect., antitrust law sect., forum com. health law 1980—), Am. Acad. Hosp. Attys., Am. Soc. Law and Medicine, Internat. Assn. Gaming Attys., Nat. Health Lawyers Assn., State Bar Nev. (mem. disciplinary comm. 1988—),. Office: Lionel Sawyer & Collins Bank Am Plz 300 S 4th St Ste 1700 Las Vegas NV 89101-6053

KENNEDY, DONALD, environmental science educator, former academic administrator; b. N.Y.C., Aug. 18, 1931; s. William Dorsey and Barbara (Bean) K.; children: Laura Page, Julia Hale; m. Robin Beth Wiseman, Nov. 27, 1987; stepchildren: Cameron Rachel, Jamie Christopher. AB, Harvard U., 1952, AM, 1954, PhD, 1956; DSc (hon.), Columbia U., Williams Coll., U. Mich., U. Ariz., U. Rochester, Reed Coll., Whitman Coll. Mem. faculty Stanford (Calif.) U., 1960-77, prof. biol. scis., 1965-77, chmn. dept., 1965-72, sr. cons. sci. and tech. policy Exec. Office of Pres., 1976, commr. FDA, 1977-79, provost, 1979-80, pres., 1980-92; prof. emeritus, Bing prof. environ. sci. Stanford U., 1992—; bd. overseers Harvard U., 1970-76; bd. dirs. Health Effects Inst., Nat. Commn. on Pub. Svc., Carnegie Commn. on Sci., Tech. and Govt. Author: Academic Duty, 1997; mem. editorial bd. Jour. Neurophysiology, 1969-75, Science, 1973-77; contbr. articles to profl. jours. Bd. dirs. Carnegie Endowment for Internat. Peace. Fellow AAAS, Am. Acad. Arts and Scis.; mem. NAS, Am. Philos. Soc. Office: Stanford U Inst for Internat Studies Encina Hall 401 Stanford CA 94305-6055

KENNEDY, DONALD DAVIDSON, JR., retired insurance company executive; b. Philadelphia, Pa., 1931. Graduate, Princeton U., Princton, N.J., 1953; JD, U. Pa., Phila., 1960. Pres., sce., dir. Providian Life & Health Ins. Co., Valley Forge, Pa. Home: 6915 Green Tree Dr Naples FL 34108-8528*

KENNEDY, EARLE JAMES, retired steel manufacturing company executive; b. St. Louis, Apr. 18, 1929; s. Earle and Aurelia (Fournie) K.; m. Marjorie Fehling, Dec. 6, 1930; children: Sharon (dec.), Earle J. III, Jeanne, Jane, Laura, Tracey. BS in Indsl. Mgmt., St. Louis U., 1951. Treas. Continental Boiler Works, St. Louis, 1951-82; pres. Westway Svc. Inc., St. Louis, 1962-95; bd. dirs., bank dir. Southside Nat. Bank, Southside Bancshares, Inc., 1978—; pres. Continental Boiler Works, St. Louis, 1982-83; pres. Grafton (Ill.) Boat Co., 1967-70; exec. v.p. The Boardman Co., Oklahoma City, 1966-82, pres., 1982-84; exec. v.p. Gulf States Fabricators, Baton Rouge, 1967-82, pres., 1982-84. Bd. dirs. Child Ctr. St. Louis Catholic Charities, 1997—.

KENNEDY, EDWARD MOORE, senator; b. Boston, Feb. 22, 1932; s. Joseph Patrick and Rose (Fitzgerald) K.; m. Joan Kennedy (div.); children: Kara Anne, Edward Moore, Patrick Joseph; m. Victoria Anne Reggie, 1992. A.B., Harvard U., 1956; postgrad., Internat. Law Sch., The Hague, Netherlands, 1958; LL.B., U. Va., 1959. Bar: Mass. 1959, U.S. Supreme Ct. 1963. Asst. dist. atty. Suffolk County, Mass., 1961-62; U.S. senator from Mass., 1962—, chmn. judiciary com., 1979-81, ranking Dem. mem. labor and human resources com., 1981—, also mem. armed service, joint econ., labor and human resources (chmn. full com., chmn. subcom. on health 1971-80) and judiciary coms., also mem. Dem. steering & coordination com. Author: Decisions for a Decade, 1968, In Critical Condition: The Crisis in America's Health Care, 1972, Our Day and Generation, 1979, (with Mark O. Hatfield) Freeze: How You Can Help Prevent Nuclear War, 1979. Pres. Joseph P. Kennedy, Jr. Found., from 1961; trustee Children's Hosp. Med. Ctr., Boston, John F. Kennedy Library, Boston Symphony (emeritus), John F. Kennedy Ctr. for Performing Arts, Robert F. Kennedy Meml. Found., Boston Coll., Mass. Gen. Hosp. Served with AUS, 1951-53. Decorated knight comdr. Order of Phoenix (Greece), grande croce Al Merito della Republica Italiana (Italy), Order el Sol (Peru); named One of 10 Outstanding Young Men, U.S. Jaycees, 1967; recipient meritorious svc. citation U.S. Com. for Refugees and Am. Immigration and Citizenship Coun., Solidarity award Nat. Conf. on Soviet Jewry, award Nat. Mil. Family Assn., 1985, Homeric award Chian Fedn., Scopus award Am. Friends Hebrew U., Hubert H. Humphrey award Leadership Conf. on Civil Rights, others. Mem. Tech. Assessment Bd., Congl. Friends of Ireland, Biomed. Ethics Bd., Arms Control Observer Group, Commn. on the Bicentennial of the U.S. Constitution, Martin Luther King Jr. Fed. Holiday Commn., NAACP. Office: US Senate 315 Russell Senate Bldg Washington DC 20510-2101*

KENNEDY, ELIZABETH, health facility administrator; b. Binghamton, N.Y., Mar. 19, 1944; d. Robert D. and Doris Beverly (Bryde) Courtright; m. Leon C. Kennedy, Aug. 29, 1964; children: Andrew, Tracey, Brian, Kristie. AAS, Ind.-Purdue U., 1986; BSN, Ind. Wesleyan U., 1996. RN, Ind.; lifetime ARC nurse. DON Summit House, Ft. Wayne, Ind., 1986-87; staff nurse Mark Souder, M.D., Auburn, Ind., 1988; instr. ARC; DON Kendallville (Ind.) Nursing Home, 1988-89, Lifecare Ctr., Lagrange, Ind., 1989-91; owner Profl. Nursing Svcs., 1989—; asst. DON Arbors at Ft. Wayne, Ind., 1991-92; nursing supr. Allen Home, Health Care & Hospice, 1993-95; DON Courtland Health and Rehab. Ctr., Ft. Wayne, 1996—; staff nurse Interim Health Care, Ft. Wayne, Ind., 1996-97; agy. nurse The Arc of N.E. Ind., 1997-98; DON The Cedars, Leo, Ind., 1998-99; owner Prof. Nursing Svc., 1989-99; clin. educator Parkview Health Sys., Ft. Wayne, Ind., 1999—; case mgr. mr/dd Ind. Case Met, Indpls., 1999—; instr. ARC., 1986, AHA CPR, 1998. Recipient Scottish Rite Nursing scholarship. Home: 6784 Covington Creek Trl Fort Wayne IN 46804-2870

KENNEDY, ELIZABETH CAROL, psychologist, educator; b. Rochester, N.Y., May 5, 1948; d. Carl Elmore and Ruth Frances (Loebs) Riggs; m. James Barry Elvin, July 29, 1967 (div. Jan. 1989); 1 child, Krista Ann; m. William Jerald Kennedy, Aug. 12, 1989 (div. Jan. 1997). AA, Broward C.C., Coconut Creek, Fla., 1986; BA, Fla. Atlantic U., 1989, MA, 1993, PhD, 1998. Paraprofl. gifted edn. Havencroft Elem. Sch., Olathe, Kans., 1980-83; asst. recreational therapist South Fla. State Hosp., Pembroke Pines, 1987-88; asst. mental health therapist Ft. Lauderdale (Fla.) Hosp., 1986-89; instr. psychology Fla. Atlantic U., Boca Raton, 1990-96; asst. prof. Southeastern Okla. State U., Durant, 1996—; rsch. asst. Fla. Atlantic U., Boca Raton, 1993-96; statis. cons. South Fla., 1994-96. Co-author: (book chpt.) Conflict in Child and Adolescent Development, 1992; contbr. articles to profl. jours. Mem. APA, Am. Psychol. Soc., Soc. for Rsch. in Child Devel., Phi Kappa Phi (scholarship 1989), Psi Chi. Avocations: scuba diving, travel, painting, skiing. Home: 5204 Creekwood Dr Durant OK 74701-1715 Office: Southeastern Okla State U Dept Psychology/Counseling Durant OK 74701-0609

KENNEDY, ELIZABETH MAE, musician; b. Medford, Mass., Oct. 16, 1949; d. Thomas Power and Anne Cecelia (Coyne) Sullivan; m. William David Kennedy, Oct. 12, 1970 (div. 1984); children: Mary Elizabeth, Jonathan Martin. AS, N.S. C.C., 1969; student, Aquinas Coll., 1991-92. Cert. liturgical musician music and liturgy. Retail sales mgmt. Jordan Marsh Co., Peabody, Mass., 1966-69; retail mgmt. Sears, Roebuck and Co., Lynn, Mass., 1969-70; asst. bookkeeper Henry Leather Co., Peabody, Mass., 1970-76; office mgr. Bartlett and Steadman Co. Inc., Marblehead, Mass., 1981-90; bandleader, performer New England Area, 1983—; music dir., contract organist St. John The Evangelist Ch., Swampscott, Mass., 1985-98; co-founder New Sch. of Music and Performing Arts, Marblehead, Mass., 1994; dir. music St. Charles Borromeo Ch., Waltham, Mass., 1998—. Organizer Devereux Neighborhood Assn.; active North Shore Piano Tchrs. Guild, 1988—, v.p., 1998—; chairperson Marblehead Festival of the Arts, 1998-99. Democrat. Roman Catholic. Avocations: reading, swimming, MIDI, computers. Home: 46 Ocean Ave Marblehead MA 01945-3616

KENNEDY, ELLEN WOODMAN, elementary and home economics educator; b. Laconia, N.H., June 23, 1950; d. Arthur Stone and Rosemary (Jackson) Woodman; m. Thomas Daniel Kennedy, July 27, 1974 (dec. Aug. 1988); children: Susan Elaine, Margaret Ann. Student, Westbrook Coll., 1968-69; BEd, Keene State Coll., 1973; MS in Elem. Edn., So. Conn. State U., 1982, postgrad. in Nutrition Edn., 1991—. Cert. tchr., N.H. Tchr. home econs. Ctrl. H.S., Manchester, N.H., 1974-75, High and Mid. Schs., West Haven, Conn., 1975-83; adult edn. tchr. Derry (N.H.) Adult Edn., 1974, 92; devel. 1st grade instr. North Sch., Londonderry, N.H., 1996—; spl. svcs. tchr. grade 1-6, spl. edn. tutor, North Sch., Londonderry. Author: New England Saturday Night Suppers, 1988. Republican. Congregationalist. Avocations: all hand embroidery, camping, doll collecting. Home and Office: 452 Mammoth Rd Londonderry NH 03053-2370

KENNEDY, EUGENE CULLEN, psychology educator, writer; b. Syracuse, N.Y., Aug. 28, 1928; s. James Donald and Gertrude Veronica (Cullen) K.; m. Sara Connor Charles, Sept. 3, 1977. AB, Maryknoll Coll., 1950; STB, Maryknoll Sem., 1953, MRE, 1954; MA, Cath. U. Am., 1958, PhD, 1962; LHD (hon.), Barat Coll., 1990. Instr. psychology Maryknoll Sem., Clarks Summit, Pa., 1955-56, Cath. U., Washington, 1959-60; prof. psychology Maryknoll Coll., Glen Ellyn, Ill., 1960-69; prof. psychology Loyola U., Chgo., 1969-95, prof. emeritus, 1995—; cons. Menninger Found., 1965-67; mem. profl. adv. bd. Chgo. Dept. Mental Health; bd. dirs., cons. King Kullen Grocery Co., 1985—, mem. exec. com., 1994—; ptnr. Associated Growth Investors, 1992—; bd. dirs. Crown Mktg. Group, Inc. Author 40 books, including Himself! The Life and Times of Richard J. Daley, 1978 (Carl Sandburg award 1978), Father's Day, 1981 (Soc. of Midland Authors fiction award 1981, Friends of Lit. award 1981, Carl Sandburg award 1981), Queen Bee, 1982, The Now and Future Church, 1984, Tomorrow's Catholics, Yesterday's Church, 1988, Fixes, 1989, Cardinal Bernardin, 1989, (with Sara Charles) Defendant, 1985, (with Sara Charles) On Becoming a Counselor, 1990, (with Sara Charles) Authority, 1996, This Man Bernadin, 1996, My Brother Joseph, 1997; author TV play: I Would Be Called John, PBS, 1987; also articles, book revs.; columnist Religious News Svc., 1991-92, 97—, Chgo. Tribune, 1992-93. Trustee U. Dayton, Ohio, 1977-86. Recipient Thomas More medal, 1972, 78, Wilbur award Religious Pub. Relations Council. Fellow Am. Psychol. Assn. (div. pres. 1975-76); mem. Authors Guild. Democrat. Roman Catholic. Home: 1300 N Lake Shore Dr Chicago IL 60610-2169 *My principal goal in all my work is to try to understand and to try to help others understand what is so human about all of us.*

KENNEDY, EUGENE PATRICK, biochemist, educator; b. Chgo., Sept. 4, 1919; s. Michael and Catherine (Frawley) K.; m. Adelaide Majewski, Oct. 27, 1943; children—Lisa Kennedy Helprin, Sheila Kennedy Violich, Katherine Kennedy Diller. BSc, DePaul U., 1941; PhD (Nutrition Found. fellow), U. Chgo., 1949, ScD (hon.), 1977; AM (hon.), Harvard U., 1960. Rsch. chemist chem. rsch. dept. Armour & Co., 1941-47; postdoctoral fellow Am. Cancer Soc., U. Calif., Berkeley, 1949-50; with Ben May Lab. Cancer Rsch., dept. biochemistry U. Chgo., 1950-56, prof. biochemistry, 1956-60; sr. postdoctoral fellow NSF, Oxford (Eng.) U., 1959-60; Hamilton Kuhn prof. biol. chemistry Harvard Med. Sch., 1960—, head dept., 1960-65; Macy scholar Cambridge U., 1976. Recipient Glycerine rsch. award, 1955; Am. Oil Chemist Soc. Lipid Rsch. award, 1970; Gairdner Found. award, 1976; Ledlie prize, 1976, Alexander von Humboldt prize, 1984; Passano Found. award, 1986, Heinrich Wieland Prize, 1986, William C. Rose Award in biochemistry. Am. Soc. Biochem. and Molecular Biology, 1992. Mem. NAS, Am. Chem. Soc. (Paul Lewis award 1958), Am. Soc. Biol. Chemists (pres. 1970-71), Am. Acad. Arts and Scis., Am. Philos. Soc. Home: 221 Mount Auburn St Cambridge MA 02138-4874 Office: Harvard Med Sch Dept Biol Chemistry Boston MA 02115

KENNEDY, EUGENE RICHARD, microbiologist, university dean; b. Scranton, Pa., July 3, 1919; s. Thomas A. and Margaret (Culkin) K.; m. Marjorie Giblin, July 24, 1945; children—Anne, Michael, Christine. BS, U. Scranton, 1941; M.S., Cath. U., 1943; Ph.D., Brown U., 1949. Diplomate Am. Bd. Microbiology. Serologist Walter Reed Army Med. Center, Washington, 1942; instr. bacteriology and immunology R.I. Hosp. Sch. of Nursing, Providence, 1946-48, Brown U., Providence, 1946-48; instr. Cath. U. Am., Washington, 1949-51, asst. prof., 1951-55, assoc. prof., 1956-66, prof. microbiology, 1966-85, prof. emeritus, 1985—, dean Sch. Arts and Scis., 1973-85. Contbr. articles to profl. jours. Served to capt. Med. Service Corps U.S. Army, 1943-46. Mem. Am. Soc. for Microbiology, AAAS, Sigma Xi, Phi Beta Kappa. Home: 15100 Interlachen Dr Apt 912 Silver Spring MD 20906-5608 Office: Cath U McCort-Ward Bldg Washington DC 20064

KENNEDY, FREDERICK MORGAN, retired secondary education educator; b. Oklahoma City, May 5, 1943; s. Fredrick Theodor and Ruthy Marie Kennedy; m. Claudette Alberta Carter, Aug. 14, 1966; children: Kimberly Michelle, Cheryl Ann. BS, Langston U., 1965; MA, Kent State U., 1979. Cert. tchr., Ohio; ordained exhorter African Meth. Episcopal Ch. Tchr. math., occupational work adjustment Cleve. City Schs., 1965-96; mem. curriculum writing com. Cleve. City Schs., 1987, 89, 92. Treas. Quinn Chapel AME Ch., Cleve., 1985-97, ch. adminstr., 1989-97. Mem. Ohio Vocat. Assn. (life), Indsl. Arts Club (membership com. 1992), Occupational Work Adjustment (instrs. div.). Democrat. Home: 17201 Dynes Ave Cleveland OH 44128-3320

KENNEDY, G. ALFRED, retired federal agency administrator; b. Woodbury, N.J., June 25, 1940; s. Bernard Herbert and Emma Eleanor (Elam) K.; 1 child (adopted), Ji-yub Lee. BA, U. Oreg., 1968; MA, Johns Hopkins U., Washington, 1977; M in Internat. Pub. Policy, Johns Hopkins U., 1982. Assoc. dir. The Fed. City Coll., Washington, 1968-71; dir. minority recruitment USIA, Washington, 1971-72; econ. programs officer USIS, Rome, 1972-76; pub. affairs officer USIS, Pusan, Republic of Korea, 1977-79; policy officer Europe Office of Edn., Cultural Affairs USIA, Washington, 1979-81, acting dep. policy office European affairs, 1982; counsel pub. affairs U.S. Mission to European Community, Brussels, 1983-88, U.S. Mission to OECD, Paris, 1988-89; dep. asst. sec. Bur. Pub. Affairs U.S. Dept State, Washington, 1989-92, sr. advisor to sec. commerce, 1993; consul gen. Am. Consulate, Toronto, 1993-96; internat. bus. cons., 1996—; mng. ptnr. Source Internat., Inc., 1997—. With U.S. Army, 1959-62. Martin Luther King fellow, 1970, Rockefeller Found. fellow, 1970. Mem. Army and Navy Club, Founders Club (Toronto, Ont. Canada), Andrews AFB Officers Club. E-mail:gakenedy@aol.com. Home and Office: 8103 Highland Meadows Dr Clinton MD 20735-1871

KENNEDY, GEORGE, actor; b. N.Y.C., Feb. 18, 1926. Films include Little Shepard of Kingdom Come, 1961, Lonely Are The Brave, 1962, The Silent Witness, 1962, Charade, 1963, The Man from the Diners' Club, 1963, Hush...Hush, Sweet Charlotte, 1964, Straight-Jacket, 1964, Island of the Blue Dolphins, 1964, McHale's Navy, 1964, The Flight of the Phoenix, 1965, In Harm's Way, 1965, Mirage, 1965, The Son's of Katie Elder, 1965, Shenandoah, 1965, The Dirty Dozen, 1967, Hurry Sundown, 1967, Cool Hand Luke, 1967 (Acad. award 1967), Bandolero!, 1968, The Boston Strangler, 1968, The Legend of Lylah Clare, 1968, The Pink Jungle, 1968, The Ballad of Josie, 1968, Guns of the Magnificent Seven, 1969, Gaily Gaily, 1969, The Good Guys and the Bad Guys, 1969, Airport, 1970, ...Tick...Tick...Tick, 1970, Zig Zag, 1970, Dirty Dingus Magee, 1970, Fool's Parade, 1971, Lost Horizon, 1973, Cahill, United States Marshall, 1973, Thunderbolt and Lightfoot, 1974, Earthquake, 1974, Airport 1975, 1975, The Eiger Sanction, 1975, The Human Factor, 1975, Airport '77, 1977, Death on the Nile, 1978, Brass Target, 1978, Mean Dog Blues, 1978, The Concord-Airport '79, 1979, The Double McGuffin, 1979, Death Ship, 1980, Just Before Dawn, 1980, Steel, 1980, Virus, 1980, Hotwire, 1980, Modern Romance, 1981, Search and Destroy, 1981, Striking Back, 1981, The Jupiter Menace, 1982, Wacko, 1983, Bolero, 1984, Chattanooga Choo Choo, 1984, A Race Breed, 1984, Savage Dawn, 1984, Rigged, 1985, The Delta Force, 1985, Radioactive Dreams, 1986, Creepshow 2, 1987, Born to Race, 1987, Private Road—No Tresspassing, 1987, Nightmare at Noon, 1988, Demonwarp, 1988, The Naked Gun, 1988, Brain Dead, 1989, Ministry of Vengeance, 1990, Naked Gun 2 1/2: The Smell of Fear, 1991, Driving Me Crazy, 1991, The Naked Gun 33 1/3: The Final Insult, 1994, Small Soldiers, 1998, Dennis the Menace Strikes Again, 1998, Men in White, 1998, also Counterforce, The Uninvited, The Terror Within, Esmerelda Bay, Hangfire, Distant Justice, (voice) Cats Don't Dance, 1997; TV movies include See How They Run, 1964, The Priest Killer, 1971, Sarge: The Badge or the Cross?, 1971, A Great American Tragedy, 1972, Deliver Us From Evil, 1973, A Cry in the Wilderness, 1974, The Blue Knight, 1975, Backstairs at the White House, 1979, The Archer—Fugitive from the Empire, 1981, The Jesse Owen's Story, 1984, International Airport, 1985, Liberty, 1986, Kenny Rogers as The Gambler II-The Legend Continues, 1987, What Price Victory, 1988, Good Cops, Bad Cops, 1990, Final Shot: The Hank Gathers Story, 1992, J.R. Returns, 1996; TV series include Sarge, 1971-72, The Blue Knight, 1975-76, Dallas, 1988-91. Served with U.S. Army, 16 years. Office: c/o Kaufman Bernstein Oberman Tivoli & Hiller 2049 Century Park E Ste 2500 Los Angeles CA 90067-3127 Address: 11573 Sumac Ln Camarillo CA 93012-8859*

KENNEDY, GEORGE DANNER, chemical company executive; b. Pitts., May 30, 1926; s. Thomas Reed and Lois (Smith) K.; m. Valerie Putis; children: Charles Reed, Jamey Kathleen, Susan Patton, Timothy Christian. BA, Williams Coll., 1948. With Scott Paper Co., 1947-52, Champion Paper Co., 1952-65; pres. Brown Co., 1965-71; exec. v.p. Internat. Minerals & Chem. Corp., Northbrook, Ill., 1971-78, pres., 1978-86; chmn. Mallinckrodt Group (formerly IMCERA), St. Louis, 1986—, CEO, 1983-91; also bd. dirs., chmn. exec. com. IMCERA (formerly Internat. Minerals & Chem. Corp.), Northbrook, Ill.; bd. dirs. Kemper Found.; chmn. nominting com. Kemper Nat.; bd. dirs., nominating com., fin. com. Scotsman Industries, Inc.; chmn. compensation com., bd. dirs. exec. com. Am. Nat. Can Co.; dir. Omni Media Systems, Inc., Great Barrington, Mass, Health Share, Acton, Mass; mng. ptnr. Berkshires Capital Investors, Willimstown, Mass. Bd. dirs. Children's Meml. Hosp. and Children's Meml. Med. Ctr.; trustee Chgo. Symphony; gov. mem. Chgo. Orch. Assn.; dir. Lyric Opera Chgo., Ctr. for Workforce Preparation and Quality Edn.; regional trustee Boys and Girls Club of Am.; mem. trustee NatCom. Against Drunk Driving. Mem. Indian Hill Club, Chgo. Club, Sleepy Hollow Country Club. Office: PO Box 559 Winnetka IL 60093-0559

KENNEDY, GEORGE HUNT, chemistry educator; b. Seattle, Apr. 24, 1936; s. George Francis and Frances (Huse) K.; m. Kay Rife, Sept. 1, 1961; children: Joseph, Jill. BS in Chemistry, U. Oreg., 1959; MS in Chemistry, Oreg. State U., 1962, PhD in Phys. Chemistry, 1966. Chemist Borden Chem. Co., Springfield, Oreg., 1957-58; rsch. chemist Chevron Rsch. Corp., Richmond, Calif., 1961-62; prof. chemistry Colo. Sch. Mines, Golden, 1965—; pres. faculty senate Colo. Sch. Mines, 1992-93. Contbr. articles to profl. jours. With USNR, 1954-62. Recipient Outstanding Tchr. award Amoco Found., 1992. Mem. Am. Chem. Soc., Internat. Oceanographic

Found., Sigma Xi, Phi Lambda Upsilon. Democrat. Avocations: fishing, hunting, mountaineering, travel. Office: Colo Sch Mines Dept Chemistry Golden CO 80401

KENNEDY, GEORGE WENDELL, prosecutor; b. Altadena, Calif., Aug. 5, 1945; s. Ernest Campbell Kennedy and Mildred (Onstott) Stuckey; m. Janet Lynn Stites, Aug. 3, 1978; children: Campbell, Britton. BA, Claremont Men's Coll., 1968; postgrad., Monterey Inst. Fgn. Studies, 1968; JD, U. So. Calif., 1971; postgrad., Nat. Coll. Dist. Attys., 1974, F.B.I. Nat. Law Inst., 1989. Bar: Calif. 1972, U.S. Dist. Ct. (no. dist.) Calif. 1972, U.S. Ct. Appeals (9th cir.) 1972. Dep. dist. atty. Santa Clara County, San Jose, Calif., 1972-87, asst. dist. atty., 1987-88, chief asst. dist. atty., 1988-90, dist. atty., 1990—. Author: California Criminal Law Practice and Procedure, 1986. Active NAACP, 1989—, police chiefs' assn. Santa Clara County, San Jose, 1990—; chair domestic violence coun. Santa Clara County, San Jose, 1990-92; bd. dirs. Salvation Army, 1993. Recipient commendation Child Advocates of Santa Clara & San Mateo Counties, 1991, Santa Clara County Bd. Suprs., 1992, Valley Med. Ctr. Found., 1992, 93; elected Ofcl. of Yr. award Am. Electronics Assn., 1998. Mem. Nat. Dist. Attys. Assn. (bd. dirs.), Calif. Dist. Attys. Assn. (bd. dirs. 1988-90, officer 1993-97, pres. 1997-98), Santa Clara County Bar Assn., Rotary Club. Avocation: sailing. Office: 70 W Hedding St 5th Flr West Wing San Jose CA 95110

KENNEDY, HAROLD EDWARD, lawyer; b. Pottstown, Pa., Oct. 18, 1927; s. Freeman S. and Alice (Brehm) K.; m. Eleanor Henry, Jan. 9, 1960; children: Kathleen, Nancy, Harold, Robert, Ellen, Anne, Susan. Student, Colgate U.; 1945-47; LLB, Syracuse U., 1952. Bar: N.Y. 1952, U.S. Dist. Ct. (no. dist.) N.Y. 1954, U.S. Supreme Ct. 1956, U.S. Dist. Ct. (so. dist.) N.Y. 1962. Ptnr. Taylor & Kennedy, Amsterdam, N.Y., 1952-59; sr. assoc. Kissam & Halpin, N.Y.C., 1959-60; vice chmn., gen. counsel, dir. mergers and acquisitions Foster Wheeler Corp., Clinton, N.J., 1960-94, legal advisor, 1994—, also bd. dirs.; bd. dirs. W.I. Refining Ltd., Compass Capital Group. Trustee First Presbyn. Ch., Orange, N.J., 1973-76, St. Barnabas Med. Ctr., 1986—, Kessler Inst. for Rehab., 1987—, vice chmn., 1992—, Union Hosp., 1994—, Beth Israel Hosp., 1996—; bd. visitors Syracuse U. Coll. of Law, 1987—. Served with USAF, 1945-47. Mem. Order of Coif, Baltusrol Golf Club, Sea Pines Country Club, Double Eagle Club. Office: Foster Wheeler Corp Perryville Corp Pk Clinton NJ 08809

KENNEDY, HARVEY EDWARD, science information publishing executive; b. Goldsboro, N.C., Oct. 2, 1928; s. Robert H. and Zilphia E. (Taylor) K.; m. Dorothy Childress, Aug. 18, 1951; children: Connie Grayce, Jeffrey Reynolds. B.A., Barton Coll., 1948; M.S., N.C. State Univ., 1952; Ph.D. in Microbiology, N.C. State U., 1954. Rsch. scientist U. N.C. Med. Ctr., Chapel Hill, 1954-58; asst. prof. Ohio State U., Columbus, 1958-61; dir. product devel. Vetco div. Johnson & Johnson, New Brunswick, N.J., 1961-67; dir. sci. affairs Biosis, Phila., 1967-75, exec. dir., 1975-80, pres., 1980-93. Editor: (spl. series) International Communication for Biomedical Research, 1980. Mem. Fahrney Medal com. Sci. and Arts com., Franklin Inst., 1985-93. Mem. Internat. Fedn. Sci. Editors (interim bd., v.p. 1980-83, 91—), Internat. Orgn. Plant Info. com. 1991-93), Am. Soc. Info. Sci., Am. Inst. Biol. Scis. (exec. com. 1983-88, pres. 1987), Coun. Biology Editors (pres. 1978-79, award for excellence in sci. communication 1990), Nat. Fedn. Abstracting and Info Svcs. (pres. 1974-75, Miles Conrad award 1986), Am. Soc. Microbiology (chmn. com. info. sci. 1976-79), Soc. for Scholarly Pub. (interim bd. 1978-81), Internat. Coun. for Sci. and Tech. Info. (pres. 1989-92). *

KENNEDY, HARVEY JOHN, JR., lawyer; b. Barnesville, Ga., Apr. 9, 1924; s. Harvey John and Marisu (Reeves) K.; m. Jean McRitchie King, Apr. 8, 1950; children: Marisu, Jean Gay. LLB, U. Ga., 1949, JD, 1969; diplomate of psychology, Colo. Christian Coll., 1973. Bar: Ga. 1948. Atty. Lamar Electric Membership Corp., Barnesville, Ga., 1948—; county atty. Lamar County, Barnesville, Ga., 1950-52, 58-60; mem. Ga. Indigent Def. Coun., 1958, Ga. Bar Assn. Bd., 1958-59, State Bar of Ga. Bd. Govs. 1980-92; agt. Govt. Appeal Local Bd. 89, 1958; city atty. City of Barnesville, Ga., 1958-65, 83, City of Milner, Ga., 1963-68. Past pres. Barnesville (Ga.) Rotary Club, 1959-60. Capt. U.S. Army, 1942-46, ETO, PTO. Decorated Bronze Star medal and Combat Infantry badge. Mem. ABA, Ga. Trial Lawyers Assn. (v.p. 1972), State Bar Ga., Ga. Assn. Plaintiff's Trial Attys. (v.p. 1968), Am. Legion (comdr. post #25), Moose (32d degree shriner). Democrat. Presbyterian. Avocations: amateur radio, fishing. Office: PO Drawer B 217 Zebulon St Barnesville GA 30204-1126

KENNEDY, HENRY H., judge. BA, Princeton U., 1970; JD, Harvard U., 1972. Judge U.S. Dist. Ct. D.C., 1997—. Office: US Dist Court for DC Barrett Prettyman Courthse 333 Constitution Ave Washington DC 20001

KENNEDY, J. JACK, JR., court administrator, bank director, lawyer; b. Abingdon, Va., June 11, 1956; s. J. Jack Sr. and Bobbie Lee (Porter) K.; m. Susan Maura Muir, June 30, 1979; children: J. Jack III, Jillian Susanne. BS, U. Va., Wise, 1978; cert. in internat. study, U. London, 1977; MA in Polit. Sci., East Tenn. State U., 1982; JD equivalent, Va. State Bar, 1982; BA in Orgnl. Mgmt., Va. Intermont Coll., 1994. Bar: Va. 1982, U.S. Dist. Ct. (we. dist.) Va. 1982, U.S. Ct. Appeals (4th cir.) 1982, U.S. Tax Ct. 1982, U.S. Ct. Claims 1982, Supreme Ct. Va. 1982, U.S Internat. Ct. Trade 1992. Mem. Va. Ho. of Dels., Richmond, 1988-91, Va. State Senate, Richmond, 1991-92; clk. Cir. Ct. for Wise County and City of Norton, Va., 1995—; bd. dirs. Black Diamond Savs. Bank, E-Commerce Today, Ltd., Kennedy & Kennedy Investment Corp., Turkey Gap Coal Co., Inc., Southwestern Va. Tech. Coun., Visit Any City.Com., Inc. State pres. Young Dems. Va., 1984-85; nat. sec. Young Dems. Am., 1985; chmn. Norton (Va.) Dem. Com., 1982-92, 95-99, 9th Congl. Dist. Dem. Com., 1985-89; del. Dem. Nat. Conv., 1976, 84, 88, 92; state chmn. Va. Assn. Local Dem. Chairmen, 1986-87; bd. dirs., chmn. Va. Land Records Mgmt. Task Force, 1997—. Named Outstanding Young Dem. Va., 1985; recipient Tech. Innovation award Va. Supreme Ct., 1997. Fellow Inst. for Ct. Mgmt., Nat. Ctr. for State Cts.; mem. ABA, Nat. Assn. for Ct. Mgmt., Va. State Bar, Va. Bar Assn., Wise County and City of Norton Bar Assn. (pres. 1997), Wise County C. of C. (chair econ. devel.), Va. Cir. Ct. Clks. Assn., Kiwanis, Phi Sigma Kappa. Baptist. Avocations: international travel, reading, Internet technology, space exploration. E-mail: jkennedy@naxs.com. Home and Office: 699 Fox Run Rd SE Norton VA 24273-2722 also: Court House PO Box 1248 Wise VA 24293-1248

KENNEDY, JACK, secondary education journalism educator; b. Iowa City, Iowa, July 12, 1950; s. John William and Barbara Fern (Guffey) K.; m. Kathleen Ann Gowey, Sept. 25, 1971; children: Lesley Kathleen, Sara Ann, Philip John. BA in English, U. Iowa, 1976, MA in Edn., 1981. Tchr., journalism adviser Regina High Sch., Iowa City, 1976-80, City High Sch., Iowa City, 1980—. With USAF, 1971-74. Nat. HS Journalism Teacher of the Yr., Dow Jones Newspaper Fund, 1993. Mem. NEA, Journalism Edn. Assn. (chair curriculum commn. 1991—), Iowa High Sch. Press Assn. (pres. 1990—), Iowa City Edn. Assn., Iowa Coun. Tchrs. English. Democrat. Avocations: reading, singing, coaching youth sports. Home: 844 Evergreen Ct Iowa City IA 52245-3541 Office: City High Sch 1900 Morningside Dr Iowa City IA 52245-4669*

KENNEDY, JACK EDWARD, lawyer; b. Queens, N.Y., Mar. 24, 1945; s. Gene Joseph and H. Virginia (Nolan) K.; m. Kathy McFarland; children: Sean Edward, Chad Everett, Mendy McFarland, Mitch McFarland, Rick Russell. AA with honors, Shasta Coll., 1965; BA, U. Calif., Chico, 1968, postgrad., 1969; JD, U. Pacific, 1975. Bar: Nev. 1977, U.S. Dist. Ct. Nev. 1978, U.S. Ct. Appeals (9th cir.) 1989, U.S. Ct. Appeals (5th cir.) 1992. Pers. group mgr. Montgomery Ward & Co., Chico, 1968-70; labor leader employee's union San Francisco, 1970-71; program developer Legal Aid Soc., Sacramento, Calif., 1971-72, Legal Ctr. for Elderly, Sacramento, 1972-75; labor/personnel dir. Washoe County Sch. Dist., Reno, Nev., 1975-86; prin. Jack E. Kennedy & Assocs., P.C., Reno, 1977—. Coro Found. grad. fellow, San Francisco, 1970. Mem. ATLA, Nev. Trial Lawyers Assn., Nev. Bar Assn., Washoe County Bar Assn., Nat. Employment Lawyers Assn., Kiwanis. Democrat. Avocations: parasailing, jet- and snow-skiing, golf, boating, tae kwon do. Home: 2845 Sagittarius Dr Reno NV 89509-3885 Office: 425 W Plumb Ln Reno NV 89509-3766 *Notable cases include: Pagni vs. State of Nev. ADA, 1995, state trooper returned to work with pay and $350,000 settlement; Am. Bank Stationary vs. Farmer, 1990, precedent-setting case in area of wrongful termination based upon expressed and implied contract; Schlang & Goodwin vs. Key Airline et al, a subs. of World Air Corp., 1988, concerning right to unionize and pub. policy safety violations; Alford vs. Sands Casino, 1988, concerning health and safety violations, sexual harassment and wrongful termination; V.H. & P.H. vs. Circus Circus, concerning inadequate security, rape of patron in room; IBEW vs. Kindred et al, concerning a union suing former members for not properly leaving the union, counter suit on freedom of associates, misrepresentation.*

KENNEDY, JACK LELAND, lawyer; b. Portland, Oreg., Jan. 30, 1924; s. Ernest E. and Lera M. (Talley) K.; m. Clara C. Hagans, June 5, 1948; children: James M., John C. Student, U.S. Maritime Commn. Acad., Southwestern U., L.A.; JD, Lewis and Clark Coll., 1951. Bar: Oreg. 1951. Pvt. practice Portland; ptnr. Kennedy & King, Portland, 1971-77, Kennedy, King & McClurg, Portland, 1977-82, Kennedy, King & Zimmer, Portland, 1982-98, Kennedy, Watts, Arellano & Ricks L.L.P., Portland, 1998—; trustee Northwestern Coll. Law, Portland; dir. Profl. Liability Fund, 1979-82. Contbr. articles to legal jours. Mem. bd. visitors Lewis and Clark Coll. With USNR, 1942-46. Recipient Disting. Grad. award Lewis and Clark Coll., 1983. Fellow Am. Coll. Trial Lawyers, Am. Bar Found. (life), Oreg. Bar Found. (charter); mem. ABA (ho. of dels. 1984-88), Oreg. State Bar (bd. govs. 1976-79, pres. 1978-79), Multnomah Bar Assn., City Club, Columbia River Yacht Club. Republican. Office: Kennedy Watts Arellano & Ricks LLP 2600 Pacwest Ctr 1211 SW 5th Ave Portland OR 97204-3713

KENNEDY, JACK S., lawyer; b. Terre Haute, Ind., Apr. 14, 1945. BA magna cum laude, Harvard U., 1967; JD, U. Va., 1972. Bar: Conn. 1972. With Robinson & Cole LLP, Hartford, mng. ptnr., 1994—. Mem. editorial bd. Va. Law Review, 1970-72. Mem. ABA (sect. bus. law), Conn. Bar Assn. (chair sect. bus. law), Order of Coif). Office: Robinson & Cole LLP Ste 26 280 Trumbull St Hartford CT 06103-3599

KENNEDY, JAMES ANDREW, chemical company executive; b. Millburn, N.J., Dec. 15, 1937; s. James Andrew and Dorothy Frances (Van Cleve) K.; m. Judith Lynne Tunstall, Jan. 26, 1974; children—Brian James, Karen Jeanne, Kevin Van Cleve. BA in Econs., Holy Cross Coll., Worcester, Mass., 1959; MBA in Fin. and Mktg., Columbia U., N.Y.C., 1962. With Nat. Starch and Chem. Co., 1967-77; from v.p. internat. divsn. to exec. v.p., dir., COO Nat. Starch and Chem. Co., Bridgewater, N.J., 1977-90; pres., CEO Nat. Starch and Chem. Corp., Bridgewater, N.J., 1990—; chmn. Nat. Starch and Chem. Corp., Bridgewater, 1996-97; bus. group pres. Unilever, 1996-97; exec. v.p., dir. Imperial Chem. Industries, Eng., 1997; chmn. Nat. Starch and Chem. Co., Bridgewater, N.J., 1997—; lectr. Notre Dame U., NYU, Pace U., Am. Mgmt. Assn., Babcock Sch. Mgmt. Wake Forest U.; bd. dirs. Unilever U.S., Inc. Trustee, chmn. bd. overseers N.J. Int. Tech. Served to lt. (j.g.) USN, 1959-61. Mem. NAM (bd. dirs.), Chem. Mfrs. Assn. (bd. dirs.). Home: 11 Crest Dr Bernardsville NJ 07924-1707 Office: Nat Starch & Chem Co 10 Finderne Ave Bridgewater NJ 08807-3355

KENNEDY, JAMES BRUCE, operations administrator; b. Rockwood, Tenn., Jan. 19, 1947; s. Byrl O. and Eva C. (Gibson) K.; m. Linda C. Thugut, Oct. 1, 1971 (div. July 1983); m. Billie K. Thompson, May 7, 1988; 1 child, Nicole S. Egan. BS in Journalism, U. Tenn., 1969; MPA, Va. Commonwealth U., 1989. Account exec. Morristown (Tenn.) Citizen-Tribune, 1969-71, Richmond (Va.) Times-Dispatch, 1971-80; dir. ops. Richmond Met. Authority, 1980—. Contbr. articles to mags. Recipient Employee of Yr. award Mayor's Commn. on Disabled, 1990. Mem. Internat. Parking Inst. (cert. adminstr. pub. parking, bd. advs. 1991-96, bd. dirs. 1996-97, 1999—, sec.-treas. 1999—), Internat. Bridge, Tunnel and Tpke. Assn., Parking Assn. Vas. (founding mem., treas. 1992-94, pres. 1994-96). Avocations: golf, collecting 1950's memoribilia. Office: Richmond Met Authority 901 E Byrd St Ste 1110 Richmond VA 23219-4071

KENNEDY, JAMES C., publishing and media executive; b. 1947; married. BBA, U. Denver, 1970. With Atlanta Newspapers, 1972-79, prodn. asst., 1972-76, exec. v.p., gen. mgr., 1976-79; pres. Grand Junction Newspapers, 1979-80; pub. Grand Junction Daily Sentinel, 1980-85; v.p. Cox newspapers div. Cox Enterprises Inc., Atlanta, 1985-86, exec. v.p., 1986-87, pres., chief oper. officer, exec. v.p., 1986-87, also chmn., 1987—; now chmn., chief exec. officer Cox Enterprises Inc., 1988—. Office: Cox Enterprises Inc PO Box 105357 Atlanta GA 30348-5357 also: 1601 W Peachtree St NE Atlanta GA 30309-2641*

KENNEDY, JAMES FREDERICK, artist; b. Sayre, Pa., Nov. 27, 1942; s. Frederick D. and Rita (Calkins) K. AAS, SUNY, Albany, 1982. Enlisted U.S. Army, 1960, discharged, 1963; commd. lt. USN, 1985, ret., 1990; computer analyst Barnett Technology, Jacksonville, Fla., 1994-95. Mem. Masons, Scottish Rite, Shriners, VFW, Am. Legion. Home: 2588 Malibu Cir Orange Park FL 32065-7591

KENNEDY, JAMES WAITE, management consultant, author; b. Belding, Mich., Sept. 23, 1937; s. Lloyd Weston and Lois (Waite) K.; m. Anna Everest; children: David, Sarah, Polly, Leif, Damian. B.A., Stanford U., 1959; P.M.D., Harvard Bus. Sch., 1969. With Foote, Cone & Belding, San Francisco and Chgo., 1959-66, Gen. Foods Corp., White Plains, N.Y., 1966-79; dir. human resources J. Walter Thompson Co., N.Y.C., 1979-83; pres. Mgmt. Team Cons., Inc., San Rafael, Calif., 1983—. Author: Getting Behind the Resume, Interviewing Today's Candidates, 1987. Mem. Harvard Bus. Sch. Club. No. Calif., Instrnl. Sys. Assn., Theta Delta Chi. Office: Mgmt Team Cons Inc 1010 B St Ste 403 San Rafael CA 94901-2921

KENNEDY, JAMES WILLIAM, JR. (SARGE KENNEDY), special education administrator, consultant; b. Santa Rosa, Calif., Oct. 6, 1940; s. James William and Kay Jean (Eaton) K.; m. Lorene Adele Dunaway, May 12, 1962 (div. Sept. 1971); children: Sean, Erin, Mark; m. Carolyn Judith Nighsonger, Mar. 30, 1972 (div. Dec. 1979); m. Patricia Carter Critchlow, Nov. 5, 1988; 1 stepchild, Joy. BA, San Francisco State U., 1964, MA, 1970. Tchr., prin., coord. spl. edn., dir. spl. edn. local plan area Napa County (Calif.) Schs., 1968-83; spl. edn. compliance cons. overseas dependent schs. Mediterranean region Dept. Def., 1983-84; adminstr. spl. edn. local plan area and dir. spl. programs Tehama County Dept. Edn., Red Bluff, Calif., 1985—. Editor Calif. Fed. Coun. Exceptional Children Jour. 1971-77, 81-83. Mem. Wilson Riles Spl. Edn. Task Force, Calif., 1981-82, Spl. Edn. Fiscal Task Force, Calif., 1987-89. Cited Outstanding Spl. Edn. Adminstr. Calif. by Spl. Edn. Adminstrs. in County Office and Calif. Coun. Exceptional Children, 1996. Mem. Coun. for Adminstrs. Spl. Edn., SELPA Adminstrs. Assn. Calif. (co-chair fin. com.), Coun. for Exceptional Children (sgt.-at-arms 1980-95), Calif. Fedn. Coun. for Exceptional Children (treas. 1992-93, Outstanding Spl. Edn. Adminstr. Calif. 1998), Spl. Edn. Adminstrs. in County Office Calif., Profl. Football rschrs. Assn., San Francisco State Alumni Assn., Phi Delta Kappa. Democrat. Avocations: sports history, pop music history, Spanish and Portuguese cultures. Office: Tehama County Dept Edn PO Box 689 Red Bluff CA 96080-0689

KENNEDY, JERRIE ANN PRESTON, public relations executive; b. Quanah, Tex.. Student, Sunset Sch. Preaching, Lubbock, Tex., 1975-78, Jo-Susan Modeling Sch., Nashville, 1984, Film Actors Lab., 1986. Co-prodr. Vincent Cirrincione & Assocs., N.Y., 1986; freelance internat. mktg. and public rels. exec. U.S., and Papua, New Guinea, 1988—; military del. NATO Allies for The French Liaison, Ft. Hood, Tex., 1992. Asst. prodr. film Legend of Johnny Kahota, 1997; author screenplay, fed. and comty. pub. spl. events prodn. U.S.A. Recipient 1st and 3d pl. awards Modeling Assn. Am., N.Y.C., 1985.

KENNEDY, JERRY WAYNE, lawyer; b. Murphy, N.C., Nov. 18, 1947; s. Almon T. and Ruby Mae (McCalla) K.; m. Maura Comerford, July 15, 1978. BA, Birmingham So. Coll., 1970; MA, Am. U., 1977; JD, Samford U., 1984; postgrad., Georgetown U., 1983-84. Bar: Ala. 1985, D.C. 1986. Press sec. Rep. Ronnie Flippo, 5th dist. Ala., 1977-80; chief of staff, legis. dir. Rep. Ben Erdreich, 6th dist. Ala., 1982-86; assoc. Heron, Burchette, Ruckert & Rothwell, Washington, 1987-90; of counsel Tuttle & Taylor, Washington, 1990-94; owner Kennedy Govt. Rels., Washington, 1995—; adj. prof. Sch. Communication, Am. U., Washington, 1979. Assoc. editor Am. Jour. Trial Advocacy, 1982-82. With USAF, 1970-74. Mem. ABA, Ala. Bar Assn., D.C. Bar Assn., Ala. State Soc. (bd. dirs.), Soc. Profl. Journalists (Sigma Delta Chi), Delta Theta Phi. Democrat. Unitarian. Home and Office: Kennedy Govt Rels 313 S Carolina Ave SE Washington DC 20003-4213

KENNEDY, JOE DAVID, JR. (JOEY KENNEDY), editor; b. Dayton, TX, Mar. 28, 1956; s. Joe David Sr. and Patricia Ann (Harper) K.; m. Veronica Elaine Pike, Feb. 2, 1980. BA, U. Ala., Birmingham, 1988; postgrad., U. Ala. Reporter gen. assignments Houma (La.) Daily Courier, 1974-76; dir. news, sports Sta. KJIN-AM/KCIL-FM, Houma, 1976-77; reporter gen. assignments Cullman (Ala.) Times, 1977-78; asst. sports editor Anniston (Ala.) Star, 1978-81; sports copy editor Birmingham News, 1981-83, asst. editor lifestyle, 1983-85, editor photography, 1985-86, Sunday editor, 1986-89, editor book revs., 1986-95, editorial writer, columnist, 1989—; book reviewer Sta. WVTM-TV, Birmingham, 1990-91. Contbr. Redbook mag., 1997, 98. Mem. Houma-Terrebonne Bicentennial Commn., 1975-76; press sec. rep. gubernatorial candidate Guy Hunt, Ala., 1978; tutor literacy Birmingham Pub. Schs. Adult Learning Ctr., 1990-91; judge J.C. Penney Golden Rule Awards for Vols., 1992; lectr. Lee Coll. Springs Art Festival, Baytown, Tex., 1992; mem. adv. bd. Sch. Journalism, U. Miss., 1992—; bd. dirs. So. Mus. Flight, 1992-93; mem. Leadership Birmingham Class, 1994-95, AIDS Care Team, 1994—; bd. dirs. A Baby's Place, 1996-97; mem. Ct. Appointed Spl. Advocates for Children, 1996—; bd. dirs. PATH Orgn. for Homeless, 1997—; deacon Southside Bapt. Ch.; reading tutor 4th graders Birmingham Pub. Schs., 1999. Named Comm. Alumnus of Yr., U. Ala., Birmingham, 1991, One of the Top 20 Grads., U. Ala., Birmingham, 1994; recipient various awards La. Press Assn., 1974-77, Ala. Press Assn., 1989-97, Ala. Sportswriters Assn., 1978-81, Hector award Troy State U., 1991, 92, 94, 95, Pulitzer prize for edtl. writing, 1991; winner Nat. Edn. Writers Assn. 1994 Ed. Press award, 1995. Avocations: Civil War history, computers, reading, writing, short wave radio. Home: 1309 Ingram Ave Birmingham AL 35213-1503 Office: Birmingham News 2200 4th Ave N Birmingham AL 35203-3840

KENNEDY, JOHN FITZGERALD, JR., lawyer, magazine editor; b. Washington, Nov. 25, 1960; s. John F. and Jacqueline Lee (Bouvier) K.; m. Carolyn Bessette, Sept. 21, 1996. B in History, Brown U., 1983; student, U. Delhi, 1985; LLB, NYU, 1989. Bar: N.Y., 1990. Intern Ctr. Democratic Policy, Washington, 1981; asst. to Larry Kieves N.Y. Commr. Bus. Devel., 1984-86; acting dep. exec. dir. 42d St. Devel. Corp., 1986; law clerk Justice Dept., Washington, 1987; intern Manatt, Phelps, Rothenberg & Philips, L.A., 1988; asst. dist. atty. Manhattan, 1989-93; editor-in-chief, co-founder George, 1995-98, pres., editor-in-chief, co-founder, 1998-99; bd. dirs. John F. Kennedy Sch. Govt., Harvard U., John F. Kennedy Libr. Found. Actor (play) Winners, 1985, (movie) Matter of Degrees, 1988. Vol. earthquake assistance, Rabginal, Guatemala, 1976; founder South African Group Edn.; mem. Juvenile Rights Clinic, NYU; vol. Spl. Olympics.; supporter John Fitzgerald Kenndy Libr., Dorchester, Mass.; co-developer Mental Retardation and Devel. Disabilities Studies Program, N.Y.C., 1988-90; head Reaching Up, N.Y., 1989-99; bd. dirs. Robin Hood Found. Avocation: wilderness sports. *Died Aug. 16, 1999; buried at sea.*

KENNEDY, JOHN HARVEY, chemistry educator; b. Oak Park, Ill., Apr. 24, 1933; s. John Harvey and Margaret Helen (Drenthe) K.; m. Joan Corinne Hipsky, June 9, 1956 (div. Mar. 1969); children: Bruce Laurence, Bryan Donald, Brent Peter, Jill Amy.; m. Victoria Jane Matthew, July 2, 1970; 1 child, Karen Anne. BS, UCLA, 1954; AM, Harvard U., 1956, PhD, 1957. Sr. research chemist E.I. du Pont de Nemours, Wilmington, Del., 1957-61; asst. prof. chemistry U. Calif., Santa Barbara, 1961-63, 67-69, assoc. prof., 1969-76, prof., 1976-93, prof. emeritus, 1993—, chmn. dept., 1982-85; assoc. prof. Boston Coll., Chestnut Hill, 1963-64; head inorganic chemistry Gen. Motors, Santa Barbara, 1964-67; cons. Eveready Battery Co., Cleve., 1983—; vis. prof. U. N.C., Chapel Hill, 1980-81, Japan Soc. Promotion of Sci., Nagoya, 1974-75, Leningrad State U., 1989, China Acad. Scis., 1990. Author: Analytical Chemistry, Principles, 1990, Analytical Chemistry, Practice, 1990; contbr. articles to profl. jours.; patentee in field. Mus. dir. Christ the King Episcopal Ch., Santa Barbara, 1982-98. Mem. Am. Chem. Soc., Electrochem. Soc. Democrat. Avocation: music. Home: 5357 Agana Dr Santa Barbara CA 93111-1601 Office: U Calif Dept Chemistry Santa Barbara CA 93106

KENNEDY, JOHN JOSEPH, bank financial officer; b. Bkyln., Jan. 28, 1948; s. John J. and Doris M. (Maguire) K.; m. Linda Graham, Sept. 27, 1969; children: John, Richard, Graham. BS, Fordham U., 1969. CPA, N.Y. Acct. Peat, Marwick, Mitchell & Co., N.Y.C., 1971-83; sr. v.p., controller Generale Bank, N.Y.C., 1984-93; sr. v.p., COO First Bank of the Americas, N.Y.C., 1994-97; gen. mgr. Banco de Bogota, N.Y.C., 1997—. Served to 1st lt. U.S. Army, 1969-71. Mem. AICPA, N.Y. State Soc. CPA's, Inst. Mgmt. Accts., Fin. Execs. Inst. Roman Catholic. Home: 29 Rockwell Cir Marlboro NJ 07746-1156 Office: Banco de Bogota 375 Park Ave Fl 3 New York NY 10152-0002

KENNEDY, JOHN PATRICK, lawyer, corporate executive; b. Houston, Oct. 2, 1943; s. Arch R. and Kathryn R. (Delahunty) K.; children: Kathleen, Elizabeth, Christina, Patrick, Lindsay. BA in Econs., U. Kans., 1965, JD, 1967; LLM, U. Mo., 1973, MBA, 1972. Bar: Kans. 1967, Mo. 1968, Ohio 1973, Wis. 1985, U.S. Supreme Ct. 1972, U.S. Dist. Ct. (we. dist.) Mo. 1972, U.S. Dist. Ct. Kans. 1967. Trial atty. Kodas, Gingerich & Stites, Kansas City, Mo., 1967-69; sr. atty. Mobay Chem. Co., Kansas City, 1969-73; v.p., gen. counsel, dir. Scotts & Sons Co., Marysville, Ohio, 1973-84; v.p., sec., gen. counsel Johnson Controls, Inc., Milw., 1984—; small bus. advisor, venture capitalist. Contbr. articles to profl. jours. Served with USAR, 1967-73. Recipient Wall St. Jour. award, 1972, Am. Jurisprudence awards, 1966-67. Mem. ABA, Ohio Bar Assn., Columbus Bar Assn., Wis. Bar Assn., Am. Corp. Counsel Assn. Democrat. Roman Catholic. Office: Johnson Controls Inc PO Box 591 5757 N Green Bay Ave Milwaukee WI 53209-4408*

KENNEDY, JOHN RAYMOND, pulp and paper company executive; b. N.Y.C., Sept. 21, 1930; s. John Raymond and Ethel R. (Leavy) K.; m. Elizabeth C. Calogerakis, Oct. 24, 1974; children: John Raymond III, James, Andrew, Paula; 1 stepson, Nicholas. B.S., Georgetown U., 1952. With Fed. Paper Bd. Co., Inc., Montvale, N.J., 1952-96; pres. Fed. Paper Bd. Co, Inc., Montvale, N.J., 1966-96; chief exec. officer Fed. Paper Bd. Co., Inc., Montvale, N.J., 1975-96, also dir.; ret. Federal Paper Bd., 1996; dir. De Vlieg-Bullard, Inc., Chase Brass Industries, Inc., Montpelier, Ohio, 1994, Internat. Paper, Purchase, N.Y., 1996—, Holnam, Inc., Dundee, Mich., 1996, Pioneer Cos., Inc., 1998. Dir. Spartech. Corp., 1997; bd. dirs. Georgetown U., Washington. Mem. Country Club of New Canaan, Devon Yacht Club, Maidstone Club, Blind Brook Club, Nat. Golf Links Am., University Club. Home: 223 Michigan Rd New Canaan CT 06840-2225 Office: JRK Financial Corporation 125 Elm St New Canaan CT 06840-5420

KENNEDY, JOHN WILLIAM, engineering company executive; b. Summit, N.J., May 20, 1956; s. William John and Jean Mary (Krutisia) K.; m. Cecelia Marie Hamrock, Dec. 26, 1981; 1 child, Sean Michael. BS with honors, North Adams State Coll., 1978; MBA with honors, Columbia Pacific U., 1987, BS in Indsl. Engring., 1988; PhD in Bus. Mgmt., LaSalle U. Cert. tchr., N.J. Tchr. Mountainside (N.J.) Sch. Dist., 1979-82, Chatham (N.J.) Boro Sch. Dist., 1982-83; plant mgr. The Chatham Club Recreation Ctr., 1982-85; ops. mgr. Coleman Equipment, Inc., Irvington, N.J., 1985-91; project mgr., acct. mgr. automated sorting systems div. Sandvik Process Systems, Totowa, N.J., 1991-95; gen. mgr. sales and engring. Barnett Industries, Irvington, N.J., 1995-96; pres., owner Multitech Assocs., Inc. & Tech. Mktg. Svcs., Inc., South Plainfield, N.J., 1996—; plant mgr., ops. mgr., cons., Madison (N.J.) Community Pool., 1971-87. Co-patentee, vacuum lifter, air logic weightless circuit; contbr. tech. articles to trade publs. Active Denville (N.J.) area Boy Scouts Am., 1984—, chmn. dist. advancement com., 1990-95—; mem. area com. Spl. Olympics, Flanders, N.J., 1987—, event dir., Morris Sussex and Warren counties, 1988—; exec. bd. Morris-Sussex Boy Scouts Am., 1996—. Named Eagle Scout Boy Scouts Am., 1970. Mem. Am. Mgmt. Assn., Inst. Indsl. Engring., Am. Soc. for Quality Control. Republican. Roman Catholic. Avocations: camping, biking, racquetball, softball, coins. Home: 198 Kings Rd Madison NJ 07940-2238 Office: Multitech Assocs Inc & Tech Mktg Svcs Inc 165A Ryan St South Plainfield NJ 07080-4206

KENNEDY, JOSEPH PATRICK, II, former congressman; b. Brighton, Mass., Sept. 24, 1952; s. Robert F. and Ethel (Skakel) K.; m. Sheila Rauch,

1979 (div.); 2 children: Joseph P. III, Matthew; m. Beth Kelly, Oct. 1993. Grad., U. Mass., Boston, 1976. Chmn., pres. Citizens' Energy Corp.; mem. 100th-105th Congress from 8th Mass. dist., 1986-98; ranking minority mem. banking & fin. svcs. subcom. on housing & cmty. devel., mem. com. on vets.' affairs 100th-105th Congress from, 8th Mass., dist. Active Can. Robert F. Kennedy Meml. Democrat. Office: 530 Atlantic Ave Boston MA 02210*

KENNEDY, JOSEPH PAUL, polymer scientist, researcher; b. Budapest, Hungary, May 18, 1928; came to U.S., 1956; s. Laszlo and Rosa (Farkas) K.; m. Ingeborg G. Hausen, Feb. 10, 1956; children—Katherine, Cynthia, Julie. PhD, U. Vienna, Austria, 1954; MBA, Rutgers U., 1961; hon. doctorate, Kossuth U., Hungary, 1989. Research fellow Sorbonne, U. Paris, 1955; research assoc. McGill U., Montreal, Que., Can., 1956; research chemist Celanese Corp., Summit, N.J., 1957-59; sr. research assoc. Esso Research Engrng. Co., Linden, N.J., 1959-70; prof. polymer sci. U. Akron, Ohio, 1970-80, disting. prof. polymer sci. and chemistry, 1980—; cons. Akron Cationic Polymer Devel. Co., 1983—. Author: Cationic Polymerization, 1975, Carbocationic Polymerization, 1982, Designed Polymers by Carbocationic Macromolecular Engineering: Theory and Practice, 1992. Named Outstanding Researcher Alumni Assn. U. Akron, 1979; recipient Morley award and medal Cleve. Am. Chem. Soc., 1982, Am. Chem. Soc. award in Polymer Chemistry, 1995. Mem. Hungarian Acad. Scis., Am. Chem. Soc. (Polymer Chemistry award 1985, Applied Polymer Sci. award 1995, George Stafford Whitby award rubber divsn. 1996). Avocation: Japanese art of the Meiji. Home: 510 Saint Andrew Akron OH 44303 Office: U Akron Inst Polymer Sci Akron OH 44325-3909

KENNEDY, JOSEPH WINSTON, lawyer; b. Marshalltown, Iowa, June 5, 1932; s. Roy Wesley and Julia Harriet (Plum) K.; m. Barbara B. Bowman, July 11, 1954 (div. June 1982); children: Kimberle Ann, Kamella Lucille; m. Paula Terry Smith, Nov. 24, 1984. BS cum laude, McPherson (Kans.) Coll., 1954; JD with honors, George Washington U., 1958. Bar: Kans. 1958, U.S. Dist Ct. Kans. 1958, U.S. Ct. Appeals (10th cir.) 1976, U.S. Supreme Ct. 1970. Spl. agt. Office of Naval Intelligence, Washington, 1954-58; assoc. Morris, Laing, Evans & Brock, Wichita, Kans., 1958-62; ptnr. Morris, Laing, Evans, Brock & Kennedy, Wichita, 1962—. Chmn. profl. divsn., atty. United Way of the Plains, Wichita, 1990-93. Recipient Best Lawyers in Am. award, 1987, 89-90, 91-92, 93-94, 95-96. Mem. ABA, Kans. Bar Assn. (bd. law examiners 1993—), Wichita Bar Assn. (bd. govs. 1964-66). Office: Morris Laing Evans Brock & Kennedy 200 W Douglas Ave Fl 4 Wichita KS 67202-3013

KENNEDY, JUDITH MARY, school psychologist; b. Custer, S.D., June 29, 1944; d. William A. and Rosaleatha K.; m. Dwane Ellis, July 3, 1993; children from a previous marriage: David R. King, Angela R. King. BS, BHSU, 1967; MS, Idaho State U., 1990, EdS, 1991. Tchr. spl. edn. Snake River Schs., Blackfoot, Idaho, 1983-88; sch. psychologist Madison Snake River, Rexburg, Idaho, 1989-91, Rapid City (S.D.) Area Schs., 1991—; cons. in field. Author: Getting to Know You, 1995, Parenting, 1998. Pres. Snake River Tchrs. Assn., 1988-89. Mem. S.D. Sch. Psychologists (pres. elect 1996-98), Evergreen Investment Club, Supien Sircle Sisters. Avocations: skiing, spirituality, reading, health. Home: 3623 Western Ave Rapid City SD 57702-5053 Office: RCAS 21 Saint Joseph St Rapid City SD 57701-2822

KENNEDY, KATHLEEN, film producer. Student, San Diego State U. With KCST, San Diego; pres. Amblin Entertainment, Universal City, Calif. Assoc. prodr.: (films) Poltergeist, 1982, Twilight Zone-The Movie, 1983, Indiana Jones and the Temple of Doom, 1984; prodr.: (films) Twister, 1996; (with Steven Spielberg) E.T. The Extra-Terrestrial, 1982 (Academy award nomination for best picture 1982); (with Quincy Jones, Frank Marshall, and Spielberg) The Color Purple, 1985 (Academy award nomination for best picture 1985); (with Marshall and Art Levinson) The Money Pit, 1986; (with Marshall and Spielberg) Empire of the Sun, 1987, Always, 1989; (with Richard Vane) Arachnophobia, 1990; (with Marshall and Gerald R. Molen) Hook, 1991; (with Robert Watts) Alive, 1993; (with Molen) Jurassic Park, 1993, (with Marshall) Milk Money, 1994; (with Clint Eastwood) The Bridges of Madison County, 1995; exec. prodr.: (films) A Dangerous Woman, 1993, Schindler's List, 1993 (Academy award for best picture 1993), Congo, 1995, The Indian in the Cupboard, 1995; (with Marshall and Spielberg) Gremlins, 1984, The Goonies, 1985, Back to the Future, 1985, Young Sherlock Holmes, 1985, *batteries not included, 1987, Dad, 1989, Back to the Future Part II, 1990, Gremlins 2: The New Batch, 1990, Back to the Future Part III, 1990, Joe Versus the Volcano, 1990, Cape Fear, 1991, We're Back! A Dinosaur's Story, 1993, Balto, 1995; (with Marshall) Fandango, 1985; (with Marshall, Spielberg, and David Kirschner) An American Tail, 1986; (with Marshall, Spielberg, Peter Guber, and Jon Peters) Innerspace, 1987; (with Spielberg) Who Framed Roger Rabbit, 1988; (with Marshall, Spielberg, and George Lucas) The Land Before Time, 1988; (with Marshall and Lucas) Indiana Jones and the Last Crusade, 1989; (with Marshall and Kirschner) An American Tail: Fievel Goes West, 1991; (with Peter Bogdanovich) Noises Off, 1992; (with Marshall and Molen) A Far Off Place, 1993; (with Molen, Kirschner, William Hanna, and Joseph Barbera) The Flintstones, 1994. *

KENNEDY, KATHLEEN ANN, faculty/nursing consultant; b. Troy, N.Y., Aug. 26, 1942; d. Joseph A. and Eleanor J. (Galligan) K. Diploma in nursing, St. Peter's Sch. Nursing, Albany, N.Y., 1963; BSN, Boston Coll., 1967; MS, Russell Sage Coll., Troy, 1980. RN, N.Y. Staff nurse St. Peter's Hosp., 1963-64; pub. health nurse Rensselaer County Health Dept., Troy, 1967-80, supervising pub. health nurse, 1969-80; assoc. DON Glens Falls (N.Y.) Hosp., 1980-83, v.p. patient svcs., 1983-95; asst. prof. Sage Coll., Troy, N.Y., 1995—; health care cons. Mem. Am. Orgn. Nurse Execs., N.Y. Orgn. Nurse Execs., N.Y. State Nurses Assn. Dist. #9, Sigma Theta Tau, Delta Pi Chpt. Office: 2 Bayberry Ln Cohoes NY 12047-2002

KENNEDY, KEN, computer science educator; b. Washington, Aug. 12, 1945; s. Kenneth Wade and Audrey Ruth K. BA in Math. summa cum laude, Rice U., 1967; MS in Math., NYU, 1969, PhD in Computer Sci., 1971. Asst. prof. dept. math. scis. Rice U., Houston, 1971-76, assoc. prof., 1976-80, prof., 1980-84, Noah Harding prof. dept. computer sci., 1985—, chmn. computer sci. program com., 1982-85, chmn. dept. computer sci., 1984-88, 90-92, dir. Computer and Info. Tech. Inst., 1986-92, dir. Ctr. for Rsch. on Parallel Computation, 1989—; vis. prof. computer sci. dept. Stanford U., 1985-86; v.p. R.M. Thrall & Assocs., Inc., 1974-81, pres., 1981-93; mem. programming langs. and implementation sub-area panel computer sci. and engrng. rsch. Div. Computer Rsch. NSF, 1975-77, mem. adv. com. for computer rsch., 1984-88, chmn., 1985-87, adv. commn. computer and info. sci. and engrng., 1995—; vis. scientist Space Shuttle Program Lead Office NASA, 1975, Dept. Computer Sci. IBM Thomas J. Watson Rsch. Ctr., Yorktown Heights, N.Y., 1978-79, cons., 1979—, Lawrence Livermore Nat. Lab., 1985—; vis. staff mem. computer div. Los Alamos Sci. Lab., 1977—; mem. exec. com. CSNET, 1984-86, computer sci. and telecom. bd., NRC, 1992-94, mem. comm. phys. scis., math. and applications, 1995-97; co-chair adv. com. high performance computin gand comm. Indo. Tech. and Next Generation Internet, 1997—; presenter numerous prof. meetings; dir. numerous masters theses, PhD dissertations. Mem. editorial bd. Jour. Parallel and Distributed Computing, 1988—, Concurrency: Practice and Experience, ACM Transactions on Software Engrng. and Methodology, 1989—; sect. editor langs. and programming Jour. Supercomputing, 1986-93; contbr. numerous chpts. to books, articles to profl. jours. Bd. dirs. Houston Soc. Performing Arts, 1986—, v.p. artistic adv., 1987—. Grantee NSF, 1973—, IBM , 1979-94, DARPA, 1987—, W.M. Keck Found., 1990-92, Office of Gov. State of Tex., 1990-95, Office Naval Rsch., 1993-96, NASA, 1993-96; Woodrow Wilson Nat. fellow, 1967-68; NSF grad. fellow, 1968-71; recipient NYU Founders Day award for Acad. Achievement, 1972. Fellow IEEE (W. Wallace McDowell award 1995), AAAS, ACM (program com. SIGPLAN nat. conf. 1982, 84, chmn. program com. principles of programming langs. confs. 1983, software sys. award com. 1983-85, chmn. 1984, chmn. program com. Supercomputing 1992); mem. Soc. Indsl. and Applied Math., Nat. Acad. Engring., Phi Beta Kappa, Sigma Xi. Home: 2238 Southgate Blvd Houston TX 77030-1121 Office: Rice U Computer Info Tech Inst PO Box 1892 Houston TX 77251-1892*

KENNEDY, KENNETH ADRIAN RAINE, biological anthropologist, forensic anthropologist; b. Oakland, Calif., June 26, 1930; s. Walter Burkhart and Margaret Miriam (Madge) K.; m. Mary Caroline Marino, Aug. 5, 1961 (div.); m. Margaret Carrick Fairlie, Aug. 10, 1969. BA, U. Calif., Berkeley, 1953, MA, 1954, PhD, 1962. Diplomate Am. Bd. Forensic Anthropology; lic. lay reader. Instr. U. Calif., 1962-63; asst. prof. anthropology Cornell U., Ithaca, N.Y., 1964-68, assoc. prof., 1968-81, prof. ecology, anthropology and Asian studies, 1981—; sec. Am. Bd. Forensic Anthropology, 1999—; cons. forensic anthropology, N.Y. State, 1964—; field rsch. in India, Pakistan, Sri Lanka, 1963—. Author 10 books; mem. editl. bd. Am. Jour. Phys. Anthropology, 1998—, acting editor-in-chief, 1985; field editor Am. Anthropologist, 1982-85; contbr. numerous articles to sci. jours. Guest White House state dinner reception for Pres. Sri Lanka, 1984. Sgt. U.S. Army, 1954-57. Grantee NSF, Smithsonian Instn., Howard Found., NEA, Am. Inst. Indian Studies, numerous others. Fellow AAAS, Am. Acad. Forensic Scis. (sec.-treas. forensic anthropology sect. 1993-94, chmn. 1994-95, chmn. phys. anthropology sect. 1994-95, T. Dale Stewart award in forensic anthropology 1987); mem. Am. Anthrop. Assn. (chmn. biol. anthropology sect. 1986-88), Am. Assn. Phys. Anthropologists (exec. bd. 1990-96, v.p. 1994-96), Cornell Rsch. Club (pres. 1978-80, 89-90), Sigma Xi (pres. 1984-85). Episcopalian. Avocations: violin, playing in chamber music groups. Office: Cornell U Ecology and Systematics Corson Hall Ithaca NY 14853-2701

KENNEDY, LAWRENCE ALLAN, mechanical engineering educator; b. Detroit, May 31, 1937; s. Clifford Earl and Emma Josephine (Muller) K.; m. Valaree J. Lockhart, Aug. 3, 1958; children: Joanne E., Julie A., Janet A., Raymond L., Jill M., Brian G. BS, U. Detroit, 1960; MS, Northwestern U., 1962, PhD, 1964. Registered profl. engr., N.Y. Chmn. dept., prof. mech. and aero. engrng. SUNY-Buffalo, 1964-83; chmn. dept. mech. engrng., prof. Ohio State U., Columbus, 1983-93, Ralph W. Kurtz disting. prof., 1992-95; dean coll. engrng. U. Ill., Chgo., 1995—; vis. assoc. prof. mech. and aero. engrng. U. Calif.-San Diego, 1968-69, VonKarman Inst., Rhode-St. Genese, Belgium, 1971-72; Goebel vis. prof. mech. and aero. engrng. U. Mich., Ann Arbor, 1980-81; cons. Cornell Aero. Lab., Buffalo, 1968-72, Tech. Adv. Service, Fort Washington, Pa., 1969—, Ashland Chem. Corp., Dublin, Ohio, 1983-90, Mech. Engring. Sci. and Application, Buffalo, 1972-83, Columbia Gas, 1987-92; vis. faculty fellow mech. and aerospace engring. Princeton U., 1994. Contbr. numerous articles on engrng. to profl. jours.; editor: Progress in Astronautics and Aeros., Vol. 58, 1978, Exptl. Thermal and Fluid Scis., 1987-95; assoc. editor Applied Mechanics Revs., 1985-88, Jour. Propulsion & Power, 1992-98. Recipient Ralph R. Teetor award 1984, AT&T Found. award, 1987, Ralph Coats Roe award, 1993; NATO fellow, 1971-72, NSF fellow, 1968-69, W.P. Murphy fellow, 1960-63; Agard lectr., 1971-72. Fellow AIAA, ASME; mem. Am. Phys. Soc., Combustion Inst., Am. Soc. Engring. Edn., Soc. of Automotive Engrs. Roman Catholic. Avocations: skiing, squash, hiking, music. Home: 24306 Turnberry Ct Naperville IL 60564-8127 Office: Coll Engring M/C 159 851 S Morgan St Chicago IL 60607-7042

KENNEDY, LINDA CAROL, art and art educator; b. Ft. Lauderdale, Fla., Dec. 19, 1942; d. Frend and Alma Eleanor (Robbins) Knarr; m. Kenneth Vincent Kennedy (div. Nov. 1975); m. John Albright Stinespring (div. Feb. 1998). BS, Ind. U., 1964; MA, U. Notre Dame, 1969; PhD in Fine Arts (Art Edn.), Tex. Tech U., 1989. Tchr. art Marion (Ind.) Cmty. Schs., 1964-65, Elkhart (Ind.) H.S. and Elkhart Meml. H.S., 1965-86; grad. tchg. asst. dept. art Tex. Tech U., Lubbock, 1986-89, part-time instr. dept. art, 1989-97, instr. Coll. Edn., 1996—; assoc. prof. art divns. comm. arts Wayland Bapt. U., Plainfield, Tex., 1997—; cons. on advanced placement art Tex. Edn. Agy., U. Tex., El Paso, Tex. Tech U., Junction; cons. Coll. Bd.; cons. for ind. sch. dists., including Ft. Worth, Austin, Pecos, Howley, Houston. Mem. Nat. Art Edn. Assn., Tex. Art Edn. Assn., Phi Kappa Phi. Home: 3709 74th St Lubbock TX 79423-1109

KENNEDY, LINDA LOUISE, secondary education educator; b. Albany, N.Y., Oct. 6, 1952; d. Robert Joseph and Ruth Irene (Bopp) Havens; m. Brian Francis Kennedy, Aug. 19, 1989 (div.). BS, SUNY, Albany, 1974, MS, 1982. Cert. secondary edn. tchr., N.Y. Tchr. math. Vincentian Inst., Albany, 1974-77, Job Corps, Glenmont, N.Y., 1977-78, Cath. Cen. High Sch., Troy, N.Y., 1978-84, Rensselaer (N.Y.) Mid. High Sch., 1984—; adj. tchr. Syracuse U., Hudson Valley C.C. Mem. Assn. Math. Tchrs. N.Y. State, Nat. Coun. Tchrs. Math., Am. Fedn. Tchrs., N.Y. State United Tchrs. (bldg. rep.), Rensselaer Tchrs. Assn. (sec. 1982-84), Delta Kappa Gamma. Roman Catholic. Avocations: reading, ceramics, tennis, walking. Home: 24 Marsdale Ct Selkirk NY 12158-9772 Office: Rensselaer Mid High Sch 555 Broadway Rensselaer NY 12144-2608

KENNEDY, MARC J., lawyer; b. Newburgh, N.Y., Mar. 2, 1945; s. Warren G. K. and Frances F. (Levinson) K.; children: Michael L., Kayla R., Shawna D. BA cum laude, Syracuse U., 1967; JD, U. Mich., 1970. Bar: N.Y. 1971. Assoc. Davies, Hardy, Ives & Lawther, N.Y.C., 1971-72, London, Buttenweiser & Chalif, N.Y.C., 1972-73, Silberfeld, Danziger & Bangser, N.Y.C., 1973; counsel Occidental Crude Sales, Inc., N.Y.C., 1974-75; v.p., gen. counsel Internat. Ore & Fertilizer Corp., N.Y.C., 1975-82; asst. gen. counsel Occidental Chem. Corp., Houston, 1982; v.p., gen. counsel Occidental Chem. Agrl. Products Inc., Tampa, Fla., 1982-87; v.p., gen counsel agrl. products group Occidental Chem. Corp., Tampa, 1987-91; assoc. gen. counsel Occidental Chem. Corp., Dallas, 1991—; faculty mentor Columbia Pacific U., Mill Valley, Calif., 1981-88. Contbr. articles to profl. jours. Trustee Bar Harbor Festival Corp., N.Y.C., 1974-87; bd. dirs. Am. Opera Repertory Co., 1982-85; mem. com. planned giving N.Y. Foundling Hosp., 1977-88; Explorer post advisor Boy Scouts Am., 1976-78. Mem. ABA (vice-chmn. com. internat. law liaison young lawyers sect. 1974-75, chmn. sub-com. proposed trade barriers to the importation of products into U.S. 1985-88, vice chmn. corp. counsel com. 1992-93, co-chmn. corp. counsel com. 1993-98), Maritime Law Assn., N.Y. State Bar Assn., Am. Corp. Counsel Assn. Office: Occidental Chem Corp PO Box 809050 Dallas TX 75380-9050

KENNEDY, MARJORIE ELLEN, librarian; b. Dauphin, Man., Can., Sept. 14, 1946; d. Stanley Harrison and Ivy Marietta (Stevens) May; m. Michael P.J. Kennedy, Apr. 3, 1980. BA, U. Sask., Regina, 1972; BLS, U. Alta., Edmonton, 1974; BEd, U. Regina, 1981. Profl. A cert. edn., Sask. Elem. sch. tchr. Indian Head (Sask) Pub. Sch., 1965-66, Elgin Sch., Weyburn, Sask., 1967-68; tchr., libr. Ctrl. Sch., Prince Albert, Sask., 1970-71; elem. sch. tchr. Vincent Massey Sch., Prince Albert, 1969-70, 72-73; children's libr. J.S. Wood br. Saskatoon (Sask.) Pub. Libr., 1974-77, asst. coord. children's svcs., 1977-79; programme head, instr. libr. tech. Kelsey Inst., Saskatoon, 1979—; head libr. and info. tech. SIAST-Kelsey Campus, Saskatoon; presenter workshops on reference materials for elem. sch. librs., storytelling and libr. programming for children, 1980—; vol. dir. Children's Lit. Workshops, Sask. Libr. Assn., 1979-80; mem. organizing com. Sask. Libr. Week, Saskatoon, 1988. Mem. Vanscoy (Sask.) and Dist. Agr. Soc., 1983-95. Named to Libr. Edn. Honor Roll ALA, 1987. Mem. Can. Libr. Assn. (instl. rep. 1984—), Sask. Libr. Assn. (insl. rep. 1984—, mem. children's sect. 1982-83), Sask. Assn. Libr. Techs. (instl. rep. 1984—), Can. Club (bd. mem. 1981-84). Mem. United Ch. Can. Avocations: antique doll restoration, porcelain doll making, antiques, pottery, gardening. Office: Kelsey Inst, Box 1520, Libr Info and Tech Program, Saskatoon, SK Canada S7K 3R5

KENNEDY, (HENRY) MARK, state supreme court judge; b. Greenville, Ala., May 5, 1952; s. D.M. and Marjorie W. Kennedy; m. Peggy W. Kennedy, Dec. 15, 1973; 1 child, Leigh Chancellor. BA, Auburn U., 1973; JD cum laude, Samford U., 1977. Bar: Ala. 1977. Clk. to presiding justice Ala. Ct. Criminal Appeals, 1977, staff atty., 1978; former judge Ala. Cir. Ct., 15th Jud. Cir.; now justice Ala. Supreme Ct., Montgomery. Mem. ABA, Ala. State Bar, Montgomery County Bar Assn., Ala. Assn. Dist. Judges. Democrat. Baptist. Office: Supreme Court of Alabama 300 Dexter Ave Montgomery AL 36104-3741*

KENNEDY, MARK ALAN, middle and secondary school educator; b. Oklahoma City, Okla., July 20, 1951; s. Millford Gordon and Lyn (Cheaney) Kennedy; m. Kim Danelle Kramer, Jan. 30, 1972; 1 child, Brianna Lynn. BA with honors, Calif. State U., 1978; postgrad., Western Sem., 1978-79, Fuller Sem., 1980-83; MEd, U. LaVerne, 1997. Cert. tchr., Calif. Sales mgr. Kennedy Investments, Ontario, Calif., 1980-83; regional v.p. A.L. Williams, Rancho Cucamonga, Calif., 1983-89; loan officer Funder's Mortgage Corp., Covina, Calif., 1989-90; math., social sci. tchr., lang. devel. specialist Ontario-Montclair Sch. Dist., 1990-96; math., social sci. tchr., lang. devel. specialist West End Cmty. Sch., 1996—, lead tchr., 1998—, acting prin., 1998-99; tchg. asst. Western Sem., Portland, Oreg., 1978-79; instr. Cmty. Inst., 1979; soccer coach DeAnza Mid. Sch., Ontario, 1990-93, core team leader, coop tchr., 1992-95, student coun. advisor, 1992-93, bilingual adv. coun., 1992-96, dist. lang. arts/social sci. trainer, 1993-94; advisor U. Calif. Riverside Honors Students' Inner City Literacy Program, 1993-95; mentor tchr. Ontario-Montclair Sch. Dist., 1994-95; cons. Inst. in Local Self Govt., Sacramento, 1994-96, Assn. Calif. Sh. Adminstrs., 1994-95; learning styles cons., 1994—; mem. sch. attendance rev. bd., 1996—; co-chair San Bernardino County Joint Program Quality Rev., chair ALT-RD curriculum team, 1998—. Author: Lessons from the Hawk, 1999; contbr. articles to profl. jours. With USN, 1971-75. Mem. ASCD, Assn. Calif. Sch. Adminstrs., Nat. Dropout Prevention Network, Phi Alpha Theta (mem. chair 1976-78). Baptist. Avocations: Hapkido, walking, German and Latin philosophy and literature, exegesis of Koine Greek, conversational Spanish. Office: West End Cmty 1135 W 4th St Ontario CA 91762-1796

KENNEDY, MARLA CATHERINE, psychologist; b. Milw., June 28, 1935; d. Raymond G. and Catherine (Wimmer) Mueller; m. William Robert Kennedy, Mar. 2, 1957; children: Joseph, Timothy, Kristin, William, Daniel. BS, Alverno, Milw., 1956; MA, U. Minn., 1983, postgrad., 1983-1989. Lic. psychologist, lic. marriage and family therapist. Intern with mentally ill and mentally retarded Met. Clin., Mpls., 1984-85; pvt. practice psychology, marriage and family therapy Mpls., 1985—; spkr. in field; part-time at Family Svc. Greater St. Paul, 1989-98; dir., co-counselor Adlerian Family Edn. Ctr., 1983-85. Contbr. articles to profl. jours. Bd. dirs. Books for Africa, 1997-98; co-founder Community Line (now First Call for Help); pres. Legions of PTAs, 1998-00; active YWCA Shelter for Women, St. Paul; vol. Rams Juvenile Justice, 1985—. Mem. Minn. Assn. Marriage and Family Therapists, Minn. Assn. Group Psychotherapists (pres. 1998-00), Alfred Adler Assn. (bd. dirs.), AAUW (bd. dirs.), New Century (bd. dirs.), Mensa, Phi Lambda Theta. Unitarian. Avocations: swimming, tennis, reading.

KENNEDY, MARLA HAMBURG, publisher, gallery director; b. Newark, Jan. 3, 1961; d. Perry Louis and Sarah (Auyash) Hamburg; m. David Dean Kennedy, July 30, 1988 (div. May 1993); 1 child, Katherine Sarah Hamburg Kennedy. BA summa cum laude, Barnard Coll., 1983. Assoc. dir. Lucio Amelio Gallery, Naples, Italy, 1984-87, Scott Hanson Gallery, N.Y.C., 1987-88; dir. Richard Green Gallery, L.A., 1988-91, Angles Gallery, Santa Monica, Calif., 1991-93, Gray Hawkins Gallery, Santa Monica, 1993-96, Howard Greenberg Gallery, N.Y.C., 1996—; pub. Picture This Pubs., N.Y.C., 1997—; cons. to art collection Leocosmo Co., Tokyo, 1991-92; writer Barbara Lee Diamonstein/Landmarks Commn., N.Y.C., 1985-87. Editor, curator: Terrae Mons, 1986, Nude in Photography, 1995, Kissing, 1996, Wedding Days, 1996 (books and exhbns.); editor/pub.: Little Angels, 1997, Little Devils, 1997. Dir. Art Night for Life, Santa Monica, 1991; fundraiser Focus on AIDS, Santa Monica, 1993-96. Mem. Nat. Arts Club. Democrat. Unitarian. Avocations: painting, ice skating, cooking, writing. Home: 110 Duane St New York NY 10007-1126 Office: Howard Greenberg Gallery 120 Wooster St New York NY 10012-5200

KENNEDY, MARY VIRGINIA, diplomat; b. Pocatello, Idaho, Sept. 5, 1946; d. Charles Millard and Martha Lorissa (Evans) K. BA, U. Denver, 1968, MA, 1969; MAT, U. Idaho, 1971. Tchr. cert. Idaho. Recreation aide ARC, South Vietnam, 1969-70; ops. officer State Dept. Ops. Ctr., Washington, 1977-78; spl. asst. amb. Philip Habib, Washington, 1979-80, Sec. State, Washington, 1980-81; econ. officer U.S. Embassy, Cairo, Egypt, 1981-84; consul Am. Consulate, Adana, Turkey, 1985-88; Pearson fellow Office Cong. Bereuter Ho. Reps., 1988-89; exec. asst. Dept. Sec. State, Washington, 1989-91; dep. chief mission Dept. State U.S. Embassy, Kuwait, 1991-93; consul gen. Am. Consulate, Karachi, Pakistan, 1994-96; dean Sch. Profl. Area Studies, Fgn. Svc. Inst., 1996-98, Coll. of Law, U. Idaho, 1998—. Bd. trustees Idaho State Hist. Soc., 1999—. Mem. Am. Fgn. Svc. Protective Assn. (bd. dirs. 1988-91), Phi Beta Kappa, Mortar Bd. Home: 944 E 8th St Moscow ID 83843-3851 address: PO Box 9735 Moscow ID 83843-0180

KENNEDY, MICHAEL JOHN, lawyer; b. Spokane, Wash., Mar. 23, 1937; s. Thomas Dennis Kennedy and Evelyn Elizabeth (Forbes) Gordon; m. Pamalee Hamilton, June 14, 1959 (div. July 1968); children: Lisa Marie, Scott Hamilton; m. Eleanore Renee Baratelli, July 14, 1968; 1 child, Anna Rosario. AB in Econs., U. Calif., Berkeley, 1959; JD, U. Calif., San Francisco, 1962. Bar: Calif. 1963, N.Y. 1976, U.S. Ct. Appeals (9th cir. 1963), U.S. Supreme Ct. 1967, U.S. Ct. Appeals (5th cir.) 1975, U.S. Ct. Appeals 2d cir.) 1977, U.S. Ct. Appeals (1st 3d and 4th cirs.) 1979, U.S. Ct. Appeals (3d and D.C. cirs.) 1982. Assoc. Hoberg & Finger, San Francisco, 1962-67; staff counsel Emergency Civil Liberties, N.Y.C., 1967-69; ptnr. Kennedy & Rhine, San Francisco, 1969-76; sole practice N.Y.C., 1976—. Served to 1st lt. U.S. Army, 1963-65. Mem. ABA, N.Y. Criminal Bar Assn., Nat. Assn. Criminal Defenders. Democrat. Roman Catholic. Club: N.Y. Athletic. Home: 1009 5th Ave New York NY 10028-0155 Office: 425 Park Ave New York NY 10022-3506

KENNEDY, MICHAEL KELLY, attorney, state representative; b. New Hampton, Iowa, Oct. 30, 1939; s. William J. and Eileen (Kelly) K.; m. Linda Weiss, Aug. 14, 1964; 1 child, Cara Kennedy Ode. BA, U. Notre Dame, 1961; JD, U. Iowa, 1968. Bar: Iowa 1968. State rep. Iowa, 1969-73. Pres. Sch. Attys., Iowa, 1985; bd. of govs. Iowa Bar, 1986-90; bd. dirs. Homestead Housing, New Hampton, 1996-99; co-chmn. Build in Faith com., New Hampton, 1996-99. Avocations: reading, golf, sports broadcasting. Home: 929 Ash Dr New Hampton IA 50659-1074 Office: Kennedy & Kennedy Kennedy Law Bldg PO Box 406 New Hampton IA 50659-0406

KENNEDY, MICHELE LYN, artist; b. Durham, N.C., Dec. 21, 1958; d. Michel Paul and Denise Helen (Francis) Richard; m. Robert Edward Kennedy, May 23, 1986; children: John Paul Jones, Catherine Elizabeth. Student, New Paltz State U., 1976-78; cert. in jewelry design, Fashion Inst. Tech., 1980; BA, Geneseo State U., 1981; studies Robert Cormier, Fenway Studio, 1987-88; studies with Henry Hensche, Cape Cod Sch. Art, 1988. Owner Kennedy Gallery, Key West, 1988—. Painting collection included in Boston Horticultural Soc., 1988, Florida Art Digest, 1996, Tribute to Caruso Key West Music Festival, 1997, Profiles of Key West. Workshop organizer U. Miami Ctr. for Autism, 1992; painting donations AIDS Help Art Auction, Key West, 1990-96. Recipient Best Gallery in Key West award Key West Citizen newspaper, 1993-98. Avocations: biking, tennis. Home and Office: Kennedy Gallery 1611 Main St West Barnstable MA 02668

KENNEDY, NANCY LOUISE, retired draftsman; b. Mar. 14, 1925; d. William Richardson and Mary Enroughty (Youmans) Humphrey; m. William Dwyer Kennedy, Sept. 3, 1952 (dec. May 1953); 1 child, Kathleen Dwyer. Student, Gulf Park Coll., 1943; B of Interior Design, Washington U., 1948. Land draftsman Carter Oil Co., Ft. Smith, Ark., 1954-60, Sinclair Oil and Gas, Oklahoma City, 1960-69, Atlantic Richfield Oil and Gas Co., Tulsa, 1969-82. Mem. Altar guild Trinity Episcopal Ch., Tulsa. Mem. Kappa Alpha Theta. Republican. Home: 6362 S 80th East Ave Apt D Tulsa OK 74133-3825

KENNEDY, NANCY MACRI, English language educator; b. Bklyn., July 26, 1959; d. Herbert Philip and Delcina Teresa (Gerrity) Macri; m. Thomas Charles Kennedy, Oct. 6, 1985; 1 child, Patrick. BA in English/Edn., Molloy Coll., 1990. Tchr. of English St. Anthony's H.S., Huntington, N.Y., 1990—. Mem. Nat. Coun. Tchrs. English, N.Y. State English Coun., Nat. Cath. Educators Am. Democrat. Roman Catholic. Office: St Anthony's H S 275 Wolf Hill Rd Melville NY 11747-1363

KENNEDY, ORIN, film company executive; b. N.Y.C., May 24, 1939; s. Solomon Fuchs and Gertrude Krex. BFA, N.Y. Sch. Interior Design, 1963. Prodn. assoc. Fries Entertainment, Los Angeles, 1976-84; exec. location mgr. Metro-Goldwyn-Mayer subs. United Artists Entertainment, Culver City, Calif., 1984-85; exec. location mgr. The Twilight Zone TV series CBS Entertainment, Los Angeles, 1985-86; exec. location mgr. LA Law TV series 20th Century Fox Film Corp., Los Angeles, 1986-94, exec. location mgr. Picket Fences TV series, 1991-96; Chicago Hope TV series, 1994—.

KENNEDY, PATRICK F., federal official; b. Chgo., June 22, 1949; m. M. Elizabeth Swope. BA, Georgetown U. Mem. Fgn. Svc., 1973; regional adminstrv. officer Fgn. Svc., Africa, 1973-74; pers. officer Bur. African Affairs, 1975-76; spl. asst. to under sec. for mgmt. Dept. of State, 1977-81; supervisory gen. svcs. officer Dept. of State, Paris, 1981-84, exec. dir., then dep. exec. sec., 1985-90; adminstrv. counselor Dept. of State, Cairo, 1991-93; asst. sec. adminstrn. Dept. of State, Washington, 1993—. Office: Dept of State Admin 2201 C St NW Rm 6330 Washington DC 20520-0001

KENNEDY, PATRICK J., congressman; b. Brighton, Mass., July 14, 1967; s. Edward M. and Joan (Bennett) K. Degree in Social Science, Providence Coll., 1991. Mem. 104th-106th Congress from 1st R.I. dist., 1995—; chmn. House Rules Com., 1992; del. 1988 Dem. Nat. Conv.; co-founder, co-chmn. Congressional Portuguese-Am. Caucus; mem. New Eng. Caucus, Congressional Caucus on Armenian Issues, Older Americans Caucus, Democratic Task Force on Tax Policy, AIDS PAC Congressioanl adv. bd., Italian-Am. Congressional Delegation; co-sponsoramendment in Older Americans Act, Higher Edn. Accumulation Program. Bd. dirs. R.I. Spl. Olympics, R.I. March of Dimes, Nat. Com. for Prevention of Child Abuse (R.I. chpt.), Big Brother R.I. Mem. R.I. Lung Assn. (bd. dirs.), R.I. Mental Health Assn. (bd. dirs.), Friends of Ireland. Address: 286 Main St Pawtucket RI 02860-2908 Office: US House Reps 312 Cannon Bldg Washington DC 20515-3901*

KENNEDY, PAUL MICHAEL, history educator; b. Wallsend, U.K., June 17, 1945; came to U.S., 1983; s. John Patrick and Margaret (Hennessy) K.; m. Catherine Urwin, Sept. 2, 1967 (dec. June 1998); children: James, John, Matthew. BA, Newcastle (Eng.) U., 1966; PhD, Oxford (Eng.) U., 1970; MA, Yale U., 1983; hon. doctorate, U. Ohio, 1989, U. New Haven, 1989, U. Newcastle, 1991, L.I. U., 1993, Union Coll., 1994, Alfred U., 1994, U. East Anglia, 1994, Conn. Coll., Quinnipiac Coll., 1999. Lectr. history U. East Anglia, U.K., 1970-74, reader, 1974-82, prof., 1982-83; Dilworth prof. history Yale U., New Haven, 1983—; dir. Internat. Security Studies, 1990—; DeVane lectr., 1992-93; Lewis lectr. Princeton U., 1990; Ford's lectr. Oxford U., 1984; Gabriel Silver lectr. Columbia U., 1988; Brodie lectr. UCLA, 1993; 1st ann. Nobel Peace lectr., Oslo, 1992; Bruno Keisky lectr., Vienna, 1994; Roskill Meml. lectr., Cambridge, 1997; rsch. asst. Sr. Basil Liddell Hart, 1966-70; vis. fellow Ins. for Advanced Study, Princeton, N.J., 1978-79; co-dir. of Secretariat to report on UN in Its Second-Half Century, 1993-96. Author, editor 13 books including Preparing for the Twenty-First Century, The Rise and Fall of Great Powers, Strategy and Diplomacy, The War Plans of the Great Powers. Recipient Wolfson prize Wolfson Found., U.K., 1989, Acqui Storia prize, Italy, 1990; fellow Alexander von Humboldt Found., 1968, 72. Fellow Royal Hist. Soc., Am. Acad. Arts and Scis., Am. Philos. Soc.; mem. Assn. Am. Historians. Roman Catholic. Home: 409 Humphrey St New Haven CT 06511-3710 Office: Yale U Internat Security Studies 34 Hillhouse Ave New Haven CT 06511-3704

KENNEDY, PRISCILLA ANN, elementary school educator; b. Chattanooga, July 23, 1941; d. Jesse Spurgeon and Agnes Adaline (Barnes) Deal; m. Steven Ray Kennedy, Aug. 16, 1964 (div. Apr. 1982); children: Cherie Michelle, Amy Heather, Matthew Steven. BA, Bob Jones U., Greenville, S.C., 1964; MA in Humanities (Theatre Arts), U. Houston, Clear Lake, 1983. Cert. elem. tchr. Tchr. grades 1 and 3 N.E. Houston Ind. Sch. Dist., 1964-67; tchr. grades 2-4 Houston Ind. Sch. Dist., 1967-69, 71-72; Chpt. I reading tchr. Pearland (Tex.) Ind. Schs., 1980-95, tchr. 2nd grade, 1995-98, tchr. drama PK-4, 1998—; Mary Kay Beauty cons., 1980-99. Mem. Young Reps. of Houston, 1968. Mem. Internat. Reading Assn., Tex. Reading Assn., Bay Area Reading Coun. (sec., v.p., pres., past pres. 1980-99), Kappa Delta Pi (Houston Alumni chpt. treas. 1994, v.p. 1995, pres. 1996, past pres. 1997). Republican. Soc. Friends. Avocations: theatre, gardening, infant swimming. Home: 213 Palm Aire Dr Friendswood TX 77546-5640

KENNEDY, R. EVAN, engineering executive, consultant, retired structural engineer; b. Worland, Wyo., Mar. 31, 1916; s. Robert Eaker and Addie Miranda (Pritchard) K.; m. Betty Lou Kaser, Feb. 3, 1945; children: Anne Louise, Carter Evan, Robert Gordon. Student, Jamestown (N.D.) Coll., 1934-35; BS in Civil Engring., U. Colo., 1938. Recorder U. S. Geol. Survey, Denver, 1938-39; jr. hydraulic engr. Colo. Water Consv. Bd., Denver, 1939-41; structural draftsman, jr. designer Am. Bridge Co., Trenton, N.J., 1941-42; stress analyst Goodyear Aircraft Corp., Akron, Ohio, 1942-44; liaison engr., group leader, sect. head Goodyear Aircraft Corp., Phoenix, 1944-46; sales rep. Luby-Sonnen Co., Madison, Wis., 1946; project engr. Rentenbach Engring. Co., Knoxville, Tenn., 1946-47; field mgr. Kaser Constrn. Co., West Des Moines, Iowa, 1947; design engr. Moffatt, Nichol & Taylor, Portland, Oreg., 1947-49, Cooper & Rose, Portland, 1949-51; chief structural engr. Barrett & Logan Architects, Portland, 1951-52; chief structural engr. Edmundson, Kochendoerfer & Kennedy A/E, Portland, 1952-53, chief engr., 1954-55, ptnr., 1955-68; mng. ptnr. Edmundson, Kochendoerfer, Kennedy-Daniel, Mann, Johnson, Mendenhall, Portland, 1968-74; v.p. Daniel, Mann, Johnson and Mendenhall, Baltimore, 1974-79; assoc. Tibbets, Abbott, McCarthy and Stratton, Washington, 1980-84; pres. Kennedy Assocs., Inc., Portland, 1984—; chmn. Seismic Design Com., Portland, 1948-50, bd. dirs., treas. Portland Bldg. Code Revisions Com., 1950-53; observer, cons. Effects Nuclear Test U.S. Dept. Commerce, Yucca Flats, Nev., 1955; instr. Oreg. Bd. Higher Edn. Architects Registration Exams., Portland, 1954-58, Engrs. Registration Exams., 1960-63; lectr. Oreg. Dental Sch. Disaster Planning, Portland, 1960-64; mem. A/E Selection Bd. U.S. Gen. Svcs. Adminstrn. NW Divsn., Auburn, Wash., 1973, Nat. Def. Exec. res. U. S. Bur. Pub. Rds., Washington, 1964-71. Contbr. articles to profl. jours. Vice chmn. Fernwood Grade Sch. PTA, Portland, 1952-53, Portland Traffic Safety Commn., 1964-74; chmn. scholarship Grant H.S. Dad's Club, Portland, 1964-67; chmn. engrs. divsn. Portland United Good Neighbors, 1965, chmn. profl. divsn., 1967, 68; pres. Portland City Club, 1968; chmn. Interfaith Housing Com., Portland, 1969-73, Dulaney Towers Condo Bd., Towson, Md., 1975-78, Dulaney Towers Maintenance Bd., 1976-78, Balt. Energy Coun., 1978, Waterford Condo. Bd., Kensington, Md., 1985-88; pres. Portland Housing Devel. Corp., Portland, 1970-74, Metrohousing, Inc., Portland, 1971-74; mem. Portland Symphonic Choir, 1958-64, Multnomah County Bldg. Code Appeals Bd., Portland, 1964, Nat. Mcpl. League, 1968-79, nat. conv. sect. convenor, 1976, 77, Mayor's Adv. Com., Portland, 1968-69, Congressman Wendell Wyatt Re-election Com., Portland, 1968; treas. Am. Plaza Condo Assn. Bd., Portland, 1991-96; mem., elder Towson Presbyn. Ch., 1974-79; bd. dirs. Chess4Success, 1996—. Recipient Meritorious Svc. award City Portland, 1952, Nat. Design Honor award HUD, Washington, 1976, Grand Design award Am. Consulting Engrs. Coun., Washington, 1996. Mem. ASCE (bd. dirs. Oreg. sect. 1953-55, Capital sect. 1980-90, sec. 1983, mem. Md. sect. 1974-90, Oreg. sect. 1990—), ASTM (chmn. NW dist. 1970), Am. Concrete Inst., Soc. Am. Mil. Engrs. (Merit award Portland Post 1973), Structural Engrs. Assn. Oreg. (founder, pres. 1949), Profl. Engrs. Oreg. (bd. dirs. 1948-74, chmn. Conv. 100 Yrs. Engring., founder Engr. Yr. award 1952), Prestressed Concrete Inst., Engring. Coun. Rsch. Inst., Consulting Engrs. Coun. Oreg. (treas. 1960, Engring. Excellence Project award 1996), Toastmasters. Republican. Home and Office: 2309 SW 1st Ave Apt 1145 Portland OR 97201-5040

KENNEDY, RAOUL DION, lawyer; b. San Jose, Calif., Feb. 6, 1944; s. Ralph Craig and Maxine Thelma (Schoemake) K.; m. Patricia Ann Bilbrey. BA, U. Pacific, 1964; JD, U. Calif., Berkeley, 1967. Bar: Calif. 1967, U.S. Supreme Ct. 1970. Assoc. Hagar, Crosby Heafey, Roach & May, Oakland, Calif., 1969-96, Morrison & Foerster, San Francisco, 1996-99, Skadden, Arps, Slate, Meagher & Flom LLP, San Francisco, Calif., 1999—. Co-author: California Expert Witness Guide, 1983, 2d edit., 1991. Fellow Am. Coll. Trial Lawyers, Internat. Soc. of Barristers; mem. Am. Bd. Trial Advocates, Internat. Acad. of Trial Lawyers, Am. Acad. Appellate Lawyers, Calif. Acad. Appellate Lawyers (pres. 1983-84). Republican. Home: 1701 Gough St San Francisco CA 94109-4419 Office: Skadden Arps Slate Meagher & Flom LLP Four Embarcadero Ctr San Francisco CA 94111

KENNEDY, RICHARD JEROME, writer; b. Jefferson City, Mo., Dec. 23, 1932; s. Donald and Mary Louise (O'Keefe) K.; m. Lillian Elsie Nance, Aug. 3, 1960; children: Joseph Troy, Matthew Cook. BS, Portland State U., 1958. Author: (novel) Amy's Eye, 1985 (Internat. Rattenfanger Lit. prize, Fed. Republic Germany 1988), also 18 children's books including Richard Kennedy: Collected Stories, 1988 and 3 musicals, including adaptation of H.C. Andersen's The Snow Queen; inclusion of stories in: The Oxford Book of Modern Fairy Tales, 1993, The Oxford Book of Children's Stories, 1993. With USAF, 1951-54. Home and Office: 415 W Olive St Newport OR 97365-3716

KENNEDY, RICHARD SYLVESTER, English educator; b. St. Paul, Oct. 13, 1920; s. William Walker Kennedy and Ellen Frances Foley; m. Ella Dickinson, Mar. 31, 1943; children: Elizabeth Ellen, Catherine Rourke, James Dickinson. BA, UCLA, 1942; MA, U. Chgo., 1947; PhD, Harvard U., 1953. Tchg. fellow Harvard U., Cambridge, Mass., 1948-50; asst. prof. U. Rochester, N.Y., 1950-57; assoc. prof. Wichita (Kans.) State U., 1957-64; prof. Temple U., Phila., 1964-88, prof. emeritus, 1988—; resident curator Casa Guidi, The Browning Mus., Florence, Italy, 1991. Author: The Window of Memory: The Literary Career of Thomas Wolfe, 1962, Dreams in the Mirror: A Biography of E.E. Cummings, 1980, Etcetera: Unpublished Poems of E.E. Cummings, 1983, Robert Browning's Asolando: The Indian Summer of a Poet, 1993, E.E. Cummings Revisited, 1994; editor: (with P. Reeves) The Notebooks of Thomas Wolfe, 1970 (Ga. Writers Assn. award 1970), Welcome to Our City: A Play in Ten Scenes, 1983, Beyond Love and Loyalty: The Letters of Thomas Wolfe and Elizabeth Nowell, Together with "No More Rivers", a Story by Thomas Wolfe, 1983, Thomas Wolfe: A Harvard Perspective, 1983, (with L. Conniff) Thomas Wolfe's Autobiographical Outline for Look Homeward Angel, 1991, Literary New Orleans, 1992, The Starwick Episodes, 1994, Selected Poems of E.E. Cummings, 1984, Literary New Orleans in the Modern World, 1998; mem. editl. bd. Am. Lit.-Duke U., Durham, N.C., 1989-90. Bd. mem. NAACP, Wichita, 1956-57. Lt. USN, 1942-46, ETO. Recipient Disting. Tchg. award Lindback Found., 1976; rsch. grantee Nat. Endowment for the Arts, 1973; Fulbright fellow U. Nijmegen, The Netherlands, 1988-89. Mem. Thomas Wolfe Soc. (pres. 1983-85, Zelda Gitlin Literary prize 1986), Soc. for the Study of So. Lit. (pres. 1988-90), N.Y. Browning Soc. (pres. 1991-96), E.E. Cummings Soc. Avocations: pottery, photography. Home: 120 Merbrook Ln Merion PA 19066 Office: Dept English Temple Univ Philadelphia PA 19122

KENNEDY, ROBERT ALAN, educational administrator; b. Benson, Minn., Sept. 29, 1946; s. William Henry and Mary Rose (Pothen) K.; m. Mary Ellen Rumpho, June 9, 1985; children: Caleb, Alex, Bryce, Curran. BS, U. Minn., 1968; PhD, U. Calif., Berkeley, 1974. Asst. prof. U. Iowa, Iowa City, 1974-78; assoc. prof. to prof. Wash. State U., Pullman, 1979-85; prof., chmn. Ohio State U., Columbus, 1987; program dir. NSF, Washington, 1987-89; v.p. res. U. Md., College Park, 1989-92; v.p. rsch., assoc. provost grad. students Tex. A&M U., College Station, 1992—. Contbr. articles to profl. jours. Office: Tex A&M U Rm 312 Adminstrn Bldg College Station TX 77843-1112

KENNEDY, ROBERT EMMET, JR., history educator; b. N.Y.C., Dec. 19, 1941; s. Robert Emmet and Jean (MacLeod) K.; m. Jane Marie McMahon, June 23, 1968; children: Mara, Gaëlle Marie, Daniel Patrick, Robert Emmet III. B.A., Johns Hopkins U., 1963; M.A., Boston Coll., 1965; Ph.D., Brandeis U., 1973. Instr. history Merrimack Coll., 1964-66; instr. history Kent State U., Ohio, 1968-69; asst.-associé U. Toulouse, France, 1969-73; asst. prof. European history George Washington U., Washington, 1973-77, assoc. prof., 1977-82, prof., 1982—. Co-editor: The Shaping of Modern France: Writings on French History since 1715, 1969; author: A Philosopher in the Age of Revolution: Destutt de Tracy and the Origins of "Ideology," 1978, A Cultural History of the French Revolution, 1989; co-author: Theatre, Opera and Audiences in Revolutionary Paris: Analysis and Repertory, 1996. Fellow Am. Council Learned Socs., 1977-78, Woodrow Wilson Internat. Ctr. for Scholars, 1983-84. Mem. Soc. French Hist. Studies, Nat. Assn. Scholars, The Hist. Soc. (bd. govs.). Roman Catholic. Office: George Washington Univ Dept History Washington DC 20052

KENNEDY, ROBERT P., civil engineer; b. Glendale, Calif., Apr. 2, 1939. BA, Stamford U., 1960, MA, 1961, PhD of Structural Engring., 1967. Rsch. engr. Northrop Corp., 1961-64; dir. mech. engring. Holmes & Narber, 1966-76; v.p. engring. divsn. Analysis Corp., 1976-80; pres. Structural Mechanics Assn., 1980-86, RPK Structrual Mechanics Consulting, Yorba Linda, Calif., 1986—. Mem. ASCE (Stephen Bechtel Energy Engr. award 1992), Nat. Acad. Engrs., Am. Concrete Inst., Earthquake Engring. Rsch. Inst. Fax: 714/777-8299. Office: RPK Structural Mechanics Cons 18971 Villa Ter Yorba Linda CA 92886-2610*

KENNEDY, ROBERT SPAYDE, electrical engineering educator; b. Augusta, Kans., Dec. 9, 1933; s. Kirk Randel and Marene Lucile (Spayde) K.; m. Eleanor Emma Stagliola, June 27, 1981; children: Carole Lesley, Nancy Allison, Nina Margret. BSEE, U. Kans., 1955; MSEE, MIT, 1957, DSc in EE, 1963. Instr. engring. MIT, Cambridge, 1958-63, asst. prof., 1963-67, assoc. prof., 1967-74, prof., 1974-94; prof. emeritus, 1994—; Dir. MIT Communication Forum, 1986-88; housemaster MacGregor House, MIT, 1985-91. Author: Fading Dispersive Communication Channels, 1968; contbr. numerous articles to jours. in field. Pres., chief pilot Quoddy Air. Fellow IEEE (pres. info. theory group 1976-77). Avocations: flight instructor, pilot. Home: 3 Green St Eastport ME 04631-1315 Office: PO Box 311 Eastport ME 04631-0311

KENNEDY, ROGER GEORGE, museum director, park service executive; b. St. Paul, Aug. 3, 1926; s. Walter J. and Elisabeth (Dean) K.; m. Frances Hefren, Aug. 23, 1958; 1 dau., Ruth. Grad., St. Paul Acad., 1944; B.A., Yale, 1949; LL.B., U. Minn., 1952. Bar: Minn. 1952, D.C. 1953. Atty. Justice Dept., 1953; corr. NBC, 1954-57; dir. Dallas Council World Affairs, 1958; spl. asst. to sec. Dept. Labor, 1959; successively asst. v.p., v.p., chmn. exec. com., dir. Northwestern Nat. Bank St. Paul, 1959-69; v.p. finance, exec. dir. Univ. Found., Minn., 1969-70; v.p. financial affairs Ford Found., N.Y.C., 1970-78; v.p. arts Ford Found., 1978-79; dir. Nat. Mus. Am. History Smithsonian Instn., Washington, 1979-92, dir. emeritus, 1993—; dir. Nat. Park Svc., Washington, 1993-97; spl. asst. to sec. HEW, 1957, cons. to sec., 1969. Author: Minnesota Houses, 1967, Men on a Moving Frontier, 1969, American Churches, 1982, Architecture, Men, Women and Money, 1985, Orders from France, 1989, Greek Revival America, 1989; editl. dir.: Smithsonian Guide to Historic America, 12 vols., 1989-90, Rediscovering America, 1990, Mission 1993, Hidden Cities, 1993, Burr, Jefferson, and Hamilton, 1999; appearances on NBC radio and TV Today, also others, 1954-57; contbr. articles to mags. and profl. jours. Served with USNR, 1944-46. Office: 855 El Caminito St Santa Fe NM 87501-2842

KENNEDY, SAMUEL VAN DYKE, III, journalism educator; b. Auburn, N.Y., July 18, 1936; s. Samuel V. Jr. and Marion Huse (Blanchard) K.; m. Bourke Larkin, Oct. 10, 1969 (div. 1994); children: Mary Morgan, Larkin Ellen, Lesley Chandler. BA, Cornell U., 1959; MA, Syracuse U., 1976, PhD, 1993. Reporter/editor The Citizen-Advertiser, Auburn, 1960-75; asst. prof. Syracuse U., N.Y., 1976-80, assoc. prof., 1980—; cons. in field, Syracuse, 1985—. Bd. dirs. Auburn Players Cmty. Theater, 1961—; trustee Osborne Meml. Assn., Auburn, 1973—. Mem. Soc. Profl. Journalists, Assn. Edn. in Journalism & Mass Comms., Am. Journalism Historians Assn., Orgn. Am. Historians. Avocation: community theater. Home: 443 Idlewood Blvd Baldwinsville NY 13027-3022 Office: Syracuse U 215 University Pl Syracuse NY 13210-2816

KENNEDY, STEPHEN DANDRIDGE, economist, researcher; b. N.Y.C., Feb. 25, 1942; s. Joseph Conrad and Frances (Midlam) K.; m. Joanna Court Bartlett, Nov. 27, 1965; children: Julia Paca, Benjamin Bartlett. AB, Harvard U., 1963; PhD, MIT, 1972. Mem. staff com. on banking and currency U.S. Ho. of Reps., Washington, 1964-66; adminstrv. asst. The Fed. Home Loan Bank Bd., Washington, 1966-67; analyst Abt Assocs., Inc., Cambridge, Mass., 1970, v.p., 1975, chief scientist, 1988—; adj. lectr. John F. Kennedy Sch. Govt., Harvard Univ., 1995. bd. trustees The Commonealth Sch., 1997—. Episcopalian. Avocations: gardening, sailing. Office: ABT Assocs Inc 55 Wheeler St Cambridge MA 02138-1192

KENNEDY, STEPHEN SMITH, hematologist, oncologist, educator; b. Byrn Mawr, Pa., June 9, 1947; s. J. Howard and Katharine (Smith) K.; m. Marion Sue Painter, Mar. 24, 1973; children: Janis Louise, Emily Katharine. BA in English Lit., Princeton U., 1969; MD, U. Va., 1973. Diplomate Am. Bd. Internal Medicine, Am. Bd. Hematology, Am. Bd. Oncology. Intern U. Iowa, 1973-74, resident internal medicine, 1974-75; resident internal medicine Dartmouth-Hitchcock Med. Ctr., 1977-78, fellow hematology, oncology, 1978-80; career hematology registrar U. Cape Town (South Africa), 1980-81; oncologist, hematologist Oncology Hematology Assoc. S.W. Va., Inc., Roanoke, 1981—; instr. clin. medicine Dartmouth-Hitchcock Med. Ctr., 1978-80; clin. asst. prof. internal medicine, U. Va., Roanoke, 1982-92, clin. assoc. prof., 1992—; chief dept. med. specialties Roanoke Meml. Hosp.; staff Cmty. Hosp. Roanoke Valley, Lewis-Gale Hosp., Alleghany Regional Hosp., Radford Cmty. Hosp., Wythe County Cmty. Hosp., Montgomery Regional Hosp., Stonewall Jackson Hosp. Contbr. articles to profl. jours. Surgeon USPHS, 1975-77. Am. Cancer Soc. fellow, 1979-80, Leukemia Rsch. Ctr. fellow U. Cape Town, South Africa, 1980-81. Fellow ACP, AMA, Am. Soc. Hematology, Am. Soc. Clin. Oncology, Roanoke Valley Acad. medicine, Med. Soc. Va. Office: Oncology Hematology Assoc SW Va Inc 2013 S Jefferson St Roanoke VA 24014-2419

KENNEDY, THOMAS J., lawyer; b. Milw., July 29, 1947; s. Frank Philip and June Marian (Smith) K.; m. Cathy Ann Cohen, Nov. 24, 1978; children: Abby, Sarah. BA, U. Wisc., 1969, JD cum laude, 1972. Bar: Wis. 1972, U.S. Dist. Ct. (ea. and we. dists.) Wis. 1972, Ariz. 1981, U.S. Dist. Ct. Ariz. 1981, U.S. Ct. Appeals (7th cir.) 1980, U.S. Ct. Appeals (9th cir.) 1981, U.S. Ct. Appeals (D.C. cir.) 1983, U.S. Supreme Ct. 1984, U.S. Ct. Appeals (11th cir.) 1986. Assoc. Goldberg, Previant, Milw., 1972-79, Brynelson, Herrick, Madison, Wisc., 1979-81; ptnr. Snell & Wilmer, Phoenix, 1981-93, Lewis and Roca, Phoenix, 1993-96; Ryley, Carlock and Applewhite, Phoenix, 1996—. Contbg. editor The Developing Labor Laws, 2d, 3d edits., The Fair Labor Standards Act. Mem. ABA, Ariz. State Bar, State Bar Wisc., Maricopa County Bar Assn. Avocations: tennis, reading, hiking.

KENNEDY, THOMAS PATRICK, financial executive; b. N.Y.C., Oct. 13, 1932; s. Andrew Francis and Marie P. (Scullen) K.; m. Mary P. Drennan, Jan. 14, 1956 (dec.); children: Thomas Patrick, Kevin M. (dec.), Michael J., Mary P. Kennedy Handsman, Deborah A. Kennedy Carter. BS, St. Peter's Coll., 1958; postgrad., Seton Hall U., 1959. Accountant Haskins & Sells CPAs, N.Y.C., 1953-54; staff Emerson Radio & TV, N.Y.C., 1957-58; various exec. positions CBS, N.Y.C., 1958-67; with Ford Found., N.Y.C., 1967; dir. fin. Pub. Broadcasting Lab., N.Y.C., 1967-69; with Children's TV Workshop (Sesame St.), N.Y.C., 1969-80, v.p. fin. and adminstrn., 1969-78, treas., 1969-78, sr. v.p., 1978-80; exec. dir. Ctr. for Non-Broadcast TV, 1980-85; pres. Tomken Mgmt., Ltd., 1980—, chmn. bd., 1983—; chmn. bd., chief exec. officer Effie Techs., Inc., 1984—; v.p., corp. fin. Jersey Capital Mkts Group, Inc., 1987-88; chief exec. officer, chmn. bd. Corp. Strategies Group, Inc., 1988-89; v.p. Vantage Securities, Inc. (co-venture with Whitehall Fin. Group), 1991-94; cons. in field; bd. advisers Franciscan Comm. Ctr.; bd. dirs., exec. dir. Ctr. for Non-Broadcast TV, 1980-85. With C.E., U.S. Army, 1954-55, Korea. Mem. Fin. Execs. Inst., Internat. Radio and TV Soc., Inst. Broadcast Fin. Mgmt., Nat. Assn. Accts., Internat. Broadcast Inst., Internat. Inst. Comm., Internat. Assn. Fin. Execs., Am. Assn. Individual Investors, Am. Legion, Korean War Vets., N.Y. Athletic Club, KC. Republican. Roman Catholic. Fax: 407-799-0812. E-mail: tompk@worldnet.att.net.

KENNEDY, WILBERT KEITH, SR., agronomy educator, retired university official; b. Vancouver, Wash., Jan. 4, 1919; s. Wilbert Parsons and Gracie Evelyn (Woolf) K.; m. Barbara Josephine Barber, Dec. 9, 1941; children: Wilbert Keith, James Clayton. BS, Wash. State U., 1940; MS in Agr., Cornell U., 1941, PhD, 1947. Asst. prof., asst. agronomist Wash. State Coll., 1947-48, assoc. prof., assoc. agronomist, 1948-49; prof. agronomy Cornell U., Ithaca, N.Y., 1949—; assoc. dir. research N.Y. State Coll. Agr., Cornell U.; also assoc. dir. Cornell U. Agr. Exptl. Sta., 1959, dir. research and dir. expt. sta., 1959-65; assoc. dean N.Y. State Coll. Agr., 1965-67, vice provost univ., 1967-72, dean, 1972-78, provost univ., 1978-84, provost emeritus, 1984—; with Atlantic Philantropic Svc. Co., Ithaca, 1988—; cons. Rockefeller Found., Kasetsart U., Thailand, 1968, Ford Found., Malaysia, 1970. Contbr. articles to profl. jours. Mem. sch. bd., Dryden, N.Y., 1953-55; exec. com. Louis Agassiz council Boy Scouts Am., 1955-70; active local Community Chest; bd. dirs. Tompkins Community Hosp., 1984-94, pres., 1986-88. Served to maj. AUS, 1942-46. Guggenheim fellow; Fulbright scholar, 1956-57; recipient N.Y. Farmers award, 1958, Merit Cert. award Am. Grassland Council, 1964. Fellow Am. Soc. Agronomy, AAAS; mem. Sigma Xi, Phi Kappa Phi, Alpha Zeta. Lodge: Rotary. Home: 410 Savage Farm Dr Ithaca NY 14850-6506

KENNEDY, W(ILBERT) KEITH, JR., electronics company executive; b. Phoenix, Ariz., Sept. 19, 1943. BSEE, MS, Cornell U., 1966, PhD, 1968. Researcher microwave solid-state devices Cornell U. and RCA Rsch. Labs., Princeton, N.J., 1964-68; researcher, leader devel. team thin-film fabrication facility Watkins-Johnson Co., Palo Alto, Calif., 1968-71, head R & D devel. dept., 1971-74, solid state div. mgr., 1974-78, also v.p., 1977, devices group v.p., 1978-86, v.p. shareowner rels. and planning coord., 1986-88, co. pres., chief exec. officer, 1988—. Contbr. articles to profl. jours. and procs. Patentee microwave power generator. Bd. dirs. CNF Transp. Inc., Joint Venture Silicon Valley; mem. exec. bd. The Ctr. for Quality Mgmt.-West, Santa Clara Valley Mfg. Group. Mem. IEEE (sr.); mem. Group Electronic Devices of IEEE, Group Microwave Theory and Techs. of IEEE, Calif. C. of C. (bd. dirs.), Phi Eta Sigma, Eta Kappa Nu, Tau Beta Phi, Phi Kappa Phi, Sigma Xi. Office: Watkins-Johnson Co 3333 Hillview Ave Palo Alto CA 94304-1223

KENNEDY, WILLIAM JAMES, pharmaceutical company executive; b. Troy, N.Y., Dec. 4, 1944; s. James Francis and Marjorie (Albrecht) K.; m. Mary Monika Silasz, July 22, 1967; children: Susan M., John R., Morgan E. BS, Siena Coll., Loudonville, N.Y., 1966; MA, Clark U., Worcester, Mass., 1969; PhD, SUNY, Buffalo, 1975. Assoc. dir. drug regulatory affairs Pfizer Pharms., N.Y.C., 1977-80; asst. dir. drug regulatory affairs Berlex Labs., Morristown, N.J., 1980-81; dir. drug regulatory affairs Kali Pharma, Elizabeth, N.J., 1981-82, GD Searle & Co., Skokie, Ill., 1982-86; v.p. drug regulatory affairs ICI Pharms. Group, Wilmington, Del., 1986-93, Zeneca Pharms. Group, Wilmington, 1993—; cons. various pharm. cos., 1981-86. Contbr. articles to profl. jours. and chpts. to books. NIH fellow, 1971-75. Mem. Pharm. Mfrs. Assn. (chmn. drug regulatory affairs com. 1991, chief negotiator Food and Drug Modernization Act legislation 1997), Del. Valley Regulatory Affairs Forum (chmn. 1988), Nat. Acad. Sci. Home: 8 Hickman St Rehoboth Beach DE 19971 Office: Zeneca Pharms Group Concord Pike New Murph Wilmington DE 19803

KENNEDY, WILLIAM JOSEPH, novelist, educator; b. Albany, N.Y., Jan. 16, 1928; s. William Joseph and Mary Elizabeth (McDonald) K.; m. Ana Daisy Dana Segarra, Jan. 31, 1957; children: Dana Elizabeth, Katherine Anne, Brendan Christopher. BA, Siena Coll., 1949; LHD (hon.), Russell Sage Coll., 1980; LittD (hon.), Siena Coll., 1984, Coll. St. Rose, 1985; ArtsD (hon.), LHD (hon.), Rensselaer Poly. Inst., 1987; LHD (hon.), L.I. U., 1989, Fordham U., 1992, Trinity Coll., 1992. Asst. sports editor, columnist Glens Falls Post Star, N.Y., 1949-50; reporter Albany Times-Union, N.Y., 1952-56, spl. writer, 1963-70; asst. mng. editor, columnist P.R. World Jour., San Juan, 1956; reporter Miami Herald, Fla., 1957; corr. Time-Life Publs. in P.R., 1957-59; reporter Knight Newspapers, 1957-59; founding mng. editor San Juan Star, 1959-61; lectr. SUNY, Albany, 1974-82, prof. English, 1983—; vis. prof. Cornell U., Ithaca, N.Y., 1982-83; founder N.Y. State Writers Inst., 1983. Author: The Ink Truck, 1969, Legs, 1975, Billy Phelan's Greatest Game, 1978, O Albany, 1983, Ironweed, 1983 (Pulitzer prize 1984, Nat. Book Critics Circle award 1984, film script 1987), Quinn's Book, 1988, Very Old Bones, 1992, Riding the Yellow Trolley Car, 1993, The Flaming Corsage, 1996, (film script with Francis Ford Coppola) The Cotton Club, 1984, (children's books with Brendan Christopher Kennedy) Charlie Malarkey and the Belly Button Machine, 1986, Charlie Malarkey and the Singing Moose, 1994, (Play) Grand View, 1996; contbr. short stories and articles to profl. jours. and mags. Served to sgt. U.S. Army, 1950-52. Recipient Creative Arts award Brandeis U., 1986, Gov. N.Y. Arts award, 1984, Comdr. Order of Arts and Letters, France, 1993; MacArthur Found. fellow, 1983, Nat. Endowment of the Arts fellow, 1981. Mem. PEN Club, Writers Guild Am. East, Am. Acad. Arts and Letters. Office: NYS Writers Inst SUNY 1400 Washington Ave Albany NY 12222*

KENNEDY, X. J. (JOSEPH KENNEDY), writer; b. Dover, N.J., Aug. 21, 1929; s. Joseph Francis and Agnes (Rauter) K.; m. Dorothy Mintzlaff, 1962; children: Kathleen, David, Matthew, Daniel, Joshua. BSc, Seton Hall U., 1950; MA, Columbia U., 1951; cert., U. Paris, France, 1956; LHD (hon.), Lawrence U., 1988; DFA (hon.), Adelphi U., 1998. Teaching fellow U. Mich., Ann Arbor, 1956-60; instr. English U. Mich., 1960-62; lectr. English Woman's Coll., U. N.C., Greensboro, 1962-63; asst. prof. English Tufts U., Medford, Mass., 1963-67; assoc. prof. Tufts U., 1967-73, prof., 1973-79; vis. lectr. Wellesley Coll., 1964, U. Calif., Irvine, 1966-67. Author: Nude Descending a Staircase, 1961, 2d edit., 1994, Introduction To Poetry, 1966, 9th edit., (with Dana Gioia) 1997, Growing into Love, 1969, Breaking and

Entering, 1971, Emily Dickinson in Southern California, 1974, Celebrations After the Death of John Brennan, 1974, (with J.E. Camp, Keith Waldrop) Three Tenors, One Vehicle, 1975, One Winter Night in August, 1975, Introduction to Fiction, 1976, (with Dana Gioia) 7th edit., 1998, Literature, 1976, (with Dana Gioia) 7th edit., 1998, The Phantom Ice Cream Man, 1979, (with Dorothy M. Kennedy) The Bedford Reader, 1982, (with Dorothy M. Kennedy and Jane Aaron) 6th edit., 1997, Did Adam Name the Vinegarroon?, 1982, French Leave: Translations, 1983, Hangover Mass, 1984, (with Dorothy M. Kennedy) Knock at a Star: a Child's Introduction to Poetry, 1982, The Owlstone Crown, 1983, The Forgetful Wishing-Well, 1985, Cross Ties: Selected Poems, 1985, Brats, 1986; (with Dorothy M. Kennedy) The Bedford Guide for College Writers, 1987, 5th edit., (with Dorothy M. Kennedy and Sylvia A. Holladay) 1999, Ghastlies, Goops and Pincushions, 1989, Fresh Brats, 1990, Winter Thunder, 1990, The Kite That Braved Old Orchard Beach., 1991, (with Dorothy M. Kennedy) Talking Like the Rain, 1992, The Beasts of Bethlehem, 1992, Dark Horses: New Poems, 1992, Drat These Brats!, 1993, The Minimus Poems, 1996, Uncle Switch, 1997, The Eagle as Wide as the World, 1997, Elympics, 1999; poetry editor: Paris Rev., 1961-64; editor: (with J.E. Camp) Mark Twain's Frontier, 1963, (with J.E. Camp, Keith Waldrop) Pegasus Descending, 1971, Messages, 1973, Tygers of Wrath: poems of hate, anger and invective, 1981; editor, pub. (with Dorothy M. Kennedy) Counter/Measures mag, 1971-74. Judge Nat. Coun. on Arts poetry book selections, 1969, 70, T.S. Eliot prize Thomas Jefferson Univ. Press, 1998, X.J. Kennedy poetry award Tex. Rev., 1998. With USN, 1951-55. Recipient Lamont Poetry award Acad. Am. Poets, Bess Hokin prize Poetry mag., 1961; Golden Rose award New Eng. Poetry Club, 1974; Los Angeles Times book award for poetry, 1985, Michael Braude award for light verse Am. Acad. and Inst. Arts and Letters, 1989, Aiken-Taylor award U. of the South, 1999; grant Nat. Council Arts and Humanities, 1967-68; Shelley Meml. award, 1970; Bread Loaf fellow in poetry Middlebury Coll., 1960; Guggenheim fellow, 1973-74; Bruern fellow in Am. civilization U. Leeds, 1974-75. Mem. Assn. Lit. Scholars and Critics, John Barton Wolgamot Soc., PEN (mem. coun. New Eng. 1996—), MLA, Poetry Soc. Am., Nat. Coun. Tchrs. English, Authors Guild, Phi Beta Kappa, Sigma Tau Delta (hon.). Home: 22 Revere St Lexington MA 02420-4424

KENNEDY-MINOTT, RODNEY, international relations educator, former ambassador; b. Portland, Oreg.; s. Joseph Albert and Gainor (Baird) Minott; children: Katharine Pardow, Rodney Glisan, Polly Berry. AB, Stanford U., 1953, MA, 1956, PhD, 1960. Instr. history Stanford U., 1960-61, asst. prof., asst. dir. history of western civilization program, 1961-62, asst. dir. summer session, 1962-63, dir. summer session, 1963-65; assoc. prof. Portland State U., 1965-66; assoc. prof., assoc. dean instrn. Calif. State U., Hayward, 1966-67, prof., 1967-77, head div. humanities, 1967-69; ambassador to Sweden and chmn. Swedish Fulbright Com., 1977-80; adj. prof. Monterey Inst. Internat. Studies, Calif., 1981; exec. v.p. Direction Internat., Washington, 1982-83; sr. research fellow Hoover Instn., 1981-82, 85—; chmn. Alpha Internat., Washington, 1983-85; sr. fellow Ctr. Internat. Rels., UCLA, 1986-90; prof. nat. security affairs tng., U.S. Naval Postgrad. Sch., Monterey, Calif., 1990—, acad. assoc. for area studies, 1995-97, asst. provost for external affairs, 1995—. Author: Peerless Patriots: The Organized Veterans and the Spirit of Americanism, 1962, The Fortress That Never Was: The Myth of Hitler's Bavarian Stronghold, 1964, The Sinking of the Lollipop: Shirley Temple v. Pete McCloskey, 1968, Regional Force Application: The Maritime Strategy and Its Affect on Nordic Stability, 1988, Tension in the North: Sweden and Nordic Security, 1989, Lonely Path to Follow: Non-aligned Sweden, United States/NATO, and the U.S.S.R., 1990. Mem. adv. bd. Ctr. for the Pacific Rim U. San Francisco, 1988-93. With U.S. Army, 1946-48, USAR, 1948-53. Mem. Am. Hist. Assn., Orgn. Am. Historians, World Affairs Coun. No. Calif., Am. Fgn. Svc. Assn. (assoc.), Marines Meml. Assn. (San Francisco), Stanford U. Faculty Club, Officer Clubs Mil. Dist. Washington D.C. Office: Dept Nat Security Affairs US Naval Postgrad Sch Monterey CA 93943

KENNEL, CHARLES FREDERICK, physics educator, government official; b. Cambridge, Mass., Aug. 20, 1939; s. Archie Clarence and Elizabeth Ann (Fitzpatrick) K.; m. Ellen Lehman; children: Matthew Bochner, Sarah Alexandra. AB (Nat. scholar), Harvard U., 1959; Ph.D. in Astrophys. Scis. (W.C. Peyton Advanced fellow 1962-63), Princeton U., 1964. Prin. rsch. scientist Avco-Everett Rsch. Lab., Mass., 1960-61, 64-67; vis. scientist Internat. Center Theoretical Physics, Trieste, Italy, 1965; faculty U. Calif., L.A., 1967-71, prof. physics, 1971-98; chmn. dept. U. Calif., 1983-86; mem. Inst. Geophysics and Planetary Physics, 1972—, acting assoc. dir. inst., 1976-77; space sci. bd. NRC, 1977-80, chmn. com. space physics, 1977-80; Fairchild prof. Calif. Inst. Tech., 1987; assoc. adminstr. NASA, Washington, 1994-96; exec. vice-chancellor UCLA, 1996-98; dir., vice-chancellor Scripps Inst. Oceanography U. Calif.-San Diego, La Jolla, 1998—; space and earth scis. adv. com. NASA, 1986-89, chmn. com. on global change rsch., adv. coun., 1998; mem. NRC Bd. Physics and Astronomy, 1987-94, chmn., 1992-94; chmn. plasma sci. NRC, DOE fusion policy adv. com., 1990; Fulbright lectr., Brazil; visitor U.S.-USSR Acads. Exch., 1988-90; disting. vis. prof. U. Alaska, 1988-93; cons. in field. Co-author: Matter in Motion, The Spirit and Evolution of Physics, 1977; co-editor: Solar System Plasma Physics, 1978. Bd. dirs. L.A. Jr. Ballet Co., 1977-83, pres., 1979-80; bd. dirs. Inst. for Theoretical Physics, Santa Barbara, Calif., 1986-90. NSF postdoctoral fellow, 1965-66, Sloan fellow, 1968-70, Fulbright scholar, 1985, Guggenheim fellow, 1987; recipient Aurelio Peccei prize Acad. Lincei, 1995, Hannes Alfven prize European Geophys. Soc., 1998. Fellow Am. Geophys. Union, Am. Phys. Soc. (pres. div. plasma physics 1989, James Clerk Maxwell prize 1997), AAAS; mem. NAS, Internat. Union Radio Sci., Internat. Acad. Astronautics.

KENNELL, RICHARD WAYNE, recording artist, business manager; b. Ft. Wayne, Ind., Aug. 11, 1952; s. John Charles and Betty June (Miller) K.; m. Leah Marie Waybright, Aug. 1, 1976. Student, Ind. U., Ft. Wayne, 1970-71, James Madison U., 1974. Rec. artist (bassist) Arista Records/Happy the Man, Reston, Va., 1974-79; rec. studio owner, producer, bus. mgr. The Inner Circle, White Plains, N.Y., 1984-96; bus. mgr. Inner Workings, Briarcliff Manor, N.Y., 1996—. Albums include Happy the Man, 1977, Crafty Hands, 1978, Better Late, 1983, Retrospective, 1989, Beginnings, 1990, Past, Present, Future, 1991, Happy the Man Live, 1994, Death's Crown, 1999, Beauty Gone Wild, 1999. Served with U.S. Army, 1971-73. Mem. ASCAP, Audio Engring. Soc., Am. Fedn. Musicians, Nat. Acad. Rec. Arts and Scis. Avocations: travel, computers, reading. Home: PO Box 122 Millwood NY 10546-0122 Office: 522 N State Rd Ste 102 Briarcliff Manor NY 10510-1536

KENNELLY, BARBARA B., former congresswoman, federal agency administrator; b. Hartford, Conn., July 10, 1936; d. John Moran and Barbara (Leary) Bailey; m. James J. Kennelly, Sept. 26, 1959 (dec. 1995); children: Eleanor Bride, Barbara Leary, Louise Moran, John Bailey. BA in Econs, Trinity Coll., Washington, 1958; grad., Harvard-Radcliffe Sch. Bus. Adminstrn., 1959; M.A. in Govt, Trinity Coll., Hartford, 1971. Mem. Hartford Ct. of Common Council, 1975-79; sec. of state State of Conn., Hartford, 1979-83; mem. 98th-105th Congresses from 1st Dist. Conn., Hartford, 1982-98; mem. ways and means com.; counselor Social Security Adminstrn., 1999—. Trustee Trinity Coll., Hartford, Conn.; previously active in numerous civic, polit., and govt. orgns. in Greater Hartford, Conn. Democrat. Roman Catholic. Office: Social Security Adminstrn 500 E St Ste 850 Washington DC 20254*

KENNELLY, SISTER KAREN MARGARET, college president; b. Graceville, Minn., Aug. 4, 1933; d. Walter John Kennelly and Clara Stella Eastman. BA, Coll. St. Catherine, St. Paul, 1956; MA, Cath. U. Am., 1958; PhD, U. Calif., Berkeley, 1962. Joined Sisters of St. Joseph of Carondelet, Roman Cath. Ch., 1954. Prof. history Coll. St. Catherine, 1962-71, acad. dean, 1971-79; exec. dir. Nat. Fedn. Carondelet Colls., U.S., 1979-82; province dir. Sisters of St. Joseph of Carondelet, St. Paul, 1982-88; pres. Mt. St. Mary's Coll., L.A., 1989—; cons. N. Cen. Accreditation Assn., Chgo., 1974-84, Ohio Bd. Regents, Columbus, 1983-89; trustee colls., hosps., Minn., Wis., Calif., 1972—; chmn. Sisters St. Joseph Coll. Consortium, 1989-93. Editor, co author: American Catholic Women, 1989; author: (with others) Women of Minnesota, 1977. Bd. dirs. Am. Coun. on Edn., 1997—, Nat. Assn. Ind. Colls. and Univs., 1997—, Assn. Cath. Colls. and Univs., 1996—, Western Region Nat. Holocaust Mus., 1997—, Assn. Am. Colls. and Univs., 1998—. Fulbright fellow, 1964, Am. Coun. Learned Socs. fellow, 1964-65. Mem. Am. Hist. Soc., Am. Cath. Hist. Soc., Medieval Acad., Am. Assn. Rsch. Historians on Medieval Spain, Nat. Assn. of Ind. Colls. and Univs. (bd. dirs. 1997—), Am. Coun. on Edn. (bd. dirs. 1997—), Assn. of Cath. Colls. and Univs. (exec. bd. 1996—). Roman Catholic. Avocations: skiing, cuisine. Home and Office: Mt St Marys Coll 12001 Chalon Rd Los Angeles CA 90049-1526

KENNER, CAROL J., federal judge. Chief bankruptcy judge for Mass., U.S. Bankruptcy Ct., Boston. Office: US Bankruptcy Ct Thomas P O'Neill Fed Bldg 10 Causeway St Rm 1101 Boston MA 02222-1009

KENNER, CAROLE ANN, nursing educator; b. Cin., Sept. 19, 1953; d. Lester O. and Betty A. Waugh. BSN, U. Cin., 1976; MSN, Ind. U., 1983, D of Nursing Sci., 1988. Staff nurse Children's Hosp. Med. Ctr., Cin., 1978, 81, 83-87, asst. head nurse, 1981-83; prof., dept. chair U. Cin., Cin., 1991—; pres. Cons. with Confidence, Inc. Instr. CPR, ARC. Fellow Am. Acad. Nursing; mem. Assn. Women's Health, Obstetric, and Neonatal Nurses (ednl. coord. Ohio chpt., coord. Greater Cin. chpt.), Nat. Assn. Neonatal Nurses (bd. dirs., dir. edn. programs 1999—, past pres.), Sigma Theta Tau. Avocations: travel, arts and crafts, music. Home: 5678 Pleasant Hill Rd Milford OH 45150-2345

KENNER, MARY ELLEN, marketing and communications executive; b. Darlington, Wis., Jan. 7, 1941; d. Horace James and Adean Elizabeth (McDonald) Smith; m. John Miller Kenner, Sept. 27, 1975. BS, Marquette U., 1963; MBA, U. West Fla., 1988. Fashion dir. spl. evenets Federated Store, Milw., 1962-63; mktg. odcl. Ohio Bell and Wis. Telephone Cos., 1963-66; coll. mktg. instr. Milw. Inst. Tech., 1966-67; advt. positions AT&T and Wis. Telephone Co., 1967-78; advtsg. dir. No. States Power Co., Mpls., 1978-83; pres. Kenner Enterprises, 1983—; adj. prof. U. West Fla., 1988-89; dir. mktg. and communications Printing Industries Am., Alexandria, Va., 1989-91; dir. mktg. and pub. rels. Am. Production & Inventory Control Soc., 1992-97; dir. mktg. Grad. Sch. U. Md. U. Coll., 1997—; adj. assoc. prof. U. Md.; mem. steering com. 1st Conf. Consumerism. Mem. Am. Mktg. Assn., Am. Soc. Assn. Execs. (cert. assn. exec.), Direct Mktg. Assn. Wash., Milw. Advtsg. Club (dir. 1969-72, sec. 1973-76), U. West Fla. Alumni Assn., Marquette U. Alumni Assn., Belleek Collectors Club. Roman Catholic. Home: 12908 Tourmaline Ter Silver Spring MD 20904-5349

KENNERKNECHT, RICHARD EUGENE, marketing executive; b. Glendale, Calif., Apr. 29, 1961; s. Richard and Sharon Mavis (Zane) K. V.p. Def. Tech. Corp. Am., 1993-96; pres. Rocky Mountain divsn. Nat. Telecom. Group, Casper, Wyo., 1996—; mktg. dir. The Uplink-Group, Mills, Wyo., 1996—; nat. sales dir. Bridge21.com, Casper, Wyo., 1998—; pres. FDC Inc., Lost Hills, Calif., 1989-91; profl. sporting clays shooter, exhbn. shooter. Mem. U.S. Sporting Assn. (mem. team U.S.A. 1988, 89, all-Am. team 1988, 89, 90, winner gold medal U.S.-French Profl. Invitational 1990, 91), U.S. Sporting Clays Assn. (mem. rules and ethics com., capt. team Perazzi), Verdugo Hills Ducks Unltd. (founding mem.), Nat. Sporting Clays Assn. (mem. nat. adv. coun. 1991-92), Olin Winchester (adv. coun. 1991-93), Calif. Waterfowl Assn. (shooting sports dir. 1992-93), Western Outdoor News (outdoor columnist 1992-93). Republican. Episcoplian. E-mail: rick@bridge21.net. Home: PO Box 1180 Mills WY 82644-1180 Office: The Uplink-Group PO Box 1180 Mills WY 82644-1180

KENNEY, BELINDA JILL FORSEMAN, electronics executive; b. Oak Ridge, Tenn., Dec. 18, 1955; d. Jack Woodrow and Betty Jean Forseman; m. Ronald Gene Kenney, Feb. 23, 1985; 1 child, Brandon. BS, U. Tenn., 1977, postgrad., 1977-78. Sales rep. Xerox Corp., Nashville, 1978-82, maj. account sales mgr., 1982-83; region sales ops. mgr. Xerox Corp., St. Louis, 1984-86; dist. sales mgr. Xerox Corp., Overland Park, Kans., 1987-89; dist. mgr. Xerox Corp., San Antonio, 1989-95; v.p. Xerox Corp., Houston, 1995-97; v.p., region gen. mgr. Bus. Svcs. Xerox Corp., Atlanta, 1998—. Active Xerox Cmty. Involvement; patron M. D. Anderson Cancer Ctr. Mem. Mensa. Lutheran. Avocations: jogging, reading, tennis, health and fitness. Office: Xerox Corp 2859 Paces Ferry Rd Atlanta GA 30339

KENNEY, DENNIS JAY, criminal justice researcher, educator; b. Kankakee, Ill., Oct. 2, 1952; s. Stan A. and Betty R. Kenney; m. Marnie Lynn Deacon, Oct. 25, 1995. BA, St. Leo Coll., 1978; MS, Rollins Coll., 1981; PhD, Rutgers U., 1986. Police sgt. City of Bartow (Fla.), Police Dept., 1974-81; asst. prof. Western Conn. State U., Danbury, 1983-87; project dir. Police Found., Washington, 1988-90; assoc. prof. U. Nebr., Omaha, 187-94; rsch. dir. Police Exec. Rsch. Forum, Washington, 1994—. Author: Crime, Fear, and the New York City Subways: The Role of Citizen Action, 1987; co-author: Organized Crime in America, 1995, Crime in the Schools: Reducing Fear and Disorder with Student Problem Solving, 1998, Police Pursuits: What We Know, 1999, Managing the Police: An Historical Look at the Future, A Conflict of Rights: Public Safety and Abortion Clinic Violence, 1999; editor: Managing Police Personnel, 1996, Managing Police Organizations, 1995, Police and Policing: Contemporary Issues, 1990, 2d edit. 1999; editor Am. Jour. of Police, 1991-95; mem. editl. bd. Police Quar., 1998—; contbr. articles to profl. jours. Mem. Am. Soc. Criminology, Acad. Criminal Justice Scis. E-mail: Dkenney@intr.net. Home: 3227 Volta Pl NW Washington DC 20007 Office: Police Exec Rsch Forum Ste # 930 1120 Connecticut Ave NW Washington DC 20036

KENNEY, DION PATRICK, business strategist, entrepreneur; b. Middletown, N.Y., Apr. 26, 1962; s. John Michel Kenney and Joan Elizabeth (Bennett) Klein. BS in Physics, Fla. State U., 1984; MS in Physics, Tex. A&M U., 1989; MBA, U. Pa., 1995. Engr. Navair-Dept. of Navy, Lakehurst, N.J., 1985-86, Stratford, Conn., 1986-87; software engr. Unisys, Houston, 1990-93; mktg. and bus. planning profl. Health Care Devel. Internat., Tarrytown, N.Y., 1993-97; coord. AHSC Group LLC, 1998; founder, pres. Cybernet Info. Systems, Yorktown Heights, N.Y., 1994—; COO AHSC Group, LLC, Tarrytown, N.Y., 1997—. Home: 8 Pkwy Dr Yorktown Heights NY 10598 Office: 777 Old Sawmill River Rd Tarrytown NY 10591

KENNEY, FRANK DEMING, lawyer; b. Chgo., Feb. 20, 1921; s. Joseph Aloysius and Mary Edith (Deming) K.; m. Virginia Stuart Banning, Feb. 12, 1944; children: Claudia Kenney Carpenter, Pamela Kenney Voetberg, Sarah Kenney Swanson, Stuart Deming Kenney. AB, U. Chgo., 1948, JD, 1949. Bar: Ill. 1948, U.S. Dist. Ct. (no. dist.) Ill. 1949. Assoc. J.O. Brown, Chgo., 1948-49; assoc., ptnr. Winston & Strawn, and predecessors, Chgo., 1949-92, ret., 1992. 1st lt. AUS, 1942-46, CBI, PTO. Mem. ABA, Ill. Bar Assn., Chgo. Bar Assn. (chmn. real property law com. 1982-83), Law Club Chgo., Fox River Valley Hunt Club, Quadrangle Club, Nat. Beagle Club Am. (bd. dirs. 1981-92), Spring Creek Basset Hunt Club (master 1977-93, chmn. bd., 1993-98, hon. chmn. bd. 1998—), Kappa Sigma (nat. housing fin. commr. for U.S. and Can., 1959-91). Republican. Roman Catholic. Home: PO Box 581 333 Old Sutton Rd Barrington IL 60010-9368 Office: Winston & Strawn 35 W Wacker Dr Ste 4200 Chicago IL 60601-1695

KENNEY, H(ARRY) WESLEY, JR., producer, director; b. Dayton, Ohio, Jan. 3, 1926; s. Harry Wesley and Minnie Ruth (Keeton) K.; m. Kay Ann Snure (div. 1964); children: Nina, Harry Wesley III, Kara; m. Heather North, May 22, 1971; 1 child, Kevin. BFA, Carnegie Inst. Tech., 1950. Dir. Fights at St. Nicks, Rocky King Detective, Night Beat Dumont Network, N.Y.C., 1950-57; producer, dir. TV shows True Story, Modern Romances NBC, N.Y.C., 1957-61; freelance dir. Omnibus, N.Y.C., 1958; dir. theater prodn. My Three Angels Totem Pole Playhouse, 1955; dir. theater prodn. The King and I Melody Fair Summer Theatre, Niagra Falls, 1959; dir. theater prodn. Twelfth Night Antioch, Yellow Springs, Ohio, 1962; dir. TV series The Doctors NBC, N.Y.C., 1964-66; exec. producer, dir. TV series Days of Our Lives NBC, Los Angeles, 1967-77; dir. TV series All in the Family CBS, Los Angeles, 1974, dir. pilots The Jeffersons, Filthy Rich, Ladies Man, Rosenthal & Jones, Side By Side, exec. producer, dir. TV series The Young and the Restless, 1981-86; producer, dir. (spl.) Miss Kline, We Love You ABC, 1974; exec. producer, dir. TV series General Hospital ABC, Los Angeles, 1987-90; freelance dir., 1990—; cons. Televisa-Mexico City UCLA Ext. Sch., 1990, guest instr. TV directing, 1975, guest instr. multiple camera directing, 1991, 93; instr. profl. seminar in TV for Televisa, 1990; guest lectr. profl. seminar dor srs. and students in drama Carnegie Mellon U., Pitts., 1990; apptd. assoc. prof. TV prodn. UCLA Sch. Theatre, Film and TV, 1993, 94, 95, 96, 97, 98, tv. prodn. Sch. Cinema and TV U. Southern Calif., 1998, 99—. Dir. closed cir. med. shows including Dr. Salk Polio Vaccine Report from U. Mich., Ann Arbor, 1956; dir. (theater prodns.) Ten Little Indians, Advent Theatre, L.A., 1991, The Best Christmas Pagaent Ever, 1993, Love Letters, W.Va. Pub. Theatre, Morgantown, 1994, Shadowlands, Tracy Roberts Theater, 1995 (Dramalogue award for Directing), Scrooge, W.Va. Pub. Theatre, 1995; dir. Sebiyophrenin: The Relapse, 3-part series; dir. (infomercials) Elements of Beauty-The Merle Norman Experience, 1993, Therapy Without Tears-The EMLA Study, 1993; dir. (series spls.) Soap Break, CBS, 1994-95 (Emmy nomination). Served with USN, 1943-46. Recipient 7 Emmy awards Acad. TV Arts and Scis. 1973, 78, 79, 82, 83, 84, 86, 13 Emmy award nominations Acad. TV Arts and Scis., 1972-88, 95. Mem. Dirs. Guild Am., Producers Guild Am., Actors Equity, Omega Delta Kappa. Avocations: athletics, tennis, traveling, bungy jumping. Home: 12996 Galewood St Studio City CA 91604-4045 *I recognize myself as an "average guy" with an average intelligence and talent and more than average patience and luck. An awareness of this fact has allowed me to accept the success I have had, always working for something better, but recognizing those shortcomings that have at times made me fail. Also because of this, thank God, I have had more than my share of happiness.*

KENNEY, JOHN JOSEPH, lawyer; b. N.Y.C., July 13, 1943; s. Joseph Charles and Regina Elizabeth (Hulbert) K.; m. Charlotte O'Brien, May 23, 1971; 1 child, Alexander Hulbert. BA, St. Michael's Coll., 1966; JD, Fordham U., 1969. Bar: N.Y. 1970, U.S. Dist. Ct. (so. dist.) N.Y. 1973, U.S. Ct. Appeals (2d cir.) 1973, U.S. Dist. Ct. (ea. dist.) N.Y. 1980, U.S. Supreme Ct. 1991. Assoc. Dunnington, Bartholow & Miller, N.Y.C., 1969-71; asst. U.S. atty. U.S. Dist. Ct. (so. dist.) N.Y., N.Y.C., 1971-80; assoc. Simpson, Thacher & Bartlett, N.Y.C., 1980-81, ptnr., 1981—. Counsel, Village of Bronxville, 1983-86; mem. Planning Bd. of Bronxville, 1992-98, counsel, 1981-83; trustee Hist. Deerfield Inc., 1992-98; bd. dirs. Citizens Crime Commn. Recipient John Marshall award U.S. Dept. Justice, 1980. Fellow Am. Coll. Trial Lawyers; mem. ABA, Fed. Bar Coun. (pres. 1994-96), Assn. Bar City N.Y. (chmn. criminal law com. 1992-95), New York County Lawyers Assn. (pres. 1996-97), N.Y. State Bar Assn. (exec. com. 1997—). Republican. Roman Catholic. Home: 8 Byway Bronxville NY 10708-4934 Office: Simpson Thacher & Bartlett 425 Lexington Ave Fl 15 New York NY 10017-3954

KENNEY, JOHN MICHEL, architect; b. N.Y.C., Oct. 22, 1938; s. John Peter and Madeline Loretta (Fuller) K.; m. Karin Suominen, Aug. 20, 1989; children: John Michel, James Brian, Dion Patrick. AAS, Orange County Community Coll., 1966; student, Columbia U., 1969. Registered arch., N.Y., N.J., Conn., Ill., Pa., Del., Ill., S.C., N.C., Ga. V.p., ptnr., dir. health facilities Perkins & Will Architects, White Plains, N.Y., 1968-81; mng. mem. AHSC Archs. P.C., Tarrytown, N.Y., 1981—; mng. mem. AHSC Group LLC; co-chmn. AHSC/Destefano and Ptnrs., Chgo.; pres. ArquInter-AHSE Europe, Madrid. Vice chmn. Orange County Dem. Coms., N.Y., 1968; chmn. Dem. Com., Middletown, N.Y., 1966-68; co-chmn. Robert Kennedy Presdl. Election Primary, Orange/Sullivan County, 1968; mem. United Hosp. Fund. Mem. AIA, Nat. Coun. Archtl. Registration Bds., N.Y. Soc. Hosp. Planning, Am. Assn. Hosp. Planners, N.Y. Acad. Scis. Democrat. Avocations: skiing, sailing, travelling. Office: AHSC Architects 777 Old Saw Mill River Rd Tarrytown NY 10591-6717

KENNEY, JOHN PATRICK, dentist; b. Joliet, Ill., July 8, 1946; s. John Edward and Nellie (Fratia) K.; m. Catherine McGehee, June 1, 1968 (separated); 1 child, David J. BS in Mktg., Christian Bros. Coll., 1968; DDS, Loyola U., Maywood, Ill., 1977, cert. in pediat. dentistry, 1979; MS in Oral Biology, Loyola U., Chgo., 1979. Diplomate Am. Bd. Forensic Odontology. Supr. passenger services Am. Airlines, Chgo., 1968-72; pvt. practice in pediatric dentistry Park Ridge, Ill., 1980—; asst. prof. pediat. dentistry Northwestern U., Chgo., 1983-97, clin. assoc. prof. pediat. dentistry, 1997-99; chief forensic odontologist Cook County Med. Examiner, 1991-97; forensic odontologist Cook County Med. Examiner, Chgo., 1984—, Kane County (Ill.) Coroner, Geneva, 1984—; cons. forensic odontologist Am. Airlines, Chgo., 1979, Midwest Express Airlines, Milw., 1985, Am. Eagle Airlines, Ind., 1995, United Express Airlines, Quincy, Ill., 1996, Comair Airlines, Mich., 1997, U.S. Army Central ID Lab., Honolulu, 1997—; mem. Nat. Disaster Med. Sys. D-Mort team USPHS. Mem. editl. bd. Jour. Forensic Scis., 1997—; contbr. articles to profl. jours. Fellow Am. Acad. Forensic Scis., Peirre Fauchard Soc., Royal Soc. Medicine; mem. ADA, Internat. Orgn. for Forensic Odonto-stomatology (v.p. 1984-87), Internat. Assn. for Identification (cert. sr. crime scene analyst 1991—), Am. Acad. Pediatric Dentists, Am. Bd. Forensic Odontology (bd. dirs., 1990—, treas. 1991-93, v.p. 1994, pres. 1995-96), Ill. State Dental Soc., Ill. Soc. Pediatric Dentists (bd. dirs. 1987-90), Chgo. Dental Soc., Kiwanis (pres. 1983-84, Disting. Pres. 1984). Office: 101 S Washington Ave Park Ridge IL 60068-4258

KENNEY, MARY ROSE, software engineer; b. Richmond, Va., Apr. 5, 1945; d. Thomas W. and Clara G. K.; m. Jeremy M. (div.). BS and MS in Math., Howard U., 1967; MS in Computer Sci., Steven's Inst., 1984. Sr. math. aide Ctr. Naval Analysis, Rosslyn, Va., 1967-77; sr. programmer analyst Control Data Corp., Rockville, Md., 1977-81; software engr. AT&T Bell Labs., Piscataway, N.J., 1981-83, software quality engr., 1983-84; software quality engr. Bellcore, Piscataway, N.J., 1984-99, Telcordia Techs., Piscataway, 1999—. Chair fundraising Youth in Sports Found., Piscataway, 1995-97; mem. fundraising com. Cmty. League Active Youth, New Brunswick, N.J., 1994, N.J. Rams, Newark, 1992-93. Mem. AAUW, NAFE, ACM, Am. Mgmt. Assn. Avocations: reading, crochet, bowling. Office: Bellcore 6 Corp Pl Piscataway NJ 08854

KENNEY, RAYMOND JOSEPH, JR., lawyer; b. Boston, Aug. 3, 1932; m. Claire L. Ducey; children: Marianne Lordi, Raymond Joseph III, Stephen V., John M. A.B. cum laude, Boston Coll., 1953, J.D., 1958. Bar: Mass. 1958, U.S. Dist. Ct. 1959, U.S. Ct. Appeals (1st cir.) 1969, U.S. Supreme Ct. 1985, U.S. Ct. Appeals (11th cir.) 1995. Mem. firm Martin, Magnuson, McCarthy & Kenney (and predecessor firms), Boston, 1958—; instr. law Mass. Dept. Edn., U. Ext., 1958-60, Boston U., 1961-66; corporator Winchester Savs. Bank, 1973—, Winchester Hosp., 1980—; lectr. continuing legal edn.; mem. Winchester Fin. Com., 1967-70, chmn., 1970-71; moderator Town of Winchester, 1972-77; chmn. Mass. Jud. Nominating Commn., 1975-77; mem. standing com. on civil rules Supreme Jud. Ct., 1977—; mem. time standards com. Mass. Superior Ct., 1990—; chmn. Mass. Clients Security Bd., 1984-87; dir. Mt. Vernon House, Winchester, 1990—. Author: Mass. Practice series (West), 1998; assoc. editor: Mass. Law Quar, 1965-72; editor-in-chief, 1973-76; contbr. articles to legal jour. Bd. dirs. Winchester chpt. ARC, 1968-71; pres. Mass. Continuing Legal Edn., 1980-83. Fellow Am. Coll. Trial Lawyers (state committeeman 1982-86), Am. Bar Found., Mass. Bar Found. (pres. 1984-88, trustee 1994-96); mem. ABA (del. 1976-78), Am. Judicature Soc. (dir. 1978-81), New Eng. Bar Assn. (pres. 1980-81), Mass. Bar Assn. (pres. 1977-78, founding chmn. sr. lawyers sect. 1999—), Middlesex Bar Assn., Mass. Def. Lawyers Assn. (Def. Lawyer of Yr. 1995), Internat. Assn. Def. Counsel, Boston Coll. Alumni Assn. (pres. 1983-84, 50th Ann. Disting. Law Alumnus award). Home: 5 Salisbury St Winchester MA 01890-2409 Office: Martin Magnuson McCarthy Kenney 101 Merrimac St Boston MA 02114-4716 *The continued well-being of society is dependent upon maintaining vitality in the law. The law must, and does, contain within itself the means to attain its own advancement, thereby preserving and enhancing that vitality. One of life's great privileges is to have been afforded the opportunity to labor in a profession which so reaches the very essence of human relationships.*

KENNEY, RICHARD JOHN, paper company finance executive; b. Evanston, Ill., Mar. 4, 1941; s. Roy H. and Marie (Weiland) K.; children: Ann, Katherine, Brian, Heather. BA, Loras Coll., Dubuque, Iowa, 1963; MBA, Ind. U., 1965. With Consolidated Papers Inc., Wisconsin Rapids, Wis., 1967—, v.p. fin., 1989-97, sr. v.p. fin., 1997—. Mem. Am. Forest & Paper Assn. (chmn. fin. mgmt. com.), Bulls Eye Country Club. Office: Consolidated Papers Inc PO Box 8050 Wisconsin Rapids WI 54495-8050*

KENNEY, RICHARD LAURENCE, poet, English language educator; b. Glens Falls, N.Y., Aug. 10, 1948; s. Laurence Augustine and Martha (Clare) K.; m. Mary Frances Hedberg, July 4, 1982; children: Hollis, Will. BA, Dartmouth Coll., 1970. Poet, 1970—; prof. U. Wash., Seattle, 1986—. Author: (poetry) The Evolution of the Flightless Bird, 1984, Orrery, 1985, The Invention of the Zero, 1993. Recipient Yale Series of Younger Poets prize Yale U. Press, 1983, Rome prize Am. Acad. and Inst. Arts and Letters, 1986, Lannan Literary award, 1994; Guggenheim Found. fellow, 1984; John

D. and Catherine MacArthur Found. fellow, 1987-92. Office: U Wash Dept English Seattle WA 98195

KENNEY, ROBERT JAMES, JR., lawyer; b. Boston, Jan. 16, 1948. BA, Harvard Coll., 1969, JD, 1972. Bar: Mass. 1972, D.C. 1976. Assoc. Hogan & Hartson, Washington, 1976-81, ptnr., 1981—. Lt. USNR, 1973-76. Recipient Federal 100 award Fed. Computer Week, 1992. Mem. Fed. Bar Assn. (chmn. govt. contracts sect. 1992-94, chmn. ADP procurement com. 1990-92, Disting. Svc. award 1990, 91, 94). Office: Hogan & Hartson 555 13th St NW Ste 800E Washington DC 20004-1161

KENNEY, THOMAS FREDERICK, broadcasting executive; b. Dearborn, Mich., Sept. 25, 1941; s. Charles B. and Grace M. (Wilson) K.; m. Beth H. Rockwood, Aug. 22, 1964; children: Sean, Blair. B.S., Mich. State U., 1964. Program mgr. Sta. WMBD-TV, Peoria, Ill., 1969-71; exec. producer Sta. WJZ-TV, Balt., 1971-73; program mgr. Sta. KFMB-TV, San Diego, 1973-75; program mgr., then dir. broadcasting ops. Sta. KHOU-TV, Houston, 1975-79; v.p., gen. mgr. KHOU-TV, 1979-84, Sta. WROC-TV, Rochester, N.Y., 1984-90; owner Santa Fe Wireless, Inc., Gainesville, Fla., 1990—; freelance TV cons., Houston, 1984. Home and Office: 1858 E Campbell Ave Gilbert AZ 85234-8228

KENNEY, THOMAS MICHAEL, publisher; b. Melrose, Mass., Mar. 4, 1947; s. James Edward and Agnes Ruth (Courtney) K.; m. Erica Marie Rizzo, June 6, 1970; children: Alexandra Beth, Edward Clarke. A.B., Dartmouth Coll., 1969; postgrad., N.Y. U. Bus. Sch. With Time Inc., 1972-76; asst. circulation dir. Time mag., 1975-76; circulation dir. Sports Illustrated mag., 1976; with Charter Publishing Co., 1976-82; pub. Redbook, 1978-79; gen. mgr. Redbook, Ladies Home Jour., Sport and Discount Merchandiser mags., 1979-80, corp. pres., 1980-82; with CBS Mags., N.Y.C., 1983-86; pub. Woman's Day, N.Y.C., 1983-85; exec. v.p. CBS Mags., 1985-86; pres. Thomas Kenney & Co., Inc., 1986-89; with The Reader's Digest Assoc., Inc., 1989-97; pres. Magazine Pub. Group, til 1997, Alnet Media L.L.C., N.Y.C., 1997—; chmn. Smithsonian Bus. Ventures, N.Y.C., 1997—; media advisor First Boston Corp., 1986—; chmn. bd. Mag. Pub. Am., 1996. Served to capt. USMCR, 1969-72. Club: Yale (N.Y.C.). Office: Allnet Media LLC 420 Lexington Ave Ste 2335 New York NY 10170

KENNEY, WILLIAM F., process engineer, safety engineer, sports official; b. N.Y.C., Sept. 27, 1933; s. William Francis and Eva (Liebl) K.; m. Mary Megna, Apr. 7, 1958 (dec. 1992); children: Kathleen, Elizabeth, Maria, Sharon, William J., Margaret, Patricia, Matthew, Brian. BSChemE, Yale U., 1955; MSChemE, Purdue U., 1956. Rsch. engr. Brookhaven Nat. Lab., Upton, N.Y., 1956-60; design prin. engr. Allied Chem Solvay Process, Syracuse, N.Y., 1960-66; rsch. engr. various tech. mgmt. Exxon Corp., N.J., 1966-94; pvt. practice Florham Pk., N.J., 1994—; cons. John Wiley Pub., Stevens Inst., Internat. Tech. Svc., 1995—. Author: Energy Conservation in Process Industry, 1984, Process Risk Management Systems, 1993; contbg. author John Wiley Pub. ency., 1994; contbr. articles to profl. jours. Coach youth sports Florham Pk. Recreation Commn., 1980-86. Mem. Internat. Assn. of Approved Basketball Ofcls. Roman Catholic. Avocations: Writing fiction and poetry, golf, tennis, jogging, reading. Home: 33 Village Rd Florham Park NJ 07932-2411

KENNEY, WILLIAM FITZGERALD, lawyer; b. San Francisco, Nov. 4, 1935; s. Lionel Fitzgerald and Ethel Constance (Brennan) K.; m. Susan Elizabeth Langfitt, May 5, 1962; children: Anne, Carol, James. BA, U. Calif.-Berkeley, 1957, JD, 1960. Bar: Calif. 1961. Assoc. Miller, Osborne Miller & Bartlett, San Mateo, Calif., 1962-64; ptnr. Tormey, Kenney & Cotchett, San Mateo, 1965-67; pres. William F. Kenney, Inc., San Mateo, 1968—; gen. ptnr. All Am. Self Storage, 1985—, Second St. Self Storage, 1990-96, Cochrane Road Self Storage, 1996—. Trustee San Mateo City Sch. Dist., 1971-79, pres., 1972-74; pres. March of Dimes, 1972-73; bd. dirs. Boys Club of San Mateo, 1972-90, Samaritan House, 1989—, Lesley Found., 1992—. With U.S. Army, 1960-62. Mem. State Bar of Calif. (taxation com. 1973-76), San Mateo County Bar Assn. (bd. dir. 1973-75), Calif. Assn. Realtors (legal affairs com. 1978—), San Mateo C. of C. (bd. dirs. 1987-93), Self Storage Assn. (we. region, pres. 1989-90, nat. bd. dirs. 1990-97, nat. v.p. 1994-95, pres. 1996), Rotary (pres. 1978-79, Elks (exalted ruler 1974-75). Republican. Roman Catholic. Home: 221 Clark Dr San Mateo CA 94402-1004 Office: 120 N El Camino Real San Mateo CA 94401-2705

KENNEY, WILLIAM JOHN, JR., real estate development executive; b. Huntington Park, Calif., Mar. 9, 1949; s. William John Sr. and Dorothy Marie (Smith) K.; m. Susan Louise Wattson, Sept. 26, 1987. BS in Econs., Calif. State U., Fullerton, 1970, BBA, 1971. Lic. real estate broker, Calif. Leasing agt. John S. Griffith, Irvine, Calif., 1972-78; dir. leasing John S. Griffith, Irvine, 1978-84; v.p. leasing John S. Griffith (now Donahue Schriber), Newport Beach, Calif., 1984-85; sr. v.p. John S. Griffith (now Donahue Schriber), Newport Beach, 1986-91, sr. v.p. devel., 1991-95; founder The Kenney Co., 1995—; speaker numerous orgns. Bd. dirs. Riverside YMCA, 1989-92. Recipient Certs. Appreciation Hemet C. of C., Riverside (Calif.) Bd. Realtors, Hemet Valley Kiwanis, Riverside Kiwanis. Mem. Calif. Bus. Properties Assn. (chmn. 1988-89, dir. 1976-96), Internat. Coun. Shopping Ctrs. (assoc., chair govt. affairs com. 1994-98), Newport Harbor Bd. Realtors (cert. appreciation), Frank Miller Club (life). Avocations: surfing, fishing, skiing. Office: The Kenney Co 824 Harbor Island Dr Newport Beach CA 92660-7228

KENNICOTT, JAMES W., lawyer; b. Latrobe, Pa., Feb. 14, 1945; s. W.L. and Alice (Hayes) K.; m. Margot Barnes, Aug. 19, 1975 (div. 1977); m. Lynne Dratler Finney, July 1, 1984 (div. 1989). AB, Syracuse (N.Y.) U., 1967; JD, U. Wyo., 1979. Bar: Utah 1979. Prin. Ski Cons., Park City, Utah, 1969—; pvt. practice Park City, 1979-87, 89—; ptnr. Kennicott & Finney, Park City, 1987-89; pvt. practice Park City, 1989—; cons. Destination Sports Specialists, Park City, 1984—; judge pro tem Utah 3d Dist. Ct., Park City, 1988—; arbitrator Am. Arbitration Assn., 1989—. Chmn. Park City Libr. Bd. 1987; bd. dirs. Park City Libr., 1985-91, Park City Handicapped Sports, 1988-94, The Counseling Inst., 1993-97, chmn., 1994-95, treas. 1995-96, mem. program com. Gov.'s Commn. on Librs. and Info. Svcs., 1990-91. Mem. Utah Bar Assn., Am. Arbitration Assn. Avocations: skiing, sailing, hiking, cycling, literature. Home and Office: PO Box 2339 Park City UT 84060-2339

KENNON, ROZMOND HERRON, physical therapist; b. Birmingham, Ala., Dec. 12, 1935; m. Gloria Oliver; children: Shawn, Rozmond Jr. BA, Talldega Coll., 1956; cert., U. Colo., 1957. Asst. chief phys. therapist St. John's Hosp., St. Paul, 1957-58, Creigthon Meml. St. Joseph's Hosp., Omaha, 1958-61; asst. chief, phys. therapist Sister Kenny Inst., Mpls., 1962, chief phys. therapy, 1962-64; cons. in phys. therapy Mt. Sinai Hosp., Mpls., 1963-70; pvt. practice, 1964. Contbr. articles to profl. jours. Bd. dirs. Southdale YMCA, Edina Human Rights, Southside Med. Ctr., Mpls., Boy Scouts Am.; bd. trustees Talladega (Ala.) Coll. Mem. Am. Phys. Therapy Assn., Am. Registry Phys. Therapists, Minn. Phys. Therapy Assn. (mem. social-econ. com., past chmn. profl. practice com., bd. dirs., past sec.). Home: 5120 Lake Crest Cir Hoover AL 35226-5027 Office: 1518 E Lake St Ste 206 Minneapolis MN 55407-1750

KENNY, DAVID, communications company professional. BS, Gen. Motors Inst.; MBA, Harvard Bus. Sch. Ptnr. Bain & Co., to 1996; vice-chmn. Bronner, Slosberg, Humphrey, Inc., 1996-97; ptnr., CEO Bronner, Slosberg, Humphrey, Inc., Boston, 1997—. Office: Bronner Slosberg Humphrey The Pruddential Tower 800 Boylston St Boston MA 02199-8001*

KENNY, EDMUND JOYCE, lawyer; b. Salem, Mass., Jan. 17, 1920; s. Jeremiah C. and Jane (Donovan) K.; m. Elizabeth Young, June 5, 1943 (dec. 1968); children: Joyce, William, Janet, Robert; m. Joan Shea, Oct. 13, 1973. BA, Boston Coll., 1940, JD, 1946; LLM, Harvard U., 1946. Bar: Mass. 1946, Ill. 1947. Mem. firm Winston & Strawn, Chgo., 1950—. Mem. Mich. Shores Club. Home: 325 Sunset Dr Northfield IL 60093-1046 Office: Winston & Strawn 35 W Wacker Dr Ste 4200 Chicago IL 60601-1695

KENNY, JOHN EDWARD, computer analyst; b. Buffalo, Oct. 28, 1945; s. Thomas Edmund and Dorthy Elizabeth (Krull) K. AAS, Erie C.C., 1972. Systems analyst Nat. Fuel Gas, Buffalo, 1969-70; programmer Svc. Systems Corp., Clarence, N.Y., 1974-77, Carborundum, Niagra Falls, N.Y., 1973-74; analyst, programmer A. Marine Midland Bank N.A., Buffalo, 1977-83; sr. analyst, programmer, project leader Empire of Am., FSA, Buffalo, 1983-85, applications project supr., 1985-89, asst. v.p. software devel., 1989-91; pres. Can.-Am. Bus. Svcs., 1991—, GPS Sys., 1995—; sr. analyst, programmer Cardinal Health Corp., Amherst, N.Y., 1995—; data processing cons. First Union Nat. Bank N.C., Elec. Data Sys. of Plano, Tex., 1996—; computer analyst Citicorp Student Loan Corp., Pittsford, N.Y., 1996-97; data processing cons. Ernst & Young LLP-Med. Mutual of Ohio, 1997—; tchr. programming langs. Advanced Tng. Ctr., Buffalo; cons. Ernst and Young yr. 2000 project Med. Mutual Ohio, 1997—. Mem. Rep. Presdl. Task Force; mem. Town of Tonawanda Conservative Com., 1980—, chmn., 1993—, chmn. N.Y. State Conservative Party, 1993-96; state committeeman 29th U.S. Congl. Dist., 1996-1999; mem. Erie County Conservative Com., 1980—, mem. exec. bd., 1994—; 911 asst. Erie County Ctrl. Police Svcs., 1995-1997. Mem. Am. Inst. Banking, Assn. Systems Mgmt., Kenton Jr. C. of C., Greater Fort Erie C. of C., Internat. Platform Assn., Smithsonian Assn., Assn. Computing Machinery, Nat. Geographic Soc., U.S. Golf Assn. (patron), Judges and police Conf. Erie County (N.Y.), Tonawanda Chmn. Men's Club, KC, Lions, Internat. Order Alhambra, World Future Soc. (profl. mem.). Republican (nat. com.). Roman Catholic. E-mail: jktg2@aol.com. Home and Office: 212 McKinley Ave Kenmore NY 14217-2438

KENNY, MARY ALICE, lawyer, law librarian; b. Evergreen Park, Ill., July 5, 1961; d. Ronald Stanley and Kathleen Regina (Fawcett) Adams; m. James Michael Kenny, Sept. 3, 1988; children: Daniel Patrick, Eileen Anne. BS, Ill. State U., 1984; JD, DePaul U., 1988; M of Libr. and Info. Sci., Rosary Coll., River Forest, Ill., 1997. Bar: Ill. 1988, U.S. Dist. Ct. (no. dist.) Ill. 1988; cert. instr. h.s. grades 6-12, Ill. Br. law libr., dir. Cook County Law Libr., Bridgeview, Ill., 1989-97; paralegal educator Am. Inst. Paralegal Studies, Oakbrook Terrace, Ill., 1990-97; pvt. practice Oak Lawn, Ill., 1992—; adj. prof. law, ref. libr. Sch. Law Libr. Loyola U., Chgo., 1998—; mem. adv. bd. Am. Inst. Paralegal Studies, Oakbrook Terrace, 1994-96. Contbg. author: Bar None: 125 Years of Women Lawyers in Illinois, (booklet) Union List of Holdings of the Branch Libraries of the Cook County Law Library, 1995, 96; contbr.: (book) Legal Research and Writing Exercises for Paralegals, 1992. Bd. dirs. Queen of Peace H.S. Alumnae Assn., Burbank, Ill., 1996—. Mem. ABA, Ill. State Bar Assn., Women's Bar Assn. Ill., DuPage Assn. Women Lawyers. Democrat. Roman Catholic. Office: 10735 S Cicero Ave # 205 Oak Lawn IL 60453-5400

KENNY, MAURICE FRANCIS, writer; b. Watertown, N.Y., Aug. 16, 1929; s. Andrew Anthony Kenny and Doris Marie (Herrick) Kenny Welch. Student, Butler U., 1950-55, NYU, 1957; Doctorate (hon.), St. Lawrence U., 1995. poet-in-residence North Country C.C., Saranac Lake, N.Y.; vis. prof. U. Okla., Norman, En'owkin Ctr., U. Victoria, B.C., Can., Paul Smith's Coll., SUNY, Potsdam; mem. panel N.Y. Found. for the Arts, N.C. Arts Coun., N.Y. State Coun. on the Arts, Arts Recognition and Talent Search for the Ednl. Testing Svc.; bd. dirs. Coord. Coun. Lit. Mags., N.Y. Found. for the Arts, WSLU-FM; coord. Iroquois Arts Festival, Saranac Lake, Writer's Week at Tupper Lake; presenter in field. Author: The Hopeless Kill, 1956, Dead Letters SSent, 1958, With Love to Lesbia, 1959, And Grieve, Lesbia, 1960, I Am The Sun, 1976, North: Poems of Home, 1979, Dancing Back Strong the Nation, 1979, Only As Far As Brooklyn, 1981, Kneading the Blood, 1981, Boston Tea Party, 1982, The Smell of Slaughter, 1982, Blackrobe: Isaac Jogues, 1982, The Mama Poems, 1985, Is Summer This Bear, 1985, Rain & Other Fictions, 1985, Between Two Rivers, 1987, Humors And/Or Not So Humorous, 1987, Selections, 1988, Last Mornings in Brooklyn, 1991, Interpreting the Indian, 1991, On Second Thought, 1991, 93, 95, Tekonwatonti: Molly Brant, 1992, Backward to Forward, 1997, Greyhounding This America, 1988, many others; co-editor Contact/II; editor, pub. Strawberry Press; poetry editor Adirondac Mag; contbr. to profl. jours. Past dir. The Little Gallery; art dir. Blue Moon Cafe, Saranac Lake. Home: Box 1029 Saranac Lake NY 12983

KENNY, PATRICK EDWARD, publishing executive; b. Alameda, Calif., July 17, 1948; s. John Roy Jr. and Ruth Margaret Kenny; m. Sylvia Grosse; children: Bryan Patrick, Katelyn Margaret, Emily Katherina. BBA, U. Iowa, 1970. Salesman Bell & Howell, New Haven, 1973-74; dist. mgr. Reader's Digest Assn., Pleasantville, N.Y., 1974-77, asst. product mgr., 1977-79, product mgr., 1979-81, sr. product mgr., 1981-84, subscription mktg. mgr., 1984-89, circulation dir., 1989-90, v.p. circulation dir., 1990-92, v.p. global circulation, 1992-94; pres. Putnam Direct Mktg. Group Ltd., Pleasantville, N.Y., 1994—. Bd. dirs. Readers Digest Fund for the Blind, 1989-94. Named Direct Marketer of Yr., Target Mktg. Mag., 1989. Mem. Direct Mktg. Assn., Mag. Pubs. of Am.

KENNY, RAY, geology and geochemistry educator, researcher; b. Chgo., June 13, 1955; m. Kerrie E. Neet, Sept. 19, 1992. BS, Northeastern Ill. U., Chgo., 1983; MS, Ariz. State U., 1986, PhD, 1991. Registered geologist, Mo. Rsch. assoc. U. Colo., Boulder, 1991-93; prof. N.Mex. Highlands U., Las Vegas, 1993—. Contbr. articles to profl. jours. Mem. AAUP, Nat. Assn. Geology Tchrs., Geol. Soc. Am., Am. Geophys. Union. Avocations: whitewater boating, backpacking, photography, cross-country skiing. Office: NMex Highlands U Dept Geology National Ave Las Vegas NV 87701

KENNY, ROBERT MARTIN, organizational development consultant. BA in Eng. and Psychology, NYU, 1972, MBA in Organizational Devel., 1987; postgrad., Saybrook Inst., 1993—. Sr. employee rels. counselor, mgmt. trainee Fed. Res. Bank, N.Y.C., 1972-73; human resources adminstr. Internat. Ctr. for Integrative Studies, N.Y.C., 1973-85; nat. human resources adminstr. Deloitte & Touche, N.Y.C., 1985-87; mgr. human resource planning Citibank, N.Y.C., 1987-88; dir. human resources The Door-A Ctr. of Alternatives and Adolescent Health Ctr., N.Y.C, 1988-94; prin. Glover Kenny Assocs., orgn. cons., N.Y.C., 1994—; mem. South Whidbey Cmty. Resilience Project, 1999—; treas., bd. dirs. Orgn. Devel. Network of Greater N.Y., 1993-96; cons. in field. Contbr. book chpts. and articles to profl. jours. Pres., bd. dirs. West 13th St. Owners, Inc., N.Y.C., 1979-84; bd. dirs. Cross-Cultural Inst., 1995-96; active nat. election campaigns, N.Y.C., 1972—. Fellow The Fetzer Inst., 1998—; Regents scholar N.Y. State Bd. Regents, 1988, Christopher Connell scholar Cathedral Coll., 1968, Saybrook Inst. scholar, 1994-97; recipient Chandra Naryansingh award for conflict resolution, 1996. Mem. APA (Sidney M. Jourard award 1995, 97, divsn. humanistic psych.), ASTD, Assn. for Transpersonal Psychology, Assn. Humanistic Psychology, Met. Assn. Applied Psychology, Soc. Human Resource Mgmt., Orgnl. Devel. Network, Scientific and Med. Network, Inst. Noetic Scis., Beta Gamma Sigma. Home and Office: 834 Woodsons Ln Langley WA 98260

KENNY, ROGER MICHAEL, executive search consultant; b. N.Y.C., Oct. 3, 1938; s. Michael F. and Mary T. (Glynn) K.; m. Carole Ann Smith, Oct. 3, 1959; children: Glynn Scott, Lynn Marie. BBA, Manhattan Coll., 1959; MBA, N.Y. U., 1961. With Port Authority of N.Y. and N.J., 1959-67, mgr. bus. ops., 1965-67; assoc. Spencer Stuart & Assocs., N.Y.C., 1967-70, v.p. West Coast ops., 1970-77; sr. v.p., ptnr. Spencer Stuart & Assocs., 1977-82, Kenny Kindler Tholke Hardy/Boardroom Cons., N.Y.C., 1982—; mng. dir. Boardroom Cons. Contbr. articles to profl. jours. Bd. overseers Conrad N. Hilton Coll. Hotel and Restaurant Mgmt. U. Houston. Mem. Nat. Assn. Corp. and Profl. Recruiters, Am. Soc. Public Adminstrs., Assn. Exec. Search Cons. (bd. dirs.), Imperial Russian Order of St. John of Jerusalem (Knights of Malta), Sky Club, Econ. Club, Westchester Country Club. Home: 33 Mt Holly Dr Rye NY 10580-1858 Office: Kenny Kindler Tholke Hardy/Boardroom Con 530 5th Ave New York NY 10036-5101 *People who are willing to experiment seem to be the most successful, at least in terms of their achievements. A completely empirical approach to life is impossible. First of all, the necessary facts aren't always available and too frequently the wrong conclusions are derived from too much empiricism.*

KENNY, SHIRLEY STRUM, university administrator; b. Tyler, Tex., Aug. 28, 1934; d. Marcus Leon and Florence (Golenternek) S.; m. Robert Wayne Kenny July 22, 1956; children: David Jack, Joel Strum, Daniel Clark, Jonathan Matthew, Sarah Elizabeth. BA, BJ, U. Tex., 1955; MA, U. Minn., 1957; PhD, U. Chgo., 1964; LHD (hon.), U. Rochester, 1988, Chonnam U., 1996. Chair English dept. U. Md., College Park, 1979-85, provost Arts and Humanities, 1979-85; pres. CUNY Queens Coll., Flushing, 1985-94, SUNY, Stony Brook, 1994—; bd. dirs. Toys 'R' Us, Computer Assocs., Chase Manhattan Met. Adv. Bd.; chair Brookhaven Sci. Assocs. Author: The Conscious Lovers, 1968, The Plays of Richard Steele, 1971, The Performers and Their Plays, 1982, The Works of George Farquhar, 2 vols.,1988; editor: British Theatre and the Other Arts, 1984; contbr. numerous articles to profl. jours. Bd. dirs. Assn. Am. Colls. and Univs., 1988-96, Goodwill of Greater N.Y., Long Island Assn. Recipient Disting. Alumnus award U. Chgo. Club Washington, 1980, Svc. and Leadership award N.Y. Urban League, 1988; named Outstanding Woman, U. Md., 1983, Outstanding Alumnus, U. Tex. Coll. Communication, 1989. Mem. Bayer Commn. Educating Undergrads, Rsch. Univ. (chair). Office: SUNY 310 Adminstrn Bldg Stony Brook NY 11790-0701

KENRICH, JOHN LEWIS, lawyer; b. Lima, Ohio, Oct. 17, 1929; s. Clarence E. and Rowena (Stroh) Katterheinrich; m. Betty Jane Roehll, May 26, 1951; children: John David, Mary Jane, Kathryn Ann, Thomas Roehll, Walter Clarence. BS, Miami U., Oxford, Ohio, 1951; LLB, U. Cin., 1953. Bar: Ohio 1953, Mass. 1969. Asst. counsel B.F. Goodrich Co., Akron, Ohio, 1956-65; asst. sec., counsel W.R. Grace & Co., Cin., 1965-68, v.p. Splty. Products Group divsn., 1970-71; corp. counsel, sec. Standex Internat. Corp., Andover, Mass., 1969-70; v.p., sec. Chemed Corp., Cin., 1971-82, sr. v.p., gen. counsel, 1982-86, exec. v.p., chief adminstrv. officer, 1986-91, ret., 1991. Trustee Better Bus. Bur., Cin., 1981-90; mem. bus. adv. coun. Miami U., 1986-88; mem. City Planning Commn., Akron, 1961-62; mem. bd. visitors Coll. Law U. Cin., 1988-92; mem. area coun. trustees Franciscan Sisters of Poor Found., Cin., 1989-93; bd. govs. Arthritis found. Southwestern Ohio chpt., 1992-95; mem. Com. on Reinvestment City of Cin., 1991-93. 1st lt. JAGC U.S. Army, 1954-56. Mem. Am. Arbitration Assn., Beta Theta Pi, Omicron Delta Kappa, Delta Sigma Pi, Phi Eta Sigma. Republican. Methodist. Home and Office: 504 Abilene Trl Cincinnati OH 45215-2515

KENRICK, CHARLES WILLIAM, lawyer; b. Chgo., June 16, 1946; s. Ralph Schwarting and Angela Augusta (Shostrom) K.; m. Patricia June Ogilvie, Dec. 27, 1969; children: Hugh, Alex, Graham, Charlotte, Blair. AB cum laude, Kenyon Coll., 1968; JD, Duquesne U., 1972. Bar: Pa. 1972, U.S. Dist. Ct. (we. dist.) Pa. 1972, U.S. Ct. Appeals (3rd cir.) 1977, U.S. Supreme Ct. 1984, U.S. Ct. Appeals (6th, 7th and 10th cirs.), 1988. From assoc. to ptnr. Dickie, McCamey & Chilcote, Pitts., 1976-98, mng. ptnr., 1993-97; with Gorr Moser Dell & Loughney, Pitts., 1997—. Articles editor Duquesne U. Law Rev., 1971; editor Pitts. Legal Jour., 1980-84. Fellow ABA, Pa. Bar Found., Allegheny Bar Found. (ho. of dels. 1980—); mem. Allegheny County Bar Assn. (bd. govs. 1984—, adminstrv. v.p. 1986—, pres.-elect 1990, pres. 1991), Internat. Assn. Def. Counsel, Kenyon Coll. Alumni Assn. Pitts. (pres. 1983-84), Duquesne U. Law Alumni Assn. (pres. 1985-86), Rivers Club, Duquesne Club, Valley Brook Club. Democrat. Office: Gorr Moser Dell & Loughney 1300 Frick Bldg 437 Grant St Pittsburgh PA 15219-6002

KENSICKI, PETER ROBERT, insurance, finance educator; b. Rockford, Ill., Oct. 10, 1944; s. Henry John and Jeanette Virginia (Zielinski) K.; m. Sally Rankin Kelsall, June 10, 1967 (div. 1978); m. Karen Louise Kroger, May 17, 1980; 1 child, Audry Amann. BBA, U. Cin., 1966; M in Ins., Ga. State U., 1968, DBA, 1972. CLU, Am. Coll., FLMI, Life Office Mgmt. Assn. Spl. agt. Northwestern Mutual Life Ins. Co., Cin., 1964-74; designer and program dir. Ga. Consumer Svcs. Program, Atlanta, 1969; asst. prof. fin. Ohio U., Athens, 1970-74; asst. v.p., dir. tng. and edn. Cin. Ins. Co., 1974-79; v.p. Am. Inst. for CPCU, Ins. Inst. of Am., Malvern, Pa., 1979-89; pres. Nat. Certification Inst., Princeton, N.J., 1983-90; prof. ins., chairholder ins. studies Ea. Ky. U., Richmond, 1989—; cons. for ins. litigation, Richmond, Ky., 1985—. Author: (textbooks) Principles of Insurance Production, 1981, rev. edit., 1986; Principles of Reinsurance, 1990, rev. edit. 1995; (trade books) The Business Insurance Handbook, 1981, How Accounting Works: A Guide for the Preplexed,. Mem. Bd. of Ethical Inquiry, Malvern, Pa., 1995—; mem. adv. com. Ward's Reports: Property Liability and Life/Health Coms., Cin., 1992—. Recipient Nat. Defense Edn. Act fellowship, U.S. Govt., Atlanta, 1966-69. Mem. CPCU Soc. (CPCU, chmn. agts. and brokers sect. 1989-94, mem. publs. com.(chmn. 1995—), Project InVEST (bd. dirs. 1989-97), Am. Soc. CLU and ChFC (ethical guidance and profl. standards com. 1992-97, Beta Gamma Sigma. $D. Roman Catholic. Avocations: cooking, reading, golf, travel. E-mail address: lpskensi@acs.eku.edu.$D. Office: Ea Ky U PO Box 25A Richmond KY 40476-0025

KENT, ALLEN, library and information sciences educator; b. N.Y.C., Oct. 24, 1921; s. Samuel and Anna (Begun) K.; m. Rosalind Kossoff, Jan. 24, 1943; children: Merryl Frances Kent Samuels, Emily Beth Kent Yeager, Jacqueline Diane Kent Maryak, Carolyn May Kent Hall. B.S. in Chemistry, CCNY, 1942. Sci. editor Intersci. Pubs., 1946-51; research assoc. Ctr. Internat. Studies, MIT, 1951-53; prin. documentation engr. Battelle Meml. Inst., Columbus, Ohio, 1953-55; asso. dir. Ctr. for Documentation and Communication Research; prof. library sci. Western Res. U., Cleve., 1955-63; dir. office communications programs, chmn. interdisciplinary doctoral program info. sci., prof. info. sci., edn. and computer sci. U. Pitts., 1963-76; Univ. Disting. Service prof. library and info. sci. and assoc. dean U. Pitts. Sch. Library and Info. Sci., 1976-91, interim dean, 1985-86, prof. emeritus, 1992; mem. mgmt. info. com. Health and Welfare Assn. Allegheny County, Pa., 1972-80; dir. Marcel Dekker, Inc., N.Y., 1978-93. Author: (with others) Machine Literature Searching, 1956, (with J. W. Perry) Documentation and Information Retrieval, 1957, Tools for Machine Literature Searching, 1958, Centralized Information Services, 1958, Mechanized Information Retrieval, 1962, 2d edit., 1966; also fgn. transls. Specialized Information Centers, 1965; Information Analysis and Retrieval, 1971, Resource Sharing in Libraries, 1977, On-Line Revolution in Libraries, 1978, Structure and Governance of Library Networks, 1979, Use of Library Materials, 1979, Information Technology, 1982; editor, co-editor numerous books in field; exec. editor: Ency. Library and Info. Sci, 1968—, Ency. Computer Sci. and Tech, 1972—, Ency. Microcomputers, 1984—, Ency. of Telecommunications, 1988—. Chmn. bd. Interuniv. Communications Council Inc., 1971-74. Served with USAAF, 1942-46. Recipient Info. Tech. Merit award Eastman Kodak Co., 1968. Fellow AAAS; mem. ALA, Assn. Computing Machinery, Am. Soc. Info. Sci. (award of merit 1977, award for Best Info. Sci. Book of Yr. 1980, Pioneer in Info. Sci. 1987), Acad. Sr. Profls. Eckerd Coll. Home: 5108 Brittany Dr S Apt 601 Saint Petersburg FL 33715-1525 *My goal has been to be useful. This entails service, dedication to my profession and to the institution which supports my work, and absolute standards of honesty.*

KENT, BARTIS MILTON, physician; b. Terrell, Tex., June 23, 1925; s. Bartis William and Annie (Smalley) K.; m. Ann L. Kiel, July 6, 1954; children: Susan Ruth, Martha Lucille, Bartis Michael. Student, So. Meth. U., 1942-44; MD, Baylor U., 1948. Diplomate Am. Bd. Internal Medicine. Intern Jefferson Davis Hosp., Houston, 1948-49; resident pathology Mass. Meml. Hosps., Boston, 1951; resident in internal medicine Baylor U., 1953-56; indsl. physician Humble Oil Co., Houston, 1949-51; instr. dept. medicine U. Iowa, 1956-58; staff physician Iowa City VA Hosp., 1956-58; practice medicine specializing in internal medicine Muskogee, Okla., 1958—; cons. Muskogee VA Hosp.; clin. asst. prof. medicine U. Okla. Sch. Medicine, 1975—. Chmn. Muskogee County chpt. Am. Nat. Red Cross, 1963-65. Served with USAF, 1951-53. Decorated Air medal. Fellow A.C.P.; mem. Indsl. Med. Assn., Soc. Nuclear Medicine, Am. Fedn. Clin. Research, Am. Heart Assn., Aerospace Medicine Assn., Am., Okla. socs. internal medicine, Muskogee C. of C. Methodist. Mason (Shriner). Home: 800 N 45th St Muskogee OK 74401-1505

KENT, BETTY DICKINSON, horsemanship educator; b. Flagstaff, Ariz., July 17, 1924; d. Walter E. Dickinson and Margaret Opal (Smith) Dickinson Langdon; m. Walter Kent, Mar. 4, 1943; children: Sherry Lee DeVillier, W. Norman, Charles H., Daniel W. Grad. pub. sch., 1942. Owner, operator Come by Chance Riding Acad., Flagstaff, 1945-65; owner, mgr. San Francisco Peaks Riding & Hunt Club, Flagstaff, 1965-75; mem. horsemanship tchg. staff No. Ariz. U., Flagstaff, 1966-75; cert. tchr. Yavapai C.C., Clarkdale, Ariz., 1979—. Contbr. articles to Western Horseman mag.; reporter, columnist The Verde Ind., Verde View; newsletter editor CVHS, 1992—. Pres. Camp Verde (Ariz.) Hist. Soc., 1990-98. Avocations: gardening, historical research.

KENT, BRUCE JONATHAN, pharmaceutical executive; b. Johnstown, Pa., Sept. 25, 1962; s. Reg and Barbara Lee (Petz) K.; m. Nan Ellen Chapple

Kent, Sept. 3, 1988; children: Alexandra Nika-Chapple, Connor Stewart-Chapple. BS in Fin., Pa. State U., 1985. Mktg. rep. Mobil Oil Corp., Phila., 1986-87; med. sales rep. Abbott Labs., Johnstown, 1987-88; med. rep. Ciba Pharms., Johnstown, 1988-90; dist. bus. mgr. Ciba Pharms., Balt., 1990-95; head managed healthcare ops. Ciba Pharms., Summit, N.J., 1995-97; dir. corp. account ops. Novartis Pharms., East Hanover, 1997-99, exec. dir., field analysis and incentives, 1999—. Republican. Evangelical. Avocations: football, golf, family activities. Home: 1115 Croton Rd Flemington NJ 08822-5608 Office: Novartis Pharms 59 Rt 10 East Hanover NJ 07936

KENT, CALVIN ALBERT, university administrator; b. Kansas City, Kans., Sept. 8, 1941; s. Homer C. Wright; m. Nita Sue Davis, Aug. 23, 1963; children: Nita Christine, Anna Elaine. BA, Baylor U., 1963; MA, U. Mo., 1965, PhD, 1967; postgrad., U. Va., 1967, Wichita State U., 1972, U. Chgo., 1975, Rice U., 1987. Instr. econs. U. Mo., Columbia, 1963-64; instr. social scis. Stevens Coll., Columbia, 1964-67; faculty U. S.D., Vermillion, 1967-78; prof. econs. U. S.D., 1973-78, dir. public fin. studies, 1971-78; Herman W. Lay prof. pvt. enterprise, dir. Center Pvt. Enterprise Baylor U., Waco, Tex., 1978-90; adminstr. Energy Info. Adminstrn., Washington, 1990-93; dean, Lewis Disting. chair bus. Coll. Bus. Marshall U., Huntington, W. Va., 1993—; exec. dir. S.D. Council on Econ. Edn., 1969-78; chief economist taxation coms. S.D. Legislature; cons. S.D. Dept. Rev. Alderman, Vermillion, 1969-78; mem. Pres.'s Adv. Com. Entrepreneurship Edn., 1983-85. Author: Indian Poverty, 1969, Taxation of Cooperative Enterprise, 1970, Death Taxes in the American States, 1974, Municipal Regulation and Franchising, 1975, Encyclopedia of Entrepreneurship, 1981, The Environment for Entrepreneurship, 1984, Entrepreneurship and the Privatization of Government, 1987, The Texas Economy, 1989, Entrepreneurship Education: Present Practices Future Direction, 1990, The Public Utilities Holding Company Act: 1935-92, 1993, Agenda for Farm Taxation, 1998; contbr. articles to profl. jours. Pres. City Coun., Vermillion, 1974-78; vice chmn. S.D. Mcpl. League, Dist. 2, 1972-74; councilman City of Huntington, W.Va., 1997—, City of Woodway, Tex., 1985-90, mayor, 1986-90; co-chair Gov.'s Commn. on Tax Fairness, 1997—; mem. Tri-State Airport Authority. Outstanding Tchr., U. S.D., 1970-72, Outstanding Prof., Baylor U., 1983; Outstanding Young Religious Leader, 1976, Disting. Prof. Baylor Sch. Bus., 1981, Piper Prof. Piper Found., 1988; recipient Freedoms Found. at Valley Forge award for excellence in pvt. enterprise edn., 1980, Sargent Americanism award, 1986, John Schramm Leadership award Nat. Assn. Econ. Edn. and Joint Coun. on Econ. Edn., NSF award, 1974, Gov.'s citation for disting. achievement, 1996. Mem. Nat. Assn. Econ. Educators (pres. 1978-80), Assn. Pvt. Enterprise Edn. (sec.-treas. 1982-90, Disting. Svc. award 1988, Outstanding Scholar award 1992, bd. dirs. 1994), Soc. Econ. Educators (sec.-treas. 1987-90, v.p. 1993, pres. 1994), Rotary, Masons. Republican. Presbyterian. Home: 133 Woodland Dr Huntington WV 25705-1349

KENT, DAVID CHARLES, lawyer; b. Shreveport, La., July 23, 1953; s. Keith C. and Louise (Goode) K.; m. Carol Elizabeth Hittson, July 3, 1976; children: John, Meredith, Robert. BA, Baylor U., 1975, JD, 1978. Bar: Tex. 1978, U.S. Dist. Ct. (no. dist.) Tex. 1980, U.S. Ct. Appeals (5th cir.) 1980, U.S. Dist. Ct. (so. and we. dists.) Tex. 1981, U.S. Ct. Appeals (11th cir.) 1981, U.S. Dist. Ct. (ea. dist.) Tex. 1981; bd. cert. civil trial law, personal injury trial law. Briefing atty. Supreme Ct. Tex., Austin, 1978-79; ptnr. Hughes & Luce L.L.P., Dallas, 1979—; bd. dirs. Law Focused Edn., Inc. Editor: Managing Scarce World Resources, 1975, Crime and Justice in America, 1976, Medical Care and Health in America, 1977, Meeting America's Energy Needs, 1978; contbr. articles to profl. jours. Coord. employee campaign United Way Dallas, 1981-90, teamwalk March of Dimes, Dallas, 1981-87; nat. exploring com. Boy Scouts Am., Irving, Tex., 1982-92. Named Outstanding Young Lawyer Dallas, Dallas Assn. Young Lawyers, 1989; recipient Cert. Recognition United Way, 1983. Mem. ABA, Tex. Bar Assn., Dallas Bar Assn. (Outstanding Com. Chair award 1998), Trial Lawyers Am., Baylor U. Alumni Assn. (scholarship com. 1980-81). Republican. Methodist. Office: Hughes & Luce LLP 1717 Main St Ste 2800 Dallas TX 75201-4685

KENT, DEBORAH WARREN, hypnotherapist, consultant, lecturer; b. N.Y.C., May 6, 1947; d. Fred Warren and Margo (Lefebre) North. BS in Spl. Edn., U. Cin., 1969; MS in Counseling, CUNY, Hunter Coll., 1973; cert. master level hypnotherapist, Am. Hypnosis Tng. Acad., Silver Spring, Md., 1987; MSW, Columbia U., 1997. Cert. clin. mental health counselor, social worker; nat. cert. counselor; nat. cert. clin. hypnotherapist. Remediation specialist, counselor, psychometrist N.Y.C. Bd. Edn., 1973-79; cons. on assessment and remediation, N.Y.C., 1979-81; prodn. mgr. The Singing Experience, N.Y.C., 1981-83; hypnotherapist Inst. for Hypnotherapy, N.Y.C., 1983-85; pvt. practice hypnotherapy and counseling, N.Y.C., 1985—; conducted workshops and seminars in clin. hypnosis, comm. skills and tng., stress mgmt.; lectr. to bus. and univs.; vocat. specialist Alternatives for Growth, N.J.; cons. vocat. case mgmt. assessment Ams. with Disabilities Act; social work cons. personal svc. unit Nat. Maritime Union, N.Y.C., chem. dependency coord., 1977—, clin. svcs. utilization rev. coord., USCG liaison. Author, columnist Ofcl. Map and Guide mag., 1990-91. Action writer Nat. Abortion Rights Action League, Washington, 1987—; co-developer Counselors Legis. Action Support System, 1989; v.p. Joint Coun. for Mental health Svcs., 1989-97. Recipient Profl. Svc. award Am. Mental Health Counselors Assn., 1992. Fellow Am. Acad. Pain Mgmt., Am. Assn. Profl. Hypnotherapists (cert.); mem. ACA, ASCD (N.Y.C. br.), NASW (N.Y.C. chpt., chem. dependency com.), Nat. Certified Counselors, Am. Mental Health Counselors Assn., Nat. Bd. Cert. Clin. Hypnotherapists (diplomate, examining bd., chairperson ethics com. 1993-97), Acad. Clin. Mental Health Counselors, Cert. Clin. Mental Health Counselors (approved clin. supr.), Nat. Soc. Neurolinguistic Programming (cert.), Am. Assn. for Assessment in Counseling (bd. dirs.), Am. Acad. Experts in Traumatic Stress (diplomate), N.Y. Mental Health Counselors Assn. (legis. rep. 1989-95, v.p. 1989-91), N.Y. Counselors Assn. (Legis. Svc. award 1991). Avocations: acting, singing, performing. Home and Office: 355 S End Ave New York NY 10280-1005

KENT, EDGAR ROBERT, JR., investment banker; b. Balt., May 28, 1941; s. E. Robert and Marian (Mueller) K.; children: E. Robert, Josephine Townsend, Louise Daniel. B.S., Princeton U., 1963; M.B.A., Columbia U., 1966; J.D., U. Md., 1975. CFA. Mng. dir. BT Alex. Brown Inc., Balt., 1968—; bd. dirs. Novatec Co. Trustee Calvert Sch., Balt., Ctr. Stage, Balt., Endowment Fund of U. Md., Balt. Cmty. Found. Home: 103 Castlewood Rd Baltimore MD 21210-1360 Office: BT Alex.Brown Inc 1 South St Baltimore MD 21202-3220

KENT, E(VERETT) ALLEN, performing arts administrator; b. Ronan, Mont., Oct. 16, 1938; s. Douglas George Kent and Fern Louise Hickman-Kent; m. Janice Gay Gustafson-Kent, June 2, 1962 (div. Mar. 1969); 1 child, Kyla Kolleen; m. Gloria Madeline Sontag-Kent, Mar. 21, 1969 (div. Apr. 6, 1990); 1 child, Patrick. BA, U. Wash., 1965, MA, 1967; PhD (abd), Wayne State U., 1974. Actor Aqua Theater, 1958, Bellevue Playbarn, 1959; actor-technician Erie Playhouse, 1960; stage mgr. KING-TV, 1965; stage mgr. sch. drama U. Wash., 1965-66; stage mgr. A Contemporary Theater, 1966; tech. dir., lighting designer Pitts. Playhouse, 1966-67; dir., designer, tech. dir., instr. Florissant Valley C.C., St. Louis, 1967-69; tech. dir. Mo. Repertory Theatre, Kansas City, 1969-70; dir., designer Ea. Washington State Coll., Cheney, 1969-73; dir. Performing Arts Ctr. U. Alaska, Anchorage, 1975-80, assoc. prof., chair dept. theater and dance, 1975-80; CEO Alaska Theatrical Svcs., Inc., Eagle River, 1974-87, KAE Enterprises, Ltd., Eagle River, 1987-90, Kent Artist Svcs., N.Y.C., 1990—; mng. dir. Denishawn Repertory Dance Co., N.Y., N.J., 1991-93; exec. dir. Jennifer Muller/The Works Dance Co., 1990-91; exec. dir., CEO Williams Ctr. for Arts, Rutherford, N.J., 1992-93; producing artistic dir. Music Theatre North, Potsdam, N.Y., 1993-94; gen. mgr. Garth Fagan Dance, Rochester, N.Y., 1995-96; salesperson Limelight Prodns., Inc., Lee, Mass., 1996-97; CEO Am. Theatrical Svcs., 1996—; artistic dir. Spokane Civic Theatre, 1971; arts and crafts specialist State of Alaska Dept. Commerce and Econ. Devel., 1974-75; lighting designer Alaska Repertory Theatre, Anchorage, 1977; lobbyist Anchorage Faculty Assn. U. Alaska, 1978-80; founder dept. theatre U. Alaska, Anchorage, 1976; arts cons. Actors Studio, Town Hall, N.Y.C., 1991; dance panelist N.J. State Coun. on Arts, 1991-93. With U.S. Army, 1961-67. Recipient Artist award Alaska State Coun. Arts, 1980. Mem. Soc. Stage Dirs. and Choreographers, Actors' Equity Assn. Roman Catholic. Avocations: hunting, fishing.

KENT, GEORGIA L., obstetrician-gynecologist, healthcare executive; b. N.Y.C., May 30, 1950; d. Harry J. and Eva R. K. BS in Biology (hons.), U. Pitts., 1971; MD, U. Pa., 1975; MBA, George Washington U., 1991. Diplomate Am. Bd. Obstetricians-Gynecologists; MD, Colo., Calif., N.Y., N.J., Pa. Sr. instr. ob-gyn. Hahnemann U., Phila., 1979-82; obstetrician-gynecologist Kaiser Group Health Assn., Washington, 1982-90; med. dir. Pacificare, Fountain Valley, Calif., 1991-93, Denver, 1993-94; v.p. med. svcs. The Prudential Ins. Co. of Am., Prudential Healthcare, Roseland, N.J., 1994-96; potter, healthcare cons. self employed, West Orange, N.J., 1997-99, Pitts., 1999—; guest lectr. U. Calif. Riverside, 1992-93, Denver U., 1993-94. Contbg. author, featured in: (book) Women in Medicine and Management: A Mentoring Guide, 1995; exhibited ceramics and pottery in N.J. Ctr. for Visual Arts Mem. Show, 1997, 98. Mem. Am. Coll. Obstetricians & Gynecologists, Am. Coll. Physician Execs. Avocations: skier, swimmer, scuba diver, greyhound rescue/adoption, potter. Office: Georgia L Kent MD 90 Sullivan Dr West Orange NJ 07052-2263

KENT, HARRY ROSS, construction executive, lay worker; b. Upland, Pa., Oct. 17, 1921; s. Bernard Cleveland and Edith Mary (Johnson) K.; m. Aurelia Naomi Canady, Jan. 15, 1945; children: Jennifer Gayle, Edith Marie. BS in Physics and Chemistry, Coll. William and Mary. Instr. physics Citadel, 1947-51; with Canady Constrn. Co., 1951-78, sec.-treas., 1960-74, pres., 1974-78; v.p. K.C. Stier & Co., Inc., 1974-78; v.p., sec. Stier, Kent and Canady, Inc., 1978—; mem. exec. coun. World Meth. Coun., 1991-96. Mem. commn. on stewardship and fin., Asbury Meml. Meth. Ch., Charleston, 1949—, treas. 1951-58, 68—, lay mem. ann. conf. 1955-70, 80—, trustee, 1963-74, chmn. long-range planning com., 1957-70, tchr. ch. sch.; mem. bd. bldg. and ch. location Charleston Dist. United Meth. Ch., 1958—, pres. bd. missions and ch. extension, 1958—, dist. trustees, 1960—, chmn. bd. dist. trustees, 1984—, chmn. bd. missions, 1975—; mem. bd. lay activities S.C. ann. conf. United Meth. Ch., 1957-96, mem. coordinating coun., 1960-68, vice-chmn. continuing com. on merger, conf. lay leader, 1970-80, chmn. equitable salary commn., 1984-88, mem. coun. on fin. and adminstrn., 1988-96, vice chair 1992-95, chair 1995-96, del. Southea. jurisdiction conf., 1960, 64, 72, 76, 80, 84, 88, 92, 96, gen. conf. 1966, 68, 70, 72, 76, 80, 84, 88, 92, gen. coun. on ministries, 1980-88, chmn. Africa sect. of advance com., mem. gen. bd. discipleship, 1988-96; conf. pres. United Meth. Men, 1984-92; mem. exec. bd. Coastal Carolina coun. Boy Scouts Am., 1960—, chmn. Charleston dist. bd., 1967; various exec. positions St. Andrew's schs. PTA, 1963-68; bd. dirs. Piedmont Nursing Ctr., 1967-82, treas. 1970-82; vice chmn. civil engring. adv. bd. Trident Tech. Coll., Charleston, 1969-71, chmn. 1970-80; pres. Charleston Boys Coun., 1982-86, 91-94, v.p. 1987-91; mem. S.C. State Licensing Bd. for Contractors, 1980—, vice chair 1989-91, chair 1992—. Lt. cmmdr. USNR, WWII. Recipient God and Country award, Scouters award, Scoutmasters Key 60 Yr. Vet. award, Silver Beaver award Boy Scouts Am., God and Svc. award United Meth. Ch./Boy Scouts Am. Mem. ASTM, Associated Gen. Contractors, Am. Phys. Soc., Am. Assn. Physics, Tchrs., Charleston Trident C. of C. Home: 2935 Doncaster Dr Charleston SC 29414-6723

KENT, HOWARD LEES, obstetrician, gynecologist; b. Norristown, Pa., Nov. 27, 1930; s. Howard Linnaeus and Margaret (Cairns) K.; m. Margaret Louise Hermanutz, Oct. 17, 1959; children: Howard Lees Jr., Lisanne, Margaret, Kristyn. AB in Zoology, U. Pa., 1953; MD, Hahnemann U., 1958. Diplomate Am. Bd. Ob-Gyn. Intern Misericordia div. Mercy Cath. Med. Ctr., Phila., 1958-59; resident Hahnemann U., 1959-62; pvt. practice Hammonton, N.J., 1964-81; prof. Thomas Jefferson U., Phila., 1982—. Author: (with others) Vaginitis/Vaginosis, 1991; editor: Proceedings-Obstetrical Society of Philadelphia, 1980-82; contbr. articles to profl. jours. Fellow Internat. Soc. for Study of Vulvovaginal Disease, Royal Soc. Medicine, Am. Coll. Ob-gyn. (key contact), Am. Coll. Surgeons, Coll. Physicians of Phila. (libr. com. 1980-89), Obstet. Soc. Phila. (asst. sec. 1978-81); mem. N.J. Ob-gyn. Soc., Vesper Club, U. Pa. Alumni. Republican. Avocations: travel, photography.

KENT, JAMES A., consulting chemical engineer, author, consultant; b. New Britain, Conn., Feb. 10, 1922; m. Anita C. Barbe, Feb. 20, 1943; children: James, David, Nicholas, Edward, Joseph. B.S. in Chem. Engring, W.Va. U., 1943, Ph.D., 1950. Registered profl. engr. Research engr. Dow Chem. Co., Midland, Mich., 1950-52; research group leader Monsanto Chem. Co., Nitro, W.Va., 1952-54; prof. chem. and nuclear engring. W.Va. U., 1954-67, assoc. dean engring., 1963-67; dean coll. engring. Mich. Tech. U., Houghton, 1967-78; dean Coll. Engring. and Sci., U. Detroit, 1978-91, cons. chem. engr., 1992—. Editor: Handbook of Industrial Chemistry, 1966, 74, 83, 92; contbr. articles to profl. jours. Mem. Gov's Adv. Com. on State Tech. Services, W. Va., 1966-67, Gov.'s Transition Team mem., 1996-97; mem. Artificial Heart Com., Nat. Heart and Lung Inst., 1968-73; adv. com. materials program Office of Tech. Assessment, 1975-77; adv. com. Mich. Transp. Research Program, 1976-80; mem. Mich. Gov.'s Planning Com. on Hazardous/Toxic Wastes, 1977-79; chmn. Mich. Gov.'s Com. to Develop State Hazardous Waste Mgmt. Plan, 1980-85. Served to 1st lt. C.E. Aus, 1943-46. Recipient numerous awards engring. and sci. hon. socs. Fellow Am. Inst. Chemists; mem. AIChE, Water Environ Fedn., Am. Soc. Engring. Edn., U.Va. U. Chem. Engring. Acad. (charter), Sigma Xi, Tau Beta Pi. Home: 898 Stewart Pl Morgantown WV 26505-1805

KENT, JEFFREY DONALD, lawyer; b. Whittier, Calif., Apr. 30, 1967; s. Michael Floyd and Cheryl Ann (Gautsche) K. BA in Econs., U. Calif., Irvine, 1989, BA in Polit. Sci., 1989; JD, Western State U., 1992. Bar: Calif. 1992, U.S. Dist. Ct. (ctrl. and ea. dists.) Calif. 1993, U.S. Dist. Ct. (so. dist.) Calif. 1995, U.S. Ct. Appeals (9th cir.) 1995, U.S. Supreme Ct. 1996. Law clk. Orange County Pub. Defender, Santa Ana, Calif., 1990-91, Orange County Dist. Atty., Santa Ana, 1991-92; assoc. Bridgman, Mordkin, Gould & Shapiro, Fountain Valley, Calif., 1993-95; ptnr. Law Offices McDonnell & Kent, Inc., La Habra, Calif., 1995—. Mem. Orange County Bar Assn., State Bar Calif., Calif. Pub. Defenders Assn., Assn. Fed. Def. Attys., Calif. Attys. for Criminal Justice, Calif. Deuce Defenders Assn., Nat. Assn. Criminal Def. Lawyers. Democrat. Avocations: travel, scuba diving. E-mail: jdkent@earthlink.net. Fax: 562 694-4280. Office: 418 E La Habra Blvd La Habra CA 90631

KENT, JEFFREY FRANKLIN, baseball player; b. Bellflower, Calif., Mar. 7, 1968. Grad., Edison H.S., Calif. Played 2d base Toronto Blue Jays, 1992; 2d baseman N.Y. Mets, 1992-96, San Francisco Giants, 1996—. Office: San Francisco Giants 3Com Park at Candlestick Pt San Francisco CA 94124*

KENT, JILL ELSPETH, academic healthcare adminstrator, lawyer; b. Detroit, June 1, 1948; d. Seymour and Grace (Edelman) K.; m. Mark Elliott Solomons, Aug. 20, 1978. BA, U. Mich., 1970; JD, George Washington U., 1975, LLM, 1979. Bar: D.C. 1975. Mgmt. intern U.S. Dept. Transp., Washington, 1971-73; staff analyst Office Mgmt. and Budget, Exec. Office of Pres., Washington, 1974-76; legis. counsel U.S. Treasury Dept., Washington, 1976-78, dir. legis. reference divsn. Healthcare Financing Adminstrn., 1978-80; sr. budget examiner Office Mgmt. and Budget, Exec. Office Pres., Washington, 1980-84; chief Treasury, Gen. Svcs. Office of Mgmt. and budget, Washington, 1984-85; dep. asst. sec. for deptl. fin. and planning U.S. Dept. Treasury, Washington, 1985-86, dep. asst. sec. for dept. fin. and mgmt., 1986-88, asst. sec. of treasury, 1988-89; CFO U.S. Dept. State, Washington, 1989-93, acting under sec. of state for mgmt., 1991; exec. devel. program Office of Mgmt. and Budget, Washington, 1984; CFO George Washington U. Med. Ctr., Washington, 1993-97; v.p. IPAC, 1997-98, The Columbus Group; pres., CEO Atlantic Threadworks Inc.; prin. Coun. Excellence in Govt., 1993—; gen. mgr. The Frogeye Co., 1995—; adj. prof. pub. policy, U. Md., 1993—. Bd. dirs. Mobile Med. Care INc., 1987-91; Trustee Newport Sch., 1988-91, Washington Civic Symphony, 1994-95; bd. dirs. China Found., 1997—; sr. counselor Atlantic Coun. U.S., 1997—. Recipient Adminstrs. award Healthcare Financing Adminstrn., 1980; named on of Top 40 Performers, Mgmt. mag., 1987, Disting. Svc. award Dept. Treasury, 1989, Am. Assn. Govt. Accts. award, 1992, Disting. Svc. award Dept. State, 1993. Mem. ABA, D.C. Bar Assn., Pres's. Coun. on Mgmt. Improvement, CFO Roundtable Healthcare Forum, Fin. Execs. Inst., Exec. Women in Govt. (treas. 1991-92, pres. 1992-93), Va. Assn. of Female Execs. (adv. coun. 1990), Coun. Excellence in Govt. (prin. 1993—). Republican. Home: 2419 California St NW Washington DC 20008-1615 Office: 2101 Wilson Blvd Arlington VA 22201-3062 *My goal has always been to contribute and make a positive impact. In my career, I have been privleged to participate in events related to the restructure of the Federal Budget, the end of the Cold War and the reevaluation in health care. It's been an outstanding return on investment.*

KENT, JOHN BRADFORD, lawyer; b. Jacksonville, Fla., Sept. 5, 1939; s. Frederick Heber and Norma Cleveland (Futch) K.; m. Monett Powers, Dec. 18, 1969; children: Monett, Susan, Sally, Katherine. AB, Yale U., 1961; JD, U. Fla., 1964; LLM in Taxation, NYU, 1965. Bar: Fla., 1964, U.S. Dist. Ct. (mid. dist.) Fla. 1965, U.S. Tax Ct., 1965, U.S. Dist. (so. dist.) Fla., 1981, Neb., 1995, U.S. Ct. Appeals (11th cir.), U.S. Supreme Ct., 1973. Assoc. Ulmer, Murchison, Kent, Ashby & Ball, Jacksonville, 1965-67; ptnr., shareholder Kent, Watts & Durden, P.A. and predecessor firms, Jacksonville, 1967-85; shareholder Carlton, Field, Ward, Emmanuel, Smith, Cutler & Kent, Jacksonville, 1985-88, Kent, Crawford & Gooding, P.A., Jacksonville, 1988—. Jacksonville Legal Aid Soc. (past bd. dirs.), Fla. Cmty. Coll (past pres., trustee), Children's Home Soc. Fla. (past pres., bd. dirs.). Mem. Nat. Assn. Theatre Owners Fla. (bd. dirs., officer 1969—), Rotary (past officer, Paul Harris Fellow). Office: Kent Crawford & Gooding PA 225 Water St Ste 900 Jacksonville FL 32202-5142

KENT, JULIE, ballet dancer, actress, model; b. Bethesda, Md., July 11, 1969; d. Charles Lindbergh and Jennifer Elsie (Machirus) Cox; m. Victor Barbee, 1996. Grad. high sch., Potomac, Md. Apprentice Am. Ballet Theatre, N.Y.C., 1985-86, mem. corps de ballet, 1986-1990, soloist, 1990-93, prin. dancer, 1993—. Starring role (film) Dancers, 1986; performed as a guest artist nationally and internationally. Recipient Prix de Lausanne Internat. Ballet competition, 1986, 1st prize at Erik Bruhn Competition in Toronto, 1993; named one of 50 Most Beautiful People, People Mag., 1993. Office: Am Ballet Theatre 890 Broadway Fl 3 New York NY 10003-1211

KENT, LINDA GAIL, dancer; b. Buffalo, Sept. 21, 1946; d. Jerol Edward and Dorismae (Kohler) K.; m. Nicholas Wolff Lyndon, June 9, 1996. BS, Juilliard Sch., 1968. Dancer Alvin Ailey Am. Dance Theater, 1968-74, then prin. dancer, 1970-74; prin. dancer Paul Taylor Dance Co., N.Y.C., 1975-89; faculty Juilliard Sch., 1984—; artist-in-residence Union Theological Seminary, N.Y. Mem. Am. Guild Mus. Artists, Actors Equity. Democrat. Unitarian. Home: 91 Payson Ave New York NY 10034-2722 Office: The Juilliard Sch Dance Divsn 60 Lincoln Center Plz New York NY 10023-6588

KENT, M. ELIZABETH, lawyer; b. N.Y.C., Nov. 17, 1943; d. Francis J. and Hannah (Bergman) K. AB, Vassar Coll. magna cum laude, 1964; AM, Harvard U., 1965, PhD, 1974; JD, Georgetown U., 1978. Bar: D.C. 1978, U.S. Dist. Ct. D.C. 1978, U.S. Ct. Appeals (D.C. cir.) 1978, U.S. Supreme Ct. 1983, U.S. Dist. Ct. Md. 1985. From lectr. to asst. prof. history U. Ala., Birmingham, 1972-74; assoc. Santarelli and Gimer, Washington, 1978; sole practice Washington, 1978—. Mem. Ripon Soc., Cambridge and Washington, 1968-93; rsch. dir. Howard M. Miller for Congress, Boston, 1972; vol. campaigns John V. Lindsay for Mayor, 1969, John V. Lindsay for Pres., 1972, John B. Anderson for Pres., 1980. Woodrow Wilson fellow 1964-65; Harvard U. fellow 1968-69. Mem. ABA, ACLU, D.C. Bar Assn., Women's Bar Assn., D.C. Assn. Criminal Def. Lawyers, Superior Ct. Trial Lawyers Assn., Nat. Women's Polit. Caucus, Phi Beta Kappa. Republican. Avocations: history, politics. Home: 35 E St NW Apt 810 Washington DC 20001-1520 Office: 601 Indiana Ave NW Ste 605 Washington DC 20004-2907

KENT, MOLLIE, writer, publishing executive, editor; b. Abilene, Tex., July 21, 1933; d. Henry Lee and Clyde Radia (Free) Summers; m. Paul Raymond Kintzinger, June 15, 1954 (div. July 1982); children: Katrina, Alice, Sarah. Student, Tulsa (Okla.) U., 1962-64, U. N.Mex., 1970-72. Lic. insurance and real estate agt., N.Mex. Owner, pub. Jemez Pub. Co., Jemez Springs, N.Mex., 1976-81, Albuquerque and Bernalillo, N.Mex., 1976-81; owner Bellwether Pub., La Plata, N.Mex., 1990-99; pub., editor S.W. Chronicle mag., La Plata, 1999—; pub., editor Jemez Mountain Views, 1976-80, Sandoval County Rev., 1977-80, Sandia Sun, 1979-81; assoc. editor, advt. mgr. Aztec (N.Mex.) Local News, 1993-98. Republican. Avocations: writing, travel, music, family. Home: PO Box 360 La Plata NM 87418-0360

KENT, PAULA, public relations, marketing and management consultant, lecturer; b. N.Y.C.; d. John and Estelle (Frye) Smith; BS, State Tchrs. Coll., Worcester, Mass., 1939; MS, Boston U., 1941; m. Stanley J. Lloyd, Jan. 23, 1943; children: Diane Adrienne Noel, Robin Michele Cheri, Kevin Christopher Kent, Gisele Nicolette Jolie. Methods engr. Internat. Bus. Machines, 1941-42; personnel dir., fashion editor Daily Jour., San Diego, also radio sta. KSDJ, 1946-48; fashion and beauty editor, columnist The San Diego Union, 1949-64; promotion dir. The San Diego Union and the Evening Tribune, 1948-71, also UCLA Extension Div. Faculty, 1961-63; pub. relations, mktg. and mgmt. cons., 1970—; v.p. La Jolla Clin. Labs., Inc., 1970-81. Lectr. mktg. workshop tour, speaker at seminars, Brussels, London, Paris, Madrid, 1972; speaker nat. and regional confs. in maj. U.S. cities; del. Nat. Fedn. Press. Women Touring Russia, 1973. Formerly active ARC, Am. Cancer Soc., Med. Aux. San Diego. Officer USN; lt. (sr.g.) USCG, 1942-45. Recipient over 158 awards 1950—, including: 39 nat., 18 western states, over 100 Calif. state awards, 13 Lulus L.A. Advt. Women's Assn., 1 local award, resulting from ann. competitions sponsored by Los Angeles Advt. Women's Club, Nat. Newspaper Publs. Assn., Calif. Press Women, Los Angeles Sales Promotion Execs. Assn., Nat. Fedn. Press Women, Editor and Pub. Mag.; recipient Outstanding Service award Boy Scouts Am., 1962, 65; civic awards City of San Diego, Distinguished Service award Investment Edn. Inst., Detroit, 1969, Golden Spear award Twin Cities Sales Promotion Execs. Assn., Mpls., 1965; Outstanding Service thru Annual Investment Clinics N.Y. Stock Exchange, 1964, L.A. Theta Sigma Phi Walter O'Malley Unique Coverage award, 1968; named Woman of Achievement San Diego, 1958, 59, 64, Woman of Valor, 1958, Woman of Year, San Diego, 1965, Woman of Achievement, Nat. Fedn. Bus. and Profl. Women's Clubs, 1966; Advt. Man of Distinction, San Diego, 1970, Don award, Legion of Portola, 1968.; fellow Boston U. 1940-41. Mem. Advt. and Sales Club San Diego (dir. 1951-71), Sales and Marketing Execs. Club San Diego (pres. 1970-71), Personnel Mgmt. Assn. (hon. mem., plaque 1963), Sales and Mktg. Execs. Internat. (dir. at large 1971-73), Sales Promotion Execs. Assn. Los Angeles (Man of Year 1965), Am. Advt. Fedn. (western region chmn. edn. com., mem. nat. edn. com. 1971-72) Nat. Newspaper Promotion Assn. (pres. Western region 1964, dir. 1968-70, chmn. western regional conv. 1964), Calif. Assn. Press Women, Nat. Fedn. Press Women, Internat. Newspaper Promotion Assn. (bd. dirs. 1971-73), Am. Mgmt. Assn. (San Diego pres's coun. bus., profl. womens' clubs outstanding svc. plaque 1969). Roman Catholic. Editor: Monthly Bull., Personnel Mgmt. Assn., 1955-59, monthly bull., Sales Execs. Club. Chmn. San Diego's Ann. Giant Sales Rally, 1953-55, 70-71, co-chmn., 1964, 65; chmn. Advt. Recognition Week Campaign, 1953-54, Nat. Unltd. Hydroplane Races, San Diego, 1953-54, sponsor rep. Evening Tribune; pub. relations advisor Nat. Mrs. Am. Pageant, honored by London Press Club Members Luncheon, 1970, San Diego 200th Anniversary celebration; producer, emcee ann. Holiday for Housewives, San Diego, 1955-60; producer, co-ordinator U. Calif., Today's World, San Diego, 1962; exec. dir., producer, dir. San Diego Ann. Golden Gloves Boxing Tournament, 1961-68; producer San Diego Ann. Metrotennis Championships, 1952-70; dir. Ann Power Boat Regatta, 1950-62; exec. dir. Ann Jr. Golf Championships; dir. Ann. Hole-in-One Tournament, 1951-70; master ceremonies, producer, emcee Gentlemen of Distinction Awards, 1967, 68, 69; producer/dir. San Diego Advt. Salesrama, 1971; producer, dir. master ceremonies San Diego Ann. Woman of Yr. Awards, 1967, 68, 69; producer/designer 34 exhibits for convs. and fairs; developed and produced A Day in San Diego for European Travel Commn., 1964; produced and emceed Ann. Boy Scout Jamboree Stage Show, 1967. Del. Nat. Fedn Press Women touring Russia. Commd. ensign, Women's Reserve, USNR, 1942, transferred USCG, served from ensign to lt. (sr.g.), 1943-46. Avocation: world travel. Office: PO Box 2243 La Jolla CA 92038-2243

KENT, PHILIP, communications executive. Pres. Turner Home Entertainment Turner Broadcasting Sys., Atlanta; pres. Turner Broadcasting Systems Internat. Inc., Atlanta. Office: Turner Broadcasting sys 1 CNN Ctr PO Box 105366 Atlanta GA 30348-5366*

KENT, RICHARD B., secondary education educator. English tchr. Mountain Valley High Sch., Rumford, Maine. Named Maine State English

Tchr. of Yr., 1993. Office: Mountain Valley High Sch Hancock St Rumford ME 04276-1599*

KENT, ROBERT B., artist, educator; b. Cleve., June 23, 1924; m. Celeste Zalk, Dec. 18, 1948; children: William, Kenneth, Brian. BA, Western Res. U., 1950, MA, 1951; postgrad, Columbia U., 1952-53; EdD, U. Calif., Berkeley, 1968. Cert. expressive therapist. Art instr. El Paso (Tex.) City Schs., 1953-54, Stockton (Calif.) Unified Schs., 1954-56, Tamalpais High Sch., Mill Valley, Calif., 1956-67; assoc. prof. U. Ga., Athens, 1967-93, emeritus, 1993—; lectr. Denmark, Sweden and Israel. Mem. editorial bd. Ill. State U. Publ.; contbr. articles to profl. jours. Mem. Am. Art Therapy Assn., Nat. Expressive Therapy Assn., World Assn. for Prevention Drug and Alcohol Abuse (internat. bd. govs.). Home: 332 Stonybrook Cir Athens GA 30605-6029

KENT, ROBERT BRYDON, law educator; b. Lowell, Mass., Dec. 2, 1921; s. Silas Stanley and Madeleine (Brydon) K.; m. Barbara Tuttle, Mar. 31, 1951; children: Robert Brydon, Dorothy Clarke, Elizabeth Montgomery, Hugh Clarke. AB, Harvard Coll., 1943; LLB, Boston U., 1949. Bar: Mass. 1948. Pvt. practice Ware, Mass., 1948-50; instr. Boston U. Sch. Law, 1950-52, asst. prof., 1952-54, prof., 1954-81; prof. law, dean U. Zambia Sch. Law, 1970-72; dir. Law Practice Inst., Zambia, 1970-71; Ford fellow in law teaching Harvard U. Law Sch., 1960-61, part-time vis. prof., 1973-74; vis. prof. Cornell Law Sch., 1980-81, prof., 1981-92, prof. emeritus, 1992—, assoc. dean, 1982-86; hon. vis. fellow Trinity Coll., Oxford U., 1976; reporter com. on civil rules Supreme Ct. R.I., Superior Ct. R.I., Dist. Ct. R.I.; cons. criminal procedure; disting. vis. prof. Roger Williams U. Sch. Law, 1997—. Author: (with Austin W. Scott) Cases and Other Materials on Civil Procedure, 1967, Rhode Island Practice: Civil Rules with Commentaries, 1969. Moderator Town of Lexington, Mass., 1965-70, selectman, 1977-81; vice chmn. Civil Liberties Union of Mass., 1966-69; exec. com. Law Assn. of Zambia, 1970-72; trustee Kimball Union Acad., pres., 1973-76. Served with U.S. Army, 1943-46. Fulbright prof. sch. law U. Zambia, 1988. Mem. Am. Law Inst. Democrat. Unitarian. Home: 1 Doran Farm Ln Lexington MA 02420-2128 Office: Cornell Law Sch Myron Taylor Hall Ithaca NY 14853

KENT, ROBERT JOHN, marine biologist; b. N.Y.C., May 20, 1948; s. Stanley Paul and Mary Katherine (Ladany) K. BA, SUNY, Buffalo, 1970; MA in Environ. Studies, SUNY, Stony Brook, 1984. Instr. Butler County Community Coll., Butler, Pa., 1975-78; coop. extension agt., 4-H natural resources specialist Cornell Coop. Extension, Riverhead, N.Y., 1978-89; sea grant program coord. N.Y. Sea Grant, Riverhead, 1989—, interim assoc. dir., 1995; adj. lectr. Marine Scis. Rsch. Ctr., SUNY, Stony Brook, 1994—. Contbr. articles to profl. publs. Recipient Epsilon Sigma Phi Outstanding Team Achievement award, 1992, Outstanding Marine Edn. Program award Coastal Extension Profls., Ithaca, 1984, 86, Outstanding Program Achievement award Cornell U., 1986, State Early Career award Epsilon Sigma Phi, 1988, Northeast Coop. Extension Dirs. award, Shoreham, N.Y., 1996. Mem. Soc. for Ecol. Restoration, Coop. Extension 4-H Agts. (spl. svc. award 1981), Nat. Marine Educators Assn. Episcopalian. Avocations: canoeing, fishing, cultural activities. E-mail: RJK13@cornell.edu. Office: New York Sea Grant 3059 Sound Ave Riverhead NY 11901-1115

KENT, ROBERTA B., literary consultant; b. N.Y.C., Sept. 7, 1945. BA magna cum laude, NYU, 1967, MA, 1969; postgrad., Princeton U., 1967-68. Asst. to head literary dept. Creative Mgmt. Assocs., N.Y.C., 1969-70; asst. to pres. Curtis Brown Ltd., N.Y.C., 1970-72, literary agt., v.p. dept. motion pictures, 1978-79; ptnr., literary agt. W.B. Agy., N.Y.C., 1972-78; literary agt., v.p. dept. motion pictures Kohner-Levy Agy., Los Angeles, 1979-81; literary agt. The Ufland Agy., Beverly Hills, Calif., 1981-83; literary agt., v.p. literary dept. S.T.E. Representation, Ltd., Beverly Hills, 1983-91; ind. cons. Cowling, Heysell, Plouse, Ingalls & Moore, Medford, Oreg., 1991-96, Black, Chapman, Webber & Stevens, Medford, Oreg., 1996-99, Frohnmayer, Deatherage, Pratt, Jamieson, Clarke & Moore, Medford, Oreg., 1999—. Mem. Phi Beta Kappa. Democrat. Avocations: camping, hiking, horseback riding. Office: 2592 E Barnett Rd Medford OR 97504

KENT, SAMUEL B., federal judge; b. 1949. BA, U. Tex., 1971, JD, 1975. Pvt. practice Royston, Rayzor, Vickery & Williams, Galveston, Tex., 1975-90; judge U.S. Dist. Ct. (so. dist.) Tex., Galveston, 1990—; adj. prof. bus. and ins. law Tex. A&M U., Galveston, 1981-86, proctor in admiralty, 1976—. Mem. Maritime Law Assn. Office: US Courthouse 601 Rosenberg St Ste 613 Galveston TX 77550-1738*

KENT, SUSAN, library director, consultant; b. N.Y.C., Mar. 18, 1944; d. Elias and Minnie (Barnett) Solomon; m. Eric Goldberg, Mar. 27, 1966 (div. Mar. 1991); children: Evan, Jessica, Joanna; m. Rolly Kent, Dec. 20, 1991. BA in English Lit. with honors, SUNY, 1965; MS, Columbia U., 1966. Libr., sr. libr. N.Y. Pub. Libr., 1965-67, br. mgr. Donnell Art Libr., 1967-68; reference libr. Paedergaat br. Bklyn. Pub. Libr., 1971-72; reference libr. Finkelstein Meml. Libr., Spring Valley, N.Y., 1974-76; coord. adult and young adult svcs. Tucson Pub. Libr., 1977-80, acting libr. dir., 1982, dep. libr. dir., 1980-87; mng. dir. Ariz. Theatre Co., Tucson and Phoenix, 1987-89; dir. Mpls. Pub. Libr. and Info. Ctr., 1990-95; city libr. L.A. Pub. Libr., 1995—; tchr. Pima C.C., Tucson, 1978, grad. libr. sch. U. Ariz., Tucson, 1978, 79; panelist Ariz. Commn. Arts, 1981-85; reviewer pub. programs NEH, 1985, 89, panelist challenge grants, 1986-89, panelist state programs, 1988; cons. to librs. and nonprofit instns., 1989-90, 92—; mem. bd. devel. and fundraising Child's Play, Phoenix, 1983; bd. dirs., mem. organizing devel. and fundraising com. Flagstaff (Ariz.) Symphony Orch., 1988; cons., presenter workshops Young Adult Svcs. divsn. ALA, 1986-88; bd. advisors UCLA Grad. Sch. Edn. and Info. Scis., 1998—; presenter in field. Contbr. articles to profl. jours. Chair arts and culture com. Tucson Tomorrow, 1981-85; bd. dirs., v.p. Ariz. Dance Theatre, 1984-86; bd. dirs. women's studies adv. coun. U. Ariz., 1985-90, Arizonans for Cultural Devel., 1987-89, YWCA Mpls., 1991-92; commr. Ariz. Commn. on Arts, 1983-87; participant Leadership Mpls., 1990-91. Fellow Sch. Libr. Sci., Columbia U., 1965-66. Mem. ALA (membership com. S.W. regional chair 1983-86, com. on appts. 1986-87, planning and budget assembly del. 1991-93, gov. coun. 1990-98, chair conf. com. 1996-97), Pub. Libr. Assn. (nominating com. 1980-82, v.p. 1986-87, pres. 1987-88, chair publs. assembly 1988-89, chair nat. conf. 1994, chair legis. com. 1994-95), Calif. Libr. Assn., Urban Librs. Coun. (exec. bd. 1994—, treas. 1996-98, vice chair/chair elect 1998, 99, chair 1999—), Libr. Adminstrn. and Mgmt. Assn. (John Cotton Dana Award com. 1994-95). Office: LA Pub Libr 630 W 5th St Los Angeles CA 90071-2002

KENT, THEODORE CHARLES, psychologist; b. June 7, 1948; m. Shirley Kent, June 7, 1948; children: Donald, Susan, Steven. *Mr. Kent is grateful that his three children turned out so well: Donald is vice-president of a high velocity internet company. Susan is a professor of anthropology at Old dominion University and Steven is a cardiologist. He is very fortunate in his marriage since his wife is such a caring person, not only to him, but as a social worker and an ombudsman. They have four lovely grandchildren. Their formula is: show love to children, keep track of them, teach them right from wrong. Their grandchildren's names are Danny, Lauren, Sam, and Julia.* BA, Yale U., 1935; MA, Columbia U., 1940, Mills Coll., 1953; PhD, U. So. Calif., 1951; DrRerumNat, Johannes Gutenberg U., Mainz, Germany, 1960. Diplomate in clin. psychology. Clin. psychologist, behavioral scientist USAF, 1951-65; chief psychologist USAF, Europe, 1956-60; head dept. behavioral sci. U. So. Colo., Pueblo, 1965-78, emeritus, 1978—; staff psychologsit Yuma Behavioral Health, Ariz., 1978-82, chief profl. svcs., 1982-83; dir. psychol. svcs. Rio Colorado Health Systems, Yuma, 1983-85; clin. psychologist, dir. mental health Ft. Yuma (Calif.) Indian Health Svc., USPHS, 1985-88; exec. dir. Human Sci. Ctr., San Diego, 1982-97. *Mr. Kent's life entailed struggle. There was struggle in finding the time he needed to write his thoughts into books. He enjoyed his clinical practice as a psychologist. One of his important insights was to see goodness as a quality evolving from the human capacity for abstraction, imagination, cognition together with a need for challenges. Singly these were products of natural selection but together this mix brought something new into the world. That is to highly value something that has no alterior gain - that exists only because it is wanted beyond survival. This represents a breakthrough in evolution.* Author: Skills in Living Together, 1983, Conflict Resolution, 1986, A Psychologist Answers Your Questions, 1987, Behind the Therapist's Notes, 1993, Mapping the Human Genome--Reality, Morality and Deity, 1995, Poems for Living, 1995, Genetic Engineering, Yes, No or Maybe--A Look At What's Ahead, 1997; author tests, including symbol arrangement test, 1952, internat. culture free non-verbal intelligence, 1957, self-other location chart, 1970, test of suffering, 1982; author plays and video Three Warriors Against Substance Abuse. Named Outstanding Prof., U. So. Colo., 1997. Fellow APA (disting. visitor undergrad. edn. program); mem. AAAS, Deutsche Gesellschaft fur Antropologie, Internat. Assn. Study of Symbols (founder, 1st pres. 1957-61), Japanese Soc. Study KTSA (hon. pres.). Home and Office: Townhouse G-64 4900 Telegraph Rd Ventura CA 93003-4131

KENT, THOMAS EDWARD, lawyer; b. Chgo., Jan. 29, 1957. BA in Sociology, U. Calif., Berkeley, 1979; JD, U. So. Calif., 1982. Bar: Calif. 1982, U.S. Dist. Ct. (cen. dist.) Calif., U.S. Dist. Ct. (no. dist.) Calif., U.S. Dist. Ct. (so. dist.) Calif., U.S. Ct. Appeals (9th cir.), U.S. Supreme Ct. Assoc. Fierstein & Sturman, L.A., 1982-87, Robinson, Diamant, Brill & Klausner, L.A., 1987-91; sole practitioner L.A., 1991—; Arbitrator L.A. County Bar Dispute Resolution Svcs. Mem. L.A. County Bar Assn., San Fernando Valley Bar Assn., Fin. Lawyers Conf., Bankruptcy Forum. FAX: 818-990-6792. Office: 16161 Ventura Blvd # 475 Encino CA 91436-2522

KENTON, JAMES ALAN, healthcare products executive; b. Chgo., Sept. 14, 1955. BBA, Loyola U., Chgo., 1977. CPA. Fin. analyst Am. Hosp. Supply Corp., McGaw Park, Ill., 1977-79, dir. planning, 1979-81, asst. controller, 1981-84, dir. fin., 1984-85; dir. new bus. devel. Kendall McGaw, Irvine, Calif., 1985-86; CFO, Intermedics Inc., Angleton, Tex., 1986-92, Eon Labs, Lake Forest, Ill., 1993-94; pres. Futuro Inc., Milford, Ohio, 1994-97, Beiersdorf Inc., Wilton, Conn., 1997—. Mem. AICPA. Office: Beiersdorf Inc 187 Danbury Rd Wilton CT 06897-4003*

KENTY, JANET ROGERS, nursing educator; b. Washington, Jan. 25, 1945; d. Howard Lewis and Alice Elizabeth (Smith) Rogers; m. Richard Donald McHugh, June 10, 1967 (div. Aug. 1978); 1 child, Kerry; m. Jay William Kenty, Aug. 5, 1978; children: Howard, Elizabeth. BSN, U. Mass. Amherst, 1967; MSN, Boston U., 1979; PhD, U. Conn., 1995. Instr. Cooley Dickinson Hosp., North Hampton, Mass., 1967-68; staff nurse Beverly (Mass.) Hosp., 1975-76; instr. Lynn (Mass.) Hosp. Sch. Nursing, 1976-78; asst. prof. Salve Regina U., Newport, R.I., 1978-85; coord. perinatal outreach edn. Women and Infants Hosp., Providence, 1985-87; vis. lectr. U. Mass., Dartmouth, 1987-95, asst. prof., 1996—. Author: (with Doenges and Moorhouse) Maternal-Newborn Care Plans, 1988. Mem. ANA, Nat. League for Nursing, R.I. Nurses Assn. (sec. dist. I 1993-95), Sigma Theta Tau, Phi Lambda Theta. Avocations: skiing, walking, in-line skating, swimming. Home: 222 Brookhaven Rd North Kingstown RI 02852-1976

KENVIN, ROGER LEE, writer, retired English educator; b. N.Y.C., May 26, 1926; s. James Marion and Gladys Irene (Macdonald) K.; m. Verna Rudd Trimble, Apr. 5, 1952; children: Brooke Trimble Kenvin Goldstein, Heather Trimble Kenvin Hietala. BA, Bowdoin Coll., 1949; MA, Harvard U., 1956; MFA, Yale U., 1959, DFA, 1961. Copywriter Crowell-Collier Pub., N.Y.C., 1950-53; tchr. Le Rosey, Rolle, Switzerland, 1953-55; prof. English, Mary Washington Coll., Fredericksburg, Va., 1959-68, chmn. dept. drama, 1970-82; prof., chmn. dept. speech and drama U. Notre Dame and St. Mary's Coll., South Bend, Ind., 1968-70; prof., chmn. dept. theatre and dance Calif. Poly. State U., San Luis Obispo, 1983-88. Author: (play) Krishnalight, 1976, (short stories) The Gaffer and Seven Fables, 1987, Harpo's Garden, 1997, The Cantabrigian Rowing Society's Saturday Night Bash, 1998, Trylons and Perispheres, 1999; contbr. short stories to lit. publs. With USN, 1944-46. Mem. Phi Beta Kappa. Home: 575 Fairview Ave Arcadia CA 91007-6736

KENYHERCZ, THOMAS MICHAEL, pharmaceutical company executive; b. Youngstown, Ohio, Jan. 6, 1950; s. William Stephen and Goldie Elizabeth (Matica) K.; m. Linda Jane Kostyshak, Mar. 20, 1973; 1 child, Craig Thomas. BS, Youngstown State U., 1971; MS, U. Cin., 1973, PhD in Analytical Chemistry (Lowenstein Schubert Twitchell fellow), 1975; postdoctoral fellow in bioanalytical chemistry, Kissinger fellow, Purdue U., 1975-77. Cert. regulatory affairs profl. Scientist, sr. scientist, mgr. prodn. support labs. Ortho Pharm. Corp., Raritan, N.J., 1977-80; dir., product devel., quality assurance and regulatory affairs Janssen Pharmaceutica Inc., Piscataway, N.J., 1980-85; pres. KROSS, Inc., Hillsborough, N.J., 1985—; founder KROSS Coatings, Inc., 1987—; Telluride Pharm. Corp., 1994—; founder, pres. Telluride Analytical Svcs. Corp., 1996—; owner Telluride Devel. Corp., 1997—; participant FDA approved Orphan Drug Devel. program, IND Treatment of Cachexic AIDS Patients, 1996. Mem. editorial bd. Jour. Automated Chemistry, 1975—. Coach basketball St. Mary's Sr. H.S., 1979-83. Recipient SBIR Rsch. award EPA Phase I and II for studies of marine contamination, 1987, 88, FDA Orphan Drug designation, 1994. Active Ctr. for Creative Living, Religious Sci. Ch. Princeton. Mem. Am. Mgmt. Assn., Am. Assn. Clin. Chemists, Am. Assn. Anti Aging Med., Am. Chem. Soc., Am. Assn. Pharm. Scientists, Am. Soc. for Quality Control, U.S.-N.I.S. C. of C., Electrochem. Soc., Parenteral Drug Assn., Pharm. Mfrs. Assn., Drug Info. Assn., Regulatory Affairs Profl. Soc., Am. Soc. Pharmacognosy, We. Electroanalytical Theoretical Soc., Licensing Execs. Soc., Aquinas Inst., Controlled Release Soc., Soc. for Biomaterials. Byzantine Catholic. Office: Telluride Compound 300 Valley Rd Bldg 278 Hillsborough NJ 08876-4059

KENYON, CARLETON WELLER, librarian; b. Lafayette, N.Y., Oct. 7, 1923; s. Herbert Abram and Esther Elizabeth (Weller) K.; m. Dora Marie Kallander, May 21, 1948; children: Garnet Eileen, Harmon Clark, Kay Adelle. A.B., Yankton Coll., 1947; M.A., U. S.D., 1950, J.D., 1950; A.M. in L.S, U. Mich., 1951. Bar: S.D. 1950. Asst. law librarian, head catalog librarian U. Nebr., 1951-52; asst. reference librarian Los Angeles County Law Library, 1952-54, head catalog librarian, 1954-60; law librarian State of Calif., Sacramento, 1960-69; became cons. Library of Congress, Washington, 1963; asso. law librarian Library of Congress, 1969-71, law librarian, 1971-89; cons. county law libraries; lectr. legal bibliography and research. Author: California County Law Library Basic List Handbook and Information of New Materials, 1967; compiler: Calif. Library Laws; assisted in compiling checklists of basic: Am. publs. and subject headings; contbr. articles and book revs. to law revs., library jours. Served with USAAC, 1943-46. Mem. ABA, State Bar S.D., Am. Assn. Law Librarians (chmn. com. on cataloging and classification 1969-71, mem. staff Law Library Inst. 1969, 71), Law Librarians Soc. Washington. Home: 4239 44th Ct NE Salem OR 97305-2117

KENYON, DAPHNE ANNE, economics educator; b. Augusta, Ga., Aug. 14, 1952; d. Lawrence Austin and Shirley (Knaus) Kenyon; m. Peter George Kachavos, Oct. 22, 1988. BA, Mich. State U., 1974; MA in Econs., U. Mich., 1976, PhD in Econs., 1980. Asst. prof. Dartmouth Coll., Hanover, N.H., 1979-83; sr. analyst U.S. Adv. Commn. on Intergovt. Relations, Washington, 1983-85; fin. economist U.S. Treasury Dept., Washington, 1985-87; sr. research assoc. Urban Inst., Washington, 1987-88; Lincoln fellow Lincoln Int. of Land Policy, Cambridge, Mass., 1988-89; asst. prof. econs. Simmons Coll., Boston, 1989-90, assoc. prof. econs., 1991-98, chair dept. econs., 1996—, prof. econs., 1998—; cons. U.S. IRS Adv. Panel, Washington, 1987—; appt. to Mass. Dept. of Revenue Adv. Group, 1991; bd. dirs. New Eng. Econ. Project, v.p., 1997-98, pres., 1999—. Assoc. editor Urban Studies, 1988-93, mem. U.S. editl. adv. com., 1993—; co-editor: Coping with Mandates, 1990, Competition Among States and Local Governments, 1991; N.H. corr. State Tax Notes, 1990; mem. editl. bd. Mass. Benchmarks, 1997—; contbr. articles to profl. jours. Mem. N.H. Gov.'s Revenue Adv. Com., Concord, 1982, 98. NSF grad. fellow, 1974. Mem. Am. Econ. Assn. (mem. com. on the status of women in econs. profession 1995-98), Nat. Tax Assn. (bd. dirs. 1996—, chair intergovernmental fiscal rels. com. 1996-98), Nat. Tax Jour. (referee Ea. Econ. Jour.). Episcopalian.

KENYON, DAVID LLOYD, architect, architectural firm executive; b. Lockport, N.Y., Sept. 9, 1952; s. F. Robert and Betty Jane (Reviere) K.; m. Susan Clair Doyle, Jan. 6, 1990; children: Sean Phillip Kenyon, Colin Doyle Kenyon. A in Civil Tech., SUNY, Utica, 1972; BArch, Syracuse U., 1975. Lic. architect, N.Y., Pa., Ariz., Calif. Oreg., Ill., Washington. Assoc. The Myrus Group, Syracuse, N.Y., 1973-79; assoc. dir. design Chase Archtl. Assocs., Syracuse, N.Y., 1978-80; prin. Kenyon Archtl. Group, Phoenix, Ariz., 1980—; cons. Nat. Trust for Historic Preservation, Washington, 1978; faculty assoc. Ariz. State U. Coll. Architecture, Tempe, Ariz., 1983-89; with nat. solar study USAID, Morocco, 1991; with mission to Malta and Morocco, OPEC, Washington, 1991-92; lectr. Assn. Construction Inspectors, 1993. Author: (textbook) A Hands on Approach to Construction Inspection, 1992. Recipient Energy Innovation award U.S. Dept. Energy, 1988, Environmental Excellence award Crescordia Valley Forward, 1991, Western Regional Design award Am. Inst. Architects, 1991, CAC Honor award, 1992. Fellow Ariz. Acad.; mem. Nat. Trust for Historic Preservation, Soc. Archtl. Historians, Internat. Conference Bldg. Officials. Office: Kenyon Jackson Architects LLC 24 W 5th St Tempe AZ 85281-3614

KENYON, DAVID V., federal judge; b. 1930; m. Mary Cramer; children: George Cramer, John Clark. B.A., U. Calif.-Berkeley, 1952; J.D., U. So. Calif., 1957. Law clk. presiding justice U.S. Dist. Ct. (cen. dist.) Calif., 1957-58; house counsel Metro-Goldwyn-Mayer, 1959-60, Nat. Theatres and TV Inc., 1960-61; pvt. practice law, 1961-71; judge Mcpl. Ct. L.A., 1971-72, L.A. Superior Ct., 1972-80; judge U.S. Dist. Ct. (cen. dist.) Calif., L.A., 1980—, sr. judge. Office: US Dist Ct 312 N Spring St Rm 2445 Los Angeles CA 90012-4701*

KENYON, EDWARD TIPTON, lawyer; b. Summit, N.J., Jan. 27, 1929; s. Theodore S. and Martha (Tipton) K.; m. Dolores Cetrule, July 11, 1953; children: David S., James N., Jonathan W., Theodore H. A.B., Harvard U., 1950; LL.B., Columbia U., 1953. Bar: N.Y. 1956, N.J. 1957. Assoc. Thacher, Proffitt, Prizer, Crawley & Wood, N.Y.C., 1955-56; law clk. to presiding judge U.S. Dist. Ct. N.J., Newark, 1956-57; assoc. Jeffers, Mountain & Franklin, Morristown, N.J., 1957-59, Bourne, Noll and Kenyon and predecessor firm, Summit, 1959-62; ptnr. Bourne, Noll and Kenyon and predecessor firm, 1962-97, of counsel, 1997—; bd. dirs. Atlantic Mgmt. Corp., 1990-98. Trustee Summit Art Ctr., 1960-72, Trinity-Pawling Sch., Pawling, N.Y., 1977—, Pingry Sch., Martinsville, N.J., 1970-97; deacon Cen. Presbyn. Ch., Summit, 1960-65, trustee, 1965-72, 87-93, pres., 1970-72, 88-91; trustee Overlook Hosp., Summit, 1967-75, pres., 1973-75; trustee Overlook Hosp. Found., 1975-84, sec., 1977-80, v.p., 1980-81, pres., 1981-84; trustee Winston Sch., Summit, 1986-93, v.p., 1987-90, pres., 1990-92; bd. dirs. Overlook Mgmt. Corp., 1988-97. With M.C., U.S. Army, 1953-55. Mem. ABA, N.Y. State Bar Assn., N.J. Bar Assn., Summit Bar Assn. (pres. 1983-84), Union County Bar Assn., Am. Coll. Trust and Estate Counsel, Am. Law Inst. Clubs: Beacon Hill (trustee 1977-81, pres. 1979-81), Edgartown Yacht Club, Harvard of N.Y.C., Harvard of N.J. (trustee 1958-69, pres. 1968-69). Home: 49 N Abels Hill Rd Chilmark MA 02535-2026 Office: 382 Springfield Ave Summit NJ 07901-2707

KENYON, ELINOR ANN, social worker; b. Otto, Tex., July 8, 1936; d. William Karl and Anna Malinda (Achelpohl) Hannusch; m. Curtis E. Kenyon; children: John Kyle, Joel Leonard. L.A., St. John's Coll., 1956; BA, Valparaiso U., 1958; MSW, U. Kans., 1961. Adoption worker/dir. Kansas City Area Office Luth. Social Svc., 1958-71; area rep. Luth. Immigration and Refugee Svc., Met. Luth. Ministry, Kansas City, Mo., 1979-83; domestic adoption worker Family and Children Svcs. of Kansas City, 1983-85; pvt. practice social worker Kansas City, 1985-87; coord. refugee family stress edn. program Cmty. Svc. Ctr., Kansas City, Kans., 1987-88; sch. social worker Turner Unified Sch. Dist., Kansas City, Kans., 1988—. Co-author: Resources for Refugee Resettlement, 1981. Mem. NASW, Kans. NEA, Coun. Exceptional Children, Kans. Assn. Sch. Social Workers, Valparaiso U. Guild. Lutheran. Office: Turner Unified Sch Dist 202 Spl Svcs Dept 800 S 55th St Kansas City KS 66106-1308

KENYON, GARY MICHAEL, gerontology educator, researcher; b. Montreal, Que., Can., June 12, 1949; s. Raymond George and Frances Evelyn (Duhault) K. B in Commerce cum laude, Loyola U., Montreal, 1970; BA, Concordia U., Montreal, 1977, MA, 1981; PhD, U. B.C., 1985. Postdoctoral fellow Andrew Norman Inst. U. So. Calif., L.A., 1985-86; postdoctoral fellow Swedish Inst. Linkoping U., Sweden, 1986-87; prof., chmn. dept. gerontology St. Thomas U., Fredericton, N.B., Can., 1987—; adj. prof. McGill U. Ctr. for Studies in Aging, Montreal; hon. rsch. assoc. U. N.B., 1996—. Author: Emergent Theories of Aging, 1988, Metaphors of Aging, 1991, Aging and Biography, 1996, Restorying Our Lives, 1997; editor jour. Gnosis, 1979-81; rev. editor Can. Jour. on Aging, 1989-90; contbr. articles to profl. jours. Can. Govt. Social Scis. and Humanities fellow, 1983-85. Mem. Gerontology Soc. Am., Can. Assn. Gerontology, N.B. Assn. Gerontology (bd. dirs.). Avocations: skiing, cooking, wines, Tai Chi (instr.), language study. Office: St Thomas U, Dept Gerontology, Fredericton, NB Canada E3B 5G3

KENYON, KENDRA SUE, organizational consultant; b. Boise, Idaho, Aug. 26, 1956; d. Francis Elwood and Patricia Ann (Sellars) K.; m. David Michael Bertsch, Feb. 16, 1972 (div. May 1979); 1 child, Shad I.; m. Curtis Sumner Van Inwegen, Sept. 1, 1997; 1 child, Cyprus Kenyon. BA in Comm., Boise State U., 1988; M in Psychol. Counseling, Idaho State U., 1991; postgrad., U. Idaho, 1996—. Nat. cert. counselor, N.Y.; lic. profl. counselor; cert. mediator. Sport psychologist Boise State U., 1990-91; dir. of therapy Northview Hosp., Boise, 1991-94; pvt. practice Boise, 1994—; pres. Orgnl. Performance Cons. Inc., Boise, 1995—; adj. prof. Boise State U., 1991-93; counselor, conflict mediator, trainer State of Idaho, Boise, 1994—; cons. Hewlett Packard, Boise, 1997-98; adv. bd. Alliance for Mentally Ill, Boise, 1995-96, Inds. Commn., Boise, 1997—. Legis. advisor Westerberg & Panter Assoc., Boise, 1995—; senate candidate Dem. Party Dist. 19, Boise, 1997; vol. counselor Alliance for Mentally Ill, Boise, 1993-94; past mem. Parents and Youth Against Drug Abuse, Boise, 1990-91. Internat. Amb. scholar Rotary Internat., 1998—; doctoral fellowship Idaho State U., 1991. Mem. ASTD, Internat. Assn. of Univ. Women, Idaho Psychol. Assn., Internat. Soc. for Performance Improvement, Idaho Assn. on Counseling and Devel., Assn. for Multi-Cultural Counseling and Tng. Democrat. Avocations: white water rafting, travel, fly fishing, hiking, skiing. Home: PO Box 343 Eagle ID 83616-0343

KENYON, KEVIN BRUCE, insurance marketing executive; b. Chgo., Apr. 16, 1952; s. Jack Scott and Dixie (Gillies) K. BS, U.S. Naval Acad., 1974. CLU; master fellow Life Mgmt. Inst. Mgr. mass mktg. Phila. Life Ins. Co., San Francisco, 1982-84; nat. mktg. dir. Transamerica Assurance Co., L.A., 1984-87; dir. mass mktg. Am. Gen. Life, N.Y.C., 1987-97; v.p. mass mktg. Am. Gen. Life Cos. Lt. USN, 1970-82. Fellow Life Office Mgmt. Assn.; mem. U.S. Naval Alumni Assn., CLU and ChFC (chair teleconfs. N.Y.C. chpt. 1995—), REBC. Democrat. Avocations: singing. Home: 114 W 27th St Apt 11 New York NY 10001-6211 Office: Am Gen Life of NY 125 Maiden Ln Fl 8 New York NY 10038-4912

KENYON, LESLIE HARRISON, architect; b. Peoria, Ill., Oct. 13, 1922; s. Fred James and Camilla (Myers) K.; m. Theo Jean Ahrends, Oct. 23, 1954. BArch, U. Mich., 1949. Lic. architect. Draftsman Holabird & Root, Chgo., 1949-50, Loebel, Scholossman & Bennett, Chgo., 1951; owner Kenyo & Assocs., Architects, Peoria, 1951—; designer Sch. div. London County Coun., 1950-51. Chmn. com. of architects and laypersons that authored Peoria I, II, III, IV, 1976-84. Bd. dirs. Youth Farm, Peoria, Peoria City Beautiful, Central Ill. Landmarks Found., Peoria, 1972—. Sgt., C.E., U.S. Army, 1943-46, PTO. Recipient Cert. of Merit, Landmarks Preservation Coun. of Ill., Hist. Preservation and Rehab. of Peoria City Hall, Peoria, 1991, Thomas H. Madigan Outstanding Achievement award Hist. Preservation and Renovation of Old Main Adminstrn. Bldg., Ill. Sch. for the Deaf, Jacksonville, 1994, Cert. of Recognition, Ill. Hist. Preservation Agy., Hist. Preservation and Renovation of Old Main Adminstrn. Bldg., Ill. Sch. for the Deaf, Jacksonville, 1994, Bldg. Beautification award Converse Mktg. from Peoria City Beautiful, Exceptional Effort in Bldg. Hist. Preservation, Peoria, 1994, Richard H. Driehaus Bricks & Mortar award Landmarks Preservation Coun. of Ill., Preservation of Mineral Springs Park Pavilion, Pekin, Ill., 1994. Mem. AIA (pres. Peoria sect., Svc. award, Ctrl. Ill. chpt. Merit award 1995). Universalist-Unitarian. Home: 100 Zig Zag Trl East Peoria IL 61611-2160 Office: Kenyon and Assoc Architects 735 N Knoxville Ave Peoria IL 61602-1063*

KENYON, PATRICIA MAE, poet; b. Belvidere, Ill., July 17, 1952; m. Henry A. Kenyon, July 1, 1984; three children; four stepchildren. tchr. jr. colls. *Patricia expresses feelings and sentiments through poetic verse. She creates poems for others to help them visualize illustrations of heritage and moments shared with family and friends. She brings memories into reality. For six years she has created personalized poems and illustrated family trees.*

She is published in seven anthologies and represents the U.S. in Poetic Voices of America, Wales, and Great Britain. She was a semi-finalist Poet of the Year for the International Society of Poets in 1997. She also enjoys public speaking. Host cable TV show. Mem. Internat. Soc. Poets. Home: 3704 W Young St Mchenry IL 60050

KENYON, REGAN CLAIR, educational research executive; b. St. Louis, Jan. 31, 1949; s. Robert Clair and Nina Naoma (Giesler) K.; m. Mary Margaret Quinlan, June 2, 1979; children: Regan Clair Jr., Moriah Quinlan. BA, U. Mo., 1969, MEd, 1973; EdD, Harvard U., 1983. Tchr. Ferguson, Mo., 1971-74; prin. Manor Sch., St. Croix, 1974-77, Country Day Sch., St. Croix, Virgin Islands, 1977-78; exec. asst. U.S. Dept. Edn., Washington, 1978-80; adminstrv. asst. Harvard U., Cambridge, Mass., 1980-81; cons. to pres. MA Higher Edn. Assistance Corp., Boston, 1981-83; pres. Secondary Sch. Admission Test Bd., Princeton, N.J., 1983—; cons. fed. and state govt. founds., Washington, 1979—; founder, pres. Princeton Inst. Ednl. Rsch., 1987—. Contbr. articles to profl. jours.; inventor, editor in field. Mem. N.J. State Bd. Edn., Trenton, N.J., 1987-91, Nat. State Bds. Edn., Washington, 1987-91. Fellow Edn. Policy for George Washington U. Inst. for Ednl. Leadership, Washington, 1978-79; Gustav Harris scholar Harvard U., 1980-83; recipient Horace Mann Prof. Contbr. citation U.S. Dept. Edn., 1980; named Disting Alumni Mo. U., 1996. Mem. Am. Ednl. Rsch. Assn., Inst. for Ednl. Leadership, Harvard Club, Nassau Club, Phi Delta Kappa. Roman Catholic. Avocations: tennis, golf, ski, fishing, hiking. Home: 5 Cedar Brook Ter Princeton NJ 08540-7407 Office: Secondary Sch Admission Test Bd CN5339 Princeton NJ 08543

KENZENKOVIC, KEVIN G., management consultant; b. Perth Amboy, N.J., Aug. 18, 1954; s. Robert John and Clare Melita (Kelly) K.; m. Carol Lynn Dorge, Apr. 22, 1989 (div. July 1996). AB in Politics, St. Joseph's U., Phila., 1976; MPA, So. Meth. U., 1978. Asst. to city mgr. City of Dallas, 1978-84; city mgr. City of Slater, Mo., 1984-86, City of Oak Ridge North, Tex., 1984-88; pres. Kenze, Inc., Lake Bluff, Ill., 1988-93, Lake Forest, 1995—; v.p., pub. fin. Norwest Investment Svcs., Inc., Milw., 1994; mem. adv. panel on transp. of hazardous materials U.S. Congress/Office of Tech. Assessment, Washington, 1985-86. Mem. Internat. City/County Mgmt. Assn., Ill. City Mgmt. Assn., Ill. Govt. Fin. Officers Assn. Roman Catholic. Avocations: badminton, reading baseball lit., golf, music. Home: 1597 N Mckinley Rd Lake Forest IL 60045-1369

KENZLE, LINDA FRY, writer, artist; b. Elkhorn, Wis., May 22, 1950; d. Marvin Delos and Ione Mae (Snyder) Fry; m. Donald Charles Kenzle; 1 child, Joshua Clay. Owner Third Coast, Williams Bay, Wis., 1975-79; artist, 1975—, cartoonist, 1978-79; editor, pub. Stylepages, 1985-88, Dollbeat, 1988-89, Greenleaf Bot. Rev., 1990-93; photographer, 1993—, illustrator, 1996—. Author: Embellishments, 1993, Dazzle, 1995, The Irresistible Bead, 1996, Pages, 1997, Gathering, 1998. Avocations: flying, travel, architecture, science, gardening. Office: PO Box 177 Fox River Grove IL 60021-0177

KEOGH, HEIDI HELEN DAKE, advocate; b. Saratoga, N.Y., July 12, 1950; d. Charles Starks and Phyllis Sylvia (Edmunds) Dake; m. Randall Frank Keogh, Nov. 3, 1973; children: Tyler Cameron, Kelly Dake. Student, U. Colo., 1972. Reception, promotions Sta. KLAK, KJAE, Lakewood, Colo., 1972-73; acct. exec. Mixed Media Advt. Agy., Denver, 1973-75; writer, mktg. Jr. League Cookbook Devel., Denver, 1986-88; chmn., coord. Colorado Cache & Creme de Colorado Cookbooks, 1988-90; speakers bur. Mile High Transplant Bank, Denver, 1983-84, Writer's Inst., U. Denver, 1988; bd. dirs. Stewart's Ice Cream Co., Inc., Jr. League, Denver. Contbr. articles to profl. jours. Fiscal officer, bd. dirs. Mile High Transplant Bank; blockworker Heart Fund and Am. Cancer Soc., Littleton, Colo., 1978—, Littleton Rep. Com., 1980-84; fundraising vol. Littleton Pub. Schs., 1980—; vol. Gathering Place, bd. dirs., 1996—, chmn. Brown Bag benefit, 1996; vol. Hearts for Life, 1991—, Oneday, 1992, Denver Ballet Guild, 1992—, Denver Ctr. Alliance, 1993—, Newborn Hope, 1980—, Girls, Inc., 1995—, Girls Hope, VOA Guild, 1996—, Le Bal de Ballet, 1998—; active The Denver Social Register and Record, 1999. Mem. Jr. League Denver (pub. rels. bd., v.p. ways and means 1989-90, planning coun./ad hoc 1990-92, sustainer spl. events 1993-94), Community Emergency Fund (chair 1991-92), Jon D. Williams Cotillion at Columbine (chmn. 1991-93), Columbine Country Club, Gamma Alpha Chi, Pi Beta Phi Alumnae Club (pres. Denver chpt. 1984-85, 93-94, alumnae adv. com. U. Colo. chpt. 1997—, bienniel conv. chmn. Denver 2001), Denver Social Register and Record. Episcopalian. Avocations: traveling, skiing, golf, family activities. Home: 63 Fairway Ln Littleton CO 80123-6648

KEOGH, JAMES, journalist; b. Platte County, Nebr., Oct. 29, 1916; s. David James and Edith (Dwyer) K.; m. Verna Pedersen, May 17, 1940; children—Kevin, Katherine Ann. Ph.B., Creighton U., 1938. Reporter Omaha World-Herald, 1938-48, city editor, 1948-51; contbg. editor Time mag., 1951-52, assoc. editor, 1952-56, sr. editor, 1956-61, asst. mng. editor, 1961-68, exec. editor, 1968; spl. asst. Pres. U.S., 1969-70; freelance writer, 1971-72; dir. USIA, 1973-77; exec. dir. The Business Roundtable, 1977-86. Author: This is Nixon, 1956, President Nixon and the Press, 1972, Centennial in Belle Haven, 1989, One of a Kind, 1995; editor: Corporate Ethics: A Prime Business Asset, 1988. Bd. dirs. The Phila. Fund, 1987—. Recipient Distinguished Nebraskan award, 1972. Clubs: Belle Haven (Greenwich, Conn.) (pres.-commodore 1967-68, 84). Home: 202 W Lyon Farm Dr Greenwich CT 06831-4353

KEOGH, KEVIN, lawyer; b. Omaha, Dec. 24, 1941; s. James Charles and Verna Marion (Pedersen) K.; m. Susan Elizabeth Mary Griffiths, Apr. 26, 1975; children: James, Caroline, Colin, Brendan. AB with honors, Holy Cross Coll., 1963; JD, Harvard U., 1966. Bar: N.Y. 1969, Conn. 1977, U.S. Ct. Appeals (2nd cir.) 1975. Assoc. Breed, Abbott & Morgan, N.Y.C., 1969-75, ptnr., 1975-88; ptnr. White & Case, N.Y.C., 1988—, exec. ptnr., 1992—. Dir. United Hosp. Fund of N.Y., 1984-88; vol. U.S. Peace Corps., Nicoya, Costa Rica, 1966-68. Mem. Am. Yacht Club (commodore 1985-86, Disting. Svc. award 1989), Yacht Racing Assn. L.I. Sound (Pres. 1983-84, Disting. Svc. award 1985), N.Y. Yacht Club (competitions com. 1990-92). Republican. Episcopalian. Home: 49 Byram Dr Greenwich CT 06830-7007 Office: White & Case Bldg Ll 1155 Avenue Of The Americas New York NY 10036-2787*

KEOGH, KEVIN, political party official. Chmn. Maine State Rep. Party, Camden. Office: Maine State Republican Party PO Box 1228 Camden ME 04843-1228

KEOGH, MARY CUDAHY, artist; b. Milw., Nov. 11, 1920; d. John and Katherine (Reed) Cudahy; m. Frank Stephen Keogh, Jan. 17, 1947 (dec. 1980); children: Mary K., Anne C., Patricia, Margaret E.; m. Warren Stringer, July 5, 1985. Student, Smith Coll., 1939-42; BFA, Milw. Downer Coll., 1944; post grad., Parsons Sch. of Design, 1945. Artist, 1969—; lectr. Woman's Club of Wis., 1977, workshops, Omaha, 1978-80, demo. Cape Coral (Fla.) Art League, 1991. One and two person shows include Lee County Alliance for the Arts, 1988, 90, 96, Barbara Mann Hall, Ft. Myers, 1992, Phillips Gallery, Sanibel, Fla., 1993, Uihlein-Peters Gallery, Milw., 1994, Alliance for the Arts, 1996, Phillips Gallery Sanibel, 1997; exhibited in group shows Sarasota Visual Arts Ctr., 1995, Fla. Artists' Group, Winter Haven, 1996, Lee County Alliance for the Arts, 1996, Women's Caucus for Art, Longboat Key, Fla., 1997, Fla. Artists Group, Venice, 1997, Venice Biennial, 1997, Phillips Gallery, 1998; represented in permanent collections U. Utah, Cedar City, Northwestern Bell, Omaha, Health Park, Ft. Myers, others. Named Best of Show, Nebr. Wesleyan Coll., Lincoln, 1981; recipient 3d place Sarasota Visual Arts Ctr., 1995, Big Arts, Sanibel, 1995, honorable mention award Venice (Fla.) Biennial, 1997, Fla. Artist Group award, Jacksonville Mus. contemporary Art, 1998. Mem. Nat. Women's Caucus for Art, Nat. Mus. Women in the Arts (charter), Fla. Artists Group. Roman Catholic. Avocations: cooking, traveling. Home and Studio: 9439 Coventry Ct Sanibel FL 33957-4231

KEOGH, RICHARD JOHN, firearms and explosives consultant; b. Woonsocket, R.I., Sept. 23, 1932; s. Michael Joseph and Dora Marie (Rumgay) K. BBA, U. Mass., 1958; MA, Pepperdine U., 1974. Lic. explosive disposal technician, Mass.; expert witness explosives and firearms, Hawaii. Commd. 2d lt. U.S. Army, 1958, advanced through grades to maj., 1967; stationed at Korea, S.C., Ala., 1958-73; ret. USAR, 1979; disposal specialist USN, Lualualei, Hawaii, 1973-76; mgmt. analyst Marine Corps Air Sta., Kaneohe Bay, Hawaii, 1976-93. Contbr. articles to profl. jours. Pres. Assn. of Owners Palms Condominium, Honolulu, 1978-80. With USAR, 1973-79. Decorated 3 Bronze Staras, 2 Purple Hearts, 2 Air medals, Cross of Gallantry, Commandants medal; recipient Founders award, Order of the Arrow Boy Scouts Am., 1989, FBI Cert. of Appreciation, 1991, Silver Beaver award Boy SScouts Am., 1994. Mem. VFW (life), DAV (life), Internat. Assn. Bomb Technicians and Investigators (life), Nat. Auto Pistol Collectors Assn., Ohio Gun Collectors Assn., Bay Colony Weapons Collectors, Hawaii Rifle Assn. (pres. 1994-96), Gun Owners Action League, Am. Legion (life), Mil. Order purple Heart (life). Avocations: rifle shooting, ammo reloading, photography. Home: 431 Nahua St Apt 203 Honolulu HI 96815-2915

KEOHANE, NANNERL OVERHOLSER, university president, political scientist; b. Blytheville, Ark., Sept. 18, 1940; d. James Arthur and Grace (McSpadden) Overholser; m. Patrick Henry III, Sept. 16, 1962 (div. May 1969); 1 child, Stephan; m. Robert Owen Keohane, Dec. 18, 1970; children: Sarah, Jonathan, Nathaniel. BA, Wellesley Coll., 1961, Oxford U., Eng., 1963; PhD, Yale U., 1967. Faculty Swarthmore Coll., Pa., 1967-73, Stanford U., Calif., 1973-81; fellow Ctr. for Advanced Study in the Behavioral Scis. Stanford U., 1978-79, 87-88; pres., prof. polit. sci. Wellesley (Mass.) Coll., 1981-93, Duke U., Durham, N.C., 1993—; bd. dirs. IBM. Author: Philosophy and the State in France: The Renaissance to the Enlightenment, 1980; co-editor: Feminist Theory: A Critique of Ideology, 1982. Trustee Colonial Williamsburg Found., 1988—, Nat. Humanities Ctr., 1993—, Doris Duke Charitable Found., 1996—. Marshall scholar, 1961-63; AAUW dissertation fellow; inducted, National Women's Hall of Fame, 1995. Fellow Am. Acad. Arts and Scis., Am. Philos. Soc.; mem. Coun. on Fgn. Rels., Saturday Club (Boston), Watauga Club (N.C.), Phi Beta Kappa. Democrat. Episcopalian. Office: Duke Univ Box 90001 207 Allen Bldg Durham NC 27708-0001

KEOHANE, ROBERT OWEN, political scientist, educator; b. Chgo., Oct. 3, 1941; s. Robert Emmet and Mary Irene (Pieters) K.; m. Nannerl Overholser, Dec. 18, 1970; children: Jonathan, Sarah, Stephan, Nathaniel. B.A., Shimer Coll., 1961; M.A., Harvard U., 1964, Ph.D., 1966. From instr. to assoc. prof. Swarthmore Coll., Pa., 1965-73; from assoc. prof. to prof. Stanford U., Calif., 1973-81; chmn. dept. polit. sci. Stanford U., 1980-81; prof. politics Brandeis U., Waltham, Mass., 1981-85; prof. govt. Harvard U., Cambridge, Mass., 1985-96, chmn., 1988-92, Stanfield prof. internat. peace, 1989-96; James B. Duke prof. polit. sci. Duke U., Durham, N.C., 1996—. Author: After Hegemony, 1984, International Institutions and State Power, 1989; co-author: Power and Interdependence, 1977, Designing Social Inquiry, 1994; co-editor: Transnational Relations and World Politics, 1972, The New European Community, 1991, Institutions for the Earth, 1993, After the Cold War, 1993, Ideas and Foreign Policy, 1993, Global Interdependence and Local Communitities, 1994, Internationalization and Domestic Politics, 1996, International Aid, 1996; editor: Neorealism and Its Critics, 1986; editor Internat. Orgn., 1974-80; contbr. articles to profl. jours. Chmn. New Democratic Coalition Delaware County, Pa., 1969-71. Recipient Sumner prize Harvard U., 1966, Grawemeyer award, 1989; fellow Ctr. Advanced Study in Behavior Scis., 1977-78 87-88; Guggenheim fellow, 1992, Frank Kenan fellow Nat. Humanities Ctr., 1995-96. Mem. Am. Acad. Arts and Scis., Am. Polit. Sci. Assn. (pres. 1999—), Am. Econ. Assn., Coun. Fgn. Rels. (Internat. Affairs fellow 1968-69), Internat. Studies Assn. (pres. 1988-89). Home: 1508 Pinecrest Rd Durham NC 27705-5817

KEOUGH, DONALD RAYMOND, investment company executive; b. Maurice, Iowa, Sept. 4, 1926; s. Leo H. and Veronica (Henkels) K.; m. Marilyn Mulhall, Sept. 10, 1949; children: Kathleen Anne, Mary Shayla, Michael Leo, Patrick John, Eileen Tracey, Clarke Robert. BS, Creighton U., 1949, LLD (hon.), 1982; LLD (hon.), U. Notre Dame, 1985, Emory U., 1993, Trinity U., Dublin, Ireland, 1993, Clarke U., 1994. With Butter-Nut Foods Co., Omaha, 1950-61; with Duncan Foods Co., Houston, 1961-67; v.p., dir. mktg. foods div. Coca-Cola Co., Atlanta, 1967-71, pres. div., 1971-73; exec. v.p. Coca-Cola USA, Atlanta, 1973-74; pres. Coca-Cola USA, 1974-76; exec. v.p. Coca-Cola Co., Atlanta, 1976-79, sr. exec. v.p., 1980-81, pres., COO, dir., 1981-93; chmn. bd. dirs. Coca-Cola Enterprises, 1986-93; advisor to bd. Coca-Cola Co., Atlanta, 1993-98; bd. dirs. Washington Post Co., H.J. Heinz Co., Home Depot, McDonald's Corp., USA Networks, Inc.; chmn. bd. Allen & Co., Inc., Atlanta, 1993—, Excalibur Technologies, Inc., 1996—. Mem. president's coun. Creighton U.; trustee emeritus U. Notre Dame and Lovett Sch. With USNR, 1944-46. Mem. Capital City Club, Piedmont Driving Club, Commerce Club, Peachtree Golf Club. Office: 200 Galleria Pky NW Ste 970 Atlanta GA 30339-5945

KEOUGH, JAMES GILLMAN, JR., minister; b. Reading, Pa., June 2, 1947; s. James Gillman Sr. and Nora (Deturck) K.; m. Dawn Eileen Wiest, Sept. 17, 1976; children: Cynthia Ann, James Michael, Wendy Sue, Danielle Lynn, Erin Mae, Bevin Leigh. BA in History Edn., Messiah Coll., Grantham, Pa., 1970; MDiv, Lancaster (Pa.) Theol. Sem., 1973; D of Ministry, Ashland (Ohio) Theol. Sem., 1980. Ordained to ministry United Ch. Christ, 1973. Minister St. Luke's United Ch. Christ, Kenhorst, Pa., 1972-75, Congl. Ch., Winchester, Va., 1975-78, 1st Congl. Ch., Newton Falls, Ohio, 1978-82, Cen. Congl. Ch., Middleboro, Mass., 1982-85; sr. minister 1st Congl. Ch., Pontiac, Mich., 1985—; founder Prayer Unlimited, Waterford, Mich., 1997—. Author: Teaching Prayer in the Local Parish, 1980, Prayer Unlimited, 1997. Mem. Oakland County Rep. Club, Mich. Rep. 500 Club; bd. dirs. Clinton Valley coun. Boy Scouts Am.; bd. dirs. Boys Clubs Am., Pontiac; pres. Somebodycares, Pontiac, 1983—. Mem. Nat. Assn. Congl. Christian Chs., S.E. Mich. Congl. Ministerium, Independence Twp. Pastors Assn., Kiwanis. Avocations: reading, hiking, fishing. Home: 3062 St Jude Dr Waterford MI 48329-4359 Office: 1st Congl Church Clarkston Rd at Pine Knob Rd PO Box 221 Clarkston MI 48347-0221

KEOUGH, WILLIAM RICHARD, English language educator; b. Boston, June 20, 1942; s. William Alexander and Rita Frances (Minahan) K. Prof. English, 1969-97; pub. Tara West, Fitchburg, 1988—. Author: Punchlines, 1990; (poetry) Any Such Greenness, 1992. Active Literacy Vols., Mass., 1980—. Mem. NEA (grantee 1979), MLA, Am. Conf. Irish Studies, Multi-Ethnic Lit. of U.S. Democrat. Avocations: writing, biking. Home: 429 Rindge Rd Fitchburg MA 01420-2024 Office: Fitchburg State Coll 160 Pearl St Fitchburg MA 01420-2631

KEOWN, MICHELE L., computer training specialist, business educator; b. Sullivan, Ill., Oct. 22, 1973; d. David A. and Cheryl D. Keown. BS, Ill. State U., 1995; MBA, Ea. Ill. U., 1999. Computer tng. specialist Lake Land Coll., Mattoon, Ill., 1996—; adj. bus. instr. Lake Land Coll., Mattoon, 1997—. Mem. ASTD, Soc. Human Resource Mgrs., MBA Assn. (sec.-treas. 1998—), Ill. C.C. Econ. Devel. Assn. E-mail: mkeown@lakeland.cc.il.us. Home: 21 Parkway Dr Sullivan IL 61951-1167 Office: Lake Land Coll 5001 Lake Land Blvd Mattoon IL 61938

KEOWN, WILLIAM ARVEL, minister, educator; b. Clinton, Ind., June 4, 1920; s. James Edward and Lula Nettie (Jackson) K.; m. Jewel Cook, Mar. 25, 1950; children: Evelyn Jewel, Deborah Anne, William S., A. Duane, Wayne A. ThB cum laude, God's Bible Sch. and Coll., Cin., 1949; MA, Butler U., Indpls., 1956; cert. in edn., Ind. State U., 1961. Ordained to ministry, 1956, Holiness, later transferred to Ch. of God (Anderson affiliation), 1957. Dean of men God's Bible Sch. and Coll., Cin., 1948-49; pastor ch. Evansville and Clinton, Ind., 1950-52; tchr. Frankfort (Ind.) Coll., 1954-57, dean of men, 1954-55; tchr. jr. high sch. Clinton, 1957-79; pastor 1st Ch. of God, Terre Haute, Ind., 1970-80, interim pastor, 1980-81, assoc. min., 1981—; basketball coach, 1967-70; instr. Ind. State Dept. Corrections, Anderson, 1979-82. With Civilian Conservation Corps., 1938-40; with U.S. Army, 1942-46. Fellow Internat. Platform Assn.; mem. Nat. Ret. Tchrs. Assn, Ind. Ret. Tchrs. Assn., Ind. Ministerial Assembly. Home and Office: 18820 S Rhodes Cir Clinton IN 47842-7208 *Applying singularity of purpose by enjoying each thing in itself in life makes apparently complex things open up to the simplicity of understanding necessary for enjoyable comprehension. I find in all disciplines (religion, science, philosophy, etc.) the interrelatedness of each to the other. That which at first appears to be totally incomprehensible responds to this view of relationships; consequently learning is fun, not drudgery.*

KEPECS, JOSEPH GOODMAN, physician, educator; b. Phila., Oct. 8, 1912; s. Jacob and Mary (Goodman) K.; m. Joan A. Epstein, Oct. 17, 1944; children—Susan, Jonathan. B.S., U. Chgo., 1935, M.D., 1937; grad., Inst. for Psychoanalysis, Chgo., 1949. Intern Cook County Hosp., Chgo., 1938-39; resident St. Elizabeth's Hosp., Washington, 1940-41; practice medicine, specializing in psychiatry Madison, Wis., 1965—; attending physician dept. psychiatry Michael Reese Hosp., Chgo., 1950-65; prof. psychiatry U. Wis., 1965-84, prof. emeritus, 1984—; lectr. Chgo. Inst. for Psychoanalysis, 1957-60, mem. faculty, 1974—; professorial lectr. dept. psychiatry U. Chgo., 1960-65. Served with AUS, 1941-46. Mem. Am. Psychoanalytic Assn., Wis. Psychoanalytic Study Group (pres. 1979-80), Am. Psychosomatic Soc., Am. Psychiat. Assn., Chgo. Psychoanalytic Soc. (pres. 1964-65). Home: 3580 Lake Mendota Dr Madison WI 53705-1473

KEPES, GYORGY, author, painter, photographer, educator; b. Selyp, Hungary, Oct. 4, 1906; came to U.S., 1937, naturalized, 1956; s. Ferene and Ilona (Fai) K.; m. Juliet Appleby, Nov. 3, 1937; children—Juliet, Imre. M.A., Royal Acad. Fine Art, 1928; self-taught in photography. Pub. in collaboration with Dan Gyorgy, Tul a Valon, 1929; ind. painter and filmmaker with Munka Art Group, Budapest, Hungary, 1929-30; exhbn., stage and graphic designer, Berlin, 1930-32, 34-36; designer studio of Laszlo Moholy-Nagy, London, 1936-37; head light and color dept. New Bauhaus, Chgo., 1937-38, Inst. Design, Chgo., 1938-43; ind. painter, photographer, tchr., U.S., 1937; prof. design North Tex. State Coll., Denton, and Bklyn. Coll., 1943-45; prof. visual design MIT, Cambridge, 1946-66, founder-dir. Ctr. for Advanced Visual Studies, 1967-70, Inst. prof., 1970-74; vis. instr. Art Dirs. Club, Chgo., 1939; vis. prof. Harvard U., Cambridge, 1965; vis. lectr. UCLA, 1969; vis. artist U. Hawaii, Honolulu, 1970; painter-in-residence Am. Acad. Rome, 1974; Bicentennial prof. U. Utah, Salt Lake City, 1975; Andrew Mellon prof. Rice U., Houston, 1976; artist-in-residence Dartmouth Coll., Hanover, N.H., 1977; Disting. Vis. Louis D. Beaumont prof. Washington U., St. Louis, 1978; Kern Inst. prof. in communications Rochester Inst. Tech. (N.Y.), 1981; exhibited paintings, Budapest, Berlin, N.Y.C., 1930-32, London, 1935-37; designed exhbn. Arts of UN, Art Inst., Chgo., 1944; designed introduction room Expn. Dest Techniques Americaines de l'Habitation et de L'Urbanisme, Paris, 1945; designer sect. Triennale de Milano, Milan, Italy, 1968. Exhbns. include Art Inst. Chgo., Katherine Kuh Gallery, San Francisco Mus. Art, Mus. Modern Art, N.Y.C., Cleve., Phila., Mus. Fine Arts, Houston, Dallas Mus. Fine Arts, Rome, Boston, London; one-man shows include: Hayden Gallery, MIT, 1978, Saidenberg Gallery, N.Y.C., 1982; group shows include: Galleria dei Levante, Munich, W.Ger., 1978, San Francisco Mus. Art (toured U.S.), 1981-82, New Gallery Contemporary Art, Cleve., 1979 (toured through 1980); represented in permanent collections: Mus. Modern Art, N.Y.C., Whitney Mus., N.Y.C., R.I. Sch. Design, Providence, Mus. Fine Arts, Boston, Fgg Art Mus., Harvard U., Cambridge, Mass., MIT, Cambridge, Art Inst. Chgo., San Francisco Mus. Modern Art, Bauhaus Archives, Berlin, Nat. Mus. Fine Arts, Budapest, Corcoran Gallery Art, Washington, Dallas Mus. Fine Arts, Houston Mus. Fine Arts, Rose Art Mus., Waltham, Mass., San Diego Fine Arts Gallery, Cleve. Mus. Art, Bklyn. Mus., Addison Gallery Am. Art, Andover, Mass.; designer stained glass windows Ikenoue Christ Ch., Tokyo, 1995; author: Language of Vision, 1944; The New Landscape in Art and Science, 1956; contbr. articles to profl. jours.; editor: Visual Arts Today, 1960, Edn. of Vision, 1965, The Nature and Art of Motion, 1965, The Structure in Art and in Science, 1965, The Man-Made Object, 1966, Module, Proportion, Symmetry, Rhythm, 1966, Sign, Image, Symbol, 1966, Arts of the Environment, 1972. Recipient medal for Dist. Contbns. to the Graphic Arts Am. Inst. Graphic Arts, 1944, 49, Purchase prize U. Ill., 1954, Soc. Typographic Arts award, Silver medal Archtl. League, 1961, Chgo. Art Dirs. Club award, 1963, Fine Arts award AIA, 1968, Colombian Bienal Coltejar award, 1972; Guggenheim fellow, 1960-61; Kepes Gyorgy Muvesz-zete named in honor in Eger, Hungary. Fellow Am. Acad. Arts and Scis.; mem. Nat. Inst. Arts and Letters.*

KEPETS, HUGH MICHAEL, artist; b. Cleve., Feb. 6, 1946; s. Nathan and Frances K. B.F.A., Carnegie Mellon U., 1968; M.F.A., Ohio U., 1972. One-man shows include, Fischbach Gallery, N.Y.C., 1974, 75, 78, Vick Gallery, Phila., 1974, 76, 77, Michael Berger Gallery, Pitts., 1975, 82, G.W. Einstein Co., Inc., N.Y.C., 1976, Graphics 1, Graphics 2, Boston, 1976, 79, Rubicon Gallery, Los Altos, Calif., 1977, New Gallery, Cleve., 1978, Women's City Club, Cleve., A.J. Wood Gallery, Phila., Carnegie-Mellon U., Pitts., 1979, Orion Editions, N.Y.C., 1980, Houghton (N.Y.) Coll., 1980, Galerie 99, Bay Harbor Islands, Fla., 1981, Cumberland Gallery, Nashville, 1983, Mattingly Baker, Dallas, 1983, Marcus/Gordon, Pitts., 1981, 85, 90, Roger Ramsay Gallery, 1984, 88, David Adamson Gallery, Washington, 1986, Randall Beck Gallery, Boston, 1986, 89, Ingrid Cusson Gallery, N.Y.C., 1989, Leo Kamen Gallery, Toronto, Can., 1990, Lyman Allyn Mus. Art, New London, Conn., 1992, David Adamson Gallery, Washington, 1992, Brenda Kroos Gallery, Cleve., 1993, 96; exhibited in group shows including, Cleve. Mus. Art, 1968, 71-79, 93—, Bklyn. Mus., 1972, 76, Asso. Am. Artists, N.Y.C., 1972, 74, Butler Inst. Am. Art, 1972, U. Pa., Phila., 1972, Espace Cardin, Paris, Michael Berger Gallery, Yale U. Art Gallery, Tyler Art Gallery, Phila., 1973, New Gallery, 1973, 74, 79, Akron (Ohio) Art Inst., 1974, Virginia Mus. Art, Richmond, Vick Gallery, 1974, Boston Mus. Fine Arts, 1975-77, 82, Phila. Print Club, Westmoreland County Art Mus., Skidmore Coll., 1975, Queens Mus., N.Y.C., Albion Coll., Lehigh U., Indpls. Mus. Art, Grand Palais-Paris, McNay Art Inst. of San Antonio, U. Mo., Kansas City, 1976, Glassboro (N.J.) State Coll., Library of Congress, 1977, Yale U. Art Gallery, 1978, Am. Acad. Arts and Letters, N.Y.C., 1978, 79, 80, Hunt Inst. for Bot. Documentation, Pitts., 1979, Md. Inst. Coll. Art, Balt., 1980, Hudson River Mus., Yonkers, N.Y., 1982, U. Pitts., 1983, Pratt Graphics Ctr., N.Y.C., 1983, Mattingly Baker Gallery, Dallas, 1984, Franklin & Marshall Coll., 1984, U. Calif.-Davis, 1985, Honolulu Acad. Art, 1985, Cleve. Mus. Art, 1985, 86, N.Y. Inst. Tech., 1985, Montgomery Coll., Rockville, Md., 1985, The Del. Art Mus., 1986; represented in permanent collections, Met. Mus. Art, N.Y.C., Cleve. Mus. Art, Phila. Mus. Fine Arts, Library of Congress, Del. Mus. Art, Indpls. Mus. Art, Harvard U. Fogg Mus., N.Y. Public Library, Worcester (Mass.) Art Mus., Yale U. Art Gallery, Minn. Mus. Art, St. Paul, R.I. Sch. Design Mus. Art, Art Inst. Chgo., U. N.C. at Chapel Hill Ackland Art Center, Utah State U., Brandeis U., Middlebury (Vt.) Coll., Kresge Art Gallery, others, also various banks and corps. including, Atlantic-Richfield Corp., N.Y.C., Johns Manville Corp., N.Y.C., FMC Corp., Chgo., AT&T, IBM, Xerox Corp., RCA, Princeton, N.J., Amarada Hess Corp., N.Y.C., Prudential Ins. Co. Am., N.Y.C., Commerce Bancshares, Kansas City, Mo., Bank of Am., San Francisco, Gen. Mills Co., N.Y.C., Westinghouse Electric Corp., Pitts., Oliver Realty, Pitts., Gen. Electric Co., N.Y.C., Chase Manhattan Bank, N.Y.C., Citicorp, N.Y.C., Rockwell Internat., Pitts., Lehman Bros., N.Y.C. Nat. Endowment for Arts grantee, 1976; Creative Artists Public Service grantee, 1975, 79-80; recipient Purchase awards Davidson Nat. Print and Drawing Competition Fashion Inst. Tech., 1976, Purchase awards Davidson Nat. Print and Drawing Competition Phila. Print Club, 1975, Cleve. Arts prize Women's City Club, 1979. Studio: 134 W 26th St New York NY 10001-6803

KEPHART, ROBERT DENNIS, publisher; b. Denver, Sept. 9, 1934; s. Robert Tennis Kephart and Myra Louise Wilson; m. Mary Sue Pair, Dec. 7, 1959 (div. 1975); 1 child, Patrick Neil. Student, U. Colo., 1953-54. Pub. Human Events, Washington, 1964-74, Libertarian Rev., Washington, 1969-72; pres., pub. Kephart Comms., Inc., Washington, 1974-81; mng. dir. Caribbean Overseas Enterprises, Largo, Fla., 1981—; dir. Agora Pub., Balt., 1997—. Recipient Lifetime Achievement in Civil Liberties award Thomas Szasz Awards Com., 1998. Mem. Newsletter Assn. Am. (Mktg. and Editl. Excellence award 1978, 79), Belleair Country Club. Avocations: painting, archaeology. E-mail: kephart@bigfoot.com. Office: Caribbean Overseas Enterprises Ltd Box 899 Indian Rocks Beach FL 33786

KEPHART, WILMER ATKINSON, JR., industrial management executive; b. Phila., May 23, 1931; s. Wilmer Atkinson and Lillian Ruth (Friel) K.; m. Mary Veronica Jernoske, June 19, 1954; children: William John, Timothy Michael. Student, Glassboro State Coll., 1950-52, U. Pa., 1958-60, Rutgers U., 1986. In standards and incentive adminstrn. Owens-Ill. Inc., Glassboro, N.J., 1969-74, mgr. quality and svc. engring., 1974-89; mgr. quality assurance Anchor Hocking Packaging, Glassboro, 1989—. Co-author: 250 Years in America, 1997. Mem. Pitman (N.J.) Planning Bd., 1979—; account exec. United Way of Gloucester County, Woodbury, N.J., 1971-73; bd. dirs. Gloucester County Hist. Soc., Woodbury, 1962-76; mem. staff Mus. Am. Glass, Wheaton Village, Millville, N.J., 1997. With USN, 1952-54. Mem.

N.J. Planing Ofcls., KC (4th deg.). Avocations: gardening, tennis, early U.S. history, travel, genealogy. Home: 608 Pitman Ave Pitman NJ 08071-1722

KEPLEY, THOMAS ALVIN, management consultant; b. Salisbury, N.C., May 28, 1928; s. Thomas Albert and Frances Roena (Lowder) K.; m. Pauline Blair, Oct. 26, 1956 (dec.); children: Alleen Jan, Vickie Lynn, Carolyn Sue, Lynda Leigh, Kaye Frances; m. Ernestine Stout, July 30, 1994. B.S., N.C. State U., 1950; postgrad., George Washington U., 1967-70. Asst. dir. trainee VA Med. Ctr., Martinsburg, W.Va., 1972-73; asst. dir. VA Med. Ctr., Marion, Ind., 1973-76, Northport, N.Y., 1976-79; dir. VA Med. Ctr., Chillicothe, Ohio, 1979-81; dep. regional dir. dept. medicine and surgery Gt. Lakes region VA, Washington, 1981-83; dir. bldg. mgmt. svc. dept. medicine and surgery VA, Washington, 1984-90; acct. rep. capitol br. Met. Life, Md., 1990-91; ins. cons., 1991-98, property tax cons., 1992-95, cost reduction cons., 1993-95; independent contractor Primerica Fin. Svcs., 1994-97; clin. assoc. Sch. Allied Health Professions, Ithaca (N.Y.) Coll., 1979-81. Mem. Ross County Health Adv. Com., Chillicothe, 1979-80; mem. Ohio Statewide Health Coordinating Council, 1980. Served with U.S. Army, 1950-52. Mem. Assn. Mil. Surgeons U.S., Rotary (Paul Harris fellow 1991—), Elks, Tau Kappa Epsilon (Beta Beta chpt.), D.C. Alumni Assn. (pres. 1994, 95). Lutheran. Home and Office: 828 Monroe Manor Rd Stevensville MD 21666-2216

KEPLINGER, (DONALD) BRUCE, lawyer; b. Kansas City, Kans., Feb. 4, 1952; s. Donald Lee and Janet Adelheit (Viets) K.; children: Mark William, Lisbeth Marie, Kristen Michelle, Kailyn Emily, Courtney Nicole; m. Carol Ann Heinz, Apr. 12, 1991. BA with highest distinction, U. Kans., 1974; JD cum laude, So. Meth. U., 1977. Bar: Kans. 1977, U.S. Dist. Ct. Kans. 1977, Mo. 1980, U.S. Ct. Appeals (10th cir.) 1985, U.S. Supreme Ct. 1989. Assoc. Clark, Mize & Linville, Salina, Kans., 1977-79, Blackwell, Sanders et al, Kansas City, Mo., 1979-82; ptnr. Payne & Jones, Overland Park, Kans., 1982-94, Norris & Keplinger, Overland Park, 1994—; master Kansas Inns of Ct.; chmn. Kansas Lawyer Svcs Corp. Contbr. articles to profl. jours. V.p. Friends of Library, Johnson County, Kans., 1980-85; deacon Village Presbyn. Ch., 1982-86. Mem. ABA, Internat. Assn. Def. Counsel, Assn. Def. Trial Attys. (state chmn. 1996—, exec. coun., 1999—), Kans. Bar Assn. (chmn. Kans. lawyer svc. corp. 1992—), Mo. Bar Assn., Kans. Assn. Def. Counsel (bd. dirs. 1990—, pres.-elect 1992-93, pres. 1993-94), Def. Rsch. Inst., Rotary Internat., Hallbrook Country Club. Republican. Avocations: reading, golf. Office: Norris & Keplinger LLC 6800 College Blvd Ste 630 Overland Park KS 66211-1556

KEPNER, JANE ELLEN, psychotherapist, educator, minister; b. Lancaster, Pa., July 13, 1948; d. Richard Darlington and Miriam Kepner; m. Raymond Earl Sparks Jr., July 23, 1969 (div. Apr. 1978); 1 child, Heather Elizabeth. AB, CCNY, 1975; MDiv, Harvard Divinity Sch., 1985. Vol. Vista, Auburn, Ala., 1967-69; creative drama tchr. East Harlem Day Care, N.Y.C., 1972-76; editl. asst. Bantam Books, Inc., N.Y.C., 1976-78; rschr. Theseus Prodns., Greenwich, Conn., 1978-82; homeless advocate Harvard Sq. Chs., Cambridge, Mass., 1984-85; cmty. organizer So. Middlesex Opportunity Coun., Marlboro, Mass., 1985-88; emergency psychiat. clinician Advocates, Inc., Framingham, Mass., 1988-89; assoc. prof. Curry Coll., Milton, Mass., 1989-90; psychologist, mental health advocate Portland (Oreg.) Health Svc., 1991-95, bd. advisors, 1992-94. Organizer emergency food pantry Marlboro City Coun., 1987; tenants rights and housing rights advocates Tenants Action Com., Marlboro, 1985-87. Pfeiffer fellow Harvard U. Div. Sch., 1983. Mem. Am. Counseling Assn., Oreg. Friends of C.G. Jung, Club 53 (bd. dirs. 1992-94), Amnesty Internat., Oreg. Coalition to Abolish the Death Penalty. Avocations: voice, hiking, gardening, biking, running.

KEPPEL, TIMOTHY ANDERSON, humanities educator, writer; b. Alamogordo, N.Mex., Oct. 21, 1955; s. Robert Alvin and Nancy (Peeler) K. BA, U. N.C., 1978; MFA, U. Calif., Irvine, 1981; PhD, Fla. State U., 1996. Social worker City of Phila., 1989-92; instr. C.C. of Phila., 1991-92, Fla. State U., Tallahassee, 1992-95; prof. lit. U. del Valle, Cali, Colombia, 1995—; cons. Consejo Nacional de Acreditación, Bogota, 1992—. Contbr. articles, over 25 short stories to profl. jours. Vol. Witness for Peace, Nicaragua, 1985. U. Calif.-Irvine Regents fellow, 1979. Mem. MLA, Coll. Lang. Assn., Phi Beta Kappa, Phi Kappa Phi. Home: 4404 Woodbridge Ct Raleigh NC 27612-3916 Office: Univ del Valle, AA25360, Cali Colombia

KEPPEL, WILLIAM JAMES, lawyer, educator, author; b. Sheboygan, Wis., Sept. 25, 1941; s. William Frederick and Anne Elizabeth (Cinealis) K.; m. Polly Holmsberg, June 26, 1965; children: Anne Rusert, Timothy, Matthew. BA, Marquette U., 1963; JD, U. Wis., Madison, 1970. Bar: Minn. 1970, U.S. Dist. Minn. 1970, U.S. Ct. Appeals (8th cir.) 1973, U.S. Dist. Ct. (we. dist.) Wis. 1979, U.S. Supreme Ct. 1979, U.S. Ct. Claims 1982. Assoc. Dorsey & Whitney, Mpls., 1970-76, ptnr., 1979-96; assoc. prof. Hamline U. Sch. Law, 1976-79, disting. practioner in residence, 1996—; instr. U. Minn. Law S ch.; adj. prof. William Mitchell Coll. Law, St. Paul; chmn., dir. Legal Advice Clinics, Ltd.; dir. Legal Assistance of Minn., Inc.; head Hennepin County Pub. Defender's Office for Misdemeanors. Author: (with Mc Farland) Minnesota Civil Practice (4 vols.), 1979, 2nd edit., 1990, Administrative Practice and Procedure, 1999; co-author, editor: Minnesota Environmental Law Handbook, 2nd edit., 1995; contbr. articles and monographs to legal jours. Lt. USN, 1963-67, Vietnam. Mem. ABA, Minn. Bar Assn. Roman Catholic. Home: 10 Luverne Ave Minneapolis MN 55419-2612 also: Hamline U Sch Law 1536 Hewitt Ave Saint Paul MN 55104

KEPPLE, THOMAS RAY, JR., college administrator; b. Pitts., Mar. 19, 1948; s. Thomas Ray and Virginia Grace (Hudson) K.; m. Jane Donaldson, Aug. 22, 1971 (dec. 1977); m. Patricia Witcher, May 24, 1994. B.A., Westminster Coll., 1970; M.B.A., Syracuse U., 1973, Ed.D., 1984. Dir. tech. tng. Morse div. Borg-Warner Corp., Ithaca, N.Y., 1970-73; dir. adminstrv. services Rhodes Coll., Memphis, 1975-81, dean adminstrv. services, 1981-86, provost, 1986-89, v.p. Univ. South, Sewanee, Tenn., 1989-98; pres. Juniata Coll., Huntingdon, Pa., 1998—; bd. dirs. Met Life Resources Retirement Adv. Bd.; chair bd. dirs. Prepaid Tuition Plan, Inc. Author: Incentive Early Retirement Programs for Faculty. Bd. dirs. Sewanee Housing Inc.; mem. exec. com. Vollintine Evergreen Community Assn., Memphis, 1976-85, pres., 1981; mem. Biomed. Research Zone Bd., 1986; sec.-treas. Health and Ednl. Facilities Bd. of Franklin County; bd. dirs. Liberty Bowl Classic. Mem. Internat. Soc. Planning and Strategic Mgmt. (v.p. communications 1984-85, pres. 1985-87), Nat. Assn. Coll. and Univ. Bus. Officers, Am. Assn. Higher Edn., Memphis Acad. Forum (pres. 1985-86), Coll. and Univ. Personnel Assn., Assn. Physical Plant Adminstrs., Omicron Delta Kappa. Presbyterian. Clubs: Univ. Club (N.Y.). Lodge: Rotary. Avocations: swimming; oil painting. E-mail: kepplet@juniatn.edu. Home: 2201 Washington St Huntingdon PA 16652-9762 Office: Juniata Coll Office of the Pres 1700 Moore St Huntingdon PA 16652-2119

KEPPLER, HERBERT, publishing company executive; b. N.Y.C., Apr. 21, 1925; s. Victor and Josephine T. (Windmann) K.; m. Louise M. Lyman, July 7, 1956; children—Kathryn Louise, Thomas Victor. B.A., Harvard, 1945. Reporter N.Y. Sun, 1948-49; with Modern Photography, N.Y.C., 1950-87; editorial dir., pub. Modern Photography, 1967-87; v.p. photog. pub. div. ABC Leisure Mags. Inc. div. ABC, N.Y.C., 1974-78; sr. v.p. photog. pub. div. ABC Leisure Mags. Inc. div. ABC, 1978-87; v.p., pub. dir. photography CBS Mags., 1987-88, Diamandis Communications Inc., 1988-90, Hachette Mags. Inc., 1990-93, Hachette Filipacchi Mags., Inc., 1993—. Author: Official 35mm Camera Rating Guide, 1957, Keppler on the Eye-Level Reflex, 1960, How to Make Better Pictures in Your Home, 1962, 124 Ways to Test Cameras, Lenses and Equipment, 1962, The Pentax Way, 1966, The Nikon-Nikkormat Way, 1976. Served to ensign USNR, 1945-46. Mem. Rolls-Royce Owners Club. Home: 119 N Highland Pl Croton On Hudson NY 10520-2113 Office: Hachette Filipacchi Mags 1633 Broadway New York NY 10019-6708

KEPPLER, RICHARD RUDOLPH, consultant, former oil company executive; b. Elizabeth, N.J., Dec. 22, 1912; s. Max Herman and Clara Elvira (Diehl) K.; m. Marjorie Edna Osterwald, June 9, 1939 (div. June 1981); children: Janet Foster, Susan Diehl; m. Katherine Gajewski, May 26, 1984 (dec. Aug. 1989). BSChemE, Princeton U., 1935; postgrad., U. Pitts. Cert. profl. engr., Mass. Safety engr. Liberty Mutual Ins. Co., N.Y.C., 1936-38; tech. svc. divsn. Exxon Corp., Elizabeth, 1938-46; tech. group head Colonial Beacon Oil Co., Everett, Mass., 1946-52; process supr. Exxon Corp., Everett, 1952-67, refinery mgr., 1968-69; ops. supr. Esso. Standard Thailand, 1969-70; R&D technician EPA Region I, Boston, 1970-71, R&D dir., 1971-83; now involved in cons. Patentee in field. Fin. com. mem. Town Winchester, Mass., town meeting mem.; vol. Hunt Hursing Home, Danvers, Mass. Mem. Exxon Annuitants, North Shore Organ Soc., Everett C. of C., Rotary. Republican. Congregational. Avocations: playing saxophone, model airplanes, woodworking. Home: 13 Cedarhill Dr Danvers MA 01923-1723

KEPPLER, WILLIAM EDMUND, multinational company executive; b. N.Y.C., June 12, 1922; s. Louis and Amelia (Koszut) K.; m. Natalie E. Lang, July 15, 1944 (dec. 1990); children: Gail, William Edmund, Jean; m. Margaret Delaney, June 20, 1992. BSChemE, Pratt Inst., 1942; MSChemE, NYU, 1944. Vice pres. Merck Sharp & Dohme, West Point, Pa., 1965-71; Vice pres. Squibb Corp., Holmdel, N.J., 1971-73; pres. Bell Mgmt., Blue Bell, Pa., 1973-74, Engel Industries, St. Louis, 1974-75; corp. sr. v.p. tech. ops./mgmt. systems Schering-Plough Corp., 1975-87; pres. Bell Mgmt., Inc., 1987—; tchr. chem. engring. Cooper Union, NYU, Bucknell U. Bd. dirs. Phila. chpt. Am. Cancer Soc., 1979; pres. Montour County (Pa.) Cerebral Palsy, 1953-57. Fellow AIChE; mem. Am. Mgmt. Assn., Whitemarsh Valley Country Club (Lafayette Hill, Pa.), Palm Beach Gardens (Fla.) Nat. Golf Club. Episcopalian. Home and Office: 407 Eagleton Cove Way Palm Bch Gdns FL 33418-8464

KERATA, JOSEPH J., secondary education educator; b. Cleve., Jan. 20, 1949; s. Joseph John and Lillian (Potocky) K.; m. Lynne E. Armington, July 20, 1990. BS in Edn., Ohio State U., 1971; MEd, Cleve. State U., 1978; postgrad., Ohio Wesleyan U., Princeton U. Tchr. sci. grades 7-8 Spellacy Jr. High Sch., Cleve., 1972-73; tchr. BSCS and gen. biology grades 10-12 Willoughby South High Sch., 1973-79; tchr. earth sci., physics, biology grades 10-12 Colegio Roosevelt, Lima, Peru, 1979-80; tchr. English adult edn. Academia Secretaria Y Typografia, Lima, 1980; tchr. gen. sci. grades 7-9 Eastlake Jr. High Sch., Willowick, Ohio, 1980-83; tchr. AP and honors biology Eastlake North High Sch., Willowick, 1983—, chair dept. sci., 1984—; mem. North Ctrl. Evaluation Team, 1978, circulum devel. and revision com., 1978, 85; judge sci. fairs several sch. dists., 1977—. Recipient Krecker Outstanding Sci. Dept. award, 1976, Outstanding Educator award Edinboro U., 1984, Sci. Tchr. of Yr. award Lubrizol Corp., 1991, Gov.'s Ednl. Leadership award, 1992, Ohio Tchr. of Yr. award, 1993; Martha Holden Jennings scholar, 1990; Woodrow Wilson Nat. fellow, 1992. Mem. NEA, Nat. Sci. Tchrs. Assn., Nat. Assn. Biology Tchrs., Ohio Edn. Assn., Ohio Acad. Sci., Willoughby-Eastlake Tchrs. Assn. (grievance chmn. 1981—), Cleve. Regional Assn. Biologists (original). Office: Eastlake North High Sch 34041 Stevens Blvd Eastlake OH 44095-2905*

KERBER, BETH-ANN, editor, reporter; b. New Brunswick, N.J., Apr. 9, 1969; d. Michael J. Gutsick and Alexis M. Messeroll; m. John F. Kerber, Aug. 17, 1991; 1 child, Sara. BS, Duquesne U., 1990. Reporter Greater Media Newspapers, E. Brunswick, N.J., 1990-93; newswriter, editor Health Resources Pub., Wall Twp., N.J., 1993-99; mng. editor Health Resources Pub., Manasquan, N.J., 1999—. Avocations: creative writing, photography, genealogy. E-mail: hrp@healthrespubs.com. Office: Health Resources Pub PO Box 456 Allenwood NJ 08720

KERBER, FRANK JOHN, diplomat; b. Indpls., June 13, 1947; s. Charles John and Romilda Ida (Molengraft) K.; m. Melanie Alice Niewoehner, July 29, 1989; 1 child, Brandon Eric Kerber. BA in Philosophy cum laude, Athenaeum of Ohio, 1969; MS, Georgetown U., 1976. Faculty coll. prep. sch. Cin., 1970-74; mgmt. cons. USAID, various locations, 1976-80; program officer USAID Mission, Tunis, Tunisia, 1980-84, Dept. of State, 1984; vice consul U.S. Consulate Gen., Winnipeg, Can., 1985-86; econ./comml. affairs officer Jordan, Lebanon and Syria, 1986-88; officer for East-West Affairs European Bur. Office of Regional Polit. and Econ. Affairs, 1988-90; A.I.D. liaison officer Bangui, Ctrl. African Republic, 1991-93; econ. officer Kingston, Jamaica, 1993-96; internat. economist Bur. Internat. Orgn. Affairs, Washington, 1996-98; spl. asst. to Amb. Schifter, 1998—. Mem. Am. Fgn. Svc. Assn. Address: 5305 Jerell Ct Burke VA 22015-1647 Office: S/SAS Dept Of State Washington DC 20521

KERBER, LINDA KAUFMAN, historian, educator; b. N.Y.C., Jan. 23, 1940; d. Harry Hagman and Dorothy (Haber) Kaufman; m. Richard Kerber, June 5, 1960; children: Ross Jeremy, Justin Seth. AB cum laude, Barnard Coll., 1960; MA, NYU, 1961; PhD, Columbia U., 1968; DHL, Grinnell Coll., 1992. Instr., asst. prof. history Stern Coll., Yeshiva U., N.Y.C., 1963-68; asst. prof. history San Jose State Coll., (Calif.), 1969-70; vis. asst. prof. history Stanford U., (Calif.), 1970-71; asst. prof. history U. Iowa, Iowa City, 1971-75, prof., 1975-85; May Brodbeck prof. U. Iowa, 1985—; vis. prof. U. Chgo., 1991-92. Author: Federalists in Dissent: Imagery and Ideology in Jeffersonian America, 1970, paperback edit., 1980, 97, Women of the Republic: Intellect and Ideology in Revolutionary America, 1980, paperback edit., 1986, Toward an Intellectual History of Women, 1997, No Constitutional Right to Be Ladies: Women and the Obligations of Citizenship, 1998; co-editor: Women's America: Refocusing the Past, 1982, 4th edit., 1995, U.S. History As Women's History, 1995; mem. editl. bd. Signs: Jour. Women in Culture and Society, Law and History Rev.; contbr. articles and book revs. to profl. jours. Fellow Danforth Found., Barnard Coll., NEH, 1976, 83-84, 94, Am. Coun. Learned Socs., 1975, Nat. Humanities Ctr., 1990-91, Guggenheim Found., 1990-91. Fellow Am. Acad. Arts and Scis.; mem. Orgn. Am. Historians (pres. 1996-97), Am. Hist. Assn., Am. Studies Assn. (pres. 1988), Am. Soc. for Legal History, Berkshire Conf. Women Historians. Jewish. Office: U Iowa Dept History Iowa City IA 52242

KERBER, RICHARD E., cardiologist; b. N.Y.C., May 10, 1939; s. Max and Pauline Kerber; m. Linda K. Kaufman; children: Ross, Justin. AB in Anthropology, Columbia U., 1960; MD, NYU, 1964. Diplomate Am. Bd. Internal Medicine, Am. Bd. Cardiology. Med. intern/resident Bellevue Hosp., N.Y.C., 1964-66; med. resident Stanford (Calif.) U. Hosp., 1968-69, cardiology fellow, 1969-71; asst. prof. internal medicine U. Iowa, Iowa City, 1971-74, assoc. prof. internal medicine, 1974-78, prof. medicine, 1978—. Editor: Echocardiography in Coronary Artery Disease, 1988. Capt. U.S. Army, 1966-68. RO1 grant NHLBI, 1995—. Fellow Am. Heart Assn. (award of Meritorious Achievement 1996), Am. Coll. Cardiology (gov. for Iowa 1976-79); mem. Am. soc. of Echocardiology (sec. 1978-80, treas. 1993-95, v.p., pres. elect 1995-97, pres. 1997—), Am. Physiology Soc., Am. Soc. for Clin. Investigation, Assn. of Univ. Cardiologists, Assn. of Am. Physicians. Office: U Iowa Dept Medicine 200 Hawkins Dr Iowa City IA 52242-1009

KERBER, RONALD LEE, industrial corporation executive; b. Lafayette, Ind., July 2, 1943; s. John Andrew Kerber and Edith Helen (McMaster) Kerkhoff; children: John, Mark, Stephen, Jacqueline. BS, Purdue U., 1965; MS, Calif Inst. Tech., 1966, PhD, 1970. Registered profl. engr., Mich. Tech. staff Aerospace Corp., Los Angeles, 1971-72; prof. Mich. State U., E. Lansing, 1969-85, assoc. dean, 1984-85; program mgr. Defense Advanced Research Projects Agy., Arlington, Va., 1983-84; dep. undersec. U.S. Dept. Defense, Washington, 1985-88; v.p. advanced systems and tech. McDonnell Douglas Corp., St. Louis, 1988-89, v.p. tech. and bus. devel., 1989-91; exec. v.p., chief tech. officer Whirlpool Corp., Benton Harbor, 1991—. Contbr. articles to profl. jours. Mem. ASME, IEEE, Am. Phys. Soc.

KERBIS, GERTRUDE LEMPP, architect; m. Walter Peterhans (dec.); m. Donald Kerbis (div. 1972); children: Julian, Lisa, Kim. BS, U. Ill.; MA, Ill. Inst. Tech.; postgrad., Grad. Sch. Design, Harvard U., 1949-50. Archtl. designer Skidmore, Owings & Merrill, Chgo., 1954-59, C.F. Murphy Assocs., Chgo., 1959-62, 65-67; pvt. practice architecture Lempp Kerbis Assocs., Chgo., 1967—; lectr. U. Ill., 1969; prof. William Rainey Harper Coll., 1970—, Washington U., St. Louis, 1977, 82, Ill. Inst. Tech., 1989-91; archtl. cons. Dept. Urban Renewal, City of Chgo.; mem. Northeastern Ill. Planning Commn., Open Land Project, Mid-North Community Orgn., Chgo. Met. Housing and Planning Council, Chgo. Mayor's Commn. for Preservation Chgo.'s Hist. Architecture; bd. dirs. Chgo. Sch. Architecture Found., 1972-76; trustee Chgo. Archtl. Assistance Ctr., Glessner House Found., Inland Architect Mag.; lectr. Art Inst. Chgo., U. N.Mex., Ill. Inst. Tech., Washington U., St. Louis, Ball State U., Muncie, Ind., U. Utah, Salt Lake City. Prin. archtl. works include U.S. Air Force Acad. dining hall, Colo., 1957, Skokie (Ill.) Pub. Library, 1959, Meadows Club, Lake Meadows, Chgo., 1959, O'Hare Internat. Airport 7 Continents Bldg, 1963; prin. developer and architect: Tennis Club, Highland Park, Ill., 1968, Watervliet, Mich. Tennis Ranch, 1970, Greenhouse Condominium, Chgo., 1976, Webster-Clark Townhouses, Chgo., 1986, Chappell Sch., 1993; exhibited at Chgo. Hist. Soc., 1984, Chgo. Mus. Sci. and Industry, 1985, Paris Exhbn. Chgo. Architects, 1985, Spertus Mus.; represented in permanent archtl. drawings collection Art Inst. Chgo. Active Art Inst. Chgo.. Recipient award for outstanding achievement in professions YWCA Met. Chgo., 1984. Fellow AIA (bd. dirs. Chgo. chpt. 1971-75, chpt. pres. 1980, nat. com. architecture, arts and recreation 1972-75, com. on design 1975-80, head subcom. inst. honors nomination); mem. Chgo. Women in Architecture (founder), Chgo. Network, Internat. Women's Forum, Arts Club Chgo., Cliff Dwellers (bd. dirs. 1987-88, pres. 1988, 89), Lambda Alpha. Office: Lempp Kerbis Assocs 172 W Burton Pl Chicago IL 60610-1310

KERBS, WAYNE ALLAN, transportation executive; b. Hoisington, Kans., Mar. 21, 1930; s. Emanuel and Mattie (Brack) K.; m. Patricia Ann Aitchison, Dec. 5, 1953; children: Jacqueline Lee Kerbs Kepler, Robert Wayne. BSEE, U. Kans., 1952; MSEE, Ohio State U., 1960; M Engring., UCLA, 1968. Test engr. Mpls.-Honeywell, 1952-54; sr. engr. Booz Allen & Hamilton, Dayton, Ohio, 1957-60; program mgr. Hughes Aircraft Co., L.A., 1960-74; pres., bd. dirs. Kerbs Industries, Inc., Los Alamitos, Calif., 1975—. Developer spacecraft devel. surveyor, 1960's, transit plan, 1996; patentee in field. Vol. PTA, Boy Scouts Am., Meth. Ch., 1952—; organizer Am. Mature Vols., L.a., 1994—; active Orange County Transp. Authority, 1994—. Lt. USN, 1954-57. Fellow Inst. for the Advancement of Engring.; mem. Soc. Automotive Engrs. (sec.), Inst. of Transp. Engrs., Elec. Automobile Assn., Advanced Transit Assn., Transp. Rsch. Bd., Am. Legion, Sigma Tau, Eta Kappa Nu, Kappa Eta Kappa. Republican. Avocations: sports, building, inventing, writing, investing.

KERCHER, DAVID MAX, mechanical engineer; b. Goshen, Ind., Nov. 18, 1931; s. Maxwell Mease and Rosemary (Harper) K.; m. Betty Noreen Raycroft, June 7, 1958; children: Kimberly S., Matthew R., Andrew D.R., Steven R., Elizabeth J., Jason R., Amy N. BSME, Purdue U., 1958; MS in Aerospace Engring., U. Cin., 1967. Engr. large jet engine divsn. GE, Cin., 1958-71, sr. engr., 1966-71, unit mgr., 1968; engr. missile and space div. GE, Burlington, Vt., 1959-60; unit mgr. gas turbine dept. GE, Schenectady, 1972-81, sr. engr., 1982; sub-sect. mgr. aircraft engine group GE, Lynn, Mass., 1983-84; sr. engr. GE Aircraft Engines, Lynn, 1985-89, prin. engr., 1989—; v.p. Sunrise Orchards, Inc., Goshen, Ind., 1996—, also bd. dirs. Contbr. articles to profl. jours.; 11 patents on gasturbine cooling. Sgt. USAF, 1950-54, USAFR, 1955-58. Mem. AIAA (sr.), ASME (gas turbine heat transfer com. 1980—, vice chmn. com. 1992-94, chmn. 1994-96), ASME Internat. Gas Turbine Inst., Am. Legion, Air Force Assn. (life), Tau Beta Pi, Pi Tau Sigma. Office: GE Aircraft Engines # 240GH 1000 Western Ave Lynn MA 01910-0001

KERCKHOFF, SYLVIA STANSBURY, mayor; b. Toledo, June 7, 1928; d. Paul William Stansbury and Lass Elizabeth Hackney; m. Alan Chester Kerckhoff, June 11, 1949; children: Steven, Sharon. BS, U. Wis., 1950; MAT, Duke U., 1960. Kindergarten tchr. Madison (Wis.) Schs., 1950-52; rsch. asst. Vanderbilt U., Nashville, 1957-58; jr. and sr. h.s. tchr. City Schs., Durham, N.C., 1959-60, 69-81; city coun. mem. City of Durham, 1981-93, mayor, 1993-99; co-chair Violence Prevention Comm., Durham, 1993-97; mem. Chamber Commerce Bd., Durham, 1993-97; founder Mayor's Univ. Adv. Coun., Durham, 1993-97; co-chair City-County Com., Durham, 1993-97. Chair N.C. League Municipalities, Transp., Comm. and Pub. Safety, 1996-97; mem. Gov.'s Transit 2000 Commn., N.C., 1996; v.p. N.C. League Women Voters, 1967-69, fin. chair, Durham League Women Voters, 1960-70; co-chair Youth Coordinating Bd., 1998—. Recipient Leadership award Duke U. med. Ctr., Durham, 1995, Durham County Women's Commn. Svc. award, 1993, Community Leadership in Arts award Durham Arts Coun., 1991; inductee DeVilbiss H.S. Hall of Fame, Toledo, 1998. Democrat. Presbyterian. Avocations: reading, tennis, music, hiking, travel. Home: 1511 Pinecrest Rd Durham NC 27705-5816

KERES, KAREN LYNNE, English language educator; b. Evanston, Ill., Oct. 22, 1945; d. Frank and Bette (Pascoe) K.; BA, St. Mary's Coll., 1967; student U. Notre Dame, 1967-68; MA, U. Iowa, 1969. Assoc. prof. English, humanities, fine arts William Rainey Harper Coll., Palatine, Ill., 1969-95, prof., 1995—, Palomar Coll., San Marcos, Calif., 1990-93; cons. bus. communications. Mem. MLA, Ill. Assn. Tchrs. English, Am. Fedn. Tchrs., Nature Conservancy, Mensa. Home: 222 Fairfield Dr Island Lake IL 60042-9622 Office: William Rainey Harper Coll Dept Liberal Arts Palatine IL 60067 *Experienced consultant in professional organizations: negotiating, multi-cultural and diversity issues. Develop and structure work force team goals for diverse employees. Written and inter-personal communication consultant.*

KERINS, FRANCIS JOSEPH, college president; b. N.Y.C., Mar. 23, 1927; s. John and Ellen (Mulrooney) K.; m. Mary Elizabeth Costigan, June 2, 1951; children: Mary Ellen Kerins Hayes, Donna (Mrs. Joseph Zelinski), John, Edward, Francis, Joseph, James. AB, St. Francis Coll., 1949; AM, St. Louis U., 1951; EdD, U. Denver, 1959; LHD, Coll. Idaho, 1983; LLD, City U., 1986. Prof., adminstr. Loretto Heights Coll., 1952-68; prof. higher edn. U. Denver, 1968-69; pres. Coll. St. Francis, Joliet, Ill., 1969-74, Carroll. Coll., Helena, Mont., 1974-89, No. Mont. Coll., Havre, 1989-90, St. Mary of the Plains Coll., Dodge City, Kans., 1990-91; commr. Western Interstate Commn. Higher Edn.; chmn. Western Ind. Colls. Fund, Commn. on Colls. Northwest Assn.; chmn. bd. Bank of Mont.; bd. dirs. Am. Council on Edn., Council Ind. Colls.; active Nat. Commn. on Higher Edn. Issues; cons. in field. Contbr. articles to profl. jours. Chmn. Lewis and Cark County Bicentennial Com., 1975—; trustee Loretto Heights Coll., 1961-67, Coll. St. Francis, 1969-74, Carroll Coll., 1974—; pres. Helena Symphony Soc., 1981—; bd. dirs. Helena YMCA, United Way; mem. Helena Airport Bd. With AUS, 1950-52. Fellow Am. Council Edn.; mem. Mont. Com. for Humanities (past chmn.), Assn. Cath. Colls. and Univs. (chmn.); mem. Helena C. of C. (bd. dir.), N.W. Assn. of Schs. and Colls. (pres.), Waterton-Glacier Internat. Peace Park Assn. (bd. dirs.), Rotary (past pres.). Roman Catholic.

KERLEY, JANICE JOHNSON, personnel executive; b. Coral Gables, Fla., Nov. 28, 1938; d. Howard Love and Lois Dean (Austin) Johnson; m. Bobby Joe Kerley, May 16, 1959; children: Janice Elisabeth Kerley Smothers, Meredith Ann Kerley Tucker. AA, Stephens Coll., 1958; B in Music Edn., U. Miami, Fla., 1960. Tchr. Dade County Pub. Schs., Miami, 1960-69; asst. to v.p. engr. Racal-Milgo, Inc., Miami, 1972-80; dir. sales and mktg. B. Joe Kerley, Realtor, Miami, 1980-83; dir. customer service, ops. mgr. Modern-Age Furniture Co., Miami, 1983-85; CEO Adecco Pers. Svcs., Greensboro, Winston-Salem, N.C., 1985—; CEO Jan-Ker, Inc., dba Adecco Pers. Svcs., Greensboro, Winston-Salem and Adecco Tech. Ctr., Greensboro, N.C. Named Small Bus. Person of Greensboro, Greensboro C. of C., 1988, Remarkable Woman of Greensboro, Greensboro Coll. Honor Soc., 1991. Mem. Am. Bus. Women's Assn. (nat. bd. dirs. 1978-79, trustee nat. scholarship fund 1978-79, named one of top ten businesswomen, 1988). Office: Adecco Tech Ctr Ste 202 7031 Albert Pick Rd Greensboro NC 27409-9522 also: 4500 Indiana Ave Ste 35 Winston Salem NC 27106-3269 also: Adecco Tech Ctr 7031 Albert Pick Rd Ste 202 Greensboro NC 27409-9522

KERMAN, ARTHUR KENT, physicist, educator; b. Montreal, May 3, 1929; s. Samuel and Ida (Birn) K.; m. Enid Ehrlich, Dec. 21, 1952; children: Ben, Daniel, Elizabeth, Melissa, James. B.Sc., McGill U., 1950; Ph.D., MIT, 1953. Mem. faculty dept. physics MIT, Cambridge, 1956, prof., 1964—, dir. Ctr. Theoretical Physics, 1976-83, dir. lab. nuclear scis., 1983-92; vis. prof. SUNY-Stony Brook, 1970-71; adj. prof. Brklyn. Coll., 1971-75; cons. Argonne Nat. Lab., 1961-83, mem. sci. and tech. adv. com., 1984-90; cons. Brookhaven Nat. Lab., 1965-81, mem. relativistic heavy ion collider policy com., 1985-95, vis. com. 1973-78, chmn. 1977; cons. Lawrence Berkeley Lab., 1975-80, mem. vis. com., 1980-83, chmn. 1981; cons. Lawrence Livermore Lab., 1964—, chmn. physical sci. advisory com. 1992-96; cons., Los Almos Sci. Lab, 1961—, mem. physics div. adv. com., 1984-96, mem. theo. div. adv. com. 1972—, mem. lansce divsn. adv. com., 1997—; cons. Nat. Bur. Standards, 1980-81, Oak Ridge Nat. Lab., 1979-85, Sandia Nat. Lab., 1998—; mem. U. Calif. Pres.'s Sci. and Academic Advisory Com. 1981-92;

mem. White House Sci. Council, 1982-85, panel on sci. and tech. in govt., 1985, fed. lab. rev. panel, 1982-83; mem. adv. com. Woods Hole Sub-panel of U.S. Dept. Energy, 1982, com. on sci., engring. and pub. policy research briefing panel on sci. frontiers and superconducting super collider Nat. Research Council, 1985, nuclear sci. adv. com. Dept. Energy and NSF, 1982-85; mem. U.S. Dept. Energy Fusion Policy Advisory Com., 1990, mem. U.S. Dept. Energy Inertial Confinement Fusion Advisory Com. 1992-96; mem. vis. com. Stanford U. Physics Dept., 1984, Yale U. Physics Dept., 1984, FONDS F.C.A.C. Comite des centres de Recherches pour le Laboratoire de Physique Nucleaire U. Montreal, 1982; Nat. Acad. Scis. panel on Inertial Confinement Fusion and Sci. Based Stockpile Stewardship, 1996-97, dirs. adv. com. Lawrence Livermore Nat. Lab., 1994-96; Ligo oversigh bd for MIT and Caltech, 1998—. Assoc. editor: Rev. Modern Physics, 1968-71. NRC fellow Calif. Inst. Tech., 1953-54, Niels Bohr Inst., Copenhagen, 1954-56; Guggenheim fellow U. Paris, 1961-62. Fellow Am. Phys. Soc. (program com. 1978-79, exec. com. div. nuclear physics 1970-72, pub. com. div. nuclear physics, Tom W. Bonner prize com. 1982-83), Am. Acad. Arts and Scis.; mem. N.Y. Acad. Scis. Office: MIT Dept Physics Rm 6-305 77 Massachusetts Ave Cambridge MA 02139-4307

KERMAN, BARRY MARTIN, ophthalmologist, educator; b. Chgo., Mar. 31, 1945; s. Harvey Nathan and Evelyn (Bialis) K.; BS, U. Ill., 1967, MD with honors, 1970. Diplomate Am. Bd. Ophthalmology; children: Gregory Jason, Jeremy Adam. Intern Harbor Gen. Hosp., Torrance, Calif., 1970-71; resident in ophthalmology Wadsworth VA Hosp., L.A., 1971-74; fellow in diseases of the retina, vitreous and choroid Jules Stein Eye Inst. UCLA, 1974-75; fellow in ophthalmic ultrasonography Edward S. Harkness Eye Inst., Columbia U., N.Y.C. and U. Iowa Hosps., Iowa City, 1975; asst. prof. ophthalmology UCLA, 1976-78, Harbor Gen. Hosp., 1976-78; asst. clin. prof. ophthalmology UCLA, 1978-83, assoc. clin. prof., 1983-95, clin. prof., 1995—, dir. ophthalmic ultrasonography lab., 1976—; cons. ophthalmologist, L.A., 1976—; chief ophthalmology Century City Hosp., 1995—; exec. bd. Am. Registry Diagnostic Med. Sonographers, 1981-87; jour. reviewer in field. With USAFR, 1971-77. Fellow Am. Acad. Ophthalmology; mem. Am. Soc. Cataract and Refractive Surgery, L.A. Soc. Ophthalmology, Am. Soc. Ophthalmic Ultrasound, Am. Assn. Ophthalmic Standardized Echography, Societas Internat. Pro Diagnostica Ultrasonica in Ophthalmic, Western Retina Study Club. Contbr. articles to profl. jours. Office: 2080 Century Park E Ste 800 Los Angeles CA 90067-2011

KERMAN, JOSEPH WILFRED, musicologist, critic; b. London, Apr. 3, 1924; U.S. citizen; married, 1946; 3 children. PhD in Music, Princeton U., 1951. Instr. music Princeton U., 1948-49; dir. grad. studies Westminster Choir Coll., 1949-51, from asst. prof. to assoc. prof., 1951-60, chmn. dept., 1961-64, 91-93; prof. music U. Calif., Berkeley, 1960—, Jerry and Evelyn Hemmings Chambers prof. music, 1985-87; C.E. Norton prof. poetry Harvard U., 1997; Heather prof. music Oxford U., 1972-74; Valentine prof. music Amherst Coll., 1988, Phi Beta Kappa, scholar, 1993. Author: Opera as Drama, 1956, rev. edit., 1989, The Elizabethan Madrigal, 1962, The Beethoven, Quartets, 1967, The Masses and Motets of William Byrd, 1981, Contemplating Music, 1985, Write All These Down, 1994, Concerto Conversations, 1999; (with others) History of Art and Music, 1968, Listen, 1972, 7th edit., 1999, The New Grove Beethoven, 1983; editor: Beethoven: Autograph Miscellany, 1970, Music at the Turn of the Century, 1970; co-editor Jour. 19th Century Music U. Calif., 1977-88. Recipient Nat. Inst. Arts and Letters award, 1956, Kinkeldey award Am. Musicol. Soc., 1970, 81, Deems Taylor award ASCAP, 1981, 95; Guggenheim fellow, 1960, Fulbright fellow, 1967, NEH fellow, 1982. Fellow Am. Acad. Arts and Scis., Brit. Acad. (corr.), Royal Musical Assn. (hon. fgn.), Am. Musicol. Soc. (hon.). Office: U Calif Berkeley Dept Music Berkeley CA 94720

KERMES, CONSTANTINE JOHN, artist, industrial designer; b. Pitts., Dec. 6, 1923; s. John Demetrios and Katina (Katerinis) K.; m. Bessie Saratopoulos, Sept. 14, 1952; children: Harriet Kermes Shuman, Kathy Kermes Dixon. BFA, Carnegie Mellon U. Designer Am.-Std. Co., Pitts., 1952-55; indsl. design cons. New Holland N.A. subs. Fiat, Modena, Italy, 1955-82; cons. designer New Holland N.A. subs. Fiat, Modena, 1982—. One man shows include Grimaldis Gallery, Balt., 1979, 80, Reading (Pa.) Mus., 1980, Jacques Seligmann Gallery, N.Y.C., 1951, 52, 54, 56, 59, 61, 64, 65, 70, 75, 78, 79, Hancock Shaker Mus., Pittsfield, Mass., 1989, Demuth Found., Lancaster, Pa., 1987, Millport Mus., Lancaster, 1989; exhibited in group shows at Butler Inst. Am. Art, Youngstown, Ohio, 1964, Pa. Watercolor Soc., 1979, 80, 91, Art 81, Washington, 1985, 91, Mus. Art, Lancaster, 1996; represented in permanent collections Storm King Art Ctr., Mountain View, N.Y., Pa. State U., Hershey (Pa.) Med. Ctr., Ford Motor Co., Pa. Hist. Mus., Hancock Shaker Mus., Mus. Art, Lancaster; illustrator Shaker Architecture, 1970; author, illustrator: American Icons, 1975; 24 patents for farm equipment designs. Recipient Am. Design Rev. award Indsl. Design mag., 1962, 64, 68, 72; design award Am. Iron and Steel Inst., 1963, 69, 73, 75, award York (Pa.) Art Assn. Mem. AHEPA (Lancaster), Pa. Watercolor Soc., Hamilton Club (Lancaster). Greek Orthodox. Home: 981 Landis Valley Rd Lancaster PA 17601-4816 Office: New Holland NA Inc 500 Diller Ave New Holland PA 17557-9301

KERMODE, (JOHN) FRANK, literary critic, educator; b. Douglas, Isle of Man, U.K., Nov. 29, 1919; s. John Pritchard and Doris (Kennedy) K. B.A., Liverpool U., 1940, M.A., 1947, D.Litt. (hon.), 1981; D.H.L. (hon.), U. Chgo., 1975; PhD (hon.), Amsterdam U., 1988, Newcastle U., 1993, Yale, 1995, U. Wesleyan, 1997, U. London, 1997. J.E. Taylor prof. English Manchester U., Eng., 1958-65; Winterstoke prof. English Bristol U., Eng., 1965-67; Lord Northcliffe prof. English Univ. Coll. London, 1967-74; King Edward VII prof. English Cambridge U., 1974-82; vis. prof. humanities Columbia U., N.Y.C., 1983, 85; Charles E. Norton prof. Harvard U., 1977-78; Henry Luce prof. Yale Y., 1994. Author numerous books including Romantic Image, 1957, Wallace Stevens, 1960, The Sense of an Ending, 1967, D.H. Lawrence, 1973, The Classic, 1975, The Genesis of Secrecy, 1979, The Art of Telling, 1983, Forms of Attention, 1985, History and Value, 1988, An Appetite for Poetry, 1989, The Uses of Error, 1991, Not Entitled, 1995, (with Anita Kermode) The Oxford Book of Letters, 1995; co-editor Encounter, 1965-67, (with Robert Alter) The Literary Guide to the Bible, 1987; editor Modern Masters Series, 1969—, Oxford Authors, 1984—. Served to lt. Royal Navy, 1940-46. Decorated officier Ordre des Arts et Sciences (France), 1973; named Knight Bachelor granted by the Queen of Eng., 1991; King's Coll. hon. fellow, 1987—. Fellow Brit. Acad., Royal Soc. Lit.; mem. Am. Acad. Arts and Scis. (hon.), Am. Acad. Arts and Letters (hon.). Home: 9 The Oast House, Pinehurst Grange Rd, Cambridge CB3 9AP, England

KERN, BERNADETTE, rehabilitation services educator, consultant; b. Boston, Apr. 26, 1957; d. Charles John and Geraldine Elizabeth (Garvey) K. BS, Bridgewater State Coll., 1979; MEd, Boston Coll., 1986; cert., Pa. Coll. Optometry, 1987. Cert. rehab. tchr. for blind and visually impaired, elem. tchr., moderate spl. needs tchr. Severe spl. needs tchr. Pilgrim Area Collaborative, Marshfield, Mass., 1979-82; resource specialist East Boston Harborside Community Sch., 1985-86; visual skill specialist VA Med. Ctr., West Haven, Conn., 1990-94; blind rehab. outpatient specialist VA Healthcare Sys., West Haven, 1994—; orientation and mobility specialist contractor Blindness and Visual Svcs., Pitts., 1989-90.; rehab. dir. Boston Aid to the Blind, 1986-90; cons. Wellmark, Westwood, Mass., 1990; adj. prof. U. Mass., Boston, 1997-98. Contbr. articles to profl. publs.; designer of Kichen for Blind and Visually Impaired, 1986; lecturer Blind Rehab. and Low Vision, 1987-90. C.C.D. tchr., St. Theckla's, North Pembroke, Mass., 1969-79; support group leader Multiple Sclerosis Soc., 1994-98. Mem. Nat. Clearinghouse on Tech. and Aging, Diabetics Educators Ea. Mass., Assn. for Edn. and Rehab. of Blind and Visually Impaired (recruiter 1986—, divsn. chair low vision 1994—). Roman Catholic. Avocations: swimming, walking. Office: VA Med Ct/124 Blind Rehab Svcs 950 Campbell Ave West Haven CT 06516-2770

KERN, BERNARD DONALD, retired educator, physicist; b. New Castle, Ind., Oct. 31, 1919; s. William Bernard and Cecile McDonald (Hudson) K.; m. Nedda Wisler Burdsall, Aug. 20, 1946; children—Richard B., Jonathan K., Arthur R. B.S., Ind. U., 1942, M.S., 1947, Ph.D., 1949. Physicist Signal Corps and Manhattan Project, Chgo., 1942-43; sr. physicist Oak Ridge Nat. Lab., 1949-50; mem. faculty U. Ky., 1950-85, prof. physics, 1958-85, chmn. dept. physics and astronomy, 1967-69, prof. emeritus, 1985; physicist U.S. Naval Radiol. Def. Lab., San Francisco, 1957-58, cons., 1957-69; prof. Inst. Teknologi Bandung (Indonesia), U Ky., State Dept. Ednl. Assistance Program, 1961- 62. Author articles on nuclear physics. Served to lt.(jg) USNR, 1943-46. Fellow Am. Phys. Soc.; mem. Am. Inst. Physics, Am. Assn. Physics Tchrs. Office: Dept Physics and Astronomy U Ky Lexington KY 40506-0012

KERN, CHARLES WILLIAM, retired university official, chemistry educator; b. Middletown, Ohio, July 13, 1935; s. Charles Albert and Charme (Bowman) K.; m. Regine Bouchard. BS, Carnegie Inst. Tech., 1957; PhD, U. Minn., 1961; postgrad., Columbia U., 1961-63. Postdoctoral fellow in chem. physics Columbia U., N.Y.C., 1961-63; asst. prof. chemistry SUNY, Stony Brook, 1964-66; adj. assoc. prof. chemistry Ohio State U., Columbus, 1966-71, adj. prof. chemistry, 1971-76, acad. vice chmn., dept. chemistry, 1972-73, prof. chemistry, 1976-80; rsch. scientist Battelle Meml. Inst., Columbus, Ohio, 1966-72, mgr. chem. physics sect., 1972-76, dir. phys. scis. program, 1973-74, inst. scientist, 1973-76, dir. Battelle Inst. program, 1976-84, cons., 1976-84; program dir. theoretical chem. physics, div. chemistry NSF, Washington, 1978-80, sr. staff assoc., computer sci. rsch. network project dir., div. math. and computer scis., 1980-83, program dir. structural chemistry and thermodynamics, acting sect. head phys. chemistry and chem. dynamics, div. chem., 1983-84, acting dir. div. chemistry, 1984-85, dep. dir. div. chemistry, 1985-86; asst. dir. gen. sci., Office of Sci. and Tech. Policy Office of the Pres., Washington, 1986; dean Ohio State U., Columbus, 1986-92; prof. chemistry Coll. Math. and Phys. Scis. Ohio State U., Columbus, 1986-92; v.p. rsch., dean Grad. Sch., Northwestern U., Evanston, Ill., 1992-93, v.p. rsch. and grad. studies, 1993-98, prof. chemistry, 1992-98, prof. emeritus, 1998—; chmn,. Sch. Many-Body Techniques in Chemistry, Seattle, 1969, Carnegie-Mellon U. Admissions Coun., 1970-72, Summer Rsch. Conf. on Theoretical Chemistry, Boulder, Colo., 1975; co-chmn. Current Biol. Problems, A Sch. for Phys. Scientists, 1977; exec. sec. NSF Dir.'s Task Force on Advanced Sci. Computing Resources, 1983-84. Assoc. editor Chem. Physics Letter, 1967-81; contbr. numerous articles to profl. jours. Mem. AAAS, Am. Chem. Soc., Am. Phys. Soc.

KERN, DONALD MICHAEL, internist; b. Belleville, Ill., Nov. 21, 1951; s. Donald Milton and Dolores Olivia (Rust) K. BS in Biology, Tulane U., 1973; MD magna cum laude, U. Brussels, 1983. ECFMG cert.; lic. Calif., Fla. Intern in surgery Berkshire Med. Ctr., Pittsfield, Mass., 1983-84; intern in psychiatry Tufts New England Med. Ctr., Boston, 1984-85; resident in internal medicine Kaiser Found. Hosp., San Francisco, 1985-87; with assoc. staff internal medicine Kaiser Permanente Med. Group, Inc., San Francisco, 1987-89; assoc. investigator AIDS Clin. Trial Unit Kaiser Permanente Med. Ctr., Stanford U., Nat. Inst. Allergy & Infectious Disease, San Francisco, 1988-90; mem. staff internal medicine Kaiser Permanente Med. Group, South San Francisco, 1989-96; mem. staff Desert Med. Group, Palm Springs, Calif., 1996—. Democrat. Roman Catholic. Avocations: theatre, ballet, traveling, 17th and 18th century French antiques.

KERN, EDNA RUTH, insurance executive; b. Rochester, N.Y., Dec. 31, 1945; d. Carl H. and Mildred B. (Fronk) McRorie; m. Charles E. Kern, Nov. 1, 1968 (div. July 1975); 1 child, Barbara Renee. BBA summa cum laude, Tex. Wesleyan Coll., 1978. CLU, ChFC. Pvt. detective Statewide Detective Agy., Orlando, Fla., 1968-78; agt. Pacific Mut. Ins., Ft. Worth, 1978-79, Conn. Mut. Ins., Ft. Worth, 1979-83; gen. agt. Gen. Am. Life Ins., Ft. Worth, 1983-85; ins. owner Kern & Assocs., Ft. Worth, 1985—; life underwriters tng. fellow Nat. Assn. Life Underwriters. Pres. All Sts. Hosp. Execs. Forum, Ft. Worth, 1986-87, Women's Health Forum, 1994-96; bd. dirs. YWCA 1984-85. Mem.Mem. Nat. Assn. Health Underwriters (registered, sec.-treas. 1990-91, Disting. Svc. award), Tex. Assn. Health Underwriters (state sec., bd. dirs. 1987-88, pres. 1988-90, Outstanding Texan of Yr. award, Hollis Roberson award), Ft. Worth Assn. Life Underwriters (bd. dirs. 1986-91, moderator 1984-86, chmn. health com. and edn. com. 1986-88), Tarrant County Assn. Health Underwriters (pres. 1986-87), Sales and Mktg. Execs. (bd. dirs. Ft. Worth chpt. 1985-87, v.p. 1986-87, sec. 1994-95, pres. 1995-96), Mensa. Republican. Avocation: community involvement. Office: Kern & Assocs PO Box 100356 Fort Worth TX 76185-0356

KERN, GEORGE CALVIN, JR., lawyer; b. Balt., Apr. 19, 1926; s. George Calvin and Alice (Gaskins) K.; m. Joan Shorell, Dec. 22, 1962; 1 child, Heath. BA, Princeton U., 1947; LLB, Yale U., 1952. Bar: N.Y. 1952. Chief U.S. Info. Ctr., Mannheim, W.Ger., 1947-48; dep. dir. pub. info. Office U.S. Mil. Govt. for Germany, Berlin and Nurnberg, 1948-49; assoc. Sullivan & Cromwell, N.Y.C., 1952-60, ptnr., 1960—; publ. Cub newspaper, Tehachapi, Calif.; bd. dirs. McJunkin Corp., Charleston, W.Va. Lt. USN, 1944-46. Home: 830 Park Ave New York NY 10021-2757 Office: Sullivan & Cromwell 125 Broad St Fl 28 New York NY 10004-2489

KERN, IRVING JOHN, retired food company executive; b. N.Y.C., Feb. 10, 1914; s. John and Min (Weitzner) Kleinberger; m. Beatrice Rubenfeld, June 22, 1941; children—John A., Arthur H., Robert M. BS, NYU, 1934, student Grad. Sch. Art and Sci., 1960-65; DHL, Mercy Coll., Dobbs Ferry, N.Y., 1980. Asst. buyer Bloomingdale's Dept. Store, N.Y.C., 1934-40; with Dellwood Foods, Inc., Yonkers, N.Y., 1945-82; pres. Dellwood Foods, Inc., 1966-77, chmn. and chief exec. officer, 1977-82; dir. Scarsdale Nat. Bank; adj. prof. polit. sci., San Diego State U., 1989-95. Mem. Cmty. Mental Health Svcs. Bd. of Westchester County, 1954-59; mem. bd. dirs., sec. Westchester County Assn., 1950-57, 76-80; exec. bd. Westchester County Better Bus. Bur., 1970-73; bd. dirs. Westchester Coalition, 1972-80, Westchester Minority Bus. Assistance Orgn., 1973-75, Milk Industry Found., 19876-82, Nat. Dairy Coun., 1979-81; bd. dirs., vice chmn. Westchester Pvt. Industry Coun., 1979-82; mil. adv. coun. Ctr. for Def. Info., 1986-97. Lt. col. AUS, 1940-45. Decorated Bronze Star. Mem. N.Y. Milk Bottlers Fedn. (pres., dir.), Met. Dairy Inst. (exec. v.p., dir.), Phi Beta Kappa, Tau Epsilon Phi.

KERN, JEAN GLOTZBACH, elementary education educator, gifted education educator; b. Fargo, N.D., Mar. 31, 1944; d. Clifford William and Edna Baker (Sullivan) Glotzbach; m. Peter Kern III, Oct. 11, 1974; 1 child, Adam Baker. BGS, Kent State U., 1973; student, SUNY, Buffalo, 1989; MEd., U. So. Fla., 1994. Cert. early childhood, elem. sch., gifted K-12, creative studies, Fla. Elem. educator Fruitville Elem. Sch., Sarasota, Fla., 1977-79, Sch. Bd. Sarasota County, Sarasota, Fla., 1977—, Ashton Elem. Sch., Sarasota, Fla., 1979-85; elem. educator gifted students Pine View Sch., Osprey, Fla., 1985-95, Bay Haven Sch. of Basics Plus, 1995; tchr. trainer Peace Corps, Cape Verde, 1996—; directing tchr. in internship program U. So, Fla., 1985—; chair elem. dept. Sarasota County Sch. Bd., 1992-93; teaching intern Dr. Donald Treffinger's Ctr. for Creative Learning, 1991, coord. Treffinger creativity project, 1992—; tchr. ESE model demonstration; spkr in field. Selby Found. grantee, 1989; Dept. Edn. grantee, 1985-86. Mem. Internat. Reading Assn. (sch. site contact person 1984—), Fla. Assn. for Gifted, Tchrs. Applying Whole Lang., Delta Kappa Gamma. Avocations: travel, reading, dieting, watching sunsets, creating. Home: 1846 W Leewynn Dr Sarasota FL 34240-9664 Office: care Peace Corp, CP 109 Corpo da Paz, Assomada Santa Catarina Cape Verde

KERN, JEROME H., lawyer; b. N.Y.C., June 1, 1937; s. Michael and Rebecca (Saltzman) K.; m. Mary Rossick; children: Jonathan Sterry, Peter M. AB, Columbia U., 1957; LLB, NYU, 1960. Law clk. to justice U.S. Ct. Appeals (2d cir.), N.Y.C., 1960-61; assoc. Simpson Thacher & Bartlett, N.Y.C., 1961-63; ptnr. Wachtell, Lipton, Rosen, Katz & Kern, N.Y.C., 1963-68; sr. and mng. ptnr. (investment banking) J.H. Kern & Co., N.Y.C., 1971-76; ptnr. Greenbaum, Wolff & Ernst, N.Y.C., 1977-82, Olwine, Connelly, Chase, O'Donnell & Weyher, N.Y.C., 1982-86; sr. ptnr., mem. exec. com. Shea & Gould, N.Y.C., 1986-91; pvt. practice Law Offices of Jerome H. Kern, N.Y.C., 1992; Baker and Botts, N.Y.C., 1992-98; vice chmn. TeleCommunications, Inc., Denver, 1998-99; CEO LinkShare Corp., Denver, N.Y.C., 1999—; adj. asst. prof. law NYU, 1964-71. Mng. editor NYU Law Rev., 1959-60. Bd. trustees NYU Law Ctr. Found.; bd. dirs. VOA Colo., Inst. for Children's Mental Disorders, City Meals-On-Wheels, N.Y.C. Root-Tilden scholar NYU, 1957-60. Mem. ABA, N.Y. State Bar Assn., Assn. Bar City N.Y.

KERN, JOHN MCDOUGALL, lawyer; b. Omaha, Nov. 28, 1946; s. Conard Lee and Agnes Rose (Brink) K.; m. Susan McDougall Kern, Oct. 15, 1977; children: Matthew, Jennifer. BA, Creighton U., 1970; JD cum laude, George Washington U., 1973. Bar: D.C. 1973, Calif. 1980, U.S. Dist. Ct. D.C. 1974, U.S. Dist Ct. (no. dist.) Calif. 1980, U.S. Dist. Ct. (ctrl. dist.) Calif. 1996, U.S. Ct. Appeals (D.C. cir.) 1974, U.S. Ct. Appeals (9th cir.) 1978; bd. cert. specialist in civil trial advocacy, Nat. Bd. Trial Advocacy. Asst. U.S. atty. criminal divsn. Office of U.S. Atty. D.C., Washington, 1973-78; asst. U.S. atty. civil divsn. Office U.S. Atty. No. Dist. Calif., San Francisco, 1978-82; v.p., dir. Crosby, Heafey, Roach & May P.C., San Francisco, Oakland, L.A., 1981—; cons. regents U. Calif., Berkeley, 1988—; faculty Nat. Inst. Trial Advocacy, 1987—; panelist Superior Ct. City and County of San Francisco Early Settlement Program, Superior Ct. Contra Cost County Bench-Bar Settlement Program; del. VI-IX Internat. AIDS Confs., 1991-93; spkr. numerous programs, confs.; lectr. in field. Contbr. abstracts, book chpt., articles to profl. jours. Mem. Am. Bd. Trial Advocates (advocate), Am. Inn of Ct., Assn. Bus. Trial Lawyers, Nat. Inst. Trial Advocacy. Office: Crosby Heafey Roach & May PC Ste 1900 4 Embarcadero Ctr San Francisco CA 94111-4106

KERN, JOHN WORTH, III, judge; b. Indpls., May 25, 1928; s. John Worth and Bernice (Winn) K.; children: John, Stephen. BA, Princeton U., 1949; LLB, Harvard U., 1952. Bar: D.C. 1953, U.S. Ct. Appeals (D.C. cir.) 1955. With, CIA, 1952-54; law clk. to chief judge U.S. Ct. Appeals D.C. Cir. Ct., 1954-55; asst. U.S. atty. D.C. Dist., Dept. Justice, Washington, 1955-59; assoc. Kilpatrick, Ballard & Beasley, Washington, 1959-65; with Dept. of Justice, Washington, 1965-68; judge D.C. Ct. Appeals, Washington, 1968-84, sr. judge, 1987—; dean Nat. Jud. Coll., Reno, 1984-87. Mem. D.C. Bar. Presbyterian. Office: DC Ct Appeals 500 Indiana Ave NW Washington DC 20001-2138

KERN, PAUL ALFRED, advertising company executive, research consultant, realtor, financial analyst; b. Hackensack, N.J., Mar. 17, 1958; s. Paul Julian and Edith Helen (Colten) K. BS in Commerce, U. Va., 1980; MBA, U. So. Calif., 1983. Sales rep. Procter & Gamble, Cin., 1980-81; rsch. svcs. mgr. Opinion Rsch., Long Beach, Calif., 1984; consumer planning supr. Dentsu, Young & Rubicam, L.A., 1984-85; rsch. exec. DJMC Advt., Inc., L.A., 1986; realtor assoc. Tarbell Realtors, Santa Ana, Calif., 1988-89; corp. pres. Jennskore, Inc., Torrance, Calif., 1989-93, also bd. dirs.; rsch. mgr. The Desert Sun, 1997-99; bd. dirs. Applicon, Inc., Hillsdale, N.J., Kernokopia, Hillsdale; cons. Venture Six Enterprises, Encino, Calif., 1985-87, DFS/Dorland, Torrance, 1986, IMI Machinery Inc., Charleston, S.C., 1987. Coach, supr. Little League Football, Alexandria, Va., 1981; active Surf and Sun Softball League (1987 champions). Recipient Most Calls Per Day award Procter and Gamble, 1980. Mem. Profl. Research Assn., Am. Mktg. Assn., Am. Film Inst., Internat. Platform Assn., U.S. Tennis Assn. (Michelob Light 4.5 Team Championship 1982), U. Va. Alumni Assn, Nat. Assn. Realtors, Calif. Assn. of Realtors, S. Bay Rd. of Realtors (Torrance-Lomita), Carson Bd. of Realtors. Club: Alta Vista Racquet. Avocations: tennis, chess, softball (S.W.A.T.S. 1987 League Champion), skiing, reading. Home and Office: 48-253 Silver Spur Trl Palm Desert CA 92260-6611

KERN, PAUL JOHN, army officer; b. Orange, N.J., June 16, 1945; s. Bruno Michael and Marjorie (Bolan) K.; m. Dolores I. Mercaldo, Aug. 28, 1971; children: Paul John Jr., Alexander Matthew. BS, U.S. Mil. Acad., 1967; MS in Mech. and Civil Engring., U. Mich., 1973; fellow nat. security, Harvard U., 1986-87. Registered profl. engr., Va. Commd. 2d lt. U.S. Army, 1967, advanced through grades to maj. gen., 1994, platoon leader, staff mem., 1967-69; troop comdr. 11th Armored Cavalry Regiment, Republic Vietnam, 1969-70; asst. prof., course dir. dept. engring. U.S. Mil. Acad., West Point, N.Y., 1973-76; ops. officer 2d bn., 33d Armor, 3d Armor Div., Kirch Goens, Fed. Republic Germany, 1976-78; br. chief Bradley Program Mgmt. Office, Warren, Mich., 1979-82; team chief reseach and devel. U.S. Army Staff, Pentagon, Washington, 1982-84; bn. comdr. 5th bn., 32d Armor, 24th Infantry Div., Ft. Stewart, Ga., 1984-86; mil. asst. Dep. under Sec. Def., Pentagon, Washington, 1987-89; comdr. 2d brigade, 24th Infantry Divsn. Saudi Arabia/Iraq, 1989-91; dir. requirements Army staff, 1991-92; asst. divsn. comdr.-maneuver, 24 Infantry Divsn. Ft. Stewart, Ga., 1992-93; mil. asst. to Sec. of Def., 1993-96; comdg. gen. 4th Inf. Divsn., Ft. Hood, Tex., 1996-97; mil. dep. to Asst. Sec. of Army Pentagon, Washington, 1997—. Co-author: Acquisition Mangers - Role and Reality, 1987. Decorated Bronze Star with 3 oak leaf clusters, Silver Star, Purple Heart with 2 oak leaf clusters, Legion of Merit. Mem. Soc. Automotive Engrs. (Teetor award 1975), Armor Assn., Assn. U.S. Army, Coun. Fgn. Rels., U.S. Naval Inst., Chi Epsilon. Roman Catholic. Avocations: sailing, woodworking, computers. Home: 3842 N Dittmar Rd Arlington VA 22207-4565*

KERN, TERRY C., judge; b. Clinton, Okla., Sept. 25, 1944; s. Elgin L. Kern and Lora Lee (Miller) Renegar; m. Charlene Heinen, Dec. 26, 1970; children: Lauren, Suzanne, Justin Hunter. BS, Okla. State U., Stillwater, 1966; JD, U. Okla., 1969. Bar: Okla. 1969, U.S. Dist. Ct. (ea. dist.) Okla. 1974, U.S. Dist. Ct. (we. dist.) Okla. 1979, U.S. Dist. Ct. (no. dist.) Okla. 1993, U.S. Ct. Appeals (10th cir.) 1979. Gen. atty. FTC, Washington, 1969-70; ptnr. Fischl, Culp, McMillin, Kern and Chaffin, Ardmore, Okla., 1971-86; founding ptnr., pres. Kern, Mordy and Sperry, Ardmore, 1986-94; dist. judge U.S. Dist. Ct. (no. dist.) Okla., Tulsa, 1994—, chief judge, 1996—. Chmn. bd. dirs. So. Okla. Meml. Hosp., Ardmore, 1989-91; vice chmn. Ardmore Devel. Authority, 1990; v.p. Perry Maxwell Intercollegiate Assn., Ardmore, 1992—. Served with USAR, 1970-75. Fellow Am. Bar Found., Okla. Bar Found. (pres. 1991, Disting. Svc. award 1992); mem. ABA, Am. Bd. Trial Advocates (Okla. chpt.), Okla. Bar Assn., W. Lee Johnson Inn of Ct. (master of bench), U. Okla. Coll. Law Assn. Democrat. Episcopal. Office: US Dist Courthouse 333 W 4th St Tulsa OK 74103-3839

KERN, WILLIAM BLIEM, JR., minister; b. Phila., Nov. 24, 1943; s. William Bliem Kern and Helen Elizabeth Kennedy; m. Ellen Eujen, Dec. 13, 1968 (div. Dec. 1972). BA, Wilmington Coll., 1967; MSc, MST, The New Seminary, 1990. Ordained min. N.Y. State Bd. Regents. Graphic design cons. to chief arch. Gibbs & Hill, N.Y.C., 1976-77; art dir. spl. projects The N.Y. Times Mag. Group, N.Y.C., 1979-80; design dir. Moving House and Home Mag., N.Y.C., 1981; assoc. art dir. Weight Watchers Mag., N.Y.C., 1982-83; market analyst The Comex Commodity Exch., N.Y.C., 1987-89; tv host, satellite psychic Internat. Satellite Nework, N.Y.C., 1991-92; min., pvt. practice spiritual counseling N.Y.C., 1990—. Author: Hail Jupiter, 1994, The Temple of Sound, 1995, The Jewel in the Lotus, 1999; performer poetry/prayer Nuc. Prayer The UN Hdqrs., 1994, Text of Amen The Great Pyramid Egypt, 1995. Mem. Am. Rsch. Ctr. in Egypt, Nat. Coun. for Geosomic Rsch., Soc. for Sci. Exploration, The Rosicsucian Soc. Am. (dir. astrology 1985—), Chakrasambara Buddhist Ctr., George Washington Lodge (treas. 1993-98). Avocations: watercolor landscape painting, Masonic education committee. E-mail: wbk@idt.net. Home: 230 Riverside Dr New York NY 10025-6172

KERNAN, BARBARA DESIND, senior government executive; b. N.Y.C., Jan. 11, 1939; d. Philip and Anne (Feuer) Desind; m. Joseph E. Kernan, Feb. 14, 1973. BA cum laude, Smith Coll., 1960; postgrad. Oxford U., 1963; MA, Harvard U., 1963; postgrad. in edn. policy George Washington U., 1980. Editor Harvard Law Sch., 1960-62; tchr. English, Newton High Sch. (Mass.), 1962-63; editor Allyn & Bacon Pubs., Boston, 1963-64; edn. assoc. Upward Bound, Edn. Assocs., Inc., Washington, 1965-68; edn. program specialist Title I, Elem. and Secondary Edn. Act, U.S. Office Edn., 1969-73; fellow Am. Polit. Sci. Assn., Senator William Proxmire and Congressman Alphonzo Bell, 1973-74; spl. asst. to dep. commr. for elem. and secondary edn. and dir. dissemination, sch. finance and analysis, U.S. Office Edn., 1975-77, chief program analysis br. div. edn. for disadvantaged, 1977-79; chief grant program coordination staff Office Dep. Commr. for Ednl. Resources, 1979-80; chief priority concerns staff Office Asst. Sec. Mgmt., U.S. Dept. Edn., Washington, 1980-81; dir. div. orgnl. devel. and analysis Office of Dep. Undersec. for Mgmt., 1981-86; Sr. Exec. Svc. candidate on spl. project to improve status of women Sec. Transp., Washington, 1983-84; inducted Sr. Exec. Svc., 1986; assoc. adminstr. for adminstrn. Nat. Hwy. Traffic Safety Adminstrn., U.S. Dept. Transp., 1986-94, career devel. leader to presdl. mgmt. interns, 1989-91; trustee Capricorn Galleries, Bethesda, Md., 1996-97; owner Philip Desind Collection, Am. Realism Fine Arts, 1997—; pres. Capricorn Galleries, Potomac, Md., 1997—. Recipient awards U.S. Office Edn., 1969, 71, 77, U.S. Dept. Edn., 1981-86, U.S. Dept. Transp., 1991, 94, Small Agy. Coun., 1990; scholarships U. Mich., 1956-58, Smith Coll., 1958-60, Harvard U., 1962-63; Am. Polit. Sci. Assn. fellow, 1973-74; Sr. Exec. fellow John F. Kennedy Sch. Govt. Harvard U., 1983. Office: Capricorn Galleries 10236 River Rd Potomac MD 20854-4905

KERNAN, JOHN WILLIAM, auto racing reporter; b. Irondale, Mo., Oct. 13, 1958. B in Journalism, U. Mo., 1986. Disk jockey Sta. KFTW-AM, Fredericktown, Mo., 1975; sports anchor Sta. KOMU-TV, Columbia, Mo., 1981-83; sports dir., anchor Sta. WDBJ-TV, Roanoke, Va., 1983-92; reports and features contbr. SpeedWeek ESPN, 1985—, host RPM 2Night, 1996—, pit reporter NASCAR Winston Cup races, 1990—. Recipient numerous awards Sta. WDBJ-TV, four award from Nat. Motorsports Press Assn., 1991 UPI So. Region Broadcast award for sports reporting, Va. AP Broadcasters award for sports coverage, 1984, 85. Office: c/o ESPN ESPN Pla Bristol CT 06010*

KERNAN, JOSEPH E., state official. BS, U. Notre Dame, 1968. Product mfg. mgr. Proctor & Gamble Co., 1976; sales exec. Schwarz Paper Co., 1976-80; city contr. South Bend, Ind., 1980-84, mayor, 1988; v.p., treas. MacWilliams Corp., 1984-88; lt. gov. State of Ind., Indpls., 1997—; bd. trustees St. Joseph Med. Ctr. Bd. dirs. St. Joseph County Spl. Olympics, Notre Dame Club, Jr. Baseball Assn., Northside L.L.; campaign cabinet United Way, 1979-82; treas. Studebaker Music Inc. Comdr. USN, 1969-75. Recipient two Purple Heart medals, two Air medals, award for Individual Excellence. *

KERNAN, PAMELA LYNNE, critical care nurse; b. Balt., June 25, 1955; d. David E. Jr. and Dottie L. (Adkins) Dell; m. Eugene Joseph Kernan, Apr. 12, 1980; children: Erin, Kristin, Kimberly, Kaitlin. Diploma, Union Meml. Hosp. Sch. Nursing, Balt., 1976; BSN, Coll. Notre Dame, Balt., 1993. RN, Md. Cert. emergency nurse. Pediatric nurse Wilson Grubb MD, Balt., 1978-80; staff nurse emergency dept. Union Meml. Hosp., Balt., 1976-93, clin. coord. night shift, 1989-90; sch. nurse County of Balt., 1993—. Mem. Emergency Nurses Assn. (Md. state pres. 1986-87, Balt. met. chpt. pres. 1983-84), Nat. Assn. Sch. Nurses, Balt. County Sch. Nurses Assn. Office: Hereford Md School 712 Corbett Rd Monkton MD 21111-1538

KERNAN, WILLIAM FRANK, lieutenant general United States Army. BA in History, Our Lady of Lake U., 1973; MA in Pers. Adminstrn., Ctrl. Mich. U.; student, Infantry Advanced Course, 1973-74, U.S. Army Command, Gen. Staff, Coll., 1978-79, U.S. Army War Coll., 1986-87. Commd. 2d lt. U.S. Army, 1968, advanced through grades to lieut. gen., 1998; platoon leader Co. D. 1st Battalion, 101st Airborne Divsn. U.S. Army, Vietnam, 1969; reconnaisance platoon leader 1st battalion, liason officer 101st Airborne Divsn. U.S. Army, Vietnam, 1969-70; comdr. hdqtrs. co. 2d battalion, 82d Airborne Divsn. Fort Bragg, N.C., 1970-71; comdr. San Antonio Dist. Recruiting Command U.S. Army, Austin, Tex., 1974-76; comdr. Hdqs. Co. 2d Battalion (Rangers), 75th Infantry, Fort Lewis, Wash., 1976-77, Co. A., 2d Battalion (Rangers), 75th Infantry, Fort Lewis, 1977-78; recorder secretariat for dept. of army selection bds., later pers. mgmt. officer, Combat Arms Divsn., U.S. Army Pers. Ctr, Alexandria, Va., 1979-81; exchange officer, rifle company comdr. 3d battalion Brit. Parachute Regiment, UK, 1981-83; exec. officer 2d battalion (airborne) to comdr. 82d Airborne Divsn., Fort Bragg, N.C., 1983-85; comdr. 3d battalion 82d Airborne Divsn., Fort Bragg, 1985-86; from dep. comdr. to comdr. 75th Ranger Regiment, Fort Benning, Ga., 1988-91; dir. for strategic plans, policies, assessments U.S. Spl. Ops. Command, McDill AFB, Fla., 1993-96; commanding gen. 101st Airborne Divsn. and Fort Campbell, Fort Campbell, Ky., 1996-98. Decorated Defense Disting. Svc. medal, Disting. Svc. medal, Legion of Merit with 3 oak leaf clusters, Bronze Star medal with V device, Bronze Star medal with oak leaf cluster, Purple heart, Meritorious Svc. medal with 3 oak leaf clusters, Air medals, Army Commednation medal with 4 oak leaf clusters, Army Achievment medal. Office: Fort Bragg Office of Commanding Gen Fort Bragg NC 28307

KERNDT, PETER REYNOLDS, physician; b. Sept. 16, 1952. MD, U. iowa, 1979; MPH, UCLA, 1996. Epidemic intelligence svc. officer USPHS Ctrs. for Disease Control and Prevention, 1985-88; dir. HIV Epidemiology Program L.A. County Dept. Health Services, L.A., 1987—. Office: 600 S Commonwealth Ave Ste 1920 Los Angeles CA 90005-4036

KERNER, FRED, book publisher, writer; b. Montreal, Can., Feb. 15, 1921; s. Sam and Vera (Goldman) K.; m. Jean Elizabeth Somerville, July 17, 1945 (div. Apr. 1951); 1 son, Jon Fredrik; m. Sally Dee Stouten, May 18, 1959; children: David, Diane. BA, Sir George Williams U. (now Concordia U.), Montreal, 1942. Mem. editl. staff Saskatoon (Can.) StarPhoenix, 1942; Asst. sports editor Montreal Gazette, 1942-44; news editor Can. Press, Montreal, Toronto, N.Y.C., 1944-50; asst. night city editor A.P., N.Y.C., 1950-57; editor Hawthorn Books, Inc., N.Y.C., 1957-58, pres., 1964-68; exec. editor Crest-Premier Books, Hall House, Fawcett World Libr., N.Y.C., 1958-63; editor-in-chief Crest-Premier Books, Fawcett World Libr., N.Y.C., 1963-64; pres. Centaur House, Inc. (pubs.), 1964-80, Paramount Securities Corp., 1965-67, Veritas Internat. Pubs., 1976—, Publishing Projects, Inc., 1967—, Communications Unltd., 1968—; editorial dir. book and ednl. divs. Reader's Digest, Can., 1968-75; v.p., pub. dir. Harlequin Enterprises Ltd., 1975-83, sr. cons. editor, 1984-96, editor emeritus, 1983—; v.p. Publitex Internat. Corp. (pubs.), 1968-75; pres. Athabaska House, 1975-77; dir. Nat. Mint, Inc., various other corps.; panelist various profl. confs.; chmn. Internat. Affairs Conf. Coll. Editors, 1965; drama festival adjudicator, 1940-48; Broadway theatrical script cons., 1948-56; speechwriter Adlai Stevenson, 1952, 56; ghostwriter Dr. Joyce Brothers, Anita Colby, Enid Haupt, and others; mem. nat. negotiating com. Am. Newspaper Guild, 1949-54, Wire Svc. Guild, 1954-57, chmn. grievance com., 1955-57. Author: (with Leonid Kotkin) Eat, Think and Be Slender, 1954, (with Walter M. Germain) The Magic Power of Your Mind, 1956, (with Joyce Brothers) Ten Days to a Successful Memory, 1957, Stress and Your Heart, 1961; pseudonym Frederick Kerr: Watch Your Weight Go Down, 1962, (with Walter M. Germain) Secrets of Your Supraconscious, 1965, (with David Goodman) What's Best for Your Child and You, 1966, (with Jesse Reid) Buy High, Sell Higher, 1966; (pseudonyum M.N. Thaler) It's Fun to Fondue, 1968, (with Ion Grumeza) Nadia, 1977, Careers in Writing, 1985, Mad About Fondue, 1986, (with Andrew Willman) Prospering Through the Coming Depression, 1986, Home Emergency Handbook and First-Aid Guide, 1990; contbg. author: Successful Writers and How They Work, 1958, Words on Paper, 1960, Overseas Press Club Cookbook, 1964, The Senior's Guide to Life in the Slow Lane, 1986, The Writer's Essential Desk Reference, 1991, 96, Lifetime: A Treasury of Uncommon Wisdoms, 1992, Chambers's Ency.; books transl. into French, German, Japanese, Portuguese, Spanish and Italian; editor: Love is a Man's Affair, 1958, Treasury of Lincoln Quotations, 1965, new edit. 1996, The Canadian Writer's Guide, 9th edit., 1985, 10th edit., 1988, 11th edit., 1992, Selling Your Short Fiction, 1992. Mem. local sch. bd., N.Y.C., 1967-68; chmn. sch. com. Westmount High Sch., 1970-72; mem. sch. com. Roslyn Sch., 1973; chmn. publs. com. Edward R. Murrow Meml. Fund; judge Dr. William Henry Drummond Nat. Poetry Contest; trustee Gibson Lit. Awards, C.A.A. Lit. Awards, Benson & Hedges Lit. Awards, CA&B Student Creative Writing Awards; bd. govs. Concordia U., 1975-79; hon. life mem. Can. Pubs. Coun.; founding mem. exec. com. Pub. Lending Rights Commn., 1986-89, vice chmn., 1988-89; founding dir. Toronto Book and Mag. Fair, bd. dirs., 1990-94. Recipient Queen's Silver Jubilee medal for contbns. to internat. pub., 1977, Allan Sangster award, 1982, Internat. Pub. award Air Can., 1982, 2 internat. awards for advertorial writing, 1990, Apex, 92 award for newsletter editing. Fellow Can. Copyright Inst. (vice chmn.), Acad. Can. Writers (vice chmn., bd. govs. 1986—); mem. European Acad. Arts, Scis. and Humanities, Orgn. Can. Authors and Pubs. (founding dir.), Can. Authors Assn. (v.p. 1972-80, founding dir. Lit. Luncheons, pres. Montreal br. 1974-75, nat. pres. 1982-83, founding editor Nat. Newsline 1982, pub. Can. Author 1982-95, hon. life, chmn. editl. adv. com. Can. Author 1978-94, chmn. grievance com. 1983-93, pub. com. 1986-92), Periodical Writers' Assn. Can. (chmn. grievance com. 1990, contracts com.), Can. Writers' Found. (bd. govs. 1982—), Assn. Am. Pubs. (hon. life), Mystery Writers Am. (editor Third Degree, co-chmn. awards com.), Writers' Union Can. (hon. life, chmn. grievance com. 1990-99, contracts com. 1990—), Soc. Profl. Journalists' Pres.'s Club, Book and Periodical Coun. (bd. govs. 1983-94), Authors Guild, Authors League Am., Internat. P.E.N., Nat. Spkrs. Assn. Am. Acad. Polit. and Social Sci., Can. Assn. Restoration of Lost Positives (pres.), Can. Soc. for Preservation of the Natural Bowtie (pres.), Sir George Williams U. Alumni Assn. (founding pres. N.Y.C. br., exec. com. 1970-75, pres. 1971-73), GeorgiAntiques (founding dir.), Avodah Honor Soc., Advt. Club, Deadline Club, Overseas Press Club, Dutch Treat Club (N.Y.C.), Toronto Press Club, Author's Club (London), Sigma Delta Chi. Home: 1405-1555 Finch Ave E, Willowdale, ON Canada M2J 4X9 Office: 55014 Fairview Mall, Willowdale, ON Canada M2J 5B9

KERNER, JOSEPH FRANK, JR., management consultant, educator; b. Cleve., Dec. 29, 1938; s. Joseph Frank Sr. and Magarat Ann (Majoris) K.; m. Marilyn Joy Long, June 14, 1964; children: Joseph, Mark, Michael, Erin. BA, Miami U., Oxford, Ohio, 1961; postgrad., Case Western Res. U., 1963-68. Dir. bus. tech. Marion (Ohio) Tech. Coll., 1969-75; mgr. benefits Cen. Net Bank, Cleve., 1975-78; mgr. compensation L.B. Foster, Pitts., 1978-80; mgr. compensation and benefits Rubbermaid, Wooster, Ohio, 1980-82; dir. compensation and benefits ChemLawn, Columbus, Ohio, 1982-84; v.p. First Nat. Bank of Commerce, New Orleans, 1984-85; instr. Bliss Coll., Columbus, 1985-88; regional v.p. Primerica Fin. Svcs., Columbus, 1985-95; pres. JFK Consultancy & Kerner Connection, Columbus, 1988—; mktg. dir. WMA Securities, 1995-97; v.p. mktg. Environ. Energy Alt. Fuel, 1995-97; mktg. advisor TAASI, 1995-98; adj. prof. Coll. Fin. Planning, 1988—; co. advisor Ohio Bus. Week, 1994—. Author: National Underwriter: Agent Exposes Himself, 1987, Pension Actuary: My Vision, 1994. Bd. dirs. Environ. Energy, Inc.; mem. Nat. Rep. Glee Club. Mem. Am. Soc. Pension Actuaries (bd. dirs. 1966-69, edn. coord. 1990—, joint bd. enrolled actuary exam. rev. com., editor Pension Actuary 1994, govtl. affairs com. 1993—, cert. fed. tax., cert. data educator), Kiwanis (immediate past pres., club builder New Albany, Ohio), Data Processing Mgmt. Assn. (faculty student chpt. of yr. 1970). Republican. Lutheran. Avocations: snow and water skiing, fishing. E-mail: JFKequal@aol.com. Home: 247 Windemere Pl Westerville OH 43082-6350

KERNER, MICHAEL PHILIP, lawyer; b. N.Y.C., July 21, 1953; s. Arthur and Rosalind (Mehr) K. BA, Antioch Coll., 1976; JD, Lewis & Clark U., 1979; LLM in Taxation with honors, Golden Gate U., 1995. Bar: Calif. 1980 (cert. specialist personal and small bus. bankruptcy law), U.S. Dist. Ct. (no. and ea. dists.) Calif. 1983, U.S. Ct. Appeals (9th cir.) 1983, U.S. Tax Ct., 1996. Staff atty. U.S. EPA, Washington, 1979-80; asst. regional counsel region 9 U.S. EPA, San Francisco, 1980-83; ptnr. Kerner, Weppner & Rosenbaum, San Francisco, 1983-95; prin. Kerner & Assocs., San Francisco, 1996—; bd. dirs. Solano County Legal Assistance, Vallejo, Calif., 1983-86; arbitrator San Francisco Superior Ct., 1991-94. Editor law rev. and law jours. Mem. San Francisco Trial Lawyers Assn., Solano County Bar Assn., Nat. Assn. Consumer Bankruptcy Attys. Democrat. Jewish. Avocations: windsurfing, snowboarding, road and mountain biking. Office: Kerner & Assocs 240 Stockton St Ste 4 San Francisco CA 94108-5306

KERNEY, THOMAS LINCOLN, II, investments and real estate professional; b. Princeton, N.J., Dec. 16, 1950; s. James Jr. and Elsie (Regan) K. BA in Journalism, Tex. Christian U., 1973. With Gloria Nilson Realtors, Princeton. Trustee James Kerney Found., Princeton, 1983—, sec., 1992-98, v.p., 1995-98, pres., 1998—; trustee Trenton Area Soup Kitchen, 1985-87, Princeton Edn. Ctr. at Blairstown, 1987-89, Princeton Child Devel. Inst., 1988-94, N.J. State Mus., 1988-94, Morven, Princeton, 1989-91, Princeton Small Animal Rescue League, 1991, treas., 1997—. Mem. Nassau Club. Roman Catholic. Home: 42 Fackler Rd Princeton NJ 08540-4706

KERNIS, AARON JAY, composer; b. Phila., Jan. 15, 1960. Attended, San Francisco Conservatory of Music, 1977-78; BMus, Manhattan Sch. Music, 1978-81; MMus, Yale U., 1983. Compositions include: (symphonies/orchestra) Mirror of Heat and Light, Cycle V-Part 2, 1984-85, Invisible Mosaic III, 1988, Symphony in Waves, 1989; (chamber/instrumental) Four Miniatures, 1977, Cycle II, 1979, Morning, 1989, Meditation (in memory of John Lennon), 1981, Suite in Three Parts for guitar, 1981, Music for Trio, Cycle IV, 1982, Suite in Three Parts for organ, 1982, Passacaglia-Variations, 1985, Invisible Mosaic I, 1985-86, Phantom Polka, 1987, Poisoned Nocturnes, 1987, Before Sleep and Dreams, 1987-90, Delicate Songs, 1988, Invisible Mosaic II, 1988, String Quartet, 1990; (vocal/choral) Six Fragments of Gertrude Stein, 1979, Stein Times Seven, 1980, Death Fugue, 1982, Cycle III, 1981, Nocture, 1982, Teach Me Thy Way, O Lord, 1982, Morningsongs, 1982-83, Dream of the Morning Sky, Cycle V-Part 1, 1982-83, America(n) (Day) Dreams, 1984, Praise Ye the Lord, 1984, I Will Lie Down, 1985, Love Scenes, 1986-87, Songs of Innocence, Books I and II, 1988-89, Brilliant Sky, 1990. Guggenheim fellow, 1985-86, N.Y. Found. for Arts fellow, 1988; NEA grantee; recipient Rome prize Am. Acad. in Rome, 1984-85, Joseph N. Bearns prize Columbia U., 1985, Tippett award. Office: Manhattan Sch of Music 120 Claremont Ave New York NY 10027-4698*

KERNOCHAN, JOHN MARSHALL, lawyer, educator; b. N.Y.C., Aug. 3, 1919; s. Marshall Rutgers and Caroline (Hatch) K. AB, Harvard U., 1942; JD, Columbia U., 1948. Bar: N.Y. 1949. Asst. dir. Legis. Drafting Research Fund Columbia U., N.Y.C., 1950-51, acting dir., 1951-52, dir., 1952-69, lectr. law, 1951-52, assoc. prof., 1952-55, prof., 1955-77, Nash prof. law, 1977-89, Nash prof. law emeritus, 1990—, exec. dir. Council for Atomic Age Studies, 1956-59, co-chmn., 1960-62, dir. Ctr. for Law and Arts, 1986—; spl. lectr., 1991—; chmn. bd. Galaxy Music Corp., 1956-89; cons. Temporary State Commn. to Study Organizational Structure of Govt. of N.Y.C., 1953; bd. dirs. E.C.Schirmer Music Co., Inc.; pres. Gaudia Music & Arts, Inc., 1987—. Author: The Legislative Process, 1980; co-author: Legal Method Cases and Materials, 1980; contbr. articles to profl. jours. Mem. civil and polit. rights com. Pres.'s Commn. on Status of Women, 1962-63; dir. emeritus Vol. Lawyers for the Arts; mem. legal and legis. com. Internat. Confedn. Socs. Authors and Composers. Mem. Assn. Bar City of N.Y. Internat. Lit. and Artistic Assn. (mem. d'honneur, internat. exec. com., mem. U.S.A. group), Copyright Soc. U.S.A. (exec. com. 1986-89), Assn. Tchrs. and Rschrs. in Intellectual Property, Com. for Lit. Property Studies. Office: Columbia U Sch Law 435 W 116th St New York NY 10027-7297

KERNODLE, LUCY HENDRICK, school system nurse; b. Rutherfordton, N.C., Oct. 7, 1947; d. Harry Vance and Elizabeth Bruce (Beavers) Hendrick; m. Harold Barker Kernodle Jr., June 8, 1968; children: Carey Elizabeth, Katherine Suzanne. BSN, Duke U., 1969. RN, N.C.; cert. sch. nurse. Generalized pub. health nurse Met. Health Dept., Nashville, 1969-71, 73-74; pediatric orientation coord. Alamance County Hosp., Burlington, N.C., 1985-90; sch. system nurse Burlington City Schs., 1990-96, Alamance-Burlington Schs., 1996—; mem. woman's health steering com. Alamance Regional Med. Ctr., 1994—. Deacon, elder, tchr. Sunday sch., youth advisor, mem. Christian edn. com. 1st Presbyn. Ch., 1977—; mem. Alamance County Svc. League, 1978-84, svc. chmn., 1983-84; mem. Alamance Caswell Med. Aux., Burlington, 1976—, pres., 1981. Mem. Profl. Educators in N.C. (bd. dirs. 1993-94), Sch. Nurse Assn. of N.C. (exec. com. 1992—, pres. 1999—), Youth Advocacy Assn., Olde Forest Racquet Club (sec., bd. dirs. 1990-93), Nat. Sch. Nurses Assn. Republican. Presbyterian. Avocations: tennis, snow skiing, sailing. Home: 639 Still Run Ln Graham NC 27253-7702 Office: Alamance-Burlington Schs 1712 Vaughn Rd Burlington NC 27217-2916

KERNODLE, ROBERT GARY, dance and exercise eucator; b. Greensboro, N.C., Sept. 30, 1953; s. Robert G. and Madge C. (Carter) K. Student, U. N.C., 1972-74, U. N.C., Greensboro, 1977-82, N.C. State U., 1975-76, N.C. Sch. of the Arts, Winston Salem, 1977. Tchr. Greensboro (N.C.) Coll., 1987-89; substitute tchr. Ctr. for Creative Leadership, 1990—; advisor, choreographer Sports Ventures, Inc., Charlotte, N.C., 1990s; mem. exec. bd., editor N.C. Dance Alliance, 1985-88. Contbr. articles to profl. jours. Avocations: poetry, abstract painting, dance, any physical activity.

KERNODLE, UNA MAE, family and consumer sciences curriculum specialist, retired secondary education educator; b. Jackson, Tenn., Mar. 4, 1947; d. James G. and Mary E. (McLemore) Sikes. B.S. in Home Econs., U. Tenn., 1969; M.Edn., U. Alaska, 1974. Tchr., head dept. vocat. edn. and electives Chugiak High Sch., Anchorage, ret.; home econs. curriculum specialist King Career Ctr., Anchorage; edn. cons. State of Alaska, Anchorage Talent Bank; presenter Gov.'s Conf. on Child Abuse, Alaska Vocat. Edn. Assn. Conf., Alaska Home Econs. Inst., 1989; state officer Alaska Home Econs.; bd. dirs. Kids Are People. Recipient Gruening award, 1989. Mem. NEA, Am. Assn. of Fam. and Consumer Scis., Am. Vocat. Assn. Democrat. Baptist. Office: Office of Career Tech 2650 E Northern Lights Blvd Anchorage AK 99508-4119

KERNS, DAVID VINCENT, lawyer; b. Salt Lake City, Jan. 29, 1917; s. Clinton Bowen and Ella Mae (Young) K.; m. Dorothea Boyd, Sept. 5, 1942; children—David V., Clinton Boyd. B.Ph., Emory U., 1937; J.D., U. Fla., 1939. Bar: Fla. 1939, U.S. Dist. Ct. (mid. dist.) Fla. 1939, U.S. Dist. Ct. (so. dist.) Fla. 1978, U.S. Dist. Ct. (no. dist.) Fla., U.S. Ct. Appeals (11th cir.) 1981, U.S. Supreme Ct. 1988. Assoc. Sutton & Reeves, Tampa, Fla., 1939-41, Fowler & White, Tampa, 1945-47; ptnr. Moran & Kerns, Tampa, 1948-49; resident atty. Fla. Road Dept., 1949-53; research asst. Supreme Ct. Fla., 1953-58; dir. Fla. Legis. Reference Bur., 1958-68, Fla. Legis. Service Bur., 1968-71, Fla. Legis. Library Services, 1971-73; gen. counsel Fla. Dept. Adminstrn., 1973-82; mem. Fla. Career Service Commn., 1983-86; spl. master Fla. Senate, 1987-96; legal cons. chief inspector gen. Fla. Gov. Office, 1995-98. Contbr. articles to profl. jours. Served with U.S. Army, 1941-45. Mem. Fla. Govt. Bar Assn. (pres. 1966, J. Ernest Webb Meml. award 1982), Fla. Bar (bd. govs. 1978-84), Tallahassee Bar Assn. (spl. dir. 1993-95). Democrat. Methodist. Home: 418 Vinnedge Ride Tallahassee FL 32303-5140

KERNS, GERTRUDE YVONNE, psychologist; b. Flint, Mich., July 25, 1931; d. Lloyd D. and Mildred C. (Ter Achter) B.; BA, Olivet Coll., 1953; MA, Wayne State U., 1958; PhD, U. Mich., 1979. Sch. psychologist Roseville (Mich.) Pub. Schs., 1958-68, Grosse Pointe (Mich.) Pub. Schs., 1968-86; pvt. practice psychology, Grosse Pointe, 1980—; instr. psychology Macomb C.C., 1959-69. Author: A Second Heartbeat, 1979. Mem. Am. Psychol. Assn., Mich. Psychol. Assn., Lakeshore Psychol. Assn. (pres. 1988-89), Psi Chi. Home: 28820 Grant St Saint Clair Shores MI 48081-3207 Office: 131 Kercheval Ave Ste 140 Grosse Pointe MI 48236-3630

KERNS, STEVE, geneticist. Pres. Universal Pig Genes, Eldora, Iowa. Office: Universal Pig Genes 30355 260th St Eldora IA 50627-8201*

KERNS, WILMER LEE, social science researcher; b. Dayton, Va., May 17, 1932; s. Lee Doil and Madeline A. (Grim) K.; m. Marian Iris May, Mar. 21, 1957 (div. 1963); children: Mark Wayne, Susan Kaye Kerns Mitchell; m. Shirley Mitchell Walton, June 19, 1965; children: Robert Todd, Lynelle Madeline, Jacob Scott Walton. AB, Trevecca Nazarene Coll., 1957; AM, U. Mich., 1960; PhD, Ohio State U., 1971. Cert. tchr., counselor, Va. Math. tchr. Norfolk (Va.) Pub. Schs., 1957-59; counselor Washington-Lee High Sch., Arlington, Va., 1960-65; social worker Arlington (Va.) County Pub. Schs., 1965-67; civil rights specialist U.S. Office Edn., Washington, 1967-69; rsch. assoc. Ohio State U., Columbus, 1969-71; assoc. regional commr. Social and Rehab. Svc., Chgo., 1971-74; planning officer Social and Rehab. Svc., Washington, 1974-75, divsn. chief, 1975-77; sr. rsch. analyst Social Security Adminstrn., Washington, 1977-97; ret., 1997. Author: Shanholtzer History and Allied Family Roots, 1980, Historical Records of Old Frederick and Hampshire Counties, Va., 1992; Frederick County, Virginia: Settlement and First Families, 1730-1830, 1995, Walton and Allied Families of Old Virginia, 2000; columnist The W.Va. Advocate, 1982-92 (Excellence in Journalism award 1992). Lay minister Truro Episcopal Ch., Fairfax, Va., 1988-91. With USN, 1950-53. Decorated Air medal; named Disting. West Virginian, Gov. of W.Va., 1989. Mem. Morgan County Hist. Soc., Winchester-Frederick County Hist. Assn. Republican. Avocations: mountain music, historical and genealogical research. Home: 4715 38th Pl N Arlington VA 22207-2914

KEROFF, WILLIAM B., advertising agency executive; b. Nashville, Apr. 28, 1943; m. Marilyn J. Keroff; children: Hilary, Meredith. MBA, Northwestern U., 1966. CEO K&R/Marc Advt., Chgo. Office: K&R/MARC 1 IBM Plz Chicago IL 60611-3586

KERPA, GARY J., computer science, consultant; b. Derby, Conn., Apr. 20, 1958; s. George B. and Marcia J. (Tiano) K. Cert., Tech. Careers Inst., West Haven, Conn., 1978. Auto. tech. Racebrook Auto., Orange, Conn., 1974-77; computer system integration cons. Lawson & Assocs., Ansonia, Conn., 1980—. Regional coord. Ams. for Perot, Dallas, 1992. Mem. ABA, Assn. Trial Lawyers Am., Aircraft Owners and Pilots Assn. Republican. Roman Catholic. Avocation: flying. Home and Office: 18 Fairview St Ansonia CT 06401-2707

KERPAN, ALLAN, government official; b. Saskatoon, Sask., Can., Dec. 9, 1954; m. Melanie Kieper, Aug. 7, 1976; children: Joshua, Tyrel, Stefanie, Danille. Farmer Saskatoon; mem. House of Commons, Ottawa, Ont., 1993—. Mem. Wheat Pool Adv. Com.; mem. Parks and Recreatoin Bd.; level III ofcl. Sask. Amateur Hockey Assn.; reg. critic Province of Sask.; justice critic Reform Party. Mem. Lions (officer), K.C. Office: House of Commons, Confedn Bldg Rm 686, Ottawa, ON Canada K1A 0A6*

KERPER, MEIKE, family violence, sex abuse and addiction educator, consultant; b. Powell, Wyo., Aug. 13, 1929; d. Wesley George and Hazel (Bowman) K.; m. R.R. Milodragovich, Dec. 25, 1963 (div. 1973); children: Dan, John, Teren, Tina, Stana. BS, U. Mont., 1973; MS, U. Ariz., 1975; postgrad., Ariz. State U., 1976-78, Columbia Pacific U., 1990—. Lic. marriage and family therapist, Oreg.; cert. domestic violence counselor, alcoholism and drug abuse counselor, mental health profl. and investigator. Family therapist Cottonwood Hill, Arvada, Colo., 1981; family program developer Turquoise Lodge, Albuquerque, 1982; co-developer abusers program Albuquerque Shelter Domestic Violence, 1984; family therapist Citizens Coun. Alcoholism and Drug Abuse, Albuquerque, 1984-86; pvt. practice cons., trainer family violence and treatment Albuquerque, 1987—; developer sex offender program Union County, Oreg. Co-author: Court Diversion Program, 1985; author Family Treatment, 1982. Lobbyist CCOPE, Santa Fe, 1983-86; bd. dirs. Union County Task Force on Domestic Violence, 1989-91; developer Choices program treatment of sex offenders and victims union, Wallowa and Baker Counties, Oreg. Recipient commendation Albuquerque Shelter Domestic Violence, 1984. Mem. Assn. for the Treatment Sexual Abusers (Ea. Oreg. rep.), Nat. Assn. Marriage and Family Therapists, PEO Club, Delta Delta Delta. Republican. Episcopalian. Avocations: art history, reading, Indian culture, swimming, public speaking. Home: 61002 Love Rd Cove OR 97824-8211

KERR, ALEXANDER DUNCAN, JR., lawyer; b. Pitts., May 6, 1943; s. Alexander Duncan Sr. and Nancy Greenleaf (Martin) K.; m. Judith Kathleen Mottl, May 25, 1969; children: Matthew Jonathan, Joshua Brandon. BS in Bus., Northwestern U., 1965, JD, 1968. Bar: Ill. 1968, Pa. 1969, U.S. Dist. Ct. (ea. dist.) Pa. 1969, U.S. Dist. Ct. (no. dist.) Ill. 1969, U.S. Ct. Appeals (3rd and 7th cirs.) 1969, U.S. Supreme Ct. 1969. Assoc. Clark, Ladner, Fontenbaugh & Young, Phila., 1968-69, 73-74; asst. U.S. atty. U.S. Dept. Justice, Chgo., 1974-79; assoc., ptnr. Keck, Mahin & Cate, Chgo., Oak Brook, Ill., 1979-90; shareholder Tishler & Wald, Ltd., Chgo., 1990—. Staff atty. Park Dist. La Grange, Ill., 1985—; active Ill. St. Andrew Soc., North Riverside, 1982—, pres., 1995-97; vestryman, lay reader, chancellor, chalice bearer Emmanuel Episcopal Ch., 1980—; mem. Pack 177, Troop 19, Order of the Arrow, Boy Scouts Am., La Grange, 1980—. With USN, 1969-75. Mem. Am. Legion, DuPage Club, Atlantis Divers. E-mail: adkerrjr@aol.com. Fax: 708-354-1208. Home: 709 S Stone Ave La Grange IL 60525-2725

KERR, ALLEN STEWART, psychologist; b. Evanston, Ill., Nov. 13, 1928; s. Charles Allen and Mildred (Latham) K.; m. Charlyn Floyd, July 19, 1952; children: Betsy Kerr Hedding, Chet, Peggy Kerr Ihinger, Cindy Kerr Levesque. BA, Brown U., 1950; D of Psychology, Forest Inst. Profl. Psychology, 1988. Lic. psychologist, Ga. Salesman Sleepeck Printing Co., Bellwood, Ill., 1953-68, v.p. sales, 1968-83; staff psychologist The Bradley Ctr., Columbus, Ga., 1988-94; sr. psychologist The Pastoral Inst., Columbus, Ga., 1994—. Lt. (j.g.) USN, 1950-53. Recipient Bell Ringer award Mental Health Assn. Columbus (Ga.), 1995. Mem. APA, Ga. Psychol. Assn., Columbus Area Psychol. Assn., Rotary (Muscogee charter mem., pres. 1997-98). Methodist. Avocations: golf, photography, writing, travel. Home: 887 Oakwood Dr Columbus GA 31904-2483 Office: The Pastoral Inst 2022 15th Ave Columbus GA 31901-1699

KERR, ALVA RAE, writer, editor, association executive, playwright; b. Borger, Tex., July 29, 1926; d. Rene Lawerence and Georgia Margaret (Jones) McDonald; m. Gary Karp, Jan. 23, 1946 (dec. 1969); children: Pamela Karp Roper, Victoria, Richard; m. Glenn Enevold Kerr, Nov. 18, 1977. Student, Wayland Coll., 1942, Grandwohl Sch. Lab. Technique, St. Louis, 1943, U. of Ams., Mex., 1970; BA, U. Houston, 1972; MA, George Washington U., 1975; postgrad., George Mason U., 1985-86, Rice U., 1990. Mem. staff DePaul Hosp., 1945-46; med. technologist Chanute Field Army AFB Extension Hosp., 1946; mem. staff Ft. Leavenworth Army Hosp., 1946,

Bronx (N.Y.) Hosp., 1947, Central Islip (N.Y.) State Hosp. Rsch. Lab., 1960; real estate broker Coldwell Banker Realtors, McLean, Va., 1975-83; writer, editor D.C. area, 1984; editor Nat. Capital chpt. Multiple Sclerosis Soc., Washington, 1984-86; editor, publ. The Will to Win, 1996; corr. sect. UN World Com. Decade of Disabled Persons, Washington, 1985-86; writer, editor Retired Officers Assn. of Houston, 1990—; lectr. Nat. Security Agy., Fort Meade, Md., 1983, Somerset Civic Assn., Fairfax, Va., 1983, B'nai Brith, McLean, 1984, also others. Playwright: The House on Dunston Road, 1992. Vol. spl. asst. on cmty. program Nat. Orgn. on Disability, Washington, 1985-86; active Soc. for Performing Arts of Harris County, 1986-88. Recipient Commendátiere for Outstanding Newsletter, Ret. Officers Assn., 1990, Cert. of Excellence 1996, 97, Award for Excellence in Newsletter Editing 1998. Mem. AAUW, Scriptwriters of Houston, Campanille Writer's Group, Assn. Adms.-Texas Navy, Houston Mus. of Natural Sci., Houston World Affairs Coun., Houston Area Retired Officers Assn. (bd. dirs. 1990—, editor Houston area newsletter), Phi Delta Gamma (pres. 1984-86). Home: 17006 Hillswind Cir Spring TX 77379-4505

KERR, ANDREW W., aerodynamics researcher; b. N.Y.C., Feb. 15, 1941. BSE in Aero. Engring., Princeton U., 1962; MSAE, U. So. Calif., 1965. With Lockheed-Calif. Co., 1963-75, group engr. rotary-wing aero/propulsion, acting mgr., rotary-wing flight scis.; chief Advanced Sys. Rsch. Office U.S. Army Aviation and Troop Command, Moffett Field, Calif., dir. aeroflightdynamics directorate, 1986—. Contbr. articles to profl. jours. Fellow Am. Helicopter Soc. (hon., mem. aerodynamics and handling qualities tech. com.); mem. Am. Inst. Aero. and Astronaut. (sr., V/STOL com.). Office: US Army Aviation and Missile Command Aeroflightdynamics Directorate MS 219-3 Ames Rsch Ctr Moffett Field CA 94035-1000*

KERR, ANTHONY ROBERT, scientist; b. Farnborough, Hants, England, Aug. 30, 1941; s. Cecil Edwin and Stella Mary (Williams) K.; m. Tanya Ross, Jan. 24, 1974; 1 child, Tristan Duncan Ross. B of Engring. with honors, U. Melbourne, Australia, 1963, M of Engring. Sci. with honors, 1967, PhD, 1969. Rsch. scientist Commonwealth Sci. & Indsl. Rsch. Orgn., Sydney, Australia, 1969-71; engr. Nat. Radio Astronomy Obs., Charlottesville, Va., 1971-74; scientist NASA Goddard Inst. Space Studies, N.Y.C., 1974-84, Nat. Radio Astronomy Obs., 1984—; vis. prof. elec. engring. U. Va., 1984—, vis. prof. astronomy, 1986—; cons. M/A-Com Microwave Assocs., Burlington, Mass., 1980-83, NASA Goddard Space Flight Ctr., Greenbelt, Md., 1987-88. Author over 50 sci. and tech. papers. Recipient Exceptional Engring. Achievement medal NASA, 1983. Fellow IEEE (mem. editorial bd. Transactions on Microwave Theory and Techniques, 1980—, Microwave prize 1978); mem. Am. Inst. Physics, Internat. Union Radio Sci. Office: Nat Radio Astronomy Obs 2015 Ivy Rd Charlottesville VA 22903-1713

KERR, BAINE PERKINS, oil company executive; b. Rusk, Tex., Aug. 24, 1919; s. James Herman and Myrta Blake (Perkins) K.; m. Mildred Pickett Caldwell, June 13, 1942; children: Baine Perkins, John Caldwell, James Robinson, Mary Blake Kerr Winters. B.A., LL.B., U. Tex. at Austin, 1942. Bar: Tex. 1942. Practiced in Houston, 1945-77; partner firm Baker & Botts, 1955-77; dir. Pennzoil Co., Houston, 1964-94, chmn. exec. com., 1972-94, pres., 1977-85, dir. emeritus, 1994—. Served with USMCR, 1942-45. Mem. Chancellors, Order of Coif, Phi Beta Kappa. Office: Esperson Bldg 808 Travis St Ste 2200 Houston TX 77002-5704*

KERR, BARBARA PROSSER, environmental researcher, education administrator; b. Asheville, N.C., Dec. 28, 1925; d. George Holcomb and Gertrude Berenice (Parker) Prosser; m. William Albert Kerr, June 18, 1950 (div. May 1959); 1 child, Diana. BA, U. Chgo., 1951; MSW, Ariz. State U., 1971. Cert. clin. social worker, psychiatry and mental health nursing. Exec. sec. Union Theol. Sem., N.Y.C., 1961-67; case worker Dept. Pub. Welfare, Wilmington, Del., 1967-69; psychiatric nurse St. Luke's Hosp. and Med. Ctr., Phoenix, 1969-70; emergency rm. social worker Marisopa Med. Ctr., Phoenix, 1971-82; dir. Kerr-Cole Sustainable Living Ctr., Taylor, Ariz., 1983—; advisor Solar Cookers Internat., Sacramento, 1993—. Author: The Expanding World of Solar Box Cookers, 1991; inventor Solar Box Cooker, 1980, Solar Wall Oven, 1986. Home: 3310 Papermill Rd Taylor AZ 85939

KERR, C(LARENCE) WILLIAM, retired university administrator; b. Greenfield, Ohio, June 19, 1923; s. Clarence Ware and Genevieve (Meyers) K. B.A., Princeton U., 1947; M.A. (Woodrow Wilson fellow), Harvard U., 1949, Ph.D. (Frederick Sheldon fellow), 1957. Instr. to asst. prof. history Kenyon Coll., 1956-59; asst. prof. history Wesleyan U., Middletown, Conn., 1959-64; lectr. Wesleyan U., 1964-73, adj. prof., 1973-93, asst. to provost, 1963-65, asst. provost, 1965-68, asso. provost, 1968-69, acting provost, 1969-70, provost, 1970-88, sec. of univ., 1972-93. Mem. AAUP, Renaissance Soc. Am., Quadrangle Club (Princeton), Signet Club (Harvard), Princeton Club (N.Y.C.), Psi Upsilon. Democrat. Presbyterian. Home: 101 High St Middletown CT 06457-3730 Office: Office of the Sec of Univ Wesleyan U Middletown CT 06459 *Died Feb. 18, 1999.*

KERR, CLARK, academic administrator emeritus; b. Stony Creek, Pa., May 17, 1911; s. Samuel William and Caroline (Clark) K.; m. Catherine Spaulding, Dec. 25, 1934; children: Clark E., Alexander W., Caroline M. BA, Swarthmore Coll., 1932, LLD, 1952; MA, Stanford U., 1933; postgrad., London Sch. Econs., 1936, 39; PhD, U. Calif., 1939; LLD, Harvard U., 1958, Princeton U., 1959, others. Traveling fellow Am. Friends Svc. Com., 1935-36; instr. econs. Antioch Coll., 1936-37; tchg. fellow U. Calif., 1937-38; Newton Booth fellow, 1938-39; acting asst. prof. labor econs. Stanford, 1939-40; asst., later assoc. prof. U. Wash., 1940-45; assoc. prof., prof., prof. emeritus, dir. Inst. Indsl. Rels., U. Calif., Berkeley, 1945-52, chancellor, 1952-58, pres., 1958-67, pres. emeritus, 1974—; chmn. Carnegie Commn. on Higher Edn., 1967-73, Carnegie Coun. Policy Studies in Higher Edn., 1974-79; vice chmn. divsns. War Labor Bd., 1943-45; nat. arbitrator Armour Co. and United Packing House Workers, 1945-52; impartial chmn. Waterfront Employers, Pacific Coast and Internat. Longshoremen's and Warehousemen's Union, 1946-47; pub. mem. Nat. WSB, 1950-51; various arbitrations in pub. utilities, newspaper, aircraft, canning, oil, local transport and other industries, 1942—; mem. adv. panel Soc. Sci. Rsch., NSF, 1953-57; chmn. Armour Automation Com., 1959-79; chmn. bd. arbitrators U.S. Postal Svc. and Nat. Assn. Letter Carriers (AFL-CIO) and Am. Postal Workers Union (AFL-CIO), 1984. Author: (with E. Wight Bakke) Unions, Management and the Public, rev. edit., 1960, 67, (with Dunlop, Harbison, Myers) Industrialism and Industrial Man, rev. edit., 1964, 73, The Uses of the University, rev. edit., 1972, 82, 95, Labor and Management in Industrial Society, 1964, Marshall, Marx and Modern Times, 1969, Labor Markets and Wage Determination: The Balkanization of Labor Markets and Other Essays, 1977, Education and National Development: Reflections from an American Perspective during a Period of Global Reassessment, 1979, The Future of Industrial Societies, 1983, (with Marian L. Gade) The Many Lives of Academic Presidents, 1986; editor: (with Paul D. Staudohar) Industrial Relations in a New Age, 1986, Economics of Labor in Industrial Society, 1986, (with Dunlop, Lester, Reynolds; editor Bruce E. Kaufman) How Labor Markets Work: Reflections on Theory and Practice, 1988, (with Marian L. Gade) The Guardians: Boards of Trustees of American Colleges and Universities, 1989, The Great Transformation in Higher Education, 1960-80, 1991, Troubled Times for American Higher Education: The 1990s and Beyond, 1994, Higher Education Cannot Escape History: Issues for the Twenty-First Century, 1994, (with Paul D. Staudohar) Labor Economics and Industrial Relations: Markets and Institutions, 1994. Trustee Rockefeller Found., 1960-76; mem. bd. mgrs. Swarthmore Coll., 1969-80, emeritus mem., 1981. Recipient Harold W. McGraw Jr. prize in Edn., 1990; named Hon. fellow London Sch. Econs. Mem. Am. Econ. Assn., Royal Econ. Assn., Am. Acad. Arts and Scis., Indsl. Rels. Rsch. Assn., Nat. Acad. Arbitrators, Phi Beta Kappa, Kappa Sigma. Mem. Soc. of Friends. Home: 8300 Buckingham Dr El Cerrito CA 94530-2530 Office: U Calif Inst Indsl Rels 2521 Channing Way # 5555 Berkeley CA 94720-5556

KERR, DAVID MILLS, state legislator; b. Pratt, Kans., May 4, 1945; s. Fred H. and Eleanor Mills (Barrett) K.; m. Mary Patricia O'Rourke, Aug. 24, 1979; children: Ryan, Daniel. BA, Kans. State U., 1968; MBA, U. Kans., 1970. Auditor Trans World Airlines, Kansas City, Mo., 1970-72, mgr. fin., 1972-76; pres. Agronomics Internat., Hutchinson, Kans., 1976-84; mem. Kans. State Senate, Topeka, 1984—, chmn. edn. com., 1992, chmn. ways and means com., chmn. joint budget com., 1995; bd. dirs. Kans. Tech. Enterprises Corp., Health Care, Inc.; chmn. Senate econ. devel. com., 1988, edn. com., 1993, Senate ways and means com., 1995; chmn. com. on econ. devel. Nat. Conf. State Legislatures; mem. Gov.'s Criminal Justice Coordinating Coun., 1988. Mem. Advanced Tech. Commn., Topeka, 1985; chmn. Task Force on Capitol Markets and Tax, Topeka, 1986; bd. dirs. Hutchinson Hosp. Corp., 1993. Named Kans. Exporter of Yr., Internat. Trade Inst., 1981. Mem. Kans. C. of C. (bd. dirs. 1983-86). Republican. Presbyterian. Avocations: travel, reading, golf, hunting, fishing. Home: 72 Willowbrook St Hutchinson KS 67502-8948 Office: PO Box 2620 Hutchinson KS 67504-2620 Office: State Senate State Capital Topeka KS 66612*

KERR, DAVID WYLIE, natural resource company executive; b. Montreal, Que., Can., Dec. 14, 1943; s. Dudley Holden and Cecilia (Maguire) K.; m. Sheryl Lee Drysdale, Nov. 1, 1969; children: Ross, Tamara. BSc, McGill U., Can., 1965, CA, 1969. Chartered acct. Touche Ross & Co., Montreal, 1965-70, Australia, 1970-72; CFO Edper Investments Ltd., Toronto, Ont., Can., 1972-78; COO Hees Internat. Corp., Toronto, 1978-85; exec. v.p. Brascan Ltd., Toronto, 1985-86; sr. v.p. strategic planning Noranda Inc., Toronto, 1986-87, pres., 1987-90, pres., CEO, 1990—, also bd. dirs.; bd. dirs. Battle Mountain Gold, Edper Brascan Corp., Falconbridge Ltd., Nexfor, Inc., Toronto, Ont. Hydro, Toronto, The Can. Life Assurance Co. Mem. Toronto Racquet Club, Granite Club, Rosedale Golf Club. Mem. United Ch. Can. Avocations: squash, hockey, golf. Office: Noranda Inc/BCE PL, 181 Bay St Ste 4100, Toronto, ON Canada M5J 2T3

KERR, DEBORAH JANE, actress; b. Helensburgh, Scotland, Sept. 30, 1921; came to U.S., 1947; d. Arthur Kerr-Trimmer; m. Anthony C. Bartley, Nov. 28, 1945 (div. 1959); children—Melanie, Francesca; m. Peter Viertel, July 23, 1960. Student, Helensburgh schs., Northumberland House Sch., Bristol. Began motion picture career in England in Major Barbara, 1940; appeared in films: Love on the Dole, Hatter's Castle, The Avengers, Perfect Strangers, I See a Dark Stranger, 1947, Black Narcissus (N.Y. Critics award), The Hucksters, Edward, My Son, King Solomon's Mines, Quo Vadis, Thunder in the East, Prisoner of Zenda, Julius Caesar, Dream Wife, Young Bess, From Here to Eternity, The End of the Affair, 1955, Proud and Profane, 1956, The King and I, 1956, Heaven Knows Mr. Alison, 1956 (N.Y. Critics Award), Bonjour Tristesse, 1958, Count Your Blessings, 1959, The Journey, 1959, Beloved Infidel, 1959, The Grass is Greener, 1960, The Sundowners, 1960 (N.Y. Critics award), The Naked Edge, 1961, Chalk Garden, 1964, Night of the Iguana, 1964, Marriage on the Rocks, 1965, Casino Royale, 1967, The Gypsy Moths, The Arrangement, The Assam Garden; appeared on stage in Heartbreak House, 1943, Gaslight (for Brit. troops in Europe), 1945, Tea and Sympathy, 1954-55, The Day After the Fair, London, 1972-73, U.S. tour, 1973—; appeared in: U.S. tour of Seascape, 1975, Long Day's Journey into Night, Los Angeles, 1977, Candida, London, 1977, The Last of Mrs. Cheney, U.S. and Can., 1978-79, The Day After the Fair, Australia, 1979; appeared on London stage in Overheard, 1981 (Recipient Sarah Siddons award as Chgo. actress of the year.); TV roles in: Witness for the Prosecution, 1982, A Woman of Substance, 1985, Reunion at Fairborough, 1985, Hold the Dream, 1986. Recipient Honorary Academy Award (for career achievement), 1994. *

KERR, DONALD MACLEAN, JR., physicist; b. Phila., Apr. 8, 1939; s. Donald MacLean and Harriet (Fell) K.; m. Alison Richards Kyle, June 10, 1961; 1 dau., Margot Kyle. B.E.E. (Nat. Merit scholar), Cornell U., 1963, M.S., 1964, Ph.D. (Ford Found. fellow, 1964-65, James Clerk Maxwell fellow 1965-66), 1966. Staff Los Alamos Nat. Lab., 1966-76, group leader, 1971-72, asst. div. leader, 1972-73, asst. dir., 1973-75, alt. energy divsn. leader, 1975-76; dep. mgr. Nev. ops. office Dept. Energy, Las Vegas, 1976-77; acting asst. sec. def. programs Dept. Energy, Washington, 1978; dep. asst. sec. def. programs Dept. Energy, 1977-79, dep. asst. sec. energy tech., 1979; dir Los Alamos Nat. Lab., 1979-85; sr. v.p. EG&G, Inc., Wellesley, Mass., 1985-88, exec. v.p., 1988-89, pres., bd. dirs., 1989-92; exec. v.p., bd. dirs. Sci. Applications Internat. Corps., San Diego, 1993-96, Info. Sys. Labs., San Diego, 1996-97; asst. dir. FBI, Washington, 1997—; mem. Navajo Sci. Com., 1974-77, Def. Sci. Bd., 1993-98; mem. sci. adv. panel U.S. Army, 1975-78; mem. engring. adv. bd. U. Nev., Las Vegas, 1976-78, Cornell U., 1985—; chmn. com. R&D Internat. Energy Agy., 1979-85; mem. nat. security adv. coun. SRI Internat., 1980-89; mem. adv. bd. U. Alaska Geophys. Inst., 1980-85; mem. sci. adv. group Joint Strategic Planning Staff, 1981-91; mem. adv. bd. Georgetown U. Ctr. Strategic Internat. Studies, 1981-87; mem. adv. com. Naval Rsch., 1982-85; mem. corp. Draper Lab., 1982-97; mem. DCI Nonproliferation Adv. Panel, 1993—; mem. bd. San Diego Tech. Coun., 1994-97; bd. dirs. Resources for the Future, Washington. Published research on plasma physics, microwave electronics, ionospheric physics, energy and nat. security. Trustee New Eng. Aquarium, 1989-93. Fellow AAAS; mem. Am. Phys. Soc., Am. Geophys. Union, Nat. Assn. Mfrs. (bd. dirs. 1986-92), Southwestern Assn. Indian Affairs, World Affairs Coun. Boston (bd. dirs. 1988-92), Atlantic Coun. (bd. dirs. 1991-97), Cosmos Club (Washington), Sigma Xi, Tau Beta Pi, Eta Kappa Nu.

KERR, FORREST DAVID, actor, writer, producer; b. Burnet, Tex., Jan. 25, 1949; s. Forrest and Dorothy Web (Dennis) K.; m. Kathleen Mable Keller, Dec. 6, 1969 (div. Mar. 1975). Student, C.C. Balt., 1970-71; AS in Bus. Adminstrn., Austin C.C., 1980; postgrad., St. Edwards U., Austin, 1980-81, Am. Acad. Dramatic Arts, Pasadena, Calif., 1990, UCLA, 1992. Control clk. Social Security Adminstrn., Balt., 1970-71; assoc. br. mgr. Fin. Am., Smyrna, Del., 1971-75; br. mgr. Investors Loan Corp., Alexandria, Va., 1865-77; mgr.-in-tng. Gt. Western Fin., Austin, 1977-78; leasing agt. Safty Kleen Corp., Austin, 1979-80; tech. staff asst. Austin C.C., 1982; mgr. main br. Jim Walter Homes Corp., Corpus Christi, Tex., 1983-84; dir. sales Royal T Homes Corp., Houston, 1985-87; gen. mgr. Conner Home Sales Corp., Houston, 1987-88, Times Manufactured Housing and Tomball (Tex.) Mobile Homes, 1988-89; asst. mgr. Florsheim Thayer McNiel, Northridge, Calif., 1990-91; apprentice editor Concorde/New Horizon Films, Venice, Calif., 1991-92; freelance writer and prodr., Thorne Pictures, Palos Verdes, Calif., 1993—; cons. Am. Cons. League, Houston, 1988-90; copy editor Fieldings Worldwide Travel Guides, Redondo Beach, Calif., 1994. Author: (screen plays) Unlikely Angel, 1990, Thunderbirds, 1992; appeared in (plays) Mousetrap, My Sister Eileen, (films) Sudden Death, Melrose Place, Man of Her Dreams, Sheriff Garrett, 1992, Graveyard Man, 1992, Chauffer, 1993, Featured Detective, 1994, Ken Osborn, 1996; assoc. prodr. (films) Thornes of Fate, 1993; (videos) Elinor Rigby, 1991, Hard Luck Woman, 1992; writer, prodr., dir. (play) The Way It Wasn't, 1989. Mem. ind. feature project, Santa Monica, Calif., 1993—; vol. Book Pals, SAG Found., L.A., 1995; founding mem. Secret Rose Theater, 1999—. With USCG, 1966-70. Mem. SAG (Screen Actors Guild awards, nominating com. L.A. 1996, conservatory 1995—, casting com. 1997—), Phi Theta Kappa. Avocations: hiking, bicycling, frisbee, billiards and pool, reading.

KERR, FREDERICK HOHMANN, health care company executive; b. Pitts., July 11, 1936; s. Nathan Frederick and Laura Marie (Hohmann) K.; m. Ethyl Nylene Bashline, 1960 (div. 1969); m. Phyllis Jensen, Aug. 21, 1970, 1 child, Linda Jean. BA, Pa. State U., 1958; MPA, U. Pitts., 1961; LLD (hon.), Luth. Coll. Health Professions, Ft. Wayne, Ind., 1996. Exec. sec. Pa. Economy League Fayette County Br., Uniontown, Pa., 1959, Armstrong County Br., Kittanning, Pa., 1959-62; exec. sec. Woodbury Tax Rsch. Conf., Sioux City, Iowa, 1962-65; pub. svc. dir. City of Sioux City, 1965-66; from asst. administr. to assoc. administr. St. Luke's Regional Med. Ctr., Sioux City, 1966-71; administr., CEO, Meml. Hosp. of Michigan City, Inc., Ind., 1971-75; pres., CEO, St. Luke's Hosp., Maumee, Ohio, 1975-86, Luth. Hosp. Ind., Luth. Coll. Health Professions, Ft. Wayne, 1986-95; v.p. for devel. Quorum Health Resources, Inc., Brentwood, Tenn., 1995—; dir. Ohio Hosp. Ins. Co., Columbus, treas. 1981-84. Trustee Ohio Hosp. Assn., Columbus, 1983-85; dir. Siouxland United Way, 1968-71, Ft. Wayne Pub. TV, 1990-94, United Way Allen County, Ft. Wayne, 1990-94; mem. Iowa Intergovtl. Rels. Com., Des Moines, 1964-67. 2nd lt. U.S. Army, 1958-59. Fellow Am. Protestant Health Assn. (vice chmn. 1988-90), Am. Hosp. Assn. (ho. dels. 1991—), ASPA (life, nat. coun. 1966-69),. Avocations: wine appreciation, golf. Home and Office: 36890 S Ridgeview Blvd Tucson AZ 85739-1260 *Being a servant is the most distinguished career of all.*

KERR, GARY ENRICO, lawyer, educator; b. Kewanee, Ill., Feb. 8, 1948; s. Roy Harrison and Marietta (Dani) K.; m. Eileen Elizabeth Straeter, Aug. 18, 1978; 1 child, Victoria Elizabeth. BA, No. Ill. U., 1970; JD, Northwestern U., Chgo., 1973. Bar: Ill. 1974, U.S. Dist. Ct. (cen. dist.) Ill. 1982, U.S. Ct. Appeals (7th cir.) 1983, U.S. Supreme Ct. 1983. Adminstrv. asst. Office Supt. Pub. Instrn. State Ill., Chgo., Springfield, 1971-74; asst. legal advisor Ill. State Bd. Edn., Springfield, 1974-78; spl. counsel Ill. State Comptroller, Springfield, 1978-79; pvt. practice Springfield, 1979—; adj. faculty Sangamon State U., Springfield, Ill., 1994; pres., dir. counsel Kerr Products, INc., Kewanee, Ill., 1980—; instr. paralegal program Robert Morris Coll., Springfield, 1992. atty. South County Democrats, Sangamon County, Ill. Fellow Ednl. Policy program Inst. Ednl. Leadership, George Washington U., 1976-77. Mem. ABA, Ill. State Bar Assn. (chmn. sch. law sect. coun. 1983-84), Sangamon County Bar Assn., Automotive Parts and Accessories Assn. (mem. govtl. affairs and internat. trade com. 1997). Avocations: snow skiing, tennis, fishing. Office: Gary Kerr Ltd 1020 S 7th St Springfield IL 62703-2417

KERR, IAN, public relations executive; b. London, Oct. 15, 1925. Diploma in journalism, London U., 1950. Reporter London, 1950-52; sr. press officer British Airways, London, 1952-58; mgr. pub. rels. Hambro Automotive Corp., 1958-62; dir. pub. rels. Renault Inc., 1962-64, Parker Pen Co., 1965-77; pres. Press Rels. Svcs. Co., 1977-88; chmn. Kerr Kelly Inc., Greenwich, Conn., 1988-93, Kerr Kelly Thompson, Greenwich, Conn., 1993-96, Emmannuel Kerr Kilsby, Stamford, Conn., 1996—. Mem. Pub. Rels. Soc. Am., Fairfield County Pub. Rels. Assn. (pres. 1982, 91, v.p. 1981, treas. 1980), IABC, Conn. Press Club (co-pres. 1985). Office: Emmannuel Kerr Kilsby 24 Richmond Hill Ave Stamford CT 06901-3647*

KERR, JAMES WILSON, engineer; b. Balt., May 21, 1921; s. James W. and Laura Virginia (Wright) K.; m. Mary Thomas Montgomery, Feb. 25, 1945 (div., dec.); children: April Kerr Miller, Catherine Kerr Wood (dec.), Wilson, Andrew; m. June Walker, Dec. 27, 1977 (div.); m. Janice White Bain, Jan. 19, 1985. BS with honors, Davidson Coll., 1942; MS, NYU., 1948; postgrad. Freiburg U., 1957-60, Brookings Inst., 1970, 75, Fed. Exec. Inst., 1982; PhD, Kennedy Western U., 1989. Commd. 2d lt. U.S. Army, 1942, advanced through grades to lt. col., 1964; with inf., World War II, Korea; electronic staff, Ft. Bragg, N.C., 1948-51; weapons rsch., N.M., 1953-57; adviser French Army, 1957-60; staff electronics, Ft. Monroe, Va., 1960-62; rsch. mgr., divsn. dir. CD, Pentagon, 1962-64, as civilian, 1964-81, asst. assoc. dir. Fed. Emergency Mgmt. Agy. for Rsch., 1981-85; sr. staff Michael Rogers, Inc., Winter Park, Fla., 1986—; dir. Mt. St. Helen's Tech. Office, 1980; v.p. Latherow & Co., Arlington, Va., 1965-86; radiol. officer Talbot County, Md., 1997—. Advanced English instr. French Army, 1957-60; cons. Am. Nat. Red Cross Mus., 1968-85, Smithsonian Instn. Dept. Postal History, 1966-85, NSF, 1976-85. Vol. fireman N.Y. State, 1946-48, Fairfax County, Va., 1969—; fire commr. Fairfax County, 1975-81, chmn., 1977-81, Orange County, Fla., 1986—, pres., 1987-90, Pike County, Ala., 1994-98; active Boy Scouts Am., in U.S., Asia and Europe, 1933—; chmn. library bd., Orangeburg, N.Y., 1946-48. Decorated Bronze Star with three oak leaf clusters, Purple Heart; recipient Silver Beaver award Boy Scouts Am., 1956, James E. West, 1994; Fulbright selectee, Japan, 1986; registered profl. engr., Calif. Fellow AAAS, Explorers Club; mem. NAS (various coms. 1962-87), Internat. Assn. Fire Chiefs (chmn. rsch. com. 1969-88, chief sci. adviser 1982-86), Fed. Fire Council, Nat. Fire Protection Assn. (chmn. hosp. disaster com. 1973-96), Presdl. Nat. Def. Exec., SAR (Fire Safety medal 1995), Black Forest Mardi Gras (Germany), Nat. Communications Club, Pentagon Officers Athletic Club, Univ. Club Fla., IEEE (sr.), Elks, Phi Beta Kappa, Gamma Sigma Epsilon, Delta Phi Alpha. Presbyn. (elder 1963—). Author: Korean-English Phrase Book, 1951; 19th Century Korea Postal Handbook, 1965, 2d edit., 1990. Editor Korean Philately mag., 1971-80, 85-95. Contbr. articles to profl. jours. Home: PO Box 1537 Easton MD 21601-1537 Office: MR Inc 199 E Welbourne Ave Winter Park FL 32789-4337

KERR, JANET SPENCE, physiologist, pharmacologist; b. New Haven, May 30, 1942; d. Alexander Pyott and Janet Blake (Conley) Spence; m. Thomas Albert Kerr Jr., July 24, 1965; children: Sarah Patterson, Matthew Spence, Timothy Marden. BA, Beaver Coll., 1964; MS, Rutgers U., 1969, PhD, 1973. Asst. prof. Rutgers U., Camden, N.J., 1973-76; rsch. assoc. U. Pa. Sch. Medicine, Phila., 1976-79; asst. prof. U. Medicine and Dentistry N.J.-Rutgers Med. Sch., New Brunswick, 1979-84; prin. rsch. scientist DuPont Pharms. Co., Wilmington, Del., 1985—; sec. Biochem. Pharmacology Discussion Group, 1997—. Contbr. articles to profl. jours. Busch fellow Rutgers U. Mem. AAAS, Am. Heart Assn., Am. Fedn. Clin. Rsch., Am. Physiol. Soc., Am. Thoracic Soc., Am. Assn. Cancer Rsch., Inflammation Rsch. Assn. (bd. dirs. 1996-98), N.Y. Acad. Scis., Sigma Xi. Office: DuPont Pharms Co Exptl Sta E400/4223 Wilmington DE 19898

KERR, KIRKLYN M., university administrator, veterinary pathologist, researcher; b. Green Bank, W.Va., May 1, 1936; married, 1957; 3 children. BS, U. W.Va., 1961, MS, 1966; DVM, Ohio State U., 1961; PhD in Vet. Pathology, Tex. A&M U., 1970. Diplomate Am. Coll. Vet. Pathology. Vet. practitioner North Side Vet. Clinic, Carlisle, Pa., 1961-62; rsch. assoc. vet. microbiology & pathology W.Va. U., Morgantown, 1962-65; form instr. to assoc. prof. vet. pathology Tex. A&M U. Coll. Vet. Medicine, 1965-72; assoc. prof. vet. pathobiology, dir. divsn. applied pathology Ohio State U. Coll. Vet. Medicine, 1972-78, dir. Ohio Agrl. Rsch. & Devel. Ctr., prof. poultry sci., 1987-91, prof. vet. preventive medicine, mem. faculty dept. preventive medicine, 1991-93; asst. dean rsch. and advanced studies, head vet. sci. La. State U. Sch. Vet. Medicine, La. State U. Agrl. Ctr., 1978-87; dean, dir. Coll. Agr. and Natural Resources U. Conn., Storrs Mansfield, 1993—. Mem. AVMA, Am. Assn. Avian Pathologists, Am. Coll. Vet. Pathologists, Farm Bur., Conn. Vet. Medicine Assn. Achievements include research in veterinary pathology, mycoplasmataceae, cancer research in animals. Office: U Conn Coll Agriculture & Natural Rsch 1376 Storrs Rd U-66 Storrs Mansfield CT 06269-4066

KERR, KLEON HARDING, former state senator, educator; b. Plain City, Utah, Apr. 26, 1911; s. William A. and Rosemond (Harding) K.; m. Katherine Abbott, Mar. 15, 1941; children: Kathleen, William A., Rebecca Rae. AS, Weber Coll., 1936; BA, George Washington U., 1939; MS, Utah State U., Logan, 1946. Tchr. Bear River H.S., Tremonton, Utah, 1940-56; prin. jr. high sch. Bear River H.S., Tremonton, 1956-60, prin., 1960-71; city justice Tremonton, 1941-46; sec. to Senator Arthur V. Watkins, 1947. Author: (poetry) Open My Eyes, 1983, We Remember, 1983, Trouble in the Amen Corner, 1985, Past Imperfect, 1988, A Helping Hand, 1990, Sound of Silence, 1991, Power Behind the Throne, 1992, Unreachable Goal?, 1993, The Only Difference, 1994, Please Boss, 1995, Beach Comber, 1995; (history) Those Who Served Box Elder County, 1984, Those Who Served Tremonton City, 1985, Diamond in the Rough, 1987, Facts of Life, 1987, Gettin' and Givin', 1989, Wells Without Water, 1996, Hand in Pocket, 1997, I Want to Come Home, 1997. Mayor Tremonton City, 1948-53; mem. Utah Local Govt. Survey Commn., 1954-55; mem. Utah Ho. of Reps., 1953-56; mem. Utah State Senate, 1957-64, chmn. appropriation com., 1959—, majority leader, 1963; mem. Utah Legis. Coun.; dist. dir. vocat. edn. Box Elder Sch. Dist. Recipient Alpha Delta Kappa award for outstanding contbn. to edn., 1982, award for outstanding contbrs. to edn. and govt. Theta Chpt. Alpha Beta Kappa, 1982, Excellence Achieved in Promotion of Tourism award, Allied Category award Utah Travel Coun., 1988, Merti award, 1993, Andy Rytting Cmty. Svc. award, 1991; named Tourism Ambassador of Month, 1986. Mem. NEA, Utah Box Elder edn. assns., Utah Sheriff's Assn. (hon.), Bear River Valley C. of C. (sec., mgr. 1955-58), Lions, Kiwanis, Phi Delta Kappa. Mem. Ch. of Jesus Christ of Latter-day Saints. Home: PO Box 246 Tremonton UT 84337-0246

KERR, MARGARET ANN, elementary education educator; b. Ashland, Ohio, Jan. 8, 1951; d. Wallace Amander and Beulah Elizabeth (Westerfield) Canfield; m. Roger William Kerr Jr., June 12, 1970; children: Robert, Thomas. BS in Edn., Ashland U., 1973; MA in Edn., LaVerne Coll., 1975. Cert. elem. tchr., reading specialist. Tchr. Ruggles-Troy Sch., Ohio, 1973-76, Nankin (Ohio) Sch., 1977-79, Mapleton Sch. Dist., 1981-82; kindergarten tchr. Mapleton Sch., 1982-92; tchr. chpt. 1 extended day kindergarten Mapleton Schs., 1992-94, reading recovery tchr., 1994—; organizer, tchr. pre-sch., 1981; coord. for active parenting Mapleton Schs., 1992-94. Treas. PTA; co-chmn, Mapleton New Bldg. Campaign; mem. Nankin Fedn. Ch., Mapleton Acad. Booster, Mapleton Sports Booster. Mem. NEA, Ohio Edn. Assn., Mapleton Edn. Assn. Avocations: reading, walking, computers, working with young people. Home: 705 State Route 302 Ashland OH 44805-9529

KERR, NANCY HELEN, psychology educator; b. L.A., June 27, 1947; d. Edmund James and Sally (Byrd) K.; m. David Foulkes, Apr. 19, 1978. BA, Stanford U., 1969; PhD, Cornell U., 1974. Asst. prof. psychology U. Wyo., Laramie, 1974-78; vis. asst. prof. psychology Emory U., Atlanta, 1978-79, vis. asst. prof. psychiatry, 1979-82; vis. asst. prof. psychology Mercer U., Macon, Ga., 1982-83; asst. prof. to prof. psychology Oglethorpe U., Atlanta, 1983—, chair div. behavioral scis., 1989-96, interim acad. dean, 1996-97, provost, 1997—. Contbr. articles to profl. jours. Recipient James McKeen Cattell award, 1990. Mem. Psychonomic Soc. Office: Oglethorpe U 4484 Peachtree Rd NE Atlanta GA 30319-2797

KERR, ROBERT JAMES, mediator, educational consultant; b. Wichita, Kans., Aug. 31, 1952; s. James Winton and Lorna Marie (Griffith) Kerr. BA in Lit., Wichita State U., 1975; MEd, Colo. State U., 1977. Cert. mediator, COR Assocs., 1995. Coord. Greek affairs Drake U., Des Moines, 1977-80; asst. dir. alumni rels. U. Colo., Boulder, 1981-84; v.p. adminstrn. Youmans & Assocs., Denver, 1984-87; sr. cons. The Midas Group, Denver, 1987-90; instr. Ctr. for Legal Studies, Golden, Colo., 1995—; sr. cons. Firstep, Golden, Colo., 1990—; cons. Leading Edge Comm., 1990, Adams Sch. Dist. 14, 1992, Mountain Solutions, 1993, The Quick Co., 1993, Western Mus. Mining and Industry, 1993, NOVA, 1993; workshop designer, facilitator Cmty. Problem Solving, U. Denver, 1992, Strategic Planning, Utah State U., 1992, Risk Mgmt., Regional Leadership Conf., Kans. City, 1993, Philanthropy and Cmty. Action, Front Range Conf., U. N.C., 1993, Planning for Academic Success, 1993, Orgnl. Planning, U. No. Colo., 1993, Goal Setting, Colo. Sch. Mines, 1993, Vol. Tng. and Goal Setting, NOVA, 1993, Strategic Planning and Goal Setting, Western Mus. Mining and Industry, 1993, Regional Mentor Program, U. Wyo., 1995, Implementing Change, Colo. Sch. Mines, 1995; coord. Greek Life U. No. Colo., 1996—. Contbr. articles and other writings to mags. and fraternity jours.; author: So You Wanna Go to College—A Guide on How to Get There, 1992, (screenplay) Second Season, 1996. Mediator Jefferson County (Colo.) Mediation Svcs., 1995; mem. steering com. Leadership Golden, 1990-92, Buffalo Bill Days Festival, 1989; mem. Resource Bank Cmty. Leadership Program, 1991—; bd. dirs. Cmty. Shares of Colo., 1992-93; coord. Greek life U. Ctr., U. No. Colo., Greeley. Recipient Cert. of Dedication Kans. Boys State program, 1969-77, Recipient of the Jefferson Cup, disting. svc. Dist. Gov. Mem. bd. gov's., Phi Kappa Delta, Omicron Delta Kappa, Sigma Phi Epsilon. Democrat. Avocations: chess, photography, astronomy, dance, travel. Home and Office: 1651 E 16th St Greeley CO 80538

KERR, ROBERT SAMUEL, III, state official; b. Oklahoma City, Oct. 12, 1950; s. Robert Samuel and LaMoyne (Cody) K.; m. Charlotte Greene, Nov. 1977; children: Robert S. IV, Kiersten. BA, Okla. U., 1973. Dir. Oklahoma Water, Inc., Oklahoma City, 1977-79; mem. Okla. Ho. of Reps., Oklahoma City, 1979-81; exec. v.p. KEPCO, Inc., Oklahoma City, 1982; ptnr. Kerr/Odom Assocs., Oklahoma City, 1983-86; lt. gov. State of Okla., 1987-91; prin. Kerr Consulting, 1991—. Mem. Interstate Oil Compact Commn., Oklahoma City, Okla. State Employment Security Bd., 1981-83; bd. dirs. Big Bros./Big Sisters of Oklahoma County, Youth Services for Oklahoma County; active Crown Heights United Meth. Ch., Oklahoma City; chmn. Okla. Dem. Party. Democrat. Office: Kerr Consulting PO Box 589 Poteau OK 74953-0589

KERR, STUART H., lawyer, think tank executive; married; one child. BA, Trinity Coll., Hartford, Conn., 1980; JD, Georgetown U., 1987. Mem. Internat. Law Inst., 1982—, exec. dir., 1988—; vis. scholar Manchester U., Eng., 1976-77. Office: Internat Law Inst 1615 New Hampshire Ave NW Washington DC 20009-2520

KERR, SYLVIA JOANN, educator; b. Detroit, June 19, 1941; d. Frederic Dilmus and Maud (Dirst) Pfeffer; widowed; children: David, Kathleen. BA, Carleton Coll., 1963; MS, U. Minn., 1966, PhD, 1968. Asst. prof. Augsburg Coll., Mpls., 1968-71; instr. Anoka Ramsey Community Coll., Coon Rapids, Minn., 1973-74; from asst. prof. to full prof. Hamline U., St. Paul, 1974—. Contbr. numerous articles to profl. jours. NIH fellow U. Minn., 1972, 74-75. Office: Hamline U Dept Biology 1536 Hewitt Ave Saint Paul MN 55104-1205

KERR, T. MICHAEL, federal official. BA, Tufts U.; M City Planning, MIT. Asst. dir. Office Office Legislation; mem. legis. staff Am. Fedn. State, County and Mcpl. Employees; mem. staff White House Office Consumer affairs, Washington; dir. Office Congl. Liaison Office of HHS Asst. Sec. for Legislation; exec. sec., dir. exec. secretariat Office of Sec. of Labor, Washington; dep. asst. sec. Workers' Compensation, Employment Stds. Adminstrn., Washington. Office: US Dept Labor 200 Constitutio Ave NW Washington DC 20210

KERR, THOMAS HENDERSON, III, electrical engineer, researcher; b. Washington, Nov. 9, 1945; s. Thomas Henderson Jr. and Norma Elaine (McAllister) K.; m. Aniece Ragland, July 5, 1975; children: Thomas Henderson IV, Stephen McAllister Pearson. BSEE magna cum laude, Howard U., 1967; MSEE, U. Iowa, 1969, PhD, 1971. Rsch. asst., 1967, 69, teaching asst., 1968; control engr. R & D Ctr. GE, Schenectady, N.Y., 1971-73; tech. staff The Analytic Sci. Corp., Reading, Mass., 1973-79; sr. analyst systems engr. Intermetrics Inc., Cambridge, Mass., 1979-86; with tech. staff Lincoln Lab. MIT, Lexington, Mass., 1986-92; CEO, prin. investigator TeK Assocs., Lexington, 1992—; cons. Nat. Security Indsl. Assn., Boston, 1979-86; instr. Northeastern U., Boston, 1990-95. Contbr. over 100 articles to profl. jours. Math. tutor Civic Ctr., Schenectady, 1971, Union Coll., Schenectady, 1972-73, Union Meth. Ch., Boston, 1973-74. Recipient NSF traineeship, 1968-70, Award for Sci./Math. Proficiency, 1963, Music Educator's award, 1963, Writing Contest award Fed. Power Commn., 1967, Western Electric award, 1965, McDonnell-Douglas award, 1966. Mem. IEEE (sr., chmn. control sys. sect. Boston 1990-92, chmn. steering com. 1992-94, vice chmn. 1995-96), IEEE Aerospace and Electronics Sys. (M. Barry Carlton award 1988), AIAA (sr.), Inst. of Nav., Am. Def. Preparedness Assn. (life), Am. Statis. Assn., Math. Assn. Am., Soc. Photogametry and Instrumentation Engrs., Assn. Computing Machinery, Sigma Xi, Tau Beta Pi, Pi Mu Epsilon, Sigma Pi Sigma, Eta Kappa Nu. Methodist. Achievements include development of automated fault detection algorithms for submarine and aircraft navigation systems; performed early GPS validation testing aboard submarine; development of decentralized Kalman filter algorithms for navigation:INS/JTIDS/GPS; simplified implementation of extended Kalman filters for target tracking; development of associated statistical tests for real time fault detection, closed-form test problems for software validation of linear systems and Kalman filters, inexpensive, commercially available Kalman filter software TK-MIP for the PC that includes on-line tutorials to lead and prompt the novice user, Cramer-Rao lower bounds for strategic radar tracking; applied decentralized 2-D Kalman filters to image restoration and multisensor fusion; performed a critical evaluation of current GPS limitations as well as its benefits; subcontracting to MITRE, XonTech, and Raytheonon national missile defense radar evaluations. Home: 11 Paul Revere Rd Lexington MA 02421-6632

KERR, THOMAS JEFFERSON, IV, academic official; b. Columbus, Ohio, Oct. 8, 1933; s. Thomas Jefferson and Ruth Glenora (Powell) K.; m. Donna Jean Lawton, June 11, 1955; children: Thomas Jefferson V, Cheryl Lee, Kathleen Anne. BS, Cornell U., 1956; MA, U. Buffalo, 1959; PhD (univ. fellow), Syracuse U., 1965; LHD (hon.), Otterbein Coll., 1984; LLD (hon.), Kendall Coll., 1996. Asst. prof., then prof. history Otterbein Coll., Westerville, Ohio, 1963-71, acting acad. dean, 1969-70, pres., 1971-84; pres. Grant Med. Ctr. Found., Columbus, 1984-89; pres. Kendall Coll., Evanston, Ill., 1990-96, pres. emeritus, 1996—; Chmn. Assn. Ind. Colls. and Univs., Ohio, 1976-78, Ohio Found. Ind. Colls., 1978-80. Mem. Greater Columbus Arts Coun., 1975-78; trustee Blue Cross Ctrl. Ohio, 1978-84, Grant Hosp., 1975-84, Ill. Restaurant Assn. Ednl. Found., 1991-96; mem. exec. com. Ill. Ind. Colls. and Univs., 1993-95; mem. Franklin County Draft Bd., 1969-71. Recipient Cokesbury Grad. Coll. Teaching award, 1963. Mem. Masons, Rotary, Phi Kappa Phi, Kappa Phi Kappa, Omicron Chi Epsilon, Phi Eta Sigma. Republican. Methodist. Home: 4890 Smoketalk Ln Westerville OH 43081-4431

KERR, WALTER BELNAP, retired missile instrumentation engineer, English language researcher, consultant; b. Salt Lake City, Oct. 14, 1926; s. Walter Affleck and Marion Adeline (Belnap) K.; m. Raida Nebeker, May 2, 1952 (dec. Mar. 1992); children: Valerie Jean Kerr Lemon, Grant Mercer, Janice Arlene Kerr Hahn, Marilyn, m. Lillian Hamilton Nelson Ettinger, Oct. 1, 1992; children: Edgar Nelson Jr., James Nelson, Patricia Nelson Hardwick, Douglas Nelson. BA in French, U. Utah, 1951, BSEE, 1955; MBA in Internat. Bus., U. So. Calif., 1972. Electrical engr. Hughes Aircraft Co., L.A., 1955-61, 67-69; missile instrumentation engr. Hercules Inc., Salt Lake City, 1961-66, 84-89, Rockwell Internat., Anaheim, Calif., 1969-70; investment broker Titan Capital Corp., L.A., Ogden, Utah, 1970-79; electrical engr. White Motor Corp., Ogden, 1979-84; tax examiner IRS, Ogden, 1990-91, ret., 1991; cons. Soc. for the Advancement of Good English, Pittsford, N.Y., 1985-86. Author: (book) Instrumentation Methods, 1963, (card) Pocket Guide to Good English, 1984; columnist Correct Corner, Cherokee Scout newspaper, 1996—; inventor. Juggler St. Benedict's Hosp., and various nursing homes, grade schs., h.s., univs., shopping ctrs. and chs., 1947—. With USN, 1945-46, 1st lt. U.S. Army, 1951-53. Mem. IEEE, The Planetary Soc., World Wildlife Fund, Soc. for the Preservation of English Lang. and Lit., Sierra Club. Republican. LDS. Avocations: tennis, juggling, planetoid research, kite flying, computing, astronomical model building. Home: 395 Messer Rd Murphy NC 28906-9197

KERR, WILLIAM ANDREW, lawyer, educator; b. Harding, W.Va., Nov. 17, 1934; s. William James and Tocie Nyle (Morris) K.; m. Elizabeth Ann McMillin, Aug. 3, 1968. AB, W.Va. U., 1955, JD, 1957; LLM, Harvard U., 1958; BD, Duke U., 1968. Bar: W.Va. 1957, Pa. 1962, Ind. 1980. Assoc. McClintic, James, Wise and Robinson, Charleston, W.Va., 1958; assoc. Schnader, Harrison, Segal and Lewis, Phila., 1961-64; asst. prof. law Cleve. State U., 1966-67, assoc. prof. law, 1967-68; assoc. prof. law Ind. U., Indpls., 1968-69, 72-74; prof. Ind. U., 1974-98, prof. emeritus, 1998—; contract atty. Indpls. Pub. Defender Agy., 1998—; asst. U.S. atty. So. Dist. Ind., Indpls., 1969-72; exec. dir. Ind. Jud. Ctr., 1974-86; dir. research Ind. Pros. Attys. Council, 1972-74; mem. Ind. Criminal Law Study Commn., 1973-89, sec., 1973-83; reporter speedy trial com. U.S. Dist. Ct. (so. dist.) Ind., 1975-84; trustee Ind. Criminal Justice Inst., 1983-86; bd. dirs. Indpls. Lawyers Commn., 1975-77, Ind. Lawyers Commn., 1980-83; mem. records mgmt. com. Ind. Supreme Ct., 1983-86. Author: Indiana Criminal Procedure: Pretrial, 1991, Indiana Criminal Procedure: Trial, 2 vols., 1998. Bd. dirs. Ch. Fedn. Greater Indpls., 1979-87. Served to capt. JAGC, USAF, 1958-61. Decorated Air Force Commendation medal; Ford Found. fellow Harvard Law Sch., 1957-58; recipient Outstanding Prof. award Students Ind. U. Sch. Law, 1974, Disting. Service award Ind. Council Juvenile Ct. Judges, 1979, Outstanding Jud. Edn. Program award Nat. Council Juvenile and Family Ct. Judges, 1985. Mem. Ind. State Bar Assn., Indpls. Bar Assn., Phila. Bar Assn., W.Va. Bar Assn., Nat. Dist. Attys. Assn., Am. Judicature Soc., Fed. Bar Assn. (Outstanding Service award Indpls. chpt. 1975), Order of Coif, Phi Beta Kappa. Office: Circle Tower Ste 1017 55 Monument Cir Indianapolis IN 46204-5901

KERR, WILLIAM T., publishing and broadcasting executive; b. Seattle, Apr. 17, 1941; m. Mary Lang, Oct. 15, 1966; 1 child, Susannah Gaskill Kerr Adler. B.A., U. Wash., 1963, Oxford U., Eng., 1965; MA, Harvard U., 1967, M.B.A., 1969. V.p. Dillon Read & Co., N.Y.C. and London, 1969-73; cons. McKinsey & Co., N.Y.C., 1973-79; v.p. New York Times Co., N.Y.C., 1979-91; pres. New York Times Mag. Group, N.Y.C., 1985-91; exec. v.p., pres. mag. group Meredith Corp., Des Moines, 1991-94, pres., chief oper. officer, bd. dirs., exec. com., 1994-96, pres., CEO, 1997-98; chmn. Meredith Corp., 1998—; bd. dirs. Storage Tek Corp., Prin. Fin. Group, Maytag Corp. Mem. Mag. Pubs. Am. (bd. dirs. 1985—, chmn. 1994-95), Century Assn. (N.Y.C.), Union Club (N.Y.C.), The Brook Club (N.Y.C.), Quogue Field Club, Wakonda Club, Des Moines Club, Reform Club (London), Litchfield Country Club. Roman Catholic. Home: PO Box 1545 Litchfield CT 06759 Office: Meredith Corp 1716 Locust St Des Moines IA 50309-3023

KERREBROCK, JACK LEO, aeronautics and astronautics engineering educator; b. Los Angeles, Feb. 6, 1928; s. Oscar A. and Florence (Hoy) K.; m. Bernice Veverka, Apr. 11, 1953; children: Christopher, Nancy, Peter. Student, U. Oreg., 1946-47; B.S., Oreg. State Coll., 1950; M.S., Yale, 1951; Ph.D., Calif. Inst. Tech., 1956. Aero. research scientist Lewis Lab., NASA, Cleve., 1951-53; research fellow Calif. Inst. Tech., 1955-56; engrng. leader Oak Ridge Nat. Lab., 1956-58; sr. research fellow Calif. Inst. Tech., 1958-60; mem. faculty M.I.T., 1960—, Richard C. Maclaurin prof. aeros. and astronautics, 1975-96, dir. Gas Turbine and Plasma Dynamics Lab., 1969-78, head div. energy conversion and propulsion, 1970-81, head dept. aeros. and astronautics, 1978-81, 83-85, assoc. dean engring., 1985-89, acting dean, 1989; assoc. adminstr. Office Aeros. and Space Tech., NASA, Washington, 1981-83; mem. Air Force Sci. Adv. Bd., 1972-88; mem. NASA Rsch. and Tech. Adv. Com., 1975-77; mem. Aeronautics and Space Engrng. Bd. NRC, 1976-81, 92-95; mem. aero adv. com. NASA, 1978-81, Nat. Commn. on Space, 1984-86; mem. Air Force Studies Bd. NRC, 1990-92, com. on Earth-Orbit Propulsion, 1991-92; mem. adv. com. Space Sta. NASA, 1987-92; chmn. com. Space Sta. NRC, 1992-95; trustee Inst. for Def. Analysis, 1984—, Aerospace Corp., 1986-88; bd. dirs. Orbital Scis. Corp., Aerodyne Rsch. Inc. Recipient Gas Turbine Power award ASME, 1971, John Leland Atwood award ASEE and AIAA, 1992; Fairchild Disting. scholar Calif. Inst. Tech., 1990. Fellow AIAA (hon.); mem. Nat. Acad. Engring., Am. Acad. Arts and Scis. Home: 108 Tower Rd Lincoln MA 01773-4403 Office: MIT 31-268 Cambridge MA 02139

KERREY, BOB (J. ROBERT KERREY), senator; b. Lincoln, Nebr., Aug. 27, 1943; s. James and Elinor K.; children: Benjamin, Lindsey. B.S. in Pharmacy, U. Nebr., 1965. Owner, founder, developer outlets in Omaha and Lincoln Grandmother's Restaurants, Omaha, 1972-75; owner, founder fitness enterprises Prairie Life Ctr., Lincoln and Omaha, Nebr.; gov. State of Nebr., Lincoln, 1983-87; ptnr. Printon, Kane & Co., Lincoln, 1987-89; U.S. Senator from Nebraska, 1989—; mem. Agrl., Nutrition & Forestry Com.; ranking minority mem. Appropriations subcom. on Treasury, Postal Svc. & Gen. Govt., select com. on Intelligence, Fin., Prodn. & Price Comptetitiveness com. Bd. dirs. Lincoln Ctr. Assn.; bd. dirs. Nebr. Easter Seal Soc. Served USN, 1966-69, Vietnam. Decorated medal of Honor; decorated Bronze Star, Purple Heart. Mem. Am. Legion, VFW, DAV, Lincoln C. of C.; mem Phi Gamma Delta. Congregationalist. Lodges: Sertoma; Lions. Office: US Senate 141 Senate Hart Bldg Washington DC 20510*

KERRICK, DAVID ELLSWORTH, lawyer; b. Caldwell, Idaho, Jan. 15, 1951; s. Charles Ellsworth and Patria (Olesen) K.; m. Juneal Casper, May 24, 1980; children: Peter Ellsworth, Beth Anne, George Ellis, Katherine Leigh. Student, Coll. of Idaho, 1969-71; BA, U. Wash., 1972; JD, U. Idaho, 1980. Bar: Idaho 1980, U.S. Dist. Ct. Idaho 1980, U.S. Ct. Appeals (9th cir.) 1981. Mem. Idaho Senate, 1990-96, majority caucus chmn., 1992-94, majority leader, 1994-96. Mem. S.W. Idaho Estate Planning Coun. Mem. ABA, Assn. Trial Lawyers Am., Idaho Bar Assn. (3d dist. pres. 1985-86), Idaho Trial Lawyers Assn., Canyon County Lawyers Assn. (pres. 1985). Republican. Presbyterian. Lodge: Elks. Avocations: skiing, photography. Office: PO Box 44 Caldwell ID 83606-0044

KERRICK, DONALD L., career officer; b. Apr. 27, 1949. Maj. gen., dep. asst. to pres. for nat. security affairs White House Staff, The White House, Washington, 1997—. Office: White House Staff Washington DC 20506

KERRIGAN, JOHN E., academic administrator. Chancellor U. Wis., Oshkosh. Office: U Wis Office of Chancellor 800 Algoma Blvd Oshkosh WI 54901-3551

KERRIGAN, MABEL BAISLEY, retired peri-operative nurse, educator; b. New Haven, July 13, 1937; d. Melville Mathew and Mary (Werle) Baisley; m. John Francis Kerrigan, June 15, 1968; children: Maureen, Elizabeth, Mary, John, Francis, Mark, William. Diploma, Hosp. St. Raphael, New Haven, 1958; BSN, U. Bridgeport, 1965. RN, cert. operating room nurse. Sch. nurse Branford (Conn.) Pub. Schs., 1980; clin. instr. Hosp. St. Raphael, 1966-68, instr. oper. rm., 1981-95, ret., 1995. Mem. Am. Assn. Operating Room Nurses (1st place writing award 1986).

KERRIGAN, NANCY, professional figure skater, former Olympic athlete; b. Woburn, Mass., Oct. 13, 1969; d. Daniel and Brenda K.; m. Jerry Solomon, 1995; 1 child, Matthew Eric Solomon. Bronze medalist World Championships, 1991, 92, Olympic Games, Albertville, France, 1992; U.S. nat. champion, 1993; silver medalist Olympic Games, Lillehammer, Norway, 1994; owner, choreographer Halloween on Ice, 1995—. Numerous commercials and product endorsements including Walt Disney Co., Reebok, Northwest Airlines, Frosted Cheerios, Ray Ban, Revlon, Aetna U.S. Healthcare, Salvino Bammers; author: (book) In My Own Words, 1996; choreographer Halloween on Ice, (video) Fairy Tales on Ice; performer: Champions on Ice Tour, 1992—; star TV spls. incl.: Dreams on Ice, Breaking the Ice, Nancy Kerrigan and friends; host Nancy Kerrigan's World of Figure Skating; starred as Sandy in Grease on Ice, 1998-99. Spokesperson Lions Club, 1994, Children's Trust Fund, 1997, Spalding Rehab. Hosp., MADD. Recipient Bronze medal World Figure Skating Championships, 1991, Silver medal, 1992, Bronze medal U.S. Pro Championships, 1997. Office: care of Star-Games Bldg 1 40 Salem St Lynnfield MA 01940

KERROS, EDWARD PAUL, stage director, playwright; b. Chgo., Oct. 15, 1954; s. Clarence and Alice (Harrington) K.; m. Sara M. Minton, June 18, 1987. BA, U. Ill., 1976. Assoc. artistic dir. Orchard Theatre, Mt. Prospect, Ill., 1984-91; resident dir. Savoy-Aires, Wilmette, Ill., 1986-89; co-artistic dir. Harlequin Players, Chgo., 1987—; resident dir. Alliance Theatre Co., Chgo., 1988-89; artistic assoc. dir. Canterbury Theatre, Michigan City, Ind., 1989—; artistic dir. HERstory Theatre, Chgo., 1996—; playwright-in-residence Papai Players, Palatine, Ill., 1989—. Dir.: (play) Same Time, Next Year, 1984, Blithe Spirit, 1989, Beyond Therapy, 1990, (mus.) In Trousers, 1988, Baby, 1989, Robber Bridegroom, 1990, Adventures of Goldilocks, 1990, Bye Bye Birdie, 1992, Nunsense, 1994, Guys and Dolls, 1996, 110 in the Shade, 1997; stage dir.: Ruddigore, 1986, The Mikado, 1987, Iolanthe, 1988, The Gondoliers, 1989, Pirates of Penzance, 1995; I Lift My Lamp, 1996. Avocations: downhill skiing, travel, photography, bicycling. Home: 4309 N Kostner Ave Chicago IL 60641-2013

KERRY, CAMERON F., lawyer; b. Washington, Sept. 6, 1950; s. Richard John and Rosemary (Forbes) K.; m. Kathy B. Weinman, June 28, 1983; children: Jessica Weinman Kerry, Laura Weinman Kerry. BA cum laude, Harvard U., 1972; JD magna cum laude, Boston Coll., 1978. Bar: Mass., D.C. Polit. cons., writer Cambridge, Mass., 1973-76; law clerk to Hon. Elbert P. Tuttle U.S. Ct. Appeals (5th cir.), Atlanta, 1978-79; assoc. Wilmer, Cutler & Pickering, Washington, 1979-82; mem. Mintz, Levin, Cohn, Ferris, Glovsky & Popeo, P.C., Boston, 1983—; adj. prof. law Suffolk U. Law Sch. Editor book chpts.; mem. Boston Coll. Law Review, 1977-78; contbr. articles to profl. jours. Campaign mgr. Paul Guzzi for Sec. State, Newton, Mass., 1974; campaign mgr. John Kerry for Lt. Gov., Boston, 1982; trustee Boston Police Found., 1993—; coop. counsel Civil Liberties Union Mass., Boston, 1985; mem. Brookline (Mass.) Dem. Town Com., 1985—. Recipient Internat. Security Mgrs. Assn. award, 1993, citation Nat. Press Photographers Assn., 1990. Mem. ABA, Mass. State Bar Assn., Boston Bar Assn., Def. Rsch. Inst. Office: Mintz Levin Cohn Ferris Glovsky and Popeo PC 1 Financial Ctr Fl 39 Boston MA 02111-2657*

KERRY, JOHN FORBES, senator; b. Denver, Dec. 11, 1943; s. Richard John and Rosemary (Forbes) K.; m. Teresa Heinz, May 25, 1995; children from previous marriage: Alexandra, Vanessa. BA, Yale U., 1966; MA, JD, Boston Coll., 1976. Bar: Mass. 1976. Nat. coordinator Vietnam Vets. Against The War, 1969-71; asst. dist. atty. Middlesex (Mass.) County, 1976-79; ptnr. firm Kerry & Sragow, Boston, 1979-82; lt. gov. State of Mass., 1982-84; U.S. senator from Mass., 1985—; chmn. Dem. Senatorial campaign com., 1986-88; mem. Fgn. Rels. Com., Fgn. Rels. subcom. Internat. Ops., Sen. Dem. Steering & Coordination Com.; mem. Com. Banking, Housing & Urban Affairs, ranking minority mem. Com. Small Bus., Select Com. on Intelligence; ranking minority mem. Commerce, Sci. & Transp. subcom. on Oceans & Fisheries. Author: The New Soldier, 1971, The New War, 1997. Democratic candidate for Congress from 5th Mass. Dist., 1972; bd. vistors Walsh Sch. Fgn. Service, Georgetown U. Served to lt. (j.g.) USNR, 1966-69. Decorated Silver Star; decorated Bronze Star with oak leaf cluster, Purple Hearts (3). Mem. Vietnam Veterans Am. (founder). Roman Catholic. Office: US Senate 304 Russell Senate Bldg Washington DC 20510-2101

KERSCHNER, LEE R(ONALD), academic administrator, political science educator; b. May 31, 1931; m. Helga Koller, June 22, 1958; children: David, Gabriel, Riza. B.A. in Polit. Sci. (Univ. fellow), Rutgers U., 1953; M.A. in Internat. Relations (Univ. fellow), Johns Hopkins U., 1958; Ph.D. in Polit. Sci. (Univ. fellow), Georgetown U., 1964. From instr. to prof. polit. sci. Calif. State U., Fullerton, 1961-69, prof., 1988—; state univ. dean Calif. State Univs. and Colls. Hdqrs., Long Beach, 1969-71, asst. exec. vice chancellor, 1971-76, vice chancellor for adminstrv. affairs, 1976-77, vice chancellor acad. affairs, 1987-92; exec. dir. Colo. Commn. on Higher Edn., Denver, 1977-83, Nat. Assn. Trade and Tech. Schs., 1983-85, Calif. Commn. on Master Plan for Higher Edn., 1985-87; interim pres. Calif. State U., Stanislaus, 1992-94, spl. asst. to the chancellor, 1994-97; exec. vice chancellor Minn. State Colls. and Univs., St. Paul, 1996-97; vice chancellor emeritus Calif. State U., 1997—; mem. Calif. Student Aid Commn., 1993-96; cons. in field. Mem. exec. com. Am. Jewish Com., Denver, 1978-83; internat. bd. dirs. Amigos de las Americas, 1982-88 (chmn. 1985-87). Served with USAF, 1954-58; col. Res., ret. Home: PO Box 748 Weimar CA 95736-0748

KERSELS, MARTIN, artist. BA in Art, UCLA, 1984, MFA in Art, 1995. One-man shows include A/B Gallery, L.A., 1993, Dan Bernier Gallery, Santa Monica, Calif., 1995, 98, Jay Gorney Modern Art, N.Y.C., 1996, Madison (Wis.) Art Ctr., 1997, Theoretical Events, Naples, Italy, 1998, Georges-Phillippe and Nathalie Vallois, Paris, 1999; group shows at Kohn Turner Gallery, L.A., 1994, Otis Parsons Gallery, L.A., 1994, Musee d'Art Moderne Ville de Paris, 1995, David Zwirner Gallery, N.Y.C., 1995, Ten in One Gallery, Chgo., 1996, Mus. Contemporary Art, Miami, 1996, Common Wealth Gallery, Madison, 1996, Mus. Contemporary Art, L.A., 1996, Stephen Wirtz Gallery, San Francisco, 1997, Whitney Mus. Am. Art, N.Y.C., 1997, Mcpl. Art Gallery, L.A., 1997, Soledad Lorenzo Gallery, Madrid, 1997, Saatchi Gallery, London, 1998, Cahors Festival, France, 1999, others; performer Sweaters, 1985, Shape of Pools Today, 1987, Kay Sir Ra Sir Ra, 1989, Weight, 1992; mem. SHRIMPS performance collaborative. Office: care Dan Bernier Gallery 6150 Wilshire Blvd Los Angeles CA 90048

KERSHAW, CAROL JEAN, psychologist; b. New Orleans, Apr. 11, 1947; d. Neal Howard and Gloria Jackson (Moss) Perkins; m. John William Wade, Aug. 20, 1983; stepchildren: Chris Wade, Stephen Wade, Tiffany Wade. BS in Secondary Edn., U. Tex., 1969; MS in Speech Communication, North Tex. State U., 1971, MEd in Counseling, 1976; EdD in Counseling, East Tex. State U., 1979. Lic. psychologist, Tex. Assoc. prof. DeVry Inst., Dallas, 1971-73; instr., counseling psychologist East Tex. State U., Commerce, 1976-78; counselor, instr. Tarrant County Jr. Coll., Hurst, Tex., 1971-74; dir. spl. svcs. Goodwill Industries, Dallas, 1974-76; marriage and family therapist, cons. mental health clinic Tex. Dept. Mental Health and Retardation, Greenville, 1977-79; asst. prof., dir. grad. program in marriage & family therapy Tex. Woman's U., Denton, 1980-83; coord. child devel. dept. Tex. Woman's U., Houston, 1983-88; pvt. practice, Inst. for Family Psychology, Houston, 1986—; co-dir. Milton H. Erickson Inst. Houston, 1986—; bd. dirs. Milton H. Erickson Inst. Tex., Houston, 1986—; internat. presenter in field. Author: Therapeutic Metaphor in the Treatment of Childhood Asthma: A Systemic Approach, Ericksonian Monographs, Vol. 2, 1986, The Couple's Hypnotic Dance, 1992, The Healing Power of the Story, Ericksonian Monographs, Vol. 9, 1994, audio Mind/Body Healing and Hypnosis, 1996; co-author: Learning to Think for an Organ, Bridges of the Bodymind, 1980, Psychotherapeutic Techniques in School Psychology, 1984, Restoring the Mind: Using Therapeutic Narrative in Psychotherapy in Ericksonian Methods, 1994. Sec. Tex. Assn. for Marriage and Family Therapy, 1978-80. Recipient Visionary award, Meritorious Svc. award Tex. Assn. for Marriage & Family Therapy, 1980. Mem. Am. Psychol. Assn., Am. Assn. for Marriage and Family Therapy (clin., approved supr.), Soc. for Exptl. & Clin. Hypnosis, Am. Soc. for Clin. Hypnosis (cert. cons., appointed to ethics com., 1996), Internat. Soc. for Clin. & Exptl. Hypnosis, Psi Chi. Democrat. Methodist. Avocations: painting, reading, exercise, writing, singing. Office: Inst for Family Psychology 2012 Bissonnet St Houston TX 77005-1647

KERSHAW, DAVID JOSEPH, process engineer; b. San Diego; s. Joseph Edward and Marie Arlene (Yezek) K. BS in Physics, San Diego State U., 1991. Data mgr. Systems Ecology Rsch. Group, San Diego, 1988-90, Naval Ocean Systems Ctr., San Diego, 1990; integration engr. San Diego State U. Found., 1990-91; software and antenna engr. SITCO, Portland, 1991-92; tech. support Computer Assocs., San Jose, Calif., 1992-93; process engr.

Intel, Santa Clara, Calif., 1993—. Author: (periodical) World Radio, 1988; editor: (directory) R4D Data Directory, 1989. Mem. Am. Inst. Physics. Achievements include design, development and testing of software for tabel tennis robot to train U.S. Olympic team; engineer manufacturing process that makes it possible to put pentiums in lap top computers, DUV overlay engr. Avocations: amateur radio, computers, physics. Office: Inter MS RN2-18 2200 Mission College Blvd Santa Clara CA 95054-1537

KERSHAW, ROBERT BARNSLEY, lawyer; b. Balt., Feb. 26, 1952; s. Harvey Barnsley Jr. and Lois Mae (Ruby) K. AB in History cum laude, Princeton U., 1974; JD with honors, U. Md., 1977. Bar: Md. 1977, U.S. Dist. Ct. Md. 1977, U.S. Ct. Appeals (4th cir.) 1977, N.Y. 1983, U.S. Dist. Ct. (so., ea. dists.) N.Y. 1983. Assoc. Ober, Kaler, Grimes & Shriver, Balt., 1977-84; founding prin. Ward, Kershaw & Minton, Balt., 1984—. Bd. dirs. Preservation Md., Inc., Balt., 1983—, pres., 1987-90; sr. warden Emmanuel Episc. Ch., Balt., 1988-90; mem. Ward, Kershaw & Minton Environ. Law Symposium Fund, 1990; chmn., pres. Md. Humanities Coun., 1997-99. Mem. ABA (vice chmn. property com., torts and ins. practice sect. 1988—), Bar. Assn. Baltimore City (treas. 1998-99), Md. Club, Princeton Club N.Y., Univ. Cottage Club. Democrat. Avocations: fly fishing, alpine skiing. Office: Ward Kershaw and Minton 113 W Monument St Baltimore MD 21201-4736

KERSHNER, IRVIN, film director; b. Phila., Apr. 29, 1923. Ed., Temple U. Fine Arts Sch., U. So. Calif. Art Ctr. Sch. Documentary filmmaker U.S. Info. Services, Mid. East, 1950-52; dir., camerman TV documentary Confidential File, 1953-55; dir., producer, writer Ophite Prodns. Dir.: (films) Stakeout on Dope Street, 1958, The Young Captives, 1959, The Hoodlum Priest, 1961, A Face in the Rain, 1963, The Luck of Ginger Coffey, 1964, A Fine Madness, 1966, The Flim-Flam Man, 1967, Loving, 1970, Up the Sandbox, 1972, S*P*Y*S, 1974, The Return of a Man Called Horse, 1978, Eyes of Laura Mars, 1978, The Empire Strikes Back, 1980, Never Say Never Again, 1983, (TV film) Raid on Entebbe, 1977 (Emmy nomination), (TV shows) The Rebel, Naked City, numerous others. Mem. Dirs. Guild Am. Address: c/o Diane Golden Silverberg, Katz, Thompson et al 11766 Wilshire Blvd #700 Los Angeles CA 90025*

KERSLAKE, KENNETH ALVIN, artist, printmaker, art educator; b. Mt. Vernon, N.Y., Mar. 8, 1930; s. Archibald and Cecilia Fox (Gotterson) K.; m. Sarah Jane Allen, Aug. 25, 1956; children: Scott Paul, Katherine Rachel. Student, Pratt Inst., 1950-53; BFA, U. Ill., 1955, MFA, 1957. Grad. asst. U. Ill.-Champaign, 1955-57; interim instr. U. Ill., Champaign, 1957-58; instr. U. Fla., Gainesville, 1958-60, asst. prof. art, 1961-68, assoc. prof., 1969-74, prof., 1974-91, Disting. Svc. prof. emeritus, 1991—; workshop lectr. U. Alaska-Fairbanks, 1982; artist-in-residence U. Mo.-Columbia, 1980, Frans Masereel Print Ctr., Kasterlee, Belgium, 1986, U. Tex., Austin; invited faculty U. Ga. Studies Abroad Program, Cortona, Italy, 1982; juror Fla. Printmakers 3rd Ann. Exhbn., 1989, Honolulu Printmakers 62nd Ann. Exhbn., 1990, Pacific States Nat. Print Exhbn., U. Hawaii, Hilo, 1992; exch. prof. Coll. of Art, Edinburgh, Scotland, 1995. Exhibited in major retrospective Impressions of Forty Years: The Prints of Kenneth A. Kerslake, Samuel P. Harn Mus. of Art, U. Fla., Gainesville, Fla., Ctr. for Arts, Vero Beach, Fla., 1997, LeMoyne Art Found., Tallahassee, Fla., 1998, U. Hawaii, Hilo, 1999, Webster U., St. Louis, Ga. Coll. and State U., Atlanta; featured in publs. including Forty American Contemporary Printmakers. Recipient Joseph Pennell award Library of Congress, 1975, Assoc. Am. Artist award Associated Am. Artist Gallery, 1979, Disting. Faculty award Fla. Blue Key-U. Fla., 1979, Tchr. Improvement Program award, 1993; named Tchr. of Yr., Coll. Fine Arts, U. Fla., 1987; grantee Tamarind Found. Inc., 1964. Mem. Soc. Am. Graphic Artists, Fla. Printmakers Soc., Samuel P. Harn Mus. Art Alliance, Boston Printmakers, Print Club Phila., So. Graphics Coun. (organized 15th ann. conf., pres. 1990-92, newsletter editor), Am. Print Alliance (exec. bd., exec. com. 1992-93). Democrat. Episcopalian. Home: 1114 NW 36th Dr Gainesville FL 32605-4945 Office: U Fla Coll Fine Arts Dept Art FAC 317 Gainesville FL 32611

KERSTETTER, MICHAEL JAMES, retired manufacturing company executive; b. Spokane, Wash., Sept. 3, 1936; s. James B. and Ruth (Marquardt) K.; m. Eileen Virginia Behm, June 26, 1955; children: Michael Stuart, Steven Douglas (dec.). AA, Long Beach (Calif.) City Coll., 1957; BSCE, Calif. State U., Long Beach, 1962, MSCE, 1968. Registered structural engr., Ca., civil engr., Ca. Process engr. Aerojet-Gen., Downey, Calif., 1955-62; design engr.Aetron div. Aerojet-Gen., Covina, Calif., 1962-64; structural engr. C.F. Braun & Co., Alhambra, Calif., 1964-69, structural engring. section head, 1969-70; engr. Conrock Co., L.A., 1970-72, asst. prodn. mgr., 1972-75, ops. mgr., 1975-79, v.p., 1979-84; exec. v.p., gen. mgr. ConAgg div. CalMat Co. (formerly Conrock Co.), L.A., 1984-89; exec. v.p. Constrn. Materials, 1989-92; retired, 1993. Pack master Cub Scouts Am., West Covina, Calif., 1976; steering com. Boy Scouts Am. Troop 443, West Covina, 1977-79. Fellow Am. Concrete Inst. (pres. So. Calif. chpt. 1984-85), Inst. Advancement Engring.; mem. Structural Engrs. Assn. So. Calif. (sec. 1979-80), Nat. Ready Mixed Concrete Assn. (bd. dirs. 1985-92), So. Calif. Rock Products Assn. (chmn. 1987-89). Clubs: Glendora (Calif.) Country.

KERSTING, EDWIN JOSEPH, retired university dean; b. Ottawa, Ohio, Nov. 4, 1919; s. Alphonse A. and Mary (Frey) K.; m. Billy Kate Walker, Mar. 23, 1946; children: Karl W., Ann L. D.V.M., Ohio State U., 1952; M.S., U. Conn., 1964. Pvt. practice vet. medicine Charleston, W.Va. and Columbus, Ohio, 1952-62; research asst. U. Conn., Storrs, 1961-62; assoc. prof. clin. vet. medicine, state extension veterinarian U. Conn., 1962-65, asst. dean resident instrn. Coll. Agr., dir. Ratcliffe Hicks Sch. Agr., 1965-66, dir. internat. programs in agr., 1965-83, dean Coll. Agr. and Natural Resources, 1966-83, dir. Storrs Agrl. Expt. Sta., dir. Conn. Coop. Extension Service, 1966-83, prof. clin. vet. medicine dept. pathobiology, 1966-85, acting dean designate proposed Sch. Vet. Medicine, 1975-81, ret., 1985; research coordinator Hartford Hosp., Conn., 1985-90, chmn. sci. rev. com., 1986-88; mem. adv. bd. to U.S. Sec. Agr. Animal Health Scis. Rsch. Program, 1978-84; bd. overseers Sch. Vet. Medicine, U. Pa.; assoc. mem. univ. bd. trustees, 1978-91, mem. adv. coun. Coll. Vet. Medicine, Cornell U., 1978-83; cons. dept. surg. rsch, 1964-85; mem. rsch. com. Hartford (Conn.) Hosp., 1985-90; cons. Hartford Hosp., 1990-96, adv. com. Northeastern Rsch. Ctr. for Wildlife Diseases, 1971-83; cons. Ministry Agr., Belize, 1968-83; adv. com. Conn. Soil Conservation Svc.; ex-officio bd. overseers Bartlett Arboretum, 1967-83. Contbr. articles to profl. publs. Pres. Conn. Lung Assn., 1977-79; exec. com. Eastern States Expn., 1968-91, emeritus mem. Conn. trustees, 1992. Served with U.S. Army, Am. Field Svc. and USCG, 1942-44. Mem. AAAS, AVMA, Royal Soc. Health, Sigma Xi, Alpha Zeta, Epsilon Sigma Phi, Gamma Sigma Delta, Phi Zeta, Phi Kappa Phi.

KERTH, LEROY T., physics educator; b. Visalia, Calif., Nov. 23, 1928; s. Lewis John and Frances (Niccolls) K.; m. Ruth Lorraine Littlefield, Nov. 19, 1950; children: Norman Lewis, Randall Thomas, Christine Jane, Bradley Niccolls. A.B. in Physics, U. Calif., Berkeley, 1950, Ph.D., 1957. Mem. staff Lawrence Berkeley Lab, U. Calif., Berkeley, 1950-59; sr. scientist Lawrence Berkeley Lab, U. Calif., 1959-61; assoc. prof. physics U. Calif., Berkeley, 1961-65, prof., 1965-93, prof. emeritus, 1993—, assoc. dean Coll. Letters and Scis., 1966-70, spl. asst. to chancellor, 1970-71, assoc. dir. for info. and computing scis. div., 1983-87, assoc. lab. dir. for gen. scis., Lawrence Berkeley Lab., 1987-89, assoc. lab. dir. sci. and tech. resources, Lawrence Berkeley Lab., 1990-92. Fellow Am. Phys. Soc. Home: 5 Los Conejos Orinda CA 94563-2214 Office: U Calif Lawrence Berkeley Lab Berkeley CA 94720

KERTZ, MARSHA HELENE, accountant, educator; b. Palo Alto, Calif., May 29, 1946; d. Joe and Ruth (Lazear) K. BSBA in Acctg., San Jose State U., 1976, MBA, 1977. CPA, Calif., cert. tax profl. Staff acct. Steven Kroff & Co., CPA's, Palo Alto, 1968-71, 73-74; contr. Rand Teleconsultancy Corp., San Francisco, 1972; auditor, sr. acct. Ben F. Priest Accountancy Corp., Mountain View, Calif., 1974-83; tchr. San Jose Unified Regional Occupation Program, San Jose, 1977; pvt. practice accounting San Jose, 1977—; lectr. San Jose State U., 1977—. Bd. dirs. San Jose State U. Coll. of Bus. Alumni Assn. Mem. AICPA, Nat. Soc. of Tax Profls., Am. Inst. Tax Studies, Am. Acctg. Assn., Calif. Soc. CPAs, San Jose State U. Coll. Bus. Alumni Assn. (bd. dirs.), Beta Alpha Psi, Beta Gamma Sigma. Democrat. Jewish. Avocations: piano, travel, art history. Home: 4544 Strawberry Park Dr San Jose CA 95129-2213 Office: San Jose State U Acctg & Fin Dept San Jose CA 95192

KERTZMAN, MITCHELL E., software company executive. LHD (hon.), U. Mass., Lowell. Founder Computer Solutions, 1974; founder, CEO Powersoft Corp., 1993; chmn. bd. dirs., CEO Sybase, Inc., Emeryville, Calif., 1995-98; pres., CEO Liberate Techs., Redwood Shores, Calif., 1998—; bd. dirs. Sybase, Inc., Shiva Corp., CNET, Interconnect Syss., Inc.; pres. Mass. Software Coun., 1994-96. Founder, chmn. Mass. Inst. New Commonwealth; mem. N.Y. State Commn. Indsl. Competitiveness, chair task force indsl. policy. Recipient Inc. Mag. and Ernst & Young's New England Entrepreneur of Yr. award, 1993, Disting. Achievement award Tech. Unit New England B'nai B'rith, 1993. Office: Liberate Techs 1000 Bridge Pkwy Redwood Shores CA 94065*

KERWIN, CORNELIUS MARTIN, dean, public affairs educator; b. Waterbury, Conn., Apr. 10, 1949; s. Daniel Vincent and Mary Catherine (Shea) K.; m. Ann D. Londe, Sept. 3, 1972; children: Michael Barnett, Alex Daniel. BA, Am. U., 1971; MA, U. R.I., 1972; PhD, Johns Hopkins U., 1978. Program asst. Johns Hopkins U., Balt., 1972-75; instr. Washington Semester Program, 1975-78; program dir. Sch Govt. and Pub. Adminstrn., Washington, 1978-80, asst. prof., 1980-84, assoc. prof., 1984-88; acting dean sch. pub. affairs Am. U., Washington, 1988-89, dean sch. pub. affairs, prof., 1989—, acting provost, 1997-98, full provost, 1998—; cons. IBM, Corp., Rockville, Md., 1984—, U.S. Fed. Energy Regulatory Commn., Washington, 1983-88, U.S. EPA, Washington, 1988—, and others. Author: Rulemaking, 1994; contbr. book chpts., conf. papers, and articles to profl. jours. Regional finalist White House Fellowship Competition, 1980. Fellow Nat. Acad. Pub. Adminstrn.; Mem. Nat. Assn. Schs. Pub. Affairs and Adminstrn. (commn. on peer rev. and accreditation 1990-93, exec. coun., 1993—), Am. Soc. Pub. Adminstrn. (bd. dirs. Nat. Capital area chpt. 1990—, chmn. sect. on pub. law and adminstrn. 1991—), Am. Polit. Sci. Assn., Smithsonian Assocs. Avocations: running, golf, tennis. Office: Am U Provost's Office 4400 Massachusetts Ave NW Washington DC 20016-8003*

KERWIN, LARKIN, retired physics educator; b. Quebec, Que., Can., June 22, 1924; m. Maria Guadalupe Turcot, 1950; 8 children. Cert. engring. studies St. Francis Xavier U., 1943, BSc summa cum laude, 1944; MSc magna cum laude, MIT, 1946; DSc magna cum laude, U. Laval, 1949; LLD (hon.), St. Francis Xavier U., 1970, U. Toronto, 1973, Concordia U., Montreal, 1976, U. Alta., 1983, U. Dalhousie, 1983, U. Moncton, 1985; DSc (hon.), U. B.C., 1973, McGill U., 1974, Meml. U. Newfoundland, 1978, U. Ottawa, 1981, Royal Mil. Coll. Can., 1982, U. Winnipeg, 1983, U. Windsor, 1984, U. Montreal, 1991; DCivil Law (hon.) Bishop's U., 1978. Teaching asst. St. Francis Xavier U., 1944; lab. demonstrator U. Toronto, 1945; rsch. physicist Geotech. Corp., Cambridge, Mass., 1945; lab. asst. physics dept. U. Laval, Quebec, 1946-48, asst. prof., 1948-51, assoc. prof., 1951-56, prof, Chair of Atomic Physics, 1956, dir. Mass. Spectrometry Lab., 1955-66, chmn. dept. physics, 1961-67; dir. Van de Graaf Accelerator Lab., 1961-72, vice-dean faculty of scis., 1967-68, acad. vice-rector, 1969-72, rector, 1972-77, prof. emeritus, 1991; pres. Assn. Univs. and Colls. Can., 1974-75, Nat. Rsch. Coun. Can., 1980-89, Can. Space Agency, 1989-92, Can. Acad. Engring., 1989-90. Author: Atomic Physics, An Introduction, 1963; mem. editorial bd. Interdisciplinary Sci. Revs. Mag., 1981—; contbr. numerous articles to profl. jours. Trustee Nat. Museums of Can., 1980-89; adv. council Ottawa chpt. Can. Soc. Weizmann Inst. Sci., 1981; Canadian rep. Versailles conf. on tech. and employment, 1982; bd. govs. Carleton U., 1983-86. Recipient Centenary medal, 1967; knight Equestrian Order of Holy Sepulchre of Jerusalem, 1970, knight comdr., 1972, comdr. with star, 1974, knight grand cross, 1980; Jubilee medal, 1977; Centenary medal of Roumania, 1977; officer Order of Can., 1978, companion, 1980; medal of Laval Alumni, 1978; Ordre du Merite, Société Saint-Jean Baptiste de Que., 1979; Gold medal, Can. Council Profl. Engrs., 1982, Officer Order of Quebec, 1987, officier Legion Honor, France, 1989; Outstanding Achievement award Govt. Can., 1987. Fellow Royal Soc. Can. (pres. 1977-78), Royal Soc. Arts, AAAS, Am. Inst. Physics; mem. Internat. Union Pure and Applied Physics (pres. 1987-91), Association Canadienne Française pour l'Avancement des Sciences (Pariseau medal 1965, Jacques Rousseau medal 1983), Am. Phys. Soc., Corp. Profl. Engrs. Que., Sociedad Mexicana Fisica, Can. Assn. Physicists (pres. 1954, Gold medal 1969), Académie des Grands Québecois.

KERWIN, MARK BRODERICK, chief financial officer, accountant; b. Boston, Oct. 1, 1957; s. Thomas Joseph and Patricia (Howley) Kerwin; m. Annemarie Lewis. BS cum laude, Boston Col., 1979; MBA, Babson Col., 1986. CPA. Audit supervisor Feeley & Driscoll, Boston, 1979-82; fin. analyst Blue Cross/Blue Shield, Boston, 1982-86; fin. mgr. Med. East Cmty. Health (now HMOBlue), Boston, 1983-86; controller, chief financial officer Emerson Col., Boston, 1986-88; assoc. v.p. Emerson Col., 1988—; treas. Nat. Acad. Television Arts & Scis., 1989-93; pres., chmn. Boston Jr. C. of C., 1984-86. Recipient Governor's award NATAS, 1990. Mem. Clover Club, Algonquin Club, Treas. Club, Jaycees (named one of Boston's ten outstanding young leaders, 1987, recipient ambassadorship, 1986). Office: Emerson Col 100 Beacon St Boston MA 02116-1501

KERWIN, WALTER THOMAS, JR., career officer, consultant; b. West Chester, Pa., June 14, 1917; s. Walter Thomas and Mary Joseph (Farra) K.; m. Barbara Walker Connell, July 10, 1940 (dec. 1980); children: Bruce Richard, Ann Walker; m. Marion Thompson McCutcheon, Oct. 27, 1984. BS, U.S. Mil. Acad., 1939; postgrad., Command and Gen. Staff Coll., 1948, Armed Forces Staff Coll., 1953, U.S. Army War Coll., 1957, Nat. War Coll., 1960; LLD (hon.), U. Akron, 1976; M in Mil. Art and Sci., Command and Gen. Staff Coll., 1978. Commd. 2nd lt. U.S. Army, 1939, advanced through grades to gen., 1973; commdg. gen. 3d armored divsn. arty. U.S. Army, Hanau, Germany, 1961-63; chief nuclear activities SHAPE NATO U.S. Army, Paris, 1963-65; commdg. gen. 3d armored divsn. U.S. Army, Frankfurt, Germany, 1965-66; asst. dep. chief staff ops. gen. staff U.S. Army, Washington, 1966-67; chief staff mil. asst. command U.S. Army, Saigon, Vietnam, 1967-68; commdg. gen. II field force Vietnam U.S. Army, Bien Hoa, 1968-69; dep. chief staff pers. gen. staff U.S. Army, Washington, 1969-72; commdg. gen. continental army command U.S. Army, Norfolk, Va., 1973; commdg. gen. forces command U.S. Army, Atlanta, 1973-74; vice chief staff U.S. Army, Washington, 1974-78; cons. Martin Marietta Corp., Bethesda, Md., 1978-94, Lockheed-Martin, 1994-97; assoc. dir. ops. Los Alamos (N.Mex.) Sci. Lab., 1953-56; bd. dirs. Gen. Employment Enterprises, Oakbrook, Ill., 1984—; mem. bd. mgrs. Army Emergency Relief, 1982—. Chmn. Army Air Force Mut. Aid Assn., Arlington, Va., 1982-97, chmn. emeritus 1997—; mem. strategy com. Army Hist. Found., 1995-97, bd. dirs., 1997—. Recipient Disting. Svc. medal Commonwealth of Pa., 1975, Outstanding Alumnus award U.S. Army War Coll., 1997, numerous mil. awards and decorations; named to Henderson Hall of Fame, West Chester, Pa., 1991, Res. Officers Assn. of U.S. Minute Man Hall of Fame, 1978. Fellow Nat. Def. U. Capstone Program (emeritus); mem. Am. Def. Preparedness Assn. (comdr. Chief award 1984), West Point Soc. (Castle-Duty Hon. Country award 1993), U.S. Field Arty. Assn. (pres.). Avocations: fishing, wilderness hiking.

KERWIN, WILLIAM JAMES, electrical engineering educator, consultant; b. Portage, Wis., Sept. 27, 1922; s. James William and Nina Elizabeth (Haight) K.; m. Madolyn Lee Lyons, Aug. 31, 1947; children: Dorothy E., Deborah K., David W. B.S., U Redlands, 1948; M.S., Stanford U., 1954, Ph.D., 1967. Aero. research scientist NACA, Moffett Field, Calif., 1948-59; chief measurements research br. NASA, Moffett Field, Calif., 1959-62, chief space tech. br., 1962-64, chief electronics research br., 1964-70; head electronics dept. Stanford Linear Accelerator Ctr., 1962; prof. elec. engring. U. Ariz., Tucson, 1969-85, prof. emeritus, 1986—. Author: (with others) Active Filters, 1970, Handbook Measurement Science, 1982, Instrumentation and Control, 1990, Handbook of Electrical Engineering, 1993, 97; contbr. articles to profl. jours.; patentee in field. Served to capt. USAAF, 1942-46. Recipient Invention NASA, 1969, 70; recipient fellow NASA, 1966-67. Fellow IEEE (Centennial medal 1984). Home: 1981 W Shalimar Way Tucson AZ 85704-1250 Office: U Ariz Dept Elec and Computer Engring Tucson AZ 85721

KERXTON, ALAN SMITH, lawyer; b. Balt., Mar. 19, 1938; s. Benjamin and Eva (Smith) K.; m. Leslie Lurie, Aug. 2, 1961; children: Amy Lynn, Susan Deborah, Katherine Diane. BA, Ohio State U., 1960, JD, 1962. Bar: DC 1963, Md. 1965. Atty. corp. reorganization br. SEC, Washington, 1963-66; pvt. practice Washington, Potomac, Md., 1966—; prin. Ezrin, West and Kerxton, Chartered, 1976-84, Dunnells and Duval, Washington, 1990-93, Holland and Knight, Washington, 1994-97; of counsel Stein, Sperling, Rockville, Md., 1998—; lectr. Cath. U. Am. Law Sch., fall 1973. With U.S. Army, 1962-63. Mem. ABA, D.C. Bar Assn., Montgomery County Bar Assn. Home: 11815 Beekman Pl Potomac MD 20854-2177 Office: 25 W Middle Ln Rockville MD 20850-2214

KERYCZYNSKYJ, LEO IHOR, lawyer, county official, educator; b. Chgo., Aug. 8, 1948; s. William and Eva (Chicz) K.; m. Alexandra Irene Okruch, July 19, 1980; 1 child, Christina Alexandra. BA, DePaul U., 1970, BS, 1970, MS in Pub. Svc., 1975; JD, No. Ill. U., 1979; postgrad., U. Ill., Chgo., 1980-82. Bar: Ill. 1981, U.S. Dist. Ct. (no. dist.) Ill. 1981, U.S. Ct. Appeals (7th cir.) 1981, U.S. Tax Ct. 1981, U.S. Ct. Claims 1982, U.S. Ct. Mil. Appeals 1982, U.S. Ct. Appeals (fed. cir.) 1983, U.S. Supreme Ct. 1984. Condemnation awards officer Cook County Treas.'s Officw, Chgo., 1972-75, adminstrv. asst., 1975-77, dep. treas., 1977-87, chief legal counsel, 1987-96, dir. fin. svcs., 1988-96; pvt. practice, 1996-98; adv. Office of Profl. Stds. Chgo. Police Dept., 1998—; adj. prof. DePaul U., Chgo., 1979-95; elected chmn. bd. dirs., Security Fed. Savs. Bank Chgo., 1992-93. Capt. Ukrainian Am. Dem. Orgn., Chgo., 1971. Recipient Outstanding Alumni award Phi Kappa Theta, 1971. Mem. ABA, Ill. State Bar Assn., Ill. Trial Law Assn., Ukrainian Am. bar Assn., Chgo. Bar Assn., Ill. Assn. County Ofcls., Internat. Assn., Clerks, Recorders, Election Ofcls. and Treas., Shore Line Interurban Hist. Soc. (bd. dirs., legal counsel 1987—, pres. and chmn., 1993-98), Theta Delta Phi. Ukrainian Catholic. Home: 2324 W Iowa St Apt 3R Chicago IL 60622-4712 Office: Office Profl Stds 1130 S Wabash Chicago IL 60605

KESEND, MICHAEL, publishing executive; b. N.Y.C., Sept. 22, 1937. BA, Syracuse U., 1959. Pres. Michael Kesend Pub. Ltd., N.Y.C., 1978—. *

KESEY, KEN, writer; b. La Hunta, Colo., Sept. 17, 1935; s. Fred and Geneva (Smith) K.; m. Norma Faye Haxby, May 20, 1956; children: Shannon, Zane, Jed (dec. 1984) Sunshine. BS, U. Oreg., 1957; postgrad., Stanford U., 1958-60. Pres. Intrepid Trips, Inc., 1964; editor, pub. mag. Spit in the Ocean, 1974—. Author: One Flew Over the Cuckoo's Nest, 1962, Sometimes a Great Notion, 1964, Garage Sale, 1973, Demon Box, 1986, Little Tricker the Squirrel Meets Big Double the Bear, 1988; co-author: Caverns, 1989, The Further Inquiry, 1990, The Sea Lion, 1991, Sailor Song, 1992; (with Ken Babbs) Last Go Round: a Real Western, 1994; author, prodr.: (play) Twister, 1995; (video and script) Twister, 1998. Address: 85829 Ridgeway Rd Pleasant Hill OR 97455-9627

KESHAVAN, MATCHERI, psychiatrist; b. Belur, Karnataka, India, May 23, 1953; came to U.S., 1985; s. Matcheri Sannaiyengar and Rama Matcheri Srinivasamurthy; m. Asha Keshavan, June 5, 1981; children: Meghana, Vidya. MB BS, Mysore Med. Coll., Karnataka, India, 1977; MD, Nat. Inst. of Mental Health, Bangalore, India, 1979. Asst. prof. psychiatry St. Johns Med. Coll., Bangalore, 1979-80; lectr. in psychiatry NIMH, Bangalore, 1980-82; IBRO rsch. fellow Internat Brain Rsch. Orgn., Vienna, Austria, 1982-83; registrar Maudsley Hosp., London, 1984-85; asst. prof. of psychiatry Wayne State U., Detroit, 1986-87; asst. prof. of psychiatry U. Pitts., 1987-91, assoc. prof., 1991—; med. dir. schizophrenia unit Western Psychiat. Inst. and Clinic, Pitts., 1988—, prof. psychiatry, 1998—. Contbr. over 100 articles to profl. publs.; author 3 books. Recipient Silver Jubilee prize Mysore U., 1977, Young Investigator award NIMH, 1989, Rsch. Scientist Devel. award, 1995—; Schizophrenia Rsch. grantee Scottish Rite Found., 1989; Internat. Brain Rsch. Orgn. scholar, 1982-83. Mem. Royal Coll. Psychiatrists (Gaskell medal 1985), Indian Psychiat. Soc. (Jayaram award), IndoAm. Psychiat. Assn. (Sci. award 1996). Hindu. Avocation: paintings and sketches. Home: 2570 Mt Royal Rd Pittsburgh PA 15217-2542 Office: Western Psychiat Inst 3811 Ohara St Pittsburgh PA 15213-2593

KESHIAN, RICHARD, lawyer; b. Arlington, Mass., Aug. 11, 1934; s. Hamayak and Takuhe (Malkesian) K.; m. Jacqueline C. Cannilla, Sept 11, 1965; children: Carolyn D., Richard M.. BS in Bus. Adminstrn., Boston U., 1956, JD, 1958. Bar: Mass. 1958. Pvt. practice law, Arlington, Mass., 1964-71; ptnr. Keshian & Reynolds, P.C., Arlington, 1971—; instr. real estate law Inst. Fin. Edn., 1976-80; instr. bus law George Washington U., Washington, 1961-63; mem. adv. bd. Coop. Bank Concord, Arlington, 1983-86; corporator Bank Five for Savs., Arlington, 1984-91; bd. dirs., gen. counsel Arlington Coop. Bank, 1978-83. Chmn. Arlington Zoning Bd. Appeals, 1972-76; pres. Arlington C. of C., 1976; v.p. Mass. Fedn. Planning Bds., 1978-85; mem. Arlington Contributory Retirement Bd., 1984—. With USMC, 1958-64; maj. Res. ret. Mem. ABA, Mass. Bar Assn., Am. Arbitration Assn. (arbitrator 1975—), Mass. Conveyancers Assn. (bd. dirs. 1996—, chmn. title standards com. 1996—), Mass. Assn. Bank Counsel (pres. 1992-95), Middlesex County Bar Assn. Democrat. Congregationalist. Home: 93 Falmouth Rd W Arlington MA 02474-1007 Office: 1040 Massachusetts Ave PO Box 440 Arlington MA 02476-0052

KESHK, MAMDOUH M. (MIKE KESHK), design engineer; b. Port Said, Egypt, Dec. 25, 1957; came to U.S., 1980; s. Mohamed Khalil and Fawiza (Fahim) K.; m. Sahar Kouta, Dec. 1, 1966. MS, Poly. U., N.Y.C., 1985. Design engr. IBM Corp., Research Triangle Park, N.C., 1985-94; sr. engr. HP, Chapel Hill, N.C., 1994-97; staff design engr. Mitsubishi Semicondr., Durham, N.C., 1997—; real estate investor MK Property Mgmt., Raleigh, 1988—. Mem. IEEE. Address: 5420 Den Heider Way Raleigh NC 27606-9583

KESKINER, ALI, psychiatrist; b. Kirsehir, Turkey, Mar. 10, 1929; came to the U.S., 1963; s. Mustafa and Ayse (Memis) K.; m. Lynne E. Hirz, Oct. 18, 1968 (div. 1982); children: Murad A., Aydin D. MD, Istanbul U., 1955; diploma in psychiatry, McGill U., 1962. Sr. intern psychiatry St. Anne's sect. Queen Mary Vets. Hosp., Montreal, Que., Can., 1958-59, resident psychiatry, 1959-60, sr. asst. resident psychiatry, 1960-61; sr. asst. resident in psychiatry Montreal Children's Hosp., 1961-62; asst. resident medicine-neurology Univ. Hosp., U. Sask., Saksatoon, Sask., Can., 1962-63; sr. rsch. scientist Mo. Inst. Psychiatry U. Mo., St. Louis, 1963-68, prof. psychiatry, 1964-76, chief behavioral rsch., 1968-75; staff psychiatrist, dir. rsch. Anclote Manor Hosp., Tarpon Springs, Fla., 1975-83; dir. rsch., staff psychiatrist VA Med. Ctr., Bay Pines, Fla., 1984-87, chief psychiatry svcs., 1988—; prof. psychiatry U. South Fla. Coll. Medicine, Tampa, 1984—; mem. rsch. com. U. South Fla. Dept. Psychiatry, Tampa, 1989—; mem. exec. com. VA Med. Ctr., 1992—; mem. sr. adv. com. Mo. Inst. Psychiatry, St. Louis, 1970-75. Contbr. chpt. to Therapeutic Studies in Therapy Resistant Schizophrenia, 1966-74; contbr. articles to profl. jours. Capt. Turkish Army, 1956-58. Grantee NIH, 1970-74; recipient Golden Eagle award Coun. on Internat. Non-Theatrical Events, 1975, 1st Place award in community mental health Nat. Mental Health Assn., 1977. Fellow Am. Psychiat. Assn. (life); mem. AAAS, N.Y. Acad. Sci., Fla. Psychiat. Soc. (various coms. 1984—), Turkish Am. Neuropsychiat. Assn. (pres. 1981-82). Office: VA Med Ctr Bay Pines FL 33504

KESLER, JAMES L., ophthalmologist; b. Vincennes, Ind., July 8, 1949; s. Richard Kesler and Bonnie L. (Perrott) Treece; m. Jana L. Blake, Aug. 29, 1970; children: Jason, Jessica. BS Biochemistry with distinction, U. Ill., 1971; MD, Washington U., 1975. Diplomate Am. Bd. Ophthalmology, Nat. Bd. Med. Examiners. Resident U. Va., Charlottesville, 1975-76, Barnes Hosp./Washington U., St. Louis, 1976-79; ophthalmologist Coastal Carolina Eye Clinic, Wilmington, N.C., 1979—; cons. in ophthalmology Duke U., 1998—. James scholar U. Ill., 1967-71. Fellow ACS (bd. dirs. N.C. chpt. 1997—), Am. Acad. Ophthalmology (councillor 1996—); mem. AMA, N.C. Med. Soc., N.C. Soc. Ophthalmology (pres. 1988), New Hanover-Pender County Med. Soc. (pres. 1991), Nat. Parliamentarian Soc., Phi Beta Kappa, Alpha Omega Alpha. Avocations: biking, tennis, baseball, basketball, reading. Office: Coastal Carolina Eye Clinic 1120 Med Ctr Dr Wilmington NC 28401

KESLER, JAY LEWIS, academic administrator; b. Barnes, Wis., Sept. 15, 1935; s. Elsie M. Campbell Kesler; m. H. Jane Smith; children: Laura, Bruce, Terri. Student, Ball State U., 1953-54; BA, Taylor U., 1958, LHD (hon.), 1982; Dr. Divinity (hon.), Barrington Coll., 1977; DD (hon.), Asbury Theol. Sem., 1984, Anderson U., 1999; HHD (hon.), Huntington Coll., 1983; LHD, John Brown U., 1987; LLD (honoris causa), Gordon Coll., 1992. Dir.

Marion (Ind.) Youth for Christ, 1955-58, crusade staff evangelist, 1959-60, dir. Ill.-Ind. region, 1960-62, dir. coll. recruitment, 1962-63, v.p. personnel, 1963-68, v.p. field coordination, 1968-73, pres., 1973-85, also bd. dirs.; pres. Taylor U., Upland, Ind., 1985—; bd. dirs. Star Fin. Group, Christianity Today, Ind. Colls. Ind., Brotherhood Mut. Ins. Co., Ind. Coll.-Univs. Inc., Christian Coll. Consortium, Nat. Assn. Evangs., Youth for Christ Internat., Youth for Christ U.S.A.; mem. bd. reference Christian Camps Inc., Coalition for Christian Colls. and Univs.; mem. adv. bd. Christian Bible Soc.; co-pastor 1st Bapt. Ch., Geneva, Ill., 1972-85; mem. faculty Billy Graham Schs. Evangelism; lectr. Staley Disting. Christian Sch. Lecture Program; gov.'s appointee to Ind. Commn. on Youth. Speaker on Family Forum (daily radio show and radio program); mem. adv. com. Campus Life mag.; author: Let's Succeed With Our Teenagers, 1973, I Never Promised You a Disneyland, 1975, The Strong Weak People, 1976, Outside Disneyland, 1977, I Want a Home with No Problems, 1977, Growing Places, 1978, Too Big to Spank, 1978, Breakthrough, 1981, Parents & Teenagers, 1984 (Gold Medallion award), Family Forum, 1984, Making Life Make Sense, 1986, Parents and Children, 1986, Being Holy, Being Human, 1988, Ten Mistakes Parents Make With Teenagers (And How to Avoid Them), 1988, Is Your Marriage Really Worth Fighting For?, 1989, Energizing Your Teenagers' Faith, 1990, Raising Responsible Kids, 1991, Grandparenting: The Agony and the Ecstasy, 1993, Challenges for the College Bound, 1994, Emotionally Healthy Teenagers, 1998; contbr. articles to profl. jours. Bd. advisors Prison Fellowship Internat., Christian Camps Inc., Christian Educators Assn. Internat., Evangelicals for Social Action, Love and Action, Venture Middle East, Internat. Com. of Reference for New Life 2000. Recipient Angel award Religion in Media, 1985, Outstanding Youth Leadership award Religious Heritage Am., 1989. Office: Taylor U Office Pres 236 W Reade Ave Upland IN 46989-1002

KESLER, JOHN A., lawyer, land developer; b. Clark County, Ill., Apr. 25, 1923; s. Hal H. and Clara (Hurst) K.; m. Maxine Ruth Weaver, May 13, 1948; children: Nicki Kesler Herrington, Bradley Weaver, John A. II. AB, Ind. State U., 1948; JD, Ind. U., 1951. Bar: Ind. 1951, Ill. 1951. Chief dep. prosecutor County Vigo, Terre Haute, Ind., 1954-58; probate commr. Cir. Ct., 1971-74; mem. ho. reps. Ind. Legis., 1969-73; asst. state atty. County Madison, Edwardsville, Ill., 1985-88; pvt. practice law Terre Haute, 1951—; pres. Wabash Valley Land Developers, Inc., Terre Haute, 1979—. Sgt. U.S. Army, 1943-46. Recipient Legion of Honor; recipient Good Govt. award West Vigo Jaycees, 1971, Civic Svc. award U.S. Jaycees, 1957, award Grand Soc. Sycamores; named Outstanding Pub. Offcl. Terre Haute Jaycees. Mem. Ill. State Bar Assn., Ind. Bar Assn., VFW, Am. Legion, United War Vets. Coun. Vigo County (past commdr.), SAR (pres.), Exchange Club (pres.), Shriners, Terre Haute Exch. Club. Democrat. Methodist. Avocations: bowling, geneology, reading. Home: 76 N Thorpe Pl West Terre Haute IN 47885-9162 Office: 219 Ohio St Terre Haute IN 47807-3420

KESLER, STEPHEN EDWARD, economic geology educator. BS with honors, U. N.C., 1962; PhD, Stanford U., 1966. Asst. prof. econ. geology La. State U., Baton Rouge, 1966-70; assoc. prof. U. Toronto, Ont., Can., 1970-77; prof. U. Mich., Ann Arbor, 1977—, assoc. chair, 1998—; vis. scientist Nat. Inst. Geography, Guatemala, 1966-69, Consejo Recursos Minerales, Mexico City, 1974-75; with Dirección General Minas, Santo Domingo, 1983-84; cons. exploration for metallic and non-metallic mineral deposits. Author: Our Finite Mineral Resources, 1975; (with others) Economic Geology of Central Dominican Republic, 1984, Mineral Resources: Economics and the Environment, 1994; assoc. editor Econ. Geology, 1981-91; mem. editorial bd. Jour. Geochem. Exploration, 1984-98. Pres. bd. trustees Lord of Light Luth. Ch., 1989-91. Fellow Geol. Soc. Am., Soc. Econ. Geologists (councillor 1983-86, internat. lectr. 1989-90, v.p. 1990-91, Thayer Lindsley lectr. 1994-95, pres. 1998-99); mem. Assn. Exploration Geochemists (councillor 1981-84), Soc. Mining Engrs. of AIME (program chmn. 1977). Lutheran. Office: U Mich Dept Geol Scis Ann Arbor MI 48109

KESSEL, BRINA, ornithologist, educator; b. Ithaca, N.Y., Nov. 20, 1925; d. Marcel and Quinta (Cattell) K.; m. Raymond B. Roof, June 19, 1957 (dec. 1968). BS (Albert R. Brand Bird Song Found. scholar), Cornell U., 1947, PhD, 1951; MS (Wis. Alumni Research Found. fellow), U. Wis.-Madison, 1949. Student asst. Patuxent Research Refuge, 1946; student teaching asst. Cornell U., 1945-47, grad. asst., 1947-48, 49-51; instr. biol. sci. U. Alaska, summer 1951, asst. prof. biol. sci., 1951-54, assoc. prof. zoology, 1954-59, prof. zoology, 1959-96, head dept. biol. scis., 1957-66; dean U. Alaska (Coll. Biol. Scis. and Renewable Resources), 1961-72, curator terrestrial vertebrate mus. collections, 1972-90, curator ornithology collection, 1990-95, adminstrv. assoc. for acad. programs, grad. and undergrad., dir. acad. advising, office of chancellor, 1973-80; sr. scientist U. Alaska, 1996—; project dir. U. Alaska ecol. investigation for AEC Project Chariot, 1959-63; ornithol. investigations NW Alaska pipeline, 1976-81, Susitna Hydroelectric Project, 1980-83. Author books, monographs; contbr. articles to profl. jours. Fellow AAAS, Am. Ornithologists' Union (v.p. 1977, pres.-elect 1990-92, pres. 1992-94), Arctic Inst. N.Am.; mem. Wilson, Cooper ornith. socs., Soc. for Northwestern Vertebrate Biology, Pacific Seabird Group, Assn. Field Ornithologists, Sigma Xi (pres. U. Alaska 1957), Phi Kappa Phi, Sigma Delta Epsilon. Office: U Alaska Mus PO Box 80211 Fairbanks AK 99708-0211

KESSEL, JOHN HOWARD, political scientist, educator; b. Dayton, Ohio, Oct. 13, 1928; s. Arthur V. and Helen (Hopkins) K.; m. Margaret Sarah Wagner, Aug. 22, 1954; children—Robert Arthur, Thomas John. Student, Purdue U., 1946-48; B.A., Ohio State U., 1950; Ph.D., Columbia U., 1958. Instr. Amherst and Mt. Holyoke colls., 1957-58; instr., asst. prof. Amherst Coll., 1958-61; asst. prof. U. Wash., 1961-65; Arthur E. Braun prof. polit. sci. Allegheny Coll., Meadville, Pa., 1965-70; prof. polit. sci. Ohio State U., Columbus, 1970-94, prof. emeritus, 1994—; vis. prof. U. Calif., San Diego, 1977, U. Wash., 1980, Am. U., 1980; vis. scholar Am. Enterprise Inst., 1980-82. Author: The Goldwater Coalition: Republican Strategies in 1964, 1968, The Domestic Presidency, 1975, Presidential Campaign Politics: Coalition Strategies and Citizen Response, 1980, 4th edit., 1992, Presidential Parties, 1984; co-editor: Micropolitics-Individual and Group Level Concepts, 1970, Theory Building and Data Analysis in the Social Sciences, 1984, Researching the Presidency: Vital Questions, New Approaches, 1993; editor Am. Jour. Polit. Sci, 1974-76; contbr. articles to profl. jours. Mem. exec. council Inter-Univ. Consortium for Polit. Research, 1964-65, 67-68; Exec. dir. Nixon-Lodge Vols. Mass., 1960; dir. arts, scis. div. Republican Nat. Com., 1963-64. Served with USN, 1950-53. Mem. Am. Polit. Sci. Assn. (exec. council 1969-71), Midwest Polit. Sci. Assn. (pres. 1978-79). Home: 516 E Schreyer Pl Columbus OH 43214-2273

KESSEL, MARK, lawyer; b. Krasnik, Poland, June 14, 1941; came to U.S., 1948; s. Leo and Erna (Friedman) K.; m. Elaine Keit, Aug. 28, 1966; children: Greer Kessel Hendricks, Robert W. BA with honors in Econs., CUNY, 1963; JD magna cum laude, Syracuse U., 1966. Bar: N.Y., Calif. Assoc. Shearman & Sterling, N.Y.C., 1971-77, ptnr., 1977—, mng. ptnr., 1990-94; bd. dirs. Heller Fin. Inc., Mus. of City of N.Y. Dir. W.M. Keck Found., L.A., 1985-86; bd. visitors Syracuse U. Coll. Law; ex-officio bd. dirs. San Francisco Psychoanalytic Inst., 1988-90. Capt. JAGC, U.S. Army, 1963-71. Mem. ABA, N.Y. State Bar, Calif. State Bar, Bar Assn. City of N.Y. Avocations: reading, running, tennis. Office: Shearman & Sterling 599 Lexington Ave Fl C2 New York NY 10022-6069

KESSEL, RICHARD GLEN, zoology educator; b. Fairfield, Iowa, July 19, 1931. BS in Chemistry summa cum laude, Parsons Coll., 1953; MS in Zoology and Physiology, U. Iowa, 1956, PhD in Zoology and Cytology, 1959; postgrad., Marine Biol. Lab., 1957. Trainee dept. anatomy Bowman Gray Sch. Medicine, Wake Forest U., 1959-60; Nat. Inst. Gen. Med. Sci. postdoctoral rsch. fellow Bowman Gray Sch. Medicine, Wake Forest U., Winston-Salem, N.C., 1960-61; instr. anatomy Bowman Gray Sch. Medicine, Wake Forest U., Winston-Salem, 1959-61, asst. prof., 1961; asst. prof. zoology U. Iowa, Iowa City, 1961-64, assoc. prof., 1964-68, prof., 1968—; vis. investigator Hopkins Marine Sta., Pacific Grove, Calif., 1966; ind. investigator Marine Biol. Lab., Woods Hole, Mass., summers 1960, 62, 64. Author: (with C.Y. Shih) Scanning Electron Microscopy in Biology: A Students' Text-Atlas of Biological Organization, 1974, (with R.H. Kardon) Tissues and Organs: A Text-Atlas of Scanning Electron Microscopy, 1979, (with C.Y. Shih) Living Images, 1982, (with R. Roberts and H. Tung) Freeze Fracture Images of Cells and Tissues, 1991, Basic Medical Histology, 1998; assoc. editor Jour. Exptl. Zoology, 1978-82; mem. editorial bd. Jour. Submicroscopic Cytology, 1980—; mem. internat. bd. editors Scanning Electron Microscopy in Biology and Medicine; contbr. articles to profl. jours., chpts. to books. Grantee USPHS, 1961-78, NSF, 1969-71, Whitehall Found., 1982-84; Bodine fellow; George Lincoln Seeley scholar; Nat Inst. Gen. Med. Sci.-USPHS, 1964-69. Mem. AAAS, Am. Soc. Cell Biology, Am. Assn. Anatomists, Electron Micros. Soc. Am., Am. Physiol. Soc., Soc. for Study of Reprodn., Am. Soc. Zoologists, Am. Inst. Biol. Sci., Soc. Devel. Biology, Sigma Xi, Phi Kappa Phi, Beta Beta Beta. Office: Univ Iowa Dept Biol Scis Iowa City IA 52242

KESSELHAUT, ARTHUR MELVYN, financial consultant; b. Newark, May 18, 1935; s. Harry and Rela (Wolk) K.; m. Nancy Slater, June 17, 1956; children—Stuart Lee, Amy Beth. B.S. in Bus. Adminstrn, Syracuse (N.Y.) U., 1958; postgrad., NYU. With Coopers & Lybrand, N.Y.C., 1958-64; treas., chief fin. officer and sr. v.p. Anchor Group, Elizabeth, N.J., 1964-79; treas., sr. v.p. also Anchor Capital Fund, Anchor Daily Income Fund, Inc., Anchor Growth Fund, Inc., Anchor Income Fund, Inc., Anchor Spectrum Fund, Inc., Fundamental Investors, Inc., Westminster Fund, Washington Nat. Fund, Inc., Anchor Pension Mgmt. Co.; sr. v.p. corp. devel. USLIFE Corp., N.Y.C., 1979-82, exec. v.p.; chief operating officer, 1982-86; pres., chief exec. officer, dir. USLIFE Equity Sales Corp, 1985-86; exec. v.p. Pacific Mut. Life Ins. Co., Newport Beach, Calif., 1986-92; chmn., CEO, bd. dirs. Pacific Equities Network, Newport Beach, Calif., 1992-93; chmn., CEO Resource Network, San Juan Capistrano, 1993—; bd. dirs. Mut. Svc. Corp., United Planners Group, So. Calif. Entrepreneurship Acad. Commr. econ. devel., City of Dana Point, Calif. With U.S. Army, 1958-60. Home: 34300 Lantern Bay Dr Villa 69 Dana Point CA 92629*

KESSELMAN, JONATHAN RHYS, economics educator, public policy researcher; b. Columbus, Ohio, Mar. 17, 1946; s. Louis C. and Jennie K.; m. Sheila Kaplan, Mar. 12, 1973; 1 child, Maresa. BA with honors, Oberlin Coll., 1968; PhD in Econs., MIT, 1972. Asst. prof. econs. U. B.C., Vancouver, Can., 1972-76, assoc. prof., 1976-81, prof., 1981—; dir. Ctr. for Rsch. on Econ. and Social Policy, Vancouver, Can., 1992—; rsch. assoc. Inst. for Rsch. on Poverty, Madison, Wis., 1974-75; vis. scholar Delhi Sch. Econs., New Delhi, 1978-79; cons. econs., 1973—; prin. investigator Equality, Security and Community Rsch. Project, 1998—. Author: Financing Canadian Unemployment Insurance, 1983, Rate Structure and Personal Taxation, 1990, General Payroll Taxes, 1997; editorial bd.: Can. Taxation: Jour. of Policy, 1979-82; contbr. numerous articles on taxation, income security, employment policy to profl. jours. Bd. dirs. Tibetan Refugee Aid Soc., Vancouver, 1980-82; mem. adv. panel Can. Ministry Employment and Immigration, Ottawa, Ont., 1982-83; mem. B.C. Econ. Policy Inst., 1983-86; trustee pension plan U. B.C., 1988-90; chmn. Musqueam Indian Band Taxation Adv. Coun., 1992-96, mem., 1996-98; mem. B.C. Premier's Forum on New Opportunities for Working and Living, 1994-95; mem. compliance adv. com. Revenue Can. Taxation, 1997—. Sr. scholar Oberlin Coll., 1967-68; NSF fellow, 1968-70; grantee U.S. Dept. Labor, 1971-72; leave fellow Can. Coun., (locat.) New Delhi, 1978-79; grantee Social Sci. and Humanities Rsch. Coun. Can., 1983-84, 90—; vis. fellow Australian Nat. U., Canberra, 1985; professorial fellow in econ. policy Res. Bank of Australia, 1985; recipient Doug Purvis award, Can. Econ. Assn., 1998. Mem. Am. Econ. Assn., Can. Econs. Assn., Can. Tax Found. Home: 4273 Musqueam Dr, Vancouver, BC Canada V6N 3R8 Office: U BC Dept Econs, 997-1873 E Mall, Vancouver, BC Canada V6T 1Z1

KESSELMAN, MARK JONATHAN, political science educator, writer; b. N.Y.C., Aug. 27, 1938; ss. Paul and Anne (Price) K. B.A., Cornell U., 1959; M.A., U. Chgo., 1963. From asst. prof. to assoc. prof. Columbia U., N.Y.C., 1965-72, prof., 1972—. Author: The Ambiguous Consensus, 1967 (with others) The Politics of Power, 1986, French Politics and Public Policy, 1980, Public Policy, The State and Socialism in France, 1985, European Politics in Transition, 1997, Comparative Politics at the Crossroads, 1997; editor: The French Workers Movement, 1984, A Union Movement for the 21st Century, 1998. Guggenheim Found. fellow, 1975, Rockefeller Found. fellow, 1980, Fulbright Sr. Rsch. scholar, 1990-91. Mem. Am. Polit. Sci. Assn., Phi Beta Kappa. Office: Columbia U Internat Affairs Bldg 420 W 118th St 7th Fl New York NY 10027-7213*

KESSEN, WILLIAM, psychologist, educator; b. Key West, Fla., Jan. 18, 1925; s. Herman Lowry and Maria Angela (Lord) K.; m. Marion Lord, June 10, 1950; children: Judith, Deborah, Anne, Peter Christopher, Andrew Lord, John Michael. B.S., U. Fla., 1948; Sc.M., Brown U., 1950; Ph.D., Yale U., 1952. Postdoctoral fellow Child Study Ctr. Yale U., 1952-54, faculty dept. psychology and Child Study Ctr., 1954-76, Eugene Higgins prof. psychology, 1976-97, chmn. dept. psychology, 1977-80, prof. pediatrics, 1978-97, acting univ. sec., 1980-81, prof. emeritus, 1997—; acting master Calhoun Coll., spring 1989. Author: (with G. Mandler) The Language of Psychology, 1959, The Child, 1965, Childhood in China, 1975, (with M.H. Bornstein) Psychological Development from Infancy, 1979; editor: Mussen's Handbook of Child Psychology, vol. 1, 1983, The Rise and Fall of Development, 1990; contbr. articles to profl. jours. Mem. Carnegie Coun. on Children, 1973-77; trustee Barnard Coll., 1983-90. With U.S. Army, 1943-46. Fellow Ctr. Advanced Study Behavioral Scis., 1959-60, Guggenheim fellow, 1970-71, Russell Sage fellow, 1989-90. Fellow Am. Psychol. Assn. (pres. div. 7 1979-80); mem. Am. Psychol. Soc., Soc. Research Child Devel., Soc. Exptl. Psychologists, Am. Acad. Arts and Scis. Home: 30 Halstead Ln Branford CT 06405-5508 Office: Yale U Dept Psychology PO Box 208205 New Haven CT 06520-8205

KESSINGER, MARGARET ANNE, medical educator; b. Beckley, W.Va., June 4, 1941; d. Clisby Theodore and Margaret Anne (Ellison) K.; m. Loyd Ernst Wegner, Nov. 27, 1971. MA, W.Va. U., 1963, MD, 1967. Diplomate Am. Bd. Internal Medicine and Med. Oncology. Internal medicine house officer U. Nebr. Med. Ctr., Omaha, 1967-70, fellow med. oncology, 1970-72, asst. prof. internal medicine, 1972-77, assoc. prof., 1977-90, prof., 1990—, assoc. chief oncology/hematology sect., 1988-91, chief oncology/hematology sect., 1991—. Contbr. articles to profl. publs. Fellow ACP; mem. Am. Assn. Cancer Edn., Am. Soc. Clin. Oncology, Am. Assn. Cancer Rsch., Internat. Soc. Exptl. Hematology, Am. Soc. Hematology, Sigma Xi, Alpha Omega Alpha. Republican. Methodist. Avocations: aviation, gardening, canning, skiing. Office: U Nebr Med Ctr 600 S 42nd St Omaha NE 68198-1002

KESSINGER, TOM G., academic administrator; b. Paterson, N.J., Mar. 24, 1941; s. Harold Caldwell and Ann (Prodehl) K.; m. Varyam K. Chawla, June 26, 1962; children: William C., Colin C. BA, Haverford Coll., 1965; AM, U. Chgo., 1967, PhD, 1972; MLitt (hon.), U. Pa., 1975. Asst. prof. U. Va., Charlottesville, 1970-73; assoc. prof. U. Pa., Phila., 1973-77; program officer Ford Found., New Delhi, India, 1977-79; rep. Jakarta, Indonesia, 1979-81; rep. S.E. Asia Ford Found., Jakarta, 1981-87; rep. India, New Delhi Ford Found., New Delhi, India, 1987-88; pres. Haverford (Pa.) Coll., 1988-96; gen. mgr. Aga Khan Trust for Culture, Geneva, Switzerland, 1996—. Author: Vilyatpur 1848-1968, 1974. Woodrow Wilson fellow, 1965, fellow Danforth Found., 1965, Nat. Def. Fgn. Lang., 1965. Democrat. Mem. Soc. of Friends. Home: 22A Ave Bouchet, Petit Saconnex, 1209 Geneva Switzerland Office: Aga Khan Trust for Culture, 1-3 Avenue de la Paix, 1211 Geneva 2, Switzerland*

KESSLER, A. D., business, financial, investment and real estate advisor, consultant, educator, lecturer, author, broadcaster, producer; b. N.Y.C., May 1, 1923; s. Morris William and Belle Miriam (Pastor) K.; m. Ruth Schwartz, Nov. 20, 1944 (div. 1974); children: Brian Lloyd, Judd Stuart, Earl Vaughn; m. Jaclyn Jeanne Sprague. Student U. Newark, 1940-41, Rutgers U., 1941-42, 46, Albright Coll., 1942, Newark Coll. Engring., 1946; PhD in Pub. Adminstrn. U. Fla., 1972; MBA, Kensington U., 1976, PhD in Mgmt. and Behavioral Psychology, 1977. Sr. cert. rev. appraiser; cert. bus. counselor; cert. exchanger; registered mortgage underwriter; registered investment advisor. Pvt. practice real estate, ins. and bus. brokerage, N.J., Pa., Fla., N.Y., Nev., Calif., Hong Kong, 1946—; pres. Armor Corp. , 1947-68; pres. Folding Carton Corp., Am., N.Y.C., 1958-68; exec. v.p. Henry Schindall Assocs., N.Y.C., 1966-67; tax rep. Calif. State Bd. Equalization, 1968-69; aviation cons. transp. div. Calif., Dept. Aeros., also pub. info. officer; 1969-71; FAA Gen. Aviation Safety Counselor; broker, mgr. La Costa (Calif.) Sales Corp., 1971-75; chmn. bd. Profl. Ednl. Found., 1975—, Timeshare Resorts Internat., 1975—, Interex, Leucadia, Calif., 1975-82, The Kessler Orgn., Rancho Santa Fe, Calif., 1975—, The Kessler Fin. Group, Fin. Ind. Inst., 1977—; pres. Ednl. Video Inst., 1978—, Fin. Planning Inst., 1975—, Rancho Santa Fe Real Estate & Land, Inc., 1975—; treas., exec. bd. dirs. Nat. Challenge Com. on Disability, 1983-90; dir. Practice Mgmt. Cons. Abacus Data Systems, 1984—; broker mgr. Rancho Sante Fe Acreage & Homes, Inc., 1987-89; mktg. dir. Commercial Real Estate Services, Rancho Santa Fe, 1987—; cons. broker Glenct. Properties Ptnrs., 1989-90; dir. U.S. Advisors, 1989—; founder Creative Real Estate Movement, 1946—; pub., editor in chief Creative Real Estate Mag., 1975—; pub. Creative Real Estate Mag. of Australia and New Zealand; founder, editor Moderator of Tape of the Month Club; founder, producer, chmn. Internat. Real Estate Expo; chmn. bd. The Brain Trust, Rancho Santa Fe, Calif., 1977—; fin. lectr. for Internat. Cruise Ships, Cunard Line, Norwegian Am. Cruises, P&O, Princess, others; lectr. life enrichment and stress mgmt. Internat. Cruise Ships; Calif. adj. faculty, prof. fin. Clayton U., St. Louis; developer, operator Barnegat Baywood Seaplane Base, Barnegat Bay, N.J.; owner, operator Skyline Airport, Hunterdon County, N.J. Scoutmaster Orange Mountain coun. Boy Scouts Am., 1955-62; harbor master N.J. Marine Patrol, 1958-67; dep. sheriff, Essex County, N.J., 1951-65; mem. pres.' adv. bd. Seton Hall U., 1961-64; chmn. Stop Smoking, 1990, Quick Study, 1990; feature broadcaster/producer Kalaidascope Radio Mag., Am. Radio Network, 1990—. Served with USAF, 1942-45. Decorated D.F.C., Air medal, Purple Heart; named to French Legion of Honor, Order of Lafayette; named a flying col, a.d.c., Gov. of Ga., 1957. Mem. Am. Soc. Editors and Pubs., Author's Guild, Internat. Platform Assn., Nat. Speakers Assn., Nat. Press Photographers Assn., Guild Assn. Airport Execs., Aviation and Space Writers Assn., Nat. Assn. of Real Estate Editors, Internat. Exchangors Assn. (founder), Air Force Assn. (dep. comdr. N.J. chpt. 1955-57). Clubs: Nat. Press, Overseas Press, La Costa Country, Cuyamaca, Rancho Santa Fe Country, Passport. Lodges: Masons, Shriners. Author: A Fortune At Your Feet, 1981, How You Can Get Rich, Stay Rich and Enjoy Being Rich, 1981, Financial Independence, 1987, The Profit, 1987, A Fortune at Your Feet in the '90s, 1994, The Midas Touch, Turning Paper Into Gold, 1994; author, instr. Your Key to Success seminar, 1988, Your Key to Creative Real Estate Success tng. program, 1996; The A to Z of Lease Purchase and 11 Other Options Training Prog.; editor: The Real Estate News Observer, 1975—; fin. editor API, 1978—; fin. columnist Money Matters, 1986—; syndicated columnist, radio and TV host of "Money Making Ideas," 1977—; songwriter: Only You, 1939, If I'm Not Home For Christmas, 1940, Franny, 1940, Flajaloppa, 1940, They've Nothing More Dear Only They've Got It Here, 1941, The Summer of Life, 1956; producer (movies) The Flight of the Cobra, Rena, We Have Your Daughters, Music Row; speaker for radio and TV as The Real Estate Answerman, 1975—; host (radio and TV show) Ask Mr. Money; conceptualist, exec. prodr. (TV show) The Trading Game, 1994; exec. prodr., moderator (TV show) A.D. Kessler's Real Estate Roundtable, 1993—. Inventor swivel seat, siptop, inflatumbrella. Home: PO Box 1144 Rancho Santa Fe CA 92067-1144

KESSLER, ALAN CRAIG, lawyer; b. Washington, Sept. 16, 1950; s. Alfred Milton and Josephine (Taub) K.; m. Gail Elaine Strauss, June 16, 1974; children: Stacy Ilana, Mark Jay, Daniel Jordan. BA with honors, U. Del., 1972; JD with honors, U. Md., 1975. Bar: Pa. 1975, U.S. Dist. Ct. (ea. dist.) Pa. 1975, U.S. Ct. Appeals (3d and 6th cirs.) 1975. Assoc. Dilworth, Paxson, Kalish, Levy & Kauffman, Phila., 1975-77, Berger & Montague, P.C., Phila., 1977-81; ptnr. Mesirov, Gelman, Jaffe, Cramer & Jamieson, Phila., 1981-91, Buchanan Ingersoll, P.C., Phila., 1991—; instr. Inst. for Paralegal Tng., Phila., 1977-96. Fin. com. Dem. City Com. Phila., 1981-84, dep. counsel, 1980-84; chmn. bd. Bldg. Stds. City of Phila., 1983-84, bd. licenses and inspections rev., 1984-91; mem. City Planning Commn., Phila., 1992-97, Presdl. Transition Team, 1992-93; commr. Lower Merion (Pa.) Twp., 1988—, Mayors Commn. Homelessness, 1990—, Mayors Com. on Spl. Svcs. Dist., 1989—; vice-chmn. Pres. Commn. on Risk Assessment and Risk Mgmt., 1993-97; bd. dirs., pres. Randolph Ct. Assn., Phila., 1980-85; bd. dirs., v.p. South St. Neighbors Assn., Phila., 1983-87, Park Towne Pl. Tenants Assn., 1977-79; bd. dirs. Support Ctr. for Child Advs., 1983-94, Phila. Indsl. Devel. Corp.; exec. com. Ctrl. Phila. Devel. Corp., 1989—, Jewish Employment Vocat. Svcs., 1989—, Phila. 2000., Supreme Ct. of Pa. Commn. on CLE, 1999—; mng. trustee Dem. Nat. Com., 1992—. Mem. ABA, Pa. Bar Assn., Phila. Bar Assn. (exec. bd. dirs. young lawyers sect., legis. liaison com., officer various coms.), Racquet Club, Radnor Valley Country Club. Democrat. Jewish. Home: 204 Daisy Ln Wynnewood PA 19096-1654 Office: Buchanan Ingersoll PC 11 Penn Ctr 14th Fl 1835 Market St Fl 13 Philadelphia PA 19103-2985

KESSLER, BERNARD MILTON, organizational and human resources development specialist; b. N.Y.C., Apr. 20, 1927; s. Irving and Yolanda (Michalovich) K.; m. Bernice Lubowsky, Dec. 26, 1948; children: Susan Beth, Mark David. BBA, CCNY, 1950; MA, NYU, 1966; PD, Fordham U., 1980; PhD, Columbia Pacific U., 1981. Cert. tchr., sch. adminstr. and supt. schs., N.Y. V.p. Al Paul Lefton Co., N.Y.C., 1950-65; elem. tchr. Greenburgh Dist. 8, Hartsdale, N.Y., 1965-67; mgr. edn. systems and services Olivetti Corp. Am., Hartsdale, 1967-71; dir. project redesign Mamaroneck (N.Y.) Pub. Schs., 1971-73; prin. Chatsworth Ave. Sch., Larchmont, N.Y., 1973-75; pres. Bernard M. Kessler Assocs., N.Y.C., 1971—; pres. exec. devel., counseling, tng. Beam Pines; exec. v.p., human resource counseling KLG Productivity Assn., Inc., N.Y.C.; cons. Xerox Corp., Stamford, Conn., 1972-73, HEW, 1970—, Citicorp, Inc., Comvestrix, Inc., 1980—, N.Y. Stock Exchange, Am. Stock Exchange, Beneficial Fin., Cigna, 1986—, ADD, 1986—, Linotype Corp., 1986—. Designer and producer packaged learning program Active Listening for Results, 1974, Stress Analysis and Control, 1983; contbr. articles to profl. jours. Chmn. bd. Artists for Environment Found., 1969-78, pres., 1978-81; past v.p. Lincoln State Acad. Store Front Sch. Served with USCGR, 1944-46. Mem. Am. Soc. Tng. and Devel. (Torch award 1979), N.Y. Acad. Scis., Orgn. Devel. Network, N.Y. Orgn. Devel. Network, Met. N.Y. Assn. Applied Psychology, Internat. Registry of Orgn. Devel. Profls., Phi Delta Kappa. Home and Office: 2213 Mohansic Ave Yorktown Heights NY 10598-3625

KESSLER, DAVID A., dean, medical educator; b. N.Y.C., May 31, 1951; married; 2 children. BA, Amherst Coll., 1973; JD, U. Chgo., 1978; MD, Harvard U., 1979; APC, NYU Sch. Bus. Food and drug law Columbia U. Sch. of Law; med. dir. Einstein-Montefiore Hosp., N.Y.C.; commr. FDA Dept. Health and Human Svcs., Rockville, Md., 1990-97; dean Yale U. Med. Sch., 1997—; mem. Inst. of Medicine; prof. pediat. and pub. health Sch. Pub. Health Yale U. Recipient ACS Medal of Honor, 1996. Office: Yale Med Sch Dean's Office 333 Cedar St New Haven CT 06510-3289

KESSLER, DIANE COOKSEY, religious organization administrator, minister; b. Jan. 8, 1947. BA in Religion, Oberlin Coll., 1969; MA in Religion and Soc., Andover Newton Theol. Sch., 1971, postgrad., 1979—; postgrad., Ecumenical Inst., World Coun. Chs., Bossey, Switzerland, 1983. Ordained to ministry United Ch. of Christ, 1983. Lobbyist Civil Liberties Union Mass., Boston, 1972; reporter The Valley Reporter, Waitsfield, Vt., 1973-74; assoc. dir. for strategy and action Mass. Coun. Chs., Boston, 1975-88, exec. dir., 1988—; del. to XV-XVI Gen. Synod, United Ch. of Christ, assoc. del. XVII-XVIII Gen. Synod; ind. preacher; speaker in field. Author: Parents and the Experts, 1974, God's Simple Gift: Meditations on Friendship and Spirituality, 1988; co-editor Encounters for Unity, 1995; also articles; mem. editl. adv. bd. Theology and Pub. Policy, 1989—, Mid-Stream, 1995—. Apptd. mem. Vt. Gov.'s Commn. on Status of Women, 1974-75; former mem. adv. bd. Mass. Dept. Revenue; active Newton Highlands Congl. Ch.; mem. coun. for ecumenism United Ch. of Christ, 1984-94, chairperson coun. 1988-89, 90-91; mem. Atty Gen.'s Adv. Com. on Pub. Charities, 1988-99; bd. dirs. Howard Benevolent Soc., 1989-95, New Eng. Holocaust Meml. Com., 1st Ch. Legacy Fund. Recipient Outstanding Woman award Coll. Club, 1990, Focolare award, 1994, Social Action Ministries award, 1995, Patron of Christian Unity award, 1998. Mem. Nat. Assn. Ecumenical Staff, Ch. Women United (exec. bd. mem.-at-large Mass. chpt., Valiant Woman award 1991), Boston Min.'s Club, The Boston Club. Office: Mass Coun Chs 14 Beacon St Ste 416 Boston MA 02108-3704

KESSLER, DIETRICH, biology educator; b. Hamilton, N.Y., May 28, 1936; s. William Conrad and Helga Martha Elizabeth (Wolfram) K.; m. Johanna Winterwerp Prins, Apr. 14, 1990; children from previous marriage: Jonathan Farley, Melissa Beth. BA with high honors, Swarthmore Coll., 1958; MS, U. Wis., 1960, PhD, 1964. Asst. prof. biology Haverford (Pa.)

Coll., 1964-70, assoc. prof., 1970-77, prof. biology, 1977-84; prof., chmn. biology Colgate U., Hamilton, N.Y., 1984-90, prof., 1990—; vis. rsch. fellow dept. genetics U. Leicester, Eng., 1990-91; vis. prof. McArdle Lab. for Cancer Rsch. U. Wis., Madison, 1988; mem. rev. panel NSF Faculty Enhancement Program Proposals, 1990, 96, instrumentation and lab. improvement program, ILI proposals, 1996, undergrad. course and curriculum devel. and faculty enhancemtnet proposals, 1996. Recipient Fulbright Research award U. Bonn, 1982-83; postdoctoral fellow Am. Cancer Soc. Brandeis U., 1966-67; NSF sci. faculty fellow Swiss Inst. for Cancer Research, Lausanne, 1971-72. Mem. Am. Soc. for Cell Biology, Mid. State Assn. Coll. and Secondary Schs. (evaluation teams for commn. on higher edn., various locations 1971-95), Coun. for Internat. Exch. of Scholars (area adv. com. for We. Europe, subcom. for Austria/Federal Republic of Germany 1988-90), Phi Beta Kappa. Office: Colgate Univ Dept Biology 13 Oak Dr Dept Biology Hamilton NY 13346-1386

KESSLER, EDWIN, meteorology educator, consultant; b. N.Y.C., Dec. 2, 1928; s. Edwin and Marie Rosa (Weil) K.; m. Lottie Catherine Menger; children: Austin Rainier, Thomas Russell. AB, Columbia Coll., 1950; MS in Meteorology, MIT, 1952, ScD in Meteorology, 1957. Chief synoptic meteorology sect. Weather Radar br. Air Force Cambridge Rsch. Lab., Bedford, Mass., 1954-61; sr. rsch. scientist Travelers Rsch. Ctr., Hartford, Conn., 1961-62, dir. atmospheric physics div., 1962-64; dir. Nat. Severe Storms Lab., Norman, Okla., 1964-86; adj. prof. U. Okla., 1964—; vis. prof. MIT, 1975-76, McGill U., Can., 1980. Editor: Thunderstorms, A Social Scientific and Technological Documentary, 3 vols., 1982, 2d edits., 1983-88, paperback edits., vol. 1, 1988, vol. 2, 1992; contbr. over 250 articles to profl. publs. State chair Common Cause, Okla., 1993—. Served with U.S. Army, 1947-48. Recipient award for outstanding authorship NOAA, 1971. Fellow AAAS, Am. Meteorol. Soc. (nat. councilor 1966-69, past mem. coms. on hurricanes, atmospheric electricity, agr. and forestry, cloud and precipitation physics, severe local storms, past chmn. com. on weather radar, cert. cons. meteorologist, Cleveland Abbe award for disting. svc. 1988); mem. AIAA (sr. mem.), Royal Meteorol. Soc. (fgn.), Am. Geophys. Union, Sigma Xi. Achievements include rsch. in agriculture and energy. Office: U Okla 100 E Boyd St Rm 684 Norman OK 73019-1000

KESSLER, FREDERICK PHILIP, labor arbitrator; b. Milw., Jan. 11, 1940; s. Frederick Philip and Marie (Schroeder) K.; m. Joan Fowler, June 26, 1966; children: Elizabeth, Anna. BA, U. Wis., 1962, LLB, 1966. State rep. Wis. Legislature, 1961-63, 65-72; atty. Nurbecker, Kessler & Kessler, Milw., 1966-72; cir. judge State of Wis., Milw., 1972-81, 86-88; labor arbitrator Milw., 1982-86, 88—; cons. Wis. Senate Nev. Legis., City of Las Vegas, 1990-96; mem. labor arbitration panels Oreg., Wis., Minn., Iowa, U.S. Virgin Islands., 1985—. Pres. Goethe Ho. of Milw., 1997—, Milw. chpt. ACLU, 1991-92; bd. dirs. World Affairs Coun., Milw., 1998—, Neighborhood Ho. of Milw., 1970-90. Mem. Wis. Bar Assn. (labor law sect. dir. 1993-94), Indsl. Rel. Rsch. Assn. (adv. bd. 1993—). Democrat. Lutheran. Home and Office: 3432 N Shepard Ave Milwaukee WI 53211

KESSLER, FREDRIC LEE, video producer, computer animation artist; b. Bklyn., Dec. 17, 1952; s. Victor and Anita Rhoda (Levy) K. BA, Syracuse U., 1974. Studio mgr., adminstrn. asst. Inter Media Arts Ctr., Huntington, N.Y., 1974-75; sr. electronic animation artist Dolphin Prodns., N.Y.C., 1975-79; pres. Musivision, Inc., N.Y.C., 1979—; cons. Computer Image Corp., Denver, 1980, RTL Prodns., Betrange, Luxembourg, 1980; prodr. Compugraph Designs/Modern Telecommunications Inc., N.Y.C., 1985-93; dir. animation svcs. Click 3X LLC, 1993-97; softimage DS artist Digital Imaging Solutions, Inc., 1998—. Computer animator (comml.) Kinney Shoes Footlocker, 1976 (Clio award 1977); producer, designer (Valentine's Day ID) MTV-S.W.A.K., 1981 (Silver award 1981), (music video) Weather Report's Swamp Cabbage, 1984, (sta. ID pkg.) Sta. WNYC-TV, 1986 (Bronze award 1987). Video Gallery Art Show Everson Mus. Art, Syracuse, 1975. Mem. Broadcast Designer's Assn., Advt. Club of N.Y. Office: Musivision Inc 185 E 85th St New York NY 10028-2140

KESSLER, GLADYS, federal judge; b. 1938. BA, Cornell U., 1959; LLB, Harvard U., 1962. Staff atty. enforcement divsn. Nat. Labor Rels. Bd., 1962-64; legis. asst. Sen. Harrison A. Willians, N.J., 1964-66, Rep. Jonathan B. Bingham, 1966-68; staff atty. office labor rels N.Y.C. Bd. Edn., 1968-69; ptnr. Berlin, Roisman and Kessler (and successor firms), 1969-77; assoc. judge D.C. Superior Ct., 1977-94; judge U.S. Dist. Ct. D.C., Washington, 1994—; asst. lectr. law sch. George Washington U., 1971-73; del. to judicial adminstrn. divsn. D.C. Superior Ct., 1985-90; mem. adv. bd. Ctr. for Dispute Settlement Inst. for Judicial Adminstrn., State Justice Inst., mem. adv. com. nat. judicial edn. project on domestic violence; mem BNA adv. bd. Alternative Dispute Resolution Report, 1987-90; mem. family law cirriculum planning com. Georgetown U.; lead judge permanency planning project Nat. Coun. Juvenile and Family Ct. Judges; chair Nat. Conf. on Bioethics, Family and the Law, D.C., 1991; mem. faculty Nat. Inst. Trial Advocacy. Contbr. articles to legal jours. Recipient Women Lawyer of Yr. award Women's Bar Assn., 1983, Svc. award D.C. Coalition Against Domestic Violence, 1987, Judicial Excellence award Trial Lawyers Assn. Washington, 1987. Fellow Am. Bar Found.; mem. ABA (judicial adminstrn. divsn., com. on bioethics and AIDS, adv. com. on youth, alcohol and drug problems, nat. adv. bd. on child support and criminal justice, individual rights and responsibilities sect.), Am. Judicature Soc. (bd. dirs. 1985-89), NOW Legal Def. and Edn. Fund, Inc., Nat. Assn. Women Judges (v.p. 1979-81, pres. 1981-82), Nat. Ctr. for State Cts. (bd. dirs. 1984-87), Women's Legal Def. Fund (founding pres. 1971), Women Judges' Fund. for Justice (bd. dirs. 1980—), Found. for Women Judges (pres. 1980-82), Pres.'s Coun. Cornell Women, Thurgood Marshall Am. Inn. Ct. Office: US Courthouse 333 Constitution Ave NW Washington DC 20001-2803*

KESSLER, HERBERT LEON, art historian, educator, university administrator; b. Chgo., July 20, 1941; s. Ben and Bertha K.; m. Johanna Zacharias, Apr. 24, 1976; 1 dau., Morisa. AB, U. Chgo., 1961; MFA, Princeton U., 1963, PhD, 1965. Asst. prof. U. Chgo., 1965-68; assoc. prof., 1968-73, prof., 1973-76, chmn. dept. art, univ. dir. fine arts, 1973-76; prof., chmn. dept. art Johns Hopkins U., Balt., 1976-89, 95-98, Charlotte Bloomberg prof. faculty arts and scis., 1984—; guest prof. Bibliotheca Hertziana, Rome, 1996-97, dean Sch. Arts and Scis., 1998—. Author: French and Flemish Illuminated Manuscripts, 1969, The Illustrated Bibles from Tours, 1977, The Cotton Genesis, 1986, The Dura Synagogue Frescoes and Christian Art, 1990, Studies in Pictorial Narrative, 1994, The Poetry and Paintings in the First Bible of Charles the Bald, 1997, The Holy Face and the paradox of Representation, 1998. Sr. fellow Dumbarton Oaks, Washington, 1980-86; Woodrow Wilson fellow; Inst. Advanced Study fellow; Am. Council Learned Socs. fellow; Am. Philos. Soc. fellow; Guggenheim fellow; fellow Am. Acad. in Rome. Fellow Medieval Acad. Am., Am. Acad. Arts & Scis.; mem. Coll. Art Assn., Phi Beta Kappa. Home: 211 Ridgewood Rd Baltimore MD 21210-2538 Office: Johns Hopkins U Baltimore MD 21218

KESSLER, JEFFREY L., lawyer; b. N.Y.C., Feb. 19, 1954; s. Milton M. and Edith H. Kessler; m. Regina T. Dessoff, May 21, 1977; children: Andrew Zalman, Leora Miriam. BA, JD summa cum laude, Columbia U., 1977. Bar: N.Y. 1978, U.S. Dist. Ct. (so. dist.) N.Y. 1978, U.S. Supreme Ct. 1985. Assoc. Weil, Gotshal & Manges, N.Y.C., 1977-85, ptnr., 1985—; adj. assoc. prof. Fordham Law Sch., 1988—; founder, bd. advisors study pvt. antitrust litig. Georgetown U., 1983-85. Bd. editors Columbia U. Law Rev., 1976-77; editor-in-chief State Antitrust Practice Statutes, 1999; contbr. numerous articles on antitrust law, sports and policy to profl. jours. Kent scholar, 1975-76, Stone scholar, 1976-77. Mem. ABA (antitrust law sect., vice-chmn. Sherman Act Sect. 2 com. 1989-90, chmn. internat. law com. 1990-94, co-chmn. pub. com. 1994-96, coun. mem. 1996—), Columbia Coll. Alumni Assn. (bd. dirs. 1996—), Phi Beta Kappa. Democrat. Jewish. Office: Weil Gotshal & Manges 767 5th Ave Fl Concl New York NY 10153-0119

KESSLER, JOAN F., lawyer; b. June 25, 1943; m. Frederick P. Kessler, Sept. 1967; 2 children. BA, U. Kans., 1961-65; postgrad., U. Wis., 1965-66; JD cum laude, Marquette U., 1968. Law clk. Hon. John W. Reynolds U.S. Dist. Ct. (ea. dist.) Wis., Milw., 1968-69; assoc. Warschafsky, Rotter & Tarnoff, Milw., 1969-71; pvt. practice Milw., 1971-74; assoc. Cook & Franke, S.C., Milw., 1974-78; U.S. atty. Eastern Dist. Wis., Milw., 1978-81; ptnr. Foley & Lardner, Milw., 1981—; lectr. profl. responsibility U. Wis. Law Sch., Marquette U. Law Sch., Milw., 1994-96; mem. bd. govs. State Bar of Wis., 1985-89, 90-92, 93-95, chair, 1993, bd. dirs. family law sect., 1991-94; mem. Jud. Coun. Wis., Madison, 1989-92; mem. Milw. Bd. Attys. Profl. Responsibility, 1979-85. Bd. dirs. Legal Aid Soc., 1974-78, v.p., 1978, Urban League, 1980-82, Women's Bus. Initiative Corp., 1989-91, Girl Scouts U.S., Milw., 1994-96; bd. dirs., pres. Voters for Choice in Wis., 1989-93. Fellow Am. Matrimonial Lawyers (bd. govs. 1990-96, v.p. 1996-99), Am. Law Inst., Am. Bar Found.; mem. ACLU (Best Lawyers in Am. 1993-98). Office: Foley & Lardner 777 E Wisconsin Ave Ste 3800 Milwaukee WI 53202-5367

KESSLER, JOHN OTTO, physicist, educator; b. Vienna, Austria, Nov. 26, 1928; came to U.S., 1940, naturalized, 1946; s. Jacques and Alice Blanca (Neuhut) K.; m. Eva M. Bondy, Sept. 9, 1950; children: Helen J., Steven J. A.B., Columbia U., 1949, Ph.D., 1953. With RCA Corp., Princeton, N.J., 1952-66; sr. mem. tech. staff RCA Corp., 1960-66, mgr. grad. recruiting, 1964-66; prof. physics U. Ariz., Tucson, 1966-93, prof. emeritus, 1994—; Vis. research asso. Princeton, 1962-64; sr. vis. fellow, vis. prof. physics U. Leeds, Eng., 1972-73, sr. vis. fellow, 1990-91; vis. prof. Technische Hogeschool Delft, Netherlands, spring 1979; Fulbright fellow dept. applied math. and theoretical physics Cambridge U., Eng., 1983-84. Contbr. articles to profl. jours. Fellow AAAS; mem. Phycological Soc. Am., Am. Phys. Soc. Achievements include patentee in field; research in low Reynolds number fluid mechanics; mechanisms of bacterial propulsion, interaction and formation of coherent swarms, leading to microturbulence; bioconvection and consumption patterns of micro-organism populations; measurement of probability densities for swimming velocity of algae and bacteria. Home: 2740 E Camino La Zorrela Tucson AZ 85718-3126 Office: U Ariz Physics Dept Bldg 81 Tucson AZ 85721

KESSLER, JOHN PAUL, JR., financial planner; b. Bronxville, N.Y., Sept. 4, 1946; s. John Paul and Helen Claire (Hopper) K. BBA in Fin., Tex. Tech. U., 1965-71. CFP; registered investment advisor. Agt. Met. Life Ins. Co., Lubbock, Tex., 1970-73; pension trust adminstr. Rep. Nat. Life, Dallas, 1973-78, Am. Founders Life, Austin, 1979-81; acct. for state appropriations Tex. State Comptr., Austin, 1981-84; fin. planner J. Paul Kessler & Assocs., Dallas, 1984-95, Pinnacle Planning Group (formerly Kessler Fin. Assocs.), Dallas, 1995—; pension cons. Kessler Fin. Group, Dallas, 1984—. Mem. Am. Mgmt. Assn., Dallas Estate Planning Coun., Dallas Employee Benefit Assn., Inst. CFPs, North Dallas Fin. Forum, Nat. Assn. Securities Dealers (registered rep.), Tex. Tech Ex-Student Assn., McKinney C. of C. Republican. Presbyterian. Avocations: golf, travel. Office: Pinnacle Planning Group PO Box 2382 Mc Kinney TX 75070-8382

KESSLER, JOHN WHITAKER, real estate developer; b. Cin., Mar. 7, 1936; s. Charles Wilmont and Elisabeth (Whitaker) K.; m. Charlotte Hamilton Power, Aug. 8, 1964; children: Catherine, Elizabeth, Jane. BS, Ohio State U., 1958. Mem. sales dept. Armstrong Cork Co., Lancaster, Pa., 1958-59; mgr. spl. products div. M & R Dietetics Labs., Columbus, Ohio, 1959-62; co-founder, mng. partner Multicon, Columbus, 1962-70; pres. Multicon Communities div. Multicon Properties, Inc., 1970-72; prin. John W. Kessler Co., Columbus, 1972—; chmn. Marsh & McLennan Real Estate Advisors Inc., 1980—, New Albany Co., 1991—; trustee Columbus Mcpl. Airport Authority; bd. dirs. Banc One Corp., Abercrombie & Fitch. Chmn. Ohio Arts and Sports Facilities Commn. Office: New Albany Co PO Box 490 New Albany OH 43054-0490

KESSLER, JUDD LEWIS, lawyer; b. Newark, Apr. 10, 1938; s. Samuel W. and Ethel S. (Shapiro) K.; m. Marian Osterweis, Jan. 7, 1979 (div. 1986); m. Carol Ann Farris, Oct. 19, 1987; 1 child, Samuel Farris. AB, Oberlin Coll., 1960; LLB, Harvard U., 1963. Bar: N.J. 1963, D.C. 1972, Md. 1989, U.S. Dist. Ct. N.J., U.S. Dist. Ct. D.C., U.S. Dist. Ct. Md., U.S. Ct. Appeals (4th cir.), U.S. Supreme Ct. 1968. Assoc. Toner, Crowley, Woelper and Vanderbilt, Newark, 1963-66; asst. gen. counsel U.S. Agy. for Internat. Devel., Washington, 1966-82; ptnr., chmn. internat. bus. practice group Porter, Wright, Morris & Arthur, Washington, 1982—. Author: (with others) Legal Aspects of Exporting, 1986; contbr. articles to profl. jours. Bd. dirs. Congregation Har Shalom, Potomac, Md., 1998—. Recipient Outstanding Career Achievement award U.S. Agy for Internat. Devel. 1982; named Presdl. Appointment to Sr. Fgn. Svc., 1982. Mem. ABA, Am. Arbitration Assn. (mem. internat. panel arbitrators 1997—), Inter-Am. Bar Assn., Inter-Am. Bar Found. (pres., 1994—), Am. Soc. Internat. Law, Fed. Bar Assn. (chmn. internat. sect. 1983-87, nat. coord. Export Legal Assistance Network 1985—, Pres.'s E Excellence Export Svc. award 1997), Cosmos Club. Office: Porter Wright Morris & Arthur 1667 K St NW Washington DC 20006-1605

KESSLER, KEITH LEON, lawyer; b. Seattle, July 18, 1947; s. Robert Lawrence and Priscilla Ellen (Allbee) K.; m. Lynn Elizabeth Eisen, Dec. 24, 1980; children: William Moore, Christopher Moore, Bradley Moore, Jamie Kessler. BA in Philosophy, U. Wash., 1969, JD, 1972. Bar: Wash. 1972, U.S. Dist. Ct. (we. dist.) Wash. 1973, U.S. Dist. Ct. (ea. dist. 1992); U.S. Ct. Appeals (9th cir.) 1973, U.S. Supreme Ct. 1975. Law clk. to Hon. Robert Finley Wash. Supreme Ct., Olympia, Wash., 1972-73; ptnr. Kessler, Tegland & Urmston, Seattle, 1973-75, Kessler & Urmston, Seattle, 1975-76, Kessler, Urmston & Sever, Seattle, 1976-77, Kessler & Sever, Seattle, 1977-79; assoc. Stritmatter & Stritmatter, Hoquiam, Wash., 1980-83; ptnr. Stritmatter, Kessler & McCauley, Hoquiam, Wash., 1983-93, Stritmatter Kessler, Hoquiam, Wash., 1993-97, Stritmatter Kessler Whelan Withey, Hoquiam, 1997—; chmn. LAW PAC, Seattle, 1991-93. Editor: Trial Evidence, 1996, author: (with others) Motor Vehicle Accident Litigation Desk Book, 1988, 1995, 97. Pres. Kairos Ctr., Aberdeen, Wash., 1984-86; co-founder Grays Harbor Support Group; bd. dir. Wash. State Head Injury Found., Bellevue, Wash., 1993-96. Recipient Founders award Wash. State Head Injury Found., 1990, Silver award United Way, 1992; Named Trial Lawyer of the Year Wash. State Trial Lawyers, 1994. Mem. Am. Bd. Trial Advocates, (pres. Wash. chpt. 1997), Wash. State Trial Lawyers Assn. (pres. 1990-91), Damage Attys. Round Table, Wash. Trial Attys. Political Forum (chmn. 1993-95), Trial Lawyers for Public Justice (state exec. com. 1994—). Office: Stritmatter Kessler Whelan Withey 413 8th St Hoquiam WA 98550-3607

KESSLER, LEONA HANOVER, interior designer; b. Phila., Sept. 15, 1925; d. Herman and Ida (Gleaner) Hanover; m. Sydney Kessler, Aug. 28, 1948; children: Andrew Louis, Todd Hanover. BS in Textile Engring., Phila. Coll. Textiles and Sci., 1948. Pvt. practice interior design and cons. Lee Kessler Interiors, Phila., 1957—; textile designer, stylist, color cons.; mem. faculty Moore Coll. Art, 1970-72, Art Inst. Phila., 1973-78, Phila. Coll. Textiles and Sci., 1978-81; juror textile design and interior design; works exhibited designer showcases, local house tours, faculty shows. Author: That Which Was Once a Warp, 1971; contbr. articles and photographs to mags. and newspapers. Recipient Graham W. Littlewood III Outstanding Alumna award Phila. Coll. Textiles Sci., 1998, Sara Tyler Wister scholar; named Alumnus of Month, Textile Engr., 1971. Mem. Am. Soc. Interior Designers (dir. Pa. East chpt. 1967-78, chpt. recognition awards 1974, 80, Nat. Medalist award 1988). Address: 101 Hawthorne Ct Wyomissing PA 19610-1028

KESSLER, LYNN ELIZABETH, state legislator; b. Seattle, Feb. 26, 1941; d. John Mathew and Kathryn (Berry) Eisen; m. Keith L. Kessler, Dec. 24, 1980; children: William John Moore, Christopher Scott Moore, Bradley Jerome Moore, Jamie. Attended, Seattle U., 1958-59. Mem. Wash. Ho. of Reps., 1993—; co-majority leader rules com. Exec. dir. United Way Grays Harbor, 1984-92; mem. adv. coun. Head Start, 1986-89, Cervical Cancer Awareness Task Force, 1990-91, vocat. adv. coun. Hoquiam High Sch., 1991—, strategic planning com. Grays Harbor Community Hosp., 1991-92, Grays Harbor Food Bank Com., 1991-92, Grays Harbor Dem. Ctrl. Com.; vice-chair Grays Harbor County Shorelines Mgmt. Bd., 1988-90; chair Disability Awareness Com., 1988-90, Youth 2000 Com., 1990-91; pres. Teenage Pregnancy, Parenting and Prevention Adv. Coun., 1989-91; v.p. Grays Harbor Econ. Devel. Coun., 1990-92; trustee Grays Harbor Coll., 1991—, Aberdeen YMCA, 1991—. Mem. Aberdeen Rotary (pres. 1993-94). Home: 62 Kessler Ln Hoquiam WA 98550-9742 Office: Wash Ho of Reps Legislative Bldg Rm 409 Olympia WA 98504

KESSLER, MICHAEL GEORGE, forensic accountant; b. Bklyn., Dec. 31, 1951; s. Anthony Vincent and Mildred Marie K.; AA, St. John's U., Jamaica, N.Y., 1971, BS, 1973, MBA, 1978; cert. advanced grad. study Pace U., 1980; m. Eloise Lita Mogel, Mar. 16, 1975; children: Jonathan, Timothy. Cert. fraud examiner, internat. investigator; diplomate Am. Bd. Forensic Accts. Cash control officer R. H. Macy's, N.Y.C., 1969-73; sr. auditor Blue Cross-Blue Shield Greater N.Y., N.Y.C., 1973-78; prin. spl. audit investigator N.Y. State Atty. Gen., N.Y.C., 1978-81, regional chief auditor investigator, 1981-83, asst. chief auditor investigator, statewide tng. officer, 1983-87; chief of investigations, N.Y. State Tax Enforcement, 1987-88; dep. insp. gen. Met. Transp. Authority, 1988-90; pres. Michael G. Kessler & Assocs., Ltd.; award of spl. recognition for unique achievement and service, N.Y.C.; cert. tchr., N.Y. State. Mem. Am. Soc. Indsl. Security, Nat. Law Enforcement Assocs., Am. Coll. Forensic Examiners, Assn. Cert. Fraud Examiners. Contbg. author HEW audit manual; author investigative auditing workpapers, medicaid fraud report for Nat. Assn. Attys. Gen., 1983, author of Kessler Report. Office: 237 Park Ave New York NY 10017-3140

KESSLER, MILTON, English language educator, poet; b. Bklyn., May 9, 1930; s. Arthur and Elizabeth (Racow) K.; m. Sonia Berer, Aug. 24, 1952; children: David Lawrence, Paula Nan, Daniel Solomon. BA magna cum laude, U. Buffalo, 1957; MA, U. Wash., 1962; postgrad., Harvard U., 1957, Ohio State U., 1959-63. Lectr. English Queens Coll., CUNY, 1963-65; faculty SUNY, Binghamton, 1965—, prof. English, 1974-99, prof. emeritus, 1999—, dir. creative writing program, 1973-75, 78-79, 85; host 1st SUNY writers' festival, 1977; exec. com. programs in arts SUNY, Binghamton, 1981-85; host 1st writers festival SUNY, 1977; vis. prof. English, U. Negev, Beersheva, Israel, 1971-72; vis. lectr., U. Haifa, Israel, 1973, vis. prof., 1981; vis. prof. U. Hawaii, 1975, U. Haifa, 1981, Antwerp U., Belgium, 1985; vis. lectr. Keio U., Tokyo, 1978—; vis. writer Jackson State Coll., Tougaloo Coll., Jackson, Miss., 1967; vis. poet in residence Tenn. Tech U., 1986; guest poet Antioch Internat. Summer Writing Seminars, Oxford, Eng., 1977-78; vis. poet Inst. Internat. Studies, Japan, 1978, also poetry readings. Author: A Road Came Once, 1963, Called Home, 1967, Woodlawn North, 1970, Sailing Too Far, 1973, The Grand Concourse, 1990, 2d edit., 1993, Riding First Car, 1995; contbr. (with others) Poems on the Underground, 1994; translator: (with Gerald E. Kadish) Love Songs and Tomb Songs of Ancient Egypt in Alcheringa, 5, 1973, (with Tateo Imamura) Random Talks of Diebutsu (Kosho Shimizu), 1979; filmmaker (with Paula Kessler) Walt Whitman: The Centennial, 1992; editor: Antwerp Studies in Literature, 1986; co-editor: Choice: A Mag. of Poetry and Graphics, 1972-81; recorded BBC Radio Programs on Whitman and Self, 1994. Robert Frost fellow in poetry Bread Loaf Conf., 1961, MacDowell Found. fellow, 1966, 79, Yaddo fellow, 1965-76, 90, Internat. fellow Keio U., Tokyo, 1978, Millay Found. fellow, 1979, fellow Va. Ctr. for Creative Arts, 1982-83, 88-89, 95; Nat. Endowment for Arts grant, 1967. Mem. Phi Beta Kappa. Jewish. Home: 315 E 68th St New York NY 10021-5692 Office: SUNY Dept English Binghamton NY 13902-6000

KESSLER, MITZI LYONS, artist; b. Charleston, S.C., May 26, 1932; d. Albert Percy and Carlotta Albertina (Drews) Lyons; m. Robert Frederick Kessler, May 3, 1952; children: Karen, Elizabeth. Student, Hollins Coll. Exhbns. include LyMoyne Art Found., Tallahassee, 1982-92, Gallery of Art, Panama City, Fla., 1986-96, Nice Art Gallery, Havana, Fla., 1994-96, Signature Gallery, Tallahassee, 1998—. Bd. dirs. Monticello (Fla.) Opera Co., 1976-82, Tallahassee Symphony Orch., 1988-95, Mus. of Art, Talahassee, 1992-98; v.p. Mus. of Art, Talahassee, 1992-93; vice moderator Christ Presbyn. Ch., Tallahassee, 1997-98, moderator Christ Presbyn. Ch. Women, 1998—. Mem. So. Watercolor Soc., Fla. Watercolor Soc., Tallahassee Watercolor Soc., The Town Club. Avocations: travel, gardening, walking, reading, music. Home: 512 Summerbrooke Dr Tallahassee FL 32312-6726

KESSLER, PETE WILLIAM, dentist; b. Paterson, N.J., Feb. 21, 1949; s. Martin and Bernice S. Kessler; m. Sue E. George, Nov. 2, 1988; children: Kasey Martin, Kelly George, Kristopher William. BA, Peabody Conservatory of Music, 1971; BS, U. Md., 1976, MS, 1978, DDS, 1982. Bassist, musician Roberta Flack, Alexandria, Va., 1970-73, Atlantic Records, N.Y.C., 1970-75; pvt. practice Balt., 1982-98, Pace, Fla., 1998-98; ret., 1998. Recorded with Fifth Dimension, Friends of Distinction, Freddy Hubbard, Village People, Crystal Gayle, Ronnie Milsap, Hulk Hogan, others. Avocations: biking, scuba diving, reading.

KESSLER, ROBERT ALLEN, data processing executive; b. N.Y.C., Feb. 2, 1940; s. Henry and Caroline Catherine (Axinger) K.; m. Marie Therese Anton, Mar. 17, 1967; children: Susanne, Mark. BA in Math., CUNY, 1961; postgrad., UCLA, 1963-64. EDP analyst Boeing Aircraft, Seattle, 1961-62; computer specialist System Devel. Corp., Santa Monica, Calif., 1962-66; mem. tech. staff Computer Scis. Corp., El Segundo, Calif., 1966-67, sr. mem. tech. staff, 1971-72, computer scientist, 1974-81; systems mgr. Xerox Data Systems, L.A., 1967-71; prin. scientist Digital Resources, Algiers, Algeria, 1972-74; sr. systems cons. Atlantic Richfield, L.A., 1981-94; computer cons., 1994—. Mem. Big. Bros. L.A., 1962-66; precinct capt. Goldwater for Pres., Santa Monica, 1964; mem. L.A. Conservacy, 1987. Mem. Assn. Computing Machinery. Avocations: racquetball, theatre, gourmet dining. Home: 6138 W 75th Pl Los Angeles CA 90045-1634 Office: Pfizer Health Solutions 2400 Broadway Santa Monica CA 90071-2201

KESSLER, ROBERT W., director license, inspections, environmental rules. BA in Urban Studies, U. Minn., St. Paul, 1974; MPA in Housing, Comty. Devel., U. So. Calif., Washington, Pub. Affairs Ctr., 1981; postgrad. studies in Project Mgmt., Program Evaluation U. Minn., 1978-94. City planner Office of the Mayor, St. Paul, Minn., 1973-74; devel. grant asst., comty. devel. divsn. City of St. Paul, 1975-80; program analyst HUD, Washington, 1980-81; asst. to chief of staff Mayor's Office City of St. Paul, 1982; comty. devel. specialist City of St. Paul, 1982-83, econ. devel. specialist neighborhood divsn., 1983-86; dir. St. Paul 503 Devel. Co., 1986-87; asst. to mayor City of St. Paul, 1987-88, dir. Mayor's info. and complaint office, 1988-90, license and permit mgr., 1990-92, dir. Office Lic., Inspections and Environ. Protection, 1992—. With U.S. Army Med. Bn., Vietnam, 1969-70. Decorated Bronze Star, U.S. Army, 1970. Mem. Internat. City/County Mgmt. Assn. (affiliate). Home: 581 Desnoyer Ave Saint Paul MN 55104-4917 Office: Lics Inspections & Environ Protection 350 Saint Peter St Saint Paul MN 55102-1514*

KESSLER, RONALD BOREK, author; b. N.Y.C., Dec. 31, 1943; s. Ernest Borek and Minuetta K.; m. Pamela Johnson Whitehead; children: Greg, Rachel Kessler. Student, Clark U., Worcester, Mass., 1962-64. Reporter Worcester Telegram, 1964; reporter, editorial writer Boston Herald, 1964-68; N.Y. bur. reporter Wall Street Jour., 1968-70; investigative reporter Washington Post, 1970-87; journalist/author, 1987—. Author: The Life Insurance Game, 1985, The Richest Man in the World: The Story of Adnan Khashoggi, 1986, Spy vs. Spy: Stalking Soviet Spies in America, 1988, Moscow Station: How the KGB Penetrated the American Embassy, 1989, The Spy in the Russian Club: How Glenn Souther Stole America's Nuclear War Plans and Escaped to Moscow, 1990, Escape from the CIA: How the CIA Won and Lost the Most Important KGB Spy Ever to Defect to the U.S., 1991, Inside the CIA: Revealing the Secrets of the World's Most Powerful Spy Agency, 1992, The FBI: Inside the World's Most Powerful Law Enforcement Agency, 1993, Inside the White House: The Hidden Lives of the Presidents and the Secrets of the World's Most Powerful Institution, 1995, The Sins of the Father: Joseph P. Kennedy and the Dynasty He Founded, 1996, Inside Congress: The Shocking Scandals, Corruption, and Abuse of Power Behind the Scenes on Capitol Hill, 1997, The Season: Inside Palm Beach and America's Richest Society, 1999. Recipient public affairs reporting award Am. Polit. Sci. Assn., 1965; citation Freedoms Found., 1966; 1st prize in newswriting UPI, 1967; Sevellon Brown Meml. award AP, 1967; sci. writers award ADA, 1968; 1st place in public service award Md.-Del.-D.C. Press Assn., 1972; outstanding series award AAUW, 1972; Bill Pryor Meml. Reporting award, 1973; Front Page award Washington-Balt. Newspaper Guild, 1973; George H. Polk Meml. award for community service, 1973; for nat. reporting, 1979; Washington Dateline award for bus. reporting Sigma Delta Chi-Soc. Profl. Journalists, 1987; 1st pl. in investigative reporting Assn. Area Bus. Publs., 1987; named Washingtonian of Yr. Washington Mag., 1972; Dow Jones Inc Newspaper Fund intern, 1964. Home and Office: 2516 Stratton Dr Potomac MD 20854-6231

KESSLER, ROSLYN MARIE, financial analyst; b. Bloomington, Ind., Dec. 5, 1953; d. Ivan Gordon and Carmen Karina (Babbensingh) Samuels; m.

Terrance Jude Kessler, Mar. 19, 1982 (div. Mar. 19, 1993); 1 child, Jude. BA in Econs., U. Rochester, 1975, MBA in Fin., 1994; BS in Acctg., SUNY, Albany, 1990. CPA, N.Y.; cert. mgmt. acct.; accredited purchasing practitioner. Staff tax acct., auditor Arthur Andersen & Co., Rochester, N.Y., 1990-92; pvt. practice pvt. practive, Rochester, N.Y., 1992; sr. buyer Xerox Corp., Rochester, N.Y., 1994—; grad. tchg. asst., 1992-94; William E. Simon Grad. Sch. Bus. Adminstrn. scholar, 1992-94. Legis. chair PTA, Winslow Elem. Sch., 1991-92, PTA Brighton H.S., 1996—; com. mem. Boy Scouts Am., Rochester, 1991-92; vol. Wesley-on-East Nursing Home, Rochester, 1992-95. Mem. Am. Fin. Assn., Inst. Cert. Mgmt. Accts., N.Y. Assn. CPA Candidates (dir. 1991-92, pres. 1992-93), Nat. Assn. Tax Practitioners, Nat. Assn. Purchasing Mgmt. Avocations: golf, statistics, futures/options, investments. Home: 499 French Rd Apt 4 Rochester NY 14618-5319

KESSLER, STEPHEN JAMES, writer, editor; b. L.A., Jan. 12, 1947; s. Jack and Nina (Ifland) K.; 1 child, Claire Kessler-Bradner. BA, Bard Coll., 1968; MA, U. Calif., Santa Cruz, 1969. Editor Green Horse Press, Santa Cruz, 1973-79; editor, pub. Alcatraz Edits., Santa Cruz, 1979-85, The Sun, Santa Cruz, 1986-89; editor The Redwood Coast Rev., Mendocino, Calif., 1999—; freelance poet, translator, essayist, journalist, 1972—. Author: (translation) Save Twilight, 1997; editor mag./anthology Alcatraz, 1979-85; contbr. essays to Poetry Flash, 1985-98.

KESSLER, STEVEN FISHER, lawyer; b. McKeesport, Pa., June 29, 1951; s. Robert and Rae (Alpern) K.; m. Susan Joyce Pearlstein, June 3, 1979; children: Matthew, Katie. BA, U. Pitts., 1973, JD, 1976. Bar: Pa. 1976, U.S. Dist. Ct. (we. dist.) Pa. 1976. Staff atty. Neighborhood Legal Services, McKeesport, Pa., 1976-79; solicitor City of McKeesport, 1980-82; sole practice, McKeesport, 1982—; solicitor McKeesport Housing Corp., 1985—; chmn. bd. dirs. McKeesport Devel. Corp., 1984—. Mem. Am. Arbitration Assn. (panel arbitrators 1981—). Democrat. Home: 1337 Foxwood Dr Monroeville PA 15146-4436 Office: 332 5th Ave Mc Keesport PA 15132-2616

KESSLER, WALLACE FRANK, school director, tour developer; b. Mar. 22, 1938; m. Susan Carol Morse, June 20, 1969 (div. Nov. 1972). BA, U. Vt., Burlington, 1959, postgrad., 1963. Cert. secondary tchr., Vt. Founder, cultural program tchr. Cutler Acad., Craftsbury, Vt., 1959-63; founder outdoor program, English dept. The Stowe (Vt.) Sch., 1963-66; asst. to headmaster, tchr. Pine Ridge Sch., Williston, Vt., 1967-71; dean of students Middlesex Coll., Stowe, 1966; founder, operator Introspect Sch., Stowe, 1972-85; headmaster Vt. Land and Sea Sch., Springfield, 1985-86; mgr. Tauck Tours, Westport, Conn., 1987—; founder, Walrus Tours Youth World Camps, Balt., 1986—; founder St. Stephen's Sch., Austin, Tex., 1996-97.; mem. scis. selection com. Vt. Acad. Arts, Montpelier, 1966-68. Avocations: bicycling, hiking, basketball, literature, conservation. Home: 1201 Robert E Lee Rd Austin TX 78704-2029 Office: Youth World Camps 10 Old Court Rd Baltimore MD 21208-4014

KESSLER, WILLIAM HENRY, architect; b. Reading, Pa., Dec. 15, 1924; s. Frederick H. and Lucia W. (Kline) K.; m. Margot Walbrecker, May 11, 1946; children: Tamara Kessler Wagner, Chevonne Kessler Patten. B.A. in Architecture, Inst. Design, Chgo., 1948; M.Arch., Harvard U., 1951. Chief designer Yamasaki, Leinweber & Hellmuth, Detroit, 1951-55; prin. William Kessler and Assos., Inc., Detroit, 1955—; adj. prof. U. Mich. Coll. Architecture. Prin. works include Center Creative Studies, Detroit, Harvard U. Sch. Pub. Health, Boston, Indsl. Tech. Inst., Ann Arbor, Mich., State of Mich. Library Museum and Archives, Detroit Sci. Center, New Detroit Gen. Hosp.-Wayne State U. Health Care Inst, Detroit. Councilman, Grosse Pointe Park, Mich., 1966-67. Served with USAAF, 1943-46. Recipient over 130 archtl. design awards. Fellow AIA (Gold medal Detroit chpt. 1974), Mich. Soc. Architects (Gold medal 1976). Home: 1013 Cadieux Rd Grosse Pointe Park MI 48230-1511 Office: Kessler Assocs Inc 409 E Jefferson Ave Ste 600 Detroit MI 48226-4322

KESSLER, WOODROW BERTRAM, family practice physician, geriatrician, educator; b. N.Y.C., Sept. 27, 1926; s. Robert Theodore and Bess Doris (Oumansky) K.; m. Anita Andar, Dec. 21, 1950; children: Rex Keith, Ginger Dale. BS, Case Western Reserve U., 1947; PhD, Rutgers U., 1951; MD, Temple U., 1962. Diplomate Am. Bd. Family Practice, Am. Bd. Geriat. Instr. U. Tex., Houston, 1951-52; rsch. assoc. Vanderbilt U., Nashville, 1952-54, E.R. Squibb, New Brunswick, N.J., 1954-58; rsch. assoc. prof. U. Miami, 1958-60, Temple U., Phila., 1960-62; med. intern Temple U. Hosp., Phila., 1962-63, med. resident, 1963; rsch. physician E.I. DuPont, Wilmington, Del., 1964-65; pvt. med. practice, 1965—; clin. assoc. prof. internal medicine Temple U. Health Scis. Ctr., 1967—; attending staff Temple U. Hosp., 1967—; dir. clin. pharmacology/investigation dept. endocrinology Temple U. Health Scis. Ctr., 1980-91; physician chief grade U.S. Dept. Vet.'s Affairs Ambulatory Care, Phila., 1994-96; Penn fellow Children's Hosp. Phila., 1977; hosp. appointments include Crozer-Chester Med. Ctr., Riddle Meml. Hosp., Coatesville VA Med. Ctr.; cons. endocrinologist Haverford (Pa.) State Hosp., 1967-69, Haverford Gen. Hosp.; cons. Hoechst Internat., A.H. Robins, Abbott Pharms., Revlon/Armour, Ciba/Geigy, Ortho Pharms., Farmitalia Urba, Milan, Merck, Sharp & Dohme, Ayerst Labs., Adria Labs., Syntex Labs., Serono Labs., Oxford Rsch. Internat., Lederle Labs., Harris Labs., AT&T, Bell Atlantic; pres., CEO Providence Med. Assocs.; pres., exec. mng. officer Providence Med. Ctr.; chmn. bd. Pa. Physicians Plan, Inc.; dir. Pa. Adminstrv. Med. Svcs.; dir. Triage Med. Svcs., Inc.; mng. dir. Wallingford Med. Ctr.; chmn. bd. Am. Health & Accident Ins. Co.; dir. Tele-Diagnostics, Inc.; med. dir. dept. mil. affairs Southeastern Pa. Vets. Ctr. Contbr. articles to profl. jours.; patentee in field of disease-tracking sys. Fellow Coll. Physicians of Phila.; mem. AMA, AAUP, Endocrine Soc., Am. Bd. Family Practice (charter), Am. Soc. Contemporary Medicine and Surgery, Drug Info. Assn., Am. Soc. Internal Medicine, Am. Acad. Family Practice, Pa. Med. Soc., N.Y. Acad. Scis., Delaware County Med. Soc., Endocrine Soc. Phila., Sigma Xi. Avocations: chess, travel. Office: TDx 415 S Providence Rd Media PA 19063-3839

KESSLER-HARRIS, ALICE, historian, educator; b. June 2, 1941. AB cum laude, Goucher Coll., 1961; MA, Rutgers U., 1963, PhD, 1968; LLD (hon.), Goucher Coll., 1991; PhD (hon.), Uppsala U., 1995. Vis. faculty Sarah Lawrence Coll., 1974-76; vis. sr. lectr. U. Warwick, 1979-80; prof. history Hofstra U., Hempstead, N.Y., 1981-88, Temple U., 1988-90, Rutgers U., New Brunswick, N.J., 1990-99, Columbia U., N.Y.C., 1999—. Author: Women Have Always Worked: An Historical Overview, 1981, Out to Work: A History of Wage-Earning Women in the United States, 1982, A Woman's Wage: Historical Meanings and Social Consequences, 1990; co-editor: Past Imperfect: Alternative Essays in American History, 1973, Women in Culture and Politics: A Century of Change, 1986, Faith of a Woman Writer: Essays in Twentieth Century Literature, 1988, Perspectives on American Labor History: The Problem of Synthesis, 1990, U.S. History as Women's History, 1995, Protecting Women: Labor Legislation in Europe, Australia and the United States, 1880-1920, 1995; contbr. articles to profl. jours. NEH fellow, 1976-77, 85-86, Rockefeller Found. fellow, 1988-89, Guggenheim fellow, 1989-90. Mem. Am. Hist. Assn., Orgn. Am. Historians, Soc. Am. Historians, Am. Studies Assn., Berkshire Conf. Women Historians, ACLU.

KESSLER-HODGSON, LEE GWENDOLYN, actress, corporate executive; b. Wellsville, N.Y., Jan. 16, 1947; d. James Hewitt and Reba Gwendolyn (Adsit) Kessler; m. Bruce Gridley, June 22, 1969 (div. Dec. 1979); m. Jeffrey Craig Hodgson, Oct. 31, 1987. BA, Grove City Coll., 1968; MA, U. Wis., 1969. Prof. Sangamon State U., Springfield, Ill., 1969-70; pers. exec. Bullock's, L.A., 1971-74; owner Brunnen Enterprises, L.A., 1982—. Author: A Child of Arthur, 1981; producer, writer play including Anais Nin: The Paris Years, 1986; appeared in TV movies, mini-series including Roots, 1978, Backstairs at The White House, 1979, Blind Ambition, 1980, Hill Street Blues, 1984-87, Murder By Reason of Insanity, 1985, Hoover, 1986, Creator, 1987, Our House, 1988, Favorite Son, 1988, Lou Grant 1983-84, Barney Miller, 1979, L.A. Law, 1990, Hunter, 1991, (screenplay) Settlers Way, 1988; (TV series) Matloc k, L.A. Law others. Knapp Prize fellow U. Wis., 1969. Mem. AFTRA, SAG, Actors Equity Assn. Republican. Mem. Ch. Scientology. Avocations: singer, directing, motivational speaking. Home: 342 Brockmont Dr Glendale CA 91202

KESTENBAUM, HAROLD LEE, lawyer; b. Bronx, N.Y., Sept. 27, 1949; s. Murray Louis and Yetta (Weiner) K.; m. Felice Gail Kravit, Aug. 11, 1973; children: Michelle, Benjamin. BA, Queens Coll., 1971; JD, U. Richmond, 1975. Bar: N.Y. 1976, N.J. 1977, U.S. Dist. Ct. (so. and ea. dist.) N.Y. Assoc. Wayne and Reiss, N.Y.C., 1975-76, Natanson, Reich and Barrison, N.Y.C., 1976-77, Goldstein and Axelrod, N.Y.C., 1977-81; pvt. practice N.Y.C. and L.I., 1981—; chmn. of the bd. Franchise It Corp., Bohemia, N.Y., 1984-89; pres., chief exec. officer Mr. Sign Franchising Corp., 1987-89; bd. dirs. Sbarro Inc., Travel Network Ltd.; cons. in field. Mem. ABA, N.Y. Bar Assn., N.J. Bar Assn., Nassau County Bar Assn. Republican. Jewish. Avocations: softball, weight training. Office: 585 Stewart Ave Ste 700 Garden City NY 11530-4785

KESTENBAUM, RICHARD, clinical and school psychologist, consultant adolescent, family and child psychology, biofeedback; b. N.Y.C., Nov. 16, 1955; s. Ralph and Evelyn (Rose) K. B.S., SUNY-Buffalo, 1977; M.A., U. Colo., Boulder, 1979, Ph.D., 1983. Cert. sch. psychologist, Colo.; lic. clin. psychologist, Colo. Staff psychologist San Luis Valley Bd. Coop. Ednl. Services, Alamosa, Colo., 1980-81; staff psychologist Jefferson County Schs., Lakewood, Colo., 1981-86; instr. U. Colo., Boulder, 1982-83; pvt. practice clin. and counseling psychology, Denver, 1983-86; staff clinician, postdoctoral intern Jefferson County Mental Health Ctr., Arvada, Colo., 1984-85; inpatient psychologist Mercy Med. Ctr., Denver, 1985, Horizon Hosp., Denver, 1985-86; instr. U. So. Maine, 1988; workshop lectr. nat., state, local confs. Mem. Rocky Flats Conversion Campaign, 1978-79; bd. dirs. Boulder County Youth Planning Council, 1979-80. Recipient Henry S. Loeb Brotherhood award, 1973; N.Y. State Regents scholar, 1973-77; State of Colo. grad. grantee, 1981-83, fellow, 1981-82. Mem. Colo. Soc. Sch. Psychologists. Home: 2882 S Gray Way Denver CO 80227-3854

KESTER, DALE EMMERT, pomologist, educator; b. Audubon, Iowa, July 28, 1922; s. Raymond and Fannie (Ditzenberger) K.; m. Daphne Dougherty; children: William Raymond, Nancy Inman. BS in Horticulture, Iowa State Coll., 1947; MS in Horticulture, U. Calif., Davis, 1949, PhD in Plant Physiology, 1951. Rsch. asst. dept pomology U. Calif., Davis, 1947-51, lectr., jr. pomologist, 1951-53, asst. prof., asst. pomologist, 1953-60, assoc. prof., assoc. pomologist, 1960-69, prof., pomologist, 1969-91, prof. emeritus, 1991—; vis. scholar dept. genetics U. Wis., Madison, 1962-63, Volcanic Rsch. Inst., Bet Dagan, Israel, 1975. Co-author: Plant Propagation: Principles and Practices, 1959, 6th revised edit., 1997; contbr. numerous articles to profl. and popular publs. 1st lt. USAF, 1943-45, ETO. Fellow Am. Soc. Hort. Sci. (Stark award 1980); mem. Internat. Plant Propagators Soc. (sec. 1961), Alpha Zeta, Gamma Sigma Delta, Phi Beta Kappa, Pi Alpha Xi. Republican. Presbyterian. Achievements include introduction of 5 almond cultivars and 2 almond rootstocks. Home: 750 Anderson Rd Davis CA 95616-3513 Office: U Calif Dept Pomology Davis CA 95616

KESTER, RANDALL BLAIR, lawyer; b. Vale, Oreg., Oct. 20, 1916; s. Bruce R. and Mabel M. (Judd) K.; m. Rachael L. Woodhouse, Oct. 20, 1940; children: Laura, Sylvia, Lynne. A.B., Willamette U., 1937; J.D., Columbia U., 1940. Bar: Oreg. 1940, U.S. Dist. Ct. Oreg. 1940, U.S. Ct. Appeals (9th cir.) 1941, U.S. Supreme Ct. 1960. Assoc., then partner firm Maguire, Shields, Morrison & Bailey, Portland, 1940-57; justice Oreg. Supreme Ct., Salem, 1957-58; partner Maguire, Shields, Morrison, Bailey & Kester, 1958-66, Maguire, Kester & Cosgrave, 1966-71, Cosgrave & Kester, Portland, 1972-78, Cosgrave, Kester, Crowe, Gidley & Lagesen, Portland, 1978-89, Cosgrave, Vergeer & Kester, Portland, 1989—; instr. Northwestern Coll. Law, 1947-56; gen. solicitor northwestern dist. U.P. R.R., 1958-79; sr. counsel UPRR Co., 1979-81. Co-author: The First Duty: History of the U.S. District Court of Oregon, 1993; contbr. articles to profl. jours. Past v.p. Portland area council Boy Scouts of Am.; past pres. Mountain Rescue and Safety Council Oreg.; past trustee Willamette U.; past bd. dirs. Oreg. Symphony Soc., Oreg. Mus. Sci. and Industry. Recipient Silver Beaver award Boy Scouts Am., 1956, alumni citation Willamette U., 1987. Fellow Am. Acad. Appellate Lawyers; mem. ABA, Am. Bar Found. (life), Multnomah Bar Assn. (past pres. 1956, Professionalism award 1991), Oreg. State Bar (treas. 1965-66, Disting. Svc. award pub. utility sect. 1991), Am. Law Inst. (life), Nat. Ski Patrol, Mt. Hood Ski Patrol (past pres.), Mazamas (past pres., climbing chmn.), Wy'east Climbers, Portland C. of C. (pres. 1973, chmn. bd. 1974), U.S. Dist. Ct. Oreg. Hist. Soc. (past pres, bd. dirs.) Oreg. Ethics Commons (co-founder, sec.), Phi Delta Phi, Beta Theta Pi, Tau Kappa Alpha. Republican. Unitarian. Clubs: Arlington (Portland), City (Portland) (v.p. 1978-80, pres. 1986-87), University (Portland), Multnomah Athletic (Portland). Home: 10075 SW Hawthorne Ln Portland OR 97225-4322 Office: Cosgrave Vergeer & Kester 121 SW Morrison St Ste 1300 Portland OR 97204-3143

KESTER, STEWART RANDOLPH, banker; b. Bronxville, N.Y., July 30, 1927; s. Robert Livingston, Jr. and Mae Anna (Jones) K.; m. Marion Fay Syrett, Sept. 23, 1950; children: Cheryl, Stewart Randolph, Valerie, Marcia. B.A., Colgate U., 1949. Sales rep. Procter & Gamble Co., N.Y.C., 1949-55; mng. ptnr. Kester Bros., Pompano Beach, Fla., 1955-86, R&S Properties, Pompano Beach, 1956-90; mng. ptnr. Fla. Coast Banks, Inc., Pompano Beach, 1973-75, vice chmn. bd., 1975-84, chmn. bd., 1984-85, chmn. exec. com., dir.; dir. Barnett Bank So. Fla. N.A., 1985-89, also bd. dirs.; with Kester Bros. Realty Inc., 1991—; pres. Crail Creek Assocs. LC, 1997—; bd. dirs. Big Sky (Mont.) Western Bank; pres. Jefferson Valley Ranch, Whitehall, Mont.; sec.-treas. Westfork Devel. Co. Inc., Big Sky, 1991-95. Vice mayor, commr., Pompano Beach, 1964-66, mayor, 1966-67; mem. Broward County Charter Commn., 1974-75; pres. United Way of Broward County, 1978-79; chmn. bd. trustees Pompano Police Edn. Fund, Inc., 1975-86; mem. exec. com. Broward chpt. NCCJ, 1983-86; bd. dirs. Ft. Lauderdale Symphony, Broward Workshop, Inc., 1981-85; founding dir., pres. Pompano Beach Bd. Trade, 1978-86; founding dir., v.p. Broward Community Found., 1985-89; bd. dirs. Big Sky Assn. for Arts, 1989-95, Vigilante Theatre Corp., 1992-94. With AUS, 1946-47. Named Outstanding Young Man Pompano Beach Jaycees, 1962; recipient Service award Ft. Lauderdale C. of C., 1975, Silver Medallion award NCCJ, 1984, Community Svc. award Pompano Beach C. of C., 1983, 85. Mem. Pompano Beach Hist. Soc., Greater Pompano Beach C. of C. (past dir.), Pompano Beach Exch. Club (past pres., charter mem., Book of Golden Deeds award 1976), Montana Hist. Soc., Custer Battlefield Mus. and Hist. Commn., Custer Battlefield Preservation Commn., Mus. of the Rockies, Buffalo Bill Hist. Ctr., Mus. of Art (Ft. Lauderdale), Sons of the Revolution (N.Y.). Republican. Presbyterian. Office: Kester Bros Realty Inc 619 E Atlantic Blvd PO Box 91 Pompano Beach FL 33061-0091

KESTERSON, DAVID BERT, English language educator; b. Springfield, Mo., Feb. 19, 1938; s. Homer Russell and Dorothy (Mace) K.; m. Cheryl Renee Monk; children: A. Todd, Chad Russell. B.S.E., S.W. Mo. State U., 1959; M.A., U. Ark., 1961, Ph.D., 1965. NDEA fellow, 1959-62; grad. teaching asst. U. Ark., Fayetteville, 1962-64; asst. prof. English N.C. State U., Raleigh, 1964-68; from asst. prof. to prof. English North Tex. State U. (name now U. North Tex.), Denton, 1968—, disting. Alumni prof., 1979, chmn. dept. English, 1981-86, assoc. dean Coll. Arts and Scis., 1986-92; sr. Fulbright lectr. U. Wûrzburg (Germany), 1985; interim dean Coll. Arts and Scis. U. North Tex., Denton, 1992-93, vice provost, 1993-98, v.p. for acad. affairs, 1998—; cons. various presses on manuscripts in Am. lit. Author: Josh Billings, 1973, Bill Nye, 1980; monograph Bill Nye: The Western Writings, 1976; editor: Studies in the Marble Faun, 1971, Critics on Poe, 1973, Critics on Mark Twain, 1973, Critical Essays on Hawthorne's The Scarlet Letter, 1988; founding editor: Hawthorne Soc. Newsletter (now Nathaniel Hawthorne Rev.), 1974-82; assoc. editor: Studies in the Novel, 1970—, Nathaniel Hawthorne Jour., 1980-82. Served with USAR, 1956-60. Recipient Mortar Bd. Outstanding Educator award, 1980; Outstanding Alumnus award S.W. Mo. State U., 1986, Disting. Grad. Alumnus award Dept. English U. Ark., 1988. Mem. Nathaniel Hawthorne Soc. (co-founder, 1st pres. 1974-76), Am. Humor Studies Assn. (pres. 1980-81), South Ctrl. MLA (exec. com. 1976-77), MLA (del. assembly 1977-80, 84-87), Melville Soc., Soc. Study So. Lit. (pres.), Mark Twain Circle, Thoreau Soc., Thomas Wolfe Soc., Fulbright Assn., POE Studies Assn., Phi Kappa Phi, Phi Beta Delta. Office: U North Tex Office PO Box 311190 Denton TX 76203-1190

KESTIN, HOWARD H., judge; b. Passaic, N.J., July 24, 1937; s. Oscar and Annette (Moichich) K.; m. Joan H. Bard, Aug. 22, 1970: children: Bette Lynn, Anita Louise. BS, St. Louis U., 1959; JD, Rutgers U., 1962; LLM, U. Va., 1995. Bar: N.J. 1962, U.S. Supreme Ct. 1965. Law sec. to assoc. justice N.J. Supreme Ct., 1962-63; dep. atty. gen. N.J., 1963-65; asst. dir. Inst. Continuing Legal Edn., Newark, 1965-66, 69-70, exec. dir., 1970-78; dir. State N.J. Legal Svcs. to Poor Program, Trenton, 1966-68; pvt. practice law Wayne, N.J., 1968-69; prof. Rutgers U., 1969-78; chief adminstrv. law judge, dir. Office Administrv. Law State N.J., 1978-83; judge family and civil law divsns. Superior Ct. N.J., Paterson, 1983-91, judge Appellate div., 1992—; adj. prof. law Seton Hall U. Sch. Law, Newark, 1972-84; counsel N.J. Family Ct. Study Commn., 1970-72. Moderator-host The Blessings of Liberty, Sta. WNBC-TV, 1971, The Right of the People, 1975. Recipient Media awards for TV series on Bill of Rights, N.J. Bar Assn./ABA, 1971. Mem. ABA (membership com. 1968-73, state legis. com. 1972-73), Am. Law Inst., N.J. Bar Assn. (chmn. adminstrv. law sect. 1972-74, chmn. young lawyers sect. 1968-69, trustee 1969-70), N.J. Supreme Ct. (chmn. com. on legal edn. and admissions to bar 1976-79, chmn. standing com. on paralegal edn. and regulation 1993—), Passaic County Bar Assn., Assn. CLE Adminstrs. (chmn. stds. and accreditation com. 1972-778, v.p. 1978). Jewish. Home: 88 Anderson Dr Wayne NJ 07470-2651 Office: Superior Ct of NJ Appellate Divsn Ct Plz N 25 Main St Hackensack NJ 07601-7015

KESTING, THEODORE, magazine editor; b. Mont Clare, Pa., Aug. 27, 1918; s. Theodore F. and Pauline (Hechler) K.; m. Jean M. Hoffman, Jan. 6, 1945 (dec.); children—Virginia Joan, Frederic, Kristin, David; m. Lorraine Williams, Mar. 4, 1968. Student, Girard Coll., 1928-36, Pa. Sch. Indsl. Arts, 1937-39, Charles Morrice Price Sch., 1940-41. Editor Curtis Pub. Co., 1936-45; editor, v.p. Sports Afield Pub. Co., Mpls., 1945-53; editor, pub. Am. Boy, 1950-53; editor Sports Afield, Hearst mags., 1956-70, Rod and Gun, 1969-70; editor at large Sports Afield, 1971—. Author: The Outdoor Encyclopedia, 1957. Home: Beaver Dam Farm Hume VA 22639 Office: 250 W 55th St New York NY 10019-5201

KESTLE, WENDELL RUSSELL, cost and economic analyst, consultant; b. Casper, Wyo., July 23, 1935; s. Philip Clayton and Ruby Maxine (Clifton) K.; m. Anne Marie Joujon-Roche, Nov. 18, 1961; children: Martha Anne, Joan Marie, Wendell Russell Jr. BA in Econs., Calif. State U., Northridge, 1961. Cost engr. Rand Corp., Santa Monica, Calif., 1961-63; mem. ops. rsch. staff Lockheed Aircraft Co., Burbank, Calif., 1963-65; mem. tech. staff Hughes Aircraft Co., El Segundo, Calif., 1965-66; sr. rsch. staff assoc. Northrop Corp., Hawthorne, Calif., 1966-69; sr. scientist Booz-Allen Applied Rsch., Inglewood, Calif., 1969-70; mgr. TRW, Inc., Redondo Beach, Calif., 1970-71; pvt. practice Carson, Calif., 1971-72; project mgr. Litton PRC, Inc., Huntsville, Ala., 1972-97; cons. in field, Washington. Author, editor sci. documents. With USN, 1952-56, Korea. Recipient letter of commendation NASA, 1976, 80, 92, 95. Mem. AAAS, Am. Econ. Assn., Ops. Rsch. Soc. of Am., Nat. Space Soc., Planetary Soc., Bot. Garden Soc. of Huntsville, Historic Huntsville Soc., Friends of the Library, Am. Legion. Roman Catholic. Home and Office: 602 Garv Cir SE Huntsville AL 35803-1608

KESTNBAUM, ALBERT S., advertising executive; b. N.Y.C., 1939; s. Nathan and Marian (Lanxner) K.; m. Roberta Anne; children: Ellen, Suzanne, Amy, David. B.A., NYU, 1959; MBA, CCNY, 1961. Sr. v.p. advt. J.B. Williams Co., N.Y.C., 1968-72; pres., chmn. bd. Parkson Advt. Agy., N.Y.C., 1972-80; pres. Chestnut Communications, Greenwich, Conn., 1980—. Mem. pub. info. com. Am. Cancer Soc. Mem. Dirs. Guild Am., Acad. TV Arts and Scis. Club: Milbrook. Office: 8 Sound Shore Dr Greenwich CT 06830-7242 *The best opportunities for success come from thorough, audacious and determined effort, in areas where your skills are most substantial, and where the potential reward is great. Often, ironically, the key ingredient to success is giving yourself permission to fail.*

KESTNER, ROBERT RICHARD, II, engineering psychologist; b. Ft. Belvoir, Va., Oct. 18, 1948; s. Robert Richard and Mary Eunice (Wooten) K.; m. Durema Joyce Hall, Dec. 27, 1970; children: James Michael, Jacob Paul. AB in Edn., U. N.C., 1970; MS in Human Sys., Fla. State U., 1975. Cert. lay spkr. United Meth. Ch. Dir. halfway house Leon County Mental Health Ctr., Tallahassee, Fla., 1973-75; dir. Crossroads Drug Treatment Program, Fayetteville, N.C., 1975-76; edn. officer 7th Army Tng. Command U.S. Army, Vilseck, Germany, 1976-78; dir. mental health ctr. 3d Squadron/2 Armed Cavalry Regiment U.S. Army, Amberg, Germany, 1979-80; chief human factors lab. Tropic Test Ctr. U.S. Army, Republic of Panama, 1985-87; engring. psychologist, project engr. U.S. Army, White Sands Missile Range, N.Mex., 1980-85, 87-96. Author/co-author test reports. Dist. commr., mem. Boy Scouts Am., Alamogordo, N.Mex., 1995-96; mayor White Sands Missile Range, N.Mex., 1981-83. With USN, 1971-73. Recipient Cross and Flame, United Meth. Ch., 1993. Mem. Human Factors Soc. (pres. Rio Grande chpt. 1983-84). Avocations: backpacking, bicycling, camping, computers, genealogy. Office: White Sands Missile Range PO Box 88 White Sands NM 88002-0088

KESTY, ROBERT EDWARD, chemical manufacturing company executive; b. Camden, N.J., Dec. 11, 1941; s. Edward Adam and Helen Dorothy (Maciejko) Krzysztanowicz; m. Louise Marie Kesty, June 12, 1976; children: Nicole Christina, Alicia Anne, Christopher Edward, Robert Edward Jr. *Daughter Nicole Christina graduated University of Delaware summa cum laude, Dean Scholar, Eugene duPont Scholarship, National Science Scholarship, IFT Scholar, Distinguished Fellow Award, Advanced Honor Certificate, Center of Agricultural Biotechnology Scholar, Student Ambassador to Russia and the Baltic States, member Alpha Lambda Delta, Phi Kappa Phi and Golden Key National Honor Society and Sigma Kappa. Attending Duke University for doctorate in Molecular and Cell Biology.Daughter Alicia Kesty received academic scholarship at Marymount University, Arlington, Virginia. Earned Girl Scout Silver Award in 1994, Gold Award in 1997; spent three weeks in England with Unity '94 Girl Guide host family. Recipient Jeremiah Award for outstanding work in Youth Ministry 1996/97. Participated Habitat for Humanity in Virginia 1996/West Virginia 1997.* Student, Purdue U., 1960-63. Tech. rep. E.F. Houghton & Co., Phila., 1963-67; rsch. chemist H. Miller Corp., Phila., 1968-72; owner, founder R.E. Kesty Inc., Medford, N.J., 1977—; semi-ret., 1993; cons. Air Products and Chems. Inc., Middlesex, N.J., 1973, Monsanto, St. Louis, 1994, Crown Tech. Inc., 1994—, Wuhan Chem. Industries, China, 1996—, Solutia Inc., St. Louis, 1997; tech. advisor EPA, Indpls., 1974-76. Contbr. articles to profl. jours.; patentee in field. Recipient Franklin and Marshall Alumni award Franklin & Marshall Coll., 1959; recipient Hearst Trophy William Randolph Hearst Found., 1959. Mem. Nat. Assn. of Corrosion Engrs., South Jersey C. of C. Roman Catholic. Avocations: sailing, skydiving, bird watching. Home: 1 Country Club Dr Medford NJ 08055 Office: RE Kesty Inc 125 Eayrestown Rd Medford NJ 08055-0342

KETCH, TINA, writer; b. Des Moines, June 19, 1952; d. Clifford and Dorothy (MacCaughey) Ketch; m. Michael Bennett, Sept. 18, 1990; children: Richard, Christopher, Timothy. PhD in Religious Scis., U. Strasbourg, France, 1987; grad., World Christian Ministries, Fresno, Calif., 1996, Profl. Career Devel. Inst., Atlanta, 1997. Writer Ketch Prodn., Lilburn, Ga., 1972—. Author: Candle Lighting Calendar, 1992—; Candle Lighting Encyclopedia, Vol. I, 1991, Vol. II, 1992, Candle Lighting Workbook, 1996, Candle Lighting Feng Shui, 1999.

KETCHAM, HENRY KING, cartoonist; b. Seattle, Mar. 14, 1920; s. Weaver Vinson and Virginia Emma (King) K.; m. Alice Louise Mahar, June 13, 1942 (dec.); 1 son, Dennis L.; m. Jo Anne Stevens, July 1, 1959 (div.); m. Rolande Praeprost, June 9, 1970; children: Dania King, Scott Henry. Student, U. Wash., 1938. Represented by Internat. Mgmt. Group Inc., Cleve. Animator, Walter Lantz Prodns., Universal Studios, Hollywood, Calif., 1938-39, Walt Disney Prodns., 1939-41, freelance cartoonist, 1946-51; creator: Dennis the Menace, 1950 (distributed by N.Am. Syndicate); also creator Half Hitch, 1971-75; donor Hank Ketcham Collection, Boston U. Librs.; author: Dennis the Menace cartoon book collections, 1954-84: I Wanna Go Home, 1965, Well, God, I Goofed Again, 1975, Someone's in the Kitchen With Dennis, 1978, (autobiography) The Merchant of Dennis, 1990, (anthology) His First 40 Years, 1991 (cons. to Warner Bros. on motion picture Dennis the Menace); illustrator Dennis the Menace, Prayers and Graces, 1993; author 1/2 hour animation spl. for TV: Mayday for Mother; designer: Dennis the Menace Playground, Monterey, Calif., 1956; fine arts exhbns. George Sherman Union Gallery-Boston U., 1994, Monterey Peninsula Mus. of Art, 1995, F.A.C.T. Gallery, Laguna Beach, 1996, Beach St. Gallery, San Francisco, 1997, Gibson Gallery, Carmel, Calif., 1997, Waterworks Visual Arts Ctr., Salisbury, N.C., 1998, Chapman Gallery, Carmel, 1998, Every Picture Tells a Story Gallery, L.A., 1999. Trustee Community Hosp. of Monterey Peninsula, 1986-95. Served as chief photographer specialist USNR, 1941-45; creative work Navy War Bond, Tng. Film Program 1942-45. Recipient Billy de Beck Award for outstanding cartoonist of yr., 1952, Silver T-Sq. award Nat. Cartoonist Soc., 1978; nominated Outstanding Comic Book Humor Cartoonist Yr., 1974. Mem. Nat. Cartoonists Soc., Phi Delta Theta. Clubs: Golf Club de Geneva; Old Baldy (Saratoga, Wyo.); Cypress Point Golf (Pebble Beach); Royal and Ancient Golf (St. Andrews, Scotland); Old Capital (bd. govs.) (Monterey, Calif.). Address: PO Box 800 Pebble Beach CA 93953-0800

KETCHAM, ORMAN WESTON, lawyer, former judge; b. Bklyn., Oct. 1, 1918; s. Walter Seymour and Arline May (Weston) K.; m. Anne Phelps Stokes, Dec. 22, 1947; children: Anne Weston Ketcham Felder, Helen Phelps Ketcham Ryan, Elizabeth Miner Ketcham Mercogliano, Susan Stokes Ketcham. BA, Princeton U., 1940; postgrad., Yale U., 1940-41, LLB, 1947, JD, 1971. Bar: D.C. 1948. With Covington & Burling, Washington, 1947-53; asst. gen. counsel Fgn. Ops. Adminstrn., Washington, 1953-55; trial atty. antitrust div. Justice Dept., 1955-57; judge Juvenile Ct. D.C., 1957-71, Superior Ct. D.C., 1971-77; sr. staff atty. Nat. Center State Cts., 1977-81; sr. fellow Washington Coll. Law Inst., 1981-83; adj. prof. law Georgetown U., 1963-67, U. Va., 1971-77, William and Mary Coll., 1978-80, Am. U., 1981-92; mem. U.S. Edn. Appeal Bd., 1982-90. acting chmn., 1984-85; mem. coun. of judges Nat. Coun. on Crime and Delinquency, 1959-75, bd. dirs., 1974-83; mem. U.S. del. UN Congress on Crime, Stockholm, 1965, Geneva, 1975; mem. Nat. Com. on Secondary Edn., 1970-74; chmn. adv. coun. to Select Com. on Crime, Ho. of Reps., 1969-70. Author: (with others) Justice for the Child, 1961, Changing Faces of Juvenile Justice, 1978, (with Monrad G. Paulsen) Cases and Materials Relating to Juvenile Courts, 1967. Washington rep. Fund for the Republic, 1953; mem. vis. com. Brookings Instn., 1971-76; bd. dirs. Children's Nat. Med. Ctr., 1987-90. Mem. ABA, Bar Assn. D.C., Am. Law Inst., Nat. Coun. Juvenile and Family Ct. Judges (pres. 1965-66), Internat. Assn. Youth Magistrates (v.p. 1966-74). Congregationalist. Clubs: Cosmos, Princeton (Washington), Chevy Chase. Home: 2 E Melrose St Chevy Chase MD 20815-4204

KETCHAM, RICHARD SCOTT, lawyer; b. Columbus, Ohio, Jan. 8, 1948; s. Victor Alvin and Dorothy Eloise (Becher) K.; m. Kim Michelle Halliburton, Apr. 7, 1984 (div. 1989); 1 child, Kate Erin; m. Christy M. Canaday, Sept. 9, 1990 (div. 1994). BS, Bowling Green (Ohio) State U., 1970; JD cum laude, Capital U., Columbus, 1974. Bar: Ohio 1974, U.S. Dist. Ct. (so. dist.) Ohio 1979. Asst. pros. atty. Franklin County (Ohio) Pros., Columbus, 1974-79; sr. asst. pros. atty. Franklin County (Ohio) Pros., 1979-84; ptnr. Ketcham & Ketcham, Columbus, 1984—; mem. task force Legal Aid Referral Project, Columbus Bar Assn. Homeless Project, 1989—. Mem. Gov.'s Task Force on Family Violence, 1984-86. Mem. Nat. Assn. Criminal Def. Lawyers, Ohio Assn. Criminal Def. Lawyers (bd. dirs. 1989—, v.p. CLE, sec.), Ctrl. Ohio Assn. Criminal Def. Lawyers (pres. 1994-95), Ohio State Bar Assn., Columbus Bar Assn. (chmn. criminal law com. 1994-95, 95-96), Franklin County Trial Lawyers. Avocations: fishing, basketball, model railroads. Home: 1937 Elmwood Ave Columbus OH 43212-1112 Office: Ketcham & Ketcham 50 W Broad St Ste 1416 Columbus OH 43215-5932

KETCHAM, WARREN ANDREW, psychologist, educator; b. Manistee, Mich., June 28, 1909; s. Perry Warren and Anna Ella (Ulrich) K.; m. Edna May Wearne, Nov. 23, 1962 (dec. Mar. 1991). BM, U. Mich., 1932, MA, 1947, PhD, 1951. Lic. psychologist Mich., Tex. Tchr. Reed City (Mich.) Pub. Schs., 1934-36, Melvindale (Mich.) Pub. Schs., 1936-38; supr. Dearborn (Mich.) Pub. Schs., 1938-43; sch. psychologist Ferndale (Mich.) Pub. Schs., 1950-53; prof., sch. psychologist U. Mich., Ann Arbor, 1953-77, prof. emeritus, 1978—; pvt. practice clin., indsl., orgnl. psychology Mich. and Tex., 1964—; cons. Am. Sch., Guatemala City, Guatemala, 1958-80. *In his younger days, he was a violin player, a student at Interlochen and a good friend of its founder. He is hired by businesses and individuals to assess potential employees and assesses employees for internal promotions. He does not find it unusual that at age 89 he is still practicing psychology which he has done for the past 37 years. He is excited over the change in business and industry trends over the past decades and has noticed a shift from people being managed by others to self-management. He is the recipient of the prestigious RHR International award for excellence in consultation. He continues to work with and guide beginning psychologists.* Sgt. U.S. Army, 1943-45, PTO. Fulbright scholar Leeds U., 1959, Hinsdale scholar U. Mich., 1951. Fellow Am. Psychol. Assn.; mem. Am. Soc. Clin. Hypnotists, Mich. Soc. Clin. Psychologists, Mich. Psychol. Assn., Nat. Registered Health Svc. Providers in Psychology. Home and Office: 608 E Lake Rd Harbor Springs MI 49740-1220

KETCHAND, ROBERT LEE, lawyer; b. Shreveport, La., Jan. 30, 1948; s. Woodrow Wilson and Attie Harriet (Chandler) K.; m. Alice Sue Adams, May 31, 1969; children: Peter Leland, Marjory Attie. BA, Baylor U., 1970; JD, Harvard U., 1973. Bar: Tex. 1973, Mass. 1973, D.C. 1981. Assoc., ptnr. Butler & Binion, Houston, 1976-85, Washington, 1981-82; shareholder Brodsky & Ketchand, Houston, 1985-88; ptnr. Webster & Sheffield, Houston, 1988-90; atty. pvt. practice, Houston, 1990-92; ptnr. Short & Ketchand, Houston, 1992—; founder, chmn. bd. dirs. Rolling Waters, d/b/a Houston Legal Clinic. Pres. Prisoner Svcs. Com. Houston, 1986; deacon South Houston Bapt. Ch., 1976—; gen. counsel, dir. Houston Met. Ministries, 1986-88; dir. Interfaith Ministries Greater Houston, 1996-98; gen. counsel Houston Bus. Roundtable, 1988—. Lt. USNR, 1973-76. Mem. ABA, Tex. Bar Assn., Houston Bar Assn. (chmn. dispute com. 1989-90). Avocations: reading, family. Home: 2707 Carolina Way Houston TX 77005-3423 Office: Short & Ketchand 11 E Greenway Plz Ste 1520 Houston TX 77046-1194

KETCHERSID, WAYNE LESTER, JR., medical technologist; b. Seattle, Oct. 16, 1946; s. Wayne Lester and Hazel May (Greene) K.; m. Wilette LaVerne Mautz, Oct. 6, 1972; 1 son, William Les. BS in Biology, Pacific Luth. U., 1976, BS in Med. Tech., 1978; MS in Adminstrn., Ctrl. Mich. U., 1990; postgrad. Kennedy Western U., 1996—. Cert. med. technologist; cert. clin. lab. dir. Nat. Cert. Agy. for Med. Lab. Pers. Staff technologist Tacoma Gen. Hosp., 1978-79, chemistry supr., 1979-81, head chemistry, 1981-83; head chemistry Multicare Med. Ctr., 1984-86, mgr., 1986-93, clin. lab. scientist, 1993—. Mem. Nat. Rep. Com. With U.S. Army, 1966-68. William E. Slaughter Found. scholar, 1975-76. Mem. Am. Soc. Clin. Lab. Sci. (cert., chmn. region IX adminstrn. 1984-94, nat. del. 1984—, vice chmn. govt. affairs com. 1991-92, chmn. 1992-93, vice chair, 1993-94, bd. trustees polit. action com. 1991-97, treas. 1994-97, nat. licensure coord. 1996—, sec./treas. bd. dirs. 1996—, nominee Mem. of Yr. 1992, Bd. Dirs. award 1994, Mendelson award 1994, Pres. award 1996), Wash. State Soc. Clin. Lab. Sci. (chmn. biochemistry sect. 1983-86, dist. pres. 1986—, co-chair ann. meeting 1996, cert. merit 1983, 84, 86, 88, pres. 1988-89, 89-90, mem. of the yr., 1990, chmn. govt. affairs com. 1991-92, chmn. 1992—, Pres.'s award 1996, 97), Am. Soc. Clin. Pathologists (med. technolgist), N.W. Med. lab. Symposium (chmn. 1986-88, 90, 92), Alpha Mu Tau. Lutheran. Contbr. articles to profl. jours. Office: 2906 S 274th Pl Auburn WA 98001-1803

KETCHLEDGE, KATHLEEN A., nurse; b. Reading, Pa., May 12, 1956; d. Charles C. and Arlene M. (Krommes) T. AS, Reading Area Community Coll., 1977. Staff nurse Community Gen. Hosp., Reading, Leigh Valley Hosp. Ctr., Allentown, Pa.; nurse mgr. skilled unit Laurel Nursing and Rehab. Ctr., Hamburg, Pa., medicare coord. infection control, 1995—, case mgr. coord., 1997-98; medicare unit coord. Orwigsburg (Pa.) Ctr., 1998—. Home: 712 N Warren St Apt 2 Orwigsburg PA 17961-1312

KETCHUM, DAVID STOREY, retired fundraising executive; b. Pitts., Sept. 28, 1920; s. Carlton G. and Mildred (Storey) K.; m. Sally Louise Doerschuk, Jan. 14, 1950; children: Louise Anne, Laura Jean. A.B., Cornell U., 1941. Sales rep. IBM Corp., 1941-42; with Ketchum, Inc., Pitts., 1945-82, pres., CEO, 1965-78, chmn. bd., 1978-82. Past pres. Hist. Soc. Western Pa., Children's Home Pitts.; former trustee Shadyside Presbyn. Ch., Pitcairn-Crabbe Found., Winchester-Thurston Sch., Presbyn.-Univ. Hosp., Animal Rescue League Western Pa.; past v.p. Coun. Chs. Pitts.; past pres. Am. Assn. Fund Raising Counsel; mem. coun. Cornell U.; former mem. Rep. Fin. Com. of Allegheny County. Capt. USAAF, 1942-45. Decorated Soldier's Medal, Bronze Star. Mem. Duquesne Club, Fox Chapel Racquet Club, Sigma Alpha Epsilon. Home: 131 Yorkshire Dr Pittsburgh PA 15208-2640

KETCHUM, JAMES ROE, curator; b. Rochester, N.Y., Mar. 15, 1939; s. George Roe and Mary Louise (Frantz) K.; m. Barbara M. Van Ness, Aug. 18, 1962; children: John Van Ness, Sarah Graham, Timothy Roe, Chester Arthur. A.B., Colgate U., 1960; postgrad., Georgetown U., 1960-61, George Washington U., 1961-62. Staff historian Dept. Interior, Washington, 1960-62; registrar The White House, Washington, 1962-63; curator The White House, 1963-70; curator U.S. Senate, Washington, 1970-95, curator emeritus, 1995—. Editor: The White House: An Historic Guide, 1962-70; contbr. numerous articles to profl. jours. and encys. Mem. Com. Preservation of White House, 1964-70; trustee U.S. Capitol Hist. Soc., 1971-79; alt. mem. Fed. Council Arts and Humanities, 1974-95; trustee Woodrow Wilson Birthplace Found., 1980—. Member Am. Assn. Museums, City Mus. Washington, Nat. Trust Historic Preservation, Theta Chi. Office: US Senate Commn Art US Capital Bldg Rm S-411 Washington DC 20510

KETCHUM, RICHARD MALCOLM, editor, writer; b. Pitts., Mar. 15, 1922; s. George and Thelma (Patton) K.; m. Barbara Jane Bray, Apr. 24, 1943; children: Liza Ketchum Murrow, Thomas Bray. BA, Yale U., 1943. Asst. to pres. Charles F. Orvis Co., Manchester, Vt., 1946-48; with USIA, 1951-56, chief visual materials divsn.; with Am. Heritage Pub. Co., Inc., 1956-74, editorial dir. book div., also v.p., dir., assoc. editor Am. Heritage mag.; co-founder, editor Blair & Ketchum's Country Jour., 1974-84. Author: Male Husbandry, 1956, American Heritage Book of Great Historic Places, 1957, The Battle for Bunker Hill, 1962, Faces from the Past, 1970, The Secret Life of the Forest, 1970, The Winter Soldiers, 1973, Will Rogers, The Man and His Times, 1973, The World of George Washington, 1974, Decisive Day, 1974, Second Cutting: Letters from the Country, 1981, The Borrowed Years, 1938-41; America on the Way to War, 1989, Saratoga: Turning Point of America's Revolutionary War, 1997, Wish You Were Here, 1997; editor: What is Communism?, 1955, What is Democracy?, 1955, American Heritage Book of the Revolution, 1958, American Heritage Book of the Pioneer Spirit, 1959, American Heritage Picture History of the Civil War (spl. Pulitzer prize citation 1961), 1960, The Horizon Book of the Renaissance, 1961, Four Days, 1964, The Original Water-Color Paintings by John James Audubon for the Birds of America. Lt. (j.g.) USNR, 1943-46. Fellow Soc. Am. Historians; mem. New England Forestry Found., Yale Club, Century Assn. Club (N.Y.C.). Home: Saddleback Farm 579 Kirby Hollow Rd Dorset VT 05251-9403

KETCHUM, ROBERT GLENN, photographer, print maker; b. L.A., Dec. 1, 1947; s. Jack Burson and Virginia (Moorhead) K. BA. cum laude, UCLA, 1970; MFA, Calif. Inst. Arts, 1974; MS (hon.), Brooks Inst. Photography, 1995. Founder, tchr. photography workshops Sun Valley Center for Arts and Humanities, 1971-73; tchr. photography Calif. Inst. Arts, 1975; curator photography Nat. Park Found., Washington, 1979-95; trustee L.A. Ctr. Photog. Studies, 1975-81, pres., 1979-81, v.p., 1981, 96—, bd. dirs.; bd. of councillors Am. Land Conservancy, 1993—; bd. trustees Alaska Conservation Found., 1994—, bd. dirs. Advocacy Arts Found., 1996-98, pres., 1998—; bd. dirs. Earth Comm. Office, 1997—, Internat. Photography Coun.; co-chair west coast coun. Aperture Found., 1996—. Author: The Hudson River and the Highlands; The Photographs of Robert Glenn Ketchum, 1985, The Tongass: Alaska's Vanishing Rain Forest, 1987, Overlooked in America: The Success and Failure of Federal Land Management, 1991, The Legacy of Wildness: A 25 Year Retrospective, 1994, Northwest Passage, 1996; author and contbg. photographer: American Photographers and the National Parks, 1981; project dir. and contbg. photographer Presidio Gateways, 1994, Threads of Light: Chinese Embroidery From Suzhou and the Photography of Robert Glenn Ketchum; one-man shows include Akron Art Mus., Ohio, 1985, 89, Santa Barbara Mus. Art, Calif., 1985, Chrysler Mus., Va., 1986, N.Y. Hist. Soc., 1987, The Hudson River Mus., N.Y., 1987, Pentax Forum Gallery, Tokyo, 1988, Fine Art Mus. of the South, Fla., 1990, Nat. Mus. Brazil, Rio de Janeiro, 1992, Am. House, Heidelburg, Germany, 1992, The Huntington Libr. and Art Collections, 1993, The Nat. Acad. Sci., 1994, Cleve. Mus. Art, 1996, Ga. Mus. Art, 1996-97, George Eastman House/Internat. Mus. Photography, Internat. Photography Hall of Fame Mus., 1997; group shows include Mpls. Inst. of Arts, 1978, White House, Washington, 1979, Friends of Photography, Calif., 1980, Nat. Mus. Am. Art, Washington, 1986, Internat. Photokina, Fed. Republic of Germany, 1986, San Francisco Mus. Art, 1987, Nat. Mus. Am. Art, 1991-94, Honolulu Acad. of the Arts, 1994, Stanford U. Art Mus., 1996, Amon Carter Mus., Ft. Worth, 1997, UCLA Fowler Mus., 1999. Recipient Ansel Adams award for conservation photography Sierra Club, 1989, UN award for outstanding environ. achievement, 1991, award of excellence for profl. achievement UCLA Alumni Assn., 1993, Chevron-Times Mirror Mag. Conservation award, 1994; rsch. grantee Ciba-Geigy, 1979, Nat. Park Found., 1978, 79, grantee Lila Acheson Wallace Fund, 1983, 85, 86, McIntosh Found., 1986-87, Akron Art Mus., 1987. Fellow The Explorer's Club; mem. Jonathan Club (resident artist), Phi Delta Theta. E-mail: peace2rth@aol.com. Home and Office: 696 Stone Canyon Rd Los Angeles CA 90077-2925

KETE, MARY LOUISE, English and American Literature educator; b. Mornstoun, N.J., Apr. 14, 1960; d. Louis Joseph and Joan Walsh Kete; m. John Harold Howe, June 22, 1985; 1 child, Madeline Eloise. BA in English cum laude, U. Vt., 1986; AM, Harvard U., 1990, PhD, 1994. Asst. prof. dept. English U. Vt., 1994—, asst. prof. grad. coll., 1995—; lectr. in field. Contbr. articles to profl. publs. Trustee Vt. Acad. of Arts and Scis., 1998—; mem. Champlain Sch. PTO, Burlington, Va., 1997—. Mem. MLA, Am. Studies Assn., Internat. Soc. for the Study of Narrative, Harriet Beecher Stowe Soc., Vt. Acad. of Arts and Scis., Ctr. for Rsch. on Vt., 19th Century Women Writers Reading Group, North Eastern MLA. Avocations: running, horse-back riding. Home: 164 Lyman Ave Burlington VT 05404 Office: U Vt Dept English Old Mill Bldg Burlington VA 05401

KETEFIAN, SHAKÉ, nursing educator; b. Beirut, Dec. 29, 1939; d. Krikor and Zaghganoush (Soghomonian) K. BSN, Am. U. Beirut, 1963; MEd, Columbia U., 1968, EdD, 1972. From asst. prof. nursing to prof. NYU Sch. Edn., Health, Nursing and Arts Professions, N.Y.C., 1972-84; dir. continuing edn. in nursing NYU, N.Y.C.; with U. Mich., 1984—; prof., assoc. dean for grad. studies, dir. doctoral and postdoctoral studies, dir. internat. affairs U. Mich. Sch. Nursing, Ann Arbor, acting dean, 1991-92. Contbr. articles to profl. jours. Fellow AAUW, Am. Acad. Nursing (governing coun.); mem. AAUP, ANA, Am. Ednl. Rsch. Assn., Am. Orgn. Nurse Execs., Midwest Nursing Rsch. Soc. (chair sci. integrity task force 1994-95), Midwest Alliance in Nursing (bd. dirs.), Mich. Nurses Assn. (bd. dirs. dist. 51), Assn. for Moral Edn., Sigma Theta Tau. Office: U Mich Sch of Nursing Ann Arbor MI 48109

KETNER, KENNETH LAINE, philosopher, educator; b. Mountain Home, Okla., Mar. 24, 1939; s. Louis Elaine and Johnnie Lucille (Hannah) K.; m. Berti Gabriella Zehetmeier, Aug. 24, 1964 (dec. Oct. 1996); 1 child, Kenneth Laine Jr. BA in Philosophy, Okla. State U., 1961, MA, 1967; MA in Folklore, UCLA, 1968; PhD in Philosophy, U. Calif., Santa Barbara, 1972. Part-time instr. Okla. State U., 1964-67; tchg. asst. U. Calif., Santa Barbara, 1969-70; mem. faculty Tex. Tech U., Lubbock, 1971—; prof. philosophy Tex. Tech U., 1977—, chmn. dept., 1979-81; founder, dir. Inst. Studies in Pragmaticism, 1972—, Charles Sanders Peirce prof. philosophy, 1981-88, Charles Sanders Peirce interdisciplinary prof., 1998—, Paul Whitfield Horn prof., 1999—; asst. prof. philosophy and folklore UCLA, summers, 1972, 74; co-organizer C.S. Peirce Bicentennial Internat. Congress, Amsterdam, Netherlands 1976; Peirce Sesquicentennial Internat. Congress, Harvard U., 1989. Author: A Critical Study of Stephen C. Pepper's Approach to Metaphysics, 1967, An Essay on the Nature of World Views, 1972, An Emendation of R.G. Collingwood's Doctrine of Absolute Presuppositions, 1973; editor, compiler: Charles Sanders Peirce: Contributions to the Nation, 4 parts, 1975, 78, 79, 87, Comprehensive Bibliography of Works of C.S. Peirce, 1977, rev. edit., 1986, Reasoning and the Logic of Things, 1993, A Thief of Peirce, 1995, His Glassy Essence: an Autobiography of C.S. Peirce, 1998; founder, gen. editor Peirce Studies, 1979—, Philosophical Inquiries, 1989—, more. Capt. USAR, 1962-64. Grantee NSF, Nat. Endowment Humanities, Am. Coun. Learned Socs. Fellow Charles S. Peirce Soc. (pres. 1973); mem. Am. Philos. Assn., Rotary, Freemason, Tau Kappa Epsilon. Democrat. Home: PO Box 65135 Lubbock TX 79464-5135 Office: Texas Tech Univ Library 304 A Lubbock TX 79409-0002

KETO, C. TSEHLOANE, historian; b. Matatiele, South Africa, Feb. 23, 1941; came to U.S. 1968; s. Victor Lentsoe and Catherine Naniwe (Mazibu) Tsehloane; children: Lefa Victor, Lefanyana James; m. Isoke K. Hajj-Mak, Apr. 1, 1994; children: John Anwar Bullock, Adika Hajj-Mak. BA, U. South Africa, Pretoria, 1963; MA, Am. U., Washington, 1966; PhD, Georgetown U., Washington, 1972. Instr. Lincoln U., Oxford, Pa., 1969-70, Elizabethtown (Pa.) Coll., 1970; asst. prof. U. Kans., Lawrence, 1970-73; assoc. prof. Temple U., Phila., 1973-91, prof., 1991—, dir. Inst. of African and African-Am. Affairs, 1985-92, dir. grad. program African-Am. Studies, 1990-95; pres. Keto Assocs., Inc., Blackwood, N.J., 1989—. Author: Aftermath of the Jameson Raid, 1980, American South African Relations, 1985, Africa Centered Perspective of History, 1989, revised edit., 1991, 93, Vision Identity and Time, 1994. Active Amnesty Internat. Mem. Am. Hist. Assn., African Studies Assn., African Heritage Studies Assn. (bd. dirs. 1988—), Nat. Coun. for Black Studies (bd. dirs. 1994—), So. Africa Rsch. Assn. (membership sec. 1976-80), Orgn. South Africans (publicity sec. 1987-89). Avocations: tennis, cycling, dancing, soccer, avianist. Home: PO Box 1851 Laurel Springs NJ 08021 Office: Temple U Dept African Am Studies Broad and Montgomery St Philadelphia PA 19104

KETRON, CARRIE SUE, secondary school educator; b. Clifton, Tex.; d. Randolph Allen and Mary (Waggoner) Ogden; m. N.M. Ketron, Aug. 4, 1984; children: John, Robert. B of Applied Arts and Scis., U. North Tex., 1990, MEd, 1993. Tchr. Duncanville (Tex.) High Sch., 1982--. Named Tchr. of Yr., Tex. Vocat. Tech. Assn., 1990, Outstanding Nat. Career & Tech. Tchr. of Yr., 1997. Mem. Golden Key Honor Soc., Am. Vocat. Assn., Cosmetology Instructors' of Pub. Schs. (parliamentarian 1989-90), Vocat. Indsl. Clubs Am. (advisor 1986-93), Iota Lambda Sigma Sigma (pres. 1995-96), Phi Theta Kappa, Alpha Chi. Baptist.

KETT, JOSEPH FRANCIS, historian, educator; b. N.Y.C., Mar. 11, 1938; s. Joseph Francis and Anne (Barry) K.; m. Eleanor Hess, June 26, 1965; children: Jennifer, John. BA magna cum laude, Coll. Holy Cross, 1959; MA, Harvard U., 1960, PhD, 1964. Instr. in history Harvard U., Cambridge, Mass., 1964-65; asst. prof. U. Va., Charlottesville, 1966-69, assoc. prof., 1970-76, prof., 1976—, chmn. dept. history, 1985-90. Author: The Formation of the American Medical Profession, 1780-1860: The role of Institutions, 1968, Rites of Passage: Adolescence in America, 1790—, 1977, The Pursuit of Knowledge Under Difficulties, 1994; co-author: The Enduring Vision, 1989, (with E. Donald Hirsch and James Trefil) Dictionary of Cultural Literacy, 1988, 2d edit., 1993; contbg. author: Cultural Literacy: What Every American Needs to Know (Hirsch), 1986; also articles. Fellow Charles Warren Ctr. Harvard U., 1969-70. Office: U Va Dept History Randall Hall Charlottesville VA 22903-3284*

KETTEL, EDWARD JOSEPH, oil company executive, retired; b. N.Y.C., Sept. 13, 1925; s. Harold J. and Evelyn M. (Melbourne) K.; student St. John's U., 1943; BA, St. Francis Coll., 1949; MA, Columbia U., 1953; m. Janet M. Johnson, Nov. 27, 1952; children: Dorothy A., David A. Ins. mgr. Arabian Am. Oil Co., 1950-56, Ethyl Corp., 1956-65; asst. treas. Atlantic Richfield Co., L.A., 1965-85, asst. treas., Chevron Corp., San Francisco, 1985-94; expert witness, 1994—; chmn. bd. Oil Ins., Ltd.; pres. Greater Pacific, Ltd.; dir. Am. S.S. Owners Mut. Protection and Indemnity Assn., Inc., Internat. Tanker Indemnity Assn., Ltd. With inf. AUS, 1943-46. Decorated Bronze Star, Purple Heart with oak leaf cluster. Mem. Am. Petroleum Inst., Mfrs. Chem. Assn., Nat. Fire Protection Assn., Risk and Ins. Mgmt. Soc., N.Y. Athletic Club, L.A. Athletic Club, Palos Verdes Country Club, Jonathan Club, Comml. Club, Ocean Colony Golf Club, Westhampton Beach Yacht Squadron, Ltd.

KETTELKAMP, DONALD BENJAMIN, retired surgeon and educator; b. Anamosa, Iowa, Jan. 21, 1930; s. Enoch George and Elsie (Norden) K.; m. Alice June Mencke, Dec. 30, 1954; children: Karen June, Lisa Marie, Suzanne D., Jonathan B.; m. Clemencia Oliveros Brandon, Apr. 28, 1989. B.A., Cornell U., Mt. Vernon, Iowa, 1952; M.D., U. Iowa, 1955, M.S., 1960. Diplomate: Am. Bd. Orthopaedic Surgery. Intern Thomas D. Dee Meml. Hosp., Ogden, Utah, 1955-56; resident orthopedic surgery U. Iowa, Iowa City, 1958-61; practice medicine specializing in orthopaedic surgery Anchorage, 1961-64; asst. prof. Albany (N.Y.) Med. Coll., 1964-66, assoc. prof., 1966-68; assoc. prof. U. Iowa, Iowa City, 1968-71; prof. U. Iowa, 1971; prof., chmn. dept. orthopaedic surgery U. Ark., Little Rock, 1971-74, Ind. U., Indpls., 1974-84; assoc. dean Tex. Tech. U., El Paso, 1984-87; exec. dir. Am. Bd. Orthopaedic Surgery, Chgo., 1986-94. Trustee Jour. Bone and Joint Surgery, 1991-96. Mem. ACS, Am. Acad. Orthopaedic Surgeons, Russell Hibbs Soc., Continental Orthopaedic Soc., Am. Soc. Surgery of Hand, Am. Orthopaedic Assn. (pres. 1989-90), Assn. Orthopaedic Chairmen (pres. 1981), Knee Soc.

KETTEMBOROUGH, CLIFFORD RUSSELL, computer scientist, consultant, manager; b. Pitesti, Arges, Romania, June 8, 1953; came to U.S., 1983; s. Petre and Constanta (Dascalu) I. MS in Math., U. Bucharest, Romania, 1976; MS in Computer Sci., West Coast U., L.A., 1985; MS in Mgmt. Info. System, West Coast U., Los Angeles, 1986; PhD in Computer and Info. Sci., Pacific We. U., 1988; MBA, U. LaVerne, 1992; PhD in Bus. Adminstrn., U. Santa Barbara, 1996; EdD in Computer Tech. in Edn., Nova Southeastern U., 1998. Lic. mathematician. Mathematician, programmer Nat. Dept. Chemistry, Bucharest, 1976-80; sr. programmer, analyst Nat. Dept. Metallurgy, Bucharest, 1980-82; sr. software engr. Xerox Corp., El Segundo, Calif., 1983-88; task mgr. Rockwell Internat., Canoga Park, Calif., 1989-91, cons., 1991-93; mgr. micro devel. Transam. Corp., L.A., 1993-95; MIS dir. Maxicare Health Plans, L.A., 1995-96; computer and info. scientist Jet Propulsion Lab.-NASA, Pasadena, Calif., 1988-89, project mgr., 1996—; adj., asst. prof. W. Coast U., Chapman U., U. Redlands, Nat. U., U. Phoenix, Union Inst., 1991—. Contbr. articles to profl. jours. Sec. Romanian Nat. Body Bldg. Com., Bucharest, 1980-82; pres., chmn. Bucharest Mcpl. Body Bldg. Com., 1978-82. Served to lt. Romanian Army, 1978. Mem. IEEE, Assn. for Computing Machinery. Republican. Avocations: soccer, body building, traveling. Home: 6004 N Walnut Grove Ave San Gabriel CA 91775-2530

KETTER, DAVID LEE, lawyer; b. Portsmouth, Ohio, Jan. 7, 1929; s. William Leslie and Dorothy Aileen (Weidner) K.; m. Beverly Jane Kinker, June 10, 1951; children—Michael David, Sandra Lee, Beth Ann, Richard Douglass. A.B., Ohio U., 1953; J.D., U. Cin., 1955. Bar: Ohio 1955, Pa. 1964. Trial lawyer Dept. Justice, Washington, 1955-56; trial lawyer Chief Counsel's Office, IRS, Pitts., 1956-62; assoc. Kirkpatrick, Pomeroy, Lockhart & Johnson, Pitts., 1962-65; ptnr. Kirkpatrick & Lockhart, Pitts., 1965-94, of counsel, 1995—. Served as sgt. USMC, 1946-47, 50-52. Mem. ABA (tax sect.), Pa. Bar Assn. (tax sect.), Allegheny County Bar Assn. (chmn. tax sect. 1964-66), Fed. Bar Assn., Estate Planning Coun. (bd. dirs. 1975-77), Pitts. Tax Club (pres. 1985-86), Order of Coif, Duquesne Club, Rivers Club, Valley Brook Country Club (sec. 1977-78). Republican. Methodist. Clubs: Duquesne, Rivers, Valley Brook Country (McMurray, Pa., sec. 1977-78). Avocations: golf; tennis; shooting. Home: 160 Canterbury Rd Mc Murray PA 15317-2802 Office: Kirkpatrick & Lockhart 1500 Oliver Building Pittsburgh PA 15222-2312

KETTER, JAMES PATRICK, accountant; b. St. Joseph, Mo., May 20, 1956; s. Melvin P. and Mildred (Gawatz) K.; m. Sharon E. Krautmann, Dec. 31, 1982; children: Patrick Jerome, Daniel Marcel, Benjamin Francis. BSBA in Finance & Acctg. magna cum laude, Marquette U., 1978. CPA, Mo., Kans.; accreditation in bus. valuation AICPA, 1998. Acct., audit mgr. Melvin Ketter, P.C., St. Joseph, 1976-84, tax specialist controlled foreign corps., 1979-84, mcpl. contract arbitrator, 1982-84; audit mgr. Coopers & Lybrand, Kansas City, Mo., 1985-86; mgr. accting. and auditing Mayer, Hoffman & McCann, Kansas City, Mo., 1986-89; mgr. Thomas King & Co., Kansas City, 1989-92; CEO JK Consulting Group, Prairie Village, Kans., 1992—; shareholder, ptnr. in charge of cons. and assurance Miller Haviland Ketter P.C., P.A. (formerly Douglas C. Miller & Co.), Westwood, Kans., 1994—; chapt., bd. dirs. and prog. chairperson, 1999—; Arts and Humanities Assn. of Johnson County, bd. dirs. and treasurers, 1999—; Harvesters, financial controller, The Commty. Food Network, 1997—. Mem. friends of Art, Kansas City, 1986, Friends of Symphony, Kansas City, 1986; account exec. United Way, 1985-87; specialist not-for-profit orgns., 1988—; mem. Friends of the Zoo, 1987, ad hoc com. on recycling City of Prairie Village, 1989—; bd dirs., sec. Corinth Hills Homes Assn., 1989-92; mem. strategic planning subcom. for city svcs., 1991—; cantor Curé of Ars Parish, 1989—, coord. of eucharistic mins., cub master Curé of Ars Cub Scout Pack; chair fin. mgmt. Vol. Leadership Coun. of the Ctr. for Mgmt. Assist., 1993—, cons., instr.; dir., fin. com. chmn. Children's Mercy Cancer Ctr., 1991-96, treas. 1993-96; adv. coun. St. Joseph Health Ctr., 1992—; mem. Leadership N.E. program Mission C. of C., 1997—. Mem. AICPA, Mo. Soc. CPAs (tax com. Kansas City chpt.), Kans. Soc. CPAs, Inst. Bus. Appraisers, Overland Park C. of C., Beta Gamma Sigma, Alpha Sigma Nu. Roman Catholic. Lodge KC. Avocations: classical literature, singing music, golf, tennis, racquetball, bicycling. Home: 5400 W 80th Shawnee Mission KS 66208 Office: 1901 W 47th Pl Ste 204 Westwood KS 66205-1834

KETTER, RONALD GEORGE, political science educator, consultant; b. Topeka, June 3, 1959; s. Elmer R. and Mary Lou (McDaniel) K. BS, Emporia (Kans.) State U., 1981; MPA, U. Tex., 1986; PhD in Polit. Sci., SUNY, Binghamton, 1996. Program evaluator GAO, Washington, 1983-86; budget and legis. analyst U.S. Exec. Office of Pres., Washington, 1987-91; asst. prof. U. Tex., El Paso, 1995-97, sr. rsch. assoc. Pub. Policy Rsch. Ctr., 1997—; lectr. U. Tex., Dallas, 1997—; cons., Grapevine, Tex., 1997—. Bd. dirs. Corning (N.Y.) Youth Ctr., 1992-93; mem. Paso del Norte Air Quality Task Force, El Paso, 1995—. Recipient Exceptional Achievement award U.S. Office Mgmt. and Budget, Washington, 1989. Mem. Am. Polit. Sci. Assn., Am. Soc. Pub. Adminstrs., Assn. Pub. Policy and Mgmt. Home: 3424 Lakeridge Dr Grapevine TX 76051-4623

KETTER, WILLIAM B., journalist, educator; b. East Grand Forks, Minn., Feb. 25, 1940; s. Joseph Stephen and Rose Mary Ketter; m. Phyllis Jane Simmons, Feb. 24, 1961; children: Catherine, Deborah, Jennifer. PhB, U. N.D., 1962. Reporter Grand Forks (N.D.) Herald, 1960-62; reporter, editor, exec. v.p. UPI, N.Y.C., 1962-78; editor, v.p. The Patriot Ledger, Quincy, Mass., 1978-98; editor op-ed section Boston Globe, 1998-99; prof. journalism, chmn. dept. Boston U., 1999—; co-chmn. media com. Mass. Supreme Jud. Ct., 1995-99. Recipient outstanding leadership award Mass. Brain Injury Assn., 1996, outstanding svc. award Mass. Supreme Jud Ct., 1998. Fellow New Eng. Acad. Journalists (chmn. 1993—, Yankee Quill award 1986, high honor 1994); mem. Am. Soc. Newspaper Editors (pres. 1995-96, Outstanding Svc. award 1996). Roman Catholic. Avocations: sailing, tennis, reading, skiing. E-mail: wbketter@bu.edu. Home: 35 Curtis St Scituate MA 02066 Office: Boston U Dept Journalism 640 Commonwealth Ave Boston MA 02215

KETTERER, ANDREW, state attorney general; b. Trenton, N.J., Jan. 17, 1949; s. Frederic and Loretta (Mehan) K.; m. Susanne Powell, 1978; 1 child, Andrew Powell. BA magna cum laude, Conn. Coll., 1971; JD, Northeastern U., 1974. Former mem. Maine Ho. of Reps.; atty. gen. State of Maine, 1995—. Chmn. Madison Dem. Town Com., Maine, 1980—; del. Somerset County Dem. Com., 1980—, Dem. State Conv., 1980-82; dir., vice chmn. Norridgewock Indsl. Com., 1982; dir. Ctrl. Maine Airport Authority, 1982—; sec., treas. Youth & Family Svcs., Skowhegan, Maine, 1980. Mem. ABA, ATLA, Maine Bar Assn., Somerset County Bar Assn., Norridgecock C. of C. (pres. 1982-83), Elks. Home: 10 Laney Rd Skowhegan ME 04976-9400 Office: Office of Atty General 6 State House Sta Augusta ME 04333-0006

KETTINGER, DAVID JOHN, broadcast executive; b. Abington, Pa., Feb. 21, 1954; s. Ralph Joseph and Mary Elizabeth (Reilly) K. Student, Villanova U., 1973-75. Disc jockey Radio Sta. WBUX, Doylestown, Pa., 1975-77; disc jockey, rschr. Radio Sta. WPST, Trenton, N.J., 1977-80; disc jockey, pub. rels. dir. Radio Sta. WKHI-FM, Ocean City, Md., 1980-81, ops. dir., program dir., 1981-82; advt. cons. sales dept., producer Agy. Voice Overs, Ocean City, 1983-89, asst. sales mgr., 1989-90; sales mgr. Stas. WWTR and WETT, Ocean City, 1990-91; sales mgr., disk jockey Radio Stas. WWTR and WETT, Ocean City, 1991-94; disc jockey Radio Sta. WQHQ-FM, Salisbury, Md., 1990-91; part-time air announcer, comml. producer, copywriter United Artist Cable TV of Ea. Shore, 1991-92; sta. mgr., with sales dept. Radio Sta. WLVW-FM and WLBW-FM, Salisbury, Md., 1994—. Vol. fireman Weldon Fire Co. (mem. fire prevention and publicity coms.), 1972-81; active Muscular Dystrophy Assn., Ocean City Power Squadron. Republican. Roman Catholic. Avocations: boating, sketching, autograph collecting, impersonations, golf. Home: 788 Ocean Pkwy Ocean Pines MD 21811-1726 Office: Stas WLVW and WLBW-FM PO Box U Salisbury MD 21802-1197

KETTLE, SALLY ANNE, consulting company executive, educator; b. Omaha, Feb. 2, 1938; d. Elaine Josephine (Winston) Smiley; m. William Frederick Kettle, July 20, 1968 (div. 1973); children: Christopher, Winston. BEd, U. Nebr., 1960, postgrad. Cert. tchr., S.C., Nebr. Tchr. Omaha Pub. Schs., Omaha, 1966-72; owner, mgr. The Rick Rack, Ltd., Lakewood, Colo., 1974-75; coord. merchandising communications 3M, St. Paul, 1978-80, sr. coord. internat. corp. comm., 1981-83; corp. dir. communications Intran Corp., St. Paul, 1984; pres. Sally Kettle & Co., Bloomington, Minn., 1985—; mem. cmty. faculty Met. State U., Mpls., 1983-90, 97—, St. Olaf Coll., Northfield, Minn., 1992-94; mem. adj. faculty U. Minn. Sch. Journalism and Mass Comm., Mpls., St. Thomas U., 1994-95, Northwestern Coll., 1998—. TV hostess City of Bloomington Cable TV, 1984-86. Co-founder Women's Resource Ctr., bd. dirs., mem. adv. bd., 1978-88; chair 13th Precinct, Bloomington, 1978-83; bd. dirs. 41st Sen. Dist., Bloomington, 1982-83; cable TV commr. Bloomington City Coun., 1984-85; pub. rels. com. U.S. Olympic Festival, 1989-90; bd. dirs. Minn. Prayer Breakfast Bd., 1984—; mem. Better Bus. Bur.; founder Ad Rev. Coun.; v.p. Christian Mgmt. Assn., Minn.; internat. com. bd. Carlson Grad. Sch. Mgmt., U. Minn.; mem. state ctrl. com. and platform commn. DFL, 1988-90; bd. dirs. Fellowship of Christian Athletes, 1988-89; pub. rels. com. '96 Billy Graham Minn. Crusade, 1996; bd. commrs. Shoreland Zoning Commn. Dakota County, Minn., 1996—. Named one of Outstanding Young Women of Am., 1965. Mem. Am. Advt. Fedn. (conf. com. 1985-87, pub. svc. com. 1986-88), Pub. Rels. Soc. Am., Advt. Fedn. Minn. (bd. dirs. 1982-86); Women's Econ. Roundtable, Internat. Platform Assn., Nat. Grad. Women's Honor Soc., Minn. Press Club (co-chair newsmaker com., bd. dirs. 1989-92), Phi Delta Gamma, Kappa Alpha Theta. Avocations: reading, sewing, entertaining, volunteering. Home: 13390 Gunflint Path Apple Valley MN 55124-7376

KETTLER, CARL FREDERICK, airline executive; b. N.Y.C., Dec. 19, 1936; s. William Henry and Martha Maria (Allmendinger) K.; m. Marianne Louis Slagboom, Dec. 19, 1970; 1 child, Patricia Heidi. BS in Aeronautics, St. Louis U., 1965; MBA, U. Calif., Berkeley, 1966. Project mgr. corp. planning Trans World Airlines, 1968-69; dir. internat. market planning Flying Tiger Ln., 1969-71; spl. asst. to U.S. Senator Henry Bellmon, 1971-74; dir. fed. affairs Air Transport Assn. Am., Washington, 1974-78; co-organizer Midway Airlines, Inc., 1974-79; asst. to pres. Airbus Industries No.Am., N.Y.C., 1978-80; vice chmn. bd. govs. Flight Safety Found., 1979-81; prtnr. Sunburst Energy Inc., Enid, Okla., 1980-82; co-founder, exec. v.p., COO Trans-Cen. Airlines, Oklahoma City, 1980—; founder T.H.E. Airline Inc., 1981; chmn., pres. Kettler Korp, Inc., 1981—; founder Kettler Komputer Svcs. Inc., 1987—, Kettler Employee Leasing Inc., 1981—; co-founder Kettler & Kettler Employment Svcs., Inc., Flemington, N.J., 1981; founder, pres. Kettler Airline Planning Svcs., Inc.; advisor to Reagan White House on Nat. Security, 1980-84; lectr. St. Louis U., 1968—; cons. aviation and internat. trade. Founder, pres. Oak Summit Sch. Hist. Soc., Citizens Against Ruining the Environ (CARE), 1985—; del. Rep. Nat. Conv., 1992. With USAF, 1955-60. Recipient Outstanding Svc. award Smithsonian Astrophys. Obs., 1959, Alumni Merit award St. Louis U., 1991. Mem. Nat. Def. Transp. Assn., Am. Inst. Aeronautics and Astronautics (air transport tech. com.), Okla. Heritage Assn., Okla. State Soc., Internat. House (Berkeley), Calif. Alumni Assn., U. Calif. at Berkeley, Ducks Unltd., Grand Nat. Quail Club (exec. com.), Capitol Hill Club, Nat. Aviation Club, Internat. Aviation Club, Wings Club, Aero Club, Alpha Eta Rho, Alpha Sigma Chi, Alpha Sigma Nu (Nat. Jesuit Scholastic Honors award, 1965), Gamma Phi Epsilon. Roman Catholic. Avocation: politics, piloting, boating, travel, writing. Home: 59 Everitts Hill Rd Flemington NJ 08822-4005

KETTLING, VIRGINIA, health facility administrator; b. Toldeo, Aug. 9, 1932; d. Charles Albert and Elizabeth (Knapp) Reuthe; m. George Kettling, June 16, 1962; children: Elys, Kandys, Gynevra, Geoff. BSN, Capital U., 1955; MA, Ohio State U., 1962. Asst. prof., dir. baccalaureate program U. Cin., 1965-71; asst. v.p., nursing dir. Bethesda Hosp. Sch. Nursing, Cin., 1971-77; clin. asst. prof. U. Wis., Milw., 1981-88; chief nurse exec. Mt. Sinai Med. Ctr., Milw., 1977-88; v.p. patient care United Samaritans Med. Ctr., Danville, Ill., 1988-97; cert. parish nurse Bethel Luth. Ch., Danville, 1997—; cons. D.A.C.C. assoc. degree program, 1998—; interim pres. Lakeview Coll. of Nursing, Danville, Ill. Named nominee Wisc. Nurse Exec. Yr. Mem. Am. Orgn. Nurse Execs., Ill. Orgn. Nurse Execs., Am. Hosp. Pub. (reviewer of books), Am. Coll. Healthcare Execs., Midwest Alliance Nursing, Exec. Club Danville. Home: 3304 Suncrest Dr Danville IL 61832-1332

KETY, SEYMOUR S(OLOMON), physiologist, neuroscientist; b. Phila., Aug. 25, 1915; s. Louis and Ethel (Snyderman) K.; m. Josephine R. Gross, June 18, 1940; children: Lawrence Philip, Roberta Frances. AB, U. Pa., 1936, MD, 1940, ScD (hon.), 1965; ScD (hon.), Loyola U., 1969, U. Ill., 1981, Mt. Sinai U., 1982, Med. Coll. Pa., 1985, Georgetown U., 1987, Washington U., 1989; MD (hon.), U. Copenhagen, 1979; ScD (hon.), U. Mich., 1991. Intern Phila. Gen. Hosp., 1940-42; NRC fellow Harvard U., 1942-43; instr. to asst. prof. pharmacology Sch. Medicine U. Pa., 1943-48; prof. clin. physiology Grad. Sch. Medicine, 1948-51; scientific dir. Nat. Insts. Mental Health and Neurol. Diseases and Blindness, 1951-56; chief Lab. Clin. Sci. NIMH, 1956-67; dir. psychiatric rsch. Mass. Gen. Hosp., 1967-77; dir. psychiatric rsch. McLean Hosp., Mass., 1977-83, psychobiologist, 1977-97, hon., 1997—; sr. scientist NIMH, 1983-96, emeritus, 1996—; Henry Phipps prof., dir. dept. psychiatry Sch. Medicine Johns Hopkins U., 1961-62; prof. psychiatry Med. Sch. Harvard U., 1967-80, prof. neurosci. Med. Sch., 1980-83, prof. emeritus neurosci. Med. Sch., 1983—; Thomas Dent Mütter lectr., Leonard Kimmelman Lecture, 1951, Eastman lectr., 1957, William Harvey Tercentenary lectr., 1957, NIH lectr., 1960, Thomas William Salmon lectr., 1961, Alvarenga Prize lectr., 1961, Acad. lectr. Am. Psychiat. Assn., 1961, Saul Korey lectr., 1964, James Arthur lectr., 1966, 3d Mental Health Research Fund lectr., London, 1965, Heinrich Waelsch lectr., 1969, Benjamin Musser lectr., 1970, Edward Mapother lectr., London, 1974, George Bishop lectr., 1975, Harvey lectr. Rockefeller U., 1975, Grass Found. lectr., 1975, Henry Maudsley lectr., London, 1978, Edward Sachar lectr., 1985; vis. prof. Coll. de France, 1966-67; fellow Ctr. Adv. Study in Behavioral Sci., 1978-79, hon. prof. Shantou U., China, 1995—. Editor-in-chief Jour. Psychiat. Research, 1959-83, founding editor, 1983—; hon. editor Jour. Cerebral Circulation and Metabolism, 1980—; contbr. sci. articles to profl. publs. Organizing com. Internat. Neurochem. Symposia, 1952-60; sci. advisory com. Mass. Gen. Hosp., 1956-60; bd. dir. Found. Fund Rsch. in Psychiatry, 1962-65; assoc. Neurosics. Rsch. Found., 1962-83; trustee Rockefeller U., 1976-85; mem. vis. com. for biology Calif. Inst. Tech., 1972-76; mem. vis. com. for psychology MIT, 1973-76; mem. overview cluster Pres.'s Biomed. Rsch. Panel, 1975-76; chmn. biosci. adv. com. NASA, 1959-60; mem. Pres.'s Panel on Mental Retardation, 1961-62. Recipient Theobald Smith award AAAS, 1948, Max Weinstein award, 1954, Disting. Svc. award HEW, 1958, Stanley Dean award, 1962, McAlpin award Nat. Assn. for Mental Health, 1972, William C. Menninger award ACP, 1976, Fromm-Reichman award, 1978, Founds. Fund Rsch. award, 1979, Passano award, 1980, Loretta Bender award, 1980, Thomas W. Salmon medal, 1982, Emil Kraepelin medal, 1984, Mihara Fund award, 1984, Disting. Alumnus award U. Pa., 1985, Ralph Gerard award, 1986, Georg Charles de Hevesy Nuclear Medicine Pioneer award, 1988, Schizophrenia Rsch. award Internat. Congress Rsch. Schizophrenia, 1989, Disting. Scientist award Nat. Assn. Rsch. Schizophrenia and Affective Disorders, 1992, Sarnat Internat. prize 1993, Lifetime Achievement award Internat. Soc. Psychiat. Genetics, 1993, Soc. Biol. Psychiatry, 1996. Disting. fellow Am. Psychiat Assn. (Disting. Svc. award 1980), Royal Coll. Psychiatrists London (hon.); fellow Am. Neurological Assn. (hon.); mem. Nat. Acad. Scis. (Kovalenko award 1973, Neurosci. award 1988), Am. Philos. Soc. (Lashley award 1992), Assn. Rsch. Nervous Mental Disease (trustee, pres. 1965, 80, Rsch. Achievement award 1980), Am. Psychopath. Assn. (pres. 1965, Paul Hoch award 1973), Soc. for Psychiat. Rsch., Am. Soc. Clin. Investigation, Am. Soc. Pharmacology and Exptl. Therapeutics, Internat. Soc. Cerebral Bld. Flow and Metabolism (hon. pres. 1980—), Soc. for Neurosci. (Grass. Found. award 1975, Ralph Gerard award 1986), Phi Beta Kappa, Sigma Xi, Alpha Omega Alpha. Achievements include devel. of techniques for measurement of total and regional human cerebral blood flow, the theoretical basis for measurement and visualization of functional activity throughout the human brain; demonstration of importance of genetic factors in the etiology of schezophrenia; first quantitative study of blood flow and oxygen consumption by the human brain. Fax: 781-320-0502. E-mail: skety@wjh.harvard.edu. Address: 10 Longwood Dr Apt 252 Westwood MA 02090-1140 also: Mailman Rsch Ctr McLean Hosp Belmont MA 02178

KEULER, ROLAND LEO, retired shoe company executive; b. Kiel, Wis., Aug. 28, 1933; s. Joseph N. and Christina (Woelfel) K.; m. Shirley Ann Johst, June 22, 1957; children: Suzanne Marie, Catherine Ann, David Richard, Carolyn Marie, Brian John and Barbara Jean (twins). BS in Acctg., Marquette U., 1959. CPA, Wis. Acct. Arthur Andersen & Co., Milw., 1959-65; sec.-treas. Napco Graphic Arts, Inc., Milw., 1965-70; contr. Weyenberg Shoe Mfg. Co. (name changed to Weyco Group, Inc.), Milw., 1970-72, treas., 1972-93, sec., 1986-93, v.p., 1993-94; cons. Project Bus., Milw., 1977-84. With U.S. Army, 1954-56. Mem. Beta Gamma Sigma, Beta Alpha Psi. Roman Catholic. Avocations: photography, woodworking, choir. Home: 720 W Fairfield Ct Milwaukee WI 53217-4133

KEUNE, RUSSELL VICTOR, architect, architectural association executive; b. Chgo., 1938; m. Ingrid Christina Friberg, 1968; 1 child, Eric Richard. BArch, U. Ill., Urbana, 1961, MArch, 1965. Registered arch., Va. Restoration arch. Nat. Park Svc., U.S. Dept. Interior, Washington, 1961-63, from staff arch. of Hist. Am. Bldgs. Survey to asst. keeper of Nat. Register Hist. Places, 1965-68; rsch. and tchg. asst. U. Ill., Urbana, 1963-65; from dir. dept. field svcs. to sr. v.p. preservation programs Nat. Trust for Hist. Preservation, Washington, 1969-83; pvt. practice, 1983-84; sr. project mgr. Geler Brown Renfrow Archs., Washington, 1984-86; v.p. for programs U.S. Com., Internat. Coun. on Monuments and Sites, Washington, 1986-93; dir. internat. rels. AIA, Washington, 1993—; mem. U.S. delegation 7th Gen. Assembly Internat. Ctr. for Study of Preservation and Restoration of Cultural Property, Rome, 1973, UNESCO Conv. Conf. on Preservation of Hist. Quars., Towns and Sites, Warsaw, Poland, 1975; mem. U.S. exch. delegation Preservation Hist. and Cultural Property, USSR, 1974; mem. task force on tourism and preservation Pacific Area Travel Assn., Macau and The Philippines, 1980, mem. task force on preservation of Chinatown, Singapore, 1985; acad. specialist on hist. preservation to Yemen Arab Republic USIA, 1989; guest lectr., spkr. numerous colls., univs., pub. agys., profl. and preservation orgns. Fellow AIA (mem. hist. resources com. 1968—, chmn. 1988-89), Internat. Coun. Monuments and Sites (bd. dirs. 1977-80, 83-86); mem. Assn. Preservation Tech. (v.p. 1974-77), Ea. Park and Monument Assn., Hist. Am. Bldgs. Survey Found. (vice chmn. 1983-93), Hist. Preservation Roundtable, Cosmos Club. Office: AIA 1735 New York Ave NW Washington DC 20006-5292

KEUSCH, CRISTINA FREXES, plastic surgeon; b. Havana, Cuba, June 7, 1958; m. BS in Biology-Chemistry summa cum laude, U. Miami, 1979; MD, Johns Hopkins U., 1983. Diplomate Am. Bd. Plastic Surgery, Am. Bd. Surgery; lic. Fla., Mass., N.Y. Resident in gen. surgery Mt. Sinai Hosp., N.Y.C., 1983-87, chief resident gen. surgery, 1987-88; resident in plastic surgery Harvard Hosp., Brigham Hosp., Children's Hosp., Boston, U., 1988-90; clin. fellow in surgery Med. Sch. Harvard U., Cambridge, Mass., 1988-90; affil. West Boca Med. Ctr., Delray Cmty. Hosp., Boca Raton (Fla.) Cmty. Hosp., Pinecrest Rehab Hosp., Boca Raton Outpatient Surgery and Laser Ctr.; presenter in field. Contbr. numerous articles to profl. jours. Fellow Am. Coll. Surgeons; mem. Am. Soc. Aesthetic Plastic Surgery, Inc., Am. Soc. Plastic and Reconstructive Surgery, Am. Soc. Laser Medicine and Surgery, Inc., Am. Cancer Soc. (mem. breast cancer task force 1992), Fla. Soc. Plastic and Reconstructive Surgery, Fla. Med. Assn., Palm Beach Soc. Plastic and Reconstructive Surgery, Southeastern Soc. Plastic and Reconstructive Surgery, Assn. Women Surgeons, Palm Beach Med. Soc., Y-Me of Fla. (physician mem. 1990), Phi Kappa Phi. Office: 950 Glades Rd Ste 3A Boca Raton FL 33431-6401

KEVAN, LARRY, chemistry educator; b. Kansas City, Mo., Dec. 12, 1938; s. Glenn Herman and Myrtle Helena (Johnson) K. BS, U. Kans., 1960; PhD, UCLA, 1963. Research assoc. U. Newcastle, England, 1963; instr. U. Chgo., 1963-65; asst. prof. chemistry U. Kans., Lawrence, 1965-67, assoc. prof., 1967-69; prof. Wayne State U., Detroit, 1969-80; Cullen prof. U. Houston, 1980—; vis. prof. U. Utah, 1971, Nagoya U., Japan, 1976, U. of Paris, 1977, Armed Forces U., Munich, 1979, Hokkaido U., Japan, 1987, U. Florence, Italy, 1987, 90; chmn. Gordon Conf. Radiation Chemistry, 1975; mem. chemistry rev. com. Brookhaven Nat. Lab., 1974-78, chmn., 1978, chemistry rev. com. Argonne Nat. Lab., 1980-86, chmn., 1982; rev. com. Nôtre Dame Radiation Lab., 1993, 94, NIH Spl. Study sects., 1982—; users com. mem. Nat. High Field Magnet Lab., 1997—. Author: Electron Spin Double Resonance Spectroscopy, 1976, Time Domain Electron Spin Resonance, 1979, Advances in Pulsed and Continuous Wave Electron Spin Resonance, 1990; also over 700 articles; editor: Radical Ions, 1968, Electron-Solvent and Anion-Solvent Interactions, 1976; mem. editl. bd. Jour. Chem. Physics, Jour. Phys. Chemistry, Radiation Physics and Chemistry, Concepts in Magnetic Resonance, Jour. Chem. Soc.-Faraday Trans., Applied Magnetic Resonance, Nucleonika, Magnetic Resonance Reviews. Guggenheim fellow, 1970-71; recipient Faculty Rsch. award Wayne State U., 1978, Rsch. award Polish Soc. Radiation Rsch., Warsaw, 1979, Rsch. award Golden Key Nat. Honor Soc., 1986, Rsch. Excellence award U. Houston, 1987, Rsch. award Sigma Xi, 1989, Marie Curie medal, 1995. Fellow AAAS, Am. Phys. Soc., Royal Soc. Chemistry (London); mem. Am. Chem. Soc. (S.E. Tex. award 1986), S.W. Catalysis Soc. (chmn. 1986-88), Internat. Zeolite Assn., Internat. ESR Soc., Internat. Soc. Magnetic Resonance. Avocations: sailboat racing, skiing, tennis, wine tasting. E-mail: Kevan@UH.EDU. Office: Univ of Houston Dept Chemistry Houston TX 77204

KEVIS, DAVID ERNEST, author; b. Phila., Sept. 10, 1942; guardian David and Eleanor Theresa (Oppermann) K. Student, Wesleyan U., Middletown, Conn., 1960-64, U. Pa., 1967-69. Cert. secondary English tchr., N.J. Author: Regards Our Customs, 1985, Constitution Storehouse, 1986, 3d edit., 1997, Letters and American Literacy, 1988, 2d edit., 1997, Advertising Advisories of Reliable Goodness, 1990, 2d edit., 1997; editor: Lifecycle Hymnbook, Christmas Caroling, 1997. Mem. Alpha Delta Phi. Avocation: church music. Home: PO Box 5 Bridgeport PA 19405-0005

KEVLES, DANIEL JEROME, history educator, writer; b. Phila., Mar. 2, 1939; s. David and Anne (Rothstein) K.; m. Bettyann Holtzmann, May 18, 1961; children: Beth Carolyn, Jonathan David. BA in Physics, Princeton U., 1960; postgrad., Oxford U., 1960-61; PhD in History, Princeton U., 1964. From asst. to prof. history Calif. Inst. Tech., Pasadena, 1964-86, Koepfli prof. humanities, 1986—, head program in sci., ethics, and pub. policy, 1987—; vis. rsch. fellow U. Sussex, Brighton, Eng., 1976; vis. prof. U. Pa., Phila., 1979, Princeton U., 1999; dir. studies Ecole des Hautes Etudes en Sciences Sociales, Paris, 1991; chmn. faculty, Calif. Inst. Tech., Pasadena, 1995-97. Author: The Physicists, 1978 (Nat. Hist. Soc. prize 1979), In the Name of Eugenics, 1985; (mag. series) Annals of Eugenics (Page One award 1985), The Baltimore Case, 1998; co-editor: The Code of Codes, 1992; contbr. articles to The New Yorker, N.Y. Rev. Books, other mags. Charles Warren fellow Harvard U., 1981-82, Ctr. for Advanced Study Behavioral Scis. fellow, 1986-87, Nat. Endowment for Humanities sr. fellow, 1981-82, Guggenheim fellow, 1983. Fellow AAAS (chmn. sect. L 1983-85), Soc. Am. Historians; mem. PEN, Author's Guild, Am. Acad. Arts and Scis., Orgn. Am. Historians, Am. Hist. Assn., History Sci. Soc. (coun 1980-82, com. publ. 1984-88, Sarton lectr. 1985), Am. Philos. Soc., Princeton Club (N.Y.C.), Century Assn., Phi Beta Kappa. Democrat. Office: Calif Inst Tech 1200 E California Blvd Pasadena CA 91106

KEVORKIAN, RICHARD, artist; b. Dearborn, Mich., Aug. 24, 1937; s. Kay and Stana (Bedeian) K.; m. Salpy Bouroujian; children: Anna, Raffi, Soseh and Ellina (twins), Serar. BFA, Richmond Profl. Inst., 1961; MFA in Painting, Calif. Coll. Arts and Crafts, 1962. Instr. drawing and painting Richard Bland Coll., Petersburg, Va., 1961-64; instr. dept. fine arts Va. Commonwealth U., Richmond, 1962-66, asst. prof. dept. painting and printmaking, 1967-69, assoc. prof., 1969-77, prof., 1967-93, prof. emeritus, 1993, chmn. dept., 1969-81. One-man exhbns. include Aaron Gallery, Washington, Marita Gilliam Gallery, Raleigh, N.C.; exhbns. include Birmingham Mus. Art, Ala., 1977, Greenville County Mus. Art, S.C., 1977, Southeastern Ctr. Contemporary Art, Winston-Salem, N.C., 1977, 78, Hunter Mus. Art, Chattanooga, 1978, Va. Mus. Fine Art, 1983, U. Tenn., Knoxville, 1983. Mem. selection bd. for visual arts Va. Ctr. for Creative Arts, Sweet Briar. Served with N.G., 1955-63. NEA individual sr. artists grantee, 1972, Va. Commonwealth U. Sch. Arts faculty creative research grantee, 1974, Nat. Endowment for Arts, Southeastern Ctr. Contemporary Arts grantee, 1976; Guggenheim fellow, 1978. Home: 7909 Rock Creek Rd Richmond VA 23229-6643

KEWALRAMANI, LAXMAN SUNDERDAS, surgeon, consultant; b. Jaipur, India, Mar. 10, 1943; came to U.S., 1970, U.S. citizen; s. Sunderdas K. and Sugnidevi Kewalramani; m. Dropadi Chellani, May 29, 1970; children: Anupama, Mukul. MB, BS, U. Rajasthn, Jaipur, 1965, M of Surgery, 1969. Diplomate Am. Bd. Phys. Medicine & Rehab., Am. Bd. Electrodiagnostic Medicine (fellow), Am. Acad. Pain Mgmt. (fellow). Fellow neurol. surgery U. Calif. Davis-Sacramento Med. Ctr., 1970-71, resident in phys. medicine and rehab., 1971-73; asst. prof. dept. phys. medicine and rehab. U. Calif., Davis, 1973-76; asst. prof. depts. phys. medicine and rehab. Baylor Coll. Medicine, Houston, 1976-79; assoc. prof. sect. rheumatology and rehab. dept. medicine sch. medicine La. State U., New Orleans, 1979-82; dir. rehab. rsch., coord. patient care La. Rehab. Inst. and Charity Hosp., New Orleans, 1979-82; pvt. practice in phys. medicine and rehab., orthopedic medicine, electrodiagnostic medicine and thermography, 1982—; med. dir. Health South Rehab. Ctr., Harahan, La., 1989-91; med. dir. rehab. unit Chalmette (La.) Med. Ctrs., 1991-92; med. dir. spine and orthopedic inst. Elmwood Med. Ctr., Jefferson, La., 1993-95; cons. rehab. medicine svc. crippled children svcs. sect. VA Hosp., 1975-76; mem. quality assurance com. Charity Hosp. and La. Rehab. Inst., New Orleans, 1979-82; presenter in field. Reviewer manuscripts, cons. editorial bd. Archives Phys. Medicine and Rehab., 1977-80; contbr. 2 chpts. to books and 96 articles to profl. jours. Cons. Cluster Living and Shared Providers, 1978; trustee New Orleans Pharmacy Mus., 1993—. Fellow Am. Acad. Phys. Medicine and Rehab. (mem. assessment diagnostic and therapeutic modalities and devices, subcom. med. practice 1985-86); mem. Am. Spinal Injury Assn., Am. Assn. Physicians India (mem. ethics and grievance com. 1992—), Am. Assn. Electrodiagnostic Medicine, Am. Assn. Electromyography and Electrodiagnosis (mem., liaison rep. to profl. stds. com. 1984—), La. State Med. Soc., La. Phys. Medicine and Rehab. Soc., Orleans Parish Med. Soc., Internat. Med. Soc. Paraplegia. Republican. Hindu. Avocations: reading, music, collecting time pieces and writing instruments. Home: 38 English Turn Ln New Orleans LA 70131 Office: 3301 St Charles Ave New Orleans LA 70115-0007

KEWIN, CYNTHIA MCLENDON, secondary education educator; b. Lexington, Ky., Aug. 25, 1957; d. William Watts and Olive Mershon (Johnson) McLendon; m. Kevin Jon Kewin, Apr. 5, 1986. BS in Speech and Drama, Asbury Coll., 1979; MEd, Georgetown U., 1987, postgrad., 1988; BA in English, U. Ky., 1989. Cert. tchr. grades 7-12. Substitute tchr. Lexington, 1979-82; tchr. Educare, Lexington, 1979—; sales and mktg. rep. Campbell House, Lexington, 1979—; word processing specialist A.B. Dick, Lexington, 1979-80; spl. agt. Am. Family Security, Lexington, 1980-81; fin. cons. Mass. Mut. Ins., Lexington, 1981-83; tchr. Fayette County Pub. Schs., Lexington, 1983—; mem. Leadership Edn., Lexington, 1996—. Bd. dirs. Tend My Sheep Ministries, Lexington; drama and choir mem. Centenary United Meth. Ch., Lexington; assoc. mem. Firefighters Assn., Lexington. Mem. NEA, Ky. Edn. Assn., Fayette County Edn. Assn., Nat. Coun. Tchrs. English, Ky. Coun. Tchrs. English, Ednl. Theater Assn. Democrat. Avocations: theater, music, sewing, landscaping, gardening. Home: 3208 Breckenwood Dr Lexington KY 40502-2912 Office: Lafayette HS 400 Reed Ln Lexington KY 40503-1200

KEWLEY, SHARON LYNN, systems analyst, consultant; b. Geneseo, Ill., Sept. 23, 1958; d. James Leslie and Geraldine (Myers) K. BBA with honors, U. Miami (Fla.), 1988. Gen. agent Varvaris & Assocs., Cedar Rapids, Iowa, 1981-84; programmer, analyst U. Miami, Coral Gables, Fla., 1984-88; systems analyst Metro Dade County, Miami, 1988-91, Nat. Coun. on Compensation Ins., Boca Raton, Fla., 1991-93; owner Boca Byte, Boca Raton, Fla., 1993—. Mem. NAFE, Kendall Jaycees, Nat. Gold Key Honor Soc., PADI Divemaster. Republican. Lutheran. Avocation: cruising, world travel, scuba diving. Office: Boca Byte PO Box 7072 Boca Raton FL 33431-0072

KEY, DANA LYNN, English education and biology educator; b. Guntersville, Ala., June 17, 1951; d. Robert L. and Verde Ray (Sparks) Porch; m.

Tom R. Key, M.D., March 23, 1977; children: Erin Michelle, Meagan Elizabeth. BS in Edn. Biology and English, Jacksonville State U., Ala., 1986, MS in Edn. Biology and English, 1990; EdS, U. Ala., 1995, EdD, 1998. Cert. secondary biology and English lang. arts tchr., Ala. Nurse Tom R. Key M.D., Gadsden, Ala.; tchr. Etowah Co. Bd. of Edn., Boaz, Ala. Ala. Sec. Em. Edn. scholar. Mem. Ala. Edn. Assn., Nat. Edn. Assn., Nat. Coun. Tchrs. English, Mid-south Rsch. Assn., Nat. Coun. Tchrs. Sci., Assn. Coll. Tchr. Educators, U. Ala. Alumni, ala. Coun. Tchrs. English, Med. Auxillary, Jacksonville State U. Alumni, Kappa Delta Pi.

KEY, JACK DAYTON, librarian; b. Enid, Okla., Feb. 24, 1934; s. Ernest Dayton and Janie (Haldeman) K.; m. Virgie Ruth Richardson, Aug. 12, 1956; children—Toni, Scot, Todd. B.A., Phillips U., Enid, Okla., 1958; M.A., U. N.Mex., 1960; M.S., U. Ill., 1962. Staff supr. Grad. Library U. Ill., 1960-62; pharmacy librarian U. Iowa, 1962-64; med. librarian Lovelace Found. for Med. Edn. and Research, Albuquerque, 1965-70; dir. Mayo Med. Ctr. Librs., Rochester, Minn., 1970-94, dir. emeritus, 1994—; prof. emeritus biomed. comm. Mayo Med. Sch.; cons. in field; participant Naval War Coll. Conf., 1979; Alberta A. Brown lectr. Western Mich. U., 1979. Author: The Origin of the Vaccine Inoculation by Edward Jenner, 1977, William Alexander Hammond (1828-1900), 1979; editor: Library Automation: The Orient and South Pacific, 1975, Automated Activities in Health Sciences Libraries, 1975-78, Classics and Other Selected Readings in Medical Librarianship, 1980, Journal of a Quest for the Elusive Doctor Arthur Conan Doyle, 1982, Medical Vanities, 1982, William A. Hammond, M.D., 1828-1900: The Publications of an American Neurologist, 1983, Classics in Cardiology, Vol. 3, 1983, Vol. 4, 1989, Medical Casebook of Dr. Arthur Conan Doyle from Practitioner to Sherlock Holmes and Beyond, 1984, Medicine, Literature and Eponyms: An Encyclopedia of Medical Eponyms Derived from Literary Characters, 1989, Conan Doyle's Tales of Medical Humanism and Values, 1992; contbr. articles to profl. jours. Served with USN, 1952-55. U. N.Mex. fellow, 1958-59, N.Mex. Library Assn. Marion Dorroh Meml. scholar, 1960, Rotary Paul Harris fellow, 1979; recipient Outstanding Hist. Writing award Minn. Medicine, 1980, Spl. Svc. award Am. Acad. Dermatology, 1992, Farthing award Baker St. Jour., 1993; decorated knight Icelandic Order of Falcon, 1980; named to Phillips U. Hall Fame, 1988. Mem. Med. Library Assn., Am. Inst. History Pharmacy, Am. Assn. History Medicine, Am. Med. Writers Assn., Am. Osler Soc. (pres. 1990-91), Mystery Writers of Am., Alcuin Soc., Baker St. Irregulars, Ampersand Club, Sigma Xi (cert. of recognition 1982). Mem. Christian Ch. (Disciples of Christ). Home: PO Box 231 54 Skyline Dr Sandia Park NM 87047-0231 Office: Mayo Clinic Rochester MN 55905

KEY, JAMES EVERETT, ophthalmologist; b. Freeport, Tex., July 19, 1944; s. James Everett and Margaret Ann (Parker) K.; m. Betty Wilson, Dec. 22, 1967; children: Peter Wilson and Courtney Brooke (twins). BA, U. Tex., 1966; MD, Baylor U., 1970. Diplomate Am. Bd. Ophthalmology. Mem. staff Coll. Medicine Baylor U., Houston, 1976-89, clin. assoc. prof. ophthalmology, 1989-93, clin. prof. ophthalmology, 1994—; chief ophthalmology St. Luke's Episcopal Hosp., Houston, 1987—. Contbr. articles to jours., chpts. to books. Trustee U. of South, Sewanee, Tenn., 1991-96, 98—. Lt. USN, 1972-73. Fellow Am. Acad. Ophthalmology; mem. AMA, Contact Lens Assn. Ophthalmologists (past pres.), Harris County Med. Assn., Tex. Ophthal. Assn. (past bd. dirs.), Houston Ophthal. Soc. (past pres.), Phi Beta Kappa. Episcopalian. Office: 6624 Fannin St Ste 2100 Houston TX 77030-2333

KEY, JANICE DIXON, physician, medical educator; b. Hickory, N.C., Aug. 14, 1954; d. Charles Dennis and Mary Louise (Edgerton) Dixon; m. L. Lyndon Key Jr., May 27, 1973; children: Rebecca Louise, Emily Edgerton. BS, U. N.C., 1976, MD, 1980. Clin. instr. Harvard Med. Sch., Boston, 1984-85; clin. assoc. prof. Sch. of Medicine, U. N.C., Greensboro, N.C., 1985-91; asst. prof. Med. U. of S.C., Charleston, S.C., 1991-98; assoc. prof. pediat. Med. U. of S.C., Charleston, 1998—. Author: Ambulatory Pediatric Care, 1992; contbr. articles to profl. jours. com. mem. S.C. Adolescent Task Force, Charleston, 1993, S.C. Dept. Edn., Columbia, 1992, S.C. Sch. Health Advisory, Columbia, 1992; co-chair Sch. Health Com., Charleston, 1992—; community adv. bd. Jr. Leaque, Charleston, 1994;. Recipient Faculty Rsch. award U. N.C., 1978. Fellow Am. Acad. Pediat.; mem. Am. Soc. Human Genetics, Soc. Adolescent Medicine (chpt. pres. 1991-98), Am. Med. Women's Assn., S.C. Med. Assn., S.C. Pediat. Med. Soc. (CME com. 1994-96), Phi Beta Kappa, Phi Eta Sigma. Democrat. Presbyterian. Office: 171 Ashley Ave Charleston SC 29425-0001

KEY, KAREN LETISHA, pharmaceutical executive; b. Sanford, N.C., Jan. 17, 1957; d. Kermit Lee and Ruth (Whitaker) K. BS in Phys. Edn., Appalachian State U., 1978; MBA, U. N.C., 1993. Profl. sales rep. Burroughs Wellcome Co., Florence, S.C., 1982-84; field trainer Burroughs Wellcome Co., Kernersville, N.C., 1984-87; field mgmt. trainee then asst. product mgr. Cardiovasculars/Antivirals/Psychotropics, Research Triangle Park, N.C., 1987-90, dist. sales mgr. psychiatry, 1990-91, asst. to sr. v.p. prodn. and engring., 1991-92, mgr. mktg. tng. and devel., 1991-92, product mgr. neuromuscular blockers, 1993-94; product mgr. Zovirax/Valtrex, 1994-95; project mgr. care mgmt. divsn. Glaxo Wellcome, Raleigh, N.C., 1995; dir. bus. ops. Glaxo Wellcome, Raleigh, 1996-98, dir. bus. devel., 1998—. Mem. Lakewood Bapt. Ch. Republican. Baptist. Avocations: golf, windsurfing, water sports. Office: Glaxo Wellcome Inc D 234 Admin Five Moore Dr Research Triangle Pk NC 27709

KEY, MARCELLA ANN, computer information specialist; b. St. Louis, Nov. 26, 1947; d. Wallace Albert and Dorothy (Croskery) F.; m. Philip Odell, Nov. 18, 1967; children: Heather Colleen, Philip Sean. BA in English magna cum laude, U. Mo., St. Louis, 1969. Info. operator Southwestern Bell Tel., St. Louis, 1965-69; army procurement intern U.S. Army Mobility Equipment Command, St. Louis, 1969-70; army contract price analyst U.S. Army Weapons Command, Rock Island, Ill., 1970-72; army data processing intern U.S. Army Mgmt. Engring. Tng. Activity, Rock Island; computer programmer U.S. Army Logistics Mgmt. System Activity, St. Louis, 1973-77; computer specialist USRCPAC, 1977, U.S. Army Logistics Mgmt. System Activity, St. Louis, 1977-80; computer specialist, cons., instr. U.S. Army Mgmt. Engring. Coll., Rock Island, 1980-88; data base adminstr. U.S. Army Aviation Troop Command, St. Louis, 1988-91; project mgr. U.S. Army Aviation and Troop Command, St. Louis, 1991-97, computer specialist Logistics Sys. Support Ctr. (LSSC), 1997—; pres., v.p., sec., Army Data Base Users' Group, Rock Island, 1982-85. Co-Author: Orgn. Study of the Automation, 1983, An Info. Mgmt. Evaluation, 1987. Guardian Treas. Jobs Daughters Bethel #5, 1986-88; dir. Epochs Bethel #2, Hazelwood, Mo., 1989-93, guardian sec., 1993-98, Bethel Guardian, 1998—; Troop com. mem. Boy Scouts Am., St. Charles, 1992-98. Mem. Army Materiel Command Data Base Users Group. Ind. Dutch Reformed. Avocations: reading, tae kwon do, water skiing, crocheting. Home: 4251 Greensboro Dr Saint Charles MO 63304-1612 Office: Logistics Sys Support Ctr 1222 Spruce St Saint Louis MO 63103-2818

KEY, MARY RITCHIE (MRS. AUDLEY E. PATTON), linguist, author, educator; b. San Diego, Mar. 19, 1924; d. George Lawrence and Iris (Lyons) Ritchie; children: Mary Helen Key Ellis, Harold Hayden Key (dec.), Thomas George Key. Student, U. Chgo., summer 1954, U. Mich., 1959; M.A., U. Tex., 1960, Ph.D., 1963; postgrad., UCLA, 1966. Asst. prof. linguistics Chapman Coll., Orange, Calif., 1963-66; asst. prof. linguistics U. Calif., Irvine, 1966-71; assoc. prof. U. Calif., 1971-78, prof., 1978—, chmn. program linguistics, 1969-71, 75-77, 87—; cons. Am. Indian langs., Spanish, in Mexico, 1946-55, S.Am., 1955-62, English dialects, 1968-74, Easter Island, 1975, Calif. Dept. Edn., 1966, 70-75, Center Applied Linguistics, Washington, 1967, 69; lectr. in field. Author: Comparative Tacanan Phonology, 1968, Male/Female Language, 1975, 2d edit., 1996, Paralanguage and Kinesics, 1975, Nonverbal Communication, 1977, The Grouping of South American Indian Languages, 1979, The Relationship of Verbal and Nonverbal Communication, 1980, Catherine the Great's Linguistic Contribution, 1980, Polynesian and American Linguistic Connections, 1984, Comparative Linguistics of South American Indian Languages, 1987, General and Amerindian Ethnolinguistics, 1989, Language Change in South American Indian Languages, 1991; founder, editor: newsletter Nonverbal Components of Communication, 1972-76; mem. editoral bd. Forum Linguisticum, 1976—, Lang. Scis., 1978—, La Linguistique, 1979—, Multilingua, 1987—; contbr. articles to profl. jours. Recipient Friends of Libr. Book award, 1976, hon. mention, Rolex awards for Enterprise, project Computerizing the Languages of the World, 1990; U. Calif. Regent's grantee, 1974, Fulbright-Hays grantee, 1975; faculty rsch. fellow, 1984-85. Mem. Linguistic Soc. Am., Am. Dialect Soc. (exec. council; regional sec. 1974-83), Internat. Reading Assn. (dir. 1968-72), Delta Kappa Gamma (local pres. 1974-76). Office: U Calif-Irvine Dept Linguistics Irvine CA 92697-5100

KEY, OTTA BISCHOF, retired educator; b. Englewood, Colo., May 19, 1907; d. Herbert and Lulu Bonita (Kitterman) Bischof; m. Elra Richard Key, Aug. 21, 1938 (dec. June 1993); children: Paul, Kathryn. BFA, Kans. U., 1933; MA, Ctrl. Mich. U., 1967. Cert. Christian educator. Tchr. Luray, Kans., 1923; elem. tchr. Luray, 1924-26; tchr. jr. h.s. Russell, Kans., 1926-29; tchr. art Meml. H.S., Lawrence, Kans., 1934-38; instr. art edn. Maryville (Mo.) U., 1937-38, Saginaw (Mich.) Valley Coll., 1957-70; ednl. asst. Meml. Presbyn. Ch., Midland, Mich., 1958-73; ednl. asst. religion dept. Millikin U., Decatur, Ill., 1976-84; student adviser Meml. H.S., Lawrence, 1934-38, dir. art exhibits, 1934-38; tchr. synod schs. Presbyn. Ch., 1955-58; mem. edn. City Ch. Coun., Decatur, Ill., 1978-84. *The three branches of the Christian Church: Roman Catholic, Christian Orthodox and Protestant discuss cooperation in various ways. The Scholarships established at McCormick and Louisville Presbyterian Seminaries emphasize good Biblical Scholarship (The Confession of 1967) which would be helpful in the discussions among the branches.* Author: Teaching Volunteers Teachers, 1984. Cooperator Decatur Ch. coun., 1976-84, Ch. Women United, Decautur, 1974-93; supporter Am. United, Washington, 1970-97, Presbyn. Ch., 1973-93. Scholarships established McCormick Presbyn. Sem., Louisville Presbyn. Sem.; recipient award Presbyn. Ch., 1958-93. Mem. Assn. of Presbyn. Ch. Educators, Assn. of Great Lakes Ch. Educators. Democrat. Ecumenical. Avocations: reading current events, ecumenical activities, visual arts, family education. Home: 2025 E Lincoln St # 1221 Bloomington IL 61701-5995

KEY, TED, cartoonist; b. Fresno, Calif., Aug. 25, 1912; s. Simon Leon and Fanny (Kahn) K.; m. Anne Elizabeth Wilkinson, Sept. 30, 1937 (dec. July 5, 1984); children: Stephen Lewis, David Edward, Peter Lawrence; m. Bonnie Williams-Cohen, Nov. 17, 1987. BA, U. Calif., Berkeley, 1933. Assoc. editor Judge mag., N.Y.C., 1937-39; radio staff writer J. Walter Thompson Advt. Agy., N.Y.C., 1939-43; cartoonist Hazel Saturday Evening Post, Phila., 1943-70, King Features Syndicate, 1969—; cartoonist, writer The Econs. Press, Inc., Fairfield, N.J., 1957—; screenwriter Walt Disney Prodns., Burbank, Calif., 1970-77. Writer, cartoonist for CBS, NBC, mags., books, newspapers; playwright (NBC radio prodn.) The Clinic (pub. in anthology Best Broadcasts Of 1939-40); creator (cartoon features) Diz and Liz for Jack and Jill mag., 1961-71, (TV series) Hazel, Peabody and Sherman for Bullwinkle and Rocky Show (TV series), 1959; writer: Hazel, NBC-TV (4 yrs.), CBS-TV (1 yr.), 1946, Here's Hazel, 1949, Many Happy Returns, 1950, If You Like Hazel, 1952, So'm I, 1953, Hazel Rides Again, 1955, Fasten Your Seat Belts, 1956, Phyllis, 1957, All Hazel, 1958, The Hazel Jubilee, 1959, The Biggest Dog in the World, 1960, Hazel Time, 1962, Life With Hazel, 1965, Diz and Liz, 1965, Squirrels in the Feeding Station, 1967, Hazel Power, 1971, Right On Hazel, 1972, Ms. Hazel, 1972, Hazel's Feline Funnies, 1982; story/screenwriter: Million Dollar Duck, The Cat From Outer Space (also wrote novel), Gus; writer: Positive Attitude Posters, 1965—, Sales Bullets, 1960—; cartoons included in New Yorker, Esquire, Look, Life, Ladies Home Jour., McCall's, Good Housekeeping, Better Homes and Gardens, People, Mademoiselle. Master sgt. Signal Corps AUS, 1943-46. Mem. Nat. Cartoonists Soc. (Best Syndicated Panel award 1977), Writers Guild Am. West. Jewish.

KEYES, ARTHUR HAWKINS, JR., architect; b. Rutland, Vt., May 26, 1917; s. Arthur Hawkins and Blanche (Emery) K.; m. Lucile Sheppard, Mar. 29, 1941; children: Arthur S., Spencer S., Janet S. A.B. cum laude, Princeton U., 1939; M.Arch., Harvard U., 1942. Partner Keyes, Lethbridge and Condon, Washington, 1956-75; partner Keyes Condon Florance (Architects), Washington, 1975-80; pres. Keyes Condon Florance (Architects), 1980-85; chmn. Keyes Condon Florance Eich Baum Esocoff King, 1985-92; chmn. emeritus, 1992—; pres. Sea Ridge Devel. Corp., Washington Bldg. Congress, 1964-65; chmn. alumni adv. council Sch. Architecture, Princeton U., 1965-73. Trustee Hist. Soc. Washington D.C. Served with USNR, 1942-46. Fellow AIA (spl. presdl. citation 1982); mem. Nat. Trust Hist. Preservation, Com. of 100 on the Fed. City. Republican. Clubs: Cosmos, Chevy Chase. Home: 11920 River Rd Potomac MD 20854-1244 also: 2605 31st St NW Washington DC 20008-3519 Office: Internat Square 1825 Eye St NW Ste 250 Washington DC 20006-5403

KEYES, BENJAMIN B., therapist; b. Alexandria, Va., Sept. 18, 1953; s. Jay F. and Harriet Edith (Champagne) K.; children: Shawn David, Jasmin Victoria. MA, U. South Fla., 1978; PhD, Internat. Coll., 1985; ThD., DMin., Zoe Coll., 1985; DD, Reeves Christian Coll., 1987. Lic. profl. counselor, Tex., mental health counselor, Fla., practitioner, cons.; nat. cert. mental health counselor; nat. cert. counselor, cert. clin. hypnotherapist. Psychologist Baker Correctional Instn., Olustee, Fla.; prof. grad. sch. Fla. Beacon Bible Coll., Largo; dir. Charis Inc., Clearwater, Fla.; dir. clin. programs partial hospitalization Rapha Inc., Pasadena, Tex.; clin. dir. Bridgework Ministry, Clearwater; pvt. practice counselor, cons.; evaluator accreditation Dept. Corrections, 1984; program dir. Manors Hosp., Largo, Fla., Medfield Hosp., Largo; CEO Daylight Partial Hospitalization Programs, St. Petersburg, Fla.; cons. psychotherapist. Co-author: Family Training Manual, 1978, E Pluribus Unum From Many to One, 1996; author: Sexuality, Learning and Teaching Modality, 1978, Christian Counseling, Substance Abuse Manual, 1985, The Spiritual Pathfinder, Qualities of an Effective Christian Counselor, 1983, A Christian Approach to Inner Healing No More Turning Away, 1985, A Christian Approach to Treating Dissociative Identity Disorder, 1997, ; contbr. articles to profl. jours. Recipient Appreciation cert. ARC, 1980-84, Youth award Trinity United Meth. Ch., 1980-81. Mem. Am. Assn. Christian Counselors, Am. Mental Health Counselors Assn., Am. Counseling Assn., Assn. Ambulatory Behavioral Healthcare, Am. Rehab. Counseling Assn., Assn. Religious and Value Issues Counseling, Christians Who Do Therapy Assn., Assn. Christian Therapists, Internat. Soc. Study of Dissociation (mem., bd. dirs. Tampa Bay chpt.), Internat. Assn. Counselors and Therapists (bd. dirs.), Fla. Ambulatory Partial Hospitalization Assn., Network of Christian Counselors, Upper Pinellas Minsterial Assn. (treas., v.p.), Assn. Ambulatoroy Behavioral Healthcare, Fla. Rehab. Assn. (past exec. bd.), Fla. Rehab. Counseling Assn. (past regional rep.), Psi Chi. Home: 2333 Feather Sound Dr #B104 Clearwater FL 33762

KEYES, CAROL JANE, nurse manager, surgical nurse; b. Madison, Wis., June 16, 1936; d. Leonard Daniel and Helen Louise (Rock) K. Diploma in Nursing, St. Mary's Sch. Nursing, 1958; BS, Boston U., 1988. RN, Wis., Mass. Staff nurse St. Mary's Med./Surg. Unit, Milw., 1958-61; staff nurse neuro unit Deaconess Hosp., Boston, 1961-62; staff nurse emergency rm. Carney Hosp., Boston, 1962-63, head nurse med. surg., 1963-64; staff nurse ICU Deaconess Hosp., Boston, 1964-66, head nurse, nurse mgr. ICU, 1966-94. Mem. AACN, Mass. Coun. Nurse Mgrs., Am. Heart Assn. Democrat. Roman Catholic. Avocations: cooking, reading, theater, entertaining, travel. Home: 151 Tremont St Apt 24U Boston MA 02111-1122

KEYES, DANIEL, author; b. N.Y.C., Aug. 9, 1927; s. William and Betty (Alicke) K.; m. Aurea Georgina Vazquez, Oct. 14, 1952; children—Hillary Ann, Leslie Joan. B.A. in Psychology, Bklyn. Coll., 1950, M.A. in English, 1961. Assoc. fiction editor Magazine Mgmt. Co., N.Y.C., 1950-52; v.p. Fenko and Keyes Photography, Inc., 1952-53; tchr. English N.Y.C. Bd. Edn., 1955-62; instr. English Wayne State U., Detroit, 1962-66; mem. faculty Ohio U., Athens, 1966—; prof. English and creative writing Ohio U., 1972-97; agt. William Morris Agy., N.Y.C., Calif. Author: (novels) Flowers for Algernon (Hugo award 1959, 66, Nebula award 1966, movie version: Charly, 1968), The Touch, 1968, The Fifth Sally, 1980, (nonfiction) The Minds of Billy Milligan, 1981 (Spl. award Mystery Writers Am., Kurd Lasswitz award, 1st prize Best Fgn. Book award 1986), Unveiling Claudia, 1986, Daniel Keyes Collected Stories, 1993 (Japan), The Milligan Wars, 1994 (Japan), Daniel Keyes Reader, 1995 (Japan), Until Death Do Us Part: The Sleeping Princess, 1998 (Japan), (TV movie) Flowers for Algernon, 1999, (non-fiction) Reliving Flowers for Algernon: A Writer's Story, 1999; supervising prodr. (TV movie) The Mad Housers, 1990. Served with U.S. Maritime Service, 1945-47. Ohio Arts Council Individual Artist fellow, 1986-87; recipient Baker Fund award 1986-87, Disting. Alumnus Honor award Bklyn. Coll. CUNY, 1988. Mem. PEN, Dramatists' Guild, Mystery Writers of Am. Office: 7491 N Federal Hwy Ste C5-110 Boca Raton FL 33487-1625

KEYES, DAVID TAYLOR, telecommunications company administrator; b. Providence, Feb. 18, 1947; s. Leonard Taylor and Alice (Whitwam) K.; m. Martha Ann Bearden, Dec. 22, 1973; children: Joshua Ryan, Caroline Louise. BBA, Fla. Internat. U., 1977; MS in Mgmt. Sci., U. Miami, 1981. Cert. quality engr. Communications technician Network Ops. AT&T, Miami, Fla., 1973-81, sales supr. Nat. Accounts, 1981-84; staff supr. Network Engring. AT&T, Atlanta, 1984-87; quality cons. Network Svc. div. AT&T, Conyers, Ga., 1987—. With USN, 1967-73, Vietnam. Mem. Am. Soc. Quality Control. Home: 4158 Azalea Ct Lithonia GA 30058-7257

KEYES, GORDON LINCOLN, history educator; b. Kearney, Ont., Can., Mar. 5, 1920; s. Arthur Beverley and Edna (File) K.; m. Mary Ferguson, June 9, 1945; children: Katherine Mary Keyes Ewing, John Thomas David. BA, U. Toronto (Ont.), 1941, MA, 1942; PhD, Princeton U., 1944. Lectr. in Greek McMaster U., Hamilton, Ont., 1941-42; asst. prof. Birmingham-So. Coll., Ala., 1945-47; faculty Victoria Coll., U. Toronto, 1947—, prof. Greek and Roman history, 1963-83, Nelles prof. ancient history, 1967-83, prof. emeritus, 1983—, also chmn. combined depts. classics, 1967-69, chmn. dept. classics, 1971-75; prin. Victoria Coll., 1976-81. Author: Christian Faith and the Interpretation of History: A Study of St. Augustine's Philosophy of History, 1966. Can. Council sr. research fellow, 1959-60. Mem. Soc. Promotion Roman Studies, Am. Philol. Assn., Classical Assn. Can. Home: 122 Orchard Dr, Thornbury, ON Canada N0H 2P0

KEYES, JAMES HENRY, manufacturing company executive; b. LaCrosse, Wis., Sept. 2, 1940; s. Donald M. and Mary M. (Nodolf) K.; m. Judith Ann Carney, Nov. 21, 1964; children: James Patrick, Kevin, Timothy. BS, Marquette U., 1962; MBA, Northwestern U., 1963. Instr. Marquette U., Milw., 1963-65; CPA Peat. Marwick & Mitchell, Milw., 1965-66; with Johnson Controls, Inc., Milw., 1967—, mgr. sys. dept., 1967-71, divsn. contr., 1971-73, corp. contr., treas., 1973-77, v.p., chief fin. officer, 1977-85, exec. v.p., 1985-86, pres., 1986—, chief operating officer, 1986-88, chief exec. officer, 1988—, also chmn.; bd. dirs. Baird Capital Devel. Fund. 1st Wis. Trust Co., LSI Logic, Inc., Universal Foods Corp. Active Milw. Symphony Orch., 1980—. Mem. Fin. Execs. Inst., Am. Inst. CPA's, Wis. Inst. CPA's., Machinery and Allied Products Inst. Office: Johnson Controls Inc PO Box 591 5757 N Green Bay Ave Milwaukee WI 53209-4408*

KEYES, JEFFREY J., lawyer. BA magna cum laude, U. Notre Dame, 1968; JD cum laude, U. Mich., 1972. Bar: Minn. 1972. Shareholder Briggs and Morgan, P.A., Mpls.; fellow Am. Coll. Trial Lawyers, Mpls.; mem. Gov.'s Task Force on Tort Reform, 1986; chmn. fed. practice com. U.S. Dist. Ct. Minn., 1990-93, chmn. adv. group on civil justice reform act U.S. Dist. Ct. Minn., 1991-93; trainer U.S. Magistrate Judges Tng. Conf. on Settlement, Mpls., 1992; lectr. numerous convs. and symposia in field. Contbr. articles to law jours. Mem. ABA (chmn. antitrust sect. franchise com. 1989-90, contbg. editor Antitrust Monograph 1987, co-editor Antitrust Sect. State Antitrust Law Handbook, Minn. chpt. 1990), Minn. State Bar Assn. (co-chair Women in the Legal Profn. task force 1996-97, chmn. civil litigation sect. 1985-86), Hennepin County Bar Assn. Office: Briggs and Morgan 2400 Ids Ctr Minneapolis MN 55402

KEYES, JOAN ROSS RAFTER, education educator, author; b. Bklyn., Aug. 12, 1924; d. Joseph W. and Hermia (Ross) Rafter; m. William Ambrose, Apr. 26, 1947 (dec.); children: William, Peter, Dion, Kenzie. BA, Adelphi U., Garden City, N.Y., 1945; MS, Long Island U., Greenvale, N.Y., 1973. Prodn. asst. CBS Radio, N.Y., 1943-44; cub news reporter Bklyn. Daily Eagle, 1945-46; advt. copywriter Gimbel's Dept. Store, N.Y., 1946-47; adj. prof. L.I. U., Greenvale, N.Y., 1984—; tchr. Port Wash. Pub. Schs., N.Y., 1970-94; lectr., cons. pub. sch. dists. nationwide, 1978—; workshop leader Tchrs. English to Speakers Other Langs. convs., 1981—. Author: Beats, Conversations in Rhythm, 1983, (video program) Now You're Talking, 1987, (computer program) Quick Talk, 1990, Oxford Picture Dictionary for Kids, 1998; contbr. articles to ednl. mags. Lectr., catechist Our Lady of Fatima Ch., Port Washington, 1987—; vol. Earthwatch, Mallorca, 1988. Australia/New Zealand ednl. grantee Port Washington Pub. Schs., 1992. Mem. Tchrs. of English to Speakers of Other Languages, Am. Fedn. of Tchrs., N.Y. State United Tchrs., Port Wash. Tchrs. Assn. Republican. Roman Catholic. Avocations: music, painting, travel, tennis, golf.

KEYES, MARGARET NAUMANN, home economics educator; b. Mt. Vernon, Iowa, Mar. 4, 1918; d. Charles Reuben and Sarah (Naumann) K. B.A., Cornell Coll., Mt. Vernon, 1939, L.H.D., 1976; M.S., U. Wis., 1951; Ph.D. (Ellen H. Richards grad. fellow), Fla. State U., 1965; H.H.D., Coe Coll., 1977. Tchr. home econs. Stanley (Iowa) High Sch., 1939-42, Washington Jr. High Sch., Clinton, Iowa, 1942-44, Clinton High Sch., 1944-50; instr. related art U. Iowa, Iowa City, 1951-57; asst. prof. related art dept. home econs. U. Iowa, 1957-68, assoc. prof., 1968-75, prof., 1975-88; research prof. U. Iowa Found., 1971-74. Author: Nineteenth Century Home Architecture Iowa City, 1967, expanded edit., 1993, Old Capitol: Portrait of an Iowa Landmark, 1988; mem. editorial bd., Home Econs. Research Jour; contbr. articles to periodicals. Mem. Terr. Hill Planning Commn. for Iowa, Terr. Hill Authority for Iowa; mem. design rev. bd. Iowa City Urban Renewal Commn.; dir. research Old Capitol Restoration Com., 1971-75; dir. Old Capitol, 1975-88; mem. Iowa State Hist. Bd., vice chmn. 1986-90, chmn., 1990-92. Recipient Peterson/Harlan award State Hist. Soc. of Iowa, 1994, Nat. History Award medal DAR, 1996; named Dist. Friend of U. Iowa Alumni Assn., 1989. Mem. Am. Home Econ. Assn. (exec. bd., chmn. art sect.), Iowa Home Econs. Assn., AAUP, Soc. Archtl. Historians, Am. Soc. Interior Designers, Interior Design Educators Council, Iowa Soc. Preservation Hist. Landmarks (dir. 1970-75), Cornell Coll. Alumni Assn. (dir. 1970-73), Nat. Trust Hist. Preservation (bd. advs. 1974-77), Internat. Fedn. Home Econs. (individual), Victorian Soc. Am. (v.p., dir. 1974-80), Iowa Centennial Meml. Found., Altrusa Club (pres. 1969-70), Phi Beta Kappa, Omicron Nu, Omicron Delta Kappa. Democrat. Presbyterian.

KEYES, MARION ALVAH, IV, manufacturing company executive; b. Bellingham, Wash., May 11, 1938; s. Marion Alvah and Winnefred Agnes (Nolte) K.; m. Loretta Jean Mattson, Nov. 17, 1962; children: Marion A., Zachary Leigh, Richard. BS in Chem. Engring., Stanford U., 1960; MSEE, U. Ill., 1968; MBA, Baldwin Wallace Coll., 1981. Registered rofl. engr., Calif., Wis., N.Y., Ill., Ohio. Tchg. asst. dept. math. Stanford U., 1958-59; tech. Stanford Aerosol Labs., 1957-59; chem. engr. Ketchikan (Alaska) Pulp Co., 1960-63; dir engring. Control Sys. divsn. Beloit (Wis.) Corp., 1963-70; gen. mgr. digital sys. divsn. Taylor Instrument Co., Rochester, N.Y., 1970-75; sr. v.p., group exec. Indsl. Products and Svcs. Group; mem. exec. operative bd. McDermott Internat. Inc., 1985-89; v.p. engring., pres. Bailey Controls Co., Wickliffe, Ohio, 1975-85, pres., CEO, 1989-90; chmn. Dcom Corp., Eastlake, Ohio, 1990-93; sr. v.p. tech. and bus. devel. process group, pres. rosemount Analytical Inc. divsn. Emerson Electric Co., St. Louis, 1993—; bd. dirs. Fibermark Corp. Author: Offshore Platform Automation, 1990; editor: A Glossary of Automatic Control Terminology, 1970; contbr. articles to profl. jours.; holder 51 U.S. and more than 100 fgn. patents. Past bd. advisors Fenn Coll. Engring., Cleve. State U.; bd. dirs. Baldwin Coll., United Cerebral Palsy, Cleve.; past prs., mem. exec. bd. N.E. Ohio coun. Boy Scouts Am.; past pres. Area 5 Boy Scouts Am. Fellow ISA (hon. life), TAPPA (Pioneer award), IEEE, Am. inst. Chemists, Instrument Soc. Am. (life hon.); mem. AIChE, Ohio Acad. Scis. (life; bd. dirs., Centennial honoree 1991, fellow), Cleve. Engring. Soc. (bd. dirs.), Soc. Am. Mil. Engrs. (life), Am. Assn. Artificial Intelligence (charter), Am. Mgmt. Assn., U.S. Automation Rsch. Coun., Am. Automatic Control Coun. (past. sec. and bd. dirs., Am. Chem. Soc., Wis. Acad. Arts, Scis. and Letters, Cleve. World Trade Assn. (Man of Yr. 1984), Canterbury Golf Club. Republican. Roman Catholic. E-mail: bud@keyes.org. Home: 8 Washington Terr Saint Louis MO 63112-1914 Office: 8000 Maryland Ave Ste 600 Clayton MO 63105-3752

KEYES, RALPH JEFFREY, writer; b. Cin., Jan. 12, 1945; s. Scott Sherman and Charlotte Esther (Shachmann) K.; m. Muriel Lee Gordon, Feb. 13, 1965; children: David, Scott. BA in History, Antioch Coll., 1967. Asst. to pub. Newsday, Garden City, N.Y., 1968-70; fellow Ctr. Studies Person, La Jolla, Calif., 1970-80; writer Phila., 1980-90; bd. trustees Antioch Writer's Workshop, Yellow Springs, 1992—. Author: We, The Lonely People, 1973,

Is There Life After High School?, 1976, The Height of Your Life, 1980, Chancing It: Why We Take Risks, 1985, TimeLock: How Life Got So Hectic and What You Can Do About It, 1991, Sons on Fathers: A Book of Men's Writings, 1992, "Nice Guys Finish Seventh": False Phrases, Spurious Sayings, and Familiar Misquotations, 1992, The Courage to Write, 1995, The Wit and Wisdom of Harry Truman, 1995, The Wit and Wisdom of Oscar Wilde, 1996; contbr. articles to mags. and newspapers. Recipient Headliner of Yr. in lit. San Diego Press Club, 1976, Citation for Nonfiction, The Athenaeum, 1985; Individual Artist's fellow Ohio Arts Coun., 1998. Mem. Author's Guild. Avocations: travel, running, watching soccer games. E-mail: ralphjk@aol.com. Home: 690 Omar Cir Yellow Springs OH 45387-1420

KEYES, RICHARD PAUL, small business owner; b. Feb. 4, 1970. AS in Bus. Adminstrn., County Coll. Morris, 1995; BA in Polit. Sci., William Paterson U., 1999. Dir. ops. Harding Pvt. Livery Svc., New Vernon, N.J., 1991—. E-mail: RK1701A@aol.com. Home: 4 East Ridge Rd Brookside NJ 07926

KEYES, ROBERT W., physicist; b. Chgo., Dec. 2, 1921; s. Lee P. and Katherine K.; m. Sophie Skadorwa, June 4, 1966; children—Andrew, Claire. B.S., U. Chgo., 1942, M.S., 1949, Ph.D., 1953. With Argonne Nat. Lab., 1946-50; staff mem. Westinghouse Research Lab., Pitts., 1953-60; mem. research staff IBM Research Lab., Yorktown Heights, N.Y., 1960—; vis. physicist Am. Phys. Soc. Vis. Indsl. Physicists Program, 1974-75, 77; vice chmn. Gordon Conf. on High Pressure Physics, 1970; chmn. Gordon Conf. on Chemistry and Physics of Microstructure Fabrication, 1976, Nat. Materials Adv. Bd. (ad hoc com. on ion implantation as a new surface treatment tech.), 1978, Internat. Conf. Heavily Doped Semiconductors, 1984; mem. Nat. Acad. Scis.-NAE-NRC evaluation panel Nat. Bur. Standards, 1970-73; cons. physics survey com., mem. statis. data panel Nat. Acad. Sci.-NRC Council Physics Survey Com., 1972; mem. data and info. panel Nat. Acad. Sci.-NRC Com. on Survey of Materials Sci. and Engring., 1974; Girling Watson vis. prof. elec. engring. U. Sydney, Fall 1996. Author: Physics of VLSI Systems, 1987; assoc. editor Revs. Modern Physics, 1976-95; corr.: Comments on Solid State Physics, 1970-85. Served with USN, 1944-46. Recipient Outstanding Contbn. award IBM, 1963. Fellow Am. Phys. Soc. (chmn. com. applications of physics 1976-78), IEEE (chmn. subcom. cultural and sci. relations 1976, mem. del. to USSR 1975, W.R.G. Baker prize 1976, awards bd. 1984-85); mem. Nat. Acad. Engring. Office: IBM PO Box 218 Yorktown Heights NY 10598-0218

KEYES, SAUNDRA ELISE, newspaper editor; b. Salt Lake City, June 28, 1945; d. Vernon Harrison and Mildred K.; m. William J. Ivey, June 13, 1969 (div. 1976). BA, U. Utah, 1966; MA, Ind. U., 1969, PhD, 1976. Tchr. Salt Lake City Pub. Schs., 1966-67; asst. prof. Fisk U., Nashville, 1971-76; reporter, city editor The Tennessean, Nashville, 1976-83; staff writer The Courier-Jour., Louisville, 1983-84; dep. mng. editor Orlando (Fla.) Sentinel, 1985-88; mng. editor Phila. Daily News, 1988-90; exec. editor, sr. v.p. Press-Telegram, Long Beach, Calif., 1991-93; mng. editor The Miami Herald, 1993-96, Contra Costa Times, 1996—. Ford Found. fellow, 1978.

KEYFITZ, NATHAN, sociologist, demographer, educator; b. Montreal, Que., Can., June 29, 1913; s. Arthur and Anna (Gerstein) K.; m. Beatrice Orkin, Oct. 8, 1939; children: Barbara Lee, Robert Norman. BS, McGill U., Montreal, 1934, LLD (hon.), 1984; PhD, U. Chgo., 1952; MA (hon.), Harvard U., 1972; LLD (hon.), U. Western Ont., 1973, U. de Montréal, 1984, McGill U., 1984, U. Alta, 1985, U. Siena, 1991, Carleton U., 1993, U. de Québec, 1993. Census clk., statistician, sr. research statistician Dominion Bur. Statistics, Govt. Can., 1936-59; dir. Colombo Plan Bur., Sri Lanka, 1956-57; prof. sociology U. Toronto, Ont., Can., 1959-63, U. Montreal, 1962-63; prof. U. Chgo., 1963-68, chmn. sociology dept., 1965-68; prof. demography U. Calif., Berkeley, 1968-72; Andelot prof. sociology and demography Harvard U., 1972-82, chmn. dept. sociology, 1978-80, emeritus, 1982—; Robert Lazarus prof. social demography Ohio State U., Columbus, 1980-84, prof. emeritus, 1984—; with Internat. Inst. Applied Systems Analysis, 1984-93; researcher Initiatives on Children, Am. Acad. Arts and Scis., Cambridge, Mass., 1994—; tech. assistance assignments, Burma, 1951, Indonesia, 1952-53, 64, 79, 85-89, Argentina, 1960, Santiago, Chile, 1963, Moscow, 1977, 85, People's Republic China, 1981; vis. fellow Stanford U., 1986. Author: Introduction to the Mathematics of Population, 1968, 2d edit., 1977, Applied Mathematical Demography, 1977, Population Change and Social Policy, 1982, (with Wilhelm Flieger) World Population Growth and Aging, 1990; contbr. articles to profl. jours. Trustee Nat. Opinion Research Ctr., 1966—. Recipient Lazarsfeld award Am. Sociol. Assn., 1990, Common Wealth award, 1991; decorated Cross of Honor for Sci., Austria, 1993; named Laureate, Internat. Union Sci. Study Population, 1997, Norberg award Population Coun. of N.Y. Fellow Royal Soc. Can., Am. Statis. Assn. (chmn. social stats. sect. 1961), Royal Statis. Soc. (hon.), Statis. Soc. of Can. (hon.); mem. NAS, Am. Acad. Arts and Scis., Can. Polit. Sci. Assn. (chmn. sociology and anthropology sect. 1961), Inter-Am. Statis. Inst., Internat. Statis. Inst., Population Assn. Am. (pres. 1969-70), Phi Beta Kappa. E-mail: keyfitz@mediaone.net. Home: 1580 Massachusetts Ave Apt 7C Cambridge MA 02138-2928 Office: Harvard U Dept Sociology Cambridge MA 02138-2928

KEYKO, GEORGE JOHN, electronics company executive; b. New Britain, Conn., May 6, 1924; s. John Simonovich and Nellie Ivanovna (Gretcha) K.; BS, Yale U., 1949; m. Anne Romanchuk, Jan. 31, 1948; children: David, Mark. Spl. rep. Lederle Labs., Conn. and N.Y., 1949-52; pres. Teacher Toys, Inc., Conn., 1952-56; sales mgr. Washington Forge, N.J., 1956-60; sales mgr. shaver divsn. Ronson Corp., Woodbridge, N.J., 1960-63; sales mgr. Caravelle and BEP divsn. Bulova Watch Co., N.Y.C., 1963-66; v.p. mktg. Technipower divsn. Benrus Watch Co., Ridgefield, Conn., 1966-68; exec. v.p. Heuer Time & Electronics Corp., Springfield, N.J., 1969, pres., 1970-75; now pres. ARK, Inc.; bd. dirs. New Products Devel. Assocs., Pasta 101 Co. Inc., Santa Barbara, Calif., Kai Gee Entertainment Taiwan, Jame Fine Chemicals, Inc., Bound Brook, N.J., Brugge Ent., Bound Brook, Ark, Inc., Westfield, N.J., A.R.K., Inc., Westfield; dir. Sark Investors Inc., Linden, N.J. Home: 931 Kimball Ave Westfield NJ 07090-1938

KEYLER, ROBERT GORDON, material handling company executive; b. Elgin, Ill., May 9, 1958; s. Robert Dean and Lois Jean (Hobbs) K.; m. Linda Jane Mendez, Sept. 21, 1988 (div. Jan. 1993). Grad., Morris County Vo-Tech., 1980. Mgr. Gardentown Ctr., Rockaway, N.J., 1976-80, Genuine Parts-NAPA, Albuquerque, 1980-88; owner G&B Enterprises, Albuquerque, 1988-91; sales rep. Parts Plus of Albuquerque, 1989-91; v.p. sales and purchasing Material Handling Specialists, Albuquerque, 1991—; cons. in field. Sponsor Youth of Unity, Albuquerque, 1980—; bd. dirs. Unity Ch., Albuquerque, 1986—, pres., 1987. Avocations: youthwork, backpacking, ballooning. Home: 11 Constellation Dr Tijeras NM 87059-8108 Office: Material Handling Specialists 3214 Los Arboles Ave NE Albuquerque NM 87107-1917

KEYLOR, WILLIAM ROBERT, humanities educator; b. Sacramento, Aug. 15, 1944; s. Robert and Thelma (Facchine) K.; m. Rheta Grenoble, Dec. 28, 1968; children: Daniel R., Justine R. BA, Stanford U., 1966; MA, Columbia U., 1967, PhD, 1971. History lectr. Rutgers U., Newark, 1970-72; from asst. to assoc. prof. Boston U., 1972-80, prof., 1980—; vis. assoc. prof. MIT, Boston, 1980; chmn. dept. history Boston U., 1988—. Author: Academy and Community The Foundation of the French Historical Profession, 1975, Jacques Bainville and the Renaissance of Royalist History in Twentieth Century France, 1979, The Twentieth-Century World: An International History, 1984, 3d edit., 1996, The Legacy of the Great War, 1997. Decorated chevalier Nat. Order Merit (French Republic); Guggenheim Found. fellow, 1978, Fulbright fellow, 1969, 86. Mem. Internat. Inst. Strategic Studies, Soc. for French Hist. Studies (pres. 1995-96, exec. bd.), Soc. for the Historians Am. Fgn. Rels. Avocations: skiing, hiking, travel. Home: 289 Woodward St Waban MA 02468-2010 Office: Boston Univ Dept History 226 Bay State Rd Dept History Boston MA 02215-1403

KEYS, ARLANDER, federal judge; b. 1943. BA, DePaul U., 1972, JD, 1975. Trial atty. Nat. Labor Rels. Bd., 1975-80; regional atty. Fed. Labor Rels. Authority, Chgo., 1980-86; adminstrv. law judge SSA, Dept. of HHS, 1986-88, chief adminstrv. law judge, 1988-95; magistrate judge U.S. Dist. Ct. (no. dist.) Ill., 1995-98, presiding magistrate judge, 1998—. With USMC, 1963-67. Mem. ABA, Fed. Bar Assn., Ill. Jud. Coun., Chgo. Bar Assn., Cook County Bar Assn., 7th Cir. Bar Assn. FAX: 312-554-8546. Office: US Dist Ct 219 S Dearborn St Rm 2578 Chicago IL 60604-1702

KEYS, LESLEE FRANCES, historic preservation planner; b. Anderson, Ind., Oct. 31, 1955; d. George Lyle and Donna Faye (Oldham) K.; m. John Albert Machnic, 1976 (div. 1997); children: Evan Benjamin, Ethan Andrew. BS, Ball State U., 1976; MA in History, Va. Tech., 1977, M in Urban and Regional Planning, 1979. Survey and inventory technician Regional Preservation Office, Dayton, Ohio, 1979, Ohio Hist. Preservation Office, Columbus, Ohio, 1980; planner Dept. Planning, Dayton, 1980-83; exec. dir. Riverside Avondale Preservation, Jacksonville, Fla., 1984-86; dir., hist. preservation analyst Jefferson County Hist. Preservation, 1986-93; mgr. Hist. Fla. Keys Preservation Bd., Key West, 1993-97; hist. resources adminstr. St. Augustine (Fla.) Regional Preservation Office, 1997—; instr. Fla. Jr. Coll., Jacksonville, 1985-86; adj. faculty U. Louisville, 1990, Barry U., 1996-97; bd. dirs. Leadership Monroe County, Fla. Author: Blueprint for Rehabilitation, 1982; editor: Historic Jefferson County, 1992. Ky. col. Hon. Order of Ky. Cols., 1989. Recipient Preservation award Dayton Coun. Neighborhoods, Dayton, 1983, Preservation award Jacksonville Hist. Landmarks Commn., Jacksonville, 1986, Svc. to Preservation award Ida Lee Willis Meml. Found., Commonwealth of Ky., 1991, award for excellence Hist. Fla. Keys Found., Key West, 1997. Mem. Am. Inst. Cert. Planners, Am. Planning Assn., Nat. Alliance Preservation Commns. (bd. dirs. 1996-98), Nat. Trust for Hist. Preservation, Fla. Trust for Hist. Preservation. Methodist. Avocations: renovating houses, distance running, reading. Office: St Augustine Regional Pres Office PO Box 4168 48 King St Saint Augustine FL 32084-4449

KEYS, MARTHA MCDOUGLE, educational administrator; b. Erie, Pa., May 20, 1938; d. Marshall and Helen (Siegel) McD. BA in English, Grove City Coll.; MEd in Counseling, U. Rochester, N.Y.; EdD, Calif. Coast U. Field supr. Calif. Sch. Profl. Psychology, 1969-75, Sonoma (Calif.) State U., 1969-75, U. Santa Clara, Calif., 1969-75; counselor, instr. Stanford (Calif.) U., 1969-75; counselor The Door, N.Y., 1975-76; lang. arts coord. Learning Skills Ctr., Coll. of New Rochelle (N.Y.), 1980-87; assoc. dir. Coun. for Internat. Understanding of Myrin Inst., 1987-89; exec. dir. Moorhead Kennedy Inst., N.Y.C., 1990-96; v.p.Moorhead Kennedy Assocs.; exec. prodr. 360 Degree Prodns., Inc.; pres. Something In Common, Inc., 1996—. Author simulations (with Moorhead Kennedy) Hostage Crisis, 1987, Death of a Dissident, 1989, Sacrilege in Talbotsville, 1990, Fire in the Forest, 1990, Hinomaru, 1992, Metalfabriken, 1993, Grocery Store, 1993, Toxic International, 1993, Atomic, 1994; (films) Cultural Baggage, 1995, Read My Lips, 1996, Sign of the Times, 1998. Home: 15915 84th Dr Jamaica NY 11432-2528

KEYS, PAUL ROSS, university dean; b. St. Louis, Mar. 21, 1940; s. Charles and Josie (Jones) K.; m. Donnielesky Harrington, May 23, 1998; children from a previous marriage, Pamela, Roderick. BS, St. Louis U., 1963, MSW, 1971; PhD, U. Wis., Milw., 1983. Exec. dir. Champaign (Ill.) Urban League, 1969; dep. dir. Concentrated Employment Program, St. Louis, 1971; asst. dir. legis. NASW, Washington, 1971-74; exec. dir. Community Svcs. Coun. Columbia, Mo., 1974-76; dir. Broward County (Fla.) Dept. of Human Svcs., 1976-78; deputy adminstr. Community Svcs. Div. State of Wis., 1978-81; prof. Hunter Coll., CUNY, 1983-94; faculty doctoral program CUNY, 1987-94; dean Coll. Health and Human Svcs., S.E. Mo. State U., Cape Girardeau, 1994—; fellow Ctr. Social Adminstrn., Hunter Coll., 1985-94. Author: New Management in Human Services, 1988, 2d edit., 1995; founding editor Jour. Multicultural Social Work, 1989—; contbr. articles to profl. jours. Pres. bd. S.E. Mo. Weed and Seed Program, Inc., 1996—; v.p. Mo. chpt. Nat. Com. to Prevent Child Abuse, 1996; bd. dirs. Cmty. Counseling Ctr. at S.E. Mo. Capt. USAF, 1963-69. Recipient Martin Luther King/Woodrow Wilson fellowship, 1970, Commendation Resolution, Mo. Gen. Assembly, 1976, GARIOA/Fulbright Rsch. fellowship, Tokyo, 1990-91, Disting. Alumni Svc. award St. Louis U. Sch. Social Svcs., 1996. Mem. Am. Pub. Welfare Assn. (exec. com. 1988), Cape Giradrdeau Downtown Rotary, Omega Psi Phi (Cmty. Svc. award 1977). Avocations: travel, computer software, jazz. Office: Coll Health and Human Svcs Southeast Mo State U Cape Girardeau MO 63701-4799

KEYSER, CHARLES LOVETT, JR., bishop; b. Greenville, S.C., Jan. 19, 1930; s. Lovett and Catherine (Howie) K.; m. Christine Dearing Crutchfield, July 6, 1955; children: Charles Jr., Christine, Catherine, Caroline. BA, U. of the South, 1951, DD (hon.), 1993; MDiv, St. Luke's Sem., 1954. Deacon, priest Diocese of Fla., Jacksonville, 1954-60; staff chaplain, tng. officer, chaplain USN, 1960-86; capt. USN, Vietnam; fleet chaplain to comdr. Europe USN, command chaplain for Marine Corp. Devel. and Edn. Command; rector Washington and Montross parishes Diocese of Va., Oak Grove, 1986-90; suffragan bishop for the Armed Forces Episcopal Ch., New York, 1990—. *

KEYSER, FRANK RAY, JR., lawyer, former governor; b. Chelsea, Vt., Aug. 17, 1927; s. Frank Ray and Ellen L. (Larkin) K.; m. Joan Friedgen, July 15, 1950; children: Christopher Scott, Carol Ellen, Frank Ray III. Student, Tufts Coll., 1946-49, LLD, 1961; LLB, Boston U., 1952; LLD, Norwich U., 1962. Bar: Vt. 1952. Practiced in Chelsea, 1952-65; mem. Vt. Ho. of Reps., 1955-59, speaker, 1959-60; gov. Vt., 1961-63; mem. Wilson & Keyser, 1952-65; v.p., pres., chmn. Vt. Marble Co., 1965-79; of counsel Kayser, Crowley, Carroll, George & Meub, P.C.; chmn., bd. dirs. Hitchcock Clinic, Ctrl., Union Mut. Ins. Co., ICI Mut. Ins. Co. Pres. Green Mountain coun. Boy Scouts Am. With USNR, World War II. Named Outstanding Young Vermonter Vt. Jr. C. of C., 1959; One of 10 Outstanding Young Men in in Nation, Jr. C. of C., 1961. Mem. ABA, Vt. Bar Assn., Vt. Golf Assn. (pres.), Am. Legion, Masons. Republican. Address: 64 Warner Ave Proctor VT 05765-1322 Office: 29 S Main St Rutland VT 05701-5014

KEYSER, JANET MARIE, pharmaceutical industry executive; b. Phila.. BS in Biology, Ursinus Coll., Collegeville, Pa., 1980. Vet. asst. Center Square (Pa.) Vet. Clinic, 1980-81; toxicology biologist Merck & Co., Inc., West Point, Pa., 1981-82, med. data coord., 1982-86, med. program coord., 1986-91, mgr. clin. quality assurance, 1991-97, assoc. dir. clin. quality assurance, 1997-98, dir. clin. quality assurance, 1998—. Mem. choir, mem. revision com. St. John's Luth. Ch., Sumneytown, Pa., 1992—. Mem. Bus. and Profl. Women's Club (sec.-treas. 1983-88), PEO. Republican. Avocations: children's sporting events, horseback riding, hiking, tennis, running. Office: Merck & Co Inc BLA-32 West Point Pike West Point PA 19486

KEYSER, RICHARD LEE, distribution company executive; b. Harrisburg, Pa., Oct. 28, 1942; s. Harold L. and Mary J. (Raup) K.; m. Mary Ellen Carter, June 20, 1964; children: Jeffrey, Jennifer. BS, U.S. Naval Acad., 1964; MBA, Harvard U., 1971. Commd. ensign USN, 1964, advanced through grades to lt., 1966; resigned, 1969; mktg.-analysis mgr. Fleetguard, Inc., Dallas, 1971-72; dir. logistics Fleetguard, Inc., Cookeville, Tenn., 1973-77; gen. mgr. parts ops. Cummins Engine Co., Inc., Columbus, Ind., 1977-83, exec. dir. mktg. ops., 1983-84; pres. NL-Hycalog, Houston, 1984-86; v.p. ops. W.W. Grainger, Inc., Chgo., 1986-87, exec. v.p., 1988-90, pres., 1991—, CEO, 1995—; bd. dirs. Morton Internat. County chmn. blood program ARC, Cookeville, 1976-77; bd. dirs. Preserve To Enjoy, Inc., Columbus, 1983-84, Irene Josselyn Clinic, Northfield, Ill., 1989-92, Lake Forest Grad. Sch. Mgmt., 1992—, Evanston Hosp. Corp., 1996—. Former lt. comdr. USNR. Fellow Am. Prodn. and Inventory Control Soc. (cert.); mem. Chgo. Club, Harvard Bus. Sch. Club Chgo. (v.p. 1988-89, pres. 1989-90), Comml. Club Chgo. Office: WW Grainger Inc 100 Grainger Pkwy Lake Forest IL 60045-5201*

KEYSER, SAMUEL JAY, linguistics educator, university official; b. July 7, 1935; s. Abraham L. and Sabina (Shaplen) K.; children: Rachel Suzanne, Beth Rebecca, Benjamin Jay Kendall. BA, George Washington U., 1956; BA with honors, Oxford (Eng.) U., 1958, MA, 1962; MA, Yale U., 1960, PhD, 1962. Mem. staff Rsch. Lab. Electronics MIT, Cambridge, 1961-62, faculty, 1965-71, mem. faculty, assoc. provost for inst. life, 1989-94, spl. asst. to the provost, 1994-98, emeritus, 1998—; faculty Univ. Coll. London, 1971-72; faculty U. Mass., Amherst, 1972-77, spl. asst. to Chancellor, 1998—, interim alcohol coord., 1999—. Co-author: English Stress: Its Form, Its Growth and Its Role in Verse, 1971, Beginning English Grammar, 1973, CV Phonology, 1983, Rule Generalization and Optionality in Language Change, 1985, (poems) Raising the Dead, 1993; author: (myths) On The Horizon, 1997; editor: (with K. Hale) The View From Building 20, 1993; editor Linguistic Inquiry, 1970—, Current Studies in Linguistics, 1972—, Linguistic Inquiry Monograph Series, 1976—. Peter de Florez chair MIT, 1989. With USAF, 1962-65. Fulbright scholar, 1956-58, sr. Fulbright scholar, 1971-72; recipient Disting. Alumnus award George Washington U., 1992. Mem. Linguistic Soc. Am., Linguistic Soc. Gt. Britain, Philol. Soc., Phi Beta Kappa. Home: 7 Frost St Cambridge MA 02140-1502 Office: Dept Linguistics & Philosophy Rm E39-353 MIT Cambridge MA 02139-4307 *People, like organizations, are very good at starting things and very bad at stopping them. This goes for projects, marriages, and careers. I have found that the best way to stop something is to start something. It makes the stopping much, much easier, at least until the last stop.*

KEYSER-FANICK, CHRISTINE LYNN, banking executive, marketing and strategic planning professional; b. Ft. Dodge, Iowa, Nov. 16, 1956; d. Archie Harlan and LaVonne Janette (Larsen) Keyser. AA, Iowa Cen. Community Coll., Ft. Dodge, 1976; BA, U. No. Iowa, 1979; MA, Drake U., 1985; grad. with honors, Sch. Bank Mktg., Boulder, Colo., 1990, Stonier Grad. Sch. Banking, U. Del., 1996. Educator Marshalltown (Iowa) Community Schs., 1979-84; v.p. LaGrave Klipfel Clarkson, Inc., Des Moines, 1985-87; pub. rels. and mktg. cons. Des Moines, 1987-88; asst. prof. Drake U., Des Moines, 1988; dir. mktg. 1st Insterstate Bank, Des Moines, 1988-89; v.p. Am. Trust & Savings Bank, Dubuque, Iowa, 1989-94; sr. v.p. San Antonio Fed. Credit Union, 1994—; speaker leadership confs. various univs., 1985—; v.p. Women in Mgmt., 1991, pres.-elect, 1992-93, pres., 1993. Contbr. articles to Iowa Commerce Mag., 1988-93. Bd. dirs. Iowa Soc. to Prevent Blindness, Des Moines, 1987-91, Dubuque Main St. Ltd., 1990-93, v.p., 1993; bd. dirs. Dubuque Symphony Orch., 1990-93, Dubuque Coun. for Diversity, 1992-94; bd. dirs., bus. devel. chair Dubuque Main St., 1991-94; mem. pub. rels. com., devel. com. San Antonio Area Coun. Girl Scouts U.S., 1994—, mem. fund devel. com., 1996—; mem. pub. rels. com., memls. com. San Antonio chpt. Am. Heart Assn., bd. dirs. Am. Heart Assoc., 1998—. Named New Bd. Mem. of Yr., Iowa Soc. to Prevent Blindness, 1988, Vol. of Yr., Iowa Main St., 1993; recipient Nat. Charlotte Danstrom Women of Achievement award, 1992. Mem. Pub. Rels. Soc. Am. (pres. Greater Dubuque chpt. 1993, v.p. 1991-92, pres. San Antonio chpt. 1997, bd. dirs. 1995—, assembly del. 1995-97, accredited), Bank Mktg. Assn. (adv. coun. 1989-93, speaker conv. 1998), Am. Mktg. Assn., ITS Inc. Mktg. Com. Advertisers of Dubuque (legis. chair 1990-93, bd. dirs. 1991-93), Dubuque Area C. of C. (membership adv. coun. 1993-94, media coord. Iowa Trade Symposium 1990, All Am. City com. 1994-95), Raddon Fin. Group (speaker 1998). Avocations: writing, volleyball, walking, bicycling. Home: 7114 Valley Trails St San Antonio TX 78250-3477 Office: San Antonio Fd Credit Union PO Box 1356 San Antonio TX 78295-1356

KEYT, DAVID, philosophy and classics educator; b. Indpls., Feb. 22, 1930; s. Herbert Coe and Hazel Marguerite (Sissman) K.; m. Christine Harwood Mullikin, June 25, 1975; children by previous marriage: Sarah, Aaron. A.B., Kenyon Coll., 1951; M.A., Cornell U., 1953, Ph.D., 1955. Instr. dept. philosophy U. Wash., 1957-60, asst. prof., 1960-64, assoc. prof., 1964-69, prof., 1969—, adj. prof. classics, 1977-79, acting chmn. dept. philosophy, 1967-68, 70, 86, winter, spring, 94, chmn. dept. philosophy, 1971-78; vis. asst. prof. dept. philosophy UCLA, 1962-63; vis. assoc. prof. Cornell U., 1968-69; vis. prof. U. Hong Kong, autumn 1987, Princeton U., autumn 1988, U. Calif., Irvine, autumn 1990. Co-editor: (with Fred D. Miller Jr.) A Companion to Aristotle's Politics, 1991; Author: Aristotle Politics, Books V, VI, 1999; contbr. articles in field to profl. jours. Served with U.S. Army, 1955-57. Inst. for Research in the Humanities fellow U. Wis., 1966-67; Ctr. for Hellenic Studies fellow, 1974-75; Inst. for Advanced Study mem., 1983-84. Mem. Am. Philos. Assn., Soc. Ancient Greek Philosophy. Home: 12032 36th Ave NE Seattle WA 98125-5637 Office: U Wash Dept Philosophy Seattle WA 98195

KEZER, PAULINE RYDER, state government executive; b. Boston, Feb. 4, 1942; d. Paul Washington and Madeline (Farmer) Ryder; m. Kenneth Ronald Kezer, Sept. 23, 1962; children: Anne Elizabeth, Pamela Lynne, Cynthia Karen. B in Psychology, Colby Coll., 1963; postgrad. Ctrl. Conn. State Coll., 1978, 83. Tutor sci. and humanities New Britain (Conn.) Schs. Teenage Parent Program, 1964-78; mem. Conn. Ho. of Reps., Hartford, 1979-85, asst. minority leader, 1981-84, asst. majority leader, 1985-86; sec. of state State of Conn., Hartford, 1991-94, asst. treas. intergovtl. affairs, 1998-99; bd. dirs. New Eng. Caucus Women Legislators, 1983-84, chmn., 1985-86; pres. Conn. Order Women Legislators, Hartford, 1981-82; mem. adv. com. Ctrl. Conn. State U. Polit. Inst., New Britain, 1983-84; mem. adv. bd. Colonial Bank, Plainville, Conn., 1980-85; CEO Hartford Ballet, 1995-97; asst. treas., dir. unclaimed property divsn. State of Conn., 1998/99. Camp dir. Girl Scout Council, 1972-81, assoc. chair, 1975-78, v.p., 1979-85, nat. bd. dirs., 1984-93 ; pres., v.p., treas., bd. dirs. YWCA, New Britain, 1971-79; chmn., sec. Inland Wetlands Com., 1972-79; chmn. State Employees Campaign for Charitable Giving, 1992; mem. Rep. Town Com., Plainville, 1977-84; exec. bd. Eastern region Council State Govts.; vol. New Britain Cancer Soc., 1980-85; bd. dirs. Collaboration for Conn.'s Children, 1985—; mem. adv. bd. Tunxis C.C., 1984—; mem. nat. rev. team Project Hometown Am., 1986; hon. chair Conn. Citizen Bee, 1992; vice chair Conn. Rep. Party, 1987-89; gov. chair, Greater Hartford United Way, 1993, 94; bd. dirs. Conn. Special Olympics, 1993-94; co-chair, founder, bd. mem. Conn. Race for the Cure, Susan G. Komen Found. for Breast Cancer Rsch., 1993-99; chmn. Conn. Sports Mus. Hall of Fame Dinner, 1994; Rep. candidate for Gov. of Conn., 1994; mem. curriculum com. women's campaign Yale U., New Haven, 1995; Bd. dirs. Combined Health Appeal Conn., 1995—; mem. Women Execs. in State Gov., 1991-98; bd. dirs., mem. faculty, v.p. Women's Campaign Sch. Yale U., 1992—; mem. bd. dirs. Conn. Combined Health Appeal, 1996, bd. nominating chair, 1995-98; mem. exec. bd. Cmty. Health Charities Conn., 1997—, nat. bd., 1999—; bd. mem. Presiding Bishops Fund for Children, 1998—. Harvard U. fellow Inst. Politics, 1990, Am. Leadership Forum fellow, 1991-92; recipient Thanks Badge and Conn. Yankee award Conn. Yankee Girl Scout council, Farmington, 1982, 79, Women Helping Women award Soroptimists, 1984—, Women of Merit award, Conn. Valley Girl Scouts, 1993, DKG award, 1994; named Outstanding Citizen, Jaycees, Plainville, Conn., 1980, Outstanding Vol., New Britain YWCA, 1978, Legislator of Yr., Conn. Valley Girl Scout coun., Hartford, 1984. Mem. Nat. Order Women Legislators (legis. chair 1986), Nat. Assn. Sec. State Regional V.P., Women Execs. in State Govt., Conn. Fedn. Rep. Women (2d v.p. 1992—), Ea. Region Coun. State Govts. (exec. bd. 1991-92), Nat. Assn. Secs. of State (exec. bd. 1991-92, Alpha Delta Pi. Republican. Episcopalian (vestryman St. Mark's Ch. 1991—). Club: Newcomers (pres. 1965-67) (New Britain).

KEZLARIAN, NANCY KAY, social services administrator, family counselor; b. Royal Oak, Mich., Aug. 26, 1948; d. Barkev A. and Nancy (Israelian) K.; m. Robert S. Vinetz, M.D., Aug. 1995. Student, U. Vienna, Austria, 1969; BA, Albion Coll., 1970; MA in Theatre and TV, U. Mich., 1971; MA in Clin. Psychology, Pepperdine U., 1992. Cert. secondary tchr., Mich., Calif.; lic. Marriage, Family, Child Counselor. Tchr. West Bloomfield Hills (Mich.) High Sch., 1971-76; tchr. ESL, L.A. Pub. Schs., 1976-80; personnel dir. Samuel Goldwyn Co., L.A., 1985-86; dir. adminstrn. and human resources (Norman Lear) Act III Communications, L.A., 1986-90; dir. programs Salvation Army Booth Meml. Ctr., L.A., 1993-94; asst. exec. dir. Florence Crittenton Ctr., L.A., 1994-96, exec. dir., 1996—; owner, mgr. KAZ, hand painted clothing co., L.A., 1980-85; mem. Screen Actors Guild. Actress My Seventeenth Summer, The Big Blue Marble, 1979 (Emmy award for childen's TV programming). Bd. dirs. Calif. Assn. Children's Homes. Named Tchr. of Yr., West Bloomfield Hills High Sch., 1976. Mem. SAG, Pers. and Indsl. Rels. Assn. (legis. rep. dist. 5 1989, 90), Calif. Assn. of Marriage and Family Therapists, L.A. Group psychtherapy Soc., Rotary Internat., Psi Chi. Avocations: writing, world mythologies, theatre, abstract artist, vegetarian chef.

KHABEER, BERYL M.A., poet, playwright, educator; b. Cleve., Jan. 7, 1952; d. Berry James and Doris Lamerle Thompson. BA, Brandeis U., 1976; MPh, Cleve. State U., 1992. Cert. tchr., Ohio. Tchr., tutor Cleve. Bd. Edn., 1985-88; tchg. asst. Cleve. State U., 1989-92; philosophy instr. Cuyahoga C.C., Cleve., 1993-94; substitute tchr. East Cleveland (Ohio) Bd. Edn., 1994, 97—; bd. dirs. New Day Press. Author: (poems) The Eighth Level of Awareness; contbr. poems to lit. publs.; author: He Calls My By the Thunder, 1998, (plays) The Way They Play House, 1970, The Souls of Men, 1970. Civil Rights scholar, 1973; recipient Playwright award ACLU, 1970,

Outstanding Achievement in Poetry award Nat. Libr. Poetry, 1994. Home: 1990 Ford Dr # 712 Cleveland OH 44106

KHACHADURIAN, AVEDIS, physician; b. Aleppo, Syria, Jan. 6, 1926; s. Khachadur and Aznive (Demirjian) K.; m. Laura Hadidian, July 27, 1961; children: Cynthia, Linda. BA, Am. U. of Beirut, 1949, MD, 1953. Resident internal medicine Am. U. of Beirut, 1953-56; fellow Postgrad. Sch. Medicine, London, 1956-57, Harvard Med. Sch., 1957-59; asst. prof. biochemistry and medicine Am. U. of Beirut, 1959-64, assoc. prof., 1964-71, prof., 1971; prof. pediatrics, dir. Clin. Research Center, Northwestern U. Med. Sch., 1971-73; prof. medicine, head div. endocrinology metabolism and nutrition U. Medicine and Dentistry N.J.-R.W. Johnson Med. Sch., Piscataway, N.J., 1973; mem. staff pediatrics Children's Meml. Hosp., Chgo.; cons. U. Chgo. Sch. Medicine. Mem. Am. Diabetes Assn., N.Y. Acad. Sci., Am. Fedn. Cin. Rsch., Am. Heart Assn., Am. Inst. Nutrition, Endocrine Soc., N.Y. Lipid Rsch. Club, Sigma Xi, Alpha Omega Alpha. Achievements include rsch. in genetics; natural history, pathogenesis and treatment of hereditary hyperlipidemias; diabetes; studies on various inborn errors of metabolism; osteoporosis.

KHADDURI, MAJID, international studies educator; b. Mosul, Iraq, Sept. 27, 1909; came to U.S., 1947, naturalized, 1954; s. Khadduri Q. and Latifa (Saati) K.; m. Majdia Dawaff, Dec. 9, 1942; children: Farid, Shirin. BA, Am. U., Beirut, 1932; PhD, U. Chgo., 1938; LHD (hon.), Johns Hopkins U., 1985; LLD (hon.), SUNY, Binghamton, 1989. Prof. higher tchrs. and law colls. Baghdad, 1938-47; vis. prof. Ind. U., 1947-48, U. Chgo., 1948-49; prof. Sch. Advanced Internat. Studies, Johns Hopkins, 1949-70, distinguished research prof., 1970-80; dir. research and edn. Middle East Inst., Washington, 1950—, bd. govs. Author: War and and Peace in the Law of Islam, 1955, Independent Iraq, 1951, Islamic Jurisprodence, 1961, Arab Contemporaries, 1973, The Islamic Conception of Justice, 1985, The Gulf War, 1988; others. Mem. Iraq del. UN Conf., San Francisco, 1945. Recipient Rockefeller research grant for book on Islamic Law of Nations, 1963; decorated Order of Rafidain (Iraq), Order of Merit (Egypt). Mem. Am. Polit. Sci. Assn., Am. Soc. Internat. Law, Shaybani Soc. Internat. Law of Washington (pres.), P.E.N. (sec. Baghdad Ctr. 1940-47, mem. N.Y. Ctr. 1968—), Acad. of Arabic Lang. (Cairo 1983), The Iraqi Acad. (Baghdad 1986), Cosmos Club (Washington). Home: 4454 Tindall St NW Washington DC 20016-2718 Office: 1740 Massachusetts Ave NW Washington DC 20036-1903

KHAIAT, LAURENT E., producer, films; b. Tel Aviv, Israel, May 25, 1968; came to U.S., 1983; s. Alain Victor and Anna Michele (Riczker) K.; m. Akemi Nakata, June 2, 1997. Exec. prodr. Los Caminantes en Vivo, L.A., 1989; prodr. The Right Way, L.A., 1990, Death Penalty, L.A., 1994; assoc. prodr. Dark Secret, L.A., 1995, Death Game, Vancouver, B.C., 1996; coprodr. La Perra de la Frontera, L.A., 1990, Gipsy, L.A., 1990, Killing American Style, L.A., 1991, Samurai Cop, N.Y.C., 1991, Eliminator, L.A., 1992; prodr., dir. Kiss of Steel, 1989; tv prodr. Little Pain, 1995. Recipient Golden Star Halo award So. Calif. Motion Picture Counsel, 1989, Lifetime Membership award, 1989, Jeanie Golden Halo Eagle award, 1989. Mem. Riviera Country Club, Newport Beach Country Club, Sodeguana Country Club, St. Andrews Golf Club. Avocations: golf, horseback riding, snow skiing, swimming, ping-pong. Office: Motion Pictures Internat 421 N Rodeo Dr # 15100 Beverly Hills CA 90210-4500

KHALEEL, RAZIUDDIN, groundwater hydrologist; b. Dhaka, Bangladesh, Nov. 10, 1945; came to U.S., 1972; s. Khaliluddin Bhuiyan and Razia (Begum) B.; m. Shaheen Fahmida Islam, Jan. 10, 1975; 1 child, Anisa Jumana. BS, Bangladesh U. Engring., 1966; MS, Asian Inst. Technology, 1970; PhD, Tex. A&M U., 1977. Postdoctoral rsch. fellow N.C. State U., Raleigh, 1977-80; asst. prof. hydrology N.Mex. Inst. Mining & Technology, Socorro, 1980-85; staff engr. Rockwell Hanford Ops., Richland, Wash., 1985-87; from prin. engr. to fellow engr. Westinghouse Hanford Co., Richland, 1987-96; cons. environ. engr. Fluor Daniel N.W., Richland, 1996—; adj. prof. Wash. State U. Tri-Cities, Richland, 1985—; hydrology cons. to UNESCO and govtl. agys., India, Japan, Taiwan, 1985-91; rschr. in groundwater hydrology. Contbr. articles to profl. jours. Pres. exec. coun. Islamic Ctr. Tri-Cities, Richland, 1993-94. Mem. Am. Geophys. Union, Sigma Xi, Phi Kappa Phi, Gamma Sigma Delta, Alpha Epsilon. Home: 2206 Davison Ave Richland WA 99352-1919 Office: Fluor Daniel NW MS B4-43 PO Box 1050 Richland WA 99352

KHALESSI, MOHAMMAD R., structural engineer, researcher; b. Yazd, Iran, Nov. 18, 1952; came to U.S., 1976; s. Mohammad-Ali and Farangis (Bahadorani) K.; m. Fariba Touhidi, Aug. 14, 1977 (div. 1984); 1 child, Ahoo; m. Mercedeh Rusty, Oct. 25, 1986; 1 child, Bobak. BS, Arya Mehr U., Tehran, Iran, 1976; MS, UCLA, 1978, PhD, 1983. Engr. C.F. Braun, Alhambra, Calif., 1980-81; rsch. engr. UCLA, 1981-83; sr. engr. Allied Signal, Torrance, Calif., 1983-87; sr. engring. splst. Boeing N.Am., Downey, Calif., 1987-97; chief technologist Mitratech Probabilistic, Fountain Valley, Calif., 1997—; bd. dirs. Advanced Probabilistic Rsch., Inc.; adv. Unicorp, VanNuys, Calif., 1995—. Contbr. articles to profl. jours. Recipient Outstanding Engring. Merit award Orange County (Calif.) Engring. Coun ., 1994. Fellow Inst. Advancement Engring.; mem. AIAA, SAE (chair subcom. probabilistic method, comm. 1994—, tech. adv. leadership coun. for probabilistic methods 1995—, Disting. Probabilistic Methods Implementations award 1996). Republican. Muslim. Achievements include pioneering work in practical application of probabilistic methods, integration of probabilistic methods with finite element technique, identification of most-probable-failure point in original space. Office: Mitratech Probabilistic LLC 11770 Warner Ave Ste 203 Fountain Valley CA 92708-2661

KHALID, SAMY, writer; b. Neuchâtel, Switzerland, Jan. 31, 1971; arrived in Can., 1971; s. Mohammed B.M. and Christiane (Sengstag) K.; m. Martine I. Leroux. BA in Translation, U. Ottawa, Ont., Can., 1992, BA in Comm., 1997. Editor, co-pres. Smartcom, Ottawa, 1992-93; translator Liberal Rsch. Bur., Ottawa, 1993-94; writer corr. Prime Min.'s Office, Ottawa, 1994-96, sr. writer French, 1996-97, spl. asst. chief of staff, 1997-98. Avocations: history, genealogy, languages.

KHALIL, MOHAMMAD ASLAM KHAN, environmental science and engineering educator, physics educator; b. Jhansi, India, Jan. 7, 1950; came to U.S., 1963; s. M. Ahsan Khan and Aleem-Un-Nisa K.; m. Giti Ara Eshraghi, June 1973; children: Kathayoon Azra, Kaviyaan Aslam. BA in Physics, Math. and Psychology, U. Minn., 1970; MS in Physics, Va. Polytechnic Inst., 1972; PhD in Physics, U. Tex., 1976; MS in Environ. Sci., Oreg. Grad. Ctr., Beaverton, 1979; PhD in Eviron. Sci., Oreg. Grad. Ctr., 1979. Teaching asst. dept. physics Va. Polytechnic Inst. and State U., 1970-71; grad. asst. dept. math. and physics U. Tex., Austin, 1971-72, teaching asst. dept. physics, 1972-73, 76, rsch. scientist asst. Ctr. for Particle Theory, 1972-76; instr. dept. physics Pacific U., Forest Grove, Oreg., 1978; rsch. asst. dept. environ. sci. Oreg. Grad. Ctr., Beaverton, 1977-79, asst. prof. dept. environ. sci., 1980-82, assoc. prof. dept. environ. sci., 1982-84, prof. dept. chem., biol. and environ. sci., 1984-86, prof. Inst. Atmospheric Sci., 1986-90, prof. dept. environ. sci. and engring., dir. Global Change Rsch. Ctr., 1990-95; prof. dept. physics Portland State U., Oreg., 1995—; owner Andarz Co., Portland, 1981—. Editor: Chemosphere: Global Change Science; mem. editl. bd. Handbook of Environ. Chemistry, Environ. Sci. and Pollution Rsch. Internat.; assoc. editor Atmospheric Environment; contbr. more than 160 articles to profl. jours. Grantee NSF, EPA, Dept. Energy, NASA. Mem. Am. Phys. Soc., Am. Chem. Soc., Am. Geophys. Union, Air and Waste Mgmt. Assn., Sigma Xi. Office: Andarz Co 9961 NW Kaiser Rd Portland OR 97231-2701 also: Portland State U Dept Physics PO Box 751 Portland OR 97207-0751

KHAN, ABDUL RAHIM, mathematics educator, researcher and author; b. Bahawalpur, Punjab, Pakistan, Jan. 1, 1953; s. Muhammad Yar and Sharaf Elahi; m. Mumtaz Perveen, Dec. 1973; 5 children. BSc in Math., Punjab U., Lahore, 1972, BSc with honours, 1973, MSc, 1974; PhD, Univ. Coll. Wales, Aberystwyth, 1983. Lectr. math. Bahauddin Zakariya U., Multan, Pakistan, 1976-84, asst. prof., 1984-88, assoc. prof., 1988—, mem. senate, 1987-90, mem. bd. math. studies, 1984—. Contbr. articles to profl. jours. Mem. Pakistan Assn. for Advancement Sci. (gen. sec. Multan chpt. 1988—), Bahauddin Zakariya U. Tchrs. Assn. (pres. 1991—), Pakistan Tchrs. Forum (fin. sec. 1991—). Avocations: music, hunting. Office: Bahauddin Zakariya U Ctr, Advanced Studies P&A Math, Multan Pakistan

KHAN, AHMED KAMAL, ambassador. Perm. rep. of Pakistan to UN N.Y.C., 1995—. Office: Perm Mission of Pakistan to UN Pakistan House 8 E 65th St New York NY 10021-7005*

KHAN, AMIR U., agricultural engineering consultant; b. Kathgodam, Uttar Pradesh, India, June 15, 1927; came to U.S., 1948; s. Abdul Rehman and Shah Khan; m. Shaheda A. Samad, Mar. 24, 1960; children: Aida, Ayesha, Mona, Omar. BS, Aligarh (India) U., 1947; MS in Gen. Agr., Mich. State U., 1949, MS in Agrl. Engring., 1952, PhD in Agrl. Engring., 1968. Mng. ptnr. Agrimac Industries, Rampur, Uttar Pradesh, 1953-58; dep. dir. Ministry of Industries, Govt. India, New Delhi, 1958-59; head agrl. machinery div. Voltas Ltd., Bombay, 1959-63; rsch. assoc. Mich. State U., East Lansing, 1964-66; head agrl. engring. dept. Internat. Rice Rsch. Inst./Ford Found., Manila, 1968-76; resident rep. Internat. Rice Rsch. Inst., Islamabad, Pakistan, 1976-82; head agrl. engring. dept. Internat. Rice Rsch. Inst., Manila, 1982-87; agrl. mechanization advisor, Nat. Agrl. Rsch. Project Winrock Internat., Giza, Egypt, 1987-94; bd. dirs. Phillipine Soc. Agrl. Engrs., 1984-86; cons. in field. Author: Rural Small Scale Industry in China, 1974, Agriculture of Egypt, 1993; contbr. over 100 articles to various publs.; holder 25 patents in agrl. machinery. Mem. Toledo Islamic Ctr., 1965—. Recipient LDC Innovation award Am. Assn. Engring. Socs., 1985, Internat. Inventors award King Gustav of Sweden, 1986. Fellow Am. Soc. Agrl. Engrs. (Kishida INternat. award 1988), Indian Soc. Agrl. Engrs. (hon. life, Commendation medal 1981), Pakistan Soc. Agrl. Engrs. (hon. life, sec.-treas. 1979, Adamjee Gold medal award 1982). Avocations: collecting antique watches, art nouveau antiques. Home: 300 Coventry Ct Perrysburg OH 43551-1269

KHAN, ARFA, radiologist, educator; b. Srinagar, Kashmir, India, Dec. 4, 1943; came to U.S., 1966; d. Ghulam Rasool and Ruqia Hayat; m. Faroque A. Khan, Apr. 16, 1966; children: Arif O., Shireen. B of Medicine, B of Surgery, Govt. Med. Coll., Kashmir, 1964. Diplomate Am. Bd. Radiology. Intern Barberton (Ohio) Citizen Hosp., 1966-67; resident in radiology L.I. Jewish Med. Ctr., New Hyde Park, N.Y., 1967-70, from instr. to assoc. prof. radiology, 1970-93, prof., 1993—, assoc. chmn. radiology, 1994—; program dir., 1995. Contbr. 50 articles to radiology jours. Mem. Am. Coll. Radiology, Am. Soc. Neuroradiology, Am. Soc. Head & Neck Radiology, Am. Soc. Thoracic Radiology, Radiol. Soc. N.Am. Democrat. Muslim. Avocations: cooking, tennis, aerobics, gardening, skiing. E-mail: khan@lij.edu. Fax: 718-343-7463.

KHAN, MASRUR ALI, nuclear and chemical engineer, physicist; b. Faridpur, Bangladesh, Sept. 24, 1949; arrived in U.S. 1971; s. Yakub Ali Khan and Mahbuba (Karim) Begum; m. Cynthia Louise Reilly, Aug. 8, 1975; children: Tarik, Alia. BS in Physics, U. Dhaka, 1971; BSChemE, U. Wis., 1974, BS in Nuclear Engring., 1976. Group leader for environ. group Commonwealth Edison Co.; with H.B. Robinson Plant; project mgr. Carolina Power and Light Co.; cons. Brunswick Steam Electric Plant, 1981-94, Pub. Svc. Electric and Gas Co., 1989-94, Pa. Power and Light Co., 1990-92; pres. Khan Consulting Svcs., Cary, N.C.; ind. safety reviewer ComEd Nuclear Sites, 1996-97; mentor Ont. Power Generation, Toronto, Can., 1998—; mgmt. cons., ind. safety reviewer N.Y. Power Authority's Design Basis Documents. Contbr. articles to profl. jours. Mem. ASME, AIChE, Am. Mgmt. Assn., Project Mgmt. Inst., Assn. for Info. and Image Mgmt., Assn. Computing Machinery, Am. Nuclear Soc. Home: 217 Brendan Choice Cary NC 27511-5508

KHAN, MOHAMMAD ASAD, geophysicist, educator, former energy minister and senator of Pakistan; b. Aima, Lahore, Pakistan, Aug. 13, 1940; came to U.S., 1964; s. Ghulam Qadir and Hajira (Karim) K.; m. Tahera Pathan, Jan. 4, 1974; 1 dau., Shehzi Samira. B.S., U. Punjab, Lahore, Pakistan, 1957, M.S., 1963; postgrad., Harvard U., 1964-65; Ph.D. (East West Center scholar), U. Hawaii, 1967. Lectr. in geophysics U. Punjab, 1963-64; asst. prof. geophysics and geodesy U. Hawaii, 1967-71, assoc. prof., 1971-74, prof., 1974—; minister of petroleum and natural resources Govt. Pakistan, 1983-86, senator, 1984-86; cabinet mem. Eonc. Coordination Commn. of the Cabinet, Govt. of Pakistan, 1983-86; chmn. internat. advisors, 1987—; chmn. Hydrocarbon Devel. Inst., Pakistan, 1984-86, Attock Oil Refinery, Pakistan, 1984-86; cabinet mem. Nat. Econ. Council, Govt. Pakistan, 1984-86; NSF and NASA fellow Summer Inst. Dynamical Astronomy at MIT, 1968-69; cabinet mem. Econ. Coord. Com. Cabinet Govt. Pakistan, 1983-86; sr. vis. scientist geodynamics Goddard Space Flight Ctr., NASA, Greenbelt, Md., 1972-74; sr. scientist Computer Scis. Corp., Silver Spring, Md., 1974-76, sr. cons., 1976-77; diplomatic minister/adviser Resource Survey and Devel. Pakistan, 1974-76; sr. resident assoc. Nat. Acad. Scis., 1972-74; leader Am. Asian Studies and Contemporary Social Problems Seminar Series, Honolulu, 1968-69. Contbr. articles to profl. publs. Chmn. East and West: A Perspective for the 80's; mem. Hawaii Environ. Council, 1979-83, chmn. exec. com., 1979-83, vice chmn., 1981-83; chmn. Pakistan Relief Fund, Honolulu, 1971. Recipient Gold medal Rawalpindi Union of Journalists, 1985, Pakistan Engring. Coun., 1985, Pakistan Assn. of Minorities, 1984, 85, Disting. Alumnus award for pofl. excellence and leadership U. Hawaii, 1995. Fellow Explorers Club; mem. Geol. Soc. U. Punjab (pres. 1962-63), Am. Geophys. Union, Pakistan Assn. Advancement Sci., Am. Geol. Inst., Am. Geophys. Union, East West Ctr. Alumni Assn. (dir. 1976-80), Internat. Alumni of East West Ctr. (exec. com., chmn. 1977-80, Disting. Alumnus award for Outstanding Career Achievements and Leadership 1984). Achievements include research in geophysics, geodetic and oceanographic applications of satellites, geodynamics, planetary interiors, global tectonics, global correlations, core-mantle boundary problems, equilibrium figures, gravity, isostasy, satellite altimetry, geodesy, earth models, geophysical exploration, ocean dynamics. Office: U Hawaii Hawaii Inst Geophysics 2525 Correa Rd Honolulu HI 96822-2219 *Most men stand the test of adversity quite well, but if you really want to test the character of a man, give him power.*

KHAN, MUNAWWAR JEHAN (MEENA), librarian, investor; b. Kathgodam, India, Apr. 13, 1942; arrived in U.S., 1963; d. Abdul Rehman and Shah Jehan (Khan) K.; m. Abdul Hafeez Khan, June 22, 1968; children: Zeenat H., Zia H., Zeba H. BA in Economics, Polit. Sci. & Geography, Aligarh (India) Muslim U., 1963; BE, U. Toledo, 1969, MLS, 1971. Libr. asst. U. Toledo, 1970-75, head info. svcs., 1975—; libr. Islamic Ctr. Toledo, 1982-93; cons. Campus Ministry, 1990-95, Masjid Saad, 1996—. Mem. ALA, AAUW, AAUP, Ohio Libr. Assn., Ohio Libr. Coun. Office: U Toledo 2801 W Bancroft St Toledo OH 43606-3328

KHAN, RASHID HUSSAIN, physician, researcher; b. Meerut, India, Mar. 28, 1939; came to U.S., 1992; s. Hamid Hussain and Maimoona Begum (Khan) K.; m. Sabiha Perveen Khan, Mar. 7, 1969. MSc, U. Karachi, 1965; PhD, U. Western Ont., 1972; MD, U. Tecnologia de Santiago, Dominican Republic, 1983. Lic. physician, N.C. Rsch. assoc. McMaster U. Med. Ctr., Hamilton, Ont., Can., 1979-80, Toronto Western Hosp., 1983-87, 90-92, U. Toronto, 1985-87, Queen's U. and Kingston (Ont.) Gen. Hosp., 1987-90; resident in medicine Mercy Cath. Med. Ctr., Darby, Pa., 1992-96, chief resident in medicine, 1996-97; physician MMC-Physicans Care, Murphy, N.C., 1997—; Contbr. articles to profl. jours.; patentee in field. Sci. fellow Am. Coll. Allergy and Immunology. Fellow Am. Coll. Allergy and Immunology; mem. AMA. Avocations: fishing, gardening, hunting, reading, computers. Home: 4270 Highway 64 W Murphy NC 28906-8110 Office: MMC-Physicians Care 5465 Highway 64 W Murphy NC 28906-8169

KHAN, RIAZ HUSSAIN, geophysicist, earth sciences educator; b. Lahore, Panjab, Pakistan, Oct. 16, 1929; came to the U.S., 1953; s. Ghulam Ahmed and Iqbal Gul Khan; m. Khlidah Haqnawaz, Sept. 13, 1950; 1 child, Asim Khan (dec.). BS, Panjab U., Lahore, 1946, MA in Earth Sci., 1949; postgrad., Rice U., 1958-60. Prof., lectr. Forman Christian Coll., Lahore, 1949-53; marine geophysicist Offshore Exploration, Inc., Houston, 1954-58; rsch. geophysicist Exxon Oil Co., Houston, 1958-60; geophysicist Robert H. Ray and Macollum Exploration and Globe U. Scis., Midland, Tex., 1960-61; rsch. geophysicist Mobil Oil Co., Dallas, 1960-63; geophys. advisor Sonatrach Nat. Oil Co., Algiers, Algeria, 1963-80; geophysicist cons. Abu Dhabi Nat. Oil Co., Abu Dhabi, United Arab Emirates, 1980-89; ret., 1990; cons. in fields of geophysics, stock market and automation, Cleve. and Dallas, 1990—; assoc. mem. Inst. Engring. in Tech., Brit. Inst. Engring. Tech., London, 1952. Avocations: international short wave radio, satellite television. Home: 1708 Waverly Ct Richardson TX 75082-3100

KHAN, SOHAIL, investment banker; b. Toronto, Ont., Can., July 19, 1972; s. Aslam and Shama Khan. MBA, Lahore U. Mgmt. Scis., Pakistan, 1996. Dir. ops. Cyrus Pharma Pvt., Ltd., Lahore, 1992-96; assoc. Citicorp, Lahore, 1996-97; asst. v.p. Citicorp, N.Y.C., 1998—. Muslem. Avocation: writing. E-mail: sohail.khan@citicorp.com. Home: 235 E 95th St New York NY 10128 Office: Citicorp 399 Park Ave New York NY 10043

KHANDEKAR, JANARDAN DINKAR, oncologist, educator; b. Indore, India, Feb. 1, 1944; came to U.S., 1971; s. Dinker and Sulaochan (Dawlae) K.; m. Amita Oomen, Aug. 28, 1971; children: Manoj, Melin. MD, MBBS, U. Indore, 1969; sabbatical, Northwestern U., Baylor U., 1992. Diplomate Am. Bd. Internal Medicine, Am. Bd. Med. Oncology. Intern M.Y. Hosp., Indore, 1967-70; resident in medicine Allegheny Gen. Hosp., Pitts., 1972-73; head divsn. med. oncology Evanston (Ill.) Hosp., 1975-98, from asst. attending physician to assoc. attending physician, 1975-79, sr. attending physician, 1979—; fellow Med. Rsch. Coun., Montréal, Que., Can., 1970-71, Tufts U., Boston, 1973-75; asst. prof. medicine Northwestern U., Chgo., 1975-80, assoc. prof., 1980-86, prof. medicine, 1986—, Kellogg/Scanlon chair in oncology, 1991-98; dir. cancer control Northwestern U. Cancer Ctr., Chgo., 1991—; assoc. dir. Kellogg Cancer Care Ctr. Evanston Hosp., 1979-87, dir., 1987—; chmn. dept. medicine Evanston Northwestern Healthcare, 1998—; active NIH Ad Hoc Com. on Nat. Prostate Cancer Program, NIH Team for Audit Clin. Trials at Yale U., Roswell Park Meml. Inst., Mayo Clinic, etc.; chmn. rsch. com. and adv. com. Searle Clin. Pharmacology Unit; sr. investigator Eastern Coop. Oncology Group, 1976-83, Community Clin. Oncology Program, 1983—; lectr. in field. Author: (with others) Radiation-Associated Thyroid Carcinoma, 1977, Adjuvant Therapy of Cancer, 1977; contbr. over 135 articles to profl. jours. Recipient cert. of merit Nat. Cancer Inst.; grantee Ill. Cancer Coun., 1983-98, Duke U., 1983-90, Nat. Cancer Inst., 1983—, Women's Health Inst., 1993, Evanston Hosp., 1993—, NIH, 1988-91, 93—. Fellow ACP (laureate); mem. AAAS, Am. Soc. Clin. Oncology, Am. Fedn. Clin. Rsch., Am. Assn. Cancer Rsch., Inst. Medicine (Chgo.). Office: Evanston Hosp 2650 Ridge Ave Evanston IL 60201-1781

KHANDKE, KAILASH, economics educator; b. Bombay, Mar. 15, 1962; came to U.S., 1986.; s. Rajaram and Kamla Khandke; m. Veena Khandke, Aug. 13, 1987; 1 child, Divya. BA, St. Xaviers Coll., Bombay, 1984; MA, U. Calif., Davis, 1989, PhD, 1993. Vis. prof. Santa Clara (Calif.) U., 1990-93, Middlebury (Vt.) Coll., 1993-95; asst. prof. Furman U., Greenville, S.C., 1995—. Author: Economics: Honors Companion, 1993. Recipient Robert E. Hughes Endowed Chair in Econs. and Bus., Furman U., 1996. Office: Furman Univ 3300 Poinsett Hwy Greenville SC 29613

KHANG, CHULSOON, economics educator; b. Kaesong City, South Korea, May 10, 1935; s. Woon-sung and Ji-chung (Lim) K.; m. Yee Yu Lau, Sept. 15, 1959; children—Kenneth, Maurice. B.A. in Econs., Mich. State U., 1959; M.A. in Econs., U. Minn.-Mpls., 1962, Ph.D. in Econs., 1965. Asst. prof. econs. San Diego State U., 1963-66; asst. prof. econs. U. Oreg., Eugene, 1966-69, assoc. prof., 1969-73, prof., 1973-97, prof. emeritus, 1997; vis. prof., research grantee U. New South Wales, Australia, 1972-73; vis. prof., Fulbright fellow Hanguk U. Fgn. Studies, Seoul, Korea, 1979; vis. prof. U. Hawaii, Honolulu, 1989. Referee, Am. Econ. Rev., Jour. Internat. Econs., Rev. Econ. Studies, Jour. Fin., Jour. Polit. Econs., Jour. Banking and Fin., Jour. Econs. and Bus., Internat. Econ. Rev. Contbr. articles to profl. jours. Mem. Eugene Area Korean Assn. (past pres.), Am. Econ. Assn. Republican. Home: 224 Edgewood Dr Port Ludlow WA 98365-9225 Office: U Oreg Dept Econs Eugene OR 97403

KHANNA, DINESH NARAIN, chemist; b. Dehra Dun, India, Feb. 2, 1955; came to U.S., 1982; s. Prem N. and Savitri (Tandon) K.; m. Achla Gupta, Oct. 25, 1983; children: Tushar, Shefali. BS in Chemistry, Dayanand Brijendra Swaroop Coll., Dehra Dun, 1974, MS in Organic Chemistry, 1976; PhD in Polymer Chemistry, Indian Inst. Tech., New Delhi, 1980. Rsch. officer Sri Ram Inst., New Delhi, 1981; postdoctoral rsch. assoc. U. Mass., Amherst, 1983-84; sr. rsch. chemist Hoechst Corp., Coventry, R.I., 1985-87; rsch. assoc. Hoechst Celanese, Coventry, 1987-89, staff chemist, 1989-92; group leader Hoechst Celanese, Branchburg, N.J., 1993-96; mgr. R & D Clariant Corp., Branchburg, 1997—; chairperson statis. symposium Hoechst Celanese, 1987, chairperson seminar program, 1987-91. Inventor, patentee in field; contbr. articles to sci. jours. Mem. Am. Chem. Soc. (divsn. polymer chemistry, divsn. polymer materials sci. and engring.), Soc. Plastic Engring. (session chairperson 1985-91, chairperson internat. symposium on polyimides 1991). E-mail: dinesh.khanna@clariant.com. Home: 7 Sutton Farm Rd Flemington NJ 08822-2725 Office: Clariant AZ Electronic Materials 70 Meister Ave Somerville NJ 08876-3440

KHANNA, FAQIR CHAND, physics educator; b. India, Jan. 23, 1935; came to U.S., 1958; s. Ram S. D. Khanna and Ram Ditti Malhotra; m. Swaraj Mukul, Jan. 16, 1966; children: Shrawan F., Varun F. BSc with honors, Panjab U., 1955, MSc with honors, 1956; PhD, Fla. State U., 1962. Sr. rsch. officer Chalk River Nuclear Labs., 1966-84; prof. physics U. Alta., Edmonton, Alta., Can., 1984—. Fellow Am. Phys. Soc. Achievements include research in subatomic physics; nuclear and particle physics; many-body physics. Office: U Alta, Theoretical Physics Inst, Edmonton, AB Canada T6G 2J1*

KHANSUR, TAWFIQ IFTEKHAR, physician, researcher, educator; b. Dacca, Bangladesh, Aug. 20, 1949; s. Salamat Ali and Jahanara (Mallick) K.; m. Nusrat Jahan Mirza, Feb. 10, 1980; children: Shad, Emaad. MD, Dacca Med. Coll., 1973. Intern Bklyn. Cumberlnad Med. Ctr., 1975-76; resident Jersey City (N.J.) Med. Ctr., 1976-78; fellow in hematology and oncology Univ. Miss. Med. Ctr., 1978-80; rsch. fellow in immunology Meml. Sloan Kettering Cancer Ctr., N.Y.C., 1980-81; attending physician, oncology svc. U. Miss. Med. Ctr., Jackson, 1981—, assoc. prof., 1988-95, prof. medicine, 1995—; chief of oncology VA Med. Ctr., Jackson, 1989—. Author numerous rsch. articles on cancer biology and treatment. Fellow ACP; mem. Am. Soc. Hematology, Am. Soc. Clin. Oncology, Am. Assn. Cancer Edn., Am. Assn. Cancer Rsch. Home: 1340 Bay Vis Brandon MS 39047-8652 Office: U Miss Med Ctr 2500 N State St Jackson MS 39216-4500

KHANZADIAN, VAHAN, tenor; b. Syracuse, N.Y., Jan. 23, 1939; s. Avedis Sarkis and Araxey (Youghian) K. B.S., U. Buffalo, 1962; postgrad., Curtis Inst. Music, Phila., 1961-63. Debut as Ruggero in La Rondine, San Francisco Spring Opera, 1968; leading roles in Wozzeck, Fra Diavolo, Les Troyens, Madama Butterfly, Lucia Di Lammermoor, Tosca; appeared throughout U.S., Can.; appeared in title role in Don Carlo, Basel, Switerland, 1992; debut as Calaf in Puccini's Turandot with Bavarian State Opera, Munich, Germany, 1995; appeared with all major opera cos., and opera festivals, including San Antonio, Ravinia, Tanglewood, Saratoga, Opera de Colombia; numerous solo recitals throughout N.Am.; appeared with symphony orchs., including Chgo., Boston, Phila., Cleve., Minn., Indpls., St. Louis, Milw., Pitts.; TV appearances include Gherman in Tchaikovsky's Queen of Spades; soloist in world premier of Menotti's Landscapes and Remembrances, PBS, 1976; leading tenor Met. Opera, 1991-99; debut as Gustavo in Un Ballo in Maschera, Met. Opera, 1993, Lyric Opera Chgo., 1993. Served with U.S. Army, 1964-65. Sullivan Found. grantee, 1971-74; Rockefeller Found. grantee, 1971-73. Address: 3604 Broadway Apt 2N New York NY 10031-3200 *My ethnic background, Armenian, with its strong Christian influence was instrumental in projecting the importance of family, religion, education, and culture. The strength and knowledge attained in this environment guided me in the arts, where I was fortunate to have had the discipline and the opportunity to pursue my goal of making a contribution in serving music.*

KHANZINA, HELEN P., English educator, translator; b. Perm, Russia, Aug. 28, 1954; came to U.S., 1995; d. Pavel L. and Dina B. Wexler; m. Yevgenii A. Khanzhin, Dec. 4, 1975 (div. Jan. 1984); 1 child, Dmitri. MA in English Lit., U. Perm, 1976; PhD in World Lit., U. St. Petersburg, 1985; assoc. prof. diploma, USSR State Com. Nat. Edn., Moscow, 1991. Asst. then assoc. prof. dept. world lit. U. Perm, 1976-95; lectr. dept. English div. continuing edn. U. Va., Charlottesville, 1996-98; interpreter Lang. Learning Enterprises, Washington, 1996—; libr. joint state govt. commn. gen. assembly Commonwealth Pa., Harrisburg, 1998—; lectr. Sch. of Humanities Pa. State U., Harrisburg and Middletown, Pa., 1999—. Author: The Making of the National Tradition in American Romantice Poetry and William Cullen Bryant's Creative Work, 1987, Genre, Mode and Style in American Romantic Poetry, 1998; editor: Problems of Method and Poetics in World Literature of the Nineteenth and Twentieth Centuries, 1995, 97; contbr. articles to profl. jours. Vis. scholar grantee USIA, 1993-94, Brit. Coun. Beatrice Ward Found., 1990. Mem. MLA, Am. Assn. Tchrs. Slavic and E. European Langs., Pa. Libr. Assn. Avocations: classical music, ballet, painting, sculpture. E-mail: ykhanzhi@legis.state.pa.us. Office: Joint State Govt Commn 108 Fin Bldg Harrisburg PA 17120

KHARE, MOHAN, chemist; b. Varanasi, India, May 15, 1942; came to U.S., 1967, naturalized, 1971; s. Dwarka Nath and Rampyari Devi Khare Srivastava; m. Meena K., Nov. 20, 1973; 1 child, Rohit. BSc, Banaras Hindu U., 1961, MSc, 1963, PhD, 1967. Rsch. assoc. U. Md., College Park, 1967-69, Oreg. State U., Corvallis, 1969-70; sr. rsch. assoc. Cornell U., Ithaca, N.Y., 1970-78; analytical specialist Hydroscience Inc., (subsidiary of Dow Chem. Co.), Knoxville, Tenn., 1978-80; tech. specialist IT Enviroscience subs. IT Corp., Knoxville, 1980-82; rsch. prof. chemistry U. Nev., Las Vegas, 1982-84, mgr. organic div. quality assurance lab. under coop. agreement with EPA, 1982-84; mgr. organic analysis lab. Environ. Monitoring Svcs. Rockwell Internat., Thousand Oaks, Calif., 1984-85; dir. environ. analytical lab. EA Engring, Sci., and Tech., Inc., Sparks, Md., 1985-87; sr. v.p. Recra Environ., Inc., Columbia, Md., 1987-89; pres., chief exec. officer Envirosystems, Inc., Columbia, 1989—; cons. to toxic and hazardous waste analytical labs.; mem. panel peer rev. Toxic Organis Lab. Contbr. articles to profl. jours. including protocols and standard oper. procedures for hazardous waste analytical program. Mem. AAAS, Am. Chem. Soc., Am. Water Works Assn., Internat. Union Pure and Applied Chemistry, Internat. Assn. of Environmental Testing Laboratory. Home: 10189 Maxine St Ellicott City MD 21042-6351 Office: Envirosystems Inc 9200 Rumsey Rd Ste 102B Columbia MD 21045-1934

KHASDAY, ALYCE FIELD, literary and film agent, psychic consultant, business owner; b. Bklyn., May 2, 1943; children: Jamie, Cortnie. Student, NYU, 1961-63; grad., La Varenne Culinary Inst. Sales mgr. Malom Lingerie, N.Y.C., 1962-66; sales coord. Sherman Underwear, N.Y.C., 1966-71; pub. rels. cons. Espon, Can., Can., 1977; organizer press confs. preventive medicine, 1977—; pres., fin. planner Greenbelt Equities, Inc., N.Y.C., 1982-84; archtl. planner, developer, pres. Kasday Design, N.Y.C., 1977-87; pres., syndicator, developer real estate, mgr. M & M Mgmt. Corp., Fla., 1984—; pres., CEO, Kombucha Magic Mushroom Farms, Inc., health beverage co., N.Y.C., N.Y.; asst. chef to Isabelle Marique, N.Y.C., Albert Jorant, Paris; founder Psychic Life Counselling, Fla., 1990—; psychic cons. various orgns. including Am. Women in Radio and T.V. Avocations: swimming, biking, skiing, French cooking. Office: 560 E 77th St Apt 520 New York NY 10162-0002 also: Kombucha Magic Mushroom Farms Inc PO Box 20717 New York NY 10021-0074

KHATAIN, KENNETH GEORGE, psychiatrist, former air force officer; b. Seattle, Oct. 11, 1953; s. Edward and LaVerne Mae (Bender) K.; children: Alanna E., Larissa E. AAS, Edmonds Community Coll., Lynnwood, Wash., 1976; BS in Molecular and Cellular Biology, U. Wash., 1978; MD, Wayne State U., 1986. Diplomate Am. Bd. Psychiatry and Neurology with qualifications in geriatric psychiatry, Nat. Bd. Med. Examiners. Resident in psychiatry Wright State U., Dayton, Ohio, 1986-90; commd. capt. USAF, 1986; advanced through grades to maj., 1992; chief inpatient psychiatry mental health svcs. Wilford Hall Med. Ctr., Lackland AFB, Tex., 1990-94; chief inpatient psychiatry VA Med. Ctr., Boise, Idaho, 1994-97; psychiatric cons. Idaho Maximum Security Prison, Boise, 1997—; psychiat. cons. Snake River Correctional Instn., Ontario, Oreg., 1999—; guest reviewer AIDS articles Psychiat. Svcs., 1988—; clin. cons. Nat. Tng. Lab. Inst., Bethel, Maine, 1989; workshop presenter, guest spkr. in field. Mem. adult edn. com. Westminster Presbyn. Ch., Dayton, 1989. Recipient physician recognition award AMA, 1989, Arnold Allen outstanding resident award Wright State U., 1990. Mem. Am. Psychiat. Assn., Tex. Soc. Psychiat. Physicians, Bexar County Psychiat. Soc., Phi Beta Kappa, Phi Theta Kappa. Avocations: jazz, rock and blues drumming, woodworking, ballroom dancing. Office: VA Med Ctr 500 W Fort St Boise ID 83702-4535

KHAYAT, ROBERT CONRAD, chancellor; b. Moss Point, Miss., Apr. 18, 1938; m. Margaret Denton; children: Margaret D. Khayat Bratt, Robert C. Jr. BA in Edn., U. Miss., 1961, JD, 1966; LLM, Yale U., 1981. Bar: Miss. 1966. With Wash. Redskins, 1960-64; pvt. practice in law, mcpl. judge City of Moss Point, Pascagoula, Miss., 1967-69; mcpl. judge City of Oxford, Miss.; pvt. practice in law Oxford, 1975-77; mem. faculty Sch. Law U. Miss., University, 1969—, vice-chancellor for univ. affairs, 1984-89, prof. law, interim dir. athletics, 1994, chancellor, 1995—; pres. NCAA Found., 1989-92. Contbr. articles to law jours. Chmn. United Fund Oxford-Lafayette County First Dr., 1971, Law Ctr. Dedication Com., 1978-79; chmn. courthouse restoration com. Lafayette County Courthouse, 1977; pres. M-Club Alumni chpt. U. Miss. Alumni Assn., 1970-71, Oxford-Lafayette County C. of C., 1973-74, Fellowship of Christian Athletes adult chpt., 1983; bd. trustees United So. Bank; tchr. young adult Sunday sch. Oxford-University United Meth. Ch. Recipient Nat. Football Found. Disting. Am. award, 1987, 89; featured in Springboard to Success sect. of 1987-88 The NFL and You; Sterling fellow Yale U., 1981; Miss. Law Jour. Endowed scholar, 1994. Mem. ABA, ATLA, Miss. State Bar, Miss. Bar Found. (trustee 1988-89), Lamar Order, Omicron Delta Kappa, Phi Delta Phi, Phi Kappa Phi. Office: U Miss Chancellor's Office 109 Lyceum University MS 38677

KHAZEI, AMIR MOHSEN, surgeon, oncologist; m. Carmeline Victoria Grace Picardi; children: Alan, Darla, Mia, Lance. BS, U. Lausanne, Switzerland, 1952, MD and Cert. d'Etudes Medicale, 1957. Diplomate Mass. Bd. Medicine, N.H. Bd. Medicine; qualified Am. Bd. Surgery. Intern Mercy Hosp., Pitts., 1957-58, resident in gen. surgery, 1957-62; fellow in surgery Lahey Clinic Found., Boston, 1962-63, assoc. staff mem. surgery and chemotherapy, 1963-67, assoc. dir. surg. rsch. lab., 1967-68; attending surgeon VA Hosp., Manchester, N.H., 1968-70; staff surgeon Cath. Med. Ctr./Elliot Hosp., Manchester, 1971—; pres., chmn. exec. com. of med. staff Cath. Med. Ctr., 1981-82, chmn. dept. surgery, 1986-87. Mem. editorial bd. Living With Cancer; co-author book; contbr. articles to profl. jours. Bd. dirs., incorporator Cath. Med. Ctr., 1981—, trustee, 1981-90; trustee Fiedlity Health Alliance Bd., Manchester, 1991-93, N.H. Nurses Found., 1991-95; pres. N.H. div. Am. Cancer Soc., 1977-79, nat. del. dir., 1982-91. Recipient of the Key ot the City of Manchester, 1981, St. George medal Am. Cancer Soc., 1982, Golden Apple award Cath. Med. Ctr., 1990, Med. Staff award N.H. Hosp. Assn., 1990, AMA Physician Regognition award, 1971—, Am. Cancer Soc. Cert. Merit for Outstanding Cancer Edn. Program, 1977, Am. Cancer Soc. Cert. Appreciation for Outstanding Uterine and Breast Cancer Detection Program, 1973-74. Fellow Am. Coll. Angiology, Internat. Coll. Angiology, Inter-Am. Coll. Physicians and Surgeons, Internat. Coll. Surgeons; mem. AMA (Physician Recognition award 1971—), Am. Fedn. Clin. Rsch., N.H. Med. Soc. (pres., chmn. exec. com. 1986-87, trustee 1992-96, pres., chmn. bd. trustees 1996-99), N.Y. Acad. Scis., Orgn. State Med. Assn. Pres.'s (life), Transplantation Soc., Hillsborough County Med. Soc. (pres. 1981-82), Am. Assn. for Cancer Edn., Soc. Laparo-endoscopic Surgeons, Am. Coll. Physician Execs., Am. Coll. Forensic Examiners. Office: Bedford Commons Bldg 3 36 Riverway Pl Bedford NH 03110-6744

KHAZEN, ALEKSANDR MOISEYEVICH, physicist; b. Russia, Feb. 28, 1933; s. Moisey M. and Isida A. (Neimark) K.; m. Rimma B. Zil'ber, Dec. 17, 1963; children: Igor, Anatoly, Irina. MSc in Thermodynamics and Electronics, Power U., 1957; MS in Math. and Mechanics, Lomonosov State U., 1962, PhD in Physics and Math., 1965. Supr. of studies of scientific rsch. lab. Inst. of Mechanics, Lomonosov State U., 1960-93. Author: The Laws of Evolution of Life and "Just Society,", 1997, 2nd edit., 1998, Introduction of the Measure of Information into the Axiomatic Basis of Mechanics, 1996, 2d edit., 1998, What is Possible and Impossible in Science or Where the Limits to Artificial Intelligence, 1988 (diploma in contest 1989), Field, Waves, Particles and their Models, 1979 (medal 1980), Interference, Lasers and Superfast-acting Computers, 1972, Modern Electronics, 1972 (medal 1980), Magnetic Elements in Electronics, 1968, Introduction into Electronics, 1968; contbr. over 100 articles to profl. jours. Mem. N.Y. Acad. Sci. Achievements include 26 patents from US, Eng., Russia, Denmark and France. E-mail: akhazen@yahoo.com. Home: 7 Village Grn Apt J Budd Lake NJ 07828-1307

KHEEL, THEODORE WOODROW, lawyer, arbitrator and mediator; b. N.Y.C., May 9, 1914; s. Samuel and Kate (Herzenstein) K.; m. Ann Sunstein, July 1, 1937; children: Ellen Jacobs, Robert J., Constance, Martha, Jane Kheel Stanley, Katherine Fleischman. AB, Cornell U., 1935, LLB, 1937. Bar: N.Y. 1937. Ptnr. Battle Fowler, 1949-82, of counsel, 1982—; pres. Earth Pledge Found., 1991—; pres. Found. for Prevention & Early Resolution of Conflict, 1994—; mem. presdl. bds. various labor disputes, 1962-66; spl. cons. Pres.'s Com. on EEO, 1962-63. Author: Transit and Arbitration, 1960, Pros and Cons of Compulsory Arbitration, 1961, How Race Relations Affect Your Business, 1963, Guide to Fair Employment Practices, 1964, Kheel on Labor Law, 1974—, Keys to Conflict Resolution, 1999. Pres. Nat. Urban League, 1956-60; mem. Pres.'s Nat. Citizens Com. for Cmty. Rels., 1964-68. Mem. Am. Arbitration Assn. (bd. dirs.). Home: 407 W 246th St Bronx NY 10471-3302 Office: 75 E 55th St Fl 5 New York NY 10022-3205

KHERA, RAJ PAL, civil and environmental engineering educator; b. Jhang, Punjab, India, Mar. 27, 1935; came to U.S., 1961; s. Dharampal and Dharamwati (Verma) K.; m. Astrid Karin Szallies; children: Kamni, Navin. Student, Tech. U., Berlin, 1960-61; MSCE, Ohio State U., 1962; PhD, Northwestern U., 1967. Registered profl. engr., N.J., N.Y. Engr. Salzgitter (Fed. Republic of Germany) Stahlbau, 1959-60, Steffen and Noele, Berlin, 1960-61; prof. civil and environ. engring. N.J. Inst. Tech., Newark, 1966—; cons. Raamot Assocs., N.Y.C., 1968-72, Converse Cons. East, West Caldwel, N.J., 1980—. Author: Geotechnology of Waste Management, 1990, 2nd edit., 1998; contbr. numerous articles to profl. jours. Fulbright fellow, 1979; named rsch. scientist German Acad. Exch., Bonn, 1980; recipient several grants including NSF, N.J. State. Fellow ASCE (mem. several coms., editor procs. 1986), Am. Soc. Engring. Edn. (mem. several coms.), Assn. Indians in Am. (v.p. 1988-90). Office: NJ Inst Tech 323 Martin Luther King Jr Blvd Newark NJ 07102-1824

KHERDIAN, DAVID, author; b. Racine, Wis., Dec. 17, 1931; s. Melkon and Veron (Dumehjian) K.; m. Kato Rozeboom, 1968 (div. 1970); m. Nonny Hogrogian, Mar. 17, 1971. BS in Philosophy, U. Wis., 1960. Lit. cons. Northwestern U., 1965; founder/editor Giligia Press, 1966-72; rarebook cons. Fresno State Coll., Calif., 1968-69; lectr. Fresno State Coll., 1969-70; ofcl. poet-in-the-schs. State of N.H., 1971; editor Ararat mag., 1971-72; dir. Two Rivers Press, Aurora, Oreg., 1978-86; poetry judge, lectr., reader of own poetry; founder, editor (with Nonny Hogrogian) The Press at Butternut Creek, 1987-88. Author: On The Death of My Father and Other Poems, 1970, Homage to Adana, 1970, Looking Over Hills, 1972, The Nonny Poems, 1974, Any Day of Your Life, 1975, Country, Cat: City, Cat, 1978, I Remember Root River, 1978, The Road From Home: The Story of an Armenian Girl (Lewis Carroll Shelf award, Boston Globe/Horn Book award, Newbery Honor Book award, Jane Addams Peace award, Banta award), 1979, The Farm, 1979, It Started With Old Man Bean, 1980, Finding Home, 1981, Taking the Soundings on Third Avenue, 1981, The Farm: Book Two, 1981, Beyond Two Rivers, 1981 (Friends of Am. Writers award), The Song in the Walnut Grove, 1982, Place of Birth, 1983, Right Now, 1983, The Mystery of the Diamond in the Wood, 1983, Root River Run, 1984, The Animal, 1984, Threads of Light: The Farm Poems Books III and IV, 1985, Bridger: The Story of a Mountain Man, 1987, Poems to an Essence Friend, 1987, A Song for Uncle Harry, 1989, the Cat's Midsummer Jamboree, 1990, The Dividing River/The Meeting Shore, 1990, On a Spaceship with Beelzebub: By a Grandson of Gurdjieff, 1990, The Great Fishing Contest, 1991, Friends: A Memoir, 1993, Juna's Journey, 1993, Asking the River, 1993, By Myself, 1993, My Racine, 1994, Lullaby for Emily, 1995, Seven Poems for Mikey, 1997, The Rose's Smile, 1997, I Called It Home, 1997, The Golden Bracelet, 1998; also bibliographies.; editor: Visions of America by the Poets of Our Time, 1973, Settling America: The Ethnic Expression of 14 Contemporary Poets, 1974, Poems Here and Now, 1976, Traveling America with Today's Poets, 1976, The Dog Writes on the Window with His Nose and Other Poems, 1977, If Dragon Flies Made Honey, 1977, I Sing the Song of Myself, 1978, Beat Voices: An Anthology of Beat Poetry, 1995; co-editor: Down at the Santa Fe Depot: 20 Fresno Poets, 1970; translator: The Pearl: Hymn of the Robe of Glory, 1979, Pigs Never See the Stars: Armenian Proverbs, 1982, Monkey: A Journey to the West, 1992, Feathers and Tails: Animal Fables From Around the World. Served with AUS, 1952-54. Office: 7121 Palm Ave Sebastopol CA 95472-4324 *The poet understands that everything is connected and all is one. This is all he really knows. But knowing this he is permitted to speak, quietly, disturbing nothing, removing nothing, revealing only the new-old relationships he has been given to see.*

KHESHGI-GENOVESE, ZAREENA, psychotherapist, educator; b. Bay Shore, N.Y., Oct. 17, 1952; d. Saeed M. and Henrietta Kheshgi; m. Thomas Anthony Genovese, Oct. 17, 1982; 1 child, Tara Anne. BSW, U. Ill., 1975; MSW, U. Ill., Chgo., 1980; D in Social Work, Loyola U., Chgo., 1993. Lic. clin. social worker. Alcoholism counselor Luth. Social Svcs., Chgo., 1978-79; inpatient psychotherapy intern Ill. State Psychiat. Inst., Chgo., 1979; psychotherapy intern Ravenswood Mental Health, Chgo., 1979-80; med. social worker Children's Meml. Hosp., Chgo., 1980-81; psychotherapist Edgewater-Uptown Mental Health, Chgo., 1981-85; pvt. practice Chgo., 1986—; psychotherapist Student Mental Health Ctr., Northwestern U., Evanston, Ill., 1988-89, Interaction Dynamics, Chgo., 1995-96; social worker Baxter Corp., Chgo., 1991-95; adj. instr. Loyola U., Chgo., 1994-95; asst. prof. Aurora (Ill.) U. Sch. Socail Work, 1995—. Guest editor Families in Society, 1997; contbr. articles to profl. jours. Recipient award Fahs-Beck Fund for Rsch. and Experimentation, N.Y.C., 1992. Mem. NASW (bd. cert. diplomate in clin. social work), Acad. Cert. Social Workers, Soc. for Social Work and Rsch. E-mail: zgenoves@aurora.edu. Office: Aurora Univ Sch Social Work 347 S Gladstone Ave Aurora IL 60506-4892

KHIM, JAY WOOK, high technology systems integration executive; b. Taegu, Korea, Oct. 22, 1940; came to U.S., 1965; s. Joon Mook and Soon E. (Lee) K. BS in Agrl. Econs., Kyung Pook U., Korea, 1963, MA in Agrl. Econs., 1966; postgrad. PhD program in Econs., U. Md., 1965-69; LLD (hon.), Randolph-Macon Coll., 1988; PhD (hon.), Kyungpook Nat. U., Republic of Korea, 1990. Mem. rsch. staff Brookings Instn., Washington, 1967-69; sr. economist NAB, Dept. of Labor, Washington, 1969-72; sr. assoc. Planning Rsch. Corp., Washington, 1972-74; chmn., CEO JWK Internat. Corp., Washington, 1974—, Internat. Trade and Investment Corp., Washington, 1977—; bd. dirs. United Bank. Author: The Third Eye, 1998; author, editor more than 100 research reports, articles for fed. govt. in fields of health, energy, def., transp., housing and internat. affairs. Bd. dirs. Fulbright Found., 1999—, Asia Soc., Washington, 1999—, George Mason Inst., George Mason U., Fairfax, Va., 1983—, United Bank, 1997—, No. Va. Cmty. Found., 1998—, Worf Trap Found. for Performing Arts, 1998—; mem. World Presidents Orgn., 1992—, chmn. Washington Met. chpt., 1994; bd. govs. U. Md. Alumni Assn.; bd. trustees Fairfax Hosp. Assn., 1986—; candidate for U.S. Congress from 11th Va. dist., 1992; chmn. fin. com. Rep. Party, Va.; commr. Small and Minority Bus. Commn., Fairfax County, 1992. Fulbright scholar, 1965, 66; recipient Sam Ill Found. award Korea, 1962, 63. Mem. Young Pres.'s Orgn., Pres. Club of Am. Mgmt. Assn., Nat. Security Assn., Am. Def. Preparedness Assn., Am. Econ. Assn., Fairfax C. of C. (bd. dirs. 1984-87), World Pres.'s Orgn. (chmn. Washington Met. chtp. 1994-95), City Club, Tower Club, Robert Trent Jones Club, Tournament of Players Club, Internat. Club (D.C.), River Bend Country Club, Fairbanks Golf and Country Club (San Diego). Office: JWK Internat Corp 7617 Little River Tpke Ste 1000 Annandale VA 22003-2689 also: 10900 Tara Rd Potomac MD 20854-1342

KHINDUKA, SHANTI KUMAR, university administrator, educator; b. Jaipur, Rajasthan, India, Dec. 22, 1933; came to U.S., 1964; s. Ram C. and Koka D. Khinduka; m. Manorama Khinduka, May 5, 1955; children: Abha, Seema. BA, Rajasthan U., 1953; MSW, Lucknow U., India, 1955, U. So. Calif., 1961; PhD, Brandeis U., 1968. Asst. prof. Lucknow U., 1955-64; assoc. social affairs office UN, N.Y.C., 1965; from assoc. to prof., asst. dean St. Louis U., 1967-74; prof. social work, dean Washington U., St. Louis, 1974—. Editor: Social Work in India, 2d edit., 1965; co-editor: Social Work in Practice, 1976, Profiles in International Social Work, 1992; chmn. edit. bd. Jour. Social Service Research, 1976—; contbr. articles to profl. jours. Bd. dirs. Council on Social Work Edn., 1978-81, commn. accreditation, 1984-88; bd. dirs. United Way of St. Louis, 1982—, Mo. Goodwill Industries, 1987—. Mem. Nat. Assn. Social Workers (chmn. symposium planning com. 1978-79, chmn. publ. com. 1985-89, 97—), Nat. Conf. Social Welfare (bd. dirs. 1979-82). Avocations: reading, travel. Home: 354 Cooperstown Dr Chesterfield MO 63017-2904 Office: Washington U G Warren Brown Sch Social Work PO Box 1196 Saint Louis MO 63188-1196

KHINOY, ANDREW, journalist; b. Apr. 12, 1915. BA, Columbia U., 1936, MS in Journalism, 1937. Copy editor, slotman, telegraph editor, news editor The Phila. Inquirer, 1937-47, asst. mng. editor, 1947-80; ret., 1980; travel writer, Phila., 1980—; disaster assistance employee (pub. affairs officer FEMA, 1982—). Mem. Soc. Profl. Journalists (bd. dirs. Phila. chpt., 1977—), Pen and Pencil Club. E-mail: akhinoy@aol.com.

KHO, EUSEBIO, surgeon; b. The Philippines, Dec. 16, 1933; came to U.S., 1964; s. Joaquin and Francisca (Chua) K.; m. Grace Casas Lim, May 24, 1964; children: Michelle Mae, April Tiffany, Bradley Jude, Jaclyn Ashley, Matthew Ryan. AA, Silliman U., The Philippines, 1955; MD, State U. Philippines, 1960. Diplomate Am. Bd. Surgery. Rotating intern Philippine Gen. Hosp., U. Philippines, 1959-60; resident gen. practice Silliman U. Med. Ctr., 1960-63; virology rschr. Van Howelling Lab. Silliman U., 1963-64; intern in surgery Francis Scott Key Med. Ctr., 1964-65, resident in gen. surgery, 1965-67; fellow in surgery Johns Hopkins, 1965-67; rsch. assoc. pediat. surgery U. Chgo. Hosps., 1967-68; resident in gen. surgery then chief resident U. Tex. Hosp., San Antonio, 1968-70; hosp. surgeon St. Anthony Hosp., Louisville, 1970-72; practice medicine specializing in surgery Scottsburg, Ind., 1972—; chmn. dept. surgery Scott County Meml. Hosp., 1973—; cons. surgeon Washington County Meml. Hosp., Salem, Ind., also Clark County Meml. Hosp., Jeffersonville, Ind., 1973—; courtesy surgeon Suburban Hosp., Louisville, 1973—; gen. surgeon 5010 U.S. Army Hosp., Louisville, 1980—. Bd. dirs. Make-A-Wish Found., Ind., 1992—. Col. M.C., USAR, 1980—, Operation Desert Storm, 1990-91. Fellow ACS, Am. Soc. Abdominal Surgeons, Am. Coll. Emergency Physicians; mem. AMA (Physician's Recognition award 1969, 72), Am. Coll. Internat. Physicians (founding mem., trustee 1974—), Ind. State Med. Assn., Ky. Med. Assn., Philippines Med. Assn. of Ind. and Ky., Surgeons in Am. (life), Assn. Philippine Practicing Physicians in Am. (life), Assn. Mil. Surgeons U.S. (life), Res. Officers Assn. U.S. (life), Mark Ravitch Surg. Assn., Bradley Aust. Surg. Soc., N.Y. Acad. Scis., Hon. Order Ky. Cols., Masons, Optimists Club. Named to Chgo. Filipino Am. Hall of Fame in medicine, 1998. Presbyterian. Home: 14 Carla Ln Scottsburg IN 47170-9707 Office: 137 E Mcclain Ave Scottsburg IN 47170-1846

KHOJASTEH, ALI, medical oncologist, hematologist; b. Shiraz, Pars, Persia, Nov. 10, 1947; came to U.S., 1974; s. Mostafa and Pari Jan (Azimi) K.; children: Artemis, Amitis. Degree, Pahlavi U., Shiraz, 1968, MD, 1974. Vice dean Sch. Medicine Shiraz U., 1980-82, chmn. med. dept. Sch. Medicine, 1982-83; chief med. oncology Ellis Fischel Cancer Ctr., Columbia, Mo., 1983-87, chmn. med. dept., 1987-90, chief of staff, 1988-89; med. dir. St. Mary Cancer Ctr., Jefferson City, Mo., 1993—; pres. Columbia Comprehensive Cancer Care Clinic and Rsch. Inst., 1990—; assoc. prof. U. Mo., Columbia, 1989—; prin. investigator Ellis Fischel CCOP, Columbia, 1988-90; chmn. Mo. Acad. Sci. Oncology, 1988-89, Mo. Cancer Pain Initiative, 1991-96; investigator Nat. Cancer Inst., 1990—; liaison Am. Coll. Surgeons, 1992—. Contbr. articles to New Eng. Jour. Medicine, Cancer, Am. Jour. Medicine, Am. Jour. Hematology, Jour. Clin. Oncol. Cancer Bull., Jour. Pain Sys. Mgmt., Can. Jour. Medicine; author: (with others) Pulmonary Medicine, Cancer and Heart, Chemotherapy Resource Book, Small Intestinal Disease. Rsch. grantee Purdue Fredrick Co., Conn., 1984—, Adria Lab., Columbus, 1988—, Glaxo Rsch. Lab., Research Triangle Park, N.C., 1988-91, Ciba-Geigy Co., 1990-93, Merrill Dow Co., 1991-95, Pfizer, 1995—, Matrix Pharm., 1996, Ross Lab., 1996, Aronex Pharm., 1997, Merck Rsch. Lab., 1997, Ligand Lab., 1997, Maxim-Pharmaceutical, 1998, Glaxo-Wellcome, 1998, Bayer Lab., 1999, Amgen, 1999, Arugon Lab., 1999. Fellow ACP, Royal Soc. Medicine (Eng.); mem. Am. Soc. Clin. Oncology, Am. Soc. Internat. Medicine, Smithsonian Soc., N.Y. Acad. Scis., Mo. Acad. Scis. (chmn. oncology sect. 1988-89), So. Med. Assn., Am. Soc. Hematology. Zoroastrian. Home: 2801 Greenbriar Dr Columbia MO 65203-3663 Office: Columbia Comprehensive Cancer Care Clinic 500 Keene St Ste 202 Columbia MO 65201-8104

KHONSARI, MICHAEL M., mechanical engineering educator; b. Aug. 17, 1957; m. Karen Sue Troy, Sept. 1, 1990. BS in Mech. Engring. with honors, U. Tex., 1978, MS in Mech. Engring., 1979, PhD in Mech. Engring., 1983. Rsch. and teaching asst. U. Tex., Austin, 1978-83; asst. prof. Ohio State U., Columbus, 1984-87; asst. prof. U. Pitts., 1988-90, assoc. prof., 1990-96; prof. So. Ill. U., Carbondale, 1996-99, prof., chmn. dept. mech. engring. and energy processes, 1996-99; Dow Chem. endowed prof. mech. engring. La. State U., Baton Rouge, La., 1999—, Dow Chem. endowed chair in rotating machinery, 1999—; mem. mech. engring. grad. com. U. Pitts., 1988-90, design interest group, 1988-96; mem. faculty ctr. motion control U. Pitts.; reviewer NSF, NASA, Am. Chem. Soc. Books, McGraw Hill Books, Addison Wesley Books, Prentice-Hall Books, Holt Rinehart and Winston Books; lectr. in field. Assoc. editor ASME Jour. Tribology, 1997—, STLE Tribology Transactions, 1990—; mem. editl. bd. Tribological Acta, 1994—; mem. editl. bd., reviewer Jour. Engring. Design Graphics, 1987—; contbr., reviewer, mem. editl. bd. adv. com. CRC Handbook of Lubrication, vol. III, 1991-93; reviewer Lubrication Engring. Jour., Wear Jour., Rheology Jour., Heat Transfer Jour., Tribology Jour., Applied Mechanics Jour.; pub. abstracts and reports; referee various jours.; contbr. articles to profl. jours. Recipient Found. award ALCOA, 1990, 91. Fellow Soc. Tribology Lubrication Engrs. (bearings com. 1985—, chmn. 1988-91, assoc. editor, rev. Tribology Transactions 1990—, assoc. editor Jour. Tribology 1997—, Presdl. Rsch. Coun. award 1993), Fell. Soc. Tribiologist and Lubrication Engs.; mem. ASME (conf. planning com. 1989-96, reviewer Jour. Tribology and conf. papers, chmn. ASME/Soc. Tribology and Lubrication Engrs. Internat. Conf. in Tribology 1996, Burt L. Newkirk award 1990), Sigma Xi. Achievements include research in thermal effects in hydrodynamic bearings, thermal effects in wet clutches, hot spot prediction in mechanical components, Thermoclastic instability, powder lubrication, multi-phase flows in bearings, friction associated with instrument pointing mechanisms operating under ultra low speeds. Office: La State U Dept Mech Engring 2508 CEBA Baton Rouge LA 70803

KHORANA, HAR GOBIND, chemist, educator; b. Raipur, India, Jan. 9, 1922; s. Shri Ganpat Rai and Shrimati Krishna (Devi) K.; m. Esther Elizabeth Sibler, 1952; children: Julia, Emilie, Dave Roy. BS, Punjab U., 1943, MS, 1945; PhD, Liverpool (Eng.) U., 1948; DSc, U. Chgo., 1967. Head organic chemistry group B.C. Rsch. Coun., 1952-60; vis. prof. Rockefeller Inst., N.Y.C., 1958—; prof. co-dir. Inst. Enzyme Rsch. U. Wis., Madison, 1960-70, prof. dept. biochemistry, 1962-70, Conrad A. Elvehjem prof. life scis., 1964-70; Alfred P. Sloan prof. biology and chemistry MIT, Cambridge, 1970—; vis. prof. Stanford U., 1964; mem. adv. bd. Biopolymers; researcher chem. methods for synthesis of nucleotides, coenzymes and nucleic acids, elucidation on the genetic code, lab. synthesis of genes, biol. membrane and light-transducing pigments. Author: Some Recent Developments in the Chemistry of Phosphate Esters of Biological Interests, 1961; mem. editorial bd.: Jour. Am. Chem. Soc, 1963—; contbr. numerous articles to profl. jours. Recipient Merck award Chem. Inst. Can., 1958, Gold medal Profl. Inst. Pub. Service Can., 1960, Dannie-Heinneman Preiz Göttingen, Germany, 1967, Remsen award Johns Hopkins U., 1968, Am. Chem. Soc. award for creative work in synthetic organic chemistry, 1968, Louisa Gross Horwitz prize, 1968, Lasker Found. award for basic med. research, 1968, Nobel prize in medicine, 1968; elected to Deutsche Akademie der Naturforscher Leopoldina HalleSaale, Germany, 1968; Overseas fellow Churchill Coll., Cambridge, Eng., 1967. Fellow Chem. Inst. Can., Am. Acad. Arts and Scis.; mem. NAS. Office: MIT 77 Massachusetts Ave Rm 68-680 Cambridge MA 02139-4307*

KHOSLA, VED MITTER, oral and maxillofacial surgeon, educator; b. Nairobi, Kenya, Jan. 13, 1926; s. Jagdish Rai and Tara V. K.; m. Santosh Ved Chabra, Oct. 11, 1952; children: Ashok M., Siddarth M. Student, U. Cambridge, 1945; L.D.S., Edinburgh Dental Hosp. and Sch., 1950, Coll. Dental Surgeons, Sask., Can., 1962. Prof. oral surgery, dir. postdoctoral studies in oral surgery Sch. Dentistry U. Calif., San Francisco, 1968—; chief oral surgery San Francisco Gen. Hosp.; lectr. oral surgery U. of Pacific, VA

Hosp.; vis. cons. Fresno County Hosp. Dental Clinic.; Mem. planning com., exec. med. com. San Francisco Gen. Hosp. Contbr. articles to profl. jours. Examiner in photography and gardening Boy Scouts Am., 1971-73, Guatemala Clinic, 1972. Granted personal coat of arms by H.M. Queen Elizabeth II, 1959. Fellow Royal Coll. Surgeons (Edinburgh), Internat. Assn. Oral Surgeons, Internat. Coll. Applied Nutrition, Internat. Coll. Dentists, Royal Soc. Health, AAAS, Am. Coll. Dentists; mem. Brit. Assn. Oral Surgeons, Am. Soc. Oral Surgeons, Am. Dental Soc. Anesthesiology, Am. Acad. Dental Radiology, Omicron Kappa Upsilon. Club: Masons. Home: 1525 Lakeview Dr Hillsborough CA 94010-7330 Office: U Calif Sch Dentistry Oral Surgery Div 3D Parnassus Ave San Francisco CA 94117-4342 *It is part of the cure to wish to be cured. With God all things are possible.*

KHOURI, ANTOUN, church administrator. Aux. bishop The Antiochian Orthodox Christian Archdiocese N.Am., Englewood, N.J. Office: Antiochian Orthodox Christian Archdiocese NAm 358 Mountain Rd Englewood NJ 07631-3798*

KHOURI, FRED JOHN, political science educator; b. Cranford, N.J., Aug. 15, 1916; s. Peter and Mary (Rizk) K.; m. Catherine McLean, June 24, 1964. Student, Union Jr. Coll., Roselle, N.J., 1934-36; B.A., Columbia U., 1938, M.A., 1939, Ph.D., 1953. Instr. Brownsville Jr. Coll. and High Sch., Tex., 1939-40; instr. polit. sci. U. Tenn., 1946-47, U. Conn., 1947-50; asst. prof. Villanova U., Pa., 1951-61, prof., 1964-86; prof. emeritus Villanova U., 1986—; vis. prof. Am. U. of Beirut, Lebanon, 1961-64; mem. Brookings Instn. Middle East Study Group, 1975-76; sr. fellow Middle East Ctr U. Pa., 1978-79, 80-81; lectr. in field. Author: The Arab States and the UN, 1954, The Arab Israeli Dilemma, 1968, 2d edit., 1976, 3d edit., 1985; assoc. editor: Jour. South Asian and Middle Eastern Studies; contbr. to books and profl. jours. Served with U.S. Army, 1941-45. Decorated Order of Cedars Lebanon. Fellow Middle East Studies Assn.; mem. Middle East Inst., Am. Polit. Sci. Assn., Am. Soc. Internat. Law, Am. Coun. for Study Islamic Socs., UN Assn. of U.S.A., World Affairs Coun., Phi Kappa Phi. Democrat. Roman Catholic. Home: 1209 W Wynnewood Rd Apt 310 Wynnewood PA 19096-2132 *Man's most desperate need is for lasting peace. Thus, ever since my military discharge in 1945, my life's aim has been to do whatever I could to promote that deeper and clearer understanding in the U.S. which is so essential to the peaceful resolution of the world's major conflicts.*

KHOURI, GEORGE GEORGE, ophthalmologist; b. Beirut, Lebanon, May 24, 1957; came to U.S., 1976; BA summa cum laude, Rollins Coll., 1978; MD, Am. U. of Beirut, 1983. Diplomate Am. Bd. Ophthalmology. Intern in internal medicine Am. U. Hosp. and Med. Ctr., Beirut, 1982-83; rsch. fellow in ocular pharmacology and physiology Wilmer Inst., Johns Hopkins Hosp., Balt., 1983-84; resident in ophthalmology U. Chgo. Hosps. and Clinics, 1984-87; clin. fellow Retina Assocs. & Schepens Eye Rsch. Inst. Mass. Eye and Ear Infirmary/Harvard Med. Sch., Boston, 1987-88; asst. prof. Tufts U. Sch. Medicine, Boston, 1988-92; staff ophthalmologist Dept. Vets. Affairs Med. Ctr., Boston, 1988-92, Malden (Mass.) Hosp., 1992-93, Melrose (Mass.)-Wakefield Hosp., 1992-93; pvt. practice West Palm Beach, Fla., 1994—; presenter in field. Contbr. articles to profl. publs. Vol. eye surgeon Aravind Eye Hosp., India, 1993, Lumbini (Nepal) Eye Hosp., 1993, Nepal Eye Hosp., Kathmandu, 1993, Lighthouse for Christ Eye Ctr., Mombasa, Kenya, 1993. Eye rsch. grantee Mass. Lions, 1992-93, VA, 1990-92. Fellow Am. Acad. Ophthalmology; mem. Am. Soc. Cataract and Refractive Surgery, Internat. Soc. Refractive Surgery. Avocations: swimming, travel, horseback riding. Office: Palm Beach Eye Ctr 1411 N Flagler Dr Ste 4100 West Palm Beach FL 33401-3411

KHOURY, GEORGE GILBERT, printing company executive, baseball association executive; b. St. Louis, July 30, 1923; s. George Michael and Dorothy (Smith) K.; m. Colleen E. Khoury Czerny, Apr. 3, 1948; children—Colleen Ann, George Gilbert. Grad. St. Louis U., 1946. Vice pres. Khoury Bros. Printing, St. Louis, 1946—; exec. dir. George Khoury Assn. Baseball Leagues, Inc., St. Louis, 1967—. Served with U.S. Army, 1943-45, NATOUSA, MTO. Decorated Purple Heart with oak leaf cluster. Roman Catholic. Office: George Khoury Assn Baseball Leagues 5400 Meramec Bottom Rd Saint Louis MO 63128-4624

KHOURY, JEHAD, research scientist; b. Tarshiha, Israel, Aug. 19, 1956; s. Adib and Massarah (Bisharah) K.; children: Adib, Wasim. BSc in Physics, Hebrew U., Jerusalem, 1978, Msc in Applied Physics, 1982; PhD, Essex U., Jerusalem, 1988. Postdoctoral Tufts U., Medford, Mass., 1989-91, rsch. scientist, 1991-93, assoc. rsch. prof., 1993-96; cons. Air Force rsch. labs. Lartec Inc., Sudbury/Concord, Mass./N.H., 1996—. Author book chpts.; contbr. numerous articles and papers to profl. jours. including Jour. Optical Soc. of Am., Optical Engring., Applied Physics. Mem. Optical Soc. Am. (coorganizer symposium 1998, tutorial lectr. ann. meeting 1996, sec. presider meetings 1996).

KHOURY, PHILIP S., social sciences educator, historian; b. Washington, D.C., Oct. 15, 1949; s. Shukry E. and Angela Mansur (Jurdak) K.; m. Mary Christina Wilson, Aug. 28, 1980. BA, Trinity Coll., 1971; PhD, Harvard U., 1980. Asst. prof. MIT, Cambridge, Mass., 1981-84; assoc. prof. Mass. Inst. Tech., Cambridge, Mass., 1984-90, prof., 1990—, assoc. dean Sch. Humanities and Social Sci., 1987-90, acting dean, 1990-91, dean, 1991—; mem. editl. bd. Jour. Interdisciplinary History, 1987—, Hist. Abstracts, 1990—, The Beirut Rev., 1991-93. Author: Urban Notables and Arab Nationalism, 1983, Syria and the French Mandate, 1987; co-editor Tribes and State Formation in the Middle East, 1990, The Modern Middle East: A Reader, 1993, Recovering Beirut: Urban Design and Post-war Reconstruction, 1993. Trustee Am. U. Beirut, 1997—, Toynbee Prize Found., 1998—, World Peace Found., 1999—; dir. Harvard Coop. Soc., 1998—. Thomas J. Watson fellow Watson Found., 1971-72; Fulbright scholar, 1976-77; Post-Doctoral Social Sci. Rsch. Coun., 1983-84; Mellon fellow Aspen Inst., 1984-85. Mem. AAAS, Am. Hist. Assn. (George Louis Beer Prize 1987), Middle East Studies Assn. (pres. 1998, dir. 1990-92, 97—), Middle East Inst., Pi Gamma Mu . Avocations: Tennis, Squash. Office: MIT Office Dean Sch Hum/Social Scis 77 Massachusetts Ave Cambridge MA 02139-4307

KHOURY, RIAD PHILIP, corporation executive, financial consultant; b. Beirut, May 27, 1935; came to U.S., 1979; s. Philip Mitri and Efrocine (Moujaes) K.; m. Samira Saade, Apr. 24, 1964; children: Philip, Marc, Serge. Graduate studies in fin. and mgmt. Ind. fin. cons. Baghdad, Iraq, 1955-58; ind. fin. investment adviser Jeddah, Saudi Arabia, 1959-61; mgr. Eastern Comml. Bank, Beirut, 1962-65; chief exec. officer United Bank of Lebanon and Pakistan, Beirut, 1965-70; vice chmn., chief exec. officer ADCOM Bank, Beirut, 1971-74; pres. Khoury Assocs. Internat., Annandale, Va., 1980—; banking and fin. cons. Lebanese Ministry Fin., Beirut, 1978-79. Recipient Officier Scientifique De L'ordre Du Merite award Le Merite, Paris, 1964, Cravate D'Honneur award Groupment Philantropique, Brussels, 1965. Avocations: tennis, swimming, trap and skeet shooting. Home and Office: 6320 Wendy Ann Ct Fairfax VA 22039-1619

KHOURY, ROBERT JOHN, international leadership management consultant; b. Torrington, Conn., Dec. 17, 1961; s. William John and Eileen Mary (Henry) K. BA in Comms., So. Conn. State U., 1984; Diploma in Engring. Tech., R.I.S.E. Inst., Nashua, N.H., 1984; MBA in Internat. Bus., N.H. Coll., 1990; postgrad. in Ednl./Corp. Leadership, U. Bridgeport, 1995—. Computer technician Apollo Computer/Hewlett Packard, Hampton, N.H., 1984-85; sales/mktg. exec. NIM-COR, Inc., Nashua, 1986-87; credit analyst Data Gen., Hooksett, N.H., 1987; internat. mgr. AAVID Engring., Laconia, N.H., 1987-91; pres., owner R.J. Khoury Global Cons., Gilford and Concord, N.H., 1991-95, Torrington, Conn., 1995-96; dir. continuing edn. Albertus Magnus Coll., New Haven, 1996—; adj. prof. N.H. Coll., Gilford, 1990-95, N.H. Tech. Coll., Laconia and Nashua, N.H., 1992-95, New Dimensions, Albertus Magnus Coll., 1996—. Mem. Fgn. Policy Assn. (charter), Am. Mgmt. Assn. Republican. Roman Catholic. Avocations: weight lifting, running, esoteric audio/video. Home and Office: 15 Commodore Pl Milford CT 06460-6521

KHOUZAM, HANI RAOUL, psychiatrist, physician, educator; b. Heliopolis, Egypt, June 5, 1950; came to U.S., 1980; s. Raoul Aniss Khouzam and Jeannette (Guindi) Roufael; m. Lynda Margaret Dickerson, Nov. 20, 1982; children: Andrea Adahlia, Andrew Amaris, Adam Yurie Alexander. MB BCh, Faculty Medicine Cairo, Egypt, 1977; MPH, Tulane U., 1981. Diplomate Am. Bd. Psychiatry and Neurology with spl. certification in Geriatric Psychiatry; cert. ednl. commn. fgn. med. grads. Med. house officer Cairo U. Teaching Hosps., 1978-79; psychiatrist Shaalan M.D., Inc., Cairo, 1979-80; rsch. scholar Okla. Med. Rsch. Found., Oklahoma City, 1982-83; resident in psychiatry U. Okla. Health Scis. Ctr., Oklahoma City, 1983-87; staff psychiatrist Okla. County Crisis Intervention Ctr., Oklahoma City, 1987-90; med. dir., inpatient psychiatry unit VA Med. Ctr., Oklahoma City, 1990-92; dir. consultation liaison psychiatry VA Med. Ctr., Manchester, N.H., 1992—; asst. prof. psychiatry dept. psychiatry and behavioral scis. Coll. Medicine U. Okla., Oklahoma City, 1987-92; staff psychiatrist VA Med. Ctr., N.H., 1992—; adj. asst. prof. psychiatry Dartmouth Med. Sch., Lebanon, N.H., 1992-95, adj. assoc. prof. psychiatry, 1995—; clin. instr. in medicine Harvard Med. Sch., Boston, 1994—. Author: Emergency Psychiatric Interventions, 1988; contbr. to profl. jours. Hubert H. Humphrey fellow in pub. health, USIA, New Orleans, 1980-81. Fellow Egyptian Sci. Soc.; mem. Egyptian Med. Assn., Am. Psychiatric Assn., N.H. Psychiatric Soc. Coptic Catholic Christian. Avocations: reading, writing, Bible study, music, stamp collecting. Home: 5 Terrace Rd Concord NH 03301-3138 Office: VA Med Ctr 718 Smyth Rd Manchester NH 03104-7004

KHOYLIAN, CAROL J., nurse; b. Winthrop, Mass., Dec. 28, 1956; d. Joseph S. Sr. and Anna R. (DeStefano) Alongi; m. Armen Khoylian, Aug. 10, 1985. Diploma, Malden (Mass.) Hosp., 1978; student, Northeastern U., Boston. RN, Mass.; cert. psychiat. and mental health nurse; cert. BLS instr., Am. Heart Assn.; cert. group therapy leader; cert. SCUBA diver. Staff nurse, operating room Malden Hosp.; office mgr. Proto-Systems Inc., Pembroke, Mass.; charge nurse Pembroke Hosp.; staff psychiat. nurse Brockton (Mass.) Hosp.; staff nurse oper. rm. South Shore Hosp. Chair shared mgmt. quality assurance com. Am. Heart Assn., 1994—; mem. Mass. Cultural Coun. Mem. Assn. Oper. Rm. Nurses, Golden Key Nat. Honor Soc. Home: 72 Forest St Pembroke MA 02359-3320

KHOZEIMEH, ISSA, electrical engineer; b. Tehran, Iran, Dec. 25, 1939; came to U.S., 1959; s. Ismail and Zohreh (Alam) K.; m. Nahid Khozeimeh; children: Lili, Nini. BSEE, George Washington U., Washington, 1966; MSEE, 1973, D in Engring., 1984, DSc in Engring. Mgmt., 1993. Registered profl. engr. Jr. engr. Potomac Electric Power Co., Washington, 1967-68; substation engr., 1968-73, design standrads engr., 1973-79, sr. engr. substation design, 1979-80; dept. head, chief elec. engr. David Volkert and Assocs., Bethesda, Md., 1980-88; mgr. Util. Svcs. Metro. Washington Airports Auth. Dulles Internat. Airport, 1988—; pres. Internat. Mktg. and Consulting Corp., Washington, 1980-82; v.p. Horizon Internat., Washington, 1982-88; pres. Forum Internat. Glen Echo, Md., 1988—. Author: An Automated Maintenance Management System for International Airports, 1993; contbr. articles to profl. jours. Recipient Sch. of Engring Svcs. award, 1976, Gen. Alumni Assn. Svc. award, 1971, George Washington U., 1976, Engr. Coun. Cert. of Appreciation, 1984, 85, Disting. Svc. award 1986, George Washington U. Alumni Assn. Disting Alumni Svc. award, 1998. Mem. IEEE (sr.), NSPE, Instrument Soc. Am., Md. Soc. Profl. Engrs. (Disting. Sr. Engr. award 1997), Washington Soc. Engrs., pres. 1998-99. Republican. Moslem. Avocations: water skiing, snow skiing, hiking, reading, publishing, lecturing, travel. Home: PO Box 557 Glen Echo MD 20812-0557 Office: Metro Washington Airports Authority Dulles Internat Airport PO Box 17045 Washington DC 20041-7045

KHRISTICH, DIMITRI, professional hockey player; b. Kiev, USSR, July 23, 1969; came to U.S., 1990.; m. Erin Khristich. Left wing Washington Capitals, 1988-92, L.A. Kings, 1996-97, Boston Bruins, 1997—. Mem. NHL All-Star Game, 1997, U.S. Olympic Hockey Team, 1998. Avocation: golf. Office: Boston Bruins 1 Fleet Ctr Ste 250 Boston MA 02114-1389*

KHURI, NICOLA NAJIB, physicist, educator; b. Beirut, Lebanon, May 27, 1933; came to U.S., 1959, naturalized, 1970; s. Najib N. and Odette (Joujou) K.; m. Elizabeth Anne Tyson, Dec. 9, 1955; children: Suzanne Odette, Najib Nicholas. B.A with high distinction, Am. U. Beirut, 1952; Ph.D., Princeton U., 1957. Asst. prof. Am. U. Beirut, 1957-58, 60-61, assoc. prof., 1961-62; mem. Inst. Advanced Study, Princeton U., 1959-60, 62-63; vis. assoc. prof. Columbia, 1963-64; assoc. prof. Rockefeller U., 1964-68, prof., 1968—; cons. Brookhaven Nat. Lab., 1963-73; mem. Carnegie Panel on U.S. Security and Arms Control, 1981-83; vis. scientist European Ctr. for Nuclear Research, Geneva, Centre d'Etudes Nucléaires, Saclay, France, Max Planck Inst. für Physik, Munich, Fed. Republic Germany. Contbr. articles to profl. jours. Trustee Am. U. Beirut. Fellow Am. Phys. Soc.; mem. Council on Fgn. Relations. Club: Century (N.Y.C.). Home: 4715 Iselin Ave Bronx NY 10471-3323 Office: Rockefeller U New York NY 10021

KIAM, VICTOR KERMIT, II, consumer products company executive; b. New Orleans, Dec. 7, 1926; s. Victor Kermit and Nanon (Newman) K.; m. Ellen Lipscher; children: Lisa, Victor III, Robin. BA, Yale U., 1948; cert. langs., U. Paris, 1949; MBA, Harvard U., 1951; DL, N.H. Coll., 1984, George Washington U., 1985; D in Sci. and Bus. Adminstrn. (hon.), Bryant Coll., 1989. Market dir. Lever Bros., N.Y.C., 1955-68; pres. Benrus Corp., Ridgefield, Conn., 1968-71, chmn., chief exec. officer, 1971-77; chmn. Friendship Collection, N.Y.C., 1977—; chief exec. officer Remington Products, Inc., Bridgeport, Conn., 1979—; chmn., CEO Remington Products, Corp., Bridgeport, Conn., 1994—; chmn. bd. dirs. First Tchr., Remington Trading Co., Japan and Hong Kong, Remington Apparel, Lady Remington, 1980—, Franzus Co., Cirrus Air Technologies, PIC Design; bd. dirs. James Madison Inst., Fla.; former owner New England Patriots; exec. in residence Wash. State U., 1987, Oxford U., 1988. Author: Going For It!, 1986, Live to Win, 1989; patentee in field; contbg. editor numerous mags. Chmn. U.S. Savs. Bonds., U. Louisville, Harding U., Nat. Sales Hall of Fame, United Way. Recipient Wharton Golden Plate award Am. Acad. Achievement, 1984, Northwood Inst. Outstanding Bus. Leader award, 1986, Kate Smith/U.S. Savs. Bonds award, 1988; named Nat. Bus. and Commerce Father of Yr. Nat. Father's Day Coun., 1982, Outstanding Entrepreneur of Yr. U. So. Calif. Sch. Bus., 1987, Man of Yr. State Police Jr. Olympics, Boston, 1989, Entrepreneur of Yr., Conn. and Western Mass., 1989. Clubs: Century (White Plains, N.Y.), Palm Beach (Fla.) Polo, Regency Whist (N.Y.C.). Office: Remington Products Inc 555 Madison Ave Fl 23D New York NY 10022-3301*

KIAMIE, DON ALBERT NAJEEB, accountant; b. Bronx, N.Y., Jan. 23, 1944; s. Samie and Carmen (Torres) K.; B.S., Fordham U., 1965; M.B.A., NYU, 1967; m. Olive F. Howell, Sept. 9, 1972; children: Matthew, Marie, Melinda. CPA, N.Y. Sr. acct. Peat, Marwick, Mitchell & Co., N.Y.C., 1967-70; asst. mgr. standards acctg. Gen. Foods Corp., N.Y.C., 1970-77; mgr. fin. reporting/planning Exxon Corp., Qwip Systems Div., N.Y.C., 1977-79; asst. controller NBC, N.Y.C., 1980-83; adj. asst. prof. acctg. Pace U., 1982—; adj. instr. Westchester Bus. Inst., 1989—; exec. v.p., CFO Windsor Mgmt. Corp. and Kiamie Related Properties, 1983—, also bd. dirs., 1987—. Mgr. Lions Babe Ruth Club, 1967-71; soccer and baseball coach Shrub Oak Athletic Club, 1983-87; pres. Pelham Babe Ruth League, 1970-71; pres. Pelham Young Rep. Club, 1970-71; v.p. Holy Spirit Parish Coun., 1977-78, chmn. teen group, 1977-78, chmn. fin. com., 1977-78; eucharistic minister, dir. youth music group Holy Rosary Ch., 1988—; soccer coach AYSO, 1988—; leader GOP 35th Dist. Town of Mt. Pleasant, N.Y., 1991—; trustee Mt. Pleasant Libr., 1994—. Mem. AICPA, N.Y. Soc. CPAs. Roman Catholic. Home: 21 Main St Hawthorne NY 10532-2017

KIANG, BARBARA NORRIS, scientific research assistant; b. Tacoma, Wash., Apr. 21, 1942; d. William Foster Norris and Sarah Louise (Ryder) Craig; m. Nelson Yuan-Sheng Kiang, Dec. 18, 1976. BA, Carleton Coll., 1963; MA, Mount Holyoke Coll., 1965. Rsch. asst. Eaton Peabody Lab., Boston, 1965-80; sr. rsch. asst. Mass. Eye & Ear Infirmary, Boston, 1980-90, lab. mgr., 1990-95, part-time rsch. asst., 1996—; part-time rsch. asst. MIT, Cambridge, 1995-96, Mass. Gen. Hosp., Boston, 1996—, Mass. Eye & Ear Infirmary, Boston, 1997—. Contbr. articles to profl. jours.

KIANG, CHING-HWA, chemical engineering educator; b. Taipei, Taiwan, Jan. 20, 1965; d. Song Kiang and Pi-Ying Huang; m. Michael William Deem, Sept. 2, 1995. BSChemE, Nat. Taiwan U., Taipei, 1987; PhD in Chemistry, Calif. Inst. Tech., 1995. Educator UCLA. Grantee NIH, 1998, UC Energy, 1998. Mem. Am. Phys. Soc., Am. Chem. Soc., Materials Rsch. Soc. Achievements include patent in field. E-mail: chk@wag.caltech.edu and chk@chem.ucla.edu. Fax: 310-206-4038. Home: 11136 Ophir Dr Los Angeles CA 90024-1945 Office: UCLA Box 951569 Los Angeles CA 90095-1569

KIBBE, JAMES WILLIAM, real estate broker; b. Bound Brook, N.J., Oct. 5, 1926; s. Orlando A. and Anna Rose (Tomb) K.; m. Bettie Brooks Dailey, June 11, 1949; children: James William Jr., Linda Jean. BS, U. Md., 1951. Salesman real estate Eig & Mc Keever, Silver Spring, Md., 1955-57, Weaver Bros., Inc., Chevy Chage Bldg., Md., 1957-70; asst. v.p. sales, leasing dept. Weaver Bros., Inc., Chevy Chage Bldg., 1970-72, mgr. sales, 1972-89, v.p., 1973-82, sr. v.p., 1983-89; sr. v.p., dir. sales The Michael Co., 1989-95; sr. v.p., dir. indsl. Barrueta, 1995-96; sr. v.p. Carey Winston/Barrueta, Bethesda, Md., 1996-98, Transwestern Carey Winston, Bethesda, 1998—; lectr. in field; chmn. Brokers and Salesmen's council, 1968-69. With USNR, 1944-46. Mem. Soc. Indsl. Office Realtors (pres. Md. and Washington chpt. 1985-86, nat. bd. dirs. 1988-90), Nat. Assn. Indsl. Officer Pks. (bd. dirs. 1987), Nat. Inst. Real Estate Brokers (state chmn. 1968-70), Nat. Assn. Realtors, New Am. Network (adv. bd. dirs. 1986-99, chmn. adv. bd. 1991-93), Md. Assn. Realtors, Washington Bd. Trade, Washington Builders Assn., D.C. Assn. Realtors, Montgomery County Bd. Realtors, Lions (started health fairs chmn. 25 yrs., Service with Integrity award). Republican. Methodist. Home: 1000 Ashland Dr Ashton MD 20861-9718 Office: Transwestern Carey Winston Ste 400A 7600 Rockledge Dr Bethesda MD 20817

KIBBE, KAY LYNN, secondary education educator, counselor; b. Sonora, Tex., Nov. 23, 1952; d. Jack Herbert and Gloria Maxine (Boswell) Kerbow; m. Robert Louis Kibbe IV, Dec. 19, 1989; 1 child, Derek Alan Holdridge. BA in English, S.W. Tex. State U., San Marcos, 1974; MEd in English, Sul Ross State U., Alpine, Tex., 1984, MEd in Counseling, 1988. Cert. profl. English educator, profl. counselor, vocat. counselor, Tex. Tchr. lang. arts Sonora Jr. High, 1975-84; tchr. English Sonora H.S., 1984-88; tchr., coach, counselor Floyd (N.Mex.) Schs., 1988-89; counselor Pampa (Tex.) Elems., 1989-93; counselor Pampa H.S., 1993-95, tchr. English, 1995—; presenter on attention deficit hyperactivity disorder Tex. Assn. Counseling, 1988—; cons. Alt. Assessments, Ea. N.Mex. U., 1984—; spice chmn. Pampa H.S., 1997-98. Faculty advisor Pampa Teen Crime Stoppers, 1997—; bd. dirs. Pampa Tchrs. Fed. Credit Union, 1993—; participant Citizens' Police Acad., Pampa, 1997; youth dir. 1st United Meth. Ch., Sonora, 1983-85. Named Tchr. of Yr. Newspapers in Edn., Liberty Newspapers, Pampa, 1997. Mem. ASCD, Nat. Coun. Tchrs. of English, Tex. Counseling Assn. Avocations: reading, raising quarter horses, old movies. Office: Pampa H S 111 E Harvester Ave Pampa TX 79065-4401

KIBBEY, HAL STEPHEN, science writer; b. West Point, N.Y., Oct. 29, 1943; s. Donald Eugene and Mary Elizabeth (Lichliter) K.; m. Martha Ann Harsanyi, Dec. 12, 1970; children: Carolyn Ann, Laura Ann. BA, Cornell U., 1965; MA, Ind. U., 1969. Rsch. asst., rsch. assoc. Ind. U., Bloomington, 1970-75, publ. editor, 1975-79, sci. writer, 1979—; free lance writer and editor, Bloomington, 1985—. Editor: Science Development: The Building of Science in Less Developed Countries, 1975. Pres. Rogers-Binford Elem. Sch. PTO, 1991-93; bd. dirs. Monroe County Civic Theater, 1995-96. Mem. ACLU, Nat. Assn. Sci. Writers, U.S. Chess Fedn. (life). Democrat. Methodist. Avocations: chess, singing, acting, writing and directing plays. Home: 1109 E Hunter Ave Bloomington IN 47401-5035 Office: Ind U Office Comm & Mktg 530 E Kirkwood Ave Bloomington IN 47408-4003

KIBBLE, EDWARD BRUCE, insurance-investment advisory company executive; b. Seattle, May 11, 1940; s. Francis Bruce and Doris Kibble; m. Carol Kibble, July 8, 1961; 3 children. BA, U. Wash., 1972. CLU. Agt. Equitable of Iowa, Seattle, 1962-72; co-founder, co-chmn. Kibble & Prentice, Inc., Seattle, 1972—; bd. dirs. Kibble & Prentice/KPI-Western Ins., Bellevue, Wash., Phoenix Savings Bank, Northwestern Trust. Contbr. articles to profl. jours. Bd. dirs. Sheldon Jackson Coll., N.W. Kidney Found., Seattle Pacific Found. Mem. Assn. for Advanced Life Underwriting, Nat. Assn. Life Underwriters (Seattle Life Underwriter of Yr. award), Million Dollar Round Table, Estate Planning Coun. Seattle (past pres.), Wash. Athletic Club, Columbia Tower Club, Rainier Club, Seattle Yacht Club, Rotary (Seattle). Republican. Avocations: sailing, skiing. Office: 600 Stewart St Ste 1000 Seattle WA 98101-1230

KIBBY, MICHAEL WILLIAM, reading educator; b. Salinas, Calif., Nov. 19, 1942; s. Hugh Evan Mosher and Hazel Kathleen (Fitzpatrick) Kibby; m. Mary Jane Stow, Nov. 28, 1964 (div. July 1983); children: Jennifer Kathleen, Andrea Jane; m. Carol Anne Bailey, Oct. 6, 1984. BS, Wayne State U., 1965; MS, U. Chgo., 1967, PhD, 1975. Tchr. Woodhaven Sch., Lansing, Mich., 1962-63; from asst. to full prof. SUNY, Buffalo, 1971—, dir. The Reading Clinic, 1971—, chmn. dept. learning and instn., 1988—. Author: Practical Steps for Informing Reading Instruction: A Diagnostic Decision Making Model, 1995. Pres., trustee Williamsville (N.Y.) Sch. Bd., 1975-88; village trustee Village of Williamsville, N.Y., 1979-88. Home: 5854 Main St Apt 801 Buffalo NY 14221-8234 Office: SUNY Buffalo Amherst NY 14260-1000*

KIBILOSKI, FLOYD TERRANCE, business and computer consultant, editor, educator; b. Coldwater, Mich., Dec. 24, 1946; s. Floyd Benedict and Lucille Henrietta (Cholaj) K.; children from a previous marriage: Sean, Angie; m. Charlene Jones, Oct. 18, 1997; children: Elizabeth, Marlene. BBA in Acctg., Western Mich. U., 1978; MA in Computer Resource Mgmt., Webster U., 1989. CPA; cert. data processor; cert. Microsoft trainer. Enlisted USAF, 1966, advanced through grades to capt., ret., 1990, acct., 1966-70, computer technician, 1970-77, acct., computer cons. Bristol Leisenring and Co., 1977-80; computer cons. USAF, U.K., 1980-85, St. Louis, 1985-90; owner, editor Louisville (Ky.) Computer Times, 1990—; adj. prof. McKendree Coll., Lebanon, Ill., 1985-90, City Colls. of Chgo., 1982-84, Embry-Riddle Aero. U., 1983-84, U. Md., 1984; chair computer sci. dept. Sullivan Coll., Louisville, 1993—, adj. prof., 1990—, motivational lectr., speaker. Author: Computer in the Audit, 1980, (human system seminar) Get the Most from Yourself, 1993. Co-founder Passionist Ctr., Louisville. Republican. Roman Catholic. Avocations: traveling, photography. Home and Office: 3206 Kings Ct Bardstown KY 40004-9489

KIBLER, DAVID BURKE, III, lawyer; b. Lakeland, Fla., Feb. 5, 1924; s. David Burke, Jr. and Bessie (Dew) K.; m. Nell Idalene Bryant, Sept. 26, 1945 (wid. Sept. 1996); children: David Burke IV, Thomas Bryant, Jacquelyn, Nancy Dew. B.A. cum laude, U. Fla., 1947, J.D., 1949; LLD (hon.), Flagler Coll., 1983, Fla. So. Coll., 1986; LHD (hon.), St. Leo Coll., 1970, Fla. State U., 1990. Bar: Fla. 1949. Since practiced in Lakeland; ptnr., chmn. Holland & Knight and predecessor, 1964-94, chmn. emeritus, 1995—; chmn., dir. Kibler Agrl. Corp.; atty. Fla. Citrus Com., 1961-65. Past pres., bd. dirs., exec. com., Lakeland United Fund; mem. Fla. Bd. Regents, 1967-76, chmn., 1969-72; past chmn. Fla. Council 100; mem., chmn. Fla. Post-secondary Edn. Com.; chmn. Fla. Postsecondary Edn. Planning Commn.; bd. dirs. U. South Fla. Found.; bd. dirs. Bok Tower Found.; pres., bd. dirs. U. Fla. Found; mem. Gov.'s High Speed Rail Commn., Gov.'s Unitary Tax Commn., Orange Bowl Com.; chmn. Lakeland Com. of 100. Served to 1st lt. AUS, 1943-46, ETO. Decorated Bronze Star with V, Purple Heart with oak leaf cluster; inducted to Tampa Bay Bus. Hall of Fame, 1992. Mem. Am., 10th Jud. Circuit bar assns., Am. Judicature Soc., Southeastern Legal Found. (legal adv. bd.), Am. Law Inst., Fla. Bar, Am. Legion, Fla. Blue Key, Alpha Tau Omega, Phi Delta Phi. Democrat. Presbyterian. Clubs: Lakeland Yacht and Country, Lone Palm Golf (Lakeland), Grasslands Golf and Country (chmn. bd.), Univ. (Tampa, Fla.). Lodge: Elks. Home: 2113 Fairmount Ave Lakeland FL 33803-3149 Office: Holland & Knight PO Box 32092-2902 92 Lake Wire Dr Lakeland FL 33815-1510*

KIBLER, RAY FRANKLIN, III, minister; b. Columbus, Ohio, Sept. 9, 1951; s. Ray F. Jr. and Evelyn B. (Wiehe) K.; m. Victoria Louise Bergstrom, June 30, 1973; children: Jonathan, Joanna. MusB, Calif. State U., Long Beach, 1974; MDiv, Luther Theol. Sem., 1977; ThM, Luther Northwestern Theol. Sem, 1987; D Ministry, Sch. Theology Claremont, 1990; postgrad., Fuller Sem. Ordained to Luth. ministry, 1979. Pastor, interim pastor Calif., 1979—; pastor Theologian program Ctr. Theol. Inquiry, 1998—; mem. faculty Luth. Bible Inst., Calif., 1992, 96—; leader in interim ministry and congregational devel., 1986—. Author: At the Crossroad: A Lutheran Confessional response to the question of what it means to believe in Jesus in today's religiously pluralistic world, 1990; contbr. articles to profl. publs.

Developer Regional Archives at Pacific Luth. Theol. Sem., Berkeley, Calif., 1980-92, Oral history project Grad. Theol. Union Faculty, 1993-98. Mem. Am. Soc. Ch. History, Luth. Hist. Conf. (bd. dirs. 1990—, membership sec.). Home: 4249 La Junta Dr Claremont CA 91711-2351 *If it will speak a word of hope for the world, the community in Christ must base its proclamation upon Scripture and upon the witness of what the historic Creeds call "the one holy catholic and apostolic Church". If it ignores its past, it lacks an authoritative word for the future.*

KIBLER, VIRGINIA MARY, economist; b. Meadville, Pa., July 30, 1960; d. Richard Dale and Jean Katherine (Brunner) K. BS in Biology, Clarion (Pa.) U., 1982, BA in Econs., 1983; MS in Natural Resource Econs., Pa. State U., 1986. Rsch. asst. Pa. Dept. Agrl. Econs., University Park, 1984-85; office mgr. League of Conservation Voters, Washington, 1986; pvt. practice econ. cons. Washington, 1986-88; economist Office of Pesticide Program EPA, Washington, 1988-91, team leader, program analyst Office of Comptroller, 1991-94, sr economist Office of Water, 1994-99; economist EPA Office of Water Mgmt., Washington, 1999—; spl. asst. U.S. Senate, Washington, 1990. Contbr. articles to profl. jours. Vol. cook So Others May Eat/Homeless Shelter, Washington, 1988—; tutor Cmty. Club, Washington, 1989-92; sec., treas. Timberwood on the Park Homeowners Assn., Wheaton, Md., 1991-93. Named one of Outstanding Young Women of Am., 1986. Mem. EPA Breakfast Club (charter chpt. 8428), Toastmasters (area gov. of yr., 1996-97, new club mentor Ariel Rios Club 1995-98, Able Toastmaster, 1997, Advanced Toastmaster, 1998, Distinguished Toastmaster, 1998). Avocations: reading, sports, history, antiques, nature. Office: EPA Office of Water 401 M St SW # 4302 Washington DC 20024-2610

KIBRIA, ESHAN, neurologist, engineer; b. Pakistan, Oct. 23, 1952; came to U.S., 1967; s. Jana Ullah and Janet Malik; m. Dorothy Kibria, Nov. 6, 1984; 4 children. BSCE, U. Engring., Lahore, Pakistan, 1964; MSCE, U. Miami, 1974; MBA, Barry U., 1980; DO, Nova Southeastern U., 1985. Registered prof. engr., Fla. Asst. prof. neurology U. South Fla., Tampa, 1990-91; assoc. Naples (Fla.) Med. Ctr., 1992-93; owner Neurology Clinics, Naples, Fla., 1992—; mem. physician adv. com. Workcare, Naples; cons. neurologist VA Outpatient Clinic, Ft. Myers, 1998-99; cons. engr. Kibria Engrs., Naples, 1992—. Author books chpts.; contbr. articles to profl. jours.; editor (newsletter) Neuro News. Avocation: gardening. Office: Neurology Clinics 11121 Health Plark S-100 Naples FL 34110

KIBRICK, ANNE, nursing educator, university dean; b. Palmer, Mass., June 1, 1919; d. Martin and Christine (Grigas) Karlon; m. Sidney Kibrick, June 16, 1949; children: Joan, John. RN, Worcester (Mass.) Hahnemann Hosp., 1941; BS, Boston U., 1945; MA, Columbia Tchrs. Coll., 1948; EdD, Harvard U., 1958; LHD (hon.), St. Joseph's Coll., Windham, Maine, 1973. Asst. edn. dir. Cushing VA Hosp., Framingham, Mass., 1948-49; asst. prof. nursing Simmons Coll., Boston, 1949-55; dir. grad. div. Boston U. Sch. Nursing, 1958-63, dean, 1963-68, prof., 1968-70; chmn. dept. nursing Boston Coll. Grad. Sch. Arts and Sci., 1970-74; founding chmn. Sch. Nursing Boston State Coll., 1974-82; founding dean Sch. Nursing U. Mass., Boston, 1974-88, prof., 1988-93, prof. emeritus, 1993—; cons. div. nursing USPHS, 1964-68; cons. Nat. Student Nurses Assn., 1985-88; mem. nat. adv. council nurse tng. USPHS, NIH, 1968-73; cons. Hebrew U.-Hadassah Med. Orgn., Jerusalem, 1971—; mem. Inst. Medicine of Nat. Acad. Scis., 1972—, mem. steering com. costs of edn. of health professions, 1972-74; mem. Nat. Med. Audiovisual Tng. Center, 1972-76, Gov.'s Com. and Area Bd. Mental Health and Mental Retardation, Nat. Commn. for Study Nursing and Nursing Edn., 1970-73; mem. faculty com., regent's external degree program in nursing SUNY, 1974-82; mem. hosp. mgmt. bd. U. Hosp., U. Mass., 1976-81; dir. Medic Alert, Am. Jour. Nursing Co.; cons. Cumberland Coll. Health Scis., New South Wales, Australia, 1986, Menoufia U., Shibin El Kom, Egypt, 1987. Mem. editorial bd. Mass. Jour. Community Health. Bd. dirs. Brookline Mental Health Assn., Met. chpt. ARC, Children's Ctr. Brookline and Greater Boston, Inc., 1984-89, Boston Health Care for Homeless, 1988-90; bd. dirs. Landy-Kaplan Nurses Coun., 1992—, treas., 1994-96; mem. Brookline Town Meeting, 1995—; mem. nat. adv. com. Hadassah Nurses Coun., 1996—. Fellow Am. Acad. Nursing; mem. Nat. Mass. Leagues Nursing (pres. 1971-73), Am. Nurses Assn., Mass. Nurses Assn. (dir. 1982-86), AIDS Internat. Info. Found. (founding mem. 1985), Mass. Nurses Found. (v.p. 1983-86), Nat. Acads. of Practice, Mass. Med. Soc. (bd. dirs. postgrad. med. inst. 1983-96, exec. com. 1989-96), Mass. Orgn. Elder Ams. (bd. dirs. 1988—), Mass. Blueprint 2000, Sigma Theta Tau, Pi Lambda Theta. Home: 381 Clinton Rd Brookline MA 02445-4146

KICE, JOHN EDWARD, engineering executive; b. Wichita, Kans., Sept. 11, 1949; s. Jack Wilbur and Anna Ruth (Jones) K.; m. Susan Pappas; children: Adam Wesley, Jason Mathew. BSBA and BS in Flour Milling Sci., Kans. State U., 1972; BS in Engring., Wichita State U., 1980. Registered profl. engr., Kans. Design engr. Kice Industries, Wichita, 1973-84, v.p. engring., 1984—; lectr. Wichita State U., 1980-86. Recipient Disting. Svc. award Assn. Operative Millers, 1988, 90, 92, 94, 96. Mem. Soc. Mfg. Engrs. Republican. Presbyterian. Achievements include patents for Positive Displacement Air Pump, Reciprocating Airlock Valve, Rotary Mixing Damper, Blade Type Mixing Damper, Conveying Air Velocity Control, Pneumatic Conveying Injector. Office: Kice Industries Inc PO Box 11388 Wichita KS 67202-0388

KICKISH, MARGARET ELIZABETH, elementary education educator; b. Atlantic City, N.J., Nov. 30, 1949; d. James Bernard and Margaret Elizabeth (Egan) Parlett; m. Robert Anthony Kickish, June 30, 1973; children: Eileen, Kathleen, Robert Jr. BS, Franciscan U., 1971; MEd, Coll. N.J., 1977. Cert. elem. educator, learning disabilities tchr. cons. Tchr. Our Lady Star of the Sea Sch., Atlantic City, N.J., 1971-75, Weymouth Twp. Elem. Sch., Dorothy, N.J., 1975-89; curriculum coord. Port Republic (N.J.) Sch., 1990-91; tchr. Brigantine (N.J.) Bd. Edn., 1991-94, supr. curriculum and instrn., 1995—; cognetics coach St. Joseph Sch., Somers Point, N.J., 1989—. Treas. PTA, Somers Point, 1987-89, pres., 1989-90; asst. coach Somers Point Softball Assn., 1991—; mem. St. Joseph Ch. Choir, Somers Point, 1985—. Mem. AAUW, NEA, ASCD, N.J. Edn. Assn. (treas. 1977-86), Prins. and Suprs. Assn., Coun. Exceptional Children, Assn. Learning Cons., Seashore Mother of Twins Club (pres. 1994-96), South Jersey Irish Cultural Soc., Kappa Delta Pi, Delta Zeta, Phi Delta Kappa. Democrat. Roman Catholic. Avocations: swimming, biking, reading, travel, crafts. Home: 526 9th St Somers Point NJ 08244-1458 Office: Brigantine Bd of Edn 301 E Evans Blvd Brigantine NJ 08203-3424

KIDD, CHARLES VINCENT, former civil servant, educator; b. Paulsboro, N.J., Jan. 22, 1914; s. Walter Stephen and Nettie (Sparks) K.; m. Blanche Facer Hoover, Aug. 27, 1938; children: David, Stephen. A.B., Princeton U., 1935; M.A. Princeton U., 1937; D. Pub. Adminstrn, Harvard U., 1957. Economist War Manpower Commn., Office War Moblzn. and Reconversion, Council Econ. Advisers, 1944-46; exec. sec. Pres.'s Sci. Research Bd., 1947; chief research planning NIH, Bethesda, Md., 1948-60; assoc. dir. NIH, 1960-64; exec. sec. fed. council sci. and tech. Office Sci. and Tech., 1964-69; exec. sec. Assn. Am. Univs., 1969-77; research prof. pub. policy George Washington U., 1978-84; program dir. AAAS, 1984-89; cons. Pan-Am. Health Orgn., 1964-74, WHO, 1958-68, Ford Found., 1960-73, UN, 1969-73, State Dept., 1970-75, NSF, 1972-80, NAS, 1979-85. Author: American Universities and Federal Research, 1959; also other books and articles on sci. and ednl. policy. Mem. U.S. del. to UN Conf. Sci. and Tech., 1964; mem. to UNESCO Conf. Sci. Policy, Karlovy Vary, 1966, to OAS Conf. Edn., Sci. and Culture, Maracay, 1968; head U.S. delegation to Castasia Conf., New Delhi, 1967; mem. Milbank Commn. for Study Higher Edn. for Pub. Health, 1973-76, U.S.-USSR Joint Group Experts in Field of Sci. Policy, 1974-77, Sci. Manpower Commn., 1975-78, Commn. Human Resources, Nat. Acad. Sci., 1975-78; Adv. com. Woodrow Wilson Sch. Princeton, 1965-67. Served as lt. (j.g.) USNR, 1944-46. Recipient Rockefeller Pub. Service award, 1955; Distinguished Service award Dept. HEW, 1964. Fellow AAAS. Clubs: Princeton (Washington); Cosmos. Home: Apt 1503 9707 Old Georgetown Rd Bethesda MD 20814-1752

KIDD, DON, bank executive; b. Crowell, Tex., Oct. 10, 1937; m. Sarrah D. Kidd; children: Vickye Faulk, Rena Shuller, Dion Kidd-Johnson. Student, San Angelo State Coll., 1961-63, So. Meth. U., 1972. Pres., CEO Western Commerce Bank, Carlsbad, N.Mex., 1973—; pres., CEO Western Bank Alamorgordo, Western Bank Clovis; pres. Western Bancshares of Carlsbad, Inc., Western Commerce Bancshares of Clovis, Inc., Western Data Svcs., Inc.; bd. dirs. Bank of the S.W. N.Mex. state sen. dist. 34, 1993—; bd. dirs. N.Mex. Ednl. Assistance Found., Carlsbad Literacy Program; bd. dirs., past pres. Carlsbad Dept. Devel.; bd. dirs., past chmn. Western States Sch. Banking, U. N.Mex., 1978-84, Guadalupe Med. Ctr., 1988-91; mem., past pres. Eddy County Sheriff's Posse; past pres. Eddy County United Way, N.Mex. State U. Bd. Regents, 1985-91. Mem. Am. Bankers Assn., N.Mex. Bankers Assn. (past pres.), Carlsbad C. of C. (bd. dirs. 1979-83, past pres.). Republican. Avocation: reading. Office: Western Commerce Bank PO Box 1358 Carlsbad NM 88221-1358

KIDD, FEDA SUTTON, elementary education educator; b. Charlottesville, Va., Apr. 7, 1953; d. Nicholas Mills Jr. and Nancy Kendall Sutton; m. Dennis Allen Kidd, June 26, 1982; children: Erin, Timothy, Daniel, David, Joseph. BS in Biology, Longwood Coll., 1975; M in Edn., U. Va., 1984. Cert. tchr.; lic. collegiate profl. tchg. Tchr. sci., caoch varsity basketball, softball, track Buckingham (Va.) Sch. Sys., 1975-78; tchr. biology and chemistry, coach Fluvanna County Sch. Sys., Va., 1978-89; mem. Fluvanna County Sch. Bd., 1991-95; elem. tchr., coach soccer, softball Open Door Christian Sch., Fluvanna, 1998—; sch. bd. rep. Health Benefits Adv. Bd. State Va., Richmond, 1994-97. Contbr. articles to profl. jours. Vice-chair Fluvanna Rep. Com., 1994-96, chmn., 1996—; chmn. 17th Rep. Senatorial Dist., 1998—. Mem. DAR (vice-regent 1998—). Republican. Baptist. Avocations: gardening, coaching, writing, reading. E-mail: ENK85@aol.com.

KIDD, HILLERY GENE, educational publisher; b. Cin., May 8, 1945; s. Herbert Kidd and Amber L. (Smith) Reed; m. Sylvia Jean Smith, Dec. 21, 1971 (div. Nov. 1980); 1 child, Shane Thomas; m. Catherine Arnold Dec. 1980 (div. 1989). Student, Austin Peay State Coll., 1963-64. Owner KIDD Contrs., Cin., 1969-72; ptnr., v.p. So. Cemeteries Svcs., Inc., Fayetteville, N.C., 1972-73; state sales dir. Life Safety Inc., Clearwater, Fla., 1975; sales mgr. Jodean Water Conditioning, Lutz, Fla., 1973-78; owner Advanced Water Sys., Largo, Fla., 1978-83; regional v.p., securities broker A.L. Williams Corp., Largo, 1983-86; rep. Uniway of Mid-East Tenn., Knoxville, 1986-92; pres., CEO H.G. KIDD Corp., Boulder City, Nev., 1993—. Author: (textbooks) Human Growth and Development, 1992, Introductory Psychology, 1993, Introductory Sociology, 1993; editor: General Biology: Microbiology, Human Anatomy and Physiology, 1993, English Composition with Essay, American Literature, 1993—, Commonalities in Nursing Care—A, 1993, Commonalities in Nursing Care—B, 1993—, Differences in Nursing Care—A, 1993—, Differences in Nursing Care—B, 1993—, Differences in Nursing Care—C, 1993—, Occupational Strategies in Nursing, 1993—. Lt. col. mil. affairs Tenn. Def. Force, Nashville, 1989-94. 1st lt. 46th Spl. Forces Co. (Airborne), U.S. Army, 1965-68. Mem. Order of DeMolay (counselor 1961-62, life mem.). Republican. Avocations: aircraft piloting, scuba diving, sport parachutist. Office: PO Box 60067 Boulder City NV 89006-0067

KIDD, JAMES LAMBERT, retired minister; b. Fall River, Mass., June 12, 1933; s. Thomas W. and Elizabeth Ann (Buckley) K.; m. O. Joann Hamilton, Sept. 12, 1953; 1 child, Pamela Elizabeth. BA, U. Mass., 1955; MDiv, Andover Newton Theol. Sem., Mass., 1959; DDiv, Chgo. Theol. Sem., 1969. Ordained to ministry United Ch. of Christ, 1958. Pastor First Congl. Ch., Pelham, N.H., 1957-61, Wellington Ave. United Ch. of Christ, Chgo., 1961-69, First Congl. Ch., Wilmete, Ill., 1969-79; sr. pastor Asylum Hill Congl. Ch., Hartford, Conn., 1979-98; ret.; vice pres. bd. dirs. Chgo. Theol. Sem., 1969-79; bd. dirs. Andover Newton Theol. Sem., 1986-97, pres. alumni/ae, 1984-85. Author: Good News from Growing Churches, 1990; contbr. articles to profl. jours. Pres. Nat. Cystic Fibrosis Rsch. Found., Chgo., 1968-70; host TV talk show Wonderful World, Chgo., 1968-70; bd. dirs. Hartford Hosp., 1995—; pres. Hartford City Wide Clergy, 1993-97. Recipient Ch. Growth award, UCC Ann. Synod, 1985, 89, Humanities award St. Joseph's Coll., West Hartford, Conn., 1998, Humanitarian award NCCJ, 1998; named Hartford Citizen of Yr., 1998. Mem. Hartford Citywide Clergy Assn. (v.p. 1990-91).

KIDD, JAMES MARION, III, allergist, immunologist, naturalist, educator; b. Baton Rouge, Dec. 15, 1950; s. James Marion Jr. and Germaine Elizabeth (Hunt) K.; m. Carolyn Ann Kelley, Apr. 29, 1981; children: Mackenzie Elizabeth, Katherine Anne. MD, La. State U., 1976. Diplomate Am. Bd. Internal Medicine, Am. Bd. Allergy and Immunology; lic. physician, La., Fla., Wis. Resident physician La. State U. Sch. Medicine, New Orleans, 1977-79; rsch. fellow Med. Coll. Wis., Milw., 1980-82; pvt. practice in allergy and immunology Allergy, Asthma, and Immunology Clinic, Baton Rouge, 1982—; clin. asst., prof. medicine La. Sch. Medicine, New Orleans, 1982—; clin. asst., prof. community medicine and pub. health Tulane U. Sch. Medicine, New Orleans, 1992—; dir. Baton Rouge Pollen Counting Sta., Nat. Allergy Bur. Fellow Am. Coll. Physicians, Am. Acad. Pediat., Am. Acad. Allergy and Immunology; mem. Royal Soc. of Medicine (U.K.), La. Allergy Soc. (pres. 1989-90, exec. sec.-treas. 1992-96), Baton Rouge Allergy Soc. (pres. 1990-95), Rotary (Paul Harris fellow). Fax: (504) 768-7642. E-mail: drjmkidd3@aol.com. Office: James M Kidd III MD 8017 Picardy Ave Baton Rouge LA 70809-3538

KIDD, JASON, professional basketball player; b. San Francisco, Mar. 23, 1973. Guard Dallas Mavericks, 1994-96, Phoenix Suns, 1996—. Active West Dallas Cmty. Ch.; formed Jason Kidd Found., Jason Kidd Basketball Scholarship Fund. Named Pac-10 Player of the Year, 1993-94; named nat. freshman of the yr. by The Sporting News and USA Today, 1993-94; voted Shick Rookie of the Year (with Grant Hill), 1994-95; tied for fourth on all-time NBA rookie impact list, 1994-95. Avocations: R&B music, movies, baseball. Office: Phoenix Suns 201 E Jefferson St Phoenix AZ 85004-2412*

KIDD, JOHN EDWARD, lawyer, corporate executive; b. Syracuse, N.Y., Jan. 17, 1936; s. Edward F. and Mary (Feczko) K.; m. Elaine Mitchell, Feb. 23, 1963; children: John Mitchell, David Alan, Cynthia Lorraine. BS in Physics, LeMoyne Coll., 1957; LLB, Georgetown U., 1961. Bar: Va. 1961, U.S. Supreme Ct. 1966, U.S. Tax Ct. 1966, N.Y. 1968, U.S. Ct. Appeals (2d cir.) 1968, U.S. Ct. Appeals (4th cir.), 1968, U.S. Dist. Ct. (so. and ea. dists.) N.Y. 1969, U.S. Dist. Ct. (no. dist. Calif.) 1980, U.S. Ct. Appeals (3d, 5th, 9th, 11th cirs.) 1981, U.S. Dist Ct. (ea. dist.) Va. 1993. Patent examiner U.S. Patent Office, Washington, 1957-60; patent advisor U.S. Navy, Washington, 1960-62; trial atty. Dept. Justice, Washington, 1963-67; counsel to Copyright Office, Washington, 1966-67; spl. counsel Dept. Justice, 1967; assoc. Kenyon & Kenyon, N.Y.C., 1967-70; assoc., ptnr. Pennie & Edmonds, N.Y.C., 1971-85, Anderson, Kill, Olick & Oshinsky, P.C., 1986-91; ptnr. Shea & Gould, 1991-94; sr. ptnr. Rogers & Wells, 1994—, exec. com. 1996—; counsel Baseball Hall of Fame, 1995—; referee 9th Jud. Dept. N.Y. Supreme Ct., 1968-69; exec., chmn. bd. E.M. Kidd, Ltd.; chmn. Symposium on Presdl. Patent Reform Commn., 1966; lectr., mem. faculty Practicing Law Inst., 1967, 1984-96; mem. Bicentennial Commn. U.S. Claims Ct., 1987-89; guest lectr. Inventor Hall of Fame, 1996-98. Contbr. writings to legal jours. Active United Fund of Westchester, Cmty. Fund of Bronxville, Westchester Coun. Boy Scouts Am.; trustee LeMoyne Coll. Alumni. Mem. ABA (lectr. 1984-94), N.Y. State Bar Assn. (chmn. spl. com. on patents and trademarks 1982-86), Fed. Cir. Bar Assn., Assn. Trial Lawyers Am., Am. Intellectual Property Assn., U.S. Trademark Assn., Copyright Soc. Am., N.Y. Intellectual Property Assn., Assn. of Bar of City of N.Y., N.Y. Patent, Licensing Exec. Soc., Delta Theta Phi. Roman Catholic. Clubs: Mahopac Country, Yale, Sky, Rockefeller. Office: Rogers & Wells LLP 200 Park Ave Fl 8E New York NY 10166-0800

KIDD, LOVETTA MONZA, music educator; b. Anniston, Ala., Jan. 13, 1943; d. Andrew Jackson and Velma Mildred (Duke) Traywick; m. Everett Wayne Kidd, Dec. 20, 1961 (dec. Dec. 1998); children: Michelle Kidd Belindo, Andy, David. Student, Okla. Coll. for Women, 1961-62, Southwestern Okla. State U., 1982-83. Pvt. piano tchr. Eva, Okla., 1967-69, Sickles, Okla., 1970-71, Dibble, Okla., 1971-78, Anadarko, Okla., 1979—; pianist First Bapt. Ch., Anadarko, 1980's. Sec. Okla. Conservative Com., Norman, 1994-95; vice chmn. Caddo County (Okla.) Rep. party, 1995-97, chmn., 1997-99; alt. del. Nat. Rep. Convention, San Diego, 1996. Mem. Okla. Fedn. Rep. Women, Concerned Women for Am., Anadarko Eagle Forum (founder, pres. 1994—), Okla.'s First Ladies, Gen. Fedn. Women's Clubs Philomathic Club (sec. 1996-98, v.p. 1998—), Okla. Fedn. Music Clubs (dist. Gold Cup chmn. 1993—), Musical Key Club (founder, pres. 1981—). Avocations: reading, gardening, needlepoint, oil painting, drawing. Home: 701 W Alabama Anadarko OK 73005

KIDD, LYNDEN LOUISE, healthcare consultant; b. Laramie, Wyo., May 7, 1959; d. David Thomas and Sally Louise (Noble) K. AA, Stephens Coll., 1979; BA in Polit. Sci., Comm., U. Wyo., 1981, JD, 1986. Adminstrv. dir. Wyo. Med. Ctr., Casper, 1986-92, v.p. med. affairs, 1992-95; consultant Next Iteration, Casper, 1995-96; assoc. APM Inc., Chgo., 1996-97; cons. Next Iteration, Phila., 1998—; search cons. Ken Clark Internatl., Princeton, 1998—. Mem. Wyo. Heritage Soc., 1987-89, Gov.'s Coun. Sports and Fitness, Wyo., 1991-96; chmn., mem. Leadership Casper, 1989-91; bd. dirs., campaign chmn. United Way, Casper, 1989-96, pres., 1994-95; bd. dirs. Casper Classic, Inc., 1989-92. Mem. Am. Health Lawyers Assn., Am. Coll. Healthcare Execs. (assoc.), Wyo. Hosp. Assn., Casper C. of C. (bd. dirs. 1991-94), Phi Alpha Delta. Avocations: volunteer work, reading, music. Home: 426 Mahogany Walk Newtown PA 18940-4212 office: Five Independence Way Ste 210 Princeton NJ 08540

KIDD, ROBERT HUGH, financial executive, accountant; b. Toronto, Ont., Can., June 1, 1944; s. Donald Alexander and Mary Isabelle K.; m. Elizabeth M. Werner; children: Donald, Scott, Suzanne. B in Commerce, U. Toronto, 1966; MBA, York U., Toronto, 1972. Chartered acct. Acct. KPMG, Toronto, 1966-72, ptnr., 1973-81; CFO, sr. v.p. George Weston Ltd., Toronto, 1981-95; chmn. Canadian Ranpart Oil & Gas Ltd., Calgary, Alberta, 1981-86; pres. Location Rsch. Co. Can. Ltd., Mississauga, Ont., 1982; CFO InContext Syss. Inc., 1995-96, Lions Gate Entertainment Corp., 1997-98; bd. dirs. Credit Suisse Can., Toronto, Canadian Bond Rating Svcs., Toronto, Proctor & Redfern Inc., Toronto; chmn. Nat. Cancer Inst. Can. fin. com., 1997-98. Author: Earnings Forecast, 1976; co-author: Terminology for Accountants, 1976. Recipient Victoria Coll. Gold medal U. Toronto, 1966, Gov. Gen.'s Gold medal Can. Inst. Chartered Accts., 1968. Fellow Inst. Chartered Accts. Ont. Avocations: skiing, swimming, boating.

KIDDA, MICHAEL LAMONT, JR., psychologist, educator; b. Jackson, Miss., May 24, 1945; s. Michael Lamont and Annie Laurie (McKeithen) K.; m. Ellen Gordon, Aug. 23, 1977; children: Patrick Gordon, John McKeithen. BA in English, Centenary Coll., Shreveport, La., 1969; MDiv, U. South, Sewanee, Tenn., 1972; MS in Social Psychology, U. Ga., 1984, PhD in Social Psychology, 1987. Youth cons. Cathedral of St. Philip, Atlanta, 1974-76; counselor All Saints' Sch., Vicksburg, Miss., 1977-79; coord. of assessment J.C. Smith U., Charlotte, N.C., 1989-94, assoc. prof. psychology, 1985—, dept. head, 1987-89, 97; corp. sec. Kidda Enterprises, 1999—; coord. Grad. Student Conf./Personality and Social Psychology, Athens, 1981; bd. trustees N.E. Ga. Area, Cmty. Resource Coun., Athens, 1980-83, v.p., 1982, tech. adminstrn., 1984; data analysis cons., Athens, 1980-85; presenter in field; corp. sec. Kidda Enterprizes, 1999. Contbr. articles to profl. jours. and to On-line and CD-Rom data bases; author newsletter ETS Higher Edn. Assessment, 1993. Adv. bd. Washington Hghts. Project, Nat. Children's Def. Fund, Charlotte, 1994; chair evaluation com. Fighting Back Against Drugs, Charlotte, 1992-94; com. mem. cub scouts pack 19 Boy Scouts Am., Huntersville, N.C., 1994—, Lions Club, 1997-99, Davidson, 1999—. Recipient Nat. Retention Excellence award Noel-Levitz Ctrs., Cross of Nails award St. Michael's Cathedral, Coventry, Eng., cert. of appreciation Washington Hts. Youth Svcs. Acad., 1997; Retention and Performance grantee Pew Charitable Trusts, 1994, Equipment grantee AT&T Found., 1991, grantee APA, 1996, United Negro Coll. Fund, 1996; Inst. Non-Traditional Ministries rsch. fellow. Mem. Am. Statis. Assn., Soc. Southeastern Social Psychologists, Lions, Sigma Xi (site coord. celebration of undergrad. rsch. 1999), Sigma Tau Delta, Psi Chi. Achievements include empirical demonstration of superiority of college-level inquiry curriculum over remediation in post-secondary education; research on effects of social control on prosocial behavior; research on causal attribution on evaluation of people with disabilities; research on effects of accepting non-reciprocal aid; devel. of relationship mapping as a curriculum assessment tool. Home: 126 Kinderston Dr Davidson NC 28036 Office: Johnson C Smith Univ 100 Beatties Ford Rd Charlotte NC 28216-5398

KIDDE, GEOFFREY CARTER, composer, flutist, music educator; b. Paris, Mar. 23, 1963; came to U.S., 1968; s. John Lyon Kidde and Constance Anson Jordan; m. Patricia Sue Kooyman, Aug. 12, 1995; children: Ethan S., Devin A. BA, Columbia U., 1985, DMA, 1995; MMus, New Eng. Conservatory, 1988. Asst. prof. U. Bridgeport (Conn.), 1996-98, head music program, 1997-98; adj. prof. St. John's U., N.Y.C., 1998—. Composer: Quest for Orch. MMC Rec., 1994. Mem. Nat. Assn. Composers (2nd prize Nat. Composers Competition 1993), League of Composers/Internat. Soc. Contemporary Music (bd. dirs., pres. 1993-95), New Eng. Conservatory Alumni Assn. (bd. dirs.).

KIDDE, JOHN LYON, investment manager; b. June 5, 1944. BA, Princeton U., 1959; postgrad. studies, Columbia U. Law Sch. Indsl. rsch. analyst Federated Employers, San Francisco, 1956-57; fin. dir. Walter Kidde S.A. do Brasil, Rio De Janeiro, 1959-60; European mgr. Walter Kidde Co., Inc., Paris, 1962-66; joint mng. dir., corp. European mgr. Walter Kidde Co., Ltd., Northolt, Eng., 1966-67; dir. internat. ops. Kidde Inc. U.S., Saddle Brook, N.J., 1967-68; v.p., dir. internat. ops. Kidde Inc. U.S., Saddle Brook, 1968-88; pres., CEO KDM Devel. Corp., Upper Montclair, N.J., 1988—; gen. ptnr. Claflin Capital II, III, IV, V & VI, VII, Boston, N. Am. Venture Capital II; bd. dirs. Tengasco, Inc., Knoxville, Pratt & Reed Corp., Bridgeport, Conn., The Futures Group, Washington, Internat. Resource Corp., Washington, Pasco Internat., Pine Brook, N.J., Asset Mgmt. Advisors, Inc., Jupiter, Fla., Juniper Ptnrs., Inc., Montclair, N.J., Australasia Inc., Cayman Island, Internat. AgriTech Resources Inc., N.Y.C., Keyes Martin Inc, East Hanover, N.J.; dir. Highland Expansion Fund Mgmt. Co., Wellesley, Mass., Princeton (N.J.) Capital Mgmt., Inc., Pax Worldwide Growth Fund, Portsmouth, USA Ctr. Com.; with Ctr. for Econ. Rsch. and Grad. Edn., Charles U., Prague; chmn. bd. Compliance Internat., Inc., Fairfield, bd. dirs. Continental Europe '92, Cayman Island. Trustee Internat. Coll. Cayman Island, Grand Cayman, Open Space Inst., N.Y.C., Stevens Inst. Tech., Hoboken, N.J., Albert Payson Terhune Found., Pompton Lakes, N.J., Fannie E. Rippel Found., Basking Ridge, N.J., Assist Inc., Peterborough, N.H.; pres. Princeton (N.J.) Reachout '56; mem. adv. bd. Whitehead Inst. Biomed. Rsch., Cambridge, Mass. With U.S. Army, 1957-58. Home: 154 Old Chester Rd Essex Fells NJ 07021-1627 Office: KDM Devel Corp 209 Cooper Ave Montclair NJ 07043-1850

KIDDER, C. ROBERT, food products executive; b. 1943. BSIE, U. Mich., 1966; MS, Iowa State U., 1968. With Ford Motor Co., Detroit, 1968-69, McKinsey & Co., N.Y.C., 1972-78, Dart Industries, 1978-80, Duracell Europe, 1980-81; with Duracell Internat. Inc., 1981-95, pres., CEO, 1988-95, past chmn., CEO; chmn., CEO Borden, Inc., Columbus, Ohio, 1995—. With USN, 1969-72. Office: Borden Inc 180 E Broad St Columbus OH 43215-3799*

KIDDER, FRED DOCKSTATER, lawyer; b. Cleve., May 22, 1922; s. Howard Lorin and Virgina (Milligan) K.; m. Eleanor (Hap) Kidder; children—Fred D. III, Barbara Anne Donelson, Jeanne Kidder-Appleton. BS with distinction, U. Akron, 1948; JD, Case Western Res. U., 1950. Bar: Ohio 1950, Tex. 1985, U.S. Dist. Ct. (no. dist.) Ohio 1950, U.S. Dist. Ct. (no. dist.) Tex. 1985. Assoc. Arter & Hadden and predecessors, Cleve., 1950-79, ptnr., 1960-79; ptnr. Jones, Day, Reavis and Pogue, Cleve., 1980-89, regional mng. ptnr. Tex., 1985-86; gen. counsel Lubrizol Corp., Cleve., 1989-92, spl. counsel, 1993—. Contbr. articles to profl. jours. Mem. Cleve. Growth Assn., Shaker Heights Citizens Com., Citizens League Cleve.; former pres. Estate Planning Coun.; co-chmn. bd. trustees Lake Erie Coll.; bd. trustees, v.p., Alzheimer's Assn., Cleve.; mem., bd. trustees Cleve. Sight Ctr.; past mem. alumni coun. U. Akron; past. corp. coun. Dallas Mus. Art; past pres. Case Western Reserve U. Law Sch. Alumni Assn.; past chmn. Shaker Heights Recreation Bd. Mem. ABA, Nat. Assn. Corp. Secs., Tex. Bar Assn., Ohio State Bar Assn., State Troopers Ohio (past sec.), Cleve. Bar Assn., Estate Planning Coun. (past pres.), Blue Coats, Soc. Benchers (past chmn.), Tax Club Cleve. (past pres.), Union Club, Pepper Pike Club (sec.), Country Club Cleve., Skating Club, Order of Coif, Ct. of Nisi Prius (former judge), Phi Eta Sigma, Beta Delta Psi, Phi Sigma Alpha, Phi Delta Theta, Phi Delta Phi. Office: The Lubrizol Corp 29400 Lakeland Blvd Wickliffe OH 44092-2298

KIDDER, JOSEPH P., city service director; b. Akron, Ohio; m. Vicki Kidder; children: Raechel, Paul. Degree in acctg., U. Akron, 1980. Ward 6 councilman City of Akron, 1984-92, svc. dir., 1992—; past chmn. budget and fin. com., Akron City Coun. Office: Office of Svc Dir Mcpl Bldg 166 S High St Akron OH 44308-1626*

KIDDER, RAY EDWARD, physicist, consultant; b. N.Y.C., Nov. 12, 1923; s. Harry Alvin and Laura Augusta (Wagner) K.; m. Marcia Loring Sprague, June 12, 1947 (div. Aug. 1975); children: Sandra Laura, David Ray, Matthew Sprague. BS, Ohio State U., 1947, MS, 1948, PhD, 1950. Physicist Calif. Rsch. Corp., La Habra, 1950-56, Lawrence Livermore Nat. Lab., Livermore, Calif., 1956—; mem. adv. bd. Inst. for Quantum Optics, Garching, Germany, 1976-90; bd. editors Nuc. Fusion IAEA, Vienna, 1979-84; cons. Sci. Applications Internat. Corp., San Diego, 1991-94; mem. hon. adv. bd. Inst. for Advanced Physics Studies, La Jolla, Calif., 1991—. Contbr. chpts. to books. With USN, 1944-46. Recipient Humboldt award Alexander von Humboldt Found., 1988. Fellow Am. Phys. Soc. (Szilard award 1993); mem. AAAS, Sigma Xi. Achievements include research in physics of nuclear weapons, inertial confinement fusion, megagauss magnetic fields, laser isotope enrichment, containment of low-yield nuclear explosions. Home: 637 E Angela St Pleasanton CA 94566-7413 Office: Lawrence Livermore Nat Lab PO Box 808 Livermore CA 94551-0808

KIDDER, (JOHN) TRACY, writer; b. N.Y.C., Nov. 12, 1945; s. Henry Maynard and Reine Marie (Tracy) K.; m. Frances Toland, Jan. 1971. AB, Harvard U., Cambridge, Mass., 1967; MFA, U. Iowa, Iowa City, 1974. Contbg. editor Atlantic Monthly, Boston, 1982—. Author: The Road to Yuba City, 1974, The Soul of a New Machine, 1981 (Pulitzer prize 1982, Am. Book award 1982), House, 1985, Among Schoolchildren, 1989 (Robert F. Kennedy book award), Old Friends, 1993; author numerous articles, short stories and book revs. Served to 1st lt. U.S. Army, 1967-69, Vietnam.

KIDDOO, ROBERT JAMES, engineering service company executive; b. Kansas City, Mo., July 8, 1936; s. Robert Leroy and Margaret Ella (Wolford) K.; m. Patricia Anne Wakefield, Apr. 17, 1957; children: Robert Michael, Stacey Margaret Kiddoo-Lee. BSBA, UCLA, 1960; MSBA, Calif. State U., Northridge, 1969; MBA, U. So. Calif., 1972, D of Bus. Adminstrn., 1978. Cert. mgmt. acct. Asst. v.p., nat. div. loan officer Crocker-Citizen's Nat. Bank, L.A., 1958-69; v.p., chief fin. officer, dir. corp. sec. Kirk-Mayer, Inc., L.A., 1969-87; prof. acctg. and MIS Calif. State U., Northridge, 1970—; region adminstr. mgr. CDI Corp.-West, Chatsworth, Calif., 1990; exec. v.p. Kirk-Mayer, Inc., L.A., 1990-92; pres. Creative Software Designs, Inc., Northridge, Calif., 1995—; univ. contr. Calif. State U., Northridge, 1997—. With U.S. Army, 1955-56. Mem. Mensa, Ltd., Beta Gamma Sigma, Beta Alpha Psi. Office: Calif State Univ Acctg and MIS Northridge CA 91330-8245

KIDERA, GEORGE JEROME, physician; b. Chgo., Apr. 29, 1913; s. Edward J. and Marie (Nadherny) K.; m. Marie A. Cuchna, Aug., 1938 (dec. Feb., 1973); children: George Peter, Kristina Alice; m. Jean Allen, Aug. 16, 1975. Student, Northwestern U., 1930-31, Crane Jr. Coll., 1931-33; BS, U. Ill., 1935, MD, 1937; postgrad., Sch. Aviation Medicine, 1942; student postgrad. sch., Cook County Hosp., 1948. Diplomate Am. Bd. Preventive Medicine. Intern West Suburban Hosp., Oak Park, Ill., 1937-38, then mem. surg. staff; regional med. dir. United Air Lines, Chgo., 1938, 46-51, med. dir., 1951-72, v.p. med. svcs., 1972-78, cons. to chmn., 1978-83; cons. Dart Industries, 1979-80; avaiation med. cons. Dart-Kraft, 1980-86, Kraft, Inc., 1986—, Premark, Internat., 1986—; cons. life scis. com. NASA, 1970—; pres. West Suburban Hosp. Interns Alumni Assn., 1949-51. Contbr. articles to profl. jours. Lt. col., flight surgeon USAAF, 1942-46. Fellow Aerospace Med. Assn. (pres. 1960, mem. exec. coun. 1963, Howard D. Edwards award 1960, Theodore C. Lyster award 1970), Am. Coll. Preventive Medicine; mem. AMA, Airline Med. Dirs. Assn. (mem. exec. coun. 1950-51, pres. 1955, award 1972), Ill. Med. Soc., Chgo. Med. Soc., Des Plaines Med. Soc., Am. Assn. Indsl. Physicians and Surgeons, Am. Med Writers Assn., Internat. Air Transport Assn., Internat. Acad. Aviation and Space Medicine (chancellor 1972-77, 1st v.p. 1977). Home and Office: 1432 Bel Aire Rd San Mateo CA 94402-3618

KIDMAN, NICOLE, actress; b. Honolulu, Hawaii, June 20, 1967; m. Tom Cruise, 1990; children: Isabella Jane Kidman, Connor Antony Kidman. Film appearences include BMX Bandits, 1983, Bush Christmas, 1983, Emerald City, 1989, Dead Calm, 1989, Days of Thunder, 1990, Flirting, 1991, Billy Bathgate, 1991 (Golden Globe Award nomination 1992), Far and Away, 1992, Malice, 1993, My Life, 1993, Batman Forever, 1995, Portrait of a Lady, 1996, To Die For, 1995 (Golden Globe award), The Peacemaker, 1997, Practical Magic, 1998, Eyes Wide Shut, 1999; TV appearances include Bangkok Hilton, 1989 (Australian Film Inst. Best Actress in Miniseries), Vietnam, 1985 (Australian Film Inst. Best Actress in Miniseries). Office: c/o Nancy Seltzer 6220 Del Valle Dr Los Angeles CA 90048*

KIEBURTZ, KARL DAVID, physician, educator, researcher; b. Seattle, Oct. 11, 1958; s. R. Bruce and Alvena B. Kieburtz; m. Victoria Frances Korth, Dec. 27, 1984. BA, Amherst Coll., 1980; MD, MPH, U. Rochester, 1985. Resident in neurology U. Rochester, N.Y., 1985-89, assoc. prof. neurology, 1989—; grant reviewer, grant prin. investigator NIH, Bethesda, 1993—; mem. exec. com. Parkinson Study Group, Rochester, 1993—; mem. sci. adv. bd. Alzheimer's Disease Coop. Study, San Diego, 1996—. Assoc. editor Neurology, 1996—; contbr. articles to profl. jours. Bd. dirs. Cmty. Health Network, Rochester, 1992-95; mem. Brighton Planning Bd., 1997—. George W. Merck tchg. scholar; Logan Clendening fellow U. Kans., 1982. Fellow Am. Acad. Neurology; mem Am. Neurol. Assn., Movement Disorder Soc., Phi Beta Kappa. Fax: 716-473-9745. Office: U Rochester Dept Neurology 1351 Mt Hope Ave Ste 220 Rochester NY 14620

KIECHEL, BARBARA BERNADETTE, vocational school educator; b. Allentown, Pa., Oct. 18, 1949; d. F. Joseph and Josephine Marie (Johnson) Mucellin; m. Gary Lee Kiechel, May 17, 1975; children: Angela, Jonathan, Marie. AA, Lehigh Carbon C.C., Schnecksville, Pa., 1969; BS, Temple U., 1978, MA, 1981. Cert. supr. comprehensive vocat. edn. tchr., Pa. Tchr. Lehigh Career & Tech. Inst., Schnecksville, 1974-81; curriculum devel. specialist Lehigh County Vocat.-Tech. Sch., Schnecksville, 1981-97, supr. curriculum and instrn., 1997—; resident leadership resource person, Temple U., Phila., 1982-83, grad. leadership devel. program, 1983-84, others. Coord. United Way Campaign, Schnecksville, 1989—, strategic planning internat. facilitator, 1994-96; asst. leader Great Valley Girl Scout Coun., Emmaus, Pa., 1989-95; ch. organist St. Francis of Assisi Ch., Allentown, Pa., 1964-75. Recipient Cert. Achievement Dept. Edn., 1990, Cert. Vol. Achievement award United Way, 1992, 94. Mem. NEA, Pa. Sch. Edn. Assn. Democrat. Avocations: gardening, hiking. Home: 5064 Jasper Rd Emmaus PA 18049-5217 Office: Lehigh County Vocat Tech 4500 Education Park Dr Schnecksville PA 18078-2501

KIECHEL, WALTER, III, editor; b. Tecumseh, Nebr.. BA, Harvard Coll., 1968, MBA, JD, 1977. Reporter, researcher Fortune Mag., 1977-78, assoc. editor, 1978-82, mem. bd. editors, 1982-88, asst. mng. editor, 1988-92, exec. editor, 1992-94, mng. editor, 1994-95; editor for bus. devel. Time, Inc., N.Y.C., 1995; editor Mgmt. Update newsletter Harvard Bus. Sch. Pub. Co.; cons. Bain & Co., 1996; pub. Harvard Bus. Rev., 1997; editl. dir. H.B.S.P. Co., 1998. With U.S. Navy. Office: 509 Madison Ave Fl 15 New York NY 10022-5501

KIECHLIN, ROBERT JEROME, retired coal company executive, financial consultant; b. N.Y.C., Nov. 2, 1919; s. Henry, Jr. and Lydia C. (Bergmann) K.; m. Regina W. Kolakowski, Oct. 6, 1951; children: Robert Jerome, Regina, William. B.S. in Acctg., NYU, 1940. C.P.A., N.Y., Mo. With Paisley & Conroy (C.P.A.s), N.Y.C., 1945-52; with N.J. Zinc Co., 1952—, asst. comptroller, 1957-61, comptroller, 1961-66, treas. and comptroller, 1966-71; controller Peabody Coal Co., St. Louis, 1971-79; v.p., controller, treas. R.L. Burns Corp., Evansville, Ind., 1979-85, Pyro Energy Corp., Evansville, Ind., 1981-85, ret.; pvt. fin. cons. coal, oil and gas industries, 1986—. Served with USNR, 1942-45, PTO. Decorated Navy Cross. Mem. AICPA, N.Y. State Soc. CPAs, Inst. Mgmt. Accts., Fin. Execs. Inst. Home: 1833 E Boonville N Harmony Evansville IN 47711

KIEF, PAUL ALLAN, lawyer; b. Montevideo, Minn., Mar. 22, 1934; s. Paul G. and Minna S. K. BA, U. Minn., 1957, LLB, 1957. Bar: Minn. 1957, U.S. Dist. Ct. Minn. 1964, U.S. Tax Ct. 1968, U.S. Supreme Ct. 1981; cert. criminal trial law specialist Nat. Bd. Trial Advocacy. Gen. practice Bemidji, Minn., 1959—; ptnr. Kief, Fuller, Baer & Wallner, Ltd., Bemidji, Minn., 1973-97; owner Paul A. Kief Law Firm, Bemidji, Minn., 1998—; pub. defender 9th Jud. Dist. Minn., Bemidji, Minn., 1966-98; pub. defender 9th Jud. Dist. Minn., 1966—, chief pub. defender, 1968-94; vol. atty. Minn. Civil Liberties Union; panel atty. Legal Svcs. Northwest Minn. Vice chmn. Beltrami County Planning Commn., 1964-68; chmn. adv. com. Gov.'s Crime Commn., 1971-77; mem. Minn. Task Force on Standards and Goals in Criminal Justice, 1975-76, Crime Victims Task Force, 1985, Jud. Selection Com., 1987, Com. on Criminal Jury Instrn. Guides, 1988-90; bd. dirs. Legal Svcs. Northwest Minn., 1990-96; capt. CAP, 1969—. Served with USAR, USNG, 1958-64. Mem. ABA, ATLA, NACDL, NAt. Bd. Trial Advocacy (cert. crim. law trial specialist 1998), Minn. Bar Assn., Minn. Trial Lawyers Assn., 15th Dist. Bar Assn. (past sec.), Beltrami County Bar Assn. (past pres.), Lawyer-Pilots Bar Assn., Minn. Assn. Criminal Def. Lawyers. Democrat. Congregationalist. Club: Toastmasters. Home: PO Box 212 Bemidji MN 56619-0212 Office: 514 America Ave NW PO Box 212 Bemidji MN 56619-0212

KIEFER, FREDERICK P., English educator; b. Providence, Jan. 3, 1945. BA, Loyola Coll., Balt., 1967; MA, Harvard U., 1968, PhD, 1972. Prof. U. Ariz., Tucson, 1973—. Author: Fortune and Elizabethan Tragedy, 1983, Writing on the Renaissance Stage, 1996. E-mail: fkiefer@u.arizona.edu. Home: 4146 E La Cienega Dr Tucson AZ 85712 Office: U Ariz English Dept Tucson AZ 85721

KIEFER, GARY, newspaper editor. Now mng. editor features Columbus (Ohio) Dispatch. Office: Columbus Dispatch 34 S 3rd St Columbus OH 43215-4241*

KIEFER, HELEN CHILTON, neurologist, psychiatrist; b. Washington; d. Frank McGlowing and Sue (Stanford) Chilton; m. John Harold Kiefer, Feb. 4, 1961 (div. July 1971); 1 child, Steven Chilton. AB in Chemistry magna cum laude, Cornell U., 1961; MS, U. Chgo., 1971, PhD in Biochemistry, 1971; MD with honors, Northwestern U., 1981. Lic. physician, Ill.; diplomate Nat. Bd. Med. Examiners. Intern psychiatry and internal medicine Michael Reese Hosp. and Med. Ctr., Chgo., 1981-82; resident neurology U. Ill. Med. Sch., Chgo., 1983-85; physicist, computer programmer physics div. Los Alamos (N.Mex.) Sci. Labs., 1965—; asst. prof. dept. biochemistry Northwestern U. Med. Sch., Chgo., 1972-78; editor Marcus Acad. Media, Chgo., 1978-81; clin. assoc. prof. dept. biochemistry Loyola Med. and Dental Sch., Chgo., 1978-81; med. staff Charter Barclay Neuropsychiat. Hosp., Chgo., 1983—; pvt. practice Chgo., 1983—; dir. med. rsch. for biotech., assoc. med. dir. high tech. Abbott Labs., Abbott Park, Ill., 1986-89; assoc. ctr. for biotechnology Northwestern U., 1992—; adj. assoc. prof. dept. biomed. engring. and grad. multidisciplinary program in neurosci. Northwestern U., Evanston, Ill., 1989-90, vis. prof., assoc. ctr. for biotech., 1992—; affiliate Internat. Human Genome Mapping Project, 1991—; vis. prof. dept. bioengring. U. Wash., Seattle, 1982-83; mem. presdl. adv. com. NIH, 1976-80; CEO, pres. The Doctor Cooks, Inc., 1995—; mem. numerous program project rev. bds., 1978-80. Woodrow Wilson fellow, NSF fellow, Danforth Found. fellow, NIH postdoctoral fellow. Mem. Assn. Clin. Scientists, N.Y. Acad. Scis., Phi Beta Kappa, Alpha Omega Alpha.

KIEFER, J. RICHARD, JR., retired corporate executive; b. Phila., Mar. 3, 1928; m. Gwendolen Clara Watkins, June 20, 1953; children: David Richard, Linda Lauretta, Nancy Ellen, Carol Gwen. BS in Chem. Engring., Drexel U., 1950; postgrad., Temple U. With McCloskey Corp., Phila., 1947-89, Valspar Corp., 1989-90; with rsch. and devel. McCloskey Corp., Phila., with customer product evaluation dept., v.p. community, industry and regulatory affairs. Mem. Friends of Acad. Vocal Arts, Olney Symphony Assn., Pa. Ballet Assn., Zool. Soc. Phila., Franklin Inst., Friends of Independence Nat. Hist. Park, Friends of Pennypack Park (vol. twilight walking tours guide); mem. Meml. Soc. Greater Phila., past pres., treas., bd. dirs.; vol. tour guide Phila. Soc. Preservation Landmarks, Phila. Cultural Coun. Recipient Sr. Statesman award Phila. Paint Industry. Mem. Phila. Paint and Coatings Assn. (past pres., past bd. dirs.), Phila. Soc. Coatings Tech. (past pres., bd. dirs., by-laws com., Liberty Bell, Tech Comm. and Benjamin Franklin awards), Fed. Soc. Coatings Tech. (hon. mem., past coun., bd. dirs., exec. com., Trigg award), Soc. Gallows Birds, N.E. High Sch. Alumni Assn. (class treas.), Masons (chmn. Trustees of the Charity Funds of Lodge, chmn. com. masonic edn., 32 degree Scottish rite, Columbia chpt. Joppa coun., high twelve past pres.), Philalethes Soc., Alpha Phi Omega, Zeta Theta (cofounder 1948). Avocations: travel, classical music, attending ballet performances, opera, theater. Home: 1027 Loney St Philadelphia PA 19111-2624

KIEFER, RENATA GERTRUD, physician, epidemiologist, economist, international health management consultant; b. Lorrach, Baden, Germany, July 4, 1946; came to U.S., 1970; d. Friedrich W. and Gertrud Anna (Keller) K.; m. James C. Bridgman. BA, Stanford U., 1963; MA, U. Calif., Berkeley, 1967; MD, U. Geneva, Switzerland, 1982; MPH, U. Calif., Berkeley, 1990. Diplomate Am. Bd. Pediatrics; cert. in environ. health, Germany. Asst. instr. dissection lab. dept. morphology U. Geneva Sch. of Medicine, Switzerland, 1979-80; interim resident dept. diagnostic radiology Univ. Hosp., Geneva, 1980, intern physician, 1982-83; clin. fellow in pediatrics Harvard Med. Sch., Boston, 1983-85; resident physician Mass. Gen. Hosp., Boston, 1983-85; sr. resident dept. pediatrics U. Calif., San Francisco, 1985-86; attending physician emergency dept. Children's Hosp. Med. Ctr., Oakland, Calif., 1986-94; fellow dept. epidemiology and internat. health U. Calif., San Francisco, 1988-90; German tech. cooperation expert tropical medicine & internat. health Inst. for Health Sci. Rsch., Asuncion, Paraguay, 1990-94, vis. prof. epidemiol. and preventive medicine, 1992—; sci. methods advisor Nat. U. Asuncion, 1994—; chief adv. rsch. and human resource devel. Health Strategies Internat.; rep. of IICS/Internat. Orgns., cons. and presenter in field; chief adviser on health projects, dir. internat. teams GTZ/Health Ministry of Colombia, 1997—. Contbr. numerous articles to profl. jours. Co-winner nat. sci. prize Paraguay Parliament, 1994; ASSU scholar Stanford U., 1962-63, Fulbright scholar, 1962-64, Internat. scholar Swedish Inst., 1968, Internat. Health scholar U. Calif., 1990; fellow AAUW, 1968; recipient award USPHS Nat. Rsch. Svc., 1989-90. Address: 6 Locksley Ave San Francisco CA 94122-3854

KIEFER, ROBERT HARRY, real estate broker; b. Tonopah, Nev., Apr. 25, 1945; s. Martin Leon and Anne Alice (Abrahamson) K.; m. Nancy Lynn Resnick, June 19, 1966; children: Courtney Martine, Reed Martin, Tyler Robert. BA in Journalism, U. Minn., 1967. V.p. mktg. Minnetonka Inc., Chaska, Minn., 1972-75; CEO Merchandising's Mktg. Inc., Mpls., 1975-79, Vet. Derm Products Inc., Mission Viejo, Calif., 1979-87; v.p., regional mgr. Calmark Devel., L.A., Las Vegas, Nev., 1987-90; prin., broker Western New Home Sales, Anaheim, Calif., 1990-94; v.p. Real Estate Dimensions, Irvine, Calif., 1994-95; prin., broker Kiefer Tract Sales & Mktg., Irvine, 1995—; mem. sales and mktg. coun. BIA, So. Calif., 1992—. Author: By Word of Mouth..., 1971. Mem. Youth Task Force South Orange County Cmty. Svc. Coun., San Clemente, Calif., 1996; mem. steering com. Surfrider Found., San Clemente, 1996; bd. dirs., mem. Jewish Cmty. Ctr., Orange County, 1996. Mem. Bldg. Industry Assn. (judge 1995-96), San Onofre Surfing Club (v.p. 1991-93), Simon Wiesenthal ctr, Anti Defamation League. Avocations: surfing, skiing, travel.

KIEFF, ELLIOTT DAN, medical educator; b. Phila., Feb. 2, 1943; s. Irving N. and Florence (Prussel) K.; m. Jacqueline Louise Silverman, June 11, 1944; children: David, Scott, Elizabeth. AB, U. Pa., 1963; MD, Johns Hopkins U., 1966; PhD, U. Chgo., 1971. Intern medicine U. Chgo., 1966-67, resident medicine, 1967-70, asst. prof. medicine, 1971-77, assoc. prof. medicine and molecular genetics, 1977-80, prof. medicine and molecular genetics, 1980-85, L. Block prof. biol. scis., 1985-87, chief infectious disease, 1971-87; Harriet Ryan Albee prof. medicine, microbiology and molecular genetics Harvard U., Boston, 1987—, chief infectious disease Brigham Hosp., 1987; chair virology Harvard U., 1991—; Meyer hon. vis. prof. U. Calif., San Francisco, 1991—. Assoc. editor Virology, 1980—, Jour. of Virology, 1982—, reviewing editor, Science, 1996—. Recipient Langer award Langer Cancer Rsch., 1983, Finland award, 1987, Ricketts award, 1996. Mem. Nat. Acad. Scis., Am. Soc. Clin. Ivestigation, Assn. Am. Physicians, Inter Urban Club. Club: Quadrangle (Chgo.); Harvard (Boston, N.Y.C.). Avocation: tennis. Home: 269 Lee St Brookline MA 02445-5914 Office: Havard Univ Med Sch 181 Longwood Ave Boston MA 02115-5804

KIEFFER, JOYCE LORETTA, health science facility administrator, educator; b. Reading, Pa., Nov. 24, 1940; d. Howard Elwood and Jane Rebecca (Wagner) Kissinger; m. Kenneth Eugene Kieffer, Nov. 17, 1962; children: Beth Gilfert, Lori Ann Kieffer-Yeich. RN, Lancaster (Pa.) Gen. Hosp. Sch. Nursing, 1961; BS, Millersville U. Cert. internat. childbirth educator. Pediatric nurse Lancaster Gen. Hosp., 1961-62; instr. obstetric nursing Harrisburg (Pa.) Hosp. Sch. Nursing, 1962-66; pvt. practice childbirth edn. Harrisburg, 1966-74; dir. parent/child edn. Harrisburg Hosp., 1974-88, assoc. program dir. WomanCare Resource Ctrs., 1988-91; program dir. Woman-Care Resource Ctrs., Pinnacle Health, 1991—; lectr. Author: To Have...To Hold - A Parent's Guide to Childbirth and Early Parenting, 1979, 82, 85, 88, 92, 96. Mem. Nat. Assn. Profls. in Women's Health, Assn. Women's Health, Obstetric, and Neonatal Nurses, Internat. Childbirth Edn. Assn. (cert.), Millersvill U. Alumni Assn., Lancaster Gen. Hosp. Alumni Assn., Sigma Theta Tau. Democrat.

KIEFFER, STEPHEN AARON, radiologist, educator; b. Mpls., Dec. 20, 1935; s. Julius Hyman and Anita Elaine (Brudnick) K.; m. Cyrile Frada Kaplan, Dec. 21, 1958; children: Alisa, Mitchell, Stuart, Paula. B.A. summa cum laude, U. Minn., 1956, B.S., 1957, M.D., 1959. Diplomate: Am. Bd. Radiology; CAQ in Neuroradiology, 1995. Intern Wadsworth VA Hosp., Los Angeles, 1959-60; resident in radiology U. Minn. Hosps., Mpls., 1960-62, 64-65, fellow in neuroradiology, 1966-68; instr. U. Minn. Med. Sch., Mpls., 1966-67; asst. prof. U. Minn. Med. Sch., 1967-68, asso. prof., 1968-72, prof., 1972-74; chief radiology service Mpls. VA Hosp., 1968-74; prof., chmn. dept. radiology SUNY-Health Sci. Ctr., Syracuse, 1974-98, chmn. governing bd. clin. practice mgmt. plan, 1985-88, mem. exec. com., 1997-98, prof. radiology, 1999—; v.p., med. bd., med. exec. com. Univ. Hosp., 1988-93; cons. Syracuse VA Med. Center, Crouse Hosp. Co-author: Introduction to Neuroradiology, 1972; co-editor: An Atlas of Cross-sectional Anatomy, 1979; contbr. numerous articles to profl. jours., also chpts. to books; editl. adv. bd. Radiology, 1980-85, assoc. editor, 1986, cons. to editor, 1987-93; cons. to editl. bd. Am. Jour. Neuroradiology, 1980-97, historian 1998—; assoc. editor: Yearbook of Radiology, 1981-86; editl. bd. RadioGraphics, 1987-93. Chmn. tech. adv. subcom. on computed tomography Ctrl. N.Y. Health Systems Agy., 1979-80; mem. tech. adv. com. on computed tomography N.Y. State Office Health Systems Mgmt., 1981; bd. dirs. Syracuse Jewish Fedn., 1975-81, 90-96, v.p., 1990-93; bd. dirs. Academic Health Profls. Ins. Assn., 1991—. Capt. M.C. U.S. Army, 1962-64. Nat. Heart Inst. trainee, 1961-62; Nat. Inst. Neurol. Diseases and Blindness fellow, 1966; James Picker Found. scholar, 1966-68. Fellow Am. Coll. Radiology (councilor 1986-92, chmn. com. on standards & accreditation, commn. on neuroradiology & MRI); mem. AMA, Am. Roentgen Ray Soc. (publs. com. 1979-84), Am. Soc. Neuroradiology (pres. 1978-79, chmn. standards for practice subcom. 1992-96, chmn. clin. outcomes rsch. subcom. 1996—), Assn. Univ. Radiologists (program com. 1985-86), Ctrl. N.Y. Radiol. Soc. (chmn. program com. 1979-82, chmn. socioeconomics com. 1994—), Ea. Neuroradiol. Soc. (pres. 1992-93), Med. Soc. State of N.Y., Minn. Radiol. Soc. (sec. 1974), Neurosurg. Soc. Am., Onondaga County Med. Soc., Radiol. Soc. N.Am. (refresher course com. 1977-82, program com. 1984-91), Soc. Chairmen Acad. Radiology Depts., N.Y. State Radiol. Soc. (v.p. 1985-86, pres. 1987-88), XVI Symposium Neuroradiologicum (v.p. 1998). Jewish. Home: 503 Standish Dr Syracuse NY 13224-2015 Office: SUNY HSC Dept Radiology 750 E Adams St Syracuse NY 13210-2306

KIEFFER, SUSAN WERNER, research geologist and development consultant; b. Warren, Pa., Nov. 17, 1942. BS in Physics and Math., Allegheny Coll., 1964; MS in Geol. Scis., Calif. Inst. Tech., 1967, PhD in Planetary Scis., 1971; DSc (hon.), Allegheny Coll., 1987. Rsch. geochemist UCLA, 1971-73, asst. prof. geology, 1973-79; geologist U.S. Geol. Survey, Flagstaff, Ariz., 1979-90; prof. geology Ariz. State U., Tempe, 1988—, Regents prof., 1991-93; prof., head dept. geol. sci. U. B.C., Vancouver, Can., 1993-95; cofounder Kieffer & Woo, Inc., Palgrave, Ont., Can., 1996—. Co-editor: (with A. Navrotsky) Microscopic to Macroscopic: Atomic Environments to Mineral Thermodynamics, 1985. Alfred P. Sloan Found. fellow, 1977-79; W.H. Mendenhall lectr., U.S. Geol. Survey, 1980; recipient Disting. Alumnus award Calif. Inst. Tech., 1982, Meritorious Svc. award Dept. Interior, 1986, Spendiarov award Soviet Acad. of Scis., 1990; MacArthur fellow, 1995—. Fellow Am. Geophys. Union, Am. Acad. Arts and Scis., Mineral. Soc. Am. (award 1980), Geol. Soc. Am. (Arthur L. Day medal 1992), Meteoritical Soc.; mem. NAS. Avocations: athletics, music. Office: Kieffer & Woo Inc, PO Box 130, Palgrave, ON Canada L0N 1P0

KIEFNER, JOHN ROBERT, JR., lawyer, educator; b. Peoria, Ill., May 31, 1946; s. John Robert and Luna Merle (Froment) K.; m. B.C. Clayton, Feb. 14, 1989; 1 child, John William. BA, Johns Hopkins U., 1968; JD, Stetson U., 1971. Bar: Fla. 1971, U.S. Ct. Appeals (D.C. cir.) 1971, U.S. Ct. Appeals (11th cir.) 1981, U.S. Supreme Ct. 1979, U.S. Ct. Mil. Appeals 1971, U.S. Tax Ct. 1981, U.S. Dist. Ct. (no. dist.) Fla. 1971, U.S. Dist. Ct. (mid. dist.) Fla. 1981. Staff atty. SEC, Washington, 1971-74, br. chief, 1974-77, regional trial counsel, 1977-82; mem. Robbins, Gaynor, Burton, Hampp, Burns, Bronstein & Shasteen, St. Petersburg, Fla., 1982-86; ptnr. Riden , Earle & Kiefner, P.A., St. Petersburg, 1986—; adj. prof. law Stetson U., St. Petersburg, 1982—. Past chmn. Combined Fed. Campaign, 1976-77. Capt. U.S. Army, 1968-76. Recipient Cert. of Merit, SEC, 1982; Charles A. Dana scholar, 1970-71. Mem. Fla. Bar Assn., ABA, St. Petersburg Bar Assn., Fla. Acad. Trial Lawyers, Am. Trial Lawyers Assn., Pinella County Trial Lawyers Assn., Fed. Bar Assn., Nat. Assn. Colls. and Univs. (recruitment com.), St. Petersburg Area C. of C., Johns Hopkins U. Alumni Assn., Masons, Shriners. Lutheran. Home: 11805 6th St E Saint Petersburg FL 33706-2918 Office: Riden Earle & Kiefner PA 100 2nd Ave S Saint Petersburg FL 33701-4360

KIEFT, GERALD NELSON, mechanical engineer; b. Chgo., Dec. 29, 1946; s. Ralph and Alice (Nelson) K.; m. Linda Louise Fank, Oct. 28, 1967; children: Gerald Nelson II, Dawn Michelle. BSME, Midwest Coll. Engring., Lombard, Ill., 1971. Sr. designer Clark Equipment Co., Aurora, Ill., 1971-73; project engr. Elgin (Ill.) Sweeper Co., 1974-86, GPI Industries, W. Chgo., Ill., 1986—. Inventor in field. Company chmn. United Way Campaign, Elgin, 1977. Presbyterian. Home: 42w192 Silver Glen Rd Saint Charles IL 60175-8339 Office: GPI Industries 1400 Powis Ct West Chicago IL 60185-6413

KIEH, GEORGE KLAY, political science educator, consultant; b. Harbel, Liberia, Mar. 2, 1956; came to U.S., 1981; s. George Klay Sr. and Madea (Johnson) K.; children: Chea, Sakon, George III, Madea, Nyonowreh. BA in Polit. Sci., U. Liberia, 1980; grad. cert., Northwestern U., 1982, MA, 1982, PhD, 1986. Lectr. polit. sci. U. Liberia, Monrovia, 1983-84, Northwestern U., Evanston, Ill., 1986-88; asst. prof. U. Memphis, Tenn., 1988-90; asst. prof. Ill. Wesleyan U., Bloomington, Ill., 1990-93, assoc. prof., 1993-95, dir. internat. studies, 1990-93; assoc. prof. Morehouse Coll., Atlanta, 1993—, founding dir. Ctr. Internat. Studies, 1993-95; adj. prof. USAF Spl. Ops. Sch., Fla., 1993—; cons. Interlink Consulting Svcs., West Palm Beach, Fla., 1995—. Author: Dependency and Foreign Policy, 1992; contbr. over 750 articles to profl. jours., book chpts. Nat. chair Liberian People's Party in Ams., 1991-95; interim nat. chair All Liberian Conf. N.Am., 1995-96, mem. monitoring bd., 1996-98. Mem. Nat. Forum Pub. Policy and Devel. (exec. dir. 1998—), Liberian Studies Assn. (bd. dirs. 1993-95), African Studies Assn., Internat. Studies Assn., Assn. Third World Studies, Acad. Coun. UN, Md. Assn. Liberia-Ga. (bd. dirs. 1998—). Methodist. Avocations: table tennis, lawn tennis, basketball. Office: Dept Polit Sci 830 Westview Dr SW Atlanta GA 30314-3773

KIEHLBAUCH, SHERYL LYNN, elementary education educator; b. Las Vegas, Apr. 6, 1950; d. William Bert and Grace (Homan) Berk; m. John Howard Kiehlbauch, Aug. 19, 1972; children: John Karl, Jason Kyle. BS, U. Nev., Las Vegas, 1972; MEd, U. Nev., 1980. Cert. tchr. K-8, reading K-12, reading improvement tchr., computer coord., reading specialist, adminstr. Data processing specialist First Nat. Bank of Nev., Las Vegas; elem. tchr. Clark County Sch. dist., Las Vegas. Named Elem. Computer Using Tchr. of the Yr., Nev., 1989, Excellence in Edn. Program recipient Presdl.

Excellence in Elem. Sci. Edn. State award Nev., 1991. Mem. Computer Using Educators Nev., So. Nev. Sci. Tchrs. Assn. (pres.), Nev. Math. Coun., PTA, Nev. State Sci. Tchrs. Assn. (pres. 1994, dist. dir., 1998—), Delta Kappa Gamma (v.p.), others.

KIEHN, MOGENS HANS, aviation engineer, consultant; b. Copenhagen, July 30, 1918; came to U.S., 1957; s. Hans-Christian and Lydia-Thea-Constans (Theill) K.; m. Ase Rasmusen, Apr. 28, 1942; children: Marianne, Hans, Lars. BS, ME, PE, Tech. Engring., Copenhagen, 1940; MS, Copenhagen, 1942; degree in Army Intelligence, Def. Indsl. Security Inst., 1972. Registered profl. engr., Ariz. Pres. Hamo Engring., Copenhagen, 1939-47, Evanston, Ill., 1958-78; engr. Sundstrand, Rockford, Ill., 1957-58; pres., owner Kiehn Internat. Engring. Co., Phoenix, 1978—; chmn., pres. ETO Internat. Engring., Phoenix, Ariz., 1978—; tech. engring. cons. Scandinavian Airlines, Sundstrand Engring., McDonnell Douglas, Ford, GM, Chrysler, Honeywell, Motorola, Gen. Electric, Hughes Aircraft; chmn. bd. Internat. Tech. Engring. Recipient 32 patents including rehab. hosp. lighting for highmast, drafting machine, tooling machinery, parts for aircraft, garbage and pollution machine, optical coupler, also others. With Finnish Army, 1939, Danish Underground, 1940-45, Morocco French Fgn. Legion, 1948-53, Vietnam. Mem. AIII, NSPE, Soc. Illuminating Engrs., Nat. Geog. Soc., Am. Fedn. Police, East Africa Wildlife Soc., Interpol Intelligence and Organized Crime Orgn., Adventures Club Denmarkk, Honors Club. Office: Kiehn Internat Tech Engring PO Box 1561 Scottsdale AZ 85252-1561

KIEKHOFER, WILLIAM HENRY, lawyer; b. Madison, Wis., June 19, 1952; s. William and Emily (Graham) K.; m. Leslie A. Cohen., Jan. 27, 1956; children: Allison Laura, Phoebe Leigh, Rachel Elizabeth. BA, U. Wis., 1976; JD, U. So. Calif., 1980. Assoc. Sidley & Austin, L.A., 1980-82, Fried & King, L.A., 1982-83, McKenna Conner & Cuneo, L.A., 1983-90, Kelley Drye & Warren LLP, L.A., 1990—. Office: Kelley Drye & Warren 777 S Figueroa St Ste 2700 Los Angeles CA 90017-5825

KIEL, BRENDA KAY, medical/surgical nurse; b. Osage, Iowa, Nov. 9, 1965; d. Leslie A. and Margaret L. (Troge) M.; m. Chad Kiel, Aug. 29, 1998. AS, N.E. Iowa Tech. Inst., 1986. Cert. ACLS, med.-surg. nurse, emergency rm. nurse, neonatal ruscitation. Staff nurse med./surg. wing St. Joseph Community Hosp., New Hampton, Iowa, 1986-98; clinic nurse Mercy Family Care Buffalo Ctr. (Iowa) Clinic, 1998—.

KIEL, FREDERICK ORIN, lawyer; b. Columbus, Feb. 22, 1942; s. Fred Otto and Helen Louise (Baird) K.; m. Vivian Lee Naff, June 2, 1963; 1 child, Aileen Vivian. AB magna cum laude, Wilmington Coll., 1963; JD, Harvard U., 1966. Bar: Ohio 1966, U.S. Supreme Ct. 1972, Ky. 1992. Assoc. Peck, Shaffer & Williams, Cin., 1966-71, ptnr., 1980-89; ptnr. Taft, Stettinius & Hollister, Cin., 1980-89; pvt. practice law Cin., 1990—; lectr. and expert witness in field; co-founder Bond Attys.' Workshop, 1976. Editor: Bond Lawyers and Bond Law: An Oral History, 1993, Bondletter, 1991—, Anderson Insights, 1992—; contbr. articles on mcpl. bond fin. to profl. jours. Arbitrator Mcpl. Securities Rulemaking Bd., 1985-92; mem. Anderson Twp. Govtl. Task Force, 1986—; sec. Anderson Twp. Greenspace Adv. Com., 1990—; rep. precinct exec. Precinct H. Anderson Twp., 1991-92, 94—; twp. atty. Anderson Twp., 1997—. Mem. Ohio State Bar Assn., Ky. Bar Assn., Cin. Bar Assn. (mem. grievance com.), Nat. Assn. Bond Lawyers (dir. 1979-84, pres. 1982-83, hon. dir. 1984—, editor The Bond Lawyer 1982—, Bond Atty.'s Workshop steering com. 1976-83, 85, scrivener com. stds. of practice 1987-89), Queen City Club, Terrace Park Country Club. Office: 1095 Nimitzview Dr Ste 103 Cincinnati OH 45230-4341

KIELAROWSKI, HENRY EDWARD, marketing executive; b. Pitts., Dec. 29, 1946; s. Henry Andrew Kielarowski and Evelyn Marie Kline Boileau; m. Lynda Blair Powell, Aug. 1971 (div. 1976); children: Amorette, Blair. BA, Duquesne U., Pitts., 1969; MA, Duquesne U., 1974, PhD, 1974. Pres. Communicators, Inc., Pitts., 1974-76; mktg. specialist McGraw-Hill, Inc., N.Y.C., 1976-81; mktg. dir. Fidelity S.A., Allison Park, Pa., 1981-86; exec. v.p. ARC Systems, Inc., Pitts., 1986-88; v.p. mktg. Providian Financial Corp., San Francisco, 1988-98; pres. La Playa Cons., Inc., San Francisco, 1999—. Author: Microcomputer Consulting in the CPA Environment, 1987; contbr. articles to profl. jours. Mem. Am. Mktg. Assn. (mktg. excellence award 1988), Direct Mktg. Assn. Democrat. Avocations: fiction writing, music, dance, travel, film making. Home: 1496 La Playa San Francisco CA 94122

KIELBORN, TERRIE LEIGH, secondary education educator; b. Miami, Fla., Sept. 25, 1955; d. Gerald and Dolores Eloise (Adams) Carter; m. Gerald Albert Kielborn, Mar. 31, 1979; children: Carl Gerald, Katie Leigh, Sarah Beth. BA in Edn., Fla. Atlantic U., 1977; MA with honors, U. South Fla., 1986; postgrad., Fla. State U. Cert. elem. and mid. sch. tchr., Fla. 6th grade sci. tchr. Belleview (Fla.) Mid. Sch.; presenter in field. Co-editor SERVE Monograph: Meaningful Science: Teachers Doing Inquiry and Teaching Science; contbr. articles to profl. jours. Chair bd. dirs. environ. edn. com. Marion County Audubon Soc., 1991, pres., 1992-93; mem. mid. sch. sci. curriculum com. Marion County, 1994-98, chair sch. adv. coun. 1993-95. Named Tchr. of Yr., 1979, 92, 94; Phi Theta Kappa scholar, 1975, Minigrants, 1990-99, Profl. Enhancement Program grantee, 1989-96, PTO grantee, Dreams grantee, 1995, Tech. grantee, 1993-95, Marion County Soil and Conservation grantee, Fla. Growers and Nurseryman grantee, Dow Chem. grantee, 1998-99, Fla. Sci. Inst. grantee, 1999; recipient NEWEST award, 1991, Sci. Grasp award Upjohn, 1992, Golden Apple award Marion County, 1992, Fla. Explorer's! Workshop award, 1995-98, Tchr. and Rschr. Update Experience (TRUE) Program award, 1997, Fla. Through a Global Lens award, Tchr. Quest Program award, 1998, Fla. Mid. Sch. Sci. Tchr. of Yr., 1997, Target Tchr. Scholarship award, 1999; nominated for presdl. award for excellence in sci., 1991, 94, 95, 96, 97, 98; Ag in the Classroom Best Idea award, 1996, Delta Exn. Outstanding Science Activity award, 1993, others; field rsch. on exotic grass of a state park, 1996. Mem. NSTA (presenter nat. conf. 1992, 95, 96, S.E. regional conf. 1993, local leader 1994), Nat. Assn. Rsch. in Sci. Tchg. (nat. conf. presenter 1996, 97), Nat. Assn. Earth Sci. Tchrs., Assn. Edn. Tchg. Scis., Fla. Assn. Earth Sci. Tchrs., Fla. Coun. Tchrs. Math. (regional bd. dirs. 1992-94, presenter state conf. 1992, 93), Fla. Assn. Sci. Tchrs. (presenter state conf. 1996, 97, 98, regional dir. Region III 1995-99), League Environ. Educators Fla., Marion Edn. Assn.-Fla. Tchrs. Profession (rep. 1986-87), Fla. Native Plant Soc. (co-v.p. Big Scrub 1992), Nat. Mid. Level Sci. Tchrs. Assn., Tchrs. Involved in Maths. Edn., Alpha Delta Kappa (sgt.-at-arms 1990-91, v.p. 1992-94), Phi Delta Kappa (rsch. rep. 1997-99), Phi Lambda Theta. Office: State Univ West Ga Middle Sch/Secondary Sci Carrollton GA 30118

KIELHORN, RICHARD WERNER, chemist; b. Berlin, Germany, June 17, 1931; s. Richard H. and Auguste (Lammek) K.; m. Anneliese Heinrich, Aug. 9, 1952; children: Anita, Margit. BS, Chem. Tech. Sch., Berlin, 1953. Lab. tech. Zoellner Werke, Berlin, 1950-57, Montrose Chem. Corp., Henderson, Nev., 1957-78; chief chemist Stauffer Chem. Corp., Henderson, 1978-88, Pioneer Chlor Alkali Co., Henderson, 1988-92; tax. cons. H&R Block, Las Vegas, Nev., 1972-96, Exec. Tax Svc., instr., 1978-95. Mem. ASTM, Am. Chem. Soc., Am. Statistical Assn., Nat. Soc. Tax Profls., Nat. Assn. Tax Practitioners. Home: 1047 Westminster Ave Las Vegas NV 89119-1825

KIELSMEIER, CATHERINE JANE, school system administrator; b. San Jose, Calif; d. Frank Delos and Catherine Doris (Sellar) MacGowan; M.S., U. So. Calif., 1964, Ph.D., 1971; m. Milton Kielsmeier; children: Catherine Louise, Barry Delos. Tchr. pub. schs. Maricopa, Calif.; sch. psychologist Campbell (Calif.) Union Sch Dist., 1961-66; asst. prof. edn. and psychology Western Oreg. State Coll., Monmouth, 1966-67, 70; asst. research prof. Oreg. System Higher Edn., Monmouth, 1967-70; dir. spl. services Pub. Schs., Santa Rosa, Calif., 1971-91; cons., 1991—. Mem. Sonoma County Council Community Services, 1974-84, bd. dirs. 1976-82, Sonoma County Orgn. for Retarded/Becoming Independent, 1978-84, bd. dirs. 1978-82; bd. dirs. Gold Ridge Sangha, 1994-97, Hosp. Chaplaincy Svcs., 1996—. Office: 7495 Poplar Dr Forestville CA 95436-9671

KIELSMEIER, JAMES CALVIN, nonprofit corporation executive; b. Elgin, Ill., Aug. 13, 1943; s. Calvin Edward and Elizabeth Margaret (Kliewer) K.; m. Deborah Constance Eng, June 23, 1979; children: Sarah Elizabeth, Christina Ann, Lauren Marie. BS, Wheaton Coll., 1965; MA, Am. U., 1972; PhD, U. Colo., 1979. Crew mem. U.S. Forest Svc., Lakeview, Ore., 1963; rsch. asst. Am. Insts. Rsch., Silver Spring, Md., 1967-69; educator St Albans Sch., Washington, 1969-72; course instr., dir. Colo. Outward Bound Sch., Denver, 1972-76; course dir. Dartmouth Coll. Outward Bound Ctr., Hanover, N.H., 1977-79; assoc. dir. Am. Youth Found., St. Louis, 1979-82; pres., CEO, founder Nat. Youth Leadership Coun., St. Paul, 1983—; asst. prof. U. Minn., —, 1984-97; edn. cons. YoungLife, 1976-78, World Concern, Kenya, Somalia, 1993-96; svc.-learning cons. Cmty. Svc. Vols., London, 1995, W. K. Kellogg Found., Battle Creek, Mich., 1996, Blandin Found., 1998, USAID, Africa, 1999—. Editor: Growing Hope: Youth Service in the Curriculum, 1991, Experiential Learning in Schools and Higher Education, 1995; contbr. articles to profl. jours. Chair Gov.'s Task Force on Svc., St. Paul, 1988-93; cons. Pres. Clinton Transition, Washington, 1992; mem. Minn. Commn. on Nat. and Cmty. Svc., St. Paul, 1994—; nat. del. Pres.'s Summit on Youth, Phila., 1997. 1st lt. U.S. Army, 1965-67, Korea. Recipient U.S. Army Commendation medal, Korea, 1967, State award Nat. Assn. Svc. and Conservation Corps., Washington, 1991; Paul Harris fellow Rotary Club Internat., Bloomington, Minn., 1997. Mem. Assn. Experiential Edn. (pres. 1983-84, Kurt Hahn award 1988), Coalition for Nat. and Cmty. Svc. (sec. 1997, pres. 1998—, mem. grantmakers forum 1998—). Presbyterian. Avocations: cross country skiing, gardening, photography. E-mail: jkiels@aol.com. Home: 1892 Tatum St Saint Paul MN 55113-5516 Office: Nat Youth Leadership Coun 1910 County Road B W Saint Paul MN 55113-5448

KIELT, RAYMOND JOHN, naval officer, dentist; b. Bklyn., Nov. 5, 1944; s. James Francis and Gladys Johanna (Nelson) K.; m. Donna Ann Luzzi, Dec. 16, 1983. BS, Fairleigh Dickinson U., 1968, DDM, 1971. Commd. lt. USN, 1971, advanced through grades to capt., 1988—; naval dental officer U.S. Marine Base Camp Lejeune, Jacksonville, N.C., 1971-73, Naval Air Sta., Roosevelt Roads, P.R., 1973-77; resident Naval Dental Sch., Bethesda, Md., 1977-79; clinic dept. head USN-AD-26 Shenandoah, Norfolk, Va., 1979-80, USN-AD-41 Yellowstone, Norfolk, 1980-81; dir. Navy Dental Clinic, Dam Neck, Va., 1981-85, 91-95, Gulfport, Miss., 1985-88, Naval Air Sta., Bermuda, 1988-91; program dir. Navy Advanced Educators in Gen. Dentistry, Norfolk, 1995-97; dental officer Navy Gen. Dentistry, Norfolk, 1997—. Mem. ADA, Acad. Gen. Dentistry (fellow 1983).

KIELY, GARRETT PAUL, publishing executive; b. Orange, N.J., Oct. 10, 1961; s. Garrett Paul Jr. and Margaret Ann (Hollywood) K.; m. Catherine Anne Mahoney, Oct. 20, 1990; children, Thomas Garrett, Julia Catherine. BA, Georgetown U., Washington, 1983. Product mgr. Springer-Verlag N.Y., N.Y.C., 1984-87; advt. and promotion mgr. St. Martin's Press, N.Y.C., 1987-88, mktg. dir., 1988-91, dir., v.p., 1991-99, pres., pub., 1999—. Office: St Martins Press 175 5th Ave Fl 2 New York NY 10010-7848

KIENBAUM, THOMAS GERD, lawyer; b. Berlin, Nov. 16, 1942; came to U.S., 1957; s. Gerd Wilhelm Kienbaum and Albertine Brigitte (Kramm) Kettler; m. Karen Smith, June 24, 1966 (div.); 1 child, Ursula; m. Elizabeth Hardy, Jan. 22, 1992. AB, U. Mich., 1965; JD magna cum laude, Wayne State U., 1968. Bar: Mich. 1968, Ill. 1991, U.S. Supreme Ct. 1983. Assoc. Dickinson, Wright, Moon, Van Dusen & Freeman, Detroit, 1968-76, ptnr., 1976-97; ptnr., founder Kienbaum Opperwall Hardy & Pelton, Detroit and Birmingham, 1997—. Contbr. legal articles to profl. publs. Bd. dirs. Wayne County Neighborhood Legal Svc., 1972-76, 87-88. Fellow ABA, State Bar of Mich. Found.; mem. Am. Judicature Soc., Coll. Labor and Employment Lawyers, State Bar Mich. (commr. 1987-96, sec. 1991-93, v.p. 1993-94, pres.-elect 1994-95, pres. 1995-96), Detroit Bar Assn. (pres. 1985-86), Barristers Assn. (pres. 1978-79), Oakland County Bar Assn., Order of the Coif. Avocations: reading, skiing, squash, sailing. Office: Kienbaum Opperwall Hardy & Pelton 325 S Old Woodward Ave Birmingham MI 48009-6202

KIENER, JOHN LESLIE, judge; b. Ft. Madison, Iowa, June 21, 1940; s. Cyril Joseph and Lucille Olive (Golden) K.; m. Carol Lynn Winston, June 4, 1966; children—Susan, Gretchen. BA cum laude, Loras Coll., 1962; JD, Drake U., 1965. Bar: Iowa 1965, Tenn. 1972, U.S. Supreme Ct. 1974. Practice, Decorah, Iowa, 1965-68; asst. atty. gen. State of Iowa, 1968-72; ptnr. firm Cantor & Kiener, 1972-80; city judge Johnson City (Tenn.), 1975-80; gen. sessions judge, Johnson City, 1980—; continuing edn. tchr., bus. law East Tenn. State U., 1975—. Mem. ABA, Tenn. Bar Assn., Washington County Bar Assn. Republican. Lodges: Rotary, Elks. Avocations: stamp collecting, genealogy. Contbr. articles to profl. jours. Home: 2403 Camelot Cir Johnson City TN 37604-2938 Office: Gen Sessions Ct Downtown Ctr Courthouse 101 E Market St Ste 7 Johnson City TN 37604-5722

KIENITZ, LADONNA TRAPP, city librarian, city official; b. Bay City, Mich.; d. Orlin D. and Mary (Stanford) Trapp; m. John Kienitz, Feb. 9, 1951 (div. Dec. 1974); children: John, Jim, Rebecca, Mary, Timothy, David. BA, Westmar Coll., 1951; MA in Libr. Sci., Dominican U., River Forest, Ill., 1970; M Mgmt., Northwestern U., 1984; JD, Western State U., Fullerton, Calif., 1995. Head libr. Woodlands Acad., Lake Forest, Ill., 1973-77; project officer North Suburban Libr. Sys., Wheeling, Ill., 1977-78; libr. dir. Lincolnwood (Ill.) Pub. Libr. Dist., 1978-86; city libr. City of Newport Beach, Calif., 1987—, dir. cmty. svcs., 1994—. Mem. ALA, Pub. Libr. Assn. (pres. 1995-96), Calif. Libr. Assn., Calif. Parks and Recreation Soc., Nat. Assn. Parks and Recreation, State Bar of Calif. Avocation: law. Office: City of Newport Beach PO Box 1768 3300 Newport Blvd Newport Beach CA 92658-8915

KIENTZ, RENEE, newspaper editor. Lifestyle editor Features Desk Houston Chronicle. Office: Houston Chronicle Pub Co 801 Texas St Houston TX 77002-2996

KIENZLE, JOHN FRED, history educator; b. Allentown, Pa., Apr. 1, 1945; s. Fred John and Florence Mary K.; m. Patricia Catherine Evertsen, Aug. 22, 1970. BA in history, Albany State U., 1967; MA in History, NYU, 1969; PhD in History, Princeton U., 1972. Retail sales clk. Floyd Bennett Stores, Patchogue, N.Y., 1960-63; cafeteria worker Albany State Dorms, 1963-67; libr. aide NYU, N.Y.C., 1967-69, Firestone Libr.,Princeton (N.J.) U., 1969-70; tchr. history Maple Hill H.S., Castleton, N.Y., 1970—. *An experienced professional educator, John Kienzle has won awards for the use of technology in instruction, was selected Schodack Schools Teacher of the Year 1996-97 and Capital District Council for the Social Studies Teacher of the Year for 1998-99. Balancing teaching and technical skills, John Kienzle has been director of media services for 30 years, managing instructional media technology from classroom applications through satellite systems to computers. He is an accomplished lecturer in photography, astronomy, travel and education.* Mem. Met. Mus. Art, 1987—, Lake Chaplain Maritime Mus., 1994—, Schodack Faculty Assn., 1970—; trustee Maple Hill H.S. Amateur Radio Club, 1975—; radio officer Rensselaer County (N.Y.) Civil Emergency Svcs., 1980—. Mem. Archaeol. Inst. Am. Republican. Roman Catholic. Avocations: sailing, flying, amateur radio, astronomy, photography. E-mail: jkienzle@albany.net. Office: Maple Hill H S 1216 Maple Hill Rd Castleton NY 12033

KIENZLE, WILLIAM XAVIER, author; b. Detroit, Sept. 11, 1928; s. Alphonso and Mary Louise (Boyle) K.; m. Javan Herman Andrews, Nov. 29, 1974. BA, Sacred Heart Sem., Detroit, 1950; postgrad., U. Detroit, 1960-63. Ordained priest Roman Cath. Ch., 1954. Priest Archdiocese of Detroit, 1954-74; editor-in-chief Mpls. Mag., 1974-77; assoc. dir. Ctr. for Contemplative Studies, Kalamazoo, 1977-78; dir. Ctr. for Contemplative Studies, Irving, Tex., 1978-79; instr. writing course St. Mary's Coll., Orchard Lake, Mich. Author: The Rosary Murders, 1979, Death Wears a Red Hat, 1980, Mind Over Murder, 1981, Assault with Intent, 1982, Shadow of Death, 1983, Kill and Tell, 1984, Sudden Death, 1985, Deathbed, 1986, Deadline for a Critic, 1987, Marked for Murder, 1988, Eminence, 1989, Masquerade, 1990, Chameleon, 1991, Body Count, 1992, Dead Wrong, 1993, Bishop As Pawn, 1994, Call No Man Father, 1995, Exit Laughing, Homicide Host Presents, 1996, Requiem for Moses, 1996, The Man Who Loved God, 1997, The Greatest Evil, 1998, No Greater Love, 1999; contbr. to Sound of a Sermon; editor-in-chief The Mich. Cath., 1962-74. Avocations: playing piano, reading, yardwork. Home and Office: PO Box 80942 Rochester MI 48308-0942

KIEREN, THOMAS HENRY, management consultant; b. Milw., July 23, 1941; s. Henry Lawrence and Hildegard (Luketell) K. BS, Holy Cross Coll., 1963; MBA, U. Chgo., 1968; postgrad., Harvard U., 1963. Mgr. Touche, Ross & Co., 1968-69; asst. v.p. Sunbeam Corp., Chgo., 1969-75; dir. bus. strategy ACF Industries, Inc., N.Y.C., 1975-78; dir. bus. and fin. planning GAF Corp., N.Y.C., 1978-82; dir. bus. planning Engelhard Corp., Edison, N.J., 1982-83; founder, pres., mng. dir. Manhattan Cons. Group, Inc., N.Y.C., 1983—; bd. dirs. Mothers Stores, Inc.; chmn. mergers and acquisitions, seminar program Exec. Enterprises, Inc., N.Y.C., 1984-87; founder, chmn. Ducks Unltd., Inc., Passaic County. Author, editor, lectr. for AMA in corp. strategy and acquisitions, 1980—; contbr. articles to profl. jours. Del. to White House conf. on small bus., Washington, 1986; mem. coun. N.Y. Philharm., 1980—; area coord., mem. fin. com. Courter for Gov. of N.J., 1989; pres. Bus. Execs. for Bush, 1988; v.p. Chgo. Symphony Jr. Governing Bd., 1968-75; founder Chgo. Symphony Soc., Ctr. for Industry and Corp. Performance, Wayne; founder, chmn. Greater Wayne Area Young Reps., Inc., 1989—; mem. Task Force on Tech. Policy Nat. Assn. Mfrs.; mem. Commn. Regulatory Reform and Govt. Waste; mem. fin. com. Whitman for Gov. of N.J. Campaign, 1993, 97, mem. Inaugural Ball com., 1998; bd. dirs. Boy Scouts Am., Cath. Charities Drug Rehab. Unit, N.J.-Straight and Narrow, Inc. Mem. U. Chgo. Bus. Sch. Alumni Assn. (bd. dirs. 1983-85), Product Devel. and Mgmt. Assn. (nat. v.p., bd. dirs., founder N.Y. chpt., Leadership award 1993), Trout Unltd., Inc. (bd. dirs. N.Y. chpt.), Holy Cross Coll. Club of N.Y., U. Club Chgo., U. Chgo. Bus. Sch. of N.Y. Club (founder, bd. dirs.), Amateur Comedy Club, Wayne Racquet Club, Fordham Grad. Sch. of Bus., Baruch Sch. of Bus. (adj. prof. of bus. strategy). Republican. Roman Catholic. Avocations: fly fishing, tennis, golf, skiing, trap shooting. Office: The Manhattan Cons Group Inc 214 E 52d St 3d Fl New York NY 10022-6903

KIERNAN, EDWIN A., JR., lawyer, corporation executive; b. N.Y.C., Aug. 2, 1926; s. Edwin A. and Helen M. (Clarke) K.; m. Ellen Mary Irving, Feb. 18, 1952; children: Robert Clarke, Katherine Waters. A.B., Columbia, 1947, J.D., 1950; LL.M., NYU, 1957. Bar: N.Y. 1950. Assoc. Simpson Thacher & Bartlett, N.Y.C., 1950-52, 54-55, Wickes, Riddell, Bloomer, Jacobi & McGuire, N.Y.C., 1956-59; atty. Western Electric Co., Inc., 1959-60; atty. Interpublic Group of Cos., Inc., N.Y.C., 1960-64, mng. atty., 1964-68, asst. sec., asst. gen. counsel, 1968-79, sec. and gen. counsel, 1980-88, v.p., 1973-81, sr. v.p., 1981-88; sec. McCann-Erickson, Inc., N.Y.C., 1962-79. Lt. (j.g.) USNR, 1944-46, 52-54. Mem. ABA, Phi Beta Kappa. Home: 1205 Par View Dr Sanibel FL 33957-6401*

KIERNAN, OWEN BURNS, educational consultant; b. Randolph, Mass., Mar. 9, 1914; s. Thomas Francis and Elizabeth (Burns) K.; m. Esther Harriet Thorley, July 13, 1940; children: Joan Ann, Nancy Elizabeth, John Albert. B.S., Bridgewater (Mass.) State Coll., 1935; M.Ed., Boston U., 1940, Sc.D. (hon.), 1968; Ed.D., Harvard U., 1950; L.H.D. (hon.), Lesley Coll., 1956; LL.D., Northeastern U., 1961; Litt.D. (hon.), Stonehill Coll., 1965; Ped.D. (hon.), R.I. Coll., 1966. Prin. Henry T. Wing High Sch., Sandwich, Mass., 1938-44; supt. schs. Wayland and Sudbury, Mass., 1944-51, Milton, 1951-57; commr. edn. State of Mass., 1957-68; exec. dir. Nat. Assn. Secondary Sch. Prins., 1969-79; dir. sch. div. McManis Assos., Inc., 1980-82; cons. Washington, 1983—; Past chmn. Mass. Bd. Edn., Mass. Bd. Vocat. Edn.; corp. mem. MIT. Trustee U. Mass.; trustee Lowell Tech. Inst., Mus. Fine Arts, Mus. Sci. Boston, Boston U.; bd. dirs. Atlantic Council U.S.; chmn. edn. com. Atlantic Treaty Assn., 1968-72; gov. bd. Atlantic Info. Centre for Tchrs., London, 1968-76; exec. com. U.S. People-to-People Program. Mem. Am. Assn. Sch. Adminstrs., New Eng., Mass. supts. assns., Council Chief State Sch. Officers (pres. 1967), Phi Delta Kappa. Home: 36 Fernbrook Ln Centerville MA 02632-2908

KIERNAN, PAUL DARLINGTON, thoracic surgeon, educator; b. Rochester, Minn., May 6, 1944; s. Paul Chapman and Elizabeth (Simpson) K.; m. Carol Lynn Harbaugh, Oct. 4, 1980; children: Paul Michael, Caroline Elizabeth, Joseph Darlington. BA, Yale U., 1967; MBA, U. Va., 1969; MD, Georgetown U., 1974. Diplomate Am. Bd. Surgery, Am. Bd. Thoracic Surgery. Intern in gen. surgery Mayo Grad. Sch. Medicine, Rochester, Minn., 1974-75, resident in gen. surgery, 1975-78, chief resident in gen. surgery, 1978-79, resident in thoracic surgery, 1979-80, chief resident in thoracic surgery, 1980, resident in cardiovasc. surgery, 1980-81, chief resident in cardiovasc. surgery, 1981, fellow in vascular surgery, 1982; pvt. practice Annandale, Va., 1982—; chief of thoracic surgery Fairfax (Va.) Hosp., 1982-94; assoc. prof. clin. surgery Georgetown U., Washington, 1982—. Author: Head and Neck Cancer, 1980; author: (with others) Cancer of the Thyroid, Cancer of the Parathyroid, An Atlas of the Surgical Techniques of O.H. Beahrs, 1985; contbr. articles to profl. jours. Trustee James F. Mitchell Found., Concord Hill Sch. Landon Sch. Mem. ACS, Am. Coll. Chest Physicians, Med. Soc. Va., Fairfax Med. Soc., Arlington Med. Soc., D.C. Md. Soc., Alexandria Med. Soc., Gen. Thoracic Surg. Club, Soc. Thoracic Surgeons, So. Thoracic Surg. Soc., Met. Washington Soc. Thoracic and Cardiovasc. Surgeons, Mayo Vascular Soc., Chesapeake Vascular Soc., Mayo Alumni Assn., Chevy Chase Club, Yale Football Y Assn., Am. Alpine Club. Roman Catholic. Home: 4704 Fort Sumner Dr Bethesda MD 20816-2467 Office: 3301 Woodburn Rd Ste 301 Annandale VA 22003-7304

KIERNAN, RICHARD FRANCIS, publisher; b. N.Y.C., Apr. 17, 1935; s. James J. and Grace (Nolan) K.; m. Jane V. Eickmeyer, Dec. 29, 1962; children: Christopher R., Peter T., Kathy Lynn. B.S., U. Conn., 1957. Salesman Med. Econs. Co., Oradell, N.J., 1963-65, sales mgr., 1965-67; gen. mgr. Med. Econs. Co., Chgo., 1967-68; pub. Med. Econs. mag., Oradell, 1970-72, sr. v.p., pub., 1990-95; sr. v.p., pub., Redbook, Annual, Med. Econs. mag., Bus. and Health mag., Drug Topics mag., Montvale, N.J., 1991—; pres. Medical Econs. Profl. Info. Svc. Group, 1995—; pub. RN Mag., Oradell, 1968-70; pres. Cliggott Pub. Co., Greenwich, Conn., 1972-75; exec. v.p. Biomed. Info. Inc., N.Y.C., 1975-79; pres. Hosp. Pubs., Inc., Secaucus, N.J., 1979-89; chmn. R.F. Kiernan Assocs., Ridgewood, N.J., 1989-90; pres., COO PISG, Med. Econs., 1994—; bd. dirs. Argus Press Holdings, USA; treas. Pharm. Adv. Council, 1979-81, pres., 1981; v.p. Devel. Med. Econs. Co. With U.S. Army, 1957-63. Mem. Pharm. Advt. Coun. (pres.), Assn. Clin. Pubs. (pres.), N.Y. Athletic Club, Ridgewood Country Club, Leland (Mich.) Country Club. Home and Office: 153 Hamilton Rd Ridgewood NJ 07450-1102

KIERSCH, GEORGE ALFRED, geological consultant, retired educator; b. Lodi, Calif., Apr. 15, 1918; s. Adolph Theodore and Viola Elizabeth (Bahmeier) K.; m. Jane J. Keith, Nov. 29, 1942; children—Dana Elizabeth Kiersch Haycock, Mary Annan, George Keith, Nancy McCandless Kiersch Bohnett. Student, Modesto Jr. Coll., 1936-37; BS and Geol. Engr., Colo. Sch. Mines, 1942; Ph.D. in Geology, U. Ariz., 1947. Geologist 79 Mining Co., Ariz., 1946-47; geologist underground explosion tests and Folsom Dam-Reservoir Project U.S. C.E., Calif., 1948-50; supervising geologist Internat. Boundary and Water Commn., U.S.-Mex., 1950-51; asst. prof. geology U. Ariz., Tucson, 1951-55, dir. Mineral Resources Survey Navajo-Hopi Indian Reservation, 1952-55; exploration mgr. resources survey So. Pacific Co., San Francisco, 1955-60; assoc. prof. geol. sci. Cornell U., Ithaca, N.Y., 1960-63, prof., 1963-79, prof. emeritus, 1979—, chmn. dept. geol. scis., 1965-71; geol. cons., Ithaca, 1960-78, Tucson, 1978—; chmn. coordinating com. on environment and natural hazards, Internat. Lithosphere Program, 1986-1991. Author: Engineering Geology, 1955, Mineral Resources of Navajo-Hopi Indian Reservations, 3 vols., 1955, Geothermal Steam-A World Wide Assessment, 1964; author: (with others) Advanced Dam Engineering, 1988; editor/author: Heritage of Engineering Geology--First Hundred Years 1888-1988 (vol. of Geol. Soc. Am.), 1991; editor: Case Histories in Engineering Geology, 4 vols., 1963-69, Engineering GeoSciences and Military Operations, 1998; mem. editorial bd. Engring. Geology/Amsterdam, 1965—. Mem. adv. coun. to bd. trustees Colo. Sch. Mines, 1962-71, pres. coms., 1990—; mem. nine coms. NAE/NAS, 1966-90; reporter coordinating com. 1 CC1 Nat. Hazards U.S. GeoDynamics Com., 1985-90. Capt. C.E., U.S. Army, 1942-45. NSF sr. postdoctoral fellow Tech. U. Vienna, 1963-64; recipient award for best article Indsl. Mktg. Mag., 1964. Fellow ASCE, Geol. Soc. Am. (chmn. div. engring. geology 1960-61, mem. U.S. nat. com. on rock mechanics 1980-86, Disting. Practice award 1986, Burwell award 1992); mem. Soc. Econ. Geologists, U.S. Com. on Large Dams, Internat. Soc. Rock Mechanics, Internat. Assn. Engring. Geologists (U.S. com. 1980-86, chmn. com. 1983-87, v.p. N.Am. 1986-90), Assn. Engring. Geologists (1st receipient Claire P. Holdredge award 1965, 93, hon. mem. 1985), Cornell Club (N.Y.C.), Statler Club, Tower Club (Ithaca), Mining Club of Southwest (Tucson). Republican. Episcopalian. Home and Office: 4750 N Camino Luz Tucson AZ 85718-5819

KIERSCHT, MARCIA SELLAND, academic administrator, psychologist; b. Rugby, N.D.; d. Osmund Harold and Cynthia (Thoresen) Selland; m. Charles M. Kierscht, Aug. 19, 1961 (div. 1972); children: Cynthia Ann, Matthew Mason. BA, U. Iowa, 1960, MA, 1962; PhD, Vanderbilt U., 1975. Lic. psychologist, Ill., Minn. Sch. psychologist South Suburban Cook County, Homewood, Ill., 1962-64, Dist. 108, Highland Park, Ill., 1964-65, Spl. Edn. Dist. Lake County Ill., Gurnee, 1966-72; psychol. examiner John F. Kennedy Ctr., George Peabody Coll., 1972-73; instr. in pediatrics Med. Sch. Vanderbilt U., Nashville, 1975-76; assoc. prof. Moorhead (Minn.) State U., 1976-80, asst. to pres., 1980-86; provost, chief exec. officer Tri-Coll. U., Fargo, N.D., 1986-90; dean grad. and profl. sch. Hood Coll., Frederick, Md., 1990-93; v.p. Consortium of Univs. of the Washington Met. Area, 1993-94; pres. Stephens Coll., Columbia, Mo., 1994—. Contbr. articles to profl. jours. V.p. Plains Art Mus., Moorhead, 1986-88; chmn. bd. govs. Fargo-Moorhead Area Found., Fargo, 1983-90; bd. dirs. United Way, Columbia, 1994—. Recipient Pembina Trail award Minn. Hist. Soc., 1994. Mem. Am. Coun. on Edn., Coun. of Fellows, Fargo C. of C., Columbia C. of C. (bd. dirs.), Montgomery County High Tech. Coun., Rotary Club (Moorhead, Columbia, Fredericktowne), Cosmos Club, Washington. Office: Office of Pres 1200 E Broadway Columbia MO 65201-4978

KIES, DAVID M., lawyer; b. N.Y.C., Jan. 25, 1944; s. Saul and Lillian (Schultz) K.; m. Emily Bardack, July 6, 1966 (div. 1985); children: Laura, Adam, Abigail; m. Anne Hayes Monteith, Oct. 7, 1990 (div. 1998); 1 child, Samuel. AB, Haverford Coll., 1965; JD, NYU, 1968. Bar: N.Y. 1968, U.S. Dist. Ct. (so. dist.) N.Y. 1969, U.S. Ct. Appeals (2d cir.) 1969. Assoc. Sullivan & Cromwell, N.Y.C., 1968-76, ptnr., 1976—; dir. London office Sullivan & Cromwell, 1992-95; dir. Imclone Systems, Inc. Former trustee Haverford Coll. Root Tilden fellow, NYU Law Sch., 1965. Mem. ABA, N.Y. State Bar Assn., Assn. Bar City of N.Y. Democrat. Jewish. Office: Sullivan & Cromwell 125 Broad St Fl 28 New York NY 10004-2489*

KIES, KENNETH J., lawyer; b. Ft. Benning, Ga., Jan. 4, 1952; s. Robert Herman K.; m. Kathleen Barbara Clark, Oct. 11, 1986. BA, Ohio U., 1974; JD, Ohio State U., 1977; MLT in Taxation, Georgetown U., 1986. Bar: Ohio 1977, U.S. Tax Ct. 1978, D.C. 1987, U.S. Supreme Ct. 1992. Assoc. Baker & Hostetler, Cleve., 1977-81; asst. minority tax counsel Com. on Ways & Means U.S. Ho. of Reps., Washington, 1981-82, chief minority tax counsel, 1982-87; ptnr. Baker & Hostetler, Washington, 1987-95; chief of staff joint com. on taxation U.S. Congress, Washington, 1995-98; mng. ptnr. Price Waterhouse Coopers, Washington, 1998—. Contbr. articles to profl. jours. Mem. Capitol Hill Club, Washington Golf and Country Club. Republican. Office: Price Waterhouse Coopers Taxation US Congress 1301 K St NW Ste 800W Washington DC 20005*

KIESEL, HARRY ALEXANDER, internist; b. Smalinikai, Lithuania, Apr. 3, 1941; came to U.S. 1949.; s. Alexander and Hedwig (Plogsties) K.; m. Irene Anna Kiesel, Sept. 19, 1964; children: Lisa Anne, Lori Jeanne. BS in Math., Drexel U., 1968, MS in Math., 1970, PhD, 1995; MD, Hahnemann U., 1975. Diplomate Am. Bd. Internal Medicine. Rsch. asst. dept. mech. engring. Drexel U., Phila., 1966-68; intern Hahnemann U., 1975-76, resident in internal medicine, 1976-78; pvt. practice, Meadowbrook, Pa., 1979—; vis. rsch. assoc. Drexel U., 1995—. Contbr. articles to profl. jours. With USN, 1958-62. Fellow ACP; mem. Am. Soc. Internal Medicine, Am. Math. Soc., Math Assn. Am. Republican. Lutheran. Avocations: music, photography, computer technology. Home: 1010 Wellington Rd Jenkintown PA 19046-3828 Office: Meadowbrook Internal Medicine Assoc 1650 Huntingdon Pike Ste 214 Meadowbrook PA 19046-8095

KIESLER, CHARLES ADOLPHUS, psychologist, academic administrator; b. St. Louis, Aug. 14, 1934; m. Teru Morton, Feb. 28, 1987; 1 child, Hugo; children from previous marriage: Tina, Thomas, Eric, Kevin. BA, Mich. State U., 1958, MA, 1960; PhD (NIMH fellow), Stanford U., 1963; D (hon.), Lucian Blaga U., Romania, 1995. Asst. prof. psychology Ohio State U., Columbus, 1963-64, Yale U., New Haven, 1964-66; assoc. prof. Yale U., 1966-70; prof., chmn. psychology U. Kans., Lawrence, 1970-75; exec. officer Am. Psychol. Assn., Washington, 1975-79; Walter Van Dyke Bingham prof. psychology Carnegie Mellon U., Pitts., 1979-85; head psychology Carnegie Mellon U., 1980-83, acting dean, 1981-82, dean Coll. Humanities and Social Scis., 1983-85; provost Vanderbilt U., 1985-92; chancellor U. Mo., Columbia, 1992-96, Weil Disting. prof. health svcs. mgmt., 1997-98; prof., sr. advisor San Diego State U., 1998—. Author: (with B.E. Collins and N. Miller) Attitude Change: A Critical Analysis of Theoretical Approaches, 1969, (with S.B. Kiesler) Conformity, 1969, The Psychology of Commitment: Experiments Linking Behavior to Belief, 1971, (with N. Cummings and G. VandenBos) Psychology and National Health Insurance: A Sourcebook, 1979, (with A.E. Sibulkin) Mental Hospitalization: Myths and Facts About a National Crisis, 1987, (with C. Simpkins) The Unnoticed Majority: Psychiatric inpatient care in general hospitals, 1993. Served with Security Service USAF, 1952-56. Recipient Disting. Alumnus award Mich. State U., 1987, Gunnar Myrdal award for Evaluation Practice Am. Evaluation Assn., 1989. Fellow AAAS, APA (Distng. Contbr. to Rsch. in Pub. Policy award 1989), Am. Psychol. Soc. (founding past pres. 1988-90); mem. AAUP, Inst. of Medicine of Nat. Acad. Scis., Sigma Xi, Psi Chi, Phi Kappa Phi. Home and Office: 3427 Mount Laurence Dr San Diego CA 92117-5649

KIESSLING, LOUISE SADLER, pediatrician, medical educator; b. Utica, N.Y.; m. Charles M. Fair. AB in Zoology, Columbia U., 1956; MA in Psychology and Counseling, Cornell U., 1969; MD, Brown U., 1976. Diplomate Am. Bd. Pediat., Nat. Bd. Med. Examiners; lic. M.D. R.I., Mass.; cert. in sch. psychology, N.Y. Intern level I, pediat. to resident level II R.I. Hosp. (Brown U.), Providence, 1976-78; resident level III, ambulatory pediat. Children's Hosp. Med. Ctr., Boston, 1978-79; neurology fellow Children's Hosp. Med. Ctr. (Harvard U.), Boston, 1979-80; dir. pediat. edn., depts. pediat. and family medicine Meml. Hosp. of R.I.; Pawtucket, 1980-96; asst. prof. pediat. and family medicine Brown U., 1981-89, assoc. prof. pediat. and family medicine, 1989-96, prof. pediat. and family medicine, 1996—; asst. physician, depts. pediat./family medicine Meml. Hosp. of R.I., 1980-84, assoc. physician, dept. family medicine, 1993—; consulting pediatrician Bradley Hosp., East Providence, R.I., 1994—; assoc. physician, dept pediat. R.I. Hosp., 1985—; pediatrician-in-chief Meml. Hosp. of R.I., 1984—; coord. Cerebral Palsy Clinic, Child Devel. Ctr., R.I. Hosp., 1980-87; instr. (part-time) Wheelock Coll., Boston, 1978-80; cons. Project Child Find, R.I. Edn. Dept., 1976-78; mem. various grant rev. bds., state and nat. levels. Contbr. numerous articles and revs. to profl. jours., chpts. to books; presenter and organizer of confs. in field; reviewer Jour. Developmental and Behavioral Pediat., 1987—. Former bd. dirs. R.I. Youth Guidance Ctr.; participant R.I. Med. Soc./R.I. Bar Assn. Partnership Against Drugs Program; mem. R.I. Spl. Edn. Adv. Com., 1993-94. United Cerebral Palsy fellow, Boston, 1978-80. Fellow Am. Acad. Pediat. (co-chmn. Com. on Children with Spl. Health Needs, R.I. chpt., 1991-98), Am. Acad. Cerebral Palsy and Developmental Medicine; mem. AMA, AAUW, Soc. for Developmental and Behavioral Pediat., Ambulatory Pediat. Assn., Nat. Tourette Syndrome Assn. (med. com. 1991—), R.I. Psychol. Assn., R.I. Med. Soc., Pawtucket Med. Soc. Office: Meml Hosp of RI Dept Pediatrics 111 Brewster St Dept Pawtucket RI 02860-4499

KIESSLING, RONALD FREDERICK, retired federal government executive; b. Cleve., Jan. 13, 1934; s. E. Oscar and Carolina Martha (Goetz) K.; m. Lois L. Nimrichter, Sept. 10, 1955 (dec. 1981); children: Elizabeth, Christopher, David; m. Jeanette Metzger, Apr. 5, 1984. Diploma, John Marshall High Sch., Cleve., 1954-90; ret., NASA Lewis Rsch. Ctr., Cleve., 1990. With NASA Lewis Rsch. Ctr., 1954—, head advanced systems/spacecraft testing sect., 1974-80, chief communications, energy and flight hardware br., 1980-82, chief materials and engine components br., 1982-85, dep. chief space tech. ops., 1985-86, dep. chief logistics mgmt. div., 1986-89. Mem. Retired and Sr. Vol. Program, adv. com. electronic tech., Akron U., 1973-89; trustee Ohio Pytian Home, Springfield, Ohio, 1998—; pres. Congregation All Saints Luth. Ch., 1997—. Sgt. USMC, 1951-54. Recipient Presdl. citation, 1971. Mem. AQP, Marine Corps League (dept. commandant 1962-64, state and local officer), NASA Suprs. Club (pres. 1976), K.P. (chancellor command 1978, grand chancellor Ohio 1993, Knight of Golden Spur, 1997, dep. supreme chancellor 1998), Am. Legion Post 421. Lutheran. Avocations: teaching, computers, photography. Home: 19 Schuberts Aly Olmsted Falls OH 44138-3027

KIEST, ALAN SCOTT, social services administrator; b. Portland, Oreg., May 14, 1949; s. Roger M. and Ellen Kiest; m. Heather L. Griffin; 1 child, Jennifer S. BA in Polit. Sci., U. Puget Sound, Tacoma, 1970; MPA, U. Wash., 1979. Welfare eligibility examiner Wash. Dept. Social and Health Services, Seattle, 1970-72, caseworker, 1972-76, service delivery coordinator, 1976-82; community svcs. office adminstr. Wash. Dept. Social and Health Svcs., Seattle, 1982—; planning commr. City of Lake Forest Park, 1989, mem. city coun., 1990—, chair city fin. com., 1992-97, vice chmn. city budget com., 1998—; mem. King County Mangaged Health Care Oversight Com., 1993-95; mem. King County Human Svcs. Roundtable, 1995—, vice chair, 1998—. Mem. Eastside Cmty. panel United Way of King County. Mem. Suburban Cities Assn., Met. King County Coun. Reg. Policy Com. Avocations: travel, music. Home: 18810 26th Ave NE Lk Forest Park WA 98155-4146 Office: Wash Dept Social & Health Svcs 14360 SE Eastgate Way Bellevue WA 98007-6462

KIEVENAAR, HENRY A., military career officer; b. Boston, June 4, 1941. BS in Bus. Adminstrn., Norwich U.; MS in Pub. Adminstrn., U. Pa., Shippensburg; grad., Command and Gen. Staff Coll., U.S. Army War Coll. Commd. 2nd lt. U.S. Army, 1964, advanced through grades to maj. gen., 1994, various positions, 1964-80; chief ops. divsn. U.S. Army Mil. Pers. Ctr., Alexandria, Va., 1980-81; comdr. 1st Bn., 35th Armor, 1st Armored Divsn. U.S. Army Europe, Germany, 1981-84, comdr. 1st Brigade, 3d Armored Divsn., 1985-87, G-3 (ops.), Vii Corps, 1987-88; asst. chief of staff, G-3 (ops.) Ctrl. Army Group Allied Command Europe, Germany, 1988-89, dep. chief staff (support), 1989-91; asst. divsn. comdr. 24th Inf. Divsn. (Mechanized) U.S. Army, Ft. Stewart, Ga., 1991-92; chief of staff V Corps U.S. Army Europe and Seventh Army, Germany, 1992-93, dep. commdg. gen. V Corps, 1993-94; comdr. Allied Command Europe Mobile Force, Germany, 1994-97; prin. dir. European and NATO Affairs Office of Asst. Sec. of Def. for Internat. Security Affairs, Washington, 1997—. Decorated Def. Disting. Svc. medal, Legion of Merit with two oak leaf clusters, Bronze Star medal with V device and three oak leaf clusters, Meritorious Svc. medal with two oak leaf clusters, Air medals with V device, Army Commendation medal with three oak leaf clusters, Army Achievement medal. Office: Office of the Asst Sec of Def Internat Security Affairs 2400 Defense Penl Washington DC 20301-2400

KIEWRA, GUSTAVE PAUL, psychologist, educator; b. Garden City Park, N.Y., July 25, 1943; s. Gustave Francis and Alice (Kozyrski) K.; m. Donna Elaine Womack, Nov. 29, 1969; children: Amy Marie, Christopher Paul, Jessica Lauren. BA, Franklin Coll., 1967; MA, Ball State U., 1968, EdD, 1972. Instr. psychology Fla. Jr. Coll., Jacksonville, 1968-70; counselor, asst. prof. counselor edn. Western Ky. U., Bowling Green, 1972-76; prof. psychology Piedmont Va. C.C., Charlottesville, 1976—; mem. psychology peer group planning com. Va. C.C. Sys., 1996; mem. bldg. com. Piedmont Va. C.C., 1993-98, planning coun., 1996—, mem. info. techs. com., 1996-98. Bd. dirs. Western Albemarle Rescue Squad, Crozet, Va., 1987, 88, Am. Lung Assn., Charlottesville, 1986-88; coord. Neighborhood Watch, Crozet, 1985-98; mem. sch. improvement com. Crozet Elem. Sch., 1990-91; mem. Piedmont (Va.) Cmty. Coll. Planning Coun., 1995-96. Recipient svc. award Piedmont Va. C.C., 1981, 86, 91, 96. Mem. APA, Va. Psychol. Assn., Am. Assn. Marriage and Family Counselors, Va. C.C. Assn. (rep. faculty affairs com. 1990-92), Faculty Profl. Assn., Internat. Platform Assn., Lions (pres. Crozet, Va. 1989-92, Key award 1991, Advancement Key award 1991, Master Key award 1992, 100% Pres. award 1990-92, Dist. Gov. Membership Growth award 1990-92, Va. Multiple Dist. 24 Achievement award 1990-92, Pres. Svc. Appreciation award 1992, Achievement award medal 1992, Melvin Jones fellow Internat. Found.), Phi Delta Kappa, Phi Theta Kappa (hon., faculty advisor 1980-88), Phi Delta Theta. Avocations: volleyball, hiking, gardening, physical conditioning, community service. Home: 1440 Birchwood Dr Crozet VA 22932-9441 Office: Piedmont Va CC 501 College Dr Charlottesville VA 22902-7589

KIFFMEYER, MARY, state official; b. Pierz, Minn., Dec. 29, 1946; m. Ralph Kiffmeyer; children: Christina, Patrick, James, John. RN, St. Gabriel's Sch. Nursing, Little Falls, Minn.; student, Anoka Ramsey C.C. RN, Minn.; cert. election judge. Co-owner med. bus.; sec. of state State of Minn., St. Paul, 1999—; guest tchr. elem. and h.s. levels in politics, home econs., phy. edn., music. Mem. bd. dirs. Monticello-Big Lake Cmty. Hosp. Dist.; treas. Monticello Big-Lake Hosp., mem. fin. com., mem. human resources, mktg. and planning coms.; statewide trainer Rep. Party of Minn.; Minn. Precinct Caucus coord., 1996, 98; past mem. and chair Big Lake Cmty. Edn. adv. Coun.; vol. ARC Bloodmobile; active various charitable/ vol. orgns.; nat. del. Rep. Party, 1992, 96, mem. nat. rules com., 1992, 96; active in local, congl., state and nat. campaigns, 1982—. Office: Office of Secretary of State 100 Constitution Ave Rm 180 Saint Paul MN 55155-1299*

KIGER, JOSEPH CHARLES, history educator; b. Kenton County, Ky., Aug. 19, 1920; s. Carl C. and Genevieve (Hoelscher) K.; m. Jean Myrick Moore, Mar. 27, 1947; children: Carl A., John J. A.B., Birmingham-So. Coll., 1943; M.A., U. Ala., 1947; Ph.D., Vanderbilt U., 1950. Teaching fellow Vanderbilt U., 1948-50; instr. history U. Ala., summer 1950, Washington U., St. Louis, 1950-51; dir. research select com. to investigate founds. U.S. Ho. of Reps., 1952; staff asso. Am. Council Edn., Washington, 1953-55; asst. dir. So. Fellowships Fund, Chapel Hill, N.C., 1955-58; asso. prof. history U. Ala., 1958-61; prof. history U. Miss., 1961—, chmn. dept. history, 1969-74, emeritus, 1990—, dir. program on founds. and Comparable orgs., 1993—; cons. non-profit orgns., also govt., 1954—. Author: Operating Principles of the Larger Foundations, 1954, (with others) Sponsored Research Policy of Colleges and Universities, 1954, American Learned Societies, 1963, (with others) A History of Mississippi, 1973; editor: Research Institutions and Learned Societies, 1982, International Encyclopedia of Foundations, 1990, Internat. Encyclopaedia of Learned Societies and Academies, 1993; co-editor: Foundations, 1984, Historiographic Review of Foundation Literature, Motivations and Perceptions, 1987. Served to capt. USMCR, 1942-46. Guggenheim fellow, 1960; grantee Russell Sage Found., 1953; grantee Rockefeller Found., 1961; grantee Am. Philos. Soc., 1964; grantee Am. Council of Learned Socs., Nat. Acad. Scis., 1980. Mem. Am. Hist. Assn., So. Hist. Assn. (life). Home: Country Club Rd Oxford MS 38655 Office: U Miss 107 Isom Hall University MS 38677

KIGER, ROBERT WILLIAM, botanist, science historian, educator; b. Washington, Oct. 4, 1940; s. William Joseph and Marian (Calvert) K.; m. Suellen Montgomery, June 11, 1968; children: David M., James R. AA with honors, Montgomery Jr. Coll., 1964; BA in Spanish with Social Scis. minor, Tulane U., 1966; MA in History, U. Md., 1971, PhD in Botany, 1972. Tchr. Poolesville Elem. Sch., Md., 1966-67; grad. teaching asst. dept. history U. Md., College Park, 1968-69, grad. teaching asst. dept. botany, 1969-70, grad. rsch. asst. dept. botany, 1969-70; assoc. editor, rsch. botanist Flora N.Am. Program dept. botany Smithsonian Inst., Washington, 1972-73; asst. dir., sr. rsch. scientist Hunt Inst. Bot. Documentation, Carnegie Mellon U., 1974-77, dir., prin. rsch. scientist, 1977—; rsch. assoc. sect. botany Carnegie Mus. Natural History, Pitts., 1978—; adj. scientist Pitts. Poison Ctr., Children's Hosp., 1990—; adj. prof. biol. scis. dept. biol. scis. Carnegie Mellon U., 1984—, history of sci. dept. history Carnegie Mellon U., 1979—; mem. internat. com. Internat. Congress Systematic and Evolutionary Biology, 1980-90, asst. treas., 1980-90, sec.-gen., 1990-96; mem. adv. com., editorial com. Flora of N.Am. Project, 1983—; cons. Chgo. Botanic Garden, Glencoe, Ill., 1980-83, 87-88, 89, Carnegie Mus. Natural History, Pitts., 1984, European Sci. Found., Stasbourg, France, 1987, Commn. Preservation and Access, Wye, Md., 1991, FBI, Martinsburg, W.Va., 1997. Editor: Memoirs of the Torrey Botanical Club, 1975-88, Huntia, 1978-92, bibliographic editor (all vols.) and taxonomic editor (various families), Flora of North America, 1987—; exec. editor Hunt Inst. publs., 1977—; contbr. articles to profl. jours. Chmn. Lawrence Meml. Award Com., 1979—; steering group Com. Organize a Flora of N.Am. Project, 1982-83; sec. for N.Am. Commn. Taxonomic Database Plant Sci. IUBS, 1986-89, working parties for devel. various standards, 1986—, program com., 1987-90, global plant species info. group, 1990—; mem. adv. com. computer databasing Mo. Botanical Garden, St. Louis, 1988-89, Rocky Mountain Flora Project, 1993—; botanical info. adv. workshop BIOSIS, Washington, 1990; chmn. judges for botany Internat. Sci. and Engring. Fair, Pitts., 1989. With USMC, 1960-61, USMCR, 1960-66. Grantee NSF, 1971-73, 78-80, 90; recipient Full Merit scholarship Montgomery Jr. Coll., 1963-64, Partial Merit scholarship Tulane U., 1964-66, NSF Grad. traineeship U. Md., 1970, Carroll E. Cox award U. Md., 1972-73. Fellow Linnean Soc. London; mem. AAAS, Botanical Soc. Am. (sec./treas. hist. sect. 1979-92, chmn. archives and history com. 1985-86), Am. Assn. Botanical Gardens and Arboreta, Am. Inst. Biol. Scis., Am. Soc. Plant Taxonomists, Internat. Assn. Plant Taxonomy, Internat. Soc. for History and Philosophy Sci., Assn. Tropical Biology, Coun. Botanical and Horticultural Librs., History Sci. Soc., Soc. Econ. Botany, Soc. Study Evolution, Soc. Systematic Biology, Torrey Botanical Club (assoc. editor 1975—), New Eng. Botanical Club. Avocations: music, model aviation, bicycling, motorcycling, photography. Home: 1183 Bucknell Dr Monroeville PA 15146-4319 Office: Carnegie Mellon U Hunt Inst Bot Documentation 5000 Forbes Ave Pittsburgh PA 15213-3890

KIGGINS, MILDRED L., telemarketing firm executive; b. Hempstead, N.Y., Sept. 14, 1927; d. Wolfgang and Hannah Ingeborg (Olsson) Weissman; m. Andrew Edward Kiggins, Jan. 8, 1962 (div. 1982); children: Daniel Mark, David Bruce. Diploma, Donovan Bus. Coll., Hackensack, N.J., 1945, Luther Coll. Acad., 1947. Exec. sec. Greenwich Engring. divsn. Am. Machine & Foundry Inc., Stamford, Conn., 1954-61; adminstrv. asst. Michael Sims Golden Crest Ins. Svcs., San Jose, Calif., 1996—; telemktg. rep. Ragtime Thrift, Inc., 1998. Tchr. Sunday sch. St. John's Luth. Ch., Stamford, 1948-50; mem. St. Timothy's Luth. Ch., San Jose. Republican. Avocations: gardening, music, sports, church activities. Home: 4644 Pinto River Ct San Jose CA 95136-2736

KIHLE, DONALD ARTHUR, lawyer; b. Noonan, N.D., Apr. 4, 1934; s. J. Arthur and Linnie W. (Ljunngren) K.; m. Judith Anne, Aug. 18, 1964; children—Kevin, Kirsten, Kathryn, Kurte. B.S. in Indsl. Engring., U. N.D., 1957; J.D., U. Okla., 1967. Bar: Okla. 1967, U.S. Dist. Cts. (we. and no. dists.) Okla. 1967, U.S. Ct. Appeals (10th cir.) 1967, U.S. Supreme Ct. 1971. Asso., Huffman, Arrington, Scheurich & Kincaid, Tulsa, 1967-71, ptnr., 1971-78; shareholder, dir., officer Arrington Kihle Gaberino & Dunn, Tulsa, 1978-97, pres., 1994-97; shareholder, dir. Gable & Gotwals, Tulsa, 1997—. Dist. chmn. Boy Scouts Am., 1983-85, cubmaster, 1986-88, coun. coms., 1988—, campiree chmn., 1990; mem. Statewide Law Day Com., 1982-86, chmn., 1983-85; trustee Brandon Hall Sch., Atlanta, 1991—, chmn., 1995—. Lt. U.S. Army, 1957-59. Recipient Silver Beaver award Boy Scouts Am. Mem. ABA, Okla. Bar Assn. (chmn. constl. bicentennial com. 1986-89), Constitution 200 (exec. com. 1986-89), Tulsa County Bar Assn., So. Hills Country Club, Q Club (scribe 1991—), Tulsa Club (bd. govs. 1987-94, pres. 1992), Order of Coif, Order of Arrow (vigil), Sigma Tau, Phi Delta Phi, Sigma Chi (Tulsa alumni pres. 1995-97). Republican. Home: 4717 S Lewis Ct Tulsa OK 74105-5135 Office: 1000 ONEOK Plz 100 W 5th St Tulsa OK 74103-4240

KIHN, HARRY, electronics engineer, manufacturing company executive; b. Tarnow, Austria, Jan. 24, 1912; came to U.S., 1920, naturalized 1927; s. Morris and Sabina K.; m. Minna Schechter, Nov., 1937; children—Michael Allan, Leslie Morris. B.S. in Elec. Engring., Cooper Union Inst. Tech., 1934; M.S. in Elec. Engring., U. Pa., 1952. Registered profl. engr., N.J. Devel. engr. Hygrade-Sylvania Co., Clifton, N.J., 1935-38; devel. engr. Ferris Instrument Co., Boonton, N.J., 1938; radio, TV research engr. RCA Mfg. Co., Camden, N.J., 1939-42; electronics, computer, defense projects and TV researcher corp. staff engr. patents and licensing RCA Labs., Princeton, N.J., 1942-75; sr. staff tech. advisor RCA Corp., 1975-77; pres. Kihn Assocs. Inc., robotics, nuclear energy, med., electronics cons., 1977—; mem. program rev. com. Office of Nuclear Waste Isolation, Dept. Energy, Washington, 1979-88; instr. electronics Rutgers U. Extension. Sr. editor Gov.'s Commn. on Sci. and Tech. Contbr. articles to profl. jours., tech. confs. Patentee in field. Vice pres. Lawrenceville Sch. Bd., 1957-60; bd. dirs. Lawrenceville Adult Sch., 1960-62, George Washington Council Boy Scouts Am.; chmn. Lawrenceville Ednl. Found., 1950-74. Recipient Microminiaturization award Miniature Precision Bearings, Inc., 1958, 2 research awards RCA Corp., 1952-56. Fellow IEEE (life, Centennial medal 1984, life mem. awards com. 1989-94); mem. NAS (materials adv. bd. 1961-62), AAAS, NSPE, N.Y. Acad. Sci., Mercer Soc. Profl. Engrs. (pres., Engr. of Yr. 1986-87), Engrs. Club of Trenton, Am. Def. Preparedness Assn., Ctrl. Jersey Engring. Coun. (chmn. 1990-91), Lions, Rotary, The Nassau Club, The Old Guard of Princeton, Sigma Xi. Home: 30 Green Ave Lawrenceville NJ 08648-1646*

KIKER, BILLY FRAZIER, economics educator; b. Elkin, N.C., Apr. 21, 1936; s. William James and Ruby Lucille (Jester) K.; m. Martha Jane Parker, Aug. 4, 1962; children: Todd, Jonathan, David. AB, Lenoir-Rhyne Coll., 1961; PhD, Tulane U., 1965. From asst. prof. to prof. Econs. U. S.C., Columbia, 1965—; Univ. Chr. prof. Dept. Econs., Columbia, 1973—; chmn. dept. U. S.C., Columbia, 1973-87, dir. Ctr. for Studies in Human Capital, 1972-75; vis. prof. U. Edinburgh, Scotland, 1973, U. Minho, Portugal, 1995, 96, Wirtschafts U., Vienna, Austria, 1997; pvt. practice cons. economist, Columbia, 1972. Author: Human Capital in Retrospect, 1968, Macroeconomic Analysis, 1974; editor: Investment in Human Capital, 1971; contbr. numerous articles to profl. jours. Fulbright scholar U. Porto, Portugal, 1988. Mem. Am. Econ. Assn., Assn. for health Svcs. Rsch., Nat. Assn. Forensic Econs. Methodist. Avocations: sailing, tennis. Home: 637 Woodland Hills Rd W Columbia SC 29210-5640 Office: U of SC Coll of Bus Admin Columbia SC 29208

KIKO, PHILIP GEORGE, lawyer; b. Massillon, Ohio, July 16, 1951; s. Willard LeRoy and Stella Jane (Schroeder) K.; m. Colleen Duffy; children: Jamie Lynn, Sarah Elizabeth, Philip George Jr., Michael Ryan. BA, Mount Union Coll., 1973; JD, George Mason Sch. Law, 1977. Bar: Va. 1977, D.C 1978, U.S. Ct. Appeals (D.C. cir.) 1978. Assoc. legal counsel, broadcast asst. Nat. Rep. Congl. Com., Washington, 1973-79; exec. asst., legis. counsel Congressman Sensenbrenner, Washington, 1979-83; assoc. counsel judiciary com. U.S. Ho. Reps., Washington, 1983-86; acting dir. policy and enforcement Office for Civil Rights U.S. Dept. Edn., Washington, 1986-87; officer, bd. dirs. Kiko Heating & Air Conditioning, Canton, Ohio, 1973-89; legis. counsel Dept. Interior, Washington, 1987-89, dir. budget and program resource mgmt., 1989-92, dep. dir. office hearings and appeals, 1992-94; assoc. adminstr. procurement and purchasing U.S. Ho. of Reps., Washington, 1995-96, dep. chief of staff/counsel sci. com., 1997-98; v.p. bd. dirs. Law Offices of Colleen Duffy Kiko P.C., 1996—; chief of staff/counsel Congressman James Sensenbrenner, 1999—; bd. dirs., sec. Pers. Dept., Arlington, Va. Mem. Arlington Rep. Com., 1978-86, 95—, Fair Housing Bd., Arlington, 1980; v.p. Arlington Hts. Citizen Assn., 1991-96; pres. St. Charles Sch. PTO, 1994—; den leader Cub Scouts, 1996—, asst. scoutmaster, 1998—; mem. St. Charles Parish Coun., 1997—. Recipient Exceptional Svc. award Sec. Interior, 1988, Presidl. Meritorious Svc. award, 1992. Mem. Va. State Bar Assn., D.C. Bar Assn. Roman Catholic. Avocations: running, hunting, fishing. Home: 3500 Arlington Blvd Arlington VA 22204-1721 Office: Office of F James Sensenbrenner US Ho of Reps 2332 Rayburn Bldg Washington DC 20515-0005

KIKOLER, STEPHEN PHILIP, lawyer; b. N.Y.C., Apr. 24, 1945; s. Sigmund and Dorothy (Javna) K.; m. Ethel Lerner, June 18, 1967; children: Jeffrey Stuart, Shari Elaine. AB, U. Mich., 1966, JD cum laude, 1969. Bar: Ill. 1969, U.S. Dist. Ct. (no. dist.) Ill. 1969, U.S. Ct. Appeals (7th cir.) 1988, U.S. Ct. Appeals (11th cir.) 1994, U.S. Ct. Mil. Appeals 1970, U.S. Supreme Ct. 1994. Assoc. Rosenthal & Schanfield, Chgo., 1969-70, 73-77, shareholder, 1977—; capt. Judge Advocate Gen.'s Corps U.S. Army, 1970-73. Mem. ABA, Am. Land Title Assn., Ill. State Bar Assn., Chgo. Bar. Assn. (real property law com., chmn. mechanics' liens subcom. 1987-89), Lake County Contractors/Devel. Assn. (chmn. com. profl. svcs. 1998—). Home: 2746 Norma Ct Glenview IL 60025-4661 Office: Rosenthal & Schanfield PC 55 E Monroe St Fl 46 Chicago IL 60603-5713

KILBANE, CATHERINE M., lawyer; b. Cleve., Apr. 10, 1963. BA cum laude, Case Western Res. U., 1984, JD cum laude, 1987. Bar: Ohio 1987. Ptnr. Baker & Hostetler, Cleve., 1997—. Mem. Delta Theta Phi. Office: Baker & Hostetler 3200 Nat City Ctr 1900 E 9th St Ste 3200 Cleveland OH 44114-3475*

KILBANE, THOMAS STANTON, lawyer; b. Cleve., Mar. 7, 1941; s. Thomas Joseph and Helen (Stanton) K.; m. Sally Conway Kilbane, June 4, 1966; children: Sarah, Thomas, Eamon, James, Carlin. BA magna cum laude, John Carroll U., 1963; JD, Northwestern U., 1966. Bar: Ohio 1966, U.S. Dist. Ct. (no. dist.) Ohio 1967, U.S. Supreme Ct. 1975, U.S. Ct. Claims 1981, U.S. Ct. Appeals (6th cir.) 1982, U.S. Ct. Appeals (3d cir.) 1990, U.S.

Ct. Appeals (5th cir.) 1998. Assoc. Squire, Sanders & Dempsey, Cleve., 1966-76, ptnr., 1976—, adminstrv. com., 1979-80, mgmt. com., 1981-83, 87-90, mng. ptnr. litigation practice area, 1991—; fed. ct. panelist U.S. Dist. Ct. (no. dist.) Ohio. Mem. editl. bd. Northwestern U. Law Rev., 1965-66. Active Rep. Presdl. Task Force. Capt. U.S. Army, 1967-69, Vietnam. Decorated Bronze Star; named Greater Cleve. Cath. Man of Yr., 1996. Fellow ABA, Am. Coll. Trial Lawyers, Internat. Acad. Trial Lawyers, Master Bencher of Anthony J. Celebrezze Inns of Ct.; mem. Ohio Bar Assn. (AAA corp. counsel com., ctr. for pub. resources constrn. com.), Greater Cleve. Bar Assn., Def. Rsch. Inst., Jud. Conf. 8th Jud. Dist. Ohio (life), Union Club, The 50 Club, The Club, Alpha Sigma Nu. Republican. Roman Catholic. Office: Squire Sanders & Dempsey 4900 Key Tower 127 Public Sq Ste 4900 Cleveland OH 44114-1304

KILBORN, PETER THURSTON, journalist; b. Providence, Apr. 7, 1939; s. John Wiggins and Eleanor Artemesia (McIntire) K.; m. Susan Holly Woodward, Jan. 29, 1966; children: David Thompson, Elizabeth Artemesia Wilhelm. BA, Trinity Coll., 1961; MSJ, Columbia U., 1962. Reporter Providence Jour.-Bulletin, 1963-64; Paris corr. McGraw-Hill World News, N.Y.C., 1966-68; reporter, writer Bus. Week Mag., N.Y.C., 1969-71, L.A. bur. chief, 1971-73; cos. editor Bus. Week, N.Y.C., 1973-74; reporter N.Y. Times, N.Y.C., 1974-75; London corr. N.Y. Times, 1975-77; editor Sunday bus. sect. N.Y. Times, N.Y.C., 1979-82; econs. editor Washington bur. N.Y. Times, 1982-83, sr. econs. corr. Washington bur., 1983-89, nat. corr. Washington bur., 1989—; bus. editor Newsweek Mag., N.Y.C., 1977-78. Trustee Trinity Coll., Hartford, Conn., 1990-96. Profl. journalism fellow Stanford U., 1968-69. Mem. U. Club (N.Y.C.). Office: The NY Times 1627 I St NW Washington DC 20006-4007

KILBOURN, LEE FERRIS, architect, specifications writer; b. L.A., Mar. 9, 1936; s. Lewis Whitman and Kathryn Mae (Lee) K.; m. Joan Priscilla Payne, June 11, 1961; children: Laurie Jane, Ellen Mae. BS in Gen. Sci., Oreg. State U., 1963; BS in Architecture, U. Oreg., 1965. Registered architect, Oreg. Specifier Wolff Zimmer Assocs., Portland, Oreg., 1965-75; specifier, assoc. Wolff Zimmer Gunsul Frasca, Portland, 1975-77; specifier, assoc. Zimmer Gunsul Frasca Partnership, Portland, 1977-81, specifier, assoc. ptnr., 1981—. Jr. warden, then sr. warden St. Stephen's Episcopal Parish, Portland. With U.S. Army, 1959-60. Fellow AIA (mem. master spec. rev. com. 1976-78, mem. documents com. 1981-89), Constrn. Specifications Inst. (mem. participating tech. documents com. 1976-78, cert. com. 1980-82, Al Hansen Meml. award Portland chpt. 1987, Frank Stanton Meml. award N.W. region 1987, chpt. pres. 1979-80); mem. Internat. Conf. Bldg. Ofcls. Home: 3178 SW Fairmount Blvd Portland OR 97201-1468 Office: Zimmer Gunsul Frasca Partnership 320 SW Oak St Ste 500 Portland OR 97204-2737

KILBOURN, WILLIAM DOUGLAS, JR., law educator; b. Colorado Springs, Colo., Dec. 9, 1924; s. William Douglas and Clara Howe (Lee) K.; m. Barbara Ruth Neff, Sept. 16, 1950; children: Jonathan VI, Katharine Ann. BA, Yale U., 1949; postgrad., Columbia U., 1949-50, LLB, 1953. Bar: Mass. 1962, Oreg. 1953, Minn. 1974. Acct. Arthur Andersen & Co., 1949-50; assoc. Davies, Biggs, Strayer, Stoel & Boley, Portland, Oreg., 1953-56; asst. prof. law U. Mont., 1956-57; assoc. prof. law U. Mo., 1957-59; prof. law, founding dir. grad. tax program Boston U., 1959-71; prof. law U. Minn., 1971-98, prof. emeritus, 1998—; dir. U. Mont. Tax Inst., 1956; of counsel Palmer & Dodge, Boston, 1964-75, Oppenheimer, Wolff & Donnelly, St. Paul and Mpls., 1980-94; mem. exec. com. Fed. Tax Inst. New Eng., 1966-72; mem. adv. com. Western New Eng. Coll. Tax Inst; vis. prof. law Duke U., 1974-75, U. Tex., 1977, Washington U., St. Louis, 1977; past ednl. advisor Tex. Execs. Inst.; lectr. in 28 states, Mex., the Caribbean, and D.C.; expert witness in field. Editor: Estate Planning and Income Taxation, 1957; contbr. articles to profl. jours. Dist. dir. United Fund, Belmont, Mass., chair fair practices com. Recipient numerous tchg. awards; Kent scholar, Stone scholar Columbia U. Law Sch. Mem. ABA (tax sect., corp. stockholder rels. com. 1962-76, chair subcom. inc. 1968-73), Boston Bar Assn. (chair tax sect. 1967-70), Boston Tax Forum, Boston Tax Coun. Avocations: tennis, botany, landscape gardening. Home: 2681 E Lake Of The Isles Pky Minneapolis MN 55408-1051

KILBOURNE, BARBARA JEAN, health and human services consultant; b. Milw., Mar. 21, 1941; d. Burton Conwell and Marjorie Janet (Tufts) K.; m. Kenneth Keith Kauffman, Feb. 10, 1962 (div. 1983). BA, U. Minn., 1972; MBA, Coll. St. Thomas, St. Paul, 1980. Adminstr. Ebenezer Soc., Mpls., 1974-85; v.p., dir. housing Walker Residence and Health Svcs., Inc., Mpls., 1985-88; exec. v.p. Oblate Ministries Health and Aging, West St. Paul, Minn., 1988-94; cons., 1995—; pres. Barbara J. Kilbourne, Ltd., 1996—; exec. dir. Cath. Health Assn. Minn., 1997-98; bd. dirs. CommonBond Resident Svcs. Corp., St. Paul, chmn., 1996-98. Author: Family Councils in Nursing Homes, 1981. Chmn. bd. dirs. LifeWorks, Eagan, Minn., 1985-96, Minn. Assn. Homes for Aging, 1991-92, Sem. Plaza, Red Wing, 1995-97; project chair Dialog 2000, Dakota County, Minn., 1988-91; bd. dirs. ARC, Mpls., 1997—, Common Bond Cmtys., 1999—, Villa Guadalupe, Chgo, chair 1999—. Mem. Minn. Rural Health Assn. (bd. dirs. 1998—). Episcopalian. Avocations: skiing, sailing, piano, golf, hiking. Home: 1021 Sibley Memorial Hwy Lilydale MN 55118-6100

KILBOURNE, EDWIN DENNIS, virologist, educator; b. Buffalo, July 10, 1920; s. Edwin I. and Elizabeth (Alward) K.; m. Joy Schmid, Dec. 20, 1952; children: Edwin Michael, Richard Schmid, Christopher Norton, Paul Alward. AB, Cornell U., 1942, MD, 1944; DSc honoris causa, Rockefeller U., 1986. Asst. Rockefeller Inst., 1948-51; mem. faculty Tulane U., 1951-55, Cornell U. Med. Coll., N.Y.C., 1955-68; prof. pub. health, dir. div. virus research Cornell U. Med. Coll., 1961-68; prof., chmn. dept. microbiology Mt. Sinai Sch. Medicine, City U. New York, 1968-86, disting. service prof., 1986—; rsch. prof. N.Y. Med. Coll., 1992—; chmn., bd. dirs. Aaron Diamond AIDS Rsch. Ctr. for the City N.Y., 1989-94. Author: (with Wilson G. Smillie) Human Ecology and Public Health, 4th edit, 1968, Influenza, 1987; Editor: The Influenza Viruses and Influenza, 1975. Mem. Health Research Council N.Y.C., 1968-75. Recipient R.E. Dyer Lectureship award NIH, 1973, Borden award Assn. Am. Med. Colls., 1974, Dowling Lectureship award, 1976, Thomas Francis Lectureship award, 1976, Nat. Acad. Scis. 1977, Harvey Lectureship award, 1978, award of distinction Cornell U. Med. Alumni Assn., 1979, acad. medal N.Y. Acad. Medicine, 1982, Jacobi Medallion award Mt. Sinai Alumni Assn., 1991, Fogarty scholar award NIH, 1992. Fellow N.Y. Acad. Scis., Am. Philos. Soc.; mem. Harvey Soc., So. Soc. Clin. Rsch., Ctrl. Soc. Clin. Rsch. (emeritus), AAAS, Am. Assn. Immunologists, Am. Acad. Microbiology, Soc. Exptl. Biology and Medicine, Am. Soc. Clin. Investigation (emeritus), N.Y. Acad. Medicine, Am. Pub. Health Assn., Assn. Am. Physicians, Am. Soc. Microbiology, Infectious Diseases Soc. Am. Rsch. and publs. on hormonal influences, genetic studies and exptl. transmission of viruses, recombinant virus vaccines especially influenza. Home: 23 Willard Ave Madison CT 06443-3202 Office: NY Med Coll Dept Microbiology/Immunology Valhalla NY 10595

KILBOURNE, KRYSTAL HEWETT, rail transportation executive; b. Sandersville, Ga., Apr. 7, 1940; d. John Ray and Kathleen (Perkins) Hewett; m. Alan Arden Kilbourne, July 1, 1961 (div. May 1972); children: Arden Alan, Keith Ray. A, U. Ga., 1960. Tchr. Massey Bus. Coll., Jacksonville, Fla., 1968-72, editor, reporter, photographer, 1968-72; asst. to pres. Luter Advt. Agy., Jacksonville, Fla., 1973-74; asst. to dir. Leukemia Soc., Jacksonville, Fla., 1975-76; asst. to pres. TeleCheck Corp., Jacksonville, Fla., 1979; mgr. customer svc. railroad ops. CSX Transp., Jacksonville, Fla., 1980—. Tuition scholar U. Ga., 1958; recipient Transp. Workers Leadership award, 1995. Mem. Nat. Assn. Railway Bus. Women, Am. Coun. Railroad Women (chair equal employment opportunity coun. 1992-94). Democrat. Presbyn. Avocations: oil painting, poetry, snorkeling, traveling, reading. Home: 4856 Deermoss Way S Jacksonville FL 32217-9306 Office: CSX Transportation 6737 Southpoint Dr S Jacksonville FL 32216-6177

KILBURG, PAUL J., federal judge; b. 1945. Bankruptcy judge U.S. Bankruptcy Ct. (no. dist.) Iowa, Cedar Rapids, 1993—. Office: 425 2d St SE Cedar Rapids IA 52407

KILBURN, EDWIN ALLEN, lawyer; b. Wenatchee, Wash., Apr. 5, 1933; s. Howard L. and Dorothy M. (Allen) K.; m. Penelope P. White, Feb. 7, 1964; children: Penelope Allen, Nancy Kitchen. BA with highest honors, Wash. State U., 1955; JD cum laude, NYU, 1958. Bar: N.Y. 1958, U.S. Supreme Ct. 1963. Assoc. Cravath, Swaine & Moore, N.Y.C., 1958, 62-68; staff, sr. group counsel ITT, N.Y.C., 1968-74, asst. gen. counsel, 1975-80, assoc. gen. counsel, 1981-95, v.p., dir. litigation, corp. policy compliance, 1982-95, ret., 1996; of counsel Stewart and Stewart, Washington, 1996-98, Wallace, King, Marraro & Branson, P.L.L.C., Washington, 1998—. Capt. JAGC, U.S. Army, 1959-62. Root Tilden Scholar. Mem. ABA (antitrust, litigation), Am. Law Inst., Troon Club (Scottsdale, Ariz.), Phi Beta Kappa. Episcopalian. Home: 513 E Bluff Dr Scottsdale AZ 85255-8171 Office: 1050 Thomas Jefferson St NW Washington DC 20007

KILBURN, H(ENRY) T(HOMAS), JR., investment banker; b. N.Y.C., Aug. 1, 1931; s. Henry Thomas and Florence (Cross) K.; m. Victoria Tyner Potter, Sept. 20, 1988. A.B., Princeton U., 1953; J.D., Columbia U., 1959. Bar: N.Y. 1959. Exec. trainee Bankers Trust Co., N.Y.C., 1953-54; assoc. Kelley Drye Newhall & Maginnes, N.Y.C., 1959-66; v.p. fin., gen. counsel W.E. Parfitt & Assocs. N.Y.C., 1967-71; assoc., then 1st v.p., sr. v.p., dir. Blyth Eastman Dillon, N.Y.C., 1972-78; exec. v.p. Blyth Eastman Dillon, N.Y.C., 1978-80; mng. dir. PaineWebber Inc., N.Y.C., 1980-88, adv. dir., 1988—; dir. PaineWebber Leasing Corp.; chmn. 1221 Assocs., Ltd. Ptnrs. 1st lt. U.S. Army, 1954-56. Mem. N.Y. Bar Assn., Securities Industry Assn. (chmn. regulated industries com. 1980-81), Links Club, Princeton Club (N.Y.C.) The Belle Haven Club. Republican. Episcopalian. Home: 48 Walsh Ln Greenwich CT 06830-7039 also: 139 E 63rd St New York NY 10021-7405 Office: Paine Webber Inc Rm 2R 1285 Avenue Of The Americas Fl Sconc New York NY 10019-6096

KILBURN, KAYE HATCH, medical educator; b. Logan, Utah, Sept. 20, 1931; d. H. Parley and Winona (Hatch) K.; m. Gerrie Griffin, June 7, 1954; children: Ann Louise, Scott Kaye, Jean Marie. BS, U. Utah, 1951, MD, 1954. Diplomate Am. Bd. Internal Medicine, Am. Bd. Preventive Medicine. Asst. prof. Med. Sch. Washington U., St. Louis, 1960-62; assoc. prof., chief of medicine Durham (N.C.) VA Hosp., 1962-69; prof., dir. environ. medicine Duke Med. Ctr., Durham, 1969-73; prof. medicine and environ. medicine U. Mo., Columbia, 1973-77; prof. medicine and cmty. medicine CUNY Mt. Siai Med. Sch., 1977-80; Ralph Edgington prof. medicine U. So. Calif. Sch. Medicine, L.A., 1980—; pres. Neurotest Inc., 1988—; pres. Workers Disease Detection Svc. Inc., 1986-95. Author: Chemical Brain Injury, 1998; editor-in-chief Archives of Environ. Health, 1986—; editor Jour. Applied Physiology, 1970-80, Environ. Rsch., 1975—, Am. Jour. Indsl. Medicine, 1980—; contbr. more than 200 articles to profl. jours. Capt. M.C., U.S. Army, 1958-60. Avocations: travel, oil painting, swimming, hunting. Home: 3250 Mesaloa Ln Pasadena CA 91107-1129 Office: U So Calif Sch Medicine 2025 Zonal Ave Los Angeles CA 90033-1034

KILBY, JACK ST. CLAIR, electrical engineer; b. Jefferson City, Mo., Nov. 8, 1923; s. Hubert St. Clair and Vina (Freitag) K.; m. Barbara Annegers, June 27, 1948; children: Ann, Janet Lee. BEE, U. Ill., 1947; MS, U. Wis., 1950; DEng (hon.), U. Miami, 1982; DSc (hon.), U. Wis., 1990; DEng (hon.), Rochester Inst. Tech., 1986; DSc (hon.), U. Ill., 1988; DSc, Rensselaer Poly. Inst., 1990; DSc (hon.), Yale U., 1996. Program mgr. Globe-Union, Inc., Milw., 1948-58; asst. v.p. Tex. Instruments, Inc., Dallas, 1958-70; self-employed inventor Dallas, 1970—; disting. prof. elec. engring. Tex. A&M U., 1978-85; inventor monolithic integrated circuit, others; cons. to govt. and industry. Served with AUS, 1943-45. Recipient Nat. Medal of Sci., 1969, 90, Ballentine medal Franklin Inst., 1967, Alumni Achievement award U. Ill., 1974, Holley medal ASME, 1982, 89; inducted into Nat. Inventors Hall of Fame, U.S. Patent Office, 1981. Fellow IEEE (Sarnoff medal 1966, Brunetti award 1978, Medal of honor 1986); mem. NAE (Zworykin medal 1975, co-recipient Charles Stark Draper prize 1989, Kyoto prize for tech. achievement 1993). Home: 7723 Midbury Dr Dallas TX 75230-3211 Office: Ste 155 6600 Lyndon B Johnson Fwy Dallas TX 75240-6531

KILDEE, DALE EDWARD, congressman; b. Flint, Mich., Sept. 16, 1929; s. Timothy Leo and Norma Alicia (Ullmer) K.; m. Gayle Heyn, Feb. 27, 1965; children: David, Laura, Paul. BA, Sacred Heart Sem., 1952; tchr.'s cert., U. Detroit, 1954; MA, U. Mich., 1961; postgrad. (Rotary Found. fellow), U. Peshawar, Pakistan, 1958-59. Tchr. U. Detroit High Sch., 1954-56; Tchr. Flint Central High Sch., 1956-64; mem. Mich. Ho. of Reps., 1964-74, Mich. Senate, 1975-76; mem. 95th-106th Congresses from 7th (now 9th) Mich. Dist., 1977—, ranking minority mem. econ. & ednl. opportunity subcom. on early childhood, youth, & families, mem. resources com., mem. congl. auto caucus, mem. edn. and the workforce com. Mem. NAACP (life), Am. Fedn. Tchrs., Urban League, Phi Delta Kappa. Lodges: K.C; Optimists. Office: US Ho of Reps 2187 Rayburn House Bldg Washington DC 20515-2209 also: 432 N Saginaw St Ste 410 Flint MI 48502-2018*

KILDUFF, BONNIE ELIZABETH, director of expositions; b. Washington, Sept. 25, 1959; d. Macolm McGreggor and Betty Kilduff. Adminstr. Aircraft Owners & Pilot Assn., Bethesda, Md., 1977-79; mktg. pub. rels., meeting planning, exec. asst. Dairy and Food Inds. Supply Assn., Rockville, Md., 1979-89; dir. expns. Packaging Machinery Mfrs. Inst., Arlington, Va., 1989—; secmem. Trade Show Adv. Coun., Denver, 1992-94. Mem. Maj. Trade Show Organizers (chmn. 1996-97), Internat. Assn. Expn. Mgrs. (cert expn. mgr., sec. found. com. 1994, mem. mktg. com. 1993—, chmn. internat. com. 1996-97), Trade Show Cur., Women in Packaging, Confedn. Organizers Packaging Expns. Avocations: art, running, painting, tennis. Office: Packaging Machinery Mfrs Inst 4350 Fairfax Dr Ste 600 Arlington VA 22203-1632

KILE, CAROL ANN, lawyer; b. Cleve., Dec. 26, 1946; d. Walter John and Leona Eleanor (Koeppen) Ripich; m. William Simons Kile, Aug. 12, 1972; children: Evan William, Warren Ripich. BA cum laude, Wittenberg U., 1968; MA, U. Ariz., 1970; JD cum laude, Cleve. State U., 1991. Bar: Ohio, 1991. Tchr. Cleve. Pub. Schs., 1969-74; children's libr. Cuyahoga County Pub. Libr., Cleve., 1976-92; clerk externship Ohio 8th Dist. Ct. Appeals, Cleve., 1991; staff atty. Legal Aid Soc. Lorain County Inc., Elyria, Ohio, 1992—; lectr. on Islamic law and constitutional history, Cleve., 1987—. Contbr. articles to profl. jours. Com. woman Rocky River (Ohio) United Meth. Ch., 1980—. Recipient award for excellence in constl. law Fed. Bar Assn., 1989, Am. Jurisprudence award in constl. law, 1989. Mem. ABA, AAUW, LWV, Ohio Bar Assn., Phi Alpha Theta. Avocations: painting, travel, volleyball.

KILE, DARRYL ANDREW, baseball player; b. Garden Grove, Calif., Dec. 2, 1968. Student, Chaffey Jr. Coll. With Houston Astros, 1987-97, Colo. Rockies, 1997—; mem. Nat. League All-Star Team, 1993. Office: Colo Rockies 2001 Blake St Denver CO 80205-2008*

KILE, KENDA JONES, educational consultant; b. Milford, Del., May 11, 1949; d. Kendal Taylor and Louisa Jane (Bennett) Jones; m. Vernon Richard Kile, Aug. 22, 1986 (div. June 1988); stepchildren: Daphne Lynne, Richard Edward. BS in Child Devel., U. Del., 1971, MEd in Elem. Reading, 1976, postgrad., 1998. Cert. reading supr., reading cons., reading specialist, learning disabilities specialist, tchr. kindergarden/nursery, special edn. tchr., Del. Kindergarten tchr. Colonial Sch. Dist., New Castle, Del., 1972-73, spl. edn. tchr., 1973-78, 1991, reading resource tchr., 1978-80, 1980-91, chpt. I coord., 1980—, elem. tchr., 1991-94, dist. lang. arts com., 1993-94, futures com., 1992-93; v.p. ednl. divsn. Get Real, Inc., L.A., 1994—; spkr. Ea. Regional Reading Conf., Wilmington, Del., 1990; facilitator, participant Assn. Computers in Edn./Computer Using Educators Leadership Inst. Del. Tech., Lewes, Del., 1990. Mem. Immanuel-on-the-Green Ch., New Castle, 1972—; vol. Army Hosp., Ft. Lee, Va., 1971-72; mem. Officer's Wives Chorus, Ft. Lee, 1971-72. Grantee Dept. Edn., 1989-91; fellow Divsn. Social Svcs., 1970. Mem. Internat. Reading Assn., Internat. Soc. Tech. in Edn., Coun. Exceptional Children, Nat. Assn. Tchrs. English, Reading Coun. No. Del., Diamond State Reading Assn., Del. State Assn. for Computers in Edn. (bd. dirs. 1989—). Democrat. Episcopalian. Avocations: needlework, reading, walking, metaphysics, water sports. Home and Office: 709 West St Laurel DE 19956-1927

KILEY, THOMAS, rehabilitation counselor; b. Mpls., Aug. 28, 1937; s. Gerald Sidney and Veronica (Roberts) K.; m. Jane Virginia Butler, Aug. 25, 1989; children: Martin, Truman, Tami, Brian. BA in English, UCLA, 1959; MS in Rehab. Counseling, San Francisco State U., 1989. Cert. rehab counselor, nat. and Hawaii. Former rsch. profl., businessman various S.E. Asian cos.; sr. social worker Episcopal Sanctuary, San Francisco, 1986-88; dir. social svcs. Hamilton Family Ctr., San Francisco, 1988-89; rehab. specialist Intracorp, Honolulu, 1989-91; pres. Heritage Counselling Svc., Honolulu, 1991—; pres. Hunter Employment Svcs., Yuma, Ariz., Brawley and Salinas, Calif., 1995—, Algo Enterprises, Yuma, 1998—. Mem. Am. Counseling Assn., Nat. Assn. Rehab. Profls. in Pvt. Sector, Am. Rehab. Counselors Assn. (profl.), Nat. Rehab. Assn., Rehab. Assn. Hawaii, Rotary, Phi Delta Kappa. Office: Heritage Counselling Svcs PO Box 893098 Mililani HI 96789-0098 also: 2450 S 4th Ave Ste 102A Yuma AZ 85364-8557

KILGARIN, KAREN, state official, public relations consultant; b. Omaha, Mar. 12, 1957; d. Bradford Michael and Verna Jane (Will) K.; m. Brian Charles Torrence, July 11, 1992; 1 child, Celeste Mattson. BA, U. Nebr., Kearney, 1979. Real estate assoc. Real Estate Assocs., Inc., Omaha, 1979-84; capital bur. chief Sta. KETV, Omaha, 1984-92; dir. comm. and publs. Nebr. Edn. Assn., Lincoln, 1995-98; dep. chief staff to gov., dir. pub. rels. State of Nebr., Lincoln, 1992-95, dir. dept. adminstrv. svcs., 1998—. Mem. Nebr. Senate, Omaha, 1980-84; trustee U. Nebr.-Kearney Found., 1992-95, mem. chancellor's adv. coun., 1995—; mem. exec. com. Nebr. Dem. Com., Lincoln, 1995—/. Recipient Oustanding Alumni award U. Nebr.-Kearney, 1993, Omaha South H.S., 1995, Wings award LWV, Omaha, 1995, President's award Nebr. Broadcasters Assn., 1995. Mem. NEA (pub. rels. coun. of states 1996-97), Soc. Profl. Journalisrts, State Edn. Editors. Presbyterian. Avocations: photography, collecting, politics. Office: Dept Adminstrv Svcs PO Box 94664 State Capitol Lincoln NE 68509-4664

KILGORE, DONALD GIBSON, JR., pathologist; b. Dallas, Nov. 21, 1927; s. Donald Gibson and Gladys (Watson) K.; m. Jean Upchurch Augur, Aug. 23, 1952; children: Michael Augur, Stephen Bassett, Phillip Arthur, Geoffrey Scott, Sharon Louise. Student, So. Meth. U., 1943-45, MD, 1949. Diplomate Am. Bd. Pathology, Am. Bd. Dermatopathology, Am. Bd. Blood Banking. Notary Pub. Intern Parkland Meml. Hosp., Dallas, 1949-50; resident in pathology Charity Hosp. La., New Orleans, 1950-54, asst. pathologist, 1952-54; pathologist Greenville (S.C.) Hosp. System, 1956—, dir. labs., 1985—; dir. labs. Greenville Meml. Hosp., 1972—; cons. pathologist St. Francis Hosp., Shriners Hosp., Greenville, Easley Baptist. Hosp.; vis. lectr. Clemson U., 1963—; asst. prof. pathology Med. U. S.C., 1968—; pres. Pathology Assocs. of Greenville, 1983—. Mem. bd. govs. S.C. Patient Compensation Fund, 1977—. Recipient Disting. Svc. award S.C. Hosp. Assn., 1976; awarded Order of The Palmetto by S.C. Gov. David M. Beasley, 1996. Fellow Coll. Am. Pathologists (life, assemblyman S.C. 1968-71), Am. Soc. Clin. Pathologists (councilor S.C. 1959-62), Am. Soc. Dermatopathology; mem. Am. Assn. Blood Banks (life, adv. coun. 1962-67, insp. committeeman Southeast dist. 1965—), AMA (ho. of dels. 1978-94), So. Med. Assn., S.C. Med. Assn., (exec. coun. 1969-76, 1978-94, pres. 1974-75; A.H. Robins award for Outstanding Cmty. Svc. 1985), Am. Soc. Cytology, Am. Coll. Nuc. Medicine, Nat. Assn. Med. Examiners, S.C. Inst. Med. Edn. and Rsch. (pres. 1974-80), S.C. Soc. Pathologists (pres. 1969-72), Richard III Soc. (co-chmn. Am. 1966-75), Am. Numis. Soc. (life), Soc. Ancient Numismatics (life), Am. Numis. Assn. (life), Blue Ridge Numis. Assn. (life), Royal Numis. Soc. (life), S.C. Numis. Assn. (life), Mensa (life), S.C. Congress Parents and Tchrs. (life), Greenville County Dental Soc. (hon. life), Greater Greenville C. of C. (pres. ednl. task force, 1965-70, elected trustee sch. dist. of Greenville County 1970-90), Greenville County Hist. Soc. (life), Hist. Greenville Found. (exec. com. 1994—, pres. 1998—), Preservation Soc. of Charleston (life), S.C. Hist. Soc. (life), Tex. State Hist. Assn. (life), Southwest Railroad Historical Soc., Thomas Wolfe Soc. (life), Medieval Acad. of Am. (life), Archeol. Inst. Am. (life), Brookgreen Gardens Found. (life), Friends of Tewkesbury Abbey (life), Canterbury Cathedral Trust in Am. (life), Assn. Friends of Lincoln Cathedral (life), U.S. Power Squadron, Confrerie des Chevaliers du Tastevin (chevalier Atlanta chpt.), Soc. Med. Friends of Wine, Wine Acad. Am. (life), Soc. Wine Educators, Les Amis du Vin (life), Confrerie de la Chaine des Rotisseurs (bailli and echanson de L'Ordre Mondial Greenville chpt.), Confrerie de Les Grapilleurs du Beaujolais (Chevalier), Epicurean Assn. of Am. (selection com.), Clan MacDuff Soc. Am. (life, exec. coun. 1980—), St. Andrews Soc. Upper S.C. (bd. govs. 1991-93), So. Meth. U. Alumni Assn. (life), Highland Park H.S. Alumni Assn. (life), Phi Eta Sigma, Phi Chi. Democrat. Presbyterian (ruling elder 1969—). Clubs: Commerce (life), Poinsett (life), Torch (pres. 1964-65), Greenville Country (life), Thirty-Nine (pres. 1981-82), Chandon. Lodge: Rotary (Paul Harris fellow 1988). Home: 129 Rockingham Rd Greenville SC 29607-3620 Office: 8 Memorial Medical Ct Greenville SC 29605-4449

KILGORE, EDWIN CARROLL, retired government official, consultant; b. Coeburn, Va., Jan. 24, 1923; s. Cecil Abram and Elizabeth Delle (Horne) K.; m. Ann Hitch, Dec. 30, 1944; children: Ashby Caroline, Elizabeth Cato. BS in Mech. Engring, Va. Inst. Poly., 1944; grad., Fed. Exec. Inst., 1969. With NASA (and predecessor), 1944-81; dep. assoc. adminstr. ops. Langley (Va.) Rsch. Ctr., 1975-76, dir. mgmt. ops., 1976-79, assoc. adminstr. mgmt. ops., 1979-81; cons. to NASA Washington, 1981—. Pres. Old Dominion U. Rsch. Found., Va. Air and Space Ctr. Recipient Outstanding Leadership award NASA, Disting. Svc. medal, Apollo Spl. Achievement award, Solid Propellant Spl. Achievement award, Roger Jones award Am. U. Va., State Sr. Tennis Champion, 1993, 94. Mem. AIAA, Pi Tau Sigma, Omicron Delta Kappa. Methodist. Club: Hampton Kiwanis (pres. 1969). Office: Acad Pub Admin Washington DC 20005

KILGORE, EUGENE STERLING, JR., surgeon; b. San Francisco, Feb. 3, 1920; s. Eugene Sterling and Mary (Kirkpatrick) K.; m. Marilynn Wines; children: Eugene Sterling, Marilynn Ann. *Son Eugene Sterling Kilgore III is the country's foremost authority on dude ranch vacations as a sure way to enjoy the beauty of mother nature and "unwind" from stress. The 5th edition of "Ranch Vacations" just published. Daughter Bee Kilgore was a superb recovery room nurse at UCSF for over 15 years, but now is renowned for organizing in every detail to perfection industrial, professional, and social meetings of any and all sizes of participants.* BS, U. Calif., Berkeley, 1941; MD, U. Calif., San Francisco, 1949. Intern in medicine Harvard service Boston City Hosp., 1949-50; intern in surgery Roosevelt Hosp., N.Y.C., 1950-51; resident gen. surgery, reconstructive hand surgery Roosevelt Hosp., 1951-55; practice medicine specializing in reconstructive hand surgery San Francisco, 1955—; asso. clin. prof. surgery U. Calif.-San Francisco, 1955-75, clin. prof., 1975-91, prof. emeritus, 1991—; chief hand surgery dept. surgery U. Calif. Hosp., also San Francisco Gen. Hosp., 1965-91; chief hand service Ft. Miley Vets. Hosp., San Francisco, 1965-91, Martinez (Calif.) Vets. Hosp., 1970-91, Livermore (Calif.) Vets. Hosp., 1965-70; chief hand service plastic surgery tng. service St. Francis Meml. Hosp., 1965-91, chief of surgery, 1979—, chief surgery emeritus, 1984—; cons. hand surgery numerous pvt. hosps., San Francisco, 1955—. Author numerous publs. in field. Served to lt. col., inf. AUS, 1941-45. Decorated Bronze Star; recipient Gold Headed Cane, AOA medal; Kaiser award for excellence in teaching U. Calif.-San Francisco Sch. Medicine, 1976, Charlotte Baer Meml. Clin. Faculty award U. Calif., 1993, Alumnus of Yr. award U. Calif. Med. Sch., 1998. Mem. AMA, ACS, Am. Assn. Surgery of Trauma, Am. Trauma Soc., Am. Soc. Surgery of Hand, Carribean Hand Soc., San Francisco Surg. Soc. (pres. 1979-80), Pacific Coast Surg. Assn., City Club. Clubs: Rotary; Bohemian (San Francisco). Office: 1199 Bush St Ste 590 San Francisco CA 94109-5976 *The road to success lies in meeting responsibility with an open, inquisitive mind and hard work, tempered with humility, kindness, time for family, for play, for the arts as well as a good laugh. The lasting measure of success is how much remains after you have gone that continues to be of value to others.**

KILGORE, J. DONALD, coroner; b. Columbus, Ga., June 14, 1930. DMS, Gupton-Jones Mortuary Coll., Nashville, 1952. Owner Kilgore Mortuary, Columbus, Ga., 1970s; coroner City of Columbus, 1977—. Chmn. Tax Assessors Bd., Columbus; sec. Med. Ctr. Hosp., Columbus; pres. East Columbus Boys Club, Heart Assn., Columbus, Sertoma, Pop Warner Football, all of Columbus, New Car Dealers Assn., Walter Richards Jr. H. PTA, Imported Cars, Inc., others; v.p., campaign dir. March of Dimes, Columbus; v.p. mental health bd., Columbus, others. Named Man of Yr., Boys Club, 1977-78. Mem. Ga. Coroner's Assn. (bd. dirs. 1977—), Masons (lt. col. Lodge 760 F&AM, State og Ga.). Office: Office of the Coroner 510 10th St Columbus GA 31902-1866*

KILGORE, JANICE KAY, musician, educator; b. Dallas, July 6, 1955; d. Jean Kendall and Dorothy Helen (King) K. Student, Oral Roberts U., 1973-76; AA, Mountain View Coll., 1979; MusB, U. North Tex., 1983, M in

Mus. Edn., 1990, doctoral studies in music performance. Cert. music tchr., Tex. Tchr. aide ESL Dallas Pub. Schs., 1979, substitute tchr., 1979-83, class piano tchr., 1983-84, choir dir./class piano instr., 1988-90, orch. tchr., 1992—; owner TNET, LLC (Telecom. Network Engring. Techs.), 1995—; asst. dir. Jazz Singers, Oral Roberts U., Tulsa, 1975-76; music dir., vocalist, keyboardist, booking agent, violist Janal, High Soc., Dallas Woodwind Ensemble Imperial String Quartet, Imperial Brass Ensemble, 1978—; music instr. Project Upward Bound, Denton, Tex., 1981; tech. Waxahachie (Tex.) Ind. Sch. Dist., 1990-92, choir dir., coord. dept. voice, orch. tchr., 1992-96; class keyboard instr. Baldwin Family Music, Dallas, 1987-89; instr. music North Lake Coll., Irving, Tex., 1990—, dir. Jazz Singers; creator, dir. numerous outdoor concerts; owner S.W. Music Enterprises. Author: British English to American English Dictionary, 1994; composer (symphonic poem) Scottish Suite, 1977, (choral work) The Wisemen, 1990; contbr. articles to mags. dir. Urbandale Christian Ch., Dallas, 1977-79, Centenary United Meth. Ch., Dallas, 1984-85, First United Meth. Ch., Midlothian, Tex., 1985-87, St. Luke United Meth. Ch., Dallas, 1989-90, First United Meth. Ch., Waxahachie, 1990-93, Trinity United Meth. Ch., Duncanville, Tex., 1993-94, Tyler St. United Meth. Ch., Dallas. Recipient Missionary Svc. award United Meth. Women, 1986. Mem. Tex. Music Educators Assn. (presenter 1994), Tex. Choral Dir. Assn., Tex. Orch. Dirs. Assn., Dallas Music Educators Assn., Denton Bach Soc., Wichita Falls Symphony Orchestra, Sherman Symphony Orchestra, Kappa Delta Pi, Pi Kappa Lambda. Republican. Avocations: interior decorating, Tae Kwon Do (greenbelt). Home: 317 Oak Meadow Ln Cedar Hill TX 75104-3283

KILGORE, JOE EVERETT, JR., army officer; b. Chattanooga, Dec. 11, 1954; s. Joe Everett and Jewell Yvonne (Nunley) K.; m. Mary Nijhuis, Aug. 21, 1982. BA in Biology, U. Tenn., Chattanooga, 1976; MS in Systems Mgmt., U. So. Calif., 1980; MA in Internat. Rels., Salve Regina Coll., Newport, R.I., 1990; MS in Nat. Security, U.S. Naval War Coll., Newport, 1990; stueent, Army War Coll., 1998-99. Cert. diving officer and civilian diving instr. Commd. 2d lt. U.S. Army, 1976, advanced through grades to lt. col., 1987; platoon leader 101st Airborne Div., Ft. Campbell, Ky., 1976-79; detachment comdr. 1st bn. 7th Spl. Forces Group, Ft. Bragg, N.C., 1980-83, co. comdr. hdqs., 1983-84; plans and ops. officer U.S. Army Western Command, Ft. Shafter, Hawaii, 1985-89; comdr. A Co., 2d bn. 1st Spl. Forces Group, Ft. Lewis, Wash., 1990-91, exec. officer 2d bn., 1991-92; commander 1st bn. 7th SFGA U.S. Army, 1995-97; chief spl. forces divsn., dir. tng. and doctrine John F. Kennedy Spl. Warfare Ctr. and Sch., 1997-98; exec. officer 1st Spl. Forces Group, 1992; inspector gen. USSOCOM, 1993; dir. tng. Down Under Divers, Waipahu, Hawaii, 1985-89; instr. scuba diving Aquidneck Island Divers, Salve Regina Coll., 1989-90. Contbr. articles to mil. and diving publs. Advisor Explorer Post 5101, Boy Scouts Am., Chattanooga, 1972-76; dir. Explorer Olymics, U. Tenn., 1975; instr. oxygen first aid Divers Alert Network, Chapel Hill, N.C., 1991; instr., disaster vol. ARC; spkr. jr. ROTC program, Oahu, Hawaii, 1985-89. Mem. NRA (life), Nat. Assn. Underwater Instrs. (life, instr.), Spl. Forces Assn. (life, membership com. 1991-92), Assn. U.S. Army, Res. Officers Assn., Am. Legon, N.Am. Fishing Club (life charter), Army War Coll. Alumni Assn. (life), N.Am. Hunting Club (life), Beta Beta Beta. Methodist. Avocations: boating, fishing, teaching scuba diving. Home: 554 Craig Rd Carlisle PA 17013-5104

KILGORE, JOHN EDWARD, JR., former petroleum company executive; b. Wichita Falls, Tex., Jan. 12, 1921; s. John Edward and Lillian (Amery) K.; m. Constance M. Brewer, May 1947; m. Emilie Smith Gilbreath, Nov. 1965; children: John Edward III, Constance Pritchett, Ralph Amery, Robert Monell, Alexander Gray; m. Annie deMontel Rassman, Oct. 25, 1986. AB, Amherst Coll., 1941; LLB, Harvard U., 1944; D in Bus, Adminstrn. (hon.), Husson Coll., 1995. Bar: Tex. 1948. Ptnr. Kilgore & Kilgore, Dallas, 1948-57, J.H. Whitney & Co., N.Y.C., 1957-68, John E. Kilgore & Co., 1968-83; founder, chmn. Cambridge Royalty Co., Petroleum Royalties Ireland Ltd., 1970-86; founder, mng. dir. Cambridge Petroleum Royalties Ltd., 1972-80; bd. dirs. TATEX. Trustee German Marshall Fund of U.S., 1978-89, Husson Coll., 1997—. With USNR, 1942-45. Mem. Union Club (N.Y.C.), Phi Beta Kappa. Office: PO Box 127 Surry ME 04684-0127

KILGORE, L(EROY) WILSON, minister; b. Elmira, N.Y., Feb. 25, 1917; s. Roy Dunning and Bertha Pearl (Bush) K.; m. Ursula Dunbar, June 27, 1940 (wid. 1960); children: Keith, Sharon, Paul, Debra; m. Lois Morse Bell, Feb. 14, 1961; children: Kristie, Richard III, Nancy, Douglas, Cynthia. BA, Colgate U., 1939; MDiv, Colgate-Rochester Div. Sch., 1942; DD (hon.), Colgate U., 1964. Ordained to ministry Presbyn. Ch., 1942. Pastor 1st Presbyn. Ch., Hartford, Conn., 1943-53; sr. pastor Lakewood Presbyn. Ch., Cleve., 1953-64, Cherry Hill Presbyn. Ch., Dearborn, Mich., 1964-72, Valley Presbyn. Ch., Scottsdale, Ariz., 1972-86; interim minister 3d Presbyn. Ch., Rochester, N.Y., 1987-88, 1st Presbyn. Ch., Tulsa, 1990-91, Kirk in the Hills Presbyn. Ch., Bloomfield Hills, Mich., 1995-96; trustee San Francisco Theol. Seminary, San Anselmo, Calif., 1978-90; mem. support agy. Presbyn. Ch. USA, 1978-86; chmn. com. on communication Presbyn. Ch. USA, 1980-82; moderator Grand Canyon Presbytery, 1986-87. Author: What a Way to Live, 1977, When the River Runs Backward 1983, 2d edit. 1989. Mem. Acad. of Parish Clergy, 1976—; trustee, pres. Westminster Village Retirement Ctr., Scottsdale, Ariz., 1990-95. Mem. Rotary. E-mail: lkresort@aol.com. Home and Office: 7800 N 65th St Paradise Valley AZ 85253

KILGORE, MEREDITH L., nurse; b. Shrevesport, La., Aug. 26, 1954; d. Robert G. and Elizabeth G. Kilgore. ASN, U. Hawaii, 1982, BA, 1992; MSPH, U. Ala., 1997; postgrad., RAND Grad. Sch., 1998—. RN. Pvt. practice musician, 1972-80; unit clk. Queen's Med. Ctr., Honolulu, 1979-83; RN Kaiser Permanente, Honolulu, 1983-94; RN, rsch. assoc. U. Ala., Birmingham, 1994-98. Contbr. articles to profl. jours. Mem. AAAS, AACN, Soc. Med. Decision Making. E-mail: kilgore@rand.org. Fax: 310-393-0411. Office: RAND Grad Sch 1700 Main St Santa Monica CA 90407-2138

KILGORE, RANDALL FREEMAN, health information services administrator; b. Birmingham, Ala., June 10, 1955; s. Isaac D.L. and Daisy Jewell (Bray) K. Student, Samford U., Birmingham, 1973-75; BS in Med. Record Adminstrn. with honors, U. Ala., 1978; postgraduate in adult edn., U. Mo., Columbia, 1980—; MRE cum laude, Midwest Bapt. Theol. Sem., Kansas City, Mo., 1991. Registered Am. Health Info. Mgmt. Assn. Asst. dir. health info. mgmt. program Stephens Coll., Columbia, Mo., 1980-82; dir. quality/risk mgmt. svcs. Boone Hosp. Ctr., Columbia, 1982-87; risk mgr. univ. hosp. U. Mo. Hosp. and Clinics, Columbia, 1987-89; coord. mktg. and adminstrv. svcs. McQuilkin, Keeling-Wallace Counseling Assocs., Inc., Columbia, 1991; dir. health info. svcs. Behavioral Health Sys. of Columbia, Kansas City, 1991—; spkr., conf. leader Univ. Hosp. Consortium, 1989, chmn. spl. com. on integration of quality assurance and risk mgmt., 1988-89; cons. Health Info. Svcs. to Charter Ridge Behavioral Health Svcs., Lexington, Ky., 1997, JCAHO Triennial Survey Preparation For Anesthesia, 1997. Mem. historic sites com. Boone County (Mo.) Hist. Soc.; com. mem. Boone County Commn. Spl. Task Force for preservation of historic and scenic roads; bd. dirs. HHosp. Industry Data Inst., 1985-88; judge Miss Columbia Pageant, 1993. Charles M. Hudson Meml. scholar, 1989, Rotary Internat. graduate fellow, 1979-80, Brandon scholar, 1990-91. Mem. Am. Health Info. Mgmt. Assn., Mo. Med. Record Assn. (nominating com., adhoc scholarship com., dir. exec. com. 1983-84, pres.-elect 1984-85), Nat. Alumni Soc. U. Ala. at Birmingham (charter, bd. dirs.), Mo. Symphony Soc., Omicron Delta Kappa. Democratic. Methodist. Home: 201 N Roby Farm Rd Rocheport MO 65279-9315 Office: Charter Behav Health Sys 200 Portland St Columbia MO 65201-6525

KILGOUR, DAVID, Canadian member of parliament; b. Winnipeg, Man., Can., Feb. 18, 1941; s. David Eckford and Mary Sophia (Russell) K.; m. Laura Mae Scott, June 22, 1974; children: Margot, Eileen, David, Hilary. Bar: B.C., 1967, Man. 1970, Alta. 1972. Candidate House of Commons, 1968, mem., 1979—; apptd. parliament sec. to govt. house leader, 1979, opposition critic for crime prevention, 1981-83, dep. critic external affairs, 1983-84, apptd. parliament sec. to min. external rels., 1984, parliament sec. to min. Indian affairs and no. devel., 1985, parliament sec. to min. transport, 1986; asst. city prosecutor Vancouver, B.C., Can., 1967-68; adv. counsel Dept. Justice, Ottawa, 1968-69; chief crown atty. Dauphin Judicial Dist., Man., 1971-72; a sr. agt. Alta. Gen. and Constl. Adv., 1972-79; dep. speaker, chmn. coms. whole house House of Commons, Ottawa, Ont., Can., 1994-97; sec. state Latin America & Africa, 1997—. Author: Uneasy Patriots: Western Canadians in Confederation, 1988, Inside Outer Canada, 1990, Betrayal: The Spy Canada Abandoned, 1994. Mem. Can. Bar Assn. Office: House of Commons, Rm 163 East Block, Ottawa, ON Canada K1A 0A6*

KILGOUR, FREDERICK GRIDLEY, librarian, educator; b. Springfield, Mass., Jan. 6, 1914; s. Edward Francis and Lillian Bess (Piper) K.; m. Eleanor Margaret Beach, Sept. 3, 1940; children: Christopher Beach, Martha, Alison, Meredith. AB, Harvard U., 1935; student, Columbia Sch. Library Service, summers 1939-41; LLD (hon.), Marietta Coll., 1980, Coll. of Wooster, 1981; DHL (hon.), Ohio State U., 1980, Denison U., 1983, U. Mo., Kansas City, 1989. Staff Harvard Coll. Library, 1935-42, OSS, 1942-45; dep. dir. office of intelligence collection and dissemination U.S. Dept. State, 1946-48; librarian Yale Med. Library, 1948-65; asso. librarian for research and devel. Yale U. Library, 1965-67; mng. editor Yale Jour. Biology and Medicine, 1949-65; lectr. in history of sci. Yale U., 1950-59, lectr. history of tech., 1961-67; fellow Davenport Coll., 1950-67; pres., exec. dir. Online Computer Library Ctr., OCLC, Inc., 1967-80, vice chmn. bd. trustees Online Computer Library Ctr., 1981-83; founder trustee Online Computer Libr. Ctr., 1984—; Disting. rsch. prof. U. N.C., Chapel Hill, 1990—. Author: Library of the Medical Institution of Yale College and Its Catalogue of 1865, 1960, The Library and Information Science CumIndex, 1975, The Evolution of the Book, 1998; co-author: Engineering in History, 1956, 90; author: Collected Papers, 2 vols., 1984; editor: Book of Bodily Exercises, 1960, Jour. Library Automation, 1968-71; contbr. to scholarly jours. Served as lt. (j.g.) USNR, 1943-45, overseas duty. Decorated Legion of Merit; recipient Margaret Mann citation in cataloging and classification, 1974, Melvil Dewey medal, 1978; Acad./Research Librarian of Year, 1979; Library Info. Tech. award, 1979, numerous others. Mem. ALA, Am. Soc. Info. Sci. (Merit award 1979), Soc. for History of Tech. Club: Cosmos (Washington). Home: 207 Carolina Meadows Villa Chapel Hill NC 27514-8500

KILGUSS, ELSIE SCHAICH, artist, gallery owner; b. Manhattan, N.Y., Aug. 4. BS in Advt., Mktg., Bryant Coll.; studied with Charles Sovek, studied with Betty Cappelli, 1968, studied with Henry Hensche, Lois Griffel; grad., R.I. Sch. Design; student, Cape Sch. Art. With Horton, Church & Goff, Advt. Agy., Providence; represented by Gallery at Chatham, Mass., 1990—; owner, instr. Studio Zwei, Wickford, R.I., 1991—. One-woman shows include Studio Zwei, Wickford, 1991—, Alfred Butler & Co., North Kingstown, 1992, Fleet Bank, North Kingstown, 1992, R.I. State House, Providence, 1993, Dodge House Gallery, Providence, 1999; two-person shows include Providence Art Club, 1991, 93, 95, 97, 98; group exhibits include Warwick (R.I.) Art Mus., 1987, 89, 91, 97, 98, Helme House, Kingston R.I., 1990, 93, 95, 97, Woods-Gerry Gallery, Providence, 1991, Wickford Art Assn. Gallery, North Kingstown, 1991, 93, 95, 97, 99, R.I. Sch. Design Mus., Providence, 1992, 94, Spring Bull Gallery, Newport, R.I., 1993, Newport Art Mus., 1990, 93, 95, 97, 99, R.I. Watercolor Soc., Pawtucket, 1993, 95, 97; represented in permanent collections Alfred Butler & Co., Carribean Villas, others; catalog covers Providence Mag., R.I. Sch. Design, Cape Cod Mag., North Kingstown Villager. Mem. Providence Art Club, R.I. Watercolor Soc., Wickford Art Assn., South County Art Assn., Newport Artist's Guild, Creative Arts Ctr., Copley Soc. (Boston), Neport Mus., Attleboro Mus., RISD Mus., Boston Mus. Fine Arts, Warwick Mus., Nat. Mus. Women in Arts, North Kingstown C. of C. E-mail: www.studiozweigallery.com. Studio: Studio Zwei Gallery 2 Main St North Kingstown RI 02852-5016

KILIAN, MICHAEL DAVID, journalist, columnist, writer; b. Toledo, July 16, 1939; s. D. Frederick and Laura Casmere (Dulski) K.; m. Pamela H. Reeves, Oct. 17, 1970; children: Eric, Colin. Student, New Sch. for Social Rsch., N.Y.C., 1957-58, U. Md., 1964. Writer Sta. KNTV, San Jose, Calif., 1960-63; reporter City News Bur., Chgo., 1965-66; reporter, asst. polit. editor Chgo. Tribune, 1966-71, editl. writer, 1971-86, editl. page columnist, 1971-86, Washington columnist, corr., cultural commentator, 1986—; commentator Sta. WBBM, CBS, 1973-82, Sta. WTTW-TV, 1975-78, Nat. Pub. Radio, 1978-79; host. "DC Jour.: CLTV News, 1995—; correspondent Roy Leonard Show, WGN, 1996-99; commentator, commentary CBC, 1996—. Author: Who Runs Chicago?, 1979, The Valkyrie Project, 1981, Who Runs Washington?, 1982, Northern Exposure, 1983, Blood of the Czars, 1984, Heavy Losses, 1985, By Order of the President, 1986, Dance on a Sinking Ship, 1988, Looker, 1991, The Last Virginia Gentleman, 1992, The Big Score, 1993, Bad Girl Blues, 1994, Postcard From Hell, 1995, Major Washington, 1998, Murder at Manassas, 1999, (comic strip) Dick Tracy, 1993—. Bd. dirs. Fund for Animals, 1976—; capt. CAP, 1976—. With U.S. Army, 1963-65. Recipient Humor Writing award UPI, 1971. Mem. White House Corrs. Assn., English Speaking Union (life), Langley Swim and Tennis Club, The Woods Club. Presbyterian. Office: Chgo Tribune 1325 G St NW Washington DC 20005-3104

KILIAN, THOMAS RANDOLPH, rural economic developer, consultant; b. Vilas, S.D., Mar. 23, 1924; s. Ward Van and Mabel Amanda (Peterson) K.; m. Lorna Jean Pearson, Aug. 27, 1949; children: James, Peter, Mary, Susan. BA, Augustana Coll., 1949; MS, Boston U., 1950; PhD, Mich. State U., 1968; student, Harvard U., 1971, 79. Dir. pub. rels. Waldorf Coll., Forest City, Iowa, 1950-52; dir. pub. rels. Augustana Coll., Sioux Falls, S.D., 1952-61, v.p. development, 1961-73, exec. v.p., 1975-82; sec. S.D. Dept. Edn./Cultural Affairs, Pierre, S.D., 1973-75; pres. N. Ctrl. Univ. Ctr., Sioux Falls, S.D., 1975-85, N. Ctrl. Univ. Ctr. C.C., Sioux Falls, S.D., 1977-85; prin. EOS Futures Group, Sioux Falls, S.D., 1985-87; dir. Rural Initiative Ctr., Sioux Falls, S.D., 1987—. Author: (book) Power Constructs, 1969, Your Way, 1996; contbr. articles to profl. jours. Pres. S.D. Heritage Fund, Pierre, 1983-95, S.D. State Hist. Soc., Pierre, 1987—, Minnehaha Century Fund, Sioux Falls, 1990—; chmn. S.D. Rev. Bd. Hist. Preservation Bd., Sioux Falls, 1992-95, Ctr. for Western Studies, Sioux Falls, 1970-95, 96—; past chmn. S.D. Pub. TV Bd., Pierre. Mem. S.D. Future Soc. (S.D. coord.). Democrat. Lutheran. Avocations: natural history, local history, archaeology, future studies. Home: 2700 S Jefferson Ave Sioux Falls SD 57105-4416 Office: Rural Initiative Ctr 1320 S Minnesota Ave Ste 210 Sioux Falls SD 57105-0657

KILIANY, MARY CATHERINE, program director, communications educator; b. Aliquippa, Pa., Mar. 28, 1964; d. Robert William and Marilyn Patricia Gray; m. Regis Paul Kiliany Jr., Sept. 14, 1996. BA in English, Pa. State U., 1986; MS in Instrnl. Leadership, Robert Morris Coll., 1996. Profl. peer tutor C.C. Beaver County, Monaca, Pa., 1989-94; instr. developmental English C.C. Beaver County, Monaca, 1990-95, supr. evening GED program, 1995-97; coord. comm. skills and tutoring ctr. Robert Morris Coll., Moon Twp., Pa., 1994—; instr. comm. skills Robert Morris Coll., Moon Twp., 1997—; advisor C.C. Challengers, Monaca, 1990-94; rschr. Robert Morris Coll., Moon Twp., 1995-96. Contbr. articles to profl. jours. Vol. team tchr. for essay writing contest Aliquippa H.S., 1995. Mem. ASCD, Pa. Assn. Devel. Educators, Golden Key. Democrat. Roman Catholic. Avocations: reading, writing, cooking, decorating. E-mail: graym@robert-morris.edu. Fax: 412-262-8600. Home: 324 Pine St Ambridge PA 15003 Office: Robert Morris Coll 881 Narrows Run Rd Moon Township PA 15108

KILKEARY, KEVIN P., hospitality executive. Pres., COO Crossroads Hospitality Co., LLC, Pitts. Office: Crossroads Hospitality Co LLC Foster Plaza Ten 680 Anderson Dr Pittsburgh PA 15220

KILKELLY, BRIAN HOLTEN, lighting company executive; b. East Orange, N.J., June 20, 1943; s. Daniel Joeseph and Mary Lorretta (Brown) K.; m. Judith Louise Kroger, May 21, 1966; children: Christopher, James. BS in Mktg., Fairleigh Dickinson U., 1968; MBA, Ga. State U., 1986. Sales rep. Thomas Lighting Div., Northern, N.J., 1965-68; mktg. svcs. Globe Inc., Hazelton, Pa., 1968-70; manpower devel./product mgr. Lithonia Lighting Div., Conyers, Ga., 1970-75; nat. market devel./southeastern mgr. Cooper Lighting Div., Atlanta, 1975-88; prin. Kilkelly Mgmt. Cons. Group, Conyers, 1988-89; partner Landmark Commercial & Investment Real Estate Inc., Conyers, 1988-95; CEO Peachtree Lighting Inc., Covington, Ga., 1988—; Bd. dirs. Tech Able Handicapped Tech. Access.; guest lectr. bus. sch. Ga. State U.; mentor GSU CMBA program; mktg. sponsor Olympic Exec. Vols., 1996. Contbr. articles to profl. jours. Active The Planning Forum, Vision 2020 Region Bd.; vol. Olympics, Atlanta, 1996; mem. permanent diaconate formation program Roman Cath. Diocese of Atlanta; lay witness renewal team, facilitator Renew 2000. With USNR, 1961-67. Mem. Nat. Assn. Realtors (Ga. chpt., comml. coun., strategic planning com.), Nat. Fire Protection Assn. (joint 101/70 com.), Illuminating Engring. Soc. (chmn. tech. com. 1975—), Japan Am. Soc., Ga. Assn. Real Estate Exchangers, KC (grand knight, 1st degree team, chmn. com., Cert. of Merit 1990), EMBA Alumni Assn. (steering com., fund raising). Republican. Roman Catholic. Avocations: walking, U.G.A. football group, teaching, youth work, church work. Home: 2377 Country Club Dr SE Conyers GA 30013-5101

KILKELLY, MARJORIE LEE, state legislator, community development official; b. Hartford, Conn., Dec. 1, 1954; d. Bruce Hamilton and Corlys Lucille (Lux) Brewer; children: Jeffrey Jr. (dec.), Robert, Sarah A.E. BS in Human Svcs., N.H. Coll., 1986, MS in Cmty. Econ. Devel., 1986; postgrad., Harvard U., 1997. Asst. to dir. Lincoln County Summer Youth Employment Program, Wiscasset, Maine, 1978; coordinator Community Food & Nutrition Program Coastal Enterprises, Inc., Wiscasset, 1978-79, Coastal Econ. Devel. Corp., Wiscasset, 1979-80; dir. Head Start Program Coastal Econ. Devel. Corp., Bath, Maine, 1980-84; asst. instr. N.H. Coll., Manchester, 1985-86; dir. Jr. Tots Wiscasset Recreation Program, 1985-88; dir. food services Boothbay Sch. Dept., Boothbay Harbor, Maine, 1985-88; owner Hurricane Hill Catering Co., Wiscasset, 1989—; mem. Maine Ho. of Reps., Augusta, 1986-96; house chair com. on agr., forestry and conservation, 1995-96; co-chmn. coastal caucus Maine Ho. of Reps., Augusta, spkr. pro tem, 1996—, candidate for speaker of house, 1992, candidate for house majority whip, 1994, chmn. agr., forestry and conservation com., 1995—; candidate Maine Senate, 1996; state senator, chmn. agriculture conservation and forestry com., island fish and wildlife com. State of Maine, 1996-98, chmn. Nat. Conf. State Legislators agr. com., 1997—; mem. Harvard state and local govt. ofcls. program Kennedy Sch. Govt., 1997—; cmty. devel. dir. Island Inst., Rockland, Maine, 1997—; community devel. dir. Island Inst., Rockland, ME, 1997—; reas. Coastal Enterprises, Inc., Rundlet Block, Wis., 1981-90; rep. to Internat. Conf. on Econ. Devel., New Delhi, 1983—; 3d Selectman Town of Wiscasset, 1993-97. Mem. planning com. Blaine House Conf. on Families, 1979-80; active Maine Human Svcs. Coun. Sta. 23, Augusta, 1980-88; Sunday sch. tchr., lectr. St. Philips Episcopal Ch., Wiscasset, 1984-85, chmn. coord. com. food bank, 1986-88, sr. warden, 1995-96; chmn. Wis. Dem. Com., 1986; nat. chmn. Schs. S.O.S. Nat. Hunger Awareness Program, Denver, 1986; mem. exec. com. Maine Rural Devel. Coun., 1995—; spkr. pro tempere 117th Legislature, 1996; candidate Main State Senate Dist. 16, 1996; chair comm. adv. panel on decommissioning Maine Yankee Nuclear Plant, 1997, mem. legis. select com.; bd. dirs. Miles Health Care, Damanscotta, Mass., 1996—, Mid Coast United Way; chmn. Citizens Adv. Panel on Decommissioning Maine Yankee Atomic Power Plant, 1997—. New England Rural fellow, Coun. State Govts. Toll fellow, Flemming fellow, 1999; grantee Maine Welfare Edn. Employment Tng. Program, 1983; Eisenhower Exch. fellowship, 1999. Mem. Bus. and Profl. Women (Maine Young Career Woman award 1989), Huntoon Hill Grange Club, Lincoln County Pomona Grange Club, Sportsmans Alliance Club of Maine, Am. Coun. Young Polit. Leaders, United Way of Mid Coast Maine (bd. mem.), Miles Hlth. Care Bd., U. Maine Bd. of Agriculture. Democrat. Episcopalian. Clubs: Maine Farm Bur., Maine State Grange. Avocations: horseback riding, gourmet cooking, fishing. Home: PO Box 180 W Alna Rd Wiscasset ME 04578-0180 Office: Maine Ho Reps State Capitol Augusta ME 04333

KILL, LAWRENCE, lawyer; b. N.Y.C., Apr. 11, 1935; s. Bernard and Dora (Laskin) K.; m. Karyl Klein, Oct. 21, 1962; children: Debra, Andrea, Brenda. BBA, CCNY, 1957; LLB cum laude, Fordham U., 1960. Bar: N.Y. 1961. Trial atty. antitrust div. U.S. Dept. Justice, Washington, 1961-66; assoc. Chadbourne & Parke, N.Y.C., 1966-72; ptnr. Anderson Kill & Olick PC, N.Y.C., 1972—. Editor-in-chief: Fordham Law Rev, 1959-60. Served with U.S. Army, 1960-61. Mem. Assn. Bar City N.Y., ABA, N.Y. State Bar assn. Home: 29 Queens Ln New Hyde Park NY 11040-1213 Office: Anderson Kill & Olick PC Ste 383 1251 Avenue Of The Americas Fl C31 New York NY 10020-1182

KILLACKEY, DOROTHY HELEN, real estate professional, former educator; b. Pitts., Mar. 29, 1927; d. Edward G. and Dorothy Marie (Krauss) Buschow; m. Feb. 5, 1949 (div. Sept. 1985); children: Thomas, Maureen, Nancy, Edward. BA, Columbia U., 1948; MS, Western Conn. State U., Danbury, 1971; 6th Yr. Profl. Deg., Western Conn. State U., 1980. Elem. tchr. Brewster (N.Y.) Pub. Schs., 1965-89; tchr. title I summer sch. Govt. Title I, Brewster, 1973-80; from real estate salesman to broker Spectra Realty, Brewster, 1983—; ch. parochial bd. dirs. St. Lawrence O'Toole Ch., Brewster, 1974-76; pres. J.F. Kennedy Sch. Union, Brewster, 1975-77. Editor J.F. Kennedy Sch. Writing Anthology, 1982-89. Mem. choir, soloist St. Lawrence O'Toole Ch., Brewster, 1970-90; mem. Historic Preservation Com., Brewster, 1991-93; vol. RSVP Program Putnam County, 1998-99; biographer Putnam County Sr. Citizens. Nancy Barrelle scholar Western Conn. State U., 1979; named Putnam County Sr. Citizen of 1999, Putnam County Execs. Mem. Phi Delta Kappa, Delta Kappa Gamma. Avocations: reading, piano, gardening. Home: 401 Stonewall Ln Brewster NY 10509-6010

KILLAM, JILL MINERVINI, oil and gas company executive; b. Pitts., Sept. 6, 1954; d. Virginio Lucien and Helen Elizabeth (Safgren) Minervini; m. Clayton Henry Killam, June 4, 1973. AAS with high honors, Eastfield Jr. Coll., Mesquite, Tex., 1974; BBA with high honors, U. Tex., Arlington, 1985. CPA, Tex. Asst. to treas. CKB & Assocs., Dallas, 1985-89, v.p., chief acctg. officer, 1989-92; v.p., CFO Box Energy Corp. (formerly OKC Ltd. Partnership), Dallas, 1992-96; v.p. fin. and adminstrn. Fremont Energy L.P., Dallas, 1997—. Mem. AICPA (Elijah Watt Sells award 1985), Tex. State Bd. Pub. Accts. (lic., Spl. award for Outstanding Achievement 1986), Tex. Soc. CPAs (state and Dallas chpt.), Petroleum Accts. Soc. Dallas, Inst. Mgmt. Accts. Republican. Roman Catholic. Avocation: water skiing. Office: Fremont Energy LP 5956 Sherry Ln Ste 1310 Dallas TX 75225-6531

KILLE, JOHN WILLIAM, JR., toxicology and biomedical product consultant; b. Tampa, Fla., June 17, 1943; s. John William and Myrtle Kille; m. Elaine Anderson; children: Amy, Lindsey, Thomas; m. Camille Ragazzo, Sept. 22, 1991; 1 stepchild, Richard. AB, Lafayette Coll., 1965; MS, Villanova U., 1968; PhD, U. Va., 1972. Diplomate Am. Bd. Toxicology. NIH rsch. trainee Worcester Found. for Exptl. Biology, 1970-72; vis. rsch scientist Cambridge U., Eng., 1972-73; rsch. fellow Cambridge (Eng.) U., 1972-73; lectr., rschr. Northwestern U., Evanston, Ill., 1974-78; group leader for drug safety Ortho Pharm. Co. divsn. Johnson & Johnson, Raritan, N.J., 1978-88; assoc. dir. product safety and regulatory affairs McNeil Splty. Products Co. divsn. Johnson & Johnson, New Brunswick, N.J., 1988-93; sr. toxicologist Cantox, Inc., Bridgewater, N.J., 1994-96; prin. J.W. Kille Assocs., Stanton, N.J., 1996—; cons. to various pharm., food and biotech. cos., and legal firms, 1994-96, Johnson & Johnson, Emisphere Techs., Inst. for Diabetes Discovery, various other internat. projects in Can., Mex., Europe and Australia, 1996—; advisor Office Tech. Assessment, U.S. Congress, 1984. Contbr. articles to sci. jours. Chmn. Family Life Edn. Com., Bloomsbury, N.J., 1985-86. Rsch. fellow Lalor Found., 1972-73, WHO, 1972-73. Mem. Genetic Toxicology Assn., Inst. Food Technologists, Regulatory Affairs Profls. Soc., Soc. Toxicology (program com. Mid-Atlantic chpt. 1996—), Teratology Soc., Mid-Atlantic Reprodn. and Teratology Assn. (pres. 1986-87). Avocations: listening to music and singing in choral groups, camping, hunting, fishing, stained glass creations. Fax: 908-236-0921. E-mail: jwkille@blast.net. Office: PO Box 69 Stanton NJ 08885-0069

KILLE, WILLARD BRONSON, III, business executive; b. Upland, Pa., Aug. 9, 1946; s. Willard Bronson Jr. and Helen Muriel (Martin) K.; m. Gail Patricia Swed, Sept. 21, 1968 (div. June 1977); 1 child, Willard Bronson IV; m. Nancy Helen Croft, July 23, 1979 (div. 1997); children: Bart C., Megan Muriel. BA, U. S.D., 1968. Mgr. Edward D. Jones & Co., Sterling, Colo., 1974-77; stock broker Paine Webber, Inc., Salt Lake City, 1977-78, A.G. Edwards & Sons, Inc., Salt Lake City, 1978-80; v.p., mgr. Underwood Neuhaus, Inc., San Antonio, 1985-86; mng. ptnr. Hampton Heights TCP, San Antonio, 1988-91; CEO, pres. Entirety, Inc., Salt Lake City, 1986-92, bus. cons., 1992—; safety officer USAF, Enid, Okla., 1982-84; tax cons. Paine Webber, Salt Lake City, 1977-78; partnership coord. Entirety, Inc., San Antonio, 1986-90; ins. cons., 1992—; mgr. Utah br. Walnut St. Securities, Salt Lake City. Dist. chmn. Boy Scouts Am., San Antonio, 1990-92; mem. high coun. Ch. of Jesus Christ of Latter Day Saints, San Antonio,

1987-89, Enid, Okla., 1982-83, Sunday sch. tchr., San Antonio, 1985-87. Capt. USMC, 1968-73; maj. USAF, 1980-85. Mem. Internat. Assn. Fin. Planners (bd. dirs. 1990-92, v.p. 1990-91, pres. 1991-92), City Club of San Antonio, Nat. Assn. Securities Dealers (prin. 1986—), Tapatio Springs Country Club. Republican. Avocations: golf, hiking, snow skiing, flying. Home: 7785 S Dolphin Cir Salt Lake City UT 84121-5678 Office: Entirety Inc PO Box 900547 Sandy UT 84090-0547

KILLEBREW, ELLEN JANE (MRS. EDWARD S. GRAVES), cardiologist; b. Tiffin, Ohio, Oct. 8, 1937; d. Joseph Arthur and Stephanie (Beriont) K.; m. Edward S. Graves, Sept. 12, 1970. BS in Biology, Bucknell U., 1959; MD, N.J. Coll. Medicine, 1965. Diplomate in cardiovasc. disease Am. Bd. Internal Medicine. Intern U. Colo., 1965-66, resident, 1966-68; cardiology fellow Pacific Med. Ctr., San Francisco, 1968-70; dir. coronary care Permanent Med. Group, Richmond, Calif., 1970-83; asst. prof. U. Calif. Med. Ctr., San Francisco, 1970-83, assoc. prof., 1983-93; clin. prof. medicine U. Calif., San Francisco, 1992—, mem. admissions panel, 1998—; admissions panel joint med. program U. Calif. San Francisco/U. Calif. Berkeley, 1998—; export med. reviewer Calif. Med. Br., 1999. Contbr. chpt. to book. Recipient Physician's Recognition award continuing med. edn., Lowell Beal award excellence in tchg., Permante Med. Group/House Staff Assn., 1992; Robert C. Kirkwood Meml. scholar in cardiology, 1970. Fellow ACP, Am. Coll. Cardiology; mem. Fedn. Clin. Rsch., Am. Heart Assn. (rsch. chmn. Contra Costa chpt. 1975—, v.p. 1980, pres. chpt. 1981-82, chmn. CPR com. Alameda chpt. 1984, pres. Oakland Piedmont br. 1995—, bd. dirs. western affiliate). Home: 30 Redding Ct Belvedere Tiburon CA 94920-1318 Office: 280 W Macarthur Blvd Oakland CA 94611-5642

KILLEBREW, JAMES ROBERT, architectural engineering firm executive; b. Okmulgee, Okla., Dec. 10, 1918; s. Robert Herman and Edith (Tyler) K.; m. Emma Herrington, Feb. 24, 1989; 1 child by previous marriage, Laura Janice. BS in Archtl. Engring., U. Tex., 1948. Registered architect, Tex. registered profl. engr., Tex. Prin. James R. Killebrew, FAIA, PE, architect, cons. engr., Granbury, Tex.; sr. structural engr. DFW Internat. Airport, 1991—; sr. cons. architect engr. Yandell-Hiller, 1989-90, Dallas-Ft. Worth Airport/Am. Airlines; sr. structural engr. Dallas-Ft. Worth Internat. Airport Bd. Prin. archtl. works include Gen. Hosp. Plainview, Tex., Vernon (Tex.) Hosp., Vernon Geriatrics Psychiat. Hosp., Wichita Gen. Hosp., Gen. Hosp. Nocona (Tex.), Sci. Bldg., Phys. Edn. Bldg., Midwestern State U., Teenage Drug Addiction Center, Vernon, Fine Arts Bldg. at Midwestern State U., AC Spark Plug Ceramics Complex-Gen. Motors Corp., Parker Sq. Savs. and Loan, Union Sq., Four Story Savs. & Loan Bldg., Wichita Falls, Sprague Electric Co., Howmet Turbine, Wichita Clutch Corp., G.H. Foster Plant, Family YMCA, SW Nat. Bank Tower; coord. measuring machine for Gen. Motors-CPC plant, Arlington, Tex. Elder Christian Ch., 1979-81. Lt. comdr. USN, 1940-45, PTO; capt. Res. (ret.). Fellow AIA (pres. Wichita Falls chpt. 1966-67, 81); mem. Nat. Soc. Profl. Engrs., Tex. Soc. Profl. Engrs. (pres. N. Tex. chpt. 1960-61), Am. Soc. Archtl. Engrs. (charter mem.), ASHRAE, Wichita Falls C. of C. (chmn. various coms.), Navy League (pres. 1967-68), Fine Art Soc. Tex. (pres. 1970, chmn. bd. 1973). Mem. Christian Ch. Club: Rotary (pres. 1983-84). Achievements include inspection for expansion of terminals, multi-story parking facilities, aircraft rescue fire fighting training facility, hangar addition, FAA technical facility and five story parking garage, DFW runway 16/34 East UPS Hdqs., Terminal 3E-B code inspection, American Airlines new 3-EA terminal 5 story parking garage, new consol. rent-a-car parking facility, JK. Home: 1906 Mill Pond Dr Grapevine TX 76051-7038 *The practice of architecture requires the efforts of many talented professionals and personnel aspiring to be professionals. No longer does one man act as master builder (or designer). If I have attained a notable degree of success, it is due to the combined efforts through many years, of all the excellent associates with which I have been fortunate to know.*

KILLEBREW, ROBERT STERLING, JR., investment manager; b. Chattanooga, Tenn., Sept. 9, 1939; s. Robert Sterling and Margaret (Kruesi) K.; m. Norma Peden, Aug. 8, 1964; children: Robert S. III, Laura H., Margaret R. BA, Yale U., 1961; MBA, U. Pa., 1964. Cer: CFA. Mem. exec. com. Robert Garrett & Sons, Balt., 1965-74; mng. dir. Alex Brown & Sons, Inc., Balt., 1974—; bd. dirs., mem. exec. com. Brock Candy Co. Chmn. bd. Enoch Pratt Free Libr., Balt., 1989-91, capital campaign Roland Park Country Sch., 1981-83. Mem. Balt. Security Analysts Soc. (pres. 1974-75), The Elkridge Club (bd. dirs.), The Niblick Soc. (bd. dirs.), West Chop Club, Royal Cinque Ports. Republican. Episcopalian. Office: Alex Brown & Sons Inc 1 South St Baltimore MD 21202-3298*

KILLEEN, EDWARD JOSEPH, actor, designer; b. New Orleans, Sept. 20, 1954; s. Joseph Henry and Teresa Mary (Gordon) K. BA in English, St. Joseph Sem. Coll., St. Benedict, La., 1976. Geophys. info. coord. Baker Hughes/Western Geophys., 1977—; designer designs and ideas, New Orleans, 1982—; state pub. rels. coord. Easter Seal Soc. La., Metairie, 1982-84; West Tex. and N.Mex. sales rep. Wang's Internat., Inc., Memphis, 1986-87; set contractor Kenner Community Theater, Metairie, La., 1987, Le Petit Theatre de Vieux Carre, New Orleans, La., 1987; design asst. Jeff. Performing Arts Soc., Metairie, 1989-92; bd. dirs. NestEGG Prodns., sec., 1998—. Graphic designer Wildlife Conclave, Tex. A&M U., 1984. Community rep. March of Dimes Birth Defects Found., New Orleans, 1980-82. Recipient Big Easy award, Best Supporting Actor award, New Orleans, 1995, Storer Boone Stage award, 1993. Avocation: carpentry. Mailing Address: PO Box 1915 Metairie LA 70004-1915

KILLEEN, JOANN, community health and critical care nurse; b. Stafford Springs, Conn., Aug. 7, 1952; d. Alfred Jr. and Frances (Lorenzetti) Sfreddo; m. Michael B. Killeen, Jr., May 3, 1975; children: Krista Erin, Kerry Ann, Gregory Michael. BSN cum laude, U. Conn., 1974. RN, Conn., Tex. Asst. supr. Waterbury (Conn.) Vis. Nurse Assn., 1975-79; staff nurse med.-surg. and ICU units Rockville (Conn.) Gen. Hosp., 1981-89; staff primary care nurse VNCC Inc., Rockville, 1989-92; nursing supr. Action Home Health Care, Lewisville, Tex., 1992; asst. dir. Action Home Health Care, 1993; dir. Arcadia Home Home, Lewisville, Tex., 1994; coord. Baylor/Irving (Tex.) Home Care, 1995-97, asst. dir. adult day svcs., 1997-99; br. mgr. Ann's Havens Hosp. VNA, Carrollton, Tex., 1999—. Office: 216 W Mulberrry St Denton TX 77777

KILLEEN, MICHAEL JOHN, lawyer; b. Washington, Oct. 5, 1949; s. James Robert and Georgia Winston (Hartwell) K.; m. Therese Ann Goeden, Oct. 6, 1984; children: John Patrick, Katherine Therese, Mary Clare, James Philip. BA, Gonzaga U., 1971, JD magna cum laude, 1977. Bar: Wash. 1977, U.S. Dist. Ct. (we. dist.) Wash. 1979, U.S. Ct. Appeals (9th cir.) 1984, U.S. Supreme Ct. 1990. Jud. clk. Wash. State Ct. Appeals, Tacoma, 1977-79; assoc. Davis Wright Tremaine, Seattle, 1979-85, ptnr., 1985—; dir. Seattle Goodwill Bd., 1987—, sec., 1998—. Author: Guide to Strike Planning, 1985, Newsroom Legal Guidebook, 1996, Employment in Washington, 1998. Mem. Gonzaga Law Bd. Advisors, Spokane, Wash., pres., 1992-96. Mem. ABA, Wash. State Bar Assn., King County Bar Assn. (treas. 1987-89, pres. award 1989). Democrat. Roman Catholic.

KILLEFER, NANCY, federal agency administrator; b. Key West, Fla., Nov. 16, 1953; m. Robert Killefer; two children. B in Econs., Vassar Coll., 1975; M in Sci. Mgmt. in Fin., MIT, 1979. Dir. McKinsey & Co., Washington; CFO, asst. sec. for mgmt. U.S. Treasury Dept., Washington. Office: US Dept Treasury 15th and Pennsylvania Ave Washington DC 20220

KILLEFFER, LOUIS MACMILLAN, advertising executive; b. Stamford, Conn., May 31, 1954; s. Robert Ayres and Josephine Bigelow (MacMillan) K.; m. Catherine Clemens Ritchie, Apr. 26, 1980; children: Alexander MacMillan, Katherine Ayres, Christian Scott. BA in Art, English, U. N.C., 1975. Account exec. Marsteller, N.Y.C., 1977-79, Grey Advt., N.Y.C., 1979-81; sr. account exec. Ally & Gargano, N.Y.C., 1981-82, account supr., 1982-84, v.p., account supr., 1984-85, v.p., mgmt. supr., 1985-87; sr. v.p., mgmt. supr. Scali McCabe Sloves, Inc., N.Y.C., 1987-90; sr. v.p., group dir. Ammirati & Puris, N.Y.C., 1990-95; exec. v.p., mng. dir. Ammirati Puris Lintas, N.Y.C., 1995-97; exec. v.p. mgmt., dir. Americas Ammirati Puris-lintas, N.Y.C., 1997—. Mem. Rowayton (Conn.) Yacht Club, Roton Point Club. Republican. Episcopalian. Office: Ammirati & Puris/Lintas One Dag Hammarskhold Plz New York NY 10017-2203*

KILLEN, CARROLL GORDEN, electronics company executive; b. Provencal, La., Mar. 22, 1919; s. Carroll Graves and Ella (Crowder) K.; m. Clara Donald Butler, Aug. 15, 1941; children: Carroll Gorden III, Margaret Karen, Lloyd Butler, Sara Elizabeth. Grad., La. State U.; B.S., La. Northwestern State Coll. Electronics engr. Magnolia Petroleum Co., Dallas, 1940-42; electronics engr. Watson Labs., Red Bank, N.J., 1942-45; chief application engr. Sprague Electric Co., North Adams, Mass., 1947-55, mgr. field engring., 1955-60, v.p. mktg. and sales, 1960-73, sr. v.p. mktg. and sales, 1973-85; v.p., gen. mgr. Tansitor Electronics, Inc., Bennington, Vt., 1985-92, dir., 1992—; dir. Cera-Mite Corp., Grafton, Wis.; cons. U.S. Dept. Def., Washington, 1949-73, U.S. Dept. Commerce, 1984-95; dir. Tantalum Internat. Study Ctr., Brussels, Belgium, 1983-85, mem. exec. com., 1983-95; pres. T.I.C., 1984-85. Author: Factors Influencing Capacitor Reliability, 1955. Chmn. Bennington Town Rep. Com., 1997—. Served to 1st lt. USAF, 1945-47, PTO. Mem. IEEE (chmn. conf. bd. 1971-74, chmn. electro conf. 1976-79, life members com., tech. activities bd., pub. rels. com.), Electronic Industries Assn. (giv. 1976—), Am. Ordinance Assn., Newcomer Soc., Nat. Security Indsl. Assn. (trustee 1980-85), Am. Mgmt. Assn., Masons, Sales Execs. Club, Bennington Town Rep. Com. (chmn. 1997—). Republican. Baptist. Avocations: gardening; woodworking; photography. Home: 511 Gage St Bennington VT 05201-1922 Office: Tansitor Electronics Inc PO Box 230 West Rd Bennington VT 05201-5017

KILLENBERG, GEORGE ANDREW, newspaper consultant, former newspaper editor; b. St. Clair County, Ill., Mar. 30, 1917; s. George W. and Lavina (Ruhl) K.; m. Therese Murphy, June 3, 1943; children: George M., Mary C., John A., Terry M., Susan M. BS, St. Louis U., 1954, MA, 1958. Engaged in pub. rels., 1935-41; mem. staff St. Louis Globe-Democrat, 1941—; city editor St. Louis Globe-Dem., 1956-66, mng. editor, 1966-79, exec. editor, 1979-84; past chmn. Mid-Am. Press Inst. Bd. dirs. Boys Town Mo., 1960-88. With AUS, 1942-46. Mem. Press Club (St. Louis, pres. 1964), Sigma Delta Chi. Roman Catholic. Home: 3042 Hatherly Dr Saint Louis MO 63121-4534

KILLGORE, LE, journalist, political columnist; b. Poughkeepsie, N.Y., Mar. 16, 1926; m. James A. Killgore, July 24, 1948; children: Lynne, Robert, Andrew. BA in Romance Langs., Skidmore Coll., 1948; postgrad., Auburn U., 1961-62. Classroom tchr. music Stare Baldwin Sch., Dallas, 1949-50, The Little Sch., Dallas, 1950-51; substitute tchr. DOD Sch., Clark AB, Philippines, 1964-65, Dayton Ohio Schs., 1966-67, Jeb Stuart High Sch., Fairfax County, Va., 1967-68; staff writer Standard-Times, San Angelo, Tex., 1972-79, sr. staff writer, 1979-83, polit. affairs editor, 1983-92; host radio pub. affairs show, polit. cons. San Angelo, 1992—; co-host radio/TV pub. affairs show. Staff writer, editor Officers Wives Club mags., Clark AB, Philippines, 1964, McClellan AFB, Calif., 1966, Panama Canal Zone, 1969-71. Recipient Overall Excellence in News Gathering award Headliners Club, 1973, Outstanding Continuous Coverage of Edn. award Tex. State Tchrs. Assn., 1977, Excellence in Health-related Reporting Tex. Med. Assn., 1977. Mem. Soc. Profl. Journalists (pres. San Angelo chpt. 1984, bd. dirs. 1986, 87, 89). Avocations: cooking, sewing, needlework, music.

KILLIAN, EDWARD JAMES, pediatrician; b. Bklyn., Nov. 14, 1927; s. Edward James and Helen Marie K.; m. Henriette Marian Killian, 1957; children: Christopher Edward, Bryan Alfred, Paul Matthew. BS, St. John's Coll., 1950; MD, SUNY, 1954. Diplomat Am. Bd. Pediatrics, Nat. Bd. Med. Examiners; lic. physician, N.Y. Intern Bklyn. Hosp., 1954-55, resident, 1955-57, attending pediatrician, 1959-61; attending pediatrician Southside Hosp., Bayshore, N.Y., 1961-93; attending pediatrician Good Samaritan Hosp., West Islip, N.Y., 1961-93, ret., 1994. Capt. USAF Med. Corps, 1957-59. Fellow Am. Acad. Pediatrics; mem. AMA, Med. Soc. State N.Y. (life), Suffolk County Med. Soc. (life), Suffolk Pediatric Soc. (emeritus). Avocations: swimming, hiking, gardening. Home: PO Box 432 English Mills Way Woodstock VT 05091

KILLIAN, GEORGE ERNEST, educational association administrator; b. Valley Stream, N.Y., Apr. 6, 1924; s. George and Reina (Moeller) K.; m. Janice E. Bachert, May 26, 1951 (dec.); children: Susan E., Sandra J.; m. Marilyn R. Killian, Sept. 1, 1984. BS in Edn., Ohio No. U., 1949; EdM, U. Buffalo, 1954; PhD in Phys. Scis., Ohio Northern U., 1989; PhD (hon.), U.S. Sports Acad., 1998. Tchr.-coach Wharton (Ohio) High Sch., 1949-51; insp. USN, Buffalo, 1951-54; dir. athletics Erie County (N.Y.) Tech. Inst., Buffalo, 1954-69; asst. prof. health, phys. edn., recreation Erie County (N.Y.) Tech. Inst., 1954-60, asso. prof., 1960-62, prof., 1962-69; exec. dir. Nat. Jr. Coll. Athletic Assn., Colorado Springs, Colo., 1969—. Editor: Juco Rev., 1960—. Served with AUS, 1943-45. Recipient Bd. Trustees award Hudson Valley C. of C., 1969, Erie County Tech. Inst., 1969, Service award Ohio No. U. Alumni, 1972, Service award Lysle Rishel Post, Am. Legion, 1982; named to Ohio No. U. Hall of Fame, 1979, Olympic Order, IOC, 1996. Mem. U.S. Olympic Com. (dir.), Internat. Olympic Com., Am. Legion, Internat. Basketball Fedn. (pres. 1990-98), Internat. U. Sports Fedn. (1st v.p. 1995), Phi Delta Kappa, Delta Sigma Phi. Clubs: Masons, Rotary. Home: 325 Rangely Dr Colorado Springs CO 80921-2655 Office: Nat Jr Coll Athletic Assn PO Box 7305 Colorado Springs CO 80933-7305

KILLIAN, LAWRENCE HARDING (LARRY H.), II (LARRY H. KILLIAN), sculptor; b. San Antonio, May 6, 1943; s. Lawrence Harding and Dorothy Louise (Wright) K.; m. Beverly Gayle Schlueder, Dec. 21, 1963 (div. 1979); children: Lawrence Harding III, Michael Ray; m. Janice Kay Nelson, June 18, 1981. Student, Tex. A&M, 1961; BS in Indsl. Arts, Southwest Tex. State, 1971, postgrad., 1971-72; postgrad., RIT Coll., 1981. Instr., job corps. and trade schs. Tex., 1971-75; owner of metal fabrication and welding bus. Austin, Tex., 1975-81; salesperson Hart Graphics, Austin, Times Printing, Random Lake, Wis., 1982-93; freelance metal sculptor Gainesville, Tex., 1991—. Exhibiting at World Trade Ctr., Dallas. Active Leadership Gainesville, 1999. Southwest Tex. State U. scholar, 1970. Mem. Tex. Sculpture Assn., Dallas Visual Arts, Gainesville Area Visual Arts, Dallas Mus. Art, Lions (pres. 1993). Avocations: antiques, real estate, travel. Home and Office: 1605 W Hwy 82 Gainesville TX 76240-2003

KILLIAN, RICHARD M., library director; b. Buffalo, Jan. 13, 1942; m. Nancy Killian; children from previous marriage: Tessa, Lee Ann. BA, SUNY, Buffalo, 1964; MA, Western Mich. U., 1965; grad. advanced mgmt. library adminstrn., Miami U., Oxford, Ohio, 1981; grad. library adminstrn. devel. program, U. Md., 1985. Various positions Buffalo and Erie County Pub. Libraries, 1963-74, asst. dep. dir., personnel officer, 1979-80; dir. Town of Tonawanda (N.Y.) Pub. Library, 1974-78; asst. city librarian, dir. pub. svcs. Denver Pub. Library, 1978-79; exec. dir. Nioga Library System, Buffalo, 1980-87; library dir. Sacramento (Calif.) Pub. Library, 1987—. Mem. ALA, Calif. Library Assn., Rotary. Home: 3501 H St Sacramento CA 95816-4501 Office: Sacramento Pub Libr Adminstrn Ctr 828 I St Sacramento CA 95814-2589*

KILLIAN, ROBERT KENNETH, former lieutenant governor; b. Hartford, Conn., Sept. 15, 1919; s. Edward F. and Annie (Nemser) K.; m. Evelyn Farnan, Dec. 7, 1942; children—Robert Kenneth, Cynthia Elaine. B.A., Union Coll., 1942; LL.B., U. Conn., 1948; LL.D., Sacred Heart U., Bridgeport, Conn., 1976, Union Coll., Schenectady, 1978. Bar: Conn. bar 1948. Since practiced in Hartford; partner firm Gould, Killian & Wynne; asst. corp. counsel Gould, Killian & Wynne, City of Hartford, 1951-54; atty. gen. State of Conn., 1967-75, lt. gov., 1975-79; chmn. Hartford Dem. Town Com., 1963-67, Hartford Civic Center and Coliseum Commn., 1980—. Trustee Nat. Jewish Hosp. and Research Center, Denver. Served with inf. AUS, 1942-46. Decorated Purple Heart; recipient numerous citations by civic and pub. service orgns. Mem. Am., Conn., Hartford County bar assns. Roman Catholic. Clubs: K.C, Elks. Home: 234 Terry Rd Hartford CT 06105-1113 Office: One Commercial Plaza Hartford CT 06103

KILLIAN, ROBERT KENNETH, JR., judge, lawyer; b. Hartford, Conn., Jan. 29, 1947; s. Robert Kenneth Sr. and Evelyn (Farnan) K.; m. Candace Korper, Oct. 6, 1979; children: Virginia, Carolyn. BA, Union U., 1969; JD, Georgetown U., 1972. Bar: Conn. 1972, U.S. Ct. Appeals (2nd cir.) 1973, D.C. 1974, U.S. Ct. Appeals (D.C. cir.) 1974. Bur. chief Sta. WTIC-AM-FM-TV, Washington, 1969-72; spl. asst. Senator Abe Ribicoff, Washington, 1972-73; atty. Gould, Killian, Wynne et al, Hartford, 1972-84; judge Conn. Probate Ct., Hartford, 1984—; atty. Killian, Donohue & Shipman, LLC, Hartford, 1985—, 1998—; spl. counsel Lt. Gov. Conn., Hartford, 1985—; mem. exec. com. Conn. Probate Assembly, 1987—, pres.-judge, 1997—; mem. investment adv. coun. State of Conn., 1995—; mem. Jud. Commn. on Attys.' Ethics, 1990—. Author: Basic Probate in Connecticut, 1990, 5th edit., 1995. Regent, U. Hartford; trustee Hartt Sch. Music; chmn. Conn. chpt. March of Dimes, 1986—; bd. dirs. Yeats Drama Found., 1989—; incorporator St. Francis Hosp. and Med. Ctr. Recipient 1st Pl. award New England Conv. Magicians, 1969; named Conn.'s Outstanding Probate Judge, Conn. Probate Assembly, 1990. Mem. ABA, Nat. Conf. Probate Judges, Conn. Bar Assn., Conn. Trial Lawyers Assn., Internat. Brotherhood Magicians, Soc. Am. Magicians (chmn. nat. conv. 1977). Democrat. Roman Catholic. Home: 83 Bloomfield Ave Hartford CT 06105-1007 Office: Killian & Donohue 363 Main St Hartford CT 06106-1885

KILLIAN, WILLIAM PAUL, industrial corporate executive; b. Sidney, Ohio, Apr. 26, 1935; s. Ray and Erie K.; m. Beverly Ann Buchanan, Sept.7, 1957; children: William, Katherine, Michael. B in Chem. Engring. with honors, Ga. Inst. Tech., 1957; M in Engring. Adminstrn. with honors, U. Utah, 1968. Chem. engr. Esso, Baton Rouge, La., 1957-58; mgr. research and devel. mfg. engring., then plant mgr. Thiokol Corp., Brigham City, Utah, 1958-68; mgr. corp. project mgmt. Masonite Corp., Chgo., 1968-70, mgr. new bus. ventures, 1970-73; mgr. strategic planning, chem. and metall. group Gen. Electric Co., Pittsfield, Mass. and Columbus, Ohio, 1973-77; v.p. corp. planning and devel. Hoover Universal Inc., Ann Arbor, Mich., 1977-85; v.p. corp. devel. Johnson Controls Inc., Milw., 1985-87, v.p. corp. devel. and strategy, 1987—; bd. dirs. Interstate Battery System of Am., Inc., Dallas, Aqua-Chem. Inc., Milw., Q.E.P. Co., Inc., Boca Raton, Fla., Gehl Co., West Bend, Wis.; spl. advisor Mason Wells Pvt. Equity Fund, Milw. Bd. advocates Skylight Opera Theatre Corp., Milw. Mem. Assn. for Corp. Growth Internat. (nat. bd. dirs., past nat. pres., past pres. Wis. chpt.), Coun. Strategic Planning Execs. of Conf. Bd. (past chmn.), Mfrs. Alliance (corp. planning coun., vice chmn.), Strategic Leadership Forum, Mensa Soc., Town Club, North Shore Racquet Club, Koseme Soc., Tau Beta Pi, Omicron Delta Kappa, Phi Kappa Phi, Pi Delta Epsilon, Phi Eta Sigma. Office: Johnson Controls Inc 5757 N Green Bay Ave Milwaukee WI 53209-4408

KILLIN, CHARLES CLARK, lawyer; b. Peoria, Ill., June 12, 1923; s. Thomas James and Marie (Clark) K. AB, U. Mich., 1947, JD, 1950. Bar: Okla. 1950. Since pvt. practice law Tulsa; ptnr. Conner & Winters, 1958-84, of counsel, 1988—. Trustee U. Tulsa, 1988—. Served with AUS, 1943-46. Fellow Am. Coll. Trust and Estates Counsel; mem. Am., Okla., Tulsa County bar assns., Theta Chi, Phi Alpha Delta. Republican. Presbyterian. Club: Rotary. Home: 2130 E 59th St Tulsa OK 74105-7004 Office: Conner & Winters 1st Place Tower 15 E 5th St Ste 3700 Tulsa OK 74103-4391

KILLINGER, KERRY KENT, bank executive; b. Des Moines, June 6, 1949; m. Debbie Roush. BBA, U. Iowa, 1970, MBA, 1971. Exec. v.p. Murphey Favre, Inc., Spokane, 1976-82; exec. v.p. fin. mgmt., investor rels., corp. mktg. Wash. Mutual, Seattle, 1983-86; sr. exec. v.p., 1986-88; pres., dir. Wash. Mutual Savs. Bank, Seattle, 1988—, chief exec. officer, 1990—, chmn. bd. dirs., 1991—; bd. dirs. Wash. Savs. League; mem. Thrift Inst. Adv. Coun. to Fed. Res. Bd., 1992-94; speaker in field. Bd. dirs. Fed. Home Loan Bank of Seattle, 1995—, Seattle Repertory Theatre, 1990—, Washington Roundtable, 1990—, Downtown Seattle Assn., 1991, Leadership Tomorrow, Seattle Found., 1992—; mem. Alliance for Edn., 1992—, chair, 1994-96, co-chmn. AIDS Walk-a-thon, Seattle, 1990; chair Partnership for Learning, 1997. Fellow Life Mgmt. Inst.; mem. Soc. Fin. Analysts, Greater Seattle C. of C. (bd. dirs. 1992—), Rotary. Office: Wash Mutual Inc PO Box 834 Seattle WA 98111-9980*

KILLINGSWORTH, MARK R., economics educator, consultant; b. Balt., Dec. 8, 1946; s. Charles C. and Beverly H. (Kritzman) K.; m. Vivienne Lynch, June 21, 1969 (dec. Mar. 25, 1994); children: Siân, Katherine; m. Cheryl G. Levine, May 25, 1997. BA in Econs., U. Mich., 1967; MPhil in Econs., Oxford U., 1969, DPhil in Econs., 1977. Asst. prof. econs. Fisk U., Nashville, 1969-76; asst. prof. econs. Barnard Coll. Columbia U., N.Y.C., 1976-78; from asst. prof. econs. to prof. econs. Rutgers U., New Brunswick, N.J., 1978—; cons. econs. U.S. Dept. Justice, U.S. Dept. Labor, U.S.E.E.O.C., 1974—. Author: Labor Supply, 1983, Economics of Comparable Worth, 1990; co-editor: Comparable Worth: Analyses and Evidence, 1989; contbr. article to profl. jour. Mem. Gov.'s Commn. Pinelands Agr., N.J., 1984-85. Rhodes Scholar, 1967. Mem. Am. Econ. Assn. (mem. editl. bd. Jour. Econ. Lit. 1987-89), Econometric Soc., Phi Beta Kappa. Avocations: opera, 20th century history. Office: Rutgers U Dept Econs New Jersey Hall New Brunswick NJ 08901

KILLION, JACK CHARLES, newspaper columnist; b. L.A., Aug. 21, 1921; s. Roger William and Anna Virginia (Moser) K.; m. Elisabeth Horn, June 29, 1947; children: Joanna Barbara, Heidi Killion Gaul, Frederick John. Student, L.A. City Coll., 1940-42. Chief of spl. branch U.S. Army Mil. Govt., Bruchsal, Baden, Germany, 1945-47; sports editor Van Nuys News, Van Nuys, Calif., 1947-48; repair supr. L.A. Dept. Water & Power, 1948-81; columnist Simi Valley Enterprise, Simi Valley, Calif., 1986—, L.A. Daily News, 1989-90. Sgt. U.S. Army, 1942-45, ETO. Decorated Hon. Membership German Severely Wounded War Vets., Pacific Battle Star, European Battle Star; Commendation for work as Chief of Spl. Branch and Denazification, Bruchsal, Baden, Germany. Mem. Mensa. Republican. Lutheran. Avocations: traveling, fishing, time spent with family. Home: 2403 Lukens Ln Simi Valley CA 93065-4909

KILLION, RICHARD JOSEPH, college official, political science educator; b. Boston, Apr. 14, 1967; s. John Francis Sr. and Edna Louise (Murphy) K.; m. KelliAnn Norden, July 24, 1993; children: Sean Patrick, Alexander Liam. BA in Econs., Stonehill Coll., 1989; MPA, George Mason U., 1994. Divsn. dir. Tele-Cons., Inc., Manassas, Va., 1989-93, TCI/Taylor, Hagerty & Assocs., Manassas, 1993-95; dir. corp. and govt. rels. Franklin Pierce Coll., Rindge, N.H., 1995-96, dir. devel., 1996-98, lectr. polit. sci., 1995—, dir. instnl. advancement, 1998—. Bd. dirs. Monadnock Children's Mus., Keene, 1995-97; exec. com. Monadnock Inst. of Nature, Place and Culture, Rindge, 1996-98; sec. Mass. State Coll. Reps., 1988-89; founding chmn. Stonehill Coll. Reps., North Easton, Mass., 1987-89; incorporator Cathedral of the Pines. Mem. Greater Peterborough C. of C. (chmn. bd.), Keene Country Club, KC, Rotary, Leadership Monadnock. Roman Catholic. Avocations: golf, reading, public policy. Home: 1 Tanner Rd Keene NH 03431-2200 Office: Franklin Pierce Coll College Rd PO Box 60 Rindge NH 03461-0060

KILLMAR, LAWRENCE E., wild animal park site curator. BSBA, Calif. Coast Univ., 1995, postgrad., 1996—. directed transp. four So. White Rhino from San Diego Zoo and Wild Animal Park to Can., 1974, to Europe, 1977; participant Gian Eland capture, Senegal, West Afirca, 1979; accompanied four Asiatic Lions to Jerusalem Zoo, 1984, others; facilitator Feline Immunodeficiency Viruses Workshop for Cheetahs, Escondido, 1995, others. Park keeper to curatorial field supr. San Diego (Calif.) Wild Animal Park, 1970-80, curator of mammals, 1982-91, gen. curator/mammal and bird collections, 1991-92, gen. curator/mammal, bird and reptile collections, 1992—. Contbr. articles to profl. jours. Fellow Am. Assn. Zoos, Parks, Aquariums; mem. Wildlife Conservation Mgmt. Com./Am. Zool. Assn., Am. Zoo and Aquarium Assn. (bd. regents 1996). Office: San Diego Wild Animal Park 15500 San Pasqual Valley Rd Escondido CA 92027-7017*

KILLORIN, EDWARD WYLLY, lawyer, tree farmer; b. Savannah, Ga., Oct. 16, 1928; s. Joseph Ignatius and Myrtle (Bell) K.; m. Virginia Melson Ware, June 15, 1957; children: Robert Ware, Edward Wylly, Joseph Rigdon. BS, Spring Hill Coll., Mobile, 1952; LLB magna cum laude, U. Ga., 1957. Bar: Ga. 1956. Pvt. practice in Atlanta, 1957—; ptnr. firm Gambrell, Russell, Killorin & Forbes, 1964-78; sr. ptnr. firm Killorin & Killorin, 1978—; lectr. Inst. Continuing Legal Edn. Ga., 1967—. Adj. prof. law Ga. State U., 1984-87. Chmn., Gov.'s Adv. Com. on Coordination State and Local Govt., 1973, Gov.'s Legal Adv. Council for Workmen's Compensation, 1974-76; bd. regents Spring Hill Coll., 1975-82, trustee, 1981-91. Served with AUS, 1946-47, 52-54. Recipient Disting. Alumnus award Spring Hill Coll., 1972. Mem. Internat., Ga. (chmn. jud. compensation com. 1976-77, chmn. legis. com. 1977-78), Atlanta Bar Assn. (editor Atlanta Lawyer 1967-70, exec. com. 1971-74, chmn. legislation com. 1978-80), D.C. Bar Assn., Am. Judicature Soc., Lawyers Club Atlanta, Atlanta Legal Aid Soc. (adv. com. 1966-70, dir. 1971-74), Nat. Legal Aid and Defender Assn., Internat. Assn. Ins. Counsel (chmn. environ. law com. 1976-78), Atlanta Lawyers

Found., Ga. Bar Found. (life), Ga. Def. Lawyers Assn. (dir. 1972-80), Ga. C. of C. (chmn. govtl. dept. 1970-75, chmn. workmen's compensation com. 1979—, Disting. Svc. award 1970-75), Def. Research Inst. (Ga. chmn. 1970-71), Spring Hill Coll. Alumni Assn. (nat. pres. 1972-74), U. Ga. Law Sch. Assn. (nat. pres. 1986-87, Disting. Svc. Scroll 1989), Ga. Forestry Assn. (life, bd. dirs. 1969—, pres. 1977-79, chmn. bd. 1979-81), Am. Forestry Assn., Demosthenian Lit. Soc. (pres. 1957), Sphinx, Blue Key, Gridiron, Phi Beta Kappa, Phi Beta Kappa Assos., Phi Kappa Phi, Phi Delta Phi, Phi Omega. Clubs: Capital City, Peachtree Golf, Commerce, Oglethorpe (Savannah), Highland Country Club (LaGrange). Roman Catholic. Contbr. articles to legal jours. Home: 436 Blackland Rd NW Atlanta GA 30342-4005 Office: Killorin & Killorin 11 Piedmont Ctr NE Atlanta GA 30305-1769

KILLORIN, ROBERT WARE, lawyer; b. Atlanta, Nov. 12, 1959; s. Edward W. and Virgina (Ware) K. AB cum laude, Duke U., 1980; JD, U. Ga., 1983. Bar: Ga. 1984, U.S. Dist. Ct. (no. dist.) Ga. 1984, U.S. Ct. Appeals (11th cir.) 1984. Ptnr. Killorin & Killorin, Atlanta, 1984—. Mem. Atlanta Bar Assn., Ga. Def. Lawyers Assn., State Bar Ga. (chair SCOPE com. 1986, young lawyers sect. legis. affairs com. 1989-91, instr. mock trial program 1989—), Ga. C. of C. (govtl. affairs com.), Internat. Assn. Def. Counsel, 11th Cir. Hist. Soc., Assn. Trial Lawyers Am., Nat. Assn. Underwater Instrs., Nat. Speliological Soc., U. Ga. Pres.'s Club, Explorer's Club. Avocations: forestry, scuba diving, basketball, tennis. Home: 5587 Benton Woods Dr NE Atlanta GA 30342-1308 Office: Robert Ware Killorin Esq 5587 Benton Woods Dr Atlanta GA 30342

KILLORIN CASWELL, MARY KATHERINE, management consultant; b. Hibbing, Minn., Nov. 20, 1951; d. Ambrose Joseph and Jean Gannon Killorin; m. Richard Whitaker Caswell, June 18, 1992. Student, Sweet Briar Coll., 1970-74; MBA, George Washington U., 1984. From lobbyist to nat. mkts. mgr. 3M, Washington, 1982-89; from sales devel. mgr. to cons. 3M, St. Paul, 1990-95, global bus. devel. mgr., 1995—. Bd. dirs. Leader Found., Washington, 1987-89. Mem. Sales and Mktg. Execs., Jr. League. Office: 3M Bldg 225-35-05 Saint Paul MN 55144

KILMAN, JAMES WILLIAM, surgeon, educator; b. Terre Haute, Ind., Jan. 22, 1931; s. Arthur and Irene (Piker) K.; m. Priscilla Margaret Jackson, June 20, 1968; children: James William, Julia Anne, Jennifer Irene. B.S., Ind. State U., 1956; M.D., Ind. U., 1960. Intern Ind.U. Med. Ctr., Indpls., 1960-61; resident surgery Ind.U. Med. Center, 1961-66, asst. prof., 1966-69, assoc. prof., 1969-73; prof. surgery Ohio State U. Coll. Medicine, 1973-91, prof. surgery emeritus, 1991—; chmn. dept. thoracic surgery Children's Hosp., 1975-91; attending surgeon Univ. Hosp., Columbus, Ohio; attending staff Children's Hosp., Columbus; pres. staff Children's Hosp., 1978; attending staff Grant Hosp., Riverside Hosp.; cons. surgeon VA Hosp., Dayton; pres. Columbus Acad. Medicine, 1977. Trustee Central Ohio Heart Assn., Acad. Medicine Edn. Found., Children's Hosp., 1978—. Served with USNR, 1951-55. USPHS Cardiovascular fellow, 1963-64; recipient Alumni Achievement award, Ind. State U., 1989. Fellow ACS, Am. Coll. Cardiology, Am. Acad. Pediats., Coll. Chest Physicians; mem. Columbus Surg. Soc. (pres. 1974, hon. mem. 1993), Columbus Acad. Medicine (coun. 1971-73), Am. Surg. Assn., Soc. U. Surgeons, Am. Assn. Thoracic Surgery, Cen. Surg. Assn., Western Surg. Assn., Soc. Vascular Surgery, Internat. Cardiovasc. Soc., Internat. Soc. Surgeons, Chest Club, Cardiovasc. Surgery Club, City Club, Palm Aire Country Club, Faculty Club, Capital Club, Columbus Athletic Club, Pickaway County Country Club, Sigma Xi, Alpha Omega Alpha. Rsch., articles infant cardiopulmonary bypass and surgery for congenital heart lesions. Home and Office: 4231 Jackson Pike Grove City OH 43123-9198 Winter Home: 7517 Fairlinks Ct Sarasota FL 34243-3846

KILMANN, RALPH HERMAN, business educator; b. N.Y.C., Oct. 5, 1946; s. Martin Herbert and Lilli (Loeb) K.; 1 child, Christopher Martin; m. Patricia C. Nalepa, Aug. 7, 1999. BS, Carnegie Mellon U., 1970; MS, Carnegie-Mellon U., 1970; PhD, UCLA, 1972. Instr. U. Pitts. Katz Grad. Sch. Bus., 1972, asst. prof., 1972-75, assoc. prof., 1975-79, prof., 1979—, George H. Love prof. orgn. and mgmt., 1991—, coord. orgnl. studies group, 1981-84, 86-89, dir. program in corp. culture, 1983—; pres. Organizational Design Cons., Pitts., 1975—. Author: Social Systems Design: Normative Theory and the MAPS Design Technology, 1977, Beyond the Quick Fix: Managing Five Tracks to Organizational Success, 1984, Managing Beyond the Quick Fix: A Completely Integrated Program for Creating and Maintaining Organizational Success, 1989, Escaping the Quick Fix Trap: How to Make Organizational Improvements That Really Last, 1989, Workbook for Implementing the Five Tracks: Vols. I and II, 1991, Logistics Manual for Implementing the Five Tracks: Planning and Organizing Workshop Sessions, 1992, Workbook for Continuous Improvement: Holographic Quality Management, 1993; co-author: Methodological Approaches to Social Science: Integrating Divergent Concepts and Theories, 1978, Corporate Tragedies: Product Tampering, Sabotage and Other Catastrophes, 1984, The Management of Organization Design: Vols. I and II, 1976, Producing Useful Knowledge for Organizations, 1983, Gaining Control of the Corporate Culture, 1985, Corporate Transformation: Revitalizing Organizations for a Competitive World, 1988, Making Organizations Competitive: Enhancing Networks and Relationships Across Traditional Boundaries, 1991, Managing Ego Energy: The Transformation of Personal Meaning into Organizational Success, 1994; mem. editorial bd. Jour. Mgmt., 1983-86, Acad. Mgmt. Exec., 1987-90, Jour. Organizational Change Mgmt., 1988—; developed Kilmann Insight Test, Learning Climate Questionnaire, Thomas-Kilmann Conflict-Mode Instrument in Ednl. Testing Svc., MAPS Design Tech. for Social Systems Design, Kilmann-Saxton Culture-Gap Survey, Kilmann's Organizational Belief Survey; contbr. chpts. to books, articles to profl. jours. Mem. Eastern Acad. Mgmt. (treas. 1975-76, dir. 1983-86), Am. Psychol. Assn., Inst. Mgmt. Scis. (1st prize Nat. Coll. Planning competition 1976), Beta Gamma Sigma, Sigma Xi. Home: 165 Millview Dr Pittsburgh PA 15238-1625 Office: U Pitts Jos M Katz Grad Sch Bus Roberto Clemente Dr Pittsburgh PA 15260 *Some live only for themselves, some sacrifice their lives for others. The space between is enjoying one's life while contributing to society. No one should have the full responsibility for saving the world, nor the complete freedom to ignore the future.*

KILMARTIN, JOSEPH FRANCIS, JR., business executive, consultant; b. New Haven, Mar. 11, 1924; s. Joseph Francis and Lauretta M. (Collins) K.; student St. Thomas Sem., 1944; BA, Holy Cross Coll., 1947; m. Gloria M. Schaffer, June 26, 1954; children: Joanne, Diane. Prodn. mgr. A.C. Gilbert Co., New Haven, 1947-49; profl. performer Broadway show Small Wonder, also TV shows Your Hit Parade, Philco Playhouse, Armstrong Circle Theatre, 1949-50; producer NBC-TV, N.Y.C., 1950-53; v.p. sales Cellomatic Corp., N.Y.C., 1953-59; sr. v.p. Transfilm Inc., N.Y.C., 1959-62, MPO Videotronics, N.Y.C., 1962-66; pres. Bus. Programs Inc., Larchmont, N.Y., 1966-75, Greenwich, Conn., 1975—; pres. Kilarnold Corp.; lectr. in field, cons. Mexican Dept. Agrarian Affairs and Colonization, 1974—. Active fund-raising Cmty. Chest, 1947-49, ARC, 1947-49, Boy Scouts Am., 1958-66, United Fund, 1970-73; mem. Congl. Adv. Bd., Presdl. Task Force, Atlantic Coun., Conn. Venture Group, Mil. Affairs Coun., Fayetteville, N.C., Harnett County Strategic Planning Commn.; bd. dirs. Lee County Arts Coun.; mem. exec. com., chmn. Lee County Rep. Party Coun.; chmn. Carolina Trace Cmty. Action Com. Recipient medal of excellence Mexican Agrarian Affairs and Colonization Dept., 1976; Golden Medallion award in bus. communication Miami Internat. Film Festival, 1978, Cmty. Developer of Yr. award Nat. Mfg. Housing Inst., 1998. Mem. Am. Mgmt. Assn., TV Execs. Soc., Pres.'s Assn. Republican. Clubs: Larchmont (N.Y.) Yacht Club, Westchester Country Club, Univ. Club (N.Y.C.), Carolina Trace Country Club, Lambs. Home: 241 Lakeview Dr Sanford NC 27330-8397

KILMER, MAURICE DOUGLAS, marketing executive; b. Flint, Mich., Sept. 14, 1928; s. John Jennings and Eleanor Minnie (Gerholz) K.; m. Vera May Passino, Mar. 30, 1950; children: Brad Douglas, Mark David, Brian John, David Scott, Karen Sue. B of Indsl. Engring., Gen. Motors Inst., 1951; MBA, U. Minn., 1969. Quality svcs. mgr. ordnance div. Honeywell, Hopkins, Minn., 1964-69; product assurance dir. peripheral ops. Honeywell, San Diego, 1969-71; pres. Convenience Systems, Inc., San Diego, 1972-75; salesman real estate Forest E. Olson Coldwell Banker, La Mesa, Calif., 1976-77; resident mgr. Forest E. Olson Coldwell Banker, Huntington Beach, Calif., 1977-78; mgmt. cons. Century 21 of the Pacific, Santa Ana, Calif., 1978-83; dir. broker svcs. Century 21 of the Pacific, Anaheim, Calif., 1983-85; exec. dir. Century 21 of S.W., Phoenix, 1985-86; sales assoc. Century 21 Rattan Realtors, San Diego, 1986-88; mgr. Rattan Realtors, San Diego, 1988-92, relocation dir., 1993-98; retired, 1998. With U.S. Army, 1951-52. Mem. Am. Soc. for Quality Control, San Diego Bd. Realtors. Republican. Avocation: playing mandolin. Home: 9074 Circle R Oaks Ln Escondido CA 92026-5926

KILMER, VAL, actor; b. Los Angeles, Dec. 31, 1959; m. Joanne Whalley, 1988 (div. 1996); 1 child, Mercedes. Educ., Hollywood's Professional Sch., Juillard. Appeared in plays Electra and Orestes, Henry IV, Part One, 1981, As You Like It, 1982, Slab Boys (Broadway Debut), 1983, Hamlet, 1988, 'Tis Pity She's A Whore, 1992; motion pictures include Top Secret!, 1984, Real Genius, 1985, Top Gun, 1986, Willow, 1988, Kill Me Again, 1989, The Doors, 1991, Thunderheart, 1991, True Romance, 1993, The Real McCoy, 1993, Tombstone, 1993, Wings of Courage, 1995, Batman Forever, 1995, Heat, 1995, The Island of Dr. Moreau, 1996, The Ghost and the Darkness, 1996, Dead Girl, 1996, The Saint, 1997, The Prince of Egypt (voice) 1998, Joe the King, 1999, At First Sight, 1999; TV appearances include The Murders in the Rue Morgue, 1986, The Man Who Broke 1,000 Chains, 1987, Gore Vidal's Billy the Kid, 1989. Office: CAA 9830 Wilshire Blvd Beverly Hills CA 90212-1804*

KILNER, URSULA BLANCHE, genealogist, writer; b. Chgo., Feb. 2, 1925; d. Frederic Russell and Blanche (Miller) Gamble; m. Glen Kilner, May 12, 1950. BA cum laude, Mt. Holyoke Coll., 1946; MA, Columbia U., 1947, postgrad., to 1951. Asst. to editor Grolier Pub., N.Y.C., 1947; mgr. Magnamusic Inc., Garrison, N.Y., 1954-55; publicity and fundraising Little Guild of St. Francis Inc., Cornwall, Conn., 1957-68; lectr. U. Conn., Torrington, 1964-66; genealogist Bird Bottom Genealogist, Salisbury, Conn., 1979—; owner, mgr. The Tenth Muse, phonograph and stereo co., 1958-60; reporter The Comml. Record, 1960-61. Author, editor: A Revolutionary Cook Book, 1985, A Cook Book for All Seasons, 1994; columnist The Voice, 1993—; book reviewer Heritage Books; contbr. articles to profl. jours. Mem. Planning and Zoning Commn., Salisbury, Conn., 1981-82. Mem. DAR (chpt. registrar), Am. Coll. Genealogists (cert. genealogist; asst. nat. registrar 1990-91), New Eng. Hist./Geneal. Soc. (life), N.Y. Geneal./Biog. Soc. (life), N.H. Soc. Genealogists (life), Conn. Soc. Genealogists, Suffolk County Hist. Soc., Nat. Soc. Huguenots (mem. adv. bd. 1993—, life, Conn. registrar 1998—), Nat. Soc. Colonial Dames XVII Century (Conn. state registrar 1995-99, organizing pres. Winthrop Fleet chpt. 1990, chpt. pres. 1999—), Nat. Soc. Colonial Dames XII Century (former Conn./Mass. rschr.), Vt. Gen. Soc., Ea. Star, Nat. Soc. Daus. Am. Colonists (Conn. registrar), Assn. Gravestone Studies, Greyhound Friends West, Inc., Piscataqua Pioneers N.H. (life), Morse Family Soc. (life), Seeley Family Soc., Van Voorhees Family Soc., Whitlock Family Soc., Ill. Geneal. Soc., Sons and Dau. First Settlers Newbury, Kewanee (Ill.) Hist. Soc. (life), Salisbury Assn., Sheffield Hist. Soc., Andover (Mass.) Hist. Soc. Avocations: knitting, lecturing, saving greyhounds, greenhouse plants. Home and Office: Bird Bottom Farm RR 1 Salisbury CT 06068-1400

KILPATRICK, CAROLYN CHEEKS, congresswoman; b. Detroit, June 25, 1945; d. Marvell and Willa Mae (Henry) Cheeks; divorced; children: Kwame, Ayanna. AS, Ferris State Coll., Big Rapids, Mich.., 1965; BS, Western Mich. U., 1972; MS in Edn., U. Mich., 1977. Tchr. Murray Wright High Sch., Detroit, 1972-78; mem. Mich. Ho. of Reps., Lansing, 1978-96; mem. 105th Congress from 15th Mich. Dist., Washington, 1997—, mem. appropriations com., Dem. whip; del. Dem. Convs., 1980, 84, 88. Rep. Detroit Substance Abuse Adv. Coun.; participant Mich. African Trade Mission, 1984, UN Internat. Women's Conf., 1986; del. participant Mich. Dept. Agr. to Nairobi (Kenya) Internat. Agr. Show, 1986. Recipient Anthony Wayne award Wayne State U., Disting. Legislator award U. Mich., Disting. Alumni award Ferris State U., Woman of Yr. award Gentlemen of Wall St., Inc., Burton-Abercrombie award 15th Dem. Congrl. dist. Mem. Nat. Orgn. 100 Black Women, Nat. Black Caucus of State Legislators (chairperson Mich. legis. session 1983-84), Nat. Order Women Legislators, Nat. Orgn. Black Elected Legis. Women (treas.). Office: House of Reps 503 Cannon House Office Bld Washington DC 20515-2215

KILPATRICK, CLIFTON WAYNE, book dealer; b. Pontiac, Mich., Nov. 16, 1949; s. Martin Laverne and Shirley Irene (Powell) Ball (dec.). Grad. high sch., Ortonville, Mich. With Royal Castle (restaurant), Miami, Fla., 1969-71, Yankee Clipper (restaurant), Ft. Lauderdale, Fla., 1971-73, Creightons (restaurant), Ft. Lauderdale, Fla., 1973-75; book collector Trivia King, Ft. Lauderdale, Fla., 1975-93. Author: Trivia Professor, 1980. Democrat. Methodist. Avocations: supplying info. to radio and TV programs. Home and Office: 2805 NW 30th Ct Oakland Park FL 33311-1331

KILPATRICK, JAMES JACKSON, JR., columnist, author; b. Oklahoma City, Nov. 1, 1920; s. James Jackson and Alma Mia (Hawley) K.; m. Marie Louise Pietri, Sept. 21, 1942 (dec. May 1997); children: Michael Sean, Christopher Hawley, Kevin Pietri; m. Marianne Means, June 19, 1998. BJ, U. Mo., 1941. Reporter Richmond (Va.) News Leader, 1941-49, chief editorial writer, 1949-51, editor, 1951-67; writer nat. syndicated columns, TV commentator. Author: The Sovereign States, 1957, The Smut Peddlers, 1960, The Southern Case for School Segregation, 1962, The Foxes' Union, 1977, (with Eugene J. McCarthy) A Political Bestiary, 1978, (with William Bake) The American South: Four Seasons of the Land, 1980, The American South: Towns and Cities, 1982, The Writer's Art, 1984, The Ear is Human, 1985, A Bestiary of Bridge, 1986, Fine Print - Reflections on the Writing Art, 1993; editor: We the States, 1964; co-editor: The Lasting South, 1957. Vice chmn. Va. Com. on Constl. Govt., 1962-68; chmn. Va. Magna Carta Com., 1965; trustee Thomas Jefferson Ctr. for Protection of Free Expression, 1990—, Supreme Ct. Hist. Soc., 1987—. Recipient medal of honor for distinguished service in journalism U. Mo., 1953; ann. award for editorial writing Sigma Delta Chi, 1954; William Allen White award U. Kans., 1979; Carr Van Anda award Ohio U., 1987; named to Okla. Hall of Fame, 1978. Fellow Soc. Profl. Journalists; mem. Nat. Conf. Editorial Writers (chmn. 1955-56), Black-Eyed Pea Soc. Am. (No. 1 Pea pro tem 1965—), Gridiron Club. Whig. Episcopalian.

KILROY, JAMES FRANCIS, educator; b. Chgo., Sept. 7, 1935; s. John Patrick and Nora (Joyce) K.; m. Mary Elizabeth Carroll, July 1, 1961; children—Maurya, James Dennis, Mark Justin. B.A., DePaul U., 1957; M.A., U. Iowa, 1961; Ph.D., U. Wis., 1965. Tchr. Pub. High Schs., Chgo., 1957-61; asst. prof. Vanderbilt U., 1965-69, assoc. prof., 1969-77, prof., 1977-84, chmn. dept. English, 1979-83, assoc. dean Grad. Sch., 1973-76; dean Coll. Arts and Scis. Tulane U., 1984-88, dean Faculty of Liberal Arts and Scis., 1988-90, provost, 1991-96, prof., 1996—. Author: James Clarence Mangan, 1970, The Playboy Riots, 1971, The Modern Irish Drama (3 vols.), 1975, 76, 78, The Playboy as Poet, 1969, The Chiastic Structure of Tennyson's In Memoriam, 1977, The Irish Short Story, 1984; co-editor: Lost Plays of the Irish Renaissance, 1970. Am. Council Learned Socs. fellow, 1967-68; Nat. Endowment Humanities fellow, 1968. Mem. MLA, Am. Com. for Irish Studies. Roman Catholic. Office: Tulane Univ Office of Provost 327 Gibson Hall New Orleans LA 70118-5698

KILROY, JOHN MICHAEL, artist, educator; b. Boston, Mar. 20, 1957. BFA, Art Inst Boston, 1978. art tchr. Quincy (Mass.) Art Assn., Lynne Art Assn., North River Art Soc., Cape Cod Sch. Art. Exhibited in shows at Tokyo Designers Gakuin Coll., 1985 (Design award 1985), 1986 (Design award 1986), So. Shore Art Assn., 1985 (award), 90 (award), North Shore Art Assn., Mass., 1987, Colorado Springs 45th Nat. Juried Show, 1989, North Shore Art Soc., Marshfield, Mass., 1997, Pierce Galleries, Inc., Hingham, Mass., 1998, Attleboro Mus. Art, 1998; represented in permanent collections at AT&T Boston Globe Collection, N.Y.C., Osborne Computer, Calif., He Mingzhang Electronic Computers, Beijing, Alaska Art and Cultural Mus., Skagway, Yankee Mag., N.H. Mem. Oil Painters Am., North River Art Soc., Knickerbocker Artists USA. Office: c/o Pierce Galleries Inc 721 Main St Hingham MA 02043

KILROY, JOHN MUIR, lawyer; b. Kansas City, Mo., Apr. 12, 1918; s. James L. and Jane Alice (Scurry) K.; m. Lorraine K. Butler, Jan. 26, 1946; children: John Muir, William Terence. Student, Kansas City Jr. Coll., 1935-37; AB, U. Kansas City, 1940; JD, U. Mo., 1942. Bar: Mo. 1942. Practice in Kansas City, 1946—; ptnr. Shughart, Thomson & Kilroy, 1948—, pres., 1977-86, chmn. bd. dirs., 1980-88, chmn. emeritus, 1988—; instr. med. jurisprudence U. Health Scis., 1973-93; panelist numerous med.-legal groups ACS, Mo. Med. Assn., Kans. U. Med. Sch., S.W. Clin. Soc. Contbr. articles to profl. jours. Chmn. bd. dirs. Kansas City Heart Assn.; mem. adv. bd. Midwest Christian Counseling Svc.; bd. dirs., pres. Della Lamb Cmty. Svc., 1991, chmn. bd. dirs., 1993; bd. dirs. Kingswood Manor, 1992-94, Mo. Meth. Found., 1993—. Named Man of Yr., Sigma Chi, 1989. Fellow Am. Coll. Trial Lawyers; mem. ABA, Mo. Bar Assn. (chmn. med. legal com.), Kansas City Bar Assn. (Litigator Emeritus award 1990), Internat. Assn. Barristers, Internat. Assn. Def. Counsel, Am. Coll. Legal Medicine, Am. Bd. Profl. Liability Attys., Fedn. Ins. Counsel, Law Soc. U. Mo., Order Barristers U. Mo., Lawyers Assn., Kansas City (pres. 1968), Kansas City C. of C., Univ. Club (v.p. 1984, pres. 1985), Indian Hills Country Club. Home: 6860 Tomahawk Rd Mission Hills KS 66208-2176 Office: Shughart Thomson & Kilroy 120 W 12th St Ste 1500 Kansas City MO 64105-1929

KILROY, WILLIAM TERRENCE, lawyer; b. Kansas City, Mo., May 24, 1950; s. John Muir and Katherine Lorraine (Butler) K.; m. Marianne Michelle Maurin, Sept. 8, 1984; children: Kyle E., Katherine A. BS, U. Kans., 1972, MA, 1974; JD, Washburn U., 1977. Bar: Mo. 1977. Assoc. Shughart, Tomson & Kilroy, Kansas City, Mo., 1977-81, mem., dir., 1981—. Contbr. articles to profl. publs. Mem. Kans. City Citizens Assn., 1980—; pres., bd. govs. Sch. Law Washburn, 1992-94, v.p. fin. 1993; with Civic Coun. of Greater Kansas City, 1999—; legal coun. Heart of Am. Coun. Boy Scouts Am., 1988-92, mem. exec. com., 1988-95, Cmty. adv. Greater Kans. City Cmty. Found. and Affiliated Trusts, 1993—; bd. dirs. Kansas City Neighborhood Alliance, 1998—, Greater Kansas City Crime Commn. Mem. Lawyers Assn. Kansas City, Kansas City Bar Assn. (chmn. civil rights com. 1984), Mo. Bar Assn., ABA (subcom. on arbitration, labor law sect. 1977—), Greater Kansas City C. of C., Univ. Club (pres. 1993-94), Kansas City Country Club. Office: Shughart Thomson & Kilroy 12 Wyandotte Plz 120 W 12th St Ste 1500 Kansas City MO 64105-1929

KILTY, JEROME TIMOTHY, playwright, stage director, actor; b. Balt., June 24, 1922; s. Harold Joseph and Irene (Zellinger) K.; m. Cavada Humphrey, May 11, 1956. B.A., Harvard U., 1949. prof. drama U. Okla., Norman, 1971, U. Tex., Austin, 1972, U. Kans., Lawrence, 1973; appointed to O'Conner Chair of Lit., Colgate U., Hamilton, N.Y., 1974-75, 91-92; instr. in drama Harvard U., Cambridge, Mass., 1983-85, 89. Co-founder, dir., actor Brattle Theatre Co., Cambridge, Mass., 1948-52; actor N.Y.C. stage and TV, 1952-57, including Relapse, 1951, Quadrille, 1952, Misalliance, 1953; played: Falstaff, Iago, City Centre, 1954; writer, actor Dear Liar, Chgo. and London, 1957 (Berlin Festival Critics award 1961, Baton Du Brigadier 1962-63, Palma D'Oro 1962-63, Stanislavsky Centenary medal 1963), dir. revival, Paris, 1974, 80, Rome, 1975, 85, for TV, Hallmark Hall of Fame, 1981, dir. Australian Premiere, 1993, Melbourne; writer, dir. for TV Ides of March, London, 1963, Long Live Life, San Francisco, 1967; dir. Marie Bell, Elisabeth Bergner, Maria Casares, Pierre Brasseur in various French, German, Italian prodns., 1962-65; assoc. dir., Am. Conservatory Theatre, San Francisco, 1966-68, Am. Shakespeare Co., Stratford, Conn., 1965-68; dir. Possibilities, N.Y.C., 1968, Sarah Ferrati in Mrs. Warren's Profession (in Italian), Rome, 1976; writer, dir. Don't Shoot Mable, It's Your Husband, 1968; writer, actor Dear Love, Boston, 1969, London, 1973, The Laffing Man, 1975; dir., actor Androcles and the Lion, 1985, Love's Labor's Lost, 1985; writer: The Little Black Book, N.Y.C., 1972, Look Away, N.Y.C.; musicals What the Devil, 1977, Barnum, 1978; play Hey Marie!, 1979; dir. Julius Caesar, San Diego Nat. Shakespeare Festival, 1979, Love's Labor's Lost, 1980, Misalliance, Denver, 1980, I, James McNeill Whistler, Hartford Stage Co., Peter Pan, Kansas City, Mo., 1985; appeared in play A Month in the Country, N.Y.C., 1979-80, Enter a Free Man, N.Y.C., 1984, Foxfire, Kansas City, Mo., 1985; mem., Hartman Theatre Co., 1981-82, 86-87, played the Doctor in Three Sisters and Ernest in Bedroom Farce; dir. Tammy Grimes in The Millionairess; star The Magistrate; mem., Am. Repertory Theatre Co., Cambridge, Mass., 1983—, created role: The King in Big River, 1983, directed, played Armado in Love's Labor's Lost, 1985, played Abel Bishop in Right You Are (If You Think So), 1988, played Don Antonio in Saturday, Sunday, Monday, 1988; played title role in King Lear, Col. Treletsky in Platonov, played James Tyrone with Claire Bloom in Long Day's Journey into Night, 1996, played Old Ekdal in Wild Duck, 1997; created role Chairman Bowman in Mastergate by Larry Gelbart, 1989, repeated role on Broadway, Criterion Theater, 1989; co-star: A Moon for the Misbegotten, Cort Theatre, N.Y.C., 1984; repeated role of Phil Hogan, Am. Repertory Theatre (Best Actor award Boston Theatre Critics 1984); mem. Hartford Stage Co., 1985-86, played in The Tempest, Twelfth Night, directed and acted in Androcles and the Lion; played Boss Mangan in Heartbreak House, Yale Repertory Theatre, 1986; dir. The Seagull, Am. Conservatory Theatre, San Francisco, 1987, The Man Who Was Peter Pan, Am. Repertory Theater, Cambridge, 1990, Arms and the Man, Alley Theater, Houston, 1995; co-star The Doctor's Dilemma, N.Y.C., 1990, played Harry Hope in The Iceman Cometh, Chgo., 1990 (Joseph Jefferson award 1991); author plays About to Begin, 1988, Margaret Sanger/Unfinished Business, 1989, The Hermit of Yalta, 1993; starred with Opera Co. of Boston in world premiere of The Balcony, 1990, Bolshoi Theatre, Moscow, 1991, starred in Gigli Concert, Court Theatre, Chgo., Spoleto Festival U.S.A., 1992, The Substance of Fire, Asolo Theatre, Sarasota, Fla., 1992, Stages Repertory Theatre, Houston, 1994, Love Letters, Asolo Theatre, 1993, King Lear, Asolo Theatre, 1993; played Horace Vandergelder in The Matchmaker, McCarter Theater, Princeton, N.J., 1994, Gov. Danforth in The Crucible, Alley Theater, Houston, 1994, King Lear, Nebr. Shakespeare Festival, 1995, Tobias in A Delicate Balance, Stages Repertory Theater, Houston, 1996. Athol Fugard's Valley Song, Arizona Theatre Co., 1997, Michael James in Playboy of the Western World, Steppenwolf Theatre, Chicago, 1998, Long Wharf Theatre, New Haven; guest starred as King Lear, Arizona State Univ., 1998. Served to capt. USAAF, 1942-46, ETO. Decorated D.F.C., Air Medal with seven clusters. Mem. Signet Soc. Club: Players (N.Y.C.). Home: PO Box 1074 Weston CT 06883-0074

KIM, CHONG LIM, political science educator; b. Seoul, Korea, July 17, 1937; came to U.S., 1962; s. Soo Myung and Chung Hwa (Moon) K.; m. Eun Hwa Park, Aug. 21, 1963; children: Bohm S., Lahn S., Lynn S. BA, Seoul Nat. U., 1960; MA, U. Oreg., 1964, PhD, 1968. Instr. U. Oreg., Eugene, 1965-67; asst. prof. U. Iowa, Iowa City, 1968-70, assoc. prof., 1970-75, prof., 1975—. Author: Legislative Connection, 1984, Legislative Process in Korea, 1981, Patterns of Recruitment, 1974; editor: Legislative Systems, 1975, Political Participation in Korea, 1980; contbr. numerous articles to profl. jours. Mem. Am. Polit. Sci. Assn., Midwest Polit. Sci. Assn. Avocations: reading, travel. Office: U Iowa Dept Polit Sci Iowa City IA 52242

KIM, DAVID SANG CHUL, publisher, evangelist, retired seminary president; b. Seoul, Republic of Korea, Nov. 9, 1915; came to U.S., 1959; m. Eui Hong Kang, Jan. 6, 1942; children: Sook Hee, Sung Soo, Hyun Soo, Young Soo, Joon Soo. BA in English Lit., Chosen Christian Coll., Seoul, 1939; postgrad., U. Wales, 1954-55, Western Conservative Bapt. Sem., 1959-61, U. Oreg., 1962-63; MA, U. Oreg., 1965; postgrad., Pacific Sch. Religion, Berkeley, Calif., 1965-66; PhD, Pacific Columbia U., 1988. Staff Chosen Rubber Industry Assn., Seoul, 1939-45; fin asst. U.S. Mil. Govt., Kunsan City, Republic of Korea, 1945-48; govt. official Ministry of Fin., Ministry of Social Affairs and Health, Ministry of Fgn. Affairs Govt. of Republic of Korea, Seoul, 1948-59; charter mem. Unification Ch., Seoul, 1954—; 1st missionary to Eng. Unification Ch., 1954-55; missionary, evangelist Unification Ch., U.S., 1959-70; supr. counseling Clearfield (Utah) Job Corps Ctr., 1966-70; founder, pres., owner The Cornerstone Press (name change to Rose of Sharon Press), 1978-85; charter mem., trustee World Relief Friendship Found., Inc. (now Internat. Relief Friendship Found., Inc.), 1974—; pres. Internat. One World Crusade Inc., 1975—; founder, United Faith, Inc., Portland, Oreg., 1970—, Global Edn. R & D Fund, Inc., 1981-96; pres. Unification Theol. Sem., 1974-94; charter mem., trustee Nat. Coun. Chs. and Social Action, 1976-96; adv. fin. supporter Global Congress of World Religions, Inc., 1978-96; charter mem. Internat. Religious Found., Inc., 1982—; v.p. Unification Thought Inst., 1989-97; founder, pres. Marriage and Family Inst. Am., 1994—; chmn. inauguration The Family Fedn. for Unification and World Peace, The Netherlands, 1996—. Author: Individual Preparation for His Coming Kingdom: Interpretation of the Principle, 1964, Victory Over Communism and the Role of Religion, 1972; editor: (book series) Day of Hope in Review, Part 1-1972-74, 1974, Part 2-1974-75, 1975, Part 3-1976-81, 1981; exec. prodr. (radio) The Unification Hour, 1975—, True Love Journey, 1993—; contbr. articles to profl. jours. Recipient Byzantine Golden medal

Am. Inst. Patristic Byzantine Studies, Inc., 1992. Address: PO Box 1755 South Rd Sta Poughkeepsie NY 12601-0755

KIM, DOOHIE, public health educator; b. Taegu, Korea, Sept. 17, 1935; s. Dong-Hoon and Hong-Dahl (Chae) K.; m. Keun-Ok Ahn, Mar. 24, 1959; children: Ji-Eoun, Ji-Kwan, Nah-Youn. BA, Kyungpook Nat. U., 1961, MA, 1963, PhD, 1970. Instr. Sch. Medicine Kyungpook Nat. U., Taegu, Korea, 1968-70, asst. prof., 1970-75, assoc. prof., 1975-78, prof., 1978-95, dir. med. libr., 1978-80, dean Sch. Pub. Health, 1990-92, 94-95, emeritus prof., 1996—; prof. and dean Sch. Medicine Dongguk U., Kyung-ju, Korea, 1995—; com. mem. Provincial Com. for Environ. Contamination, Taegu, Korea, 1975-79; adv. mem. Taegu Supervising Corp. for Korean Indsl. Safety, 1985—. Author: Environmental Sanitation, 1975, Introduction of Health Science, 1989, Practice of School Health, 1979, Making Health for Prolonging Life, 1994. Adv. mem. Provincial Policy Com. of Kyungpook-do Korea, Taegu, 1979-81, Policy Com. Taegu City, 1981-83. Maj. Korean mil., 1964-67. Recipient Letters of Commendation, Prime Ministry Korea, 1963, Minister of Helath and Social Affairs of Korea, Seoul, 1985, Pres. of Kyungpook Nat. U., Taegu, 1987. Mem. APHA, Am. Coll. Preventive Medicine (internat. mem.), Korean Soc. Preventive Medicine (pres. 1987-89, Plaque 1990), Korean Indsl. Health Assn. (leader Kyungpook br. 1974-80), Internat. Commn. Occupl. Health, Korean Soc. Agrl. Medicine and Rural Health (pres. 1994-96). Home: Lombard Mantion 2-101, 1-3 Sooseoung 2ka, Taegu 706-032, Republic of Korea Office: The Dongguk Univ Sch Medicine, 707 Suck-jang Dong Kyung-ju, Kyung 780-714, Republic of Korea

KIM, E. HAN, finance and business administration educator; b. Seoul, Korea, May 27, 1946; came to U.S., 1966; s. Chang Yoon and Young Ja (Chung) K.; m. Tack Han, June 14, 1969; children—Juliane H., Elaine H., Deborah H. BS, U. Rochester, 1969; MBA, Cornell U., 1971; PhD, SUNY-Buffalo, 1975. Asst. prof. Ohio State U., Columbus, 1975-77, assoc. prof., 1979-80; assoc. prof., then prof. fin. and bus. adminstrn. U. Mich., Ann Arbor, 1980-84, Fred M. Taylor Disting. prof., 1984—, chmn. dept. fin., 1988-91; dir. Mitsui Life Fin. Rsch. Ctr., 1990—; vis. assoc. prof. U. Chgo., 1978-79; vis. rsch. fellow Korea Devel. Inst., 1986-87; econ. cons. Govt. of Korea, 1985-87, 98; Cycle and Carriage vis. prof. Nat. U. Singapore, 1989; Yamaichi prof. econs. U. Tokyo, 1990-91; cons. Bank of Korea, 1985, U.S. Dept. Treasury, IRS, 1988-94, World Bank, 1989-91, 93, Posco, 1995-98, Korea Stock Exch., 1997-98; co-chair Citizens for Econ. Freedom, 1997—; bd. dirs. Found. Rsch. in Internat. Banking and Fin. Assoc. editor Jour. Fin., 1979-83, 88-92, Fin. Rev., 1982—, Internat. Jour. Fin., 1990—, Internat. Rev. Fin. Analysis, 1990-92, Rev. No. Am. Jour. of Econs. and Fin., 1990—, Rev. Quantitative Fin. and Acctg., 1990—, Pacific Basin Fin. Jour., 1991-96; edit. bd. Jour. Bus. Rsch., 1977—; adv. bd. Asia-Pacific Jour. Mgmt., 1990-96, Jour. Asian Bus., 1996—; contbr. articles to profl. jours. Mem. Korea-Am. Econ. Assn. (sec. gen. 1985, v.p. 1986, pres. 1996), Am. Econ. Assn., Am. Fin. Assn., Western Fin. Assn. Avocation: tennis, golf. Office: U Mich Sch Bus Adminstrn Ann Arbor MI 48109

KIM, E. KITAI, pathologist; b. Sangjoo, Kyungbook, Republic of Korea, June 5, 1933; came to U.S., 1966; s. Byung O. and Soon A. (Park) K.; m. Chung Ok Roh, Apr. 3, 1960; children: Steve Ho-Suk, David Hyun-Min. Pre-med., Seoul Nat. U., 1954, MD, 1958. Diplomate Am. Bd. Pathology. Resident, tchg. fellow Case-We. Res. U. Hosp., Cleve., 1966-72; asst. prof., assoc. prof. Med. Coll. Ohio, Toledo, 1972-89, prof. pathology, 1989—. Author: Surgical Pathology with Cytology Correlation, 1992, (book chpt.) Gastrointestinal Cancer, 1989. Capt. Korean M.C., 1958-64. Recipient Brilliant Citizens' award Seoul City Govt., 1995. Fellow Coll. Am. Pathologists, Internat. Acad. Pathology, Internat. Acad. Cytology; mem. Am. Soc. Cytology. Avocations: golf, indoor exercise, reading. Office: Med Coll Ohio 3000 Arlington Ave Toledo OH 43614-2595

KIM, EARNEST JAE-HYUN, import and export company executive; b. Seoul, Korea, Dec. 9, 1938; s. Chang-Nyun and Gui-Nim (Yun) K.; m. Jung-Ki Eun, Mar. 25, 1967; children: Yoo-Kyoung, Ja-Hong, Yung-Ju, Do-Hyung. Degree, Hanyang U., 1961; postgrad., Sung Kyun Kwan U., 1975. Reporter Daily Econ. News, Seoul, 1966-74; exec. dir. STAF Corp., Seoul, 1975-82; dir. Korea Fedn. Handicrafts Coops., Seoul, 1979-82; pres. Buenos Amigos, Inc., Laredo, Tex., 1982-95, Buenos Hermanos L.L., 1992—, Nueva Moda Mundo, Mexico City, Mex., 1990—, Buenos Amigos de Mex. S.A., 1994—, Amiguitas S.A. de C.V., Mexico City, 1995—. Inventor, patentee Method of Casting, Method of Jewelry Making. Recipient Spl. Congl. Recognition, Congressman Albert Bustamante, 1988, Cert. of Excellence, Senator Judith Zaffirini, 1983, Cert. of Appreciation, Mayor of Laredo, 1988, Cert. of Appreciation, Am. Legion, 1988, recognition award of achievement and contbn. Ministry Commerce, Industry and Energy Korea, 1999. Mem. Laredo C. of C., Korean Assn. Mex. (pres. 1998-99), Korean C. of C. (v.p. nat. chpt. 1999-01), Overseas Korean Trade Assn. (bd. dirs. 1999-01), Lions (v.p. Laredo 1991—, pres. award 1989), Laredo Country club. Buddhist. Avocation: golf. Home: 413 Chevy Chase Dr Laredo TX 78041-2702 Office: Amiguitas SA de CV, Carmen 58 Col Centro, Mexico City 06020, Mexico

KIM, GEUN-EUN, surgeon, educator; b. Seoul, Korea, 1941; came to U.S., 1965; s. Doo-Man and Ki-Ok; m. Eun-Kyung Choi; children: Catherine, Judy. MD, Seoul Nat. U., 1965. Cert. in surgery. Intern Einstein Med. Ctr., Phila., 1965-66, resident, 1966-70; fellow in vascular surgery NYU Med. Ctr., 1970; with Beth Israel Hosp., N.Y.C., Downtown Hosp.; clin. prof. surgery N.Y. Med. Coll.; vis. prof. surgery Coll. Medicine, Ulsan U., Seoul; dir. Ctr. for Vascular Disease, Asan Med. Ctr. Fellow ACS; mem. Assn. for Acad. Surgery, Internat. Cardiovasc. Soc., N.Y. Soc. Surgery, Ea. Vascular Soc., Korean Surg. Soc. (hon.). E-mail: gekim7@www.AMC.Seoul.Kr. Office: Ctr Vascular Disease, Asan Med Ctr, Song Pa Ku Seoul Korea

KIM, HAN PYONG, dentist, researcher; b. Seoul, Korea, May 2, 1945; s. Koe Jin and Jung Bok (Park) K.; m. Young Sook Yoon, Apr. 27, 1974; 1 child, Sung Mo. MA, DDS, Seoul Nat. U., 1975; PhD, Yonsei U., Seoul, 1982; MA, Monterey Inst. Internat. Study, 1996. Prof. Yonsei U., Seoul, 1977-84; vis. scholar UCLA, 1982; project rschr. for health care sys. Korea Dental Assn., Seoul, 1988-92; mem. bd. health ins. Nat. HIC, Seoul, 1990-92. Mem. Pres.'s Leadership Circle, Washington, 1995. Avocations: golf, fishing, photography. Home: 3125 Hermitage Pebble Beach CA 93953

KIM, IH CHIN, pediatrician; b. Seoul, Korea, Aug. 6, 1925; s. Young Whan and Young Ho (Cho) K.; came to U.S., 1953, naturalized, 1965; MD, Seoul Nat. U., 1950; student Yon Sei U., 1944-46; postgrad. U. Pa., 1954-55; m. Helen Fern Wagner, Mar. 15, 1957 (dec.); children: Catherine Joy Kim Smith, Stephen Thomas. Diplomate Am. Bd. Pediatrics. Intern, Transp. Hosps., Seoul and Pusan, Korea, 1950-51; resident in pediatrics Pusan Children's Charity Hosp., 1951-53, Children's Hosp. Phila., 1953-55, fellow in pediatric gastroenterology, 1955-58, research assoc., 1958-67, med. staff, 1963-67; practice medicine, specializing in pediatrics, Easton, Pa., 1965—, Phillipsburg, N.J., 1971—; staff dept. pediatrics Hahnemann Med. Coll. and Hosp., Phila., 1967-96, Easton Hosp., 1965—, Warren Hosp., Phillipsburg, N.J., 1966—, chief dept. pediatrics, 1978-90; clin. asst. prof. pediatrics Hahnemann Med. Coll., Phila., 1971-96. Contbr. articles to med. jours., Fellow Am. Acad. Pediatrics; mem. AMA, Country Club Northampton County. Presbyterian. Address: 6 Ivy Ct Easton PA 18045-5816 Office: 545 Heckman St Phillipsburg NJ 08865-2600

KIM, JAE TAIK, educator; b. Seoul, Korea, Oct. 3, 1933; came to the U.S., 1961; s. Hee Joon and Soon Ra Hong Kim; m. Yang Ja Yoon, Aug. 14, 1962; 1 child, Glenn V. BA, Yonsei U., Seoul, 1961; MPA, U. So. Calif., L.A., 1965, PhD, 1971. MPA coord. West Point Off-Campus Program, 1978-94; prof. John Jay Coll., CUNY, N.Y.C., 1991—; bd. dirs. Cho Hung Bank. Editor: New Reading in Public Administration, 1980; contbr. articles to ency. Chmn. bd. dirs. N.Y. State Adv. Coun. on Ethnic Affairs, 1979-81; rsch. cons., bd. mem. Tri-State Asian Profile, United Way, N.Y., 1979-80; mem. adv. coun. U.S. Commn. on Civil Rights, N.Y., 1980-85; mem. cultural awareness curriculum adv. com. N.Y.C. Police Dept., 1989-90; pres. Korean-Am. Assn. Greater N.Y., 1992-94. Recipient Ellis Island medal of honor Nat. Ethnic Coalition Orgns., N.Y.C., 1994, Spl. award Asian Am. Higher Edn. Coun., N.Y.C., 1994, Pres. Nat. award Republic Korea, Seoul, 1995; named Man of Compassion, Inst. Jewish Humanities, N.Y.C., 1994. E-mail: JTYJKim@aol.com. Home: 108 Pershing Rd Englewood Cliffs NJ 07632

KIM, JAEGWON, philosophy educator; b. Taegu, Korea, Sept. 12, 1934; came to U.S., 1955, naturalized, 1966; m. Sylvia Hughes, June 18, 1961; 1 child, Justin Lee. AB, Dartmouth Coll., 1958; PhD, Princeton U., 1962. Instr. philosophy Swarthmore Coll., 1961-63; asst. prof. philosophy Brown U., 1963-67, vis. prof., 1975, William Perry Faunce prof. philosophy, 1987—; chair dept. Borwn U., 1990-99; assoc. prof. philosophy U. Mich., 1967-70, prof., 1971-87, chmn. dept., 1979-87, Roy Wood Sellars Prof. Philosophy, 1986-87; assoc. prof. Cornell U., 1970-71; prof. Johns Hopkins U., 1977-78; vis. prof. Stanford U., 1967; Fulbright lectr., Republic of Korea, 1984. Author: Supervenience and Mind, 1993, Philosophy of Mind, 1996, Mind in a Physical World, 1998; contbr. numerous articles to profl. publs.; editor: (with Alvin I. Goldman) Values and Morals, 1978, (with A. Beckermann and H. Flohr) Emergence or Reduction?, 1992 (with E. Sosa) A Companion to Metaphysics, 1995. Fellow Am. Coun. Learned Soc., 1980-81, NEH, 1985; NSF grantee, 1977-79. Mem. Am. Philos. Assn. (chmn. com. on status and future of profession 1976-81, mem. bd. officers 1976-81, 88-90, v.p. ctrl. divsn. 1987-88, pres. 1988-89), Philosophy of Sci. Assn. (mem. governing bd. 1979-81), Am. Acad. Arts and Scis., Coun. Philos. Studies. Office: Brown U Dept Philosophy Providence RI 02912

KIM, JAI BIN, civil engineering educator; b. Seoul, Korea, May 17, 1934; came to U.S., 1955; s. M.Y. and Y.W. Kim; m. Yung Ja Hong, June 17, 1960; children: Clara A., Vivian T., Robert H., Patricia A. BSCE, Oreg. State U., 1959, MSCE, 1960; PhD in Civil Engring., U. Md., 1965. Registered profl. engr., Pa., Md., N.J., Va., Conn. Chief rsch. engr. D.C. Govt. Dept. Hwys. and Traffic, Washington, 1964-66; asst. prof. Bucknell U., Lewisburg, Pa., 1966-72, assoc. prof., 1972-77, prof., 1977—, chmn. civil engring., 1977—; pres. structural cons. co. BKLB, Inc., Lewisburg, 1982—. Patentee in field. Mem. ASCE (mem. com. 1982—), Transp. Rsch. Bd. (com. on bridge constrn. 1988—). Republican. Office: Bucknell U Dept Civil Engring Moore Ave Lewisburg PA 17837

KIM, JAI SOO, physics educator; b. Taegu, Korea, Nov. 1, 1925; came to U.S., 1958, naturalized, 1963; s. Wan Sup and Chanam (Whang) K.; m. Hai Kyou Kim, Nov. 2, 1952; children: Kami, Tomi, Kihyun, Himi. BSc in Physics, Seoul Nat. U., Korea, 1949; MS in Physics, U. Sask., Can., 1957, PhD, 1958. Asst. prof. physics Clarkson U., Potsdam, N.Y., 1958-59; asst. prof. physics U. Idaho, Moscow, 1959-62, assoc. prof., 1962-65, prof., 1965-67; prof. atmospheric sci. and physics SUNY, Albany, 1967-95, chmn. dept. atmospheric sci., 1969-76; emeritus prof., 1995—; rep. Univ. Corp. for Atmospheric Research SUNY, Albany, 1970-76; cons. Korean Studies Program SUNY, Stony Brook, 1983-85; vis. prof. Advanced Inst. Sci. and Tech., Seoul, Korea, 1983; cons. U.S. Army Research Office, 1978-79, Battelle Meml. Inst., 1978-81, Environ. One Corp., 1978-84, N.Y. State Environ. Conservation Dept., 1976-82, Norlite Corp., 1982-84, Korean Antarctic Program, 1988—. Contbr. articles to profl. jours. Mem. Am. Inst. Physics, Am. Geophys. Union, Sigma Xi. Home: 22 Westover Rd Slingerlands NY 12159-3646 Office: 1400 Washington Ave Albany NY 12222-0100

KIM, JAMES JOO-JIN, electronics company executive; b. Seoul, Korea, Jan. 8, 1936; came to U.S., 1955, naturalized, 1971; s. Hyang-Soo and Seung-Ye (Oh) K.; m. Agnes Chungsook Kil, Dec. 30, 1961; children—Susan, David, John. Student, Seoul Nat. U. Coll. Law, 1954-55; B.S., U. Pa., 1959, M.A., 1961, postgrad., 1961-63; D in Comml. Sci. (hon.), Villanova U., 1990. Asst. prof. econs. Villanova (Pa.) U., 1964-70; founder, pres. AMKOR Electronics, Inc., West Chester, Pa., 1970-80; chmn., chief exec. officer AMKOR Tech. Inc., 1980—, chmn., CEO, 1998—; founder, dir. Electronics Boutique Holding Corp.; bd. dirs. Forté Sys., Inc., WLSI Tech., Inc., CFM Techs. Inc.; chmn. Anam Group (Korea), 1992—. Trustee U. Pa. Recipient award Pres. Park/Chung Hee, Republic of Korea, 1979, award Pres. Roh/Tae Woo, Republic of Korea, 1990. Mem. Union League Club (Phila.), Beta Gamma Sigma. Office: AMKOR Tech Inc 1345 Enterprise Dr West Chester PA 19380-5930

KIM, JAMES JUPYUNG, surgeon, orthopedist, medical educator; b. Seoul, Dec. 4, 1943; m. Janet Young Hee, Nov. 22, 1971; children: Daniel, Erica. MD, Seoul Nat. U., 1968, Seoul Nat. U., 1968. Diplomate Am. Acad. Orthopedic Surgeons. Intern St. Francis Hosp., Miami Beach, Fla.; resident Mt. Sinai Med. Ctr., Miami Beach; clin. asst. prof. Med. Sch. U. Miami. Mem. AMA, Miami Orthopedic Soc., Fla. Med. Assn., Dade County Med. Assn. Presbyterian. Avocations: golf. Office: James J Kim MD 7400 N Kendall Dr Miami FL 33156-7706

KIM, JAY, former congressman; b. Korea, 1939; m. June, 1961; children: Richard, Kathy, Eugene. BS, U. So. Calif., MCE; MPA, Calif. State U. Coun. mem. City of Diamond Bar, Calif., 1990, mayor, 1991; mem. 103rd Congress from 41st dist. Calif., 1993-98; pres., founder Jaykim Engrs. Inc. Recipient Outstanding Achievement in Bus. and Community Devel. award, Engr. of Yr. award, Caballero de Distinction award, Engr. Bus. of the Yr. award, others. Republican. Methodist. Address: Ste 201 374 Maple Ave Vienna VA 22180*

KIM, JOHN CHAN KYU, electrical engineer; b. Tokyo, June 15, 1935; came to U.S., 1958; s. Ke Jun and Young Sok Kim; m. Tong-Rahn Chu, Sept. 11, 1965; children: Janet M., William H., Douglas S. Student, Seoul Nat. U., 1954-57; BSEE, Tri-State U., 1959; MSEE, Mich. State U., 1960, PhD in Elec. Engring., 1962. Instr. Tri-State U., Angola, Ind., 1961-62; sr. rsch. engr. Systems Rsch. Labs., Inc., Dayton, Ohio, 1962-64, Honeywell, Inc., Mpls., 1964-65; sr. staff engr. E-System Inc., Falls Church, Va., 1965-69; head analysis sect., C3 dept. TRW, Inc., Fairfax, Va., 1969-74, sr. staff engr., systems engring. lab., 1974-79, mgr. undersea surveillance dept., 1979-81, asst. project mgr. WWMCCS Support Project, 1981-85, dep. project mgr., Navy Comms. Project, 1985-88, advanced systems mgr., Navy Systems Ops., 1988-92, sr. staff engr., Air Traffic Control Systems Project, 1992-95, tech. fellow, 1995—. Author: Naval Shipboard Communications Systems, 1994. Bd. dirs. Vol. Ctr. of Fairfax (Va.) County, 1992—; scoutmaster Boy Scouts Am., McLean, 1983-84; nat. judge Mathcounts, Alexandria, Va., 1996—; engring. and devel. com. Air Traffic Control Assn. Mem. IEEE, Armed Forces Comms. and Electronics Assn., Nat. Security Industry Assn., Air Traffic Control Assn. Methodist. Avocations: cycling, swimming, carpentry. Home: 8006 Snowpine Way Mc Lean VA 22102-2420 Office: TRW Inc 475 School St SW Washington DC 20024-2711

KIM, JOUNG-IM, communication educator, consultant; b. Taejon, Choongnam, Republic of Korea, May 8, 1947; came to U.S., 1975; d. Yong-Kap Kim and Im-Soon Nam; m. James Andrew Palmore, Jr., Jan. 21, 1989 (div. Nov. 1993). BA in Libr. Sci., Yonsei U., Seoul, Korea, 1970, postgrad., 1974-75; postgrad., U. Hawaii at Manoa, 1975, MA in Sociology, 1978; PhD in Comm., Stanford U., 1986. Rschr. Korean Inst. Family Planning, Seoul, 1974-75; spl. resource person UN/East-West Ctr., Honolulu, 1976; rsch. asst. East-West Ctr., Honolulu, 1977-78; rsch., teaching asst. Stanford U., Calif., 1979-83, instr., 1984; asst. prof. U. Hawaii at Manoa, Honolulu, 1984-95, assoc. prof., 1995—; cons. UN Econ. and Social Commn. for Asia and Pacific, Bangkok, 1979, 84-86, 89, 90-92; cons. UN Devel. Program, Devel. Tng. Comm. Planning, Bangkok, 1984, UN Population Funds, N.Y.C., 1991, 92; mem. faculty communication and info. scis. doctoral program U. Hawaii at Manoa, Honolulu, mem. faculty Ctr. Korean Studies. Contbr. articles to profl. jours., monographs, and chpts. to books. Grantee East-West Ctr., 1972, 75-78; Population Libr. fellow U. N.C., 1973; Stanford U. fellow, 1978-79, 83, 84. Mem. Internat. Comm. Assn., Internat. Network for Social Network Analysis. Avocations: dancing, listening to music, flower arranging, reading, swimming. Office: U Hawaii at Manoa 2560 Campus Rd # 336 Honolulu HI 96822-2217

KIM, KWANG-IEL, psychiatrist, educator; b. Pyungyang, Dem. Peoples Rep. Korea, Dec. 6, 1936; s. Insong and Youngbok (Chie) K.; m. Haeshin Kim, May 10, 1965; children: Daeho, Sora, Yongho. MD, Seoul Nat. U., 1961, M in Med. Scis., 1963, PhD in Med. Sci., 1967. Clin. rschr., instr. neuropsychiatry Seoul Nat. U. Hosp., 1968-71; chief dept. psychiatry Seoul Mcpl. Hosp., 1969-71; chmn., assoc. prof. Kyung Hee U., Seoul, 1971-75; chmn., prof. Hanyang U., Seoul, 1975-97, pres. Mental Health Rsch. Inst., 1975-88, 97-99; supt. Kuri Hosp. Hanyang U., 1999—; cons. The Women's Hotline and Sexual Violence Hotline, Seoul, 1985—, Nat. Annuity Corp., Seoul, 1989—; med. advisor The Korean Automobile Accident Ins., Seoul, 1988—, Upjohn Pharmaceutica, Seoul, 1989—, Asiana Airline, Seoul, 1995—, Samsung Marine and Accident Ins., Seoul, 1995—. Author: Psychoanalytic Study of Korean Traditional Culture, 1983 (award 1984); editor: Family Violence: The Fact and Counteract, 1988; editor-in-chief Jour. Korean Neuropsychiat. Assn., 1989-95; mem. editl. bd. Children and Youth Svcs. Rev., 1990—; contbr. articles to profl. jours. Mem. deliberations com. Korean Broadcasting Comm., Seoul, 1988-91. Capt. Korean Army, 1961-66. Recipient Best Sci. Publ. prize Korean Med. News, 1973. Mem. Korean Neuropsychiat. Assn. (pres. 1985-86, trustee, chmn. 1986-87, Byokbong prize 1993), Korean Cultural Anthropology Assn., World Psychiat. Assn. (transcultural psychiat. com. 1983—, Wyeth-Ayerst award 1989), Coun. Korean Med. Inst. (deliberations com. 1989—), Korean Acad. Sci. Tech. (acting mem.). Home: Pyungchang-dong 175-7 1-106, Seoul 110-12, Republic of Korea Office: Hanyang U Kuri Hosp, Dept Neuropsychiatry, Kuri 471-020, Republic of Korea

KIM, LILLIAN G. LEE, retired administrative assistant; b. Toishan, Canton, China, June 17, 1919; came to the U.S., 1921; d. Yick You and Lucy Yu Oy (Louie) Lee; m. Herman Hom Kim, Oct. 12, 1941. *Lillian Kim's siblings are Jane Lee Hahn (1st husband, James, 2nd, Walter B. brothers) Thomas and Ingeborg Lee; Walter (Wally) and Anna May Wong Lee; Paul and Thelma Stewart Lee. Her nieces are Mariyln Johnson, Barbara Fitzgerald, Jane E. Everich, Susan A. Considine, Monica Lee Hafner. Nephews are James W. Hahn, Douglas P. Lee, Stewart C. Lee, Eric Grant Lee and Roger Alan Lee. Her great-nephews and great-nieces include Sean M. Considine, Patrick S. Everich, Ryan L. Everich, Jessica Lee Considine, Jordan E. Considine, Megan E. Lee, Justin Alexander Lee, Rachel Hope Lee, Connor Benjamin Lee, Brandon Michael Lee, as well as other half-nephews/ nieces, and greats.* Cert., Ea. U., 1941. Stenographer, sec. Peabody Book Shop, Balt., 1937-38; sec. Prisoners Aid Assn., Balt., 1938-41; sec. Civilian Def. Exec. Office Balt. Mcpl. Govt., 1942-44, sec. to safety dir., 1944-48; sec.-stenographer, asst. supr. stenography divsn. Ctrl. Payroll Bur., 1948-64, adminstrv. sec., supr. adminstrv. sect., 1964-77; ret., 1977; ctrl. payroll councilwoman Classified Mcpl. Employee Assn., Balt., 1949-77, columnist Hall Light, 1950-77; chmn. ret. employee group CHICA-Combined Health/ Industry Comb. Appeal and United Way, Balt., 1970-77; bd. dirs. Women's Civic League; pres., bd. dirs. AARP (Rodgers Forge Chpt. 2360), 1997—; lectr. in field. *Chinese immigration specialist who worked for repeal of 105 quota and liberalizaton of immigration laws. Reunited relatives living in Hoi Ping, Bock Suey, and Toi Shan with families in the U.S. Toishanese/ Cantonese interpreter. Liaison between Chinese families and public. Community volunteer. Established social ties between the public and their Chinese neighbors by coordinating Grace and St. Peter's annual Chinese Lunar New Year Festival. Recognitions, awards include: Outstanding Woman of the Week; Baltimore's Best Silver and Blue award; Outstanding Baltimorean; Outstanding Service in Promoting International Relations; Carnation Volunteerism award; Outstanding Service in Teaching Chinese Language and Culture; GERI award; Star Spangled Banner Essay award.* Author: (with Lee Yick You and Louie Yu Oy) Early Baltimore Chinese Families, 1976, Chinese Americans-A Part of America, 1977; Letters to the Editor: Tien Nien Poems, Lectures, and Speeches, Gnin-Gnin's China: Our Heritage, 1980, Grace and St. Peter's Chinese Church School (founders Frances L. and Florence M. "Daisy" Marshall), Chinese Traditions, Customs, and Festivals; edit. publ. Wah Kue Sim Mon (bilingual news bull.), 1998, Tien Nien Chatter; columnist Towson Times; freelance writer Senior Digest. organizor Chinese Young People's Fellowship, 1946-65; founder, exec. sec. Grace & St. Peter's Chinese Lang. Sch., Balt., 1954-73, dir., prin., 1974—; vestrywoman Grace & St. Peter's Ch., Balt., mem. parish activity planning, 1969—, sec. bd. trustees Grace & St. Peter's Sch., Balt., 1980-86; trustee, 1987-90; exec. bd. Boy Scouts Am., 1978-95; mem., bd. dirs. Women's Civic League, 1979-82, exec. bd., 1999; Chinese interpreter of Am. laws, social security taxes, federal and state taxes to Chinese; represented Chinese immigrants in cts. as a vol. Recipient Gold 13 medal WJZ-TV Channel 13, Exec. Citation Humanitarian award Baltimore County, Golden Rule award JC Penney's, Best of Towson, 1998, First Place Best Vol. award Readers of Towson Times, 1998; Congratulatory Honors award Club 88 Tchrs. of Lyndhurst Elem. Sch. No. 88), 1999, award for outstanding svc. tchg. and promoting lang., culture, tradition, and history Coordination Coun. for N.Am. Affairs, Dist. Svc. to Balt. Chinese Cmty. award Orgn. of Chinese Ams.-Balt. Chpt. Mem. AARP (pub. rels. dir., bd. dirs.), Episcopal Asiamerica Ministry (parish rep. 1975-93, diocesan rep. 1994—), Nat. Soc. D.A.R. (medal of hon.). Democrat. Episcopalian. Avocations: community service, gardening, bowling, reading. Home: 524 Anneslie Rd Baltimore MD 21212-2009 Office: Grace & St Peters Chinese Lang Sch 707 Park Ave Baltimore MD 21201-4703

KIM, MI JA, dean; b. Seoul, Jan. 23, 1940; came to U.S., 1966; d. Si Hyung and Jung Kwon (Ahn) Lee; m. Heung Soo Kim, Jan. 14, 1964; children: Yoon Hi and Joseph. BS in Nursing, Yon Sei U., Seoul, 1962; PhD in Physiology, U. Ill., Chgo., 1975; JD (hon.), North Park Coll., 1995. Staff nurse Severance Hosp., Seoul, 1962-63; health nurse Am. Embassy, Seoul, 1963-66; asst. prof. Coll. Nursing/Univ. Ill., Chgo., 1975-79, assoc. prof., 1979-84, prof., 1984—, assoc. dean for rsch. dir. of grad. studies and assoc. dean acad. affairs, 1984-88, acting dean, 1988-89, dean, 1989-95, vice chancellor for rsch. and dean of grad. coll., 1995—; cons. Levine Assocs., Kensington, Md., 1989—, Bd. Regents Higher Edn., Boston, 1989, Nat. Ctr. Nursing Rsch., Bethesda, Md., 1987-91, 1996—; mem. nat. adv. coun. Nat. Inst. Nursing Rsch., Nat. Inst. of Health, 1996-2000; mem. forum Future of Academic Medicine, Am. Assn. Med. Colls., 1996-99; secretariat World Health Orgn. Collaborating Ctrs. for Nursing and Midwifery Devel., 1988-94; active White House health professions review group Heath Care Reform, 1993. Mem. adv. bd. Health of the Pub., PEW Charitable Trust, Robert Wood Johnson found., 1992-96; profl. review group mem. WHite House, 1993; adv. coun. Ctr. Bioethics and human Dignity, 1994. Named 100 Most Influential Women in Chgo., Chgo. Tribune, 1991, Univ. Scholar, U. Ill., 1985-88, Outstanding Nurse Educator, Korean Nurses Assn., Seoul, 1983; recipient Disting. Health and Edn. award Midwest Cmty. Coun. Chgo., 1994, Book of Yr. award Am. Jour. Nursing, 1984, Golden Apple award, students of Coll. Nursing, U. Ill., 1976, 78. Fellow Am. Acad. Nursing; mem. North Am. Nursing Diagnosis (bd. dirs. 1985—), Am. Thoracic Soc., Chgo. Lung Assn. (bd. dirs. 1977—, Leadership Recognition award 1996), Chgo. Heart Assn. (bd. govs. 1980-88), Am. Physiol. Soc., Internat. Leadership Inst. (adv. coun. 1998—), Sigma Theta Tau (Disting. lectr. 1987, Mary Tolle Wright award for Excellence in Leadership, 1997). Avocation: golf. Office: U Ill Chgo Rm 310AOB 1737 W Polk St # 672 Chicago IL 60612-7224

KIM, MICHAEL CHARLES, lawyer; b. Honolulu, Mar. 9, 1950; s. Harold Dai You and Maria Adrienne K. Student, Gonzaga U., 1967-70; BA, U. Hawaii, 1971; JD, Northwestern U., 1976. Bar: Ill. 1977, U.S. Dist. Ct. (no. dist.) Ill. 1977, U.S. Ct. Appeals (7th cir.) 1981, U.S. Supreme Ct. 1986. Assoc. counsel Nat. Assn. Realtors, Chgo., 1977-78; assoc. Rudnick & Wolfe, Chgo., 1978-83, Rudd & Assocs., Hoffman Estates, Ill., 1983-85; ptnr. Rudd & Kim, Hoffman Estates and Chgo., 1985-87; prin. Michael C. Kim & Assocs., Chgo. and Schaumburg, Ill., 1987-88; ptnr. Martin, Craig, Chester & Sonnenschein, Chgo. and Schaumburg, 1988-91; sr. ptnr. Arnstein & Lehr, Chgo. and Hoffman Estates, 1991—; gen. counsel Assn. Sheridan Condo-Coop Owners, Chgo., 1988—; adj. prof. John Marshall Law Sch., Chgo. Author column Apt. and Condo News, 1984-87; co-author Historical and Practice Notes; contbr. articles to profl. jours. Bd. dirs. Astor Villa Condo Assn., Chgo., 1987-91, treas. 1987-89. Mem. ABA, Chgo. Bar Assn. (chmn condominium law subcom. 1990-92, chmn. real property legis. subcom. 1995-97, vice chmn. real property law com., 1998—), Ill. State Bar Assn. (real estate law sect. coun. 1990-94, corp. and securities law sect. coun. 1990-92), Asian Am. Bar Assn. Greater Chgo. Area (bd. dirs. 1987-88, 90-91), Cmty. Assns. Inst. Ill. (bd. dirs. 1990-92, pres. 1992), Coll. Cmty. Assn. Lawyers (bd. govs. 1994-98), Univ. Club (Chgo.). Avocations: squash, photography, travel. Office: Arnstein & Lehr 120 S Riverside Plz Ste 1200 Chicago IL 60606-3910

KIM, MINSEONG, economics educator; b. Pusan, Korea, May 17, 1963; s. Hyung-Kun Kim and Mi-Hye Cho; m. Yeonwook Im, Nov. 24, 1990; children: Danny Taewoon, Lynette. BA, Seoul Nat. U., 1986; PhD, Brown U., 1996. Asst. prof. U. Pitts., 1996—. Contbr.: (book) The Political Economy of Conflict and Appropriation, 1996; contbr. articles to profl. jours. Susan Kamins fellow Brown U., 1992, rsch. fellow, 1993, Alfred Sloan fellow, 1995. Office: U Pitts Dept Econs 4S01 Forbes Quad Pittsburgh PA 15260

KIM, MOON HYUN, physician, educator; b. Seoul, Korea, Nov. 30, 1934; s. Jae Hang and Kum Chu (Choi) K.; m. Yong Cha Pak, June 20, 1964; children: Peter, Edward. M.D., Yonsei U., 1960. Diplomate: Am. Bd. Ob-Gyn. (examiner 1979—). Sr. instr. Ob-Gyn Yonsei U., Seoul, 1967-68; intern Md. Gen. Hosp., Balt., 1961-62; resident in Ob-Gyn Cleve. Met. Gen. Hosp., 1962-66; fellow in reproductive endocrinology U. Wash., Seattle, 1966-67, U. Toronto, Ont., Can., 1968-70; asst. prof. Ob-Gyn, also chief endocrinology and infertility U. Chgo., 1970-74; asso. prof. Ob-Gyn Ohio State U., Columbus, 1974-78; prof. Ohio State U., 1978-92, chief div. reproductive endocrinology, 1974-92, vice chmn. dept. ob-gyn, 1982-96; Richard L. Meiling chair in ob-gyn., Ohio State U., 1987-98; prof. U. Calif., Irvine, 1998—. Contbg. author books; contbr. articles to profl. jours. Recipient McClintock award U. Chgo., 1975; named Prof. of Yr. Ohio State U., 1976; recipient Clin. Teaching award, 1980. Fellow Am. Coll. Ob-Gyn; mem. Am. Gynecol. and Obstetric Soc., Korean Med. Assn., Am. Fertility Soc., Chgo. Gynecol. Soc., Endocrine Soc., Soc. Study Reprodn., Soc. Gynecol. Investigation. Home: 24 Whistler Ct Irvine CA 92612-4069 Office: Univ Calif Irvine Med Ctr 101 The City Dr Bldg 22A Orange CA 92868

KIM, PAUL DAVID, emergency medical administrator; b. Schenectady, N.Y., Nov. 25, 1957; s. Hyung Rin and Eleanora (Pallante) K.; m. Jean Penna, Nov. 11, 1988; 1 child, Melissa. BS in Psychology, Fordham U., 1980; MD, U. Juarez City, Mex., 1985. Med. asst. Office of Dr. Surendra Nevatia, Glens Falls, N.Y., 1985-86; counselor adolescent mental health Four Winds Hosp., Saratoga Springs, N.Y., 1986-88; asst. chief med. adminstrn. svc. Stratton Dept. VA Med. Ctr., Albany, N.Y., 1989-96, area mgr. office emergency med. preparedness, 1996—; pres., founder SK Consulting, Inc., Pittsfield, Mass., 1993—. Mem. editl. adv. bd. MEDSAFE, Inc., 1995—; contbr. articles to healthcare jours. Vol. mem. Bousquet Ski Patrol. Mem. Am. Coll. Health Care Execs., Nat. Ski Patrol, New Eng. Assn. Ind. Healthcare Cons., N.Y. State Emergency Mgrs. (com. mem. 1996—). Republican. Roman Catholic. Office: Dept VA Med Ctr 113 Holland Ave Albany NY 12208-3410*

KIM, PETER SUNGBAI, biochemistry educator; b. Atlanta, Apr. 27, 1958; s. Mi Heh (Ryu) K.; m. Kathryn H. Spitzer; children: Michael, Jeremy, Alexander. AB magna cum laude with distinction, Cornell U., 1979; PhD, Stanford U., 1985. Whitehead fellow Whitehead Inst., Cambridge, 1985-88, assoc. mem., 1988-92, mem., 1992—; asst. prof. biology MIT, Cambridge, 1988-92, assoc. prof., 1992-95, prof., 1995—; asst. investigator Howard Hughes Med. Inst., Cambridge, 1990-93, assoc. investigator, 1993-97, investigator, 1997—. Recipient Excellence in Chemistry award ICI Pharms., 1989, Walter J. Johnson prize Jour. Molecular Biology, 1989, Nat. Acad. Sci. Molecular Biology award, 1993, Eli Lilly Biol. Chemistry award Am. Chem. Soc., 1994, DuPont Merck Young Investigator award Protein Soc., 1994, Ho-Am prize for basic sci. Ho-Am. Found., 1998, Hans Neurath award The Protein Soc., 1999. Fellow Biophys. Soc., Am. Acad. Microbiology; mem. NAS, Korean Acad. of Sci. and Tech. Office: MIT/Whitehead Inst 9 Cambridge Ctr Cambridge MA 02142-1401

KIM, PYUNG-SOO, martial arts educator; b. Seoul, Korea, Dec. 4, 1939; came to U.S., 1968; s. Chong Won and Duk In (Lee) Kim; m. Sonnya Park Kim; children: Sean Kim, Tasha Kim. BA in Russian Lang. and Lit., Han Kuk U. Fgn. Studies, Seoul, 1963. 10th degree Black Belt, 1994. Founder Kong Soo Do Club, Joong Ang H.S., Seoul, 1954, Kwon Bop Martial Arts Club, Han Kuk U. Fgn. Studies, Seoul, 1957-63; tchr. Spl. Police Detachment Korean Pres., 1958; tchr. hand-to-hand combat tng. Republic of Korea Army, 8th Divsn., 1961-63; founder Korean Tae Kwon/Karate Acad., Seoul, 1963; chief instr. Kang Duk Won Martial Arts Assn., Seoul, 1964, 8th U.S. Army and HQ I Corps, 1964-67; founder Kim Soo Coll. Tae Kwon-Karate, Houston, 1968, ChaYon-Ryu, Houston, 1970—; founding pres. Byung in Martial Arts Friendship Assn., Houston, 1994-97; lectr. in field; faculty martial arts instr. U. Houston and Rice U., 1970—; Tae Kwon Do coord. U.S. Olympic Festival '86, Houston; fight choreographer Houston Grand Opera, 1986; presdl. appt. to Com. on Unification of Korea, 1986-93; advisor World Martial Arts Coun., 1990. Editor, corr. Black Belt Mag., 1964-67; author: Palgue 1,2,3, 1973, Palgue 4,5,6, 1974, Palgue 7 & 8: Black Belt Requirements, 1976, History of ChaYon-Ryu, 1990. Recipient citation for contbn. to elevating Korean nat. image in world Korean Govt., 1970, Leadership commendation Mayor Kathy Whitmire, 1987, commendation U.S. Pres. Bill Clinton, 1993, 98, Ednl. Leadership citation Gov. Ann Richards, 1993, Gov. G.W. Bush, 1998, Leadership commendation Mayor Bob Lanier, 1993, Lifetime Achievement award of honor World karate Union Hall of Fame, 1997; named Best Karate Instr. in Houston, Houston Press, 1990, Grandmaster of the Yr., Tex. Martial Arts Hall of Fame, Man of Yr. Am. All-Open Hall of Fame, 1991, World Karate Union Hall of Fame, Internat. Martial Arts Hall of Fame, 1997. Avocation: golf. Office: ChaYon-Ryu Internat Martial Arts Assn 1740 Jacquelyn Dr Houston TX 77055-3604

KIM, SANG KOO, pastor, educator; b. Joongwon, Choongbuk, Korea, July 22, 1938; came to U.S., 1978; s. Seyong and Sun (Shin) K.; m. Sunok Lee, Oct. 3, 1969; children: James Han, Grace Jong. BA, Korea U., Seoul, 1964; MDiv, Presbyn. Theol. Sem., Seoul, 1966; D Ministry, San Francisco Theol. Sem., 1981. Ordained to ministry 33th Daejon Presbytery Presbyn. Ch., 1968. Sr. pastor Seattle Korean Presbyn. Ch., 1980-88, Dong Shin Presbyn. Ch., Fullerton, Calif., 1988—; moderator Western Presbytery in U.S.A., La., 1983-84; prof. Faith Evang. Sem., Federalway, Wash., 1983-88, K.P.C.A. Presbyn. Sem., L.A., 1988—; vice moderator K.P.C.A., 1995; moderator Korean Presbyn. Ch. in Am., 1995-96. Author: The Core Theory of Salvation, 1993. Democrat. Home: 5777 Los Arcos Way Buena Park CA 90620-2724 Office: Dong Shin Presbyn Ch 2121 E Wilshire Ave Fullerton CA 92831-4159*

KIM, SANG U., gastroenterologist; b. Aug. 16, 1963. BSEE, U. Wash., 1986, MD, 1990. Diplomate Am. Bd. Internal Medicine, sub-bd. Gastroenterology. Resident in internal medicine U. Wash. Med. Ctr., Seattle, 1990-93, fellow in gastroenterology, 1993-95; pvt. practice Gastrointestinal and Liver Clinic of Edmonds, Wash., 1995—. Office: Gastrointestinal & Liver Clinic Edmonds 21616 76th Ave W Ste 207 Edmonds WA 98026-7512

KIM, SE JUNG, civil engineer; b. Seoul, Korea, Aug. 29, 1931; came to U.S., 1968, naturalized, 1973; s. Ki Yong and Soon Dong (Cha) K.; m. Yong Ok Son, Mar. 26, 1961; children: Dohi, Ginny. BS, Seoul Nat. U., 1957. Registered profl. engr., N.Y. Civil engr. U.S. Army C.E., Seoul, 1957-65; project mgr. Ghana State Constrn. Corp., Accra, 1965-68; sr. civil engr. Howard, Needles, Tammen & Bergendoff, N.Y.C., 1968-75; ptnr. Solar Engr. and Builders, Spring Valley, N.Y., 1975-79; sr. civil engr. TAMS Consultants, Inc., N.Y.C., 1979—. Mem. NSPE, Am. Water Works Assn., Seoul Nat. U. Coll. Engring. Alumni Assn. (pres. N.Y. chpt. 1984). Home: 68 Minuteman Cir Orangeburg NY 10962-2721 Office: TAMS Consultants Inc 655 3rd Ave Fl 3 New York NY 10017-5627

KIM, SOOK CHA, artist; b. Choong-Joo, Korea, Mar. 30, 1940; came to U.S., 1973; d. Kyung Nam Chai and Choon Yi Lim; m. Myung Hak Kim, Dec. 5, 1967; 1 child, Young Kyoon. Student, Seoul Nat. U.; BFA, Hong-Ik U., 1965, MFA, 1967. Owner Morning Star Art Gallery, Washington, 1995—. Featured artist New Art Internat. 1997 Edit. Recipient Gold medal--Art Addiction Internat. prize Most Talented Artists Competition, Sweden, 1997. Home: 6540 Braddock Rd Alexandria VA 22312 Office: Morning Star Art Gallery 600 T St NW Washington DC 20001

KIM, SOO-RYONG, investment banker; b. Pusan, Republic of Korea, Feb. 7, 1951; came to U.S., 1985; s. Yang-Soo and Soon-Ah (Park) K.; m. Hye-Boon Chung, Nov. 1, 1976; children: Eugenie, Suhgenie. BBA, Dong-A U., Pusan, 1979; MBA, U. Pa., 1987. Clk. Korea Exchange Bank, Pusan, 1970-73, sect. chief, 1976-78; interpreter/sec. I Corps (ROK/US), Uijeongbu, Republic of Korea, 1974-75; head mktg. dept. Mfrs. Hanover Trust Co., Seoul, Republic of Korea, 1979-85; v.p., area mgr. Korea/Taiwan N.Y.C., 1985-88; investment officer, investment mgmt. group Mfrs. Hanover Trust Co., N.Y.C., 1988—, mgr. syndication/distbn. dept. alternative investment mgmt. group, 1989-90; mgr. investment project developing markets group corp. fin. dept. Mfrs. Hanover Trust Co.; mng. dir., head far east divsn. and utility/telecom divsn. Chemical Securities Asia Ltd., Hong Kong, 1992-95; mng. dir. Chase Manhattan Bank, Seoul, Korea, 1995-98; adv. to chmn., fin. supr. commn. Rep. of Korea, Seoul, Korea, 1998—; adv. to chmn. Korea Life Ins. Co. Ltd., 1998—; pres., CEO Meridien Ptnrs. LLC, 1998—. Author: MHT Seoul Business Manual, 1985, Restructuring Strategies for Leading Banks of Korea, 1998; co-author: MHT AIM Group Policies and Manual. Mgr. Little League Baseball, Tobias, Korean Presbyn. Ch., N.J. Mem. Am. Mgmt. Assn., Korean Baseball Assn. Ea. USA (chmn. 1989—, coach 1987-88). Presbyterian. Avocation: baseball, golf. Home: 19 Villa Dr Bridgewater NJ 08807-5664 Office: Meridian Ptnrs LLC 19 Villa Dr Bridgewater NJ 08807

KIM, SUNG YUP, diplomat; b. Pusan, Republic of Korea, Apr. 25, 1945; s. Kwang Bok Kim and Myo Ok Park; m. Ke Soon, June 1, 1974; children: Sang Yoon, Sang In. BA, Korea U., Seoul, 1970; MD, Seoul Nat. U., 1972. Dir. Asian bur. Ministry of Fgn. Affairs, Seoul, 1989-90, sr. coord. planning and budget, 1995-97; diplomatic advisor to spkr. Nat. Assembly, Seoul, 1990-92; counsellor Korean Embassy, Denmark, 1992-93; charge d'affaires, counsellor Korean Embassy, Tel-Aviv, 19939-95; consul gen. Korean Embassy, Washington, 1997—. Office: Korean Embassy 2320 Massachusetts Ave NW Washington DC 20008

KIM, SUNG-HOU, chemistry educator, biophysical and biological chemist; b. Taegu, Korea, Dec. 12, 1937; s. Yong-Tai and Ok-Kum (Choi) K.; m. Rosalind Yuan, July 27, 1968; children: Christopher Sang Jai, Jonathan Sang-Joon. B.S., Seoul Nat. U., 1960, M.S., 1962; Ph.D., U. Pitts., 1966. Teaching asst. in chemistry Seoul Nat. U., 1960-62; lectr. chemistry Kun-Kook U., Seoul, 1960-62; research asst. dept. crystallography U. Pitts., 1963-66; research assoc. MIT, Cambridge, 1966-70, sr. research scientist, 1970-72; asst. prof. Duke U., Durham, N.C., 1972-73, assoc. prof., 1974-78; prof. chemistry U. Calif.-Berkeley, 1978—, Miller research prof., 1983-84; faculty sr. scientist Lawrence Berkeley Lab., 1979—, dir. div. structural biology, 1989—; exch. prof. Peking U., 1982; vis. prof. U. Paris, 1986; mem. adv. group biophysics and biophys. chemistry A Study sect. NIH, 1976-80; co-chmn. nucleic acids Gordon Research Conf., 1983; chmn. curriculum planning com. U.S. Nat. Com. for Crystallography, 1983-84. Mem. editorial bd. Jour. Biol. Chemistry, 1979-83, Nucleic Acid Research, 1983-85, Annual Rev. of Biophysics and Biomolecular Structure, 1989-93; sci. rev. bd. Howard Hughes Med. Inst., 1995—; contbr. articles to profl. jours. Awarded Presdl. Svc. Merit medal (Republic of Korea), 1985; recipient Sidhu award Pitts. Diffraction Conf., 1970, Rsch. Career Devel. award NIH, 1976-79, E.O. Lawrence award, 1987, Javits Neurosci. Investigator award HHS, 1988, Princess Takamatsu Cancer Found. award, 1989; Woo-Nam scholar Woo-Nam Found., Korea, 1959; Fulbright fellow, 1962; Guggenheim fellow, 1985-86; Ho-Am prize in sci., Samsung Found., Seoul, 1993. Fellow Am. Acad. Arts and Sci., 1994; mem. NAS, 1994, Am. Soc. Biol. Chemists, Am. Chem. Soc., Am. Crystallographic Assn., AAAS, Korean Scientists and Engrs. in Am. Home: 1080 Country Club Dr Moraga CA 94556-1924 Office: U Calif Dept Chemistry Berkeley CA 94720*

KIM, WAN HEE, electrical engineering educator, business executive; b. Osan, Korea, May 24, 1926; came to U.S., 1953, naturalized, 1962; s. Sang Chul and Duck Hyung (Chong) K.; m. Chung Sook Noh, Jan. 23, 1960; children: Millie, Richard K. B.E., Seoul Nat. U., 1950; M.S. in Elec. Engring, U. Utah, 1954, Ph.D., 1956. Research asst. U. Ill., Urbana, 1955-56; research staff IBM Research Ctr., Poughkeepsie, N.Y., 1956-57; asst. prof. Columbia U., N.Y.C., 1957-59; assoc. prof. Columbia U., 1959-63, prof. elec. engring., 1963-78; chmn., CEO Tech. Assessment Corp. Internat., 1991—; chmn. Tech. Cons., Inc., N.Y.C., 1962-69; chmn. KOMKOR Am., Inc., N.Y.C., 1970-72; spl. advisor for the pres. and govt. Republic of Korea, 1967-79; advisor Korea Advanced Inst. Sci., Seoul, 1971-73; chmn. Korea Inst. Electronics Tech., 1977-81; mem. bd. Korea Telecommunication Electric Rsch. Inst., 1977-81; pres. WHK Engring. Corp. Am., 1982-84, WHK Electronics Inc., 1982-84; chmn., chief exec. officer Industries Assn. Electronic Korea, 1978-81; chmn. WHK Industries Inc., 1984-88, AEA Corp., WHK-FJF&M Assocs., 1988-89; pres. Asian Electronics Union, 1979-83; pub. Electronic Times of Korea, 1982-83, Dr. Kim Report on Korea, 1988—; cons. The World Bank, Washington, other indsl. orgns.; chmn., CEO Tech. Assessment Corp. Internat. (TACI), 1991—. Author: (with R.T. Chien) Topological Analysis and Synthesis of Communication Networks, 1962, (with H.E. Meadows) Modern Network Analysis, 1970; pub.: The Dr. Kim Report on Korea, 1988—; also numerous articles. U.S. rep. on U.S.-Japan Scientists Coop. Program.; trustee U.S.-Asia Inst., Washington, 1984-88. Served with Korean Army, 1950-53. Decorated Bronze Star; recipient Achievement medal U.S.-Asia Inst., Industry medal Republic of Korea, 1989; Guggenheim grantee, 1964, NSF rsch. grantee, 1958-78. Fellow IEEE, Union Radio Scientifique Internat. (mem. U.S. nat. com. Commn. Band C 1963-78), Sigma Xi, Tau Beta Pi. Honorarily named the father of Korean electronics industry for his contbrn. to promotion of industry. Home: PO Box 778 Palo Alto CA 94302-0778 Office: 1250 Oakmead Pkwy Ste 210 Sunnyvale CA 94086-4037 *Be prepared five minutes earlier than others.*

KIM, YONG CHOON, philosopher, theologian, educator; b. Kyongju, Korea, Jan. 1, 1935; came to U.S., 1958, naturalized, 1972; s. Chang Ho and Chung Ja (Choe) K.; m. Joyce Chungja Whang, Dec. 18, 1965; 1 dau., Grace. B.A., Belhaven Coll., Jackson, Miss., 1960; Th.M., Westminster Theol. Sem., Phila., 1964; Ph.D., Temple U., 1969. Asst. prof. Asian studies York Coll., Pa., 1969-70; asst. prof. philosophy and religion Cleve. State U., 1970-71; asst. prof. philosophy U. R.I., Kingston, 1971-74, assoc. prof., 1974-79, prof., 1979—; founder, dir. Korean-Am. Christian Studies Inst., 1981—. Author: Oriental Thought, 1973, The Ch'ondogyo Concept of Man: An Essence of Korean Thought, 1978; editl. adv. bd. Dictionary World Philosophy, 1997—. Korean Culture and Arts Found. grantee, 1977; Korea Found. fellow, 1992. Mem. Assn. Asian Studies, Am. Acad. Religion, Soc. for Asian and Comparative Philosophy, AAUP, Korean-Am. Univ. Profs. Assn. (dir. Eastern region 1986-90, 97—, chair law and ethics com. 1990-96). Home: 134 Parkwood Dr Kingston RI 02881-1600 Office: Univ RI Dept Philosophy Kingston RI 02881

KIM, YOON BERM, immunologist, educator; b. Pyongnam, Korea, Apr. 25, 1929; came to U.S., 1959, naturalized, 1975; s. Sang Sun and Yang Rang (Lee) K.; m. Soon Cha Kim, Feb. 23, 1959; children: John, Jean, Paul. *Son John H. Kim, BA 1982, Yale University; MD 1990, The Chicago Medical School; Internship and Residency in Obstetrics and Gynecology, Women's and Infants' Hospital, Brown University School of Medicine 1990-94; Clinical Instructor OBG, Brown University School of Medicine 1994-95. Fellow, Reproductive Endocrinology and Infertility, Reproductive Endocrinology Center, UCSF School of Medicine 1995-97. Practice OBG, DuKane Obstetrics and Gynecology Ltd., 1997—. Daughter Jean M. Kim, BA 1984, Yale University; JD 1987, Boston College Law School; Corporate Attorney 1987—. Does non-profit work and church ministry. Son Paul J. Kim, BS 1990, Brown University; MD 1995, University of Illinois (Chicago), College of Medicine; Residency in Family Practice.* M.D., Seoul Nat. U., 1958; Ph.D., U. Minn., 1965. Intern Univ. Hosp. Seoul Nat. U., 1958-59; asst. prof. microbiology U. Minn., Mpls., 1965-70, assoc. prof., 1970-73; mem., head lab. ontogeny of immune system Sloan Kettering Inst. Cancer Research, Rye, N.Y., 1973-83; prof. immunology Cornell U. Grad. Sch. Med. Scis., N.Y.C., 1973-83; chmn. immunology unit Cornell U. Grad. Sch. Med. Scis., 1980-82; prof. microbiology, immunology and medicine, chmn. dept. micorbiology and immunology Finch U. Health Scis., Chgo. Med. Sch., 1983—, acting dean Sch. Grad. and Postdoctoral Studies, 1994-95; mem. Lobund adv. bd. U. Notre Dame, 1977-88. Contbr. numerous articles on immunology to profl. jours. Recipient rsch. career devel. award USPHS, 1968-73, Morris Parker Rsch. award U. Health Scis., Chgo. Med. Sch., 1984. Fellow Am. Acad. Microbiology; mem. AAAS, Assn. Gnotobiotics (pres.), Internat. Assn. for Gnotobiology (founding), Am. Assn. Immunologists, Am. Soc. Microbiology, Am. Assn. Pathologists, Korean-Am. Med. Assn., N.Y. Acad. Scis., Soc. for Leucocyte Biology, Internat. Soc. Devel. Comparative Immunology, Harvey Soc., Internat. Soc. Interferon and Cytokine Rsch., Chgo. Assn. Immunologists (pres.), Assn. Med. Sch. Microbiology and Immunology Chairs, Internat. Endotoxin Soc. (charter), Soc. Natural Immunity (charter), Sigma Xi, Alpha Omega Alpha. Achievements include discovery of the unique germfree dolostrum-deprived immunologically "virgin" piglet model used to investigate ontogenic development and regulation of the immune system including T/B lymphocytes, natural killer/killer cells, and macrophages; research on ontogeny and regulation of immune system, immunochemistry and biology of bacterial toxins, host-parasite relationships and gnotobiology. Home: 313 Weatherford Ct Lake Bluff IL 60044-1905 Office: Finch U Health Scis Chgo Med Sch 3333 Green Bay Rd North Chicago IL 60064-3037

KIM, YOUNG KIL, aerospace engineer; b. Pusan, Korea, June 18, 1956; came to U.S., 1984; naturalized, 1988; s. Tae Hyun and Myong Ok (Shin) K.; m. Susan Katherine Hong, July 16, 1981; children: Steven Charles, Christina Kay. BS, Seoul Nat. U., Rep. of Korea, 1979; MS, Ga. Inst. Tech., 1985, PhD in Aerospace Engring., 1991. Rsch. engr. Korean Inst. Aero. Tech. Korean Air Lines, Seoul, 1978-84; vis. rsch. engr. Agy. for Def. Devel., Daedog, Republic of Korea, 1981-82; rsch. assoc. Univs. Space Rsch. Assn., Huntsville, Ala., 1991-93; rsch. engr. U. Ala. Rsch. Inst., Huntsville, 1993-96; sr. rsch. engr. U. Ala. in Huntsville Rsch. Inst., 1996—. Mem. AIAA, Korean-Am. Scientists and Engrs. Assn. Roman Catholic. Avocations: tennis, golf. Home: 9010 Cannstatt Dr SE Huntsville AL 35802-3716 Office: U Ala in Huntsville Rsch Inst Huntsville AL 35899

KIM, YOUNGMIN, English educator; b. Seoul, Korea, Apr. 1, 1954; s. Juhwi and Gwisaeng Lee K.; m. Myung-Hye Huh, Nov. 23, 1979. BA in English, Han Kuk U. Fgn. Studies, Seoul, Korea, 1978, MA in English, 1980; PhD in English, U. Mo., 1991. Teaching asst. Han Kuk U. Fgn. Studies, Seoul, Korea, 1978-80, lectr., 1980-83; rsch. asst. U. Ga., Athens, 1984-86, teaching asst., 1986-87; asst. prof. Dongguk U., Seoul, 1991-95, assoc. prof., 1995—; vis. asst. prof. Cornell U., Ithaca, N.Y., 1998-99. Author: Yeats and Open Form, 1991, Ezra Pound, 1998. Rsch. grantee Min. Fgn. AFfairs, Ottawa, Can., 1996, 98, Korea Rsch. Found., Seoul, 1997, Teaching fellow, 1998; Asian scholar IASIL, Tokyo, 1995. Mem. Yeats Soc. Korea (v.p. 1992-95). Presbyterian. Avocations: travel, hiking, climbing mountains, singing. Home: 316 Highland Rd Apts #C106 Ithaca NY 14850 Office: Cornell U Dept Asian Studies 338 ROckefeller Hall Ithaca NY 14853

KIM, ZAEZEUNG, allergist, immunologist, educator; b. Hamhung, Korea, Feb. 21, 1929; came to U.S., 1967; s. Suh and Suyeo (Hahn) K.; m. Youngju Kim, June 2, 1961; children: Keungsuk, Maria. Student, Hamhung Med. Coll., Korea, 1946-50; MD, Seoul U., Korea, 1960; PhD in Immunology, U. Cologne, Fed. Republic of Germany, 1968. Diplomate Am. Bd. Allergy and Immunology. Intern Seoul Nat. U. Hosp., 1960-61, resident in medicine, 1961-63; resident in medicine Heidelberg U. Hosp., Fed. Republic of Germany, 1963-64; research fellow Max-Planck Inst., Cologne, 1965-67; fellow in hematology U. Tex., Houston, 1967-68; resident in allergy and immunology Temple U. Hosp., Phila., 1968-69; fellow in medicine Ohio State U., Columbus, 1969-71; instr. medicine Med. Coll. Wis., Milw., 1972-75, asst. prof., 1975-78, assoc. clin. prof., 1978—; practice medicine specializing in allergy and immunology Racine, Wis. Contbr. articles to profl. jours. Fellow Am. Acad. Allergy and Immunology, Am. Coll. Allergists; mem. AMA. Home: 461 W Sunnyview Dr Apt 13 Oak Creek WI 53154-3893 Office: 461 W Sunnyview Dr Apt 13 Oak Creek WI 53154-3893

KIMBALL, ANNE SPOFFORD, French language educator; b. Bangor, Maine, July 2, 1937; d. Spofford Harris and Marian Stevens Kimball. BA, Mt. Holyoke Coll., 1959; MA in Tchg., Harvard U., 1960; MA, Middlebury Sch. French, Paris, 1961; PhD, U. wis., 1969. Asst. U. de Lille, France, 1960-61; instr., then asst. prof. Mt. Holyoke Coll., South Hadley, Mass., 1963-74, assoc. dean studies, 1974-75; acad. dean., assoc. prof. French Randolph-Macon Woman's Coll., Lynchburg, Va., 1975-82, assoc. prof., then prof. French, 1982-99, Dana prof. French, 1999—. Author: Max Jacob: Lettres a Marcel Jouhandeau, 1979, 31 Jours en France, 1984, Max Jacob: Lettres a Nino Frank, 1989, Max Jacob: Lettres a Pierre Minet, 1990. Pres., v.p., program chair, bd. dirs. Alliance Française, Lynchburg, 1976—. Recipient award Fulbright Found., 1960-61, 61-62, 83-84, Young Humanist award NEH, 1981-82, award Am. Coun. on Learned Socs., 1988-89, Am. Philos. Soc., 1988-89, 97-98; Danforth fellow 1965-66, 66-67. Mem. MLA, FLAVA, Am. Assn. Tchrs. French, Soc. des Amis de Max Jacob, Soc. des Amis de Jean Cocteau, Soc. des Amis de Jean Paulhan. Democrat. Unitarian. Avocations: bell ringing, duplicate bridge, hiking, kayaking, travel. E-mail: akimball@rmwc.edu. Home: HC 77 262 B Shore Rd Hancock ME 04640 Office: Randolph-Macon Woman's Coll 2500 Rivermont Ave Lynchburg VA 24503

KIMBALL, BRUCE ARNOLD, soil scientist; b. Aitkin, Minn., Sept. 27, 1941; s. Robert Clinton and Rica (Barneveld) K.; m. Laurel Sue Hanway, Aug. 20, 1966; children: Britt, Rica, Megan. BS, U. Minn., 1963; MS, Iowa State U., 1965; PhD, Cornell U., 1970. Soil scientist USDA-Agrl. Rsch. Svc. U.S. Water Conservation Lab., Phoenix, 1969-90, rsch. leader Environ. and Plant Dynamics Rsch. Group, 1990—. Editor: Impact of Carbon Dioxide, Trace Gases and Climate Change on Global Agriculture, 1990; co-editor: Carbon Dioxide Enrichment of Greenhouse Crops, 1986; contbr. articles to profl. jours. Fellow Am. Soc. Agronomy (chmn. program div. A3 1988, assoc. editor 1977-83, bd. dirs. 1994-97), Soil Sci. Soc. Am.; mem. AAAS. Avocations: computers, biking. Office: US Water Conservation Lab 4331 E Broadway Rd Phoenix AZ 85040-8832

KIMBALL, CATHERINE D., state supreme court justice. Former judge La. Dist. Ct. (18th dist.); now assoc. justice Supreme Ct. of La. Office: 301 Loyola Ave New Orleans LA 70112-1814

KIMBALL, CLYDE WILLIAM, physicist, educator; b. Laurium, Mich., Apr. 20, 1928; s. Clyde D. and Gertrude M. (O'Neil) K. B.S. in Engring. Physics, Mich. Coll. Mining and Tech., 1950, M.S., 1952; Ph.D. in Physics, St. Louis U., 1959. Staff scientist aeronautronic div. Ford Co., 1960-62; assoc. physicist Argonne Nat. Lab., Ill., 1962-64; prof. physics No. Ill. U., De Kalb, 1964—, Presdl. rsch. chair, 1982-86; rsch. prof. No. Ill. U., 1986-88, disting. prof., 1989—; advisor to pres. sci. and tech. No. Ill. U., De Kalb, 1982-88; program dir. low temperature physics Materials Research Div., NSF, Washington, 1978-79; chair, bd. govs. Consortium for Advanced Radiation Sources, 1994—; exec. com. Basic Energy Sci. Synchrotron Rsch. Ctr., 1994—. Contbr. articles to profl. jours. Served with U.S. Army, 1952-54. Fellow Am. Phys. Soc.; mem. AAAS, Am. Assn. Physics Tchrs., Sigma Xi. Home: PO Box 842 Dekalb IL 60115 Office: No Ill U Dept Physics Faraday West 217 Dekalb IL 60115

KIMBALL, DONALD ROBERT, food company executive; b. Anderson, Ind., Mar. 4, 1938; s. Robert Martin and Mary Lucille (Gibson) K.; m. Mari-Anne Talbot, Apr. 6, 1985; children: Randy, Rick, Sharon-Lee, Douglas, David. BS in Agr., Purdue U., 1960. Registered profl. sanitarian, Ind. Pub. health sanitarian Div. Dairy Products, Ind. Bd. Health, LaPorte, 1962-66; milk sanitation rating officer Div. Dairy Products, Ind. Bd. Health, Indpls., 1966-75; chief milk sanitation rating officer Div. Dairy Products, Ind. Bd. Health, 1973-75, dir., 1975-87; dir. regulatory affairs Dean Foods Co., Rockford, Ill., 1987—, dir. farm rels., 1990-99. Contbr. articles to profl. jours. Capt. U.S. Army, 1960-68. Recipient Disting. Svc. award, Midwest Dairy Products Assn., 1988. Mem. Internat. Assn. Milk, Food, Environ. Sanitarians, Nat. Conf. Interstate Milk Shipments (MMSR com., coun. III), Assn. Food and Drug Ofcls., Dairy Practices Coun., Conf. Food Protection (coun. I), Ill. Food Safety Task Force. Methodist. Avocations: bicycling, hiking. Office: Dean Foods Co Technical Ctr PO Box 7005 Rockford IL 61125-7005

KIMBALL, EDWARD LAWRENCE, law educator, lawyer; b. Safford, Ariz., Sept. 23, 1930; s. Spencer Woolley and Camilla (Eyring) K.; m. Evelyn Bee Madsen, June 9, 1954; children: Christian Edward, Paula, Mary, Miles Spencer, Jordan Andrew, Joseph Ellsworth, Sarah Camilla. BS, U. Utah, 1953, LLB, 1955; LLM, U. Pa., 1959, SJD, 1962. Bar: Utah 1955, Wis. 1971. Law clk. Utah Supreme Ct., 1955; mem. faculty U. Mont., 1956-62, asso. prof. law, 1960-62; mem. faculty U. Wis. at Madison, 1962-73, prof. law, 1967-73; prof. law Brigham Young U., Provo, Utah, 1973-95, Wilkinson prof. law, 1982-95, prof. law emeritus, 1996—. Author: (with others) Criminal Justice Administration, 1969, rev. edit., 1982, Spencer W. Kimball, 1977, Programmed Materials on Problems in Evidence, 1978, Camilla, 1980, The Teachings of Spencer W. Kimball, 1982, The Story of Spencer W. Kimball: A Short Man, A Long Stride, 1985, The Writings of Camilla Eyring Kimball, 1988, Frank J. Remington: Contributions to Criminal Justice, 1994, (with Boyce) Utah Evidence Law, 1996; mem. editorial bd. Brigham Young U. Studies, 1970-75, 85-92, The Carpenter, 1969-73. Mem. spl. rev. bd. Wis. Dept. Health and Social Svcs., 1970-73; mem. Utah Bd. Pardons and Paroles, 1979-83, pro tem 1988-95; dist. committeeman Four Lakes coun. Boy Scouts Am., 1965-72; trustee Sunstone Found., 1988-91. Bicentennial fellow U. Pa., 1955-56; Rockefeller fellow U. Wis., 1961-62. Mem. Utah Bar Assn., Order of Coif, Phi Beta Kappa, Phi Kappa Phi,

Lambda Delta Sigma, Delta Phi Kappa, Phi Delta Phi. Mem. Ch. Jesus Christ Latter-day Saints (bishop). Office: Brigham Young U Law Sch Provo UT 84602

KIMBALL, GEORGE EDWARD, III, sports columnist; b. Grass Valley, Calif., Dec. 20, 1943; s. George Edward and Rita Sue (Laslie) K.; m. Sarah Ann Kimball; children: Darcy Maeve, George E. IV. Student, Mass. Bay C.C., U. Kans.; postgrad. in Creative Writing, U. Iowa. Sports editor Boston Phoenix, 1970-79; sports columnist Boston Herald, 1980—; spl. U.S. corr. Irish Times; featured sports columnist N.Y. Post, 1993. Author: (novel) Only Skin Deep, (non-fiction) Sunday's Fools; co-host SportsCall, Sta. WRKO, 1986-87, Old Colony Sports Network, 1996-97; appeared numerous TV programs; contbr. articles to mags., poetry to numerous anthologies. Dem. candidate for sheriff, Douglas County, Kans., 1970. Recipient Best Sports Column award United Press Internat., 1984, 86, Nat Fleischer award for Excellence in Boxing Journalism Boxing Writers Assn., 1985, Best Golf Column award Golf Writers Assn., 1992; named Boston's Best Sports Columnist Boston Mag., 1987. Mem. South Shore Country Club (Hugham), The European Club (senate Brittas Bay, Ireland). Office: News Group Boston Inc PO Box 2096 One Herald Sq Boston MA 02106*

KIMBALL, HARRY RAYMOND, medical association executive, educator; b. L.A., 1937. MD, Wash. U., 1962. Intern King County Hosp., Seattle, 1962-63; resident in internal medicine U. Wash. Hosps., Seattle, 1963-64, 67-68; fellow infectious diseases NIH Hosps., Bethesda, Md., 1964-67; pres. Am. Bd. Internal Medicine, Phila. Office: Am Bd Internal Med 510 Walnut St Ste 1700 Philadelphia PA 19106-3699*

KIMBALL, LYNN JEROME, historian; b. La Junta, Colo., Sept. 21, 1943; s. Stanley Jerome and Ruth Estelle (Wilson) K.; m. Kathleen May Seker Mitchell, Nov. 13, 1965 (div. Mar. 1974); children: Scott, Lori, Todd; m. Dorothy Jean Bumar, Dec. 15, 1984; children: Donald, Wendy. BS, U.S. Naval Acad., Annapolis, Md., 1965; MS, U.S. Naval Postgrad. Sch., Monterey, Calif., 1971. Commd. USMC, 1965, advanced through grades to lt. col.; dir. plans & policies Joint Spl. Ops. Command USMC, Ft. Bragg, N.C., 1980-83; ops. officer 3d Marine Divsn. USMC, Okinawa, Japan, 1983-84; battalion comdr. Marine Corps Base USMC, Camp Lejeune, N.C., 1984-87; def. attache Am. Embassy, Santo Domingo, Dominican Republic, 1988-90; dir. ops. and tng. Marine Corps Base USMC, Camp Lejeune, 1990-91, dir. environ. tng. Marine Corps Base, 1991-92; ret. USMC, 1991; writer, historian, 1992—; vis. lectr. Profl. Mil. Edn., Camp Lejeune, 1990—. Columnist Jacksonville Daily News, 1996—, Tideland News, 1996—, Richlands Advertiser, 1996—; author: Battle of New River, 1996, Diary of J.Q.A. Morris, 1997; contbr. articles to profl. jours. Adv. bd. Onslow County Bd. Tourism, Jacksonville, N.C., 1995—, Onslow County Mus., 1995—. Mem. Marine Corps Assn., U.S. Naval Inst., Sons Confederate Vets., Marine Corps Historical Found., Onslow Hist. Soc., Civil War Roundtable Eastern N.C. Republican. Baptist. Avocations: weight training, bicycling, scuba diving, Civil War histo. Home: 227 Creedmoor Rd Jacksonville NC 28546-6028

KIMBALL, MARC KENNEDY, press secretary; b. Ely, Minn., Nov. 9, 1960; s. Robert W. and Susan (Cady) K.; m. Michele Heigle, Oct. 5, 1991; children: Adam C., Amanda R. BA in Journalism, U. Minn., 1983. Reporter Minn. Daily, Mpls., 1983-85; tchr. English Helena Sch., Tsuchiura, Japan, 1984-85; dep. press. sec. U.S. Rep. Gerry Sikorski, Fridley, Minn., 1985-89; press. sec. U.S. Rep. Byron Dorgan, Washington, 1989-92, U.S. Senator Byron Dorgan, Washington, 1992-94; press. sec. Ho. Budget Comm., Washington, 1994-95, minority press sec., 1995-97; press sec. U.S. Rep. Martin Sabo, Washington, 1997-98, U.S. Sen. Thomas Daschle, Washigton, 98-. Democrat. Lutheran. Avocations: hockey, soccer. Home: 5809 Clapham Rd Alexandria VA 22315-5626 Office: US Sen Thomas A. Daschle 509 SHOB Washington DC 20510-4103*

KIMBALL, MARK DOUGLAS, lawyer; b. Seattle, May 26, 1959; s. Frederick Burton and Merry Doris (Bredenberg) K. BA, U. Wash., 1979, JD, 1982. Bar: Wash. 1983, U.S. Dist. Ct. (we. dist.) Wash. 1985. Lawyer pvt. practice, Bellevue, Wash., 1983—. Editor: (books) Oregon Revised Statutes Annotated. Mem. Wash. State Bar Assn., Progressive Animal Welfare Soc. Republican. Presbyterian. Office: Mark Douglas Kimball PS 10655 NE 4th St Ste 400 Bellevue WA 98004-5086

KIMBALL, RICHARD ARTHUR, JR., lawyer; b. N.Y.C., Feb. 3, 1930; s. Richard Arthur and Josephine (Dodge) K.; m. Hopeton Drake Kneeland, Dec. 22, 1956; children: George J., Samuel W., Sylvia K. Perry. BA, Yale U., 1952, LLB, 1958. Assoc. Debevoise, Plimpton & McLean, N.Y.C., 1958-61; asst. treas. Morgan Guaranty Trust Co., N.Y.C., 1961-63; assoc. Debevoise, Plimpton, Lyons & Gates, N.Y.C., 1963-69; ptnr. Hughes Hubbard & Reed, N.Y.C., 1970-92, counsel, 1993—. Bd. dirs. English-Speaking Union of U.S., N.Y.C., 1985-97, N.Y. br. English-Speaking Union, 1965-89, chmn., 1993-94; pres. Yale Glee Club Assocs., New Haven, 1980-85, Dutchess Land Conservancy, Milbrook, 1988—, chmn., 1997—, The Nature Conservancy, Lower Hudson chpt., 1991-94. 1st lt. U.S. Army, 1953-55. Fellow Am. Coll. Trust and Estate Counsel; mem. ABA, N.Y. State Bar Assn., Assn. Bar City N.Y., Century Assn. (N.Y.C., treas. 1983-89), Yale Club (N.Y.C.). Office: Hughes Hubbard & Reed 1 Battery Park Plz Fl 12 New York NY 10004-1482

KIMBERLIN, SAM OWEN, JR., financial institutions consultant; b. Wichita Falls, Tex., Feb. 4, 1928; s. Sam Owen and Mary Ruth (Crowell) K.; m. Alison Gray, Dec. 20, 1955; children: S. Scott, David Winston. BBA, U. Tex., Austin, 1951, LLB, 1953; grad. Grad. Sch. Banking, Rutgers U., 1972. Bar: Tex. 1953. First asst. Office Dist. Atty., Austin, 1953-54; asst. atty. gen. Office Atty. Gen. State Tex., Austin, 1955; gen. counsel Tex. Dept. Banking, Austin, 1956-62; exec. dir. Assn. State Chartered Banks in Tex., Austin, 1962-64; exec. v.p. Tex. Bankers Assn., Austin, 1964-88; mng. dir. TBA Svcs. Co., Inc., Austin, 1988-90; cons. Austin Trust Co., 1990—, Thornhill Securities, Inc., Austin, 1990—; chmn. devel. bd. Austin Trust Co., 1991—. Author: Banking in Texas, 1972 (honors award 1972); co-author: Fight Your Texas Tax Appraisal and Win, 1997. Mem. adv. coun. on property tax cons. Tex. Dept. Licensing and Regulation, 1996—; chmn. appraisal rev. bd. Travis Ctrl. Appraisal Dist., 1995-96; trustee S.F. Austin High Continuing Edn. Found. With USMC, 1946-48. Mem. Am. Soc. Assn. Execs., Tex. Assn. Bank Counsel, Adms. Club, Headliners Club, Tarry House Lodge. Methodist. Avocations: tennis, skiing. Home: 3503 Scenic Hills Dr Austin TX 78703-1044 Office: PO Box 5930 Austin TX 78763-5930

KIMBERLING, JOHN FARRELL, retired lawyer; b. Shelbyville, Ind., Nov. 15, 1926; s. James Farrell and Phyllis (Casady) K. B of Naval Sci. and Tactics, Purdue U., 1946; AB, Ind. U., 1947, JD, 1950. Bar: Ind. 1950, Calif. 1954. Assoc. Bracken, Gray, DeFur & Voran, 1950-51; assoc. Lillick McHose & Charles, and predecessor firms, 1953-63, ptnr., 1963-86; ptnr. Dewey Ballantine, L.A., 1986-89. Bd. visitors Ind. U. Sch. Law, 1987—; bd. dirs. Ind. U. Found., 1988—. Lt. (j.g.) USNR, 1951-53. Fellow Am. Coll. Trial Lawyers; mem. ABA (charter mem. litigation sect.), State Bar Calif., L.A. Bar Assn., L.A. Jr. C. of C. (past pres.), Beta Theta Pi, Phi Delta Phi. Democrat. Clubs: California, Chancery, Lincoln. Home: 1180 Los Robles Dr Palm Springs CA 92262-4124 *My goal in life is and has been to do the very best of which I am capable in my professional life and in helping to make my community a better place in which to work and live.*

KIMBERLY, JOHN ROBERT, management educator, consultant; b. New Haven, Sept. 16, 1942; s. John T. and Beatrice (Branch) K.; m. Barbara Lenox Christy, June 27, 1970; children: Laura Lenox, John Fowler, Nina-Charlotte Marie. BA, Yale U., 1964; MS, Cornell U., 1967, PhD, 1970. Asst. prof. sociology U. Ill., Champaign/Urbana, 1970-74; vis. fellow Ecole Polytechnique, Paris, 1975-76; from asst. to assoc. prof. Sch. Mgmt. Yale U., New Haven, 1977-82; from assoc. to full prof. Wharton Sch., U. Pa., Phila., 1983—, Henry Bower prof., 1989—; rsch. prof. Ecole Polytechnique, Paris, 1989-91; cons. OECD, 1975—, Office Tech. Assessment U.S. Congress, 1982-84, Robert Wood Johnson Found., Princeton, N.J., 1984-85; mem. health care tech. study sect. HHS, Washington, 1986-89. Author: The End of an Illusion, 1984, Cases in Health Policy and Management, 1985, The Migration of Managerial Innovation, 1993; editor: The Organization Life Cycle, 1980, Managing Organizational Transitions, 1984; contbr. articles to profl. jours. Bd. dirs. Wissahickon Hospice, Phila., 1985—, Chestnut Hill Hosp. Health Care, 1992—, Bach Festival Phila., 1992—, Community Fin. Bancorp, 1993—. Grantee HCA Found., Nashville, 1984-86, HHS, Washington, 1986—, Commonwealth Found., N.Y.C., 1986-87, Robert Wood Johnson Found., Princeton, 1986-87, Kaiser Family Found., 1994-96; Salmon and Rameau fellow INSEAD, Fountainbleau, France, 1996—. Mem. Am. Sociol. Assn., Acad. of Mgmt., Am. Pub. Health Assn. Avocations: restoration of antique cars and boats, tennis, skiing. Office: U Pa Wharton Sch Philadelphia PA 19104

KIMBERLY, WILLIAM ESSICK, investment banker; b. Neenah, Wis., Mar. 19, 1933; s. John Robbins and Elizabeth McFarland (Essick) K.; m. Elena Guajardo, Nov. 27, 1965; children: Essicka Amelia, Ariadne Elena, Dagny Maria. Student Williams Coll., 1951-52, U. Wis., 1953-54. Sr v.p. Kimberly-Clark Corp, Neenah, Wis., 1959-83; prin. W.E. Kimberly Investments, Neenah, 1983-85; pres. Kimberly, Brunell, & Lehmann, Inc., Washington, 1986-88; pres. The Manchester Group Ltd., Washington, 1989-92; chmn. NAZTEC Internat. Group, Inc., 1992—; bd. dirs. UOL Pub., Inc., Sytel, Inc., Kimberly Gallery of Art Inc. With USNR, 1956-58. Trustee, Pan Am. Devel. Found., Asheville Sch. Republican. Episcopalian. Club: Met. (Washington). Avocations: auto racing, art, baseball, music. Office: Naztec Internat Group Inc 6723 Whittier Ave Ste 200 Mc Lean VA 22101-4533

KIMBLE, JAMES A., management consultant, accountant; b. Owosso, Mich., June 16, 1937; s. Gaylord Browning and Iva I. (Ansted) K.; children from previous marriage: Kim, Katherine, Kerri, Charles; m. Anne Park, June 13, 1970; 1 child, Jeffrey. BBA, U. Toledo, 1959. With The PM Group Toledo Inc., 1961—, v.p., 1964-90, pres., 1990—; mem. Accreditation Coun. Accountancy, 1975, Accreditation Coun. Taxation, 1984; bd. dirs. Black and Skaggs Assocs., chmn. bd., 1994; bd. dirs. Nat. Assn. Health Care Cons., Inc., 1992-95. Pres. Citizens for Metroparks, Toledo, 1976-77; v.p., commr. Met. Park Dist., 1977-86; pres. Metroparks, Toledo, 1986-94; chmn. July spl. events Toledo Sesquicentennial, 1987; bd. dirs. Stone Oak Village, Ohio, 1998—, Assistance Dogs of Am., 1998—. Recipient Treasury Card IRS, 1976. Mem. Soc. Profl. Bus. Cons. (bd. dirs. 1977-80, cert.), Inst. Cert. Profl. Bus. Cons., Black & Skaggs Assocs. Republican. Avocations: fishing, travel, photography, genealogy. Office: The PM Group Toledo Inc 3150 N Republic Blvd Toledo OH 43615-1524

KIMBLE, JUDITH E., molecular biologist, cell biologist; b. Providence, Apr. 24, 1949. BA, U. Calif., Berkeley, 1971; PhD, U. Colo., 1978; postgrad., U. Wis., 1978-82. Asst. prof. to assoc. prof. U. Wis., 1983-92; prof. molecular biology, biochemistry U. Wisc., Madison, 1992—, prof. med. genetics, 1994—; investigator Med. Genetics, 1994—, Howard Hughes Med. Inst., Md., 1994—. Mem. NAS, Am. Acad. Arts and Sci., Am. Soc. Cell Biology, Am. Soc. Biochemistry and Molecular Biology, Genetic Soc. Office: HHMI/Dept Biochemistry U Wisc-Madison 433 Babcock Dr Madison WI 53706-1544*

KIMBLE, MELINDA L., environmental administrator; m. James R. Phippard; 4 stepchildren. B in Econs., U. Denver; M in Econs., Harvard U. Fgn. svc. officer Dept. of State, Washington, 1971-89, sr. fgn. svc. officer, 1989-93, min. counselor, 1993-97; dep. asst. sec. Bur. Internat. Orgn. Affairs, Dept. of State, 1993-97, prin. dep. asst. sec. Oceans and Internat. Environ. and Sci. Affairs, 1997—. Recipient award Global Alliance for Women's Health, Internat. Honor award U.S. Dept. Agr. Office: Dept of State Oceans Internat Environ 2201 C St NW Washington DC 20520-0001

KIMBLE, WILLIAM EARL, lawyer; b. Denver, May 4, 1926; s. George Wilbur and Grace (Fick) K.; m. Jean M. Cayia, Dec. 27, 1950; children: Mark, Cary, Timothy, Stephen, Philip, Peter, Michael. LL.B., U. Ariz., 1951. Bar: Ariz. 1951. Spl. agt. FBI, 1951-52; pvt. practice Bisbee, 1952-60, Tucson, 1962—; judge Superior Ct. Ariz., 1960-62; ptnr. Kimble, Nelson, Audilett, McDonough & Molla, 1962—; Commr. Ariz. Oil and Gas Commn., 1958-60; adj. prof. law U. Ariz. Coll. Law, 1962-86. Author: The Consumer Product Safety Act, 1973, Products Liability, 1977; sr. editor Consumer Products Alert newsletter, 1980-81; editor, pub. In Def. of Elec. Accidents newsletter, 1993—. Founder Naval War Coll. Found.; Rep. nominee Ariz. atty. gen., 1956; Rep. nominee Ariz. U.S. Congress, 1964. Served with USNR, 1944-46. Fellow Am. Coll. Trial Lawyers; mem. Sigma Chi, Phi Alpha Delta. Home: 95 N Camino Miramonte Tucson AZ 85716-4945 Office: Kimble Nelson Audilett McDonough & Molla Ste 500 335 N Wilmot Rd Tucson AZ 85711-2636

KIMBRELL, DEBORAH ANN, geneticist, educator; b. San Angelo, Tex., July 22, 1950; d. Billy Lee and Dorothy (Babish) K.; m. S. Ingemar C. Olsson, June 15, 1991. BA in Biology and Psychology with honors, Mills Coll., 1972; PhD in Genetics, U. Calif., Berkeley, 1985. Rsch. technician dept. respiration physiology Max Planck Inst. Exptl. Medicine, Göttingen, Germany, 1973-74; NIH predoctoral trainee dept. genetics U. Calif., Berkeley, 1979-85; Am. Cancer Soc. postdoctoral fellow dept. genetics U. Cambridge, Eng., 1985-88; Swedish MRC vis. scientist fellow dept. microbiology U. Stockholm, 1988-90; asst. prof. dept. biology and Inst. Molecular Biology, U. Houston, 1991-98; sr. faculty fellow dept. biochemistry and cell biology Rice U., Houston, 1998—. Contbr. articles to profl. jours. Pres. Rsch. and Scholarship Fund grantee U. Houston, 1991, 92-93; grantee Houston Coastal Ctr., 1992-98, Am. Cancer Soc., 1993—. Mem. AAAS, Genetics Soc. Am. Office: Rice Univ Dept Biochemistry and Cell Biology Houston TX 77005-1892

KIMBRELL, LEONARD BUELL, retired art history educator, art appraiser; b. Archibald, La., Aug. 3, 1922; s. Lee Baines and Jessie Mae (Wilson) K.; m. Betty Evelyn Davis, Dec. 30, 1942; children: Anna Kathryn, Rebecca Lynn Bogorad. BA, La. State No. Coll., Natchitoches, 1942; MS, U. Oreg., 1950, MFA, 1954; PhD, State U. Iowa, 1965. Tchr. Roseburg (Oreg.) H.S., 1946-48, Parkrose H.S., Portland, Oreg., 1952-54; asst. prof. art history Eastern Oreg. Coll., LaGrande, 1955-61; prof. art history Portland State U., 1961-93, prof. emeritus, 1993—; art appraiser Portland, 1991—. Co-author: McCosh, 1985; contbr. articles to Artweek Northwest Mag., and other publs.; paintings and lithographs in collections at U. Oreg. Mus. and Portland Art Mus. Sgt. U.S. Army, 1942-46, ETO. Recipient rsch. grant Kress Found., Art in the Pacific Northwest, 1968. Democrat. Avocations: painter, lithographer, writer. Home: 1785 SW Montgomery Dr Portland OR 97201-2482

KIMBRELL, ODELL CULP, JR., physician; b. Spartanburg, S.C., May 2, 1927; s. Odell Culp and Leona (Nicholas) K.; m. Etta Lou; children from former marriage: Odell Culp III, Cynthia Anne. A.B., Duke U., 1947, M.D., U. Pa., 1951. Diplomate: Am. Bd. Internal Medicine, Am. Bd. Life Ins. Medicine. Intern Med. Coll. Va., Richmond, 1951-52, resident in internal medicine, 1954-56; sr. resident in internal medicine VA Hosp., Phila., 1956-57; practice medicine specializing in internal medicine and endocrinology Gallipolis, Ohio, 1957-60; practice medicine specializing in internal medicine and endocrinology Raleigh, N.C., 1960-93, practice ins. medicine, 1967—; mem. hon. staff Wake Med. Ctr.; clin. prof. medicine U.N.C. Med. Sch., 1970-90; med. dir. Pa. Life Ins. Co. Contbr. articles to med. jours. Bd. dirs. Wake County Hosp. System Inc., Raleigh, 1971-81, sec., 1973-74, chmn., 1974-76; bd. dirs. Wake Health Facilities and Service Inc., 1975-81, pres., 1975-76; chmn. Wake County Heart Fund, 1961; deacon Hudson Meml. Presbyn. Ch., Raleigh, 1971-73. Served with USAF, 1952-54. Fellow ACP; mem. AMA, N.C. Med. Soc., Wake County Med Soc., Am. Soc. Internal Medicine, N.C. Soc. Internal Medicine, Am. Acad. Ins. Med., Mid-Atlantic Med. Dirs. Club (pres. 1979-80, 92). Democrat. Lodge: Lions. Home: 1905 Hunting Ridge Rd Raleigh NC 27615-5515 Office: 2610 Wycliff Rd Raleigh NC 27607-3063 *Serving through devoted application of mind, body and spirit.*

KIMBRELL, WILLARD DUKE, textile company executive; b. Gaston County, N.C., Dec. 28, 1924; s. Curtis C. and Carolyn (Carter) K.; m. Dorothy Rhyne, Feb. 9, 1932; 3 children. BS in Textiles, N.C. State Coll., 1949; PhD, U. N.C., Charlotte. Various positions Parkdale Mills, Inc., Gastonia, N.C., 1938—, CEO, 1961—; bd. dirs. Am. Textile Mfg., Inman Mills; pres. Gaston Cmty. Found. Trustee Bowman Gray Sch. Medicine, U. N.C.; dir. YMCA, Gastonia. With USAF. Mem. Am. Yarn Spinners Assn. (pres.), N.C. Textile Mfrs. Assn. (pres.). Republican. Office: Parkdale Mills Inc 1630 W Garrison Blvd PO Box 1787 Gastonia NC 28053-1787*

KIMBRIEL-EGUIA, SUSAN, engineering planner; b. San Francisco, July 22, 1949; d. Scott Slaughter and Kathleen (Edens) Smith; m. Floyd Thomas Kimbriel; 1 child, John Thomas; m. Candelario Eguia, Feb. 14, 1991; 1 child, Daniel. Engrng. planner, sys. adminstr. various mainframe and PC based sys. Northrop Aircraft, Hawthorne, Calif., 1982-91; owner, operator Susie's Day Care, Palmdale, Calif., 1995—; PC cons. Moselle Ins. Corp., North Hollywood, Calif., 1989-96, Northrop Aircraft, 1991-96. Avocations: handcrafts, gardening, skating, biking, computer graphics.

KIMBROUGH, LORELEI, elementary education educator; b. Chgo.; d. Paul and Lina (Higgs) Bobbett; children: Denise, Devi, Paul, Jeri Lynn. BS in Edn., Ill. State U., 1947; postgrad., DePaul U., Chgo. U., others. Cert. tchr., Ill. Tchr. of Latin and English Greensboro (N.C.) Pub. Schs.; spl. edn. tchr. Chgo. State Hosp./Reed Zone Ctr., Chgo., Jewish Children's Bur., Chgo.; elem. tchr. Chgo. Bd. of Edn., Pasadena (Calif.) High Sch.; English tchr. Malala H.S., Madang, 1993-94; tchr. jr. H.S. Cathedral Chapel Cath. Sch., 1995-96, Holy Trinity Sch., L.A., 1998—; tutor to fgn. students. Missionary worker L.A. Archdiocese, Papua New Guinea; vol. ARC, Solheim Luth. Home, Glendale Meml. Hosp. Recipient four-year scholarship State of Ill., Chgo. Musical Coll. award. Mem. Nat. Coun. Tchrs. of English, Ill. Coun. of Social Studies, Nat. Coun. Social Studies.

KIMBROUGH, ROBERT AVERYT, lawyer; b. Sarasota, Fla., Nov. 2, 1933; s. Verman T. and Edith (Averyt) K.; m. Emilie Hudson, Aug. 24, 1957; children: James E., Robert A. Jr. BS, Davidson Coll., 1955; LLB to JD, U. Fla., 1960. Bar: Fla. 1960, U.S. Dist. Ct. Fla. 1962. Pvt. practice, Sarasota, 1960—. Chmn., bd. trustees, Ringling Sch. Art & Design, Sarasota, 1983-85; chmn. Sarasota Welfare Home Inc., 1986-89; pres. Fla. West Coast Symphony, Sarasota, 1986-90. Recipient Champion Higher Edn. in Fla., Ind. Coll. and Univs. of Fla., 1984-85, Alumnus of Yr. award Phi Delta Theta, 1997. Mem. ABA, Fla. Bar, Sarasota County Bar Assn., Sarasota Yacht Club, Kiwanis. Republican. Presbyterian. Avocations: flying, fishing, boating. Home: 7100 S Gator Creek Blvd Sarasota FL 34241-9729 Office: 1530 Cross St Sarasota FL 34236-7015

KIMBROUGH, ROBERT COOKE, III, infectious diseases physician; b. Washington, Nov. 26, 1941; s. Robert Cooke Jr. and Victoria Walton (Fitz Gerald) K.; m. Susan Jane Brackney (div.); children: Susan Fitz Gerald Kimbrough Gilson, Robert Cooke IV; m. Susan Kay Utterback, Apr. 11, 1974; children: John Williams, Bradley Warren. BS, U. Kans., 1963; MD, U. Kans., 1969. Diplomate Am. Bd. Internal Medicine. Intern, resident Baylor Coll. Medicine, Houston, 1969-73; chief resident St. Luke's Episcopal Hosp., Houston, 1972; fellow in infectious disease Baylor Coll. Medicine, 1972-74, U. Oreg. Med. Sch., Portland, 1974-75; instr. infectious diseases U. Oreg. Health Scis. Ctr., Portland, 1975-79; from asst. prof. to assoc. prof. infectious diseases Oreg. Health Scis. U., Portland, 1979-89; pvt. practice The Ferrell-Duncan Clinic, Inc., Springfield, Mo., 1989-93; prof. infectious diseases Tex. Tech. U. Health Scis. Ctr., Lubbock, 1993—, clerkship dir. of internal medicine, 1998—. Reviewer Archives Internal Medicine, Jour. Infectious Diseases, Clin. Infectious Diseases, Annals Internal Medicine. Fellow ACP (chmn. assoc. com. 1984, 85, v.p. Oreg. chpt. 1986, pres. 1987-89, Howard P. Lewis tchg. award 1988), Infectious Diseases Soc. Am.; mem. AMA, Am. Fedn. Clin. Rsch., Am. Soc. Microbiology, Am. Assn. History of Medicine, Am. Osler Soc., Oreg. Med. Assn. (chmn. nominating com. 1985, chmn. pharmacy liaison com. 1986-89, trustee 1987-89, profl. cons. com. 1987-89), Multnomah County Med. Soc. (chmn. strategic planning com. 1985, sec. 1986, v.p. 1987, pres.-elect 1988), Tex. Med. Assn., Lubbock Med. Soc., Garza Med. Soc., Crosby County Med. Soc.,. Avocations: trap shooting, medical history. Home: 3109 80th St Lubbock TX 79423-2022 Office: TTUHSC Dept Medicine 3601 4th St Lubbock TX 79430-0001

KIMBROUGH, WALTER MARK, university activities director; b. Apr. 22, 1967. BS, U. Ga., 1989; MS, Miami U., Oxford, Ohio, 1991; PhD, Ga. State U., 1996. Coord. Greek life Emory U., Atlanta, 1992-95; dir. new student programs Ga. State U., Atlanta, 1995-96; dir. student activities Old Dominion U., Norfolk, Va., 1997—. E-mail: wkimbrou@odu.edu. Home: 107 Westover Ave # 104 Norfolk VA 23507

KIMBROUGH, WILLIAM ADAMS, JR., lawyer; b. Selma, Ala., July 21, 1935; s. William Adams and Elizabeth (Bradford) K.; m. Kay Lindsey, Dec. 28, 1958; children: Mary Elizabeth, William Adams. BA (Union Carbide scholar), U. of South, 1957; LLB, U. Ala., 1961. Corr. Nat. Carbon Co., Chgo., 1957-58; mem. Lindsey & Christopher, Butler, Ala., 1961; asst. U.S. atty., 1962-65; gen. atty. Gulf, Mobile & Ohio R.R. Co., Mobile, Ala., 1965-70; mem. Stockman, Bedsole & Kimbrough, Mobile, 1970-76, Adams, Adams & Kimbrough, Grove Hill, Ala., 1976-77; U.S. atty. So. Dist. Ala., Mobile, 1977-81; mem. Turner, Onderdonk, Kimbrough & Howell, PA, Mobile, 1981—. Mem. Ala. State Dem. Exec. Com., 1966-70, Mobile County Dem. Exec. Com., 1991—. With U.S. Army, 1958, 61-62. Mem. ABA, Ala. Bar Assn., Mobile County Bar Assn. (pres. 1996), Am. Coll. Trial Lawyers, Nat. Assn. Former U.S. Attys., Nat. Assn. Criminal Def. Attys., Ala. Trial Lawyers Assn., Bienville Club, Country Club of Mobile, Omicron Delta Kappa. Methodist. Office: 1359 Dauphin St Mobile AL 36604-2140

KIMCHUK, AMY LYNN, mathematics educator; b. Jan. 14, 1969. AAS, C.C. of Phila., 1989; BS in Math., Gwynedd Mercy Coll., 1993; MA in Math., Villanova U., 1996. Night auditor Rittenhouse Hotel and Condo, Phila., 1993-97; instr. math. Raritan Valley C.C., Somerville, N.J., 1997-98; instr. math., computer sci. Univ.of Scis. in Phila., 1998—; adj. instr. math. Camden County Coll., Blackwood, N.J., 1994-97. E-mail: a.kimchu@usip.edu. Office: 600 S 43d St Philadelphia PA 19104-4495

KIME, J. WILLIAM, career officer, engineer, ship management executiv; b. Greensboro, N.C., July 15, 1934; m. Valerie Jean Hiddlestone., Aug. 5, 1980; 1 child, James. Grad., Balt. City Coll., 1951, USCG Acad., 1957, Indsl. Coll. Armed Forces, 1977; MS, MIT, 1964. Registered profl. engr., Mass. Commd. ensign USCG, 1957, advanced through grades to adm., 1990; with CGC Casco, Loran Sta. Wake Island, 1960, CG Hdqs., Washington; prin. U.S. negotiator Internat. Maritime Orgn., London; 1st engring. officer CGC Boutwell, Boston; asst. chief merchant marine tech. divsn. CG Hdqs., Washington, 1977-78, dep. chief Office Marine Environ. & Systems, 1981-82, chief Office Marine Safety, Security and Environ. Protection, 1984-88, comdt., 1990-94; commdg. officer Marine Safety Office, Balt., 1978-81; chief ops. divsn. 7th CG Dist., Miami, 1982-84; comdr. 11th CG Dist., Long Beach, Calif., 1988-90; retired USCG, 1994; chmn., CEO Interocean Ugland Mgmt. Group, Voorhes, N.J, 1994—. Decorated Def. DSM, Transp. DSM, Army DSM, Navy DSM, Air Force DSM, CGDSM, Def. Superior Svc. medal, Legion of Merit. Fellow Soc. Naval Archs. and Marine Engrs. (hon. life, pres. 1992-94, Vice Adm. Jerry Land medal 1990, UN World Maritime prize 1993); mem. Am. Soc. Naval Engring., Tau Beta Pi, Sigma Xi. Address: 7423 Pink Wood Ct Columbia MD 21046-1219*

KIMELMAN, ADAM S., journalist; b. N.Y.C., Apr. 16, 1975; s. David J. and Roni J. Kimelman. BA in Comms., Monmouth U., 1997. Copy editor Asbury Park Press, Neptune, N.J., 1997—; mng. editor, sports editor The Outlook, West Long Branch, N.J., 1994-95, editor-in-chief, 1996-97. Mem. N.J. Comm. Assn. Avocations: sports, writing, reading. Home: 138 Briar Ct Marlton NJ 08053

KIMERER, NEIL BANARD, SR., retired psychiatrist, educator; b. Wauseon, Ohio, Jan. 13, 1918; s. William and Ruby (Upp) K.; m. Ellen Jane Scott, May 22, 1943; children: Susan Leigh, Neil Banard, Brian Scott, Sandra Lynn. BS, U. Toledo, 1941; MD, U. Chgo., 1944; postgrad. (fellow), Menninger Sch., 1947-50. Diplomate Am. Bd. Psychiatry and Neurology. Intern Emanuel Hosp., Portland, Oreg., 1944; resident psychiatry Winter VA Hosp., Topeka, 1947-50; asst. physician Central State Hosp., Norman, Okla., 1950; cons. Central State Hosp., 1955-98; chief out-patient psychiat. clinic U. Okla. Sch. Medicine, Oklahoma City, 1951-53; instr. dept. psychiatry, neurology and behavioral scis. U. Okla. Sch. Medicine, 1953-61, assoc. prof., 1961-69, clin. prof., 1969-85, clin. prof. emeritus, 1985-98; practice medicine specializing in psychiatry Oklahoma City, 1953-98; med. dir. Oklahoma City Mental Health Clinic, 1953-68; chmn. dept. psychiatry Bapt. Med. Ctr. Okla., 1979-83; ret., 1998. Author: To Get and Beget, 1971, revised, 1996, Independence Means Swim or Sink, 1995; contbr. articles in field to profl. jours. Mem. exec. com. Okla. Family Life Assn., 1958-60; bd. dirs.

Oklahoma City Jr. Symphony Soc., 1959. Served as pfc ASTP, 1943-44; to capt. M.C. AUS, 1945-47. Fellow Am. Psychiat. Assn. (life); mem. AMA (life), Okla. Med. Assn., Oklahoma County Med. Soc., Oklahoma City Clin. Soc., AAAS, Alpha Kappa Kappa (pres. Nu chpt. 1943). Lodge: Rotary. Home: 2800 NW 25th St Oklahoma City OK 73107-2228

KIMES, BEVERLY RAE, editor, writer; b. Aurora, Ill., Aug. 17, 1939; d. Raymond Lionel and Grace Florence (Perrin) K.; m. James H. Cox, July 6, 1984. BS, U. Ill., 1961; MA in Journalism, Pa. State U., 1963. Dir. publicity Mateer Playhouse, Neff's Mills, Pa., 1962, Pavillion Theatre, University Park, Pa., 1963; asst. editor Automobile Quar. Publs., N.Y.C., Princeton, N.J., 1963-64, assoc. editor, 1965-66, mng. editor, 1967-74, editor, 1975-81; editor The Classic Car, 1981—. bd. corporators Mus. Transp., Brookline, Mass.; bd. trustees Nat. Automotive History Collection, Detroit Pub. Libr. Recipient Thomas McKean trophy, 1983, 85, 86, Moto award Nat. Assn. Automotive Journalists, 1984, 85, 86, 97, Benz award, 1994, Disting. Svc. Citation Automotive Hall of Fame, 1993. Mem. Internat. Motor Press Assn., Milestone Car Soc. (bd. dirs.), Soc. Automotive Historians, (pres. 1987-89, Cugnot award 1978-79, 83, 85-86, Friend of Automotive History award 1985). Author: The Classic Tradition of the Lincoln Motor Car, 1968, (with R.M. Langworth) Oldsmobile: The First Seventy-Five Years, 1972; The Cars That Henry Ford Built, 1978; (with Rene Dreyfus) My Two Lives, 1983; (with Robert C. Ackerson) Chevrolet: A History from 1911, 84; The Standard Catalog of American Cars 1805-1942, 1985; The Star and the Laurel: The Centennial History of Daimler, Mercedes and Benz, 1986; editor: Great Cars and Grand Marques, 1976; Packard: History of the Motor Car and theCompany, 1979; Automobile Quarterly's Handbook of Automotive Hobbies, 1981, The Classic Car: The Ultimate Book About the World's Grandest Automobiles, 1990.

KIMM, SUE YOUNG SOOK, academic administrator, researcher; b. Seoul, Republic of Korea, Feb. 11, 1938; came to U.S., 1956.; d. Lloyd C. and Diana Duk-Sil (Cha) K.; m. Seymour Grufferman, Dec. 23, 1967. AB, Bryn Mawr (Pa.) Coll., 1960; MD, Yale U., 1964; MPH, Harvard U., 1968, MS, 1974. Diplomate Nat. Bd. Med. Examiners, Am. Bd. Pediatrics, Am. Coll. Epidemiology. Intern, then resident in pediatrics Children's Hosp. Med. Ctr., Boston, 1964-66; resident in pediatrics Case-Western Res. U. Hosp., Cleve., 1966-67; cons. pediatrician Tokyo Sanitarium Hosp., 1969-71; chief of pediatrics, asst. prof. Gondar Pub. Health Coll. Haile Sellassie I. U., Gondar, Ethiopia, 1971-73; fellow Ctr. for Community Health & Med. Care Harvard U., Boston, 1974-75; asst. prof. pediatrics Sch. of Medicine Duke U., Durham, N.C., 1976-87; acting chief nutrition rsch. sect. Nat. Heart, Lung & Blood Inst. NIH, Bethesda, Md., 1985-87; asst. v.p. for health promotion Health Scis. Ctr. U. Pitts., 1987-91; assoc. prof. dept. clin. epidemiology/preventive medicine Sch. Medicine, U. Pitts., 1987-97; prof. dept. family medicine/clin. epidemiology U. Pitt., 1977—; cons. Nat. Heart, Lung & Blood Inst.-NIH, Bethesda, 1987—; grant reviewer NIH, Bethesda, 1987—; mem. Nat. Cancer Inst. Rev. Subcom., Bethesda, 1998—. Contbr. articles to med. jours. Vol. physician AMA, South Vietnam, 1968; cons. family health project Pitts. Urban League, 1989. Harvard U. fellow, 1974-75; Bryn Mawr Coll., Yale U. scholar, 1956-60; recipient Cert. of Appreciation, NIH, 1987. Fellow Am. Heart Assn. (epidemiology coun.); mem. Am. Coll. Epidemiology, Preventive Cardiology Soc., Internat. Fedn. for Preventive Cardiology, No. Am. Assn. for Study of Obesity, Pitts. Athletic Assn., Dandie Dinmont Terrier Club. Avocations: decorative arts, horticulture. Home: 432 Morewood Ave Pittsburgh PA 15213-1814 Office: U Pitts Sch Medicine M200 Scaife Hall Pittsburgh PA 15261-2002

KIMME, ERNEST GODFREY, communications engineer; b. Long Beach, Calif., June 7, 1929; s. Ernest Godfrey and Lura Elizabeth (Dake) K.; BA cum laude, Pomona Coll., 1952; MA, U. Minn., 1954, PhD, 1955; m. Margaret Jeanne Bolen, Dec. 10, 1978; children by previous marriage: Ernest G., Elizabeth E., Karl Frederick. Mem. grad. faculty Oreg. State U., Corvallis, 1955-57; mem. tech. staff Bell Telephone Labs., Murray Hill, N.J., 1957-65, supr. mobile radio rsch. lab., 1962-65; head applied sci. dept. Collins Radio Co., Newport Beach, Calif., 1965-72; rsch. engr. Northrop Electronics, Hawthorne, Calif., 1972-74; sr. staff engr. Interstate Electronics Corp., Anaheim, Calif., 1974-79; dir. advanced systems, dir. advanced comm. systems, tech. dir. spl. comm. programs Gould Navcomm Systems, El Monte, Calif., 1979-82; pres. Cobit, Inc, 1982-84; tech. staff Gen. Rsch. Corp., Santa Barbara, 1984-87; v.p. engring. Starfind, Inc., Laguna Niguel, Calif., 1987-88; dir. engring. R&D Unit Instruments, Orange, Calif., 1988-89; staff scientist Brunswick Def. Systems, Costa Mesa, Calif., 1989-90; v.p. engring. Redband Techs., Inc., 1990-96; adj. prof. U. Redlands, Golden Gate Univ., 1989—; adj. faculty math. U. Redlands Whitehead Coll., 1990—, Chapman U., 1997—. Contbr. articles to profl. jours. Mem. AAAS, Aircraft Owners and Pilots Assn., Exptl. Aircraft Assn., Phi Beta Kappa, Sigma Xi. Home: 301 N Starfire St Anaheim CA 92807-2928

KIMMEL, FRANK EDWARD, engineer; b. Chgo., May 7, 1924; s. Frank and Marie Christine (Kviz) K.; m. Irene Emily Homolka, Oct. 7, 1950; children: Lynn, Frank, Richard. BSME, Ill. Inst. of Technology, 1945; MS in Indsl. Mgmt., Loyola U., 1967. Dept. head mfg. engring. Western Electric Hawthorne Works, Chgo., 1946-72; dir. indsl. engring. Gen. Dynamics, Clayton, Mo., 1973-78; mfg. engring. resources mgr. G.D. Searle, Skokie, Ill., 1978-81; engring. resources svcs. cons. Owner of Home Office Bus., Naperville, Ill., 1981-87; gen. engr. Def. Supply Agy., Chgo., 1987-96; cons. Naperville, Ill., 1996—. Patentee in field; contbr. articles to profl. jours. Mem. Village Planning Bd., Naperville, 1959-60. Mem. Western Soc. Engrs. (mem. chmn. 1968-69), Blue Key Nat. Honor Fraternity. Avocations: defense supply productivity improvement specialist, indsl. profit improvement quality expert, cost reduction consultant. Home: 8 S 264 Wehrli Rd Naperville IL 60540-9460

KIMMEL, HERBERT DAVID, psychology educator; b. N.Y.C., May 22, 1927; s. Max and Lillian (Neuwirth) K.; m. Barbara B. Ellis; children: Elinor, Ann Kimmel Ritter, Jean, Tracy. BS, U. Fla., 1948; MA, NYU, 1951; PhD, U. So. Calif., 1958. Lic. psychologist, Fla. Sch. psychometrist William S. Hart Union High Sch., Newhall, Calif., 1950-52; rsch. asst., rsch. assoc., project dir. Mgmt. and Mktg. Rsch. Corp., Human Factors Rsch., 1953-58; asst. prof., then assoc. prof. psychology U. Fla., Gainesville, 1958-65; prof. psychology Ohio U., Athens, 1965-68; prof. psychology U. So. Fla., Tampa, 1968-86, chmn. dept. psychology, 1968-72, disting. rsch. prof., 1986-93, disting. rsch. prof. emeritus, 1993—; disting. vis. prof. U. Tulsa, fall 1976; vis. prof. psychology U. P.R., summer 1963, Duke U., spring 1961; vis. scientist Human Factors Rsch., Inc., summer 1964; gastprof. U. Giessen, summer, 1982; prof. U. Trier, 1987—, mem. sci. adv. bd. Ctr. Rsch. in Psychobiology and Psychosomatics, 1994—. Author: Experimental Principles and Design in Psychology, 1970, Experimental Psychopathology, 1971, Biofeedback and Self-Regulation, 1979, The Orienting Reflex in Humans, 1979; author chpts. to books; masthead cons. editor Jour. Exptl. Psychology, 1960-74; mem. editorial bd. Behavior Therapy and Exptl. Psychiatry, 1976—, Jour. Behavioral Assessment, 1979—, Jour. Clin. and Cons. Psychology, 1981-88; mem. editorial bd. Pavlovian Jour. of Biol. Scis., 1976—, mng. editor, 1978-83; ad hoc editor for various publs. in field; contbr. articles for profl. jours. Recipient A. von Humboldt Sr. Scientist award U. Tuebingen, 1980-81; grantee NIMH, 1959-72, Office Naval Rsch., 1960-61, U.S. Office Edn., 1969-70, Nat. Libr. Medicine, 1973-76, U.S. Army Med. Rsch. and Devel. Command, 1974-83, NSF, 1976-78, German Rsch. Soc., 1983. Fellow APA; mem. N.Y. Acad. Scis., Southeastern Psychol. Assn., Psychonomic Soc., Psychometric Soc., Soc. for Philosophy and Psychology (pres. 1977-78), Pavlovian Soc. (2d v.p. 1980, 1st v.p. 1981, pres. 1982, exec. com. 1983—). Home: 1931 Woodbury Blvd Houston TX 77030

KIMMEL, MAREK, biomathematician, educator; b. Gliwice, Poland, Sept. 17, 1953; came to U.S., 1982; s. Zbigniew and Janina (Rybicka) K.; m. Barbara Stankiewicz, June 27, 1981; children: Jan, Katarzyna. MS, Silesian Tech. U., Gliwice, 1977, PhD, 1980. Asst. prof. Silesian Tech. U., 1977-82, Sloan-Kettering Inst., N.Y.C., 1982-90; assoc. prof. dept. stats. Rice U., Houston, 1990-94, prof., 1994—; habilitation in math. scis. Jagiellonean U., 1997; cons. rsch. divsn. IBM, Yorktown Heights, N.Y., 1989—; chmn. dept. stats. Rice U., Houston, 1996-99. Co-editor: Mathematical Population Dynamics, 1991, 95, 98; contbr. over 100 articles to profl. jours. including Jour. Theoretical Biology, Biometrics, Genetics. Grantee Nat. Cancer Inst., 1985, NSF, 1989-98, NIH, 1995—. Fellow Am. Statis. Assn.; mem. Inst. Math. Stats., Soc. for Mathematical Biology, Cell Kinetics Soc. Roman Catholic. Achievements include research on the statistical model of natural history of lung cancer; mathematical model of unequal division of cells; methods of estimation of cell cycle kinetics; mathematical model of gene amplification; population genetics of microsatellite loci. Office: Rice U Dept Stats PO Box 1892 Houston TX 77251-1892

KIMMEL, MARK, writer, retired venture capital company executive; b. Denver, Feb. 15, 1940; s. Earl Henry and Gerry Claire Kimmel; m. Gloria J. Danielewicz, Jan. 29, 1966 (div.); children: Kenton, Kristopher; m. Heidi J. Moller, Sept. 5, 1999. BSEE, U. Colo., 1963, BS in Mktg., 1963; MBA in Fin., U. So. Calif., 1966. Sales engr., market rsch. analyst 3M Co., Calif. and Minn., 1963-70; mktg. mgr. Am. Computer and Comms., Calif., 1970-71; mgr. new bus. devel. Motorola, Inc., Schaumburg, Ill., 1971-76; v.p. corp. devel. Nat. City Lines, Denver, 1976-77; pres. Enervest, Inc., Denver, 1977-84; gen. ptnr. Columbia Venture Fund Ltd., 1983-91, Columbine Venture Fund II, 1983-91, Columbine Venture Mgmt. I, 1983-91, Columbine Venture Mgmt. II, 1983-91; pres. columbine Venture Mgmt. Inc., 1983-91, Paradigm Ptnrs., Inc., 1992-96. Mem. Nat. Assn. Small Bus. Invesetment Cos. (past bd. govs.), Venture Capital Assn. Colo. (past chmn.). Home and Office: 3757 Telluride Cir Boulder CO 80303-7423

KIMMEL, MORTON RICHARD, lawyer; b. N.Y.C., Nov. 10, 1940; s. Benjamin Bert and Sylvia (Alabaster) K.; m. Marcia Harriet LaPotin, Sept. 10, 1967; children: Wayne Douglas, Michelle Wendy, Karen Paige, Larry Keith. BA, Temple U., 1962; JD, George Washington U., 1965. Bar: Del. 1965, D.C. 1966. Law clk. Del. Superior Ct., Wilmington, 1965-66; ptnr. Kimmel, Carter, Roman & Peltz P.A., Wilmington, 1970—; supr. Del. Justices of the Peace, 1970-72; rep. State Farm Ins. Co., 1968-90, trustee lawyers' fund for client protection, 1985-97; arbitrator and mediator; lectr. in fields of criminal law, ins. law, personal injury law, law office mgmt., trial practice, ethics, professionalism, mediation and arbitration, 1970—. Author: You Can Do It, 1973, Emergency Medicine, 1982, Delaware Arbitration Manual, 1984, The Delaware Bar in the 20th Century, 1994. Mem. ATLA, Am. Bd. Trial Advs., Del. Trial Lawyers Assn., Fedn. Ins. Counsel, Def. Rsch. Inst. (chmn. Del. 1976-77). Democrat. Jewish. Avocations: sports, reading. Office: Kimmel Carter Roman & Peltz PA 913 N Market St Wilmington DE 19801-3019

KIMMELMAN, GREGORY M., television producer and director; b. Phila., Mar. 4, 1947; s. Bernard and Lorene (Lawrence) K.; child from previous marriage, Joshua; m. Susan Jane Goldstein, Feb. 6, 1988. BS, Am. U., Washington, 1969; MS, Columbia U., 1971; student, New Sch., N.Y.C., 1978. Prin. Golden Lion Entertainment, N.Y.C., 1978-81; pres. G.K. Film Enterprises, N.Y.C., 1981-84; mktg. dir. Reuters Internat., N.Y.C., 1984-88; CABLE-READY v.p. internat. mktg. Ashley Entertainment, N.Y.C., 1988-92; cable-ready v.p. internat. mktg. Global Telemedia, N.Y.C., 1992—; cons. GMK, Inc., N.Y.C., 1986—. Actor Washington Theatre Cub, 1969, Columbia U. Theatre, 1967, Smithsonian Inst., 1966; dir. indsl. film North Am. Philips, 1989; producer record album Shooting Star, 1979; producer home video Tennis Kinetics With Martina Navratilova, 1986, 1996 and 1997 N.Y. Emmy Awards, Visit of Pope Paul Video, 1995; producer, dir. TV program Bright Idea, 1989; producer TV program Second Challenge, 1983, Point in Time with Edwin Newman, 1988, CBS Eye on People, 1998. Mem. Dirs. Guild Am., Internat. TV Assn., Soc. Satellite Profls., Acad. TV Arts and Scis. (bd. govs.). Avocations: gourmet cooking, internat. travel, music collecting. Home: 15 Patchen Ln Weston CT 06883-1943

KIMMEY, JAMES RICHARD, JR., medical educator, consultant; b. Boscobel, Wis., Jan. 26, 1935; s. James Richard and Frances Dale (Parnell) K.; m. Sarah Webster Eastman, June 21, 1958; children—Elisabeth Webster, James Richard III. BS, U. Wis., 1957, MS, 1959, MD, 1961; MPH, U. Calif. at Berkeley, 1967. Diplomate: Am. Bd. Preventive Medicine. Intern Univ. Hosps., Cleve., 1961-62; med. resident Univ. Hosp., Madison, 1962-63; served from surgeon to med. dir. USPHS, 1963-68, chief kidney disease br., 1964-66; regional health dir. USPHS, N.Y., 1967-68; exec. dir. Community Health Inc., N.Y.C., 1968-70, Am. Pub. Health Assn., 1970-73; sec. Health Policy Council Wis., 1973-75; pres. James R. Kimmey Assos., Inc., 1975-85; dir. Midwest Center for Health Planning, 1976-79; exec. dir. Inst. Health Planning, 1979-87; adj. assoc. prof. Columbia Sch. Public Health, 1968-75; adj. prof. N.Y. U., 1968-70; lectr. Johns Hopkins, 1971-73; clin. instr. U. Wis., 1974-87; pres. Inst. Health Planning, 1979-86; prof. of pub. health and dir. Ctr. for Health Services Edn. and Research, St. Louis U. Med. Ctr., 1987-91; dean Sch. Pub. Health, St. Louis U., 1991-93, v.p. health scis., 1993-98, exec. v.p., 1998—. Editor: The Nation's Health, 1972-73; mng. editor: Am. Jour. Pub. Health, 1970-73; editorial adv. bd.: Health Cost Mgmt., 1983-87; Contbr. articles to profl. jours. Pres. World Fedn. Pub. Health Assns., 1972-73; bd. dirs. Internat. Union Health Edn., 1970-73; mem. sci. adv. bd. Gorgas Inst., 1970-73. Decorated USPHS Commendation medal, 1968. Fellow APHA (governing coun. 1978-81, 83-87, 89—, chmn. cmty. health planning sect. 1979-80), Am. Coll. Preventive Medicine; mem. Am. Health Planning Assn. (dir. 1974-75, 77-78, corp. sec. 1977-78, pres. 1980-81, Richard H. Schlesinger award 1978, James R. Kimmey award 1994), Am. Coll. Health Adminstrs., Mo. Pub. Health Assn. (Mo. Communicator of Yr. award 1994), Prospective Payment Assessment Commn. (commr. 1991-97), Phi Eta Sigma, Alpha Omega Alpha, Delta Omega, Alpha Sigma Nu. Democrat. Episcopalian. Home: 1614 S 18th St Saint Louis MO 63104-2504 Office: DuBourg Hall 221 N Grand Blvd Saint Louis MO 63103-2006

KIMMICH, CHRISTOPH MARTIN, academic administrator, educator; b. Dresden, Jan. 16, 1939; s. Emil and Dora (Dreher) K.; m. Flora Graham Horne, July 10, 1965. BA, Haverford Coll., 1961; DPhil, U. Oxford, Eng., 1964. Asst. then assoc. prof. Columbia U., N.Y.C., 1965-73; assoc. then full prof. Bklyn. Coll., CUNY, 1973—, assoc. provost, 1984-88, provost, v.p. acad. affairs, 1988-97; interim chancellor CUNY, N.Y.C., 1997—; v.p. bd. dirs. rsch. and devel. fedn. Bklyn. Coll., 1989—, chmn. bd. dirs. rsch. found. of CUNY, 1997—. Author: The Free City, 1968, Germany and the League of Nations, 1976, German Foreign Policy: 1918-1945, 1981, 2d edit., 1991. Trustee St. Antony's Coll. Trust, N.Y.C., 1978—; bd. dirs. Northeastern Sci. Found., Troy, 1987-98, Coll. Cmty. Svcs., Inc., Bklyn., 1988-95, bd. trustees Cranbury Pub. Libr., 1997—. Fulbright scholar, 1961; Internat. Affairs fellow, 1974; Guggenheim fellow, 1983. Mem. Phi Beta Kappa. Home: 183 Plainsboro Rd Cranbury NJ 08512-2603 Office: CUNY Office of the Chancellor 535 E 80th St New York NY 10021-0795

KIMMICH, JON BRADFORD, computer science program executive; b. Lancaster, Pa., Aug. 8, 1964; s. John Howard and Alice (Ingram) K. BS in Computer Sci., Ind. U. Pa., 1986; MS in Computer Sci., Ohio State U., 1988; MBA, Seattle U., 1993. Developer Microsoft, Redmond, Wash., 1988-93, lead program mgr., sr. producer, 1993-97, product planner, 1997—; dir. PKT Found. Contbr. articles to profl. jours. Trustee PKT Found. Mem. IEEE (Computer Soc.), Assn. for Computing Machinery, Acad. Interactive Arts and Scis., Internat. Interactive Comms. Soc., Am. Film Inst. Achievements include 7 patents pending. Home: 1442 W Lake Sammamish Pkwy SE Bellevue WA 98008-5218 Office: Microsoft Corp 1 Microsoft Way Redmond WA 98052-8300

KIMMITT, JOSEPH STANLEY, political consultant; b. Lewistown, Mont., Apr. 5, 1918; s. Joseph Henry Kimmitt and Margaret Bowe; m. Eunice Leona Wegener, Mar. 20, 1947; children: Robert, Kathleen, Jay, Tom, Mark, Mary, Judy. Student, U. Mont., 1940-41; BS, Utah State U., 1960; LLD (hon.), Mont. Tech., 1977. Commd. 2d lt. U.S. Army, 1942, advanced through grades to col., ret., 1966; adminstrv. asst. to majority leader U.S. Senate, Washington, 1966, sec. for majority, 1966-77, sec. of the senate, 1977-81; v.p. govt. affairs Hughes Helicopter Co., Washington, 1981-84; asst. to pres. for govt. affairs McDonnell Douglas Helicopter Co., Washington, 1984-97; ptnr. Kimmitt, Coates & McCarthy, Washington; bd. dirs. Mont. Energy, Butte, Mont., U. Mont. Found., Missoula. Local pres., state v.p. Jaycees, Logan, Utah, 1958; bd. mem. March of Dimes, Arlington, Va.; bd. advisors Dem. Leadership Coun., Washington. Recipient various mil. awards U.S. Army, 1941-66. Mem. KC, Assn. U.S. Army (bd. dirs.), Nat. Def. Indsl. Assn. (bd. dirs.). Democrat. Roman Catholic. Home: 6004 Copely Ln Mc Lean VA 22101-2507 Office: Kimmitt Coates & McCarthy 1730 M St NW Ste 911 Washington DC 20036-4512

KIMMITT, ROBERT MICHAEL, lawyer, banker, diplomat; b. Logan, Utah, Dec. 19, 1947; s. Joseph Stanley and Eunice L. (Wegener) K.; m. Holly Sutherland, May 19, 1979; children: Kathleen, Robert, William, Thomas, Margaret. BS, U.S. Mil. Acad., 1969; JD, Georgetown U., 1977. Bar: D.C. 1977. Commd. 2d lt. U.S. Army, 1969, advanced through grades to maj., 1982, served in Vietnam, 1970-71; brig. gen. USAR, 1996—; law clk. U.S. Ct. Appeals, Washington, 1977-78; sr. staff mem. NSC, Washington, 1978-83, dep. asst. to Pres. for nat. security affairs and exec. sec. and gen. counsel, 1983-85; gen. counsel U.S. Dept. Treasury, Washington, 1985-87; ptnr. Sidley & Austin, Washington, 1987-89; undersec. for polit. affairs Dept. State, Washington, 1988-91, ambassador to Germany, 1991-93; mng. dir. Lehman Bros., Washington, N.Y.C., 1993-97; sr. ptnr. Wilmer, Cutler & Pickering, Washington, 1997—; U.S. mem. Panel of Arbitrators, Internat. Ctr. for Settlement of Investment Disputes, 1988-89. Bd. dirs. Mannesmann AG, Siemens AG, Allianz Life Ins. Co. N.Am., Big Flower Holdings, United Def. Industries, German Marshall Fund, Atlantic Coun., Mike Mansfield Found., Am. Coun. on Germany, Am. Inst. for Contemporary German Studies, U.S. Group Coun., BMW AG. Decorated Bronze star (3), Purple Heart, Air medal, Vietnamese Cross of Gallantry, German Svc. Cross, German Army Cross in Gold; recipient Arthur Flemming award Downtown Jaycees, 1987, Alexander Hamilton award U.S. Dept. Treasury, 1987, Presdl. Citizens medal, 1991, Def. Disting. Civilian Svc. medal, 1993. Mem. Am. Acad. Diplomacy, Assn. Grads. U.S. Mil. Acad. (trustee 1976-82), Coun. Fgn. Rels. Roman Catholic. Office: Wilmer Cutler & Pickering 2445 M St NW Washington DC 20037-1420

KIMNACH, MYRON WILLIAM, botanist, horticulturist, consultant; b. Los Angeles, Dec. 26, 1922; s. Elmer Edward and Ida (Johnson) K.; m. Maria Jaeger, Nov. 17, 1961. Grad. h.s. Asst. mgr. U. Calif. Botanic Garden, Berkeley, 1951-62; curator Huntington Bot. Gardens, San Marino, 1962-88; now book-dealer Monrovia, Calif. Contbr. articles profl. jours. Pres., bd. dirs. Palm Soc., 1976-78. With USCG, 1943-46. Fellow Cactus and Succulent Soc. Am. (pres. 1970-71, bd. dirs. 1968-74, editor jour. 1993—). Home and Office: 509 Bradbury Rd Monrovia CA 91016

KIMPORT, DAVID LLOYD, lawyer; b. Hot Springs, S.D., Nov. 28, 1945; s. Ralph E. and Ruth N. (Hutchinson) K.; m. Barbara H. Buggert, Apr. 2, 1976; children: Katrina Elizabeth, Rebecca Helen, Susanna Ruth. AB summa cum laude, Bowdoin Coll., 1968; postgrad., Imperial Coll., U. London, 1970-71; JD, Stanford U., 1975. Bar: Calif. 1975, U.S. Supreme Ct. 1978. Assoc. Baker & McKenzie, San Francisco, 1975-82, ptnr., 1982-90; ptnr. Nossaman, Guthner, Knox & Elliot, 1990—. Active San Francisco Planning and Urban Rsch., 1978—, The Family, 1987—. Served with U.S. Army, 1968-70. Mem. ABA, San Francisco Bar Assn., Commonwealth Club of Calif., Phi Beta Kappa. Democrat. Episcopalian. Office: Nossaman Guthner Knox & Elliott 50 California St Fl 34 San Francisco CA 94111-4624

KIMPTON, BILL, hotel executive; b. Kansas City, Mo.. BS in Econs., Northwestern U.; grad., U. Chgo. Chmn. Kimpton Hotel and Restaurant Group, Inc., San Francisco, 1981—. Office: Kimpton Hotel and Restaurant Group Inc 222 Kearny St #200 San Francisco CA 94108

KIMPTON, DAVID RAYMOND, natural resource consultant, writer; b. Twin Falls, Idaho, Feb. 19, 1942; s. Lloyd and Retura (Robins) K.; m. Joanna Peak, June 2, 1984; foster children: Donnie, Derrick, Dustin. BS in Forestry, U. Idaho, 1964. Forester U.S. Forest Svc., Panguitch, Utah, 1966-68; with dept. interdisciplinary natural resources U.S. Forest Svc., Ely, Nev., 1968-71; with dept. interdisciplinary natural resources U.S. Forest Svc., Stanley, Idaho, 1971-72, dist. ranger, 1972-78; dist. ranger U.S. Forest Svc., Mountain City, Nev., 1978-84; natural resource cons. Idaho, 1984-92; range conservationist U.S. Forest Svc., Stanley, Idaho, 1992-93; program mgr. natural resources Sawtooth Nat. Recreation Area, Stanley, Idaho, 1993-97; conservationist pvt. practice, 1997—; incident comdr. U.S. Forest Svc., Western States, 1978-86; botanist pvt. and govtl., Idaho, Nev., 1985-92; naturalist schs., pvt., govt., Idaho, Nev., 1988—. bd. dirs. Salmon River Emergency Med. Clinic, Stanley, Idaho, 1984-86, v.p., 1987-92; bd. dirs., v.p. Idaho Mountain Health Clinics, Boise, 1985-92. Author Mining Law jour., 1990; author Life Saving Rescue mag., 1989. Pres. Meth. Youth Found., Twin Falls, 1960—; treas., v.p. Chrisman Bd. Dirs., Moscow, Idaho, 1960-63; bd. dirs. Vol. Fire Dept., Ely, 1968-71, Sawtooth Valley Meditation Chapel, 1974-76, Stanley Cmty. Bldg., 1977-78; mem. Sawtooth Valley Assn, Stanley, 1971-72, Vol. Fire Dept. Stanley, 1975-78, Mountain Search and Rescue, Stanley, 1972-78, Coalition of Taxpayers, Stanley, 1990-95. With U.S. Army, 1965-66, Vietnam. Named Outstanding Young Men Am., Bd. Nat. Advs., 1971, Outstanding Mem., White Pine Jaycees, 1969. Mem. Idaho Wildlife, Sawtooth Wildlife Coun. Mem. Christian Ch. Avocations: botany, wildlife, naturalist, backpacking, hunting. Home: PO Box 32 Stanley ID 83278-0032

KIMSEY, WILLIAM L., diversified financial services company executive. Co-chmn. bd. dirs. Ernst & Young, LLP, N.Y.C.; CEO Ernst & Young Internat., N.Y.C. Office: Ernst & Young LLP 787 7th Ave New York NY 10019-6018*

KIMURA, DOREEN, psychology educator, researcher; b. Winnipeg, Man., Can.; 1 child, Charlotte Vanderwolf. BA, McGill U., Montreal, Que., Can., 1956, MA, 1957, PhD, 1961; LLD (hon.), Simon Fraser U., 1993, Queen's U., 1999. Lectr. Sir George Williams U. (now Concordia U.), Montreal, 1960-61; rsch. assoc. otol. rsch. lab. UCLA Med. Ctr., 1962-63; rsch. assoc. Coll. Medicine, McMaster U., Hamilton, Ont., 1964-67; assoc. prof. psychology U. Western Ont., London, 1967-74, prof., 1974-98; prof. emeritus, 1998—; coord. clin. neuropsychology program U. Western Ont., London, 1983-97; sr. clin. neuropsychology Univ. Hosp., London, 1975-83; vis. prof. psychology Simon Fraser U., 1998—. Author: Neuromotor Mechanisms in Human Communication, 1993, Sex and Cognition, 1999; contbr. numerous articles to profl. jours. Recipient Outstanding Sci. Achievement award Can. Assn. Women in Sci., 1986, John Dewan award Ont. Mental Health Found., 1992; fellow Montreal Neurol. Inst., 1960-61, Geigy fellow Kantonsspital, Zürich, Switzerland, 1963-64. Fellow Royal Soc. Can., Can. Psychol. Assn. (Disting. Contbns. to Sci. award 1985); mem. Internat. Neuropsychol. Symposium. Office: Simon Fraser U, Dept Psychology, Burnaby, BC Canada V5A 1S6

KIMURA, HIROSHI, periodontist; b. Nishio City, Japan, June 8, 1966; came to U.S., 1975; s. Shoji and Kiyoko K. BA, Boston U., 1989; DMD, Tufts U., 1993. Clin. instr. Tufts U., Boston, 1993-95; assoc. periodontist N.Y.C., 1995-97, Omicare Internat., N.Y.C., 1995-97; ptnr. Overseas Japanese Family Medicine, N.Y.C., 1997—; owner Periodontics & Dental Implants, N.Y.C., 1997—. Mem. ADA (assoc.), Am. Acad. Periodontology (assoc.), Am. Acad. Osscointegation (assoc.), N.Y. Dental Soc., Japanese Med. Soc. Am. (bd. dirs. 1997—), Delta Sigma Delta. Avocations: violin, soccer, travel, teaching, reading. Office: Periodontics & Dental Implants NY 30 Central Park S Ste 3D New York NY 10019

KIMURA, MIYOSHI, statistics educator, researcher; b. Ena-shi, Gifu-ken, Japan, Aug. 22, 1947; s. Masaru and Toshiko (Kato) K.; m. Hiroko Nakatsuru, May 17, 1974; children: Shogo, Ayako. BSc, Nagoya (Japan) U., 1970; MSc, Kyushu U., Fukuoka, Japan, 1973, DSc, 1988. Asst. prof. Nanzan U., Nagoya, Japan, 1975-82, assoc. prof., 1982-90, prof., 1990—, course leader Grad. Sch., 1992-96, head dept. info. sys. and quantitative scis., 1999—; vis. rschr. Stanford (Calif.) U., 1980-81, U. Wash., Seattle, 1991, U. Sheffield, U.K., 1997-98; course leader Grad. Sch., Nanzan U., Nagoya, 1992-96; head dept. of info. systems and quantitative scis. Nanzan U., Nagoya, 1999—. Contbr. articles to profl. jours. Rsch. grantee Nitto Scholarship Found., Nagoya, 1986, Japan Securities Scholarship Found., Tokyo, 1989, Hori Info. Sci. Scholarship Found., Nagoya, 1995. Avocation: tennis. Home: 22 1-Chome, Ryokuen-nishi, Gifu-Ken Kakamigahara-shi 509-0116, Japan Office: Nanzan Univ, 18 Yamazato-cho, Showa-ku, Nagoya 466-8673, Japan

KIMZEY, LORENE MILLER, endocrinology nurse; b. Indpls., Dec. 20, 1943; d. James Loren and Imogene Faye (Nicely) Miller; m. Charles H. Kimzey, Jr., Jan. 2, 1963; 1 child, Charles Clinton. BSN with distinction, George Mason U., 1976, MEd, 1991. RN, Va.; cert. in reproductive endocrinology and infertility. Staff asst. Congressman Jerry Pettis, Washington, 1967-68, Congressman John Wold, Washington, 1968-69, Office of

Sec. of Health, Edn. and Welfare, Washington, 1970-73; clin. nurse NIH, Bethesda, Md., 1977-81, 83—; nurse NICU Sibley Meml. Hosp., Washington, 1981-83; instr. reproductive endocrinology Nursing Dept.; instr. Living With Diabetes, NIH, Bethesda, 1989-98, regulatory health proj. mgr., 7DA, 1998—; spkr. in field. Contbr. articles to Imprint mag., Am. Acad. Ambulatory Nursing Newsletter, Sterility and Fertility, also others. Vol. staff FISH, Fairfax, Va., 1984-90; unit fundraiser Am. Diabetes Assn., No. Va., 1994. Recipient Outstanding Cmty. Chmn. award NIH, 1988, Clin. Excellence award, 1989, Svc. Chief's award, 1994, Nurse of Yr. award, 1995, Ednl. Excellence award, 1995. Mem. Va. Nurses Assn., Endocrine Nurses Assn. (chm. edn. and rsch. com., Rsch. award 1995), George Mason Alumni Assn. Baptist. Avocations: gourmet cooking, swing dancing. Home: 1313 Ingleside Ave Mc Lean VA 22101-2829 Office: 7DA 9201 Corporate Blvd Rockville MD 20850

KINAKA, WILLIAM TATSUO, lawyer; b. Lahaina, Hawaii, Apr. 4, 1940; s. Toshio and Natsumi (Hirouji) K.; m. Jeanette Louisa Ramos, Nov. 23, 1968; children: Kimberly H., Kristine N.Y. BA in Polit. Sci., Whittier Coll., 1962; MA in Internat. Rels., Am. U., 1964, JD, 1973. Bar: D.C. 1975, U.S. Ct. Appeals (D.C. cir.) 1975, U.S. Dist. Ct. D.C. 1975, U.S. Tax Ct. 1975, U.S. Ct. Mil. Appeals 1975, Hawaii 1976, U.S. Dist. Ct. Hawaii 1976, U.S. Ct. Appeals (9th cir.) 1976. Career trainee CIA, Langley, Va., 1966; legis. asst. Sen. Hiram L. Fong, Washington, 1966-76; assoc. Ueoka & Luna, Wailuku, Hawaii, 1977-85; pvt. practice law Wailuku, Hawaii, 1985—; grand jury counsel 2d Cir. Ct., 1985-86; ct. arbitrator, 1989—; legal cons. Hale Mahaolu Elderly Housing, Kahului, 1976—. Active Dem. Party of Hawaii, Wailuku, 1988-89; pres. Nat. Eagle Scout Assn. of Boy Scouts Am., Wailuku, 1983-91; bd. dirs. Wailuku Main St. Assn., 1988-94, Maui Adult Day Care Ctr., Puunene, 1978—; Maui coun. Boy Scouts of Am., 1983—; pres., bd. dirs. Maui Youth Intervention Program, Inc., 1993—. Mem. Hawaii Bar Assn., Maui Bar Assn., Maui Japanese C. of C., Maui C. of C., Nat. Eagle Scout Assn. (pres. Wailuku 1983-91). United Ch. of Christ. Avocations: scouting, gardening, swimming, poetry writing. Home: 639 Pio Dr Wailuku HI 96793-2622 Office: 24 N Church St Ste 207 Wailuku HI 96793-1606

KINASEWITZ, GARY THEODORE, medical educator; b. N.Y.C., Aug. 17, 1946; m. Kathlee Anne O'Sullivan, Aug. 16, 1969; children: Amanda, Judith, Gregory. BS, Boston Coll., 1968, MEd, 1969; MD, Wayne State U., 1973. Diplomate Am. Bd. Internal Medicine. Rsch. assoc. U. Pa., Phila., 1978-79, asst. prof. medicine, 1979-80; asst. prof. medicine La. State U. Med. Ctr., Shreveport, 1980-83, assoc. prof. medicine and physiology, 1983-88; coord., cardiovascular rsch. N.W. La. Biomed. Rsch. Ctr., Shreveport, 1987-88; prof. medicine and physiology La. State U. Med. Ctr., Shreveport, 1988; prof. medicine and physiology Okla. U. Health Scis. Ctr., Oklahoma City, 1988—, chief pulmonary and crit. care medicine, 1988—; mem. cardiovascular biology Okla. Med. Rsch. Found., Oklahoma City, 1994—; mem. rsch. adv. com. N.W. La. Biomed. Rsch. Found., 1985-88; univ. rep. Am. Fedn. Clin. Rsch., 1984-87. Author: (book) Pulmonary Function Testing: Principles and Practice, 1984. Bd. dirs. Am. Heart Assn., La., 1983-87, Am. Lung Assn., Okla., 1991—. Recipient Albert Hyman award Am. Heart Assn., La., 1981. Fellow Am. Coll. Chest Physicians (pathophysiology adv. com. 1983-86), Am. Coll. Physicians; mem. Am. Thoracic Soc. (coun. of chpt. reps. 1992-95), So. Soc. for Clin. Investigation, Cen. Soc. Clin. Rsch., Am. Physiol. Soc., Alpha Omega Alpha. Office: Univ Okla Health Scis Ctr 920 Stanton L Young Blvd Rm 3sp Oklahoma City OK 73104-5020

KINBERG, JUDY, television producer, director; b. Freeport, N.Y., Sept. 15, 1948; d. Jack H. and Rose M. (Schwartz) K. BA, Hofstra U., 1970. Prodn. asst. various programs including Camera Three CBS TV, N.Y.C., 1970-75; assoc. producer PBS-WNET/Dance in America, N.Y.C., 1975-76, producer, 1977—. NBC co-producer: He Makes Me Feel Like Dancin', 1984 (Acad. award, Emmy award, Chgo. Internat. Film Festival Silver Hugo, CINE Golden Eagle award, Christopher awards); producer: PBS Dance in America: The Feld Ballet, 1979, The Green Table (with Joffrey Ballet), 1982, The Magic Flute (with N.Y.C. Ballet), 1983, San Francisco Ballet: A Song for Dead Warriors, 1984, A Choreographer's Notebook: Stravinsky Piano Ballets by Peter Martins, 1984, Balanchine, Parts I and II, 1984 (27th Ann. Internat. Film and TV awards of N.Y., gold medal Chgo. Internat. Film Festival Silver Plaque Monitor award, Emmy nomination), San Francisco Ballet in Cinderella, 1985 (Internat. Film and TV Festival of N.Y. gold medal, CINE Golden Eagle award, Parent's Choice award), Mark Morris, 1986 (CINE Golden Eagle award, Am. Film & Video Festival Red Ribbon award, Emmy nomination), Choreography by Jerome Robbins, 1986 (Chgo. Internat. Film Festival Silver Hugo, CINE Golden Eagle award), Dance Theatre of Harlem in A Streetcar Named Desire, 1986 (Chgo. Internat. Film Festival Silver Hugo), In Memory of...A Ballet by Jerome Robbins, 1987 (Chgo. Internat. Film Festival Silver Hugo, CINE Golden Eagle award), Agnes, the Indomitable de Mille, 1987 (Emmy award, Chgo. Internat. Film Festival Silver Hugo, CINE Golden Eagle award), Paul Taylor: Roses and Last Look, 1988, Balanchine and Cunningham: An Evening at Am. Ballet Theatre, 1988, La Sylphide (with the Pa./Milw. Ballet), 1989, A Night at The Joffrey, 1989, (Emmy nomination, Gold medal Internat. Film and TV Festival of N.Y., Best Video Creation IMZ Video Danse Awards), The Search for Nijinsky's Rite of Spring, 1989 (producer/dir., Best Documentary IMZ Video Danse Awards, Internat. Film & TV Festival N.Y. Bronze medal), Baryshnikov Dances Balanchine, 1989 (Emmy nomination, finalist Internat. Film and TV Festival of N.Y.), Paul Taylor's Speaking in Tongues (Gold medal Internat. Film and TV Festival N.Y. Gold Plaque award Chgo. Internat. Film Festival), 1991, The Hard Nut with Mark Morris Dance Group, 1992 (Gold medal Internat. Film and TV Festival of N.Y., Emmy nomination), Balanchine Celebration, 1993 (Emmy nomination), The Wrecker's Ball, Three Dances by Paul Taylor, 1996 (Rose d'or de Montreaux Festival finalist); producer, dir. Bob Fosse/Steam Heat, 1990 (Emmy award, Ohio State award, Chgo. Film Festival Silver Plaque, Festival Internat. du Film Sur L'Art), A Tudor Evening with Am. Ballet Theatre, 1990, Balanchine in Am. with the N.Y.C. Ballet, 1990, Ballerinas: Dances by Peter Martins, 1991, A Renaissance Revisited, 1996 (N.Y. Festivals finalist award), (documentary) Variety and Virtuosity/American Ballet Theatre Now, 1998; producer PBS Great Performances: Out of Our Fathers' House, 1978 ; co-producer PBS Dance in America: Pilobolus Dance Theatre, 1977, Trailblazers of Modern Dance, 1977 (1st pl. 9th Ann. Dance Film and Video Festival), San Francisco Ballet: Romeo and Juliet, 1978, Choreography by Balanchine, Part III, 1978 (Chgo. Internat. Film Festival Silver Plaque, Emmy nomination), Choreography by Balanchine, Part IV, 1979 (Emmy award), The Martha Graham Dance Company: Clytemnestra, 1979 (Chgo. Internat. Film Festival Golden Hugo), Two Duets with Choreography by Jerome Robbins and Peter Martins, 1980, Nureyev and the Joffrey Ballet: In Tribute to Nijinsky, 1981 (Peabody award 1981, Emmy nomination), The Tempest: Live with the San Francisco Ballet, 1981, L'Enfant et Les Sortileges, 1981, Paul Taylor: Three Modern Classics, 1982, Paul Taylor: Two Landmark Dances, 1982, Bournonville Dances (with mems. of N.Y.C. Ballet), 1982; co-producer PBS Theater in America: When Hell Freezes Over I'll Skate, 1979; prodr., dir. PBS Great Performances: The World of Jim Henson, 1994 (Parents Choice honor, 1995). Mem. Dirs.' Guild Am., Acad. TV Arts and Scis. Office: WNET/Dance In America 450 W 33rd St New York NY 10001*

KINCADE, DORIS HELSING, apparel marketing educator; b. Roanoke, Va., Nov. 15, 1951; d. Carl Edward and Katherine Elizabeth (May) Helsing; m. William James Kincade, June 10, 1972. BS, East Carolina U., 1973, MS in Home Econs., 1974; PhD, U. N.C., Greensboro, 1988. Lectr. Peace Coll., Raleigh, N.C., 1974-78, dept. coord., 1978-86; market analyst HKH Partners, Research Triangle Park, N.C., 1982—; asst. statistician Cone Mills Corp., Greensboro, N.C., 1987-88; lectr. U. N.C., Greensboro, 1988-89; asst. prof. Auburn U., Ala., 1989-92; asst. prof. Va. Poly. Inst. and State U., Blacksburg, Va., 1992-96, assoc. prof., 1996—; cons. Triangle L & C, Rsch. Triangle Pk., 1986-93, S.E. Region Ala. Apparel Mfrs., 1990-92; mem. New Century Coun., 1993-95; rsch. reviewer Internat. Textile and Apparel Assn., Am. Collegiate Retailing Assn., Flexible Automationa and Intelligent Mfg.; guest lectr. East Carolina U., 1983. Contbr. articles to profl. jours. Grantee Rayon/Acetate Coun. N.Y., 1989, Russell Corp., 1990, Vanity Fair Corp., 1992, J.C. Penney Retail Rsch., 1992, Vol. Inter-Industry Coun. Stds., 1993, Va. Tech. Found., 1995, Human Resources Collaboration, 1996, Reach Out, 1998; fellow Textile Clothing Tech. Corp., Nat. Apparel Rsch. Ctr. Mem. Am. Collegiate Retailing Assn., Assn. Family and Consumer Scis., Internat. Textile and Apparel Assn. (ITAA academic/industry com. chair, reviewer, bd. dirs. pub. Clothing and Textile Rsch. Jour.), Textile Apparel Linkage Coun., Phi Kappa Phi, Phi Upsilon Omicron, Kappa Omicron Nu. Avocations: apparel design & production, hiking, boating. Office: 109 Wallace Hall Va Poly Inst and State U Blacksburg VA 24061-0410

KINCAID, CYNTHIA JUNE, school psychologist; b. Libertyville, Ill., May 17, 1971; d. Herbert Jackson and Mary Patricia (Daidone) K. BA magna cum laude, Ea. Ill. U., 1993. Cert. sch. psychologist, Ill. Instr. family parenting program Coll. Lake County, Grayslake, Ill., 1995—; sch. psychologist Mundelein (Ill.) Elem. Sch. Dist. #75, 1996—. Mem. Nat. Assn. Sch. Psychologists, Ill. Sch. Psychologists Assn. Home: 520 Ames St Libertyville IL 60048-2610 Office: Mundelein Elem Sch Dist 75 330 N California Ave Mundelein IL 60060-2099

KINCAID, ELSIE ELIZABETH, educational therapist; b. Vernon, Tex., Nov. 29, 1929; d. Richard Oscar Paul and Bertha Rosanna (Quast) Schuetze; m. Richard Warren Kincaid, June 1, 1949; children: Carol Jean, Richard Warren, Sandra Elizabeth, Robert Rendall. AA, Del Mar Coll., 1949; BS magna cum laude, Tex. Agrl. and Industry U., 1976; MS, Corpus Christi (Tex.) State U., 1978; PhD, Columbia Pacific U., 1985. Dir., diagnostician, edn. therapist Corpus Christi Acad. Devel. Services, 1979-80; dir., diagnostician, ednl. therapist Corpus Christi Acad. Devel. Svcs., Corpus Christi, 1980-86; diagnostician, ednl. therapist Acad. Devel. Svcs., Corpus Christi, 1987; ednl. therapist Clinic for Learning Disabilities, Dallas, 1989; pvt. practice McKinney and Dallas, Tex., 1990-92, Plano, Tex., 1992-98, McKinney and Plano, Tex., 1998—; spl. edn. substitute tchr. Corpus Christi Ind. Sch. Dist., 1986-88. Author: Reasoning Process As Early Intervention for Reading Disability, 1985, The Preschool Diagnostic Development Screening Test, 1987. V.p. Symphony Guild Corpus Christi, 1973; bd. dirs. Ada Wilson Hosp. for Children, Corpus Christi, 1986-89, Samaritan Counseling Ctr. of Coastal Bend, 1987-89 (v.p. 1988), Holy Family Sch., McKinney, 1990-92, 99—; mem. adv. bd. "Any Baby Can" Project, Corpus Christi, 1988-89; mem. High Risk Infant Task Force, Art Mus. So. Tex. and Corpus Christi, 1988-89; vol. Collin County Community Food Pantry, 1990-91; mem. McKinney Rep. Womens Club, McKinney Symphony Orch. Guild, St. Peters Episcopal Ch. Women (v.p.), Diocesan Conviction (chmn. N. Dallas E.C.W.). Mem. Jennete Hammer Guild (pres. 1984-85), CPA Wives (pres. 1970), Mental Health Assn. Collin County, Estate Garden Club (pres. 1981), Daus. of King (v.p. 1986-88), EnAvant Club (reporter), Kappa Delta Pi, Beta Sigma Phi. Republican. Episcopalian. Avocations: tennis, bridge, golf. Home and Office: 2034 Hillcrest Ct Mc Kinney TX 75070-4010

KINCAID, JAMAICA, writer; b. St. John's, Antigua and Barbuda, May 25, 1949; came to U.S., 1966; d. Annie Richardson; m. Allen Shawn; 2 children. Student pub. schs., St. John's; hon. degree, Williams Coll., 1991, L.I. Coll., 1991, Amherst Coll., 1995, Bard Coll., 1997, Middlebury Coll., 1998. Author: At the Bottom of the River, 1983 (Morton Dauwen Zabel award Am. Acad. and Inst. of Arts and Letters 1984), Annie John, 1985, A Small Place, 1988, Lucy, 1990, Autobiography of My Mother, 1996, My Brother, 1997; editor: My Favorite Plant, 1998. *

KINCAID, JOHN, political science educator, editor; b. Phila., May 5, 1946; s. John and Louise M. (Berger) K.; children: Karen Louise, Sarah Jeanenne. B.A., Temple U., 1967, Ph.D., 1981; M.A., U. Wis., 1968. Instr., St. Peter's Coll., Jersey City, 1969-70; dir. Phoenix Peace Ctr., Ariz., 1970-72; v.p., treas. Pentagon Papers Fund for Civil Liberties, Los Angeles, 1972-73; instr. Temple U., Phila., 1975-79; asst. prof. North Tex. State U., Denton, 1979-84; assoc. prof. U. North Tex., Denton, 1984-86; dir. research U.S. Adv. Commn. on Intergovtl. Relations, Washington, 1986-87; exec. dir. U.S. Adv. Commn. on Intergovtl. Relations, Washington, 1987-94; Robert B. and Helen S. Meyner prof. govt. and pub. svce., Lafayette Coll., Easton, Pa., 1994—; dir. Meyner Ctr. for study of state and local govt., Lafayette Coll., 1994—; research fellow Ctr. for Study Federalism, Phila., 1982-85. Editor and contbr.: Political Culture, Public Policy and the American States, 1982; Covenant, Polity, and Constitutionalism, 1983; The Covenant Connection: Federal Theology and the Origins of Modern Politics, 1988, Competition among States and Local Governments, 1991. Editor: The Covenant Letter, 1979-92; Publius: The Journal of Federalism, 1981—; editor: State Government and Politics book series, 1983—. Contbr. articles to profl. jours. Recipient numerous grants NEH, Earhart Found., Ford Found., Fund for Improvement Postsecondary Edn., North Tex. State U., Nat. Inst. Edn., USIA. Mem. Southwestern Polit. Sci. Assn. (v.p., program chmn. 1984-86, pres. 1993-94), Am. Polit. Sci. Assn., Nat. Acad. Pub. Adminstrn., Acad. Polit. Sci. Episcopalian. Avocation: stamp collecting. Office: Meyner Ctr Lafayette Coll Easton PA 18042-1785

KINCAID, MARILYN COBURN, medical educator; b. Bennington, Vt., July 14, 1947; d. E. Robert and Jean A. (Flagg) Coburn; m. William Louis Kincaid, Dec. 21, 1970. AB, Mt. Holyoke Coll., 1969; MD, St. Louis U., 1975. Cert. Am. Bd. Ophthalmology, Am. Bd. Pathology. Asst. prof. ophthalmology & pathology U. Tex., San Antonio, 1982-86; assoc. prof. ophthalmology & pathology U. Mich. Med. Sch., Ann Arbor, 1986-87; assoc. prof. ophthalmology & pathology St. Louis U. Sch. Medicine, 1989-94, prof., 1994—; bd. dirs. Singular Vision Outreach, St. Louis. Author (book) Intraocular Lenses, 1989; contbr. articles to profl. jours. Fellow Am. Acad. Ophthalmology (Honor award 1990), Coll. Am. Pathologists; mem. Am. Assn. Ophthalmic Pathologists (sec.-treas. 1983-86). Avocations: sewing, embroidery. Office: St Louis U The Eye Inst 1755 S Grand Blvd Saint Louis MO 63104-1540

KINCAID, PAUL KENT, public relations professional; b. Topeka, Kans., Oct. 13, 1952; s. E. Leon and Darlene A. (Schrader) K.; m. Janet Lynn Wilenzick, Nov. 8, 1975; children: Jennifer Elizabeth, Brian Christopher. BS in Mass Communications, Phillips U. Asst. news bur. dir. Phillips U., Enid, Okla., 1975-76; news bur. dir. Emporia (Kans.) State U., 1976-77, dir. univ. rels., 1977-86; dir. univ. rels. S.W. Mo. State U., Springfield, 1986-94, assoc. v.p. for univ. advancement, dir. univ. rels., 1994—, also coord. govtl. rels., 1993—. Bd. dirs. Visually Impaired Presch., Springfield, 1989-93, pres. bd. dirs., 1990-92; active Springfield Area C. of C., 1986—. Mem. Pub. Rels. Soc. Am. (accredited), Soc. Profl. Journalists, Coun. for Advancement and Support Edn. (recipient several awards 1976—), Pub. Rels. of the Ozarks, Springfield Advt. Assn., Leadership Springfield Alumni Assn. Avocations: family, tennis, golf, management theory and practice. Home: 3154 W Tracy Ct Springfield MO 65807-3184 Office: SW Mo State U 901 S National Ave Springfield MO 65804-0088

KINCAID, SHERRIE LYNN, clinical research and surgical intensive care unit nurse; b. Dallas, Aug. 14, 1959; d. Daryl B. and Betty J. (Mayo) Cordell; 1 child, John Christopher Riley. BS, Tex. Woman's U., 1983, MA, 1990. RN, Tex.; CCRN. Staff nurse Meth. Med. Ctr., Dallas, 1982-86; clinician Home Health Svcs. of Dallas, 1987; regional dir. Redicare Health Svcs. Co., Dallas, 1988; clin. dir. Home Health Svcs. II, Inc., Dallas, 1988-90; staff nurse II St. Paul Med. Ctr., Dallas, 1991-95; sr. rsch. nurse U. Tex. Southwestern Med. Ctr., Dallas, 1993-98; ICU staff nurse Zale Lipshy U. Hosp., 1995—; assoc. clin. scientist DuPont Pharms., Wilmington, Del., 1998—. Nurse, ARC. Mem. AACN, Am. Bus. Women's Assn. (past pres.), Tex. Woman's U. Alumnae Assn., Assn. Clin. Rsch. Profls., Drug Info. Assn. Home: 431 Everest Cedar Hill TX 75104

KINCAID, STEVEN RANDALL, marketing professional; b. Oklahoma City, July 19, 1953; s. William Calvin Hoover and Mary Elizabeth (Cochran) K. *Father William Kincaid was a United States Marine and a district sales manager for Southwestern Bell Telephone. He was also an avid fisherman, musician and baseball enthusiast. Mother Mary Beth was active in church and music. Sister Marilyn is an attorney and Vice President and Regulatory Counsel for Compliance of a life insurance company. Marilyn travels extensively, enjoys music, sports and literature and actively promotes animal rights. Daughter Rachel is a gifted student and artist, reads voraciously, plays baseball and is a Girl Scout. Son David is also a gifted student, plays baseball and is an active Boy Scout.* BA, Okla. State U., 1975; MA, U. Ill., 1977, PhD, 1980. Rsch. analyst Gen. Foods Corp., White Plains, N.Y., 1980-82; rsch. assoc. Opinion Rsch. Corp., Princeton, N.J., 1982-85, rsch. dir., 1985-86, rsch. exec., 1986-87, account exec., 1989-91; cons. John Hancock Life Ins. Co., Boston, 1987-88, dir. rsch., 1988-89; dir. rsch. Prudential Ins. Co., Newark, 1991-93; sr. assoc. Abt Assocs., Cambridge, Mass., 1993-95; pres. Kincaid Assocs., Boxford, Mass., 1995-98; v.p. Fidelity Investments, Boston, 1998—. Named Eagle Scout Boy Scouts Am., 1968. Mem. Am. Assn. Pub. Opinion Research, Am. Polit. Sci. Assn., Applied Polit. Sci. Study Group. (charter), Mktg. Sci. Inst. (trustee), Phi Kappa Phi. Democrat. Methodist. Office: Fidelity Investments 100 Summer St Boston MA 02110-2116

KINCAID, TINA, entertainer, producer; b. Lenoir, N.C., Dec. 24, 1959; d. Joseph George and Betty Gail (Prestwood) K.; m. Stephen Kim Cretella, June 11, 1988 (div. May 1994); m. Timothy Alexander Williams, Aug. 15, 1998. Student, Am. Theater Arts, 1979-81. Entertainer, 1979—; TV producer, actor Video Record Albums of Am., Pasadena, Calif., 1980-83; v.p. sales, mktg. prodns. Amity Sales Inc., Hudson, N.C., 1980—; co-founder, producer, singer T'NT Entertainments, Inc., Pasadena, 1981-83; founder, pres. ProductVision, Inc., L.A., 1984-86; co-founder, v.p. prodns. Kincaid Enterprises, Morganton, N.C., 1988-89; founder, owner VAT Pub., Hudson, 1989—; cons. Mary Kay Cosmetics, Hudson, 1989—; co-founder, v.p., performer Rappin' Grandmas, Inc!, Hickory, N.C., 1991—; founder, owner Gingerbread Treasures, Hudson, 1992—; owner Charmingly Yours, Hudson, 1995—; entertainer, singer The Troy Cory China Goodwill Concert Tour, 1991; co-founder www.starbeanies.com., Hudson, 1998—. Actor, author TV spl. Catching Christmas, 1981; singer, author album Isn't A Shame, 1990, The Real Country, 1990; co-songwriter album/CD: Dancing Across the Finish Line, 1995; author, editor: The Wedding Book, 1990, Recipes for Love, 1991. Mem. SAG. Republican. Mem. Christian Ch. Avocations: dancing, writing, photography, art, travel. Home: 4491 Magnolia Ln Hudson NC 28638-8708

KINCAIDE, DONALD LEWIS, political science educator; b. Mar. 18, 1956. BA, Mississippi Valley State U., 1974; MA, Kans. State U., 1979. Prof. polit. sci. Mississippi Valley State U., Itta Bena, Miss., 1979—. Home: 831 Bryant St Grenada MS 38901

KINCHEN, THOMAS ALEXANDER, college president; b. Thomasville, Ga., Dec. 28, 1946; s. George H. and Annie L. (Castleberry) K.; m. Ruth Ann Hunter, Aug. 27, 1967; children: Alex, Lisa Ann. AB summa cum laude, Ga. So. Coll., 1969; MEd, U. Ga., 1975; MDiv, New Orleans Bapt. Theol. Sem., 1979, EdD, 1982. Pastor several chs., 1972-76; v.p. New Orleans Bapt. Theol. Sem., 1982-86; exec. dir., treas. W.Va. Conv. So. Bapt., Scott Depot, 1986-90; pres. Fla. Bapt. Theol. Coll., Graceville, 1990—. Editor Laos: All the People of God, 1984; contbr. articles to profl. jours. Bd. dirs. Area Devel. Coun., Graceville, 1991; mem. edn. commn. So. Bapt. Conv., 1992—; pres. bd. dirs. Jackson County Devel. Coun., 1996. Mem. So. Bapt. Adult Edn. Assn. (pres. 1996-98, v.p. 1994-96), Graceville C. of C. (pres. 1993), Kiwanis, Phi Kappa Phi, Alpha Psi Omega. Avocations: golfing, fishing, woodworking. Office: Fla Bapt Theol Coll 5400 College Dr Graceville FL 32440-3306

KIND, GABRIEL MATTHEW, plastic surgeon; b. Evanston, Ill., Apr. 11, 1961; s. Joshua Benjamin and Phyllis Barbara K.; m. Elizabeth Ann, May 25, 1986; children: Joseph Andrew, Emily Ann. BA, Dartmouth Coll., 1982; MD, Northwe. U., 1986. Diplomate Am. Bd. Surgery, Am. Bd. Plastic Surgery; cert. added qualification surgery of hand. Intern then resident Rush-Presbyn.-St. Luke's Med. Ctr., Chgo., 1986-91; resident in plastic surgery Northwestern U. Med. Ctr., Chgo., 1991-94; fellow in hand and microsurgery Buncke Clinic, San Francisco, 1994-95, asst. dir., 1995—. Contbr. articles to profl. jours. Fellow ACS; mem. AMA, Am. Soc. Plastic and Reconstructive Surgery, Am. Soc. Reconstructive Microsurgery. E-mail: gkind@yahoo.com. Office: 45 Castro St San Francisco CA 94114

KIND, JOSHUA B., history educator; b. Phila., Nov. 5, 1933; s. Abraham and Sarah (Singer) K. BA, U. Pa., 1955; PhD, Columbia U., 1967. Instr. art history Northwestern U., Evanston, Ill., 1959-62; instr. humanities U. Chgo., 1962-65, Ill. Inst. of Technology, Chgo., 1965-69; prof. art history No. Ill. U., DeKalb, 1969—; adj. prof. art history Sch. of The Art Inst. of Chgo., 1964-76. Office: No Ill Univ 216 Anderson Hall Dekalb IL 60115-2294

KIND, KENNETH WAYNE, lawyer, real estate broker; b. Missoula, Mont., Apr. 1, 1948; s. Joseph Bruce and Elinor Joy (Smith) K.; m. Diane Lucille Jozaitis, Aug. 28, 1971; children: Kirstin Amber, Kenneth Warner. BA, Calif. State U.-Northridge, 1973; JD, Calif. Western U., 1976. Bar: Calif. 1976, U.S. Dist. Ct. (ea., so., no. dists.) Calif., 1976, U.S. Cir. Ct. Appeals (9th cir.); lic. NASCAR driver, 1987. Mem. celebrity security staff Brownstone Am., Beverly Hills, Calif., 1970-76; tchr. Army and Navy Acad., Carlsbad, Calif., 1975-76; real estate broker, Bakersfield, Calif., 1978—; sole practice, Bakersfield, 1976—; lectr. mechanic's lien laws, Calif., 1983—. Staff writer Calif. Western Law Jour., 1975. Sgt. U.S. Army, 1967-70. Mem. ABA, VFW, Nat. Order Barristers, Rancheros Visitadores. Libertarian. Office: 4042 Patton Way Bakersfield CA 93308

KIND, PHYLLIS, art gallery owner. BS in Chemistry, U. Pa., 1954, PhD in Phys. Chemistry, 1956; MA in English, U. Chgo., 1965. Mem. staff mdse. control Macy's, New York, N.Y., 1948-53; social worker N.Y.C. Dept. Welfare, 1954; 3d grade tchr. N.Y.C. Bd. Edn., 1956-59; various positions Chgo. Bd. Edn., 1960-67; owner Phyllis Kind Gallery, Chgo., 1967, N.Y.C., 1975—. Office: Phyllis Kind Gallery 136 Greene St New York NY 10012-3202*

KIND, RON, congressman; b. La Crosse, Wis.; s. Elroy and Greta Kind; m. Tawni Kind; 1 child, Johnny. Degree with honors, Harvard U., 1985; M, London Sch. Econs.; JD, U. Minn. Formerly with Quarles and Brady, Milw.; past prosecutor La Crosse County, numerous counties, Wis.; mem. 105th-106th Congress from 3d Wis. dist., 1996—, mem. house edn. and workforce com., resources com., mem. freshman bipartisan campaign fin. reform task force; active Freshman Bipartisan Campaign Fin. Reform Task Force; co-founder Upper Miss. River Congl. Caucus. Active Boys' and Girls' Club, La Crosse YMCA; bd. dirs. Coulee Coun. Alcohol or Other Drug Abuse. Mem. New Dem. Network, La Crosse Optimists Club. Lutheran. Office: 1713 Longworth Bldg Washington DC 20515-4903*

KINDBERG, SHIRLEY JANE, pediatrician; b. Newark, Feb. 4, 1936; d. John Bertil and Mabel Jacoba (deJonge) K.; m. Charles Dale Coln, May 12, 1962; children: Sara, Eric, Lois, Ruth, Mary. BS, Wheaton Coll., 1957; MD, Baylor U., 1961. Intern Tex. Children's Hosp., Houston, 1961-62; resident Children's Med. Ctr., Dallas, 1962-63; fellow in pediat. pulmonary disease U. Tex. S.W. Med. Sch., Dallas, 1963-64, fellow in pediat. infectious disease, 1965-67; pvt. practice gen. pediat. Dallas, 1969-81, pvt. practice newborns, 1981—. Active Northwest Bible Ch., 1972—. Fellow Am. Acad. Pediat.; mem. Tex. Pediat. Soc., Dallas Symphony Assn., The Dallas Opera. Republican. Avocations: cooking, travel, music. Office: 3600 Gaston Ave Ste 406 Dallas TX 75246-1804

KINDEL, JAMES HORACE, JR., lawyer; b. L.A., Nov. 8, 1913; s. James Horace and Philipina (Butte) K.; children: William, Mary, Robert, John. AB, UCLA, 1934; LLB, Loyola U., Los Angeles, 1940. Bar: Calif. 1941; CPA, Calif. Pvt. practice law Kindel & Anderson, L.A., Calif., 1945-96; of counsel McKenna & Cuneo, L.A., 1997—; ret. ptnr. Coopers-Lybrand; officer, dir., co-owner R.J. Noble Co., Orange, Calif., 1950—; co-owner sand and gravel and poultry bus., Guatemala; co-owner Sunnymead Poultry Ranch, Calif. Trustee UCLA Found. Mem. ABA, L.A. Bar Assn., Orange County Bar Assn., State Bar Calif., AICPA, Chancery Club, Calif. Club, Phi Delta Phi, Theta Xi. Home: 800 W 1st St Apt 2405 Los Angeles CA 90012-2432 Office: 444 S Flower St Fl 7 Los Angeles CA 90071-2901

KINDERWATER, DIANE, state official. BA in Broadcast Journalism, U. Wis. Promotions and mktg. dir., prodr., nat. sales mgr.; media advisor, press sec. N.Mex. Legislature; press sec. Office Gov. Gary Johnson, Santa Fe, 1994—. Fax: 505-986-4364. Office: Office Gov State Capitol Bldg Rm 300 Santa Fe NM 87503

KINDERWATER, JOSEPH C. (JACK KINDERWATER), publishing company executive; b. Milw., Aug. 5, 1922; s. Joseph Charles and Ida (Noll) K.; m. Jacqueline Shirley Marsh, 1948; children—Mark, Mary Jo, Nancy, Scott, Diane. B.A., U. Minn., 1948. Advt. copywriter C. Derosier Inc., St. Paul, 1948-50; account exec. David Advt. Agy., St. Paul, 1950-53; advt. rep.

The Webb Pub. Co., St. Paul, 1953-63, advt. sales mgr., 1963-68, advt. dir., 1968-78, v.p., pub., 1979-87, exec. v.p., 1987-88, chmn., pres., 1988-89; pub. cons., 1990—; v.p. Midwest Unit Farm Publs., 1979-84, pres., 1985-88. Bd. dirs. Nat. Audit Bur. Circulation, 1985-89, Better Bus. Bur. Minn., St. Paul, 1985-89; fund vol. Am. Heart Assn., St. Paul, 1983-85, Children's Hosp., St. Paul, 1975; instr. Jr. Achievement, St. Paul, 1970-75; bus. exec. rsch. com. U. Minn., 1966. With USAAF, 1943-46; ETO. Mem. Northwest Farm Equipment Assn. (pres. 1984-87), Nat. Agr. Mktg. Assn. (v.p. 1976-77), State Farm Mag. Pubs. Assn. (dir. 1980-89), Agr. Pub. Assn. (bd. dirs. 1981-89), St. Paul Advt. Club (pres. 1974-76), Am. Advt. Fedn. (Cleo award 1965, dist. gov. 1965-69). Roman Catholic. Clubs: Minn. Press, Midland Hills Country, St. Paul Athletic, Minn. Advt. Home: 2680 Oxford St N Saint Paul MN 55113-2089 Office: 708 N 1st St Ste 343 Minneapolis MN 55401-1133

KINDIG, DAVID A., medical educator; b. May 19, 1940; m. 1962; 3 children. BA, Carleton Coll., 1962; MD, U. Chgo., 1968, PhD, 1968. Intern Dept. Pediatrics U. Chgo., 1968-69; from resident to chief resident Dept. Ped. & Social Medicine Montefiore Hosp. & Med. Ctr., N.Y.C., 1969-71; dir., Divsn. Prof. Svcs. Nat. Health Svcs. Corp., HEW, 1971-73; co-dir. Inst. Health Team Devel. Montefiore Hosp. & Med. Ctr., 1973-74; dept. dir. Bur. Health Manpower HEW, 1974-76; dir. Montefiore Hosp. & Med. Ctr., 1976-80; vice chancellor health science U. Wis., Madison, 1980-85; dir. programs health mgmt. Sch. Medicine, 1985-94; prof. prev. medicine U. Wis., Madison, 1980—; dir. Wis. Network Health Policy Res., 1994—; program coord. Montefiore Hosp. & Med. Ctr., 1969-70; instr. Dept. Cmty. Health Albert Einstein Coll. Medicine, 1970-71, assoc. prof., 1978-80; acting med. dir. Martin Luther King Jr. Neighborhood Health Ctr., 1970-71; mem. bd. dirs. Rural Prod. Project, Robert Wood Johnson Found., 1975-79; sr. prog. cons., 1979-82; mem. bd.d irs. Am. Med. Student Assn. Found., 1984-86; chair Wis. Govt. Task Force AIDS, 1985-86; vis. prof. health mgmt. Shanghi Second Med. U., 1987—, Beijing Med. U., Sch. Pub. Health, 1988—. Mem. Inst. Med. Nat. Acad. Sci., Assn. Health Svc. Rsch. (treas. 1993-96, pres. elect 1996), Am. Coll. Physician Execs., Soc. Med. Adminstrn. Home: 720 E Gorham Apt 406 Madison WI 53703 Office: 500 Preventive Medicine 610 Walnut St Rm 758 Madison WI 53705*

KINDIG, FRED EUGENE, statistics educator, arbitrator; b. York, Pa., Sept. 5, 1920; s. Fred E. and Hattie (Keller) K.; m. Marie M. Doyle (dec. 1971); children: Pamela M., Bonita K., Gretchen A., Suzanne J.; m. Grace L. Mathison, Aug. 19, 1972 (dec. 1979); m. Susan S. Friend, Mar. 16, 1980. B.S., Pa. State U., 1942; M.S., U. Pitts., 1947, Ph.D., 1951. Indsl. engr., supr. Westinghouse Electric Corp., Pitts., 1942-51; asst. to exec. v. p. Phoenix Glass, Monaca, Pa., 1951-53; asst. and assoc. prof. U. Pitts., 1953-62; prof., coordinator quantitative methods Ohio State U., Columbus, 1962-81; prof. emeritus Ohio State U., 1981—; labor mgmt. arbitrator, 1953—. Author: Fundamentals of Statistical Controls and Fundamentals of Linear Programming, 1956; Contbr. articles to profl. jours. Pres. PTA, various times; mem. Franklin County 648 Bd., 1979-82; trustee, chmn. bd. trustees Columbus State Community Coll., 1982-92; trustee emeritus, 1992—. Mem. Am. Inst. Decision Scis. (v.p. 1969-71), Am. Arbitration Assn., Nat. Acad. Arbitrators, Am. Soc. Quality Control, Inst. Math. Stats., Am. Statis. Assn., Indsl. Relations Research Assn., Ops. Research Soc. Am., Soc. Profls. In Dispute Resolution, Alpha Sigma Phi, Tau Beta Pi, Beta Gamma Sigma. Clubs: Brookside Country, Univ. Home: 213 St Antoine St Columbus OH 43085-2242 Office: 207 St Jacques St Columbus OH 43085-2227 *Although fate plays an important role, perseverance, absolute honesty, basic integrity, and the highest of moral standards make for an unbeatable combination.*

KINDLEBERGER, CHARLES P., II, economist, educator; b. N.Y.C., Oct. 12, 1910; s. E. Crosby and Elizabeth Randall (McIlvaine) K.; m. Sarah Bache Miles, May 1, 1937; children: Charles P., Richard S., Sarah, E. Randall. AB, U. Pa., 1932, DS (hon.), 1984; AM, Columbia U., 1934, PhD, 1937; Dr. h.c., U. Paris, 1966, U. Ghent, 1975, U. Pa., 1984; Dr. rer.pol. h.c., U. Basle, 1997. Research in internat. trade and fin. Fed. Res. Bank N.Y., 1936-39, Bank Internat. Settlements, 1939-40, Bd. Govs. FRS, 1940-42; Am. sec. Joint Econ. Com. U.S. and Can., 1941-42; served with OSS, Washington, 1942-44, 45; chief div. German and Austrian Econ. Affairs, Dept. State, Washington, 1945-48; assoc. prof. econs. MIT, 1948-51, prof., 1951-76, prof. emeritus, 1976—, chmn. faculty, 1965-67; vis. prof. econs. Brandeis U., 1983-87; cons. fellow Brit. Acad. Author: International Short-Term Capital Movements, 1937, The Dollar Shortage, 1950, International Economics, 1953, rev. edits., 1973, 78, The Terms of Trade, 1956, Economics Development, 1958, rev. edits., 1965, 77, Foreign Trade and the National Economy, 1962, Economic Growth of France and Britain, 1851-1950, 1964, Europe and the Dollar, 1966, Postwar European Growth, 1967, American Business Abroad, 1969, Power and Money, 1970; editor: The International Corporation, 1970, The World in Depression, 1929-39, 1973, rev. edit., 1986, Economic Response, 1978, Manias, Panics and Crashes, 1978, 3d edit., 1996, International Money, 1981, A Financial History of Western Europe, 1984, rev. edit., 1993, Multinational Excursions, 1984, Keynesianism vs Monetarism, 1985, Marshall Plan Days, 1987, International Capital Movements, 1987, International Economic Order, 1988, The German Economy, 1945-47: Charles P. Kindleberger's Letters from the Field, 1989, Economic Laws and Economy History, 1989, Historical Economics, Art or Science?, 1990, The Life of an Economist: An Autobiography, 1991, Mariners and Markets, 1992, The World Economy and National Finance in Historical Perspective, 1995, World Economic Primacy, 1500-1990, 1996, Centralization vs. Pluralism, 1996, Essays in History, Financial, Economic, Personal, 1999. Intelligence officer 12th Army Group, 1944-45; disch. rank of maj., Gen. Staff Corps. Decorated Legion of Merit, Bronze Star; recipient Harms prize Institut für Weltwirtschaft, Kiel, 1978. Fellow Am. Econ. Assn. (disting., v.p. 1966, pres. 1985), Brit. Acad. (corr.); mem. Am. Acad. Arts and Scis., Am. Philos. Soc., Phi Beta Kappa, Delta Psi. Episcopalian. Home: Brookhaven at Lexington A-406 1010 Waltham St Lexington MA 02421-8044

KINDLUND, NEWTON CARLTON, retail executive; b. Detroit, Mich., June 25, 1940; s. Newton K. and Virginia M. (Rolf) K.; m. Nancy J. Peck, Jan. 28, 1962; children: Anne Kirsten, Erika Page; m. Joanne Weber Kindlund, May 29, 1974; 1 child, Darien F. BA, Mich. State U., 1963; postgrad., Boston Coll., 1969; student, U. Pa., 1977. Nat. sales mgr. Vesely Co., Inc., Lapeer, Mich., 1963-68; v.p. sales and mktg. Midas Internat. Corp., Chgo., 1968-70; pres. Recreation Enterprise Corp., Gainesville, Fla., 1970-73, N.C. Kindlund & Assoc., Glenville, N.C., 1974-75; regional v.p. Recreational Vehicle Industry Assn., Washington, 1976-77; founder, pres. Holiday of Orlando (Fla.), Inc., 1977-85, Holiday RV Rental/Leasing, Orlando, 1985-90; bd. chmn., founder, pres. Holiday RV Superstores, Inc., Orlando, 1987—; pres. Holiday RV Superstores of N.Mex., Inc., Holiday RV Assurance Svcs., Inc. of Ariz., Holiday RV Superstores of S.C., Inc., Holiday RV Superstores West, Inc., Holiday RV Superstores of Mich., Inc.; bd. dirs. Recreational Vehicle Industry Assn., Chgo., 1970-72, Cen. Fla. World Trade Coun., Orlando, 1985-87; adv. bd. Trailer Life Publs., 1985-90. Contbr. articles to profl. jours. Founding bd. mem. Fla. Recreational Vehicle Trade Assn., Tampa, 1978; bd. dirs. Ctrl. Fla. Better Bus.Bur., Winter Park, 1994-95; adv. bd. Crummer Sch. of Bus., Rollins Coll., Winter Park, Fla., 1998; judge Students in Free Enterprise, Clearwater, Fla., 1998. Recipient Small Bus. Person of Yr. award Small Bus. Adminstrn., State of Fla., 1982, Entrepreneur of Yr. award Ernst & Young, Inc., Tampa, 1990, 100 award Miami Herald, 1992, 93, semi-finalist Jim Moran Entreprenurial Excellance award Fla. State U., 1996; named one of 500 fastest growing pvt. cos. Inc. Mag., 1983, one of top 150 Fla. pub. corps. Fla. Travel mag., 1993, one of Fla. top 100 cos. Orlando Metro 100, 1993, Industry Exec. of Yr., RV News Mag., 1995. Mem. Fla. RV Trade Assn. (founding mem., bd. dirs. 1987-90), Family Motor Coach Assn. (adv. bd. 1990—), Nat. RV Bus. Assn. (adv. bd. 1989-90), Recreational Vehicle Rental Assn. (nat. chmn. 1992, 93), Recreational Vehicle Dealers Assn. (exec. bd. 1992, 93), Orlando C. of C. (bd. dirs., exec. com. 1984-88, Silver 100 award 1992). Republican. Episcopalian. Avocations: skiing, golf, sailing. Home: 280 Stirling Ave Winter Park FL 32789-5747 Office: Holiday RV Superstores Inc 7851 Greenbriar Pky Orlando FL 32819-8926

KINDNESS, THOMAS NORMAN, former congressman, lawyer, consultant; b. Knoxville, Tenn., Aug. 26, 1929; s. Norman Garden and Christine (Gunn) K.; m. Averil J. Stoneback, Jan. 7, 1984; children by previous marriage: Sharon L., David T., Glen J., Adam B. AB, U. Md., 1951; LLB, George Washington U., 1953. Bar: D.C. 1954. Practiced in Washington, 1954-57; asst. counsel legal dept. Champion Internat. Corp., Hamilton, Ohio, 1957-73; mayor Hamilton, 1964-67; mem. city council, 1968-69; mem. Ohio Ho. of Reps. from 58th Dist., 1971-74; previous mem. 94th-99th Congresses from 8th Ohio Dist.; now pvt. practice law, govtl. affairs cons. Washington.

KINDRICK, ROBERT LEROY, academic administrator, dean, English educator; b. Kansas City, Mo., Aug. 17, 1942; s. Robert William and Waneta LeVeta (Lobdell) K.; B.A., Park Coll., 1964; M.A., U. Mo., Kansas City, 1967; Ph.D., U. Tex., 1971; m. Carolyn Jean Reed, Aug. 20, 1965. Instr., Central Mo. State U., Warrenburg, 1967-69, asst. prof., 1969-73, assoc. prof., 1973-78, prof. English, 1978-80, head dept. English, 1975-80; dean Coll. Arts and Scis., also prof. English, Western Ill. U., Macomb, 1980-84; v.p. acad. affairs, prof. English, Emporia State U., Kans., 1984-87; provost, v.p. acad. affairs, prof. English, Eastern Ill. U., Charleston, 1987-91; provost, v.p. acad. affairs, dean grad. studies, dean grad. sch., prof. English U. Mont., 1991—. Chmn. bd. dirs. Mo. Com. for Humanities, 1979-80, Ill. Humanities Coun., 1991. Pres. Park Coll. Young Dems., 1963; v.p. Mo. Young Dems., Jefferson City, 1964; campus coordinator United Way, Macomb, Ill., 1983; mem. study com. Emporia Arts Council, 1985-86; mem. NFL Edn. Adv. Bd., 1995—. U. Tex. fellow, 1965-66; Am. Council Learned Socs. travel grantee, 1975; Nat. Endowment for Humanities summer fellow, 1977; Medieval Acad. Am. grantee, 1976; Mo. Com. Humanities grantee, 1975-84; Assn. Scottish Lit. Studies grantee, 1979. Mem. Mo. Assn. Depts. English (pres. 1978-80), Mo. Philological Assn. (founding pres. 1975-77), Medieval Assn. Midwest (councillor 1977—, ex officio bd. 1980—, v.p. 1987-88, exec. sec. 1988—), Ill. Medieval Assn. (founding exec. sec. 1983-93), Mid-Am. Medieval Assn., Rocky Mountain MLA, Assn. Scottish Lt. Studies, Early English Text Soc., Société Rencesvals, Medieval Acad. N.Am. (exec. sec. com. on ctrs. and regional assns.), Internat. Arthurian Soc., Sigma Tau Delta, Phi Kappa Phi. Club: Rotary (editor Warrensburg club). Author: Robert Henryson, 1979; A New Classical Rhetoric, 1980, Henryson and the Medieval Arts of Rhetoric, 1993, William Matthews on Caxton and Malory, 1997, The Poems of Robert Henryson, 1997; editor: Teaching the Middle Ages, 1981—; editor Studies in Medieval and Renaissance Teaching, 1975-80; contbr. articles to profl. jours. Home: 342 Eddy Ave Missoula MT 59801-4334 Office: U Mont Main Hall Missoula MT 59812

KINDSCHI, GEORGE WILLIAM, pathologist; b. Rochester, Minn., May 2, 1940; s. Leslie and Signe (Smedal) K.; m. Claire Elizabeth McCann, June 8, 1968; four children. BA, U. Wis., 1962, MD, 1968, MS, 1981. Diplomate Am. Bd. Pathology, Am. Bd. Dermatology, Am. Bd. Med. Mgmt. Med. intern USN, Great Lakes, Ill., 1968-69; resident in pathology USN, Bethesda, Md., 1969-73; dir. labs. USN, Great Lakes, 1973-76, The Monroe (Wis.) Clinic, 1976—. Capt. MC USNR, ret. Fellow Am. Assn. Dermatopathology, Coll. Am. Pathologists; mem. Am. Med. Soc., Wis. State Med. Soc., Kiwanis Internat. Avocations: reading, writing, old radio, classical music, coin collecting. Home: N2702 Greenbush Rd Monroe WI 53566-9431

KINDT, JOHN WARREN, SR., lawyer, educator, consultant; b. Oak Park, Ill., May 24, 1950; s. Warren Frederick and Lois Jeannette (Woelffer) K.; m. Anne Marie Johnson, Apr. 17, 1982; children: John Warren Jr., James Roy Frederick. AB, Coll. William and Mary, 1972; JD, U. Ga., 1976, MBA, 1977; LLM, U. Va., 1978, SJD, 1981. Bar: D.C. 1976, Ga. 1976, Va. 1977. Advisor to Gov. of Va., 1971-72; congl. asst. to Congressman M. Caldwell Butler, 1972-73; cons. White House staff, 1976-77; asst. prof. U. Ill., 1978-81, assoc. prof., 1981-85, prof., 1985—; cons. 3d UN Conf. on Law of the Sea; lectr. U. Ill. Exec. MBA Program. Author: Marine Pollution and the Law of the Sea, 4 vols., 1986, 2 vols., 1988, 92, Economic Impacts of Legalized Gambling, 1994; contbr. articles to profl. jours. Caucus chmn., del. White House Conf. on Youth, 1970; co-chmn. Va. Gov.'s Adv. Council on Youth, 1971; mem. Athens (Ga.) Legal Aid Soc., 1975-76. Rotary fellow, 1979-80; Smithsonian ABA/ELI scholar, 1981; sr. fellow London Sch. of Econs., 1985-86. Mem. Am. Soc. Internat. Law, D.C. Bar Assn., Va. Bar Assn., Ga. Bar Assn. Home: 801 Brookside Ln Mahomet IL 61853-9545 Office: U Ill 350 Commerce W Champaign IL 61820

KINDT, THOMAS JAMES, chemist; b. Cin., May 18, 1939; s. James Michael and Barbara Katherine (Mayer) K.; m. Marie Louise Robinson, Sept. 5, 1964; children: Rachel Mary, James Thomas. BA cum laude, Thomas More Coll., Covington, Ky., 1963; PhD, U. Ill., 1967. Asst. rsch. scientist City of Hope Med. Ctr., Duarte, Calif., 1967-70; asst. prof. Rockefeller U., N.Y.C., 1970-73; assoc. prof. Rockefeller U., 1973-77, acting head lab. immunology/immunochemistry, 1975-78; vis. scientist Institut Pasteur, Paris, 1982-83; chief lab. immunogenetics NIH, Bethesda, Md., 1977—; dir. divsn. intramural rsch. Nat. Inst. Allergy and Infectious Diseases, NIH, Bethesda, Md., 1995—; adj. prof. Cornell U. Med. Coll., N.Y.C., 1973-78, Georgetown U., Washington, 1982—; sci. adv. Oncor Inc., Gaithersburg, Md., 1984—; mem. sci. adv. bd. Innovir Inc. N.Y.C., 1990—. Dep. editor Jour. Immunology, 1987-92; assoc. editor FASEB Jour., 1992—; N.Am. editor Rsch. in Immunology, 1990—; co-author: Antibody Enigma, 1984; contbr. articles to profl. jours.; patentee in field. Adv. com. Multiple Sclerosis Found., N.Y.C., 1984-92. With USN, 1957-59. Recipient Awd. for Exceptional Achievement, Asst. Sec. for Health, 1985. Mem. Am. Heart Assn., Am. Soc. Biol. Chemists, Am. Assn. Immunology, Am. Soc. Microbiology, Harvey Soc. Democrat. Roman Catholic. Home: 8313 Still Spring Ct Bethesda MD 20817-2727 Office: NIH NIAID Bldg 10 Rm 4A31 MSC 1356 10 Center Dr Bethesda MD 20892-1356*

KINDZRED, DIANA, communications company executive; b. Chgo., Apr. 13, 1946; d. Bernell and Katherine L. (Gee) K. Student, Northwestern U., 1970-73; cert. in bio-med. scis., U. Chgo. Med. Ctr., 1998. Owner, pres. Kindzred & Co. Comm., Chgo., 1978—; bd. dirs. WomanMade Gallery. Contbr. articles to profl. jours.; author numerous poems. Co-founder midwest div. Am. Sephardi Fedn., Evanston, Ill., 1990; coord. Amnesty Internat., Evanston, 1991. With U.S. Army, 1964-67. Recipient Award for Poetry Nat. Libr. of Poetry, 1996, Cmty. Svc. award Fred Hampton Scholarship Fund, 1990, Fundraising award Jewish United Fund, 1994. Democrat. Jewish. Avocations: international travel, writing, lecturing. Home and Office: 1530 N Sedgwick St #306 Chicago IL 60610 Office: Kindzred & Co Comm 1440 S Indiana Ave Apt 1004 Chicago IL 60605-2841

KINEE-KROHN, PATRICIA, special education educator; b. Phila.; d. William J. and Lillian L. (Long) K.; m. Eugene J. Krohn, July 21, 1995. BS, Westchester State Coll., 1982; AB, Immaculata Coll., 1988; MEd, St. Joseph's U., 1992. Cert. spl. edn. tchr., elem. edn. tchr., reading specialist. Spl. edn. tchr. Holly Hills Elem., Mt. Holly, N.J., 1982-84; elem. edn. tchr. St. James Elem. Sch., Falls Church, Va., 1987-88, Most Blessed Sacrament, Phila., 1988-90; spl. edn. tchr. Kingsway Learning Ctr., Haddonfield, N.J., 1991-97; spl. day class instr. learning handicapped Vannoy Elem. Sch., Castro Valley, Calif., 1997-98; program specialist Kingsway Learning Ctr., Haddonfield, N.J., 1998—; instr. Immaculata (Pa.) Coll., 1994-97, 98—, Chestnut Hill Coll., 1996-97; in-svc. devel. Gesu Sch., Phila., 1994-97, reading cons., 1992-97; tutor Progressive Edn. Svcs., Sewel, N.J., 1993-95. Vol. Trinity Hospice, Runnemede, N.J., 1993-97; CCD instr. Annunciation Cath. Ch., Bellmawr, N.J., 1994-95. Mem. Internat. Reading Assn., So. Jersey Reading Assn., Alpha Zeta (v.p. 1993-95). Avocations: cross stitching, bowling, reading. Home: PO Box 1183 Haddonfield NJ 08033-0716 Office: Kingsway Learning Ctr 144 Kings Hwy W Haddonfield NJ 08033-2190

KINER, RALPH MCPHERRAN, sports commentator, former baseball player; b. Santa Rita, N.Mex., Oct. 27, 1922; m. DiAnn Shugart, Dec. 1982; children: Michael, Scott, Kathryn; adopted children: Tracee, Kim; 1 stepdaughter, Candice Beck. Attended, Pasadena City Coll. Baseball player Pitts. Pirates, 1946-53, Chgo. Cubs, 1953-54, Cleve. Indians, 1955; gen. mgr. San Diego Padres (Pacific Coast League); announcer Chgo. White Sox, N.Y. Mets., WWOR-TV, 1962—. Pilot USN. Recipient By Saam award, 1985; elected to Baseball Hall of Fame, 1975, Pa. Hall of Fame, N.Y. Mets Hall of Fame. Office: care NY Mets William A Shea Stadium 12310 Roosevelt Ave Flushing NY 11368-1600

KING, ALGIN BRADDY, marketing educator; b. Latta, S.C., Jan. 19, 1927; s. Dewey Algin and Elizabeth (Braddy) K.; m. Barbara I. Kelley, Nov. 29, 1997: children: Drucilla Ratcliff, Martha Louise. BA in Retailing and Polit Sci. cum laude, U. S.C., 1947; MS, NYU, 1953; PhD, Ohio State U., 1966. Exec. trainee Sears, Roebuck & Co., 1948-48; instr. retailing U. S.C., 1948-51; chief econ. analysis br. dist. OPS, 1951-53; exec. dir. Columbia (S.C.) Mchts. Assn., 1953-54; asst. prof. Tex. A&M U., 1954-55; mem. faculty Coll. William and Mary, 1955-72, prof. bus. adminstrn., 1959-72, dir. Bur. Bus. Research, 1959-63, assoc. dean Sch. Bus. Adminstrn., 1968-72; prof., dean Ctrl. Conn. State U. Sch. Bus., Avon, 1972-73; prof., head dept. bus. and econs. James Madison U., 1973-74; prof., dean Western Carolina U. Sch. Bus., Cullowhee, N.C., 1974-76; prof. mktg. and mgmt. Christopher Newport U., Newport News, Va., 1976-87, dean Sch. Bus. Adminstrn. and Econs., 1977-87; prof., chmn. dept. mktg. Towson (Md.) State U. Sch. Bus. and Econs., 1987—; pres. Bus. and Adminstrv. Cons. Ltd. (mgmt. and mktg. cons.); teaching asst. Ohio State U., 1963-64; professorial lectr. George Washington U.; mgmt. cons. CSC, U.S. Army. Author: (with others) Hampton Waterfront Economic Study, 1967, The Source Book of Economics, 1973, Management Perceptions, 1976, International Marketing by Dabringer & Muellach Instrn. Manual, 1991; contbr. chpts. to books and articles to profl. jours. Mem. finance resource group Conn. Council Higher Edn., 1972-73; mem. U.S. Senatorial Bus. Adv. Bd. W.T. Grant Retailing scholar, 1947. Mem. Am. Mktg. Assn., Acad. Mgmt., Am. Inst. Decision Scis., Rotary, Phi Beta Kappa. Methodist.

KING, ALLEN B., company executive. Pres. Universal Corp., Richmond, Va., pres., COO. Office: Universal Leaf Tobacco Co Inc 1501 N Hamilton St Richmond VA 23230-6003*

KING, ALONZO, artistic director, choreographer. Student, Sch. Am. Ballet, Am. ballet theatre Sch., Harkness House Ballet Arts. Art dir. Lines Contemporary Ballet, San Francisco, 1982—; master tchr. working with Les Ballets de Monte-Carlo, London's Ballet Rambert, Nat. Ballet of Can., N.C. Sch. of Arts, San Francisco Ballet; inaugurator San Francisco Inst. Choreography, 1982; performer Bella Lewitzsky Dance Co., DTH. Commd. to create and stage ballets for The Joffrey Ballet, Dance Theatre of Harlem; ballets in repertoires of Frankfurt Ballet, Dresden Ballet, BalletMet, Washington Ballet, Hong Kong Ballet; choreographer for Les Ballets de Monte-Carlo; choreogrpaher for prima ballerine Natalia Makarova, Patrick Swazye; original works choreographed include Ocean (3 Isadora Duncan Dance award 1994 for outstanding achievement in choreography, original score and co. performance)), Rock, 1995, Signs and Wonders, Rain Dreaming, Stealing Light, Without Wax, 1990, others. Mem. panels Nat. Endowment for Arts, Calif. Arts Coun., City of Columbus Arts Coun., Lila Wallace-Reader's Digest Arts Ptnrs. Program; former art commr. City and County of San Francisco. Nat. Endowment for Arts Chroeographer's fellow. Office: Lines Contemporary Ballet 50 Oak St Fl 4 San Francisco CA 94102-6011

KING, AMANDA ARNETTE, elementary school educator; b. Conway, S.C., Feb. 6, 1951; d. James Hilton and Maisie (Dunn) Arnette; m. Roachel Dent King III, Dec. 31, 1972; children: Roachel Dent IV, Amanda Catherine. AB, Coker Coll., 1973; MEd of Early Childhood Edn., U. S.C., 1997. Tchr. Darlington (S.C.) County Sch. Dist., 1972-75, 78-81, James F. Byrnes Acad., Florence, S.C., 1981-88, Darlington County Sch. Dist., 1988—. Mem. Society Hill (S.C.) Rescue Squad, Woodmen of World, Palmetto Project; bd. dirs., vice chmn. Darlington County Libr. Sys.; bd. dirs. Mental Health Assn. Darlington County. Recipient Golden Apple award, 1993-94, Tchr. of the Yr. award James F. Byrnes Acad., 1988, Rosenwald/St. David's Elem. Sch., 1990, 93, 97; named Star Tchr. Time Warner Cable, 1998. Mem. S.C. Coun. Tchrs. Math., Internat. Reading Assn., Palmetto State Tchrs. Assn. (mem. com.), Coker Coll. Alumni Assn. (2d v.p. 1988—, Outstanding Alumni com. 1989-90, 93—), Pilot Club (Hartsville, S.C.). Baptist. Home: PO Box 58 Society Hill SC 29593-0058

KING, AMY CATHRYNE PATTERSON, mathematics educator, researcher; b. Douglas, Wyo., Dec. 30, 1928; d. John Francis and Mabel Eloise (Wear) Patterson; m. Don R. King, Aug. 8, 1949 (dec. 1985). BS, U. Mo., 1949; MA, U. Wichita, 1960; PhD, U. Ky., 1970. Tchr. Goddard (Kans.) Pub. Schs., 1956-58, U. Wichita, 1960-62; asst. instr. U. Kans., Lawrence, 1962-65; instr. Washburn U., Topeka, 1966-67; teaching asst. U. Ky., Lexington, 1967-70; prof. math. Ea. Ky. U., Richmond, 1970—; presenter at various confs. Author: instr.'s manual for College Algebra, 1981; (with Cecil B. Read) Pathways to Probability, 1963; contbr. (with others) articles to profl. jours. Departmental rep. for United Way, 1983; pres. Cokesbury Sunday Sch., Centenary United Meth. Ch., 1995-96. Recipient Award in Teaching, Ea. Ky. U., Richmond, 1982, Ea. Ky. U. Found. Professorship, 1993. Mem. Am. Math. Soc., Math. Assn. Am. (mem. various coms., 1st award for Disting. Coll. or Univ. Teaching 1992), Nat. Coun. Tchrs. Math., Assn. for Women of Math., Ky. Coun. Tchrs. Math. (Maths. Edn. Svc. and Achievement award 1998), Women in Math. Edn., Ky. Acad. Computer Users' Group, AAUP (treas. local chpt. 1984-86), Pi Mu. Epsilon, Kappa Mu Epsilon, Pi Lambda Theta, Sigma Delta Pi, Delta Kappa Gamma (pres. Omicron chpt., 1994-96), Sigma Xi. Phi Kappa Phi. Methodist. Office: Ea Ky Univ Wallace Bldg #313 Richmond KY 40475-3133

KING, ANDRE RICHARDSON, architectural graphic designer; b. Chgo., July 30, 1931; s. Earl James and Margie Verdetta (Doyle) K.; children: Jandra Maria, Andre Etienne; m. Sally M. Ryan, Sept. 19, 1980. Student, Chgo. Tech. Coll., 1956-57, U. Chgo., 1956-59; B.A.E., Art Inst. Chgo., 1959; grad., Gemological Inst. Am., 1992. ARK, Archtl. & Environ. Graphic Design Firm est., 1982—; With Skidmore, Owings & Merrill, Chgo., 1956-82; ind. designer, cons., 1982—. Mem. alumni bd. Chgo. Art Inst. Served with USAF, 1951-55. Recipient Design award Art Inst. Chgo., 1959, DESI award, 1982; Hon. consul of Barbados, W.I., 1971—. Mem. AIA (assoc.), Am. Inst. Graphic Designers, Soc. Environ. Graphic Designers, Soc. Topographic Arts, Chgo. Soc. Communicating Arts, Art Dirs. Club of Chgo. (pres. 1979-80, 80-82), Art Inst. Chgo. Alumni (bd. dirs.), Arts Club of Chgo., Consular Corps of Chgo., Sigma Pi Phi, Beta Boule. Home: 6700 S Oglesby Ave Chicago IL 60649-1301 Office: 220 S State St Ste 2200 Chicago IL 60604-2103 *To provide creative excellence for the future through my works.*

KING, ANGUS S., JR., governor of Maine; b. Mar. 31, 1944; m. Mary J. Herman; children: Angus III, Duncan, James, Benjamin, Molly. BA, Dartmouth Coll., 1966; JD, U. Pa., 1969. Bar: Maine 1969. Staff atty. Pine Tree Legal Assistance, Showhegan, Maine, 1969-72; chief counsel Office Senator William D. Hathaway U.S. Senate Subcom. on Alcoholism and Narcotics, Washington, 1972-75; former ptnr. Smith, Lloyd & King, Brunswick, Maine; gov. State of Maine, Augusta, 1995—; TV host Maine Watch, Maine Pub. Broadcasting Network, 20 yrs.; v.p., gen. counsel Swift River/Hafslund Co., 1983; founder, pres. N.E. Energy Mgmt. Inc., 1989-94. Office: Office of Gov 1 State House Sta Augusta ME 04333-0001*

KING, ANTHONY GABRIEL, museum administrator; b. Needham, Mass., June 13, 1953; s. Henry Brazell and Ottilie Rosena (Sandrock) K.; m. Debra Harte, Oct. 3, 1981; children: Courtney, Michael, Shannon, Megan. BS, Springfield (Mass.) Coll., 1976; MA, NYU, 1978. Curatorial asst. Mus. of Am. Indian, N.Y.C., 1975-76; asst. dir. Bronx County Hist. Soc., N.Y.C., 1976-79; exec. dir. Berkshire County Hist. Soc., Pittsfield, Mass., 1979-83; dir. Wash. Hist. Soc., Tacoma, 1983-86, Onondaga Hist. Assn., Syracuse, N.Y., 1986-89; dep. dir. Worcester (Mass.) Art Mus., 1989-98; treas. N.E. Mus. Assn., 1990-94, pres., 1994-96; dir. ops. and fin. Clark Art Inst., Williamstown, Mass., 1998—; adj. faculty museum adminstrn. Harvard U., adj. faculty art history and we. civilization Emmanuel Coll., Boston, 1992—; guest lectr. Tufts U. Grad. Sch. Mem. preservation adv. bd. State of Wash., Olympia, 1984-86, mem. hist. records adv. bd., 1984-86; pres. Tacoma Centennial Com., 1983-84; chmn. Pittsfield Hist. Commn., 1981-83, Pittsfield Civic Ctr. Commn., 1982-82; mem. Steering com. Mass. Arts Advocacy Com., Boston, 1979-83. Mem. Am. Assn. State and Local History, Am. Assn. Mus. (bd. dirs.), Wash. Mus. Assn. Democrat. Roman Catholic. Avocation: rugby football. Office: Clark Art Inst 225 South St Williamstown MA 01267-2891

KING, ARTHUR R., JR., education educator, researcher; b. Portland, Oreg., Dec. 17, 1921. BA, U. Wash., 1943; MA, Stanford U., 1951, EdD, 1955. Tchr., counselor Punahou Sch., Honolulu, 1946-49; rsch. assoc. Stanford (Calif.) U., 1949-51; dir. curricular svcs. Sonoma County Schs., Calif., 1951-55; assoc. prof. edn. Claremont Grad. Sch., Claremont, Calif., 1955-65; prof. edn. U. Hawaii, Honolulu, 1965—, dir. Curriculum Rsch. &

Devel. Group, 1966—, rschr. Edn. Rsch. and Devel. Ctr., 1966-74; prin. investigator, editor courses Hawaii State Dept. Edn.; head Ocean Project, 1979-90; co-founder Pacific Cir. Consortium. Author: (with John A. Brownell) The Curriculum and the Disciplines of Knowledge: A Theory of Curriculum Practice, 1966; contbr. articles to profl. jours. Served USN, WWII; capt., USNR, ret. Office: U Hawaii at Manoa Curriculum Rsch & Devel Group 1776 University Ave Honolulu HI 96822-2463

KING, B. B. (RILEY B. KING), singer, guitarist; b. Itta Bene, Miss., Sept. 16, 1925. LHD (hon.), Tougaloo (Miss.) Coll., 1973; MusD (hon.), Yale U., 1977, Berklee Coll. of Music, 1982; D of Fine Arts, Rhodes Coll. of Memphis, 1990. Began teaching self guitar, 1945; later studied, Schillinger System; past disc jockey and singer Memphis radio stas., internat. appearances throughout world, recs. on, RPM, Crown, Bullet, Kent, ABC Records, ABC/Dunhill Records.; Founding mem., John F. Kennedy Performing Arts Center, 1971, toured, Russia, 1979 (Recipient more than 25 awards as best singer and/or guitarist, including Grammy award 1970); albums include: Back in the Alley, B.B. King in London, Do the Boogie!, Completely Well, Electric B.B.-His Best, The Fabulous B.B. King, Guess Who, Heart and Soul, Live at Cook County Jail, Six Silver Strings, 1985, King of the Blues, 1989, Indianola Mississippi Seeds, 1989, Live at San Quentin, 1990 (Grammy award), Blues is King, 1990, Live at the Apollo, 1991 (Grammy award), Live at the Regal, 1991, Spotlight on Lucille, 1992, There is Always One More Time, 1992, Singin' the Blues, 1993, On the Road with B.B. King: An Interactive Autobiography, 1996, (guest appearance) Six Pack, 1993; guest artist with U2's Rattle and Hum, 1988, Deuces Wild, 1997; subject, collaborator: B.B. King, 1970, B.B. King Blues Guitar, 1970, B.B. King Songbook, 1971, B.B. King, The World's Greatest Living Blues Artist, Blues Guitar, A Method by B.B. King, 1973; performance at closing ceremonies Summer Olympics, Atlanta, Ga., 1996; author: (autobiography, with David Ritz) Blues All Around Me, 1996 (2d prize 8th Ann. Ralph J. Gleason Music Book awards). Co-founder Found. Advancement Inmate Rehab. and Recreation, 1972—; founding mem. Kennedy Performing Arts Ctr. Recipient Humanitarian award Fed. Bur. Prisons, 1972; Humanitarian award B'nai B'rith Music and Performance Lodge, N.Y.C., 1973; Gallery of Greats and Best Blues Guitarist, 1974; Artist of the Decade and Humanitarian award Record World mag., 1974; Best Blues Singer Nat. Assn. TV and Radio Announcers, 1974; Hall of Fame and Best Blues Vocalist and Guitarist Ebony mag., 1974; Grammy award Best Traditional Blues Rec., 1986; Grammy Lifetime Achievement award, 1987; Grammy award Best Rhythm & Blues Vocal Performance, Male, 1970, Best Ethnic of Traditional Recording, 1981, Best Traditional Blues Recording, 1983, 85, Best Traditional Blues Album for Blues Summit, 1993; co-recipient Grammy award for Best Rock Instrumental Performance, 1996; recipient Hall of Fame award Nat. Assn. for Campus Activities, 1986; recipient Presdl. medal of the Arts, 1990; Songwriter's Hall of Fame Lifetime Achievement award, 1991, Orville H. Gibson Lifetime Achievement award Gibson Guitar Co.; Nat. award of distinction U. Miss., 1992; Kennedy Ctr. Honors, 1995; recipient W.C. Handy award Blues Found., 1983, 85, 87, 88, 91, Lifetime Achievement award, 1997; MTV Video Music award for Best Video from a Film, 1988-89, Image awards NAACP, 1975, 81, 93, Pioneer in Music award Nat. Assn. Black Owned Broadcasters, 1997; Living Legend award Trumpet Awards, 1997, Golden Mike award NATRA, 1969, 74; Nat. Heritage fellow Nat. Endowment of the Arts, 1991; inducted into Blues Found. Hall of Fame, 1980, Rock and Roll Hall of Fame, 1987; named Blues Act of Yr., Performance Award Polls, 1985, 87, 88; named to Rock Walk, 1989, Amsterdam Walk of Fame, 1989, Hollywood Walk of Fame, 1990; named Best Blues Instrumentalist, Ebony Mag., 1974-75, Best Male Blues Singer, 1974-75, Blues Guitarist of Yr., Guitar Player Mag., 1970-74, Most Outstanding Blues Singer, Living Blues Mag., 1993-94, 96-97, Blues Artist of Yr., 1994. Office: care Sidney A SeidenbergInc 1414 Avenue Of The Americas New York NY 10019-2514 *I would say to all people, but maybe to young people especially— black and white or whatever color— follow your own feelings and trust them; find out what you want to do and do it, and then practice it and practice it every day of your life and keep becoming what you are, despite any hardships and obstacles you meet.**

KING, BETSY, professional golfer; b. Reading, Pa., Aug. 13, 1955. Winner U.S. Open-Women, 1989, 1990, LPGA, 1992; 3d ranked woman LPGA Tour, 1992; LPGA tour victories include: Orlando Classic, 1984, Columbia Savings Classic, 1984, Henredon Classic, 1986, Rail Charity Classic, 1986, 88, Tucson Open, 1987, Dinah Shore Invitational, 1987, McDonald's Classic, 1987, Atlantic City Classic, 1987, Kemper Open, 1988, Cellular One-Ping Championship, 1988, Jamaica Classic, 1989, Nabisco Dinah Shore, 1990, U.S. Women's Open, 1989, 1990, Corning Classic, 1991, Mazda Championship, 1992, ShopRite Classic, 1995, Corestates Betsy King Classic, 1997, Solheim Cup, 1998. Inductee LPGA Hall of Fame, 1995. LPGA leading money winner, 1984, 89, 93. Office: LPGA 100 International Golf Dr Daytona Beach FL 32124-1092*

KING, BETTY D., state senate employee; b. Port Arthur, Tex., Nov. 27, 1926. Sec. Tex. State Senate, Austin, 1977—. Office: Rl Senate State Capitol PO Box 2910 2E.22 Austin TX 78768-2910

KING, BILLIE JEAN MOFFITT, former professional tennis player; b. Long Beach, Calif., Nov. 22, 1943; d. Willard J. Moffitt; m. Larry King, Sept. 17, 1965. Student, Calif. State U. at Los Angeles, 1961-64. Amateur tennis player, 1958-67, profl., 1968—; mem. Tennis Challenge Series, 1977, 78; dir., ofcl. spokesperson World TeamTennis, Chgo., 1985—; commentator, analyst Wimbledon and other tennis events HBO, N.Y.C.; Singles champion tournaments Wimbledon, 1966-68, 72, 73, 75, U.S. Open, 1967, 71, 72, 74, U.S. Hardcourt, 1966, Italian Open, 1970, West German Open, 1971, Australian Open, 1968, South African Open, 1966, 67, 69, U.S. Indoor, 1966-68, 71, U.S. Clay Court, 1971, French Open, 1972, Avon, 1980; doubles champion Wimbledon, 1961, 62, 65, 67, 68, 70-73, U.S. Open, 1965, 67, 74, 80, French, 1972, Italian, 1970, South African, 1967-70, Bridgestone, 1976, Virginia Slims, 1974, 76; mixed doubles champion Wimbledon, 1967, 71, 73, U.S. Open, 1967, 71, 73, French, 1967, 70, South African, 1967, Australian, 1968; winner 29 Virginia Slims singles titles, 1970-77, 4 Colgate titles, 1977, Fedn. Cup, 1963-67, 76-79, Wightman Cup, 1961-67, 70, 77, 78; World Tennis Team All-Star, 3 times; host Colgate women's sports TV spl. The Lady is a Champ, 1975; co-founder, dir. Kingdom, Inc., San Mateo, Calif.; sports commentator ABC-TV, 1975-78; co-founder, pub. WomenSports mag., 1974—; founder Women's Tennis Assn., 1973; first woman commr. (Team Tennis League) profl. sports history, 1984; TV commentator HBO-Sports Wimbledon coverage; capt. Fed. Cup for USA, 1995; cons. Virginia Slims World Championship Series; bd. dirs. Challenger Ctr.; amb. Adventures in Movement Charity; coach Fed. Cup Women's Tennis Team, 1995-96, USA Olympic Women's Tennis Team, 1996; nat. spokesperson Literary Vols. Am.; tennis tchr. to profls. Author: Tennis to Win, 1970, (with Kim Chapin) Billie Jean, 1974, (with Cynthia Starr) We Have Come a Long Way, The Story of Women's Tennis, 1988. Named Sportsperson of Yr., Sports Illustrated, 1972; Woman Athlete of Yr., A.P., 1967, 73, Top Woman Athlete of Yr., 1972; Woman of Yr., Time mag., 1976, One of 10 Most Powerful Women in Am., Harper's Bazaar, 1977, One of 25 Most Influential Women in Am., World Almanac, 1977, One of 100 Most Important Ams. of 20th Century, Life mag., 1990; named to Internat. Tennis Hall of Fame, 1987, Nat. Women's Hall of Fame, 1990; Lifetime Achievement award, March of Dimes, 1994. Office: World Team Tennis 445 N Wells Chicago IL 60610*

KING, BILLY, sports team executive; b. Jan. 23, 1966. Degree in polit. sci., Duke U., 1988. Color analyst ESPN; asst. Ill. State U.; asst. coach Ind. Pacers; v.p. basketball adminstrn. Phila. 76ers, 1997-98, gen. mgr., 1998—. Office: c/o Phila 76ers 1st Union Ctr Philadelphia PA 19148*

KING, CARL EDWARD, employee screening executive; b. Pine Bluff, Ark., June 19, 1940; s. Carl B. King and Claudia Marie (Fulbright) Ingham; m. Jonna Sue DeWeese, Mar., 1964 (div. Nov. 1974); 1 child, Grant Edward; m. Paula Honor Finnell, Mar. 6, 1975. LLB, La Salle Extension U., 1971; BS in Criminal Justice, U. Nebr., Omaha, 1978; M in Bus. Mgmt., Cen. Mich. U., 1979. Enlisted USMC, 1957, commd. 2d lt., 1969, advanced through grades to maj., 1981; ops. officer, co. commdr. Mil. Police Co., Okinawa, Japan, 1973-74; asst. provost marshal USMC, Barstow, Calif., 1975; provost marshal USMC, Beaufort, S.C., 1975-77, Kaneohe Bay, Hawaii, 1978-81; ret. USMC, 1981; salesman Smith Protective Services, Houston, 1981-82, mgr. investigations div., sales mgr., 1982-83, v.p. mktg., 1983-84; co-founder, CEO Team Bldg. Systems, Houston, 1984—; pres., CEO, founder WNCK, Inc., Houston, 1992—; founder Insights-Corp. Selection Systems, Inc., Houston, 1992—; CEO Insights-Corp. Selection Systems, WNCK, Inc. Mem. loss prevention adv. bd. U. Houston, 1986—. Decorated Bronze Star, Purple Heart with oak leaf cluster. Mem. FBI Nat. Acad., Internat. Assn. Chiefs of Police, Am. Soc. Indsl. Security, Nat. Order Battlefield Commns., Marine Mustang Assn. Republican. Methodist. Avocations: reading, snow skiing, jogging. E-mail: carl@insights-inc.com. Home: 16 Diamond Oak Ct The Woodlands TX 77381-2820 Office: Insights Corp Selections Sys 600 Kenrick Dr Ste A2 Houston TX 77060-3631

KING, CAROLE, songwriter, singer; b. Bklyn., Feb. 9, 1942; m. Gerry Goffin; m. Charles Larkey; m. Rick Evers; m. Rick Sorensen, 1982; children: Louise, Sherry, Molly, Levi. Student, Queens Coll. Co-writer (with Gerry Goffin) numerous songs, 1960-68, including Will You Still Love Me Tomorrow?, He's a Rebel, Go Away, Little Girl, Up on the Roof, Natural Woman, The Locomotion, Take Good Care of My Baby, It's Too Late; albums include Tapestry, 1971 (4 Grammy awards), Simple Things, Pearls: Songs of Goffin and King, Wrap Around Joy, 1974, One To One, 1982, Speeding Time, 1983, Legacy, 1989; off-Broadway theater appearance in A Minor Incident, 1989; Broadway appearance inBlood Brothers, 1994. Inducted in Rock & Roll Hall of Fame, 1990. Office: Free Flow Prodns Inc PO Box 161897 Austin TX 78716-1897 also: care Atlantic Records 75 Rockefeller Plz New York NY 10019-6908

KING, CAROLYN DINEEN, federal judge; b. Syracuse, N.Y., Jan. 30, 1938; d. Robert E. and Carolyn E. (Bareham) Dineen; children: James Randall, Philip Randall, Stephen Randall; m. John L. King, Jan. 1, 1988. A.B. summa cum laude, Smith Coll., 1959; LL.B., Yale U., 1962. Bar: D.C. 1962, Tex. 1963. Assoc. Fulbright & Jaworski, Houston, 1962-72; ptnr. Childs, Fortenbach, Beck & Guyton, Houston, 1972-78, Sullivan, Bailey, King, Randall & Sabom, Houston, 1978-79; circuit judge U.S. Ct. Appeals (5th cir.), Houston, 1979—, chief judge, 1999—. Trustee, mem. exec. com., treas. Houston Ballet Found., 1967-70; trustee, mem. exec. com., chmn. bd. trustees U. St. Thomas, 1988-98; mem. Houston dist. adv. coun. SBA, 1972-76; mem. Dallas regional panel Pres.'s Commn. White House Fellowships, 1972-76, mem. commn., 1977; bd. dirs. Houston chpt. Am. Heart Assn., 1978-79; nat. trustee Palmer Drug Abuse Program, 1978-79; trustee, sec., treas., chmn. audit com., fin. com., mem. mgmt. com. United Way Tex. Gulf Coast, 1979-85. Mem. ABA, Fed. Bar Assn., Am. Law Inst. (coun. 1991—, chmn. membership com. 1997—), State Bar Tex., Houston Bar Assn. Roman Catholic. Office: US Ct Appeals 11020 US Courthouse 515 Rusk St Houston TX 77002-2600

KING, CARY JUDSON, III, chemical engineer, educator, university official; b. Ft. Monmouth, N.J., Sept. 27, 1934; s. Cary Judson and Mary Margaret (Forbes) K., Jr.; m. Jeanne Antoinette Yorke, June 22, 1957; children: Mary Elizabeth, Cary Judson IV, Catherine Jeanne. B. Engring., Yale, 1956; S.M., Mass. Inst. Tech., 1958, Sc.D., 1960. Asst. prof. chem. engring. MIT, Cambridge, 1959-63; dir. Bayway Sta. Sch. Chem. Engring. Practice, Linden, N.J., 1959-61; asst. prof. chem. engring. U. Calif., Berkeley, 1963-66, assoc. prof., 1966-69, prof., 1969—, vice chmn. dept. chem. engring., 1967-72, chmn., 1972-81, dean Coll. Chemistry, 1981-87, provost profl. schs. and colls., 1987-94; vice provost for rsch. U. Calif. Sys., Oakland, 1994-96, interim provost, sr. v.p. acad. affairs, 1995-96, provost, sr. v.p. acad. affairs, 1996—; cons. Procter & Gamble Co., 1969-87; bd. dirs. Coun. for Chem. Rsch., chmn., 1989. Author: Separation Processes, 1971, 80, Freeze Drying of Foods, 1971; contbr. numerous articles to profl. jours.; patentee in field. Active Boy Scouts Am., 1947-86; pres. Kensington Community Council, 1972-73, dir., 1970-73. Recipient Malcolm E. Pruitt award Coun. for Chem. Rsch., 1990. Mem. AIChE (Inst. lectr. 1973, Food, Pharm. and Bioengring Divsn. award 1975, William H. Walker award 1976, Warren K. Lewis award 1990, bd. dirs. 1987-89, Clarence G. Gerhold award 1992); mem. AAAS, Nat. Acad. Engring., Am. Soc. Engring. Edn. (George Westinghouse award 1978), Am. Chem. Soc. (Separations Sci. and Tech. award 1997). Home: 7 Kensington Ct Kensington CA 94707-1009 Office: U Calif Office of Pres 1111 Franklin St Fl 12 Oakland CA 94607-5201

KING, CHARLES BENJAMIN, minister; b. Gasburg, Va., Oct. 20, 1942; s. James Skelton and Frances (Walton) K.; m. Patsy Mitchell, Sept. 11, 1965; children: James A., Katherine A. BA, Randolph-Macon Coll., 1964; MDiv, Duke U., 1967; cert. clin. pastoral edn., Med. Coll. Va., 1969. Ordained to ministry Meth. Ch. as deacon, 1965, as elder, 1969. Student pastor Bethel United Meth., Hanover, Va., 1963-64; youth dir. Noland Meml. United Meth. Ch., Newport News, Va., 1964; student minister 1st United Meth. Ch., Graham, N.C., 1965-67; minister St. Peter's United Meth. Ch., Montpelier, Va., 1967-70; minister of evangelism Trinity United Meth. Ch., Richmond, Va., 1970-72; minister Courtland (Va.) United Meth. Ch., 1972-76; sr. minister Westover Hills United Meth. Ch., Richmond, 1976-80, Christ United Meth. Ch., Norfolk, Va., 1980-84; assoc. dir. leadership devel. Va. United Meth. Conf., Richmond, 1984-89, dir. evangelism, 1989-94; supt. Farmville dist., 1994—. Author: Jesus the Christ, 1978; co-author: Revealing Christ: Sharing the Faith. Recipient Lifetime Membership award United Meth. Women, 1976, Growth Plus award Bd. of Discipleship, 1990. *The great challenge of Christian evangelism: "Where there is vision...there is risk. Where there is risk...there is witness. Where there is witness...there is Gospel (Good News of Jesus Christ). Where there is Gospel...there is hope."*

KING, CHARLES HOMER, manufacturing executive; b. Chgo., July 30, 1938; s. Merle Marine and (Searge) K.; m. Kathie Theiss, May 5, 1984; children: Dennis, Denise, Patricia, Justin. BS in Mgmt. and Mktg., Louisville U., 1967; MA in Computer Data Mgmt., Webster U., Jeffersonville, Ind., 1983. Cert. resource mgmt., prodn. and inventory mgmt. Materials mgr. Internat. Harvester Co., Louisville, 1977-84; material requirements planning mgr. Navistar Internat. Corp., Springfield, Ohio, 1984-91, sys. and shop fl. mgr., 1991-97; materials mgr. Master Industries, Inc., 1998—. Mem. Fraternal Order of Eagles, Springfield Model Airplain Club. Republican. Methodist. Home: 5546 Auburn Dr Greenville OH 45331

KING, CHARLES MARK, dentist, educator; b. Ft. Benning, Ga., Mar. 15, 1952; s. Charles Ray and Marilyn Anita (Alexander) K.; children: Kelley Michelle, Kevin Marcus, Mark Alexander. BS, U. Ala., 1973, MS, 1977, DMD, 1981, JD, Birmingham Sch. Law, 1997. Cert. Pain Management Practitioner, 1992. Lab. technician Med. Lab. Assn., Birmingham, Ala., 1973-74; rsch. asst. dept. surgery Univ. Hosp., Birmingham, 1974-76, dept. anesthesiology, 1976-78; gen. practice dentistry, Birmingham, 1981—; clin. instr. U. Ala. Sch. Dentistry, Birmingham, 1982-89; mem. bd. advisors Dist. Dental Assts. Soc., 1984-90. Contbr. articles to profl. jours. Lt. col. Ala. Army NG. Named Best Clin. Instr., Student Body U. Ala. Sch. Dentistry 1985. Mem. Acad. Pain Management, Acad. Gen. Dentistry, Assn. Mil. Surgeons U.S., Nat. Assn. Doctors, Scottish Rite, Shriners, Masons, Delta Sigma Delta. Republican. Baptist. Avocations: archery, martial arts, hunting, water sports, flying. Masons, Shriners. Office: PO Box 94805 Birmingham AL 35220-4805

KING, CHARLES ROSS, physician; b. Nevada, Iowa, Aug. 22, 1925; s. Carl Russell and Dorothy Sarah (Mills) K.; m. Frances Pamela Carter, Jan. 8, 1949; children—Deborah Diane, Carter Ross, Charles Conrad, Corbin Kent. Student, Butler U., 1943; BS in Bus., Ind. U., 1948, MD, 1964. Diplomate Am. Bd. Family Practice. Dep. dir. Ind. Pub. Works and Supply, 1949-52; salesman Knox Coal Corp., 1952-59; rotating intern Marion County Gen. Hosp., Indpls., 1964-65; family practice medicine Anderson, Ind., 1965—; sec.-treas. staff Cmty. Hosp., 1969-72, pres.-elect, dir., chief medicine, 1973—, bd. dirs., 1973-75; sec.-treas. St. John's Hosp., 1968-69, chief medicine, 1972-73, chief pediatrics, 1977—; bd. dirs. Rolling Hills Convalescnet Ctr., 1968-73; pres. Profl. Ctr. Lab., 1965—; vice chmn. Madison County Bd. Health, 1966-69, chmn., 1986—; chmn. bd. dirs. Star Fin. Bank, Anderson. Bd. dirs. Family Svc. Madison County, 1968-69, Madison County Assn. Mentally Retarded, 1972-76, Anderson Fine Arts Ctr., 1996—; chmn. bd. dirs. Anderson Downtown Devel. Corp., 1980—; mem. Paramont Restoration Steering Com., 1994—; trustee, sec.-tread. St. John's Med. Ctr., 1989—; mem. exec. com. Madison United Way Fund, vice-chmn., 1995, chmn., 1996; mem. exec. com. Stop Teen Pregnancy Program, 1995—; exec. commr. Health Search Madison County, 1995—. With U.S. Army, 1944-46. Recipient Dr. James Macholtz award Spl. Olympics, 1986—. Fellow Royal Soc. Health, Am. Acad. Family Practice (charter); mem. AMA (numerous Physicians Recognition awards), Ind. Med. Assn., Pan Am. Med. Assn., Am. Acad. Gen. Practice, Madison County Med. Soc. (pres. 1970), 9th Dist. Med. Soc. (sec.-treas. 1968), Anderson C. of C. (bd. dirs. 1979-82), Indpls. Mus. Art (corp. mem.), Anderson Country Club (bd. dirs. 1976-79), Phi Delta Theta (pres. Alumni Assn. 1952), Phi Chi. Methodist. Club: Anderson Country (bd. dirs. 1976-79). Home: 920 N Madison Ave Anderson IN 46011-1208 Office: 1933 Chase St Anderson IN 46016-4238

KING, CHARLES THOMAS, retired school superintendent, educator; b. Coatsville, Pa., July 19, 1911; s. John Henry and Estella (Orr) K. m. Dorothy Eckman, Nov. 30, 1933; children: Marilyn Mae, Kenneth Alan, Donald Edwin. BS, West Chester State Coll., 1932; EdM, Temple U., 1944; EdD, Rutgers U., 1957. Tchr. West Pottsgrove Twp. Sch., Stowe, Pa., 1933-35; tchr. Haverford Twp. Sch., Havertown, Pa., 1935-38, dir. elem. health and phys. edn., 1938-42; prin. Llanerch Sch., Havertown, Pa., 1942-45; supervising prin. West Pottsgrove Twp. Sch., Stowe, Pa., 1945-47; prin. Glenwood and Short Hills Schs., Millburn, N.J., 1947-51, asst. to supt., 1951-59, asst. supt., 1959-62, supt., 1962-74; mem. state adv. council on Handicapped 1968-72; mem. state cert. appeals com., 1972-74. Pres. Millburn Cmty. Coun., 1954-56; bd. dirs. Millburn Pub. Libr., 1962-74 Millburn Twp. Com.; chmn. N.J. Coun. Econ. Edn., 1972-74; deacon Congl. Ch., 1963-66; chmn. Pilgrim Congl. Ch., 1993-97. Recipient Cmty. Svc. award Millburn Twp. Com., 1995. Mem. Essex County Supts. Roundtable (chmn. 1965-66), West Chester State Coll. Alumni Assn. (chpt. pres. 1981-83, Disting. Alumni award 1982), Millburn Coaches Assn. (Man of Yr. award 1989), Rotary (pres. 1957-58, bd. dirs. 1996—, Paul Harris fellow 1986, Svc. Above Self plaque 1989), Millburn Old Guard (pres. 1997), Phi Delta Kappa (chpt. pres. 1959-60, emeritus 1974). Home: 470 W Riverview Cir Reno NV 89509

KING, CHAROLETTE ELAINE, retired career officer; b. Baker, Oreg., Apr. 10, 1945; d. Melvin Howard and Rella Maxine (Gwilliam) Wright; m. Craig Seldon King, April 14, 1965; children: Andrea Karen, Diana Susan. Clerical positions various firms, Idaho, Va., Conn., 1964-71; nursing sec. VA, San Diego, 1974-77; sec. USN, Agana, Guam, 1972-73; procurement clk. USN, Bremerton, Wash., 1977-80; procurement clk. USN, San Diego, 1980, support svcs. supr., 1980-83, div. dir., 1983-87, program analyst, 1987-93, adminstrv. officer, 1993-96, mgmt. analyst, 1996. Recipient Model Agy. cup USN, San Diego, 1986. Republican. Avocations: reading, camping, sewing, writing, quilting.

KING, CHRIS ALLEN, military officer; b. Brunswick, Maine, Feb. 7, 1960; s. Donald King and Marjorie Marilyn (Gaddis) Edwards; m. Margaret Anne Murtz, Mar. 23, 1990; children: Sarah Anne, Lisa Marie. BS, U.S. Mil. Acad., 1983; MPA, Princeton U., 1992. Commd. 2d lt. U.S. Army, 1983, advanced through grades to lt. col., 1999; platoon leader, then troop co. exec. officer U.S. Army, Bamberg, Germany, 1984-86; squadron adj., then troop comdr. U.S. Army, Bindlach, Germany, 1987-90; from battalion ops. officer to battalion exec. officer U.S. Army, Ft. Riley, Kans., 1996-98; spl. asst. to chief legis. liaison U.S. Army, Pentagon, 1998—; asst. prof. dept. social scis. U.S. Mil. Acad., West Point, N.Y., 1992-95. Deacon Manhattan (Kans.) 1st Presbyn. Ch., 1997-98; cmty. mayor West Point Mayor's program, 1994-95. Mem. U.S. Army Armor Assn. (order of St. George award 1995), Assn. of U.S. Army, Phi Kappa Phi. Avocation: backpacking.

KING, CLARENCE CARLETON, II, healthcare executive; b. Asheville, N.C., June 12, 1956; s. Clarence Carleton King and Betty Ann (Barker) Haddon; m. Janet Susan Kerly, Aug. 20, 1983; 1 child, Douglas Carleton. BBA summa cum laude, Ga. State U., 1978; M in Health Adminstrn., Duke U., 1980. Hosp. adminstr. Hosp. Affiliates Internat., Nashville, 1980-81, Hosp. Corp. of Am., Nashville, 1981-86; v.p. devel. Carle Care HMO, Carle Clinic, Urbana, Ill., 1986-88; COO Health Alliance Med. Plans, Urbana, 1988-90, CEO, 1990-95; exec. dir. Prudential Health Care-North Tex., Dallas, 1995-97, v.p. health plan ops., 1997—; bd. dirs. Ill. Assn. HMOs, Chgo., 1990-91; bd. dirs., pres. Carle Employees Fed. Credit Union, Urbana, Ill., 1990-93; bd. dirs., vice chmn. Ill. HMO Guaranty Assn., Chgo., 1990-95. Vol. Prudential's Vol. Day, Dallas, 1996-97. Mem. Tex. Healthcare Coun. (bd. dirs. Austin 1996-97), Am. Coll. Healthcare Execs. Republican. Baptist. Avocations: golf, skiing, basketball, travel. Office: Prudential Health Care North Tex 4100 Alpha Rd Ste 400 Dallas TX 75244-4327

KING, CLARK CHAPMAN, JR., lawyer; b. Quincy, Ill., May 18, 1929; s. Clark Chapman and Miriam Doris (Decker) K.; m. Joyce Jepson Jones, Jan. 5, 1955; children: Clark Chapman III, Jeffrey L., Stephen D., Carolyn Ann. BA cum laude, Amherst Coll., 1951; LLB, Harvard U., 1954. Bar: Ill. 1955, U.S. Dist. Ct. (no. dist.) 1955, (mid. dist.) Ill. 1960, U.S. Ct. Appeals (7th) 1957, (5th) 1982, (11th) 1985, (6th) 1984, U.S. Supreme Ct. 1977. Asst. atty. gen. State of Ill., Springfield, 1954, spl. asst. atty. gen., 1957-60; assoc. Robertson, Kepner, Springfield, 1957-60, Hough, Young & Coale, Chgo., 1960-61; ptnr. Lord, Bissell & Brook, Chgo., 1961-94, of counsel, 1994—. Active Northbrook Civic Assn.; vice-chmn. Cook County Young Reps., Chgo., 1960; area chmn. Northfield Twp. Rep. Orgn., 1960-70. Sgt. U.S. Army, 1954-57. Mem. Chgo. Bar Assn., Internat. Bar Assn., Agrl. Bar Assn. Avocations: fishing, hunting. Office: Lord Bissell & Brook 115 S La Salle St Ste 3200 Chicago IL 60603-3972

KING, CLAUDIA LOUAN, film producer, lecturer; b. Merced, Calif., May 1, 1940; d. Alvin Cecil and Thelma May (Matthew) K.; m. Douglas McLean, July 10, 1965 (div. 1975); children: Kia Gabrielle, Kendra Sue. BA, U. Calif., 1963; MA, Ind. U., 1969. Lectr. U. Fla., Gainesville, 1969-70; asst. prof. U. Nev., Las Vegas, 1973-79; producer Source 17 Prodns., Santa Monica, Calif., 1979-85; freelance producer Chico, Calif., 1985—. Author: Life Mastery: A Self-Esteem Handbook for Adults and Children, 1994, (screenplays) The Garden of Eden, 1983, My Sister's Keeper, 1986, (documentary) The Evolution of Women, 1988, 92 (short stories) In the Realm of the Invisible, 1991; prodr.: Rape is Everybody's Concern, 1978, Los Angeles Personally Yours, 1986; pub. Light Paths Communications, 1994—. Mem. Chico Annie's Com. for Dramatic Arts, 1996. Carnegie grantee, 1969; Nev. Endowment for Humanities grantee, 1978. Mem. Women in Film, Coll. Art Assn. Democrat. Avocation: camping. Home: PO Box 3576 Chico CA 95927-3576

KING, CORETTA SCOTT (MRS. MARTIN LUTHER KING, JR.), educational association administrator, lecturer, writer, concert singer; b. Marion, Ala., Apr. 27, 1927; d. Obidiah and Bernice (McMurray) Scott; m. Martin Luther King, Jr., June 18, 1953 (dec. Apr. 1968); children: Yolanda Denise, Martin Luther III, Dexter Scott, Bernice Albertine. A.B., Antioch Coll., 1951; Mus.B., New Eng. Conservatory Music, 1954, Mus.D., 1971; L.H.D., Boston U., 1969, Marymount-Manhattan Coll., 1969, Morehouse Coll., 1970; H.H.D., Brandeis U., 1969, Wilberforce U., 1970, Bethune-Cookman Coll., 1970, Princeton U., 1970; LL.D., Bates Coll., 1971. Voice instr. Morris Brown Coll., Atlanta, 1962; commentator CNN, Atlanta, 1980—; lectr., writer; founding pres., chief exec. officer Martin Luther King Jr. Ctr. for Nonviolent Social Change Inc. Author: My Life With Martin Luther King, Jr., 1969; contbr. articles to mags.; syndicated newspaper columnist N.Y. Times Syndication Sales Corp., 1986-90, United Features Syndicate, 1990-94; concert debut, Springfield, Ohio, 1948; numerous concerts throughout U.S., concerts, India, 1959, performances, Freedom Concert. Del. to White House Conf. Children and Youth, 1960; sponsor Com. for Sane Nuclear Policy, Com. on Responsibility, Moblzn. to End War in Viet Nam, 1966, 67, Margaret Sanger Meml. Found.; mem. So. Rural Action Project, Inc.; pres. Martin Luther King, Jr. Found.; chmn. Commn. on Econ. Justice for Women; mem. exec. com. Nat. Com. Inquiry; co-chmn. Clergy and Laymen Concerned about Vietnam, Nat. Com. for Full Employment, 1974; pres. Martin Luther King Jr. Center for Nonviolent Social Change; co-chairperson Nat. Com. Full Employment; mem. exec. bd. Nat. Health Ins. Com.; active YWCA; bd. dirs. So. Christian Leadership Conf., Martin Luther King, Jr. Found. Gt. Britain; trustee Robert F. Kennedy Meml. Found., Ebenezer Bapt. Ch. Recipient Outstanding Citizenship award Montgomery (Ala.) Improvement Assn., 1959, Merit award St. Louis Argus, 1960, Distinguished Achievement award Nat. Orgn. Colored Women's Clubs, 1962, Louise Waterman Wise award Am. Jewish Congress Women's Aux., 1963, Myrtle Wreath award Cleve. Hadassah, 1965, award for excellence in field human relations Soc. Family of May, 1968, Universal Love award Premio San Valentine Com., 1968, Wateler Peace prize, 1968, Dag Hammarskjold award, 1969, Pacem in Terris award Internat. Overseas Service Found., 1969, Leadership for Freedom award Roosevelt U., 1971, Martin Luther King Meml. medal Coll. City N.Y., 1971, Internat. Viareggio award, 1971, numerous others; named Woman of Year Utility Club N.Y.C., 1962, Woman of Year Nat. Assn. Radio and TV Announcers, 1968, UAW Social Justice award, 1980. Mem. Nat. Council Negro Women (Ann. Brotherhood award 1957), Women Strike for Peace (del. disarmament conf. Geneva, Switzerland 1962, citation for work in peace and freedom 1963), Women's Internat. League for Peace and Freedom, NAACP, United Ch. Women (bd. mgrs.), Alpha Kappa Alpha (hon.). Baptist (mem. choir, guild adviser). Club: Links (Human Dignity and Human Rights award Norfolk chpt. 1964). Address: Martin Luther King Jr Ctr 449 Auburn Ave NE Atlanta GA 30312-1503*

KING, DANIEL CARLETON, physician assistant, air force officer, consultant; b. Toledo, Mar. 26, 1961; s. William Forrest and Susanne Shirley (Krohn) K.; 1 child, William Robert Hotop. BS, U. Nebr., Omaha, 1993, MPAS, 1998. Cert. Nat. Commn. on Cert. Physician Assts. Enlisted man USAF, 1984, advanced through grades to capt., 1997; allergy technician 7th Med. Group, Caswell AFB, Tex., 1984-87; allergy technician 7100st Combat Support Wing Med. Ctr., Wiesbaden, Germany, 1987-89, non-commd. officer in charge, 1989-91; staff physician asst. 355th Med. Ops. Group, Tucson, 1993-97, team chief clin. svcs. package air transportable hosp., 1994-96, dir. continuing med. edn., 1995-97; staff physician asst., mem. exec. com. of med. staff 52d Med. Ops. Group, Spang Dahlem Air Base, Germany, 1997—; dep. cons. 52d FW for Nuclear Weapons Pers. Reliability, Spang Dahlem Air Base, Germany, 1997—. Health care provider to homeless vets. Tucson VA Hosp., 1995-96. Fellow Am. Acad. Physician Assts.; mem. Soc. Air Force Physician Assts. Mem. UNity Ch. 010Avocations: collecting antique maps, photography, mountain climbing and hiking, bicycling. Home: PSC 9 Box 3365 APO AE 09123 Office: 52d Med Ops Group SGOMF-C APO AE 09123

KING, DARRYL ERIC, filmmaker, director; b. Phila., Nov. 30, 1965; s. Martin Earl and Lottie Virgina (Williams) K. BA, Penn State U., 1988. Dir. video Alpha Internat. Records, Phila., 1991-94; dir., pres. Full Circle Films Prodn., Phila., 1991-97; dir., prodr. Visually Yours Inc., Phila., 1992-96, More Flavor Inc., Phila., 1992-96; Author: (scripts) Colur By Number, 1993, Till Death Do Us Part; (poet) Edge of Twillight, 1995. Mem. Black Filmmakers Orgn., Phila. Film Festival. Avocations: study God's word, writing, poetry, songs. Home: 2006 Widener Pl Philadelphia PA 19138-2454

KING, DAVID ROY, lawyer; b. N.Y.C., Jan. 5, 1950; s. Joseph S. and Doris (Kagan) K.; m. Eunice Searles, Aug. 22, 1971; children: Mark B., Anna M. BA, U. Pa., 1971; JD, Harvard U., 1974. Bar: Pa. 1974, U.S. Dist Ct. (ea. dist.) Pa. 1974. Assoc. Morgan, Lewis & Bockius LLP, Phila., 1974-81, ptnr., 1981—. Office: Morgan Lewis & Bockius LLP 1701 Market St Philadelphia PA 19103-2921

KING, DAVID STEVEN, quality control executive; b. Easton, Pa., May 16, 1960; s. Carl Stanley and Verna Marilyn (Frey) K. BS in Stats., Va. Poly. Inst. and State U., 1982. Cert. statistician, quality engr., reliability engr., quality auditor, quality mgr., ISO 9000 lead assessor, quality assurance profl. Quality and product design engr. SIECOR Corp., Hickory, N.C., 1982-86; quality supr. Alcatel Cable Systems, Fordyce, Ark., 1987-89; quality assurance mgr. Aeroquip Corp., Heber Springs, Ark., 1989-90; quality control mgr. Progress Lighting, Cowpens, S.C., 1990-92; quality mgr. Dana Corp., Greenville, S.C., 1993-95; quality engr. Std. Products, Spartanburg, S.C., 1995—. Mem. Am. Soc. for Quality Control, Am. Stats. Assn., ASTM. Home: 11 Vale St Spartanburg SC 29301-5543

KING, DEBORAH SIMPKIN, music, voice educator; b. Manchester, Tenn., July 9, 1954; d. William Edward and Peggy Lou (Little) Simpkin; m. Gordon Wesley King, Aug. 19, 1975; children: Patrick King, Michael King. Studied with Carapetyan, others, 1971-91; MusB, Tex. Christian U., 1976; MusM, North Tex. State U., 1981; studied with James Rives-Jones, 1989; Mus D, U. North Tex., 1990. High sch. voice tchr. Tex., 1976-77; tchg. fellow North Tex. State U., Denton, 1980-85; elem. gifted prog. music instr. All Saints' Cathedral Day Sch., Ft. Worth, 1987-88; music hist. lectr. U. North Tex., Denton, 1988-91; interim prof. Tarrant County Jr. Coll., 1990; asst. prof., coord. choral and vocal studies Grad. Studies Jersey City State Coll., 1991-95; founder, artistic dir. Schola Cantorum on Hudson, 1992—; asst. prof. choral, vocal music Kutztown (Pa.) U., 1996-97; owner voice studios, N.Y.C., Jersey City, N.J., Montclair, N.J., 1995—. Author: (with others) Twentieth-Century Conductors, 1999; editor: A Blow Anthology, 1996; alto soloist All Saints' Episcopal Cathedral, Ft. Worth, 1973-88; guest, co-conductor The Choir of the Episcopal Diocese, Ft. Worth, Tex., 1988, 1990-91; mem. various profl. chorales; appeared in numerous (oratorio, recital) solo appearances, choral/vocal workshops, clinics, adjudications, 1980—. Bd. dirs. Hudson County Friends of Art and Music, 1992—; music dir., choral adjudicator, clinician St. John's Episcopal Ch., Montclair, N.J., 1994—. Named valedictorian Tex. Christian U., 1976; recipient grad. dean's scholarly comm. dissertation award U. North Tex., 1990. Mem. Nat. Assn. for Tchrs. of Singing, Am. Choral Dir.'s Assn. (bd. dirs. N.J. chpt.), Am. Musicological Soc., Choral Am., Soc. for Seventeenth-Century Music, Conductors' Guild, Coll. Music Soc., Alpha Lambda Delta, Pi Kappa Lambda. Democrat. Episcopalian. Avocations: hiking, running, herb gardening, low fat cooking. Home: 3 Washington Dr Apt B West Paterson NJ 07424-3110

KING, DIANE AVERBACH, education educator; b. Phila., Mar. 28, 1925; d. Louis and Mollie (Chaplick) Averbach; m. Leon King, Nov. 30, 1946; childen: Cheryl, Elliot, Louis. BA, U. Pa., 1945; MA, Dropsie Coll., 1970, PhD, 1979; D Pedagogy (hon.), Jewish Theol. Sem., N.Y.C., 1987. Tchr. Germantown Jewish Ctr., Phila., 1950-67; ednl. cons. Grath Coll., Phila., 1963-87; acting dir. Ctrl. Agy. for Jewish Edn., Melrose Park, Pa., 1987-88, assoc. dir., 1988-89; assoc. prof. edn. Gratz Coll., Melrose Park, 1979—; bd. dirs. Averbach Ctrl. Agy. for Jewish Edn., Melrose Park, 1990—, Phila. Jewish Archives, 1992—; writer curriculum materials for Jewish schs. Contbg. author: Jewish Life in Philadelphia (1830-1940), 1983, Philadelphia Jewish Life (1940-1985), 1986; contbr. to ency. Recipient humanitarian award Fedn. Jewish Agys., 1983, lifetime achievement award Jewish Educators Assembly-Behrman House Pubs., 1998. Mem. Phi Beta Kappa. Home: 4030 Woodruff Rd Lafayette Hill PA 19444-1618

KING, DON, boxing promoter; b. Cleve., Aug. 20, 1931; s. Clarence and Hattie K.; m. Henrietta King; children: Deborah, Carl, Eric. Boxing promoter, 1972—; owner Don King Prodns., Inc., Fla., 1974—; promoter various fighters including Muhammud Ali, Sugar Ray Leonard, Mike Tyson, Ken Norton, Joe Frazier, Larry Holmes, Roberto Duran, George Foreman. Office: care Don King Prodns Inc 501 Fairway Dr Deerfield Beach FL 33441-1865*

KING, DOROTHY JACKSON, psychologist, marriage-family counselor, therapist; b. Dundee, Miss., Dec. 13, 1955; d. Allan Jackson and Cliftee (Miller) Davis; m. Savoid Lester King, Jan. 27, 1979; children: Darren, Ranando. MDiv, Emmanuel Sch. Religion, Johnson City, Tenn., 1989; M Counseling, Evangel Sch. Religion, Monroe, La., 1990; PhD in Philosophy, Friends Christian U., Merced, Calif., 1992. Ordained, 1985. Assoc. pastor St. Andrew's Meth. Ch., Memphis; pastor Limestone and Jonesborough Chs., Johnson City, Tenn.; physician asst. Drs Motley and Medlock, Memphis; dean Bethel Bible Coll. and Sem., Jonesboro, Ark.; family advocacy rep. USN and Hawaii Family Ct., Honolulu; mem. child abuse adv. bd. Makalapa Abuse Com., Honolulu. Author: Psychological Development in Minorities, 1993, Women on Fire for God: Old and New Testament, 1997, Dealing with Stress and Drug Abuse in the Family, 1997, Impact of Stress Upon God's People and the Utilization of Prayer, 1997, Understanding the Bible: Genesis Eternal Life Through Jesus Christ; contbr. articles to various publs. Lt. USN. Fellow ACA; mem. Am. Mental Health Assn., Assn. Marriage and Family Counselors, Multicultural Assn., Am. Assn. Profl. Hypnotherapists, Assn. Clin. Pastoral Edn. Avocations: chess, horseback riding, fishing, bowling. Address: 4103 Cornerstone Dr Jonesboro AR 72401-7823

KING, DUANE HAROLD, museum administrator; b. Bristol, Tenn., May 18, 1947. BA, U. Tenn., 1969; MA, U. Ga., 1972, PhD, 1975. Dir. Mus. Cherokee (N.C.) Nation, 1975-82; exec. dir. Cherokee Nat. Hist. Soc., Tahlequah, Okla., 1982-87, Mid. Oreg. Indian Hist. Soc., Warm Springs, 1987-90; asst. dir. George Gustav Heye Ctr. Nat. Mus. Am. Indian, N.Y.C., 1990-95; exec. dir. Southwest Mus., L.A., 1995—; chmn. adv. com. Trail of Tears Nat. Hist. Trail Nat. Park Svc., 1991—; bd. trustees mem. Inst. Am. Indian and Alaska Native Culture and Arts Devel., Santa Fe, 1988—; exec. dir. Friends of Sequoyah Found. of Ea. Band Cherokee Indians, 1989-90; periodic cons. Cherokee Nation of Okla., 1989-94, Mus. Cherokee Indian, 1985—, Walt Disney Imagineering, Glendale, Calif., 1994; hist. advisor KUSA-TV, Denver, 1994-95; Sequoyah prof. We. Caroiina U., Cullowhee, N.C., 1995, adj. asst. prof. dept. sociology and anthropology, 1976-82; adj. prof. divsn. arts and humanities Northeastern State U., Tahlequah, 1986-87; vis. asst. prof. dept. anthropology U. Tenn., Knoxville, 1974-82; asst. prof. dept. sociology and anthropology U. Tenn., Chattanooga, 1974-76. Contbr. video documentaries and articles to profl. jours. Recipient Spl. Achievement and Exceptional Svc. awards (6) Smithsonian Instn., 1992-95, Gold award Nat. Park Svc., 1995, Svc. award Confederated Tribes Warm Springs, 1990, Performance award Cherokee Nation Okla., 1985, Mayor's Merit award for exceptional achievements City of Knoxville, 1983, Disting. Svc. award Ea. Band Cherokee Indians, 1982, Vol. Svc. award Save the Children Found., 1982. Fax: 213 224-8223. Home: 311 Santa Rosa Rd Arcadia CA 91007-3040 Office: Southwest Museum PO Box 41558 Los Angeles CA 90041-0558*

KING, EDWARD C., judge. Chief justice Supreme Ct. Federated States Micronesia, Ponape. Office: Supreme Ct Federated States Micronesia PO Box P5-J Kolonia Pohnpei FM 96941

KING, EDWARD LOUIS, retired chemistry educator; b. Grand Forks, N.D., Mar. 15, 1920; s. Edward Louis and Beatrice (Nicholson) K.; m. Joy Kerler, Dec. 20, 1952; children: Paul, Marcia (dec.). Student, Long Beach (Calif.) Jr. Coll., 1938-41; B.S., U. Calif., Berkeley, 1942, Ph.D., 1945. Research chemist Manhattan Project, U. Cal., Berkeley, 1942-46; mem. chemistry faculty Harvard, 1946-48, U. Wis., 1948-62, U. Colo., Boulder, 1963-90; chmn. dept. chemistry U. Colo., 1970-72. Author: How Chemical Reactions Occur, 1963, Chemistry, 1979; Editor: Inorganic Chemistry, 1964-68. Guggenheim fellow, 1957-58. Mem. Am. Chem. Soc., Phi Beta Kappa, Sigma Xi. Office: U Colo Dept Chemistry PO Box 215 Boulder CO 80309-0215

KING, EDWARD WILLIAM, retired transportation executive; b. North Fork, W.Va., Jan. 29, 1923; s. Edward Ward and Myrtle (Charlton) K.; m. Mary Elizabeth Preston, Oct. 31, 1947 (dec. 1976); children: Edward William Jr., Elizabeth King Brown, Mary King Sullivan; m. Martha Lee Corns Mather, Apr. 7, 1977. Edn., Va. Poly. Inst., Washington and Lee U., U. Tenn.-Knoxville. Pres., treas. Mason & Dixon Lines, Inc., Kingsport, Tenn., until 1974, chmn. bd., treas., 1974—; pres., treas. Crown Enterprises, Inc.; treas. Mason & Dixon Tank Lines, Inc.; chmn. Regular Common Carrier Conf., 1966-67; dir. Kingsport Nat. Bank, Kingsport Fed. Savs. & Loan. Seal sale chmn. Sullivan County TB Assn.; mem. Kingsport Bd. Edn.; dir., sec.-treas. Holston Valley Hosp., 1956-79; trustee East Tenn. State U. Found. Named Young Man of Yr. Kingsport Jaycees, 1958. Mem. Am. Trucking Assn. (Tenn. v.p., trustee ATA Found.), Trucking Employers, Tenn. Motor Transport Assn. (pres. 1957-58), Kingsport C. of C. (v.p.). Presbyterian. Clubs: Ridgefields Country (Kingsport); Kingsport Civitan (pres.).

KING, ELAINE A., curator, art historian, critic; b. Oak Park, Ill., Apr. 12, 1947; d. Casimir Stanley and Catherine Mary (Chemle) Czerwien. BS, No. Ill. U., 1968, MA, 1974; PhD, Northwestern U., 1986. Intern George Eastman House, Rochester, N.Y., 1977; lectr. history of photography Northwestern U., Evanston, Ill., 1977-81; curator Dittmar Meml. Gallery, Evanston, 1978-81; dir. Artemesia Gallery, Chgo., 1976-77, Carnegie-Mellon Art Gallery, Pitts., 1985-91; prof. critical theory and history of art Carnegie Mellon U., Pitts., 1981—; bd. dirs. Mountain Lake Criticism Conf., Blacksburg, Va., 1982-91; ind. curator, 1991—; exhbn. rev. panel Pa. Coun. on Arts, 1991; exec. dir., chief curator Contemporary Art Ctr., Cin., 1993-95; guest curator Pitts. Cultural Trust, 1992, 93, 95, 96; 10 year Retrospective of Diane Samuels, Mcpl. Gallery of Hungary, Györ, bd. dirs. Mid-Am. Coll. Art Assn.; panel chair Midwest CAA Conf., 1997; co-coord. Watson Festival, 1996—; adj. prof. U. Cin., 1994; art critic-in-residence U. Ariz., Tucson; Am. guest curator Hungarian Bienale Exhbn. II, Györ, 1993, Master Graphic Arts Bienale IV, 1995, 97, 99; panelist NEA Visual Arts, 1993; grant reviewer Inst. Mus. Sci., Washington, 1994, Ohio Arts Coun. fellowship and grant evaluator, 1994-95; mem. organizing com. Midwest Mus. Con., 1994-95; Am. rep. Inter Arts Spring 1996 Budapest (Hungary) Crossroads, Am. critic rep. AICA Conf. The Edge, Zagreb, Croatia, Chair Coll. Arts Assoc. Com. disting. exhbn. award, 1995-98, AICA conf. ctrl. European cross-roads, 1996, 97, XXXIII Congress Internat. Art Critics, Warsaw, Poland, 1999. Curator, author: The Figure As Fiction, 1993, Alfred DeCredico: Drawings, 1985-93, Emily Cheng: Monoprints, 1994, (exhbn. catalogues) Barry LeVa: 1966-88, Mel Bochner: 1973-85, Elizabeth Murray: Drawings: 1980-86, Michael Gitlin: Sculpture & Drawings, 1990, New Generations: Chgo., 1990, New Generations: N.Y., 1991, Magdalena Jetalova, 1991, Martin Puryear: Sculpture & Drawings, 1987, Abstraction/Abstraction, Tishan Hsu, Paintings, Drawings & Sculpture, 1987, N.Y. Painting Today, Michel Gerand: Drawings and Site Works, 1989, Drawings and Sculpture, 1990, Art in the Age of Information, 1993, Five Artists at the Airport: Insights into Public Art, 1992, Martha Rosler: In Place of the Public, 1994, Shari Zolla, 1997, Lyzabeth Sallan: 2 Installations, Light Into Art: From Video to Virtual Reality (also booklet), David Humphrey: Paintings and Drawings 1987-95 (also catalogue), others; author: The Misunderstood Patron, The National Endowment for the Arts; free lance art critic, Grapheion Tema Celeste, & Sculpture, Cin. Enquirer; Grapheion; Art on Paper, art critic in residence Delaware Contemporary Ctr. for the Arts, 1992, Mid-Atlantic Arts Fellow, 1991, No. Ill. U., 1997; corr. critic, regional editor Diaglogue, Columbus, Ohio, 1984-89; corr. critic Sculpture; contbr. articles to profl. jours. Active Dem. Party, Evanston, Ill., ward judge, 1977-78, precinct capt., 1977. Recipient Hunt Art award, 1977; Art Critics fellow Pa. Coun. on Arts, 1985, 89, 95, 99, rsch. fellow Smithsonian Inst., 1998; faculty rsch. grantee, 1985, 87, 89-90, 96—, Grant Trust for Mutual Understanding, Rockefeller Found., 1994, Thendora Found., 1995; mem. tech. com., cmty. program scholar Pa. Humanities Coun., 1997; sr. rsch. fellow Smithsonian Instn., 1999—. Mem. Coll. Art Assn., Am. Assn. Mus., Assn. Historians Am. Art, Internat. Assn. Art Critics (Am. sect.), Art Table. Avocations: cooking, gardening, tennis, swimming, sailing. Fax: 412-521-8576. E-mail: eK06@andrew.cmu.edu. Office: Carnegie Mellon U Coll Fine Arts Pittsburgh PA 15213

KING, FELTON, bishop. Bishop Ch. of God in Christ, Phoenix. Office: Emmanuel Ch of God in Christ 1537 W Buckeye Rd Phoenix AZ 85007*

KING, FRANK WILLIAM, writer; b. Port Huron, Mich., Oct. 1, 1922; s. William Ernest and Catherine Theresa (Smith) K.; student U. Utah, 1963-65, Santa Monica City Coll., 1941, 48-49; BA, Marylhurst Coll., 1979; MA, U. Portland, 1982; m. Carma Morrison Sellers, Sept. 16, 1961; children: Rosanne, Jeanine Nell, Melanie, Lisa June; one stepson, Michael Sellers. Air traffic contr. FAA, Salt Lake City, Albuquerque and Boise, Idaho; 1949-65, info. officer Western Region, L.A., 1965-68; pub. affairs officer L.A. Dist. C.E., U.S. Army, 1968-69, Walla Walla (Wash.), 1969-77, N. Pacific div., Portland, Oreg., 1977-79; dir. pub. rels. U. Portland, 1979-80; adj. asst. prof. comm. U. Portland, 1982-83; instr. Portland (Oreg.) C.C., 1980-87; freelance writer, 1960—. Exec. asst. L.A. Fed. Exec. Bd., 1965-67; chmn. Walla Walla County Alcoholism Adminstrv. Bd., 1974-75; vice-chmn. Walla Walla County Human Services Adminstrv. Bd., 1976-78, chmn., 1977-78. Served with USMCR, 1942-45. Decorated Air medal; William Randolph Hearst scholar, 1965. Mem. Soc. Profl. Journalists, Pub. Relations Soc. Am. (accredited), Kappa Tau Alpha. Democrat. Roman Catholic. Home and Office: 310 N Fawn Dr Otis OR 97368-9323

KING, FREDERIC, health services management executive, educator; b. N.Y.C., May 9, 1937; s. Benjamin and JEanne (Fritz) K.; m. Linda Ann IDell, Mar. 27, 1976; children from previous marriage: Coby Allen, Allison Beth, Iosa Robyn, Daniel Seth. *Mr. King is pursuing his avid interest as a master image artist in photography, jewelry design and is authoring a book. Wife Linda is an accomplished creative artisan who is on sabbatical from her first love, teaching. At Ohr Eliyahu Academy, she became a legend as a compassionate and gifted teacher. Fred and Linda are dedicated to the Jewish community and their Orthodox Jewish lifestyle. They currently share their country home with four dogs and seven cats and look forward to frequent visits from their beautiful grandchildren who reside with their very special parents, Anna and Yehuda in Jerusalem.* BBA cum laude, CUNY, 1958. Dir. adminstrn. Albert Einstein Coll. Medicine, Bronx, 1970-72; assoc. v.p. health affairs Tulane Med. Ctr., New Orleans, 1972-77; dir. fin. Mt. Sinai Med. Ctr., N.Y.C., 1977-78; v.p. fin. Cedars-Sinai Med. Ctr., L.A., 1978-82; pres. Vascular Diagnostic Svcs., Inc., Woodland Hills, Calif., 1982-84; exec. dir. South Bay Ind. Physician sMed. Group, Inc., Torrance, Calif., 1984-98; ret., 1998; assoc. adj. prof. Tulane U. Sch. Pub. Health; asst. prof. Mt. Sinai Med. Ctr.; instr. Pierce Coll., L.A. Bd. dirs. Ohr Eliyahu Acad., chmn.; bd. dirs. AMHO Pacific Region; pres. Torah Learning Ctr. Young Israel Venice. With U.S. Army, 1959-62. Mem. Healthcare Forum, Am. Hosp. Assn., PRes.'s Assn., Calif. Assn. Hosps. and Health Systems. Republican. Home: W75 N749 Tower Ave Cedarburg WI 53012-1024

KING, FREDERICK ALEXANDER, neuroscientist, educator; b. Paterson, N.J., Oct. 3, 1925; s. James Aloysius and Louise Bisset (Gallant) K.; m. Sally Wolff King; children: Alexander Karell, Elizabeth Gallant. AB, Stanford U., 1953; AM, Johns Hopkins U., 1955, PhD, 1956. Instr. psychology Johns Hopkins U., 1954-56; asst. prof. psychiatry Ohio State U., 1957-59; mem. faculty Coll. Medicine, U. Fla., 1959-78, asst., then asso. prof., then prof. neurosurgery, 1965-69, prof., chmn. dept. neurosci., 1969-78; dir./co-dir. Center Neurobiol. Scis., 1964-78; dir. Yerkes Regional Primate Rsch. Ctr., rsch. prof. neurobiology, prof. anatomy and cell biology, psychology, assoc. dean Sch. Medicine Emory U., Atlanta, 1978-94, dir. emeritus Yerkes Regional Primate Rsch. Ctr., 1994—; prof. emeritus neurosci Emory U., 1994—; prof. emeritus anatomy and cell biology Emory U. Sch. Medicine, 1996—; adj. prof. psychology Emory and Ga. Inst. Tech.; mem. adv. com. Primate Research Centers, NIH, 1969-73; mem. psychobiology adv. panel, biol. and med. scis. div. NSF, 1963-67, cons. med. and biol. scis., 1967-70; chmn. research scientist devel. rev. com. NIMH, 1969-70, 75-78, chmn. com. for coordination and communication for dirs. in biol. research tng. programs, 1972-78; sec.-treas. Fla. Anat. Bd., 1969-71; vice chmn. bd. sci. advisers Yerkes Regional Primate Research Center, 1974-78; mem. brain scis. com. NRC-Nat. Acad. Scis., 1974-78; mem. internat. sci. adv. bd. Nat. Mus. Kenya, 1983—; mem. com. for nat. survey of lab. animals NAS, 1985-88, also ILAR com. Gen. editor: Handbook of Behavioral Neurobiology, 7 vols, 1972-85; Contbr. articles to profl. jours. Served with USNR, 1943-46, 51. John Carrol Fulton scholar, 1953-55; NIH rsch. fellow, 1955-56; NIMH spl. fellow Inst. Physiology, U. Pisa (Italy) Faculty Medicine, 1961-62. Mem. Internat. Neuropsychology Soc. (sec.-treas.), Soc. Neurosci. (chmn. com. on edn., chair com. on animals in rsch. 1987, chair subcom. primates in rsch. 1983-90), Am. Psychol. Assn. (chmn. membership com. divsn. physiol. and comparative psychology, chmn. com. for animal rsch. and experimentation, bd. sci. affairs, spl. citation for leadership in sci. psychology 1984, pres. divsn. comparative and physiol. psychology 1989-90), Am. Assn. for Accreditation of Lab. Animal Care (bd. trustees 1987-90), Nat. Assn. Biomed. Rsch. (bd. dirs. 1987-89), Incurably Ill for Animal Rsch. (bd. advisors 1987-89, bd. dirs. 1989-96), Americans for Med. Progress (bd. dirs. 1990-95), NIH (adv. com. to dir. 1991-94). Home: 2681 Galahad Dr NE Atlanta GA 30345-3626 Office: Emory U Yerkes Regional Primate Rsch Ctr Atlanta GA 30322*

KING, G. ROGER, lawyer; b. Ashland, Ohio, Sept. 16, 1946. BS, Miami U., 1968; JD, Cornell U., 1971. Bar: Ohio 1971, D.C. 1972. Legis. asst. U.S. Senator Robert Taft Jr., Washington, 1971-73; profl. staff counsel Labor and Human Resources Com., U.S. Senate, Washington, 1973-74; ptnr. Jones, Day, Reavis & Pogue, Columbus, Ohio. Office: Jones Day Reavis & Pogue 1900 Huntington Ctr Columbus OH 43215-6103

KING, GARR MICHAEL, federal judge; b. Pocatello, Idaho, Jan. 28, 1936; s. Warren I. King and Geraldine E. (Hanlon) Appleby; m. Mary Jo Rieber, Feb. 2, 1957; children: Mary, Michael, Matthew, James, Margaret, John, David. Student, U. Utah, 1957-59; LLB, Lewis and Clark Coll., 1963. Bar: Oreg. 1963, U.S. Dist. Ct. Oreg. 1965, U.S. Ct. Appeals (9th cir.) 1975, U.S. Supreme Ct. 1971. Dep. dist. atty. Multnomah County Dist. Atty.'s Office, Portland, Oreg., 1963-66; assoc. Morrison, Bailey, Dunn, Carney & Miller, Portland, 1966-71; ptnr. Kennedy & King, Portland, 1971-77, Kennedy, King & McClurg, Portland, 1977-82, Kennedy, King & Zimmer, Portland, 1982-98; judge U.S. Dist. Ct. Oreg., Portland, 1998—. Active various pvt. sch. and ch. bds. Served as sgt. USMC, 1954-57. Fellow Am. Coll. Trial Lawyers (regent 1995-98), Am. Bar Found.; mem. ABA, Oreg. Bar Assn., Multnomah County Bar Assn. (pres. 1975), Jud. Conf. 9th Cir. (del.), Northwestern Coll. Law Alumni Assn. (pres.), Multnomah Athletic Club. Democrat. Roman Catholic. Avocations: tennis, reading, gardening. Office: 907 US Courthouse 1000 SW 3rd Ave Portland OR 97204

KING, GEORGE, academic administrator. Pres. Sawyer Coll. Bus., Cleveland Heights, Ohio. Office: Sawyer Coll Bus Cleveland Heights OH 44118

KING, GEORGE H., judge. AB, UCLA, 1971; JD, U. So. Calif., L.A., 1974. Judge U.S. Dist. Ct. (cen. dist.) Calif., 1995—. Office: Roybal Fed Bldg Ste 670 255 E Temple St Los Angeles CA 90012

KING, GEORGE RALEIGH, manufacturing company executive; b. Benton Harbor, Mich., May 13, 1931; s. Maurice Peter and Opal Ruth (Hart) King; m. Phyllis Stratton, Apr. 10, 1950; children: Paula King Zang, Angela King Young, Philip. Student Adrian Coll., 1950-51. Cert. purchasing profl. exec. status. With Kirsch Co., Sturgis, Mich., 1951—, data processing trainee, 1951-53, data processing mgr., 1953-59, asst. purchasing agt., 1959-62, purchasing agt., 1962-68, asst. dir. purchasing, 1968-71, dir. purchasing, 1971—. Author: Rods & Rings, 1972. Elder, 1st Presbyterian Ch., Sturgis, 1970; pres. Sturgis Civic Players, 1972. Recipient citation Boy Scouts Am., 1966, Jr. Achievement, 1967; nominated candidate for adminstr. Fed. Procurement Policy, Reagan Adminstrn., Washington, 1980. Mem. Am. Purchasing Soc. (pres. 1979-81), Nat. Assn. Purchasing Mgmt., Southwestern Purchasing Assn. Clubs: Klinger Lake Country, Exchange (pres. Sturgis 1959, dist. gov. dist and nat. clubs 1961). Masons, Elks. Home: 1804 Lakeshore Dr Apt 16 Saint Joseph MI 49085-1616

KING, GEORGEANN CAMARDA, elementary education educator; b. N.Y.C., Aug. 5, 1966; d. Leonard Thomas and Theresa (Gentile) Camarda; m. Robert Michael King, Oct. 16, 1994. BA, Rutgers U., 1988, MEd, 1990. Tchrs. asst. Bridgewater (N.J.) - Raritan Sch. dist., 1991; tchr. 3d grade Mountain Lakes (N.J.) Bd. Edn., 1991—; tchr. art Morris Plains (N.J.) Country Day Sch., 1994, 95; tutor Cmty. Families, Mountain Lakes, 1992-93. Avocations: painting, reading, cooking, travel, writing. Office: Wildwood Elem Sch Glen and Kenilworth Rds Mountain Lakes NJ 07046

KING, (LENARD) GLEN, broadcasting educator, composer; b. N.Y.C., Oct. 13, 1935; s. Lawrence Herbert and Marcea Helen (Berger) K.; m. Margaret Elizabeth Gabler, Aug. 26, 1989. BA, Calif. State U., L.A., 1960, MFA, 1964. Prodn. asst. Sta. KABC-TV, L.A., 1963-64; news asst. Sta. KTLA-TV, L.A., 1964-65; disc jockey Sta. KUTE, L.A., 1965-66, Sta. KFOX, L.A., 1966; instr. theater arts Elizabeth Seton Coll., Yonkers, N.Y., 1966-67; assoc. prof. broadcasting West L.A. Coll., Culver City, Calif., 1977-84; prof. broadcasting Los Angeles Valley Coll., Van Nuys, Calif., 1985—; founder Silver Kat Music BMI, 1985—; supr. student cable internships West L.A. Coll., Culver City, Calif., 1980-85; designer broadcasting and TV aesthetics and documentary curriculums area colls.; owner, mgr. Silver Kat Music Pub. affiliate Broadcast Music Inc.; broadcast cons. CBS News, 1991, KMNY, 1992; prodr., dir. Pub. Access TV Adelphia Cable Co., Charlottesville, 1996-98, dir. M.S. Telethon, 1996-98. Composer popular, country and gospel songs, 1976—. With USN, 1953-56, Republic of Korea. Winner internat. competition Song Writers Hall of Fame and N.Y. Music Pubs. Group, 1985; recipient 1st prize Am. Song Festival, L.A., 1976, Grand prize, 1979. Mem. BMI (affiliate), Nat. Acad. Songwriters (profl.), Nat. Music Pubs. Assn., Songwriters Assn. Am., Gospel Music Assn. (profl.), Nashville Songwriters Assn Internat. (profl.), Charlottesville Area Songwriters Assn. (founder). Avocations: music, antiques, automobiles. E-mail: glen@silverkat.com.

KING, GLYNDA BOWMAN, state legislator; b. Chattanooga, July 5, 1946; d. William Cass and Johnnie Olivan (Griffin) Bowman; m. Thomas Wayland King, Jan. 12, 1963; children: Denise Schon, Kelly Todd. Grad. high sch., Tyner, Tenn. Exec. dir. Regions 8 and 10 Mental Health, Mental Retardation and Substance Abuse Bds., spl. projects coord. Ga. Dept. Human Resources; spl. projects coord. Ga. Dept. Human Resources, Divsn. Mental Helath, Mental Retardation and Substance Abuse. Mem. Clayton County (Ga.) Drug Adv. Com., 1976—, Ga. Arts Caucus, Atlanta, 1991—, Clayton County Disabilities Early Intervention for Families and Children; bd. dirs. Clayton County Bd. Edn., 1983-89, Gov.'s Commn. on Mental Health, Mental Retardation and Substance Abuse, Atlanta, 1992—, Leadership Clayton; state rep. Ga. Gen. Assembly, Atlanta, 1991-92; mem. success by six coun. United Way, Atlanta, 1992—; hon. life mem. E.J. Swint Elem. Sch. PTA, 1979—. Recipient Founders award 16th Dist. Ga. PTA, 1985, Pub. Policy-Lay Advocacy award Mental Health Assn. of Ga., 1993. Mem. Mental Health Assn. Met. Atlanta (pres. 1992-93), Clayton County C. of C., Southlake Kiwanis. Democrat. Baptist. Home: 3263 Lake Jodeco Rd Jonesboro GA 30236-5343

KING, GUNDAR JULIAN, retired university dean; b. Riga, Latvia, Apr. 19, 1926; came to U.S., 1950, naturalized, 1954; s. Attis K. and Austra (Dale) Kenins: m. Valda K. Andersons, Sept. 18, 1954; children: John T., Marita A. Student, J.W. Goethe U., Frankfurt, Germany, 1946-48; BBA, U. Oreg., 1956; MBA, Stanford U., 1958, PhD, 1964; DSc (hon.), Riga Tech. U., 1991; D Habil. Oecon., Latvian Sci. Coun., 1992. Asst. field supr. Internat. Refugee Orgn., Frankfurt, 1948-50; br. office mfr. Williams Form Engring. Corp., Portland, Oreg., 1952-54; project mgr. Market Rsch. Assocs., Palo Alto, Calif., 1958-60; asst. prof., assoc. prof. Pacific Luth. U., 1960-66, prof., 1966—, dean Sch. Bus. Adminstrn., 1970-90; vis. prof. mgmt. U.S. Naval Postgrad. Sch., 1971-72, San Francisco State U., 1980, 1987-88; internat. econ. mem. Latvian Acad. Scis., 1990—; regent Estonian Bus. Sch., 1991-99; vis. prof. Riga Tech. U., 1993-97. Author: Economic Policies in Occupied Latvia, 1965; contbr. articles to profl. publs. Mem. Gov.'s Com. on Reorgn. Wash. State Govt., 1965-88; mem. study group on pricing U.S. Commn. Govt. Procurement, 1971-72; pres. N.W. Univs. Bus. Adminstrn. Conf., 1965-66. With AUS, 1950-52. Fulbright-Hayes scholar, Thailand, 1988, Fulbright scholar, Latvia, 1993-94. Mem. AAUP (past chpt. pres.), Am. Mktg. Assn. (past chpt. pres.), Assn. Advancement Baltic Studies (pres. 1970), Western Assn. Collegiate Schs. Bus. (pres. 1971), Latvian Acad. Scis., Alpha Kappa Psi, Beta Gamma Sigma. Home: PO Box 44401 Tacoma WA 98444-0401 Office: Pacific Lutheran U Tacoma WA 98447

KING, GWENDOLYN S., retired utility company executive, former federal official; b. East Orange, N.J.; d. Frank M. and Henryne (Walker) Stewart; m. Colbert I. King. BA cum laude, Howard U., 1962; postgrad., George Washington U.; hon. doctorate, U. Md., 1990, U. New Haven, 1992. Legis. asst. to Sen. John Heinz Washington, 1978-79; dir. Commonwealth of Pa. Office, Washington, 1979-86; dep. asst. to the pres. and dir. Office Intergovtl. Affairs The White House, Washington, 1986-88; commr. Adv. Commn. on Intergovtl. Rels.; mem. Interagency Com. Women's Bus. Enterprise; dir. The White House Task Force on P.R.; exec. v.p. Gogol & Assocs., 1988-89; commr. Social Security Adminstrn., Balt., 1989-92; sr. v.p. corp. and pub. affairs PECO Energy Corp., Phila., 1992-98; bd. dirs. Lockheed Martin, Monsanto Co., Marsh & McLennan Cos. Bd. dirs.Fox Chase Cancer Ctr., Nat. Adoption Ctr. Recipient Drum Major for Justice award So. Christian Leadership Conf., 1990, Alumni award Howard U., 1991, Black Achievement Bus. and Fin. award Ebony Mag., 1992. Office: 1506 Hamilton St NW Washington DC 20011-3858

KING, HENRY LAWRENCE, lawyer; b. N.Y.C., Apr. 29, 1928; s. H. Abraham and Henrietta (Prentky) K.; m. Barbara Hope, 1949 (dec. May 1962); children: Elizabeth King Robertson, Patricia King Cantlay, Matthew Harrison.; m. Alice Mary Sturges, Aug. 1, 1963 (div. 1978); children: Katherine Masury King Baccile, Andrew Lawrence, Eleanor Sturges; m. Margaret Gram, Feb. 14, 1981. AB, Columbia U., 1948; LLB, Yale U., 1951. Bar: N.Y. 1952, U.S. Supreme Ct., other fed. cts. 1952. With Davis Polk & Wardwell, N.Y.C., 1951—, ptnr., 1961—, mng. ptnr., chmn., 1982-96. Mng. editor Yale Law Jour., 1951. Trustee, chmn. bd. Columbia U., 1983-95, chmn. emeritus, 1995—; chmn. bd. Columbia Presbyn. adv. coun.; pres. Assn. Alumni Columbia Coll., 1966-68, Alumni Fedn. Columbia U., 1973-75; chmn. Coll. Fund, 1972-73; pres. Yale Law Sch. Assn., 1984-86, chmn., 1986-88; bd. dirs. Citizen's Com. for N.Y.C., Inc., N.Y.C. Ctr. Music and Drama, Inc., Am. Skin Assn., Fishers Island Devel. Co., Fund for Modern Cts., Vols. of Legal Svc., Inc., Episcopal Charities, Columbia-Cornell Care, Inc.; vestryman Trinity Ch. N.Y., 1991-98; coun. Mcpl. Art Soc.; trustee Chapin Sch., 1977-89, Columbia U. Press, 1978-92. Recipient Columbia Alumni medal for conspicuous service, 1968, John Jay award, 1992. Fellow Am. Coll. Trial Lawyers; mem. ABA, Coun. on Fgn. Rels., Am. Law Inst., N.Y. State Bar Assn. (pres. 1988-89), Assn. Bar City N.Y., Am. Judicature Soc., N.Y. Acad. Medicine (bd. dirs., trustee), Fishers Island Club, Century Assn., Union Club (N.Y.C.), Jupiter Island Club, Blind Brook Club, Fisher Island Yacht Club. Home: 115 E 67th St New York NY 10021-5901 also: 61 Links Rd Hobe Sound FL 33455-2318 Office: Davis Polk & Wardwell 450 Lexington Ave New York NY 10017-3911

KING, HENRY SPENCER, III, lawyer; b. Charlotte, N.C., Feb. 7, 1941; s. Henry Spencer Jr. and Janie Pauline (Jenkins) K.; m. Ellen Frost Hayne, Aug. 31, 1963; children: Cheryl King Hay, Ann Lunsford King. BA with honors, Furman U., 1963; JD cum laude, U. S.C., 1968. Bar: S.C. 1963. Atty. Butler, Means, Evins & Browne, Spartanburg, S.C., 1968-78; ptnr. King and Hray, Spartanburg, 1978-92; shareholder Leatherwood Walker Todd & Mann, P.C., Greenville & Spartanburg, 1992—; city atty. City of Spartanburg, 1987—. Lt. col. U.S. Army, 1963-65. Mem. ABA, S.C. Bar Assn., Spartanburg Bar Assn., Internat. Assn. Def. Counsel, S.C. Def. Trial Attys. (past bd. dirs.), Def. Rsch. Inst., Spartanburg County Club (bd. dirs. 1982-86), Rotary Club, Sertoma (Sertoman of Yr. 1978). E-mail: hking.@lwtmlaw.com. Home: 3 Cateswood Dr Spartanburg SC 29302-3464 Office: Leatherwood Walker et al 1451 E Main St Spartanburg SC 29307-2245

KING, INDLE GIFFORD, industrial designer, educator; b. Seattle, Oct. 23, 1934; s. Indle Frank and Phyllis (Kenney) K.; m. Rosalie Rosso, Sept. 10, 1960; children: Indle Gifford Jr., Paige Phyllis. BA, U. Wash., 1960, MA, 1968. Indsl. designer Hewlett-Packard, Palo Alto, Calif., 1961-63; mgr. indsl. design Sanborn Co., Boston, 1963-65; mgr. corp. design Fluke Corp., Everett, Wash., 1965-97; prof. indsl. design Western Wash. U., Bellingham, 1985—; pres., CEO Teaque Inc., 1998—; judge nat. and internat. competitions; cons. in field. Contbr. articles to profl. jours.; designer patents in field. Coach Mercer Island (Wash.) Boys' Soccer Assn., 1972-77; pres. Mercer Island PTA, 1973; advisor Jr. Achievement, Seattle, 1975-78. Recognized as leading one of Am.'s Top 40 Design Driven Cos., ID Jour., 1999. Mem. Idsl. Design Soc. Am. (Alcoa award 1965, v.p. Seattle chpt. 1986-88), Mercer Island Country Club. Office: 14727 NE 87th St Redmond WA 98052-6500

KING, IVAN ROBERT, astronomy educator; b. Far Rockaway, N.Y., June 25, 1927; s. Myram and Anne (Franzblau) K.; m. Alice Greene, Nov. 21, 1952 (div. 1982); children: David, Lucy, Adam, Jane. AB, Hamilton Coll., 1946; AM, Harvard U., 1947, PhD, 1952. Instr. astronomy Harvard U., 1951-52; mathematician Perkin-Elmer Corp., Norwalk, Conn., 1951-52; methods analyst U.S. Dept. Def., Washington, 1954-56; with U. Ill., 1956-64; assoc. prof. astronomy U. Calif., Berkeley, 1964-66, prof., 1966-93, chmn. astronomy dept., 1967-70, prof. emeritus, 1993—; mem. faint object camera team Hubble Space Telescope. Contbr. numerous articles to sci. jours. Served with USNR, 1952-54. Fellow AAAS (chmn. astronomy sect. 1974), NAS, Am. Acad. Arts & Scis., Am. Astron. Soc. (councillor 1963-66, chmn. div. dynamical astronomy 1972-73, pres. 1978-80), Internat. Astron. Union. Rsch. study of stellar systems. Office: U Calif Dept Astronomy Berkeley CA 94720

KING, J. B., medical device company executive, lawyer. AB, Ind. U., 1951; LLB, Mich. U., 1954. Bar: Ind. 1954, Mich. 1954. Atty., ptnr. Baker & Daniels, 1954-87; v.p., gen. counsel Eli Lilly and Co., Indpls., 1987-95, Guidant Corp., Indpls., 1995—; bd. dirs. Ind. Corp. Survey Commn., Bank One, Indpls, Indpls. Water Co.; conf. bd. Coun. Chief Legal Officers. Mem. bd. govs. Riley Meml. Assn. Fellow Ind. Bar Found.; mem. ABA, Ind. State Bar Assn., Indpls. Bar Assn., 7th Cir. Bar Assn., Nat. Tax Assn. (com. on multistate taxation), Assn. Gen. Counsel, Ind. Legal Found. (bd. dirs.), Ind. Fiscal Policy Inst. (bd. govs.), Ind. Corp.Survey Commn. Home: 602 Plum Nearly Ln Apt B Wilmington NC 28403-8480 Office: Guidant Corp PO Box 44906 Indianapolis IN 46244-0906*

KING, J. BRADLEY, lawyer; b. Noblesville, Ind., Sept. 2, 1957; s. Charles Joseph and Marina (Davis) K. BA in History & Polit. Sci. with honors, Ind. U., 1978; JD, Coll. of William and Mary, 1981. Bar: Calif. 1981, Ind. 1985. Pvt. practice cons. to local govts. Indpls., 1982-85; staff atty. Legislative Svcs. Agy., State of Ind., Indpls., 1985-90; asst. corp. counsel, chief lobbyist at gen. assembly City of Indpls., 1990-92; gen. counsel State of Ind. Election Commn., Indpls., 1992—; del. Ind. State Conv., 1998. Sr. warden, vestryman Episcopal Ch. of All Sts., Indpls., 1989-91, 93-96; asst. state party rules Ind. Rep. State Com., Indpls., 1997, chair Ind. presdl. electors meeting, 1996. Named Election Adminstr. of Yr.; Ballot Access News, 1997; named to Order of Ky. Cols. Phi Beta Kappa, 1977. Avocations: singing, walking. Office: Ind Election Commn 302 W Washington St Ste E-204 Indianapolis IN 46204-2767

KING, JACK A., lawyer; b. Lafayette, Ind., July 29, 1936; s. Noah C. and Mabel E. (Pierce) K.; m. Mary S. King, Dec. 10, 1960; children: Jeffrey A., Janice D., Julie D. BS in Fin., Ind. U., 1958, JD, 1961. Bar: Ind. 1961. Ptnr. Ball, Eggleston, King & Bumbleburg, Lafayette, 1961-70; judge Superior Ct. 2 of Tippecanoe County, Ind., 1970-78; v.p., assoc. gen. counsel Superior Ct. 2 of Tippecanoe County, 1979, v.p., gen. counsel, asst. sec., 1980-85; v.p., counsel Sentry Ctr. West, 1981-85; asst. gen. counsel Sentry Corp., 1979-85; v.p., gen. counsel, asst. sec. Gt. S.W. Fire Ins. Co., 1980-85, Gt. S.W. Surplus Lines Ins. Co., 1981-85; v.p., gen. counsel Dairyland County Mut. Ins. Co. Tex., 1980-85; v.p. legal, asst. sec. Scottsdale Ins. Co., 1985-95; asst. sec. Nat. Casualty Co., 1985-95; v.p. legal, asst. sec. Scottsdale Indemnity Co., 1992-95; sr. v.p., gen. coun. TIG Excess & Surplus Lines, Inc., 1995-96; v.p. Ariz. Ins. Info. Assn., 1988-96; exec. dir. Ariz. Ins. Guaranty Funds, 1998—; bd. dirs. Countrywide Ins. Co.; cons., mediator and arbitrator, 1996-97; exec. com. Ariz. Joint Underwriting Plan, 1980-81; mem. Ariz. Property & Casualty Ins. Commn., 1985-86, vice-chmn., 1986; mem. Ariz. Study Commn. on Ins., 1986-87, Ariz. Task Force on Ct. Orgn. and Adminstrn., 1988-89; adv. com. Ariz. Ho. Rep. Majority Leaders, 1989, Ariz. Dept. Ins. Fraud Unit, 1997-97. Contbr. to The Law of Competitive Business Practices, 2d edit. Bd. dirs. Scottsdale Art Ctr. Assn., 1981-84. Mem. ABA, Ind. Bar Assn., Maricopa County Bar Assn. Office: 3443 N Central Ave Ste 1000 Phoenix AZ 85012-2209

KING, JACK HOWELL, transportation engineering executive; b. Jackson, Tenn., Mar. 1, 1952; s. Thomas Thaddeus and Lula Janette (Upchurch) K.; m. Nancy Lynne Herring, Apr. 1, 1989; 1 child, Melissa Lynne. BCE, U. Tenn., 1975, MCE, 1976. Registered profl. engr., Tenn., Fla. City traffic engr. City Cleve., Tenn., 1976-78; v.p. Cen. Distbrs., Inc., Jackson, Tenn., 1977-91; traffic studies engr. City of Tampa, Fla., 1978-79, asst. traffic engr., 1979-81, city traffic engr., 1981-84; dept. head hwy. design Watson and Co., Tampa, 1984-85; dept. head transp. engr. Greenhorne and O'Mara, Inc., Tampa, 1985-89; dist. roadway design engr. Fla. Dept. Transp., Tampa, 1990-93, dist. project mgmt. adminstr., 1993-98, dir. of prodn., 1998—. Mem. Inst. Transp. Engrs. (chmn. awards com. Fla. sect. 1988-90, dir. 1982-84). Methodist. Avocations: golf, tennis, football, world travel. Home: 4615 W Lowell Ave Tampa FL 33629-7628 Office: Fla Dept Transp 11201 Mckinley Dr N Tampa FL 33612-6456

KING, JAMES ANDREW, protective services educator and administrator; b. Corinth, Miss., Apr. 26, 1948; s. Doyal Andrew and Martha Lee (Ridings) K.; m. Hannelore Martha Wanner, Feb. 5, 1970; 1 child, Karl Joseph. B Pub. Adminstrn., Nat. U., San Diego, 1982, M Forensic Sci., 1983; PhD in Criminology, U. Ky., 1986. Cert. criminologist, protection specialist. Commd. U.S. Army, 1966, criminal investigator, instr., 1966-76, ret., 1976; commd. USN, 1977, criminal investigator, instr., 1977-91, ret., 1991; prof. criminal justice Nat. U., 1983-88; protective svc. specialist NATO, 1989-91; exec. dir. Internat. Assn. Personal Protection Agts., Brighton, Tenn., 1991—; cons. various nat. and internat. orgns., 1989—. Author: Providing Protective Services, 1989. Decorated Bronze Star (2), Purple Heart (2), Air medal, Cross Gallantry, Govt. Vietnam; named Ky. Col., Gov. State Ky., 1976, Knight Chevalier, Police Hall Fame, 1994, Legion Honor award, 1994. Mem. Spl. Forces Assn., Lambda Alpha Epsilon. Office: IAPPA 458 W Kenwood Brighton TN 38011-6294

KING, JAMES CECIL, Medievalist, educator; b. Uniontown, Pa., Sept. 14, 1924; s. Joseph Herbert and Eliza Ann (Kelley) K.; m. Diana Hanbury, Sept. 5, 1952 (div. Apr. 1958); children—Christopher Hanbury, Sheila Anne. B.A., George Washington U., 1949, M.A., 1950, Ph.D., 1954. Master for French, German and Latin St. Albans Sch. for Boys, Washington, 1952-55; asst. prof. German George Washington U., 1955-60, assoc. prof., 1960-65, prof., 1965-90, prof. emeritus, 1990—; researcher Langs.-of-the-World Archives, 1960-61. Editor (with Petrus W. Tax) of series Die Werke Notkers des Deutschen, 1972—. Served with U.S. Army, 1943-46. German Acad. Exchange Service grantee, 1963. Mem. Linguistic Soc. Am., Medieval Acad. Am., Am. Assn. Tchrs. German, MLA, Am. Goethe Soc., Soc. Germanic Philology, AAUP, Phi Beta Kappa. Anglican. Home: 9296 Bailey Ln Fairfax VA 22031-1930

KING, JAMES EDWARD, museum director; b. Escanaba, Mich., July 23, 1940; s. G. Willard and Grace (Magee) K.; m. Frances Bartos, Jan. 15, 1973; 1 child, Scott E. BS, Alma Coll., 1962; MS, U. N.Mex., 1964; PhD, U. Ariz., 1972. Lab asst. in biology Alma Coll., Mich., 1960-62; rsch. asst. dept. biology U. N.Mex., Albuquerque, 1962-64; teaching asst. dept. botany and plant pathology Mich. State U., East Lansing, 1964-66; plant industry inspector Mich. Dept. Agriculture, Lansing, 1966-68; rsch. asst. dept. geochronology U. Ariz., Tucson, 1968-71, rsch. assoc. dept. geoscis., 1971-72; assoc. curator paleobotany Ill. State Mus., Springfield, 1972-78, head sci. sects. and full curator, 1978-85, asst. dir. for sci., 1985-87; adj. assoc. prof. dept. geology U. Ill., Urbana, 1979-88; dir. Carnegie Mus. Natural History, Pitts., 1987-96, Cleve. Mus. Natural History, 1996—; adj. prof. biology Sangamon State U., Springfield, Ill., 1983-87; adj. rsch. scientist Hunt Inst. Bot. Documentation, Carnegie Mellon U., Pitts., 1988—; adj. prof. dept. geology and planetary sci., U. Pitts., 1988-96; vis. scientist in residence Alma (Mich.) Coll., 1985. Author sci. papers on topics related to geology and paleobotany; mem. editorial bd. Jour. Archaeol. Sci., 1980-87. Bd. dirs. Western Pa. Conservancy, 1996-97, Allegheny Land Trust, 1995-96; trustee Chagrin River Watershed Ptnrs., 1997—; mem. exec. com. Univ. Cir., Inc., 1996—. Fellow Ill. State Acad. Sci. (pres. 1981-82); mem. Am. Assn. Mus. (bd. dirs. 1994-97), Am. Quaternary Assn., (treas., exec. com. 1976-84), Am. Assn. Stratigraphic Palynologists, Assn. Sci. Mus. Dirs. (v.p. 1992-93, pres. 1993-96), Assn. Systematics Collections (v.p. 1989-91, pres. 1991-93), Sigma Xi (pres. Springfield chpt. 1985-86). Office: Cleve Mus Natural History 1 Wade Oval University Cir Cleveland OH 44106-1767

KING, JAMES LAWRENCE, federal judge; b. Miami, Fla., Dec. 20, 1927; s. James Lawrence and Viola (Clodfelter) K.; m. Mary Frances Kapa, June 1, 1961; children—Lawrence Daniel, Kathryn Ann, Karen Ann, Mary Virginia. BA in Edn., U. Fla., 1949, JD, 1953; LHD (hon.), St. Thomas U., 1992. Bar: Fla. 1953. Assoc. Sibley & Davis, Miami, Fla., 1953-57; ptnr. Sibley Giblin King & Levenson, Miami, 1957-64; judge 11th Jud. Cir. Dade County, Miami, 1964-70; temp. assoc. justice Supreme Ct. Fla., 1965; temp. assoc. judge Fla. Ct. Appeals (2d, 3d and 4th dist.), 1965-68; judge U.S. Dist. Ct. (so. dist.) Fla., Miami, 1970-84, chief judge, 1984-91, sr. judge, 1991—; temp. judge U.S. Ct. Appeals 5th cir., 1977-78; mem. Jud. Conf. U.S., 1984-87, mem. adv. commn. jud. activities, 1973-76, mem. joint commn. code jud. conduct, 1974-76, mem. commn. to consider stds. for admission to practice in fed. cts., 1976-79, chmn. implementation com. for admission attys. to fed. practice, 1979-85, mem. com. bankruptcy legis., 1977-78; mem. Jud. Conf. U.S., 1984-87; mem. Jud. Coun. 11th Cir., 1989-92; pres. 5th cir. U.S. Dist. Judges Assn., 1977-78; chief judge U.S. Dist. Ct. C.Z., 1977-78; long range planning commn. Fed. Judiciary, 1991-95. Mem. state exec. council U. Fla., 1956-59; mem. Bd. Control Fla. Governing State Univs. and Colls., 1964. Served to 1st lt. USAF, 1953-55. Recipient Outstanding Alumnus award U. Fla. Law Rev., 1980. Mem. Fla. Bar Assn. (pres. jr. bar 1963-64, bd. govs. 1958-63, Merit award young lawyer sect. 1967), ABA, Am. Law Inst., Inst. Jud. Adminstrn., Fla. Blue Key, Pi Kappa Tau, Phi Delta Phi. Democrat. Home: 11950 SW 67th Ct Miami FL 33156-4756 Office: James King Fed Justice Bldg 99 NE 4th St Rm 1127 Miami FL 33132-2139*

KING, JAMES NEDWED, construction company executive, lawyer; b. Chgo., July 9, 1947; s. Ralph C. and Marie (Nedwed) K.; m. Ellen Josephine Carpenter, Jan. 29, 1977; children: Cynthia Marie, Michelle Ellen. BBA, U. Notre Dame, 1969; JD, U. N.Mex., 1972. Bar: N.Mex. 1972. Pres. Bradbury & Stamm Constrn. Co., Albuquerque, 1972—; bd. dirs. Associated Gen. Constructors; dir. Albuquerque Econ. Devel. Corp. Mem. N.Mex. Amigos. Home: 13731 Apache Plume Pl NE Albuquerque NM 87111 Office: Bradbury & Stamm Constrn Co PO Box 10850 Albuquerque NM 87184-0850

KING, JANE CUDLIP COBLENTZ, volunteer educator; b. Iron Mountain, Mich., May 4, 1922; d. William Stacey and Mary Elva (Martin) Cudlip; m. George Samuel Coblentz, June 8, 1942 (dec. June 1989); children: Bruce Harper, Keith George, Nancy Allison Coblentz Patch; m. James E. King, August 23, 1991 (dec. Jan. 1994). BA, Mills Coll., 1942. Mem. Sch. Resource and Career Guidance Vols., Inc., Atherton, Calif., 1965-69, pres., CEO, 1969—; part-time exec. asst. to dean of admissions Mills Coll., 1994—. Proofreader, contbr., campus liaison Mills Coll. Quarterly mag. Life gov. Royal Children's Hosp., Melbourne, Australia, 1963—; pres. United Menlo Park (Calif.) Homeowner's Assn., 1994—; nat. pres. Mills Coll. Alumnae Assn., 1969-73, bd. trustees, 1975-83; bd. govs. Mills Coll. Alumnae Assn., 1966-73, 75-83, 98—. Named Vol. of Yr., Sequoia Union H.S. Dist., 1988, Disting. Woman Mid-Peninsula (forerunner San Mateo County Women's Hall of Fame), 1975; recipient Golden Acorn award for Outstanding Svc., Menlo Park C. of C., 1991. Mem. AAUW (Menlo-Atherton br. pres. 1994-96, v.p. programs 1996-97, editor Directory and Acorn, 1994—), Atherlons, Palo Alto (Calif.) Area Mills Coll. Club (pres. 1986), Phi Beta Kappa. Episcopalian. Avocations: reading, gardening. Office: Menlo-Atherton HS Resource-Career Guid Vols 555 Middlefield Rd Atherton CA 94027-3400

KING, JANE LOUISE, artist; b. South Bend, Ind., Aug. 9, 1951; d. Bill and Anne Luciel (Hopkins) Berta; m. Gerald William King Jr., July 7, 1973; children: Kelly Anne, Dinah Jolene. Student, Ind. U., South Bend, 1969-70, Ind. U., 1970-71; BFA, Ohio State U., 1973. Ind. artist Colo., 1974—; instr. Sangre de Cristo Art Ctr., Pueblo, Colo., 1982, Art Studio, Longmont, Colo., 1989. Exhibited oil and pastel paintings in numerous group shows including 5th Ann. Internat. Exhibit Kans. Pastel Soc., 10th and 22nd Ann. Pastel Soc. Am., N.Y., Colo. State Fairs, Poudre Valley Art League; prin. works represented in numerous pvt. collections; contbr. poems to At Days End, 1994. Leader 4-H Club, Longmont, 1986—; sec. Longmont Artists Guild Gallery, 1988-89, bd. dirs., 1989; supt. 1st Bapt. Ch., Longmont, 1990-91. Mem. Colo. Artists Assn. (area 1 rep. 1994), Longmont Artists Guild (Grumbacher award 1992), Longmont Arts Coun., Knickerbocker Artists N.Y., Audubon Artists N.Y. Republican. Avocations: gardening, skiing, horseback riding, music, reading. Home: 1508 Kempton Ct Longmont CO 80501-6716

KING, JANET CARLSON, nutrition educator, researcher; b. Red Oak, Iowa, Oct. 3, 1941; d. Paul Emil and Norma Carolina (Anderson) Carlson; m. Charles Talmadge King, Dec. 25, 1967; children: Matthew, Samuel. BS, Iowa State U., 1963; PhD, U. Calif., Berkeley, 1972. Dietitian Fitzsimmons Gen. Hosp., Denver, 1964-67; NIH postdoctoral fellow dept. nutrition sci. U. Calif., Berkeley, 1972-73, asst. prof. nutrition dept. nutrition sci., 1973-78, assoc. prof. nutrition dept. nutrition sci., 1978-83, prof. nutrition dept. nutrition sci., 1983—, chair dept. nutrition sci., 1988-94; dir. USDA Western Human Nutrition Rsch.Ctr., San Francisco, 1995—; Frances E. Fischer Meml. nutrition lectr. Am. Dietetic Assn. Found., 1985, Lotte Arnrich Nutrition lectr. Iowa State U., 1985; Massee lectr. N.D., 1991, Lydia J. Roberts lectr. U. Chgo., 1995, Virginia A. Beal lectr. U. Mass., 1998; vis. prof. U. Calif., Davis, 1998—. Contbr. articles to Jour. Am. Diet. Assn., Am. Jour. Clin. Nutrition, Jour. Nutrition, Nutrition Rsch., Obstetrics and Gynecology, Brit. Jour. Obstetrics and Gynaecology. Recipient Lederle Labs. award in human nutrition Am. Inst. Nutrition, 1989, Internat. award in human nutrition, 1996. Mem. AAAS, Nat. Acad. Scis. Inst. Medicine, Am. Dietetic Assn., Am. Inst. Nutrition, Am. Soc. Clin. Nutrition. Office: USDA Western Human Nutrition Rsch Ctr Univ Calif Davis CA 95616

KING, JANET FELLAND, family nurse practitioner; b. Ann Arbor, Mich., May 5, 1947; d. Robert Marcy and Marjorie Marie (Sherman) Felland; m. William Curtis Runyon, May 20, 1967 (div. May 8, 1972); m. Robert Allen King, Oct. 26, 1974; 1 child, Stephen Tremain King. Student, U. Mich., 1965-67, Earlham Coll., 1968-69; BSN, Ball State U., 1971; MNSc, U. Ark., 1976. RN, Idaho. Med. surg. nurse McCullough-Hyde Meml. Hosp., Oxford, Ohio, 1971-72; migrant health nurse Colo. Dept. Health, Lamar, 1972-74; pub. health nurse City Health Dept., Little Rock, 1974-75; family nurse practitioner Idaho Migrant Coun., Burley, 1976-81; pub. health nurse South Ctrl. Dist. Health, Burley, 1981-82; family nurse practitioner Family Health Svcs., Burley, 1982—; treas. Mini Cassia Child Protection Team, Burley, 1982—; mem. Idaho Health Profl. Loan Repayment Bd., Pocatello, 1992—. Vol., nurse and deacon Diocese of Honduras, Roatan, 1990; archdeacon Diocese of Idaho, 1990—, mem. standing com., 1997—; trustee Episcopal Camp & Conf. Bd., 1991—; hospice vol., 1994—. Named Woman of Progress, Bus. and Profl. Women, 1981-82; recipient Outstanding Clinician Achievement award N.W. Primary Care Assn., 1992. Mem. Idaho Nurses Assn. (regional rep. 1982-84), Sigma Theta Tau. Episcopalian. Avocations: cross country skiing, hiking. Home: 678 E 400 N Rupert ID 83350-9460 Office: Family Health Svcs 2311 Park Ave Ste 11 Burley ID 83318-2170

KING, JOHN CHARLES PETER, newspaper editor; b. Vancouver, B.C., Can., Dec. 13, 1949; s. Charles Frederick Michael and Pauline Ida (Trueb) K.; m. Jennifer Winsor; children: Sheila, James. B.A., York U., 1973. Mem. staff The Globe and Mail Ltd., Toronto, Can., 1970—, night city editor, 1973-75; bur. chief Ottawa, Can., 1975-78; nat. editor Toronto, 1978-81; bur. chief Washington, 1981-84; assoc. editor Report on Bus., Toronto, 1984-87, exec. editor, 1987-93; dep. mng. editor The Globe and Mail, 1993-99, prodn. mgr., 1999—. Spanish lang. fellow Nat. Press Found., 1987; Thomson scholar, 1987. Office: 164 Pearson Ave, Toronto, ON Canada M6R 1G5

KING, JOHN ETHELBERT, JR., education educator, former academic administrator; b. Oklahoma City, July 29, 1913; s. John Ethelbert and Iosa (Koontz) K.; m. Glennie Beanland, Dec. 25, 1936; children: Wynetka Ann King Reynolds, Rebecca Ferriss King Stevens. BA, N. Tex. State U., 1932; MS, U. Ark., 1937; PhD, Cornell U., 1941; LLD (hon.), Coll. of Ozarks, 1965; LHD (hon.), No. Mich. U., 1966, U. S.C., 1989. Latin tchr., coach Frisco (Tex.) Pub. High Sch., 1933-35; missionary to Native Ams. Presbyn. Ch. U.S.A., Okla., Ariz., 1938-43; asst. prof. N.Y. State Coll. Agr., Cornell U., Ithaca, 1945-47; acad. dean, provost, prof. U. Minn., Duluth, 1947-53; pres., prof. Emporia (Kans.) U., 1953-66; prof., pres. U. Wyo., Laramie, 1966-67; prof., chmn. dept. So. Ill. U., Carbondale, 1967-83; Disting. vis. prof., interim dean U. S.C., Columbia, 1984-90; ednl. adviser Civilian Conservation Corps, U.S. Forest Svc., Ozone, Ark., 1935-37; mentor Assn. Governing Bds. Univs. and Coll., Washington, 1977-90. Editor: Work and the College Student, 1967, Money, Marbles and Chalk, 1978. Life trustee U. Ozarks, Clarksville, Ark., 1965—. Officer USN, 1943-45, PTO. Recipient Disting. Alumnus award N. Tex. U., Denton, 1965, U. Ark., Fayetteville, 1983. Mem. NEA (life), Am. Assn. Colls. Tchr. Edn. (pres. 1966-67), Rotary, Blue Key, Omicron Delta Kappa, Lambda Chi Alpha, Sphinx Club, Phi Delta Kappa. Democrat. Avocations: native Am. studies, western U.S. history. Office: U SC Coll Edn Columbia SC 29208

KING, JOHN JOSEPH, manufacturing company executive; b. Toledo, Jan. 12, 1924; s. Walter and Frances (Gwozd) Kawecka; m. Joy G. Mohler, Jan. 28, 1950; children: Catherine M., Carolyn S., David J., Michael R., Mark A.R. BSME magna cum laude, U. Toledo, 1957, MS in Indsl. Engring., 1961. Registered profl. engr., Ohio. Draftsman, Tecumseh Products Co., 1941-42; die designer Bingham Stamping Co., 1942-46; tool designer Spicer Mfg. Co., 1946-47; product designer Am. Floor Surfacing Co., 1947-50; founder, mgr. engr. Kent Industries, 1950-52; mech. engr. Owens Ill. Inc., Toledo, 1953-63; mgr. rsch. and devel. Permaglass Inc., Genoa, Ohio, 1963-69; founder, pres. Ashur Inc., Rossford, Ohio, 1969—, also chmn. bd. dirs. Patentee in field. Mem. Am. Ceramic Soc., Soc. Mfg. Engrs., Phi Kappa Phi, Tau Beta Pi. Republican. Roman Catholic. Clubs: Devils Lake Yacht.

Lodges: KC, Eagles. Home: 1111 W Elm Tree Rd Rossford OH 43460-1338 Office: Ashur Inc 28663 Glenwood Rd Perrysburg OH 43551-3011

KING, JOHN LANE, retired lawyer; b. Bellefontaine, Ohio, Oct. 24, 1924; s. John D. and Mabel L. (Nipken) K.; m. Eileen R. Hickey, Oct. 28, 1950; children: Sara K. Decarlo, John Lane, Mary L. King Garland, Anne E. BS., Ohio State U., 1947; J.D., U. Mich., 1950. Bar: Mich. 1951, Ohio 1950. Asst. atty. gen. State of Ohio, Columbus, State of Ohio, 1950; mem. staff Office Regional Counsel, IRS, Detroit, 1950-53; mem. Berry Moorman, B.C., Detroit, 1953-97; ret., 1997. Councilman, City of Grosse Pointe (Mich.), 1967-71, mayor, 1971-79; bd. dirs. Sacred Heart Rehab. Ctr., Adult Well-Being Svcs.; trustee Herbert Pointing Found., Clarence and Grace Chamberlin Found., Bon SEcours Hosp. Found. Mem. ABA, Mich. Bar Assn., Detroit Athletic Club, Detroit Country Club, Cardinal Club, Cooley Club, Sr. Men's Club Grosse Pointe, Phi Alpha Delta. Home: 15 Wellington Pl Grosse Pointe MI 48230-1919

KING, JOHN QUILL TAYLOR, science center administrator, college administrator emeritus; b. Memphis, Sept. 25, 1921; s. John Q. Taylor and Alice (Woodson) Johnson; m. Marcet Hines, June 28, 1942 (dec. Mar. 1995); children: John Q. Taylor, Clinton Allen, Marjon Alicia, Stuart Hines. BA, Fisk U., 1941, LHD (hon.), 1980; grad., Landig Coll. Mortuary Sci., 1942; BS, Huston-Tillotson Coll., 1947, DSc (hon.), 1988; MS, DePaul U., 1950; PhD, U. Tex., 1957; LLD (hon.), Southwestern U., 1970, St. Edward's U., 1976; LHD (hon.), Austin Coll., 1978. Mortician King-Tears Mortuary, Inc., Austin, Tex., 1946-84; pres. King-Tears Mortuary, Inc., Austin, 1984—; with Huston-Tillotson Coll., Austin, 1947—, prof. math., 1952-65, dean, 1960-65, pres., 1965-87, chancellor, pres., 1987-88, chancellor and pres. emeritus, 1988—, dir., chair Ctr. Advancement Sci., Engring. and Tech., 1988—; mem. exec. council Ind. Colls. and Univs. Tex., 1965-82; vis. scientist Tex. Acad. Sci., 1960-67; mem. coop. writing com. Pitman Pub. Corp., 1956, 58, 60, 62; adv. dir. Chase Bank of Tex., Austin. Author: (with wife) The Story of Twenty-Three Famous Negro Americans, 1967, Famous Black Americans, 1975; booklet Mary McLeod Bethune: A Woman of Vision; contbr. numerous articles to religious and profl. jours. Div. officer Boy Scouts Am., 1956-60, 78—; peace edn. com. Am. Friends Service Com., 1959-66; mem. Austin com. USO, 1960-72, Austin-Bergstrom AFB Community Council; mem. gen. bd. edn. United Meth. Ch., 1960-72, 88—; mem. Tex. Conf. Chs., 1963-76; exec. com. South Central Jurisdictional Bd. Christian Social Concerns, 1968-72; pres. Gen. Council on Ministries, 1972-80; del. Meth. Gen. and Jurisdictional Confs., 1956, 60, 64, 66, 67, 68, 70, 72, 76, 80, 84, 88; chmn. Austin-Travis County Community Relations Council; bd. dirs. Wesley Found., U. Tex., 1953-69, Texas So. U., 1960-69, Tex. Conf. Chs., 1963-78, Child and Family Service, 1964-70, Tex. Mental Health Assn., 1955-67, Austin chpt. NCCJ, Tex. Meth. Student Movement, 1960-70, Community Council of Austin and Travis County, 1966-72, Eden Home for the Aged, 1967-74, Travis County unit Am. Cancer Soc., 1963-69, United Fund of Austin and Travis County, 1965-70; trustee Austin Coll., 1979—; mem. Tex. Statewide Health Coordinating Council, 1978-80; mem. Austin CSC, 1975-81, chmn., 1978-81; mem. Gov.'s Com. Aging, 1971-78; adv. bd. Big Bros. of Austin; adv. com. Perkins Sch. Theology, So. Meth. U., Regional Med. Program Tex.; bd. dirs. Amistad Research Ctr., 1972-88, New Life Inst., Inc., 1993; trustee Fisk U., 1965-77; mem. adv. com. Command and Gen. Staff Coll., 1977-80, chmn., 1980; mem. Centennial Commn., U. Tex., Austin; trustee, sec. Found. for Ins. Regulatory Studies in Tex., 1992; presdl. appointee Tex. Funeral Svc. Commn., 1997—; pres. bd. dirs. Heritage Intervention Programs, Inc. Capt. AUS, 1942-46, maj. gen. AUS (ret.), lt. gen. Tex. State Guard. Recipient Carl Bredt award U. Tex. Coll. Edn., 1970, Disting. Svc. award Tex. Luth. Coll., 1976, Martin Luther King Humanitarian award, 1983, Roy Wilkins Meritorious award NAACP, 1982, Arthur B. De Witty award Austin br. NAACP, 1985, Citizen of Yr. award Omega Psi Phi, 1987, Mil./Edn. award Nat. Assn. Negro Bus. and Profl. Women's Clubs, Inc., 1989, Whitney M. Young, Jr. award Austin Area Urban League, 1990, Disting. Alumnus award Ex-students' Assn. U. Tex. at Austin, 1990, Philanthropist of Yr. award Nat. Soc. Fund Raising Execs., Greater Austin chpt., 1991, Man of Yr. award Ind. Funeral Dirs. Tex., 1994, George Washington Honor medal Freedoms Found. at Valley Forge, 1994. Mem. Am. Statis. Assn., Nat. Assn. for Industry-Edn. Cooperation (bd. dirs. 1980—), Nat. Inst. Sci., Philos. Soc. Tex., Austin C. of C. (v.p., bd. dirs. 1966-69, vice chmn. 1968-69, Minority Adv. of Yr. award 1989), Austin Coun. Fgn. Affairs (trustee), Masons (33 degree), Shriners, Kiwanis, Phi Beta Kappa, Sigma Pi Phi, Delta Pi Epsilon, Epsilon Nu Delta, Alpha Phi Alpha (Frederick D. Patterson award 1988, Legacy award 1997, Hall of Fame 1997), Phi Delta Kappa, Alpha Kappa Mu. United Methodist.

KING, JOSEPH, JR., government administrator, educator; b. Charleston, W.Va., June 8, 1950; s. Joseph and Jessie Ree (May) K.; m. Linda Streeter, Sept. 4, 1986. BA, Ohio State U., 1972; MS, Xavier U., 1975; EdD, U. Cin., 1982; diploma, U.S. Army War Coll., 1999. Investigator U.S. EEOC, Cin., 1976-79; tng. officer U.S. EEOC, Washington, 1979-82; EEO advisor U.S. Army, Washington, 1982-84; EEO officer U.S. Army, Giessen, Germany, 1984-86, Nurenburg, Germany, 1986-89; dir. EEO U.S. Army, St. Louis, 1989—; dir. The King Group, St. Louis, 1989—; prof. Boston U., 1984-89, Webster U., 1989—; cons. in field. Author: Discretionary Equality, 1982. Unit commr. Boy Scouts Am., St. Louis, 1990; congrl. intern. Congrl. Black Caucus, Washington, 1980. Sgt. USAF, 1979-82. Mem. ASTD, Am. Mgmt. Assn., Soc. Human Resource Mgmt., Soc. for Profls. in Dispute Resolution. Independent. Avocations: jogging, fitness, martial arts. Home: 4520 Chouteau Ave Saint Louis MO 63110-1518 Office: USAR Personnel Command 9700 Page Ave Saint Louis MO 63132-1547

KING, JOSEPH BERTRAM, architect; b. Greenville, S.C., Sept. 14, 1924; s. Joseph A. and Bertram (Kerns) K.; m. Julia Nelson Hipps, Aug. 2, 1945; children: Allen, David, Thomas. Student, Memphis State Coll., 1943; B in Arch. Engring., N.C. State U., 1949. Prin. J. Bertram King, Asheville, N.C., 1952-94; Chmn. Planning and Zoning Commn., Asheville, 1966—; vice chmn. Met. Planning Bd., 1966-74. Prin. works include Humanities, Social Sci., Art and Mgmt. bldgs., residence hall, student center, U. N.C.-Asheville, occupational edn. bldg, Asheville High Sch., Bank of Asheville, Madison County High Sch, City-County Central Library Bldg, Reynolds High Sch, Sealtest Dairies. Bd. dirs. United Fund; Bd. dirs. N.C. Design Found., mem., 1983-87. Served as pilot USAAF, 1942-45, ETO. Decorated Air medal with 2 oak leaf clusters.; Recipient various archtl. honor awards. Fellow A.I.A. (pres. N.C. chpt. 1973); mem. N.C. Bd. Architecture (past pres.), Asheville C. of C. (past pres. 1972), Tau Beta Pi, Sigma Pi Alpha, Phi Kappa Phi. Home: 222 Country Club Rd Asheville NC 28804-2608

KING, JOSHUA ADAM, plastic surgeon; b. Englewood, N.J., Feb. 6, 1963. BS, Union Coll., 1985; MD, Albandy Med. Coll., 1987. Plastic surgeon Albany Plastic & Reconstructive Surgery, N.Y., 1995—; asst. clin. prof. Albany Med. Coll., N.Y., 1995—. Office: Albany Plastic & Reconstructive Surg Ctr 4 Executive Park Dr Albany NY 12203

KING, JOY RAINEY, poet, retired medical secretary; b. Memphis, Aug. 5, 1939; d. Roy Henry and Margaret (Irvin) Rainey; m. Guy Robert King, Dec. 24, 1956; children: William Lonnie, Cheryl King Ramsey. Grad., Whitehaven H.S., Memphis, 1957. Sec. Gen. Telephone Co., Sumter, S.C., 1957-59; med. sec. L.H. Brisco, MD, Tupelo, Miss., 1963-69, James Ballard, MD, Tupelo, 1969-73; with First Nat. Bank of Southaven, Miss., 1973-79. Author: From the Gazebo; contbr. poetry to Best Poems of 1995, Best Poems of 1996, Upsouth mag., Parnassus of World Poets, Sparrow Internat., Amber, others; poetry pub. in China, N.S., Croatia, India, Italy, Finland and Belgium; poem featured in Baseball Hall of Fame. Recipient Editor's Choice award, 1993, 94, Nat. Library of Poetry award, 1995, 96, hon. mention Longfellow Poetry Awards, President's recognition lit. excellence Nat. Authors Registry, 1999, Pres. Recognition of Lit. Excellence, Natl. Author's Registry, 1999, Poet of Month award. Mem. Internat. Soc. Poets, The Poets Guild, Internat. Poetry Hall of Fame, So. Ill. Writers Guild (sec. 1996-98). Baptist.

KING, KAREN KAY, petroleum company executive; b. May 1, 1942. B in Liberal Studies, U. Okla., 1995, postgrad. Supply logistics aide Phillips Petroleum Co., Bartlesville, Okla., 1986—. E-mail: kkking@ppco.com.

KING, KAY SUE, investment company executive; b. Indpls., Sept. 14, 1948; d. George W. and Nadine M. K.; 1 child, Christopher G. Student, U. Ariz., 1966-70; BS in Edn., Ind. U., 1971; MA in Speech Communication, U. Hawaii, 1974. Tchr. Indpls. High Schs., 1971-1973; sec., treas. G. W. King Co., Indpls., 1974—; domestic sales mgr. Regal Travel, Indpls., 1975-90; pres., bd. dirs. K.S. King, Inc., Indpls., 1977—; mng. ptnr. K.S. King Co., Indpls., 1982—. Mem. pub. rels. com. Indpls. Zoolog. Xoc., 1976-85; vol. Indpls Humane Soc., 1966—, Indpls. Aid to Zoo Horse Show, 1974-78, Save the Ducks campaign, Indpls., 1978, Pan Am. Games Olympic Sports Com., Indpls., 1981-82; tchr. Sunday sch. Meridian St. Methodist Ch., Indpls., 1988-90. Elected Festival Princess 500 Festival Assn., Indpls., 1968. Mem. Internat. Assn. Bus. Communicators, Internat. Wildlife Fedn., Indpls. Zool. Soc. (charter), Indpls. Pub. Libr., Indpls. Children's Mus., Indpls. Ski Club, U. Ariz. Alumni Assn., Ind. Univ. Alumni Assn., Channel 20, Riviera Club, Lilly Pool, Meridian Hills Country Club, Delta Delta Delta. Avocations: swimming, reading, skiing, horseback riding, animals, children. Home: 702 Holliday Ln Indianapolis IN 46260-3589 Office: King Co 5665 N Meridian St Indianapolis IN 46208-1502

KING, KAY WANDER, design educator, fashion designer, consultant; b. Houston, Oct. 16, 1937; d. Aretas Robert and Verna Elizabeth (Klann) Wander; m. George Ronald King, Feb. 21, 1960; 1 child, Collin Wander. BA, U. North Tex., 1959; M of Liberal Arts, Houston Bapt. U., 1991. Fashion designer Kabro Houston, Inc., 1959-66, Joe Frank, Inc., Houston, 1966-68; fashion dir. Foley's, Houston, 1968-70; prin. Kay King Designer/Cons., Houston, 1970—; chair fashion dept. Houston C.C., 1981-97, chair fashion and interior design depts., 1997—; cultural exchange prof. of fashion design Jinan, China; mem. adv. bd. Spring (Tex.) Ind. Sch. Dist. Tech. Edn., 1990—; bd. dirs. Make it Yourself with Wool, Tex., nat. judge, 1997; Tex. Workforce Edn. Course Manual Facilitator, 1997-98; site evaluator Tex. Coord. Bd. for Higher Edn., 1994, 99. Designer Mrs. Am., 1966, Houston Oilers Cheerleaders, 1968-92, Astroworld and The Astrodome, 1968-69, Brian Boru Opera, 1991, Design Industries Found. Fighting AIDS, 1994-96, Houston Comets, 1997. Chair Gulf Coast area United Cerebral Palsy Telethon, 1981; chair Whiteley Endowment Scholarship Awards, Houston, 1990-93, Sickle Cell Found., Houston, 1995-99; adminstr. Bedichek Faculty Devel. Grants, 1995-96; pres. Spring Br. Ind. Sch. Dist. Coun., PTAs, Houston, 1987-88; bd. dirs. Houston C.C. Found., 1988-93, Mus. Fine Arts Costume Inst., Houston, 1991—, acquisitions com., 1993—. Recipient Yellow Rose of Tex., Gov. Tex., 1982, Nat. Inst. for Staff and Orgnl. Devel. Tchg. Excellence award U. Tex., 1993, Award of Excellence, Houston C.C. Faculty Assn. Coun., 1995, Fin. Advisors' Excellence in Cmty. Leadership award Am. Express, 1996, Innovation award Houston C.C., 1996, Chancellor's Medallion award, 1996, Tony Chee Tchg. Excellence award, 1996, Bedichek Outstanding Cmty. Svc. award, 1997, Athena award Sickle Cell Assn., 1997, Fine Arts Fashion award Mus. Fine Arts Houston, 1999; named Woman to Watch, Houston Woman mag., 1991, Woman of Excellence, Fedn. Houston Profl. Women, 1992; Bedichek Faculty Devel. grantee, 1986, 89, 90, 93, 94; Women's Archives honoree U. of Houston, 1998-99. Mem. Nat. PTA (life, hon., coun. pres. 1987-88), Costume Soc. Am. (awards chair 1992-93, exec. bd. dirs., sec. 1993—), Tex. Jr. Coll. Tchrs. Assn. (sect. chair 1990-92), Fashion Group Internat. (bd. dirs. 1969—, cultural exch. chair 1965-71, regional dir. 1969-70, program dir., chair career conf. 1994, retail chair 1995, Keynote address 1997), Houston C.C. Women Adminstrs. Assn. (bd. dirs. 1993-95, v.p. 1994-95, Star award 1989, Keynote address 1996), Houston Fashion Designers Assn. (charter, publicity chair 1989-93, v.p. bd. dirs. 1993-97), Fedn. Houston Profl. Women (bd. dirs., program dir. 1993, adminstrv. sec. 1994, pres.-elect 1995, pres. 1996, past pres. 1997, travel chair 1998-99, charter mem. Classy Clown Corps 1994—), Zeta Tau Alpha (charity showhouse chair 1985, Nat. Cert. of Merit 1986). Avocations: opera, ballet, travel, graphic computer design, professional football. Office: Houston CC System 1300 Holman St # 325A Houston TX 77004-3834

KING, KENNETH PAUL, secondary education educator; b. Omaha, Oct. 28, 1960; s. Richard Carlyle King and Karen (Cushman) Cheyney; m. Tina Anne, July 6, 1990; 1 child, Marshall. BS, Iowa State U., 1986; MS in Edn., No. Ill. U., 1991, EdD, 1998. Cert. secondary edn., Iowa, adminstrv., Ill. Writer, editor Quaransan Group, Northbrook, Ill., 1991; tchr. physics Sch. Dist. #46, Elgin, Ill., 1986-95; grad. asst. No. Ill. U., DeKalb, 1995—, instr. sci. teacing methods, 1996-98, asst. prof. curriculum and instrn., 1998—; developer of telecomms. applications for elem. edn. Camp dir. Boys Scouts of Am., St. Charles, Ill., 1992, 96, sect. dir. nat. camping sch., Kansas City, Mo., 1983-92, 96. Recipient U. Chgo. Teaching Commendation award, 1993. Mem. ASCD, Nat. Assn. Rsch. Sci. Tchg., Assn. for Rsch. in Edn., Ill. Assn. for Supervision and Curriculum Devel., Assn. for the Edn. of Tchrs. of Sci. Avocations: camping, scout leader, music, film, book collecting. Home: 128 Delcy Dr Dekalb IL 60115-1902 Office: No Ill U Gabel Hall Dekalb IL 60115

KING, KENNETH VERNON, JR., pharmacist; b. Lexington, Miss., Dec. 17, 1950; s. Kenneth Vernon Sr. and Louise (Jordan) K.; m. Janis Marie Guynes, June 12, 1976 (dec.); children: Kenneth V. King III, Nanette Marie King Tucker, Jason Guynes King. AA, Holmes Jr. Coll., 1971; BS in Pharmacy, U. Miss., 1973; cert. sterile compounding dosage units, Profl. Compounding Ctrs. Am., Houston, 1993. Registered pharmacist, Miss., Pa.; cert. in sterile aseptic compounding medicinal units, vaccination adminstrn. Am. Pharm. Assn., Ctrs. Disease Control. Pharmacist Barretts Drug Store, Greenwood, Miss., 1973-74, Eckerd Drugs, Greenwood, 1974-76, 77-88, Medi-Save Drugs Ellis Isle, Jackson, Miss., 1976; pharmacist Eckerd Drugs, Pearl, Miss., 1988-90, Jackson, 1990-92; compounding pharmacist Marty's Discount Drugs, Flowood, Miss., 1992-96, co-owner, 1996—; cons. Stat-Home Hospice care of Miss., Grace House of Jackson, 1992—, Hospice Care Found., Vicksburg, Miss., 1993-94, So. Care In-Patient Hospice, Brookhaven, Miss., 1998—, Family Care Hospice, Brandon, Miss., 1998—; cons. Whispering Pines Hospice (inpatient), 1992—, Hospice of Ctrl. Miss. (outpatient), 1993—, So. Care In-Patient Hospice, Brookhaven, Miss. 1998—, Family Care Hospice, Brandon, Miss., 1998—; owner, contractor, rschr., cons. Profl. Pharm. Svcs. in Miss., Jackson; owner Pharmakan Inc., Pharmakeus Inc.; clin. pharmacy instr. U. Miss. Sch. Pharmacy, Oxford, 1985-92, 95—, external residency instr., 1996—; tchr. environ. illness VA Hosp.; hospice pharmacist, cons., 1992—; mem. Profl. Compounding Corp. Am., Houston, P2C2 Profl. Care, Inc., Houston; co-writer compounding criteria Miss. State Bd. Pharmacy, Pharmacy Practice Act, 1993, co-investigator prescribing protocols, 1994; participant AIDS Update '96 for Delta Region (Miss., Ark. and La.), Jackson, 1996; opening spkr. PCCA Nat. Conv. on Hospice Practice, 1996; presenter in field; co-panelist, author HCFA waiver for reimbursement pharmacy cons. svcs. by Medicaid; chmn. Miss. HIV/AID Assembly Health Care Provider Network, 1997-98; tech. cons. Profl. Pharmacy Compouding Ctrs. Am., 1998—; cons. credentialing Astha specialty practice Am. Pharm. Assn. 1998; tchr. bio-med. ethics Grad. Theol. Union Ch. Divinity Sch. of the Pacific, Berkeley. Advisor Leflore County 4-H, Greenwood, 1974-76; aux. patrolman Greenwood Police Dept., 1982-86; drug identification specialist Greenwood Aux. Police Dept., 1984-85; pres., founder Human Ecology Action League Miss., Inc., 1988—, bd. dirs. 1991—, advt. coord., Atlanta, 1989%, sec., 1984—; coord. Environ. Assocs. Jack Eckerd, Inc., 1990-92; mem. Rainbow Whole Food Coop., 1989—; coord. regional support svcs. HEAL Inc., 1989—; mem. IACP Ethics Com.; mem. Episcopal Discity of Calif. Trinity Parish, San Francisco. Recipient Innovative Pharmacist of Yr. award Miss. Pharm. Assn., 1997. Aem. Internat. Assn. Compounding Pharmacist, Environ. Coalition of Miss. (co-founder), Environ. Assocs. of Jack Eckerd Inc. (coord.), Miss. Soc. Cons. Pharmacists. Mem. Word of Life Ch. Achievements include research in experimental, investigational dosage forms for hospice patients. Office: Profl Pharm Svcs 1050 B2 N Flowood Dr Jackson MS 39208

KING, K(IMBERLY) N(ELSON), computer science educator; b. Apr. 28, 1953; s. Paul Ellsworth and Marcelia Jeannette King; m. Cynthia Ann Stormes, Sept. 5, 1981 (div. Nov. 1991); m. Susan Ann Cole, Aug. 9, 1996. BS with highest honors, Case Western Res. U., 1975; MS, Yale U., 1976; PhD, U. Calif., Berkeley, 1980. Asst. prof. info. and computer sci. Ga. Inst. Tech., Atlanta, 1980-86, rsch. scientist, 1986-87; assoc. prof. math. and computer sci. Ga. State U., Atlanta, 1987—; cons. Norfolk So. Rwy., 1991. Author: Modula-2: A Complete Guide, 1988, C Programming: A Modern Approach, 1996; columnist Jour. Pascal, Ada, and Modula-2, 1989-90; contbr. articles to profl. jours. Vol. Ga. Radio Reading Svc., Atlanta, 1989—. Grad. fellow NSF, 1975-78; NSF grantee, 1981-84. Mem. AAUP, IEEE Computer Soc., Assn. for Computing Machinery (chmn. program com. 36th annual southeast conf. 1998), Tau Beta Pi. Office: Ga State U Computer Sci Atlanta GA 30303

KING, KRIS, professional hockey player; b. Bracebridge, Ont., Can., Feb. 18, 1966. Hockey player Washington Capitals, 1984-87, Detroit Red Wings, 1987-90, N.Y. Rangers, 1990-91, Phoenix Coyotes (formerly Winnipeg Jets), 1992-97, Toronto Maple Leafs, 1997—. Named Winner King Clancy trophy, NHL, 1996. Office: Phoenix Coyotes, Air Canada Ctr, 40 Bay St Ste 300, Toronto, ON Canada M5J 2X2*

KING, L. ELLIS, civil engineer, educator, consultant; b. Jamestown, N.C., Aug. 21, 1939; s. Lee Bolen and Juanita Ethel (Hodgin) K.; m. Rachel Sale Garrett, Oct. 1, 1960. BSCE, N.C. State U., 1961; DEng, U. Calif., Berkeley, 1967. Registered profl. engr., N.C.; ACTAR cert. traffic accident reconstructionist. Asst. prof. W.Va. U., Morgantown, 1967-72, assoc. prof., 1972-73; assoc. prof. U. Colo., Denver, 1973-75; prof. Wayne State U., Detroit, 1975-76; prof., chmn. dept. civil engring. U. N.C., Charlotte, 1976-95; prof. civil engring., 1995—; forensic engring. expert to numerous attys. and corps., 1967—. Contbr. chpts. to books, articles to profl. jours. NSF trainee, 1965-67. Fellow ASCE (Walter L. Huber prize 1973), Inst. Transp. Engrs.; mem. Nat. Soc. Profl. Engrs., Nat. Acad. Forensic Engrs., Am. Soc. Engring. Edn., Transp. Rsch. Bd., Human Factors and Ergonomics Soc. Home: 100 Wrenwood Ln Charlotte NC 28211-1833 Office: U NC Charlotte Dept Civil Engring Charlotte NC 28223

KING, LARRY (LARRY ZEIGER), broadcaster, radio personality; b. Bklyn., Nov. 19, 1933; s. Eddie and Jennie Zeiger; m. Alene Akins, 1961 (div. 1963), remarried 1967 (div. 1971); 1 child, Chaia; m. Sharon Lepore, 1976 (div. 1982); m. Julia Alexander, Oct. 7, 1989; 1 child, Andy. Disc jockey various radio stas. Miami, Fla., 1957-71; freelance writer, broadcaster, 1972-75; radio personality Sta. WIOD, Miami, 1975-78; writer entertainment sects. Miami Herald, 7 yrs.; radio talk show host The Larry King Show, 1978—; host 1990 Goodwill Games; Columnist USA Today, Sporting News; host sta. WLA-TV Let's Talk, Washington. Appeared in films Ghostbusters, 1984, Lost in America, 1985; author: Larry King, Tell It To The King, (with B. D. Colen) Mr. King, You're Having a Heart Attack, 1989, Larry King: Tell Me More, When You're From Brooklyn, Everything Else Is Toyko, 1992, (with Mark Stencel) On the Line: The New Road to the White House, 1993. Chmn. Larry King Cardiac Found; hon. trustee Am. Women in Radio and TV Com.; mem. Washington Ctr. for Politics and Journalism, The Read-Am. Adv. Bd., Hart Assist Found. Bd. Recipient Radio award Nat. Assn. Broadcasters, 1985, Jack Anderson Investigative Reporting award, 1985, Peabody award for Larry King Show U. Ga. Sch. Journalism, 1987, award for Larry King Live shows Awards for Cablecasting, 1987, 88, 89, also for excellence in cable TV, 1990, Marconi award Nat. Assn. Broadcasters, 1990; named Best Radio Talk Show Host Washington Jour. Rev., 1986, Broadcaster of Yr. Internat. Radio and TV Soc., 1989; named to Emerson Hall of Fame, Broadcasters Hall of Fame, 1992, Man Of Yr. Am. Heart Assn., 1992. Mem. Friars Club. Office: CNN Larry King Live 820 1st St NE Washington DC 20002-4243*

KING, LARRY L., playwright, actor; b. Putnam, Tex., Jan. 1, 1929; s. Clyde Clayton and Cora Lee (Clark) K.; m. Jeanne Casey, Nov. 25, 1950 (div. Nov. 1964); children: Alexandria, Kerri Lee, Bradley Clayton; m. Rosemarie Courmaris, Feb. 20, 1965 (dec.); m. Barbara Sue Blaine, May 6, 1978; children: Lindsay Allison, Blaine Carlton. Student, Tex. Tech U., 1949-50. Oil field worker El Paso Natural Gas Co., Jal, N.Mex. and Midland, Tex., 1943-45; reporter Hobbs (N.Mex.) Daily Flare, 1949, Midland Reporter-Telegram, 1950-52, Odessa (Tex.) Am., 1952-54; adminstrv. asst. U.S. Congress, Washington, 1954-64; freelance writer Washington, 1964—; pres. Texhouse Corp., Washington, 1979—; Ferris prof. journalism and polit. sci. Princeton (N.J.) U., 1973-75; Disting. Lyndon B. Johnson lectr. Southwest Tex. State University, 1991. Author: (books) The One-Eyed Man, 1966, . . . And Other Dirty Stories, 1968, Confessions of a White Racist, 1971, The Old Man and Lesser Mortals, 1974, Wheeling and Dealing, 1978, Of Outlaws, Con Men, Whores, Politicians and Other Artists, 1980, The Whorehouse Papers, 1981, That Terrible Night Santa Got Lost in the Woods, 1981, None But a Blockhead: On Being a Writer, 1986, Warning: Writer At Work, 1986, Because of Lozo Brown, 1988, True Facts, Tall Tales, and Pure Fiction, 1997, Reflections In A Bloodshot Eye: A Writer's Life in Letters, 1999, (plays) The Best Little Whorehouse in Texas, 1978, The Kingfish, 1979, The Night Hank Williams Died, 1986, The Golden Shadows Old West Museum, 1987, Christmas: 1933, 1987, The Best Little Whorehouse Goes Public, 1994, The Dead Presidents' Club, 1995; also numerous articles; starred in: The Best Little Whorehouse in Texas (on Broadway), 1979, The Night Hank Williams Died (off-Broadway), 1989; contbg. editor Harper's, 1967-71, New Times, 1974-77, Tex. Monthly, 1973-78, Tex. Observer, 1964-74. Sgt. AUS, 1946-49. Recipient Stanley Walker Journalism award Tex. Inst. of Letters, 1972, Tony award League of N.Y. Theatres and Producers, 1978-79, Mary Goldwater award Theatre Lobby, 1988, Helen Hayes award, 1989; elected to Tex. Walk of Stars, 1988; Nieman fellow Harvard U., 1969-70, Duke U. fellow, 1975-76. Mem. Authors Guild, PEN, Writers Guild Am. East, Actors Equity Assn., Nat. Acad. TV Arts and Scis. (Emmy award 1981), Nat. Writers Union, Screenwriters Guild East, Dramatists Guild, Sandhills Club (Monahans, Tex.), Pelican Club (Odessa), Mystic Knights of the Sea. Democrat. Avocations: breeding show dogs, singing opera, ballet dancing. *I have always avoided strong drink and evil companions.*

KING, LAURA JANE, librarian, genealogist; b. Pemberville, Ohio, Jan. 19, 1947; d. Richard D. and Jessie Florence (Brown) Zepernick; m. Bruce William King, June 17, 1972; 1 child, Christian Andrew. BA, Bowling Green (Ohio) State U., 1969, MEd, 1976; MLS Kent State U., 1995. Cert. geneal. lectr. County extension agt. home econs. Ohio Coop. Extension Svc., Paulding County, 1970-77; asst. dir., historian Pemberville Pub. Libr., asst. dir., br. coord.; mem. PRIDE com., vocat. home econs. dept. Paulding Exempted Village, 1975—; instr. genealogy Continuing Edn. Bowling Green State U., Eastwood Sch. Dist. Cmty. Edn. Mem. Paulding County Bicentennial Commn., 1975-77; organist 1st Presbyn. Ch., Pemberville, ruling elder, ch. historian; state chmn. Friends of Libr., 1992-95; advisor 4-H. Recipient Tenure award Coop. Extension Svc., 1975; mem. Wood County Citizen's Com. for Bicentennial of U.S. Constn. and NW Ordinance; mem. Wood County Literacy Bd.; mem. Pemberville Sch. Adv. Com.; past sr. state historian Children of Am. Revolution; past pres. Eastwood Local Schs. Band Boosters. Mem. ALA, Mary Sherman Hayes Soc. (sr. v.p.), Flag of the U.S. of Am. (sr. state chmn., sr. state registrar 1994—, sr. state chmn. govt. studies, 1998—), Libr. Adminstrn. and Mgmt. Assn., Children of the Am. Revolution, Ohio Geneal. Soc. (pres. Wood County chpt. 1978-80, chmn. pub. rels. chmn. 1982-83, chmn. First Families of Wood County com., state program chmn. ann. conf. 1991, 95, state chmn. History Writing Contest 1993, trustee 1995—), Berks County Geneal. Soc., Palatines to Am., DAR (vice regent chpt. 1975-77, regent chpt. 1979-83, registrar chpt. 1985—, state vice chmn. pages 1978-80, state chmn. lineage rsch. 1980-87, state and divsn. outstanding jr. mem. 1980, state chmn. membership commn. 1983-87, state recording sec. 1987-89, state corr. sec. 1989-92, area spkr.'s staff, state chmn. Friends of the Libr. 1992-95, chpt. libr. 1998—), U.S. Daus. of 1812 (chmn. state insignia), First Families Ohio, Daus. Union Vets., Nat. Soc. Magna Charta Dames, Colonial Dames 17th Century, Daus. Am. Colonists (chpt. regent 1986—, state chmn. pub. rels., 1987, chmn. mideast region pub. rels.), Bus. and Profl. Women's Club (pres. Paulding 1975-76, v.p. 1974-75), Ohio Libr. Assn., Coun. Ohio Genealogists (v.p. 1992), Colonial Order Crown of Charlemagne, SAR (medal of Appreciation). Club: Order Eastern Star. Corr. docent DAR Mus., Washington. Home: 14553 N River Rd Pemberville OH 43450-9797

KING, LAWRENCE PHILIP, lawyer, educator; b. Schenectady, N.Y., Jan. 16, 1929; s. Louis D. and Sonia K.; children—David J. Kaufman, Deborah J. King. B.S.S., CCNY, 1950; LL.B., NYU, 1953; LL.M., U. Mich., 1957. Bar: N.Y. 1954, U.S. Supreme Ct. 1963. Atty. Paramount Pictures Corp., N.Y.C., 1955-56; asst. prof. law Wayne State U., 1957-59; asst. prof. NYU, 1959-61, assoc. prof., 1961-63, prof., 1963—, Charles Seligson prof. law, 1979—, assoc. dean Sch. Law, 1973-77; of counsel Wachtell, Lipton, Rosen & Katz, N.Y.C.; cons. Commn. to Study Bankruptcy Law U.S., 1970-73, advisor nat. bankruptcy rev. com., 1996-97; assoc. reporter adv. com. on bankruptcy rules U.S. Jud. Conf., 1968-76, reporter, 1979-83, mem. adv. com. on bankruptcy rules, 1983-92; vis. faculty law Hebrew U., Jerusalem,

1971, 87, 94, Haifa U., 1994, 96, 97, 98, 99, Tel Aviv U., 1987, 94, Temple U. Sch. Law, U. Calif. Law Sch., Berkeley; lectr. Bar Ilan U., U. Stockholm, U. Innsbruck, Fed. Ct. Author: (with R. Duesenberg) Sales and Bulk Transfers Under the U.C.C., 1966, supplement, 1997, (with M. Cook) Creditors Rights, Debtor's Protection and Bankruptcy, Cases and Materials, 1985, 2d edit., 1989, 3d edit., 1997; contbr. articles, book revs. to legal jours.; editor-in-chief: Collier on Bankruptcy, 1964, 15th edit. rev., 1979—; co-editor-in-chief: Collier Bankruptcy Practice Guide, 1981—. Trustee Village of Saltaire (N.Y.), 1980-84, mayor, 1984-86, acting justice, 1988—. Recipient NYU Law Alumni Achievement award, 1976, NYU Law Alumni 25-Yr. Faculty Svc. award, 1984, legal teaching award, 1993, award Bankruptcy Lawyers divsn. UJA-Fedn., 1984, Man of Yr. award Comml. Law League Am., 1969, Disting. Svc. award Am. Coll. Bankruptcy, 1997. Mem. ABA, N.Y. State Bar Assn., Assn. of Bar of City of N.Y., Nat. Bankruptcy Conf., Am. Law Inst. Office: NYU Sch Law 40 Washington Sq S New York NY 10012-1005

KING, LELAND W., architect; b. Battle Creek, Mich., Dec. 17, 1907; s. Leland Wiggins and Elizabeth Gale (Arnold) K.; m. Hametia Fielder, Nov. 29, 1934; children: Sheryl Letia, Louisa Sands. Student, Ga. Sch. Tech., 1927, Armour Inst. Tech. (Chgo. Art Inst., Beaux Arts Design), 1928-29. Registered architect, Colo., Ariz., N.Y., Calif., Nat. Council Archtl. Registration Bds. Archtl. draftsman, designer indsl., sch., hosp. and residential projects Ga., Ill., Mich., Wis., 1925-32; supr. architect's office U.S. Treasury, 1935-37; field insp. diplomatic and consular bldgs. Dept. State, 1937-40, in Scandinavia, Balkans, Europe, Middle East, C. and S. Am.; asso. chief Fgn. Bldg. Ops. Dept. State, 1941-51; dir. and supervising architect, 1952-54; in charge U.S. diplomatic and consular bldg. design and constrn., worldwide; cons. Bd. Edn. White Fish Bay, Milw., 1931-32; tech. adviser to U.S. del. UNESCO Hdqrs. Bldg., Paris, 1952-53; exec. sec. Fgn. Service Bldgs. Com., U.S. Congress, 1952-54; gen. archtl. and indsl. design as asso. Norman Bel Geddes, 1954-55; asso. with James Gordon Carr (Architect), 1956; v.p., dir. architecture Pereira and Luckman, 1956-59; supervising archt. Ampex Corp., 1959-62; pvt. archtl. practice as Leland King, FAIA, 1961—; sr. partner King/Reif & Assos. (architecture and planning), Menlo Park, Calif.; Chmn. archtl. and constrn. engrng. panel research, adv. council to postmaster gen., 1967, 68; dir., supervising architect U.S. Embassy projects, 1937-54, honor awards Stockholm, Paris, 1953, Memorex project, Santa Clara, Calif., 1972, Mission Control Air Force, 1982; chmn. Bodega Harbour Design Rev. Com. Works exhibited U.S. State Dept., Mus. Modern Art, N.Y.C., 1953, Octagon, 1954, San Jose Mus., 1980. Recipient McGraw-Hill Top Ten Plants award, 1971. Fellow AIA (honor award 1955, chpt. award 1974), Cosmos Club (Washington). Home: 21218 Heron Dr Bodega Harbour Bodega Bay CA 94923

KING, LEON, financial services executive; b. Phila., 1921; s. Abraham and Ethel (Walton) K.; m. Diane Averbach, Nov. 30, 1946; children: Cheryl, Elliot, Louis. BS in Econs, Wharton Sch., U. Pa., 1945; grad. with honors, Bank Adminstrn. Inst., 1970. CPA, Pa. Pub. acct., 1946-52; contr. hotel divsn. Bankers Securities Corp., 1952-57; contr. Sun-Ray Drug Co., 1957-60, Bellevue Stratford Hotel, 1960-64; with Indsl. Valley Bank and Trust Co., Phila., 1964-83; exec. v.p. Indsl. Valley Bank and Trust Co., 1973-83; with Indsl. Valley Title Ins. Co., Phila., 1964-86, chmn. bd., 1983-86; pres. Bancshares Inc., 1987-97; gen. ptnr. King Assocs. Ltd. Partnership, 1996—; pvt. practice, 1987—. Mem. AICPA, Pa. Inst. CPAs, Beta Gamma Sigma. Home: 4030 Woodruff Rd Lafayette Hill PA 19444-1618 *Always be polite and courteous. Treat all people the same regardless of rank, station, or position. We are all human beings and each deserves civility and respect. From a small child to a chief of state, from a beggar to a captain of industry, all should be treated in the same friendly and courteous way.*

KING, LESLIE JOHN, geography educator; b. Christchurch, N.Z., Nov. 10, 1934; s. Lawrence Charles and Phyllis Ivy (Walter) K.; m. Doreen Mercia Brown, Oct. 22, 1960; children—Loren A., Andrew Brett. B.A., U. N.Z., 1955, M.A., 1957; Ph.D., U. Iowa, 1960. Lectr. U. N.Z., 1960-62; asst. prof. McGill U., Montreal, Que., 1962-65; prof. geography Ohio State U., 1964-70, McMaster U., Hamilton, Ont., Can., 1970—. Author: Readings in Economic Geography, 1968, Statistical Analysis in Geography, 1969, Cities, Space and Behavior, 1978, Central Place Theory, 1984. Recipient Fulbright travel award, 1957. Fellow Royal Soc. Can.; mem. Assn. Am. Geographers (Distinguished Service award 1976). Home: RR 3, Dundas, ON Canada L9H 5E3 Office: McMaster U, Hamilton, ON Canada

KING, LINDA CAROL, music educator; b. Littlefield, Tex., Apr. 17, 1947; d. Doyce Oren and Billie Maxine (Spann) Hutto; m. Herbert Eugene King, June 11, 1971 (dec. Aug. 1996); children: Joel, Heather, Whitney. BS, U. N. Tex., 1969; MEd, Tex. Tech. U., 1971. Tchr. Posey Elem. Sch., Lubbock, 1969-73; pvt. piano tchr. Lubbock, 1969—; tchr. Wright Elem., Lubbock, 1984-96; tchr. piano lab. Cavazos Jr. High, Lubbock, 1996—. Author: From Magnolia to Mesquite, 1996. Mem. Tex. State Tchrs. Assn., Lubbock Music Tchrs. Assn., Delta Zeta. Baptist. Avocations: sewing, cooking, gardening. Home: 6608 1st St Lubbock TX 79416-3704

KING, LINDA ORR, museum director; b. Washington, June 21, 1948; d. William Baxter and Jayne (Reiser) Orr; m. James McClain King (dec. Aug. 1997); children: David, Adam, Lindsay. BA, La. State U., 1970, MA in Fine Arts, 1971. Fine arts history asst. La. State U., Baton Rouge, 1967-70, grad. asst., 1970-71; assoc. curator La. State Mus., New Orleans, 1971-74; curator Coastal Ga. Hist. Soc./Mus. Coastal History, St. Simons Island, 1984-87; dir. Coastal Ga. Hist. Soc., St. Simons Island, 1987—. Co-editor: (photograph essay) George Francois Mugnier, 1975. Pres. Glynn County Soc. of St. Vincent de Paul, 1990-94; mem. Glynn County Courthouse Renovation Com., 1989—; Ga. state dir. S.E. Mus. Conf., 1990-94, also membership chair; mem. adv. coun. Brunswick Downtown Devel. Authority; mem. Leadership Glynn, 1992; mem. Commn. on Preservation of Ga. State Capitol; chmn. adv. coun. on hist. preservation Coastal Regional Devel. Ctr., 1987-98, chmn., 1996-98. Recipient Kellogg Career Enhancement award Kellogg Found., 1989, Leadership award Southeastern Mus. Conf., 1995; Internat. Partnership Among Museums fellow to Sierra Leone, 1992. Mem. Ga. Assn. Mus. and Galleries (treas. 1987-89, Mus. Profl. of Yr. 1993), Coastal Mus. Assn. (treas. 1987-89), Am. Assn. Mus., Low Country Mus. Network (treas. 1993—). Roman Catholic. Office: St Simons Island Lighthouse Mus PO Box 21136 Saint Simons GA 31522

KING, LLEWELLYN WILLINGS, publisher, lecturer, journalist, commentator; b. Bulawayo, Zimbabwe, Oct. 6, 1939; came to U.S., 1963; s. Herbert Willings and Dorothy Ann (Hooper) K. Student, Churchill Coll., 1951-55; DSc in Engring. (hon.), Stevens Inst. of Tech., 1995, PhD (hon.). City editor The Citizen, Harare, Zimbabwe, 1958-60; sub-editor Ind. TV News, London, 1960-61, Sunday Mirror, London, 1961-63; copy editor N.Y. Herald Tribune, N.Y.C., 1963-64; pres. Sovereign Assocs., N.Y.C., 1964-66; editor wire desk Washington Daily News, 1966-69; asst. editor Washington Post, 1969-70; reporter McGraw Hill, Washington, 1970-73; chmn. King Pub. Group, Washington, 1973—; founder Women NOW mag., N.Y.C., 1965; pres. Washington-Balt. Newspaper Guild, 1967-70; host cable TV program The Bull and the Bear; host radio program White House Chronicle. Contbr. articles to profl. jours. Mem. Aircraft Owners and Pilots Assn., Nat. Prss, St. James's Club, London Press Club. Avocations: flying, horseback riding, boating. Office: King Pub Group 627 National Press Building Washington DC 20045-1601

KING, LLOYD, federal judge. BA, UCLA, 1958; LLB, U. Calif., Berkeley, 1965. With Rothschild, Phelan, King & Montali, San Francisco, 1965-75; bankruptcy judge no. dist. U.S. Dist. Ct. Calif.; apptd. chief bankruptcy judge U.S. Dist. Ct. Hawaii, 1992. Mem. FBA, Maritime Law Assn. Office: 1132 Bishop St Ste 250L Honolulu HI 96813-2830

KING, LOWELL RESTELL, pediatric urologist; b. Salem, Ohio, Feb. 28, 1932; s. Lowell Waldo and Vesta Ethylwin (Snyder) K.; m. Mary Elizabeth Hill, July 9, 1960 (div. 1991); children—Andrew Restell, Erika Lillie. BA, Johns Hopkins U., 1953, MD, 1956. Intern Johns Hopkins Hosp., Balt., 1956-57; resident in urology Johns Hopkins Hosp., 1957-62; asst. prof. urology Johns Hopkins U., 1962-63; asst. prof. urology Northwestern U., 1963-67, assoc. prof., 1967-70, prof., 1970-81, prof. urology and surgery, 1974-81; prof. urology and pediatrics Duke U., Durham, N.C., 1981-97, prof. emeritus, 1997; prof. surgery/urology U. N.Mex., Albuquerque, 1997—; prof., chmn. dept. urology Presbyn.-St. Luke's Hosp., 1968-70; surgeon-in-chief Children's Meml. Hosp., Chgo., 1974-80. Author: (with P.P. Kelalis) Clinical Pediatric Urology, 1976, 3d edit., 1992, Bladder Replacement and Continent Urology Diversion, 1986, 2d edit., 1991, Urologic Surgery in the Neonate and Young Infant, 1992, Reconstructive Urology, 1992, Urologic Surgery in Infants and Children, 1997; cons. editor Urology; editor profl. jours.; contbr. articles to sci. jours. Vestryman, sr. warden Ch. of Our Savior, 1974-80; bd. dirs. Gads Hill Settlement House, 1969-73. Recipient Gold medal All India Urologic Congress, 1996, Gold medal Mex. Coll. Urology, 1991. Mem. AMA, Am. Urol. Assn. (career achievement award 1996), Am. Acad. Pediats. (chmn. sect. urology 1969-72, sec. 1972-76, Urology medal 1992), Soc. Pediat. Urology (pres. 1983), Soc. U. Urologists, Am. Assn. Genitourinary Surgeons, Clin. Soc. Genitourinary Surgeons (pres. 1996). Republican. Episcopalian. Home: 2012 Dietz Pl NW Albuquerque NM 87107-3220 Office: U NMex Health Scis Ctr Sch Medicine Dept Surgery Divsn Urology 2211 Lomas Blvd NE Albuquerque NM 87106-2745

KING, LUCY JANE, psychiatrist, health facility administrator; b. Vandalia, Ill., Dec. 23, 1932; d. Ira and Lucy Jane (Harris) K. AB, Washington U., St. Louis, 1954, MD, 1958. Diplomate Am. Bd. Psychiatry and Neurology, subspecialty Addiction Psychiatry. From instr. to assoc. prof. psychiatry dept. Washington U., 1963-74; prof. dept. psychiatry Med. Coll. of Va., Richmond, 1974-79; clin. prof. dept. psychiatry George Washington U., Washington, 1981-84, Ind. U. Med. Sch., 1994—; mem. editorial bd. Annals of Clin. Psychiatry, 1989—. Author: (with others) Psychiatry in Primary Care, 1983; contbr. articles to profl. jours. Fellow Am. Psychiat. Assn.; mem. Am. Acad. Clin. Psychiatrists, Am. Med. Women's Assn., Am. Acad. Addiction Psychiatry, Am. Soc. Addiction Medicine (cert., dual diagnosis com. 1990—). Avocation: history. Office: Midtown CMHC 1001 W 10th St Indianapolis IN 46202-2859*

KING, LYNDEL IRENE SAUNDERS, art museum director; b. Enid, Okla., June 10, 1943; d. Leslie Jay and Jennie Irene (Duggan) Saunders; m. Blaine Larman King, June 12, 1965. B.A., U. Kans., Lawrence, 1965; M.A., U. Minn.-Mpls., 1971, Ph.D., 1982. Dir. Univ. Art Mus., U. Minn.-Mpls., 1979—; dir. exhbns. and mus. programs Control Data Corp., 1979, 80-81; exhbn. coordinator Nat. Gallery of Art, Washington, 1980. Recipient Cultural Contbn. of Yr. award Mpls. C. of C., 1978; Honor award Minn. Soc. Architects, 1979. Mem. Assn. Art Mus. Dirs., Art Mus. Assn. Am. (v.p. bd. dirs. 1984-89), Assn. Coll. and Univ. Mus. and Galleries (v.p. 1989-92), Am. Assn. Mus., Internat. Coun. Mus., Upper Midwest Conservation Assn. (pres. bd. dirs. 1980—), Minn. Assn. Mus. (steering com. 1982), Am. Fedn. Arts Bd. Home: 326 W 50th St Minneapolis MN 55419-1247 Office: Weisman Art Mus 333 E River Rd Minneapolis MN 55455-0367*

KING, M. JEAN, association executive; b. Cleve., May 5, 1930. BS in Med. Tech., U. Del., 1960, MS in Microbiology, 1960. Med. technologist Del. Hosp., Wilmington, 1950-60; staff microbiologist Wilmington Gen. Hosp., 1960-61, Episcopal Hosp., Phila., 1961-68; mem. faculty dept. microbiology Temple. U. Med. Sch., 1966-68; staff microbiologist Crozier Chester (Pa.) Med. Ctr., 1969-71; designer Parkinson's Walker Dog Pilot Program, U. Pa. Hosp., Phila., 1997; founder Ind. Dogs, Inc., Chadds Ford, Pa., 1984, pres., 1986—; pres. Akbash Dogs Internat., 1987; speaker rehab. hosps., svc. orgns., self help groups, radio and TV. Theater pipe organ concert artist Longwood Gardens, Kennett Square, Pa., Dickenson Theater Organ Soc., Wilmington, Del., Sunnybrook Ballroom, Pottsdown, Pa., Marietta (Pa.) Theater, Phoenixville (Pa.) Theater. founder Parkinsans Walker Dog Pilot Program, U. Pa. Hosp. Recipient award Delta Soc., Am. Animal Hosp. Assn., Gaines Dog Food, 1987-88, Work with Handicapped Population citation Pres. George Bush, 1990, Poor Richard Pro Bono award, 1994; named to Hall of Fame, U. Del., 1988. Mem. Am. Akbash Dog Assn. (pres. emeritus), Delta Soc., Del. County C. of C., Beta Beta Beta. Home: 14 Maple Ln Chadds Ford PA 19317-9201 Office: Independence Knoll 146 Stateline Rd Chadds Ford PA 19317-9047

KING, MARCIA, management consultant; b. Lewiston, Maine, Aug. 4, 1940; d. Daniel Alden and Clarice Evelyn (Curtis) Barrell; m. Howard P. Lowell, Feb. 15, 1969 (div. 1980); m. Richard G. King Jr., Aug., 1980. BS, U. Maine, 1965; MSLS, Simmons Coll., 1967. Reference, field advisory and bookmobile libr. Maine State Libr., Augusta, 1965-69; dir. Lithgow Pub. Libr., Augusta, 1969-72; exec. sec. Maine Libr. Adv. Com., Maine State Libr., 1972-73; dir. Wayland (Mass.) Free Pub. Libr., 1973-76; state libr. State of Oreg., Salem, 1976-82; dir. Tucson Pub. Libr., 1982-91; mgmt. cons. King Assocs., Tucson, 1991—. Past chmn. bd. dirs. Tucson United Way; past chmn. adv. bd. com. Sta. KUAT (PBS-TV and Radio); mem. adv. bd. Resources for Women, Inc.; bd. dirs., past chmn. Salvation Army. Mem. ALA, Nat. Ctr. for Non-Profit Bds. Unitarian. Office: King Assocs 7130 N Camino Caballos Tucson AZ 85743

KING, MARGARET ANN, communications educator; b. Marion, Ind., Feb. 27, 1936; d. Paul Milton and Janet Mary (Broderick) Burke; m. Charles Claude King, Aug. 25, 1956; children: C. Kevin, Elizabeth Ann, Paul S., Margaret C. Student, Ohio Dominican, 1953-56, U. Kans., 1980-81; BA in Communication, Purdue U., 1986, MA in Pub. Communication, 1990. Regional rep. Indpls. Juv. Justice Task Force, 1984-85; vis. instr. dept. communication Purdue U., West Lafayette, Ind., 1992-96; v.p. King Mktg. Cons., Inc., 1996—; bd. mem. Vis. Nurse Home Health Svcs. Contbr. chpt. to book. Grad. mem. Leadership Lafayette, 1983. Purdue U. fellow, 1986-87. Mem. AAUW, Speech Comm. Assn. Am., Ctrl. States Comm. Assn. (conf. presenter 1989), Golden Key, Phi Kappa Phi. Republican. Roman Catholic. Avocations: poetry writing, vocal and piano music. Home: 7938 Wild Orchard Ln Cincinnati OH 45242-4309 *Personal philosophy: Ignorance is its own reward.*

KING, MARGARET LEAH, history educator; b. N.Y.C., Oct. 16, 1947; d. Reno C. and Marie (Ackerman) King; m. Robert E. Kessler, Nov. 12, 1976; children: David King Kessler, Jeremy King Kessler. BA, Sarah Lawrence Coll., 1967; MA, Stanford U., 1968, PhD, 1972. Asst. prof. dept. history Calif. State Coll., Fullerton, 1969-70; asst. prof. Bklyn. Coll., 1972-76, assoc. prof., 1976-86; prof. Bklyn. Coll. and Grad. Ctr., CUNY, 1987—; Disting. guest prof. Centre for Reformation and Renaissance Studies, U. Toronto, 1995. Author: Venetian Humanism in an Age of Patrician Dominance, 1986, Women of the Renaissance, 1991, The Death of the Child Valerio Marcello, 1994; contbr. articles to profl. jours.; mem. editorial bds. Recipient Howard R. Marraro prize Am. Cath. Hist. Assn., 1986, Am. Hist. Assn., 1996, Tow award for distinction in scholarship Bklyn. Coll., 1994-95; fellow Danforth Found., 1967-72, Woodrow Wilson Found., 1967-68, Am. Coun. Learned Socs., 1977-78, NEH, 1986-87; grantee Am. Coun. Learned Socs., 1976, Gladys Krieble Delmas Found., 1977-78, 80-81, 90, Am. Philos. Soc., 1979, 90, NEH, 1984. Mem. Am. Hist. Assn. (Howard and Helen Mararro prize 1996), Renaissance Soc. Am. (exec. dir. 1988-95, editor Renaissance Quar. 1984-88, 97—). Home: 324 Beverly Rd Douglaston NY 11363-1125 Office: Bklyn Coll Dept History 2900 Bedford Ave Brooklyn NY 11210-2814

KING, MARIAN EMMA, health and physical education educator; b. Miami, Fla., Aug. 6, 1949; d. Daniel Huffman and Emma (Smith) K. BS, Fla. State U., 1971; MS, Ga. State U., 1977, EdS, 1983; EdD, Nova Southeastern U., 1996. Cert. health and phys. edn. tchr., Ga. Tchr. Howard H.S., Atlanta City, 1971-76, Washington H.S., Atlanta City, 1976-77, Northside H.S., 1977-91, North Atlanta H.S., 1991—; cons. Measurement Inc. Sponsor Easter Seal Shoot-Out, Atlanta, 1980-86, Am. Cancer Soc. Gt. Am. Smoke-Out, Atlanta, 1987-98, March of Dimes Walk Am., Atlanta, 1987-98, Diabetes Walk-A-Thon, Atlanta, 1990-98; worksite wellness coord. UNICEF Bike-A-Thon, 1989—, sponsor, 1990-91; first aid instr. and vol. ARC; host Mindbusters Sta. WPBA, 1996—. Named Region 6AAA Coach of Yr., 1984, 85, Atlanta Area III Tchr. of Yr., 1989, Ga. Phys. Educator of Yr., 1990, Drug Free Schs., 1992-96, N. Atlanta Tchr. of Yr., 1996-97; grantee NAPPS, 1990-94. Mem. AAHPERD (chmn. so. dist. secondary phys. edn. coun. 1992-93, Ga. del. 1993, So. Dist. Secondary Phys. Edn. Tchr. of Yr. award 1990), Nat. Assn. Health Educators, Nat. Assn. for Sport and Phys. Edn., Nat. Assn. for Girls and Women in Sports, Assn. Advancement Health Edn., Ga. Assn. for Health, Phys. Edn., Recreation and Dance (comm. appointee 1993-94), Kappa Delta Pi. Avocations: travel, camping, snow and water skiing, scuba diving. Home: 4085 White Oak Ln SW Lilburn GA 30047-2248 Office: North Atlanta High Sch 2875 Northside Dr NW Atlanta GA 30305-2807

KING, MARVIN, research executive; b. N.Y.C., Apr. 23, 1940; s. Alexander M. and Frances (Dombeck) K.; m. Carole Hedi Breindel, Dec. 10, 1961; 1 child, Sarah Meryl. BEE, The City Coll., 1961; MS, Polytechnic U., 1963; Eng. Sc. D, Columbia U., 1966. Electrophysicist ITT Fed. Labs., Nutley, N.J., 1962-64; engr., sci. Columbia U. Electronics Rsch. Lab., N.Y.C., 1964-67; various positions Riverside Rsch. Inst., N.Y.C., 1967-84, v.p for rsch., 1984-87, exec. v.p., 1987-90, pres., 1990—; cons. U.S. Army, Ft. Monmouth, N.J., 1967, Harris Corp., Ann Arbor, Mich., 1970, Flow Rsch., Inc., Kent, Wash., 1973. Patentee in field. Participant N.Y. Acad. Medicine Commn. Biomed. R&D, 1991-93; active N.Y.C. Partnership Tech. Exec. Coun., 1992-95. Mem. IEEE, Optical Soc. Am. Avocations: cinema, classical music, calligraphy, investing, computers. Office: Riverside Rsch Inst 330 W 42nd St Rm 902 New York NY 10036-6991*

KING, MARY ANN, secondary education educator; b. Jacksonville, N.C., June 22, 1961; d. Hiram and Dorothy N. (Roberts) K. AS in Horticulture, Abraham Baldwin Agrl. Coll., Tifton, Ga., 1982; AS in Edn., South Ga. Coll., 1984; BS in Edn., Ga. So. Coll., 1986. Lic. social sci. tchr., Ga. Tchr. social sci. Ware County High Sch., Waycross, Ga., 1986-94; tchr. social studies Alpha Ctr., Waycross, Ga., 1994-98, Wave County H.S., Waycross, Ga., 1998—. Named Outstanding Educator Waycross (Ga.) Jaycees, 1988-89, Tchr. of Yr., 1995. Mem. Nat. Coun. Social Studies, Ga. Assn. Educators, Waycross Area Community Theatre, Breakfast Exch. Club., Delta Kappa Gamma. Baptist. Avocations: walking, gardening, exercising, reading. Home: 6560 Hidoma Ln Millwood GA 31552-9793

KING, MARY-CLAIRE, geneticist, educator; b. Evanston, Ill., Feb. 27, 1946; m. 1973; 1 child, Emily King Colwell. BA in Math., Carleton Coll., 1966; PhD in Genetics, U. Calif., Berkeley, 1973. Am. Cancer Soc. prof. medicine and genetics U. Wash., Seattle, 1995—; mem. bd. sci. counselors Nat. Cancer Inst.; cons. Com. for Investigation of Disappearance of Persons, Govt. Argentina, Buenos Aires, 1984—. Contbr. more than 150 articles to profl. jours. Recipient Alumni Achievement award Carleton Coll. Mem. AAAS, Am. Soc. Human Genetics, Soc. Epidemiologic Research, Inst. Medicine, Phi Beta Kappa, Sigma Xi. Office: U Wash Depts Medicine and Genetics 1959 NE Pacific Seattle WA 98195-7720

KING, MAXWELL CLARK, academic administrator; b. Ft. Pierce, Fla., Jan. 1, 1928; s. Hiram and Ida (Chandler) K.; m. Doris W. King, Jan. 29, 1953; children: Maxwell Clark II, Pamela King Jones, Carol, Russell E., Dori King Bell. BS, Auburn (Ala.) U., 1950; MS in Edn., U. Fla., 1954, EdD, 1956; postgrad., U. Tex., 1958-59. Tchr. St. Lucie County High Sch., Ft. Pierce, 1950-51; prin. Dan McCarty High Sch., Ft. Pierce, 1956-60; pres. Indian River Community Coll., Ft. Pierce, 1960-68, Brevard Community Coll., Cocoa, Fla., 1968—; cons. overseas liaison com. Am. Coun. on Edn., India, 1978; chmn. C.C.'s for Internat. Devel., Cocoa, 1976—, Fla. Gov.'s Summer Colls. Coun., Tallahassee, 1988-90; mem. exec. com. S. Regional Edn. Bd., Atlanta, 1987-91; bd. dirs. Am. Bank South, Merritt Island, Fla. Contbr. articles to profl. jours. Bd. dirs. United Way Brevard County, Cocoa, 1969—, Eugene Wuesthoff Meml. Hosp., Rockledge, Fla., 1970—; chmn. bd. dirs. Wuesthoff Health Svcs., Rockledge, 1986—. 1st lt. U.S. Army, 1951-53. Recipient Norm Keller Disting. Svc. award Melbourne Jaycees, 1986, Patrick Henry medal Mil. Order World Wars, 1986, Thomas J. Peters Nat. Leadership award U. Tex., 1989, Eileen Tosney Outstanding Am. Community-Univ. Adminstr., Am. Assn. Univ. Adminstrs., 1989; named laureate Brevard Bus. Leadership Hall of Fame, Jr. Achievement, Cocoa, 1988; Fulbright scholar, India, 1979-81, Republic of China, 1987. Mem. Assn. Community Coll. Trustees (Nation's Outstanding Community Coll. Pres. award 1976), Am. Assn. Community and Jr. Colls. (bd. dirs. 1978-81), Fla. Assn. Colls. and Univs. (pres. 1971-72), Fla. Assn. Community Colls. (pres. 1965-66), Nat. Pres. Acad. (chmn. 1975-76), Cocoa Beach Area C. of C. (bd. dirs. 1988-91), Kappa Delta Pi, Phi Delta Kappa. Avocations: golf, reading. Office: Brevard Community Coll District President's Office Clearlake Rd. Cocoa FL 32922

KING, MAXWELL E. P., newspaper editor; married; two children. Grad., Harvard U., 1967. Began journalism career at Louisville Courier-Journal, Providence Journal; City Hall reporter Phila. Inquirer, 1972-74, city editor, from 1974, then various newsroom mgmt. positions, including asst. mng. editor, assoc. mng. editor, v.p. consumer mktg. and distbn., 1987-88, sr. v.p. div., 1988-90, editor, exec. v.p., 1990-98; staff writer Forbes Mag., N.Y.C., 1977-78; exec. dir. Heinz Endowments, Pitts., 1998—. Office: Howard Heinz Endowment 625 Liberty Ave Pittsburgh PA 15222-3115*

KING, MICHAEL, syndicated programs distributing company executive; s. Charles King. BA in Mktg., Fairleigh Dickinson U., 1971. Advt. salesman Sta. WORC, Worcester, Mass.; from sales mgr. to part owner Sta. WAAF-FM, Worcester; pres., CEO, King World Prodns., N.Y.C., 1977—. Office: 12400 Wilshire Blvd Ste 1200 Los Angeles CA 90025-1058*

KING, MICHAEL HOWARD, lawyer; b. Chgo., Mar. 10, 1943; s. Warren and Betty (Fine) K.; m. Candice M. King, Aug. 18, 1968; children—Andrew, Julie. B.S. Washington U., St. Louis 1967, J.D. 1970. Bar: Ill. 1970, U.S. Dist. Ct. (no. dist.) Ill. 1970, U.S. Dist. Ct. (ea. dist.) Wis. 1972, U.S. Ct. Appeals (7th cir.) 1974, U.S. Ct. Appeals (5th cir.) 1979, U.S. Supreme Ct. 1975, U.S. Ct. Appeals (3d cir.) 1983, U.S. Tax Ct. 1987, U.S. Ct. Appeals (10th cir.) 1987, U.S. Dist. Ct. (no. dist.) Calif. 1987, U.S. Dist. Ct. Nebr. 1988, U.S. Dist. Ct. (ctrl. dist.) Ill. 1992, U.S. Dist. Ct. (no. dist.) N.Y. 1992, U.S. Ct. Appeals (2nd cir.) 1994. Spl. atty. organized crime, racketeering sect. U.S. Dept. Justice, Washington, 1970-73; asst. U.S. atty. No. Dist. Ill., Chgo., 1973-75; assoc. Antonow & Fink, Chgo., 1976, ptnr., 1977-79; ptnr. Ross & Hardies, Chgo., 1979-95; chmn. Bd. Commr. Office of State Appellate Defender. Co-author Model Jury Instructions in Criminal Antitrust Cases, 1982, Handbook on Antitrust Grand Jury Investigations, 1988. Bd. dirs. Chgo. Youth Ctrs., 1977-82; trustee Cove Sch., 1984-88, the Goodman Theatre, 1993—. Mem. ABA (litigation sect., antitrust sect., criminal practice procedure com.), Ill. Bar Assn., Chgo. Bar Assn. (judiciary com., antitrust com.), Am. Judicature Soc., Fed. Bar Assn., Assn. Trial Lawyers Am., Mid-Am. Club (bd. govs.), Econ. Club, Phi Delta Phi, Alpha Epsilon Pi. Home: 2025 Windy Hill Ln Highland Park IL 60035-4233 Office: Ross & Hardies 150 N Michigan Ave Ste 2500 Chicago IL 60601-7567

KING, MICHAEL JOHN, sanitarian; b. Newark, July 26, 1951. BA, Montclair (N.J.) State Coll., 1974. Sr. sanitarian Warren County (N.J.) Health Dept., 1979—; coord. Warren County Sludge Health and Environ. Task Force. Founder, chmn. Phillipsburg Riverview Orgn., 1989—, Riverview Arts Ctr., 1991—, Riverview Conservancy, 1990—, RiverFest, 1990—; founder Pohatcong Projects Com. to preserve Pohatcong Grasslands and endangered bird species. Mem. N.J. Environ. Health Assn. (bd. dirs. 1990-94). Avocations: birdwatching, hiking, traveling. Office: Phillipsburg Riverview Orgn 68 S Main St Phillipsburg NJ 08865-2360

KING, MICHAEL PEARSON, writer, English educator; b. Peterbourugh, Eng., Nov. 6, 1957; came to U.S., 1959; s. Van Lewis King and Emily Jane (Pearson) Harvey; m. Sarah Margaret Nusser, Aug. 27, 1983; children: Laura, Benjamin. BA, U. Wis., 1979; MA, Iowa State U., 1987. Maintenance supr. Madison (Wis.) Club, 1980-81; asst. mgr. Ballantines Cafeterias, Cary, N.C., 1981-82; prodn. mgr. Court Reporting Svcs., Raleigh, N.C., 1982-85; tchg. asst. English dept. Iowa State U., Ames, 1986-87; adj. prof. Upper Iowa U., West Des Moines, 1988—; instr. Des Moines Area C.C., Boone, Iowa, 1988-89; instr. English dept. Iowa State U., Ames, 1989, 96; writer free lance, Ames, Iowa, 1986—; item writer Am. Coll. Testing Program, Iowa City, Iowa, 1988. Author: short stories in various mags. including; Alternative Fiction and Poetry, 1988, Asylum, 1988, EOTU Mag. of Exptl. Fiction, 1989, Lactuca, 1992, Satire, 1995. Bd. dirs. Children's Svcs. of Ctrl. Iowa, Ames, 1993-96, chair pers. com. 1993-95, fin. com. 1995-96; bd. sec. 1994-95, treas. 1995-96; Dir. at large Edwards Neighborhood Assn., Ames, 1996-97. Home and Office: 310 Westwood Dr Ames IA 50014-3562

KING, NANCY, communications educator; b. Blytheville, Ark., May 10, 1945; d. Willie Lee and Janie (Jones) Garrett; m. Perry King, June 17, 1967; children: Perry Jr., Tiffany, Christopher. BA in Speech Communication, Calif. State U., L.A., 1974, MA in Speech Communication, 1981; MA in Psychology, Chapman U., 1998. Asst. supr. Pacific Telegraph & Telephone, 1968-70; computer operator West Coast Community Exch. Fenton & Lavine,

L.A., 1970-71; computer operator So. Gas Co., L.A., 1972-81, communication cons., 1982—; devel. lang. specialist Charles Drew Headstart Program, L.A.; assoc. prof. speech dept. Marymount Coll., Rancho Palos Verdes, Calif., 1986—; speechwriter various regional ofcls.; instr. Calif. State U., L.A., 1979-86; mem. Calif. Libr. Svcs. Bd., 1984-94, pres., 1988-89, 90-91; mem. Calif. Libr. Networking Task Force, 1985—, Calif. Librs. Adv. Bd., 1984-94, Orange County Friends of Libr. Found., 1988-94, Calif. Alliance for Literacy Task Force, 1988, 89; faculty coord. Webster U., 1996—; intern counselor Am. Inst. Family Counselors, 1997. Contbr. articles to profl. jours. Co-chmn. black coun. Orange County Hist. and Cultural Found., pres. bd., 1992; campaign mgr. Fran Williams for Santa Ana City Coun. Mem. NEA, Nat. Speech Communication Assn., Western Speech Communication Assn., Am. Fedn. Tchrs., AAUW, L.A. Southcentral Planning Coun. (bd. dirs.). Republican. Roman Catholic. Office: Marymount Coll 30800 Palos Verdes Dr W Palos Verdes Peninsula CA 90274

KING, NATHANIEL BREGMAN, aviation construction company executive; b. N.Y.C., June 13, 1957; s. Jonathan and Cynthia (Bregman) K.; m. Jean King, 1978 (div. 1984); 1 child, Jonathan Wesley. Grad. in constrn. mgmt., U. Houston, 1985. Constrn. supt. Brookstone Corp., Houston, 1980-87; facility mgr. Continental Airlines, Houston, 1987-89; sr. project mgr. Am. Airlines, Dallas, 1989-93; spl. advisor P.R. Ports Authority, San Juan, 1993-94; cons. King & Assocs., San Juan, 1994; dir. O'Brien-Kreitzberg, Ft. Lauderdale, Fla., 1994—; frequent spkr. on aviation devel. in U.S. and Caribbean. Mem. Clear Lake (Tex.) Shores City Coun., 1986-87. Mem. Am. Assn. Airport Execs., Aviation Coun. Internat. Office: O'Brien-Kreitzberg Inc 1700 E Las Olas Blvd Ste 308 Fort Lauderdale FL 33301-2408

KING, NICK, magazine editor. Editor The Boston Globe Mag. Office: Boston Globe Globe Newspaper Co PO Box 2378 Boston MA 02107-2378

KING, NINA DAVIS, journalist; b. Coco Solo, Panama, May 7, 1941; d. James White and Ruth (Steele) Davis. B.A. in French, U. N.C., 1963, M.A. in Comparative Lit. (Chancellors fellow), 1967; Ph.D. in English, Wayne State U., 1973. Lectr. Queens Coll., 1970-73; copy editor Newsday, L.I., N.Y., 1973-76; asst. news editor Newsday, 1976-77, asst. book rev. editor, 1977-79, book rev. editor, 1979-88; book editor The Washington Post, 1988—. Author: (with R. Winks) Crimes of the Scene: A Mystery Novel Guide for the International Traveler, 1997. Mem. Nat. Book Critics Circle, Phi Beta Kappa. Office: The Washington Post 1150 15th St NW Washington DC 20071-0002

KING, NORAH MCCANN, federal judge; b. Steubenville, Ohio, Aug. 13, 1949; d. Charles Bernard and Frances Marcella (Krumm) McCann; m. Tunney Lee King, Mar. 22, 1975; children: Catherine, Colin, Hilary, Adrienne. BA cum laude, Rosary Coll., 1971; JD summa cum laude, Ohio State U., 1975. Bar: Ohio 1975, So. Dist. of Ohio 1980. Law clerk U.S. Dist. Ct., Columbus, Ohio, 1975-79; counsel Frost, King, Freytag & Carpenter, Columbus, Ohio, 1979-82; asst. prof. Ohio State U., Columbus, Ohio, 1980-82; U.S. magistrate judge U.S. Dist. Ct., Columbus, Ohio, 1982—. Recipient award of merit Columbus Bar Assn., 1990. Mem. Coun. U.S. Magistrate Judges, Fed. Bar Assn. Office: US Dist Ct 85 Marconi Blvd Rm 235 Columbus OH 43215-2837

KING, OLIN B., electronics systems company executive; b. Sandersville, Ga., 1934; married. BS, N. Ga. Coll., 1953. With RCA Corp., 1956-57, Army Ballistic Missile Agy., 1957-60, Marshall Space Flight Ctr., 1960-61; pres. SCI Systems, Inc., Huntsville, Ala., 1966-81, chmn. bd., CEO, past pres., past dir. Served to capt. U.S. Army, 1954-56. Office: SCI Systems Inc PO Box 1000 Huntsville AL 35807-4001*

KING, ORDIE HERBERT, JR., oral pathologist; b. Memphis, Aug. 11, 1933; s. Ordie Herbert and Hazel (Eaton) K.; m. Violette Papagianis, Mar. 21, 1974; children: Catherine Ann, Alexander Carlos; children by previous marriage: Anna LaVelle, Ordie Herbert III. BS, Memphis State U., 1957; DDS, U. Tenn., 1959, PhD, 1965. Diplomate Am. Bd. Oral Pathology. USPHS postdoctoral fellow U. Tenn., 1960-62, rsch. assoc. dept. pathology, 1963-65, asst. prof. pathology, 1965; resident oral pathology U. Tenn., City of Memphis Hosps., 1962-63; asst. prof. pathology Northwestern U., 1966; assoc. prof. oral pathology St. Louis U., 1967-69, prof., 1969-70, chmn. dept., 1967-70, chmn. dept. dentistry univ. hosps., 1967-70; acting chmn., vis. assoc. prof. oral pathology Washington U., St. Louis, 1969-70; prof. oral pathology, assoc. prof. pathology W.Va. U., Morgantown, 1970-74, prof. pathology, 1974, dir. Cytopathology Lab., Med. Ctr., 1971-74; prof. pathology So. Ill. U. Sch. Dental Medicine, Alton, 1974-97; chmn. dept. diagnostic specialties So. Ill. U., Edwardsville, 1979-92; clin. prof. pathology Washington U. Sch. Dental Medicine, St. Louis, 1979-80; dir. So. Ill. Pathology Lab., Ltd., Godfrey, Ill., 1977—; dental cons. to chief med. examiner State of Tenn., 1963-65; mem. exec. com. St. Louis U. Hosps., 1967-70; mem. med. staff West Tenn. Cancer Clinic, 1962-65, W.Va. U. Hosp., 1970-74; mem. med./dental staff dept pathology Alton (Ill.) Meml. Hosp., 1986—; cons. VA Hosp., Clarksville, W.Va., 1973-74; dental cons. St. Louis County Med. Examiner, 1968-70; cons. cancer control program Nat. Ctr. for Chronic Disease Control, USPHS, 1967-70; mem. Mo. Bd. Dental Splty. Examiners, 1982-84. Fellow Am. Acad. Oral Pathology; mem. Am. Soc. Cytology, ADA, Am. Cancer Soc. (bd. dirs. W.Va. div. 1972-74), Tenn. Walking Horse Breeders and Exhibitors Assn., Spotted Saddle Horse Breeders and Exhibitors Assn., Delta Sigma Delta, Kappa Alpha, Phi Rho Sigma, Omicron Kappa Upsilon. Home: 6111 Vollmer Ln Godfrey IL 62035-1062 Office: So Ill Path Lab Ltd Godfrey IL 62035

KING, PATRICIA ANN, law educator; b. Norfolk, Va., June 12, 1942; d. Addison A. and Grayce (Wood) K.; m. Roger W. Wilkins, Feb. 21, 1981; 1 child, Elizabeth. BA, Wheaton Coll., 1963; JD, Harvard U., 1969. Bar: D.C. 1969, U.S. Supreme Ct. 1980. Spl. asst. to chair EEOC, Washington, 1969-71; dep. dir. civil rights office HEW, Washington, 1971-73; prof. law Georgetown Law Ctr., Washington, 1973—; adj. prof. Sch. Hygiene and Pub. Health Johns Hopkins U., 1990—; bd. dirs. Wheaton Coll., Womens Legal Defense Fund. Co-author: Law, Science and Medicine, 1984; contbr. articles to profl. jours. Chmn. Redevelopment Land Agy., Washington, 1976-80. Fellow Hastings Ctr.; mem. Am. Soc. Law and Medicine, Am. Law Inst., Inst. Medicine. Office: Georgetown Law Ctr 600 New Jersey Ave NW Washington DC 20001-2075*

KING, PAULA JEAN, nursing administrator. MS, CCRC, Boston U., 1973. Thanatology clin. specialist R.I. Hosp., 1978-84, asst. dir. med. nursing, 1984-89; asst. dir./clin. rsch. coord. Clin. Rsch. Programs Ltd., Attleboro, Mass., 1989-94; pres. JM Clin. Trials, Inc., Swansea, Mass., 1994—. Mem. ANA (cabinet-nursing practice), ANA Coun. Clin. Nurse Specialists, Am. Nurses Found., Am. Nurses Found. Century Club, R.I. State Nurses Assn., Internat. Congress Death and Dying, Assocs. Clin. Pharmacology, Collaborative Clin. Rsch., Drug Info. Assn., Sigma Theta Tau. Home: 966 Walnut St Fall River MA 02720-5334

KING, PETER COTTERILL, former utilities executive; b. White Plains, N.Y., Aug. 23, 1930; s. Robert Cotterill and Ruth (McKeown) K.; m. Nancy English, June 28, 1958; children: Margot E., Philip M., Sabrina P. B.S., U.S. Mil. Acad., 1952; M.B.A., U. Pa., 1958; seminar cert., Harvard, 1968. Commd. 2d lt. U.S. Army, 1952, advanced through grades to 1st lt., 1956; resigned, 1956; col. (Res.); systems engr. IBM Research Ctr., Yorktown Heights, N.Y., 1958-62; v.p. Security Bank & Trust Co., Lawton, Okla., 1962-69; pres. Security Broadcasting Corp., Lawton, 1964-69; adminstr. Southwestern Power Adminstrn., Dept. Interior, 1969-77; pres. EDG Energy Mgmt., Inc., Tulsa, 1977-80; assoc. The Dorchester Cos., Tulsa, 1980-82; dir. First State Financial, Inc., 1982-98. Chmn. United Way campaign, Lawton, 1968; chmn. Okla. Arts and Humanities Council, 1970-72; mem. Lawton City Council, 1968-69; bd. dirs. Tulsa Arts and Humanities Council; trustee Nat. Electric Reliability Council, 1975-77. Mem. Tulsa C. of C. Republican. Episcopalian. Home and Office: 1123 E 18th St Tulsa OK 74120-7408

KING, PETER D., psychiatrist, educator, real estate developer; b. Chgo., Feb. 20, 1927; s. Ralph DeWitt and Jane Munn (Spear) K.; m. Harriet Virginia Morse, Dec. 16, 1950 (div. Sept. 1968); children: Katherine V. Wangsgard, Dana Hutchins, Kevin Allison; m. Patricia Hopson, Jan. 1, 1969 (div. Apr. 1972); m. Simone Misook Cho, Oct. 25, 1974; 1 child, Carol Denise. BA with spl. honors, U. Chgo., 1950, BS, 1954, MD, 1954; PhD, So. Calif. Psychoanal. Inst., 1967. Diplomate psychiatry Am. Bd. Psychiatry and Neurology. Rsch. assoc. hematology U. Chgo. (Ill.) Clinics, 1951-54; resident in psychiatry Warren (Pa.) State Hosp., 1955-58; clin. dir., dir. rsch. Madison (Ind.) State Hosp., 1958-59; USPHS fellow in child psychiatry Reiss-Davis Child Ctr., L.A., 1959-61; asst. prof. psychiatry and behavioral sci. UCLA Med. Ctr., L.A., 1961-67; clin. prof. psychiatry and behavioral sci. U. So. Calif. Sch. Medicine, L.A., Calif., 1967—; pres. King Devel. Corp., Encino, Calif., 1978-98; pvt. practice psychiatry Encino, 1962-96, Sherman Oaks, Calif., 1996—; staff psychiatrist Calif. Dept. Corrections, 1996—; founder Coagulation Lab., U. Chgo. (Ill.) Clinics, 1952-54; founder Mental Health Clinic, Altoona, Pa., 1958; med. dir. Madre de Vida Inst., Tarzana, Calif., 1962; cons. on immunology Euvita/Eudyna, L.A., 1994-95, founder Formula 2001, 1994-95. *Author of Hypnosis and Schizophrenia (J.Nerv.Ment.Dis., 1957), and Early Infantile Autism (J.Child Pschiat., 1975), Dr. King explains how autism and schizophrenia develop. Mother-infant "bonding-dissonance" in first months causes certain infants to enter a trance in the case of schizophrenia and to struggle and be put down in that of autism. In both, developing brains are severely affected (King, Reconcil. Of Biol. & Exper., Proc. 16th Int.Cong.Psychother., Seoul: August, 1994, p. 470). Schizophrenics withdraw and hypnosis from within causes symptoms. Autistics push away from others and non-human world substitutes for nurture, causing a repertory of unusual symptoms which consumes them and drives others away.* Author: The Principle of Truth, 1960, Studies on Early Infantile Autism, 1973, Collected Poetry, 1975; contbr. chpts. to books and articles to profl. jours. Cpl. USAAF, 1945-47. Shurtleff scholar U. Chgo. (Ill.) Sch. Medicine, 1951-54; recipient Spl. award Citizens of Altoona, 1958, 3d pl. award Nat. Libr. Poetry, 1997. Fellow Am. Psychiat. Assn., Am. Acad. Psychoanalysis, Am. Group Psychotherapy Assn.; mem. ACLU, NOW, So. Calif. Psychoanalytic Inst. (chair faculty selection 1993-96, Franz Alexander prize), Coun. for a Livable World. Achievements include research on the study of sleep; hypnosis theory of schizophrenia; effects of therapy, drugs and electroshock on schizophrenia; autism; and others. Avocations: civil rights, computers, body building, triathlon, writing. Home: 3757 Crownridge Dr Sherman Oaks CA 91403-4820 Office: 3757 Crownridge Dr Ste 101 Sherman Oaks CA 91403-4820

KING, PETER JOSEPH, JR., retired gas company executive; b. Concord, N.H., Aug. 5, 1921; s. Peter Joseph and Helen (Hallinan) K.; m. Louise Lynch, Sept. 11, 1948; children: Anne, Peter. B.S., Georgetown U., 1942; LL.B., Harvard U., 1948, postgrad. Advanced Mgmt. Program, 1966. Bar: N.H. 1949, Mass. 1950, Colo. 1973. Practice law N.H., 1948-51; with AEC, 1952-53; with Colo. Interstate Gas Co., Colorado Springs, 1953-86, pres., chief operating officer, dir., 1977-85, vice chmn., 1985-86, also bd. dirs. Bd. dirs. Myron Stratton Home, Colorado Springs, 1974-93; mem. Colo. Transp. Commn., 1987-95, chmn., 1991-92. 1st lt. AUS, 1942-45, 51-52. Mem. Garden of the Gods Club, El Paso Club. Roman Catholic. Home: 7 Chase Ln Colorado Springs CO 80906-4205

KING, PETER THOMAS, congressman, lawyer; m. Rosemary King; children: Sean, Erin. Grad., St. Francis Coll., 1965; JD, U. Notre Dame, 1968. Atty.; town councilman Town of Hempstead, N.Y., 1977-81; comptr. Nassau County, N.Y., 1981-93; mem. 103d-106th Congresses from 3rd N.Y. dist., Washington, 1993—; spl. asst. to Chief Dep. Nassau County Exec.; gen counsel to Nassau Regional Off-Track Betting Corp.; chief dep. Nassau County Atty.; Acting County Atty. Chmn. Town Bd. Com. on Conservation and Waterways. Recipient cert. of achievement for excellence in fin. reporting (7 yrs) Gov. Fin. Officers Assn., cert. of honor Long Island Com. for Soviet Jewry, Alumni Achievement award St. Francis Coll., Huey award Vets. of Viet Nam War. Mem. Am. Legion, Vets. Corps of 69th Infantry, Knights of Columbus (named Citizen of the Yr.), Sons of Italy. Republican. Roman Catholic. Office: US Ho of Reps 403 Cannon Bldg Washington DC 20515-3203

KING, PHILIP GORDON, public relations consultant; b. Ely, Minn., Apr. 11, 1922; s. Herbert Sidney and Ruth Marie (Trimble) K.; m. Onriette Lebron, Feb. 23, 1957; children: Gordon Rivard, Philip David, Bernardine Victoria. A in Bus., Ely Jr. Coll., 1942; BS, Northwestern U., 1948, MA, 1950; postgrad. Columbia U., 1950-51. Tech. dir. Columbia U. Theater, 1950-51, Houston (Tex.) Playhouse, 1951-52, Civic Light Opera, Grand Rapids, Mich., 1952-54; editor/publicist CBS/TV Network, L.A., 1954-60; v.p. Pat McDermott Co., N.Y.C., 1960-62; pub. info. dir. Sta. WCBS-TV, N.Y.C., 1962-65; pub. rels. cons. NEA, N.Y.C., 1965-68, dir. press, radio and TV rels., Washington, 1968-72, pub. info. mgr., 1972-83; pres. King Communications, Washington, 1983-88, Warren, Vt., 1988—; grad. lectr. CCNY, 1962-64; pub. rels. cons. NEA, Washington, 1983-88, Prentice Hall Inc., Englewood, Cliffs, N.J., 1984, Assn. Supervision and Curriculum Devel., 1984-88, Phi Delta Kappa Internat., 1984-89, Green Mountain Cultural Ctr., 1988—, Internat. TV and Film Festival N.Y., 1988—, League of Vt. Writers, 1989—, The Valley Reporter, 1994—. Capt. U.S. Army, 1942-46, ETO. Mem. NEA, Am. Assn. Pub. Rels. Execs., Edn. Writers Assn. Democrat. Presbyterian.

KING, PHILIP JEROME, internet retailer, music business consultant; b. Ft. Benning, Ga., May 29, 1954; m. Jennie Louise Walker, Apr. 23, 1994 (div. Mar. 1999). Exec. v.p. Melton's Pro Sound, Atlanta, 1993-96; pres., CEO Bailey Park 45 Co., Atlanta, 1995—; pres., CEO Ga. Music Industry Assn., Atlanta, 1995-98, pres. emeritus; area mgr. Amazon.com, New Castle, Del., 1999—. Recipient Commendation, Mayor Bill Campbell, 1996, 98, Dedication to Atlanta Music Cmty. Commendation, Gov. Zell Miller, 1996, 98. Mem. Nat. Acad. Rec. Arts And Scis., Ga. Music Industry Assn. Avocations: songwriting, singing. Office: Bailey Park 45 Co PO Box 52203 Atlanta GA 30355-0203

KING, R. PETER, science educator, academic center director; b. Springs, Transvaal, South Africa, Mar. 12, 1938; came to U.S., 1990; s. Frank H. and Rose M. (Seeley) K.; m. July 29, 1961; children: Jeremy P., Andrew J., Janet M. BSc, U. Witwatersrand, Johannesburg, 1958, MSc, 1962; PhD, U. Manchester, Eng., 1963. Lectr. U. Witwatersrand, 1963-65, U. Natal, Durban, South Africa, 1965-73, U. Manchester, 1973-74; prof. U. Witwatersrand, 1974-90, U. Utah, Salt Lake City, 1990—; dir. communtion ctr. U. Utah, 1990—; mem. Prime Minister's Sci. Adv. Coun., South Africa, 1979. Editor: Principles of Flotation, 1982; contbr. articles to profl. jours. Fellow South African Inst. Mining and Metallurgy (pres. 1983-84); mem. Soc. Mining, Metallurgy and Exploration, Soc. Indsl. and Applied Math. Home: 2055 E 1300 S Salt Lake City UT 84108-2241 Office: U Utah Rm 412 135 S 1460 E Salt Lake City UT 84112-0114*

KING, RAY JOHN, electrical engineer; b. Montrose, Colo., Jan. 1, 1933; s. John Frank and Grace (Rankin) K.; m. Diane M. Henney, June 20, 1964; children: Karl V., Kristin J. BS in Electronic Engring., Ind. Inst. Tech., 1956, BS in Elec. Engring., 1957; MS, U. Colo., 1960, PhD, 1965. Instr. Ind. Inst. Tech., 1956-58, asst. prof., 1960-62, acting chmn. dept. electronics, 1960-62; research asso. U. Colo., 1962-65; research assoc. U. Ill., 1965; assoc. prof. elec. engring. U. Wis., Madison, 1965-69; prof. U. Wis., 1969-82, assoc. dept. chmn. for research and grad. affairs, 1977-79; staff rsch. engr. Lawrence Livermore Nat. Lab. (Calif.), 1982-90, sr. scientist high power microwaves program, 1989-90; co-founder KDC Tech. Corp., 1983, v.p., 1990—, cons.; vis. Erskine fellow U. Canterbury, N.Z., 1977; guest prof., Fulbright scholar Tech. U. Denmark, 1973-74. Author: Microwave Homodyne Systems, 1978; contbr. articles to profl. jours.; patentee in field. NSF Faculty fellow, 1962-65. Fellow IEEE; mem. IEEE Soc. on Antennas and Propagation (adminstrv. com. 1989-91, chmn. wave propagation stds. com. 1986-89, gen. chmn. symposium 1989), IEEE Soc. Microwave Theory and Techniques, IEEE Soc. Instrumentation and Measurements, Forest Products Soc., Electromagnetics Acad., Internat. Sci. Radio Union (commns. A, B, F), Sigma Xi, Iota Tau Kappa, Sigma Phi Delta. Home: 2595 Raven Rd Pleasanton CA 94566-4605 Office: KDC Tech Corp 2011 Research Dr Livermore CA 94550-3803

KING, REATHA CLARK, community foundation executive; m. N. Judge King Jr.; children: N. Judge III, Scott. BS in Chemistry and Math., Clark Coll., 1958; PhD in Chemistry, U. Chgo., 1960; MBA, Columbia U., 1977; doctorate (hon.), Smith Coll., 1993, S.C. State U., 1995. Rsch. chemist Nat. Bur. Standards, Washington, 1963-68; mem. chemistry faculty York Coll. CUNY, Jamaica, 1968-77, assoc. dean divsn. natural scis. and math., 1970-74, assoc. dean acad. affairs, 1974-77; pres. Met. State U., St. Paul, Mpls., 1977-88; pres., exec. dir. Gen. Mills Found., Mpls., 1988—; bd. dirs. Minn. Mut. Ins. Co., St. Paul, H.B. Fuller Co., St. Paul, N.W. Corp., Mpls.; cons., spkr. in field. Contbr. numerous articles to profl. jours. Bd. dirs. Coun. on Founds., Washington, Minn. Coun. on Found., H.B. Fuller Co. Found., St. Paul, Corp. Nat. and Cmty. Svc., vice-chair; chair corp. adv. coun. ARC; bd. overseers Clark Atlanta U.; mem. ministers and missionaries benefit bd. Am. Bapt. Ch., N.Y.C. Recipient Sisterhood award for disting. humanitarian svc. Nat. Conf. Christian and Jews, 1993, Woman of Distinction award St. Croix Valley Girl Scouts, 1995. Mem. NAACP (cmty. svc. award in edn. 1994), Delta Sigma Theta. Home: 110 1st Ave NE Apt 403 Minneapolis MN 55413-2261 Office: Gen Mills Found PO Box 1113 Minneapolis MN 55440-1113*

KING, RICHARD ALLEN, lawyer; b. St. Joseph, Mo., July 4, 1944; s. Allen Welden and Lola (Donelson) K.; m. Deedee Gershenson, Apr. 19, 1986; children from previous marriage: Mary, Suzanne, Allen. BA, U. Mo., Columbia, 1966, JD cum laude, 1968. Bar: Mo. 1968. Law clk. Office of Chief Counsel, IRS, 1967; assoc. Reese, Constance, Slayton, Stewart & Stewart, Independence, Mo., 1968-73; ptnr. Constance, Slayton, Stewart & King, Independence, 1973-80, Cochran, Kramer, Kapke, Willerth & King, Independence, 1980-81; exec. asst. to gov. State of Mo., Jefferson City, 1981-82; dir. revenue State of Mo., 1982-85; ptnr. Smith, Gill, Fisher and Butts, Inc., Kansas City, Mo., 1985-87, Wirken & King, Kansas City, 1988-93, King, Hershey, Coleman, Koch & Stone, Kansas City, Mo., 1993—; asst. city counselor City of Independence, 1968-69, mayor, 1974-78; vice chmn. Nat. Conf. Rep. Mayors, 1975-77; chmn. Mo. Gov.'s Task Force on Cmty. Crime Prevention, 1975-76; chmn. Kansas City Pub. Improvements Adv. Com., 1991-96; chmn. KC Team Effort, 1991-95; pres. Good Govt. League, Independence, 1972-73; mem. Mo. Commn. Human Rights, 1973-74; bd. dirs. Multistate Tax Commn., 1983-85, Chrisman Sawyer Bank, 1989-95. Contbr. articles to profl. jours. Bd. dirs. Am. Cancer Soc., Independence, 1973-79, chmn. crusade, 1973; bd. dirs. Independence Boys Club, 1972-79, Independence Cmty. Assn. Arts, 1973-76, Independence Sanitarium and Hosp., 1974-78, Jefferson City Meml. Hosp., 1981-85, NE Jackson County Mental Health Ctr., 1978-80, Greater Kansas City Nat. Coun. on Alcoholism, 1978-81, Am. Legion Boys State Mo., 1975—, Jefferson City United Way, 1982-85, Jackson County Hist. Soc., 1999—; pres. Friends U. Mo. Truman Campus, 1979-80, Kansas City Consensus, 1989-90; trustee Harry S. Truman Scholarship Found., 1975-78, Kansas City U., 1979-80, Andrew Drumm Inst., 1990—, pres. bd. trustees, 1992-94. Capt. U.S. Army, 1969-72. Recipient Outstanding Young Man of Mo. award Mo. Jaycees, 1975, award Mo. Inst. Pub. Adminstrn., 1983. Mem. ABA, Mo. Bar Assn., Ea. Jackson County Bar Assn., Kansas City Bar Assn. (chmn. real estate law com. 1988-89), Nat. Assn. Bond Lawyers, Internat. Assn. Gaming Attys., Independence C. of C. (pres. 1980-81), Order of Coif, Phi Delta Phi, Beta Theta Pi. Unitarian. Home: 206 E 30th St Kansas City MO 64108-3213 Office: King Hershey Coleman Koch & Stone 2345 Grand Blvd Ste 2100 Kansas City MO 64108-2619 *There is nothing in life as important as living. "Success" is an objective which all too often deprives its pursuer of the satisfaction he or she seeks. That satisfaction lies in meaningful personal relationships, spiritual communion with a Higher Power, and appreciation for the meaning and purpose of life.*

KING, RICHARD HOOD, newspaper executive; b. Boston, Jan. 24, 1934; s. Gilbert and Frances (Hood) K.; m. Reta Schoonmaker, July 25, 1959; children: D. Whitney, Richard H. Jr., Nanci A. A.B., Harvard U., 1955, M.B.A., 1961. Mgr. acctg. Hitchiner Mfg. Co., Inc., Milford, N.H., 1963-68; div. contr. Hitchiner Mfg. Co., Inc., Wallingford, Conn., 1968-71; sec., treas. Smyth Mfg. Co., Inc., Bloomfield, Conn., 1971-72; v.p. fin. Progressive Trade Corp., Glastonbury, Conn., 1972-73; v.p., treas. Hartford Courant Co., Conn., 1973-85, v.p., asst. to gen. mgr., 1986-90, v.p. adminstrn., 1990-96, ret., 1996. Treas. Hartford Courant Found., 1974-96, trustee, 1993-98; v.p., sec., bd. dirs. Better Bus. Bur., Hartford, 1978; bd. dirs. Camp Tourtant, Inc., 1980-96, treas., 1980-96; bd. dirs. Conn. Prison Assn., 1984-91, treas., 1985, chmn. bd. dirs., 1986-89; bd. dirs. Hartford Symphony Orch., 1990-98; bd. dirs., regional v.p. Conn. Audubon Soc., 1991-92, chmn., 1993-95, chmn. emeritus, 1995-98, bd. overseers, 1998—; bd. dirs. Penikese Island Sch., 1998—. Lt. (j.g.) USNR, 1955-57. Mem. Fin. Execs. Inst. (treas. Hartford chpt. 1980-81, sec. 1981-82, v.p. 1982-83, pres. 1983-84), Conn. Daily Newspapers Assn. (treas. 1992, 1st v.p. 1993-95, pres. 1995, exec. dir., lobbyist 1996—), Glastonbury C. of C. (treas., exec. bd. dirs. 1991-94), Hartford Club, Harvard-Radcliffe Club No. Conn. (v.p. 1989-90, pres. 1990-92), Chapoquoit Yacht Club (West Falmouth, Mass., treas. 1973-74). Home: 11 Snug Harbor Ln PO Box 456 West Falmouth MA 02574-0456 Office: 118 Oak St Hartford CT 06106-1514

KING, RICHARD MAURICE, JR., consultant; b. Wilmington, N.C., Jan. 15, 1935; s. Richard Maurice Sr. and Eleanor (Watson) K.; m. Edith Page Stevenson, Dec. 26, 1960 (dec. Dec. 1979); 1 child, Eleanor King Bohanon. BS in Math., U. N.C., 1956. Statis. engr. E.I. duPont de Nemours, Parlin, N.J., 1956-59; statis. cons., computer group mgr. Am. Cyanamid, Stamford, Conn., 1959-71; various positions in computer mktg. and product mgmt. Xerox Corp., various locations, 1971-87; nat. account mgr. Delphax Sys., Randolph, Mass., 1988-90; product market mgr. Bull Printing Sys., Wellesley, Mass., 1990-91; pres. Logical Imaging Solutions, Santa Ana, Calif., 1993-95; cons. Ptnrs. Cons. Svcs., Laguna Niguel, Calif., 1991-93, 96—. Home: 30902 Clubhouse Dr 4D Laguna Niguel CA 92677

KING, ROBERT BRUCE, federal judge; b. White Sulphur Springs, W.Va., Jan. 29, 1940; m. Julia Kay Doak, Apr. 16, 1965. BA, W.Va. U., 1961; JD, W.Va. Coll. of Law, 1968. Bar: W.Va. 1968, U.S. Dist. Ct. (so. dist.) W.Va. 1968, U.S. Ct. Appeals W.Va. 1968, U.S. Ct. Appeals (4th cir.) 1970, U.S. Dist. Ct. (no. dist.) W.Va. 1972, U.S. Supreme Ct. 1974, U.S. Dist. Ct. (ea. dist.) Ky. 1975, U.S. Claims Ct. 1985, U.S. Tax Ct. 1991. Asst. mgr. Sam Snead All-Am. Golf Course, Sharpes, Fla., summer 1965; rsch. asst. State and Cmty. Planning Office, Office of R&D, W.Va. U., Morgantown, 1966-68; law clk. Chief Judge John A. Field, Jr. U.S. Dist. Ct. (so. dist.) W.Va., Charleston, 1968-69; assoc. Haynes and Ford, Lewisburg, W.Va., 1969-70; asst. U.S. atty. So. Dist. of W.Va., Charleston, 1970-74; assoc. Spilman, Thomas, Battle and Klostermeyer, Charleston, 1975, ptnr., 1976-77, 81; U.S. atty. So. Dist. of W.Va., Charleston, 1977-81; ptnr. King Allen Guthrie & McHugh, 1981-98; judge U.S. Ct. Appeals (4th cir.), Richmond, Va., 1998—. Mem. Jud. Investigation Commn. of W.Va., 1990-94; vis. com. Coll. of Law of W.Va. U., 1997—. Patrick Duffy Koontz scholar. Fellow Am. Coll. Trial Lawyers; mem. ABA, W.Va. Bar Assn., Kanawha County Bar Assn., Greenbrier County Bar Assn.,U.S. Golf Assn., W.Va. Golf Assn., W.Va. U. Alumni Assn., W.Va. Law Sch. Assn., Fellows of the Am. Bar Found., Jud. Conf. of 4th Cir. Ct. Appeals, Am. Bd. Trial Advocates (W. Va. chpt. pres. 1986-90), Nat. Assn. Criminal Def. Lawyers, Order of the Coif, Pi Sigma Alpha, Phi Alpha Theta. Presbyterian. Office: c/o Fourth Circuit Clk 1100 E Main St Richmond VA 23219*

KING, ROBERT CHARLES, biologist, educator; b. N.Y.C., June 3, 1928; s. Charles James and Amanda (McCutchen) K. B.S., Yale U., 1948, Ph.D., 1952. Scientist biology dept. Brookhaven Nat. Lab., 1951-55; mem. faculty Northwestern U., 1956—, prof. biology, 1964—; chmn. 8th Brookhaven Symposium in Biology, 1955; vis. investigator, fellow Rockefeller U., 1959; NSF sr. postdoctoral fellow U. Edinburgh, Scotland, 1958, Commonwealth Sci. and Indsl. Research Orgn. Div. Entomology, Canberra, Australia, 1963, Sericultural Expt. Sta., Tokyo, Japan, 1970. Author: Genetics, 2d edit., 1965, A Dictionary of Genetics, 5th edit., 1997, (with W.D. Stansfield) Ovarian Development in Drosophila melanogaster, 1970, also numerous papers; editor: Handbook of Genetics Series, 5 vols., (with H. Akai) Insect Ultrastructure, 2 vols., 1982. Fellow AAAS; mem. Am. Soc. Zoologists, Histochem. Soc., Am. Soc. Cell Biology (treas. 1972-75), Electron Microscopy Soc. Am., Genetics Soc. Am., Am. Soc. Naturalists, Soc. Devel. Biology, Entomol. Soc. Am., Genetics Soc. Can., Genetics Soc. Korea, Sigma Xi (pres. Northwestern U. chpt. 1966-67). Home: 2890 Fredric Ct Northbrook IL 60062-7504 Office: Northwestern U Dept Biochemistry & Molec Bio Evanston IL 60208

KING, ROBERT COTTON, professional society consultant; b. Mpls., Jan. 8, 1931; s. George Herbert and Helen (Morse) K.; m. Arlene Catherine Wortman, May 28, 1955; children: Robert Cotton, Mary Louise, Katharine Ann. BA, U. Minn., 1954; grad. Advanced Mgmt. Program, Harvard Bus.

Sch., 1974. Mgr. Morris (Minn.) C. of C., 1957-59, Fergus Falls (Minn.) C. of C., 1959-62; editor Fergus Falls Daily Jour., 1962-65; editorial writer Mpls. Tribune, 1965-67; asst. mng. editor Mpls. Star, 1967-68, mng. editor, 1969-72, editor, 1972-75, v.p. advt., 1975-79; pres. Info. Pubs., Inc., Mpls., 1979-80; group v.p. Mpls. Star and Star Tribune Co., 1980-82; pres. Downtown Council of Mpls., 1983-88; assn. cons., 1988—. Bd. dirs. Edina (Minn.) Little League Baseball, 1969-73, Downtown YMCA, 1977-79, Minn. Better Bus. Bur., 1978-82; bd. dirs. Cath. Bull., 1978-90, treas., 1979-90. 1st lt. AUS, 1955-57. Profl. Journalism fellow Stanford, 1968. Mem. Minn. A.P. (pres. 1973), Minn. Advt. Fedn. (dir. 1978-79), Kiwanis (pres. 1978), Sigma Delta Chi. Episcopalian. Home: 5809 Oaklawn Ave Minneapolis MN 55424-1919*

KING, ROBERT DAVID, insurance company executive; b. Providence, Jan. 21, 1950; s. Wendell Sherman and Eileen (Alward) K.; m. Bonita Jean Finlay, Aug. 7, 1971; children: Michael D., Rebecca A., Jennifer L. BA, U. Conn., 1971. CPCU. Underwriter Liberty Mut. Ins. Co., Boston, 1971-75, supervising underwriter, 1975-77; asst. mgr. Liberty Mut. Ins. Co., Chgo., 1977-81, mgr. bus. lines underwriting, 1982-84, div. underwriting mgr., 1984-88; asst. v.p. Liberty Mut. Ins. Co., Boston, 1988-89, v.p., mgr. support ops., 1989—. Mem. Soc. CPCU's, Ins. Inst. Am. (assoc. in risk mgmt., underwriting, mgmt., rsch. and planning). Roman Catholic. Avocations: running, canoeing. Home: 70 Maryland St Marshfield MA 02050-6221 Office: Liberty Mut Ins Co 175 Berkeley St Boston MA 02116-5066

KING, ROBERT EDWARD, retired pharmacy educator; b. Zanesville, Ohio, Dec. 27, 1923; s. Ray Harrison and Edna Elizabeth (Bowman) K.; m. Jane Wanner Klein, Aug. 12, 1950; children: Susan J., Timothy P., Peter R., Christina A., Jonathan D. BS in Pharmacy, Ohio State U., 1944; PhD in Pharmaceutical Chemistry, U. Minn., 1948. Rsch. assoc. Merck Sharp & Dohme, West Point, Pa., 1948-61; prof. pharmacy Phila. Coll. Pharmacy and Sci., 1961-86, prof. emeritus, 1986—; Author: Remington's Pharmaceutical Sciences, 1965-85; editor: (jour.) Parenteral Drug Assn., 1966-78. Republican. Episcopalian. Avocations: reading, gardening. Home: 3475 Aquetong Rd Doylestown PA 18901-9233

KING, ROBERT HENRY, minister, church denomination executive, former educator; b. Sunny South, Ala., Apr. 1, 1922; s. Henry C. and Della S. (Bettis) K.; m. Edna Jean McCord, June 1, 1949; children: Jocelyn, Jann, Roger. BD, Immanuel Luth. Sem., Greensboro, N.C., 1949; MEd, U. Pitts., 1956; MA, Ind. U., 1968, PhD, 1969. Ordained to ministry Luth. Ch.—Mo. Synod, 1949. Pastor Victory Luth. Ch., Youngstown, Ohio, 1949-57, St. Philip Luth. Ch., Chgo., 1957-65; asst. prof. Concordia Tchrs. Coll., River Forest, Ill., 1968-70; prof. edn. Lincoln U., Jefferson City, Mo., 1970-87; v.p. Luth. Ch.—Mo. Synod, St. Louis, 1986—; pastor Pilgrim Luth. Ch., Freedom, Mo., 1977-97; dir. lay ministry Concordia Coll., Selma, Ala., 1987-90; vis. instr. Concordia Sem., St. Louis, 1989—; dir. workshop Obot Idim Sem., Nigeria, 1990. Contbr. articles to religious jours. Mem. Jefferson City Sch. Bd., 1973-76. Lilly Found. fellow, 1965. Mem. Am. Assn. Adult Continuing Edn., Mo. Assn. Adult Continuing Edn., Phi Delta Kappa. Office: 901 Roland Ct Jefferson City MO 65101-3576

KING, ROBERT LEROY, business administration educator; b. Decatur, Ga., Jan. 22, 1931; s. John Todd and Charlotte (Stringer) K.; m. Helen Butler Leaptrott, Mar. 25, 1956; children: Robert Todd, Keith Alan, John Christopher. BBA, U. Ga., 1952; MA, Mich. State U., 1953, PhD, 1960; Dr. honoris causa, Oskar Lange Acad. Econs., Wroclaw, Poland, 1992. Asst. prof. mktg. U. S.C., Columbia, 1957-61, assoc. prof., 1961-65; prof. mktg. Va. Poly. Inst. and State U., Blacksburg, 1965-82, head dept., 1969-76; prof. bus. adminstrn., head dept. The Citadel, Charleston, S.C., 1982-85, Robert A. Jolley chair bus. adminstrn., 1985-90; dir. internat. bus. studies, prof. mktg. U. Richmond, 1990-96, prof. emeritus, 1996—; cons. in field; vis. researcher Warsaw Tech. U., Acad. Econs. in Wroclaw (Poland); overseas tchr. in field. Maj. USAR, 1953-76. Grantee Ford Found., 1964-65, Va. Poly. Inst. and State U., 1979-82, Citadel Devel. Found., 1982-90. With AUS, 1953-55; maj. Res. Mem. Am. Acad. Advt. (exec. sec. 1986—, book rev. editor Jour. Advt. 1983-94), Am. Mktg. Assn., Acad. Mktg. Sci. (bd. govs. 1988-94, chmn. bd. govs. 1988-90, v.p. fin., treas. 1986-88), Assn. for Consumer Rsch., Acad. Internat. Bus., Am. Assn. for Advancement Slavic Studies, Decision Scis. Inst., So. Conf. Slavic Studies, So. Mktg. Assn. (pres. 1972-73), Delta Sigma Pi, Omicron Delta Epsilon, Omicron Delta Kappa, Beta Gamma Sigma. Baptist. Author: An Annotated Index to the Proceedings of the American Marketing Association Educators' Conferences, 1973, 80; Procs: Southern Marketing Association 1973 Conference, 1974; Marketing and the New Science of Planning, 1969, Retailing: Theory and Practice for the 21st Century, 1985, Marketing in an Environment of Change, 1986, Minority Marketing: Issues and Prospects, 1987, Retailing: Its Present and Future, 1988, Proceedings of the 1988 Conference of the Academy of International Business Southeast U.S. Region, Marketing: Positioning for the 1990's, 1989, Marketing: Toward the Twenty-First Century, 1991, Retailing: Reflections, Insights and Forecasts, 1991, Developments in Marketing Science, Vol. XIV, 1991, Marketing: Perspectives for the 1990s, 1992, Minority Marketing: Research Perspectives for the 1990s, 1993, Retailing: Theories and Practices for Today and Tomorrow, 1994; Retailing: End of a Century and a Look to the Futrue, 1997; contbr. numerous articles to profl jours. Avocations: photography, classical music, history, travel. Home: 2440 Edgeview Ln Midlothian VA 23113-9618 Office: American Academy of Advertising Sch Bus Univ of Richmond Richmond VA 23173

KING, ROBERT LUCIEN, lawyer; b. Petaluma, Calif., Aug. 9, 1936; s. John Joseph and Ramona Margaret (Thorson) K.; m. Suzanne Nanette Parre, May 18, 1956 (div. 1973); children: Renee Michelle, Candyce Lynn, Danielle Louise, Benjamin Robert; m. Linda Diane Carey, Mar. 15, 1974 (div. 1981); 1 child, Debra; m. J'an See, Oct. 27, 1984 (div. 1989); 1 child, Jonathan F.; m. Marilyn Collins, June 15, 1991. AB in Philosophy, Stanford U., 1958, JD, 1960. Bar: Calif., N.Y. 1961. Asst. U.S. atty. U.S. Atty's. Office (so. dist.), N.Y.C., 1964-67; assoc. Debevoise & Plimpton, N.Y.C., 1960-64, 67-70, ptnr., 1970—; mng. ptnr. Debevoise & Plimpton, L.A., 1989-95; lectr. Practicing Law Inst., N.Y.C., ABA, Asia/Pacific Ctr. for Resolution of Internat. Bus. Disputes, CPR Inst. for Dispute Resolution. Fellow Am. Coll. Trial Lawyers; mem. ABA, Assn. Bar City N.Y., Calif. Bar Assn. Democrat. Avocation: poetry. Home: 16 Lockwood Rd Scarsdale NY 10583-5302

KING, ROBERT THOMAS, editor, free-lance writer; b. Hillside, N.J., Oct. 29, 1930; s. Philip Arthur and Lucy (Davis) K.; m. Fredericka Bredow, 1978. Ed., Emmanuel Coll., Cambridge, Eng., 1948-50; BA, Birmingham (Eng.) U., 1955; postgrad., Shakespeare Inst., Stratford-Upon-Avon, Eng., 1955-56. Trainee Oxford U. Press, N.Y.C., 1957-59; chief copy editor NYU Press, 1959-61, editor, 1961-63, mng. editor, 1963-66; dir. U. S.C. Press, Columbia, 1966-84. Contbr. articles to profl. jours., mags., newspapers. Recipient Lucy Hampton Bostick award, 1978. Mem. Am. Assn. Univ. Presses (bd. dirs. 1972-74, chmn. goals and long-range problems com.), Andiron Club, Grolier Club, Torch Club (Columbia). Episcopalian (dir. The Episcopalian, vestry, lic. lay reader). Home: PO Box 477 Winnsboro SC 29180-0477

KING, ROBERT WANDELL, writer; b. Denver, Dec. 7, 1937; s. Wendell Benton and Elizabeth Johnson King; m. Helen Jane LaMar (div.); children: Lisa, Lynn, Lawrence; m. Elizabeth A. Franklin. BA in English, U. Iowa, 1959, PhD in English, 1965; MA in Am. Lit., Colo. State U., 1961. Asst. prof. U. Alaska, Fairbanks, 1965-68; assoc. prof. to prof. U. N.D., Grand Forks, 1968-95; vis. prof. U. Nebr., Lincoln, 1996—. Author: Standing Around Outside, 1979, A Circle of Land, 1990, Learning American, 1998. Democrat. E-mail: rKing@unlserve.unl.edu. Home: 1930 Dakota St Lincoln NE 68502 Office: Dept of English U Nebr Box 88033 Lincoln NE 68588-0333

KING, ROBERT WILSON, gubernatorial staff member; b. Newport, R.I., Sept. 25, 1954. BA in Lit., Boston U., 1977. With Sta. WBUR-FM, Boston, 1976-77; pub. affairs dir. Sta. KDLG-AM, Dillingham, Alaska, 1978-79, news dir., 1979-94; comm. dir. Knowles for Gov. Campaign, 1994; press sec. Office Gov. Tony Knowles, Juneau, Alaska, 1994. Bd. dirs. Juneau Symphony, Alaska Hist. Soc. E-mail: BobúKing@gov.state.ak.us. Home: 419 Kennedy St Juneau AK 99801 Office: PO Box 110001 Juneau AK 99811

KING, ROGER M., syndicated programs distributing company executive; s. Charles King; m. Raemali King; children: Kellie, Anna Rose, Lucinda Monroe. Former newspaper sales rep., mgr. radio sta., sales mgr. TV sta.; with King World Prodns., N.Y.C., chmn., 1977—. Office: King World Prodns 1700 Broadway Fl 33 New York NY 10019-5905*

KING, RONALD BAKER, federal judge; b. San Antonio, Aug. 16, 1953; s. Donald Dick and Elaine (Baker) K.; m. Cynthia Sauer, June 7, 1975; children: Karen Elizabeth, Ronald Baker Jr., Kelsey Ann. BA, So. Meth. U., 1974; JD, U. Tex., 1977. Bar: Tex. 1977, U.S. Dist. Ct. (we. dist.) Tex. 1980, U.S. Ct. Appeals (5th cir.) 1981, U.S. Tax Ct. 1985. Briefing atty. Supreme Ct. Tex., Austin, 1977-78; assoc. Foster, Lewis, Langley, Gardner & Banack Inc., San Antonio, 1978-82, ptnr., 1982-88; judge U.S. Bankruptcy Ct. (we. dist.) Tex., San Antonio, 1988—. Mem. Tex. Bar Assn. Presbyterian. Avocations: piano, basketball, tennis, water sports. Home: 1702 Hounds Rise St San Antonio TX 78248-1206 Office: US Bankruptcy Ct PO Box 1439 San Antonio TX 78295-1439

KING, RONALD L., state official, English educator; b. South Boston, Va., Jan. 3, 1958; s. Roy L. and Linda Gail (Lawrence) K. BA in English, James Madison U., 1980, MA in English, 1988. Cert. Pub. Purchasing Officer, Nat. Inst. Govt. Purchasing; lic. contracting officer, Commonwealth of Va. Buyer Leggett Dept. Store, South Boston, 1981-87; sr. buyer U. Va., Charlottesville, 1987; buyer Va. Commonwealth U., Richmond, 1987-89; procurement mgr. Va. Mus. Fine Arts, Richmond, 1989-94; state sr. procurement specialist Va. Divsn. Purchases and Supply, Richmond, 1994-95, state procurement rev. analyst, 1995—; adj. faculty, dept. English, Va. Commonwealth U., 1988—. Mem. arts com. Centenary United Meth. Ch., Richmond, 1993—; block capt. West of the Blvd. Civic Assn., Richmond, 1994—. Mem. Assn. Govtl. Purchasing (at-large bd. mem. 1996-97), Nat. Inst. Govtl. Purchasing (del. to Russia/Estonia con. 1992), Capital Area Purchasing Assn. (pres. 1995—), adv. bd. James Madison U. Founders Soc., 1998. Avocations: travel, reading. Office: PO Box 1199 805 E Broad St Richmond VA 23219-1926

KING, RONOLD WYETH PERCIVAL, physics educator; b. Williamstown, Mass., Sept. 19, 1905; s. James Percival and Edith Marianne Beate (Seyerlen) K.; m. Justine Merrell, June 22, 1937 (dec. Aug. 1990); 1 son, Christopher Merrell; m. Mary M. Govoni, June 1, 1991. A.B., U. Rochester, 1927, S.M., 1929; Ph.D., U. Wis., 1932; student, U. Munich, Germany, 1928-29, Cornell U., 1929-30. Asst. in physics U. Rochester, 1927-28; Am.-German exchange student, 1929-30; White fellow in physics Cornell U., 1929-30; U. fellow in elec. engring. U. Wis., 1930-32, research asst., 1932-34; instr. physics Lafayette Coll., 1934-36, asst. prof., 1936-37; Guggenheim fellow Berlin, Germany, 1937-38; with Harvard U., 1938—, successively instr., asst. prof., assoc. prof., 1938-46, prof. applied physics, 1946-72, prof. emeritus, 1972—; cons. electromagnetics and antennas, 1972—. Author: Electromagnetic Engineering, Vol. 1, 1945, 2d edit, Fundamental Electromagnetic Theory, 1963, Transmission Lines, Antennas and Wave Guides, (with A.H. Wing and H.R. Mimmo), 1945, 2d edit., 1965, Transmission-Line Theory, 1955, 2d edit., 1965, Theory of Linear Antennas, 1956, (with T.T. Wu) Scattering and Diffraction of Waves, 1959, (with R.B. Mack and S.S. Sandler) Arrays of Cylindrical Dipoles, 1968, (with C.W. Harrison, Jr.) Antennas and Waves: A Modern Approach, 1969, Tables of Antenna Characteristics, 1971, (with G.S. Smith et al) Antennas in Matter, 1981 (with S. Prasad) Fundamental Electromagnetic Theory and Applications, 1986, (with M. Owens and T.T. Wu) Lateral Electromagnetic Waves Theory and Applications to Communications, Geophysical Exploration and Remote Sensing, 1992; also articles in field. Guggenheim fellow Europe, 1937, 58, IBM scholar Northeastern U., 1985; recipient Disting. Service citation U. Wis., 1973, Pender award U. Pa., 1986. Fellow IEEE (Centennial medal 1984, Grad. Edn. award 1997), AAAS, Am. Acad. Arts and Scis., Am. Phys. Soc.; mem. IEEE Antennas and Propagation Soc. (Disting. Achievement award 1991), AAUP, Internat. Sci. Radio Union, Bavarian Acad. Sci. (contbg. mem.), Phi Beta Kappa, Sigma Xi. Home: 92 Hillcrest Pky Winchester MA 01890-1440 Office: Gordon McKay Lab 9 Oxford St Cambridge MA 02138-2901

KING, ROSALYN MERCITA, social science researcher; b. Jacksonville, Fla., Aug. 16, 1948; d. Morris Charles and Marie (Coleman) K. BS, Howard U., 1970, MA, 1972; EdD, Harvard U., 1979. Dir. police youth project NCCJ, Washington, 1970-73; placement coord. U. North Fla., Jacksonville, 1973-74, instr., student support counselor, 1973-75; career edn. program coord. Roxbury/Harvard Sch. Program, Cambridge, Mass., 1976; rsch. analyst Spl. Commn. on Unequal Ednl. Opportunity Mass. Ho. of Reps., Boston, 1977; program coord. Freedom House, Inc., Roxbury, Mass., 1977-78; sr. program assoc. Expand Assocs., Inc., Silver Spring, Md., 1979; sr. assoc., dir. rsch. Mark Battle Assocs., Inc., Washington, 1980; dir. planning, program devel. and tech. assistance PUSH-Excel Inst. Research and Tng., Washington, 1981; rsch. assoc. So. Ctr. Studies in Pub. Policy Clark Coll., Atlanta, 1981-84; pres. Info. Rsch. Network Svc., Alexandria, Va., 1984—, Bathshua's Greetings, Alexandria, 1988—; asst. prof. psychology Loudoun Campus No. Va. C.C., Sterling, Va., 1996—; chief racial stats. U.S. Bur. Census, Washington, 1988; vis. prof. psychology Coppin State Coll., Balt., 1989-90; faculty rsch. assoc. U. Md., College Park, 1990-91; adj. lectr. dept. psychology George Mason U., Fairfax, Va., 1991—; adj. prof. psychology Prince George's C.C., Andrews AFB, 1991-94, Mary Washington Coll., Fredericksburg, Va., 1992-93, Catonsville (Md.) C.C., 1991-94, lectr., 1994-96; sr. pub. health analyst Agy. for HIV/AIDS Commn. Pub. Health, Washington, 1992-94; adj. prof. psychology and chair Ctr. for Tchg. Excellence No. Va. Region, No. Va. C.C., Loudoun campus, Sterling, Va., 1996—. Contbr. articles to profl. jours. Mem. Soc. for the Tchg. of Psychology, Psi Chi, Phi Delta Kappa.

KING, ROSEMARY ANN, air force officer; b. Erie, Pa., Dec. 2, 1966; d. Thomas Leonard and Dolores Ann (Sikora) King. BS, U.S. Air Force Acad., 1988; MLA, Harvard Extension Sch., 1992; postgrad., Ariz. State U., 1997—. Commd. 2d lt. USAF, 1988, advanced through grades to maj., 1995; aquisition officer Onizuka Air Stn., USAF, Sunnyvale, Calif., 1995-97. Asst. editor War, Lit. and Arts, 1992-95; book reviewer; author conf. papers. Participant, asst. Spl. Olympics, Colo., 1993-94; mem. Citizen's Project, Colo., 1992-95; child sponsor Children's Internat., Calif., 1992—; vol. Ann. Art/Wine Festival, Calif., 1995—. Fulbright Hays scholar, 1994; Air Force grantee, 1993. Mem. Assn. Grads., Virginia Woolf Soc., Air Force Assn. Democrat. Unitarian Universalist. Avocations: soccer, jogging, reading, socializing.

KING, ROSEMARY KRANYAK, pediatrics nurse; b. Phila., Nov. 29, 1965; d. John S. and Rosemary (Jones) Kranyak; m. Scott T. King, Mar. 28,1992; children: Michael, David. BSN, Widener U., Chester, Pa., 1988. PALS Cert. Pediatric nurse Kennedy Meml. Hosps., Stratford, N.J., 1988-89, New Era Nursing Inc., Stratford, 1989-90; asst. head nurse Va. Pediatrics & Adolescents, Springfield, 1990-92; pediatric nurse Meth. Hosp., Sacramento, 1992-96.

KING, RUFUS, lawyer; b. Seattle, Mar. 25, 1917; s. Rufus Gunn and Marian (Towle) K.; m. Janice L. Chase, June 15, 1941 (div. June 1951); children: Rufus III, Agnes S.; m. Elvine R. Rankine, Nov. 23, 1973. A.B., Princeton U., 1938; postgrad., Stanford U., 1940-41; J.D., Yale U., 1943. Bar: N.Y. 1944, D.C. 1948, Md. 1953. Instr. Princeton U., 1938-39; partner Rice & King, Washington, 1953-64; pvt. practice Washington, 1964-75; partner King & Newmyer, Washington, 1977-83; of counsel Berliner & Maloney, Washington, from 1983, Berliner, Corcoran & Rowe, 1989—; counsel Senate Crime Com., 1951, also other congl. coms.; cons. Nat. Commn. Law Enforcement and Adminstrn. Justice.; Chmn. joint com. on narcotic drugs Am. Bar Assn. and AMA, 1956—; dir. Drug Policy Found., 1988-89, Nat. Orgn. for Reform of Marijuana Laws. Author: You and I, 1940, Manifesto, 1947, Gambling and Organized Crime, 1968, The Drug Hangup, 1971, Stop the Drug War Now, 1991; Contbr. articles to profl. and popular jours. Pres. Montgomery County Community Psychiat. Clinic. Recipient award Drug Policy Found., 1989, Lifetime Achievement award, Assn. Drug Reform Orgns., 1998, svc. award Nat. Orgn. for Reform Marijuana Laws, 1999. Mem. ABA (chmn. criminal law sect. 1957-60, sec. 1954-57, mem. ho. of dels. 1960-66, chmn. spl. com. atomic attack 1962—, del. sect. individual rights, mem. spl. com. on standards for adminstrn. criminal justice), N.Y. State Bar Assn., Md. Bar Assn., Bar Assn. D.C., Am. Law Inst. (life). Clubs: Princeton (N.Y.C.); Metropolitan (Washington). Home: 3524 Williamsburg Ln NW Washington DC 20008-1207 Office: 1101 17th St NW Washington DC 20036-4704

KING, SAM B., III, legislative staff member. BA in Polit. Sci., U. S.C. Field rep. Charles D. Ravenel for Gov. Campaign, 1974; campaign mgr. William Howell for State Senate, 1975; upstate dir. U.S. Senator Ernest F. Hollings, 1977-89; state dir. U.S. Senator Ernest F. Hollings, Columbia, S.C., 1989—. Office: Strom Thurmond Fed Bldg 1835 Assembly St Rm 1551 Columbia SC 29201

KING, SHARON LOUISE, lawyer; b. Ft. Wayne, Ind., Jan. 12, 1932. AB, Mt. Holyoke Coll., 1954; JD with distinction, Valparaiso U., 1957; LLM in Taxation, Georgetown U., 1961. Bar: Ind. 1957, D.C. 1958, Ill. 1962. Trial atty. tax divsn. U.S. Dept. Justice, 1958-62; sr. counsel Sidley & Austin, Chgo. Bd. dirs. Lawyer's Com. for Better Housing, Inc. Fellow Am. Coll. Tax Counsel; mem. ABA (chmn. com. closely-held corps. taxation sect. 1979-81, regulated pub. utilities com. taxation sect. 1982-83, coun. dir. taxation sect. 1983-86), Chgo. Bar Assn. (bd. mgrs. 1973-75, chmn. fed. tax com. 1983-84), Ill. State Bar Assn. (counsel dir. sect. fed. taxation 1989-91), Women's Bar Assn. Ill. (bd. dirs. Found., v.p. Found., dir. scholarship). Office: Sidley & Austin 1 First Natl Plz Chicago IL 60603-2003

KING, SHELDON SELIG, medical center administrator, educator; b. N.Y.C., Aug. 28, 1931; s. Benjamin and Jeanne (Fritz) K.; m. Ruth Arden Zeller, June 26, 1955 (div. 1987); children: Tracy Elizabeth, Meredith Ellen, Adam Bradley; m. Xenia Tonesk, 1988. A.B., NYU, 1952; M.S., Yale U., 1957. Adminstrv. intern Montefiore Hosp., N.Y.C., 1952, 55; adminstrv. asst. Mt. Sinai Hosp., N.Y.C., 1957-60; asst. dir. Mt. Sinai Hosp., 1960-66, dir. planning, 1966-68; exec. dir. Albert Einstein Coll. Medicine-Bronx Mcpl. Hosp. Ctr., Bronx, N.Y., 1968-72; asst. prof. Albert Einstein Coll. Medicine, N.Y.C., 1968-72; dir. hosps. and clinics Univ. Hosp., assoc. clin. prof. U. Calif., San Diego, 1972-81; acting head div. health care scis., dept. community medicine U. Calif. (Sch. Medicine), 1978-81; assoc. v.p. Stanford U., 1981-85, clin. assoc. prof. dept. community, family and preventive medicine; exec. v.p. Stanford U. Hosp., 1981-85, pres., 1986-89; pres. Cedars-Sinai Med. Ctr., L.A., 1989-94; exec. v.p., pres. ea. region Salick Health Care, Inc., L.A., 1994—, pres. eastern region, 1996-98; interim dir. UCLA Med. Ctr., 1995; mem. adminstrv. bd. coun. teaching hosps., 1981-86, chmn. adminstrv. bd., 1985; preceptor George Washington U., Ithaca Coll., Yale U., U. Mo., CUNY; chmn. health care com. San Diego County Immigration Coun., 1974-77; adv. coun. Calif. Health Facilities Commn., 1977-82; chmn. ad hoc bd. advs. Am. Bd. Internal Medicine, 1985-91; bd. dirs. Nat. Com. Quality Health Care, chmn., 1993-94; mem. exec. com. St. Joseph Health Sys., 1990-94; bd. dirs. Am. Health Properties, acting chmn. 1996—; nat. adv. com. Robert Wood Johnson Exec. Nurse Fellows Program, 1998—. Mem. editorial adv. bd.: Who's Who in Health Care, 1977; mem. editorial bd. Jour. Med. Edn, 1979-84. Bd. dirs. hosp. coun. San Diego and Imperial Counties, 1974-77, treas., 1976, pres., 1977; bd. dirs. United Way San Diego, 1975-80, B'rith Milah Bd., Vol. Hosps. Am., 1990-94, mem. exec. com., 1991-93; mem. Accreditation Coun. for grad. med. edn., 1987-90, Prospective Payment Assessment Commn., 1987-90, Inst. of Medicine, 1988—; mem. nat. adv. com. Robert Wood Johnson Exec. Nurse Fellows Program, 1998—. With AUS, 1952-55. Fellow Am. Coll. Health Care Execs., Am. Pub. Health Assn., Am. Hosp. Assn. (governing coun. Met. sect. 1983-86, coun. on fin. 1987, ho. of dels. 1987-89), Calif. Hosp. Assn. (trustee 1978-81), Am. Podiatric Med. Assn. (project coun. 2000 1985-86), Healthcare Rsch. and Devel. Inst. (bd. dirs., chmn. 1993-97). Home: Apt 27G 17352 Sunset Blvd Apt 505D Pacific Palisades CA 90272-4116 Address: Salick Health Care 8201 Beverly Blvd Los Angeles CA 90048-4505

KING, STEPHEN EDWIN, novelist, screenwriter, director; b. Portland, Maine, Sept. 21, 1947; s. Donald and Nellie Ruth (Pillsbury) K.; m. Tabitha Jane Spruce, Jan. 2, 1971; children: Naomi Rachel, Joseph Hillstrom, Owen Phillip. B.S., U. Maine, 1970. Tchr. English Hampden (Maine) Acad., 1971-73; writer in residence U. Maine at Orono, 1978-79. Novels include Carrie, 1974, 'Salem's Lot, 1975, The Shining, 1976, The Stand, 1978, The Dead Zone, 1979, Firestarter, 1980, Danse Macabre, 1981, Cujo, 1981, Different Seasons, 1982, The Dark Tower: The Gunslinger, 1982, Christine, 1983, Pet Sematary, 1983, The Talisman, 1984, Cycle of the Werewolf, 1985, Skeleton Crew, 1986, It, 1986, The Eyes of the Dragon, 1987, Misery, 1987, The Dark Tower: The Drawing of the Three, 1987, The Tommyknockers, 1987, The Dark Half, 1989, The Stand (uncut), 1990, Four Past Midnight, 1990, The Dark Tower III: The Waste Lands, 1991, Needful Things, 1991, Gerald's Game, 1992, Dolores Claiborne, 1992, Insomnia, 1994, Rose Madder, 1995, Desperation, 1996, The Green Mile (serial), 1996, Bag of Bones, 1997, Wizard & Glass, 1997, The Girl Who Loved Tom Gordon, 1999, Storm of the Century, 1999; short story Night Shift (collection), 1978, Nightmares and Dreamscapes, 1993, Creepshow (comic), 1982, The Plant (self pub.), 1983, 1984, My Pretty Pony, 1988, Dolan's Cadillac, 1989, Six Stories, 1997; author numerous other short stories; (as Richard Bachman) Rage, 1977, The Long Walk, 1979, Roadwork, 1981, The Running Man, 1982, Thinner, 1984, Insomnia, 1993, The Regulators, 1996; author numerous short story screenplays; writer, creator TV program "Stephen King's Golden Years", 1991; film director: Maximum Overdrive, 1986; original screenplay: Sleepwalkers, 1991; actor: Knightriders, 1981, Creepshow, 1982, Maximum Overdrive, 1986, Creepshow II, 1988, The Shawshank Redemption, 1995 (USC Scriptor Awd. 1995); creator, writer (TV mini-series) The Stand, 1994, Storm of the Century, 1999 (mini-series). Mem. Author's Guild Am., Screen Artists Guild, Screen Writers of Am., Writer's Guild. Democrat. Office: 49 Florida Ave Bangor ME 04401*

KING, STEPHEN MILES, public administration educator; b. Dec. 5, 1960. BS in Polit. Sci., Kearney State Coll., 1983; MA in Polit. Sci., U. Mo., 1984, PhD in Polit. Sci., 1990. Asst. prof. polit. sci. Wash. State U., Pullman, 1989-91; asst. prog. govt. Oral Roberts U., Tulsa, 1991-98; assoc. prof. pub. adminstrn. Regent U., Virginia Beach, Va., 1998—. E-mail: smking@regent.edu. Office: 1000 Regent University Dr Virginia Beach VA 23464

KING, STEVE MASON, judge, lawyer; b. Graham, Tex., Dec. 17, 1951; s. Beverly W. and Chloe (Stalcup) K.; m. Julia Ellen Milford, Mar. 30, 1974; children: Cassandra, Mason. BA cum laude, U. Tex., 1974; JD, Baylor U., 1976. Bar: Tex. 1977, U.S. Dist. Ct. (no. dist.) Tex. 1978, U.S. Ct. Appeals (5th cir.) 1981, U.S. Supreme Ct. 1981, U.S. Tax Ct. 1984, U.S. Dist. Ct. (ea. dist.) Tex. 1989. Assoc. Byrom, Butcher & Moore, Ft. Worth, 1977-78, Garrett & Stahala, Ft. Worth, 1978-83; ptnr. Garrett, Stahala & King, Ft. Worth, 1983-86, Epstein, Becker, Borsody & Green, Ft. Worth, 1986-87; pvt. practice Ft. Worth, 1987-94; judge Tarrant County Probate Ct. # 1, Ft. Worth, 1994—; mem. nominating com. Nat. Coll. of Probate Judges, 1999, chair nominating com., 1999, co-chair membership com. 1999; faculty Tex. Coll. of Probate Judges; mem. Tex. Guardianship Manual Revision Com.; mem. Tex. Supreme Ct. Commn. Info. Tech., 1997—. Note contbr.: The Handbook of Tex., 3rd edit. Trustee Buckner Bapt. Benevolences, Dallas, 1981—; parliamentarian Bapt. Gen. Conv. Tex., 1988-90; dir. Dispute Resolution Svcs. Tarrant County, Chisholm Trail Roundup, dir., v.p.; head Ramrod Fort Worth Herd Outriders; mem. Fort Worth Sesquicentennial Celebration History Commn.; chair Tarrant County Judges Info. Tech. & Records Commn. Fellow Tex. Bar Found.; mem. State Bar Tex., Tarrant County Bar Assn. (chair history and archives com.), Tarrant County Probate Bar Assn. (bd. dirs., pres. 1993-94), Magna Carta Barons (Somerset chpt.), Ft. Worth Club, Phi Delta Phi. Avocations: woodworking, history, genealogy. Office: Tarrant County Courthouse Rm 260A 100 W Weatherford St Fort Worth TX 76102-2115

KING, STEVEN HAROLD, health physicist; b. Stamford, Conn., June 27, 1959; s. Richard H. and Joan W. (Weaver) K.; m. Kim Yvonne Bulmer, June 18, 1983; children: Christopher K., Brandon S., Arielle L. BA, SUNY, Buffalo, 1981, MA, 1983. Asst. health physicist Milton S. Hershey Med. Ctr. Pa. State U., Hershey, 1983-86, assoc. health physicist, 1986—, laser safety officer, 1989—; grad. program com. mem. Pa. State U., Harrisburg, Pa., 1989—. Author: (with others) Handbook of Management of Radiation Protection Programs, 1991; contbr. articles to profl. jours. Mem. Am. Assn. Physicists in Medicine, Am. Nuclear Soc., Health Physics Soc. (chair admissions com. 1989-91, pres. Susquehanna Valley chpt. 1989-90). Office: Milton S Hershey Med Ctr 500 University Dr Hershey PA 17033-2391

KING, SUSAN BENNETT, retired glass company executive; b. Sioux City, Iowa, Apr. 29, 1940; d. Francis Moffatt Bennett and Marjorie (Rittenhouse) Sillin; divorced. AB, Duke U., 1962. Legis. asst. U.S. Senate, Washington, 1963-66; dir. Nat. Com. for Effective Congress, Washington, 1967-71, Ctr. Pub. Financing of Election, Washington, 1972-75; exec. asst. to chmn. Fed. Election Commn., Washington, 1975-77; chmn. U.S. Consumer Product Safety Commn., Washington, 1978-81; dir. consumer affairs Corning (N.Y.) Glass Works, 1982, v.p. corp. communications, 1983-86; pres. Steuben Glass, N.Y.C., 1987-92; sr. v.p. corp. affairs Corning Inc., 1992-94; consumer affairs del. OECD, Paris, 1980-81; bd. dirs. Coca-Cola Corp., Guidant Corp., Health Effects Inst.; leader in residence Terry Sanford Inst. Pub. Policy, Duke U., Durham, N.C. Trustee Duke U., Durham, N.C., 1987—, Eurasia Found., Washington, Nat. Pub. Radio Found. Fellow Inst. Politics, Harvard U., 1981, Sanford Inst. Pub. Policy, Duke U., 1995-97. Mem. Nat. Consumers League (pres. 1984-85).

KING, TERRY LEE, statistician, mathematician; b. Akron, Iowa, Feb. 24, 1945; s. Stanley W. and Hazel M. (Peck) K.; m. Carol Elizabeth Glass, June 12, 1971; children: Kevin, Shawn, Heather. BA cum laude, Westmar Coll., 1967, U. Iowa, 1969; PhD, Pa. State U., 1980. Instr. Thiel Coll., Greenville, Pa., 1969-71; statistician Desmatics Inc., State College, Pa., 1975-79; instr. Frostburg (Md.) State Coll., 1979-81, assoc. prof. math./stats., 1981-89; chmn. dept. math./stats. N.W. Mo. State U., Maryville, 1988-93, prof. math. and stats., 1989—. Editl. collaborator Current Index to Statistics, 1980-89. Deacon, active in music program First Bapt. Ch. Mem. Am. Statis. Assn. (membership com. 1982-84, mem. com. on stats. and disability 1995-97, newsletter editor statis. edn. sect. 1997—), Math. Assn. Am. (vice-chair Mo. sect. 1990-91, chmn. 1991-92, past chair 1992-93), Biometric Soc., Gideon Internat., Rotary Internat. (Maryville chpt., program chair 1995-96, sec. 1996—), Phi Kappa Phi, Kappa Mu Epsilon, Pi Mu Epsilon. Office: NW Mo State U 800 University Dr Maryville MO 64468-6015

KING, TERRY SCOT, engineering educator; b. Muscatine, Iowa, June 17, 1952; s. Robert Lloyd and Norma June (Slater) K.; m. Kathleen Ellen Kuster, Mar. 27, 1976; children: Andrew Lewis, Jonathan Patrick. BS, Iowa State U., 1975; PhD, MIT, 1979. Rsch. engr. Exxon Chem. Co., Baton Rouge, La., 1979-81, sr. engr., 1981-82; asst. prof. Iowa State U., Ames, 1982-86, assoc. prof., 1986-90, prof. engring., 1990-97, chair dept., 1990-97; dean of engring. Kans. State U., Manhattan, 1997—; bd. dirs. Nantech, Manhattan. Contbr. more than 60 articles to profl. jours.; patentee in field. Bd. dirs. Kans. State U. Rsch. Found., Manhattan, 1997—, Kans. State U. Found., Manhattan, 1997—. Office: 146 Rathbone Hall Manhattan KS 66506-5200

KING, THOMAS, physician, physiology educator; b. Shanghai, China, June 1, 1934; came to U.S., 1965; s. Tung Ming and Yen Vee (Sung) K.; m. Amy Penn, July 15, 1959; children: Susan, Caroline. MB, Ch.B., U. Edinburgh, Scotland, 1959, MD, 1963. Asst. prof. medicine Cornell U. Med. Ctr., N.Y.C., 1970-73, assoc. prof. medicine, 1973—, acting chief div. pulmonary and critical care medicine, 1982-85, 91-93, assoc. prof. physiology and biophysics, 1975—. Recipient Pulmonary Acad. award Nat. Heart & Lung Inst., 1972-77. Fellow Royal Coll. Physicians London, Am. Coll. Chest Physicians; mem. N.Y. Trudeau Soc. (pres. 1978-79), Chinese-Am. Med. Soc. (pres. 1984-85), Am. Thoracic Soc., Med. Rsch. Soc. of U.K., Am. Fedn. Clin. Rsch., Am. Physiology Soc. Office: Cornell U Med Ctr 520 E 70th St # 505 New York NY 10021-9800

KING, W. DAVID, federal judge. BS, Murray State U., 1967; JD, U. Ky., 1972. Pvt. practice Paducah, Ky.; magistrate judge U.S. Dist. Ct. (we. dist.) Ky., Pacudah, 1979—. With U.S. Army, 1968-70. Fax: (502) 442-6481. Office: US Dist Ct We Dist Ky 105 Federal Bldg Paducah KY 40201

KING, WARREN R., federal judge. Grad., Rensselaer Polytech. Inst.; JD, Am. U.; LLM, Yale U. Atty. U.S. Dist. Ct. D.C.; chief grand jury/intake divsn., dep. and acting chief divsn. Superior Ct. Washington; with Office of Improvements in Adminstrn. of Justice U.S. Dept. Justice; assoc. judge Superior Ct. D.C., Washington, 1981-81, U.S. Ct. Appeals (D.C. cir.), Washington, 1991—; mem. faculty Antioch Sch. Law, 1975—; mem. staff Atty. Gen.'s task force on violent crime; mem. hearing com. Bd. Profl. Responsibility. With USN. Office: Dist of Columbia Court of Appeals 500 Indiana Ave NW Rm 6000 Washington DC 20001-2131*

KING, WAYNE DOUGLAS, former state senator; b. Boston, Nov. 24, 1955; s. Roger Franklin and Roberta (Dixon) K.; m. Alice Vartanian, Dec. 21, 1985; 1 child, Zachary. BS, U. N.H., 1977, MEd, 1980. Assoc. King Realty Inc., Campton, N.H., 1977-90; mem. N.H. Ho. of Reps., Concord, 1983-88, N.H. Senate, Concord, 1989-94; pres. Moosewood Mktg., 1993—. Dem. candidate for gov. State of N.H., 1994. Address: PO Box 500 Rumney NH 03266-0500

KING, WAYNE EDGAR, educator, journalist; b. McDowell County, N.C., Mar. 31, 1939; s. Weldon Edgar and Mary (Hixon) K.; m. Nina Davis, (div. June 1978); m. Paula Theodore Carroll, July 16, 1984. BA in Journalism, U. N.C., 1964. Reporter, editor The Detroit Free Press, 1964-69; editor, bur. chief, corr. The N.Y. Times, N.Y.C., 1969-93; dir. journalism program Wake Forest U., Winston-Salem, N.C., 1993—. Mem. editl. bd. Acad. Mag., Washington, 1996—. Recipient Pulitzer prize, 1968. Mem. AAUP, Torch Club. Home: 2200 Allen Easley Dr Apt 6-i Winston Salem NC 27106-4631

KING, WILLARD FAHRENKAMP (MRS. EDMUND LUDWIG KING), Spanish language educator; b. Roswell, N.Mex., July 13, 1924; d. W.F. and Willard (Pickerill) Fahrenkamp; m. Edmund Ludwig King, Jan. 29, 1951. Student, Tex. Christian U., 1940-41; B.A., U. Tex., 1943, M.A., 1946; Ph.D., Brown U., 1957. Instr. Spanish U. Tex., 1946-47, 49-50; instr. Spanish Brown U., 1950-51; instr. Spanish Bryn Mawr (Pa.) Coll., 1958-60, asst. prof., 1960-64, assoc. prof., 1964-70, prof. Spanish, 1970—, Dorothy Nepper Marshall prof. Hispanic studies, 1976—, chmn. dept. Spanish, 1964-89, dir. Hispanic studies program, 1971-92; corporator Internat. Inst. in Spain, resident dir., 1991-93. Author: Prosa novelística y academias literarias en el siglo XVII, 1963, Juan Ruiz de Alarcón, letrado y dramaturgo, 1989; also articles; editor, translator: Lope de Vega, El Caballero de Olmedo, 1972; translator: Amèrico Castro, The Spaniards, 1971; editor, commentator Agustín Moreto, El desdén, con el desdén, 1996. Guggenheim fellow, 1965-66. Mem. MLA, Renaissance Soc. Am., Phi Beta Kappa. Home: 171 Western Way Princeton NJ 08540-7207 Office: Thomas Libr Bryn Mawr Coll Bryn Mawr PA 19010

KING, WILLIAM BRADLEY, emergency medicine physician; b. Owensboro, Ky., July 17, 1958; s. Lee Bradley and Betty (Hamilton) K.; m. Valerie Susan Russell, Dec. 21, 1985 (div. June 1997); children: Kelsey, Kayla, Kylie. BS, U. Ky., 1981; MS, U. Louisville, 1985, MD, 1989. Diplomate Am. Bd. Emergency Medicine. Intern U. Louisville Affil. Hosps., 89-90, resident emergency medicine, 90-92; physician Ky. Emergency Medicine Physicians Assocs., P.S.C., Louisville, 1992-95; asst. clin. prof. emergency medicine U. Louisville, 1995—; physician Norton Health Care, Louisville, 1995—; staff physician emergency dept. Bapt. East Hosp., 1999—; chmn. dept. emergency medicine Alliant Health Sys., 1995-97, vice chmn., 1998. Fellow Am. Coll. Emergency Physicians (sec.-treas. 1998—; v.p. Ky. chpt. 1999), Am. Acad. Emergency Medicine; mem. Am. Coll. Emergency Physicians, Ky. Med. Assn., Jefferson County Med. Soc. Avocations: weight training, running, golf, tennis. Home: 9498 Longwood Cir Louisville KY 40223 Office: Norton Healthcare 200 E Chestnut St Louisville KY 40202-1800*

KING, WILLIAM BRUCE, lawyer; b. Boston, June 3, 1932; s. Gilbert and Frances (Hood) K.; m. Sheila Malone, July 9, 1955; children: Stephen Bruce, Rachel Creath, Christopher Bruce. A.B., Harvard U., 1954, LL.B., 1959. Bar: Mass. 1959. Assoc. firm Goodwin, Procter & Hoar LLP, Boston, 1959-67, ptnr., 1968—; prin. William B. King P.C., 1981—; mem. bd. investment Cambridge Savs. Bank, 1973—, trustee, 1969—, corporator, 1965—; sec. Bradley Real Estate, Inc., 1963—; trustee Cambridge Heritage Trust, 1984—; dir. mem. exec. com. Cambridge Fin. Group, Inc., 1998—, Cambridge Appleton Trust, N.A., 1999—. Author: (with others) Real Estate Investment Trusts: Structures, Analysis, and Strategy, 1997. Trustee Buckingham Browne and Nichols Sch., 1970-76, sec., 1970-73, vice chmn., 1974-76; mem. Cambridge (Mass.) Hist. Commn., 1973—, vice chmn., 1973-86, chmn., 1986—; pres Cambridge Civic Assn., 1963-65; bd. govs. Nat. Assn. Real Estate Investment Trusts, 1982-88, chmn. state regulation subcom. of govt. rels. com., 1989-91. Served with USN, 1954-56. Recipient 4th Ann. Industry Leadership award Nat. Assn. Real Estate Investment Trusts, 1995. Mem. ABA, Mass. Bar Assn., Boston Bar Assn., Cambridge-Arlington-Belmont Bar Assn. (pres. 1974-75). Home: 25 Hurlbut St Cambridge MA 02138-1603 Office: Exchange Pl Boston MA 02109-2803

KING, WILLIAM COLLINS, oil company executive; b. Pitts., Aug. 11, 1921; s. William Raffington and Anne Blatchford (Collins) K.; m. Carolyn Ottilie Thorne, Sept. 1, 1951; children: William R., John Thorne, Louise R., Andrew C. BSChemE, Carnegie-Mellon U., 1943; MSChemE, MIT, 1948. With Gulf Rsch. & Devel. Co. div. Gulf Oil Corp., Pitts., 1948-55, with chems. dept., 1955-57, dir. market rsch. and econ. planning chems. dept., 1957-63, world wide coord. chem. ops., 1963-67, v.p. chem. ops. in Europe and Middle East, 1967-72, dir. corp. policy analysis, 1972-80, v.p. corp. planning, 1980-85; bd. dirs. Fertiberia, S.A., Spain, Rio Gulf Petrolquimica, S.A., Spain, Kuwait Chem. Fertilizer Co., Kuwait; spkr., 1975—, participant nat. and local programs, participant local radio programs. Contbr. articles to profl. publs. Bd. dirs. Hist. Soc. We. Pa., 1977—, pres., trustee, 1986-90, trustee emeritus, 1999, chmn., 1990-97, vile chmn., 1998— (honored with William Collins King Atrium of Senator John Heinz Pitts. Regional History Ctr., 1996); v.p., bd. dirs. Civic Light Opera Co., Pitts., 1978-86 (Golden Hall of Fame, 1996); councillor of the Atlantic Coun. of the U.S., 1985-93. Served with C.E., U.S. Army, 1944-46, CBI. Recipient Alumni Merit award Carnegie Mellon U., 1998. Fellow Am. Chem. Soc.; mem. N.Am. Soc. Corp. Planning (bd. dir. chpt. 1982-85), Strategic Mgmt. Soc., Coun. Planning Execs. (conf. bd.), Am. Inst. Chem. Engrs. Clubs: Duquesne; Fox Chapel Racquet, Fox Chapel Golf (Pitts.). *Do all that you do in that way most likely to enhance the self esteem of others.*

KING, WILLIAM RICHARD, business educator, consultant; b. McKeesport, Pa., Dec. 24, 1938; s. Dewey Clark and Cambria Edith (Jones) K.; m. Fay Eileen Bickerton, June 20, 1958; children: James David, Suzan Lorain, Cambria H.L. B.S. with honors, Pa. State U., 1960; M.S. Case Inst. Tech, 1962, Ph.D., 1964. Indsl. engr. Pitts. Steel Co., 1960; instr., research fellow, research asst. Case Inst. Tech., 1960-64; asst. prof. ops. research, 1964-65; asst. prof. stats. and ops. research Air Force Inst. Tech., 1965-67; assoc. prof. bus. adminstrn. U. Pitts., 1967-69, prof., 1969-85, univ. prof., 1986—, dir. doctoral program, 1971-74, dir. Strategic Mgmt. Inst., 1980-85; on leave as profl. staff mem. U.S. Senate Budget Com., 1976-77; v.p., dir. Cleland-King, Inc., 1969-85; mgmt. cons.; chmn. Internat. Conf. on Info. Systems Profl. Corp., 1987-88; vis. prof. U. Auckland, New Zealand, 1994, Nat. U. of Singapore, 1997, City U. of Hong Kong, 1997, 98. Author: Quantitative Analysis for Marketing Management, 1967, Probablilty for Management Decisions, 1968, (with David Cleland) Systems Analysis and Project Management, 1968 (McKinsey Found. award 1969), 3d edit., 1983, Management: a Systems Approach, 1972, Marketing Management Information Systems, 1977, (with David Cleland) Strategic Planning and Policy, 1978, (with John Grant) The Logic of Strategic Planning, 1982; also articles in profl. jours.; editor: (with David Cleland) Systems, Organizations, Analysis, Management, 1969, Project Management Handbook, 1983, 2d edit., 1989 (Inst. Indsl. Engrs. Book of Yr. award 1984); (with Gerald Zaltman) Marketing Scientific and Technical Information, 1979, (with D. I. Cleland) Strategic Planning and Management Handbook, 1987, (with P. Gray, E. McLean and H. Watson) Management of Information Systems, 1989, 2nd edit., 1994, (with V Sethi) Organizational Transformation Through Business Process Reengineering, 1998; assoc. editor: Strategic Mgmt. Jour., 1985-89, Mgmt. Sci., 1971-89, MIS Quar., 1980-82, editor-in-chief, 1983-85; area editor: Internat. Jour. Info. and Mgmt. Scis.; cons. editor Prentice Hall Info. Mgmt. Series; mem. editorial adv. bd. Omega: the Internat. Jour. of Mgmt. Sci., Info. Systems Rsch., Jour. Global Info. Mgmt., Jour. Mgmt. Info. Sys., Jour. Global Info. Tech. Mgmt., Jour. Market-Focused Mgmt., Info. Sys. Mgmt., IEEE Transactions on Engring. Mgmt., Encyclopedia Info. Sys. Active YMCA, YMHA; v.p., dir. Pitts. Commerce Inst., 1971-80; bd. dirs. Western Pa. Montessori Sch., 1968-71, pres., 1968-69. Served to 1st lt. USAF, 1965-67. Ford Found. Systems research fellow, 1960-62; Travelers Ins. Co. research fellow, 1963-64, External Examiner City U. of Hong Kong, 1996—; Alumni Meml. scholar Pa. State U., 1956-60. Fellow AAAS, Decision Sci. Inst.; mem. Planning Forum, Ops. Rsch. Soc. Am., Acad. Mgmt., Strategic Mgmt. Soc., Inst. Mgmt. Scis. (v.p. 1986-89, pres. 1989-90), Assn. Info. Sys. (pres. 1995), Assn. Computing Machinery, Am. Mktg. Assn., Soc. Info. Mgmt., World Future Soc., Tau Beta Pi, Beta Gamma Sigma, Alpha Pi Mu, Sigma Tau. Office: Katz Grad Sch Bus U Pitts Pittsburgh PA 15260

KING, WILLIAM STEWART, II, public relations executive; b. Neptune, N.J., Nov. 8, 1954; s. William Stewart and Helen Irene (Moysiuk) K.; m. Shelley Ann Bundy, July 17, 1983; children: Bentley, Hallie. BA, Morris Harvey Coll., 1976. Sports info. dir. Morris Harvey Coll., Charleston, W.Va., 1974-76; asst. promotions dir. Tulane U., New Orleans, 1977; pub. relations dir. Milw. Bucks NBA, 1977—; mem. NBA Pub. Rels. Adv. Bd. Editor Milw. Bucks Media Guide, 1977-99, HOOP game program, 1977-99. Bd. dirs. Midwest Athletes Against Childhood Cancer Fund, Make-A-Wish Found. of Wis. Avocation: professional jet ski racer. Home: 39214 Lakeview Ln Oconomowoc WI 53066-1960 Office: Milw Bucks 1001 N 4th St Milwaukee WI 53203-1314

KING, WILLIAM TERRY, retired manufacturing company executive; b. Cleve., Dec. 3, 1943; s. William T. and Marion (Rothweiler) K.; m. Judith Ann Cervantes, Oct. 22, 1943; children: Kimberly, Kelly. BSC, St. Louis U., 1968. Contr. for Can. and Latin Am., Monsanto Co., St. Louis, 1977-82, mgr. internat. fin., 1982-84, dir. ops. analysis, 1984-86, asst. contr., 1986-88, asst. controller, 1993-97; ret., 1997; v.p., contr. Fisher Controls Internat. Inc., Clayton, Mo., 1988-92. Mem. Com. to Elect A.J. Cervantes, St. Louis, 1964-65; v.p. adv. bd. dirs., exec. com., chmn. fin. and planning com. St. Mary's Health Ctr. Mem. Inst. Mgmt. Acctg. (cert.). Republican. Roman Catholic. Avocations: golf, fishing, gardening. Home: 16643 Sterling Pointe Ct Chesterfield MO 63005-4509

KING CALKINS, CAROL COLEMAN, health sciences administrator; b. L.A., May 31, 1949; d. Harold S. and Gladys (Blumenthal) Coleman; 1 child, Katrina Elizabeth King; m. Michael Steven Calkins, Oct. 10, 1987. BA in Psychology, U. Colo., 1972, postgrad., 1998—; MBA, U. No. Colo., 1982. Dir. group living Nat. Jewish Ctr. Immunology and Respiratory Medicine, Denver, 1980-82; dir. clin. support svcs. Nat. Jewish Ctr. Immunology and Respiratory Medicine, 1982-83, dir. spl. projects, 1983-84, asst. dir. adminstrv. svcs., 1984, dir. adminstrv. svcs., 1984-95; dir. facilities ops. U. Colo. Health Scis. Ctr., Denver, 1995—; chair purchasing and contract subcom. Denver Health and Hosps. New Authority, 1994-96; speaker in field. Recorder improvement process coun. Jefferson County (Colo.) Schs., 1989. Mem. Colo. Hosp. Assn. Risk Mgrs., Am. Coll. Healthcare Execs., Assn. Commuter Transp. (v.p. Rocky Mountain chpt. 1992), Rocky Mountain Assn. Higher Edn. Facilities Officers, Pi Alpha Alpha. Avocations: weight training, horseback riding, hiking. Office: 4200 E 9th Ave Denver CO 80220-3706

KINGDOM, ROGER, olympic athlete; b. Vienna, Ga., Aug. 26, 1962; 1 child, Jierra Brianne. Grad., U. Pitts., 1983. Track & field athlete; winner gold medal Pan-Am Games, 1983; winner gold medal 110m hurdles Olmympic Summer Games, 1984, 88; ranked No. 1 in world Track & Field News, 1985, 89, 90. Holder world record 12.92. Office: c/o USA Track & Field Ste 140 1 RCA Dome Indianapolis IN 45225*

KINGDON, HENRY SHANNON, physician, biochemist, educator, executive; b. Puunene, Maui, Hawaii, July 2, 1934; s. Robert Wells and Anna Catherine (McCune) K.; m. Mary Lee Colman, June 22, 1957 (dec. Aug. 28, 1983); children: Holly, Catherine, Henry Colman; m. Jodi Kremiller, Jan. 26, 1985. AB in Chemistry, Oberlin Coll., 1956; MD, Western Res. U., 1963, PhD in Biochemistry, 1963; postgrad., U. Wash., 1962-63. Intern Univ. Hosp., Seattle, 1963-64; resident U. Wash. Affiliated Hosps., Seattle, 1964-65; practice medicine specializing in internal medicine Chgo., 1967-72, Chapel Hill, N.C., 1973-81; asst. prof. medicine and biochemistry U. Chgo., 1967-71, asso. prof., 1971-73, acting chmn. dept. medicine, summer 1971, dir. med. internship program, 1971-72; prof. medicine and biochemistry U. N.C., Chapel Hill, 1973-81; med. dir. Hyland Therapeutics div. Travenol Labs., Glendale, Calif., 1981-84; v.p., med. dir. Hyland div. Baxter Healthcare Corp., Glendale, Calif., 1984-90, v.p., gen. mgr., 1990-91; v.p. sci. affairs, chief med. officer Blood Therapy Group Baxter Healthcare Corp., Deerfield, Ill., 1991-93; v.p., med. dir. Gene Therapy Unit Baxter Biotech., Deerfield, 1993-95; v.p. tech. affairs Baxter Biotech., Deerfield, 1995—; bd. dirs. Immuno AG. Contbr. articles on mechanisms of blood coagulation, primary structure of proteins, and on regulation of anabolic nitrogen metabolism to profl. jours. Served with USPHS, 1965-67. Guggenheim Meml. Found. fellow, 1972-73; NIH grantee, 1957-59, 69-81. Mem. Am. Soc. Biol. Chemists, Am. Soc. Hematology, Internat. Soc. Thrombosis and Haemostasis, Central Soc. Clin. Research, So. Soc. Clin. Research, Phi Beta Kappa, Sigma Xi. Achievements include methods developed regarding eliminating AIDS and hepatitis infectivity from blood products; several patents pending. Home: Rte 1 Box 98 Drummond WI 54832 Office: Baxter Biotech LC IV-1 1627 Lake Cook Rd Deerfield IL 60015-5214 *Look it up; write it down; be on time; do a little extra.*

KINGDON, JOHN WELLS, political science educator; b. Wisconsin Rapids, Wis., Oct. 28, 1940; s. Robert Wells and Catherine (McCune) K.; m. Kirsten Berg, June 16, 1965; children: James, Tor. BA, Oberlin Coll., 1962; MA, U. Wis., 1963, PhD, 1965. Asst. prof. polit. sci. U. Mich., Ann Arbor, 1965-70, assoc. prof., 1970-75, prof., 1975-98, prof. emeritus, 1998—, chmn. dept. polit. sci., 1982-87. Author: Candidates for Office, 1968, Congressmen's Voting Decisions, 1973, 3d rev. edit., 1989, Agendas, Alternatives and Public Policies, 1984, 2d edit., 1995, America the Unusual, 1998. NSF grantee, 1978-82, Soc. Sci. Research Council grantee, 1969-70; Guggenheim fellow, 1979-80, Ctr. for Advanced Study in Behaviorial Scis. fellow, 1987-88. Fellow Am. Acad. Arts and Scis.; mem. Midwest Polit. Sci. Assn. (pres. 1987-88). Office: U Mich Dept Polit Sci Ann Arbor MI 48109

KINGERY, SANDRA LYNN, Spanish language educator, translator; b. Urbana, Ill., Nov. 22, 1964; d. Ross Alan and Phyllis (May) Kingery Martin; m. Miguel Angel Delgado, June 19, 1992. BA in Polit. Sci., Philosophy, Lawrence U., Appleton, Wis., 1986; certificado, U. Barcelona, Spain, 1987; MA in Spanish, U. Wis., 1989, PhD in Spanish, 1996. Lectr., tchg. asst. U. Wis., Madison, 1987-94; asst. prof. Lycoming Coll., Williamsport, Pa., 1994-96, 98—, Wake Forest U., Winston-Salem, N.C., 1996-97; internat. adv. com. Lycoming Coll., Williamsport, Pa., 1994-96, curriculum devel. com., 1995-96, judicial bd., 1995-96, faculty exec. coun., freshman seminar com., substance abuse com., 1998—, mid. states task force, 1999—. Mem. AAUW, MLA, Am. Assn. Tchrs. of Spanish and Portugese, Phi Sigma Iota, Spanish Club, Scholars Coun. Avocations: international travel, reading, biking, aerobics. Office: Lycoming Coll PO Box 2 Williamsport PA 17701

KING-GARNER, MIRIA, elementary education educator; b. Gadsden, Ala., May 29, 1949; d. Carl Jr. and Joyce Elrod (Gore) King; m. James Rickey Garner, June 2, 1968; 1 child, Micah. BS in Edn., Auburn U., 1972; MA, U. Ala., 1975, AA, 1981; Master's Endorsement in Adminstrn., 1995. Tchr. 6th-8th grades Etowah County Bd. Edn., Gadsden; asst. prin. Sardis H.S. Named Etowah County System Elem. Tchr. of Yr., 1988-89; inducted in Tchr. Hall of Fame (elem.) 1989. Mem. NEA, Ala. Edn. Assn., Etowah Edn. Assn., Delta Kappa Gamma.

KINGHAM, RICHARD FRANK, lawyer; b. Lafayette, Ind., Aug. 2, 1946; s. James R. and Loretta C. (Hoenigke) K.; m. Justine Frances McClung, July 6, 1968; 1 child, Richard Patterson. BA, George Washington U., 1968; JD, U. Va., 1973. Bar: D.C. 1973, U.S. Dist. Ct. D.C. 1974, U.S. Ct. Appeals (8th cir.) 1977, U.S. Supreme Ct. 1977, U.S. Ct. Appeals (5th cir.) 1980; registered fgn. lawyer Law Soc. Eng. and Wales, 1994. Editorial asst. Washington Star, 1964-68, 69-70; assoc. Covington & Burling, Washington, 1973-81, ptnr., 1981—, mng. ptnr. London office, 1996—; lectr. law U. Va., Charlottesville, 1977-90; mem. com. issues and priorities new vaccine devel. Inst. Medicine, NAS, 1983-86, Nat. Adv. Allergy and Infectious Diseases Coun. NIH, 1988-92, adv. bd. World Pharms. Report, 1990-96; mem. World Health Org. Coun. Internat. Orgns. Med. Scis. Working Party Comm. in Pharmacovigilance, 1997—. Articles editor U. Va. law rev., 1972-73; contbr. articles to profl. jours. Treas., mem. parochial ch. coun. St. Peter's Ch. Eaton Sq., London, 1998—. Mem. AAAS, ABA, Brussels Pharm. Law Group, Drug Info. Assn., Food and Drug Law Inst., European Soc. Pharmacovigilance, Food Law Group (U.K.), Soc. Vertebrate Paleontology, European Forum for Good Clin. Practice, Order of the Coif, Reform Club (London). Republican. Episcopalian. Avocation: vertebrate paleontology. Home: 26 Walpole St, London SW3 4QS, England also: PO Box 7566 Washington DC 20044-7566 Office: Leconfield House, Curzon St, London W1Y 8AS, England also: Covington & Burling PO Box 7566 1201 Pennsylvania Ave NW Washington DC 20044

KING HOOKHAM, ELEANOR, artist; b. Marlow, Okla., Apr. 5, 1909; d. William Frank Sr. and Sara Caroline (Smith) King; m. George Lawrence Salley, July 9, 1934 (div. Mar. 1940); 1 child, Jane King Salley; m. Robert Ernest Hookham, Nov. 5, 1943 (dec. Aug. 1989); children: Tarrant K., Robert Peyton. Student, Oklahoma City Coll.; Doctorate (hon.), Cultural Acad. de France, Paris, 1980; DA (hon.), Elmhurst Coll., 1987. Pvt. art tchr. Elmhurst, Ill., 1946-83; hon. chairperson Elmhurst Art Mus., 1997—. One-woman shows include Montross Gallery, N.Y.C., 1939, 41, Wheaton (Ill.) Pub. Libr., 1956, Concordia Sr. Coll., Fort Wayne, Ind., 1959, Galerie Internat., N.Y.C., yearly 1950-65, Pensacola (Fla.) Art Mus., 1969, Galerie Marcel Bernheim, Paris, yearly 1965-74, Galerie Bernheim-Jeune, Paris, yearly, 1985-92; works exhibited in group shows at Leonard Clayton Gallery, N.Y.C., 1938, Montross Gallery, N.Y.C., 1942, Johnson Gallery, Chgo., 1959, 60, 61, Ill. State Art Mus., Springfield, 1964, Internat. Fedns. Cultureelle Feminine Musée d'Art Moderne, Medaille D'Argent, 1968; author: Creative Art and the Subconscious, 1979, Complete Color Theory, 1979. Founder Elmhurst Fine Arts and Civic Ctr. Found., 1974, pres. 1974-92, chmn. bd., 1992-97; founder Elmhurst Art Mus., 1981, pres., 1981-91; co-founder Elmhurst Artist Guild. Recipient Nat. award Elmhurst Art Mus., 1998. Mem. Elmhurst Artists' Guild (co-founder, hon. life, pres. 1951-53), found. Elmhurst Art Mus. Episcopalian. Avocations: golfing, swimming. Home and Office: Eleanor King Studio 289 Adelia St Elmhurst IL 60126-3537

KINGMAN, DONG, artist, educator; b. Oakland, Calif., Apr. 1, 1911; s. Dong Chuan-Fee and Lew Shee K.; m. Wong Shee, Sept. 1929 (dec. June 1954); children—Eddie, Dong Kingman Jr.; m. Helena Kuo, Sept. 1956. Student, Lingnan, Hong Kong, 1924-26; LHD (hon.), Acad. Art Coll., San Franciso, 1987. Tchr. art San Diego Art Gallery, 1941-43; tchr. Famous Artists Schs., Westport, Conn., Columbia U., Hunter Coll.; Lectr. tour around world sponsored by internat. cultural exchange program Dept. State, 1954. Represented in permanent collections, Whitney Mus. Am. Art, Am. Acad. Arts and Letters, Bklyn. Mus., Toledo Mus. Art, Joslyn Art Mus., Omaha, Mus. Fine Arts, Boston, Met. Mus. Art, Mus. Modern Art, N.Y.C., U. Nebr., Wadsworth Atheneum, Bloomington (Ill.) Art Assn., San Francisco Mus., Mills Coll., De Young Mus., Albert Bender Collection, Eleanor Roosevelt Collection, Chgo. Art Inst., N.Y. State Tchrs. Coll., Springfield (Ill.) Art Assn., Cranbrook Acad. Art, Butler Art Inst., Ft. Wayne Mus., Addison Gallery, U.S. Dept. State, many others; executed murals, Bank of Calif., San Francisco, N.Y. Hilton Hotel, R.H. Macy & Co., Franklin Sq., N.Y., Boca Raton Hotel, Fla., Hyatt Regency Hotel, Hong Kong, Ambassador Hotel, Kowloon, Hong Kong, Lincoln Savs. Bank, N.Y.C.; illustrator: The Bamboo Gate (Vanya Oakes), 1946, China's Story (Enid LaMonte Meadowcroft), 1946, Nightingale (Andersen), 1948, Johnny Hong in Chinatown (Clyde Robert Bulla), 1952, Caen's and Kingman's San Francisco (Herb Caen), 1964, City on the Golden Hill (Herb Caen), 1967; author: (with Helena Kuo Kingman) Dong Kingman's Watercolors, 1980, Paint the Yellow Tiger, 1991; Painted: (with Helena Kuo Kingman) title paintings for 55 Days at Peking, movie title paints for Flower Drum Song, 1964, movie poster Universal Studio Tour. Served in U.S. Army. Recipient award Chgo. Internat. Watercolor Exhbn., 1944, Gold medal of honor Audubon Artists Exhbn. 1946, award, 1956; Joseph Pennel Meml. medal Phila. Watercolor Club, 1950, award, 1968; Watercolor prize Pa. Acad., 1953, Am. Watercolor Soc. award, 1956, 60, 62-65, 67, 72, High Wings Medal award, 1973, V.K. McCracken Young award, 1976, Ford-Times award, 1978, Barse Miller Meml. award, 1979, Dolphin Medal award, 1987; 150th Anniversary Gold Medal award Nat. Acad. Design, 1975, Walter Bigg Meml. award, 1977; Key to City of Omaha, 1980, Key to City of Cin., 1980; San Diego Watercolor Soc. prize, 1984, 1st prize for Ch. No. 1, San

Francisco Art Assn., 1936; named Hon. Admiral of Navy, Omaha, 1979, Hon. Citizen of Louisville, 1980, Hon. Capt. of Belle of Louisville, 1980, Man of Yr. Chinatown Planning Coun., N.Y.C., 1981, Man of Yr. Oakland (Calif.) Chinese Community Coun., 1985, Man of Yr. Rotary Club 1991, Man of Yr. Chinese Affirmative Action, San Francisco, 1991, Guest of Honor for Opening Internat. Book Fair, Hong Kong, 1991, judge Miss Universe and Miss U.S.A., 1963-85; Guggenheim fellow, 1942-43. Home: 21 W 58th St New York NY 10019-1604

KINGMAN, ELIZABETH YELM, anthropologist; b. Lafayette, Ind., Oct. 15, 1911; d. Charles Walter and Mary Irene (Weakley) Yelm; m. Eugene Lingman, June 10, 1939; children: Mixie Kingman Eddy, Elizabeth Ann Kingman. BA, U. Denver, 1933; MA, 1935. Asst. in anthropology U. Denver, 1932-34; mus. asst. Ranger Naturalist Staff Mesa Verde Nat. Park, Colo., 1934-38; asst. to husband in curatorial work Indian art exhibits Philbrook Art Ctr., Tulsa, 1939-42, Joslyn Art Mus., Omaha, 1947-69; tutor humnaities dept. U. Omaha, 1947-50; cjhn. bd. govs. Pi Beta Phi Settlement Sch., Gatlinburg, Tenn., 1969-72, Joslyn Art Mus., Omaha, 1947-50; tutor humanities dept. U. Omaha, 1947-50; chmn. bd. govs. Pi Beta Phi Settlement Sch., Gatlinburg, Tenn., 1969-72; asst. to husband in exhibit design mus. Tex. Tech. U., 1970-75; bibliographer Internat. Ctr. ARid and Semi-Arid Land Studies, 1974-75; libr. Sch. Am. Rsch., Santa Fe, N.Mex., 1978-86; rsch. assoc., 1986-98. V.p. Santa Fe Corral of the Westerners, 1985-86. Mem. AAUW, LWV, Archeol. Inst. Am. (v.p. Santa Fe chpt. 1981-83), Santa Fe Hist. Soc. (sec. 1981-83). Home: 604 Sunset St Santa Fe NM 87501-1118 Office: Sch Am Rsch 660 Garcia St Santa Fe NM 87501-2858

KINGMAN, WILLIAM LOCKWOOD, financial consultant; b. Medford, Mass., Aug. 21, 1930; s. Henry Eugene and Helen Elizabeth (Crandell) K.; m. Nancy Barbara Dean, Mar. 27, 1954; children: Lawrence Eugene, Celena Elizabeth. Grad., Middlesex Sch., Concord, Mass., 1949; BA in Econs., Yale U., 1953. With Franklin Mgmt. Corp., Boston, 1956-88, v.p., 1960-66, exec. v.p., 1966-68, vice chmn., 1968-71, chmn., 1971-88; also bd. dirs.; with Franklin Mgmt. Corp., N.Y.C., 1959-71, v.p., dir., 1960-71; exec. v.p., dir. Appleton Ptnrs. Inc., Boston, 1989—; chmn. audit com. Middlesex Savs. Banks, 1961-88, trustee, 1959—, mem. bd. investment, 1988—; trustee New England Fund (now Sentinel Balanced Fund), 1961-73; bd. dirs. Sigma Capital Shares Inc. (now Sentinel Aggressive Growth Fund). Mem. Acton Rep. Com., 1960-72, Acton Fin. Com., 1972-77, Acton Water Dist. Fin. Com., 1982—; mem. corp. Emerson Hosp., Concord, Mass., 1960-76, 92—, trustee, 1961-71; trustee The Fenn Sch., Concord, 1967-77, treas., 1969-77; trustee Charlestown (Mass.) Armed Svcs. YMCA, 1978—, v.p., 1988-93; bd. dirs. Boston Port, Seaman's Aid Soc., 1981—, pres., 1991-93. Lt. (j.g.) USNR, 1953-56; lt. (s.g.) ret. Mem. Navy League U.S. Republican. Unitarian. Clubs: Union (Boston), Wardroom (Boston); Nashoba Valley Hunt, Old Northbridge Hounds. E-mail: wkingman@appletonpartners.com. Home: 65 Esterbrook Rd Acton MA 01720-5701 Office: Appleton Ptnrs Inc 45 Milk St Boston MA 02109-5105

KINGON, JACQUELINE GOLDWYN (JACKIE KINGON), artist; b. June 18, 1940. BA, Sch. Visual Art, N.Y.C., 1980. Artist Kingon Art Studio, N.Y.C., 1992—. Artist: solo exhibitions include: Visual Arts Gallery, N.Y.C., (drawings), 1980, Open Loft, N.Y.C., 1981, Andrea Ruggieri Gallery, Washington, 1987, U.S. Embassy, Brussels, 1989; works shown in group exhbns. include: Visual Arts Gallery, N.Y.C., 1980, Jack Tilton Gallery, A More Store, Colab, N.Y.C., 1983-84, Arlington (Va.) Arts Ctr., 1985, Corocoran Gallery, Washington, 1985, W.P.A. Washington Projects for the Arts, 1985-86, Gallery K, Washington, 1986, Anton Gallery, Washington, 1986, Adrea Ruggieri Gallery, Washington, 1986, Coun. for Artistic Expression, Port Authority N.Y., 1993-95, Tribeca Towers: Art in Residence, Art Initiative, N.Y.C., 1994, Penine Hart, N.Y.C., 1995, Deep Space Gallery, You Win, N.Y.C., 1996, Donahue/Sosinski Art, Pools of Light, N.Y.C., 1997, Mus. Contemporary Art/Colaciello Armour Gallery, Artists' Responses to the Gulf War, W. Palm Beach, Fla., 1998, Donahus/Sosinski World Artists for Tibet, N.Y.C., 1998. Recipient Outstanding Student award Sch. Visual Arts, N.Y.C., 1980. Address: 44 Gramercy Park North New York NY 10050 Studio: Kingon Art Studio 32 Union Sq E New York NY 10003

KINGSBERY, WALTON WAITS, JR., retired accounting firm executive; b. Evergreen, Ala., June 25, 1928; s. Walton Waits and Alpha Lee (Eaton) K.; m. Helen Elizabeth Clayton, Mar. 21, 1953; children: Walton Waits, III, J. Clayton, Peter C. BS with honors, U. Ala., 1950. CPA, N.J., N.Y., Calif., Ohio. With Price Waterhouse & Co., 1950-88; mng. partner Price Waterhouse & Co., Cleve., 1977-82; mem. policy bd. Price Waterhouse & Co., 1979-87; mng. ptnr. Western area Price Waterhouse & Co., Los Angeles, 1982-87, mem. mgmt. com., 1982-85; mem. bus. adv. bd. Bateman Eichler, Hill Richards, L.A., 1988-90, Employee Office of Atty. Gen. N.J., 1988-95; mem. adv. bd. N.J. Bur. Securities, 1993—, N.J. Supreme Ct. Com. on Unauthorized Practice of Law, 1990-99; commr. N.J. Commn. to Deter Criminal Activity; dir. N.J. Citizens Against Crime, Inc. Author booklets, papers in field. Chmn. Shrewsbury (N.J.) Planning Bd., 1972; bd. dirs. Greater Cleve. Growth Assn., 1978-82; trustee Beech Brook, 1979, Cleve. Playhouse, 1980; clk. Village of Hunting Valley, Ohio; planning bd. Spring Lake, N.J., 1997—; mem. N.J. Commn. to Deter Criminal Activity. Served with AUS, 1950-53. Mem. AICPA, SAR, Nat. Assn. Accts., Ohio Soc. CPAs, N.J. Soc. CPAs, N.Y. Soc. CPAs, Calif. Soc. CPAs, Bluecoats, Newcomen Soc. N.Am., Cleve. Country Club, Union Club, Cleve. Racquet Club, Duquesne Club (Pitts.), Fifty Club, Calif. Club, Jonathan Club, Lincoln Club (L.A.), Univ. Club (N.Y.C.), Spring Lake Golf Club (trustee, exec. com., com. chmn., treas.), 200 Club, Beverly Hills Country Club (bd. govs.). *From a small town in Alabama to partner of Price Waterhouse in New York, then board member, management committee, head of the Cleveland office, then the west coast practice was a long, interesting road made easier by professional mentors, a loving wife and an understanding family.*

KINGSBURY, JOHN MERRIAM, botanist, educator; b. Boston, July 4, 1928; s. Willis Albert and Constance Elizabeth (Merriam) K.; m. Louise Arnold Gerken, June 6, 1956; 1 dau., Joanna Merriam. B.S., U. Mass., 1950; A.M., Harvard U., 1952, Ph.D., 1954; Sc.D. (hon.), Dickinson Coll., 1985. Instr. Brandeis U., Waltham, Mass., 1953-54; mem. faculty N.Y. State Coll. Agr. and Life Scis., Cornell U., Ithaca, N.Y., 1954—, prof. botany, 1970-83; prof. botany emeritus N.Y. State Coll. Agr. and Life Scis., Cornell U., 1983—; prof. clin. scis. Coll. Vet. Medicine, Cornell U., 1978-83, dir. arboretum and bot. garden, 1982-83; instr. Marine Biol. Lab., Woods Hole, Mass., summers 1958-61; founding dir. Shoals Marine Lab., 1972-79; adj. prof. U. N.H., 1976-78; cons. Upstate Med. Ctr., Syracuse, N.Y., 1977-86; instr. Aquavet course Cornell U. - U. Pa., 1978-98; lectr. Cornell U. Adult U., 1978-99; proprietor Bullbrier Press, 1983—; lectr. Columbus project Sta. WGBH/Pub. Broadcasting Svc., Boston, 1990; mem. endowment com. Shoals Marine Lab., 1992-96, chmn., 1992-94; vis. faculty U. Tasmania, Australia, 1980. Author: Poisonous Plants of the United States and Canada, 1964, Deadly Harvest—A Guide to Common Poisonous Plants, 1965, Seaweeds of Cape Cod and the Islands, 1969, rev. edit., 1997, The Rocky Shore, 1970, Oil and Water: The New Hampshire Story, 1975, 200 Conspicuous, Unusual, or Economically Important Tropical Plants of the Caribbean, 1988, Here's How We'll Do It—An Informal History of the Construction of the Shoals Marine Laboratory, 1991; mem. editl. bd. Cornell U. Press, 1985-86. NSF faculty fellow, 1958; Fulbright sr. scholar, 1980; recipient Profile Svc. award U. N.H., 1998. Fellow Am. Acad. Vet. and Comparative Toxicology (hon.); m. Bullard Meml. Farm Assn. (clk. 1978—, pres. 1990-94), Sea Edn. Assn. (trustee 1977-92, pres. 1982-87), Marine Biol. Lab. (life), Nature Conservancy (trustee N.Y. state bd. 1983-90), Audubon Soc. (lectr. Mass. chpt. 1987-89), Mass. Soc. Cin., Sigma Xi, Phi Zeta. Office: Cornell U 135A Guterman Lab Ithaca NY 14853-5903

KINGSBURY, MICHAEL BRYANT, organist, retired elementary and secondary education educator; b. Wilmington, N.C., Dec. 25, 1933; s. Walter Russell and Olga Loretta (Lewis) K. BA, Emory U., 1957; MA, Atlanta U., 1978. Cert. mid. sch. sci. tchr., sci. tchr. K-12, social studies tchr., Ga. Tchr. Bouldercrest Elem. Sch., Atlanta, 1958-62; sci. tchr. Northcutt Elem. Sch., College Park, Ga., 1962-66, G.P. Babb Jr. H.S., Forest Park, Ga., 1966-84, Pointe South Mid. Sch., Jonesboro, Ga., 1984-94; organist, choir master Episcopal and Cath. Chs., Atlanta and Decatur, Ga., 1955—; organist, dir. Cath. music Ft. McPherson/U.S. Army, Atlanta, 1994—. Author, editor: Laboratory Manual for Earth Science, 1970. Bd. dirs. Camelot Homeowners Assn., Jonesboro, 1978-84; patron Atlanta Symphony Orch., 1992—; lector St. Luke's Episcopal Ch. Recipient Ritter Music award Atlanta Pub. Schs., 1951, Cmty. Svc. award Clayton County Ret. Tchrs., 1998, Service Playing cert. Am. Guild Organists, others; NSF grant, 1970. Mem. Clayton County Ret. Tchrs. Assn. (pres. 1996—), Ga. Ret. Tchrs. Assn., Am. Guild of Organists (membership com. 1958—), Atlanta Music Club. Democrat. Episcopalian. Avocations: walking, bicycle riding, collecting southern writings and Gone with the Wind memorabilia. Home: 2669 Lake Jodeco Dr Jonesboro GA 30236-5355 Office: Ft McPherson US Army Lee St Atlanta GA 30330

KINGSEED, COLE CHRISTIAN, military officer, history educator; b. Charleston, S.C., Aug. 27, 1949; s. William B. and Marilyn J. (Harney) K.; m. Leslie Grover, Aug. 4, 1953; children: John, Maura. BA, U. Dayton, 1971; MA, Ohio State U., 1980, PhD, 1983. Commd. 2d lt. U.S. Army, 1971, advanced through grades to col.; bat. comdr. 25th Infantry Divsn., Schofield Barracks, Hawaii, 1988-90; assoc. prof. U.S. Mil. Acad., West Point, N.Y., 1992—; adj. faculty Naval War Coll., Newport, R.I., 1991-92, Mount Saint Mary Coll., Newburgh, N.Y., 1993—. Author: Eisenhower and the Suez Crisis of 1956, 1995. Mem. Soc. of Historians for Am. Fgn. Rels., Naval Inst. Roman Catholic. Avocations: reading, sports, stamp collecting. Office: Dept History US Military Acad West Point NY 10996

KINGSEED, WYATT, city official; b. Columbus, Ohio, Jan. 7, 1956. BS, Miami U., Oxford, Ohio, 1978; MPA, Ohio State U., 1980. Intern fin. dept., City of Columbus, 1979-80; budget analyst fin. dept., 1980-82, debt analyst, 1982-86, budget dir., 1987-89, asst. dir., 1990-91; dir. fin. dept. City of Columbus, 1992—. Mem. Gov. Fin. Assn. of Am. Office: Fin Dept/City Hall 90 W Broad St Columbus OH 43215-9000*

KINGSLAKE, RUDOLF, retired optical designer; b. London, Aug. 28, 1903; came to U.S., 1929; s. Martin and Margaret (Higham) K.; m. Hilda G. Conrady, Sept. 14, 1929; children: David C., Alan H. (dec.). BSc, Imperial Coll., London, 1924, MSc, 1926, DSc, 1950; DSc (hon.), U. Rochester, 1986. Prof. U. Rochester, N.Y., 1929-37, 68-83; optical designer Eastman Kodak Co., Rochester, 1937-68. Author: Lenses in Photography, 1951, 2d edit., 1963, Lens Design Fundamentals, 1978, Optical Systems Design, 1983, A History of the Photographic Lens, 1989, Optics in Photography, 1992; also numerous articles. Named Engr. of Yr., Rochester Engring. Soc., 1978. Fellow Soc. Motion Picture and TV Engrs. (Progress medal 1964), Soc. Photographic Scientists and Engrs.; mem. Optical Soc. Am. (hon., pres. 1947-49, Ives medal 1973), Soc. Photog. Instrumentation Engrs. (life). Home: 1570 East Ave Apt 120 Rochester NY 14610-1635

KINGSLEY, BEN, actor; b. Scarborough, Eng., Dec. 31, 1943; s. Rahimtulla Harji and Anna Lyna (Goodman) Bhanji; children: Edmund William Macaulay, Ferdinand James Macaulay, Thomas Alexis, Jasmin Anna. M.A. (hon.), Salford U. Assoc. artist Royal Shakespeare Co., Eng., 1968—. Appeared in plays including Hamlet, 1975-76, Othello, 1985-86, Edmund Kean, 1981-83; films include Gandhi, 1981 (Acad. award 1992), Betrayal, 1982, Turtle Diary, 1984, Sleeps Six, 1984, Harem, 1985, Maurice, 1987, Testimony, 1987, Pascali's Island, 1988, Without a Clue, 1988, Slipstream, 1989, The Children, 1990, Una Vita Scellerata, 1990, The Fifth Monkey, 1990, L'Amour Necessaire, 1991, Bugsy, 1991, Sneakers, 1992, Dave, 1993, Innocent Moves, 1993, Searching for Bobby Fisher, 1993, Schindler's List, 1993, Death and the Maiden, 1994, Species, 1994, Twelfth Night: Or What You Will, 1996, The Assignment, 1997, Photographing Fairies, 1997, Parking Shots, 1998, The Confession, 1999; (TV movies) Camille, 1984, Murderers Among Us: The Simon Weisenthall Story, 1988 (Disting. Svc. award 1989), Joseph, 1995, Moses, 1996, Weapons of Mass Distraction, 1997, The Tale of Sweeny Todd, 1998, Alice in Wonderland, 1999; (TV series) Oxbridge Blues, 1986, Crime and Punishment, 1998; (TV spls.) Silas Marner, 1987. Recipient Padma Shri award Govt. of India, 1984, Grammy award. 1984, Oscar award, 1983; named Best Actor and Best Newcomer Brit. Acad. Film and TV Arts, 1982, Best Actor Standard Film Awards, London, 1983. Mem. Brit. Acad. Film and TV Arts, Acad. Motion Picture Arts and Scis. (Golden Camera Berlin award, Evening Standard Film award for Best Actor for Schindler's List 1995). Office: care ICM 8942 Wilshire Blvd Beverly Hills CA 90211-1934*

KINGSLEY, JAMES GORDON, healthcare executive; b. Houston, Nov. 22, 1933; s. James Gordon and Blanche Sybil (Payne) K.; m. Martha Elizabeth Sasser, Aug. 24, 1956 (div. 1992); children: Gordon Alan, Craig Emerson; m. Suzanne H. Patterson, Oct. 30, 1993; 1 child, Aaron T. AB, Miss. Coll., 1955; MA, U. Mo., 1956; BD, ThD, New Orleans Bapt. Theol. Sem., 1960, 65; HHD (hon.), Mercer U., 1980; LittD (hon.), Seinan Gakuin U., Japan, 1989; postgrad., U. Louisville, 1968-69, Nat. U. Ireland, 1970, Harvard U., 1976. Asst. prof. Miss. Coll., 1956-58; instr. Tulane U., 1958-60; asst. prof. William Jewell Coll., Liberty, Mo., 1960-62; assoc. prof. Ky. So. Coll., Louisville, 1964-67, prof., 1967-69; prof. lit. and religion William Jewell Coll., 1969-93, dean, 1976-80, pres., 1980-93; v.p. Health Midwest, Kansas City, Mo., 1994-95, 96—; dep. dir. Nelson-Atkins Mus. of Art, 1995-96; vis. fellow Cambridge (Eng.) U., 1988. Author: A Time for Openness, 1973, Frontiers, 1983, Conversations with Leaders for a New Millenium, 1991, A Place Called Grace, 1993; contbr. articles to profl. jours. LaRue fellow, 1976. Mem. English Speaking Union, Burren Conservancy, Friends of the Bog, Cambridge Soc. Episcopalian. Home: Lakewood 402 NE Point Dr Lees Summit MO 64064-1561 Office: Health Midwest 2310 E Meyer Blvd Kansas City MO 64132-1136

KINGSLEY, JEAN-PIERRE, government official; b. Ottawa, Ont., Can., July 12, 1943; s. Oscar and Françoise (Charette-Bertrand) K.; m. Suzanne Potvin, Aug. 19, 1967; children: Marie-France, Justin, Michèle. B. Comm., U. Ottawa, 1965, M.A. in Hosp. Adminstrn., 1969. Programmer IBM, Ottawa-Hull, 1965-66; field supr. Travelers Ins., Ottawa-Hull, 1966-67; chief hosps. Dept. Vets.' Affairs Govt. Can., Ottawa-Hull, 1969-71, profl. officer Can. Mortgage & Housing Corp., 1971; assoc. exec. dir. and exec. dir. Charles Camsell Hosp., Edmonton, Alta., Can., 1971-73; prin. exec. officer Office of Dep. Min. Health and Welfare, Dept. Nat. Health and Welfare Govt. of Can., Ottawa-Hull, 1973-74, group chief, Treasury Bd. Secretariat, 1974-76; dir. gen. audit br. Pub. Svc. Commn., Ottawa-Hull, 1976-77; pres., CEO Ottawa Gen. Hosp., 1977-81; dep. sec., Ministry of State for Social Devel. Govt. of Canada, Ottawa-Hull, 1981-84, dep. sec. pers. policy, Treasury Bd. Secretariat, 1984-87, asst. dep. registrar gen. Dept. Consumer and Corp. Affairs, 1987-90; chief electoral officer Parliament of Can., Ottawa, 1990—; chmn. Monfort Hosp., 1981-90; bd. dirs. Internation Found. for Election Sys., Inst. for Democracy and Electoral Assistance. Avocations: music, community activities, windsurfing, carpentry, swimming. Home: 404A-62 Donald St, Ottawa, ON Canada K1K 1N2 Office: Elections Canada, 257 Slater St, Ottawa, ON Canada K1A OM6

KINGSLEY, JOHN MCCALL, JR., manufacturing company executive; b. Berlin, Dec. 1, 1931; s. John McCall and Elizabeth (Curry) K.; m. Ines Hinckeldeyn, 1967; children—John M. III, Kate Alexandra. B.A., Yale, 1953; M.B.A., Harvard, 1955. CPA, N.Y. Sr. staff acct. Price Waterhouse & Co. (C.P.A.'s), N.Y.C., 1957-62; assoc. Dillon, Read & Co., Inc., N.Y.C., 1962-65; v.p. fin. Gen. Host Corp., N.Y.C., 1966-69; v.p. corp. fin. F.S. Smithers & Co., Inc., 1970-71; exec. v.p. Sturm, Ruger & Co., Inc., Southport, Conn., 1971-96; dir. Sturm, Ruger & Co., Inc., Stamford, Conn., 1971—; pres. Kingsley Cons., LLC, 1997—. With AUS, 1955-57. Mem. N.Y. State Soc. CPA's, Econ. Club N.Y., Round Hill Club, Maidstone Club ((East Hampton, N.Y.). Republican. Episcopalian. Home: 16 Will Merry Ln Greenwich CT 06831-3338 Office: 111 Prospect St Stamford CT 06901-1208

KINGSLEY, JOHN PIERSALL, lawyer; b. Catskill, N.Y., Apr. 22, 1938; s. John Willis and Emma (Piersall) K.; children: Jessica Skiba, Matthew Pyms. BA, Drew U., 1960; LLB, Syracuse U., 1963. Bar: N.Y. 1966. Claims person Travelers Ins. Co., Albany, N.Y., 1963-67; examiner Travelers Ins. Co., Hartford, Conn., 1967-68; supr. Travelers Ins. Co., N.Y.C., 1968-69; assoc. J. Richard Williams, Albany, 1969-70, Mahoney & Williams, Esquires, Albany, 1970-74; ptnr. Williams & Kingsley, Esquires, Albany, 1974-77, Harvey and Harvey, Mumford & Kingsley, Esquires, Albany, 1977-87, Kingsley and Towne, Esquires, Albany and Catskill, N.Y., 1987-98; prin. John P. Kingsley P.C., Albany and Catskill, 1999—. Mem. Shaker Mus., Old Chatham, N.Y., 1988—, Columbia County Coaching Assn., 1986—; bd. dirs. Olana Hist. Site, Hudson, N.Y., 1986—. Mem. N.Y. State Bar Assn., Greene County Bar Assn., Capital Dist. Trial Lawyers Assn., Am. Trial Lawyers Assn., Nat. Beagle Club (bd. dirs.), Old Chatham Hunt Club (master of beagle hounds). Avocations: beagling, tennis, hunting, fox hunting. Office: John P Kingsley PC 329 Main St Catskill NY 12414-1823 also: John P Kingsley PC 18 Computer Dr W Albany NY 12205-1616

KINGSLEY, JUDITH, artist; b. N.Y.C.; d. Fred and Minna Evelyn (Weisman) Gladstone; m. Theodore Kingsley, Oct. 26, 1950 (dec. May 1964); children: Ellen Kingsley Hirschfeld, Melinda Kingsley Nester; m. John Fitting Jr., Apr. 9, 1976 (dec. Dec. 1997). Student, Syracuse U., 1948-49, Adelphi U., 1949-50, Pratt Inst., Art Students League, N.Y.C., Nat. Acad. Fine Arts, Positano Art Inst., Italy, 1972, China Inst., N.Y.C., 1977. Solo shows include Galerie Internat., N.Y.C., 1969, Weiner Gallery, N.Y.C., 1970, Palm Beach Gallery, 1971, Lobster Pot Gallery, Nantucket, Mass., 1972, Crystal House Gallery, Miami Beach, Fla., 1973, Springfield (Ill.) Art Assn., 1975, East River Savs. Bank Gallery, Rockefeller Ctr., N.Y., 1976, Bergdorf Goodman Art Gallery, N.Y.C., 1977, Adelphi U. Art Gallery, Garden City, N.Y., 1978, Multiple Images Gallery, Palm Beach, Fla., 1982, Valand Gallery, Naples, Fla., 1983, La Galeria De Santa Fe, N.Mex., 1984, Reece Gallery, N.Y.C., 1979-80, Nelson Rockefeller Collection, N.Y.C., 1981-82, L'Atelier Gallery, Piermont, N.Y., 1991-92, Jain Marunouchi Gallery, N.Y.C., 1995-96, G.G. Rein Gallery, Houston, 1995-96, The Darvish Collection, Naples, Fla., 1995-98, Hofburg Palace Exhibit, Vienna, Austria, 1993, No. Trust Bank, Naples, 1998, Naples Art Gallery, 1998-99, Artsforum Gallery, N.Y.C., 1998. Sec. bd. dirs. N.Y. Artists Equity, 1984-93. Recipient Morilla Oil award New Rochelle Art Assn., 1973. Mem. English Speaking Union, Marco Island Art Assn., Collier Athletic Club, Island Country Club, Marco Bay Yacht Club. Avocations: golf, tennis, swimming, yachting. Home and Office: 311 Nassau Ct Marco Island FL 34145-4013

KINGSLEY, LINDA S., corporation counsel. BA, State U. of N.Y., 1976; JD, Albany U., 1993. Bar: N.Y. State. Corp. counsel City Hall, Rochester, N.Y., 1994—. Mem. TMLA, N.Y. State Bar Assn. (second vice chair, municipal law sec.). Office: City Hall Office of the City Council 30 Church St Rm 400A Rochester NY 14614-1224*

KINGSLEY, NATHAN, journalist, consultant, educator; b. N.Y.C., Nov. 20, 1926; m. Cynthia Jean Kirkpatrick, June 20, 1950; 1 child, Alexandra Marjorie Jane. BS, CCNY, 1948; MA in Polit. Sci., Columbia U., 1977. Reporter, corr. N.Y. Herald Tribune, N.Y.C., 1946-55, assoc. mng. editor, 1963-65; mng. editor news svc. Herald Tribune News Svc., N.Y.C., 1955-59; mng. editor Internat. Herald Tribune, Paris, France, 1959-63; dir. news Radio Free Europe and Radio Liberty, Munich, 1965-72; spl. corr. radio and TV CBS News, Germany, 1966-72; dep. dir. for programming Voice of Am., 1972-74; v.p., sec. Radio Free Europe and Radio Liberty, Munich and Wash., 1976-80; spl. asst. to asst. sec. state U.S. Dept. State, Washington, 1974-76, pub. and congl. affairs dir., 1986-91; sr. editor spl. project U.S. News and World Report, Washington, 1980-84; chief of corrs. Washington Times, 1984-86; cons., writer Total Comm. Internat., Washington, 1991—; prof. Manship chair La. State U., Baton Rouge, 1996-97; chmn. bd. dirs. Parkway Comm., Inc., Washington, 1980-84; adj. assoc. prof. media and govt. George Washington U., 1990-93. Author: (with others) The Future of Journalism, 1993. Co-chmn. Music for the World Found., Washington, 1993-95. With USN, 1944-46. Poynter fellow Yale U., 1979. Mem. Lansdowne Club, Nat. Press Club, Overseas Press Club (Spot Coverage award 1972), Fed. City Club. Avocations: amateur radio broadcaster, antique book collector. Home and Office: 4217 Leland St Chevy Chase MD 20815-6048

KINGSLEY, PATRICIA, public relations executive; b. Gastonia, N.C., May 7, 1932; d. Robert Henry and Marjorie (Norment) Ratchford; m. Walter Kingsley, Apr. 1, 1966 (div. 1978); 1 child, Janis Susan. Student, Winthrop Coll., 1950-51. Publicist Fountainebleau Hotel, Miami Beach, Fla., 1952; exec. asst. ZIV TV, N.Y.C., 1953-58; publicist Rogers & Cowan, L.A. and N.Y.C., 1960-71; ptnr. Pickwick Pub. Rels., L.A., 1971-80, PMK Pub. Rels., L.A., 1980—; adv. com. Women's Action for Nuclear Disarmament, Arlington, Mass., 1983—. Democrat. Office: PMK Pub Rels Inc 955 Carrillo Dr Ste 200 West Hollywood CA 90048-5400

KINGSLEY, ROBERT THOMAS, developer; b. Johnson City, N.Y., Apr. 26, 1953; s. Carmen M. and Geraldine R. (Crossett) K.; m. Dana Alice Winne, Feb. 5, 1987 (div. May 1993); children: Frank Robert, Robin Lee. AAS in Mktg. and Sales, Broome C.C., Binghamton, N.Y., 1978, AAS in Paralegal, 1980; BS in Mgmt., SUNY, Binghamton, 1981; postgrad, William Howard Taft U., 1998—. Assoc. dir. U.S. Squash Assn., Bala Cynwyd, Pa., 1988-91; dir. pub. support and health edn. svcs. ARC, Binghamton, 1992—; CEO King Enterprises, Binghamton, 1981—. Mem. Leadership Broome, Binghamton, 1996-97; com. mem. Project Pride, Binghamton, 1997. Mem. A Ctr. for the Resolution of Dispute, NRA (life), Nat. Soc. Fund Raising Execs. Avocations: squash, fly fishing, aviation. Office: PO Box 1214 Binghamton NY 13902-1214

KINGSMILL, T. HARTLEY, JR., federal judge; b. 1921. BS, Loyola U., New Orleans, 1942, LLB, 1948. Pvt. practice, 1948-71; bankruptcy judge U.S. Dist. Ct. (ea. dist.) La., New Orleans, 1971—. With USN, 1942-46. Fax: (504) 589-2245. Office: US Dist Ct (ea dist) La 501 Magazine St Rm 710 New Orleans LA 70103

KINGSOLVER, BARBARA ELLEN, writer; b. Annapolis, Md., Apr. 8, 1955; d. Wendell and Virginia (Henry) K.; m. Steven Hopp; 2 children. BA, DePauw U., 1977; MS, U. Ariz., 1981; LittD (hon.), DePauw U., 1994. Sci. writer U. Ariz., Tucson, 1981-85; free-lance journalist Tucson, 1985-87, novelist, 1987—; book reviewer N.Y. Times, 1988—, L.A. Times, 1989—. Author: The Bean Trees, 1988 (ALA award 1988), Homeland and Other Stories, 1969 (ALA award 1990), Holding the Line: Women in the Great Arizona Mine Strike of 1983, 89, Animal Dreams, 1990 (PEN West Fiction award 1991, Edward Abbey Ecofiction award 1991), Another America, 1992, Pigs in Heaven, 1993 (L.A. Times Fiction prize 1993, Mountains and Plains Fiction award 1993, Western Heritage award 1993, ABBY Honor Book 1994), Essays, High Tide in Tucson, 1995, The Poisonwood Bible, 1998. Recipient Feature-writing award Ariz. Press Club, 1986; citation of accomplishment UN Nat. Coun. of Women, 1989; Woodrow Wilson Found./Lila Wallace fellow, 1992-93. Mem. PEN Ctr. USA West, Nat. Writers Union, Phi Beta Kappa. Avocations: human rights, environmental conservation, gardening, natural history. Office: PO Box 31870 Tucson AZ 85751-1870 also: care Harper Collins 10 E 53rd St New York NY 10022*

KINGSTON, ALEX(ANDRA), actress; b. London, Mar. 11, 1963. T.V. and movie actress. Appeared in T.V. films Foreign Affairs, 1993, The Infiltrator, 1995, Weapons of Mass Distraction, 1997; films include The Cook, The Thief, His Wife & Her Lover, 1989, Carrington, 1995, Virtual Encounters 2, 1998, Croupier, 1998, This Space Between Us, 1999, Moll Flanders, 1999, Essex Boys, 1999; T.V. series include The Knock, 1994, ER, 1997—. Recipient SAG award for Outstanding Performance by Ensemble in a Drama Series, 1994. Office: c/o The Gersh Agy 232 N Canon Dr Beverly Hills CA 90210*

KINGSTON, JACK, congressman; b. Bryan, Tex., 1955; m. Libby Kingston; children: Betsy, John, Ann, Jim. BA in Economics, U. Ga. Salesman, v.p. Palmer & Cay Carswell Ins. Co., 1979-92; mem. Ga. State Ho. Reps., 1985-93, 103rd to 105th Congresses from 1st Ga. Dist., 1993—; mem. Ways and Means Com., 1985-93, Appropriations Com., Congl. Rural Caucus Exec. Bd., 1993—, chmn. Theme Team (house Rep. comm. team). Vol. Hospice, United Way; mem. Atlantic Coast Conservation Assn., Isle of Hope Community Assn. Recipient Guardian of Small Bus. award Nat. Fed. of Ind. Bus., 1992, Sound Dollar award Free Cong. Found., 1994, Golden Bulldog award mems. 103rd , 104th cong., 1994, 96, Golden Eagle award Nat. Security Caucus, 1994, cert. recognition inspector. gen. Criminal Investigator Acad., 1994, plaque of appreciation Camden county bd. realtors, 1995, disting. cit. award Armstrong state coll., 1996, merit award the Seniors Coalition, 1996, comm. police award city of Statesboro, 1997, numerous others. Mem. Am. Legislative Exchange Coun., Soc. Chartered Property and Casualty Underwriters, Solomon's Lodge F&AM, Rotary (Paul Harris fellow). Republican. Episcopal. Office: US Ho Reps 1507 Longworth HOB Washington DC 20515

KINGSTON, MAXINE HONG, author; b. Stockton, Calif., Oct. 27, 1940; d. Tom and Ying Lan (Chew) Hong; m. Earll Kingston, Nov. 23, 1962; 1 child, Joseph Lawrence. BA, U. Calif., Berkeley, 1962; D degree (hon.), Ea. Mich. U., 1988, Colby Coll., 1990, Brandeis U., 1991, U. Mass., 1991. Tchr. English, Sunset High Sch., Hayward, Calif., 1965-66, Kahuku (Hawaii) High Sch., 1967, Kahaluu (Hawaii) Drop-In Sch., 1968, Kailua (Hawaii) High Sch., 1969, Honolulu Bus. Coll., 1969, Mid-Pacific Inst., Honolulu, 1970-77; prof. English, vis. writer U. Hawaii, Honolulu, 1977; Thelma McCandless Disting. Prof. Eastern Mich. U., Ypsilanti, 1986, Chancellor's Disting. Prof. U. Calif., Berkeley, 1990—. Author: The Woman Warrior: Memoirs of a Girlhood Among Ghosts, 1976 (Nat. Book Critics Cir. award for non-fiction; cited by Time mag., N.Y. Times Book Rev. and Asian Mail as one of best books of yr. and decade), China Men, 1981 (Nat. Book award; runner-up for Pulitzer prize, Nat. Book Critics Cir. award nominee 1988), Hawai' One Summer, 1987 (Western Books Exhbn. Book award, Book Builders West Book award), Tripmaster Monkey-His Fake Book, 1989 (PEN USA West award in Fiction), Through the Black Curtain, 1988; contbr. short stories, articles and poems to mags. and jours., including Iowa Rev., The New Yorker, Am. Heritage, Redbook, Mother Jones, Caliban, Mich. Quarterly, Ms., The Hungry Mind Rev., N.Y. Times, L.A. Times, Zyzzyva; prodr. The Woman Warrior, Berkeley Repertory Co., 1994, The Huntington Theater, Boston, 1994, The Mark Taper Forum, L.A., 1995; host: (TV series) Journey to the West, 1994; subject of documentaries Talking Story, Stories My Country Told Me, Writers and Places; interviews on Dick Cavett, Bill Moyers, Ken Burns' The West, The News Hour with Jim Lehrer. Guggenheim fellow, 1981; recipient Nat. Endowment for the Arts Writers award, 1980, 82, Mademoiselle mag. award, 1977, Anisfield Wolf Book award, 1978, Calif. Arts Commn. award, 1981, Hawaii award for lit., 1982, Calif. Gov.'s award art, 1989, Major Book Collection award Brandeis U. Nat. Women's Com., 1990, award lit. Am. Acad. & Inst. Arts & Letters, 1990, Lila Wallace Reader's Digest Writing award, 1992, Spl. Achievement Oakland Bus. Arts award, 1994; named Living Treasure Hawaii, 1980, Woman of Yr. Asian Pacific Women's Network, 1981, Cyril Magnin award for Outstanding Achievement in the Arts, 1996, Disting. Artists award The Music Ctr. of L.A. County, 1996, Nat. Humanities medal NEH, 1997, Fred Cody Lifetime Achievement award, 1998, John Dos Passos prize for lit., 1998. Mem. Am. Acad. Arts and Scis. Office: Univ Calif Dept English 322 Wheeler Hall Berkeley CA 94720-1030

KINGSTON, ROBERT HILDRETH, engineering educator; b. Somerville, Mass., Feb. 13, 1928; s. Alexander Haddon and Martha (Aitcheson) K.; m. Ruth Ahara, Apr. 19, 1952; children, Robert E., Susan E., Margaret K. Tivey, Katherine A. BS, MIT, 1948, MS, 1948, PhD, 1951. Mem. tech. staff Bell Labs., Murray Hill, N.J., 1951-52; mem. staff MIT Lincoln Lab., Lexington, Mass., 1952-88, head optics div., 1969-72, group leader, 1959-69, 72-77; group leader MIT Lincoln Lab., Lexington, 1984-87; adj. prof. dept. elec. engring. MIT, 1985-90, sr. lectr., 1990-94; vis. assoc. prof. Stanford U., Palo Alto, Calif., 1964-65; chmn. Dept. Def. Spl. Group, Optical Masers, Washington, 1962-66; lectr. Tsinghua U., Beijing, 1987; vis. prof. Imperial Coll. Sci., Tech. and Medicine, U. London, 1990, Tufts U., Medford, Mass., 1993—. Author: Detection of Optical and Infrared Radiation, 1978, Chinese transl., 1984, Optical Sources, Detectors, and Systems, 1995; editor: Semiconductor Surface Physics, 1957, Jour. of Quantum Electronics, 1965-70; contbr. numerous articles to sci. jours.; patentee in field. Mem. Lexington, Mass. Town Meeting, 1958-77; chmn. Capital Expenditures Commn., Lexington, 1962-64; pres. Lexington Bicentennial Band, 1989-90; trumpet Lexington Moonlighters Dance Band, Waltham Soft Touch Dance Band. Fellow IEEE (Centennial medal 1984), Am. Phys. Soc., Optical Soc. Am.; mem. NAE. Home and Office: 4 Field Rd Lexington MA 02421-8015*

KINIGAKIS, PANAGIOTIS, research scientist, engineer, author; b. Chanea, Greece, July 11, 1949; s. John and Evangelia (Vozinakis) K.; m. Kalliopi Paleologos, July 31, 1977; children: Evangelia, Maria Anna. BS, Superior Agrl. Sch., Athens, Greece, 1971, MS, 1973; MS in Food Sci., Rutgers U., 1979. Packaging devel. specialist Am. Cyanamid Co., Clifton, N.J., 1979-81; sr. packaging engr. Warner Lambert Co., Morris Plains, N.J., 1981-83; tech. svcs. supr. M&M Mars Inc., Hackettstown, N.J., 1983-87; sr. tech. prin. Kraft Foods Inc., Glenview, Ill., 1987—; agrl. engr. Food Agrl. Orgn. div. of UN, Chanea, 1975-77. Patentee pkg. equipment and mfg. systems; contbr. articles to profl. jours. Advisor Greek Orthodox Youth Assn., Randolph, N.J., 1986, Hamilton, N.J., 1990. Mem. ASM, TAPPI, Internat. Materials Info. soc., Inst. Food Tech., Inst. Packaging Profls. (cert.), Soc. Plastics Engrs., N.Y. Acad. Scis. Greek Orthodox. Avocations: volleyball, soccer, tennis, scuba diving. Home: 2631 Deering Bay Dr Naperville IL 60564 Office: Kraft Foods Inc 801 Waukegan Rd Glenview IL 60025

KINKADE, KATE, magazine editor, insurance executive; b. N.Y.C., Jan. 22, 1951; d. Joel M. and Peeta S. (Sherman) Sandleman; m. Patrick Ramsey, June 27, 1981; children: Jamaa Ramsey, Kikanza Ramsey. BS in Speech, Emerson Coll., Boston, 1972; postgrad., Am. Coll., Bryn Mawr, Pa. CLU. Mgr. sales Equitable Life Ins., L.A., 1973-76; agy. v.p. Lincoln Nat. Life Ins. Co., Encino, Calif., 1976-80; chief exec. officer TIME Fin. Svcs., Reseda, Calif., 1980—; editor-in-chief Calif. Broker, Burbank, Calif., 1981—; exec. v.p. Life Underwriters Assn., Encino, 1978-81. Contbr. articles to profl. jours. Treas., trustee Labor Community Strategy Ctr., L.A. Recipient Asst. Prodn. awards Equitable Life, 1973, 77, Lincoln Nat. Life, 1978, 80, Pacific Mut. Life, 1983. Mem. Assn. CLU's. Avocations: model trains, whitewater rafting, dancing. Office: TIME Fin 20301 Ventura Blvd #310 Woodland Hills CA 91364

KINKEL, R. JOHN, research company executive, educator; b. Fond du Lac, Wis., Nov. 9, 1940; s. Reuben and Miriam (McKone) K.; m. Norma Castro Josef, Mar. 28, 1979; children: Jonathan, Danielle. BA, St. Joseph's Coll., Rensselaer, Inc., 1964; MA, Marquette U., 1975; PhD, Ohio State U., 1980. Tchr., counselor St. Bonaventure's, Detroit, 1964-77; asst. prof. U. Mich., Flint, 1980-86; mem. grad faculty Wayne State U., Detroit, 1987-93; pres. Research and Cons. Svcs., Inc., Grosse Pointe, Mich., 1993—. Author article and chpt. Involved in voter registration Mich. Coalition, Detroit, 1972. Mem. Am. Sociol. Assn., DeLaSalle Dads Club. Democrat. Roman Catholic. Avocations: running, writing, home repairs. Home: 13910 Silent Woods Dr Shelby Township MI 48315-4295

KINLAW, DENNIS FRANKLIN, clergyman, society executive; b. Lumberton, N.C., June 26, 1922; s. Wade Hampton and Sally (Burney) K.; m. Elsie Blake, Dec. 31, 1943; children: Elizabeth Kinlaw Coppedge, Dennis Franklin Jr., Katherine Kinlaw Key, Susan Kinlaw Masters, Sally Kinlaw Babcock. BA, Asbury Coll., 1943, LHD (hon.), 1980; MDiv, Asbury Theol. Sem., 1946; MA, Brandeis U., 1961, PhD, 1967; LLD (hon.), Houghton Coll., 1971; DD (hon.), 1990. Ordained deacon N.C. Conf. United Meth. Ch., 1949, ordained elder, 1951; transferred to Ky. Conf., 1969, ret., 1984. Pastor Meth. Ch., Faison, 1949-53, Loudenville (N.Y.) Community Ch., 1955-61; assoc. prof., prof. Old Testament langs. and lit. Asbury Theol. Sem., Wilmore, Ky., 1963-68, prof. bibl. theology, 1982-83; pres. Asbury Coll., Wilmore, 1968-81, 86-92; founder, pres. Francis Asbury soc., Wilmore, 1982—; pres. Francis Asbury Soc., Wilmore, 1982—; vis. prof. Seoul (Republic of Korea) Theol. Coll.; bd. dirs. Christianity Today, Carol Stream, Ill., Ludhiana Christian Med. Bd., N.Y.C.; mem. Lausanne Commn. on World Evangelism, Theol. Commn. of World Evang. Fellowship; chmn. bd. OMS Internat., Greenwood, Ind. Author: Preaching in the Spirit, 1985; contbr. commentaries in bibl. publs. Recipient Alumnus award Asbury Theol. Sem., 1961. Fellow Christianity Today Inst.; mem. Soc. Bibl. Lit. and Exegesis, Wesley Theol. Soc., Evang. Theol. Soc. Home: 140 Lowry Ln Wilmore KY 40390-1219 Office: Francis Asbury Soc PO Box 7 Wilmore KY 40390-0007*

KINLEY, DAVID, physical therapist, acupuncturist; b. Newark, Dec. 16, 1935; m. Helen Sandra Wehrle, Mar. 14, 1958; children: Sandra, Deborah, Denise. D Mechanotherapy, Easton Coll., 1970; postgrad in trad. Chinese acupuncture, Tri State Inst., 1979-82. Lic. in acupuncture, phys. therapy and massage; cert. in hypnosis, biofeedback, touch for health. Pvt. massage practice Newark, 1957-60; pvt. phys. therapy practice Cranford, N.J., 1960-63; founder, massage instr., phys. therapist, acupuncturist, hypnotherapist Kinley Comprehensive Ctr. for Acupuncture and Phys. Therapy, Clark, N.J., 1963—; cons. in phys. therapy Vis. Nurse Assn., 1970; practice in biofeedback, 1972; established ctr. for phys. therapy and rehab., Elizabeth, N.J.; clin. affiliate N.Y. State Phys. Therapy Coll., 1982; cons. in acupuncture and phys. therapy Sunny Isles Med. Ctr., Miami Beach, Fla., 1982, pain mgmt. No. Miami Inst. Fla.; founder Kinley Comprehensive Ctr. for Acupuncture/ Phys. Therapy, Fla.; asst. in preparation of licensing legis. for N.J. Acupuncture; mem. acupuncture examining bd. N.J. Bd. Med. Examiners. Recipient Lydia Hayes achievement award, 1957. Mem. N.J. State Phys. Therapy Assn. (officer 1959—, pres. 1993, exec. dir., bd.dirs., sr. advisor), Am. Acupuncture Assn. and Oriental Medicine (pres. Acupuncture and Moxibustion Assn. 1973-87), Assn. Applied Psycho Physiology and Biofeedback, Internat. Soc. Profl. Hypnotist, Internat. Soc. Myomassethics, Fla. State Massage Assn., Fla. State Acupuncture Assn., Am. Acad. Environ. Medicine, N.J. Acupuncture Assn. (pres. 1991-93). Avocations: outdoors, swimming, boating, travel, reading. Home and Office: Kinley Inst 668 Raritan Rd Clark NJ 07066-2232

KINLEY, JOHN JAMES, government official; b. Lunenburg, N.S., Can., Sept. 23, 1925; s. John James and Lila Evelyn (Young) K.; m. Grace Elizabeth MacPherson, Dec. 18, 1954; children: Paula, Peter, Edward, Shona. BS, Dalhousie U., Halifax, N.S., 1946; B.Engring., Tech. U. N.S., Halifax, 1948, Dr.Engring., 1995; MS in Bus. and Engring. Adminstrn., MIT, 1950. Registered profl. engr., N.S. Owner Interlaken Farm, Lunenburg, 1971—; lt. gov. Province of N.S., Halifax, 1994—; mem. ministers adv. bd. Can. Mil. Colls., Dept. Nat. Def., 1979-81; mem. Atlantic Devel. Coun., 1973-76, Dept. Regional Econ. Expansion, 1969-74. Pres. Lunenburg Bd. of Trade, 1965-66, Assoc. South Shore Bd. of Trade, 1967-71. Lt. comdr. Can. Navy, 1943-45. Decorated Atlantic Star , War medal, 1943-45, Can. Forces Decoration; recipient Can. Vol. Svc. medal Dept. Nat. Def. Can., Can. 125 medal Govt. Can., 1992. Mem. Can. Foundry Assn. (charter, dir. 1976-79), Offshore Trade Assn. N.S. (chmn. 1988-89), Royal Can. Legion (br. pres. 1968), Navy League of Can. (nat. pres. 1980-82, nat. chair 1982-85), Masons. Avocations: philately, swimming, hiking, golf, sailing. Office: Government House, 1451 Barrington St, Halifax, NS Canada B3J 1Z2

KINLEY, LOREN DHUE, museum director; b. Tillamook, Oreg., Feb. 1, 1920; s. Henry Raymond and Flora (Phillips) McK.; m. Mary Eileen Sessions, May 22, 1942; children: Candace Eileen, Scott Dhu, Kevin Loren, Laurie Lee, Maris Colleen. Student, Oreg. State U., U. Oreg.; D.Sc., U. Portland, 1973. Advt. mgr. Headlight Herald, Tillamook, 1946; partner Kenwood Press, Tillamook, 1949; dir. Oreg. Mus. Sci. and Industry, Portland, 1960-78; chief exec. officer Oreg. Mus. Sci. and Industry, 1978—; bd. dirs. Fred Hutchinson Cancer Rsch. Ctr. Found., Oreg. Mus. Sci. and Industry; for Portland ops. mgr. Office of Devel. Oreg. State U. Mayor of Tillamook, 1954-60; pres. Leukemia Assn. Oreg. Inc., 1983—; bd. dirs. St. Mary's Acad., 1993—; bd. trustees Oreg. Mus. Sci. and Industry; mem. Oreg. State U Found. Served with AUS, World War II, ETO, MTO. Decorated Bronze Star with oak leaf cluster; named 1st Citizen of Oreg., 1951; recipient award Oreg. Mus. Sci. and Industry, 1965, Elsie M.B. Naumberg award as outstanding sci. mus. dir., 1968, citation for outstanding svc. Oreg. Acad. Sci., 1971, Aubrey Watzek award Lewis and Clark Coll., 1973; named alumni of yr. Oreg. State U., 1999, recipient heart of gold award, 1999. Mem. Assn. Sci. and Tech. Ctrs. Am. (pres. 1973—), League Oreg. Cities (past pres.), Kappa Sigma. Republican. Home and Office: 11925 SW Belvidere Pl Portland OR 97225-5805

KINLIN, DONALD JAMES, lawyer; b. Boston, Nov. 29, 1938; s. Joseph Edward and Ruth Claire (Byrne) K.; m. Donna C. McGrath, Nov. 29, 1959; children: Karen J., Donald J., Joseph P., Kevin S. BS in Acctg., Syracuse U., 1968, MBA, 1970; JD, U. Nebr., 1975. Bar: Nebr. 1976, Ohio 1982, U.S. Supreme Ct. 1979, U.S. Claims Ct. 1982, U.S. Tax Ct. 1982, U.S. Ct. Appeals (5th and fed. cirs.) 1982. Atty. USAF, Mather AFB, Calif., 1976-78; sr. trial atty. Air Force Contract Law Ctr., Wright-Patterson AFB, Ohio, 1978-86, dep. dir., 1986-87; ptnr. Smith & Schnacke, Dayton, Ohio, 1987-89, Thompson, Hine and Flory, Dayton, 1989—; mem. adv. bd. Fed. Publs. Inc. Govt. Contract Costs, Pricing & Acctg. Report. Contbr. articles to legal jours. Pres. Forest Ridge Assn., Dayton, 1984-96; sec., gen. counsel U.S. Air and Trade Show, 1995-98, chmn., 1998—; bd. dirs. Nat. Aviation Hall of Fame, 1998—. Mem. ABA (chmn. sect. pub. contract law 1993-94, sec., budget and fin. officer sect., coun. mem., chmn. fed. procurement divsn., vice chmn. acct., cost and pricing com., truth in negotiations com., chmn. cost Acctg. stas. subcom.), Fed. Bar Assn., Ohio Bar Assn., Nebr. Bar Assn. (bd. dirs. U.S. Air and Trade show 1994—), Contracts Appeals Bar Assn. (bd. govs. 1998—). Avocation: travel. Office: Thompson Hine & Flory LLP PO Box 8801 2000 Courthouse Pla NE Dayton OH 45401-8801

KINMAN, GARY, company executive. Owner, CEO Kinman Assocs., Inc. Office: Kinman Assocs Inc 7300 Industrial Pkwy Plain City OH 43064-8788*

KINNAIRD, SUSAN MARIE, special education educator; b. Grosse Pointe, Mich., May 3, 1954; d. William Burl and Ida Mae (Diehl) Cunningham; m. Henry Wayne Kinnaird Jr., Nov. 30, 1985. BA in Edn., Wayne State U., 1978; MA in Ednl. Adminstrn., U. Houston at Clear Lake, 1990. Cert. elem. tchr., spl. edn. tchr., spl. edn. supr., instrnl. supr., Tex. Parent trainer Dept. Mental Health, Warren, Mich., 1977-78; spl. edn. tchr. Houston Ind. Sch. Dist., 1978-95, spl. edn. coord., 1995—. Asst. coach Spl. Olympics, Houston, 1982, 84, 88-91; bell choir mem. Cen. Presbyn. Ch., Houston, 1979—. Grantee Houston Bus. Com. for Ednl. Excellence 1991, 92. Mem. Coun. for Exceptional Children (chpt. 100 newsletter editor 1990-92, sec. 1992-93, pres.-elect 1993-94, pres. 1994-95). Roman Catholic. Avocations: sewing, handcrafts, music, reading, travel. Home: 4111 Mona Lee Ln Houston TX 77080-1768 Office: Houston Ind Sch Dist SW Dist Office 5827 Chimney Rock Rd Houston TX 77081-2714

KINNAMON, RON, administrator; b. Dallas, Apr. 9, 1937; s. David Ernest and Gladys Lucile (Page) K.; m. Sally Ann Stromberg, June 7, 1958; children: Scott Roger, Randall Lee, Jeffrey Craig. BA, So. Meth. U., 1959; MS, George Williams Coll., 1960. Camp dir. YMCA Camp Grady Spruce, Dallas, 1960-63; br. dir. Richardson (Tex.) YMCA, 1963-69; region assoc. Southwest Region UMCA, Dallas, 1969-73; CEO Miami (Fla.) YMCA, 1973-76; nat. field exec. Southeast Field, Atlanta, 1976-83, West Field, San Francisco, 1983-90; asst. nat. exec. dir. YMCA of USA, Chgo., 1990-98; retired, 1998; v.p. America's Promise, 1998—; vice chair Character Counts Coalition, Marina del Rey, Calif., 1994—; bd. dirs. Josephson Inst. of Ethics, 1997—; mem. steering com. Connect Am., Washington, 1996—; mem. program com. Points of Light Found., Washington, 1992-96, mem. program com.; mem. nat. adv. coun. Forum Early Childhood Devel., Kansas City, 1996—; bd. dirs. Josephson Inst. Ethics. Author: Camp Leadership Focus, 1974, co-author: The YMCA and Drug Abuse, 1971; editor: Managing YMCA Resources, 1976. Bd. dirs. George Willian Coll. Aurora (Ill.) U., 1994-98, Uhlich Children's Home, Chgo., 1991—, vice chair, 1993-96; coun. mem. St. Pails United Ch. Christ, Chgo., 1996—. Recipient Disting. Svc. award Kiwanis Club, Richardson, 1969. Mem. Assn. Profl. Dirs. (William Stahl award 1975). Avocations: camping, biking, computer, cooking, travel. E-mail: rkinna@aol.com. Home: 2650 N Lakeview Ave Apt 3010 Chicago IL 60614-1825

KINNAN, TIMOTHY ALAN, air force officer; b. Tacoma, Apr. 24, 1948; s. Henry Wallace and Marjorie Gladys (Ahrendt) K.; m. Sue E. Kelley, June 6, 1970; children: Jennifer, Emily. BS, USAF Acad., 1970; MS in Astronautical-Aero. Engring., Purdue U., 1971; postgrad., Armed Forces Staff Coll., Norfolk, Va., 1981; disting. grad., Nat. War Coll., Washington, 1990. Commd. 2d lt. USAF, 1970, advanced through grades to maj. gen., 1996; air staff action officer Directorate Programs and Evaluation, Washington, 1981-83; exec. officer to vice comdr. Tactical Air Command, Langley AFB, Va., 1983-84; pilot, F-15C and ops. officer 94th Tactical Fighter Squadron, Langley AFB, 1984-85; comdr. 318th Fighter Interceptor Squadron, McChord AFB, Wash., 1985-87; dir. ops. 475th weapons evaluation group, dep. comdr. ops. 325th Tactical Tng. Wing, Tyndall AFB, Fla., 1987-89; exec. officer to chief staff SHAPE, Mons, Belgium, 1990-92; comdr. 401st Fighter Wing, Aviano Air Base, Italy, 1992-93; mil. asst. to sec. air force USAF, Washington, 1993-94; comdr. 347th Wing Moody AFB, Ga., 1994-96; deputy comdr. 5th Allied Tactical Air Force, Vicenza, Italy, 1996-97; commandant Air War Coll. USAF, Maxwell AFB, Ala., 1997-98, comdr. Doctrine Ctr., 1998—. Contbr. articles to mil. publs. Decorated Defense Distg. Svc. medal, Def. Superior Svc. medal, Legion of Merit with oak leaf cluster, Air medal; recipient 1st Risner Trophy, USAF, 1977. Mem. Air Force Assn., USAF Acad. Assn. Grads., Nat. War Coll. Alumni Assn. Methodist. Avocations: jogging, computers. Home: 341 Sequoia Dr Maxwell AFB AL 36113-1210 Office: 325 Chennault Cir Ste 113 Maxwell AFB AL 36112-6427

KINNARD, WILLIAM JAMES, JR., retired pharmacy educator; b. Wilmington, Del., Apr. 18, 1932; s. William J. and Helen F. (Ossenkemper) K.; m. Dolores F. Malia, July 18, 1959. B.S., U. Pitts., 1953, M.S., 1955; Ph.D., Purdue U., 1957. From instr. to prof. U. Pitts., 1957-68; prof. pharmacology, dean Sch. Pharmacy U. Md., Balt., 1968-89, dean Grad. Sch., acting vice chancellor grad. studies and research, 1985, acting pres., 1989-90; acting asst. chancellor U. Md. System, 1991, prof. pharm. practice and sci., 1992-97; chmn. bd. U.S. Pharmacopeial Conv., 1975-85; nat. pharm. cons. surgeon gen. USAF, 1983-89; mem. Am. Coun. Pharm. Edn., 1986-92, v.p., 1990-92. Contbr. jours. in field. Fellow Am. Found. Pharm. Edn., 1954-57; recipient Honors Achievement award Angiology Research Fedn., 1960-65; Disting. Alumnus award U. Pitts. Sch. Pharmacy, 1973, Purdue U. Sch. Pharmacy, 1985. Fellow Am. Coll. Clin. Pharmacology, AAAS, Acad. Pharm. Sci.; mem. Am. Pharm. Assn., Inst. Medicine of Nat. Acad. Scis., Am. Assn. Coll. of Pharmacy (pres. 1976-77), Rho Chi. Lutheran. Home: 4000 N Charles St Baltimore MD 21218-1760

KINNE, FRANCES BARTLETT, chancellor emeritus; b. Story City, Iowa; d. Charles Morton and Bertha (Olson) Bartlett; m. Harry L. Kinne, Jr. (dec.); m. M. Worthington Bordley, Jr. (dec.). *Frances Bartlett Kinne, Ph.D. is the daughter of Charles and Bertha Bartlett. Both parents initiated their careers as educators. Charles was later the Editor-Publisher of the Story City Herald (Iowa) in the early years of the Century. Bertha was a founding librarian, serving for 43 years. In 1995, the Bertha Bartlett Public Library was dedicated to her memory. Brother Charles was an honor student, musician, and star athlete. Maternal Grandparents immigrated from Norway. Paternal Grandparents' lineage descends from Josiah Bartlett, first Governor of New Hampshire and a signer of the Declaration of Independence.* Student, U. No. Iowa; B of Music Edn., Drake U., M. of Music Edn., DFA (hon.), 1981, hon. degree; PhD cum laude, U. Frankfurt, Fed. Republic of Germany, 1957; LHD (hon.), Wagner Coll., N.Y.; LLD (hon.), Lenoir Rhyne Coll.; DHL (hon.), Jacksonville U., 1995; LLD (hon.), Flagler Coll. Tchr. music Kelley (Iowa) Consol. Sch.; supr. music Boxholm (Iowa) Consol. Sch., Des Moines pub. schs.; sr. hostess Camp Crowder, Mo.; dir. recreation VA, Wadsworth, Kans.; lectr. music, English and Western culture Tsuda Coll., Tokyo; cons. music U.S. Army Gen. Hdqrs., Tokyo; mem. faculty Jacksonville (Fla.) U., 1958—, Disting. Univ. prof., 1961-62, prof. music and humanities, 1963—, dean, founder Coll. Fine Arts, interim pres., 1979, pres., 1979-89, chancellor, 1989-94; chancellor emeritus, 1995—; past chmn. Ind. Colls. and Univs. Fla.; mem. adv. coun. Nat. Soc. Arts and Letters; hon. mem. staff Mayo Clinic, Jacksonville; corporator Charles Schepens Eye Rsch. Inst. of Harvard U., Cambridge, Mass. Author: A Comparative Study of British Traditional and American Indigenous Ballads, 1958; contbr. chpt. to book and articles to profl. jours. Bd. govs. Drake U.; bd. dirs. (hon.) Jacksonville Symphony Assn., Bert Thomas Scholarship Found., Doug Milne Found., Jacksonville U.; bd. dirs., exec. com. Eye Rsch. Found.; mem., then chmn. adv. bd. Ronald McDonald House; past mem. bd. govs. Jacksonville C. of C., past v.p. Recipient hon. awards Bus. and Profl. Women's Clubs, 1962, Disting. Svc. award Drake U., 1966, 1st Fla. Gov.'s award for achievement in arts, 1972, EVE award in edn., 1973, Arts Assembly Individual award, 1978-79, Roast award Soc. for Prevention of Blindness, 1980, Brotherhood award NCCJ, 1981, Top Mgmt. award Jacksonville Sales and Mktg. Execs., 1981, Alumni Achievement award U. No. Iowa, Ann. Burton C. Bryan award, Pub. Svc. award Physicians Edn. Network, Freedom Found. Valley Forge Brotherhood of NCCJ award, Disting. Svc. award Fla. Soc. Ophthalmology, Women of Achievement award 1st Coast Bus. and Profl. Women's Club Jacksonville, Disting. Educator award Internat. Longshoremen's Assn., Hope award Nat. Multiple Sclerosis Soc., Disting. Am. award Nat. Football Fedn., Fla. State Mus. Tchrs. award, Outstanding Civic Leader award Civic Roundtable of Jacksonville, Vol. Jacksonville 2d Ann. Bernard Gregory Servant Leader award; named Eve of Decade, Elaine Gordon Lifetime Achievement award Fla. Fedn. Bus. and Profl. Women, 1996; inducted into Fla. Women's Hall of Fame, Outstanding Svc. to Theatre Edn. Fla. Assn. for Theatre Edn.; hon. mem. 3d Armored Divsn., U.S. Army; day named in her honor Women's Club of Jacksonville and other orgns.; one of six women featured on History Week posters apptd. by Mayor Jacksonville; bldgs. named in honor: Frances Bartlett Kinne Univ. Ctr. Jacksonville U., Frances Bartlett Kinne Alumni and Devel. Ctr. Drake U. Mem. AAUW, Nat. Music Tchrs. Assn., Fla. Music Tchr. Assn., Music Educators Nat. Conf., Fla. Music Edn. Assn. (past bd. dirs.), Assn. Am. Colls. (past bd. govs., exec. com.), Friday Musicale (life), Fla. Coll. Music Edn. Assn. (past pres., v.p.), Delius Assn. of Fla. (life), Nat. Assn. Schs. Music (past chmn. region 7), Fine Arts Forum (hon.), Ind. Colls. and Univs. of Fla. (past chmn., 1st woman chmn.), So. Acad. Letters, Arts and Scis., Internat. Coun. Fine Arts Deans (past chmn., 1st woman chmn.), Fla. Women's Hall of Fame (Gov.'s First award), Jacksonville Women's Network Inner Wheel, Nat. Soc. Arts and Letters (adv. coun.), P.E.O., Green Key (hon.), Ret. Officers Assn. (hon. mem. Mayport chpt.), St. John's Dinner Club (past pres.), Exch. Club (Golden Deeds award), River Club (1st woman mem.), Rotary (one of 1st two women elected bd. dirs. Jacksonville chpt., Paul Harris fellow, pres. elect 2000—), Alpha Xi Delta, Mu Phi Epsilon (Elizabeth Mathias award, judge internat. music edn. award), Alpha Psi Omega (hon.), Alpha Kappa Pi (hon.), Alpha Kappa Psi (hon.), Beta Gamma Sigma, Omicron Delta Kappa (hon.), Alpha Xi Delta (Woman of Distinction award). Fax: 904-646-4904. Home: 4032 Mission Hills Cir W Jacksonville FL 32225-4635 *It has been a delightful challenge to amalgamate my career with happy experience as a U.S. Army wife - as a young bride assigned to China and evacuated to Occupied Japan - in pursuit of my Ph.D. at the University of Frankfurt in Occupied Germany (the lone American student) as a professor, dean, president chancellor and now Chan. Emer. of Jacksonville University.*

KINNEAR, GREG, actor, producer; b. Ind., June 17, 1963. Wit Armed Forces Radio, Athens, Greece. Appeared on TV series College Mad House, 1989, The Best of the Worst, 1991, Talk Soup, 1991-94, Later with Greg Kinnear, 1994—, TV movies What Price Victory, 1988, Murder in Mississippi, 1990, Dillinger, 1991, Based on an Untrue Story, 1993, TV spl. Spring Series, 1993, films, Blankman, 1994, Sabrina, 1995, Dear God, 1996, A Smile Like Yours, 1997, As Good As It Gets, 1997, You've Got Mail, 1998; co-exec. prodr. TV series The Best of the Worst, 1991; exec. prodr. Talk Soup, 1991-94, Later with Greg Kinnear, 1994—. *

KINNEAR, JAMES WESLEY, III, retired petroleum company executive; b. Pitts., Mar. 21, 1928; s. James Wesley and Susan (Jenkins) K.; m. Mary Tullis, June 17, 1950; children: Robin Wood (Mrs. David Bruce Anderson), Susan (Mrs. Charles Neul), James Wesley IV, William M. BS with distinction, U.S. Naval Acad., 1950. With Texaco, Inc., 1954—; sales mgr. Texaco, Inc., Hawaii, 1959-63; div. sales mgr. Texaco, Inc., L.A., 1963-64; asst. to vice chmn. bd. dirs. Texaco, Inc., N.Y.C., 1964-65, asst. to chmn. bd. dirs., gen. mgr. marine dept., 1965, v.p. supply and distbn., 1966-70, sr. v.p. strategic planning, 1970-71, sr. v.p. worldwide refining, petrochems., supply and distbn., 1971-72, sr. v.p. world wide mktg., also in charge internat. marine ops. and petrochems., 1972-76, sr. v.p. internat. marine and aviation sales petrochem. dept., marine dept., mktg. and refining in Europe, 1976-78, dir., 1977—, exec. v.p., 1978-83; pres. Texaco USA Texaco, Inc., 1982-84; vice chmn. bd. dirs. Texaco, Inc., White Plains, 1983-86, pres., chief exec. officer, 1987-93; ret., 1993; bd. dirs. Corning Inc., Asarco Inc., Paine Webber Group. Chmn. bd. dirs. Met. Opera Assn., Inc.; bd. overseers Meml. Sloan-Kettering Cancer Ctr.; bd. mgrs. N.Y. Bot. Garden. Named Hon. Dir., Am. Petroleum Inst. Mem. Bus. Coun., U.S. Naval Inst., Round Hill Club, Blind Brook Club, Verbank Hunting Club, Brook Club, Iron City Fishing Club, Augusta, Nat. Golf Club. Episcopalian. Home: 149 Taconic Rd Greenwich CT 06831-3113 Office: PO Box 120 4 Stamford Plz Stamford CT 06904*

KINNEAR, JOHN KENYON, JR., architect; b. Bklyn., Aug. 9, 1948; s. John Kenyon and Helen (Knowlton) K.; m. Alice Taylor, Jan. 30, 1971 (div. July 1982); m. Donna Manheim, Nov. 27, 1982. BArch, Pratt Inst., 1972. Registered arch., N.Y., Conn.; cert. Nat. Coun. Archtl. Registration Bds. Prin. Janko Rasic Assocs. Architects, N.Y.C., 1972—; chmn. archtl. adv. com. Town of Ridgefield, Conn. Recipient Monsanto DOC Nat. Design award, 1993. Mem. AIA, Nat. Trust for Hist. Preservation, Am. Friends of the Georgian Group (bd. dirs.), Nelson Soc., Soc. for Nautical Rsch.,

Sandanona Hare Hounds. Am. Friends of the Georgian Soc. (v.p.). Avocations: horseback riding, historic ship modeling. Home: 90 Cains Hill Rd Ridgefield CT 06877-4209 Office: Janko Rasic Assocs Archts 109 E 37th St New York NY 10016-3040

KINNEBREW, JACKSON METCALFE, lawyer; b. Oklahoma City, June 29, 1941; s. Jackson A. and Mary Lucille (Metcalfe) K.; m. Carole A. Vadner, Sept. 23, 1967; children: Scott, Sarah. BBA in Acctg., U. Okla., 1963; JD, So. Meth. U., 1967, LLM in Taxation, 1973. Bar: Tex. 1968, U.S. Dist. Ct. (no. dist.) Tex. 1968, U.S. Tax Ct. 1970, U.S. Ct. Appeals (5th cir.) 1971, U.S. Supreme Ct. 1971; CPA, Tex. Assoc. Strasburger & Price, Dallas, 1968-74, ptnr., 1975-98, of counsel, 1999—; lectr. Wills and Probate Inst., 1980, 81, 83, 89, Practicing Law Inst., 1983, Southwestern Legal Found. (bd. trustees 1987—). Contbr. legal articles to profl. jours. Gen. counsel Communities Found. of Tex., Inc., Dallas, 1987—; fund raising chmn. Boy Scouts Am., Dallas, 1984-86; chmn. legacy com. Am. Cancer Soc., Dallas, 1978-82. Lt. U.S. Army, 1963-65. Fellow Am. Coll. Trust and Estate Counsel (state chmn. 1984-89, bd. regents 1988-94, membership selection com. 1993-99), Internat. Acad. Estate and Trust Law (academician 1990—); mem. ABA (subcom. chmn. 1979), State Tex. Bar Assn. (lectr. 1981, 82), Dallas Bar Assn. (chmn. probate sect. 1985), Tex. Soc. CPAs, Dallas Estate Planning Coun. (pres. 1985, program v.p. 1984, treas. 1982, sec. 1981), Tex. Bd. Legal Specialization (cert.). Avocations: golf, sports, bridge. Office: Strasburger & Price LLP 4300 Bank of America Plz 901 Main St Ste 4300 Dallas TX 75202-3794

KINNELL, GALWAY, poet, translator; b. Providence, Feb. 1, 1927; s. James Scott and Elizabeth (Mills) K.; children: Maud, Fergus. AB summa cum laude, Princeton U., 1948; MA, U. Rochester, 1949. Instr. English Alfred U., N.Y., 1949-51; dir. liberal arts program U. Chgo., 1951-55; Am. lectr. U. Grenoble, France, 1956-57; Fulbright lectr. U. Iran, Teheran, 1959-60; adj. assoc. prof. Columbia U., N.Y.C., 1972, adj. prof., 1974, 76; Citizens' prof. U. Hawaii at Manoa, Honolulu, 1979-81; dir. writing program NYU, N.Y.C., 1981-84, Samuel F.B. Morse prof. arts and scis., 1985-92, Erich Maria Remarque prof. creative writing, 1992—; lectr. summer session U. Nice, France, 1957; vis. prof. Queens Coll. of CUNY, 1971, Pitts. Poetry Forum, 1971, Brandeis U., 1974, Skidmore Coll., 1975, U. Del., 1978; poet-in-residence Juniata Coll., 1964, Reed Coll., 1966-67, Colo. State U., 1968, U. Wash., 1968, U. Calif., Irvine, 1968-69, U. Iowa, 1978, Holy Cross Coll., 1977; vis. poet Sarah Lawrence Coll., 1972-78, Princeton U., 1976; resident writer Deya Inst., Mallorca, Spain, 1969-70; vis. writer Macquarie U., Sydney, Australia, 1979; dir. Squaw Valley Cmty. of Writers, 1979—. Author: (poetry) What a Kingdom It Was, 1960, Flower Herding on Mount Monadnock, 1964, Body Rags, 1968, Poems of Night, 1968, The Hen Flower, 1969, First Poems: 1946-1954, 1970, The Shoes of Wandering, 1971, The Book of Nightmares, 1971, The Avenue Bearing the Initial of Christ into the New World: Poems 1946-1964, 1974, Mortal Acts, Mortal Words, 1980, Selected Poems, 1982 (Nat. Book award for poetry 1983, Pulitzer Prize for poetry 1983), The Fundamental Project of Technology, 1983, The Past, 1985, When One Has Lived a Long Time Alone, 1990, Imperfect Thirst, 1994; (novels) Black Light, 1966; (children's) How the Alligator Missed Breakfast, 1982; (non-fiction) The Poetics of the Physical World, 1969, Walking Down the Stairs: Selections from Interviews, 1978, Thoughts Occasioned by the Most Insignificant of All Human Events, 1982, Remarks on Accepting the American Book Award, 1984; translator: Rene Hardy's Bitter Victory, 1956, Henri Lehmann's Pre-Columbian Ceramics, 1962, The Poems of Francois Villon, 1965, Yves Bonnefoy's On The Motion and Immobility of Douve, 1968 (Cecil Hemley Poetry prize Ohio U. Pr. 1968), Yvan Goll's The Lackawanna Elegy, 1970, Yves Bonnefoy's Early Poems, 1947-1959, 1990, The Essential Rilke, 1999; editor: The Essential Whitman, 1987. Fulbright scholar, 1955-56; Guggenheim fellow, 1961-62, 74-75; grantee Ford Found., 1955, Nat. Inst. Arts and Letters, 1962, Rockefeller Found., 1962-63, 68; Amy Lowell travelling fellow, 1969-70, MacArthur fellow, 1984; recipient Longview Found. award, 1962, Bess Hokin prize Poetry Mag., 1965, Eunice Tietjens prize Poetry Mag., 1966, Ingram Merrill Found. award, 1969, Brandeis U. Creative Arts award, 1969, Shelley prize Poetry Soc. Am., 1974, Medal of Merit Nat. Inst. Arts and Letters, 1975, Landon Translation prize, 1979; named Vt. State Poet, 1989-93. Mem. Nat. Acad. and Inst. Arts and Letters, Am. Acad. Arts and Sci. Office: New York Univ Dept of English New York NY 10003-6607

KINNEN, EDWIN, electrical engineer, educator; b. Buffalo, Mar. 9, 1925; s. Albert J. and Anna M. (Kumpf) K.; m. Ellen S. Underwood, Nov. 29, 1952; children—Susan, Janet, Peter, Andrew. B.S., U. Buffalo, 1949; M.S., Yale U., 1950; Ph.D., Purdue U., 1957. Registered profl. elec. engr., N.Y. Research engr. Westinghouse Research Lab., Pitts., 1950-55; instr. U. Pitts., 1953-55, Purdue U., West Lafayette, Ind., 1955-59; asst. prof. U. Minn., Mpls., 1959-63; prof. elec. engring. U. Rochester, N.Y., 1963-92; dept. chmn. U. Rochester, 1989-92, prof. emeritus, sr. scientist, 1992—; cons. Minneapolis-Honeywell, 1960-63, Washington Sci. Industries, 1960-63, Control Data Corp., Mpls., 1962-63, Eastman Kodak, 1977-78. Contbr. more than 80 tech. papers to profl. jours.; patentee in field. Served with U.S. Army, 1943-45; ETO. Westinghouse fellow, 1955-57; Japan Soc. for Promotion Sci. fellow, 1970; NIH Spl. fellow, 1971, Paul Harris fellow, 1991; Netherland Sci. Research scientist, 1978, 81; recipient William Roger Merit award March of Dimes, Genesse Valley Chpt., 1983. Mem. IEEE (sr.), Rehab. Engring. Soc. N.Am., Biomed Engring. Soc. (founding), Sigma Xi. Presbyterian. Home: 6 Rainberry Pittsford NY 14534-4426 Office: Univ Rochester Dept Elec Engring Rochester NY 14627

KINNEY, ARTHUR FREDERICK, literary history educator, author, editor; b. Cortland, N.Y., Sept. 5, 1933; s. Arthur F. and Gladys (Mudge) K. BA magna cum laude, Syracuse U., 1955; MS, Columbia U., 1956; PhD, U. Mich., 1963. Instr. Yale U., New Haven, Conn., 1963-66; asst. prof. U. Mass., Amherst, 1966-69, assoc. prof., 1969-73, prof., 1973-85, Copeland Prof., 1985—; adj. prof. Clark U., 1973—, NYU, 1992—; dir. Mass. Ctr. for Renaissance Studies, Amherst; spkr. in field. Author over 20 books including: Humanist Poetics, 1986, Continental Humanist Poetics, 1989, John Skelton: Priest as Poet, 1987; editor: Renaissance Historicism, 1987, Elizabethan Backgrounds, 1974, revised edit. 1990, Rogues, Vagabonds, and Sturdy Beggars, 1973, 2nd edit. 1990; editor English Literary Renaissance jour., (book series) Twayne English Authors Series-Renaissance, Massachusetts Studies in Early Modern Culture; editorial bd. several jours.; editorial cons. in field. With AUS, 1956-58. Recipient Disting. Tchg. award U. Mass., 1990, Chancellor's medal, 1985, Univ. Rsch. fellowship, 1976; named Fulbright fellow, Christ Ch., Oxford U., 1977-78, Sr. Huntington Libr. fellow, 1973-74, 78, 83, Sr. NEH fellow, 1973-74, 87-88, Sr. Folger Shakespeare Libr. fellow, 1974, 90, 92. Mem. MLA (pres. coun. of editors of learned jours. 1971-73, 81-83), Shakespeare Assn. Am. (trustee 1995—), Renaissance Soc. Am. (coun. mem.), Renaissance English Text Soc. (pres. 1985—), Sixteenth-Century Studies Conf. Avocation: published photographer, jazz. Home: 25 Hunters Hill Cir Amherst MA 01002-3116 Office: English Dept U Mass Amherst Amherst MA 01003 also: Ctr Renaissance Studies PO Box 2300 Amherst MA 01004-2300

KINNEY, EARL ROBERT, mutual funds company executive; b. Burnham, Maine, Apr. 12, 1917; s. Harry E. and Ethel (Vose) K.; m. Margaret Velie Thatcher, Apr. 23, 1977; children: Jeanie Elizabeth, Earl Robert, Isabella Alice. A.B., Bates Coll., 1939; postgrad., Harvard U. Grad. Sch., 1940. Founder, North Atlantic Pack Co., Bar Harbor, Maine, 1941; pres. North Atlantic Pack Co., 1941-42, treas., dir., 1941-64; with Gorton Corp. (became subs. Gen. Mills, Inc. 1968), 1954-68, pres., 1958-68; v.p. Gen. Mills, Inc., 1968-69, exec. v.p., 1969-73, chief fin. officer, 1970-73, pres., chief operating officer, 1973-77, chmn. bd., 1977-81; pres., chief exec. officer IDS Mut. Fund Group, Mpls., 1982-87; bd. dirs. Idexx Labs., Inc. Trustee Bates Coll., also chmn. alumni drives, 1960-64. Office: 4900 IDS Ctr Minneapolis MN 55402

KINNEY, HARRISON BURTON, writer; b. Mars Hill, Maine, Aug. 16, 1921; s. Charles Stephen K. and Blanche Perkins Gosline Clark; m. Doris Getsinger, Feb., 1952 (div. July 26, 1985); children: Susan Edith, Barbara Lee, Joanne Leslie, John Harrison. BA, Washington & Lee U., 1947; MA, Columbia U., 1949. Reporter New Yorker Mag., N.Y.C., 1949-54; articles editor McCall's Mag., N.Y.C., 1955-58; freelance writer Croton-on-Hudson, N.Y., 1958-60; bus. writer IBM Corp., Armonk, N.Y., 1960-86; freelance writer, 1986—. Author: (children's book) The Lonesome Bear, 1949, The Last Supper of Leonardo da Vinci, 1953, Has Anybody Seen My Father?, 1960, (children's book) The Kangaroo in the Attic, 1960, James Thurber: His Life and Times, 1995; contbr. articles, short stories to The Saturday Evening Post, Collier's, Woman's Home Companion, Reader's Digest, Woman's Day, Good Housekeeping, McCalls, Redbook, others. Capt. med. adminstrv. corps U.S. Army, 1943-46. Home: 11 Terry Hill Rd Carmel NY 10512-6105

KINNEY, JANIS MARIE, librarian, consultant, storyteller; b. Cresson, Pa., Dec. 26, 1935; d. Cecil and Ruth Ellen (Moyer) Powell; m. James Leroy Kinney; 1 child, Janis Cecilia. BS in Libr. Sci., Clarion U., 1957; MEd in Curriculum and Instrn., Pa. State U., 1987. Librarian N. Huntingdon Sch. Dist., Irwin, Pa., 1957-58, Greater Gallitzin (Pa.) Schs., 1959-61, Hollidaysburg (Pa.) Area Sch. Dist., 1961-90; storyteller Altoona, Pa., 1990—; chair Allegheny Storytellers of Pa., 1991—; rostered artist Pa. Coun. on the Arts in Edn. Program; cons. various sch. dists.; cons. Old Bedford Village Storytelling Festival, Bedford, Pa., West Overton Village Tellabration. Author/producer audio cassettes; featured teller Corn Island Storytelling Festivals, Louisville; contbr. articles to profl. jours. Active Blair County Arts Found., Altoona, 1991—, Blair County Tourist & Conv. Bur., 1992—, Blair County Hist. Soc., 1994—; Pa. Rural Arts Alliance, 1992—. Mem. Internat. Order E.A.R.S., Nat. Storytelling Assn., Allegheny Storytellers Pa. (founder). Avocations: reading, bicycling, hiking, travel. Home and Office: 1900 16th Ave Altoona PA 16601-2502

KINNEY, JOHN FRANCIS, bishop; b. Oelwein, Iowa, June 11, 1937; s. John F. and Marie B. (McCarty) K. Student, St. Paul Sem., 1957-63, N.Am. Coll., Rome, 1968-71; J.C.D., Pontifical Lateran U., 1971. Ordained priest Roman Catholic Ch., 1963. Assoc. pastor Ch. of St. Thomas, Mpls., 1963-66; vice chancellor of St. Paul and Mpls. Diocese, 1966-73; assoc. pastor Cathedral, St. Paul, 1971-74, chancellor, 1973; pastor Ch. of St. Leonard, St. Paul, from 1974; titular bishop of Caorle and aux. bishop Archdiocese of St. Paul and Mpls., 1977-82; bishop Diocese of Bismark, N.D., 1982-95, Diocese of St. Cloud, Minn., 1995—. Mem. Canon Law Soc. Am. Roman Catholic. Office: Chancery Office PO Box 1248 Saint Cloud MN 56302-1248*

KINNEY, KATHY, actress; b. Stevens Point, Wis., Nov. 3, 1954; d. Harold and Marian Kinney. Student, U. Wis. Actress playing Mimi Bobeck on The Drew Carey Show ABC-TV, 1995—. Appearances include (films) Parting Glances, 1986, Scrooged, 1988, Arachnophobia, 1990, Stanley and Iris, 1990, The Linguini Incident, 1991, Mr. Jones, 1993, This Boy's Life, 1993, (TV series) Newhart, 1989-90, Grand, 1990, (TV episodes) The Larry Sanders Show, 1992, Seinfeld, 1992, Lois and Clark: The New Adventures of Superman, 1996, (TV movies) Inherit the Wind, 1988, Promised a Miracle, 1988, (TV spls.) Tag Team, 1991, presenter The Eighteenth Ann. Cable Ace Awards, 1996; also various stage appearances. Avocations: restoring old lamps, reading. Office: care The Drew Carey Show Warner Bros TV 4000 Warner Blvd Burbank CA 91522-0001

KINNEY, KENNETH PARRISH, retired banker; b. Kansas City, Mo., Aug. 5, 1921; s. Wayne William and Dorothy Fay (Parrish) K.; m. Madeline Shriver Brennan, Aug. 2, 1947 (dec. Sept. 1983); children—Ann, Frank, Catherine, William, Madeline, Ellen, Robert; m. Terese Ann Bargen-Cagney, May 25, 1985. A.B., Princeton U., 1943; postgrad., Grad. Sch. Bus. Adminstrn., NYU, 1949-51. Sub-acct. Nat. City Bank N.Y., N.Y.C., 1946-50; asst. mgr. Chem. Bank, N.Y.C., 1950-55; sr. v.p. No. Trust Co., Chgo., 1955-86. Bd. dirs. Hinsdale (Ill.) Libr. Bd., 1985-91, Gt. Books Found., Chgo., 1997—. 1st lt. A.C., U.S. Army, 1943-46, ETO. Mem. Bankers Assn. Fgn. Trade (pres. 1969-70), Chgo. Council Fgn. Rels. (treas. 1967-70), Chgo. Com., Union League Club (Chgo.), Hinsdale Golf Club. Home: 633 S County Line Rd Hinsdale IL 60521-4726

KINNEY, LINFORD NELSON, retired army officer; b. Newton, N.J., Sept. 11, 1937; s. Sidney Ayers and Edna Louella (Winfield) K.; m. Joyce Arlene Souder, May 1, 1987. BSBA, Pa. Mil. Coll., 1959; postgrad., Golden Gate Coll., 1967. Commd. 2d lt. U.S. Army, 1959, advanced through grades to col., 1981; pers. officer Mil. Pers. Ctr., Washington, 1974-76; mem. staff Dept. Army, Pentagon, Washington, 1976-77; comdr. U.S. Army Port, Pusan, Korea, 1977-78; dir. hdwrs. MTMC, Washington, 1979-83; dir. New Cumberland (Pa.) Army Depot, 1983-87; comdr. MTMC Terminal Command Far East, Seoul, South Korea, 1987-89; ret., 1989; pres. Beaumont Sq. Homeowners Assn., Mechanicsburg, Pa., 1990—; mem. Cen. Pa. Coun., CAI. Vol. Internat. Exec. Svc. Corps., Stamford, Conn., 1990—; mem. Comp Plan Com., Hampden Twp., 1991, sr. logistics analyst, 1992-98; mem. Hampden Twp. Planning Commn. Decorated Bronze Star, Legion of Merit, Def. Superior Svc. Medal, Meritorious Svc. Medal (3). Mem. Nat. Def. Transp. Assn., Assn. U.S. Army, Ret. Officers Assn., Am. Philatelic Soc., Bur. Issues Assn., Am. Legion, Mil. Order World Wars, Mil. Order Fgn. Wars, Army Transp. Regtl. Assn., Army Transp. Mus. Found., Army Transp. Assn. Vietnam, Theta Chi. Republican. Methodist. Avocations: stamps, reading. Home: 1050 Tunberry Ct Mechanicsburg PA 17055-9100

KINNEY, LISA FRANCES, lawyer; b. Laramie, Wyo., Mar. 13, 1951; d. Irvin Wayne and Phyllis (Poe) K.; m. Rodney Philip Lang, Feb. 5, 1971; children: Cambria Helen, Shelby Robert, Eli Wayne. BA, U. Wyo., 1973, JD, 1986; MLS, U. Oreg., 1975. Reference libr. U. Wyo. Sci. Libr., Laramie, 1975-76; outreach dir. Albany County Libr., Laramie, 1975-76, dir., 1977-83; mem. Wyo. State Senate, Laramie, 1984-94, minority leader, 1992-94, with documentation office Am. Heritage Ctr. U. Wyo., 1991-94; assoc. Corthell & King, Laramie, 1994-96, shareholder, 1996—; owner Summit Bar Rev., 1987—. Author: (with Rodney Lang) Civil Rights of the Developmentally Disabled, 1986; (with Rodney Lang and Phyllis Kinney) Manual For Families with Emotionally Disturbed and Mentally Ill Relatives, 1988, rev. 1991, 99; Lobby For Your Library; Know What Works, 1992; contbr. articles to profl. jours; editor, compiler pub. relations directory for ALA, 1982. Bd. dirs. Big Bros./Big Sisters, Laramie, 1980-83, Children's Mus., 1993-97; bd. dirs. Am. Heritage Ctr., 1993-97; bd. dirs. Citizen of the Century, 1997—, govt. chmn., 1997—. Recipient Beginning Young Profl. award Mt. Plains Libr. Assn., 1980; named Outstanding Wyo. Libr. Wyo. Libr. Assn., 1977, Outstanding Young Woman State of Wyo., 1980, Arts and Scis. Disting. Alumni award U. Wyo., 1997. Mem. ABA, Nat. Confs. of State Legislatures (various coms. 1985-90), Laramie Area C. of C. (bd. dirs. 1996—, pres. 1999, Top Hand award 1997), Zonta, Rotary. Democrat. Avocations: photography, dance, reading, travel, languages. Home: 2358 Jefferson St Laramie WY 82070-6420 Office: Corthell & King PC 221 S 2nd St Laramie WY 82070-3610

KINNEY, MARK BALDWIN, fellowship executive, educator; b. Bangor, Maine, Dec. 27, 1944; s. Gerald Lewis and Virginia (Baldwin) K.; m. Nancy Pearson Kinney, June 6, 1964; children: Kathryn Louise Hahn, William Kinney. BA, U. Maine, Orono, 1962-66; MA, George Peabody Coll. for Tchrs, Nashville, 1970-71; PhD, George Peabody Coll. for Tchrs, 1971-76. Tchr. math. Herman (Maine) Sch. Dist., 1967-70; rsch. assoc. Inst. of Gerontology U. Mich., 1974-76; asst. prof. U. Toledo, 1976-80, dir. off-campus edn., 1985-86, dir. student svcs., 1986-87, assoc. prof., 1980—, dir. Ctr. for Internat. Studies and Programs, 1995-96, Lisle fellow (fellowship pres.), 1984-89; exec. dir. Lisle Fellowship, Temperance, Mich., 1989—; vis. lectr. Ea. Mich. U., Ypsilanti, 1973-75; cons. GM Corp., Toledo, Saginaw, 1990-94, U. Toledo Corp, 1993-94. Author: Staff Training in Geriatric Institutions, 1975, Skills in Interpersonal Comm., 1983, Exercises for the Older Adult, 1988, Empower Ourselves and Others, 1994. George Peabody Coll. Tchg. doctoral fellow U.S. Office of Edn., 1971-72. Mem. Phi Delta Kappa. Avocations: sailing, swimming, skiing, singing, boat building. E-mail: mkinney@utnet.utoledo.edu. Office: Lisle Fellowship 433 W Sterns Rd Temperance MI 48182-9568

KINNEY, RALEIGH EARL, artist; b. Brainerd, Minn., Mar. 11, 1938; s. Earl Martin and Nancy Ann (Wolleat) K.; m. Darlene Joyce Fox, Sept. 12, 1964; children: Rodney Eric, Aaron Weston. BS, St. Cloud (Minn.) State U., 1965, MA, 1968. Cert. tchr. Art tchr. St. Cloud Jr. High Sch., 1965-70; art tchr., dept. chmn. St. Cloud Sr. High Sch., 1970-80; ind. instr. watercolor workshop, 1980—. Contbg. artist North Light Pub., 1993, 94. Served with USN, 1957-61. Named Artist of Yr. Phoenix C. of C., 1987. Mem. Ariz. Watercolor Soc. (signature), Midwest Watercolor Soc. (v.p. 1976-77, signature), Plein Air Painters Am. Republican. Avocation: photography. Home: 506 W Pebble Beach Dr Tempe AZ 85282-4827

KINNEY, RICHARD GORDON, lawyer, educator; b. Chgo., May 8, 1939; s. Michael James Sr. and Blanche Marie (Gill) K.; m. Katherine Choffen, Dec. 26, 1969; 1 child, Richard Greg. BSEE, U. Ill., 1961; JD, U. Chgo., 1964. Bar: Ill. 1964, U.S. Ct. Customs and Patent Appeals 1975, U.S. Supreme Ct. 1970, U.S. Ct. Appeals (fed. cir.) 1982. With patent dept. Zenith Radio Corp., Chgo., 1963-64, Borg-Warner Corp., Chgo., 1968-73; divsn. patent counsel Baxter Travenol Labs., Inc., Deerfield, Ill., 1973-76; prin. Law Offices of Richard G. Kinney, Chgo. and Merrillville, Ind., 1976-95; pres. Richard G. Kinney, P.C., 1995-98; lawyer, educator; b. Chgo., May 8, 1939; s. Michael James, Sr., and Blanche Marie (Gill) K.; m. Katherine Choffen, Dec. 26, 1969; 1 son, Richard Greg. BSEE, U. Ill., 1961; JD, U. Chgo., 1964. Bar: Ill. 1964, U.S. Ct. Customs and Patent Appeals, 1975, U.S. Supreme Ct. 1970, U.S. Ct. Appeals (fed. cir.) 1982. With patent dept. Zenith Radio Corp., Chgo., 1963-64; with patent dept. Borg-Warner Corp., Chgo., 1968-73; div. patent counsel Baxter Travenol Labs., Inc., Deerfield, Ill., 1973-76; Law Offices of Richard G. Kinney, Chgo. and Merrillville, Ind., 1976; Rep. candidate Ill. State Senate, 1976; chmn. 6th Congl. Dist. Citizens for Goldwater-Miller, 1964. Mem. Ind. Bar Assn. Roman Catholic. Rep. candidate Ill. State Senate, 1976; chmn. 6th Congrl. Dist. Citizens for Goldwater-Miller, 1964. Mem. Ind. Bar Assn. Roman Catholic. Office: Richard G Kinney PO Box 11119 Merrillville IN 46411-1119

KINNEY, ROBERT BRUCE, mechanical engineering educator; b. Joplin, Mo., July 20, 1937; s. William Marion and Olive Frances (Smith) K.; m. Carol Stewart, Jan. 29, 1961; children—Rodney, David, Linda. B.S., U. Calif.-Berkeley, 1959, M.S., 1961; Ph.D., U. Minn., 1965. Sr. research engr. United Aircraft Research Labs., East Hartford, Conn., 1965-68; assoc. prof. mech. engring. U. Ariz., Tucson, 1968-78, prof., 1978-87, assoc. dept. head, 1980-83; prof. emeritus U. Ariz., 1987—. Alexander von Humboldt grantee, 1976-77. Mem. Tau Beta Pi, Phi Kappa Phi. Office: U Ariz Dept Mech Engring Tucson AZ 85721

KINNEY, STEPHEN HOYT, JR., lawyer; b. Albuquerque, Feb. 27, 1948; s. Stephen Hoyt and Harriet May (Gadsden) K.; m. Leslie vanLiew, June 10, 1972; 1 child, Erin. B.S., MIT, 1970; J.D., Harvard U., 1973. Bar: N.Y. 1974, U.S. Dist. Ct. (so. dist.) N.Y. 1974, U.S. Dist. Ct. (ea. dist.) N.Y. 1974, U.S. Dist. Ct. (no. dist.) N.Y. 1978, U.S. Ct. Apls. (2d cir.) 1975, U.S. Supreme Ct. 1982. Programmer, analyst MIT, 1968-70; law clk. N.J. Organized Crime Unit, Trenton, 1972; assoc. Reid & Priest, N.Y.C., 1973-85, sr. atty., 1985-86, ptnr. 1986-98; ptnr. Thelen Reid & Priest LLP, N.Y.C., 1998—. Author, editor: Outline of Arbitration, 1984; contbr. articles to jour. in field. Authored computer programs. Mem. ABA, N.Y. State Bar Assn. Club: MB Yacht (Port Washington, N.Y.). Office: Thelen Reid & Priest 40 W 57th St Fl 28 New York NY 10019-4001

KINNEY, THOMAS J., adult education educator. BA in Psychology, Syracuse U., 1968; MSW in Mgmt., SUNY, Albany, 1974. Dir. profl. development program, Nelson A. Rockefeller coll. pub. affairs and policy U. Albany, SUNY, 1976-99, spl. asst. to provost, 1997-99; with UP of Edn. Premier Health Alliance, Chgo., 1999—; mem. Task Force N.Y. State Work Force 21st Century; mem. SUNY 2000 Task Group Social Svcs.; dir. Ctr. Profl. Devel. and Continuing Edn. Rsch., chmn. quality forum Rockefeller Coll. Press; prof. Russian Acad. Edn.; co-founder Russian-Am. Ctr. Adult and Continuing Edn., Moscow; mem. task force employee assistance programs N.Y. State Assembly; mem. implementation adv. com. WorkKeys project Am. Coll. Testing; presenter in field. Editor Jour. Continuing Social Work Edn. Named Continuing Educator of Yr., Continuing Edn. Assn. N.Y., 1988; named to Internat. Adult and Continuing Hall of Fame, 1996. Fellow N.Y. State Acad. Pub. Adminstrn.; mem. Am. Assn. Adult and Continuing Edn. (treas., past chair commn. continuing profl. edn., Outstanding Svc. medallion 1994, pres. 1999—), Nat. Univ. Continuing Edn. Assn. (chair divsn. continuing edn. professions, mem. fin. com., mem. task force displaced profls.). Office: U P Edn Premier Inc 3 Westbrook Corp Ctr Westchester IL 60154

KINNEY, WILLIAM LIGHT, JR., newspaper editor, publisher; b. Bennettsville, S.C., Oct. 26, 1933; s. William Light and Annie Laurie (Mayer) K.; m. Margaret Rene Pegues, Mar. 21, 1964; children: Elisabeth Mayer Kinney McNiel, William Light III (dec.). BS, Wofford Coll., 1954, LHD, 1999; BA in Journalism, U. S.C., 1977. Copy editor The State, Columbia, S.C., 1955-58; reporter Marlboro Herald-Advocate, Bennettsville, 1958-59, advt. mgr., 1959-60, bus. mgr., 1960-65, mng. editor, 1965-70, editor, pub., 1970—; pres. Marlboro Pub. Co. Inc., 1970—; sec. Marlboro Savs. & Loan Assn., Bennettsville, 1970-82, First Nat. Bank of S.C., Bennettsville, 1973-84; mem. adv. bd. S.C. Nat. Bank, Bennettsville, 1984-94, Wachovia Bank, 1994—; sec., mem. adv. bd. Security Fed. Savs. & Loan, 1982-90, bd. dirs., 1984-89; pres. Greater Pee Dee Press Inc., 1972-82, Bennettsville Parking and Devel. Co., 1964; v.p. Hamlet (N.C.) News Inc., 1973-82. Editor, pub.: Three Who Dared, 1960, Sherman's March—A Review, 1961. Pres. United Fund, Bennettsville, 1963-64; chmn. Marlboro County com. S.C. Tricentennial, 1970, U.S. Bicentennial, 1974—; councilman, mayor pro tem City of Bennettsville, 1967-69; mem. Marlboro County Devel. Bd., 1958-81; bd. dirs. Kinney Found., 1971—, chmn. bd. dirs., 1975-99; bd. dirs. Indian Mus. of Carolinas, 1972—; trustee Whipple Found., 1979—, chmn., 1981—; trustee S.C. Press Found., 1978-93, vice chmn., 1985-92, chmn., 1992-93; trustee Neil Monroe Trust Fund, 1965-91, chmn., 1977-91; mem. adv. bd. SBA, 1962-64; chmn. fin. com. 1st Meth. Ch., 1985-87, staff parish com. chmn., 1990-92; mem. Chancel Choir, 1951—; trustee S.C. Meth. Adv., 1968-78, S.C. Hall of Fame, 1980-88, v.p., 1980-82; dir. S.C. Confedn. Local Hist. Socs., 1974-75, treas., 1975-78, v.p., 1979, pres., 1980-82; warden St. David's Soc., 1978-80, pres., 1980-81; chmn. Jennings-Brown House Restoration, 1974-76, Bennettsville Downtown Commn., 1977-82; v.p. Bennettsville Downtown Devel. Assn., 1993—; trustee Am. Folklife Ctr., Washington, 1982—, chmn. 1987, 92-93, 98—, vice chmn., 1990-92; mem. S.C. Archives and History Commn., 1987—, vice chmn., 1988-90, 98—, chmn., 1990-93; mem. S.C. Rev. Bd. for Nat. Register of Hist. Places, 1988—, chmn., 1990—, S.C. State Devel. Bd., 1993; bd. dirs. Friends Brookgreen Gardens, 1991-97, pres., 1993-96, trustee, 1993-96; mem. bd. visitors Coker Coll., 1986-89; bd. dirs. S.C. Com. for Humanities, 1981-85, Pawleys Island Civic Assn., 1979—, Palmetto Trails, 1993-97; trustee Scotia Village Retirement Cmty., 1995—; v.p. Marlboro Civic Ctr. Found., 1994—. Named Bennettsville and S.C. Young Man of Yr., 1961, S.C. Amb. for Econ. Devel., 1990, Knight of Justice of the Order of St. John, Knights of Malta, Sovereign Order of St. John of Jerusalem, 1995—. Mem. SAR, Nat. Trust for Historic Preservation (bd. advisors So. Region 1997—) S.C. Press Assn. (pres. 1972-73), Palmetto Conservation Found. (dir. 1997—), Marlboro County Hist. Preservation Com. (chmn. 1986-96), S.C. C. of C. (bd. dirs. 1964-68, 75-78), Bennettsville C. of C. (bd. dirs. 1964-67, 75-78), Bennettsville Jaycees (pres. 1962), S.C. Jaycees (v.p. 1963, nat. dir. 1964), Marlboro Hist. Soc. (bd. dirs. 1967-79, pres. 1975-79, Govs. award for lifetime achievement in historic preservation 1996), U. S.C. Soc. (bd. dirs. 1972-82, vice chmn. 1977-82), Wofford Coll. Alumni Assn. (bd. dirs. 1968-72), Marlboro Country Club, Marlboro Cotillion (pres. 1984-86), Nat. Debutante Cotillion (sponsor 1987-95), Sans Souci Club (pres. 1980-82), Rotary (bd. dirs. 1968-70, pres. 1970-72), Phi Beta Kappa, Sigma Alpha Epsilon, Sigma Delta Chi. Home: Magnolia PO Box 656 Bennettsville SC 29512-0656 Office: Shiness 100 Fayetteville Ave Bennettsville SC 29512-4022 *"Service to humanity is the best work of life" is a tenet of the Jaycee Creed that still drives me to work through my avocations as well as my vocation to help make my community, state and nation better than I found. These efforts have broadened my horizons, enriched my life and heightened my spirit. I recommend active service to one's home community, state and nation to all.*

KINNISON, ROBERT WHEELOCK, retired accountant; b. Des Moines, Sept. 17, 1914; s. Virgil R. and Sopha J. (Jackson) K.; m. Randi Hjelle, Oct. 28, 1971; children—Paul F., Hazel Jo Lewis. B.S. in Acctg., U. Wyo., 1940. C.P.A., Wyo., Colo. Ptnr. 24 hour auto service, Laramie, Wyo., 1945-59; pvt. practice acctg., Laramie, Wyo., 1963-71, Las Vegas, Nev., 1972-74, Westminster, Colo., 1974-76, Ft. Collins, Colo., 1976-97; ret., 1997. Served with U.S. Army, 1941-45; PTO. Mem. Wyo. Soc. C.P.A.s, Am. Legion (past comdr.), Laramie Soc. C.P.A.s (pres. 1966), VFW. Clubs: Laramie Optimist (pres. 1950), Sertoma. Home: PO Box 168 Fort Collins CO 80522-0168

KINNISON, WILLIAM ANDREW, retired university president; b. Springfield, Ohio, Feb. 10, 1932; s. Errett Lowell and Audrey Muriel (Smith) K.; m. Lenore Belle Morris, June 11, 1960; children—William Errett, Linda

Elise, Amy Elisabeth. A.B., Wittenberg U., 1954, B.S. in Edn., 1955; M.A., U. Wis., 1963; Ph.D. (1st Flesher fellow), Ohio State U., 1967; postgrad., Harvard U. Inst. Ednl. Mgmt., 1970; LL.D., Calif. Luth. Coll., 1983; Th.D., John Carroll U., 1983; LLD, Lenoir-Rhyne Coll., 1987; LHD, Capital U., 1995. Asst. dean admissions Wittenberg U., Springfield, 1958-65; asst. to pres. Wittenberg U., 1967-70, v.p. for univ. affairs, 1970-73, v.p. adminstrn., 1973, pres., 1974-95, pres. emeritus, 1995—. Author: Samuel Shellabarger: Lawyer, Jurist, Legislator, 1969, Building Sullivant's Pyramid: An Administrative History of the Ohio State University, 1970, Concise History of Wittenberg University, 1976, An American Seminary, 1980, Springfield and Clark County: an Illustrated History, 1985, also articles. Asst. to dir. Sch. Edn. Ohio State U., Columbus, 1965-67; past chmn. Assn. Ind. Colls. and Univs. Ohio; trustee Ohio Found. Ind. Colls., 1974-95, vice chair bd. trustees, 1995; chmn. standing com. Luth. World Ministries, 1976-82; mem. exec. coun. Luth. Ch. in Am., 1978-86; mem., chmn. Commn. for a New Luth. Ch., 1982-86; bd. dirs. Am. Assn. Colls., 1982-84. With U.S. Army, 1956-58. Mem. Clark County Hist. Soc. (trustee 1963—), Orgn. Am. Historians, Blue Key, Phi Beta Kappa, Phi Delta Kappa, Kappa Phi Kappa, Pi Sigma Alpha, Tau Kappa Alpha, Delta Sigma Phi, Omicron Delta Kappa. Clubs: Cosmos, Rotary. Home: 1820 Timberline Dr Springfield OH 45504-1236

KINO, GORDON STANLEY, electrical engineering educator; b. Melbourne, Australia, June 15, 1928; came to U.S., 1951, naturalized, 1967; s. William Hector and Sybil (Cohen) K.; m. Dorothy Beryl Lovelace, Oct. 30, 1955; 1 child, Carol Ann. B.Sc. with 1st class honours in Math, London (Eng.) U., 1948, M.Sc. in Math, 1950; Ph.D. in Elec. Engring, Stanford U., 1955. Jr. scientist Mullard Research Lab., Salford, Surrey, Eng., 1947-51; research asst., then research assoc. Stanford U., 1951-55, research assoc., 1957-61, mem. faculty, 1961—, prof. elec. engring., 1965—, assoc. dean facilities and planning Sch. Engring., 1986-92, assoc. chmn. elec. engring., 1984-88, W.M. Keck Found. chair engring., 1992-97, W.M. Keck Found. chair engring. emeritus, 1997—; dir. Ginzton Lab., 1994-96; mem. tech. staff Bell Telephone Labs., 1955-57; cons. to industry, 1957—. Author: (with Kirstein, Waters) Space Charge Flow, 1968, Acoustic Devices, 1987, (with Corle) Confocal Scanning Optical Microscopy and Related Imaging Systems, 1996; also numerous papers on microwave tubes; electron optics, plasma physics, bulk effects in semiconductors, acoustic surface waves, acoustic imaging, optical microscopy, fiber optics, non-destructive testing, optical storage. Guggenheim fellow, 1967-68; recipient Applied Research Achievement award Am. Soc. Non-destructive Testing, 1986. Fellow IEEE (Centennial medal, Sonics and Ultrasonics Group Achievement award 1984), Am. Phys. Soc., AAAS; mem. Nat. Acad. Engring. Inventor Kino electron gun, 1959; co-inventor real-time scanning optical microscope, 1987, solid immersion lens, 1989, microfabricated miniature microscope, 1995. Home: 867 Cedro Way Stanford CA 94305-1002

KINOSHITA, TOICHIRO, physicist; b. Tokyo, Japan, Jan. 23, 1925; came to U.S., 1952; s. Tsutomu and Fumi (Ueda) K.; m. Masako Matsuoka, Oct. 14, 1951; children: Kay, June, Ray. BS, Tokyo U., 1947, PhD, 1952. Mem. Inst. for Advanced Study, Princeton, N.J., 1952-54; postdoctoral fellow Columbia U., N.Y.C., 1954-55; rsch. assoc. Cornell U., Ithaca, N.Y., 1955-58, asst. prof., 1958-60, assoc. prof., 1960-63, prof., 1963-92, Goldwin Smith prof., 1992-95, Goldwin Smith prof. emeritus, 1995—; mem. tech. adv. panel U.S. Dept. Energy, Washington, 1982-83; com. fundamental constants Nat. Rsch. Coun., Washington, 1984-86. Author: Quantum Electrodynamics, 1990; contbr. over 100 articles to profl. jours. Guggenheim fellow, 1973-74; recipient Sun-Amco medal Internat. Union Phys. & Applied Sci., 1998. Fellow NAS, AAAS, Am. Physical Soc. (Recipient J.J. Sakurai prize 1990). Democrat. Home: 5 Winthrop Pl Ithaca NY 14850-1740 Office: Cornell U Newman Lab Ithaca NY 14853

KINOSZ, DONALD LEE, quality consultant; b. Pitts., Dec. 7, 1940; s. Michael and Pearl (Buckner) K.; m. Deborah Michele Reed, June 2, 1978; children: Brigitte, Brenda, Wayne Casey. BS, U. Pitts., 1966, MBA, 1995. Process engr. Alcoa Tech. Ctr., Alcoa Center, Pa., 1966-76, Alcoa, Tenn., 1976-79; mgr. Alcoa Tech. Ctr., Alcoa Center, Pa., 1979-81, pers. mgr., 1981-83, chem. mgr., 1983-85, ceramics mgr., 1985-88, mgr. quality, 1988-94; cons. Quality Assoc. Inc., 1994—; prodn. mgr. Anderson County Works, Palestine, Tex., 1978-79; mem. adv. bd. U. Pitts., 1988-94. City councilman City of Lower Burrell, Pa., 1980-88. Fellow Am. Inst. Chemists; mem. Am. Soc. Quality Control, Indsl. Rsch. Inst. (chmn. quality dirs. network), Quality Dirs. Network (founder, past chair), Strongland C. of C. (bd. dirs. 1985—), Pa. Quality Leadership Found. (sr. examiner 1994), Sigma Xi, Beta Gamma Sigma. Achievements include patents in anti-pollution method, electrolytic production of magnesium, production of magnesium chloride, regeneration of activated carbon having materials adsorbed thereon, flow control baffles for molton salt electrolysis, metal production, disposal of waste gasses from production of aluminum chloride, electrolytic furnace lining, method of preparing an electrolytic cell for operation, situ cleaning of electrolytic cells, treatment of offgas from aluminum chloride production. Home: 491 Dakota Dr Lower Burrell PA 15068-3305 Office: Quality Assocs Inc 3401 Windy Hill Dr Lower Burrell PA 15068-2201

KINS, JURIS, lawyer; b. Jelgava, Latvia, Apr. 24, 1942; came to U.S., 1949; s. Arnolds and Zenta (Dunis) K.; m. Olita Gita Kakis, Oct. 11, 1969; children: Aleksis A., Mikus N. BSChemE, U. Wis., 1964; MSChemE, U. Mich., 1965; JD, U. Wis., 1969. Bar: Wis. 1969, Ill. 1969. Assoc. ptnr. Chadwell & Kayser, Ltd., Chgo., 1969-90; ptnr. Vedder, Price, Kaufman & Kammholz, Chgo., 1990-93; Abramson & Fox, Chgo., 1993—. Pres. Latvian Peoples Support Group, Chgo., 1991—. Mem. ABA, Chgo. Bar Assn., Ill. Bar Assn., Wis. Bar Assn., Latvian Bar Assn. Avocations: tennis, skiing. Office: Abramson & Fox One E Wacker Dr Ste 3800 Chicago IL 60601

KINSBRUNER, JAY, history educator; b. N.Y.C., Jan. 10, 1939; s. Mac and Florence (Reitman) K.; m. Karen Hillman, Mar. 14, 1972; children: Jennifer, Mieca. BA, Syracuse U., 1960; PhD, N.Y.U., 1964. Instr. Nassau County Coll., Garden City, N.Y., 1964-65; asst. to prof. Queens Coll. CUNY, Flushing, 1965—; vis. scholar Inst. Caribbean Studies, Rio Piedras, P.R., 1984; mem. nat. screening com. for Fulbright Program, 1999—. Author: Independence in Spanish America, 1994, Not of Pure Blood, 1996. Fulbright lectr. Fulbright Commn., Venezuela, 1967. Mem. Am. Hist. Assn., Conf. on Latin Am. History, L.Am. Studies Assn. Home: 43 Jones Dr Highland Mills NY 10930-2714 Office: Queens Coll Flushing NY 11367

KINSELLA, RALPH ALOYSIUS, JR., physician; b. St. Louis, June 4, 1919; s. Ralph A. and Mabel Lamb (Downey) K.; m. Margaret Neville Boyle, Aug. 9, 1947; children: Ralph Aloysius, III, Mary, John, Eileen, Michael, Margaret, Matthew, Charles. AB, St. Louis U., 1939, MD, 1943. Diplomate: Am. Bd. Internal Medicine. Intern Presbyn. Hosp., N.Y.C., 1943; postgrad. St. Louis U., 1946-47, mem. faculty, 1948-95, prof. medicine, 1972-95, emeritus prof., 1995—; chief unit II St. Louis U. Med. Service, St. Louis City Hosp., 1958-80, med. dir., 1980-85; med. dir. St. Louis Univ. Hosp., 1985-95; pres. Inst. Med. Edn. and Rsch., St. Louis, 1972-95. Served with U.S. Army, 1944-46. Charles H. Nielson fellow, 1947-48; John and Mary Markle scholar, 1948-53. Fellow ACP, AAAS; mem. St. Louis Soc. Internal Medicine, St. Louis Med. Soc., Mo. Med. Soc., Endocrine Soc., Central Soc. Clin. Rsch., AMA, N.Y. Acad. Scis., Univ. Club, Sigma Xi. Roman Catholic. Rsch. in steroid hormonal biochemistry. Home: 53 Hanley Downs Saint Louis MO 63117-1366

KINSELLA, WILLIAM PATRICK, author, educator; b. Edmonton, Alta., Can., May 25, 1935; s. John Matthew and Olive Mary (Elliott) K.; m. Mildred Irene Clay, Sept. 10, 1965 (div. 1978); children: Shannon, Lyndsey, Erin; m. Ann Ilene Knight, Dec. 30, 1978 (div. 1997). BA, U. Victoria, B.C., Can., 1974; MFA, U. Iowa, 1978; DLitt, Laurentian U., Sudbury, Ont., Can., 1990, U. Victoria, 1991. Prof. U. Calgary, Alta., Can., 1978-83; freelance author Chilliwack, B.C., Can., 1983—. Author: Dance Me Outside, 1977, Scars, 1978, Shoeless Joe Jackson Comes to Iowa, 1980, Born Indian, 1981, Shoeless Joe, 1982, Mocassin Telegraph, 1983, The Thrill of Grass, 1984, The Alligator Report, 1985, The Iowa Baseball Confederacy, 1986, The Fencepost Chronicles, 1986, Five Stories, 1987, Red Wolf, Red Wolf, 1987, The Further Adventures of Slugger McBatt, 1988 (reissued as Go The Distance, 1995), The Miss Hobbema Pageant, 1989, Two Spirits Soar: The Art of Allen Sapp, 1990, Box Socials, 1991; co-author: (poetry with Ann Knight) The Rainbow Warehouse, 1989, Even At This Distance, 1994, The Dixon Cornbelt League, 1993, Brother Frank's Gospel Hour, 1994, The Winter Helen Dropped By, 1995, If Wishes Were Horses, 1996, The Secret of the Northern Lights, 1998, Magic Time, 1998. Houghton Mifflin Lit. fellow, 1982; recipient Fiction award Can. Authors Assn., 1982, Vancouver Writing award, 1987, Stephen Leacock medal, 1987; decorated Order of Can., 1994; named Author of Yr., Can. Libr. Assn., 1987. Mem. Enoch Emery Soc. Office: 9442 Nowell, Chilliwack, BC Canada V2P 4X7 Address: PO Box 2162 Blaine WA 98231-2162

KINSER, CYNTHIA D., state supreme court justice; b. Pennington Gap, Dec. 20, 1951; d. Morris and Velda (Myers) Fannon; m. H. Allen Kinser, Jr., March 17, 1974; children: Charles Adam, Terah Diane. Student, Univ. of Ga., 1970-71; BA, Univ. of Tenn., 1974; JD, Univ. of Va., 1977. Bar: Va. 1977, U.S. Dist. Ct. (we. dist.) Va. 1977, U.S. Ct. Appeals (4th cir.) 1977, U.S. Supreme Ct. 1988. Law clk. to Judge Glen M. Williams U.S. Dist. Ct., 1977-78; pvt. law practice, 1978-90; commonwealth's atty. Lee County, Va., 1980-83; magistrate judge U.S. Dist. Ct. (we. dist.) Va., Abingdon, 1990-98; justice Va. Supreme Ct., Richmond, 1998—; trustee Chapter 7 Panel, U.S. Bankruptcy Ct., 1979-90. Mem. Va. Bar Assn., Va. Trial Lawyers Assn., Am. Bar Assn. Methodist. Office: Supreme Court PO Box 457 Pennington Gap VA 24277-0457*

KINSER, KATHERINE ANNE, lawyer; b. Russellville, Ark., Apr. 25, 1954; d. Thomas Kinser and Nancy (Seminatore) Barber; m. Frank W. Sullivan III, Aug. 19, 1988. BA, U. Ark., Little Rock, 1979; JD, So. Meth. U., 1984. Bar: Tex. 1984, U.S. Supreme Ct. 1990; cert. family law specialist, Tex. Assoc. Michael F. Pezzulli, P.C., Dallas, 1984-86; pvt. practice, Dallas, 1986; ptnr. McCurley, Kinser, McCurley & Nelson, L.L.P., Dallas, 1986—; speaker in field. Contbr. articles to legal publs. Fellow Am. Acad. Matrimonial Lawyers; mem. ABA, State Bar Tex. (family law coun.), Tex. Acad. Family Law Specialists, Tarrant County Family Law Bar Assn., Dallas Bar Assn. (family law sect., sec. 1988-89, v.p. 1990-91, pres. 1991-92, mock trial com. 1987—), Sports Lawyers Assn., Phi Alpha Delta. Avocation: scuba diving. Office: Ste 4242 1202 Elm St Dallas TX 75202-3907

KINSER, RICHARD EDWARD, management consultant; b. L.A., May 14, 1936; s. Edward Lee and M. Yvonne (Withers) K.; m. Suzanne Carol Logan, Mar. 22, 1958. BA in Econs., Stanford U., 1958. Mgr. U.S. Steel Corp., San Francisco, 1958-65; v.p. Booz-Allen & Hamilton, Inc., 1965-78; sr. v.p., bd. dirs. William H. Clark Assocs., Inc., San Francisco, 1979-81; dep. dir. presdl. personnel The White House, Washington, 1981-83; mng. ptnr. Gould & McCoy, Inc., 1983-86; pres. Kinser & Assoc., N.Y.C., 1986—; exec. dir. Turn Around Mgmt. program European Bank for Reconstruction and Devel. Bd. dirs. San Francisco Bicentennial Com., 1976; vice chancellor's advisor Oxford U. Fellow Aspen Inst.; mem. White House Fellows Commn., Stanford Alumni Assn., Econ. Club, Capitol Hill Club. Republican. Home: 415 E 54th St New York NY 10022-5101 Office: Fl 36 515 Madison Ave Fl 36 New York NY 10022-5403

KINSEY, DAVID JONATHAN, state official, meteorologist; b. Richmond, Va., Nov. 19, 1954; s. Ralph Elsworth and Barbara Ann (Snead) K.; m. Elizabeth Rose Hughson, Oct. 6, 1979 (separated May 1998); children: Rachel Elizabeth, David Jonathan Jr. BS, Va. Commonwealth U., 1987; AD in Weather Tech., C.C. USAF, Colorado Springs, 1989; MBA, Averett Coll., 1997. Coastal resources program analyst Va. Coun. Environment, Richmond, 1987-88; chief weather station ops. 200th. Weather Flight Va. Air N.G., Richmond, 1988—; environ. program analyst Va. Coun. Environment, 1988-90, environ. program planner, 1990-91; policy analyst Va. Dept. Air Pollution Ctrl., Richmond, 1991-96; pres. Dad's Pads, Richmond, 1997—; environ. program mgr. Va. Dept. Environ. Quality, Richmond, 1996—; dir. Met. Washington Air Quality Com., 1997—, Endzone Ptnrs., 1997—; dir. Ridefinders, Richmond, 1996—; cons. Electric Vehicle Partnership, Richmond, 1997—. Pres., v.p. Va. Commonwealth U. Alumni Bd., Richmond, 1987-89; dir. Richmond Road Runners Club, 1990—; asst. cubmaster Cub Scout Pack 777, Richmond, 1994-96, asst. scoutmaster Troop 715, 1996-98. Presbyterian. Avocations: distance running, writing, inventing. Home: 3003 Park Ave Richmond VA 23221 Office: Va Dept of Environmental Quality 629 E Main St Richmond VA 23219-2429

KINSEY, DOUGLAS PAUL, insurance agent, financial planner; b. Dayton, Ohio, Sept. 15, 1960; s. Paul Richard and Violet Louise (Hinders) K.; m. Jenny Ann Leist, Nov. 5, 1988; 1 child, Austin Douglas. BA, Ohio State U., 1983. CFP; cert. ins. counselor. Sales rep. L.M. Berry & Co., Dayton, Ohio, 1983-86; field rep. Superior Ins., Atlanta, 1986-87; ins. agent Pottinger & Co., Dayton, 1987-90, Brower Ins., Dayton, 1990—; mem. supervisory bd. Heartland Fed. Credit Union, Dayton, 1995-98; pres. Montgomery Ptnrs., Dayton, 1990-98. Fin. chmn., vestryman St. Paul's Episcopal Ch.; dist. fin. chmn. Boys Scouts Am., Dayton, 1994-95. Mem. Kettering-Oakwood C. of C. (mem. legislative com. 1996—), Inst. Cert. Fin. Planners, Inst. Ind. Ins. Agts. Assn. Dayton (bd. dirs. 1993—), Ohio State U. Alumni Assn. Montgomery County (pres. 1994-96), Rotary (Oakwood chpt. dir. internat. svc. 1998-98, Paul Harris fellow), Masons, Elks. Republican. Episcopalian. Avocations: fly fishing, skiing, bicycling, golf, reading. Office: Brower Ins 110 N Main St Ste 1400 Dayton OH 45402-1786

KINSEY, JAMES LLOYD, chemist, educator; b. Paris, Tex., Oct. 15, 1934; s. Lloyd King and Elaine Mills K.; m. Berma McDowell, July 28, 1962; children: Victoria, Samuel, Adam. B.A., Rice U., 1956, Ph.D., 1959; NSF fellow, U. Uppsala, Sweden, 1959-60; postdoctoral fellow, U. Calif., Berkeley, 1960-62. Asst. prof. dept. chemistry M.I.T., 1962-67, asso. prof., 1967-74, prof., 1974-88, chmn. dept., 1977-82; D.R. Bullard-Welch Found. prof. sci. Rice U., Houston, 1988—; dean natural scis., 1988-98; interim provost Rice U., Houston, 1993-94; cons. Los Alamos Nat. Labs., external rev. com. chemistry and laser sci. div., 1983-89; Miller rsch. fellow, 1960-62; mem. NAS-NRC Bd. Chem. Scis., 1980-83, co-chmn., 1981-83; mem. steering com. U.S. Army Basic Sci. Rsch.-NRC, 1981-86; mem. oversight rev. com. chemistry div., NSF, 1989; mem. vis. com. for divsn. chemistry and chem. engring. Calif. Inst. Tech., 1999—; mem. com. of chemistry facilities and infrastructure U. Calif.-Berkeley, 1992-93; mem. corps. vis. com. for dept. chemistry MIT, 1994—; vis. com. for chemistry Stanford U., 1993-96. Assoc. editor Jour. Chem. Physics, 1981-84; mem. editorial adv. bd. Jour. Phys. Chemistry, 1984-88, Ann. Rev. Phys. Chemistry, 1985-89; mem. adv. editorial bd. Chem. Physics Letters, 1992-97; mem. Coun. of Am. Acad. of Arts and Scis., 1997—; contbr. articles to profl. jours. Recipient E.O. Lawrence award U.S. Dept. Energy, 1987; Alfred P. Sloan fellow, 1964-68, Guggenheim fellow, 1969-70. Earle K. Plyler Prize, Am. Physical Soc. 1995. Fellow AAAS, Am. Phys. Soc. (exec. com. divsn. chem. physics 1985-88), Am. Acad. Arts and Scis.; mem. NAS, Am. Chem. Soc. (chmn. divsn. phys. chemistry 1985, Nobel Laureate Signature award for grad. edn. 1990), Sigma Xi. E-mail: jlkinsey@rice.edu. Office: Rice U MS-600 PO Box 1892 Houston TX 77251-1892

KINSEY, JONI LOUISE, art history educator; b. Grand Forks, N.D., Nov. 19, 1958; d. Barry Allan and Carmen Louise Kinsey. BFA, U. Tulsa, 1981; MA, Washington U., 1984, PhD, 1989. Vis. asst. prof. Washington U., St. Louis, 1989-91; asst. prof. U. Iowa, Iowa City, 1991-97, assoc. prof., 1997—. Author: Thomas Moran and the Surveying of the American West, 1992, Plain Pictures: Images of the American Prairie, 1996 (Kayden Nat. Book award 1997), The Majesty of the Grand Canyon: 150 Years in Art, 1998; contbr. articles to profl. jours. Bd. dirs. Friends of Hist. Preservation, Iowa City, 1992—, pres., 1996-99. Smithsonian Predoctoral fellow Smithsonian Instn., Nat. Mus. Am. Art, Washington, 1987-88; travel to collections grantee Nat. Endowment for the Humanities, 1992, Exhbn. Planning grantee Nat. Endowment for the Humanities, 1995. Fellow Ctr. for Great Plains Studies-U. Nebr. (assoc.); mem. Am. Studies Assn., Coll. Art Assn., Assn. Historians Am. Art, Western Hist. Assn., Midwest Art History Assn. Democrat. Unitarian. Avocations: old house restoration, travel, sailing, reading. Office: U Iowa Sch Art/Art History 120 Riverside Side Iowa City IA 52242

KINSEY, MARK A., government official; b. Phoenix, 1958. AB, Ariz. State U., MA, PhD in Econs. Rsch. asst., instr. econs. Ariz. State U. Coll. Bus., Tempe; sr. fin. economist Treasury Dept., Washington, 1990-94; dep. dir. Office Fed. Housing Enterprise Oversight, HUD, Washington, 1994-97, acting dir., 1997—. Fax: 202-414-3823. Office: Office Fed Housing Enterprise Oversight 1700 G St NW Washington DC 20552-0003*

KINSINGER, JACK BURL, chemist, educator; b. Akron, Ohio, June 23, 1925; s. William Franklin and Idelle (Althaus) K.; m. Addie Jean Parker, Sept. 2, 1946 (div. 1987); children: Paul Craig, Amy Jo; m. Gladys Styles Johnston, 1997. BA, Hiram Coll., 1948; MS, Cornell U., 1951; PhD, U. Pa., 1958. Group leader rsch. Rohm & Haas Co., Phila., 1951-56; from asst. prof. to prof. chemistry Mich. State U., East Lansing, 1957-82, assoc. chmn. dept. chemistry, 1965-69, chmn. dept., 1969-75, asst. v.p. rsch. and devel., 1977, assoc. provost, 1977-82; prof. chemistry Ariz. State U., Tempe, 1982-87, v.p. acad. affairs, 1982-87; pres., CEO, Chgo. Osteo. Health Systems and Midwestern U., 1987-96; ret.; cons. Union Carbide Co., 1958-80, vice chmn. div. polymer chemistry, 1966-68, chmn., 1969; dir. chemistry div. NSF, 1975-77; trustee Kirksville Osteo. Med. Coll., 1984-87, Ariz. State U. Res. Park; exec. com. Fed. Independent Ill. Colls. and Univs., 1993-95. Editor computer symposium Jour. Polymer Sci., 1968. 2nd lt. USAAF, 1943-45. Recipient Disting. Alumnus award Hiram Coll., 1984. Fellow AAAS; mem. Am. Chem. Soc., Coun. Chem. Rsch. (vice chair exec. com. 1980-81). Home: 33 Red Fox Ln Kearney NE 68847-7611

KINSINGER, ROBERT EARL, property company executive, educational consultant; b. Chgo., Aug. 5, 1923; s. Elmer John and Frances Louise (Ballenger) K.; m. Sylvia Kading, May 20, 1950; children: William, Candace, Lisa. A.B., Stanford U., 1948, M.A., 1951; Ed.D., Columbia U., 1958; LL.D., Simpson Coll., 1977; L.H.D., Hahnemann U.; Litt.D., Thomas Jefferson U., 1986. Staff mem. U.S. del. 3d Gen. Assembly UN, Paris, France, 1948; regional field rep., mgr. chpt. and regional blood center ARC, Boise, Ida., 1949-56; lectr. Columbia U., 1956, Queens Coll., 1957; ednl. cons. Nat. League Nursing, 1957-60; dir. health careers project USNY, 1960-66; program dir. W.K. Kellogg Found., Battle Creek, Mich., 1966-70, v.p., 1970-83; chmn. Ednl. Services for the Professions, Inc., 1983-87; pres. Kinland Properties; cons. in field; vice-chmn., adv. coun. Mich. Comprehensive Health Planning Bd.; chmn. Commn. on Physicians Assts.; dir. Jossey-Bass Inc., Publs., 1982-89; dir., chmn., trustee, exec. com. Fielding Inst., 1985-92, 95—; adv. com. Corp. Cmty. Coll. TV; trustee Aviation Safety Inst. Author: Education for Health Technicians-An Overview, 1965; co-author: Clinical Nursing Instruction by Television, 1965; Editor: Career Opportunities for Health Technicians, 1971. Chmn. bd. overseers U. of State of N.Y. Regents Coll.; mem. exec. com. Commn. for a Nation of Lifelong Learners. Lt. USNR, World War II. Recipient commn. of honor SUNY, Farmingdale, 1970; Man of Yr. award Nat. Council Community Services, 1971; Honors of Soc. award Am. Soc. Allied Health Professions. Fellow Am. Soc. Allied Health Profls.; mem. Village West Yacht Club. Avocation: hot-air balloons (piloted first balloon flight over the Magnetic North Pole 1994). Home and Office: 21901 Confidence Rd Twain Harte CA 95383-9688 *While the "Golden Rule" should always guide one's relationships, of equal importance is steadfast delivery of what you promise to yourself and to others, and a constant effort to exceed the original promise.*

KINSKI, NASTASSJA (NASTASSJA NAKSZYNSKI), actress; b. Berlin, Jan. 24, 1960; d. Klaus G. and Ruth Brigitte (Tocki) K.; m. Ibrahim Moussa, 1984; children: Aljosha, Sonja Leila, Kenia Niambi Jones. Film debut: Falsche Bewegung, 1975; appeared in films: To the Devil a Daughter, 1976, Passion Flower Hotel, Stay As You Are, 1979, Tess, 1981 (Golden Globe award 1981), One from the Heart, 1981, Cat People, 1982, Exposed, 1983, The Moon in the Gutter, Unfaithfully Yours, 1983, Symphony of Love, 1983, Hotel New Hampshire, 1984, Paris, Texas, 1984, Maria's Lovers, 1985, Revolution, 1985, Torrents of Spring, 1988, Night Sun, 1989, Dawn, 1990, The Insulted & the Injured, 1990, Faraway, So Close, 1994, Terminal Velocity, 1994, Somebody is Waiting, 1996, One Night Stand, 1997, Little Boy Blue, 1997, Fathers' Day, 1997, Susan's Plan, 1998, The Lost Son, 1998, Savior, 1998, Friends and Neighbors, 1998, The Magic of Marciano, 1999, The Intruder, 1999, The Los Son, 1999, Town and Country, 1999; appeard in TV miniseries The Ring, 1996, Bella Mafia, 1997. Recipient Bundespreis (German film award) for Symphony of Love, 1983. Office: William Morris Agency care Peter Levine 151 S El Camino Dr Beverly Hills CA 90212-2775*

KINSLER, BRUCE WHITNEY, air traffic controller, consultant, air traffic control engineer, air defense engineer, air traffic control automation specialist, branch manager; b. Ukiah, Calif., Jan. 11, 1947; s. John Arthur and Mary Helen (Hudson) K.; m. Mickey Kinsler, Apr. 1, 1969 (div. Nov. 1976); 1 child, Arthur Todd; m. Segundina L. Pangilinan, May 27, 1978; 1 stepchild, Stephanie Lizarraga. AA, El Camino Coll., 1979; BA, Calif. State U., Long Beach, 1984. Air traffic controller FAA, various locations, 1971-81; cen. sta. mgr. Times Mirror Security Communications, Irvine, Calif., 1982-84; supr. office services Law Offices Paul, Hastings, Janofsky & Walker, L.A., 1984-85; air traffic control cons. Hughes Aircraft Co., Fullerton, Calif., 1985-88; engr., scientist space sta. div. McDonnell Douglas, Huntington Beach, Calif., 1989-90; ATC/ADGE sr. sys. engr. Hughes Aircraft Co., Fullerton, Calif., 1990-97; air traffic control automation specialist FAA, San Diego, 1997—, br. mgr. ASR11,9,8,7 radar program, 1999—; mem. citizens adv. com. Calif. Dept. Transp., Sacramento, 1982—. Author air traffic control tng. manuals, air def. manuals. Res. detective sheriff Orange County, 1991—. With USNR, 1986—. Recipient Plankholder, USN Meml. Mem. Nat. Air Traffic Com. (nat. com.), Shelby Am. Auto Club, Human Factors Soc. (pres. Orange County chpt.), Nat. Corvette Mus. (founding mem.). Republican. Avocations: sports cars, phys. fitness. Home: 32145 Camino Nunez Temecula CA 92592

KINSLEY, MICHAEL E., magazine editor; b. Detroit, Mar. 9, 1951; s. George and Lillian (Margolis) K. AB, Harvard U., 1972, JD, 1977; postgrad., Magdalen Coll., Oxford U., Eng., 1972-74. Bar: D.C. Mng. editor The Washington Monthly, 1975; mng. editor The New Republic, Washington, 1976-79, editor, 1979-81, 85-89, sr. editor, 1989-95; editor Harper's Mag., N.Y.C., 1981-83; Am. Survey editor The Economist, London, Eng., 1988-89; contbg. writer Time mag., 1987—; co-host CNN Crossfire, 1989-95. Editor Slate Mag., 1996—. Office: Slate Magazine One Microsoft Way Redmond WA 98052

KINSLEY, WILLIAM BENTON, literature educator; b. Montpelier, Vt., Sept. 11, 1934; emigrated to Can., 1965; s. Benton Rufus and Ann Magadline (Finnegan) K.; m. Therese Huang, Dec. 30, 1964 (dec. Mar. 1996); children: Anne-Marie, Claire, Eliane. Student, Wesleyan U., 1952-55; B.A., U. Toronto, (Ont., Can.), 1958; postgrad., U. Lyon, France, 1959; Ph.D., Yale U., 1965. Instr. St. Michael's Coll., Winooski, Vt., 1958-59, U. Rochester, N.Y., 1963-64; asst. prof. English lit. U. Montreal, Que., Can., 1965-71, assoc. prof., 1971-81, prof., 1981—, chmn. dept. etudes anglaises, 1970-71, 75-79, 90-91, 98-99. Editor: Contexts 2: The Rape of the Lock, 1979. Warden St. Pascal-Baylon Catholic Ch., Montreal, 1981-84. Can. council fellow, 1972-73. Mem. MLA, Am. Soc. Eighteenth Century Studies (pres. English 1974-75), Can. Soc. Eighteenth Century Studies, Assn. Can. Coll. and Univ. Tchrs. English, Can. Comparative Lit. Assn. Home: 3782 Kent Ave, Montreal, PQ Canada H3S 1N3 Office: U Montreal Etudes Anglaises, Case Postale 6128 Sta A, Montreal, PQ Canada H3C 3J7

KINSLOW, MARGIE ANN, volunteer worker; b. Salt Lake City, Dec. 7, 1931; d. Diamond and Sarah (Chipman) Wendelboe; m. James Ferol Kinslow, Apr. 6, 1954 (dec. July 1982). Student, U. Utah, 1949-53. Jr. vol. chmn. various hosps., Okla., Mont., Colo., 1967-87; pres. Ch. Woman's Orgn., Bartlesville, Okla., 1968; fin. advisor, jr. v.p., vol. chmn. Swedish Med. Ctr., Englewood, 1971-92; pres. Delta Gamma Alumnae, Denver, 1975-76; jr. vol. chair Colo. Assn. Hosp. Aux., Denver, 1977-82, 2d v.p., 1982-84; transp. chair, master class chmn. Rocky Mountain Regional Auditions, Met. Opera, Denver, 1986—. Office vol. Rep. Office, Billings, Mont., 1969-70, Colo. Senator, Denver, 1974-76; vol. various polit. candidates, Denver, 1974-90; various offices Newcomers, Okla., Mont. and Colo., 1967-75. Recipient Stellar award, 1979, Cable award, 1991. Mem. PEO, Gen. Fedn. of Women's Clubs (bd. dirs. 1994—, corr. sec. Western region), Colo. Gen. Fedn. of Women's Clubs (pres. 1994-96, various offices 1986-94), Denver Lyric Opera Guild, Cherry Creek Woman's Club (pres. 1985, Hoby corp. bd. 1997—), Littleton Rep. Women's Club. Episcopalian. Avocations: bridge, travel, people, the arts.

KINSMAN, ROBERT DONALD, art museum administrator, cartoonist; b. Bridgeport, Conn., Sept. 13, 1929; s. Cummings Sanborn and Sarah Elizabeth (Barton) K.; m. Patricia Ann Mulreed, Oct. 3, 1953. B.S., Columbia U., 1958, M.A. in Art History, 1966, A.B.D. in Art History.

Asst. curator Nat. Gallery Art, Washington, 1961-62; instr. art history Mary Washington Coll., U. Va., Fredericksburg, 1962-63, asst. prof. art history, dir. duPont Art Galleries, 1966-68; curator contemporary art Detroit Inst. Arts, 1963-65; asst. prof. art history SUNY, Albany, 1968-77; dir. Sheldon Swope Art Gallery, Terre Haute, Ind., 1978-85, Met. Mus. and Art Ctr., Coral Gables, Fla., 1985-86, Mus. Cartoon Art, Rye Brook, N.Y., 1987-88; freelance cartoonist, writer, 1988—. Contbr. articles to profl. jours. Bd. dirs. Arts Illiana, Inc., 1981-85. With U.S. Army, 1951-53. Mem. Am. Assn. Museums, Coll. Art Assn. Am. Home: 32 Bouton St E Apt 3 Stamford CT 06907-1651

KINSMAN, ROBERT PRESTON, biomedical plastics engineer; b. Cambridge, Mass., July 25, 1949; s. Fred Nelson and Myra Roxanne (Preston) K. BS in Plastics Engring., U. Mass., Lowell, 1971; MBA, Pepperdine U., Malibu, Calif., 1982. Cert. biomed. engr., Calif.; lic. real estate sales person, Calif. Product devel. engr., plastics divsn. Gen. Tire Corp., Lawrence, Mass., 1976-77; mfg. engr. Am. Edwards Labs. divsn. Am. Hosp. Supply Corp., Irvine, Calif., 1978-80, sr. engr., 1981-82; mfg. engring. mgr. Edwards Labs., Inc. subs. Am. Hosp. Supply Corp., Añasco, P.R., 1983; project mgr. Baxter Edwards Critical Care divsn. Baxter Healthcare Corp., Irvine, 1984-87, engring. and prodn. mgr., 1987-93; pres. Kinsman & Assocs., Irvine, Calif., 1993—; expert/auditor Med. Device Certification GmbH, Memmingen, Germany, 1995—; dir. engring. CardioVascular Dynamics, Inc., Irvine, 1997—; mem. mgmt. adv. panel Modern Plastics mag., N.Y.C., 1979-80; elected Nat. Hon. Soc., 1967. Vol. worker VA, Bedford, Mass., 1967-71; instr. first aid ARC, N.D., Mass., Calif., 1971-82; pres., bd. dirs. Lakes Homeowners Assn., Irvine, 1985-91; chmn., bd. dirs., newsletter editor Paradise Park Owners Assn., Las Vegas, Nev., 1988—; bd. dirs. Orange County (Calif.) divsn. Am. Heart Assn., 1991—, chmn. devel. com., 1993-95, v.p. bd. dirs., 1993-94, chmn.-elect bd. dirs., 1994-95, chmn. bd. dirs., 1995-96, adv. coun. rep., 1994-96, immediate past chmn. bd. dirs., 1996-97, mem. nominating com., 1995—; mem. steering com. Heart and Sole Classic fundraiser, 1988—, event chmn., 1991-92, mem. devel. com. Calif. affiliate, 1993-95. Capt. USAF, 1971-75, USAFR, 1975-81. Recipient Cert. of Appreciation, VA, 1971, Am. Heart Assn., 1991-95, Outstanding Svc. award., 1996; selected Community Hero Torchbearer 1996 Olympic Games, United Way Am. and Atlanta Com. for Olympic Games. Baxter/Allegiance Found. Community Svc . grantee, Deerfield, Ill., 1992, 93. Mem. Soc. Plastics Engrs. (sr., Mem. of Month So. Calif. sect. 1989), Soc. Mfg. Engrs. (sr.), Am. Mgmt. Assn., Am. Soc. Quality, Arnold Air Soc. (comptr. 1969, pledge tng. officer 1970), Plastics Acad., Demolay, Profl. Ski Instrs. Am., Mensa, Am. Legion, Elks, Phi Gamma Psi. Avocations: skiing, scuba diving, marathon running, golfing, music. Office: Kinsman & Assocs 4790 Irvine Blvd Ste 105-289 Irvine CA 92620-1973

KINSMAN, SARAH MARKHAM, investment company executive; b. L.A., Oct. 1, 1951; d. Robert Starr and Barbara Ann (Yates) K.; m. Kevin H. Olsen, Oct. 15, 1984 (div.); 1 child, Robert Kinsman. AB, UCLA, 1973; MBA, Harvard U., Boston, 1976. Acct. officer Citibank's World Corp. Group, N.Y.C., 1976-79; fin. mgr. Union Pacific Corp., N.Y.C., 1980-86; v.p., sr. transactor Citibank, N.A., N.Y.C., 1986-88; v.p. Bank N.Y., N.Y.C., 1988-92; sr. v.p. GE Capital, N.Y.C., 1992—. Com. chmn. Jr. League, N.Y.C., 1988—; mem. women's com. Am. Cancer Soc., N.Y.C., 1988-90; den leader Boy Scouts Am. Mem. Assn. for Corp. Growth, Women's Harvard Bus. Sch. Club N.Y.C., Harvard Bus. Sch. Club N.Y.C., Harvard Bus. Sch. Club N.J., Phi Beta Kappa. Avocations: horseback riding, gardening, travel, reading, dancing. Home: 2 Rowlands Rd Flemington NJ 08822-7020 Office: GE Capital 335 Madison Ave Fl 12 New York NY 10017-4669

KINSOLVING, AUGUSTUS BLAGDEN, lawyer; b. Boston, Jan. 19, 1940; s. Arthur Lee and Mary Kemp (Blagden) K.; m. Monique Berard, Dec. 21, 1974; children: Isabelle, Arthur. BA, Yale U., 1961; MA, Oxford U., 1963; LLB, Harvard U., 1965. Bar: N.Y. 1965. Assoc. Davis Polk & Wardwell, N.Y.C., 1965-70; v.p. Donaldson Lufkin & Jenrette Inc., N.Y.C., 1970-74; currently v.p., gen. counsel Asarco Inc., N.Y.C., 1975—; bd. dirs. So. Peru Copper Corp. Trustee Down Town Assn., 1975-91. Rhodes scholar, 1961. Mem. Am. Assn. Rhodes Scholars (dir. Claremont, Calif. chpt. 1975-90), Coun. of the Ams. (adv. bd. 1991—), Nat. Ctr. for State Cts. (corp. counsel com. 1997—). Club: N.Y. Yacht. Avocation: sailing. Office: ASARCO Inc 180 Maiden Ln Fl 22 New York NY 10038-4991

KINSOLVING, CHARLES MCILVAINE, JR., marketing executive, communications investor; b. N.Y.C., Jan. 27, 1927; s. Charles McIlvaine and Florence Natalie (Hogg) K.; m. Coral May Eaton, July 13, 1963 (dec. Jan. 1988); m. Jolie Brockman Hammer, Apr. 26, 1993 (dec. Aug. 1995); m. Jacqueline Wolf Vogelstein, Aug. 22, 1998. Student, U. Paris, 1948; AB, U. Pa., 1949; postgrad., Harvard Med. Sch., 1949-50, Columbia U., 1951-53. Stockholder relations AT&T, N.Y.C., 1950-51; rsch. assoc. Young & Rubicam Inc., N.Y.C., 1951-53; asst. mgr. media rsch. McCann-Erickson Inc., N.Y.C., 1953-58; mgr. plans devel. Nat. Broadcasting Co., N.Y.C., 1958-60; v.p., mktg. new tech., Newspaper Adv. Bur., N.Y.C., 1960-87, sr. v.p. mktg. group, 1987-92; ind. comm. investor, N.Y.C., 1992—; media cons. U.K., Belgium, South Africa; speaker Internat. Fedn. of Editors of Jours. Contbr. articles to profl. jours. Dem. candidate for State Assembly, Manhattan, 1954, 98; 1st vice chmn. N.Y. County Dem. Exec. Com., N.Y.C., 1963-71; mem., chmn. Planning Bd. #6 Manhattan, N.Y.C., 1969-84. Served with U.S. Army, 1945-46. Mem. Am. Mktg. Assn., Am. Assn. Pub. Opinion Rsch., Nat. Cable TV Assn., Am. Newspaper Pubs. Assn. (tech. com. 1983-92, telecomm. com. 1982-92), Union Club, Century Assn., Dutch Treat Club (bd. govs. 1994—), City Club (v.p. 1987-89), Coffee House Club (bd. dirs. 1984—), St. Anthony Club of Phila., St. Paul's Sch. Alumni Assn. (exec. com. 1994—, v.p. 1995—), Phi Beta Kappa, Delta Psi. Episcopalian. Avocations: travel, photography, philately. Home: 1172 Park Ave New York NY 10128-1213

KINSOLVING, SYLVIA CROCKETT, musician, educator; b. Berkeley, Calif., Sept. 30, 1931; d. Harold Waldo and Louise (Effinger) Crockett; m. Charles Lester Kinsolving, Dec. 18, 1953; children: Laura Louise, Thomas Philip, Kathleen Susan. AA in Voice, Piano magna cum laude, No. Va. Community Coll., 1983; BA, U. Calif., Berkeley, 1953. Solo vocalist various chs. Va., 1982—; pvt. tchr. piano Vienna, Va., 1983—; singer, soloist Unity Ch., Oakton, Va., 1980—, St. Andrew's Anglican Ch., Alexandria, Va., 1985—; active numerous local musical prodns., 1959—. Tour leader Vienna Newcomers, 1980. Mem. PEO, U. Calif. Alumni Club, Fairfax West Music Fellowship (sec. 1990—), Phi Theta Kappa, Pi Beta Phi. Democrat. Episcopalian. Avocations: walking, swimming, music, reading. Home: 1517 Beulah Rd Vienna VA 22182-1417

KINSTLER, EVERETT RAYMOND, artist; b. N.Y.C., Aug. 5, 1926; s. Joseph E. and Essie K.; m. Lea C. Nation, June 23, 1958 (div. 1984); children: Katherine G., Dana C.; m. Peggy Chartier, 1996. Ed., Art Students League, N.Y.C., 1943-45; hon. doctorate, Rollins Coll., 1983. Started career as illustrator N.Y.C., 1943; began specializing in portraiture, 1955; instr. Art Students League, N.Y.C., 1969-74. Portraits include over 35 U.S. cabinet officers, ofcl. White House portrait former Pres. Gerald R. Ford, former Pres. Ronald Reagan, J. Edgar Hoover, Richard K. Mellon, Mrs. Irenée duPont, Jr., Kurt Waldheim, sec.-gen. UN, Casper Weinberger, sec. of def., William Casey, dir. CIA, Cyrus Vance, sec. of state, Astronaut Alan B. Shepard, Jr., William Bowen, pres. Princeton U., James Cagney, John D. Rockefeller III, Byron Nelson, Frank Cary, pres. IBM, Charles Scribner, Jr., John Wayne, John Kemeny, pres. Dartmouth Coll., William Simon, sec. Treasury, Elliot Richardson, ambassador to Gt. Britain, Tennessee Williams, John Connally, gov. of Tex., Charles Brown, CH., ATT, Russel Long, U.S. Senator, Morris Udall, mem. U.S. Congress, Katharine Hepburn, Gregory Peck, former Pres. Richard M. Nixon; Bartlett Gramatti, pres. Yale U., George P. Shultz, former U.S. Sec. of State, Paul Newman, Thomas Kean, former Gov. N.J., former Pres. George Bush, Arthur Ashe, Tony Bennett, Carol Burnett, Elizabeth Dole, Betty Ford, Lady Bird Johnson, William Webster, former dir. CIA, Harry Blackmun, U.S. Supreme Ct. Justice, former U.S. Sec. of State Warren Christopher, Placido Domingo, President Bill Clinton, Gene Hackman, also numerous others; represented in permanent collections, Butler Inst. Am. Art, Nat. Portrait Gallery, Washington, Nat. Acad. Design, Mus. City N.Y., Met. Mus. Art, N.Y.C., The Pentagon, Am. Embassy, Paris, Carnegie Mus., N.Y. Stock Exchange, Bklyn. Mus., White House, Smithsonian Instn., numerous colls., univs., bus. firms; Author: Painting Portraits, 1971, Painting Faces, Figures, Landscapes, 1981. Recipient Artists' Fellowship Medal, 1986, Nat. Arts Club medal, 1993, Allied Artists medal, 1997. Mem. Allied Artists Am. (dir. 1958-60), Artists Fellowships, Inc. (pres. 1967-70), Am. Watercolor Soc., Pastel Soc. Am., Audubon Artists, NAD, Actor's Fund Am. (life). Clubs: Century Assn. (N.Y.C.), Lotos (N.Y.C.) (life), Nat. Arts (N.Y.C.) (v.p.), Dutch Treat (N.Y.C.); Players (life). Office: care Nat Arts Club 15 Gramercy Park S New York NY 10003-1705

KINSTLINGER, JACK, engineering executive, consultant; b. Antwerp, Belgium, Mar. 2, 1931; came to U.S., 1939; s. Joseph and Rose (Lichtblau) K.; m. Marilyn Wiseman, July 16, 1967; children: Michael, Jeremy. BSCE, Rensselaer Polytechnic Inst., 1952; MSCE, MIT, 1954. Registered profl. engr., N.Y., Pa., Wash., N.H., Colo., Del., Md., Mass., Fla., N.J. Assoc. Tippetts, Abbett, McCarthy, Stratton, N.Y.C., 1957-68; dep. sec. Pa. Dept. Transp., Harrisburg, 1968-75; state hwy. dir. State of Colo., Denver, 1975-82; v.p. Daniel-Mann-Johnson-Mendenhall, Denver, 1982-84; CEO, chmn. bd. dirs. KCI Techs., Inc., Balt., 1984—; adv. coun. U. Md. Bd. dirs. Am. Jewish Com., Balt.; chmn. CE Adv. Bd. Rensselaer Poly. Inst.; chmn. subcom. Md. Coun. on Mgmt. and Productivity; chmn. Marylanders for Effective and Safe Hwys. Fellow ASCE, Am. Cons. Engrs. Coun.; mem. Am. Inst. Cert. Planners, Engring. Soc. Balt., Greater Balt. Com., Greater Washington Bd. Trade , B&O Railroad Mus. (bd. dirs.), Am. Rds. and Transp. Builders Assn. (vice chair, bd. dirs.), High Speed Ground Transp. Assn. (bd. dirs.). Office: KCI Techs Inc 10 N Park Dr Hunt Valley MD 21030-1841*

KINT, ARNE TONIS, industrial engineer, mechanical engineer; b. Tallinn, Harjumaa, Estonia, Nov. 2, 1932; came to U.S., 1957; s. Tônis Kint and Salme (Redlich) K.; m. Saima Kärp, Aug. 30, 1964. BS in Mech. Engring., Stockholm Tekniska Inst., 1954; BS in Indsl. Engring., Ga. Tech., 1960; MS in Indsl. Engring., U. Calif., 1963. Registered profl. indsl. engr., Calif.; cert. profl. materials handling and mgmt., Mich. Mech. engr. Philips Neon Co., Stockholm, 1954-57; student indsl. engr. Weirton (W. Va.) Steel Co., 1959; plant, foundry engr. H.C. Macaulay Foundry Co., Inc., Berkeley, Calif., 1960-67; indsl. engring. project leader Matson Navigation Co., San Francisco, 1967-69; area indsl. engr. Interpace Corp., Pitts., 1969-72; cons. indsl. engr. Oakland, Calif., 1972-73; work design, analysis supr. Truck Divsn. Internat. Harvester Co., Inc., San Leandro, Calif., 1973-75; sr. systems project engr. Engineered Sys. & Devel. Corp., Santa Clara and San Jose, Calif., 1975-89; cons. ind. engr. Applied Engring. and Design, Inc., San Jose, Calif., 1989-90; project engr. Jacobs Engring. Group, Martinez, Calif., 1990-92; cons. ind. engr. Indsl. Engring. USA, Oakland, Calif., 1992-98; cons. to pres. Fabricated Metals, Inc., San Leandro, Calif., 1998-99; project mgr. Mason West, Inc., San Francisco Airport Extension of Bay Area Rapid Transit, Millbrae, Calif., 1999—. Bd. dirs. Estonian Info. Ctr., Stockholm, 1946-75; pres. Estonian League of Liberation, San Francisco, 1968-73. Decorated Gold Svc. medal Estonian Nat. Found., 1971. Mem. Estonian Soc. San Francisco (pres. 1962, 63), Swedish Am. C. of C., Estonian Ski Club. Avocations: skiing, boating, hunting, travel, fishing. Home: 312 Alta Vista Ave Oakland CA 94610-1941

KINTNER, PHILIP L., history educator; b. Canton, Ohio, Jan. 23, 1926; s. William Wagner and Effie (Erwin) K.; m. Anne Genung, Dec. 27, 1951; children: Karen, Judith, Jennifer. BA, Wooster Coll., 1950; MA, Yale U., 1952, PhD, 1958. Instr. Trinity Coll., Hartford, Conn., 1954-56, Reed Coll., Portland, Oreg., 1957-58; instr. Trinity Coll., 1958-59, asst. prof., 1959-64; vis. assoc. prof. U. Iowa, Iowa City, 1964-65; assoc. prof. Grinnell (Iowa) Coll., 1964-69; coll. entrance bd. exam commissioner European History, Princeton, N.J., 1968-70; chief reader advanced placement European history, 1969-72; ACM prof. Florence (Italy) Program, 1989-90; prof. Grinnell Coll., 1970-96, Rosenthal prof. humanities, 1976-96; prof. emeritus, 1996—. With U.S. Army, 1944-46. Recipient numerous travel/study grants for rsch. in Germany. Mem. Sixteenth Century Studies Conf. Avocations: woodworking, gardening, cooking, mineral hunting. Home: 1126 Summer St Grinnell IA 50112-1751 Office: Grinnell Coll PO Box 805 Grinnell IA 50112-0805

KINTNER, TREVA CARPENTER, retired education educator; b. Topeka, Ind., Apr. 27, 1920; d. Adrian and Elizabeth (Burns) Carpenter; m. Loren D. Kintner, Aug. 25, 1946; children: Susan, David. BS, Manchester Coll., North Manchester, Ind., 1944; MS, U. Mo., 1952. Tchr. pub. schs. Milford, Ind., 1944-45, Wakarusa, Ind., 1945-46, Pickerington, Ohio, 1947-48; instr. U. Mo., Columbia, 1952-54; asst. prof. foods U. Mo., 1968-86; ret.; prof. Prince of Songkaa U. Pattani, Thailand, 1986. Contbr. articles to profl. jours. Bd. dirs. Citrus coun. Girl Scouts U.S., 1995—. Recipient U. Mo. Alumni award, 1998; U. Mo. scholar, 1981. Mem. AAUW (pres. 1987-89), Kissimmee Women's Club (pres. 1991, 92), Kissimmee Garden Club, Ret. Tchrs. Assn. (pres. 1989-91), Sigma Xi, Gamma Sigma Delta (award of merit 1986), Phi Upsilon Omicron (nat. coun. 1989-92, Ednl. Found. 1996-98), Delta Kappa Gamma. Address: 2775 Orchid Ln Kissimmee FL 34744-3015

KINTSCH, WALTER, psychology educator, director; b. Temesvar, Romania, May 30, 1932; came to U.S., 1955; s. Christof and Irene (Hollerbach) K.; m. Eileen Hoover, June 27, 1959; children: Anja, Julia. PhD, U. Kans., 1960. Prof. U. Colo., Boulder, 1968—. Editor: Psychol. Rev., 1989-94; author books. Office: U Colo Dept of Psychology Institute of Cognitive Science Boulder CO 80309-0345

KINTZEL, ROGER, publisher; b. July 9, 1943. Pub. Altanta Constn., 1995—. Office: Atlanta Constn 72 Marietta St NW Atlanta GA 30303

KINTZELE, JOHN ALFRED, lawyer; b. Denver, Aug. 16, 1936; s. Louis Richard and Adele H. Kintzele; children: John A., Marcia A., Elizabeth A.; m. Suzanne Hinsberger; stepchildren: William Karp III, Christopher Karp. BS in Bus., U. Colo., 1958, LLB, 1961. Bar: Colo. bar 1961. Assoc. James B. Radetsky, Denver, 1962-63; pvt. practice law Denver, 1963—; corp. officer, dir. Kintzele, Inc.; rep. 10th cir. U.S. Ct. of Claims Bar. Chmn. Colo. Lawyer Referral Service, 1978-83, Election commr., Denver, 1975-79, 83-86. Mem. ABA, Colo. Bar Assn., Denver Bar Assn., Am. Judicature Soc. Democrat. Roman Catholic. Home: 10604 E Powers Dr Englewood CO 80111-3957 Office: 1317 Delaware St Denver CO 80204-2704

KINZER, JAMES RAYMOND, retired pipeline company executive; b. Pampa, Tex., Sept. 14, 1928; s. William Graham and Leota (Gott) K.; m. Billy June Chesher, June 30, 1956 (dec.); children—Mark William, Kandia Ann, Karen June, Kourtney Margaret, John Richard. B.B.A., So. Methodist U., 1950, LL.B., 1952. Bar: Tex. bar 1952. Asso. firm Locke, Purnell, Boren, Laney & Neely, Dallas, 1955-59; counsel Tex. Industries, Inc., 1960-63; atty. Mobil Oil Corp., 1964-65; asst. gen. counsel Mobil Pipe Line Co., Dallas, 1966-70; gen. counsel Mobil Pipe Line Co., 1970-92. Served with AUS, 1952-55. Roman Catholic.

KINZER, JOSEPH W., military officer. BA in History, U. Tampa; MS in Pub. Adminstrn., Shippensburg U.; grad., U.S. Army Command/Gen. Staff, U.S. Army War Coll. Commd. 2d lt. U.S. Army, 1964, advanced through grades to lt. gen., 1996; ret., 1998; co. tactical officer, regimental S-1/S-4, 4th regiment U.S. Mil. Acad., West Point, N.Y., 1974-77; exec. officer 1st bn., 506th infantry, 101st airborne divsn. Ft. Campbell, Ky., 1977-78; dep. asst. chief of staff G-3, 101st airborne divsn. Ft. Campbell, 1979-80, asst. chief of staff G-3, 82d airborne divsn., 1980-83; asst. chief of staff G-3, 82 airborne divsn. Ft. Bragg, N.C., 1984-85; comdr. 3d assault brigade, 101st airborne divsn. Ft. Campbell, 1986-88; asst. divsn. comdr. 82d airborne divsn. Ft. Bragg, 1988-90; dir. ops., readiness and mobilization Office Dep. Chief of Staff for Ops. and Plans, U.S. Army, Washington, 1993-94; dep. comdg. gen. 5th U.S. Army, Ft. Sam Houston, Tex., 1994-96, comdg. gen., 1996-98. Decorated Def. Disting. Svc. medal, Disting. Svc. medal with oak leaf cluster, Legion of Merit with 2 oak leaf clusters, Bronze star with V device and 2 oak leaf clusters. E-mail: jkinzer941@aol.com.

KINZER, WILLIAM LUTHER, lawyer; b. Mifflintown, Pa., Jan. 25, 1929; s. John Raymond and Ethel Naomi (Sellers) K.; m. Ann Marie Rosato, May 3, 1958; children: Karen, Carolyn, Cynthia, Matthew, Mark. BA, Dickinson Coll., Carlisle, Pa., 1950; LLB, Temple U., 1956; LLM, Georgetown U., 1961. Bar: D.C. 1957, Ga. 1962. Atty. IRS, Washington, 1956-62; assoc. Powell, Goldstein, Frazer & Murphy, Atlanta, 1962-65, ptnr., 1965—; Author miscellaneous tax articles, 2 BNA Tax Portfolios. Capt. USAF, 1951-53. Mem. ABA (com. chmn. 1987-89), Fed. Bar Assn., Ga. Bar Assn., Atlanta Bar Assn., Atlanta Tax Forum (pres. 1980, trustee 1978-81), Cherokee Town and Country Club (Atlanta). Roman Catholic. Avocation: golf. Home: 904 Spring Valley Woodstock GA 30189 Office: Powell Goldstein Frazer & Murphy 191 Peachtree St NE Ste 16 Atlanta GA 30303-1740

KINZIE, DANIEL JOSEPH, biomedical engineer; b. Chapel Hill, N.C., June 28, 1966; s. Joseph Lee and Jeannie Lillian (Jones) K. BS in Mech. Engring. and Materials Sci., MIT, 1988; MS, Stanford U., 1989; postgrad., Washington U., 1996—. Sr. engr. space systems div. Gen. Dynamics, San Diego, 1989-93; Whitaker Rsch. fellow U. Wash., Seattle, 1994-96; rsch. fellow Washington U. Sch. Medicine, 1996—. Contbr. articles to profl. jours. MacDonald fellow Stanford U., 1988, Guggenheim fellow Princeton U., 1988, Fgn. Lang. fellow NSF, 1989. Mem. AIAA, ASME, AMA, Mo. Soc. Family Practice Physicians, Wilderness Medicine Soc., Biomed. Engring. Soc., Pi Tau Sigma, Sigma Xi. Lutheran. Achievements include development of new sol-gel processing technique for Barium-Yttrium-Cuprate high temperature superconductor powder, quench heaters for SSC superconducting dipole magnets, superconducting x-ray lithography light source magnet; modeling and experimental analyses on high-energy phosphate metabolism in the heart.

KINZIE, JEANNIE JONES, radiation oncologist, nuclear medicine physician; b. Great Falls, Mont., Mar. 14, 1940; d. James Wayne and Lillian Alice (Young) Jones; m. Joseph Lee Kinzie, Mar. 26, 1965 (div. Sept. 1982); 1 child, Daniel Joseph; m. Johnson Wachira, Oct. 7, 1991. Student, Oreg. State U., 1960; BS, Mont. State U., 1961; MD, Washington U., 1965; MBA, U. Phoenix, 1997. Diplomate Am. Bd. Radiology; diplomate Am. Bd. Nuclear Medicine; cert. advanced master gardener Colo. State U., 1997. Intern. in surgery U. N.C., Chapel Hill, 1965-66; resident in therapeutic radiology Washington U., St. Louis, 1968-71, instr. in radiology, 1971-73; asst. prof. in radiology Med. Coll. of Wis., Milw., 1973-75; asst. prof. in radiology U. Chgo., 1975-78, assoc. prof. in radiology, 1978-80; assoc. prof. of radiation oncology Wayne State U., Detroit, 1980-85; prof. radiology U. Colo., Denver, 1985-95; dir. radiation oncology U. Hosp., Denver, 1985-91; cons. Denver Vets. Hosp., Denver Gen. Hosp., Rose Med. Ctr., FDA Ctr. for Devices and Radiologic Health, Denver; sci. adv. bd. Cancer League Colo., 1985-88; examiner Am. Bd. Radiology, 1985-88; adv. physician Colo. Med. Found., 1988—; chmn. faculty promotion com. U. Colo. Health Scis. Ctr., 1988-89. Assoc. editor Internat. Jour. Radiation Oncology Biology and Physics, 1985-95; contbr. articles to profl. jours.; chpts. to books. Mem. Faith Bible Chapel Ch. NIH grantee, 1973-75; Am. Coll. Radiology fellow, 1984; fellow nuclear medicine U. Colo., 1996-98. Mem. AMA, Colo. Med. Soc., Denver Med. Soc. (del. to Colo. Med. Soc. Ho. of Dels. 1989—), Am. Coll. Radiology, Colo. Radiol. Soc., Metabolic Bone Disease Soc. Colo., Soc. Nuclear Medicine, Rocky Mountain Oncology Soc. (bd. dirs. 1989-93, pres. 1991-93), Am. Soc. Therapeutic Radiologists, Am. Cancer Soc. (bd. dirs. Denver unit 1986-87), Am. Soc. Clin. Oncology, Wilderness Med. Soc., Xeriscape Colo. Republican. Avocations: stamp collecting, cross country skiing, gardening, rug latching, mountain climbing. Home: PO Box 2767 Evergreen CO 80437-2767 Office: Nuclear Medicine Box A034 4200 E 9th Ave Denver CO 80262

KINZIE, RAYMOND WYANT, banker, lawyer; b. Chgo., Oct. 20, 1930; s. Raymond Allen and Florence (Wyant) K.; m. Dorothy Cherry Beek, Sept. 17, 1955; children: Diana K. Wieczorek, Dorothy K. Tedeschi, Raymond Wyant Jr., Susan Hawthorne (dec.). BA, Carleton Coll., 1952; LLB, Yale U., 1955, JD, 1964. Bar: Ill. 1956, U.S. Dist. Ct. (no. dist.) Ill. 1959, U.S. Ct. Appeals (7th cir.) 1961, U.S. Supreme Ct. 1964. Assoc. McBride and Baker, Chgo., 1955-56; atty. Continental Ill. Nat. Bank & Trust Co. (now Bank Am. Chgo.), Chgo., 1956-59; trust officer Lake View Trust and Savs. Bank, Chgo., 1959-65, asst. v.p. loans and credit, 1965-71, v.p., trust officer, 1971-82, sr. v.p., sr. trust officer, 1982-88; sr. v.p., sr. trust officer LaSalle Bank Lake View subs. Algemene Bank Nederland (now known as ABN-AMRO Bank), Chgo., 1988-90; sr. v.p. trust svcs. ABN-AMRO Bank subs. LaSalle Nat. Trust, N.A., Chgo., 1990-92; sr. v.p. wealth mgmt. group Lasalle Nat. Trust, N.A., Chgo., 1993-97; sr. v.p. Wealth Mgmt. Group LaSalle Nat. Bank, Chgo., 1997-98; cons. LaSalle Nat. Bank, 1998—; bd. dirs. Land Trust Coun. Ill., Chgo.; mem. adv. bd. Nat. Coll. Edn. (Lewis U.), Evanston, Ill., 1975—; commentator radio editl. rebuttals Sta. WBBM; talk shows commentator WLS. Contbr. to Time, Newsweek, Chgo. Tribune, Chgo. Sun Times, Crain's Chgo. Bus., other profl. publs. Bd. dirs., sec.-treas. Ravenswood Hosp. Med. ctr., Chgo., 1975-85; bd. dirs., sec. Ravenswood Health Care Found., 1975-80. Mem. Am. Mgmt. Assn., Ill. State Bar Assn., Chgo. Bar Assn., Chgo. Estate Planning Coun., Land Trust Coun. Ill. Home: 1027 N Marion St Oak Park IL 60302-1374 Office: LaSalle Nat Bank 3201 N Ashland Ave Chicago IL 60657-2107 *Motto: Alle Anfang ist Schwer (All beginning is difficult.). A happy home, a career that's fun plus health and wealth and time enough to enjoy them is paradise found on earth - greater pleasure than these will not be found even in the Elysian Fields.*

KINZLER, THOMAS BENJAMIN, lawyer; b. N.Y.C., June 19, 1950; s. David and Rhoda Lenore (Wolgel) K.; m. Carol Ada Loebel, Aug. 24, 1975; children: Katherine Diane, David James. BA, Columbia Coll., 1971; JD, Boston U., 1975. Bar: N.Y. 1976, U.S. Dist. Ct. (no., so., ea. and we. dists.) N.Y. 1976, U.S. Ct. Appeals (2d cir.) 1976. Assoc. Kreindler, Relkin & Goldberg, N.Y.C., 1975-77, Arthur, Dry & Kalish, N.Y.C., 1977-80; assoc. Kelley Drye & Warren, N.Y.C., 1980-85, ptnr., 1985—. Mem. ABA, Assn. of the Bar City of N.Y.C. (products liability com. 1983-86, com. on state legis. 1978-80). Office: Kelley Drye & Warren 101 Park Ave New York NY 10178-0002

KINZLEY, COLLEEN ELIZABETH, zoological park curator; b. Leonardo, N.J., May 2, 1965. BA, Calif. State U., Hayward, 1984. Gen. animal keeper Phoenix Zoo, 1983-86, Brookfield Zoo, Chgo., 1986-90; sr. animal keeper Oakland (Calif.) Zoo, Calif., 1990-91; sr. animal mgmt. curator Knowlton Zoo, Oakland, Calif., 1991—. Mem. Am. Zool. Assn., Am. Assn. Animal Keepers, Elephant Mgrs. Assn.

KINZLY, ROBERT EDWARD, engineering company executive; b. North Tonawanda, N.Y., July 4, 1939; s. Robert William Kinzly and Ruth Elizabeth (Burgin) Kinzly-Bund; m. Brenda Deuel Lutz, Oct. 12, 1963; children: Michael Robert, Jennifer Ann. BA, SUNY, Buffalo, 1961; MS, Cornell U., 1964. Engr. Calspan Corp., Buffalo, 1963-67, sect. head, 1968-69, br. head, 1970-75; pres. SCIPAR, Inc., Buffalo, 1975-96; chmn. working group Am. Nat. Standards Inst., N.Y.C., 1969-72. Patentee in field. Mem. Assn. Old Crows (bd. dirs. 1982-92), Phi Beta Kappa, Sigma Xi. Republican. Presbyterian. Office: SCIPAR Inc PO Box 400 Buffalo NY 14231-0400

KIO, STEPHEN HRE, minister; b. Haka, Chin State, Burma, Mar. 19, 1937; came to U.S., 1979; s. Sang and Kawl (Dong) Fen; m. Klem Kyin Kio, Apr. 26, 1964; children: Van, Zalal, Lal, Dede. BA, U. Rangoon, Burma, 1960; BD, Serampore Coll., West Bengal, India, 1963; MA, Emory U., 1980, PhD, 1984. Lectr. Zomi Bapt. Theol. Sem., Falam, Burma, 1963-64; sr. pastor Falam (Chin State) Bapt. Ch., 1964-73; prin. Zomi Bapt. Theol. Sem., Falam, Burma, 1977-78; bible translator old testament Falam Bapt. Assn., 1973-78; bible translator new testament Falam Bapt. Assn., Atlanta, 1979-85; translations cons. United Bible Socs., Guam, 1986—; com. mem. Asia-Pacific Reg. Translation Com., Hong Kong, 1980—; treas. Zomi Bapt. Conv., 1964-77; sr. pastor Haka Bapt. Ch., 1978-79. Author: Church History, 1974, Pastoral Works 1966, N.T. Introduction, 1976. Mem. Bible Soc. Micronesia (bd. dirs. 1986—), United Bible Socs. (com. new readers selection 1987—), Soc. Bibl. Lit. Fax: 671-653-2053. Home: Perez Acres 129-25 Gollo Ct Yigo GU 96929-2301 *I have never applied for or desired to hold high position. Rather I aimed at little jobs and yet do it well. If I make a difference in small things, life would be worthwhile.*

KIPA, ALBERT ALEXANDER, foreign language and literature educator; b. Kiev, Ukraine, Sept. 10, 1939; came to U.S., 1951; s. Wadym and Alla (Divishek) K.; m. Oksana A. Smulka, June 4, 1966; children: Marko W., Dimitri O. BA, CCNY, 1962; AM, U. Pa., 1964, PhD, 1972. Lectr. CCNY, N.Y.C., 1962; teaching fellow U. Pa., Phila., 1962-64, Albert-Ludwigs U., Freiburg, Germany, 1964-65; from instr. to asst. prof. to assoc. prof. Muhlenberg Coll., Allentown, Pa., 1966-79, prof., 1979—, dir. humanities program, 1981-83, head dept. fgn. langs. and lits., 1989-93, 97—, J. & F.

Saeger prof. comparative lit., 1996—. Author: Gerhart Hauptmann in Russia, 1974; co-editor, author: Probleme der Komparatistik und Interpretation, 1978, Aufnahme-Weitergabe: Literarische Impulse um Lessing und Goethe, 1982; contbr. articles to profl. jours. Mem. Nat. Adv. Coun. on Ethnic Heritage Studies, Washington, 1980-82; pres. bd. dirs. Ukrainian Heritage Sch., Phila., 1984-94. Fulbright grantee, 1964, 81; study grantee NEH, 1978. Mem. MLA (del. assembly 1983-85), Am. Assn. Tchrs. of German (pres. chpt. pres. assembly 1974), Pa. State Modern Lang. Assn. (pres. 1990-92), Shevchenko Sci. Soc., Ukrainian Acad. of Arts & Scis. (v.p. 1998—). Avocations: piano, philately. Office: Muhlenberg Coll 2400 W Chew St Allentown PA 18104-5564

KIPER, MEL, sports commentator; b. July 25, 1950; married; 1 child. Student, Essex C.C., Balt. Expert analyst NFL draft ESPN, 1984—; contbr. SportsCenter ESPN; pres. Draft Publs., 1981—. Office: ESPN 935 Middle St No 2 Bristol CT 06010

KIPLINGER, KNIGHT A., journalist, publisher; b. Washington, Feb. 24, 1948; s. Austin Huntington and Mary Louise (Cobb) K. BA, Cornell U., 1969; postgrad., Princeton U., 1969-70. Reporter Montgomery County Sentinel, Rockville, Md., 1970; Washington corr. Griffin-Larrabee News Bur., Washington, 1970-73, bur. mgr., 1976-78; Washington bur. chief, chief news svc. Ottaway Newspapers div. Dow Jones & Co., Washington, 1978-83; with Kiplinger Washington Editors, Washington, 1983—, v.p. for publs., 1983-89, exec . v.p., 1989-92, pres., 1992—; assoc. editor The Kiplinger Washington Letter, Washington, 1983—; editor in chief Kiplinger's Personal Fin. Mag., Washington, 1985—, pub., 1988—. Co-author: Washington Now, 1975, The New American Boom, 1986, America in the Global '90s, 1989. Bd. dirs. Oratorio Soc. Washington, 1975-85, chmn., 1991—; mem. adv. bd. Levine Sch. Music, Washington, 1975—, Mount Vernon Ladies' Assn., 1986-92—; mem. nat. adv. bd. Nat. Mus. Women in the Arts, Washington, 1988-92; trustee Greater Washington Rsch. Ctr., 1992—. Mem. Soc. Profl. Journalists, Soc. Am. Bus. Editors and Writers, Nat. Press Club. Office: Kiplinger Washington Editors 1729 H St NW Washington DC 20006-3904

KIPNIS, DAVID MORRIS, physician, educator; b. Balt., May 23, 1927; s. Rubin and Anna (Mizen) K.; m. Paula Jane Levin, Aug. 16, 1953; children—Lynne, Laura, Robert. A.B., Johns Hopkins U., 1945, M.A., 1949; M.D., U. Md., 1951. Intern Johns Hopkins Hosp., 1951-52; resident Duke Hosp., Durham, N.C., 1952-54, U. Md. Hosp., 1954-55; asst. prof. medicine Washington U. Sch. Medicine, St. Louis, 1958-63; asso. prof. Washington U. Sch. Medicine, 1963-65, prof., 1965—, Busch prof., chmn. dept. medicine, 1973-92; disting. univ. prof. of medicine Washington U. Sch. of Medicine, St. Louis, 1992—; asst. physician Barnes Hosp., asso. physician, 1963-72, physician-in-chief, 1973-93, distinguished Univ Prof; Chmn. endocrine study sect. NIH, 1963-64, mem. diabetes tng. program com., 1970—; chmn. Nat. Diabetes Adv. Bd. Editor: Diabetes, 1973; Asso. editor: Am. Jour. Medicine, 1973; Editorial bd.: Am. Jour. Med. Scis; Contbr. articles to profl. jours. Served with AUS, 1945-46. Markle scholar in med. scis., 1957-62; Banting lectr. Brit. Diabetes Assn., 1972. Mem. NAS (coun. 1997—), Am. Soc. Clin. Investigation, Assn. Am. Physicians (Kober medal 1994), Am. Fedn. Clin. Rsch., Am. Diabetes Assn. (Lilly award 1965, Banting medal 1977, Best medal 1981), Endocrine Soc. (Oppenheimer award 1965), Am. Soc. Biol. Chemists, Am. Acad. Arts and Scis., Inst. Medicine. Home: 7200 Wydown Blvd Saint Louis MO 63105-3023 Office: Barnes Hosp Dept Medicine PO Box 8212 660 S Euclid Ave Saint Louis MO 63110-1010

KIPNIS, NAHUM S., science educator; b. Malin, Ukraine, Sept. 12, 1937; came to U.S., 1979; s. Shaya and Mina (Roitblat) K.; m. Berta M. Kamenir, Jan. 15, 1959; children: Alexander, Constantine. MS in Physics, Math., Zhitomir Pedagogical Inst., Ukraine, 1960; PhD in History of Sci., U. Minn., 1984. Tchr. physics High Sch., Ukraine, 1960-65; asst. prof. Inst. for Mining Engring., St. Petersburg, Russia, 1965-79; postdoctoral fellow U. Minn., Mpls., 1984-85; sci. educator Bakken Libr. and Mus., Mpls., 1986-98; pvt. practice sci. edn. cons. Mpls., 1998—. Author: History of the Principle of Interference of Light, 1991, Rediscovering Optics, 1992; contbr. articles to profl. jours. Mem. Am. Assn. Physics Tchrs., History of Sci. Soc.

KIPNISS, ROBERT, artist; b. N.Y.C., Feb. 1, 1931; s. Sam and Stella Anita K.; m. Jean Elizabeth Prutton, July 6, 1954 (div. 1982); children: Max, Ivan, Ruby, Benjamin; m. Laurie Lisle, 1994. Student, Wittenberg Coll., 1948-50; PhD (hon.), Wittenberg U., 1980; BA, U. Iowa, 1952, MFA, 1954; PhD (hon.), Ill. Coll., 1989. One man exhbns. include Museo de Arte Moderno, Cali, Columbia, 1977, Kalamazoo Art Inst., Canton Art Inst., Enatsu Galerie, Tokyo, Gallery New World, Dusseldorf, Germany, Redfern Gallery, London, Venable Neslage, Washington, Hexton Gallery, N.Y.C.; represented in permanent collections Chgo. Art Inst., Whitney Mus. Am. Art, N.Y.C., Nat. Collection Fine Arts, Libr. of Congress, L.A. County Mus., Detroit Inst. Art, Cleve. Mus., N.Y. Pub. Libr., Butler Art Inst., De Young Mus., Indpls. Mus. Art, Portland Mus. Art, Yale Mus., New Haven, Conn., Brit. Mus., London, The Fitz William Mus., Cambridge, U.K., New Orleans Mus. Art, Met. Mus. Art. Served with U.S. Army, 1956-58. Recipient Ralph Fabri prize in lithography Nat. Acad. Design, 1976, James R. Marsh Meml. award in lithography Audubon Artists, 1978, Charles M. Lea prize Print Club Phila., 1978, prize for lithography Soc. Am. Graphic Artists, 1979, Medal of Honor in Graphics Audubon Artists, 1983, Childe Hassam purchase award Am. Acad. Arts and Letters, 1988, The Cannon prize Nat. Acad. Design, 1999, Graphics award Boston Printmakers, 1999, Daniel Serra-Badue Meml. award Audiovision Artists, 1998. Mem. Nat. Acad. Design, The Century Assn., Soc. Am. Graphics Artists, Royal Soc. Painter Printmakers (London), The Boston Printmakers.

KIPPENHAN, CHARLES JACOB, mechanical engineer, retired educator; b. Middle Amana, Iowa, Nov. 8, 1919; s. Adam John and Emilia (Heinemann) K.; m. Jane Elizabeth Munsinger, Dec. 18, 1941; children—Judith Evans (Mrs. James R. Halstead II), Kurt Alfred. B.S. in Mech. Engring. State U. Iowa, 1940, M.S., 1946, Ph.D., 1948. Instr. mech. engring. State U. Iowa, 1941-42; from asst. prof. mech. engring. to prof., head dept. Washington U., St. Louis, 1948-64; prof. mech. engring. U. Wash., Seattle, 1963-88; chmn. dept. mech. engring. U. Wash., 1964-73, adj. prof. architecture, 1973-88; prof. emeritus, 1988; cons. to industry, 1949—. Contbr. profl. jours. Served to lt. USN, 1942-46. AEC-Am. Soc. Engring. Edn. fellow nuclear energy seminar Cornell U., summer 1959, direct energy conversion U. Ill., summer 1963; NSF sci. tchr. fellow TH Munich, Germany, 1960-61. Mem. ASHRAE, Am. Soc. Engring. Edn., ASME, Sigma Xi, Theta Tau, Pi Tau Sigma, Tau Beta Pi. Home: 3908 NE 38th St Seattle WA 98105-5416

KIPPER, BARBARA LEVY, corporate executive; b. Chgo., July 16, 1942; d. Charles and Ruth (Doctoroff) Levy; m. David A. Kipper, Sept. 9, 1974; children: Talia Rose, Tamar Judith. BA, U. Mich., 1964. Reporter Chgo. Sun-Times, 1964-67; photo editor Cosmopolitan Mag., N.Y.C., 1969-71; vice chmn. Chas Levy Co., Chgo., 1984-86, chmn., 1986—. Chmn. Spertus Inst. Jewish Studies; trustee Chgo. Hist. Soc. Recipient Deborah award Com. Women's Equality, Am. Jewish Congress, 1992, Shap Shapiro Human Rels. award The Anti-Defamation League of B'nai B'rith, Personal PAC's Leadership award, 1996; named Nat. Soc. Fund Raising Exec.'s Disting. Philanthropist, 1995. Mem. Com. of 200, Coun. on Founds., Chgo. Coun. on Fgn. Rels., Chgo. Network, Women's Issues Network, The Standard Club, Execs. Club of Chgo., Econ. Club of Chgo. Jewish. Office: Chas Levy Co 1200 N North Branch St Chicago IL 60622-2410*

KIPPERT, ROBERT JOHN, JR., lawyer; b. Detroit, Aug. 29, 1952; s. Robert John Sr. and Jeanne Marcella (DeYonker) K.; m. Dorothy Marie Cunningham, Oct. 28, 1978 (div. June 1988); 1 child, Cristie; m. Kim Denise Katherine Greenman, Feb. 10, 1990. BBA, U. Mich., 1974; JD, Wayne State U., 1977, LLM in Taxation, 1994. Bar: Mich. 1979; CPA. Tax staff acct. Arthur Young & Co., Bloomfield Hills, Mich., 1977-78; tax staff sr., mgr. McEndaffer, Hoke & Bernhard, P.C., Bloomfield Hills, 1978-84; tax supr. Cen. Transport, Inc., Sterling Heights, Mich., 1984-85; tax atty. Chrysler Fin. Corp., Southfield, Mich., 1985-89, mgr. non-income taxes and licensing, 1989-95, staff tax counsel, 1995-99, sr. tax couns., 1999—. Charter pres. Sterling Heights Jaycees. Mem. AICPA, ABA, Mich. Bar Assn., Mich. Assn. CPA's, Am. Arbitration Assn. (panel mem.). Republican. Roman Catholic. Avocations: softball, basketball officiating, music. Home: 2740 Apache Tr Wixom MI 48393-2122 Office: Chrysler Fin Co LLC 27777 Franklin Rd Southfield MI 48034-2337

KIPPING, HANS F., dermatologist; b. Chgo., Jan. 8, 1924; s. Johaanes and Johannah (Rauch) K.; m. Rosemary New, Jan. 3, 1928 (dec.); children: Susan, John, David. MD, U. Buffalo, 1947. Intern, Buffalo Gen. Hosp., N.Y., 1947-48, resident in indsl. medicine, Millard Fillmore Hosp., Buffalo, 1948-49; resident in dermatology E.J. Meyer Meml. Hosp., Buffalo, 1953-56; practice medicine specializing in dermatology, Buffalo, 1956—; clin. prof. dermatology SUNY-Buffalo; attending dermatologist Erie County Health Care Ctr., 1979; dermatologist Buffalo Gen. Hosp., cons. dermatology Roswell Park Meml. Inst., 1980—; cons., lectr. in field. Contbr. articles, research studies to profl. jours. Served to capt. USAF, 1950-52. Fellow Am. Soc. Dermatopathology; mem. Assn. Profs. Dermatology, AMA, Soc. Investigative Dermatology, Am. Acad. Dermatology, Dermatology Found., Toronto Dermatology Soc., Buffalo-Rochester Dermatology Soc. (pres. 1962-63), N.Y. State Dermatology Soc. (pres. 1974-75). Republican. Methodist. Club: Youngstown Yacht. Home: 192 Castlebrook Ln Buffalo NY 14221-4475 Office: 4444 Main St Buffalo NY 14226-4420

KIPPUR, MERRIE MARGOLIN, lawyer; b. Denver, July 24, 1962; d. Morton Leonard and Bonnie (Seldin) Margolin; m. Bruce R. Kippur, Sept. 7, 1986. BA, Colo. Coll., 1983; JD, U. Colo., 1986. Bar: Colo. 1986, U.S. Dist. Ct. Colo. 1986, U.S. Ct. Appeals (10th cir.) 1987. Assoc. Sterling & Miller, Denver, 1985-88, McKenna & Cuneo, Denver, 1989-94; sr. v.p., gen. counsel, dir. First United Bank, Denver, 1994-96; prin. Merrie Margolin Kippur Assocs., PC, Denver, 1997—; lectr. in field. Author: Student Improvement in the 1980's, 1984; (with others) Ethical Considerations in Bankruptcy, 1985, Partnership Bankruptcy, 1986, Colorado Methods of Practise, 1988. Contract liaison Jr. League Denver, 1992-94; bd. dirs. Bylaws Parliamentarian, 1994-95, planning coun., 1995-96, nominating com., 1996-97, facilitator, 1996-97, facilitator co-chair, 1997-98, v.p. planning, 1998-99, exec. v.p. membership-tng., 1999—. Mem. ABA, Nat. Network Estate Planning Attys., Colo. Bar Assn., Denver Bar Assn., Gamma Phi Beta, Phi Delta Phi, Pi Gamma Mu. Democrat. Avocations: reading, scuba diving, wine collecting.

KIRALY, BÈLA KÀLMÀN, retired history educator, Hungarian army officer; b. Kaposvar, Hungary, Apr. 12, 1912; came to U.S., 1956; s. József and Lutz Etelka Kiraly; m. Sarolta Gömbös, Dec. 6, 1947 (div. Aug. 1955); adopted children: Ference, Miklos, Sarolta Szendrey. BA, Ludovika Mil. Acad., Budapest, Hungary, 1935; MA, Gen. Staff Acad., Budapest, 1942, Columbia U., 1958; PhD, Columbia U., 1962; D in Mil. Sci. (hon.), Zrinyi Miklo's Mil. Acad., Budapest, 1994; LHD (hon.), Bklyn. Coll., 1994. With Hungarian Army, 1930-56, advanced through grades to col. gen., 1948-51; imprisoned by communists, Budapest, 1951-56; mem.-in-exile Hungarian Com., N.Y.C., 1957-66; from instr. to prof. history Bklyn. Coll., CUNY, 1962-82, prof. emeritus, 1982—; pres. Atlantic Rsch. & Publs. Inc., Highland Lakes, N.J., 1984—; col. gen. Hungarian Army, Budapest, 1992—; mem. Hungarian Parliament, Budapest, 1990-94. Author: Hungary in the Late 18th Century, 1969, Ferenc Deak, 1975, The First War between Socialist States, 1981; editor-in-chief: Atlantic Studies on Society in Change, 105 books, 1982—. Named Ky. col. State of Ky., 1960, Tchr. of Yr., Bklyn. Coll., 1964; recipient award of merit U.S. Mil. Acad., 1982, Righteous Among Nations award Yad Vashem, Jerusalem, 1993; fellow Columbia U. faculty seminar, 1975. Mem. Am. Hist. Assn., World Fedn. Hungarian Historians (co-pres. 1992). Democrat. Roman Catholic. Avocation: pigeon breeding. Home and Office: Atlantic Rsch & Publ Inc PO Box 568 Highland Lakes NJ 07422-0568

KIRALY, KARCH (CHARLES KIRALY), professional volleyball player; b. Jackson, Mich., 1960; s. Laszlo and Toni (Iffland) K.; m. Janna Miller, 1986. BS in Biochemistry, UCLA, 1983. Mem. U.S. Nat. Team, 1981-89; profl. beach volleyball player, 1983—. Recipient Gold medal Olympic team 1984, 1988, capt. team and MVP 1988 team, over 125 profl. career titles; named NCAA All-American, 1979, 80, 81, 82; MVP (twice) NCAA Tournament, Gold medalist Beach Volleyball, 1996; World's Best Volleyball Player by Internat. Volleyball Fedn., 1986, 88; mem. nat. team 1985 World Cup, 1986 World Championship. Led UCLA 3 NCAA Championships; first professional volleyball player who grossed over two million dollars in career earnings. Office: Assn Volleyball Profls 330 Washington Blvd Ste 600 Marina Del Rey CA 90292*

KIRBY, ALLAN PRICE, JR., investment company executive; b. Wilkes-Barre, Pa., June 18, 1931; s. Allan Price and Marian (Sutherland) K.; children: Jessie Ann, Allan Price III, Slater Baran, Coray Sutherland, Milan Stanton. Grad., Morristown Sch., 1949; BA, Lafayette Coll., 1953. Pres. Liberty Sq., Inc., Mendham, N.J.; dir., chmn. exec. com. Alleghany Corp.; chmn. bd. dirs. A.P. Kirby Jr. Found. Inc.; bd. dirs. Chgo. Title Corp.; chmn. bd. mgrs. Allan P. Kirby Ctr. for Free Enterprise and Entrepreneurship. Trustee Fred M. and Jessie A. Kirby Episcopal House, Wilkes U.; trustee, treas. Angeline Elizabeth Kirby Meml. Health Ctr. Lt. (j.g.) USNR, 1953-55. Mem. Delta Kappa Epsilon. Clubs: Mendham (N.J.) Golf and Tennis; Morris County Golf (Convent, N.J.); Yale (N.Y.C.); Black River Fish and Game (Pottersville, N.J.). Office: 14 E Main St PO Box 90 Mendham NJ 07945-0090

KIRBY, BRENDA JEAN, critical care nurse; b. Silver City, N.Mex., June 23, 1968; d. Scott Lawrence and Ruth Leola (Ellis) K. ADN, Ea. N.Mex. U., Clovis, 1988; BSN, West Tex. State U., 1990. RN, Tex. Staff nurse High Plains Bapt. Hosp., Amarillo, Tex. Mem. AACN, Am. Heart Assn. Home: 608 7th Ave Canyon TX 79015-4314

KIRBY, BRENDAN TIMOTHY, security system specialist, entrepreneur; b. Brookline, Mass., May 3, 1945; s. Robert Edward and pauline Eleanor (Tighe) K. BA, Boston U., 1968; grad., USAF Air U., Squadron Officer Sch., 1998. Maintenance support clk. USPS, Boston, 1973-96. Mem. Internat. Assn. Chiefs Police (assoc.), Internat. Assn. Ct. Officers and Svcs. Inc., Am. Indsl. Hygiene Assn., Am. Def. Preparedness Assn., Naval Enlisted Res. Assn., Nat. Sheriff's Assn., Internat. Narcotic Enforcement Officers Assn., Narcotic Enforcement Officers Assn. of Conn., Am. Philatelic Soc., am. Soc. Indsl. Security, Nat. Environ. Health Assn. Home: 68 Trevalley Rd Revere MA 02151-2760

KIRBY, CAROL BINGHAM, Spanish language educator; b. Oct. 12, 1946. BA, U. Akron, 1967; MA, U. Wis., 1969; PhD, U. Ky., 1977. Prof. Purdue U., West Lafayette, Ind., 1975-83, Slippery Rock (Pa.) U., 1983-85, Buffalo State Coll., 1985—.

KIRBY, DIANNA LEA, broadcast executive; b. Lincoln, Ill., June 27, 1956; d. Raymond Burnell and Patricia JoAnn (Bartle) Kirby. AA, Springfield (Ill.) Coll., 1976; U. Ill., Sangamon State U., Springfield, 1979. With broadcast svcs. Sangamon State U., 1977-80; traffic dir. Sta. WIL-FM, St. Louis, 1980-85; ops. dir. Sta. KCLC Lindenwood Coll., St. Charles, Mo., 1985-86; radio sta. mgr. St. Louis C.C. at Flo Valley, St. Louis, 1986—. Former sec.-treas., bd. dirs. When in Need of Svc. Bowling Club, 1982-97. Mem. Am. Bus. Women's Assn. (sec. regional conf. 1990-92, Woman of Yr. 1986, 92), St. Charles Women's Bowling Assn. (bd. dirs. 1993—, assoc. 2nd v.p. 1996—), Nat. Broadcasting Soc./Alpha Epsilon Rho (nat. v.p. 1995-98, coord. nat. conv. 1987, 93, chmn. nat. project on Tourette syndrome 1984-92, dir. regional conv. 1989-91, 94, Nat. Outstanding Mem. 1986, Nat. Honor Lifetime Mem. 1990). Office: St Louis CC Sta KCFV 3400 Pershall Rd Saint Louis MO 63135-1408

KIRBY, DOROTHY MANVILLE, social worker; b. Burke, S.D., Oct. 23, 1917; d. Charles Vietz and Gail Lorena (Coonen) Manville; m. Sigmund Kirby, July 11, 1941 (div. 1969); children; Paul Howard, Robert Charles. BA, Wayne State U., 1970, MSW, 1972. Cert. social worker, Mich.; lic. marriage and family therapist, Mich. Pvt. practice social work Allen Park, Mich., 1973—; conduct seminars on stress, personal effectiveness and communication for various orgns., hosps. and bus. Pres. Allen Park Symphony Orch., 1990-92. Mem. AAUW, Am. Group Psychotherapy Assn., Nat. Assn. Social Workers (clin.), Nat. Assn. Marriage and Family Counseling, Mich. Assn. Marriage and Family Counseling (sec. 1982), LWV (pres. Allen Park 1965-66). Presbyterian. Lodge: Soroptimists. Avocation: playing violin. Home and Office: 15720 Wick Rd Allen Park MI 48101-1535

KIRBY, FRED MORGAN, II, corporation executive; b. Wilkes Barre, Pa., Nov. 23, 1919; s. Allan P. and Marian G. (Sutherland) K.; m. A. Walker Dillard, Apr. 30, 1949; children: Alice Kirby Horton, Fred Morgan III, Dillard, Jefferson. Grad., Lawrenceville Sch., 1938; A.B., Lafayette Coll., Easton, Pa., 1942; postgrad., Harvard U., 1947; LLD, Lafayette Coll., 1984; postgrad., Drew U., 1997; LLD, St. Joseph's U., 1981. From v.p. to pres., bd. dirs. Allan Corp., 1953-75; pres., chmn. bd. dirs. Filtration Engrs., Inc., 1951-56; dir. Alleghany Corp., 1958-61, 63—, v.p., 1961, exec. v.p., 1963-67, chmn. bd., 1967—, pres., 1968-77, mem. exec. com., 1968—; bd. dirs. World Minerals, Inc. Pres., dir. F.M. Kirby Found., Inc.; dir. United Cerebral Palsy Rsch. & Edn. Found., Inc., Nat. Football Found. and Coll. Hall of Fame, Inc. Served to lt. (s.g.) USNR, 1942-46. Recipient 25th Anniversary citation NCAA, 1966, Silver Anniversary All-Am. award Sports Illustrated, 1966, Gold medal Pa. Soc., 1982, Internat. Swimming Hall of Fame, 1989. Mem. Westmoreland Club, (Pa.), Spring Valley Hounds (N.J.), Treyburn Country Club (N.C.), Morris County Golf Club (N.J.), Zeta Psi. Office: PO Box 151 17 Dehart St Morristown NJ 07963-0150

KIRBY, HARMON E., ambassador; b. Hamilton, Ohio, Jan. 27, 1934; s. Cecil and Julia Catherine (Tucker) K.; m. Françoise Rolande Chatelain, Dec. 26, 1963; children: Caroline Patricia, Christopher Harmon. AB, Harvard U., 1952; MA, George Washington U., 1977. With pers. and labor rels. Diamond Nat. Corp., Middletown, Ohio, 1959-60; exec. asst. to exec. v.p. Hudson Pulp and Paper Co., N.Y.C., 1960-61; joined Fgn. Svc., Dept. State, 1961; vice consul U.S. Mission, Geneva, 1961-63, U.S. Consulate Gen., Madras, India, 1964-66; internat. rels. officer Dept. State, 1966-69; polit. officer U.S. Embassy, New Delhi, 1969-72; turkish desk officer Dept. State, 1974-76; polit. counselor U.S. Mission to the European Cmtys., Brussels, 1976-79; counselor, dep. chief of mission U.S. Embassy, Khartoum, 1979-81; sr. seminar Nat. and Internat. Affairs, Washington, 1981-82; dir. Pakistan/Afghanistan/Bangladesh affairs, 1982-84; min.-counselor dep. chief of mission U.S. Embassy, Rabat, Morocco, 1984-87; dir. UN polit. affairs Dept. State, Washington, 1987-89; amb. to Togo, 1990-94. Bd. dirs. Internat. Eye Found. Mem. Am. Fgn. Svc. Assn., Phi Beta Kappa. Avocations: travel, photography, tennis, swimming. Home: 6811 Barrett Ln Bethesda MD 20814-1205

KIRBY, H(ARRY) SCOTT, priest; b. Richmond, Va., May 6, 1938; s. William Alphus and Lucille Viola (Patterson) K.; m. Heather Patricia Roberts, June 22, 1963; children: Cheryl Christine, Robert Bruce. BA, U. Richmond, 1960; MDiv, Gen. Theol. Sem., N.Y.C., 1963. Ordained priest Episcopal Ch., 1963. Asst. to rector Cathedral of St. Luke and St. Paul, Charleston, S.C., 1963; curate Ch. of the Advent, Kenmore, N.Y., 1963-66; rector Ch. of St. John the Bapt., Dunkirk, N.Y., 1966-73, Ch. of St. John on the Mountain, Bernardsville, N.J., 1973-79; canon Christ Ch. Cathedral, Salina, Kans., 1979-89; dean Christ Ch. Cathedral, Eau Claire, Wis., 1989—; devel. cons. St. Francis Acad., Salina, 1991; chmn. long range planning Diocese of Eau Claire, 1989—, dean Chippewa Valley, 1990-96, mem. coun. of advice to the pres., ho. of deps., 1994—, chair com. on state of the ch., 1994-97; mem. com. t elect presiding bishop; chaplain Eau Claire Police Dept. Contbr. articles to mags. Bd. dirs. Presiding Bishop's Fund for World Relief. Recipient Bishop's Svc. award Diocese of Western Kans., 1980. Mem. Anglican Soc. Home: 1712 Lehman St Eau Claire WI 54701-7524 Office: Christ Ch Cathedral 510 S Farwell St Eau Claire WI 54701-3723

KIRBY, JAMES EDMUND, JR., theology educator; b. Wheeler, Tex., June 24, 1933; s. James Edmund and Mamie (Helton) K.; m. Patty Ray Boothe, July 22, 1955; children: David Edmund, Patrick Boothe. B.A. cum laude, McMurry Coll., 1954; B.D., Perkins Sch. Theology, 1957, S.T.M., 1959; Ph.D., Drew U., 1963; postgrad., Cambridge (Eng.) U., 1957-58. Ordained to ministry United Meth. Ch., 1959; pastor First Meth. Ch., Roby, Tex., 1958-59, Milford (Pa.) Meth. Ch., 1960-61; asst. prof. Bible, McMurry Coll., Abilene, Tex., 1959-60; asst. prof. religion Sweet Briar Coll., Va., 1963-67; prof. religion, head dept. religion Okla. State U., Stillwater, 1967-70; head Sch. Humanistic Studies, 1970-76; dean, Prof. Ch. History Sch. Theology, Drew U., Madison, N.J., 1976-81; dean Perkins Sch. Theology So. Meth. U., Dallas, 1981-94, pres. ad interim, 1994-95, prof. ch. history, 1995—; teaching asst. Drew Theol. Sem., Madison, N.J., 1960-61; cons. bd. missions United Meth. Ch., South Africa, 1968. Co-author: The Methodists, 1996; contbr. articles to profl. jours.; bd. dirs., pres. Wesley Works Editl. Project. John M. Moore fellow, 1957-58; Dempster fellow, 1962. Mem. Am. Acad. Religion, Soc. Values in Higher Edn., Am. Soc. Ch. History, Alpha Chi, Omicron Delta Kappa. Home: 9235 Windy Crest Dr Dallas TX 75243-6222 Office: So Meth U Selecman Hall Perkins Sch Theology Dallas TX 75275

KIRBY, JOHN JOSEPH, JR., lawyer; b. Washington, Oct. 22, 1939; s. John Joseph and Rose Elizabeth (Mangan) K.; m. Dynda L. Andrews, June 24, 1980; children: John Pickens, Timothy James, Perrin Patricia Lucia. BA, Fordham Coll., 1961; BA (Rhodes scholar), Oxford U., 1964, MA, 1967; LLB, U. Va., 1966. Bar: Va. 1966, N.Y. 1969. Asst. prof. law U. Va., 1966-67; spl. asst. civil rights divsn. U.S. Dept. Justice, Washington, 1967-68; assoc. Mudge Rose Guthrie Alexander & Ferdon, N.Y.C., 1968-70, ptnr., 1971-95, chmn., 1991-95; ptnr. Latham & Watkins, N.Y.C., 1995—; dep. dir. Pres.'s Commn. on Campus Unrest, 1970; bd. dirs. Georgetown U., 1976-92, Fordham U., 1994—. Bd. dirs. Merton Coll. Charitable Corp., 1995—, Fund for Modern Cts., 1998—. Mem. ABA, Assn. Bar City N.Y., Va. State Bar, D.C. Bar. Home: 1148 5th Ave New York NY 10128-0807 also: 64 Beach Rd Westhampton Beach NY 11978-2339 Office: 885 3rd Ave Ste 1000 New York NY 10022-4834

KIRBY, JOHN THOMAS, comparative literature educator; b. New Haven, May 9, 1955; s. Edward Joseph and Mildred Jean (Howard) K.; children: Susannah Leigh, David Alexander. AB cum laude, U. N.C., 1977, MA, 1981, PhD, 1985. Asst. prof. classics Smith Coll., Northampton, Mass., 1985-87; asst. prof. to prof. classics and comparative lit. Purdue U., West Lafayette, Ind., 1987—, chair classics, 1988-94, chair comparative lit., 1994—; editl. cons. Purdue U. Press, Yale U. Press, U. Calif. Press; cons. U. Okla., 1997, U. Notre Dame, 1998. Author: The Rhetoric of Cicero's Pro Cluentio, 1990; editor: The Comparative Reader: A Handlist of Basic Reading in Comparative Literature, 1998; assoc. editor Romance Langs. Ann.; mem. editl. bd. Argumentation and Advocacy; author ency. articles and entries; contbr. chpts. to books, articles to profl. jours. Recipient several awards; NEH fellow, 1991; Purdue Rsch. Found. grantee, 1990, 91; Morris House fellow Smith Coll., 1986; Robert E. Frane Meml. scholar, 1985; Morehead scholar U. N.C., 1973-77. Mem. MLA, Am. Comparative Lit. Assn., Am. Philol. Assn., Calif. Classical Assn., Classical Assn. Middle West and South (mem. exec. com.), Am. Soc. for the History of Rhetoric, Phi Beta Kappa, Phi Eta Sigma. Avocations: Renaissance and Baroque music. Office: Purdue U 1354 Stanley Coulter Hall West Lafayette IN 47907-1945

KIRBY, KENT BRUCE, artist, educator; b. Fargo, N.D., Dec. 31, 1934; s. Harold Ely and Vida Nicola (Vennerstrom) K.; m. Lynn Rennetha Schutte, Sept. 1, 1956 (div. 1981); children: Kalin Louise, Jeffrey Bruce, Kristin Beth; m. Carrie Anne Parks, 1983. B.A., Carleton Coll., 1956; M.A., U. N.D., 1959; M.F.A., U. Mich., 1970. Tchr. Benjamin Franklin Jr. High Sch., Fargo, 1956-59; instr. in art, acting head dept. art Muskingum Coll., 1959-61; instr. Wilkes Coll., 1961-62; faculty art Alma (Mich.) Coll., 1962-90, prof., 1971—, chmn. dept. art and design, 1962—, chmn. div. fine arts, 1973-75, Charles A. Dana prof. art, 1976. One-man shows Grad Rapids Art Mus., 1981, U. N.Mex., 1980, Ctr. for Creative Studies, Detroit, 1982, Ctrl. Mich. U., Mt. Pleasant, 1990, New Eng. Sch. Photography, Boston, 1992; group shows include, 2d Internat. Exhbn. Prints and Drawings, Wesleyan U., 1982, Color Print U.S.A., Tex. Tech. U., Lubbock, 1983, 20th Bradley Nat. Print and Drawing Exhbn., 1985, 4th Rockford Internat. Biennale, 1985, Nat. Invitational Print Exhbn., U. Ala., 1988; exhibited Nat. Mus. Am. History, Washington, 1988-89, Stockton Nat. Print and Drawing Exhbn., Haggin Mus. of Art, 1990, " A Decade of Mich. Printmaking", Detroit Inst. of Art, 1992, Nat. Small Print Exhbn., U. of Wis., Parkside, 1994, 95, 97, Fla. Nat., 1997; represented in permanent collections, Chgo. Art Inst., Detroit Art Inst., Smithsonian Inst., Brit. Mus., London; author: Studio Collotype: Continuous Tone Printing for the Artist, Printmaker and Photographer, 1988. Chmn. museums com., council mem. Mich. State Council for Arts, 1966-68. research fellow Newberry Library, 1974; Mich.

Council for Arts grantee, 1975, 78; Nat. Endowment for Arts grantee, 1976. Mem. AAUP, Coll. Art Assn., Mid-Am. Print Coun. Home: 9667 W Van Buren Rd Riverdale MI 48877-9707

KIRBY, LE GRAND CARNEY, III, lawyer, accountant; b. Dallas, Feb. 25, 1941; s. Le Grand C. and Michie V. (Moore) K.; m. Jane Marie Daniel, June 14, 1958; children: Le Grand C. IV, Kimberli K., Kristina K. BBA, So. Meth. U., 1963, LLB, 1965. Bar: Tex. 1965; CPA, Tex. From staff acct. to ptnr. Arthur Young & Co., Dallas, 1965-80; ptnr., dir. litigation support Arthur Young & Co. (name now Ernst & Young), Dallas, 1983—; dep. chief acct. SEC, Washington, 1980-83; adv. counsel Fin. Reporting Inst., L.A., 1982—. Mem. ABA (acctg. and law com. 1983—), State Bar Tex. (securities com.), Am. Inst. CPA's, Tex. Soc. CPA's, Nat. Assn. Corp. Dirs. (pres. Dallas chpt. 1985-89), D.C. CPA's. Office: Ernst & Young LLP Ste 1500 2121 San Jacinto St Dallas TX 75201-6714

KIRBY, MARY WEEKS, elementary education educator, reading specialist; b. Cheverly, Md., Nov. 23, 1947; d. Isaac Ralph and Dorothea (Huppert) Weeks; m. William Charlie Kirby, Feb. 14, 1976 (div. Mar. 1997); children: Joie, Fatimah, Tariq. B in Music Edn., James Madison U., 1969; MEd, Va. Commonwealth U., 1976; cert. Writers' Digest Sch., 1988. Cert. tchr. of music, reading and elem., Va. Music instr. Charles City County Schs., Providence Forge, Va., 1969-70, Hanover Learning Ctr., Va., 1970-72; sales cons. Boykins's Music Shop, Richmond, Va., 1972-74; elem. tchr. New Kent Pub. Schs., Va., 1974-98, writing cons., 1980—; libr. Blue Grass (Va.) Book Bank, 1998—; libr. aide Highland County Pub. Libr., Monterey, Va., 1998—; presenter ednl. and reading workshops, 1980-82, 95. Sponsor Young Authors' Workshop, New Kent, 1985-98; co-chmn., presenter Parents Anonymous of Va., 1984-88; trustee Islamic Ctr. of Va., 1985-88, sec., 1981-85, prin. Islamic Sch., 1995-98; active Boy Scouts Am., Girl Scouts U.S., U.S. Naval Sea Cadet Corps. Mem. NEA, New Kent Edn. Assn. (officer 1977-81, 90-92, 94-95), Va. Edn. Assn., Internat. Reading Assn., Va. State Reading Assn., Richmond Area Reading Council (sec. 1982-83, bd. dirs. 1992—), Sigma Alpha Iota (life). Avocations: needlework, reading, swimming. Home: PO Box 211 Monterey VA 24465

KIRBY, ORVILLE EDWARD, potter, painter, sculptor; b. Wichita, Kans., Jan. 31, 1912; s. Charlie and Elizabeth J. (Sage) K. Student, U. Utah, 1935-36, U. So. Calif., L.A., 1934-35, St. Paul Sch. Fine Art, 1933-34. Owner Orville Kirby Pottery, L.A., 1941-47; owner Sleepy Hollow Pottery, Laguna Beach, Calif., 1948-54, Monroe, Utah, 1955—. Republican. Mormon. Avocation: collecting old coins. Home and Office: 95 W Center St Monroe UT 84754-4159

KIRBY, PRISCILLA CROSBY, dietitian; b. Dallas, Mar. 7, 1955; d. Frank Miller and Maydene (Cook) Crosby; m. Robert Darden Kirby, Sept. 27, 1980; children: Sarah Elizabeth, Bethany Jane; foster child: Leigh. BS, Purdue U., 1977. Registered dietitian. Dietetic intern Mass. Gen. Hosp., Boston, 1977-78; clin. registered dietitian Logansport (Ind.) Meml. Hosp., 1979-82, S.E. Ala. Med. Ctr., Dothan, 1990-91; cons. health care facilities Kirby & Assocs., Winamac, Ind., 1984-87, Abbeville, Ala., 1987—; clin. registered dietition SAMC, Dothan, 1998—; community projects chair Western Ind. Dietetic Assn., Lafayette, 1979-80; nutrition dir. Campe Seale Harris, Ala., 1989-96, bd. dirs., 1992-96. Reporter Appris Study Guild, Abbeville, 1989-90, pres.-elect, 1990-91, pres., 1991-92; dir. mission friends 1st Bapt. Ch., 1989-91. Mem. Am. Dietetic Assn., So. Ala. Dietetic Assn. (pres. 1990-92), Dietitians Health Care Facilities (cons.), Henry County Health Coun., Am. Heart Assn., Ala. Dietetic Assn. (bd. dirs. 1990—, pres. bd. dirs. 1994-98). Republican. Avocations: creative memories albums.

KIRBY, RONALD EUGENE, fish and wildlife research administrator; b. Angola, Ind., Nov. 26, 1947; s. Robert Waye and Lorraine Alice (Hoag) K.; m. Dona J. Kirby; children: Cyrus Robert, William Emil, Peter Waye, Joshua M. Brosten, Emily A. Brosten, Andrew J. Brosten. BS, Duke U., 1969; MA, So. Ill. U., 1973; PhD, U. Minn., 1976. Staff biologist Coop. Wildlife Rsch. Lab., So. Ill. U., Carbondale, 1969-72; collaborating biologist U.S. Forest Svc., St. Paul and Cass Lake, Minn., 1970-72; rsch. biologist Antarctic Rsch. Program NSF, McMurdo Station, Antarctica, 1974; NIH rsch. trainee dept. ecology and behavioral biology U. Minn., Mpls., 1972-76; wildlife biologist, Patuxent Wildlife Rsch. Ctr. U.S. Fish and Wildlife Svc., Laurel, Md., 1976-80; population mgmt. specialist div. refuge mgmt. U.S. Fish and Wildlife Svc., Washington, 1980-82, rsch. coord. Nat. Wildlife Refuge System, 1982-83; regional assistance biologist, office info. transfer U.S. Fish and Wildlife Svc., Ft. Collins, Colo., 1983-88; leader info. transfer sect. U.S. Fish and Wildlife Svc., Ft. Collins, 1988-90; asst. dir. No. Prairie Wildlife Rsch. Ctr., Jamestown, N.D., 1991-92, dir., 1993; dir. U.S. Nat. Biol. Svc. No. Prairie Sci. Ctr., Jamestown, N.D., 1993-96; dir. U.S. Geol. Survey No. Prairie Wildlife Rsch. Ctr., Jamestown, N.D., 1997—; mem. waterfowl adv. com. Minn. Dept. Natural Resources, St. Paul, 1970-72; mem. black duck subcom. Atlantic Flyway Coun., 1976-80; mem. tech. sect. Central Flyway, 1991—. Contbr. to numerous profl. publs; editorial referee, sci. jours. and profl. reports. Active, Boy Scouts Am., 1984—. Grantee, AEC, 1972-76. Mem. The Wildlife Soc., Lambda Chi Alpha. Avocations: hiking, camping, bird watching, motorcycling, hunting. Office: No Prairie Wildlife Rsch Ctr US Geol Survey 8711 37th St SE Jamestown ND 58401-9736

KIRBY, RUSSELL STEPHEN, epidemiologist, statistician, geographer; b. New Haven, June 8, 1954; s. Frank Eugene and Emily (Baruch) K.; m. Elizabeth Margaret Ivens, July 9, 1977; children: Rachel Anne, Amelia Jeanne, Jocelyn Eileen. BA, U. Wis., 1974, MS, 1977, PhD, 1981, MS, 1991. Lectr. U. Wis., Madison, 1980, 82-83; rsch. analyst 3 Wis. Ctr. for Health Stats., Madison, 1981-83, rsch. analyst 5, 1983-85, rsch. analyst 6 maternal and child health statistician, 1985-88; sr. rsch. analyst maternal and child health Ark. Ctr. Health Statistics, Little Rock, 1988-91; instr. dept. pediatrics U. Ark. Med. Scis., Little Rock, 1989-93, asst. prof., 1993-96; assoc. prof. dept. ob.-gyn. Milw. Clin. Campus U. Wis. Med. Sch., 1996—; vis. asst. prof. Beloit Coll., 1987-88; adj. asst. prof. U. Ark., Little Rock, 1988-95; sci. dir. Ark. Reproductive Health Monitoring System, 1991-94, dir., 1994-96, cons., 1996—. Bd. editors: Jour. Perinatology, book rev. editor, 1997—; contbr. articles to profl. jours. Recipient Callon-Leonard award Wis. Assn. for Perinatal Care, 1994, Fraternalist of Yr. award Ct. Razorback Ind. Order Foresters, 1996, Byron L. Hawks award Ark. Perinatal Assn., 1995; named Vol. of Yr. SE chpt. Wis. March of Dimes Birth Defects Found., 1998, Outstanding Advocate for Maternal and Child Health Wis. Maternal and Child Health Coalition, 1999. Fellow Am. Coll. Epidemiology; mem. APHA, Assn. Am. Geographers (life), Agrl. History Soc. (life), So. Hist. Soc. (life), Wis. Assn. for Perinatal Care (bd. dirs. 1996—, pres. elect 1998—, pres. 1999—), Ark. Perinatal Assn. (pres. 1991-92), Soc. for Epidemiologic Rsch., Nat. Perinatal Assn. (bd. dirs. 1990-92, 95-98, ann. conf. chair 1999), Nat Birth Defects Prevention Network (pres. 1999), Midwest Soc. for Pediatric Rsch., Soc. for Pediatric Epidemiologic Rsch., Teratology Soc. Avocations: camping, writing book reviews, computer cartography and graphics, used books. E-mail: r-kirby@whin.net. Home: 5654 N Santa Monica Blvd Whitefish Bay WI 53217-4714 Office: SSMC Dept Ob-Gyn PO Box 342 Milwaukee WI 53201-0342

KIRBY, SARAH ANN VAN DEVENTER, aerospace engineer; b. Champaign, Ill., Mar. 10, 1961; d. David Bruce Kirby and Florence May Van Deventer. BS in Aerospace Engring., U. Mich., 1983; MEd, U. Houston, Clear Lake, 1989. Space systems ops. engr. NASA/JSC-MOD, Houston, 1983—. Contbr. articles to profl. jours. Bd. dirs. Hidden Cove Homeowners Assn., Friendswood, Tex., 1991-96. Mem. AIAA (sr.). Avocations: genealogy, theology, tutoring math, softball, golf. Home: 45 Hideaway Dr Friendswood TX 77546-4868 Office: NASA JSC Mail Code DF83 Houston TX 77058

KIRBY, WILLIAM JOSEPH, corporation executive; b. Balt., Sept. 23, 1937; s. William J. and Marjorie M. (Wagner) K.; M. Catherine Gordon Craig, June 17, 1961; William Joseph III, Andrew Craig, David Francis. BA, Pa. State U., 1959; MS in Indsl. and Labor Rels., Cornell U., 1961; AMP, Harvard U., 1981. Mgmt. trainee Bell Telephone of Pa., Phila., 1961; employee benefits staff asst. Avisun Corp., Phila., 1961-62; recruiting mgr. Am. Viscose Corp., Phila., 1962-64; personnel mgr. FMC Film & Packaging, Fredericksburg, Va., 1964-69; dir. personnel adminstrn. FMC Machinery Group, Chgo., 1969-72; dir. personnel FMC Corp., Chgo., 1972-76, v.p. personnel, 1976-85; v.p. adminstrn. FMC Corp., 1985—, sr. v.p., 1994; bd. dirs. Met. Planning Coun., Chgo.; mem. policy bd. dirs. U. Wyo. Inst. for Environ. and Natural Resource. Trustee, chmn. acad. and student affairs com., mem. exec. com. Roosevelt U., Chgo.; mem. collections and rsch. com. Field Mus., Chgo. Fellow Nat. Acad. Human Resources; mem. Labor Policy Assn. (bd. dirs., mem. exec. com.), Bus. Roundtable (employee relations com.), Personnel Roundtable, Mid-Am. Club, Harvard Club, Glen View Club, Economic Club, Chgo. Club. Republican. Episcopalian. Office: FMC Corp 200 E Randolph St Ste 6700 Chicago IL 60601-6662

KIRCH, DARRELL GENE, dean; b. Denver, May 3, 1949; m. Deborah M. Kirch; children: Samantha M., Madeline A. BA in Philosophy, U. Colo., 1973, MD magna cum laude, 1977. Diplomate Am. Bd. Psychiatry and Neurology, Nat. Bd. Med. Examiners. Resident in psychiatry U. Colo. Health Scis. Ctr., Denver, 1977-82; med. staff fellow adult psychiatry br. NIMH, Washington, 1982-84, sr. staff fellow neuropsychiatry br., 1984-87, med. dir. neuropsychiat. Rsch. Hosp., 1987-89, chief unit on neurobehavioral studies, 1989-92; dep. scientific dir. NIMH, Bethesda, Md., 1992-93; prof. sch. grad. studies, prof. dept. psychiatry Med. Coll. Ga., Augusta, 1994—, dean sch. medicine, 1994—; dir. Robert Wood Johnson Found. Generalist Initiative Implementation Grant Med. Coll. Ga., 1994—, chair VA Med. Ctr. Dean's Com., 1994—; chair adv. bd. Ga. Radiation Therapy Ctr., Augusta, 1994—; mem. clin. enterprise exec. com. Med. Coll. Ga., 1994—, chair clin. enterprise coun., 1994—, mem. exec. com., bd. trustees physicians practice group, 1994—, mem. exec. com. med. and dental staff, 1994—; merit reviewer rsch. svc. U.S. Dept. VA, Washington, 1989—; examiner Am. Bd. Psychiatry and Neurology, Deerfield, Ill., 1985—; many others. Reviewer numerous profl. jours.; assoc. editor: Psychopharmacology Bull., 1990—, Schizophrenia Bull., 1989—. Capt. USPHS, 1986-94. Decorated Commendation medal. Mem. AAAS, AMA, Am. Psychiat. Assn., Am. Soc. Clin. Psychopharmacology, Assn. for Acad. Psychiatry, Ga. Psychiat. Physicians Assn., Internat. Soc. for Psychiatric Genetics, Med. Assn. Ga., Richmond County Med. Soc., Soc. for Neurosci., Soc. Biol. Psychiatry. Home: 8 Winged Foot Dr Augusta GA 30907-9140 Office: Med Coll Ga Sch Medicine Office of Dean Augusta GA 30912-4750*

KIRCH, PATRICK VINTON, anthropology educator, archaeologist; b. Honolulu, July 7, 1950; s. Harold William and Barbara Ver (MacGarvin) K.; m. Debra Connelly, Mar. 3, 1979 (div. 1990); m. Therese Babineau, Feb. 6, 1994. BA, U. Pa., 1971; MPhil, Yale U., 1974, PhD, 1975. Assoc. anthropologist Bishop Mus., Honolulu, 1975-76, anthropologist, 1976-82, head archaeology div., 1982-84, asst. chmn. anthropology, 1983-84; dir., assoc. prof. Burke Mus. U. Wash., Seattle, 1984-87, prof., 1987-89; prof. U. Calif., Berkeley, 1989—, prof. anthropology, endowed chair, 1994—; curator Hearst Mus. Anthropology, 1989—; adj. faculty U. Hawaii, Honolulu, 1979-84; mem. lasting legacy com. Wash. State Centennial Commn., 1986-88; pres. Soc. Hawaiian Archaeology, 1980-81. Author: The Anthropology of History in the Kingdom of Hawaii, 1992, Feathered Gods and Fishhooks, 1985, Evolution of the Polynesian Chiefdoms, 1984, The Wet and the Dry, 1994, The Lapita Peoples, 1996, Legacy of the Landscape, 1996; editor: Island Societies, 1986, Historical Ecology in the Pacific Islands, 1997; contbr. articles to profl. pubs. Recipient J.I. Staley prize in anthropology Sch. Am. Rsch., 1998; grantee NSF, 1974, 76, 77, 82, 87, 88, 89, 93, 96, 98, NEA, 1985, NEH, 1988, Hawaii Com. for Humanities, 1981, rsch. grantee Nat. Geog. Soc., 1986, 89, 96; fellow Ctr. for Advanced Study in Behavioral Scis., 1997-98. Fellow AAAS, NAS (John J. Carty medal for the advancement of sci. 1997), Am. Acad. Arts and Scis., Am. Anthrop. Assn., Am. Philos. Soc., Calif. Acad. Scis.; mem. Assn. Field Archaeology, Polynesian Soc., Sigma Xi. Democrat. Avocation: cross country skiing. Office: U Calif Dept Anthropology 232 Kroeber Hall Berkeley CA 94720-3710*

KIRCHER, JOHN JOSEPH, law educator; b. Milw., July 26, 1938; s. Joseph John and Martha Marie (Jach) K.; m. Marcia Susan Adamkiewicz, Aug. 26, 1961; children: Joseph John, Mary Kathryn. BA, Marquette U., 1960, JD, 1963. Bar: Wis. 1963, U.S. Dist. Ct. (ea. dist.) Wis. 1963, U.S. Ct. Appeals (7th cir.) 1992. Sole practice, Port Washington, Wis., 1963-66; with Def. Research Inst., Milw., 1966-80, research dir., 1972-80; with Marquette U., 1970—, prof. law, 1980—, assoc. dean acad. affairs, 1992-93; chmn. Wis. Jud. Council, 1981-83. Author: (with J.D. Ghiardi) Punitive Damages: Law and Practice, 1981; editor: Federation of Insurance and Corporate Counsel Quarterly; mem. editorial bd. Def. Law Jour.; contbr. articles to profl. jours. Recipient Teaching Excellence award Marquette U., 1986, Disting. Service award Def. Research Inst., 1980, Marquette Law Rev. Editors' award, 1988. Mem. ABA (Robert B. McKay Professor award 1993), Am. Law Inst., Wis. Bar Assn., Wis. Supreme Ct. Bd. of Bar Examiners (vice-chair 1989-91, chair 1992), Am. Judicature Soc., Nat. Sports Law Inst. (adv. com. 1989—), Assn. Internationale de Droit des Assurances, Scribes. Roman Catholic. Office: PO Box 1881 Milwaukee WI 53201-1881

KIRCHHEIMER, ARTHUR E(DWARD), lawyer, business executive; b. N.Y.C., June 26, 1931; s. Arthur and Lena K.; m. Esther A. Jordan, Sept. 11, 1965. B.A., Syracuse U., 1952, LL.B., 1954. Bar: N.Y. 1954, Calif. 1973. Ptnr. Block, Kirchheimer, Lemax & Failmezger, Syracuse, N.Y., 1954-70; corp. counsel Norwich Pharmacal Co., N.Y., 1970-72; sr. v.p., gen. counsel Wickes Cos., Inc., San Diego, 1972-84; prin. Arthur E. Kirchheimer, Inc., P.C., San Diego, 1984-90; writer, cons. in bus. matters La Jolla, Calif., 1990—; sec., dir. Corp. Fin. Council San Diego, 1975. Pres. Mental Health Assn. Onondaga County, 1970; chmn. Manlius (N.Y.) Planning Commn., 1969-72; mem. Alternatives to Litigation Spl. Panel, 1984—; mem. San Diego County Grand Jury, 1991-92. Mem. ABA, Calif. Bar Assn. Home and Office: 2876 Palomino Cir La Jolla CA 92037-7066

KIRCHHOFF, FREDERICK THOMAS, academic administrator, dean; b. Jacksonville, fla., Nov. 11, 1942; s. Frederick Thomas and Ruth Love (Thigpenn) K. AB, Harvard U., 1964, AM, 1965, PhD, 1969. Prof. English Ind. U.-Purdue U., Ft. Wayne, 1969-95, chmn. dept. English and linguistics, 1988-94; dean Met. State U. Coll. Arts and Scis., St. Paul, 1994—. Author: William Morris, 1979, John Ruskin, 1984, William Morris: The Construction of a Male Self, 1856-1872, 1984. Bd. dirs. Ft. Wayne Cinema Ctr., 1992-94. Mem. Midwest Victorian Studies Assn. (pres. 1995-97). Home: 3846 Richfield Rd Minneapolis MN 55410-1222 Office: Met State U 700 7th St E Saint Paul MN 55106-5003

KIRCHHOFF, MARY VIRGINIA, city council member; b. Wilson Creek, Mo., Jan. 30, 1926; d. Ashley Chester and Ollie Flora (Alexander) Mixon; m. John Joseph Kirchhoff, May, 23, 1948; children: John E., Mary Karen. BA in Fine Arts, Tex. Christian U., 1969. Speaker Nat. Parkinson's Disease Assn., West Tex., Lubbock, Tex., 1996—; city council mem. Plainview, Tex., 1990—; dep. chmn., Rep. Party State of Tex., elected senatorial # 30 com. woman State Rep. Com., 1972-78; elected to supts. cabinet Plainview Ind. Sch. Dist., 1990-92; city council rep. Canadian Mcpl. Water Authority, Plainview, Tex., 1995—; bd. dirs. Hale County Appraisal Dist., Plainview, 1995—; bd. dirs. Unger Meml. Lib., Plainview, 1992-96; advisor to chmn. dist. 18 State Bd. Edn., Tex., 1994, appomted by Commnrs. Ct. to the Plainview Hosp. Authority Bd., 1999; spkr. in field. Contbr. articles to profl. jours. Organizer summer youth program SCOPE; officer Girl Scouts U.S., 1963-67; mem. airport bd., 1994-96; bd. dirs. Plainview Recycling Beautification, 1995—; elder 1st Christian Ch., 1997—; vol. reader, listener La Mesa Elem. Sch., 1998—. Named Tex. Outstanding Rep. Woman, Rep. Party. Mem. Lions Club Internat., Retired Tchrs. Assn., Tex. Mcpl. League, DAR (Daughters of Amer. Revolution), West Tex. C. of C. (elected 1st woman to exec. bd. 1965), Jr. Svc. League (pres., 1953-62), Women's Club (pres., charter mem., 1953-63), Delta Kappa Gamma (organizer Kappa Xi chpt., pres. 1984), Pi Beta Phi (charter). Avocations: philanthropy, travel, writing. Home: 1000 S Broadway St Plainview TX 79072-8644

KIRCHHOFF, MICHAEL KENT, economic development executive; b. Effingham, Ill., Apr. 3, 1963; s. Robert D. and Violet M. (Baumann) K; m. Lynn Reilly, May 27, 1989; 1 child, Amelia Elizabeth. BA in Econ., East Ill. U., 1986, BS in Bus., 1986; postgrad., U. Okla., 1995. Cert. Ill. Assessing Officer. Owner, mgmt. cons. Spectrum Cons., Springfield, 1985-90; intern govs. office Ill. Dept. Revenue, Springfield, 1986-87, property tax analyst, 1987-89; econ. devel. prof. Dept. Commerce and Community Affairs, Springfield, 1989-92; data analyst Ill. Dept. Pub. Aid, Springfield, 1992; mkt. devel. rschr. Ill. Power Co., Decatur, 1992-95; joint purchasing coord. State of Ill., Springfield, 1995-96; owner Phoenix Assocs., Springfield, 1995-96; exec. dir. Tuscola (Ill.) Area Improvement Assn., 1996-97, program mgr. Mainstreet Tuscola, 1996-97; exec. dir. Jacksonville (Ill.) Area Econ. Devel. Coun., 1997—. Asst. scoutmaster, asst. explorer advisor, scoutmaster, dist. chmn. Okaw dist. Boy Scouts Am., 1997, chmn. honest Abe dist., 1998—, exec. bd. mem. Abraham Lincoln coun.; mem. Big Bros./Big Sisters, I-Search for Children, Project Safeplace; v.p. Sangamon County Reps., Operation Snowball; treas., bd. dirs. Ctrl. Ill. Youth Svc. Bur.; bd. dirs. Ctrl. Ill. Workforce Prep.; vice chair Douglas County Tourism Com.; advisor Tuscola Tourism Com.; mem. Ill. Enterprise Zone Assn., Nat. Main St. Network, mem. Ill. Rural Ptnrs.. membership chair, 1998—; bd. dirs. Jacksonville Main St., 1998—, Day Care Ctr., 1999—. Recipient Charles Carter Meml. award InterFraternity Coun., 1984. Mem. Am. Soc. Pub. Adminstrn., Am. Econ. Devel. Coun., Nat. Coun. for Urban Econ. Devel., Cmty. Devel. Soc., Ill. Devel. Coun. (chmn. govt. affairs com.), Mid-Am. Econ. Devel. Coun., Jacksonville Area Indsl. Corp. (sec. 1997—), Acad. Polit. Sci., Mid Am. InterFraternity Coun. Assn. (Outstanding State Coord. 1984, Outstanding Area V.P. 1985), Nat. Trust for Hist. Preservation, Springfield Jaycees, Jacksonville Country Club, Kiwanis, Order of Omega, Omicron Delta Epsilon, Beta Sigma Psi. Lutheran. Home: 1225 W College Ave Jacksonville IL 62650-2214 Office: Jacksonville Area Econ Devel Coun 200 W Douglas Ave Jacksonville IL 62650-2012

KIRCHICK, CALVIN B., lawyer; b. N.Y.C., Apr. 6, 1946; s. Jean Kirchick; m. Judith Madian, Apr. 28, 1968; children: Ross, Lisa, Joelle. BA magna cum laude, U. Mich., 1968, JD magna cum laude, 1972. Assoc. Baker & Hostetler, Cleve., 1972-81, ptnr., 1982—. Contbr. articles to profl. jours. Endowment counsel Coun. Jewish Fedns., N.Y.C., 1976-90, Cleve., 1996—; rec. sec. Green Rd. Synagogue, Beachwood, Ohio, 1982-85, trustee, 1981-86; founding trustee, v.p. Internat. Coun. Dati Tzioni Schs., 1994—; founding trustee Solomon Schecter Day Sch. leve., 1978-85; trustee Jewish Nat. Fund Cleve., 1984-94; co-founder, trustee Fuchs Bet Sefer Mizrachi, Cleve., 1984—. Angell scholar U. Mich., 1966. Fellow Am. Coll. Trust and Estate Coun.; mem. ABA (generation skipping transfer tax com. legis. and regulations planning and drafting 1988—, charitable deduction com. legis. 1987—, GSST com. 1987—, estate and gift tax com. 1987—), Ohio State Bar Assn., Greater Cleve. Bar Assn. (probate and trust law sect. com. 1987—), Phi Beta Kappa, Phi Kappa Phi, Order of Coif; mem. ACTEC (com. on Charitable Giving, 1995—). Republican. Jewish. Avocations: bicycling, skiing, swimming, modern history, Jewish religious studies. Office: Baker & Hostetler 3200 Nat City Ctr 1900 E 9th St Ste 3200 Cleveland OH 44114-3475*

KIRCHICK, WILLIAM DEAN, lawyer; b. Oceanside, N.Y., Nov. 20, 1950; s. Julian Gilbert and Jean (Kostinsky) K.; m. Carol Bonnie Rudnick, May 29, 1977; children: James Rory, Jeffrey Scott. BA in Polit. Sci. magna cum laude, U. Mich., 1973; JD cum laude, Boston Coll., 1976. Bar: Mass. 1978, Ill. 1976, U.S. Dist. Ct. Mass. 1978, U.S. Ct. Appeals (1st cir.) 1978, U.S. Tax Ct. 1976, U.S. Supreme Ct. 1982; accredited estate planner designation. Assoc. Arnstein, Gluck, Lehr & Milligan, Chgo., 1976-77; assoc., ptnr. Peabody & Brown, Boston, 1977-88; ptnr. Bingham Dana LLP, Boston, 1988—; mem. Boston Probate and Estate Planning Forum, 1987—, program events coord., 1989-90, moderator, 1990-91; mem. Boston Estate Planning Coun., 1986—, mem. exec. com., 1988-91, sec. 1995-96, treas., 1996-97, v.p. 1997-98, pres.-elect, 1998—; mem. Norfolk and Plymouth Bus. and Estate Planning Coun., 1990—; mem. Planned Giving Group of New Eng., Inc., 1997—; mem. curriculum adv. com. for Mass. Continuing Legal Edn., Inc. Contbg. author: Estate Planning and Drafting Techniques, 1987, Basic Drafting of Wills and Trusts in Massachusetts, 1988, Practical Estate Planning Techniques in Massachusetts, 1989, Estate and Protective Planning Techniques in Massachusetts, 1990, How to Complete Estate Tax Returns, 1994; contbr. articles to profl. jours. Chmn. young lawyers team spl. events com. Combined Jewish Philanthropies of Greater Boston, Inc., 1982-84, chmn. young lawyers team, 1984-85, mem. lawyers team cabinet, 1985-89, 91-94. Recipient Campaign Leadership award Combined Jewish Philanthropies of Greater Boston, Inc., 1984. Fellow Am. Coll. Trust and Estate Counsel; mem. ABA (mem. sect. probate, trusts and real property), Mass. Bar Assn. (mem. tax sect. exec. com. 1989-92, probate sect. exec. com. 1992-93), Boston Bar Assn. (mem. estate planning com. 1981—, chmn. 1984-88, chmn. subcom. to study income, gift and estate tax proposals of Tax Reform Act of 1986 1985-86, chmn. subcom. on proposed temporary regulations concerning Chpt. 13 Internal Revenue Code 1988-89, mem. probate sect. 1978—), U. Mich. Club Greater Boston, Boston Coll. Law Sch. Alumni Assn. Phi Beta Kappa, Phis Eta Sigma. Avocations: jogging, swimming, walking. Office: Bingham Dana LLP 150 Federal St Fl 15 Boston MA 02110-1726

KIRCHKNOPF, MATTHEW BELA, research laboratory manager; b. Yonkers, N.Y., Jan. 25, 1960; s. Matthew and Mary. (Nemeth) K.; m. Gloria N. Muscardin, Mar. 5, 1994. BSME, Northeastern U., 1983; MBA, U. Md., 1993. Project/program mgr. Naval Rsch. Lab., Washington, 1985—. With USCGR, 1986—. Republican. Roman Catholic. Avocations: jogging, skiing, sports, golf, aerobics. E-mail: matthewúkirchknopf@king-crab.nrl.navy.mil. Home: 5917 Berwyn Rd Berwyn Heights MD 20740

KIRCHMAN, CHARLES VINCENT, lawyer; b. Washington, June 28, 1935; s. Floyd Vincent and Dorothy Johanna (Johnson) K.; m. Erika Ottilie Knoeppel, July 4, 1959; children: Mark C., Eric H., Charles E. BA, U. Md., 1959; JD, George Washington U., 1962. Bar: D.C. 1962, Md. 1970. Security specialist Adj. Gen's. Office U.S. Army, 1962-64; sole practice Washington, 1964-70, Wheaton, Md., 1970-73; ptnr. Andrews & Schick, Waldorf, Md., 1973-77; sole practice Wheaton, Md., 1977-92; ptnr. Kirchman & Kirchman, Wheaton, 1992—. Home: 14801 Notley Rd Silver Spring MD 20905-5837 Office: 11141 Georgia Ave Wheaton MD 20902-4637

KIRCHMAN, ERIC HANS, lawyer; b. Washington, May 2, 1962; s. Charles Vincent and Erika Ottilie (Knoeppel) K.; m. Hillary Bronkie Hutson, Apr. 19, 1991; children: Erika B., Thomas E. BA, Univ. Md., 1985; JD, Univ. Balt., 1990. Bar: Md. 1990, U.S. Dist. Ct. Md. 1991. Assoc. Hillel Abrams, Rockville, Md., 1990-92; ptnr. Kirchman & Kirchman, Wheaton, Md., 1992—; of counsel Md. Coun. for Gifted and Talented Children, Inc., Silver Spring, 1994. With U.S. Army Reserve, 1985-98. Mem. ATLA, Md. Criminal Def. Attys. Assn., Montgomery County Bar Assn. Office: Kirchman & Kirchman 11141 Georgia Ave Ste 403 Wheaton MD 20902-4659

KIRCHNER, JAKE, publishing executive. Editor PC Mag., N.Y.C. Office: PC Mag-Ziff Davis Publ Co 28 E 28th St New York NY 10016-7930*

KIRCHNER, JAMES WILLIAM, retired electrical engineer; b. Cleve., Oct. 17, 1920; s. William Sebastian and Marcella Louise (Stuart) K.; m. Eda Christene Landfear, June 11, 1950 (dec. May 1977); children: Kathleen Ann Kirchner Duda, Susan Lynn Kirchner Buonpane. BS in Elec. Engring., Ohio U., 1950, MS, 1951. Registered profl. engr., Ohio. Instr. elec. engring. Ohio U., Athens, 1950-52; mgr. liaison engring. Lear Siegler Inc., Maple Heights, Ohio, 1952-64; coordinator engring. services Case Western Res. U., Cleve., 1964-72, gen. mgr. Med. Ctr. Co. (CWRU), 1972-91; ret., 1991; sec. of corp. Thermagon, Inc., Cleve., 1992. Mem. Portage County Republican Exec. Com., 1961-62; treas. PTA, Aurora, Ohio, 1963-65, v.p., 1965-66; mem. The Ch. in Aurora, 1956—. Served with USAAF, 1942-45, PTO. Mem. NSPE (life), IEEE (life), Ohio Soc. Profl. Engrs. (life), Cleve. Engring. Soc. (chmn. environ. com. 1976), Am. Soc. Engring. Edn. (life). Home: Reserves of Aurora 535 Treetop Ct Aurora OH 44202-7317

KIRCHNER, JOHN ALBERT, retired otolaryngology educator; b. Waynesboro, Pa., Mar. 27, 1915; s. Francis Edward and Jessie Cecilia (Cameron) K.; m. Aline Legault, Oct. 11, 1947; children: John C., Thomas L., Paul E., Marie Cecile, Christine A. MD, U. Va., 1940; MS, Yale U., 1952. Intern Charity Hosp., New Orleans, 1940-41; resident in otolaryngology Johns Hopkins Hosp., 1946-50; mem. faculty Sch. Medicine Yale U., New Haven, 1951—, prof. otolaryngology, 1962-85, prof. emeritus, 1985—; with Conn. Acad. of Arts and Scis., 1999—; rsch. cons. NIH, 1966; spl. rschr. pathology and physiology of larynx and pharynx NINCDS. Editor: Yearbook Ear, Nose and Throat, 1969-75. Capt. inf. AUS, 1942-46. Decorated Bronze Star.; recipient Harris P. Mosher rsch. award Am. Trilogical Soc., 1958, Semon medal in laryngology U. London, 1981; Commonwealth Fund fellow, 1963-64, fellow Silliman Coll., Yale U., 1977—. Mem. Am. Laryngol. Assn. (pres. 1979-80, Casselberry award 1966,

Newcomb award 1969, de Roaldes medal 1985, Merit award 1988), Am. Acad. Otolaryngology (v.p. 1978-79), Am. Laryngol., Rhinol. and Otolaryn. Soc. (pres. 1981-82), Am. Assn. Head and Neck Surgery (pres. 1977-78), New Eng. Otolaryn. Soc. (pres. 1965-66), European Laryngological Soc. (hon.), Japan Broncho-Esophagological Soc. (hon.), German Soc. Otolaryngology, Head and Neck Surgery (corr.), Italian Soc. Otolaryn. (corr.), Coll. Oto-Rhino-Laryngologium Amicitae Sacrum. Home: 12 Rimmon Hill Rd Woodbridge CT 06525-1324 Office: Yale Sch Medicine Dept Surgery 333 Cedar St PO Box 208041 New Haven CT 06520-8041

KIRCHNER, LISA BETH, vocalist, actress; b. L.A.; d. Leon and Gertrude (Schoenberg) K. BA, Sarah Lawrence Coll., N.Y., 1975. Picture rschr. McGraw-Hill, 1985-87, John Wiley & Sons, 1988, Simon & Schuster/Globe Book Co., 1988-91, Chelsea House Pubs., 1987-94, Oxford Univ. Press, 1992—, Facts on File, 1997, Greenwood Pub. Co., 1997, Lazard Freres, 1998—; songwriter, BMI. Broadway appearances include The Three Penny Opera, 1975, The Human Comedy, 1985; off-Broadway appearances include the Radiant City, 1993, Hotel for Criminals, 1974, The American Imagination, others; TV shows include Songs From the Heart, Another World, The Guiding Light, As The World Turns, others; films include Little White Truth, 1995, Something Cool; appearances at White House and Gracie Mansion; performed as back-up singer and featured soloist with Judy Collins (numerous TV appearances). Mem. AFTRA, SAG, Equity. Avocations: painting, crafts, poetry.

KIRCHNER, PETER THOMAS, nuclear medicine physician, educator, consultant; b. July 2, 1939; s. Elek and Julia (Kossy) K.; m. Mary Coleman Kirchner, Dec. 18, 1965; children: David, Annette, Julie. BA Physics, Yale U., 1960; MD, Columbia U., 1964. Diplomate Am. Bd. Internal Medicine, Am. Bd. Nuclear Medicine. Intern, then resident, chief resident in internal medicine Nat. Naval Med. Ctr., Bethesda, Md., 1964-70; fellow in nuclear medicine Johns Hopkins U., Balt., 1970-72; head nuclear medicine Nat. Naval Med. Ctr., Bethesda, Md., 1972-77; asst. prof. radiology George Washington U., Washington, 1974-77; assoc. dir. nuclear medicine U. Chgo., 1978-81, assoc. prof. radiology, 1977-81; assoc. prof. radiology U. Iowa, Iowa City, 1981-84, prof. radiology, 1984—, prof. medicine, 1989—; dir. nuclear medicine U. Iowa Hosps. and Clinics, Iowa City, 1981-98; IPA contractee Dept. of Edn., Germantown, Md., 1998—; mem. radiology study sect. NIH, 1995—; mem. rev. com. on edn. programs in nuclear medicine technology, 1996—; bd. dirs. joint rev. com. Nuclear Medicine Tech., exec. com., 1997—; mem. nat. adv. com. Nat. Isotope Ctr., DOE, 1996—. Editor Nuclear Medicine Review Syllabus, 1980; co-editor Nuclear Medicine Self Study I, 1988, Self Study II, 1996; author more than 80 sci. articles, 12 book chpts. Ea. Iowa alumni schs.com. chair Yale U., 1989-94. Capt. USNR, 1963-92. Out Svc. Tng. grantee USN, 1970; recipient Von Hevessy award Hungarian Soc. Nuclear Medicine, 1993. Fellow ACP, Am. Coll. Nuc. Physicians (chair quality assurance and practice cert. com. 1993-95, bd. regents 1993—), Am. Coll. Radiology, Am. Bd. Nuc. Medicine (sec. 1992-94, chair exam. com. 1991-94, vice chair 1994, 95), Radiol. Soc. N.Am. (sci. program com. 1992-98), Inst. Clin. Positron Emission Tomography (bd. dirs. 1992-97, pres. 1993-94), Soc. Nuc. Medicine (exec. com. 1988-93, bd. dirs. 1993-97, house of dels. 1993—, chair sci. program com. 1988-90, v.p. 1992-93, pres. 1995-96, gen. program chair 1999—, trustee 1981-89). Avocation: tennis. Office: Dept of Edn Med Scis Divsn Germantown MD 20874

KIRGIS, FREDERIC LEE, law educator; b. Washington, Dec. 29, 1934; s. Frederic Lee Sr. and Kathryn Alice (Burrows) K.; children: Julianne, Paul Frederic. B.A., Yale U., 1957; J.D., U. Calif.-Berkeley, 1960. Bar: Colo. 1961, D.C. 1964, Va. 1983. Atty. Covington & Burling, Washington, 1964-67; from asst. prof. to prof. law U. Colo., Boulder, 1967-73; prof. law UCLA, 1973-78; prof. law Washington & Lee U., Lexington, Va., 1978—, dir. Frances Lewis Law Ctr., 1978-83, dean law sch., 1983-88. Author: International Organizations in their Legal Setting, 1977, 2d edit. 1993, Prior Consultation in International Law, 1983; contbr. articles to profl. jours. Pres. Maury River Soccer Club, Lexington, 1978-85. Served to capt. USAF, 1961-64. Recipient Deak award 1974; research fellow NATO, Brussels, 1978. Mem. Am. Soc. Internat. Law (v.p. 1985-87, sec. 1994—), Am. Law Inst., Internat. Law Assn. (Am. br.), Am. Jour. Internat. Law (bd. editors 1984-96, 98—), State Bar Va., Order of Coif. Democrat. Presbyterian. Home: 15 Grey Dove Rd Lexington VA 24450-2269 Office: Washington and Lee U Sch of Law Lexington VA 24450

KIRIAKOPOULOS, GEORGE CONSTANTINE, dentist; b. Derby, Conn., June 3, 1926; s. Constantine Elias and Rose (Yerontakis) K.; AA, U. Paris (France), 1947; AB, Bklyn. Coll., 1950; DDS, Columbia, 1954; m. Virginia Demos, June 3, 1956; 1 dau., Stephanie. Pvt. practice gen. dentistry, Fort Lee, N.J., 1955—; assoc. dir. dept. dentistry St. Giles Hosp., Bklyn., 1955-60; attending dept. oral surgery Lenox Hill Hosp., N.Y.C., 1956-60, adj. oral surgeon, 1960-64; assoc. prof., then prof. dept. pedodontics Columbia, 1956—; attending in dentistry Presbyn. Hosp., 1986—; mem. adv. com. Columbia Presbyn. Hosp. Med. Ctr.; mem. adv. com. to dean Sch. Dental and Oral Surgery Columbia U. Served with AUS, 1943-46. Decorated Bronze Star, Silver Star, D.S.M.; recipient Medal of Meritorious Service, Lenox Hill Hosp., 1964. Fellow Royal Soc. Health; mem. ADA, Am. Assn. Hosp. Dentists, N.Y. State Dental Soc., Columbia U. Alumni Assn., Psi Omega. Greek Orthodox (pres. Parish Coun., Cathedral St. John, Tenafly, 1980-83). Author: Your Child's Teeth - the Layman's View, 1966; Who Wants to Be a Dentist?, 1968; The Modern Thermopylae—Battle of Crete, May 1941, 1978; Portrait of a Cretan Hero, 1978; Cyprus and the Polish Connection, 1980; Ten Days to Destiny, 1985, Paperback edit., 1986, The Nazi Occupation of Crete: 1941-45, 1995, others. Home: 2205 Mackay Ave Fort Lee NJ 07024-5034 Office: 415 West St Fort Lee NJ 07024-5010

KIRICK, DANIEL JOHN, agronomist; b. Port Jervis, N.Y., Nov. 8, 1953; s. Daniel and Mary Theresa Kirick; m. Jean Marie Guse, Sept. 27, 1986; children: Nicholas, John, Kristina. BA in Biology, History, U. Minn., Duluth, 1976; BS in Agronomy, U. Minn., St. Paul, 1977. Cert. profl. agronomist. Agronomist Delft (Minn.) Farm Chems., 1978, Skelly Fertilizer, Trimont, Minn., 1978-80, Mower County Svc. Co., Sargeant, Minn., 1980-86, Cenex Supply, Ellis, S.D., 1986-88, Rice (Minn.) Farm Supply, 1988-91, Kirick Agronomy Svcs., St. Cloud, Minn., 1992—. Mem. Comty. Edn. Devel. Adv. Coun., Sauk Rapids, Minn., 1990-94, Youth Devel. Bd., Sauk Rapids, 1990, Benton County Ext. Com., 1993-98, Ctrl. Minn. Forage Coun., 1994—. Mem. AAAS, Weed Sci. Soc. Am., Soil Sci. Soc. Am., Crop Sci. Soc. Am., Am. Soc. Agronomy. Roman Catholic. Home: PO Box 206 Rice MN 56367-0206 Office: Kirick Agronomy Svcs 9144 County Rd 4 Saint Joseph MN 56374

KIRILA, CAROL ELIZABETH, osteopathic physician; b. Mount Clemens, Mich., Oct. 28, 1952; d. Andrew William and Mary Margaret (Schmeltz) K. Diploma, Rsch. Med. Ctr. Sch. Nursing, Kansas City, Mo., 1974; BS in Biology, U. Mo., Kansas City, 1987; DO, U. Health Scis.-Coll. Osteo., 1991. RN, Mo. Lab. asst. Lakeside Hosp., Kansas City, 1969-74, RN, inservice instr., 1976-87, part time staff nurse, relief supr., 1988-91; staff nurse Children's Mercy Hosp., Kansas City, 1974, U. Health Scis. Hosp., Kansas City, 1974-76, Rsch. Med. Ctr., Kansas City, 1976; part time staff nurse Kendallwood Pvt. Duty, 1988-91; intern Still Regional Med. Ctr., Jefferson City, Mo., 1991-92; resident internal medicine U. of Mo. Kansas City Sch. of Medicine, 1992-95; staff physician Internal Medicine Assn. St. Joseph, Mo., 1995-96, Permante Med. Group, Kansas City, Mo., 1996-98; mem. faculty U. of Health Scis., Coll. Osteo. Medicine, 1998—. Catechumenate sponsor St. James Ch., Kansas City, 1982; mem. Manheim Park Neighborhood Assn., Kansas City, 1982-91. Recipient cert. of recognition U. Health Scis. Coll. Osteo. Medicine, 1988-89, Outstanding Svc. and Achievement award U. Mo.-Kansas City, 1986. Mem. Am. Osteo. Assn. Democrat. Episcopalian. Avocations: plants, reading, music, cooking, fitness. Home: 217 W 99th St Kansas City MO 64114-4170

KIRK, BALLARD HARRY THURSTON, architect; b. Williamsport, Pa., Apr. 1, 1929; s. Ballard and Ada May (DeLaney) K.; m. Vera Elizabeth Kitchener, Mar. 13, 1951; children: Lisa Lee, Kira Alexandria, Dayna Allison, Courtlandt Blaine. BArch, Ohio State U., 1959. Pres. Kirk Assocs., Architects, Columbus, Ohio, 1963—; mem. Ohio Bd. Bldg. Standards, Columbus, 1973-78, 92—; pres. Nat. Coun. Archtl. Registration Bds., Washington, 1983-84, Ohio Bd. Examiners Architects, Columbus, 1973—; bd. dirs. Nat. Archtl. Accrediting Bd., Washington, 1986-89. Mem. AIA (bd. dirs. Columbus chpt. 1988-92), Coll. of Fellows. Republican. Mem. Brethern Ch. Home: 2459 Tremont Rd Columbus OH 43221-3727 Office: Kirk Assoc Architects 2459 Tremont Rd Columbus OH 43221-3727

KIRK, CAROL, lawyer; b. Henry, Ill., Dec. 23, 1937; d. Howard P. and Mildred Root McQuilkin; m. Robert James Kirk, Aug. 20, 1961; children: Kathleen, Nancy, Sally. BS in Music Edn., U. Ill., 1960; JD, Ind. U., Indpls., 1989. Bar: Ind. 1989. Pvt. piano tchr., 1957-85, pub. sch. music tchr., 1960-62; dir. Ind. State Ethics Commn., Indpls., 1989-97; atty. and investigator Disciplinary Commn., Supreme Ct. Ind., Indpls., 1997—; pres. Coun. on Govtl. Ethics Laws, (Internat.), 1993-94. Exec. editor Articles & Prodn. Ind. Law Rev., 1988-89. Mem. Met. Devel. Commn., Indpls., 1982-87; chairperson Pub. Radio Adv. Bd., Indpls., 1983-84, treas. Cmty. Svc. Coun., Indpls., 1988-91. Invitee to Nat. 4H Congress, Chgo., 1956; named 4H Family of Yr., Washington Twp., 4-H, Indpls., 1980, Vol. of Week, Voluntary Action Ctr., Indpls., 1980. Mem. LWV (pres. Indpls. 1979-83), Ind. Bar Assn., Indpls. Bar Assn., Phi Alpha Delta, Mu Phi Epsilon. Avocation: choir singing. Office: Discip Commn Supreme Ct Ind 115 W Washington St Indianapolis IN 46204

KIRK, CASSIUS LAMB, JR., lawyer, investor; b. Bozeman, Mont., June 8, 1929; s. Cassius Lamb and Gertrude Violet (McCarthy) K.; AB, Stanford U., 1951; JD, U. Calif., Berkeley, 1954. Bar: Calif. 1955. Assoc. firm Cooley, Godward, Castro, Huddleson & Tatum, San Francisco, 1956-60; staff counsel for bus. affairs Stanford U., 1960-78; chief bus. officer, staff counsel Menlo Sch. and Coll., Atherton, Calif., 1978-81; chmn. Eberli-Kirk Properties, Inc. (doing bus. as Just Closets), Menlo Park, 1981-94; mem. summer faculty Coll. Bus. Adminstrn. U. Calif., Santa Barbara, 1967-73; past mem. adv. bd. Allied Arts Guild, Menlo Park; past nat. vice chmn. Stanford U. Annual Fund; past v.p. Palo Alto C. of C. With U.S. Army, 1954-56. Mem. VFW, Stanford Faculty Club, Order of Coif, Phi Alpha Delta. Republican. Home and Office: 1330 University Dr Apt 52 Menlo Park CA 94025-4241

KIRK, COLLEEN JEAN, retired conductor, educator; b. Champaign, Ill., Sept. 7, 1918; d. Bonum Lee and Anna Catherine (Hoffert) K. B.S. with high honors, U. Ill., 1940, M.S., 1945; Ed.D., Columbia U., 1953. Tchr. music public schs. Danvers, Ill., 1940-44, Watseka, Ill., 1944-45; instr. Univ. High Sch., Urbana, Ill., 1945-49; asst. prof. edn. and music U. Ill., 1949-58, asso. prof., 1958-64, prof., 1964-70; prof. Fla. State U., Tallahassee, 1970-90; condr. choral union Fla. State U., 1970-90; choral clinician, condr., adjudicator. Dir. music Wesley United Meth. Ch., Urbana, 1947-70; dir. jr. chorus, Ill. Summer Youth Music, Urbana, 1963-71; co-dir. Fla. Honors Choral Ensemble, Tallahassee, 1980-81; dir. Fla. Jr. High Sch. Choral Ensemble, Tallahassee, 1983; author: (with others) Modern Methods in Elementary Education, 1959; (with Harold Decker) Choral Conducting: Focus on Communication, 1988, Choral Music Education in America (1892-1992), 1992; contbr. numerous articles to Choral Jour. Recipient Pres.'s Award for Excellence in Teaching, Fla. State U., 1979, Disting. Svc. award U. Ill. Sch. Music Alumni Assn., 1991; named to Fla. Music Educators Hall of Fame, 1992. Mem. Am. Choral Dirs. Assn. (life, pres. So. divsn. 1971-75, nat. pres. 1981-83, Wayne Hugoboom award for Disting. Svc. 1988, Harold A. Decker Choral award 1981, So. divsn. conv. award Excellence in Choral Art, 1994), Am. Choral Found., Inc., Music Educators Nat. Conf., Assn. Profl. Vocal Emsembles, Fla. Music Educators Assn., Internat. Fedn. Choral Music, AAUP, Coll. Music Soc., Fla. Vocal Assn., Fla. Coll. Music Educators Assn., Sonneck Soc., Pi Kappa Lamdba, Kappa Delta Pi, Sigma Alpha Iota.

KIRK, CONSTANCE CARROLL, health educator; b. Pittsburg, Kans., Sept. 20, 1945; d. Leland Raymond K. and Ruth Nadine (Johnson) Graves. BS, Colo. State U., 1967; MS, U. Colo., 1976; EdD, U. No. Colo., 1980. Instr. N.Mex. Highlands U., Las Vegas, 1968-69; tchr., coach Madison (Wis.) East High Sch., 1969-71, Waunakee (Wis.) High Sch., 1972-74; exercise specialist The Conditioning Spa, Greeley, Colo., 1977-79; founder, owner Weight Dynamics, Greeley, Colo., 1981—; tchr. U. Wis., Oshkosh, 1985-89; assoc. prof. U. Wis., Whitewater, 1989—. Author: Taming the Diet Dragon, 1994; contbr. articles to profl. jours. Mem. Nat. Wellness Inst., Inst. Neotic Sci., World Wildlife Fund, U.S. Humane Soc. Avocations: Yoga, hiking, pets. Home: 381 W Ann St Whitewater WI 53190-1918 Office: U Wis Whitewater WI 53190

KIRK, DONALD, journalist; b. New Brunswick, N.J., May 7, 1938; s. Rudolf and Clara (Marburg) K.; m. Susanne Smith, May 31, 1965 (div.); m. Emiko Hayashi, Dec. 12, 1985; children: James Paul, John Winston. AB, Princeton U., 1959; MA, U. Chgo., 1965; postgrad. (Ford Found. fellow), Columbia U., 1964-65. Reporter Chgo. Sun-Times, 1960-61, N.Y. Post, 1961-64; free lance corr., writer, 1965—; Asia corr. Washington Star, 1967-70; Far East corr. Chgo. Tribune, 1971-74, N.Y. and UN corr., 1975-76; world editor, spl. corr. USA Today, 1982-90; vis. fellow Cornell U., Ithaca, N.Y., 1986-88; Fulbright rschr., Philippines, 1995-96. Author: Wider War: The Struggle for Cambodia, Thailand and Laos, 1971, Tell It To The Dead: Memories of a War, 1975, Korean Dynasty: Hyundai and Chung Ju Young, 1994, Tell It To The Dead: Stories of a War, 1996, Looted: The Philippines After the Bases, Business Guide to the Philippines, 1998. Recipient Page One award Chgo. Newspaper Guild, 1960; citations Overseas Press Club, 1967, 72, 73, Best Asia article award 1974; George Polk Meml. award for fgn. reporting, 1975, Fulbright scholar, New Delhi, India, 1962-63; Edward R. Murrow fellow Coun. Fgn. Rels., N.Y.C., 1974-75. Mem. Am. Soc. Journalists and Authors, Soc. Profl. Journalists. Clubs: Nat. Press (Washington); Overseas Press (N.Y.C.); Fgn. Corrs. (Hong Kong); Internat. House of Japan. Home: 4343 Davenport St NW Washington DC 20016-4513

KIRK, DONALD EVAN, electrical engineering educator, dean; b. Balt., Apr. 4, 1937; m. Judith Ann Sand, Sept. 4, 1962; children: Kara Diane, Valerie Susan, Dana Elizabeth. BSEE, Worcester Poly. Inst., 1959; MSEE, Naval Postgrad. Sch., Monterey, Calif., 1961; PhD in Elec. Engring., U. Ill., 1965. From asst. to full prof. Naval Postgrad. Sch., Monterey, Calif., 1965-87; assoc. dean engring. San Jose (Calif.) State U., 1987-90, prof. elec. engring., 1990-93, dean engring., 1994—; vis. scientist MIT Lincoln Lab., Lexington, Mass., 1981-82; program officer NSF, Arlington, Va., 1993-94. Author: Optimal Control Theory: An Introduction, 1970; co-author: First Principles of Discrete Systems and Digital Signal Processing, 1988, Contemporary Linear Systems, 1994. Bd. dirs. Carmel (Calif.) Sanitary Dist., 1973-77. Fellow IEEE, ASEE; mem. Sigma Xi, Tau Beta Pi, Eta Kappa Nu. Office: College Engring San Jose State Univ San Jose CA 95192-0080

KIRK, DONALD JAMES, accounting educator, consultant; b. Cleve., Nov. 28, 1932; s. John James and Helen Anna (Pilskaln) K.; children: J. Alexander, Bruce D.; m. Mary Mimi Colgage Bullock, Jan. 31, 1998. BA, Yale U., 1959; MBA, NYU, 1961; LLD (hon.), Lycoming Coll., 1979. Acct. Price Waterhouse & Co., N.Y.C., London and Washington, 1959-73; ptnr. Price Waterhouse & Co., 1967-73; from mem. to chmn. Fin. Acctg. Stds. Bd., Stamford, Conn., 1973-86; prof. acctg. Columbia U. Grad. Sch. Bus., N.Y.C., 1987-94, exec.-in-residence, 1995—; dir. Gen. Re Corp., 1987-98; trustee Fidelity Group Mut. Funds, 1987—, Valuation Rsch. Corp., 1993-95; pub. gov. Nat. Assn. Securities Dealers, Inc., 1996—. Officer, bd. dirs. Urban League of Southwestern Fairfield County, Conn., 1971-77; mem. Greenwich (Conn.) Rep. Town Mtg., 1971-77, Greenwich Bd. of Estimate and Taxation, 1977-89; bd. dirs. Nat. Arts Stabilization fund, 1983—, chmn., 1995—, bd. overseers NYU Schs. Bus., 1985-89; bd. trustees The Greenwich Hosp. Assn., 1989—, chmn., 1996—, Greenwich Found. for Comty. Gifts, 1991-93; bd. dirs. Yale-New Haven Health Sys., 1998—. Recipient Alumni Achievement award NYU Grad. Sch. Bus. Adminstrn., 1980; named to Acctg. Hall of Fame Ohio State U., 1996. Mem. AICPA (governing coun. 1987-90, pub. oversight bd. of SEC practice sect. 1995—, gold medal award for disting. svc. 1986), Am. Acctg. Assn., Fin. Execs. Inst. (bd. dirs. N.Y.C. 1990-94), Yale Alumni Assn. Greenwich (bd. dirs. 1988-91), Stanwich Club (past pres.), Yale Club N.Y.C. Office: Columbia U 600 Uris Hall Grad Sch Bus New York NY 10027

KIRK, EDGAR LEE, musician, educator; b. Harrisburg, Pa., May 28, 1923; s. Arthur Lee and Bertha May (Berthel) K.; m. Ellen Calhoun Gray, June 18, 1947; children: Arthur Lee, Douglas Gray. MusB, Eastman Sch. Music, U. Rochester, 1947, MusM, 1948, PhD, 1957. Mem. faculty Mich. State U., East Lansing, 1948-89, now emeritus, prof. bassoon, chmn. applied music, 1973-89, chmn. grad. studies, 1978-87, dir. admissions dept. music, 1982, assoc. chmn., 1987-88; prof. bassoon Eastman Sch. Music, U. Rochester, summers, 1954-65; instr. bassoon Interlochen Arts Acad., 1975-79. Bassoonist, Rochester (N.Y.) Philharmonic Orch., 1946-47, 54-55, staff bassoonist, radio sta. WHAM, Rochester, 1947-48, 1st bassoonist, Lansing (Mich.) Symphony Orch., 1960-73, 87-89, mem., Richards Woodwind Quintet, 1965-88; Rec. artist: Wind Quintets of Peter Muller, Crystal Records, Anton Reicha, Wind Quintets Opus 99, No. 2 and Opus 100, No. 6, Mus. Heritage Soc. With U.S. Army, 1943-46. Mem. Internat. Double Reed Soc. (pres. 1973-74). Home: 1281 Scott Dr East Lansing MI 48823-5213

KIRK, GARY VINCENT, investment advisor; b. Wausau, Wis., Jan. 15, 1943; s. Kenneth Robinson and Mary (Fisher) K.; m. Cynthia Kimberly Monroe, Dec. 21, 1966; children: Alisa Kimberly, Randolph Monroe. BS in Chem. Engring., U. Wis., 1965; MBA, Stanford U., 1967. Analyst Nat. Air Pollution Control Adminstrn., Pub. Health Svc., Washington, 1967-69; fin. analyst Memorex Corp., Santa Clara, Calif., 1969-71; ptnr. Robertson, Colman, Siebel & Weisel, San Francisco, 1971-78; pres. Siebel Capital Mgmt., Inc., Larkspur, Calif., 1978-84, exec. v.p., 1984-90; prin. Wood Island Assocs., Inc., Larkspur, Calif., 1992-98, pres., 1993-98; sr. v.p. U.S. Trust, Larkspur, Calif., 1998—. Deacon Menlo Park (Calif.) Presbyn. Ch., 1976-78; trustee St. Marks Sch. Bd., San Rafael, Calif., 1985-88. Lt. (j.g.) USPHS, 1967-69. Mem. Marin Country Club. Avocations: tennis, golf, bridge. Home: 40 Carnoustie Dr Novato CA 94949-5850 Office: US Trust 80 E Sir Francis Drake Blvd Larkspur CA 94939-1709

KIRK, GERALD ARTHUR, nuclear radiologist; b. L.A., Jan. 20, 1940; s. Arthur H. and Aural (Roderick) K.; m. Cherie J. Hutson, Dec. 27, 1965; children: Shannon Richard, Joel Daryn. BA in Physics, La Sierra Coll., 1962; MD, Loma Linda U., 1967. Intern Deaconess Hosp., Spokane, Wash., 1967-68; staff physician Empress Zandith Meml. Hosp., Addis Ababa, Ethiopia, 1968-69; pvt. practice Simi Valley, Calif., 1969-70; resident in radiology Loma Linda (Calif.) Med. Ctr., 1972-75, dir. sect. nuclear radiology, 1975—. Maj. USPHS, 1970-72. Home: 1341 Pine Knolls Cres Redlands CA 92373-6545 Office: Loma Linda U Dept Nuclear Radiology 11234 Anderson St Dept Nuclear Loma Linda CA 92354-2871

KIRK, HENRY PORT, academic administrator; b. Clearfield, Pa., Dec. 20, 1935; s. Henry P. and Ann (H.) K.; m. Mattie F., Feb. 11, 1956 (dec. July 1996); children: Mary Ann, Rebecca; m. Jenny Sheldon, Dec. 13, 1997. BA, Geneva Coll., 1958; MA, U. Denver, 1963; EdD, U. Southern Calif., 1973. Counselor, ednl. Columbia Coll., Columbia, Mo., 1963-65; dean Huron (S.D.) Coll., 1965-66; assoc. dean Calif. State U., L.A., 1966-70; dean El Camino Coll., Torrance, Calif., 1970-81; v.p. Pasadena (Calif.) City Coll., 1981-86; pres. Centralia (Wash.) Coll., 1986—. Contbr. articles to profl. jours. Mem. hist. commn., City Chehalis, 1990, pres. econ. devel. coun., 1992; campaign chmn., United Way, Centralia, 1989-90. Recipient PTK Bennett Disting. Pres. award, 1990; Exemplary Contbn. to Resource Devel. award Nat. Coun. Resource Devel., 1993. Mem. Wash. Assn. Community Colls. (pres. 1998-99), C. of C. (pres. 1998) Torrance Rotary Club (pres. 1987-88), Centralia Rotary Club (pres. 1990-91), Phi Theta Kappa, Phi Delta Kappa. Presbyterian. Avocation: antique restoration. Office: Centralia Coll 600 W Locust St Centralia WA 98531-4035

KIRK, JAMES ALLEN, mechanical engineering educator; b. Cleve., Nov. 3, 1944; s. Charles J. and Helen T. (Tulas) K.; m. Cynthia L. Ambler, Feb. 6, 1976; 1 child, Heather E. BSEE, Ohio U., 1967; MSME, MIT, 1969, PhD, 1972. Rsch. engr. Ford Motor Co., Dearborn, Mich., 1966-67; rsch. assoc. MIT, Cambridge, Mass., 1968-72; asst. prof. mech. engring. U. Md., College Park, 1972-77, assoc. prof. mech. engring., 1977-86, prof. mech. engring., 1986-98, prof. emeritus mech. engring., 1998—; pres. Flywheel Sys., Inc., 1997—; pres. FARE, Inc., College Park, Md. 1988—; owner Kirk Cons. Co., College Park, Md., 1977-88. Author: Scientific Automobile Accident Reconstruction, 1992, Vehicle Dynamics and Tire Forces, 1993, Forensic Engineering, 1993; contbr. articles to profl. jours. Mem. ASME, ASM Internat., Am. Soc. Engring. Edn. (Dow Outstanding Young Faculty award 1977), Soc. Automotive Engring. (Ralph Teetor award 1975), Nat. Assn. Profl. Accident Reconstrn. Specialists. Achievements include designed magnetically suspended flywheel for NASA and emergency stopping system for U.S. capitol-house subway system. Home: 7210 Windsor Ln Hyattsville MD 20782-1045 Office: Fare Inc 4321 Hartwick Rd Ste 116 College Park MD 20740-3210

KIRK, JAMES GRAHAM, pastor; b. Alameda, Calif., Jan. 9, 1937; s. Roy and Helen Graham (Thomson) K.; m. Sandra J. Killam Aug. 24, 1958 (div. 1985); m. Elizabeth Juliana Dittmer, Sept. 26, 1987; children: John Graham Kirk, Eric William Villegas, James Keith Kirk. AB, Lewis & Clark Coll., 1958; BD, San Francisco Theol. Seminary, 1961; postgrad., Heidelberg U., 1961-64; STD, San Francisco Theol. Seminary, 1980. Ordained to ministry Presbyn. Ch., 1964. Pastor St. Mark Presbyn. Ch., Newport Beach, Calif., 1968-73; dir. adv. coun. Discipleship and Worship, N.Y.C., 1973-85; co-pastor First Presbyn. Ch., Kalamazoo, Mich., 1985-86; interim pastor Cen. Presbyn. Ch., Lafayette, Ind., 1986-88; pastor Harundale Presbyn. Ch., Glen Burnie, Md., 1988—; del. Conf. on Renewal of Congregations, World Coun. of Chs., Crete, Greece, 1981, Conf. on Inter-religious Prayer, Bangalore, India, 1996; vice moderator Presbytery of Balt., 1997-98. Author: When We Gather (3 vols.), 1983-86, Meditations for Lent, 1988, Meditations for Advent, 1989. Trustee Bd. of Edn., Cresskil, N.J., 1977-85; mem. Md. Juvenile Justice Adv. Coun., 1996—; bd. dirs. Hospice of the Chesapeake, 1997—; moderator Presbytery of Balt., 1998-99. Mem. Rotary (trustee Glen Burnie chpt. 1990—, pres. 1995-96, Paul Harris fellow 1997, Disting. Svc. award 1997), Masons (chaplain 1965-67). Office: Harundale Presbyn Ch 1020 East Way Glen Burnie MD 21060-7303 *Life is a journey along faith's trail. Led by God's Spirit we seek to avoid the pitfalls, detours and hazards that hinder our faithful response to Christ's call, "come, follow me!".*

KIRK, JOHN MAC GREGOR, lawyer; b. Flint, Mich., Mar. 9, 1938; s. R. Dean and Berenice E. (Mac Gregor) K.; m. Carol Lasko, June 8, 1971; children: John M. Jr., Caroline Dwyer. BA, Washington & Lee U., 1960, LLB, 1962; LLM in Taxation, NYU, 1967. Bar: Mich. 1962, U.S. Ct. Mil. Appeals 1966, U.S. Supreme Ct. 1966, U.S. Tax Ct. 1969, U.S. Dist. Ct. (ea. dist.) Mich. 1982, U.S. Ct. Appeals (6th cir.) 1983. Trial atty. tax divsn. U.S. Dept. Justice, Washington, 1967-72; assoc. Boyer & Briggs, Bloomfield Hills, Mich., 1972-74; ptnr. Butler, Long, Gust, Klein & Van Zile, Detroit, 1975-78; mem. Meyer, Kirk, Snyder & Safford P.L.L.C., Bloomfield Hills, 1978—. Mem., past pres. Friends of Baldwin Pub. Libr., Birmingham, Mich., 1972—. Mem. ABA, State Bar Mich., Oakland County Bar Assn., Detroit Bar Assn., Birmingham Rotary, Walloon Yacht Club (treas., past commodore 1960—). Republican. Presbyterian. Home: 4350 Yale Ct Bloomfield Hills MI 48302-1669 Office: Meyer Kirk Snyder and Safford PLLC 100 W Long Lake Rd Ste 100 Bloomfield Hills MI 48304-2773

KIRK, PATRICK LAINE, lawyer; b. South Bend, Ind., May 12, 1948; s. Jerry W. and Vivian E. (Evans) K.; m. Cheryl A. Ensminger, Dec. 30, 1967; children: Kevin P., Travis S. BA, Valparaiso U., 1970, JD, 1973. Bar: N.Y. 1974, U.S. Dist. Ct. (no. dist.) N.Y. 1977, U.S. Supreme Ct. 1986. Ptnr. Grilli & Kirk, Herkimer, N.Y., 1974-89; asst. dist. atty. Herkimer County, Herkimer, N.Y., 1976-78; chief asst. dist. atty. Herkimer County, 1978-86, 1978-86, dist. atty., 1986-91, county judge and county surrogate, 1992—; acting justice Supreme Ct. of N.Y., 1997—; counsel Herkimer Cen. Sch., 1974-76; asst. counsel Village of Herkimer, N.Y., 1981-89; lectr. Police Tng. Sch., Utica, N.Y., 1979-91, Arson Seminar, 1987, Rape Crisis Tng.; tchr. Herkimer County C.C., 1981; criminal justice com. Nat. Conf. State Trial Ct. Judges. Advisor Law Explorer Post, Herkimer, 1974-76; bd. dirs. Martin Luther Home, Clinton, N.Y., 1980, Herkimer County Drug Task Force; chmn. sect. Mohawk Valley United Fund, Ilion, N.Y., 1985; mem. Arson Task Force, 1986-91. Mem. ABA (N.Y. del. to nat. conf. of spl. court judges 1995), N.Y. State Bar Assn. (jud. adminstrn. com.), Internat. Narcotics Enforcement Officers Assn., Drug Enforcement Assn. N.Y. (v.p. 1990-91), N.Y. State County Judges Assn., N.Y. State Surrogate Judges Assn., Am. Judges Assn., Elks. Republican. Lutheran. Home: 840 W German St Herkimer NY 13350-2136 Office: Herkimer County Courthouse Herkimer NY 13350

KIRK, PAUL GRATTAN, JR., lawyer, former political organization official; b. Newton, Mass., Jan. 18, 1938; m. Gail Loudermilk. AB, Harvard U., 1960, LLB, 1964. Bar: Mass. 1965, U.S. Dist. Ct. Mass. 1967, D.C. 1975,

U.S. Supreme Ct. 1976. Asst. dist. atty. Middlesex County, Cambridge, Mass., 1966; assoc. Maloney, Gallagher & Kirk, Boston, 1966-69; staff counsel U.S. Senate, Washington, 1969-77; ptnr. Sullivan & Worcester, Boston, 1977-90, of counsel, 1990—; chmn. Kirk & Assocs., Inc., Boston, 1997—; treas. Democratic Nat. Com., Washington, 1983-85; chmn. Dem. Nat. Com., 1985-89; co-chmn. Commn. on Presdl. Debates, 1987—, Nat. Student-Parent Mock Election, 1989; vis. lectr. Mass. Continuing Legal Edn. Program, John F. Kennedy Sch. Govt., Harvard U., Boston Coll., Coll. William and Mary, New Eng. Law Inst., others; bd. dirs. Hartford Fin. Svcs. Group, Inc., Hartford Life, Inc., Rayonier, Inc., Bradley Real Estate Corp. Chmn. bd. dirs. John F. Kennedy Libr. Found.; trustee Stonehill Coll., St. Sebastian's Sch., others; chmn. nominating com. Harvard Bd. Overseers, 1993-94; chmn. bd. dirs. Nat. Dem. Inst. for Internat. Affairs. Roman Catholic. Avocation: sports activities. Office: Sullivan & Worcester 1 Post Office Sq Ste 2300 Boston MA 02109-2129 also: Kirk & Assocs Inc 1 Post Office Sq Ste 2400 Boston MA 02109-2103

KIRK, REA HELENE (REA HELENE GLAZER), special education educator; b. N.Y.C., Nov. 17, 1944; d. Benjamin and Lillian (Kellis) Glazer; 3 stepdaughters. BA, UCLA, 1966; MA, Ea. Mont. Coll., 1981; EdD, U. So. Calif., 1995. Life cert. spl. edn. tchr., Calif., Mont. Spl. edn. tchr. L.A., 1966-73; clin. sec. speech and lang. clinic Missoula, Mont., 1973-75; spl. edn. tchr. Missoula, Gt. Falls, Mont., 1975-82; br. mgr. YWCA of L.A., Beverly Hills, Calif., 1989-91; sch. adminstrn., ednl. coord. Adv. Schs. of Calif., 1991-94; dir. Woman's Resource Ctr., Gt. Falls, Mont., 1981-82, Battered Woman's Shelter, Rock Springs, Wyo., 1982-84, Battered Victims Program, Sweetwater County, Wyo., 1984-88, Battered Woman's Program, San Gabriel Valley, Calif., 1988; dir. Spl. Edn., Pasadena, 1994-96, prin., 1995; asst. prof. U. Wis., Platteville, 1996—; mem. Wyo. Commn. on Aging, Rock Springs; mem. Cmty. Action Bd. City of L.A. pres., bd. dirs. battered woman's shelter, Gt. Falls; pres. Women's Resource Ctr., Gt. Falls, Religious Congregation, Rock Springs; founder, advisor Rape Action Line, Gt. Falls; founder Jewish religious svcs., Missoula; 4-H leader; hostess Friendship Force; Friendship Force ambassador, Wyo., Fed. Republic Germany, Italy; mem. YWCA Mont. and Wyo.; v.p. Coun. Devel. Disabilities, Wis.; bd. dirs. Coun. Children with Behavior Disorders, Wis. Recipient Gladys Byron scholar U. So. Calif., 1993, Dept. Edn. scholar U. So. Calif., 1994, honors Missoula 4-H; recognized as signigicant Wyo. woman as social justice reformer and peace activist Sweetwater County, Wyo.; nominated Wyo. Woman of the Yr., 1981, 82; honored by L.A. Mayor Bradley for Anti-Poverty work. Mem. Coun. for Exceptional Children (v.p. Gt. Falls 1981-82, bd. dirs., Professionally Recognized Spl. Educator 1998), Assn. for Children with Learning Disabilities (Named Outstanding Mem. 1982), Phi Delta Kappa, Delta Kappa Gamma, Psi Chi, Pi Lamda Theta.

KIRK, RICHARD DILLON, lawyer; b. Washington, Jan. 23, 1953; s. William Edward and Mary Elizabeth (Dillon) K.; m. Bridget Louise Stillwagon, June 27, 1981; children: Catherine Dillon, Suzanne Grace. AB, Georgetown U., 1975; JD, U. Va., 1978. Bar: Del. 1978, U.S. Dist. Ct. Del. 1980, U.S. Ct. Appeals (3rd cir.) 1984, U.S. Supreme Ct. 1984. Law clk. Del. Supreme Ct., Wilmington, 1978-79; assoc. Richards, Layton & Finger, Wilmington, 1979-82; dep. atty. gen. Del. Dept. Justice, Wilmington, 1982-84; assoc. Morris, James, Hitchens & Williams, Wilmington, 1984-86, ptnr., 1987—. Mem. Del. State Bar Assn. (pres. 1993-94, New Lawyers Disting. Svc. award 1988). Democrat. Roman Catholic. Office: Morris James Hitchens & Williams 222 Delaware Ave Wilmington DE 19801-1621

KIRK, RON, mayor, lawyer; m. Matrice Ellis; children: Elizabeth Alexandria, Catherine Victoria. BA with honors in Polit. Sci. and Sociology, Austin Coll., 1976; JD, U. Tex., 1979. Legis. asst. Senator Lloyd Bentsen, Washington, 1981-83; asst. city atty., chief lobbyist City of Dallas, 1983-89, mayor, 1995—; shareholder Johnson & Gibbs, P.C., Dallas, 1989-94; ptnr. Gardere & Wynne, L.L.P., Dallas, 1994—; sec. of state State of Tex., Austin, 1994-95; mem. Gen. Svcs. Commn. Tex., 1992-94, chmn., 1993. Active Big Bros./Big Sisters of Dallas, 1986-92; adv. trustee Schreiner Coll., 1988-90; chair South Dallas/Fair Park Trust Fund Adv. Bd., 1990-91; bd. trustees Austin Coll., 1991—; mem. exec. com. Dallas Regional Mobility Coalition, 1992-94; bd. dirs. State Fair of Tex., 1993—; active North Tex. Food Bank, 1985-90, Leadership Dallas Alumni Assn., 1986—, Dallas Assembly, 1990—, Dallas Dem. Forum, 1990-93, Dallas Helps, 1990-91, Mus. African-Am. Life and Culture, 1991—, St. Luke Community United Meth. Ch., Dallas. Recipient Vol. of Yr. award Big Bros./Big Sisters Met. Dallas, 1992; named Citizen of Yr., Omega Psi Phi, 1994. Mem. ABA, Nat. Bar Assn., State Bar Tex., J.L. Turner Legal Assn. (C.B. Bunkley Cmty. Svc. award 1994), Austin Coll. Alumni Assn. (Disting. Alumni award 1992). Office: City Hall 1500 Marilla St Dallas TX 75201-6300*

KIRK, RONALD, mayor; b. Austin, Tex.; m. Matrice Ellis; children: Elizabeth Alexandria, Catherine Victoria. BA in Polit. Sci./Sociology, Austin Coll.; JD, U. Tex., 1979. Ptnr. Gardere and Wynne, LLP; sec. of state, legis. aide for U.S. Sen. Lloyd Bentsen; asst. city atty., chief lobbyist City of Dallas, 1983-89; mayor Dallas, 1995—; mem. adv. bd., chair standing com. on urban econ. policy U.S. Conf. Mayors; appointee Fed. Adv. Commn. on Electronic Commerce; co-chair Nat. League of Cities' Election '96 task force; chair Tex.' Gen. Svc. Commn.; bd. dirs. Brinker Internat. Pres. Dallas Zool. Soc.; chair South Dallas/Fair Park Trust Fund Adv. Bd.; mem. bd. trustees Austin Coll.; chmn. bd. Hart Global Leaders Forum for So. Meth. U. Recipient Martin Luther King Justice award Dallas Bar Assn.; named Vol. of Yr., Big Bros./Big Sisters of Met. Dallas, Father of Yr., YMCA, 1998. Office: 1500 Marilla St Dallas TX 75201

KIRK, SHERWOOD, librarian; b. Kermit, W.Va., July 12, 1924; s. James Douglas and Magdalene (Elkins) K.; m. Ora Ward, Jan. 9, 1958; children: Diana, James Sherwood, Philip Lindsey. Student, Mich. State U., 1944; A.B., U. Ky., 1949; postgrad., U. Ill., 1949-50. Student asst. U. Ky., 1946-49; circulation asst. U. Ill., 1949-51; head reference and circulation Marshall U., 1951-52; sr. asst., agrl. libr. U. Neb., 1952-54; spl. project asst. Nat. Agr. Libr., Washington, 1954-55; reference asst., liaison loan div. Libr. Congress, 1955-56, catalog asst., 1956-57; coord. pub. libr. svcs. Ky. Dept. Librs., Frankfort, 1957-63; asst. state libr. Ky. Dept. Librs., 1963-69; state libr. Fla., 1969-71; assoc. dir. libr. ops. Ill. State Libr., Springfield, 1971-82; exec. dir. Western Ill. Libr. System, Monmouth, 1982-94; delivery cons. Alliance Libr. Sys., 1994-95, Galesburg, Ill., 1994-95; dir. Aledo-Mercer Carnegie Pub. Libr. Dist., 1996—; Mem. Ky. Gov.'s Planning Com. on Librs., 1968; chmn. Fla. Sec. of State's Com. Libr. Svc. to State Govt., 1970; adv. com. libr. svcs. and constrn. Fla. State Libr.; bd. dirs. Friends of Lincoln Libr., Springfield, Ill., 1977—; sec. Resource Sharing Alliance West Central Ill.; mem. Adv. Com. on Edn. in Ill. Author publs. Mem. Ill. State Libr. subcom. for Pub. Libr. Svcs.; Ill. State Libr. Scholarship Com.; pres. Ill. Book Pac. Recipient plaque for outstanding libr. Ky. Libr. Trustee Assn., 1968. Mem. ALA (coun. 1967-69), Ky. Libr. Assn. (pres. 1965-66), Fla. Libr. Assn., Ill. Libr. Assn. (chmn. local arrangement 1974, conv., mem. Bicentennial, com. 1974—, legis.-libr. devel. com., Robert R. McClarren legis. award 1990, chair pub. policy com. 1991), Assn. State Libr. Agys. Methodist (adminstrv. bd.). Clubs: Mason (Frankfort) (Shriner), Optimist (Frankfort); Springfield Lit. (pres. 1972). Home: 6 Edwardian Ct Monmouth IL 61462-1485

KIRK, SUSANNE SMITH, editor; b. Washington; d. Harold Clair and Theodora Smith; m. Donald Kirk, May 31, 1965 (div. 1985); m. Samuel Alexander Tomlinson III, June 24, 1989. Student Kaiserin-Theophanu Sch., Cologne, W.Ger., 1958; AB, Smith Coll., 1963; cert. Goethe Inst., Berlin, 1963; MS, Columbia U., 1965. Reporter, South China Morning Post, Hong Kong, 1965-67; corr. German News Agy., Saigon, Vietnam, 1968-69; editor Charles Tuttle Pubs., Tokyo, 1972-74; freelance journalist, 1965-74; asst. editor Charles Scribner's Sons (now Scribner divsn. Simon & Schuster), N.Y.C., 1975, editor, 1976-80, asst. v.p., 1977-98, fgn. rights dir., 1978-82, sr. editor, 1980-85, exec. editor, 1985-98, v.p., sr. editor, 1998—. Speaker various writers' confs. Contbr. articles to newspapers. Mem. Mystery Writers Am., Crime Writers Assn. (U.K.), Internat. Assn. Crime Writers, Snarks Ltd. (N.Y.C., v.p. 1983-84, pres. 1985-86), Smith Coll. Club (N.Y.C.), Pilgrimage Garden Club (Natchez). Home: PO Box 2056 Natchez MS 39121-2056 Office: Scribner Simon & Schuster 1230 Avenue Of The Americas New York NY 10020-1513

KIRK, THOMAS, chiropractor; b. Aug. 3, 1965. DC, Life U., Marietta, Ga., 1995. Ptnr. Humber-Kirk Clinic, College Park, Ga., 1995—. Office: 5640 Old National Hwy College Park GA 30349-3834

KIRK, THOMAS GARRETT, JR., librarian; b. Phila., Aug. 2, 1943; s. Thomas Garrett and Bertha (C.) K.; m. Elizabeth B. Walter, Aug. 29, 1964; children: Jennifer E., Cynthia M., Kristen A. BA, Earlham Coll., Richmond, Ind., 1965; MA, Ind. U., 1969; postgrad., Drexel U., 1987-88. Sci. libr. Earlham Coll., 1965-79; libr. cons. Richmond, Ind., 1972—; acting dir. librs. U. Wis., Parkside, Kenosha, 1979-80; dir. libr. Berea (Ky.) Coll., 1980-87, prof., 1987-94; dir. libr. Earlham (Ind.) Coll., 1994—; vis. instr. Ind. U. Libr. Sch., summers 1977, 78; bd. dirs SOLINET, 1981-84, 85-86, treas., 1982-84; bd. dirs. Ky. Libr. Network, 1985-87, 91-93, OCLC Users Coun., 1986-92, Pvt. Acad. Libr. Network Ind., v.p. 1995-96, pres., 1996-97; adv. bd. OCLC Coll. and Univ. Librs., 1995-98. Author: Library Research Guide to Biology, 1978; editor: Course-related Library and Literature Instruction, 1979, Increasing the Teaching Role of Academic Libraries, 1984; editl. bd. Coll. and Rsch. Librs., 1996—, Internet Reference Svcs. Quar., 1996—. Mem. ALA (coun. 1986-90), Assn. Coll. Rsch. Librs. (v.p., pres.-elect 1992-93, pres. 1993-94, 94-95, exec. com. 1984-85, 86-90, 92-95, rep. to Coalition for Networked Info. 1990-95, Miriam Dudley Bibliographic Instrn. Libr. of Yr. award 1984), Ind. Libr. Fedn., Ky. Libr. Assn. (Acad. Libr. of Yr. award 1984), Phi Kappa Phi. Mem. Soc. of Friends. Office: Earlham Coll Lilly Libr Richmond IN 47374

KIRK, THOMAS KENT, research scientist; b. Minden, La., Oct. 13, 1940; s. William Thomas and Wilda Inez (Gilstrap) K.; m. Celeste Hanson; children by previous marriage: Sharon Denise, Deborah Katherine, Sandra Kay. BS, La. Tech. U., 1962; MS, N.C. State U., 1964, PhD, 1968; postdoctoral, Chalmers Inst. Tech., Sweden, 1968-70. Rsch. microbiologist Forest Products Lab. USDA, Madison, Wis., 1970-80, project leader, 1980-85, dir. Inst. for Microbiol. and Biochem. Tech., 1985-96; prof. bacteriology U. Wis., Madison, 1996—; prof. dept. bacteriology U. Wis., 1982—; adj. prof. dept. wood and paper sci. N.C. State U., Raleigh, 1975—; vis. prof. Wood Rsch. Inst., Kyoto U., Uji, Japan, 1979-80. Contbr. more than 200 sci. papers and articles to profl. publs.; patentee in field. Recipient Marcus Wallenberg prize, Falun, Sweden, 1985. Fellow Internat. Acad. Wood Sci. (v.p. 1995—); mem. NAS, TAPPI (prize and medal R&D div. 1986), Am. Soc. Microbiology, Am. Chem. Soc. (Marvin J. Johnson Microbial and Biochemical Technology award 1993). Home: 3145 Timber Ln Verona WI 53593-9057 Office: U Wis Dept Bacteriology EB Fred Hall Madison WI 53706*

KIRKBRIDE, PATRICIA CAPELL, educational administrator; b. Piedmont, S.C., Jan. 4, 1935; d. Lawrence Marion and Mattie Sue (Bishop) Capell; m. Roger E. Kirkbride, Mar. 14, 1981 (dec. Oct. 1985). Student, N. Va. C.C., Leesburg, 1973-75; AS, U. Md., 1981; cert. in property mgmt., Greenville Tech. Coll. Cert. assn. exec. Am. Soc. Assn. Execs. With Nat. Assn. Affiliations, Washington, 1964-82; exec. dir. Fla. Phys. Therapy Assn., Orlando, 1982-86; exec. v.p. Ctrl. Fla. Multi Housing Assn., Orlando, 1986-88; property mgr. Knight Austin Corp., Richmond, Va., 1988-90; dir. devel., edn. Phys. Therapy Rehab. Svcs., Fort Walton Beach, Fla., 1991-95; dir. bus., program devel. Profl. Health Educators, Inc., St. Petersburg, Fla., 1995-96; sr. v.p., COO Acad. Continuing Edn., Boca Raton, Fla., 1996—. Mem. Okaloosa County Coordinating Coun., 1992-95; mem. organizing, founding com. Okaloosa Med. Assistance Clinic, 1993, pub. chmn., 1993-95, bd. dirs., 1994-95; chmn. Okaloosa County Children's Health Fair, 1994-95; mem. planning com. Jingle Bell Run for Arthritis, 1993-94. Mem. Am. Bus. Women's Assn., Fort Walton Beach C. of C. (bd. dirs. 1995, chmn. health care com. 1995), Eagles Auxiliary (editor, 1992-94, v.p., 1994-95, pres. 1994, aerie chaplain 1998-99). Republican. Episcopalian. Office: Nat Acad Continuing Edn 751 Park Commerce # 106/108 Boca Raton FL 33487

KIRKBY, MAURICE ANTHONY, oil company executive; b. Southwell, Notts, U.K., Apr. 12, 1929; emigrated to Can., 1983; s. George Sydney and Rose (Marson) K.; m. Muriel Beatrice Longmire, 1954; children: Peter Michael, Susan Margaret. B.A. with 1st class honors in Mech. Sci., King's Coll., Cambridge, Eng., 1952, M.A., 1955. Chief petroleum engr. Brit. Petroleum Co. p.l.c., London, 1969-74, gen. mgr. exploration and prodn. dept., 1976-80, dirs.' support staff, 1982-83; gen. mgr. BP Petroleum Devel., Aberdeen, Scotland, 1974-76; sr. v.p. oil and gas Standard Oil Co., Cleve., 1980-82; pres., chief exec. officer, dir. BP Can. Inc., Calgary, Alta., Can., 1983-88; chmn., chief exec. officer Hope Brook Gold Inc., Calgary, Alta., Can., 1986-88; dep. chmn. N.Am. Gas Investment Trust, London, 1989-95; bd. dirs. Ensign Oil and Gas Inc., U.S.A. Contbr. articles to profl. jours. Mem. Bus. Council on Nat. Issues, Ottawa, Ont., Can., 1983-88. Served with RAF, 1947-49. Fellow Inst. Mining and Metallurgy (dir. 1980), Royal Acad. Engring.; mem. Inst. Mech. Engrs., Soc. Petroleum Engrs. (dir. 1980, 81-83).

KIRK-DUGGAN, MICHAEL ALLAN, retired law and computer sciences educator; b. Stevens Point, Wis., Dec. 15, 1931; s. Frank E. and Dorothy Ada (Darrow) Duggan; married July 1956 (div. Jan. 1981); children: Michelle, Cheryl, Michael, Christopher, Robert, Siobhan, Mary; m. Cheryl Ann Kirk, Jan. 1, 1983. BS in Math, Coll. Holy Cross, 1953; postgrad., U. Minn., 1953-56; JD, LLB, Boston Coll., 1956; M in Patent Law, Georgetown U., 1959. Bar: Mass. 1956, U.S. Supreme Ct. 1961; qualified trial/def. counsel Gen. Cts. Martial, 1965; cert. cmty. based conflict resolution, 1994. Sr. engr. Sylvania Programming Lab., Needham, Mass., 1960-61; trial atty. antitrust divsn. U.S. Dept. Justice, 1961-67; asst. prof. econs. Whittemore Sch., U. N.H., Durham, 1967-69; comdr. U.S. Naval Intelligence Res., 1956-78; adminstrv. judge Atomic Safety and Licensing Bd. Panel, Washington, 1972-89; prof. bus. law and computer scis. U. Tex., Austin, 1969-93, prof. emeritus, 1993—; apptd. adv. procurator Tribunal, Diocese of Raleigh, 1995-97; editor-in-chief Computing Revs., N.Y.C., 1969-74. Author: Antitrust & U.S. Supreme Court, 1829-1984, 1984, Computer Utility, 1972, Law and the Computer, 1973, Paul Robeson Movies and Discography, 1999; contbr. numerous articles to profl. jours. Head Profs. for Johnson, Durham, 1968; eucharistic min., lector St. Columba Cath. Ch., Oakland, Calif., 1997—; del. Tex. Dem. Com., Austin, 1972—; IRS Vol. Income Tax Assistance, 1993-97; mem. Gospel Choir, 1993—. Mem. Mensa, Friend of Bill W. Democrat. Avocations: computer guru/hacker, semi-pro photographer, choral. Home: 4872 Reno Ln Richmond CA 94803-3850

KIRKEGAARD, R. LAWRENCE, architectural acoustician; b. Denver, Dec. 11, 1937; s. Raymond Lawrence and Frances Jean (Stocking) K.; m. Joslyn Ann Hills, Mar 23, 1959; children: Dana Lawrence, Jonathan Eric, Bradford Andrew. AB cum laude, Harvard U., 1960, MArch, 1964. Cons. archtl. acoustics Bolt, Beranek & Newman, Cambridge, Mass., 1962-64; supervisory cons., regional mgr. Chgo., 1964-75; pres., prin. cons. R. Lawrence Kirkegaard & Assocs., Inc., Downers Grove, Ill., 1976—; Frequent panelist for Nat. Endowment for Arts Design Arts Challenge Grant program. Prin. archtl. acoustics works: new projects include new Concert Hall for Tanglewood, Ordway Music Theatre, St. Paul, new performing arts cts. in Denver, Fort Lauderdale, Charlotte, N.C., Maui, Portand, Oreg., L.A., Greenville, S.C., Cin., New Concert Hall for Atlanta, Ga.; internat. projects include performing arts ctrs. in Taipei and Tainan, Taiwan, Bergamo, Italy, Edmonton, remodeling of the Tyl Theatre, Prague, Royal Philharmonic Hall, Liverpool, Eng., Barbican Concert Hall, London, Maison de Musique, Toulose, France; remodeling projects include Carnegie Hall (post-renovation), Orch. Hall, Chgo., Davies Symphony Hall, San Francisco, Heinz Hall, Pitts., Mahaffey Theatre, St. Petersburg, Fla., Guthrie Theatre, Oreg. Shakespeare Festival, Stratford Shakespeare Festival, Ont., Young Peoples' Theatre, Toronto; new schs. of music include Rice U., Northwestern U., U. Ala., Iowa State U., Pacific Luth. U., Red Deer Coll., Alta., Cin. Convervatory Mus., Luther Coll., N.D. State U.; remodeling projects include U. Chgo., Carleton Coll., Oberlin Conservatory. Co-founder Chestnut Hill Mental Health Ctr., Greenville, S.C. Mem. AIA (hon., nat. com. on arts and recreation), Acoustical Soc. Am., Harvard Grad. Sch. Design Alumni Coun., U.S. Inst. Theatre Tech., Am. Symphony Orch. League, Harvard Club (Chgo.). Home: 5200 Brookbank Rd Downers Grove IL 60515-4544 Office: 4910 Main St Downers Grove IL 60515-3611

KIRKER, WILLIAM GEORGE, health facility administrator; b. New Castle, Pa., June 4, 1951; s. Clifford George and Mary Gretta (Jackson) K.; m. Connie L. Telesz, Sept. 25, 1982. BS in Edn., Slippery Rock (Pa.) U., 1973, MS in Adminstrn., 1992. Reporter/photographer New Castle (Pa.) News, 1973-78; assoc. editor Arby's Inc., Youngstown, Ohio, 1978; editor/writer Fishers Big Wheel, Inc., New Castle, 1978-81; resource devel. dir. The Bair Found., New Wilmington, Pa., 1981-88; dir. advancement svcs. Slippery Rock U., 1988-99; dir. devel. Children's Inst., Pitts., 1999—. Mem. budget/allocation com. Lawrence County United Way, New Castle, 1995-97; mem. strategic planning com. Wilmington Area Sch. Dist., 1993; mem. Leadership Lawrence County, 1996-97; host family Children of Chernobyl Charitable Fund, 1996—; v.p., sch. dir. Rhema Christian Acad., 1997—; local coord. Coun. Internat. Ednl. Exch., 1998—; mem. adv. bd. Cmty. Svc. Learning Inst., 1999—; mem. Pitts. Planned Giving Coun. Recipaient Outstanding Student Paper award Internat. Acad. Bus. Disciplines, 1992. Mem. Assn. Profl. Rschrs. Advt. (pres. 1990-98, founding mem., svc. award com. 1996, co-chmn. internat. conf. 1997), Nat. Soc. Fund Raising Execs., Lawrence County C. of C. (dir. 1996-97), Slippery Rock U. Alumni Assn. (bd. dris. 1999—). Republican. Avocations: golf, organic gardening, tennis, photography. Home: RR 3 Box 203A Volant PA 16156-8601 Office: Children's Inst 6301 Northumberland St Pittsburgh PA 15217-1396

KIRKGAARD, VALERIE ANNE, writer, producer, consultant; b. Merced, Calif., Aug. 18, 1940; d. Basil Stuart and Audrey (Thompson) Coghlan; m. Alonzo Bryson Kirkgaard, Oct. 6, 1962 (div. Aug. 1963); children: Jennifer Alexandra, John Erik. AA, Santa Monica City Coll., 1961; BA, UCLA, 1968; M of Counseling, Goddard Coll., L.A., 1982; M. of Enlightenment, Sci. of Mind Ch., San Diego, 1992. Bd. dirs., care organizer Norwalk State Hosp., L.A., 1976-78; liaison to bd. dirs. Gay and Lesbian Cmty. Svcs. Ctr., 1976-79; therapist in pvt. practice, Pasadena, Pacific Palisades, Calif., 1979-98; ear coner; cable host, prodr. Waking Up In America, 1989—; radio host/prodr. Wake Up America, 1987-92; radio host, prodr. Terry Cole Whittaker; radio prodr./host Open Forum, Waking Up In America, others; spkr. in field. Author: Breakfast At Bob's, 1982, Take Two Breaths and Call Me in the Morning, 1988; environ. editor United Fitness Mag., 1992; columnist Hollywood Times, 1976, Century City News, 1990-92, others; inventor; author numerous articles; numerous appearances and interviews. Olympic Torch relayer Olympic Com., Santa Fe Springs, Calif., 1984. Mem. NOW, Calif. Assn. Marriage Family and Child Counselors, Women's Mus. of Art, Los Angeles County Mus. Art, World Vision, World Affairs Coun., The Hunger Project, Cousteau Soc., Mus. of Tolerance, Greater L.A. Press Club, Scriptwriters Network, Pacific Palisades C. of C., Roar Found. Avocations: polo, horseback riding, hiking, racquetball, reading, gardening. Home: 811 Fernwood Pacific Dr Topanga CA 90290 Office: The Coning Co 869 Via De La Paz Ste F Pacific Palisades CA 90272

KIRKHAM, JAMES ALVIN, manufacturing executive; b. Sumner County, Tenn., June 18, 1935; s. Shirley Barnes and Ouida Redempta (Bursby) K.; m. Shirley Ann Clouse, Sept. 3, 1954; children: Denise Anne, James Alvin II, Hughe Allan. Welder Ind. Wire Co., 1952-54; driver Arthur Lowe Cigar & Candy Co., 1954-56; time study Insley Mfg. Co., 1957; salesman Am. Chicle Co., 1958-59; mgr. Ace Battery, Inc., Indpls., 1967—; v.p. L P Industries, Inc., Indpls., 1977—; pres. Rubber Recycling Corp., 1989—; ptnr. TKT Leasing, Indpls., 1978—, LDJ Leasing, Indpls., 1979—, Vets. Interstate Plan, Inc. Sec. Johnson County Pk. Bd.; bd. dirs. English Ave. Boys Club, State 4-H Horse and Pony Orgn.; pres. bd. dirs. Ind. Horse Coun. Found., Inc.; pres. PTO, Clark Twp. Sch. Dist.; v.p. Johnson County 4-H Fairboard; active Boy Scouts Am.; chmn. fundraising equestrian events 10th Pan Am. Games; treas. Ind. Horse Coun. Inc. Recipient Golden Boy award Indpls. Boys Club Alumni Assn., 1970; named Outstanding Show Mgr., Ind. State Fair, 1971; named to Ind. Horseman Hall of Fame, 1998. Mem. Am. Horse Show Assn., Ind. Saddle Horse Assn., Ind. Motor Truck Assn., Indpls. Motor Truck Assn., U.S. C. of C., Indpls. C. of C., Masons, Shriners, Moose Lodge, Ind. Pony Exhibitors Club, Am. Hackney Club, Ind. Pony of Am. Club, Ind. Shetland Pony Breeders Club. Home: 1213 N Matthews Rd Greenwood IN 46143-8343 Office: 2166 Bluff Rd Indianapolis IN 46225-1983

KIRKHAM, M. B., plant physiologist, educator; b. Cedar Rapids, Iowa; d. Don and Mary Elizabeth (Erwin) K. BA with honors, Wellesley Coll.; MS, U. Wis., PhD. Cert. profl. agronomist. Plant physiologist U.S. EPA, Cin., 1973-74; asst. prof. U. Mass., Amherst, 1974-76, Okla. State U., Stillwater, 1976-80; from assoc. prof. to prof. Kans. State U., Manhattan, 1980—; guest lectr. Inst. Water Conservancy and Hydroelectric Power Rsch., Inst. Farm Irrigation Rsch., China, 1985, Inst. Exptl. Agronomy, Italy, 1989, Agrl. U. Wageningen, Inst. for Soil Fertility, Haren, The Netherlands, 1991, Massey U., New Zealand, 1991, Lincoln U., New Zealand, 1998, HortResearch, Palmerston North, New Zealand, 1998; William A. Albrecht seminar spkr. U. Mo., 1994; vis. scholar Biol. Labs., Harvard U., 1990; vis. scientist environ. physics sect. dept. sci and indsl. rsch., Palmerston North, New Zealand, 1991, Environ. and Risk Mgmt. Group, 1998, Landcare Rsch., Crown Rsch. Inst. New Zealand, Lincoln, 1998, HortResearch, The Horticulture and Food Rsch. Inst. New Zealand, Ltd., Palmerston North, 1998; participant Internat. Grassland Congress, New Zealand, 15th and 16th Internat. Congress of Soil Sci., Apaculco, Mex. and Montpelier, France, 13th Internat. Soil Tillage Rsch. Orgn. Conf., Aalborg, Denmark; spkr. Internat. Conf. Vadose Zone Hydrology, Davis, Calif., 1995, 4th Congress European Soc. for Agronomy, Veldhoven, The Netherlands, 1996, Internat. Workshop Characterization and Measurement of Hydraulic Properties of Unsaturated Soil, Riverside, Calif., 1997, Internat. Symposium on Plant Growth and Environ., Seoul, 1993, 16th Internat. Congress of soil Sci., Montpelier, France, 1998, Internat. Conf. Vadose Zone Hydrology, Davis, Calif., 1995; peer rev. panel mem. USDA/Nat. Rsch. Initiative, Washington, 1994. Cons. editor Plant and Soil Jour., 1979—; mem. editl. bd. Field Crops Rsch. Jour., 1983-91, Soil Sci., 1997—, Jour. Crop Prodn., 1998—; mem. editl. adv. bd. Trends in Agrl. Scis.-Agronomy, 1992—; contbr. numerous articles and papers to sci. jours.$dd papers to sci. jours. Recipient Best Reviewer award Water Resources Engring. divsn. Jour. Irrigation and Drainage Engring., ASCE, 1996; NSF postdoctoral fellow U. Wis., 1971-73, Nat. Def. Edn. Art fellowship, E.I. du Pont de Nemours and Co. summer faculty fellow, 1976, grantee NSF, USDA, Office Water Rsch. and Tech., U.S. Dept. Energy, Dept. Sci. and Indsl. Rsch., New Zealand; invited paper Internat. Grasslands Congress, New Zealand. Fellow AAAS, Am. Soc. Agronomy (editorial bd. 1985-90), Soil Sci. Soc. Am. (travel grantee to internat. congress Japan 1990), Royal Meteorol. Soc., Crop Sci. Soc. Am. (editorial bd. 1980-84); mem. Am. Soc. Plant Physiology (editorial bd. 1982-87), Am. Soc. Horticultural Sci., Internat. Soil Tillage Rsch. Organ., Internat. Soil Sci. Soc. (elected 1st vice chmn. commn. soil physics 1994-98), Bot. Soc. Am., Am. Meteorol. Soc., Société Française de Physiologie Végétale, Japanese Soc. Plant Physiology, Scandinavian Soc. Plant Physiology, N.Y. Acad. Sci., Soc. for Exptl. Biology (London), Growth Regulator Soc. Am., Water Environment Fedn., Phi Kappa Phi, Gamma Sigma Delta, Sigma Xi (sec. Kans. State U. chpt. 1997-99). Home: 1420 Mccain Ln Apt 244 Manhattan KS 66502-4680 Office: Kans State U Dept Agronomy Throckmorton Hall Manhattan KS 66505-5501

KIRKIEN-RZESZOTARSKI, ALICJA MARIA, academic administrator, researcher, educator; b. Lodz, Poland; came to U.S., 1965; d. Leszek Tadeusz and Francesca Irene (Mortkowicz) Kirkien. MSChemE, Polish U. Coll., London, 1951; PhD, U. London, 1955. Asst. prof. chemistry U. W.I., Jamaica, 1956-59, assoc. prof., 1959-61; assoc. prof. U. W.I., Trinidad, 1961-65; assoc. prof. Trinity Coll., Washington, 1966-68, prof. chemistry, 1968-92, chair chemistry dept., 1969-91, prof. emeritus, 1992—; sr. rsch. assoc. George Washington U. Med. Ctr., Washington, 1984. One person show at Trinity Coll., Washington, 1994; watercolors and oils exhibited in show at Sorrento, Italy, 1994, 96, Karistos, Greece, 1993, Cade Gallery, Anne Arundel Coll., Arnold, Md., 1998; contbr. numerous articles to profl. publs. Sec., treas. Polish Vets. Assn., Washington, 1981-83. Named one of Outstanding Educators of Am., 1973, 75; sr. rsch. fellow Univ. Coll., 1965-66, 71, U. Calif., Santa Barbara, 1967. Fellow Royal Inst. Chem. (Gt. Britain); mem. Md. Fedn. Art (Critics Choice award for pottery 1992), Am. Chem. Soc. (adv. bd. Chem. and Engring. News 1978-81), Chem. Soc. Gt. Britain, Polish Inst. Arts and Scis. of N.Y., Phi Beta Kappa. Republican. Roman Catholic. Avocations: graphic painting, and ceramics. Home: 407 Buckspur Ct Millersville MD 21108-1764 Office: Trinity Coll 125 Michigan Ave NW Washington DC 20010-2916

KIRKLAND, ALFRED YOUNGES, SR., federal judge; b. Elgin, Ill., 1917; s. Alfred and Elizabeth (Younges) K.; m. Gwendolyn E. Muntz, June 14, 1941; children: Pamela E. Kirkland Jensen, Alfred Younges Jr., James

Muntz. BA, U. Ill., 1941, JD, 1943. Bar: Ill. 1943. Assoc. Mayer, Meyer, Austrian & Platt, Chgo., 1943; sr. ptnr. Kirkland, Brady, McQueen, Martin & Callahan and predecessor firms, Elgin, 1951-73; spl. asst. atty. gen. State of Ill., 1969-73; judge 16th Cir. Ct. Ill., 1973-74; judge U.S. Dist. Ct. (no. dist.) Ill., 1974-79, sr. judge, 1979—; mem. Coun. Practicing Lawyers U. Ill. Law Forum, 1969—, mem. adv. bd., 1972-73, mem. adv. coun. continuing legal edn., 1959-62; chmn. Ill. Def. Rsch. Inst., 1965-66. Outdoor editor: Elgin Daily Courier-News, Kewanee Star-Courier; fishing editor: Midwest Outdoors Mag. Pres. Elgin YMCA, 1963, chmn. bd. trustees, 1995—. 2d lt. inf. AUS, 1943-46. Fellow Am. Coll. Trial Lawyers, Am. Bar Found.; mem. ABA (ho. of dels. 1967-70), Ill. State Bar Assn. (pres. 1968-69), Chgo. Bar Assn., Kane County Bar Assn. (pres. 1961-62), Elgin Bar Assn. (pres. 1951-52), Am. Judicature Soc. (bd. dirs. 1967—), Ill. Bar Found. (bd. dirs. 1961-69), Ill. Def. Counsel (bd. dirs. 1966-69), Soc. Trial Lawyers, Legal Club Chgo., Law Club Chgo., Internat. Assn. Ins. Counsel, Fed. Ins. Counsel, Assn. Ins. Counsel, Outdoor Writers Assn. Am. (gen. counsel), Assn. Gt. Lakes Outdoor Writers (v.p., bd. dirs.), Ill. C. of C. (bd. dirs. 1969-70), Phi Delta Phi, Sigma Nu. Republican. Congregationalist. Clubs: Elgin Country (pres. 1956), Cosmopolitan Internat. (past pres., judge advocate). Lodges: Elks, Moose. Home: 2421 Tall Oaks Dr Elgin IL 60123-4844

KIRKLAND, BRYANT MAYS, clergyman; b. Essex, Conn., May 2, 1914; s. Henry Burnham and Helen Josephine (Mays) K.; m. Bernice Eleanor Tanis, Aug. 19, 1937 (dec. Mar. 1996); children: Nancy Tanis (Mrs. Tom L. Thompson), Elinor Ann (Mrs. Donald C. McFerren), Virginia Lee (Mrs. Laird James Stuart); m. Lola Mae Shiflet, May 30, 1998. AB, Wheaton Coll., 1935; ThB, Princeton Theol. Sem., 1938; ThM, Eastern Bapt. Theol. Sem., Phila., 1946; DD (hon.), Beaver Coll., 1949, Lafayette Coll., 1962, Denison U., 1964; LLD (hon.), U. Tulsa, 1962; STD (hon.), Parson Coll., 1966, Hastings Coll., 1989; LittD (hon.), Washington and Jefferson Coll., 1968; LHD (hon.), Lebanon Valley Coll., 1983. Ordained to ministry Presbyn. Ch., 1938; pastor Pa., 38-46, N.J., 1946-57, Tulsa, 1957-62; pastor Fifth Ave. Presbyn. Ch., N.Y.C., 1962-87, elected minister emeritus, 1987—; pres., chief exec. officer Am. Bible Soc., N.Y.C., 1989-91; interim min. Nat. Presbyn. Ch., Washington, 1991-93; interim min. 1st Presbyn. Ch., Moorestown, N.J., 1993-94, Malvern, Pa., 1994-96; v.p. John Templeton Found., Radnor, Pa., 1996-98; vis. lectr. homiletics Princeton Theol. Sem., 1951-56, 64-85, 87—; overseas guest lectr. U.S. Armed Forces, U.S. Army Chaplain Sch., 1965, 68, 71, 74, 81, 87, 88-94; Berger lectr., 1968, Swartley lectr., 1969, T.J. and Inez Raney lectr., 1969, Logan lectr., 1971, Royster lectr. 1976, 80, Staley lectr., 1978, 81, B. Cobb lectr., 1982, George A. Buttrick lectr., 1983, 85, Otis lectr., 1984; disting. adj. prof. Ea. Bapt. Theol. Sem.; mem. Commn. Ecumenical Mission and Rels., Presbyn. Ch., 1949-62, Commn. on Continuing Edn., 1967; mem. coun. Nat. Presbyn. Ch. Ctr., Washington, 1962-65. Author: Growing in Christian Faith, 1963, Home Before Dark, 1965, 1986, Living in a Zig Zag Age, 1972, Experiencing God in Unexpected Ways, 1978, Pattern For Faith, 1982. rev. edit., 1992; contbg. author: Evangelical Sermons of Our Day, 1959, Year of Evangelism in Local Church, 196O. Trustee Beaver Coll., U. Tulsa; trustee John M. Templeton Found., 1991—, v.p., 1996-98; trustee, v.p. Religion in Am. Life, 1991—; pres. bd. trustees Princeton Theol. Sem.; trustee, v.p. bd. Ctr. Theol. Inquiry, Princeton. Recipient Disting. Alumni award Princeton Theol. Sem., 1988, Legion of Merit, Chapel Four Chaplains, 1989, Alumni Disting. Svcs. award Wheaton (Ill.) Coll., 1994; named Clergyman of Yr., Religious Heritage Am., 1975. Mem. Am. Bible Soc. (sr. trustee), Princeton Club (N.Y.C.), Nassau Club. Address: 1122 Stover Shop Rd Churchville VA 24421-2124

KIRKLAND, GEOFFREY ALAN, motion picture production designer; b. Derby, Eng., Oct. 7, 1939; came to U.S., 1980; s. Cyril George and Florence Kathleen Kirkland; m. Elspeth Mary Kennedy, Mar. 23, 1970. AA, Royal Coll. of Art, London, 1961. Designer BBC, London, 1961-66; freelance art dir. London, 1966-75; freelance prodn. designer L.A., 1975—. Prodn. designer: (films) Bugsy Malone, 1975 (British Film Academy award 1975), Midnight Express, 1978, Fame, 1980, Shoot the Moon, 1982, The Right Stuff, 1983 (Academy award nomination best art direction 1983), Birdy, 1984, Leonard Part 6, 1987, Journey to the Center of the Earth, 1987, Mississippi Burning, 1988, Wildfire, 1989, Come See the Paradise, 1990, Renaissance Man, 1994, Space Jam, 1996, Desperate Measures, 1998, Angela's Ashes, 1998.

KIRKLAND, GERRY PAUL, sales executive; b. Muscatine, Iowa, June 22, 1943; s. Paul L. and Mary (Shelter) K.; m. Carol Godske; children: Steffanie, Kevin, Kara, Peter. Student, Rockhurst Coll., 1961-64; MBA, Calif. Coast U., 1996. Prodn. supr. Deere & Co., East Moline, Ill., 1964-71; loan officer Security State Bank, Bettendorf, Iowa, 1971-73; worldwide prodn. mgr. J.I. Case, Racine, Wis., 1973-86; v.p. mktg. and sales The Prime Mover Co., Muscatine, 1986-90; gen. mgr. Nissan Indsl. Equip. Co., Schaumburg, Ill., 1990-93; with Pettibone Corp., Schaumburg, Ill., 1993—; v.p. internat. ops. Pettibone Corp., Lisle, Ill., 1993-96; pres. CTR Mfg., Union Grove, N.C., 1996—; sr. v.p., gen. mgr. Blount, Inc., 1999—; pres. CTR Mfg., Inc., Union Grove, N.C.; bd. dirs. Backwaters Gamblers Ski Club, Rock Island, Ill., 1987-90; mem. pres.'s coun. Purdue U. Bd. dirs. Crime Stoppers, Muscatine, 1987-90; Rep. county and state del., Muscatine, 1988; active opns. edn. Muscatine Sch. Dist.; bd. dirs. Muscatine High Sch. Boosters; pres. Northwestern U. Parents Coun., 1983-87; mem. Purdue U. Parents Adv. Coun.; chmn. Sleepy Hollow Plan Commn., 1993—. Mem. Indsl. Truck Assn. (bd. dirs.), Am. Barefoot Water Ski Assn. (bd. dirs.), Rotary. Republican. Avocations: golf, boating, water skiing. Fax: 919-269-4452. Home: 153 Pin Oak Ln Mooresville NC 28117-7501 Office: Blount Inc 535 Mack Todd Rd Zebulon NC 27597

KIRKLAND, JOHN DAVID, oil and gas company executive, lawyer; b. McAllen, Tex., June 6, 1933; s. O.D. and Daisy (Donohoe) K.; m. Ann Wales, June 15, 1957 (div. Feb. 1985); children: David, Solace, Robert; m. Kate Sayen, May 15, 1993. BA, Yale U., 1955, LLB, 1958. Bar: Tex. 1958. Atty. Baker, Botts, Shepherd & Coates, Houston, 1958-67; v.p. in charge fin. Pennzoil Co., Houston, 1967-73, exec. v.p., dir., 1973-78; dir. exec. edn. Jones Sch. Mgmt. and Adminstrn. Rice U., Houston, 1978-79; vice chmn., dir. Sandefer Oil & Gas, Inc., Houston, 1980; exec. v.p., dir. Roy M Huffington, Inc., Houston, 1980-86; chmn. Heritage Trust Co., Houston, 1986-89; chmn., CEO Antara Resources Inc., Houston, 1996—; bd. dirs. Mesa Petroleum Co., 1967-73, Jupiter Corp., 1962-67, Downtown Bank, 1965-70, Pogo, Inc., 1970-77, Plato, Inc., 1973-78. Pres. Houston Ballet Found., 1972-74, trustee, 1979—, chmn., 1979-84; treas., chmn. fin. com. United Way of Houston, 1983-84; trustee Chinquapin Sch., 1991-94; bd. dirs. Houston chpt. Juvenile Diabetes Found., 1995-97. Mem. Tex. Bar Assn. Home: 2433 Stanmore Dr Houston TX 77019-3423 Office: Antara Resources Inc 1100 Louisiana St Ste 3500 Houston TX 77002-5274

KIRKLAND, JOHN LEONARD, lawyer; b. Elgin, Ill., Aug. 8, 1926; s. Alfred Hines and Elizabeth Aurelia (Younges) K.; m. Harriet Grose, Oct. 14, 1950; children—Karen Emily Kirkland Lazos, Kevin Grose, Robert John, Melissa Caroline Kirkland Glyman. B.A., Lake Forest Coll., 1948; JD, Chgo.-Kent Coll. Law, 1952. Bar: Ill. 1951, U.S. Dist. Ct. (no. dist.) Ill. 1952. Assoc. Hinshaw, Culbertson, Moelmann, Hoban & Fuller, Chgo., 1952-60, ptnr., 1960-90, mng. ptnr., 1979-84; of counsel Hinshaw and Culbertson, Chgo., 1991—; lectr. Inst. Continuing Legal Edn. on Ins. Law, 1968-75. Mem. Cook County Zoning Bd. Appeals, Ill., 1968-73; mem. Arlington Heights Zoning Bd. Appeals, Ill., 1961-68, chmn., 1965-68. Served with USN, 1944-46. Fellow Am. Bar Found., Am. Coll. Trial Lawyers; mem. Ill. State Bar Assn. (bd. govs. 1975-79, editor The Policy ins. law publ. 1976-90), Soc. Trial Lawyers, Trial Lawyers Club Chgo. (pres. 1961), Fedn. Ins. Counsel, Union League Club (Chgo.), Big Foot Country Club (Lake Geneva, Wis., pres. 1978-79). Home: 7040 Pelican Bay Blvd # D303 Naples FL 34108-7549 Office: Hinshaw & Culbertson 222 N La Salle St Ste 300 Chicago IL 60601-1081

KIRKLAND, JOSEPH J., research chemist; b. Winter Garden, Fla., May 24, 1925; s. Joe J. and Bertye (Porcher), K.; m. Ann Winston Driskell, June 25, 1949 (div.); children—Kent, Kerry, Celeste; m. Karin R. Monson, Sept. 30, 1983; children—Mark, Holly. A.B., Emory U., 1948, M.S., 1949; D.Sci. (hon.), 1974; Ph.D., U. Va., 1953. Chemist, Hercules Co., Wilmington, Del., 1949-50; research chemist E.I. DuPont De Nemours & Co., Wilmington, 1953-92; v.p. R&D, Rockland Techs., Inc., Newport, Del., 1992-97; mgr. Zorbax R&D, Hewlett-Packard Co., Newport, 1997—; vis. prof. U. Del., 1978-82. Co-author: Introduction to Modern Liquid Chromatography, 1974, 2d edition 1979, Modern Size Exclusion Liquid Chromatography, 1979, Practical HPLC Method Development, 1988, 2d edit., 1997; editor: Modern Practice of Liquid Chromatography, 1971. Served with USN, 1944-46; Asia. Recipient Torbern Bergman medal Swedish Chem. Soc. 1982; DuPont Fellow, 1988. Mem. Am. Chem. Soc. (award in chromatography 1972, Anachem award Detroit sect. 1979, Dela. sect. award 1988), Chromatography Forum of Del. Valley (chmn. 1971-72, Dal Nogare award 1974), Ea. Analytical award Achievements in Separation Sci., 1993, DuPont Lavoisier award, 1997, Chromatography Soc. award (U.K.), 1997. Office: Hewlett Packard-Newport 538 First State Blvd Newport DE 19804-3552

KIRKLAND, JUDY JOYLENE, computer specialist; b. Great Falls, Mont., June 16, 1952; d. Howard Harold and Marvelle Ann (Plummer) Scoones; m. Paul M. Kirkland, May 22, 1976 (div. Feb. 1982); 1 child, William Howard. Cert in Acctg. Data Processing, Helena (Mont.) Vo-Tech Ctr., 1975; BS in Home Econs., Mont. State U., 1986. Adminstrv. asst. State of Mont., Helena, 1979-82; work/study sec. Mont. State U., Bozeman, 1982-86; title ins. clk. Am. Title, Billings, Mont., 1986-87; legal sec. Corner Pockets of Am., Billings, 1987-89; word processing operator Mont. State U., Bozeman, 1989-92; temporary sec. Tenera, Idaho Falls, Idaho, 1992-94, Express Svcs./INEL, Idaho Falls, 1995-96; adminstrv./sales asst. TCI Media Svcs., Idaho Falls, 1996-97; customer svc. rep. fin. Idaho Innovation Ctr., Idaho Falls, 1997—, quickbooks profl. advisor, 1998—; sec., dir. Musicians West Inc., Pocatello, Idaho, 1994—; computer trainer Computer Tng. Wheels, Idaho Falls, 1992-93; adminstrv. asst. Summer Music Festival, Pocatello, 1994-95. Graphic artist posters, brochures, programs Musicians West, 1st Presbyn. Ch., Idaho Falls Symphony Chorale, Mark Neiwirth, Brian Wilhour, 1992—. Crisis line counselor Bozeman Help Ctr., 1985-86; team mem. Life Tng. various locations, 1988-93; music vol. 1st Presbyn. Ch., Idaho Falls, 1996-97; adult CPR/1st aid cert. ARC, Idaho Falls, 1996—. Mem. Idaho Falls Symphony Chorale, Westminster Choir, Tau Pi Phi, Alpha Psi Omega. Avocation: piano, music theory/composition, yoga, spirituality, reading. Home: PO Box 52098 Idaho Falls ID 83405-2098 Office: Idaho Innovation Ctr 2300 N Yellowstone Hwy Idaho Falls ID 83401-1662

KIRKLAND, (JOSEPH) LANE, labor union official; b. Camden, S.C., Mar. 12, 1922; s. Randolph Withers and Louise (Richardson) K.; m. Edith Draper Hollyday, June 10, 1944 (div. 1972); children: Blair, Lucy, Louise, Edith, Katherine; m. Irena Neumann, Jan. 19, 1973. Student, Newberry (S.C.) Coll., 1940; grad., U.S. Mcht. Marine Acad., 1942; BS, Georgetown U. Sch. Fgn. Svc., 1948; LLD (hon.), Duke U., Princeton U., Dartmouth Coll., Columbia U., CUNY, Holy Cross Coll., U. S.C., U. Haifa, Hofstra U. Lic. master mariner. Deck officer U.S. Merchant Marine, 1941-46; nautical scientist Hydrographic Office Navy Dept., 1947-48; mem. rsch. staff AFL, 1948-53; asst. dir. dept. social security AFL-CIO, 1953-58; dir. rsch. and edn. Internat. Union Operating Engrs., 1958-60; exec. asst. to pres. AFL-CIO, 1961-69, sec.-treas., 1969-79, pres., 1979-95; ret., 1995; mem. Blue Ribbon Def. Panel.; mem. Commn. on Founds. and Pvt. Philanthropy, 1969-70, Pres.'s Commn. CIA Activities within U.S., 1975, Nat. Commn. on Productivity, 1971-74; mem. gen. adv. com. ACDA, 1974-81; mem. Presdl. Commn. on Fin. Structure and Regulation, 1970-72. Bd. dirs. Polish Am. Enterprise Fund, Freedom House. Recipient Disting. Pub. Svc. medal Dept. Def., Washington, Presdl. Citizen's medal U.S. Pres., Washington, Presdl. medal of Freedom U.S. Pres., Washington, Order of Merit Pres. Hungary, Order of Francisco de Miranda Pres. Venezuela, Order of Merit Poland. Mem. Internat. Orgn. Masters, Mates and Pilots., Coun. Fgn. Rels. Democrat. Episcopalian. Office: George Meany Ctr Labor Studies 10000 New Hampshire Ave Silver Spring MD 20903-1706*

KIRKLAND, LORENZO LEVON, football player; b. Lamar, S.C., Feb. 17, 1969. Student, Clemson U. Linebacker Pitts. Steelers, 1992—. Named to Pro Bowl, 1996. Office: Three Rivers Stadium 300 Stadium Cir Pittsburgh PA 15212-5729*

KIRKLEY, D. CHRISTINE, non-profit organization administrator; b. Horton, Ala., Aug. 28, 1932; d. Vester Boyd and Josephine Prumrytle (Parrish) K.; m. Jack Stanley I, July 4, 1952; 1 child, Jack Stanley II. Student, U. Ala., 1951-52, Samford U., 1963-65, Cathedral Coll., 1982. Svr. rep. South Ctrl. Bell, Birmingham, Ala., 1984—; dir. Helpline Christian Outreach Ministries Inc, Birmingham, 1991—. Area mgr. Operating Blessing, Birmingham, 1989—; mem. Christian Helplines Internat., 1990—, sec. exec. com., 1994—. Mem. Telephone Pioneers Am. (fund raiser 1976-78, pres. 1979, cmty. edn. coord. 1982-83, drug abuse chairperson 1982-83), Internat. Platform Assn., Kiwanis. Mem. Assemby of God Ch. Avocations: reading, bowling, crocheting, swimming. Office: Helpline Christian Outreach Ministries Inc 8 Roebuck Dr Birmingham AL 35215-8046

KIRKLEY, JAMES FRANKLIN, religion and ethics educator; b. Balt., July 1, 1951; s. James Straughn and Helen Maxine (Smith) K.; m. Roberta Parker Welch, June 7, 1975 (div. Mar. 1987); children: Adam James, Andrew David, Luke Robert. BSBA, Bucknell U., 1973; MDiv, Gordon-Conwell Theol. Sem., 1977; PhD in Theology and Ethics, Duke U., 1989. Area dir., youth pastor Young Life/First Bapt. Ch., New Martinsville, W.Va., 1977-78; area dir. Young Life, Rochester, N.Y., 1978-81; pastor Cornerstone Bapt. Ch., Rochester, 1981-82; self-employed painting contractor Rochester, 1982-83; self-employed home improvement contractor Durham, N.C., 1983-89; instr. philosophy and ethics Durhan C.C., 1989-91; asst. prof. religion and ethics Shaw U., Raleigh, N.C., 1991—; pres. faculty senate Shaw U., 1995-97; faculty cons. Crossroads, Wynnewood, Pa., 1993—. Trustee Shaw U., 1996-97; commr. N.C. H.S. Lacrosse Assn., 1996—; bd. dirs. N.C. Lacrosse Found., 1996—; bd. dirs., founder Bull City Lacrosse, Durham, 1994—; coach South Team Nat. North-South H.S. Lacrosse All Star Game, 1998. Named Coach of Yr. N.C. Interscholastic Lacrosse Assn., 1994, Coach of Yr. N.C. H.S. Lacrosse Assn., 1998. Mem. AAUP, Am. Acad. Religion, Soc. Christian Ethics, U.S. Lacrosse Coaches Assn., U.S. Lacrosse Found. Home: 5121 Lazywood Ln Durham NC 27712-9794 Office: Shaw U 118 E South St Raleigh NC 27601-2399

KIRKLEY-BEY, MARIE LOPEZ, state legislator; b. New Britain, Conn.; widowed. Grad. high sch., New Britain, Conn. Mem. Conn. Ho. of Reps., Hartford. Mem. Women in Leadership, Hartford YWCA, Ctr. for Cmty. Change, Alcohol and Drug Recovery Ctr. Recipient Nat. Vol. award Aetna Life and Casualty. Mem. Nat. Black Caucus. Address: 39 Ashley St Hartford CT 06105-1402 Office: Conn Ho of Reps State Capitol Hartford CT 06106*

KIRKLIN, JOHN WEBSTER, surgeon; b. Muncie, Ind., Aug. 5, 1917; m. Margaret Katherine; 3 children. BA summa cum laude, U. Minn., 1938; MD magna cum laude, Harvard U., 1942; MD (hon.), U. Munich, 1961; DSc (hon.), Hamline U., 1966, U. Ala., Birmingham, 1978, Ind. U., Bloomington, 1983; hon. degree, U. Bordeaux, France, 1982, Universidad de la República, Uruguay, 1982. Diplomate: Am. Bd. Surgery, Am. Bd. Thoracic Surgery (mem. exam. and tng. programs coms.). Intern Hosp. U. Pa., 1942-43; resident in surgery Mayo Clinic and Mayo Grad. Sch. Medicine, Rochester, Minn., 1943-44, 46-48, first asst. in surgery, 1949-50, chmn. dept. surgery, 1964-66; asst. resident in surgery Children's Hosp., Boston, 1948-49; surgeon Mayo Clinic, 1950-66, instr. surgery, 1951-53, asst. prof., 1953-57, asso. prof., 1957-60, prof., 1960-66, bd. govs., 1965-66; surgeon-in-chief U. Ala., Birmingham, 1966-82; Fay Fletcher Kerner prof. surgery U. Ala.-Birmingham Sch. Medicine and Med. Ctr., 1966—; assoc. chief staffy U. Ala.-Birmingham Hosps., 1966—; chmn. dept. surgery U. Ala.-Birmingham Sch. Medicine and Med. Ctr., 1966-82, dir. div. cardiothoracic surgery, dir. Congenital Heart Disease Research and Tng. Ctr., 1982-84, prof. surgery, 1990; mem. task force on prevention and treatment of cardiovascular disease in the young Nat. Heart, Lung and Blood Inst., 1977-78; mem. policy adv. bd. for coronary artery surgery, mem. adv. com. crippled children services regional program NIH. Author: (with R.B. Karp) The Tetralogy of Fallot from a Surgical Viewpoint, 1970, (with others) Cardiac Surgery and the Conduction System, 1983; contbr. articles to profl. publs.; editorial bd.: Am. Heart Jour, 1964-76, Am. Jour. Cardiology, 1974-80, Circulation, 1967-78, Jour. Thoracic and Cardiovascular Surgery, 1971-83, Year Book Cardiovascular Medicine and Surgery; corr. mem. editorial bd.: European Jour. Intensive Care Medicine, 1974—; former editorial bd.: Jour. French Soc. Thoracic Surgery. Served to capt. U.S. Army, 1944-46. Fellow Royal Australasian Coll. Surgeons (hon.), Royal Coll. Surgeons Ireland (hon.), Royal Coll. Surgeons Edinburgh (hon.), Royal Coll. Surgeons Eng. (hon.), Assn. Surgeons Gt. Britain and Ireland (hon.); mem. AAUP, AMA, ACS, Ala. Acad. Sci., Ala. Heart Assn., Am. Acad. Pediatrics, Am. Assn. Thoracic Surgery (pres. 1978-79), Am. Coll. Cardiology (v.p. bd. govs. 1973-74), Am. Heart Assn., Am. Soc. Artificial Internal Organs, Am. Soc. Critical Care Medicine, Am. Surg. Assn. (recorder 1967-71), Birmingham Surg. Soc., Cardiac Soc. Australia and N.Z. (corr.), Deutsche Gesellschaft Fur Chirurgie, Harvard Med. Alumni Assn., Internat. Surg. Group, Jefferson County Med. Soc., Mayo Found. Alumni Assn., Nat. Acad. Scis., N.Y. Acad. Scis., Royal Soc. Medicine (affiliate), Soc. Clin. Surgery, Soc. Critical Care Medicine, Soc. Surg. Chairmen, Soc. Thoracic Surgeons, Soc. Univ. Surgeons, Soc. Vascular Surgery, So. Soc. Clin. Investigation, So. Surg. Assn., Surg. Biology Club, European Soc. Cardiovascular Surgery (hon.), Mexican Soc. Cardiology (hon.), N.Y. Soc. Thoracic Surgery (hon.). Office: U Ala Sch Medicine & Med Ctr Dept Surgery Birmingham AL 35294*

KIRKORIAN, DONALD GEORGE, college official, management consultant; b. San Mateo, Calif., Nov. 30, 1938; s. George and Alice (Sergius) K. BA, San Jose State U., 1961, MA, 1966, postgrad., 1968; postgrad., Stanford U., 1961, U. So. Calif., 1966; PhD, Northwestern U., 1972. Producer Sta. KNTV, San Jose, Calif., 1961; tchr. L.A. City Schs., 1963; instrnl. TV coord. Fremont Union High Sch. Dist., Sunnyvale, Calif., 1963-73; assoc. dean instrn. learning resources Solano C.C., Suisun City, Calif., 1973-85, dean instrnl. services, 1985-89, dean learning resources and staff devel., 1989-99; exec. dir. Learning Resources Assn. of Calif. Cmty. Colls., 1976—; owner, pres. Kirkorian and Assocs., Suisun City; field cons. Nat. Assn. Edn. Broadcasters, 1966-68; adj. faculty San Jose State U., 1968-69, U. Calif., Santa Cruz, 1970-73, U. Calif., Davis, 1973-76; chmn. Bay Area TV Consortium, 1976-77, 86-87; mem. adv. panel Speech Comm. Assn./Am. Theater Assn. tchr. preparation in speech., comm., theater and media, N.Y.C., 1973-77. Author: Staffing Information Handbook, 1990, National Learning Resources Directory, 1991, 93; editor: Media Memo, 1973-80, Intercom: The Newsletter for Calif. Community Coll. Librs., 1974-75, Update, 1980-90, Exploring the Benicia State Recreation Area, 1977, California History Resource Materials, 1977, Time Management, 1980; contbr. articles to profl. jours. Chmn. Solano County Media Adv. Com., 1974-76; bd. dirs. Napa-Solano United Way, 1980-82; mem. adv. bd. Calif. Youth Authority, 1986-93. Mem. Nat. Assn. Ednl. Broadcasters, Assn. for Edn. Comm. and Tech., Broadcast Edn. Assn., Calif. Assn. Ednl. Media and Tech. (treas.), Western Ednl. Soc. for Telecomm. (bd. dirs. 1973-75, pres. 1976-77, State Chancellor's com. on Telecomm. 1982-86), Learning Resources Assn. Calif. Comm. Colls. (sec.-treas., pres.), Assn. Calif. C.C. Adminstrs. (bd. dirs. 1985-91), Cmty. Coll. Instrnl. Network. Home: 1655 Rockville Rd Suisun City CA 94585-1373 Office: PO Box 298 Fairfield CA 94533-0029

KIRKPATRICK, ANDREW BOOTH, JR., lawyer; b. Asheville, N.C., Jan. 16, 1929; s. Andrew Booth and Gertrude Elizabeth (Ingle) K.; m. Frances Gordon Cone, Oct. 9, 1954; children: Christine, Melissa, Charles. B.S. cum laude, Davidson Coll., 1949; LL.B. magna cum laude, Harvard U., 1954. Bar: Del. 1954, Fla. 1955. Law clk. U.S. Ct. Appeals 3d Circuit, 1954-55; assoc. firm Morris, Nichols, Arsht & Tunnell, Wilmington, Del., 1955-58; ptnr. Morris, Nichols, Arsht & Tunnell, 1958-95, of counsel, 1995—; chmn. censor com. Supreme Ct. Del., 1970-78. Trustee, chmn. bd. U. Del.; trustee Unidel Found., Inc.; dir. Wilmington Trust Co.; pres. Young Republicans of New Castle County, 1957-58; chmn. Kennett Pike Assn., Wilmington, 1967-68; chmn. Gov.'s Commn. on Organized Crime, 1972-73; trustee Tatnall Sch., Inc., 1972-82. Served to 1st lt. inf. U.S. Army, 1951-53. Fellow Am. Coll. Trial Lawyers, Am. Bar Found.; mem. ABA, Del. Bar Assn. (pres. 1978-79), Am. Law Inst., Wilmington Club, Wilmington Country Club, Vicmead Hunt Club, Phi Beta Kappa. Presbyterian. Home: 9 Barley Mill Dr Wilmington DE 19807-2217 Office: Morris Nichols Arsht & Tunnell PO Box 1347 Wilmington DE 19899-1347

KIRKPATRICK, ANNE SAUNDERS, systems analyst; b. Birmingham, Mich., July 4, 1938; d. Stanley Rathbun and Esther (Casteel) Saunders; children: Elizabeth, Martha, Robert, Sarah. Student, Wellesley Coll., 1956-57, Laval U., Quebec City, Can., 1958, U. Ariz., 1958-59; BA in Philosophy, U. Mich., 1961. Systems engr. IBM, Chgo., 1962-64; sr. analyst Commonwealth Edison Co., Chgo., 1981-97. Treas. Taproot Reps., DuPage County, Ill., 1977-80; pres. Hinsdale (Ill.) Women's Rep. Club, 1978-81. Club: Wellesley of Chgo. (bd. dirs. 1972-73). Home: 222 E Chestnut St Unit 8B Chicago IL 60611-2376

KIRKPATRICK, CARL KIMMEL, prosecutor; b. Kingsport, Tenn., Aug. 2, 1936; s. Carl Kimmel and Alice (Rowland) K.; m. Barbara G. Kirkpatrick, Aug. 7, 1992; 1 child, Carl Kimmel III. BA, Vanderbilt U., 1959, JD, 1962. Bar: Tenn. 1962, U.S. Dist. Ct. (ea. dist.) Tenn. 1964. Pvt. practice Kingsport, 1962-66; asst. dist. atty. 20th Jud. Dist. Sullivan County, Tenn., 1963-64; dist. atty. gen. 2d Jud. Dist. Tenn., 1966-93; U.S. atty. U.S. Dept. of Justice, Knoxville, Tenn. Recipient Disting. Svc. award Am. Legion, 1979, Community Achievement award Kingsport Times News, 1973, Law Enforcement award Optimist Club, 1973, 79. Mem. Nat. Dist. Attys. Assn. (bd. dirs. 1983-93), Knoxville Bar Assn., Phi Delta Phi. Democrat. Baptist. Avocations: motorcycle riding, sport shooting, gardening. Office: US Attys Office 800 Market St Ste 211 Knoxville TN 37902-2342

KIRKPATRICK, CHARLES HARVEY, physician, immunology researcher; b. Topeka, Nov. 5, 1931; s. Hazen Leon and Clarice Opal (Privott) K.; m. Janice Faye Fosha, July 11, 1959; children: Heather, Michael, Brian. BA, U. Kans., 1954; MD, U. Kans., Kansas City, 1958. Diplomate Am. Bd. Internal Medicine, Am. Bd. Allergy and Immunology. Asst. prof. U. Kans., Kansas City, 1965-68, assoc. prof., 1967; sr. investigator Nat. Inst. Allergy and Infectious Diseases, NIH, Bethesda, Md., 1968-79; dir. allergy and clin. immunology Nat. Jewish Ctr., Denver, 1979-93; prof. U. Colo., Denver, 1979—; dir. rsch. Innovative Therapeutics, Inc., 1993-96; pres. Cytokine Sci., Inc., Denver, 1996-99; active NIH study sects., Bethesda. Editor: 4 books; contbr. numerous articles to profl. jours. NIH research grantee, 1981-86. Fellow ACP, Am. Acad. Allergy and Immunology, Molecular Med. Soc.; mem. Am. Soc. Clin. Investigation, Am. Assn. Immunologists. Episcopalian. Avocations: enology, antique corkscrews, antique automobiles. Home: 295 Leyden St Denver CO 80220-5951 Office: Cytokine Scis Inc 1899 Gaylord St Denver CO 80206-1210

KIRKPATRICK, CLAYTON, former newspaper executive; b. Waterman, Ill., Jan. 8, 1915; s. Clayton Matteson and Mable Rose (Swift) K.; m. Thelma Marie De Mott, Feb. 13, 1943 (dec. Dec. 1998); children: Pamela Marie Kirkpatrick Foy, Bruce, Eileen Bea Kirkpatrick Vaughan, James Walter. AB, U. Ill., 1937. Reporter City News Bur., Chgo., 1938; mem. staff Chgo. Tribune, 1938—, day city editor, 1958-61, city editor, 1961-63, asst. mng. editor, 1963-65, mng. editor, 1965-67, exec. editor, 1967-69, editor, 1969-79; v.p. Chgo. Tribune Co., 1967-77, exec. v.p., 1977-79, pres., 1979-81, chmn., 1981; ret., 1981. U.S. del. 19th Gen. Conf., UNESCO, Nairobi, 1976; life trustee Rush-Presbyn.-St. Luke's Med. Ctr.; trustee Robert R. McCormick Trusts, 1976-90. With USAAF, 1942-45. Decorated Bronze Star medal; recipient Elijah Parish Lovejoy award Colby Coll., 1978; William Allen White award U. Kans., 1977; Fourth Estate award Nat. Press Club, 1979. Mem. Chgo. Club, Tavern Club, Comml. Club, Glen Oak Country Club, Phi Beta Kappa, Sigma Delta Chi. Republican. Methodist. Home: 471 Stagecoach Run Glen Ellyn IL 60137-3740

KIRKPATRICK, DAVID WARREN, educational researcher, writer; b. Bennington, Vt., Apr. 19, 1929; s. David Warren and Minerva Kirkpatrick. BS in Edn., North Adams (Mass.) State Coll, 1959; MA in History, Lehigh U., 1964. Cert. social studies tchr., Mass., Pa. High sch. history tchr. Easton (Pa.) Area Sch. Dist., 1961-71; pres. Pa. State Edn. Assn., Harrisburg, 1969-71; comms. dir. Pa. Gov., Harrisburg, 1971-73; cons., sr. staff mem. Pa. Senate Edn. Commn., Harrisburg, 1973-77; sr. staff mem. Pa. Senate and Rural Affairs Commn., 1977-80; exec. dir. Assn. Pa. State Colls. and Univs., Harrisburg, 1980-85; comms. dir. Pa. Auditor Gen., Harrisburg, 1985-86; exec. dir. Pa. Assn. Rural and Small Schs., Harrisburg, 1987-91, The Reach Alliance, Harrisburg, 1992-95; ednl. rschr., writer, cons. Harrisburg, 1995—; bd. dirs. Pa. Sch. Employees Retirement System, Harrisburg, 1971-73; founder Pa. Rural Coalition, Harrisburg, 1980—, bd. dirs., 1980-87, chmn., 1980-82; mem. consumer adv. coun. Pa. Pub. Utlity Commn., 1983-87, chmn., 1985-87; sr. fellow Allegheny Inst., Pitts., 1998—. Author: Choice in Schooling, 1990, School Choice: The Idea That Will Not Die,

1997; columnist; contbr. articles to profl. jours. and newsletters. Pub. rels. chair Vote Yes for Water, Harrisburg, 1981; participant in numerous polit. campaigns. Named Alumnus of Yr., North Adams State Coll., 1971; Disting. fellow The Blum Ctr., Marquette U., 1995—; Wm. Robertson Coe fellow Stanford U., 1965; Grad. scholar Lehigh U., 1959-61. Fellow Pub. Svc. Rsch. F/TN. Avocations: reading, travel, music collection. Home: 2323 Rudy Rd Harrisburg PA 17104-2025

KIRKPATRICK, DOROTHY ANN, early childhood education educator, former nurse; b. Columbus, Ga., Aug. 10, 1934; d. Marcellus McCluster and Tommie (Williams) Ballard; m. Garland Penn Kirkpatrick, Jan. 31, 1958; children: Garland Penn, Dawn Annette. RN Diploma, Mercy Sch. of Nursing, 1955; BA, DePaul U., 1980; MEd, Loyola U., 1983. RN, Mich. Pediatric nurse Michael Reese Hosp., Chgo., 1955-57; head nurse U. Ill. Rsch. and Edn. Hosp., Chgo., 1957-59; nurse educator Northwestern Meml. Hosp., Chgo., 1982-84; childcare specialist Ann Arbor (Mich.) Pub. Schs., 1989-92, cons., 1992—; infant/toddler specialist, early childhood educator Ctr. for Devel. and Learning Problems, Ann Arbor, 1992—; pvt. practice as infant/toddler specialist, nurse educator for children with learning disabilities, 1995—; cons. Chgo. City-Wide Coll., 1985-88, Nat. Assn. Edn. Young Children, Chgo. and Ann Arbor, 1985—; mem. adv. bd. Early Childhood Dirs. Assn., Ann Arbor, 1989—; mem. Early On Infant/Toddler State Referral Sys., 1994; co-chair U. Mich. Turner African Am. Svc. Coun., 1994. Contbr. articles to profl. jours. Vol. Am. Cancer Soc., Chgo., 1965-70, Human Rights Commn., Ann Arbor, 1990-93, Ind. Voters League, Chgo., 1970-87, Family Support and Tutoring Programs, Chgo., 1970-88; supporter Children's Def. Fund; mem. New Hope Bapt. Ch., Ann Arbor. Recipient Disting. Svc. award Rockwell Gardens Headstart Tchrs., 1988. Fellow Nat. Ctr. for Clin. Infant Programs, Zero to Three; mem. Chgo. Assn. Edn. Young Children, Washtenaw Assn. Edn. Young Children, Nat. Black Child Devel. Inst. Avocations: antique collecting, hobby farm, fishing.

KIRKPATRICK, EDWARD SCOTT, physicist; b. Wilmington, Del., Dec. 12, 1941; s. Edward Crane and Mary McChesney (Scott) K.; m. Daphna Weinshall, 1994; 1 chld, Yael K. AB in Physics, Princeton U., 1963; PhD, Harvard U., 1969. Postdoctoral fellow James Franck Inst., U. Chgo., 1969-71; mem. rsch. staff IBM Rsch., Yorktown Heights, N.Y., 1971—, mgr. theoretical physics, 1977-79, mgr. low temperature physics, 1979-81, mgr. VLSI design, 1981-84, mgr. advanced work stations, 1986-93, sr. mgr. multimedia architecture lab., 1995—; mgr. system design IBM Communication Group, White Plains, N.Y., 1984-86; vis. prof. SUNY, Stonybrook, 1976, U. Paris, 1978, 98, Hebrew U., Jerusalem, 1993; mem. IBM Acad. Tech., 1992—, tech. coun., 1994-96. Contbr. articles on percolation theory, spin glasses, simulated annealing for optimization and complexity to jours. in field. Fellow IEEE, AAAS, Am. Phys. Soc. (Applications of Physics prize 1986); mem. Westchester Flying Club (Purchase, N.Y., engring. officer). Avocations: flying, camping. Office: IBM Rsch Ctr Rt 134 Yorktown Heights NY 10598*

KIRKPATRICK, EDWARD THOMSON, college administrator, mechanical engineer; b. Cranbrook, B.C., Can., Jan. 15, 1925; came to U.S., 1954, naturalized, 1981; s. John Thomson and Mary Pauline (Jones) K.; m. Barbara Jane Kelsberg, May 22, 1948; children—Allan, Karen, Ann, Keith. B.A. in Sci., U. B.C., 1947; M.S., Carnegie Inst. Tech., 1956, Ph.D., 1958. Registered profl. engr., N.Y., Ohio. Sales engr., mgr. F.D. Bolton, Ltd., Vancouver, B.C., 1948-54; asst. prof. Carnegie Inst. Tech., Pitts., 1954-58; dept. head U. Toledo, 1958-63; engring. dean Rochester Inst. Tech., N.Y., 1963-71; pres. Wentworth Inst. Tech., Boston, 1971-90. Author: 1620 Fortran II-D Program, 1963. Contbr. articles to profl. publs. Recipient Outstanding Civilian Service medal U.S. Army, 1971. Fellow Am. Soc. Engring. Edn. (bd. dirs. 1982-86); mem. ASME, Nat. Soc. Profl. Engrs. Republican. Episcopalian. Avocations: homebuilt aircraft, flying, foreign travel. Home: 40 Radcliffe Rd Weston MA 02493-1024 Office: Wentworth Inst Tech Office of Pres 550 Huntington Ave Boston MA 02115-5998

KIRKPATRICK, FRANCIS H(UBBARD), JR., biophysicist, intellectual property practitioner, consultant; b. Laurel Hill, N.C., Nov. 7, 1943; s. Francis Hubbard and Jean Orr (Murray) K.; m. Cornelia Ewart Goodreds, Aug. 30, 1969; 1 child, Adam Bane. BA in Physics, Harvard Coll., 1964; PhD in Biophysics, Stanford U., 1970. Registered U.S. patent agent, 1992. Postdoctoral intern Biophysics Program, Wash. State U., Pullman, 1969-71; postdoctoral fellow dept. radiation biology and biophysics U. Rochester (N.Y.) Sch. Medicine, 1972-74, asst. prof. dept. radiation biology and biophysics, 1974-80; lab. mgr. Pall Corp., Glen Cove, N.Y., 1980-82, mgr. biotech. rsch., 1982-84; tech. dir. FMC BioProducts, Rockland, Maine, 1984-93; dir. intellectual property Focal, Inc., Lexington, Mass., 1993—; mem. Genetics Small Bus. Innovative Rsch. Spl. Study Sect., 1988—; cons., lectr. in field. Contbr. articles to sci. jours.; patentee in field. Pres. South-East Area Coalition, Rochester, 1977. Recipient Rsch. Career Devel. award NIH, 1975-80; competitive fellow NIH, 1967, 72; grantee NIH, 1974-80, U.S. Dept. Energy, 1975-80. Mem. Biophys. Soc., Optical Soc. Am., Am. Chem. Soc., Am. Soc. Biochemistry and Molecular Biology, Patent and Trademark Office Soc. Avocations: gardening, real estate development. Home: 37 Clover Hill Dr Chelmsford MA 01824-2611 Office: Focal Inc 4 Maguire Rd Lexington MA 02421-3105*

KIRKPATRICK, FRANK GLOYD, minister, religion educator; b. Washington, Aug. 4, 1942; s. George Gloyd and Amy Mary (Cook) K.; m. Elizabeth Alden Murray, June 11, 1966; children: Amy, Daniel. BA, Trinity Coll., 1964; MA, Columbia U., Union Theol. Sem., N.Y.C., 1966; PhD, Brown U., 1970. Ordained to ministry Episcopal Ch., 1973. Prof. religion Trinity Coll., Hartford, Conn., 1969—; parish assoc. Trinity Ch., Hartford, 1973-79; chair Peace and Justice Commn., Diocese of Conn., 1980-82, examining chaplains com. Common Ministry, 1982-88, Commn. on Ministry, 1988-91; bd. dirs. Episcopal Ch., Yale U., New Haven, 1985-87. Author: Community, 1986; co-author: Living Issues in Ethics, 1982; contbr. articles to profl. jours. mem. Conn. Freeze Campaign, Hartford, 1980—. Mem. Am. Acad. Religion (pres. New Eng. chpt. 1990-91), Christian Conf. Conn., Episcopal Peace Fellowship. Democrat. Home: 154 Clearfield Rd Wethersfield CT 06109-3219 Office: Trinity Coll 300 Summit St Hartford CT 06106-3100

KIRKPATRICK, GARLAND PENN, pediatrician; b. Chgo., Aug. 23, 1932; s. Merrill Stanley and Nellie Florene (Douglas) K; m. Dorothy Ann McCluster, Jan. 31, 1958; children: Garland Penn, Dawn Annette. Ab, Talladega (Ala.) Coll., 1954; BS, U. Ill., Chgo., 1956, MD, 1958. Diplomate Am. Bd. Pediatrics. Fellow in devel. and behavioral pediatrics U. N.C., Chapel Hill; clin. instr. pediatrics U. Ill. Coll. Medicine, Chgo., 1959-64; pvt. practice pediatrics Kirkpatrick & Germain, Chgo., 1963-89; clin. asst. prof. pediatrics U. Chgo., 1983; clin. assoc. prof. pediatrics Northwestern Med. Sch., Chgo., 1985; clin. asst. prof. pediatrics U. Mich. Sch. Medicine, Ann Arbor, 1995, asst. clin. prof. pediatrics, 1996—; chmn. dept. pediatrics USAF Hosp., Richards Gebour AFB, 1961-63; cons. Chgo. Bd. Edn., 1983-84; spkr. in field. Contbr. articles to profl. jours. Fellow Am. Acad. Pediatrics (exec. com. Ill. chpt. 1984); mem. AMA, Nat. Med. Assn., Soc. for Behavioral and Devel. Pediatrics. Baptist. Avocations: chess, gardening, reading, music: classical, jazz and gospel. Home: 1365 Folkstone Ct Ann Arbor MI 48105-2845 Office: U Mich Panahi & Assocs 4870 W Clark Rd Ypsilanti MI 48197-1104

KIRKPATRICK, JAYNE F., director public affairs. BA in English, Elon Coll., 1975; MA in English Lit., Duke U., 1978; student, U. N.C. Dir. pub. affairs Pub. Transit Assn., Washington, 1982—. Mem. N.C. Govt. Info. Offices, Raleigh Pub. Rels. Soc. Office: Raleigh Municipal Bldg Public Affairs Office Rm 506 Raleigh NC 27602*

KIRKPATRICK, JEANE DUANE JORDAN, political scientist, government official; b. Duncan, Okla., Nov. 19, 1926; d. Welcher F. and Leona (Kile) Jordan; m. Evron M. Kirkpatrick, Feb. 20, 1955; children: Douglas Jordan, John Evron, Stuart Alan. AA, Stephens Coll., 1946; AB, Barnard Coll., 1948; MA, Columbia U., 1950, PhD, 1968; postgrad. (French govt. fellow), Inst. Polit. Sci., U. Paris, 1952-53; LHD (hon.), Georgetown U., 1981, U. Pitts., 1981, U. Charleston, 1982, Hebrew U., 1982, Colo. Sch. Mines, 1983, St. John's U., 1983, Universidad Francisco Marroquin, Guatemala, 1985, Coll. of William and Mary, 1986, U. Mich., 1988, Syracuse U., 1994; hon. degree, Loyola U., Chgo., 1996. Asst. prof. polit. sci. Trinity Coll., 1962-67; assoc. prof. polit. sci. Georgetown U., Washington, 1967-73, prof., 1973—, Leavey prof., 1978—; sr. fellow Am. Enterprise Inst. for Pub. Policy Rsch., 1977—; mem. cabinet U.S. permanent rep. to UN, 1981-85. Author: Elections USA, 1956, Perspectives, 1962, The Strategy of Deception: A Study in World-Wide Communist Tactics, 1963, Mass Behavior in Battle and Captivity, 1968, Leader and Vanguard in Mass Society; The Peronist Movement in Argentina, 1971, Political Woman, 1974, The New Presidential Elite, 1976, Dismantling the Parties: Reflections on Party Reform and Party Decomposition, 1978, The Reagan Phenomenon, 1983, Dictatorships and Double Standards, 1982, Legitimacy and Force (2 vols.), 1988, The Withering Away of the Totalitarian State, 1990; syndicated columnist, 1985-97; contbr. articles to profl. jours.; editor, contbr. various pubs. Trustee Helen Dwight Reid Ednl. Found., 1972—, pres., 1990—. Recipient Disting. Alumna award Stephens Coll., 1978, B'nai B'rith Humanitarian award, 1982, Award of the Commonwealth Fund, 1983, Gold medal VFW, 1984, French Prix Politique, 1984, Dept. Def. Disting. Pub. Svc. medal, 1985, Bronze Palm, 1992, Disting. Svc. medal Mayor of N.Y.C., 1985, Presdl. Medal of Freedom, 1985, Jamestown Freedom award, 1990, Centennial medal Nat. Soc. DAR, 1991, Disting. Svc. award USO, 1994, Laureate of the Lincoln Acad. of Ill., Medallion of Lincoln, 1996, Jerusalem 3000 award, 1996. Mem. Internat. Polit. Sci. Assn. (exec. coun.), Am. Polit. Sci. Assn. (Hubert Humphrey award 1988), So. Polit. Sci. Assn. Office: Am Enterprise Inst 1150 17th St NW Washington DC 20036-4603 *My experience demonstrates to my satisfaction that it is both possible and feasible for women in our times to successfully combine traditional and professional roles, that it is not necessary to ape men's career patterns,— -starting early and keeping one's nose to a particular grindstone, but that, instead, one can do quite different things at different stages of one's life. All that is required is a little luck and a lot of work.*

KIRKPATRICK, JOHN ALGER, organic chemist, food scientist; b. Drexell Hills, Pa., May 2, 1930; s. John Bolan and Gertrude Laura (Alger) K.; m. Helen M. Thompson, Sept. 10, 1961 (dec. Aug. 1966); m. Lois Arlene Fekelman, Feb. 15, 1969; 1 child (dec.). BS in Biochemistry, Pa. State U., 1959; MS in Food Sci., Rutgers U., 1995. Rsch. chemist in lipids and flavors Campbell Soup Co., Camden, N.J., 1960-90; food scientist Du Pont/Con Agra Ventures, Wilmington, Del., 1991-93; environ. chemist Pa. Dept. Envrion. Protection S.E. Regional Field Office/Solid Waste Mgmt., Conshohocken, 1993—. With U.S. Army, 1952-53, ETO. Mem. Inst. Food Technologists (profl.), Am. Chem. Soc., Soc. Mayflower Descendents of Pa. Lutheran. Avocations: camping, square and round dancing, travel. Office: Pa Dept Environ Protection Southeast Regional Field Of 555 E North Ln Ste 6010 Conshohocken PA 19428-2233

KIRKPATRICK, JOHN ELSON, oil company executive, retired naval reserve officer; b. Oklahoma City, Feb. 13, 1908; s. Elmer Elsworth and Claudia (Spencer) K.; m. Eleanor Blake, June 20, 1932; 1 child, Joan Elson. Student, U.S. Mil. Acad., 1925-26; BS, U.S. Naval Acad., 1931; postgrad., Harvard U. Grad. Sch. Bus. Adminstrn., 1935-36; LLD, Oklahoma City U., 1963; HHD, Bethany Nazarene Coll., 1967. Founder, v.p., treas. Allied Steel Products Corp., Tulsa, 1936-41; v.p., treas. Kirkpatrick & Bale Oil Co., Oklahoma City, 1945-50; ptnr. Kirkpatrick Oil Co., Oklahoma City, 1950-95; emeritus dir., Bank One, Okla. Hon. chmn. Kirkpatrick Found.; hon. consul Republic of Korea, 1974—; life trustee Okla. Zool. Soc.; mem. life bd., donor bldg. Oklahoma City Art Mus.; mem. Okla. Heritage Assn., Allied Arts Found.; hon. dir. Okla. State Fair; former mem. sr. adv. bd. Frontiers of Sci. Found.; hon. chmn. bd. dirs.; past pres. Presbyn. Homes; founder, bd. dirs. Oklahoma City Cmty. Found.; former mem. Bus. Com. for Arts, Inc.; hon. chmn. Lyric Theatre Okla.; hon. life trustee, dir. emeritus Nat. Cowboy Hall of Fame and Western Heritage Ctr.; trustee Falcon Found.; donor Kirkpatrick Auditorium at Oklahoma City U., 1965; dir. Kirkpatrick Sci. and Air Space Mus. at Omniplex; mem. adv. bd. Okla. Health Scis. Ctr.; hon. trustee Tulsa Cmty. Found. Decorated Bronze Star with V; recipient Disting. Svc. award Okla. U., 1959, Sweet Success vol. award, 1998, Nat. Brotherhood citation NCCJ, 1962, AIA award, 1963, Outstanding Okla. Oil Man award Okla. Petroleum Coun., 1974, Merit award Okla. Hosp. Assn., 1974, Esquire/Bus. Com. for the Arts award, 1974, 75, Evergreen Disting. Svc. award for Pub. Service, 1982, Okla. Charitable Achiever awards cert. of recognition Pearl M. & Julia J. Harmon Found., 1988, Patrick Henry medal Mil. Order of World Wars Okla. City chpt., 1989, Ptnrs. award World Neighbors, 1991, Henry G. Bennett Distng. Svc. award Okla. State U., 1992, Achievement award Okla. City Fedn. of Colored Womens Clubs, 1992; named to Okla. Hall of Fame, 1962, Okla. Commerce and Industry Hall of Fame, 1985, Wall of Fame Okla. City Pub. Sch. Found., 1990, Humanitarian award Nat. Arthritis Found. Okla. Chpt., 1993; named Outstanding Philanthropist, Okla. chapter Nat. Soc. Fund Raising Execs., 1986, Arts Advocate of Yr., SW Theatre Assn. Performing Arts for Children Divsn., 1993, Disting. Philanthropy award Am. Assn. Mus., 1995, Disting. Friends award Okla. City U., 1997; donor Kirkpatrick Ctr. bldg. Okla. Ctr. Sci. and Arts, 1978; dedicated in his name John E. Kirkpatrick Horticulture Ctr. at Okla. State U. Tech. br., 1990; recognized by Profl. Photographers of Am. Inc. for meritorious contributions to profl. photography Nat. award; recipient John E. Kirkpatrick Humanitarian Oklahoma City Rotary, 1994; honored by Kappa Sigma; inductee The Okla. Mil. Hall of Fame, 1999. Mem. Ind. Petroleum Assn. (past dir.), Oklahoma City C.of C. (life dir.), Okla. Hist. Soc. (dir. emeritus), Okla. County Hist. Soc. (Cardinal Svc. award 1989), Harvard Area Group, Asia Soc. Okla. (Civic Leader award 1991), 45th Inf. Divsn. Mus. (hon. life, bd. dirs.), Assn. Grads. USAF Acad. (hon.). Clubs: Economic, Men's Dinner, Rotary, Oklahoma City Petroleum (pres. 1959-60). Home: PO Box 268822 Oklahoma City OK 73126-8822 Office: Kirkpatrick Oil Co PO Box 268822 Oklahoma City OK 73126-8822

KIRKPATRICK, JOHN GILDERSLEEVE, lawyer; b. Toronto, Ont., Can., Jan. 28, 1917; s. Herbert Rutherfoord and Edna (Nelles) K.; m. Irena Groten, June 24, 1944; children—Xenia, Kathleen, Patricia. B.Sc., McGill U., 1939, B.C.L., 1942. Bar: Que. 1943, created Queen's Counsel 1961. Counsel, formerly ptnr. Ogilvy, Renault (and predecessors), Montreal, 1943—. Anglican. Home: 4444 Sherbrooke St W, Apt 507, Montreal, PQ Canada H3Z 1E4 Office: 1981 McGill College Ave, Suite 1100, Montreal, PQ Canada H3A 3C1

KIRKPATRICK, RICHARD ALAN, internist; b. Rochester, Minn., Jan. 17, 1947; s. Neal R. and Ethel C. (Hull) K.; m. Susan Baxter; children: James N., Ronald S., David B., Mary J., Scott B., Christina Marie. BA in Chemistry with honors, U. Wash., 1968, BS in Psychology, 1968, MD, 1972. Diplomate Am. Bd. Internal Medicine. Intern, resident in internal medicine Mayo Grad. Sch., Rochester, 1972-76, spl. resident in biomed. communications, 1974-75; pvt. practice specializing in internal medicine Longview, Wash., 1976—; founding ptnr. Internal Medicine Clinic of Longview, 1977, Kirkpatrick Family Care, Longview, 1996; mem. clin. faculty U. Wash.; dir. cardiac rehab. program St. John's Hosp.; sec. The Physicians Alliance. Editor: Drug Therapy Abstracts, Wash. Internists; mem. editorial adv. bd. Your Patient and Cancer, Primary Care and Cancer; weekly med. TV talk show host, 1978—; contbr. articles to med. jours. Bd. dirs., v.p. Columbia Theatre for Performing Arts; mem. City Coun., Longview; mem. S.W. Wash. Symphony; bd. dirs. S.W. Wash. Youth Symphony; pres., bd. dirs. Sta. KLTV. Named to Hall of Fame, Lower Columbia Coll., 1996. Fellow ACP (gov.'s coun., sec. Washington chpt.); mem. Wash. State Soc. Internal Medicine (trustee, past pres.), Am. Geriatrics Soc., Am. Soc. Echocardiography, Am. Soc. Internal Medicine, Wash. Med. Assn. (mem. com.), Am. Cancer Soc. (local bd. dirs.), Am. Soc. Clin. Oncology, AMA, Am. Med. Writers Assn. Office: Washington Way at Civic Ctr Longview WA 98632

KIRKPATRICK, ROBERT HUGH, communications executive; b. Kingston, N.Y., Mar. 3, 1954; s. Oscar Hugh and Ann (Page) K.; m. Debra Cook, Oct. 25, 1986; 1 child, Page. BA in Polit. Sci. with high honors, SUNY, Oneonta, 1977; M in Pub. and Pvt. Mgmt., Yale U., 1979. Cert. pvt. pilot. Policy analyst edn. com. N.Y. State Assembly, 1977; mgr. mktg. Cummins Engine Co., Columbus, Ind., 1980-81, mgr. mktg. ops., 1982-83, dir. electronics mktg., 1984-86, dir. bus. devel. Svc. Products Co. subs., 1987-89; pres. Intelesis Inc., Columbus, 1989-97, CEO, 1996-97; pres. transp. and power divsn. AFFINA Corp., Columbus, 1998—; cons. in field, New Haven, 1978-79. Contbr. articles to bus. jours. Trustee SUNY, Albany, 1975-76; pres. Student Assn. of State Univ., Inc., 1975-76, v.p. 1974-75; pres. Columbus Arts Guild, 1981-82; treas. San Souci, Inc., Columbus, 1983-85; mem. allocations com. United Way, 1990-92; mem. City Transp. Commn., Oneonta, N.Y., 1973-74; bd. dirs. Leadership Bartholomew County Alumni Assn., 1991-92; bd. dirs. Young Mothers' Ednl. Devel., Inc., 1994-96; adminstrv. bd. First United Meth. Ch., 1994-96, trustee 1997-99; exec. com. ABC-Stewart Montessori Sch., 1996—, sec. 1997. Mem. Assn. Telemessaging Svcs. Internat. (bd. dirs. 1993-95, v.p., sec. 1994-95), CADCOM Egt. Owners Assn. (bd. dirs. 1994-96, v.p. 95-96), Yale Club Ind. (treas. 1981-85), Ind. Vocat. Tech. Coll. Found. (Columbus bd. dirs. 1991-93), Rotary (bd. dirs. 1994—, pres. 1996-97, treas. 1997-99). Methodist. Home: 3973 W Wood Lake Ln Columbus IN 47201-8235 Office: AFFINA Corp PO Box 622 Columbus IN 47202-0622

KIRKPATRICK, R(OBERT) JAMES, geology educator; b. Schenectady, N.Y., Dec. 31, 1946; s. Robert James and Audrey (Rech) K.; m. Susan A. Wilson, Sept. 4, 1968 (div. 1984); children: Gregory Robert, Geoffrey Stephen; m. Carol A. Hanna, Sept. 3, 1985. AB, Cornell U., 1968; PhD, U. Ill., 1972. Asst. U.S. Geol. Survey, Denver, 1968; rsch. and teaching asst. U. Ill., Urbana, 1968-72, asst. prof. dept. geology, 1978-80, assoc. prof., 1980-83, prof., 1983-88, prof., head dept., 1988-97, exec. assoc. dean Coll. Liberal Arts & Scis., 1997—; sr. rsch. geologist prodn. rsch. div. Exxon, Houston, 1972-73; rsch. fellow in geophysics Harvard U., Cambridge, 1973-75; asst. rsch. geologist Scripps Instn. Oceanography, La Jolla, Calif., 1976-78; mem. ocean crust panel Joint Oceanographic Instns. for Deep Earth Studies, 1977-78, active margin panel, 1978, downhole measurements panel, 1977-78; cons. various corps. Editor: Initial Reports of the Deep Sea Drilling Project, Vols. 46 and 55, 1979, 80; co-editor: Kinetics of Geochemical Processes, 1981; assoc. editor American Mineralogist, 1987-90; contbr. over 160 articles to profl. jours. Overseas fellow Churchill Coll., Eng., 1985-86; rsch. grantee NSF, 1977—, various other orgns., 1978—. Fellow Geol. Soc. Am., Mineral. Soc. Am. (councillor 1990-93); mem. Am. Geophys. Union (VGP award com. 1985-88, chmn. 1986-88), Am. Cer. Soc., Internat. Mineral. Assn. (alt. U.S. del. 1982, coord. com. 1986 meeting, chmn. program com. 1986, U.S. rep. Commn. on Crystal Growth, v.p. 1986-90, sec. Commn. on Mineral Physics 1986-91). Office: U Ill Dept Geology Urbana IL 61801

KIRKPATRICK, WILLIS F., state banking and securities administrator; b. Caldwell, Idaho; m. Phyllis Galloway; 3 children. Grad., Coll. Idaho, 1957; postgrad., U. Oreg., 1957-59. Dist. mgr. Chrysler Corp., Dodge Divsn., Spokane, Wash.; staff Walston & Co. Investment Brokers, Spokane, Wash.; examiner State of Alaska Divsn. Banking, Securities and Corps., Juneau, 1969-73, dir., 1973, 81—; mgr. Juneau offices Alaska Fed. Savings and Loan, 1974-81; apptd. acting commr. dept. commerce and econ. devel., State of Alaska, during 3 gov. transitions, 1981—. Past pres. Juneau Children's Receiving Home, Southeast Alaska Coun. Boy Scouts Am. Mem. Juneau Downtown Rotary Club (pres. 1978-79, cmty. svc. chmn. Alaska-Whitehorse dist.). Office: State of Alaska Dept Commerce Divsn Banking PO Box 110807 Juneau AK 99811-0807

KIRKSEY, AVANELLE, nutrition educator; b. Mulberry, Ark., Mar. 23, 1926. BS, U. Ark., Fayetteville, 1947; MS, U. Tenn., Knoxville, 1950; PhD, Pa. State U., 1961; postdoctoral, U. Calif., Davis, 1976; DSc honoris causa, Purdue U., 1997. Assoc. prof. Ark. Polytechnic U., Russellville, 1950-55; research asst. Pa. State U., University Park, 1956-58, fellow Gen. Foods, 1958-60; assoc. prof. Purdue U., West Lafayette, Ind., 1961-69, prof. nutrition, 1970-85; disting. prof. Purdue U., West Lafayette, 1985-96, disting. prof. emeritus, 1997; prin. investigator nutrition project in rural Egypt; coord. nutrition program Indonesian Univs., 1987-91. Contbr. articles to profl. jours. Recipient Borden award Am. Home Econs. Assn., 1980. Fellow Am. Inst. Nutrition (Lederle award 1994); mem. N.Y. Acad. Scis., Phi Kappa Phi, Sigma Xi. Office: Purdue U Dept Food Nutrition West Lafayette IN 47907 Home: 4900 Park Ave Ste 306 Fort Smith AR 72903-1402

KIRKWOOD, DAVID HERBERT WADDINGTON, Canadian government official; b. Toronto, Ont., Can., Aug. 8, 1924; s. William Alexander and Mossie May (Waddington) K.; m. Diana Thistle Gill, June 6, 1953; children: Peter, Gill, Melissa, John. B.A., U. Toronto, 1945, M.A., 1950. Research physicist Can. Atomic Energy Program, Chalk River, Ont., Canada, 1945-48; fgn. service officer Can. Dept. External Affairs, Ottawa, Ont., 1950-69; asst. sec. to cabinet Privy Council Office, Ottawa, 1969-72; asst. dep. minister Dept. Nat. Def., Ottawa, 1972-75; sr. asst. dep. minister Dept. Transport, Ottawa, 1975-78; chmn. Anti Dumping Tribunal, Ottawa, 1978-80; dep. minister Services Dept. Supply and Services, Ottawa, 1980-83; dep. minister Can. Dept. Nat. Health and Welfare, Ottawa, 1983-86; pres. Can. Mediterranean Inst., Ottawa, 1986-90; apptd. chmn. environ. assessment panel on air transp. devel. in So. Ontario, 1990-94; chmn. environ. assessment panel on decommissioning of Elliot Lake Uranium Mines, 1993-96. Bd. dirs. Can. Med. Inst., 1986-96, Royal Can. Geog. Soc., 1987-97, Hospice of All Sts., 1987-97. Home: Apt 1B, 260 Metcalfe St, Ottawa, ON Canada K2P 1R6

KIRKWOOD, JAMES MACE, pharmaceutical benefit management company executive; b. Chgo., Sept. 19, 1942; s. Robert Charles and Helen Maxine (Butler) K.; m. Anne Naylor, June 21, 1965 (div. Oct. 1972); m. Nancy Lynne Slessman, Oct. 4, 1986; children, Jocelyn Anne, Colin James. BS in Pharmacy, U. Pitts., 1965; D in Pharmacy (hon.), U. Pitts., 1981. Lic. pharmacist Pa., Md., Del., Va., N.J., W.Va., Maine, Ohio, Nev.; cert. analyst Walter V. Clarke Activity Vector Analysis. Pharmacy, store mgr. Sun Drug Co., Greensburg, Pa., 1966-72; owner Profl. Bldg. Pharmacy, Greensburg, 1972-74; pharmacy area supr. Keystone Stores, Lebanon, Pa., 1974-76; dir. profl. placement Rite Aid, Balt., 1976-80; pharmacy dist. mgr. Grand Union Corp., Elwood Park, N.J., 1980-81; dir. pharmacy ops. White Shield Stores, Camp Hill, Pa., 1981-85; mgr. loss prevention White Shield Stores, Camp Hill, 1981-85; from pharmacy supr. to corp. supr. 3d party ops. Rite Aid, N.J., Pa., 1985-89; dir. profl. pers. Rite Aid Corp., Harrisburg, Pa., 1989-93; mgr. bus. re-engring. Rite Aid Corp., Harrisburg, 1993-94; mgr. Strategic Bus. Solutions, 1994-95; v.p. profl. svcs. MediClaim Inc., Lemoyne, Pa., 1995—; adj. instr. U. Pitts. Sch. Pharmacy, 1989—; founder, v.p. Ednl. Horizons, Hershey, Pa., 1995—; cons. Rivercrest Ctr., Mont Clar, Pa., 1982—, Hanover Surgicenter, 1991—, ASA Cons., Lemoyne, Pa., 1995—, Managed Care Rx, Camp Hill, 1996. Recipient U. Pitts. Sch. Pharmacy Disting. Alumni award, 1994, named Vol. of Yr., 1995. Mem. Am. Soc. Cons. Pharmacists, Ctrl. Pa. Pitts. Club (pres. 1990-92), U. Pa. Alumni Assn. (mem. strategic planning com., bd. dirs.), Pitts. Band Alumni Assn. (pres. 1992-93), U. Pitts. Alumni Coun., Pa. Pharmacy Assn., U. Pitts. 1787 Soc., N.Y. Skyliners, Reading Buccaneer Alumni Assn., Capitol Area Pharmacy Assn., Lions, Rotary, Westshoremen Alumni Assn., U. Club of Pitts., Brandermill Country Club. Republican. Lutheran. Avocations: scuba, music, theater, reading. Home: 394 Rising Sun Ln Millersburg PA 17061-1456 Office: Medi-Claim Inc 20 Erford Rd Lemoyne PA 17043-1163

KIRKWOOD, JOHN ROBERT, neuroradiologist; b. Albany, N.Y., Mar. 19, 1941; s. John Kinloch and Rita Arline (Schwick) K.; m. Norma Starr Miller, June 17, 1967 (dec. Mar. 1973); 1 child, Timothy; m. Gale Arcuni Duncan, Aug. 3, 1974; children: James Duncan, Christopher, Allison. BA in Psychology magna cum laude, Yale U., 1963, MD, 1967. Diplomate Am. Bd. Med. Examiners; diplomate in diagnostic radiology and neuroradiology Am. Bd. Radiology. Intern Children's Hosp. Med. Ctr., Boston, 1967-68; resident in diagnostic radiology U. Calif. Med. Ctr., San Francisco, 1968-71; fellow, instr. neuroradiology Brigham Hosp., Boston, 1971-72; chief neuroradiology Walter Reed Army Med. Ctr., Washington, 1972-73; asst. prof. radiology George Washington U. Hosp., Washington, 1973-74; from asst. prof. to assoc. prof. radiology Tufts U. Sch. Medicine, Boston, 1974—; vice chmn. dept. radiology, Baystate Med. Ctr., Springfield, Mass., 1987-95; pres. Radiology and Imaging, Inc., Springfield, 1995-97; chmn. dept. radiology Baystate Med. Ctr., Springfield, 1997—. Author: Essentials of Neuroimaging 1990, 2d edit., 1995; contbr. rsch. articles to profl. jours. Major U.S. Army, 1972-73. Fellow Am. Coll. Radiology; mem. AMA, Am. Soc. Neuroradiology, Mass. Radiology Soc. (sec. 1995, v.p. 1998, pres.-elect 1999). Avocations: sailing, skiing, golf, art, music. Office: Radiology and Imaging Inc 780 Chestnut St Springfield MA 01107-1610

KIRKWOOD, MAURICE RICHARD, banker; b. Tipton, Ind., Dec. 24, 1920; s. Walter Bryan and Lettie (Cooper) K.; m. Anne Elizabeth Smith, Aug. 30, 1942; children—Candace Lynn, Susan Kay. B.S. with distinction, Ind. U., 1942, M.S., 1943. Instr. Ind. U., 1942-43; gen. mgr. Stars & Stripes, Darmstadt, Germany, 1946-52; v.p. Fidelity Bank & Trust Co., Indpls., 1952-59; v.p., cashier, sec. to bd. Am. Fletcher Nat. Bank and Trust Co.,

Indpls., 1959—; sec., dir. 101 Monument Corp., 1966-70; guest lectr. Ind. U. Bus. Sch., 1954—; v.p., sec. Am. Fletcher Corp., 1975—; sec. Indpls. Clearing House, 1956-57; dir., instr. Am. Inst. Banking, 1959-61; sec., dir. Ind. Dept. Fin. Instns., 1965—; sec. to adv. com. of banking comptroller of the currency; v.p., dir. Wells Landing Assn., Inc., 1987—; dir. Beach Walker Villas Assn., Inc., 1992—. Author: National Bank and the Future, 1962. Treas. Muscular Dysthrophy Assn., 1959-64; treas. P.T.A., 1958-60; dist. chmn. United Fund, 1957; mem. regional adv. com. to Comptroller Currency, 1970-72; Bd. dirs. Meth. Home for Aged, Franklin, Ind.; bd. dirs., sec. Am. Fletcher Found. Served to 1st lt. AUS, 1943-46. Recipient Meritorious Civilian Svc. award Dept. Army, 1952; award of Appreciation Office Comptr. of Currency, 1962; Sagamore of the Wabash Gov. of Ind., 1986. Mem. Robert Morris Assos. (bd. dirs. 1965-69, chmn. bd. regents Comml. Lending Sch. 1968—, pres. Ohio Valley chpt. 1963-64, Distinguished Service award 1974), Ind. U. Sch. Bus. Alumni Assn. (dir. 1965-69), Nat. Assn. Accountants, Indpls. C. of C., Ind. Traffic Safety Found., Indpls. Civic Progress Assn., Ind. Credit Men's Assn., Sigma Nu, Beta Gamma Sigma, Phi Eta Sigma, Delta Sigma Pi. Methodist. Clubs: Hillcrest Country, Ind. U. Varsity, Ind. U. Men's, Columbia (Indpls.); Timuquana Country (Jacksonville, Fla.). Home and Office: c/o Mrs LD Sheetz 2224 Turnberry Ln Fort Wayne IN 46804-9353

KIRKWOOD, ROBERT KEITH, applied physicist; b. Santa Monica, Calif., Mar. 10, 1961; s. Robert Lord and Patricia Cathrine (Keith) K.; m. Kimberly DeNeve Saunders, May 2, 1991; 1 child, Rebekah Marie. BS, UCLA, 1982, MS, 1984; PhD, MIT, 1989. Rsch. asst. dept. elec. engring. UCLA, 1982-84; mem. tech. staff TRW Space and Tech. Group, Redondo Beach, Calif., 1984-85; rsch. asst. MIT, Cambridge, 1985-89, vis. scientist Plasma Fusion Ctr., 1992-94; postdoctoral fellow Calif. Inst. Tech., Pasadena, 1989-91; rsch. assoc. geophysics div. Air Force Phillips Lab., Hanscom AFB, Mass., 1991-92, physicist, 1992-94; physicist Lawrence Livermore (Calif.) Lab., 1994—. Contbr. articles to Nuclear Fusion, Physics of Plasmas, Rev. Sci. Instruments, Physics Letters A, Physical Review Letters. Recipient Rsch. Associateship award NRC, 1991; postdoctoral fellow Dept. Energy, 1989; doctoral fellow TRW Space and Tech. Group, 1985. Mem. Am. Phys. Soc. (Simon Ramo award in plasma physics 1991), Am. Geophys. Union. Achievements include development of wave transmission diagnostics for plasmas and demonstration of the interaction between multiple laser beams in plasmas. Office: Lawrence Livermore Lab L-473 PO Box 808 Livermore CA 94551-0808

KIRMAN, CHARLES GARY, photojournalist; b. Chgo., Feb. 2, 1949; s. Irving A. and Sylvia Lea K.; m. Heidemarie Mocker, Nov. 15, 1976 (div.); children: Christian, Courtney. BS in Profl. Photography, Rochester (N.Y.) Inst. Tech., 1972. Staff photographer Chgo. Sun-Times, 1972-81; pres. European Beauty Culture Coll., Phoenix, 1982-86; owner Phoenician Grill, Phoenix, 1987-88; admissions dir. Al Collins Graphic Design Sch., Tempe, Ariz., 1988-92; staff photographer Ventura County (Calif.) Newspapers, 1992—. With USNR, 1966-68. Recipient Nat. Headliner award for spot news photography, 1977; named Ill. Press Photographer of Year, 1975, Chgo. Press Photographer of Year, 1974. Mem. Ill. Press Photographers Assn., Chgo. Press Photographers Assn., Nat. Headliner Club. Home: 1505 Visiala St Oxnard CA 93035 Office: 5250 Ralston St Ventura CA 93003-7318

KIRMSE, SISTER ANNE-MARIE ROSE, nun, educator, researcher; b. Bklyn., Sept. 23, 1941; d. Frank Joseph Sr. and Anna (Keck) K. BA in English cum laude, St. Francis Coll., 1972; MA in Theology with honors, Providence Coll., 1975; PhD in Theology, Fordham U., 1989. Joined Sisters of St. Dominic, Roman Cath. Ch., 1960; cert. elem. tchr., N.Y. Tchr. elem. sch. Diocese Bklyn., 1962-73; instr. adult edn. Diocese Rockville Centre, N.Y., 1974—; dir. religious edn. St. Anthony Padua Parish, East Northport, N.Y., 1975-83; dir. spiritual programs Diocese of Rockville Centre, 1979—; demonstration tchr. Paulist Press, N.Y.C., 1968-70; cons. Elem. Sch. Catechetical Assocs., Bklyn., 1971-73; mem. adj. faculty grad. program Sem. Immaculate Conception, Huntington, N.Y., 1979-80; adj. instr. Molloy Coll., Rockville Centre, 1985, St. Joseph's Coll., Patchogue, N.Y., 1990-91; adj. asst. prof. Ignatius Coll., Bronx, N.Y., 1996-98, Fordham Coll. Liberal Studies, 1998—; asst. to Rev. Avery Dulles, Fordham U., Bronx, 1988—, rsch. assoc. Laurence J. McGinley chair in religion and society, 1989—. Recipient Kerygma award Diocese of Rockville Centre, 1980; Dominican scholar Providence Coll., 1973, Presdl. scholar Fordham U., 1988; McGinley fellow Fordham U., 1988. Mem. Cath. Theol. Soc. Am., Coll. Theology Soc., Amnesty Internat., Kiwanis (pres. Fordham U. 1997-99). Democrat. Roman Catholic. Avocations: swimming, needlework, cooking, traveling, reading. Office: Fordham U Keating Hall 322 Bronx NY 10458 *With Saint Irenaeus, I believe that "the glory of God is a person fully alive!" Life is meant to be lived to the full, with passion and extravagance, with commitment and the courage of one's convictions. As with love, the more of our lives we give away, the more life we find we have.*

KIRNA, HANS CHRISTIAN, lawyer, consultant; b. N.Y.C., Sept. 16, 1956; s. Hans H. and Ingrid D. (Korjus) K.; m. Eileen T. Barrett, June 19, 1993. BA cum laude, Upsala Coll., 1978; MA in Anthropology, New Sch. for Social Rsch., 1982; JD, CUNY, 1986. Indexer H.W. Wilson, Bronx, N.Y., 1986-87; claim counsel Am. Internat. Group, N.Y.C., 1987-94; cons. Willcox, Inc., N.Y.C., 1994-97; broker Guy Carpenter, N.Y.C., 1997-98; sr. claims atty. Risk Enterprise Mgmt. (Zurich Ins.), N.Y.C., 1998—. Author: Sam's Strange Friend, 1994; rschr.: (by Dr. Sid Harring) Crow Dog's Case, 1994; artist: prin. works include painting of Christ and 4 disciples, St. Gabriel and Michael's Orthodox Ch., Stroudsburg, Pa.; composer piano pieces. Active Great Neck (N.Y.) Rep. Club, 1980-81, Congl. Ch. of Manhasset, 1987-96. Mem. Am. Anthrop. Assn. Avocations: artist, collector of art, antiques, runner. Home: 25 Cypress Dr Denville NJ 07834-1709

KIRRER, ERNEST DOUGLAS, physician. BA, NYU, 1971; MD, U. Antwerp, 1982. Diplomat Am. Bd. Family Practice. Resident in family practice St. Mary Hosp., Hoboken, N.J., 1982-85; attending physician Gen. Hosp. Ctr. Passaic, N.J., 1986—, chief divsn. family practice, 1997—. Fellow Am. Acad. Family PRactice; mem. Med. Soc. N.J., PAssaic County Med. Soc. Office: 40 Union Ave Clifton NJ 07011-2219

KIRSCH, A(NTHONY) THOMAS, anthropology and Asian studies educator, researcher; b. Syracuse, N.Y., May 29, 1930; s. Henry Gilbert and Florence May (Sheehan) K.; m. Ingrid Olsen-Tjensvold, Dec. 20, 1968 (div. June 1983); m. Yohko Tsuji, July 31, 1984. BA in Anthropology and Sociology, Syracuse U., 1952, MA in Sociology, 1959; PhD in Social Anthropology, Harvard U., 1967. Asst. prof. anthropology Princeton U., N.J., 1966-70; assoc. prof. anthropology and Asian studies Cornell U., Ithaca, N.Y., 1970-78, prof., 1978—, chair anthropology dept., 1971-74, 78-79, 82-85, 88-90, acting chair Asian studies dept., 1981; assoc. dir. Cornell Thailand Project, Ithaca, 1973—; chair anthropology rev. com. Coun. for Internat. Exch. Scholars, Washington, 1987-90; Fulbright lectr., cons., Thailand, 1985-86. Author: (monograph) Feasting and Social Oscillation, 1973; co-author: The Human Direction, 1970, 3d edit., 1980, in Japanese, 1975; co-editor: Change and Persistence in Thai Culture, 1975; editor/contbr. Jour. Asian Studies; mem. edit. bd./corr. Jour. S.E. Asian Studies, Singapore, 1986—. Cons. Fgn. Svc. Inst., Washington, 1987-88. With U.S. Army, 1953-55. Predoctoral fellow NIMH, Harvard U., 1960-66, sr. fellow NEH, Harvard U., 1974-75; rsch. grantee NIMH, Thailand, 1962-64; Fulbright rsch. grantee Dept. Edn., Thailand, 1992. Fellow Am. Anthrop. Assn.; mem. Am. Ethnol. Soc., Assn. for Asian Studies (exec. bd.-Thailand, Laos, Cambodia studies group 1983-86, S.E. Asia regional coun. 1984-87), The Siam Soc. (life). Avocations: cooking, eating, classic films. Office: Cornell U Dept Anthropology 265 Mcgraw Hall Ithaca NY 14853-4601

KIRSCH, ARTHUR WILLIAM, investment consultant; b. Bklyn., Jan. 22, 1941; s. Joseph and Helen (Silverstein) K.; m. Isabel Leader, Sept. 20, 1965 (div. 1980); children: Deborah Beth, Gabrielle, Alexandra, Andrew; m. Denise McLaughlin, May 15, 1982. B.A., Washington Sq. Coll., NYU, 1962; postgrad., Grad. Sch. Pub. Adminstrn., NYU, 1962-68. Program budget dir. N.Y.C. Human Resources Adminstrn., 1966-68; sr. assoc. E.F. Shelley & Co., N.Y.C., 1968-73; v.p. Citibank, N.A., N.Y.C., 1973-80; sr. mng. dir. Marine Midland Bank, N.A., N.Y.C., 1980-91; pres. Paradigm Mgmt. Inc., N.Y.C., 1991-93; sr. mgr. Pricewaterhouse Coopers, N.Y.C., 1993—; pres., dir. Kirsch Bros., Inc., Bklyn., 1978—. Author: (with William Grinker and Don Cooke) Climbing the Job Ladder, 1968, (with Cooke) Upgrading the Work Force, 1971, Manpower Services in the Workplace, 1980. Served with U.S. Army, 1962-65. Office: Coopers & Lybrand 1301 Avenue Of The Americas New York NY 10019-6022

KIRSCH, DONALD, financial consultant, author; b. N.Y.C., Oct. 9, 1931; s. William and Eva (Wasserman) K.; m. Dorothy Ann Tejw, June 6, 1959; children: Mark Adam, Karen Rebecca Hoffman, Jonathan Bradford. *Wife Dorothy, writer/publisher (Who's Who of American Women); son Mark, partner (litigation) Rogers & Wells (New York), winner of multi-awards as an assistant U.S. attorney, married to TV reporter/anchor Debby Feyerich; daughter Karen, M.D. (pathologist), three boys (Joshua, Zachary, Joseph), married to award-winning oncologist Dr. Anthony D. Hoffman, practitioner/researcher (second name on second paper on AIDS); son Jonathan, vice president and senior securities analyst International Netherlands Group, previously with Bear Stearns & Co.* BS, NYU, 1952. Editorial staffer Wall Street Jour., N.Y.C., 1952-53; writer AP, N.Y.C., 1954-55; pres. Wall Street Cons., N.Y.C., 1955—; chmn. Wall St. Group, Calif., Inc., Los Angeles, 1963—; chmn., pres. The Wall Street Group, Inc., N.Y.C., 1959—; adj. assoc. prof. NYU Grad. Sch. Arts and Sci., 1974-79; founding chmn. Typesetting Products, Inc., Talleres Graficos de Interamericanos, Inc., San Juan, P.R., 1962-80; chmn. Eurofinancing Ltd., 1968; bd. dirs. Co*star Entertainment Inc., MedNet Inc. (chmn. strategic planning com.), Medi-Mail Inc., Dialscan Systems, Audiofidelity Enterprises Inc., Interstate Nat. Dealers Svcs., Inc. *More than 40 years in finance and journalism. Created first national financial public relations firm in U.S. (1959), Canada (1961), Europe (1968); noted for introducing new concepts, including first or early Wall Street entries in CATV, mobile homes, nursing, publicly-owned hospitals, controlled release medical technologies, year 2000 software, medical practice management, first FDA-approved DNA cancer diagnostic, amongst others. Introduced and taught first university program on financial and economic journalism, wrote first book on subject, now widely used in newsrooms and journalism programs. Conceived "Sidewalks of New York" Annual Award Dinner for Big Brothers of New York.* Author: FInancial and Economic Journalism: Analysis Interpretation and Reporting, 1978 (Librarians Assn. award 1978), Investor Relations for the Over-the-Counter or Newly Public Company, (with others) The Handbook of Investor Relations; contbr. numerous articles to profl. jours. Trustee Nat. Symphony Orch. of the John F. Kennedy Ctr. for Performing Arts, treas. bd. trustees, 1996-98; trustee Big Bros.; mem. bd. mgrs. Episcopal Social Svcs., N.Y. Mem. N.Y. Soc. Security Analysts, Met. Pres'. Orgn., Young Pres. Orgn. (chmn. met. chpt. 1976-77), Chief Execs. Orgn., Am. Assocs. Royal Acad. Trust (mem. nat. coun.), Econs. Club N.Y., Friar's Club, The Metropolitan (N.Y.C.), Masons. Office: The Wall St Group Inc 32 E 57th St New York NY 10022-2513

KIRSCH, JEFFREY SCOTT, securities executive; b. Chgo., Nov. 11, 1947; s. Norton M. and Estelle (Kaufman) K.; m. Jodi Lynn Spak, May 20, 1985; children: Alexandra J., Jonathan Peter. BSBA, Babson Coll., 1970. V.p. Auto Gard Inc., Chgo., 1970-90; securities dealer Chgo. Bd. Option Exchange, 1973—, mem. arbitration com., 1978-79, mem. system and facilities com., 1980-81; pres. Kirsch Inc., Chgo., 1981—; pres. one-hr. photo systems Fromex, Chgo., 1981—. Bd. dirs. Young Men's Jewish Council, Chgo., 1978; mem. New Warrior Chgo., counselor Hales Franciscan H.S., Chgo. Mem. Automotive Parts and Accessories Assn., Babson Coll. Alumni Com. Club: Standard (Chgo.). Avocations: boating, tennis, polo, racquetball, windsurfing. Home: 442 W Wellington Ave Chicago IL 60657-5804 Office: First Option Chgo 440 S La Salle St Chicago IL 60605-1028 also: Fromex Inc 188 W Washington St Chicago IL 60602-2306 also: 40 W Lake St Leo Burnett Bldg Chicago IL 60601

KIRSCH, LAURENCE STEPHEN, lawyer; b. Washington, July 20, 1957; s. Ben and Bertha (Gomberg) K.; m. Celia Goldman, Aug. 19, 1979; children: Rachel Miriam, Max David. BAS, MS, U. Pa., 1979; JD, Harvard U., 1982. Bar: D.C. 1982, U.S. Ct. Appeals (3d cir.) 1983, (5th cir.) 1997, U.S. Dist. Ct. D.C. 1985, U.S. Ct. Appeals (D.C. cir.) 1985, U.S. Supreme Ct. 1987; registered environ. assessor, Calif. 1988. Law clk. to presiding judge Pa. Dist. Ct., Phila., 1982-83; vis. asst. prof. law U. Bridgeport (Conn.) Law Sch., 1983-84; assoc. Cadwalader, Wickersham & Taft, Washington, 1984-90, ptnr., 1991—; chmn. steering coms. Superfund. *Mr. Kirsch is an environmental litigator, counselor and transactional attorney. His litigation victories include three appellate decisions overturning site listings on the National Priorities List, including the first such decision in the history of the Superfund program, and opinions on the interaction of bankruptcy and environmental law. He negotiates with government agencies and private parties, advises on environmental implications of real estate and corporate transactions, and performs environmental assessments. Mr. Kirsch lectures widely on environmental law subjects and taught a law school course on Law, Science and Technology. He was interviewed as an expert in environmental law by CBS News, the MacNeil-Lehrer Report, and numerous radio shows and newspapers.* Editor-in-chief Indoor Pollution Law Report, 1987-91; mng. editor Harvard Environ. Law Rev., 1981-82; contbr. articles to profl. jours. Mem. ABA, Fed. Bar Assn., AAAS, Air Pollution Control Assn. (indoor air quality com.), Environ. Law Inst., Nat. Inst. Bldg. Scis. (indoor air quality com.), Am. Soc. Testing and Measurement (indoor air quality com.), Phi Beta Kappa. Home: 7212 Longwood Dr Bethesda MD 20817-2122 Office: Cadwalader Wickersham & Taft Ste 700 1333 New Hampshire Ave NW Washington DC 20036-1574

KIRSCH, MARILYN, artist; b. Mar. 21, 1950. BFA, Mass. Coll. Art, 1972; MFA, Sch. Mus. Fine Arts, Boston, 1976. Solo exhbns. include The Germantown Acad. Arts Ctr. Gallery, Ft. Washington, Pa., 1998, Phila. Art Alliance Members' Gallery, 1999, DeBottis Gallery, West Chester, Pa., 1999, Akar Architecture & Design, Iowa City, 1999; group exhbns. include N.C. Mus. Art, Raleigh, 1975, Inst. Contemporary Art, Boston, 1975, Nielsen Gallery, Boston, 1976, The Katonah (N.Y.) Gallery, 1977, Univ. Art Mus., Santa Barbara, Calif., 1978, Bertha Urdang Gallery, N.Y.C., 1978, Art in the Armory, Phila., 1990, Jessica Berwind Gallery, Phila., 1987, 88, 90, 93, 94, Phila. Art Alliance, 1988, 97; represented numerous pvt. and corp. collections. E-mail: kirsch@mipg.upenn.edu. Studio: 2113 Pine St Philadelphia PA 19103-6513

KIRSCH, NORMAN MAYNARD, clergyman; b. Bismarck, N.D., May 23, 1941; s. Jacob and Lydia (Siewert) K.; m. Judith L. Anderson, Aug. 14, 1964; children: Monica, Rachel. BA, Yankton Coll., 1963; MDiv, Chgo. Theol. Sem., 1967; D Ministry, Drew U., 1985. Ordained minister United Ch. of Christ, 1967. Pastor Congregational United Ch., Eureka, Kans., 1967-69; pastor St. John's United Ch., Owosso, Mich., 1969-83, Wyandotte, Mich., 1983—; moderator Detroit Met. Assn., 1994-95, Mich. Conf. United Ch., East Lansing, 1994-96; pres. Evangelical Homes of Mich., Detroit, 1994-96. Mem. Masons, Kiwanis. Office: St John United Ch of Christ 2744 4th St Wyandotte MI 48192-5808

KIRSCHBAUM, JAMES LOUIS, real estate company administrator; b. Missoula, Mont., Oct. 19, 1940; s. Louis Elsworth and Margaret Marie (Lloyd) K.; m. Marilyn Jean McCann, Sept. 5, 1964; children: Kristyn Marie, Heidi Maureen. Student Ea. Wash. U., 1958-61, Whitworth Coll., 1963-65. V.p. Far West Securities, Spokane, 1963-73, Columbia Mortgage, Spokane and Portland, Oreg., 1973-75; regional v.p. Sherwood & Roberts, Spokane, 1975-80; pres., CEO Bancshares Mortgage, Spokane, 1980-86; exec. v.p. Seafirst Bank, Seattle, 1986-90; pres., CEO Security Properties Investments Inc., Seattle, 1991-93; v.p. Insignia Fin. Group, Inc., 1993-94; exec. v.p. Source Capital Corp., Spokane, 1994—; chmn. Housing Fin. Commn. State of Wash., Seattle, 1983-87; chmn. real estate com. Wash. State Investment Bd., 1991-93. Trustee Ea. Wash. U., Cheney, 1987—; chmn. Leadership Spokane, 1983; pres. United Way, Spokane County, 1984; bd. dirs. Nat. Multihousing Coun., 1992-93. 1st lt. USAR, 1961-68. Republican. Lutheran. Home: 6819 S Highland Park Dr Spokane WA 99223-6200*

KIRSCHBAUM, MYRON, lawyer; b. N.Y.C., Nov. 20, 1949; s. Jonas and Doris (Rose) K.; m. Esther Weiner, June 23, 1971; children: Rachel, Shoshana Stein, Yisrael. BA, Yeshiva U., 1971; JD, Harvard U., 1974. Bar: N.Y. 1975, U.S. Dist. Ct. (so. dist.) N.Y. 1975, U.S. Dist. Ct. (no. dist.) Calif. 1989, U.S. Ct. Appeals (2d cir.) 1975, U.S. Ct. Appeals (9th cir.) 1990, U.S. Ct. Appeals (fed. cir.) 1994. Law clk. U.S. Ct. Appeals (2d cir.), N.Y.C., 1974-75; assoc. Kaye, Scholer, Fierman, Hays & Handler, N.Y.C., 1975-82, ptnr., 1983—. Editor Harvard Law Rev., 1972-73, case and comment editor, 1973-74. Bd. dirs. Coalition for Soviet Jewry, N.Y.C., 1985—; bd. trustees Rofel Internat., Boston, 1999—. Mem. ABA, Assn. of the Bar of City of N.Y. Office: Kaye Scholer Fierman Hays & Handler 425 Park Ave New York NY 10022-3506

KIRSCHENBAUM, BLOSSOM S., educator of English language; b. N.Y.C., May 28, 1933; d. Avram Len Baruch Mordchai and Bia (Astor-Kranzel) S.; m. Baruch David Kirschenbaum, Nov. 27, 1952 (div. July, 1996); children: Jenner Diana, Abram Eugene, Helena April. BA, Hunter Coll. (now CUNY), 1957; MA, Brown U., 1972, PhD, 1976. Instr. humanities, coord. English MIT, Cambridge, Mass., 1975-76; lectr. dept. and writing labs. Southeastern Mass. U. (now campus of Mass. U.), North Dartmouth, 1976-78; lectr. English dept. R.I. Sch. of Design, Providence, R.I., 1964-65, 77-79, Clark U., Worcester, Mass., 1983-86; rschr. dept. comparative lit. Brown U., Providence, R.I., 1983-98; lectr. Italian dept. U. R.I., Providence, 1990; lectr. English as a Fgn. Lang., Brown U. Summer Program, Providence, 1988, 89, 90. Contbg. editor Jewish Spectator, edited in Israel, published in France, 1998—; contbr. to Encyclopedia of Continental Women Writers, 1991, Jewish-American Women Writers, 1994, Contemporary Jewish-American Novelists, 1997, Contemporary Jewish-American Peers, 1999; translated several works from Italian to English, 1976-99; contbr. articles to fgn. lang. mags. and jours. Sec. to bd. dirs. Stop Wasting Abandoned Property, Providence, R.I., 1979-92; mem. ACLU. Recipient scholarship Yivo Weinrich Summer Inst., N.Y.C., 1986; grantee: R.I. State Coun. for Arts, 1978, 79, 83, R.I. State Coun. for Humanities, 1977. Mem. MLA, N.E. MLA, League for Yiddish (N.Y.C.), Am. Italian Hist. Assn., PEN (N.Y. Ctr.), Mendele. Avocation: writing double dactyls (prize winner). E-mail: Blossom Kirschenbaum@Brown.edu. Home: 169 Congdon St Providence RI 02906-1460

KIRSCHENBAUM, HOWARD, educator; b. N.Y.C., Oct. 6, 1944; s. Abraham Irving and Theone (Hamburger) K.; m. Barbara Linell Glaser, Mar. 2, 1972 (div. 1985); 1 child, Kimara Linell; m. Mary M. Rapp, July 30, 1988. BA, New Sch. for Social Rsch., 1966; MS, Temple U., 1968, EdD, 1975. Tchr. Abington (Pa.) H.S., 1966-68, New Lincoln Sch., N.Y.C., 1968-69; instr. Temple U., Phila., 1969-71; exec. dir. Nat. Humanistic Edn. Ctr., Upper Jay, N.Y., 1971-77, Sagamore Inst., Raquette Lake, N.Y., 1977-90; pres. Values Assocs., Rochester, N.Y., 1990-97; prof. Warner Grad. Sch. Edn. U. Rochester, 1997—; adj. faculty SUNY Brockport, 1992-97; dir. White Pine Camp Mus., Paul Smiths, N.Y., 1994-97. Author: 100 Ways to Enhance Values and Morality in Schools and Youth Settings, 1995, On Becoming Carl Rogers, 1979, 20 others; co-author: Values Clarification, 1972, 3rd edit., 1995; contbr. articles to profl. jours. Founder, pres. Adirondack Archtl. Heritage, Keeseville, N.Y., 1990-97; bd. dirs., v.p. Adirondack Nature Conservancy and Land Trust, Keene Valley, N.Y. Mem. ASCD, Author's Guild, Am. Ednl. Rsch. Assn., Nat. Assn. Ptnrs. in Edn., Character Edn. Partnership, Nat. Eagle Scout Assn. Avocations: hiking, travel, historic preservation. Office: Warner Grad Sch Edn Univ Rochester Rochester NY 14627

KIRSCHENMAN, KARL AARON, editor; b. Ridgecrest, Calif., Apr. 27, 1969; s. Karl Lewis Kirschenman and Carol Elaine (Spargo) Reid. BS, No. Ariz. U., Flagstaff, 1994. Supr. comml. prodn. KNAZ-TV, Flagstaff, 1992-93; prodn. mgr., editor Envision Prodns., Sedona, Ariz., 1993-95; freelance editor Studio City, Calif., 1995-96; asst. editor The Post Group, Hollywood, Calif., 1995-97; editor Digital Magic, Santa Monica, Calif., 1997—. Office: Digital Magic 3000 W Olympic Blvd Santa Monica CA 90277

KIRSCHENMANN, HENRY GEORGE, JR., management consultant, former government official, accountant; b. Bklyn., June 11, 1930; s. Henry Godfrey and Eva Helen (Gellert) K.; m. Pam Hirst, Feb. 3, 1957; children—Victoria Mary, Henry George III, Ronald William. BS, Md. U., 1958; MPA, Am. U., 1977. CPA; cert. gov. fin. mgr. Mem. auditor staff Price Waterhouse & Co., Washington, 1959-61; mem. auditor staff U.S. Army Audit Agy., Winston-Salem, N.C., 1962-64; mem. internal auditor staff Martin-Marietta Co., Orlando, Fla., 1961-62; various fin. and adminstrv. positions HEW, Washington, 1964-80; dep. asst. sec. HHS, Washington, 1980-88; assoc. cons. KPMG, Peat, Marwick, Washington, 1988—; bd. dirs., assoc. dir. tng. Pub. Service Inst., Silver Spring, Md., 1969-73; exec. dir. Nat. Edn. Inst., Rockville, Md., 1984—; pres. H.G. Kirschenmann & Assocs., 1990—; instr. U. Va. Sch. Continuing Edn., Fairfax; lectr. in field. Pres. Support Groups, Inc., 1994—; dir. Soc. Not for Profit Orgns. and Cmtys., Inc., 1994—. Recipient Superior Svc. award HHS, 1970, Disting. Svc. award, 1982, Presdl. Rank award, 1988. Mem. Am. Inst. CPAs, Md. Assn. CPAs, Soc. Rsch. Adminstrs., Nat. Grants Mgmt. Assn. (bd. dirs., bus. officer 1997—), Assn. Govt. Accts. (recognition of achievement 1968, 72, 77), Inst. Cost Analysis (bd. dirs. 1981-84), Pi Alpha Alpha. Democrat. Roman Catholic. Avocations: private pilot; sports; tropical fish; theater.

KIRSCHNER, BARBARA STARRELS, pediatric gastroenterologist; b. Phila., Mar. 23, 1941; m. Robert H. Kirschner. M.D., Woman's Med. Coll. of Pa., 1967. Diplomate Am. Bd. Pediatrics; cert. in pediatric gastroenterology and nutrition. Intern, U. Chgo., 1967-68, resident, 1968-70; Wyler Children's Hosp., U. Chgo., 1984—, assoc. prof. pediatrics, 1984-88; prof. pediatrics and medicine, 1988—, mem. com. on nutrition and nutritional biology. Contbr. articles to profl. jours. Pediatric Gastroenterology fellow U. Chgo., 1975-77; recipient Davidson award in pediatric gastroenterology Acad. Pediatrics, 1993. Mem. Am. Gastroenterologic Assn., N.Am. Soc. Pediatric Gastroenterology, Soc. Pediatric Rsch., Alpha Omega Alpha. Office: U Chgo Med Ctr 5825 S Maryland Ave # 4065 Chicago IL 60637-5417

KIRSCHNER, RICHARD MICHAEL, naturopathic physician, speaker, author; b. Cin., Sept. 27, 1949; s. Alan George and Lois (Dickey) K.; 1 child, Aden Netanya; m. Lindea Bowe. BS in Human Biology, Kans. Newman Coll., 1979; D in Naturopathic Medicine, Nat. Coll. Naturopathic Medicine, 1981. Vice pres. D. Kirschner & Son, Inc., Newport, Ky., 1974-77; co-owner, mgr. Sunshine Ranch Arabian Horses, Melbourne, Ky., 1975-77; pvt. practice Portland, Oreg., 1981-83, Ashland, Oreg., 1983—; seminar leader, trainer Inst. for Meta-Linguistics, Portland, 1981-84; cons. Nat. Elec. Contractors Assn., So. Oreg., 1985-86, United Telephone N.W., 1986; spkr. Ford Motor Co., Blue Cross-Blue Shield, Balfour Corp., NEA, AT&T, Triad Sys., Supercuts, 1986-89, Hewlett-Packard, Pepsi Co., George Bush Co., 1990-91, Goodwill Industries Am., Motorola, 1992, The Homestead T.V.A., Federated Ambulatory Surg. Assn., V.H.A. Satellite Broadcast, 1993, Oreg. Dept. Edn., Anaheim Meml. Hosp., 1994, Inc. 500 Conf., U.S. C. of C., Inst. Indsl. Engrs., 1995, EDS, ASFSA, Safeco Ins., Fairfax County, Va.; spkr., trainer Careertrack Seminars, Boulder, Colo., 1986-93; owner, spkr., trainer R & R Prodns., Ashland, Oreg., 1984—. Co-author: audio tape seminar How to Deal with Difficult People, 1987, video tape seminar, 1988, interactive CD-Rom The Leadership Series: Difficult People, 1997, others; author: (audio tape seminar) How to Find and Keep a Mate, 1988, (videotape seminar) How to Find a Mate, 1990, The Happiness of Pursuit, 1994, (videotape seminar) How to Deal with Difficult People, Vol. II, 1992, (book) Dealing With People You Can't Stand, 1994, Digital Publishing on e World, Discussions of Problem People and Happiness, 1995, (7 vol. video series) Telecare: Exceptional Service on the Phone, 1998, (book) Life By Design, 1999. Spokesman Rogue Valley PBS, 1986, 87. Mem. Am. Assn. Naturopathic Physicians (bd. dirs., chmn. pub. affairs 1989-93, bd. dirs. 1995—, Webmaster, 1996—), Wilderness Soc., Internat. Platform Assn. Republican. Office: R&R Prodns PO Box 896 Ashland OR 97520-0030

KIRSCHNER, RUTH BRIN, elementary education educator; b. Mpls., Mar. 12, 1924; d. Sigman and Leah (Chazankin) Brin; m. Norman Bernard Kirschner, June 19, 1949; children: Sally Jo Kirschner Minsberg, William Arthur. BS cum laude, U. Minn., 1946. Primary tchr. Robert Fulton Sch., Mpls., 1946-52; elem. tchr. St. Louis Park (Minn.) Schs., 1962—; tchr. religious sch. Adath Jeshurun Synagogue, Mpls., 1946-83, Bnai Emet Synagoguue, St. Louis Park, 1989—; primary tchr. Latch Key, Mpls., 1986-88; nursery sch. tchr. Westwood Luth. Ch., St. Louis Park, 1989—; customer svc. rep. Am. Automobile Assn., St. Louis Park, 1985—. Sec. 4th Dist. Dem. Com., St. Louis Park, 1986-90; state del. St. Louis Park Dem. Com., 1986, 88, 90; mem. Cmty. Rels. coun. St. Louis Park, 1986-88; mem. St. Louis Park Charter Commn., 1997—; pres. Friends of St. Louis Park Libr.,

1987-88, sec., 1990—; pres. St. Louis Park Friends, 1991-92, 93-94; del. to 44th Dist. Dem. Farmer Labor Exec. Bd.; alt. to 5th Dist. Dem. Farmer Labor ctrl. com., del. to conv., 1998; apptd. mem. charter commn. St. Louis Park, 1993—; mem. Visions, 1994; bd. dirs. Suburban Alliance, 1994. Mem. AAUW (sec.-treas. 1970-72, parliamentarian 1974-76), Lioness (pres. Lyn-Lake 1995—, v.p. 1993-95), Alpha Delta Kappa (state scholarship chmn. 1988-90, sec. Gamma chpt. 1990—). Jewish. Avocations: reading, music, embroidery, telling stories, travel. Home: 3135 Colorado Ave S Minneapolis MN 55416-2050

KIRSCHNER, STANLEY, chemist; b. N.Y.C., Dec. 17, 1927; s. Abraham and Rebecca K.; m. Esther Green, June 11, 1950; children—Susan Joyce, Daniel Ross. BS magna cum laude, Bklyn. Coll., 1950; AM, Harvard U., 1952; PhD, U. Ill., 1954. Research chemist Monsanto Chem. Co., Everett, Mass., 1951; teaching asst. in chemistry Harvard U., 1950-52, U. Ill., Urbana, 1952-54; mem. faculty dept. chemistry Wayne State U., Detroit, 1954—; prof. Wayne State U., 1960—, prof. emeritus, 1992—; vis. prof. U. London, 1963-64, U. Florence, Italy, 1976, U. Sao Paulo, Brazil, 1969, Tohoku U., Sendai, Japan, 1978, Tech. U. Lisbon, Portugal, 1984, U. Porto, Portugal, 1984. Author: Advances in the Chemistry of Coordination Compounds, 1961, Coordination Chemistry, 1969, Inorganic Syntheses, Vol. 23, 1985; contbr. articles to profl. jours. Served with USN, 1945-46. Recipient Pres.'s award for excellence in teaching Wayne State U., 1979, Gold award Engring. Soc. of Detroit, 1995, Heyrovsky medal Czechoslovak Acad. Scis., 1978, Catalyst award in chem. edn. Chem. Mfrs. Assn., 1984, Faculty Svc. award Wayne State U. Alumni Assn., 1986; fellow Fulbright Found., 1963-64, NSF, 1963-64, Ford Found., 1969-70. Fellow AAAS, Am. Inst. Chemists, N.Y. Acad. Scis.; mem. AAUP, Am. Chem. Soc. (chmn. divsn. edn., bd. dirs. 1985-93, Henry Hill award 1995, Brazilian Acad. Scis., Internat. Conf. Coordination Chemistry (permanent sec. 1966-89, emeritus 1990), Internat. Union Pure and Applied Chemistry (com. nomenclature of inorganic chemistry 1991-93), Chem. Soc. Chile (hon.), Chem. Soc. (London). Home: 25615 Parkwood Dr Huntington Wd MI 48070-1424 Office: Dept Chemistry Wayne State Univ Detroit MI 48202

KIRSCHSTEIN, RUTH LILLIAN, physician; b. Bklyn., Oct. 12, 1926; d. Julius and Elizabeth (Berm) K.; m. Alan S. Rabson, June 11, 1950; 1 child, Arnold. B.A. magna cum laude, L.I. U., 1947; M.D., Tulane U., 1951, LL.D. (hon.), 1997; D.Sc. (hon.), Mt. Sinai Sch. Medicine, 1984; LL.D. (hon.), Atlanta U., 1985; DSc (hon.), Med. Coll. Ohio, 1986; LHD (hon.), L.I. U., 1991; PhD (hon.), Tulane U., 1997. Intern Kings County Hosp., Bklyn., 1951-52; resident pathology VA Hosp., Atlanta, Providence Hosp., Detroit, Clin. Ctr., NIH, Bethesda, Md., 1952-57; fellow Nat. Heart Inst. Tulane U., 1953-54; asst. dir. div. biologics standards NIH, 1971-72; dep. dir. Bur. Biologics, FDA, 1972-73, dep. assoc. commr. sci., 1973-74; dir. Nat. Inst. Gen. Med. Scis., 1974-93; acting assoc. dir. woman's health NIH, Bethesda, 1974-93; acting dir. NIH, 1993, dep. dir., 1993—; mem. Found. Advanced Edn. Scis.; chmn. grants peer rev. study team NIH; mem. Inst. Medicine, NAS, 1982—; co-chair, sec. Spl. Emphasis Oversight Com. on Sci. and Tech., 1989—; co-chair PHS Coordinating Com. on Women's Health Issues, 1990—; mem. Office of Tech. Assessment Adv. Com. on Basic Rsch., 1989—. Recipient Superior Svc. award, 1980, Presdl. Disting. Exec. Rank award, 1985, 95, Pub. Svc. award Fedn. Am. Socs. for Exptl. Biology, 1993, Nat. Pub. Svc. award Am. Soc. Pub. Adminstrn./Nat. Acad. Pub. Adminstrn., 1994, Roger W. Jones award for exec. leadership Am. U., 1994, Georgeanna Seegar Jones Women's Health Lifetime Achievement award, 1995. Mem. AMA (Dr. Nathan Davis award 1990), NAS-IOM, Am. Assn. Immunologists, Am. Assn. Pathologists, Am. Soc. Microbiology, Am. Acad. Arts and Scis., Inst. Medicine. Home: 6 West Dr Bethesda MD 20814-1510 Office: NIH Shannon Bldg Rm 126 1 Center Dr MSC 0148 Bethesda MD 20892-0148

KIRSH, MICHAEL ALAN, financial estate planner; b. Bklyn., Aug. 3, 1952; s. Lawrence and Pauline (Goldberg) K.; m. Marcia Beth Fabrikant, Sept. 11, 1976; children: Jordana Erin, Ross Morgan. Grad. high sch., Bklyn. CFP; CLU; accredited estate planner. Prin. Kirsh Fin. Svcs., Inc., N.Y.C., 1978—. Mem. Nat. Assn. Estate Planners, Nat. Assn. Life Underwriters, Inst. CFPs, Am. Soc. CLU and ChFC, Assn. Advanced Life Underwriting, Million Dollar Roundtable (Honor Roll, Top of the Table award), The Internat. Forum. Republican. Jewish. Avocations: tennis, skiing, reading. Office: 425 Park Ave New York NY 10022-3506

KIRSHBAUM, HOWARD M., judge, arbitrator; b. Oberlin, Ohio, Sept. 19, 1938; s. Joseph and Gertrude (Morris) K.; m. Priscilla Joy Parmakian, Aug. 15, 1964; children—Audra Lee, Andrew William. B.A., Yale U., 1960; A.B., Cambridge U., 1962, M.A., 1966; LL.B., Harvard U., 1965. Ptnr. Zarlengo and Kirshbaum, Denver, 1969-75; judge Denver Dist. Ct., Denver, 1975-80, Colo. Ct. Appeals, Denver, 1980-83; justice Colo. Supreme Ct., Denver, 1983-97; arbiter Jud. Arbiter Group, Inc., Denver, 1997—, sr. judge, 1997—; adj. prof. law U. Denver, 1970—; dir. Am. Law Inst. Phila., Am. Judicature Soc., Chgo., Colo. Jud. Inst. Denver, 1979-89; pres. Colo. Legal Care Soc., Denver, 1974-75. Bd. dirs. Young Artists Orch., Denver, 1976-85; pres. Community Arts Symphony, Englewood, Colo., 1972-74; dir. Denver Opportunity, Inc., Denver, 1972-74; vice-chmn. Denver Council on Arts and Humanities, 1969. Mem. ABA (standing com. pub. edn.), Colo. Bar Assn., Denver Bar Assn. (trustee 1981-83), Soc. Profls. in Dispute Resolution. Avocations: music performance; tennis. Office: Jud Arbiter Group Inc 1601 Blake St Ste 400 Denver CO 80202-1328

KIRSHBAUM, JON ALAN, information systems consultant, retired educational administrator; b. L.A., Nov. 5, 1942; s. George Alexander and Mary Elizabeth (Ball) K.; m. Anne Nofrey, Aug. 11, 1961 (div.); 1 child, Warren Ashley (dec.); m. Linda Louise Carl, Dec. 15, 1976; stepchildren: Gary Nicholas, Grant Adam. *Father George Kirshbaum, BS 1939, Wharton, MBA 1967, University of Chicago, AMP 1968, Harvard, retired insurance executive in Sequim, Washington, appeared in Who's Who in Finance and Industry, 1975-76. Mother Mary (Ball) Kirshbaum, 1933 graduate of Salem (Ohio) High School, served as assistant librarian at Salem Public Library, research librarian at University of Pennsylvania, and reference librarian at Lockheed during World War II. A dedicated American Field Service Chairperson from 1959-60 in the San Fernando Valley (California), she also founded "Forget Me Not" gift shop at Blue Hill (Maine) Hospital in the late 1970s.* BS in Comprehensive Mktg., No. Ill. U., 1965, MBA in Fin., 1971, postgrad., 1988-93; MDiv, McCormick Theol. Seminary, Chgo., 1980. Cert. chief sch. bus. ofcl. IRD sales/DPD br. office adminstr. IBM Corp., Chgo., 1965-67; systems analyst/sr. assoc. planner IBM Corp., Endicott, N.Y., 1967-71; seminary asst. Lincoln Park Presbyn. Ch., Chgo., 1972-73; team/project leader Chgo. Pub. Schs., 1974-89, data base adminstr., 1989-92, supr. desktop pub., 1992-94, core team mem., Time re-engring. project, 1994-95; project leader Info. Technologies, Chgo., 1995-96; prin. cons. Keane, Inc., Lisle, Ill., 1996—; freelance travel writer, 1998—. Mng. editor: Today's Traveler Mag., Chgo., 1991-92, exec. editor/v.p. mktg., 1992-97. Mem. DuPage County (Ill.) Geneal. Soc. (bd. dirs. 1986-89, pres. 1989-90), DuPage County Hist. Soc., Glen Ellyn (Ill.) Hist. Soc., Morton Arboretum, Salem (Ohio) Hist. Soc., Project Mgmt. Inst. (midwest chpt.), Soc. Profl. Journalists, Chgo. Headline Club, N.Am. Travel Journalists Assn. (regional v.p. 1993-94), Vernon County (Mo.) Hist. Soc., U.S. Lighthouse Soc. (New Dungeness chpt.), The Nature Conservancy, Rainshadow Natural Sci. Found., The Wheaton History Ctr. Presbyterian. Avocations: fishing, genealogy, photography, travel. Office: Keane Inc Lisle IL 60532

KIRSHBAUM, LAURENCE J., book publishing executive. Degree, U. Mich., 1966. Reporter Newsweek Mag., Detroit & San Francisco, 1966-69; asst. sales mgr. Random House, 1970-74; dir. mktg. Ballantine Books, 1970-74; from v.p. mktg. to pres. Warner Books, Warner Pub. Svcs., 1974-82; v.p., circulation dir. Conde Nast Pubs., 1982-83; pub., COO Warner Books, 1983-84, pres., 1984—. Co-author: Is the Library Burning?, 1970. Office: Warner Books Inc 1271 Avenue Of The Americas New York NY 10020-1300*

KIRSHENBAUM, JERRY, editor, journalist; b. Benton Harbor, Mich., Aug. 30, 1938; s. Milton and Frieda K.; m. Susan White, Nov. 24, 1968; 1 child, David. BS, Northwestern U., 1960; MA, U. Mich., 1963. Reporter Mpls. Tribune, 1963-66; writer Time Mag., N.Y.C., 1966-69; writer Sports Illustrated Mag., N.Y.C., 1969-80, sr. editor, 1980-85, asst. mng. editor, 1985-97, spl. contbr., 1997—. Office: Sports Illustrated Mag 1271 Avenue Of The Americas New York NY 10020-1300

KIRSHENBAUM, RICHARD IRVING, public health physician; b. Bklyn., Aug. 19, 1933; s. Joseph and Anne (Hantman) K.; m. Jean Shicher, Aug. 17, 1957; children: Miriam, Susan, Rachel. AB, Temple U., 1955; DO, Phila. Coll. Osteo. Medicine, 1959; MPH, Columbia U., 1971. Diplomate Am. Bd. Preventive Medicine. Resident intern Met. Hosp., Phila., 1959-60; pvt. practice medicine Bklyn., 1960-70; resident in pub. health N.Y.C. Dept. Health, 1970-73, pub. health physician, 1973-81, regional health dir. for Queens County, 1977-80, chief epidemiologist for Manhattan Borough, 1980-81; pub. health physician N.Y. State Dept. Health, N.Y.C., 1981-98; retired, 1998. Contbr. articles to profl. jours. Lt. col. Med. Corps N.Y. Army NG, 1981-91, USAR, 1991-93. Recipient Physician's Recognition award AMA 1973, 76, 79, 82, 85, 88, 90, 93, 96, 98. Fellow Am. Coll. Preventive Medicine. Home: 313 Whitman Dr Brooklyn NY 11234-6935

KIRSHNER, LEWIS A., psychiatrist; b. Phila., Apr. 16, 1940; s. Jacob J. and Estelle (Varbalow) K.; divorced; children: Adam J., Benjamin R. BA, Wesleyan U., Middletown, Conn., 1961; MD, Jefferson Med. Coll., Phila., 1965. Diplomate Am. Bd. Psychiatry. Resident in psychiatry Albert Einstein Coll. Medicine, Bronx, N.Y., 1969-73; resident in adolescent psychiatry Harvard U. Health Svc., 1973; dir inpatient psychiatry Mt. Auburn Hosp., Cambridge, Mass., 1974-79; med. dir. Met. Beaverbrook Mental Health Ctr., Watertown, Mass., 1979-80; chief mental health Harvard Cmty. Health Plan, Wellesley, Mass., 1980-89; pvt. practice specializing in psychoanalysis, 1982—; acad. psychiatrist VA Med. Ctr./Harvard South Shore Program, Brockton, Mass., 1993—; psychiatrist Mass. Mental Health Ctr., Boston, 1993—; tng. and supervising analyst Boston Psychoanalytic Inst., 1993—; mem. faculty Mass. Inst. Psychoanalysis, 1994—; assoc. clin. prof. Harvard med. Sch., 1997—; vis. prof. U. Lyon, France, 1998-99. Contbr. articles to profl. jours. Maj. USAF, 1969-71. Fellow Am. Psychiat. Assn.; mem. Am. Psychoanalytic Assn, Boston Psychoanalytic Soc., Soc. for Psychotherapy Rsch., Recontres de Ville Cerf (dir. d'enseignement 1998—), Sigma Xi, Alpha Omega Alpha. Office: 306 Harvard St Cambridge MA 02139-2211

KIRSHNER, NORMAN, pharmacologist, researcher, educator; b. Wilkes-Barre, Pa., Sept. 21, 1923; s. Samuel and Marie (Frank) K.; m. Annette Grossman, Feb. 14, 1962; children: Naomi Lynn, Susan Laura, Miriam Amy. B.S., U. Scranton, 1947; M.S., Pa. State U., 1951, Ph.D., 1952. Asst. prof. biochemistry Duke U., 1957-66, assoc. prof., 1966-70, prof., 1970—, chmn. dept. pharmacology, 1977-88, prof. emeritus, 1993—; mem. study sect. NSF, NIH, Washington; cons. Roche Inst., Nutley, N.J. Contbr. numerous articles to profl. jours.; editor: Molecular Pharmacology, 1978-82. Served with U.S. Army, 1943-45, ETO, PTO. NIH grantee, 1957—; NSF grantee. Mem. Am. Soc. Biol. Chemists, Am. Soc. Pharmacology and Exptl. Therapeutics, Am. Soc. Neurochemistry. Democrat. Jewish. Office: Duke Univ Dept Pharmacology Durham NC 27710

KIRSLIS, PETER ANDRE CHRISTOPHER, computer science research and development specialist; b. Cambridge, Mass., Feb. 9, 1954; s. Peter Gabriel and Stephanie Leona (Szymczak) K. BA in Applied Math. cum laude, Harvard U., 1975; MS in Computer Sci., U. Ill., 1977, PhD in Computer Sci., 1986. Mem. tech. staff AT&T Bell Labs., Murray Hill, N.J., 1978-81, Denver, 1986-96; mem. tech. staff Lucent Tech. Bell Labs., Denver, 1996—; rsch. analyst U. Ill., Urbana, 1981-86; tech. staff mem. Digital Tech., Inc., Champaign, 1982, Interactive Systems Corp., Estes Park, Colo., 1983. Co-author (chpt. in book) A Distributed Unix System, 1987; contbr. articles to profl. jours. Mem. IEEE Computer Soc., U.S. Amateur Ballroom Dance Assn. (winner various competitions 1980—), Assn. Computing Machinery, Rocky Mountain Harvard U. Alumni Assn. (chmn. scholarship 1987-89). Avocations: ballroom dancing, skiing, hiking. Office: AT&T Bell Labs 11900 Pecos St Denver CO 80234-2797

KIRSNER, JOSEPH BARNETT, physician, educator; b. Boston, Sept. 21, 1909; s. Harris and Ida (Waiser) K.; m. Minnie Schneider, Jan. 6, 1934; 1 son, Robert S. MD, Tufts U., 1933; PhD in Biol. Scis., U. Chgo., 1942; DSc (hon.), Tufts U., 1993. Intern Woodlawn Hosp., Chgo., 1933-34; resident in internal medicine Woodlawn Hosp., 1934-35; asst. in medicine U. Chgo., 1935-37, from asst. prof. to assoc. prof., 1937-51, prof., 1951—, Louis Block Distinguished Service prof. medicine, 1968—, chief of staff, also dep. dean for med. affairs, 1970-76; Cons. NIH, 1956-69; hon. pres. Gastrointestinal Research Found., 1961—; Mem. drug efficacy adv. com. to NRC; chmn. adv. group Nat. Commn. on Digestive Diseases, 1978; chmn. emeritus sci. adv. com. Nat. Found. Ileitis and Colitis. Editor, author: Inflammatory Bowel Disease, 4th edit., 1995, The Growth of Gastroenterologic Knowledge During the 20th Century, 1994, Early Days of American Gastroenterology, 1996; contbr. more than 675 articles to profl. publs. Served with M.C. AUS, 1943-46, ETO; PTO. Recipient Julius Friedenwald medal disting. work gastroenterology, 1975, Horatio Alger award, 1979, hon. Gold Key for Disting. Service U. Chgo. Med. Alumni Assn., 1979, Alumni medal U. Chgo. Alumni Assn., 1989, Disting. Educator award Am. Gastroenterological Assn., 1999; Joseph B. Kirsner award for excellence in rsch. in clin. gastroenterology established in his honor, Am. Gastroent. Assn., 1990; G. Brohée lectr. World Cong. Gastroenterology, 1994, Laureate award Lincoln Acad. Ill. Mem. Am. Assn. Physicians, ACP (master, John Phillips award), Am. Gastroent. Assn. (past pres., governing bd.), Am. Gastroscopic Soc. (past pres.), Am. Soc. Gastrointestinal Endoscopy (Rudolf Schindler award), Am. Soc. Clin. Investigation, Ctrl. Soc. Clin. Rsch., Chgo. Soc. Internal Medicine (past pres.), Inst. Medicine Chgo. (George H. Coleman medal). Rsch. in gastrointestinal disorders, inflammatory disease of gastrointestinal tract. Home: 5805 S Dorchester Ave Chicago IL 60637-1730 Office: U Chgo Med Ctr 5841 S Maryland Ave Chicago IL 60637-1463 *We need a return to higher standards, personally and professionally. Striving for personal excellence and achievement promotes universal excellence and peace.*

KIRSNER, ROBERT SHNEIDER, Dutch and Afrikaans educator; b. Chgo., Oct. 18, 1941; s. Joseph B. and Minnie (Shneider) K.; married, July 14, 1968; children: Rachel, Daniel. BA in Chemistry with honors, Oberlin Coll., 1962; MA in Gen. Linguistics, Columbia U., 1968, PhD in Gen. Linguistics with distinction, 1972. Preceptor linguistics Columbia U., N.Y.C., 1970-71; from asst. prof. to assoc. prof. Dutch and Afrikaans UCLA, 1972-89, prof., 1989—; lectr. in linguistics Columbia U., N.Y.C., 1971-72; pres. Netherlandic studies program UCLA, chair dept. curriculum com., mem. departmental com. Germanic lang. instrn., mem. acad. senate faculty welfare com., mem. undergraduate courses and curricula, mem. libr. com. Editor: Low Countries and Beyond, 1993; mem. editl. bd. Tydskrif vir Nederlands en Afrikaans, Publications of the American Association for Netherlandic Studies, Tijdschrift voor Nederlands en Afrikaans; mem. adv. bd. Functions of Language; mem. adv. bd. linguistics Algemene Nederlandse Spraakkunst. Fulbright Fellow, 1968-69; Columbia U. Pres.'s fellow, 1969-70; U. Calif. Regents' Faculty fellow, 1974; fellow-in-residence Netherlands Inst. Advanced Study Humanities and Social Scis., 1979-80; NSF grantee, 1980-83; Sr. Fulbright Rsch. scholar, 1984; Visitor's fellow Netherlands Orgn. Advancement Pure Rsch., 1984; vis. scholar Netherlands Inst. Advanced Study, 1984; Am. Philos. Soc. grantee, 1988; Visitor's fellow South African Coun. Humanities Rsch., 1992; Visitor's fellow Netherlands Orgn. Sci. Rsch., 1995. Mem. Internat. Assn. Dutch Studies, Internat. Cognitive Linguistics Assn., Internat. Pragmatics Assn., So. African Assn. Dutch Studies, Linguistic Soc. Netherlands, Am. Assn. Netherlandic Studies, Linguistic Soc. Am. Office: UCLA Dept Germanic Langs Box 951539 212 Royce Hall Los Angeles CA 90095-1539

KIRST, MICHAEL WEILE, education educator, researcher; b. West-treading, Pa., Aug. 1, 1939; s. Russell and Marian (Weile) K.; m. Wdndy Burdsall, Sept. 6, 1975; children: Michael, Anne. AB summa cum laude, Dartmouth Coll., 1961; MPA, Harvard U., 1963, PhD, 1964. Budget examiner U.S. Bur. Budgets, Office of Edn., Washington, 1964-64; assoc. dir. President's comsn. on White House fellows Nat. Adv. Coun. on Edn. Disadvantaged Children, Washington, 1966; dir. program planning and evaluation Bur. Elem. and Secondary Edn., U.S. Office Edn., Washington, 1967; staff dir. U.S. Senate Subcommittee Manpower, Employment and Poverty, Washington, 1968-69; with Ca. State Bd. Edn., Sacramento, 1975-77, pres., 1977-81; prof. edn. Stanford (Calif.) U., 1969—; prin. investigator Policy Analysis for Calif. Edn., Berkeley, 1984—, Ctr. Policy Rsch. in Edn., Rutgers U., Stanford U., Mich. State U., 1984—, Reform Up Close, 1988-92; chmn. bd. comparative studies in edn. U.S. Nat. Acad. Scis., 1994—. Author: Government Without Passing Laws, 1969, (with Frederick Wirt) The Political Web of American Schools, 1972, revised, 1975, republished as Political and Social Foundations of Education, (with Joel Berke) Federal Aid to Education: Who Governs, Who Benefits, 1972, (with W. Garms) Revising School Finance in Florida, 1973, (with others) State School Finance Alternatives, 1975, (with others) Contemporary Issues in Education: perspectives from Australia and U.S.A., 1983, (with others) Who Controls Our Schools: American Values in Conflict, 1984, (with Frederick Wirt) Schools in Conflict: Political Turbulence in American Education, 1982, 3d edit., 1992, Political Dynamic of American Education, 1997; editor: The Politics of Education at the Local, State, and Federal Levels, 1970, State, School and Politics, 1972; author numerous monographs; contbr. numerous articles to profl. jours., newspapers and mags. Pres. Calif. State Bd. Edn., Sacramento, 1977-80. Mem. NAS (chmn. bd. international comparative studies in edn.), Nat. Acad. Edn., Am. Edn. Rsch. Assn. (v.p.), Internat. Acad. Edn., Phi Beta Kappa. Office: Stanford U Sch Edn MC 3096 Stanford CA 94305

KIRSTEUER, ERNST KARL EBERHART, biologist, curator; b. Vienna, Austria, Sept. 28, 1933; came to U.S., 1965; s. Ernst and Barbara (Reichhalter) K.; m. Erika Stepnitz, Jan. 18, 1958. Ph.D. (research fellow 1958-60), U. Vienna, 1961. Instr. U. Vienna, 1961-62; prof. marine biology U. Cumana, Venezuela, 1963-65; asst. curator Am. Mus. Natural History, N.Y.C., 1965-70; assoc. curator Am. Mus. Natural History, 1970-75, curator, 1975-87, chmn., 1977-84, ret., 1987. Contbr. articles in field to profl. jours. NSF grantee, 1968-71.

KIRTLEY, HATTIE MAE, retired real estate broker; b. Ludlow, Okla., July 9, 1934; d. Adam Marion and Hattie Ethel (Buttler) Williams; m. Albert David Kirtley, Aug. 21, 1954; children: Sharon Ann, Gary Dean. BS in Secondary Edn., Northwest Mo. State U., 1970; postgrad., Mo. Western, 1972. Cert. Mo. realestate salesperson. Waitress Greyhound Bus Depot, Wichita, Kans., 1951; telephone operator S.W. Bell Telephone Co., Wichita, 1952; key punch operator Cudahy Packing Co., Wichita, 1954, Kans. Gas & Electric Co., Wichita, 1955, Kans. State Income Tax Bur., Topeka, 1956, M.F.A. Dairy Breeders, Springfield, Mo., 1957; tchr. vocat. home econs. South Holt High Sch., Oregon, Mo., 1969-70; tchr. various schs., Cosby, Denton, Mo., Kans., 1971-72, 72-74; real estate salesperson St. Joseph, Mo., 1980-82, 82-84, Savannah, Mo., 1984—. Charter mem. Riverview Bapt. Ch., Wichita, Kans., 1951, Sharon Bapt. Ch., 1952, Kings Hwy. Bapt. Ch., 1953. Baptist. Avocations: travel, cooking, playing piano, sewing.

KIRTLEY, JANE ELIZABETH, professional society administrator, lawyer; b. Indpls., Nov. 7, 1953; d. William Raymond and Faye Marie (Price) K.; m. Stephen Jon Cribari, May 8, 1985. BS in Journalism, Northwestern U., 1975, MS in Journalism, 1976; JD, Vanderbilt U., 1979. Bar: N.Y. 1980, D.C. 1982, Va. 1995, U.S. Dist. Ct. (we. dist.) N.Y. 1980, U.S. Dist. Ct. D.C. 1982, U.S. Ct. Claims 1982, U.S. Ct. Appeals (4th cir.) 1982, U.S. Ct. Appeals (D.C. cir.) 1985, U.S. Ct. Appeals (10th cir.) 1996, U.S. Ct. Appeals (5th cir.) 1997, U.S. Ct. Appeals (6th cir.) 1998, U.S. Ct. Appeals (6th and 11th cir.) 1998, U.S. Supreme Ct. 1985. Assoc. Nixon, Hargrave, Devans & Doyle, Rochester, N.Y., 1979-81, Washington, 1981-84; exec. dir. Reporters Com. for Freedom of Press, Arlington, Va., 1985—; mem. adj. faculty Am. U. Sch. Comm., 1988-98. Exec. articles editor Vanderbilt U. Jour. Transnat. Law, 1978-79; editor: The News Media and the Law, 1985—, The First Amendment Handbook, 1987, 4th edit., 1995, Agents of Discovery, 1991, 93, 95, Pressing Issues, 1998—; columnist NEPA Bull., 1988—, Virginia's Press, 1991—, Am. Journalism Rev., 1995—, W.Va.'s Press, 1997—, Tenn. Press, 1997—; mem. editl. bd. Govt. Info. Quar., Comm. Law and Policy. Bd. dirs. Student Press Law Ctr., Arlington, Va.; mem. steering com. Libel Def. Resource Ctr., N.Y.C.; adv. bd. Pa. Ctr. for the 1st Amendment, University Park, Freedom Forum 1st Amendment Ctr., Nashville. Mem. ABA, N.Y. State Bar Assn., D.C. Bar Assn., Va. State Bar Assn., Sigma Delta Chi. Home: 724 Franklin St Alexandria VA 22314-4104 Office: Reporters Com 1815 No Fort Myer Dr Ste 900 Arlington VA 22209

KIRTON, ORLANDO CECILIO, surgeon, educator; b. Gamboa, Panama, Sept. 14, 1958; s. Leafton and Ruth Isabel (Atkinson) K.; m. Jillian Euphemia, July 4, 1987; children: Phillip, Briana, Emily. BA in Biochemistry, Brown U., 1978; MD cum laude, Harvard U., 1983. Diplomate Am. Bd. Surgery. Intern SUNY Health Sci Ctr., Bklyn., 1983-84; resident in surgery SUNY, Bklyn., 1984-85, 87-89, chief resident in surgery, 1989-90; clin. instr., rsch. fellow dept. pathology Children's Hosp., Boston, 1985-87; fellow surg. critical care dept. surgery Jackson Meml. Hosp./U. Miami Sch. Medicine, 1990-91; fellow surgery trauma Jackson Meml. Hosp./U. Miami, 1991-92, med. dir. advanced trauma life support, 1996—; asst. prof. clin. surgery dept. surgery U. Miami, 1992-97, assoc. prof. surgery, 1997-99; assoc. dir. surg. intensive care Jackson Meml. Med. Ctr., 1992—; assoc. dir. dept. surgery Hartford (Conn.) Hosp., 1999—; assoc. prof. surgery, assoc. program dir. dept. surgery U. Conn. Health Ctr., Hartford, 1999—; attending physician trauma & surg. care Jackson Meml. Hosp., 1992—, mem. faculty gen. surg. & trauma critical care, 1992—, mem. faculty anesthesia critical care, 1992—, attending nutritional and metabolic support svcs., 1993—, attending physician dept. hyperbaric medicine, 1995—; attending surgeon VA Hosp., Miami, 1995—; med. dir. trauma ICU Jackson Meml. Med. Ctr., 1997—. Cons. editor Chest, 1996—; contbr. articles to profl. jours. Spkr. 4th Ann. Black History Month program Miami Arena, 1995; mem. Dade County Trauma adv. com., 1996—. Maj. U.S. Army Res., 1992—. Recipient H. Quillian Jones award Fla. Com. Trauma, 1991, Disting. Svc. award South Fla. Coalition Black Trade Unionists, 1993, DuPont Critical Care Rsch. award Am. Coll. Chest Physicians, 1995, Young Investigator award, 1993; grantee Nat. Rsch. Svc., 1985-87, Merck & Co., 1993, Zeneca Pharms., 1995—; rsch. fellow N.Y. Dept. Health, 1979. Fellow ACS (candidate group 1984-92), Am. Coll. Critical Care Medicine; mem. AMA, Nat. Med. Assn., Am. Trauma Soc., Am. Assn. Surgery Trauma, Assn. Acad. Surgeons, Soc. Critical Care Medicine (abstract reviewer 1994-96, editor surg. sect. newsletter 1995—), So. Med. Assn., Eastern Assn. Surgery Trauma, Assn. Surg. Edn., Alpha Omega Alpha. Office: Hartford Hosp Dept Surgery PO Box 5037 80 Seymour St # B501C Hartford CT 06102-5037*

KIRVEN, TIMOTHY J., lawyer; b. Buffalo, Wyo., May 26, 1949; s. William J. and Ellen F. (Farrell) K.; m. Elizabeth J. Adams, Oct. 31, 1970; 1 child, Kristen B. BA in English, U. Notre Dame, 1971; JD, U. Wyo., 1974. Bar: Wyo. Ptnr. Kirven & Kirven, PC, Buffalo, 1974—. Author Rocky Mountain Mineral Law, 1982. Mem. Johnson County Libr. Br., Buffalo. Mem. ABA, Wyo. State Bar (v.p. 1997—), Johnson County Bar Assn., KC (G.K. treas. 1992-96), Western States Bar Conf. (pres.-elect 1997—), Rotary (pres. Buffalo club 1988-89, YEP chmn. 1993—). Home: PO Box C Buffalo WY 82834-0060 Office: Kirven and Kirven PC PO Box 640 104 Fort St Buffalo WY 82834-0640*

KIRWAN, KATHARYN GRACE (MRS. GERALD BOURKE KIRWAN, JR.), retail executive; b. Monroe, Wash., Dec. 1, 1913; d. Walter Samuel and Bertha Ella (Shrum) Camp; m. Gerald Bourke Kirwan Jr., Jan. 13, 1945. Student, U. Puget Sound, 1933-34; BA, BS, Tex. Woman's U., 1937; postgrad., U. Wash., 1941. Libr. Brady (Tex.) Sr. High Sch., 1937-38, McCamey (Tex.) Sr. High Sch., 1938-43; mgr. Milady's Frock Shop, Monroe, 1946-62, owner, mgr., 1962-93. Meml. chmn. Monroe chpt. Am. Cancer Soc., 1961-93; mem. Snohomish County Police Svcs. Action Coun., 1971; mem. Monroe Pub. Libr. Bd., 1950-65, pres. bd., 1964-65; mem. Monroe City Coun., 1969-73; mayor City of Monroe, 1974-81; commr. Snohomish County Hosp. dist. 1, 1970-90, chmn. bd. commrs., 1980-90; mem. East Snohomish County Health Planning Com., 1979-81; mem. Snohomish County Law and Justice Planning Com., 1974-78, Snohomish County Econ. Devel. Coun., 1975-81, Snohomish County Pub. Utility Dist. Citizens Adv. Task Force, 1983; sr. warden Ch. of Our Saviour, Monroe, 1976-77, 89, sr. warden, 1976-77, 89-90; mem. Monroe Breast Cancer Screening Project community planning group Fred Hutchinson Cancer Rsch. Ctrs., 1991-93. With USNR, 1943-46. Mem. AAUW, U.S. Naval Inst., Ret. Officers Assn., Naval Res. Assn., Bus. and Profl. Women's Club (2d v.p. 1980-82, pres. 1983-84), Washington Gens., Snohomish County Pharm. Aux., C. of C. (pres. 1972), Valley Gen. Hosp. Guild (pres. 1994, 95, 96), Valley Gen. Hosp. Found. (sec. 1993-97). Episcopalian. Home: 538 S Blakeley St Monroe WA 98272-2402

KIRWAN, R. DEWITT, lawyer; b. Albany, Calif., Aug. 30, 1942; s. Patrick William and Lucille Anne (Vartanian) K.; m. Betty-Jane Elias, June 29, 1969 (div. 1982); children: Katherine DeWitt, Andrew Elias; m. Nancy Jane

Evers, Oct. 27, 1984; 1 child, Fletcher Evers. BA, U. Calif., Berkeley, 1966; JD, U. San Francisco, 1969. Bar: Calif. 1971, U.S. Dist. Ct. (ctrl. dist.) Calif. 1971, U.S. Ct. Appeals (9th cir.) 1971. Assoc. Schell & Delamer, L.A., 1971-73; ptnr. Lillick & McHose, L.A., 1973-90, Pillsbury Madison & Sutro, L.A., 1990-98, Akin, Gump, Strauss, Hauer & Feld, L.A., 1998—. Chmn., exec. bd. dirs. U. Calif., Berkeley, 1988-97, trustee U. Calif. Berkeley Found., 1995-98; bd. dirs., trustee Pacific Crest Outward Bound Sch.; bd. dirs. L.A. Philharm. Assn., 1985-89, pres., 1986-88, mem. bus. and profl. com.; bd. dirs. Pasadena (Calif.) Symphony Assn., 1978-82. Capt. USAR, 1966-71. Mem. ABA, Am. Bd. Trial Advs., Calif. Club. Democrat. Roman Catholic. Avocations: fly fishing, mountaineering, hunting, skiing. Office: Akin Gump Strauss Hauer & Feld 2029 Century Park E Ste 2600 Los Angeles CA 90067-3012

KIRWAN, WILLIAM ENGLISH, II, mathematics educator, university official; b. Louisville, Apr. 14, 1938; s. Albert Dennis and Elizabeth (Heil) K.; m. Patricia Ann Harper, Aug. 27, 1960; children: William English, III, Ann Elizabeth. B.A., U. Ky., 1960; M.S. (NDEA fellow 1960-63), Rutgers U., 1962, Ph.D., 1964. Instr. Rutgers U., 1963-64; mem. faculty U. Md., College Park, 1964, prof. math., 1972, chmn. dept., 1977-81, vice chancellor for acad. affairs, 1981-86, provost, 1986-88, acting pres., 1988-89, pres., 1989-98; pres. Ohio State U., Columbus, 1998—; vis. lectr. London U., 1966-67; program dir. NSF, 1975-76. Contbr. articles to profl. jours. Mem. adv. bd. Montgomery County (Md.), 1975-79; chmn. MS 2000 Com. for NRC; bd. dirs. Greater Washington YMCA, 1994—, Nat. Assn. State Univs. and Land Grant Colls., 1995—, World Trade Ctr. Inst., 1990—. Decorated officer Order of King Leopold II (Belgium); named Disting. Alumnus, U. Ky., 1989. Mem. Am. Math. Soc. (coun. 1980-82, editor Proc., 1977-82), Math. Assn. Am., Am. Assn. Colls. and Univs. (bd. dirs. 1993—), Coun. for the Internat. Exch. of Scholars (bd. dirs. 1994—), NCAA (pres. commn. 1995—). Office: Ohio State U 190 N Oval Mall 205 Bricker Columbus OH 43210-1209*

KIRWIN, KENNETH FRANCIS, law educator; b. Morris, Minn., May 10, 1941; s. Francis B. and Dorothy A. (McNally) K.; m. Phyllis J. Hills, June 2, 1962; children—David, Mark, Robert. B.A., St. John's U., 1963; J.D., U. Minn., 1966. Bar: Minn. 1966, U.S. Dist. Ct. Minn. 1968, U.S. Ct. Appeals (8th cir.) 1969. Law clk. to assoc. justice Supreme Ct., Minn., 1966-67; assoc. Lindquist & Vennum, Mpls., 1967-70; prof. law William Mitchell Coll. Law, St. Paul, 1970—; staff dir. Uniform Rules Criminal Procedure, 1971-74, reporter, 1982-87; reporter Uniform Victims of Crime Act, 1991-92; adj. prof. U. Minn. Law Sch., 1977, 80; active Minn. Lawyers Profl. Responsibility Bd., 1975-81, Minn. Bd. Continuing Legal Edn., 1975-83. Author: (with Maynard E. Pirsig) Cases and Materials on Professional Responsibility, 1984. Mem. Ramsey County Bar Assn., Minn. State Bar Assn., ABA (mem. standing com. on discipline 1983-89), Am. Law Inst. Home: 1418 Brookshire Ct New Brighton MN 55112-6390 Office: William Mitchell Coll Law 875 Summit Ave Saint Paul MN 55105-3030

KIS, MIROSLAV MIRKO, minister, religion educator; b. Miklusevci, Croatia, Yugoslavia, Nov. 6, 1942; came to U.S., 1974; s. Andrija and Natalija (Pap) K.; m. Brenda Starr Bond, Aug. 22, 1971; children: Richard Andrej, Adam Daniel. BA, Seminarie Adventiste, France, 1973; MDiv, Andrews U., Berrien Springs, Mich., 1976; PhD, McGill, Montreal, Que., Can., 1983. Ordained to ministry Seventh-day Adventist Ch., 1979. Pastor, intern Seventh-Day Adventist Ch., France, 1972-73; assoc. pastor Seventh-Day Adventist Ch., San Pedro, Calif., 1973-74; pastor Seventh-Day Adventist Ch., Montreal, 1976-79, 81-83; asst. prof. Can. Union Coll., College Heights, Alta., Can., 1979-81; assoc. prof. Christian ethics Andrews U., Berrien Springs, Mich., 1983-91, chmn. dept. theology and Christian philosophy, 1986—, prof. Christian ethics, 1991—; trustee Loma Linda (Calif.) Bioethics Com., 1985-90. Sgt. Yugoslavia mil, 1961-63. Mem. Soc. Christian Ethics, Am. Acad. Religion, Andrews Soc. Religious Studies. Office: Seventh-day Adventist Theol Sem Andrews U Berrien Springs MI 49104

KISABETH, TIM CHARLES, obstetrician, gynecologist; b. Fostoria, Ohio, Oct. 29, 1957; s. Donald C. and Doris J. (Smith) K. BA in Chemistry, Capital U., 1979; MD, Ohio State U., 1982. Diplomate Nat. Bd. Med. Examiners, Am. Bd. Obstetrics and Gynecology. Resident in ob-gyn Oakwood Hosp., Dearborn, Mich., 1982-86; chief resident Oakwood Hosp., Dearborn, 1985-86; pvt. practice Alton, Ill., 1986—; lab. dir. Alton Multispecialists, 1995—; also bd. dirs.; chmn. ob-gyn. dept. Alton (Ill.) Meml. Hosp., 1991-93, 95-97; chmn. ob-gyn dept. St. Anthony's Hosp., Alton, Ill., 1999—. Mem. Greater Alton-Twin River Growth Assn., 1987—; bd. dirs. Pride, Inc., 1992—, chmn. Alton Lake com., 1993-95. Fellow Am. Coll. Ob-Gyn.; mem. AMA (del. resident sect. 1984-86, del. yhoung physicians sect. 1990-92), Ill. Med. Soc. (ho. of dels. 1987—, young physicians com. 1987-92, com. on pub. rels. and membership 1992—), Madison County Med. Soc. (pres. 1994-95), Am. Fertility Soc., Masons DeMolay (Legion of Honor award 1988), Alton Waterski Club. Lutheran. Avocations: travel, photography. Home: 3312 Rosenberg Ln Godfrey IL 62035-1172 Office: Alton Multispecialists Ltd 2 Saint Anthonys Way Ste 111 Alton IL 62002-4569

KISAK, PAUL FRANCIS, engineering company executive; b. Pitts., July 15, 1956; s. Paul F. and Catherine M. (Svaranowic) K.; married. BSE in Nuclear Engring., Engring. Physics and Engring. Sci., U. Mich., 1982; MBA, Ea. Mich. U., 1984; postgrad., U. Va., 1986, George Washington U., 1985-87, UCLA, Naval Postgrad. Sch., Argonne Nat. Lab., Los Alamos Nat. Lab., Sandia Nat. lab., Lawrence Livermore Nat. Lab. Lic. realtor, contractor. Intelligence officer, engr. CIA, Langley, Va., 1983-86; engr., diplomat U.S. Dept. of State, Washington, 1986-87; engr., program mgr. Space Applications Corp., Vienna, Va., 1987-88; founder, pres. KKI, Inc., Middletown, Va., 1986—; sr. scientist, program mgr. Info. Tech. & Application Corp., Reston, 1987-89; cons. devel. PFK Enterprises, Washington, 1986—; pub., editor, author, mem. mgmt. adv. group CIA; mem. working group Strategic Def. Initiative, 1986—; ind. pub., editor, writer. Holder software copyrights and trademarks. Caseworker U.S. Senator John Glenn, Columbus, Ohio, 1979; trustee League of Student Orgns.; del. Loudoun County Rep. Nat. Party, 1988—. Ea. Mich. U. scholar, Ohio State U. scholar; recipient Presdl. Sports awards, George P. Schultz U.S. Dept. State Tribute of Appreciation award; named to NRA Legion of Honor. Mem. AIAA, ASME, Internat. Soc. Profl. Engrs., Am. Phys. Soc., Am. Math. Soc., Am. Nuc. Soc., Am. Astronautical Soc., Am. Mgmt. Soc., Assn. MBA Execs., Am. Fedn. Ret. Intelligence Officers, Bioengring. Soc., Mensa, Intertel, Texnikoi, Camelopard Socs., Naval Intelligence Profls., Marine Corp. League Det.# 890, ISPE, Beta Gamma Sigma, Pi Mu Epsilon. Avocations: flying, reading, sports, movies, woodworking.

KISBER, MATTHEW HARRIS, state legislator; b. Jackson, Tenn., Jan. 31, 1960; m. Elizabeth Paige Lowe, Nov. 6, 1993. BA in Polit. Sci., Vanderbilt U., 1982. Photojournalist Jackson Sun, Inc., 1978-81; from asst. ops. mgr. to v.p. ops. Kisber's Dept. Stores, Inc., 1982-91; mem. Tenn. Ho. Reps., Nashville, 1982—, chmn. fin., ways and means com., 1997—; pres., treas., chmn. bd. dirs. Jackson Photo Supply, Inc., 1983-87; v.p. for bus. devel. First Tenn. Bank, N.A.; pres., chmn. bd. dirs. Vineyard's Gifts, Inc. Bd. dirs. Jackson Area Coun. on Alcohol and Drug Dependency, Jackson Family YMCA, Jackson Area Symphony Assn., United Negro Coll. Fund; mem. youth legislature Tenn. YMCA, 1978—, legis. dir., 1982—, advisor Tenn. delegation to conf. on nat. affairs; active Am. Coun. Young Polit. Leaders, del. to Japan, 1987. Recipient Friend of Edn. award, Jackson Edn. Assn., 1987; So. Legis. Conf. scholar, 1989; Jim Spradley award for Econ. Deve. Ten. Indsl. Deve. Coun., 1995. Mem. So. Legis. Conf. (exec. com. 1996—, mgmt. com. 1997—, vice chmn. fiscal affairs and govt. ops. com. 1998,), Nat. conf. of State Legislatives (vice-chmn. econ. devel. and culture com., 1998), Jackson Area C. of C., Vanderbilt U. Alumni Assn., Vanderbilt Nat. Commodore Club (bd. dirs. 1986-94). Home: 74A Tall Oaks Dr Jackson TN 38305-4507 Office: State of Tenn 33 Legislative Plz Nashville TN 37243

KISCADEN, SHEILA M., state legislator; b. St. Paul, Apr. 21, 1946; d. Harvey Richard and Bea Mae (Conway) Martineau; m. Richard Craig Kiscaden, Sept. 12, 1970; children: Michael, Karen. BS in Edn., U. Minn., 1969; MS in Pub. Adminstrn., U. So. Calif., L.A., 1986. Tchr. So. St. Paul Secondary Schs., Minn., 1969-70, Jobs 70, Rochester, Minn., 1970-71; regional coord. Planned Parenthood, Rochester, Minn., 1971-76; vol. svc. coord. Olmsted County, Rochester, Minn., 1977-80, human svc. planner, 1980-82, legis. liaison, 1982-85; prin. Cons. Collaborator, Rochester, Minn., 1987—; senator Minn. State Senate, St. Paul, 1992—. Bd. dirs. Ability Bldg. Ctr. Found. Bd., Rochester, Minn., 1989-94, Dyslexia Inst. Minn., Rochester, Minn., 1989-94; team leader Global Vols., 1989—. Fulbright scholar, 1970. Mem. Phi Beta Kappa. Republican. Home: 724 11th St SW Rochester MN 55902-6339 Office: Minn State Senate 143 State Office Bldg Saint Paul MN 55155-1288*

KISCHUK, RICHARD KARL, insurance company executive; b. Detroit, Mar. 14, 1949; s. Russell and Aubrey Ann (Artt) K.; m. Sandra Jean Dierkes, June 26, 1971; children: Robert Charles, Kirsten Grace, Erin Michelle, Danielle Laraine, Russell Olan, Erika Anne. BS, U. Mich., 1969, M in Actuarial Sci., 1971; MS in Bus. Adminstrn., Ind. U., 1979. Enrolled actuary. Actuarial trainee Lincoln Nat. Life, Ft. Wayne, Ind., 1971-72, actuarial asst., 1972-1973, asst. actuary, 1973-77, asst. v.p., 1977-80, 2d v.p., 1980-82; v.p. Lincoln Nat. Corp., Ft. Wayne, Ind., 1982-86; v.p., dir. Lincoln Nat. Health and Casualty Ins. Co., 1985-87, Lincoln Nat. Life Reins. Co., 1985-87, Lincoln Nat. Adminstrv. Service; chief operating officer, dir. Lincoln Intermediaries, Inc., 1985-87, Spl. Pooled Risk Adminstrs., Inc., 1985-87, Underwriters and Mgmt. Services, Inc., 1985-87; pres. Crown Point Mgmt. Cons., Inc., 1987—, Bavefficient Solutions, Inc., 1998—. Mem. editorial adv. bd. CLU Jour., 1983-91; contbr. articles to profl. jours. Fellow Soc Actuaries (chmn. fin. reporting sect. 1982-85, bd. govs. 1986-89), mem. Am. Acad. Actuaries. Avocations: camping, backpacking, canoing, photography. Office: Crown Point Mgmt Cons Inc PO Box 355 Pendleton IN 46064-0355

KISE, JAMES NELSON, architect, urban planner; b. Trenton, May 2, 1937; s. Charles Richard and Gladys May (Doll) K.; m. Rachel Bok, Dec. 20, 1958 (div.); children: Jefferson Bok, Charles Curtis; m. Sarah Ludlow Ogden Smith, June 15, 1974; children: Laura Ludlow Susanna, Anthony Lawrence Triplett. BArch, U. Pa., 1959, MArch, 1963, M in City Planning, 1964; postgrad., U. Rome, 1959-60. Registered architect, Pa., N.J., Maine, Del. New town planner Harvard-MIT Joint Ctr. of Urban Studies Ciudad Guayana Project, Caracas, Venezuala, 1961-62; ctr. city planner Phila. City Planning Commn., 1962-66; project dir. Wallace McHarg Roberts & Todd, Phila., 1966-67; dir. urban design ctr. Nat. Urban Coalition (formerly Urban Am., Inc.), Washington, 1967-70; ptnr. Kise Straw & Kolodner, Phila., 1970—; lectr. U. Pa., 1962-67, 95—; adj. instr. urban design Drexel U., 1974-76; dir. Curtis Pub. Co., 1970-75. Work includes master plans for Schukill River Park, Phila., 1965, Downtown Harrisburg, Pa., 1975, Sadat City, Egypt, 1977, Acad. Ctr. for Performing Arts, 1981, Atlantic City Master Plan, 1986, South Broad St. Design, Phila., 1991, Schuylkill Heritage Corridor Plan, 1995, Lakewood Ranch Town Ctr. Plan, Fla., 1996, Independence Mall Masterplan, 1997. Bd. dirs. Settlement Music Sch., 1963-83, Phila. Mus. Art, 1975—, Ebenezer Maxwell Mansion, 1980-93, mem. adv. bd., 1993—; bd. dirs. Ctrl. Phila. Devel. Corp., 1989—, The Found. for Arch., Preservation Pa., 1991—, Phila. Soc. Preservation of Landmarks, 1993—, Fleisher Art Meml., 1970, pres., 1982-94; bd. dirs. Washington Cmty. Sch. Music, 1967-70, pres. bd., 1968-70. Mem. AIA, Am. Inst. Planners, Phila. Club, Phila. Cricket Club, Franklin Inn, Tau Sigma Delta. Democrat. Episcopalian. Home: Lane's End 3031 W School House Ln Philadelphia PA 19144-5431 Office: 123 S Broad St Ste 1270 Philadelphia PA 19109-1028

KISER, GLENN AUGUSTUS, retired pediatrician, investor; b. Bessemer City, N.C., July 13, 1917; s. Augustus B. and May (Carpenter) K.; m. Katherine Parham, June 13, 1941 (dec. 1972); m. Muriel Coykendall, Feb. 4, 1973. BS, Duke U., 1941, MD, 1941. Diplomate Nat. Bd. Med. Examiners. Resident physician Duke Hosp., Durham, N.C., 1946-48, Johns Hopkins U., Balt., 1946; pvt. practice Salisbury, N.C., 1947-55; ret. Salisbury, 1955—; founder stockholder Food Lion, Inc.; med. cons. State of N.C., Raleigh, 1961-64, 75-76, New River Mental Health Ctr., Boone, N.C., 1976-77; chief pediat. dept. Rowan Meml. Hosp., Salisbury, 1947-55, chief of staff, 1951-52, pres. Watauga County (N.C.) Med. Soc., 1978. Mem. bd. advisors Chowan Coll., Murfreesboro, N.C., 1977-78; trustee Rowan Regional Med. Ctr. Found., Salisbury, Kiser Med. Office Bldg. at Rowan Regional Med. Ctr., Kiser Welcome Ctr. at Duke U. Children's Hosp. Surgeon USPHS, 1941-46. Recipient Exemplary Life Svc. award Catawba Coll., 1995, N.C.'s Philanthropist of Yr. award, 1996, Order of the Long Leaf Pine award State of N.C., 1996; named alisbury's Man of Yr., 1998. Mem. AMA, N.C. Med. Soc., Pinnacle Club Duke Med. Ctr. (charter), Duke Med. Ctr. Alumni Assn. (coun. 1988), Duke U. Founders Soc., Lions (dep. dist. gov. N.C. chpt. 1959, James B. Duke Soc., pres. Milford Hills chpt. 1959, zone chmn. 1959, dep. dist. gov. 1960, internat. amb. 1961), Salisbury Country Club. Presbyterian. Avocations: photography, music, alumni activities, boating, cycling. Home: 728 Klumac Rd Apt 138C Salisbury NC 28144-5716

KISER, JACKSON L., federal judge; b. Welch, W.Va., June 24, 1929; m. Carole Gorman; children: Jackson, William, John Michael, Elizabeth Carol. B.A., Concord Coll., 1951; J.D., Washington and Lee U., 1952. Bar: Va. Asst. U.S. atty. Western Dist. Va., 1958-61; assoc., then ptnr. R.R. Young, Young, Kiser, Haskins, Mann, Gregory & Young P.C., Martinsville, Va., 1961-82; judge U.S. Dist. Ct. (we. dist.) Va., 1982-93, chief judge, 1993-97, sr. judge, 1997—. Mem. Martinsville City Sch. Bd., 1971-77. With JAGC U.S. Army, 1952-55, capt. Res., 1955-61. Mem. Am. Coll. Trial Lawyers (state com.), Va. Bar Assn. (exec. com.), Va. State Bar, Va. Trial Lawyers Assn., 4th Cir. Jud. Conf. (permanent), Martinsville-Henry County Bar Assn., Order of Coif. Office: US Dist Ct PO Box 3326 700 Main St Danville VA 24543-3326

KISER, KAREN MAUREEN, medical technologist, educator; b. St. Louis, Sept. 28, 1951; d. Arthur John and Elizabeth M. (Boyer) Meier; m. Winston Kiser, July 21, 1973; children: Cynthia Kay, Jessica Lea. BS in Med. Tech., S.E. Mo. State U., 1973; MA in Health Care Edn., Cen. Mich. U., 1984. Part-time lab. asst. Luth. Med. Ctr., St. Louis, 1970-71; part-time lab. technician Jewish Hosp., St. Louis, 1972-73, med. technologist, 1973-77; prof., edn. coord. St. Louis C.C. at Forest Park, 1977—; on-site surveyor Nat. Accrediting Agy. for Clin. Lab. Sci., Chgo., 1986, 94, 96; self-study reviewer, 1994, 95, 99; reviewer F.A. Davis, 1995, W.B. Saunders Co., Phila., 1986-91; spkr. in field. Leader Girl Scouts U.S., 1986-90, 91-92, co-leader, 1990-97; assoc. advisor Explorer Scouts, 1978-81; capt. United Way, St. Louis, 1989, 90, 93; vol. Mastodon State Hist. Site, 1998—. Recipient Emerson Electric award for Teaching Excellence, 1993, Gov.'s award for Excellence in Teaching, 1993. Mem. NEA, Am. Org. for Clin. Lab. Sci., Mo. Soc. for Clin. Lab. Sci., Am. Soc. for Microbiology, Mo. Edn. Assn., Mo. Assn. Cmty. and Jr. Colls., Am. Soc. Clin. Pathologists. Office: Saint Louis CC 5600 Oakland Ave Saint Louis MO 63110-1316

KISER, M.L., computer programmer; b. Lexington, Ky., Oct. 28, 1957. AA, Fugazzi Jr. Coll., 1985. Systems analyst/programmer Chandler Med. Ctr. U. Ky., Lexington, 1997-99. Mem. Nat. Mus. of Am. Indian, Ky. Hist. Soc., John Wayne Cancer Found. (life).

KISER, MOSE, III, small business owner; b. Raleigh, N.C., Nov. 14, 1956; s. Mose Jr. and Joyce Ann (Carpenter) K.; m. Jean Louise Charles, May 15, 1982; children: Taylor Forbes, Margaret Stewart. BA in Psychology, N.C. State U., 1980. Sales trainee Odell Sentry Hardware, Greensboro, N.C., 1980, Wrangler Menswear, Greensboro, 1981-82; sales rep. Wrangler Menswear, Knoxville, Tenn., 1982-84; pres., owner, operator AuraTech, Inc., Greensboro, 1986—; bd. dirs. Greensboro Ice Sports. Adult dir. Greensboro Ice Sports, Inc., 1990; mem. Greensboro Sports Coun., 1990, also bd. dirs. Mem. HemoCue Assn. Regional Distbrs., Health Industry Distbrs. Assn., Biomktg. assn., N.C. State U. Athletic Aid Assn., Greensboro Sports Coun., N.C. State U. Alumni Assn., Greesboro Country Club. Republican. Methodist. Avocations: ice hockey, golf, running. Home: 3106 Solara Tree Greensboro NC 27410-9053 Office: AuraTech Inc 7349 W Friendly Ave Greensboro NC 27410-6255

KISER, NAGIKO SATO, retired librarian; b. Taipei, Republic of China, Aug. 7, 1923; came to U.S., 1950; d. Takeichi and Kinue (Sōma) Sato; m. Virgil Kiser, Dec. 4, 1979 (dec. Mar. 1981). Secondary teaching credential, Tsuda Coll., Tokyo, 1945; BA in Journalism, Trinity U., 1953; BFA, Ohio State U., 1956, MA in Art History, 1959; MLS, cert. in library media, SUNY, Albany, 1974. Cert. community coll. librarian, Calif., cert. jr. coll. tchr., Calif., cert. secondary edn. tchr., Calif., cert. tchr. library media specialist and art, N.Y. Pub. rels. reporter The Mainichi Newspapers, Osaka, Japan, 1945-50; contract interpreter U.S. Dept. State, Washington, 1956-58, 66-67; resource specialist Richmond (Calif.) Unified Sch. Dist., 1968-69; editing supr. CTB/McGraw-Hill, Monterey, Calif., 1969-71; multimedia specialist Monterey Peninsula Unified Sch. Dist., 1975-77; librarian Nishimachi Internat. Sch., Tokyo, 1979-80, Sacramento City Unified Sch. Dist., 1977-79, 81-85; sr. librarian Camarillo (Calif.) State Hosp. and Devel. Ctr., 1985-93. Editor: Short Form Test of Academic Aptitude, 1970, Prescriptive Mathematics Inventory, 1970, Tests of Basic Experience, 1970. Mem. Calif. State Supt.'s Regional Coun. on Asian Pacific Affairs, Sacramento, 1984-91. Library Media Specialist Tng. Program scholar U.S. Office Edn., 1974. Fellow Internat. Biog. Assn. (life); mem. ALA, Am. Biog. Inst. (life, dep. gov. 1988—), Libr. Congress (nat. mem.), Calif. Libr. Assn., Med. Libr. Assn., Asunaro Shogai Kyoiku Kondankai (Lifetime Edn. Promoting Assn., Japan), The Mus. Soc., Internat. House of Japan, Matsuyama Sacramento Sister City Corp., Japanese Am. Citizens League, Japanese Am. Nat. Mus., Japanese Am. Cultural and Cmty. Ctr., Ikenobo Ikebana Soc. Am., L.A. Hototogisu Haiku Assn., Ventura County Archeol. Soc., Internat. Platform Assn., Internat. Soc. Poets. Mem. Christian Science Ch. Avocations: flower arranging, ballroom dance, classical music. Office: Camarillo State Hosp & Devel Ctr Profl Libr PO Box 6022 Camarillo CA 93011-6022

KISER, ROBERTA KATHERINE, medical records administrator, education educator; b. Alton, Ill., Aug. 13, 1938; d. Stephen Robert and Virginia Elizabeth (Lasher) Golden; m. James Robert Crisman, sept. 6, 1958 (div. May 1971); 1 child, Robert Glenn; m. James Earl Kiser, Dec. 19, 1971; 1 child, James Jacob. BEd, So. Ill. U., 1960. Cert. tchr., Ill., Calif. Librarian Oaklawn (Ill.) Elem. Sch., 1960-62, Alsip (Ill.) Elem. Sch., 1966-69; tchr. Desert Sands Unified Sch. Dist., Indio, Calif., 1969-79; prin. Mothercare Infant Sch., Rancho Mirage, Calif., 1980-89; substitute tchr. Greater Coachella Valley Sch., Calif., 1989-91; med. acct. Desert Health Care, Bermuda Dunes, Calif., 1990-92; mentor tchr., computing, typing skills Wilde Woode Children's Ctr., Palm Springs, Calif., 1990-92; chiropractic asst. Rapp Chiropractic Health Ctr, Palm Desert, Calif., 1992-93; sr. med. records clk. Eisenhower Med. Ctr., Rancho Mirage, 1993—. V.p. Palm Desert (Calif.) Community Ch. Montessori Sch. Bd., 1982-85. Republican. Avocation: handbell ensemble musician. Home: 39-575 Keenan Dr Rancho Mirage CA 92270-3610 Office: Eisenhower Med Ctr 39000 Bob Hope Dr Rancho Mirage CA 92270-3221

KISER, STEPHEN, artist, educator; b. Koloa, Hawaii, Feb. 4, 1944; s. Mary A. Kiser; m. Kathleen A. Cahill, Jan. 14, 1973; children: Lisa, Kari. Cert., Brooks Inst. Photography, 1965; BA, San Jose State U., 1976, MA, 1978. Freelance photojournalist, 1964-66, 72-74; photographer Pace Publs., L.A. and N.Y.C., 1966-68; exec. and artistic dir. Tidewater Young Performers, Norfolk, Va., 1968-69; owner Steve Kiser Prodns., Orange, Calif., 1970-72; coord. dir. Ctr. for Creative Arts and Scis., San Francisco, 1976-78; owner Steve Kiser Studios, Palo Alto, Calif., 1995—; assoc. prof. Foothill Coll., Los Altos Hills, Calif., 1996—; trustee, v.p. Am. Indian Contemporary Arts, San Francisco, 1988—. Exhibiting artist with numerous one man and group shows, 1970—. Event coord. Calif. Winter Spl. Olympics, Momouth, Calif., 1975-80; v.p. Hands Across the Water, U.S./Indonesia, 1984-93; advisor Leadership Mid-Peninsula, 1995. With USN, 1968-69. Fellow Rotary, Brazil, 1970; Arts fellow for Contemporary Native Am. Artist, Ednl. Found. Am., 1996. Mem. Am. Soc. Media. Photographers, Internat. Sculpture Assn., Soc. for Photog. Edn., Coll. Art Assn., Hale Naua III. Avocation: exploring new places and concepts. Home: 3302 Vernon Ter Palo Alto CA 94303-4203 Office: 4000 Middlefield Rd # 3 Palo Alto CA 94303-4739

KISER, THELMA KAY, analytical chemist; b. Oakridge, Tenn., Oct. 9, 1944; d. Lawrence T. and Sally Lura (Clay) K. BA in Biology, Emory & Henry Coll., 1968; BS in Chemistry, East Tenn. State U., 1979; postgrad., Ohio State U., 1981, 83, U. Cin., 1986, 87. Cert. collegeate profl. tchr. Tchr. Dickenson County Schs., Clintwood, Va., 1975-78; lab. mgr., rsch. scientist Mead Imaging div. Mead Corp., Dayton, Ohio, 1979-90; group leader, chem. control Marion Merrell Dow, Cin., 1990-95; sr. R&D chemist, mgr. IQC Arcade Inc., Chattanooga, Tenn., 1995—. Contbr. chpt. to book on photopolymers; patentee in field. Vol. counselor Scioto-Paint Valley Crisis Ctr., Chillicothe, Ohio, 1980-84; founding mem. Mead Imaging Hiking Club, Chillicothe, Dayton, 1982-86. Mem. AAAS, Am. Chem. Soc., Ohio Acad. Sci., Soc. for Tech. Communications. Avocations: playing classical piano, hiking, writing non-fiction/poetry, natural history collecting. Office: Arcade Inc 1600 E Main St Chattanooga TN 37404-5036

KISH, ELISSA ANNE, educational administrator, consultant; b. Bklyn., Sept. 29, 1934; d. Robert Joseph and Yolanda Filomina (Romano) Lucadamo; m. Joseph Laurence Kish Jr., Oct. 16, 1955; children: Grace Edna Kish, Joseph Robert, Frances Caroline Kish Burrell. BA, CUNY, 1956; EdM, Rutgers U., 1965. Elem. tchr. N.Y. City Pub. Schs., Bklyn., 1956-57, U.S. Army Dependent Schs., Hanau, West Germany, 1958, Piscataway (N.J.) Pub. Schs., 1961-62, New Brunswick (N.J.) Pub. Schs., 1965, 71-76; vice prin. Hopatcong (N.J.) Pub. Schs., 1977-78; asst. supt. Dunellen (N.J.) Pub. Schs., 1978-80; supr. K-12 instrn. Elmwood Park (N.J.) Pub. Schs., 1980-90; interim high sch. adminstr. Dunellen Pub. Schs., 1991-92; adminstr. ctrl. office Elmwood Park Pub. Schs., 1992-96; cons. Newark Pub. Schs., 1976-77; evaluator Middle States Assn., Navesink, N.J., 1988; cons. State U. N.Y., Garden City, 1992, Mt. Vernon Pub. Schs., N.Y., 1992; mem. fine arts & humanities coun. Town of Wareham, Mass., 1996—. Author: Nutrition Program For Schools, 1979; contbng. author: Curriculum & Values: An Inquiry, 1976. Mem. strategic planning team Town of Elmwood Park, 1993-95; officer, mem. Westfield Coll. Women's Club, Westfield, N.J., 1969-92; founder, 1st pres. Vocational Adv. Coun., Elmwood Park, 1980-90; trustee Christopher Montessori Acad., Westfield, 1968-72. Recipient numerous grants for rsch. and curriculum devel., 1979—. Mem. ASCD, NEA, Elmwood Park Prins. and Suprs. Assn. (pres. 1989-90), Elmwood Park Adminstrs. Assn. (pres. 1986-89), Nat. Geographic Soc., Smithsonian Assocs., Kappa Delta Pi, Alpha Epsilon Phi. Avocations: theatre, opera. Home and office: 1309 San Miguel Ln Fort Myers FL 33903-1541

KISH, GEORGE FRANKLIN, thoracic and cardiovascular surgeon; b. Toledo, Ohio, Mar. 30, 1944; s. George F. and Ann (Kucharski) K.; m. Joann Mata Kish, Mar. 16, 1968; children: Jeremy, Nathan. BS, Ohio State U., 1966, MD, 1970. Surg. intern George Washington U. Med. Ctr., 1970-71, surg. resident, 1971-74, surg. rsch. fellow, 1974-75, chief surg. resident, 1975-76, thoracic and cardiovascular surgery resident, 1976-78; asst. prof. surgery W.Va. U. Med. Ctr., Morgantown, 1978-80; cardiovascular surgery D'Angelo Clinic, Erie, Pa., 1980—; chief cardiovascular surgery Hamot Med. Ctr., Erie, 1982-93. Contbg. author International Trends in General Thoracic Surgery, Vol. 7, 1991; contbr. articles to profl. jours. Dr. I.S. Grisoff fellow cardiovascular surgery George Washington U., 1974-75; affiliate rsch. grantee Am. Heart Assn., W.Va. Med. Ctr., 1979. Fellow ACS, Internat. Soc. Cardiovascular Surgeons, Soc. Thoracic Surgeons, Am. Coll. Cardiology, Am. Coll. Chest Physicians, Southeastern Surg. Congress, Internat. Coll. Angiology. Avocation: down hill skiing. Fax: 814-456-1859. Home: 218 Frontier Dr Erie PA 16505-2506 Office: D'Angelo Clinic 104 E 2nd St Ste 701 Erie PA 16507-1591

KISHEL, GREGORY FRANCIS, federal judge; b. Virginia, Minn., Jan. 26, 1951. AB, Cornell U., 1973; JD, Boston Coll., 1977. Bar: Minn. 1978, U.S. Dist. Ct. Minn. 1978, U.S. Ct. Appeals (8th cir.) 1978, Wis. 1985, U.S. Dist. Ct. (we. dist.) Wis. 1985. Staff atty. Legal Aid Svc. of N.E. Minn., Duluth, 1978-81; pvt. practice law Duluth, 1981-86; judge U.S. Bankruptcy Ct., St. Paul, 1986—; part-time judge U.S. Bankruptcy Ct., Duluth, 1984-86. Mem. ABA, Nat. Conf. Bankruptcy Judges, Minn. Bar Assn., Wis. State Bar Assn., Polish Geneal. Soc. Minn. (pres. 1996—). Office: US Bankruptcy Ct 316 Robert St N Ste 210 Saint Paul MN 55101-1487

KISHIMOTO, YUJI, architect, educator; b. Tokyo, Nov. 6, 1938; s. Hideo and Miyo (Anesaki) K.; m. Toshiko Mitsumori, Oct. 22, 1970; 1 child, Kyo. BArch, Waseda U., 1963; MArch, Harvard U., 1965; EdM, U. Mass., 1976. Registered architect. Designer Vincent G. Kling Assocs., Phila., 1966-67; design critic Boston Archtl. Ctr., 1966-69; instr. R.I. Sch. of Design, Providence, 1966-70; prtnr. Design Collaboratives, Boston, 1967-71; instr. Deerfield (Mass.) Acad., 1971-76; asst. prof. U. Hawaii, Honolulu, 1976-78; assoc. prof. Va. Poly. Inst. and State U., Blacksburg, 1978-80;

assoc. prof. Clemson (S.C.) U., 1980-87, prof., 1987—; pvt. practice, 1985—; urban design cons. Boston Redevel. Authority, 1966-67; design cons. Commonwealth Architects, Boston, 1966-68, Hawaii Group Architects, Honolulu, 1978; S.C. Amb. for Econ. Devel., 1989; co-coord. Clemson U./Hiroshima U. Exch. Program, 1991—; mem. Greenville City Chamber Sci. and Tech. Com., 1991-96; coord. internat. program Clemson U., 1994—, spl. asst. to pres. for US-Japan rels., 1996—, exec. dir. US-Japan Alliance, 1996-97, exec. dir., 1998—; dir. Clemson U.-FIA Exch. Program, 1998—. Oil and acrylic paintings exhbtd. George Walter Vincent Smith Art Mus., Springfield, Mass., 1974 (Springfield Art League award), one-man show Hilson Gallery Deerfield (Mass.) Acad., 1972 and 3-man show, 1971; exhbn. collaborative painting with David Chamberlain Duet, 1997, Brooks Performing Arts Ctr., Clemson U., 1997, 98, Peace Performing Arts Ctr., Founders Gallery, 1997-98, Laura Knott Art Gallery, Bradford, Mass., 1998, James and Raymond Assocs. Gallery, 1998; contbr. articles to profl. jours. V.p. Clemson Area Internat. Friendship, Clemson, 1985-89; spl. asst. to pres. Clemson U. for U.S.-Japan rels., 1996—; bd. dirs. Greenville Internat. Sister City, 1997—, Christ Ch. Episcopal Sch., Greenville, S.C., 1997—, trustee, 1997—. Harvard U. fellow, 1964; travel grantee Asia Found., 1964, Deerfield Acad., 1972, 74; rsch. grantee Va. Poly. Inst. and State U., 1979, Clemson U., 1981, Clemson U. Provost, 1982; Clemson U. Innovation Fund grantee, 1989; named S.C. Ambassador for Econ. Devel., 1989; recipient Harlan McClure award, 1996, 97. Mem. AIA, Assn. Collegiate Schs. Architecture N.Am. (chmn. ASCA-Japan com. 1992—, Japan liaison com.), Archtl. Inst. Japan, S.C. AIA, Japan Inst. Architects, Japan-Am. Assn. Western S.C. (pres. 1988-90, v.p. 1990—), Western S.C. Torch Club Internat. (sec. and pres.-elect 1993-94, pres. 1994-95), Sertoma (v.p. Clemson Club 1986-87). Avocations: classical guitar and lute (performed at numerous recitals, 1972—), painting, running marathons. Home: 101 Hickory Ridge Ct Central SC 29630-9450 Office: Clemson Coll Arch Lee Hall Clemson U Clemson SC 29634-0503

KISKA, TIMOTHY OLIN, newspaper columnist; b. Detroit, July 26, 1952; s. Edward Frederick and Mary Clare (Barnhart) K.; m. Patricia Irene Anstett, May 23, 1981; children: Caitlin, Amy, Eric. BA, Wayne State U., 1980, MA, 1995. Mem. staff Detroit Free Press, 1970-74, reporter, 1974-85, automotive writer, 1985-87; columnist Detroit News, 1987—; mem. student newspaper publs. bd. Wayne State U., 1994-97. Author: Detroit's Powers and Personalities, 1989; contbr. articles to AutoWeek, Automobile, 1985—. Mem. TV Critics Assn. Home: 20050 Marford Ct Grosse Pointe MI 48236-2324 Office: Detroit News 615 W Lafayette Blvd Detroit MI 48226-3197

KISKADDEN, ROBERT MORGAN, artist, educator; b. Tulsa, Dec. 6, 1918; s. William Walter and Irene Sylvia (Price) K.; m. Barbara Jane Meyer, Dec. 23, 1948; children: Kathryn Ann Kiskadden McMurray, Jayne Ann Kiskadden Bechtel. BFA, U. Kans., 1947; MA, Ohio Wesleyan U., 1949. Tchg. fellow Ohio Wesleyan U., Delaware, 1947-49; asst. prof. art Wichita (Kans.) Mcpl. U., 1949-57; assoc. prof. art Wichita State U., 1958-66, prof. art, 1967-68, prof. and acting chmn., 1969, prof., chmn. dept. art, 1970, asst. dean divsn. art, 1971-84, prof., asst. dean emeritus, 1984—. One man shows include Ohio Wesleyan, Delaware, 1949, Estes Park, Colo., 1950, 51, Wichita State U., 1958, Petroleum Club, Wichita, 1958, Hutchinson (Kans.) Art Assn., 1961, 77, Studio Gallery, Topeka, 1962, Wichita Art Mus., 1965, Melody Art Mart, Paducah, Ky., 1966, Wichita State Bank, 1967, Hays (Kans.) State Coll., 1967, Wichita Art Assn., 1972, 84, Bethel Coll., Newton, Kans., 1974, Ellington Gallery, Wichita, 1979, Carmel (Calif.) Fine Art Gallery, 1988, Mus. of the S.W., Midland, Tex., 1993; exhibited in group shows at U. Wichita Gallery, 1949, 60, William Rockhill Nelson Gallery, Kansas City, 1952-55, 57, 59, 63, Wichita Art Mus., 1953-70, Mulvane Art Mus., 1957, 72, 74, Blue Door Gallery, Taos, N.Mex., 1958, Mus. N.Mex., Santa Fe, 1959, Springfield (Mo.) Art Mus., 1965, U. Tex.-El Paso, 1969, Sacred Heart Coll., 1969, So. State Coll., Springfield, S.D., 1971, Birger Sandzen Meml. Gallery, Lindsborg, 1981, McFarland Gallery, Wichita, 1969, Raven Art Gallery, Wichita, 1972, Ulrich Mus., 1977, 79, Ellington Gallery Oils and Watercolors, Wichita, 1979, annually Wichita Art Assn., Wichita State U., others; works in permanent collections Am. Embassy, Cairo, Peking U., others; contbr., worked on Joan Miro Mosaic Project facade of Ulrich Mus. Art, 1976-78. Chmn. bdlg. com. McKnight Art Ctr., Wichita, 1974; ex-officio mem. Wichita Art Mus., Wichita Art Assn.; adv. coun. Kans. Cultural Arts Commn., Topeka, 1969, 75. Sgt. C.E. U.S. Army, 1942-45. Recipient numerous awards of merit, best of show, cash, purchase awards, popular, hon. mention, 1st, 2d, 3rd prizes, 1949-93; Kiskadden Scholarship for Studio Art Majors established by Wichata State U., 1984—. Mem. Srs. in Retirement, Chisholm Trail Antique Gun Assn. (life), Wichita Art Assn. (adv. bd.), Wichita Artist Guild (past pres., bd. dirs.), Kans. Watercolor Soc. (charter), Kans. Acad. Oil Painters (charter), Nat. Assn. Mus., Nat. Cowboy Hall of Fame, Sigma Alpha Epsilon. Avocations: golf, fly fishing.

KISKER, CARL THOMAS, physician, medical educator. B.A., Johns Hopkins U., 1958; M.D., U. Cin. Coll. Medicine, 1962. Diplomate Am. Bd. Pediatrics, Am. Bd. Pediatric Hematology-Oncology. Lic. physician Ohio, Iowa. Intern U. Oreg. Coll. Medicine, 1962-63; sr. asst. surgeon NIH, 1963-65; jr. resident pediat. Children's Hosp., Cin., 1965-66; sr. resident pediat. Children's Hosp., 1966-67, fellow pediat. hematology, 1967-69, asst. attending pediatrician, 1968-69, attending pediatrician, 1969-73, dir. hemophilia project, 1971-73, dir. clin. hematology lab., 1972-73; asst. prof. pediat. U. Cin., 1969-72, assoc. prof. pediat., 1972-73; assoc. prof. pediat. U. Iowa, Iowa City, 1973-79; dir. divsn. pediat. hematology-oncology U. Iowa, 1973-97, prof. pediat., 1979—; med. lectr. various student and profl. groups; active mem. Pediat. Hematology-Oncology Group, Cin., Children's Cancer Study Group, L.A.; pres. Midwest Blood Club.; mem. adv. coun. Nat. Hemophilia Ctrs., 1979—.$D. Mem. editl bd. Pediat. Today; contbr. numerous sci. papers to profl. jours. and chpts. in books. Mem. Iowa Found. Fund Raising Com. Lederle Med. Student Rsch. fellow, 1959; recipient state and fed. grants. Mem. Am. Soc. Hematology, Mid-west Soc. for Pediat. RSch., Am. Fedn. for Clin. RSch., Am. Heart Assn., Internat. Soc. Thrombosis and Haemostasis (sub-com. on neonatal hemostasis), Ctrl. Soc. for Pediat. Rsch., Soc. Pediat. Rsch., Johnson County Med. Soc., Prairie Region Affiliated Blood Svcs., Am. Pediat. Soc. Office: Univ of Iowa Hosp 2520 Jcp Iowa City IA 52242

KISLAK, JEAN HART, art director; b. Mineola, N.Y.; d. Frank Ernest and Isabelle Tayor (Ellis) Hart; m. William I. Herendeen, Aug. 23, 1952 (div. Feb. 1956); m. Louis G. Johnson, Jan. 31, 1959 (div. Feb. 1975); 1 child, Jennifer Taylor Johnson; m. Jay Kislak, Apr. 7, 1985. Student Peace Jr. Coll., Raleigh, N.C., Queens Coll., Charlotte, N.C. With Storer Broadcasting Co., Miami, Fla.; with S.E. Banks N.A., Miami, Fla., 1974-84, art dir., 1974-84; mem. Gov. Fla. Panel Visual Arts, 1980, Dade County Art in Pub. Places, 1979-81; art cons., 1974—; internat. rep. Christies, Inc., 1998—. Bd. dirs. Viscaya Mus., Miami, 1963, Beaux Arts, U. Miami, 1968, Theatre Art Patrons, Miami, 1965, NEH (Fla.), 1992; trustee Dade County Zool. Soc., 1988—, Miami Art Mus., Barry Coll. Charter Sch.; mem. Bacardi Imports Art Bd., 1983-89, 98—, Fla. State Bd. Art Coun., 1987, Miami Art Mus. (formerly Dade County Ctr. for the Arts Bd.), 1989-99, bd. dirs. Nat. Wildflower Assn., 1991; mem. exec. bd. Zoological Soc. Fla., 1994; mem. Fla. Humanities Bd., 1994. Recipient Gov. Fla. award art, 1976, 79, Miami Dade Pub. Library award, 1978, Bus. Com. for Arts award, 1975-79, WPBT Pub. TV award, 1976, 77, 80, Lowe Gallery, U. Miami cert. recognition, 1980, Dade County Art in Pub. Places cert. recognition, 1981, 82. Mem. 1805 Club (hon. v.p. 1993—), Kislak Found. (bd. dirs. 1997—). Address: 720 NE 69th St Miami FL 33138-5738

KISLIK, RICHARD WILLIAM, publishing executive; b. N.Y.C., Oct. 31, 1927; s. Louis K. and Isabelle (Deutelbaum) K.; m. Audrey Gerber, June 19, 1949; children: Nancy J., Andrew R., Laurie S., Wendy J. AB, Harvard U., 1948, MBA, 1949. Rsch. asst. Bus. Sch. Harvard U., 1949-50; asst. contr. Maidenform Brassiere Co., 1950-54; contr. Doubleday & Co., Inc., 1954-60; treas., dir. Ziff-Davis Pub. Co., 1960-61; v.p. fin., dir. Random House, Inc., 1961-68; cons., 1968; v.p. Intext Ednl. Pubs., Inc., 1968-69, pres., 1969—; exec. v.p. Intext, Inc., 1970-71, pres., 1971-77, chmn. bd., chief exec. officer, 1972-80, cons., 1980; pres., dir. W.H. Smith Pubs. Inc., 1981-86; pvt. practice, 1986—; v.p. M. Evans & Co., 1987; bd. dirs., v.p. fin. Chelsea Green Pub. Co., White River Junction, Vt. Mem. Players Club, Dutch Treat Club, Harvard Club (N.Y.C.), Pubs. Lunch Club, Harvard Bus. Sch. Club Greater N.Y. Home: 176 E 71st St New York NY 10021-5159

KISMARIC, CAROLE LEE, editor, writer, book packaging company executive; b. Orange, N.J., Apr. 28, 1942; d. John Joseph and Alice Felicia (Gruskos) K.; m. Charles Vincent Mikolaycak, Oct. 1, 1970. BA in Psychology, Pa. State U., 1964. Reporter, writer Parkersburg News, W. Va., summers 1960, 61; reporter, writer UPI, Columbus, Ohio, summer 1962; writer Conde Nast Publs., N.Y.C., 1964; picture editor, assoc. editor Time Life Book Div., N.Y.C., 1965-75; editorial dir. Aperture, Inc., N.Y.C., 1976-85; freelance pub. cons., editor, writer N.Y.C., 1985—; co-founder, co-owner book packaging co. Lookout Books, N.Y.C., 1990—; founder Lookout with Marvin Heiferman, comms. co.; mem. visual arts and policy panels NEA, Washington, 1977-81, 93; tchr. grad. sch. photography program Sch. Visual Arts, N.Y.C., 1990—. Author: Duel of the Ironclads, 1969, The Boy Who Tried to Cheat Death, 1971, The Rumor of Pavel and Paali, 1988, A Gift From Saint Nicholas, 1988, Forced Out: The Agony of the Refugee in Our Time, 1989, I'm So Happy, 1990, My Day, 1993, Talking Pictures, 1994, Growing Up With Dick and Jane: Living and Learning and American Dream, 1996, Love is Blind, 1996, Dick Clark's American Bandstand, 1997, Flaming Creature: The Life and Times of Jack Smith, 1997, Self-Portrait: John Coplans, 1997, The Mysterious Case of Nancy Drew and the Hardy Boys, 1998, The Art of the X-Files, 1998, Big Dogs, Little Dogs, 1998, To the Rescue: Eight Artists in an Archive, 1999; author, editor: The Photography Catalogue, 1976; contbr. numerous articles to profl. jours.; assoc. curator From the Picture Press, Mus. Modern Art, 1973; co-curator traveling exhbns. L.A. Mcpl. Art Gallery: Forced Out in Time, 1989-93, Internat. Ctr. of Photography, Talking Pictures, 1994-97, Mus. Modern Art: Fame After Photography, 1999. Recipient award Communications Graphics Assn., 1971, 72; Book of Yr. award Am. Inst. Graphic Arts, 1974, 75, 91. Avocation: traveling. Home: 64 E 91st St New York NY 10128-1359 Office: Lookout Books 1024 6th Ave New York NY 10018-5415

KISNER, JACOB, poet, editor, publisher; b. Chelsea, Mass., Apr. 30, 1926; s. Louis and Sarah (Kotel) K.; m. Gladys Selma Feinstein, May 29, 1947; 1 child, Lesley Kisner Cafarelli. Student, Calvin Coolidge Coll., 1945-46, Burdett Coll., 1943-45, Harvard U. Extension, 1944-48, Mass. State Univ. Extension, 1944-50, Cambridge Ctr. for Adult Edn., 1946-51. With Boston Am. advt. dept., 1943; Sunday dept. writer Boston Globe, 1943-45; local news editor Jewish Advocate, Boston, 1945-46; founder, editor, pub. Dorchester (Mass.) Herald, 1946-47; copywriter Harold Cabot & Co. Advt. Agy., Boston, 1948; trade reporter Fairchild News Svc., Boston, 1948-49; with Boston Pub. Libr. Cataloguing Dept., 1949; sr. proof-reader Rec. and Statis Corp., Boston, 1950-54; participant NBC Comedy Writers Devel. Project, 1956; editor Crossroads, Toronto, Ont., Can., 1964-67; Am. editor View, Can., 1967—; rsch. dir. N.Y. bur. Moneytree Publs., N.Y.C., 1972—; stamp and autograph dealer, 1973-82; owner, operator Penthouse F Stamps, 1982—; discoverer Lord and Taylor find of Finnish postal hist.; free-lance writer, 1943—. Author: (plays) First Came Paula, 1954, Speak of the Devil, 1955, The Monkey's Tail, 1956; (TV plays): The Late Mr. Honeywell, 1957, A World Apart, 1957; (poetry) I Am Hephaestus, 1966; numerous pub. articles, revs., rsch. on stamps and postal hist.; contbr. poetry to various lit. jours. and anthologies. Saxophonist, leader big band Jack Kenton, 1943-46; philatelic journalist; discussion moderator Great Books Found., Boston, 1948-51; judge of poetry contests, Rochester, N.Y., also N.Y. Poetry Forum, 1969—; sec. Am.-European Friendship Assn., 1948-51; chmn. Nat. Poetry Day Com., 1970; N.Y. State dir. and N.Y.C. chmn. World Poetry Day Com., 1971—; v.p., bd. dirs., incorporator N.Y. Poetry Forum, 1973-75; founder postmaster Park Ave Local Post, 1978—. Recipient Spl. Commendation for poem on death of Martin Luther King, Jr., So. Christian Leadership Conf., 1968, World Peace award Ky. State Poetry Soc., 1970, Gold Medal award Internat. Poets' Shrine, Hollywood, 1971, Radio award for Poetry of Superior Broadcast Quality, Sta. WEFG-FM, Winchester, Va., 1970, Spl. Citation award Poetry Pageant, 1970, Writer's Digest award, 1971. Mem. Am. Newspaper Guild, Acad. Am. Poets (founder), Wilson MacDonald Poetry Soc. Can. (exec. com. 1967-77, v.p. 1977—), Am. Philatelic Soc., Trans-Miss. Philatelic Soc., Soc. Philatelic Ams., Soc. Israel Philatelists, Am. Revue Assn., Confederate Stamp Alliance, United Postal Stationery Soc., Scandinavian Collectors Club, Perfins Club, Am. Philatelic Rsch. Libr., Scandinavian Philatelic Libr. Soc. Calif., N.Mex. Philatelic Assn., Finnish Study Group. Address: Penthouse F 254 Park Ave S Ph F New York NY 10010-7208

KISNER, WENDELL HOWARD, JR., plastic surgeon; b. L.A., Dec. 5, 1939; s. Wendell Howard Sr. and Jennie Junkin Kisner; m. Jane Johnsey, June 26, 1957; children: Wendell, Aaron, Meg, Walter. BS, Tulane U., 1961, MD, 1965. Diplomate Am. Bd. Plastic and Reconstructive Surgery. Intern in surgery U. Kans. Med. Ctr., 1965-66; resident in gen. surgery LDS Hosp., Salt Lake City, 1966-67, Ochsner Clinic, New Orleans, 1969-71; resident in plastic surgery U. Miss., 1971-72; chief resident in plastic surgery U. Tenn., 1972-73; pvt. practice Salem, Oreg., 1973-75, Baton Rouge, 1975—; rsch. fellowship microvascular surgery Ochsner Clinic, 1970; instr. surgery U. Miss., 1971-72, U. Tenn., 1972-73; clin. instr. surgery U. Oreg., 1973-75; clin. asst. prof. plastic surgery dept. surgery La. State U. Med. Sch., 1975—; lectr. in field. Contbr. articles to profl. jours.; author of poetry. Meet physician, head NCAA Track and Field Championship, Baton Rouge, 1982, 87; charter mem., bd. mem. Baton Rouge Opera, 1983; bd. mem. Baton Rouge Symphony, 1998—. Capt. USAF, 1967-69. Mem. Am. Assn. Hand Surgery, Am. Coll. Surgeons, Am. Soc. Plastic and Reconstructive Surgeons (sports medicine com., mktg. com., panel mem. sports injuries 1986), Southeastern Soc. Plastic and Reconstructive Surgeons (chmn. pub. rels. com., historian 1990-91, trustee 1992-94, asst. sec. 1994-96, v.p. 1996-97, pres.-elect 1997-98, pres. 1998-99), Baton Rouge Surg. Soc. (pres. 1989), Costa Rica Plastic Surgery Soc. (corr.), La. Soc. Plastic Surgery, La. State Med. Soc., East Baton Rouge Parish Med. Soc., Surg. Assn. La., Undersea and Hyperbaric Med. Soc., Am. Coll. Hyperbaric Medicine, Am. Soc. Aesthetic Plastic Surgery, U.S. Olympic Sports Medicine Soc., Krewe Bacchus. Avocations: hunting, fishing, golfing, camping, herpetology. E-mail: trotman@earthlink.net. Office: 7777 Hennessy Blvd Ste 8002 Baton Rouge LA 70808-4368

KISON, CAROL, nursing educator, critical care nurse; b. Milw.. Diploma, Sacred Heart; AAS, Milw. Area Tech. Coll.; BSN, Alverno Coll.; MSN, Clayton U., 1986; MSM, Cardinal Stritch, 1987; MSN, U. Wis., Milw., 1990; PhD in Health Svcs., Walden U., Minn. RN, Wis. Adj. asst. prof. nursing Marian Coll., Fond du Lac, Wis.; DON long-term care U. Wis., Milw. Mem. ANA, AACN, Nat. League for Nursing, WND, GMAC, Wis. Nurses Assn., Doctorate Assn. N.Y. Educators, Sigma Theta Tau.

KISOR, HENRY DU BOIS, newspaper editor, critic, columnist; b. Ridgewood, N.J., Aug. 17, 1940; s. Manown and Judith (Du Bois) K.; m. Deborah L. Abbott, June 24, 1967; children: Colin, Conan. BA, Trinity Coll., 1962, LittD (hon.), 1991; MS in Journalism, Northwestern U., 1964. Copy editor Wilmington News-Jour. (Del.), 1964-65; copy editor Chgo. Daily News, 1965-73, book editor, 1973-78; book editor Chgo. Sun-Times, 1978—; adj. prof. Medill Sch. Journalism Northwestern U., Evanston, Ill., 1979-82. Author: What's That Pig Outdoors?: A Memoir of Deafness, 1990, Zephyr: Tracking a Dream Across America, 1994, Flight of the Gin Fiz; Midlife at 4,500 Feet, 1997. Bd. dirs. Chgo. Hearing Soc., 1975-76. Recipient Stick-O-Type award Chgo. Newspaper Guild, 1981, 85, Outstanding Achievement award Ill. UPI, 1983, 85, 1st pl. award Ill. UPI columns divsn., 1985, James Friend Meml. Critic award Friends of Lit., 1988, Best Non-fiction award, 1991; finalist Pulitzer Prize nomination in criticism Columbia U., 1981; NEH seminar fellow, 1978. Office: Chgo Sun-Times 401 N Wabash Ave Chicago IL 60611-5642

KISS, TIBOR, military attache; b. Kasbarat, Hungary, Mar. 26, 1945; s. Irme Kiss and Gizella Ferenczi; m. Katalin Csutora's, July 4, 1970; children: Viktoria, Tibor. Student, Mil. Acad., Szentendre, Hungary, 1967; cert. German tchr., Coll. Juha'sz Gyula, Szeged, Hungary, 1967; degree in econs. and fgn. trade, U. Econ. Sci., Budapest, Hungary, 1979. Desk officer Gen. Staff, Budapest, 1967-73, 74-76, 78-85; head dept. Gen. Staff, Budapest, 1989-92, dir., 1993-95; ops. officer ICCS, Saigon, Vietnam, 1973-74; sec. to DAO Hungarian Embassy, London, 1976-78; mil. and air attache Hungarian Embassy, Helsinki; dep. gen. dir. Mil. Intelligence, Budapest, 1993-95; def., mil. and air attache Hungarian Embassy, Washington, 1998—. Brig. gen. Hungarian Army, 1951. Recipient Degree of Order of Finnish Lion, Pres. of Finland, 1989. Office: Hungarian Embassy 3910 Shoemaker St Washington DC 20008

KISSA, KARL MARTIN, electrical engineer; b. Wilmington, Del., June 5, 1961; s. Erik and Selma (Tamm) K. BS, Duke U., 1982; MEE, U. Del., 1986, PhD, 1989. Tech. staff C.S. Draper Lab., Cambridge, Mass., 1989-94; photonic device engr. United Techs. Photonics, Bloomfield, Conn., 1994-95; sr. optical engr. Uniphase Telecom. Products, Bloomfield, 1995—. Vol. Harvard Sq. Meals Program, Cambridge, Mass., 1991-94. Mem. IEEE, Phi Beta Kappa, Tau Beta Pi, Eta Kappa Nu. Episcopalian. Home: 9 Rebecca Ln Simsbury CT 06070-1424 Office: Uniphase Telecom Products 1289 Blue Hills Ave Bloomfield CT 06002-1302

KISSANE, JAMES DONALD, English literature educator; b. Pocatello, Idaho, June 21, 1930; s. Donald P. and Leedice Irene (McAnelly) K.; m. Nancy Jane Duke, June 8, 1952; children: Alan, John, Peter, Emily. BA, Grinnell Coll., 1952; PhD, Johns Hopkins U., 1956. Asst. prof. English Grinnell (Iowa) Coll., 1956-60, assoc. prof., 1960-65, prof., 1965—, Carter-Adams prof. lit., 1972-89, Routt prof. lit., 1989—; vis. prof. English U. Ky., 1971-72. Author: (with S.P. Zitner and M.M. Liberman) A Preface to Literary Analysis, 1964, The Practice of Criticism, 1966, Alfred Tennyson, 1970; contbr. articles to various publs. Mem. Phi Beta Kappa.

KISSANE, MARY ELIZABETH, communications executive, consultant; b. Westchester, N.Y.; d. Thomas Patrick and Marion (O'Shea) K. BA cum laude, Iona Coll., 1982, MS in Corp. Comms. with honors, 1990; JD, N.Y. Law Sch., 1996. Asst. to CFO Aspen Systems Corp., 1984; account supr. Charles Barker, Inc., 1984-86; communications mgr. BET Fin., Inc., 1987; assoc. Bliss, Barefoot & Assocs., 1988; asst. v.p. Georgeson & Co., 1989-92, v.p., 1992-95, dir. investor rels. divsn., 1995-98; sr. mng. dir. Hill and Knowlton, 1998—; adj. asst. prof. mass comm. Grad. Sch. Arts Sci., Iona Coll., New Rochelle, N.Y. Author: Global Gadflies: Applications and Implications of U.S. - Style Corporate Government Abroad, 1997; mem. N.Y. Law Sch. Jour. Internat. and Comparative Law, 1994-95. Recipient Am. Jurisprudional prizes for legal writing and rsch., 1992-93. Office: Hill and Knowlton Inc 466 Lexington Ave New York NY 10017-3140

KISSANE, SHARON FLORENCE, writer, consultant, educator; b. Chgo., July 2, 1940; d. Bruno William and Agnes Evelyn (Payne) Mrotek; m. James Quin Kissane, July 2, 1966 (dec. June 1989); children: Laura Janine Ehrke, Elaine Marie Kissane. BA, De Paul U., 1962; MA, Northwestern U., 1963; PhD, Loyola U., 1970. Cert. tchr., Ill. Tchr. Notre Dame H.S., Chgo., 1959-61, Our Lady of Solace Sch., Chgo., 1961-62; tech. writer, editor Commerce Clearing House, Chgo., 1962-63; tchr. U. Ill., Chgo., 1963-66; mgr. Amalgamated Ins. Co., Chgo., 1966-68; writer Herald Newspapers, Des Plaines, Ill., 1968-69; assoc. dir. Montague Coll. Psycho-Ednl. Clinic, Chgo., 1970-72; dir. Learning Ctr., libr. Stevenson Elem. Sch., Des Plaines, 1972-73; dir. Park Ridge (Ill.) Reading Ctr., 1973-78; pres. Kissane Comms. Ltd., Barrington, Ill., 1979—; learning disabilities specialist Montessori Sch., Lake Forest, Ill. Author: What is Child Abuse?, 1993, Gang Awareness, 1995; co-author: Polish Biographical Dictionary, 1992, Career Success for People With Physical Disabilities, 1996, Autobiography of Mousie Garner, Vaudeville Stooge; contbr. articles to profl. jours. Bd. dirs. Barrington (Ill.) Children's Choir, 1984-85, LA FEP Student Exch. Program, Barrington, 1983-84, Barrington Area United Way, Operation Smile Internat., Chgo.; mem. task force Dist. # 220, Barrington, 1983-86; founding mem. Barrington Area Arts Coun., 1980, Park Ridge Hist. Soc., 1972; mem. curriculum com. Barrington H.S., 1981-84; elections judge South Barrington Precinct, 1989—. Recipient Dale Carnegie Speech scholarship Jr. Achievement, 1958; named Hon. Citizen of Korea, 1965; recipient Citte del sol, Italy. Mem. Nat. Assn. Women Bus. Owners (bd. dirs. 1982-83), Internat. Platform Assn., MIT Forum, Barrington Profl. Women, Midwest Soc. Profl. Cons., Phi Delta Kappa, Kappa Gamma Pi. Republican. Avocations: painting, post-card art, music, sports. Office: Kissane Comms Ltd 15 Turning Shore Dr South Barrington IL 60010-9597

KISSEBERTH, PAUL BARTO, retired publishing executive; b. Tiffin, Ohio, July 5, 1932; s. Roscoe Paul and Mary Margaret (Barto) K.; m. Ann Capps Grinton, June 26, 1954; children: Mary, Katharine, Michael, John. B.A., Ohio Wesleyan U., 1954. With McGraw Hill Inc., 1956-89; Western field sales mgr. Fleet Owner Mag., Chgo., 1974-76; advt. sales mgr. Fleet Owner Mag., N.Y.C., 1976-78, pub., 1978-89, v.p., pub., 1986-89; chmn. McGraw-Hill Pubs., 1981-82; v.p., assoc. pub. Aviation Week & Space Tech., 1987-89; sr. v.p., pub. Fleet Owner Mag., FM Bus. Publs., 1989; pres. transp. and trucking divsn. Fleet Owner Mag., FM Bus. Publs., N.Y.C., 1989-91; pub. Fleet Owner mag. Intertec Pub. Inc., White Plains, N.Y., 1992-96; ret., 1996. Lay leader First United Methodist Ch., Stamford, Conn., 1980-83. Served to 1st lt. USAF, 1954-56. Mem. Associated Bus. Press, Beta Theta Pi. Home: 39 Happy Hill Rd Stamford CT 06903-1203

KISSEL, HOWARD WILLIAM, drama critic; b. Milw., Oct. 29, 1942; s. Leo and Ruth (Miletzky) K.; m. Christine Buck, May 5, 1974. BA, Columbia U., 1964; MS in Journalism, Northwestern U., 1966. Arts editor Women's Wear Daily, N.Y.C., 1971-86; drama critic N.Y. Daily News, 1986-97, columnist, 1997—; juror Pulitzer Prize for Drama, 1994; bd. dirs. Theater Devel. Fund.; adj. prof. Marymount Manhattan, 1998—. Author: David Merrick, The Abominable Showman; Dictionary of Literary Biography, 1982-97. Named to Hall of Achievement Northwestern U., 1997. Mem. N.Y. Drama Critics Circle (pres. 1984-86), N.Y. Film Critics Circle (chmn. 1975, 82), Players Club. Jewish. Home: 275 Central Park W New York NY 10024-3015 Office: NY Daily News Inc 450 W 33rd St Fl 3 New York NY 10001-2681

KISSEL, JOHN THOMAS, neurologist; b. Cin., Dec. 20, 1953; s. Raymond Bernard and Mary Catherine K.; m. Margaret Emily Jones, June 10, 1978; children: Emily Catherine, James David, Andrew Thomas. BS cum laude, Northwestern U., 1974, MD, 1978. Diplomate Am. Bd. Psychiatry and Neurology, Nat. Bd. Med. Examiners. Intern in internal medicine Ohio State U., Columbus, 1978-79, clin. neuromuscular fellow, 1979-82, rsch. fellow, 1983-85, from asst. to assoc. prof. neurology, 1985-97, prof. neurology, 1997—; resident in neurology Barnes Hosp., St. Louis, 1979-82. Co-author: Peripheral Neuropathy, vol. 1, 1994, Handbook of Clinical Neurology, vol. 19, 1992, Current Therapy in Neurological Disease, 1993, Immunology of Neuromuscular Disease, 1994, Neurobase, 1994, rev., 1996, Neuroimmunology, 1998; co-editor: Seminars in Neurology, Myopathies, 1998; ad hoc jour. reviewer Jour. Neurol. Scis., Archives Neurology; presenter in field; prin. investigator; referee numerous jours. Med. adv. com. Muscular Dystrophy Assn., 1998—. Fellow Am. Acad. Neurology (S. Weir Mitchell award, Founders award, mem. numerous coms.); mem. Am. Neurol. Assn., Ctrl. Ohio Neurol. Soc., Ctrl. Soc. Neurol. Rsch. (pres. 1997-99), Alpha Omega Alpha. E-mail: kissel.2@osu.edu. Office: Ohio State U Med Ctr 1654 Upham Dr Columbus OH 43210

KISSEL, PETER CHARLES, lawyer; b. Watertown, N.Y., Sept. 29, 1947; s. Laurence Haas and Catherine Cantwell (Weldon) K.; m. Sharon Darlene Murphy, June 14, 1970. AB, Syracuse U., 1969; JD, Am. U., 1972. Bar: D.C. 1973, U.S. Ct. Claims 1976, U.S. Dist. Ct. D.C. 1979, U.S. Ct. Appeals (9th cir.) 1979, U.S. Ct. Appeals (D.C. cir.) 1983, U.S. Ct. Appeals (3d cir.) 1986, U.S. Ct. Appeals (5th cir.) 1988, U.S. Supreme Ct. 1978. Atty.-advisor Fed. Power Commn., Washington, 1972-74; atty. pub. utilities, 1974-77; assoc. O'Connor & Hannan, Washington, 1977-79, ptnr., 1979-87; ptnr. Baller Hammett, Washington, 1987-93; ptnr., CFO, Grammer, Kissel, Robbins, Skancke & Edwards, Washington, 1993—; co-bus. mgr. Energy Law Jour., Washington, 1981, asst. editor, 1982-89, bus. mgr., 1989-92. Contbr. articles to profl. jours. Mem. vestry St. Patrick's Episcopal Ch., Washington, 1975-78, 82-85, 86-90, chmn. ann. fundraising campaign, 1987-89; bd. dirs. Episcopal Caring Response to AIDS Inc., 1988-93, v.p., 1990-91, pres., 1992, mem. exec. com., 1990-93; bd. dirs. PRISM, 1996-97, Foun. of the Energy Law Jour., 1990-92. Recipient Spl. award Fed. Power Commn., 1973. Mem. Bar Assn. D.C., Fed. Energy Bar Assn. (vice-chmn. com. on publs. 1984-85, chmn. com. on hydroelectric regulation 1991-92), Nat. Hydropower Assn., John Sherman Myers Soc. (Washington Coll. Law), Syracuse U. Soc. Fellows, Syracuse U. Washington adv. bd., Phi Kappa Psi. Democrat. Episcopalian. Avocations: gardening, American history, Irish history. Home: 5604 Utah Ave NW Washington DC 20015-1230 Office: Grammer Kissel Robbins Skancke & Edwards 1225 I St NW Ste 1225 Washington DC 20005-5939

KISSEL, RICHARD JOHN, lawyer; b. Chgo., Nov. 27, 1936; s. John and Anne T. (Unichowski) K.; m. Donna Lou Heidersbach, Feb. 11, 1961; children—Roy Warren, David Todd, Audrey Anne. B.A., Northwestern U., 1958; J.D., Northwestern U.-Chgo., 1961. Assoc. Peterson, Lowrey, Rall, Barber & Ross, Chgo., 1961-65; div. counsel Abbott Labs., North Chicago, Ill., 1965-70; mem. Pollution Control Bd., Chgo., 1970-72; adminstrv. asst. Gov.'s Staff, Chgo., 1972; ptnr. Martin, Craig, Chester & Sonnenschein, Chgo., 1973-88; ptnr. Gardner, Carton & Douglas, 1988—, vice chmn. exec. com., 1989-94, chmn. mgmt. com., 1996-98; adj. prof. U. Ill. Sch. Pub. Health, Chgo., 1973-76; instr. Kent. Sch. Law, Ill. Inst. Tech., Chgo., 1974-78; mem. vis. com. Northwestern U. Law Sch., 1996—. Recipient Ill. award IAWA, 1996. Contbr. articles to legal jours. Fellow Internat. Soc. Barristers; mem. Ill. State Bar Assn., Chgo. Bar Assn., Ill. State C. of C. (chmn. environ. affairs 1973-76), Com. on Cts. for 21st Century. Roman Catholic. Club: Knollwood (gov. 1976-82) (Lake Forest). Office: Gardner Carton & Douglas 321 N Clark St Ste 3000 Chicago IL 60610-4762

KISSEL, WILLIAM THORN, JR., sculptor; b. Feb. 6, 1920; s. William Thorn and Frances A. (Dallett) K.; m. Barbara Eldred Case, June 17, 1943 (dec. June 1978); children: William Thorn III (dec.), Michael C. Grad., Choate Sch., 1939; BA, Harvard U., 1944; postgrad., Pa. Acad. Fine Arts, 1951-53; grad., Barnes Found., 1953, Rinehart Grad. Sch. Sculpture, Balt., 1958; BFA (hon.), Md. Inst. Coll. Art, 1996. T. Exhibited sculpture Lever House, N.Y.C., N.A.D., N.Y.C., Balt. Sculptor's Exhibit, York, Pa., Beverly, Mass., Gloucester, Woodmere Gallery, Germantown, Pa.; represented in pvt. collections, U.S.; executed large granite meml., Montclair, N.J.; also many animal sculpture studies and commns. Pilot, lt. (j.g.) USNR, 1942-45. Recipient Mass. Sculptor's award Regional Exhibit, 1958, Speyer award NAD, 1966, 68, Am. Artists Profl. League award, 1966; fellow Pa. Acad. Fine Arts, 1951-53. Fellow Am. Artists Profl. League, Nat. Sculpture Soc. Republican. Episcopalian. Home: 223 Greenspring Valley Rd Owings Mills MD 21117-4118

KISSINGER, HENRY ALFRED, former secretary of state, international consulting company executive; b. Fuerth, Germany, May 27, 1923; came to U.S., 1938, naturalized, 1943; s. Louis and Paula (Stern) K.; m. Ann Fleischer, Feb. 6, 1949 (div. 1964); children: Elizabeth, David; m. Nancy Maginnes, Mar. 30, 1974. A.B. summa cum laude, Harvard U., 1950, M.A., 1952, Ph.D., 1954. Exec. dir. Harvard Internat. Seminar, 1951-69; mem. faculty dept. govt., Ctr. for Internat. Affairs Harvard U., 1954-69; dir. def. studies program Harvard Internat. Seminar, 1958-69, assoc. prof. govt., 1959-62, prof., 1962-69; faculty Ctr. Internat. Affairs, Harvard U., 1960-69; asst. to Pres. for Nat. Security Affairs, 1969-75; Sec. of State, 1973-77; founder, chmn. Kissinger Assocs., Inc., N.Y.C.; chmn. Nat. Bipartisan Commn. on Ctrl. Am., 1983-84; mem. internat. adv. com. Chase Bank; study dir. nuclear weapons and fgn. policy Coun. Fgn. Rels, 1955-56; dir. spl. studies project Rockefeller Bros. Fund, Inc., 1956-58; cons. Ops. Rsch. Office, 1950-61; cons. to dir. Psychol. Strategy Bd., 1952; cons. Ops. Coordinating Bd., 1955, Weapons Systems Evaluation Group, 1959-60, Dept. State, 1965-69; trustee Ctr. Strategic and Internat. Studies; hon. chmn. World Cup USA, 1994. Author: Nuclear Weapons and Foreign Policy, 1957, A World Restored: Castlereagh, Metternich and the Restoration of Peace, 1812-22, 1957, The Necessity for Choice: Prospects of American Foreign Policy, 1961, The Troubled Partnership: A Reappraisal of the Atlantic Alliance, 1965, White House Years, 1979, For the Record, 1981, Years of Upheaval, 1982, Observations: Selected Speeches and Essays, 1984, Diplomacy, 1994, Years of Renewal, 1999; Editor: Problems of National Strategy: A Book of Readings, 1965, Confluence, An Internat. Forum, 1951-58; contbr. to profl. jours. Trustee Met. Mus. Art, N.Y.C., 1978—. Served with AUS, 1943-46. Recipient citation Overseas Press Club, 1958, Woodrow Wilson prize for best book fields of govt., politics, internat. affairs, 1958, Disting. Pub. Svc. award Am. Inst. Pub. Svc., 1973, Nobel Peace prize, 1973, Presdl. Medal of Freedom, 1977, Medal of Liberty, 1986; named Hon. Knight Comdr. of St. Michael and St. George, 1995; Guggenheim fellow, 1965-66. Mem. Am. Polit. Sci. Assn., Council Fgn. Relations, Am. Acad. Arts and Scis., Phi Beta Kappa. Clubs: Metropolitan (Washington); Century, River Club, Brook Club (N.Y.C.), Bohemian (San Francisco).

KISSINGER, WALTER BERNHARD, automotive test and service equipment manufacturing executive; b. Furth, Germany, June 21, 1924; came to U.S., 1938, naturalized, 1939; s. Louis and Paula (Stern) K.; m. Eugenie Van Drooge, July 4, 1958; children: William, Thomas, Dana Marie, John. B.A., Princeton U., 1951; M.B.A., Harvard U., 1953. Asst. to v.p. fgn. operations Gen. Tire & Rubber Co., Akron, Ohio, 1953-56; pres. Advanced Vacuum Products Co., Stamford, Conn., 1957-62; exec. v.p., dir. Glass-tite Industries, Providence, 1960-62; asst. to pres. Jerrold Corp., 1963-64; exec. v.p., Chmn. exec. com., dir. Jervis Corp., Hicksville, N.Y., 1964-68; chmn., pres., chief exec. officer Allen Group Inc., Melville, N.Y., 1969-88; pres. WBK Assocs., Melville, N.Y., 1988—; chmn. bd. of the Long Island Res. Inst., Melville, NY, 1992—; vice chmn. bd. of trustees & chmn. of academic affairs comm., Hofstra U. dir. Kissinger Family Found., mem. bd. Stony Brook Found.; served to capt. AUS, 1943-46, 50. Decorated Commendation medal. Club: Princeton of New York. Home: Lower Dr Huntington Ba NY 11743 also: Lazy K Ranch Divide CO 80814 Office: WBK Assocs 200 Broadhollow Rd Melville NY 11747-4806*

KISSLING, FRED RALPH, JR., publishing executive, insurance agency executive; b. Nashville, Feb. 10, 1930; s. Fred Ralph and Sarah Elizabeth (FitzGerald) K.; m. Mary Jane Gallaher; children: Sarah FitzGerald, Jayne Kirkpatrick. BA, Vanderbilt U., 1952, MA, 1958. Spl. agt. Northwestern Mut. Life Ins. Co., Nashville, 1953-58, gen. agt., Lexington, Ky., 1962-80; gen. agt. New Eng. Mut. Life Ins. Co., 1981-87; mgr. life dept. Bennett & Edwards, Kingsport, Tenn., 1958-62; pres. Employee Benefit Cons., Inc., Lexington, 1961—; owner Lexington House, Inc., 1966—, Kennington Assocs., 1967—; prin. Kissling Orgn. 1980—, pub. Leader's mag., 1967—, editor, 1996—; owner, editor Fin. and Estate Planners Quar., 1993—; owner and pub. Financial Services Advisor, 1993—, Fraternal Monitor, 1999—; owner, pub., editor Probe Pub. Inc., 1997—. Author: Sell and Grow Rich, 1966; editor: Questionnaire in Pension Planning, 1970, Questionnaire in Estate Planning, 1971. Adv. bd. Salvation Army, Lexington, 1971—, chmn., 1988-91; gen. chmn. United Way of Blue Grass, 1975, bd. dirs., 1975-78, 80-83; trustee, chmn. bd. Lexington Children's Theatre, 1979-81, pres., 1981-83. Mem. Am. Soc. CLU's (chpt. pres. 1969-70, 80-81, regional v.p. 1971-73), Ky. Gen. Agts. and Mgrs. Assn. (pres. 1965-66), Million Dollar Round Table (life mem., v.p., program chmn. 1976), Assn. for Advanced Underwriting (bd. dirs. 1976-84, pres. 1982-83), Am. Soc. Pension Actuaries (bd. dirs. 1971-78, pres. 1974), Nat. Assn. of Estate Planning Councils (bd. dirs. 1986-92, pres. 1989-90), U. Akron Sales Insts., (adv. dir. 1996—), Am. Philatelic Soc., Sigma Chi, Lexington Club, Iroquois Hunt Club, Lafayette Club, Spindletop Hall, Masons, Shriners. Office: 98 Dennis Dr Lexington KY 40503-2915

KISSLING, HELEN GREY, elementary education educator; b. Houston, Feb. 9, 1949; d. Harvey Grey Glover and Lucille Helen (Risch) Heflin and adoptive father Emmett Dorsey Heflin; m. Chris David Kissling, Nov. 1, 1969 (div. Sept. 1997); children: Christian Anthony, Stephanie Annette. BA in Liberal Arts, Calif. State U., Fresno, 1985. Multiple subjects credential, Calif. First grade tchr. Hanford (Calif.) Elem. Sch. Dist., 1985-95, 96-99, tchr. kindergarten, 1995-96. Mem. NEA, Calif. Kindergarten Tchrs., Calif. Tchrs. Assn., Hanford Elem. Tchrs. Assn. Mem. Assembly of God. Avocations: reading, horseback riding, computers.

KISSLINGER, CARL, geophysicist, educator; b. St. Louis, Aug. 30, 1926; s. Fred and Emma (Tobias) K.; m. Millicent Ann Thorson, Mar. 27, 1948; children: Susan, Karen, Ellen, Pamela, Jerome. B.S., St. Louis U., 1947, M.S., 1949, Ph.D., 1952. Faculty St. Louis U., 1949-72, prof. geophysics, geophys. engring., 1961-72, chmn. dept. earth and atmostpheric scis., 1963-72; prof. geophysics U. Colo., Boulder, 1972-94; dir. Coop. Inst. for Rsch. in Environ. Sci., 1972-79, 93-94; emeritus U. Colo., Boulder, 1994—; UNESCO expert in seismology, chief tech. adviser Internat. Inst. Seismology and Earthquake Engring., Tokyo, 1966-67; chmn. com. seismology NRC-Nat. Acad. Scis., 1970-72; mem. U.S. Geodynamics Com., 1975-78; U.S. nat. corr. Internat. Assn. Seismology and Physics of Earth's Interior, 1970-72; mem. Internat. Union Geodesy and Geophysics, bur., 1975-83, v.p., 1983-91; mem. Gov.'s Sci. Adv. Council, State of Colo., 1973-77, com. on scholarly communication with People's Republic of China, Nat. Acad. Scis., 1977-81, NRC/Nat. Acad. Scis. adv. com. to U.S. Geol. Survey, 1983-88; governing bd. Am. Inst. Physics, 1989-95; chair NRC/Nat. Acad. Scis. panel on seismic hazard evaluation, 1992-96. Recipient Alumni Merit award St. Louis U., 1976, Alexander von Humboldt Found. Sr. U.S. Scientist award, 1979, U.S. Geol. Survey's John Wesley Powell award, 1992, Disting. Svc. award U. Colo., 1993, Commemorative medal USSR Acad. Scis., 1985. Fellow Am. Geophys. Union (bd. dirs. sect. seismology 1970-72, fgn. sec. 1974-84), Geol. Soc. Am., Assn. Exploration Geophysics (India), AAAS; mem. Soc. Exploration Geophysicists, Seismol. Soc. Am. (dir. 1968-74, pres. 1972-73), Austrian Acad. Sci. (corr.), Phi Beta Kappa, Sigma Xi. Club: Cosmos. Home: 4165 Caddo Pky Boulder CO 80303-3602

KISTER, JAMES MILTON, retired mathematician, educator; b. Cleve., June 29, 1930; s. James Leonard and Katherine Alice (Sherrick) K.; m. Susan Spence, 1956; 1 dau., Karen Lynn; m. Jane Bridge; 1978. BA, Coll. of Wooster, 1952; MA, U. Wis., 1956, PhD, 1959. Rsch. asst. Los Alamos (N.Mex.) Sci. Lab., 1953-55; mem. faculty U. Mich., Ann Arbor, 1959-98, prof. math., 1966-98, chmn. dept., 1971-73; ret., 1998; assoc. Office Naval Rsch., U. Va., 1960-61; mem. Inst. Advanced Study, Princeton, N.J., 1962-64; vis. prof. UCLA, 1967; vis. fellow Clare Hall, Cambridge (Eng.) U., 1970; vis. mem. Institut des Hautes Etudes Scientifique, 1974; vis. prof. U. Calif. at Berkeley, summer 1975; vis. fellow Wolfson Coll., Oxford U., 1977, 85-86. Assoc. editor: Duke Math. Jour., 1972-75; assoc. editor: Mich. Math. Jour, 1976-78, mng. editor, 1978, 82-88. Hon. rsch. fellow Univ. Coll., London, 1993. Mem. Am. Math. Soc., Math. Assn. Am.

KISTIAKOWSKY, VERA, physics researcher, educator; b. Princeton, N.J., Sept. 9, 1928; d. George Bogdan and Hildegard (Moebius) K.; m. Gerhard Emil Fischer, June 16, 1951 (div. 1970); children: Marc Laurenz Fischer, Karen Marie Fischer. A.B., Mt. Holyoke Coll., 1948, Sc.D. (hon.), 1978; Ph.D., U. Calif.-Berkeley, 1952. Staff scientist U.S. Naval Rsch. Def. Lab., San Francisco, 1952-53; fellow U. Calif.-Berkeley, 1953-54; rsch. assoc. Columbia U., N.Y.C., 1954-57, instr., 1957-59; asst. prof. Brandeis U., Waltham, Mass., 1959-62, adj. assoc. prof., 1962-63; staff mem. MIT, Cambridge, 1963-69, sr. rsch. scientist, 1969-72; prof. physics, 1972-94; prof. emerita, 1994—. Author: Atomic Energy, 1959; One Way Is Down, 1967; contbr. articles on nuclear and elem. particle physics and astrophysics to profl. jours. Dir. Coun. for a Liveable World, 1983—, dir. Edn. Fund., 1983—, pres., 1997—. Recipient Centennial award Mt. Holyoke Coll., 1972. Fellow AAAS, Am. Phys. Soc. (councilor 1974-77); mem. Assn. for Women in Sci. (pres. 1982-83), Phi Beta Kappa (vis. scholar 1983-84, senator 1988-96), Sigma Xi (lectr. 1990-92). Office: MIT 77 Massachusetts Ave Rm 6-108 Cambridge MA 02139-4307

KISTNER, DAVID HAROLD, biology educator; b. Cin., July 30, 1931; s. Harold Adolf and Hilda (Gick) K.; m. Alzada A. Carlisle, Aug. 8, 1957; children—Alzada H., Kymry Marie Carlisle. A.B., U. Chgo., 1952, B.S., 1956, Ph.D., 1957. Instr. U. Rochester, 1957-59; instr., asst. prof. biology Calif. State U., Chico, 1959-64, assoc. prof., 1964-67, prof., 1967-92, prof. emeritus, 1992—; rsch. assoc. Field Mus. Natural History, 1967—, Atlantica Ecol. Rsch. Sta., Salisbury, Zimbabwe, 1970-95; CEO Kistner family Trust, 1982—; dir. Shinner Inst. Study Interrelated Insects, 1968-75; cons.-developer DowAgro Scis., Indpls. Author: (with others) Social Insects, Vols. 1-3; editor Sociobiology, 1975—; contbr. articles to profl. jours. Patron Am. Mus. Natural History; life mem. Republican Nat. Com., 1980—. Recipient Outstanding Prof. award Calif. State Univs. and Colls., L.A., 1976; John Simon Guggenheim Meml. Found. fellow, 1965-66; grantee NSF, 1960-92, Am. Philos. Soc., 1972, Nat. Geog. Soc., 1988. Fellow Explorers Club, Calif. Acad. Scis.; mem. AAUP, AAAS, Entomol. Soc. Am., Pacific Coast Entomol. Soc., Kans. Entomol. Soc., Am. Soc. Naturalists, Am. Soc. Zoologists, Soc. Study of Systematic Zoology, Internat. Soc. Study of Social Insects, Mus. Nat. Hist. (life), Chico State Coll. Assocs. (charter). Home: 3 Canterbury Cir Chico CA 95926-2411

KIT, SAUL, biochemist, educator; b. Passaic, N.J., Nov. 25, 1920; s. Isadore and Minnie (Darvick) K.; m. Dorothy Anken, Sept. 28, 1945; children: Sally, Malon, Gordon. A.B., U. Calif.-Berkeley, 1948, Ph.D., 1951. Post-doctoral fellow U. Chgo., 1951-52; rsch. assoc. biochemistry dept. U. Tex./M.D. Anderson Hosp. and Tumor Inst., Houston, 1953-55, asst. biochemist dept. biochemistry, 1956-57, assoc. biochemist, 1957-60, biochemist and chief sect. nucleoprotein metabolism, 1961-62; asst. clin. prof. biochemistry Baylor U. Coll. Medicine, Houston, 1956-57, assoc. clin. prof., 1957-58, vis. prof. virology and epidemiology dept., spring 1962, prof. biochemistry and head divsn. biochem. virology, 1962-92, prof. emeritus, 1993—; vis. prof. Inst. Venez Olano, Caracas, Venezuela, 1971, U. Buenos Aires, 1971, Calouste Gulbenkian Found., Lisbon, 1973; disting. vis. prof. La Trobe U., Victoria, Australia, 1982; mem. del. U.S.-Soviet Health Exch. in Virology, 1967; mem. del. on indsl. biochemistry Program to People's Republic of China, 1990; chmn. pathobiol. chemistry study sect., 1975-79; cons. NIH, 1970-92; sci. adv. bd. Am. Genetics Internat., Inc., 1981-84, Novagene Inc., 1983—. Assoc. editor: Cancer Research, 1960-79; mem. editorial bd. Intervirology, 1972-85, Internat. Jour. Cancer, 1964-90; contbr. 250 articles to profl. jours.; holder 12 U.S. patents, 14 fgn. patents in field. With AUS, 1942-46. Recipient Rsch. Career award NIH, 1962-88, Disting. Inventor of 1987 award Intellectual Property Owners, Inc. Mem. Am. Soc. Cell Biology (treas. 1965-68, pres. 1970), Am. Assn. Cancer Rsch. (pres. S.W. sect. 1965-66), Am. Soc. Biol. Chemists, Am. Chem. Soc., Am. Soc. Microbiology, Am. Soc. Virology, Argentine Soc. Virology (corr.), Am. Assn. Vet. Lab. Diagnostics. Home: 11935 Wink Rd Houston TX 77024-7134

KITABCHI, ABBAS EQBAL, medical educator; b. Tehran, Iran, Aug. 28, 1933; 4 children. BS, Cornell Coll., 1954; MS, U. Okla., Oklahoma City, 1956, PhD in Med. Scis., 1958, postgrad., 1958-60, MD, 1965. Diplomate internal medicine Am. Bd. Internal Medicine. Grad. asst., rsch. fellow dept. physiology U. Okla. Med. Ctr., Oklahoma City, 1954-56; rsch. assoc. Okla. Med. Rsch. Inst., Oklahoma City, 1960-61, biochemist, 1961-65; intern VA Hosp. and U. Okla. Med. Ctr., Oklahoma City, 1965-66; instr., sr. fellow endocrinology dept. medicine U. Wash., Seattle, 1966-68; attending staff U. Tenn. Hosps., Memphis, 1968—; asst. prof. medicine U. Tenn., Memphis, 1968-71, assoc. prof. medicine, 1971-73, prof. medicine, 1973—, assoc. prof. biochemistry, 1968-72, prof. biochemistry, 1972—, chief divsn. endocrinology and metabolism, 1973—, program dir. Clin. Rsch. Ctr., 1973-92; sr. investigator biochemistry sect. Okla. Med. Rsch. Found., Oklahoma City, 1965-66; assoc. chief of staff for rsch. and edn. VA Med. Ctr., Memphis, 1968-73, chief labs. endocrinology and metabolism, 1968-75, assoc. chief sect. metabolism, med. svc., 1969-75; chief Endocrine and Diabetic Clinics, Regional Med. Ctr., Memphis, 1973—; ad hoc reviewer NSF Rsch. Grants, 1974—, Gen. Clin. Rsch. Ctr., 1976—; program dir. NIH Tng. Grant in Endocrinology, Metabolism and Diabetes, 1978-81; v.p., bd. dirs. Nat. Pituitary Found., 1980-90; mem. steering com. Diabetes Control and Complications Trial, Nat. Inst. Arthritis, Diabetes, Digestive and Kidney Diseases, 1982-90, mem. stds. and methods com., 1982-85, mem. treatment com., 1985-90, mem. diabetes prevention program, 1992—, mem. intervention com., 1992—, mem. ancillary study com., 1994—; bd. dirs. Nat. Assn. Clin. Rsch. Ctr. Program Dirs., 1983-84; mem. ad hoc com. biomed. scis. study sect. NIH Fogarty Internat. Fellowships, 1986-87; others; cons. in endocrinology and attending physician U. Tenn. Bowld Hosp., Memphis, 1983—, VA Med. Ctr., Memphis, 1983—, Bapt. Meml. Hosp., Memphis, 1983—, Meth. Hosp., Memphis, 1983—, Le Bonheur Childrens Hosp., Memphis, 1983—. Assoc. editor Hormone Secreting Pituitary Tumors, 1982, The Hypothalamus, 1983; mem. editl. bd. Jour. Clin. Endocrinology and Metabolism, 1976-79, Capsules and Comments, 1977-82, Diabetes, 1981-87, Endocrinology, 1984-88, Diabetes Care, 1995-97; guest reviewer Am. Jour. Med. Scis., Am. Jour. Medicine, Am. Jour. Physiology, Annals Internal Medicine, Diabetes, Diabetes Care, Diabetologia, Jour. Am. Geriatric Soc., Jour. Biol. Chemistry, Jour. Clin. Endocrinology and Metabolism, Jour. Clin. Investigation, Metabolism, New Eng. Jour. Medicine. Fellow ACP; mem. Am. Soc. Clin. Endocrinologists, Am. Fedn. for Clin. Rsch., Assn. Am. Physicians, Am. Soc. for Clin. Investigation, Am. Soc. for Biochemistry and Molecular Biology, Am. Inst. Nutrition, Am. Diabetes Assn. (nat. rsch. com. 1978-81), Endocrine Soc., Ctrl. Soc. for Clin. Rsch. (sub-specialty chmn. 1975), So. Soc. for Clin. Investigation (sub-specialty chmn. 1974, 98), Tenn. Diabetes Prevention and Control Program, Tenn. Diabetes Assn. (pres. 1973-74, 92), Memphis and Mid-South Med. Soc., Memphis Acad. Internal Medicine, Alpha Omega Alpha, Sigma Xi. Office: U Tenn Memphis 951 Court Ave Rm 335M Memphis TN 38103-2813

KITADA, SHINICHI, biochemist; b. Osaka, Japan, Dec. 9, 1948; came to U.S., 1975; s. Koichi and Asako Kitada. MD, Kyoto U., 1973; MS in Biol. Chemistry, UCLA, 1977, PhD, 1979. Intern Kyoto U. Hosp., Japan, 1973-74; resident physician Chest Disease Research Inst., 1974-75; rsch. scholar lab. nuclear medicine and radiation biology UCLA, 1979-87, rsch. scholar Jules Stein Eye Inst., 1988-91; rsch. biochemist La Jolla (Calif.) Cancer Rsch. Found., 1992—. Author papers in field. Japan Soc. Promotion Sci. fellow 1975-76. Mem. Am. Oil Chemists Soc., N.Y. Acad. Scis., Sigma Xi. Home: 920 Kline St Ste 301 La Jolla CA 92037-4320 Office: The Burnham Inst 10901 N Torrey Pines Rd La Jolla CA 92037-1062

KITAGAWA, AUDREY EMIKO, sprititual leader, former lawyer; b. Honolulu, Mar. 31, 1951; s. Yonoichi and Yoshiko (Nagaishi) K. B.A. cum laude, U. So. Calif., 1973; J.D., Boston Coll., 1976. Bar: Hawaii, 1977, U.S. Dist. Ct. Hawaii, 1977. Assoc., Rice, Lee & Wong, Honolulu, 1977-80; pvt. practice, Honolulu, 1980-96; head Sri Ramakrishna Spiritual Family, 1996—. Mem. Historic Hawaii Found., 1984. Mem. Hawaii Bar Assn., ABA, Honolulu Club. Republican. Office: 740 8th Ave Honolulu HI 96816-2112

KITAMURA, MICHAEL, state director; b. Honolulu, Apr. 30, 1954. BA in English, U. Oreg.; JD, Antioch Sch. Law. State dir. Office of Senator Daniel K. Akaka, Honolulu, 1991—. Office: Prince Kuhio Fed Bldg Rm 3-106 PO Box 5014 300 Ala Moana Blvd Honolulu HI 96850-4977

KITAO, T. KAORI, art history educator; b. Tokyo, Jan. 30, 1933; came to the U.S., 1952; d. Harumichi and Aiko (Yoshida) K.; 1 child, Giulio K. BA, U. Calif., Berkeley, 1958, MA, 1961; PhD, Harvard U., 1966. Asst. prof. RISD, Providence, 1963-66; asst. prof. Swarthmore (Pa.) Coll., 1966-68, assoc. prof., 1968-75, prof., chairperson art dept., 1975-81, prof. art history, 1981-93, William R. Kenan prof., 1993—; v.p. Internat. Soc. for the Comparative Study Civilizations, 1980-84. Andrew Mellon grantee, 1977-78, Sloan Found. grantee, 1986; NEH Younger Humanist fellow, 1973-74. Mem. Soc. Archtl. Historians. Office: Swarthmore Coll 500 College Ave Ste 2 Swarthmore PA 19081-1390

KITCH, EDMUND WELLS, lawyer, educator, private investor; b. Wichita, Kans., Nov. 3, 1939; s. Paul R. and Josephine (Pridmore) K.; m. Joanne Steiner, Dec. 1, 1966 (div. 1976); 1 child, Sarah; m. Alison Lauter, Jan. 29, 1978; children: Andrew, Whitney. BA, Yale U., 1961; JD, U. Chgo., 1964. Bar: Kans. 1964, Ill. 1966, U.S. Supreme Ct. 1973, Va. 1986. Asst. prof. law Ind. U., 1964-65; mem. faculty U. Chgo., 1965-82, prof., 1971-82; prof., mem. Ctr. Advanced Studies U. Va., Charlottesville, 1982-85, Joseph M. Hartfield prof., 1985—, Sullivan and Cromwell rsch. prof., 1996-99; vis. prof. Bklyn. Law Sch., 1995; Jack N. Pritzger Disting. vis. prof. of law Northwestern U., 1996; spl. asst. solicitor gen. U.S. Dept. Justice, 1973-74; exec. dir. Adv. Com. on Procedural Reform CAB, 1975-76; reporter Com. on Pattern Jury Instruction, Ill. Supreme Ct., 1966-69; mem. com. on pub.-pvt. sector rels. in vaccine innovation Inst. of Medicine, NAS, 1982-85, mem. com. on evaluation polio vaccine, 1987-88. Author: (with Harvey Perlman) Intellectual Property, 5th edit., 1997; Regulation, Federalism and Interstate Commerce, 1981. Contbr. articles to profl. jours. Mem. Va. Bar Assn., Am. Law Inst., Order of Coif, Phi Beta Kappa. Office: U Va Sch Law 580 Massie Rd Charlottesville VA 22903-1738

KITCH, FREDERICK DAVID, advertising executive; b. Chgo., Sept. 7, 1928; s. John Raymond and Mary Minerva (Wheeler) K.; m. Beverly Jane West, Nov. 24, 1976; children: William Mark, Stephen Neal, Michael Bruce Hile. BS in Journalism, Northwestern U., 1951. Mgmt. tng. Swift & Co., Chgo., 1954-55; dept. head Swift & Co., Evansville, Ind., 1955-57; account exec. Keller-Crescent Co., Evansville, Ind., 1957-60, sr. account exec., 1960-65, v.p. account supervision, 1965-72, v.p. direct client services, 1972-80, exec. v.p. client services, 1980-86, exec. v.p. mktg. and sales, 1986-93, also bd. dirs., ret., 1993; founder, chmn. Kitch & Schreiber, Inc., Evansville, 1994—. Past pres. bd. dirs. Evansville Rescue Mission, 1981-97; pres. Welborn Hosp. Found., Evansville, 1984-91, Operation City Beautiful, Evansville, 1985-87; sec., treas. Vanderburgh County Redevel. Authority; v.p. Oak Meadow Homeowners Assn. Served to lt. U.S. Army, 1951-53. Recipient Silver Medal Tri State Advt. Club, 1980. Mem. Affiliated Advt. Internat. (sec.-treas.), 1980, Evansville Country Club (bd. dirs.). Republican. Episcopalian. Avocations: tennis, golf. Home: 50 Oak Meadow Rd Evansville IN 47711-9286 Office: Kitch & Schreiber Inc 320 NW King Jr Blvd Evansville IN 47735

KITCHEN, BRENT A., airport executive; b. Topeka, Sept. 2, 1945. Student, Kans. State U.; BS in Aviation Mgmt., Embry-Riddle Aero. U., 1973. Airport mgr. City of Manhattan, Kans., 1973-78; asst. airport dir. Cedar Rapids, Iowa, 1978-81, Des Moines, 1981-86; dep. dir. airport facilities Tulsa Airport Authority, 1986-88; airports dir. Tulsa Airport Authority, Tulsa, OK, 1988—; director Tulsa Intl. Airport, Tulsa, OK, 1988-. Served U.S. Army, Viet Nam. Office: Tulsa Internat Airport Authority PO Box 581838 Tulsa OK 74158-1838*

KITCHEN, CHARLES WILLIAM, lawyer; b. July 17, 1926; s. Karl K. and Lucille W. (Keynes) K.; m. Mary Applegate, July 22, 1950; children: Kenneth K., Guy R., Anne Kitchen Campbell. BA, Western Res. U., 1948, JD, 1950. Bar: Ohio 1950, U.S. Dist. Ct. Ohio 1952, U.S. Ct. Appeals (6th cir.) 1972, U.S. Supreme Ct. 1981. Ptnr. Kitchen, Derry & Barnhouse Co., LPA, Cleve., 1950-97, sr. ptnr., 1997, ret., 1997; life mem., exec. com. 8th Jud. Dist. Ct., 1988-91. Mem. Regional Coun. on Alcoholism, 1981-86, chmn., 1985-86; bd. dirs. Scarborough Hall, 1992-94. With A.C., U.S. Army, 1944-45. Fellow Internat. Acad. Trial Lawyers; mem. ABA (sect. tort and ins. practice, sec. litigation), Am. Arbitration Assn. (panelist 1961-91), Cleve. Assn. Civil Trial Attys. (pres. 1971-72), Ohio Assn. Civil Trial Attys. (pres. 1975-76), Greater Cleve. Bar Assn. (chmn. med.-legal com. 1974-75, chmn. lawyers assistance program 1981-83, chmn. mentor com. 1988-95, jud. campaign com. chmn. 1993-95, ttustee 1984-87), Am. Legion, Order of Coif, Beta Theta Pi, Phi Delta Phi. Presbyterian. Home: 401 Bounty Way Apt 242 Avon Lake OH 44012-2482 Address: 8755 E Old Spanish Terr Dr Tucson AZ 85710

KITCHEN, DENIS LEE, publisher, artist; b. Milw., Aug. 27, 1946; s. Benjamin Luther Kitchen and Margaretha (Margert) Riley; m. Irene Nonnweiler (div. 1976); children: Sheena Heather, Scarlet Denise; m. Holly Brooks (div. 1992); m. Stacey Ann Pollard, May 18, 1996; 1 child, Alexa. BS in Journalism, U. Wis., Milw., 1968. Founder, pub., pres. Kitchen Sink Press, Northampton, Mass., 1969-99; founder, pres., chmn. Comic Book Legal Def. Fund, Inc., Northampton, 1986—; pres. Denis Kitchen Art Agy., Shutesbury, Mass., 1987—, Kitchen Sink Merchandising, Inc., Northampton, 1992—, Disappearing Inc., Northampton, 1997—. Author: The Oddly Compelling Art of Denis Kitchen, 1998; contbr. to numerous publs. Recipient Small Press Pioneer award Ann. Industry awards, 1995, Pub. of Yr. award Staros Reports, 1996, numerous others. Avocations: collecting cartoon art and vintage jukeboxes, stone wall building, topical postcards, comic art history. Home: 62 Sand Hill Rd Shutesbury MA 01072-9705 Office: Kitchen Sink Merchandising Inc 76 Pleasant St Northampton MA 01060-3909

KITCHEN, ELLEN CARLEEN, municipal official; b. Great Bend, Kans., Aug. 17, 1959; d. George Dewey and Bonnie Mae (Naugle) Horman; m. Michael William Kitchen, Feb. 28, 1981; 1 child, Ashley Lynn. Legal sec. degree, Cape Metro Bus. Coll., Cape Girardeau, Mo., 1978. Clk. FBI, Washington, 1979; sec. First Crown Fin. Corp., Cape Girardeau, 1980-81; sec. Chaffee (Mo.) Housing Authority, 1981-93, exec. dir., 1994—. Mem. Nat. Assn. Housing and Redevel. Ofcls. (cert. mgr. pub. housing), Chaffee PTO (treas. 1992-95, sec. 1995-96, 2d v.p. 1996-97), Country C.B. Club Chaffee (treas. 1996-97, sec. 1993-95). Office: Chaffee Housing Authority 904 S 2nd St Chaffee MO 63740-1209

KITCHEN, JOHN MARTIN, historian, educator; b. Nottingham, Eng., Dec. 21, 1936; s. John Sutherland and Margaret Helen (Pearson) K. BA with honors, U. London, 1963, PhD, 1966. Mem. Cambridge Group Population Studies, Eng., 1965-66; mem. faculty Simon Fraser U., Burnaby, B.C., Can., 1966—. Author: The German Officer Corps 1890-1914, 1968, A Military History of Germany, 1975, Fascism, 1976, The Silent Dictatorship, 1976, The Political Economy of Germany 1815-1914, 1979, The Coming of

Austrian Fascism, 1980, Germany in the Age of Total War, 1981, British Policy Towards the Soviet Union During the Second World War, 1986, The Origins of the Cold War in Comparative Perspective, 1988, Europe Between the Wars, 1988, A World in Flames, 1990, Empire and After: A Short History of the British Empire and Commonwealth, 1994, Nazi Germany at War, 1994, The Cambridge Illustrated History of Germany, 1996, Empire and Commonwealth, 1996. Fellow Inter-Univ. Seminar on Armed Forces and Soc. Fellow Royal Hist. Soc., Royal Soc. Can. Office: Simon Fraser U, Dept History, Burnaby, BC Canada V5A 1S6

KITCHEN, PAUL HOWARD, hockey historian; b. Toronto, Ont., Can., Nov. 14, 1937; s. Percy Floyd and Mary Henrietta (Price) K.; m. Anne Margaret Heaney, Aug. 23, 1963; children: Kevin, Peter. BA, Carleton U., 1963; BLS, U. B.C., 1964. Librarian Nat. Library Can., Ottawa, 1964-66, chief bibliography div., 1966-70, spl. asst to nat. librarian, 1970-72, liaison officer govt. libraries, 1972-75; exec. dir. Can. Library Assn., Ottawa, 1975-85; pres. Paul Kitchen and Assocs., Ottawa, 1986-98; dir. Book and Periodical Devel. Council, Toronto, 1975-85. Ann. contbr. Am. Library Assn. Yearbook, 1975-85. Mem. Soc. for Internat. Hockey History Rsch. (pres. 1998—).

KITCHENS, FREDERICK LYNTON, JR., insurance company executive; b. Detroit, Sept. 30, 1940; s. Frederick Lynton and Madeline Dorothy (Jacobs) K.; m. Carol Ann Crane, Dec. 22, 1961; children: Frederick Lynton, Anne LeBaron, Susan Elizabeth. BA, Mich. State U., 1962. CPCU. Mgr. underwriting Royal Ins. Co., N.Y.C., 1968-70; asst. to pres. Grow, Keller, Englebert & Freese, Detroit, 1970-71; v.p. Dobson McOmber, Inc., Ann Arbor, Mich., 1971-73; exec. v.p. Hylant MacLean, Inc., Toledo, 1973-83; chmn., chief exec. officer Cherokee Ins. Co., Nashville, 1983-84; chmn. Coastal Plains Ins., Jacksonville, Fla., 1984-92; exec. v.p., dir. Brown & Brown, Inc., Jacksonville, 1992—; instr. Coll. Ins., N.Y.C., 1969-70. Trustee Jacksonville Country Day Sch., 1985-90, Hope Haven Children's Clinic, 1988-91; dir. Jacksonville Commodores League; mem. Fla. Aviation Adv. Coun., 1990-94, Leadership Jacksonville, 1991. Capt. U.S. Army, 1962-67, Vietnam. Decorated Bronze Star; recipient Commendation medal NATO, 1965. Mem. Jacksonville C. of C. (community devel. bd. 1986), Lloyd's of London (underwriting mem.), L.A. Yacht Club (commodore 1989-90), Fla. Yacht Club, Safari Club Internat. (dir., pres. north Fla. chpt. 1990-92). Republican. Presbyterian. Avocations: flying, safari hunting. Office: Brown & Brown PO Box 17548 Jacksonville FL 32245-7548

KITCHENS, JOYCE ELLEN, lawyer, assistant county guardian; b. Jesup, Ga., Oct. 8, 1948; d. Arthur Ellis and Ray Lucille (Burton) K.; m. Larry Keith Brumfield, Aug. 23, 1969 (div. July 1973); m. Jerry Baxter Barnes; stepchildren: Craig Randall Barnes, Suzanne Cynthia Barnes. BA in English Lit., Purdue U., 1970, MA in English Lit., 1972; JD, Emory U., 1982. Bar: Ga. 1982, U.S. Dist. Ct. (no. dist.) Ga. 1982, U.S. Dist. Ct. (mid. dist.) Ga. 1992, U.S. Ct. Appeals (11th cir.) 1982, U.S. Ct. Mil. Appeals 1996, U.S. Tax Ct. 1995. Staff atty. Dept. Vet. Affairs, Atlanta, 1982-89, asst. dist. counsel, 1989-91; pvt. practice Atlanta, 1991—; cons. Fedn. Hwy. Adminstrn., Atlanta, 1993—; adj. faculty Emory U. Sch. Law. Mem. Fed. Bar Assn. (pres. Atlanta chpt. 1991-92, 11th cir. officer 1992-98, dep. sec. 1998-99), Ansley Kiwanis (past pres. 1992-93, Disting. Svc. award 1991). Democrat. Presbyterian. Avocations: reading, travel, adventure. Office: PO Box 53278 Atlanta GA 30355-1278

KITCHENS, WILLIAM H., lawyer; b. Newnan, Ga., Aug. 3, 1948. BA with high honors, Emory U., 1970; JD, U. Ga., 1973. Bar: Ga. 1973. Ptnr. Arnall Golden & Gregory, LLP, Atlanta; adj. prof. food and drug law Emory U. Sch. Law, 1979—. Notes editor Ga. Law Review, 1972-73; mem. editl. adv bd. Food and Drug Law Jour., 1981-87, 96—; author: Georgia Jurisprudence Environmental Law, 1995, 96, The Georgia Environmental Law Handbook, 1996, FDA Regulation of Tissue Engineering in Synthetic Biodegradable Polymer Scaffolds, 1997; contbr. articles to profl. jours. Mem. ABA, Am Judicature Soc., State Bar Ga., Lawyers Club Atlanta, Atlanta Bar Assn, Omicron Delta Kappa. Office: Arnall Golden & Gregory LLP 1201 W Peachtree St NW Ste 2800 Atlanta GA 30309-3450

KITCHIN, JAMES D., III, obstetrician-gynecologist, educator; b. Newport News, Va., 1931. MD, U. Va., 1960. Gen. med., surg. intern U. Va., Charlottesville, 1960-61, resident in ob-gyn, 1961-65, asst. prof. ob-gyn, 1967-71, assoc. prof., 1971-81, prof., 1981—; mem. staff U. Va. Hosp., 1967—; rsch. fellow div. endocrinology and infertility, dept. ob-gyn, U. Wash., Seattle, 1965-67. Lt. (j.g.) USNR, 1953-56. Mem. AMA. Office: U Va Health Sci Ctr Dept Ob-Gyn PO Box 387 Charlottesville VA 22809

KITE, JOSEPH HIRAM, JR., microbiologist, educator; b. Decatur, Ga., Nov. 11, 1926; s. Joseph Hiram and Lulie (Hatch) K.; m. Jane Pascale, Aug. 6, 1970. AB, Emory U., 1948; MS, U. Tenn., 1954; PhD, U. Mich., 1959. Med. technician in bacteriology Communicable Disease Ctr., Atlanta, 1950-51, VA Hosp., 1951-52; rsch. assoc. U. Buffalo, 1958-59, instr., 1959-63; asst. prof. bacteriology and immunology SUNY-Buffalo, 1963-68, assoc. prof. microbiology, 1968-72, prof. microbiology, 1972—; sci. del. Citizen Amb. Program People to People Internat.; mem. sci. adv. bd. Infectech, Inc., Sharon, Pa . Contbr. articles to med. jours., chpts. to med. textbooks. Served with AUS, 1945-46. Mem. Am. Assn. Immunologists, Am. Soc. Microbiology, Tissue Culture Assn., AAAS, N.Y. Acad. Scis. Methodist. Subspecialties: Immunology (medicine); Microbiology (medicine). Current work: tuberculosis and autoimmune diseases; teaching medical, dental and graduate students; research on mechanisms of protective immunity to Mycobacterium tuberculosis, and autoimmune regulation in thyroiditis. Home: 108 Chasewood Ln East Amherst NY 14051-1888 Office: Med Sch SUNY Dept Microbiology Buffalo NY 14214

KITE, STEVEN B., lawyer; b. Chgo., May 30, 1949; s. Ben and Dolores (Braver) K.; m. Catherine Lapinski, Jan. 13, 1980; children: David, Julia. BA, U. Ill., 1971; JD, Harvard U., 1974. Bar: Ga. 1974, U.S. Dist. Ct. Ga. 1974, U.S. Ct. Appeals (5th and 11th cirs.) 1981, Ill. 1985, Fla. 1986. Ptnr. Kutak, Rock & Campbell, Atlanta, 1974-84, Gardner, Carton & Douglas, Chgo., 1984—. Author, editor: Law For Elderly, 1978; author: Tax-Exempt Financing for Health Care Organizations, 1996; co-author: Bond Financing, 1994. Bd. dirs. Atlanta Legal Aid Soc., 1979-84; trustee Sr. Citizens Met. Atlanta, 1980-83. Mem. ABA, Ill. Bar Assn., State Bar Ga., Chgo. Bar Assn., Fla. Bar Assn., Nat. Assn. Bond Lawyers. Avocations: travel, sports, reading. Office: Gardner Carton & Douglas Quaker Tower 321 N Clark St Ste 3400 Chicago IL 60610-4795

KITE, THOMAS O., JR., professional golfer; b. Austin, Tex., Dec. 9, 1949; m. Christy Kite; 3 children. Student, U. Tex. mem. Ryder Cup Team, 1979, 81,83,85,87,89,93., Capt., 1997. Named PGA Rookie of Yr., 1973, PGA Player of Yr., 1989; winner Air New Zealand Open, 1974, European Open (Eur), 1980, Oki Pro-Am (Spain), 1996; winner numerous golf tournaments including Bicentennial, 1976, B.C. Open, 1978, Inverrary Open, 1981, Bay Hill Open, 1982, Tournament Players Championship, 1985, 89, 91, Western Open, 1986, Kemper Open, 1987, Nestle Invitational, 1989, Nabisco Championship, 1989, Atlanta Classic, 1992, U.S. Open, 1992, L.A. Open, 1993; recipient Vardon trophy, 1981, 82,. PGA leading money winner, 1981, 89. *

KITE, WILLIAM MCDOUGALL, lawyer; b. Buffalo, N.Y., Aug. 25, 1923; s. William Henry and Susanna (McDougall) K.; m. Margaret Maupin Wulsin, Apr. 15, 1950; children: Margaret, William Jr., Thomas, Matthew. AB, Princeton U., 1945; LLB, Harvard U., 1949. Bar: Ohio 1949, U.S. Dist. Ct. (so. dist.) Ohio 1949. Assoc. Cottle, Campbell, Druffel & Hogan, Cin., 1949-56; ptnr. Cohen, Todd, Kite & Stanford, Cin., 1956—; bd. dirs. Midland Co., Cin.; bd. dirs., sec. Camargo Hunt, Inc.; pres., gen. mgr. Camargo Stables, Inc.; mem. pres.'s adv. coun. Berea Coll., 1993—. Mayor City of Indian Hill (Ohio), 1971-75; bd. mem. Cin. Hist. Soc., 1973-82; pres., bd. dirs. Coun. Alcoholism of S.W. Ohio, 1975-77; bd. dirs. Shawn Womack Dance Project, Friends Spl. Treatment Ctr., Children's Hosp.; chmn. bd. dirs. Maple Knoll Hosp. and Home, Cin., 1958-62, Cin. Country Day Sch., 1982-86; pres. Planned Parenthood Assn., Cin., 1978-82; trustee Cin. Country Day Sch. Found.; ruling elder Glendale Indian Hill and Presbyn. Chs.; mem. Bd. Tax Appeals, Indian Hill. Lt. USN, 1942-46, PTO, 1950-52, Korea. Mem. ABA (bd. dirs.), Ohio Bar Assn. (bd. dirs.), Cin. Bar Assn. (diversity com. 1993—). Presbyterian. Avocations: horseback riding, swimming, sailing. Home: 9645 Cunningham Rd Cincinnati OH 45243-1621 Office: Cohen Todd Kite & Stanford 525 Vine St Ste 16 Cincinnati OH 45202-3121

KITFIELD, JAMES CRAWFORD, foreign policy correspondent, writer; b. Atlanta, Feb. 2, 1956; s. David Brewster and Ruste Kitfield. B in Journalism, U. Ga., 1979. Asst. editor Overseas Life Mag., Frankfurt, Germany, 1979-82, mng. editor, 1982-85; sr. editor Mil. Forum Mag., Washington, 1986-89; assoc. editor Govt. Exec. Mag., Washington, 1990-94; corr. Nat. Journal Way, Washington, 1994—. Author: Prodigal Soldiers, 1995. Recipient Journalism award Gerald Ford Libr., 1990, 95, Jesse H. Neal award Assn. Bus. Pub., 1987. Office: Nat Jour Mag 1501 M St NW Washington DC 20005-1700

KITNER, DAVID N., lawyer; b. Brownwood, Tex., Aug. 25, 1948. BA, Rice U., 1970; JD with honors, U. Tex., 1973. Bar: Tex. 1973; bd. cert. labor and employment law, Tex. Bd. Specialization. Mem. Strasburger & Price L.L.P., Dallas; instr. trial advocacy So. Meth. U., 1982-86. Fellow Am. Coll. Trial Lawyers; mem. ABA, Tex. Assn. Def. Counsel, Dallas Bar Assn., Order Coif, Defense Rsch. Inst.; fellow Tex. Bar Found. Office: Strasburger & Price LLP 901 Main St Ste 4300 Dallas TX 75202-3714

KITNER, HAROLD, artist, educator; b. Cleve., May 18, 1921; s. Isaac and Frieda Kitner; m. Joyce Lapaz, Nov. 30, 1946; children: Jon, Ann, Kathi. MA, Case Western Res. U., 1947; postgrad., Cleve. Inst. Art, Ohio U., Cleve. Coll., Washington and Lee U.; D Equivalency, Kent State U., 1949. Chmn. fine arts Kent (Ohio) State U., 1950-74, dean Honors Coll., 1970-72, prof. emeritus, 1980. One-man shows include Cleve. Mus., Kent State U. Mus., Libr. Congress; represented in permanent collections at Akron Art Mus., Canton Art Inst., Cleve. Mus., Dayton Art Inst., Akron U., Kent State U. Negotiator, pres. faculty union AAUP, Kent., 1977-80; founder Blossom Festival Sch., Cleve., 1967. Jewish. Home: 9161 E Bay Harbor Dr Bay Harbor Islands FL 33154

KITO, TERUO, former international trading company executive; b. Nagoya, Japan, Jan. 27, 1932; came to U.S., 1963; s. Otomaro and Hatsu (Mizuno) K.; m. Eiko Kito, Mar. 3, 1966; 1 child, Teruyo. M in Econs., Hitoshubashi U., 1954. With Mitsui & Co. Ltd., Tokyo, 1954-63, gen. mgr., 1966-73, sr. gen. mgr., 1979-83; asst. gen. mgr. Mitsui & Co. (USA), Inc., N.Y.C., 1963-66; sr. gen. mgr. Mitsui & Co. (USA), Inc., L.A., 1973-79; v.p., regional gen. mgr. Mitsui & Co. (USA), Inc., Seattle, 1983-85; sr. v.p., chief operating officer Mitsui & Co. (USA), Inc., N.Y.C., 1985-89; pres., chief exec. officer Intermgmt. of N.Y., Inc., N.Y.C., 1990—. Mem. Scarsdale Country Club, Nippon Club, Sky Club. Avocations: traveling overseas, golf. Office: Intermgmt of NY Inc 420 Lexington Ave Rm 2360 New York NY 10170-2360*

KITOWSKI, VINCENT JOSEPH, medical consultant, former physical medicine and rehabilitation physician; b. San Antonio, July 14, 1920; s. Casimir B. and Ruth Ruby (Sien) K.; m. Winifred Ann Maloney, Dec. 28, 1946; 1 child, Oona Colleen. BS, U. Tex., 1946; MD, Baylor U., 1950. Gen. practice San Antonio, 1950-56; with ARAMCO, Dhahran, Saudi Arabia, 1956-59; resident Baylor Coll. Medicine, Houston, 1959-62; with VA Hosp., Richmond, Va., 1962-64; chief phys. medicine and rehab. VA Hosp., Kerrville, Tex., 1964-65; with Baylor Med. Coll., Houston, 1965-86; ret., 1986; cons. Vis. Nurse Assn., Houston. Contbg. author: Rehabilitation in Ischemie Heart Disease, 1983, Medical Rehabilitation, 1985; contbr. articles to profl. jours. 1st lt. U.S. Army Air Corps, 1942-45, ETO. Fellow Am. Coll. Phys. Medicine and Rehab. Avocations: gardening, music, piano. Office: 12426 Huntingwick Dr Houston TX 77024-4906

KITSOS, CONSTANTINE NICHOLAS, plastic surgeon; b. Athens, Greece, Aug. 10, 1938; came to U.S., 1946; s. Nicholas E. and Bessie H. Kitsos; children: Katie, Kristina, Nicholas. MD, U. Wash., 1964. Diplomate Am. Bd. Surgery, Am. Bd. Plastic Surgery. Pvt. practice Miami, Fla. Capt. M.C., U.S. Army, 1965-67. Mem. Am. Soc. Plastic and Reconstructive Surgeons. Greek Orthodox. Office: 9000 NE 2d Ave Miami FL 33138

KITT, OLGA, artist; b. N.Y.C., July 29, 1929; d. Elias and Mary (Opiela) K.; m. Nicholas Rawluk, Aug. 6, 1955 (div. 1960); 1 child, Wade. BA, Queens Coll., 1951; MA, State U. Iowa, 1952; studied with Meyer Schapiro, N.Y.C., 1954; studied with Hans Hofmann, N.Y.C., Provincetown, 1954-55; postgrad., Inst. Fine Arts, NYU, 1955, NYU, 1960-62; studied with Robert Beverly Hale, N.Y.C., 1979. Gallery asst. Chappellier Gallery, N.Y.C., 1952-53; asst. to Walter Pach N.Y., 1953-56; teaching asst. CCNY, 1953-58; tchr. art N.Y., 1962-80. One-person shows include CCNY, 1957, Manhattan Coll., Riverdale, N.Y., 1980, Blackout Gallery, N.Y.C., 1997; exhibited in group shows at Whitney Mus., N.Y.C., 1954, Bronx County Hist. Soc., 1978, Mus. Modern Art, N.Y.C., 1978, Art Students League, N.Y.C., 1979, Bronx Mus. Arts, 1979; represented in permanent collections including Bronx Arts Ensemble, Riverdale Press, Riverdale YM-YWHA, U. Iowa, Iowa City, Fordham U., Fordham Prep. Sch., Hostos Coll., N.Y.C., Harris Sch. of Art, Tenn.; represented in pvt. collections. Home: 5610 Netherland Ave Bronx NY 10471-1703 Studio: 495 S Broadway Yonkers NY 10705-3221

KITT, WALTER, psychiatrist; b. N.Y.C., Dec. 18, 1925; s. Elias and Mary (Opiela) K.; m. Terry Escorcia, May 15, 1955 (dec. 1974); 1 child, Gregory; m. Sally Anderson Chappell, June 22, 1977. Student, CCNY, 1942-44; AB magna cum laude, Syracuse U., 1948; MD, Chgo. Med. Sch., 1952. Diplomate Am. Bd. Psychiatry and Neurology. Resident Neuropsychiat. Inst., Chgo., 1953-56; practice medicine specializing in psychiatry Chgo., 1956-64, Munster, Ind., 1963-80; psychiatrist Lakeside VA Med. Ctr., Chgo., 1981-92; practice medicine specializing in psychiatry Park Ridge, Ill., 1992-96, Schaumburg, Ill., 1996-97; acting chief psychiat. svcs. Lakeside VA Med. Ctr., Chgo., 1986-87; ret., 1998; asst. prof. clin. psychiatry U. Ill. Med. Ctr., Chgo., 1958-64, Northwestern U., Chgo., 1974-96; chmn. divsn. psychiatry Our Lady of Mercy Hosp., Dyer, Ind., 1970-72. Mem. Am. Psychiat. Assn. Home: 3750 N Lake Shore Dr Chicago IL 60613-4238

KITTEL, CHARLES, physicist, educator emeritus; b. N.Y.C., July 18, 1916; s. George Paul and Helen Kittel; m. Muriel Agnes Lister, June 23, 1938; children: Ruth, Peter, Timothy. BA, Cambridge (Eng.) U., 1938, MA, 1993; PhD, U. Wis., 1941. Research physicist Bur. Ordnance, head USN team attached to Brit. Admiralty Helensburgh, Scotland, 1940-42; supr. Submarine Ops. Research Grp. USN, Washington, 1943-45; research assoc. MIT, Cambridge, 1945-47; research physicist Bell Labs., Murray Hill, N.J., 1947-51; prof. physics U. Calif., Berkeley, 1951-78, prof. emeritus, 1978—; cons. E.I. Du Pont & Co., RCA, Westinghouse Corp., Hughes Aircraft Co., Chevron Corp., numerous others. Author: Introduction to Solid State Physics, 7th edit., 1996, (with H. Kroemer) Thermal Physics, 2d edit., 1980, Quantum Theory of Solids, rev. edit., 1987. Guggenheim fellow, 1947, 57, 64, Miller fellow, U. Calif., 1959, 60; recipient Disting. Tchrs. award, U. Calif. Berkeley, 1972. Fellow Am. Acad. Arts and Scis., Am. Phys. Soc. (Oliver Buckley Solid State Physics prize 1957, coun. 1958-62); mem. NAS, Am. Assn. Physics Tchrs. (Oersted medal 1978), Am. Inst. Physics (bd. govs. 1954-58). Avocation: vigneron. E-mail: kittel@uclink4.berkeley.edu. Office: U Calif Dept Physics Berkeley CA 94720-7300

KITTELSEN, RODNEY OLIN, lawyer; b. Albany, Wis., Mar. 11, 1917; s. Olen B. and Nellie Winifred (Atkinson) K.; m. Pearle M. Haldiman, Oct. 12, 1940; children: Gregory S., James E., Bradley J. PhB, U. Wis., 1939, LLB, 1940. Spl. agt. FBI, Washington, 1940-46; ptnr. Kittelsen, Barry, Ross, Wellington & Thompson, Monroe, Wis., 1946—; dist. atty. Green County, Monroe, 1947-53; pres. State Bar Wis., Madison, 1976-77, 83-85; dir. Wis. Law Found., Madison, 1992—. Pres. Monroe Police and Fire Commn., 1947—; legal counsel X-FBI Inc., Quantico, Va., 1986—; mem. Am. Coll. Trust and Estate Coun., Chgo., 1983—. Recipient Outstanding Citizen award Monroe Jaycees, 1977, Outstanding Svc. award Albany FFA, 1991, Disting. Svc. award U. Wis. Law Sch., 1995, Disting. Svc. award U. Wis. Law Alumni Assn., 1995. Fellow Am. Bar Found., Wis. Bar Assn. (pres. 1976-77, 83-85, Goldberg award 1990), Wis. Bar Found. (pres. 1985). Home: 708 26th Ave Monroe WI 53566-1620 Office: 916 17th Ave Monroe WI 53566-2003

KITTERMAN, JOAN FRANCES, education educator; b. Muncie, Ind., July 27, 1951; d. Thomas Harvey and Ruth (Jackson) K. BS in Elem. Edn. magna cum laude, Ball State U., 1973, MA in Elem. Edn., 1976, EdD in Spl. Edn., 1984. Cert. gen. elem. edn., reading; cert. tchr. learning disabled/neurologically impaired, Ind. Tchr. phys. edn. and music Morrison Christian Schs., Taiwan, 1973-74, tchr. 4th grade, 1974-75; title I reading tchr. Blackford County Schs., Hartford City, Ind., 1976-77, Liberty-Perry Community Schs., Selma, Ind., 1977-81; doctoral fellow Ball State U., Muncie, Ind., 1981-83; asst. prof. English as a fgn. lang. Seoul (Korea) Theol. Sem., 1984-86; asst. prof. spl. edn. and reading Ohio No. U., Ada, 1986-88; asst. prof. grad. studies Georgetown (Ky.) Coll., 1988-90, interim dean grad. studies, 1990-91, dean grad. edn., 1991-93; assoc. prof. edn. Ind. Wesleyan U., Marion, 1993-94; assoc. prof. edn. Taylor U., Upland, Ind., 1994—, chair edn. dept., 1996—; prof. edn., dir. tchr. edn. Taylor U., Upland, 1997—; workshop presenter in field. Mem. Coun. for Exceptional Children, Internat. Reading Assn., TESOL, Phi Delta Kappa. Avocations: reading, cross-stitching. Office: Taylor U 236 W Reade Ave Upland IN 46989-1002

KITTLE, CHARLES FREDERICK, surgeon; b. Athens, Ohio, Oct. 24, 1921; s. Frederick F. and Ida (Falls) K.; m. Jeane Mignon Groenier, 1945 (div. 1973); children: Candace Mignon, Bradley Dean, Leslie Jeane, Brian David; m. Ann Catherine Bates, 1981. AB with honors, Ohio U., Athens, 1942, LLD, 1967; MD with honors, U. Chgo., 1945; MS in Surgery, U. Kans., 1950. Diplomate Am. Bd. Surgery, Am. Bd. Thoracic Surgery (mem. bd. 1967-75, chmn. 1973-75). Intern U. Chgo. Clinics, 1945-46; resident gen. and thoracic surgery U. Kans. Med. Center, 1948-52; spl. tng. radio-isotopes for med. use Oak Ridge Inst. Nuclear Studies, 1950, cons. med. div., 1950-55; mem. faculty U. Kans. Sch. Medicine, 1950-66; assoc. prof. surgery, lectr. history medicine, 1959-66; cons. thoracic surgery VA Hosp., Wadsworth, Kans., 1954-57; cons. gen. surgery VA Hosp., 1957-60; attending gen. surgery VA Hosp. Kansas City, Mo., 1954-66, Wichita, Kans., 1955-62; prof. surgery, head sect. thoracic and cardiovascular surgery U. Chgo. Clinics, 1966-72; prof. surgery, dir. thoracic surgery sect. Rush Med. Coll. and Presbyn.-St. Luke's Hosp., 1973-92, prof. emeritus, 1992—; dir. Rush Cancer Ctr., 1978-86; mem. staff McNeal Hosp., Berwyn, Ill., 1986-92; cons. Mcpl. TB Sanatorium, Chgo., 1968-74, Hines VA Hosp., Maywood, Ill., 1973-92; spl. rsch. cardiovascular surgery, control of blood flow. Served as lt. (j.g.) USNR, 1946-48. Clin. fellow Am. Cancer Soc., 1950-52; Markle scholar med. scis., 1952-58. Mem. AAAS, ACS (bd. dirs. Kans. 1965-68), Am. Assn. History Medicine, Am. Assn. Thoracic Surgery, Am. Coll. Cardiology (bd. dirs. Kans. 1963-66), Chgo. Surg. Soc. (pres. 1972-73), Am. Heart Assn. (chmn. program com. cardiovasc. surgery 1965-88, exec. com. cardiovasc. surgery coun. 1962-74, chmn. coun. 1972-74), Am. Physiol. Assn., Cen. Surg. Soc., Chgo. Med. Soc., Am. Surg. Assn., Internat. Cardiovasc. Soc. (sec. 1965-71), Internat. Soc. Surgery, Soc. Med. Hist. (pres. Chgo. 1983-85), N.J. Thoracic Surgery Soc., Ill. Thoracic Surgery Soc. (pres. 1983-84), Soc. Clin. Surgery, Soc. Surg. Oncology, Soc. Vascular Surgery, Soc. Univ. Surgeons (pres. 1966-67), Soc. Thoracic Surgery, Univ. Village Assn. (bd. dirs. 1986-89, pres. 1989), Arthur Conan Doyle Soc., Caxton Club, Chgo. Literary Club, Hounds of Baskerville, Chgo. Lit. Club (pres. 1999—), Grolier Club, Phi Beta Kappa, Sigma Xi, Alpha Omega Alpha. Home: 856 S Laflin St Chicago IL 60607-4026

KITTLE, JOSEPH S., science administrator, consultant; b. Clarksburg, W.Va., June 19, 1939; s. Harry Maurice and Florence Louise (Stealey) K.; m. Mary B. Kittle, Dec. 27, 1961; children: Adam, Andrew. BS, The Citadel, Charleston, S.C.; MBA, Auburn U., 1973. Lt. col. USAF, 1961-81; sr. assoc. CACI, Aarlington, Va., 1981-83; pres. Synergetics, Alexandria, Va., 1983-89; bus. devel. dir. Aeroflex Sys. Divsn., Mclean, 1988-89; program devel. dir. S.W. Rsch. Inst., San Antonio, 1989—; program dir. Resource Cons., Mclean, Va., 1983-87; mem. faculty continuous engring studies U. Tex., Austin, 1996—. mem. vestry, warden St. Mark's Ch., Alexandria, 1961-81; cmty. leader Cub Scouts, Alexandria, 1975-80; music dir. Shrine Mt. Family Conf., 1978—; vol. Samm Homeless Shelter, San Antonio, 1992—, bd. dirs.; mentor Holmes Bus. Careers H.S., 1993-96. Mem. Am. Def. Prepardness Assn., World Trade Assn., Plaza Club. Episcopalian. Avocations: music, guitar, soccer, skiing. Home: 103 Ivy Ln San Antonio TX 78209-5446 Office: SW Rsch Inst PO Box 28510 San Antonio TX 78228-0510

KITTLESON, HENRY MARSHALL, lawyer; b. Tampa, Fla., May 13, 1929; s. Edgar O. and Ardath (Ayers) K.; m. Barbara Clark, Mar. 20, 1954; 1 dau., Laura Helen. BS with high honors, U. Fla., 1951, JD with high honors, 1953. Bar: Fla. 1953. Ptnr. Holland & Knight, Lakeland and Bartow, Fla., 1955—; mem. adv. bd. Fla. Fed. Savs. & Loan Assn., 1974-86; mem. Fla. Law Revision Commn., 1967-76, vice chmn., 1969-71; mem. Gov.'s Property Rights Study Commn., 1974-75, Nat. Conf. Commrs. Uniform State Laws, 1982—. Mem. council U. Fla. Law Center, 1974-77. Served to maj. USAF, 1953-55. Fellow Am. Bar Found.; mem. ABA (chmn. standing com. on ethic and profl. responsibility 1980-81), Am. Law Inst., Am. Coll. Real Estate Lawyers, Fla. Bar (chmn. standing com. profl. ethics 1965-66, tort litigation rev. commn. 1983-84), Blue Key, Sigma Phi Epsilon, Phi Delta Phi, Phi Kappa Phi, Beta Gamma Sigma, Lakeland Yacht and Country Club. Presbyterian. Home: 5334 Woodhaven Ln Lakeland FL 33813-2656 Office: Holland & Knight PO Box 32092 92 Lake Wire Dr Lakeland FL 33815-1510

KITTLITZ, LINDA GALE, small business owner; b. Waco, Tex., Jan. 22, 1949; d. Rudolf Gottlieb and Lena Hulda (Landgraf) K. BA in Art, Tex. Tech. U., 1971. Sales rep. Taylor Pub. Co., San Francisco and Dallas, 1972-73, Internat. Playtex Corp., San Francisco, 1974-76, Faberge Inc., San Francisco, 1976-78, Soflens div. Bausch and Lomb Co., San Francisco, 1978-81, Ben Rickert Inc., San Francisco, 1981-86; mfr.'s sales rep. Dearing Sales, San Francisco, 1986-87; sales rep. Golden West Envelope Co., San Francisco, 1987-89; sales assoc. R.G. Creations, Inc., San Francisco, 1989-90; owner, mgr. Linda Kittlitz & Assocs. (Custom Packaging and Printing Solutions), San Francisco, 1990—. Mem. NAFE. Democrat. Baptist. Avocation: walking.

KITTO, FRANKLIN CURTIS, computer systems specialist; b. Salt Lake City, Nov. 18, 1954; s. Curtis Eugene and Margaret (Ipson) K.; m. Collette Madsen, Sept. 16, 1982; children: Melissa Erin, Heather Elise, Stephen Curtis. BA, Brigham Young U., 1978, MA, 1980. Tv sta. operator Sta. KBYU-TV, Provo, Utah, 1973-78; grad. teaching asst. Brigham Young Univ., 1978-80; cable TV system operator Instructional Media U. Utah, Salt Lake City, 1980-82, data processing mgr., 1982-83, media supr., 1983-85, bus. mgr., 1985-87; dir. computer systems tng. MegaWest Systems, Inc., Salt Lake City, 1987-90, dir. new product devel., 1990-91, mgr. tng. and installation, 1991-93, mgr. rsch. and devel., 1993; tng. and installation mgr. Total Solutions, American Fork, Utah, 1993-95, tng., support and installation mgr., 1995; EDI programmer Megawest Systems, Inc., Salt Lake City, 1996; EDI supervisor Companion Technologies (formerly Megawest Systems, Inc.), Midvale, Utah, 1996—. Recipient Kiwanis Freedom Leadership award, Salt Lake City, 1970, Golden Microphone award Brigham Young U., 1978. Mem. Assn. Ednl. Communications and Tech., Utah Pick Users Group (sec. 1983-87, pres. 1987-89, treas. 1989-90), Am. Soc. Tng. and Devel., Assn. for Computer Tng. and Support, Phi Eta Sigma, Kappa Tau Alpha. Mormon. Home: 10931 S Avila Dr Sandy UT 84094-5965 Office: Companion Techs Utah 6975 Union Park Ctr Ste 500 Midvale UT 84047-6026

KITTO, JOHN BUCK, JR., mechanical engineer; b. Evanston, Ill., Dec. 22, 1952; s. John Buck and Marie (Comstock) K.; children: Christopher Daniel, Andrew Comstock. BSME, Lehigh U., 1975; MBA, U. Akron, 1980. Reg. profl. engr., Ohio, Pa. Sr. engr. McDermott Tech. Inc. subs. Babcock & Wilcox Co., Alliance, Ohio, 1975-80, research engr., 1980-81, program mgr., 1981-94, bus. devel. specialist, 1995-99; bus. devel. mgr. The Babcock and Wilcox Co., Barberton, Ohio, 1999—. Editor: Heat Exchangers for Two Phase Flow, 1983, Two-Phase Heat Exchanger, 1985, Maldistribution of Flow, 1987, Steam: Its Generation and Use, 1992; author and patentee in field. Fellow ASME (chmn. chpt. 1983-84, chmn. exec. com. of heat transfer divsn. 1992-93, v.p. region V 1992-95, officer bd. comms. 1991-95, sr. v.p. 1995-98, mem. bd. govs. 1998—, Prime Movers award 1992, Dedicated Svc. award 1992, George Westinghouse Silver medal 1991); mem. NSPE (Young Engr. of Yr. award 1986), AIChE, Air Waste Mgmt. Assn., Tau Beta Pi, Pi Tau Sigma, Beta Gamma Sigma, Sigma Iota Epsilon. Republican. Avocations: reading, hiking, board games, coaching soccer. Fax: 330-860-1409. Home: Apt 9 1785 Beechwood Ave NE North Canton OH 44720 Office: B&W Svc Co PO Box 665 90 E Tuscarawas Ave Barberton OH 44203-0665

KITTREDGE, JOHN KENDALL, retired insurance company executive; b. Pitts., July 7, 1927; s. Richard Carlyle and Velma (Null) K.; m. Elizabeth Delo, May 26, 1951 (dec. June 1998); children: Amy, Carol. BA, Williams Coll., 1948. With Prudential Ins. Co. Am., 1948-65, v.p., 1965-73, sr. v.p., 1973-77, exec. v.p., 1977-88; chmn. Prudential Real Estate Affiliates, 1987, Prudential Property and Casualty Co., 1978-82, Prudential Reins. Co., 1978-87. Mem. N.J. Bd. Higher Edn., 1971-73; bd. dirs. Mental Health Assn., Essex County, 1968-72; trustee Coll. Medicine and Dentistry N.J., 1970-79, chmn., 1971-78; trustee Employee Benefit Rsch. Inst., chmn., 1986-87 ; mem. bd. overseers U. Pa. Sch. Nursing, 1982—; mem. Fed. coun. on Grad. Med. Edn., 1986-88; bd. dirs. Am. Acad. Actuaries, 1989-91. Fellow Soc. Actuaries; mem. Am. Acad. Actuaries, Inst. of Medicine, Phi Beta Kappa. Home: 878 Pinehurst Dr Chapel Hill NC 27514-6532

KITTRELL, MARIE BECKNER, retired educator; b. Winchester, Ky., Oct. 25, 1905; d. Lucien and Marie Daviess (Warren) Beckner; m. James Bingham Kittrell, June 23, 1928 (dec.); children: James Bingham Jr., Marie Beckner Kitrell Lynn, Lucien Cartwright (dec.), Lucy Hunter Kittrell Combs. BA, U. Ky., 1926. Social editor Winchester newspaper, 1925, 26, 27; senate clerk revisions law com. Washington, 1927-28; sch. tchr.; sec. to supt. schs., editor sch. newspaper Ludlow, Ky., 1927; writer, producer, hostess TV show, 1957-71; hostess mgr. Thomas Hunt Morgan House, Lexington, 1967-69. Freelance writer. Pres. Jr. League Lexington, 1936-40, Young Women's Rep. Club; originator, pres. Jr. League Horse Show, Lexington, 1937-41; nat. adv. com. mem. women's fair N.Y. World's Fair, 1939; mem. Bd. Child Guidance Svc., Bd. Manchester Cmty. Ctr., Lexington, adv. bd. Ky. Hist. Markers Program, Fayette County Com. Ky. Civil War Centennial Commn.; chair program arrangements Lexington & Fayette County Sesqui-Centennial Ky. Statehood, 1942. Named May Queen Ct. Mem. League Am. Pen Women, Monday Club, Ky. Hist. Soc., U. Ky. Alumni Assn., Filson Club (life), Colonial Dames Am. (past pres., registrar), Delta Delta Delta. Presbyterian. Avocations: piano, stampl collecting, ballroom dancing.

KITTRELL, PAMELA R., lawyer; b. Athens, Ga., June 15, 1965; d. John Edison and Anne (Hagins) K. AB summa cum laude, U. Miami, 1987; JD, U. Mich., 1990. Bar: Fla. 1990, U.S. Dist. Ct. (so. dist.) Fla. 1991, D.C. 1992, Colo. 1994, U.S, Ct. Appeals (11th cir.) 1994, U.S. Dist. CT. (mid. dist.) Fla. 1995. Assoc. Stearns, Weaver, Miller, Weissler, Alhadeff & Sitterson, PA, Miami, 1990-93; sr. assoc. Cooney, Mattson, Lance, Blackburn, Richards & O'Connor, P.A., Ft. Lauderdale, Fla., 1994-98. Mem. Fla. Bar (appellate practice and advocacy sec.), Broward County Bar Assn., Fla. Def. Lawyers Assn. Democrat.

KITTRIE, NICHOLAS N(ORBERT NEHEMIAH), law educator, international consultant, author; b. en route Bilgoraj, Poland, Mar. 26, 1930; (parents Brit. citizens); came to U.S., 1944; s. S.K. Kronenbergh and Perla F. (Ver Standig) K.; m. Sara Yudovic de Burak, June 1, 1962; children: Orde Felicien, Norda Nicole, Zachary McNair. Student, U. Cairo, 1946, U. London, 1947; LLB, U. Kans., 1950, MA, 1951; postgrad., U. Chgo., 1954-55; LLM, Georgetown U., 1963, SJD, 1968. Bar: Kans. 1953, D.C. 1958, U.S. Supreme Ct. Rsch. asst. U. London, 1947; instr. Western civilization dept. U. Kans., 1948-50; legal analyst Kans. Govt. Rsch. Ctr., 1951-54; asst. to dir. legis. svc. ABA, 1955-56, project dir., 1956-58; rsch. assoc. Yale Law Sch., 1958; legal asst. to U.S. Senator Wiley, 1959; counsel to U.S. Senator Estes Kefauver, antitrust and monopoly subcom. U.S. Senate, 1959-62; ptnr. DeGrazia & Kittrie, Washington, 1962-67; prof. criminal and comparative law Washington Coll. Law, Am. U., 1963—, dir. Inst. for Advanced Studies in Justice, 1970-78, dean, 1977-79, Mooers scholar and prof. law, 1983—, prof., 1994—; univ. prof. Am. U., Washington, 1994—; dir. Inst. Law and Policy, 1980—; lectr. U. Ottawa, summer 1966; rsch. scholar Univs. Warsaw and Berlin, summers 1967, 68; rsch. assoc. Ctr. Studies Criminal Justice U. Chgo., 1967-68; dir. Law and Policy Inst., Jerusalem, summers 1970-76, Inst. Law and Mass Media, 1978—; chmn. Eleanor Roosevelt Inst. for Justice and Peace, 1989—; vis. fellow Inst. Advanced Legal Rsch. U. London, 1973-74, Nat. Inst. Justice U.S. Dept. Justice, 1979-80; vis. prof. London Sch. Econs., 1974; cons. Pres.'s Commn. Marijuana and Drug Abuse, 1972, v.p.'s commn. to combat terrorism, 1985; permanent rep. of AIDP to UN Social and Econs. Coun., 1975—; mem. task force on role of psychology in criminal justice Am. Psychol. Assn., 1975-76; dir. 1st Washington Devel. Corp., Bank of Chios, Athens, Greece; dir., gen. counsel Liberty House Investments; v.p. Nickal Corp.; chmn. KVK Communications Ltd. Author: International Legal Responsibility for Colonial People, 1951, Survey of Adminstration of Criminal Justice, 1956, (with others) The Mentally Disabled and the Law, 1959, The Right to be Different: Deviance and Enforced Law, 1971, The Comparative Law of Israel and the Middle East, 1971, The Real Estate Settlement Process and Its Cost, 1972, Crescent and Star: Arab-Israeli Perspectives on the Middle East Conflict, 1972, The Juvenile Drug Offender, 1972, Medicine, Law and Public Policy, 1975, Sanctions, Sentencing and Corrections, 1981, The Tree of Liberty: Rebellion and Political Crime in America, 1986, 2d edit., 1998, The Uncertain Future: Gorbachev's Eastern Bloc, 1988, The War Against Authority: From the Crisis of Legitimacy to a New Social Contract, 1995, Rebels With a Cause: The Minds and Morality of Political Offenders, 1999; chmn. editorial bd. Jour. Criminology, 1973-75, Justice mag., 1973-75; mem. editorial bd. Law and Human Behavior, 1976-80; mem. editorial adv. bd. The Washington Times; mem. exec. bd. Paragon House Pubs.; sr. cons. U.S. News and World Report Books; contbr. articles to profl. jours. Chmn. UN Alliance for Crime Prevention and Criminal Justice, 1976—, sci. com. U. Messina, Italy; mem. senate Am. U., 1964-72. Served with Brit. Middle East Command, 1944-45. Raymond fellow U. Chgo., 1954-55; rsch. fellow Yale Law Sch., 1955; sr. fellow NEH, 1973-74. Mem. ABA, AAAS (mem. coun. 1972—), Am. Soc. Criminology (pres. 1975), Internat. Assn. Penal Law (v.p. Am. sect., sec.-gen. 1975-80), Internat. Assn. Comparative Pub. Law (bd. dirs. 1976—), Am. Soc. Pub. Adminstrn., Am. Judicature Soc., Am. Soc. Internat. Law, Internat. Inst. Space Law, Inter-Am. Bar Assn., Kans. Bar Assn., D.C. Bar Assn., Rose Haven Yacht Club (bd. dirs., Cosmos Club, Phi Delta Phi (Sam Green award 1989), Pi Sigma Alpha. Home: 6908 Ayr Ln Bethesda MD 20817-4902 also: 42427 Cochran Mill Rd Leesburg VA 20175-4617 Office: Am U Sch Law 4801 Massachusetts Ave NW Ste 354 Washington DC 20016

KITTROSS, JOHN MICHAEL, retired communications educator; b. N.Y.C., Apr. 25, 1929; s. John H. and Lucile S. (Vossen) K.; m. Sally Sprague, Dec. 27, 1951; children—David M., Julia Ann. AB, Antioch Coll., 1951; MS, Boston U., 1952; PhD, U. Ill., 1960. Various positions broadcasting, summer stock, motion picture prodn., 1946-52; rsch. asst. U. Ill. Inst. Comm. Rsch., Urbana, 1955-59; from instr. to assoc. prof. dept. telecomm. U. So. Calif., 1959-68; prof. comm. Temple U., 1968-85, asst. dean Sch. Comm. and Theater, 1971-73, assoc. dean, 1973-80; dean Emerson Coll., Boston, 1985, provost, v.p. acad. affairs, 1985-87, prof. dept. mass comm., 1987-93; vis. prof., dir. Temple U. Sch. Comms. and Theater London Programme, 1994; mng. dir. K E G Assocs., 1995—. Author: Television Frequency Allocation Policy in the United States, 1979; co-author: Stay Tuned: A Concise History of American Broadcasting, 1978, 2d edit., 1990, Controversies in Media Ethics, 1996, 2d edit., 1999; editor: Free and Fair: Courtroom Access and the Fairness Doctrine, 1970, Jour. Broadcasting, 1960-72, Documents in American Telecommunications Policy, 1977, Administration of American Telecommunications Policy, 1981; co-editor, editor: Media Ethics, 1989—; compiler: Bibliography of Theses and Dissertations in Broadcasting, 1920-73, 1978; contbg. editor: Comm. Booknotes Quar., 1997—; contbr. articles to profl. jours. Trustee Upper Moreland Free Pub. Library, 1976-82. Served with AUS, 1952-54. Mem. AAUP, Broadcast Edn. Assn. (Disting. Broadcast Edn. award 1990), Assn. Edn. in Journalism and Mass Comm., Radio-TV News Dirs. Assn., Soc. Profl. Journalists, ACLU. Unitarian (trustee ch. 1966-68). Home: 164 High St Acton MA 01720-4218

KITTS, JUDITH PATE, English educator; b. Fayetteville, N.C., Feb. 14, 1944; d. Herbert William and Sarah Elizabeth (Turner) Pate; m. John I. Kitts, Jr. (div. May 1978); 1 child, Lesley Kathleen. BA, U. N.C., Greensboro, 1966; MA, U. N.C., Chapel Hill, 1968. English tchr. DeKalb County Schs., Atlanta, 1968-72, Memphis City Schs., 1975—. creative writing tchr. U. Tenn. Summer Scholars, Memphis, 1995. Mem. Nat. Coun. Tchrs. English, Memphis Acoustic Music Assn. Democrat. Avocations: traveling, reading, music, rafting, pottery. Home: 1662 Carruthers Pl Memphis TN 38112-5208

KITTS, THOMAS MICHAEL, English language educator, writer; b. Staten Island, N.Y., Oct. 5, 1955; s. Richard John and Anna (Cornette) K.; m. Cynthia Casciola-Kitts, June 25, 1977; children: Dylan, Holly. BA, St. John's U., 1977; MA, NYU, 1979, PhD, 1991. Tchr. English Corpus Christi Sch., N.Y.C., 1977-79, Rice H.S., N.Y.C., 1979-80; asst. dir. alumni rels. St. John's U., Jamaica, N.Y., 1980-82, dir. alumni rels., 1982-91, asst. prof. English, 1991-97, assoc. prof., 1997—; Presenter in field. Author: The Theatrical Life of George Henry Boker, 1994, (play) Gypsies, 1987, (manual) DiYann's Literature, 1997, American Tradition in Literature, 1999; contbr. articles to profl. jours. Mem. MLA, Am. Popular Culture Assn., Northeast MLA, Dramatists Guild, Victorian Soc. Am., Mid-Atlantic Popular Culture Assn. Roman Catholic. Avocations: music, sports, theatre. Office: St John's U 8000 Utopia Pkwy Jamaica NY 11432-1343

KITZ, RICHARD JOHN, anesthesiologist, educator; b. Oshkosh, Wis., Mar. 25, 1929; s. Edward G. and Lona M. (Schneider) K.; m. Jeanne Hogan, Feb. 27, 1954; 1 child, Anne Marie. BS, Marquette U., 1951, MD, 1954; MA (hon.), Harvard U. Med. Sch., 1969. Diplomate: Am. Bd. Anesthesiology (dir.). Intern in surgery Columbia U., 1954-55; resident in surgery, 1956-57; resident in anesthesiology Columbia U., 1958-60, instr. in anesthesiology, 1960-61, NIH spl. rsch. fellow, 1961-62, asst. prof. anesthesiology, 1962-66, assoc. prof., 1966-69; prof. rsch. and tchg. in anesthesia Harvard U.-MIT, co-dir. divsn. health scis. tech., 1985-91; anaesthetist-in-chief Mass. Gen. Hosp., Boston, 1969-94; prof. Harvard U. Med. Sch., 1969-70, Henry Isaiah Dorr prof. anaesthesia, 1970-98, Henry Isaiah Dorr Disting. prof., 1998—, faculty dean clin. affairs, 1994—; cons. FDA; prin. investigator Harvard Anaesthesia Rsch. and Rsch. Tng. Ctr., 1969-93. Contbr. numerous articles, rev. to profl. publs.; editor: (with E.M. Papper) Uptake and Distribution of Anesthetic Agents, 1963, (with M.B. Laver) Scientific Basis of Anesthesia; editor-in-chief Jour. Clin. Anesthesia, 1987-95. Served with M.C. USN, 1955-57. Fellow Coll. Anesthesiologists; mem. NAS, Inst. Medicine, AMA, Assn. Univ. Anesthetists, Am. Soc. Anesthesiologists, Mass. Soc. Anesthesiologists, Royal Coll. Surgeons Ireland (hon. mem. faculty anesthetists), Royal Coll. Anesthetists Eng. (hon.), German Soc. Anesthesiologists and Intensive Care (hon.), Japan Soc. Anesthesiologists (hon.), Australian Soc. Anesthetists (hon.), Harvard Club (Boston), Beverly Yacht Club, Blue Water Sailing Club. Roman Catholic. Home: 6 Pond St Dover MA 02030-2432 Office: Mass Gen Hosp Dept Anesthesia Boston MA 02114

KITZES, WILLIAM FREDRIC, lawyer, safety analyst, consultant; b. Bklyn., Nov. 24, 1950; s. David Louis and Rhoda Rachel (Feldman) K; m. Sandra Shimasaki, Apr. 7, 1979: children: Justin, Dana. BA, U. Wis., 1972; JD, Am. U., 1975. Bar: D.C. 1977. Legal advisor on product recalls U.S. Consumer Products Safety Commn., Washington, 1975-77, program mgr., 1977-80, regulatory counsel, 1980-81; v.p., gen. mgr. Inst. for Safety Analysis, Rockville, Md., 1981-83; prin. Consumer Safety Assocs., Potomac, Md., Boca Raton, Fla., 1983—; cons. Toro Co., Bloomington, Minn., 1987, Vendo Co., Fresno, Calif., 1987, Nat. Assn. Attys. Gens., Washington, 1987, Arctic Cat, Inc., thief River Falls, Minn., 1995—, Global Furniture, Toronto, Ont., 1997, Product Safety Online, Boca Raton, 1997—. Counsel Friends of Charlie Gilchrist, Montgomery County, Md., 1983; chmn. Fla. Consumers Coun., 1995—. Recipient silver medal for meritorious svc. U.S. Consumer Products Safety Commn., 1976. Mem. Am. Soc. Safety Engrs., Human Factors Soc., System Safety Soc., Nat. Safety Coun., Internat. Consumer Product Health and Safety Orgn. Home and Office: Consumer Safety Assocs Consumer Safety Assocs 4501 NW 25th Way Boca Raton FL 33434-2506

KITZHABER, JOHN ALBERT, governor, physician, former state senator; b. Colfax, Wash., Mar. 5, 1947; s. Albert Raymond and Annabel Reed (Wetzel) K. BA, Dartmouth Coll., 1969; MD, U. Oreg., 1973. Intern Gen. Rose Meml. Hosp., Denver, 1976-77; Emergency physician Mercy Hosp., Roseburg, Oreg., 1974-75; mem. Oreg. Ho. of Reps., 1979-81; mem. Oreg. Senate, 1981-95, pres., 1985, 87, 89, 91; gov. State of Oregon, 1995—; assoc. prof. Oreg. Health Sci. U., 1986—. Mem. Am. Coll. Emergency Physicians, Douglas County Med. Soc., Physicians for Social Responsibility, Am. Council Young Polit. Leaders, Oreg. Trout. Democrat. Office: Office of the Gov State Capitol Bldg Rm 254 Salem OR 97310

KITZIS, GARY DAVID, periodontist, educator; b. Bklyn., Apr. 2, 1953. BA in Biology, Adelphi U., 1975; DMD, U. Fla., 1979; C.A.G.S. in Periodonics, Boston U., 1984, C.A.G.S. in Prosthodontics, 1986. Diplomate Am. Bd. Periodontology. Pvt. practice gen. dentistry Atlanta, 1980-82; pvt. practice periodontist, prosthodontist Woodbury, N.Y., 1986—; assoc. prof. periodontics SUNY Sch. Dental Medicine, Stony Brook, 1986—. Contbr. articles to profl. jours. Fellow Acad. Gen. Dentistry, Suffolk Acad. Medicine, Am. Coll. Prosthodontists (assoc.); mem. Am. Acad. Periodontology, Acad. Osseointegration, N.Y. Acad. Scis., ADA, Suffolk County Dental Soc. (bd. dels. 1988—), Long Island Soc. for Osseointegration (membership com. 1988-91, v.p. 1991-93), Am. Acad. Gold Foil Operators, Northeastern Soc. Periodontists. Achievements include determination of the accuracy of dental articulator interchange ability; patent on stress distributing dental implant. Office: 156 Plainview Rd Woodbury NY 11797-2807

KITZKE, EUGENE DAVID, research management executive; b. Milw., Sept. 2, 1923; s. Leo R. and Regina R. (Tomczyk) K.; m. Lorraine Grace Shummon, Sept. 2, 1946; children: Mary Victoria, Paul Simon, Patrice Lynn, Jerome Peter. B.S., Marquette U., 1945, M.S., 1947. Instr. microbiology St. Mary's Sch. Nursing, Grand Rapids, Mich., 1946-47; assoc. prof. Aquinas Coll., 1947-51; lab researcher S.C. Johnson & Son, Inc., Racine, Wis., 1951-57, research mgr., 1957-76, v.p. corp. research and devel., 1976-81; pres. Oak Crete Block Corp., South Milwaukee, Wis., 1980—; developer Wind Crest Subdiv., Wind Lake, Wis., 1993; asst. clin. prof. dept. environ. medicine Med. Coll. Wis., Milw., 1973-81; owner Danel Enterprise, South Milwaukee; bd. dirs. Songcards, Inc.; judge Marquette U. Sci. Fair. Author: For the Next Generation, 1986; patentee (in field); contbr. articles to tech. jours., fiction and poetry to mags. Mem. Pres.' Council Alverno Coll., 1979-87. Recipient H.F. Johnson Cmty. Svc. award, 1996; Disting. Scholar Marquette U., 1995. Mem. Palm Soc. (exec. bd., past pres.), AAAS, History of Sci. Soc., Sigma Xi, Phi Sigma, Sigma Tau Delta. Roman Catholic. Home: 616 Aspen St South Milwaukee WI 53172-1702 Office: PO Box 413 South Milwaukee WI 53172-0413 Office: 7101 S Pennsylvania Ave Oak Creek WI 53154-2439 *Honor thyself. Be in control. Be paid.*

KITZMILLER, HOWARD LAWRENCE, lawyer; b. Shippensburg, Pa., May 6, 1930; s. Franklin Leroy and Emma Corrinna (Bedford) K.; m. Shirley Mae Pine, Apr. 4, 1953; children: David Lawrence, Diane May. BA summa cum laude, Dickinson Coll., 1951; JD, Dickinson Sch. of Law, 1954; LLM, George Washington U., 1958. Bar: Pa. 1955, D.C. 1984. Commr. U.S. Ct. Mil. Appeals, Washington, 1958-59; various positions to assoc. gen. counsel FCC, Washington, 1959-80; various positions to sr. v.p. and sec. Washington Mgmt. Corp., 1983—. Editor Dickinson Law Rev., 1954. Deacon, elder Westminster Presbyn. Ch., Alexandria, Va.; bd. dirs. S.E. Fairfax Devel. Corp., Fairfax County, Va., 1977, also past pres.; various positions including pres., parents adv. coun., bd. assocs., trustee, investment com. Randolph-Macon Coll., Ashland, Va., 1984-95. Capt. JAGC, U.S. Army, 1955-58. Mem. ABA, FBA, City Club Washington, Masons, Phi Beta Kappa. Republican.

KITZMILLER, WILLIAM MICHAEL, government official; b. Bryn Mawr, Pa., Mar. 29, 1931; s. Richard Dale Kitzmiller and Virginia Hanford (Jones) Hedges; m. Lynn Grey Fisher, Dec. 31, 1955; children—Virginia Grey, Elizabeth Curtiss, Katherine Dale. B.A., Yale U., 1954, postgrad., 1956-57. Account exec. Selvage & Lee, Inc., N.Y.C., 1959-65; legis. asst. Congressman Richard L. Ottinger, Washington, 1965-68; press asst. V.P. Hubert H. Humphrey, Washington, 1968; pub. affairs dir. Nat. Commn. on Product Safety, Washington, 1968; exec. dir. Grassroots, Inc., Washington, 1968-71; exec. sec. Rep. Ogden R. Reid, Washington, 1971-74; freelance writer, 1974-75; communications dir. Westchester County, White Plains, NY., 1975-76; staff coordinator Com. on Energy and Commerce U.S. Ho. of Reps., Washington, 1976-83, staff dir. Com. on Energy and Commerce, 1983-90; ptnr. Johnson Smith Dover Kitzmiller & Stewart, Washington, 1990—. Author: What Every Woman Should Know About the Environment: A Guide to Global Housekeeping, 1970; Citizen Action: Vital Force for Change, 1971; United State Trade Relations with Japan and China, 1979, 2d edit., 1983; editor: Energy and Helium: A Crisis in Future Energy Technology, 1979, China's Economic Development and U.S. Trade Interests, 1985, editorial dir. com. history project, 1986; editorial dir. Legis. Jour. of Com. of Commerce and Mfrs., 1988; contbr. artices to profl. jours. Mem. Sea Space Symposium (chmn., Emerald award 1988), Elizabethan Club, U. Club of Washington. Democrat. Avocations: sailing; chess; scuba diving. Home: 6109 Franklin Gibson Rd Tracys Landing MD 20779-2301 Office: Johnson Smith Dover Kitzmiller 1300 Connecticut Ave NW Ste 600 Washington DC 20036-1710

KIVELSON, MARGARET GALLAND, physicist; b. N.Y.C., Oct. 21, 1928; d. Walter Isaac and Madeleine (Wiener) Galland; m. Daniel Kivelson, Aug. 15, 1949; children: Steven Allan, Valerie Ann. AB, Radcliffe Coll., 1950, AM, 1951, PhD, 1957. Cons. Rand Corp., Santa Monica, Calif., 1956-69; asst. to geophysicist UCLA, 1967-83, prof., 1983—, also chmn. dept. earth and space scis., 1984-87; prin. investigator of magnetometer, Galileo Mission, Jet Propulsion Lab., Pasadena, Calif., 1977—; overseer Harvard Coll., 1977-83; mem. adv. coun. NASA, 1987-93; chair atmospheric adv. com. NSF, 1986-89, Com. Solar and Space Physics, 1977-86, com. planetary exploration, 1986-87, com. solar terrestial phys., 1989-92; mem. adv. com. geoscis. NSF. Editor: The Solar System: Observations and Interpretations, 1986; co-editor: Introduction to Space Physics, 1995; contbr. articlels to profl. jours. Named Woman of Yr., L.A. Mus. Sci. and Industry, 1979, Woman of Sci., UCLA, 1984; recipient Grad. Soc. medal Radcliffe Coll., 1983, 350th Anniversary Alumni medal Harvard U. Fellow AAAS, NAS, Am. Geophysics Union, Am. Acad. Arts and Scis.; mem. Am. Phys. Soc., Am. Astron. Soc., Internat. Inst. Astronautics (corr. mem.). Office: UCLA Dept Earth & Space Scis 6847 Slichter Los Angeles CA 90095-1567

KIVENSON, GILBERT, engineering consultant, patent agent; b. Pitts., Dec. 5, 1920; s. Samuel and Anne (Bortnicker) K. BSChemE, Carnegie Mellon U., 1942; MSChemE, U. Pitts., 1947. Registered profl. engr., Calif. Fellow Mellon Inst. Indsl. Rsch., Pitts., 1944-54; engr. Westinghouse Electric Co., Pitts., 1955-68; sr. engr. Rockwell North Am. Aviation, L.A, 1971-73, 76-79, J.B. Lansing, L.A, 1980-81; cons., patent agent L.A., 1980—. Author: Industrial Stroboscopy, 1965, Durability & Reliability In Engineering Design, 1971, Art & Science of Inventing, 1977, 2d edit., 1982. Avocations: sailing, cycling, golf. Home: 22030 Wyandotte St Canoga Park CA 91303-1118

KIVETTE, RUTH MONTGOMERY, English language educator; b. Union City, N.J., Jan. 10, 1926; d. Joseph and Margaret Eliza (Ditty) Montgomery; m. Everett McNeill Kivette, Oct. 23, 1954. AB, Barnard Coll., 1948; AM, Columbia U., 1950, PhD, 1960; BD, Union Theol. Sem., N.Y.C., 1954; J.D., Fordham U. Law Sch., 1985. Asst. prof. Davis and Elkins Coll., Elkins, W.Va., 1950-52; lectr. Barnard Coll., N.Y.C., 1952-55, 57-61, asst. prof., 1961-67, assoc. prof., 1967-74, prof. English, 1974-92, prof. emeritus, 1992—; chmn. dept. Barnard Coll., 1977-79, 85-88. Kent fellow, 1954; Lilly postdoctoral fellow in religion, 1963; Folger Library fellow, 1966; Mellon grantee, 1983. Mem. AAUP, AAUW, MLA, Law and Humanities Inst., Milton Soc. Am. Office: Columbia U Barnard Coll New York NY 10027*

KIVIKOSKI, ASKO ILMARI, obstetrician/gynecologist; b. Helsinki, Finland, Aug. 3, 1932; came to U.S., 1984; MD, U. Turku, Finland, 1958, DSc, 1967. Diplomate Am. Bd. Ob-gyn. Intern U. Turku, 1962, resident in ob/gyn., 1962-65, asst. prof., 1966-76; resident in surgery City Hosp., Turku, 1965-66; researcher Washington U., St. Louis, 1971-72; fellow in perinatology Mt. Sinai Hosp., N.Y.C., 1978-79; head dept. ob/gyn. Ctrl. hosp., Lahti, Finland, 1976-84; staff Barnes Hosp., St. Louis, 1984-87, 97—; chief gynecol. svcs. St. Louis Regional Med. Ctr., 1987-97; asst. prof. Washington U., St. Louis, 1984-92, assoc. prof., 1992—. Mem. Am. Coll. Obstetricians/Gynecologists, Am. Inst. Ultrasound in Medicine, N.Y. Acad. Sci. Office: Washington Univ Sch Medicine Dept Ob/gyn 4911 Barnes-Jewish Hosp Plz Saint Louis MO 63110-1036

KIYOTA, HEIDE PAULINE, clinical psychologist; b. Bamberg, Germany, July 6, 1942; came to U.S., 1970; d. Fritz and Marcella (Schropfer) S.; m. Ronald Masaki Kiyota, Dec. 26, 1982; children: Heather E., Catherine M., Michelle H. BS, U. Md., 1975, MA, 1979; PhD, U. Hawaii, 1986. Lic. psychologist, Hawaii; accelerated hypnotherapy cert. The Wellness Inst., 1996. Counselor-trainee Regional Inst. for Children & Adolescents, Balt., 1976-77; supr.-counselor Multiple Offender Alcoholism Program, Balt., 1977-80; therapist-intern VA, Honolulu, 1983-84; clin. psychologist Kalihi-Palama Counseling Svcs., Honolulu, 1987-89; pvt. practice psychologist Honolulu, 1988—; presenter in field. Contbr. articles to profl. jours. Mem. Am. Psychol. Assn., Hawaii Psychol. Assn., Phi Kappa Phi. Home: 1812 Nahenahe Pl Wahiawa HI 96786-2627 Office: 410 Kilani Ave Ste 219 Wahiawa HI 96786

KIZER, CAROLYN ASHLEY, poet, educator; b. Spokane, Wash., Dec. 10, 1925; d. Benjamin Hamilton and M. (Ashley) K.; m. Stimson Bullitt, Jan., 1948 (div.); children: Ashley Ann, Scott, Jill Hamilton; m. John Marshall Woodbridge, Apr. 11, 1975. BA, Sarah Lawrence Coll., 1945; postgrad. (Chinese govt. fellow in comparative lit.), Columbia U., 1946-47; studied poetry with Theodore Roethke, U. Wash., 1953-54; LittD (hon.), Whitman Coll., 1986, St. Andrew's Coll., 1989, Mills Coll., 1990, Wash. State U., 1991. Specialist in lit. U.S. Dept. State, Pakistan, 1964-65; first dir. lit. programs Nat. Endowment for Arts, 1966-70; poet-in-residence U. N.C. at Chapel Hill, 1970-74; Hurst Prof. Lit. Washington U., St. Louis, 1971; lectr. Spring Lecture Series Barnard Coll., 1972; acting dir. grad. writing program Columbia, 1972; poet-in-residence Ohio U., 1974; vis. poet Iowa Writer's Workshop, 1975; prof. U. Md., 1976-77; poet-in-residence, disting. vis. lectr. Centre Coll., Ky., 1979; disting. vis. poet East Wash. U., 1980; Elliston prof. poetry U. Cin., 1981; Bingham disting. prof. U. Louisville, Ky., 1982; disting. vis. poet Bucknell U., Pa., 1982; vis. poet SUNY, Albany, 1982; prof. Columbia U. Sch. Arts, 1982; prof. poetry Stanford U., 1986; sr. fellow in humanities Princeton U., 1986; vis. prof. writing U. Ariz., 1989, 90, U. Calif., Davis, 1991; Coal Royalty chair U. Ala., 1995; participant Internat. Poetry Festivals, London, 1960, 70, Yugoslavia, 1969, 70, Pakistan, 1969, Rotterdam, Netherlands, 1970, Knokke-le-Zut, Belgium, 1970, Bordeaux, 1992, Dublin, 1993, Glasgow, 1994; sr. fellow humanities council Princeton U., 1986. Author: Poems, 1959, The Ungrateful Garden, 1961, Knock Upon Silence, 1965, Midnight Was My Cry, 1971, Mermaids in the Basement: Poems for Women, 1984 (Gov.'s award State of Wash. 1985, San Francisco Arts Commn. award 1986), Yin: New Poems, 1984 (Pulitzer prize in poetry 1985), The Nearness of You, 1987 (Theodore Roethke prize, 1988); Proses: On Poems & Poets, 1994, Picking & Choosing: Prose on Prose, 1995, Harping On: Poems 1985-1995, 1996; editor: Woman Poet: The West, 1980, Leaving Taos, 1981, The Essential Clare, 1993, 100 Great Poems by Women, 1995; translator Carrying Over, 1988; founder, editor: Poetry N.W., 1959-65; contbr. poems, articles to Am. and Brit. jours. Recipient award Am. Acad. and Inst. Arts and Letters, 1985, Pres.'s medal Ea. Washington U., 1988, 4 Gov.'s award State of Wash., 1965, 85, 95, 98, Silver medal Commonwealth Club, 1997, Aiken Taylor prize Sewanee Rev., 1998. Mem. PEN, Amnesty Internat., Poetry Soc. Am. (Masefield prize 1983, Frost medal 1988), Acad. Am. Poets (chancellor 1995-99). Episcopalian. Address: 19772 8th St E Sonoma CA 95476-3849*

KIZER, JOHN OSCAR, lawyer; b. Wheeling, W.Va., Mar. 6, 1913; s. Edwin O. and Laura E. (Dennis) K.; m. Lillian Taylor Cart, Sept. 15, 1934; children: Nora Kizer Bell, Stephen. AB, W.Va. U., 1934, LLB, 1936. Bar: W.Va. 1936. Dir. safety responsibility dept. W.Va. Rd. Commn., 1936-39; assoc. Clark, Woodroe & Butts, Charleston, W.Va., 1939; ptnr. Campbell, Love, Woodroe & Kizer and predecessor firms, Charleston, 1939-75, Love, Wise, Robinson & Woodroe, Charleston, 1976-83, Love, Wise & Woodroe, Charleston, 1983-89, Kay, Casto, Chaney, Love & Wise, Charleston, 1989—; gen. receiver Cir. Ct. Kanawha County, 1953-98; dir. emeritus Charleston Nat. Bank. Bd. dirs., past pres., co-incorporatpr Children's Mus., Charleston; co-incorporator Sunrise Found.; bd. dirs. Daywood Found. Recipient Spl. Achievement award for Pub. Svc. W.Va. U. Coll. of Law, 1991, W.Va. Bar Assn. Lifetime Achievement award, 1998. Mem. ABA, W.Va. Bar Assn., W.Va. State Bar (chmn. com. legis. 1960-71, mem. com. legal ethics, 1964-84, chmn. 1968-84), Berry Hills Country Club, Delta Tau Delta. Presbyterian. Home: 2506 Kanawha Ave SE Charleston WV 25304-1026 Office: Kay Casto Chaney Love & Wise 1600 Bank One Ctr Charleston WV 25301-2723

KIZER, KENNETH WAYNE, physician, educator, administrator; b. Decatur, Ind., May 28, 1951; s. Homer Martin Kizer and Ellen Hope Howland; m. Suzanne A. Stoddard, Aug. 26, 1972; children: Kelli Christina, Kimberly Casey. BS with honors, Stanford U., 1972; MD with honors, MPH in Epidemiology, UCLA, 1976. Rotating internship Naval Regional Med. Ctr., Portsmouth, Va., 1977; undersea medicine fellowship Naval Undersea Med. Inst., Groton, Conn., 1977; resident in diagnostic radiology U. Calif, San Francisco, 1980-81, resident in occupational medicine, 1982-83; firefighter, physician; dir. Emergency Med. Svcs. Authority State of Calif., 1983-84; chief dep. dir. and chief of pub. health Calif. Dept. Health Svcs., Sacramento, 1984-85, dir., 1985-91; prof., chmn. dept. community and internat. health U. Calif., Davis, 1991-94; undersec. for health Dept. Vets. Affairs, Washington, 1994—; dir. Health Sys. Internat., Inc., 1994-97; educator, researcher, consultant in field. Contbr. numerous articles to profl. jours., chpts. to books. Chair Black Infant Health Leadership Com., Calif., 1989-91, Lyme Disease Steering Group, AIDS Vaccine Rsch. and Devel. Adv. Com., 1986-91, Calif. Radiation Emergency Screening Team, 1988-91, Interagency Task Force for Oversight of Dept. of Energy Facilities in Calif., 1989-90, Hazardous Waste Appeal Bd., 1990; co-chair Calif. AIDS Leadership Com.; mem. Diving Control Bd. U. Calif., 1980-91, Gov.'s Emergency Ops. Exec. Coun., 1984-91, Governing Bd. Calif YMCA Model Legislature Program, 1986-90, Chem. Emergency Planning and Response Commn., 1988-90; chair S.W. Low Level Radioactive Waste Compact Commn., 1990-91, tobacco edn. oversight com. State Calif., 1990-91, exec. com. San Francisco Bay Area Youth Excellence Initiative, 1989-90, mgmt. com. Santa Monica Bay Restoration Project, 1987-91; former mem. Gov's Task Force on Toxics, Waste and Tech., 1985-86; former sec. commn. emergency med. svcs. State of Calif., 1984; bd. dirs. Calif. Wellness Found., 1992—, Matthews Found., 1991-94, Ctr. for AIDS Rsch., Edn. and Svcs., 1992-94, Infection Control Coun., 1991-94; mem. adv. bd. Preventive Sports Medicine Inst., 1991-94. Lt. USN, 1976-80. Recipient Humanitarian Svc. medal Dept. of Def., 1979, Spl. Recognition award No. Calif. Emergency Med. Care Coun., 1984, Golden State Med. Assn., 1986, Calif. Div. Am. Lung Assn., 1988, Calif. Health Fedn., 1988, cert. of Recognition Calif. Asian Pacific Health Coalition, 1989, Spl. Achievement award Calif. Emergency Physician Med. Group, 1989, Jean Spencer Felton award for Excellence in Scientific Writing, 1989, spl. awards from March of Dimes, Am. Cancer Soc., Calif. State Senate, Calif. Conf. Local Health Officers, others, 1991—, Healthcare Heroes award Calif. State Assembly, 1996, Cert. of Recognition award, 1996, Dr. Nathan Davis award AMA, 1998, Literacy Achievement award Am. Coll. Physician Execs., 1998, Founders award Wilderness Medical Soc., 1998; named Toll fellow Coun. State G ovts., 1987. Fellow Am. Coll. Preventive Medicine, Am. Coll. Emergency Physicians, Am. Coll. Occupational Medicine, Am. Acad. Clin. Toxicology, Royal Soc. Health, Royal Soc. Medicine, Am. Coll. Med. Toxicology, Explorers Club; mem. APHA, Internat. Soc. Toxinology, Am. Coll. Physician Execs., South Pacific Underwater Med. Soc., Wilderness Med. Soc., Undersea and Hyperbaric Med. Soc., Nat. Soc. YMCA Youth Govs., Nat. Assn. Underwater Instrs. (Outstanding Contribution to Diving award 1984), Delta Tau Delta (Beta Rho chpt. Hall of Fame 1987), Alpha Omega Alpha, Delta Omega. Republican. Avocations: scuba diving, hiking and backpacking, photography, racquet sports, book collecting. Office: Dept Vets Affairs 810 Vermont Ave NW Rm 800 Washington DC 20420-0001

KIZZIAR, JANET WRIGHT, psychologist, author, lecturer; b. Independence, Kans.; d. John L. and Thelma (Rooks) Wright; m. Mark Kizziar. BA, U. Tulsa, 1961, MA, 1964, EdD, 1969. Sch. psychologist Tulsa Pub. Schs.; pvt. practice psychology Tulsa, 1969-78, Bartlesville, Okla., 1978-88; lectr. univs., corps., health spas, 1989—. Co-host: Psychologists' Corner program, Sta. KOTV, Tulsa.; author: (with Judy W. Hagedorn) Gemini: The Psychology and Phenomena of Twins, 1975, Search for Acceptance: The Adolescent and Self Esteem, 1979. Sponsor Youth Crisis Intervention Telephone Center, 1972-74; bd. dirs. March of Dimes, Child Protection Team, Women and Children in Crisis, United Fund, YMCA Fund, Mental Health of Washington County, Alternative H.S.; edn. dir. appt. Gov.'s Commn. on Violence Against Women, Pub. Awarness Com., 1996, Women's Found. Fresh Start Women's Found., 1995. Named Disting. Alumni U. Tulsa, Outstanding Young Woman of Okla. Mem. APA, NOW, Internat. Twins Assn. (pres. 1976-77). Home: 9427 N 87th Way Scottsdale AZ 85258-1913 Office: PO Box 5227 Scottsdale AZ 85261-5227

KJELDAAS, TERJE, JR., physics educator emeritus; b. Oslo, Norway, Oct. 24, 1924; came to U.S., 1940; s. Terje and Mimi Helene (Hansen) K.; m. Sigrid Seland Moeller, June 17, 1950; children—Ingrid, John. B.S., Poly. Inst. Bklyn., 1948; A.M., Columbia, 1949; Ph.D., U. Pitts., 1959. Rsch. engr. Westinghouse Elec. Rsch. Labs., Churchill Boro, Pa., 1950-59; prof. physics Poly. U. N.Y., 1959-89, head dept., 1977-80; prof. emeritus, 1989; cons. Served with USAAF, 1943-46. Mem. Am. Phys. Soc. Home: 50 Fort Pl Staten Island NY 10301-2415 Office: Poly U Six Metrotech Ctr Brooklyn NY 11201-2990

KJELLBERG, ANN C., editor; b. Boston, Jan. 11, 1962; d. Raymond N. and Judith (Priestley) K. BA, Yale U., 1984. Asst. to exec. editor Farrar, Strauss & Giroux, N.Y.C., 1986-87, asst. editor, 1987; asst. to the editor N.Y. Rev. of Books, N.Y.C., 1988-93; Am. editor Artes, Stockholm, Sweden, 1993-95; asst. editor N.Y. Rev. of Books, N.Y.C., 1993—. Mem. comms. com. Am. Friends Svc. Com., Phila., 1991—; lit. exec. Estate of Joseph Brodsky. Office: NY Rev of Books 1755 Broadway New York NY 10019-3743

KJELLBERG, BETTY J., association administrator; b. Lynwood, Calif., Sept. 24, 1947; d. Albert Ray Ferguson and Virginia Louise (Kanavos) Wanderman; m. T.H. Kjellberg, Dec. 8, 1973. BA, Calif. State Coll., L.A., 1969; MS in LS, U. So. Calif., 1971; MBA, Ariz. State U., 1982; M of Aviation Mgmt., Embry Riddle Aero. U., Daytona Beach, Fla., 1990. Cert. assn. exec.; lic. pvt. pilot. Dir. health sci. libr. Good Samaritan Med. Ctr., Phoenix, 1971-83; adminstrv. dir. Greater Phoenix Cmty. Clin. Oncology Program, Phoenix, 1983-85; med. staff svcs. adminstr. Good Samaritan Regional Med. Ctr., Phoenix, 1985-88; exec. dir. Ariz. Psychol. Assn., Scottsdale, 1989-98; owner Assn. Solutions, LLC, Scottsdale, 1998—; chair Coun. of Execs. of State and Provincial Psychol. Assns., Washington, 1995-96, mem. exec. com., 1993-96. Bd. dirs. Scottsdale Leadership Inc., 1995—, treas., 1996; precinct committeeman Rep. Party, Scottsdale, 1986-90; mem. City of Scottsdale Airport Adv. Commn., 1994—; pub. mem. Good Samaritan Regional Med. Ctr. Instnl. Rev. Bd., Phoenix, 1994—, Ariz. Supreme Ct. Jud. Performance Rev. Team, Phoenix, 1994-95; mem. adv. com. City of Scottsdale CityShape 2020, 1995. Mem. Am. Soc. Assn. Execs., Ariz. Soc. Assn. Execs., Ariz. Pilots Assn. (bd. dirs. 1986-94), Soroptimist Internat. of Phoenix, Las Rancheras Rep. Women, Am. Assoc. U. Women, (Scottsdale Br.). Office: Ariz Psychol Assn 6210 E Thomas Rd Ste 209 Scottsdale AZ 85251-7044

KJOK, SOLVEIG, artist, art historian, linguist; b. Lillehammer, Norway, Mar. 16, 1968; d. Erik and Ingunn (Haugsrud) K. BA in French Lit., U. Vienna, Austria, 1991; M in French Lit., U. Paris, 1992; MA in Romance Lang. and Lit., U. Cin., 1993, MA in Art History, 1996; MFA in Painting, Parsons Sch. Design, N.Y.C., 1998. Graphic designer Agence Karen, Paris, 1988; tchg. asst. art history U. Cin., 1995-96, dir. ind. studies of Norwegian lang./culture, 1993-96; resident Larroque Artists' Colony, Urt, France, 1997-98; tchg. asst. painting Parsons Sch. Design, N.Y.C., 1997-98; lectr. in field. Contbr. articles to profl. jours.; translator: French/Norwegian, Paris, 1988; Spanish/Norwegian translator/interpretor Medellin, Bogota, Colombia, 1993; translator English, German novels, articles, short stories into Norwegian, various pub. houses, 1985—; one-woman shows include Brodie Gallery, Cin., 1996, Kreditkassen, Bagn, Norway, 1987; exhibited in group shows at Gjensidigegården, Fagernes, Norway, 1985, Valdrestunet, Bagn, 1987, Art et Dessin, Paris, 1988, Mus. of U. Medellin, 1993, KZF Gallery, Cin., 1994, 840 Gallery, Cin., 1995, 96, Machina dell'Arte, Cin., 1996, Schoharie County Arts Coun., 1996, Gallery Alexy, Phila., 1996, Glenn Eure's Ghost Fleet Gallery, Nags Head, N.C., 1996, Amos Joseph Fine Art, Santa Fe, 1996, N.J. Ctr. Visual Arts, 1997, Pleiades Gallery, N.Y.C., 1997, Viridian Artists, Inc., 1997, Akademie der bildenden Künste Munich, 1997, A.I.R. Gallery, N.Y.C., 1997, Artists' Space, N.Y.C., 1997, Brenda Taylor Gallery, N.Y.C., 1998, Cmty. Cultural Ctr., Phila., 1998, Manefisken Galleri, Oslo, 1998, Valdres Kunstforening's Gallery, Norway, 1998, PS 122 Gallery, N.Y.C., 1998, Cameron/Weiland Gallery, N.Y.C., 1998, Galeri Steen, Oslo, Norway, 1999, others; works in pvt. and pub. collections. Mem. Cin. Artists Group Effort, 1994—. Recipient Alpha Kappa Alpha Grad. Merit award; grantee Ga. Rotary Student Program, 1989, Lise & Arnfinn Heje's Legacy, Oslo, 1990, Thom Wilhelmsen's award, Oslo, 1991, Knut Hamsun's Legacy, Oslo, 1992, Olav and Lizzie Juvkam's legacy, 1990-94, Einar Storsveen's Legacy, 1992-94; Cin. Women's Club scholar, 1995, U. Cin. scholar, 1993-96, Parsons scholar, 1997-98; AAUW fellow, 1997-98; Joahn Jorgen Brochs Legat. grant, 1998, Rsch. grant Astrup-Fearnley, Oslo, 1996, Thesis Rsch. grant Astrup-Fearnley Found., Oslo, 1996, Artist grant Norwegian Ministry Culture, 1998; recipient Edwin Gould Found. award Nat. Arts Club, N.Y.C., 1998, Excellence in Drawing award Internat. Icarus Exhbn., 1998, Spl. Gallery prize Contemporary Realism III Exhibit, Phila., 1998, others. Mem. Internat. Assn. Univ. Women, Coll. Art Assn., Norwegian Soc. Young Artists, Norwegian Visual Artists, Drawing Assn. Norway. Avocation: long distance running. Home: 44 Eagle St Brooklyn NY 11222-1013

KJOS, VICTORIA ANN, lawyer; b. Fargo, N.D., Sept. 17, 1953; d. Orville I. and Annie J. (Tanberg) K. BA, Minot State U., 1974; JD, U. N.D., 1977. Bar: Ariz. 1978. Assoc. Jack E. Evans, Ltd., Phoenix, 1977-78, pension and ins. cons., 1978-79; dep. state treas. State of N.D., Bismarck, 1979-80; freelance cons. Phoenix, 1980-81, Anchorage, 1981-82; asst. v.p., v.p., mgr. trust dept. Great Western Bank, Phoenix, 1982-84; assoc. Robert A. Jensen P.C., Phoenix, 1984-86; ptnr. Jensen & Kjos, P.C., Phoenix, 1986-89; assoc. Allen, Kimerer & LaVelle, Phoenix, 1989-90, ptnr., 1990-91; dir. The Yoga and Fitness Inst., Phoenix, 1994-97; lectr. in domestic relations. Contbr. articles to profl. jours. Bd. dirs. Arthritis Found., Phoenix, 1986-89, v.p. for chpt. devel., 1988-89; bd. dirs. Ariz. Yoga Assn., 1993-95, v.p., 1993-95. Mem. ABA, ATLA, Ariz. Bar Assn. (exec. coun. family law sect. 1988-91), Maricopa Bar Assn. (sec. family law com. 1988-89, pres. family law com. 1989-90, judge pro tem 1989-91), Ariz. Trial Lawyers Assn.

KLAAS, NICHOLAS PAUL, management and technical consultant; b. Kieler, Wis., June 25, 1925; s. Paul Francis and Ida Klaas; m. Ruth Elizabeth Barry, Nov. 5, 1949; children: Paul, Patricia, Kathleen, James. BA, Loras Coll., 1945; PhD, U. Notre Dame, 1948. Registered to practice before U.S. Patent Office, 1970. Product mgr. Rohm & Haas Co., Phila., 1948-52; mgr. research and devel. 3M Co., St. Paul, 1952-65; exec. v.p., dir. Wyomissing Corp., West Reading, Pa., 1965-71; group v.p. chems. GAF Corp., N.Y.C., 1971-77; gen. mgr. splty. chems. Ga. Pacific Corp., Portland, Oreg., 1977; pres. J.T. Baker Chem. Co., Phillipsburg, N.J., 1977-84; chmn. bd. J.T. Baker B.V., Deventer, Netherlands, 1978-84; pres. Klaas Assocs. Inc., 1984—; adj. prof. chemistry San Diego State U., 1985-98; mem. bd. visitors U. N.C., Asheville, 1986-91, Council for Chem. Research, 1987-98. Patentee in field; contbr. articles to profl. jours. Trustee St. Joseph Hosp., Reading, Pa., 1968-71; bd. regents Loras Coll., Dubuque, Iowa, 1974-76. Mem. AAAS, Synthetic Organic Chem. Mfg. Assn. (dir. 1974-77), Asphalt Roofing Mfrs. Assn. (dir. 1974-77), Am. Chem. Soc. Club: Smoke Rise. Home: 51 Hoot Owl Ter Butler NJ 07405-2409

KLAAS, PAUL BARRY, lawyer; b. St. Paul, Aug. 9, 1952; s. N. Paul and Ruth Elizabeth (Barry) K.; m. Barbara Ann Bockhaus, July 30, 1977; children: James, Ann, Brian. AB, Dartmouth Coll., 1974; JD, Harvard U., 1977. Bar: Minn. 1977, U.S. Dist. Ct. Minn. 1977, U.S. Ct. Appeals (8th cir.) 1979, U.S. Ct. Appeals (10th cir.) 1980, U.S. Supreme Ct. 1982, U.S. Ct. Appeals (9th cir.) 1989, U.S. Ct. Appeals (fed. cir.) 1994. Assoc. Dorsey & Whitney, Mpls., 1977-82; ptnr. Dorsey & Whitney, 1983—; chair Tech. and Intellectual Property Litigation practice group; adj. prof. William Mitchell Coll Law, St. Paul, 1980-85. Office: Dorsey & Whitney Pillsbury Ctr S 220 S 6th St Ste 2200 Minneapolis MN 55402-1498

KLAERNER, CURTIS MAURICE, former oil company executive; b. Fredericksburg, Tex., Sept. 7, 1920; s. Elgin and Irene (Wagner) K.; m. Aileen E. Eitt, Sept. 4, 1942; children: Sherilyn Kay, Curtis Elgin. B.S. in Chem. Engring, U. Tex., 1942; grad. program sr. execs., Mass. Inst. Tech., 1956. Process engr., then chief process engr. Magnolia Petroleum Co., 1942-53; refinery mgr., then mgr. Eastern region mfg. Socony Mobil Oil Co., 1953-59; regional exec., then regional v.p. Mobil Internat. Oil Co., 1959-61; pres. Mobil Inner Europe, Geneva, Switzerland, 1962-65; corp. v.p. charge marine transp. and internat. sales Socony Mobil Oil Co., 1965-69; exec. v.p. internat. div. Mobil Oil Corp., 1969-72, pres., 1972-79, also exec. v.p., dir., mem. exec. com. corp.; vice chmn., dir. Commonwealth Oil Refining Co., San Antonio, 1979; pres., chief operating officer Commonwealth Oil Refining Co., 1979-83; ret., 1983; pres. Klaerner Enterprises, 1984—; vice chmn. Weed Instrument Co.; dir. Belgian Refining Corp., Antwerp, 1984—, W.I. Oil Corp., Antigua, 1984—, Nat. Petroleum Ltd., Bermuda, 1986—; mem. adv. coun. Engring. Found., U. Tex., Austin. Recipient Disting. Grad. award Coll. Engring., U. Tex., 1983. Mem. Coun. Fgn. Rels., Phi Eta Sigma, Omega Chi Epsilon, Phi Kappa Sigma. Republican. Episcopalian. Clubs: Circumnavigators (N.Y.C.); Oak Hills Country, Optimists, Exchange , Petroleum (San Antonio). Home: 144 Cas Hills Dr San Antonio TX 78213-3322

KLAES, JAMES GRAHAM, III, advertising executive; b. Mt. Vernon, N.Y., Nov. 21, 1945; s. James Graham, Jr. and Frances Imelda (Barker) K.; m. Geraldine Margaret Romitti, Jan. 27, 1968 (div. Dec. 1984); children: Ian Christopher, Brian Jeremy. BA in English, U. San Francisco, 1968. Writer, prodr. White & Shuford Advt., El Paso, Dallas, 1971-73, Mithoff Advt., El Paso, 1973-75, Chapman Advt., El Paso, 1976-78; creative dir., prodr. Paragon Advt., El Paso, 1978-79; prodr., news reporter KDBC-TV, El Paso, 1980-83; creative dir., prodr. Knight & Co. Advt., El Paso, 1983-84; mgr., prodr. RXL-Pulitzer, Spokane, Wash., 1995-97; writer El Paso Inc., 1997—. Dir., prodr. (TV show) Contact, KDBC-TV, El Paso, 1980-82; prodr., writer (video) The Murals of El Paso, 1993, Carlos Callejo Fresco, 1995; host (TV show) Mayor's Spotlight, Paragon TV, El Paso, 1997-99; assignment editor KVIA-TV News, El Paso, 1999—. Bd. dirs. El Paso Tourist Attractions Promotions, 1983-88, Mexican Food Capitol of World, El Paso, 1985-90, Goodwill Industries, 1990-96, El Paso Ctr. Children, 1991-97. With U.S. Army, 1968-70, Germany. Mem. Advt. Fedn. El Paso (Topps award 1973, Vision award 1993). Avocations: rock climbing, archaeology, local history, arts. Email: jimklaes@aol.com.

KLAFTER, CARY IRA, lawyer; b. Chgo., Sept. 15, 1948; s. Herman Nicholas and Bernice Rose (Maremont) K.; m. Kathleen Ann Kerr, July 21, 1974; children: Anastasia, Benjamin, Eileen. BA, Mich. State U., 1968, MS, 1971; JD, U. Chgo., 1972. Bar: Calif. 1972. Assoc. Morrison & Foerster, San Francisco, 1972-79, ptnr., 1979-96; dir. corp. affairs legal dept. Intel Corp., 1996—; lectr. law Stanford Law Sch., 1990—. Capt. USAR, 1971-78. Mem. Great No. Rlwy. Hist. Soc.

KLAFTER, CRAIG EVAN, university administrator, legal historian; b. N.Y.C., Aug. 2, 1958; s. Gerald and Lenore (Schiener) K.; m. Catriona Susan Walker, Aug. 24, 1985. BA with honors, U. Chgo., 1980, MA, 1983; DPhil, Oxford (Eng.) U., 1991. Lectr. Am. history and instns. U. Manchester, Eng., 1990-91; lectr. modern history U. Southampton, Eng., 1991-92, rsch. fellow modern history, 1992-93; assoc. historian Jud. Br. U.S., Washington, 1993-94; adj. prof. law Boston U., 1994—, asst. to prov., 1994-95, asst. to pres., 1995—. Author: Reason Over Precedents: Origins of American Legal Thought, 1993, Essays on English Law and the American Experience, 1994, Legal Practice Management and Quality Standards, 1995. V.p., treas., trustee St. Catherine's Coll. (Oxford) Found., Washington, 1993—; mem. convocation Oxford U. Fellow St. George Tucker Soc.; mem. Oxford Soc., Am. Soc. Legal History, Hist. Soc. Avocations: skiing, squash, swimming. Home: 66 Kenrick St Brighton MA 02135-3805 Office: Boston U 145 Bay State Rd Boston MA 02215-1708

KLAGHOLZ, LEO F., state agency administrator. BA in Psychology, LaSalle Coll., 1966; MA in Edn., Cath. U. of Am., 1970, PhD in Curriculum and Instrn., 1973. Past dir. divsn. tchr. preparation and certification State of N.J. Dept. Edn., Trenton, asst. commr. divsn. acad. programs and standards, 1993, commr. of edn., 1994—; former tchr., prin.; past adminstr. N.J. Dept. Higher Edn., Trenton State Coll.; developer Alt. Cert. Program.

KLAHR, GARY PETER, lawyer; b. N.Y.C., July 9, 1942; s. Fred and Frieda (Garson) K. Student, Ariz. State U., 1958-61; LL.B. with high honors, U. Ariz., 1964. Bar: Ariz. 1967, U.S. Dist. Ct. Ariz. 1967. Assoc. Brazlin & Greene, Phoenix, 1967-68; sr. ptnr. Gary Peter Klahr, P.C., Phoenix, 1967-68. Asst. editor Ariz. Law Rev., 1963-64; contbr. articles to profl. jours. bd. dirs. CODAMA, 1975-89, pres., 1980-81; bd. dirs. Tumbleweed Runaway Ctr., 1972-76; bd. dirs., corp. sec. Internat. Found. Anti-Cancer Drug Discovery; chmn. Citizens Criminal Justice Commn., 1977-78; co-chmn. delinquency subcom. Phoenix Forward Task force; vol. referee Juvenile Ct., 1969; vol. adult probation officer; vol. counselor youth programs Dept. of Corrections, Phoenix; ex-officio mem., spl. cons. Phoenix Youth Commn.; mem. citizen adv. coun. Phoenix Union H.S. Dist., 1985-90, 95—, co-chmn. 1998—, elected governing bd., 1991-95, v.p., 1992-95, co-chmn. citizens adv. com., 1970-72; mem. rev. bd. Phoenix Police Dept., 1985-94; bd. dirs. Metro Youth Ctr., 1986-87, Svc./Employment/Redevel. (SER) Jobs for Progress, Phoenix, 1985-90, pres., 1986-87, East McDowell Youth Assn., 1992-94; v.p. local chpt. City of Hope, 1985-86; Justice of the Peace pro tem Maricopa County Cts., 1985-89; juvenile hearing officer Maricopa County Juvenile Ct., 1985-89; v.p., co-founder Cmty. Leadership for Youth Devel. (CLYDE); del. Phoenix Together Town Hall on Youth Crime, 1982. Named 1 of 3 Outstanding Young Men of Phoenix Phoenix C. of C., 1969; recipient Disting. Citizen award Ariz. chpt. ACLU, 1976. Mem. ACLU (v.p. ctrl. chpt. Ariz. 1990-95, pres. 1995—, mem. state bd.), Ariz. State Bar (past sec., bd. dirs. young lawyers sect., co-chmn. unauthorized practice com. 1988-89, mem. other coms.), Maricopa County Bar Assn. (past sec., bd. dirs. young lawyers sec., vice-chmn. juvenile practice com. 1998—), Am. Judicature Soc., Jewish Children's and Family Svc., Common Cause, NAACP, Ariz. ConsumersCoun., Phoenix Jaycees, Order of the Coif, Phi Alpha Delta. Democrat. Jewish. Office: 917 W McDowell Rd Phoenix AZ 85007

KLAHR, SAULO, physician, educator; b. Santander, Colombia, June 8, 1935; came to U.S., 1961, naturalized, 1970; s. Herman and Raquel (Konigsberg) K.; m. Carol Declue, Dec. 29, 1965; children: James Herman, Robert David. B.A., Colegio Santa Librada, Cali, Colombia, 1954; M.D., U. Nat., Bogota, Colombia, 1959. Intern Hosp. San Juan de Dios, Bogota, 1958-59; resident U. Hosp., Cali, 1959-61; mem. faculty Washington U. Sch. Medicine, St. Louis, 1966—, prof. medicine, 1972-86, Joseph Friedman prof. renal disease, 1986-91, Simon prof. medicine, co-chmn. dept., 1991-97, dir. renal div., 1972-91; physician in chief Jewish Hosp., St. Louis, 1991-96; assoc. physician Barnes Hosp., 1972-75, physician, 1975-96; physician Barnes-Jewish Hosp., 1996—; established investigator Am. Heart Assn., 1968-73; mem. adv. com. artificial kidney chronic uremia program USPHS, 1971—; bd. dirs. Eastern Mo. Kidney Found., 1973-75, chmn. med. adv. bd., 1973-74; rsch. com. Mo. Heart Assn., 1973-80, chmn., 1980-81; sci. adv. bd. Nat. Kidney Found., 1978, chmn., 1983-84, chmn. rsch. and fellowship com., 1979-81, v.p., 1986-88, pres., 1988-90; mem. gen. medicine B study sect. USPHS, 1979-83, chmn. gen. medicine B study sect., 1981-83; mem. cardiovascular and renal rev. group FDA, mem. VA Merit Rev. Bd. Nephrology, 1984-87, chmn., 1986-87; chmn. rsch. com. adv. bd. kidney, urology Nat. Inst. Diabetes and Digestive and Kidney Diseases, 1991-92, chmn. adv. bd., 1992-93; mem. adv. coun. Inst. Diabetes, Digestive Diseases and Kidney Diseases, 1995-98. Editor: Contemporary Nephrology, Chronic Renal Disease, Nutrition and the Kidney; editor in chief Am. Jour. Kidney Diseases, 1992-96; mem. editorial bd. Am. Jour. Nephrology, Am. Jour. Physiology and Renal and Electrolyte, Kidney and Body Fluids in Health and Disease, Internat. Jour. Pediatric Nephrology; assoc. editor Jour. Clin. Investigation; editor Kidney Internat., 1997—; contbr. articles to profl. jours., book chpts. USPHS postdoctoral fellow, 1961-63; recipient David M. Hume award Nat. Kidney Found., 1992, Thomas Addis medal Internat. Soc. Nutrition and Renal Metabolism, 1996. Fellow ACP, AAAS, Australian, Chilean, Colombian and Italian Socs. Nephrology (hon.); mem. Am. Soc. Nephrology (councillor 1980-81, sec.-treas. 1981-84, pres. 1985-86), Am. Soc. Clin. Investigation, Am. Physiol. Soc., Biophys. Soc., N.Y. Acad. Scis., Am. Soc. Renal Biochemistry and Metabolism (pres. 1982-84), Ctrl. Soc. Clin. Rsch., Soc. Exptl. Biology and Medicine, Assn. Am. Physicians, Soc. Gen. Physiologists, Internat. Soc. Nephrology (councillor 1987-95, mem. mgmt. com. 1987-95, chmn. program com. Sydney meeting 1997, mem. exec. com. 1997—), Sigma Xi, Alpha Omega Alpha. Home: 11544 Ladue Rd Saint Louis MO 63141-8341 Office: Barnes-Jewish Hosp Washington U Med Ctr 216 S Kings Hwy Blvd Saint Louis MO 63110*

KLAIN, RONALD ALAN, lawyer; b. Indpls., Aug. 8, 1961; s. Stanley Hugh and Sarann (Horwitz) K.; m. Monica Medina, June 22, 1986; children: Hannah, Michael, Daniel. BA, Georgetown U., 1983; JD, Harvard U., 1987. Bar: Pa., 1992. Law clk. Hon. Byron R. White, Washington, 1987-89; spl. asst. Senate Judiciary Com., Washington, 1986-87; chief counsel Senate Judiciacy Com., Washington, 1989-92; dir. Washington issues Clinton/Gore Campaign, 1992; assoc. counsel to Pres. The White House, Washington, 1993-94; chief of staff for Atty. Gen., Dept. Justice, Washington, 1994-95; staff dir. Senate Dem. Leadership Commn., Washington, 1995; chief of staff Vice President Gore, The White House, Washington, 1995—. Commr. Pres.'s Commn. on Fed. Appointments Process, Washington, 1990. Democrat. Jewish. Home: 3408 Taylor St Chevy Chase MD 20815-4024

KLAITS, JOSEPH A., education program director, historian; b. N.Y.C., Sept. 23, 1942; s. Julius Klaits and Beatrice Spielman; m. Sondra G. Stein; m. Barrie Gelbhaus; children: Frederick, Alexander. AB, Columbia U., 1964; MA, U. Minn., 1966, PhD, 1970. Prof. history Oakland U., Rochester, Mich., 1969-91; dir. Jennings Randolph Program for Internat. Peace U.S. Inst. Peace, Washington, 1991—; vis. prof. history Cath. U. Am., Washington, 1982-83; Fulbright program acad. liaison U.S. Info. Agy., Washington, 1983-86; cons. Woodrow Wilson Internat. Ctr. for Scholars, Washington, 1985-91, U.S. Info. Agy., Washington, 1988. Author: Servants of Satan: The Age of the Witch Hunts, 1985, Printed Propaganda under Louis XIV: Absolute Monarchy and Public Opinion, 1976; editor: Liberty/Liberti: The French and American Experiences, 1991, The Global Ramifications of the French Revolution, 1994. E-mail: joeúklaits@usip.org. Fax: 202-429-6063. Home: 2737 Woodley Pl NW Washington DC 20008 Office: US Inst Peace 1200 17th St NW Washington DC 20036

KLAKEG, CLAYTON HAROLD, cardiologist; b. Big Woods, Minn., Mar. 31, 1920; s. Knute O. and Agnes (Folvik) K.; student Concordia Coll., Moorhead, Minn., 1938-40; BS, N.D. State U., 1942; BS in Medicine, N.D. U., 1943; M.D., Temple U., 1945; MS in Medicine and Physiology, U. Minn.-Mayo Found., 1954; children: Julie Ann, Robert Clayton, Richard Scott. Intern, Med. Ctr., Jersey City, 1945-46; mem. staff VA Hosp., Fargo, N.D., 1948-51; fellow in medicine and cardiology Mayo Found., Rochester, Minn., 1951-55; internist, cardiologist Sansum Med. Clinic Inc., Santa Barbara, Calif., 1955—; mem. staff Cottage Hosp., St. Francis Hosp. Bd. dirs. Sansum Med. Rsch. Found., pres., 1990. Served to capt. M.C., USAF, 1946-48. Diplomate Am. Bd. Internal Medicine. Fellow ACP, Am. Coll. Cardiology, Am. Coll. Chest Physicians, Am. Heart Assn. (mem. council on clin. cardiology); mem. Calif. Heart Assn. (pres. 1971-72, Meritorious Service award 1968, Disting. Service award 1972, Disting. Achievement award 1975), Santa Barbara County Heart Assn. (pres. 1959-60, Disting. Service award 1958, Disting. Achievement award 1971), Calif. Med. Assn., Los Angeles Acad. Medicine, Santa Barbara County Med. Assn., Mayo Clinic Alumni Assn., Santa Barbara Soc. Internal Medicine (pres. 1963), Sigma Xi, Phi Beta Pi. Republican. Lutheran. Club: Channel City. Contbr. articles to profl. jours. Home: 5956 Trudi Dr Santa Barbara CA 93117-2175 Office: Sansum Med Clinic Inc PO Box 1239 Santa Barbara CA 93102-1239

KLAMM DE BETAS, ULLRICH, investor; b. Frankfurt, Germany, Aug. 21, 1939; s. Wulf H. and Ursula (Grosse) K.; m. Susan McGuigan Murphy, Dec. 3, 1976. MA in Econs., Christian-Albrechts U., Kiel, Germany, 1962; PhD in Econs. summa cum laude, U. Paris, Sorbonne, 1965; postgrad., Harvard U., 1966. Account supr. Ogilvy & Mather, Inc., Lausanne, Switzerland, 1967-68; v.p. Auerbach, Pollak & Richardson, Inc., N.Y.C., 1968-75, chmn., CEO, 1975-83; chmn., CEO CTH, Inc., N.Y.C., 1993—; pres., CEO Hosp. Diagnostic Equipment Corp., N.Y.C., 1987—; mng. mem. Lucero Capital, LLC, N.Y.C. Author: The Potentials and Pitfalls of Acquisitions, 1972; author, editor: Building in the Mid-1970's, 1973. Dir. Nat. Oncology Found., Ft. Lauderdale, 1994—. Named to All-Am. Analysts Team Institutional Investor mag., 1971. Office: 120 W 44th St New York NY 10036-4011

KLAMMER, JOSEPH FRANCIS, management consultant; b. Omaha, Mar. 25, 1925; s. Aloys Arcadius and Sophie (Nadolny) K. BS, Creighton U., 1948; MBA, Stanford U., 1950; cert. in polit. econs. Grad. Inst. Internat. Studies, U. Geneva, 1951. Cert. mgmt. cons. Adminstrv. analyst Chevron Corp., San Francisco, 1952-53; staff asst. Enron Corp., Omaha, 1953-57; mgmt. cons. Cresap, McCormick and Paget, Inc., N.Y.C., 1957-75; v.p., mgr. San Francisco region Cresap, McCormick and Paget, Inc., 1968-75, bd. dirs.; mgmt. cons., prin. J.F. Klammer Assocs., San Francisco, 1975—; CEO, pres. Isabelle Towers Homeowners Assn., 1993-94, bd. dirs., 1993-94, mem. fin. com., 1994-95, mem. rules com., 1995-96, mem. fin. com., 1996—; past bd. dirs. Conard House. Apptd. and attended U.S. Mil. Acad., West Point, N.Y. 1st lt. USAAF, 1943-46, lt. col. USAF, ret. Recipient Sovereign Mil. Hospitaller Order of St. John of Jerusalem of Rhodes and of Malta, Alumni Merit award Creighton U. Coll. Arts and Scis., 1998. Mem. Omaha Club, Knights of Malta, Alpha Sigma Nu. Republican. Roman Catholic. Home: 1998 Broadway San Francisco CA 94109-2281 Office: 1850 Union St San Francisco CA 94123-4309

KLAMON, LAWRENCE PAINE, lawyer; b. St. Louis, Mar. 17, 1937; s. Joseph Martin and Rose (Schimel) K.; m. Jo Ann Karen Beatty, Nov. 1957 (div. Feb. 1974); children: Stephen Robert, Karen Jean, Lawrence Paine; m. Frances Ann Estes, Mar. 1980. A.B., Washington U., St. Louis, 1958; J.D., Yale U., 1961. Bar: N.Y. 1964, Ga. 1992. Confidential asst. Office Sec. Def., Washington, 1961-62; spl. asst. to gen. counsel Office Sec. Def., 1962-63; asso. Cravath, Swaine & Moore, N.Y.C., 1963-67; v.p., gen. counsel Fuqua Industries, Inc., Atlanta, 1967-73; sr. v.p. fin. and adminstrn. Fuqua Industries, Inc., 1971-81, pres., 1981-89, chief exec. officer, 1989-91; chmn., 1991; sr. counsel Alston & Bird, Atlanta, 1991-95; pres., CEO Fuqua Enterprises, Inc., Atlanta, 1995-97; chmn. Gov.'s Internat. Adv. Coun., 1992-95. Mem. bd. editors Yale Law Jour., 1959-61. Mem. ABA, Assn. Bar City N.Y., Atlanta Bar Assn., State Bar Ga., Atlanta C. of C. (bd. dirs.), Order of Coif, Phi Beta Kappa, Omicron Delta Kappa. Home: 2665 Dellwood Dr NW Atlanta GA 30305-3519

KLAPER, MARTIN JAY, lawyer; b. Chgo., Jan. 12, 1947; s. Carl and Kate F. (Friedman) K.; m. Julia Warner, Nov. 14, 1973. B.S. in Bus. summa cum laude, Ind. U., 1969, J.D. summa cum laude, 1971. Bar: Ind. 1971, U.S. Dist. Ct. (no. and so. dists.) Ind. 1971, U.S. Ct. Appeals (7th cir.) 1972, U.S. Supreme Ct. 1979. Law clk. to justice U.S. Ct. Appeals (7th cir.), 1971-72; ptnr. Ice Miller Donadio & Ryan, Indpls., 1972—. Mem. ABA, Ind. Bar Assn. Office: Ice Miller Donadio & Ryan 1 Am Sq Box 82001 Indianapolis IN 46282

KLAPPER, BYRON D., financial company executive; b. N.Y.C., May 2, 1938; s. Irving and Lottie K.; m. Karin I. Klapper, June 28, 1964; children: Kimberly, Lonn-Eric. *Wife Karin, counsels young women at Planned Parenthood on managing their reproductive lives, suggesting options, possibilities, and positive choices. Her priorities are as a wife, mother, and devoted daughter. Daughter Kimberly Isleen excels in lodging industry with a reputation as turnaround specialist, making high-visibility properties showcases of efficiency and profitability. Son Lonn-Eric, on graduating Kent State University, married Dana Richmond, stayed in Ohio and started a family. Lonn is an insurance industry executive specializing in annuities and retirement.* BS in Journalism, U. Kans., 1964; cert. Wharton Sch., U. Pa., 1974. Reporter Topeka (Kans.) Daily Capitol, 1963, U.P.I., Kansas City, Mo.; editor Am. Cyanamid Co., Wayne, N.J., 1964-67; media rels. staff Bethlehem Steel Corp., N.Y.C., 1968; speech writer Burlington Ind., Inc., N.Y.C., 1969; reporter Wall St Jour., N.Y.C., 1970-80; sr. v.p. Std. and Poors Corp., N.Y.C., 1980-90; mng. dir. Fitch Investors Svc., N.Y.C., 1990-98, Am. Capital Access, Inc., 1998—; columnist skiing Morritown Daily Record, 1988—, Editor-in-chief, SnoSports., Internet Ski Mag.; bd. dirs. Powell Techs., Inc., Visions West, Inc. Contbg. editor Barron's N.Y.C., 1967-69; pub. S&P's Creditweek, 1981—; publ. Creditweek Internat., 1983, Mcpl. Bond Book, 1984, S&P's Creditwire, 1986. Recipient Nat. Journalism award, William Randolph Hearst Found., 1960, 62, New Products award, McGraw Hill, 1986. Mem. Ea. Ski Writers Assn. (dir. 1985-91), Govt. Fin. Officers Assn., Pub. Securities Assn., Bond Market Assn., Downtown Athletic Club, Fgn. Corres. Club Japan (hon.), N.Am. Ski Journalists Assn. (dir. 1998—). Avocations: writing, photography, skiing, computers, triathalon. Home: 37 Tara Ln Montville NJ 07045-9699

KLAPPER, MOLLY, lawyer, educator; b. Berlin, Germany; came to U.S., 1950; d. Elias and Ciporah (Weber) Teicher; m. Jacob Klapper; children: Rachelle Hannah, Robert David. BA, CUNY, MA, 1964; PhD, NYU, 1974; JD, Rutgers U., 1987. Bar: N.J. 1987, U.S. Dist. Ct. N.J. 1987, N.Y. 1989, U.S. Dist. Ct. (so. and ea. dists.) N.Y. 1989, D.C. 1989, U.S. Supreme Ct. 1991, U.S. Ct. Appeals (2d cir.) 1992. Prof. English Bronx C.C., CUNY, 1974-84; law intern U.S. Dist. Ct. N.J., Newark, 1987; law sec. to presiding judge appellate div. N.J. Supreme Ct., Springfield, 1987-88; assoc. Wilson, Elser, Moskowitz, Edelman and Dicker, N.Y.C., 1988-96; adminstrv. law judge Dept. Finance, N.Y.C., 1997—. Author: The German Literary Influence on Byron, 1974, 2d edit., 1975, The German Literary Influence on Shelley, 1975; contbr. to profl. publs. NEH fellow, 1978; grantee Am. Philos. Soc., 1976. Mem. ABA (bankruptcy com.), N.Y. Bar Assn. (bankruptcy com.), D.C. Bar Assn. Avocations: bicycling, skiing, roller skating, walking, hiking. Office: Wilson Elser Moskowitz Edelman and Dicker 720 Ft Washington Ave New York NY 10040-3708

KLAPPERICH, FRANK LAWRENCE, JR., investment banker; b. Oak Park, Ill., Oct. 11, 1934; s. Frank Lawrence and Marjorie (Doan) K.; m. Margaret Monroe Touborg, Mar. 9, 1957; children: Margaret Friis, Susan Doane, Frank Lawrence III, Elizabeth Monroe. AB, Princeton U., 1956; MBA, Harvard U., 1961, postgrad., 1979. With Kidder, Peabody & Co., Inc., Chgo., 1961—; v.p. Kidder, Peabody & Co., Inc., 1964—, dir., 1972-86, mng. dir., 1986-88, sr. v.p., 1988-90, ret., 1990; pres. Charter Capital Corp., 1991—; bd. dirs. T.C. Mfg. Co., Inc. Governing mem. Emeritus Coun. Luth. Gen. Health Sys., Orchestral Assn. Chgo. Symphony Orch., 1995—; vice chmn. governing mems., 1996-98. Mem. Investment Analysts Soc. Chgo., Securities Industry Assn. (chmn. Ctrl. States dist. 1986-87), Inst. Chartered Fin. Analysts, Harvard Bus. Sch. Assn. Chgo., Princeton Club (Chgo., pres. 1970-71), Charter Club (governing bd. 1987-97), Chgo. Club, Mid-Day Club (trustee 1987-90), Bond Club (pres. 1983-84), Econ. Club, Harvard Club (Chgo.), Harvard Club of Naples (Fla. bd. dirs. 1999), Princeton Club (N.Y.C.), Indian Hill Club (Winnetka, Ill.), Hole-in-the-Wall Golf Club (Naples, Fla.). Home: 345 Woodley Rd Winnetka IL 60093-3740 Office: 125 S Wacker Dr Ste 300 Chicago IL 60606-4402

KLARE, GEORGE ROGER, psychology educator; b. Mpls., Apr. 17, 1922; s. George C. and Lee (Launer) K.; m. Julia Marie Price Matson, Dec. 24, 1946; children: Deborah, Roger, Barbara. Student, U. Nebr., 1940-41, U. Minn., 1941-43, U. Mo., 1943; B.A., U. Minn., 1946, M.A., 1947, Ph.D., 1950. Instr. U. Minn., 1948-50; staff psychologist Psychol. Corp., N.Y.C., 1950-51; research assoc. U. Ill., 1952-54; asst. prof. dept. psychology Ohio U., Athens, 1954-57; assoc. prof. Ohio U., 1957-62, prof., 1962-79, Disting. prof., 1979-89, Disting. prof. emeritus, 1989—, chmn. dept., 1959-63, acting dean Coll. Arts and Sci., 1965, 85-86, dean, 1966-71, media coordinator, 1972-75, acting assoc. provost for grad. and research programs, 1986-87; research assoc. Harvard U., 1968-69; vis. prof. State U. N.Y. at Stony Brook, 1971-72, U. Iowa, 1979-80; staff mem. N.Y.C. Writers Conf., 1956-57; cons., lectr. Nat. Project Agr. Communication, 1957-59, Com. on World Literacy and Christian Lit., 1958-62; exec. asst., sr. rsch. engr. Autonetics, 1960-61; cons. Resources Devel. Corp., 1962-65, Boston Pub. Sch., 1968, D.C. Heath Co., 1971, Western Electric, 1973, Westinghouse, 1975, Human Resources Rsch. Orgn., 1978-79, U.S. Navy, 1975, Armed Svcs. Readability Rsch., 1975, Center for Ednl. Exptl., Devel. and Evaluation, 1978-79, 81, U.S. Army, 1979, Bell System Center for Tech. Edn., 1975-80, Time, Inc., 1977-79, AT&T, 1979-81, 83,84, Coll. Osteo Medicine, Ohio U., 1987-89; lectr. Open Univ., Eng., 1975, NATO Conf. Visual Presentation of Info., The Netherlands, 1978, Beijing Normal U., 1990. Author: (with Byron Buck) Know Your Reader, 1954, The Measurement of Readability, 1963, (with Paul A. Games) Elementary Statistics: Data Analysis for the Behavioral Sciences, 1967, A Manual for Readable Writing, 1975, 4th edit., 1980, How to Write Readable English, 1985, Assessing Readability-Citation Classic, 1988; mem. editorial bd. Info. Design Jour., 1979—, Instrl. Sci., 1975-93, Reading Tchr., 1981-82, Reading Rsch. and Instrn., 1985-87, The Literacy Dictionary, 1993 (invited essay 1995). Served to 1st lt. USAAF, 1943-45. Decorated Air medal, Purple Heart; Fulbright travel grantee U.S.-U.K. Ednl. Commn. to Open U., 1977-81. Fellow Am. Psychol. Assn.; mem. Nat. Reading Conf. (invited address 1975, Oscar Causey award for outstanding contbns. to reading research 1981), Internat. Reading Assn. (elected to Hall of Fame 1997), Am. Ednl. Research Assn., Phi Beta Kappa, Delta Phi Lambda, Psi Chi, Phi Delta Kappa. Home and Office: 5 Pleasantview Dr Athens OH 45701-1447

KLARE, MICHAEL THOMAS, social science educator, program director; b. N.Y.C., Oct. 14, 1942; s. Charles and Mildred (Smith) K. BA, Columbia U., 1963, MA, 1968; postgrad., Yale U., 1963-65; PhD, Union Inst., 1976. Instr. Parsons Sch. Design, N.Y.C., 1967-70; research dir. N.Am. Congress on Latin Am., Berkeley, Calif., 1970-76; vis. lectr. Tufts U., 1973; vis. fellow Center of Internat. Studies, Princeton U., 1976-77; fellow Inst. Policy Studies, Washington, 1977-84; prof. peace & world security studies Hampshire Coll., Amherst, Mass., 1985—, dir. 5 colls. program in peace and world security studies, 1985—; vis. assoc. prof. of peace studies Wellesley Coll., 1992-93; def. corr. The Nation, 1983—. Author: War Without End, 1973, Supplying Repression, 1978, Beyond the Vietnam Syndrome, 1981, American Arms Supermarket, 1985, Rogue States and Nuclear Outlaws, 1995; co-author: A Scourge of Guns, 1996; editor: Peace and World Security Studies: A Curriculum Guide, 6th edit., 1994; co-editor: Low Intensity Warfare, 1988, Peace and World Security Studies: A Curriculum Guide, 5th edit., 1989, World Security: Challenges for a New Century, 1991, 3d edit., 1998, Lethal Commerce: The Global Trade in Small Arms and Light Weapons, 1995; contbg. editor Current History. Bd. dirs. Arms Control Assn., 1994—, Ednl. Found. for Nuclear Sci., 1993—. Mem. Internat. Studies Assn., Peace Studies Assn., Am. Acad. Arts and Scis. (internat. security studies com.). Home: 17 Columbus Ave Northampton MA 01060-4252 Office: Hampshire Coll Sch Social Sci Amherst MA 01002

KLARFELD, JONATHAN MICHAEL, journalism educator; b. Springfield, Mass., Dec. 11, 1937; m. Patricia Holland, Sept. 7, 1974; children: Victoria, Alexander. AB, Colgate U., 1960. Reporter, editor Holyoke (Mass.) Transcript-Telegram, 1962-65, UPI, Springfield, Boston, 1965-66, Boston Globe, 1966-68; press sec. Boston Parks/Redevel. Auth., 1968-70; reporter, writer Boston Record-Am., 1970-72; mgr. pub. info. Mass. Blue Cross, 1972-74; assoc. professor journalism Boston U., 1975—, dir. print journalism, 1979-96, dir. print and online journalism program, 1996—; editl. cons. Lawyers Weekly Pubs., Boston, Lansing, Mich., Richmond, Va., Providence, 1983-92; press analyst Oxbow Corp., West Palm Beach, Fla., 1984-96; news media critic/columnist Boston Herald, 1994, 95; cons. in libel and invasion of privacy cases. Contbr. articles to numerous newspapers, periodicals. Mem. New England Gilbert & Sullivan Soc., Sorcerers Rugby Club (pres. 1974-80), Newton Squash and Tennis Club (bd. govs. 1999—), New Eng. Gilbert and Sullivan Soc., Delta Kappa Epsilon. Unitarian. Avocations: squash, tennis, Gilbert and Sullivan. Office: Boston U Sch Journalism Boston MA 02215

KLARFELD, PETER JAMES, lawyer; b. Holyoke, Mass., Aug. 19, 1947; s. David Nathan and Gloria (Belsky) K.; m. Mary Myrtle, July 7, 1985; children: Peter Marcus (dec.), Mary Elizabeth, Louis Edward. BA, U. Va., 1969, JD, 1973; MA, U. Chgo., 1970. Bar: Va. 1973, D.C. 1975, U.S. Dist. Ct. D.C. 1977, U.S. Dist. Ct. (ea. dist.) Va. 1977, U.S. Supreme Ct. 1977, U.S. Ct. Appeals (4th cir.) 1978, U.S. Ct. Appeals (3rd & 9th cirs.) 1986, U.S. Ct. Appeals (2d cir.) 1998, U.S. Dist. Ct. (ea. dist.) Wis. 1987, U.S. Dist. Ct. (no. dist.) Calif. 1990. Law clk. to Hon. Robert R. Merhige, Jr. U.S. Dist. Ct. (ea. dist.) Va., Richmond, 1973-74; atty., advisor office of legal counsel U.S. Dept. Justice, Washington, 1974-76; ptnr. Brownstein Zeidman & Lore, Washington, 1977-96, Wiley, Rein and Fielding, Washington, 1996—. Editor: Covenants Against Competition in Franchise Agreements, 1992; contbr. articles to profl. jours. Trustee Dalkon Shield Other Claimants Trust, Richmond, 1990-96, chmn., 1991-96. Mem. ABA. Home: 434 E Columbia St Falls Church VA 22046-3501 Office: Wiley Rein & Fielding 1776 K St NW Washington DC 20006-2304

KLARICH, DAVID JOHN, lawyer, state senator; b. Hamilton, Ohio, July 17, 1963; s. Victor Martin and Janet Dawn (Carlson) K.; m. Cheryl Ruth O'Donnell, June 18, 1988. BA in Biology and Chemistry, U. Mo., 1985; MA in Pub. Policy, Regent U., 1990, JD, 1990. Bar: Mo. 1990. State rep. 92d and 94th dists. Mo. Ho. of Reps., Jefferson City, 1990—; 26th dist. State Senate, Mo., 1994—; with Riezman and Blitz, PC, Clayton, Mo., 1995—. Active West County Rep. Orgn., Franklin and Washington County Reps., St. Louis Young Reps., Coll. Reps., Pachyderms; trustee Logan Coll. Chiropractic, 1998. Recipient Adminstrn. of Justice award Jud. Conf. Mo., 1991, Mo. Bar award, 1993, 97, Mo. Hosp. Assn. award, 1995; named Mo. Bar Outstanding Legis. of Yr., 1996, Voice of Bus. award Assoc. Industries, 1998. Mem. Bar Assn. Met. St. Louis, Young Lawyers Assn., Vol. Lawyers Assn., St. Louis Lawyers Assn., Mo. Assn. Trial Attys., ABA, St. Louis Eagle Scout Assn., Nat. Eagle Scout Assn., Jaycees, Lions, Mo. C. of C. (Spirit of Enterprise award 1997), Theta Xi. Mem. Assembly of God Ch. Office: Riezman and Blitz PC 7700 Bonhomme Ave Fl 7 Clayton MO 63105-1924

KLARMAN, HERBERT ELIAS, economist, educator; b. Chmielnik, Poland, Dec. 21, 1916; came to U.S., 1929, naturalized, 1929; s. Joseph Louis and Helen (Klarman) K.; m. Mary A. Monk, 1967; children: Seth Andrew, Michael Joseph. A.B., Columbia U., 1939; M.A., U. Wis., 1941, Ph.D., 1946. Economist nat. income divsn. Dept. Commerce, 1946-47; asst. prof. econs. Bklyn. Coll., 1947-48; asst., then assoc. dir. Hosp. Coun. Greater N.Y., 1949-51, 52-62; asst. dir. N.Y. State Hosp. Study, Columbia U., 1948-49; med. economist Nat. Security Resources Bd., 1951-52; mem. faculty Johns Hopkins U., 1962-69, prof. public health adminstrn. and polit. economy, 1965-69; prof. environ. medicine and community health Downstate Med. Center, SUNY, 1969-70; prof. econs. NYU Grad. Sch. Public Adminstrn., N.Y.C., 1970-82; sr. assoc. Johns Hopkins U. Sch. Hygiene and Pub. Health, 1982—; mem. health services rsch. study sect. NIH, 1962-66; chmn. planning com. 2d Conf. on Econs. Health, 1967-69; mem. U.S. Nat. Com. on Vital and Health Stats., 1967-71, N.Y. State Health Adv. Council, 1976-83; mem. spl. med. adv. group VA, 1977-81; mem. Inst. Medicine, Nat. Acad. Scis., 1971. Author: Hospital Care in New York City, 1963, Economics of Health, 1965; also articles, chpts. in books.; editor: Empirical Studies in Health Economics, 1970. Served to capt. AUS, 1942-46. Recipient 1st Norman A. Welch Meml. award, 1965, Disting. Career award in health svcs. rsch. Assn. for Health Svcs. Rsch., 1989; Guggenheim fellow, 1976-77. Fellow AAAS, Am. Public Health Assn.; mem. Am. Econ. Assn., Am. Statis. Assn., Royal Econ. Soc., Phi Beta Kappa. Home: 1 E University Pky Baltimore MD 21218-2451

KLASERNER, JAMES, publishing executive. Gen. mgr. Expo Group, Cin. Office: Expo Group 431 Ohio Pike Ste S104 Cincinnati OH 45255-3637*

KLASKO, HERBERT RONALD, lawyer, law educator, writer; b. Phila., Nov. 26, 1949; s. Leon Louis and Estelle Lorraine (Baratz) K.; m. Marjorie Ann Becker, Aug. 27, 1977; children: Brett Andrew, Kelli Lynn. BA, Lehigh U., 1971; JD, U. Pa., 1974. Bar: Pa. 1974, U.S. Dist. Ct. (ea. dist.) Pa. 1974, U.S. Ct. Appeals (3d cir.) 1981. Assoc. Fox, Rothschild, O'Brien & Frankel, Phila., 1974-75; ptnr., chmn. immigration dept. Abrahams & Loewenstein, Phila., 1975-88, Dechert, Price & Rhoads, Phila., 1988—; instr., mem. adv. bd. Inst. for Paralegal Tng., Phila., 1974-81; instr. Temple Law Sch. Grad. Legal Studies, Phila., 1984; adj. prof. Villanova U. Law Sch., Pa., 1985-90. Co-author: (with Matthew Bender and Hope Frye) Employer's Immigration Compliance Guide, 1985; bd. editors: Immigration Law and Procedure Reporter. Exec. committeeman, bd. dirs. Jewish Community Rels. Coun., Phila., 1977—; chmn. exec. com., com. on unprosecuted Nazi war criminals Nat. Jewish Community Rels. Adv. Coun., N.Y.C., 1983-90; v.p. Hebrew Immigrant Aid Soc., Phila., 1977—; pres. Coun. of Tenants Assn., Southeastern Pa., 1980-81. Recipient Legion of Honor award Chapel of Four Chaplains, 1977. Mem. ABA (coordinating com. on immigration), Phila. Bar Assn., Am. Immigration Lawyers Assn. (chmn. Phila. chpt. 1980-82, bd. govs. 1980—, nat. sec. 1984-85, 2d v.p. 1985-86, 1st v.p. 1986-87, pres.-elect 1987-88, pres. 1988-89, exec. com. 1984-90, 96—, gen. counsel, 1996—), Am. Immigration Law Found. (bd. dirs. 1987-90). Avocations: politics, sports, traveling, organizations. Office: Dechert Price & Rhoads 4000 Bell Atlantic Tower 1717 Arch St Ste 3 Philadelphia PA 19103-2793

KLASS, MORTON, anthropology educator, consultant; b. Bklyn., June 24, 1927; s. David A. and Millie (Fisher) K.; m. Sheila Solomon, May 2, 1953; children: Perri Elizabeth, David Arnold, Judith Alexandra. B.A., Bklyn. Coll., 1955; Ph.D., Columbia U., 1959. Mem. faculty Bennington Coll., Vt., 1959-64; vis. asst. prof. Columbia U., N.Y.C., 1962-65; assoc. prof. Barnard Coll., N.Y.C., 1965-69, prof. anthropology, 1969-96, prof. emeritus of anthropology, 1997—; dir. So. Asian Inst. Columbia U., N.Y.C., 1982-85; vis. lectr. Fgn. Service Inst., Dept. State, Washington, 1966-76. Author: East Indians in Trinidad, 1961, 2d edit., 1988, From Field to Factory, 1978, 2d edit., 1996, Caste: The Emergence of the South Asian Social System, 1980, 2d edit., 1998, Singing with Sai Baba: The Politics of Revitalization in Trinidad, 1991, 2d edit., 1996, Ordered Universes: Approaches to the Anthropology of Religion, 1995; co-author: (with H. Hellman) The Kinds of Mankind, 1971, (with M. Weisgrau) Across the Boundaries of Belief: Contemporary Issues in the Anthropology of Religion, 1999. With U.S. Mcht. Marine, 1945-48. Am. Council Learned Socs. grantee, 1971-72; Social Sci. Research Council fellow, 1957-58; recipient Clark F. Ansley award Columbia U. Press, 1959. Fellow Am. Anthrop. Assn.; mem. Royal Anthrop. Inst. Gt. Britain and Ireland.

KLASS, PHILIP JULIAN, technical journalist, electrical engineer; b. Des Moines, Nov. 8, 1919; s. Raymond N. and Ann (Traxler) K.; m. Nadya Boriss Boboschevska. BSEE, Iowa State U., 1941. Engr. GE, Schenectady, N.Y., 1941-52; sr. avionics editor Aviation Week & Space Tech., N.Y.C., 1952-58; sr. avionics editor Aviation Week & Space Tech., Washington, 1958-86, contbg. avionics editor, 1986—. Author: UFOs—Identified, 1968, Secret Sentries in Space, 1971, UFOs—Explained, 1975, UFOs: The Public Deceived, 1983, UFO—Abductions: A Dangerous Game, 1988, The REAL Roswell Crashed-Saucer Cover-up, 1997. Recipient writing awards Aviation/Space Writers Assn., 1973, 75, 77, 80, Lauren D. Lyman award, 1989, Profl. Achievement in Engrng. award Iowa State U., 1988, aerospace journalist award Royal Aero. Soc., 1998, Boeing Decade of Excellence award for lifetime achievement, Royal Aeronautical Soc., 1998; asteroid named in his honor, 1999. Fellow IEEE, Com. Sci. Investigation Claims of Paranormal (founder); mem. Nat. Press Club. Home and Office: 404 N St SW Washington DC 20024-3702

KLASSEK, CHRISTINE PAULETTE, behavioral scientist; b. Chgo., Dec. 28, 1947; d. Walter and Pauline (Bogolin) Strom; m. Alexander George Klassek, June 14, 1969; 1 child, Margaret Mary. BA in Applied Behavioral Sci., Nat. Louis U., 1989, cert. in leadership, 1993. Asst. juvenile libr. Bolingbrook (Ill.) Fountaindale Libr., 1974-79; behavior modification counselor, dir. vol. svcs. J.P. Kennedy Sch. for Exceptional Children, Palos Park, Ill., 1982-86; tchr. spl. edn. Little Friends Orgn., Downers Grove, Ill., 1986-89; program dir. Carmelite Carefree Village, Darien, Ill., 1989-97, adminstrv. liaison, 1997—; bd. mem. Benedictine Univ. Adv. Bd. for Sr. Programs and Issues, 1996; dep. registrar for Carefree Village, Dupage County, 1998; notary public, 1999—. Treas. Young Democrats Will County, 1972; chmn., pres. bd. dirs. Dem. Women's Com. DuPage Twp., Ill., 1973-76; leader Campfire Girls Assn.; mem. adv. coun. case mgmt. Little Friends Assn., 1988; cert. pastoral min. care St. Charles Borromeo Pastoral Ctr.; vol. Pub. Action to Deliver Svc., Helping Hands Rehab. Ctr., Ray Graham; active Cath. Coun. Women; bd. dirs., mem. human rels. com. J.P. Kennedy Sch. Exceptional Children, 1985-86; notary public. Recipient Cert. of Appreciation, Am. Cancer Soc., 1991, Achievement award Life Svcs. Network Ill., 1995, DuPage County Consortium Intergenerational Task Force, 1996. Mem. LWV, Assn. Sr. Svc. Providers, Ill. Activity Profl. Assn., Surburban Activity Therapists Assn., Notary Public Assn. Am., Jaycees. Roman Catholic. Avocations: arts and crafts, reading, walking, classical music, writing poetry. Home: 240 Davis Ln Bolingbrook IL 60440-2369 Office: Carmelite Carefree Village 8419 Bailey Rd Darien IL 60561-5361

KLASSEN, PETER JAMES, academic administrator, history educator; b. Crowfoot, Alta., Can., Dec. 18, 1930; came to U.S., 1955; s. John C. and Elizabeth (Martens) K.; m. Nancy Jo Cooprider, Aug. 1, 1959; children: Kenton, Kevin, Bryan. BA, also cert., U. B.C., Can., 1955; MA, U. So. Calif., 1958, PhD, 1962. Cert. secondary tchr. Lectr. U. So. Calif., Los Angeles, 1957-62; prof. history Fresno (Calif.) Pacific Coll., 1962-66; prof. history Calif. State U., Fresno, 1966—, dean sch. social scis., 1979-97, dir. internat. programs, 1992—. Author: The Economics of Anabaptism, 1964, Europe in the Reformation, 1979, Reformation: Change and Stability, 1980, A Homeland for Strangers, 1989; contbr. articles to jours. Pres. West Fresno Home Improvement Assn., 1966-70, Fresno Sister Cities Coun., 1987-90; mem. Calif. Coun. for Humanities, 1987-92. Research grantee Deutscher Akademischer Austauschdienst, 1975. Mem. Am. Hist. Assn., Am. Soc. Ch. History, Fresno City and County Hist. Soc. (pres. 1983-85), Soc. Reformation Rsch., German Studies Assn., Sixteenth Century Studies Assn., Assn. Advancement Slavic Studies, Golden Key, Phi Alpha Theta, Phi Kappa Phi, Phi Beta Delta. Home: 1838 S Bundy Dr Fresno CA 93727-6201 Office: Internat Program Calif State U Fresno CA 93740

KLATELL, JACK, dentist; b. N.Y.C., July 15, 1918; s. Meyer and Jennie (Merin) Klatsky; m. Arline Bragin, Aug. 9, 1944; children: Robert E., David A. Dental. B.S., Coll. City N.Y., 1938; D.D.S., Columbia U., 1941. Intern Mt. Sinai Hosp., N.Y.C., 1941-42; sr. resident dental and oral surgery Seaview Hosp., S.I., N.Y., 1942-43; pvt. practice dentistry N.Y.C., 1943-93; dir. dept. dentistry, dentist-in-chief Mt. Sinai Hosp., 1965—; assoc. clin. prof. N.Y.U. Coll. Dentistry, 1967—; prof. dentistry Mt. Sinai Sch. Medicine, 1966—, also chmn. dept.; clin. prof. dentistry Columbia U. Sch. Dental and Oral Surgery, 1994—; cons. Bronx VA Hosp., 1972—, Goldwater Meml. Hosp., 1974-80. Author: The Mt. Sinai Medical Center Family Guide to Dental Health; contbr. profl. jours. Served to capt. Dental Corps AUS, 1943-46. Fellow Acad. Gen. Dentistry Internat. Coll. Dentists, Am. Coll. Dentists (life); mem. ADA (life), Am. Acad. Oral Pathology, N.Y. Inst. Clin. Oral Pathology, Met. Conf. Hosp. Dental Chiefs, Am. Assn. Hosp. Dentists, Phi Beta Kappa, Omicron Kappa Upsilon, Alpha Omega. Home: 8 E 83rd St New York NY 10028-0418

KLATELL, ROBERT EDWARD, lawyer, electronics company executive; b. Tampa, Fla., Dec. 11, 1945; s. Jack S. and Arla M. (Bragin) K.; m. Penelope E. Manegan, June 14, 1970; children—Christopher J., James M., Jeremy N. B.A., Williams Coll., 1968; J.D., NYU, 1971. Bar: N.Y. 1972. Asso. Kramer, Lowenstein, Nessen, Kamin & Soll, N.Y.C., 1970-76; gen. counsel Arrow Electronics, Inc., N.Y.C., 1976—; v.p. Arrow Electronics, Inc., 1979-88, sr. v.p., 1988-93, treas., 1990-96; CFO, 1992-96; exec. v.p. Arrow Electronics, Inc., Melville, N.Y., 1993—. Mem. ABA, Assn. Bar City N.Y., Fin. Execs. Inst. Office: Arrow Electronics Inc 25 Hub Dr Melville NY 11747-3509

KLAUBERG, WILLIAM JOSEPH, technical services company executive; b. N.Y.C., June 30, 1926; s. Leo V. and Marian (Casey) K.; m. Kathleen Kelly, Feb. 18, 1950; children: Christine Anne, Kathleen Noel, Angela Ellen, William Jr. BS in nautical sci., Merchant Marine Acad., 1947; BS in fgn. svc., Georgetown U., 1949. Mgr. US Lines, Inc., Japan, 1949-65; v.p. US Lines, Inc., Tokyo, 1965-68; v.p. European Div. US Lines, Inc., London, 1968-71; v.p. West Coast Div. US Lines, Inc., San Francisco, 1971-73; v.p. East Coast Div. US Lines, Inc., N.Y.C., 1973-81; project mgr. Vinnell Corp., Balt., 1981-82; v.p. Vinnell Corp., Fairfax, Va., 1982-83; exec. v.p. Vinnell Corp., Fairfax, 1983-88, pres., CEO, 1988-93, chmn., chief exec. officer, 1993-94; chmn., 1994-97. Lt. (j.g.) USNR, 1947-52.

KLAUDER, JOHN RIDER, physics educator; b. Reading, Pa., Jan. 24, 1932; s. David Streeper and Jean (Rider) K.; m. Robertha Howell, Sept. 11, 1953 (div. 1980); children: Karol Jean, Katherine Jane, Kim Ann, John Christopher; m. Agnes Nadasdi, July 26, 1980; 1 child, Jennifer Ann. BS, U. Calif., Berkeley, 1953; MS, Stevens Inst. Tech., 1956; PhD, Princeton U., 1959. Mem. tech. staff, then dept. head AT&T Bell Labs., Murray Hill, N.J., 1953-88; prof. depts. math. and physics U. Fla., Gainesville, 1988—; cons. Los Alamos (N.Mex.) Nat. Lab., 1978-89. Co-author: Fundamentals of Quantum Optics, 1968, Coherent States, 1985; editor Jour. Math. Phys., 1979-86. Fellow AAAS, Am. Phys. Soc.; mem. Internat. Assn. Math. and Physics (pres. 1988-91), Internat. Union Pure and Applied Physics (assoc. sec. gen. 1984-90). Office: U Fla Dept Math/Physics Gainesville FL 32611

KLAUS, CHARLES, retired lawyer; b. Freiburg, Baden, Germany, Feb. 11, 1935; came to U.S., 1939; children: Charles, Kathryn, Richard. BA, Cornell U., 1956, MBA, JD with distinction, 1961; postdoctoral, Case Western Res. U., 1964, Lakeland Community Coll., 1976. Bar: Ohio 1961, U.S. Dist. Ct. (no. dist.) Ohio 1962. Assoc. Baker & Hostetler, Cleve., 1961-71, ptnr., 1972-94, retired, 1995. Past hon. trustee and pres. Cleve. Music Sch. Settlement; past trustee Cleve. Audubon Soc.; past trustee, sec. Cleve. Area Arts

Coun., Lake Erie Opera Theatre, N.E. Ohio chpt. Arthritis Found.; former mem. Group Svc. Coun. Welfare Fedn. Cleve.; corp. mem. The Holden Arboretum. Recipient Award of Merit, Cleve. Audubon Soc., 1979. Mem. Millard Fillmore Soc., Order of Coif, Phi Kappa Phi. Clubs: Rowfant (past sec.), Kirtland Country (dir., sec., Willoughby, Ohio).

KLAUS, KENNETH SHELDON, choral conductor, vocalist, music educator; b. Baton Rouge, La., Oct. 1, 1952; s. Kenneth Blanchard and Marian Ida (Fyler) K.; m. Phebe Darlene Arceneaux, Aug. 16, 1975; children: Christopher Fyler, Michael Calvin, Rachel Elizabeth. MusB, La. State U., 1974, MusM, 1976, PhD, 1983. Bass soloist St. James Episcopal Ch., Baton Rouge, summer 1972; dir. music Blackwater United Meth. Ch., Baker, La., 1972-79; interim dir. music Goodwood Bapt. Ch., Baton Rouge, summer 1980; dir. music First United Meth. Ch., Brookhaven, Miss., 1981-84, Houma, La., 1985—; violist Baton Rouge Symphony Orch., 1971-79; dir. choral music Copiah-Lincoln C.C., Wesson, Miss., 1979-84; dir. choral activities, assoc. prof. music Nicholls State U., Thibodaux, La., 1984—; vocal soloist New Orleans Opera, Miss. Opera, Baton Rouge Symphony, Concert Choir New Orleans, Chorale Acadienne, Jefferson Performing Arts Soc., La. Sinfonietta, also others; choral music clinician various high schs. and jr. high schs. in La. and Miss., ch. music workshops; adjudicator dist. and regional choral festivals in La. and Miss.; solo/ensemble festivals in La. and Miss.; condr. various choirs. Author: Chamber Music for Solo Voice and Instruments, 1960-89, 1994; contbr. book, music, and CD revs. The Choral Jour., 1985—. Bd. dirs. Thibodaux Playhouse, Inc., 1987-89, Nicholls State U. United Meth. Campus Ministry. Mem. Fellowship United Meths. in Music and Worship Arts (rep. La. conf. Acadiana dist.), Nat. Assn. Tchrs. Singing (Miss. artist award 1980), Am. Choral Dirs. Assn. (La. student activities chmn. 1985-93, chmn. La. vocal jazz and show choir 1993-97, La. ch. music chair 1997—), Music Educators Nat. Conf., La. Music Educators Assn., Music Tchrs. Nat. Assn. (nat. cert. voice tchr.), La. Music Tchrs. Assn., Phi Kappa Phi, Phi Mu Alpha Sinfonia, Pi Kappa Lambda. Home: 419 Cedar Tree Dr Thibodaux LA 70301-5728 Office: Nicholls State U Dept Music Thibodaux LA 70310 *As we go through this life, God help us not to become prisoners of our own minds.*

KLAUS, SUZANNE LYNNE, horticulturist, production specialist; b. Kansas City, Mo., May 2, 1956; d. John Wallace and Shirley Jane (Hoffman) K.; m. William D. Luebbert, Nov. 4, 1989. BS in Agr., U. Mo., 1978, MS in Horticulture, 1980. Prodn. mgr., owner John Klaus & Sons Greenhouses, Greenwood, Mo., 1972—; tchr. horticulture Longview C.C., Lee's Summit, Mo., 1979-81, 99—; guest spkr., panel mem. Mo. State Florists Convs., 1981, 92, 86, 89; guest spkr. St. Louis Growers Assn., 1985, Ohio Florists' Conf., 1986, Ball's Grow Show, 1987, Kans. State Growers Conf., 1988. Floriculture judge for nat. conv. Future Farmers Am., 1984-98. Mem. Mo. State Florists' Assn. (bd. dirs. 1980-89, res. 1987-88), Floral Acad. Mo. (bd. dirs. 1986-87, pres.-elect 1988-89), Nat. Assn. Women in Horticulture (pres. 1989-90), Ohio Florists' Assn., Pointsettia Growers Assn., Nemokan Floral Assn. (bd. dirs. 1987-89). Republican. Roman Catholic. Avocations: swimming, water skiing, computer science, aerobics, piano and organ playing. Home: PO Box 376 Greenwood MO 64034-0376

KLAUS, WILLIAM ROBERT, lawyer; b. Phila., Jan. 19, 1926; s. William Anthony and Amanda (Pusey) K.; m. Janet Lois Scoggins, Aug. 18, 1951; 1 child, Kenneth Springfield. LLB, Temple U., 1951. Bar: Pa. 1952. Assoc. Pepper, Hamilton & Scheetz, Phila., 1952-59, ptnr., 1959-96, chmn. emeritus, 1995—; bd. dirs. Westmoreland Coal Co., Colorado Springs, Pa. Warehousing Co., Phila., Acer Engring. & Cons., Lancaster, Pa. Co-author: Practical Guide to U.C.C., 1969. Chmn. Phila. Comm. Legal Svcs., Inc., 1966-83, Phila. Legal Assistance Corp., 1995—. Staff sgt. U.S. Army, 1943-46, ETO. Faculty fellow U. Pa. Law Sch., 1973. Mem. ABA (chmn. com. legal aid 1978-79), Nat. Legal Aid Defenders Assn. (pres. 1978), Pa. Bar Assn., Phila. Bar Assn. (chancellor 1974), Phila. Club (chmn. house com. 1979—), Little Egg Harbor Yacht Club (commodore 1991), Merion Cricket Club. Avocations: skiing, sailing, archeology, music, antiques. Office: Pepper Hamilton Plc 18th And The Pky Philadelphia PA 19103-2977

KLAUSEN, RAYMOND, sculptor, television and theatre production designer; b. Jamaica, N.Y., May 29, 1939; s. Jens and Ane Kathrine (Jensen) K. BA, Hofstra U., 1961; MA in Art, NYU, 1963; MFA in Theatre Design, Yale U., 1967. Prodn. designer TV and theater, 1972-89; Hoffman eminent scholar prof. theatre, Fla. State U., 1993—. Theatrical set designer, 1967—, freelance TV art dir., 1970—; designer sets for numerous TV series, individual spls. for Sammy Davis Jr., Elvis Presley, Neil Diamond, Bing Crosby, Perry Como, Jackie Gleason, Cher, Smothers Brothers, Pearl Bailey, The Muppets, Natalie Cole, plus the Kennedy Ctr. Honors, Omnibus, AFI Tributes to Bette Davis, John Huston, Fred Astaire, Jimmy Stewart, Henry Fonda, Alfred Hitchcock and Elizabeth Taylor, also Nat. Tours for Lionel Richie, Kenny Rogers, Julio Iglesias, Travis Tritt, Bally's Casino Prodns. Jubilee!, Night of 100 Stars, The Tony Awards, The Am. Music Awards Show (24 times), The Academy Awards Show (9 times), Freidrick Stadt Palast, Berlin, Comedy Tonight (Broadway), (series) Vibe; solo exhbns. include LBJ Gallery, Newport Beach, Calif., 1990, Wade Gallery, L.A., 1991, Gallery Sanyo, Tokyo, 1991, 92, Ruth Bachofner Gallery, L.A., 1992, 95, Fla. State U. Mus., Tallahassee, 1993,; group exhbns. include Zantman Galleries, Carmel, Calif., 1991, Long Beach (Calif.) Mus. Art, 1992, Ward-Nasse Gallery, N.Y.C., 1992, Ettinger Gallery, Laguna Beach, Calif., Boise (Idaho) State U. Art Gallery, 1993, LACE, L.A., 1993, Alder Gallery, Eugene, Or., 1993, Clara Kott Von Storch Gallery, Mich., 1993, Michael Stone Collection, Va., 1993, San Diego Art Inst., Calif., 1993, Roy G. Biv Gallery, Palm Springs, Calif., 1994, Palm Springs Desert Mus., Calif., 1994, La Quinta Sculpture Park, La Quinta, Calif., 1994, Quietude Garden Gallery, East Brunswick, N.J., 1995, Hunter Mus. Am. Art, Chatanooga, Tenn., 1995, SUNY Plattsburg Art Mus., 1995, San Bernadino Coungy Mus., Calif., 1995, Paris Gibson Mus., Great Falls, Mont., 1995, Eva Cohen Gallery, Chgo., Ill., 1995, D.O.C.S. Gallery, New Orleans, 1997. With U.S. Army, 1962-63. Bates Travel fellow Europe, 1967; TDK Corp. grantee, 1991, 92; recipient 3 Nat. Acad. TV Arts and Sci. Emmy awards for Cher series, 1976, Acad. awards, 1982, 83, nominations for 1980, 91 Acad. Awards and Lynda Carter's Celebration, 1981, Kennedy Ctr. Honors, 1984, 86, Am. Music Awards, 1985, 90, Happy Birthday Hollywood, 1987, Acad. awards, 1991, 96. Home: 310 S Swall Dr Apt 503 Los Angeles CA 90048-3094 Office: 342 W 85th St Apt 4A New York NY 10024-3253 also: 325 S Swall Dr Apt 503 Los Angeles CA 90048-3078

KLAUSMEYER, DAVID MICHAEL, scientific instruments manufacturing company executive; b. Indpls., Aug. 29, 1934; s. David M. and V. Jane (Donnellan) K.; m. Julie Ann Johnson, Oct. 29, 1955; children: Kathleen M., Kevin M., Gregory J. BSS, Georgetown U., 1955. Asst. to pres. White Cons. Ind., Cleve., 1957; auditor Ernst & Ernst, Cleve., 1957-59; pres. Photopipe, Inc., Cleve., 1960-63; v.p. McGregor & Werner Internat., Inc., Washington, 1964-70; internat. cons. Stratford of Tex., Houston, 1971-72; pres. FLR Corp., Houston, 1972-74, Southwest Cons., Houston, 1981-86, Imaging Products, Houston, 1987-90; pres. Nanodyanmics, Inc., N.Y.C., 1988—, also bd. dirs.; pres. Corp. Devel., Houston, 1974-81; ptnr. Klausmeyer & Assoc., Houston, 1970—; dir. U.S. investment banking G.H. Securities, Grand Cayman Island, 1995—, dir. Pharm. Labs. Inc., Arlington, Tex.; bd. dirs. S.W. Venture Reification, Houston, TWK Techs., Charlotte, N.C.; pres. Arsenal Stallions, Inc., 1997—; mng. ptnr. Millcreek Farms, 1992—. Bd. dirs. Catholic Endowment Found. Galveston-Houston, 1999—. With USCG, 1955-57. Republican. Roman Catholic. Home: 288 Litchfield Ln Houston TX 77024-6035 Office: Nanodynamics Inc 10878 Westheimer Rd # 178 Houston TX 77042-3202

KLAUSNER, JACK DANIEL, lawyer; b. N.Y.C., July 31, 1945; s. Burt and Marjory (Brown) K.; m. Dale Arlene Kreis, July 1, 1968; children: Andrew Russell, Mark Raymond. BS in Bus., Miami U., Oxford, Ohio, 1967; JD, U. Fla., 1969. Bar: N.Y. 1971, Ariz. 1975, U.S. Dist. Ct. Ariz. 1975, U.S. Ct. Appeals (9th cir.) 1975, U.S. Supreme Ct. 1975. Assoc. counsel John P. McGuire & Co., Inc., N.Y.C., 1970-71; assoc. atty. Hahn & Hessen, N.Y.C., 1971-72; gen. counsel Equilease Corp., N.Y.C., 1972-74; assoc. Burch & Cracchiolo, Phoenix, 1974-78; ptnr. Burch & Cracchiolo, 1978-98; judge pro tem Maricopa County Superior Ct., 1990—, Ariz. Ct. Appeals, 1992—; ptnr. Warner Angle Roper & Hallam, Phoenix, 1998—. Bd. dirs. Santos Soccer Club, Phoenix, 1989-90; bd. dirs., pres. south Bank Soccer Club, Tempe, 1987-88. Home: 1390 W Island Cir Chandler AZ 85248-3700 Office: Warner Angel Roper & Hallam 3550 N Central Ave Ste 1500 Phoenix AZ 85012-2105

KLAUSNER, RICHARD D., federal agency administrator, cell biologist; b. New York, N.Y., Dec. 22, 1951. BS, Yale U., 1973; MD, Duke U. Med. Sch., 1976. Rsch. assoc. Harvard Med. Sch., 1977-79; rscher., med. officer, mathematical biology program Nat. Insts. Health, Bethesda, Md., 1979-84; branch chief, cell biology, metabolism branch Nat. Inst. of Child Health and Human Develop., Bethesda, Md., 1984-95; dir. Nat. Cancer Inst., Bethesda, Md., 1995—; chrm., Scientific Advisory Bd., Ariad Pharmaceuticals, 1991. Medicine, 1976; numerous articles in prof. journals. Recipient Meritorious Svc. Award, 1986, PHS, Damashek Prize, 1992, Am. Soc. for Hematology; mem. 1993 Nat. Acad. Sciences. Mem. Am. Soc. for Clinical Investigation (1994—), Inst. Medicine. Office: Nat Cancer Inst Bldg 31 Rm 11A48 31 Center Dr MSC 2590 Bethesda MD 20892-2590*

KLAUSNER, ROBERT DAVID, facial, plastic and cosmetic surgeon; b. Indpls., Oct. 1, 1962. BA, U. Pa., 1984, MD, 1988. Diplomate Am. Bd. Otolaryngology, Am. Bd. Facial Plastic and Reconstructive Surgery, Am. Bd. Otolaryngology, Head and Neck Surgery. Intern U. Pa., Phila., 1988-89; resident otolaryngology, head, neck surgery Hosp. U. Pa., Phila., 1989-93; fellow plastic reconstructive surgery McCollough Plastic Surgery Ctr., Birmingham, Ala., 1994-95; physician Carle Ctr. for Cosmetic Surgery, Champaign, Ill., 1998—. Office: 1702 S Mattis Ave Champaign IL 61821-5469

KLAUSNER, SAMUEL ZUNDEL, sociologist, educator; b. Bklyn., Dec. 19, 1923; s. Edward Solomon and Bertha (Adler) K.; m. Bracha Turgeman, Oct. 26, 1948 (div. 1960); children: Rina Ellen Klausner Spence, Jonathan David; m. Madeleine Suringar, Feb. 20, 1964 (div. 1982); children: Daphne Klausner Genyk, Tamar; m. Roberta Sands, Nov. 26, 1992. BS, NYU, 1947; MA, Columbia U., 1951, EdD, 1952, PhD, 1963. Cert. psychologist, N.Y., D.C. Lectr. edn. CCNY, 1951-52, 55-57; lectr. sociology Columbia U., 1957-63; instr. psychology Hebrew U., Jerusalem, 1952-53; lectr. religion and psychiatry Union Theol. Sem., 1961-63; assoc. prof. sociology U. Pa., Phila., 1967-70, prof., 1970-96; dir. Ctr. for Rsch. on the Acts of Man, 1971-88, chmn. grad. group in sociology, 1984-86; prof. emeritus U. Pa., Phila., 1996—; clin. psychologist Govt. Mental Hosp., Jerusalem, 1954-55; program dir. Bur. Applied Social Rsch., Columbia U., 1956-61; sr. rsch. assoc. Bur. Social Sci. Rsch., Washington, 1964-67; exec. sec. Soc. for Study of Religion, 1964-70; cons. U.S. Dept. Commerce, 1968-69, U.S. Naval Chaplains Sch., 1973-81, Nat. Libr. Medicine, 1969, NRC, 1967-81, others; vis. prof. Al Mansoura U., Egypt, 1983, Muhammad V. Univ., Morocco, 1986. Author: Psychiatry and Religion, 1964, The Quest for Self-Control, 1965, The Study of Total Societies, 1967, Why Man Takes Chances, 1968, Society and Its Physical Environment, 1970, On Man in His Environment, 1971, Eskimo Capitalists, 1981; author, editor: The Nationalization of the Social Sciences, 1986; also articles. With USAAC, 1943-45; with Israel Air Force, 1947-48. Ford Found. area rsch. fellow, 1952-53; Fulbright scholar, 1983. Mem. APA, AAAS, Am. Sociol. Assn., Am. Vets. Israel (nat. pres. 1998—), Assn. Sociol. Study of Jewry (pres. 1980), Soc. Sci. Study of Religion (v.p. 1974). Jewish. Home: 7055 Greenhill Rd Philadelphia PA 19151-2322 Office: Univ Pa Dept Sociology Philadelphia PA 19104 *My ideals of social conduct have not been designed to assist in attaining professional success. Judaism is a central guiding reference and though I may deviate from its principles in my daily behavior for reasons of good sense and self interest, they remain normative. My professional station arises from an obsession with the requirements of scholarship. A willingness to be critical of current social institutions has brought social attention but not professional advancement.*

KLAUSS, KENNETH KARL, composer, educator; b. Parkston, S.D., Apr. 8, 1923; s. Christian and Paulina (Engel) K. *Kenneth Klauss's family has a music tradition. His maternal uncle, violinist Carl Engel, taught at Union College, Lincoln, Nebraska. Engel Hall, on campus, is a music building dedicated to his memory. His sister, pianist Mabel Klauss Anderson, toured in the early 1920s with a Chatauqua group out of Lincoln which was under the leadership of Thurlow Lieurance, an early researcher of the music of Native Americans.* MusB in Composition, U. So. Calif., 1946. Tchr. composition and piano L.A., 1946-50; composer Lester Horton Theater, L.A., 1949-50; tchr. music San Francisco, 1950-61; composer, educator L.A., 1961—; lectr. in music for dance Idyllwild (Calif.) Sch. Music and Arts, 1967-74; lectr. in music history So. Calif. Inst. Architecture, Santa Monica, 1970-76; composer in residence Perry/Mansfield Camp, Steamboat Springs, Colo., 1966; guest performer, composer, lectr. Libr. Congress, Am. U., Washington, 1996. *The Klauss Archive will serve as a reference source for the universities and colleges of southeastern South Dakota. It consists of an extended collection of manuscripts, memorabilia, recordings, scores, and technical and historical books dealing with music and art. The James Art Museum displays an impressive collection of the paintings of Bernard James, a native of Dayton, Tennessee. Both the Archive and the Museum are housed in an historic (1904) building, First and Main Streets, Parkston.* Composer: (opera) Fall of the House of Usher, 1952; author, composer: (poetry/music orchestration) Story of the World Volumes I to VIII, 1952-86, 86-96. Founder, patron Klauss/James Archive and Art Mus., Parkston, 1995—. Recipient hon. mention opera competition Ohio U., Athens, 1954. Democrat. Avocations: history, poetry. Home: 440 Wren Dr Los Angeles CA 90065-5040

KLAVITER, HELEN LOTHROP, magazine editor; b. Lima, Ohio, Mar. 5, 1944; d. Eugene H. and Jean (Walters) Lothrop; m. Douglas B. Klaviter, June 7, 1969 (div. 1982); 1 child, Elizabeth. B.A., Cornell Coll., Mt. Vernon, Iowa, 1966. Communication specialist Coop. Extension Service, Urbana, Ill., 1969-71; mng. editor Poetry Mag., Chgo., 1973—; editorial cons. Harper & Row, N.Y.C., 1983-87. Bd. dirs. Ill. Theatre Ctr., 1989-95, St. Clement's Open Pantry, 1990—, Episc. Diocese of Chgo. Hunger Commn., 1992—, Comms. Commn., 1993—. Episcopalian. Office: Poetry Mag Modern Poetry Assn 60 W Walton St Chicago IL 60610-7324

KLAW, BARBARA VAN DOREN, author, editor; b. N.Y.C., Sept. 17, 1920; d. Carl and Irita (Bradford) Van Doren; m. Spencer Klaw, July 5, 1941; children: Joanna Klaw Schultz, Susan Klaw (Del Tredici), Rebecca Klaw (Feldman), Margaret Klaw (Metcalfe). B.A., Vassar Coll., 1941. Writer-researcher OWI, Washington, 1942-43; reporter N.Y. Post, 1943-45; free-lance editor, writer, 1945-63; editor Am. Heritage mag., N.Y.C., 1963-88. Author: One Summer, 1936, One Winter, 1938, A Pony Named Nubbin, 1939, Joan and Michael, 1941, all under pseudonym Martin Gale; under pseudonym Eleanor Benton: The Complete Book of Etiquette, 1956; Camp Follower, 1944; editor folklore anthology, 1960. Home: 280 Cream Hill Rd West Cornwall CT 06796-1207

KLAW, SPENCER, writer, editor, educator; b. N.Y.C., Jan. 13, 1920; s. Alonzo and Alma (Ash) K.; m. Barbara Van Doren, July 5, 1941; children: Joanna Klaw Schultz, Susan Klaw (Del Tredici), Rebecca Klaw (Feldman), Margaret Klaw (Metcalfe). A.B., Harvard U., 1941. Reporter San Francisco Chronicle, 1941; Washington corr. Raleigh (N.C.) News and Observer, and United Press, 1941-43; reporter United Press, N.Y.C., 1946, The New Yorker, 1947-52; asst. to Sunday editor New York Herald Tribune, 1952-54; assoc. editor Fortune, 1954-60; free-lance writer, 1960—; lectr. in journalism U. Calif., Berkeley, 1968-69, Grad. Sch. Journalism, Columbia U., N.Y.C., 1970-87; editor Columbia Journalism Rev., 1980-89. Author: The New Brahmins: Scientific Life in America, 1968, The Great American Medicine Show, 1975, Without Sin: The Life and Death of the Oneida Community, 1993; contbr. to publs. including American Heritage, Esquire, Fortune, Saturday Evening Post, Natural History, Playboy, Harper's, The Reporter. With U.S. Army, 1943-45. Home and Office: 280 Cream Hill Rd West Cornwall CT 06796-1207

KLAWITER, DONALD CASIMIR, lawyer; b. Phila., Feb. 26, 1950; s. Joseph C. and Frances J. (Koniecki) K.; m. Marie M. Gabuzda, Jan. 2, 1982; children: Joseph, Jeffrey. BA, MA, U. Pa., 1972, JD, 1975. Bar: Pa. 1975, U.S. Supreme Ct. 1979, D.C. 1987, U.S. Dist. Ct. D.C. 1987, U.S. Ct. Appeals (4th and 8th crcts.) 1988, U.S. Ct. Appeals (9th crct.) 1993. Trial atty. antitrust div. U.S. Dept. Justice, Phila., 1975-78; spl. asst. operations antitrust div. U.S. Dept. Justice, Washington, 1978-80; chief antitrust U.S. Dept. Justice, Dallas, 1980-82; sr. trial atty. U.S. Dept. Justice, Washington, 1982-86; of counsel Morgan, Lewis & Bockius, Washington, 1986-88, ptnr., 1988—. Mem. ABA (litigation, antitrust law and criminal justice sects., chair criminal practice and procedure com. sect. antitrust law 1995-97, mem. governing coun. sect. antitrust law 1997—, editl. bd. mem. Antitrust Law Devel. IV 1994-97). Roman Catholic. Home: 5930 Munson Ct Falls Church VA 22041-2443 Office: Morgan Lewis & Bockius 1800 M St NW Washington DC 20036-5802

KLAYMAN, BARRY MARTIN, lawyer; b. Montclair, N.J., Sept. 26, 1952; s. Max M. and Sylvia (Cohen) K.; m. Anna Kornbrot, June 8, 1975; children: Alison Melissa, Matthew Daniel. BA magna cum laude, Columbia U., 1974; JD cum laude, Harvard U., 1977. Bar: Pa. 1977, U.S. Dist. Ct. (ea. dist.) Pa. 1977, U.S. Ct. Appeals (3d cir.) 1978, Del. 1998. From assoc. to ptnr. Wolf, Block, Schorr & Solis-Cohen LLP, Phila., 1977—. Contbr. articles to profl. jours. Bd. dirs. Akiba Hebrew Acad., 1991—, sec., 1994-95, v.p., 1995-96, 98—, treas. 1996-98; mem. com. on nat. and overseas svcs. Fedn. Jewish Agys., 1991—. Mem. ABA (litig. sect., torts and ins. practice sect.), Del. Bar Assn., Phila. Bar Assn., Pa. Bar Assn., Assn. Trial Lawyers Am., B'nai B'rith Youth Orgn. (bd. dirs. Phila. region 1984—, chmn. 1991-95, mem. internat. youth commn. 1991—, exec. com., 1996—), B'nai B'rith (coun. v.p. 1996-97, mem. Justice Lodge 1992—), Phi Beta Kappa. Office: Wolf Block Schorr & Solis-Cohen LLP 920 King St Ste 300 Wilmington DE 19801-3300

KLEBANOFF, SEYMOUR JOSEPH, medical educator; b. Toronto, Ont., Can., Feb. 3, 1927; s. Eli Samuel and Ann Klebanoff; m. Evelyn Norma Silver, June 3, 1951; children: Carolyn, Mark. MD, U. Toronto, 1951; PhD in Biochemistry, U. London, 1954. Intern Toronto Gen. Hosp., 1951-52; postdoctoral fellow dept. path. chemistry U. Toronto, 1954-57; postdoctoral fellow Rockefeller U., N.Y.C., 1957-62; assoc. prof. medicine U. Washington, Seattle, 1962-68, prof., 1968—; mem. adv. coun. Nat. Inst. Allergy and Infectious Diseases, NIH, 1987-90. Author: The Neutrophil, 1978; contbr. over 200 articles to profl. jours. Recipient Merit award NIH, 1988, Mayo Soley award Western Soc. for Clin. Investigation, 1991, Bristol-Myers Squibb award for Disting. Achievement in Infectious Disease Rsch., 1995. Fellow AAAS; mem. NAS, Am. Soc. Clin. Investigation, Am. Soc. Biol. Chemists, Assn. Am. Physicians, Infectious Diseases Soc. Am. (Bristol award 1993), Endocrine Soc., Soc. for Leukocyte Biology (Marie T. Bonazinga rsch. award 1985), Inst. of Medicine, Am. Acad. Arts and Scis. Home: 509 Mcgilvra Blvd E Seattle WA 98112-5047 Office: U Wash Dept Medicine Div Al & Infectious Disease PO Box 357185 Seattle WA 98195-7185

KLEBBA, RAYMOND ALLEN, property manager; b. Chgo., Apr. 16, 1934; s. Raymond Aloysius and Marie Cecelia (Tobin) K.; m. Barbara Ann Gurbal, Oct. 7, 1961; children: Anne, Daniel, Mary, Theresa. Student, Loyola U., Chgo., 1954-56; cert. property mgr., Inst. Real Estate Mgmt., 1970. Corr., rep. Western R.R. Assn., Chgo., 1956-61; pres. Midland Warehouse, Chgo., 1961-68; v.p., gen. mgr. Strobeck, Reiss Sch. Mgmt. Co., Chgo., 1968-70, real estate mgr. and broker, 1970-83; v.p., dir. Mid-Am. Nat. Bank, Chgo., 1983-90; br. mgr. Bank of Highwood/Deerfield, Ill., 1990-94; v.p. sales First Colonial Mortgage Corp., Chgo., 1994-95; bus. mgr. St. Matthias Parish, Chgo., 1995—. Mem. ERA Tempo Realty, Inc., Chgo. Bd. Realtors (vice chmn. comml. and indsl. leasing property mgmt. coun.), Inst. Real Estate Mgmt. (life, chmn. chpt. of yr. com. 1975-76), Rotary, Moose. Avocations: bowling, golf, gardening, treasure hunting, fishing. Home: 4933 N Leavitt St Chicago IL 60625-1308

KLEBER, HERBERT DAVID, psychiatrist, educator; b. Pitts., June 19, 1934; s. Max J. and Dorothea (Schulman) K.; m. Joan Louise Fox, Sept. 9, 1956 (div. Jan. 1988); children: Elizabeth, Marc, Pamela. BA in Psychology cum laude, Dartmouth Coll., 1956; MD, Jefferson Med. Coll., 1960; MA (hon.), Yale U., 1975; PhD (hon.), N.Y. Med. Coll., 1990. Lederle rsch. fellow Jefferson Med. Coll., 1959-60; rotating intern Health Ctr. Hosps. of U. Pitts., 1960-61; resident in psychiatry Yale U., New Haven, 1961-64; surgeon, chief receiving svc. USPHS Hosp., Lexington, Ky., 1964-66; asst. chief Hill-West Haven divsn. Conn. Mental Health Ctr., 1966-67, outpatient and admissions coord., 1967-68, dir., founder drug dependence unit, 1968-75, dir. substance abuse treatment unit, 1975-89; exec. dir. psychiatry emergency rm. svc. Yale-New Haven Hosp., 1967-68; from asst. prof. to assoc. prof. Yale U. Sch. Medicine, New Haven, 1966-75; prof. Yale U., 1975-91; exec. v.p., med. dir. Ctr. on Addiction and Substance Abuse Columbia U., 1992—; prof., dir. divsn. substance abuse N.Y. State Psychiat. Inst., 1991—; prof. psychiatry Columbia U. Coll. Phys. and Surg., N.Y.C., 1991—; attending psychiatrist Columbia-Presbyn. Med. Ctr., 1992—; U.S. presdl. appointee Office Nat. Drug Control Policy, dep. dir., 1989-91; founder APT Foudn., Inc., 1970, CEO, 1982-89; dir. NIDA Clin. Rsch. Ctr. for Treatment of Opioid and Cocaine Abuse, Yale U., 1986-89, dir. rsch. tng. fellowship in substance abuse, 1988-89; mem. drug abuse adv. com. FDA, 1987-90; mem. bd. of sci. counselors Addiction Rsch. Ctr, Nat. Inst. on Drug Abuse, 1982-85; mem. exec. instns. rev. groups NIMH and Nat Inst. on Drug Abuse; Nolan D.C. Lewis vis. prof. Carrier Found., 1985; lectr. and presenter in field. Contbr. chpts.: Opiate Addiction: Origins and Treatment, 1973, Treatment Aspect of Drug Dependence, 1978, Clinical Psychiatric Medicine, 1981, Cocaine: Scientific and Social Dimensions, 1992, Drugs, Alcohol and Tobacco: Making the Science and Policy Connections, several others; editor: APA Treatment Manual for Substance Abuse Disorders, APA Textbook of Substance Abuse Treatment, Clinician's Guide to Cocaine Abuse Treatment; (with others) APA Textbook-Treatment of Psychiatric Disorders: Treatment of Substance Abuse; assoc. editor Am. Jour. Drug and Alcohol Abuse and Addictive Behaviors, mem. edit. bd.; rsch. editor Jour. Substance Abuse Treatment, mem. edit. bd. Am. Jour. Addictions, Advances in Alcohol Actions/Misuse, Harvard Rev. of Psychiatry; edit. cons. Archives Gen. Psychiatry, Conn. Medicine, Med. Letter, Jour. Maintenance in the Addictions, Sci.; contbr. over 200 articles to profl. jours. Exec. com. Com. on Problems of Drug Dependence, Inc.; co-chmn. Mayor's Task Force on Drugs, City of New Haven; mem. adv. bd. Rand Drug Policy Rsch. Ctr.; mem. Gov.'s Drug Adv. Coun., State of Conn., 1970-76; mem. nat. adv. coun. Nat. Inst. of Drug Abuse, Alcohol, Drug Abuse and Mental Health Adminstrn., 1975-79, NIMH, 1977-79. Recipient Meritorious Svc. award Lapides Found., 1979, Families in Action Drug Prevention award, 1990, Gov.'s award for outstanding svc. in field of substance abuse State of Conn., 1987, Nyswander and Dole award, 1986, Alcohol, Drug Abuse, Mental Health Agy. award for pub. svc., 1986. Fellow ACP, Am. Psychiat. Assn. (mem. coun. on addiction, cons. joint commn. on pub. affairs, task force on benzodiazepine dependency, Gold award 1975, Found.'s Fund prize 1981), Am. Coll. Neuropsychopharmacology (Eddy award of Coll. on Problems of Drug Dependence 1995), N.Y. Acad. Medicine, Am. Acad. Psychiatrists in Alcoholism and Addictions (founding, Founders award 1987); mem. Inst. of Medicine (substance abuse coverage com., medication devel. for substance abuse com.). Republican. Jewish. Avocations: swimming, cross-country skiing. Office: Columbia U Coll Phys/Surgns 1051 Riverside Dr New York NY 10032-2603

KLECK, ROBERT ELDON, psychology educator; b. Archbold, Ohio, Aug. 3, 1937. AB in Philosophy, Denison U., 1959; PhD in Social Psychology, Stanford (Calif.) U., 1963. Postdoctoral fellow Stanford U., 1963-64; asst. prof. Williams Coll., Williamstown, Mass., 1964-66; asst. to assoc. prof. Dartmouth Coll., Hanover, N.H., 1966-75, prof. psychology, 1975—, John Sloan Dickey Third Century Prof. of Social Scis., 1985-90, chmn. dept. psychology, 1993—; vis. rsch. prof. Boy's Town Ctr. Study of Youth Devel., Stanford U., 1974-75; cons. VA Stroke Project, 1983—, Disadvantaged Children in N.H., 1974, Bur. Devel. Disabilities, Concord, N.H., 1975-80, Crotchet Mountain Rehab. Ctr., 1973, Abilities, Inc., Albertson, N.Y., 1979-81, Can. Rsch. Coun., NSF, USPHS; faculty sponsore USPHS Post-doctoral fellowship, 1977-78. Cons. editor Jour. Personality and Social Psychology, 1974-78, assoc. editor 1971-72; mem. editorial bd. Jour. Nonverbal Behavior, 1990-93; mem. editorial adv. bd. Action for Children's TV, 1975-79; editorial cons.various jours.; contbr. articles to profl. jours. Danforth fellow, 1959-63; Gen. Motors scholar, 1955-59. Mem. Am. Psychol. Soc., Internat. Soc. Rsch. on Emotion, Soc. Experimental Social Psychology, New Eng. Psychol. Assn., New Eng. Soc. Psychol. Assn., Soc. Kent and Danforth Fellows, Sigma Xi, Phi Beta kappa. Home: 28 Low Rd Hanover NH 03755-2207 Office: Dartmouth Coll Dept Of Psychology Hanover NH 03755

KLECKNER, DEAN RALPH, trade association executive; b. Riceville, Iowa, Oct. 7, 1932; s. Ralph Burton and Grace Mary (Lenth) K.; m. Natalie Leone Kitzmann, June 7, 1953; children: Mark, Scott, Kirk, Rhonda,

Lisa. LLD (hon.), Wartburg Coll., 1986. Sec. Floyd County (Iowa) Farm Bur., 1959, county orgn. dir., 1959-60, pres., 1960-62, voting del., 1962, dist. II dir., 1963-66; v.p. Iowa Farm Bur. Fedn., Des Moines, 1966-75, pres., 1975-86, also bd. dirs.; pres. Am. Farm Bur. Fedn., Park Ridge, Ill., 1986—; bd. dirs. U.S. Meat Export Fedn., Denver, 1980—, mem. food and agr. com. and adv. com. for trade negotiations, Washington, 1987—; mem. Nat. Econ. Commn., Washington, 1988-89; bd. dirs. First Interstate of Iowa. Mem. Iowans Right to Work, 1978—, Nat. Inst. for Rural Health, Des Moines, 1986—; mem. adv. com. dean's coun. Iowa State U., Ames, 1987—. Named Outstanding Young Farmer Iowa Jaycees, 1967. Office: Am Farm Bur Fedn 225 W Touhy Ave Park Ridge IL 60068-4202*

KLECKNER, ROBERT A., accounting firm executive; b. 1935. BS, U. Dayton; MBA, Ohio State U. With Grant Thornton Internat., Chgo., 1957—, now mng. dir., internat. Office: Grant Thornton Internat One Prudential Plz Fl 8 Chicago IL 60601*

KLECKNER, ROBERT GEORGE, JR., lawyer; b. Reading, Pa., Mar. 14, 1932; s. Robert George and Elizabeth (Endlich) K.; m. Carol Espie, June 15, 1955; children: Anthony Savage, Susan Duffield. BA, Yale U., 1954; LLB, U. Pa., 1959. Bar: Pa. 1960, N.Y. 1964. Pvt. practice Reading, 1960-63; assoc. Sullivan & Cromwell, N.Y.C., 1963-70; house counsel Goldman, Sachs & Co., N.Y.C., 1970-78; cons. N.Y.C., 1978-80; house counsel Johnson & Higgins, N.Y.C., 1980-97; sr. atty. legal dept. Marsh & McLennan Cos., Inc., N.Y.C., 1997; ret., 1997. 1st lt. USAR, 1955-57, Korea. Mem. ABA, Assn. Bar City N.Y., Berks County (Pa.) Bar Assn., Union Club, Univ. Club, Phi Beta Kappa. Republican. Lutheran. Home: 80 East End Ave New York NY 10028-8004

KLECKNER, SIMONE MARIE, law librarian; b. Bucharest, Romania, Mar. 7, 1927; came to U.S., 1966; d. George Vrabiescu and Clementa (Cionea) Radian; m. Rudolf Kleckner, Apr. 23, 1960. JD, Bucharest U., 1953; MLS, Columbia U., 1969; LLM, NYU, 1973. Asst. curator NYU Sch. Law Libr., 1969-74; legal libr. UN Dag Hammarskjold Libr., N.Y.C., 1975-86, chief reference and biblio. sect., 1986-87; chief libr. U.S. Ct. Internat. Trade, N.Y.C., 1987-96. Author: International Legal Bibliography, 1983, Settlement of Disputes in International Law Bibliography, 1985; translator Penal Code of the Romanian Social Republic, 1976; lic, 1976; compiler UN Juridical Yearbook, 1974-84. Pres. ad hoc com. Orgn. Romanian Democracy, 1997—. Mem. Am. Soc. Internat. Law, Am. Fgn. Law Assn. Republican. Ea. Orthodox. Avocation: travel. Home: 110 W 69th St New York NY 10023-5116

KLECKNER, WILLARD RICHARDS, electrical engineer, consultant, educator; b. Plainfield, N.J., Sept. 29, 1937; s. Willard Ralph and Gladys Alta (Richards) K.; m. Linda Re Kleckner; 1 child, Tamara Lee. BSEE, Pa. State U., 1959, BSBA, 1959, MBA, 1976; LLB, La Salle U., 1965; PhD in Bus. Adminstrn. and Engring., Calif. Western U., 1980. Cons. engr. Kleckner Enterprises, Whitehall, Pa., 1961-65, Hazleton, Pa., 1975-78; labor rels. mgr. Eaton Corp., Phila., 1965-73; dir. labor rels. Beverage Mgmt. Corp., Columbus, Ohio, 1973-75; dir. adminstrn. Penn-Dixie Industries, Inc., Nazareth, Pa., 1978-81; v.p. adminstrn. Merrick Corp., Roseland, N.J., 1981-83; dir. engring., rsch. devel. AquaScis. Internat., Inc., Lincoln Park, N.J., 1988-90; cons. elec., environ. safety and R&D engr. Kleckner Assocs., Hibernia, 1990-93; prin., indsl. hygienist, safety engr., environ. engr. Kleckner Enterprises, Inc., Long Valley, N.J., 1993-95, Oxford Environ., Inc., Pine Brook, N.J., 1994-95, Kleckner Enterprises, Inc., Lecanto, Fla., 1995—; lectr. on indsl. rels. and safety, 1975—; lectr. on low frequency electromagnetic field radiation; cons. Country Oaks Inn, Lecanto, Fla., 1995—. Contbr. articles to profl. jours. Instr., lectr. on safety and environ., 1977—, on internal and external electronic security equipment, 1975—, on water tech., 1988. With USN, 1955-61. Mem. IEEE (sr.), APA, Am. Arbitration Assn., Am. Soc. Safety Engrs., Am. Engring. Assn., Am. Paramedic Assn., Assn. Locksmiths Am., Assn. Energy Engrs., Am. Indsl. Hygiene Assn., Nat. Registry of Environ. Profls., NASA, Pa. State U. Alumni Assn. Republican. Presbyterian. Office: Kleckner Enterprises Inc PO Box 189 Lecanto FL 34460-0189

KLECZKA, GERALD D., congressman; b. Milwaukee, Wis., Nov. 26, 1943; m. Bonnie L. Scott, 1978. Ed., U. Wis., Milw. Mem. Wis. Assembly, 1968-74; mem. Wis. Senate, 1974-84, 98th-106th Congresses from 4th Wis. dist., Washington, D.C., 1984—; mem. ways and means com., ways and means health subcom. Mem. Wis. Dem. Com., Milwaukee County Dem. Com., 19th Assembly Dist. Dem. Com. Unit; del. Dem. Nat. Conv., 1980, 84, 88. With Air N.G., 1963-69. Mem. LaFarge Lifelong Learning Inst., Thomas More Found., Polish Nat. Alliance-Milk. Soc., Polish Am. Congress. Office: 2301 Rayburn Bldg Washington DC 20515-4904*

KLEDIS, JAREL EMANUEL, sculptor; b. Cherokee, Iowa, July 28, 1949; s. John Manuel and Lucille Clarace (Johnson) K.; m. Sherry Ann Beminio, Aug. 23, 1969 (div. June 1981); children: Kyle, Candace. AA, Iowa Ctrl. C.C., Ft. Dodge, 1969; BS in Art Edn., N.W. Mo. State U., 1972; MA, Ft. Hays U., 1975. Instr. art Warrensburg (Mo.) Sch., 1972-74; prof. art Buena Vista U., Storm Lake, Iowa, 1980-84; prof. art, dir. gallery Westman Coll., Lemars, Iowa, 1983-84; freelance sculptor Denver, 1984-87, Lemars, 1987—; judge art contest Lemars Iowa Art Coun., 1983. One-man show at Sanford Mus., Cherokee, 1983; commd. works include sculpture at Iowa Ctrl. C.C., 1977, Black Mt., N.C., 1994, Western U., Callowee, N.C., 1995, Quietude Sculpture Garden, New Brunswick, N.J., 1995-98, Witherspoon Gallery, Greensboro, N.C., 1996, Western Carolina Agrl. Ctr., 1997; sculpture in permanent collection of River Sculpture Park Chattanooga. Advisor Ft. Dodge Pk. Sys., 1977. Winner sculpture contests at U. N.C., 1994, Western U., 1995. Avocation: reading. Home: 164 Maney Branch Rd Weaverville NC 28787-9715

KLEE, CAROL ANNE, foreign language educator; b. Royal Oak, Mich., Sept. 6, 1953; d. Lewis Emil and Anne Perna (Marino) K.; m. Luis Alberto Ramos-García, Dec. 30, 1987; 1 child, Camille Anne Ramos-Klee. BA, Coll. Wooster, 1975; MA, U. Tex., 1980, PhD, 1984. Rsch. asst. S.W. Ednl. Devel. Lab., Austin, Tex., 1980-83; asst. prof. U. Ill., Urbana-Champaign, 1983-85; asst. prof. U. Minn., Mpls., 1985-90, assoc. prof., 1990—. Editor: Sociolinguistics of the Spanish Speaking World, 1991, Faces in a Crowd: The Individual Learner in Mulisection Courses, 1994; editor Hispanic Linguistics, 1988-95; contbr. articles to profl. jours. Mem. MLA, Am. Coun. on the Tchg. Fgn. Langs., Am. Assn. U. Suprs., Coords. and Dirs. Lang. Programs (pres. 1996-97), Am. Assn. Tchrs. Spanish and Portuguese (exec. coun. 1994-96), Minn. Coun. on the Tchg. Fgn. Langs. (adv. bd. 1986-88, Emma Birkmaier award 1997), Phi Beta Kappa. Office: U Minn Dept Spanish & Portuguese 34 Folwell Hall Minneapolis MN 55455

KLEE, CLAUDE BLENC, medical researcher. MD, U. Marsailles, France, 1959. Chief lab. chemistry, chief protein biochemistry sect. Nat. Cancer Inst., 1974—. Recipient Women's Excellence in Sciences award Fedn. Am. Soc. for Exerimental Biology, 1997. Mem. Inst. Med.-Nat. Acad. Sci. Office: Nat Cancer Inst-Biochem Lab 9000 Rockville Pike Bethesda MD 20892-0001*

KLEE, VICTOR LA RUE, mathematician, educator; b. San Francisco, Sept. 18, 1925; s. Victor La Rue and Mildred (Muller) K.; m. Elizabeth Bliss; children—Wendy Pamela, Barbara Christine, Susan Lisette, Heidi Elizabeth; m. Joann Polack, Mar. 17, 1985. B.A., Pomona Coll., 1945, D.Sc. (hon.), 1965; Ph.D., U. Va., 1949; Dr. honoris causa, U. Liège, Belgium, 1984, U. Trier, Germany, 1995. Asst. prof. U. Va., 1949-53; NRC fellow Inst. for Advanced Study, 1951-52; asst. prof. U. Wash., Seattle, 1953-54, assoc. prof., 1954-57, prof. math., 1957-97, adj. prof. computer sci., 1974-97, prof. applied math., 1976-84; prof. emeritus, 1998—; vis. asso. prof. UCLA, 1955-56; vis. prof. U. Colo., 1971, U. Victoria, 1975, U. Western Australia, 1979; cons. IBM Watson Research Center, 1972; cons. to industry; mem. Math. Scis. Research Inst., 1985-86; sr. fellow Inst. for Math. and its Applications, 1987. Co-author: Combinatorial Geometry in the Plane, 1963, Old and New Unsolved Problems in Plane Geometry and Number Theory, 1991; contbr. more than 200 articles to profl. jours. Recipient Rsch. prize U. Va., 1952, Vollum award for disting. accomplishment in sci. and tech. Reed Coll., 1982, David Prescott Burrows Outstanding Disting. Achievement award Pomona Coll., 1988, Max Planck rsch. prize, 1992; NSF sr. postdoctoral fellow, Sloan Found. fellow U. Copenhagen, 1958-60, fellow Ctr. Advanced Study in Behavioral Scis., 1975-76, Guggenheim fellow, Humboldt award U. Erlangen-Nürnberg, 1980-81, Fulbright fellow U. Trier, 1992. Fellow AAAS (chmn. sect. A 1975), Am. Acad. Arts and Scis.; mem. Am. Math. Soc. (assoc. sec. 1955-58, mem. exec. com. 1969-70), Math. Assn. Am. (pres. 1971-73, L.R. Ford award 1972, Disting. Svc. award 1977, C.B. Allendoerfer award 1980, 99), Soc. Indsl. and Applied Math. (mem. coun. 1966-68), Assn. Computing Machinery, Math. Programming Soc., Internat. Linear Algebra Soc., Phi Beta Kappa, Sigma Xi (nat. lectr. 1969). Home: 13706 39th Ave NE Seattle WA 98125-3810 Office: U Wash Dept Math PO Box 354350 Seattle WA 98195-4350

KLEEBLATT, NORMAN L., museum curator. AB in Art History, Rutgers U., 1971; diploma in conservation, NYU, 1975, MA, 1975. Conservator The Jewish Mus., N.Y.C., 1975-80, curator collections/conservator, 1981-87, curator collections, 1987-94, Susan and Elihu Rose curator fine arts, 1995—; mem. sci. coun. Mus. Art and History of Judaism; planning cons. Nat. Found. Jewish Culture, 1995; surveyor mus. assessment program Am. Assn. Mus., 1993; mem. acad. com. Bernard Manekin Inst. Jewish Art, 1989-90; adj. instr. Bernard Manekin Inst. Jewish Art, Jewish Theol. Sem. Am., 1988-95; cons. Montclair (N.J.) Art Mus., 1975, Congregation Adath Jeshurun, Elkins Park, Pa., 1988-89; advisor N.Y. State Coun. on Arts, 1982, field rep., 1984; curatorial cons. N.Y. Pub. Lib., 1984; mem. program com. Coun. Am. Jewish Mus. Contbg. author: Gonn Mosny: Atmen und Malen, 1989, The Encyclopedia of Jewish-American History and Culture, 1992, Pre-Raphaelite Art in its European Context, 1995, L'Affaire Dreyfus de A & Z: histoire et dictionnaire, 1994, L'Affaire Dreyfus et l'opinion publique en France et à l'étranger, 1995, Diaspora and Modern Visual Culture: Representing African and Jewish Diaspora, 1998; reviewer in field. Recipient Hon. Mention, Henry Allen Moe Prize, 1985, 88, Nat. Jewish Book award, 1992, Second prize Henry Allen Moe Prize, 1992, Présidence d'honneur Com. Sci. Soc. Internat. d'Histoire de l'Affaire Dreyfus, 1994—; post-grad. fellow Nat. Mus. Fellowship Act, 1975-76; fellow mus. profls. Nat. Endowment Arts, 1996. Mem. Internat. Assn. Art Critics (Am. sect.), Am. Assn. Mus., Coll. Art Assn. Office: The Jewish Mus 1109 5th Ave New York NY 10128

KLEEMAN, CHARLES RICHARD, medical educator, nephrologist, researcher; b. L.A., Aug. 19, 1923; m. 1945; 3 children. BS, U. Calif., 1944, MD, 1947. Rotating intern San Francisco City Hosp., 1947-48; asst. resident pathology Mallory Inst.-Boston City Hosp., 1948-49; resident in medicine Newington VA Hosp., 1949-51; from instr. to asst. prof. metabolism Yale U. Sch. Medicine, 1953-56; from assoc. clin. prof. to assoc. prof. UCLA Sch. Medicine, L.A., 1956-64, prof., dir. divsn. medicine Cedars-Sinai Med Ctr., 1964-74, prof. divsn. nephrology, 1975-94, prof. emeritus, 1994—; nephrologist VA Med. Ctr., West L.A., 1993—; prof. medicine, dept. chief Hadassah Med. Sch.-Hebrew U., Israel, 1972-75; vis. prof. Beilinson Hosp.-Tel Aviv U., 1968, St. Francis Hosp., Honolulu, 1968, U. Queensland, 1966; chief metabolic sect. VA Hosp., L.A. 1956-60, cons., 1962—. Upjohn-Endocrine Soc. scholar U. London, 1960-61. Mem. AMA, Am. Physiol. Soc., Inst. Medicine-NAS, Am. Soc. Clin. Investigators, Endocrine Soc. ckleeman@ucla.edu. Office: VAMC West LA Dept Med Div Nephr W111L Wilshire and Sawtelee Blvds Los Angeles CA 90073

KLEEMAN, MICHAEL JEFFREY, telecommunications and computer consultant; b. Santa Monica, Calif., July 13, 1949; s. Eugene Stanley and Sylvia (Liebman) K.; m. Janet Louise Depree, Jan. 1, 1977 (div. June 1981); m. Veronica K. Napoles, May 5, 1985; 1 child, Samuel Andres. AB in Psychology, Syracuse U., 1970; MA in Psychology, Claremont Grad. Sch., 1975, postgrad., 1975-78. Asst. v.p. Fairleigh Dickinson U., Rutherford, N.J., 1970-71; research dir., back unit Casa Colina Hosp., Pomona, Calif., 1973-75; assoc. researcher U. Calif., San Francisco, 1975-77; project dir. Teknekron Inc., Berkeley, Calif. and Washington, 1977-80; tech. mgr. 3 Mile Island Class Action Berger & Montague, Phila., 1980-81; mgr.-systems Systems Applications Inc., San Rafael, Calif., 1981-82; mgr.-overseas Sprint (Internat.), Burlingame, Calif., 1982-83; dir. planning Med. Retirement Communities, Larkspur, Calif., 1984-85; dir. telecommunications Arthur D. Little Inc., San Francisco, 1985-89; dir. Comms. Planning, Kentfield, Calif., 1990-94; v.p. Hill Arts & Entertainment, Emeryville, Calif., 1990-93; founder, bd. dirs. San Francisco-Moslow Teleport/SFMT, Inc. (now Global Telesys. Group, Inc.), 1987-92; dir. MCGI, San Rafael, Calif., 1992-94; v.p. Boston Consulting Group, San Francisco, 1994—; bd. dirs. AVT Corp., Seattle, 1988-91. Author: PC LAN Primer, 1987; contbg. editor Adminstrv. Mgmt. Mag., 1985-90; contbr. articles to profl. jours.; patentee in field. Cons. United Way of Bay Area, San Francisco, 1977-79; mem. adv. bd. Found. for Arts of Peace, Berkeley, 1984-89; cons., advisor Inst. for Global Comm., San Francisco, 1986-89, Ark Found., Bolinas, Calif., 1985-86; tech. lead Project Calif., Calif. Coun. on Sci. and Tech., 1992-93; bd. dirs. eTrust, 1997—; bd. govs. strategy com. ARC, Washington, 1998—. Mem. AAAS, IEEE, Assn. Computing Machinery, Am. Psychol. Assn.. West Point Inn Assn (bd. dirs.). Jewish. Avocations: rowing, photography, poetry. Office: BCG 2 Embarcadero Ctr San Francisco CA 94111-3823

KLEEMAN, NANCY GRAY ERVIN, special education educator; b. Boston, Feb. 19, 1946; d. John Wesley and Harriet Elizabeth (Teuchert) Ervin; m. Brian Carlton Kleeman, June 27, 1969. BA, Calif. State U., Northridge, 1969; MS, Calif. State U., Long Beach, 1976, Calif. State U., Long Beach, 1976; cert. resource specialist, Calif. State U., Long Beach, 1982. Cert. spl. edn., learning disabilities and resource specialist tchr., Calif. Tchr. spl. edn., resource specialist Downey (Calif.) Unified Sch. Dist., 1972-86; tchr. spl. day class Irvine (Calif.) Sch. Dist., 1986—; tutor in field; spkr. Commn. for Handicapped, L.A., 1975; advisor Com. to Downey Unified Sch. Dist., 1976-82; owner ISIS Design Publs. Author: Rhyme Your Times, 1990; author numerous greeting cards. Vol. sec. UN, L.A., 1980-83; vol. coord., art dir., educator Sierra Vista Mid. Sch., Irvine, 1986-88; liaison Tustin (Calif.) Manor Convalscent Home and Regents Point Retirement Home, Irvine, 1988—; fundraiser Ronald McDonald House, Orange, Calif.; mem. Nat. Young Svc., Washington; vol. Sr. Cheer Project, 1984—, Vets. Cheer Project, 1996—. Recipient award Concerned Students Orgn., Downey, 1984; named Tchr. Yr. Sierra Vista Middle Sch., 1988. Mem. NEA, Irvine Tchrs. Assn., Calif. Tchrs. Assn., Dogs for the Blind, Nat. Hist. Soc. Avocations: restoring antique carousel horses, figure skating, canoeing, numerology. Office: Irvine Unified Sch Dist 2 Liberty Irvine CA 92620-2536

KLEER, NORMA VESTA, retired critical care nurse; b. London, Apr. 23, 1933; d. Harold N. and Julia Bonanova (Ball-Dale) Wragg; divorced; children: Valerie Mainguy, David. Diploma, Torbay (South Devon, Eng.) Hosp., 1954, St. Francis Hosp., Trenton, N.J., 1964. Lic. healthcare risk mgr.; cert. legal cons. Critical care nursing mgr. Bayfront Med. Ctr., St. Petersburg, Fla.; dir. nursing PRN Inc., St. Petersburg, Am. Healthcare Mgmt., St. Petersburg; nursing coord. Care Plus Inc. Hi-Tech. Home Infusion Co., Fla.; case mgr., DON Bayada Nurses Home Care Specialists, St. Petersburg, Fla.; dir. nurses Nurses PRN, Tampa Bay, Fla.; ret., 1998; pioneer in devel. of EMS Sys., Pinellas Co. Mem. Fla. Emergency Nurses Assn. (founder, 1st pres.).

KLEHFOTH, JAY GORDON, publisher, writer, consultant; b. Richmond, Ind., June 8, 1945; s. Gordon Walter and Mary (Emery) K.; m. Barbara Lynn Mauzy, Feb. 14, 1985; children: Jennifer Lynn Klehfoth Hollandbeck, Alexander Jay. BS, Ind. U., 1967; postgrad., Miami U., 1967-71. Mfg. analyst/fin. specialist Philco-Ford, Connersville, Ind., 1968-71, mgr. profit analysis, 1971-73, mgr. product/price analysis, 1973-76; sr. fin. analyst-internat. Ford Motor (World Hdqrs.), Dearborn, Mich., 1976-78; sr. fin. analyst-diversified products, 1978-79, cons. to pres., sr. v.p.s, 1979-81; asst. v.p. fin./strategic planning W.R. Grace (Grace Energy), Dallas, 1981-92; pres. Yesteryear Enterprises, Inc., Dallas, 1993—; guest lectr. Cornell U. Grad. Sch., Elmira, N.Y., 1981. Author, editor The Vintage Ford mag., 1989— (Golden Quill award). Served to lt. USAF, 1968-71. Mem. Model T Ford Club Am. (officer 1989—). Fax: 972-783-0575. E-mail: jay@mtf-ca.com. Home: 10315 Cimmaron Trl Dallas TX 75243-2519

KLEHR, HARVEY, political science educator; b. Newark, Dec. 25, 1945; s. Samuel and Shirley (Brummer) K.; m. Elizabeth Turner, July 29, 1970 (dec. Nov. 1995); children: Benjamin, Gabriel, Joshua; m. Marcia Steinberg, May 17, 1998; 1 child, Aaron. BA, Franklin & Marshall Coll., 1967; PhD, U. N.C., 1971. Prof. Emory U., Atlanta, 1971-85, Samuel Candler Dobbs prof. politics, 1985-96, Andrew Mellon prof. politics and history, 1996—. Author: Amerasia Spy Case, 1996, Secret World of American Communism, 1995, Verona: Decoding Soviet Espionage, 1999. Recipient Alumni citation Franklin & Marshall Coll., 1985. Office: Emory U Dept Polit Sci Atlanta GA 30032

KLEI, THOMAS RAY, parasitology educator; b. Detroit, Dec. 11, 1942; s. Rosemary K.; 1 child, Catherine. BS, N. Mich. U., Marquette, 1965; PhD, Wayne State U., Detroit, 1971; vis. scientist, Queensland Inst. Med. Rsch., Brisbane, Australia. Postdoc. fellow U. Ga., Athens, 1971-73; asst. prof. Millersville (Pa.) State Coll., 1973-75, U. Ga., Athens, 1973-75; asst. prof. La. State U., Baton Rouge, 1975-77, assoc. prof., 1977-82, prof., 1982-92, Boyd prof., 1992—; vis. scientist Queensland Inst. Med. Rsch., Brisbane, Australia, 1997. Office: La State U Sch Vet Medicine Baton Rouge LA 70803

KLEIM, E. DENISE, city official; b. Modesto, Calif., July 8, 1953; d. Edward Melvin and Eleanora Kleim; m. Christopher Corich, Aug. 11, 1985; children: Aaron Christopher Corich-Kleim, Paige Eleanora Corich-Kleim. BA in Econs. cum laude, San Jose State U., 1975; M.Mgmt., Willamette U., 1982. Mgmt. asst. Urban Renewal Agy. City of Salem, Oreg., 1976-78, grant adminstr. dept. cmty. devel., 1978-80, asst. to dir. dept. cmty. devel., 1981-84, lobbyist, 1980-83; sr. mgmt. analyst Bur. Bldgs., City of Portland, Oreg., 1984-86, adminstrv. mgr., 1986-99, mgr. adminstrv. svcs. divsn. Office Planning and Devel. Rev., 1999—. Mem. planning com. Emergency Ops. Ctr., Portland, 1992—; mem. noise control program adv. com. Dept. Environ. Quality, State of Oreg., Salem, 1982-84; mem. cmty. housing resources bd. Salem Bd. Realtors, 1981-83; mem. employee benefits adv. com. mgmt. rep. City of Portland, 1989-94; v.p. Montclair After Sch. Care Assn., Portland, 1995-96; mem. Atkinson Soc., Salem, 1995-97; cmty. meeting coord. Dist. Atty. campaign, Marion County, Oreg., 1983; program dir. oreg. Women's Polit. Caucus, 1981-82, treas., 1980-81. Mem. Oreg. Bldg. Ofcls. Assn. (strategic planning com. 1996, edn. com. 1990—), City Club of Portland (ballot measure study com. 1987). Office: City of Portland Office Planning-Devel Rev 1120 SW 5th Ave Portland OR 97204-1914

KLEIMAN, ALAN BOYD, artist; b. Bklyn., Feb. 20, 1938; s. Louis and Alfreda (Belowsky) K.; m. Audrey Barbara Code, Feb. 9, 1963; 1 dau., Andrea Kristin. B.F.A., Va. Commonwealth U., 1951; M.F.A., Cranbrook Acad. Art, 1953. Asst. publicity dir. Artist Tenents Assn., 1960-67; v.p. Grand St. Artist Group, 1970-75; chmn. Soho Artifacts, 1971-75. Author: Painting Provincetown Water, 1961, Investigations into the Light of Red Color, 1968, Light, Dazzle and Glow, 1970; one-man show includes Elizabeth Harrisi Gallery, N.Y.C., 1995, Ohara Gallery, N.Y.C., 1996, Robert Steel Gallery, N.Y.C., 1997; group shows include Nexus Gallery, Boston, 1959, Betty Parsons Gallery, N.Y.C., 1961, 79, Sun Gallery, 1962, New Gallery, Provincetown, Mass., 1961-62, Marino, N.Y.C., 1966, Warren Benedek, N.Y.C., 1972, Landmark Gallery, N.Y.C., 1975-76, Renaissance Soc., Chgo., 1979, Art U.S.A. '80, U.S., Can., Sweden, Siegel Gallery, N.Y.C., 1983, Michael Walls Gallery, N.Y.C., 1989, Robert Steel Gallery, N.Y.C., 1997; represented in permanent collections Mus. Modern Art, Whitney Mus., Am. Arts, Met. Mus. Art, N.Y.C., Carnegie Mus., Pitts., Boston Mus. Fine Arts, William Patterson Coll., Wayne, N.J.; 169 self portraits at Clocktower, N.Y.C., 1985—; retrospective 1960-86 at P.S.I., N.Y.C., 1986. Served with U.S. Army, 1953-55. Recipient 1st prize Boston Arts Festival, 1954; N.Y. State Council Arts grantee, 1977-78; Curtral Council Found. awardee, 1978; Esther and Adolph Gottleib Found. grantee, 1985, Pollack-Krasner Found. grantee, 1987. Mem. Theatre of Artists League (v.p. 1972), Orgn. Ind. Artists, Am. Abstract Artists, Nat. Endowment for Arts. *My creative drive has at times thrived on procrastination, anger, jealousy, rage, talent and plain hard work. Balancing emotion and intelligence make the tension expressed in my painting. I want to make more and better art.**

KLEIMAN, BERNARD, lawyer; b. Chgo., Jan. 26, 1928; s. Isadore and Pearl (Wikoff) K.; m. Gloria Baime, Nov. 15, 1986; children—Leslie, David. B.S., Purdue U., 1951; J.D., Northwestern U., 1954. Bar: Ill. 1954. Practice law in assn. with Abraham W. Brussell, 1957-60; dist. counsel United Steel Workers Am., 1960-65, spl. counsel, 1997—, gen. counsel, 1965-97; ptnr. Kleiman, Cornfield & Feldman, Chgo., 1960-75; prin. B. Kleiman (P.C.), 1976-77, Kleiman, Whitney, Wolfe & Elfenbaum, P.C., 1978—; Mem. collective bargaining coms. for nat. labor negotiations in basic steel, aluminum, tire and can mfg. industries. Contbr. articles to legal jours. Served with U.S. Army, 1946-48. Mem. ABA, Ill. Bar Assn., Chgo. Bar Assn., Cook County Bar Assn.

KLEIMAN, DAVID HAROLD, lawyer; b. Kendallville, Ind., Apr. 2, 1934; s. Isadore and Pearl (Wikoff) K.; m. Meta Dene Freeman, July 6, 1958; children: Gary, Andrew, Scott, Matthew. BS, Purdue U., 1956; JD, Northwestern U., 1959. Bar: Ind. 1959. Assoc. firm Bamberger & Feibleman, Indpls., 1959-61; ptnr. Bagal, Talesnick & Kleiman, Indpls., 1961-73, Dann Pecar Newman & Kleiman, Indpls., 1973—; dep. pros. atty., 1961-62; counsel Met. Devel. Commn., 1965-75; Ind. Heartland Coordinating Commn., 1975-81. Editor: Jour. of Air Law and Commerce, 1958-59. Chmn. Young Leadership Coun., 1967; v.p. Indpls. Hebrew Congregation, 1973; pres. Jewish Cmty. Ctr. Assn., 1972-75; pres. Jewish Welfare Fedn., 1981-84; v.p. United Way Ctrl. Ind., 1982-86, pres., 1986, chmn. bd. dirs., 1987; bd. dirs. Jewish Fedn., 1972—, Ind. Symphony Soc., 1991-96; bd. dirs. Ind. Repertory Theatre, 1986—, pres. 1991-94. Recipient Young Leadership award, 1968, Isadore Fiebleman Man of Yr. award, 1987, Mossler Cmty. Svc. award, 1988, Chalfie Cmty. Svc. award, 1998. Mem. ABA, Ind. State Bar Assn., Indpls. Bar Assn., Comml. Law League Am., Columbia Club, Skyline Club (bd. dirs. 1993—), B'nai B'rith, Broadmoor Country Club. Office: Dann Pecar Newman & Kleiman One American Square Box 82008 Indianapolis IN 46282

KLEIMAN, DEVRA GAIL, zoologist, zoological park research scientist; b. N.Y.C., Nov. 15, 1942. BS in Biopsychology, U. Chgo., 1964; PhD in Zoology, U. London, 1969. Rsch. asst. Wellcome Inst. Comparative Physiology, Zool. Soc. London, 1965-69; NIMH postdoctoral fellow Inst. Animal Behavior, Rutgers U., N.J., 1970-71; rsch. assoc. Smithsonian Instn., 1970-72; reproduction zoologist Nat. Zool. Pk., Smithsonian Instn., Washington, 1972-79, acting head dept. zool. rsch., 1979-81, head dept. zool. rsch., 1981-96, acting asst. dir. animal programs, 1983-84, asst. dir. rsch. ednl. activities, 1984-85, asst. dir. rsch., 1985-96, sr. rsch. scientist, 1997—; adj. asst. prof. dept. Psychology George Washington U., 1974-77; adj. asst. prof. dept. Zoology U. Md., 1979-84, adj. prof., 1984—; studbook keeper International Studbook for Leontopithecus rosalia, 1974-84; grant reviewer NIMH, 1977, 81, NSF, 1978, 79; adj. prof. Biology George Mason U., Fairfax, Va., 1980-82; U.S. del. com. Internat. Ethological Conf., 1980-86; mem. bd. fellowships and grants Smithsonian Instn., 1982-84, chair rsch. policy com., 1984-86; mem. species survival plan mgmt. com. L. r. chrysomelas, 1985—, L. r. chrysopygus, 1986—; scientific adv. com. Jersey Wildlife Preservation Trust, 1986—; co-studbook keeper Giant Panda Ailuropoda melanoleuca, 1988-96; chair species survival plan giant panda, 1993-96; ad hoc reviewer behavioral and neuroscis. studies sect. NIH, 1988; adv. bd. program on zoos Sta. WQED, 1990; presenter numerous confs. Mem. editorial bd. International Zoo Yearbook, 1977—, Carnivore, 1977-81, Zoo Biology, 1982-99; consulting editor Am. Jour. Primatology, 1983-91; chief editor Wild Mammals in Captivity, 1983-96; field editor Jour. Soc. conservation Biology, 1986—; contbr. articles to profl. jours. Bd. dirs. Scientists Ctr. Animal Welfare, 1984-86; trustee Dian Fossey Gorilla Fund, 1990-95. Recipient Women in Sci. and Engring. award NSF, 1987, award for Disting. Achievement Soc. Conservation Biology, 1988, Outstanding Svc. award Am. Zoo and Aquarium Assn., 1993. Fellow AAAS, Animal Behavior Soc. (sec. 1977-80, pres. 1983—); mem. Am. Assn. Zool. Pks. and Aquariums (species coord., internal mgmt. com. L. r. rosalia, species survival plan subcom. 1986-90, vice chair Giant Panda task force 1988-92, chair 1992-93, mem New World Primate TAG, Cheetah SSP, Brazil FIG, Reintro. adv. group, rsch. coord. group 1991—, chair behavior and husbandry adv. group 1992-93), World Conservation Union (mem. SSC primate specialist group 1983—, SSC reintro./specialist group 1988—, vice-chair primates 1989—), Consortium Aquariums, Univs. and Zoos (adv. com. 1986—), Internat. Soc. Endangered Cats (rsch. adv. bd. 1988-91), Sigma Xi. Office: National Zoological Park 3000 Connecticut Ave NW Washington DC 20008-2509

KLEIMAN, KEITH JEFFREY, computer consultant; b. Hackensack, N.J., June 1, 1972; s. Morton Lester and Ruth (Carrasco) K.; m. Heidi Lee Griep, Oct. 25, 1997. BS in Mgmt. Sci. and Info. Systems, Pa. State U., 1996. Info. systems specialist Advent Assocs., Inc., State College, Pa., 1996-97; info. tech. support profl. instr. The Computer Learning Ctr., Cherry Hill, N.J., 1997-98; tech. support profl. Computer Aid Inc., Wilmington, Del., 1998—. Presbyterian. Home: Apt 21 B 4 700 Lower State Rd North Wales PA 19454

KLEIMAN, KELLY (RUTH B.), non-profit organization consultant, lawyer; b. Balt., Feb. 17, 1955; d. Allen and Jeanette (Albert) K.; m. Ronald D. Falzone, Sept. 4, 1978 (div. Sept. 1989). AB, U. Chgo., 1975, JD, 1979. Bar: Ill. 1979. Dep. dir. Pub. Funding for the Arts, Chgo., 1978-79; assoc. Rudnick & Wolfe, Chgo., 1979-81; asst. dean Chgo. Kent Coll. Law, Chgo., 1981-86; exec. dir. Chgo. Children's Choir, 1986-87; prin. NFP Cons., Chgo., 1987—; mem. faculty Bus. and Profl. Inst., Coll. of DuPage, 1989-97. Contbr. articles to profl. jours., including Chgo. Philanthropy mag. Mem. tech. assistance com. Chgo. Women in Philanthropy, 1992-95; vol. reader Rec. for Blind, Chgo., 1992—; bd. dirs. Lincoln-Belmont YMCA, Chgo., 1992-95. Mem. Assn. Cons. to Nonprofits (bd. dirs. 1989—, pres. 1998-2000). Democrat. Jewish. Avocations: writing fiction, theater directing. Home and Office: NFP Cons 2103 N Seminary Ave Apt 16 Chicago IL 60614-4176

KLEIMAN, MACKLEN, manufacturing company executive; b. Boston, Aug. 15, 1913; s. Samuel and Anna (Kaufman) K.; m. Ida Maletz Kleiman; children: Steven Lawrence, Terry Sue. BSEE, MIT, 1935. Pres., CEO Lynn (Mass.) Screw Corp., 1950—. 2d lt. U.S. Army. Mem. Rotary. Avocation: gardening. Home: 4 Coolidge Rd Marblehead MA 01945-2827

KLEIMAN, VIVIAN ABBE, filmmaker; b. Phila., Oct. 11, 1950; d. Philip and Hilda (Kramer) K. BA, U. Calif., 1974. Filmmaker; lectr. Grad. Program in Documentary Film Stanford U., 1995-99; bd. dirs. Cultural Rsch. and Comm., Berkeley, Calif., Catticus Corp., Berkeley; founding dir. Jewish Film Festival, Berkeley, 1981-85, Frameline, San Francisco, 1985—; pres. Signifyin' Works, Berkeley, 1991—; v.p. Film Arts Found., San Francisco, 1983-93; cinematographer Tongues Untied, 1989. Producer, dir. films including Judy Chicago: The Birth Project, 1985, Ein Stehaufmannchen, 1991, My Body's My Business, 1992; co-producer films including Routes of Exile: A Moroccan Jewish Odyssey, 1982, California Gold, 1984, Color Adjustment, 1992, Roam Sweet Home, 1996, (with Michael Chandler) Forgotten Fires, 1998; assoc. producer The Disney Channel, 1982-83; rschr. for various films including A Woman Named Golda, 1982. Recipient George Foster Peabody award Sundance Film Festival, Outstanding Achievement award Internat. Documentary Assn., Nat. Emmy award nominee, The Eric Barnouw awards Orgn. Am. Historians, Red ribbon Am. Film and Video Festival, Best of Festival award Black Maria Festival, Black Internat. Cinema Berlin, Gold Plaque, Social/Polit. Documentary Chgo. Internat. Film Festival, N.C. Silver Juror's prize. Mem. Assn. of Ind. Vdeo and Film, Film Arts Found., Internat. Documentary Assn. Office: 2600 10th St Berkeley CA 94710-2522

KLEIN, ABRAHAM, physics educator, researcher; b. Bklyn., Jan. 10, 1927; s. Philip and Ida (Warshofsky) K.; m. Murielle Pollack, June 22, 1950; children—Julia, Hilary. B.A., Bklyn. Coll., 1947; M.A., Harvard U., 1948, Ph.D., 1950; DSc (hon.), U. Frankfort, 1995. Instr. physics Harvard U., Cambridge, Mass., 1950-52, jr. fellow, 1952-55; assoc. prof. physics U. Pa., Phila., 1955-58, prof., 1958-94, prof. emeritus, 1994—; vis. prof. U. Paris, 1961-62, Princeton U., N.J., 1969-70, MIT, Cambridge, 1975-76, Yale U., New Haven, 1983; disting. vis. prof., Drexel U., 1994—. Assoc. editor Phys. Rev., 1965-68; contbr. articles to profl. jours. Served with USAF, 1946. Sr. postdoctoral fellow NSF, 1961-62, fellow Alfred P. Sloan Found., 1961-63, Guggenheim Found., 1975; recipient Disting. Alumnus award Bklyn. Coll., 1966, Hunboldt Sr. Scientist award, 1987, 95. Fellow Am. Phys. Soc.; mem. AAUP, Am. Assn. Physics Tchrs. Avocations: gardening, theatre, films, reading. Home: 1313 Morris Rd Wynnewood PA 19096-2448 Office: U Pa Dept Physics 209 S 33rd St Dept Physics Philadelphia PA 19104-6317

KLEIN, ARNOLD SPENCER, lawyer; b. N.Y.C., Mar. 10, 1951; s. Paul and Ethel (Cooper) K.; m. Arlene Sandra Feinberg, Aug. 14, 1977; children: Jeffrey Daniel, Rachel Pauli. BA, SUNY, Stony Brook, 1974; JD cum laude, N.Y. Law Sch., 1977. Bar: N.Y. 1978, Fla. 1984, U.S. Dist. Ct. (so. and ea. dists.) N.Y., U.S. Dist. Ct. (so. dist.) Fla., U.S. Ct. Appeals (2d cir.), U.S. Supreme Ct. Mem. Kelley, Drye & Warren, N.Y.C., 1977-85, ptnr., 1986-94; ptnr. Meltzer, Lippe, Goldstein & Schlissel, P.C., Mineola, N.Y., 1994—. Mem. ABA, N.Y. State Bar Assn., Nassau County Bar Assn. Office: Meltzer Lippe 190 Willis Ave Mineola NY 11501-2693

KLEIN, ARNOLD WILLIAM, dermatologist; b. Mt. Clemens, Mich., Feb. 27, 1945; s. David Klein; m. Malvina Kraemer. BA, U. Pa., 1967, MD, 1971. Intern Cedars-Sinai Med. Ctr., Los Angeles, 1971-72; resident in dermatology Hosp. U. Pa., Phila., 1972-73, U. Calif., Los Angeles, 1973-75; pvt. practice dermatology Beverly Hills, Calif., 1975—; clin. prof. dermatology/medicine U. Calif. Ctr. for Health Scis; mem. med. staff Cedars-Sinai Med. Ctr.; asst. clin. prof. dermatology Stanford U., 1982-89; asst. clin. prof. to clin. prof. dermatology/medicine, UCLA; mem. Calif. State Adv. Com. on Malpractice, 1983-89; med. adv. bd. Skin Cancer Found., Lupus Found. Am., Collagen Corp., Botox adv. bd., Allergan; presenter seminars in field. Assoc. editor Jour. Dermatologic Surgery and Oncology; reviewer Jour. Sexually Transmitted Diseases, Jour. Am. Acad. Dermatology; mem. editorial bd. Men's Fitness mag., Shape mag., Jour. Dermatologic Surgery and Oncology, Archives of Dermatology; contbr. numerous articles to med. jours. Mem. AMA, Calif. Med. Assn., Am. Soc. Dermatologic Surgery, Internat. Soc. Dermatologic Surgery, Am. Assn. Cosmetic Surgeons, Assn. Sci. Advisors, Los Angeles Med. Assn., Am. Coll. Chemosurgery, Met. Dermatology Soc., Am. Acad. Dermatology, Dermatology Found., Scleroderma Found., Internat. Psoriasis Rsch. Inst., Lupus Found., Discovery Fund for Eye Rsch. (dir.), Hereditary Disease Found. (dir.), Jennifer Jones Simon Found. (trustee), Am. Venereal Disease Assn., Soc. Cosmetic Chemists, AFTRA, Los Angeles Mus. Contemporary Art (founder), Dance Gallery Los Angeles (founder), Am. Found. AIDS Research (founder, dir.), Children's Mus. L.A. (founder), Friars Club, Phi Beta Kappa, Sigma Tau Sigma, Delphos. Office: 435 N Roxbury Dr Ste 204 Beverly Hills CA 90210-5004 *The sincerest form of respect is trust. Being a Physician is all about serving this trust. Also, it is about dedication, observation, obsession and creative intelligence. Who and what I am...where I begin and where I end...is all about being a physician.*

KLEIN, ARTHUR, foundation executive; b. Phila., June 27, 1934; s. Philip and Esther (Moyerman) K.; m. Marilyn A. Burnett, Mar. 12, 1961 (dec. Dec. 1990); children: Joshua, Rebecca Rose Clark, Alexander, Judith Amy. AB, Haverford Coll., 1955; MS, U. Pa., 1958; DHL, Combs Coll. Music, Bryn Mawr, Pa., 1983. Editor Phila. Jewish Times, 1958-71; pres. Rittenhouse Found., Phila., 1963-96, chmn., 1996—; pres. Phila. Meml. Park, 1965-85, Gt. Valley Pet Cemetery, Frazer, Pa., 1968-85, Bristol Gardens, Inc. (Pa.), 1981—; trustee Mikveh Israel Cemetery Trust, Phila., 1977—. Pres. Phila. Jaycees, 1961, Ctr. City Residents Assn., Phila., 1963; chmn. Phila. Art Alliance, 1968-71; trustee The Provincial Found., Phila., 1965—, Friends of Independence Nat. Hist. Park, 1989-96; exec. bd. Com. of Seventy, 1989—; hon. v.p. Temble Beth Zion-Beth Israel; trustee Combs Coll. Music, Bryn Mawr, Pa., 1983-85, Pa. Coll. Podiatric Medicine, Phila., 1983-98; mem. bd. visitors Sch. Podiatric Medicine Temple U., 1998—. Treas. Found. Big Bros., Big Sisters of Am., 1989—, Independence Hall Preservation Fund, 1991-99, pres., 1992—; treas. Big Bros./Big Sisters of Am., 1976-94, sec. Am. Revolution Patriots Fund, 1992—; chmn. bd. trustees Harcum Jr. Coll., Bryn Mawr, 1982-95, trustee 1976—; committeeman 8th Ward Republican Exec. Com., Phila., 1979—; bd. dirs. Mann Ctr. Performing Arts, 1989-98, Pan Am. Assn., 1991-96, English Speaking Union Phila., 1991-96. Recipient Eyerman award Pa. Jr. C. of C., 1962. Mem. Soc. Profl. Journalists (pres. Phila. chpt. 1968), Jewish Cemetery Assn. Phila. (pres. 1970), Locust Club, Plays and Players, Franklin Inn Club, Barnegat Light Yacht Club. Republican. Home: 2023 Pine St Philadelphia PA 19103-6522 Office: The Rittenhouse Found 225 S 15th St Ste 2034 Philadelphia PA 19102-3979

KLEIN, BENJAMIN, economics educator, consultant; b. N.Y.C., Jan. 29, 1943; s. Hyman and Beartha (Kristel) K.; m. Lynne Schneider; children: Franz, Emily, Amanda. ABA in Philosophy, Bklyn. Coll., 1964; MA in Econs., U. Chgo., 1967, PhD in Econs., 1970. Asst. prof. UCLA, 1968-72, assoc. prof., 1973-78, prof. econs., 1978—; faculty research fellow Nat. Bur. Econs., N.Y.C., 1971-72, research assoc., 1976-77; pres. Econ. Analysis Corp., Los Angeles, 1980—; vis. prof. U. Wash., Seattle, 1978; cons. FTC, Washington, 1976-86, bd. govs. FRS, Washington, 1973-75. Contbr. articles to profl. jours. Ford Found. fellow, 1967-68, Scaiffe Found. fellow, 1975-76, Law and Econs. fellow U. Chgo. Law Sch., 1979; grantee Sloan Found., 1981-87; recipient amn. prize for disting. scholarship in law and econs. U. Miami Law and Econ. Ctr., 1978-79. ann. award for best articles Western Econ. Assn., 1979. Mem. Am. Econs. Assn. Office: UCLA Dept Econs 405 Hilgard Ave Los Angeles CA 90095-9000

KLEIN, BERNARD, publishing company executive; b. N.Y.C., Sept. 20, 1921; s. Joseph J. and Anna (Wolfe) K.; m. Betty Stecher, Feb. 17, 1946; children: Cheryl Rona, Barry Todd, Cindy Ann. B.A., CCNY, 1942. Founder, pres. U.S. List Co., Boca Raton, Fla., 1946—; founder, pres., chief editor B. Klein Publs., Delray Beach, Fla., 1953—; cons. direct mail advt. and reference book pub. to pubs., industry, 1950—. Author: all biennials Ency. of American Indian, 1954—; Guide to American Directories. Served with AUS, 1942-45, ETO. Mem. Direct Mail Advt. Assn. Lodge: Masons. Home: 12727 Coral Lakes Dr Boynton Beach FL 33437-4143

KLEIN, BERNARD JOSEPH, management specialist; b. 1945. Employee State of Calif., L.A., 1968-72, City of L.A., 1969-79, Atlantic Richfield, L.A., 1979-84; pres. Klein & Assocs. Inc., New Orleans, La., 1984-89, Klein Ainswrth & Co., Inc., New Orleans, 1989—; mng. ptnr. Astoria Gertna Belle Partnr, Metaire, La., 1992—. Address: 100 Mariners Blvd Ste 9 Mandeville LA 70448-6897*

KLEIN, BILL, legislative staff member; m. Lori Gillen, 1995; 1 child, Gwen. BA in Polit. Sci., George Washington U., 1981; MA in Nat. Security Studies, Georgetown U., 1997. With Pa. Senator Arlen Specter; legis. dir. U.S. Rep. Lawrence Coughlin, Congresswoman Tillie Fowler, 1993—. Recipient Fla. Disting. Svc. medal for exceptionally meritorious svc. Gov. Fla., 1996. Fax: 202-225-9318. Office: Congresswoman Tillie K Fowler 106 Cannon Bldg Washington DC 20515

KLEIN, CALVIN RICHARD, fashion designer; b. N.Y.C., Nov. 19, 1942; s. Leo and Flore (Stern) K.; m. Jayne Centre, Apr. 26, 1964 (div. 1974); 1 dau., Marci; m. Kelly Rector, Sept. 1986. A.A., Fashion Inst. Tech., 1962. Pres., designer Calvin Klein, N.Y.C., 1969—; critic Parsons Sch. Design; critic, cons. Fashion Inst. Tech., dir., 1975—. Recipient Coty award, 1973, 74, 75, Woolmark award for Career Achievement, 1987; named Outstanding Am. talent in women's fashion design Coun. Fashion Designers of Am., 1981, 83, 87; Womenswear/Menswear Designer of the Year, Coun. Fashion Designers of Am., 1993. Mem. Council Fashion Designers, Mus. Modern Art, Met. Mus. Art, Whitney Mus., Guggenheim Mus. Office: Calvin Klein Inc 205 W 39th St Fl 17 New York NY 10018-3102*

KLEIN, CHARLOTTE CONRAD, public relations executive; b. Detroit, June 20, 1923; d. Joseph and Bessie (Brown) K. BA, UCLA, 1945. Corr. UPI, Los Angeles, 1945-46; staff writer CBS, Los Angeles, 1946-47; publicist David O. Selznick Studios, Culver City, Calif., 1947-49, Foladare and Associs., Los Angeles, 1949-51; publicist to v.p. Edward Gottlieb & Assocs., N.Y.C., 1951-62; v.p. to sr. v.p. Harshe Rotman & Druck, N.Y.C., 1962-78; dir. press/govt. affairs Sta. WNET-TV, N.Y.C., 1978-79; pres. Charlotte C. Klein Assocs., N.Y.C., 1979-84; sr. v.p., group supr. Porter Novelli, N.Y.C., 1984-89; prin. Charlotte Klein Assocs., N.Y.C., 1989—; adj. prof. pub. rels. NYU; bd. dirs. U.S. Trademark Assn., 1959-62, Am. Arbitration Assn., 1970-80 (exec. com. 1980-82). Contbr. articles to profl. jours. Bd. dirs. Manhattan chpt. Am. Cancer Soc., 1988-92. Recipient Cine Golden Eagle, 1977, Matrix award Women in Communications, 1975. Mem. Pub. Rels. Soc. Am. (accredited; pres. N.Y. chpt. 1985-86, Silver Anvil award 1978, John Hill award 1988), Women's Forum (bd. dirs. N.Y. chpt. 1986-87, 96-98), Internat. Women's Forum (leadership com. chair dialogue for democracy 1993-98, co-chair task force on violence against women globally, 1998—), Women Execs. in Pub. Rels. (pres. 1965). Avocations: painting, stamp collecting, tennis, kite flying.

KLEIN, CHRISTOPHER CARNAHAN, economist; b. Anniston, Ala., July 5, 1953; s. Wallace Carnahan and Frances Luvona (Meaders) K.; m. Vicki Lynn Brown, May 7, 1983; children: Hannah Marie Brown, Colin Christopher Brown. BA in Econs., U. Ala., 1976; PhD in Econs., U. N.C., 1980. Economist FTC, Washington, 1980-86; economist Tenn. Pub. Svc. Commn., Nashville, 1986-93, rsch. dir., 1993-94, dir. utility rate div., 1994-95; chief utility rate divsn. Tenn. Regulatory Authority, Nashville, 1995-97, chief econ. analysis divsn., 1997—; mem. adj. faculty Mid. Tenn. State U., Murfreesboro, 1990-94; adj. assoc. prof. Vanderbilt U., 1998—; mem. Fed.-State Joint Bd. Staff, 1994-96; mem. rsch. adv. com. Nat. Regulatory Rsch. Inst., Columbus, Ohio, 1990-95, chmn., 1993-95; mem. staff subcom. on gas Nat. Assn. Regulatory Utility Commrs., 1990-94. Contbr. articles to profl. jurs. Recipient cert. of commendation FTC, 1985. Mem. Am. Econ. Assn., So. Econ. Assn., Indsl. Orgn. Soc., Transp. and Pub. Utilities Group, Alpha Pi Mu. Avocations: writing poetry, tube hi-fi, photography. Office: Tenn Regulatory Authority 460 James Robertson Pkwy Nashville TN 37243-0505

KLEIN, CHRISTOPHER M., federal judge; b. Sacramento, 1946. BA, MA, Brown U., 1969; JD, MBA, U. Chgo., 1976. Trial atty. U.S. Dept. Justice, 1978-80; with Cleary, Gottlieb, Steen & Hamilton, 1980-83; dep. gen. counsel Nat. Rd. Passener Corp., 1983-87; apptd. bankruptcy judge ea. dist. U.S. Dist. Ct. Calif., 1988. Lt. col. USMC, 1969-79. Office: 650 Capitol Mall 8308 US Courthouse Sacramento CA 95814

KLEIN, CHUCK, private investigator; b. Cin., Mar. 20, 1942; s. Charles H. and Ruth Emily (Becker) K.; m. Annette Margolis Levine, Aug. 18, 1996; children: Trey, Jay, Todd, Amy, Brad. LLB, Blackstone Law Sch., 1972. Cert. police officer, Ohio; cert. fire fighter, Ind.; cert. firearms instr. NRA; lic. pvt. investigator. Firearms editor P.I. Mag., Toledo, Ohio, 1988—; contbg. editor GUNS and Weapons for Law Enforcement, N.Y.C., 1990—. Author: (fiction) Circa 1957, 1990, (non-fiction) Instinct Combat Shooting, 1986, Klein's Firearm Manual, 1997, Klein's C.C.W. Handbook, 1998, (fiction) The Power of God, 1999. Mem. Fairfield Sportsman Assn., Kiwanis. Avocations: golf, skeet.

KLEIN, DANIEL E., JR., federal judge; b. 1934. BA, Union Coll., 1956; LLB, U. Md., 1964, JD, 1969. Bar: Md. 1964. Law clk. to Judge Prendergast Supreme Bench Balt., 1963-64; law clk. to Hon. Edward S. Northrop, U.S. Dist. Ct. for Dist. Md., 1964-65; ptnr. Klein & Harlan and predecessors, Balt., 1965-78; magistrate judge for Md., U.S. Magistrate Ct., Balt., 1978—. With USAF, 1956-60; mem. Md. Air N.G., 1962-82. Office: 830 US Courthouse 101 W Lombard St Ste 830 Baltimore MD 21201-2693

KLEIN, DEBORAH RAE, health facility administrator; b. Detroit, Mar. 29, 1951; d. Chester Anthony and E. Jacquelyn (Hollenbeck) Simpson; m. Robert Joseph Klein, Apr. 15, 1977; 1 child, Jeffrey. BS in Nursing, Mich. State U., 1974; MS in Health Adminstrn., U. Houston, 1984. Grad. nurse St. Mary's Hosp., Livonia, Mich., 1974; RN U.S. Army, Ft. Polk, La., 1974-78; DON Byrd Meml. Hosp., Leesville, La., 1978-79, Alvin (Tex.) Cmty. Hosp., 1979-83; adminstrn. resident Katy (Tex.) Med. Ctr., 1983-84, DON, 1984-85, COO, DON, 1985-90; v.p. Doctors' Hosp., Tulsa, 1990-97; dir. ops. improvement Okla. divsn. Columbia HCA, 1997-98; v.p., COO SouthCrest Hosp., Tulsa, Okla., 1998—; cons. in field; diplomat Am. Coll. Healthcare Execs. Sec., treas. Sam Houston coun. Boy Scouts Am., 1984-88. Capt. U.S. Army, 1972-78. Republican. Roman Catholic. Avocation: reading. Home: 8823 E 62nd Ct Tulsa OK 74133-1307 Office: SouthCrest Hosp 8801 S 101st Ave E Tulsa OK 74133

KLEIN, DENNIS ALLAN, language educator, writer; b. N.Y.C., Oct. 19, 1943; s. Gordon David and Bertha (Berman) K. BS, U. Kans., 1965, MA, 1967; PhD, U. Mass., 1973. Prof. Spanish U. S.D., Vermillion, 1976—. Author: Peter Shaffer, Boston, 1979, Peter and Anthony Shaffer: A Reference Guide, 1982, Blood Wedding, Yerma and The House of Bernarda Alba: Federico Garcia Lorca's Tragic Trilogy, 1991, Peter Shaffer, rev. edit., 1993; contbr. author: Garcia Lorca: A Selectively Annotated Bibliography of Criticism, 1979, Garcia Lorca: An Annotated Primary Bibliography, 1982, Women Writers of Spanish America: An Annotated Bio-Bibliographical Guide, 1987, Peter Shaffer: A Casebook, 1991, Dictionary of the Literature of the Iberian Penisula, 1993, Latin Am. Jewish Writers: A Critical Dictionary, 1997; contbr. numerous articles to profl. jours. Grantee NEH, 1979, 84, 93, 94, 95, Exxon Found., 1981, Bush Found., 1989, Office Rsch., 1992. Mem. MLA (head hispanic bibliographer, 1970—). Jewish. Office: U SD 414 E Clark St Vermillion SD 57069-2307

KLEIN, DONALD FRANKLIN, psychiatrist, scientist, educator; b. N.Y.C., Sept. 4, 1928; s. Jesse and Rose K.; m. Rachel Gittelman, Dec. 29, 1968; children: Beth, Geri, Hilary, Michelle, Erika. BA magna cum laude, Colby Coll., Waterville, Maine, 1947; MD, SUNY, Bklyn., 1952. Rotating intern USPHS Hosp., S.I., N.Y., 1952-53; resident in psychiatry Creedmoor State Hosp., 1953-54, 56-58; dir. rsch. and evaluation, dept. psychiatry L.I. Jewish-Hillside Med. Center, 1972-76; prof. psychiatry SUNY Med. Sch., Stony Brook, 1972-76; dir. rsch. and therapeutics N.Y. State Psychiat. Inst., N.Y.C., 1976—; attending psychiatrist Presbyn. Hosp., N.Y.C., 1977—; prof. psychiatry Columbia U. Coll. Physicians and Surgeons, N.Y.C., 1978—; chmn. clin. psychopharmacology study sect. NIMH, 1973-75; sr. sci. advisor Alcohol Drug Abuse Mental Health Adminstrn., 1989-91; cons. Nat. Inst. Drug Abuse, 1991—, Nat. Inst. Alcoholism and Alcohol Abuse, 1996—. Co-author: Diagnosis and Drug Treatment of Psychiatric Disorders: Adults and Children, 2d edit., 1980, Mind, Mood and Medicine, 1981, Understanding Depression, 1993; co-editor: Critical Issues in Psychiatric Diagnosis, 1978, Anxiety: New Research and Changing Concepts, 1980; contbr. articles to med. jours. Sr. asst. surgeon USPHS, 1954-56. Recipient A.E. Bennett Neuropsychiat. Rsch. award, 1964, Found.'s Fund prize for rsch. in psychiatry Am. Psychiat. Assn., 1988, Gold medal Soc. Biol. Psychiatry, 1990, Heinz Lehmann award N.Y. State Office of Mental Health, 1991, Thomas W. Salmon award, 1993. Fellow Psychiat. Rsch. Soc., Am. Psychopathol. Assn. (past pres., Hamilton award 1980), Am. Coll. Neuropsychopharmacology (life, past pres., Paul Hoch award 1991), Royal Coll. Psychiatry (founding); mem. Am. Soc. Clin. Psychopharmacology (pres. 1993-97, v.p. 1997—). Home: 1016 5th Ave Apt 14D New York NY 10028-0132 Office: NY State Psychiat Inst 1051 Riverside Dr New York NY 10032-2603 also: 182 E 79th St Ste E New York NY 10021-0422

KLEIN, DYANN LESLIE, theater properties company executive; b. Clifton, N.J.; d. Alfred L. and Florence (Staff) K.; divorced. BA, Ohio State U., 1973; postgrad., Rutgers U., 1976, Sch. Visual Arts, 1983-86. Art therapist Jackson Meml. Hosp., Miami, Fla., 1973-74; prodn. asst. Dom Albi Assocs., N.Y.C., 1974-75; freelance prodn. asst. N.Y.C., 1975-76, freelance designer and stylist, 1976-80; pres. Props For Today, Inc., N.Y.C, 1980—; owner Famous Furnishings, Inc., retail celebrity home furnishings, N.Y.C, 1997—; guest spkr. Fashion Inst. of Tech., N.Y.C., 1987, mem. faculty; bd. dirs. Tipps Directory, N.Y.C. Mem. NAFE, Internat. Home Furnishings Assn., N.Y. Women in Film and TV, Pro New York. Jewish. Avocations: watercoloring, tennis, skiing, design, antiques. Office: Props For Today Inc 330 W 34th St New York NY 10001-2406

KLEIN, EDWARD JOEL, editor, author, lecturer; b. Yonkers, N.Y., Oct. 19, 1936; s. Meyer I. and Gertrude (Axelrod) K.; m. Emiko Oshikiri, June 25, 1963 (div. 1975); children: Karen, Alec; m. Tessa Namuth, Mar. 20, 1978 (div. 1981); m. Dolores Jones Barrett, Oct. 24, 1987. B.S., Columbia U., 1960, M.S., 1961. Copy boy, feature writer N.Y. Daily News, N.Y.C., 1957-60; reporter World Telegram & Sun, N.Y.C., 1960-61; reporter, editor Japan Times, Toyko, 1961-63; fgn. corr. UPI, Tokyo, 1963-64; editor The Shipping and Trade News, Toyko, 1964-65; assoc. editor Newsweek Mag., N.Y.C., 1965-69, fgn. editor, 1969-76, asst. mng. editor, 1976-77; editor N.Y. Times Mag., N.Y.C., 1977-87; contbg. editor Vanity Fair, N.Y.C., 1988—; Parade, N.Y.C., 1991—. Author: (with Robert Littell and Richard Chesnoff) If Israel Lost the War, 1969, The Parachutists, 1981, All Too Human: The Love Story of Jack and Jackie Kennedy, 1996, Just Jackie: Her Private Years, 1998; editor: (with Don Erickson) About Men. Mem. Coun. on Fgn. Rels., PEN Am. Ctr., Am. Motorcyclist Assn., Overseas Press Club Am. (bd. govs.).

KLEIN, ELAINE CHARLOTTE, educational administrator; b. Herreid, S.D., June 14, 1939; d. Herman F. and Minnie (Weigum) K.; 1 child, Erika Katherine. BA, U. Puget Sound, 1961; MA, U. Wash., 1964; Cert. Adminstr., Seattle U., 1976; postgrad., Western Wash. U., 1986. Cert. secondary sch. adminstr., Wash., K-12 tchr., Wash. Tchr. Edmonds Sch. Dist., Lynnwood, Wash., 1961-77; asst. prin. Meadowdale Jr. H.S., Lynnwood, Wash., 1977-80; asst. prin. Mountlake Terrace (Wash.) H.S., 1981-93, prin., 1993-97; exec. dir. cmty. svcs. Frederick County Pub. Schs., Frederick, Md., 1997—; adj. faculty Heritage Inst., Antioch U., Seattle Pacific U., Western Wash. U.; instr. Mt. St. Mary's Coll., Emmitsburg, Md.; cons. Am. Coll. Testing Passport Portfolio, Iowa City, 1995-97; workshop presenter. Author: (chpt.) ACT Manual for Administrators, 1997; grant writer. Pres. Pacific N.W. region Internat. Tng. in Comm., Alaska, B.C., Wash., 1993-94. Recipient Award for Excellence in Edn. award Wash. State Legislature, 1997; named Wash. State Prin. of Yr., 1997. Mem. ASCD, Nat. Assn. Secondary Sch. Prins. and Affiliates, Rotary (Mountlake Terrace pres. 1996-97). Methodist. Avocations: public speaking, reading, traveling, advocating for public schools. Office: Frederick County Pub Schs 115 E Church St Frederick MD 21701-5403

KLEIN, (MARY) ELEANOR, retired clinical social worker; b. Luzon, Philippines, Dec. 13, 1919; came to U.S., 1921; (parents Am. citizens); d. Roy Edgar and Edith Lillian Hay; m. Edward George Klein, June 24, 1955. BA, Pacific Union Coll., 1946; MSW, U. So. Calif., 1953. Lic. clin. social worker. Social worker White Meml. Hosp., Los Angeles, 1948-56; clin. social worker UCLA Hosp. Clinics, 1956-65, supr. social worker, 1965-67, assoc. dir., 1967-73, dir., 1973-82. Bd. dirs., treas. Los Amigos de la Humanidad, U. So. Calif. Sch. Social Work; hon. life mem. bd. dirs. Calif. div. Am. Cancer Soc., mem. vol. bd. Calif. div., 1964—, del. nat. dir., 1980-84, chmn. residential crusade for Orange County (Calif.) unit, 1985-86; bd. dirs. Vol. Exchange, 1988-97, sec., 1991-96, v.p., 1996-97; v.p. Dem. Club West Orange County, 1996-98, pres., 1998-99. Recipient Disting. Alumni award Los Amigos de la Humanidad, 1984, Outstanding Performance award UCLA Hosp., 1968, various service awards Am. Cancer Soc., 1972-88. Fellow Soc. Clin. Social Work; mem. APHA, NASW (charter), Am. Hosp. Assn., Soc. Social Work Leadership in Health Care (formerly Soc. Hosp. Social Work Dirs.) (nat. pres. 1981, bd. dirs. 1978-82, life mem. local chpt.), Assn. Oncology Social Work (charter). Democrat. Unitarian. Avocations: travel, gardening. Home: 1661 Texas Cir Costa Mesa CA 92626-2238

KLEIN, EMILEE, professional golfer; b. Santa Monica, Calif., June 11, 1974. Student, Ariz. State U. With LPGA, 1994—. Named two-time All-American, 1993, 94, Collegiate Player of the Year, 1994. Winner PING/Welch's Championship, 1995, Weetabix Women's British Open, 1995; recorded four top-20 finishes in 1995; third place Rolex Rookie of the Year standings, 1995. Office: LPGA 100 International Golf Dr Daytona Beach FL 32124-1092 also: Callaway Golf 2285 Rutherford Rd Carlsbad CA 92008-8815*

KLEIN, ERIC ALAN, surgical oncologist, urologist; b. Bristol, pa., Dec. 25, 1955; s. Milton and Sylvia Klein; m. Susan Kerins, Dec. 27, 1980; 1 child, Mira Lamson. Student, Johns Hopkins U., 1973-77; MD, U. Pitts., 1981. Diplomate Am. Bd. Urology, Nat. Bd. Med. Examiners. Intern Cleve. Clinic Found., 1981-82, resident, 1982-86; fellow Meml. Sloan Kettering Cancer Ctr., N.Y.C., 1986-89; head sect. urol. oncology dept. urology Cleve. Clinic Found., 1989—; mem. editl. bd. the Prostate Jour., 1997—, Molecullar Urology, 1997—. Editor: Renal Cell Carcinoma: Immunotherapy, 1993, biology of Renal Cell Carcinoma, 1995, Management of Prostate Cancer, 1999; assoc. editor Seminars in Urologic Oncology, 1994—; contbr. articles to profl. jours. Trustee-at-large Ohio divsn. Am. Cancer Soc., 1996. Internat. travelling fellow Cleve. Clinic, 1986. Fellow ACS; mem. Am. Urol. Assn. (exam. com. 1988—, Internat. Acad. Exch. award 1994), Soc. Urol. Oncology (exec. com. 1998—), Am. Soc. Clin. Oncology, Am. Assn. Cancer Rsch., Soc. Internat. Urology. Avocations: photography, 20th Century history. E-mail: Kleine@ccf.org. Office: Cleve Clinic Dept Urology Desk A 100 9500 Euclid Ave Cleveland OH 44195

KLEIN, ESTHER MOYERMAN (MRS. PHILIP KLEIN), author; b. Phila., Nov. 3, 1907; d. Louis and Rebecca (Feldman) Moyerman; m. Philip Klein, Apr. 26, 1930; children: Arthur, Karen Louise Klein Mannes. BS, Temple U., 1929, HHD (hon.), 1980; student, U. London, 1954. Feature writer Pub. Ledger Syndicate, 1928-29, Pub. Ledger, Evening Bull., Phila. Record, 1929-32; editor Art Alliance Bull., 1945-49; commentator Sta. WPEN, 1949-74; del. Internat. Conf. Residential Adult Edn., Holland, 1957, Germany, 1959; participant in first workshop Residential Adult Edn. for Adult Edn. Assn. U.S., 1954. Author: A Guidebook to Jewish Phila., 1965, History and Guidebook of Fairmount Park, 1974. Mem. Gov.'s Commn. on Charitable Orgns., 1969—; organizer Rittenhouse Sq. Women's Com. for Phila. Orch., 1953, bicentennial women's com. Friends Nat. Independence Hist. Park; chmn. bicentennial program Beth Zion - Beth Israel Congregation; bd. dirs. Rittenhouse Found., Univ. City Sci. Ctr.; historian, archivist Walnut St. Theatre; co-founder Long Beach Is. Found. Arts and Scis., N.J.; Named Disting. Dau. Pa.; recipient Gimbel Phila. award, 1975, awards Alumnae Girls High Sch., Phila. Art Alliance, Temple U., City Coun. Phila., Colonial Hist. Soc.; Klein Recital Hall at Temple U., Esther M. Klein Art Gallery named in her honor; Esther M. Klein Way street named in her honor by Mayor Pendell, 1998. Mem. Temple U. Alumni (honored at 80th ann. 1964), Phila. High Sch. for Girls Alumnae. Address: One Rittenhouse Sq Philadelphia PA 19103-5228

KLEIN, FAY MAGID, health administrator; b. Chgo., Jan. 12, 1929; d. Victor and Rose (Begun) Magid; m. Jerome G. Klein, June 27, 1948 (div. 1970); children: Leslie Susan Janik, Debra Lynne Maslov; m. Manuel Chait, Aug. 28, 1994. BA in English, UCLA, 1961; MA in Pub. Adminstrn., U. So. Calif., 1971. Cert. health adminstrn. Supr. social workers Los Angeles County, 1961-65; program specialist Econ. and Youth Opportunity Agy., L.A., 1965-69; sr. health planner Model Cities, L.A., 1971-72; dir. prepaid health plan Westland Health Svcs., L.A., 1972-74; exec. dir. Coastal Region Health Consortium, L.A., 1974-76; grants and legis. cons. Jewish Fed. Council of L.A., 1976-79; planning coun. Jewish Fed. Couns. of So. Fla., Palm Beach to Miami, 1979-82; adminstrv. dir. program in kidney diseases Dept. Medicine UCLA, 1982-84; exec. dir. west coast Israel Cancer Rsch. Fund, L.A., 1984-94; cons. to non-profit orgns. Santa Monica, 1994—; cons. Arthritis Found., L.A., 1984, Bus. Action Ctr., L.A., 1982, Vis. Nurses Assn., L.A., 1982. Charter mem. Los Angeles County Mus. of Art, Mus. of Contemporary Art, L.A.; cons. L.A. Mcpl. Art Gallery, 1979; mem. UCLA/Armand Hammer Mus. Fellow U.S. Pub. Health, U. So. Calif., 1970-71. Mem. Am. Pub. Health, UCLA Alumni Assn. (life), U. So. Calif. Alumni Assn. (life).

KLEIN, FREDA, retired state agency administrator; b. Seattle, May 17, 1920; d. Joseph and Julia (Caplan) Vinikow; m. Jerry Jerome Klein, Oct. 20, 1946; children: Jan Susan Klein Waples, Kerry Joseph, Robin Jo Klein. BA, U. Wash., 1942; MS, U. Nev., Las Vega, 1969, EdD, 1978. Owner, mgr. Smart Shop, Provo, Utah, 1958-60, Small Fry Shop, Las Vegas, 1961-66; vocat. counselor, test adminstr. Nev. Employment Security Dept., Las Vegas, 1966-77, local office mgr., 1978-95; ret., 1995. Contbr. articles to profl. jours.; screenwriter, 1995-98. Exec. bd. Pvt. Industry Coun., Las Vegas, 1988—, Interstate Conf. on Employment Security Agys., Nev., 1988-90, Area Coordinating Com. for Econ. Devel., Las Vegas, 1988—; vol. Ctr. for Bus. and Econ. Rsch., U. Nev., Las Vegas. Recipient Achievement award Nev. Bus. Svc., 1990, Cert. of Spl. Congl. Recognition, 1992; named Outstanding Woman, Goodwill Industries sci. and rsch. divsn., 1977. Mem. AAUW, Internat. Assn. Pers. in Employment Security, U. Nev. Las Vegas Alumni Assn., Henderson C. of C. (exec. bd. 1986—), Soroptimist Internat. (pres. 1987-88), Phi Kappa Phi (scholastic hon.). Avocations: hiking, swimming, writing. Home: 2830 Phoenix St Las Vegas NV 89121-1312

KLEIN, GABRIELLA SONJA, retired communications executive; b. Chgo., Apr. 11, 1938; d. Frank E. Vosicky and Sonja (Kosner) Becvar; m. Donald J. Klein. BA in Comm. and Bus. Mgmt., Alverno Coll., 1983. Editor, owner Fox Lake (Wis.) Rep., 1962-65, McFarland (Wis.) Comty. Life and Monona Cmty. Herald, 1966-69; bur. reporter Waukeshau (Wis.) Daily Freeman, 1969-71; mem. cmty. rels. staff Waukeshau County Tech. Coll., Pewaukee, Wis., 1971-73; pub. rels. specialist JI Case Co., Racine, Wis., 1973-75; corp. publs. editor JI Case Co., Racine, 1975-80; v.p., bd. dirs. publs. Image Mgmt. Valley View Ctr., Milw., 1980-82; pres. Comm. Concepts Unltd., Racine, 1983-98; ret., 1998; mem. comty. com. Racine Unified Sch. Bd. Past pres. Big Bros./Big Sisters Racine County; v.p. devel. Girl Scouts U.S., Racine County; bd. dirs. Racine Comty. Found., Racine County Youth as Resources. Recipient awards Wis. Press Assn., Nat. Fedn. Press Women; named Wis. Woman Entrepreneur of Yr., 1985, Vol. of Yr. Racine Area United Way, 1994, Woman of Distinction Bus., Racine YWCA, 1995. Mem. Internat. Assn. Bus. Communicators (accredited, bd. dirs. 1982-85, various awards), Soc. Profl. Journalists, Ad Club of Racine (silver medal 1998). Home: 3045 Chatham St Racine WI 53402-4001

KLEIN, GAIL BETH MARANTZ, freelance writer, dog breeder; b. Bklyn., Dec. 1, 1946; d. Herbert and Florence (Dresner) Marantz; m. Harvey Leon Klein, Mar. 17, 1979. AB cum laude, U. Miami, Coral Gables, Fla., 1968, MEd, 1969, MBA, 1977. Cert. residential contractor, Fla.; notary pub. Asst. dir. student activities Miami-Dade Community Coll., 1969-79, instr. photography for mentally retarded adults, 1974, acting dir. student activities, 1976, acting advisor student publs., 1979; dog breeder Vizcaya Shepherds, Palm Beach Gardens, Fla., 1979—; trainer Dog Obedience and Conformation Show Handling, West Palm Beach, 1980—; owner, CEO Word Master Profl. Comm.; freelance writer WordMaster Profl. Comms.; mgr. proposal devel., specialist Profl. Food-Svc. Mgmt., Inc., 1994-97; spl. projects-ops., Chartwells, 1997-98; proposal and resource libr. mgmt., proposal writer Wackenhut Corp., Inc., 1998—; cons., speaker in field; appeared on various radio talk shows. Editor (booklet) 1978 Consumers Guide to Banking, 1978, (newsletter) Newsletter of German Shepherd Dog Club Ft. Lauderdale, Inc., 1980-83, Sunshine State Shepherd, 1988-89; contbr. articles to newspapers and mags. Chair spl. events com. Third Century U.S.A., Dade County, Fla., 1976; mem. adv. com., mktg. cons. YWCA of Greater Miami, 1976-79; mem. comty. rels. com. Greater Miami Jewish Fedn., 1976-79; mem. Met. Miami Art Ctr., 1977-79; vice chair, chair appeals bd. Palm Beach County Animal Care and Control, 1989-97, mem. pet overpopulation com., 1991-93; co-developer, co-adminstr. OFA Verifications for German Shepherd Dogs, 1985—; pub. info. coord. Am. Kennel Club, Palm Beach County, 1991-94. Recipient Job Training Partnership Act Employee of Yr. award State of Fla., 1994. Mem. Assn. Proposal Mgmt. Profls., Nat. Assn. Dog Obedience Instrs., Conformation Judges Assn. Fla., Inc., Palm Beach Users Group, Am. Sewing Guild, German Shepherd Dog Club Am., Inc. (hip dysplasia/orthopedic com. 1987-89), German Shepherd Dog Club of Can., Inc., German Shepherd Dog Club of Greater Miami (bd. dirs. 1981-82, 89-94, rec. sec. 1977-78, corr. sec. 1978-80, life), Jupiter-Tequesta Dog Club, Inc. (pres. 1984-85, bd. dirs., various other offices, Gaines Sportsmanship award 1993), Obedience Tng. Club Palm Beach County, Inc. (AKC Cmty. Achievement Merit award 1994), Wolf Song of Alaska (grant/proposal writer), Hadassah (life), Treasure Coast German Shepherd Dog Club (charter), Fla. Freelance Writers Assn., Alpha Lambda Delta, Epsilon Tau Lambda, Phi Kappa Phi, Mortar Board. Republican. Jewish. Avocations: reading, computers, crafts, photography, sewing. Home: 12956 Mallard Creek Dr Palm Beach Gardens FL 33418-8662

KLEIN, GARNER FRANKLIN, cardiologist, internist; b. San Pedro, Calif., June 21, 1933; s. John William and Anna Louise K.; m. Nancy Shank, Aug. 19, 1985; children: Kevin Wayne, Samuel Kyle, Lisa K., Garner F. BA in Biology, North Tex. State U., 1953; MA in Anatomy, U. Tex. Med. Br., Galveston, 1956, MD, 1958. Diplomate Am. Bd. Internal Medicine. Intern U.S. Naval Hosp., Camp Pendleton, Calif., 1958-59; resident in internal medicine VA Hosp./Southwestern Med. Sch., Dallas, 1962-66; cardiologist Valley Diagnostic Clinic, Harlingen, Tex., 1966—; cardiologist Valley Bapt. Med. Ctr., Harlingen, 1966—, chief med. staff, 1994-96; pres. Valley Diagnostic Med. and Surg. Clinic, 1992-96; cons. in cardiology Dolly Vinsant Meml. Hosp., San Benito, Tex., 1966—, South Tex. Hosp., Harlingen, 1966—; med. dir. Harlingen and San Benito Emergency Med. Svc., 1991—, Los Fresnos (Tex.) Emergency Med. Svc., 1992—, Valley Diagnostic Clin., 1996—, Los Fresnos Rural Health Clin., 1996—. Mem. Wesley United Meth. Ch., Harlingen. Lt. comdr. M.C., U.S. Navy, 1958-66. Named Profl. Vol. of Yr., Tex. affiliate Am. Heart Assn., 1983. Fellow ACP, Am. Coll. Cardiology; mem. Tex. Soc. Internal Medicine (Ambassador Leadership award 1998), Am. Heart Assn. (pres. Tex. affil. 1980-81), Cameron-Willacy County Med. Soc. (pres. 1978), Sigma Xi, Alpha Omega Alpha. Avocations: hunting, fishing, gardening. Office: Valley Diagnostic Clin 2200 Haine Dr Harlingen TX 78550-8549

KLEIN, GEORGE D., geologist, executive; b. Den Haag, Netherlands, Jan. 21, 1933; came to U.S., 1947, naturalized, 1955; s. Alfred and Doris (deVries) K.; m. Suyon Chong, Sept. 23, 1994. BA, Wesleyan U., 1954; MA, U. Kans., 1957; PhD, Yale U., 1960. Rsch. sedimentologist Sinclair Research Inc., 1960-61; asst. prof. geology U. Pitts., 1961-63; from asst. prof. to assoc. prof. U. Pa., 1963-69; prof. U. Ill., Urbana, 1970-93, prof. emeritus, 1993—; pres. N.J. Marine Scis. Consortium, Ft. Hancock, N.J., 1993-96; dir. N.J. Sea Grant Coll. program, 1993-96; prin., pres. George D. Klein & Assocs., Matawan, N.J., 1996-98; pres. Klein/Chong, Inc., Matawan, N.J., 1996-98, SED-STRAT Geosci. Cons., Houston, 1998—; vis. fellow Wolfson Coll. Oxford U., 1969; vis. prof. geology U. Calif., Berkeley, 1970; vis. prof. oceanography Oreg. State U., 1974, Seoul Nat. U., 1980, U. Tokyo, 1983; CIC vis. exchange prof. geophys. sci. U. Chgo., 1979-80; vis. prof. geophysics U. Utrecht, 1988; vis. prof. sedimentary geology Vrije U. of Amsterdam, The Netherlands, 1989; chief scientist Deep Sea Drilling Project Leg 58, 1977-78; continuing edn. lectr.; assoc. Ctr. Advanced Studies U. Ill., 1974, 83; co-dir. project Pangea of Global Sedimentary Geology program, 1991-93. Author: Sandstone Depositional Models for Exploration for Fossil Fuels, 3d edit, 1985, Clastic Tidal Facies, 1977, Holocene Tidal Sedimentation, 1976; assoc. editor Geol. Soc. Am. Bull., 1975-81, Jour. Geodynamics, 1992-93; cons. editor: McGraw-Hill Ency. of Sci. and Yearbook, 1977-89; chief cons. adv. editor: CEPCO div. Burgess Pub. Co, 1979-81; series editor: Geol. Sci. Monographs, Internat. Human Resources Devel. Corp. Press, Inc., 1981-87, Sedimentary Geology, Prentice-Hall Inc., 1988—; mem. editorial bd. Geology, 1973-75, 88-91, Sedimentary Geology, 1985-89; mng. editor Sedimentology, Earth Scis. Revs., 1987-92. Bd. dirs. The Jersey Shore Partnership, Inc., 1993-96; commr. N.J. Beach Erosion Commn., 1994-98. Recipient Outstanding Paper award Jour. Sedimentary Petrology, 1970, Erasmus Haworth Disting. Alumnus award in geology, U. Kans., 1980, Citation of Recognition Ill. Ho. Reps.; Sr. Rsch. fellow Japan Soc. for Promotion of Sci., 1983, Sr. Fulbright Rsch. fellow, The Netherlands, 1989; Outstanding Geology Faculty mem. U. Ill. Geology Grad. Student Assn., 1983; grantee NSF, NOAA. Fellow Geol. Soc. Am. (chmn. divsn. sedimentary geology 1985-86); mem. Am. Geophys. Union, Am. Inst. Profl. Geologists, Soc. for Sedimentary Geology, Am. Assn. Petroleum Geologists, Soc. Exploration Geophysicists, Houston Geol. Soc. Home: PO Box 42188 Houston TX 77242-2188 Office: SED-STRAT Geoscience Cons PO Box 41288 Houston TX 77241-1288

KLEIN, GEORGE ROBERT, periodical distribution company executive; b. Washington, Pa., Sept. 28, 1909; s. George Ruttman and Virginia R. (Hickey) K.; m. Mary Elizabeth Fisher, Jan. 28, 1939. BA, Ohio Weslyan U., 1930; BS, MIT, 1932. Pres. George R. Klein News Co., Shaker Heights, Ohio, 1940—. Chmn. bd. trustees Ch. of the Saviour, United Meth., 1960-81; vice chmn., trustee St. Luke's Hosp., 1965—; v.p. bd. mgrs. Cen. YMCA, 1946-71; trustee Christian Residences Found., 1965-77, Goodwill Industries Cleve., 1967-70, Ch. of the Saviour Found., 1962—, N.E. Ohio Conf. Meth. Ch., 1965—, Cleve. Zool. Soc., 1970—, Mus. Arts Assn., 1973—, Play House Found., 1972—, Ohio Weslyan U., 1971—, Univ. Circle Found., 1974—; trustee, pres. Cleve. Play House Theatre; mem. Welfare Fedn. Manpower Commn., 1971-74; pres. Ohio Weslyan U. Assocs., 1960-62; trustee Cleve. Inst. Music, 1987—, Dunham Tavern Mus., 1982—, Ohioana Libr. Assn., 1987-96; mem. Ohio Arts Coun., 1980-85. Served with USN, 1943-46. Mem. Nat. Bur. Ind. Pubs. and Periodical Distbrs. Assn. (past pres.), Mid-Am. Periodical Distbrs. Assn. (past pres.), Mag. Distbrs. Research Project Group (past pres.), Nat. Council Periodical Distbrs. Assn. (past dir.), Ind. Periodical Distbrs. Great Lakes (past pres.), Cleve. Engrng. Soc., Canterbury Golf Club, Skating Club, City Club, Everglades Club (Palm Beach), Rowfant Club, Univ. Club, Union Club, Kiwanis, Sigma Pi Sigma, Pi Mu Epsilon, Omicron Delta Kappa. Home: 23699 Shaker Blvd Cleveland OH 44122-2606

KLEIN, GERHART LEOPOLD, public relations executive; b. Phila., July 24, 1948; s. Joseph G. and Liselotte M. (Peschke) K.; m. Anne Sceia, July 19, 1976. BS cum laude, Temple U., 1970, JD, 1980. Bar: Pa. 1980, N.J. 1980, U.S. Dist. Ct. (ea. dist.) Pa. 1980, U.S. Dist. Ct. N.J. 1980, U.S. Ct. Appeals (3d cir.) 1982, U.S. Supreme Ct. 1985, U.S. Tax Ct. 1985. News anchor WAMS, Wilmington, Del., 1967-68; news anchor, disc jockey WRCP AM & FM, Phila., 1968-70, news dir., 1970; editor, writer, reporter, news anchor WCAU (CBS) Radio, Phila., 1970-72; dir. pub. info., press sec. Pa. Dept. Pub. Welfare, Harrisburg, 1972-73; freelance journalist Phila., 1973-75; asst. editor Focus Mag., Phila., 1974-75; editor, writer, reporter, news anchor KYW Newsradio, Phila., 1975-77; atty. Montgomery, McCracken, Walker & Rhoads, Phila., 1980-85; v.p., gen. mgr. to exec. v.p. Anne Klein & Assocs., Inc., Marlton, N.J., 1985—. Mem. Environ. Commn., Mt. Laurel Twp., N.J., 1988-92; mem. water quality com. Old Taunton Colony Club, 1995—. Recipient Phila. Trial Lawyers Assn. Barrister award, 1980. Mem. Pub. Rels. Soc. Am. (chmn. task force on ethics bd. confidentiality 1991-92, mem. body of knowledge bd. 1994-98, author PR Law Sect. of Accreditation Handbook 1990, Phila. chpt. Pepperpot award 1986, Presdl. citation 1991, 92), Pub. Rels. Soc. Am. Counselors Acad. (chmn. tech. com.), Pub. Rels. Profls. So. N.J. (treas. 1990-92), Soc. Profl. Journalists, Broadcast Pioneers, Pinnacle Worldwide (treas. 1994-96, pres.-elect 1996-98, pres. 1998—). Office: Anne Klein & Assocs Inc 3 Greentree Ctr Ste 200 Marlton NJ 08053-3215

KLEIN, HAROLD PAUL, microbiologist; b. N.Y.C., Apr. 1, 1921; Alexander and Lillyan (Pal) K.; m. Gloria Nancy Dolgov, Nov. 14, 1942; children—Susan Ann, Judith Ellen. B.A., Bklyn. Coll., 1942; Ph.D., U. Calif., Berkeley, 1950. Am. Cancer Soc. fellow Mass. Gen. Hosp., Boston, 1950-51; instr. microbiology U. Wash., Seattle, 1951-54; asst. prof. U. Wash., 1954-55; asst. prof. biology Brandeis U., Waltham, Mass., 1955-56; assoc. prof. Brandeis U., 1956-60, prof., 1960-63, chmn. dept. biology, 1956-63; vis. prof. bacteriology U. Calif., Berkeley, 1960-61; div. chief exobiology, dir. life scis. Ames Research Center, NASA, Mountain View, Calif., 1963-84; scientist-in-residence Santa Clara U., Calif., 1984-95; sr. rsch. scientist SETI Inst., Mountain View, Calif., 1984—; mem. U.S.-USSSR Working Group in Space Biology and Medicine, 1971-84; investigator US/USSR Cosmos 936 flight, 1975, Cosmos 1129 flight, 1979; leader biology team Viking Mars Mission, 1976; mem. space sci. bd. NAS, 1984-89; participating scientist USSR Mars 1996 flight. Mem. editorial bd. Origins of Life, 1970-89. Served with U.S. Army, 1943-46. NSF Sr. Postdoctoral fellow, 1963; grantee NIH, 1955-63; NSF, 1957-63. Mem. Internat. Soc. Study Origin of Life, Am. Soc. Biol. Chemists, Internat. Astronautical Fedn., Phi Beta Kappa. Home: 1022 N California Ave Palo Alto CA 94303-3123 Office: SETI Inst Mountain View CA 94043

KLEIN, HARVEY, physician, educator; b. N.Y.C., Aug. 29, 1937; s. Emanuel and Rose (Sanderman) K.; m. Phyllis Levine, Sept. 22, 1963; children: Laura, Daniel. SB, U. Chgo., 1959; MD, Harvard U., 1963. Diplomate Am. Bd. Internal Medicine. Intern N.Y.-Cornell, N.Y.C., 1963-64, asst. resident, 1964-65, sr. resident, 1967-68, chief resident, 1968-69, fellow in medicine, 1969-70; asst. prof. medicine Cornell U. Med. Coll., N.Y.C., 1970-75, assoc. prof., 1975-88, William S. Paley prof. clin. medicine, 1992—. Capt. USAF, 1965-67. Office: Cornell U Med Coll 525 E 68th St New York NY 10021-4873

KLEIN, HENRY, architect; b. Cham, Germany, Sept. 6, 1920; came to U.S., 1939; s. Fred and Hedwig (Weiskopf) K.; m. Phyllis Harvey, Dec. 27, 1952; children: Vincent, Paul, David. Student, Inst. Rauch, Lausanne, Switzerland, 1936-38; BArch, Cornell U., 1943. Registered architect, Oreg., Wash. Designer Office of Pietro Belluschi, Architect, Portland, Oreg., 1948-51; architect Henry Klein Partnership, Architects, Mt. Vernon, Wash., 1952—. Bd. dirs. Wash. Pks. Found., Seattle, 1977-92, Mus. N.W. Art, 1988-95. With U.S. Army, 1943-46. Recipient Louis Sullivan award Internat. Union Bricklayers and Allied Craftsmen, 1981; Presdl. Design award Nat. Endowment Arts, 1988; George A. and Eliza Howard Found. fellow. Fellow AIA (Seattle chpt. medal 1995). Jewish. Home: 21625 Little Mountain Rd Mount Vernon WA 98274-8311 Office: Henry Klein Partnership 314 Pine St Mount Vernon WA 98273-3852

KLEIN, HERBERT GEORGE, newspaper editor; b. L.A., Apr. 1, 1918; s. George and Amy (Cordes) K.; m. Marjorie Galbraith, Nov. 1, 1941; children: Joanne L. (Mrs. Robert Mayne), Patricia A. (Mrs. John Root). AB, U. So. Calif., 1940; Hon. Doctorate, U. San Diego, 1989. Reporter Alhambra (Calif.) Post-Advocate, 1940-42, news editor, 1946-50; spl. corr. Copley Newspapers, 1946-50, Washington corr., 1950; with San Diego Union, 1950-68, editl. writer, 1950-52, editl. page editor, 1952-56, assoc. editor, 1956-57, exec. editor, 1957-58, editor, 1959-68; mgr. communications Nixon for Pres. Campaign, 1968-69; dir. comm. Exec. Br., U.S. Govt., 1969-73; v.p. corp. rels. Metromedia, Inc., 1973-77; media cons., 1977-80; editor-in-chief, v.p. Copley Newspapers, Inc., San Diego, 1980—; publicity dir. Eisenhower-Nixon campaign in Calif., 1952; asst. press. sec. V.P. Nixon campaign, 1956; press sec. Nixon campaign, 1958; spl. asst., press sec. to Nixon, 1959-61; press sec. Nixon Gov. campaign, 1962; dir. comm. Nixon presdl. campaign, 1968; mem. Advt. Coun., N.Y. Author: Making It Perfectly Clear, 1980. Trustee U. So. Calif.; past chmn. Holiday Bowl; bd. dirs. Clair Burgener Found., Greater San Diego Internat. Sports Coun.; mem. com. Super Bowl XXII and XXXII; chair internat. com. Scripps Health and Sci. Found.; active Olympic Tng. Site Com.; bd. dirs. San Diego Econ. Devel. Com. With USNR, 1942-46; comdr. Res. Recipient Fourth Estate award U. So. Calif., 1947, Alumnus of Yr. award U. So. Calif., 1971, Gen. Alumni Merit award, 1977, Spl. Svc. to Journalism award, 1969, Headliner of Yr. award L.A. Press Club, 1971, San Diego State U. First Fourth Estate award, 1986, Golden Man award Boys and Girls Club, 1994, Newspaper Exec. of Yr. award Calif. Press Assn., 1994; named Community Champion, Hall of Champions, 1993. Mem. Am. Soc. Newspaper Editors (past dir.), Calif. Press Assn., Pub. Rels. Seminar, Gen. Alumni U. So. Calif. (past pres.), Alhambra Jr. C. of C. (past pres.), Greater San Diego C. of C. (mem. exec. com.), Bohemian Club, Fairbanks Country Club, Kiwanis, Rotary (hon.), Sigma Delta Chi (chmn. nat. com., chmn. gen. activities nat. conv. 1958), Scripps Inst. (chair internat com.), Delta Chi. Presbyterian. Home: 5110 Saddlery Sq PO Box 8935 Rancho Santa Fe CA 92067-8935 Office: Copley Press Inc 350 Camino De La Reina San Diego CA 92108-3003 *As I look back on a lifetime in journalism and politics, the thesis which has most effected my career has been a desire to be a thoughtful "man in the arena". To leave a legacy, you cannot be bland. I believe one must develop a philosophy endowed with principle which allows him to take a stand, popular or not, on issues in which he or she believes.*

KLEIN, HOWARD BRUCE, lawyer, law educator; b. Pitts., Pa, Feb. 28, 1950; s. Elmer and Natalie (Rosenzweig) K.; m. Lonnie Jean Wilets, Dec. 12, 1977; children: Zachary B., Eli H. Student, Northwestern U., 1968-69; BA, U. Wis., 1972; JD, Georgetown U., 1976. Bar: Wis. 1976, Pa. 1981, U.S. Ct. Appeals D.C., 1978, U.S. Dist. Ct. Pa. 1981, U.S. Ct. Appeals (3rd cir.) 1982, U.S. Supreme Ct. 1983. Law clk. to justice Robert Hansen Wis. Supreme Ct., Madison, 1976-77; asst. atty. gen. dept. justice State of Wis., 1977-80; chief criminal divsn. U.S. Atty.'s Office, Phila., 1980-87; ptnr. Blank, Rome & McCauley, Phila., 1987-96, chmn. litigation dept., 1991-94; prin. Law Offices of Howard Bruce Klein, Phila., 1996—; dir. in house tng. Am. Law Inst.-ABA, 1996—; regional, nat. instr. Nat. Inst. Trial Advocacy, Phila. and Boulder, Colo., 1987—; lectr. introduction to trial advocacy, evidence Temple U., Phila., 1984—; instr. Atty. Gen. Advocacy Inst., Washington, 1983-87; lectr. pub. corruption and trial advocacy; cons. Pa. Valley Neighborhood Assn., 1984—. Contbr. to profl. jours. Advisor Phila. Police Dept. Reform Commn., 1986—; campaign issues dir. Pa. Atty. Gen. campaign, Phila., 1988, 92; bd. dirs. Citizens Crime Commn. Delaware Valley, Phila. Mem. Fed. Bar Assn. (chmn. criminal law com.), Phila. Bar Assn., Wis. Bar Assn., D.C. Bar Assn., U.S. Attys. Alumni Assn. (co-founder, exec. bd.), Vesper Club (Phila.). Democrat. Jewish. Avocations: swimming, basketball, hiking. Office: 1700 Market St Ste 2632 Philadelphia PA 19103-3903

KLEIN, IRMA MOLLIGAN, career development educator, consultant; b. New Orleans, Jan. 5, 1936; d. Harry Joseph and Gesina Frances (Bauer) Molligan; m. John Vincent Chelena (dec. 1978); 1 child, Joseph William; m. Chris George Klein, Aug. 14, 1965. BS in Bus. Augustine Coll., postgrad. Mktg. Inst., Chgo., Loyola U., Chgo., Realtors Inst., Baton Rouge. Mgr. Stan Weber & Assocs., Metairie, La., 1971-75; tng. dir., 1975-81; cons. Coldwell Banker Comml. Co., New Orleans, 1981; dir. career devel. Coldwell Banker Residential Co., New Orleans, 1982-85; pres. Irma Klein Career Devel., Inc., Les Quarante Ecolieres, 1994-95; pres. Klein Enterprises, Inc., 1994—; instr. U. New Orleans, Bonnabel H.S., Realtors Inst., La. Real Estate Commn. Author: Career Development, 1982; Training Manual, 1978, Obtaining Listings, 1986, Participative Marketing, 1986, Marketing & Servicing Listings, 1987, Designing Training Curriculum, 1987, Participative Management. Active Friends of Longue Vue Gardens, La. Hist. Assn. Meml. Hall Found. Mem. La. Realtors Assn. (bd. dirs. 1973-74, grad. Realtors Inst. 1976), Jefferson Bd. Realtors (v.p. 1984), Edn. and Resources (cert., pres. La. chpt.), Rsch. Club of New Orleans (pres. 1984-85), Realtors Nat. Mktg. Inst. (amb. Tex. and La. 1985—, Outstanding Achievement award 1985, cert. broker 1980, residential specialist 1977), Nat. Assn. Realtors (nat. conv. speaker 1986), CRB (pres. La. chpt. 1982-83, chmn. edn.), CRS (pres. La. chpt. 1988-90), Forty Scholars Soc., Am. Dental Assts. Assn., Les Quarante Ecolieres (pres. 1994-96). Republican. Roman Catholic. Clubs: Antique Study Group, Confederate Lit. (New Orleans) (pres.), Rsch. (New Orleans), Metairie Woman's (sec. 1997-99, pres.-elect 1999—), Odyssey Ho. La.. Avocation: antiques.

KLEIN, IRWIN GRANT, lawyer; b. Bklyn., June 6, 1949; s. Melvin Morton and Gladys (Mandel) K.; m. Charlene Elena Perez, July 31, 1988; children: Robert Matthew Perez, Gabriella Margaux Perez. BS, U. Wis., 1971; JD, Vt. Law Sch., 1977. Bar: N.Y., 1977, U.S. Dist. Ct. (so. & ea. dist.) N.Y., 1977, Vt., 1977, U.S. Supreme Ct., 1988. Assoc. atty. Hein, Waters, Klein & Zurkow, Far Rockaway, N.Y., 1977-78; asst. dist. atty. Queens County Dist. Atty., Kew Gardens, N.Y., 1979-82; ptnr. Hein, Waters & Klein, Cedarhurst, 1982-89, 1991—, Lapp & Klein, Cedarhurst, N.Y., 1989-91. Mem. Vt. Law Rev., N.Y. State Defenders Assn., N.Y. State Bar Assn., Nassau County Bar Assn., Queens County Bar Assn., Phi Delta Phi. Office: Hein Waters & Klein 123 Grove Ave Cedarhurst NY 11516-2302

KLEIN, JEFFREY, editor-in-chief; b. Scranton, Pa., Jan. 15, 1948; s. Harold and Helen (Blum) K.; m. Judith Weinstein, Aug. 9, 1971 (dec. Aug. 1996); children: Jacob, Jonah. BA, Columbia U., 1969; MA, San Francisco State U., 1973. Instr. various colls., 1972-75; editor Mother Jones Mag., San Francisco, 1976-81; editor-in-chief San Francisco Mag., 1981-82; founder, editor San Jose (Calif.) Mercury News West mag., 1983-92; editor-in-chief Mother Jones Mag., San Francisco, 1992—; cons. Parenting Mag., San Francisco, 1984; contbg. editor Calif. Mag., L.A., 1980s. Author: The Black Hole Affair, 1991; contbr. articles to profl. jours. Office: Mother Jones Mag 731 Market St Ste 600 San Francisco CA 94103-2027*

KLEIN, JEFFREY HOWARD, oncologist, internist; b. Cleve., Jan. 24, 1943; s. Joseph Bart and Tillie Alice Klein; m. Nancy Klein, June 5, 1971; 1 child, Bart Edward. BS in Medicine, Northwestern U., 1966, MD, 1968. Diplomate Am. Bd. Internal Medicine, Am. Bd. Med. Oncology. Intern Cleve. Met. Gen. Hosp., 1968-69, resident, 1969-70; resident Rush-Presbyn. St. Luke's Med. Ctr., Chgo., 1970-71, Am. Cancer Soc. clin. fellow, 1971-72; pvt. practice internist, oncologist Lombard Med. Group, Thousand Oaks, Calif., 1974—; also bd. dirs. Lombard Med. Group, Thousand Oaks; chief of medicine Los Robles Regional Med. Ctr., Thousand Oaks, 1976-77, chief of staff, 1979-81; trustee Columbia/Los Robles Med. Ctr., Thousand Oaks, 1995-98. Maj. USAF, 1972-74. Mem. Am. Soc. Clin. Oncology, So. Calif. Acad. Clin. Oncology (charter), Phi Beta Kappa, Pi Kappa Epsilon, Alpha Omega Alpha. Avocations: philosophy, tennis, skiing, music. Office: Lombard Med Group Inc 2230 Lynn Rd Thousand Oaks CA 91360-1901

KLEIN, JEFFREY PETER, advertising agency executive; b. N.Y.C., June 29, 1943; s. Seymour M. and Ruth (Liberman) K. B.A., Colgate U., 1965; M.B.A., Columbia U., 1967. Exec., Mr. Ephram, Inc., N.Y.C., 1967-69; account exec. Thomson-Leeds Co., 1969-79; officer M.K.B. Group, Inc., N.Y.C., 1979—. Trustee, com. chmn. Collegiate Sch., N.Y.C., 1976-85, 91-98, pres. bd. trustees 1994-98; bd. dirs., com. chmn. 92nd Street YMHA, 1980—; pres. Bertha & Isaac Liberman Found., 1983—; chmn. bd. dirs. N.Y. Chamber Symphony, 1993—; mem. Point-of-Purchase Advt. Inst., Inc. Mem. Contemporary Arts Coun., Architecture and Design Com., Conservation Com., Mus. Modern Art. Clubs: Sunningdale Country (bd. dirs. 1980-

85) (Scarsdale, N.Y.); Harmonie, Colgate (N.Y.C.). Avocations: golfing, photography, travel, reading. Home: 480 Park Ave New York NY 10022-1613 Office: MKB Group Inc 200 Park Ave S 1018 New York NY 10003-2332

KLEIN, JEFFREY S., lawyer, media executive; b. Los Angeles, Apr. 15, 1953; s. Norman and Shirlee Klein; m. Karyn Kitson, Sept. 29, 1984; 3 children. BA suma cum laude, Claremont Mens Coll., 1975; M in Journalism, Columbia U., 1978; JD, Stanford U., 1980. Assoc. Kaplan, Livingston, Goodwin, Berkowitz & Selvin, Beverly Hills, Calif., 1980-81, Garey, Mason & Sloane, Santa Monica, Calif., 1981-83; weekly contbr. UPI-Radio, L.A., 1983-84; sr. staff counsel Times Mirror, 1983-87, asst. to pres., 1987-90; asst. to pub. L.A. Times, 1989-91; pres. L.A. Times Valley and Ventura County edits., 1991-96; v.p. L.A. Times, 1991-96, sr. v.p. consumer mktg., 1996-97, sr. v.p., gen. mgr. news, 1997—; pres., CEO Calif. Cmty. News Corp., 1995-97; adj. prof. journalism U. So. Calif., 1985-87; adv. Gov. Bruce Babbitt, Phoenix, 1980. Author weekly column Legal View, L.A. Times, 1985-93, various book revs. Bd. dirs. Found. for Am. Commn., Gould Ctr. for Humanities, Claremont McKenna Coll. Recipient Angel award Vol. League of San Fernando Valley, Disting. Cmty. Svc. award Anti-Defamation League, 1994, Visionary award United Way North Angeles Region, 1995, Premiere Parents award March of Dimes, 1996. Mem. Calif. Bar Assn. Office: LA Times Times Mirror Square Los Angeles CA 90053

KLEIN, JEROME OSIAS, pediatrician, educator; b. N.Y.C., Feb. 10, 1931; s. Max N. and Elizabeth (Schlanger) K.; m. Linda Sue Breskin,June 19, 1955; children: Andrea, Bennett, Adam. AB, Union Coll., 1952; MD, Yale U., 1956. Diplomate Am. Bd. Pediatrics. Intern U. Minn. Hosps., Mpls., 1956-67; residnt in pediatrics Boston City Hosp., 1959-61, assoc. dir. pediatrics, 1967-72, dir. pediatric infectious diseases, 1973-96; vice chmn. acad. affairs dept. pediats. Boston Med. Ctr., 1996—; assoc. prof. pediatrics Harvard U. Med. Sch., Boston, 1967-74; prof. Boston U. Sch. Medicine, 1974; lectr. Harvard U. Med. Sch., Boston, 1974—; cons. dept. pediats. Mass. Gen. Hosp., 1970-74; cons. adv. com. on vaccines and biologics, FDA, 1983-85. Author/editor: (with J.S. Remington) Infectious Diseases of the Fetus and Newborn Infant, 1976, 4th edit., 1995; author: (with C.C. Bluestone) Otitis Media in Infants and Children, 1987, 2d edit., 1995; editor: Report of the Committee on Infectious Diseases, Am. Acad. Pediats., 19th edit.; assoc. editor Revs. of Infectious Diseases, 1978-89, Pediat. Infectious Diseases Jour., 1982-92; contbr. numerous articles on rsch. in infectious diseases of children to profl. jours. Asst. surgeon, USPHS, 1957-59. Peabody fellow, Harvard U., 1963-64; grantee Nat. Inst. Allergy and Infectious Diseases. Mem. Am. Acad. Pediats. (com. on infectious diseases 1974-82), Infectious Diseases Soc. Am. (councillor 1980-83, treas. 1987-92, disting. physician award 1995, Bristol award 1995), Phi Beta Kappa, Alpha Omega Alpha. Office: Boston Medical Center Maxwell Finland Lab Infectious Diseases Boston MA 02118

KLEIN, JERRY EMANUEL, insurance and financial planning executive; b. Cin., Apr. 4, 1933; s. Milton H. and Ida S. (Dunsker) K.; m. Arlene Ruth Rosen, July 3, 1957 (dec. Nov. 1974); children: Marjorie, Bradley, Amy; m. Nancy Cohen Han, Aug. 7, 1982. BMech. Engring., Cornell U., 1956; MBA, Ohio State U., 1959. CLU, ChFC. Fin. engring. Avco Electronics, Cin., 1959-61; spl. agt. Northwestern Mut. Life of Milw., Cin., 1961—. Vice chmn. Am. Jewish Com., 1978; pres. Social Health Assn., 1964-66, Jewish Vocat. Svc., 1978-80, Cancer Family Care, 1981-83; chmn. fin. com. Jewish Fedn., 1981-83, treas., mem. exec. com., 1981-84; bd. dirs. Children Psychiat. Ctr., 1973-86, Jewish Family Svc., 1984-94, Jewish Vocat. Svc., 1964-92, Cin. Jewish Fedn., 1972-92, Halom House, 1992, treas., 1998—; chmn. NILB Scholarship Com., 1985—; bd. dirs. Cin. Radio Reading Svc., 1997; bd. dirs. Cin. Assn. Blind, 1999—. 1st lt. USAF, 1956-58. Recipient Kate S. Mack award Jewish Fedn., 1975, Human Rels. award NCCJ, 1992. Mem. Million Dollar Round Table (life), Nat. Assn. Life Underwriters, Estate Planning Coun. Cin., Assn. CLUs. Jewish. Office: Northwestern Mut Life 312 Walnut St Ste 2200 Cincinnati OH 45202-4029

KLEIN, JERRY LEE, SR., religion educator, minister; b. Walters, Okla., Oct. 25, 1947; s. Rudolf Anton and Mable Eula (Elliott) K.; m. Jane Ellen Keeth, Apr. 20, 1969; children: Jerry, Jr., John. AA, Cameron U., 1967; BA, Okla. Christian Univ. of Sci. and Arts, 1969; MA, Harding U., 1974; postgrad., N.Y. Inst., 1988-91. Instr. Bible, Henderson State Coll., Arkadelphia, Ark., 1970-71; pulpit min. Ch. of Christ, Comanche, Okla., 1971-75; instr. Greek Prairie Hill Sch. of Bible, Comanche, 1974-75; pulpit minister Main St. Ch. of Christ, Lockney, Tex., 1975-82; prof. religion Amarillo (Tex.) Coll., 1982-95, instr. part-time, 1995—; dir. Amarillo Bible Chair, 1982-94; min. Comanche Trail Ch. of Christ, Amarillo, 1995—; tchr. Bible, Caprock H.S., Amarillo, 1995-96; edn. dir. Mountain Terrace Ch. of Christ, Memphis, Tenn., 1969-70, San Jacinto Ch. of Christ, Amarillo, 1984-89; campus coun. Amarillo Coll., 1982-94, chaplain, 1990-91; steering com. Amazing Grace Campaign, Amarillo, 1990. Author: Training Leaders for Christ I, 1998, Training Leaders for Christ II, 1998, True Worship, 1989, (children's songs) Bible Teachers Mailbox, 1988; contbr. articles to religious jours. Dir. vols. Ark. Children's Colony, Arkadelphia, 1970-71; bd. dirs. VICA, Tascosa H.S., 1983-94; city chmn. Heart Fund and Kidney Found., Comanche, 1974-75; cubmaster Boy Scouts Am., Lockney, 1978-82; coach Little League Baseball, Lockney, 1978-82; mem. child welfare bd., Floyd County, Tex., 1980-82. Recipient spl. citation Ark. Children's Colony, 1971, certs. appreciation Tex. Dept. Health, 1982, Tex. Dept. Human Resources, 1983; named Favorite Prof. Bapt. Student Union, Amarillo Coll., 1989, 93. Mem. Soc. Bibl. Lit., Am. Acad. Religion, Lions (pres. Comanche 1974-75), Rotary, Kappa Chi (sponsor 1982-95). Republican. Home: 5614 Purdue St Amarillo TX 79109-5823 Office: Comanche Trail Ch of Christ 2700 E 34th Ave Amarillo TX 79103-4700 *Life itself can't give me joy—unless I really will it. Life just gives me time and space—it's up to me to fill it.*

KLEIN, JIM, company executive. Pres. Oakwood Corp. Housing, L.A., 1996—. Office: Oakwood Corp Housing 2222 Corinth Ave Los Angeles CA 90064

KLEIN, JOAN DEMPSEY, judge; b. San Jose, Calif., Aug. 18, 1924; d. Edward Joseph and Estelle (Kottinger) Dempsey; m. Donrad Lee Klein, Mar. 16, 1963; children: Marc Dempsey Gross, Brad Hunter Gross; stepchildren: Karen Beth , Susan Linda. BA, San Diego State Coll., 1948; LLB, UCLA, 1955. Bar: Calif. 1955, U.S. Supreme Ct. 1964. Dep. atty gen., trial lawyer State of Calif., 1955-63; judge L.A. Mcpl. Ct., 1963-75, presiding judge, 1974; mem. L.A. Superior Ct., 1974-78; presiding justice Calif. Ct. Appeals, L.A., 1978—; prof. jud. adminstrn. U. So. Calif. 1974-75; mem. Calif. Coun. on Criminal Justice, 1970-74, Jud. Criminal Justice Planning Com., 1974-76; del. Nat. Adv. Commn. Criminal Justice Standards and Goals, Washington, 1973; chmn. adv. com. Calif. Hwy. Patrol, 1976; participant S. Am. Lecture Tour Internat. Communication Agy. Mem. adv. bd. Girls Week L.A. City Schs., Gifted Children's Assn., San Fernando Valley, Vol. League San Fernando Valley. Named Alumna of Yr. Law Sch. UCLA, 1963, Angel of Distinction L.A. Cen. City Assn., 1969, Woman of Achievement Calif. Fedn. Bus. and Profl. Women's Club, 1973, Mcpl. Ct. Judge of Yr. Calif. Trial Lawyers, 1973, Woman of Yr. L.A. Times, 1975; recipient Profl. Achievement award UCLA Alumni Assn., 1975, Myrtle Wreath award Hadassah, 1977, Community Woman of Achievement award Big Sisters L.A., 1979, cert. merit from Gov. Brown, 1979, Portrait in Excellence award B'nai Brith Women, Woman of the Yr. award Met. News, 1992, Woman of Vision award Valley Presbyn. Hosp., 1991. Mem. Internat. Fedn. Women Lawyers, Nat. Assn. Women Judges (founding and current pres.), Calif. Women Lawyers (pres. 1975), Calif. Judges Assn., L.A. County Bar Assn., Women Lawyers Assn., Bus. and Profl. Women's Club. (L.A. chpt.), Legion Lex. U. Soc. Calif., UCLA Law Sch. Alumni Assn. (past pres.). Democrat. Office: Ct Appeals 300 S Spring St Los Angeles CA 90013-1230

KLEIN, JOSEPH MARK, retired mining company executive; b. N.Y.C., Nov. 9, 1921; s. Erwin Wolffe and Ada (Black) K.; m. Betty Evelyn Northington, Dec. 24, 1948; children: Kathryn Ann, Elizabeth Ellen, Joseph Mark, Jr., Timothy Northington. Certificate in fgn. trade, Am. Grad Sch. Internat. Mgmt., 1947; D Internat Laws (hon.), Am. Grad. Sch. Internat. Mgmt., 1993. Vice pres. internat. ops. Clary Corp., San Gabriel, Calif., 1948-60; dir. Clary Corp., 1967-70; dir. internat. ops. Remington Rand Corp., N.Y.C., 1961-62; pres. NBC Internat. Ltd.; v.p. NBC News, N.Y.C., 1962-66; exec. v.p., dir. Cyprus Mines Corp., Los Angeles, 1966-79; chmn. bd. Hawaiian Cement Corp., 1969-79; ret. pres., dir. Pluess-Staufer Industries, Inc., Los Angeles, 1979-91, sr. fin. cons., bd. dirs., 1991—; dir. Mission Ins. Group, Inc.; mem. Pres.'s Export Expansion Council, 1971-74; Vice-chmn. bd. trustees Am. Grad. Sch. Internat. Mgmt., 1975-83, chmn. bd. trustees, 1983-88. Served to capt. U.S. Army, 1940-46. Decorated Silver Star, Bronze Star, Purple Heart, Croix de Guerre; recipient Jonas B. Mayer Outstanding Alumni Assn. award Am. Grad. Sch. Internat. Mgmt., 1974, So. Calif. Alumni Assn. award, 1974. Mem. AIME, Ret. Officers Assn. (pres. dir. west L.A. area chpt.), Town Hall, Mil. Order Purple Heart (comdr. Ariz. 1949-50, Hollywood chpt. 1987-88), Am. Legion (state post comdr. 1990-91, svc. officer 1991—), Riviera Country Club, Elks. Republican. Presbyterian. Home: 1071 Villa View Dr Pacific Palisades CA 90272-3949

KLEIN, JOSEPH MICHELMAN, musical director; b. Sharon, Mass., July 16, 1936; s. Henry H. and Esther (Michelman) K.; m. Mary A. Morford, May 1, 1964; children: Christopher, Michael, Joshua. Grad. pvt. studies, Tanglewood, Mass., 1957; BA, Columbia U., 1958; studies with Nadia Boulanger, Paris, 1959-60. Formerly chmn. music dept. Horace Mann Sch., N.Y.C.; dir. Columbia U. Bands, N.Y.C., 1984-86; prof. music theatre Syracuse U., 1986-89; music faculty Trinity Sch., N.Y.C., 1984-86. Arranger-pianist CBS radio and TV; music coach Bing Crosby Family, Hollywood Palace TV Show; musical dir. Seagram Liquor, McDonald's Hamburgers, Toyota, indsls.; arrived in Calif. star-sys. theatres including Ben Kapen's Melodyland, Hyatt Music Theatre, Circle Star Theatre, Carousel Theatre, also L.A. Civic Light Opera; musical dir. nat. co. Man of La Mancha, 1967-70; condr. (Broadway prodns.) Johnny Johnson, 1971, Lost in the Stars, 1972, Man of La Mancha, 1972, Cyrano, 1974, Sacramento Music Circus, 1975-80, Pippin, 1977, On the Twentieth Century, 1979, Jones Beach, 1981; musical dir. Radio City Music Hall, N.Y.C., 1982-85, A Chorus Line, Nat. Tour, 1989-93, Radio City Music Hall Spectacular Nat. Tour, 1993-95, A Chorus Line European Tour, 1995-96, I Do! I Do! (with Donna McKechnie), Queen's Theatre, N.Y.C., 1997. Mem. NARAS, Am. Fedn. Musicans, Actors Equity, Soc. Stage Dirs. and Choreographers. Home: 28 W 87th St New York NY 10024-3534

KLEIN, JUDAH B., retired lawyer; b. Bklyn., Feb. 9, 1923; s. Kolman Karl and Gladys Ruth (Edelson)) K.; m. Paula Berk, Nov. 8, 1953; 1 child, Caryn Ann. BS, U. Md., 1947; LLB, Bklyn. Law Sch., 1950. Bar: N.Y. 1951, U.S. Dist. Ct. (so. and ea. dists.) N.Y. Ptnr. Klein & Klein, N.Y.C., 1952-58; gen. counsel Paragon Industries Inc., Mineola, N.Y., 1959-70; pvt. practice, 1970-71; asst. chief counsel, sr. v.p. The Title Guarantee Co., N.Y.C., 1972-79; v.p., gen. counsel LTIC Assoc., Inc., N.Y.C., 1979-93; ret., 1993; lawyer; b. Bklyn., Feb. 9, 1923; s. Kolman Karl and Gladys Ruth (Edelson) K.; m. Paula Berk, Nov. 8, 1953; 1 dau., Caryn Ann. B.S., U. Md., 1947; LL.B., Bklyn. Law Sch., 1950. Bar: N.Y. 1951, U.S. Dist. Ct. (so. and ea. dists.) N.Y. Ptnr. Klein & Klein, N.Y.C., 1952-58; gen. counsel Paragon Industries Inc., Mineola, N.Y., 1959-70; sole practice, 1970-71; asst. chief counsel, sr. v.p. The Title Guarantee Co., N.Y.C., 1972-79; v.p., gen. counsel LTIC Assoc., Inc., N.Y.C., 1979—, ret. Served to 1st lt. U.S. Army, 1943-46, 51-52. Mem. ABA, Assn. Bar City of N.Y., Nassau County Bar Assn., Am. Coll. Real Estate Lawyers, N.Y. State Bar Assn. Jewish. Club: Masons. 1st lt. U.S. Army, 1943-46, 51-52. Mem. ABA, Assn. Bar City N.Y., Nassau County Bar Assn., Am. Coll. Real Estate Lawyers, N.Y. State Bar Assn., Masons. Jewish.

KLEIN, JULIA MEREDITH, newspaper reporter; b. Phila., Dec. 11, 1955; d. Abraham and Murielle (Pollack) K. BA magna cum laude, Harvard U., 1977. Copy editor J.B. Lippincott, Phila., 1977; features reporter The Oakland Press, Pontiac, Mich., 1978; freelance writer, researcher, editorial cons., 1978—; reporter The Phila. Inquirer, 1983—. Nat. Arts Journalism Program fellow, 1996-97, John J. McCloy fellow in journalism, 1998. Mem. Soc. Profl. Journalists, Phi Beta Kappa. Home: 307 Monroe St Philadelphia PA 19147-3211 Office: Phila Inquirer 400 N Broad St PO Box 8263 Philadelphia PA 19101-8263

KLEIN, KAREN K., federal judge. Magistrate judge U.S. Dist. Ct. N.D., Fargo. Fax: 701-239-5270. Office: 655 First Ave N Fargo ND 58102

KLEIN, KENNETH, orchestra conductor, educator; b. L.A., Sept. 5, 1939; s. Samuel Raymond and Hildegarde (Shire) K.; m. Leslie Marie Jaen, Apr. 30, 1978; 1 child, David Stewart Alan. MusB, U. So. Calif., 1963; studied with Nadia Boulanger, Paris, 1966-67; studied with Fritz Zweig, L.A., 1959-77; studied with R. Lert, Am. Symphony Orch. League Inst., 1963, 64; studied with Izler Solomon, Aspen Music Festival, 1961; studied with Friedelind Wagner, Bayreuth Festival, Germany, 1966. Music dir. Guadalajara (Jalisco, Mex.) Symphony Orch., 1967-78, Nassau Symphony, Garden City, L.I., 1980-86, Waterville Valley (N.H.) Festival, 1985, 86, Santa Cruz (Calif.) Symphony, 1981-85, S.D. Symphony, Sioux Falls, 1983-89, N.Y. Virtuosi Chamber Symphony, N.Y.C., 1982—; guest condr. London Symphony Orch., London Philharmonic, Royal Philharmonic, Philharmonia Orch., Orch. Nat. de France, Suisse Romande, Vienna Symphony, Casals Festival, Montreux Festival, Moscow Philharmonic and P.R. Symphony, Nat. Symphony Mex., Bolshoi Ballet, Stuttgart Ballet, N.Y.C. Ballet. Condr. (recordings) Music From Mex., 1979, 93, Serenade to Music, 1987, Skyscrapers, 1987 (Fanfare Mag. Want List 1988), Mozart Album, 1990, Copland: Orch. Works, 1990, Violin Album: Glazunon Tchakovski, 1990, Morton Gould Am. Salute, 1991, Ravel, Saint-Saens, Sierra Album, 1994; recordings for EMI/ANGEL, Vox, ASV, Unicorn-Kanchana, Collins Classics, Pickwick, Ribbonwood, Albany Records; apptd. chamber orch. Sylvia and Deany Kaye Playhouse, 1998; debut Vienna's Musikverein, 1997-98. Recipient 1st prize Coleman Chamber Music Soc., 1963, Gold medal Mex. Am. Inst., 1978, Venturesome Programming award ASCAP, 1984, 85. Mem. Am. Symphony Orch. League, Conductor's Guild. Avocation: tennis. Office: Jeffrey James Arts Consulting 316 Pacific St Massapequa Park NY 11762-1807*

KLEIN, LAWRENCE ALLEN, accounting educator; b. Harrisburg, Pa., Jan. 14, 1946; s. Samuel Edward and Ella Violet (Loeb) K. AB, Franklin and Marshall Coll., 1969; MBA, Pa. State U., 1974, PHD, 1978. Adminstrv. asst. dept. acctg. and mgmt. info. systems Pa. State U., State College, 1975-76; asst. prof. acctg. U. Houston, 1978-79, U. Wyo., Laramie, 1982-84; asst. prof. bus. adminstrn. Franklin & Marshall Coll., Lancaster, Pa., 1979-82; assoc. prof. accountancy Bentley Coll., Waltham, Mass., 1984—; vis. prof. econ. and mgmt. Vesalius Coll., Brussels, 1996; presenter in field. Author study guides for books in field; co-editor conf. procs., 1976. Program/conf. coord. N.E. Am. Acctg. Assn., State College, 1976; mem. small bus. coun. Laramie Area C. of C., 1973-74. With USAF, 1969-70. Grantee Am. Acctg. Assn., Hasking & Sells Found. Mem. AAUP, NRA (life), AARP, Nat. Retired Tchrs. Assn., Inst. Mgmt. Accts. (I. Wayne Keller award, Ray E. Longnecker award 1980, Cert. Merit Manuscript award), Am. Acctg. Assn. (Sectional Best Paper award 1987), Inst. Internal Auditors, Decision Scis. Inst. (chmn. acctg. track N.E. sect. 1992), Mass. Soc. CPAs (acad. assoc.), Fin. Execs. Inst., Assn. for Pvt. Enterprise Edn., Am. Legion (life), Am. Inst. Physics, U.S. Golf Assn., U.S. Tennis Assn. (life), Elks (permanent benefactor), Marine Meml. Club (perpetual benefactor), Jewish War Vets. (life), Beta Gamma Sigma, Beta Alpha Psi, Omicron Delta Kappa. Democrat. Jewish. Avocations: tennis, golf, reading. Home: 76C Charlesbank Way # C Waltham MA 02453-2512

KLEIN, LAWRENCE ROBERT, economist, educator; b. Omaha, Sept. 14, 1920; s. Leo Byron and Blanche (Monheit) K.; m. Sonia Adelson, Feb. 15, 1947; children: Hannah, Rebecca, Rachel, Jonathan. B.A., U. Calif.-Berkeley, 1942; Ph.D., MIT, 1944; M.A., Lincoln Coll., Oxford U., 1957; LL.D. (hon.), U. Mich., 1977, Dickinson Coll., 1981; Sc.D. (hon.), Widener Coll., 1977, Elizabethtown Coll., 1981, Ball State U., 1982, Technion, 1982, U. Nebr., 1983; Dr. honoris causa, U. Vienna, 1977; Dr.Ed., Villanova U., 1978; Dr. (h.c.), Bonn U., 1974, Free U. Brussels, 1979, U. Paris, 1979, U. Madrid, 1980. Faculty U. Chgo., 1944-47; research assoc. Nat. Bur. Econ. Research, 1948-50; faculty U. Mich., 1949-54; research assoc. Survey Research Center, 1949-54, Oxford Inst. Stats., 1954-58; faculty U. Pa., Phila., 1958—, prof., 1958—, Univ. prof., 1964—, Benjamin Franklin prof., 1968—; now prof. econs. and emeritus U. Pa.; vis. prof. Osaka U., Japan, 1960, U. Colo., 1962, CUNY, 1962-63, 82, Hebrew U., 1964, Princeton U., 1966, Stanford U., summer 1968, U. Copenhagen, 1974; Ford vis. prof. U. Calif. at Berkeley, 1968, Inst. for Advanced Studies, Vienna, 1970, 74; cons. Canadian Govt., 1947, UNCTAD, 1966, 67, 75, 77, 80, McMillan Co., 1965-74, E.I. du Pont de Nemours, 1966-68, State of N.Y., 1969, AT&T, 1969, Fed. Res. Bd., 1973, UNIDO, 1973-75, Congl. Budget Office, 1977—, Council Econ. Advisers, 1977-80; chmn. bd. trustees Wharton Econometric Forecasting Assocs., Inc., 1969-80, chmn. profl. bd., 1980—; trustee Maurice Falk Inst. for Econ. Research, Israel, 1969-75; adv. council Inst. Advanced Studies, Vienna, 1977—; chmn. econ. adv. com. Gov. of Pa., 1976-78; mem. com. on prices Fed. Res. Bd., 1968-70; prin. investigator econometric model project Brookings Instn., 1963-72, Project LINK, 1968—; sr. adviser Brookings Panel on Econ. Activity, 1970—; mem. adv. com. Inst. Internat. Econs., 1983; coordinator Jimmy Carter's Econ. Task Force, 1976; mem. adv. bd. Strategic Studies Center, Stanford Research Inst., 1974-76. Author: The Keynesian Revolution, 1947, Textbook of Econometrics, 1953, An Econometric Model of the United States, 1929-1952, 1955, Wharton Econometric Forecasting Model, 1967, Essay on the Theory of Economic Prediction, 1968, An Introduction to Econometric Forecasting and Forecasting Models, 1980; Author-editor: Brookings Quar. Econometric Model of U.S.; Ecometric Model Performance, 1976, Lectures in Econometrics, 1983; Editor: Internat. Econ. Rev, 1959-65; asso. editor, 1965—; Editorial bd.: Empirical Econs, 1976—. Recipient William F. Butler award N.Y. Assn. Bus. Economists, 1975; Golden Slipper Club award, 1977; Pres.'s medal U. Pa., 1980; Alfred Nobel Meml. prize in econs., 1980. Fellow Econometric Soc. (past pres.), Am. Acad. Arts and Scis., Nat. Assn. Bus. Economists; mem. Am. Philos. Soc., Nat. Acad. Scis., Social Sci. Rsch. Coun. (fellow 1945-46, 47-48, com. econ. stability, dir. 1971-76), Am. Econ. Assn. (John Bates Clark medalist 1959, exec. com. 1966-68, pres. 1977), Eastern Econ. Assn. (pres. 1974-76). Office: U Pa Mc Neil Bldg Rm 335 3718 Locust Walk Philadelphia PA 19104-6209*

KLEIN, LINDA ANN, lawyer; b. N.Y.C., Nov. 7, 1959; d. Gerald Ira Klein and Sandra Florence (Kimmel) Fishman; m. Michael S. Neuren, Sept. 23, 1985. BA cum laude, Union Coll., 1980; JD, Washington & Lee U., 1983. Bar: Ga. 1983, D.C. 1984, U.S. Dist. Ct. (no. and mid. dist.) Ga. 1985, U.S. Ct. Appeals (11th cir.) 1986. Assoc. Nall & Miller, Atlanta, 1983-86, Martin, Cavan & Andersen, Atlanta, 1986-90; ptnr. Martin, Cavan & Andersen, 1990-93, Gambrell & Stolz, 1993—; instr. Nat. Ctr. Paralegal Tng., Atlanta, 1986. Mem. ABA (editor Trial Techniques newsletter 1989, vice-chmn. trial techniques com. 1989-90, chair 1991-92, vice chair fidelity and surety com. 1994-97, mem. coun. tort and ins. practice sect. 1998—, chair ann. meeting 1996-97, ho. of dels. 1998—, exec. coun. nat. conf. of bar pres. 1998—), State Bar of Ga. (vice chair profl. liability com., chair study com. on rules of practice 1987—, bd. govs. 1989—, mem. exec. com. 1992—, sec. 1994-96, pres. 1997-98), Nat. Conf. Bar Pres. (exec. coun. 1998—), Inst. for CLE (chair Ga. br. 1998—), Atlanta Bar Assn. (bd. dirs. Atlanta Coun. on Young Lawyers 1986-89, chair commn. on uniform rules of ct. 1986), Coun. of Superior Cts. Judges (ex-officio uniform rules com.), Phi Alpha Delta, Pi Sigma Alpha.

KLEIN, LUELLA VOOGD, obstetrics-gynecology educator; b. Walker, Iowa, Oct. 24, 1924; d. Elmer DeWitt and Leah (Stunkard) Bare; m. Alfred O. Colquitt. BA, U. Iowa, 1947, MD, 1949. Diplomate Am. Bd. Ob-Gyn (gen. bd. dirs., bd. dirs. div. maternal-fetal medicine). Intern Western Res. U., Cleve., 1949-50; resident in medicine, surgery and ob-gyn Cleve. City Hosp., 1950-55; U.S. Sr. Fulbright Rsch. scholar U. London Postgrad. Med. Sch., 1955-57; obstetric cons. Ga. Dept. Pub. Health, Atlanta, 1958-60; pvt. practice Atlanta, 1960-65; asst. dir. clin. rsch. Bristol Labs., Syracuse, N.Y., 1965-67; prof., dir. maternal and infant care project Emory U. Grady Meml. Hosp., Atlanta, 1967—; co-dir. Regional Perinatal Ctr., Charles Howard Candler prof., chmn. dept. ob-gyn Emory U. Sch. Medicine, Atlanta, 1986-93; bd. dirs. Alan Guttmacher Inst., N.Y.C., chmn., vice-chmn.; Maternal and Child Health Care governing coun. Am. Hosp. Assn., Chgo.; chmn. FDA Ob-Gyn Device Com., Washington, 1986-88. Recipient Elizabeth Blackwell award Am. Women's Med. Assn., 1986, Atlanta Woman History Maker award Am. Women's Assn., 1987, Daggett Harvey award Chgo. Maternity Ctr., Northwestern U., 1991, 40th Anniversary award FIGO, 1994. Fellow Am. Coll. Obstetricians and Gynecologists (pres., v.p., asst. sec. 1982-85, Disting. Svc. award 1994); mem. AMA, Ga. Obstet. and Gynecol. Soc. (pres.), Atlanta Obstet. and Gynecol. Soc. (pres.), Med. Assn. Ga. (chair maternal and child health care com.), Inst. Medicine, Marietta Country Club (Marietta, Ga.). Office: Grady Meml Hosp Dept Gyn/Ob 69 Butler St SE Atlanta GA 30303-3033*

KLEIN, LYNN ELLEN, artist; b. San Francisco, Apr. 14, 1950. BA in Studio Arts, U. Minn., 1974, MFA in Design, 1976. Instr. art edn. U. Minn., Mpls., 1976-78, lectr. in design, 1974-84; vis. artist U. Iowa, Ames, 1984—; resident Cité Internat. des Arts, Paris, summer 1998. One woman shows include Rochester (Minn.) Fine Arts Ctr., 1976, Northrup Gallery, U. Minn., Mpls., 1976, Allrich Gallery, San Francisco, 1982, 88, Coffman Gallery, U. Minn., 1982, The Print Club, Phila., 1985, Foster-White Gallery, Seattle, 1989, Carolyn Ruff Gallery, Mpls., 1994; exhibited in group shows Mpls. Inst. of Arts, Minn. Artist Exhbn. Program, 1976, Franklin Inst. of Sci. Mus., Phila., 1984, Franklin Inst. Sci. Mus. Lensless Photo, 1984, Photo Influences on Other Media Minn. Mus. Art, St. Paul, 1990, Textile Arts Internat., 1990, San Francisco Bay Area Women Artists Mentors, San Francisco, 1994, USART San Francisco Internat. Art Expo, I. Wolk Gallery, St. Helena, Calif., 1996, Robert Green Fine Arts, Mill Valley, Calif., 1996, Craftsman's Guild and Calif. Heritage Gallery, 1998, Ren Brown Collection, Bodega Bay, Calif., 1998, Gensler Architecture-Material Matters, San Francisco, 1998; represented in permanent collections Mpls. Inst. of Arts, Oakland (Calif.) Mus., Bibliotéque Nationale, Dept. des Estampes et de lá Photographie, Paris, Phila. Mus. Art, Walker Art Ctr., Mpls., Achenbach Found., Fine Arts Mus. San Francisco. Recipient J.D. Phelan award World Print Coun., 1983; Minn. State Arts Bd. Grantee, 1978; Photography fellow, St. Paul, 1984; Rockefeller Found. fellow, Am. Ctr., 1984-86, Jerome Found. Printmaking fellow, Kala Inst., Berkeley, 1989. Mem. Achenbach Graphic Arts Coun., Calif. Soc. of Printmakers.

KLEIN, MARC S., newspaper editor and publisher; b. Feb. 16, 1949; married; 2 children. BA in Journalism, Pa. State U., 1970. Bur. chief Courier-Post, Camden, N.J., 1970-75; asst. mng. editor Phila. Bull., 1975-81; editor Jewish Exponent, Phila., 1981-83; editor, pub. Jewish Bull. of No. Calif., San Francisco, 1984—; publ. Jewish Cmty. Online. Past pres. Temple Israel, Alameda; former bd. dirs. Oakland-Piedmont Jewish Community Ctr. Recipient 1st place awards Phila. Press Assn., 1973, 1st place award N.J. Press Assn., 1973; Wall St. Jour. Newspaper Fund intern, fellow, 1969. Mem. Am. Jewish Press Assn. (pres.), Soc. Profl. Journalists (past bd. dirs.). Office: 225 Bush St Ste 1480 San Francisco CA 94104-4216

KLEIN, MARILYN (LYNN), interior designer, volunteer; b. Bklyn., Oct. 11, 1929; d. Abraham M. and Ella (Goldwasser) Feinberg; m. Richard S. Klein, Sept. 11, 1949; children: Adrienne, Neil, Paula. BA in English Edn., Fairleigh Dickenson U., Teaneck, N.J., 1949; postgrad., NYU Sch. Drama, N.Y.C., 1950. Interior designer Kleins Furniture Co., Corona, N.Y., 1965-85; interior designer Dede Goldman Interiors, Port Washington, N.Y., 1985-92, Glen Cove, N.Y., 1985-92, Freeport, Bahamas, 1992-98. Founder, exec. Elmont (N.Y.) Jewish Ctr., 1955-80; founder, sisterhood pres. Luis de Torres Synagogue, Freeport, 1950-96; exec. v.p. Hadassah Fla. Atlantic, 1992—; past fundraiser, pres. Simcha of Aberdeen, chair Woman of Valor event Fla. Atlantic region, 1997, keeper of gate. Named Queen Esther, Elmont Jewish Ctr., 1967, Woman of Valor, Hadassah, Fla., 1997, Woman of Yr. Hadasah, 1997; recipient awards United Jewish Appeal, Israel Bonds, Fedn. Jewish Philanthropis, Elmont, 1975. Mem. B'nai Brith. Home: 7411 Hearth Stone Ave Boynton Beach FL 33437-2924 Office: Fla Atlantic Region Hadassah 5341 W Atlantic Ave Ste 305 Delray Beach FL 33484-8166

KLEIN, MARK PAUL, real estate developer; b. Champaign, Ill., Apr. 27, 1943; s. George and Mary Klein; m. Libby Klein; children: Marnee, Meredith. BBA, U. Pa., Phila., 1976; MBA, Drexel U., 1979. Owner Klein Real Estate, Newtown Square, Pa., 1977—; prof. St. Joseph U., Phila., 1981, Pa. State U., Media, 1986, Polley U., Newtown Square, 1988-97. Comdr. CAP, 1970; bd. dirs. Buxmont Ballet Co., New Hope, Pa., 1980, Simon Milles Sales Co., Phila., 1987, Victoria Mills Co., Springfield, Pa., 1996. With USN, 1966-68. Avocations: sailing, skiing. Home: 105 Deer Ln Newtown Square PA 19073-4307 Office: Klein Real Estate 105 Deer Ln Newtown Square PA 19073-4307

KLEIN, MARTIN, ocean engineering consultant; b. N.Y.C.; s. Allen and Muriel (Seidman) K.; children: Allen Jameson, Robyn Marie. SBEE, MIT, 1962. Program mgr. sonar systems EG&G Internat., Bedford, Mass., 1962-67; pres. Klein Assocs., Inc., Salem, N.H., 1968-89; cons. Andover, Mass., 1989—; mem. mgmt. coun. Project Urquhart (Loch Ness), London, 1992—; mem. bd. advisors B.Engring. Tech. program U. N.H., Durham, 1988—, Acad. Applied Sci., Concord, N.H., 1982—; mem. adv. bd. MIT Sea Grant, Cambridge, 1989—; bd. dirs. Marine Archaeol. and Hist. Rsch. Inst., Elliot, Maine, 1990-98; pres. The Bear Trap Investment Co., 1995-96; mem. vis. com. R.S. Peabody Mus. Archaeology, 1995-98; assoc. mem. Adv. Coun. Underwater Archaeology, 1992—. Contbr. articles to mags. Minister search com., publicity dir. Unitarian Universalist Ch., Andover, 1990-91, chair publicity com., 1991-93; trustee Andover Pub. Libr., 1992-98. Recipient Small Bus. Person of Yr. award SBA, 1983. Fellow Marine Tech. Soc. (dir. budget and fin. 1991-93, chair fellows com. 1998-99), Explorers Club; mem. IEEE, Acoustical Soc. Am., Am. Bonsai Soc. (v.p. 1993-95, pres. 1995-97). Achievements include patents in field; development of first commercially successful side scan sonar.

KLEIN, MARTIN JESSE, physicist, educator, science historian; b. N.Y.C., June 25, 1924; s. Adolph and Mary (Neuman) K.; m. Miriam June Levin, Oct. 28, 1945 (div. 1973); children: Rona F., Sarah M. Klein Zaino, Nancy R. Klein; m. Linda L. Booz, Oct. 8, 1980; 1 child, Abigail M. AB, Columbia U., 1942, MA, 1944; PhD, MIT, 1948. With OSRD for USN, 1944-45; research asso. physics Mass. Inst. Tech., 1946-49; instr. physics Case Inst. Tech., 1949-51, asst. prof., 1951-55, assoc. prof., 1955-60, prof., 1960-67, acting dept. head, 1966-67; prof. history physics Yale U., 1967-74, Eugene Higgins prof. history physics and prof. physics, 1974-91, 95—, Bass prof. history sci., prof. physics, 1991-95, chmn. dept. history sci., 1971-74; William Clyde De Vane prof., 1978-81; Van der Waals guest prof. U. Amsterdam, 1974, Pieter Zeeman guest prof., 1993; vis. prof. Harvard U., 1989-90, Rockefeller U., 1975, adj. prof. 1976-79. Author: Paul Ehrenfest, Vol. I: The Making of a Theoretical Physicist, 1970; editor: Collected Scientific Papers of Paul Ehrenfest, 1959; sr. editor The Collected Papers of Albert Einstein, 1988-97; editorial adviser Ency. Brit, 1956-76; translator: Letters on Wave Mechanics, 1967; contbr. articles to profl. jours. NRC fellow Dublin (Ireland) Inst. Advanced Studies, 1952-53; Guggenheim fellow Leyden, Netherlands, 1958-59; Guggenheim fellow Yale, 1967-68. Fellow Am. Acad. Arts and Scis., Am. Phys. Soc.; mem. NAS, AAUP, History of Sci. Soc., Am. Assn. Physics Tchrs., Internat. Acad. History of Scis., Phi Beta Kappa, Sigma Xi. Home: 44 N Lake Dr Apt B-1 Hamden CT 06517-2419 Office: Yale U Dept Physics PO Box 208120 New Haven CT 06520-8120

KLEIN, MARTIN SAMUEL, management consulting executive; b. N.Y.C., Dec. 8, 1932; s. David and Dorothy (Manheim) K.; m. Elizabeth Jann Perks, Dec. 19, 1964 (dec. Aug. 1994); children: Sarah Madeline, Dorothy Ann. AB, Harvard U., 1954, MBA, 1962. V.p. United Rsch., Cambridge, Mass., 1962-69, Boston Cons. Group, 1969-73; pres. Instl. Strategy Assocs., Belmont, Mass., 1973—; cons. Brookings Instn., Washington, 1963-64. Author: (with others) Impact of Transportation on Development, 1964, Combining Public Health Nursing Agencies, 1964. Contbr. articles to profl. jours. Bd. dirs. Vis. Nurse Assn., Boston, 1972-82, Harvard Cmty. Health Plan, Boston, 1978-93; vice chmn. Harvard Cmty. Health Plan Found., 1986-93, Cambridge Ctr. for Adult Edn., 1983-85; sec.-treas. Ctr. for Effective Philanthropy, Cambridge, 1982-98. Sr. fellow, trustee Cheswick Ctr., 1980—; trustee Mt. Auburn Hosp., Cambridge, 1995—, Big Sister Assn. Greater Boston, 1996—; counsellor to bd. trustees Aga Khan U., Karachi, Pakistan, 1993—; Harvard Coll. scholar, 1954, Fulbright scholar, Australia, 1954-55, George F. Baker scholar Harvard Bus. Sch., 1962. Mem. Am. Hosp. Assn. (com. on governance). Jewish. Clubs: Harvard (N.Y.C.), (Boston); Belmont Hill (treas. 1979-80) (Belmont, Mass.), Harvard Travellers Club (Boston). Office: Instl Strategy Assocs Inc PO Box 108 43 Village Hill Rd Belmont MA 02478-2117

KLEIN, MARY ANN, English educator; b. San Antonio, July 8, 1944; d. Joseph Archibald and Mary Ann (McMurrough) K.; m. Joseph Anthony Messina. BA, Incarnate Word Coll., 1965; MA, U. Dallas; PhD, Marquette U., 1973. Cert. secondary tchr., Tex. Tchr. Jefferson Davis Jr. H.S., San Antonio, 1965-67; prof. English Quincy (Ill.) U., 1972—, chair dept. English, 1982-89, chair divsn. lang., lit. and comms., 1997—; cons., evaluator North Ctrl. Assn., Chgo., 1996—; mem. summer seminar NEH, 1975, 80. Contbr. articles, poetry, revs. to profl. publs. Bd. dirs. Family Svcs., Quincy, Quincy Soc. Fine Arts, Quincy LWV; v.p. bd. dirs. Quincy Civic Music Assn. Midwest Faculty Seminar Occasional fellow U. Chgo., 1990. Mem. MLA, Midwest MLA, Nat. Coun. Tchrs. English, Ill. Assn. Tchrs. English, Midwest Victorian Studies Assn. (bd. dirs.), Ill. Medieval Assn. Avocations: reading, writing, gardening, travel, photography. E-mail: kleinma@quincy.edu. Home: 2100 Aldo Blvd Quincy IL 62301 Office: Quincy U 1900 College Ave Quincy IL 62301

KLEIN, MELVYN NORMAN, lawyer, investment executive; b. Chgo., Dec. 27, 1941; s. Harry H. and Bertha M. (Gleicher) K.; m. Annette Lorraine Grossman, Mar. 13, 1976; children: Jacqueline Anne, Jenna Katherine. Student, London (Eng.) Sch. Econs. and Polit. Sci., 1962; BA in Econs. with highest honors, Colgate U., 1963; JD, Columbia U., 1966; postgrad., Johns Hopkins Sch. Advanced Internati. Studies, 1966-67; LHD (hon.), Tex. A&M U., Corpus Christi, 1997. Bar: D.C. 1968, Tex. 1980. Legis. asst. Rep. Sidney Yates, Washington, 1966; assoc. McKinsey & Co., Washington, 1967-68; sr. v.p. Donaldson, Lufkin and Jenrette, Inc., N.Y.C., 1969-77; counsel Brownstein, Zeidman & Schomer, Washington, 1978-93; sole practice Corpus Christi, 1979—; spl. counsel United Techs. Corp., 1985; bd. dirs. Anixter Internat., Quexco, Bayou Steel Corp., Am. Med. Internat., Sante Fe Energy Resources, Cockrell Oil Corp., Hanover Compressor Corp.; sr. investment adv. Sprout Capital Group III, 1977-87; gen. ptnr. GKH Ptnrs., L.P., 1987—; pres. Jakk Holding Corp., 1991—; adj. prof. bus. Tex. A&M U., Corpus Christi; mem. adv. com. internat. econ. policy, U.S. Sec. State, 1999. Guest columnist Corpus Christi Caller-Times newspaper, 1980—. Active v.p. Hubert Humphrey presdl. campaign, 1968; mem., chmn. Corpus Christi Bus. Devel. Comm., 1979-86; chmn. bd. govs. Art Mus. South Tex.; bd. dirs. S. Tex. Ednl. Broadcasting System, 1984-86; mem. exec. com. Pres.'s Pvt. Sector Study of Cost Control in Fed. Govt.; mem. internat. bd. advisors Columbia U. Sch. Internat. Affairs. Mem. ABA, World Pres.'s Orgn., Horatio Alger Assn. Disting. Ams., Am. Bus. Conf. (founding mem., chmn. capital formation and tax policy com. 1980-86), D.C. Bar Assn., State Bar Tex., Young Pres. Orgn., Philosophical Soc. Tex. Clubs: Corpus Christi Yacht, Corpus Christi Country, River Oaks Country (Houston), Corpus Christi Town, Standard (Chgo.). Lodge: Rotary. Home: 210 Jackson Pl Corpus Christi TX 78411-1216 Office: GKH Ptnrs 200 W Madison St Ste 3800 Chicago IL 60606-3414

KLEIN, MICHAEL CLARENCE, lawyer; b. Kearney, Nebr., July 16, 1952; s. Milton N. and Mary E. (Moore) K.; m. Jacqueline A. McGuigan, Aug. 14, 1971; children—Andrew M., Benjamin P., Molly E., Katherine A. B.A., Kearney State Coll., 1974; J.D., U. Nebr., 1977. Bar: Nebr. 1977, U.S. Dist. Ct. Nebr. 1977, U.S. Supreme Ct. 1987. Ptnr., Anderson, Klein, Peterson & Swan, Holdrege, Nebr., 1977—; chmn. 10th Jud. Dist. Mental Health Board, Holdrege, 1981—. Editor Nebr. Law Rev., 1975-77. Bd. dirs. Child Saving Inst., Omaha, Phelps County Community Found., Holdrege, Nebr. Mem. ABA, Nebr. Bar Assn., 10th Jud. Dist. Bar Assn. (sec. 1981-82), Phelps County Bar Assn. (pres. 1981). Republican. Roman Catholic. Lodge: Elks. Home: 820 Hancock St Holdrege NE 68949-2146 Office: Anderson Klein Peterson & Swan 417 East Ave Holdrege NE 68949-2216

KLEIN, MICHAEL D., lawyer; b. Wilkes-Barre, Pa., June 9, 1951. BA magna cum laude, King's Coll., 1973; JD, Dickinson Coll., 1976. Bar: Pa. 1976, U.S. Ct. Appeals (3rd cir.) 1984, U.S. Dist. Ct. (mid. dist.) Pa. 1984, U.S. Dist Ct. (ea. dist.) Pa. 1994. Asst. atty. gen. Commonwealth of Pa., Harrisburg, 1976-82; mgr. corp. affairs, corp. sec. Pa. Am. Water Co., Hershey, 1982-89; ptnr. LeBoeuf, Lamb, Greene & MacRae LLP, Harrisburg, Pa., 1991—. Mem. Pa. Bar Assn., Am. Water Works Assn. Office: LeBoeuf Lamb PO Box 12105 200 N 3rd St Ste 300 Harrisburg PA 17101-1511

KLEIN, MICHAEL ELIHU, physician; b. N.Y.C., Apr. 6, 1946; s. Leo and Edith (Rigrod) K.; m. Elizabeth Angela McGehee, Oct. 8, 1988; children: Michael, Debra, Daniel. BA, Wesleyan U., Middletown, Conn., 1967; MD, Yale U., 1972, MPH, 1972. Diplomate in internal medicine and hematology Am. Bd. Internal Medicine. Asst. dir. hematology U. Md., Balt., 1979-83; sr. investigator U. Md. Cancer Ctr., Balt., 1979-83; pvt. practice specializing in hematology/oncology Cowley Assocs., Camp Hill, Pa., 1983-97, Ctrl. Pa. Hematology & Oncology, Lemoyne, 1997—; cons. in hematology and oncology Polyclinic Hosp., Harrisburg, Pa., 1983—, Holy Spirit Hosp., Camp Hill, 1983—. Author: Political Dynamics National Health Insurance in New York, 1972; contbr. articles to profl. jours., chpts. to books. Founder, bd. dirs. Number Nine, New Haven, 1971. Comdr. lt. USPHS, 1974-77. Mem. AMA, Am. Soc. Clin. Research, Am. Soc. Clin. Oncology, Am. Soc. Hematology, Am. Legion, Balt. Blood Club (pres. 1979-83). Avocations: stamp collecting, baseball, reading. Office: Ctrl Pa Hematology & Oncology Ste 100 50 N 12th St Lemoyne PA 17043

KLEIN, MICHAEL JEFFREY, consumer products company executive; b. Balt., Apr. 12, 1955; s. Ralph Lincoln and Shirley M. (Snyderman) K.; m. Clara Lynn Berger; children: Samuel B., Jacob I. BS in Fin., U. Md., 1977. V.p. Klein's Super Markets, Forest Hill, Md., 1977—; v.p. Forest Hill Lanes, 1985—; ptnr. Colgate Investments, Forest Hill, 1977—. Trustee Harford Day Sch., Bel Air, Md., 1995—; mem. partnership bd. United Way Harford County, 1997; vol. Am. Cancer Soc., Bel Air, 1982-83. Democrat. Avocations: golf, baseball, travel. Office: Klein's Super Markets 2011 Klein Plaza Dr Ste 2 Forest Hill MD 21050-2603

KLEIN, MICHAEL LAWRENCE, research chemist, educator; b. London, Mar. 13, 1940; s. Julius and Bessie (Bloomberg) K.; m. Brenda May Woodman, June 3, 1962; children—Paula Denise, Rachel Anne. B.Sc., Bristol U., Eng., 1961; Ph.D., Bristol U., 1964. Research fellow CIBA-GEIGEY, Genoa, Italy, 1964-65; research fellow Imperial Chem. Industries (UK), Bristol, Eng., 1965-67; research assoc. Rutgers U., New Brunswick, N.J., 1967-68; research officer NRC of Can., Ottawa, Ont., 1968-87; prof. chemistry U. Pa., Phila., 1987-91; William Smith prof. chemistry 1991, 1991-93; Hepburn prof. phys. scis., 1993—; part-time prof. chemistry Mc Master U., Hamilton, Ont., 1977-89; mem. internat. relations com. Natural Scis. and Engring. Research Council, Ottawa, 1982-84, mem. NSERC chem. panel, 1985-86, NSF panels, 1993—, NIH panels, 1996, 97, 99; vis. prof., Paris, Lyon, France, Kyoto, Japan, Amsterdam, Canberra, Australia, Florence, Italy; fellow commoner Trinity Coll., Cambridge, Eng., 1985-86; dir. NSF Materials Rsch. Lab., 1993-96, NSF MRSEC, 1996—; Miller prof. U. Calif., Berkeley, 1997, Linnett prof. U. Cambridge. Editor: Rare Gas Solids, Vol. I, 1976, Vol. II, 1977, Inert Gases, 1984; mem. editl. bd. Chem. Physics, 1986—, Physics Reports, 1986—, Jour. Phys. Chemistry, 1990-95, Molecular Physics, 1992—, Computational Materials Sci., 1992—, Jour. Chem. Soc. Farady Trans., 1993-98, Jour. Phys. Condensed Matter, 1994-97, Phys. Chemistry Chem. Physics, 1999—; contbr. numerous articles to profl. jours. IBM World Trade fellow, 1970, Guggenheim fellow, 1989, Humboldt fellow, 1995; grantee Natural Scis. and Engring. Rsch. Coun., 1979-89, NSF, 1988—, NIH, 1988—. Fellow Royal Soc. Can., Chem. Inst. Can., Am. Phys. Soc. (Rahman prize 1999); mem. Am. Chem. Soc. (Phila. Sect. award 1998), Royal Soc. Chemistry (U.K.). Home: 133 W Atlantic Blvd Ocean City NJ 08226-4603 Office: U Pa Dept Chemistry Philadelphia PA 19104-6323

KLEIN, MICHAEL ROGER, lawyer, business executive; b. N.Y.C., Apr. 10, 1942; s. Jesse and Stephanie (Siegel) K.; m. Diane Atkinson, July 4, 1967 (div. June 1974); m. Joan Ilona Fabry, Feb. 19, 1977; children: Nicholas Jesse, Alexander Fabry. BBA, U. Miami, Coral Gables, Fla., 1963, JD, 1966; LLM, Harvard U., 1967. Bar: Fla. 1966, D.C., 1969, U.S. Dist. Ct. (D.C. cir.) 1970, U.S. Supreme Ct., 1970. Asst. prof. law La. State U., Baton Rouge, 1967-69; assoc. Wilmer, Cutler & Pickering, Washington, 1969-74, ptnr., 1974—; pres. Zenith Gallery, Inc., Washington, 1978—; chmn. LePavillon of D.C., Washington, 1983-89, CoStar Group Inc., Bethesda, Md., 1988—; bd. dirs. Perini Corp., SRA Internat. Inc., Comml. Mortgage Trading Forum LLC, Structured Fin. Advisors LLC. Author: Eminent Domain, 1969; contbr. articles to profl. jours. Trustee Ctr. for Law in the Pub. Interest, L.A., 1975-91, Am. Himalayan Found., 1996—; chmn. bd. trustees Advocates for Pub. Interest, Washington, 1986-89; dir. Support Ctr. of D.C., Inc., 1991-95. Mem. Am. Law Inst. Jewish. Office: Wilmer Cutler & Pickering 2445 M St NW Washington DC 20037-1427

KLEIN, MILES VINCENT, physics educator; b. Cleve., Mar. 9, 1933; s. Max Ralph and Isabelle (Benjamin) K.; m. Barbara Judith Pincus, Sept. 2, 1956; children: Cynthia Klein-Banai, Gail. BS, Northwestern U., 1954; PhD, Cornell U., 1961. NSF postdoctoral fellow Max Planck Inst., Stuttgart, Germany, 1961; prof. U. Ill., Urbana, 1962—. Co-author: Optics, 1986; contbr. articles to profl. jours. A.P. Sloan Found. fellow, 1963. Fellow AAAS, Am. Phys. Soc. (Frank Isakson prize 1990), Am. Acad. Arts and Scis.; mem. IEEE (Sr.), Materials Rsch. Soc., Nat. Acad. Scis. Office: U Ill Sci & Tech 104 S Goodwin Ave Urbana IL 61801-2902

KLEIN, MILTON MARTIN, history educator; b. N.Y.C., Aug. 15, 1917; s. Edward and Margaret (Greenfield) K.; m. Margaret Gordon, Aug. 25, 1963; children: Edward Gordon, Peter Gordon. B.S.S., CCNY, 1937, M.S. in Edn., 1939; Ph.D., Columbia U., 1954. Historian, USAAF, 1944-47; tchr. N.Y.C. pub. schs., 1947-57; vis. prof. Columbia U., summers 1959, 60, lectr. history, 1954-58; prof. history, chmn. dept. L.I. U., 1958-62, dean Coll. Liberal Arts and Sci., 1962-66; dean grad. studies and research SUNY-Fredonia, 1966-69; prof. history U. Tenn., 1969-84, alumni disting. service prof., 1977-84, Lindsay Young prof., 1980-84, prof. emeritus, 1984—, univ. historian, 1988-97; Walter E. Meyer vis. prof. N.Y. U. Law Sch., 1976-77; chmn. Columbia U. Faculty Seminar on Early Am. History and Culture, 1971-72. Author: Social Studies for the Academically Talented Student, 1960, The Politics of Diversity: Essays in the History of Colonial New York, 1974, New York in the American Revolution: A Bibliography, 1974, The American Whig: William Livingston of New York, 1990, 93, Vol. Moments: Vignettes of the History the University of Tennessee, 1794-1994, 1994; also numerous articles; editor: Independent Reflector (William Livingston), 1963, A History of the American Colonies, 13 vols., 1973-86, New York-The Centennial Years, 1676-1976, 1976, Courts and Law in Early New York, 1978, The Twilight of British Rule in Revolutionary America: The New York Letter Book of General James Robertson, 1983, North America in Colonial Times, 4 vols., 1998; mem. editl. bd. Am. Jour. Legal History, 1970-76, N.Y. History, 1973—, Soundings, 1985—, U. Tenn. Press, 1972-75, Presidl. Studies Quar., 1992-96; adv. editor: Eighteenth-Century Studies, 1975-83, 93-95; adv. bd. America: History and Life, 1982-96. Served to lt. col. USAF Res. Recipient Outstanding Teaching award U. Tenn. Alumni, 1974, Kerr History prize N.Y. State Hist. Assn., 1975, 92, Articles prize Am. Soc. 18th Century Studies, 1976; Fulbright lectr. U. Canterbury, Christchurch, N.Z., 1962; Ford Found. traveling fellow, 1955-56, Lilly Found.-Clements Libr. fellow, 1961; Am. Philos. Soc. grantee, 1973. Mem. Am. Hist. Assn., Orgn. Am. Historians, Am. Soc. 18th Century Studies (articles prize 1976), Southeastern Am. Soc. 18th Century Studies (dir. 1978-81, v.p. 1982-84, pres. 1984-85), AAUP (nat. council 1978-80), Am. Soc. Legal History (chmn. membership com. 1969-74, dir. 1971-76, 84-86, sec. 1975-77, v.p. 1978-80, pres. 1980-82), Am. Antiquarian Soc., Mass. Hist. Soc., Phi Beta Kappa, Sigma Alpha Mu, Phi Alpha Theta, Phi Kappa Phi, Omicron Delta Kappa, Golden Key. Home: 7103 Rotherwood Dr Knoxville TN 37919-7413

KLEIN, MORTON, industrial engineer, educator; b. N.Y.C., Aug. 9, 1925; s. Norbert and Lottie (Wigdor) K.; m. Gloria Ritterband, July 31, 1949; children: Lisa, Melanie. B.S.M.E., Duke U., 1946; M.S., Columbia U., 1952, D.Engring. Sci., 1957. Engr. Picatinny Arsenal, Dover, N.J., 1950-54; instr. Sch. Engring and Applied Sci., Columbia U., N.Y.C., 1956; asst. prof. Sch. Engring and Applied Sci., Columbia U., 1957-61, asso. prof., 1961-69, prof. indsl. engring, ops. rsch., 1969—, chmn. dept. indsl. engring. and ops. research, 1982-85, 94-95; cons. to industry, govt. Author: (with Cyrus Derman) Probability and Statistical Inference for Engineers, 1959; editor: Managment Science, 1960-77; rsch. and publs. on prodn. planning, scheduling early cancer detection examinations, network flows and statis. quality control. Served with USN, 1943-46. Mem. Am. Inst. Indls. Engrs., Pi Tau Sigma, Alpha Pi Mu, Omega Rho. Office: Columbia U 301 SW Mudd # A New York NY 10027

KLEIN, NEIL CHARLES, physician; b. N.Y.C., Jan. 6, 1935; s. Martin and Jeannette F. (Pazow) K.; divorced; children: Lisa, Susie, David; m. Phyllis Klein, Nov. 26, 1989. AB, Columbia U., 1956; MD, Cornell U., 1960. Diplomate Am. Bd. Internal Medicine, Am. Bd. Gastroenterology, Nat. Bd. Med. Examiners. Intern N.Y. Hosp., 1960-61, resident, 1964-67; fellow in medicine Cornell Med. Coll., 1965-67, clin. instr. in medicine, 1967-70, asst. clin. prof. medicine, 1970-77; assoc. clin. prof. medicine N.Y. Med. Coll., 1977-84; clin. prof. medicine N.Y. Med. Coll., 1984—; asst. clin. attending physician N.Y. Hosp., 1970-77, St. Joseph's Hosp., Stamford, Conn., 1967-72; from asst. to assoc. attending physician Stamford (Conn.) Hosp., 1967—, assoc. chief medicine, 1972-75, chief divsn. gastroenterology, 1978-84. Bd. dirs. Conn. Med. Ins. Co., 1988—, fin. com., 1988—, sec., 1990—; bd. dirs. Stamford Health Network, 1987-93, chmn. fin. com., 1994—; mem. sci. adv. coun. Fairfield-Westchester Ileitis-Colitis Found., 1982—; mem. Commn. of Aging, Stamford, 1971-82. Fellow ACP, Am. Coll. Gastroenterology, Royal Soc. Tropical Medicine and Hygiene; mem. Fairfield County Med. Assn. (trustee 1980-87, chmn. bd. trustees 1984-85, pres. 1985-86), Conn. State Med. Assn., Am. Soc. Gastrointestinal Endoscopy, Am. Fedn. Clin. Rsch., Am. Gastrointestinal Assn., Cornell Med. Coll. Alumni Assn. (pres. 1976-78, sr. advisor 1978—), Stamford Med. Soc. (pres. 1990-91). Office: Stamford Med Group 1450 Washington Blvd Stamford CT 06902-2451

KLEIN, OTTO G., III, lawyer; b. Berkeley, Calif., Dec. 7, 1950. BA, U. Wash., 1973; JD, Yale U., 1976. Bar: Wash. 1976. Mem. Summit Law Group, Seattle, 1997—. Office: Summit Law Group 1505 Westlake Ave N Ste 300 Seattle WA 98109-3050*

KLEIN, PAUL E., lawyer; b. N.Y.C., Apr. 26, 1934. AB, Cornell U., 1956; JD, Harvard U., 1960. Bar: Mich. 1960, Ill. 1965, N.Y. 1967, U.S. Supreme Ct. 1977, U.S. Ct. Appeals (2d cir.) 1980. Atty. Dow Chem. Co., Midland, Mich., 1960-65; assoc. Gunther & Choka, Chgo., 1965-66; atty. Esso Rsch. & Engring. Co., Linden, N.J., 1966-67; sr. mng. editor Matthew Bender & Co., N.Y.C., 1967-72; assoc. gen. counsel N.Y. Life Ins. Co., N.Y.C., 1972-80, v.p., assoc. gen. counsel, 1980-84; v.p., counsel Huggins Fin. Svcs., Inc., N.Y.C., 1984-86; exec. corp. tax. div. Ernst & Young, N.Y.C., 1986-95; pvt. practice White Plains, N.Y., 1995—; adj. asst. prof. L.I. U., 1972-79, adj. assoc. prof., 1979-80; adj. assoc. prof. acctg. and taxation, Fordham U. at Lincoln Ctr. grad. sch. of bus. adminstrn., 1995—. Former columnist Jour. Real Estate Taxation; writer; editor. Mem. ABA (past chmn. subcom. on life ins. products/ins. cos. com., sect. taxation), Assn. Bar City N.Y. (past chair subcom. on life and health ins. of the com. on ins. law), Assn. Life Ins. Counsel (sec.-treas. 1979-83, bd. govs. 1983-87), N.Y. State Bar Assn. Office: 58 Midchester Ave White Plains NY 10606-3817

KLEIN, PERRY IAN, electronics engineer; b. Balt., Nov. 15, 1942; s. Samuel C. and Vivian (Elkin) K.; m. Susan Shurberg, June 20, 1965; 1 child, Sherry. BSEE, U. Pa., 1964, MSE, 1965, PhD in Engring., 1968. Mem. tech. staff Comms. Satellite Corp., Washington, 1968-71; pres., gen. mgr. Radio Amateur Satellite Corp., Washington, 1971-80; v.p. Washington Cable Sys., Inc., 1979—; pres. Shurberg-Klein Found., Washington, 1997—; founder Radio Amateur Satellite Corp., Washington, 1969. Patentee in field. Dir. Md. Brass Ensemble, 1986—. Mem. IEEE (sr.). Avocations: amateur radio, composing music. Home: 700 7th St SW Washington DC 20024 Office: Washington Cable 700 7th St SW Washington DC 20024

KLEIN, PETER, theatrical producer; b. Timisoara, Rumania, July 22, 1945; s. Andrew and Ari (Wiener) K.; m. Phyllis Urman, June 23, 1978; children: Nadia, Alexis. BA, Baruch Coll., New York, 1973. Tour mgr. Hurok Concerts, N.Y.C., 1969-74; founder/pres. Living Arts, N.Y.C., 1973—; bd. dirs. Spectra Arts, N.Y.C., Ballet Manhattan, N.Y.C.; founder Opera Nazionale Italiana, Rome, 1986—. Organized White House concert of Andres Segovia for Jimmy Carter, 1979; prodns. in Europe include: A Chorus Line, West Side Story, Ain't Misbehavin'; prodr. The Gershwins' "Porgy and Bess" world tour, 1992—. Avocations: tennis, basketball, skiing. Office: Living Arts Inc 250 W 57th St Ste 2401 New York NY 10107-2402

KLEIN, PETER MARTIN, lawyer, retired transportation company executive; b. N.Y.C., June 2, 1934; s. Saul and Esther (Goldstein) K.; m. Ellen Judith Matlick, June 18, 1961; children: Amy Lynn, Steven Ezra. AB, Columbia U., 1956, JD, 1962. Bar: N.Y. 1962, D.C. 1964, U.S. Supreme Ct. 1966. Asst. proctor Columbia U., 1959-62; asst. counsel Mil. Sea Transp. Svc., Office Gen. Counsel, Dept. Navy, Washington, 1962-65; trial atty. civil div. U.S. Dept. Justice, N.Y.C., 1966-69; gen. atty. Sea-Land Svc., Inc., Menlo Park, N.J., 1969-76, v.p., gen. counsel, sec., 1976-79; v.p., gen. counsel, sec. Sea-Land Industries, Inc., Menlo Park, 1979-84; assoc. gen. counsel R.J. Reynolds Industries, Inc., Winston-Salem, N.C., 1978-84; sr. v.p., gen. counsel, sec. Sea-Land Svc., Inc. (formerly Sea-Land Corp.), Charlotte, N.C., 1984-94, sr. v.p.-law, sec., 1994-95, ret., 1996—; mem. adv. com. on pvt. internat. law Dept. State, 1974-95; mem. U.S. delegation UN Conf. of Trade and Devel., UN Commn. on Internat. Trade Law, 1975-76, trade regulation adv. bd. Bur. Nat. Affairs, 1986-88; alt. mem. N.Am. coun. London Ct. of Internat. Arbitration, 1988-95. Trustee Jewish Edn. Assn. Met. N.J., 1973-76; trustee Temple B'nai Abraham of Essex County, N.J., 1973—, v.p., 1976-81, pres. 1981-83; mem. Essex County Dems. Com., 1986-88; mem. Livingston Twp. Planning Bd., 1996—, vice chmn. 1997—. With USN, 1956-59, Antarctica. Mem. ABA, FBA, Am. Maritime Assn. (bd. dirs., chmn. coms. on law and legis. 1974-78), Am. Polar Soc., Navy League U.S. (life), U.S. Naval Inst. (life), N.Y. State Bar Assn., D.C. Bar Assn., Internat. Bar Assn., Maritime Law Assn. Home: 22 Sandalwood Dr Livingston NJ 07039-1409

KLEIN, PETER WILLIAM, lawyer, corporate officer, investment company executive; b. Lorain, Ohio, Sept. 22, 1955; s. Warren Martin Klein and Barbara (Lesser) Pomeroy; m. Jennifer Lynn Ungers, Aug. 3, 1984. Student, U. Sussex, 1975-76; BA, Albion Coll., 1976; JD, Cleve. Marshall Coll. Law, 1981; LLM, NYU, 1982. Bar: Ohio 1981, Ill. 1984. Assoc. Guren, Merritt, Feibel, Sogg & Cohen, Cleve., 1982-84, Siegan, Barbakoff, Gomberg & Gordon, Ltd., Chgo., 1984-86; mng. dir., gen. counsel Trivest Inc., Miami, Fla., 1986—. Mem. ABA (taxation sect., corp. sect., banking and bus. law). Home: 3618 Palmetto Ave Miami FL 33133-6221 Office: Trivest Inc 2665 S Bayshore Dr Ste 800 Miami FL 33133-5401

KLEIN, PHILIP ALEXANDER, economist; b. Austin, Tex., Oct. 8, 1927; s. David Ballin and Rose (Schaffer) K.; m. Margaret A. McCormack, May 20, 1961; children—Kathleen Monico, Alan Schaffer. B.A., U. Tex., 1948, M.A., 1949; Ph.D., U. Calif., Berkeley, 1958. Instr. Carleton Coll., Northfield, Minn., spring 1955; mem. faculty Pa. State U., State College, 1955—, prof. econs., 1965—; rsch. assoc. Nat. Bur. Econ. Rsch., 1955-70, 73-79, Ctr. Internat. Bus. Cycle Rsch., Columbia U., 1979-96, Econ. Cycle Rsch. Inst., 1996—; vis. prof. San Francisco State U., summer 1963, U. Hawaii, summer 1967, Inst. Européen D'Adminstrn. des Affairs, Fontainbleau, France, 1963-64, 65, 66, 67, U. Osijek, Yugoslavia, 1970, Mills Coll., spring 1982; acad. visitor London Sch. Econs., 1973-74, 81; disting. Fulbright fellow U. Siena, Italy, 1989; adj. scholar Am. Enterprises Inst., Washington, 1976—; cons. UN, Ctr. Devel. Planning Projections Policies, 1973, OECD, Paris, 1978-81, EEC, Brussels, 1979-82, World Bank, Washington, 1986, 87, 88. Mem. editorial bd. Internat. Jour. Forecasting, 1986—, Jour. Econ. Issues, 1976-81, 85-87; author books in field; contbr. articles to profl. jours., chpts. to books. With M.C., AUS, 1946-47. Recipient Distinction in Social Scis. award Pa. State U., 1981; Fulbright fellow France, 1963, Yugoslavia, 1970, Italy, 1989. Mem. Econs. Assn., Assn. Evolutionary Econs. (pres. 1977, Veblen-Commons award 1990), Assn. Comparative Econs., Phi Beta Kappa (pres. chpt. 1981). Home: 719 S Sparks St State College PA 16801-4114 Office: Pa State U Dept Econs 516 Kern Grad Bldg University Park PA 16802

KLEIN, PHILIPP HILLEL, electronic materials consultant; b. N.Y.C., Sept. 14, 1926; s. Raphael and Lillian Rae (Wald) K.; m. Charlotte Feuerstein, June 21, 1953; children: Joshua David, Daniel William, Jonathan Henry. BS in Chemistry, Syracuse U., 1948, MS in Phys. Chemistry, 1951, PhD in Phys. Chemistry, 1953. Rsch. assoc. Knolls Atomic Power Lab., Schenectady, N.Y., 1952-56; phys. chemist GE Electronics Lab., Syracuse, N.Y., 1956-61; mem. rsch. staff Sperry Rand Rsch. Ctr., Sudbury, Mass., 1961-66; rsch. chemist NASA Electronics Rsch. Ctr., Cambridge, Mass., 1966-70; sect. head U.S. Naval Rsch. Lab., Washington, 1970-87, rsch. cons., 1987-90; prin. Philipp Klein Cons., Washington, 1990—. Assoc. editor Materials Letters, 1985-89; editor Advanced Energy Conversion, 1962; contbr. articles to profl. jours. With USNR 1945-46. Fellow Am. Inst.

Chemists; mem. IEEE (life, chmn. com. on solid state devices 1962-63), Am. Ceramic Soc. (electronics com. 1968-70), Am. Assn. for Crystal Growth (program chmn. 1985-87), Am. Phys. Soc., Sigma Xi. Achievements include patents on the purification of fluorides, preparation of laser hosts, and deposition of silicon carbide shapes. Office: Philipp Klein Cons 2017 Hillyer Pl NW Washington DC 20009-1005

KLEIN, REYNOLD ANTHONY, marketing professional; b. L.A., Nov. 6, 1956; s. Lawrence and Betty Isabelle Klein. BA, Bard Coll., 1978; MBA, Vanderbilt U., 1985. Mktg., media coord. Rosapepe, Powers & Spanos, Washington, 1981-82; sr. media planner Enicson Mktg. Comm., Nashville, 1985-87; dir. strategic planning Crow, Montgomery & Clark, Canton, Ohio, 1987-88; acct. exec. The Tombras Group, Knoxville, Tenn., 1989-94; acct. supr. Cranford Johnson Robinson Woods, Little Rock, 1994-97, dir. strategic mktg., 1997—. Literacy tutor vol. Nashville pub. schs., 1985-86, Knoxville (Tenn.) area literacy prog., 1990; mem. coord. com. east Tenn. book drive for east Europe, 1993-94. Mem. Internat. Assn. Bus. Comm., Am. Mktg. Assn. (sec. Czechmate project 1991-92, v.p. outreach Knoxville chpt. 1992-93). Office: Cranford Johnson Robinson Woods 303 W Capitol Ave Little Rock AR 72201-3531

KLEIN, ROBERT, manufacturing company executive; b. Phila., Dec. 3, 1924; s. Julius and Eleanor (Arons) K.; m. Judith Auritt, June 30, 1946; children: William J., Sally G., Anne L. BA, Pa. State U., 1948. From indsl. engr. to pres. Caloric Corp., Topton, Pa., 1948-69; pres. Samuel Klein Corp., Alburtis, Pa., 1969-74, Alliance Wall Corp., Atlanta, 1963-78; chmn. bd. Alliance Wall Corp., 1978-85, dir., 1985-87; chmn. bd. Eichler Wood Products Co., Laury's Station, Pa., 1971-78; dir. John M. Spiegel Co., Allentown, Pa., 1972-78; mng. dir. Alliance Europe, Genk, Belgium, 1971-85; gen. mgr. Alliance Europe, 1985-87; bd. dirs., v.p. Nat. Bank Topton, 1960-67; mng. dir. Alliance Pentagon, Odense, Denmark, 1972-85; trustee Albert Einstein Med. Ctr., Phila., 1989-99. Chmn. adv. com. Good Shepherd Home Workshop, 1967-85; mem. bd. assocs. Muhlenberg Coll., 1969—, pres. bd. assocs., 1969-70, trustee, 1970-82, life trustee, 1982; trustee Jewish Fedn., Allentown, 1970-74, 78-81, Boca Raton, Fla. and Phila., 1990; bd. dirs. Porcelain Enamel Inst., 1974-89, treas. 1986-89, Nat. Foundry Assn.; pres. alumni trustees, sec. Coll. Bus. Adminstrn., Pa. State U., 1977-85, pres. Alumni Assn., 1987-89; mem. exec. bd. Disting. Alumni Assn., Penn State, 1997; vice chmn. nat. campaign, 1998—, pres.-elect, 1999— With USMCR, 1943-45. Decorated Purple Heart; recipient Alumni Achievement award Muhlenberg Coll., 1976, Alumni Achievement award Pa. State U., 1978, Disting. Alumni award, 1994; Alumni fellow Pa. State U., 1981. Home: # 9015 500 SE 5th Ave Boca Raton FL 33432 *Work hard, think smart, and work with and encourage your associates. Always remember that every decision you make includes and affects people. This should not decrease aggressiveness but instead make your decisions "people sensitive."*

KLEIN, ROBERT EDWARD, publishing company executive, educator; b. Cin., Dec. 27, 1926; s. Albert and Elisabeth (Muschnau) K.; m. Nancy Minter, May 28, 1958; children: Robert Schuyler, Elisabeth Susan. AB, Kenyon Coll., 1950; MBA, Cornell U., 1952; AM, U. Chgo., 1969, PhD, 1983. CEO Market Power, Inc., Chgo., 1964; dist. mgr. McGraw Hill Co., Chgo., 1969-88; v.p. sales Plastics Today, 1988-90; pres. Klein Assocs., 1990—; cons. U.S. Dept. Justice, 1967-71, Time/Life Books, 1980, Time Life History of WWII; lectr. in Soviet history Barat Coll., 1970-72; dept. assoc. history Northwestern U., Evanston, Ill., 1986—; prof. European, German and bus. and mil. history Loyola U., Chgo., 1988—. Author: J.F. C. Fuller and the Tank, 1983. Mem. Com. for Near East Understanding. With U.S. Army, 1944-45. Grolier scholar, 1952. Mem. VFW, Am. Legion, Masons, Beta Theta Pi. Roman Catholic. Home: 1030 Greenleaf Ave Wilmette IL 60091-2707

KLEIN, ROBERT MAJER, retired bank executive; b. N.Y.C., Apr. 1, 1940; s. Nicholas and Helen (Elias) K.; Susan R. Feder, Apr. 14, 1962; children: David, Eric. BA, Syracuse U., 1961. V.p. Merrill Lynch, N.Y.C., 1962-80, Donaldson Lufkin & Jennrette, N.Y.C., 1980-83, Paine Weber, N.Y.C., 1983-84; sr. v.p., dep. gen. mgr. Compagnie Fin. de CIC et de l'Union Europeenne, N.Y.C., 1984-94; ret., 1994. Avocations: game fishing, collecting early 20th century Am. art.

KLEIN, ROBERT MARSHALL, lawyer; b. Chgo., Mar. 21, 1957; s. Ronald Shevre and Jacqueline Carol (Margolin) K.; m. Cynthia Lynn Martin, Dec. 2, 1983; children: Brian, David, Jacob. BBA, U. Wis., 1979, JD, 1982. Bar: Wis. 1982, U.S. Dist. Ct. (we. dist.) Wis. 1982, Ill. 1982, U.S. Dist. Ct. (no. dist.) Ill. 1982, U.S. Ct. Appeals (7th cir.) 1982, U.S. Supreme Ct. 1985. Assoc. Laner, Muchin, Donbrow, Becker, Levin & Tominberg, Ltd., Chgo., 1982-88, ptnr., 1988-95; ptnr. Coffield, Ungaretti & Harris, Chgo., 1995-96, Klein, Dub & Holleb, Chgo., 1997—; mem. Ill. Atty. Registration and Disciplinary Commn., Ill. Supreme Ct., Chgo., 1987-94. Contbr. articles to profl. jours. Mem. Ill. Bar Assn. (employee benefits sect. coun. 1989—, chmn. 1993-94), Chgo. Bar Assn., Internat. Found. Employee Benefit Plans, Mensa. Avocations: swimming, piano, coin collecting. Home: 1152 Norman Ln Deerfield IL 60015-3114 Office: Klein Dub & Holleb 222 N La Salle St Ste 1900 Chicago IL 60601-1102

KLEIN, ROBERTA PHYLLIS, writer, editor, consultant to architects and designers; b. Columbus, Ohio, Dec. 26, 1934. Student U. Pitts., U. Miami. Exec. editor Fla. Designers Quar., Miami, 1978-83; editor-in-chief On Design mag., 1983-84; dir. Sunshine State Bank, South Miami, Fla., 1978-85; design writer Sunshine Mag., Ft. Lauderdale Sun Sentinel; former contbg. editor So. Accents Mag.; contbg. writer Restaurant Bus. Mag., 1987-91, stringer Money Mag., 1988; editor Fla. Real Estate Mag., 1991-92; editor, writer Fla. Architecture Mag., 1992—; contbr. Architectural Digest, Veranda Mag.; lectr. Purdue U., Ill., Inst. Bus. Designers, Am. Soc. Interior Designers. Contbr. to Fla. Design Mag., Architecture Mag., So. Fla. Bus., Jour., Fla. Real Estate Jour. Recipient Editl. awards Am. Soc. Interior Designers, Miami/Ft. Lauderdale, 1978, Inst. Bus. Designers, Fla. chpt., Miami, 1979, Interior Design Guild, Miami, 1981; Editl./Pictorial award AIA, Miami/Ft. Lauderdale chpt., 1980, Addy awards, 1977.

KLEIN, ROSALYN FINKELSTEIN, social worker; b. N.Y.C., Dec. 4, 1946; d. Philip and Hilda (Myers) Finkelstein; m. Edward R. Klein, June 14, 1970; children: Brian, Dana, Jennifer. BA, Hunter Coll., 1970; MA, NYU, 1973; MSW, Fordham U., 1983. Lic. clin. social worker, Conn.; diplomate Am. Bd. Examiners Clin. Social Work; cert. clin. supr. Acad. Cert. Social Workers; cert. speech and lang. pathologist. Speech pathologist N.Y.C. Bd. Edn., Bklyn., 1970-74, Princeton (N.J.) Med. Ctr., 1974-76; clin. supr. So. Conn. State U., New Haven, 1977; speech pathologist Easter Seal Rehab., Meriden, Conn., 1977-79; social worker Greenwich (Conn.) Dept. Social Svc., 1983—; social worker Milford (Conn.) Mental Health Ctr., 1985-86, Jewish Family Svc., Greenwich, 1995—; field instr. Fordham U., 1987—; mem. future planning com., operating com., mem. supervisory com., conflict mediation com. Greenwich Dept. Social Svcs., 1995—. Mem. Hadassah, Orange, 1976-94, Dem. Town Com., Greenwich, 1996-97; treas. Sisterhood/Synagogue, Orange, 1984-86. Mem. Conn. Soc. Clin. Social Workers. Avocations: walking, traveling, reading, theater.

KLEIN, SAMI WEINER, librarian; b. Worcester, Mass., July 6, 1939; d. Phillip and Barbara Rose (Ginsberg) Weiner; m. Eugene Robert Klein, Oct. 22, 1961; children: Pamela, Jeffrey, Elizabeth. BS, Simmons Coll., 1961; MLS, U. Md., 1973; postgrad., Johns Hopkins U., 1976-78. Chemist Hercules, Wilmington, Del., 1961-62, FDA, Washington, 1965-66; libr. NSWC, White Oak, Md., 1973-78; chief Hdqs. Libr. EPA, Washington, 1978-82; chief rsch. info. svcs. Nat. Inst. Svcs. and Tech., Gaithersburg, Md., 1982-95; chief rsch. libr. and info. program, rsch. libr. Nat. Inst. Stds. and Tech., Gaithersburg, Md., 1995-99; retired Nat. Inst. Svcs. and Tech., Gaithersburg, Md., 1999; cons. in field; mem. librs. exec. coun. Met. Washington Coun. of Govts., 1981-82; elected mem. com. Fed. Libr. Info. Ctr., 1993-95, chair, budget and fin. working group, 1994-98. Editor OIS Sci.-Tech Info, 1982-95; mem. editorial bd. Assn. Ofcly. Analyt. Chemists, 1985-92, Sci. and Tech. Librs., 1996—. Fed. govt. rep. Inst. for Sci. Info. Internat. Users Group, 1985-86; mem. edn. com. Fed. Libr. and Info. Ctr. Com., 1987-91. Recipient Gold medal Am. Soc. Chemists, 1961, Engring. award Govt. Inidustry Data Exch. Program, 1997. Mem. ALA (sec.-treas. Fed. Librs. Round Table 1983-84, rep. to NTIS 1984-90, bd. dirs. 1986-89, v.p. 1991, pres. 1991-92, nominations chair 1992-93, scholar 1994-96, chair privatization com. 1995-97, chair co-awards com. 1996—, 1st FLRT Disting. Svc. award 1995), Spl. Librs. Assn. (treas. info.-tech. group 1986-87, student loan com. 1984-85), D.C. Law Librs. Soc. (NIST v.p. standards com. for women 1988, pres. 1989, bd. dirs. Constar Credit Union 1994—), Fed. Libr. and Info. Network (exec. adv. com. 1989-91, sec. 1989, vice chair 1990-91), Jewish Mus. Md. (bd. dirs. 1999—), Beta Phi Mu. Democrat. Jewish. Home: 11041 Woodelves Way Columbia MD 21044-1002

KLEIN, SAMUEL EDWIN, lawyer; b. Phila., Apr. 17, 1946; s. Morris and Lillian (Hess) K.; m. Rebekah Susan Rosenberg, Aug. 28, 1971; children: Jared Noah, Zoe Aliyah. BBA, Temple U., 1968, JD, 1971. Bar: U.S. Supreme Ct., U.S. Ct. Appeals (3rd cir.), U.S. Dist. Ct. (ea. dist.) Pa. 1971. Law clk. U.S. Dist. Ct. (ea. dist.), Phila., 1971; atty. Kohn, Klein, Nast & Graf, P.C., Phila., 1972-92, Dechert Price & Rhodes, Phila., 1992—. Author: Media Survival Kit, 1986, 89, 94. Dir. ACLU Phila. Chpt., 1988-93; pres., bd. trustees Springside Sch., Phila. Sgt. USAF, 1968-72. Recipient First Amendment award Soc. Profl. Journalists, 1981, Fund for Religious Liberty award Am. Jewish Congress, 1998. Fellow Am. Coll. of Trial Lawyers; mem. ABA. Avocations: reading, tennis, cycling. Home: 8204 Seminole St Philadelphia PA 19118-3930 Office: Dechert Price & Rhoads 4000 Bell Atlantic Tower 1717 Arch St Ste 3 Philadelphia PA 19103-2793

KLEIN, SHELDON, computational linguist, educator; b. Chgo., May 15, 1935; s. Joseph and Bertha (Stone) K.; m. Carol Wallace, Oct. 20, 1955; 1 child, Jahna (Mrs. Paul N. Antoniades). B.A. in Anthropology, U. Calif., Berkeley, 1956, Ph.D. in Linguistics, 1963. With Artificial Intelligence Research Group, System Devel. Corp., Santa Monica, Calif., 1961-64; asst. prof. linguistics and computer sci. Carnegie-Mellon U., Pitts., 1964-66; assoc. prof. computer sci. and linguistics U. Wis., Madison, 1966-73, prof., 1973—, chmn. dept. linguistics, 1974-76; vis. dir. studies L'Ecole des hautes etudes en sciences sociales, Paris, 1976-77; vis. prof. Fakultät für Linguistik und Literaturwissenschaft, U. Bielefeld, Fed. Republic Germany, 1977-78; vis. fellow Clare Hall and Dept. Archaeology U. Cambridge, 1988; life mem. Clare Hall, 1988—; linguistic fieldwork with Kawaiisu Indians, U. Calif. Survey of Calif. Indian Langs., Cen. Calif., 1958, Wenner-Gren Found. Anthrop. Research, 1981-86; archaelogical fieldwork, Kebara cave, Mt. Carmel, Israel, 1990; cons. System Devel. Corp., 1965, 67. Contbr. articles to books and profl. jours. Life mem. in residence Clare Hall, Cambridge U., 1995. NSF grantee, 1969-73; Internat. Rsch. and Exchs. Bd. sr. scholar Soviet Ministry of Higher Edn., Fgn. Langs. Inst., Moscow, 1973. Fellow Am. Anthrop. Assn., Royal Anthrop. Inst. Gt. Britain and Ireland; mem. Am. Assn. Artificial Intelligence, Assn. Computational Linguistics, Cognitive Sci. Soc., Soc. Study on Indigenous Langs. of Americas, Linguistics Soc. Am. (life mem. 1997), Soc. Linguistic Anthropology, Sigma Xi. Office: U Wis Dept Computer Sci 1210 W Dayton St Madison WI 53706-1613

KLEIN, SNIRA L(UBOVSKY), Hebrew language and literature educator; came to U.S., 1959, naturalized, 1974; d. Avraham and Devora (Unger) Lubovsky; m. Earl H. Klein, Dec. 25, 1975. Tchr. cert., Tchrs. Seminar, Netanya, Israel, 1956; B. Rel. Edn., U. Judaism, 1961, M in Hebrew Lit., 1963; BA, Calif. State U., Northridge, 1966; MA, UCLA, 1971, PhD, 1983. Tchg. asst. UCLA, 1969-71; instr., continuing edn. U. Judaism, L.A., 1971-76, 94—, instr., 1975-84; vis. lectr. UCLA, 1985-91; adj. asst. prof. U. Judaism, 1984-94. Mem. Assn. for Jewish Studies, Nat. Assn. of Profs. of Hebrew, World Union of Jewish Studies. Jewish. Avocations: gardening, music. Office: U Judaism 15600 Mulholland Dr Los Angeles CA 90077-1519

KLEIN, STACY LYNN, educator; b. Framingham, Mass., Aug. 17, 1970; d. Stuart Matthew and Sheryl G. AA, Palm Beach C.C., 1990; BS in Adminstrn. Studies, Nova U., 1992; MIBA, Nova Southeastern U., 1994. Office mgr. Unitech Mgmt., Hollywood, Fla., 1993-95; prodr. Image Com, Inc., Ft. Lauderdale, Fla., 1994-96; admissions counselor Keiser Coll., Ft. Lauderdale, Fla., 1996-97; univ. rep. Nova Southeastern U., Ft. Lauderdale, Fla., 1997-99, student advisor, 1999—; adj. faculty Fla. Nat. Coll., Miami, 1999—, Broward C.C., Ft. Lauderdale, 1999—. Avocations: sailing, biking, tennis. Home: 16175 Golfclub Rd #108 Weston FL 33326 Office: Nova Southeastern U 3301 College Ave Fort Lauderdale FL 33314

KLEIN, STEPHEN THOMAS, performing arts executive; b. Cleve., Mar. 9, 1947; s. Howard B. and Lilly (Gatchell) K.; m. Mary Ussery, Nov. 19, 1972; children—William Howard, Sarah Katherine. B.F.A., Boston U., 1970. Orch. Mgr. Cleve. Orch., 1978-82; exec. dir. Denver Symphony Orch., Colo., 1982-85, Nat. Symphony Orch., Washington, 1985-94; mng. dir. Pitts. Pub. Theater, 1994—.

KLEIN, T(HEODORE) E(IBON) D(ONALD), writer; b. N.Y.C., July 15, 1947; s. Richard and Norma (Kashins) K. A.B., Brown U., 1969; M.F.A., Columbia U., 1972. Asst. story editor Paramount Pictures, N.Y.C., 1972-75; editor-in-chief Twilight Zone Mag., N.Y.C., 1981-86; editor CrimeBeat mag., N.Y.C., 1991-93; editor mag. Sci-Fi Entertainment, Herndon, Va., 1995. Author: (novel) The Ceremonies, 1984, (story collection) Dark Gods, 1985; screenwriter: (feature film) Trauma, 1994; contbr. fiction to anthologies; author articles in mags., newspapers. Recipient novel award Brit. Fantasy Soc., 1985, novella award World Fantasy Soc., 1986. Mem. Phi Beta Kappa. Home: 210 W 89th St New York NY 10024-1805

KLEIN, VERLE WESLEY, corporate executive, retired naval officer; b. Stickney, S.D., Apr. 7, 1933; s. Albert and Kate (Noteboom) K.; children by previous marriage: Pamela Louise, Janice Lynn; m. Marjorie Nancy Hagan, Apr. 29, 1989; 1 child, Tia Leigh. BS, U.S. Naval Postgrad. Sch., 1962; MBA, George Washington U., 1975. Commd. ensign U.S. Navy, 1954, advanced through grades to rear adm., 1980; assigned to (Patrol Squadron 22), 1955-58; flight instr. (Naval Air Sta.), Corpus Christi, Tex., 1958-60; with (Air Antisubmarine Squadron 22), 1963-65; test pilot (Naval Air Test Center), Patuxent River, Md., 1967-69; comdg. officer (Light Attack Squadron 4), 1969-70; ops. officer (USS Wasp), 1971-72; asst. aviation comdr. detailer (Bur. Naval Personnel), 1972-74; head major procurement programs and budgeting br. (Naval Material Command), 1975-76; exec. asst. and naval aide to asst. sec. (Dept. Navy), 1976-78; comdr. (Naval Air Station), Patuxent River, 1978-80; dep. dir. Office Budgets and Reports, also fiscal mgmt. div. (Office of Chief Naval Ops.), 1980-85; v.p. BDM Corp., McLean, Va., 1985-87; cons., 1987—. Decorated Silver Star, Legion of Merit with four gold stars, D.F.C., 24 Air medals with two gold stars, Navy Commendation medal, Gallantry Cross Republic Vietnam, numerous others. Mem. Am. Soc. Mil. Comptrollers. Home: 6824 Greywalls Ln Raleigh NC 27614-9729

KLEIN, WOODY, writer, editor, educator; b. N.Y.C., Dec. 17, 1929; s. Albert Maurice and Fannie Joan (Lichtblau) K.; m. Audrey Lehman; children: Wendy, James. BA, Dartmouth Coll., 1951; MS, Columbia U., 1952. Reporter Washington Post, 1954-56; reporter, columnist N.Y. World Telegram & Sun, N.Y.C., 1956-65; press sec. Mayor John V. Lindsay, N.Y.C., 1965-68; dir. corp. publs. IBM, Armonk, N.Y., 1968-92; editor Westport (Conn.) News Brooks Cmty. Newspapers, 1992-98; author-in-residence Westport Hist. Soc., 1998—; pres. Woody Klein Assocs., Westport; adj. prof. journalism NYU, 1960-66, U. Bridgeport, Conn., 1968-76, Fairfield (Conn.) U., 1980-90, Iona Coll., New Rochelle, N.Y., 1998—. author: Let in the Sun, 1964, Lindsay's Promise, 1970; contbr. numerous articles to newspapers, mags., profl. jours. V.p. United Way of Westport/Weston, Conn., 1985-90; mem. Rep. Town Meeting, Westport, 1971-73. Recipient award for disting. reporting Sigma Delta Chi, 1960, Page One award Newspaper Guild N.Y., 1960, award Newspaper Reporters Assn., 1961, N.Y. Philanthropic League, 1961, NCCJ, 1965, Excellence award IBM, 1987, 88, 89 (2), Pultzer Prize nomination, 1996. Mem. Soc. Profl. Journalists (1st Pl. award 1994), New Eng. Press Assn. (1st Pl. award 1996), Rotary, Conn. Press Club (award 1993-97, 1st Pl. award 1993, 94). Avocations: tennis, classical music., sketching. Home and Office: 12 Blue Ribbon Dr Westport CT 06880-2218

KLEINBARD, EDWARD D., lawyer; b. N.Y.C., Nov. 6, 1951; s. Martin L. and Joan K.; m. Norma F. Cirincione, Oct. 17, 1947. BA, MA, Brown U., 1973; JD, Yale U., 1976. Bar: N.Y. 1977. Ptnr. Cleary, Gottlieb, Steen & Hamilton, N.Y.C. Book rev., article editor Yale Law Jour., 1975-76; contbr. articles to profl. jours. Fellow Am. Coll. Tax Counsel; mem. ABA, N.Y. State Bar Assn. (co-chmn. fin. instruments com. 1989-91), Assn. Bar City of N.Y., Am. Assn. Fin. Engrs. (bd. advisors). Office: Cleary Gottlieb Steen & Hamilton 1 Liberty Plz Fl 38 New York NY 10006-1470

KLEINBERG, DAVID LEWIS, education administrator; b. San Francisco, Feb. 28, 1943; s. Moe and Lilyan (Abrams) K.; m. Gay Buros, Mar. 21, 1970 (div. 1983); children—Leah, Rebecca; m. Patrice Ellen Greenwood, Apr. 29, 1984; stepchildren: Aaron, Brian, Jesse. B.A., San Francisco State U., 1970. Prodr. Sta. KTVU TV, Oakland, Calif., 1978-79, 89-90; writer, editor San Francisco Chronicle, 1960-80, editor Sunday Datebook, 1980-94; co-dir. Bay Area Classic Learning, San Francisco, 1994—. Served with U.S. Army, 1965-67, Vietnam. Decorated Bronze Star. Jewish. Avocation: basketball, post card collecting, stand-up comic. Home and Office: 287 Sussex St San Francisco CA 94131-2936

KLEINBERG, HOWARD J., newspaper columnist; b. N.Y.C., Oct. 23, 1932; s. Benjamin and Ruth (Wile) K.; m. Natalie Bernstein, Feb. 22, 1953; children: Linda Kleinberg Landy, Eliot, Eileen Kleinberg Newmark, David. Student pub. schs. Mem. staff Miami (Fla.) News, 1950-65, 66-88, mng. editor, 1968-76, editor, 1976-88; nat. columnist Cox Newspapers, Miami, 1988—; history columnist Miami Herald, 1989—. Author: Miami, The Way We Were, 1985, The Great Florida Hurricane and Disaster, 1993, Miami Beach, A History, 1994. Mem. Orange Bowl Com. Served with AUS, 1953-55, Korea. Recipient 1st pl. award Fla. Edn. Assn., 1985, Miami Urban League Black Awareness award, 1975, 1st pl. awards for column writing, Cox Newspapers, 1987, 88.

KLEINBERG, JUDITH G., lawyer, children's advocate; b. Hartford, Conn., Jan. 28, 1946; d. Burleigh B. and Ruth (Leven) Greenberg; m. James Paul Kleinberg, Aug. 30, 1970; children: Alexander, Lauren. BA cum laude, U. Mich., 1968; JD, U. Calif., Berkeley, 1971. Atty. pvt. practice, San Francisco, 1971-74; legal affairs reporter comml. and pub. TV, San Francisco, 1974-76; prof. law Mills Coll., Oakland, Calif., 1977-84; chief of staff The Global Fund for Women, Los Altos, Calif., 1987-88; pub. interest atty., non-profit corp. law/orgn. specialist alternative dispute resolution Palo Alto, Calif., 1988-94; exec. dir. Kids in Common: A Children & Families Collaborative, San Jose, Calif., 1994—; chair Am. Promise, Silicon Valley, 1997—; arbitrator/mediator, legal adv. for abortion rights, women and children's rights and environ. groups, Santa Clara County and Calif., 1980—; speaker in field; chair Am.'s Promise - Silicon Valley. Mem. bd. editors Calif. Law Rev., 1969-71. Mem. steering com. lawyers coun. No. Calif. sect. ACLU, bd. dirs., 1990-92; founder, chairperson No. Calif. Friends of Pediat. AIDS Found.; past pres. Com. for Green Foothills; mem. legis. and steering coms. Calif. Coalition for Childhood Immunization, 1995—; mem. Calif. Children's Advs. Roundtable, 1995—; bd. dirs. Palo Alto SAFE, Support Network for Battered Women, 1990-92, Palo Alto Coun. PTAs, Leadership Midpeninsula, 1994-96; pres. Palo Alto Stanford divsn. Am. Heart Assn., 1994-95; v.p. Assn. for Sr. Day Health, 1994-95; founder Safer Summer Project; pres., legal counsel Calif. Abortion and Reproductive Rights Action League, 1980-86. Recipient Calif. Pks. and Recreation Soc. Merit award, 1995, World of People award Girl Scouts Am., Santa Clara County, 1996. Mem. Nat. Assn. Child Advocates, Calif. Women Lawyers (v.p. 1986-88).

KLEINBERG, LAWRENCE H., food industry executive; b. N.Y.C., Dec. 20, 1943; s. Paul and Gertrude (Voron) K.; m. Lois Helene Kass, June 10, 1967; children: Brian Andrew, Rachel Adele. B.A. in Econs., Adelphi U., 1965, M.B.A., 1969. Analyst, Pfizer, Inc., N.Y.C., 1965-69; various fin. mgmt. positions Beech-Nut, Inc., N.Y.C., 1969-73; v.p., controller Life Savers, Inc., N.Y.C., 1973-79, sr. v.p. fin., 1979-83, exec. v.p., 1983, pres., 1984, div. pres. Nabisco Brands, Inc., 1984-87; v.p., corp. controller Nabisco Brands, Inc., Parsippany, N.J., 1987-88; sr. v.p. fin. Nabisco Foods Group, Parsippany, N.J., 1988-94; sr. v.p. planning Nabisco, Inc., Parsippany, 1995-96; pvt. investor, cons., 1996—.

KLEINBERG, MARVIN H., lawyer; b. N.Y.C., Aug. 17, 1927; s. Herman and Lillian (Grossman) K.; m. Irene Aertker, July 7, 1962; children—Sarah Elizabeth, Ethan Chaim, Joel Victor. BA in Physics, UCLA, 1949; JD, U. Calif., Berkeley, 1953. Bar: Calif. 1954, also U.S. Patent Office, U.S. Supreme Ct. 1954. Dep. pub. defender Los Angeles County, 1954; patent atty. RCA, Camden, N.J., 1955-57, Litton Industries, Inc., Beverly Hills, Calif., 1957-61; patent counsel Modal Systems Inc., La Jolla, Calif., 1961-63; mem. firm Golove & Kleinberg, Los Angeles, 1963-70, Golove, Kleinberg & Morganstern, Los Angeles, 1970-72, Kleinberg, Morganstern & Scholnick, Los Angeles, 1973-76, Kleinberg, Morganstern, Scholnick & Mann, Beverly Hills, 1976-79; sole practice Marvin H. Kleinberg, Inc., Beverly Hills, 1979-84; ptnr. Arant, Kleinberg & Lerner, 1985-93, Arant, Kleinberg, Lerner & Ram, 1993-95, Arant, Kleinberg, Lerner & Ram, LLP, L.A., 1996-97, Kleinberg & Lerner, LLP, 1998—; adj. lectr. patent law, mem. Innovation Clinic Adv. Council Franklin Pierce Law Center, Concord, N.H., 1975—; adv. council PTC Research Found., 1981; dir., sec. Digem, Inc., Los Angeles. Active YMCA Indian Guides, 1974-79; pres. Opportunity Houses Inc., Riverside, Calif., 1973-76, UCLA Class of '49, 1979-84; co-chairperson Sholem Ednl. Inst., Los Angeles, 1974-75; chief referee Region 58, Am. Youth Soccer Orgn., 1976-84; dir. Dental Med. Diagnostic Sys., Inc., 1996—. Sgt. AUS, 1946-47. Mem. ABA, Los Angeles Intellectual Property Law Assn., Los Angeles County Bar Assn., Am. Intellectual Property Law Assn., Zeta Beta Tau. Home: 3901 Cody Rd Sherman Oaks CA 91403-5022 Office: Kleinberg & Lerner LLP 2049 Century Park E Ste 1080 Los Angeles CA 90067-3112

KLEINBERG, NORMAN CHARLES, lawyer; b. Phila., July 18, 1946; s. Frank and Mildred Brosnan (Hill) K.; m. Marcia Sue Topperman, Jan. 31, 1971; children—Lauren Blythe, Joanna Leigh. A.B., Tufts U., 1968; J.D., Columbia U., 1972. Bar: N.Y. 1973, U.S. Supreme Ct., U.S. Ct. Appeals (1st, 2d, 3d and 4th cirs.), U.S. Dist. Ct. (so. and ea. dists.) N.Y., U.S. Tax Ct., U.D. Dist. Ct. (ea. dist.) Wis., U.S. Dist. Ct. (no. dist.) Calif., U.S. Dist. Ct. (ea. dist.) Mich. Law clk. to judge U.S. Dist. Ct. (so. dist.) N.Y., N.Y.C., 1972-74; assoc. Hughes Hubbard & Reed, N.Y.C., 1974-80, ptnr., 1980—. Articles editor Columbia Jour. Law and Social Problems, 1971-72. Served to staff sgt. USAR, 1968-74. Fellow Am. Coll. Trial Lawyers; mem. ABA, Fed. Bar Coun., Assn. of Bar of City of N.Y. (com. on state cts. of superior jurisdiction, com. profl. responsibility, com. profl. and judicial ethics, com. on judiciary, coun. on jud. adminstrn.), Internat. Bar Assn., N.Y. State Bar Assn., Def. Rsch. Inst. Home: 460 E 79th St New York NY 10021-1443 Office: Hughes Hubbard & Reed 1 Battery Park Plz Fl 12 New York NY 10004-1482

KLEINDIENST, RICHARD GORDON, lawyer; b. Winslow, Ariz., Aug. 1923; s. Alfred and Gladys (Love) K.; m. Margaret Dunbar, Sept. 3, 1948; children: Alfred Dunbar, Wallace Heath, Anne Lucile, Carolyn Love. AB magna cum laude, Harvard U., 1947, LLB, 1950; LLD, Susquehanna U. Bar: Ariz. 1950. Dep. atty. gen. Dept. Justice, 1969-72, atty. gen., 1972-73; past mem. bd. Small Bus. Devel. Ctr., Office Econ. Opportunity. Author: Justice, The Memoirs of an Attorney General, 1985. Mem. Ariz. Ho. of Reps. from Maricopa County, 1953-54; chmn. Ariz. Young Republican League, 1955, Ariz. Rep. Com., 1956-60, 61- 63; mem. Rep. Nat. Com., 1956-60, 61, 63; nat. dir. field operations Goldwater Pres. com., 1964; candidate for gov. Ariz., 1964; nat. dir. field operations Nixon for Pres. Com., 1968; gen. counsel Rep. Nat. Com., 1968; past mem. Ariz., Am. heart assns., Nat. Symphony Orch. Served to lt. USAAF, World War II. Mem. FBA (pres. 1974—), Phi Beta Kappa, Sigma Alpha Epsilon. Clubs: Thunderbirds, Arizona (Phoenix); Burning Tree (Bethesda, Md.). Office: 3103 W Crest View Dr Prescott AZ 86305-5001

KLEINE, HERMAN, economist; b. N.Y.C., Mar. 6, 1920; s. Max and Fannie (Schechter) K.; m. Paula Stein, June 16, 1962; children—Joseph, Michael. B.S., State U. N.Y. at Albany, 1941; M.A., Clark U., 1942, Ph.D., 1951. Researcher for Nat. Indsl. Conf. Bd., 1946; instr. to asst. prof. Worcester Polytech. Inst., 1946-49; economist ECA, Mut. Security Agy., The Hague, Netherlands, 1949-53; internat. relations and econs. FOA, ICA, Washington, 1953-57; dir. U.S. Ops. Mission to Ethiopia, ICA, 1957-59, asst. dep. dir. for ops., 1959-61; Nat. War Coll., 1961-62; AID adviser U.S. Mission to UN, N.Y.C., 1962-64; dep. asst. adminstr. for Africa AID, Washington, 1964-67; dep. dir. U.S. AID mission to Brazil, 1967-69; asso. U.S. coordinator Alliance for Progress, 1969-70; dep. U.S. coordinator, asst. adminstr. Latin Am. Bur. AID, Washington, 1971-76; advisor to controller Interam. Devel. Bank, 1976-84; dir. internship programs Ctr. Immigration

Policy and Refugee Assistance, Georgetown U., 1984-86; cons., mediator, 1986—; mem. U.S. delegation UN Gen. Assembly, 1962, 63. Served from pvt. to capt. USAAF, 1942-46. Recipient AID Distinguished honor award, 1973, Adminstrs. Distinguished Career Service award, 1976, Superior Honor award Dept. State, 1976, Distinguished Alumnus award State U. N.Y. at Albany, 1977; duPont fellow, 1948; named to Hempstead, N.Y. Sch. Dist. Hall Fame, 1986. Mem. Kappa Phi Kappa. Jewish. Home and Office: 7305 Burdette Ct Bethesda MD 20817-2907

KLEINER, ARNOLD JOEL, television station executive; b. N.Y.C., Apr. 7, 1943; s. Leo and Hannah K.; m. Carol Dunn, Aug. 15, 1965; children: Kim, Kerri, Keith. BBA, Pace Coll., 1967. Acct. exec. KDKA Radio, Pitts., 1968-69, WJZ-TV, Balt., 1969-71; sales mgr. TVAR (Group W), N.Y.C., 1974-75; acct. exec. TVAR, Chgo., 1971-72; sales mgr. WBZ-TV, Boston, 1972-74; gen. sales mgr. WJZ-TV, Balt., 1975-78; dir. sales WPVI-TV, Phila., 1978-81; v.p., gen. mgr. WMAR-TV, Balt., 1981—; pres., gen. mgr. KABC-TV, L.A., 1996—. Chmn. media rels. com. United Way Ctrl. Md., Balt., 1982-84; co-chmn. Md. reg. NCCJ, 1986-90, sr. co-chair, 1990-91; bd. dirs. Levindale, Balt., 1982-84; mem. adv. bd. Md. Fedn. Parents for Drug Free Use, Balt., 1986—, William Donald Schaefer Ctr. for Pub. Policy, Balt., 1986—; chmn. edn. com. Greater Balt. Com., 1986—, bd. dirs., 1989—, pres. chamber divsn., 1991—, Coll. of Notre Dame, Md., 1989—; mem. Mayor's Coord. Com. on Criminal Justice, Balt., 1983-88, Variety Club of Md., 1984, Johns Hopkins Children Ctr.'s Devel. Com., 1984—; bd. dirs. Balt. Reads, Inc., Greater Balt. Com.; chmn. adv. com. Mayor's Office Internat. Programs; bd. dirs. Alvin Ailey Dance Theater Found. of Md., Inc., 1990—. Recipient Victorine Q. Adams Humanitarian award, Am. Men's ORT Cmty. Achievement award, 1986. Mem. Md./D.C. Broadcasters Assn. (dir. 1984), TV Bur. Advt. (sales adv. com. 1975-78), Advt. Assn. of Balt., Advt. Club of Balt., Balt. Jewish Coun. (bd. dirs., mem. exec. com. 1985—), Nat. Assn. Broadcasters. Office: Sta KABC-TV 4151 Prospect Ave Los Angeles CA 90027-4524*

KLEINER, DIANA ELIZABETH EDELMAN, art history educator, administrator; b. N.Y.C., Sept. 18, 1947; d. Morton Henry and Hilda Rachel (Wyner) Edelman; m. Fred S. Kleiner, Dec. 22, 1972; 1 child, Alexander Mark. BA magna cum laude, Smith Coll., 1969; MA, MPhil, Columbia U., 1970, 74, PhD, 1976; MA (hon.), Yale U., 1989. Lectr., asst. prof. U. Va., Charlottesville, 1975-76, 76-78; vis. asst. prof. U. Mass., Boston, 1979; Mellon faculty fellow Harvard U., Cambridge, Mass., 1979-80; asst. prof. Yale U., New Haven, 1980-82, assoc. prof., 1982-89; fellow Whitney Humanities Ctr., Yale U., New Haven, 1984-87; master Pierson Coll., Yale U., New Haven, 1986-87; dir. grad. studies dept. history of art Yale U., New Haven, 1988-90; prof. history of art and classics Yale U., New Haven, 1989-95, dir. grad. studies dept. classics, 1991-94, chair dept. classics, 1994-95, Dunham prof. classics and history of art, 1995—, dep. provost for the arts, 1995—; adv. bd. Archaeol. News, Tallahassee, 1980—, Am. Jour. Archaeology, Boston, 1985-98; mem., chair program for ann. meetings com. Archaeol. Inst. Am., Boston, 1988-93. Author: Roman Group Portraiture, 1977, The Monument of Philopappos in Athens, 1983, Roman Imperial Funerary Altars with Portraits, 1987, Roman Sculpture, 1992, paperback edit., 1994; editor: I, Claudia: Women in Ancient Rome, 1996, I Claudia II: Further Reflections on Women in Ancient Rome, 1999. Bd. dirs. Westville Cmty. Nursery Sch., New Haven, 1989-90, The Foote Sch., New Haven, 1994—. Grantee: Am. Coun. Learned Socs., 1979, NEH, 1980, 95, Am. Philos. Soc. 1982, The John Paul Getty Trust, 1992. Mem. Archaeol. Inst. Am., Am. Philol. Assn., Coll. Art Assn., Am. Numismatic Soc. Home: 102 Rimmon Rd Woodbridge CT 06525-1941

KLEINER, ELAINE LAURA, English literature educator; b. Portland, Oreg., May 2, 1942; d. Eugene Michael and Florence Isabelle (Hoffman) K. *Elaine's great grandfather, Henry Jenkins, was an artist and also served with the Company H of the 117th Illinois Volunteer Infantry in the Civil War. His daughter, Annie Ardner, the descendent of Welsh, Irish, and German ancestors, was born in Indiana. Annie's daughter Carrie, a daughter of Union Veterans of the Civil War, married John Hoffman, the son of an Iowa farmer. John's son, Johnny, won several ribbons, seven battle stars, the Purple Star, and the French Croix de Guerre in World War II. He served as attache to the U.S. Embassy in Rome for three years.* BA, Oreg. State U., 1964; MA, U. Chgo., 1966, PhD, 1971. Tchg. asst. U. Wis., Madison, 1966-67; instr. English Wis. State U., Whitewater, 1966, 67; asst. prof. English Ind. State U., Terre Haute, 1969-76, assoc. prof., 1976-81, acting dir. honors, 1977-78, dir. univ. studies, 1976-85, prof. English, 1981—; mng. editor Sci.-Fiction Studies, Terre Haute, 1967-69. Author: This Sacred Earth and Other Poems, 1997, Beside Great Waters: Poems of the Highlands and Islands, 1997; co-editor: Sacramental Acts: The Love Poems of Kenneth Rexroth, 1997. Mem., patron Terre Haute Choral Assn., 1980—; bd. dirs. United Ministries for Higher Edn., Terre Haute, 1978-85. Fulbright sr. scholar USIA, Romania, 1989; NEH summer fellow, 1979; Ind. Arts Commn. grantee, 1983, Ind. Humanities grantee, 1985. Mem. Assn. for Sci. and Culture, Assn. Tchrs. Tech. Writing, Ind. Coll. English Assn., Soc. for Romanian Studies, Ind. Tchrs. of Writing, Ind. Writers Assn. Democrat. Eastern Orthodox. Avocations: sailing, creative writing, cycling, swimming, hiking. Home: 1531 S 6th St Terre Haute IN 47802-1607 Office: Ind State U Root Hall 207 Terre Haute IN 47809

KLEINER, FRED SCOTT, art historian, archaeologist, educator, editor; b. N.Y.C., Apr. 29, 1948; m. Diana Elizabeth Edelman, Dec. 22, 1972; 1 child, Alexander Mark. BA with honors, U. Pa., 1968; MA, Columbia U., 1969, PhD, 1973. Agora fellow Am. Sch. Classical Studies, Athens, Greece, 1973-75; asst. prof. art history and archaeology U. Va., Charlottesville, 1975-78; asst. prof. Boston U., 1978-81, assoc. prof., 1981-86, prof., 1986—, dir. grad. studies dept. art history, 1979-81, 99—, chmn. dept. art history, 1981-85, sr. fellow Soc. Fellows Humanities, 1985-86; excavator, Cosa, Italy, 1969-70; vis. prof. Yale U., New Haven, 1997. Author: Greek and Roman Coins in the Athenian Agora, 1976, The Early Cistophoric Coinage, 1977, Mediaeval and Modern Coins in the Athenian Agora, 1978, The Arch of Nero in Rome, 1985, Art through the Ages, 10th edit., 1995; editor-in-chief Am. Jour. Archaeology, 1985-98; mem. adv. bd. Archaeol. News, 1980—; contbr. articles to profl. jours.; contbr. to other books, encyclopedias and exhbn. catalogues. Bd. dirs. Yale Youth Hockey Assn., 1994-97, v.p., 1996-97; co-founder, mgr. Conn. Ice Dogs, 1997—. Grantee Am. Philos. Soc., 1971, 80, Am. Coun. Learned Socs., 1978, 82; Guggenheim fellow, 1988-89. Fellow Am. Numismatic Soc. (mem. publs. com. 1982-91, trustee 1989-91); mem. Archaeol. Inst. Am. (chmn. fellowship com. 1985, mem. pubs. com. 1985-98), Coll. Art Assn. (mem. Morey Book award com., 1999—). E-mail: fsk@bu.edu. Home: 102 Rimmon Rd Woodbridge CT 06525-1941 Office: Boston U Dept Art History Boston MA 02215

KLEINER, RICHARD ARTHUR, writer, editor; b. N.Y.C., Mar. 9, 1921; s. Israel Simon and Alma (Kempner) K.; m. Hortensia Rivas, Aug. 7, 1954; children: Katherine Evert, Cynthia Smetana, Peter. Litt.B., Rutgers U., 1942. With Newspaper Enterprise Assn., Cleve., 1947-49, N.Y.C., 1949-64, L.A., 1964-86; sr. editor Newspaper Enterprise Assn., 1977-85; West Coast dir. United Media Prodns., 1982-85; columnist United Media, 1986—; mem. journalism faculty Calif. State Coll., Long Beach, 1975-77, UCLA, 1977-82, Coll. of Desert, 1986-88; columnist Weekly Packet, Blue Hill, Maine, 1991-95. Author: books, including E.S.P. and the Stars, 1970, Index of Initials and Acronyms, 1971, Take One, 1974, The Two of Us, 1976, Hollywood's Greatest Love Stories, 1976, Please Don't Shoot My Dog, 1981, (with Alice Faye) Growing Older but Staying Younger, 1990, Rock Hudson: Friend of Mine, 1990; book editor: The Desert Sun, 1986-93. Served with U.S. Army, 1942-46. Address: 32094 Via Buena San Juan Capistrano CA 92675-3823

KLEINFELD, ANDREW JAY, federal judge; b. 1945. BA magna cum laude, Wesleyan U., 1966; JD cum laude, Harvard U., 1969. Law clk. Alaska Supreme Ct., 1969-71; U.S. magistrate U.S. Dist. Ct. Alaska, Fairbanks, 1971-74; pvt. practice law Fairbanks, 1971-86; judge U.S. Dist. Ct. Alaska, Anchorage, 1986-91, U.S. Ct. Appeals (9th cir.), San Francisco, 1991—. Contbr. articles to profl. jours. Mem. Alaska Bar Assn. (pres. 1982-83, bd. govs. 1981-84), Tanana Valley Bar Assn. (pres. 1974-75), Phi Beta Kappa. Republican. Office: US Ct Appeals 9th Cir Courthouse Sq 250 Cushman St Ste 3-a Fairbanks AK 99701-4665

KLEINFELD, ERWIN, mathematician, educator; b. Vienna, Austria, Apr. 19, 1927; came to U.S., 1940; s. Lazar and Gina (Schönbach) K.; m. Margaret Morgan, July 2, 1968; children—Barbara, David. B.S., CCNY, 1948; M.A., U. Pa., 1949; Ph.D., U. Wis., 1951. Instr. U. Chgo., 1951-53; asst. prof. Ohio State U., 1953-56, asso. prof., 1957-60, prof., 1960-62; prof. math. Syracuse U., 1962-67, U. Hawaii, 1967-68, U. Iowa, 1968—; vis. lectr. Yale, 1956-57; cons. Nat. Bur. Standards, summer 1953; research specialist U. Conn., summer 1955; research mathematician Bowdoin Coll., summer 1957; research asso. Cornell U., summer 1958, U. Calif. at Los Angeles, summer 1959, Stanford, summer 1960, Inst. Def. Analysis, summer 1961, 62, AID-India, summer 1964, 65; vis. prof. Emory U., 1976-77; Cons. Edn. IX Project, World Bank, U. Indonesia, 1985-86, Mucia/Ind. U.-(ITM) Shah Alam, Malaysia Project, 1988-89. Editorial bd. Jour. Algebra-Academic Press; cons. editor, Merrill Pub. Co.-Div. Bell & Howell. Contbr. articles research jours. Served with AUS, 1945-46. Wis. Alumni Rsch. Found. fellow, 1949-51, vis. rsch. fellow U. New Eng., Australia, 1992; grantee U.S. Army Rsch. Office, 1955-70, NSF, 1970-75. Mem. Am. Math. Soc., Sigma Xi. Office: Univ Iowa Math Dept Iowa City IA 52242-1419

KLEINFELDER, CAROLE, lacrosse head coach. Head lacrosse coach Harvard U., Cambridge, Mass., 1978—; dir. pub. World Under-19 Lacrosse Tournament, Havertown, Pa., 1996; lacrosse player U.S. Nat. Team. Named Nat. Coach of the Yr. NCAA, 1990. Mem. U.S. Women's Lacrosse Assn. (pres. 1992-94). Office: Harvard Univ The Murr Ctr 65 N Harvard St Boston MA 02163-1012*

KLEINGARTNER, ARCHIE, founding dean, educator; b. Gackle, N.D., Aug. 10, 1936; s. Emanuel and Ottile (Kuhn) K.; m. Dorothy Jean Hanselmann, Sept. 21, 1957; children: Elizabeth, Thomas. BA, U. Minn., 1959; MS, U. Oreg., 1961; PhD, U. Wis., 1965. Asst. and assoc. prof. UCLA, 1964-69, assoc. dean, chmn., 1969-71, prof., 1971-75, 83—, dir. entertainment mgmt. program, 1988—; founding dean Sch. Pub. Policy and Social Rsch. UCLA, Berkeley, 1994—; v.p. U. Calif. Sys., Berkeley, 1975-83; cons. in field, 1967—; arbitrator in field, 1971—. Mem. labor mgmt. disputes panel City of L.A., 1978—. With U.S. Army, 1954-56. Mem. London Sch. Econs., Alpha Kappa Psi. Republican. Methodist. Avocations: tennis, biking, gardening. Home: 13014 Brentwood Ter Los Angeles CA 90049-4807 Office: UCLA Sch Pub Policy and Social Rsch PO Box 951656 Los Angeles CA 90095-1656

KLEINHENZ, CHRISTOPHER, foreign language educator, researcher; b. Indpls., Dec. 29, 1941; s. John Emory and Louise Eleanor (Ross); m. Margaret Ellen Zechiel, Aug. 1, 1964; children: Steven Russell, Michael Thomas. BA, Ind. U., 1964, MA, 1966, PhD, 1969. Asst. prof., dir. Bologna program Ind. U., 1970-71; instr. U. Wis., Madison, 1968-69, asst. prof., 1969-70, asst. prof., dept. French and Italian, 1971-75, assoc. prof., 1975-80, chmn. medieval studies program, 1975-80, 81-84, 89-95, 96—, prof., 1980—, chmn. dept., 1985-88; dir. devel. grant NEH, Madison, 1976-79, co-dir. rsch. tools grant, 1980-84. Author: The Early Italian Sonnet, 1986; editor: Medieval Manuscripts and Textual Criticism, 1976, Medieval Studies in North America, 1982, Garland Studies in Medieval Literature, 1986—, Dante Studies, 1988—; co-editor: Saint Augustine the Bishop: A Book of Essays, 1994, Garland Medieval Casebooks, 1991—, Fearful Hope: Approaching the New Millenium, 1999; chmn. editorial bd. Medieval Acad. Reprints for Teaching, 1981-93; bibliographer MLA, N.Y.C., 1981-88, BIGLLI, Rome, 1994—, Dante Studies, 1984—; book rev. editor Italica, 1984-93; translator: Dante Alighieri, Il Fiore and the Detto d'Amore, 1999. Chmn. com. on ctrs. and regional assns. Medieval Acad., 1993-99. Newberry Libr./NEH grantee, 1988-89. Mem. Medieval Assn. of Midwest (pres. 1984-85), Dante Soc. Am. (mem. coun. 1985-91), Am. Boccaccio Assn. (v.p. 1987-93, pres. 1993-97), Am. Assn. Tchrs. of Italian (v.p. 1993-98, pres. 1999). Avocations: sports, stamp collecting, photography, travel. Home: 2247 Fox Ave Madison WI 53711-1922 Office: U Wis Dept French and Italian 1220 Linden Dr Madison WI 53706-1525

KLEINKNECHT, KENNETH SAMUEL, retired aerospace company executive, former federal space agency official; b. Washington, July 24, 1919; s. Christian Frederick and Nell May (Barr) K.; m. Patricia Jean Todd, May 24, 1947; children: Linda May, Patricia Ann, Frederick William. B.S.M.E., Purdue U., 1942. Project engr. NACA Lewis Research Center, Cleve., 1942-51; aero. research scientist NASA Flight Research Ctr., Edwards AFB, Calif., 1951-59; successively mgr. Mercury Project, dep. mgr. Gemini Program, mgr. command and service modules NASA Johnson Space Ctr., 1959-70, mgr. Skylab Program,, 1970-74; dir. flight ops. NASA Johnson Space Ctr., Houston, 1974-76; asst. mgr. Orbiter Project NASA Johnson Space Ctr., 1976-77; head constrn. space shuttle orbiter NASA Johnson Space Center, 1979-81; dep. assoc. adminstr. for space transp. systems European ops. to European Space Agy., Paris NASA Hdqrs., Washington, 1977-79; mgr. program engrng., sr. space transp. system tech. adviser Denver div. Martin Marietta Aerospace, 1981-83, mgr. mfg. procurement and testing, 1983-84, dir. design to cost/productivity Space Sta. Project, 1984-88; mgr. laser project Zenith Star Program, 1988-90, ret., 1990. Exec. bd. Sam Houston Area council Boy Scouts Am., Houston, 1972-77. Recipient (with others) Group Achievement award for Mercury Project NASA, 1962, NASA medal for outstanding leadership Pres. of U.S., 1963, 81, John J. Montgomery award San Diego chpt. Nat. Soc. Aerospace Profls., 1963, with others) Group Achievement award for X-15 Research Airplane Flight Test Orgn., 1964, for Gemini Program, 1966, NASA Exceptional Service medal, 1969, NASA Disting. Service medal, 1969, 73. Fellow Am. Astron. Soc. (W. Randolph Lovelace II award 1975); assoc. fellow AIAA; mem. Internat. Acad. Astronautics. Club: Masons. Home: 825 Front Range Rd Littleton CO 80120-4005 *As a member of the team that made lunar and space shuttle missions successes, I believe that my "formula for success" is one part high goal and one hundred parts persistence. I have always believed in establishing principles, high ideals of conduct as structures to direct our lives. It is voluntary total dedication to valid ideals, attention to detail, discipline and accepting accountability that will bring success on every level. To reach beyond one's present grasp is to assure ever higher attainments in the future.*

KLEINKORT, JOSEPH ALEXIUS, physical therapist, consultant; b. Bronxville, N.Y., Jan. 28, 1946; s. Joseph P. and Marie C. (Richter) K.; m. Kathleen J. Kleinkort, Oct. 3, 1953; children: Pat, Mike, Kelly, Kristin, Kevin. BS in Phys. Therapy, St. Louis U., 1968; MA in Psychology, Ball State U., 1977; PhD (hon.), Medicina Alternativa, Copenhagen, 1983; PhD in Safety Mgmt., Western States U., 1998. Registered safety dir. World Safety Orgn.; registered phys. therapist, Tex., Fla. Dir. phys. therapy Phys. Therapy, Inc., Ft. Lauderdale, Fla., 1970-72; commd. officer USAF, 1972; dir. phys. therapy USAF Hosp.-Barksdale, Bossier City, La., 1972-74, USAF Hosp.-Torrejone, Madrid, 1974-78; asst. dir. Wilford Hall Med. Ctr., San Antonio, 1980-83; res. at rank of maj. USAF, 1983; pres. Chronic Pain Assn., Inc., San Antonio, 1983-88; exec. dir. Ft. Worth Back Inst., 1988-90; pres. Joseph A. Kleinkort, P.C., Roanoke, Tex., 1983—; sr. v.p., 1995-96, exec. v.p., 1996—, COO, 1997—; cons. Dynatronics Corp., Salt Lake City, 1985—; bd. dirs. Magnetherapy, Inc., Sci. Cons. Magnetherapy; mem. Applied Biomed. Rsch. Inst., 1996—; v.p. clin. rsch. Health Rsch. and Clin. Assoc., 1996—; COO Worksteps Inc., 1997—. Author: Therapeutic Medical Devices, 1983, Thermal Agents Rehabilitation, 1985, Laser Application Technology, 1986. Precinct judge, San Antonio, 1988; precinct chmn. Denton County Rep. Party, 1996-98; bd. dirs. Arlington Philharm. Symphony, 1993-94; elder First Bapt. Ch., Roanoke, 1996—. Recipient Alumni Merit award St. Louis U., 1983; named Outstanding Phys. Therapist of Tex., Tex. Phys. Therapy Bd., 1985. Fellow Am. Coll. Orthopedics (membership sec. 1988-90), mem. Internat. soc. Lasers in Medicine and Sci., Am. Assn. Phys. Medicine and Rehab., Am. Phys. Therapy Assn., Tex. Phys. Therapy Assn., Am. Platform Soc. Avocations: sailor, gospel teacher. Home and Office: 303 Inverness Dr Roanoke TX 76262-5561

KLEINMAIER, JUDITH MARIE RADDANT, journalist; b. Clintonville, Wis., Aug. 18, 1947; d. Kenneth Charles and Winnifred Charlotte (Breed) Raddant; m. Stephen W. Kleinmaier, Dec. 21, 1968; children: Bryan, Karen, Daniel. BA with honors, Marquette U., 1969. Copy editor Milw. Jour., 1969-70; publs. editor State Hist. Soc. Wis., Madison, 1970-73; pub. info. coord. S. Ctrl. Libr. System, Madison, 1980-87; copy editor The Capital Times, Madison, 1987—, copy desk chief, 1988—, mem. editl. bd., 1990—. Pres. bd. dirs. Cmty. Housing and Svcs., Madison, 1994-97, bd. dirs. 1992—; vol., coord. of vols. for partnership The Capital Times and Wright Mid. Sch., 1997—. Mem. Soc. Profl. Journalists, LWV (past bd. dirs. and study com. chmn. Dane County chpt.), Alpha Sigma Nu. Home: 325 Cheyenne Trl Madison WI 53705-4702 Office: The Capital Times Box 8060 1901 Fish Hatchery Rd Madison WI 53708

KLEINMAN, ANDREW YOUNG, plastic surgeon; b. Bklyn., July 2, 1953; s. Hyman Jack and Ruth Young K.; m. Elizabeth Wofsey, June 3, 1979 (div. 1998); children: Julia, Alexander. BS, MIT, 1975; MD, U. Rochester, 1979. Gen. surg. resident George Washington U. Hosp., Washington, 1979-81; resident in surgery Harvard Surg. NEDH, Boston, 1981-82; rsch. fellow Mass. Gen. Hosp., Boston, 1982-83; resident in plastic surgery Baylor Coll. Medicine, Houston, 1983-85; pvt. practice New Rochelle, N.Y., 1985—. Mem. Med. Soc. (Westchester, N.Y. chpt., bd. dirs. 1997—, chmn. peer rev. 1997—), Am. Soc. Plastic and Reconstructive Surgery, Med. Soc. State N.Y., Phi Beta Kappa, Phi Lambda Upsilon. Avocations: sailing, audiophile. E-mail: AKleinman@aol.com. Office: 175 Memorial Hwy New Rochelle NY 10801

KLEINMAN, ARTHUR MICHAEL, medical anthropologist, psychiatrist, educator; b. N.Y.C., Mar. 11, 1941; s. Marcia F. (Kaplan) K.; m. Joan Andrea Ryman, Mar. 20, 1965; children: Peter John, Anna Simone. A.B., Stanford U., 1962, M.D., 1967; M.A., Harvard U., 1974. Diplomate: Nat. Bd. Med. Examiners, Am. Bd. Neurology and Psychiatry. Med. intern Yale-New Haven Hosp., 1967-68; surgeon USPHS, Bethesda, Md., Taiwan, 1968-70; resident in psychiatry Mass. Gen. Hosp., Boston, 1972-75; assoc. prof. U. Wash., Seattle, 1976-79, prof. psychiatry and anthrology, 1979-82; prof. med. anthropology and psychiatry Harvard U., Cambridge, Mass., 1982—, chmn. dept. social medicine, dir. Ctr. for Study Culture and Medicine, 1991—, Maude and Lillian Presley prof. med. anthropology, 1993—; co-chair com. on culture, health and devel. Social Sci. Rsch. Coun. Author: Patients and Healers in the Context of Culture, 1980 (Wellcome medal Royal Anthrop. Inst.), Social Origins of Distress and Disease, 1986, The Illness Narratives, 1988, Rethinking Psychiatry, 1988; co-editor: Relevance of Social Science for Medicine, 1981, Culture and Depression, 1985, Pain as Human Experience, 1992; editor-in-chief: Culture, Medicine and Psychiatry: A Jour. of Internat. Cross-Cultural Rsch., 1976-86. Recipient Rsch. award NIMH, 1977-79, Rockefeller Found., 1983-86, 88-89, NSF,1983-86, R.W. Johnson Found., 1988-89; grantee NIMH, 1984—, Carnegie Corp., 1990-92, MacArthur Found., 1992-94, Rockefeller Found., 1992-94; Guggenheim fellow, 1992. Fellow AAAS, Am. Psychiat. Assn., Am. Anthrop. Assn., Inst. Medicine of Nat. Acad. Scis. (chmn. com. on chronic pain, illness behavior and disability), Royal Anthrop. Inst., Am. Acad. Arts and Scis. Office: Harvard U 330 William James Hall 33 Kirkland St Cambridge MA 02138-2044*

KLEINMAN, BURTON HOWARD, real estate investor; b. Chgo., Nov. 19, 1923; s. Eli I. and Pearl (Cohan) K.; m. Shirley A. Freyer, Sept. 6, 1950 (div. Oct. 1969); children: Kim, Lauri. BS in Engring., U.S. Naval Acad., 1948. Commd. ensign USN, 1948, resigned, 1949; v.p. C.F. Corp., Chgo., 1958-80, pres., 1980-85; owner B.H. Kleinman Co., Northfield, Ill., 1955—. Bd. dirs. United Way Northfield, 1970-72, North Shore Mental Health Assn., 1978-82. Mem. Northfield C. of C. (bd. dirs. 1976-81), Kenosha Pilots Assn. Republican. Unitarian. Clubs: Deerfield Singles (pres. 1974-75), Winnetka Tennis Assn., Ridge & Valley Tennis. Avocations: tennis, scuba diving, sailing, flying. Home: 570 Happ Rd Northfield IL 60093-1112 Office: BH Kleinman Co 456 W Frontage Rd Northfield IL 60093-3038

KLEINMAN, CHARLES STEPHAN, physician, medical educator; b. N.Y.C., Mar. 12, 1947; s. Meyer and Dora (Levine) K.; m. Jessica Sue Pollack, June 14, 1969; children: Ari David, Joshua Michael. BA, NYU, 1967; MA, Rutgers U., 1968; MD, N.Y. Med. Coll., 1972; MA (hon.), Yale U., 1986. Diplomate Am. Bd. Pediatrics. Instr. pediatrics Cornell U. Med. Coll., N.Y.C., 1974-76; asst. prof. pediatrics Yale U., New Haven, 1977-81, assoc. prof., 1981-86, prof. pediatrics, diagnostic imaging and ob-gyn., 1986—; chief pediatric cardiology Yale U./Yale-New Haven Med. Ctr., New Haven, 1986—. Office: Yale Sch Medicine Sect Pediatric Cardiology 333 Cedar St New Haven CT 06520-8064*

KLEINMAN, GEORGE, commodities executive; b. Bklyn., Aug. 10, 1951; s. Herman and Helen Kleinman; m. Sherri Ellen Meadow; children: Kevin, Craig. BS in Bus., Ohio State U., 1973; MBA in Fin., Hofstra U., 1975. Product mgr. Mead Johnson Labs., Evansville, Ind., 1974-77; sr. v.p. commodities Merrill Lynch, Mpls., 1977-83; pres. Commodity Resource Corp., Mpls., 1983—; pvt. practice futures and options cons., 1991—; bd. dirs. K&W Cattle Co., Ainsworth, Nebr.; mem. COMEX divsn. N.Y. Mercantile Exch. Author: Mastering Commodity Futures and Options, 1998; columnist, Farm Week, Agweek, Fin. Times, Consensus. Mem. Nat. Futures Assn., Mpls. Grain Exch. (past bd. dirs.), Delta Sigma Pi. Avocations: skiing, racquetball. Office: Commodity Resource Corp PO Box 8700 Incline Village NV 89452-8700

KLEINMAN, R. E., mathematician, educator; b. N.Y.C., July 27, 1929; married; 2 children. BA, NYU, 1950; MA, U. Mich., 1951; PhD in Applied Math., Delft U. Tech., 1961. Rsch. asst. in math. U. Mich., Ann Arbor, 1951-53, rsch. assoc., 1955-58, from assoc. rsch. mathematician to rsch. mathematician, 1959-68; assoc. prof. U. Del., Newark, 1968-72, prof. math., 1972-95, Unidel prof., 1995—; vis. prof. math. U. Strathclyde, 1972, 82, Delft U. Tech., 1987, 96, U. Paris, 1993, CNRS, 1993, U. Nice-Sophia Antipolis, France, 1994; vis. scientist David Taylor Naval Ship R&D Ctr., 1982, Naval Rsch. Lab., 1986. Recipient fellowships and grants. Fellow IEEE; mem. Am. Math. Soc., Edinburgh Math. Soc., Gesellschaft Angewandte Math. and Mech., Soc. Indsl. and applied Math., Internat. Sci. Radio Union. Office: University of Delaware Dept Math Sciences 501 Ewing Hall Newark DE 19716*

KLEINROCK, LEONARD, computer scientist; b. N.Y.C., June 13, 1934; s. Bernard and Anne (Schoenfeld) K.; m. Stella Schuler, Dec. 1, 1967; children: Nancy S., Martin C. BEE, CCNY, 1957, DSc (hon.), 1997; MS, MIT, 1959, PhD, 1963; DS (hon.), CCNY, 1997. Asst. elec. engr. Photobell Co. Inc., 1951-57; rsch. engr. Lincoln Labs., MIT, 1957-63; mem. faculty UCLA, 1963—, prof. computer sci., 1970—, chairperson dept., 1991-94, co-chairperson dept., 1994-95; co-founder Linkabit Corp., 1968-69, pres., 1995; CEO, chmn. Tech. Transfer Inst., 1976—; pres. Nomadix LLC, 1995—; cons. in field, prin. investigator govt. contracts; Disting. lectr. UCLA, 1994; chair Realizing the Info. Future: The Internet and Beyond, 1994. Author: Queueing Systems, Vol. I, 1975, Vol. II, 1976, Communication Nets: Stochastic Message Flow and Delay, 1964, Solutions Manual for Queueing Systems, Vol. I, 1982, Vol. II, 1986, Queueing Systems: Problems and Solutions, 1996; also articles. Recipient Paper award ICC, 1978, Leonard G. Abraham paper award Communications Soc., 1975, Outstanding Faculty Mem. award UCLA Engring. Grad. Students Assn., 1966, Townsend Harris medal CCNY, 1982, L.M. Ericsson Prize Sweden, 1982, 12th Marconi award, 1986, Monie A. Ferst award Sigma Xi, 1997; Guggenheim fellow, 1971-72. Fellow IEEE (Disting. lectr. 1973, 76); mem. NAE, Ops. Rsch. Soc. Am. (Lancaster prize 1976), Assn. Computing Machinery (SIG com. award 1990), Internat. Fedn. Info. Processes Sys. (Harry H. Goode award 1996), Amateur Athletic Union. Jewish. Avocations: karate, hiking, jogging, swimming. Home: 318 N Rockingham Ave Los Angeles CA 90049-2636 Office: UCLA Dept Computer Sci 405 Hilgard Ave 3732 Boelter Hall Los Angeles CA 90095-1596

KLEINROCK, ROBERT ALLEN, physician; b. Bronx, N.Y., July 25, 1950; s. Morris and Pearl (Schwartz) K.; m. Marie Louise Swinehart, Aug. 13, 1979. BS, CCNY, 1970; MD, NYU, 1974. Diplomate Am. Bd. Pediats. Pediat. intern Children's Hosp. San Francisco, 1974-75, resident, 1975-77; pediatrician Permanente Med. Group, Vallejo, Calif., 1977—. Avocation: Grateful Dead rock music. Office: Permanente Med Group 975 Sereno Dr Vallejo CA 94589-2441

KLEINROCK, VIRGINIA BARRY, public relations executive; b. Boston, Nov. 5, 1947; d. Robert Edmund and Anne Marie (Crowley) Barry; m. Lewis James Kleinrock, Dec. 15, 1984. AS, Garland Jr. Coll., Boston, 1967; BS, East Carolina U., 1969; MS, Simmons Coll., 1973; postgrad. Sch. Bus. Communications, Boston U., 1973, 86, 88. Tchr. Somerville (Mass.) Pub. Schs., 1969-70; tchr. Newton (Mass.) Pub. Schs., 1970-84, career edn. program coord., 1978-83; pres. Infinite Energy, Belmont, Mass., 1982-95; prin. The Kleinrock Group, Naples, Fla., 1996—; cons. McKnight Pub. Co.,

Bloomington, Ill., 1976-82; publicity coord./intern Impact Communications, Boston, 1982. Contbr. articles to profl. jours. Recipient Commendation for Excellence for Pilot Occupational Training Program, New Eng. Assn. of Schs. and Colls., 1969. Mem. Pub. Rels. Soc. Am., Counselors Acad., The Fashion Group, Fla. Pub. Rels. Assn., Advt. Fedn. of S.W. Fla., Internat. Platform Assn., Internat. Women's Writing Guild, Pub. Rels. Assn. of Collier County, Naples C. of C., Naples Press Club. Office: The Kleinrock Group 853 Vanderbilt Beach Rd Ste 10 Naples FL 34108-8746

KLEINSCHNITZ, BARBARA JOY, oil company executive, consultant; b. Granite Falls, Minn., Aug. 25, 1944; d. Arthur William and Joy Ardys (Roe) Green; m. Charles Lewis Kleinschnitz, Dec. 28, 1963 (div.); 1 child, Katheryn JoAnn Kleinschnitz Hartsock. BBA, U. Denver, 1983; student, Colo. Women's Coll. Leadman Schlumberger Well Services, Denver, 1968-76; supr., log processing Scientific Software-Intercomp, Denver, 1976-82; tech. cons. Tech. Log Analysis, Inc., Lakewood, Colo., 1982-83; customer support mgr. Energy Systems Tech., Inc., Englewood, Colo., 1983-86; cons. technical Littleton, Colo., 1986-87; documentation specialist Q.C. Data, Inc., 1987-91; tng. specialist Advanced Data Concepts, Ft. Collins, Colo., 1991-93; tech. writer Computer Data Sys., Inc., Ft. Collins, 1993-97; instr. Inst. Bus. & Med. Careers, Inc., Ft. Collins, 1997—; tech. writer Mgmt. Tech. Inc., Ft. Collins, 1998—; cons. Tech. Log Analysis, Inc., Denver, 1983-89, Energy Systems Tech., 1986-93. Vol. Denver Police Reserve, 1973-75. Mem. NOW, NAFE, Assn. Women Geoscientists, Soc. Profl. Well Log Analysts (bd. dirs. 1989-90, v.p. 1990-91), Denver Well Log Soc. (bd. dirs. 1986-87, v.p. 1987-88, pres. 1988-89). Democrat. Roman Catholic. Avocations: raquetball, swimming, video cassette recordings, internet. Home: 1130 Muirfield Way Fort Collins CO 80525-9144 Office: 1201 Oakridge Dr Ste 300 Fort Collins CO 80525-5596

KLEINSMITH, BRUCE JOHN See NUTZLE, FUTZIE

KLEINWALD, MARTIN (MARTIN LITTLEFIELD), book publishing executive; b. N.Y.C., 1940; children: Susanne Camilleri, Lisa Wolf. Pres., CEO Vantage Press, Inc., N.Y.C. Office: Vantage Press Inc 516 W 34th St Fl 6 New York NY 10001-1395*

KLEINWORTH, EDWARD J., agricultural company executive. Pres. St. Ansgar Mills, Inc. Office: St Ansgar Mills Inc PO Box 370 Saint Ansgar IA 50472-0370*

KLEISER, (JOHN) RANDAL, motion picture director; b. Lebanon, Pa., July 20, 1946; s. John Raymond and Harriet Kelly (Means) K. B.A., U. So. Calif., 1964, M.A., 1974. Dir.: (films) Grease, 1978, The Blue Lagoon, 1980, Summer Lovers, 1982, Grandview U.S.A., 1984, Flight of the Navigator, 1986, Big Top Pee Wee, 1988, Getting It Right, 1989, White Fang, 1990, Honey I Blew Up the Kid, 1992, It's My Party, 1996, (Disneyland Theme Parks) Honey I Shrunk the Audience 3-D, 1993; exec. prodr. North Shore, 1987, Return to the Blue Lagoon, 1990, (TV shows) New York News, 1996, All Together Now, 1975, Dawn: Portrait of a Teenage Runaway, 1976, The Boy in the Plastic Bubble, 1977, The Gathering, 1978 (Emmy nomination best dir. 1978), Marcus Welby, M.D., The Rookies, Starsky and Hutch, Family, 1973-77, (short subjects) Foot Fetish, 1974, Peege, 1973, Portrait of Grandpa Doc, 1977. Office: Randal Kleiser Prodns 500 S Buena Vista St # 262 Burbank CA 91521-0001 Office: ICM care Jim Wiatt 8942 Wilshire Blvd Beverly Hills CA 90211-1934*

KLEISNER, FRED, hotel executive. Chmn., pres., COO Westin Hotels & Resorts, Seattle; pres., COO Starwoods Hotels & Resorts, White Plains, N.Y. Office: Starwoods Hotel & Resorts The Westin Bldg 777 Westchester Ave White Plains NY 10604*

KLEISNER, TED J., museum director; b. Chgo., Sept. 5, 1944. Student, U. Denver. Pres., mng. dir. Pres.'s Cottage Mus./The Greenbrier, 1987—. Office: 300 W. Main St White Sulphur Springs WV 24986*

KLEMA, ERNEST DONALD, nuclear physicist, educator; b. Wilson, Kan., Oct. 4, 1920; s. William W. and Mary Bess (Vopat) K.; m. Virginia Clyde Carlock, May 23, 1953; children: Donald David, Catherine Marion. A.B. in Chemistry, U. Kans., 1941, M.A. in Physics, 1942; postgrad., Princeton U., 1942, U. Ill., 1946-49; Ph.D. in Physics, Rice U., 1951. Staff scientist Los Alamos Sci. Lab., 1943-46; sr. physicist Oak Ridge Nat. Lab., 1950-56, prin. physicist, 1958; assoc. prof. nuclear engring. U. Mich., 1956-58; prof. nuclear engring. Northwestern U., 1959-68, chmn. dept. engring. scis., 1960-66; prof. engring. sci. Tufts U., 1968-86, dean Coll. Engring., 1968-73, adj. prof. internat. politics Fletcher Sch. Law and Diplomacy, 1973-83, dean emeritus, prof. emeritus Coll. of Engring., 1987—; vis. scholar physics Harvard U., 1985-86; chmn. subcom. on neutron standards and measurements NRC, 1958-62; del. Internat. Atomic Energy Agy. symposium neutron detection, dosimetry and standardiazation, Harwell, Eng., 1962; cons. Oak Ridge Nat. Lab., Argonne Nat. Lab. Author articles fission cross-sects., gamma-gamma angular correlations, empirical nuclear models, thermal neutron measurements, semi-conductor radiation detectors. Fellow Am. Phys. Soc., Am Nuclear Soc.; mem. IEEE (sr.), Phi Beta Kappa, Sigma Xi, Pi Mu Epsilon, Alpha Chi Sigma. Clubs: Harbor (Seal Harbor, Me.). Patentee purification hydrogen-argon mixtures.

KLEMA, MARY KULIFAY, nurse; b. Poland, Ohio, Dec. 26, 1938; d. Joseph Thomas and Mary Ann (Ziga) K.; m. Michael Augustine Klema, Feb. 11, 1961 (div. Feb. 1978); children: Michael, Johanna, Joseph. BSN, Ursuline Coll., 1984. RN, Ohio. Coord. discharge, risk mgmt. cons. The St. Paul, Westlake, Ohio, 1986-93; home care nurse, mgr. clin. stats., Medicare educator Cleve. Clinic Found., 1993-97; case mgr. InterCare Network, Bay Village, Ohio, 1997—. Contbg. author: (book chpt.) Home Care, 1996. Mem. investment group, treas. civic series Women's City Club, Cleve., 1998. Mem. Am. Assn. for Continuity of Care, Ohio Continuity of Care, N.E. Ohio Case Mgmt. Soc., Sigma Theta Tau (past founding pres.). Republican. Roman Catholic. Home: 2441 Saybrook Rd University Heights OH 44118-4440

KLEMANN, GILBERT LACY, II, lawyer; b. New Rochelle, N.Y., July 26, 1950; s. N. Robert and Rosemary Virginia (Gerard) K.; m. Patricia Louise Hild, June 16, 1973; children: Tricia Rosemary, Gilbert Hild. AB, Coll. Holy Cross, 1972; JD, Fordham U., 1975. Bar: N.Y. 1976, U.S. Dist. Ct. (so. and ea. dists.) N.Y. 1976, Conn. 1988, U.S. Supreme Ct. 1991. Assoc. Chadbourne, Parke, Whiteside & Wolff, N.Y.C., 1975-83; ptnr. Chadbourne & Parke (formerly Chadbourne, Parke, Whiteside & Wolff), N.Y.C., 1983-90; sr. v.p., gen. counsel Fortune Brands, Inc. (formerly Am. Brands Inc.), Old Greenwich, Conn., 1991-97, exec. v.p. strategic and legal affairs, 1998; exec. v.p. corp., mem. bd. dis. Fortune Brands, Inc. (formerly Am. Brands Inc.), Old Greenwich, 1999—. Editor Fordham Law Rev., 1974-75. Mem. Conn. Bar Assn., Greenwich (Conn.) Country Club, Nassau Club (Princeton, N.J.). Republican. Roman Catholic. Avocation: golf. Home: 25 Hope Farm Rd Greenwich CT 06830-3331 Office: Fortune Brands Inc 1700 E Putnam Ave Old Greenwich CT 06870-1321*

KLEMENS, PAUL GUSTAV, physicist, educator; b. Vienna, Austria, May 24, 1925; came to U.S., 1959, naturalized, 1968; s. Walter and Ida (Klug) K.; m. Ruth Hannah Wiener, July 30, 1950; children: Michael Walter, Susan Margaret. BSc, U. Sydney, 1946, MSc, 1948; PhD, Oxford U., 1950. With Nat. Standards Lab., Sydney, Australia, 1950-59; research officer Nat. Standards Lab., 1950-52, sr. research officer, 1952-57, prin. research officer, 1957-59; physicist Westinghouse Research Lab., Pitts., 1959-64; mgr. transport properties of solids dept. Westinghouse Research Lab., 1964-67; prof. physics U. Conn., 1967-91, prof. emeritus, 1991—, head dept. physics, 1967-74; vis. prof. Leiden (The Netherlands) U., 1963-64, City U., London, 1989, U. Nottingham, Eng., 1992; mem. adv. bd. on heat Nat. Bur. Standards, 1967-70, mem. adv. bd. on cryogenics, 1974-79; mem. governing bd. Internat. Thermal Conductivity Confs., 1973—; mem. adv. bd. associateship program NRC, 1983-87; mem. standing com. on accreditation Conn. Bd. Higher Edn., 1980-86; cons. Los Alamos Nat. Lab., 1972-97. Contbr. articles to sci. jours. Recipient Y.S. Touloukian award Heat Transfer div. ASME, 1988. Fellow Am. Phys. Soc.; mem. Conn. Acad. Sci. and Engring. Clubs: Cosmos Washington. Home: 21 Timber Dr Storrs-Mansfield CT 06268-1210 Office: U Conn Dept Physics Storrs Mansfield CT 06269-3046

KLEMENS, THOMAS LLOYD, editor; b. Pitts., Mar. 28, 1952; s. Robert F. and Ann E. (Lacy) K.; m. Norreen McLellan, Aug. 4, 1973; children: Jonathan, Zachary. BFA, Carnegie-Mellon U., 1974; BSCE, U. Pitts., 1983; postgrad., Roosevelt U., Chgo., 1990-91. Registered profl. engr., Ill. Choir dir., tchr. Wellsville (Ohio) H.S., 1975-76; asst. band dir., tchr. North Hills H.S., Ross Twp., Pa., 1976-79; field engr. S.J. Groves & Sons, Pitts., 1983; structural engr. Sargent & Lundy, Chgo., 1983-87; field engr. Structural Preservation Systems, Inc., Margate, N.J., 1987; project mgr. Northwest Group, Inc., West Chicago, Ill., 1987; engr., purchasing agt. L.J. Keefe Co., Mt. Prospect, Ill., 1987-89; from assoc. editor to editor Hwy. & Heavy Constrn. Cahners Pub., Des Plaines, Ill., 1989-91, editor Hwy. & Heavy Constrn. Products, 1991-93, sr. editor Consulting/Specifying Engr., 1993-94; instr. Motorola U., 1996—; mem. com. on constrn. equipment Transp. Rsch. Bd., Washington, 1991-93; co-owner Wordwright, Palatine, Ill., 1993—; adj. faculty William Rainey Harper Coll., Palatine, Ill., 1997—. Author Hwy. and Heavy Constrn., 1989-91, editor, 1991-92; author, editor Infrastructure, 1992-93; sr. editor Cons./Specifying Engr., 1993-94; editor PM Engr., Bus. News Pub., 1994-96, Plumbing Engr., TMB Pub., 1996—. Mem. ASCE, Soc. for Tech. Comm., Am. Soc. Plumbing Engrs., Soc. Fire Protection Engrs. Office: 1838 Techny Ct Northbrook IL 60062-5474

KLEMENT, VERA, artist; b. Gdansk, Dec. 14, 1929; d. Klement and Rose (Rakovchik) Shapiro; divorced; 1 son, Max Klement Shapey. Cert. in fine arts, Cooper Union Sch. Art and Architecture, 1950. Prof. art U. Chgo., 1969-95. One woman shows include RoKo Gallery, N.Y.C., 1958, 60, Bridge Gallery, N.Y.C., 1965, Artemisia Gallery, Chgo., 1974, Chicago Gallery, 1976, Marianne Deson Gallery, 1979, 81, Goethe Inst., 1981, CDS Gallery, N.Y.C., 1981, 84, Roy Boyd Gallery, Chgo., 1983, 85, 87, 89, 90, 91, 92, 93, Spertus Mus., Chgo., 1987, retrospective exhbn., 1953-86, Renaissance Soc., Chgo., 1987, Brody's Gallery, Washington, 1992, Fassbender Gallery, Chgo., 1994, 95, 96, 97, Chgo. Cultural Ctr., 1999; group shows include Mus. Modern Art, N.Y.C., 1954, 55, Bklyn. Mus., 1950-60, Dallas Mus. Fine Arts, 1954, Tate Gallery, London, 1956, Museo de Arte Moderno, Barcelona, Spain, 1955, Musee d'Arte Moderne, Paris, 1955, U. Ky., 1959, Art Inst. Chgo., 1967, Walker Art Center, Mpls., 1977, U. Mo., 1978, Detroit Inst. Arts, 1978, Ukrainian Inst. Art, Chgo., 1978, Jewish Mus., N.Y.C., 1982, Kunstverein, Munich, Germany, 1987, Amerika Haus, Berlin, 1987, Terra Mus. Am. Art, Chgo., 1988, Corcoran Gallery, Washington, 1994, Cultural Ctr., Chgo., 1994, former IBM Gallery, N.Y.C., 1995, Va. Beach Ctr. Arts, 1995, Fischer Art Gallery at U. So. Calif., 1995, Portland (Oreg.) Mus. Art, Evanston (Ill.) Art Ctr., Mus. Contemporary Art, Chgo., 1996, Block Gallery Northwestern U., Evanston, Ill., 1996, many others; represented in permanent collections Mus. Modern Art, N.Y.C., Phila. Mus. Art, Print Club, Phila., Ill. State Mus., Springfield, U. Tex., Nat. Mus. Am. Art, Washington, Jewish Mus., N.Y.C., Art Inst. Chgo., Philip Morris, N.Y.C., Smart Mus. U. Chgo., Sch. Social Svc. Adminstrn. U. Chgo., Mus. Contemporary Art, Chgo., Mary & Leigh Block Gallery, Evanston, Ill., Mus. Art U. Ariz., Tucson; also pvt. collections. Recipient Pollock/Krasner Found. award, 1998, others; Louis Comfort Tiffany Found. fellow, 1954, Guggenheim fellow, 1981-82, Nat. Endowment for the Arts fellow, 1987; Ill. Arts Coun. grantee, 1988.

KLEMIN, LAWRENCE R., lawyer; b. New Rockford, N.D., Mar. 31, 1945; s. Lawrence R. Klemin and Carol M. (Cook) Roaldson; m. Rita R. DiPalma, Sept. 2, 1970; children: Laura K., Peter L. BA in English, U. N.D., 1967, JD with distinction, 1978. Bar: N.D. 1978, U.S. Dist. Ct. N.D. 1978, U.S. Ct. Appeals (8th cir.) 1987, U.S. Supreme Ct. 1988. Hearing officer N.D. Employment Security Bur., Bismarck, 1971-75; assoc. Atkinson & Dwyer, Bismarck, 1978-81; ptnr. Atkinson, Dwyer & Klemin, Bismarck, 1981-82, Dwyer & Klemin, Bismarck, 1982-86; pres. Lawrence R. Klemin, P.C., Bismarck, 1986-92, Bucklin & Klemin, P.C., Bismarck, 1992-96, Bucklin, Klemin & McBride, P.C., Bismarck, 1996—; pres. Title and Escrow Co., Bismarck, 1988-98, Litigation Svcs., Inc., Bismarck, 1995—; state rep. N.D. legis assembly, 1998—; mem. state adv. coun. N.D. Office Adminstrv. Hearings, Bismarck, 1993-98; lectr. on real property law Nat. Bus. Inst., 1989—. Author, editor Civil Practice of North Dakota, 1993—. Bd. dirs. N.D. March of Dimes, Bismarck, 1994—; mem. Corpus Christi Parish Coun., Bismarck, 1996—. With U.S. Army, 1967-70, Vietnam. Mem. State Bar Assn. N.D. (chair adminstrv. law com. 1996-98), N.D. Land Title Assn. (legis. com. 1990-99), Bismarck Mandan C. of C. (bd. dirs. 1996-98), Optimist Internat. (bd. dirs. 1985-86), Elks, Eagles, Am. Legion. Roman Catholic. Avocations: antique auto restoration, astronomy, camping. Home: 1709 Montego Dr Bismarck ND 58501-0856 Office: Bucklin Klemin & McBride PC 400 E Broadway #500 PO Box 955 Bismarck ND 58502-0955

KLEMM, WILLIAM RAYMOND, career officer; b. Washington, June 11, 1947; s. Richard and Jean K.; m. Nancy Knox, Oct. 25, 1969; children: Richard, Keith. BS with honors, Widener U., 1969; student res. officer candidate tng., U.S. Naval Acad., 1968; MBA, Rensselaer Poly. Inst., 1974; exec. edn. program, Duke U.; program mgrs. course, Def. Sys. Mgmt. Coll., Ft. Belvoir, Va. Commd. ensign U.S. Navy, 1969, advanced through grades to rear adm., engring. duty officer, 1971, auxs. officer, main propulsion asst. USS La Salle, boilers officer, chief engr. USS John F. Kennedy; sr. ship supt., docking officer Norfolk (Va.) Naval Shipyard U.S. Navy, Portsmouth, Va.; from FF7-7 constrn. sup. to repair officer Supr. Shipbldg. Conversion and Repair, Bath, Maine; type desk officer on staff Comdr. Naval Air Force U.S. Atlantic Fleet; officer in charge planning and engring. repairs, alterations Bremerton, Wash.; repair, planning, prodn. officer Puget Sound Naval Shipyard Bremerton; dep. program mgr., officer in charge Naval Sea Sys. Cmd. advanced indsl. mgmt. site, Portsmouth, Va.; 98th comdr. Norfolk Naval Shipyard; dep. comdr. Naval Shipyard, SUPSHIP mgmt. and field activity support directorate Naval Sea Sys. Cmd.; chief naval ops., dir. indsl. capability Maintenance Policy and Acquisition Logistics Divsn. With USNR, 1964-69. Decorated Legion of Merit, Meritorious Svc. medal (3), Navy Commendation medal.

KLEMME, CARL WILLIAM, banker; b. Ft. Wayne, Ind., Sept. 11, 1928; s. Ludwig and Marianne (Rupil) K.; m. Ann Elise Wichman, Sept. 11, 1954; children: Ellen Elise Taylor, Sarah Ann Venizelos, Carl Andrew. BS, Yale U., 1950; MBA, NYU, 1956; postgrad. mgmt., Harvard U., 1971. With Morgan Guaranty Trust Co., N.Y.C., 1950-80, v.p., 1961-70, sr. v.p., 1970-72, exec. v.p., 1972-80; exec. v.p. Russell Reynolds Assocs., Inc., N.Y.C., 1981-82, Nat. Westminster Bancorp, N.Y.C., 1982-93; arbitrator NASD, N.Y.C., 1975—; mgmt. cons. Nat. Exec. Svc. Corps., N.Y.C., Internat. Exec. Svc. Corps, Stamford, Conn. Mem. Millburn Bd. Edn., 1967-73; trustee Howard U., 1975-91, Millburn (N.J.) Pub. Libr., 1979-84, Wittenberg U., 1983-96, New Eyes for the Needy, 1980-86, Twp. Beautification League, 1998—; bd. dirs. Downtown-Lower Manhattan Assn., 1972-80; bd. dirs. Bank Adminstrn. Inst., 1975-81, chmn., 1979-80. With U.S. Army, 1950-52. Mem. Phi Beta Kappa. Republican. Episcopalian. Home: 35 Woodfield Dr Short Hills NJ 07078-1609

KLEMME, MINNIE DOROTHY, writer; b. Murdock, Nebr., May 2, 1912; d. Henry and Henrietta (Heberlein) K. Student, Wesleyan U., 1937-38. Author: (poetry book) Ideals Poets, 1985, Cloth of My Dreams, 1995; contbr. poetry to profl. jours. Named Ideals Best Loved Poet, Ideals Mag., Nashville, 1983, Am. Poet Assn. Poet of Merit, Am. Poetry Soc., Santa Cruz, Calif., 1989. Mem. Nat. Libr. Poetry, Nebr. Writers Guild. Home: 30312 Highway 1 Murdock NE 68407-2240

KLEMP, HAROLD, minister, writer. Student, U. Ind. Spiritual leader Eckankar Religion of the Light and Sound of God, Mpls., 1981—; spkr. in field. Author: The Wind of Change, 1980, Soul Travelers of the Far Country, 1987, Child in the Wilderness, 1989, The Living Word, Books 1 and 2, 1989, 96, The Book of ECK Parables, Vols. 1-4, 1986, 88, 91, 94, The Spiritual Exercises of ECK, 1993, Ask the Master, Books 1 and 2, 1993, 94, The Dream Master, 1993, We Come as Eagles, 1994, The Drumbeat of Time, 1995, The Slow Burning Love of God, 1996, The Easy Way Discourses, 1992, The ECK Dream 1 Discourses, 1987, The ECK Dream 2 Discourses, 1989, The Master 3 Discourses, 1994, Letters of Light & Sound 1 and 2, 1991, 94, A Modern Prophet Answers Your Key Questions About Life, 1998. Office: Eckankar PO Box 27300 Minneapolis MN 55427-0300

KLEMPERER, WILLIAM, chemistry educator; b. N.Y.C., Oct. 6, 1927; s. Paul and Margit (Freund) K.; m. Elizabeth Cole, Jan. 12, 1949; children: Joyce Hillary, Paul, Wendy Judith. AB, Harvard U., 1950; PhD, U. Calif., Berkeley, 1954; DSc, U. Chgo., 1996. Instr. chemistry Harvard U., Cambridge, Mass., 1954-57, asst. prof., 1957-61, assoc. prof., 1961-65, prof., 1965—; asst. dir. NSF, Washington, 1979-81; vis. scientist Bell Telephone Lab., 1963-83; Evans lectr. Ohio State U., 1981, Pratt lectr. U. Va., 1984, Rollefson lectr. U. Calif., 1985, Oesper lectr. U. Cin., 1987, Kolthoff lectr. U. Minn., 1987, Mary E. Kapp lectr. Va. Commonwealth U., 1987, Linus Pauling Disting. lectr. Oreg. State U., 1988, Harry Emmett Gunning lectr. U. Alta., Can., 1988, Fritz London Meml. lectr. Duke U., 1989, Hinshelwood lectr. Oxford U., Eng., 1989, Neckers lectr. So. Ill. U., 1990, George C. Pimentel meml. lectr. U. Calif., Berkeley, 1992, Joe L. Franklin meml. lectr. Rice U., 1994, E.K.C. Lee Fellowship lectr. U. Calif., Irvine, 1994; Richard C. Lord lectr. MIT, Cambridge, Mass., 1997; Bernstein lectr. UCLA, 1997. Served with A.C., USN, 1944-46. Recipient Wetherill medal Franklin Inst., 1978, Disting. Svc. medal NSF, 1981, Bomem Michelson award The Coblentz Soc., 1990, Remsen award Am. Chem. Soc. Md. sect., 1992, Faraday Medal and Lectureship Royal Soc. Chemistry, 1995. Fellow Am. Phys. Soc. (Earle Plyler prize 1983); mem. NAS, Am. Acad. Arts and Scis., Am. Chem. Soc. (Irving Langmuir award 1980, Peter Debye award 1994). Home: 53 Shattuck Rd Watertown MA 02472-1310 Office: Harvard U Dept Chemistry and Chem Biology 12 Oxford St Cambridge MA 02138-2902

KLEMPNER, MARK STEVEN JOEL, physician, research scientist, educator; b. Utica, N.Y., Jan. 18, 1949; s. Ben and Goldie (Rockoff) K.; m. Frances Borger, Sept. 9, 1979; children: Samuel Jacob, Jesse Maxwell, Hannah Rachel. Student, Tulane U., 1966-69; MD, Cornell U. Med. Coll., 1973. Diplomate Nat. Bd. Med. Examiners, Am. Bd. Internal Medicine, Am. Bd. Internal Medicine Subspecialty Infectious Disease. From intern to resident Mass. Gen. Hosp., Boston, 1973-75; clinical assoc. Nat. Inst. Health, Bethesda, Md., 1975-78; infectious disease cons. U.S.N. Med. Ctr., Bethesda, Md., 1976-78; asst prof. med. Tufts U. Sch. Med., Boston, Mass., 1978-83; asst. physician New England Med. Ctr., Boston, Mass., 1978-83; assoc. prof. med., assoc. prof., prof. medicine Tufts U. Sch. of Medicine, Boston, 1983—, Louisa C. Endicott prof. medicine, assoc. physician-in-chief, vice-chmn. for scientific affairs; co-dir. HIV-Hemophilia Ctr.; assoc. editor Yearbook Infectious diseases; editl. bd. Am. Jour. of Medicine, Antimicrobial Agents & Chemotherapy, Jour. Spirochetal and Tick Borne Diseases; reviewer Jour. Infectious Diseases, Jour. Clin. Infestigation, New Eng. Jour. Medicine, Jour. Leukocyte Biology, Inflammation, Jour. I. Contbr. articles to numerous profl. jours. With USPHS, 1978—. Tulane U. scholar, Teagle scholar Cornell U. Med. Coll.; recipient Dean William Mecklenburg Polk Prize in Medicine, Cornell U. Med. Coll., Excellence in Teaching award Tufts U. Sch. of Medicine. Mem. AAAS, ACP, Am. Soc. Microbiology, Infectious Diseases Soc. Am. (Squibb award 1994), Infections Diseases Soc. Am. (Abbot Achievement award), Am. Fedn. Clin. Rsch., Am. Soc. Clin. Investigation, Am. Bd. Internal Medicine (bd. dirs., chmn. subsplty. bd. infectious diseases), Assn. of Am. Physicians, Assn. of Subspecialty Profs. (sec.-treas. 1996, pres. 1998—), Phi Eta Sigma, Alpha Omega Alpha. Office: New Eng Med Ctr Dept Med Divsn Infectious Disea Boston MA 02111

KLENE, MARY JEAN, English educator; b. Hannibal, Mo., Sept. 8, 1929; d. Othmar Carl and Ada Blanche (Ridder) K. BA, St. Mary's Coll., Notre Dame, Ind., 1959; MA, Notre Dame U., 1966; PhD, U. Toronto, Ont., Can., 1970. Tchr. St. Mary's Sch., Alexandria, Va., 1951-53; H.S. tchr. high schs., South Bend, Ind., 1953—; tchr., counselor Sisters of the Holy Cross, Notre Dame, Ind., 1961-63; H.S. tchr. h.s., Flint, Mich., 1963-64; dean students St. Mary's Acad., South Bend, 1964-65; lectr. St. Mary's Coll., Notre Dame, 1965—; chair dept. English, St. Mary's Coll., 1973-78, 80-85. Editor, transcriber: The Southwell-Sibthorpe Commonplace Book, 1997 (Josephine A. Roberts award for Best Edition), Instructor's Guide for the Slide Set Shakespeare: New Productions, 1975-80, The Royal Shakespeare Company, 1981; contbr. articles to books, jours. in field. Fellow NEH, 1978-79, 1980, 83-84, Faculty fellow Lilly Endowment, London, 1985-86. Mem. MLA, Renaissance English Text Soc., Renaissance Soc. Am., Shakespeare Assn. Am. Avocations: swimming, designing Shakespeare multimedia programs. Office: St Mary's Coll Notre Dame IN 46556

KLENK, JAMES ANDREW, lawyer; b. Evergreen Park, Ill., July 18, 1949; s. Paul Theodore and Joan (Launspach) K.; m. Carol Evans, Aug. 26, 1972; children: Paul Andrew, Matthew Evans. BA, Beloit Coll., 1971; JD, U. Wis., 1974. Bar: Ill. 1974, Wis. 1974, U.S. Supreme Ct. 1978. Law clk. to Judge Thomas E. Fairchild U.S. Ct. Appeals (7th cir.), Chgo., 1974-75; assoc. Kirkland & Ellis, Chgo., 1975-78; ptnr. Reuben & Proctor, Chgo., 1978-86, Isham, Lincoln & Beale, Chgo., 1986-88, Sonnenschein, Nath & Rosenthal, Chgo., 1988—. Articles editor Wis. Law Rev. Mem. ABA (litigation sect., torts and ins. practice sect., bus. law sect.), Ill. Bar Assn. (anti-trust law sect., litigation sect., torts and ins. practice sect., intellectual prop.), Libel Def. Resource Ctr. (def. counsel sect.), Order of Coif, Phi Beta Kappa. Office: Sonnenschein Nath & Rosenthal 8000 Sears Tower Chicago IL 60606

KLENK, ROSEMARY ELLEN, pediatrician; b. Pitts., June 16, 1948; d. Joseph Albert and Frieda (Roppolo) Meisner; m. Kenneth Klenk, June 26, 1977; children: Kara, Jacob, Caitlin, David, Colin, Kevin. BA in History, U. Rochester, 1970; BSN, Columbia U., 1972; MD, Cornell U., 1980. Diplomate Nat. Bd. Med. Examiners, Am. Bd. Pediat.; RN. Ptnr., pvt. practice New England Pediat., Stamford, Conn., 1983—; bd. dirs. So. Conn. Child Guidance Ctr.; med. bd. Stamford (Conn.) Hosp.; part-time instr. Coll. Physicians & Surgeons Columbia U., 1983—; attending physician Stamford Hosp. Contbr. articles to profl. jours. Fellow Am. Acad. Pediat.; mem. Conn. State Med. Soc., Fairfield County Med. Soc. Office: New England Pediatrics 166 W Broad St Ste 103 Stamford CT 06902-3661*

KLENK, TIMOTHY CARVER, lawyer; b. Glen Cove, N.Y., Apr. 29, 1939; s. Horace I. and Laura (Dugan) K.; m. Ann Ruth Schuessler, 1961 (dec. 1966); 1 child, Carolyn; m. Margaret Jo Garrett, Aug. 30, 1969. AB, Wheaton Coll., 196l; JD, Northwestern U., 1967. Bar: Ill. 1967, U.S. Dist. Ct. (no. dist.) Ill. 1968, U.S. Dist. Ct. (cen. dist.) Wis. 1976, U.S. Dist. Ct. (cen. dist.) Ill. 198l, U.S. Ct. Appeals (7th cir.) 1979, U.S. Supreme Ct. 1980. Systems engr. IBM, N.Y.C., 1961-62; assoc. Kirkland & Ellis, Chgo., 1967-70; assoc. Pope, Ballard, Shepard & Fowle Ltd., Chgo., 1970-74, ptnr., 1974-77, dir., 1977-94, mng. dir., 1993-94; ptnr. Ross & Hardies, Chgo., 1994—. Bd. dirs. Living Bibles Internat. U.S., Naperville, Ill., 1983-91, also v.p. 1st lt. U.S. Army, 1962-64. Mem. ABA, Ill. Bar Assn., 7th Cir. Bar Assn., Am. Judicature Soc., Christian Legal Soc. (bd. dirs. 1986—, pres. 1988-90), Am. Arbitration Assn. (arbitrator), Order of Coif. Republican. Avocations: flying, water sports, skiing. Office: Ross & Hardies 150 N Michigan Ave Ste 2500 Chicago IL 60601-7567

KLENNERT, DANIEL CHARLES, artist; b. Crookston, Minn., June 5, 1950; s. Charles George and LaVaun Joyce Klennert; m. Beverly Ann Frisvold, June 18, 1971 (div. Nov. 1988); 1 child, Amie Ann Klennert Dutson. Grad. H.S. art advisor Puyallup (Wash.) Arts Down Town. Art exhibits include Cowboy/Indian Nation Art Show, Canaby, Oreg., 1992, Twin Cranes Gallery, Seattle, 1992, Cowboy/Indian Nation Art Show, Bellevue, Wash., 1993, Earth Day Fest, Sea-Tac (Wash.) Mall, 1993, Harvest Festival, Portland, Oreg., 1993, Seattle, 1993, Scottsdale (Ariz.) Mall Show, 1993, Mill Ave. Arts Fest, Tempe, Ariz., 1994, Country Jam U.S.A., Queen Creek, Ariz., 1994, Grand Junction, Colo., 1994, West Fest, Santa Fe, 1994, Artisans Galleria, Sedona, Ariz., 1994, Fremont Arts and Crafts Fair, Seattle, 1995-98, KMS Fin./Art Exhibit, Seattle, 1996, Greenwood Art Walk, Seattle, 1996, St. of Dreams, Puyallup and Fife, 1997, 98, Fall City, Wash., 1997, North Kitsap Arts & Crafts, Poulsbo, Wash., 1996, Peace Arch Celebration, Blaine, Wash., 1996, Bellevue Sculpture Exhbn., 1996-97, Internat. Sculpture Exhbn., Blaine, 1998, many others; civic displays include Woodland Pk. Zoo, Seattle, 1988, Bear Creek Bus. Pk., Seattle, 1989, Downtown Ellensburg, Wash., 1991, 93, 95, 96, 97, 98, Kent (Wash.) Sr. Ctr., 1995, 96, Walnut Ave. Mall, Sun Valley, Idaho, 1995-96, Downtown Toppenish, Wash., others. With U.S. Army. Avocations: dumpster diving, junk collecting, litter removal, art, creating scu pture. E-mail: irondan@nwl-ink. Home: 404 Prospect Ave W Kent WA 98031 Studio: 22410 SR 706 E Ashford WA 98330

KLEPINGER, JOHN WILLIAM, trailer manufacturing company executive; b. Lafayette, Ind., Feb. 7, 1945; s. John Franklin and R. Wanda (North) K.; m. Mary Patricia Duffy, May 1, 1976; 1 child, Nicholas Patrick. BS,

Ball State U., 1967, MA, 1968. Sales engr. CTS Corp., Elkhart, Ind., 1969-70; exec. v.p. Woodlawn Products Corp., Elkhart, 1970-78; v.p. Period Ind., Henderson, Ky., 1976-78, Sotebeer Constrn. Co., Inc., Elkhart, 1978-81; gen. mgr. Wells Industries Inc., Ogden, Utah, 1981—, Wells Cargo, Inc., Phoenix, 1995—; regional dir. Zion's First Nat. Bank, Ogden, 1986—. Bd. dirs. St. Benedict's Hosp., Ogden, 1986-94, chmn., 1987-94; bd. dirs. Weber County Indsl. Devel. Corp., Nat. Job Tng. Partnership Inc., 1986-89; mem. Weber-Morgan Pvt. Industry Coun., 1983-96, Utah Job Tng. Coordinating Coun., 1988-96, chmn. 1993-94. Named Ogden Bus. Man of Yr., Weber County Sch. Dist., 1984. Mem. Nat. Assn. Trailer Mfrs. (bd. dirs., vice chmn. 1994-95, chmn. 1995-97, sec., treas. 1998—), Weber County Prodn. Mgrs. Assn. (pres. 1984-85, 92-93), Nat. Assn. Pvt. Industry Couns. (bd. dirs. 1986-96, pres. 1988-92), Nat. Alliance Bus. (bd. dirs. 1987-90), Ogden Area C. of C. (bd. dirs. 1986-96, treas. 1986-89), Phoenix C. of C., Exch. Club (bd. dirs. Ogden 1984-86). Roman Catholic. Avocations: finance, community service, leadership, sports, travel. Home: 5181 Aztec Dr Ogden UT 84403-4606 Office: Wells Industries Inc PO Box 1619 Ogden UT 84402-1619

KLEPONIS, JEROME ALBERT, dentist; b. Ashland, Pa., July 26, 1955; s. Albert Francis and Anna Mae Catherine (Burns) K. BS in Biology summa cum laude, Allentown Coll. St. Francis de Sales, 1977; DMD, U. Pa., 1981. Resident in gen. dentistry Geisinger Med. Ctr., Danville, Pa., 1981-82; assoc. Office of Dr. Stephen D. Eingorn, Bethlehem, Pa., 1982-83; dir. dental svcs. Lock Haven (Pa.) Hosp., 1983-86; sr. staff dentist Tri-Town Med. Ctr., Williamstown, Pa., 1986-87; dir. dental svcs. Embreeville Ctr., Coatesville, Pa., 1987-92, Danville (Pa.) State Hosp., 1992—. Vol. Chester County Buddies, West Chester, Pa., 1990-92; CPR instr. Am. Heart Assn., 1989—; mem. leadership com. Cardinal Brennan Jr./Sr. H.S., 1994—, co-chmn. 1996-97, chmn. 1998, ann. appeal, mem. select com., 1996—; mem. pres.'s coun. Allentown Coll., 1991—, mem. capital campaign alumni steering com., 1996-97. Recipient Alumni Svc. award Allentown Coll., 1993, Alumni Achievement award, 1997, Disting. Alumni award Cardinal Brennan Jr./Sr. H.S., 1998. Fellow Am. Assn. Hosp. Dentists, Acad. Gen. Dentistry, Acad. Dentistry for Persons with Disabilities (chairperson ad hoc com. on mental health 1995—, bd. dir. 1998—); mem. ADA (vol. PEERS network 1995—), Am. Soc. Geriatric Dentistry, Pa. Dental Assn., Dental Soc. of Chester County and Delaware County, Am. Soc. Dentistry for Children, Am. Soc. Forensic Odontology, Am. Assn. Mental Retardation, Elks, Am. Hose Co., Am. Legion Sons of Vets., Allentown Coll. Alumni Assn. (bd. dirs. 1983-94, sec. bd. dirs. 1985-87, pres. bd. dirs. 1991-94), Psi Omega (editor Zeta chpt. 1979-81). Roman Catholic. Avocations: traveling, photography, journalism, hiking. Home: 1201 Arch St Ashland PA 17921-1213 Office: Danville State Hosp 200 State Hosp Dr Danville PA 17821-9198

KLEPPA, OLE J., chemistry educator; b. Oslo, Feb. 4, 1920; married; 2 children. MS, Norwegian Inst. Tech., 1946, DS, 1956. Union Carbon and Carbide postdoctoral fellow, instr. U. Chgo. Inst. Study of Metals, 1948-50; rsch. supr. divsn. chemistry and metallurgy Norwegian Def. Rsch. Establishment, 1950-51; asst. prof. U. Chgo., 1952-57, assoc. prof., 1958-62, prof. dept. chemistry, 1962-90, prof. dept. geophysical scis., 1968-90, prof. emeritus, 1990—, assoc. dir. James Franck Inst., 1968-71, dir., 1971-77, dir. materials rsch. lab., 1984-87; cons. Argonne Nat. Lab., 1959-71; dir. The Calorimetry Conf., 1963-69, chmn., 1966-67; vis. prof. Japan Soc. Promotion of Sci., 1975, U. Paris, Orsay, 1977; presenter confs. in field. Bd. editors Jour. Chem. Physics, 1965-67, Jour. Chem. Thermodynamics, 1981-87, Jour. Phase Equilibria, 1995—; contbr. articles to profl. jours. Recipient Huffman Meml. award, 1982, U.S. Sr. Sci. Humboldt award, 1983-84. Fellow AAAS, Am. Soc. Metals; mem. Am. Chem. Soc., Am. Ceramic Soc., Soc. Norwegian Engrs., Royal Norwegian Soc. Sci. and Letters, Norwegian Acad. Tech. Scis., Minerals, Metals, and Materials Soc. (Hume-Rothery award 1994). Achievements include pioneering development of new technique of high-temperature oxide melt solution calorimetery; being the first person to extensively apply the Calvét-type twin microcalorimeter in high temperature thermochemistry; originator of a novel high-temperature reaction calorimeter suitable for continuous use at temperatures up to about 1500K; applying new calorimeter in extensive studies of binary alloys of early transition metals and rare earth metals with Group VIII transition metals and with noble metals. Office: U Chgo James Franck Inst 5640 S Ellis Ave Chicago IL 60637-1433

KLEPPE, JOAN MARIE, entertainment executive; b. Lomira, Wis., Aug. 22, 1925; d. George Jacob and Susan Elizabeth (Welsch) Steiner; m. Albert Whitney Wellander, June 10, 1950 (div. Mar. 1960); children: Thomas A., Alan G., Barbara Sue; m. Willard Earl Kleppe, Sept. 18, 1978 (dec. Mar. 1988). Degree magna cum laude, Fond du Lac (Wis.) Comml Coll., 1943; BS in Music Edn., U. Wis., 1947; postgrad., Second City, Chgo., 1976-78. Cert. exec. sec., Ill. Adminstrv. asst. to pres. Canvas Products Corp., Fond du Lac, Wis., 1947-50; jr. exec. corp. offices Sears, Roebuck and Co., Chgo., 1950-54; exec. dir. Lake View Citizens' Coun., Chgo., 1963-67; exec. sec. Chgo. Police Dept., 1967-72, founder, dir. boys' a capella choir, 1970-72; polygraph interviewer, reporter Inst. Lie Detection, Chgo., 1972-75; exec. sec., adminstrv. asst. Electro Brand, Inc. importers, Chgo., 1975-80, Gen. Instrument Corp., Chgo., 1980-85; founder, exec. dir., musician Spring Valley Concert Band, Schaumburg, Ill., 1994—; entertainer St. Andrew Players, Chgo., 1965-74; trombonist Ukrainian Cathedral Concert Band, Chgo., 1968-70; performer, dir., costumer St. Marcelline Prodns., Inc., Schaumburg, 1989-95; performer, bd. dirs. Silver Foxes Theatrical Troupe, Streamwood, Ill., 1992-96. Author, dir. children's theatrical prodns. Let Freedom Ring, 1966, A Fractured Fairy Tale, 1967; author: Kids 'n' Kops, 1997; writer, dir. musical comedy Talent, of Chorus, 1989, Puttin' on the Bits, 1990; composer music anthem Chgo.: I Will, 1970; columnist Chgo. police dept. publ. The Star, 1968-72. Coord. neighborhood groups Lake View Citizens Coun., Chgo., 1963-67; sec., youth liaison youth com. Chgo. Police Dept., 1967-72; founding mem. Schaumburg Arts Collective, 1996—; mem., liaison Schaumburg Sister Cities, 1995—; coord. benefit performances; bd. dirs. St. Marcelline Prodns.; mem. Prairie Center Arts Found., 1997—, Assn. Concert Bands, Inc., 1998—. U. Wis. scholar, 1943, Pi Rho Zeta scholar, 1942; named Vol. of Yr. Kiwanis, 1970, Most Valuable Civilian Employee Chgo. Police Dept., 1970. Republican. Roman Catholic. Avocations: acting in community theater, freelance writing, costume design, singing, fishing. Home: 9 Dartford Ln Schaumburg IL 60194-3924 Office: Spring Valley Concert Band Inc PO Box 68901 Schaumburg IL 60168-0901

KLEPPE, JOHN ARTHUR, electrical engineering educator, business executive; b. Oakland, Calif., Feb. 21, 1939; s. Arthur William and Musa (Anderson) K.; m. Julianna Marie Galli, Aug. 12, 1961; children: John Frederick, Johanna Beth, Judith Anne. BSEE, U. Nev., 1961, MSEE, 1967; PhD, U. Calif., Davis, 1970. Registered profl. engr., Nev., Calif. Prof. elec. engring. U. Nev., Reno, 1970—, dir. Engring. Research and Devel., 1976-88; pres., research cons. Sci. Engring. Instruments, Inc., Reno, 1968-97; pres. Klepco, Inc., 1976—; cons.; chief engr. NSF weather expdn. to Antarctica, 1977; del. White House Conf. Small Bus., 1980. Author: (textbook) Engineering Applications of Acoustics, 1989; contbr. articles, papers to publs. and confs. around the world. Served to lt. C.E. USN, 1961-65. Recipient Outstanding Engring. Achievement award for Nev., 1981, 84; Inventor of Yr. award, 1985. Mem. IEEE, Nev. Innovation and Tech. Coun. (pres. 1981-93, pres. 1996-97), Sigma Xi, Tau Beta Pi. E-mail: kleppe@ee.unr.edu. Home: 2425 Greensboro Dr Reno NV 89509-5707 Office: SEI 1275 Kleppe Ln Ste 14 Sparks NV 89431-6499

KLEPPE, SHIRLEY R. KLEIN, artist; b. Sedalia, Mo., Sept. 29, 1946; d. Benjamin Eades Klein and Clara Louise Shirley; m. Stephen Douglas Kleppe, Nov. 22, 1968; children: Clinton Douglas, Nicole Lynne. BS in Edn., Ctrl. Mo. State U., 1967; postgrad., Ariz. State U., 1988. Art tchr. Benton County R#1 Sch. Dist., Cole Camp, Mo., 1967-68, Turner (Kans.) Unified Sch. Dist., 1968-69; graphic designer Menorah Med. Ctr., Kansas City, Mo., 1969-70; freelance graphic designer, illustrator Kansas City, 1970-75; advt. dir. Gorges Wholesale Meats, inc., Harlingen, Tex., 1975-76; art instr. City of Phoenix, 1979-82; advt. dir. Ariz. Restaurant Sys. Inc., Scottsdale, 1998—; sponsor vis. artist program Ctrl. Mo. State U., Warrensburg, 1993—; pres. Outrageous Red Inc., Scottsdale, Ariz., 1994—; exclusive jewelry vendor Sonic Corp., Oklahoma City, 1997—. Exhibited in shows at Western Fedn. Watercolor Socs., El Cajon, Calif., 1990 (Best of Show), Salmagundi Club, N.Y.C., 1990 (Thomas Moran award for watercolor), Rocky Mountain Nat. Watermedia, Golden, Colo., 1994 (3d Pl. award), Ky. Watercolor Soc., 1995 (Top award for watercolor); contbr. watercolor painting articles to profl. publs. Pres. Edmond (Okla.) Iris Soc., 1986-87. Mem. Nat. Watercolor Soc. (2d pl. award 1997), Watercolor West, Pa. Watercolor Soc., Ky. Watercolor Soc., Western Fedn. Watercolor Socs., Ariz. Watercolor Soc. (Royal Scorpion mem.), Ariz. Artists Guild (v.p. membership 1983-84, scholarship chmn. 1990-95, bldg. fund 1998—), Western Colo. Watercolor Soc. (Past Pres. award 1992, 97). Avocations: gardening, cooking, snow and water skiing, hiking, photography. Home and Office: 8210 E Tether Trl Scottsdale AZ 85255-1424

KLEPPER, CAROL HERDMAN, mental health therapist; b. Wagner, S.D., July 17, 1933; d. Forrest Glenwood and Augusta Wilhamina (Mills) Herdman; m. Albert Raymond Klepper, May 14, 1955; children: James David, Leesa Lynn, Krista Patrice. BS in Psychology cum laude, South Oreg. State Coll., 1987; MS in Counseling, Oreg. State U., 1989. Nat. cert. counselor, lic. profl. counselor; cert. diplomate in psychotherapy. Dir. counseling Klamath Hospice, Klamath Falls, Oreg., 1990-91; staff therapist Klamath Mental Health Ctr., 1991-94; in-house counselor Wednesday's Child, 1995—, title 19 supv., 1996—; data rschr. Rich Pickett and Co., Klamath Falls, 1986-90; pre-commitment investigator Klamath Mental Health Ctr., 1991-94; EPSDT coord. County of Klamath, 1991-94. Mem. youth svcs. team local mid-schs., Klamath Falls, 1992-94; juv. fire-setters network Klamath Falls Fire Dist. #1, 1992-95; head start health bd., Klamath Falls, 1991—, RAPP Team Mem., 1995—; program therapist KAP, 1998—. Mem. Psi Chi. Home and Office: 8926 Highway 66 Klamath Falls OR 97601-9519

KLEPPER, ELIZABETH LEE, physiologist; b. Memphis, Mar. 8, 1936; d. George Madden and Margaret Elizabeth (Lee) K. BA, Vanderbilt U., 1958; MA, Duke U., 1963, PhD, 1966. Research scientist Commonwealth Sci. and Indsl. Research Orgn., Griffith, Australia, 1966-68, Battelle Northwest Lab., Richland, Wash., 1972-76; asst. prof. Auburn (Ala.) U., 1968-72; Plant physiologist USDA Agrl. Research Service, Pendleton, Oreg., 1976-85, research leader, 1985-96. Assoc. editor Crop Sci., 1977-80, 88-90, tech. editor, 1990-92, editor, 1992-95; mem. editl. bd. Plant Physiology, 1977-92, Irrigation Sci., 1987-92; mem. editl. adv. bd. Field Crops Rsch., 1983-91; contbr. articles to profl. jours., chpts. to books. Marshall scholar British Govt., 1958-59; NSF fellow, 1964-66. Fellow AAAS, Crop Sci. Soc. Am. (fellows com. 1989-91, pres.-elect 1995-96, pres. 1996-97, past pres. 1997-98), Soil Sci. Soc. Am. (fellows com. 1986-88), Am. Soc. Agronomy (monograph com. 1983-90, bd. dirs. 1995-98); mem. Sigma Xi. Home: 1454 SW 45th Pendleton OR 97801 Office: USDA Argl Rsch Svc PO Box 370 Pendleton OR 97801-0370

KLEPPER, ROBERT KENNETH, writer, silent film historian, journalist; b. Springfield, Mo., Nov. 11, 1966; s. Kenneth Herbert and Altha Ann (Shumate) K. Reference asst. Pensacola (Fla.) Pub. Libr., 1983-84; office worker Pensacola Tax Collector Office, 1984-85; purchasing agt. asst. Gen. Oceanics, Miami, 1992-93; historian, writer various publs., 1993-99; reviewer books and videos relating to silent era The Silents Majority Internet Website, 1996; reviewer videos Classic Images and Films of the Golden Age, 1996—; dist. historian Future Bus. Leaders Am., 1983-84, pres., 1984-85, mem. Fla. Future Bus. Leaders Am. State Exec. Coun. Author: Silent Films on Video, 1996, Silent Film Reviews, 1999; co-prodr. (video) Nurse Marjorie (1920), 1997, (video) The Ghost of Rosy Taylor (1918), 1998, Hail the Woman (1921); wrote introduction Little Mary Sunshine (1916); contbr. articles to jours. Vol. Body Positive, People with AIDS Coalition, Miami, Fla., 1992-93; vol. receptionist Escambia AIDS Svcs., Pensacola, 1994-95; mem. Silent Film Soc., Atlanta, 1994-95; sec. ACLU N.W. Fla, 1988; vol. worker Lois Benson for Congress, Pensacola, 1995. Named Outstanding Dist. Pres., Fla. state chpt. FBLA, 1985, Internat. Man of Yr. 1998-99. Mem. Friends of Marion Davies Fan Club, Libr. Congress (nat. mem. 1999), Am. Film Inst. Republican. Avocations: watching silent films, collecting movie memorabilia, drug and alcohol rehab counseling. Home: 1500 N 65th Ave Lot 3 Pensacola FL 32506-3917

KLEPPER, ROBERT RUSH, plant physiologist; b. Sculthorpe AFB, Norfolk, Wales, Nov. 8, 1957; came to U.S., 1958; s. Norman Eugene and Rosalind Violet (Rush) K.; m. Laurene Kay Wycoff, June 25, 1991; children: April Kaylynn, Candace Rose. AS, Iowa Lakes C.C., Estherville, Iowa, 1987; BS, Buena Vista Coll., Storm Lake, Iowa, 1990; MS, Iowa State U., 1992; PhD, Columbia Pacific U., San Rafael, Calif., 1994. Mgr. Milford (Iowa) Nursery, 1985-89; rsch. assoc. Iowa State U., Ames, 1989-90; adj. prof. Iowa Ctrl. C.C., Storm Lake, 1992—; dir. R&D TransAgra Internat., Storm Lake, 1990-97; prof. biology and chemistry Iowa Lakes C.C., Estherville, 1997—; ind. cons., Linn Grove, Iowa, 1991—; sci. advisor Mus. Sci., Boston, 1994—; sci. day advisor Buena Vista U., Storm Lake, 1990—, adj. prof., 1996—; adj. prof. Iowa Lakes C.C., Spencer, 1994—, prof., Emmetsburg, 1997—. Mem. Plant Growth Regulator Soc. Am., Am. Soc. Plant Physiologists, Coun. Agrl. Sci. and Tech., Am. Soc. Agronomy. Avocations: playing guitar, riding bike, hiking, reading. E-mail: rklepper@ilcc.cc.ia.us. Home: 4476 100th Ave Linn Grove IA 51033-7545 Office: Iowa Lakes Cmty Coll 300 S 18th St Estherville IA 51334

KLEPPNER, DANIEL, physicist, educator; b. N.Y.C., Dec. 16, 1932; s. Otto and Beatrice (Taub) K.; m. Beatrice Spencer; children: Paul, Sofie, Andrew. BS, Williams Coll., 1953; BA, Cambridge (Eng.) U., 1955; PhD, Harvard U., 1959. Asst. prof. physics Harvard U., Cambridge, Mass., 1962-66; assoc. prof. MIT, Cambridge, 1966-73, prof., 1974—, Lester Wolfe prof. physics, 1986—, assoc. dir. Rsch. Lab. of Electronics, 1987—. Author: Introduction to Mechanics, 1973, Quick Calculus, 1986. Recipient Oersted medal, AAPT, 1996. Fellow Am. Phys. Soc. (Davisson-Germer prize 1986, Julius Edgar Lilienfeld prize 1991), AAAS, Optical Soc. Am. (William F. Meggars award 1991), Am. Acad. Arts and Scis.; mem. NAS, Am. Assn. Physics Tchrs. (Oersted medal). Office: MIT Dept Physics 77 Mass Ave Rm 26237 Cambridge MA 02139-4307

KLESIUS, PHILLIP HARRY, microbiologist, researcher; b. Phila., Mar. 1, 1938; s. Phillip M. and Mary Hoagen (Plummer) K.; m. Patricia Ann Wood, Oct. 31, 1969; children—Stephen, Patrick. B.S., Fla. So. U., Lakeland, 1961; M.S., Northwestern State U., Natchitoches, La., 1963; Ph.D., U. Tex., Austin, 1966; postgrad., U. Calif.-San Francisco, 1967. Hon. diplomate Am. Coll. Vet. Microbiologists. Asst. prof. microbiology U. Tex., Austin, 1967-68; asst. prof microbiology U. Ariz., Tucson, 1968-72; asst. chief strep sect. USPHS, Fort Collins, Colo., 1972-73; research microbiologist U.S. Dept. Agr., Auburn, Ala., 1973-82, dir., 1982—; adj. prof. Auburn U., 1974—; adj. assoc. prof. Med. Coll. S.C., Charleston, 1975—; visting prof. Tuskegee Inst., Ala., 1974—. Contbr. articles to profl. jours. Named USDA Scientist of Yr., 1994. Fellow Am. Acad. Microbiology, Am. Assn. Vet. Immunologists (dir. 1985—), Am. Assn. Vet. Pathologists, Am. Assn. Vet. Parasitologists, Am. Soc. Microbiologists. Home: 828 Heard Ave Auburn AL 36830-6222 Office: Fish Diseases and Parasites Rsch Lab PO Box 952 Auburn AL 36831-0952

KLETT, EDWIN LEE, lawyer; b. Clearfield, Pa., Dec. 8, 1935; s. John L. and Gertrude Elizabeth (Larson) K.; m. Janis Lynn Gibson; children: David, Lauren, Krista, Kirklin, Keenan. BS in Commerce and Finance, Bucknell U., 1957; JD, Dickinson Sch. Law, Carlisle, Pa., 1962. Bar: Pa. 1963, U.S. Dist. Ct. (we. dist.) Pa. 1963, U.S. Ct. Appeals (3d cir.) 1967, U.S. Ct. Appeals (6th cir.) 1985, U.S. Supreme Ct. 1983. Assoc. Eckert, Seamans, Cherin & Mellott, Pitts., 1962, ptnr., 1969; sr. ptnr., chmn. Klett Lieber Rooney & Schorling, Pitts., 1989—; trustee Dickinson Sch. Law, 1982—; mem. civil procedural rules com. Pa. Supreme Ct., 1986—, vice chair, 1989-92, chair, 1993—. Mem. Pa. State Transp. Adv. Bd., Harrisburg, Pa., 1985-88, Rep. State Fin. Com., Harrisburg, 1986-91, Allegheny County Rep. Fin. Com., Pitts., 1987-92. Fellow Internat. Acad. Trial Lawyers, Am. Coll. Trial Lawyers (Pa. state com. 1994—, state chair 1996-98), Am. Bd. Trial Advs., Am. Bar Found., Am. Bar Inst., Pa. Bar Found., Alletheny County Bar Found.; mem. ABA (ho. dels. 1999), Am. Bd. Trial Advs., Acad. Trial Lawyers Allegheny County (bd. govs. 1986-88, pres. 1988-89), Am. Judicature Soc., Allegheny County Bar (bd. govs. 1989-92, 99—, pres.-elect 1999—). Home: 151 Ordale Blvd Pittsburgh PA 15228-1525 Office: Klett Lieber Rooney & Schorling 40th Fl 1 Oxford Ct Fl 40 Pittsburgh PA 15219-1407

KLETT, GORDON A., retired savings and loan association executive; b. Galva, Iowa, Apr. 29, 1925; s. Ernest and Frieda (Gutknecht) K.; m. Edna Mae Klett, June 11, 1950; children: Joel G., Kristin F., Andrea E. B.A., Valparaiso U., 1949; M.A., UCLA, 1951. With U.S. Weather Bur., St. Paul, 1941-42; vis. lectr. U. Ceylon, Colombo, 1951-52; fgn. service officer U.S. Dept. State, Mex., 1956-58; with Glendale (Calif.) Fed. Savs. and Loan Assn., 1953-56, 59-84, pres., chief operating officer, 1980-84. Served with USAAF, 1943-46.

KLEVAN, ROBERT BRUCE, music educator; b. Lodi, Calif., May 12, 1953; s. Stanley P. and Mary C. (Canepa) K.; m. Norma D. Taylor, May 26, 1974; children: Rebecca, Roxanne, Anthony. MusB summa cum laude, U. Pacific, 1975, MusM, 1981; PhD in Music, U. Tex., 1993. Cert. tchr. music, Calif. Dir. mus. Marysville (Calif.) H.S., 1975-77, Robert Louis Stevenson Sch., Pebble Beach, Calif., 1977—; fine arts chmn. Robert Louis Stevenson Sch., Pebble Beach, 1986—, summer camp dir., 1995—. Contbr. articles to profl. jours.; dir. wind ensemble U. Calif., Santa Cruz, 1994—. Founding mem. Monterey Jazz Festival Edn. Com., 1983; bd. dirs. Chamber Music Soc., Carmel, Calif., 1992-94. Recipient Youth Leadership award Elks, Stockton, Calif., 1971. Mem. Ctrl. Coast Section Music Educators (bd. dirs., chmn. medals com. 1994—), Calif. Orch. Dirs. Assn. (pres. 1994-96), Internat. Assn. Jazz Educators, Am. Choral Dirs. Assn., Calif. Music Educators Assn. (Outstanding Music Educator award 1993), Music Educators Nat. Conf. Avocations: fencing, swimming, writing, watersports. Office: PO Box 657 Pebble Beach CA 93953-0657

KLEVEN, MARGUERITE, state senator. Mem. S.D. Senate, Pierre, 1995—, mem. appropriations com., chmn. govt. ops. and audit com. Republican.

KLEWANS, SAMUEL N., lawyer; b. Lock Haven, Pa., Mar. 2, 1941; s. Morris and Ruth N. K.; children: Richard Bennett, Ruth Elise, Paul Henry, Margo Ilene. A.B., U. Pa., 1963; J.D., Am. U., 1966. Bar: Va. 1966, U.S. Dist. Ct. (ea. dist.) Va. 1966, U.S. Dist. Ct. D.C. 1967, U.S. Ct. Appeals D.C. 1967, U.S. Ct. Appeals (4th cir.) 1967, U.S. Supreme Ct. 1971. Law clk., U.S. Dist. Ct. Ea. Dist. Va. 1966-67; ptnr. Fried, Fried & Klewans, Springfield, Va., 1970-86; prin. Klewans & Assocs., 1986-91; shareholder/atty. Grad, Logan & Klewans, P.C., 1991—; lectr. No. Va. Inst. Continuing Med. Edn., No. Va. Ctr. Quality and Health Edn. Contbr. articles to profl. jours. Served to 1st lt. JAGC-USAR, 1966-72. Mem. Fairfax County Bar Assn. (ethics and grievance com. 1971-72, mem. 75-76, courts com. 1975-76; jud. selection com. 1979-82, chmn. 1981-82), Va. State Bar (mem. disciplinary bd. 1976-84, vice chmn. 1982-83, chmn. 1983-84, lectr. continuing legal edn., professionalism faculty), Practice Resource Group (lectr.). Office: 1421 Prince St Alexandria VA 22314-2805

KLEWENO, GILBERT H., lawyer; b. Endicott, Wash., Mar. 21, 1933; s. Melvin Lawrence and Anna (Lust) K.; m. Virginia Symms, Dec. 28, 1958; children: Stanley, Douglas, Phillip. BA, U. Wash., 1955; LLR, U. Idaho, 1959. Bar: Wash. 1960. Assoc. Read & Church, Vancouver, Wash., 1960-68, Boettcher, LaLonde & Kleweno, Vancouver, Wash., 1968—; part-time U.S. Magistrate Judge, 1979. Chmn. Bd. Adjustors, Vancouver, Civil Svc. Commn., Vancouver. Mem. Wash. State Bar Assn., Elks, Gyro Club. Office: Boettcher LaLonde Kleweno 610 Esther St Vancouver WA 98660-3022*

KLEY, JOHN ARTHUR, banker; b. Jericho, N.Y., Oct. 24, 1921; s. John and Annie (Upton) K.; m. Florence Elizabeth Cannon, Sept. 1, 1945 (dec. Apr. 1983); 1 dau., Martha Anne; m. Edna C. Dornhoefer, June 1984 (div. June 1987); m. Lorelei W. Lasecki. Apr. 1989. Grad., Stonier Grad. Sch. Banking, Rutgers U., 1952; B.P.S., Pace U., 1974. With Washington Irving Trust Co. (and successor County Trust Co.), White Plains, N.Y., 1937-76; asst. treas., asst. v.p., v.p. Washington Irving Trust Co. (and successor County Trust Co.), 1947-57, exec. v.p., 1957-60, pres., 1960-72, chmn. bd., 1972-76; v.p. Bank N.Y. Co., 1968-74, vice chmn., 1974-77; dir. Bank of N.Y., 1973-77. Past chmn. bd. trustees, trustee emeritus Westchester Community Coll.; past pres., chmn. Westchester Community Coll. Found.; past pres. Legal Aid Soc. West County; past chmn. bd. regents Stonier Grad. Sch. Banking, Rutgers U. Served from pvt. to maj. USAAF, 1942-46; lt. col. Res. Recipient Leffinqwell medal, 1960. Mem. ABA (com. on mechanization of check handling, chmn. tech. com. 1954-64, N.Y. State Bankers Assn. (pres. 1969-70, The Pelican Bay Club (Naples, Fla.), Imperial Golf Club (Naples), Whippoorwill Club (Armonk, N.Y.). Episcopalian. Home: 7515 Pelican Bay Blvd Apt 303 Naples FL 34108-6518

KLIBANOV, ALEXANDER MAXIM, chemistry and biotechnology educator, researcher; b. Moscow, July 15, 1949; U.S., 1977, naturalized, 1983; s. Maxim and Eugenia (Tomas) K.; m. Margarita Romanycheva, Apr. 21, 1972; 1 child, Tanya. MS, Moscow U., 1971, PhD, 1974. Rsch. chemist Moscow U., 1974-77; postgrad. rsch. chemist U. Calif.-San Diego, 1978-79; asst. prof. applied biological sci. dept. MIT, Cambridge, 1979-83, H.L. Doherty prof., 1981-83, assoc. prof., 1983-87, prof., 1987-88, prof. chemistry dept., 1988—; cons. in field. Contbr. over 200 articles to profl. jours.; mem. editl. bd. Applied Biochemistry and Biotech, 1981—, Advances Biochem. Engring./Biotechnol., 1985—, Chimicaoggi, 1986—, Biocatalysis, 1988—, Applied Biocatalysis, 1989—, Biotechnology Progress, 1990—, Jour. Molecular Catalysis-Enzymatic, 1995—, Biotech. and Bioengring., 1998—. Recipient Internat. Enzyme Engring. prize Engring. Found., 1993; grantee numerous orgns. Fellow Am. Inst. Med. and Biol. Engring. (founding); mem. NAS, NAE, Am. Chem. Soc. (Leo Friend award 1986, Ipatieff prize 1989, Marvin J. Johnson award 1991, Arthur C. Cope Scholar award, 1993), Am. Soc. Biochemistry and Molecular Biol. Home: 45 The Ledges Rd Newton MA 02459-2072 Office: MIT Bldg 56-579 Cambridge MA 02139-4301

KLIEBHAN, SISTER M(ARY) CAMILLE, academic administrator; b. Milw., Apr. 4, 1923; d. Alfred Sebastian and Mae Eileen (McNamara) K. Student, Cardinal Stritch Coll., Milw., 1945-48; B.A., Cath. Sisters Coll., Washington, 1949; M.A., Cath. U. Am., 1951, Ph.D., 1955. Joined Sisters of St. Francis of Assisi, Roman Catholic Ch., 1945; legal sec. Spence and Hanley (attys.), Milw., 1941-45; instr. edn. Cardinal Stritch Coll., 1955-62, assoc. prof., 1962-68, prof., 1968—, head dept. edn., 1962-67, dean students, 1962-64, chmn. grad. div., 1964-69, v.p. for acad. and student affairs, 1969-74, pres., also bd. dirs., 1974-91, chancellor, 1991—. Bd. dirs. Goals for Milw. 2000, 1980-83; treas. Wis. Found. Ind. Colls., 1974-79, 87-90, v.p., 1979-81, pres., 1981-83; bd. dirs. DePaul Hosp., 1982-91, Sacred Heart Sch. Theology, 1983—, Viterbo Coll., 1990-98, Milw. Cath. Home, 1991—, St. Ann Ctr. for Intergenerational Care, 1991—, Wis. Psychoanalytic Found., 1989-96, St. Coletta's of Mass., 1995-98, Internat. Inst. Wis., 1984-94, Milw. Achiever Program, Inc., 1983—, Franciscan Pilgrimage Programs, Inc., 1997—, Friends of Internat. Inst. Wis., 1994—, Mental Health Assn. Milwaukee County, 1983-87, Pub. Policy Forum, 1987-90, Better Bus. Bur. of Wis. Inc., 1989—, YWCA Greater Milw., 1996—, St. Camillus Campus, 1996—, mem. adv. bd., 1989-96; mem. TEMPO, 1982—, bd. dirs., 1986-89; bd. govs. Wis. Policy Rsch. Inst., 1987-97. Mem. Am. Psychol. Assn., Rotary Club of Milw. (v.p., pres. elect 1992-93, pres. 1993-94), St. Mary's Acad. Alumnae Assn., Phi Delta Kappa, Delta Epsilon Sigma, Psi Chi, Delta Kappa Gamma, Kappa Delta Pi. *It is because of my faith that I can meet every condition with courage.*

KLIEFOTH, A(RTHUR) BERNHARD, III, neurosurgeon; b. San Antonio, Nov. 26, 1942; S. Arthur Bernhard, Jr. and Pauline (Gray) K.; m. Ingrid R. Kunde, Apr. 22, 1968; children: Karena, Tanya. AB in Chemistry, Princeton U., 1965; MD, U. Tex., 1970. Diplomate Am. Bd. Neurol. Surgery. Intern Naval Hosp., Oakland, Calif., 1970-71; resident gen. surgery Naval Hosp., San Diego, 1972-73; neurosurg. tchr. Washington U., St. Louis, 1973-78; rsch. fellow dept. radiation scis. Washington U., 1977-78; commd. ensign USN, 1969, advanced through grades to comdr., 1977; staff neurosurgeon Naval Regional Med. Ctr., Oakland, 1978-81; resigned, 1981; capt. USNR, 1985; practice medicine specializing in neurosurgery Knoxville, Tenn., 1981—; mem. staff U. Tenn Hosp., St. Mary's Hosp.; chmn. dept. surgery, 1989-90; clin. assoc. prof. surgery U. Tenn.; bd. dirs. Tenn. Donor Svcs., Cole Neurosci. Found., Knoxville Donor Svcs. Pres. Princeton Alumni Assn. Knoxville and Eastern Tenn. Fellow ACS, Stroke Coun. Am. Heart Assn.; mem. AMA, Am. Assn. Neurol. Surgeons, Am. Soc. Stereotactic and Functional Neurosurgery, Tenn. Neurosurg. Soc., World Soc. Stereotactic and Functional Neurosurgery, Congress Neurol. Surgeons, So. Neurosurg. Soc., So. Med. Assn., Tenn. Med. Assn., Knoxville Acad. Medicine, San Francisco Neurol. Soc., Soc. Med. Cons. to Armed Forces, Assn. Mil. Surgeons U.S., Soc. Neurosci. Office: 939 E Emerald Ave Ste 905 Knoxville TN 37917-4578 Also: PO Box 51648 Knoxville TN 37950-1648

KLIEN, WOLFGANG JOSEF, architect; b. Hollabrunn, Austria, Sept. 29, 1942; s. Josef and Maria (Kainz) K.; Dipl. Ing., Vienna Tech. U., 1967; m. Jean M. Klien; children: Christina Olga, Angelika Maria. Designer, E. Donau, Architect, Vienna, 1968; with C. Nitschke & Assos., Architects, Columbus, Ohio, 1968-71; project architect GSAS Architects, Phoenix, 1971-75, 77-78; prodn. architect Harry Glueck, Vienna, 1976-77; v.p. architecture Am. Indian Engring. Inc., Phoenix, 1978-81; pres. S.W. Estate Group, Inc., real estate devel., San Diego, 1980-82; pres., tech. dir., branch mgr. Ariz. br. office SEG-S.W. Estate Group, Inc., Phoenix, 1982-86; prin. Klien & Assoc., Architecture, Planning, Devel. Cons., Phoenix, 1986—, Atlantic-Pacific Trading Corp., Internat. Trade, Phoenix, 1986-88; pres., gen. mgr. Polybau, Inc., Hayward, Calif., 1988-90; pres. Libra Cons., Inc., Phoenix, 1989—; ptnr. Heart Devel. Co., LLC, dBa Heart Homes, 1993-96; v.p. Sunrise Custom Homes, Inc., 1995—. founder, pres. SOS-Children's Villages of Ariz., Inc., 1998—. Recipient Great Silver Medal of Merit, Republic of Austria, 1993. Mem. AIA, Austro-Am. Coun. West, Austrian Soc. Ariz. (founder 1985, v.p. 1985-86, pres. 1987—). Roman Catholic. Home and Office: 11797 E Casitas Del Rio Dr Scottsdale AZ 85255

KLIESCH, WILLIAM FRANK, physician; b. Franklinton, La., Nov. 4, 1928; s. Edward Granville and Elsie Jeni (Sylvest) K.; m. May Virginia Reid, Dec. 17, 1955; children: Thomas Karl, William August, John Francis. BS, La. State U., 1949, MD, 1953. Intern Valley Forge Hosp., Phoenixville, Pa., 1953-54; intern in med. rsch. Charity Hosp., New Orleans, 1956-57; resident, fellow in internal medicine Ochsner Found. Hosp., New Orleans, 1957-59; pvt. practice New Orleans, 1959-69, Jackson, Miss., 1969—; dir. spinal injury svc. Miss. Meth. Rehab. Ctr., Jackson, 1980—. Capt. U.S Air Force, 1953-56. Fellow Am. Coll. Emergency Physicians; mem. Am. Spinal Injury Assn., Internat. Paraplegia Soc. Episcopalian. Avocations: gardening, farming. Home: 8892 Gary Rd Jackson MS 39212-9732 Office: Miss State Hosp Whitfield MS 39193

KLIEWER, KENNETH LEE, computational scientist, research administrator; b. Mountain Lake, Minn., Dec. 31, 1935; s. Henry Gerhard and Susan (Epp) K.; m. Kathleen Kay Zimmermann, Aug. 30, 1959; children—Steven Anthony, Lisa Jo, Christopher Lee. B.S. in Elec. Engring., U. Minn., 1957, M.S.E.E., 1959; Ph.D. in Physics, U. Ill., 1964. Asst. prof., assoc. prof., prof. dept. physics Iowa State U., Ames, 1963-81; assoc. physicist, physicist, sr. physicist Ames Lab.-Dept. Energy, 1963-81, program dir. solid state physics, 1974-78, assoc. dir. sci. and tech., 1978-81; assoc. lab. dir. for phys. research Argonne (Ill.) Nat. Lab., 1981-86, dir. advanced photon source design project, 1983-86; dean Sch. Sci. Purdue U., West Lafayette, Ind., 1986-91; asst. v.p. for rsch., 1991-92; dir. ctr. computational scis. Oak Ridge (Tenn.) Nat. Lab., 1992—; guest prof. U. Hamburg and Deutsches Electronen Synchrotron (DESY), Fed. Republic Germany, 1972-73, Free U. Berlin, 1974, Fritz Haber Inst., Berlin, 1975; vis. scientist Rockwell Internat. Sci. Ctr., Thousand Oaks, Calif., 1976; temporary program officer Dept. Energy, Washington, 1979-80; cons., Argonne Nat. Lab.; mem. fusion policy adv. com. Dept. Energy, 1990-91. Editor: (with others) Non-Traditional Approaches to the Study of the Solid-Electrolyte Interface, 1980; contbr. articles to profl. jours. Illini fellow U. Ill., 1959-61; U.S. Steel Found. fellow, 1961-63. Fellow Am. Phys. Soc. (exec. com. div. condensed matter physics 1980-82), AAAS, Sigma Xi, Eta Kappa Nu, Tau Beta Pi. Home: 165 Whippoorwill Dr Oak Ridge TN 37830-8646

KLIGER, MILTON RICHARD, financial services executive; b. N.Y.C., Sept. 26, 1922; s. David and Sadie (Zelikow) K.; m. Ruth Salkind, Jan. 30, 1944 (dec. July 1991); children: Alan S., Sandra F.; m. Gladys Duarte, Sept. 26, 1992. BBA, Bernard Baruch Coll., 1947. Acct. Shipowners Agy. Inc., N.Y.C., 1946-48; chief acct. Am.-Israeli Shipping Co. Inc., N.Y.C., 1948-53; exec. v.p. Maritime Overseas Corp., N.Y.C., 1953-87, also bd. dirs.; sr. v.p., treas. Overseas Shipholding Group Inc., N.Y.C., 1970-87, also bd. dirs.; sr. v.p. Argent Group, Ltd., N.Y.C., 1988-89; pres. Milton Kliger Mgmt. Svcs., Inc., N.Y.C., 1989-93, Marine Equity Corp., N.Y.C., 1990—. Home: 3530 Mystic Pointe Dr Apt 701 Aventura FL 33180-4526

KLIGERMAN, MORTON M., radiologist; b. Phila., Dec. 26, 1917; s. Samuel and Dorothy (Medvene) K.; m. Barbara B. Coleman, Mar. 14, 1956; children: Hilary, Thomas A., Valli á Court. B.S., Temple U., 1938, M.D., 1941, M.Sc., 1948; M.A. (hon.), Yale U., 1958; D.F.A. (hon.), New Sch. Music, 1985; MA (hon.), U. Pa., 1986. Instr. radiology Temple U., Phila., 1947-48, Columbia U., N.Y.C., 1948-50; asst. prof. radiology Columbia U., 1950-53, assoc. prof., 1953-58; Robert E. Hunter prof. radiology, chmn. dept. radiology Yale U., New Haven; also radiologist-in-chief Yale-New Haven Hosp., 1958-72; dir. Cancer Research and Treatment Center U. N.Mex., Albuquerque, 1972-80, prof. radiology, 1972-80; asst. dir. for radiation therapy Los Alamos Sci. Lab., 1972-80; chief div. radiation oncology Bernalillo County Med. Center, Albuquerque, 1972-80; prof. radiation oncology U. Pa., Phila., 1980—, Henry K. Pancoast prof. research oncology, 1984-88; prof. emeritus, 1988—; cons. on staff Presbyn. Hosp., Lovelace-Bataan Med. Center, St. Joseph Hosp., VA Hosp., all Albuquerque, Los Alamos Med. Center. Contbr. articles to profl. jours. Bd. dirs. Santa Fe Opera, 1975-80, mem. nat. adv. bd., 1980-89; bd. dirs. Santa Fe Opera Found., 1976-80, also pres.; bd. dirs. N.Mex. divsn. Am. Cancer Soc., 1972-76, Phila. divsn., 1985-89, Pa. Ballet, 1985-89; bd. advisors Annenberg Ctr., U. Pa., 1987—, Phila. Scholar Fund, 1992—. With M.C., U.S. Army, 1944-47. Recipient Disting. Alumni award Temple U., 1964; Silver Medallion Columbia U., 1967; Grubbe Gold Medal award Chgo. Med. Soc.-Chgo. Radiol. Soc., 1976; Disting. Alumnus award Temple U. Med. Sch., 1986; named Med. Alumnus of Yr. Temple U. Med. Sch., 1989. Fellow Am. Coll. Radiology, Coll. Physicians Phila.; mem. Pa. Med. Soc., Philadelphia County Med. Soc., Am. Assn. Cancer Rsch., Am. Radium Soc. (v.p. 1976-77, pres. 1982-83, Janeway medal 1981), Am. Soc. Therapeutic Radiologists (pres. 1968-69, Gold medal 1982), Am. Legion, Alpha Omega Alpha. Home: 220 W Rittenhouse Sq Philadelphia PA 19103-5737 Office: Hosp of Univ Pa Dept Radiation Oncology 3400 Spruce St Philadelphia PA 19104-4204

KLIGFIELD, PAUL DAVID, physician, medicine educator; b. N.Y.C., Dec. 20, 1945; s. Irving and Yetta (Blumenstein) K.; m. Mary Susan Winters, Dec. 16, 1978; 1 child, Benjamin Winters. BA, Queens Coll., N.Y.C., 1966; B in Med. Sci., Dartmouth Coll., 1968; MD, Harvard U., 1970. Diplomate Am. Bd. Internal Medicine, Am. Bd. Cardiovascular Diseases. Intern and resident in medicine Beth Israel Hosp., Boston, 1970-72; rsch. fellow St. Georges Hosp., London, 1972-73; fellow in cardiology N.Y. Hosp., 1973-75, dir. cardiac graphics lab., 1977—; asst. prof. medicine Med. Coll., Cornell U., N.Y.C., 1977-83, assoc. prof., 1983-92, prof., 1992—; cons. Rockefeller U. Hosp., N.Y.C., 1977—. Contbr. articles to profl. jours. Lt. comdr. USNR, 1975-77. Fellow Am. Coll. Cardiology, N.Y. Acad. Medicine (trustee 1990-97), N.Y. Cardiologic Soc. (sec.-treas. 1997—); mem. Am. Osler Soc. (pres. 1991-92), N.Y. Heart Assn. (bd. dirs. 1988-94), Internat. Soc. for Computerized Electrocardiography (bd. dirs. 1984—), Grolier Club. Office: Cornell Med Ctr 525 E 68th St New York NY 10021-4873

KLIGLER, ROGER MICHAEL, physician; b. N.Y.C., Jan. 10, 1952; s. Seymour Hyman and Gloria Kligler; m. Catherine Mary Whelan, Dec. 3, 1978; children: Benjamin, David, Laura. BS, Dickinson Coll., 1974; MD, Georgetown U., 1978. Diplomate Am. Bd. Internal Medicine. Intern internal medicine North Shore U. Hosp., Manhasset, N.Y., 1978-79; resident primary care internal medicine U. Calif., Davis, 1979-81; physician David Burns MD, PC, Little Falls, N.Y., 1982-83; physician Brodgewater Goddard Park Med. Assoc., Brockton, Mass., 1983—, utilization rev. coord., asst. med. dir., v.p. med. affairs, 1996—. Office: Bridgewater Goddard Park Med Assocs 1 Pearl St Brockton MA 02301-2800*

KLIMA, MARTHA SCANLAN, state legislator; b. Balt., Dec. 3, 1938; d. Thomas Moore and Catherine A. Scanlan; m. James Patrick Klima Jr., Apr. 8, 1961; children: Jennifer, J. Patrick III, Andrew. AA, Villa Julie Coll., 1958. Med. stenographer U. Md. Med. Sch., Balt., 1958-63; mem. appropriations com. Md. Ho. of Dels., Annapolis, 1982—; sec. Cen. Md. Health Systems Agy., 1981-83; commr. State Planning Commn., State of Md., 1983—. Del. Rep. Nat. Conv. Dallas, 1984; bd. dirs. Greater Balt. Med. Ctr., Towson, 1986-91, Md. Spl. Olympics, 1987—. Named Freshman of Yr., Ho. of Dels., 1984, Woman of Yr. Towsontowne Bus. and Profl. Women's Club; recipient Gov.'s Citation for Outstanding Svc. to Citizens of Md., 1988, Pub. Svc. award for Outstanding Support to Balt. Assn. Retarded Citizens, Inc., 1994, Legis. award Balt. County Commn. on Disabilities, 1994. Mem. Am. Legis. Exchange Coun. (state chmn. 1987-97, chmn. Telecomm. and Info. Tech. Task Force, Outstanding State Legislator award 1994), Women Legis. Md., Congress of PTA's (hon. life), Balt. County C. of C. (Merit award 1981). Republican. Roman Catholic. Avocations: fishing, walking, boating. Home: 1403 Newport Pl Lutherville Timonium MD 21093-5920 Office: Ho Reps State Capital Annapolis MD 21401

KLIMA, ROGER RADIM, physiatrist; b. Prague, Czechoslovakia; came to U.S., 1982, naturalized, 1988; s. Josef and Radka Klima. BA, Zatlanka Coll., Prague, 1971; MD, Charles U., Prague, 1978. Diplomate Am. Bd. Phys. Medicine and Rehab., Am. Bd. Electrodiagnostic Medicine. Resident in surgery Charles U., 1978-79, resident in orthopedic surgery, 1979-81; fellow, clin. clk. Beverly Hills Med. Ctr. and Cedars-Sinai Med. Ctr., L.A., 1984-86; resident in surgery U. Medicine and Dentistry-N.J. Med. Sch., Newark, 1986-87; resident in phys. medicine and rehab. U. Medicine and Dentistry-N.J. Med. Sch./Kessler Inst., Newark and West Orange, 1987-90; mem. phys. medicine and rehab. faculty Stanford (Calif.) U. and affiliated hosps., 1990—; dir. phys. medicine and rehab. outpatient svcs. Palo Alto (Calif.) VA Health Care Sys., 1992—, also co-dir. comprehensive pain mgmt.; clin. instr. in phys. medicine and rehab. U. Medicine and Dentistry-N.J.Med. Sch., 1989-90; clin. instr. in phys., medicine and rehab. Stanford U. Sch. Medicine, 1990-96, asst. prof., 1996—. Contbr. articles to profl. jours. Recipient first ann. Thompson Humanitarian award Stanford U. Phys. Medicine and Rehab., 1994, 97. Mem. Am. Acad. Phys. Medicine and Rehab. (liaison resident physician coun. 1989-90), Assn. Acad. Physiatrists, Am. Assn. Electrodiagnostic Medicine. Office: Stanford U Med Ctr Divsn Phys Medicine and Rehab Rm NC 104 Stanford CA 94305

KLIMAN, GERALD BURT, electrical engineer; b. Boston, July 28, 1931; s. Milford and Minnie (Savits) K.; m. Edith Vivian Moses, Aug. 21, 1960; children: Jonathan Meir, Daniel Joseph. SB, MIT, 1955, SM, 1959, ScD, 1965. Electronics technician meteorology dept. MIT, Cambridge, 1950-55, instr., tchg. asst. elec. engring. dept., 1957-65; asst. prof. elec. engring. Rensselaer Poly. Inst., Troy, N.Y., 1965-71; elec. engr. transp. divsn. GE, Erie, Pa., 1971-76; elec. engr. Advanced Nuclear Systems GE, San Jose, Calif., 1976-78, Corp. Rsch. and Devel. GE, Schenectady, N.Y., 1978—. Assoc. editor Electric Machines and Power Systems Jours., 1976—; contbr. articles to profl. jours. Mem. exec. bd. Interfaith Community, Schenectady, 1983; pres., v.p., concertmaster Music Co. Orch., Schenectady, 1978—; chmn. Agudat Achim Sch. Com., Schenectady, 1990-91; Capt. USAF, 1955-57. Fellow IEEE, mem. Sigma Xi, Tau Beta Pi, Eta Kappa Nu. Achievements include 42 patents on electromagnetic pumps, permanent magnet motors, incipient fault diagnostics, electron beam and laser cutting, switched reluctance motors, high speed motors and superconducting magnets. Office: GE Corp Rsch and Devel PO Box 8 Schenectady NY 12301-0008

KLIMENT, ROBERT MICHAEL, architect; b. Prague, Czechoslovakia, June 9, 1933; came to U.S., 1950; s. Felix and Sophie (Baltinester) K.; m. Janet McClure, Sept. 12, 1959 (div. 1968); 1 child, Nicholas McClure; m. Frances Halsband, May 1, 1971; 1 child, Alexander Halsband. BA, Yale U., 1954, MArch, 1959. Registered architect Penn., N.Y., N.J., Mass., Conn., Ohio, Va., D.C., N.C., N.H., Md.; cert. Nat. Coun. Archtl. Registration Bds. Architect Mitchell/Giurgola Architects, Phila., 1961-66; architect, assoc. Mitchell/Giurgola Architects, N.Y.C., 1967-71; ptnr. R.M. Kliment Architect, N.Y.C., 1972-78, R.M. Kliment & Frances Halsband Architects, N.Y.C., 1978—; instr. U. Pa., Phila., 1963-66, vis. prof., 1972-73; asst. prof. Columbia U., N.Y.C., 1966-70, vis. prof., 1977, 84; vis. prof. MIT, Cambridge, Mass., 1970, Yale U., New Haven, 1972-74, N.C. State U., Raleigh, 1978, Rice U., Houston, 1979, U. Va., Charlottesville, 1979-80, Harvard U., Cambridge, 1980-81. Works include Computer Sci. Bldg. Princeton U. (Nat. Honor award AIA 1994), U. Va. Life Scis. Bldg., Columbia U. Computer Scis. Bldg. (Nat. Honor award AIA 1987, award NYSAA 1985, Tucker award Bldg. Stone Inst. 1985, other awards), Mercantile Exch. Bldg., N.Y. (Bard award for excellence in architecture City Club N.Y. 1989), Burke Chemistry Bldg., Dartmouth Coll., Adelbert Adminstrn. Bldg., Case Western Res. U. (AIA Nat. honor award 1994), Sudikoff Computer Sci. Bldg., Dartmouth Coll., MTA/L.I. R.R. Entrance Bldg., Penn Sta., N.Y. (Bard award for excellence in architecture City Club N.Y. 1995, AIA nat. honor award 1996, NYSAA & NYC AIA awards 1995), Ebert Art Ctr., Coll. of Wooster; exhibited in group shows at Bklyn. Mus., 1977, The Drawing Ctr., 1977, Cooper Hewitt Mus., 1977-78, Mus. Finnish Architecture, Helsinki, Finland, 1980, Harvard Grad. Sch. Design, 1981, NAD, 1981, 87, Smith Coll. Mus. Art, 1981, Rice U. Farrish Hall Gallery, 1983, Columbia U. Low Libr., 1986, Parrish Art Mus., 1987, German Architecture Mus., Frankfurt, 1989, Rotunda Gallery, Bklyn., 1995. With U.S. Army, 1955-57. Fulbright scholar, Italy, 1959-60; AIA Archtl. Firm award, 1997, Medal of Honor NYC AIA, 1998. Fellow AIA, Century Assn. Office: R M Kliment & Frances Halsband Architects 255 W 26th St New York NY 10001-8001

KLIMENT, STEPHEN ALEXANDER, architect, editor, journalist; b. May 24, 1930; s. Felix and Sophia (Baltinester) K.; m. Felicia Drury, Dec. 24, 1957; children: Pamela Drury, Jennifer Anne. *Spouse Felicia Drury Kliment obtained a Bachelor's degree in history and philosophy from Barnard College and a Bachelor of Science degree from Teacher's College, Columbia University. She is a professor in the Special Education Department of the City College of the City University of New York, and a math specialist for the New York City Board of Education. She conducts statistical research studies which identify the relationship between diet and the social andacademic behavior of students in the classroom.* Student, Ecole Speciale d'Architecture, Paris, 1948-49; BArch, MIT, 1953; MFA, Princeton U., 1957. Draftsman Jean Labatut, Princeton, N.J., 1957; designer Skidmore, Owings & Merrill, N.Y.C., 1957-59, Reeb-Draz Assos., Cleve., 1959-60; editor Archtl. and Engring. News, 1961-69; v.p. Caudill Rowlett Scott, N.Y.C., 1969-72; architect, cons., 1972-78; editor in chief Advt. & Pub. News, 1978-80; exec. editor Whitney Libr. of Design, 1981-85; v.p., editorial dir. Practice Mgmt. Assocs., Ltd., 1985-87; editor scientific and tech. div. John Wiley & Sons, 1987-90; editor Archtl. Record, 1990-96; architect, editl. cons., 1996—; lectr. U. Oreg., Carnegie-Mellon U., U. Ariz., Yale U., Harvard U., Washington U., St. Louis, U. Tex., U. Nebr., Ariz. State U., N.C. State U., Tex. A&M U.; adj. prof. Sch. of Architecture and Environ. Studies, CUNY, 1997—. Author: Writing for Design Professionals, 1998, Creative Communications for a Successful Design Practice, Into the Mainstream: Syllabus for a Barrier-Free Environment, Architectural Sketching and Rendering: Techniques for Designers and Artists; (with R.H. McNulty) Neighborhood Conservation; editor: Design Principal's Report and Design Firm Management and Administration Report, 1998—; contbr. articles to profl. jours. Bd. dirs. Bldg. Research Inst., 1969-71; chmn. adv. Council Princeton Sch. Architecture and Urban Planning, 1973-84. With AUS, 1953-55. Fellow AIA, Univ. Club (N.Y.C.). Episcopalian. Home and Office: 1255 5th Ave New York NY 10029-3850

KLIMP, JACK W., military officer; b. Kalamazoo, Mich., Sept. 9, 1945; m. Catherine Anne Durst; children: Catherine Ashley, Elizabeth Anne. BS, U.S. Naval Acad., 1968, MA pub. adminstrn.; grad., Amphibious Warfare Sch. Platoon commander, co. exec. officer, co. commander Co G.2d Battalion 1st Marine; chief of staff 1st Marine Divsn. Headquarters Detachment, Twentynine Palms, Calif., 1992; brigadier gen., 1993; commanding gen. Marine Corps. Recruit Depot, Parris Island, S.C., 1993-95, major gen., 1995-98; commanding gen. Manpower and Reserve Affairs, lt. gen. Marine Corp Recruiting Command, Quantico, Va., 1998—. Decorated Def. Superior Svc. medal, Legion of Merit, Bronze Star medal with Combat V, Def. Meritorious Svc. medal, Jt. Svc. Commendation medal, Navy Commendation medal, Navy Achievement medal, Combat Action Ribbon, Korean Order of Nat. Security Merit Samil medal. Office: Manpower and Reserve Affairs 3280 Russell Rd Quantico VA 22134

KLINCK, CYNTHIA ANNE, library director; b. Salamanaca, N.Y., Nov. 1, 1948; d. William James and Marjorie Irene (Woodruff) K.; m. Andrew Clavert Humphries, Nov. 26, 1983. BS, Ball State U., 1970; MLS, U. Ky., 1976. Reference/ young adult libr. Bartholomew County Libr., Columbus, Ind., 1970-74; dir. Paul Sawyier Pub. Libr., Frankfort, Ky., 1974-78, Washington-Centerville Pub. Libr., Dayton, Ohio, 1978—; libr. bldg. cons.; mem. OPLIN Task Force. Contbr. articles to profl. mags. Bd. dirs. Bluegrass Comty. Action Agy., Frankfort, Ky., 1971-73; founder, bd. dirs. FACTS, Inc. (info. & referral), Frankfort, 1972-74; co-founder, bd. dirs. Seniors, Inc., Dayton, Ohio, 1980-81, 91—; trustee, officer South Comty., Inc. Mental Health Ctr., Dayton, 1980-89; pres. Miami Valley Librs.; mem. govt. affairs com. Ohio Libr. Coun. Mem. ALA, Am. Soc. for Info. Sci., Am. Soc. for Pers. Adminstrn., Ohio Libr. Assn. (chmn. legis. com.), South Metro C. of C. (bd. dirs.), Rotary Internat. (bd. dirs.). Office: Washington-Centerville Pub Libr 111 W Spring Valley Pike Dayton OH 45458-3761

KLINCK, JAMES WILLIAM, insurance company executive; b. Kitchener, Ont., Can., Dec. 12, 1951; s. Armand Adam and Imogene (Sim) K.; m. Viola Mary Wright, Sept. 17, 1977; childen: David James, Bonnie Ann. B in Math. with honors, U. Waterloo, Ont., Can., 1974. Cert. info. sys. profl. V.p., chief info. officer Metlife-Can. Ops., Ottawa, Ont., Can., 1991-96; v.p. applications devel. Met. Life, N.Y.C., 1996—. Named One of Top 10 Can. Chief Info. Officers Toronto, 1994. Mem. Can. Info. Processing Soc. Home: 18 Le Parc Ct West Windsor NJ 08550 Office: Met Life Ins Co One Madison Ave New York NY 10010

KLINDT, JOYCE ANN, plastic surgeon; b. Aug. 27, 1949. BA, U. Wis.; MD, Mt. Sinai U. Attending plastic surgeon L.I. Surgeons, Melville, N.Y., Smith Sea Hosp., Bayshore, N.Y., Good Samaritan Hosp., West Islip, N.Y.

KLINDT, STEVEN, art museum director; b. Davenport, Iowa, Dec. 18, 1947. BA in Art, U. Iowa, 1971, MA in Photography, 1974. Dir. Evanston (Ill.) Art Ctr., 1976-79, Mus. Contemporary Photography and Columbia Coll. Art Gallery, Chgo., 1979-84, Tweed Mus. Art, Duluth, Minn., 1984-89; exec. dir. The Queens Mus. of Art, Queens, N.Y., 1989-92; assoc. dir. Mus. of the City of N.Y., 1992-94; exec. dir. Morris Mus., Morristown, N.J., 1994—; adj. prof. NYU, 1992—; pres., bd. dirs. Upper Midwest Conservation Assn, Mpls., 1986-87; commr. Duluth Pub. Arts Commn., 1986-87; panelist Minn. State Arts Bd., St. Paul, 1985-87. Editor: (exhibition catalogues) Nathan Lerner: Fifty Years of Photographic Inquiry, 1984, Minnesota Sculpture Collections, 1988, The Tweed Museum of Art: 30 Years, 1988. Pres. bd. dirs. N.J. Assn. Mus., 1995—, N.J. Art Pride, 1995—. Mem. Assn. Art Mus. Dirs., Cliff Dwellers Club (Chgo.), Park Ave. Club (Florham Park, N.J.). Office: Morris Mus 6 Normandy Heights Rd Morristown NJ 07960-4627

KLINE, ALLEN HABER, JR., lawyer; b. Houston, June 17, 1954; s. Allen H. Sr. and Maude Rose (Brown) K.; m. Barbara Ann Byrd, July 24, 1982; children: Allison Ashley, Allen III. BA, U. Denver, 1976; JD, U. Miami, 1979. Bar: Tex. 1980, U.S. Dist. Ct. (so. dist.) Tex. 1980, U.S. Ct. Appeals (5th cir.) 1980, U.S. Ct. Appeals (11th cir.) 1983, U.S. Supreme Ct. 1985; bd. cert. personal injury trial law Tex. Bd. Legal Specialization. Sole practice Houston, 1980—. Mem. Houston Bar Assn., Coll. of the State Bar of Tex. Club: City Wide (Houston) (life). Avocations: tennis, water, snow skiing. Office: 440 Louisiana St Ste 2120 Houston TX 77002-4205

KLINE, BARBARA A., nursing case manager; b. Pitts., July 11, 1958; d. Robert T. and Janet (Falkenstein) K. BSN, Cedar Crest Coll., Allentown, Pa., 1982; MSA in Health Adminstrn., West Chester U., 1988; postgrad., U. Pa., 1995—, U. Pa. Cert. med.-surg. nurse, ACLS. Staff nurse Crozer-Chester Med. Ctr., Upland, Pa.; primary nurse Paoli (Pa.) Meml. Hosp.; mktg. dept. liaison U. Pa. Med. Ctr.; clin. resource mgr. adminstrn. Hosp. of U. Pa., Phila., 1994—. Named Nurse of Hope, Am. Cancer Soc., 1984.

KLINE, BONITA ANN, middle school guidance counselor, educator; b. Charleroi, Pa., Sept. 25, 1952; d. Milton Paul Kobaly and Ann Marie (Gohosky) George; m. Dennis Charles Kline, Aug. 8, 1981. BS in Elem. Edn., U. Pitts., 1973; MEd, Calif. (Pa.) U., 1986; postgrad., U. Pitts., 1986—. Cert. elem. tchr., Pa., elem. guidance counselor, Pa., elem. prin., Pa., secondary guidance counselor, Pa., asst. supt., Pa. Juvenile probation officer Westmoreland County Court System, Greensburg, Pa., 1974; elem. tchr. Belle Vernon (Pa.) Area Sch. Dist., 1975—. Mem. Ea. Pa. Profl. Womens Group, Tri-State Area Sch. Study Coun., PTO. Democrat. Roman Catholic. Avocations: reading, fishing, traveling, swimming, gardening. Home: 1415 Willowbrook Rd Belle Vernon PA 15012-9616 Office: Belle Vernon Area Sch Dist 250 Crest Ave Belle Vernon PA 15012

KLINE, CAROLE JUNE, special education educator; b. Youngstown, Ohio, June 16, 1947; d. Stephen and Mary (Kuzniak) Yourst; m. Ronald Edward Kline, Aug. 3, 1968; children: Christopher John, Melinda Marie. BS in Elem. Edn., Kent State U., 1968, MEd in Spl. Edn., 1970; postgrad., L.I. U., 1987. Cert. tchr. spl. edn., elem. and nursery sch., N.Y. Libr. I reference rm. Kent (Ohio) State U., 1968; intermediate EMR tchr. Niles (Ohio) City Schs., 1969-75; tchr. elem. spl. edn. Fulton (N.Y.) City Schs., 1984-88; subs. tchr. Baldwinsville (N.Y.) Ctrl. Schs., 1982-84, resource tchr. jr. h.s., 1984, resource and spl. edn. tchr. jr. h.s., 1988—; homebound instr. Baldwinsville Ctrl. Schs., 1988—, inclusion com., 1998—; adv. bd. OCM BOCES Career Exploration Program, 1997—. Bd. dirs. Seneca Gardens Homeowners Assn., Baldwinsville, 1998—, Baldwinsville Comty. Band, 1988-97, Baldwinsville Cmty. Connection, 1995-97, steering com., 1996. Mem. NEA, Nat. Edn. Assn. N.Y. (del. 1993, 94, 95, 96), Baldwinsville Tchr.'s Assn. (exec. com. 1990-97, bldg. rep. 1988-97), Coun. for Exceptional Children (rsch. divsn. 1990-97), Coun. for Children With Behavioral Disorders (divsn. for learning disabilities 1990-97), Kent State Alumni Assn. Democrat. Roman Catholic. Avocations: floral design, boating, needlework. Home: 1607 S Ivy Trl Baldwinsville NY 13027-9047 Office: Durgee Jr High Sch E Oneida St Baldwinsville NY 13027

KLINE, CELESTE MARIE, librarian; b. Daggett, Mich., July 25, 1945; d. Lamiel Bernard and Martha Elizabeth Kline; divorced; 1 child, Tanya Gypsy. Profl. lifetime libr. cert., Wash.; cert. profl. libr., Mich. Coord. children's svcs. Peter White Pub. Libr., Marquette, Mich., 1972-75, Josephine County Libr. Sys., Grants Pass, Oreg., 1975-80; head Ill. Valley br. Josephine County Libr. Sys., Cave Junction, Oreg., 1980-85; head reference/ adult brs. Josephine County Libr. Sys., Grants Pass, 1985-91, libr. dir., 1991-92; libr. dir. Ellensburg (Wash.) Pub. Libr., 1992—; chair children's sect. Oreg. Libr. Assn., 1980-82; sec. So. Oreg. Libr. Fedn., 1981-83, pres., 1983-85. Bd. dirs. Kittitas County Bd. Health Adv. Com., Ellensburg, 1998—, Comty. Health and Safety Network, Ellensburg, 1997-99; mem. Friends of the Libr., 1992—, Interagy. Coun., Ellensburg, 1992—. Mem. LWV, Wash. Libr. Assn., Rotary Club Ellensburg. Roman Catholic. Avocations: traveling, reading, church activities, family, Internet. E-mail: klinec@epl.eburg.com. Office: Ellensburg Pub Libr 209 N Ruby St Ellensburg WA 98926

KLINE, DAVID ADAM, lawyer, educator, writer; b. Keota, Okla., Sept. 27, 1923; s. David Adam and Lucy Leila (Wood) K.; m. Ruthela Deal, Aug. 25, 1947; children: Steven, Timothy, Ruthanna. Student Oklahoma City U., 1945-47; JD, Okla. U., 1950. Bar: Okla. 1949. Law clk., spl. master U.S. Dist. Ct., Okla., 1952-61; 1st asst. U.S. atty. Western Dist. Okla., 1961-69; judge Western Dist. Okla., U.S. Bankruptcy Ct., Oklahoma City, 1969-82; pres. Nat. Conf. Bankruptcy Judges 1977-78; sr. shareholder Kline & Kline, Oklahoma City, 1983—; mem. arbitration panel program U.S. Dist. Ct. (we. dist.) Okla., 1985— mem. faculty Fed. Jud. Ctr., Washington, Nat. Seminar Bankruptcy Judges, 1971-86; adj. prof. law Oklahoma City U., 1980-84; cons. Norton Bankruptcy Law and Practice, 1986, Callaghan & Co. Digest editor Am. Bankruptcy Law jour., 1974-77; contbg. author Cowans Bankruptcy Law and Practice, 1983, interim and 1986 edit.; contbg. co-writer Briefcase, 1988—; author: A Little Book (A New Thing in the Earth), 1993, A Little Book II (The Blood of the Lion), 1995, A Little Book III (The Revelation), 1997, A Little Book IV (A Still Small Voice), 1998; bd. dirs. Consumer Credit Counseling Svc. Ctr., Okla., 1971—, chmn. 1992. Fellow Am. Coll. Bankruptcy. Office: Kline & Kline 720 NE 63rd St Oklahoma City OK 73105-6405

KLINE, DAVID GELLINGER, neurosurgery educator; b. Phila., Oct. 13, 1934; s. David Francis and Lois Ann (Gellinger) K.; m. Carol Anne Loewen, Mar. 1, 1958 (div.); children: Susan, Robert, Nancy. AB in Chemistry, U. Pa., 1956, MD, 1960. Diplomate Am. Bd. Neurol. Surgery (sec.-treas. 1978-83, chmn. 1983-84, adv. bd. 1984-90, chmn. 50th anniversary celebration 1990). Intern and resident in gen. surgery U. Mich., Ann Arbor, 1960-62; research investigator Walter Reed Army Inst. Research and Walter Reed Gen. Hosp., 1962-64; resident in neurosurgery and teaching instr. U. Mich., Ann Arbor, 1964-67; instr. neurosurgery and surgery Sch. Medicine La. State U., New Orleans, 1967-68, asst. prof., 1968-70, assoc. prof., 1970-75, prof.,

1976, head sect. of neurosurgery, 1971, chmn. dept. neurosurgery, 1976—, Boyd prof., chmn. neurosurgery, 1995—; cons. USPHS Health Center Hosp., New Orleans VA Hosp., Kessler AFB Hosp.-Lederle Labs.; vis. investigator Delta Regional Primate Center, Covington; mem. Am. Bd. Med. Specialists, 1978-86, mem. residency rev. com., 1977-84; lectr. in field. Contbr. articles to sci. jours., also mem. numerous editorial bds. Capt. M.C. AUS, 1962-64. Recipient Frederick Coller Surg. prize, 1967; numerous grants. Mem. AMA, ACS, Orleans Parish Med. Society, La. State Med. Soc., New Orleans Neurol. Soc., Am. Acad. Neurol. Surgery, Soc. Neurol. Surgeons (treas. 1986-91, v.p. 1994-95, pres. 1996-97), So. Neurol. Surgery Soc. (sec. 1976-79, pres. 1985-86), Am. Assn. Neurol. Surgeons (bd. dirs. 1985-89), Soc. Univ. Neurosurgeons, Congress Neurol. Surgeons, Assn. Acad. Surgery, Surg. Biol. Club II, Soc. Univ. Surgeons, Sunderland Soc. (pres. 1981), Phi Beta Kappa, Kappa Sigma, Phi Chi. Episcopalian (vestry and lay reader). Home: 307 Fairway Dr New Orleans LA 70124-1020 Office: La State U Med Ctr 1542 Tulane Ave New Orleans LA 70112-2825 *Success, whether defined by the individual who believes he or she has achieved it or 'granted' by others has little meaning unless it is accompanied by happiness. To have both, one must not only enjoy his or her life's work but also life as a whole and particularly people and specifically working hard with and interacting well with others. Honesty about one's own efforts as well as those of others, a large measure of perseverance, a sense of humor, and a degree of courage as well as a certain amount of realistic optimism are very necessary to survive let alone flourish.*

KLINE, DAVID JONATHAN, video producer; b. Greer, S.C., Oct. 26, 1972; s. William Leon and Elizabeth Jane (Schubert) K. BS in Cinema and Video Prodn., Bob Jones U., 1995, MA in Cinema and Video Prodn., 1997. Asst. prodr. TV Prodns. Bob Jones U., Greenville, S.C., 1995—. Republican. Baptist. Avocations: reading, Macintosh computers. Home: A-210 CVA 1647 Wade Hampton Blvd Greenville SC 29614-2000 Office: Bob Jones U TV Prodns 1700 Wade Hampton Blvd Greenville SC 29614-0001

KLINE, DENNY LEE, hazardous devices and explosives consultant; b. Boston, Jan. 31, 1939; s. Francis Marion and Sylvia Lee (Denny) K.; m. Sadie Mae Thompson, June 14, 1963; 1 child, Hank Von. Student, Vanderbilt U., 1957-58, Mid. Ga. Coll., 1959-61; BS, Ga. So. Coll., 1963; M. Forensic Sci., George WashingtonU., 1981. Cert. explosives and hazardous devices specialist. Tchr., coach football Harlem (Ga.) High Sch., 1963-65; tchr., coach Butler High Sch., Augusta, Ga., 1966-69; spl. agt., supr. FBI, Newark, 1970-76; supr.-examiner lab. explosives unit FBI, Washington, 1976-88; spl. investigator background investigation contract svc. FBI, 1995—; faculty instr. forensic sci. tng. and rsch. unit FBI Acad., Quantico, Va., 1988-90; pres., chief exec. officer ETA Consultants, Inc., Stafford, Va., 1990—; cons. Nuclear Diagnostic Sys., Inc., Lorton, Va., 1991-93; cons., v.p. Gen. Nucleonics, Tucson, 1994; course dir. anti-terrist assistance U.S. Dept. State, Baton, Rouge, 1990—; mem. exch. faculty Police Staff Coll., Bramshill, Eng., 1989; bomb technician FBI Hazardous Devices sch., Huntsville, Ala., 1976—; spl. investigator background investigation contract svcs. program FBI, 1995—. Contbr. articles to profl. jours. Mem. Internat. Assn. Bomb Technicians and Investigators, Am. Soc. for Indsl. Security, Internat. Assn. Chiefs of Police, Assn. Former Spl. Agts. of the FBI. Episcopalian. Avocations: golf, tennis, fishing, sailing. Office: ETA Cons Inc 1335 Aquia Dr Stafford VA 22554-2037

KLINE, EUGENE MONROE, lawyer; b. N.Y.C., May 22, 1914; s. Lewis R. and Hattie (Wachter) K.; m. Harriet Meyer, July 2, 1939; children: Robert A., Thomas R. AB, Columbia U., 1933, LLB, 1935. Bar: N.Y. 1935, U.S. Dist. Ct. (so. dist.) N.Y. 1945, U.S. Dist. Cr. (ea. dist.) N.Y. 1955, U.S. Supreme Ct. 1973. Atty. Charter Rev. Commn., N.Y.C., 1935; assoc. Greenbaum, Wolf & Ernst, N.Y.C., 1935-37, Wagner, Quillinin and Rifkind, N.Y.C., 1937-40; atty. SEC, N.Y.C. and Washington, 1941-43; from assoc. to ptnr. Phillips Nizer Benjamin Krim & Ballon, LLP, N.Y.C., 1943—; bd. dirs. Bill Blass, Ltd., N.Y.C. With U.S. Army, 1943. Home: 390 Heathcote Rd Scarsdale NY 10583-7538 Office: Phillips Nizer Benjamin Krim & Ballon LLP 666 5th Ave New York NY 10103-0001

KLINE, FAITH ELIZABETH, college official; b. Lake Charles, La., Dec. 22, 1937; d. Walter Raymond and Erma Ruth (Gilbert) McClung; m. George Ellis Kline, Nov. 26, 1959; children: Alexandra M., George E. IV, Elizabeth A. BA, So. Nazarene U., 1960. Owner, ptnr. Country Peddler Gift Shop, Jackson, Mich., 1972-75; asst. dir. admissions Spring Arbor (Mich.) Coll., 1976-80; exec. sec. to pres. Camp Internat., Inc., Jackson, Mich., 1980-85; registered rep. IDS/Am. Express, Jackson, 1985-86; investment broker A. G. Edwards & Sons, Inc., Jackson, 1986-89; dir., trust and investment svcs., corp. asst. sec. The Free Meth. Found., Spring Arbor, 1989-92; adminstr. trusts and investments Hillsdale (Mich.) Coll., 1992—; mem. Jackson County (Mich.) Hosp. Fin. Authority, 1987-92; pres. Hearthstone Enterprises, Inc., 1996—; co-owner Idyll Hour Coffeehouse, Spring Arbor, Mich., 1997—. Author: The Klines of Evanston: 1848 to 1968, 1970. Trustee Concord (Mich.) Bd. Edn., 1979-95, v.p., 1991-93, pres., 1993-94; sec. Jackson County (Mich.) County Reps., 1984-85, mem. exec. com., 1993-96; mem. Spring Arbor Twp. Hist. Com., Jackson Area Estate Planning Coun.; mem. Nat. Com. on Planned Giving, 1993—. Methodist. Avocation: 19th Century American antiques. Home: 9023 Hammond Rd Concord MI 49237-9781 Office: Hillsdale Coll 33 E College St Hillsdale MI 49242-1205

KLINE, FRANK MENEFEE, psychiatrist; b. Cumberland, Md., May 14, 1928; s. Frank Huber and Margaret (Menefee) K.; m. Shirley Steinmetz, June 27, 1953; children: Frank F., Margaret L. BS, U. Md., 1950, MD, 1952; PhD, So. Calif. Psychoanalytic Ins., 1977. Diplomate Am. Bd. Psychiatry and Neurology (examiner 1970—). Intern Cin. Gen. Hosp., 1952-53; resident Brentwood VA Med. Ctr., West L.A., 1955-58; Regional chief West Cen. Mental Svc., L.A. County Dept. Mental Health, L.A., 1967-68; assoc. dir. adult psychiatry out-patient dept. L.A. County, U. So. Calif. Med. Ctr., 1968-77, acting dir. adult psychiatric dept., 1977-78; chief psychiatry VA Med. Ctr., Long Beach, Calif., 1977-91; assoc. prof. U. So. Calif., clin. prof., prof. emeritus, 1992—; clin. prof., vice-chair U. Calif., Irvine, 1978-91, prof. emeritus, 1995—; clin. prof. Drew King, 1992—, MS; reviewer Hosp. Comty. Psychiatry, 1978—, Am. Jour. Psychiatry, 1978—, Readings, 1995—. Editor: A Handbook of Group Psychotherapy, 1983. 1st lt. M.C., U.S. Army, 1953-55. Fax: 310-325-3941. Office: 24 Sorrel Ln Rolling Hills Estates CA 90274

KLINE, FRED WALTER, retired communications company executive; b. Oakland, Calif., May 17, 1918; s. Walter E. and Jean M. Kline; m. Verna Marie Taylor, Dec. 27, 1952; children—Kathleen, Nora, Fred Walter. B.A. in Calif. History, U. Calif.-Berkeley, 1940. With Walter E. Kline & Assocs. and successor Fred Kline Agy., Inc., from 1937; chmn. bd., pres. Kline Communications Corp., Los Angeles, 1956-96, ret., 1996; pres. Capitol News Service. Commr. Los Angeles County Fire Services Commn., Calif. Motion Picture Devel. Council; cons., advisor Calif. Film Commn.; former fed. civil def. liaison; developer state-wide paramedic rescue program; Calif. chmn. Office of Asst. Sec. Def.; mem. Calif. Com. for Employer Support of Guard and Res.; mem. Los Angeles Film Com. Served with USAAF, World War II; brig. gen. Calif. Mil. Dept. Recipient Inter-Racial award City of Los Angeles, 1963, named Man of Yr., 1964. Mem. Acad. Motion Picture Arts and Scis., Radio and TV News Assn. So. Calif., Pub. Relations Soc. Am., Calif. Newspaper Pubs. Assn., Cath. Press Council (founding mem.), Pacific Pioneer Broadcasters, Footprinters Internat., Am. Mil. Govt. Assn. (past pres.), Navy League, Calif. State Police Officers Assn., Internat. Assn. Profl. Firefighters (hon. life), Peace Officers Assn. Los Angeles County (life), Internat. Assn. Chiefs of Police, Internat. Assn. Fire Chiefs, Calif. Fire Chiefs Assn., Fire Marshals Assn. N.Am., Nat. Fire Protection Assn., Nat. Fin. Writers Assn., Hollywood C. of C., Nat. Fire Sci. Acad., Calif. State Mil. Forces, Calif. Pubs. Assn., So. Calif. Cable Club. Sigma Delta Chi. Clubs: Greater Los Angeles Press, Media (Los Angeles), Sacramento Press. Columnist Calif. newspapers. Office: 1180 Weber Way Sacramento CA 95822-1840

KLINE, GEORGE LOUIS, author, translator, retired philosophy and literature educator; b. Galesburg, Ill., Mar. 3, 1921; s. Allen Sides and Wahneta (Burner) K.; m. Virginia Harrington Hardy, Apr. 17, 1943; children: Brenda Marie, Jeffrey Allen, Christina Hardy (Mrs. Francis C. Hanak). Student, Boston U., 1938-41; A.B. with honors, Columbia Coll., 1947; M.A., Columbia U., 1948, Ph.D., 1950. Instr. philosophy Columbia U., 1950-52, 53-54, asst. prof., 1954-60; vis. asst. prof. U. Chgo., 1952-53; assoc. prof. philosophy and Russian Bryn Mawr Coll., 1960-66, prof. philosophy, 1966-81, Milton C. Nahm prof. philosophy, 1981-91, chmn. dept., 1977-82, chmn. dept. Russian, 1990-91, Milton C. Nahm prof. emeritus of philosophy, 1991—, Katharine E. McBride prof. of philosophy, 1992-93; lectr. Free U., West Berlin, Heidelberg U., Marburg U., Germany, London Sch. Econs. and Polit. Sci., Mid East Tech. U., Ankara, Turkey, Oxford (Eng.) U., Queens U., Belfast, Trinity Coll., Dublin, U. Belgrade, U. Zagreb, Yugoslavia, U. P.R., Uppsala U., Sweden; participant internat. confs. Austria, Can., Denmark, France, Germany, The Netherlands, Italy, Mex., Eng., Scotland, Russia. Author: Spinoza in Soviet Philosophy, 1952, reprint, 1981, Religious and Anti-Religious Thought in Russia, 1968; co-author: Continuity and Change in Russian and Soviet Thought, 1955, Marx and the Western World, 1967, Hegel and the Philosophy of Religion, 1970, Sartre: A Collection of Critical Essays, 1971, Hegel and the History of Philosophy, 1974, Dissent in The USSR: Politics, Ideology, and People, 1975, Speculum Spinozanum, 1977, Western Philosophical Systems in Russian Literature, 1979, Vico and Marx: Affinities and Contrasts, 1983, Nineteenth Century Religious Thought in the West, 1985, Spinoza nel 350 anniversario della nascita, 1985, Hegel and Whitehead: Contemporary Perspectives on Systematic Philosophy, 1986, George Lukács and His World: A Reassessment, 1987, Dictionary of Literary Biography Yearbook, 1987, 88, Europa und die Folgen: Castelgandolfo-Gespräche, 1987, 88, Hegel and His Critics, 1989, Brodsky's Poetics and Aesthetics, 1990, Spinoza: Issues and Directions, 1990, Histoire de la littérature russe, 1990, The Trotsky Reappraisal, 1992, Metaphysics as Foundation: Essays in Honor of Ivor Leclerc, 1992, Philosophical Imagination and Cultural Memory, 1993, Hryhorij Savyč Skovoroda: An Anthology of Critical Articles, 1994, Phenomenology and Skepticism: Essays in Honor of James M. Edie, 1996, Russian Religious Thought, 1996, Iosif Brodskii: Trudy i dni, 1998; works translated into numerous fgn. languages; translator: History of Russian Philosophy (V.V. Zenkovsky), 2 vols, 1953, Boris Pasternak: Seven Poems, 1969, 2d edit., 1972, Joseph Brodsky: Selected Poems, 1973; co-translator: A Part of Speech (Joseph Brodsky), 1980, To Urania (Joseph Brodsky), 1988; editor: Soviet Education, 1957, Alfred North Whitehead: Essays on his Philosophy, 1963, reprint 1989; editor, contbr.: European Philosophy Today, 1965; co-editor, contbr.: Russian Philosophy, 3 vols, 1965, 2d edit., 1969, reprint, 1976, 84, Explorations in Whitehead's Philosophy, 1983, Philosophical Sovietology, 1988; co-editor Jour. Philosophy, 1959-64, cons. editor, 1964-78; cons. editor Ency. Philosophy, 1962-67, Studies in Soviet Thought (now Studies in East European Thought), 1962—, Jour. Value Inquiry, 1967—, Process Studies, 1970—, Soviet Union, 1975-80, Philosophy Research Archives (now Jour. Philos. Rsch.), 1975—, Jour. History of Ideas, 1976-86, 88-98, Slavic Review, 1977-79, Soviet Studies in Philosophy (now Russian Studies in Philosophy), 1987—, History of Philosophy Quar., 1990-93, Skepsis, 1990—; Symposion: A Journal of Russian Thought, 1996—; cons. editor philosophy Current Digest of Soviet Press, 1961-64; contbr. numerous articles to nat. and internat. jours. and reference works. Served with USAAF, 1942-45. Decorated D.F.C; Cutting traveling fellow Paris, 1949-50; Fulbright fellow Paris, 1950, 79; Ford fellow Paris, 1954-55; Rockefeller fellow USSR and East Europe, 1960; Nat. Endowment for Humanities sr. fellow, 1970-71; Guggenheim fellow, 1978-79. Mem. Am. Philos. Assn. (exec. com. Ea. div. 1990-93), Metaphys. Soc. Am. (councillor 1969-71, 78-82, v.p. 1984-85, pres. 1985-86, del. to Am. Coun. Learned Socs., 1994-97), Philosophy Edn. Soc. (pub. Rev. Metaphys., dir. 1966-90), Soc. Phenomenology and Existential Philosophy, Am. Assn. Advancement Slavic Studies (dir. 1972-75), Hegel Soc. Am. (councillor 1968-70, 74-78, v.p. 1971-73, pres. 1984-86), Soc. Advancement Am. Philosophy, PEN, Phi Beta Kappa. Home: 632 Valley View Rd Ardmore PA 19003-1029

KLINE, GEORGE WILLIAM, II, television producer; b. San Antonio, July 5, 1949; s. Robert Walter and Adelaide McCall (Carter) K.; m. Kristin Scheffey, Mar. 5, 1977; children: Amanda Dupree, George William III, Luke Carter. BA, Austin Coll., 1971. Road mgr. Kris Kristofferson, N.Y.C., 1971-73; producer Sta. KERA-TV (PBS affiliate), Dallas, 1973-75; ind. producer Strongbow Prodns., L.A., 1975-77; producer Bill Stokes Assocs., Dallas, 1977-78; exec. producer Tannebring Rose Assocs., Dallas, 1978-82; pres. Geo. Kline Co., Inc., Dallas, 1982—; bd. dirs. U.S.A. Film Festival, Dallas, 1986-89; bd. dirs., v.p. Motion Picture Producers Tex., 1988—. Chmn. bd. Addison (Tex.) Airport, 1986; bd. dirs. St. Michael Sch., Dallas, 1990—, Episcopal Children's Found., 1997—, St. Michael Found., 1997—; vestryman St. Michael and All Angels Ch., 1992—. Recipient award Comm. Arts mag., 1982; gold award Internat. Film and TV Festival, N.Y., 1983, 87-88, silver award, 1987; award Art Dirs. Club N.Y., 1983; gold award for best 30 second comml. Dallas Advt. League, 1986, 3 gold Addys, 2 silver Addys, 1987, silver Addy, gold Addy, 1992; Matrix award Women in Comm., 1987, Best of Show award 10th Dist. Addys., 1988, Mobius award, Chgo., 1991, gold award Houston Internat. Film Festival. Mem. Motion Picture Prodns. Tex. (v.p.), Assn. Ind. Comml. Prodns., Highland Pk. League, Egypt Exploration Soc. (London), Am. Rsch. Ctr. in Egypt, Balboa de Mazatlan S.A., Dallas Press Club, River Crest Country Club (Ft. Worth), Steeplechase Club (Ft. Worth), Dallas Country Club. Episcopalian. Office: George Kline Co Inc 3009 Maple Ave Dallas TX 75201-1294

KLINE, HOWARD JAY, cardiologist, educator; b. White Plains, N.Y., Nov. 5, 1932; s. Raymond Kline and Rose Plane; divorced; children: Michael, Ethan; m. Ellen Sawamura, June 13, 1987; 1 child, Christopher. BS, Dickinson Coll., 1954; MD, N.Y. Med. Coll., 1958. Intern San Francisco Gen. Hosp., 1958-59; resident Mt. Sinai Hosp., N.Y.C., 1959-61; sr. resident U. Calif. Med. Ctr., San Francisco, 1961-62; cardiology fellow Mt. Sinai Hosp., N.Y.C., 1962-64; dir. cardiology training program St. Mary's Hosp., San Francisco, 1970-90, Calif. Pacific Med. Ctr., San Francisco, 1992—; clin. prof. medicine and cardiology U. Calif. Med. Ctr., San Francisco, 1984—; vis. prof. Nihon U., Tokyo, 1986. Editor (jours.) Hosp. Practice, Cardiology, 1992—; contbr. articles to Hosp. Practice. Lt. col. U.S. Med. Corps, 1967-69. Fellow ACP, Am. Heart Assn., Am. Coll. Cardiology, Am. Coll. Chest Physicians; mem. Burkes Tennis Club. Avocations: painting, reading, running, skiing, tennis. Office: 2100 Webster St Ste 516 San Francisco CA 94115-2382

KLINE, J. PETER, hotel executive. BS in Hotel Adminstrn., Cornell U., MS in Acctg. CPA, Tex. With Laventhol & Horwath, ptnr., mgr. cons. divsn. Tex., 1976-80; founding ptnr. Harvey Hotel Co., Dallas, 1981—; pres., CEO Bristol Hotels & Resorts, Dallas; chmn., CEO Bristol Hotels & Resorts, Addison, Tex., 1998. Mem. N.Y. Hospitality Coun.; bd. dirs. North Tex. Commn.; adv. bd. U. North Tex., U. Tex.-Dallas Sch. Mgmt.; co-chmn. 2d Ann. Cornell U. Conf. on Hospitality Ind. Strategy, 1998. Mem. Internat. Assn. Holiday Inss, U.S. C. of C. (mem. regulatory affairs and econ. policy coms.). Office: Bristol Hotel Co 14285 Midway Rd # 340 Addison TX 75001-3621*

KLINE, JACOB, biomedical engineering educator; b. Boston, Aug. 3, 1917; s. Joseph and Jennie (Goldman) K.; m. Barbara Fine, Dec. 22, 1957; children: David, Jonathan, Pamela. B.S., MIT, 1942, M.S., 1951; Ph.D. (NSF fellow), Iowa State U., 1962. Cert. clin. engr. Electronics engr. Internat. Tel. & Tel. Co., Newark, 1942-46; chief video sect. optical rsch. lab. Boston U., 1946-48; rsch. asst. MIT, 1948-51, rsch. engr., 1951-52; mem. faculty U. R.I., Kingston, 1952-66; assoc. prof. engring. U. R.I., 1956-60, dir. bio-med. engring. program, 1962-66; prof. biomed. engring., dir. biomed. engring. program U. Miami, Coral Gables, Fla., 1966-79; chmn. dept. biomed. engring. U. Miami, 1979—; cons. lab. for criminal investigation U. R.I., 1952-66; cons., tech. advisor to attys. on elec. and biomed. problems, 1952—; cons. on relaxation therapy Lab. for Clin. Physiology, Chgo., 1949-53, on labotomy rsch. Boston Psychopathol. Hosp., 1949-53, on orthodontic rsch. Tufts U. Dental Sch., 1951-53; cons. Venice (Fla.) Hosp., St. Francis Hosp., Miami Beach, Fla., Children's Hosp., Miami, Miami Heart Hosp., Miami Beach, Tex. Tech. U. Med. Sci. Ctr., Odessa, 1966—; cons. Lab. for Clin. Physiology, Chgo., 1949-53, Boston Psychiatric Hosp., 1949-53, Venice Hosp., Fla., St. Francis Hosp., Miami, Childrens Hosp., Miami, Miami Heart Hosp., Jackson Meml. Hosp., Miami, 1966—, Tex. Tech. Med. Sci. Ctr., Odessa, 1996—. Author: Biomedical Foundation for Biomedical Engineers, 1976, Handbook for Biomedical Engineers, 1987 (translated into Chinese 1991); contbr. articles to profl. jours.; patentee hydrogel surface of urol. prosthesis. NASA/Am. Soc. Engring. Edn. fellow, summers, 1965, 66. Fellow Am. Acad. Dental Electrosurgery, AAAS; mem. IEEE (dir. 1943—), Am. Soc. Artificial Organs, Am. Assn. Advancement Med. Instrumentation (chmn. bd. trustees AAMI Found. 1982-85). Patentee myocardial prosthetic device. Office: U Miami Coll Engring Coral Gables FL 33124

KLINE, JAMES EDGAR, actor; b. Beach Grove, Ind., Feb. 22, 1932; s. Charles Raymond and Edna Marie (Pollack) K.; m. Phyliss Dawn Schneider, Nov. 8, 1952; children: Timson, James Jr., Peggy, Daniel, Andrew, Mary, Jon. lectr. in field; judge Nat. Prospectors and Treasure Convention, 1989-90. Appeared in films Coming Home, 1978, Comes A Horseman, 1979, Electric Horseman, 1980, China Syndrome, 1981, Tom Horn, 1982, Weekend in the Country, 1997, It's My Party, 1997, City of Angels, 1998, various other films, TV programs, commls.; author: Where to Find Gold in Southern California, 1975, Where to Find Gold in the Desert, 1977, Where to Find Gold in Nevada, 1985, How to Find Gold, 1997, Gold Rush (childrens), 1998, Follow the Padres (childrens), 1999; other mag. articles and short stories. With U.S. Army, 1952-53. Recipient Cert. of Achievement, Am. Cancer Soc., 1977, Disneyland, 1983, City of Anaheim, 1984, also various schs.

KLINE, JAMES EDWARD, lawyer; b. Fremont, Ohio, Aug. 3, 1941; s. Walter J. and Sophia Kline; m. Mary Ann Bruening, Aug. 29, 1964; children: Laura Anne Kline, Matthew Thomas, Jennifer Sue. BS in Social Sci., John Carroll U., 1963; JD, Ohio State U., 1966; postgrad., Stanford U., 1991. Bar: Ohio, 1966, N.C., 1989, U.S. Tax. Ct., 1983. Assoc. Eastman, Stichter, Smith & Bergman, Toledo, 1966-70; ptnr. Eastman, Stichter, Smith & Bergman (name now Eastman & Smith), Toledo, 1970-84, Shumaker, Loop & Kendrick, Toledo, 1984-88; v.p., gen. counsel Aeroquip-Vickers, Inc. (formerly Trinova Corp.), Toledo, 1989—; corp. sec. Sheller-Globe Corp., 1977-84; adj. prof. U. Toledo Coll. Law, 1988-94; bd. dirs. Plastic Techs., Inc. Author: (with Robert Seaver) Ohio Corporation Law, 1988. Trustee Kidney Found. of Northwestern Ohio, Inc., 1972-81, pres., 1979-80; bd. dirs. Toledo Botanical Garden (formerly Crosby Gardens), 1974-80, pres., 1977-79; bd. dirs. Toledo Zool. Soc., 1983-96, pres., 1991-93; bd. dirs. Toledo Area Regional Transit Authority, 1984-90, pres., 1987-88; bd. dirs. Home Away From Home, Inc. (Ronald McDonald House NW Ohio), 1983-88; trustee Toledo Symphony Orch., 1981—, St. John's H.S., 1988-91, Ohio Found. Ind. Colls., 1991—; trustee Lourdes Coll., 1988-96, chmn., 1994-96. Fellow Ohio Bar Found.; mem. ABA, Nat. Assn. Corp. Dirs., Ohio Bar Assn. (corp. law com. 1977—, chmn. 1983-86), Toledo Bar Assn., Mfrs. Alliance (chair Law Coun. II 1997—), Toledo Area C. of C. (trustee 1994—), Inverness Club, Toledo Club (trustee 1990-97), Stone Oak Country Club, Ottawa Skeet Club, Answer Club. Roman Catholic. Home: 216 Treetop Pl Holland OH 43528-8451 Office: Aeroquip-Vickers Inc 3000 Strayer Rd Maumee OH 43537-0050

KLINE, JERRY ROBERT, government official, ecologist; b. Mpls., May 20, 1932; s. Frederick Andrew and Margaret (Wicklund) K.; m. Alice Nell Reed, Sept. 4, 1954; chilren: Steven, Jennifer, Robert, Neil, Daniel. BS, U. Minn., 1957; MS, 1960, PhD, 1964. Postdoctoral rsch. assn. Argonne Nat. Lab., Ill., 1964-65; group leader rsch., 1968-74; scientist, dir. Rainforest Project P. R. Nuclear Ctr., 1965-68; sr. scientist Nuclear Regulatory Commn., Washington, 1974-80; adminstrv. judge, 1980-98. Contbr. articles to profl. jours., chpts. to books. Bd. dirs. Cedar Ln. Unitarian Ch. (chmn.); with U.S. Army. 1950-53. NRC Spl. Achievement, 1979. Mem. Nature Conservancy,Sigma Xi. Avocations: travel, gardening. Home: 13624 Middlevale Ln Silver Spring MD 20906-2123

KLINE, JOEL D., pastor; b. Dixon, Ill., Sept. 4, 1950; s. Harvey Swope and Ruth Evelyn (Zimmerman) K.; m. Janice Elaine Keeney, Aug. 30, 1970; children: Joshua D., Jesse A., Jill E. BA in Sociology, Elizabethtown (Pa.) Coll., 1971; MDiv, Bethany Theol. Sem., Oak Brook, Ill., 1975, DMin, 1983. Ordained to ministry Ch. Brethren., 1975. Pastor Big Swatara Ch. of the Brethren, Hummelstown, Pa., 1975-86; sr. pastor Beacon Hts. Ch. of the Brethren, Ft. Wayne, Ind., 1986—; Bd. dirs. No. Ind. dist. Ch. of the Brethren, Napanee, 1987-93, chmn. dist. min. commn., 1990-91, moderator, 1992-93; chmn. ann. conf. com. Ethics in Ministry, Ch. of the Brethren, 1991-92. Author: Reaching Out in Word and Deed, 1988, Growing in Christian Discipleship, 1990. Bd. dirs. Vincent House, Ft. Wayne, 1990—; co-chair Allen County CROP Walk, Ft. Wayne, 1996-98, chair 1999; bd. dirs. Assoc. Chs. of Ft. Wayne and Allen County, 1995—; mem. coordinating com. Pastors Uniting, 1996—. Charles E. Merrill fellowship Harvard Divinity Sch., 1999. Avocations: reading, walking, family activities. Home: 2704 Whitegate Dr Fort Wayne IN 46805-2435 Office: Beacon Hts Ch of the Brethren 2810 Beacon St Fort Wayne IN 46805-2802

KLINE, JOHN ALVIN, academic administrator; b. Marshalltown, Iowa, July 24, 1939; s. Laurence Alvin Kline and Kathryn White; m. Ann Louise Henry; children: Teri, Marc, David, Nanette, Melissa. BS, Iowa State U., 1967; MS, U. Iowa, 1968, PhD, 1970. Sr. exec. service, U.S. Govt. Asst. prof. speech U. N.Mex., Albuquerque, 1970-71; assoc. prof. speech communication U. Mo., Columbia, 1971-75; dean communication skills Air U., Maxwell AFB, Ala., 1975-82, ednl. adv., 1982-86, dir. academic affairs, 1986-92; sr. exec. provost Air U., 1992—. Author: Guide to Air Force Speaking, 1980, Speaking Effectively, 1989, Listening Effectively, 1996; co-author: Orientations to Interpersonal Communication, 1976; contbr. articles to profl. jours. Named Outstanding Tchr. Cen. States Speech Assn., 1972, Fed. Employee of Yr. Montgomery Fed. Adminstrs., 1979; recipient Award for Meritorious Civilian Svc., 1985, Decoration for Exceptional Civilian Svc., 1988; NDEA Title IV fellow U. Iowa, 1967-70. Mem. Speech Communication Assn., Air Force Assn., Phi Delta Kappa. Methodist. Lodge: Rotary. Home: 8418 Shaffer Ridge Ct Montgomery AL 36117-7402 Office: AU/CA 55 S Lemay Plz Maxwell AFB AL 36112-6335

KLINE, JOHN CHARLES, painter, educator; b. Bryn Mawr, Pa., Mar. 16, 1972; s. Franklyn Richard and Marilyn (Campbell) K.; m. Christine Malone, May 12, 1995. AA, Delaware County C.C., Upper Darby, Pa., 1993; student, Pa. Acad. Fine Arts, Phila., 1993-94. Artist-in-residence Country Day Sch. of the Sacred Heart, Bryn Mawr, 1995; tchr. Am. Milou Studio, Bala Cynwyd, Pa., 1996—. Exhibited in one-man show at Country Day Sch. of the Sacred Heart, 1995, Agora Gallery, N.Y.C., 1999; exhibited in group shows at Mus. Am. Art of the Pa. Acad. Fine Arts, Phila., 1997, Wayne Art Ctr., 1998, Ann. Juried Mems. Exhbn., Chester Springs, Pa., 1998; art work for CD cover Frankie and the Fashions, 1996. Quaker. Avocations: drumming, writing, woodworking, photography. Home: 129 Hickory Ln Bryn Mawr PA 19010-1017 Office: Country Day Sch Sacred Heart 480 Bryn Mawr Ave Bryn Mawr PA 19010 also: Country Day Sch Sacred Heart 480 Bryn Mawr Ave Bryn Mawr PA 19010

KLINE, JOHN WILLIAM, retired air force officer, management consultant; b. Zanesville, Ohio, June 26, 1919; s. Gerry William and Lillian Elizabeth (Scheiderer) K.; m. Katherine Edmond Winton, Oct. 24, 1942; children: Susan Isabel (Mrs. John Farris Morehead), Flora Edmond (Mrs. Richard Crandall Creighton), Elizabeth Gerry. Student, Ohio U., 1937-40; grad., Primary, Basic and Advanced Flying Schs., 1941, Air Command and Staff Sch., 1949, Air War Coll., 1959; B.A., La. Tech. U., 1971. Commd. 2d lt. USAAF, 1941; advanced through grades to maj. gen. USAF, 1965; comdr. (2d Bomb Wing), Hunter AFB, Ga., 1961-63, (397th Bomb Wing), Dow AFB, Maine, 1963-64; dir. operations, chief staff Hdqrs. 8th Air Force, Westover AFB, Mass., 1964-66; vice comdr. 3d Air Div., Andersen AFB, Guam, 1966-68; asst. dep. chief staff ops. Hdqrs. SAC, Offutt AFB, Nebr., 1968-69; vice-comdr. 2d Air Force, Barksdale AFB, La., 1969-72; ret., 1972; v.p., mgmt. cons. Paul R. Ray, Inc., Ft. Worth, 1972—; pres. Mapotec, Inc., Daytona Beach, Fla., 1974, Precision Aerial Surveys, Inc., 1975-85; v.p. ops. Aero Service, Houston, 1976-80, v.p. new ventures and planning, 1980-82; advisor INTEC Sys., Inc., 1994—. Decorated D.S.M., Legion of Merit with 3 oak leaf clusters, Air medal with oak leaf cluster, Air Force Commendation medal; Air Force Distinguished Service Order Republic Vietnam). Mem. Beta Theta Pi. Presbyterian. Club: Champions Golf (Houston). Home: 1038 Townplace St Houston TX 77057-1942

KLINE, KENNETH ALAN, mechanical engineering educator; b. Chgo., July 11, 1939; s. George Lester and Beverly Gretchen (Hanson) K.; m. Nancy Ann Bixler, June 25, 1960; children: Lisa Suzanne, John Kenneth, Jeffery Eastbury, Gretchen Mary. BS, U. Minn., 1961, PhD, 1965. Rsch. asst. U. Minn., Mpls., 1961-62, rsch. fellow, 1962-65; sr. rsch. engr. Esso Prodn. Rsch. Co., Houston, 1965-66; assoc. prof. Wayne State U., Detroit, 1966-73, prof. mech. engring., 1973—, interim chair dept. mech. engring.,

1986-87, chair, 1987-95, interim dean of engring., 1996—, chair mech. engring., 1997—; cons. Ford Motor Co., Detroit, 1976—, vis. scientist, 1984-85; vis. prof. U. Munich, 1972-73. Editor Proc. 6th Internat. Conf. Vehicle Structures, 1986; contbr. articles to profl. jours. Patentee ops. in submarine wells, layng pipes in water. Rep. precinct del., Grosse Pointe Park, Mich., 1982-84; vol. Grosee Pointe Neighborhood Club, 1973-82. A.P. Sloan Found. nat. scholar, 1959-61; NSF fellow 1961-64, NASA fellow 1964-65; recipient Sr. U.S. Sci. award Alexander von Humboldt-Stiftung, Fed. Republic Germany, 1972; prin. investigator NSF Rsch. Experiences for Undergrad. Sites, 1995—. Fellow ASME (chair 1974-75, 89-91, program chair winter ann. meeting 1993, gen. chair internat. mech. engring. congress & expo. 1994, nat. nominating com. 1997—, chair nat. dept. heads com., 1998—), AIAA, Soc. Automotive Engrs. (chair 1984-86, Forest R. McFarland award 1993), Soc. Rheology, Engring. Soc. (vice chair Detroit 1988—). Avocations: bird watching, tree farming, reading, swimming. Office: Wayne State U Engring Rm 2105 Detroit MI 48202

KLINE, KEVIN DELANEY, actor; b. St. Louis, Oct. 24, 1947; s. Robert Joseph and Peggy (Kirk) K.; m. Phoebe Cates, Mar. 5, 1989; 2 children: Owen, Greta. BA in Speech and Theatre, Ind. U.; adv. program diploma, Juilliard Sch. Drama Divsn., N.Y.C., 1972. Founding mem. The Acting Co., N.Y.C., 1972-76; apptd. artistic assoc. N.Y. Shakespeare Festival, 1993. Actor Broadway prodns.: On the Twentieth Century, 1978 (Tony award), Loose Ends, 1979, Pirates of Penzance, 1980 (Tony award, Obie award), Arms and the Man, 1985; off-Broadway: Richard III, 1983, Henry V, 1984, Hamlet, 1986 (Obie award), Much Ado About Nothing; actor, dir. off-Broadway: Hamlet, 1990; actor, dir. TV special: Hamlet, 1990; motion picture appearances include: Sophie's Choice, 1982, Pirates of Penzance, 1983, The Big Chill, 1983, Silverado, 1985, Violets are Blue, 1985, Cry Freedom, 1987, A Fish Called Wanda, 1988 (Academy award Best Supporting Actor 1989), The January Man, 1989, I Love You To Death, 1989, Soapdish, 1991, Grand Canyon, 1991, Consenting Adults, 1991, Chaplin, 1992, Dave, 1993, George Balanchine's The Nutcracker (voice only), 1993, Princess Caraboo, 1994, French Kiss, 1995, Looking for Richard, 1996, The Hunchback of Notre Dame (voice only), 1996, Fierce Creatures, 1997, In & Out, 1997, The IG Storm, 1997, Fierce Creatures, 1997, A Midsummer Night's Dream, 1999, Wild Wild West, 1999; TV guest appearance Cheers, 1982; dir. Hamlet, 1990. Office: William Morris Agy 1325 Avenue of the Americas New York NY 10019-6026*

KLINE, LEE B., architect; b. Renton, Wash., Feb. 2, 1914; s. Abraham McCubbin and Pearl (Davidson) K.; m. Martha Myers, Aug. 29, 1936 (div. Oct. 1995); children—Patricia, Joanne Louise Kline Kresse; m. Marilyn Gibson, May 7, 1997. B.Arch., U. So. Calif., 1937. Draftsman, designer, 1937-43; pvt. archtl. practice Los Angeles, 1943—; instr. engring. extension U. Calif., 1947-53; mem. panel arbitrators Am. Arbitration Assn., 1964—. Pres. LaCanada Irrigation Dist., 1966-96, dir., 1963-96; bd. dirs. Foothill Mcpl. Water Dist., 1980-96, LaCanada br. ARC, 1959-81. Recipient Disting. Service citation Calif. council AIA, 1960, honor awards AIA, 1957, 59, Sch. of Month awards Nation's Schools, 1964, 71. Fellow AIA (pres. Pasadena chpt. 1957, pres. Calif. council 1959). Home: 526 W Huntington Dr Unit F Arcadia CA 91007-3443 Office: Kline Enterprises Inc 969 Colorado Blvd Los Angeles CA 90041-1773

KLINE, LOWRY F., lawyer. Sr. v.p., gen. counsel Coca-Cola Enterprises, Atlanta, now exec. v.p., gen. counsel. Office: CocaCola Enterprises 2500 Windy Ridge Pkwy SE Atlanta GA 30339-5677*

KLINE, MICHAEL J., lawyer; b. Phila., Nov. 5, 1944. BS summa cum laude, U. Pa., 1966, JD cum laude, 1969. Bar: Pa. 1969, N.J. 1976. Atty. Fox, Rothschild, O'Brien & Frankel, Lawrenceville, N.J. Author: Introduction to Corporate Law, 1978. Gen. counsel Deborah Heart and Lung Ctr. and Deborah Hosp. Found., Browns Mills, N.J., 1976—; pres. Jewish Geriatric Home, Cherry Hill, N.J., 1991-93; pub. mem. Adv. Grad. Med. Edn. Coun. N.J., 1990—. Mem. ABA, Am. Acad. Hosp. Attys., Nat. Assn. Bond Lawyers, N.J. State Bar Assn., N.J. Soc. Hosp. Attys., Mercer County Bar Assn. Office: Fox Rothschild O'Brien & Frankel Princeton Pike Corp Ctr 997 Lenox Dr Bldg 3 Lawrenceville NJ 08648-2317*

KLINE, NORMAN DOUGLAS, federal judge; b. Lynn, Mass., Dec. 28, 1930; s. Samuel and Ida (Luff) K.; m. Betty Toba Feldman, Feb. 27, 1966; children: Sarah, Samuel. AB, Harvard Coll., 1952, postgrad., 1952-53; JD, Boston U., 1959. Bar: Mass. 1959. Pvt. practice Boston, 1959-60; atty. U.S. Dept. Army, Cleve., 1960; trial atty. FMC, Washington, 1960-72, adminstrv. law judge, 1972-92, chief adminstrv. law judge, 1992—. With U.S. Army, 1953-55. Mem. Fed. Adminstrv. Law Judges Conf. Avocations: classical music, collecting CDs. Office: Fed Maritime Commn 800 N Capitol St NW Washington DC 20573

KLINE, PRISCILLA MACKENZIE, nursing educator; b. Elgin, Ill., Sept. 25, 1944; d. Gordon Innes and Esther May (Brooks) Mackenzie; m. Ellis Lee Kline, June 12, 1965; children: Heather, Heidi. BSN, U. Ill., 1965, MSN, 1969; EdD, Clemson (S.C.) U., 1987. RN, S.C. Project dir. Alzheimer's Community Edn. Project; pvt. practice Clemson; psychiat. nurse transitional care program Elgin State Hosp., 1967-68; lectr. psychiat. nursing Sacramento State Coll., 1968-69; in-svc. coord. Woodland (Calif.) Meml. Hosp., 1969-71; asst. prof. psychiat. nursing Edinboro (Pa.) State Coll., 1974-78; assoc. prof. Clemson U. Coll. Nursing, 1988-95, assoc. dean, 1988-93, acting head dept. profl. svcs., 1991-93; prof. emerita, 1996—; nurse psychotherapist Clemson U. Coll. Nursing. Contbr. numerous articles to profl. jours. Vol. nurse Hospice of Anderson, S.C.; leader Girl Scouts U.S., 1976-89; mem. Alzheimer's adv. com. S.C. Commn. on Aging, 1987—, chair, 1989—. Recipient merit award AAUP, 1984, Centennial Outstanding Grad. award Clemson U. Coll. Edn., 1989, Award of Excellence S.C. League for Nursing, 1996. Mem. ANA (Pres.'s award S.C. chpt. 1993), Nat. League Nursing, S.C. League Nursing (Excellence award 1996), So. Nursing Rsch. Soc., S.C. Gerontol. Soc., Sigma Theta Tau (internat. treas. 1991-93, 93-95, Excellence in Nursing award 1993), Sigma Theta Tau Found. (chair, bd. dirs. 1994-95, treas. 1995—, 75th Anniversary Disting. Lectr. 1995—). Home: 203 N Elm St Pendleton SC 29670-1731

KLINE, RAYMOND ADAM, professional organization executive; b. New Ringgold, Pa., Sept. 14, 1926; s. Raymond Adam and Helen Marie (Herb) K.; m. Jeanelle Batley, Apr. 26, 1958; children—Robin Jeanelle, Raymond Ashley. AB, Lebanon Valley Coll., 1950, LLD (hon.), 1990; LLB, George Washington U., 1957, JD (hon.), 1982. Bar: D.C. 1958. Mgmt. analyst Army Missile Command, Huntsville, Ala., 1958-61; chief mgmt. devel. office Marshall Space Flight Ctr., Huntsville, 1961-66; asst. assoc. adminstr. for systems mgmt. NASA Hdqrs., Washington, 1967-75, asst. adminstr. instl. mgmt., 1975-77, assoc. adminstr. mgmt. ops, 1977-79; dep. adminstr. GSA, 1979-84, acting adminstr., 1981, 1984-85; pres. Nat. Acad. Pub. Adminstrn., 1985-92; instr. in polit. sci. U. Ala., 1958-63. Served with U.S. Army, 1944-46, 50-51. Mem. D.C. Bar, Phi Delta Phi, Pi Gamma Mu. Home: 15432 Carrolton Rd Rockville MD 20853-1703

KLINE, RICHARD STEPHEN, public relations executive; b. Brookline, Mass., June 20, 1948; s. Paul and Helen (Chartoff) K.; m. Carroll Potter, (dec. Apr. 1984); m. Sharon Tate, June 16, 1985; stepchildren: Allison, Kevin. BA, U. Mass., 1970. Reporter, photographer Worcester (Mass.) Telegram & Gazette, 1970-71; account exec. Wenger-Michael Advt., L.A., 1971; pub. rels. dir. Oakland (Calif.) Symphony Orch., 1972; asst. v.p., dir. promotions Gt. Western Savs. and Loan, Beverly Hills, Calif., 1972-75; v.p., dir. mktg. Union Fed. Savs. and Loan, L.A., 1975-78; chmn. bd. dirs. Berkhemer & Kline, L.A., 1978-88, Berkhemer Kline Golin/Harris, L.A., 1988-93; COO Golin/Harris Comm., Chgo., 1992-95; pres. Shandwick U.S.A., N.Y.C., N.Y., 1995-96, Kline Consulting Group, L.A., 1997; exec. v.p. Fleishman-Hillard, Inc., L.A., 1997—; former instr. Am. Savs. and Loan Inst.; bd. dirs. Golin/Harris Communications; exec. com. Santa Barbara Old Spanish Days Fiesta Rodeo, 1992. Past pres., mem. exec. com. Big Bros. L.A.; bd. dirs. Am. Cancer Soc., L.A., Solvang (Calif.) TheatreFest; mem. Town Hall Forum, L.A.; commr. Parks and Recreation, City of Oakland, 1973-74; bd. dirs. United Way, 1988-93, TheaterFest, 1990-94.. Recipient Pres.'s Club award Big Bros. Greater L.A., 1987, 88, Best in West Pub. Svc. award Am. Advt. Fedn., San Francisco, 1975. Mem. Nat. Investor Rels. Inst., Pub. Rels. Soc. Am. (Disting. Cmty. Svc. award 1987), Internat. Assn. Bus. Communicators, Motor Press Guild, Newcomen Soc., Nat. Cattlemen's Assn., Calif. Cattlemen's Assn., Am. Quarter Horse Assn., Rancheros Visitadores, Vaqueros de Los Ranchos, Publicity Club L.A., Jonathan Club. Avocation: horseback riding, fishing. Office: Fleishman-Hillard Inc 515 S Flower St Ste 700 Los Angeles CA 90071-2209

KLINE, ROBERT H., foundation administrator; b. Dixon, Ill., Aug. 12, 1920; m. Jean Grace Pollard; children: Robert MacDonald Kline, John Woodson Kline, Jeanie Pollard Kline, Mary Kline Moran, Thomas Peyton Kline, James Douglas Kline. Attended, U.S. Navy Midshipman Sch. at Notre Dame U., 1943; BS in Chemistry, Beloit (Wis.) Coll., 1942. Pub. info. officer military sea transp. svc. U.S. Navy, 1950-53, ret. lt. comdr.; reporter, feature writer Rittman (Ohio) Press, 1946-47, Wilmington (N.C.) News, 1947-48, Richmond News Leader, 1948-50; promotion mgr. Norfolk Newspapers, 1953-56; acct. exec. Cargill, Wilson & Acree (Advtg. Agy.), 1956-59; prin. Robert Kline & Co. Advtg. Agy., Richmond, Va., 1959; founder Southeastern Inst. Rsch., 1964; founder, chmn. U.S. Hist. Soc., Richmond, Va., 1974—. Editor: (books) The Patriots, Generation of Genius, Down to the Sea with Jack Woodson, Masterpieces Best Loved Paintings of American Museums; designer: (logos) City of Richmond, Chesapeake Bay Bridge Tunnel, Smithfield Foods, Engineers Club of Richmond. Founder, former chmn. Richmond First Homes Program for the Homeless; former dir. Richmond Urban League; former chmn. bd. vis. St. Gertrude H.S.; dir. Va. Refugee and Immigration Svc.; former chmn. St. Joseph's Villa adv. bd., Richmond; eucharistic min. St. Bridget's Cath. Ch. With USN, 1943-46, 50-53, PTO. Recipient Maritime Svc. award Propeller Club. Mem. PRSA (founder, former dir. Thomas Jefferson chpt., 2 Silver Anvil awards, Advtg. Person of the Yr. 1962), Am. Mktg. Assn. (founder, former pres. Richmond chpt.), Advtg. Club of Richmond (former pres.). Office: US Historical Soc 1st and Main Sts Richmond VA 23219*

KLINE, RONALD R., history and technology educator; b. Oswego, Kans., Apr. 21, 1947; s. Raymond O. and Donna L. Kline; m. Gloria Hughes, Dec. 1969 (div. July 1973); m. Margaret M. Motz, Apr. 15, 1976; stepchildren: David Marcotte, Melissa, Michele, Margot, Maggie. BSEE, Kans State U., 1969; MS in History and Sci., U. Wis., 1979, PhD in Sci., 1983. Field engr. GE, Pittsfield, Mass., 1969-77; dir. history ctr. IEEE, N.Y.C., 1984-87; asst. prof. history and tech. Cornell U., Ithaca, N.Y., 1987-93, assoc. prof., 1993—. Author: Stewarts, 1992; contbr. articles to various jours. Mem. IEEE (editor tech. 1995-97), Soc. for History Tech. (adv. editor Tech. and Culture 1998—, chmn. prize coms. 1997, 98, editl. excellence awards 1996, 97, 98), History of Sci. Soc. (adv. editor Isis 1996-98), Orgn. Am. Historians. Office: Cornell U 394 Rhodes Hall Ithaca NY 14850

KLINE, SIDNEY DELONG, JR., lawyer; b. West Reading, Pa., Mar. 25, 1932; s. Sidney D. and Leona Clarice (Barkalow) K.; m. Barbara Phyllis James, Dec. 31, 1955; children: Allison S. McCanney, Leslie S. Davidson, Lisa P. Gallen. BA, Dickinson Coll., 1954, LLD, 1998; JD with honors, The Dickinson Law Sch., 1956, LLD, 1994. Bar: Pa. 1956, U.S. Dist. Ct. (ea. dist.) Pa. 1961, U.S. Supreme Ct. 1967. Assoc. Stevens & Lee, Reading, Pa., 1958-62, ptnr., shareholder, 1963-97, pres., 1977-93, chmn., 1993-97, counsel, 1998—; bd. dirs. Reading Eagle Co. Pres., United Way of Berks County, Reading, 1972-74, campaign chmn., 1986; bd. dirs. Reading Ctr. City Devel. Fund, 1976—, pres., 1992-97; trustee Dickinson Sch. Law, 1978—, sec., 1988—; trustee Dickinson Coll., 1979—, chmn., 1990-98. Served with U.S. Army, 1956-58. Recipient Doran award United Way Berks County, 1978, Richard J. Caron Cmty. Svc. award Caron Found., 1993, Thun Cmty. Svc. award, 1995. Fellow Am. Coll. Trust and Estate Coun., Nat. Soc. Fund Raising Execs. (Outstanding Vol. Fund Raiser Greater Northeastern Pa. chpt. 1992), Pa. Bar Assn., Berks County Bar Assn., Berkshire Country Club (Reading), Moselem Springs Golf Club (Fleetwood, Pa.), The Club at Pelican Bay (Naples, Fla.). Republican. Lutheran. Office: PO Box 679 111 N 6th St Reading PA 19603-0679

KLINE, SUSAN ANDERSON, medical school official and dean, internist; b. Dallas, June 4, 1937; d. Kenneth Kirby and Frances Annette (Demorest) Anderson; m. Edward Mahon Kline, Dec. 26, 1964 (dec. July 1990). BA, Ohio U., 1959; MD, Northwestern U., 1963. Diplomate Am. Bd. Internal Medicine, Nat. Bd. Med. Examiners (bd. dirs. 1977-81). Dir. cardiac catheterization lab. The New York Hosp., 1971-80; assoc. dean student affairs Cornell U. Med. Coll., N.Y.C., 1974-78; assoc. dean admissions and student affairs Cornell Med. Sch., Ithaca, N.Y., 1978-80; mgr. occupl. med. programs GE Co., 1980-84; sr. assoc. dean student affairs N.Y. Med. Coll., Valhalla, 1984-94, interim dean, v.p. med. affairs, 1994-96, exec. vice dean acad. affairs, vice provost univ. student affairs, 1996—; bd. dirs. Nat. Residency Matching Program, 1996—, chmn. unmatched student com., 1998—; mem. test com. Ednl. Commn. on Fgn. Med. Grads., Phila., 1985-92; mem. U.S. med. licensing exam. test accommodations com. Nat. Bd. Med. Examiners, Phila., 1992-97; chmn. adv. com. Electronic Residency Application Svc., 1996—; mem. Liaison Com. on Med. Edn., 1998—, ad hoc subcom. for the review of accreditation standards, 1998—. Bd. visitors Coll. Arts, Ohio U., Athens, 1981-91; bd. dirs. Burke Rehab. Hosp., White Plains, N.Y., 1997—. Recipient Leaders of the Future award Nat. Coun. Women, N.Y.C., 1978, Cert. of Appreciation, Ohio U., 1978. Fellow Am. Coll. Cardiology; mem. Am. Heart Assn. (fellow coun. on clin. cardiology), N.Y. Cardiologists Soc., Am. Assn. Med. Colls. (chmn. N.E. group on student affairs, chmn. 1989-93), Cruising Club Am., Alpha Omega Alpha. Avocation: sailing. Home: 561 Pequot Ave Southport CT 06490-1366 Office: New York Medical College Sunshine Cottage Valhalla NY 10595

KLINE, SYBIL ROSE, researcher; b. San Francisco; d. Samuel Henry and Louise (Holdforth) K. BA, Humboldt U., 1972, MA in Psychology, 1975; PhD, U. Calif., Santa Cruz, 1996. Lic. ednl. psychologist; Cert. sch. psychologist, bilingual cert. Sch. psychologist Monterey (Calif.) Peninsula Unified Sch. Dist., 1980-81, Oak Grove Unified Sch. Dist., San Jose, Calif., 1981-82, Santa Cruz (Calif.) County Office of Edn., 1982-83, Santa Cruz City Schs., 1983-96; cons. psychologist San Jose Unified Sch. Dist., 1992; practitioner, researcher, connection coord. U. Calif. Santa Cruz Ctr. for Rsch. on Cultural Diversity, 1992-96, Santa Cruz (Calif.) City Schs., 1982-96; rschr. prin. investigator Alternative Assessment Project, CREDE, UCSC, US Dept. Edn.; lecturer edn. dept., UCSC, 1998. Author: PASS S Dynamic Assessment, 1995, One-Minute Attention Test, 1995; co-author: (manual) Guidelines for the Linguistically and Culturally Different Exceptional Student, 1987. Regents fellow U. Calif., Santa Cruz, 1990; grantee Dept. Edn.; Fellow Office Bilingual Edn. and Minority Lang. Affairs, 1993-96. Mem. APA, Nat. Assn. Sch. Psychologists, Am. Edn. Rsch. Assn., Soc. Rsch. in Child Devel., Coun. Exceptional Children (divsn. culturally/linguistically diverse learners), Calif. Assn. Sch. Psychologists (multicultural com., Psychologist of Yr. 1986). Office: Univ Calif CREOE Santa Cruz CA 95064

KLINE, SYRIL LEVIN, writer, columnist, reporter, educational consultant, commentator, theatre critic; b. Washington, Oct. 19, 1953; d. Irvin and Blanche (Hewitt) Levin; m. Raymond B. Lessans (div.); children: Seth Adam Lessans, Jonathan Rafael Lessans; m. Peter Lee Kline, Dec. 28, 1989. BS, U. Md., 1975. Cert. integrative learning master facilitator, 1990. Tchr. Hebrew Washington Hebrew Congregation, 1974-80; sec., realtor Colquitt-Carruthers Inc., Montgomery County, Md., 1974-80; adminstrv. asst. Bd. Jewish Edn., Silver Spring, Md., 1980-81; tchr. presch. and kindergarten Children's Learning Ctr., Rockville, Md., 1982-89; curriculum designer, dir. integrative learning Nat. Acad. Integrative Learning, Rochester, N.Y., 1990-92; ednl. cons. Integra Learning Systems, South Bend, Ind., 1992—; freelance radio and print writer South Bend, 1992—; ednl. cons. Integrative Learning Systems, Damascus, Md., 1988-89; ind. cons., course designer Prince George's County (Md.) Libr., 1989, North Syracuse (N.Y.) Schs., 1989-92, Oswego (N.Y.) Cmty. Schs., 1989-92, Xerox, Rochester, N.Y., 1990-92, Eastman Kodak, Rochester, 1990-92, Penn Yann (N.Y.) Schs., 1991, Utica (N.Y.) Schs., 1991, City of Rochester Schs., 1991, Bellcore, Elizabeth, N.J., 1991, Alliant Tech Sys., St. Paul, 1991, Paramus (N.J.) Cmty. Schs., 1992, Govt. Can., 1992, Project Read, San Francisco, 1992, Sandia Labs, Santa Fe, 1992, City of Elkhart, Ind., 1992-94, Trinity Corp., Joliet, Ill., 1995, Scottsdale Mall, South Bend, 1995, Pathfinders, Plymouth, Ind., 1996; assessment designer Integra Learning Systems, 1995. Co-author: (novel) The Butterfly Dreams, 1998; featured commentator Sta. WVPE, 1995-98; reporter, staff writer Action Line column for South Bend Tribune; soprano Ind. Opera North. Spkr., presenter Little Bear Child Abuse Prevention Program, Madison Ctr. Hosp., South Bend, 1993-95; vol. fundraiser Jewish Fedn. St. Joseph Valley, South Bend, 1995-96; mem. com., writer, presenter Holocaust Commemoration; actress, dir. Osceola Players, South Bend Civic Theatre; cantorial soloist Temple Beth El, South Bend, 1997, poet, 1996. Mem. Hadassah (life, corres. sec. 1994-95), Omicron Nu. Democrat. Avocations: radio commercial voices, singing, theatre, pets, travel. Home: 19109 Johnson Rd South Bend IN 46614-5461

KLINE, TIMOTHY DEAL, lawyer; b. Oklahoma City, July 16, 1949; s. David Adam and Ruthela (Deal) K.; m. Alyssa Lipp Krysler, Aug. 29, 1985. BA, U. Okla., 1971, JD, 1976. Bar: Okla. 1976, U.S. Dist. Ct. (we. dist.) Okla. 1977, U.S. Ct. Appeals (10th cir.) 1977; cert. in bus. bankruptcy law and consumer bankruptcy Am. Bankruptcy Bd. of Certification. Law clk. to presiding justice U.S. Dist. Ct. (we. dist.) Okla., Oklahoma City, 1976-80; assoc. Linn, Helms, Kirk & Burkett, Oklahoma City, 1980-83; ptnr. Kline & Kline, Oklahoma City, 1983—; adj. prof. law Oklahoma City U., 1980-84, 90. Mem. Am. Coll. Bankruptcy, Okla. County Bar Assn. (pres. 1998-99), Phi Delta Phi. Democrat. Office: Kline & Kline 720 NE 63rd St Oklahoma City OK 73105-6405

KLINE, VICKI ANN, investment consultant; b. Monterey, Tenn., Oct. 26, 1948; d. William John and Betty (Coleman) Harden; children: David, John, Lori, Lisa, Daniel. BS in Acctg., Nova U., 1983; MBA, Kent State U., 1994. CPA, Ohio; CFP; cert. personal fin. specialist. Internal auditor Roadway Svc., Akron, Ohio, 1984-85; acctg. mgr. A. Schulman Inc., Fairlawn, Ohio, 1985-93; investment cons. Butler Wick & Co., Inc., Kent, Ohio, 1993—. Mem. AICPA, Ohio Soc. CPAs, Inst. Mgmt. Accts., Inst. CFPs, Women's Network. Home: 1282 Congress Lake Rd Mogadore OH 44260-9690 Office: Butler Wick & Co Inc 149 N Water St Kent OH 44240-2418

KLINEDINST, DUNCAN STEWART, lawyer; b. Washington, July 10, 1952; s. David Moulson and Mary Stewart (Coxe) K.; m. Mary Rose Bartelloni, June 29, 1990; children: Catherine Anne, Caroline Stewart. BA, Washington and Lee U., 1974; JD, U. Va., 1978. Bar: D.C. 1978, Va. 1987. Investment analyst The Riggs Nat. Bank, Washington, 1974-75; assoc. Hogan & Hartson, Washington, 1978-86; ptnr. Hogan & Hartson, McLean, Va., 1987—. Chmn. Washington and Lee Alumni Admissions Com., Washington, 1983-90; v.p. Washington and Lee Alumni Fraternity Coun., Lexington, Va., 1991-93; mem. vestry St. John's Episcopal Ch., McLean, Va., 1997—. Mem. Va. Bar Assn., Washington and Lee U. Alumni Assn., U. Va. Alumni Assn., Century Club, Phi Beta Kappa, Omicron Delta Epsilon, Phi Kappa Psi. Episcopalian. Office: Hogan & Hartson 8300 Greensboro Dr Ste 1100 Mc Lean VA 22102-3609*

KLINEDINST, JOHN DAVID, lawyer; b. Washington, Jan. 20, 1950; s. David Moulson and Mary Stewart (Coxe) K.; m. Cynthia Lynn DuBain, Aug. 15, 1981. BA cum laude in History, Washington and Lee U., 1971, JD, 1978; MBA in Fin. and Investments, George Washington U., 1975. Bar: Calif. 1979, U.S. Dist. Ct. (so. dist.) Calif. 1979, U.S. Ct. Appeals (9th cir.) 1987. With comml. lending dept. 1st Nat. Bank Md., Montgomery County, 1971-74; assoc. Ludecke, McGrath & Denton, San Diego, 1979-80; ptnr. Whitney & Klinedinst, San Diego, 1980-83, Klinedinst & Meiser, San Diego, 1983-86; mng. ptnr. Klinedinst, Fliehman & McKillop, San Diego, 1986—. Mem. law coun. Washington and Lee U., 1993-97, vice chmn. law campaign, 1991-94; vice chmn. bd. dirs. ARC of San Diego/Imperial, 1991-97; pres. House Corp. Calif. Lamda, Phi Kappa Psi, 1999—. Recipient Disting. Alumnus award Washington and Lee U., 1993. Mem. ABA, Calif. Bar Assn., San Diego Bar Assn., San Diego Def. Lawyers, Washington Soc. (bd. dirs. 1997—), Washington and Lee U. Alumni Assn. (bd. dirs. 1986-90, pres. 1989-90), Washington and Lee U. Club (pres. San Diego chpt. 1980-87), La Jolla Beach and Tennis Club, Fairbanks Ranch Country Club, Phi Kappa Psi. Republican. Episcopalian. Home: 6226 Via Dos Valles Rancho Santa Fe CA 92067-9999 Office: Klinedinst Fliehman & McKillop 501 W Broadway Ste 600 San Diego CA 92101-3584

KLINEDINST, THOMAS JOHN, JR., insurance agency executive; b. Cin., Aug. 2, 1942; s. Thomas John and Betty Ann (Broeman) K.; m. Diana Lowry McCarroll; children: Thomas John III, Margaret Lucie, George Calvin. BA, Georgetown U., 1965. Spl. agt. Fidelity & Deposit Co. Md., Cleve., 1965-67; account exec. Thomas E. Wood, Inc., Cin., 1967-71, asst. v.p., 1971-73, v.p., 1973-79, exec. v.p., 1979-87, pres., 1987-95, pres., chmn., CEO, 1995—, also bd. dirs.; cons. Airport Operators Coun. Internat., Washington, 1979-95; pres. Ohio CAP Ins. Co., Ltd., 1988—; dir. Star Banc Corp., 1993—, Star Bank Cinti, 1993—, Employers Resource Assn., 1994—, Franciscan Health Sys. of Ohio Valley, 1994—, chmn., 1997; exec. com. USI Ins. Svc. Corp., 1995—. Pres. Travelers Aid-Internat. Inst., Cin., 1980-84; pres.-elect Fedn. Cath. Cmty. Charities, Cin., 1980-81; pres. Terrace Park Swim Club, Cin., 1980-82; trustee Cin. Better Bus. Bur., 1991—, dir. Project Encor, 1991—; bd. dirs. Hamilton County Hosp. Commn., 1996, chmn., 1997;. Named Young Agt. of Yr., Cin. Ins. Bd., 1977. Mem. Coun. Ins. Agts. and Brokers (mem. bd. dirs. 1984-94), Ind. Ins. Agts. Assn. Ohio, Cin. Ins. Bd. (trustee 1980-85, pres. 1984-85), Queen City Club, Cin. Country Club, Friars Club (pres. 1974-78, Friars award 1977), Rotary. Republican. Roman Catholic. Office: Thomas E Wood Inc 312 Elm St Fl 24 Cincinnati OH 45202-2739

KLINEFELTER, JAMES LOUIS, lawyer; b. L.A., Oct. 8, 1925; s. Theron Albert and Anna Marie (Coffey) K.; m. Joanne Wright, Dec. 26, 1957 (div.); children: Patricia Anne, Jeanne Marie, Christopher Wright; m. Mary Lynn S. Klinefelter, Aug. 19, 1971; 1 child, Mary Katherine. BA, U. Ala., 1949, LLB, 1951. Bar: Ala. 1951, U.S. Dist. Ct. (no. dist.) Ala. 1959, U.S. Ct. Appeals (11th cir.) 1983. Regional claims rep. State Farm Mut. Auto Ins. Co., Anniston, Ala., 1951-54; ptnr. Burnham & Klinefelter, Anniston, 1954—; mem. adv. com. Supreme Ct. Ala. Mem. Ala. Dem. Exec. Com., 1964—, chmn. legis. rev. com., 1964—; past chmn. Calhoun County Dem. Exec. Com., 1964—. Lt. (j.g.) USNR, 1943-46. Mem. ABA, Assn. Def. Trial Attys., Ala. Bar Assn. (mem. task force on jud. selection, mem. long-range planning task force), Calhoun County Bar Assn., Ala. Def. Lawyers Assn. (past pres.), Ala. Law Inst. (bd. dirs.), Ala. Sch. Bd. Attys. (past pres.), Internat. Assn. Def. Counsel, Kiwanis (past pres.), Anniston Country Club, Phi Kappa Sigma, Phi Alpha Theta. Avocations: tennis, swimming, reading. Home: 1412 Christine Ave Anniston AL 36207-3924 Office: Burnham & Klinefelter So Trust Nat Bank Bldg PO Box 1618 Anniston AL 36202-1618 *When obligations or obnoxious tasks are accepted gratefully as opportunities, one's life can be turned about, and bitterness and resentment changed into joyful satisfaction. Hard tasks are the food of growth.*

KLINETOB, CARSON WAYNE, retired physical therapist; b. Berwick, Pa., Feb. 8, 1922; s. Dalbys Bryan and Margaret Jeannette (Hampton) K.; m. Edna Mae Ginader; children: Sandra Lynne, Diane Beth. BS, East Stroudsburg U., 1946; cert. phys. therapy, U. Pa., 1948; postgrad., NYU, Kingston, Pa., 1949. Lic. phys. therapist Pa., Ill., Wis., Ala. Staff phys. therapis VA Hosp., Wilkes-Barre, Pa., 1948, chief phys. therapist, 1949; chief phys. therapist Downey (Ill.) VA Hosp., 1953; owner Phys. Rehab. Ctr., Waukegan, Ill., 1955-60; co-owner, bd. dirs. Tri W-G Inc., Valley City, N.D., 1968-86; phys. therapist Wausau (Wis.) Med. Ctr., 1969—; ret. Contbr. articles to profl. jours. With U.S. Army, 1943-45, ETO. Mem. Am. Phys. Therapy Assn., Wis. Phys. Therapy Assn., Am. Legion, DAV (life), Masons, Shriners, Acacia. Avocations: golf, sports.

KLING, MERLE, political scientist, university official; b. Russia, June 15, 1919; came to U.S., 1921, naturalized, 1927; s. Saul and Dina (Hoffman) K.; m. Ann Ruth Yasgur, Jan. 1, 1948 (dec. June 1976); 1 child, Arnold Saul; m. Sandra Perlman, Aug. 26, 1978 (dec. Aug. 1990). A.B., Washington U., St. Louis, 1940, M.A., 1941, Ph.D., 1949; D.Hum., Washington U., 1983; LL.D., Mercy Coll., 1985. Mem. faculty Washington U., 1946—, asst. prof. polit. sci., 1950-54, asso. prof., 1954-61, prof., 1961-83, prof. emeritus, 1983—; dean Washington U. (Faculty Arts and Scis.), 1966-69, 73-76, provost, 1976-79, exec. vice chancellor, provost, 1979-83, acting chmn. dept. polit. sci., 1970-71; pres. Mercy Coll., Dobbs Ferry, N.Y., 1984-85; vis. prof. U. Ill., 1961; research asso. Center Internat. Studies, Princeton U., 1964-65. Author: The Soviet Theory of Internationalism, 1952, A Mexican Interest Group in Action, 1961; contbr. articles to profl. jours. Served with AUS, 1942-45. Merle Kling professorship of Modern Letters established in honor, Washington U., 1983. Mem. Am. Polit. Sci. Assn. (council 1967-69), Midwest Polit. Sci. Assn. (editor jour. 1965-66, pres. 1969-70), Phi Beta

Kappa, Alpha Kappa Delta, Omicron Delta Kappa. Home: 20 N Kingshighway Blvd Saint Louis MO 63108-1366

KLING, PHRADIE (PHRADIE KLING GOLD), small business owner; b. N.Y.C., July 2, 1933; d. Samuel A. and Mary Leah (Cohen) K.; m. Lee M. Gold, Sept. 5, 1955 (div. 1976); children: Judith Eileen, Laura Susan, Stephen Samuel, James David. BA, Cornell U., 1955; MA in Human Genetics, Sarah Lawrence Coll., 1971. Genetic counselor assoc. Coll. Medicine and Dentistry N.J., Newark, 1970-73; assoc. genetic counselor Sarah Lawrence Coll., Bronxville, N.Y., 1970-73; genetic counselor N.Y. Fertility Rsch. Found., N.Y.C., 1971-73; staff assoc., genetic counselor depts. pediatrics, ob-gyn and neurology Columbia U. Coll. Physicians and Surgeons, N.Y.C., 1973-78; asst. in genetics St. Luke's Hosp. Ctr., N.Y.C., 1977-79; health program assoc. Conn. Dept. Health Svcs., Hartford, 1978-84; edn. cons. Conn. Traumatic Brain Injury Assn., Rocky Hill, 1984-85; office mgr. Anderson Turf Irrigation Inc., Plainville, Conn., 1986-92; owner, mgr. KlingWorks, contract adminstrn., Avon, Conn., 1992—; speaker, instr. on health and health ethics issues, Conn., N.Y., N.J., 1971-85; dir. confs. on genetics and traumatic brain injury, 1980-85; project dir. ednl. field testing Biol. Scis. Curriculum Study, 1981-83; scientist AAAS Sci.-by-Mail, 1991—. Mem. Farmington River Watershed Assn., Simsbury, Conn., 1988—; docent Sci. Mus. Conn., West Hartford, 1989-90. Recipient citation for dedicated svc. Conn. Safety Belt Coalition, 1985. Mem. Am. Human Genetics Soc., Bus. and Profl. Microcomputer Users Group (bd. dirs.), Conn. Assn. for Jungian Psychology (bd. dirs.), Am. Mensa (chpt. coord. gifted children 1985—). Avocations: computer genealogy, canoeing, swimming, music. Home and Office: 33 Hunter Rd Avon CT 06001-3618

KLING, S(TEPHEN) LEE, banker; b. St. Louis, Dec. 22, 1928; m. Ann Hemingway (div. 1958); m. Rosalyn H. Kling, May 3, 1962; children: Stephen L., Frank Frederick, Lee C., Allan B. BBA, Washington U., St. Louis, 1950. Chmn. bd., CEO Landmark Bancshares Corp., St. Louis, 1974-91; asst. spl. counselor on inflation White House, Washington, 1978-79; adv. vice-chmn. bd. U.S. divsn. Reed Stenhouse, Inc., Washington, 1978-79; chmn. bd. Kling Rechter & Co., 1991—; bd. dirs. Union Planters Corp., Memphis, Hanover Direct Inc., N.Y.C., Falcon Products, Inc., St. Louis, Bernard Chaus Inc., N.Y.C., Nat. Beverage Co., Ft. Lauderdale, Fla., Top Air Mfg. Co., Parkersburg, Iowa, Electro Rent Corp., L.A. Trustee Mo. Hist. Soc., St. Louis, Barnes-Jewish Found., St. Louis and Coro Midwestern area, NCCJ, St. Louis, St. Louis Symphony, The Moog Oral Sch., St. Louis, Trumam Libr. Inst., Independence, Mo., St. Louis Zoo Found., St. Louis U.-Mo., Chancellors Coun., St. Louis; fin. chmn. Dem. Nat. Com., 1974-77; treas. Dem. Nat. Conv., 1976; nat. treas. Carter-Mondale Re-election Com., Gephardt for Pres. Com.; co-chmn. Citizens Com. for Ratification of Panama Canal Treaties; U.S. econ. advisor representing pvt. sector during peace negotiations between Israel and Egypt, 1979; co-chmn. Coalition for Enactment of Caribbean Basin Initiative Legis., 1982-83; apptd. to Def. Base Closure and Realignment Commn., 1995, Mo. State Hwy. and Transp. Commn., 1995, chmn., 1997. Mem. Sr. Execs. Orgn., Burning Tree Club, 1925 F St. Club, Standard Club (Chgo.), Westwood Country Club, Legends Country Club. Home: Grayling Farm 5751 Robertsville Rd Villa Ridge MO 63089-2535 Home: 1401 S Brentwood Blvd Saint Louis MO 63144-1440

KLING, WILLIAM, economist, retired foreign service officer; b. N.Y.C., May 8, 1915; s. Irving and Sophie (Kling) K.; m. Suzanne Kaufman (M.D.), June 28, 1940; children: Robert Irving, Michael Paul, Virginia Airini Susan. B.S., CCNY, 1937; M.S., Mass. State Coll., 1938; Ph.D., Clark U., 1943. Grad. asst. Mass. State Coll., 1937-38, Clark U., 1938-39; instr. CCNY, 1939-40; agrl. economist Dept. Agr., also War Food Adminstrn., 1940-45; agrl. attache Bucharest, Rumania, Budapest, Hungary, Belgrade, Yugoslavia, Sofia, Bu, Albania, 1945-47; first sec., consul Am. embassy, London, 1948-54; 1st sec., consul Am. embassy, Wellington, New Zealand, 1954-60; assigned Dept. of State, Washington, 1960-68; chief div. of functional intelligence Dept. of State, 1961-63, dep. dir. and acting dir. Office of Functional and External Research, 1962-63, econ. adviser to asst sec. for African Affairs, 1963-66, dep. dir. econ. affairs Office Inter African Affairs, 1966-68; dir. govt. affairs Uniroyal, Inc., Washington, 1968-73; Washington rep. Am. Soybean Assn., 1973-79; prin. William Kling Assos. (consultants), Falls Church, Va., 1979—; cons. Japanese Fedn. Agrl. Coop. Assns., 1979; dir. econs. and stats. div. Distilled Spirits Council U.S., Inc., Washington, 1979-86, dir. industry stats. div., 1986-97; mem. Nat. Def. Exec. Rsc., 1970—; cons. Fed. Emergency Mgmt. Agy., 1970—; mem. export policy task force U.S. C. of C., 1978-79, mem. multilateral trade negotiation task force and chmn. agr. subgroup, 1978-79. Editor: DISCUS UPC News, Annual Statis, Rev. Distilled Spirits Industry, Pub. Revenues from Alcohol Beverages, Tax Briefs, 1980-85, Retail Outlets for the Sale of Distilled Spirits, 1992, 97, Distilled Spirits Brand Directory, 1993, 95, 97; contbr. articles to profl. jours. Recipient Meritorious Honor award State Dept., 1968. Mem. Am. Fgn. Service Assn., Soc. Govt. Economists., Diplomatic and Consular Officers Ret. Clubs: Nat. Economists, Internat. Economists. Home and Office: 6434 Lakeview Dr Lake Barcroft Falls Church VA 22041

KLING, WILLIAM HUGH, broadcasting executive; b. St. Paul, Apr. 29, 1942; s. William Conrad and Helen A. (Leonard) K.; m. Sarah Margaret Baldwin, Sept. 25, 1976. B.A. in Economics, St. John's U., 1964; postgrad., Boston U., 1964-66. Pres. Minn. Pub. Radio, Inc., St. Paul, 1966—, Greenspring Co., 1986—; founding dir. Nat. Pub. Radio, 1968-70, dir., 1977-80; founding pres. Public Radio Internat., 1982-86; vice chmn. Pub. Radio Internat., 1986-93; bd. dirs. St. Paul Cos., Wenger Corp., Irwin Fin.; mem. various fund bds. Capital Group Am. Funds. Bd. dirs. Minn. Orch., 1987-93; trustee J.L. Found., 1988—; bd. dirs., chmn. Fitzgerald Theater Corp., 1983—; mem. The James Madison Coun. of Libr. of Congress, 1992-94. Recipient Edward R. Murrow award, 1981, award for Excellence Channels Mag., 1987; named Twin Citian of Yr., Twin Citian mag., 1987, Disting. Minnesotan, 1995. Mem. Mpls. Club, Minn. Club. Office: Minn Pub Radio Inc 45 7th St E Saint Paul MN 55101-2274

KLINGELE, JANINE MARIE, nursing administrator; b. St. Paul, Apr. 4, 1947; d. Robert Claire and Janet Mae (Kelly) Emerson; m. Lawrence Thomas Klingele, Aug. 8, 1969; children: Maria, Brenda, Paul, David, John. BSN, Coll. of St. Catherine, 1969. Cert. nursing adminstrn. ANCC. Charge nurse, relief supr. Southview Acres Nursing Home, South Saint Paul, Minn., 1974-76; charge nurse ICU Ransom Meml. Hosp., Ottawa, Kans., 1980-86, relief supr., 1982-86, orientation dir., 1984-86, head nurse med.-surg., 1984-86, co-instr. for health careers secondary edn., 1986-88, asst. dir. nursing, 1986-92, chmn. nursing quality assurance, 1986-90; dir. patient svcs. Ransom Meml. Hosp., Ottawa, 1992-96; pvt. duty mgr. St. Lukes/Shawnee Mission Health Care Sys., 1997-98; ob-gyn. clin. head nurse KU Physicians, Inc., 1998—; presenter of continuing edn. Kans. Fedn. of LPN, Topeka, 1991; co-presenter Am. Soc. Hosp. Pharmacists, Washington, 1992. Mem. Sacred Heart Musical Liturgists, Ottawa, 1990—; presenter Continuing Edn. on Health Care and Ethical Issues, 1994, Continuing Edn. Kans. Assn. Risk and Quality Mgrs., 1995, Midwest Bioethics, Continuing Edn. for Nursing on Spirit-ful Care: Ethical Issues, 1996; past trustee Franklin County Mental Health Clinic. Mem. ANA, Kans. State Nurses Assn. (appointed mem. coun. on edn. 1992-96), Kans. Orgn. Nursing Execs., Sigma Theta Tau. Roman Catholic. Avocations: crochet, music, family activities, cooking. Home: 3930 Iowa Ln Ottawa KS 66067-8028 Office: OBGyn Clinic 5300 Bell 3901 Rainbow Blvd Kansas City KS 66160

KLINGENSMITH, ARTHUR PAUL, business and personal development consultant; b. L.A., May 23, 1949; s. Paul Arthur and Hermine Elinore K.; m. Donna J. Bellucci, Apr. 26, 1976 (div. Jan. 1981). AA in Social Sci., Indian Valley Jr. Coll., 1976; BA in Indsl. Psychology, San Francisco State U., 1979; MA in Indsl. Psychology, Columbia Pacific U., 1980. Enlisted USAF, Biloxi, Miss.; advanced through grades to staff sgt. USAF; instr. radio ops. USAF, Biloxi, 1968-72; air traffic control operator USAF, Hamilton AFB Novato, Calif., 1972-74; resigned USAF, 1974; elec. technician Calif. Dept. Transp., Oakland, 1975-78; right of way agt. Calif. Dept. Transp., San Francisco, 1978-85; sr. right of way agt. Calif. Dept. Transp., Sacramento, 1985-87, computer researcher, 1985-87; v.p., cons. Associated Right of Way Svcs., Inc., 1989-92; pvt. practice relocation and redevel. cons., 1987-96, bus. and pers. devel. cons., 1996—. V.p. bd. dirs. PAST Found. Mem. Inst. Noetic Scis., World Future Soc. Republican. Avocations: automobile restoration, painting, writing. Home and Office: Arthur P Klingensmith & Assocs PO Box 574 Sausalito CA 94966-0574

KLINGENSMITH, MIKE, publishing executive. Publisher Entertainment Weekly Mag.; pres. Sports Illustrated, N.Y.C., 1997—. Office: Sports Illustrated Time & Life Bldg 1271 Avenue Of The Americas New York NY 10020-1300*

KLINGENSTEIN, FREDERICK ADLER, investment banking executive; b. N.Y.C., Apr. 13, 1931; s. Joseph and Esther (Adler) K.; m. Sharon Moore Lowe, July 2, 1932; children: Kathy Klingenstein, Susan Klingenstein, Lucy Brody, Amy Pollinger. BA, Yale U., 1953; postgrad., Harvard U. Sch. Bus., 1953-54; LHD, St. Lawrence U., 1986. Chmn., chief exec. officer Wertheim & Co., N.Y.C., 1972-86; co-chmn. Wertheim-Schroder & Co. Inc., N.Y.C., 1986-88; chmn. Klingenstein, Fields & W. L.P., 1989—. Chmn. Mt. Sinai Med. Ctr., N.Y.C., 1986-95; trustee Am. Mus. Natural History, N.Y.C., 1965—, St. Lawrence U., Canton, N.Y., 1979-85; pres. Rye County Day Sch., Rye, N.Y., 1980-84. Served to 1st lt. arty. U.S. Army, 1954-56. Office: Klingenstein Fields & Co LP 787 7th Ave New York NY 10019-6018*

KLINGENSTEIN, R. JAMES, physician; b. N.Y.C., Oct. 30, 1948; s. Paul and Selma (Feldman) K.; m. Susanne Klingenstein, 1993; 1 child, Rachel J. AB magna cum laude, Case Western Res. U., 1970; MD with honors, NYU, 1974; JD, Boston Coll., 1989; student, Harvard Sch Pub. Health, 1988. Intern Mt. Sinai Hosp., N.Y.C., 1974-75, resident, 1975-76; resident Bellevue Hosp., N.Y.C., 1976-77; clin. assoc. immunology br. Nat. Cancer Inst. NIH, HEW, Bethesda, Md., 1977-79; fellow in gastroenterology Mass. Gen Hosp., Boston, 1979—; clin. research fellow Harvard U., Boston, 1979-82; clin. assoc. medicine Mass. Gen. Hosp., 1982—; instr. in medicine Harvard Med. Sch., 1982-83, Tufts U. Sch. Medicine, 1983-87; asst. prof. Tufts U., 1987—. Assoc. editor: Internat. Jour. of Risk and Safety in Medicine; contbr. articles to profl. jours. Fellow ACP; mem. Am. Gastroenterol. Assn., Phi Bbeta Kappa. Home: 2000 Washington St Ste 543 Newton MA 02462-1608 Office: Mass Gen Hosp GI Unit Boston MA 02114

KLINGER, ALLEN, engineering and applied science educator; b. N.Y.C., Apr. 2, 1937; s. Benjamin and Evelyne Klinger; m. Judith Theresa Flesch, Aug. 31, 1958 (div. Dec. 1980); children: Deborah, Richard; m. Dorothy Joy Fisher, Feb. 14, 1988; stepchildren: Elisa, Laura, Kevin. BEE, The Cooper Union, 1957; MS, Calif. Inst. Tech., 1958; PhD, U. Calif., Berkeley, 1966. Mem. tech. staff Hughes Aircraft Co., Culver City, Calif., 1957; teaching asst. Calif. Inst. Tech., Pasadena, 1957-58; electronics engr. ITT Labs., Nutley, N.J., 1958-59; electronics system engr. System Devel. Corp., Santa Monica, Calif., 1959-62; rsch. asst. U. Calif. Electronics Rsch. Lab., Berkeley, 1962-64; sr. rsch. engr. Jet Propulsion Lab., Pasadena, Calif., 1964-65; researcher Rand Corp., Santa Monica, Calif., 1965-67; prof. UCLA, 1967—; mem. L.A. County Data Processing and Telecom. Adv. Com., 1994-95; cons. in pattern recognition, image analysis, computer systems and math. modeling; expert witness, 1990—. Author: Data Structures, in Ency. Phys. Sci. and Tech., 1989; editor: Soviet Image Pattern Recognition Research, 1989, Human Machine Interactive Systems, 1991; co-editor: Data Structures, Pattern Recognition and Computer Graphics, 1977 Structured Computer Vision, 1980; contbr. chpts. to books. Fulbright fellow India, 1990. Fellow IEEE (Disting vis. 1975-76, 88-90). Office: UCLA Computer Sci Dept 3531-H Boelter Hall Los Angeles CA 90095-1596

KLINGER, DONALD E., educator; b. San Francisco, Oct. 27, 1946; s. Evans N. K. and ruth Biebesheimer; m. Janette Kettmann, July 2, 1988; childrne: Chris Fanning, Amy, Heidi Warden, John. BA in Polit. Sci., U. Calif., 1968; MA in Govt., George Washington U., 1971; PhD in Pub. Adminstrn., U. So. Calif., 1974. Mgmt. intern, staffing scientist U.S. Office Personnel Mgmt. (U.S. Civil Svc. Commn.), Washington, 1968-73; asst. prof. Ind. U. Sch. Pub. & Environ. Affairs, Indpls., 1974-80; prof. pub. adminstrn. Fla. Internat. U. Coll. Urban & Pub. Affairs, Miami, 1980—; cons. in field. Author: La Administracisn de Personal en el Sector Pzblico: Contextos y Estrategias, 1998, Workplace Drug Abuse and AIDS, 1991; co-author: (with John Nalbandian) Public Personnel Management: Contexts and Strategies, 4th edit., 1998. Fulbright scholar, 1994. Mem. Am. Soc. Pub. Adminstrn., Am. Rev. pub. Adminstrn., Internat. Personnel Mgmt. Assn., Phi Beta Kappa. Avocations: music, backpacking, cooking. Office: Fla Inernat U Bldg AC 3000 NE 151st St North Miami FL 33181-3600

KLINGER, DOUGLAS EVAN, money management executive; b. Phila., Dec. 22, 1964; s. Norman Ashton and Sondra Ann Klinger; m. Jennifer Ann Dobrota, Apr. 11, 1992. BA in Econs. and Finance, Trinity Coll., Hartford, Conn., 1986. Mem. instnl. brokerage Kidder Peabody and Co. Inc., Hartford, 1984-86; credit analyst Provident Nat. Bank, Phila., 1986-87, relationship mgr. PNC Fin. Corp., 1987-88; dir. corp. markets PNC Instnl. Mgmt. Corp., Wilmington, Del., 1988-90; v.p., dir. corp. markets mgmt. Provident Instnl. Mgmt. Corp., Lehman/Provident IFG, Wilmington, Del., 1990-92; mng. dir. PNC Bank Investment Mgmt. & Rsch., Phila., 1993-98; dir. mktg. PNC Funds, Phila., 1993-98; pres. Cigna Health Svcs., Bloomfield, Conn., 1998—. Mentor Free Enterprise Fellowships Program. Mem. Trinity Club Phila., Skytop Club, St. A Club of Phila., Pa. Horticultural Soc., U.S. Treasury Mgmt. Assn. Avocations: sailing, fishing, skiing, gardening, reading. Home: 2 Grant Estate Rd West Simsbury CT 06092-2100 Office: Cigna Corp 900 Cottage Grove Rd Bloomfield CT 06002*

KLINGER, MARILYN SYDNEY, lawyer; b. N.Y.C., Aug. 14, 1953; d. Victor and Lillyan Judith (Hollinger) K. BS, U. Santa Clara, 1975; JD, U. Calif., Hastings, 1978. Bar: Calif. 1978. Assoc. Chickering & Gregory, San Francisco, 1978-81, Steefel, Levitt & Weiss, San Francisco, 1981-82, Sedgwick, Detert, Moran & Arnold, San Francisco and L.A., 1982-87; ptnr. Sedgwick, Detert, Moran & Arnold, San Francisco, 1988-98, L.A., 1998—; guest lectr. Stanford U. Sch. Engring. Vol. atty. Lawyers Commn. on Urban Affairs, San Francisco, 1978-80. Mem. ABA (tort and ins. practice sect., surety and fidelity com., constrn. forum, pub. contracts sect.), Internat. Assn. Def. Counsel (chmn. fidelity and surety com. 1996-98), Nat. Assn. Bond Claims, Surety Claims Inst. (spkr.), No. Calif. Surety Underwriters Assn., No. Calif. Surety Claims Assn. (lectr., pres. 1989-90), Surety Assn. L.A. (spkr.). Avocations: reading, hiking, golf. Home: 939 15th St #10 Santa Monica CA 90403 Office: Sedgwick Detert Moran & Arnold 801 S Figueroa St 18th Fl Los Angeles CA 90017-3716

KLINGERMAN, KAREN NINA, elementary school educator, teacher consultant, course coordinator; b. Rahway, N.J., Sept. 12, 1952; d. Nelson Randolph and Alma Margaret (Magnani) Terry; m. William Robert Klingerman, May 25, 1975; children: Bryan William, Brad Nelson. BS in Secondary Edn., Bloomsburg (Pa.) U., 1974; MEd, Trenton State Coll., 1977; Elem. Edn. Cert., Holy Family Coll., Phila., 1992. Cert. secondary edn. educator, elem. edn. educator, Pa. Tchr. Bensalem (Pa.) Sch. Dist., 1974—; tchr. cons., course coord. Pa. Writing Project West Chester (Pa.) U., 1988—. Contbr. articles to Pa. Writing Project Newsletter. Educators adv. bd. Mercer Mus./Bucks County Hist. Soc., Doylestown, Pa., 1993—. Recipient Bucks County IU # 22 grant, 1986, Award for Innovative Teaching, Pa. State Educators Assn., 1988. Fellow Pa. Writing Project; mem. NEA, Nat. Coun. Tchrs. English, Pa. State Edn. Assn. Avocations: colonial crafts, antiques, downhill skiing, sports spectator, summers at Jersey shore. Home: 49 Sharon Dr Richboro PA 18954-1049 Office: Bensalem Sch Dist 3000 Donallen Dr Bensalem PA 19020-1829

KLINGERMAN, ROBERT HARVEY, manufacturing company executive; b. Freeland, Pa., Nov. 10, 1939; s. Thomas Van and Emma Yeager (Hoffman) K.; m. Eleanor Jean Deemer, Aug. 31, 1963; children: Jeffrey Allen, Timothy Scott. BS in Chem. Engring., Lehigh U., 1961. Sr. applications engr. Elliott Co. div. Carrier Corp., Jeannette, Pa., 1961-66; project mgr. Stokes div. Pennwalt Corp., Phila., 1966-70, Cragmet Corp., Rancocas, N.J., 1970-74; v.p. engring. Cheston Co. (now Consarc Corp.), Rancocas, 1974-78; dir. ops. Inducto Heat, Madison Heights, Mich., 1978-82; pres. W.J. Savage Co., Knoxville, Tenn., 1982—, also bd. dirs.; bd. dirs. Metl-Saw, Inc., Benecia, Calif. Patentee in field. Mem. Abrasive Engring. Soc., Am. Soc. Metals, Nat. Machine Tool Bldrs., Soc. Mfg. Engrs. Republican. Methodist. Avocations: little theater, gourmet cooking. Home: 700 Chateaugay Rd Knoxville TN 37923-2014 also: WJ Savage Co 1 Hopkins St Knoxville TN 37921

KLINGHOFFER, DAVID, journalist; b. Santa Monica, Calif., Oct. 31, 1965; s. Paul and Carol (Bernstein) Kaye. AB magna cum laude, Brown U., 1987. Film and TV critic Washington Times, 1990-92; editl. asst. Nat. Rev., N.Y.C., 1987, asst. book editor, 1987-89, lit. editor, 1992-98, sr. editor, 1998—. Jewish. Office: Nat Review 215 Lexington Ave New York NY 10016-6023*

KLINGHOFFER, JUNE FLORENCE, physician, educator; b. Phila., Feb. 12, 1921; d. Harry and Esther (Uram) K.; m. Sidney U. Wenger, June 24, 1947; 1 child, Robert Klinghoffer Wenger. BA, U. Pa., 1941; MD, Woman's Med. Coll. Pa., Phila., 1945. Diplomate Am. Bd. Internal Medicine, Am. Bd. Rheumatology. Intern , then resident Albert Einstein Med. Ctr., Phila., 1945-47; fellow in pathology Woman's Med. Coll. Pa., 1947-48; prof. medicine Med. Coll. Pa., Phila., 1969—, Ethel Russell Morris prof. medicine, 1987—. Contbr. articles to med. jours. Recipient Lindback award for disting. teaching, 1965, Alumnae Achievement award Med. Coll. Pa., 1978. Fellow ACP, Phila. Coll. Physicians; mem. AMA, AAUP, Am. Med. Women's Assn., Assn. Am. Med. Colls., Am. Coll. Rheumatology, Alpha Omega Alpha. Home: 356 Meadow Ln Merion Station PA 19066-1331 Office: Med Coll Pa 3300 Henry Ave Philadelphia PA 19129-1191

KLINGLE, PHILIP ANTHONY, law librarian; b. Bklyn., July 24, 1950; s. Lorin Russell and Therese Margaret (Meehan) K.; m. Rachelle Phyllis Miller, Nov. 20, 1977; children: David Adam, Michael Matthew, Anne Elizabeth. BA, Fordham U., 1971; MA, NYU, 1973; MS, Columbia U., 1976. Asst. reference libr. N.Y. Hist. Soc., N.Y.C., 1973-77; libr. Bklyn. Pub. Libr., 1977-78; reference libr., asst. prof. John Jay Coll. Criminal Justice CUNY, 1978-81; libr. Inst. Jud. Adminstrn. Sch. of Law NYU, 1981-82; sr. law libr. ct. libr. N.Y. State Supreme Ct., S.I., 1982—. Editor: jour. The Literature of Criminal Justice, 1980-81, IJA Report, 1981-82. Mem. ALA, Am. Assn. Law Librs., Law Libr. Assn. Greater N.Y., Libr. Assn. CUNY (mem. exec. coun. 1978-81). Office: NY State Supreme Ct Libr Richmond County Courthouse Staten Island NY 10301

KLINGMAN, JOHN PHILIP, architect, educator; b. Phila., July 31, 1947; s. John Philip and Ethel Iva (Serfas) K. BSCE, Tufts U., 1969; postgrad., Stanford U., 1969-70; MArch, U. Oreg., 1983. Registered architect, La. Constrn. coord., project mgr. Payette Assocs., Inc., Boston, 1972-81; mem. design team Fairchild Biochemistry Bldg. Harvard U., 1977-88; project architect LaBouisse & Waggonner Inc. Architects, New Orleans, 1986-89; cons. architect Waggonner & Ball, Inc. Architects, New Orleans, 1990-96; design, planning and preservation U.S. Customhouse, New Orleans, 1996—; asst. prof. Sch. Architecture Tulane U., New Orleans, 1983-90, assoc. prof., 1990-96, prof., 1996—, assoc. dean, 1991-93; mem. archtl. rev. com. Historic Dists. Landmarks Commn., 1995—. Co-editor: Talk About Architecture: A Century of Architectural Education at Tulane, 1993. Recipient GSA Honor award for customhouse projects, 1996. Avocation: wood sculpture. Home: 1309 Harmony St New Orleans LA 70115-3424 Office: Tulane U Sch Architecture New Orleans LA 70118

KLINGSBERG, DAVID, lawyer; b. N.Y.C., Feb. 4, 1934; m. Fran Sue Morganstern, Aug. 16, 1959; 3 children. LL.B., Yale U., 1957; B.S., NYU, 1954. Bar: N.Y. 1958. Law clk. to U.S. Dist. Judge, N.Y., 1957-58; atty. U.S. Dept. Justice, Office Dep. Atty. Gen., Washington, 1958-59; asst. U.S. atty. criminal div. So. Dist. N.Y., 1959-61; chief appellate atty. U.S. Atty. Office, N.Y., 1961-62; assoc. Kaye, Scholer, Fierman, Hays and Handler, N.Y.C., 1962-65; ptnr., chmn. exec. com. Kaye, Scholer, Fierman, Hays and Handler, 1966—. Contbr. articles to legal jours.; mem. editorial bd. Yale Law Jour, 1956-57. Fellow Am. Coll. Trial Lawyers, Am. Bar Found.; mem. ABA, Assn. Bar City N.Y. (chmn. anti-trust and trade regulation com. 1986-89, mem. com. on diversity in legal profession 1998—, Thurgood Marshall award for representation in death sentence cases 1998), N.Y. State Bar Assn., Fed. Bar Coun., Def. Rsch. Inst. Office: Kaye Scholer Fierman Hays & Handler LLP 425 Park Ave New York NY 10022-3506

KLINK, FREDRIC J., lawyer; b. N.Y.C., Oct. 4, 1933; s. Frederick Carl and Sophia Adelaide (Wolf) K.; m. Sandra Scott, 1979; children: Christopher, Charles; stepchildren: Kirsten Morehouse, Trina Morehouse. A.B., Columbia U., 1955, LL.B., 1960. Bar: N.Y. 1960. Practiced in N.Y.C.; ptnr. firm Dechert, Price & Rhoads, 1989—. Editor: Columbia U. Law Rev, 1959-60. Served as lt. (j.g.) USNR, 1955-57. Mem. Am. Law Inst., Am., Internat., N.Y. C. bar assns. Home: Wilson Point 11 Hilltop Rd Norwalk CT 06854-5001 Office: Dechert Price & Rhoads 30 Rockefeller Plz Fl 22 New York NY 10112-2200*

KLINK, KARIN ELIZABETH, medical communications company executive, writer; b. Nov. 12, 1937; d. Nils Gustaf and Mary Josephine (Crowley) Hernblad; m. Fredric J. Klink, Nov. 28, 1958 (div. Apr., 1979); children: Christopher Frederick, Charles Gustaf. BA in Geology, Barnard Coll., 1958; MFA in Film Making, Columbia U., 1963; MS in Counseling and Art Therapy, U. Bridgeport, 1977. grad. cert. in corp. video Fairfield U., 1983. Film editor, writer Eye Gate House, N.Y.C., 1966-68; sr. editor Starting Tomorrow, N.Y.C., 1968-70; dir. creative therapies Hall-Brooke Hosp., Westport, Conn., 1978-83; mgr. editorial devel. New Eng. Advt. Assn., Norwalk, Conn., 1984-85; editorial dir. Logical Communications, Norwalk, 1985; pres. Creative Word & Image, Rowayton, Conn., 1985—; freelance med. writer, editor for various cos., 1984—. Artist; author films, filmstrips and videotapes; designer, animator The Stage Evolves, 1964; writer, photographer slide tapes, 1985. Sec., bd. dirs. aerial photographer Preserve the Wetlands, Rowayton, 1983-91; bd. dirs. Inst. Visual Artists, Silvermine Guild, New Canaan, Conn., 1984—. Mem. Am. Med. Writers Assn. (sec./treas. bd. dirs. N.Y. chpt. 1989-90, treas., 1990-93, del. to nat. meetings 1990-97, recipient disting. svc. award 1992, pres.-elect 1993-94, pres. 1994-95, exec. com., adminstr. pub. rels. 1995-96, adminstr. chpts. 1996-97, Fellow award 1996), Am. Art Therapy Assn. (profl.), Silvermine Guild Artists (artist mem., various awards), So. Conn. Art Therapy Assn. (art therapist, pres. 1982-83). Democrat. Episcopalian. Avocations: drawing, painting aerial photography, sailing, painted Easter egg in White House collection at Smithsonian Inst. Home and Office: 13 Sammis St Norwalk CT 06853-1514

KLINK, ROBERT MICHAEL, consulting engineer, management consultant, financial consultant, property developer; b. Hamilton, Ind., Sept. 5, 1939; s. Robert Eli and Marie Ann Klink; m. Jessie Joyce Plummer, Sept. 10, 1960 (dec. Feb. 1966); children: Kevin Mark, Kent Michael, Kelly Martin, Kris Montgomery, Jeffrey Arthur. Student, Tri State Coll., Angola, Ind., 1957; degree in Hwy. Engring., Purdue U., 1959; cert. in grad. sch. mgmt., Harvard U., 1976. Cert. behavioral cons. Hwy. engr. Ind. State Hwy. Commn., Ft. Wayne, 1959-65; staff engr. Cities Svc. Oil Co., Inc., South Bend, Ind., 1965-66; client svcs. mgr., asst. to v.p. Clyde E. Williams & Assocs., South Bend, 1966-72; pres. Alpha Devel. Corp., South Bend, 1970-72; sr. v.p., CFO Snell Environ. Group, Inc., Lansing, Mich., 1972-77; pres. Klink Devel. Co., Dayton, Ohio, 1972-91; pres., chmn. Solar GeoThermo Energy Systems, Inc., Dayton, 1982—; pres., mng. ptnr. Klink Enterprises Co., Dayton, 1977—; pres., chmn. bd. Design Enterprise, Ltd., Dayton, 1977-91; chmn., pres. Cons. Info. Agy., Chattanooga, 1991—; bd. dirs. Pono Kai Resort, Kapaa, Kauai, Hawaii, Imperial Hawaii, Honolulu; cons. World Bank/USAID, Dacca, Bangladesh, Country of Brazil, Rio de Janeiro; cons. engr., mgmt. cons., project developer, cons. to govtl. agys. and Fortune 500 cos.; lectr., spkr. in field. Patentee Solar and Geo Thermo Energy System; co-author: Water Handling Handbook, 1977. Trustee Centerville (Ohio) Cmty. Ch., 1982-88, Okemos (Mich.) Cmty. Ch., 1972-77; mem. The Presdl. Roundtable, Washington, 1989—, Rep. Senatorial Inner Circle, Washington, 1985—, Nat. Rep. Congrl. Com., 1986—, The Presidents Assn.; tchr. Woodland Park Bapt. Ch., Chattanooga. Recipient Outstanding Citizen award Am. Legion, Butler, Ind., 1953, Resolution of Appreciation Centerville City Coun., 1978, Resolution of Appreciation Greene County, 1989; named Hon. Citizen of Tenn., Nashville, 1989. Mem. Am. Water Works Assn. (life), Nat. Water Pollution Control Fedn., Profl. Svcs. Mgmt. Assn. (com. chair), Soc. for Mktg. Profl. Svcs. (com. chair), Ind. Hoosier Assocs., Ohio Early Birds. Christian and Missionary Alliance. Avocations: gardening, landscaping, woodworking, classic automobiles, golf.

KLINK, RON, congressman, reporter, newscaster; b. 1951; m. Linda Hogan; children: Matthew, Juliana. Broadcast newsman ctrl., southwest Pa., W.V., Ohio; TV news reporter, anchorman KDKA-TV, Pitts., 1978-92; ptnr. Dagwood's, Pitts.; mem. 103rd-106th Congress from 4th Pa. dist., Washington, D.C., 1993—. Vol. local fire dept.; bd. dirs. Vocat. Tech. High Sch.; active com. on commerce, subcom. on telecom., trade and consumer protection, and energy and power, and oversight and investigations. Democrat.

Mem. United Ch. of Christ. Office: US Ho of Reps 2448 Rayburn Washington DC 20515-3804

KLINKENBERG, HILKA ELISABETH, etiquette/protocol expert, author, speaker; b. Bremen, Fed. Republic Germany, July 20, 1946; came to U.S., 1976; d. Lorenz and Agatha Margarete (Bohlen) K. BA, U. Toronto, Ont., Can., 1968. Mng. dir. Etiquette Internat., N.Y.C., 1989—; media spokesperson Am. Express Gift Checks. Author: At Ease...Professionally, 1992; contbr. monthly columns to Agenda New York Mag., Horsesmouth.com. Vol. Vol. Svcs. for Children, N.Y.C., 1979-83, Helpline Telephone Crisis Counseling, N.Y.C., 1984-86; fund raising com. mem. Westchester Assn. for Retarded Citizens, White Plains, N.Y., 1991; fashion show coord. Guild for the Blind, N.Y.C., 1990. Mem. ASTD, NAFE, Americas Soc., The Global Bus. Assn., Nat. Spkrs. Assn., Women in Comm., Mid-Atlantic Club N.Y.C., The Univ. Club. Avocations: painting, skiing, cycling, gardening, golf. Office: Etiquette Internat 254 E 68th St New York NY 10021-6012

KLINKER, SHEILA ANN J., state legislator, middle school educator; m. Victor Klinker; children: Kerri, Kevin, Kelly. BS in Edn., Purdue U., MS in Elem. Edn., MS in Adminstrn. and Supervision. Outreach liaison Purdue U. Sch. Edn., 1982—; state rep. Ind. Ho. of Reps., Indpls., 1982—. Mem. St. Mary's Cathedral Parish; 1st woman appointee Tippecanoe Area Plan Commn.; bd. dirs. Lafayette Symphony, Opera de Lafayette, Tippecanoe County Chid Care, Purdue Musical Orgn.; past chairwoman pub. svc. divsn. United Way. Recipient Outstanding Svc. award Ind. Advocates for Children, Legis. award Assn. of BPW's Outstanding Woman in Politics, Woman of Distinction award Sycamore Girl Scout Coun., Salute to Women in Politics award, Outstanding Svc. for Pub. Interest award Ind. Optometric Assn., Pres.'s Spl. Svc. award Ind. Soc. Profl. Land Surveyors, Spl. Recognition award Ind. Chpt. NASW, Legis. Efforts Recognition award Ind. Residential Facilities Assn., Ind. Assn. for Counseling and Devel., Tippecanoe Arts Fedn. award, Purdue U. Musical Orgn. Alumni award, Marriage and Family Therapists Svc. award, 1998, Social Workers Svc. award, 1998, Ind. Assn. for Gifted Leadership award, 1998. Mem. Bus. and Profl. Women's Assn., Lafayette C. of C. (edn. com.), Delta Kappa Gamma, Phi Delta Kappa, Kappa Alpha Theta (mem. adv. bd.). Democrat. Home: 633 Kossuth St Lafayette IN 47905-1444 Office: Ind Ho of Reps State House Third Fl Indianapolis IN 46204*

KLINMAN, JUDITH POLLOCK, biochemist, educator; b. Phila., Apr. 17, 1941; d. Edward and Sylvia (Fitterman) Pollock; m. Norman R. Klinman, July 3, 1963 (div. 1978); children: Andrew, Douglas. BA, U. Pa., 1962; PhD, 1966. Postdoct. fellow Weizmann Inst. Sci., Rehovoth, Israel, 1966-67; postdoct. assoc. Inst. Cancer Rsch., Phila., 1968-70; rsch. assoc., 1970-72, asst. mem., 1972-77, assoc. mem., 1977-78; asst. prof. biophysics U. Pa., Phila., 1974-78; assoc. profl. chemistry U. Calif., Berkeley, 1978-82; prof., 1982—; mem. ad hoc biochemistry and phys. biochemistry study sects. NIH, 1977-84, phys. biochemistry study sect., 1984-88. Mem. editl. bd. Jour. Biol. Chemistry, 1979-84, Biofactors, 1991-98, European Jour. Biochemistry, 1991-95, Biochemistry, 1993—, Ann. Rev. of Biochemistry, 1996—; contbr. articles to profl. jours. Fellow NSF, 1964, NIH, 1964-66, Guggenheim fellow, 1988-89. Mem. Am. Chmn. Soc. (exec. coun. biol. dvisn. 1982-85, chmn. nominating com. 1987-88, program chair 1991-92, Repligen award 1994), NAS, Am. Acad. Arts and Scis., Am. Soc. Biochemistry and Molecular Biology (membership com. 1984-86, pub. affairs com. 1987-94, program com. 1995, pres.-elect 1997, pres. 1998), Sigma Xi. Office: U Calif Dept Chemistry Berkeley CA 94720

KLINMAN, NORMAN RALPH, immunologist, medical educator; b. Phila., Mar. 23, 1937; s. William and Miriam (Ralph) K.; m. Linda A. Sherman, June 18, 1978; children—Andrew, Douglas, Theodore, Matthew. A.B., Haverford (Pa.) Coll., 1958; M.D., Jefferson Med. Coll., Phila., 1962; Ph.D. (Helen Hay Whitney Found. research fellow 1963-66), U. Pa., 1965. Fellow in immunology U. Pa. Med. Sch., 1962-66, Weizman Inst., Tel Aviv, 1966-67, Nat. Inst. Med. Research, London, 1967-68; mem. faculty U. Pa. Med. Sch., 1968-78, prof. pathology, 1975-78; prof. dept. immunology The Scripps Rsch. Inst., La Jolla, Calif., 1978—; adj. prof. U. Calif., San Diego; cons. NIH, 1975-78; mem. sci. adv. bd. Hybritech, 1981-86, Baxter, 1985—; mem. NIH Aging Rev. Com., 1982-85, I UIS Nomenclature Com., 1983-87; mem. fellowship screening com. ACS, Calif. div., 1983-85. Author articles in field, chpts. in books; assoc. editor: Immunochemistry, 1970-74, Jour. Immunology, 1972-76, Developmental and Comparative Immunology, 1982-86, Jour. Molecular and Cellular Immunology, 1983—, Internat. Revs. of Immunology, 1984—, Jour. Exptl. Zoology, 1985-87, Aging: Immunological and Infectious Diseases, 1987-95; adv. editor: Jour. Exptl. Medicine; editor: B Lymphocytes in the Immune Response. Am. Cancer Soc. research scholar, 1966-68; recipient USPHS Career Devel. award, 1970-75, Parke-Davis award, 1976, NIH Merit award 1987. Mem. Am. Assn. Immunologists, Am. Assn. Exptl. Pathologists, Gerontology Soc. Am., Internat. Soc. Developmental and Comparative Immunology. Home: 7766 Hillside Dr La Jolla CA 92037-3944 Office: 10666 N Torrey Pines Rd La Jolla CA 92037-1027

KLINT, RONALD VERNON, math educator, financial consultant; b. Chgo., Feb. 11, 1939; s. Charles W. and Claire P. (Buente) K.; m. Carol L. Rodningen, Oct. 13, 1984; children: Matthew, Andrew. AA, Glendale (Calif.) C.C., 1958; BA, UCLA, 1960; MA, Calif. State U., L.A., 1964. Cert. tchr. and admin., Calif. Math instr. Glendale Schs., 1961—; pres. Prof. Edn. of Glendale (Calif.), 1967-70; mentor tchr. Glendale Schs., 1988-94. Vol. Glendale Rep. Party, various time. Mem. Foothill Math. Coun., Calif. Math Coun. Avocations: gardening, photography. Home: 4400 Ramsdell Ave La Crescenta CA 91214-3461

KLIPHARDT, RAYMOND A., engineering educator; b. Chgo., Mar. 18, 1917; s. Adolph Lewis and Hortense Marietta (Brandt) K.; m. Rhoda Joan Anderson, May 5, 1945; children: Janis Kliphardt Emery, Judith Kliphardt Ecklund, Jill Kliphardt White, Joan Kliphardt Quinn, Jennifer Kliphardt Miller. B.S., Ill. Inst. Tech., Chgo., 1938, M.S., 1948. Instr. North Park Coll., Chgo., 1938-43; asst. prof. Northwestern U., Evanston, Ill., 1945-51, assoc. prof., 1952-63, prof. engrng. scis., 1964-87, prof. emeritus, 1987—, dir. U. Khartoum project, 1964-68, dir. focus program, 1975-78, chmn. engrng. scis. and applied maths. dept., 1978-87; cons. applied maths. div. Argonne Nat. Lab., Lemont, Ill., 1962-63; cons. on patent litigation Kirkland and Ellis, Chgo., 1976-77. Author: Analytical Graphics, 1957; Program Design in Fortran IV, 1970. Mem. bd. edn. Morton Grove, Ill., 1952-55, Niles Twp., Ill., 1957-58. Served as ensign USNR, 1943-45. Recipient Western Electric Fund award for excellence in instrn. of engrng. students, Am. Soc. Engring. Edn., 1967. Office: Northwestern U Technol Inst Evanston IL 60208

KLIPPING, ROBERT SAMUEL, geophysicist; b. Glaston, N.D., Dec. 5, 1928; s. Roy Samuel and Marie (Peterson) K.; m. Gayle Cleone Swanson, Sept. 29, 1951; children: Barbara, Sharon, Joan. BS in Geology, Colo. Coll., Colorado Springs, 1953. Geophys. computer scientist Gen. Geophys. Co., Denver, 1953-57; geophys. supr. Mandrel Indsl. Inc., Denver, 1957-65, area mgr., 1965-69; geophys. Pennzoil Co., Denver, 1969-72, exploration mgr., 1972-78; geophys. cons., owner Klipping & Assocs., Denver, 1978—. Author: American Association of Petroleum Geologists, 1976, Montana Geological Society, 1978. Staff sgt. U.S. Army, 1946-48. Mem. Am. Assn. Petroleum Geologists, Soc. Exploration Geophysicists, Denver Geophys. Soc. (treas. 1972-73, sec. 1973-74). Republican. Methodist. Avocations: woodworking, antique cars, golf, fishing. Home: 14645 Sterling Rd Colorado Springs CO 80921-2618 Office: Klipping & Assocs 518 17th St Denver CO 80202-4130

KLIPPSTATTER, KURT L., conductor, music director; b. Graz, Austria, Dec. 17, 1934; s. Karl and Karoline K.; m. Mignon Dunn, July 24, 1972. Guest faculty mem. Memphis State U., 1973-76; dir. orchestral activities HARTT Sch. Music, Hartford, Conn., 1977-90; dir. Ill. Opera Theatre, U. Ill., Urbana, 1990—; faculty Israel Vocal Arts Inst. Tel Aviv & Internat. Inst. Vocal Art, Chiari, Italy, 1982—. Condr., music coach numerous theatres, orchs., Austria, West Germany, U.S., Mex., France, Poland, 1954—; artistic dir., Memphis Opera Theatre, 1972-76, music dir., Ark. Symphony, Little Rock, 1973-80, Greater Trenton Symphony, 1984-91; Music columnist: Ark. Democrat, 1979-80. Mem. Opera Am., Condrs. Guild.

KLIPSTEIN, ROBERT ALAN, lawyer; b. N.Y.C., Sept. 23, 1936; s. Harold David and Hyacinth (Levin) K. AB, Columbia U., 1957, JD, 1960; LLM in Taxation, NYU, 1965. Bar: N.Y. 1960, U.S. Supreme Ct. 1964. Practice law, N.Y.C., 1961—; assoc. Saxe Bacon & O'Shea, 1961, Rosenman, Colin, Kaye, Petschek & Freund, 1962-63; law sec. to justice N.Y. County Supreme Ct., 1963-64; assoc. Bernays & Eisner, 1965-70; ptnr. Eisner, Klipstein & Klipstein, 1971-77; ptnr. Danziger, Bangser, Klipstein, Goldsmith, Greenwald & Weiss (name now Bangser Klein Rocca & Blum), 1977-92; counsel Sullivan & Donovan, 1992—; arbitrator City of N.Y. Small Claims Ct., 1971—. Served with U.S. Army, 1960-62. Mem. ABA, N.Y. State Bar Assn., Assn. Bar City of N.Y., N.Y. County Lawyers Assn., Am. Immigration Lawyers Assn., Westchester County Bar Assn., Am. Judges Assn., Phi Alpha Delta. Club: Univ. Glee (N.Y.C.). Home: 401 E 74th St Apt 6G New York NY 10021-3931 Office: Sullivan & Donovan LLP 415 Madison Ave New York NY 10017-1111

KLIR, GEORGE JIRI, systems science educator; b. Prague, Czechoslovakia, Apr. 22, 1932; came to U.S., 1966, naturalized, 1972; s. Jan and Emilie (Přitasilová) K.; m. Milena Řeholová, Jan. 26, 1962; children: Jane, John. MEEE, Czech Tech. U., Prague, 1957; PhD, Czechoslovak Acad. Scis., Prague, 1964; D (hon.), Prague U. Econs., Prague, 1994, Tech. U. in Brno, Moravia, 1997, Czech Tech. U., Prague, 1998. Rsch. fellow Inst. Computer Research, Prague, 1960-64; lectr. U. Baghdad, Iraq, 1964-66, UCLA, 1966-68; assoc. prof. Fairleigh Dickinson U., 1968-69; assoc. prof. Sch. Advanced Tech., SUNY, Binghamton, 1969-72, prof. systems sci., 1972—, disting. prof. T.J. Watson Sch., 1984—, chmn. dept. systems sci., 1977-94; dir. Internat. Conf. Applied Gen. Systems Rsch., 1977, Ctr. for Intelligent Systems, T.J. Watson Sch., 1995—. Author: Cybernetic Modelling, 1967, An Approach to General Systems Theory, 1969, Methodology of Switching Circuits, 1972, Architecture of Systems Problem Solving, 1985, Fuzzy Sets, Uncertainty, and Information, 1988, Facets of Systems Science, 1991, Fuzzy Measure Theory, 1992, Fuzzy Sets and Fuzzy Logic, 1995, Uncertainty-Based Information, 1998; author, co-author or editor other books; editor-in-chief: Book Series on Basic and Applied General Systems Research, 1978-82, Book Series on Frontiers in System Science: Implications for the Social Sciences, 1978-84, International Jour. Gen. Systems, 1974—, IFSR Book Series on Systems Science and Engineering, 1984—; mem. editl. bds. other profl. jours.; contbr. numerous articles to profl. jours. Recipient award for outstanding contbns. Austrian Soc. Cybernetics, 1976, award Netherland Soc. Systems Rsch., 1976, Bernard Bolzano gold medal in math. scis. Czech Acad. Scis., 1994, Lotfi A. Zadeh Best Paper award, 1994, Disting. Leadership award ISSS, 1994, SUNY award for excellence in rsch., 1996, award for highest achievement in scholarship Simon Bolivar U. in Caracas, 1997; IBM rsch. fellow, 1969, Netherlands Inst. Advanced Studies fellow, 1975-76, 82-83, Japan Soc. for Promotion of Sci. fellow, 1980. Fellow IEEE (life), Internat. Fuzzy Systems Assn(pres. 1993-95); mem. AAAS, Internat. Soc. Sys. Scis. (mng. dir., v.p. 1978-80, pres. 1980-81, disting. leadership award 1994), Internat. Fedn. Sys. Rsch. (pres. 1980-84), N.Am. Fuzzy Info. Procession Soc. (pres. 1988-91). Home: 401 Manchester Rd Vestal NY 13850-3606 Office: SUNY/Dept Sys Sci/Indsl Eng Thomas J Watson Sch Engring and Applied Sci Binghamton NY 13902-6000 *The main force behind my intellectual development has been my passion for discovery and integration in science and technology. The most precious values in professional life are for me scientific honesty and tolerance.*

KLITZING, KLAUS VON, research facility administrator, physicist; b. Schroda, June 28, 1943; s. Bogislav and Anny (Ulbrich) von K.; m. Renate Falkenberg, May 27, 1971; children: Andreas, Christine, Thomas. Diploma, Tech. U. Braunschweig, 1969; Ph.D., U. Wuerzburg, 1972; Habilitation, 1978. Faculty mem. Tech. U., Munich, 1980-84; dir. Max Planck Inst. für Festkörperforschung, Stuttgart, Fed. Republic Germany, 1985—. Recipient Nobel prize in physics Royal Swedish Acad. Sci., 1985. Office: Max Planck Inst Feskörperforschung, Heisenbergstr 1, D-70569 Stuttgart Germany

KLITZKE, THEODORE ELMER, former college dean, arts consultant; b. Chgo., Nov. 4, 1915; s. John Frederick and Edith (Bachmann) K.; m. Margaret Bridget Gaughan, Feb. 23, 1946; children: Annetta, Margaret. B.F.A., Chgo. Art Inst., 1940; B.A., U. Chgo., 1941, Ph.D., 1953; D.F.A. (hon.), Kansas City Art Inst., 1980, Md. Inst., Coll. Art, 1982. Instr. art history U. Chgo., 1946-47; edn. adviser U.S. Armed Forces in Germany, Nurnberg, 1948-51; asst. prof. art history N.Y. State Coll. Ceramics, SUNY, Alfred, 1953-59; prof. art history, chmn. dept. U. Ala., 1959-68; v.p. acad. affairs, dean Md. Inst., Coll. Art, 1968-82, pres., 1977-78; pres. Balt. News Network, 1989-97; mem. accessions com. Balt. Mus. Art, 1979-82. Author: Melville Price Retrospective, 1970; contbg. author: Festschrift Ulrich Middeldorf, 1968, Lothar Strauch: 1907-91, Plastik und Graphik, 1993; contbr. articles to profl. jours. Bd. dirs. Ala. chpt. ACLU, 1965-68; bd. dirs. S.W. Ala. Self-Help Housing, 1966-68. Served with AUS, 1942-46. Recipient First Annual Peace and Freedom award Democratic Student Orgn., U. Ala., 1968; citation Civil Liberties Union Ala. Mem. AAUP, Southeastern Coll. Art Conf. (pres. 1961-62), Coll. Art Assn., Nat. Assn. Schs. Art (dir. 1971-74, mem. commn. on accreditation 1975-78, treas. 1980-82, fellow 1981), Print and Drawing Soc. of Balt. Mus. Art (pres. 1974-76), Union Ind. Colls. Art (chmn. planning com. 1977-80), Am. Studies Assn., Coll. Art Assn. Am., Johns Hopkins Club (Balt.). Home: 7918 Sherwood Ave Baltimore MD 21204-3600

KLITZMAN, BRUCE, physiologist, plastic surgery educator, researcher; b. Dayton, Ohio, Nov. 4, 1951; m. Hardee Burt Brown; children: Rachel Hardee, Page Hardee. BS in Biomed. Engring. cum laude, Duke U., 1974; PhD, U. Va., 1979. Rsch. assoc. physiology U. Ariz. Coll. Medicine, Tucson, 1979-81; asst. prof. physiology, biophysics La. State U. Sch. Medicine, Shreveport, 1981-85; assoc. prof., 1985; dir. plastic surgery rsch. labs., asst. rsch. prof. surgery, assoc. prof. cell biology and biochem. engring. Duke U. Med. Ctr., Durham, N.C., 1985—; adj. prof. biomed. engring. La. Tech. U., Ruston, 1982-86; session chmn. Third, Fourth and Fifth World Congresses for Microcirculation, 1984, 87, 91; speaker, lectr. various symposia and seminars. Contbr. articles to profl. jours., chpts. to books; assoc. editor Jour. Reconstructive Microsurgery; editl. bd. Cell Transplantation, Am. Jour. Physiology, Jour. Reconstructive Microsurgery, Microvascular Rsch., Microcirculation. Recipient Instl. Nat. Rsch. Svc. award NIH, 1974-81, Machiko-Kuno Med. Student Rsch. award, U. N.C. at Chapel Hill, 1992, first prize investigator category, Plastic Surgery Ednl. Found., 1988; fellow U. Va., 1979, NATO, 1980; grantee Am. Heart Assn., 1982-85, NIH, 1985—. Mem. Am. Physiol. Soc., Am. Heart Assn. (circulation coun. 1984, grantee 1982-85, rsch. com. La. chpt. 1985), Am. Soc. Reconstructive Microsurgery (chmn. sci. session), Microcirculatory Soc. (sec. 1993-97, program com. 1983-84, mem. com. 1984-87, pres. 1998-99), Soc. Biomaterials, Plastic Surgery Rsch. Coun. (sci. adv. bd. 1998), European Soc. Microcirculation (travel award 1980), Internat. Soc. Oxygen Transport to Tissue. E-mail address: Klitz@duke.edu. Home: 3015 Wade Rd Durham NC 27705-5630 Office: Duke U Med Ctr Plastic Surgery Rsch Lab PO Box 3906 Durham NC 27710

KLITZMAN, ROBERT LLOYD, physician, author; b. N.Y.C., July 1, 1958; s. Joseph Arthur and Joan Marilyn (Kahn) K. AB, Princeton U., 1980; MD, Yale U., 1985. Diplomate Am. Bd. Psychiatry and Neurology. Rsch. asst. Nat. Inst. Health, Bethesda, Md., 1980-81; researcher Papua New Guinea Inst. Med. Rsch., 1980-81; intern The N.Y. Hosp. Cornell U. Med. Ctr., N.Y.C., 1985-86, resident, 1986-89; fellow Columbia Presbyn. Med. Ctr., N.Y.C., 1989-96, asst. prof. clin. psychiatry, 1996—; vis. scholar Russel Sage Found., 1999—. Author: A Year-long Night, 1989, In a House of Dreams and Glass, 1995, Being Positive: The Lives of Men and Women with HIV, 1997, The Trembling Mountain, 1998; contbr. articles to profl. jours., chpts. to books. Recipient Keese prize Yale U., 1985; Robert Wood Johnson Found. clin. scholar U. Pa., 1991-93, MacDowell Colony fellow, 1991, Dupont fellow, 1982, Burroughs-Wellcome fellow Am. Psychiat. Assn., 1987, Aaron Diamond Found. fellow, 1993-96, Merck Co. Found. fellow Corp. of Yaddo, 1994; Picker-Commonwealth scholar, 1996-98; NIMH Career Devel. awardee, 1996-99. Mem. PEN, Am. Psychiat. Assn. (mem. N.Y. County dist. br. com. on AIDS 1989—, commn. on AIDS 1988-89, steering com. of AIDS edn. project 1987-88).

KLOBASA, JOHN ANTHONY, lawyer; b. St. Louis, Feb. 15, 1951; s. Alan R. and Virginia (Yager) K.; m. Kathleen L. Davlan, June 15, 1979. BA in Econs., Emory U., 1972; JD, Wash. U., 1975. Bar: Mo. 1975, U.S. Dist. Ct. (ea. dist.) Mo. 1975, U.S. Ct. Appeals (8th cir.) 1976, U.S. Supreme Ct. 1979, U.S. Tax Ct. 1981, U.S. Ct. Appeals (9th cir.) 1990, U.S. Ct. Appeals (10th cir.) 1993. Assoc. Kohn, Shands, Elbert, Gianoulakis & Gilium, St. Louis, 1975-80; ptnr. Kohn, Shands, Elbert, Gianoulakis & Giljum, St. Louis, 1981—. Spl. counsel City of Town and Country, Mo., 1987; spl. counsel City of Des Peres, Mo., 1987, alderman, 1989-91. Mem. ABA, Mo. Bar Assn., Met. St. Louis Bar Assn., Order of Coif, Phi Beta Kappa. Republican. Office: Kohn Shands Elbert Gianoulakis & Giljum LLP 1 Mercantile Ctr Fl 24 Saint Louis MO 63101-1643*

KLOBE, TOM, art gallery director; b. Mpls., Nov. 26, 1940; s. Charles S. and Lorna (Effertz) K.; m. Delmarie Pauline Motta, June 21, 1975. BFA, U. Hawaii, 1964, MFA, 1968; postgrad., UCLA, 1972-73. Vol. peace corps Alang, Iran, 1964-66; tchr. Calif. State U., Fullerton, 1969-72, Santa Ana (Calif.) Coll., 1972-77, Orange Coast Coll., Costa Mesa, Calif., 1974-77, Golden West Coll., Huntington Beach, Calif., 1976-77; art gallery dir. U. Hawaii, Honolulu, 1977—; acting dir. Downey (Calif.) Mus. Art, 1976; cons. Judiciary History Mus., Honolulu, 1982-96, Maui (Hawaii) Arts and Cultural Ctr., 1984-94, curator Kāia Wai Ola: This Living Water, 1994; exhibit designer Inst. for Astronomy, Honolulu, 1983-86; exhibit design cons. Japanese Cultural Ctr. Hawaii, 1993—; juror Print Casebooks; project coord. Crossings '97, France, Hawaii. Recipient Best in Exhbn. Design award Print Casebooks, 1984, 86, 88, Vol. Svc. award City of Downey, 1977; Exhbn. grantee NEA, 1979—, State Found. Culture and the Arts, 1977—. Mem. Hawaii Mus. Assn., Nat. Assn. Mus. Exhbn. Roman Catholic. Office: U Hawaii Art Gallery 2535 The Mall Honolulu HI 96822-2233 *Personal philosophy: Nothing is impossible. Believe in yourself and in each other. Each of us has the ability to shape our destiny.*

KLOBERDANZ, TIMOTHY J., educator in social sciences, writer. MA, Colo. State U., 1974; PhD, Ind. U., 1986. Folklore archivist Ind. U., Bloomington, 1980-81; assoc. prof. anthropology N.D. State U., Fargo, 1987—; dept. chair anthropogy and sociology, N.D. State U., Fargo, 1990-93,. tjklober@plains.nodak.edu. Office: 310 28th Ave N Fargo ND 58102-1941

KLOBUCHAR, MYRNA NILAN, English educator; b. Saint Cloud, Minn., July 11, 1948; d. Martin and Myrna (Lehnan) N. BS, St. Cloud State U., 1970, MA, U. Minn., 1976, BS, U. Wis., 1979; PhD, U. Minn., 1992. Tchr. English, curriculum coord. K-12 Hopkins (Minn.) Pub. Schs., 1970—. Mem. Nat. Coun. Tchrs. English, Minn. Coun. Tchrs. English. Home: 10715 57th Ave N Plymouth MN 55442-1658

KLOCEK, MARK C., manufacturing specialist; b. Syracuse, N.Y., May 15, 1961; s. Stanley L. Sr. and Joyce M. (Clark) K.; divorced; children: Zachary C. Klocek, Stephen P. Pace. Set up man UTC Carrier Corp., Dewitt, N.Y., 1988—. With USCG., 1978-84. Mem. Sheet Metal Workers, Nat. Smokers Alliance. Avocations: auto body repair, environmental conservation, masonry, antique refinishing, carpentry.

KLOCK, JOHN HENRY, lawyer; b. Gouverneur, N.Y., Mar. 29, 1944; s. John F. and Patricia M. (Chateau) K.; m. Connie E. McLaughlin, May 31, 1969; children: Thomas, Jacqueline. BA, St. Bonaventure U., 1966; postgrad., U. Va., 1967; MA, NYU, 1970; JD, Rutgers U., 1976. Bar: N.J. 1976, U.S. Dist. Ct. N.J. 1976, N.Y. 1977, U.S. Ct. Appeals (3d cir.) 1979, U.S. Dist. Ct. (ea. dist.) N.Y. 1981, U.S. Supreme Ct. 1981, U.S. Dist. Ct. (so. dist.) N.Y. 1982, U.S. Dist. Ct. (no. dist.) N.Y. 1988; cert. civil trial atty. N.J. Law clk. to judge U.S. Dist. Ct. N.J., Newark, 1976-77; assoc. Gibbons, Del Deo, Dolan, Griffinger & Vecchione, Newark, 1977-83, ptnr., 1983—. Author: New Jersey Practice Court Rules (4th edit.), vol. 1, 1A, 2, 2A, 1992, New Jersey Practice Evidence Rules, vol. 2B, 2C, 2d edit., 1994, New Jersey Practice Trial Lawyers Manual, vol. 20, 1999; contbr. articles to profl. jours; patentee quick release automatic chaulk gun. Mem. U.S. Supreme Ct. Hist. Soc., Scotch Plains (N.J.) Hist. Soc., 1983, N.J. Hist. Soc., Plainfield Country Club. Mem. ABA, N.J. Bar Assn., N.Y. Bar Assn. Roman Catholic. Avocations: golf, gardening. Home: 1800 Lake Ave Scotch Plains NJ 07076-2920

KLOCK, JOSEPH PETER, JR., lawyer; b. Phila., Mar. 14, 1949; s. Joseph Peter and Mary Dorothy (Fornace) K.; m. Susan Marie Girsch, Mar. 17, 1979; children: Susan Elizabeth, Kathleen Marie, Robert Charles, Peter Joseph II. BA, LaSalle Coll., 1970; JD, U. Miami, Fla., 1973. Bar: Fla. 1973, Pa. 1973, D.C. 1978. Ptnr. Steel, Hector & Davis LLP, Miami, Fla., 1977-79; adminstrv. ptnr. Steel, Hector & Davis, Miami, 1978-82, chmn., mng. ptnr., 1983—; gen. counsel, chief legal officer Flo-Sun, Inc., 1991—; adj. prof. U. Miami Law Sch., 1974-84; bd. dirs. Nat. Beverage Corp., Premier Hotel Corp., Fla. Partnership for the Americas, FTAA Adminstrv. Secretariat, Inc., St. Thomas Human Rights Inst.; mem. Fed. Jud. Nominating Com. of Fla., 1993-97. Trustee Belen Jesuit Prep. Sch., Barry U. Collins Ctr., Miami Art Mus.; trustee Fundacion Mir, 1989-98; chmn. bd. trustees Carrollton Sch. Fellow Am. Bar Found.; mem. ABA (chmn. Caribbean law com. internat. law sect. 1991-92), Fla. Bar (chmn. civil procedure rules com. 1979-82), D.C. Bar, Dade County Bar Assn., Assn. Bar City of N.Y., Am. Law Inst., Am. Assn. Sovereign Mil. Order Malta, Iron Arrow Honor Soc., Westview Country Club, Sailfish Club Palm Beach, Govs. Club West Palm Beach, Miami City Club (pres. 1994-97), Phi Alpha Delta, Phi Kappa Phi, Omicron Delta Kappa. Democrat. Roman Catholic. Home: 5095 SW 82nd St Miami FL 33143-8503 Office: 200 S Biscayne Blvd Fl 41 Miami FL 33131-2310 also: Ste 316 340 Royal Poinciana Way Palm Beach FL 33480-4020

KLOCK, STEVEN WAYNE, engineering executive; b. Deadwood, S.D., Apr. 16, 1954; s. Earl Leroy and Irma Helena (Neamy) K.; m. Robin Ann Barney, June 25, 1982; children: Tana, Renee, Thomas, Stephanie. Cert., Denver Inst. Tech., 1974; BS, S.D. Sch. Mines and Tech., 1992; MBA, U. S.D., 1997. Test tech. Magnetic Peripherals Inc., Rapid City, S.D., 1974-76, group leader, 1976-81, test engring. tech., 1981-87; process engring. technician SCI Sys., Rapid City, 1987-92, quotes adminstr., 1992-97, test engring. technician, 1997-99, devel. engr., 1999—. Mem. S.D. Emergency Med. Technician Assn. Democrat. Avocations: computers, restoring early Mustangs. Office: SCI Systems 222 Disk Dr Rapid City SD 57701-7805

KLODOWSKI, HARRY FRANCIS, JR., lawyer; b. Pitts., June 18, 1954; s. Harry F. and Nancy (Coll) K.; m. Amy Martha Auslander, Nov. 12, 1983; children: Deborah, Daniel. BA, SUNY, Buffalo, 1976, JD, 1979. Bar: Pa. 1979, U.S. Dist. Ct. (we. dist.) Pa. 1979, U.S. Tax Ct. 1979, U.S. Ct. Appeals (3d cir.) 1979. Assoc., then ptnr. Berkman, Ruslander, Pohl, Lieber & Engel, Pitts., 1979-88; prin. Doepken, Keevican & Weiss, P.C., Pitts., 1988-93, Picadio McCall Kane & Norton, Pitts., 1993-94; pvt. practice, Pitts., 1994—. Assoc. editor Pitts. Legal Jour., 1979—; contbr. articles to profl. jours. Mem. ABA, Pa. Bar Assn., Allegheny County Bar Assn. (chmn. environ. law sect. 1997), Environ. Law Inst. (assoc.), Air and Waste Mgmt. Assn. (chmn. pub. info. com. 1996—), Rivers Club. Avocations: skiing, racquetball. Home: 615 Sandy Hill Rd Valencia PA 16059-2731 Office: 330 Grant St Ste 3321 Pittsburgh PA 15219-2202

KLODT, GERALD JOSEPH, office product development executive; b. Ottumwa, Iowa, Feb. 6, 1949; s. Edward William and Isabelle Margaret (Herrmann) K.; m. Menzi Louise Behrnd, May 26, 1979. BFA, U. Iowa, 1971, MA, 1972; MFA, U. Ill., 1974, U. Wis., 1979. Designer Tevcin, Inc., Perry, Iowa, 1972-75; assoc. designer William Stumpf & Assocs., Middleton, Wis., 1975-77; prof. design U. Wis., Madison, 1977-84; pres., chief exec. officer Klodt & Assocs., Madison, 1977—; engr. Fel-Pro Energy Inc., Lake Geneva, Wis., 1982-83; v.p. research and devel., product engring., product design, product packaging, product quality W.T. Rogers Co., div. Newell, Madison, 1984-91; dir. for product and graphic design Nordic Design Ltd. subs. of Nordic Group of Cos. Corp., Baraboo, Wis., 1994-95; cons. engr. Linton Assocs., Chesieres, Switzerland, 1984; project dir., engr. U.S. Dept. Energy, Madison, 1980-83; bd. dirs. XYTE Inc., v.p., 1999. Author: Earth Sheltered Housing, 1985; mech. and design patentee for office products, creator The Klodt Collection. Bd. dirs. Energy Idea Exchange, Madison, 1978-80; mem. Wis. State Resources Advisory Panel, 1978-80; leader, educator Am. Youth Found., Camp Miniwanca, Mich., 1977. Named Tchr Yr. dept. engrng. and applied sci. U. Wis., 1982. Mem. Kappa Sigma. Home: 7422 Longmeadow Rd Madison WI 53717-1067 Office: Klodt & Assocs 7422 Longmeadow Rd Madison WI 53717-1067

KLOEHN, RALPH ANTHONY, plastic surgeon; b. Milw., Dec. 18, 1932; s. Ralph Charles and Virginia Mary (Kosak) K.; m. Mary Theresa Landers, Nov. 4, 1961; Children: Colleen, Gregory, Kristine, Patricia, Timothy, Philip, Michelle. BS, Marquette U., 1954, MD, 1958. Diplomate Am. Bd. Plastic Surgery. Rotating intern Charity Hosp. La., New Orleans, 1958-59; gen. surgery resident Marquette U. Hosps., Milw., 1961-65; resident in plastic and maxillofacial surgery U. Tex. Med. Br., Galveston, 1965-68; fellowship in plastic and reconstructive surgery African Med. Rsch. Found., Nairobi, Kenya, 1968-69; pvt. practice medicine specializing in plastic surgery Milw., 1969—; med. cons. McGhan Med. Corp., Santa Barbara, Calif., Mentor/Sonique Surg. Sys., Santa Barbara. Contbr. articles to profl. jours. Lt. USNR, 1959-61. Fellow ACS, Internat. Coll. Surgeons; mem. AMA, Am. Soc. Aesthetic Plastic Surgery, Am. Soc. Plastic and Reconstructive Surgery, Am. Soc. Maxillofacial Surgeons, Can. Soc. Aesthetic for (Cosmetic) Plastic Surgery. Republican. Roman Catholic. Avocations: photography, sports fishing. Home: N14 W 30082 High Ridge Rd # 5 Pewaukee WI 53072 Office: Affiliated Cosmetic and Plastic Surgeons 2323 N Mayfair Rd Ste 503 Milwaukee WI 53226-1507 *Personal philosophy: I try to live each moment as an investment for eternity by doing my best in every activity undertaken.*

KLOEPPER, DAVID ALAN, management consultant; b. Colby, Kans., Dec. 8, 1945; s. Robert Mayer and Justine (Peterson) K.; m. Evelyn Maria Gritzbach, June 27, 1969. BS in Metallurgy, MIT. Process devel. engr. Grumman Aerospace, Bethpage, N.Y., 1968-72; mgr. svc. engring. Hilti, Inc., Stamford, Conn., 1972-79; nat. sales mgr. F & S Cen. Mfg., Bklyn., 1979-82; v.p. ops. and adminstrn. Imperial Bolt & Mfg. Co., South Plainfield, N.J., 1982-85; nat. sales mgr. Indsl. Bolt & Nut, Irvington, N.J., 1985-86, T.A. & D.A. Troy, Fairfield, N.J., 1986-87; project mgr. Don Aux Assocs., Hasbrouck Heights, N.J., 1987—, practice leader, 1992—. Pres. Van Vorst Park Neighborhood Assn., Jersey City, 1981-82. Republican. Avocations: movies, classical music. Home: 308 Varick St Jersey City NJ 07302-3404 Office: Don Aux Assocs 777 Terrace Ave Hasbrouck Heights NJ 07604-3110

KLOER, PHILIP BALDWIN, television critic; b. Honolulu, Sept. 13, 1955; s. Baldwin Ernest and Betty Louise (Burger) K.; m. Heather Ann Windsor, May 14, 1976; 1 child, Amanda Cynthia. BA, Ind. U., 1976. Writer Stillwater (Okla.) News-Press, 1976-78; film critic, columnist Fla. Times-Union, Jacksonville, 1978-85; arts editor Atlanta Constitution, 1985-87, TV critic, 1987—. Contbr. TV Guide, 1990. Recipient Olive Br. award Ctr. for War, Peace & Media, NYU, 1991, finalist Green Eyeshade award Sigma Delta Chi, 1986; named TV Critic of Yr., Nat. TV Movie Festival, 1990, Critic of Yr., Fla. Soc. Newspaper Editors, 1985. Office: Atlanta Constitution 72 Marietta St NW Atlanta GA 30303-2804

KLOESS, LAWRENCE HERMAN, JR., lawyer; b. Mamaroneck, N.Y., Jan. 30, 1927; s. Lawrence H. and Harriette Adelia (Holly) K.; m. Eugenia Ann Underwood, Nov. 19, 1931; children: Lawrence H. III, Price Mentzel, Branch Donelson, David Holly. AB, U. Ala., 1954, JD, 1956; grad., Air War Coll., 1976, Nat. Def. U., 1977, Nat. Def. U., 1977. Bar: Ala. 1956, U.S. dist. Ct. (no. dist.) Ala. 1956, U.S. Ct. Appeals (5th cir.) 1957, U.S. Ct. Mil. Appeals 1971, U.S. Supreme Ct. 1971, U.S. Ct. Appeals (11th cir.) 1981. Sole practice Birmingham, Ala., 1956-60, 62-66; corp. counsel Bankers Fire and Marine Ins. Co., 1961-62; dist. counsel for Ala. Office Dist. Counsel U.S. Dept. Vets. Affairs, Montgomery, 1966-95. Contbr. articles on law to profl. jours. Vice chmn. Salvation Army adv. bd., 1981, mem. bd., 1978-81; mem. nat. conf. bar pres.'s ABA, 1981—; mem. adminstrn. bd. Frazer Meml. United Meth. Ch., 1987-90, 92—; mem. adv. coun. Ret. and Sr. Vol. Program, Montgomery, 1997—. Col. Judge Adv. Gen. USAFR, 1954-86, ret. Bd. dirs., sec. Air Force Judge Adv. Gen. Sch. Found., 1996—. Decorated Legion of Merti, Meritorious Svc. medal with oak leaf cluster, Commendation medal; named Outstanding Judge Advocate USAFR, 1977, 79. Mem. ABA (nat. conf. bar. pres. 1981—), Ala. State Bar Assn. (chmn. editl. adv. bd. Ala. Lawyer 1975-79, editl. bd. 1970-82, character and fitness com., chmn. law day com. 1973, chmn. citizen edn. com. 1974, CLE adv. com. 1983), Ala. Law Found. (trustee), Montgomery County Bar Assn. (chmn. law day com. 1972, chmn. state bar liaison com. 1975, chmn. bd. dirs. 1977, bd. dirs. 1979, chmn. and editor Montgomery County Bar Jour., ABA Merit award 1979-80, v.p. 1980, pres. 1981), Fed. Bar Assn. (pres. Montgomery Fed. Bar Assn. 1973), Citizens Conf. on Ala. Ct. (exec. com., sponsor of new jud. article to state constn. 1973), Citizens Conf. on Criminal and Juvenile Justice (mem. staff 1974), Farrah Law Soc., REs. Officers Assn. of U.S. (chpt. pres. 1978, state pres. 1982), Air Force Ret. Judge Adv. Assn., Ret. Officers Assn. (life), Air War Coll. Alumni Assn. (life), Sigma Delta Kappa (pres. U. Ala. chpt.), Theta Chi (Outstanding Alumni award 1976), Montgomery Capital Rotary Club (pres. 1979, Paul Harris fellow), Montgomery Rotary Club (v.p. 1996, pres. 1998), Maxwell-Gunter Officers (Montgomery), Capital City Club, Montgomery Country Club, Blue Gray Cols. Assn., Mystic Soc. (Krewe of phantom host), Hon. Order Ky. Cols., Svc. Corps. of Ret. Execs. Assn. (bd. dirs. 1996—), Ala. Soc. for Cripple Children and Adults (bd. mem.), English Speaking Union (bd. dirs. 1997—). Republican. Home: 7157 Pine Crest Dr Montgomery AL 36117-7413

KLOHN, EARLE JARDINE, engineering company executive, consultant; b. Winnipeg, Man., Can., Aug. 14, 1927; s. August Frank and Florence (McLeod) K.; m. Beryl MacRae, Aug. 8, 1950 (dec. Nov. 19, 1963); children: James Kimberley, Douglas Alan, Barbara Marjorie; m. Lorna Charles, Oct. 2, 1964; 1 child, Michael. BSCE with distinction, U. Alta., Edmonton, Can., 1950, MSCE, 1952. Registered profl. civil engr., Can. Found. engr. O.J. Porter & Co. Ltd., Sacramento, Calif., 1950, R.M. Hardy and Assocs. Ltd., Edmonton, 1951; found. engr. Klohn Leonoff Ltd., Vancouver, 1952-55, sr. engr., 1955-60; ptnr. Klohn Leonoff Ltd., Richmond, B.C., Can., 1960, pres., 1970-87, chmn., CEO, 1987-93; pres., CEO Klohn-Crippen Cons. Ltd., Vancouver, B.C., 1988-97, chmn. emeritus, 1997—; past chmn. Can. Nat. Com. on Large Dams; past mem. com. on tailing dams Internat. Commn. on Large Dams; mem. numerous cons. rev. bds. for earthfill dams; geotech. cons. Revelstoke Dam, Site C Dam, Stikine-Iskut devel. for BC Hydro, numerous others; internat. cons. design and constrn. tailing dams; past chmn. Vancouver Geotech. Group; presenter papers at various seminars, profl. meetings and confs. Contbr. numerous articles to profl. publs. Recipient Alfred A. Raymond award Raymond Internat., 1960, Legget award Can. Geotech. Soc., 1990, McPartland Meml. medal, 1992, Pub. Paper award Can. Dam Safety Assn., 1995. Fellow ASCE, Engring. Inst. Can. (past chmn. Vancouver br., Leonard medal 1972), Can. Acad. Engring.; mem. Assn. Cons. Engrs. Can., Can. Inst. Mining and Metallurgy, Assn. Profl. Engrs. B.C. (Meritorious Achievement award 1982), Wash. Soc. Profl. Engrs., Minn. Soc. Profl. Engrs., Yukon Terr. Soc. Prof. Engrs., Alaska Soc. Profl. Engrs., Colo. Soc. Profl. Engrs., Wyo. Soc. Profl. Engrs., Can. Sect. Internat. Soc. Soil Mechanics and Found. Engring., Morgan Creek Go. and Country Club (Surrey, B.C.). Mem. United Ch. Can. Office: Klohn-Crippen Cons Ltd, 510 Burrard St Ste 600, Vancouver, BC Canada V6C 3A8

KLOHR, JOANNE CAROL, nurse; b. Punxsutawney, Pa., June 18, 1966; d. Samuel Joseph and Carole Ann (Peace) Ishman; m. George Frederick Klohr, Jr., Sept. 23, 1989; 1 child, Ashley Nicole. Diploma in Nursing, Conemaugh Valley Meml. Hosp., Johnstown, Pa., 1987. Cert. BLS, ACLS; cert. in med./surg. nursing; RN, Pa. Staff nurse med./surg. Punxsutawney Hosp., 1987-89, staff nurse emergency rm., ICU, 1989-91, nursing supr., 1991-98, ICU staff nurse, 1998—. Mem. NLN (advocacy), Punxsutawney Nurses Club. Democrat. Avocations: reading, playing piano, knitting, needlework. Home: 2 Lewis St Punxsutawney PA 15767-1518 Office: Punxsutawney Area Hosp 81 Hillcrest Dr Punxsutawney PA 15767-2605

KLOMBERS, NORMAN, retired podiatrist, association executive; b. N.Y.C., Jan. 28, 1923; s. Moe and Lillian K.; m. Gloria Evelyn Piatek, Jan. 16, 1955; children: Lee Alan, Robin Sheri. Grad., Coll. Arts and Scis., L.I. U., 1942; D.P.M. cum laude, N.Y. Coll. Podiatric Medicine, 1944. Diplomate: Am. Bd. Podiatric Orthopedics, Am. Bd. Podiatric Pub. Health. Practice podiatric medicine N.Y.C., 1944-68; dir. profl. services Podiatry Soc. N.Y., 1968-78; dir. dept. sci. affairs Am. Podiatric Med. Assn., Washington, 1978-80; exec. dir. Am. Podiatric Med. Assn., 1980-89, ret., 1989; exec. dir. Anxiety Disorders Assn. Am., Rockville, Md., 1990-93; ret., 1993; faculty N.Y. Coll. Podiatric Medicine, 1944-78. Named Disting. Practitioner, Nat. Acad. of Practice, 1986. Fellow Am. Coll. Foot Orthopedists.

KLONGLAN, GERALD EDWARD, sociology educator; b. Nevada, Iowa, Apr. 1, 1936; s. Bernie R. and Willene Rebecca (Maland) K.; m. Donna Eileen Becvar, June 29, 1960; children: Jason, Suzanne. B.S., Iowa State U., 1958, M.S., 1962, Ph.D., 1963. Mem. faculty Iowa State U., Ames, 1963—, prof. sociology, 1972—, chmn. dept. sociology and anthropology, 1976-90, interim assoc. dean Coll. Sci. and Humanities, 1988-89; asst. dir. Iowa Agr. and Home Econ. Expt. Sta., 1990—; assoc. dean nat. programs Coll. Agr., 1995—; staff sociologist U.S. Dept. Agr., Coop. State Rsch. Svc., Washington, DC, 1991-93; evaluation rschr. AID, Malawi, 1967, project cons., Ghana, 1976; ednl. cons. King Saud U., Saudi Arabia, 1981-83, Peking U., People's Republic of China, 1984-85; project implementor U. Zambia, Lusaka, 1982-83; family rsch., Norway, 1988, Czech Republic, 1995; project dir. mgmt. tng. Czech Republic and Slovak Republic, 1991-96; project dir. agr. rsch., Russia, Ukraine, other countries of former Soviet Union, 1992—. Author: Social Indicators, 1972; (research monographs) Adoption Diffusion of Ideas, 1967; Creating Interorganizational Coordination, 1975, Communication Policy, 1983. Vol. scientist Am. Cancer Soc., 1969—; bd. dirs. Luth. Campus Ministry, Ames, 1972-78, chmn. bd., 1974-76; pres. Bethesda Luth. Ch., Ames, 1994-95. Recipient Wilton Park award Iowa State U., 1983. Mem. Rural Sociol. Soc. (coun. 1974-76, 91-92, v.p. 1977-78, pres. 1985-86), Am. Sociol. Assn. (com. on internat. sociology 1993-96), Midwest Sociol. Soc. (tng. com. 1975-78), Sigma Xi (pres. Iowa State U. chpt. 1983-84). Home: 1622 Maxwell Ave Ames IA 50010-5536 Office: Iowa State U Coll Agr 137 Curtiss Hall Ames IA 50011-1070

KLONSKY, BRUCE GARY, educator; b. N.Y.C., Sept. 30, 1950; s. Sam and Gertrude (Dogin) K. AB in Psychology, Lehman Col., 1971; MA in Psychology, Fordham U., 1973, PhD in Psychology, 1978. Tchg. fellow Fordham U., Bronx, N.Y., 1974-76; vis. asst. prof. W.Va. U., Morgantown, 1978-79; prof. SUNY, Fredonia, 1979—; vis. rsch. assoc. Purdue U., West Lafayette, Ind., 1988-89; vis. scholar Inst. for Rsch. on Human Devel. U. Ill., Urbana, 1988-89; vis. prof. W.Va. U., Morgantown, 1995-96; cons. editor Jour. Genetic Psychology, Washington, 1986—; cons. Chautauqua Opportunities, Dunkirk, N.Y., 1995—; co-tchr. workshop on aggression, expression and mgmt. Chautauqua County Family Day Care Providers, Fredonia, 1994. Contbr. chpts. to books, articles to profl. jours. Vol., cons. Fredonia Hotline for Rape and Battering, 1985-87. Recipient rsch. grant SUNY Rsch. Found., 1982, rsch. opportunity award NSF, 1988-89; Evaluation and Assessment grantee U.S. HHS. Mem. APA, Am. Psychology Soc., Am. Edn. Rsch. Assn., Am. Sociol. Assn., Assn. for Advancement of Applied Sport Psychology, Soc. for Rsch. in Child Devel., Soc. for Advancement of Social Psychology, Assn. for Study of Play, Sigma Xi, Psi Chi. Office: SUNY Psychology Dept Thompson Hall W339 Fredonia NY 14063

KLOOSTER, JUDSON, academic administrator, dentistry educator; b. La Combe, Alta., Can., Dec. 24, 1925; s. Henry J. and Evelyn Mae (Eglin) K.; m. Arlene Jean Madsen, Nov. 28, 1948; children: Cherylin Klooster Peach, Lynette Carol Tibbetts, Terrill Ann Klooster McClanahan Hannum. Student, Andrews U., 1942-43, Pacific Union Coll., 1943-44; DDS, U. Pacific, 1947; MMS, Tulane U., 1968. Pvt. practice dentistry San Francisco, 1947-49, Escondido, Calif., 1949-67; part-time mem. faculty Loma Linda (Calif.) U. Sch. Dentistry, 1956-67, full-time prof. restorative dentistry, 1967—, dir. continuing edn., 1968-72, dean, 1971-94, dean emeritus, 1994—, emeritus prof. dentistry, 1997—; mem. faculty U. Pacific Sch. Dentistry, 1947-49; cons. USPHS, VA. Treas. Am. Fund for Dental Health, 1987-89, v.p. 1990-91, pres., 1992-93. Lt. Dental Corps USNR, 1953-55. Fellow Am. Coll. Dentists, Internat. Coll. Dentists (councillor); mem. ADA, Calif. Dental Assn. (chmn. coun. dental edn. 1972-75), Tri-County Dental Soc. (ex officio dir. 1971-94, pres.-elect 1978-79, pres. 1979-80), Rotary (pres. San Bernardino S. club 1977-78), Xi Psi Phi. Republican. Mem. Seventh Day Adventist Ch. (elder 1969—). Home: 25131 Crestview Dr Loma Linda CA 92354-3508 Office: Loma Linda U Sch Dentistry Ctr Dental Rsch Loma Linda CA 92350

KLOOSTERHUIS, ROBERT JOHN, publishing association company executive; b. Kalamazoo, Aug. 22, 1932. BA, Emmanuel Missionary Coll., Berrien Springs, Mich., 1954; MA, Andrews U., Berrien Springs, 1965. Ordained minister Seventh-day Adventist Ch., 1966; lic. pilot. Pres. Franco-Haitian Sem., Port-au-Prince, Haiti, 1960-61; sec.-treas. Franco-Haitian Union, Port-au-Prince, 1961-64; pastor Ill. Conf., Brookfield, 1965-70, youth ministries stewardship dir., 1970-76; pres. Franco-Haitian Union, Port-au-Prince, 1976-80, African Indian Ocean Divsn., Abidjan, Ivory Coast, 1980-85; gen. v.p. Gen. Conf. Seventh-day Adventists, Silver Spring, Md., 1985—; chmn. bd. Pacific Press Pub. Assn., Nampa, Idaho, 1985—. Office: Pacific Press PO Box 5353 Nampa ID 83653-5353*

KLOPACK, KENNETH BARTHON, art educator, artist; b. Chgo., Dec. 31, 1949; s. Barthon R. Klopack and Cecilia L. (Wojtkiewicz) Wojcik; m. Gaye Lee Green, Feb. 12, 1971; children: Kristin, Lauren, Kenneth B. BA in Art Edn., Northeastern Ill. U., 1971, MA in Spl. Edn. Gifted, 1989. Cert. art edn. K-12, Ill.; cert. type 75 adminstrn., Ill. Art educator Funston Elem. Sch. Chgo. Pub. Schs., 1972—; part-time art educator Sch of the Art Inst., Chgo., 1997—; tchr. to tchr. presenter Chgo. Found. for Edn., 1994—; artist mem. Artists of Rogers Park, Chgo., 1997—, Galerie de Hamptons, West Hamptons Beach, L.I., N.Y., 1994—. Author, illustrator: (book) Show Off Your Art, 1984; polit. cartoonist Nadig Newspapers, 1978—. Recipient Golden Apple award for tchg. Golden Apple Found., 1989, Kohl Internat. Tchg. award Kohl Found., 1993; named Art Educator of Yr., Ill. Art Edn. Assn., 1996; grantee for edn. N.Y. Stock Exch., 1994. Mem. Art Inst. Chgo., Mus. Contemporary Art, Chgo. Artist's Coalition. Avocations: running, sports, reading. Home: 4443 N Tripp Ave Chicago IL 60630-4207

KLOPF, GORDON JOHN, educational consultant, former college dean; b. Milw., Jan. 10, 1917; s. Milton and Lillian (Spiegler) K. BS, U. Wis., 1939, MA, 1941, PhD, 1950; postgrad., U. Mich.; LHD (hon.), Bank St. Coll. of Edn., 1998. Tchr., counselor pub. schs. Burlington, Wis., 1939-41; counselor men's activities, instr. speech Wayne U., 1942-47; coord. student activities summer insts. for sch. counselors U. Wis., Madison, 1947-51; prof. tng. personnel, guidance workers serving with AUS, U.S. Dept. State, Am. Council on Edn. project Tokyo U., Kyoto U., Kyushu U., Japan, 1951-52; dean students coll. for tchrs. SUNY, 1952-59; ednl. specialist in guidance Dept. State, Japan, 1954; assoc. prof. edn., dept. guidance, student personnel adminstrn. Tchrs. Coll., Columbia U., N.Y.C., 1958-64; asst. to pres., chmn. guidance programs Bank Street Coll. Edn., N.Y.C., 1964-69, dean of faculties, provost, 1965-80, dean emeritus, 1980-85, dean Ctr. for Leadership devel., dir. Sch. and Gen. Ledership and Supervision Program, disting. specialist in ednl. leadership, 1980-85; pres. Gordon J. Klopf, ednl. cons., N.Y.C., 1983—; continuing edn. cons. Fall River (Mass.) Pub. Schs., 1979-89, Kennesaw State Coll., 1985-94; cons. U.S. Office Edn., Washington, 1964-81, P.R. Dept. Instrn., 1965—, Mendoza Found., Ministry of Edn., Venezuela, 1971-80; clin. prof. gerontology, Southampton campus L.I. U.; mem. U.S. Planning Com. and UN World chairperson for Internat. Yr. of Older Persons, 1999, chair 1998—; UN-NGO chair UN Internat. Yr. of Older Person, 1999; mem. U.S. NGO Com. for U.S. Internat. Year. Author: Student Leadership and Government, 1949, rev., 1955; Planning Student Activities in the High School, 1950; College Student Government, 1960, Teacher Education In a Social Context, 1967, Perspectives On Learning, 1967, New Careers in the American School, 1968, New Careers and Roles in Education, 1968, Teams for Learning, 1969; The Principal and Staff Development in the School, 1976; co-author: The School as Locus of Advocacy for All Children, 1987; author-editor: Education Before Five, 1977; co-author: Mentoring, 1982, The School Principal and Special Education, 1982; co-author numerous other works in field. editor: Operational Studies in Guidance, 1962, Orientation, 1963, Encounter and Dialogue, 1963, Student Personnel Work in the Future, 1966, Jour. Research and Devel. in Edn., Vol. 5, No. 3, 1972; editor, chmn. The Role and Preparation of the Counselor in the Secondary School, 1963; adv. editor Brit. Young Children's Ency., 16 vols., 1970; chair UN-NGO Com. on Internat. Yr. of the Older Person, 1998. Past chmn. adv. coun. U.S. Student Assn.; nat. chmn. Project Follow Through, 1967-68; trustee U.S. Com. for UNICEF, 1971-81, chmn. edn. com., 1975-80, chairperson bd. Action for Children, chmn. non-govt. orgn. edn. working group, 1988—, chairperson DPI-Non Govt. Orgn., exec. com. UN, 1990-96, co-chairperson UNICEF Forum on Children in Ctrl. Am., 1993-94; trustee Bklyn. Children's Mus., 1980-89; bd. dirs. Daytop Inc., 1973—; trustee Hampton Day Sch., 1975-94, pres. 1984-86, chmn. evaluation com., 1995; mem. coun. The Hayground Sch., Bridgehampton, N.Y.; mem. edn. Parish Art Mus., Southampton; v.p., program chmn. Elem. Sch. Ctr., N.Y., pres. 1985-87, v.p., 1987-90, bd. dirs.; pres., bd. dirs. chairperson Morningside Heights Housing Corp. Program; program chair, bd. dirs. Morningside Heights Retirement and Health Svcs., chmn. UN-NGO, 1999, UNICEF working NCO group in edn. Brown U. scholar, 1995-97. Mem. N.Y. State Deans Assn. (research chmn., past v.p.), Am. Personnel and Guidance Assn., Western N.Y. Personnel and Guidance Assn. (past pres.), AAUP, Am. Coll. Personnel Assn., Buffalo World Hospitality Assn. (past chmn.). Home: 70 La Salle St Apt 4B New York NY 10027-4705 also: Jason's Ln PO Box 1208 East Hampton NY 11937-0996

KLOPFENSTEIN, PHILIP ARTHUR, high school educator; b. Lake Odessa, Mich., Apr. 28, 1937; s. Glendull Carl and Bernice (Shumway) K.; m. Anna Jo Davis, Aug. 24, 1960. B.A., Mich. State U., 1961; M.A., Western Mich. U., 1964; arts adminstrn. cert., Harvard U., 1970; postgrad., Henderson State U., 1990-91. Cert. tchr., Mich. Faculty mem. U. Ark., Little Rock, 1965-68; tchr. Ark. Ednl. TV, Conway, 1969-70; dir. Southeast Ark. Arts and Scis. Ctr., Pine Bluff, 1970-76, Augusta Richmond County Mus., (Ga.), 1977-79, Montgomery Mus. Fine Arts, (Ala.), 1979-82; v.p., devel. officer Found. Hist. Research and Reclamation, Montgomery, Ala., 1982-88; adj. prof. Auburn U., 1984-88; cons. Endright Svcs., Inc., 1983-89; tchr. Glenwood H.S., 1989—; fed. programs coord. Centerpoint H.S. (merger two dists.), 1997—. Served with U.S. Army, 1957-59. USIA grantee, 1980. Mem. Southeastern Mus. Conf., Three Rivers Art Guild (chmn. guild bd. 1989-95). Home: PO Box 890 Glenwood AR 71943-1388

KLOPFENSTEIN, REX CARTER, electrical engineer; b. Pittsfield, Mass., Mar. 3, 1938; s. Glenn A. and Jasimine V. (Carter) K.; m. Linda Gilgore, Oct. 6, 1962; children: Mark W., Eric G. BSEE, U. Conn., 1959; MEE, Syracuse U., 1963. Engr. GE, Syracuse, N.Y., 1959-63; lab. mgr. Melpar Divsn. E Sys., Falls Church, Va., 1963-70; mgr. hardware engring. Logicon Inc., Fairfax, Va., 1977-78; software and test mgr. Acuity Sys. Inc., Reston, Va., 1978-81; engring. mgr. AMF Electronic Rsch. Lab., Sterling, Va., 1981-82; tech. staff The MITRE Corp., McLean, Va., 1970-77, lead engr., 1982-96; lead engr. Mitretek Sys., Inc., McLean, Va., 1996—; sec. tech. com. X3K5 Am. Nat. Standards Inst., Washington, 1992-94. Co-author: Microcomputer Design and Application, 1977; contbr. articles to profl. jours. Mem. Rep. Nat. Com., chmn. honor roll, 1997. Fellow Washington Acad. Scis. (bd. mgrs. 1996-98, pres.-elect 1998, pres. 1999—); mem. IEEE (No. Va. sect. sec. 1991-92, vice-chmn., treas. 1992-93, chmn. 1993-94, nat. area coun. vice-chmn. 1994-95, chmn. 1995-96, assoc. editor, editor 1998—, web site mgr. 1997—), Assn. for Computing Machinery, Tau Beta Pi, Chi Phi. Avocation: photography. Home: 4224 Worcester Dr Fairfax VA 22032-1140 Office: Mitretek Systems Inc 7525 Colshire Dr Ste 600 Mc Lean VA 22102-7400

KLOPFLEISCH, STEPHANIE SQUANCE, social services agency administrator; B.A., Pomona Coll., 1962; M.S.W., UCLA, 1966; m. Randall Klopfleisch, June 27, 1970; children—Elizabeth, Jennifer, Matthew. Social worker, Los Angeles County, 1963-67; program dir. day care, vol. services Los Angeles County, 1968-71; div. chief children's services Dept. Public Social Services, Los Angeles County, 1971-73, dir. bur. of social services, 1973-79; chief dep. dir. Dept. Community Services, Los Angeles County, 1979-95; interim dir. Cmty. & Sr. Svcs., Los Angeles County, 1996-97, dir. 1998—; with Area 10 Devel. Disabilities, 1981-82; bd. dirs. Los Angeles Fed. Emergency Mgmt. Act, 1985-91, pres., 1987; bd. dirs. Los Angeles Shelter Partnership, Pomona Coll. Assocs., 1988—. Mem. Calif. Commn. on Family Planning, 1976-79; mem. Los Angeles Commn. Children's Instns., 1977-78; bd. dirs. United Way Info., 1978-79; chmn. Los Angeles County Internat. Yr. of Child Commn., 1978-79; bd. govs. Sch. Social Welfare, UCLA, 1981-84; bd. dirs. Calif. Soc. Welfare Archives, 1999—. Mem. Nat. Assn. Social Workers, L.A. Philhamonic Affiliates, 1995, Soroptimist Internat. (bd. dirs. 1989—, pres. L.A. chpt. 1993).

KLOPMAN, GILLES, chemistry educator; b. Brussels, Belgium, Feb. 24, 1933; came to U.S., 1965; s. Alge and Brana (Brendel) Klopman; m. Malvina Pantiel, Sept. 5, 1957. BA, Athenee d'Ixelles (Belgium), 1952; lic. chemistry, U. Brussels, 1956; D.Chemistry, 1960. Rsch. scientist Cyanamid European Rsch. Inst., Geneva, Switzerland, 1960-67; postdoctoral fellow U. Tex., 1964-65; assoc. prof. Case Western Res. U., Cleve., 1967-69, prof. chemistry, 1969—, chmn. dept., 1981-86, interim dean sci. and math., 1986-88, C.F. Mabery prof. of rsch., chmn. dept., 1988-95; v.p. Biofor, Ltd., PA, 1986-95; pres. Discovery Software Inc., 1991-93, Multicase, Inc., 1995—. Recipient Kahlbaum prize Swiss Chem. Soc., 1971; grantee NSF, NIH, EPA, PRF, ONR. Mem. Am. Chem. Soc. (Morley medal 1993), Brit. Chem. Soc. Belgium Chem. Soc. (Stas Spring medal 1960), Swiss Chem. Soc., AAUP, Sigma Xi. Author: All Valence Electrons SCF Calculations, 1970; Chemical Reactivity and Reaction Paths, 1974; contbr. articles to profl. jours. Home: 22 Hyde Park Cleveland OH 44122-7536 Office: Case Western Res U 10900 Euclid Ave Cleveland OH 44106-1712

KLORES, DAN, public relations executive. Pres. Dan Klores Assocs., Inc., N.Y.C. Office: Dan Klores Assocs Inc 386 Park Ave S Fl 10 New York NY 10016-8804*

KLOS, JEROME JOHN, lawyer; b. LaCrosse, Wis., Jan. 17, 1927; s. Charles and Edna S. (Wagner) K.; m. Mary M. Hamilton, July 26, 1958; children—Bryant H., Geoffrey W. B.S., U. Wis., 1948, J.D., 1950. Bar: Wis. 1950. Pres. Klos, Flynn and Papenfuss, LaCrosse, Wis., 1950—; bd. dirs. Union State Bank, West Salem, Wis. Mem. LaCrosse County Bd., 1957-74, vice chmn., 1972-74; pub. adminstr. La Crosse County, 1962-73; bd. dirs. West Salem Area Growth, Inc., La Crosse Area Growth, Inc.; trustee Sander and McKinly Scholarship Funds of West Salem Sch. Dist. Fellow Am. Coll. Real Estate Lawyers, Am. Coll. Probate Counsel; mem. ABA, Wis. Bar Assn. Lodges: Elks, K.C. Home: 346 N Leonard St West Salem WI 54669-1238 Office: 800 Lynn Tower Bldg La Crosse WI 54601

KLOSE, CHARLOTTE ANN, insurance agency owner; b. Mankato, Minn., Oct. 22, 1939; d. Jerome John and Drusilla Lucille (Wiegert) Kunkel; m. Gerhard Klose, Aug. 12, 1961; children: Karin Anne, Susan Marie. BA in English, Coll. St. Benedict, St. Joseph, Minn., 1961; MA in English, Nazareth Coll., Rochester, N.Y., 1967, MS in Edn., 1977. CLU, ChFC, The Am. Coll., Bryn Mawr, Pa., 1988; CPCU, CPCU Soc., Malvern, Pa., 1995. H.s. Latin and English tchr. Richfield (Minn.) Pub. Schs., 1961-63; h.s. English and reading tchr. Rochester City Schs., 1963-81; owner State Farm Ins. Agy., Penfield, N.Y., 1981—; presenter regional conf. State Farm Ins. Cos., Albany, N.Y., 1997; presenter Nat. Conf. Students for Responsible Bus., Evanston, Ill., 1996; mem. adv. com. women and gender studies divsn. Colgate Rochester Divinity Sch., 1995—; presenter Theol. Inst., Colgate Rochester Divinity Sch., 1997. Contbr. articles to profl. jours. Mem. edn. coms. Penfield Schs., 1972-78; mem. steering com. Women's Resource Ctr., YWCA, Rochester, 1989-91; mem. Goals for a Greater Rochester, 1991-93; pres. Rochester Women's Network, 1991-92, bd. dirs. 1988-94; bd. dirs. Susan B. Anthony House, 1997—. Mem. CLU Assn. (bd. dirs. 1989-91), Rochester Life Underwriters Assn. (1994-96), CPCU Assn., Penfield Bus. Assn., Penfield Rotary (com. chair 1989-95). Roman Catholic. Avocations: travel, writing, reading, wine tasting, swimming. Home: 70 Thorntree Cir Penfield NY 14526-1224 Office: State Farm Ins Cos 1844 Penfield Rd Ste 3 Penfield NY 14526-1491

KLOSINSKI, LEONARD FRANK, mathematics educator; b. Michigan City, Ind., July 16, 1938; s. Frank and Helen (Podgorna) K.;. BS, U. Santa Clara, 1961; MA, Oreg. State U., 1963. Programmer NASA Ames Rsch. Ctr., Mountain View, Calif., 1963; instr. math. Santa Clara (Calif.) U., 1964-68, asst. prof., 1968-76, assoc. prof., 1976—; dir. Nat. Sci. Found. Insts., 1969-74; mng. editor, treas. Fibonacci Assn., 1975-80; dir. William Lowell Putnam Math. Competition, 1978—. Author: Santa Clara Silver Anniversary Contest Book/ Problems and Solutions of the University of Santa Clara High School Mathematics Contests, 1985, Students' Solutions Manual to Accompany Lynn E. Garner's Calculus and Analytical Geometry, 1988; editor: William Lowell Putnam Mathematical Competition Problems and Solutions, 1965-84, 1985; contbr. articles to profl. jours. Mem. Math. Assn. Am. (coun. on competitions 1992—, Putnam prize com. 1975—, adv. bd. Math. Horizons 1993—, sec.-treas. No. Calif. sect. 1979—, vice-chair No. Calif. sect. 1999, award for disting. coll. or univ. tchg. math. No. Calif. sect. 1999). Democrat. Roman Catholic. Avocation: art collecting. Office: Santa Clara U Math Dept Santa Clara CA 95053

KLOSK, RUSSELL MARTIN, human resources executive; b. N.Y.C., Sept. 23, 1969; s. Michael J. Klosk and Laurie Beth (Wendel) Gazzale; m. Carolyn E. Ford. BA, U. So. Calif., 1991. Acct. exec., exec. recruiter Culver Personnel Svcs., Sherman Oaks, Calif., 1991-92; acct. mgr., exec. recruiter Culver Personnel Svcs., Sherman Oaks, 1992; asst. br. mgr., exec. recruiter Culver Personnel Svcs., Marina Del Rey, 1992-94; asst. br. mgr., exec. recruiter accts. exec. search MIS Search/Accts. on Call (divsn. Adecco A), Burbank, 1994; br. mgr., exec. recruiter accts. exec. search MIS Search/Accts. on Call (divsn. Adecco A), Bellevue, Wash., 1994-95; exec. recruiter Accent Multilangue (divsn. of Adecco SA), N.Y., 1995-96; corp. recruiter, staffing Strategic Support Union, Electronic Data Syss., Florham Park, N.J., 1996-97; mgr. profl. staffing Price Waterhouse Coopers, LLP, N.Y.C., 1997-98; human resources/recruiting mgr. Microsoft Corp., Washington, 1998; dir. corp. recruiting Gannett Co., Inc., Washington, Va., 1999—; career transition advisor cmty. outreach YMCA, Bernardsville, N.J., 1997; projects A.V.E. No. Va. Tech. Coun., 1998, 99. Event coord. Rep. Party Somerset County, Somerville, N.J., 1996, 97, Arlington County, Va., 1998—. Mem. Am. Mgmt. Assn., Soc. Human Resources Mgmt., Human Resources Assn. Nat. Capital Area, U. So. Calif. Nations Capital Alumni Club (v.p.), U. So. Calif. Gen. Alumni Assn., Magnolia Lodge (Master Mason), Phi Alpha Delta, Kappa Alpha Order, Order of Omega. Avocations: scuba diving, softball, golf, reading, travel. Office: Gannett Co Inc 1100 Wilson Blvd Ste 2100 Arlington VA 22209-2299

KLOSKA, RONALD FRANK, manufacturing company executive; b. Grand Rapids, Mich., Oct. 24, 1933; s. Frank B. and Catherine (Hilaski) K.; m. Mary F. Minick, Sept. 7, 1957; children: Kathleen Ann, Elizabeth Marie, Ronald Francis, Mary Josephine, Carolyn Louise. Student, St. Joseph Sem., Grand Rapids, Mich., 1947-53; PhB, U. Montreal, Que., Can., 1955; MBA, U. Mich., 1957. Staff acct. Coopers & Lybrand, Niles, Mich., 1957, staff to sr. acct., 1960-63; treas. Skyline Corp., Elkhart, Ind., 1963, v.p., treas., 1964-67, exec. v.p. fin., 1967-74, pres., 1974-85, pres., chief ops. officer, 1985-91, vice chmn., chief adminstrn. officer, 1991-95, vice chmn., CEO, chief adminstrn. officer, 1995-98; vice chmn., CEO Skyline Corp., Elkhart, 1998—. With U.S. Army, 1957-60. Mem. Mich. Soc. CPAs, Ind. Soc. CPAs, South Bend Country Club. Roman Catholic. Home: 1329 E Woodside St South Bend IN 46614-1455 Office: Skyline Corp 2520 Bypass Rd Elkhart IN 46514-1584

KLOSNER, JEROME MARTIN, mechanical engineer, educator; b. N.Y.C., Mar. 23, 1928; s. Morris and Minnie (Gotchkofsky) K.; m. Naomi Beth Certner, May 31, 1965; children—Michael Robert, Lise Helaine, Marc Alexander. B.C.E., Coll. City N.Y., 1948; M.S., Columbia, 1950; Ph.D., Poly. Inst. Bklyn., 1959. Sr. structures engr. Republic Aviation Corp., Farmingdale, N.Y., 1952-56; sr. scientist Avco Research & Advanced Devel. Div., Wilmington, Mass., 1956, cons., 1956-67; research assoc. Poly. Inst. Bklyn., 1956-59, asst. prof., 1959-62, assoc. prof., 1962-67, prof. applied mechanics, 1967—; cons. Gen. Applied Sci. Labs., Inc., L.I., N.Y., 1959, FTC, Washington, 1963, Ingersoll-Rand Corp. Research Center, Princeton, N.J., 1966, Technautics Corp., N.Y.C., 1968-69, Weidlinger Assocs., N.Y.C., 1976—, Hazeltine, L.I., 1985-87, Beltran, Inc., N.Y.C., 1986-92, Multiline Tech., 1987; vis. mem. Courant Inst. Math. Scis., N.Y.U., 1966-67; Mem. Nat. Research council com. on Recommendations for U.S. Army Basic Sci. Research, 1976-79, 85-88. Reviewer, contbr. articles profl. jours. Fellow AIAA (assoc.), ASCE, ASME; mem. Acoustical Soc. Am., Sigma Xi, Sigma Gamma Tau. Office: Polytech U Dept Mech & Aerospace Engring Rte 110 Farmingdale NY 11735

KLOSOWSKI-GOROMBEI, DEBORAH ANN, nursing administrator, flight nurse; b. Chgo.; d. Timothy Joseph Sr. and Rose J. (Garbel) Klosowski; m. James Thomas Gorombei, Apr. 3, 1993. BSN with honors, Loyola U., Chgo.; MS, Purdue U. Calumet, 1995. RN, Ill., Ind., Ariz.; cert. PALS, BLS, ACLS, ATLS, Neonatal Resuscitation Program, Flight Nurse Advanced Trauma Course. Staff nurse ER St. Margaret Mercy Hosp., Hammond, Ind., 1989-95; staff nurse SICU U. Chgo., 1990-92; supr. St. Francis Hosp., Blue Island, Ill., 1993; renal nurse clinician WSKC, Blue Island, 1993-94; chief flight nurse (fixed wing) West Chgo., Ill., 1995; asst. mgr. clin. ops. med. ICU, Christ Hosp., Oak Lawn, Ill., 1995-96; adminstrv. dir., chief flight nurse aeromed. network U. Chgo., 1997-99; chief flight nurse LifeNet Air Med. Transport, 1999—; nurse educator/cons., bd. dirs. Allied Health Care Resources, Olympia Fields, Ill.; speaker in field. Co-investigator for publs. in field. Nurse ARC, Lamont, Ill., 1991; campaign asst. for politician, Chgo., 1988. Recipient Washington Square Health Found., 1988-90, Pres.'s Medallion for Nursing, 1990, Donald S. Powers Nursing Talent award, 1994-95; named to St. Francis H.S. Hall of Fame. Mem. Emergency Nurses Assn., U.S. Parachuting Assn., Nat. Flight Nurses Assn., So. Ariz. Search and Rescue Assn., Alpha Sigma Nu, Sigma Theta Tau (rsch. grantee Mu Omega chpt. 1998). Roman Catholic. Avocations: skydiving, car shows, auto racing, photography, research. Office: LifeNet Air Med Transport Ste 200 1550 S Alma Sch Rd Mesa AZ 85210

KLOSSON, MICHAEL, foreign service officer; b. Washington, Aug. 22, 1949; s. Boris Hansen and Harriet Fraser (Cheston) K.; m. Bonita L. Bender; children: Emily C., Karen Lee Bender. B.A., Hamilton Coll., 1971; M.P.A., Woodrow Wilson Sch., Princeton U., 1974; M.A., Princeton U., 1975. Asst. lectr. Hong Kong Baptist Coll., 1971-72; commd. fgn. service officer Dept. State, 1975; staff asst. to asst. sec. of state for East Asian affairs Dept. State, Washington, 1975-77; Chinese Lang. trainee Fgn. Service Inst., Taichung, Taiwan, 1977-78; polit. officer Am. embassy, Taipei, Taiwan, 1978-80; polit. officer office Japanese affairs Dept. State, Washington, 1980-81, spl. asst. to sec. of state, 1981-83; Pearson fellow U.S. Senate, 1983-84; dep. dir. for polit. affairs Office European Security and Polit. Affairs Dept. State, Washington, 1984-87, dir., secretariat staff, 1987-90; dep. chief of mission Am. Embassy, Stockholm, 1990-92, chargé d'affaires, 1992-93; charge d'affaires Am. Embassy, The Hague, 1993-94, dep. chief of mission, 1994-96; dep. asst. sec. of state for legis. affairs Dept. of State, Washington, 1996—. Herbert H. Lehman fellow, 1971, Winston Churchill fellow, 1972-74. Mem. Am. Fgn. Svc. Assn., Phi Beta Kappa. Office: Dept State Bur Legis Affairs Rm 7261 Washington DC 20520

KLOSTERMAN, ALBERT LEONARD, technical development business executive, mechanical engineer; b. Cin., Oct. 22, 1942; s. Albert Clement and Mary J. Klosterman; m. Lynne Marie Gabelein, Jan. 4, 1964; children: Scott, Lance, Kimberly, Brad. BSMechE, U. Cin., 1965, MSMechE, 1968, PhD, 1971. Instr. U. Cin., 1966-70, adj. assoc. prof., 1974—; project mgr. Structural Dynamics Rsch. Corp., Milford, Ohio, 1970-72, mem. tech. staff, 1972-73, dir. tech. staff, 1973-78, v.p., gen. mgr., 1978-83, sr. v.p., chief tech. officer, gen. mgr., 1983-95; sr. v.p., chief scientist, 1995—; mem. exec. steering com. Initial Graphics Exchange System/Product Data Exch. Speification of Nat. Standards Bd., Gaithersburg, Md., 1984—. Mem. editorial bd. Internat. Jour. Vehicle Design, 1979—. Recipient Disting. Alumnus award U. Cin., 1988. Mem. Assn. Computing Machinery, ASME (assoc.), Phi Kappa Theta. Republican. Roman Catholic. Home: 5444 Forest Ridge Cir Milford OH 45150-2821 Office: Structural Dynamics Rsch Corp 2000 Eastman Dr Milford OH 45150-2712*

KLOTMAN, ROBERT HOWARD, music educator; b. Cleve., Nov. 22, 1918; s. Louis Klotman and Pearl (Warshawsky) Kaplan; m. Phyllis Helen Rauch, Apr. 4, 1943; children: Janet Lynn, Paul Evan. BS in Music Edn., Ohio No. U., 1940; MA in Music, Case-Western Res. U., 1950; EdD, Columbia U., 1956; MusD (hon.), Ohio No. U., 1984. Supr. music pub. schs. Dola, Ohio, 1940-42; tchr. instrumental, vocal music pub. schs. Euclid, Ohio, 1942, 46; tchr. instrumental music pub. schs. Cleveland Heights, Ohio, 1946-59; dir. music edn. pub. schs. Akron, Ohio, 1959-63; divisional dir. music edn. pub. schs. Detroit, 1963-69; prof., chmn. dept. music edn. Ind. U., Bloomington, 1969-87, prof. emeritus, 1987—; vis. prof. Shanghai Conservatory of Music, 1985, U. Alta., Edmonton, Can., summer 1991; guest lectr. U. Bar-Ilan, Israel, 1984; ednl. dir. firm Scherl & Roth (string importers), Cleve., 1956-70; mem. adv. bd. Contemporary Music Project, Ford Found., 1964-65; ednl. cons. Summy-Birchard Co. (music pubs.); mem. bicentennial com. J. C. Penney Co., 1974-76. Condr., Akron Youth Symphony Orch., 1959-63, Bloomington Youth Symphony Orch., 1969-75, Terre Haute Youth Symphony, 1992, Great Lake Music Camp Orch., 1982-96; author: Learning to Teach Through Playing: String Techniques and Pedagogy, 1971, The School Music Administrator and Supervisor: Catalysts for Change in Music Education, 1973, Teaching Strings, 1988, 2d. edit. 1996, (with others) Humanities Through the Black Experience, Foundations of Music Education, 1983, 2d edit., 1988; co-author: Administrating and Supervising Music, 1991; contbg. author: Ency. of Edn., 1971; editor: Orch. News, 1959-70; mem. editorial bd. Music Educators Jour., 1962-64, Instrumentalist, 1974—; editor (with others) Scheduling Music Classes, 1968; editor, contbg. author: Music Performance Trust Funds Guide; composer: Action with Strings, 1962, Renaissance Suite, 1964, String Literature for Expanding Technique, 1973. Bd. dirs., sec. Ind. U. Credit Union, 1974-87; chmn. ednl. com. Chamber Music Am., 1993-95; chmn. Hall of Fame com. MENC, 1998—. With inf. AUS, 1942-46, ETO, PTO. Recipient citation Nat. Assn. Negro Musicians Inc., 1966, citation Black Music Caucas, 1978, Outstanding Hoosier Musician award, 1986, Disting. Service award Am. String Tchrs. Assn., 1987, Sagamore of the Wabash Govs. award, 1991. Mem. Chamber Music Am. (chair edn. com. 1993-95), Am. String Tchrs. Assn. (pres. 1962-64, dir. pubs. 1985-94, chmn. past pres. coun. 1998—), Music Educators Nat. Conf. (chmn. commn. on tchr. edn. 1968-72, pres. 1976-78, Disting. Svc. award 1989, Hall of Fame com. 1996—), Rotary, Phi Mu Alpha Sinfonia, Phi Delta Kappa. Democrat. Jewish. Avocations: tennis, swimming, reading mystery novels. Home: 2740 S Spicewood Ln Bloomington IN 47401-4347 Office: Ind U Sch Music Bloomington IN 47405

KLOTSCHE, CHARLES MARTIN, real estate development company executive, writer; b. Milw., Jan. 30, 1941; s. J.M. and Roberta; m. Christine Klotsche, Feb. 13, 1972; children: Lyna, Kelly. BA in Econs., Babson Coll., 1962; MBA in Fin., U. Wis., Milw., 1968. Account exec. Harris-Upham and Co., 1963-65; pres. Sante Fe Equities, Inc., 1978—; chmn. bd. First Equity Corp., 1980—; pres. N.Am. Yachtshares, Inc., 1981—, Pan Am. Publs., Inc., 1982—, Trans Pacific Investments, Inc., 1986—; chmn. bd., CEO Klotsche Properties, Inc., 1983—; pres., CEO Pacific Continental Holdings, Inc., 1992—, Blue Moon Charter Co., 1992—; CEO Pan Am. Press, Inc., 1996—; adv. dir. Bank of Santa Fe; bd. dirs. Visa Internat. Bank, Granada; lectr. Marquette U., 1967, Babson Coll., 1991, U. Calif., Irvine, 1992, Santa Monica Coll., 1993. Author: The Encumbered Perceptive and the Intrepid, 1978, The Real Estate Revolution, 1979, Real Estate Investing, A Practical Guide to Wealth Building Secrets, 1980, Real Estate Syndications, the Complete Handbook, 1983, Real EState Development and Finance Handbook, 1986, The 49th Vibration, 1989, Color Medicine, 1993, Omega Point, 1993, Delta Raven Four, 1994, The Silent Victims, 1997, Travels with Charlie, 1997, Continents in the Must, 1997 (screenplays) Capture, 1996, Provenduce, 1997; travel writer Christian Sci. Monitor, 1988; featured in numerous profl. and popular mags. Bd. dirs. N.Mex. Spl. Olympics for Mentally Retarded, Orch. Santa Fe, Santa Fe Assn. Retarded Citizens, St. Elizabeth Shelter; pres. Santa Fe Bus. Cmty. for Arts, 1986—. Served with Officer Corps USMC, 1964-67. Recipient 3 nat. awards for excellence Nat. Assn. Homebuilders. Mem. U.S. Mortgage Brokers Assn., Nat. Assn. Realtors, Urban Land Inst., N.Mex. Gen. Contractors Assn., Rocky Mountain Outdoor Writers and Photographers Assn., Internat. Assn. Resort Developers, Timesharing Internat., Rotary. Republican. Lutheran. Office: PO Box 1043 Sausalito CA 94966-1043

KLOTSCHE, JOHN CHESTER, lawyer; b. Milw., June 18, 1942; s. Johannes Martin and Roberta (Roberts) K.; m. Christine Elizabeth Nelson, May 12, 1975; children: Karissa Faith, Jason Martin, Jonathan William. BS, U. Ariz., 1964; JD, U. Wis., 1967. Bar: Wis. 1967, Ill. 1968, U.S. Dist. Ct. (no. dist.) Ill. 1968, U.S. Ct. Appeals (7th cir.) 1970, Tex. 1987, U.S. Supreme Ct. 1987, U.S. Ct. Appeals (5th cir.) 1989, U.S. Dist. Ct. (no. dist.) Tex. 1990, U.S. Ct. Appeals (6th cir.), U.S. Claims Ct., U.S. Tax Ct. Law clk. to presiding justice Wis. Supreme Ct., Madison, 1967-68; assoc. Baker & McKenzie, Chgo., 1968-73, ptnr., 1973-87; ptnr. Baker & McKenzie, Dallas, 1987-93, L.A., 1993-94, Palo Alto, 1994—. Contbr. articles to profl. jours. Named Order of Coif. Mem. ABA, Ill. Bar Assn., Wis. Bar Assn., Tex. Bar Assn., Phi Delta Phi. Office: Baker & McKenzie 660 Hansen Way Palo Alto CA 94304-1044

KLOTT, DAVID LEE, lawyer; b. Vicksburg, Miss., Dec. 10, 1941; s. Isadore and Dorothy (Lipson) K.; m. Maren J. Randrup, May 25, 1975. BBA summa cum laude, Northwestern U., 1963; JD cum laude, Harvard U., 1966. Bar: Calif. 1966, U.S. Ct. Claims. 1968, U.S. Supreme Ct. 1971, U.S. Tax Ct. 1973, U.S. Ct. Appeals (Fed. cir.) 1982. Ptnr. Pillsbury, Madison & Sutro, San Francisco, 1966—; mem. tax adv. group to sub-chpt. C J and K, Am. Law Inst.; tchr. Calif. Continuing Edn. of Bar, Practising Law Inst., Hastings Law Sch., San Francisco; bd. dirs. and counsel Marin Wine and Food Soc. Commentator Calif. Nonprofit Corp. Law; bd. dirs. Joan Shorenstein Barone Found. for Harvard, The Phyllis J. Shorenstein Fund for the Asian Art Mus. San Francisco; counsel Drum Found. Mem. ABA (tax exempt fin. com.), Calif. State Bar Assn. (tax sect.), San Francisco Bar Assn., Am.-Korean Taekwondo Friendship Assn. (1st dan-black belt), Harvard Club, Northwestern Club, Olympic Club, City Club San Francisco (founding mem.), Bay Club (charter mem.), Harbor Point Racquet and Beach Club, Internat. Wine and Food Soc. (bd. dirs., exec. com., bd. govs. Ams.), Beta Gamma Sigma, Beta Alpha Psi (pres. local chpt.). Office: Pillsbury Madison & Sutro 235 Montgomery St Ste 1616 San Francisco CA 94104-2902

KLOTTER, JAMES C., historian, educator; b. Lexington, Ky., Jan. 17, 1947; s. John Charles K. and Marjorie Virginia (Gibson) Gabbard; m. Freda Jean Campbell, Dec. 28, 1966; children: Karen, Christopher, Katherine. BA, U. Ky., 1968, MA, 1969, PhD, 1975; LittD, Ea. Ky. U., 1997, Union Coll., 1998. Rsch. analyst Ky. Hist. Soc., Frankfort, 1973-75, asst. editor, 1975-78, mng. editor, 1978-80, state historian, 1980-88, asst. dir., 1988-90, dir., state historian, 1990-98; state historian, prof. history Georgetown Coll., 1998—; chmn. bd. dirs. Farmers State Bank, Booneville, Ky.; bd. dirs. Hyden (Ky.) Middlefork Fin.; bd. dirs., bd. govs. Frontier Nursing Svc., Hyden, 1991-96. Author: William Goebel: The Politics of Wrath, 1977, co-author: A New History of Kentucky, 1997; editor: Our Kentucky: Study of Blue Grass State, 1992. Sec. Ky. Civil War Roundtable, Lexington, 1984-94, pres. 1994—. Mem. So. Historian Assn., Ky. Assn. Tchrs. History (pres. 1986-87), Ky. Coun. on Archives (chmn. 1980-81), Ky. Oral History Commn. Bd., Ky. Hist. Soc., U. Ky. Libr. Assn. (pres. 1984-85), Filson Club. Office: 400 E College St # 244 Georgetown KY 40324-1628

KLOTTER, JOHN CHARLES, retired legal educator; b. Louisville, Nov. 6, 1918; s. John J. and Lillie R. (Fischer) K.; m. Jane Riddle, Nov. 2, 1954 (dec.); children: James C., Douglas A., Ronald L. AB, Western Ky. U., 1941; JD, U. Ky., 1948. Bar: Ky. 1948, U.S. Supreme Ct. 1967. Tchr. pub. schs. Louisville, 1941-42; spl. agt. FBI, 1948-50; legal officer Ky. State Police, 1951-52; dir. divsn. probation and parole State of Ky., Frankfort, 1952-56; assoc. dir. So. Police Inst., U. Louisville, 1957-71, dir. So. Police Inst., prof., dean Sch. Justice Adminstrn., So. Police Inst., 1971-81; Editorial dir. criminal justice text series W.H. Anderson Co., 1970-76; chmn. Louisville-Jefferson County Criminal Justice Commn., 1974-76; mem. Ky. Crime Commn., 1971-75, Ky. Law Enforcement Coun., 1971-81, Atty. Gen.'s Prosecutors Adv. Coun., 1970-82. Author: Techniques for Police Instructors, 1963; (with Kanovitz) Constitutional Law, 1968, 8th edit., 1998, Criminal Evidence, 1971, 6th edit., 1999, Legal Guide for Police, 1978, 5th edit., 1998, Criminal Justice Instructional Techniques, 1979, Legal Aspects of Private Security, 1981, Criminal Law, 1983, 6th edit., 1997. Capt. U.S. Army, 1942-46; col. Res. ret. Ford Found. grantee, 1968. Mem. Ky., Louisville bar assns., Res. Officers Assn., Soc. Former Spl. Agts. FBI. Home: 2103 Starmont Rd Louisville KY 40207-1140

KLOTZ, CHARLES RODGER, shipping company executive; b. Englewood, N.J., Apr. 14, 1942; s. George Edward and Beryl Edith (Culingford) K.; m. Deborah Goodwin, June 25, 1966; children: Christine, Suzanne. BS, Trinity Coll., Hartford, Conn., 1964; MBA, Dartmouth Coll., 1966. Officer Bank of Boston Corp., 1969-85; pres., chief exec. officer Gulf Resources & Chem. Corp., Boston, 1985-89; also bd. dirs. Gulf Resources & Chem. Corp.; chmn. bd., CEO Spartan Madison Corp., 1991—; chmn. bd. G.L. Holdings Corp., 1988—; chief exec. officer, chmn. bd. Gotaas Larsen Shipping Corp., 1988-97, also bd. dirs. Lt. USCG, 1966-69. Mem. Flyfisher's Club (London), Wellesley Country Club, Coral Beach and Tennis Club (Bermuda), Algonquin Club. Episcopalian. Office: Bingham Dana & Gould 150 Federal St Fl 15 Boston MA 02110-1726

KLOTZ, FLORENCE, costume designer; b. N.Y.C.; d. Philip K. and Hannah Kraus. Student, Parsons Sch. Design, 1941. Designer: Broadway shows Take Her She's Mine, 1960, Never Too Late, 1962, Nobody Loves An Albatross, 1963, On An Open Roof, 1963, Owl and the Pussycat, 1964, One by One, 1964, Mating Dance, 1965, The Best Laid Plans, 1966, Superman, 1966, Paris Is Out, 1970, Norman Is That You, 1970, Legends, Follies, 1971 (Drama Desk award, Tony award), A Little Night Music, 1973 (Drama Desk award, Tony award), Side By Side Sondheim, 1975, Pacific Overtures, 1976 (Drama Desk award, Tony award, Los Angeles Critic Circle award), On the 20th Century, 1978 (Drama Desk award), Broadway Broadway, Dancin' In The Streets, 1982, Grind, 1984 (Tony award), Jerry's Girls, 1985; (ballet-jazz opus) Antique Epagraph, N.Y.C.; Broadway musicals Rags, 1986, Roza, 1987; Ctr. prodns. Carousel, 1956, Oklahoma, 1956, Annie Get Your Gun, 1956, 4 Baggatelle; movies Something for Everyone, 1969, A Little Night Music, 1976 (Oscar nomination, Los Angeles Critic Circle award); ice shows John Curry's Ice Dancing, 1979; Broadway musical A Doll's Life; ballet 8 Lines, 1986, I'm Old Fashioned (Jerome Robbins), Ives Songs (Jerome Robbins), City of Angels, 1989 (Tony award nominee, Outer Critics Circle award), Kiss of the Spider Woman, 1989 (Tony award 1989, Drama Desk award 1989), Show Boat, Toronto, Can., 1993, Broadway, 1994-95 (N.Y. Outer Critics Cirlce award 1995, Drama Desk award 1995, Tony award 1995, Theatre L.A. Ovation award 1997, Jessie award 1996), Whistle Down the Wind, 1996. Recipient Life Achievement award Theatre Crafts Internat., 1994, L.A. Ovation award, 1997, award NAACP, 1997, Dramalogue, 1997, L.A. DRama Desk, 1997; inducted into Theatre Hall of Fame, 1997. Democrat. Home: 1050 Park Ave New York NY 10028-1031

KLOTZ, IRVING MYRON, chemist, educator; b. Chgo., Jan. 22, 1916; s. Frank and Mollie (Nasatir) K.; m. Mary Sue Hanlon, Aug. 7, 1966; children: Edward, Audie Jeanne, David. B.S., U. Chgo., 1937, Ph.D., 1940. Rsch. assoc. in chemistry Northwestern U., 1940-42, instr., 1942- 46, asst. prof., 1946-47, assoc. prof., 1947-50, prof., 1950-63, Morrison prof. chemistry, 1963-86, prof. emeritus, 1986—; Lalor fellow Marine Biol. Lab., Woods Hole, Mass., 1947-48, corp. mem., 1947—, trustee, 1957-65. Author: Chemical Thermodynamics, 4th rev. edit., 1986, 5th rev. edit., 1994, Energies in Biochemical Reactions, rev. edit., 1967, Introduction to Biomolecular Energetics, 1986, Diamond Dealers, Feather Merchants, 1986; Ligand-Receptor Energetics: A Guide for the Perplexed, 1997; contbr. articles to sci. and other jours. Recipient Army-Navy cert. of appreciation for wartime research, 1948, William C. Rose award biochem. Am. Soc. Biochem. and Molecular Biology, 1993. Fellow Royal Soc. Medicine, Am. Acad. Arts and Scis., AAAS; mem. Nat. Acad. Scis., Am. Soc. Biochemistry and Molecular Biology, Am. Chem. Soc. (Eli Lilly award 1949, Midwest award 1970), Phi Beta Kappa, Sigma Xi, Phi Lambda Upsilon, Alpha Chi Sigma. Home: 2515 Pioneer Rd Evanston IL 60201-2203

KLOTZ, LOUIS HERMAN, structural engineer, educator, consultant; b. Elizabeth, N.J., May 21, 1928; s. Herman Martin and Edna Theresa (Kloepfer) K.; m. Virginia Helen Roll, Apr. 3, 1966 (dec. Oct. 1995); Emily Louise, Jennifer-Claire Virginia. *Louis Klotz serves on the Planning Committees of the local chapter of the American Cancer Society for the "Making Strides Against Breast Cancer" and "Relay for Life" events. He walks these events and the Boston Marathon Jimmy Fund Walk to raise money to battle cancer. Daughter Emily Klotz, BA 1990 Wellesley College, PhD in Immunology 1997 University of Chicago has a post-doctoral appointment at the National Cancer Institute, Bethesda, Maryland. Daughter Jennifer-Claire Klotz, BA 1992 Mount Holyoke College, MS in Agricultural Economics, 1996 Purdue University is with the U.S. Department of Agriculture, Washington, DC.* BSCE, Pa. State U., 1951; MCE, N.Y.U., 1956; PhD, Rutgers U., 1967. Registered profl. engr., N.J., N.H. Structural engr. various firms, N.Y., N.J. metro area, N.Y., N.J., 1951-65; asst. prof. civil engring. U. N.H., Durham, 1965-69, assoc. prof. civil engring., 1969-86, chmn. dept. civil engring., 1971-74; spl. projects dir. ASCE, N.Y.C., 1986-87; cons. Klotz Assocs., Inc., New Castle, N.H., 1987-88; project mgr. Universal Engring. Corp., Boston, 1988-91; exec. dir. New Eng. States Earthquake Consortium, 1991-94; pres. Klotz Consultants Group, Inc., New Castle, N.H., 1994—; cons., evaluator Office of Energy Related Inventions, Gaithersburg, Md., 1978—; mem. energy policy adv. group N.H. Ho. of Reps., Concord, 1979-82; founding mem. N.H. Legis. Acad. Sci. & Tech., Concord, 1980-83. Editor: Energy Sources, The Promises and Problems, 1980; author: Users Manual Small Hydroelectric Financial/Economic Analysis, 1983; (monograph) Water Power, Its Promises and Problems; contbr. articles to Procs. of 1st Internat. Conf. on Computing in Civil Engring., Hydro Rev. Advisor Environ. Protection div. N.H. State Atty. Gen.'s Office, Concord, 1972-76; mem. New Castle (N.H.) Budget Com., 1977-79; tech. reviewer N.E. Appropriate Tech. Small Grants program Dept. Energy, Boston, 1979-80; bd. dirs. Family Svcs. Assn. Portsmouth, 1995-98, Seacoast Hospice, 1996-98. Ford Found fellow, 1962-65, Ford Found. grant, 1968, Systems Design fellow, NASA, Assn. for Engring. Edn., Houston, 1975; named Gen. Acctg. Office Faculty Fellow, U.S. Gen. Acctg. Office, Washington, 1975-76. Mem. AAAS, ASCE (com. on coordination outside ASCE 1978-86), Am. Assn. Engring. Edn., N.Y. Acad. Scis. Republican. Episcopalian. Home: 90 Mainmast Cir New Castle NH 03854 Office: Klotz Consultants Group Inc PO Box 204 New Castle NH 03854-0204

KLOTZ, WENDY LYNNETT, analytical chemist; b. Lebanon, Pa., June 15, 1966; d. William Lewis and Helen Irene (Schrader) Unger; m. Brian Lee Klotz, Sept. 29, 1990. BS, Delaware Valley Coll., Doylestown, Pa., 1988; postgrad., LaSalle U., Phila., 1989-92, Villanova U., 1992—. Cert. chemist. Chemist Rohm and Haas Co., Bristol, Pa., 1987-89; scientist Rohm and Haas Co., Spring House, Pa., 1989—. Active advertising The Hunger Project, Bucks County, Pa., 1986. Mem. AAAS, Am. Inst. Chemists (Outstanding Senior award 1988), Am. Chem. Soc. (Analytical Chemistry Undergraduate award 1987), Sigma Xi. Office: Rohm and Haas Co PO Box 904 727 Norristown Rd Spring House PA 19477-0904

KLOWDEN, MICHAEL LOUIS, lawyer; b. Chgo., Apr. 7, 1945; s. Roy and Esther (Siegel) K.; m. Patricia A. Doede, June 15, 1968; children: Kevin B., Deborah C. AB, U. Chgo., 1967; JD, Harvard U., 1970. Bar: Calif. 1971. From assoc. to ptnr. Mitchell, Silberberg & Knupp, L.A., 1970-78; mng. ptnr. Morgan, Lewis & Bockius, L.A., 1978-95; vice chmn. Jefferies Group, Inc. and Jefferies Co., Inc., L.A., 1995-96, pres., COO, 1996—; bd. dirs. Jefferies Group, Inc., L.A. Trustee U. Chgo., 1986—. Office: Jefferies Group Inc 11100 Santa Monica Blvd Los Angeles CA 90025-3384

KLOZE, IDA IRIS, lawyer; d. Max and Bertha (Samet) K. A.A., George Washington U., 1944, AB, 1947; LLB, U. Md., 1926; JD, 1967. Bar: Md. 1927, U.S. Supreme Ct. 1949. Sole practice, Balt., 1927-34; dep. collector IRS, Balt., 1934-39; with GAO, 1943-45, War Assets Adminstrn., 1945-49, Labor Dept., 1950-53, FTC Antitrust Divsn., 1956-71; vol. atty. Pro Bono Law Litigation Divsn. Pub. Citizen, Washington, 1972-76; ret. Mem. Mrs. Rosalyn Carter's Com. Mental Health; exec. sec. Commn. for Prevention Infantile Paralysis, Balt., 1940-42; lobbyist Md. Legis., U.S. Congress for Equal Rights Amendment Constitution; rep. Indsl. Coun. Nat. Womens Party, Balt., 1940-42; sec. Citizen's Commn. Md., Balt., 1935-39; trial atty. Fed. Trade Commn., U.S. Anti-Trust Divsn. Mem. ABA, Women's Bar Assn. (v.p. Balt. 1928-32), Profl. Women's Coun. (pres. 1928-33), Nat. Women's Party (lobbyist, co-chmn. campaign com. Md. for re-election FDR for 4th term, legal asst. life mem. 1951—), Fed. Bar Assn. (rec. sec., mem. nat. coun., sec. com. gen. counsels 1951-52).

KLUCK, CLARENCE JOSEPH, physician; b. Stevens Point, Wis., June 20, 1929; s. Joseph Bernard and Mildred Lorraine (Helminiak) K.; divorced; children: Paul Bernard, Annette Louise Kluck Winston, David John, Maureen Ellen. BS in Med. Sci., U. Wis., 1951, MD, 1954. Resident San Joaquin Hosp., French Camp, Calif., 1955-56; asst. instr. medicine Ohio State U., Columbus, 1958-60; physician, chief of medicine Redford Med. Ctr., Detroit, 1960-69; practice medicine specializing in internal medicine Denver, 1969-83; med. dir. Atlantic Richfield Co., Denver, 1983-85; corp. med. dir. Cyprus Minerals Co., Englewood, Colo., 1985-92; pres. Kluck Med. Assocs., Englewood, 1992—; bd. dirs. Climbo Catering, Detroit, 1967-69, Met. Labs., Denver, 1970-81, Provost, Inc., Denver, 1985-92; pres., CEO, chmn. bd. Corpcare, Inc., Englewood, 1992-97; CEO, pres. Corpcare Med. Assocs., P.C., 1992-97; pres. Denver Occupational and Aviation Medicine Clinic, P.C., 1995—. Contbr. articles to profl. jours. Served to capt. U.S. Army, 1956-58. Recipient Century Club award Boy Scouts Am., 1972.

Fellow Am. Occupational Med. Assn., Am. Coll. Occupational and Environ. Medicine, Am. Coll. Occupational Medicine; mem. Am. Acad. Occupational Medicine, Rocky Mountain Acad. Occupational Medicine (bd. dirs. 1985-88), Arapahoe County Med. Soc., Denver Med. Soc. (bd. dirs. 1973-74, council mem. 1981-87), Colo. Med. Soc. (del. 1973-74, 81-87), Am. Mining Congress Health Commn., Am. Soc. Internal Medicine, Colo. Soc. Internal Medicine. Roman Catholic. Clubs: Flatirons (Boulder, Colo.); Metropolitan. Avocations: fishing, hiking, skiing, flying, golf. Office: 3700 Havana St Ste 200 Denver CO 80239-3242

KLUCK, EDWARD PAUL, chief of police; b. Irvington, N.J., Oct. 8, 1946; s. Arthur and Dolores (Wesoloski) K.; m. Theresa Helen Moore, May 11, 1973. Grad., FBI Acad., Avantico, Va., 1979. Chief of police Madison, N.J. Vol. Project Cmty. Aide, Madison, 1976—; mem. Madison Alliance Drug Use, 1990—. Staff sgt. USAF, 1965-69. Mem. Internat. Chiefs of Police Assn., N.J. Pub. Mgrs. Assn., FBI Nat. Graduates, Madison Golf Club. Office: Borough of Madison Police Dept 50 Kings Rd Madison NJ 07940-2592

KLUCKING, GAIL MARIE, educator; b. Trenton, N.J., Feb. 17, 1958; d. Laurence Patrick and Christine Thelma Minnick;l m. Tony Baugn Klucking, June 5, 1987; 1 child, Sara. BA, Mo. Bapt. Coll., 1984; MPA, Troy State U., 1991; MPhil, U. Oxford, England, 1993; postgrad., Auburn U., 1998—. Instr. English Kubaski H.S., Okinawa, Japan, 1987-89; founding dir., com. mem. Taylor Rd. Kindergarten, Montgomery, Ala., 1988—; adj. instr. Auburn U., Montgomery, 1993—; field rep. European Region Troy State U., Upper Heyford, England, 1990-91; adv. 21st century adminstr. evaluatin program task force State of Ala., Dept. Edn., Taylor Rd. Edn. Adhoc Com., Montgomery. Sunday sch. tchr. O'Fallon (Ill.) Bapt. Ch., 1980-85, Taylor Rd. Bapt. Ch., 1994-99; coach Spl. Olympics, Seattle, 1987; pres. Student Govt. Assn., Mo. Bapt. Coll., 1984. With USAF, 1985-87. Mem. Am. Soc. Pub. Adminstrn., Phi Sigma Alpha. Republican. Avocations: fitness training, reading.

KLUCZYNSKI, JANET, computer company marketing executive; b. Chgo., Aug. 5, 1955; d. Thomas Edward and Melanie Irene (Lakoma) K. BA in English cum laude, Dartmouth Coll., 1977; M in Mgmt., Kellogg Grad. Sch. Mgmt., 1980. Asst. product dir. McNeil Consumer Products Co. div. Johnson & Johnson, Ft. Washington, Pa., 1980-83; mktg. rep. IBM, Boston, 1984-87; assoc. cons. corp. competitive analysis Digital Equipment Corp., West Concord, Mass., 1987-88; mktg. programs mgr. Stratus Computer, Inc., Marlboro, Mass., 1988-95; dir. mktg. Cmty. Stream Internat. (name changed to Corp. Software & Tech., Inc.), Norwood, Mass., 1996—. Alumnae admissions interviewer Dartmouth Coll., class officer, 1992-97; mem. Jr. League Boston, 1984-89; English tutor, fundraiser, mem. bus. leaders bd. One with One, Brighton, Mass., 1986—. Mem. Kellogg Alumni Club of Boston (bd. dirs. 1991-95). Democrat. Roman Catholic. Avocations: tennis, curling, spectator sports, the Arts, travel. Home: 15 Westminster Ave Lexington MA 02420-2815

KLUEPFEL, DIETER, microbiologist; b. Darmstadt, Fed. Republic Germany, Oct. 7, 1930; s. Max and Ute Maria (Paqué) K.; m. Jane MacMillan, Dec. 26, 1959 (div. 1975); children: Alexandra, Mark; m. Hélène Sasseville, June 25, 1983. Diploma sci. nat., ETH, Zurich, Switzerland, 1954, D. Natural Sci., 1957. Postdoctoral fellow Nat. Rsch. Coun. Can., Ottawa, 1957-59; rsch. scientist Lepetit Spa, Milan, Italy, 1959-61, head lab., 1961-65; sr. rsch. scientist Ayerst Labs., Montreal, Que., Can., 1965-70, rsch. assoc., 1970-75; rsch. prof. Inst. A. Frappier U. du Que., Laval, 1975-99, prof. emeritus, 1999—; dir. Applied Microbiology Rsch. Ctr., Laval, 1989-98. Assoc. editor Can. Jour. Microbiology, 1978-88; contbr. articles to profl. jours. Boehringer-Mannheim Award of Can. Soc. of Microbiologists, 1998. Mem. Can. Soc. Microbiologist (pres. appl. sect. 1980-82), Am. Soc. Microbiology, Soc. Indsl. Microbiology. Achievements include rsch. publs. and patents in industrial microbiology and biotechnology; in process development of biobleaching of paper pulp enzyme technology; research in regulation of hemi cellulases genes in actinomycetes and on structure-function of these enzymes. Home: 2314 Grand Blvd, Montreal, PQ Canada H4B 2W9 Office: Inst Armand Frappier, 531 Blvd des Prairies, Laval, PQ Canada 47N 4Z3

KLUES, JACK, communications executive. Exec. v.p. worldwide media svcs. Leo Burnett Co., Inc., Chgo.; CEO StarCom Worldwide, Chgo., 1999—. Office: Leo Burnett Co Inc 35 W Wacker Dr Chicago IL 60601-1648*

KLUG, AARON, molecular biologist; b. Aug. 11, 1926; s. Lazar and Bella (Silin) K.; m. Liebe Bobrow, 1948; 2 children. B.Sc., U. Witwatersrand; M.Sc., U. Cape Town; PhD, DSc, Cambridge U.; DSc (hon.), U. Chgo., 1978, Columbia U., 1978; D (hon.), U. Strasbourg, 1978; DSc (hon.), Stockholm U., 1980, U. Witwatersrand, 1984, Hebrew U., Jerusalem, 1984, Hull U., 1985, U. St. Andrews, 1987, U. Western Ont., 1991, Warwick U., 1994, Capetwon U., 1997; D Litt, Cambridge U., 1998. Jr. lectr., 1947-48; rsch. student Cavendish Lab. Cambridge (Eng.) U., 1949-52; Rouse-Ball rsch. student Trinity Coll., 1949-52; Colloid Sci. dept., 1953; Nuffield rsch. fellow Birkbeck Coll., London, 1954-57, dir. virus structure rsch. group, 1958-61; mem. staff Med. Rsch. Coun. Lab. Molecular Biology, Cambridge U., 1962—, joint head div. structural studies, 1978-86, dir., 1986-96; Leeuwenhoek lectr. Royal Soc., 1973; Dunham lectr. Harvard U. Med. Sch., 1975; Harvey lectr., N.Y.C., 1979, Lane lectr. Stanford U., 1983; Silliman lectr. Yale U., 1985; Cetus lectr. Berkeley U., 1986; Pauli lectr., Zürich, 1986; Nishina Meml. lectr., Tokyo, 1986; J. T. Baker lectr. Cornell U., 1987; Jean Weigle lectr., Geneva, 1989, Steenbock lectr. U. Wis., Madison, 1989; Innovators in Biochem. lectr. U. Va., Richmond, 1990; Calbiochem. lectr. U. Calif., San Diego, 1991. Contbr. articles to sci. jours. Recipient Heineken prize Royal Netherlands Acad. Sci., 1979, Louisa Gross Horwitz prize Columbia U., 1981, Nobel prize in chemistry, 1982, Gold medal of Merit, U. cape Town, 1983, Copley medal Royal Soc., 1985, Harden medal Biochem. Soc., 1985; Knight, 1988, Order of Merit, 1995. Fellow Royal Soc. (pres. 1995—), Peterhouse (Cambridge hon.), Royal Coll. Physn, (hon., Baly medal 1987), Royal Coll. Pathologists (hon.), Trinity Coll. (Cambridge, hon.), Birkbeck Coll. (London, hon.); mem. Am. Acad. Arts and Scis. (fgn. hon.), French Acad. Scis. (fgn. assoc.), Max-Planck-Gesellschaft (fgn. assoc.), NAS (fgn. assoc.), Am. Philos. Soc. (fgn. mem.). Office: Med Rsch Coun Lab Molecular Biology, Cambridge CB2 2QH, England

KLUG, MICHAEL GREGORY, scientist; b. Indpls., Oct. 11, 1967; s. James Charles and Janet Mae K.; m. Dagmar M. Kube, Aug. 18, 1995. BS in Biology, Ind. U., 1989, PhD, 1996. Predoctoral fellow Am. Heart Assn., Ind. affiliate, Indpls., 1991-94; rsch. scholar Ind. U. Sch. Medicine, Indpls., 1994-95; postdoctoral fellow Eli Lilly & Co., Indpls., 1997—. Contbr. articles to profl. jours., chpt. to book. Monsey fellow for summer rsch. Ind. U. Sch. Medicine, Indpls., 1989; recipient Paul Nicoll award Am. Heart Assn.-Ind. affiliate, Indpls., 1992. Mem. AAAS, Am. Physiol. Soc., Tissue Engrng. Soc., Phi Beta Kappa. Avocations: running, reading, bicycling, travel. Office: Eli Lilly & Co R&D Labs Lilly Corp Ctr Mail Drop 0520 Indianapolis IN 46285

KLUG, SCOTT LEO, former congressman; b. Milwaukee, Wis., Jan. 16, 1953; s. Ralph William Klug and Josephine (Farrell) Weber; m. Tess Summers, Mar. 4, 1978; children: Keefe, Brett, Collin Phillip. BA, Lawrence U., 1975; MS in Journalism, Northwestern U., 1976; MBA, U. Wis., 1990. Reporter TV sta. Wausau, Wis., 1976-78; reporter Sta. KING-TV, Seattle, 1978-81; investigative reporter Sta. WJLA-TV, Washington, 1981-88; anchor, reporter Sta. WKOW-TV, Madison, Wis., 1988-90; v.p. pub. fin. dept. Blunt, Ellis & Loewi, Madison, 1990; mem. 102nd-105th U.S. Congress from 2d Wis. dist., Washington, D.C., 1991-98; mem. commerce com. 102nd-105th U.S. Congress from 2d Wis. dist.; publ., CEO Wis. Trails, Madison, 1999—; pub. affairs counsel Foley and Lardner, Washington, 1999—. Reporter, producer documentaries (Emmy awards 1989, 90). Named Nat. Humanitarian of Yr., Humane Soc., 1986; John McCloy fellow Columbia U. Sch. Journalism, 1987. Republican. Avocations: tennis, basketball, cooking. Office: Wis Trails PO Box 5650 Madison WI 53705-0650 also: Foley & Lardner Washington Harbour 3000 K St NW Washington DC 20007-5109*

KLUGE, HOLGER, retired bank executive; b. Hamburg, Germany, Mar. 11, 1942; married; 2 children. BComm with honors, Sir George Williams Univ., Montreal, 1971; MBA with honors, Sophia U., Tokyo, 1977. Mem. branch ops. staff Can. Imperial Bank of Commerce, Montreal, 1959-81, v.p. Asia Pacific ops., 1981-84, sr. v.p. internat. ops., 1984-86, exec. v.p. support svcs. Corp. Bank, 1986-88, exec. v.p. Eastern Can., Europe, Mid. East, Africa and Latin Am. Corp. Bank, 1988-90, exec. v.p. internat., 1990, pres. Personal and Comml. Bank (formerly Individual Bank), 1990-99, bd. dirs., 1992-99, dir. corp. coun. on youth in the economy, ret., 1999; bd. dirs. Husky Oil Ltd.; chmn., dir. Can. Imperial Bank of Commerce West Indies Holdings Ltd., CEF Holdings, Ltd., TAL Investment Counsel, Ltd. Bd. dirs., chmn. bd. Can. Youth Bus. Found. Mem. Can. Banking Assn. (vice chmn.). Office: Can Imperial Bank Commerce, Commerce Court, Toronto, ON Canada M5L 1A2

KLUGE, JOHN WERNER, broadcasting and advertising executive; b. Chemnitz, Germany, Sept. 21, 1914; s. Fritz and Gertrude (Donj) K.; children—Samantha, Joseph B. Student, Wayne U.; B.A. (4 year honor scholar), Columbia, 1937. Vice pres., sales mgr. Otten Bros., Inc., Detroit, 1937-41; pres., dir. radio sta. WGAY, Silver Spring, Md., 1946-59, St. Louis Broadcasting Corp., Brentwood, Mo., 1953-58, Pitts. Broadcasting Co., 1954-59; pres., treas., dir. Capitol Broadcasting Co., Nashville, 1954-59, Asso. Broadcasters, Inc., Ft. Worth-Dallas, 1957-59; partner Western N.Y. Broadcasting Co., Buffalo, 1957-60; pres., dir. Washington Planagraph Co., 1956-60, Mid.-Fla. Radio Corp., Orlando, 1952-59; treas., dir. Mid-Fla. Television Corp., 1957-60; owner Kluge Investment Co., Washington, 1956-60; partner Nashton Properties, Nashville, 1954-60, Texworth Investment Co., Ft. Worth, 1957-60; chmn. bd. Seaboard Service System, Inc., 1957-58; chm. bd., pres., CEO Metromedia Inc., Secaucus, N.J., 1959-86; former gen. ptnr., chm. bd., pres., CEO Metromedia Co.; now chmn. and pres. Metromedia Co., East Rutherford, N.J.; now pres., chmn. bd. Benale Holdings Corp., Dallas; also chmn., dir. LDDS Comm., Jackson, Miss.; investor, operator N.Y./N.J. Metro Stars, Secaucus, N.J., 1995; pres. New Eng. Fritos, Boston, 1947-55, N.Y. Inst. Dietetics, N.Y.C., 1953-60; chmn. bd., pres., dir. Metromedia, Inc., N.Y.C., Metromedia, Inc. (including met. broadcasting div., world wide broadcasting div. and Foster & Kleiser div., outdoor advt.); chmn. bd., treas., dir. Kluge, Finkelstein & Co. (food brokers), Balt.; chmn. bd., treas. Tri-Suburban Broadcasting Corp., Washington, Kluge & Co.; chmn. bd., pres., treas. Washington, Silver City Sales Co., Washington; dir. Marriott-Hot Shoppes, Inc., Chock Full O' Nuts Corp., Nat. Bank Md., Waldorf Astoria Corp., Just One Break, Inc., Belding Heminway Co., Inc.; mem. adv. council Mfrs. Hanover Trust Co.; Mem. Washington Bd. Trade. Bd. dirs. Brand Names Found., Inc., Shubert Found.; v.p., bd. dirs. United Cerebral Palsy Research and Ednl. Found., 1972—; trustee Strang Clinic Miliken U.; bd. govs. N.Y. Coll. Osteo. Medicine. Served to capt. U.S. Army, 1941-45. Mem. Nat. Food Brokers Assn., Washington Food Brokers Assn. (pres. 1958), Grocery Wheels Washington, Grocery Mfrs. Reps. Washington, Advt. Club Washington, Nat. Assn. Radio and Television Broadcasters, Advt. Council N.Y.C., Nat. Sugar Brokers Assn. Clubs: Army and Navy (Washington), University (Washington), Figure Skating (Washington), National Capital Skeet and Trap (Washington), Broadcasters (Washington); Metropolitan (N.Y.C.), Columbia Associates (N.Y.C.), University (N.Y.C.); Olympic (San Francisco); Marco Polo (N.H. gov.). Office: Metromedia One Meadowlands Plaza East Rutherford NJ 07073*

KLUGE, STEVE, secondary education educator. Sci. tchr. Foxlane High Sch., Bedford, N.Y., 1987—; project coord. Morgenthau Nature Conservancy. Developed AP course in physical geology. Recipient Outstanding Earth Sci. Tchr. award, 1992. Office: Fox Lane High Sch PO Box 390 Rte 172 S Bedford Rd Bedford NY 10506*

KLUGER, RICHARD, author, editor; b. Paterson, N.J., Sept. 18, 1934; s. David and Ida (Abramson) K.; m. Phyllis Schlain, Mar. 23, 1957; children—Matthew Harold, Leonard Theodore. A.B. cum laude, Princeton, 1956. Copy editor Wall St. Jour., 1956-57; editor, pub. County Citizen, New City, N.Y., 1958-60; staff writer N.Y. Post, 1960-61; asso. editor Forbes mag., 1962; gen. books editor N.Y. Herald Tribune, 1962-63, book editor, 1963-66; editor Book Week, 1963-66; sr. editor Simon and Schuster, 1966-68, mng. editor, 1968, exec. editor, 1968-70; editor-in-chief Atheneum Pubs., 1970-71; pres., pub. Charterhouse Books, 1971-73. Author: When the Bough Breaks, 1964, National Anthem, 1969, Simple Justice, 1976, Members of the Tribe, 1977, Star Witness, 1979, Un-American Activities, 1982, The Paper: The Life and Death of the New York Herald Tribune, 1986, The Sheriff of Nottingham, 1992, Ashes to Ashes: America's Hundred-Year Cigarette War, 1996; co-author: (with Phyllis Kluger) Good Goods, 1982, Royal Poinciana, 1988. Recipient George Polk award, 1987, Pulitzer prize Gen. Non-Fiction, 1997; Nat. Am. Book Non-Fiction award nominee, 1976, 86, Nat. Book Critics Cir. award nominee, 1997. Home: 7 Queens Ln Pennington NJ 08534

KLUGER, RUTH, German language educator, editor; b. Vienna, Austria, Oct. 30, 1931; came to U.S., 1947, naturalized, 1952; d. Viktor and Alma (Gredinger) Kluger Hirschel; m. Werner T. Angress, Mar. 1952 (div. 1962); children: Percy, Dan. BA, Hunter Coll., 1950; MA, U. Calif.-Berkeley, 1952, PhD, 1967. Asst. prof. German lang. and lit. Case Western Res. U., 1966-70; assoc. prof. U. Kans., Lawrence, 1970-73; assoc. prof. U. Va., Charlottesville, 1973-75, prof., 1975-76; prof. U. Calif.-Irvine, 1976-80, 86-88, dir. Göttingen Study Ctr., Edn. Abroad Program, 1988-90; prof. Princeton U., 1980-86; editor German Quar., 1977-84. Author: The Early German Epigram: A Study in Baroque Poetry, 1971, Weiter leben Eine Jugend, 1992, Katastrophen, Uber Deutsche Literatur, 1994, Frauen lesen anders, 1996; corr. editor Simon Wiesenthal Ctr. Ann., 1987; contbr. articles to profl. jous. Recipient Rauriser Literaturpreis, 1993, Grimmelshausen-Preis, 1993, Niedersachsen Preis, 1993, Marie-Louise-Kaschnitz preis, 1994, Heine-Preis, 1997; ACLS fellow, 1978. Mem. MLA (exec. coun. 1978-82), Am. Assn. Tchrs. German (exec. coun. 1976-81), Deutsche Akademie für Sprache und Dichtung, Lessing Soc. (pres. 1977-79), PEN Club. Democrat. Jewish. Home: 62 Whitman Ct Irvine CA 92612-4066 Office: U Calif Dept German Irvine CA 92612

KLUGMAN, JACK, actor; b. Phila., Apr. 27, 1922; s. Max and Rose K.; m. Brett Somers, 1966 (separated); children: David, Adam. Student, Carnegie Inst. Tech., Am. Theatre Wing, N.Y.C. Film appearances include Timetable, 1956, Twelve Angry Men, 1957, Cry Terror, 1958, The Scarface Mob, 1962, The Days of Wine and Roses, 1963, I Could Go on Singing, 1963, Act One, 1963, Yellow Canary, 1963, Hail Mafia, 1965, The Detective, 1968, The Split, 1968, Goodbye Columbus, 1969, Who Says I Can't Ride a Rainbow, 1971, Two Minute Warning, 1976, Dear God, 1996; TV series: Harris Against the World, 1964-65, The Odd Couple, 1970-75 (Emmy award 1971, 73), Quincy, 1976-83, You Again, 1986-87; other TV appearances include: Naked City, The Twilight Zone, The Defenders (Emmy award 1964); TV movies Fame is the Name of the Game, 1966, Poor Devil, 1973, The Underground Man, 1974, One of My Wives is Missing, 1976, Around the World in 80 Days, 1989, The Odd Couple: Together Again, 1993, Parallel Lives, 1994; N.Y. stage debut in Stevedore, Equity Library Theatre, 1949; Broadway debut in Golden Boy, 1952; other stage appearances include Gypsy, 1959, The Sudden and Accidental Re-education of Horse Johnson, 1968, I'm Not Rappaport, 1987, Three Men on a Horse, 1993; appears in summer stock. Winner Emmy award, 1963, 71, 73. Mem. AFTRA, SAG, Actors Equity. Office: S Klein Associates 20300 Ventura Blvd Ste 215 Woodland Hills CA 91364-2497

KLUGMAN, PETER JAY, psychologist, consultant; b. Bklyn., May 19, 1942; s. Joseph and Shirley (Rich) K.; m. Marthanne Hamlin, Oct. 29, 1964 (dec. Dec. 1979). BA, U. Miami, 1964, MEd, 1965; MA, U. Fla., 1974, PhD, 1978. Diplomate Am. Acad. Pain Mgmt.; lic. psychologist, N.J., Pa. Commd. 2d lt. U.S. Army, 1966, advanced through grades to lt. col., 1983, ret., 1986; chief Community Mental Health Svc., Ft. Dix, N.J., 1976-86; clin. dir. Biofeedback Ctr. of South Jersey, Willingboro, N.J., 1986-99; pres. Orgnl. Potential, Medford, N.J., 1986-99; cons. Pub. Svc. Electric and Gas, N.J., 1984—, Office Surgeon Gen. U.S. Army, 1986—, USAF, 1994—. Contbr. articles to profl. jours. Bd. dirs. Girl Scouts of South Jersey Pines, 1989—, Lenape Regional High Sch. Bd. Edn., N.J.; v.p. Medford Bd. Edn., N.J. Decorated Bronze Star, Legion of Merit, Army Commendation medal, Vietnam Svc. medal, Acheivement medal, Dept. of the Army Civilian. Mem. APA, N.J. Psychol. Assn. (South Jersey rep. 1990-93), South Jersey Psychol. Assn. (bd. dirs. 1989-93). Jewish. Office: Orgnl Potential PO Box 1551 Medford NJ 08055-6551

KLUGMAN, STEPHAN CRAIG, newspaper editor; b. Fargo, N.D., May 11, 1945; s. Ted and Charlotte (Olson) K.; m. Julie Sue Terpening, Sept. 18, 1971; children: Josh, Carrie. BA in Journalism, Ind. U., 1967. Copy editor Chgo. Sun-Times, 1967-68, asst. telegraph editor, 1968-72, telegraph editor, 1972-74, city editor, 1974-76, asst. mng. editor features, 1976-78; asst. prof. Medill Sch. Journalism, Northwestern U., Evanston, Ill., 1978-79, dir. undergrad. studies, 1979-82; editor Jour.-Gazette, Ft. Wayne, Ind., 1982—. Mem. Am. Soc. Newspaper Editors. Office: Jour-Gazette 600 W Main St Fort Wayne IN 46802-1408

KLUKA, DARLENE ANN, human performance educator, researcher; b. Berwyn, Ill., Oct. 6, 1950; d. Aloysius Louis and Lillian (Malkovsky) K. BA, Ill. State U., 1972, MA, 1976; PhD, Tex. Woman's U., 1985. Educator, coach Fenton High Sch., Bensenville, Ill., 1972-73, New Trier East High Sch., Winnetka, Ill., 1973-80; coach Bradley Univ., Peoria, Ill., 1980-82; grad. teaching asst. Tex. Woman's Univ., Denton, 1982-85; prof. Newberry (S.C.) Coll., 1985-86; prof., rschr., dir. Human Performance Ctr., Grambling (La.) State U., 1986-90; asst. prof. human studies and sport adminstrn. U. Ala., Birmingham, 1990-94, rschr., dir. Motor Behavior and Sports Vision Lab., 1990-94; dir. grad. program U. Ctrl. Okla., Edmond, 1994-97; assoc. prof., health and physical edn. coord. Grambling State U., La., 1997—; head of del. Internat. Olympic Acad., Olympia Greece, 1990; dep. del. U.S. Olympic Com., 1996—; adv. bd. Women's Sports Found., 1992—; U.S.A. Volleyball Sports Medicine and Performance Commn., 1994—; bd. dirs. U.S.A. Volleyball, v.p. mem. rels. and human resources, 1996—. Author: Visual Skill Enhancement for Sport Exercises, 1989, Volleyball Drills, 1990, Volleyball, 4th edit., 2000, Motor Behavior: From Learning to Performance, 1999; founding co-editor Internat. Jour. Sports Vision, 1991-97; founding editor Internat. Jour. Volleyball Rsch., 1997—; mem. editl. bd. Coaching Volleyball Jour., 1988—. Recipient Rsch. award So. Assn. Phys. Edn. Coll. Women, 1994, 96, U.S. Volleyball Leader award, 1998, Joseph Andera Rsch. award Internat. Acad. of SportsVision, 1999, Disting. Svc. award AAALF Internat. Rels. Coun., 1999; Disting. Achievements award Ill. State U. Alumni Assn., 1997. Mem. AAHPERD (rsch. fellow, Taylor Dodson Young Profl. award so. dist. 1991, bd. govs. 1993-96), AAUP (Disting. scholar award 1997), Nat. Assn. for Girls and Women in Sport (bd. dirs., exec. com. 1989-92, 93-96, pres. 1990-91, Honor award 1996), Internat. Coun. for Sport Sci. and Phys. Edn. (exec. bd. 1997—, editl. bd. 1998—), Internat. Acad. Sports Vision (adv. bd. 1989-98, v.p. 1993—), Internat. Coun. for Health, Phys. Edn. and Recreation Sport and Dance (Disting. Scholar in Sport award 1995), Women's Sports Found. (internat. com. 1993—, Pres.'s award 1996), Internat. Assn. Phys. Edn. and Sports for Girls and Women, Girls and Women in Sport (rep. to exec. bd. Internat. Coun. Sport Sci. and Physical Edn. 1996—). Roman Catholic. Avocations: jogging, photography, collecting Olympic Games memorabilia.

KLUMPP, BARBARA ANNE, quality assurance and utilization review executive; b. N.Y.C., Mar. 16, 1955; d. John Jr. and Dorothy (Alzinger) K.; m. Howard C. Schadt Jr., Oct. 11, 1981; 1 child, John Howard Klumpp Schadt. BSN, Adelphi U., 1977, MSN, 1982; MBA, Century U., 1996. RN, N.Y.; cert. in nursing adminstrn.; cert. profl. healthcare quality, cert. profl. utilization rev.; cert. in nursing care mgmt.; cert. case mgmt. Staff nurse South Nassau Hosp., Oceanside, N.Y., 1978; vis. nurse Vis. Nurse Svc. N.Y., Flushing, 1978-84; nurse supr. Health Svcs. at Home, Commack, N.Y., 1983-87, Long Beach (N.Y.) Hosp., 1987-89; adminstr. United Presbyn. Residence, Woodbury, N.Y., 1989-91; v.p. pediatrics DSI Home Care, Baldwin, N.Y., 1991-92; adminstr. TQM Family Care CHHA, Hicksville, N.Y., 1992-94; dir. managed care Am. Life and Health Ins. Co., Hicksville, 1994-95; regional patient mgr. U.S. Health Care, Uniondale, N.Y., 1995-97; sr. mgr. Heritage N.Y. Med. Group, Garden City, N.Y., 1997-98; performance improvement coord. N. Shore- LIJ Health Sys., 1998—; mem. profl. adv. com. Winthrop U. Hosp., Mineola, N.Y., 1989-91, Franklin Hosp. Med. Ctr., Valley Stream, N.Y., 1989-91, L.I. Care at Home, East Meadow, N.Y., 1993—. Mem. ANA, N.Y. State Nurses Assn., Nat. Assn. for Health Care Quality, Home Care Assn. N.Y. State, Nat. League for Nursing (advisor infection control 1994), Case Mgmt. Soc. Am. Home: 1622 Dewey Ave North Bellmore NY 11710

KLUMPP, STEPHEN PAUL, architect; b. Rochester, N.Y., Nov. 4, 1952; s. Oscar Edward and Mary Elizabeth (Ladue) K.; m. Cheryl Anne Miller, May 17, 1986; 1 child, Andrew Ozcy. BArch, Ill. Inst. Tech., 1975. Registered architect, Ill., N.Y.; cert. Nat. Coun. Archtl. Registration Bds. Designer Communica Internat., LaGrange, Ill., 1975-76; ptnr. Schiller & Frank Architects, Wheeling, Ill., 1976-85; project architect Archiplan Internat., Rolling Meadows, Ill., 1985-91; pres., owner Ar-K-Teks Unltd., Ltd., Wheeling, 1981—. Pres. East-Fowler Adv. Coun., Chgo., 1973-75. Recipient Gold and Bronze Key award Chgo. Home Builders Assn., 1996, Remodeling award Better Homes and Gardens, 1994, Preservation award Highland Park, 1993. Mem. AIA, Bldg. Ofcls. and Code Adminstrs. Internat., Nat. Space Soc., Nat. Soc. Hist. Preservation, Frank Lloyd Wright Home and Studio Found., Wheeling C. of C. Avocations: genealogy, carpentry, computers, video production. Home: 300 11th St Wheeling IL 60090-2716 Office: Ar-K-Teks Unltd Ltd 300 11th St Wheeling IL 60090-2716

KLUNGNESS, ELIZABETH JANE, publisher, writer, retired accountant; b. Indpls., Apr. 25, 1924; d. Robert Andrew and Mary (Van Gorder) Butler; m. Walter James Hicks, Aug. 24, 1946 (div. Jan. 1970); children: Pamela K. Hicks, Jerry L. Hicks; m. James Gregory Klungness, July 10, 1971. Student, Arthur Jordon Conservatory, Indpls., 1942-44, Butler U., Indpls., 1945-48. Clk. Eli Lilly, William H. Block Dept. Store, Bridgeport Brass, Indpls., 1943-48; pub. acct. Ind., Tex., Wash., Oreg., 1948-67; agt. IRS, Longview, Wash., 1967-72; pvt. practice Tower Acctg., Castle Rock, Wash., 1973-75; writer, editor Tower Enterprises, Yuma, Ariz., 1975-89; pub. Tower Enterprises, Vista, Calif., 1989—; book reviewer Bremerton (Wash.) Sun, 1957-60, Yuma Sun, 1981-83; instr. Chehalis (Wash.) Jr. Coll., 1970-71, Ariz. Western U., 1983-84; spkr. in field. Author: Prisoners in Petticoats, 1993; author, pub.: Century House Cookbook, 1981, Non-Golfer's Cookbook, 1982, Tax Tips for Writers, 1994, 95, 96, 97, 98, 99, Grandma, I Want to Write, 1994; editor: Northwoods Jour. Revs.; contbr. articles to jours.; editor, pub.: Writer's News, 1994—. Recipient 1st pl. fiction award Coun. for Arts, Carlsbad, Calif., 1993, 1st pl. award PEN/Dorothy Daniels, 1993. Mem. Philanthropic Ednl. Orgn., Nat. Writers Assn., Sisters in Crime, Soc. S.W. Authors, Pi Bet Phi. Avocations: mentoring writers, reading. Home and Office: 2130 Sunset Dr Spc 47 Vista CA 92083-4516

KLUNZINGER, THOMAS EDWARD, writer, actor, director, township treasurer; b. Ann Arbor, Mich., Sept. 11, 1944; s. Willard Reuben and Katherine Eileen (McCurdy) K.; BA cum laude in Advt., Mich. State U., 1966. Copywriter Campbell-Ewald Advt. Co., Detroit, 1966-70; travel cons. Moorman's Travel Service, Detroit, 1973-74; media dir. Taylor for Congress campaign, East Lansing, Mich., 1974; comms. specialist House Republican Staff, Lansing, Mich., 1975-80; trustee Meridian Twp., Ingham County, Mich., 1980-84; vice chmn. Econ. Devel. Corp., 1982-84; compliance officer The Eyde Co., Lansing, 1985-88; legis. aide Mich. Ho. of Reps., Lansing, 1988-90; comm. officer Mich. Capital Healthcare, 1994-96. Mem. Ingham County Rep. Com., 1976—, sec., 1986-88, 91-92, 96, Mich. Rep. State Com., 1981-85, 6th Dist. Rep. Com. sec., 1989-93; mem. Ingham County Bd. Canvassers, 1993-96; treas. Meridian Twp., 1996—; bd. dirs. Capital Area Transp. Authority. Author: Chester!, 1981; Heavy Lady, 1983; Double Standards, 1985; A Villa in Unadilla, 1985, Losing It, 1987, The Wizards of Kyshtym/Deine Kleine Beine, 1988, Lounge Lizards/Managing Gran, 1989, Like A Brother, 1989, Loose Dogs Will Bite, 1990, Beloved Friend, 1990, To Be Announced, 1991, Okemos Passing, 1992, Song of the Whale, 1993, Mimsy Borogroves and the Tooth Fairy, 1993, What About the Hungarian?, 1995, The Passion of Richard II, 1996, The Hunchback of Notre Dame, 1997, Out at Home, 1998, The Real Boy's Pirate Show, 1998. Mem. Dramatists Guild; pres. Riverwalk Theatre, 1990-92, sec. 1993-95. Mem. Am. Numis. Assn., Mich. Numis. Soc. (sec. 1991-96, editor 1993—). Address: PO Box 16231 Lansing MI 48901-6231

KLURFELD, JAMES MICHAEL, journalist; b. N.Y.C., May 15, 1945; s. Herman and Jeanette (Garfield) K.; m. Judith E. Freiband, July 23, 1967; children: Jennifer, Jason. B.A., Syracuse U., 1967. Tchr. N.Y. Bd. Edn., 1967-68; reporter Newsday, Melville, N.Y., 1968-73; Albany bur. chief Newsday, 1973-76, Washington bur. chief, 1981-86, assoc. editor, 1986-87, editor editorial pages, 1987—, v.p., 1998—. Recipient Pulitzer prize, 1969, Award for Nat. Corr. Sigma Delta Chi, 1983, Disting. Writing award Am. Soc. Newspapers Editors, 1987. Office: Newsday Inc 235 Pinelawn Rd Melville NY 11747-4250

KLUTTZ, HENRY G., principal. Prin. West Rowan High Sch., Mt. Ulla, N.C., 1985—. Recipient Blue Ribbon Sch. award U.S. Dept. Edn., 1990-91. Office: W Rowan High Sch 8050 Highway 801 Mount Ulla NC 28125*

KLUTZ, ANTHONY ALOYSIUS, JR., health, safety and environmental manager; b. Wilkes-Barre, Pa., Dec. 2, 1954; s. Anthony A. Klutz and Matilda (Konopka) Weigand; m. LetaMarie A. Rydzewski, July 15, 1978; children: Athena Marie, Anthony A. III. BS, Kings Coll., Wilkes-Barre, 1976; MS, Rensselaer Poly. Inst., 1978; MBA, Clemson U., 1988. Material devel. engr. Sangamo Capacitor-Schlumberger, Pickens, S.C., 1978-87, product devel. engr., 1986-87; mgr. process engring. Sangamo Weston-Schlumberger, West Union, S.C., 1987-90; safety and environ. mgr. Schlumberger Industries, West Union, 1990-94, health, safety and environ. mgr. Electricity N.Am., 1994-98, health, safety environ. N. Am., 1998—. Vice chmn. Oconee County Local Emergency Planning Com., Walhalla, S.C., 1988—; mem. coun. Holy Cross Parish, Pickens, 1986-87. Mem. Am. Vacuum Soc., Electro Chem. Soc., Am. Soc. Materials, S.C. C. of C. (tech. com.), Mgmt. Club (pres. 1985, 92, v.p. 1991), KC (Knight of Mo. award Pickens 1988, Grand Knight 1994-97). Avocations: reading, computing, travel. Home: 398 Chinquapin Rd Easley SC 29640-7053 Office: Sangamo Weston-Schlumberger Hwy 11 West Union SC 29696-9610

KLYBERG, ALBERT THOMAS, historical society administrator; b. Hackensack, N.J., Aug. 8, 1940. AB, Coll. Wooster, 1962; postgrad., U. Mich. Asst. curator manuscripts William L. Clements Libr., Ann Arbor, Mich., 1963-68; libr. R.I. Hist. Soc., Providence, 1968-69, exec. dir., 1969—; adj. prof. history U. R.I., 1974-93, Providence Coll., 1986-93; acting exec. dir. Heritage Harbor; project mgr. Woonsocket Visitors Ctr., Mus. Work and Culture. Compiler, bibliographer March of America series Univ. Microfilms, Inc., 1966; editor R.I. History; project dir. Papers of Gen. Nathanael Greene. Mem. R.I. Hist. Soc. Office: RI Hist Soc 110 Benevolent St Providence RI 02906-3152

KMET, REBECCA EUGENIA PATTERSON, pharmacist; b. June 17, 1948; d. Eugene Roberts and Ruth Winn (Pettis) Patterson; m. Joseph Paul Kmet, 1969. BS in Pharmacy, U. Ariz., 1971; MBA, Nat. U., 1981. Pharmacist Santa Monica (Calif.) Bldg. Profl. Pharmacy, 1972-73, Vets. Hosp., West Los Angeles, Calif., 1973-74, Kaiser Med. Ctr., San Diego, 1979-82, Farmersville Drug Store, Farmersville, Calif., 1991-95; relief pharmacist various locations, 1995—. Community svc. vol; cmty. activist; mem. Eagle Forum. Lt. USN, 1975-78. Recipient Presdl. Achievement award Rep. Party Nat. Congl. com. Mem. DAR, Navy League, Naval Hist. Found., U.S. English, Eagle Forum, Rho Chi, Kappa Epsilon. Avocations: theology, reading, writing, antiqueing, gardening. Home: PO Box 42557 Tucson AZ 85733-2557

KMETZ, DONALD R., retired academic administrator. Dean Sch. Medicine U. Louisville, 1981-98; ret., v.p. health affairs, 1992-98; ret. Office: U Louisville Sch Medicine Health Scis Ctr 323 E Chestnut St Louisville KY 40202-1823

KMIEC, DOUGLAS WILLIAM, government official, law educator, columnist; b. Chgo., Sept. 24, 1951; s. Walter and Beatrice (Neumann) K.; m. Carolyn Keenan, June 2, 1973; children: Keenan, Katherine, Kiley, Kolleen, Kloe. BA, Northwestern U., 1973; JD, U. So. Calif., L.A., 1976. Bar: Ill. 1976, Calif. 1980, U.S. Supreme Ct. 1986. Assoc. Vedder, Price, et al, Chgo., 1976-78; prof. law Valparaiso U., Ind., 1978-80, Notre Dame U., 1980-99; Carusa family chair in law Pepperdine U., 1999—; dir. Thomas J. White Ctr. on Law and Govt., 1983-88; dep. asst., atty. gen. Office of Legal Counsel, Dept. Justice, Washington, 1985-87; asst. atty. gen., 1988-89; vis. scholar Stanford U., 1985; spl. asst. to sec. HUD, Washington, 1982-83; disting. chair Dorothy & Leonard Straus, Pepperdine U. Sch. Law, 1995-96, 97-98; mem. pres.'s Commn. on Manufactured Housing, Washington, 1984-85, 89—; mem. adv. com. Civil Rights Commn., bd. trustees Housing Allowance Program, Ind., 1983-85; state chmn. Scholars for Reagan and Bush, Ind., 1984. Author: Recharting Criminal Procedure, 1984, Zoning and Planning Desk Book, 1986, The Attorney General's Lawyer, 1992, Cease-fire on the Family, 1995; host, exec. prodr. Forefront TV series WNIT-TV, 1984-85; radio commentator The American Family Perspective, 1994-96; columnist Chgo. Tribune, 1996—. Recipient Clark Boardman prize, 1983, 87, 90, Disting. Svc. award HUD, 1983, Disting. Svc. award Dept. Justice, 1987, Edmund J. Randolph award Dept. Justice, 1989; White House fellow, Washington, 1982-83, 40th Anniversary Fulbright Disting. fellow, 1987. Mem. U.S. Supreme Ct. Bar, Ill. Bar Assn., Calif. Bar Assn., Notre Dame Club (Washington). Republican. Roman Catholic. Office: Pepperdine U Sch of Law Malibu CA 90265

KMIEC, EDWARD URBAN, bishop; b. Trenton, N.J., June 4, 1936. Ed. s. John Kmiec and Thecla (Czupta) St. Charles Coll., Catonsville, Md., 1956; St. Mary's Sem., Balt., 1958; S.T.L. Gregorian U., Rome. 1962, Ordained priest Roman Cath. Ch., Dec. 20, 1961; ordained titular bishop of Simidicca and aux. bishop of Trenton, 1982-92; bishop of Nashville, 1992—. Address: The Catholic Center 2400 21st Ave S Nashville TN 37212-5302

KMIOTEK-WELSH, JACQUELINE, lawyer; b. Bklyn., Dec. 31, 1959; d. Casimir Edward and Anna Catherine Kmiotek; m. James Winfield Welsh III. BA, St. John's U., N.Y.C., 1981, JD, 1983; MBA, NYU, 1991. Bar: N.Y. 1984, U.S. Dist. Ct. (so. and ea. dists.) N.Y. 1984, U.S. Dist. Ct. (we. dist.) N.Y. 1992, U.S. Supreme Ct. 1989. Asst. counsel N.Y. Job Devel. Auth., 1984-85; assoc. Squadron, Ellenoff, Pleasant & Lehrer, N.Y.C., 1985; assoc. atty. N.Y. Power Authority, 1985-86, atty., 1986-90, sr. atty., 1990—. Fellow N.Y. Bar Found., N.Y. State Bar Assn. (mem. Ho. of Dels. 1993-96, exec. com. young lawyers sect. 1993-97, pub. utility law com. 1994—, chair young lawyers sect., com. profl. svc. project on women subcom. 1994-96, chair young lawyers sect. com. on pub. svcs. and pro-bono project on disaster legal assistance 1994-95, mem. 1995-96, mem. com. 1995—, mem. internat. law and practice sect. com. on U.S.-Can. law 1994—, young lawyer divsn. pub. utility law com.), Am. Bar Found.; mem. ABA (fellow young lawyers divsn., liaison pub. contract law sect. 1988-90, exec. com. 1988-89, vice-chmn. 1989-91, chmn. 1991—, young lawyers divsn. pub. utility law com., internat. law exec. com. 1989-91, mem. govt. lawyers exec. com. 1990-91, liaison coord. group on energy law 1990-92, coord. group energy law 1992-95, mem. com. sect. of real property, probate & trust law 1995-97, liaison ABA Jour. 1992-95, mem. Ho. of Dels. 1993-96, vice chair bylaws com. govt. and pub. sector lawyer's divsn. 1993-95, vice chmn. young lawyer divn. publs. com. 1995-96, vice chair women in the profession com. 1994-95, judge awards of achievement com. 1992-95, mem. exec. coun. young lawyer's divsn. 1993-95, 4th dist. rep., mem. membership com. sect. real property probate trust law, 1995-96, liaison, 1995-97, vice chair publ. com. 1995-96, mem. editl. bd. sect. pub. utility comm. transp. law 1996—), Fed. Energy Bar Assn., Phi Alpha Delta. Office: NY Power Authority 1633 Broadway New York NY 10019-6708

KNABE, GEORGE WILLIAM, JR., pathologist, educator; b. Grand Rapids, Mich., June 29, 1924; s. George William and Dorothy Emma (Fischofer) K., m. Lorine Jeanette Moffit, Jan. 16, 1954; children: Katharine J., Elizabeth J., Ann C., Dorothy M. Student, Mich. State U., 1942-43, The Citadel, Charleston, SC, 1943-44, Johns Hopkins U., 1944-45; MD, U. Md., 1949. Diplomate Am. Bd. Pathology. Intern Balt. City Hosp., 1949-50; resident pathology Cleve. Clin. Found., 1950-51, Henry Ford Hosp., Detroit, 1953-54; chief lab. svc. VA Ctr., Dayton, Ohio, 1955-57; vis. prof. pathology U. El Salvador Sch. Medicine, 1957-59; asst. prof. pathology U. P.R. Sch. Medicine, 1959-60; prof., chmn. dept. pathology Sch. Medicine, U. S.D., 1960-68, dean., 1967-72; dir. med. edn. St. Luke's Hosp., Duluth, 1972-78; prof. pathology U. Minn.-Duluth Sch. Medicine, 1972—, assoc. dean clin. affairs., 1972-76; chief. dept. pathology Virginia (Minn.) Regional Med. Ctr., 1978—; bd. dirs Health Sys. Agy. of Western Lake Superior, Duluth 1975-82, No. Lakes Health Care Consortium, 1984—, U. Minn. Health and Med. Sch. Adv. Groups 1972—. 1st lt. to capt. M.C., USAF, 1951-53; surgeon to capt., USPHS Res., 1957—. Mem. AMA, U.S. and Can. Acad. Pathology, Am. Soc. Clin. Pathologists, Coll. Am. Pathologists. Avocations: art, horticulture, photography. Home: 1008 S 7th Ave Virginia MN 55792-3151 Office: Va Regional Med Ctr 901 9th St N Virginia MN 55792-2325

KNACHEL, PHILIP ATHERTON, librarian; b. Indpls., June 23, 1926; s. Firman F. and Mary Esther (Atherton) K.; m. Pierrette Annie Roy, July 1, 1955; children—Sylvette, Eric. B.S., Northwestern U., 1948; cert., Institut de Tours, France, 1951; M.A., Johns Hopkins U., 1952, Ph.D., 1954; M.S.L.S., Syracuse U., 1959; Litt.D. (hon.), Amherst Coll., 1984. Instr. history Hunter Coll., N.Y.C., 1954-57; historian Rome Air Devel. Ctr., N.Y., 1957-59; chief tech. services Folger Shakespeare Library, Washington, 1959-61, asst. dir., to 1969, assoc. dir., 1969-93; freelance French translator, 1993—; adj. prof. history U. Md., College Park, 1967-69; French translator cons. Author: England and the Fronde, 1967; editor: Eikon Basilike, 1966, The Case of the Commonwealth of England Stated, 1967. Served with USN, 1944-46. Mem. ALA, Am. Translators Assn. Club: Cosmos (Washington). Avocations: piano, travel. Home: 5807 Phoenix Dr Bethesda MD 20817-3401

KNAG, PAUL EVERETT, lawyer; b. Flushing, N.Y., Feb. 26, 1948; s. Howard Alf and Charlotte (Rausch) K.; m. Maryann McCaffrey, June 27, 1970; children: Paul Everett, Peter, Kathleen, John. BA magna cum laude, Queens Coll., 1967; JD cum laude, Harvard U., 1970. Bar: N.Y. 1970, Conn. 1971, D.C. 1983. Law clk. U.S. Ct. Appeals (2nd cir.), N.Y.C., 1970-71; assoc. Cummings & Lockwood, Stamford, Conn., 1971-79; ptnr. Cummings & Lockwood, Stamford, 1979—. Mem. Conn. Bar Assn., Stamford Bar Assn., Nat. Health Lawyers Assn., Conn. Health Lawyers Assn., Officer's Club Hartford, Dunes Club (Naragansett, R.I.), Middlesex Club Darien, Harvard Club Fairfield County (treas.), Quinnipiack Club. Republican. Office: Cummings & Lockwood 4 Stamford Plz PO Box 120 Stamford CT 06904

KNAPP, ALBERT BRUCE, gastroenterologist; b. N.Y.C., Aug. 9, 1955; s. Russell Sage and Bettina (Liebowitz) K.; m. Alice Anne Cohen, Sept. 7, 1986. BA, Columbia Coll., 1975, MD, 1979. Intern, resident Albert Einstein Med. Ctr., N.Y.C., 1979-82; fellow in gastroenterology Harvard Med. Sch., Boston, 1982-85; assoc. attending Lenox Hill Hosp., N.Y.C., 1985—, St. Vincent's Hosp., N.Y.C., 1985—; asst. prof. NYU Med. Sch., N.Y.C., 1990—. Author textbook in field, 1982; contbr. numerous articles to profl. jours. Trustee N.Y. Police Found., N.Y.C., 1991—. NIH rsch. grantee, 1982. Fellow ACP (jour. reviewer Annals of Internal Medicine 1985—); mem. Am. Gastroenterol. Assn. (jour. reviewer Gastroenterology 1985—), Am. Assn. Gastrointestinal Endoscopy, Am. Assn. for Study of Liver Disease (Rsch. award 1984). Office: 21 E 29th St New York NY 10016-7405

KNAPP, ANDREW C., political association administrator. BA in Internat. Rels., Mich. State U., 1995. With Engler for Gov., Lansing, Mich., 1993-94, Consumers Energy, Lansing, 1995; polit. dir. Rep. Govs. Assn., Washington, 1995—. Republican. E-mail: aknapp@rnchq.org. Office: Rep Govs Assn 310 1st St SE Washington DC 20003

KNAPP, BARBARA ALLISON, financial services, oncological nurse consultant; b. Boston, May 30, 1936; d. Henry Philip and Mary Veronica (Norton) Frank; m. John Northcott Knapp, July 27, 1963 (dec. June 12, 1994); children: Linda, David, Diana; m. James M. Nikrant, June 20, 1998. BSN, Hood Coll., 1959; MA, U. Iowa Sch. of Nursing, 1981. Instr. Mass.Gen. Hosp. Sch. of Nursing, Boston, 1959-63; acting dir. Aga Khan Hosp., Nairobi, Kenya, East Africa, 1963-65; dir. dept. of pt. edn. Mercy Hosp., Cedar Rapids, Iowa, 1975-78; clin. nurse specialist dept. otolaryngology U. Iowa Hosp. and Clinics, Iowa City, 1981-84; clin. nurse specialist in oncology U. Iowa Hosp. and Clinics, Iowa City, 1992-94; clin. nurse specialist in surgical nursing U. Chgo. Med. Ctr., 1984-92; nursing cons., chmn. CEO SCI Fin. Group Inc., Cedar Rapids, 1994—; mem. bd. accreditation Nat. League for Nursing N.Y.C., 1993-96; mem. adv. bd. Mercy Hosp. Women's Health Ctr., 1994—. Dir., editor: (instructive films) Preoperative Teaching Film, 1976 (Am. Hosp. Assn. Film of the Yr. 1976), Learning About Diabetes, 1978, Head and Neck Postoperative Care, 1984, Psychosocial Effects of Head and Neck Cancer, 1984. Bd. dirs. United Way, Cedar Rapids, 1994—, Cedar Rapids Symphony Orch., 1994—, YMCA, Cedar Rapids, Meth-Wick Retirement Cmty., Jr. Achievement, 1996—; trustee Mt. Mercy Coll. (v. chmn. bd.), YMCA, 1996—. Mem. Am. Cancer Soc., Oncology Nursing Soc., Cedar Rapids C. of C. (dir. 1996—), Rotary Internat., Sigma Theta Tau. Roman Catholic. Avocations: reading, travel, skiing, golf, tennis. Home: 307 Crescent St SE Cedar Rapids IA 52403-1731

KNAPP, CANDACE LOUISE, sculptor; b. Benton Harbor, Mich., Feb. 28, 1948; d. Claire Warren and Frances Mary (Collins) K.; m. Björn Andrén, Mar. 3, 1988. BFA, Cleve. Inst. Art, 1971; MFA, U. Ill., 1974. Sculptures exhibited in numerous galleries; represented in permanent collections including Northwood Inst. Collection, West Palm Beach, Fla., Malone & Hyde, Memphis, Mobil Oil Co., Stockholm, HageGården Music Ctr., Edane, Sweden, others; included in book Contemporary American Women Sculptors; numerous commns. including St. Vincent de Paul Cath. Ch., Arlington, Tex., Padre Pio Found., Cromwell, Conn., Temple Emanuel, Dallas, West Haven, Conn., Tampa (Fla.) Gen. Hosp., Pub. Art Commn. City of St. Petersburg, Fla. Helen Greene Perry traveling scholar, 1971. Mem. Assn. Fla. Liturgical Artists (co-founder). Fax: 813-654-6572.

KNAPP, CHARLES BOYNTON, economist, educator, institute president; b. Ames, Iowa, Aug. 13, 1946; s. Albert B. and Anne Marie (Taff) K.; m. Lynne Vickers, Aug. 25, 1967; 1 dau., Amanda. B.S., Iowa State U., 1968; M.A., Ph.D., U. Wis., 1972. Asst. prof. econs., research assoc. Ctr. for Study of Human Resources, U. Tex., Austin, 1972-76; spl. asst. to Sec. of Labor Dept. Labor, Washington, 1977-79, dep. asst. sec. labor, 1979-81; assoc. prof. pub. policy George Washington U., 1981-82; assoc. prof. econs. Tulane U., New Orleans, 1982-87, sr. v.p., 1982-85, exec. v.p., 1985-87; pres., prof. econs. U. Ga., Athens, 1987-97; pres. Aspen Inst., 1997—; bd. dirs. AFLAC Inc. Contbr. articles to profl. jours. Office: Aspen Inst Ste 700 #1 DuPont Cir Washington DC 20036

KNAPP, CHARLES LINCOLN, law educator; b. Zanesville, Ohio, Oct. 22, 1935; s. James Lincoln and Laura Alma (Richardson) K.; m. Beverley Earle Trott, Aug. 23, 1958 (dec. 1995); children: Jennifer Lynn, Liza Beth. BA, Denison U., 1956; JD, NYU, 1960. Bar: N.Y. 1961. Assoc. Paul, Weiss, Rifkind, Wharton & Garrison, N.Y.C., 1960-64; asst. prof. law NYU Law Sch., N.Y.C., 1964-67, assoc. prof., 1967-70, prof. law, 1970-88, Max E. Greenberg prof. contract law, 1988-98, Max E. Greenberg prof. emeritus contract law, 1998—, assoc. dean, 1977-82; vis. prof. law U. Ariz. Law Sch., Tucson, 1973, Harvard U. Law Sch., Cambridge, Mass., 1974-75, Hastings Coll. Law, San Francisco, 1996-97, disting. prof. law, 1998—. Author: Problems in Contract Law, 1976, (with N. Crystal and H. Prince) 4th edit., 1999; editor-in-chief: Commercial Damages, 1986. Mem. Am. Law Inst., Order Coif, Phi Beta Kappa. Office: Hastings Coll Law 200 Mcallister St San Francisco CA 94102-4707

KNAPP, CLEON TALBOYS, business executive; b. Los Angeles, Apr. 28, 1937; s. Cleon T. and Sally (Brasfield) K.; m. Elizabeth Ann Wood, Mar. 17, 1979; children: Jeffrey James, Brian Patrick, Aaron Bradley, Laura Ann. Student, UCLA, 1955-58. With John C. Brasfield Pub. Corp. (purchased co. in 1965, changed name to Knapp Comm Corp. 1977, sold to Condé Nast Publs. in 1993); pres. Talwood Corp., Knapp Found., L.A.; Bd. dirs., bd. trustees Santa Fe Opera, Fulfillment Fund; bd. visitors John E. Anderson Grad. Sch. of Mgmt., UCLA; chmn. bd. trustees Art Ctr. Coll. Design. Mem. Bel Air Country Club, Regency Club, Country Club of the Rockies, Eagle Springs Golf Club. Office: Talwood Corp 10100 Santa Monica Blvd Los Angeles CA 90067-4100

KNAPP, DAVID ALLAN, pharmaceutical educator, researcher; b. Cleve., Feb. 25, 1938; s. Frederick Allan and Ethel R. (Ogden) K.; m. Deanne Evander, June 2, 1962; 1 child, Wendy Kay Knapp Steagall. BS, Purdue U., 1960, MS, 1962, PhD, 1965. Lic. pharmacist. Asst. prof. Coll. Pharmacy Ohio State U., Columbus, 1964-67, assoc. prof., 1967-71; assoc. prof., now prof. Sch. Pharmacy U. Md., Balt., 1971—, assoc. dean grad. edn. and rsch., 1981-83, chmn. dept. pharm. practice and adminstrn. sci., 1987-91, dir. Ctr. on Drugs and Pub. Policy, 1987-96, acting dean Sch. Pharmacy, 1989-91, dean, 1991—; vis. scholar U. Mich. Sch. Pub. Health, 1970-71; intramural researcher Nat. Ctr. for Health Svc. Rsch., Dept. HHS, Hyattsville, Md., 1978; scholar in residence Am. Assn. Colls. Pharmacy, Alexandria, Va., 1986-87. Author: Pharmacy Drugs and Medical Care, 5 edits., 1972-92; contbr. articles to profl. jours. Recipient numerous grants and contracts. Fellow AAAS, APHA, Am. Assn. Pharm. Scientists, Am. Found. Pharm. Edn. (bd. dirs. 1994-96, exec. com. 1995-96); mem. Am. Assn. Colls. Pharmacy (bd. dirs. 1986-89, 93-96, Volwiler Rsch. Gold medal 1986, pres. 1994-95, commn. to stimulate change in pharm. edn. 1989-95, commn. future grad. edn. pharm. scis. 1996—), Am. Pharm. Assn. (rsch. achievement award 1984), Am. Soc. Hosp. Pharmacists (commn. on goals 1996, com. credentialing 1996—), Sigma Xi, Rho Chi. Unitarian. Office: Sch Pharmacy U Md 20 N Pine St Baltimore MD 21201-1142*

KNAPP, DAVID HEBARD, banker; b. N.Y.C., May 22, 1938; s. Alfred John and Doris (Hebard) K.; m. Letitia Lykes, Aug. 18, 1959; children—Genevieve, Christopher, Breckenridge. B.A., Williams Coll. With Rotan, Mosle, Houston, 1960-62; asst. cashier, mgr. credit dept. Fannin Bank, Houston, 1962-64, asst. v.p. comml. loans, 1964-66, v.p. comml. loans, 1968-70, vice chmn. bd., 1970-82; co-chmn. exec. com. Interfirst Bank Fannin, 1982-83; devel. loan officer AID, Rio de Janeiro, Brazil, 1966-68; pres. Penta Internat., Inc., Houston, 1979-82; dir. Lykes Bros. Inc., Tampa, Fla., First Fla. Banks, Tampa, Interocean Steamship Co., Tampa, Lykes Bros. Steamship Co., New Orleans. Trustee St. Lukes Episcopal Hosp., Houston, St. John's Sch., Urban Affairs Corp.; trustee Armand Bayou Nature Center, Pasadena, Tex., pres., 1977-79. Club: Houston Country (Houston). Home: 2328 Timber Ln Houston TX 77027-4129 Office: 2807 Bammel Ln Houston TX 77098-1105

KNAPP, DENNIS RAYMOND, federal judge; b. Buffalo, W.Va., May 13, 1912; s. Amon Lee and Ora Alice (Forbes) K.; m. Helen Ewers Jordan, June 1, 1935; children: Mary F., Margaret Ann, Dennis Raymond. AB, W.Va. Inst. Tech., 1932, LLD, 1972; AM, W.Va. U., 1934, LLB, 1940. Bar: W.Va. 1940. High sch. tchr. Putnam County, W.Va., 1932-35; supt. schs., 1935-37; practiced in Nitro, 1940-56; judge Ct. of Common Pleas, Kanawha County, W.Va., 1957-70; U.S. dist. judge for So. Dist. W.Va., Charleston, 1970-93, sr. judge, 1993—; Vice pres., dir. Bank of Nitro, 1949-70; v.p. Hygeia, Inc., 1968-70. Bd. dirs. Goodwill Industries, Inc., 1968-70; adv. bd. Marshall U., Huntington, W.Va. With AUS, 1944-46. Named Alumnus of Year W.Va. Inst. Tech., 1967. Mem. Am., W.Va. bar assns., W.Va. Jud. Assn., W.Va. Tech. Coll. Alumni Assn. (pres. 1968). Republican. Methodist. Home: 800 Sweetwater Island Cir Longwood FL 32779-2345 Office: US Courthouse PO Box 2546 Charleston WV 25329-2546*

KNAPP, DONALD ROY, musician, educator; b. Mpls., Dec. 26, 1919; s. Roy Cecil and Nellie Anette (Johnson) K.; m. Loretto C. Downes, June 5, 1960 (dec. 1975); m. Kimberly J. Carr, May 9, 1977 (div. 1980); 1 child, Deidre. Student Met. Sch. Music, Voss Bus. Coll. Percussionist Sauter-Finegan Band, N.Y.C., 1962-64, Shubert Theater, Chgo., 1970-75, Arie Crown Theater, Chgo., 1975-77, mus. show Annie, N.Y.C., 1978-82, Lyric Opera of Chgo., 1955-57; prof. percussion Met. Sch. Music, Chgo., 1945-48; instr. percussion Roy C. Knapp Sch. Percussion, Chgo., 1948-52; played in Broadway musicals including original prodns. of West Side Story, Hello Dolly, Guys and Dolls, Gypsy, Kismet, Cabaret, Can Can, Fiddler on the Roof. Served with USN, 1941-45, PTO. Mem. Chgo. Fedn. Musicians (bd. dirs. 1983-86, sec.-treas. Local 10-208 1993—), Musicians Union of Greater N.Y.C., Musicians Union of Los Angeles. Republican. Lodges: Masons, K.T., Shriners (band). Home: 2909 N Sheridan Rd Apt 704 Chicago IL 60657-5939

KNAPP, EDWARD ALAN, retired government administrator, scientist; b. Salem, Oreg., Mar. 7, 1932; s. Gardner and Lucille (Moore) K.; m. Jean Elaine Hartwell, June 27, 1954; children: Sandra, David, Robert, Mary. A.B., Pomona Coll., 1954; Ph.D., U. Calif., Berkeley, 1958; D.Sc. (hon.), Pomona Coll., 1984, Bucknell U., 1984. With Los Alamos Sci. Lab., U. Calif., 1958-82, dir. accelerator tech. div., 1977-82; asst. dir., then dir. NSF, Washington, 1982-84; sr. fellow Los Alamos Nat. Lab., 1984; pres. Univs. Rsch. Assn., Washington, 1985-89; sr. fellow Los Alamos Nat. Lab., 1990, dir. Los Alamos meson physics facility, 1990-91; pres. Santa Fe Inst., 1991-96, prof., 1996; cons. in field. Contbr. articles to profl. jours. Fellow AAAS, Am. Phys. Soc.; mem. IEEE, Sigma Xi. Methodist. Office: Santa Fe Inst 1399 Hyde Park Rd Santa Fe NM 87501-8943*

KNAPP, GEORGE GRIFF PRATHER, insurance consultant, arbitrator; b. New Rochelle, N.Y., June 26, 1923; s. Griff Prather and Lucy Chadbourne (Norvell) K.; m. Eva Witte, May 30, 1953; children: Edward, Wesley, Helen, Elizabeth. B.A., Harvard U., 1945; postgrad., Law Sch., 1946. With Chubb & Son, N.Y.C., 1947-88; mgr. personal lines dept. Chubb & Son, 1966-73, asst. to pres., 1973, Can. zone officer, 1974-78, N.Y. zone officer, 1978-83, sr. v.p., 1968-88, nat. producer liaison, 1984-88; sr. v.p. Fed. Ins. Co., 1968-88, dir., 1970-88; exec. dir. Excess Line Assn. N.Y., 1988-90; cons. ins. advisor Westchster County vol. hosp.; arbitrator for major property/casualty ins. co. Gov. Lawrence Hosp., 1968-75. Served with U.S. Army, 1943-46. Republican. Roman Catholic. Clubs: Harvard (N.Y.C.); Bronxville Field. Home: 22 Elm Ln Bronxville NY 10708-1939

KNAPP, GEORGE M., lawyer; b. Inglewood, Calif., June 19, 1954. BA magna cum laude, UCLA, 1975; JD, George Washington U., 1978. Bar: Calif. 1978, D.C. 1979. Law clk. to Hon. Jon G. Lotis Fed. Energy Regulatory Commn., 1978-79, dep. asst. gen. counsel, 1980; ptnr. Coudert Bros., Washington. Mem. ABA (vice chmn. alt. energy sources com. sect. of environ., energy, and resources, 1980-85, chmn. 1985-89, mem. coun. 1989-92, chmn. membership com. 1992-94, chmn. strategic planning com. 1994-96, vice chmn. sect. 1996-97, chmn.-elect sect. 1997-98, chmn. sect. 1998-99), State Bar Calif., D.C. Bar, Fed. Energy Bar Assn. (chmn. program com. 1991-92, chmn. internat. energy transactions com. 1995-97), Phi Beta Kappa. Office: Coudert Bros 1627 I St NW Washington DC 20006-4007

KNAPP, GEORGE ROBERT, investment executive, business advisor, lawyer; b. Bethlehem, Pa., Oct. 8, 1947; s. Donald Albert and Adelaide Marie (Shogren) K.; children: Katherine, Laura, Sarah; m. Susan Jane Rutter. BA, Colgate U., 1969; JD, Harvard U., 1972. Bar: Pa. 1973, U.S. Dist. Ct. (we. dist.) Pa. 1973. Assoc. Kirkpatrick & Lockhart, Pitts., 1972-78, ptnr., 1978-96; pres. Stonewood Capital Mgmt., Pitts., 1996—; pres., bd. dirs. Tippins Industries, Pitts., 1996—; bd. dirs. On Target Commn., Inc., Pitts., TMC Investment Co. (Del.), Newbold Corp. (Va.), Emglo Products, Inc., Johnstown, Pa. Hon. consul Kingdom of Denmark, 1995—. Mem. Duquesne Club (Pitts.), Valleybrook Country Club (Pitts.). Republican. Presbyterian. Avocations: travel, music, athletics. Office: Tippins Industries Inc 1090 Freeport Rd Pittsburgh PA 15238-3102*

KNAPP, HOWARD RAYMOND, internist, clinical pharmacologist; b. Red Bank, N.J., Oct. 5, 1949; s. Howard Raymond and Jane Marie (Ray) K.; m. Brenda Louise Carr, 1984; 1 child, Matthew. AB in Biology, Washington U., St. Louis, 1971; MD, Vanderbilt U., 1977, PhD in Pharmacology, 1984. Diplomate Am. Bd. Internal Medicine; lic., Iowa, Tenn. Asst. prof. medicine and pharmacology Vanderbilt U., Nashville, 1984-89, assoc. prof., 1990; assoc. prof. internal medicine and pharmacology U. Iowa, Iowa city, 1990-97, prof. internal medicine and pharmacology, 1997—, assoc. dir. NIH Clin. Rsch. Ctr.; mem. NIH Nutrition Study Sect., Bethesda, Md., 1994-96; cons. pharm. firms, grant orgns. and govtl. entities; mem. applied pharmacol. task force Nat. Bd. Med. Examiners, 1997—. Editor-in-chief Lipids, 1995—; contbr. numerous articles to profl. jours., chpts. to books. Grantee NIH, Am. Heart Assn., others. Fellow ACP, Am. Heart Assn. (vascular biol. rsch. rev. com. 1993-95, arteriosclerosis coun.); mem. Ctrl. Soc. for Clin. Rsch. (chair clin. pharmacol. sect. 1992-95), Am. Soc. for Clin. Pharmacology and Therapeutics. Achievements include first demonstration that calcium ionophores stimulate eicosanoid synthesis; first evidence that N-3 fatty acids reduce platelet activation and blood pressure in patients; first demonstration of the effects of 5-lipoxygenase inhibition in humans. Office: U Iowa Div Clin Pharm Dept Int Med C31-P Gen Hosp Iowa City IA 52242

KNAPP, JAMES IAN KEITH, judge; b. Bklyn., Apr. 6, 1943; s. Charles Townsend and Christine (Grange) K.; m. Joan Elizabeth Cunningham, June 10, 1967 (div. Mar. 1971); 1 child, Jennifer Elizabeth; m. Carol Jean Brown, July 14, 1981; children: Michelle Christine, David Michael Keith. AB cum laude, Harvard U., 1964; JD, U. Colo., 1967; M in Law in Taxation, Georgetown U., 1989. Bar: Colo. 1967, Calif. 1968, U.S. Supreme Ct. 1983, D.C. 1986, Ohio 1995. Dep. dist. atty. County of L.A., 1968-79; head dep. dist. atty. Pomona br. office, 1979-82; dep. asst. atty. gen. criminal divsn. U.S. Dept. Justice, Washington, 1982-86, dep. assoc. atty. gen., 1986-87, dep. asst. atty. gen. tax divsn., 1988-89, acting asst. atty. gen. tax divsn., 1989, acting dep. chief organized crime sect. criminal divsn., 1989-91, dep. dir., asset forfeiture office criminal divsn., 1991-94; adminstrv. law judge Social Security Adminstrn., 1994—. Editor: California Uniform Crime Charging Standards and Manual, 1975. Vice chmn. Young Reps. Nat. Fedn., 1973-75; pres. Calif. Young Reps., 1975-77; mem. exec. com. Rep. State Ctrl. Com., Calif., 1975-77. Mem. Calif. Bar Assn., D.C. Bar Assn., Dayton Bar Assn. Episcopalian. Avocations: travel; reading. Office: Office of Hearings & Appeals 110 N Main St Ste 800 Dayton OH 45402-1786

KNAPP, JOHN WILLIAMS, retired college president; b. Dec. 9, 1932; m. Margaret Lee Dickerson, Mar. 16, 1957; children: Katherine, John Jr., Elizabeth. BS, Va. Mil. Inst., 1954; MS, Johns Hopkins U., 1962, PhD, 1965. Engr. Concrete Pipe & Products, Co., Richmond, 1958-59; from instr. to prof. civil engring. Va. Mil. Inst., Lexington, 1959-84, head civil engring. dept., 1966-71, 82-84, dean faculty, 1984-89, supr. pres., 1989-95; ret., 1995; chmn. bd. Maury Svc. Authority, Lexington, 1970-84; dir. local adv. bd. Crestar Bank, Lexington, 1989-95. Co-author: Introduction to Hydrology, 3d edit., 1989. Lt. U.S. Army, 1954-58; maj. gen. USAR. Recipient Edn. award Halliburton Found., 1978, Bliss medal Soc. Mil. Engrs., 1979. Fellow ASCE; mem. NSPE, Am. Acad. Environ. Engrs., Sigma Xi, Phi Kappa Phi, Tau Beta Pi. Episcopalian. Home: 212 Barclay Ln Lexington VA 24450-2006*

KNAPP, LONNIE TROY, elementary education educator; b. Charles City, Iowa, Dec. 2, 1948; s. Troy Leroy and Anna Mildred (Conner) K.; m. Nancy Maureen Godfrey, Aug. 19, 1972; children: Eric Lonnie, Jamie Troy, Dusty Mack. BA, U. No. Iowa, 1972. Elem. tchr. Clear Lake, Iowa, 1972-92, Palm Springs (Calif.) Unified Sch. Dist., 1992—. Contbr. articles to profl. jours. Recipient Outstanding Tchr. award, Conservation Tchr. award, Iowa, North Cen. U.S. Mem. NEA, Iowa Edn. Assn., Calif. Tchrs. Assn., Clear Lake Edn. Assn. (various offices).

KNAPP, MADONNA FAYE, property manager, administrator; b. Greenup, Ill., Nov. 13, 1933; d. Rella James Packer and Ruth Evelyn (Mills) Lam; m. Carl E. Helmick, Feb. 8, 1953 (div.); children: Carl E. Jr., Cheryl A. Helmick Pease, Madonna J. Helmick Zelazny, Timothy J.; m. Glenn E. Knapp, Sept. 24, 1984 (dec. 1997). Grad. high sch., Champaign, Ill. Notary pub., Ind. Justice of peace, Ill., 1957-61; owner, mgr. Feathercrafts, Champaign, Ill., 1961-64; hostess Town and Country Steak House, Champaign/Urbana, Ill., 1966-68; leasing agt. Pinehurse Village Apts., Indpls., 1976-78, Shortridge Mobile Home Park, Indpls., 1978-79; adminstr. Kingston Square Homes, Inc., Indpls., 1981—. Precinct committeewoman Champaign Dem. Com., 1966-67; mem. Indpls. Dem. Com., 1970, 91-92. Recipient letter of accomodation State's Atty. Piatt County, 1961, others. Mem. Midwest Assn. HUD Mng. Agts., Fraternal Order Police. Democrat. Methodist. Avocations: oil painting, crafts, doll collecting, speaking and instructing painting and crafts. Home: 7216 Twin Oaks Dr Indianapolis IN 46226-5722 Office: Kingston Square Homes Inc 7171 Twin Oaks Dr Indianapolis IN 46226-5719

KNAPP, MARK LANE, communications educator, consultant; b. Kansas City, Mo., July 12, 1938; s. Herbert H. and Mary Ellen (Coleman) K.; m. Cynthia Lackie Dennis, Jan. 27, 1963 (div. Aug. 1974); children: Hilary A. Cellard, Eric C.; m. Lillian J. Davis, Aug. 8, 1975; 1 child, Avery K. Davis. BS, U. Kans., 1962, MA, 1963; PhD, Pa. State U., 1966. From instr. to asst. prof. U. Wis., Milw., 1965-70; from assoc. prof. to prof. Purdue U., West Lafayette, Ind., 1970-80; prof. SUNY, New Paltz, N.Y., 1980-83; disting. vis. prof. U. Vt., Burlington, 1983; vis. prof. U. Tex., Austin, 1983-85, sr. lectr., 1985-87, prof., 1987-89, Jesse H. Jones Centennial prof. in comm., 1989—; cons., lectr. in field. Author: Nonverbal Communication in Human Interaction, 1972, 4th edit. (with J. Hall), 1997, Japanese edit., 1979, Spanish edit., 1980, Social Intercourse: From Greeting to Goodbye, 1978, Essentials of Nonverbal Communication, 1980, Interpersonal Communication and Human Relationships, 1984, 3d edit. (with A. Vangelisti), 1996, (with J.C. McCroskey and C.E. Larson), An Introduction to Interpersonal Communication, 1971; editor: (with G.R. Miller) Handbook of Interpersonal Communication, 1985, 2d edit., 1994; contbr. articles to profl. jours., chpts. to books. With U.S. Army, 1957-59. Recipient Outstanding Young Tchr. award Ctrl. States Speech Assn., 1969; Ea. Comm. Assn. scholar, 1982-83. Fellow Internat. Comm. Assn. (pres. 1975-76); mem. Nat. Comm. Assn. (pres. 1989-90, Golden Anniversary award 1974, Disting. Scholar award 1993, Robert J. Kibler Meml. award 1993), Assn. Comm. Adminstrs. (pres. 1997), Coun. Comm. Assns. (vice chair 1997). Achievements include research in interpersonal communication, nonverbal communication, communication in developing and deteriorating relationships, communication and the process of aging, communication behavior in organizational settings. Home: 5804 Rising Hills Dr Austin TX 78759-5513 Office: U Tex Dept Speech Comm Austin TX 78712

KNAPP, MILDRED FLORENCE, retired social worker; b. Detroit, Apr. 15, 1932; d. Edwin Frederick and Florence Josephine (Antaya) K.; BBA, U. Mich., 1954, MA in Cmty. and Adult Edn. (Mott Found. fellow 1964), 1964, MSW (HEW grantee 1966), 1967. Dist. dir. Girl Scouts Met. Detroit, 1954-63; planning asst. Coun. Social Agys. Flint and Genessee County, 1965; sch. social worker Detroit Pub. Schs., 1967-98; field instr. grad. social workers. Mem. alumnae bd. govs. U. Mich., 1972-75, scholarship chmn., 1969-70, 76-80, chair spl. com. women's athletics, 1972-75, class agt. fund raising Sch. Bus. Adminstrn., 1978-79; mem. Founders Soc. Detroit Inst. Art, 1969—, Friends Children's Mus. Detroit, 1978—, Women's Assn., Detroit Symphony Orch., 1982-89, Mich. Humane Soc., 1991—; vol. Coun. Detroit Symphony Orch., 1990—; trustee, fin. chmn. Children's Mus. Recipient Appreciation cert. Mem. Nat. Assn. Social Workers, Acad. Cert. Social Workers, Nat. Cmty. Edn. Assn. (charter), Sch. Social Work Assn. Am. (charter), Outdoor Edn. and Camping Coun. (charter), Mich. Sch. Social Workers Assn. (pres. 1980-81), Detroit Sch. Social Workers Assn. (past pres.), Detroit Assn. U. Mich. Women (pres. 1980-82), Detroit Fedn. Tchrs., Madame Alexander Doll Club. Methodist. Home: 702 Lakepointe St Grosse Pointe MI 48230-1706

KNAPP, PATRICK, women's basketball coach; m. Maggie Knapp; children: Melanie Lynne, Patrick. BS, Widener Coll., 1975. Coach Bishop McDevitt H.S., Phila., 1976-80; asst. coach U. Notre Dame, 1980-83; women's basketball coach N.Mex. State U., 1983-86; head coach women's basketball Georgetown U., Washington, 1986—. Office: Georgetown U Women's Athletics Dept 37th & O Street NW Washington DC 20057-1956*

KNAPP, PEGGY DURDA, international company administrator; b. Mpls., Jan. 2, 1944; d. Joseph and Dolores Catherine Durda; m. Bobby Lee Knapp, Apr. 16, 1966 (div. Febr. 1973); 1 child, Noelle Catherine. Attended, U. Minn., Mpls., 1961-64, Christian Life Sch. Theology, 1996—. Stewardess Northwest Airlines, Mpls., 1964-66; sales mgr. LDS, Dallas; aeration ind. internat. dir. Chaska, Minn. Divsn.; mem. bd. dirs. Joseph Durda Found., Mpls. Vol. Minn. AIDS Project, Mpls., 1993-95, Parkland Hosp., Dallas, 1986-88; Christian Ch. counselor, 1998—; vol. pre-sch. spl. needs children, 1997—; lic. min., treas. bd. dirs. Heart's Cry Internat. Ministry, 1999. Mem. Nat. Assn. Golf Supts., Nat. Golf Found., Assn. Women Execs. Republican. Avocations: reading, painting, crafts, floral design. Home: 4946 Devonshire Cir Excelsior MN 55331-9329 Office: Aeration Industries Inc. 4100 Peavey Rd Chaska MN 55318-2344

KNAPP, RICHARD MAITLAND, association executive; b. Hartford, Conn., July 23, 1941; s. Maitl K.; m. Elizabeth Burgoyne, Apr. 1969; children—Heather, Peter. B.A., Marietta (Ohio) Coll., 1963; M.A., U. Iowa, 1965, Ph.D. in Hosp. and Health Adminstrn, 1968. Trainee USPHS, 1964-65; Project dir. Teaching Hosp. Info. Ctr., Council of Teaching Hosps., Assn. Am. Med. Colls., Washington, 1968-69; dir. div. teaching hosps. Assn. Am. Med. Colls., Washington, 1969-73, dir. dept. teaching hosps., 1973-87, sr. v.p., 1987-93, exec. v.p., 1994—; mem. adv. com. ambulatory dental services program Robert Wood Johnson Hosp., 1978-83; bd. dirs. Nat. Assn. Biomed. Rsch., chmn. exec. com. 1993-95; chmn. exec. com. Ad Hoc Group for Med. Rsch., 1992—. Contbr. articles to profl. jours.; mem. editorial bd. Inquiry, 1983-88. Bd. dirs. Hosp. Fund, Inc., 1984—; adv. com. The Commonwealth Fund Exec. Nurse Devel. Program, 1984-93; trustee Inova Health Sys. Bd., 1986—, chmn., 1999—; trustee Inova Health Care Svcs. Bd., 1982-98, chmn. 1993-98; mem. operating bd. Fairfax Hosp., 1987-92, sec. bd., 1987-89, chmn. bd., 1990-92; mem. vestry St. Anne's Episc. Ch., Reston, Va., 1979-83. Mem. Assn. Univ. Programs in Health Adminstrn., Am. Hosp. Assn., NAS Inst. Medicine, Delta Upsilon, Cosmos Club, Hidden Creek Country Club. Office: Assn Am Med Colls 2450 N St NW Washington DC 20037-1167

KNAPP, ROBERT CHARLES, retired obstetrics and gynecology educator; b. N.Y.C., Jan. 19, 1927; s. Jack and Hilda (Knapp); m. Miriam Hermanos, Nov., 1955; children: Louise, Jennifer, Michael. A.B., Columbia U., 1949; M.D., SUNY Downstate Med. Center, Bklyn., 1953; M.A., Harvard U., 1982. Diplomate: Am. Bd. Ob-Gyn. Intern Kings County Hosp., Bklyn., 1953-54; resident Kings County Hosp., 1954-58; instr. ob-gyn SUNY, Bklyn., 1958-62; Am. Cancer Soc. fellow SUNY, 1962-63, asst. prof. ob-gyn, 1962-63; asst. prof. Cornell U., 1963-69, assoc. prof., 1969-70; chmn. dept. ob-gyn. Nassau County Med. Center, East Meadow, N.Y., 1967-70; assoc. prof. ob-gyn. Harvard Med. Sch., Boston, 1970-75, William H. Baker prof. gynecology, 1975-93, William H. Baker prof. emeritus, 1993—; asso. chief of staff Boston Hosp. for Women, 1975-80; dir. gynecology surgery and oncology Brigham and Women's Hosp., Boston, 1980-89; dir. gynecology Sidney Farber Cancer Inst., 1975-89. Served with U.S. Army, 1944-46. Fellow ACOG, ACS; mem. AAAS, Am. Soc. Clin. Oncology, Am. Fedn. Clin. Rsch., Obstet. Soc. Boston, Am. Radium Soc., Boston Surg. Soc. Soc. Gynecologic Oncology, Am. Assn. for Cancer Rsch., Soc. Surg. Oncologists, Internat. Soc. Gynecologic Oncologists. Home: 20 Sutton Pl S New York NY 10022-4165

KNAPP, ROLAND B., rear admiral United States Navy; b. Nov. 7. Commd. ensign USN, advanced in grades to rear admiral; dir. fleet maintenance U.S. Atlantic Fleet USN, Norfolk, Va., 1997—. Office: USN Atlantic Fleet Maintenance 1562 Mitscher Ave Ste 250 Norfolk VA 23551-2401*

KNAPP, ROSALIND ANN, lawyer; b. Washington, Aug. 15, 1945; d. Joseph Burke and Hilary (Eaves) K.; B.A., Stanford U., 1967, J.D., 1973. Admitted to Calif. bar, 1973, D.C. bar, 1980; with Dept. Transp., Washington, 1973—, asst. gen. counsel legislation, 1979-81, dep. gen. counsel, 1981—. Mem. D.C. Bar Assn., Calif. Bar Assn. Office: Dept Transp Office of the General Counsel 400 7th St SW Washington DC 20590-0003

KNAPP, STEPHEN ALBERT, artist; b. Worcester, Mass., Oct. 15, 1947; s. Walter Edwin and Antoinette Blake K.; m. Frances Deane Nichols, Jan. 23, 1971; children: Sarah Anne, Jonathan Andrew. BA, Hamilton Coll., 1969. Artist Worcester, Mass., 1971—. Editor: (book) The Art of Glass, 1998; contbr. articles to profl. jours.; selected art commns. include: Royal Caribbean Cruise Lines, 1996, 97, Harnischfeger Industries, Milw., 1996, 98, CNA Ins. Co., Chgo., 1996, Sprint, Washington, 1996, Disney's Contemporary Resort, Lake Buena Vista, Fla., 1995, Lotus Devel. Corp., Cambridge, Mass., 1995, numerous others. Bd. dirs. Social Svc. Planning Corp., 1985-88, Worcester Area Assn. Retarded Children, 1976-82; mem. Elm Park adv. com., Worcester, 1988-90. Achievements include extensive work with factories, developing kiln-formed glass on an archtl. scale, and working in cast glass, bronze, and welded steel; devel. new techniques in metal etching and fabrication, new glazing techniques for large scale ceramic murals. Avocations: bicycling, hiking, cross country skiing, music.

KNAPP, THOMAS EDWIN, sculptor, painter; b. Gillette, Wyo., Sept. 28, 1925; s. Chester M. and Georgia Mabel (Blankenship) K.; m. Dorothy Wellborn; children: Gordon, Kathy, Dan, Kent, Keith. Student, Santa Rosa Jr. Coll., 1952-53; A.A., Calif. Coll. Arts and Crafts, 1953-54; student, Art Ctr. Sch., Los Angeles, 1954-55. Animation artist Walt Disney Studios, Burbank, Calif., 1954-56, Portrait & Hobby Camera Shops, WyoFoto Studies, Cody, Wyo., 1956-64; owner Rocky Mountain Land Devel. Corp., Cody, Wyo., 1965-66; comml. artist Mountain States Telephone Co., Albuquerque, 1966-69; lectr. at art seminars. Exhibited one-man shows, Cody County Art League, 1968, Jamison Gallery, Santa Fe, 1969, Mesilla Gallery, 1971, Inn of Mountain Gods, Mescalero Apache Reservation, N.Mex., Mountain Oyster Club, Tucson, joint shows, Rosquist Gallery, Tucson, (with Michael Coleman), Zantman Gallery, Palm Desert Calif.; one and two person shows nationally with Dorothy Bell Knapp through 1988; group shows, Saddleback Inn, Santa Ana, Calif., Zantman Gallery, Carmel, Calif., Borglum Meml. Sculpture Exhbn. Nat. Cowboy Hall of Fame, Oklahoma City, 1975-76, Maxwell Gallery, San Francisco, 1975; represented permanent collections, Whitney Gallery Western Art, Cody, Senator Quinn Meml. Auditorium, Spencer, Mass., Heritage Mus., Anchorage, Indpls. Mus. Art, Mescalero Tribe, N.Mex.; works include Dance of the Mountain Spirits (Blue Ribbon award 1976), Laguna Eagle dancer (spl. award 1974, Blue Ribbon Los Angeles Indian Art Show, 1975-76), Santa Clara Buffalo dancer (Spl. award San Antonio Indian Nat. show 1974, Spl. award Los Angeles Indian show 1976), Mandan chieftan (Spl. award San Diego Indian show 1974, Spl. award Los Angeles Indian show 1976); commd. to sculpt bronze statue of Tex. ranger Capt. Bill McMurrey, now in Tex. Ranger Mus., San Antonio, bronze Giant Galapagos Tortoise in collection of Gladys Porter Zoo, Brownsville, Tex., Meijer Found., Grand Rapids, Mich., El Paso Mus. of Art, Mus. of Native Am. Cultures, Spokane, Wash., Cherokee Nat. Hist. Mus., Talequah, Okla., Diamond M. Found. Mus., Snyder, Tex., Buffalo Bill Hist. Ctr., Cody, Wyoming; Tex. Ranger (horseback) in bronze installed El Paso Mus. Art, 1989; commissioned giant Galapagos Tortoise in bronze for installation Sculpture Pk., Loveland, Colo., Giant Galapagos Tortoise Bronze Installed, 1998, Juarez Park, San Miguel de Allende Mexico, 1990, 16-foot bronze endangered salt water crocodile for Gladys Porter Zoo, Brownsville, Tex., 1998, heroic size bronze commd. for Rose Bowl, Tournament of Roses, 1992, heroic size Cahuilla Indian woman The Reed Gatherer, Waring Plaza, Palm Desert, Calif. Active Boy Scouts Am., 1947-68, World Wildlife Fund. Served with USN, World War II, Korea. Decorated Air medal; recipient Order Arrow award Boy Scout Am., 1968. Mem. Mensa, N.Y. Zool. Soc. Home and Office: PO Box 430144 Laredo TX 78043-0144

KNAPP, WHITMAN, federal judge; b. N.Y.C., Feb. 24, 1909; s. Wallace Percy and Caroline Morgan (Miller) K.; m. Ann Fallert, May 17, 1962; 1 son, Gregory Wallace; children by previous marriage—Whitman Everett, Caroline Miller (Mrs. Edward M. W. Hines), Marion Elizabeth. Grad., Choate Sch., 1927; BA, Yale, 1931; LLB, Harvard U., 1934; LLD (hon.), CUNY City Coll., 1992. Bar: N.Y. 1935. With firm Cadwalader, Wickersham & Taft, N.Y.C., 1935-37; dep. asst. dist. atty. N.Y.C., 1937-41; with firm Donovan, Leisure, Newton & Lumbard, N.Y.C., 1941; mem. staff dist. atty. N.Y.C., 1942-50; chief indictment bd., 1942-44, chief, appeal bur., 1944-50; partner firm Barrett Knapp Smith Schapiro & Simon (and predecessors), 1950-72; U.S. dist. judge So. Dist. N.Y., 1972-87, sr. dist. judge, 1987—; spl. counsel N.Y. State Youth Commn., 1950-53; Waterfront Commn. N.Y. Harbor, 1953-54; mem. temp. commn. revision N.Y. State penal law and criminal code, 1964-69; chmn. Knapp Commn. to Investigate Allegations of Police Corruption in N.Y.C., 1969-72; gen. counsel Urban League Greater N.Y., 1970-72. Editor: Harvard Law Rev, 1933-34. Sec. Community Council Greater N.Y., 1952-58; pres. Dalton Schs., N.Y.C., 1950-53, Youth House, 1967-68; Trustee Univ. Settlement, 1945-64, Moblzn. for Youth, 1965-70. Mem. ABA, Am. Law Inst., Am. Bar Found., Am. Coll. Trial Lawyers, Assn. Bar City N.Y. (sec. 1946-49, chmn. exec. com. 1971-72). Office: 1201 US Courthouse 40 Foley Sq New York NY 10007-1502

KNAPPMAN, ELIZABETH FROST See FROST-KNAPPMAN, (LINDA) ELIZABETH

KNAPTON, DAVID ROBERT, city planner; b. Providence, R.I., Apr. 15, 1945; s. Ernest John and Jocelyn (Babbitt) K. BA, Princeton U., 1968, MFA, 1971. Instr. Temple U., Phila., 1972-79; city planner Phila. City Planning Commn., 1980—. Bd. mgrs. Germantown Boys & Girls Club, Phila., 1977—; dir. Boys & Girls Clubs Met. Phila., 1982—; mem. vestry, rector's warden St. Peter's Ch., Germantown, 1993—; dir. Historic Rittenhousetown, Phila., 1996—. Woodrow Wilson fellow, 1968; grantee in humanities Nat. Def. Edn. Act, 1968-71, travel and rsch. grantee Kress Found., 1971. Fellow Princeton Terrace Club (bd. govs. 1980—); mem. Am. Planning Assn. Democrat. Episcopalian. Avocations: gardening, chamber music. Home: 128 W Washington Ln Philadelphia PA 19144-2614 Office: Phila City Planning Commn 1515 Arch St. Philadelphia PA 19102-1921

KNAUER, GEORG NICOLAUS, classical philologist; b. Hamburg, Germany, Feb. 26, 1926; came to U.S., 1975; s. Georg A. and Ilse M. (Groothoff) K.; m. Elfriede Regina Overhoff, Aug. 3, 1951; 1 child, Georg Lorenz. DrPhil, U. Hamburg, 1952. Research asst. Thesaurus Linguae Latinae, Munich, Germany, 1952-54; assistent Freie U., Berlin, 1954-61; privatdozent Freie U., 1961-64, assoc. prof., 1964-66, prof., 1966-74; prof. classical studies U. Pa., Phila., 1975-88, prof. emeritus, 1988—; chmn. dept. classical studies U. Pa., 1978-79, 80-82, 85-88; resident The Rockefeller Found., Bellagio Study and Conf. Ctr., Como, Italy, 1989; fellow Herzog August Bibliothek, Wolfenbüttel, Germany, 1991, 97; Brit. Council scholar U. London, 1957-58; vis. prof. Yale U., 1965-66; Nellie Wallace lectr. Oxford (Eng.) U., 1969; mem. Inst. Advanced Study, Princeton, N.J., 1973-74; vis. prof. Columbia U., fall 1976; mem. Notgemeinschaft für eine freie Universität, Berlin, 1969-90; mem. Bund Freiheit der Wissenschaft, Bonn, 1970—; mem. Internat. Council on Future of Univ., N.Y.C. Author: Psalmenzitate in Augustins Konfessionen, 1955, 2d edit. under title Three Studies, 1987, Die Aeneis und Homer, 1964, 2d edit. 1979. Served with German Army, 1944-45. Guggenheim fellow, 1979-80; NEH fellow, 1984-85; vis. scholar Am. Acad., Rome, 1979-80, 90, 97, resident in classics, 1985. Mem. Am. Philol. Assn., Berliner Wissenschaftliche Gesellschaft, Am. Renaissance Soc. Home: The Quadrangle Apt 3314 3300 Darby Rd Haverford PA 19041-1070 Office: U Pa Dept of Classical Studies Logan Hall Philadelphia PA 19104-6304

KNAUER, JAMES PHILIP, physicist; b. Sandusky, Ohio, May 12, 1950; s. William David Sr. and Alice Roselyn (Mowry) K.; m. Susan Diana Holmes, Apr. 8, 1974. BS, MIT, 1972; MS, U. Hawaii, 1974, PhD, 1977. Rsch. asst. MIT, Cambridge, Mass., 1971-72; grad. teaching asst. U. Hawaii, Honolulu, 1972-74, 74-77; rsch. investigator U. Pa., Phila., 1977-78; jr. researcher U. Hawaii, 1978-79; assoc. rsch. scientist Lockheed Missiles & Space Co., Palo Alto, Calif., 1979-86, rsch. scientist, 1979-86; scientist Lab. for Laser Energetics U. Rochester (N.Y.), 1986—; mgr. Nat. Laser Users Facility, Rochester, 1986-96. Leader 4-H Club, Monroe County, N.Y., 1987—. Recipient award for Excellence in Plasma Physics Research Am. Physical Society, 1995. Mem. Am. Phys. Soc. (Award for Excellence in Plasma Physics Rsch., 1995), Am. Endurance Ride Conf., Eastern Competitive Trail Ride Assn., N.Y. State Horse Coun., Sigma Xi. Republican. Avocation: horseback riding. Office: Nat Laser Users Facility Univ of Rochester 250 E River Rd Rochester NY 14623-1212

KNAUER, LEON THOMAS, lawyer; b. N.Y.C., July 16, 1932; s. Lawrence R. and Loretta M. (Trainor) K.; m. Traude Kunz, Sept. 11, 1976; children: Robert A., Katrine M. BS in Math., Fordham U., 1954; JD, Georgetown U., 1961. Bar: Conn. 1961, D.C. 1961, U.S. Supreme Ct. 1965. Law clk. U.S. Dist. Ct. (D.C.), 1960-61; assoc. Wilkinson, Barker & Knauer LLP, Washington, 1961-68, ptnr., 1968-82; ptnr. Wilkinson, Barker & Knauer, LLP, Washington, 1982—; instr. Georgetown U. Law Center, 1964-65. Editor: Telecommunications Act Handbook: A Complete Reference for Business, 1996, Telecommunications Act of 1996-A Domestic and International Prospective for Business, 1998. Pres. Catholic Apostolic Mass Media, 1974-76, Knights of Malta, 1979—. Lt. USMC, 1954-57. Recipient award for outstanding legal svc. in media area NAACP, 1973, Officer's Cross for legal svcs. to Austria, 1992. Mem. Fed. Comms. Bar Assn. (editor Comms. Bar Jour. 1960-69, treas. 1980-82, mem. exec. com. 1982-84), Washington Golf and County Club, Cosmos Club Washington, Fordham U. Alumni of Washington (pres. 1982-85). Republican. Roman Catholic. Office: 2300 N St NW #700 Washington DC 20037-1122

KNAUER, VIRGINIA HARRINGTON (MRS. WILHELM F. KNAUER), consumer consultant, former government official; b. Phila., Mar. 28, 1915; d. Herman Winfield and Helen (Harrington) Wright; m. Wilhelm F. Knauer, Jan. 27, 1940; children: Wilhelm F., Valerie H. (Mrs. I. Townsend Burden III). BFA, U. Pa., 1937; grad., Pa. Acad. Fine Arts, 1937; postgrad., Royal Acad. Fine Arts, Florence, Italy, 1938-39; LL.D. (hon.), Phila. Coll. Textiles and Sci., St. Francis de Sales, Widener Coll., Chester, Pa., Tufts U.; Litt.D. (hon.), Drexel U.; L.H.D. (hon.), Russell Sage Coll., Pa. Coll. Podiatric Medicine; L.H.D., Jacksonville U.; LLD (hon.), U. Pa., 1971. Dir. Pa. Bur. Consumer Protection, 1968-69; spl. asst. to Pres. for consumer affairs The White House, 1969-77; dir. U.S. Office Consumer Affairs, Washington, 1971-77, 81-88; spl. adv. to Pres. for consumer affairs The White House, 1981-88; chair ABRH Inc., Washington, 1988-91; consumer cons. Haney and Knauer, Inc., Washington, 1991-93; pres. Virginia Knauer & Assocs., Inc., Washington, 1977-81; chmn. Coun. for Advancement of Consumer Policy, 1979-81; U.S. rep., vice chmn. consumer policy com. OECD, 1970-77, 81-88; mem. Coun. Wage and Price Stability, 1974-77; Councilman-at-large, Phila., 1960-68; vice-chmn. Philadelphia County Rep. Com., 1958-77; pres. Phila. Congress Rep. Women's Councils, 1958-77; dir. Pa. Coun. Rep. Women, 1963-80; founder N.E. Phila. Coun. Rep. Women, pres., 1956-68. Bd. dirs. Hannah Penn House, 1956—, v.p., 1971; chmn. Knauer Found. Hist. Preservation; nat. chmn. to promote no fault automobile ins. Project New Start, 1988-91. Recipient Gimbel-Phila. award, 1977, Ind. Achievement in Govt. award Soc. Consumer Affairs Profls., 1983; named Disting. Dau. Pa., 1969; named to Disting. Women's Com., Northwood U., 1997. Mem. Nat. Trust Hist. Preservation, AARP, Annapolis Ctr. (bd. dirs.), Consumers for World Trade (bd. dirs.), Zeta Tau Alpha, Kappa Delta Epsilon (hon.). Episcopalian.

KNAUS, JONATHAN CHARLES, manufacturing executive; b. Jacksonville, Fla., June 27, 1963; s. Vincent Leo and Jeanne Marie (Holloway) K.; m. Victoria Anatolyevna Koneva, Apr. 25, 1992; children: Christopher Jonathan, Nicole Marie. BS in Commerce, Washington and Lee U., 1985. CPA, Va.; cert. internal auditor; cert. in fin. mgmt.; cert. mgmt. acct. Sr. staff acct. Marriott Corp., Bethesda, Md., 1987-88, supr. lease accts., 1988-89; internal audit supr. Caterair Internat., Bethesda, Md., 1989-91; fin. controller JV Aeromar Caterair Internat., Moscow, 1991-93, fin. dir. JV Aeromar, 1993-94; fin. dir. Unisys Corp., Moscow, 1994-95, Eastman Kodak Co., Moscow, 1996—. Mem. Va. Beach Jaycees, 1986-87. Named Jaycee of Quarter Fall 87 Herndon (Va.) Jaycees, 1987. Republican. Roman Catholic. Avocations: fgn. langs. including fluent Russian. Home: c/o 666 Fifth Ave Ste 572 Box 178 New York NY 10103 Office: Kodak AO, 1 Mosfilmovskaya Bldg 3, Moscow 119858, Russia

KNAUSS, JOHN ATKINSON, former federal agency administrator, oceanographer, educator, former university dean; b. Detroit, Sept. 1, 1925; s. Karl Ernst and Loise (Atkinson) K.; m. Marilyn Mattson, Sept. 6, 1954; children: Karl, William. BS, MIT, 1946; MS, U. Mich., 1949; PhD, U. Calif., 1959; DSc (hon.), U R.I., 1992. Oceanographer Navy Electronics Lab, San Diego, 1947, Office Naval Rsch., 1949-51, Scripps Instn. Oceanography, 1951-52, 55-62; prof. Grad. Sch. Oceanography, U. R.I., Narragansett, 1962-90, dean, 1962-87, provost for marine affairs, 1969-82, v.p. marine programs, 1982-87, prof., dean emeritus, 1990—; undersecretary for oceans and atmosphere Dept. Commerce, Washington, 1989-93; adminstr. Nat. Oceanic and Atmospheric Adminstrn., Washington, 1989-93; U.S. commr. Internat. Whaling Commn., 1991-93; rsch. assoc. Scripps Inst. Oceanography U. Calif., San Diego, 1993—; leader 10 oceanographic expdns to study oceanic circulation, 1955-65; chair U.S. phys.-chem. panel Internat. Indian Ocean Expdn., 1959-62; mem. Pres's. Commn. on Marine Scis., Engring. and Resources, 1967-68; mem. State Dept. Pub. Adv. Com. on Law of Sea, 1970-82; chair sr. adv. com. on environ. scis. Ctr. for Energy and Environ. Rsch., U. P.R., 1977-80; mem. Nat. Adv. Com. on Oceans and Atmosphere, 1978-85, vice chair, 1979-81, chair 1981-85; chair bd. govs. Joint Oceanographic Instns., Inc., 1978-80; co-founder Law of Sea Inst., mem. exec. bd. 1965-76, 82-87; bd. dirs. Coun. for Ocean Law, 1983-89, 94—; chair marine divsn. Nat. Assn. State U. and Land Grant Colls., 1984-85; chair Joint Oceanographic Instns. for Deep Earth Sampling, 1984-86; bd. dirs. Harbor Br. Oceanographic Instn., 1987-89; 1st vice chmn. Intergovernmental Oceanographic Commn., 1991-93; mem. bd. trustees Bermuda Biological Sta. for Rsch., 1995—; chair ocean rsch. adv. panel Nat. Oceanographic Rsch. Leadership Coun., 1998—. U.S. Congress renamed its Sea Grant fellowship the Dean John A. Knauss Fellowship program in 1987. With USNR, 1943-46, 53-54. Named to R.I. Heritage Hall of Fame, 1983; recipient Albatross award Am. Miscellaneous Soc., 1959, Nat. Sea Grant award, 1974. Fellow AAAS (v.p. 1972-73), Am. Geophys. Union (pres. oceanography sect. 1965-67, pres-elect 1996-98, pres. 1998-2000, Ocean Sci. award 1988); mem. Am. Meteorol. Soc. (coun. 1980-82). Home: 2634 Ellentown Rd La Jolla CA 92037-1147 also: 2634 Ellentown Rd La Jolla CA 92037

KNAUSS, ROBERT LYNN, international business educator, corporate executive; b. Detroit, Mar. 24, 1931; s. Karl Ernst and Loise (Atkinson) K.; m. Angela Tirola Lawson, Feb. 21, 1973; children by previous marriage: Robert B., Charles H., Katherine E.; 1 stepson, Ian T. Lawson. AB, Harvard U., 1952; JD, U. Mich., 1957. Bar: Calif., Tenn., Tex. Assoc. Pillsbury, Madison & Sutro, San Francisco, 1958-60; prof. law U. Mich., 1960-72, v.p. student svcs., 1970-72; dean, prof. law Vanderbilt U., Nashville, 1972-79; dean U. Houston Law Ctr., 1981-93, disting. univ. prof., 1981-95; vis. prof. law Vt. Law Sch., South Royalton, Amos Tuck Sch. Bus. Adminstrn., Dartmouth Coll., Hanover, N.H., 1979-81; chmn. CEO Baltic Internat. USA/Inc., 1994—; chmn. bd. dirs. Philips Svcs. Corp., 1998—; bd. dirs. Mex. Fund, Equus II, Inc., AIRO Catering Svcs. Editor: Small Business Financing, 4 vols., 1966, Securities Regulation Sourcebook, 1970-71, (with others) Cases and Materials on Enterprise Organizations, 1987; contbr. articles to profl. jours. Regent Nat. Coll. Dist. Attys., 1981-95. Lt. (j.g.) USNR, 1952-55. Fellow Tex. Bar Found., Am. Bar Found; mem. Calif. Bar Assn., Tenn. Bar Assn., Tex. Bar Assn. (chmn. corp. coun. sect. 1991), Am. Law Inst. (life), Order of Coif. Home: PO Box 40 Three Creek Ranch Burton TX 77835-0040 Office: 5151 San Felipe Ste 1661 Houston TX 77056

KNAUSS, WOLFGANG GUSTAV, engineering educator. Prof. aeronautics and applied sci. Calif. Inst. Tech., Pasadena. Editor: (with E. Emri) Mechanics of Time-Dependent Materials. Fellow ASME, Soc. Exptl. Mechanics (Murray medal 1995, chmn. divsn. for time dependent material behavior), Am. Acad. Mechanics, Inst. for the Advancement of Engring.; mem. AIAA, Nat. Acad. Engring., Russian Acad. Natural Scis. (fgn., Kapitsa medal), Internat. (Russian Acad. Engring. (corr.), The Adhesion Soc., Soc. Rheology, Soc. for the Advancement Sci., Sigma Xi. Office: Calif Inst of Tech Div Engring & Applied Sci Mail Code 105 50 Pasadena CA 91125

KNAUST, CLARA DOSS, retired elementary school educator; b. Freistatt, Mo., Feb. 18, 1922; d. John Fredrick and Hedwig Louise (Brockschmidt) Doss; m. Donald Knaust, July 7, 1946 (dec.); children: Karen Louise, Ramona Elizabeth, Heidi Marie. BS in Edn., S.W. Mo. State U., 1969. Elem. tchr. Trinity Luth. Sch., Freistatt, 1942-46; tchr. kindergarten Trinity Luth Ch., Springfield, Mo., 1961-65, Redeemer Luth Ch., Springfield, 1962-63, 66-69; tchr. kindergarten Springfield R-12 Sch. System, 1969-70, 73-84, elem. tchr., 1970-73; elem. and kindergarten tchr. Springfield Luth. Sch., 1984-88; mem. planning bd. Early Childhood Conf., U. Mo., Columbia, 1977-80. Pres. Springfield Gen. Hosp. Guild, 1969-71; local and zone pres. Luth. Women's Missionary League, Springfield, 1986-94; historian Trinity Luth. Ch., 1985-94; chair bd. edn. Grace Luth. Ch., Tulsa. Mem. Assn. for Childhood Edn. Internat. (br. state pres. 1980-84, president's coun. 1983-85, Hall of Fame plaque 1988, state pres. 1989-93), Springfield Edn. Assn. (life), Springfield Luth. Sch. Assn. (pres. 1992-94), S.W. Dist. Kindergarten Assn. (pres. 1978-79), Alpha Delta Kappa. Avocations: painting, crafts, collecting, music. Home: Univ Club 1722 S Carson Ave Apt 1710 Tulsa OK 74119-4641

KNEAVEL, ANN CALLANAN, humanities educator, communications consultant; b. Balt., Oct. 29, 1946; d. James Michael and Ann (Ijams) Callanan; m. Thomas Charles Kneavel, Jr., Dec. 18, 1970; children: Meredith Elizabeth, Thomas Charles III, Rebecca Ann. BA, Coll. Notre Dame Md., 1968; MA in Am. Lit., U. Md., 1970; PhD in Modern Brit. Lit., U. Ottawa, Ont., Can., 1979. Instr. U. Md., College Park, 1968-71, U. Ottawa, 1971-72, Wilmington (Del.) Coll., 1976-79, Del. Tech. and C.C., Dover, 1975-79; asst. prof. Widener U., Chester, Pa., 1981-82; prof. Goldey-Beacom Coll., Wilmington, Del., 1981—; dir. satellite campuses Total Quality Master's Program, Falmouth, Mass., 1995—. Contbr. articles to profl. jours. Trustee Hockessin (Del.) Pub. Libr., 1981-93, Alpha Tau Omega Fraternity, Wilmington, 1994—; mem. Friends of Hockessin Libr., 1981—. Mem. MLA, Nat. Coun. Tchrs. English, Conf. on Christianity and Lit., Am. Culture Assn., C.C. Humanities Assn., Alpha Chi (faculty sponsor, Svc. award 1994). Roman Catholic. Home: 7 Arthur Dr Hockessin DE 19707-1012 Office: Goldey-Beacom Coll 4701 Limestone Rd Wilmington DE 19808-1927

KNEAVEL, THOMAS CHARLES, JR., psychologist; b. Balt., Oct. 30, 1941; s. Thomas Charles and Caroline Frances (Noha) K.; m. Ann Callanan, Dec. 18, 1970; children: Meredith, Thomas, Rebecca. BS, Loyola Coll., Balt., 1963, MEd, 1968; PhD, U. Ottawa, 1979. Diplomate Am. Bd. Forensic Examiners; lic. psychologist, Del. Tchr. Ridge Sch., Towsen, Md., 1961-65; psychologist Balt. City Schs., 1965-69; clin. psychologist D.C. Children's Ctr., Laurel, Md., 1969-70; cons. Joseph House, Balt., 1969-70; psychology intern Child Study Ctr. U. Ottawa, 1970-71; psychology intern Child Diagnostic and Devel. Clinic Children's Hosp. of Ea. Ont., Ottawa, 1971-72; sch. psychologist Cape Henlopen Sch. Dist., Nassau, Del., 1972-79; psychologist Comty. Mental Health Clinic, Beebe Hosp., Lewes, Del., 1973-79; program dir. child crisis unit Terry Children's Psychiat. Ctr., New Castle, Del., 1979-86, chief psychologist, 1982-86; pvt. practice, 1983—; mem. adj. faculty dept. psychiatry and human behavior Thomas Jefferson U. Med. Sch., 1980-86; psychologist Christina Sch. Dist., 1986-98; clin. cons. Turnabout Counseling Ctr., Seaford, Del., 1987-91; clin. dir. adolescent programs Meadow Wood Hosp., New Castle, Del., 1993-94; dir. psychol. svcs. Med. Ctr. Del. Dept. Adolescent Medicine 1st State Sch., 1995-99; cons. on compulsive gambling to dir. divsn. mental health, frequent nat. presenter on treating oppositional disorders in children and adolescents, 1980-82; apptd. by Gov. DuPont and Gov. Castle to Del. Devel. Disabilities Planning Coun., 1982-94, vice chmn., 1983-85, chmn., 1985-87; mem. citizens adv. bd. Comty. Mental Health Clinic, Beebe Hosp., 1974-79; state rep. Nat. Assn. Devel. Disabilities, Washington, 1984-87, mem. child devel. com.; mem. state genetics adv. coun. A.I. DuPont Inst. and State of Del., 1986-90; apptd. by Gov. Castle to State Bd. Psychol. Examiners, 1989, v.p., 1991-92, pres., 1992-94; bd. dirs. Falmouth Inst. Quality Sys. Mgmt., 1997—; mem. Eagle Scouts. Mem. APA, Del. Psychol. Assn., Falmouth Inst. Quality Sys. Mgmt. (bd. dirs.), Nat. Assn. Sch. Psychologists (charter), Del. Sch. Psychologists Assn. (pres. 1976-77), Del. Psychol. Inc. (bd. dirs. 1987-89). Roman Catholic. E-mail: docneavel@aol.com. Home: 7 Arthur Dr Hockessin DE 19707-1012 Office: 1701 Augustine Cut Off Wilmington DE 19803-4415

KNEBEL, CONSTANCE, potter, ceramicist; b. Nov. 2, 1934. Student, Northeastern U., 1953-54, Boston Sch. Art, 1954-55. Asst. to editor Esquire Mag., N.Y.C., 1961-70; photographer Time, Inc., N.Y.C., 1971-83; freelance potter, ceramicist Honolulu, 1983-97, Canaan, N.Y., 1997—. E-mail: cknebel@taconic.net. Home: 271 Tunnel Hill Rd Canaan NY 12029-2706

KNEBEL, DONALD EARL, lawyer; b. Logansport, Ind., May 26, 1946; s. Everett Earl and Ethel Josephina (Hultgren) K.; m. Joan Elizabeth Vest, June 5, 1976 (div. 1980); 1 child, Mary Elizabeth. BEE with highest distinction, Purdue U., 1968; JD magna cum laude, Harvard U., 1974. Bar: Ind. 1974, U.S. Ct. Appeals (7th cir.) 1980, U.S. Ct. Appeals (3rd cir.) 1986, U.S. Ct. Appeals (6th cir.) 1987, U.S. Ct. Appeals (fed. cir.) 1988. Assoc. Barnes, Hickam, Pantzer & Boyd, Indpls., 1974-81; ptnr. Barnes & Thornburg, Indpls., 1981—. Contbr. articles on intellectual property, antitrust and distbn. law to profl. publs. Trustee Indpls. Civic Theatre, 1986-95, chmn., 1988-91, hon. trustee, 1995—. Mem. ABA, Ind. Bar Assn., Indpls. Bar Assn., 7th Cir. Bar Assn., Kiwanis (pres. 1991-92), Columbia Club. Office: Barnes & Thornburg 11 S Meridian St Indianapolis IN 46204-3506

KNEBEL, JACK GILLEN, lawyer; b. Washington, Jan. 28, 1939; s. Fletcher and Amalia Eleanor (Rauppius) K.; m. Linda Karin Ropertz, Feb. 22, 1963; children: Hollis Anne (dec.), Lauren Beth. BA, Yale Coll., 1960; LLB, Harvard U., 1966. Bar: Calif. 1966, U.S. Dist. Ct. (no. dist.) Calif. 1966, U.S. Ct. Appeals (9th cir.) 1966. Assoc. McCutchen, Doyle, Brown & Enersen, San Francisco, 1966-74, ptnr., 1974-94, of counsel, 1994—; lectr. in law Stanford Law Sch., 1998—; mem. exec. com. San Francisco Lawyers Com. for Urban Affairs, 1991-93; mem. adv. coun. Hastings Coll. Trial Advocacy, San Francisco, 1981-91, chair, 1990-91; mediator, arbitrator Am. Arbitration Assn., 1989—; mem. ARTEMA, 1999—. Bd. dirs., pres. Orinda (Calif.) Assn., 1972-74, Sea Ranch (Calif.) Assn., 1978-79; co-chmn. Citizens to Preserve Orinda, 1983-85. Lt. (j.g.) USN, 1960-66. Fellow Am. Coll. Trial Lawyers (mem. com. on fed. rules civ. pro 1990-93); mem. ABA, Maritime Law Assn. of U.S. Democrat. Home: PO Box 220 Islesboro ME 04848 Office: McCutchen Doyle Brown & Enersen Ste 1800 Three Embarcadero Ctr San Francisco CA 94111

KNEBEL, JOHN ALBERT, lawyer, former government official; b. Tulsa, Oct. 4, 1936; s. John Albert and Florence Julia (Friend) K.; m. Zenia Irene Marks, June 6, 1959; children—Carrie, John Albert III, Clemens. B.S., U.S. Mil. Acad., 1959; M.A. in Econs, Creighton U., 1962; J.D., Am. U., 1965. Bar: D.C. bar 1966, U.S. Ct. Appeals bar 1966. Asst. to Rep. J.E. Wharton of N.Y., Washington, 1963-64; asso. mem. law firm Howrey, Simon, Baker & Murchison, Washington, 1965-68; asst. counsel Com. on Agr., U.S. Ho. Reps., Washington, 1968-71; gen. counsel SBA, Washington, 1971-74, U.S. Dept. Agr., Washington, 1973-75; under sec. Dept. Agr., 1975-76, sec. of agr., 1976-77; ptnr. firm Baker & McKenzie, Washington, 1977-86; pres. Am. Mining Congress, Washington, 1986-95; exec. v.p. Nat. Assn. Broadcasters, Washington, 1995—. Served to 1st lt. USAF, 1959-62. Mem. Fed. Bar Assn. (past pres.), Am., D.C. bar assns., Delta Theta Phi, Omicron Delta Gamma. Home: 1418 Laburnum St Mc Lean VA 22101-2523 Office: Nat Assn Boradcasters 1771 N St NW Ste 500 Washington DC 20036-2891*

KNECHT, BEN HARROLD, surgeon; b. Rapid City, S.D., May 3, 1938; m. Jane Bowles, Aug. 27, 1961; children: John, Janelle. BA, U. S.D., 1960; MD, U. Iowa, 1964; cert. total quality mgmt., U. Wash., 1998. Diplomate Am. Bd. Surgery. Intern Los Angeles County Gen. Hosp., 1964-65; resident in surgery U. Iowa Sch. Medicine, Iowa City, 1968-72; surgeon Wenatchee (Wash.) Valley Clinic, 1972—; med. dir. Cascade Hosp. and Surgery Ctr., 1997—; chmn. med. informatics Wen Valley Clinic, 1995—, chmn. gen.-vasc. surg. dept., 1996—; dir. emergency rm. Ctrl. Wash. Hosp., Wenatchee, 1972-79, chmn. libr., 1976-86, chief surgery, 1983-86; chmn. claims rev. panel Wash. State Med. Assn., Seattle, 1979-82, prof. liability com. risk mgmt., 1985-90; clin. prof. surgery U. Wash.; mem. adv. risk mgmt. com. Wash. State Physicians Ins. Subscribers, 1990-98, regional adv. com. Nat. Libr. Medicine, 1991-93. Fundraiser Cen. Wash. Hosp. Found., 1987; del. Gov.'s Conf. on Librs., 1991; bd. dirs. United Way, 1974-77; mem. founding bd. Cascade Unitarian Fellowship, 1986-88; mem. ad hoc com. on tchg./learning Wenatchoe H.S., 1999—; post leader Med. Explorers, 1973-76. Lt. comdr. USN, 1965-68, Vietnam. Mem. AMA (alt. del. 1985-87, del. 1988-98, surg. caucus exec. com. 1991-94), ACS (bd. dirs. Wash. chpt. 1981-84), Am. Coll. Physician Execs., Am. Soc. Quality, North Pacific Surg. Assn., Wash. State Med. Assn. (trustee 1979-98), Chelan-Douglas County Med. Soc., Am. Soc. Gen. Surgery (founding bd. 1994—, bd. dir.1992—), Rotary (chmn. youth com. 1976-78), Alpha Tau Omega. Avocations: snow and water skiing, reading, hiking, computing. Office: Wenatchee Valley Clinic 820 N Chelan Ave Wenatchee WA 98801-2028

KNECHT, JAMES HERBERT, lawyer; b. Los Angeles, Aug. 5, 1925; s. James Herbert and Gertrude Martha (Morris) K.; m. Margaret Paton Vreeland, Jan. 3, 1953 (dec. 1994); children—Susan, Thomas Paton, Carol. BS, UCLA, 1947; LLB, U. So. Calif., 1957. Bar: Calif. bar 1957, U.S. Supreme Ct. bar 1969. Mem. firm Forster, Gemmill & Farmer, Los Angeles, 1957-84; sole practice, 1985—; chmn. bd. Templeton (Calif.) Nat. Bank, 1992-95. Fellow Am. Bar Found. (life); mem. ABA, San Luis Obispo County Bar Assn., Legion Lex, Caltech Assocs., L.A. Area C. of C. (dir. 1979-83), Beta Theta Pi. Home: 5030 Vineyard Dr Paso Robles CA 93446-9682 Office: PO Box 2280 Paso Robles CA 93447-2280

KNECHT, RICHARD ARDEN, family practitioner; b. Grand Rapids, Mar. 7, 1929; s. Fredrick William and Eva Rae (Blakley) K.; m. Joan Matson, Dec. 26, 1951 (div. 1975); children: Richard Arden, Karrie Jo, Jeffrey Paul; m. Patricia Irene Gilmore, Aug. 14, 1976; 1 child, Kimberly Kahler. BS, U. Mich., 1951, MD, 1955. Diplomate Am. Bd. Family Practice, Am. Bd. Geriatric Medicine; cert. med. dir. Intern St. Mary Hosp., Grand Rapids, Mich., 1955-56; pvt. practice, Indian River, Mich., 1956—. Fellow Am. Acad. Family Physicians, Am. Geriatric Soc., Royal Soc. Medicine; mem. Mich. Med. Soc. (com. on aging 1988—), Mich. Acad. Family Practice (chmn. com. on aging 1986-88, pub.'s award 1988), Mich. Med. Dirs. Assn. (pres. 1996-97). Avocations: archaeology, motorcycling, geology, hunting, fishing. Home and Office: PO Box 130 125 Morgan St Fife Lake MI 49633

KNECHT, WILLIAM L., lawyer; b. Lock Haven, Pa., Jan. 15, 1946; s. Clair N. and Betty R. (Harter) K.; m. Margaret E. O'Malley, June 10, 1972; children: William E., Jennifer M. BA, Pa. State U., 1967; JD, Dickinson Sch. Law, 1970. Bar: Pa. 1970, U.S. Supreme Ct. 1976, U.S. Tax Ct. 1981, U.S. Dist. Ct. (middle dist.) Pa. 1973, Ct. Common Pleas 1970. Assoc. McCormick, Lynn, Reeder, Nichols & Sarno, Williamsport, Pa., 1973-76; ptnr. McCormick, Reeder, Nichols, Bahl, Knecht & Person, Williamsport, 1976-96, McCormick Law Firm, Williamsport, 1996—; bankruptcy trustee U.S. Justice Dept., Williamsport, Pa., 1978-91. Editor Lycoming Reporter, 1976—. 1st lt. U.S. Army, 1971-73. Mem. ABA, Pa. Bar Assn., Lycoming County Law Assn. (exec. com. 1976—), Lycoming Law Assn. (pres. 1995), Ross Club. Republican. United Ch. of Christ. Avocations: stamps and first day cover collecting. Home: 253 Lincoln Ave Williamsport PA 17701-2237 Office: McCormick Law Firm PO Box 577 835 W 4th St Williamsport PA 17703-0577

KNEE, STANLEY LA MOYNE, protective services official; married; 4 children. B in Criminal Justice, Calif. State U., Fullerton, 1977; grad., FBI Nat. Acad., 1982, Calif. Peach Officers Stds. and Tng. Command Coll., 1986; M in Criminal Justice, Calif. State U., Long Beach, 1987. From patrol officer to field sgt. Garden Grove (Calif.) Police Dept., 1969-78, lt., 1978-81, capt., 1981-88; Chief of Police, National City (Calif.) Police Dept., 1988-92, Garden Grove Police Dept., 1992-97, Austin Police Dept., 1997—; instr. Calif. State U., Fullerton, 1993-97; guest lectr. in field; cons. to various orgns. Lt. U.S. Army, 1967-69, Vietnam. Decorated 2 Bronze Stars; recipient Svc. Appreciation award Orange County Korean C. of C., 1992, Outstanding Pub. Adminstr., Orange County chpt. Am. Soc. Pub. Adminstrn., 1994, Humanitarian award Orange County Human Rels. Commn., 1995, Cmty. Svc. award Orange County chpt. 100 Black Men, 1996, Cmty. Svc. Support award Garden Grove Interfaith Coun., 1997. Mem. Internat. Assn. Chiefs of Police, Police Exec. Rsch. Forum, Major City Chiefs Assn., FBI Nat. Acad., Tex. Police Chief's Assn., Command Coll. Alumni Assn., Law Enforcement Intelligence Unit. FAX: 512-480-5279. Office: Police Dept Austin 1715 E Eighth St Austin TX 78701-3397

KNEE, STEPHEN H., lawyer; b. Newark, Oct. 15, 1940; s. Simon E. and Mollie (Liest) K.; m. Carole Leibowitz, Feb. 17, 1984; children: Robert A., David E., Dana R. AB, Duke U., 1962; JD, N.Y.U., 1965. Bar: N.J. 1965, N.Y. 1981, U.S. Ct. Appeals (3rd cir.) 1981, U.S. Supreme Ct. 1969, U.S. Dist. Ct. (so. dist.) N.Y. 1999. Law sec. Superior Ct. of N.J., Paterson, 1965-66; ptnr. Stryker, Tams & Dill, LLP, Newark, 1966-98, Saiber Schlesinger Satz & Goldstein, LLC, Newark, 1998—. Author: Buying and Selling Businesses, 1996. Trustee N.J. Shakespeare Festival, 1988—, sec.; trustee Jewish Family Services of Metrowest, 1988—. Mem. ABA (com. on negotiated acquistions, subcom. on uniform securities act of state regulation of securities com.), N.J. Bar Assn. (dir. corp. and bus. law sect. 1979—, chmn. 1984-86, program com. 1991-97), Inst. for Continuing Legal Edn. (mem. adv. com. 1980—), Essex County Bar Assn., Am. Coll. Investment Counsel, Nat. Assn. Bond Lawyers. Office: Saiber Schlesinger Et Al & Goldstein LLC One Gateway Ctr Newark NJ 07102

KNEEDLER, ALVIN RICHARD, college president; b. Ruffsdale, Pa., Apr. 8, 1943; s. Alvin Raymond and Louise (Mac Innes) K.; m. Suzette Gallagher, June 17, 1967; children: Eric, Rebecca. AB, Franklin and Marshall Coll., 1965; MA in French Language and Lit., U. Pa., 1967, PhD in French Language and Lit., 1970; cert. in Ednl. Mgmt., Harvard U., 1975; DHL (hon.), Tohoku Gakuin U., 1993. Instr. French Franklin and Marshall Coll., Lancaster, Pa., 1968-70, asst. prof. French, 1970-72, asst. to dean, 1971-74, asst. to pres., 1974-77, sec. coll., 1977-79, v.p. adminstrn., 1979-84, v.p. devel., 1984-88, sec. bd. trustees, 1974-88, pres., 1988—; mem. exec. com. Assn. Ind. Colls. and Univs. of Pa., 1989—, chmn., 1996-97; bd. dirs. Nat. Assn. Ind. Colls. and Univs., 1998—, exec. com., 1999, chair policy & pub. rels. com., 1999. Mem. Lancaster City Planning Commn., 1980-85, chmn., 1983-85; mem. adv. bd. PRIME, Inc., 1991—; v.p., bd. dirs. Hist. Preservation Trust, Lancaster, 1984-87; sec., bd. dirs. Pa. Sch. Arts, Lancaster, 1985-89; bd. dirs. St. Joseph Hosp., 1991-95, Lancaster Area Arts Coun., 1967-91, Louise Von Hess Found. for Med. Edn., 1990—, Urban League Lancaster County, 1991-93, United Way, 1993—, Lancaster Alliance, 1998—; chmn. Cmty. Cultural Planning Com., 1989-90; mem. Downtown Task Force, 1989-90; trustee Kiski Sch., 1988-95; chmn. exec. bd. Commonwealth Partnerships, 1997-98. Mem. Am. Assn. Tchrs. French, Am. Soc. for 18th Century Studies, Lancaster C. of C. and Industry (bd. dirs. 1990-92), Phi Beta Kappa, Phi Alpha Theta. Republican. Presbyterian. Home: 1416 Newton Rd Lancaster PA 17603-2461 Office: Franklin and Marshall Coll PO Box 3003 Lancaster PA 17604-3003

KNEELAND, DOUGLAS EUGENE, retired newspaper editor; b. Lincoln, Maine, July 27, 1929; s. Vernis Bruce and Sadie Jane (Curtis) K.; m. Anne Packard Libby, Sept. 8, 1951 (dec. Nov. 1989); children: Debra Jo Kneeland Wentz, Libby Kneeland Williams, Bruce, Wayne; m. Barbara Jordan Lees, May 24, 1997. B.A. in Journalism, U. Maine, 1953. Reporter Bangor Daily News, Maine, 1951-53, Worcester Telegram, Mass., 1953-56; city editor, news editor Lorain Jour., Ohio, 1956-59; copy editor, nat. corr., dep. nat. editor N.Y. Times, N.Y.C., Kansas City, San Francisco and Chgo., 1959-81; nat.-fgn. editor Chgo. Tribune, 1981-82, assoc. mng. editor, 1982-87, assoc. editor, 1987-90, pub. editor, 1990-93; vis. lectr. journalism U. Maine, Orono, 1993—; columnist Lincoln News, Maine, 1995—. Served with AUS, 1947-49, Korea, Japan. Home: RR 2 Box 15 Lincoln ME 04457-9601

KNEEN, JAMES RUSSELL, health care administrator; b. Kalamazoo, Dec. 16, 1955; s. Russell Packard and Joyce Elaine (Knapper) K.; m. Peggy Jo Howard, Aug. 4, 1979; children: Benjamin Russell, Katherine Elaine. BA, Alma Coll., 1978; MHA, U. Mo., 1982. Systems analyst Bronson Meth. Hosp., Kalamazoo, 1976-79; cons. U. Mo., Columbia, 1979-81; adminstrv. resident Meth. Hosp. Ind., Indpls., 1981-82; div. dir. psychiat. care svcs. Parkview Meml. Hosp., Ft. Wayne, Ind., 1982-88; exec. v.p. Meml. Hosp., Ocomonowoc, Wis., 1988-90; exec. dir. Meml. Hosp. Found., Oconomowoc, 1988-90; pres., CEO Fostoria (Ohio) Community Hosp., 1990-94; pres. United Health Partnership, Toledo, 1995—. Bd. dirs. Washington House Alcoholism Treatment Ctr., 1983-88; bd. dirs., sec.-treas. Parkview Regional Outreach, 1985-88; bd. dirs., pres. Seneca County chpt. Am. Cancer Soc. Fellow Am. Coll. Healthcare Execs.; mem. Am. Hosp. Assn., Wis. Hosp. Assn. (coun. on health care delivery systems), Regent's Adv. Coun. Wis. (bd. dirs.), Ohio Hosp. Assn. (various coms.), Rotary (bd. dirs. Fostoria chpt). Office: United Health Ptrn 2200 Jefferson Ave Toledo OH 43624-1120

KNEIPPER, RICHARD KEITH, lawyer; b. Kenosha, Wis., June 18, 1943; s. Richard F. and Esther E. (Beaster) K.; m. Sherry Hayes, Dec. 16, 1977; children: Ryan Hayes, Lindsey Merrill. BS, Washington and Lee U., 1965; JD, Cornell U., 1968. Bar: Tex. 1982, U.S. Dist. Ct. (so. dist.) N.Y. 1968, U.S. Ct. Appeals (2d cir.) 1971. Atty. Chadbourne & Parke, N.Y.C., 1968-81, Jones, Day, Reavis & Pogue, Dallas, 1981—; adv. com. Nat. Mus. Am., Smithsonian, Nat. Arts Edn. Initiative, Nat. Mus. Am. Art, Smithsonian Instn. Contbr. numerous articles to profl. jours. Bd. trustees, The Dallas Parks Found.; mem. profl adv. group Save Outdoor Sculpture!; chmn. Dallas Adopt-A-Monument; bd. dirs., mem. new bus. task force, mem. internat task force Health Industry Coun. Dallas-Ft. Worth Region. Mem. ABA, N.Y. Bar Assn., Tex. Bar Assn., Tex. Sculpture Assn., Assn. Bar City of N.Y. Episcopal. Office: Jones Day Reavis & Pogue 2300 Trammell Crow Ctr 2001 Ross Ave Ste 2000 Dallas TX 75201-2958

KNEISEL, EDMUND M., lawyer; b. Atlanta, Feb. 21, 1946; s. John F. and Mary E. (Moore) K.; m. Leslie A. Jones, June 19, 1976; 1 child, Mary Kathleen. AB, Duke U., 1968; JD, U. Ga., 1974. Bar: Ga. 1974, U.S. Dist. Ct. (no. and mid. dists.) Ga. 1976, U.S. Ct. Appeals (4th, 5th, 6th and 11th cirs.) 1976, U.S. Supreme Ct. 1984. Law clk. to Hon. R.C. Freeman U.S. Dist. Ct. (no. dist.) Ga., Atlanta, 1974-76; assoc. Kilpatrick & Cody, Atlanta, 1976-82; ptnr. Kilpatrick Stockton LLP, 1982—. Mng. editor Ga. Law Rev., Athens, 1973-74; contbr. articles to profl. jours. Lt. USNR, 1968-71. Mem. ABA, Lawyers Club Atlanta, Druid Hills Golf Club. Office: Kilpatrick Stockton LLP 1100 Peachtree St NE Ste 2800 Atlanta GA 30309-4501

KNELL, GARY EVAN, media executive, lawyer; b. Sacramento, Feb. 27, 1954; s. David J. and Gertrude A. (Milkes) K.; m. Kim Larson, Oct. 18, 1981; children: Dwight M., Savannah B., Lucia L., Maya E. BA, UCLA, 1975; JD, Loyola U., L.A., 1978. Bar: Calif. 1978. Asst. counsel sub-com. on intergovtl. relations U.S. Senate Govt. Affairs Com., Washington, 1978-79; counsel sub-com. on adminstrv. practice and procedure U.S. Senate Judiciary Com., Washington, 1979-81; spl. asst. to v.p., gen. counsel Sta. WNET-TV, N.Y.C., 1981-82, dir. telecommunications, 1982-84, sr. v.p., gen. counsel, 1984-89; v.p., dir. legal affairs Children's TV Workshop, N.Y.C., 1989-93, exec. v.p. corp. affairs, 1993-96, exec. v.p. ops.; mktg. dir., mgr. pub. co.; guest lectr. Harvard U. Sch. Edn., Assn. Bar City of N.Y., Promax, Media Law Inst. Contbr. articles to profl. jours. Bd. dirs. Bklyn. Conservatory Music. Mem. ABA (communications law sect. 1987—), Fed. Comm. Bar Assn. *

KNELLER, JOHN WILLIAM, retired French language and literature educator; b. Oldham, Eng., Oct. 15, 1916; s. John William and Margaret Ann (Truslove) K.; m. Alice Bowerman Hart, Apr. 30, 1943; 1 dau., Linda Hart. AB, Clark U., 1938, LittD, 1970; AM, Yale U., 1948, PhD, 1950; French Govt. and Fulbright fellow, U. Paris, France, 1949-50. Asst. in instrn. Yale U., 1947-49; instr. French Oberlin Coll., 1950-52, asst. prof., 1952-55, assoc. prof., 1955-59, prof. French, 1959-65, chmn. dept. Romance langs., 1958-65; dean Oberlin Coll. (Coll. Arts and Scis.), 1967-68, provost, 1965-69; pres. Bklyn. Coll., 1969-79, pres. emeritus, 1979—; univ. prof. humanities and arts Hunter Coll. and Grad. Ctr., CUNY, 1979-95, prof. emeritus, 1995—; mng. editor French Rev., 1962-65, editor-in-chief, 1965-68; co-chair bd. dirs. Henri Peyre Inst. for the Humanities, 1980—; cons. NEH; chmn. subcom. on enrollment goals and projections N.Y. State Edn.; Commr.'s Adv. Coun. on Higher Edn., Adv. Coun. on Higher Edn. Co-author: Initiation au francais, 1963, Introduction a la poesie francaise, 1962; assoc. editor Yale French Studies, 1948-50; contbr. articles to jours. in field. Bd. dirs. Independence Savs. Bank. With AUS, 1942-46. Decorated comdr. Ordre des Palmes Académiques (France). Mem. Am. Assn. Tchrs. French (exec. council 1962-68), Modern Lang. Assn. (exec. council 1965-69), Yale Grad. Sch. Assn. (exec. com. 1967, 71), Bklyn. C. of C. (dir.), Kappa Delta Pi (hon.), Alpha Sigma Lambda (hon.). Clubs: Century (N.Y.C.), Yale (N.Y.C.), Southport Racquet. Office: CUNY Grad Ctr 33 W 42nd St New York NY 10036-8099

KNEPPER, EUGENE ARTHUR, realtor; b. Sioux Falls, S.D., Oct. 8, 1926; s. Arlie John and May (Crone) K.; B.S.C. in Acctg., Drake U., Des Moines, 1951; m. LaNel Strong, May 7, 1948 (div. Sept. 1996); children—Kenton Todd, Kristin Rene. Acct., G.L. Yager, pub. acct., Estherville, Iowa, 1951-52; auditor R.L. Meriwether, C.P.A., Des Moines, 1952-53; acct. govt. renegotiation dept. Collins Radio Co., Cedar Rapids, Iowa, 1953-54; head acctg. dept. Hawkeye Rubber Mfg. Co., Cedar Rapids, 1954-56; asst. controller United Fire & Casualty Ins. Co., Cedar Rapids, 1956-58; sales assoc. Equitable Life Assurance Soc. U.S., Cedar Rapids, 1958-59; controller Gaddis Enterprises, Inc., Cedar Rapids, 1959-61; owner Estherville Laundry Co., 1959-64; sales assoc., comml. investment div. mgr. Tommy Tucker Realty Co., Cedar Rapids, 1961-74; owner Real Estate Investment Planning Assocs., Cedar Rapids, 1974—; treas. Investment Properties Inc., 1994—; controlling ptnr. numerous real estate syndicates; cons. in field, fin. speaker; guest lectr. Kirkwood Community Coll., Cedar Rapids, Mt. Mercy Coll., Cedar Rapids, Cornell Coll., Mt. Vernon; creative financing instr. Iowa Real Estate Commn.-Iowa Assn. Realtors. Patron Cedar Rapids Symphony, 1983-86, treas., mem. exec. com., bd. dirs. Oak Hill-Jackson Outreach Fund, 1970-83, pres., 1973-74; bd. dirs. Consumer Credit Counseling Service Cedar Rapids-Marion Area, 1974-80, pres., 1974-80; mem. pub. rels. com., vol, Cedar Valley Habitat for Humanity, contbr. newsletter, 1991-95, mental health adv. vol., 1991—. Served with USNR, 1945-46. Recipient Storm Manuscript award, 1976. Mem. Nat. Assn. Realtors (state mcpl. legis. com., subcom. on multi-family housing), Iowa Assn. Realtors (pres. comml. investment div. 1973, 80, named life mem.; state legis. com., savs. and loan formation feasibility com., mcpl. and county legis. com.), Nat. Assn. Accountants, Nat. Inst. Real Estate Brokers (membership chmn. Iowa 1972-

73), Real Estate Securities and Syndication Inst. (small group investment council, steering com. 1985, vice chmn. regional officers and state officers devel. com., gov. Iowa div., regional v.p.), Cedar Rapids Bd. Realtors, Internat. Platform Assn., Internat. Inst. Valuers. Methodist. Clubs: Cedar Rapids Optimist (past chmn. boys work com.); Eastern Iowa Execs. (dir., pres. 1981-82). Contbr. articles to profl. jours. Home: 283 Tomahawk Trl SE Cedar Rapids IA 52403-2037

KNEPPER, GEORGE W., history educator; b. Akron, Ohio, Jan. 15, 1926; s. George W. and Grace (Darling) K.; m. Phyllis Watkins, Aug. 21, 1949; children—Susan Lynne, John Arthur. B.A., U. Akron, 1948; M.A., U. Mich., 1950, Ph.D., 1954. Mem. faculty U. Akron, 1948-49, 54-92, assoc. prof. history, head dept., 1959-62; dean U. Akron (Coll. Liberal Arts), 1962-67, prof. history, 1964-88, disting. prof. history, 1988-92. Author: New Lamps for Old, One Hundred Years of Urban Higher Education at the University of Akron, 1970, An Ohio Portrait, 1976, Akron: City at the Summit, 1981, Ohio and Its People, 1989, Summit's Glory: Sketches of Buchtel Coll. and the University of Akron, 1990; editor: Travels in the Southland; The Journal of Lucius Verus Bierce 1822-23, 1966. Served to ensign USNR, 1943-46. Fulbright fellow U. London, Eng., 1953-54. Mem. Am., So. hist. assns., Orgn. Am. Historians, Ohio Acad. History, Omicron Delta Kappa, Alpha Tau Omega, Phi Alpha Theta, Alpha Sigma Lambda. Home: 88 Ridge Side Ct Munroe Falls OH 44262-1076 Office: Univ Akron Coll Liberal Arts Dept History Akron OH 44325

KNEPPER, RONALD ALAN, sculptor, educator; b. Ft. Wayne, Ind., May 9, 1955; s. Robert Lester and Janet Vera (Dressler) K.; m. Melissa Waters, Sept. 8, 1972 (div. Sept. 1977); children: Jennifer Lynn Knepper Tyson, Angelique Mae; m. Carol Brentegani Ferreira Dos Santos, Mar. 30, 1985; 1 child, Francesca Brentegani. BFA, Ind. U., 1982; MA, N.Mex. State U., 1985; MFA, Mills Coll., 1987. Vis. artist Biola U., La Mirada, Calif., 1986, Kent Inst. Art and Design, Canterbury, Eng., 1989, Hacettepe U., Ankara, Turkey, 1990; guest lectr. Bilkent U., Ankara, Turkey, 1989-90; adj. prof. Ind.-Purdue U., Ft. Wayne, 1992; dir. Kouros Gallery, N.Y.C., 1994-95; instr. Parsons Sch. Design, N.Y.C., 1995—; mem. gallery adv. bd. Mills Coll, Oakland, Calif., 1985-87; freshman advisor Bilkent U., 1989-90; edn. co-chair Names Project AIDS Quilt, Ft. Wayne, 1994. Group exbhns. include Ft. Wayne Mus. Art, 1993, South Bend (Ind.) Regional Mus. Art, 1993, Indpls. Mus. Art, 1994, Artists Space Gallery, 1994, Kouros Gallery, 1995, 96; represented in permanent collections Trinity English Luth. Ch., Concordia Luth. Seminary Libr., N.Mex. State U. Art Gallery, Zion Luth. Ch., Artworks Gallery, Palo Alto Group Women Collectors, Mills Coll. Art Gallery, Urart Sanat Galerisi, Siyah/Beyaz Sculpture Garden, GAllery Nev Sculpture Garden, Bilkent U., Haceteppe U. Art instr. Blaising Social Svcs., New Haven, Ind., 1993. With USN, 1972-73. Recipient grant Pollock-Krasner, 1992-92, fellowship Arts United Greater Ft. Wayne, 1992-93, residency Sculpture Space, Inc., 1994. Mem. Internat. Sculpture Ctr. Democrat. Lutheran. Avocations: photography, travel, music. Home: 186 Pinehurst Ave Apt 5A New York NY 10033-1730

KNER, ANDREW PETER, art director; b. Budapest, Hungary, Apr. 11, 1935; s. Albert and Susan (Gellert) K.; m. Carol Stevens, Sept. 16, 1961; children: Anne, Peter. BA, Yale U., 1957, MFA, 1959. Asst. art dir. Time, Inc., N.Y.C., 1961-63; asst. promotion dir. Look mag., N.Y.C., 1963-65; promotion art dir. Esquire mag., N.Y.C., 1965-69; exec. promotion dir. N.Y. Times, N.Y.C., 1969-84; creative dir. for promotion Backer Spielvogel Bates, N.Y.C., 1984-90; creative dir. R.C. Publs., N.Y.C., 1990—; art dir. Print Mag., N.Y.C., 1963—; advisor Nat. Endowment for the Arts, Washington, 1975-81. 1st lt. U.S. Army, 1958-60. Mem. Art Dirs. Club (pres. 1983-85, 7 Gold medals 1975-86, Cert. of Merit, 1965-88), Am. Inst. Graphic Arts (bd. dirs. 1981-83, Distinctive Merit award 1965-88), N.Y. Art Dirs. Club (pres. N.Y.C. chpt. 1983-85), Yale Club. Democrat. Home: 147 E 18th St New York NY 10003-2477 Office: Print Mag 104 5th Ave Fl 19 New York NY 10011-6988*

KNESEL, ERNEST ARTHUR, JR., diagnostic company executive; b. New Orleans, Dec. 11, 1945; s. Ernest Arthur and Catherine Charlotte (Maier) K.; m. Lavina Lynn Menge, June 2, 1968; children: Eric Ernest, Tami Lynn, Bradley William. Student, Armstrong Coll., 1963-64; BS, Fairleigh Dickinson U., 1968, MS, 1970. Cert. clin. chemist. Technologist Am. Biol. Control Lab., Tenefly, N.J., 1966-68; sr. technologist Englewood (N.J.) Hosp., 1968-69; founder, v.p. Biomed. Reference Labs., Inc., Burlington, N.C., 1969-82; sr. v.p. Roche Biomed. Labs., Inc., Burlington, 1982-95; pres., founder Roche Image Analysis Sys., Inc., Elon College, N.C., 1989-96; exec. v.p., founder Autocyte, Inc., Elon College, 1996—. Inventor serum filter/dispenser vial, automated aliquoting system, cyto-rich automated cytology preparation system and simultaneous machine and human interactive cytology evaluation system. Mem. Am. Assn. Clin. Chemistry, Am. Soc. Clin. Pathologists (assoc.). Roman Catholic. Avocation: magic. Office: AutoCyte Inc PO Box 1029 Burlington NC 27216-1029

KNEZ, BRIAN, publishing executive. Pres., CEO Harcourt Brace & Co., Chestnut Hill, Mass. Office: Harcourt Brace & Co 27 Boylston St PO Box 1000 Chestnut Hill MA 02167*

KNEZEVICH, JANICE A., critical care nurse; b. Ann Arbor, Mich., Nov. 10, 1960; d. Charles Oliver Kennon and Donna (May) Cisco; m. Mark P. Knezevich, July 16, 1982; children: Branden Bosko, Eric Michael. Diploma, Toledo Hosp. Sch. Nursing, 1982. Cert. gerontol. nurse ANCC. Staff nurse neurology unit Toledo Hosp., 1982-83; staff nurse telemetry unit, charge nurse ICU/CCU Mercy/Meml. Hosp., Monroe, Mich., 1985-90; quality assurance nurse, nursing supr. Staff Builders Home Health Care, Monroe, 1990-95; insvc. dir., quality mgmt. specialist Greenbrook Manor, Monroe, 1983-85, insvc. coord. quality assurance, infection control nurse, 1995—, also asst. dir. nursing, 1998—. Mem. Mich. Soc. Infection Control. Home: 2447 10th St Monroe MI 48162-4332

KNEZO, GENEVIEVE JOHANNA, science and technology policy researcher; b. Elizabeth, N.J., Aug. 8, 1942; d. John and Genevieve (Sadowski) K.; 1 child, Alexandra M. AB in Polit. Sci., Douglass Coll., Rutgers U., 1964; MA in Sci., Tech. and Pub. Policy, George Washington U., 1981; grad., Nat. Def. U., 1989. With Congl. Rsch. Svc., Libr. of Congress, Washington, 1967—, specialist in sci. and tech., 1979—, head sci., rsch. and tech. sect., 1986-88, sr. level specialist in sci. and tech. policy, 1991—. Author profl. publs. Mem. Phi Beta Kappa, Pi Sigma Alpha. Avocations: whitewater canoeing, hiking, gymnastics, classical music, community volunteer activities. Home: 606 Oakley Pl Alexandria VA 22302-3611 Office: Libr of Congress Congl Rsch Svc Sci Technology & Medicine Divsn Washington DC 20540-7490

KNICELY, CARROLL FRANKLIN, publishing executive; b. Staunton, Va., Dec. 8, 1928; s. Bernard Clyde and Violet Iona Phillips-K.; m. Evelyn Virginia Furr, Feb. 4, 1948; children: Kaye Gaines, Brenda Kramer, Beverley White, Carroll Jr., Daryl. BS, Barry U., 1982. Bus. mgr. News-Virginian, Waynesboro, Va., 1952-57; pres., pub. Glasgow (Ky.) Daily Times, 1957-76, Associated Pubs., Glasgow, 1960—; regent Western Ky. U., Bowling Green, 1976-80; cons. Aquila Mut. Funds, N.Y.C., 1988-98, trustee, 1998—; chmn. Vision 2020, Inc., Bowling Green, Ky., 1998—. *Over forty years of newspaper publishing, real estate development, community activism, local regional and statewide economic development activity. Pioneered newspaper transition from letterpress to offset. Published first daily newspaper east of Mississippi by web offset with cold type in 1958. Founded Cave City Convention Center. In 1979 negotiated relocation of GM Corvette assembly plant from St. Louis to Bowling Green, Kentucky. In 1985 pursued and personally negotiated location of Toyota assembly plant at Georgetown, Kentucky, resulting in an influx of over 100 Japanese plants which greatly enhanced Kentucky's economic standing. In 1994 named to Barry University Hall-of-Fame and received Tim Carter Distinguished Service Award.* Dir. Citizens TransFin./Star Bank, Glasgow & Bowling Green, 1976-98; commr. commerce Commonwealth of Ky., Frankfort, 1979-80, sec. of commerce, 1983-88; postmaster U.S. Postal Svc., Glasgow, 1965-67; mem. Barren River Area Devel. Dist., 1994; trustee Campbellsville (Ky.) U. 1997. Mem. Ky. Press Assn. (pres. 1978-79), Glasgow C. of C. (pres. 1978-79), Rotarian, Mason. Baptist. Avocations: cycling, travel, writing. E-mail: srknicely@glasgow-ky.com. Home: 505 Augusta Cir Glasgow KY 42141 Office: Associated Pubs Inc 211 S Green St PO Box 335 Glasgow KY 42142

KNICKERBOCKER, ROBERT PLATT, JR., lawyer; b. Hartford, Conn., Sept. 23, 1944; s. Robert P. and Audrey Jane (Stempel) K.; m. Kathleen A. Sakal (div. May 1985); children: Sarah, Abigail, Jonathan; m. Barbara Denise Whinnem, Oct. 3, 1987. BA, Cornell U., 1966; JD, U. Conn., 1969. Bar: Conn. 1969, U.S. Dist. Ct. Conn. 1969, U.S. Ct. Appeals (2d cir.) 1970. Law clk. to presiding justice Conn. Supreme Ct., Hartford, 1968-69; ptnr. Day, Berry & Howard, Hartford, 1969—; mem. State Implementation Plan Regulation Adv. Commn., 1979-90. Chmn. Town Plan and Zoning Commn., Glastonbury, Conn., 1975-79, Glastonbury Bd. Edn., 1982-86. Mem. Conn. Bar Assn., Greater Hartford C. of C. (state legis. com.). Republican. Episcopalian. Office: Day Berry & Howard Cityplace Hartford CT 06103-3499

KNICKREHM, GLENN ALLEN, management executive; b. L.A., Mar. 27, 1948; s. Allen F. and Evelyn Knickrehm. B.A. magna cum laude, Occidental Coll., 1971; B.S., Columbia U., 1971, M.B.A., 1973. Analyst, Exxon Co., N.Y.C. and La., 1971-72; cons. Boston Cons. Group, Boston and Munich, 1973-77; mgr. Boston Cons. Group, Boston, 1977-83; pres., chmn. Our Market Supermarket, Inc., 1980-81; pres. Bay Resource Corp., 1983—; chmn. Apex Internat. Alloys, Inc., 1986-89; dir. Vanalco, Inc., 1987—; pres. Mashamoquet Holdings, Inc., 1995—; adv. Beach Brook Prodns., 1995—; pres. Constellation Prodns., Inc., 1996—. Dir. New Eng. Theater Guild, Inc., 1985-89, Samuel Bronfman fellow, 1972. Mem. Soc. Preservation New Eng. Antiquities, Boston Athenaeum, Columbia U. Faculty Club, Phi Beta Kappa, Tau Beta Pi, Beta Gamma Sigma, Sigma Pi Sigma, Pi Mu Epsilon, Kappa Mu Epsilon. Office: 1280 Massachusetts Ave Cambridge MA 02138-3840

KNIEF, HELEN JANETT, artist; b. Bklyn., July 16, 1907; d. Charles Martin and Madeleine Elizabeth (Bollinger) Dreyer; m. Frederick Knief Jan. 19, 1931 (dec.); 1 chld, Frederick D. Student, Pratt Inst., Phoenix Sch. Design, Art Students League, Bklyn. Mus. Art. Painter in impressionist style. Exhibited works in numerous shows, including Academy Gallery, Bklyn. Mus., Country Art Gallery, Westbury and Locust Valley, N.Y., Lever House; works in numerous collections; painted numerous commd. portraits. Awards in clude 1st prizes in portrait painting and in landscape oils. Mem. Art League Nassau County, Malverne Art League, Long Beach Art Assn., others. Address: 1601 SE 24th Rd # 311 Ocala FL 34471-6003

KNIERIM, STEPHEN DALE, minister; b. Dayton, Ohio, Oct. 20, 1951; s. Paul and Eva Alice (Hall) K.; m. Marilyn Kay Miller, July 18, 1981; 1 child, David. BSBA, Grace Coll., 1975; cert. in Bibl. studies, Grace Sem., 1977. Asst. pastor Brookville (Ohio) Grace Brethren Ch., 1977; pastor Clayton (Ohio) Grace Brethren Ch., 1977-84, Aleppo (Pa.) Brethren Ch., 1984-89, Living Ch. of Five Mile, Cin., 1989-93, Oakland Christian Ch., Russiaville, Ind., 1993—. Named one of Outstanding Young Men Am., 1985. Republican. Home and Office: 200 S Co Rd 1280W Russiaville IN 46979

KNIERIM, WILLIS M., educator; b. Sept. 20, 1940. BA, U. Colo., 1963; MPA, U. Colo., Denver, 1971; postgrad., Northwe. U., Am. U., Johns Hopkins U., U. Wyo. Tchr., curriculum coord. Boulder Valley Schs., 1963-96; tchr., adminstr. Colegio Bolivar, Cali, Colombia, 1964-65; pres. Boulder Valley Edn. Assn., 1987-91; bd. dirs. Learning to Read. Bd. dirs. United Way. Mem. Colo. Edn. Assn., C. of C. E-mail: knierim1@aol.com. Home: 2290 Nicholl St Boulder CO 80304

KNIES, PAUL HENRY, former life insurance company executive; b. Columbus, Ohio, Jan. 28, 1918; s. Daniel and Eva (Schneider) K.; m. Evadna Johnson, Mar. 16, 1941; children: Barbara Ann (Mrs. H. Michael Sell), Philip L., Paul R. B.A., Ohio State U., 1940. With Met. Life Ins. Co., 1940-80, controller, 1964-80, sr. v.p., mem. exec. com., 1971-80. Author: Knies Family in the United States, 1994. Trustee Valley Hosp., Ridgewood, N.J., Citizens Budget Commn., N.Y.C., 1975-80. Served with arty. AUS, 1942-45. Fellow Soc. Actuaries; mem. Fin. Execs. Inst. (treas. 1974-80), Inst. Internal Auditors, Fin. Execs. Research Found. (treas. 1972-80), Phi Beta Kappa. Home: 1912 Clear Ct Columbia MO 65203-5844

KNIES, ROBERT CARL, JR., critical care nurse; b. Wilkes-Barre, Pa., Sept. 7, 1960; s. Robert Carl and Alice Ann (Swartman) K.; m. Lisa Ann Stumhofer, May 17, 1986. Diploma, St. Joseph Hosp. Sch. Nursing, Reading, Pa., 1983; BSN, Pa. State U., 1990; MSN, Villanova U., 1996. Cert. emergency nurse, CPR instr., emergency med. technician, instr., ACLS. Staff nurse St. Joseph Hosp., Reading, 1983-84; clin. nurse community Gen. Hosp., Reading, 1984-89; nurse Med. Pers. Pool, Allentown, Pa., 1989-91, Pottstown (Pa.) Meml. Med. Ctr., 1990-96; clin. nurse specialist emergency svcs. Health Sys. Minn., 1996—; nurse Hospice of Twin Cities, 1997-98—; adj. faculty Reading Area C.C., 1991-95. Mem. Nat. Assn. Clin. Nurse Specialists (bd. dirs. 1999—), Emergency Nurses Assn. (pres.-elect Twin-Cities chpt., chairperson nat. govt. affairs), Sigma Theta Tau, Alpha Sigma Lambda.

KNIESCHE, THOMAS WERNER, German language educator; b. Cologne, Germany, Feb. 20, 1960; came to the U.S., 1985; s. Oskar Werner and Anni (Pretzsch) K.; m. Sigrid Berka, May 23, 1991; 1 child, Christopher. Staatsexamen, U. Cologne, 1985; MA, Washington U., 1986; PhD, U. Calif., Santa Barbara, 1990. Vis. asst. prof. German studies Brown U., Providence, 1990-91, asst. prof., 1991-96, assoc. prof., 1996—; vis. asst. prof. Franklin & Marshall Coll., Lancaster, Pa., 1991. Author: Die Genealogie der Post-Apokalypse, 1991; editor: Dancing on the Volcano: Essays on the Culture of the Weimar Republic, 1994. Mem. MLA, Am. Assn. Tchrs. German. Office: Brown Univ Box 1979 190 Hope St Providence RI 02912-9037

KNIESLER, FREDERICK CORNELIUS, retired municipal official; b. Trenton, N.J., Feb. 2, 1930; s. Frederick Edward and Mary Ellen (Hanheen) K.; m. Bernice Rottkamp, Aug. 17, 1929; children: Frederick C. Jr., Christopher D., Gregory B., Maria E. AA, Rider U., 1970, BS, 1973, MA, 1980. Lic. pub. acct. N.J.; cert. mcpl. fin. officer N.J. Spl. dep. clk. Monmouth County, N.J., 1969-75; project coor., sec. treas Manasquan River Regional Sewerage Auth., N.J., 1975-77; from clk. bd. chosen freeholders to dep. county clk. Monmouth County, 1977-82; asst. commr. N.J. Dept. Labor, 1982-90; twp. adminstr. Manalapan Twp., 1990-94; dep. commr. N.J. Dept. Labor, 1994-97; commr. Monmouth County Bd. Parks & Recreation, 1991—; past chair policy com. N.J. Unemployment Ins. Reemployment Demonstration Project, Mgmt. Com. Disability Automated Benefits sys., evaluation com. Mail Claims Pilot Program; past mem. Gov.'s Mgmt. Improvement Program. Twp. clk. Upper Freehold Twp., N.J., 1954-57, treas., 1975-86; county chmn. Rep. Com., Monmouth County, 1981-86, mcpl. chmn. Upper Freehold; del. Rep. Nat. Convention, Kansas City, 1976. Served in USAR, 1949-81. Recipient Pres.'s Disting. Svc. award N.J. State League of Municipalities. Mem. Am. Soc. Profl. Adminstrs., Nat. Assn. Govt. Labor Ofcls. (pres. 1996-97), Interstate Conf. Employment Security Adminstrs. (sec. 1987-89), N.J. Conf. of Mayors (charter), Assn. U.S. Army, Internat. Assn. Employees in Employment Security. Republican. Roman Catholic. Avocations: Thomas Merton, collecting AM flyer trains, gray iron toy soldiers. E-mail: Kniesler1@aol.com.

KNIFFEN, DONALD AVERY, astrophysicist, educator, researcher; b. Kalamazoo, Apr. 27, 1933; s. Frerick Bowerman and Eva Virginia (Arp) K.; m. Janis Kay Nesom, June 14, 1952; children: Karyol Kniffen Poole, Donald Avery Jr., Kimberly Kniffen Giesbrecht. BS magna cum laude, La. State U., 1959; AM, Washington U., St. Louis, 1960; PhD, Cath. U. Am., 1967. Astrophysicist Goddard Space Flight Ctr., NASA, Greenbelt, Md., 1960-91; lectr. physics U. Md., College Park, 1978-87; project scientist Compton Gamma Ray Obs., 1979-91; William W. Elliott prof., chmn. dept. physics and astronomy Hampden-Sydney Coll., Va., 1991—; vis. scientist NASA/USRA, Greenbelt, 1997-98; astrophysics cons. NASA/HSTX, NASA/USRA 1991-98, vis. sr. scientist, NASA Headquarters, 1999—, Awarded Medal for Outstanding Leadership NASA, 1992, recipient Laurel Award, Space/Missiles, Aviation Week & Space Tech., 1991. Contbr. articles to profl. jours. Served with USN, 1952-56. Fellow Royal Astron. Soc.; mem. AAUP, Am. Phys. Soc., Am. Astron. Soc., Internat. Astron. Union, Sigma Xi. Democrat. Avocations: travel; reading, gardening. Home: 2814 Andy Court Crofton MD 21114-3157 Office: Hampden-Sydney Coll Dept Physics Hampden Sydney VA 23943 also: Code SR NASA Headquarters Office of Space Scis Washington DC 20546

KNIFFEN, JAN ROGERS, finance executive; b. Herrin, Ill., Sept. 19, 1948; s. Paul Rogers and Evelyn Rose (Manering) K.; m. Janet Ann Rohn, Aug. 27, 1975; children: Julie Ann Meyer, Natalie Ann Meyer. Student, U. Ill., 1966-68; BS in Journalism, So. Ill. U., 1968-71; MBA in Fln., Lindenwood Coll., 1975-78; post-grad., St. Louis U., 1985—. Mgmt. trainee ACF Industries, St. Charles, Mo., 1972-73, order inquiry rep., 1973-75, sr. market analyst, 1975-77, sr. planner strategic planning, 1977-79; mgr. leasing, sales adminstrn. ACF Industries, Earth City, Mo., 1979-81, dir. bus. planning, estimating, and scheduling, 1981-83, asst. treas., 1983-85; asst. treas. May Dept. Stores Co., St. Louis, 1985-86, v.p., treas., 1986-91, sr. v.p., treas., 1991—; adj. prof. bus. adminstrn. Lindenwood Coll., 1978—; fin. advisor Job Network, St. Louis, 1987. Bd. mgrs. St. Charles (Mo.) County YMCA, 1981-86; bd. overseers Lindenwood Coll., 1986-93, bd. dirs., 1993—, alumni coun., 1983-86. Capt. USAF, 1970-75. Republican. Presbyterian. Club: Noon Day (St. Louis). Avocation: distance running. Office: May Dept Stores Co 611 Olive St Saint Louis MO 63101-1721

KNIFFIN, PAULA SICHEL, insurance sales executive; b. N.Y.C., Oct. 2, 1941; d. Harold M. and Edith (Sachnoff) Sichel; m. Richrd G. Kniffin, Aug. 3, 1963; children: Douglas, Kelly. BA, Bucknell U., 1963. CLU; cert. fin. planner. Tchr. New Cumberland (Pa.) Jr. High Sch., 1963-64, Meadowbrook Jr. High Sch., East Meadow, N.Y., 1964-67; real estate salesperson Claire Sobel Real Estate, Syosset, N.Y., 1979-80; sales force recruiter Mut. of N.Y. Life Ins. Co., Jericho, 1981-82; head of life and health ins. dept., employee benefit cons. The Viking Agy., Inc., Syosset, N.Y., 1983—. Mem. Soc. of Fin. PRofls., Internat. Assn. Fin. Planners, Women Life Underwriters Conf. (pres. 1988-89), Nassau Life Underwriters Assn. (bd. dirs. 1988-89), Ladies Golf Com. (chair 1990-93), Nassau Country Club, Mayacoo Lakes Country Club. Republican. Avocations: golf, tennis, bridge, reading. Office: The Viking Agy 117 Oak Dr Syosset NY 11791-4625

KNIGHT, ALICE DOROTHY TIRRELL, state legislator; b. Manchester, N.H., July 14, 1903; d. Nathan Arthur and Clara (Stiles) Tirrell; m. Norman Knight, Nov. 15, 1952. B.A., U. N.H., 1925, postgrad., 1933; postgrad. Boston U., 1941-42. Tchr. Newton Falls (N.Y.) High Sch., 1925-26; prin. Oswegatchie (N.Y.) Union Sch., 1926-27, Bartlett Sch., Goffstown, N.H., 1932-35; home lighting specialist Pub. Svc. Co. N.H., Manchester, 1935-39; tchr. merchandising Mt. Ida Jr. Coll., Newton Centre, Mass., 1939-45; home svc. dir. Boyd Corp., Portland, Maine, 1945-47; dist. home economist Frigidaire Sales Corp., Boston, 1948-64; mem. N.H. Ho. of Reps., 1967-74, 76-78, 80-90; rep to N.H. Gen. Ct., 1967-91; mem. joint legis. com. on elderly affairs, 1983-87; pres. Greater Manchester Community Concert Assn., 1985-87; co-chmn. Goffstown Bicentennial Com. of the Constn., 1986—. Mem. budget com. Town of Goffstown, 1966-72; mem. Gov.'s Adv. Com. Alcoholism, 1972-73, 74-78, Statewide Health Coordinating Coun., 1977-78, N.H. Hist. Soc.; past pres. bd. dirs. Hillsborough County North Cancer Soc.; bd. dirs. N.H. Cancer Soc. Recipient award N.H. Program on Alcohol and Drug Abuse, 1971, 75, Gov.'s Recognition award Hillsborough County, 1986, Pub. Svc.award Union Pomona Grange, 1987. Mem. Nat. Home Fashions League (pres. 1957-58), Nat. Order State Legislators, Vis. Nurses Assn. (bd. dirs. Greater Manchester chpt. 1981-87), N.H. Coun. World Affairs, Nat. Grange (life), DAR (regent 1974-76), Nat. Order Women Legislators (treas. 1968-71), Manchester Bus. and Profl. Women (pres. 1972-74), Nat. Soc. New Eng. Women, Order Eastern Star (life), Soroptimist (life, Boston), Goffstown Unity Club, Goffstown Garden Club (pres. 1976-78), Goffstown Shirley Club (pres. 1977-78), Goffstown Hist. Soc. (life). Republican.

KNIGHT, ANDREW KONG, visual artist, educator; b. Seattle, July 5, 1964; s. Richard Ivan Cook and Clara Kun Nai Kong; m. Julie Anne McLean, Feb. 2, 1991. Student, Calif. Coll. Arts and Crafts, 1978; BFA, San Francisco Art Inst., 1986; postgrad., Nat. U., 1996. Cert. tchr., Calif. Staff illustrator Western Ind. Bankers, Oakland, Calif., 1984-88, Western assn. Equipment Lessors, Oakland, 1989-94; art educator Kenneth C. Aikin Cmty. Ctr., Castro Valley, Calif., 1986-96; art educator, mural supr. Hayward (Calif.) Unified Sch. Dist., 1992—; freelance illustrator Miller Freeman Pubs., San Francisco, Hewlett Packard, Palo Alto, Calif., New United Motor Co., Fremont, Calif., 1983—, Island/Mercury Records, N.Y.C.; guest lectr. Stanford U., Palo Alto, 1996, Calif. State U., Hayward, 1992-96; spkr. in field. Exhibited in at Art of Calif., 1993, 94 (Silver award 1993, Gold award 1994), Am. Illustration 13, 1994 (award), Airbrush-Action Mag. (1st Pl. Fine Art award 1993), 3 Dimensional Art Dirs. and Illustrators Awards Show, 1996 (Gold award). Mem. adv. Hayward Arts Coun., 1994-95. Mem. NEA, Nat. Assn. Artists' Orgns., Calif. Tchrs. Assn., Precita Eyes Muralists. Home: 5181 Chesney Glen Dr Castro Valley CA 94552-5514

KNIGHT, ARTHUR WINFIELD, English educator; b. San Francisco, Dec. 29, 1937; s. Walter Arthur and Irja Blomquist K.; m. Glee Marquardt, Sept. 27, 1966 (dec. Oct. 1975); m. Kit Duell, Aug. 25, 1976; 1 child, Tiffany Carolyn. BA, San Francisco State U., 1960, MA, 1962. Tchr. English Anderson (Calif.) Union H.S., 1963-64; instr. journalism Riverside (Calif.) City Coll., 1964-65; instr. English Delta Coll., University Center, Mich., 1965-66; prof. English California U. Pa., 1966-93; film critic Anderson Valley Advertiser, Boonville, Calif., 1992—; adj. pro. prof. studies U. San Francisco, 1995—. Author:All Together, Shift, 1972, Who Moved Among the Others as They Walked, 1974, The Secret Life of Jesse James, 1996, The Darkness Starts Up Where You Stand, 1996, The Cruelist Month, 1997, Johnnie D., 1999; author of poems; contbr. articles to profl. jours.; producer (plays) King of the Beatniks, 1985, 88, 93, Blue Earth, 1986, The Abused, 1986, Burning Daylight, 1987. Recipient 1st Pl. prize Joycean Lively Arts Guild, East Douglas, Mass., 1982. Mem. Western Writers Am. Avocation: photography. Office: PO Box 2580 Petaluma CA 94953

KNIGHT, ATHELIA WILHELMENIA, journalist; b. Portsmouth, Va., Oct. 15, 1950; d. Daniel Dennis and Adell Virginia (Savage) K. B.A. with honors in English, Norfolk State Coll., 1973; M.A. with honors in Journalism, Ohio State U., 1974. Cert. tchr., Va. Aide D.C. Coop. Extension Service, 1969-72; sub. tchr. Portsmouth Pub. Schs., 1973; reporter Virginian Pilot, Norfolk, 1973, Chgo. Tribune, 1974; met. desk reporter Washington Post, 1975-81, investigative reporter, 1981-94, sports writer, 1994—; lectr. high schs., colls. Recipient Mark Twain award, 1982, 87, Front Page award Washington-Balt. Newspaper Guild, 1982, Nat. award for edn. Edn. Writers Assn., 1987, Pub. Svc. award Md.-Del.-D.C. Press Assn., 1990, 93, 1st Pl. award for spot news, 1997; Ohio State U. fellow, 1974, Nieman fellow Harvard U., 1985-86. Mem. Women in Comm., Nat. Assn. Black Journalists, Washington-Balt. Newspaper Guild, Investigative Reporters and Editors. Baptist. Home: 1425 4th St SW Apt A803 Washington DC 20024-2225 Office: Washington Post 1150 15th St NW Washington DC 20071-0002

KNIGHT, AUBREY KEVIN, vocational education educator; b. Oxford, Miss., May 2, 1947; s. Kenneth and Katherine (Bishop) K.; m. Bonnie Faye Cagle, Jan. 9, 1970; children: Aubrey Kenneth, Allen Keith. Grad., NRI Sch. Electronics, Washington, 1980; student, Itawamba C.C., Tupelo, Miss., 1987, Miss. State U., Starkville, 1988, 89, Northwest C.C., Oxford, Miss., 1988-89, 93-94. Owner and technician Yocona Electronics, Oxford, 1979-87; electronics instr. Oxford-Lafayette Bus. and Indsl. Complex, 1987-97; instr. Millsaps Vocat. Ctr., Starkville, Miss., 1997—. Mem. Miss. Assn. Electronics Instrs. (pres. 1990-92), Miss. Trade and Tech. Assn. (2d v.p. 1991-92, 1st v.p. 1992-93, pres. 1993-94), Miss Vocat. Indsl. Clubs of Am. (pres., Miss. bd. dirs. 1994-95), Miss. Assn. Vocat. Educators, Mississippians for Emergency Medicine, Miss. Emergency Med. Tech. Assn., Miss. Law Enforcement Officers Assn. Baptist. Avocations: gardening, computers. Office: Millsaps Vocational Ctr. 805 Louisville Rd Starkville MS 39759-3752

KNIGHT, BETTY ANN, county commissioner; b. Brunswick, Mo., Sept. 2, 1947; d. George William and Elizabeth (Miles) James; m. William M. Knight, Jan. 26, 1969; children: Michelle Ann, Carrie Shea. BS, U. Mo., 1969. Cert. real estate agt., Mo.; cert. securities specialist Nat. Assn. Securities Dealers; cert. ins. agt., Mo. Real estate agt. ERA MH Realty, Platte City, Mo., 1984-85; paraplanner IDS Fin. Svcs., Platte City, Mo., 1986-89; dep. treas. Platte County, 1989-94, presiding commr., 1995—; treas., bd dirs. James' Pecan Farms, Inc., Brunswick, Mo., 1969—; bd. dirs. U. Mo. Ext. Coun., Platte City, 1995-99, Kansas City Internat./Northland C. of C., Kansas City, Clay/Platte Devel. Coun., Kansas City; chmn. Emergency

Preparedness, Platte County, 1995—; bd. dirs. Mid-Am. Regional Coun., Kansas City, 1995—, 1st vice chair, 1997-98, chair, 1999—; bd. dirs. Mo. Assn. Counties, Jefferson City, 1995—, treas., 1998, 3d v.p., 1999. Arts chmn. Platte City Elem. PTA, 1984-89; leader Brownie Troop, Platte City, 1985-86; mem. Platte City Bus. and Profl. Women, 1987-90; mem. Mo./Nat. Rep. Parties, 1989—, Federated Rep. Women, Platte County, 1990—, Platte Rep. Assn., 1989—, Eleemonsynary Soc., Platte County, 1993—; bd. dirs. Platte County Econ. Devel. Coun., Kansas City, 1995—, Platte County Sch. Bd., 1992-95, Platte City Plan and Zoning, 1991; bd. dirs., sec. Platte City Ath. Assn., 1990-92; active Synergy Svcs. Comm. Adv. Bd., St. Luke's Northland Strategic Planning Adv. Bd. Mem. Mo. County Commrs., N.W. Commrs., Platte County Women's Exch. (pres., treas. 1989—, Leadership award 1992, Woman of Yr. 1993), Platte County Hist. Soc., Parkville Rotary, 1st Class County Caucus, U. Mo. Alumni Assn., Parkville Fine Arts Assn. Methodist. Avocations: collector (eggs, elephants, Republican memoribilia), travel, sports (Kansas City Chiefs and Univ. Mo. Tigers). Home: PO Box 1188 Platte City MO 64079-1188

KNIGHT, BOB, college basketball coach; b. Massilon, Ohio, Oct. 25, 1940; s. Carroll and Hazel (Henthorne) K.; m. Nancy Lou Knight, Apr. 17, 1963 (div.); m. Karen Edgar, 1988. BS, Ohio State U., 1962. Asst. coach Cuyahoga Falls (Ohio) High Sch., 1962-63; freshman coach U.S. Mil. Acad., West Point, N.Y., 1963-65; head basketball coach U.S. Mil. Acad., 1965-71, Ind. U., Bloomington, 1971—; speaker clinics in field; condr. tng. clinics for coaches and players. Trustee Naismith Meml. Basketball Hall of Fame. Served with U.S. Army. Recipient Big Ten Coach-of-Year award, 1973, 75, 76, 81, 89; named unanimously Nat. Coach of Year, 1975, 89, Nat. Coach of Yr. AP and Basketball Weekly, 1976; recipient appreciation plaque from team, 1979. Mem. Nat. Assn. Basketball Coaches (bd. dirs.). Methodist. Coached U.S. team to gold medal 1984 Olympics; coached Ind. U. to NCAA Championship, 1976, 81, 87; college basketball's winningest active coach (one of only 12 NCAA coaches to have won 700 or more games). Office: Indiana Univ Basketball Office Assembly Hall Bloomington IN 47408*

KNIGHT, CHERYL DUBOIS, library director; b. Mar. 2, 1950. BA, SUNY, New Paltz, 1973; MSLS, L.I. U., 1988. Head children's svcs. Hicksville (N.Y.) Pub. Libr., 1987-92; libr. dir. Brandywine Cmty. Libr., Topton, Pa., 1997—. E-mail: brandypl@ptd.net. Office: 220 Kulps Rd Barto PA 19504

KNIGHT, CHRISTOPHER NICHOLS, lawyer; b. New Haven, Sept. 7, 1946; s. Douglas Maitland and Grace Wallace (Nichols) K.; m. Emily Byrn Turner, Oct. 20, 1979; children: Ethan Douglas, Benjamin Walker Lester, Christopher N. Jr. BA, Yale U., 1968; JD, Duke U., 1971. Bar: Wis. 1971, U.S. Dist. Ct. (ea. dist.) Wis. 1973, U.S. Ct. Appeals (7th cir.) 1977, N.C. 1979, U.S. Dist. Ct. (mid. dist.) N.C. 1979, Minn., 1980, U.S. Supreme Ct. 1980, U.S. Ct. Appeals (4th, 8th cirs.) 1980, U.S. Dist. Ct. Minn. 1980, Ill. 1982, N.Y., 1996. Assoc. Quarles & Brady, Milw., 1971-78, ptnr., 1978-79; ptnr. Smith Helms Mulliss & Moore, Greensboro, N.C., 1979-80, Kutak Rock, Mpls., 1980-82, Isham Lincoln & Beale, Chgo., 1982-88, Hopkins & Sutter, Chgo., 1988—. Mem. ABA, Ill. State Bar Assn., Minn. State Bar Assn., N.Y. State Bar Assn., N.C. State Bar Assn., State Bar Wis., Nat. Assn. Bond Lawyers. Congregationalist. Office: Hopkins & Sutter Three First National Plz Chicago IL 60602

KNIGHT, CONSTANCE BRACKEN, writer, realtor, corporate executive; b. Detroit, Oct. 30, 1937; d. Thomas Francis and Margaret (Kearney) Bracken; m. James Edwards Knight, June 14, 1958 (div. Feb. 1968); children: Constance Lynne Knight Campbell, James Seaton, Keith Bracken. Student, Barry Coll., 1955-56, Fla. State U., 1958-60; AA, Marymount Coll., 1957. Columnist, feature writer Miami Herald, Ft. Lauderdale, Fla., 1954-55, 79-80; pub. rels. dir. Lauderdale Beach Hotel, 1965-67; columnist, feature writer Ft. Lauderdale News/Sun-Sentinel, 1980-81; owner Connie Knight and Assoc. Pub. Rels., Ft. Lauderdale, 1981-85; editor, pub. Vail (Colo.) Mag., 1986-89, contbg. freelance writer, 1989—; editorial cons. Vail Valley Mag., 1993; pres. Knight Enterprises, Vail, 1994—; instr. Colo. Mountain Coll., Vail, 1979. Mem. Planning and Environ. Commn., Vail, 1990-92, Vail Licensing Authority, 1995—. Mem. N.Am. Ski Journalists (treas. 1990-93). E-mail: cknight@vail.net. Fax #: (970) 476-3615. Office: 385 Gore Creek Dr Ste 201 Vail CO 81657-3606

KNIGHT, DAN PHILLIP, marketing executive; b. Rentz, Ga., Aug. 14, 1941; s. Daniel Prentice and Tommie Lou (Mullis) K.; m. Doris Kathleen McCleskey, July 20, 1963; children: Dana, Kirsten, Delana, Kiesha. BJ, U. Ga., 1963; JD, Atlanta Law Sch., 1967. Sales analyst Ford Motor Co., East Point, Ga., 1963-66; pub. rels., program dir. Ga. Heart Assn., Atlanta, 1966-68; pub. rels. dir., editor Ga. Mcpl. Assn., Atlanta, 1968-69; dir. advt., pub. rels. John H. Harland Co., Atlanta, 1969-72; dir. pub. rels. Burger King Corp., Miami, Fla., 1972-73; account exec. Grey Advt., N.Y.C., 1973-76; v.p. Pringle, Dixon, Pringle, Atlanta, 1976-79; dir. field ops. Habersham Plantation Corp., Toccoa, Ga., 1979-83; pres. Knight & Assocs., Baldwin, Ga., 1983-95; prof. Bauder Coll., Atlanta, 1996-98, prof. ESL instrn. and consulting, 1999—; com. chmn. Atlanta Advt. Club, 1969-72. Editor Urban Ga. mag., 1968-69. Sec. Alpharetta (Ga.) Planning Commn., 1970-72; com. chmn. MIA Crusade Project 4th of July parade, Atlanta, 1970. Recipient Outstanding Com. Chmn. award MIA Crusade Project, 1970; named one of Outstanding Young Men in Am., U.S. C. of C., 1971. Mem. Am. Mktg. Assn. (profl.), Alpharetta Jaycees (v.p. 1968-69, officer 1967-71, outstanding pub. speaker award 1970, disting. svc. award 1971). Republican. Baptist. Avocations: golf, writing, basketball, acting, travel.

KNIGHT, DEIDRE ELISE MOSTELLER, literary agent; b. Atlanta, July 12, 1966; d. J. Ford Mosteller Jr. and Eleanor (Brannon) Mosteller Knight; m. Judson David Knight, June 15, 1991. Student, Mary Washington Coll., 1984-88. Asst. prodn. coord. VanDerkloot Film and TV, Atlanta, 1988-89; freelance prodn. coord. Atlanta, 1989-90; producer's asst. for In The Heat of The Night MGM/UA, Covington, Ga., 1990-91; sales exec. Diamond Data, Woodstock, Ga., 1991-96; lit. agt. Knight Agy., Atlanta, 1996—. Film reviewer Lakeside Ledger newspaper, 1995-96. Deacon Life Ctr. Ministries, Dunwoody, Ga., 1993-96. Mem. Romance Writers Am., Assn. Authors' Reps., Authors' Guild. Avocations: musician, films, books, writing. Office: Knight Agy PO Box 550648 Atlanta GA 30355-3148

KNIGHT, DIANE, special education educator; b. De Ridder, La., Dec. 2, 1955. BS, McNeese State U., 1976; MEd, Northwestern State U., Natchitoches, La., 1980, EdD, 1986. Cert. tchr., La., Ga. Tchr. English Vernon Parish Sch. Bd., Leesville, La., 1976-77; tchr. spl. edn. Natchitoches Parish Sch. Bd., La., 1978-80; ednl. diagnostician Natchitoches Parish Sch. Bd., 1985-88; tchr. spl. edn. Sabine Parish Sch. Bd., Many, La., 1983-85; dir. pupil appraisal Red River Parish Sch. Bd., Coushatta, La., 1988-89; asst. prof. Ga. Southwestern Coll., Americus, 1989-90, U. Southwestern La., Lafayette, 1990-95; assoc. prof. U. Ga., Athens, 1995-96; ednl. diagnostician Spl. Sch. Dist. 1, 1996—; ednl. cons. and evaluator, Lafayette, 1990-95, Athens, Ga., 1995-96, Baton Rouge, 1996—; presenter in field. Contbr. articles to profl. jours. Mem. Am. Coll. of Forensic Examiners, La. Assn. Evaluators, Coun. for Exceptional Children (learning disabilities divsn., tchr. edn. divsn., La. state sec., v.p.), Rotary, Phi Delta Kappa. Republican. Mem. Unity Ch. Home: 962 Ridgepoint Ct Baton Rouge LA 70810 Office: ARDC-Hunt Correctional Ctr Spl Sch Dist # 1 PO Box 174 Saint Gabriel LA 70776-0174

KNIGHT, DORIS RATHBUN, retired government and history educator; b. N.Y.C., Feb. 22, 1936; d. Rober E. and Armenia (Bertoli) Rathbun; m. Paul R. Knight, Apr. 19, 1958; 1 child, Roger. BA, U. Mass., 1957, MA, 1962, postgrad., 1962-63, 72-73. Editl. asst. Merriam-Webster Unabridged Dictionary, 3d edit., Springfield, Mass., 1958-60; prof., chair social sci. divsn. Holyoke (Mass.) C.C., 1963-94. Guest columnist Jour.-Tribune, Biddeford, Maine, 1994-97. Mem., chair planning bd. Northampton, Mass., 1977-82; mem. planning bds. Southampton, Mass., 1983-92, Kennebunkport, Maine, 1995—, vice chmn., 1998-99; vice chair Dem. Town Com., Southampton, 1990-94; vice chair R.S.V.P. So. Maine Adv. Coun., 1998-99, chair, 1999—. Mem. Newcomers Club (pres. 1997-98). Avocations: reading, writing, travel, local history research.

KNIGHT, DOUGLAS MAITLAND, educational administrator, optical executive; b. Cambridge, Mass., June 8, 1921; s. Claude Rupert and Fanny Sarah Douglas (Brown) K.; m. Grace Wallace Nichols, Oct. 31, 1942; children: Christopher, Douglas Maitland, Thomas, Stephen. AB, Yale U., 1942, MA, 1944, PhD, 1946; LLD (hon.), Ripon Coll., Knox Coll., Davidson Coll., 1963, U. N.C., 1965, Ctr. Coll., 1973, Ohio Wesleyan U., 1971; LHD (hon.), Lawrence U., 1964, Carleton Coll., 1966; LittD (hon.), St. Norbert Coll., Wake Forest Coll., 1964. Instr. English, Yale U., 1946-47, asst. prof., 1947-53; vis. asst. prof. English, U. Calif., Berkeley, summer 1949; Morse rsch. fellow, 1951-52; pres. Lawrence U., Appleton, Wis., 1953-63; pres. Duke U., Durham, N.C., 1963-69, pres. emeritus, 1992—; v.p. divsn. ednl. devel. RCA, N.Y.C., 1969-71, v.p. divsn. edn. svcs., 1971-72, staff v.p. edn. and community rels., 1972-73, cons., 1973-75; pres. RCA, Iran, 1971-72, dir., 1971-73; pres. Social Econ. and Ednl. Devel., Inc., 1973-76; pres. Questar Corp., 1976-99, chmn., 1999; assoc. fellow Saybrook Coll., Yale U., 1954—; U.S. del. SEATO Conf. Asian U. Pres., Pakistan, 1961; mem. nat. commn. UNESCO, 1965-67; chmn. Nat. Adv. Commn. Librs., 1966-68; advisor Imperial Orgn. for Social Svc., Govt. of Iran; mem. Nat. Commn. Sci. and Engring. Manpower, 1959-61. Author: Pope and the Heroic Tradition, 1951, (poetry) The Dark Gate, 1971, Journeys in Time, 1993; editor, contbr.: The Federal Government and Higher Education, 1960, Iliad and Odyssey, Twickenham edit., 1967, Medical Ventures and the University, 1967, Libraries at Large, Tradition, Innovation and the National Interest, 1970, Street of Dreams: The Nature and Legacy of the 1960's, 1989, Education and the Civil Order: A Memoir of the Woodrow Wilson National Fellowship Foundation, 1996, The Dancer and the Dance, Encounter in Education 1938-1998, 1999; co-inventor the Questar long-distance microscope, 1981. Trustee Edward W. Hazen Found., 1951-63; corp. mem. MIT, 1965-70; bd. dirs., chmn. Woodrow Wilson Nat. Fellowship Found., 1957-93, emeritus, 1993—; bd. dirs. CEEB, 1955-59, Catalyst, 1961-73, United Negro Coll. Fund, 1967-72, Near East Found., 1975-84, Internat. Schs. Svcs., 1976-82, Solebury Sch., 1975-83; program chmn. Salzburg Seminar, 1971, mem. adv. coun., 1997; founding trustee Questar Libr. Sci. and Art, 1982—, pres., 1996-99, emeritus, 1999—; pres. Delaware River Mill Soc., 1992-97, emeritus, 1997. Mem. Am. Assn. Advancement of Humanities (bd. dirs. 1979-83), Grolier Club, Century Assn. (N.Y.C.), Cosmos Club (Washington), Elizabethan Club, Berzelius (New Haven), Phi Beta Kappa. Home: 68 Upper Creek Rd Stockton NJ 08559-1205 Office: Questar Corp 6204 Ingham Rd New Hope PA 18938-9663

KNIGHT, EDWARD HOWDEN, retired hospital administrator; b. Vancouver, B.C., Can., Apr. 13, 1933; s. Edward Allen and Helen Blackley (Howden) K.; m. Glenda Carol Wiggins, Mar. 6, 1964; children: Carolyn, Patricia, Brett. B of Commerce, diploma in hosp. adminstrn., U. B.C., 1956. Adminstrv. asst. Vancouver Gen. Hosp., 1956-57; adminstr. Prince Rupert Gen. Hosp., 1957-61, Red Deer Gen. Hosp., 1961-72, Dr. Richard Parsons Aux. Hosp., 1963-72, Valley Park Manor Nursing Home, 1969-72; dep. exec. dir. Calgary (Alta.) Gen. Hosp., 1972-74, exec. dir., 1974-83, pres., 1983-88; pres. E.H. Knight & Assocs. Inc., Calgary, 1988-92; lectr. Red Deer Coll., 1968-72; adj. asst. prof. faculty medicine U. Calgary, 1978-91; trustee Alta. Blue Cross Plan, 1963-68; mem. Fed. Task Force on Cost of Health Services in Can., 1969. Recipient Queen's Silver Jubilee medal, 1977. Fellow Can. Coll. of Health Service Execs. (dir. 1972-74, founding charter mem.), Am. Coll. Healthcare Execs. (regent for Alta. 1973-76, 79-82); mem. Can. Hosp. Assn. (dir. 1981-83), Alta. Hosp. Assn. (dir. 1977-84, pres. 1983), Assn. Can. Teaching Hosps. (pres. 1986-87), Phi Delta Theta. Clubs: Red Deer, Kinsmen (pres. 1971-72), Glencoe. Lodge: Rotary. Home: 820 Windridge Cir San Marcos CA 92069-7917

KNIGHT, EDWARD R., judge, lawyer, educator, psychologist; b. Milw., Oct. 5, 1917; s. Harry and Lillian (Bachman) K.; m. Judith A. Weidberg, July 6, 1941; 1 child, Barbara Jane. AB, U. Wis., 1940, JD, 1941; AM, NYU, 1942, PhD, 1943. Bar: Wis. 1941, N.J. 1976; diplomate Am. Bd. Profl. Psychology. Master Oxford Sch., Pleasantville, N.J., 1941, psychologist, 1942, head psychologist, 1943, asst. headmaster, 1945-47, headmaster, 1947-73, emeritus, 1973—; U.S. magistrate judge, 1976—; judge Mcpl. Ct., Margate City, N.J., 1976-81; ptnr. Fox, Rothschild, O'Brien & Frankel, Atlantic City, N.J.; dir. First Fidelity Bank, 1950-90. Pres., bd. govs. Atlantic City Med. Ctr., 1973-87, chmn. emeritus, 1987—; chmn. Master Planning Bd., Egg Harbor Twp., N.J., 1961-73; chmn. Atlantic County (N.J.) Charter Study Commn., 1973-74, vice. chmn. Bd. of Atlanticare, 1993—. Author: Self-Discipline and Academic Failure; mem. editl. bd. Parental Delinquency; contbr. articles on edn. and psychology to profl. jours. Capt., USAAF, 1943-45; personnel com., personnel div. ATSC, Wright Field. Fellow APA (sch. psychologists div.); mem. Ea. N.J. psychol. assns., Nat. Assn. Ind. Schs., N.J. Assn. Sch. Psychologists, Interam. Soc. Psychology, Boarding Sch. Headmasters Assn. Mid. States (pres. 1966-67), Wis. Alumni Assn., U. Wis. Mem. Union (life), Atlanticare Health Sys. (vice-chmn. bd.), Phi Delta Kappa, Kappa Delta Pi. Home: 7 N Thurlow Ave Margate City NJ 08402-1213 Office: US Dist Ct 1300 Atlantic Ave Fl 5 Atlantic City NJ 08401-7207

KNIGHT, EDWARD S., lawyer, federal official; b. Amarillo, Tex., Jan. 20, 1951; m. Amy Knight; 1 child, Travis. BA in Latin Am. Studies with honors, U. Tex., Austin, 1973; JD, U. Tex., 1976. Bar: Tex., D.C., Supreme Ct. With Akin, Gump, Strauss, Hauer and Feld, Washington, 1978-82, ptnr., 1982-93; exec. sect., sr. adv. to sec. Treasury U.S. Dept. Treasury, Washington, 1993-94, gen. counsel, 1994-99; exec. v.p., chief legal officer NASD, Washington, 1999—. Mem. ABA, Supreme Ct. Bar Assn., D.C. Bar Assn., Tex. Bar Assn. Office: NADS 1735 K St NW Washington DC 20006*

KNIGHT, FRANK BARDSLEY, mathematics educator; b. Chgo., Oct. 11, 1933; s. Frank Hyneman and Ethel Eunice (Verry) K.; m. Ingeborg G. Belz, Aug. 30, 1971; children: Marion A., Marc A., Ellen D. B.A., Cornell U., 1955; Ph.D., Princeton U., 1959. Instr. math. U. Minn., Mpls., 1960-61, asst. prof., 1962-63; asst. prof. math. U. Ill., Urbana, 1964-66, assoc. prof., 1967-71; prof. U. Ill, Urbana, 1971-91, prof. emeritus, 1991—. Author: Essentials of Brownian Motion and Diffusion, 1981, Essays on the Prediction Process, 1981, Foundations of the Prediction Process, 1992. Sloan fellow, 1968-71; NSF grantee, 1981-89. Mem. Am. Math. Soc., Inst. Math. Stats., Am. Alpine Club. Office: U Ill 1409 W Green St Urbana IL 61801-2943

KNIGHT, FRANK JAMES, pharmaceutical marketing professional; b. L.A., July 17, 1947; s. George Orlando Jr. and Virginia Clarabelle (Seig) K.; m. Mary Jane Vargo, Aug. 7, 1977 (div. July 1989); children: Cheryl Lynne, Michael Scott; m. Barbara Lorrene Garlick, June 19, 1993. BS, Okla. State U., 1970. Mktg. rep. Mobil Oil Corp., N.Y.C., 1971-73; sales rep. Monarch Crown Corp., N.Y.C., 1974-78; territory mgr. V.H. Monette, Inc., Smithfield, Va., 1978-81; profl. rep. Dermik Labs., Blue Bell, Pa., 1981-83; sr. profl. oncology specialist Novartis Oncology, East Hanover, N.J., 1983—. Capt. U.S. Army, 1970. Mem. Am. Motorcycle Assn., Harley Owners Group (safety officer, road capt.). Home: 8768 Banyan St Alta Loma CA 91701-3355 Office: Novartis Pharmaceuticals 59 State Route 10 East Hanover NJ 07936-1005

KNIGHT, FRANKLIN W., history educator; b. Mile Gully, Manchester, Jamaica, Jan. 10, 1942; came to U.S., 1964; s. Willis Jefferson and Irick May (Sanderson) K.; m. Ingeborg Bauer, June 11, 1965; children: Michael, Brian, Nadine. BA with honors, U. West Indies, Jamaica, 1964; MA, U. Wis., 1965, PhD, 1969. From asst. to assoc. prof. SUNY, Stony Brook, 1968-73; assoc. prof. Johns Hopkins U., Balt., 1973-77, prof., 1977-91, Stulman prof. History, 1991—, dir. Latin Am. Studies Program, 1992-95; v.p. Latin Am. Studies Assn., 1997-98; pres., 1998-00. Author: Slave Society in Cuba, 1970 (Black Acad. award 1971), The Caribbean, 1990; co-editor: The Modern Caribbean, 1989, Atlantic Port Cities, 1991; editor: Caribbean Slave Societies, 1997. Active Md. Quincentenary Com., 1992. Named Disting. Grad. U. West Indies, Jamaica, 1992. Mem. Am. Hist. Assn., Latin Am. Studies Assn., Assn. Caribbean Historians. Office: Johns Hopkins U 3400 N Charles St Baltimore MD 21218-2680

KNIGHT, FRED BARROWS, forester, entomologist, educator; b. Waterville, Maine, Dec. 12, 1925; s. Stephen Cecil and Mildred Evelyn (Barrows) K.; m. Jane Wooster, Dec. 18, 1945; children: Mary Jane Knight Cushman, Susan L. Knight Hughes, James Wooster. BS with distinction, U. Maine, 1949; M in Forestry, Duke U., 1950, D in Forestry, 1956. Lic. forester, Maine. With Bur. Entomology and Plant Quarantine, U.S. Dept. Agr., Asheville, N.C., 1950-51; rsch. entomologist Forest Service, Ft. Collins, Colo., 1951-60; assoc. prof. to prof., chmn. dept. U. Mich., Ann Arbor, 1960-72; prof. forest resources, dir. Sch. Forest Resources, U. Maine, Orono, 1972-82; Dwight B. Demeritt prof. forest resources Sch. Forest Resources, U. Maine, 1972-90, interim dean Coll. Forest Resources, 1982-83, assoc. dean, 1983-88, acting dean, 1986-88, dean, 1988-90, dean, prof. emeritus in forestry, 1991—; dir. seven Islands Land Co., 1984-97; mem. State Bd. Licensing Prof. Foresters, 1990-98. Author: Principles of Forest Entomology, 4th edit., 1965, 5th edit., 80; also numerous articles. Comdr. USNR, 1943-85, ret., 1985. Fellow AAAS, Soc. Am. Forester (assoc. editor, past sect. officer); mem. Entomol. Soc. Am., Am. Forestry Assn., Soc. Les Voyageurs, Sigma Xi, Phi Kappa Phi (pres. U. Maine chpt. 1991-93), Alpha Zeta, Xi Sigma Pi. Congregationalist. Home: 395 Main St Orono ME 04473-1322

KNIGHT, GARY, lawyer, educator, publisher, trader; b. St. Joseph, Mo., Dec. 8, 1939; s. Herbert S. and Iris (Crawford) K.; m. Rebecca Emelie Forrester, Nov. 24, 1962; children: Kevin Crawford, David Forrester, Jonathan Gary. Student, Westminster Coll., 1957-59; AB in Polit. Sci., Stanford U., 1961; JD, So. Meth. U., 1964. Bar: Calif. 1965. Assoc. Nossaman, Thompson, Waters and Moss, L.A., 1964-68; mem. faculty La. State U. Law Center, Baton Rouge, 1968-85; assoc. prof. La. State U. Law Center, 1971-75, prof. law, 1975-85, Campanile prof. marine resources law, 1971-85; owner Jonathan Pub. Co., 1981—, Global Tech. Trading, Austin, Tex., 1994—; mem. adv. com. on law of sea Nat. Security Council Inter-Agy. Law of Sea Group, 1972-81; cons. CIA, 1977-85; mem. Gulf of Mex. Fishery Mgmt. Coun., 1981-84. Author: The Future of International Fisheries Management, 1975, Managing the Sea's Living Resources, 1977, The International Law of the Sea: Cases, Documents and Readings, 1991, Marine Fisheries Management Reporter, 1981-94; assoc. editor: Ocean Development and International Law: A Jour. of Marine Affairs, 1972-85. Mem. ABA (com. on law of sea 1971-80, com. marine resources 1967-71), Am. Soc. Internat. Law (bd. rev. and devel. 1975-80, panel on law of sea 1972-80), Internat. Law Assn. (com. on law of sea 1974-81), Law of Sea Inst. (exec. bd. 1975-81), Order of Coif, Phi Alpha Delta, Omicron Delta Kappa, Beta Theta Pi. Home: 3604 Pinnacle Rd Austin TX 78746-7417 Office: Jonathan Pub 3939 Bee Caves Rd Ste 200 Austin TX 78746-6429

KNIGHT, GARY CHARLES, mechanical engineer; b. Bartlesville, Okla., Nov. 15, 1950; s. Charles Robert and Elizabeth India (Brown) K.; m. Lisa Jo Martin, Sept. 12, 1981; children: Amanda Joann, Gary Michael. BSME, U. Tulsa, 1981. Registered profl. engr., Okla.; commd. inspector Nat. Bd. Boiler and Pressure Vessel Inspectors. Results engr. I Pub. Svc. Co. Okla., Tulsa, 1981-83, results engr. II, 1983-88, results engr. III, 1988-89, maintenance supr., 1989-90, maintenance supt., 1990-92, asst. sta. mgr., 1992, sta. mgr., 1992-97; dir. prodn. S.W. region Ctrl. and S.W. Svcs., Inc., Dallas, 1997—. With U.S. Army, 1970-73, Vietnam. Mem. ASME, NSPE, Okla. Soc. Profl. Engrs. Republican. Home: 500 Overhill Dr Allen TX 75013-8519 Office: Ctrl and SW Svcs Inc 1616 Woodall Rodgers Fwy Dallas TX 75202-1234

KNIGHT, GLADYS (MARIA), singer; b. Atlanta, May 28, 1944; d. Merald, Sr. and Elizabeth (Woods) K.; m. Barry Hankerson, Oct. 1974 (div. 1979); 1 son, Shanga; children from previous marriage: Kenya, James. Grad., Coll.; Degree (hon.), Shaw U. Author: lyrics Way Back Home, others; first pub. recital, Mt. Mariah Bapt. Ch., Atlanta, 1948; toured with Morris Brown Choir, 1950-53, recitals local chs. and schs., 1950-53; winner grand prize Ted Mack's Amateur Hour 1952; jazz vocalist, Lloyd Terry Jazz Ltd., 1959-61, mem. Gladys Knight and the Pips (formerly Pips Quartet), 1953—, concert appearances in Eng., 1967, 72, 73, 76, Australia, Japan, Hong Kong, Manila, 1976; rec. artist, Brunswick, 1957-61, Fury, 1961-62, Everlast, 1963, Maxx and Bell, 1964-66, Motown, 1966-73, Buddah, Capitol, Columbia, MCA, 1988; albums with the Pips include Best of Gladys Knight and the Pips, All the Great Hits, If I Were Your Woman, 1989, Soul Survivors: The Best of Gladys Knight and the Pips 1973-1988, 1990, Blue Lights in the Basement, 1996, Imagination, 1996, The Lost Live Albums, 1996; solo album Good Woman, 1991; TV appearance Charlie & Co., 1985; produced, appeared in HBO film Sisters in the Name of Love, 1986. Winner 6 gold Buddah records, 1 gold, 1 platinum Buddah album; 4 Grammy awards; named Top Female Vocalist, Blues and Soul mag. 1972; spl. award Washington City Coun. for inspiration to youth in city, 1972; other awards include Clio, AGVA, NAACP Image, Ebony Music, Cashbox, Billboard, Record World, Rolling Stone, Ladies Home Jour., Am. Music award (with Pips), 1984, 1988, Core award B'nai B'rith award; inducted into Rock and Roll Hall of Fame, 1996. Address: care Shakeji Inc. 3945 E Patrick Ln Ste E Las Vegas NV 89119 also: Jimmy Newman Mgmt 2110 E Flamingo Rd Ste 300 Las Vegas NV 89119-5193 also: RCA 1133 6th Ave New York NY 10036-6710

KNIGHT, H. STUART, law enforcement official, consultant; b. Sault St. Marie, Ont., Can., Jan. 6, 1921; s. Alexander G. and Muriel C. (Breathwaite) K.; m. Betty Cooley, June 29, 1946; children: Suzanne Cawley, Bill, Bob, John, Barbara Powell. BS, Mich. State U., 1948; postgrad., Princeton U., 1965-66. With U.S. Secret Svc., Washington, 1950-82, dir., 1973-82; vice chmn. Guardsmark Inc., Memphis, 1984—; v.p. Interpol, Paris, 1974-81; disting. faculty fellow Fed. Execs. Inst., Charlottesville, Va., 1981; mem. adv. bd. Am. Products Devel. Co.; mem. steering com. Ctr. for Strategic and Internat. Studies. Bd. dirs. Falls Church (Va.) Homeowners Assn., 1982-84; bd. dirs., pres. INKODE Govt. Sys.; mem. lottery bd. State of Va. Staff sgt. U.S. Army, 1942-46, PTO. Decorated Silver Star, Bronze Star, Purple Heart; recipient Mr. Sam award Touchdown Club, Washington, 1979; named original mem. Gallery of Fame, Mich. State U. Mem. Internat. Assn. Chiefs of Police (life, mem. bd. officers 1974-81), Nat. Sheriffs Assn. (life), Civitan. Avocations: bicycling, golf, puzzles. Office: Guardsmark Inc 22 S 2nd St Memphis TN 38103-2695

KNIGHT, HERBERT BORWELL, manufacturing company executive; b. Oak Park, Ill., July 4, 1928; s. Herbert Alfred and Bessie Carne (Borwell) K.; m. Nancy Gordon, June 29, 1963; children: Sharon and Tom (twins). A.B., Dartmouth Coll., 1951, M.B.A., 1952. V.p. mktg. B.K. Johl, Allsteel Equipment Co., Aurora, Ill., 1966-69; asst. to pres. Bliss & Laughlin Industries, Oak Brook, Ill., 1969-71; sr. v.p. First Health-Care, Chgo., 1972-75; pres. Newport News Indsl. Corp., Va., 1975-80; dir. planning Tenneco Inc., Houston, 1980-86; treas., owner A.E. Bogott & Sons, Inc., Sterling, Ill., 1988-98; bd. dirs. First Chgo.-Oak Park; CEO, mem. adv. bd. Alpha Venture Capital, Chgo. Former mem. bd. overseers C. Everett Koop Inst., Dartmouth Med. Sch., Hanover, N.H.; trustee Rush Presbyn. St. Lukes Hosp., Chgo., Copley Hosp., Aurora, Ill. Episcopalian. Clubs: Econ., Union League (Chgo.), Geneva Golf, Dunham Woods Riding Club, Eagle Brook Country Club.

KNIGHT, J. VERNON, medicine and microbiology educator; b. Osceola, Mo., Sept. 6, 1917; m. Elizabeth Gordon; 4 children. AB, William Jewell Coll., 1939, DSc (hon.), 1982; MD, Harvard U., 1943. Diplomate Am. Bd. Internal Medicine. Intern Mass. Meml. Hosp., Boston, 1943; resident Cornell U.-N.Y. Hosp. Med. Ctr., N.Y.C., 1946-47, from asst. in medicine to asst. prof., 1948-54; assoc. prof. medicine Vanderbilt U. Sch. Medicine, Nashville, 1954-59; clin. dir. Nat. Inst. Allergy and Infectious Diseases, NIH, Bethesda, Md., 1959-66; prof., chmn. dept. microbiology and immunology Baylor Coll. Medicine, Houston, 1966-88, prof. infectious disease sect. dept. medicine, 1966-87, prof. biotech., dir. Ctr. for Biotech., 1989-94, prof., acting chmn. dept. molecular physiology-biophysics, 1994—, Kyle and Josephine Morrow disting. prof., 1984; sr. attending physician Meth. Hosp., Houston, 1966—; attending physician Ben Taub Gen Hosp., Houston, 1966—; physician, cons. VA Hosp., Houston; bd. dirs. Viratek, Inc., Costa Mesa, Calif., 1980-94; mem. med. scis. rev. panel to NASA, Am. Inst. Biol. Scis., 1976-80; profl. cons. U.S. Army Med. Rsch. Inst. Infectious Diseases, 1962-81. Patentee on small particle aerosol generator for treatment respiratory disease including lungs; patentee for small particle aerosol liposome and liposome-drug combinations for med. use. Bd. dirs. Contemporary Arts Mus., Houston, 1977-82, Gorgas Meml. Inst. Tropical and Preventive Medicine, Washington, 1977-91. With M.C., USN, 1944-46, ETO. Recipient Guy R. Odum, Jr. award M.D. Anderson Hosp. and Tumor Inst., 1986; Disting. Svc. Prof. award Baylor Coll. Medicine, 1986, Disting. Faculty award, 1987. Mem. ACP, Am. Clin. and Cllimatol. Assn., Am. Fedn. for Clin. Rsch., Am. Soc. for Clin. Investigation, Am. Soc. for Microbiology, Am. Soc. for Virology, Assn. Am. Physicians, Assn. Med. Sch. Microbiology Chairmen (pres. 1981), Infectious Diseases Soc. Am.

(emeritus), Internat. Assn. Aerobiology, Internat. Leprosy Assn., Soc. for Exptl. Biology and Medicine, Tex. Med. Assn., Harris County Med. Soc., Sigma Xi, Alpha Omega Alpha. Office: Baylor Coll Medicine 1 Baylor Plz Rm 410B Houston TX 77030-3411

KNIGHT, JAMES ATWOOD, consulting executive; b. Providence, Apr. 26, 1954; s. Richard Brayton and Louise (Atwood) K.; m. Cynthia Forbes Olney, June 11, 1983; children: Hilary Atwood, James Atwood Jr., Remington Forbes, William Olney, Elsie Lawson. BS, Boston U., 1975; MBA, Dartmouth Coll., 1984. Sr. assoc. Strategic Decisions Group, Menlo Park, Calif., 1984-88; mgr. Apple Computer, Cupertino, Calif., 1988-90; with Holt, Chgo., 1990, Boston Cons. Group, Chgo., 1991-95; v.p. SCA Consulting L.L.C., Chgo., 1995-97, mng. ptnr., 1997—. Author: Value Based Management, 1997; contbr. chpt. to book. Avocations: skiing, squash. Home: 606 Tiverton Rd Lake Forest IL 60045-1655 Office: SCA Consulting LLC 200 W Madison St Ste 1900 Chicago IL 60606-3416

KNIGHT, JANET ANN, elementary education educator; b. Covina, Calif., July 22, 1937; d. Arnold M. and Thelma (Lyle) Ostrum; m. Ronald L. Knight, Sept. 14, 1957; children: Barbara Lynne, Susan Kaye. BA in Edn., Cen. Wash. U., 1979; MA in Edn., Heritage Coll., 1992. Cert. elem, secondary tchr., Wash. 2nd grade tchr. Kennewick (Wash.) Pub. Schs., 1980-81, 1st grade tchr., 1981-85, 3rd grade tchr., 1985-93, 4th grade tchr., 1993—; lang. arts dist. com. Kennewick Sch. Dist., 1985-89, curriculum, instrn. com., 1989-92, dist. curriculum and instruction renewal cycle for learning excellence, 1992-94, dist. assessment com., 1992-95. Mem. Richland (Wash.) Light Opera Co., 1963-75. Mem. NEA, ASCD, Wash. Edn. Assn., Kennewick Edn. Assn., Wash. Orgn. Reading Devel., Benton County Coun. of Internat. Reading Assn., Order of Rainbow for Girls, Sigma Tau Alpha. Episcopalian. Avocations: Petit Basset Griffon Vendeen show dogs, ceramics, golf, photography, reading. Home: 120 Heather Ln Richland WA 99352-9155 Office: Westgate Elem Sch 2514 W 4th Ave Kennewick WA 99336-3115

KNIGHT, JEFFREY LIN, lawyer, corporation executive; b. Evansville, Ind., Sept. 21, 1959; s. Jack T. and Ruth (Rogers) K.; m. Erin Elizabeth Hostettler, Dec. 18, 1982; children: Kathryn Ruth, Abigail Rebekah, Margaret Rachel, Caroline Elizabeth. BS, U. Evansville, 1981; JD, U. Ind., Indpls., 1984. Bar: Ind. 1984. Assoc. Clark, Statham, McCray, Thomas & Krohn, Evansville, 1984-85, Frank, Collins & Stephens, Evansville, 1985-88; v.p., sec., treas., gen. counsel Pacific Press & Shear, Inc., Mt. Carmel, Ill., 1988-90; gen. mgr. Pacific Press & Shear, Inc., 1991-93; corp. sec., gen. counsel Old Nat. Bancorp, 1993—. Mentor Evansville Vanderburgh Sch. Corp., 1984-87; campaign chmn. Hostettler For Congress Com., 1994, 96, 98. Mem. Ind. Bar Assn., Evansville Bar Assn., Am. Soc. Corp. Secs., Optimists (sec. 1987-88, v.p. 1988-89). Republican. Baptist. Avocations: golf, tennis. Home: 330 Largo Ct Evansville IN 47712-7616

KNIGHT, JEFFREY RICHARD, small business owner; b. Salt Lake City, Apr. 22, 1962; s. Richard M. and Donna H. (Hallman) K.; m. Carrie Lyn Jackson. BBA, Calif. State Poly. Inst. U., 1984, MBA, 1986. owner KD Enterprises, 1995—; pres. Lockheed Martin Activities Coordinating Com., Camarillo, 1991-93. With Lockheed Martin, Camarillo, Calif., 1985-96; prin. engr. DirecTV, quality assurance mgr., 1996—; owner, KD Enterprises, pres. Co. Activities Coordinating Com., Camarillo, 1991-93. Treas. Hillcrest Park Home Owners Assn., 1990-92, pres., 1992-93; chmn. Calif. State Poly. Inst. U. Rose Float Com., 1984-85. Mem. Thailand Darts Assn., Rose Float Alumni Assn. (treas. 1985-86, bd. dirs. 1987-88, pres. 1991-93, historian/archivist 1994—, chmn. 50th float activities com.), Nat. Employee Svcs. and Recreation Assn. (pres. Gold Coast chpt. 1994-95), Toastmasters Internat. (chpt. treas. 1996, v.p. pub. rels. 1996, Competent Toastmaster award 1996). Republican. Avocations: philately, softball, darts. Home: 2143 Saxe Ct Thousand Oaks CA 91360-3148

KNIGHT, JOHN ALLAN, clergyman, philosophy and religion educator; b. Mineral Wells, Tex., Nov. 8, 1931; s. John Lee and Beulah Mae (Bounds) K.; m. Justine Anne Rushing, Aug. 22, 1958; children—John Allan, James Alden, Judith Anne. B.A., Bethany Nazarene Coll., 1952; M.A., Okla. U., 1954; B.D., Vanderbilt U., 1957, Ph.D., 1966. Ordained to ministry Ch. of Nazarene, 1954; pastor Tenn. Dist. Ch. of Nazarene, 1953-61, 71-72; prof., chmn. dept. philosophy and religion Trevecca Nazarene Coll., Nashville, 1957-69; chmn. dept. philosophy and religion Mt. Vernon (Ohio) Nazarene Coll., 1969-71, pres., 1972-75; pastor Grace Nazarene Ch., Nashville, 1971-72; pres. Bethany (Okla.) Nazarene Coll., 1976-85; gen. supt. Internat. Ch. of the Nazarene, 1985—, vice chair Bd. Gen. Supts., 1990-92, chair Bd. Gen. Supts., 1992-94; coordinator U.S. Govt. Project Studying Possible Coop. Ventures for Tenn. Colls. and Univs., 1969; mem. gen. bd. Internat. Ch. of Nazarene, 1980-85. Author: Commentary on Philippians, 1968, The Holiness Pilgrimage, 1971, In His Likeness, 1976, Beacon Bible Expositions, Vol. 9, 1985, What the Bible Says About Tongues - Speaking, 1988; co-author: Sanctify Them -- That the World May Know, 1987; co-author: Go -- Preach, The Preaching Event in the 90s; author: All Loves Excelling, 1995; editor-in-chief: Herald of Holiness, Kansas City, Mo., 1975-76. Pres. bd. govs. Okla. Ind. Coll. Found., 1979-81. Recipient Lily Found. Theology award Vanderbilt U., 1958-59; Carré fellow Vanderbilt U., 1960-62. Mem. Soc. Sci. Study Religion, Am. Acad. Religion, Wesley Theol. Soc. (pres. 1979), Evang. Theol. Assn. Club: Kiwanis Internat. Home: PO Box 368 Bethany OK 73008-0368 Office: Internat Ch of the Nazarene 6401 Paseo Blvd Kansas City MO 64131-1213

KNIGHT, JOHN FRANCIS, insurance company executive; b. N.Y.C., Sept. 30, 1919; s. Samuel F. and Abigail (Sullivan) K.; m. Marilyn Rockefeller, Oct. 30, 1948; children: Jeffrey J., Melanie K. Eggers, John Mark, Jane M., James M. B.B.A. cum laude, St. John's U., 1952. With Republic Fin. Svcs. Inc., Republic Ins. Group, Dallas, 1939-88; agy. supr. Republic Fin. Svcs. Inc., Republic Ins. Group, 1950-56, asst. v.p., 1956-60, v.p., 1960-67, sr. v.p., 1967-69, exec. v.p., 1969-71, sr. exec. v.p., 1971-72, pres., 1972-83, vice chmn., bd. dirs., 1983-88. Served to maj. AUS, 1942-46. Decorated Bronze Star. Republican. Roman Catholic. Home: 16 Coolidge St Malverne NY 11565-1808

KNIGHT, JOHN K., aeronautics director; b. Vicksburg, Miss.; m. Rose (Thornton) K., 1960; children: Tim, Todd. U. Ark., Little Rock. cert. flight instr. Asst. dir. Ark. dept. of Aeronautics, Little rock, 1988-92, dir., 1992—. Baptist. Avocations: quarter horses, flying. Office: Ark Dept of Aeronautics 3d Floor One Airport Dr Little Rock AR 72202

KNIGHT, KENNETH VINCENT, leisure company executive, entrepreneur, venture capitalist; b. Jersey City, Mar. 30, 1944; s. Julian (Konopacki) and Ellen (Gordon) Knight; m. Karen Keenan, June 1, 1968 (div. June 1978); 1 child, Karisa M.; m. Maria H. Herrera, June 17, 1983; children: Alexander, Maria B., Christina M. Student, Northwestern Coll., Iowa, 1962-65; BS in Mgmt., N.Y. Inst. Tech., 1966; MBA, Nova Southeastern U., 1976; grad., Officer Candidate Sch., FARNG, 1968. Mgr., customer/corp. rels. Cavanaugh Corp., Miami, Fla., 1966-68; asst. dir. corp. svcs. Burger King Corp., Miami, 1968-70; asst. to sr. v.p. investor rels. Deltona Corp., Miami, 1970-74; dir. corp./investor rels. Gen. Devel. Corp., GDV Corp., Miami and N.Y.C., 1974-78; v.p. resort affiliations, stockholder Interval Internat., Miami, 1978-79, sr. v.p. mktg., 1979-82, exec. v.p., chief ops., 1983-84; pres., chief ops. Interval Internat. & Worldex, Miami, 1984-87, pres. and major shareholder, 1987-89, vice chmn., 1989-92; founder, gen. ptnr. Leisure Fund, Ltd., Miami, 1992—; founder, chmn., CEO Leisurecorp Internat., 1992—, Leisure Fund Assoc., L.P., Nev., 1995—; pres. MKH Mgmt., Inc., Miami, 1995—; co-founder Worldex Corp., Miami, 1982-92, Worldex Travel Ctrs., 1983-92, Leaguestar Pl., London, 1988-92; co-founder Worldex Corp., Denver and L.A., Worldex Europe Ltd., London, Intercambico Internationales de Vacienes, SA, Mexico City, 1985-92, Leisurecorp Internat., 1992—; mem. bd. advisors Property Planning, Inc., 1972-75, Interval Internat., 1975-78, Ecotourism Natureshare Assn., Stowe, Vt., 1990, Vacation Accommodation Directory, Inc., Tampa, 1992, Condo Network, Inc., Kansas City, 1992, Brentwood Equities, L.A., 1993-95, Chiralt Corp./Erose Capital, L.A., 1997—, Voice Track Corp., Dallas, 1997, Century Found., also others; bd. govs. Nova Southeastern U. Grad. Sch. Bus. and Entrepreneurship, 1992—, trustee, 1994—, vice chmn. devel., 1998—, also mem. adv. bd.; mem. spkrs. forum, Dave Thomas's Ambs. Enterprise Program, Nova Southeastern U., 1995, bd. dirs. South Fla. Alumni, 1996—, vice chmn. strategy planning com., 1998—; mem. Farquar Undergrad. Pres. Search Com., 1998, bd. trustees audit com., 1998—; mem. Fla. Venture Forum, Fla. Internat. U., 1995—, Small Bus. Devel. Ctr., U. Ctrl. Fla., 1996—, Assoc. Gov. Bds. Univs. and Colls., 1995—; trustee pvt. trust. Founder: (mags.) The Leisure Society, Dreamweavers; exec. pub.: (newspaper) Timesharing Times, 1980, (mag.) Timeshare Traveler, 1984-90, Directory Resorts, 1980-90; mem. editl. bd. Vacation Industry Rev., 1985— (most traveled exec. 1984, spkr. worldwide); author: Best Use for Resort Condominiums, 1972, Time Sharing—What It Is and How It Works, 1974. Soccar asst. St. Thomas Episcopal Ch., 1995; Cub scout den leader Pack 336, Boy Scouts Am., 1996. 1st lt. Fla. Army N.G., 1966-93, ret. Recipient Achievers award Fla. Trend mag., 1983, 88, Inc. 500 award Inc. mag., 1984, The Capital award Nat. Leadership Coun., 1991, Nova U. Alumni award, 1992; named Fla.'s Best Internat. Co., Prestige Internat. mag., 1985, Alumni of Yr., Nova Southeastern U., 1993. Roman Catholic. Avocations: experimental and adventure travel, cruising, scuba diving, boating, skiing. Office: Leisure Corp Internat World Trade Ctr 80 SW 8th St Miami FL 33130-3003

KNIGHT, KIT MARIE, poet, writer, movie critic; b. North Kingston, R.I., Sept. 21, 1952; d. Basil Arthur and Helen (Swerdi) Duell; m. Arthur Winfield Knight, Aug. 25, 1976; 1 child, Tiffany Carolyn. BA in Comm., California U. Pa., 1975. Co-editor, co-pub. the unspeakable visions of the individual, lit. mag., California, 1976-84; poet, columnist Russian River News, weekly newspaper, Guerneville, Calif., 1988-92; poet, columnist, film critic Russian River Times, Guerneville, 1987-98. Author: (book of poetry) Women of Wanted Men, 1994 (Perry award James-Younger Gang 1995); co-editor: (anthologies) The Beat Diary, 1977, The Beat Angels, 1982, The Beat Vision, 1987, Kerouac and The Beats, 1988. Docent Petaluma (Calif.) Hist. Libr. and Mus., 1998-99. Mem. North Bay Civil War Roundtable (charter). Avocation: research and writing about The War Between the States. Home and Office: PO Box 2580 Petaluma CA 94953

KNIGHT, LESTER B., healthcare company executive; b. N.Y.C., May 15, 1958. B of Indsl. Engring., Cornell U.; M of Bus., Cornell Johnson Sch. of Mgmt. Various positions Baxter Internat. Inc., 1981-90, corp. v.p., 1990-92, exec. v.p., 1992-96; chmn. bd. CEO, Allegiance Corp., 1996-99; vice chmn. Cardinal Health Inc., 1999—; bd. dirs. Health Industry Mfrs. Assn., Evanston Hosp. Corp., Jr. Achievement of Chgo., The Baxter Allegiance Found., Evanston Northwestern Healthcare. Trustee Northwestern U., Lincoln Found. for Bus. Excellence. Mem. Comml. Club Chgo., Chgo. Club, Chgo. Commonwealth Club, Chgo. Coun. on Fgn. Rels., Econ. Club Chgo., Bus. Roundtable (Mid-Am. com.). Office: Allegiance Corp 1430 Waukegan Rd Mc Gaw Park IL 60085-6726*

KNIGHT, NORMAN, philanthropist, former broadcast executive; b. July 24, 1924; m. Susannah Howard Andre, Aug. 26, 1944; children: Norman Scott, Randolph Howard, Jeffrey Bryant, Robert Andre. LLD (hon.), Northeastern U.; DBA (hon.), Nathaniel Hawthorne Coll.; DCS (hon.), Merrimack Coll.; DHL (hon.), Suffolk U.; DCC (hon.), Anna Maria Coll. News reporter, scriptwriter Sta. WEW, WIL, WTMV, 1938-41; Announcer, host-producer Sta. WTMV, 1942; announcer, promotion mgr., news reporting continuity dir. Sta. KTHS, 1943; announcer Sta. WMC, 1943; announcer, news writer, reporter, salesman Sta. WMMN, 1944; gen. mgr. Sta. WAJR, 1944-46; Eastern dir. sta. relations MBS, 1946-49; v.p. sales, advt. and promotion Sponsor Publs., Inc., 1950-53; gen. mgr. Sta. WABD (now WNYW-TV), 1953-54; exec. v.p., gen. mgr. Yankee Network div. RKO Teleradio Pictures, Inc. (operating Yankee Network WNAC, WRKO, WNAC-TV); also dir. Yankee Network; v.p. RKO Teleradio Pictures, 1954-56; pres. Yankee div. RKO Teleradio Pictures, Inc., 1957-60, Yankee div. RKO Gen., Inc., 1958-60; treas., chmn. Knight Sales, Inc.; chmn., treas. Knight Radio, Inc. (WEZF, WGIR and WGIR-FM), Knight Broadcasting N.H, Inc. (WHEB-FM, WXHT, WTMN); pres., treas. Knight Communications Corp. (WTAG and WSRS); chmn. Caribbean Communications Corp. Established first complete TV sta.: pub. affairs film unit which produced Brotherhood Series: River of Life, Wershmeitz (only film 1956 Hungarian revolt), Suffer the Little Children, Breast Cancer, over 100 porgrams Dangers of Apathy; TV documentaries, 1953-60; Author: (sales techniques radio/TV) The Cause of All Mankind, (film and TV) A Storm is Always a Challenge, Awake America, others. Radio-TV chmn. United Fund Greater Boston, Mass. Cancer Soc., ARC chpt. Met. Boston, Met. Boston chpt. ARC; bus. chmn. Easter Seal Soc.; radio chmn. Salvation Army; dir. Strawberry Banke; bd. dirs. New Eng. Nephrosis Found.; pres., founder New Eng. Kidney Disease Found.; pres. Norman Knight Charitable Found.; trustee Mass. Bd. Regional Community Colls., Agassiz Village Camps, Crippled Children's Non-Sectarian Fund, Boys and Girls Camps, Inc.; mem. nat. council, exec. com. New Eng. council Boy Scouts Am.; exec. com., dir. Rescue, Inc.; exec. com. The Jimmy Fund; exec. com., trustee Children's Cancer Research Found., Dana Farber Cancer Inst.; mem. fin. com. Com. Econ. Devel.; mem. devel. council Boston U.; mem. pres.'s council Boston Coll.; bd. dirs. Freedoms Found.; also nat. co-chmn. Am. Freedom Center. Recipient Americanism award Am. Heritage Com., 1959, awards from VFW, Am. Legion, Amvets, Am. Legion Aux., 1959-60, award for contbn. to radio and TV industry Alpha Epsilon Rho; Golden Mike award Broadcasters Found., 1996; named one of ten Outstanding Youngn Men, Boston Jr. C. of C., 1956, Man of Yr., Italian-Am. Police Assn., Humanitarian award ARC, 1998; Norman Knight Hyperbaric Medicine Ctr., Mass. Eye and Ear Infirmary established in his name, 1999. Mem. Radio-TV Execs. Soc., Young Pres.'s Orgn., Broadcast Pioneers, AIM, Alpha Epsilon Rho. Clubs: Variety (Boston); Broadcasting Execs. New Eng, 100 of Mass. (co-founder, pres., dir.), 100 of N.H. (life), Univ. Office: 63 Bay State Rd Boston MA 02215-1802

KNIGHT, PATRICIA MARIE, optics researcher; b. Schnectady, N.Y., Jan. 25, 1952; d. Donald Orlin and Mary Ann K. BS in Engring. Sci., Ariz. State U., 1974, MSChemE, 1976; PhD in Biomed. Engring., U. Utah, 1983. Teaching and rsch. asst. Ariz. State U., Tempe, 1974-76; product devel. engr. Am. Med. Optics, Irvine, Calif., 1976-79, mgr. materials rsch., 1983-87; rsch. asst. U. Utah, Salt Lake City, 1979-83; dir. materials rsch. Allergan Med. Optics, Irvine, 1987-88, dir. rsch., 1988-91, v.p. rsch., devel. and engring., 1991—; Contbr. articles to profl. jours. Mem. Soc. Biomaterials, Am. Chem. Soc., Soc. Women Engrs., Assn. Rsch. in Vision and Opthalmology, Biomed. Engring. Soc. Avocations: photography, skiing, golf. Office: Allergan Inc PO Box 19534 Irvine CA 92623-9534

KNIGHT, PHILIP H(AMPSON), shoe manufacturing company executive; b. Portland, Oreg., Feb. 24, 1938; s. William W. and Lota (Hatfield) K.; m. Penelope Parks, Sept. 13, 1968; children: Matthew, Travis. B.B.A., U. Oreg.; M.B.A., Stanford U. C.P.A., Oreg. Chmn., chief exec. officer, past pres. Nike, Inc., Beaverton, Oreg., 1967—. Bd. dirs. U.S.-Asian Bus. Coun., Washington, 1st lt. AUS, 1959-60. Named Oreg. Businessman of Yr., 1982, One of 1988's Best Mgrs., Bus. Week Magazine. Mem. AICPA. Republican. Episcopalian. Office: Nike Inc One Bowerman Dr Beaverton OR 97005-6453

KNIGHT, RALPH H., consumer products company executive; b. 1949. MBA, U. Ga., 1972. Acct. Deloite & Touche, Atlanta, 1972-77; with Food Giant, Atlanta, 1977-84, Air Atlanta (Ga.), 1985, Atlanta (Ga.) Beverage Co., 1985-92; sr. v.p., CFO Red Food Stores, Inc., Chattanooga, 1992-94; v.p., CFO, COO Chattanooga Neighborhood Enterprise, 1995—. Office: Chattanooga Neighborhood Enterprise 535 Chestnut St Ste 100 Chattanooga TN 37402-4927*

KNIGHT, (CHARLES) RAY, professional sports team executive; b. New Albany, Ga., Dec. 28, 1952; m. Nancy Lopez. Mgr. Cin. Reds, to 97; with ESPN Sports, N.Y.C., 1997—. Named N.L. Comeback Player of the Yr., The Sporting News, 1986. Office: ESPN 605 3d Ave New York NY 10158-0180*

KNIGHT, REBECCA JEAN, secondary education educator; b. Oklahoma City, Nov. 8, 1949; d. G.B. and Lillian Pearl (Wright) Williams; m. Ronnie Dean Knight, Mar. 1, 1968; children: Ronald Chad, Dustin Ryan. BS, East Tex. State U., 1972, postgrad., 1989-92. Cert. tchr., Tex. Tchr.'s aide Bailey Inglish Elem., Bonham, Tex., 1971; tchr. Bonham H.S., 1973—. Mem. ins. com. Bonham Ind. Sch. Dist., 1975—, dist. site based com., 1992-93, campus site based com., 1993-98; tchr. adult Sunday sch. Ch. of God, Lannius, Tex., 1990—, tchr. teenage Sunday sch., 1969-90. Mem. NEA, Assn. Tex. Profl. Educators, Nat. Coun. Tchrs. of English, Tex. State Tchrs. Assn., Alpha Chi. Avocations: gardening, computers, walking, sewing, decorating.

KNIGHT, ROBERT EDWARD, banker; b. Alliance, Nebr., Nov. 27, 1941; s. Edward McKean and Ruth (McDuffee) K.; m. Eva Sophia Youngstom, Aug. 12, 1966. BA, Yale U., 1963; MA, Harvard U., 1965, PhD, 1968. Asst. prof. U.S. Naval Acad., Annapolis, Md., 1966-68; lectr. U. Md., 1967-68; fin. economist Fed. Res. Bank of Kansas City (Mo.), 1968-70, research officer, economist, 1971-76, asst. v.p., sec., 1977, v.p., sec., 1978-79; pres. Alliance (Nebr.) Nat. Bank, 1979-94, also chmn., 1983-94; pres. Robert Knight Assocs., banking and econ. cons., Cheyenne, 1979—; chmn. Eldred Found., 1985—; vis. prof., chair banking and fin. E. Tenn. State U., Johnson City, 1988; mem. faculty Stonier Grad. Sch. Banking, 1972—, Colo. Grad. Sch. Banking, 1975-82, Am. Inst. Banking, U. Mo., Kansas City, 1971-79, Prochnow Grad. Sch. Banking, U. Wis.; mem. extended learning faculty Park Coll., 1996—; mem. Coun. for Excellence for Bur. Bus. Rsch. U. Nebr., Lincoln, 1991-94, mem. Grad. Sch. Arts & Scis Coun., Harvard, 1994—; chmn. Taxable Mcpl. Bondholders Protective Com., 1991-94. Trustee, 1984-85, Knox Presbyn. Ch., Overland Park, Kans., 1965-69; bd. regents Nat. Comml. Lending Sch., 1980-83; mem. Downtown Improvement Com., Alliance, 1981-94; trustee U. Nebr. Found.; bd. dirs. Stonier Grad. Sch. Banking, Box Butte County Devel. Commn., Nebr. Com. for Humanities, 1986-90; mem. fin. com. United Meth. Ch., Alliance, 1982-85, trustee, 1990-93; Box Butte County Indsl. Devel. Bd., 1987-94; mem. Nebr. Com. for the Humanities, 1986-90. Woodrow Wilson fellow, 1963-64. Mem. Am. Econ. Assn., Am. Fin. Assn., So. Econ. Assn., Nebr. Bankers Assn. (com. state legis. 1980-81, com. comml. loans and investments 1986-87), Am. Inst. Banking (state com. for Nebr. 1980-83), Am. Bankers Assn. (econ. adv. com. 1980-83, cmty. bank leadership coun.), Western Econ. Assn., Econometric Soc., Rotary, Masons. Contbr. articles to profl. jours. Home and Office: 429 W 5th Ave Cheyenne WY 82001-1249

KNIGHT, ROBERT G., mayor, investment banker; b. Wichita, Kans., July 31, 1941; s. Edwar G. and Melba (Barbour) K.; m. Jane Carol Benedick, Aug. 12, 1967; children—Jennifer, Amy, Kristin. B.A., Wichita State U. Rep. First Securities Co., Wichita, Kans., 1970-76, v.p., 1984—; v.p. Mid-Continent Mcpls., Wichita, Kans., 1977-82, Ranson & Co., Wichita, Kans., 1982-84; mayor City of Wichita, 1980-81, 84—. Trustee Salvation Army, Wichita, 1980—, Urban Ministeries, Wichita, 1980—, Southwestern Coll., Winfield, Kans., 1980—; bd. dirs. Kans. Water Authority, Topeka, 1983—; commr. City of Wichita, 1979—. Served with USMCR, 1962-66. Recipient award of honor Concerned Citizens for Community Standards, 1982. Mem. Nat. League Cities, Kans. League Municipalities. Republican. Methodist. Avocation: sports. Office: Mayors Office City Hall 1st Fl 455 N Main St Wichita KS 67202-1600*

KNIGHT, SANDRA NORTON, civil engineer; b. Chattanooga, Mar. 2, 1962; d. Johnny Lee Norton and Wanda Dean (Pledger) Weaver; m. Donald Lauaghn Knight, Oct. 24, 1992. Student, Chattanooga State Tech. C.C., 1980-82; BSCE, U. Tenn., 1986; postgrad., Fla. State U., 1990. Registered profl. engr., Tenn. Traffice engr. technician City of Knoxville; project mgr. Fla. Dept. Transp., Tallahassee, 1987-93, Cook & Spencer Cons., Chattanooga, 1993-96; engr. design mgr. City of Chattanooga, 1996; county engr. Bradley County, Cleveland, Tenn., 1996—. Bldg. inspector Town of Decatur, Tenn., 1996—, alderman, 1995-99. Mem. ASCE (sec.-treas. 1994-95, v.p. 1995-96, pres. 1996-97, v.p. Tenn. sect. 1998-99, sec. Tenn. sect. 1998-99, Young Engr. of Yr. 1991, 96, 97), TSPE (sec. Chattanooga chpt. 1998-99, v.p. 1999-2000). Republican. Baptist. Avocations: Siberian huskies, reading. Office: Bradley County Engr PO Box 1167 Cleveland TN 37364-1167

KNIGHT, THOMAS JEFFERSON, JR., computer consultant, trainer; b. San Antonio, Oct. 21, 1955; s. Thomas Jefferson and Martha Lena (Craig) K.; m. Lois Ann Simmons, July 13, 1985 (div. Jan. 1993); 1 child, Thomas Jefferson III. BS, Baylor U., 1978; M. Pub. Adminstrn., Golden Gate U., 1988. Commd. 2d lt. USAF, 1978, advanced thru grades to capt., 1988; chief of adminstrn. USAF 780th Radar Squadron, Fortuna AFB, N.D., 1978-79; squadron sect. comdr. USAF 325th Component Repair Squadron, Tyndall AFB, Fla., 1979-82; protocol officer USAF HQ Tactical Air Command, Langley AFB, Va., 1982-85; exec. officer USAF 487th Tactical Missile Wing, Comiso AS, Italy, 1985-86, USAF 57th Fighter Weapons Wing, Nellis AFB, Nev., 1986-90; resigned, 1990; cons., Waco, Tex., 1990; dir. tech. svcs. Entré Computer Ctr., Waco, 1990—. Local commr. Panama City (Fla.) Boy Scouts Am., 1979-80. Mem. Air Force Assn. Presbyterian.

KNIGHT, TOWNSEND JONES, lawyer; b. N.Y.C., Aug. 10, 1928; s. Jesse and Marguerite H. (Jones) K.; m. Elise Heck; children: Margaret Knight Dudley, Elise Knight Wallace, Jessica Knight Casoni. BS, Harvard U., 1949; JD, Columbia U., 1952. Bar: N.Y. 1952. Assoc. Curtis, Mallet-Prevost, Colt & Mosle, N.Y.C., 1953-65, ptnr., 1965—. Trustee Audrey Cohen Coll., N.Y.C., 1969—, Cold Spring Harbor (N.Y.) Lab., 1970-76, 82-88, 89-95, hon. trustee, 1995—; dir. Friends Ivory & Sime Trust Co., 1995—. Mem. ABA, N.Y. State Bar Assn., Assn. of Bar of City of N.Y., Downtown Assn., Harvard Club, Cold Spring Harbor Beach Club. Episcopalian. Avocation: photography. Office: Curtis Mallet-Prevost Colt 101 Park Ave New York NY 10178

KNIGHT, V. C., manufacturing executive; b. Landess, Ind., Aug. 12, 1904; s. Charles and Daisie (Farr) K.; m. Velma Cain, June 30, 1926; children: James, Marilyn. Student, Ind. State U., 1921-24; Ph.D. in Bus. Adminstrn., Adrian Coll., 1977, Hillsdale Coll., 1983. With McCray Refrigerator Co., 1926-47; v.p. ops.; exec. v.p. Betz Corp., Hammond, Ind., 1947-51; with Addison Products Co., 1951—, now chmn. bd.; Past trustee Adrian Coll., present trustee emeritus. Office: Addison Products Co 215 Talbot St Addison MI 49220

KNIGHT, VICK, JR., author, educator, counselor; b. Lakewood, Ohio, Apr. 6, 1928; s. Vick Ralph and Janice (Higgins) K. BS, U. So. Calif., 1952; MA, L.S. State Coll., 1956; postgrad. Whittier Coll., 1959-61, Long Beach State Coll., 1960-61, Calif. State Coll.-Fullerton, 1961-64, Claremont U., 1963-65, UCLA, 1993-98; EdD, Calif. Coast U., 1991, postgrad, UCLA, 1993-98; m. Beverly Joyce McKeighan, Apr. 14, 1949 (div. 1973); children: Stephen Foster, Mary Ann; m. Carolyn Schlee, June 6, 1981; children: Kathy, Meri. Producer-dir. Here Comes Tom Harmon radio series ABC, Hollywood, Calif., 1947-50; tchr., vice-prin. Ranchito Sch. Dist., Pico Rivera, Calif., 1952-59; prin. Kraemer Intermediate Sch., Placentia, Calif., 1959-64; dir. instructional svcs. Placentia Unified Sch. Dist., 1964-65, asst. supt., 1965-71; program dir. World Vista Travel Svcs., 1970-72; dir. grad. extension La Verne Coll., 1971-73; v.p. Nat. Gen. West Investments, 1971-74; bd. dir. community rels. and devel. Childrens Hosp. of Orange County (Calif.), 1974-84; sr. dir. curriculum and edn. svcs. Elsinore Union High Sch. Dist., Lake Elsinore, Calif., 1985-88; exec. dir. Elsinore Valley Community Devel. Corp., 1989-92; dean Sch. Edn. Newport U., Newport Beach, Calif., 1992-96; pres. Aristan Assocs.; bd. dirs. Key Records, Hollywood. Dist. chmn. Valencia Coun. Boy Scouts Am.; chmn. Cancer Soc. Ptnrs. of Ams., also chmn. Sister City Com.; chmn. Community Chest Drives; chmn. adv. com. Esperenza Hosp.; mem. Educare; hon. life mem. Calif. PTA. Bd. dirs. U. Calif.-Irvine Friends of Library, pres., 1975-77; bd. trustees Lake Elsinore Unified Sch. Dist., 1991, pres. 1993-99; bd. dirs. Muckenthaler Cultural Groups Found.; chmn. bd. William Claude Fields Found. Club. With USN, 1946-48. Recipient Disting. Citizen award Whittier Coll., 1960; Educator of Yr. award Orange County Press Club, 1971, Author and Book award U. Calif., 1973, Children's Lit. award Calif. State U.-Fullerton, 1979, Bronze Pelican award Boy Scouts Am.; named Canyon Lake Man of the Yr., 1994; mem. NEA, ASCAP, Nat. Sch. Pub. Rels. Assn. (regional v.p.), U.S. Jr. C. of C. (bd. dir., Young Man of Calif. 1959), Calif. Jr. C. of C. (state v.p.), Pico Rivera Jr. C. of C. (pres.), Canyon Lake C. of C. (pres. 1998), Audubon Soc., Western Soc. Naturalists, Calif. Tchrs. Assn., Internat. Platform Assn., Soc. Children's Book Writers, Authors Guild, Authors League Am., Anti-Slubberdegullion Soc., Bank Dicks, Assn. Hosp. Devel., Art Experience, Good Bears of World, Los Compadres con Libros, Blue Key, Skull and Dagger, Les Amis du Vin, Phi Sigma Kappa, Alpha Delta Sigma, E Clampus Vitus, Theta Nu Epsilon, Kiwanian (pres.), Master Mason, Canyon Lake Home Owners Club (pres. 1989-91), West Atwood Yacht (commodore) Club. Writer weekly Nature Notebook newspaper columns, 1957—, wine columnist Riverside Press-Enterprise, 1991—, S. Coast Wines Mag.; fine arts editor

Placentia Courier; editor curriculum guides: New Math., Lang. Arts, Social Scis., Pub. Rels., Biol. Sci. Substitute Tchrs; author: (ecology textbooks) It's Our World; It's Our Future; It's Our Choice, Snakes of Hawaii, Earle the Squirrel, Night the Crayons Talked; My Word!; Send for Haym Salomon!, Joby and the Wishing Well; Twilight of the Animal Kingdom; A Tale of Twos, Who's Zoo, A Navel Salute, Friend or Enema?, John Sevier: Citizen Soldier, Toasting Temecula Wines, A Rainforest Adventure, also math. instrn. units; contbr. articles to various jours. Home: 22597 Canyon Lake Dr S Canyon Lake CA 92587-7595

KNIGHT, W. DONALD, JR., lawyer; b. Macon, Miss., May 30, 1941. BA summa cum laude, Miss. State U., 1961; MA, Emory U., 1963; LLB, U. Va., 1967. Bar: Ga. 1967. Ptnr. King & Spalding, Atlanta, 1974; mem. adv. bd. N.Am. Free Trade & Investment Report. Co-author: Structuring Foreign Investment in U.S. Real Estate, 1982; editorial bd.: Va. Law Review; editorial advisory bd.: Tax Mgmt. Internat. Jour., 1981—; contbr. editor: Intertax (internat. tax review). Mem. ABA, Atlanta Bar Assn., Internat. Bar Assn., Internat. Fiscal Assn., Raven Soc., Order of the Coif, Omicron Delta Kappa. Office: King & Spalding 191 Peachtree St NE Atlanta GA 30303-1740*

KNIGHT, WALKER LEIGH, editor, publisher, clergyman; b. Henderson, Ky., Feb. 6, 1924; s. Cooksey Bennett and Rowena (Henderson) K.; m. Iva Nell Moseley, Nov. 10, 1943; children: Walker Leigh, Kenneth Wayne, Nelda Denise, Emily Jill. BA, Baylor U., 1949. Reporter Henderson Gleanor and Jour., 1942; ordained to ministry Bapt. Ch., 1948; pastor in Dale, Tex., 1948-49; editor Falls County Record, Marlin, Tex., 1948-49; assoc. editor Bapt. Std., Dallas, 1950-59; editl. dir. So. Bapt. Home Mission Bd., Atlanta; also editor Missions U.S.A. mag. and Atlanta bur. chief Bapt. Press News Service So. Bapt. Home Mission Bd., 1959-83; editor, pub. Bapts. Today (formerly SBC Today), 1983-89, pub., 1989-93, pub. emeritus, 1994—; editor The Whitsitt Jour., 1995-98. Author: Panama, The Land Between, 1965, Struggle for Integrity, 1969, See How Love Works, 1971, Seven Beginnings, 1976, Chaplaincy, Love on the Line, 1978, Tell the People, 1986; contbr. to Southern Baptists Observed, 1992, Struggle for the Soul of the SBC, 1993. With USAAF, 1943-45. Home: 1008 Forrest Blvd Decatur GA 30030-4732 Office: 403 W Ponce de Leon Decatur GA 30030-2445

KNIGHT, WALTER DAVID, physics educator; b. N.Y.C., Oct. 14, 1919; s. Walter David and Ruth Della (Hubbard) K.; m. Elizabeth Lewis Wiggins, Apr. 7, 1945 (div. July, 1972) children—Margaret Benton, Jonathan Goodnow; m. Sara Frances Pattershall, July 27, 1972; 1 child, Nathaniel Nims. A.B., Middlebury Coll., 1941; M.A., Duke U., 1943, Ph.D. in physics, 1950; D.Sc. (hon.), Middlebury Coll., 1976; Dr. h.c., Ecole Polytech. Fed. de Lausanne, Switzerland, 1983. Instr. Trinity Coll., Hartford, Conn., 1946-50; asst. to assoc. prof. U. Calif.-Berkeley, 1950-61, prof., 1961-90, prof. emeritus, 1990—; asst. to assoc. dean Coll. Letters and Sci., Berkeley, Calif., 1959-63, dean, 1967-72; prof. Miller Inst., Berkeley, 1979-80; vis. disting. prof. Niels Bohr Inst., 1988; vis. prof. Fed. Polytech Sch., Lausanne, Switzerland, 1980; Sackler Disting. lectr. chemistry U. Tel Aviv, 1989. Author: (with C. Kittel, M.A. Ruderman) Mechanics, 1964; contbr. articles to profl. jours. Served to lt. (j.g.) USNR, 1944-46. Fellow Alfred P. Sloan Found., 1956-57, Guggenheim Found., 1961, Oxford U., 1983-84. Fellow Am. Phys. Soc., AAAS; mem. Nat. Acad. Scis., European Phys. Soc., Am. Acad. Arts and Scis., Sigma Xi. Avocations: music, gardening. Home: 972 Creston Rd Berkeley CA 94708-1544 Office: U Calif 366 La Conte Hall 7300 Physics Dept Berkeley CA 94720*

KNIGHT, WILLIAM EDWARD, university administrator, educator; b. Warren, Ohio, June 6, 1965; s. William E. and Laverne (Readman) K.; m. Adriene J. Kelly, Dec. 12, 1992. BS in Edn., Kent (Ohio) State U., 1987, MEd, 1989, PhD, 1992. Coord. acad. assessment and evaluation svcs. regional campus Kent State U., 1990-92; vis. scholar U. Mich., Ann Arbor, 1992; asst. prof. ednl. leadership Ga. So. U., Statesboro, 1993-96, asst. dir. instl. rsch. and planning, 1993-95, dir. instl. rsch., 1995-96; asst. prof. higher edn., dir. instl. rsch. Bowling Green (Ohio) State U., 1996—. Mem. Assn. for Instl. Rsch., Ohio Assn. for Instl. Rsch. Office: Bowling Green State U 301 McFall Bowling Green OH 43403

KNIGHT, WILLIAM J. (PETE KNIGHT), state senator, retired air force officer; b. Noblesville, Ind., Nov. 18, 1929; s. William T. and Mary Emma (Illyes) K.; m. Helena A Stone, June 7, 1958; children: William Peter, David, Stephen; m. Gail A. Johnson, Sept. 3, 1983. BS, Air Force Inst. Tech., 1958; student, Indsl. Coll. Armed Forces, 1973-74. Commd. 2d lt. USAF, 1953, advanced through grades to col., 1971; fighter pilot Kinross AFB, Mich., 1953-56; exptl. test pilot Edwards AFB, Calif., 1958-69; exptl. test pilot, Viet Nam, 1969-70; dir. test and deployment F-15 program, 1976; dir. Flight Attack System Program Office, 1977-79; vice comdr. Air Force Flight Test Ctr. Edwards AFB, 1979-82; ret. USAF, 1982; mayor City of Palmdale, Calif., 1988-92; mem. Calif. Assembly, Sacramento, 1992-96, Calif. Senate, Sacramento, 1996—; v.p. Eidetics Internat., Torrance, Calif., 1988-92. Decorated D.F.C. with 2 oak leaf clusters, Legion of Merit with 2 oak leaf clusters, Air medal with 11 oak leaf clusters, Astronauts Wings; recipient Octave Chanute award, 1968, Harmon Internat. trophy, 1968, citation of honor Air Force Assn., 1969 winner Allison Jet Trophy Race, 1954; named to Nat. Aviation Hall of Fame, 1988, Lancaster Aerospace Walk of Honor, 1990, Internat. Space Hall of Fame, 1998. Fellow AIAA (assoc.), Soc. Exptl. Test Pilots (past pres.); mem. Air Force Assn., Internat. Order of Characters, Aerospace Primus Club, Daedalians, Elks, Shriners. Holder world's speed record for winged aircraft, 4520 m.p.h., 1967. Home: 220 Eagle Ln Palmdale CA 93551-3613 Office: 2196 State Capital Sacramento CA 95814

KNIGHT, WILLIAM V., geologist; b. Moundsville, W.Va., May 23, 1927; s. Marion Eugene and Alma (Bonar) K.; m. Martha Ashworth, Dec. 27, 1951; children: William Harold, James Frederick, Robert Bruce. Student, W.Va. U.; BS in Geology, Ohio State U.; MS, U. Tulsa. Registered geologist; chartered geologist, U.K.; cert. profl. geologist; European Geologist. Tchr. U. Tulsa; owner geologic consulting co.; exec. dir. Am. Inst. Profl. Geologists, 1989—. Named Disting. West Virginian, 1996. Mem. Am. Inst. Profl. Geologists (charter, sect. pres.), Am. Assn. Petroleum Geologists, Soc. Exploration Geophysicists, Assn. Ground Water Scientists and Engrs., Assn. Engring. Geologists, Geol. Soc. London, Tulsa Geol. Soc. (hon.). Office: Am Inst Profl Geologists 7828 Vance Dr Ste 103 Arvada CO 80003-2125*

KNIGHTS, EDWIN MUNROE, pathologist; b. Providence, Dec. 25, 1924; s. Edwin Munroe and Viola Ruth (Koreb) K.; m. Ruth Lindsay Currie, Sept. 23, 1961; children—Edwin B., Jessie B., Ross D., David J. A.B., Brown U., 1948; M.D., Cornell U., 1948. Intern Bellevue Hosp., N.Y.C., 1948-49; resident in pathology R.I. Hosp., Providence, 1949-50, Henry Ford Hosp, Detroit, 1952-54; assoc. pathologist Harper Hosp., Detroit, 1954; dir. labs. Hurley Hosp., Flint, Mich., 1957-62, Providence Hosp., Southfield, Mich., 1963-75; dir. Northland Oakland Med. Labs., Southfield, Mich., 1964—, Bio Sci. Labs., Detroit, 1975-85, Smith Kline Bio-Sci. Labs., Detroit, 1985-89; dir. labs. Kern Hosp., Warren, Mich., 1977-81; pres. Coll. Terr. Inc., Flint, Mich., 1968—; dir. Performance Assurance Profls., Bloomfield Hills, 1988-94; pres. Life Sci. Inc., Flint, 1971-72, Vet. Med. Labs., 1973-75; clin. prof. pathology Mich. State U., 1974-75; rep. Comprehensive Health Planning Council S.E. Mich., 1973-85, trustee, 1986-87; mem. lab peer rev. com. Mich Dept. Social Services, 1979-84; med. dir. Smith Kline Beecham Labs., Detroit, 1990-92, Nat. Health Labs., Flint, Mich., 1992-94; pres. Life Sci. Inc., Grantham, 1996—; pathologist Project Hope, Indonesia and Vietnam, 1961, Peru, 1962, Ecuador, 1964. Author: Ultramicro Methods for Clinical Laboratories, 1957, 2d edit., 1962; editor: Minicomputers in the Clinical Laboratory, 1970, Lifelines, 1971-75; contbg. editor Jour. Foot Surgery, 1983-89; contbr. numerous articles to profl. jours.; patentee in field. Mem. adv. coun. New Eng. Hist. Geneal. Soc.; mem. long range planning com. Ea. Cmty. Assn. Served to lt. USN, 1944-46, 50-52, ETO, Korea. USPHS grantee, 1957-66. Fellow ACP, Coll. Am. Pathologists, Am.Soc. Clin. Pathologists (Mich. councillor 1966-68); mem. AMA, Oakland County Med. Soc. (pres. 1974), Mich. Soc. Pathologists (pres. 1970, del. Mich. State Med. Soc. 1986-93), Internat. Acad. Pathology, Mich. State Med. Soc., Assn. Clin. Scientists, Gen. Soc. Mayflower Descs., Roger Williams Family Assn. Home and Office: 164 Top O'World Rd Box 1303 Grantham NH 03753-1303

KNIGHTS, RONALD MICHAEL, business educator; b. Bronx, N.Y., Mar. 6, 1943; s. Nehemiah and Eramae (Williams) K.; m. Mimi A. Beauman, July 26, 1980 (dec. May 1991); children: Veronica, Varron. BBA, U. N.Mex., 1968, M of Vocat. Counseling, 1972, PhD in Counseling Psychology, 1976. Sr. counselor Office of Manpower and Devel., Albuquerque, 1968-72; pers. counselor employe adv. City of Albuquerque, 1972-79; mgr. employee rels. RMS/Citicorp., Englewood, Colo., 1979-81; asst. prof. mgmt. Sch. Bus. Met. State Coll., Denver, 1982-89, assoc. prof. mgmt., Sch. Bus., 1989-96, prof. mgmt., Sch. Bus., 1996—; mem. minority affairs adv. coun. U. Colo., Denver,; cons. U.S. West Comms., Denver, 1987-88, Pioneer Steel-Tube Distbrs., Henderson, Colo., 1989-90, Colo. Dept. Transp., Denver, 1995—; co-founder, pres. African-Am. Leadership Inst., Denver, 1990—, pres., 1998—; designer, developer Bus. and Tech. Asst. for Women and Minorities in Constrn. Industry, 1994. With USAF, 1969-75. Recipient Minority Intern Advsior award State Farm Ins. Co., 1989, Black History Month award U.S. HUD, 1995; named African Am. Who Makes a Difference, Urban Spectrum Newspaper, 1991. Mem. Am. Jour. Case Rsch., N.Am. Case Rsch. Assn., Soc. Case Rsch. Democrat. Roman Catholic. Avocations: reading, jogging. Home: 3126 Clayton St Denver CO 80205-4228

KNILANS, MICHAEL JEROME, supermarkets executive; b. Columbus, Ohio, Mar. 3, 1927; s. Alfred Sidney and Bernice (Meyers) K.; m. Anne Eberhardt, June 15, 1947; children: Michael, Kyleen, Christine, Timothy, Suzanne. BS, Ohio State U., 1949. With Big Bear Stores Co., Columbus, 1942-89, mdse. mgr., 1952-61, v.p., 1961-70, exec. v.p., 1970-76, pres., 1976-89, also dir.; bd. dirs. Price Chopper Supermarkets, Schenectady, N.Y. Chmn. bd. Ohio Workers Compensation Bd., 1989-95; bd. dirs. Children's Hosp., Columbus, Mt. Carmel Coll. Nursing, Columbus; v.p. East Ctr. region Boy Scouts Am. With USNR, 1944-46, PTO. Mem. Ohio Coun. Retail Mchts. (treas.), Better Bus. Bur. (pres. 1978), C. of C., Masons, Shriners, Jesters, Rotary (pres. 1981—, dist. gov. 1993-94). Republican. Home: 1119 Kingsdale Ter Columbus OH 43220-4946

KNIPLING, EDWARD FRED, retired research entomologist, agricultural administrator; b. Port Lavaca, Tex., Mar. 20, 1909; s. Henry John and Hulda Lena (Rasch) K.; m. Phoebe Rebecca Hall; children: Edwina, Anita, Edward B., Gary D., Ronald R. B.S., Tex. A&M U., 1930; M.S., Iowa State U., 1932, Ph.D., 1947; D.Sc. (hon.), Catawba Coll., 1962, N.D. State U., 1970, Clemson U., 1972. With USDA, various locations, 1931-73; dir. entomology research div. USDA, Beltsville, Md., 1953-73. Author: Principles of Insect Population Suppression, 1979, Principles of Insect Parasitism Analysis from New Perspectives, 1992; contbr. more than 200 articles to profl. jours. Recipient Nat. Medal Sci., 1966, Rockefeller Pub. Svcs. award, 1966, Pres.'s award for Disting. Fed. Civilian Svc., 1971, World Food prize World Food Prize Found., 1992, Sci. and Tech. Found. Japan prize, 1995; named to Agrl. Rsch. Svc. Sci. Hall of Fame. Fellow Entomol. Soc. Am. (pres. 1952); mem. NAS, Am. Acad. Arts and Scis. Club: Cosmos. Avocations: bow and arrow hunting; fishing; hiking. Home: 2623 Military Rd Arlington VA 22207-5117*

KNIPPERS, DIANE LEMASTERS, association president; b. Rushville, Ind., Jan. 6, 1952; m. Edward C. Knippers, Jr. BA in History, Asbury Coll., 1972; MA in Sociology, U. Tenn., 1974. Teaching asst. U. Tenn., 1972-73; assoc. editor, asst. editor, editorial asst. Good News Mag., 1974-80, assoc. exec. sec., editor, 1980-82; exec. v.p., deputy dir., program dir., dir. orgn. IRD, 1982-93; pres. Inst. Religion and Democracy, 1993—. Office: Inst Religion and Democracy 1521 16th St NW Ste 300 Washington DC 20036-1463

KNIPSCHEER, CAROL S., English language educator; b. Aug. 27, 1951. BA in History, French, Secondary Edn., Carroll Coll., Waukesha, Wis., 1973; MA in ESL, U. Ill., 1978. Instr. EFL Peace Corps, Ivory Coast, 1973-75; instr. ESL and French Urbana (Ill.) Pub. Schs., 1976-79; coord. English for tech. purposes Agy. for Agrl. R&D Insts., Bogor, Indonesia, 1981-84; dist. coord. ESL Conway (Ark.) Pub. Schs., 1987-90; dir. intensive English program U. Ctrl. Ark., Conway, 1991—. Email: carolk@ecom.uca.edu. Office: U Ctrl Ark Internat Programs 109 S Minton Hall Conway AR 72035

KNIPSCHILD, ROBERT, artist, educator; b. Freeport, Ill., Aug. 17, 1927; s. Leon Francis and Alice (Walsh) K.; m. Patricia Ann O'Connor, Sept. 1, 1949; children—Abby Clare Knipschild Weber, Amy Louise Knipschild Wermeling, John Eliot, Jill Anne Knipschild Harsch, Sarah Kate. B.A., U. Wis., 1950; M.F.A., Cranbrook Acad. Art, 1951. Tchr. Balt. Mus. Art, 1951-52, Am. U., 1952, U. Conn., 1954-56, U. Wis., 1956-60, U. Iowa, 1960-66; prof. art, dir. grad. studies fine arts U. Cin., 1966-90, prof. emeritus fine arts, 1990—. Exhbns. include, Mus. Modern Art, Whitney Mus., Met. Mus., Corcoran Mus., Boston Mus., Carnegie Inst., also in Europe, Japan and Australia. Served with AUS, 1945-47. Office: 1159 Hill Crest Rd Cincinnati OH 45224-3223

KNISELY, DOUGLAS CHARLES, accountant; b. Cleve., May 7, 1948; s. Victor D. and Lydia (Sichau) K.; m. Ruth Hedges, Dec. 24, 1971; children: Brent, Megan, Amanda. BS, Ohio State U., 1971; MBA, Capital U., 1981. CPA, cert. fin. planner, Ohio. Draftsman A.H. Sichau, Architect, Brook Park, Ohio, 1971-73; auditor E.C. Redman, CPA, Columbus, Ohio, 1973-76; ptnr. Bolon, Hart & Turley, Columbus, 1976-80; prin. Bolon, Hart & Buehler, Columbus, 1980-92; pres. Controllership Svcs. & Fin. Planning, Inc., Columbus, 1992—; trustee Gamma Tau Corp., Columbus, 1974; adj. prof. acctg. Columbus State Community Coll., 1993-98. Mem., past pres. St. John's Evang. Luth. Ch.; bd. dirs., treas. Luth. Sr. City, 1986-90; mission interpreter Am. Luth. Ch., Mpls., 1985-87; bd. dirs. Luth. Social Svcs. Ctrl. Ohio, 1990-92, Fitness Gymnastic Ctr. Found., 1998—; treas. So. Ohio Synod Evang. Luth. Ch. in Am., 1994-98. Named one of Outstanding Young Men of Am., 1978, Disting. Citizen, Ohio Ho. of Reps., 1994. Mem. Am. Inst. CPA's, Ohio Soc. CPAs (bd. dirs. 1990-93). Club: Toastmasters (pres. Midday chpt. 1980-81, Outstanding Area Gov. 1982). Home: 5875 Grove City Rd Grove City OH 43123-9509 Office: Controllership Svcs & Fin Planning 65 E State St Ste 1000 Columbus OH 43215-4216

KNISELY, RALPH FRANKLIN, retired microbiologist; b. Altoona, Pa., Mar. 30, 1927; s. Calvin Ross and Freida Pauline (Neher) K.; m. Joan Marie Fitzgerald, Jan. 29, 1949 (div. 1955); 1 child, Patricia Ann; m. Ann Martin, May 21, 1960. BS, Pa. State U., 1953, postgrad., 1953. Bacteriologist Altoona Hosp., 1953-56, adminstrv. asst. to pathologist, 1957-59; microbiologist Chem. Corps Dept. Army, Ft. Detrick, Md., 1959-72; rsch. microbiologist Edgewood Arsenal, Aberdeen Proving Ground, Md., 1972-86. Contbg. author: Rapid Identification of Biological Agents, 1966; contbr. articles to Jour. Bacteriology, European Jour. Microbiology. Pres. Eastview Civic Assn., Frederick, Md., 1968-69. With USN, 1945-46, 50-51; capt. Res. ret., 1945-87. Mem. Am. Soc. for Microbiology (emeritus), Rsch. Soc. Am. (emeritus), Assn. Mil. Surgeons U.S. (life), N.Y. Acad. Sci. (emeritus), Ret. Officer's Assn. (chpt. v.p. 1969-70), AARP (bd. dirs. chpt. 636 1989-90, 97-98, chpt. pres. 1995-96), Fleet Res. Assn., Nat. Assn. Ret. Fed. Employees (pres. chpt. 409 1995-97, bd. dirs. 1997-98), Internat. Platform Assn., Nat. Sojourners (pres. chpt. 354 1965, 81, sec. 1986—), George Washington Masonic Stamp Club (pres. 1978-80, sec. 1988-98), Knisely Reunion Assn. (pres., historian 1994-95), Am. Legion, Am. Philatelic Soc. (life), Masonic Rsch. Soc., Philalethes Soc., Quatuor Coronati Corr. Cir. (London), Sampson WWII Vets. (Md. dir., exec. trustee), Legion of Honor, Hagerstown Shrine Club, Masons, Shriners, Elks, Tall Cedars of Lebanon. Republican. Lutheran. Avocations: family genealogy, amateur radio. Home: 7400 Skyline Dr Frederick MD 21702-3652

KNISELY, ROBERT A., federal agency administrator; b. Chgo., Mar. 19, 1940; m. Marty Beyer, 1974; two children. AB, Harvard Coll., 1962; JD, Georgetown U., 1972. Bar: D.C. 1973. Ops. rsch. analyst Dept. of Def., 1964-65; sys. analyst Ctr. for Naval Analyses, 1965-67; CAP monitoring staff Office Econ. Opportunity, 1967-69; chief evaluation and urban sys. br. Ctr. for Cmty. Planning Dept. Health, Edn. and Welfare, 1969-72; dir. cmty. mgmt. sys. divsn., chair urban info. sys. Dept. Housing and Urban Devel., 1972-73; sr. atty. adviser Office of Gen. Counsel, Fed. Energy Adminstrn., 1973-74; dep. gen. counsel, staff dir. Presdl. Clemency Bd., The White House, 1974-75; dir. Office Program Evaluation Dept. Commerce, 1975-77; dir. Office Planning and Budget Sys. Dept. Energy, 1977-78; dep. exec. dir. Consumer Product Safety Commn., 1979-81; exec. asst. to the dir. ACTION, 1981-82; dep. chair mgmt. Nat. Endowment for the Arts, 1982-84; sr. mem. corp. devel. Sys. Rsch. and Applications Co., 1984-89; dep. asst. sec. for budget and programs, 1989-91; spl. asst. to the sec. and dir. Drug Enforcement and Program Compliance, 1991-92; dep. dir. resources bur. transp. stats. Dept. Transp., 1992—, dep. dir.. regulatory rev., nat. performance rev. Office of Vice Pres., 1995—. With USMCR, 1962-67. Avocations: scuba diving, photography. Office: Dept Transp 400 7th St SW Washington DC 20590

KNISKERN, JOSEPH WARREN, lawyer; b. Coral Gables, Fla., July 7, 1951; s. Kenneth Felix and Elise (Scofield) K.; m. Cheryl Rybka. BSBA, U. Fla., 1973, JD cum laude, 1976. Bar: Fla. 1976; cert. real estate atty., Fla.; cert. family mediator, Fla.; registered real estate salesperson, Fla. Assoc. Smathers & Thompson, Miami, Fla., 1976-83, ptnr., 1983-87; ptnr. Kelley Drye & Warren, Miami, 1987-93; pvt. practice Coral Gables, Fla., 1993—; authorized agt. Attys. Title Ins. Fund, Lawyers Title Ins. Corp. Author: When the Vow Breaks: A Survival and Recovery Guide for Christians Facing Divorce, 1993, Courting Disaster: What Runaway Litigation is Costing You and What Can Be Done to Stop the Fallout, 1995. Trustee Miami-Gables Ch. of Christ, 1979-86. Mem. ABA, Fla. Bar, Dade County Bar Assn., Christian Legal Soc., Cmty. Assns. Inst., Inst. for Christian Conciliation, Am. Assn. Christian Counselors. Republican. Office: 1550 Madruga Ave Ste 332 Coral Gables FL 33146-3071

KNIZESKI, JUSTINE ESTELLE, insurance company executive; b. Glen Cove, N.Y., June 4, 1954; d. John Martin and Elsie Beatrice (Gozelski) Knizeski. BA, Conn. Coll., 1976; M. Mgmt., Northwestern U., 1981. Customer svc. supr. Brunswick Savs., Freeport, Maine, 1977-79; investment analyst Bankers Life and Casualty Co., Chgo., 1980-83; dir. corp. planning and analysis, 1983-87; dir. budgets, cost acctg. Blue Cross/Blue Shield of Ill., 1987-97; dir. planning, budgets and analysis, 1997—. Chmn. bd. dirs. Alternatives, Inc., Chgo., 1984-87, vice chmn., 1987-91, sec., 1991-92, bd. dirs., 1983-84, mem. ad hoc fin. com., 1998-99; mem. Chgo. Coun. Fgn. Rels., 1984-85. Mem. Planning Forum. Avocations: sailing, bicycling, traveling, painting.

KNOBBE, LOUIS JOSEPH, lawyer; b. Carroll, Iowa, Apr. 6, 1932; s. Louis C. and Elsie M. (Praeger) K.; m. Jeanette M. Sganga, Apr. 3, 1954; children: Louis, Michael, Nancy, John, Catherine. BSEE, Iowa State U., 1953; JD, Loyola U., L.A., 1959. Bar: Calif. 1960, U.S. Supreme Ct. 1963; U.S. Patent and Trademark Office. Tech. staff Bell Telephone Labs., 1953-54; patent engr. GE, Washington, 1955-56, N.Am. Aviation, Downey, Calif., 1956-59; patent lawyer Beckman Instruments, Fullerton, Calif., 1959-62; co-founder, ptnr. Knobbe, Martens, Olson & Bear, Newport Beach, Calif., 1962—; lectr. Am. Intellectual Property Law Assn., Computer Law Assn., Inc., L.A. Intellectual Property Law Assn., San Diego Bar Assn., Orange County Patent Law Assn.; adj. prof. Sch. Law U. San Diego, 1987—. Co-author: Attorney's Guide to Trade Secrets, 1972, 2d edit., 1996, How to Handle Basic Patent, 1992; contbg. author: Using Intellectual Property Rights to Protect Domestic Markets, 1986; contbr. articles to profl. jours. Bd. dirs. Orange County (Calif.) Performing Arts Ctr., 1975-83, Orange County chpt. Assn. Corp. Growth; past pres. Philharmonic Soc. Orange County; bd. mem., past v.p. Opera Pacific, Orange County. Fellow Inst. Advancement Engring.; mem. ABA, IEEE (past chmn. Orange County sect., Centennial medal 1984), Am. Intellectual Property Law Assn., Am. Arbitration Soc. (mem. panel neutrals), State Bar Calif., Orange County Bar Assn. (mem. civil mediation panel), Orange County Patent Law Assn., San Diego Patent Law Assn., Licensing Execs. Soc., Santa Ana North Rotary, First Friday Friars, Pacific Club, Balboa Yacht Club, Phi Kappa Phi, Tau Beta Pi, Eta Kappa Nu. Avocations: boating, still and video photography, travel and exploration in Lake Powell, Death Valley, deserts of Arizona and Baja, California. Office: 620 Newport Center Dr Fl 16 Newport Beach CA 92660-6420

KNOBEL, DALE THOMAS, history educator, university administrator; b. East Cleveland, Ohio, Sept. 14, 1949; s. Harry Spencer and Gwynne Ann (Thomas) K.; m. Tina Hess Jamieson, June 19, 1971; children: Allison Hess, Matthew Winsper. BA, Yale U., 1971; PhD, Northwestern U., 1976. Asst. prof. history Northwestern U., Evanston, Ill., 1976-77, Tex. A&M U., College Station, 1977-84; assoc. prof. history Tex. A&M U., 1984—, dir. univ. hons. prog., 1987-92, exec. dir. honors programs and acad. scholarships, 1992—, interim assoc. provost for undergrad. programs, 1995-96. Book rev. editor Jour. of the Early Republic, 1987-89; editor Forum for Honors; author: Paddy and the Republic: Ethnicity and Nationality in Antebellum America, 1985; co-author: Prejudice, 1982; contbr. articles to profl. jours. Exec. committeeman Brazos County Dem. Party, Bryan, Tex., 1984—; chmn. Bryan Hist. Landmark Commn., 1987-93; trustee Bryan Pub. Libr., 1989-92, Brazos Valley Mus. of Natural History, 1994—. Am. Assn. State and Local History grantee, 1984; NEH grantee, 1978; NSF grantee, 1972-74; W.K. Kellogg Found. grantee, 1985-87. Mem. Nat. Collegiate Hons. Coun. (exec. com.), Great Plains Reg. Hons. Coun., Orgn. Am. Historians, Immigration History Soc., Soc. for Hist. of the Early Am. Republic, Am. Conf. on Irish Studies, Phi Kappa Phi, Phi Beta Delta. Methodist. Home: 204 Broadway W Granville OH 43023-1120 Office: Tex A&M U Univ Honors Program College Station TX 77843

KNOBELSDORFF, KRISTINA LOUISE MARIE, English language educator; b. Boston; d. Adam J. and Kerry M. (Nash) K. BA, Trinity Coll., Hartford, Conn., 1986; postgrad., Lyme Acad. Fine Arts, Old Lyme, Conn., 1989-92; MA in Liberal Studies, Albertus Magnus Coll., 1995; postgrad., U. Conn., 1998—. Staff asst. Monitor Radio, Boston, 19986-87; editl. asst. anesthesiology dept. Yale U., New Haven, 1989-91; ops. planning coord. Chesebrough-Ponds USA, Clinton, Conn., 1992-94; coord. Can. ops. Chesebrough-Ponds USA, Clinton, 1994; grad. asst. Albertus Magnus Coll., New Haven, 1994-95; editl. asst. Blackbirch Press, Woodbridge, Conn., 1996-97; lect. English Albertus Magnus Coll., 1997-98. Exhibited in group show Killingworth Art Show, 1989 (Best in Show award). Tutor ESL, Westbrook, Conn.; vol. Christmas in April, Hartford, 1995. Mem. Kappa Gamma Pi. Avocations: oil painting, drawing, horseback riding, travel, tennis. Home: 21 Great Hammock Rd Old Saybrook CT 06475-2003

KNOBLACH, JAMES MICHAEL, state represenative; b. St. Cloud, Minn., Nov. 5, 1957; s. Marcellus Peter and Vivian Joyce (Lundgren) K.; m. Janet Helena Hughes, Sept. 3, 1988; children: Daniel, Laura. BS in Econs. and Bus. Adminstrn., St. John's U., 1979; MBA, Harvard U., 1981; MA in Am. Govt., Georgetown U., 1987. CPA, Minn.; cert. real estate broker. Gen. mgr. Chem-Waste Control divsn. MediSense, Inc., Mpls., 1983-85; pres. North Star Direct, St. Cloud, Minn., 1987-94, North Star Resources, St. Cloud, 1995—; state rep. Minn. Ho. of Reps., St. Cloud, 1995—, asst. majority leader, chair capital investment com.; dir. Advanced UroSci., White Bear Lake, Minn., 1995—, Harbinger Med., Eden Prairie, 1996—. Dir. Ctrl. Minn. Boy Scouts, St. Cloud, 1994—. Republican. Avocations: mountain climbing, running. Office: Minn House of Reps 100 Constitution Ave Saint Paul MN 55155-1232

KNOBLAUCH, EDWARD CHARLES, baseball player; b. Houston, July 7, 1968. Ed., Tex. A&M U. Second baseman Minn. Twins, 1991-98, N.Y. Yankees, 1998—. Named Am. League Rookie of Yr., The Sporting News, 1991, Baseball Writers Am., 1991; named to Am. League All-Star Team, 1992, 94, 96. Office: NY Yankees Yankee Stadium 161st St and River Ave Bronx NY 10451*

KNOBLAUCH, MARK GEORGE, librarian, consultant; b. Ft. Wayne, Ind., Oct. 8, 1947; s. Marcus George and Helen Edna (Helmke) K. B.A., Valparaiso U., 1969; A.M.L.S., U. Mich., 1970. Cataloger Chgo. Pub. Library, 1970-73, head serials dept., 1973-78, head acquisitions div., 1978-84, dir. tech. svcs., 1985-91, dir. collection mgmt., 1992-96; dep. exec. dir. Pub. Libr. Assoc., 1997-99; columnist Arts Sect., Chgo. Tribune newspaper, 1981-91. Contbr. articles to profl. jours. Judge U.S. Indsl. Film Festival, Chgo., 1976-90; chmn. 1st St. Paul's Luth. Ch., Chgo., 1979-83; bd. dirs. Printer's Row Book Fair, 1986—. Mem. ALA, Ill. Library Assn., Assn. Library Collections & Tech. Svcs. (exec. bd. 1990), Beta Phi Mu. Home: 435 W Surf St Chicago IL 60657-6132*

KNOBLE, WILLIAM AVERY, government finance officer, accountant; b. Fountain Hill, Pa., Jan. 22, 1948; s. Thomas Barber and Hazel Leola

(Hefner) K.; m. Constance Haig Whipple, May 23, 1973 (div. Jan. 12, 1990); children: Gretchen Haig, Adrienne Avery. BSBA, Susquehanna U., 1970. CPA, Fla.; cert. govt. fin. officer. Fin. officer Charlotte County Dist. Sch. Bd., Port Charlotte, Fla., 1975-82; fin. dir. City of Punta Gorda, Fla., 1982-87, Charlotte County Fla. Clk. of Cir. Ct., Port Charlotte, 1987—. Mem. AICPAs, Govt. Fin. Officers Assn., Fla. Inst. CPAs, Fla. Govt. Fin. Officer Assn., S.W. Fla. Govt. Fin. Officer Assn. Avocations: fishing, freshwater, saltwater. Office: Charlotte County Clk Circuit Ct 18500 Murdock Cir Punta Gorda FL 33948-1068

KNOBLER, ALFRED EVERETT, ceramic engineer, manufacturing company executive, publisher; b. N.Y.C., Mar. 4, 1915; s. Samuel and Mildred (Weisz) K.; children—Peter Stephen, Joanna Gabin. B.S. in Ceramic Engring, Va. Poly. Inst., 1938. Engr. U.S. War Dept., Phila., 1942-44; Fed. Tel. & Tel. U.S. War Dept., N.Y.C., 1944-45; CEO Pilgrim Glass Corp., Ceredo, W.Va., 1949—; pres. Knobler Internat. Ltd., Moonachie, N.J., 1950—, Knobler Energy Assocs., Inc., West Hamlin, W.Va., 1976—. Home: 301 W 57th St New York NY 10019-3114 Office: Knobler Internat Ltd 225 5th Ave New York NY 10010-1102

KNOBLOCH, FERDINAND J., psychiatrist, educator; b. Prague, Czechoslovakia, Aug. 15, 1916; emigrated to Can., 1970; s. Ferdin and Marie (Verunac) K.; m. Susana Hartman (dec. 1944 victim of Holocaust); m. Jirina Skorkovska, Sept. 5, 1947; children: Katerina, Yohana. Maturity degree, Realgymnasium, Prague, 1927-35; student med. sch., Charles U., Prague, 1935-46; psychoanalytic tng., 1945-53. Successively lectr., asst. prof., assoc. prof. psychiatry Charles U., 1946-70; mem. faculty U. B.C., Vancouver, Can., 1970—; prof. psychiatry U. B.C., Vancouver, 1971-83, prof. emeritus, 1983—; clin. dir. Day House Univ. Hosp., 1972-90; vis. prof. U. Havana, 1963, U. Ill., Chgo., 1968-69, Columbia U., 1969-70, Albert Einstein Med. Coll., 1970; pres. European seminar mental health and family WHO, 1961, 3d Internat. Congress Psychodrama, 1968; co-chmn. Internat. Symposium Non-Verbal Aspects and Techniques of Psychotherapy, 1974; hon. dir. psychodrama Moreno Inst., N.Y.C., 1974. Author: (with Jirina Knobloch) Forensic Psychiatry, 1967 (award Czechoslovak Med. Soc. 1968), Psychotherapy, 1968, Neurosis and You, 1962, 63, 68, Integrated Psychotherapy, 1979 (transl. into German 1983, Japanese 1984, Czech 1993, Chinese, 1995); contbr. articles on psychotherapy integration, psychology of music and evolutionary psychology to profl. jours. Mem. Czechoslovak Soc. Advancement Psychoanalysis and Integration of Psychotherapy (pres. 1968-72), Am. Acad. Psychoanalysis, Polish Psychiat. Assn. (corr.), Am. Psychiat. Assn., Can. Psychiat. Assn., Am. Group Psychotherapy Assn., Can. Soc. for Integrated Psychotherapy and Psychoanalysis (pres. 1972—), World Psychiat. Assn. (co-chmn. sect. psychotherapy 1983-93, chmn. 1993-96). Political prisoner of Gestapo, 1943-45. Home and Office: 4137 W 12th Ave, Vancouver, BC Canada V6R 2P5

KNOBLOCH, IRVING WILLIAM, retired biology educator, author; b. Buffalo, Mar. 1, 1907; s. Johann Philipp and Henrietta Georgia (Linke) K.; m. Natalie Agatha Mueller, Dec. 28, 1934; children: Karen Gail, Keith Rickard, Craig Geoffrey. BA, SUNY, Buffalo, 1930, MA, 1932; PhD, Iowa State U., 1942. Wildlife specialist U.S. Dept. Interior, Red House, N.Y., 1933-37; asst. prof. biology SUNY, Buffalo, 1942-45; from asst. prof. to prof. Mich. State U., East Lansing, 1945-76; freelance writer East Lansing, 1976—. Author: Ferns etc. Chihuahua, Mexico, 1962, Prelim List Plant Coll. Mexico, 1983, Livable Planets Hard to Find, 1995, others; editor: Readings in Biological Science, 3 edits., 1948-75; contbr. over 150 articles to profl. jours. Grantee NSF, 1964-67, Ford Found., 1967-71, Mich. State U., 1967-69, Sigma Xi. Mem. AAUP (v.p. and pres. local), Am. Fern Soc. (nat. v.p. and pres. 1968-70), Bot. Soc. Am. (chmn. teaching sect. 1968-69), Hardy Fern Found., Nature Conservancy, Mich. Nature Assn., Am. Inst. Biol. Sci., Nat. Wildlife Fedn., Sierra Club, Mich. Bot. Club, Planned Parenthood, Zero Population Growth, Greenpeace, World Wildlife Fund, others. Republican. Avocation: gardening. Home: 2530 Marfitt Rd Apt 319 East Lansing MI 48823-6303

KNODERER, DAVID LETTERFLY, artist, educator; b. Portland, Ind., Feb. 8, 1953; s. William Henry and Arleen Gladys (Reuse) K. Apprentice Sign Shop, Longwood, Fla., 1973-74; signmaker, lettering artist, gold leaf gilder, muralist Sarasota, Fla., 1974-96; resident artist Lazydays RV Superctr., Tampa, Fla., 1996—. Participant Sarasota Unity Artist First Ann. Show, 1995, 2d Ann. Artists Show, 1997. Winner 1986 Signs of the Times Design Competition, 1986. Mem. Soc. Gilders, Am. Acad. Equine Artists, Family Motor Coach Assn., Circus Hist. Soc. Avocations: dressage and Haute Ecole horsemanship. Home: 4111 El Shaddiai Sq Plant City FL 33565

KNOEBEL, SUZANNE BUCKNER, cardiologist, medical educator; b. Ft. Wayne, Ind., Dec. 13, 1926; d. Doster and Marie (Lewis) Buckner. A.B., Goucher Coll., 1948; M.D., Ind. U.-Indpls., 1960. Diplomate: Am. Bd. Internal Medicine. Asst. prof. medicine Ind. U., Indpls., 1966-69, assoc. prof., 1969-72, prof., 1972-77, Krannert prof., 1977—; asst. dean rsch. Ind. U., Indpls., 1975-85; assoc. dir. Krannert Inst. Cardiology, Indpls., 1974-90; asst. chief cardiology sect. Richard L. Roudebush VA Med. Ctr., Indpls., 1982-90; editor-in-chief ACC Current Jour. Rev., 1992—. Fellow Am. Coll. Cardiology (v.p. 1980-81, pres. 1982-83); mem. Am. Fedn. Clin. Research, Assn. Univ. Cardiologists. Office: Ind U Sch Medicine 1111 W 10th St Indianapolis IN 46202-4800

KNOEDLER, ELMER L., retired chemical engineer; b. Gloucester, N.J., Feb. 12, 1912; s. Elmer L. and Carolyn (Belle) K.; m. Mabel Dyer Todd, Jan. 15, 1966; children: Dianne, Homer. ME, Cornell U., 1934, MS, 1936; PhD, Columbia, 1952. Registered profl. engr., 3 states. With Atlantic Mfg. Co., 1934-35; asst. supt. charge Davis Emergency Equipment Co., 1937-38; charge research and devel. metal powder process Metals Disintegrating Co., 1939-41, cons. chem. engr., sr. field engr., 1941-82; partner Sheppard T. Powell & Assocs., Balt.; Past mem. Md. Bd. for Registration Engrs. and Land Surveyors. Contbr. numerous articles tech., profl. jours. Fellow Am. Inst. Chemists, ASME (past chmn. com. water conditioning and indsl. waste); mem. Am. Inst. Chem. Engrs. (chmn. Balt. sect. 1953), Am. Chem. Soc., Am. Inst. Cons. Engrs., Sigma Xi, Phi Lambda Upsilon. Home: 400 Avinger Ln Apt 321 Davidson NC 28036-9759 Office: 1915 Aliceanna St Baltimore MD 21231-3014

KNOELL, NANCY JEANNE, kindergarten educator; b. Boone, Iowa, Dec. 12, 1941; d. Wallace Knute and Dorothy Althea (Walker) Johnson; m. Gerald Dwain Brown, June 21, 1970 (div. Dec. 1987); children: Renae Jeanne, Arlan Gerald; m. Lawrence Hubert Knoell, Oct. 19, 1991. BS, Gustavus Adolphus Coll., 1963; postgrad., Hamlin U., U. Minn., Coll. St. Thomas. Cert. tchr. elem. K-6, Minn. Tchr. kindergarten Rochester (Minn.) Pub. Schs., 1963-66, Robbinsdale Area Ind. Sch. Dist. 281, New Hope, Minn., 1966—; mem. sci. design team Robbinsdale Area Ind. Sch. Dist. 281, New Hope; mentor to 1st year tchr., 1995-96. Mem. Am. Fedn. Tchrs., Assn. Childhood Edn. Internat. (bldg. rep., sec., pres. Robbinsdale br.), Delta Kappa Gamma. Lutheran. Avocations: ballroom dancing, running, golf, roses, piano. Home: 8209 Toledo Ave N Brooklyn Park MN 55443-2228 Office: Neill Elem Sch 6600 27th Ave N Minneapolis MN 55427-3042

KNOEPFLMACHER, ULRICH CAMILLUS, literature educator; b. Munich, Germany, June 26, 1931; U.S. citizen; s. George A. and Hilde (Weiss) K.; married; 4 children. AB, U. Calif., Berkeley, 1955, MA, 1957; PhD, Princeton U., 1961. From instr. to assoc. prof. U. Calif., Berkeley, 1961-69, Humanities Rsch. prof., 1966-67, 77; asst. dean U. Calif. Coll. Letters and Sciences, Berkeley, 1967-71; prof. U. Calif., Berkeley, 1969-79; prof. English Princeton U., 1979—, now William and Annie S. Paton Found. prof. ancient and modern lit.; vis. prof. Harvard U., 1971; Grad. prof. Tulsa U., 1979, Bread Loaf Sch. English, 1981, 83, 85, 87, NYU, 1982, Johns Hopkins U., 1983; adv. bd. Publs. MLA, 1977-81, SEL, 1979— VIJ, 1982—, Children's Lit., 1987—; dir. NEH summer seminars, 1975, 84, 86, 89, 90, 91, 95, 99. Author: Religious Humanism and the Victorian Novel, 1965, George Eliot's Early Novels: The Limits of Realism, 1968, Laughter and Despair: Readings in Ten Novels of the Victorian Era, 1971, Emily Bronte's Wuthering Heights, 1988, Wuthering Heights: A Study, 1994, Ventures into Childland: Victorians, Fairy Tales, and Femininity, 1998; editor: Francis Newman: Phases of Faith, 1970; co-editor: Nature and the Victorian Imagination, 1977, The Endurance of Frankenstein: Essays on Mary Shelley's Novel, 1978, Forbidden Journeys: Fairy Tales and Fantasies by Victorian Women Writers, 1992, Cross-Writing the Child and the Adult, 1997, George MacDonald's Fairy Tales, 1999; cons. editor Teaching Children's Literature: Issues, Pedagogy, Resources, 1992; edit. bd. publs. MLA, 1981-83. Recipient Disting. Tchg. award Acad. Senate U. Calif., 1977; Am. Coun. Learned Soc. fellow, 1965, Guggenheim fellow, 1969-70, 87-88, sr. fellow NEH, 1972-73, 91-92, sr. fellow Humanities Coun., Princeton U., 1975, Rockefeller Found. sr. fellow, 1983-84, Nat. Humanities Ctr. fellow, 1996. Mem. MLA, Nat. Coun. Tchrs. English, N.E. Victorian Assn., Children's Lit. Assn. Office: Princeton U Dept English McCosh Hall Princeton NJ 08544-1016

KNOKE, DAVID HARMON, sociology educator; b. Phila., Mar. 4, 1947; s. Donald Glenn and Frances Harriet (Dunn) K.; m. Joann Margaret Robar, Aug. 29, 1970; 1 child, Margaret Frances. BA, U. Mich., 1969, MSW, 1971, PhD, 1972; MA, U. Chgo., 1970. Asst. prof. sociology Ind. U., Bloomington, 1972-75, assoc. prof., 1975-81, prof., 1981-85, dir. Inst. Social Rsch. and Ctr. for Survey Rsch., 1982-84; prof. sociology U. Minn., Mpls., 1985—, chmn., 1989-92, undergrad. dir., 1995-98, grad. dir., 1998—; mem. sociology program rev. panel NSF, 1981-83; mem. sociology rev. panel Fulbright Scholars, 1993-95; mem. sociology com. Grad. Records Exams., 1998-2000. Author: Change and Continuity in American Politics, 1976, (with Peter J. Burke) Log-Linear Models, 1980, (with James R. Wood) Organized for Action, 1981, (with George W. Bohrnstedt) Statistics for Social Data Analysis, 1982, 3d edit., 1994, (with James H. Kuklinski) Network Analysis, 1982, (with Edward O. Laumann) The Organizational State, 1987, Organizing for Collective Action, 1990, Political Networks, 1990, (with George W. Bohrnstedt) Basic Social Statistics, 1991, (with Franz Pappi, Jeffrey Broadbent and Yutaka Tsujinaka) Comparing Policy Networks, 1996, (with Arne Kalleberg, Peter Marsden and Joe Spaeth) Organizations in America, 1996, (with Peter Capelli, Laurie Bassi, Harry Katz, Paul Osterman and Michael Useem) Change at Work, 1997. Recipient NIMH Rsch. Scientist Devel. award, 1977-82; 11 rsch. grants NSF; Nat. Merit scholar, 1965-69, Fulbright Sr. Rsch. scholar, Germany, 1989, scholar of the Coll. U. Minn., 1996-99; Ctr. for Advanced Study in the Behavioral Scis. fellow, 1992-93. Mem. Am. Sociol. Assn. (chair orgns. and occupation sect. 1992-93), Sociol. Rsch. Assn., Internat. Network for Social Network Analysis, European Group for Orgnl. Studies. Unitarian. Home: 7305 Wooddale Ave S Minneapolis MN 55435-4157 Office: U Minn Dept Sociology Minneapolis MN 55455

KNOLL, ANDREW HERBERT, biology educator; b. West Reading, Pa., Apr. 23, 1951; s. Robert Samuel and Anna Augusta (Meyer) K.; m. Marsha Craig, June 22, 1974; children: Kirsten C., Robert A. BA with highest honors, Lehigh U., 1973; MA, Harvard U., 1974, PhD, 1977; PhD (hon.), Uppsala U., Sweden, 1996; DSc (hon.), Lehigh U., 1998. Asst. prof. geology Oberlin Coll., Ohio, 1977-82; assoc. prof. Harvard U., Cambridge, Mass., 1982-85, prof. biology, 1985—; curator bot. mus. Harvard U., Cambridge, 1985—, prof. earth and planetary sci., 1985—, chmn. dept. organismic and evolutionary biology, 1992-98; mem. com. on planetary biology U.S. Space Sci. Bd., 1982-88, NRC Bd. on Earth Scis., 1987-88, 92-95, space studies bd., 1989-90, 97—; Crosby vis. lectr. MIT, 1999. Assoc. editor Paleobiology, 1980-92, Precambrian Rsch., 1985—, Trends in Ecology and Evolution, 1987-92, Rev. of Palaeobotany and Palynology, 1987—, Am. Jour. Sci., 1990—, Geology, 1992-98, Palaios, 1996—, Palaeography Palacoclimatology Palaeocology, 1997—, Internat. Jour. Plant Scis., 1998—; contbr. articles to profl. publs. Bd. dirs. U.S. Nat. Mus. Nat. Hist., 1993-97. Vis. fellow Gonville and Caius Coll., Cambridge, England, 1991-92, fellow Geol. Soc. Am., Linnean Soc., London, Am. Acad. Arts and Scis., 1987, Guggenheim, 1987, Am. Assoc. Adv. Sci.; recipient Walcott medal Nat. Acad. Scis., 1987. Fellow AAAS; mem. NAS, Bot. Soc. Am., Am. Philos. Soc., Paleontol. Soc. (Schuchert award 1987), Soc. Study Evolution, Phi Beta Kappa, Sigma Xi. Avocations: travel, reading, cooking, choral music. Office: Harvard Univ Botanical Museum 26 Oxford St Cambridge MA 02138-2902

KNOLL, FLORENCE SCHUST, architect, designer; b. Saginaw, Mich., May 24, 1917; d. Frederick E. and M. Haisting Schust; m. Hans G. Knoll, July 1, 1946 (dec. 1955); m. Harry Hood Bassett, June 22, 1958 (dec. 1991). Student, Cranbrook Art Acad., Bloomfield Hills, Mich., 1935-37, Archtl. Assn., London, 1938-39; B.Arch., Ill. Inst. Tech., Chgo., 1941; D.F.A. (hon.), Parsons Sch. Design, 1979. Archtl. draftsman, designer Gropius & Breuer, Boston, 1941; design dir. Knoll Planning Unit, 1942-55; pres. Knoll Internat., N.Y.C., 1955-65; pvt. practice architecture and designer Coconut Grove, Fla., 1965—. Recipient Ill. Inst. Tech. Hall of Fame award, 1982; recipient Athena award R.I. Sch. Design, 1982, others. Mem. AIA (recipient Gold medal for indsl. arts 1961), Indsl. Designers Am. (hon.).

KNOLL, GREGG A., artist, printmaker, educator; b. Milw., May 10, 1949; s. Gilbert Alan and Helen A. (Burek) K. BFA with honors, Layton Sch. Art & Design, 1973; MA, U. Iowa, 1977, MFA, 1979. Founder and master printer Green River Press, Iowa City, 1976—, profl. artist, 1985—; founder hand-papermaking facility U. Iowa, Iowa City, 1979-84; vis. artist (faculty) U. Iowa, 1979-84; juror Graham Scholarship com. U. Iowa, 1980-83; head press restoration team Smithsonian Instn., Washington, 1982; cons. Grand Valley State Coll., Allendale, Mich., 1984; participant watercolor workshops Wustum Mus. Fine Arts, Racine, Wis., 1990, Mount Mercy Coll., Cedar Rapids, 1976, Sioux City Art Ctr., 1977. Exhibited in group shows at Chautauqua (N.Y.) Art Assn. Galleries, 1978, Cheney Cowles Meml. Mus., SPokane, Wash., 1979, Farthing Art Gallery, Boon, N.C., 1980, Nicolet Coll. and Tech. Inst., Rhinelander, Wis., 1989, Wustum Mus. Fine Arts, 1989, Wausau (Wis.) Ctr. for Visual Arts, 1991, Eau Claire (Wis.) Regional Arts Ctr., 1993, Regional Art Exhbn., Kenosha, Wis., 1993, Appalachian State U., Boone, N.C., 1995, North Valley Art League Gallery, Redding, Calif., 1996, others; represented in permanent collections at L.L. Pelling Co., Iowa City, U. Iowa hosps. and clinics, U. Iowa Mus. Art, Northwestern Mutual Ins. Co., Milw., Wustum Mus. Fine Arts; author: (with others) Papermaking, 1977, Handmade Paper Today, 1979. Recipient Grumbacher Gold Medallion Merchandise award Wustum Mus. Fine Arts, 1989, 2d Pl. award 1998, Mary Ann Naczinski Meml. Purchase award, 1989, S.C. Johnson Wax Purchase award, 1990, 1st Place award 7th Annual Regional Art Exhbn. Gallery Ten, Rockford, Ill., 1993, Northern Nat. Art Competition Rotary Club, 1993; grantee U. Iowa, 1975. Mem. U. Iowa Alumni Assn., Coll. Art Assn. Am., Milw. Art Mus. Avocations: billiards, fishing, archaeology, astronomy. Office: Green River Press PO Box 356 South Milwaukee WI 53172-0356

KNOLL, JAMES LEWIS, lawyer; b. Chgo., Oct. 5, 1942. AB, Brown U., 1964; JD, U. Chgo., 1967. Bar: Ill. 1967, Oreg. 1971, Wash. 1984, Alaska 1993. Mediator, arbitrator Portland, Oreg.; adj. prof. law Northwestern Sc. Law, Lewis and Clark Coll., 1982-91. Mem. ABA (mem. TIPS coun. 1989-92, chair property ins. com. 1984-85, mem. fidelity surety com., chair comml. tort com. 1985-86), Oreg. State Bar (editor 2 vol. text on ins. 1983, 96), Wash. State Bar, Oreg. Assn. Def. Coun. (pres. 1984). Office: 1500 SW Taylor St Portland OR 97205-1819*

KNOLL, M.J., college administrator; b. Rockville Centre, N.Y., Dec. 19, 1966; d. Edward Vincent and Rose Mary Knoll; m. Chris Finn, Oct. 5, 1996. BA, U. N.H., 1989; postgrad., Northeastern U. Admissions counselor Pine Manor Coll., Chestnut Hill, Mass., asst. dir. admissions, assoc. dir. admissions; sr. assoc. dir. admissions Northeastern U., Boston; dir. admissions Bentley Coll., Waltham, Mass. Coord. visuals for Against the Tide swim Mass. Breast Cancer Coalition, Boston, 1996, 97, 98; runner Susan B. Komen Breast Cancer Run, Newton, Mass., 1996, 97. Mem. Nat. Assn. Coll. Admissions Counseling, New Eng. Assn. Coll. Admissions Counseling, Speak Out. Democrat. Avocations: running, sewing, reading, writing, interior design/renovation. E-mail: mknoll@bentley.edu.

KNOLL, ROBERT EDWIN, English educator; b. Libery, Nebr., Feb. 3, 1922; s. Louis Jarrett and Marie (von Goetz) K.; m. Virginia Elizabeth Koehler, June 29, 1953; children: Elizabeth, Sarah, Benjamin. BA, U. Nebr., 1943; MA, U. Minn., 1947, PhD, 1950. From asst. prof. to prof. English U. Nebr., Lincoln, 1950-90, George Holmes prof., 1980-88, Paula and D.B. Varner prof., 1988-90, Varner prof. emeritus, 1990—; founding fellow centennial ednl. program A. Cluster Coll., 1969-72. Author: Prairie University, A History of the University of Nebraska, 1995 (cert. Am. Assn. State and Local History 1997); editor: McAlmon and the Lost Generation, 1962, Landmark edit., 1976, Ben Jonson's Plays, An Introduction, 1964, Christopher Marlowe, 1969, Conversations with Morris Wright, 1977, Weldon Kees and the Midcentury Generation, Letters 1935-1955, 1986. Bd. govs. Villa Cather Pioeer Meml., 1974—. 1st lt. U.S. Army, 1943-46. Woods fellow Warburg Inst., London, 1959-60; Fulbright prof., Graz, Austria, 1966-67; fellow Nat. Humanities Inst., Yale U., 1977-78; named Nebr. Prof. of Yr., 1988, Nebraskan of Yr., Rotary, 1989; recipient award for tchg. Coun. for Advancement and Support of Edn., 1988, others. Mem. AAUP, MLA, Nat. Coun. Tchrs. English, Shakespeare Assn. Am. (founding trustee 1972-96), Phi Beta Kappa. Democrat. Presbyterian. Home: 2818 S 24th St Lincoln NE 68502-4907 Office: U Nebr Dept English Lincoln NE 68558-0333

KNOLL, WILLIAM LEE, animation director; b. Long Beach, Calif., July 9, 1948; s. Robert B. aned Virginia M. (Humphrey) K.; m. Susan D. Spafford Johnson, May 28, 1971 (div. Dec. 1976); m. Linda L. Gill, July 18, 1981; 1 child, Tracy Lynn. BA, San Diego State U., 1974. Mem. Motion Picture Screen Cartoonists, North Hollywood, Calif., 1976—; asst. animator DePatie-Freleng, Van Nuys, Calif., 1976-80, Hanna-Barbera, North Hollywood, 1980-86; FX animator Boss Films, Marina del Rey, Calif., 1986; dir. Marvel Prodns., Van Nuys, 1986-87; timing dir. D.I.C., Burbank, Calif., 1988-91, Warner Bros. Animation, Sherman Oaks, Calif., 1991-96, Dreamworks, Inc., Encino, Calif., 1996-97, Walt Disney TV Animation, North Hollywood, Calif., 1998—; mem. adv. com. for animation devel. Mt. San Antonio Coll., 1996—. Animator: (animated program) Ziggy's Gift, 1982 (Emmy award 1982-83); dir.: (animated program) Muppet Babies, 1986 (Emmy award 1986-87); timing dir.: (animated program) Animaniacs, 1995 (Emmy award 1995-96), (children's program) Animaniacs, 1995 (Emmy award 1995-96). Chmn. Animal Control Commn., South Pasadena, 1983-84; v.p. Booster's Club, South Pasadena, 1983-84; pres. Covina (Calif.) Am. Little League, 1989, 90; candidate Covina Unified Sch. Dist. Sch. Bd., 1995, mem. bd., 1999—. Recipient Certs. of Appreciation, City of South Pasadena, 1984, Covina Firefighters, 1996, Cert. of Recognition City of Covina, 1995. Mem. NATAS, Aztec Athletic Found., Covina Breakfast Lions (pres. 1988—, Lion of Yr. 1995, 96), Lions Internat. Youth Exch. (dist. chmn. 1991-94, govenor 1993), Lambda Chi Alpha Alumni. Avocations: golf, reading, charitable activities. Home: 2412 E Rio Verde Dr West Covina CA 91791-2140 Office: Disney TV Animation 5200 Lankershim Blvd Ste 600 North Hollywood CA 91601-3100

KNOLLE, MARY ANNE ERICSON, psychotherapist, business communications consultant; b. Kilgore, Tex., Jan. 7, 1941; d. Evert Eric and Frances Leone (Scott) Ericson; children by previous marraige: Clay Claflin, Sunny Claflin; m. John W. Knolle, Mar. 14, 1980; children: Sara Anne, Evelyn. BA, North Tex. U., 1962; MA in Comm., U. Tex., 1968; postgrad., UCLS, 1964-66; MA in Psychology, Houston Bapt. U., 1989. Editor co. publs. Gt. S.W. Life Ins. Co., 1962; prof. U. Balt., 1968, Miami (Fla.) Dade Coll., 1968, Savannah (Ga.) State Coll., 1969, U. Houston, 1972-76; dir. pub. rels. Alvin (Tex.) Coll., 1970-72; founder, pres. Panorama Programs, Houston, 1972-76; coord. mgmt. devel. tng. Brown & Root, Inc., Houston, 1970-79; divsn. founder, mgr. mgmt. and orgnl. devel. sys. Diversified Human Resources Group, Inc., Houston, 1979—, Panorama Cons., 1980—; pres., therapist Stepfamily Support Ctr., Inc., Houston, 1989—; founder, pres. Panorama Mgmt. Inst., Houston, 1979—; cons. moot ct. U. Tex. Law Sch., 1965—; judge regional speech contest Houston Jaycees; instr. Houston C.C., Alvin C.C., U. Balt., Savannah St. Coll.; moderator Christian Parenting Class; co-founder Family Mediation Ctr.; mem. Faculty Bus. Cons. Houston, Inc. Recipient Blockbuster award United Way, 1979. Mem. ASTD, Med. Psychol. and Legal Soc. (organizing founder 1992—), MFamily Bus. Ptnrs., Alvin C. of C. (chmn. edn. com.), Houston City Club, Alpha Delta Pi (past pres. alumnae). Presbyterian. E-mail: maknolle@hotmail.com. Office: 5959 West Loop S Ste 600 Bellaire TX 77401-2406

KNOLLENBERG, JOSEPH (JOE KNOLLENBERG), congressman; b. Ill., 1934; m. Sandie Knollenberg; children: Martin, Stephen. Student, Eastern Ill. U. CLU. Agent, owner ins. co., 1960-93; mem. 103d-106th Congresses from 11th Mich. Dist., 1993—, mem. appropriations com., mem. econ. and ednl. opportunity com., mem. edn. and the workforce, stds. of offcl. conduct coms. Past chmn., Birmingham Cable TV Community Adv. Bd., 18th Dist. Rep. Com., Rep. Com. Oakland County, 1978-86; past pres. St. Bede's Parish Coun., Evergreen Sch. PTA (Birmingham Sch. Dist.), Bloomfield Glens Homeowner's Assn., Cranbrook Homeowner's Assn.; past coord. Southfield Ad Hoc Park and Recreation Devel. Com.; past mem. Southfield Mayor's Wage and Salary Com.; chmn. Candidate Assistance Com./State Com., Oakland County Campaign, 1978; former regional/vice chair 17th Dist. Com., 1975-77; mem. Rep. State Com; exec. com. mem. and fin. com. Rep. Com. Oakland County; founder, mem. Rep. Leadership Com. Oakland County, 1984—; mem. Allstate Ins. Co's P.A.C.; del. Rep. Nat. Conv., 1980; del. to every state convention since 1974. Named chmn. of one of the top twenty-five counties in the country by Rep. Nat. Com. Mem. Am. Soc. Chartered Life Underwriters, Detroit Assn. Life Underwriters, Oakland County Lincoln Rep. Club, Troy C. of C. (current vice chmn.). Office: US Ho Reps 1511 Longsworth HOB Washington DC 20515-2211*

KNOLLER, GUY DAVID, lawyer; b. N.Y.C., July 23, 1946; s. Charles and Odette Knoller; children: Jennifer Judy, Geoffrey David. BA cum laude, Bloomfield (N.J.) Coll., 1968; JD cum laude, Ariz. State U., 1971. Bar: Ariz. 1971, U.S. Dist. Ct. Ariz. 1971, U.S. Sup. Ct. 1976. Trial atty. atty. gen.'s hons. program Dept. Justice, 1971-72; atty., adv., NLRB, 1972-73, field atty. region 28, Phoenix, 1972-74; assoc. Powers, Ehrenreich, Boutell & Kurn, Phoenix, 1974-79; ptnr. Froimson & Knoller, Phoenix, 1979-81; sole practice, Phoenix, 1981-84; ptnr. Fannin, Terry & Hay, P.A., 1984-85; sole practice, Phoenix, 1985—; of counsel Burns & Burns. Mem. bd. visitors Ariz. State U. Coll. Law, 1975-76; pres. Ariz. Theatre Guild, 1990, 91. Fellow Ariz. Bar Found.; mem. ABA, State Bar Ariz. (chmn. labor relations sect. 1977-78), Ariz. State U. Coll. Law Alumni Assn. (pres. 1977). Office: 3550 N Central Ave Ste 1401 Phoenix AZ 85012-2112

KNOP, CHARLES MILTON, electrical engineer; b. Chgo., Feb. 18, 1931; s. Frank and Rose (Hajek) K.; m. Christine Bernadette Koziol, June 3, 1977. BSEE, Ill. Inst. Tech., Chgo., 1954, MSEE, 1960, PhD in Elec. Engring., 1963. Elec. engr. various R&D, aircraft cos., 1954-68; mgr. R&D Andrew Corp., Orland Park, Ill., 1968-85, chief scientist, dir. antenna rsch., 1985—; cons. in field. Contbr. over 60 articles to profl. jours.; holder 10 patents. Fellow IEEE. Roman Catholic. Avocations: classical music, financial market analysis. Home: 12041 Rambling Rd Lockport IL 60441-7869 Office: 10500 153rd St Orland Park IL 60462-3071

KNOPF, ALFRED, JR., retired publisher; b. White Plains, N.Y., June 17, 1918; s. Alfred A. and Blanche (Wolf) K.; m. Alice Laine, July 27, 1952; children—Alison, Susan, David. Grad., Phillips Exeter Acad., 1937; A.B., Union Coll., Schenectady, 1942. With Atheneum Pubs., N.Y.C., 1959-88; chmn. bd. Atheneum Pubs., 1964-88; vis. chmn. Scribner Book Cos.; sr. v.p. MacMillan Pub. Co. (ret.). Capt. USAAF, 1941-45. Mem. Delta Upsilon. Clubs: Dutch Treat (N.Y.C.); Tavern (Chgo.). Home: Bayberry Rdg Westport CT 06880

KNOPF, BARRY ABRAHAM, lawyer; b. Passaic, N.J., May 11, 1946; s. Edward and Sonia (Sameth) K.; children: Elisa, Scott. Student, Rutgers U., 1968, JD, 1972. Bar: N.J. 1972, U.S. Dist. Ct. N.J. 1972, U.S. Tax Ct. 1975, U.S. Supreme Ct. 1975, U.S. Ct. Appeals (3d cir.) 1981; cert. civil trial atty. Nat. Bd. Trial Advocacy, N.J. Supreme Ct. Assoc. Cohn & Lifland, Saddle Brook, N.J., 1972-75, ptnr., 1975—; instr. N.J. Inst. for Continuing Legal Edn., 1982—, Nat. Inst. Trial Advocacy, 1989—. Co-author: Professional Negligence, Law of Malpractice in New Jersey, 1979, 2d edit., 1984, 3d edit., 1990, 4th edit., 1996, Personal Injury Litigation Practice in New Jersey, 1990, Civil Trial Preparation, Practical skills Series, 1992, 2d edit., 1996; New Jersey Product Liability Law, 1994. V.p. Temple Beth Tikvah, Wayne, N.J., 1985-93, pres. 1993-95. Home: 1014 Smith Manor Blvd West Orange NJ 07052-4103 Office: Cohn Lifland Pearlman Herrmann & Knopf Park 80 West 1 Saddle Brook Rochelle Park NJ 07662

KNOPF, KENYON ALFRED, economist, educator; b. Cleve., Nov. 24, 1921; s. Harold C. and Emma A. (Underwood) K.; m. Madelyn Lee Siddy Trebilcock, Mar. 28, 1953; children—Kristin Lee, Mary George. A.B.

magna cum laude with high honors in Econs., Kenyon Coll., 1942; M.A. in Econs.; Ph.D., Harvard U., 1949; LLD (hon.), Kenyon Coll., 1993. Mem. faculty Grinnell Coll., 1949-67, prof. econs., 1960-67, Jentzen prof., 1961-67, chmn. dept., 1958-60, chmn. div. social studies, 1962-64, chmn. faculty, 1964-67; dean coll. Whitman Coll., Walla Walla, Wash., 1967-70; prof. econs. Whitman Coll., 1967-89, Hollon Parker prof. econs., 1985-89, prof. emeritus, 1989—, provost, 1970-81, dean faculty, 1970-78, acting pres., 1974-75; pub. interest dir. Fed. Home Loan Bank, Seattle, 1976-83; mem. council undergrad. assessment program Ednl. Testing Service, 1977-80. Author: (with Robert H. Haveman) The Market System, 4th edit, 1981; A Lexicon of Economics, 1991; editor: Introduction to Economics Series (9 vols.), 1966, 2d edit., 1970-71; co-editor: (with James H. Strauss) The Teaching of Elementary Economics, 1960. Mem. youth coun. City of Grinnell, 1957-59; bd. dirs. Walla Walla United Fund, 1968-76, pres. 1973; mem. Walla Walla County Mental Health bd., 1968-75; mem. Walla Walla Civil Svc. Commn., 1978-84, chmn., 1981-84, councilman City of Grinnell, 1964-67; pres. Walla Walla County Human Svcs. Adminstrv. Bd., 1975-77; mem. Iowa adv. coun. SBA; tax aide AARP/IRS Tax Counseling for Elderly, 1987-98, local coord., 1990-91, assoc. dist. coord. S.E. Wash., 1991-94, assoc. dist. coord. tng., 1994-98; bd. dirs. Shelter Bay Cmty., Inc., 1995—, v.p. 1995-97, pres., 1997—. Social Sci. Rsch. Coun. grantee, 1951-52. Mem. Am. Conf. Acad. Deans (exec. com. 1970-77, chmn. 1975), Am. Econ. Assn., Indsl. Rels. Rsch. Assn., Am. Assn. Ret. Persons, Kiwanis, Phi Beta Kappa, Delta Tau Delta. Office: 223 Skagit Way La Conner WA 98257-9602

KNOPMAN, DAVID S., neurologist; b. Phila., Oct. 6, 1950. AB, Dartmouth Coll., 1972; MD, U. Minn., 1975. Diplomate Am. Bd. Psychiatry and Neurology. Intern Hennepin County Med. Ctr., 1975-76; resident U. Minn., 1976-79; asst. prof. neurology U. Minn., Mpls., 1980-86, assoc. prof. neurology, 1986-98, prof., 1998—; dir. Alzheimer's Disease Clinic, U. Minn. Physicians, Mpls., 1983—; co-dir. Alzheimer Ctr., Mpls. Neurosci. Inst., Abbott-Northwestern Hosp., Mpls., 1995—. Office: U Minn Dept Neurology Minneapolis MN 55455-0361

KNOPMAN, DEBRA SARA, hydrologist, policy analyst; b. Phila., Aug. 13, 1953; d. Harold L. and Minnette (Smulyan) Knopman; m. Donald Weightman, Sept. 29, 1985; children: Leah Alana, David Atwood. BA, Wellesley Coll., 1975; MSCE, MIT, 1978; PhD, Johns Hopkins U., 1986. Sci. writer and editor Washington, 1975-78; legis. asst. Daniel P. Moynihan, Washington, 1979-80; prof. staff mem. U.S. Senate Com. on Environ. and Pub. Works, Washington, 1980-83; student asst., office of groundwater U.S. Geol. Survey, Reston, Va., 1984-85, rsch. hydrologist, nat. rsch. program, 1985-86, hydrologist, br. of systems analysis, 1987-91, chief, br. or systems analysis, 1991-93; dep. asst. sec. water and sci. Dept. Interior, 1993-95; dir. Progressive Policy Inst. Ctr. for Innovation and Environ., 1995—; mem. Nuclear Waste Tech. Rev. Bd., 1997—. Editor: Scientific Research in Israel, 1976; editor Geophysics News, 1990-92; contbr. articles to profl. jours. Mem. commn. on geoscis., environment and resources NRC, 1995-98. Henry R. Luce Found. scholar, Taiwan, 1978-79. Mem. Am. Geophys. Union (chair pub. info. com. 1990-92). Democrat. Jewish. Office: Progressive Policy Inst Ctr for Innovation and Environ 600 Pennsylvania Ave SE Ste 400 Washington DC 20003-4350*

KNOPOFF, LEON, geophysics educator; b. L.A., July 1, 1925; s. Max and Ray (Singer) K.; m. Joanne Van Cleef, Apr. 9, 1961; children—Katherine Alexandra, Rachel Anne, Michael Van Cleef. Student, Los Angeles City Coll., 1941-42; B.S. in Elec Engring, Calif. Inst. Tech., 1944, M.S. in Physics, 1946, Ph.D. in Physics, 1949. Asst., then assoc. prof. physics Miami U., Oxford, Ohio, 1948-50; mem. faculty UCLA, 1950—, prof. physics, 1961—, prof. geophysics, 1959—, rsch. musicologist, 1963—; assoc. dir. Inst. Geophysics and Planetary Physics, 1972-86; prof. geophysics Calif. Inst. Tech., 1962-63, research assoc. seismology, 1963-64; vis. prof. Technische Hochschule, Karlsruhe, Germany, 1966, Harvard U., 1972, U. Chile, Santiago, 1973; Chmn. U.S. Nat. Upper Mantle Com., 1963-71; sec. Internat. Upper Mantle Com., 1963-71; chmn. com. math. geophysics Internat. Union Geodesy and Geophysics, 1971-75; mem. Internat. Union Geodesy and Geophysics (U.S. nat. com.), 1973-75; vis. prof. U. Trieste, 1984. Recipient Wiechert medal German Geophys. Soc., 1978; Gold medal Royal Astron. Soc., 1979; NSF sr. postdoctoral fellow Cambridge (Eng.) U., 1960-61; Guggenheim Found. fellow, 1976-77; Selwyn Coll. Cambridge U. fellow. Fellow AAAS, Am. Acad. Arts and Scis., Royal Astron. Soc. (Jeffreys lectr.), Am. Geophys. Union (Gutenberg lectr. 1992), Nat. Acad. Scis., Seismol. Soc. Am. (hon., medal 1990); mem. Am. Phys. Soc., Am. Philosophical Soc., Phi Beta Kappa (hon.). Office: U Calif Dept Physics Los Angeles CA 90095

KNOPP, MARVIN ISADORE, mathematics educator; b. Chgo., Jan. 4, 1933; s. Mitshel and Minnie (Isr起el) K.; m. Josephine Zadovsky, June 9, 1957 (div. 1998); children: Seth David, Yudah Benjamin, Abby Alissa, Elana Melissa. B.S., U. Ill., 1954, A.M., 1955, Ph.D., 1958. Rsch. mathematician Space Tech. Labs., L.A., 1958-59; NSF postdoctoral fellow Inst. Advanced Study, Princeton, N.J., 1959-60; asst. prof. U. Wis., 1960-62, assoc. prof., 1962-67, prof., 1967-72; mathematician Nat. Bur. Standards, Washington, 1963-64; vis. prof. U. Basel, Switzerland, 1968-69; prof. U. Ill., Chgo., 1970-76, Temple U., Phila., 1976—, Bryn Mawr (Pa.) Coll., 1988-89; Mem. Inst. Advanced Study, Princeton, N.J., 1975, 78, 88; vis. prof. Ohio State U., spring 1979. Author: Theory of Area, 1969, Modular Functions in Analytic Number Theory, 1970, 2d edit., 1993; editor Ill. Jour. Math., 1971-78, The Ramanujan Jour., 1995—, Procs. of Conf. in Analytic Number Theory, 1981, others; contbr. articles to profl. jours. NSF grantee, 1960-90, Fulbright-Hays grantee NRC, 1975-76, Nat. Security Agy. grantee, 1990-93. Mem. Am. Math. Soc., London Math. Soc. Democrat. Jewish. Home: 410 Lancaster Ave Apt 221 Haverford PA 19041-1326 Office: Temple U Dept Math Philadelphia PA 19122

KNORR, JOHN CHRISTIAN, entertainment executive, bandleader, producer; b. Crissey, Ohio, May 24, 1921; s. Reinhold Alfred and Mary (Rieth) K.; m. Jane Lucy Hammer, Nov. 8, 1941; children: Gerald William, Janice Grace Knorr Wilcox. Student, Ohio No. U., 1940-41. Violin soloist with Helen O'Connell, 1934-35; reed sideman Jimmy Dorsey, Les Brown and Sonny Dunham orchs., 1939-48; mem. theater pit orchs. and club shows, Ohio, 1949-57; leader Johnny Knorr Orch., Toledo, 1958—; mgr. Centennial Ter.; owner Johnny Knorr Entertainment Agy.; bandleader, show producer; mem. Royal Ct. of Jesters #21, 1987. Recs. include Live at Franklin Park Mall, 1973, Let's Go Dancing, 1979, encore, 1984, (TV spl.) An Era of Swing, 1973, Live at Centennial Terrace, 1986, Let's Dance, 1989, Oh Johnny, 1997. Trustee Presbyn. Ch. Served to cpl. AUS, 1944-45. Recipient outstanding dance band citations, Chgo., 1966, Des Moines, 1968, Las Vegas, 1969, Nat. Ballroom Operators Assn., Omaha, 1970, Entertainment Operators Assn., 1973; named Grand Duke of Toledo, King of the Hoboes, 1975; named to First Libbey H.S. Hall of Fame, 1994; winner in instrumental category Peoples Choice Awards for Performing Arts, 1997; inducted into Lake Erie West People's Choice Awards Hall of Fame, 1999. Mem. Am. Fedn. Musicians, Am. Legion, Exch. Club, Circus Fans Am., Masons, Shriners, Ind. Order Foresters. Home and Office: 1751 Fallbrook Rd Toledo OH 43614-3251

KNORTZ, HERBERT CHARLES, retired conglomerate company executive; b. Bklyn., Mar. 31, 1921; s. John Walter and Elizabeth (Grotyohann) K.; m. Lorraine Marion Kraut, Aug. 12, 1949; children: Steven Holbrook, Elizabeth Alyn, David Cartwright. BBA, St. Johns U., 1946, DCS (hon.), 1977; MBA, NYU, 1949. C.P.A., N.Y. Supervising clk. Bklyn. Trust Co., 1938-43; with Price Waterhouse & Co., N.Y.C., 1945-51; supr. standard costs Lever Bros. Co., 1951-55; mgr. cost dept. Crown Cork & Seal Co., 1955-56; asst. comptroller Royal McBee Corp., 1956-60; controller Mack Trucks, Inc., 1960-61; dep. comptroller ITT Corp., 1961-63, v.p., comptroller, 1963-66, sr. v.p., comptroller, 1966-73, exec. v.p., comptroller, 1973-85, exec. v.p., 1985-86; ptnr. Cortina Shops, 1957-60, Lewisboro Tennis Club, 1971-72; trustee Corp. Property Investors, 1973-91; bd. dirs., nominating com., audit com. Xtra Corp., 1990-99; lectr. profl. meetings. Contbr. to jours.; also Financial Executives Handbook; Editor: Food for Thought. Trustee Vincent Ross Research Found.; mem. bus. adv. bd. St. John's U. Served with USAAF, 1943-45. Mem. Fin. Execs. Inst. (v.p. research found., mem. internat. com.), Am. Mgmt. Assn. (gen. mgmt. council, audit com., trustee), Am. Contract Bridge League, Am. Inst. C.P.A.s, Nat. Assn. Accountants (nat. pres. 1985-86, nat. chmn. 1986-87), Inst. Mgmt. Accounting (bd. regents), Internat. Assn. Fin. Exec. Insts., Acad. Acctg. Historians, Delta Mu Delta, Beta Alpha Psi, Beta Gamma Sigma. Clubs: Economics, Accountants, Board Room, Armonk Tennis, Flint River Forests. Home: 14 Manor Rd Ridgefield CT 06877-4908 *The weak pursuit of small goals by little people produces little progress; but the intense pursuit of great goals by little people can achieve surprisingly great gains.*

KNORTZ, WALTER ROBERT, accountant, former insurance company executive; b. Bklyn., July 15, 1919; s. John Walter and Elizabeth Anna (Grotyohann) K.; m. Muriel Clancy, Oct. 14, 1950 (dec.); children: Deborah Ann, Kenneth Robert, Pamela Jane; m. Dorothy E. Lauterborn, Nov. 17, 1962. B.B.A., St. Johns U., 1942; M.B.A., N.Y. U., 1949. Former registered prin. Nat. Assn. Securities Dealers. C.P.A., N.Y. Acct. Consol. Edison Co., N.Y.C., 1936-45; mng. acct. S.D. Leidersdorf & Co., N.Y.C., 1945-53; with Equitable Life Assurance Soc. of U.S., N.Y.C., 1953-82; 2d v.p. Equitable Life Assurance Soc. of U.S., 1969-73, v.p., assoc. controller, 1973-75, v.p., fin. officer investment ops., 1975-82; asst. treas., treas. Equitable Life Holding Corp., 1971-75; comptroller Equitable Life Mortgage & Realty Investors, 1970-75; v.p., treas. Equitable Life Community Enterprises Corp., 1970-75, Student Life Funding, Inc., 1970-75; v.p., dir. Equico Lessors, Inc., Mpls., 1974-78; v.p. Equico Securities, Inc., 1970-80, Planters Devel. Corp., St. Louis, 1972-81; mem. Phila. Stock Exchange, Inc., 1971-78. Pres. Leisure Towne Civic League, 1983-84, treas., 1985-86; mem. bldg. fund com. Holy Eucharist Ch., chmn. fin. com., 1984-89. Served with AUS, 1942-45. Mem. AICPA, Tax Execs. Inst., Fin. Execs. Inst. Roman Catholic. Home: 41 Finchley Ct Southampton NJ 08088-1006

KNOSPE, WILLIAM HERBERT, medical educator; b. Oak Park, Ill., May 26, 1929; s. Herbert Henry and Dora Isabel (Spruce) K.; m. Adris M. Nelson, June 19, 1954. B.A., U. Ill., Chgo. and Urbana, 1951; B.S., U. Ill., 1952; M.D., U. Ill., Chgo., 1954; M.S. in Radiation Biology, U. Rochester, 1962. Diplomate Am. Bd. Internal Medicine and Subspecialty Bd. on Hematology. Rotating intern Upstate Med. Ctr. Hosps-SUNY-Syracuse, 1954-55; resident in medicine Ill. Central Hosp., Chgo., 1955-56, VA Research Hosp-Northwestern U. Med. Sch., Chgo., 1956-58; investigator radiation biology Walter Reed Army Inst. Research, Washington, 1962-64; investigator hematology, asst. chief dept. hematology Walter Reed Army Inst. Research, 1964-66; attending physician med. service Walter Reed Gen. Hosp., Washington, 1963-64, fellow in hematology, 1964-65; asst. chief hematology service, chief hematology clinic Walter Reed Army Inst. of Rsch., Washington, 1964-66; asst. attending staff physician Presbyn. St. Luke's Hosp., Chgo., 1967-68, asst. dir. hematology radiohematology lab., 1967-74, assoc. attending staff physician, 1968-74, sr. attending staff physician, 1974—; asst. prof. medicine U. Ill.-Chgo., 1967-69, assoc. prof., 1969-72; assoc. prof. medicine Rush Med. Coll., Chgo., 1971-74, prof. medicine, 1974—; dir. sect. hematology Rush-Presbyn.-St. Luke's Med. Ctr., Chgo., 1974-93; Elodia Kehm prof. hematology Rush-Med. Coll., Chgo., 1986-94, prof. emeritus, 1994—; prof. medicine U. N.Mex., Albuquerque, 1994—; speaker at profl. confs. U.S. and abroad; vis. prof. medicine dept. hematology U. Basel, Switzerland, 1980-81, Cancer Ctr., U. N.Mex., 1992-93. Contbr. numerous articles to profl. publs. Trustee Ill. chpt. Leukemia Soc. Am., 1977-88, v.p., 1979-80; trustee Bishop Anderson House (Rush-Presbyn.-St. Luke's Med. Ctr.), 1980-94. Served to capt. M.C., USAR, 1958-61, to lt. col., U.S. Army, 1961-66. Fellow ACP; mem. Am. Fedn. Clin. Research, AMA, Am. Soc. Hematology, Am. Soc. Clin. Oncology, Central Soc. Clin. Research, Chgo. Med. Soc., Inst. Medicine Chgo., Internat. Soc. Exptl. Hematology, Radiation Research Soc., Southeastern Cancer Study Group, Polycythemia Vera Study Group, Eastern Coop. Oncology Group, Ill. State Med. Soc., Assn. Hematology-Oncology Program Dirs., Sigma Xi. Club: Chgo. Literary. Office: 310 Big Horn Ridge Dr NE Albuquerque NM 87122-1455

KNOTT, DOUGLAS RONALD, college dean, agricultural sciences educator, researcher; b. Fraser Mills, B.C., Can., Nov. 10, 1927; s. Ronald David and Florence Emily (Keeping) K.; m. Joan Madeline Hollinshead, Sept. 2, 1950; children: Holly Ann, Heather Lynn, Ronald Kenneth, Douglas James (dec.). BSA, U. B.C., 1948; MS, U. Wis., 1949, PhD, 1952. Asst. prof. U. Sask., Saskatoon, 1952-56, assoc. prof., 1956-65, prof., 1965-93, head dept. crop sci., 1965-75, assoc. dean rsch. Coll. Agr., 1988-93; prof. emeritus, 1993—. Author: The Wheat Rusts—Breeding for Resistance, 1989; also numerous papers. Named to Saskatchewan Agr. Hall of Fame. Fellow Am. Soc. Agronomy, Agrl. Inst. Can.; mem. Can. Soc. Agronomy, Genetics Soc. Can. Mem. United Ch. of Can. Avocations: squash, tennis. Office: U Sask Dept Plant Scis, 51 Campus Dr, Saskatoon, SK Canada S7N 5A8

KNOTT, JACK H., political science educator, administrator; b. Grand Rapids, Mich., June 14, 1947; s. Harold George and Alice (June) K.; m. Vicki Lynn Bergsma, June 6, 1969; children: Michael, Lisa, Alex. BA, Calvin Coll., 1969; MA, Johns Hopkins U., 1971; PhD, U. Calif., Berkeley, 1977. Lectr. U. Calif., Berkeley, 1977-78; prof. polit. sci. Mich. State U., East Lansing, 1978-97, dir. Inst. Pub. Policy, 1987-97; prof. polit. sci. U. Ill., Champaign-Urbana, 1997—, dir. Inst. Govt. and Pub. Affairs, 1997—; mem. adv. bd. Consortium for Internat. Earth Sci. Info., Saginaw, Mich., 1994-96, Ill. Issues Mag., Springfield, 1997—. Author: Managing the German Economy, 1980, Zero Base Budgeting, 1981, Reforming Bureaucracy, 1987; mem. editl. bd. Pub. Adminstrn. Rev., 1995-97. Sci. Ctr. fellow, Berlin, 1974-76; Russell Sage Found. fellow, 1981-82; grantee Kellogg Found., 1994—, U.S. AID/Mott Found., 1995-97. Mem. Am. Polit. Sci. Assn., Pub. Adminstrn. Soc. (bd. dirs.), Assn. Pub. Policy and Mgmt., Union League Club (Chgo.), Mich. Athletic Club. Avocations: skiing, tennis, handball, hiking/mountain climbing. Email: JHKNOTT@UIUC.EDU. Office: U Ill Inst of Govt 1007 W Nevada St Urbana IL 61801

KNOTT, JOHN RAY, JR., language professional, educator; b. Memphis, July 9, 1937; s. John Ray and Wilma (Henshaw) K.; m. Anne Percy, Dec. 5, 1959; children: Catherine, Ellen, Walker, Anne. A.B., Yale U., 1959, Carnegie fellow, 1960; Ph.D., Harvard U., 1965. Instr. Harvard U., 1965-67; mem. faculty U. Mich., Ann Arbor, 1967—; prof. English U. Mich., 1976—, chmn. dept., 1982-87, assoc. dean Coll. Arts and Scis., 1977-80, acting dean Coll. Arts and Scis., 1980-81, interim dir. Inst. for Humanities, 1987-88; dir. region IV Mellon Fellowship Selection Com., 1989-94. Author: Milton's Pastoral Vision, 1971, The Sword of the Spirit, 1980, Discourses of Martyrdom in English Literature, 1563-1694, 1993; editor: The Triumph of Style, 1967, Mirrors: An Introduction to Literature, rev. edit., 1987; contbr. articles on Abbey, Berry, Browne, Bunyan, Fox, Foxe, Milton, and Spenser to scholarly jours. Woodrow Wilson fellow, 1960-61; NEH fellow, 1974. Mem. MLA, Milton Soc., Renaissance Soc. Am., Sierra Club. Office: Univ Mich Dept English Ann Arbor MI 48109

KNOTT, JOHN ROBERT, mathematics educator; b. Dale, Ind., June 24, 1937; s. Hilary Francis and Eunice Meriba (Heichelbech) K.; m. Mary Elizabeth Bockting, July 26, 1958; children: Susan, Lisa, Thomas. AB, Depauw U., 1959; MS, So. Ill. U., 1963; EdD, Ind. U., 1973. Tchr. math. North High Sch., Evansville, Ind., 1959-68; prof. math. U. Evansville, Evansville, 1968-70, Ind. State U., Evansville, 1966-68; assoc. instr. math. Ind. U., Bloomington, 1970-71; prof. math. U. Evansville, Evansville, 1971—; faculty athletics rep. NCAA, 1977—; math. dept. chmn. U. Evansville, 1983-94. Mem. Nat. Coun. Tchrs. of Math., Math. Assn. Am., Phi Delta Kappa (chpt. pres. 1981-82), Phi Kappa Phi. Democrat. Roman Catholic. Office: U Evansville 1800 Lincoln Ave Evansville IN 47714-1506

KNOTT, KENNETH, engineering educator, consultant; b. Dudley, Worcestershire, Eng., Mar. 6, 1929; came to U.S., 1977; s. John Peter Grainger and Sarah (Turner) K.; m. Margaret Knott, Apr. 22, 1957; children: DiLwyn John, Tracy James. Diploma in Grad. Studies, Engring. Prodn., U. Birmingham at Edgbaston, Eng., 1956; MS in Indsl. Engring., Pa. State U., 1966; PhD in Engring. Prodn., Tech. U. Loughborough, Eng., 1983. Apprentice British Thompson Houston Co. Ltd., Birmingham, 1944-48, Coventry, Eng., 1948-50; design draftsman New Conveyor Co. Ltd., Smethwick, Eng., 1952-53; tech. asst. to gen. mgr. N. Hingley and Sons, Netherton, Eng., 1953-55; prodn. engr. Chubb and Sons, Ltd., Wolverhampton, Eng., 1955-56; plant mgr. John Morris Electrical Engring., Bilston, Eng., 1956; lectr. in prodn. engring. Dudley and Staffordshire Tech. Coll., Dudley, Eng., 1956-63; instr. in indsl. engring. Pa. State U., State College, 1963-66; mng. dir. Maynard Tng. Ctr., Birmingham, 1966-70, Kenneth Knott Ltd., Birmingham, 1966-77, Work Study Contract Svcs., Birmingham, 1970-77; asst. prof. indsl. and mgmt. systems engring. Pa. State U., 1977-84, assoc. prof. indsl. and mgmt. engring., 1984-87, prof. indsl. and mgmt. engring., 1987-95, emeritus prof. indsl. engring., 1996—; mem. editorial bd. Internat. Jour. Prodn. Rsch., Loughborough, 1984—; mem. robotics sub-com. Welding Rsch. Coun., N.Y.C., 1977-79, welding processes sub-com., 1977-83; mem. com. maintenance in mfg. Nat. Mfg. Engring. Ctr., Ann Arbor, Mich., 1989-90. Author: Job Analysis Procedure Manual, 1970, (with others) A Comparison of Alternative Time Slotting Systems for Indirect Time Standards Work Measurement, 1986, An Analytical Approach to Designing and Testing Time Slotting Systems, 1986; co-author: Laboratory Manual Manufacturing Processes, 1965, Principles and Practice of MTM-2, 1970, Principles and Practice of MTM-3, 1971, Manufacturing Processes Associate Degree Program, 1980; editor Metods Time Measurement Jour., 1982-90; contbr. tech. papers to profl. jours. Recipient AT&T Found. Outstanding Teaching award Am. Soc. Engring. Edn., 1991, Lenhard Teaching fellowship Lenhardt Ctr. Innovative Teaching Pa. State U., 1992. Fellow Inst. Indsl. Engrs. (panel rsch. in work measurement work measurement and methods engring. divsn. 1981-83, assoc. editor IIE Transactions 1982-92, program chmn. 1983-87, rsch. chmn. 1984-89, reorganization com. 1988, divsn. dir. 1982-83, honors chmn. 1991—, pres. Ctrl. Pa. chpt. 1982-83, Phil Carroll award 1986, Tech. Innovation in Indsl. Engring. award 1993), World Acad. Productivity Sci.; mem. NSPE, Am. Soc. Quality Control. Soc. Am. Magicians, Pa. Soc. Profl. Engrs., Fedn. Productivity Scis. (hon., London), Methods Time Measurement Assn. (editor Methods Time Measurement Jour., chmn. midland region United Kingdom divsn. 1967-72, internat. com. investigation into Application Handbook Requirements 1970, tech. panel United Kingdom divsn. 1969-77, tng. and qualifications com.), Soc. Mfg. Engrs. (continuing edn. chmn. Ctrl. Pa. chpt. 1987, sec. 1993—), Internat. Brotherhood Magicians, Sigma Xi, Alpha Pi Mu. Avocation: magic. Home: PO Box 234 Pine Grove Mills PA 16868-0234 Office: Pa State U 207 Hammond Bldg University Park PA 16802-1401

KNOTT, WILLIAM ALAN, library director, library management and building consultant; b. Muscatine, Iowa, Oct. 4, 1942; s. Edward Marlan and Dorothy Mae (Holzhauer) K.; m. Mary Farrell, Aug. 23, 1969; children: Andrew Jerome, Sarah Louise. BA in English, U. Iowa, 1967, MA in L.S., 1968. Asst. dir. Ottumwa (Iowa) Pub. Libr., 1968-69; libr. cons. Iowa State Libr., Des Moines, 1968-69; dir. Hutchinson (Kans.) Pub. Libr. and S. Cen. Kans. Libr. System, Hutchinson, 1969-71; dir. Jefferson County Pub. Libr., Lakewood, Colo., 1971—. Served with U.S. Army, 1965-67. Mem. ALA, Colo. Libr. Assn. Author: Books by Mail: A Guide, 1973; co-author: A Phased Approach to Library Automation, 1969; editor: Conservation Catalog, 1982. Office: Jefferson County Pub Libr 10200 W 20th Ave Lakewood CO 80215-1402

KNOTTS, DON, actor; b. Morgantown, W.Va., July 21, 1924; s. William Jesse and Elsie (Moore) K.; m. Kathryn Metz, Dec. 27, 1947 (div.); children: Karen Ann, Thomas Allen; m. Loralee Czuchna (div.), Oct. 12, 1974. B.A., W.Va. U., 1948. Appeared on Broadway in No Time for Sergeants, 1955-56; other stage appearences include A Good Look at Boney Kern, Last of the Red Hot Lovers, Mind with the Dirty Man; with Steve Allen Show, 1956-60; played Barney Fife TV series Andy Griffith, 1960-65 (5 Emmy awards for Outstanding Performance in a Supporting Role), also Don Knotts Show, 1970-71, Three's Company, 1979-84, What A Country!, 1987, recurring role in series Matlock; TV movies include I Love a Mystery, 1973, Return to Mayberry, 1986; film appearances include No Time for Sergeants, 1958, Wake Me When It's Over, 1960, The Last Time I Saw Archie, 1961, It's a Mad, Mad, Mad, Mad World, 1963, Move Over Darling, 1963, The Incredible Mr. Limpet, 1964, The Ghost and Mr. Chicken, 1966, The Reluctant Astronaut, 1967, The Shakiest Gun in the West, 1968, The Love God, 1969, How to Frame a Figg, 1971, The Apple Dumpling Gang, 1975, No Deposit, No Return, 1976, Gus, 1976, Herbie Goes to Monte Carlo, 1977, Hot Lead, Cold Feet, 1978, The Prize Fighter, 1979, The Apple Dumpling Gang Rides Again, 1979, Cannonball Run II, 1984, Pinocchio and the Emperor of the Night, 1987 (voice only), Big Bully, 1995, Cats Don't Dance, 1997, Baywatch: White Thunder at Glacier Bay, 1998; author: The Barney Fife Guide to Life, Love, and Self-defense, 1993, Pleasantville, 1998; TV series Doug, 1991; TV guest appearances Many Loves of Dobie Gillis, 1959, The Andy Williams Show, 1962-69, Newhart, Step by Step, 1991, Burke's Law, 1994, others. Office: The Barry Freed Co Ste 400 2040 Avenue Of The Stars Los Angeles CA 90067-4713*

KNOTTS, FRANK BARRY, physician, surgeon; b. St. Louis, Jan. 27, 1948; s. Frank Louis and Anna Lee (Amerman) K.; m. Wendy Diane Lautz Horton (div.); children: Ryan Matthew, Kara Luan; m. Denise Marie Stern, Aug. 26, 1984. BA in Physics, Johns Hopkins U., 1969; PhD in Molecular Biology, UCLA, 1974, MD, 1975. Diplomate Am. Bd. Surgery with subspecialties in gen. surgery and surg. crit. care. Mem. Rotary. Avocations: flying, scuba, skiing, software devel. Home: 26029 Edinborough Cir Perrysburg OH 43551-9545 Office: St Vincent Mercy Med Ctr 2409 Cherry St MOB 303 Toledo OH 43608

KNOTTS, GLENN R(ICHARD), foundation administrator; b. East Chicago, Ind., May 16, 1934; s. V. Raymond and Opal Ione (Alexander) K. B.S., Purdue U., 1956, M.S., 1960, Ph.D., 1968; M.S., Ind. U., 1964; Dr. Med. Sci. (hon.), Union Coll., 1975; Sc.D. (hon.), Ricker Coll., 1975. Mem. profl. staff Bapt. Meml. Hosp., San Antonio, 1957-60; instr. chemistry San Antonio Coll., 1958-60; adminstrv. asst. AMA, Chgo., 1960-61, research assoc., 1961-62, dir. advt. eval., div. sci. activities, 1963-69; exec. dir. Am. Sch. Health Assn., Kent, Ohio, 1969-72; vis. disting. prof. health sci. Kent State U., 1969-72, prof., mem. grad. faculty dept. allied health scis., 1972-75, coordinator grad. studies and research, 1975; editor-in-chief, prof. med. journalism U. Tex. M.D. Anderson Cancer Ctr., Houston, 1975-85, head dept. med. info. and publs., 1975-79, dir. div. ednl. resources, 1979-85; dir. devel. U. Tex. Health Sci. Ctr. at Houston, 1985-88; prof. U. Tex. Grad. Sch. Biomed. Scis., 1983—; adj. prof. dept. journalism Coll. Communications U. Tex.-Austin, 1984—; exec. dir. Hermann Eye Fund, Houston, 1989—; vis. prof. health edn. Madison Coll., Va., summer 1965, Union Coll., Ky., summers 1965, 66, 69; vis. prof. health edn. Utah State U., summer 1965; vis. lectr. Ind. U., 1965-66; vis. lectr. pharmacology Purdue U., 1968-69; vis. prof. Pahlavi U. Med. Sch., Iran, summer 1970; adj. prof. allied health scis. Kent State U., 1975—; prof. dept. biomed. communications U. Tex. Sch. Allied Health Scis., Houston, 1976—; prof. dept. behavioral scis. U. Tex. Sch. Pub. Health, 1977—; cons. health scis. communications, 1969—; pres. Health Scis. Inst., 1973—; mem. exec. com. Internat. Union Sch. and Univ. Health and Medicine, Paris, 1969-72. Co-author various texts and filmstrips on health sci.; contbr. numerous articles to profl. jours.; cons. editor: Clin. Pediatrics, 1971—; contbg. editor: Annals of Allergy, 1972—; exec. editor: Cancer Bull., 1976-85; mem. numerous editorial bds. Bd. dirs. Med. Arts Pub. Found., Houston, 1977-80, Art League of Houston, 1986-88, Delia Stewart Dance Co., Houston, 1988-90; mem. adv. bd. World Meetings Inc., 1971-80, bd. trustees Mus. Art Am. West, 1987-89; trustee Houston Mus. Natural Sci., 1987-89. Served with U.S. Army, 1956-58. Recipient Gold medal French-Am. Allergy Soc., 1973; named Disting. Alumni Purdue U., 1999. Fellow Am. Pub. Health Assn., Am. Sch. Health Assn. (mem. exec. com. 1968-72, editor Jour. Sch. Health 1975-76, Disting. Service award 1973), Am. Inst. Chemists, Royal Soc. Health; mem. Internat. Union Health Edn., AAHPER, Am. Acad. Pharm. Scis., Am. Med. Writers Assn., Am. Pharm. Assn., AAUP, Am. Chem. Soc., AAAS, AMA, Purdue U. Alumni Assn., Ind. U. Alumni Assn., Union Coll. Alumni Assn., Ricker Coll. Alumni Assn., Sigma Xi, Rho Chi, Sigma Delta Chi, Eta Sigma Gamma, Phi Delta Kappa, Kappa Psi. Republican. Presbyterian. Clubs: Marines Meml. (San Francisco); Univ. Faculty; Doctors (Houston), Pelican (Galveston, Tex.). Lodge: Rotary. Home: PO Box 20787 Houston TX 77225-0787 Office: Hermann Eye Fund 6411 Fannin St Houston TX 77030-1501

KNOTTS, ROBERT LEE, insurance executive; b. Thornton, W.Va., Jan. 14, 1942; s. James Bailey and Lena Louise (Jacobs) K.; m. Dottie Lue Watts, Aug. 20, 1967; children: Brice Alan, Lance Eric, Chandra Marie. ChFC, CLU. Sales, truck driver Wholesale Grocery, Grafton, W.Va., 1960-67; lineman, crew leader Monongahelia Power Co., Grafton, 1967-78; agt., registered rep. N.Y. Life Ins., N.Y. Life Ins. & Annuity Corp., Charleston, W.Va., 1978—, NYLIFE Securities Corp., Charleston, 1978—; sec. bd. dirs. Grafton Homes, Inc., 1990-97. V.P. Taylor County Econ. Devel. Authority, Grafton, 1985-87; pres. Taylor Devel. Group, Inc., Grafton, 1987—. With

USMC, 1960-64. V.p. Taylor County Econ Devel. Authority, Grafton, 1985-87, pres. Taylor Devel. Group, Inc., 1987—; treas. Taylor County Dem. Exec. Com., 1990-98. With USMC, 1960-64. Mem. Nat. Assn. Life Underwriters, Fairmont Assn. Life Underwriters, North Ctrl. W.Va. Chartered Fin. Cons., N. Ctrl. W.Va. Estate Planning Coun., Grafton Rotary (pres. 1979-81, 95-96, pres. edn. endowment 1991-96). Methodist. Office: NY Life Ins Co PO Box 599 Grafton WV 26354-0599

KNOUSE, BRENDA LEE (WEIKEL), critical care, medical/surgical nurse; b. Shamokin, Pa., June 6, 1963; d. Andrew Henry and Mary Alice (Wagner) Reich; married April, 1995; children: Nicholas E. Jr., Katie. Diploma in nursing, Lancaster (Pa.) Gen. Hosp., 1984; ADN, Franklin and Marshall Coll., Lancaster, 1984. RN, Pa.; cert. in ACLS. Staff nurse Mountain View Manor Nursing Home, Trevorton, Pa., 1984-86; staff nurse telemetry unit Sunbury (Pa.) Community Hosp., 1986—; staff nurse Dr. Michael R. Green, Sunbury, 1994-96; nurse PRN pool Susquehanna Health Sys., Williamsport, Pa., 1996-97; staff nurse telemetry unit Geisinger Med. Ctr., Danville, Pa., 1997—; team coord. telemetry unit Pa. State Geisinger Health Sys., Danville, 1999—. Office: a State Geisinger Health Sys 100 Academy Ave Danville PA 17822

KNOWLER, ROBERT GENE, county treasurer; b. New Sharon, Iowa, June 29, 1936; s. Clifford and Blanche L. (Stephen) K. Owner Bob Knowler's Black Night, Sioux City, Iowa, 1967-82; pres. Curtis Media Corp., Sioux City and Dallas, 1983-94; treas. Woodbury County, Sioux City, 1995—. Chmn. bd. dirs. Morningside Coll., Sioux City, 1972-84, Boys Club of Sioux City, 1975-90; vice chmn. Sioux City C. of C., 1975-80; pres. Siouxland All-Am. Band, Sioux City, 1988. Named to Order of Morningside, Morningside Coll., 1984. Mem. Rotary Internat. (exec. sec. 1992—, Paul Harris fellow 1990), Masons, Shriners. Republican. Methodist. Avocations: flying, trombone, antique autos. Home: 4001 Old Lakeport Rd Sioux City IA 51106-9510 Office: Woodbury County Courthouse 620 Douglas St Sioux City IA 51101-1246

KNOWLES, CHARLES TIMOTHY, lawyer, state legislator; b. Providence, Aug. 21, 1949; s. Charles Timothy and Olga (Dower) K.; m. Sandra J. Bellem; children: Justin, Jennifer. BA, U. R.I., 1971; JD cum laude, New England Sch. Law, 1977. Bar: R.I., U.S. Dist. Ct. (R.I.), U.S. Supreme Ct. Assoc. Robinson & Resnick, Warwick, R.I., 1977-79, Haronian & Paquin, Warwick, 1979-84; ptnr. Knowles & Bissonnette, Warwick, 1984—; mem. R.I. Ho. of Reps., Providence, 1989-97, chmn. jud. com., 1993-97; retired. Sec. Narragansett (R.I.) Dem. Cen. Com., 1982-93; vice-chmn. Narragansett Zoning Bd., 1982-88; vice chmn. Narragansett Little League, 1982-88. 1st lt. U.S. Army, 1971-73; col. R.I. ARNG, 1974—, brig. comdr., 1997—. Mem. R.I. Bar Assn., Am. Legion, Save the Bay, Lions, St. Andrew's Alumni Assn. (sec.). Episcopalian. Home: 56 Fowler St North Kingstown RI 02852-5010 Office: Knowles and Bissonnette 3214 Post Rd Warwick RI 02886-7129

KNOWLES, CHRISTOPHER ALLAN, healthcare executive; b. Washington, Oct. 24, 1949; s. Charles Edward and Eleanor Patricia (Murphy) K.; m. Mary Margaret O'Loughlin, Feb. 14, 1988; children: Sean Christopher, James Charles, Thomas Patrick. BA, U. Nebr., 1975; MPA, Drake U., Des Moines, 1982; postgrad., Fordham U., 1987-91. Adminstrv. asst. to dir. Nebr. Dept. Water Resources, Lincoln, 1976-78; environ. planner Iowa Natural Resources Council, Des Moines, 1978-81, Md. Environ. Trust, Balt., 1982; fin. analyst Norwest Corp., Des Moines, 1982-83; asst. dir., dir. fin. Hospice of Cen. Iowa, Des Moines, 1983-85; assoc. dir. home health svcs. dept. Hackensack Med. Ctr., N.J., 1985-86; fiscal mgr. Family Health Ctr. Montefiore Med. Ctr., N.Y.C., 1986-87; assoc. dir. and adminstr. Comprehensive Family Care Ctr., Albert Einstein Coll., N.Y.C., 1987-88; exec. dir. Hospice Care of L.I., 1988; assoc. dir. Bronx-Lebanon Hosp., N.Y.C., 1989; chmn., chief exec. officer Knowles Econometrics, Inc., Pelham Manor, N.Y., 1990-91; asst. controller N.Y.C. Health & Hosps. Corp., 1990; dep. dir. Coalition Vol. Mental Health Agys., N.Y.C., 1990-91; dir. Vis. Nurse Svc., Martha's Vineyard Cmty. Svcs., Oak Bluffs, Mass., 1991—; chief economist Knowles Econometrics, Vineyard Haven, Mass., 1994-96; pres. The Wintertide Coffeehouse, Inc., Vineyard Haven, Mass., 1993-94; treas. AIDS Alliance of Martha's Vineyard (Mass.), Inc., 1992-93; chmn. Dukes County (Mass.) Health and Human Svcs. Adv. Com., 1995-96. Chmn. Barnstable County (Mass.) Health Human Svc. Adv. Com., 1999—. U.S. Dept. Edn. grantee, 1981-82. Mem. Pi Sigma Alpha, Pi Alpha Alpha. Democrat. Episcopalian. Avocation: sailing. Office: PO Box 369 Vineyard Haven MA 02568-0369

KNOWLES, EDDIE ADE, dean; b. May 3, 1946. BA, Lincoln U., 1970; MA, Columbia U., 1973; PhD, U. Albany, 1998. Asst. dir. Coll. Discovery Program, Bronx C.C., 1970-73, dir. Coll. Discovery Program,, 1973-74; asst. prof. Hostos C.C., Bronx, 1974-75; asst. dean Rensselaer Coll., Troy, 1977-79, dean minority affairs, 1979-82, dean of students, 1982—. E-mail: KNOWLE@RPI.EDU.

KNOWLES, EDWARD F(RANK), architect; b. Bklyn., Aug. 12, 1929; s. Frank W. and Isabel (Leudesdorff) K.; m. Barbara Lee DuPree, Mar. 14, 1953; children: Christopher, Sarah, Mary, Emily. BArch, Pratt Inst., 1951. Registered architect, N.Y. Pvt. practice in architecture N.Y.C., 1960—; ptnr. Macfayden & Knowles, N.Y.C., 1965-68; instr. architecture Pratt Inst., 1959-60, Cooper Union Coll., N.Y.C., 1960-64, Columbia U., N.Y.C., 1965-66; cons. N.Y. State Council Arts, Bklyn. Inst., Man and Sci., San Francisco, Arts Resources Devel. Com., Richmond Found., N.Y.C. Dept. Parks. Prin. works include Holy Trinity Episc. Ch., Hicksville, N.Y., Manhattan Sch. of Music, Bklyn. Acad. Music, The Leperc Space Lobby Restoration, City Ctr. of Music and Drama, new Boston City Hall, The Drawing Ctr., N.Y.C., Pine Manor Jr. Coll., 21 McGill Club, Toronto, IBM World Trade Corp., Myron Minskoff, MCA Broadcasting, First Rock Fin. Corp., Equilease Corp., Litton Industries, McDonough, Marcus, Cohn and Tretter, Fleischman Shopping Ctr., Naples, Fla., Exotic Gardens, East Norwich, L.I., N.Y., Duff's Restaurant, N.Y.C., Abel's Restaurant, Newark, N.J., Casey's Restaurant, N.Y.C., Ferdinand Coudert residence, Lowell Nesbitt residence, Catherine Cahill and William Bernhard residence, Mr. and Mrs. Henry Stifel residence, Mr. and Mrs. Harvey Lichtenstein residence, Luigo de la Huerta residence, Harvey Smith residence, Wallace Forbes residence, Guido diBenedetto residence, Dorothea Tanning residence, Alvin Friedman-Klein residence, Hamilton Fish Kean residence, Baron Lambert chalet, Gstaad, Switzerland, Altman residence, N.Y.C., Gillespie residence, Prout's Neck, Maine, Robert residence, Nantucket, Phyllis Vineyard residence, Ont., Mr. and Mrs. Robert Greenhill residences, Moosehead Lake, Maine, Fla., Nantucket, Alison Flemer residence, Vieques. Mem. Rembrandt Club (Bklyn.). Office: 127 W 56th St New York NY 10019-3809 *Significant architecture must express the emotional factors of the problem in addition to the obvious requirements of program, site, budget, and structure, or it ceases to be an art form. The rejection of any of the phenomena that are experienced at any point in history is short-sighted.*

KNOWLES, ELIZABETH PRINGLE, art museum director; b. Decatur, Ill., Jan. 9, 1943; d. William Bull and Elizabeth E. (Pillsbury) P.; m. Joseph E. Knowles; 1 child, Elizabeth Bakewell. BA in Humanities with honors, Stanford, 1964; MA in Art History, U. Calif., Santa Barbara, 1968; grad., Mus. Mgmt. Inst., 1984. Cert. jr. coll. tchr., Calif. Instr. art history Murray State U., Murray, Ky., 1967-68; instr. art history Santa Barbara Art Inst., 1969, Santa Barbara City Coll., 1969-70, 76-78; from staff coord. docents to curator edn. Santa Barbara Mus. Art, 1974-86; assoc. dir. Meml. Art Gallery, Rochester, N.Y., 1986-88; instr. mus. studies Calif. State U., Long Beach, 1989; exec. dir. Lyman Allyn Art Mus., New London, Conn., 1989-95; pres. Only In Conn. Spl. Interest Tours, Chester, 1995-97; supr. mus. edn. programs Mystic (Conn.) Seaport Mus., 1996—; instr. continuing edn. Santa Barbara City Coll., 1973-86. Contbr. essays to art catalogues. Board dirs., chmn. Met. Transit Dist., Santa Barbara, 1978-80; founding pres. Santa Barbara Contemporary Arts Forum, Santa Barbara, 1976-78; commr. Santa Barbara City Planning Commn., 1975-77. Kellogg Found. fellow Smithsonian Inst., 1985. Mem. Am. Assn. Mus. (treas. edn. com. 1986-88), Coll. Art Assn., New Eng. Mus. Assn. (v.p. 1993-95).

KNOWLES, EM CLAIRE, dean; b. Sacramento, June 6, 1952; d. Sidney Stanley and Almeana Early K. BA, U. Calif., Davis, 1973; MLS, U. Calif., Berkeley, 1974; MPA, Calif. State U., 1974; DA, Simmons Coll., 1988. Data collector regional svcs. faculty study U. Calif., Berkeley, 1974, team leader spl. projects, 1975; libr., coord. shields libr. U. Calif., Davis, 1975-88; asst. dean grad. sch. libr. & info. scis. Simmons Coll., Boston, 1988—; co-chair examining com. Boston Pub. Libr., 1996-98. V.p. Greater Boston Inter U. Coun., 1998—. Mem. ALA (sec. black caucus 1985-89), Assn. Libr. & Info. Sci. Educators, Streetwise Investment Club (parliamentarian 1998—), Women's Nat. Book Assn. (adv. bd. 1990-99), Nat. Black MBA Assn. (design team, Leaders of Tomorrow 1993—). Methodist. Avocations: reading, aerobics, travel, community service. Office: Simmons Coll - GS LIS 300 The Fenway Boston MA 02115-9858

KNOWLES, HARRY, communications executive. Adminstr. Ain't-it-cool-news.com Website, Austin, Tex. Office: PO Box 180011 Austin TX 78718-0011*

KNOWLES, HARRY JAY, internet personality; b. May 12, 1971; s. Jay Knowles. Founder, owner website Ain't It Cool News, 1996—; salesman vintage film memorabilia. Office: PO Box 180011 Austin TX 78718-0011*

KNOWLES, JAMES KENYON, applied mechanics educator; b. Cleve., Apr. 14, 1931; s. Newton Talbot and Allyan (Gray) K.; m. Jacqueline De Bolt, Nov. 26, 1952; children: John Kenyon, Jeffrey Gray, James Talbot. SB in Math., MIT, 1952, PhD, 1957; DSc (hon.), Nat. U. Ireland, 1985. Instr. math. MIT, Cambridge, 1957-58; asst. prof. applied mechanics Calif. Inst. Tech., Pasadena, 1958-61, assoc. prof., 1961-65, prof. applied mechanics, 1965—, William R. Kenan Jr. prof., 1991—, William R. Kenan Jr. prof. emeritus, 1996—; vis. prof. MIT, 1993-94; cons. in field. Contbr. articles to profl. jours. Recipient Eringen medal Soc. Engring. Sci., 1991. Fellow ASME, AAAS, Am. Acad. Mechanics. Home: 522 Michillinda Way Sierra Madre CA 91024-1066 Office: Calif Inst Tech Div Engring & Applied Sci 104-44 1201 E California Pasadena CA 91125-0001

KNOWLES, JOCELYN WAGNER, health writer, women's health specialist; b. N.Y.C., Feb. 22, 1918; d. Frederick and Violet Alice (Swain) W.; m. Clive Dorman Knowles, 1950 (div. 1959); 1 child, Katherine Miranda. Student, London Sch. Econs., 1938; BS, Columbia U., 1939, MA, 1940; MPH, UCLA, 1970. Exec. dir. Nat. Physicians Forum, Inc., N.Y.C., 1945-49; West Coast editor Nat. Foremen's Inst. Prentice-Hall Co., L.A., 1959-68; writer, editor The Female Patient mag., 1980-81; dir. Planned Parenthood of S.W., Silver City, N.Mex., 1981-83; freelance writer, 1977—; asst. to pres., lit. agt. Writers House, Inc., N.Y.C., 1989-92; book critic Kirkus Revs., 1989-90, Book of the Month Club, 1991—, Pubs. Weekly, 1991-98. Contbr. articles to med. and consumer mags.; staff bookreviewer L.A. Times. First woman organizer Brotherhood of Railway Trainmen, 1945-47; publicist Farmers Union of Iowa, Des Moines, 1951, Golden Gate Arboretum, San Francisco, 1976; bd. dirs. Nat. Womens Health Network, 1981-85; apptd. to Sarasota (Fla.) Commn. on Status of Women, 1994-96; sec. Sarasota County Health Care Campaign, 1996-98, Howard County (Md.) Commn. on Women, 1999—. NIH grantee U. Calif., L.A., 1968-70; Va. Ctr. for the Arts fellow, Charlottesville, 1976, Woolrich fellow Columbia U., N.Y.C., 1977, Wurlitzer Found. fellow, Taos, N.Mex., 1981. Jewish.

KNOWLES, JOHN, author; b. Fairmount, W.Va., Sept. 16, 1926; s. James Myron and Mary Beatrice (Shea) K. BA, Yale U., 1949. Reporter Hartford (Conn.) Courant, 1950-52; assoc. editor Holiday mag., N.Y.C., 1956-60; writer in residence U. N.C., Chapel Hill, 1963-64, Princeton (N.J.) U., 1968-69. Author: A Separate Peace, 1960 (Richard and Hinda Rosenthal Found. award Am. Acad. and Inst. Arts and Letters 1960, William Faulkner Found. award 1960), Morning in Antibes, 1962, Double Vision: American Thoughts Abroad, 1964, Indian Summer, 1966, Phineas: Six Stories, 1968, The Paragon, 1971, Spreading Fires, 1974, A Vein of Riches, 1978, Peace Breaks Out, 1981, A Stolen Past, 1983, The Private Life of Axie Reed, 1986. Recipient Nat. Assn. Ind. Schs. award 1961. Office: care E P Dutton PO Box 120939 Bergenfield NJ 07621*

KNOWLES, MARJORIE FINE, lawyer, educator, dean; b. Bklyn., July 4, 1939; d. Jesse J. and Roslyn (Leff) Fine; m. Ralph I. Knowles, Jr., June 3, 1972. BA, Smith Coll., 1960; LLB, Harvard U., 1965. Bar: Ala., N.Y., D.C. Teaching fellow Harvard U., 1963-64; law clk. to judge U.S. Dist. Ct. (so. dist.), N.Y., 1965-66; asst. U.S. atty. U.S. Atty.'s Office, N.Y.C., 1966-67; asst. dist. atty. N.Y. County Dist. Atty., N.Y.C., 1967-70; exec. dir. Joint Found. Support, Inc., N.Y.C., 1970-72; asst. gen. counsel HEW, Washington, 1978-79; insp. gen. U.S. Dept. Labor, Washington, 1979-80; assoc. prof. U. Ala. Sch. Law, Tuscaloosa, 1972-75, prof., 1975-86, assoc. dean, 1982-84; law prof., dean Ga. State U. Coll. Law, Atlanta, 1986-91, law prof., 1986—; cons. Ford Found., N.Y.C., 1973—, trustee Coll. Retirement Equities Fund, N.Y.C., 1983—; mem. exec. com. Conf. on Women and the Constn., 1986-88; mem. com. on continuing profl. edn. Am. Law Inst.-ABA, 1987-93. Contbr. articles to profl. jours. Am. Council Edn. fellow, 1976-77, Aspen Inst. fellow, Rockefeller Found., 1976. Mem. ABA (chmn. new deans workshop 1988), Ala. State Bar Assn., N.Y. State Bar Assn., D.C. Bar Assn., Am. Law Inst. Office: Ga State U Coll Law University Plz Atlanta GA 30303

KNOWLES, RICHARD ALAN JOHN, English language educator; b. Southbridge, Mass., May 17, 1935; s. Clarence Fay and Mildred Elizabeth (Branniff) K.; m. Jane Marie Boyle, Sept. 1, 1958; children: Jonathan Edwards, Katherine Mary. BA magna cum laude, Tufts U., 1956; MA, U. Pa., 1958, PhD, 1963. Physics asst. Tufts U., Medford, Mass., 1954-56; asst. instr. English U. Pa., Phila., 1956-60; from asst. prof. to prof. U. Wis., Madison, 1962-90, Dickson-Bascom prof. humanities, 1990—; vis. lectr. U. Pa., 1967, George Washington U., Am. U., 1969, Cath. U., Washington, 1985; manuscript reader various univs., 1965—; cons. Am. Players Theater, Spring Green, Wis., 1980-83; poetry judge Brittingham Poetry Prize, Madison, 1986—, NEH referee, panelist, Washington, 1988—. Author: (with others) Shakespeare Variorum Handbook, 1971; editor: (with others) English Renaissance Drama, 1978; editor: New Variorum As You Like It, 1977; co-editor New Variorum Shakespeare, 1978—; mem. editl. bd. Shakespeare Notes, 1996—. Officer, producer Madison Savoyards, Wis., 1978—; pres. Friends U. Wis. Librs., Madison, 1982-84. Folger Libr. fellow, Washington, 1968, Guggenheim fellow, N.Y., 1976-77; NEH fellow 1983-87; Rsch. fellow Humanities Rsch. Inst., Madison, 1990. Mem. MLA, Shakespeare Assn. Am., Internat. Assn. Univ. Profs. English, Assn. Lit. Critics and Scholars, Nakoma Country Club. Democrat. Avocations: theater, chamber music, opera, gardening, carpentry. Home: 2226 Commonwealth Ave Madison WI 53705-5302 Office: U Wis Dept English 600 N Park St Madison WI 53706-1403

KNOWLES, RICHARD NORRIS, chemist; b. Wilmington, Del., Aug. 8, 1935; s. Francis and Dorothy Edith L.; m. Alice Keith Pfohl, Aug. 30, 1957 (div. May 1987); children: Elizabeth Nelson, Dorothy Lawrence, Cynthia Norris; m. Claire Elaine Frerichs, Dec. 31, 1988. BS, Oberlin Coll., 1957; PhD, U. Rochester, 1961. With DuPont Co., Wilmington, Del., 1960-96; asst. works mgr. Chambers Works, N.J., 1980-83; mgr. Niagara Falls (N.Y.) Plant, 1983, Belle (W.Va.) Plant, 1987-95; dir. cmty. awareness emergency response & industry outreach Wilmington, 1995-96; work with Chem. Mfrs. Assn. in Responsible Care; assoc. Dalmau Network; prin. Richard M. Knowles & Assocs. Contbr. articles to profl. jours.; patentee (40) in field; featured in The New Pioneers, 1998. Elder Westminster Presbyn. Ch.; bd. dirs. Nat. Inst. Chem. Studies, Berkana Inst. Recipient Chem. Emergency Planning and Preparedness Ptnr. award EPA, 1995, 96. Mem. Am. Chem. Soc., Assn. Quality and Patricipation, Audubon Soc., Sierra Club, Nature Conservancy (DuPont Agrl. Products Crystal award 1991), Almost Heaven Hammered Dulcimer Soc. Achievements include 40 patents in field. Office: 6989 Rebecca Dr Niagara Falls NY 14304-3050

KNOWLES, THOMAS WILLIAM, business educator, consultant; b. Chgo., June 2, 1941; s. Thomas Houlding and Dorothy (Lovell) K.; m. Fay Rosemary Bailey, June 18, 1966; children: Jennifer Lynn, Julie Bailey (dec.). BSChemE, Purdue U., 1963; MBA, U. Chgo., 1966, PhD, 1971. Prodn. engr. Lever Bros. Co., Hammond, Ind., 1963-64; prof. ops. mgmt. and mgmt. sci. Stuart Sch. Bus. Ill. Inst. Tech., Chgo., 1969—; vis. assoc. prof. U. Chgo. Grad. Sch. Bus., 1988; pres. Thomas W. Knowles and Associs., Inc., Olympia Fields., Ill., 1976—. Author: Management Science: Building and Using Models, 1989; contbr. articles to profl. jours. Treas. BZ chpt. Sigma No Alumni Assn., 1967-73, Com. for Legis. Reform, Ill., 1978-80, Compassionate Friends, Ill., 1980-90; pres., v.p. Rich Twp. (Ill.) Reps., 1973-74; del. Rep. Nat. Conv., New Orleans, 1988; trustee Rich Twp., 1981-89, supr., 1989-93. Mem. Decision Scis. Inst. (Stanley T. Hardy award 1989), Inst. for Ops. Rsch. and Mgmt. Sci. (chmn. Chgo. 1975-78), Math. Programming Soc., Prodn. and Ops. Mgmt. Soc., Beta Gamma Sigma, Tau Beta Pi. Avocations: reading, fishing, travel, genealogy, boating. Home: 20440 Hellenic Dr Olympia Fields IL 60461-1438 Office: Stuart Sch Bus Ill Inst Tech 565 W Adams St Chicago IL 60661-3613

KNOWLES, TONY, governor; b. Tulsa, Jan. 1, 1943; m. Susan Morris; children: Devon, Lucas, Sara. BA in Econs., Yale U., 1968. Owner, mgr. The Works, Anchorage, 1968—, Downtown Deli, Anchorage, 1978—; mayor Municipality of Anchorage, 1981-87; now gov. State of Alaska, 1994—. Mem. citizen's com. to develop comprehensive plan for growth and devel., Anchorage, 1972; mem. Borough Assembly, Anchorage, 1975-79; bd. dirs. Fairview Cmty. Ctr., March of Dimes, Pub. TV Sta. KAKM, numerous sports facilities coms. Served with U.S. Army, 1961-65, Vietnam. Mem. Anchorage C. of C. (bd. dirs.). Office: Office of the Governor PO Box 110001 Juneau AK 99811-0001

KNOWLES, VIRGINIA LYNN, gerontology services educator; b. Logan, W.Va., July 28, 1950; d. Ronald Lee and Betty Ann (Claypool) Cook; m. John Michael Knowles, July 31, 1971 (div. 1997); children: Jennifer Lee, Jason Edward. BSN, W.Va. U., 1972. Lic. nursing home adminstr., W.Va. Coord. health occupations Wyo. County Vocat.-Tech. Ctr., Pineville, W.Va.; quality assurance coord. Glenwood Park Retirement Village., Princeton, W.Va.; chmn. vocat. nursing skill competition W.Va. State, 1988; condr. statewide workshops on electronic data submission Health Care Fin. Assn., 1998; Beta-tested computer med. records program for long-term care, 1998. Author first state-approved curriculum for new Sch. Practical Nursing, Pineville. Mem. W.Va. Health Care Assn. (quality assurance com. 1996-97), Am. Assn. of Nurse Assessment Coords. (charter). Address: 35 Lees Mobile Home Park Princeton WV 24740-2443

KNOWLES, WILLIAM LEROY (BILL KNOWLES), television news producer, journalism educator; b. L.A., June 23, 1935; s. Leroy Edwin and Thelma Mabel (Armstrong) K.; children from previous marriage: Frank, Irene, Daniel, Joseph, Ted; m. Sharon Weaver, Dec. 28, 1990. B.A. in Journalism, San Jose State Coll., 1959; postgrad., U. So. Calif., 1962-63. Reporter, photographer, producer KSL-TV, Salt Lake City, 1963-65; producer, editor, writer WLS-TV, Chgo., 1965-70; news writer ABC News, Washington, 1970-71; asso. producer ABC News, 1971-75, ops. producer, 1975-77; So. bur. chief ABC News, Atlanta, 1977-81; Washington bur. chief ABC News, 1981-82, West Coast bur. chief, 1982-85; prof. U. Mont., Missoula, 1986—; jazz writer and historian; v.p., co-owner Present Past Productions, Inc.; adv. U. Mont. Student Documentary Unit. Served with U.S. Army, 1959-62. Decorated Commendation medal; Gannett fellow Ind. U., 1987; Media Mgmt. fellow Poynter Inst. Media Studies, 1988. Mem. Assn. for Edn. in Journalism (head radio-TV divsn. 1995-96). Office: U Mont Sch Journalism Missoula MT 59812

KNOWLTON, ALEXANDER WHITNEY, graphic designer; b. Port Chester, N.Y., Oct. 28, 1963; s. Eber Asire and Rosamond Ann (Ross) K. BFA, Sch. Visual Arts, N.Y.C., 1987. Designer Russek Advt., N.Y.C., 1987; assoc. art dir. Spy Mag., N.Y.C., 1987-89; sr. designer Alexander Isley Design, N.Y.C., 1989-93, Parham Smith, N.Y.C., 1993; art dir. Spy Mag., N.Y.C., 1993-94; pres. Best Design Inc., N.Y.C., 1994—; art dir. CBS/Fox Video, N.Y.C., 1994; instr Sch. Visual Arts, 1994-96. Recipient The Billie award Billboard Mag., 1994, Gold award Broadcast Designers Gold award, 1995, and numerous other awards from orgns. including AIGA, Creativity How Mag., Soc. Pub. Designers, TDC. Mem. Type Dirs. Club, Am. Inst. Graphic Arts, Village Dive Club. Avocations: scuba, figure drawing, photography, skiing. Office: Best Deisgn Inc 27 W 24th St #10D New York NY 10010

KNOWLTON, AUSTIN E. (DUTCH KNOWLTON), professional football team executive. BS, Ohio State U. Owner Knowlton Constrn. Co., ARGA Co.; majority owner Cin. Reds (Major Leagues), 1970's; chmn. bd. The Cin. Bengals (NFL). Office: Cin Bengals 200 Cinergy Stadium Cincinnati OH 45202 also: Cin Bengals One Bengals Dr Cincinnati OH 45204*

KNOWLTON, EDGAR COLBY, JR., linguist, educator; b. Delaware, Ohio, Sept. 14, 1921; s. Edgar Colby and Mildred (Hunt) K. A.B., Harvard U., 1941, A.M., 1942; Ph.D., Stanford U., 1959. Instr. U. Hawaii, Honolulu, 1948-53; asst. prof. European langs. U. Hawaii, 1954-59, assoc. prof., 1959-65, prof., 1965-88, acting chmn. dept. European langs. and lit., 1984-86, prof. emeritus, 1988—; lectr., Acad. of Lifelong Learning, U. of Hawaii, 1998, vis. prof. linguistics U. Malaya, Kuala Lumpur, 1962-64; music reviewer Honolulu Advertiser, 1957-61; exec. dir. Hawaii Coun. on Portugese Heritage, 1991-93, Enumerator, U.S. Census Bureau, 1999. Author: Esteban Echeverria, 1986; co-author: V. Blasco Ibáñez, 1972; translator: Francisco de Sá de Meneses, The Conquest of Malacca, 1971, Almeida Garrett, Camoëns, 1972, Casimiro de Abreu, Camoëns and the Man of Java, 1972, Machado de Assis, You, Love, and Love Alone, 1972, Almeida Garrett, Afonso de Albuquerque, 1977, Gina Sobrero, Espatriata: An Italian Baroness in Hawaii 1887, 1991; compiler: Portuguese Immigrants to Hawaii, 1993; Portuguese Athletes of Hawaii, 1993, Portuguese in Hawaii Before 1878, 1995; contbr. articles to profl. jours. Mem. program com. Hawaiian Hist. Soc., 1961-62. Served with USNR, 1944-46, 51-52. Recipient Translation prize, Lisbon, 1973, Fulbright award U. Cen. de Venezuela, 1975. Mem. MLA (mem. bibliography com. 1969-82), Am. Assn. Tchrs. Spanish and Portuguese, Am. Assn. Tchrs. Spanish (pres. Hawaii chpt. 1964-65), Puerto Rican Heritage Soc. Hawaii (hon.), Phi Beta Kappa, Sigma Delta Pi. Home: PO Box 11426 Honolulu HI 96828-0426

KNOWLTON, GRACE FARRAR, sculptor, photographer, painter; b. Buffalo, Mar. 15, 1932; d. Frank Neff and Esther Sargeant (Norton) Farrar; m. Winthrop Knowlton, July 8, 1960 (div. 80); children: Eliza, Samantha. B.A., Smith Coll., 1954; M.A., Columbia U., 1981. Asst. to curator of graphic arts Nat. Gallery of Art, Washington, 1955-57; tchr. art Arlington Pub. Schs., Va., 1957-60; sculptor, photographer, painter, 1960—. Exhbns. include Hirschl & Adler Modern, N.Y.C., 1995, 97. Home and Studio: 67 Ludlow Ln Palisades NY 10964-1606

KNOWLTON, KEVIN CHARLES, lawyer; b. Syracuse, N.Y., Oct. 19, 1957; s. Erwin Leslie and Arlene Grace (Morgan) K.; m. Lois Jean Clair, July 21, 1979; children: Andrew, Keith, Lauren. BA cum laude, Houghton Coll., 1979; JD, Syracuse U., 1982. Bar: Fla. 1982, U.S. Dist. Ct. (mid. dist.) Fla. 1982, U.S. Ct. Appeals (11th cir.) 1982, U.S. Supreme Ct. 1986. Law clk. to judge 2nd Dist. Ct. Appeals, Lakeland, Fla., 1982-85; ptnr. Peterson & Myers P.A., Lakeland, 1985—, mgmt. com. Treas. Phoenix (N.Y.) Rep. Com., 1980-82, Planning Bd., 1980-82, Town of Schroeppel Planning Bd., 1980-82; chmn. bd. dirs. Lakeland Christian Sch.; chmn. pres.'s adv. coun. on excellence Houghton Coll.; chmn. exec. bd. dirs. Lake Morton Cmty. Ch., 1995—, elder; mem. instnl. rev. bd. Lakeland Regional Med. Ctr., mem. ethics com. N.Y. State Regents scholar 1975-79. Mem. ABA, Assn. Trial Lawyers Am., Fla. Bar Assn., Lakeland Bar Assn. (chmn. law day legal forum 1986), Fla. Acad. Healthcare Attys., Am. Health Lawyers Assn., Christian Legal Soc., Houghton Coll. Alumni Assn. (pres. Orlando, Fla. chpt. 1985, 91—), Willson Inn of Ct., Lakeland Yacht and Country Club, Phi Alpha Theta. Avocations: basketball, snow skiing. Home: 839 Heathercrest Lakeland FL 33813-1240 Office: Peterson & Myers PA 100 E Main St Lakeland FL 33801-4655

KNOWLTON, LESLIE BROOKS, journalist; b. Orange, N.J., July 18, 1952; d. Bruce Douglas and Elizabeth (Snow) Knowlton; m. Charles Gottlieb Herzog, Dec. 27, 1979 (div. 1992); 1 child, Siri Whitney Herzog. BA, U. Conn., 1977; MA, Calif. State U., Long beach, 1983; postgrad., City Coll., 1998—. Dir. rsch. Grubb & Ellis Co., Newport Beach, Calif., 1985-87; reporter Orange County Businessweek, Irvine, Calif., 1987-89; reporter/desk asst. L.A. Times, Costa Mesa, Calif., 1989-90; free lance journalist L.A. Times, N.Y.C., 1989-99; staff writer N.Y. Daily News, 1999—. U. Conn. Faculty scholar, 1976, Univ. scholar, 1976. Mem. Am. Soc. Journalists and Authors, Author's Guild, Nat. Writers Union, N.Y. Newswomen's Club, Deer Isle Yacht Club, Phi Kappa Phi, Psi Chi. Avocations: fiction, boating, hiking. Home: 339 W 87th St Apt 1 New York NY 10024-2639 Office: 450 W 33rd St New York NY 10001

KNOWLTON, NANCY, biologist; b. Evanston, Ill., May 30, 1949; d. Archa Osborn and Aline (Mahnken) K.; m. Jeremy Bradford Cook Jackson; 1 child, Rebecca Knowlton. AB, Harvard U., 1971; PhD, U. Calif., Berkeley, 1978. Asst. prof. biology Yale U., New Haven, 1979-84, assoc. prof., 1984; biologist Smithsonian Tropical Rsch. Inst., Panama, Republic of Panama, 1985—; prof. Scripps Instn. Oceanography U. Calif., San Diego, 1997—; panelist animal learning and behavior NSF, Washington, 1989-92; vis. scholar Wolfson Coll., Oxford (Eng.) U., 1990-91, Zoology Inst., U. Basel, Switzerland, 1996-97. Editor Am. Scientist, 1981-90, Evolution, 1995-97. NATO postdoctoral fellow NSF, Liverpool, Cambridge, Eng., 1978-79; Aldo Leopold Leadership fellow, 1999. Mem. AAAS (coun. del. sect. on biol. scis., com. on coun. affairs), Ecol. Soc. Am., Soc. Study Evolution. Office: Univ of Calif-San Diego SIO La Jolla CA 92093

KNOWLTON, THOMAS A., retired food products executive; b. Toronto, Ont., Can., June 16, 1946; s. William George and Grace K.; m. Janice Elizabeth Knowlton, June 8, 1968; children: Kimberly, Tricia, Jeffrey, Andrea. B.A., U. Windsor, Ont., 1968, M.B.A., 1970. Brand mgr. Colgate Palmolive, Toronto, 1970-73; product mgr. Gen. Foods, Toronto, 1973-75; v.p., dir. client services Leo Burnett, Toronto, 1975-79; sr. v.p. mktg. and sales Kellogg Salada Can. Inc., Rexdale, Ont., 1979-82, pres., chief exec. officer, 1983-88; v.p. Kellogg Co., 1984—; mng. dir. Kellogg Co. of Gt. Britain Ltd., 1989-90, chmn., 1990-94, exec. v.p., area dir. Europe, 1992-94; corp. exec. v.p., pres. Kellogg N.Am., 1994-99; ret., 1998; bd. dirs. Wm. Wrigley Jr. Co. Mem. Young Pres.'s Orgn., York Downs Golf and Country Club (Unionville, Ont.), Gull Lake Country Club (Richland, Mich.). Home: 123 Cheltanham Ave, Toronto, ON Canada 57692JA Home: 123 Cheltenham Ave, Toronto, ON Canada M4N 1R1

KNOWLTON, WILLIAM ALLEN, political and military consultant, educator; b. Weston, Mass., June 19, 1920; s. Frank Warren and Isabelle (Riese) K.; m. Marjorie Adams Downey, Nov. 27, 1943; children: William Allen, Davis Downey, Timothy Riese, Hollister Knowlton Petraeus. BS, U.S. Mil. Acad., 1943; MA, Columbia U., 1957; grad., Nat. War Coll., 1960; LLD (hon.), Akron U., 1972. Commd. 2d lt. U.S. Army, 1943, advanced through grades to gen., 1976; with 7th Armored Div., World War II, Army Gen. Staff, 1947-49, SHAPE, France, 1951-54; assoc. prof. social scis. U.S. Mil. Acad., 1955-58, supt., 1970-74; bn. comdr. 3d Armored Cav. Regt., 1958-59; mil. attache Tunisia, 1961-63; brig. comdr. Ft. Knox, Ky., 1963-64; with Office Chief Staff U.S. Army, 1964-65; mil. asst. to spl. asst. to sec. and dept. sec. def. Office Sec. Def., 1965-66; sec. Joint Staff, dir. pacification support, dep. asst. chief staff for civil ops. revolutionary devel. support U.S. Mil. Assistance Command, Vietnam, 1966-67; asst. div. comdr. 9th Inf. Div., Vietnam, 1968; sec. gen. staff Office Chief Staff U.S. Army, 1968-70; chief staff hdqrs. U.S. European Command, Stuttgart, W.Ger., 1974-76; comdr. Allied Land Forces Southeast Europe, Izmir, Turkey, 1976-77; U.S. rep. NATO Mil. Com., Brussels, 1977-80; ret., 1980; cons. on internat. affairs and strategic intelligence R & D Assocs., Marina del Rey, Calif.; sr. assoc. Burdeshaw Assocs. Ltd., 1981-91; dir. Aeronca Inc., 1982-86, Chubb Corp., Fed. Ins. Co., Vigilant Ins. Co., Chubb Life Am., 1983-93; sr. fellow CAPSTONE course Nat. Def. U., 1984-95, sr. fellow emeritus CAPSTONE course, 1995—; sr. rsch. fellow Inst. Advanced Technology U. Tex., Austin, 1998—; lectr. Am. U., 1995—. Contbr.: Ency. Americana and nat. mags. Trustee Davis and Elkins Coll., 1982-90. Decorated Def. D.S.M., Army D.S.M., Silver Star with 2 oak leaf clusters, Legion of Merit with oak leaf cluster, D.F.C., Bronze Star with V device, Air medal with 9 oak leaf clusters, Army Commendation medal with oak leaf cluster, knight comdr. cross Order Merit W. Ger., officer Legion of Honor France, Vietnamese Nat. Order and Gallantry Cross with palm; recipient George Washington honor medal Freedoms Found., Valley Forge, 1957, 58, Lemnitzer award, 1994; named Hon. Col. Regiment, 40th armor Berlin. Mem. Am. Mil. Inst., 7th Armored Divsn. Assn. (hon. pres.), Coun. Fgn. Rels., Soc. Mayflower Descs., Washington Inst. Fgn. Affairs (v.p. 1998), S.R., Soc. Colonial Wars, Univ. Club (N.Y.C.), Army and Navy Club (Washington), Phi Kappa Phi. Home: 4520 4th Rd N Arlington VA 22203-2343

KNOX, BRIAN VICTOR, newspaper publisher and editor; b. Madison, Wis., May 2, 1951; s. William David and Jane (Shaw) K.; m. Terrie Lynn Wyrick, Aug. 23, 1984; children: Jessica, Paris, Gillian, Brian. Editor, pub. Daily Jefferson County Union, Ft. Atkinson, Wis., 1977—; v.p. ops. W.D. Hoard & Sons Co., Ft. Atkinson, 1981—; editor, pub. Hometown News LLP, Ft. Atkinson, 1991—; pres. South Ctrl. Publs., Stoughton, Wis., 1997—. Mem. Ft. Atkinson Sch. Bd., 1988-94. Mem. Wis. Newspaper Assn. (bd. dirs. 1998—). Republican. Episcopalian. Avocations: cross country skiing, book collecting, dairy farming. Office: WD Hoard & Sons Co 28 Milwaukee Ave E Fort Atkinson WI 53538

KNOX, CHARLES COURTENAYE, composer; b. Atlanta, Apr. 19, 1929; s. Charles Courtenaye and Janet (Ryder) K.; m. Ruth Elizabeth McSwain, Aug. 31, 1954. BFA, U. Ga., 1951; MMus, Ind. U., 1955, PhD, 1962. Prin. trombone Atlanta Symphony, 1949-51; assoc. prof. music Miss. Coll., Clinton, 1955-65; prof. music Ga. State U., Atlanta, 1965-95. Composer: Workshop, 1995, Voluntary on Hyfrydol, 1978, Clouds Are Not Spheres, 1994, Music for Brass and Piano, 1982, 2002, 1998, Semordnilap, 1991, Rivers Run Through It, 1997. Mem. ASCAP, Am. Music Ctr., Am. Composers Forum. Presbyn. E-mail: cknox@gsu.edu. Home: 482 Page Ave NE Atlanta GA 30307-1730

KNOX, CHARLES GRAHAM, lawyer; b. Erie, Pa., June 10, 1948; s. William Wallace and Agnes Ruth (Graham) K.; m. Jill Ann Poole, Mar. 22, 1975; children: Stephanie Marie, William Wallace II. BA, Williams Coll., 1970; JD, U. Mich., 1973. Bar: Pa. 1973, U.S. Dist. Ct. (we. dist.) Pa. 1973. Assoc. Buchanan Ingersoll P.C., Pitts., 1972-81, shareholder, 1981-97; ptnr. Marcus & Shapira, LLP, Pitts., 1997—. Pres., bd. trustees Parkwood United Presbyn. Ch., Allison Park, Pa., 1991. Mem. ABA, Pa. Bar Assn., Allegheny County Bar Assn. Home: 4230 Wembleton Dr Allison Park PA 15101-1564 Office: Marcus & Shapira LLP 301 Grant St Ste 35 Pittsburgh PA 15219-1407

KNOX, CHARLES MILTON, purchasing agent, consultant; b. Tuscola, Ill., Mar. 1, 1937; s. Paul F. and Fern E. (Ewing) K.; m. Caryl A. Lossman, June 26, 1960; children: Ann E. Kendzior, Jeffrey C. BS, Ill. Wesleyan U., 1959; grad., CMI Mgmt. Inst. Cert. life purchasing mgr. Exec. trainee Carson Pirie Scott & Co., Peoria, Ill., 1959-62; owner Knox True Value Hardware, Villa Grove, Ill., 1962-85; contract adminstr. Ill. Sec. of State, Springfield, 1985-87; sr. buyer U. Ill., Urbana, 1987—; pres. Profl. Purchasing Cons., Villa Grove, 1991—; guest lectr. Parkland C.C., 1993. Editor: University of Illinois Contract Procedures Manual, 1994; co-author: History of Villa Grove, 1987, History of Douglas County, 1984, Illinois Secretary of State Contract Procedures, 1986; city, ch. and county hist. publs. Rep. area campaign coord. Sec. of State, 1986, state rep., 1992; committeeman Rep. Ctrl. Com., 1992, 94, 96, 98; county chmn. Douglas County Rep. Ctrl. Com., 1994, 96, 98; county coord. Congrl. Campaign, 1994, 96, 98; pres. Libr. Dist., 1980-89, v.p., 1989—; bd. dirs. County Mus. With USNR, 1955-63. Recipient Outstanding Buyer of Yr. award U. Ill., 1989, 90, 92. Mem. Ill. Assn. Pub. Purchasing Ofcls. (Mgr. of Yr. 1994), Ill. Rep. County Chmns. Assn., Ill. State Hist. Soc., Douglas County Geneal. Soc. (v.p. 1984), Masons, Rotary (pres. 1963, dir. 1964, 65, 66), Alpha Kappa Psi, Tau Kappa Epsilon. Republican. Methodist. Avocations: genealogy, history. Home: 100 Hickory Ln Villa Grove IL 61956-1607 Office: U Ill Purchasing Divsn 1321 S Oak St Champaign IL 61820-6903

KNOX, ELIZABETH LOUISE, community volunteer, travel consultant; b. Forest Hills, N.Y.; d. Frederick Conrad and Emma M. Wissel; m. Rudolph T. Haas Jr., Feb. 1944 (div. June 1955); 1 child, Rudolph T. III; m. James Henry Knox, Aug. 22, 1956 (dec. Feb. 1987); children: Julie Frances, Alice Carrie. Student, Hunter Coll. Ret. co-owner Del Mar (Calif.) Travel Bur. Mem. bd. trustees Salk Inst., La Jolla, 1994—; co-chair Salk Inst. Coun., 1995—; v.p. women's assn., 1969-70, pres., 1970-72, trustee, 1981-82, chmn. Andy Williams golf tournament benefit, 1969-70, chmn. 30th anniversary com., 1990-92; co-chmn. fashion show benefit Bishop's Sch., La Jolla, 1967, chmn., 1968, trustee, devel. chmn., 1971—, v.p., 1980-82, pres., 1982-86, headmaster's adv. coun., 1986—; bd. dirs. women's aux. Scripps Meml. Hosp., La Jolla, 1963-64, co-chmn. candlelight ball, 1963; charter mem. La Jolla unit Children's Hosp., San Diego, 1956, chmn. ways and means La Jolla unit, 1956-59, chmn. 10th annual fair benefit, 1963, pres. La Jolla unit, 1965, bd. dirs. women's auxiliary, 1962-64, chmn. San Diego stadium premiere benefit, 1967; bd. regents Calif. Luth. Univ., 1994—. Recipient Nat. Lane Bryant award, 1966, Woman of Valor award Temple Beth Israel, 1967, Jonas Salk award of Congress Salk Inst., 1972, Pres.'s award Women's Assn./Salk Inst., 1978, Woman of Dedication award San Diego Door of Hope Aux./Salvation Army, 1986. Mem. La Jolla Beach and Tennis Club, Del Mar Turf Club. Home: 2688 Hidden Valley Rd La Jolla CA 92037-4025

KNOX, GEORGE L(EVI), III, consumer products company executive; b. Indpls., Sept. 6, 1943; s. George L. II and Yvonne M. (Wright) K.; m. B. Gail Reed, Jan. 1, 1979; children: Reed H.W., Gillian S.G. BS in Polit. Sci., Tuskegee U., 1967; MBA, Harvard U., 1975. Fgn. service officer Dept. State, Washington and Tokyo, 1968-73; assoc. McKinsey & Co., N.Y.C. and Tokyo, 1975-77; mgr. internal cons. Philip Morris Inc., N.Y.C., 1977-79, mgr. fin. relations, 1979-83, dir. fin. relations and adminstrn., 1983-85; dir. communications Philip Morris Mgmt. Corp., N.Y.C., 1985-87; staff v.p. pub. affairs Philip Morris Cos. Inc., N.Y.C., 1987-90, v.p. pub. affairs, 1990-95, v.p. corp. affairs strategy and comm., 1995—. Mem. Civilian Pub. Affairs Com. U.S. Mil. Acad., West Point, N.Y., 1988; trustee Studio Mus. in Harlem, N.Y.C., 1979; bd. dirs. So. Ctr. for Internat. Studies; dir. Am. Ballet Theater, 1995. Mem. Nat. Investor Relations Inst. Democrat. Episcopal. Avocations: squash, reading. Office: Philip Morris Cos Inc 120 Park Ave New York NY 10017-5592

KNOX, HAVOLYN CROCKER, financial consultant; b. Charlotte, N.C., Oct. 20, 1937; d. Earl Reid and Etta Lorain (Wylie) Crocker; m. Charles Eugene Knox, July 20, 1963 (div. 1981); children: Charles Eugene Jr., Sandra Leigh. Cert. Stenography, U. N.C., Greensboro, 1956. ChFC, CLU. Exec. sec. Stellings-Gossett Theatres, Inc., Charlotte, 1956-57; legal sec. McDougle, Ervin, Horack & Snepp, Charlotte, 1957, Pierce, Wardlow, Knox & Caudle, Charlotte, 1957-63; adminstrv. asst. Charlotte-Mecklenburg Planning Commn., 1980; exec. asst. Conn. Mut. Life Ins. Co., Charlotte, 1981-86; assoc. The Hinrichs Fin. Group, Charlotte, 1986-91, Lyn Knox & Assocs., Charlotte, 1991—. Ops. dir. Eddie Knox for Mayor campaign, Charlotte; campaign mgr. Herb Spaugh for City Coun., Charlotte, 1981, 83, 85; registration chmn. Kemper Open Golf Tournament, Charlotte, 1976-79; pres. The Legal Aux., Charlotte, 1972-73; bd. dirs. Oratorio Singers of Charlotte, 1986-93. Recipient William Danforth Found. award, 1955. Mem. Am. Soc. CLU and ChFC (bd. dirs. Charlotte chpt. 1994-95),harlotte Estate Planning Coun., Charlotte Civitan Club. Republican. Presbyterian. Avocations: piano, reading, golf. Home: 2331 Carmel Rd Charlotte NC 28226-6322 Office: Lyn Knox & Assocs PO Box 4115 Charlotte NC 28226-0099

KNOX, JAMES EDWIN, lawyer; b. Evanston, Ill., July 2, 1937; s. James Edwin and Marjorie Eleanor (Williams) K.; m. Rita Lucille Torres, June 30, 1973; children: James Edwin III, Kirsten M., Katherine E., Miranda G. BA in Polit. Sci., State U. Iowa, 1959; JD, Drake U., 1961. Bar: Iowa 1961, Ill. 1962, Tex. 1982. Law clk. to Justice Tom C. Clark, U.S. Supreme Ct., 1961-62; assoc., then ptnr. Isham, Lincoln & Beale, Chgo., 1962-70; v.p. law Northwest Industries, Inc., Chgo., 1970-80; exec. v.p., gen. counsel Lone Star Steel Co., Dallas, 1980-86; sr. v.p. law Anixter Internat. Inc., Chgo., 1986—; ptnr. Mayer, Brown & Platt, Chgo., 1992-96; gen. counsel Antec Corp., 1996—; instr. contracts and labor law Chgo. Kent Coll. Law 1964-69; arbitrator Nat. Ry. Adjustment Bd., 1967-68. Mem. ABA, Ill. Bar Assn., Phi Beta Kappa, Order of Coif, Phi Eta Sigma. Office: Anixter Internat Inc 2 N Riverside Plz Chicago IL 60606-2600

KNOX, JAMES MARSHALL, lawyer; b. Chgo., Jan. 12, 1944; s. Edwin John and Shirley Lucille (Collett) K.; m. Janine Foster, July 18, 1964; children: Erik M., Christian S. BA, U. Ill., 1968; MA in Libr. Sci., Rosary Coll., 1973; JD, DePaul Coll. of Law, 1979. Bar: Ill. 1979, U.S. Dist. Ct. (no. dist.) Ill. 1979, U.S. Ct. Appeals (7th cir.) 1980. Head reference Northbrook (Ill.) Pub. Libr., 1973-76; asst. dir. hdqrs. Jackson (Miss.) Met. Libr. Sys., 1976-77; assoc., Fishman & Fishman, Ltd., Chgo., 1979-91; prin. Law Office James M. Knox, 1991—; gen. counsel Deerfield (Ill.) Pub. Libr., 1994—. Commr. Evanston Preservation Commn., 1991-98. Mem. ABA, Ill. State Bar Assn., Ill. Trial Lawyer's Assn., Chgo. Bar Assn., U. Ill. Alumni Assn. (dir. 1986-91). Home: 1305 Lincoln St Evanston IL 60201-2334 Office: Law Offices 3700 Three 1st National Plz Chicago IL 60602

KNOX, LANCE LETHBRIDGE, venture capital executive; b. Hartford, Conn., Sept. 25, 1944; s. Robert Chester and Leonice Katherine (Merrels) K.; children: Michele Merrels, Elizabeth McVarish; m. Mary E. Lambert, 1981. BA, Williams Coll., 1966; MBA, NYU, 1970. Asst. cashier Citibank, N.A., N.Y.C., 1968-70, asst. v.p., 1970-72, v.p., 1972-74, sr. credit officer, 1973-74; v.p. fin. GATX Corp., Chgo., 1974-77; pvt. investor venture capital, 1978—; pres., bd. dirs. The Lethbridge Group Inc., Chgo.; pres. Bistrot Zinc, Chgo., Brio, Chgo. Bd. dirs. Better Govt. Assn.; trustee Kingswood-Oxford Sch., West Hartford. Office: 3342 N Southport Ave Chicago IL 60657-1439

KNOX, RICHARD ALBERT, journalist; b. Lafayette, Ind., Aug. 5, 1946; s. Albert L. and Ruth (Powell) K.; m. Jean Harbour McBee, Jan. 1, 1978; children: Elizabeth Gray, Sarah Harbour. BA, U. Ill., Urbana, 1968; MS, Columbia U., 1969. Health and med. writer The Boston Globe, 1969—; syndicated writer Knight-Ridder News Svc., 1983-93, N.Y. Times News Svc., 1993—. Author: Germany's Health System: One Nation United with Health Care for All, 1993; author chpts. to books; contbr. articles to profl. jours. Active The Boston Cecilia, 1970—. NEH fellow Stanford U., 1978-79, Advanced Studies in Pub. Health fellow Harvard U., 1990-91; recipient Howard W. Blakeslee award Am. Heart Assn., 1978, Pub. Svc. in AIDS Edn. Gov. award Mass., 1988. Home: 27 Wellesley Park Boston MA 02124-2134 Office: Boston Globe 135 Morrissey Blvd Boston MA 02125-3338*

KNOX, RICHARD DOUGLAS, JR., healthcare executive; b. Bethesda, Md., Mar. 22, 1950; s. Richard D. Sr. and Margaret L. (Liming) K. BS, Va. Commonwealth U., 1973. CPA, Va. From staff mem. to sr. mgr. KPMG Peat Marwick, Richmond, Va., 1973-81; sr. mgr. KPMG Peat Marwick, Norfolk, Va., 1981-86; v.p., CIO Children's Hosp. of King's Daus., Norfolk, Va., 1986-88, sr. v.p. fin., CFO, 1988—; treas. Internat. Ctr. for Children's Health, Norfolk, 1992—; bd. dirs. Ctr. for Pediatric Rsch., Norfolk, 1993—; sec.-treas. Network for Pediatric Care, Norfolk, 1989—; treas. Children's Health Network, Norfolk, 1994—; sec. Pediatric Faculty Assocs., Norfolk, 1994-97; treas. Barry Robinson Ctr., Norfolk, 1994—, Children's Med. Group (sec. treas.), Norfolk, 1996—; mem. bus. adv. Norfolk State U., 1993-97; bd. dirs. The Planning Coun., Norfolk, Vol. Hampton Roads, Norfolk, pres., 1998—; bd. dirs. Shared Hosp. Svcs., Portsmouth, Va., chmn. Long Range Planning com. 1996—; bd. dirs. Access HomeCare, Virginia Beach, Va., Nat. Assn. Children's Hosps., chmn. Champus com., Alexandria, 1992—; chmn. acctg. adv. coun. Old Dominion U., Norfolk, 1996—. Mem. AICPA, Va. Soc. CPA's, Healthcare Fin. Mgmt. Assn. Episcopalian. Avocations: boating, diving. Home: 700 55th St Virginia Beach VA 23451-2220 Office: Childrens Hosp of Kings Daus 601 Childrens Ln Norfolk VA 23507-1910

KNOX, ROBERT ARTHUR, oceanographer, academic administrator; b. Washington, Jan. 15, 1943; s. James Milton and Virginia Matilda (Ernst) K.; m. Dorothy Chapin Hall, June 18, 1966; children: Leila Elizabeth, James Chapin. AB, Amherst Coll., 1964; PhD, MIT/Woods Hole Oceanographic Inst, 1971. Rsch. assoc. MIT, Cambridge, 1971-73; asst. rsch. oceanographer Scripps Inst. Oceanography/U. Calif. San Diego, La Jolla, 1973-81, acad. adminstr., 1980-90, assoc. rsch. oceanographer, 1981-86, rsch. oceanographer, 1986—, acting chair, chair ocean rsch. divsn., 1988-89, dir. physical oceanography rsch. divsn., 1989-91, assoc. dir., 1992—; sr. vis. fellow Wolfson Coll., Oxford U., England, 1983. Contbr. articles to profl. jours. Coach, coord., v.p., pres. Del Mar (Calif.) Youth Soccer Club, 1981-90. Ford Found. fellow MIT, 1964-65. Mem. Am. Geophysical Union, Am. Meteorological Soc., Oceanography Soc., Phi Beta Kappa, Sigma Xi. Avocations: sailing, soccer. Home: 13019 Long Boat Way Del Mar CA 92014-3831 Office: Scripps Inst Oceanography UCSD 0210 9500 Gilman Dr La Jolla CA 92093-5003*

KNOX, ROBERT BURNS, religious organization administrator; b. Concord, N.H., Feb. 26, 1917; s. Ralph Burns Knox and Ruby Aileen (Gillette) Dixon; m. Barbara Macauley Lovejoy, July 4, 1941; children: Robert B. Jr., Karen Lovejoy Knox Campbell. BA, U. N.H., 1941; MA, George Washington U., 1956; Ministry Program, U. of the South, 1981. Lic. lay min. Episcopal Ch. Cadet USAF, 1940, Col., 1970; chief of order dept. RCA Distbn. Corp., San Antonio, 1972-76, 77-79; staff mem. St. George Episcopal Ch., San Antonio, 1979—; bd. dirs., treas. Order of St. Luke the Physician, Sch. Pastoral Care. Mem. interparish com. for Evangelism, San Antonio, 1987-89, compensation com. for Episcopal Diocese West Tex., 1990-93, armed forces com., 1993-96. Recipient Legion of Merit with oak leaf cluster, others. Episcopalian. Avocations: spectator sports, Hi-Fi Jazz recordings, stamps. Home: 10614 Mt Ida San Antonio TX 78213-1738 *Joy and sadness are constants in our lives on earth. Throughout childhood and our adult lives we face ups and downs, never having been promised, and not experiencing, only the good life. But through it all, faith and trust in our Lord God brings us through those cycles and prepares us for the unknown life hereafter.*

KNOX, ROBERT SEIPLE, physicist, educator; b. Franklin, N.J., July 13, 1931; s. Harvey Stoll and Laura (Seiple) K.; m. Myrta I. Borges, Sept. 1, 1954; children: Bruce Robert, Wayne Harvey, Lee Benjamin. B.S. in Engring. Physics, Lehigh U., 1953; Ph.D. in Physics and Optics, U. Rochester, 1958. Research asso. U. Ill., 1958-59; research asst. prof., 1959-60; mem. faculty U. Rochester, N.Y., 1960—; assoc. prof. dept. physics U. Rochester, 1963-68, prof., 1968-97; sr. scientist Lab. for Laser Energetics, 1985—; chmn. dept. physics and astronomy U. Rochester, 1969-74, assoc. dean spl. programs Coll. Arts and Scis., 1982-87, prof. emeritus, faculty sr. assoc., 1997—; cons. solid state sci. divsn. Argonne Nat. Lab., 1959-69, Naval Rsch. Lab., 1960-70; NSF Sr. fellow U. Leiden, 1967-68; rschr. on atomic spectra and structure, absorption and luminescence spectra ionic and molecular crystals, photosynthesis theory picosecond spectroscopy. Author: Theory of Excitons, 1963, (with A. Gold) Symmetry in the Solid State, 1964, (with D.L. Dexter) Excitons, 1965; also articles. Fellow Japan Soc. Promotion of Sci. fellow Kyoto U., 1979, Royal Soc. Guest Rsch. fellow, Fulbright fellow Imperial Coll. (London), 1993. Fellow Am. Phys. Soc. (Biol. Physics prize 1994), Am. Soc. Photobiology, Am. Assn. Physics Tchrs., Biophys. Soc. Office: U Rochester Dept Physics & Astronomy Rochester NY 14627-0171

KNOX, ROGER, zoological park administrator; b. Ark., Sept. 28, 1937. BA in Psychology, U. Ark., 1961. Chmn., CEO Federated Dept. Stores Foleys, Houston, 1963-83, Goldsmith Dept. Stores, Houston, 1983-87; pres. Memphis Zoo and Aquarium, 1988—. Office: Memphis Zoo and Aquarium 2000 Galloway Ave Memphis TN 38112-5033*

KNOX, SUSAN MARIE, paralegal; b. Crystal Lake, Ill., Oct. 7, 1941; d. Vernon J. and Hazel A. (Heimer) K. BA, Loretto Heights Coll., 1961; cert. paralegal, Roosevelt U., 1984. Legal sec. Wildman Harrold Allen & Dixon, Chgo., 1979-82; legal asst. Bishop, Callas & Wagner, Crystal Lake, 1982-84; legal sec., paralegal Karon, Morrison & Savikas, Chgo., 1984-86; legal asst. Wildman Harrold Allen & Dixon, Chgo., 1986-87; pres., owner Consider A Concierge, Crystal Lake, 1988—, Paralegal/Courier Svcs. of No. Ill., Crystal Lake, 1990—. Mem. Ill. State Bar Assn. Democrat. Roman Catholic. Avocations: golf, bridge, legal research and reading about global current events. Home: 520 Devonshire Ln Crystal Lake IL 60014-7537 Office: ParalegalCourier Svc No Ill PO Box 1696 Crystal Lake IL 60039-1696

KNOX, VENERRIA L., municipal or county official. BS in Journalism, Northwestern U., 1978; M in Adminstrn., Willamette U., 1980. Asst. to dep. treas. Treasury Dept. State of Oreg., Salem, 1979-80; fin. analyst Pacific Power, Portland, Oreg., 1980-83; fin. officer Security Pacific Bank, Seattle, 1983-85; legis. analyst City of Seattle, 1985-87, mgr. fin. and govt. ops., 1987-91, dep. dir., program support divsn. dir. Dept. Housing, 1991-93, dir. Dept. Housing and Human Svcs., 1994-99, dir. human svcs. dept., 1999—. Mem. U.S. Conf. City Human Svc. Ofcls., Nat. Cmty. Devel. Assn., Nat. Forum Black Pub. Adminstrs., African-Am. Young Women's Braintrust. Office: Human Svcs Dept-DO Dept Housing & Human Svcs 618 2nd Ave 6th Fl Seattle WA 98104-2222*

KNOX, WENDALL J., management consultant. BA in Social Rels., Harvard U.; postgrad., MIT. Dir. urban econs. practice Abt Assocs., Cambridge, Mass., 1973-83, dir. bus. rsch. and cons. practice, 1983-92, pres., CEO, 1993—; bd. dirs. Ea. Bank; adv. bd. Commonwealth Capital Ventures, BankBoston Devel. Co.; trustee Ea. Enterprises. Bd. dirs. Brigham and Women's Hosp., The Partnership, Biomed. Scis. Career Project, Corp. for Bus. Work and Learning, United Way of Mass. Bay. Mem. Greater Boston C. of C. (bd. dirs.). Office: Abt Assocs Inc 55 Wheeler St Cambridge MA 02138

KNOX, WILLIAM ARTHUR, judge; b. Fargo, N.D., Jan. 8, 1945. BS, N.D. State U., 1966; JD, U. Minn., 1968. Law specialist USCG, Boston and Juneau, Alaska, 1968-72; prof. U. Mo. Sch. Law, Columbia, 1972-85; magistrate judge U.S. Cts., Jefferson City, Mo., 1985—. Author: (books) Federal Criminal Forms, 1993, Missouri Criminal Practice, 1995. Lt. comdr. USCGR. Office: 131 W High St Jefferson City MO 65101

KNOX, WILLIAM DAVID, publishing company executive; b. Sault Ste. Marie, Mich., June 9, 1920; s. Victor A. and Bertha V. (Byers) K.; m. Jane Edith Shaw, June 15, 1941; children: Georgia Knox Mode, William David, Randall S., Brian V. BS, Mich. State U., 1941; postgrad., Harvard U., 1943-44; LLD (hon.), U. Wis., 1973. Youth editor Hoard's Dairyman mag., W.D. Hoard & Sons Co., Fort Atkinson, Wis., 1941-42; assoc. editor Hoard's Dairyman mag., W.D. Hoard & Sons Co., 1946-49, editor, 1949—, pres., treas., gen. mgr., 1972—; pres. Nat. Brucellosis Com., 1955-66, chmn. Wis. com., 1951-60; mem. nat. agrl. adv. com., 1961-62, nat. adv. com. on trade negotiations, 1976-82; bd. dirs. First Am. Bank and Trust, D.C.I. Mktg., Inc. Pres. Fort Atkinson Bd. Edn., 1948-59; bd. visitors U. Wis., 1979-84; trustee University Research Park, Inc., 1984-93; bd. dirs. Wis. Taxpayers Alliance, 1976—. Lt. USNR, 1942-46. Recipient Disting. Service award Nat. Brucellosis Com., 1957, Disting. Service award Pure Milk Assn., 1966, Disting. Service award Am. Dairy Sci. Assn., 1970, Disting. Service award Wis. Farm Bur. Fedn., 1974, Disting. Service award Nat. Assn. Animal Breeders, 1981, Disting. Service award Nat. Assn. Livestock Records, 1983, Dist. Svc. award Wis. Agri-Bus. Coun., 1992, Disting Svc. award Nat. Agri-Mktg. Assn., 1992, Outstandin ANR Patriarch award Alumni assn. Coll. of Agr. and Natural Resources, Mich. State U., 1992; service citations Fla. Dairy Farmers Fedn., 1962; service citations Wis. Farm Bur. Fedn., 1956; service citations Nat. Plant Food Council, 1963; service citations Dairy Council Central Ga., 1967; Nat. 4-H Alumni award, 1965; Mich. State U. Distinguished Alumnus award, 1966; named Tri-State Man of Yr., 1966; Milw. Milk Producers Assn. Man of Yr., 1976; recipient Mid-Am. Dairymen Salute award, 1977. Fellow Am. Dairy Sci. Assn.; mem. Agrl. Publs. Assn. (pres. 1979-81), Am. Newspaper Pubs. Assn., Am. Veterinary Med. Assn. (hon.), Am. Jersey Cattle Club (hon.), Am. Agrl. Econs. Assn., Wis. Veterinary Med. Assn. (hon.), Rotary (Internat. Service citation 1956), Alpha Gamma Rho, Alpha Zeta (Centennial Honor Roll award 1997). Republican. Episcopalian. Home: 703 Robert St Fort Atkinson WI 53538-1150 Office: Hoard's Dairyman W D Hoard & Sons Co PO Box 801 Fort Atkinson WI 53538-0801

KNUDSEN, JAMES GEORGE, chemical engineer, educator; b. Youngstown, Can., Mar. 27, 1920; s. James Skov and Rose Maude (Ray) K.; m. Joyce Mildred Renville, July 7, 1947; children—Kathryn Lee, Shelley Lynne. B.S. in Chem. Engring., U. Alta., 1943, M.S. in Phys. Chemistry, 1944; Ph.D. in Chem. Engring., U. Mich., 1949. Faculty Oreg. State U., Corvallis, 1949—, asst. prof., 1949-53, assoc. prof., 1953-57, prof. chem. engring., 1957-86, prof. emeritus, 1986—; asst. dean engring. Oreg. State U., 1959-70, assoc. dean engring., 1970-81; cons. heat transfer and fluid mechanics. Co-author: Fluid Dynamics and Heat Transfer, 1958; contbr. articles to profl. publs. NSF sr. postdoctoral fellow, 1961-62; Battelle sci. fellow, 1974. Mem. AIChE (pres. 1980, Founders award 1977, D.Q. Kern award 1983), Am. Chem. Soc. Home: 3220 NW Crest Dr Corvallis OR 97330-1807 Office: Oregon State University Corvallis OR 97331*

KNUDSEN, JOHN ROLAND, retired mathematics educator, consultant; b. Bklyn., July 12, 1916; s. Johan Sevrin and Ingeborg (Roland) K.; m. Ruth Ida Strube, June 7, 1942; children: John Karl, Thomas Paul. BS cum laude, NYU, 1937, PhD, 1951; postgrad., Johns Hopkins U., 1937-39. Teaching fellow Johns Hopkins U., Balt., 1937-39; asst. prof. math. NYU, N.Y.C., 1939-57, assoc. prof. math., 1957-72, prof. math., 1972; tech. staff mem. AT&T Bell Labs, Holmdel, N.J., 1972-83; ret., 1983; cons. AT&T Bell Labs, Murray Hill, N.J., 1957-64, Holmdel, N.J., 1968-72, 83-87; vis. prof. Bangalore (India) Univ., 1968. Co-author: Real Variables, 1969. Mem. Math. Assn. Am., Am. Math. Soc., Phi Beta Kappa. Home: 10105 Jupiter Hills Dr Austin TX 78747-1322

KNUDSEN, KERMIT BRUCE, physician; b. Mpls., Sept. 16, 1931; m. Karen Hansen, Mar. 27, 1954; children: Peter, Mark, John, Lisa, Karen. BS, Lawrence Coll., 1952; MD, U. Ill., 1956. Diplomate Am. Bd. Internal Medicine, Am. Bd. Gastroenterology. Intern St. Louis City Hosp., 1956-57; resident in internal medicine Henry Ford Hosp., Detroit, 1959-62, fellow in gastroenterology, 1962-63; cheif gastroenterology Wilford Hall USAF Hosp., San Antonio, 1963-67; pvt. practice specializing in internal medicine Boulder, Colo., 1967-68; gastroenterologist Scott & White Clinic and Hosp., Temple, Tex., 1968-96, dir. gastroenterology divsn., 1972-74, chmn. edn. dept., 1974-78, assoc. clinic bd., 1973-92, chmn. dept. internal medicine, 1979-92, pres., 1979-92; chief of staff Scott & White Meml. Hosp., Temple, 1979-92; dir. Ctr. for Outcomes Studies Scott & Whtie Clinic and Hosp., Temple, Tex., 1992-96; assoc. dean Tex. A&M U., Temple, 1975-79, prof. internal medicine, 1979-96; bd. dirs. Temple Indsl. Found., pres., 1985; bd. dirs. N.C.N. Bank, Temple. Bd. dirs. Temple Econ. Devel. Commn., 1985-88, Health Sys. Minn., Stratis Health. Fellow ACP; mem. Am. Gastroent. Assn., AMA, Am. Group Practice assn. (trustee 1983-90, sec. 1986-87, v.p. 1988, pres.-elect 1989, pres., 1989-90), Tex. Med. Assn., Alpha Omega Alpha. Lutheran. Home: 66 Ponderosa Park Dr Durango CO 81301 Office: Scott & White Clinic 2401 S 31st St Temple TX 76508-0001

KNUDSEN, LAURA GEORGIA, linguist; b. Kenosha, Wis., Sept. 21, 1969; d. Richard Dennis and Georgia Elizabeth (Perrin) Wright; m. Martin Christian Knudsen, Aug. 20, 1994. BA in Linguistics, Ind. U., 1991, MA in Linguistics, 1996. Linguist Ind. U., Bloomington, 1987—, tchr. ESL, Ctr. for English Lang. Tng., 1995—; tchr. ESL Aichi U., Toyohashi, Japan, 1998; presenter in field;. Contbr. articles to profl. jours. Fulbright scholar IIE, Budapest, 1996-97; FLAS fellow U.S. Dept. Edn., Ind. U., 1993-94, GANN fellow, 1991-92. Mem. Linguistic Soc. Am., Ind. U. Linguistic Club (sec. 1996, pres. 1998), INTESOL. Avocation: Aikido. Office: Ind U Dept Linguistics Memorial Hall 317 Bloomington IN 47405

KNUDSEN, RAYMOND BARNETT, clergyman, association executive, author; b. Denver, Nov. 11, 1919; s. Franklin Ole and Julia (Nielsen) K.; m. Edna Mae Nielsen, Jan. 26, 1940 (dec. Mar. 1992); children: Raymond Barnett, Silas John, Mark Allen, Ann Delight Knudsen Semotan; m. Virginia Harris Foster, Apr. 23, 1994. Student, Coll. Emporia, 1937-38, Wheaton Coll., 1938-39; BA, U. Denver, 1941; ThM, McCormick Theol. Sem., 1948; postgrad., U. Chgo., 1948; DD, Burton Coll., 1955, LLD, 1964; ThD, Miami Bible Inst., 1987. Ordained to ministry Presbyn. Ch., 1948. Co-founder Knudsen Printing Co., Denver, 1928; pastor 1st Presbyn. Ch., Akron, Colo., 1937-39, 8th Ave. Presbyn. Ch., Denver, 1939-40; dir. Martin M. Post Larger Parish, Logansport, Ind., 1941-44; asst. Faith Presbyn. Ch., Chgo., 1945; pastor 1st Presbyn. Ch., Warsaw, Ill., 1946-52, 5th Presbyn. Ch., Springfield, Ill., 1952-63; sr. pastor Webb Horton Meml. Presbyn. Ch., Middletown, N.Y., 1963-70; exec. dir. for donor support Nat. Coun. Chs. of Christ in U.S.A., 1970-71, asst. gen. sec., 1971-77; pres. Nat. Consultation on Fin. Devel., 1977-85, chmn., 1985-88, chmn. emeritus, 1988—; chmn. bd. dirs. Eleemysonary Publ. Co., Marlboro, N.J., 1995—; lectr. philosophy Orange County (N.Y.) C.C., 1964-70, Lectures Internat., 1994—, Norwegian Am. Cruise Line, 1996—; chaplain Moore McCormick Cruise Line, 1965, Holland Am. Lines, 1994—, Celebrity Cruise Line, 1995—, Crown Princess Cruise Line, 1996—; instr. Drew U. Sch. Theology, 1978-86, Perkins Sch. Theology So. Meth. U., 1986—; chmn. broadcasting press Synod of Ill., Presbyn. Ch., 1954-60, mem. gen. council, 1954-62; chmn. founding com. Ill. Presbyn. Home, Springfield, 1954; pres. Middletown Council Chs., 1967-69; chmn. Fifty Million Dollar Fund, Hudson River Presbytery, 1964-70; pres. Webb Horton Presbyn. Assocs.; v.p. Inst. Activation Research.; cons. Episc. Diocese of Pitts., 1977-85, Orthodox Ch. in Am., 1978-88, Christian Meth. Episc. Ch., 1983-88, Hawaii conf. United Ch. of Christ, 1983-86, Asbury Hills Camp, 1983-86; cons. Fla. Council of Chs., 1986—, Pitts. Experiment, 1987-88, Jesus Fellowship, Inc., 1987-93, 1st Bapt. Ch., Washington, 1987-90, Cornstone Consultation, 1990—, Higher Dimensions, Tulsa, 1990, David M. Wright M.D. Found., Richmond, Va., 1991, Alfalit, Inc., Miami, Fla., 1991, Abundant Life, Richmond, 1991; chaplain Ann Norton Sculpture Gardens, Inc., 1993—. Author: The Trinity, 1936, New Models for Financing the Local Church, 1974, 2d edit., 1985, New Models for Creative Giving, 1976, 2d edit., 1985, Models for Ministry, 1976, Developing Dynamic Stewardship, 1977, The Workbook, 1977, New Models for Church Administration, 1979, Steward Enlistment and Commitment, 1986, Let Your Money Do the Talking, 1987, From "Commitment?" to "Commitment!", 1987, Wiltshire Village Cookbook, 1993, 20 Seconds, 1995, The Word and Words Made Fresh Vols. I & II, 1999; mem. rev. bd. Antenna, 1963-90; contbr. religious columns to publs.; syndicated newspaper column The Counselor. Mem. Middletown Narcotics Guidance Coun., 1969-70; pres. bd. dirs. Occupations, Inc., 1964-69, treas., 1969-71, pres. emeritus, 1976—; bd. dirs. Aid to Retarded Children N.Y., 1963-66, United Presbyn. Student Found., 1962-70, Presbyn. Sr. Svcs., N.Y.C., 1981-85, Presbyn. Panel, 1981-87, Christian Collegiate Schs., Richmond, 1991; mem. exec. bd. Orange County chpt. Aid to Retarded Children; trustee Orange County Workshop for Disabled, 1963, Homemaker Svc. Orange County; pres. bd. trustees Camp Townsend, 1964-70; active Pres. Clin. Nat. Steering Com., 1995—. Recipient Author citation N.J. Inst. Tech., 1980, Cert. for Outstanding Ministry, Wheaton Coll., 1991; Dr. Raymond B. and Edna M. Knudsen ann. lectureship established in honor, 1992; Edna Mae Knudsen Meml. Fund established to fin. Knudsen Libr. and Needy Students at McCormick Theol. Sem., 1992; Dr. Raymond B., Edna M. Knudsen and Virginia F. Librs. established 1st Presbyn. Ch., West Palm Beach, Fla., 1990 and Palms West Presbyn. Ch., Loxahatchee, Fla. Mem. Nat. Temperance League (hon. v.p. chmn. nominating com. 1961-62), Alcohol Edn. Found. (bd. dirs.), Counselor Assn. Inc. (pres. 1954-82, chmn. bd. dirs. Ill. Soc. 1955-88, chmn. emeritus 1988—), Greenview Shores Civic Assn. (founder, pres. Fla. Soc. 1990-92), Lectures Internat., Masons, Rotary (chmn. internat. contacts). Home and Office: 1457 Brampton Cv Wellington FL 33414-8962 *We live in a global village in the shadow of a friendly, fatherly God. Through the structures of time and circumstances we move into the future and instead of closed doors we discover new directions, alternate routes, and challenging frontiers to bring us into each tomorrow. We discover the significance of selves as we lose ourselves in service to others. Through the interweaving of lives through the warp of generations and the woof of others we become a part of the fabric of time upon which the future stands with hope and promise.*

KNUDSEN, RUDOLPH EDGAR, JR., insurance company executive; b. Far Rockaway, N.Y., July 18, 1939; s. Rudolph Edgar and Katherine Elizabeth (Benham) K.; m. Margaret Rebecca Vreeland, June 10, 1961; children—Peter, Kathryn. AB, Columbia Coll., 1961. Programmer Met. Life Ins. Co., N.Y.C., 1961-65, Am. Life Ins. Co. N.Y., N.Y.C., 1965-70; 2d v.p. Am. Life Ins. Co. N.Y., 1971-72, v.p., 1973—. Served with USAR, 1961-62. Methodist. Club: Broken Sound. Home: 2436 NW 63rd St Boca Raton FL 33496-3626 Office: Mut of Am Life Ins Co 1150 Broken Sound Pkwy NW Boca Raton FL 33487-3525

KNUDSEN, WILLIAM CLAIRE, geophysicist; b. Provo, Utah, Dec. 12, 1925; s. Nels William and Julia A. (Brown) K.; m. Ruth Crandall, Aug. 31, 1948; children: Linda, Ruthanne, Guy, Grant. B.S., Brigham Young U., 1950; M.S., U. Wis., 1952, Ph.D., 1954. Sr. rsch. physicist Calif. Rsch. Corp., La Habra, 1954-62; staff scientist Lockheed Palo Alto Rsch. Lab., Palo Alto, Calif., 1962-84, Knudsen Geophys. Rsch. Inc., Monte Sereno, Calif., 1984-95. Patentee in field. Served with Signal Corps U.S. Army, 1944-46. Mem. Am. Geophys. Union, Sigma Xi. Mem. LDS Ch.

KNUDSON, ALFRED GEORGE, JR., medical geneticist; b. Los Angeles, Aug. 9, 1922; s. Alfred George and Mary Gladys (Galvin) K.; m. Anna T. Meadows, June 20, 1977; children by previous marriage: Linda, Nancy, Dorene. B.S., Calif. Inst. Tech., 1944, Ph.D., 1956; M.D., Columbia U., 1947. Chmn. dept. pediatrics City of Hope Med. Center, Duarte, Calif., 1956-62; chmn. dept. biology City of Hope Med. Center, 1962-66; assoc. dean Health Sci. Center, SUNY, Stony Brook, 1966-69; dean Grad. Sch. Biomed. Scis., U. Tex. Health Sci. Center, Houston, 1970-76; dir. Inst. Cancer Research, Fox Chase Cancer Center, Phila., 1976-83, sr. mem., 1976—, disting. sci., 1992—, pres., 1980-82; mem. Assembly Life Scis., NRC, 1975-81. Author: Genetics and Disease, 1965; contbr. articles to profl. jours. Recipient Charles S. Mott prize GM Cancer Rsch. Found., 1988, medal of honor Am. Cancr Soc. 1989, Charles Rodolphe Brupbacher Found. prize, 1995, Gairdner Found Internat. award, 1997, Albert Lasker Clin. Med. Rsch. award Lasker Found., 1998. Fellow AAAS; mem. NAS, Am. Philos. Soc., Am. Acad. Arts and Scis., Internat. Soc. Pediatric Oncology, Am. Soc. Human Genetics (pres. 1978, Allan award 1991), Assn. Am. Physicians, Am. Pediatrics Soc., Am. Assn. Cancer Rsch. Achievements include research in genetics of human cancer. Office: Inst Cancer Rsch 7701 Burholme Ave Philadelphia PA 19111-2412

KNUDSON, HARRY EDWARD, JR., retired electrical manufacturing company executive; b. N.Y.C., Dec. 30, 1921; s. Harry Edward and Helen (Jones) K.; m. Anne Howland, Sept. 21, 1944; children—Anne, Erik. B.S. in Elec. Engring, Bucknell U., 1947. Cadet engr. Phila. Electric Co., 1947; with Fed. Pacific Electric Co., Newark, 1947-80; exec. v.p. Fed. Pacific Electric Co., 1970-76, pres., 1976-80; also dir., corp. v.p. parent co. Reliance Electric Co., 1979-80; v.p; gen. mgr. distbn. and control GTE Products Corp., Danvers, Mass., 1980-84, ret. Bd. dirs. Trenton Psychiat. Hosp., 1995-98. Served with USNR, 1943-46. Mem. Nat. Elec. Mfrs. Assn. (chmn. bd. govs., mem. officers com.), Elec. Mfrs. Club, Phi Kappa Psi, Kappa Eta Nu. Methodist. Home: 608 Johnston Dr Watchung NJ 07060-6467

KNUDSON, RUTHANN, environmental consultant; b. Milw., Oct. 24, 1941; d. Sidney Olaus and Clara Ruth (Tappe) K. BA magna cum laude, U. Minn., 1963, MA, 1966; PhD, Wash. State U., 1973; postgrad., U. Idaho, 1988. Seasonal ranger Nat. Park Svc., Bandelier Nat. Monument, N.Mex., 1963; instr. U. No. Colo., Greeley, 1966-68; asst. rsch. prof. U. Idaho, Moscow, 1974-79, assoc. rsch. prof., 1979-81; dir. cultural resource svcs. Woodward Clude Cons., San Francisco, 1981-86, v.p., shareholder, 1985-88; archaeologists Nat. Park Svc., Washington, 1990-96; supr. Agate Fossil Beds Nat. Monument, 1996—; prin. Knudson Assoc. (formerly Paleo-Designs), 1974%; vis. asst. prof. Wright State U., Dayton, Ohio, 1974; cons. Am. Folklife Ctr., Washington, 1981-83, NRC, Washington, 1982, 83; resource cons. Calif. Heritage Task Force, 1983-94, Office Tech. Assessment, Washington, 1986; Woodward lectr., 1985. Author: Cambria Village Ceramics, 1967; Organizational Variability in Late Paleo-Indian Assemblages, 1983, Contemporary Cultural Resource Mamangement, 1986; co-editor: The Public Trust and the First Americans, 1995, The 10, 000 year old Libbick Artifact Assemblage, 1998. Bd. dirs. Preservation Action, Washington, 1980*85, 89-90, Californians for Preservation Action, 1981-82; sec.-treas. Idaho NOW, 1977-78. Recipient Preservation award Nat. Conf. State Historic Preservation Officers, 1981, Conservation award Am. Soc. Conservation Archaeology, 1981. Mem. Soc. Applied Anthropoligy, Am. Anthropol. Assn. (Margaret Mead award 1983), Soc. Am. Archaeology (exec. bd. 1979-81, exec. com. 1983-85, legis. coord. 1979-82, chmn. com. pub. archaeology 1980-82, 84-85), Women's Coun. Energy & Environ. (bd. dirs. 1994-96), Soc. Vert. Paleontology, Phi Beta Kappa. Home: 343 River Rd Harrison NE 69346-2734 Office: Agate Fossil Beds Nat Monument 301 River Rd Harrison NE 69346-2734

KNUDSON, THOMAS JEFFERY, journalist; b. Manning, Iowa, July 6, 1953; s. Melvin Jake and Coreen Rose (Nickum) K. B.A. in Journalism, Iowa State U., 1980. Reporter/intern Wall Street Jour., Chgo., summer 1979; staff writer Des Moines Register, 1980-99; sr. writer Sacramento (Calif.) Bee, 1999—. Office: Sacramento Bee PO Box 15779 Sacramento CA 95852-0779

KNUDTSON, DIANE MARIE, elementary education educator; b. Urbana, Ill., Nov. 13, 1970; d. Ronald Erwin Walters and Lorine Marie Pearson; m. Dean Leon Knudtson, July 16, 1994; 1 child, Rachel Marie. BA, Carthage Coll., 1993; MA, Lesley U., 1997. Cert. 1-8 tchr., K-8 spl. edn. tchr., Wis. Spl. edn. educator Bain Elem. Sch., Kenosha, Wis., from 1994; tchr. Whittier Elem. Sch., Pleasant Prairie, Wis.; tutor Bain-Best Plus, Kenosha, 1993-94. Home: 23717 65th St Salem WI 53168-9642 Office: Whittier Elem Sch 8452 Copper Rd Pleasant Prairie WI 53158

KNUDTSON, NANCY ANN, family nurse practitioner; b. Spencer, Iowa, Nov. 29, 1962; d. Ronald Arthur and Willa May (Nagel) Moeller; m. Donald Wayne Knudtson, Sept. 6, 1987. BSN, U. Iowa, 1986; MS, S.D. State U., 1995. RN, Iowa; cert. family nurse practitioner ANCC. Nurse orthopedic, surg. St. Mary's Hosp., Rochester, Minn., 1986-87; nurse med./surg. North Iowa Med. Ctr., Mason City, 1987-88; nurse ICU, critical care unit Naeve Hosp., Albert Lea, Minn., 1988-90, St. Joseph Mercy Hosp., Mason City, 1990-91; clinic supr. Lake Mills and Northwood, Iowa, 1991-93; office nurse Lake Mills and Northwood, Iowa, 1991-95; family nurse practitioner Lake Mills (Iowa) Clinic Mayo Health Sys., 1995—. Mem. Am. Acad. Nurse Practitioners, S.E. Minn. Nurse Practitioners, Iowa Assn. Nurse Practitioners, Sigma Theta Tau. Home: 222 482nd St Lake Mills IA 50450-8032

KNUE, JOSEPH, writer, historian; b. Denver, Mar. 18, 1952; s. Joseph Edward Jr. and Edythe Marie (McCracken) K.; m. Marna Jean Benjamin, June 20, 1980; stepchildren: Miriamah Saba Turpin, Jesse N. Saba. BA, Colo. State U., 1974. Adminstrv. asst. N.D. State Hwy. Dept., Bismarck, 1975-76; writer, 1976—; vis. writer Bismarck State Coll., 1997; invitee Regional Authors Autograph Party, Augustana Coll. Ctr. for Western Studies, Sioux Falls, S.D., 1997. Author: Of Time and the Prairie, 1988, Big Game in North Dakota, 1991 (award Am. Libr. Assn. 1992), North Dakota Wildlife Viewing Guide, 1992 (award Am. Libr. Assn. 1992), Nebraska Wildlife Viewing Guide, 1997; co-author: Feathers from the Prairie, 1989. Mem. Phi Beta Kappa. Avocations: fine woodworking, antiques restoration, classic auto restoration. Home: 110 City # 4 San Antonio TX 78204-1343

KNUE, PAUL FREDERICK, newspaper editor; b. Lawrenceburg, Ind., July 11, 1947; s. Paul F. and Neil (Beadel) K.; m. Elizabeth Wegner, Sept. 6, 1969; children: Amy, Katherine. BS in Journalism and English, Murray State U., 1969. Mng. editor Evansville Press, Ind., 1975-79; editor Ky. Post, Covington, 1979-83, Cin. Post., 1983—. Trustee Scripps Howard Found. Mem. Am. Soc. Newspaper Editors, AP Mng. Editors Assn., AP Soc. Ohio (trustee). Home: PO Box 30067 Cincinnati OH 45230-0067 Office: E W Scripps Co 125 E Court St Cincinnati OH 45202-1212

KNULL, ERHARD, minister; b. Radomsko, Poland, June 25, 1929; came to U.S., 1952.; s. Richard and Martha (Kamchen) K.; m. Lydia Penno, July 21, 1956; children: Carmen Ruth Knull Bloomster, Ralph Erhard Carl. BA, Sioux Falls Coll., 1960; BD, No. Am. Bapt. Seminary, 1961; post grad., U. Tuebingen, Fed. Republic Germany, 1961-62; MA, Kent state U., 1973; MDiv, North Am. Bapt. Seminary, 1984; postgrad., Chaplain Tng. Sch., St. Louis, 1974, Samaritan Counseling Ctr., Lakewood, Ohio, 1982-83. Ordained to ministry Bapt. Ch, 1963; cert. VA chaplain, Washington. Min. Rosenfeld Bapt. Ch., Drake, N.D., 1962-65, Missionary Bapt. Ch., Parma, Ohio, 1965-69; lectr. Kent (Ohio) State U., 1969; sr. staff chaplain Louis Stokes Cleve. Dept. of Veterans Affairs Med. Ctr., Brecksville, 1970—; chaplain, counselor DVA Community Outreach program, Cleve., 1978—. Contbr. articles to profl. jours. Active Parma Heights Bapt. Ch., also tchr., advisor men's fellowship. Mem. North Am. Bapt. Conf. (endorsed chaplain), North Am. Bapt. Sem. Alumni Assn. Baptist. Avocations: reading, bicycling, traveling, walking, gardening. Office: Louis Stokes Cleve Med Ctr Dept Vets Affairs 10000 Brecksville Rd Dept Vets Cleveland OH 44141-3204

KNUPP, RALPH, publishing company executive. Sr. v.p. human resources Reed Elsevier, Inc., Newton, Mass. Office: Reed Elsevier Inc 275 Washington St Newton MA 02458-1646

KNUTESON, MILES GENE, advertising executive; b. Wisconsin Rapids, Wis., Aug. 18, 1952; s. Kenneth Thomas and Myrtle Lucille (Knoll) K.; m. Christine Marie Coleman, Aug. 18, 1979; children: Katherine Marie, Emily Melissa. BS, U. Wis., Stevens Point, 1974. News reporter Sta. WHBY, Appleton, Wis., 1974-77; account exec. Sta. WHBY, Appleton, 1977-79; gen. sales mgr. Sta. WAPL, Appleton, 1979-80, Stas. WHBY, WAPL-FM, Appleton, 1980-81, Sta. WGEE, Green Bay, Wis., 1981-83; v.p., gen. mgr. Stas. KIOA/KDWZ-FM, Des Moines, 1983-88; v.p. sales, mktg. Midwest Communications, Inc., Des Moines, 1988-89; gen. sales mgr. Sta. WMEE/WQHK, Ft. Wayne, Ind., 1988-89, Stas. WTTS/WGCL, Bloomington, Ind., 1989-90; v.p., gen. mgr. Stas. WFHR/WGLX, Wisconsin Rapids, Wis., 1990—. Bd. dirs. United Way, Wisconsin Rapids, 1991-92, campaign chairperson, 1992, pres., 1994; chmn. adv. bd. Salvation Army, Appleton, 1981-83, mem. adv. bd., Bloomington; chmn. Distributive Edn. Adv. Bd., 1980, chmn. pub. rels. com., Des Moines, 1987. Recipient Pub. Affairs award N.W. Broadcast News Assn., 1976, Sch. Bell award Wis. Edn. Assn. Coun., 1976. Mem. Des Moines Radio Broadcasters Assn. (v.p., sec., chmn.), Wis. Broadcasters Assn. (bd. dirs. 1995—), Fox Cities C. of C. (amb.), Wisconsin Rapids Area C. of C. (bd. dirs. 1994—, chmn. 1996), Rotary (bd. dirs. Wisconsin Rapids chpt. 1995—). Lutheran. Avocations: golf, gardening. Home: 5411 Barberry Dr Wisconsin Rapids WI 54494-1524

KNUTH, DONALD ERVIN, computer sciences educator; b. Milw., Jan. 10, 1938; s. Ervin Henry and Louise Marie (Bohning) K.; m. Jill Carter, June 24, 1961; children: John Martin, Jennifer Sierra. BS, MS, Case Inst. Tech., 1960; PhD, Calif. Inst. Tech., 1963; DSc (hon.), Case Western Res. U., 1980, Luther Coll., Decorah, Iowa, 1985, Lawrence U., 1985, Muhlenberg Coll., 1986, U. Pa., 1986, U. Rochester, 1986, SUNY, Stony Brook, 1987, Valparaiso U., 1988, Oxford (Eng.) U., 1988, Brown U., 1988, Grinnell Coll., 1989, Dartmouth Coll., 1990, Concordia U., Montréal, 1991, Adelphi U., 1993, Masaryk U., Brno, 1996, Duke U., 1998, St. Andrews U., 1998; Docteur, U. Paris-Sud, Orsay, 1986; Marne-la-Vallée, 1993; D Tech., Royal Inst. Tech., Stockholm, 1991; Pochetnogo Doktora, St. Petersburg U., Russia, 1992. Asst. prof. Calif. Inst. Tech., Pasadena, 1963-66, assoc. prof., 1966-68; prof. Stanford (Calif.) U., 1968-92, prof. emeritus, 1993—; cons. Burroughs Corp., Pasadena, 1960-68. Author: The Art of Computer Programming, 1968 (Steele prize 1987), Computers and Typesetting, 1986. Guggenheim Found. fellow, 1972-73; recipient Nat. medal of Sci., Pres. James Carter, 1979, Disting. Alumni award Calif. Inst. Tech., 1978, Priestly award Dickinson Coll., 1981, Franklin medal, 1988, J.D. Warnier prize, 1989, Adelsköld medal Swedish Acad. Scis., 1994, Harvey prize Israel Institute of Technology, 1995, Kyoto prize Inamori Found., 1996. Fellow Am. Acad. Arts and Scis.; mem. IEEE (hon., McDowell award 1980, Computer Pioneer award 1982, von Neumann medal 1995), NAS, Nat. Acad. Engring., Assn. for Computing Machinery (Grace Murray Hopper award 1971, Alan M. Turing award 1974, Computer Sci. Edn. award 1986, Software Sys. award 1986), Acad. Sci. (fgn. assoc. Paris, Oslo and Munich). Fellow, The Computer Mus. Lutheran. Avocation: playing pipe organ. Office: Stanford Univ Computer Scis Dept Stanford CA 94305-9045

KNUTH, ELDON LUVERNE, engineering educator; b. Luana, Iowa, May 10, 1925; s. Alvin W. and Amanda M. (Becker) K.; m. Marie O. Parrat, Sept. 10, 1954 (div. 1973); children: Stephen B., Dale L., Margot O., Lynette M.; m. Margaret I. Nicholson, Dec. 30, 1973. B.S., Purdue U., 1949, M.S., 1950; Ph.D. (Guggenheim fellow), Calif. Inst. Tech., 1953. Aerothermodynamics group leader Aerophysics Devel. Corp., 1953-56; asso. research engr. dept. engring. UCLA, 1956-59, asso. prof. engring., 1960-65, prof. engring. and applied sci., 1965-91, prof. emeritus, 1991—, head chem., nuclear thermal div. dept. engring., 1963-65, chmn. energy kinetics dept., 1969-75, head molecular-beam lab., 1961-88; Gen. chmn. Heat Transfer and Fluid Mechanics Inst., 1959; vis. scientist, von Humboldt fellow Max-Planck Inst. für Strömungsforschung, Göttingen, Fed. Republic Germany, 1975-76. Author: Introduction to Statistical Thermodynamics, 1966; also numerous articles. Served with AUS, 1943-45. Mem. AIAA, Am. Soc. Engring. Edn., Am. Inst. Chem. Engrs., Combustion Inst., Soc. Engring. Sci., AAAS, Am. Phys. Soc., Am. Vacuum Soc., Sigma Xi, Tau Beta Pi, Gamma Alpha Rho, Pi Tau Sigma, Sigma Delta Chi, Pi Kappa Phi. Club: Gimlet (Lafayette, Ind.). Patentee radial-flow molecular pump. Home: 18085 Boris Dr Encino CA 91316-4350

KNUTH, ERIC JOSEPH, lawyer; b. Detroit, Oct. 25, 1964; s. Harold Joseph and Mary Kay (Werthmann) K.; m. Toni Lynn Yopps, Dec. 19, 1987; children: Cory, Kelsey, Christa. BS, No. Mich. U., 1987; JD cum laude, Thomas Cooley Law Sch., Lansing, Mich., 1990. Bar: Mich. 1991, U.S. Dist. Ct. (ea. and we. dists.) Mich. 1991, U.S. Ct. Appeals (6th cir.) 1992, U.S. Dist. Ct. (ea. dist.) Wis. 1994. Law clk. Reid & Reid Law Firm, Lansing, Mich., 1987-90; rsch. atty. Mich. Ct. of Appeals, Detroit, 1990; atty. Mouw & Celello, Iron Mountain, Mich., 1991-97, Bernstein & Bernstein, 1997-99, Law Offices of Christopher Varjabedian, P.C., 1999—; mem. Cooley-Am. Bar Assn. Nat. Trial Team, Lansing, 1989-90; instr. Thomas Cooley-Legal Methods Course, Lansing, 1990. Recipient Am. Jurisprudence Book award-Advocacy, Lawyers Coop., 1989, Am. Jurisprudence Book award-Sales, 1990, Merit award Gun Control, 1990, Disting. Student award Cooley Law Sch., 1990. Mem. ABA, ATLA, State Bar of Mich., Dickinson County Bar Assn. Democrat. Roman Catholic. Avocations: volleyball, hunting, softball.

KNUTH, MONA MAY, nursing administrator, educator; b. Sugar Grove, Ill., June 16, 1912; d. Ruel Horace and Hazel (Graham) Mighell; m. Martin H. Knuth, Nov. 5, 1940 (dec. Sept. 1990); 1 child, Kim M. (dec.). Diploma, Copley Meml. Sch. Nursing, Aurora, Ill., 1932; BA in Psychology, Aurora U., 1976. Instr., staff devel. dept. Copley Meml. Hosp., Aurora, 1970-80; adminstr. Galena Blvd. Nursing Home, Aurora, 1953-64; DON St. Joseph Mercy Hosp., Aurora, 1964-70; vol., staff devel. dept. Copley Meml. Hosp., Aurora, 1980—.

KNUTSEN, ALAN PAUL, pediatrician, allergist, immunologist; b. Mpls., July 21, 1948; s. Donald Richard and Shirley Marie (Erickson) K.; children: Laura Joelle, Brian A., Benjamin C., Elizabeth G., Katherine M., Amy S. BA, U. Calif., Riverside, 1971; MD, St. Louis U., 1975. Resident pediatrics St. Louis U. Med. Ctr., 1975-78; fellow allergy Duke U. Med. Ctr., Durham, N.C., 1978-80, 1980-93; dir. St. Louis U. Med. Ctr., 1985—; prof. St. Louis U., 1993—, 1993—; mem. credentials com. St. Louis U. Med. Ctr., 1980—, infectious disease com., 1980—; dir. diagnostic pediatric immunology lab, 1983—; cons. NIOSH, 1984. Contbr. articles to profl. jours. Mem. Am. Acad. Allergy/Immunology, Southwestern Allergy Assn., Clin. Immunology Soc., Mo. State Allergy Assn., So. Pediatric Rsch., Phi Beta Kappa, Alpha Omega Alpha. Democrat. Presbyterian. Home: 437 California Ave Saint Louis MO 63119-3119 Office: St Louis U Pediatric Rsch Inst 1465 S Grand Blvd Saint Louis MO 63104-1003

KNUTSON, DAVID HARRY, retired lawyer, banker; b. St. Paul, Dec. 17, 1934; s. Harry E. and Violet I. (Ekberg) K.; m. Kirsten Birgit Eriksen, Aug. 20, 1977; 1 child, Clara Elizabeth. AB cum laude, Harvard U., 1956, LLB, 1961; LLM in Corp. Law, NYU, 1990, LLM in Taxation, 1994. Bar: Minn. 1962, N.Y. 1963. Assoc. Lord, Day & Lord, N.Y.C., 1962-69; staff atty. Freeport Minerals Co., N.Y.C., 1969-70, asst. sec., 1970-75, sec., 1975-85, v.p., 1984-85, sr. atty., 1985-86; sec. Freeport-McMoRan Inc., N.Y.C., 1980-85; v.p., sr. assoc. counsel The Chase Manhattan Bank, N.Y.C., 1986-96, securities law counsel, 1992-96; dir., treas. Roxbury Land Trust, Inc. Am.-Scandinavian Found. fellow U. Copenhagen, Fulbright travel grantee, 1961-62. Mem. Assn. of Bar of City of N.Y., ABA, Harvard Club of N.Y.C. Lutheran. Home: 201 E 79th St Apt 10A New York NY 10021-0836 also: Weekends 45 Davenport Rd Roxbury CT 06783-1001

KNUTSON, DAVID LEE, lawyer, state senator; b. Mpls., Nov. 24, 1959; s. Howard Arthur and Jerroldine Margo (Sundby) K.; m. Laurie Sjoquist, June 25, 1983; children: Ann Marie, Timothy David. BA, St. Olaf Coll., 1982; JD, William Mitchell Coll. Law, 1986. Bar: Minn. 1986, U.S. Dist. Ct. Minn. 1986, U.S. Ct. Appeals (8th cir.) 1987, U.S. Tax Ct. 1989. Pvt. practice Burnsville, Minn., 1986—; mem. Minn. State Senate Dist. 36, 1993—, asst. minority leader, 1995—. Bd. dirs. Our Saviour's Shelter for Homeless, Mpls., 1988-90, City Task Force on Arts, Burnsville, 1988, Legal Assistance Dakota County, Ltd., 1994—, Dakota County Tech. Coll. Found., 1994—; bd. dirs. Minn. Valley YMCA, 1988—, chmn., 1991-93. Named one of Ten Outstanding Young Minnesotans, Minn. Jaycees, 1993; recipient Lake Conf. Disting. Alumni award, 1996, Pro Bono Publico award Legal Svcs. Coalition, 1998. Mem. Minn. Bar Assn., Dakota County Bar Assn., Burnsville Jaycees (bd. dirs. 1988-90), Apple Valley C. of C., Burnsville C. of C. (bd. dirs. 1990-92), Burnsville Breakfast Rotary. Republican. Avocation: reading, travel, sports. Office: Knutson Law Office 100 Ames Bus Ctr 2500 W County Rd 42 Burnsville MN 55337

KNUTSON, ROGER CRAIG, marketing and sales professional, inventor; b. Omaha, Mar. 5, 1952; s. Roy Victor and Charlotte Ann (Rosa) K. B of Physics, BS in Math., U. Minn., 1975. Mgr., founder Ecumenical Coffeehouse, Omaha, 1967-69; instr. SCUBA, coach swim team City of Mpls., City of Omaha, 1969-75; qualifications test dir. aerospace divsn. Control Data Corp., Bloomington, Minn., 1974-77; regional product specialist GenRad Inc., Schaumburg, Ill., 1977-80; dist. mgr. Computervision, Indpls., 1980-91; owner, founder Computer Aided Tools and Svc., Indpls., 1991-94; sr. sales rep. MacNeal Schwendler Corp., Indpls., 1994-96; chief technologist, founder Magitech Inc., Indpls., 1995, also bd. dirs.; product data mgmt. maj. account exec., exec. br. mgr. Structural Dynamics Rsch. Corp., Indpls., 1996—. Patentee in field of environ. conservation and edn. Commr. Boy Scouts Am. Recipient Commendation for Heroism City of Mpls., 1974, Double Ruby award Nat. Forensic League, 1969. Mem. MENSA, Intertel Soc. Avocations: collector of antiques, minerals and fossils, aquatics, SCUBA, theoretical physics, sports, home of America's most extensive pending collection of shells. Home: 6444 Dover Rd Indianapolis IN 46220-4554

KNUTSON, RONALD DALE, economist, educator, academic adminstrator; b. Montevideo, Minn., July 12, 1940; s. Claus and Alice (Peterson) K.; m. Sharron DeGree, Sept. 16, 1961; children: Scott, Ryan, Nicole. B.S., U. Minn., 1962, Ph.D., 1967; M.S., Pa. State U., 1963. Prof. Purdue U., 1967-73; staff economist Agrl. Mktg. Service, USDA, Washington, 1971-73; adminstr. Farmer Coop. Service, 1973-75; prof. dept. agrl. econs. Tex. A&M U., 1975—, dir. Agrl. Food Policy Ctr., 1989—; econ. cons. Kraft, Borden Inc., Sun-Diamond, Am. Bankers Assn., Milk Industry Found., GAO, U.S. Dept. Justice, Am. Farm Bur. Fedn., White House Food and Nutrition Study, NAS, U.S. Congress, Nat. Commn. on Productivity Exec. Office Pres.; project leader Rural Devel. Policy; chmn. milk pricing adv. com. U.S. Dept. Agr.; mem. Pres. Reagan's Transition Task Force for Agr., 1980-81; mem. agrl. policy adv. com. Sec. Agr. and Trade Rep., 1980-87; bd. dirs. Farm Found. Author: (with J.B. Penn and B.L. Flinchbaugh) Agricultural and Food Policy, 4th edit., 1997. Recipient Lifetime Achievement award So. Agrl. Econs. Assn., 1995, Faculty Disting. Achievement award in Ext., 1984, Faculty Disting. Achievement award in Tchg., 1998 Assn. Former Students of Tex. A&M U. Mem. Am. Agrl. Econs. Assn., So. Agrl. Econ. Assn. Home: 1011 Rose Cir College Station TX 77840-2327 Office: Tex A&M U Dept Agrl Food Policy Ctr College Station TX 77843

KNUTZEN, MARTHA LORRAINE, lawyer; b. Bellingham, Wash., Aug. 28, 1956. BA in Polit. Sci., Scripps Coll., 1978; MA in Polit. Sci, Practical Politics, U. San Francisco, 1981, JD, 1981. Bar: Calif. Lawyer, mgr. legal computer support svcs. San Francisco, 1981—. Staff mem. Barbara Boxer for Senate Campaign, 1992; mem. San Francisco Citizens' Adv. Com. on Elections, 1994—; pres. Harvey Milk Lesbian/Gay/Bisexual Dem. Club, 1995; 3rd vice chair Dem. Party, San Francisco, 1992—; chair San Francisco Human Rights Commn., 1996—; comty. organizer; assisted in founding and developing a lesbian rights advocacy orgn.; participant in many polit. campaigns as vol., 1986—. Recipient Harvey Milk Lesbian/Gay Bisexual Dem. Club Vol. of Yr. award, 1994, Civil Rights Leadership award, 1996, Alice B. Toklas Lesbian/Gay Dem. Club Vol. of Yr. award, 1997. Home: 109 Bartlett St Apt 301 San Francisco CA 94110-3087 Office: Office of Atty Gen 50 Fremont St San Francisco CA 94105-2230*

KNYCHA, JOSEF, journalist; b. Summerside, P.E.I., Can., Apr. 19, 1953; s. Michael Stanley and Marjorie Mary (Gallant) K. Student pub. schs., Auburn, N.S., Can. Reporter Halifax Herald Ltd., N.S., 1971-81; editor The Mirror, Cameron Publs., Kentville, N.S., 1981-82, editor The Register, 1982-84; bus./markets/automotive editor Star-Phoenix, Saskatoon, Sask., Can., 1984-89, asst. news editor, 1990-96; exec. editor World of Wheels Pub. Inc., Toronto, Can., 1996—; editor Cross Country Publs., Brandon Man., 1989-90. Southam fellow U. Toronto. Mem. Automobile Journalists Assn. Can. (past pres.). Office: World of Wheels Pub Inc 1200 Markham Rd Ste 300, Scarborough, ON Canada M1H 3C3

KO, WEN-HSIUNG, electrical engineering educator; b. Shang-Hong, Fukien, China, Apr. 12, 1923; came to U.S., 1954, naturalized, 1963; s. Sing-Ming and Sou-Yu (Kao) K.; m. Christina Chen, Oct. 12, 1957; children: Kathleen, Janet, Linda, Alexander. BSEE, Nat. Amoy U., Fukien, China, 1946; MS, Case Inst. Tech., 1956, PhD, 1959. Engr., then sr. engr. Taiwan Telecommunication Adminstrn., 1946-54; mem. faculty Case Inst. Tech., Cleve., 1956-93; prof. elec. and biomed. engring. Case Western Res. U., Cleve., 1967-93, prof. emeritus, 1994—, dir. engring. design center, 1970-82; pres., prin. Wen H. Ko & Assocs., Cleve., 1996—; cons. NSF, N.Am. Mfg. Co., NIH, 1966-82; rschr. in med. implant electronics, telemetry and stimulation, microsensors and microactators, micro-electro-mech.-sys. Recipient career achievement award Transducer Internat. Conf., Chgo., 1997. Fellow IEEE, AIMBE; mem. Instrument Soc. Am., Bio-Med. Engring. Soc., Sigma Xi, Eta Kappa Nu. Home: 1356 Forest Hills Blvd Cleveland OH 44118-1359 Office: Case Western Res U Electronics Design Ctr Cleveland OH 44106

KOART, NELLIE HART, real estate investor and executive; b. San Luis Obispo, Calif., Jan. 3, 1930; d. Will Carleton and Nellie Malchen (Cash) Hart; m. William Harold Koart, Jr., June 16, 1951 (dec. 1976); children: Kristen Marie Kittle, Matthew William. Student Whittier Coll., 1947-49; BA, U. Calif.-Santa Barbara, 1952; MA, Los Angeles State Coll., 1957. Life diploma elem. edn., Calif. Farm worker Hart Farms, Montebello, Calif., 1940-48; play leader Los Angeles County Parks and Recreation, East Los Angeles, Rosemead, Calif., 1948-51; elem. tchr. Potrero Heights Sch. Dist., South San Gabriel, Calif., 1951-55, vice prin., 1955-57; real estate salesman William Koart Real Estate, Goleta, Calif., 1963-76, real estate investor KO-ART Enterprises, Goleta, 1976—, pres. Wm. Koart Constrn. Co., Inc., Goleta, 1975-91; real estate sales person Joseph McGeever Realty Co., Goleta, 1976-91; adv. bd. Bank of Montecito, Santa Barbara, Calif., 1983—. Editor: Reflections, 1972. Charter mem. Calif. Regents program Calif. Fedn. Republican Women, 1989; treas. Santa Barbara County Fedn. Republican Women, Alamar-Hope Ranch, 1981-82, treas. County Bd., 1983-84, auditor, 1985, 96, 97; treas. Com. to Recall Hone, Maschke and Shewczyk, Goleta, 1984; treas. Santa Barbara County Lincoln Club, 1983-87, bd. dirs., 1983-93; assoc. mem. state central com. Calif. Republican Party, 1985-87. Mem. Santa Barbara Apartment Assn., Antique Automobile Club of Am. (sec.-treas. Santa Barbara 1980-84), Serena Cove Owners Assn. (sec.-treas, bd. dirs 1990—), Goleta Bus. Roundtable Advisory Group. Clubs: Moderate Republican Majority, Alamar - Hope Ranch republican Women's Club, GALS Republican Women's Club, Santa Barbara Women's Club, Channel City Club, Santa Barbara County Lincoln Club, Santa Barbara County Tax-Payers Assn. Avocations: swimming, numismatics, geneology, college and professional football. Office: KO-ART Enterprises PO Box 310 Goleta CA 93116-0310

KOBAK, ALFRED JULIAN, JR., obstetrician, gynecologist; b. Chgo., Feb. 10, 1935; s. Alfred J. and Rose B. (Baron) K.; m. Sue B. Stein, May 3, 1959; children: William, Steven, Jane, Deborah. *Son William Koback is Assistant Professor Obstetrics and Gynecology at University of Southern California and Chief of Gynecology at the University Hospital of the University of Southern California. Son Steve is father of daughter Sara. Daughter Jane is owner of Lake and Land Outfitters of Valparaiso, Indiana. Daughter Deborah has recently married Daniel Nielson of Washington, D.C. Sue (Stein) Koback is associated with Advertising Concepts, Inc. of Valparaiso, Indiana. Steve is a manager at Intel Corporation, Portland, Oregon. Deborah is manager of corporate relations for the World Resources Institute.* BS, U. Ill., 1957, MD, 1959. Diplomate Am. Bd. Ob-Gyn. Intern Michael Reese Hosp., Chgo., 1959-60; resident Cook County Hosp., 1960-62, 64-65; practice medicine specializing in ob-gyn. Valparaiso, Ind., 1965—; mem. med. staff Porter Meml. Hosp., Valparaiso, 1965—, pres., 1981-82; asst. clin. prof. ob-gyn Ind. U.; clin. instr. ob-gyn Rush Med. Sch., Chgo.; pres. Ob-Gyn Assocs., Valparaiso, 1970—. Contbr. articles to med. jours. Bd. dirs. Northwest Ind. Jewish Fedn., 1970-84, Porter County Bd. Health, 1991—, pres., 1997. Served to capt. USAF, 1962-64. Fellow ACS, Internat. Coll. Surgeons, Am. Coll. Ob-Gyn.; mem. AMA, Am. Soc. for Reproductive Medicine, Ind. Med. Assn., Ctrl. Assn. Obstetricians and Gynecologists, Porter County Med. Soc. (pres. 1979, 86), Chgo. Gynecol. Soc. (v.p. 1998-99), Sand Creek Club. Republican. Office: 1101 Glendale Blvd Valparaiso IN 46383-3724

KOBAK, JAMES BENEDICT, management consultant; b. St. Louis, Mar. 4, 1921; s. Edgar and Evelyn (Hubert) K.; m. Hope McEldowney, June 13, 1942; children: James Benedict, John D. (dec.), Thomas M. BS, Harvard U., 1942; postgrad. in accounting, Pace Coll., 1946-49. CPA, N.Y., La., Union S.Africa. Assoc. J.K. Lasser & Co., N.Y.C., 1946-71; partner J.K. Lasser & Co., 1954-64, adminstrv. partner, 1964-71; internat. adminstrv. partner Lasser, Harmood Banner, Dunwoody, N.Y.C., 1964-71; pres. James B. Kobak & Co., Darien, Conn., 1971—; ptnr. James B. Kobak Bus. Models Co., 1972-82; founder Kobak Open. Chmn. mag. com.; mem. bus. com. Nat. council Boy Scouts Am.; co-founder, sec.-treas. John D. Kobak Appalachian Edn. Found., Darien; trustee Hill Sch., Pottstown, Pa. Served to capt., F.A. AUS, 1942-46. Mem. AICPA, N.Y. State Soc. CPAs, Transvall Soc. Accts., Harvard Club (N.Y.C.), Wee Burn Country Club (Darien), Hapenny Bay Beach Club (St. Croix), Carambola Golf Club, St. Croix Country Club. Home and Office: 4 Mansfield Pl Darien CT 06820-2814 Home: Sweet Lime Village # 29 Kingshill VI 00850*

KOBAYASHI, ALBERT SATOSHI, mechanical engineering educator; b. Chgo., Dec. 9, 1924; s. Toshiyuki and Taka (Torii) K.; m. Elizabeth Midori Oba, Sept. 24, 1953; children: Dori Kobayashi Ogami, Tina, Laura. BS in Engring., U. Tokyo, 1947; MSME, U. Wash., 1952; PhD, Ill. Inst. Tech., 1958. Position II engr. Konishiroku Photo Industry, Tokyo, 1947-50; design engr. Ill. Tools Works, Chgo., 1953-55; rsch. engr. Armour Rsch. Found., Ill. Inst. Tech., Chgo., 1955-58; from asst. prof. to assoc. prof. dept. mech. engring. U. Wash., Seattle, 1958-64, prof., 1964-97, Boeing Pennell prof. structural mechanics, 1988-95, prof. emeritus, 1997—; coll. faculty assoc. The Boeing Co., Seattle, 1958-76; cons. Math. Sci. Northwest, Bellevue, Wash., 1962-82, UN Development Program, N.Y., 1984; vis. scholar U. Tokyo, 1969, 77; program dir. mech., structural and materials engring. div. NSF, 1987-88. Contbr. over 440 papers to Fracture Mechanics, Exptl. Mechanics Biomechanics and numerical analysis. Recipient F. G. Tatnell award Soc. Exptl. Stress Analysis, 1973, B.J. Lazan award, 1981, R. E. Peterson award, 1983, William Murray Lecture medal, 1983, Burlington Resources Found. Faculty Achievement award, 1992, M. M. Frocht award, 1995, G. E. Sr. Rsch. award Am. Soc. Engring. Edn., 1995, Disting. Alumni award Univ. Student Club (UW), 1997; decorated Order of Rising Sun, gold rays with neck ribbons Emperor of Japan, 1997. Fellow ASME, Soc. Exptl. Mechanics (hon. life mem., pres. 1989-90); mem. NAE, ASTM, Am. Ceramic Soc. Home: 15420 62nd Pl NE Kenmore WA 98028-4312 Office: U Wash Dept Mech Engring Box 352600 Seattle WA 98195-2600

KOBAYASHI, HERBERT SHIN, electrical engineer; b. Webster, Tex., Feb. 6, 1929; s. Mitsutaro and Moto Kobayashi; m. Haruko Orita; children: June, Naomi, Ken. BSEE, U. Houston, 1951; MSEE, U. Mich., 1958, MS in Indsl. Engring., 1969. Design engr. SIE, Houston, 1960-61; design engr. Boeing Aerospace, Huntsville, Ala., 1961-62, New Orleans, 1962; design engr. Lockheed Electronics, Houston, 1963; aerospace technologist NASA, Houston, 1963-89; pres. Kobayashi Inc., Webster, Tex., 1960—. Mem. planning and zoning commn., Webster, 1993-94. With U.S. Army, 1954-56. Mem. IEEE, AIAA. Patentee in field. Home: 1428 Fm 528 Rd Webster TX 77598-4702

KOBAYASHI, NORITAKE, business educator; b. Tokyo, Feb. 23, 1932; s. Daijyo and Makiko (Tadokoro) K.; m. Mieko Mary Margaret Nishino, May 21, 1960; children: Norikazu, Sumiko, Kumiko. AB cum laude, Harvard U., 1953, postgrad., 1953-54; LLB, Keio U., Japan, 1954, PhD, 1973. Lectr. Keio U., Tokyo, 1956-62; assoc. prof. Keio U., Yokohama, Japan, 1962-73, prof. Grad. Sch. Bus. Adminstrn., 1973-96, dir. sch. bus., 1980-83, dean Grad. Sch. Bus. Adminstrn., 1987-91; Mitsubishi chair, prof. Keio U., Tokyo, 1991-96, prof. emeritus, 1996—; dean, The Coll. of Cross-Cultural Communication and Business Shukutoku U., Saitama, Japan, Japan, 1996—; vis. prof. Ind. U., Bloomington, 1968, Asian Inst. Mgmt., Philippines, 1970, Internat. Mgmt. Inst., Geneva, 1974; bd. dirs. Mazda Motor Corp., 1980-96, Bosch Japan K.K. 1992—; sr. advisor Calpis Ajinomoto Dannone Co. Ltd., 1991—. Author: Joint Venture in Japan, 1967, The World of Japanese Business, 1969, International Business, 1972, Japanese Multinational Enterprises, 1980, Management, A Global Perspective, 1997. Trustee emeritus Brown U.; mem. adv. bd. Carnegie Bosch Found. Recipient Mgmt. Sci. Pub. Prize Nihon Keiei Kyokai, 1981. Fellow Acad. Internat. Bus.; Workshop to Study Motivational Enterprises (pres.); mem. Comparative Law Assn. Japan, Mgmt. Assn. Japan, Am. Acad. Polit. and Social Sci., Japan-Am. Soc., Keio U. Alumni Assn., Tokyo-Am. Club, Harvard Club, Tokyo Club. Home: 9-13 Shirokane 4-chome, Minato-ku, Tokyo 108-0072, Japan Office: Shukutoku Univ, 1150-1 Fujikubo Miyoshi, Irumagun 354-0042, Japan

KOBAYASHI, RIKI, chemical engineer, educator; b. Webster, Tex., May 13, 1924; s. Mitsutaro and Moto (Shigeta) K.; m. Barbara Joan Stevens, June 1, 1957; children: James Brock, Alec Stevens; m. Lee Mary Parker Lovejoy; children: Susan, Anne. BSChemE, Rice U., 1944; MS, U. Mich., 1947, PhD in Chem. Engring., 1951. Faculty dept. chem. engring. Rice U., Houston, 1951-94, Louis Calder prof., 1967-94, prof. emeritus, 1994—; D.L. Katz disting. lectr. U. Mich., 1975; hon. chmn., honoree Symposia on Thermodynamics, Chromatography & Transport Phenomena, Am. Inst. Chem. Engrs. Spring Meeting, 1987; plenary lectr. Chemicon '89 Trivandrum, India; Lindsay disting. lectr. Tex. A&M U., 1985; cons. in field. Author: (with others) Handbook of Natural Gas Engineering, 1959; Contbr. over articles to profl. jours. Served with AUS, 1945-46. Recipient Meritorious award Cyrogenic Engring. Conf. Com., 1966, 1st Donald L. Katz award Gas Processors Assn., 1985, Outstanding Engring. Alumni award Rice U., 1985; Japan Soc. Promotion of Sci. fellow, 1985. Fellow AICE, Am. Inst. Chemists; mem. AIME, NAE, Am. Inst. Physics, Am. Chem. Soc., Japan Inst. Chem. Engring. (hon.), Nat. Acad. Engring., Sigma Xi, Alpha Chi Sigma, Tau Beta Pi, Phi Lambda Upsilon, Phi Kappa Phi. Unitarian. Achievements include co-invention of diffl. kinetics. Home: 348 Piney Point Rd Houston TX 77024-6506 Office: Rice U MS 362 PO Box 1892 Houston TX 77251-1892

KOBAYASHI, SEIEI, English literature educator; b. Maebashi, Gunma, Japan, Nov. 22, 1941; s. Mokuhei and Shizuko (Yamada) K.; m. Chieko Ohto, Apr. 4, 1970; children: Shigehisa, Naoki. BA, U. Tokyo, 1965, MA, 1969. Lectr. Kyoritsu Women's Jr. Coll., Tokyo, 1970-74, asst. prof., 1974-80; asst. prof. Hosei U., Tokyo, 1980-81, prof., 1981-93; prof. English lit. Chuo U., Tokyo, 1994—. Author: An Essay on Shakespeare's History Plays, 1981; contbg. author: The Discourse of Vision-The Meeting Point of Popular Culture and Art (ed. Y. Midzunoe), 1994, Essays on World Modern Drama (ed. M. Osada), 1996, Celtic Illusion (ed. Y. Midzunoe), 1998; co-editor: Kadokawa—Scott Foresman English-Japanese Dictionary, 1992. Mem. English Lit. Soc. Japan, Shakespeare Soc. Japan, Renaissance Inst. Avocations: music, photography. Office: Chuo U Faculty Sci & Tech, 1-13-27 Kasuga, Bunkyo 112-0003, Japan

KOBAYASHI, SUSUMU, supercomputer company executive; b. Kumamoto, Japan, Apr. 3, 1939; s. Senkichiro and Michiko Kobayashi. BS, Tokyo Inst. Tech., 1963. Programmer Osaka (Japan) Gas Co., Ltd., 1963-65, C. Itoh Computing Services Co., Ltd., Tokyo, 1965-67; applications analyst, systems engr. Control Data Far East, Inc., Tokyo, 1967-75; asst. gen. mgr. systems dept. JMA Systems, Inc., Tokyo, 1975-79; dir. Nuclear Data Corp., Tokyo, 1979-89, Yokogawa Supertek Corp., Tokyo, 1989-90; tech. advisor sales div. Yokogawa Cray ELS Ltd., Tokyo, 1990-92; tech. advisor Cray Rsch. Japan Ltd., Tokyo, 1990-96; advisor The Tsukuba Press Ltd., Tsukuba-shi, Japan, 1996-97; pres. Tera Computer Japan, Tokyo, 1997—. Translator, editor: Fortran 4 (D.D. McCracken), 1968, Lisp 1.5 Primer (C. Weissman), 1970, A Few Good Men from Univac, (D.E. Lundstrom), 1992, The Official Computer Widow's (and Widower's) Handbook (by Experts on Computer Widow/Widowerhood), 1992, Future Computer Opportunities (Jack Dunning), 1993, Enabling Technologies for Petaflops Computing (T. Sterling, P. Messina, P.H. Smith), 1997, The Supermen, (Charles J. Murray), 1998; contbr. articles to electronics mags. Mem. Assn. Computing Machinery, IEEE, Inc., Japan Math. Soc., Japan Info. Processing Soc., Am. Assn. for Artificial Intelligence. Avocations: motoring, audio/visual. Home: 85-2-206 Migawa 2-chome, Mito Ibaraki 310-0912, Japan

KOBAYASHI, YUTAKA, biochemist, consultant; b. San Francisco, Mar. 11, 1924; s. Harutoyo and Haru (Murata) K.; m. Martha Kitaoka, Aug. 21, 1954 (dec. 1979); children: Andrew Yutaka, David Haruo, Thomas Sachio; m. E. Maureen Byrne, Dec. 29, 1982. BA, Iowa State Coll., 1946, MS, 1950; PhD, U. Iowa, 1953. Rsch. fellow Northwestern Med. Sch., Chgo., 1953-57; scientist/sr. scientist Worcester Found. for Exptl. Biology, Shrewsbury, Mass., 1957-74; mgr. applications lab. New Eng. Nuclear/DuPont, Boston, 1974-85; pres. Ko-By Assocs., Wellesley, Mass., 1985—; cons. Ko-By Assocs., Wellesley, 1985—. Co-author: (book) Biological Applications on Liquid Scintillation Counting, 1974; contbr. articles to profl. jours. Mem. Am. Chem. Soc., Am. Soc. for Biochemistry and Molecular Biology, Am. Soc. for Pharmacology and Exptl. Therapeutics, Am. Nat. Standards Inst. (accredited stds. com. N42 on radiation instrumentation), Sigma Xi, Phi Lambda Upsilon. Avocations: tennis, fishing. Home and Office: 60 Audubon Rd Wellesley MA 02481-2828

KOBDISH, GEORGE CHARLES, lawyer; b. Casper, Wyo., June 30, 1950; s. Richard Matthew and Jo Earl (Uttz) K.; m. Mary Ellen Griffith, Jan. 24, 1969; children: George Charles, Jr., Kelly Rebecca, Kimberlee Nelle. BBA with honors, U. Tex., 1971, JD, 1974. Bar: Tex. 1974, U.S. Dist. Ct. (no. dist.) Tex. 1975. Asst. atty. gen. State of Tex., Austin, 1974-76; assoc. McCall, Parkhurst & Horton LLP, Dallas, 1976-80, ptnr., 1981—; lawyer; b. Casper, Wyo., June 30, 1950; s. Richard Matthew and Jo Earl (Uttz) K.; m. Mary Ellen Griffith, Jan. 24, 1969; children: George Charles, Jr., Kelly Rebecca, Kimberlee Nelle. BBA with honors, U. Tex., 1971, JD, 1974. Bar: Tex. 1974, U.S. Dist. Ct. (no. dist.) Tex. 1975. Asst. atty. gen. State of Tex., Austin, 1974-76; assoc. McCall, Parkhurst & Horton L.L.P., Dallas, 1976-80, ptnr., 1981—. Bd. dirs., North Dallas Shared Ministries, pres., 1996-98. Mem. Nat. Assn. Bond Lawyers, Tex. Bar Assn., Dallas Bar Assn., Royal Oaks Country Club, Tower Club, Dallas Friday Group, Serra Club of Dallas (bd. dirs., pres. 1998—), Phi Delta Theta. Roman Catholic. Bd. dirs. North Dallas Shared Ministries, pres. 1996-98. Mem. Nat. Assn. Bond Lawyers, Tex. Bar Assn., Dallas Bar Assn., Royal Oaks Country Club, Tower Club, Dallas Friday Group, Serra Club of Dallas (bd. dirs., pres. 1998—), Phi Delta Theta. Roman Catholic. Home: 9206 Arbor Branch Dr Dallas TX 75243-6308 Office: McCall Parkhurst & Horton LLP 717 N Harwood St Ste 900 Dallas TX 75201-6586

KOBE, LAN, medical physicist; b. Semarang, Indonesia; naturalized; d. O.G. and L.N. (The) Kobe. BS in Physics, IKIP U., Bandung, Indonesia, 1964, MS in Physics, 1967; MS in Med. Physics and Biophysics, U. Calif.-Berkeley, 1975. Physics instr. Sch. Engring., Tarumanegara U., Jakarta, Indonesia, 1968-72; research fellow dept. radiation oncology U. Calif.-San Francisco, 1975-77; clin. physicist in residence dept. radiation oncology UCLA, 1977-78, asst. hosp. radiation physicist, 1978-80, hosp. radiation physicist, 1980—; instr. radiation oncology physics to resident physicians and med. physics graduate students. Contbr. sci. papers to profl. publs. Newhouse grantee U. Calif.-Berkeley, 1974-75, grantee dean grad. div. U. Calif.-Berkeley, 1975; recipient Pres. Work Study award U. Calif., Berkeley, 1974-75, Employee of Month award UCLA, 1983, Outstanding Service award, 1986, devel. Achievement award, 1988, Ptnrs. in Excellence award UCLA, 1996. Mem. Am. Soc. for Therapeutic Radiology and Oncology, Am. Assn. Physicists in Medicine (nat. and So. Calif. chpts.), Am. Bd. Radiology (cert.), Am. Assn. Individual Investors (life). Office: UCLA Dept Radiation Oncology 200 Ucla Medical Plz Ste B265 Los Angeles CA 90095-8344

KOBER, JANE, lawyer; b. Shamokin, Pa., May 17, 1943; d. Jeno Daniel and Angela Agnes (Kogut) DiRienzo; m. Arthur Kober, June 20, 1970 (div. 1975). AB, Pa. State U., 1965; MA, U. Chgo., 1966; JD, Case Western Res. U., 1974. Bar: Ohio, N.Y. Lectr. U. Baghdad, Iraq, 1966-67; editor, cons. Ernst & Young, Washington, 1968-70; law clk. to Hon. William K. Thomas, U.S. Dist. Ct. for No. Dist. Ohio, Cleve., 1974-75; atty., ptnr. Squire, Sanders & Dempsey, Cleve. and N.Y.C., 1975-87; ptnr. Shea & Gould, N.Y.C., 1987-89, LeBoeuf, Lamb, Greene & MacRae, L.L.P., N.Y.C., 1989—. Mem. Union Club Cleve. Office: LeBoeuf Lamb Greene MacRae 125 W 55th St New York NY 10019-5369*

KOBERT, JOEL A., lawyer; b. Newark, Oct. 4, 1943. BA, Norwich U., 1965; JD, Howard U., 1968. Bar: D.C. 1968, N.J. 1971. Atty. U.S. Dept. Justice, Washington, 1968; ptnr. Courter, Kobert, Laufer & Cohen P.C., Hackettstown, N.J.; active Supreme Ct. Ad Hoc Com. on Legal Svcs. 1982-88, Supreme Ct. Com. on Interests and Trust Accts., 1984-86, Supreme Ct. Com. on Computerization of Ct. System, 1984-86; chmn. bd. trustees Interest on Lawyers Trust Accts., 1988-91. Capt. U.S. Army, 1968-70. Reginald Heber Smith fellow, 1970-71. Fellow Am. Bar Found.; mem. ABA (mem. dist XIII ethics com. 1982-86), D.C. Bar, N.J. State Bar Assn. (treas. 1987, sec. 1988, 2d v.p. 1989, 1st v.p. 1990, pres. elect 1991, pres. 1992, bd. trustees 1981-87, bd. trustees N.J. Lawyer, bd trustees N.J. State Bar Found., 1986-93, mem. ops. com. 1985-91, chmn. com. law adminstrn. and econs. 1981-86, mem. membership com., 1986-87, mem. com. fin. and ops, 1990-93, mem. travel com. 1990-93), N.J. League Mcpl. Attys. Office: Courter Kobert Laufer & Cohen PC 1001 County Road 517 Ste 1 Hackettstown NJ 07840-2785

KOBETZ, RICHARD WILLIAM, criminologist, consultant; b. Chgo., Oct. 23, 1933; s. Nestor Joseph and Mary (Zurek) K.; m. Eleanore Marian Sever, Oct. 8, 1960; children: Kevin, Kimberly and Candice (twins). AA, Chgo. City Jr. Coll., 1959; student, Ill. Tchrs. Coll., 1964-66; MS in Pub. Adminstrn., Ill. Inst. Tech., 1968; D of Pub. Adminstrn., Nova U., 1978. Diplomate Am. Bd. Forensic Examiners; cert. personal protection specialist. Police officer Winnetka (Ill.) Police Dept., 1954-55; from police officer to sgt. to lt. Chgo. Police Dept., 1955-68; asst. dir. Internat. Assn. Chiefs of Police, Washington, 1968-79; exec. dir., trainer, cons. Exec. Protection Inst., Berryville, Va., 1979—; dir., trainer, cons. North Mountain Pines Tng. Ctr., Winchester, Va., 1979—; security cons. numerous U.S. corps., 1979—; active various security and enforcement agys., 1979—. Author: The Police Role and Juvenile Delinquency, 1971, Juvenile Justice Administration, 1973, Target Terrorism: Providing Protective Services, 1979, Providing Executive Protection, 1990, Vol. II, 1994; contbr. articles to profl. jours., chpts. to books. Acad. Security Educators and Trainers disting. fellow, 1987. Mem. Acad. Security Educators and Trainers (pres., v.p. 1982—), Internat. Assn. Chiefs of Police (Achievement award 1979), Am. Soc. Indsl. Security, Am. Soc. Criminology, Am. Soc. for Pub. Adminstrn. Republican. Roman Catholic. Club: Nine Lives Assocs. (Berryville) (exec. sec. 1978—). Avocations: canoeing, skeet shooting, hiking, travel. Home and Office: Highlander Lodge Journey's End RR 1 Box 332 Bluemont VA 20135-9301

KOBLENTZ, ROBERT ALAN, lawyer; b. Columbus, Ohio, Aug. 20, 1946; s. Maurice Charles and Martha (Levelle) K.; m. Kathryn Anderson, Oct. 20, 1973; children: Maureen, Robert. BA, Ohio State U., 1967, JD, 1970. Bar: Ohio 1970, U.S. Dist. Ct. (so. dist.) Ohio 1971, U.S. Supreme Ct. 1992. Legal rsch. Bancroft-Whitney Co., San Francisco, 1970-71; atty. Tracy, DeLibera, Lyons & Collins, Columbus, 1971-78, DeLibera, Lyons, Koblentz & Scott, Columbus, 1978-80, Scott, Koblentz & Binau, Columbus, 1980-86; pvt. practice Columbus, 1986—. Bd. dirs. Friends of WOSU, Columbus, 1982-88, Opera Columbus, 1984-87, Upper Arlington Civic Assn., Columbus, 1988-90. Mem. ABA, Ohio State Bar Assn. (del. family law section 1979—), Ohio Acad. Trial Lawyers (chmn. family law sect. 1983), Columbus Bar Assn. (chmn. family law com. 1976-78), Franklin County Trial Lawyers (pres. 1985-86). Office: 35 E Livingston Ave Columbus OH 43215-5768

KOBLENZ, MICHAEL ROBERT, lawyer; b. Newark, Apr. 9, 1948; s. Herman and Esther (Weisman) K.; m. Bonnie Jane Berman, Dec. 22, 1973; children: Adam, Alexander, Elizabeth. B.A., George Washington U., 1969, LL.M., 1974; J.D., Am. U., 1972. Bar: N.J. 1972, D.C. 1973, N.Y. 1980, U.S. Dist. Ct. N.J. 1972, U.S. Dist. Ct. D.C. 1973, U.S. Dist. Ct. (so. dist.) N.Y. 1980, U.S. Ct. Appeals (7th cir.) 1976, U.S. Ct. Claims 1973, U.S. Tax Ct. 1973, U.S. Mil. Ct. Appeals 1974. Atty., U.S. Dept. Justice, Washington, 1972-75; lectr. Am. U., 1975-78; spl. asst. U.S. atty. Office of U.S. Atty., Chgo., 1976-78; atty. Commodity Futures Trading Commn., Washington, 1975-77; spl. counsel, 1977, asst. dir., 1977-78; regional counsel, N.Y.C., 1978-80; assoc. Rein, Mound & Cotton, N.Y.C., 1980-82, ptnr., Mound, Cotton & Wollan (and predecessor firms), 1983—. Contbr. articles to legal jours. Mem. bd. appeals Village of Flower Hill, Manhasset, N.Y., 1983-84, trustee, 1984-86; trustee Village of East Hills, 1988—, Dep. Mayor, 1993-94, Mayor, 1994—; mem. Roslyn Little League, 1991—, bd. dirs., 1992. Recipient Cert. of Appreciation for Outstanding Service U.S. Commodity Futures Trading Commn., 1977. Home: East Hills 20 Hemlock Dr Roslyn NY 11576-2303 Office: Mound Cotton & Wollan 1 Battery Park Plz New York NY 10004-1405

KOBLER, JOHN, writer; b. Mt. Vernon, N.Y., Jan. 7, 1910; s. Albert John and Mignon (Sommers) K.; m. Adele Palmer, Jan. 7, 1932 (div. 1945); children—Albert John III, Lynn (Mrs. James Hannon Jr.); m. Ruth Margaret Low, Apr. 5, 1945 (div. 1963); children—Karen, Andrea; m. Evelyn Cummins, Feb. 10, 1966 (div.); m. Rita Stein, Jan. 27, 1984. B.A., Williams Coll., 1931. Newspaper reporter N.Y. Evening Jour.; fgn. corr. INS, Universal Syndicate; reporter-feature writer King Features, N.Y. Daily Mirror, 1931-39; editor PM, 1940-42; civilian intelligence officer AUS, North Africa, 1943-44, Italy, 1943-44, France, 1943-44; attached Am. Embassy, Paris, 1945-46; assoc. editor Life, 1946-47; freelance contbr. New Yorker, 1947-57, Life, 1947-57, Saturday Evening Post, 1947-57, Colliers, 1947-57, others, 1947-57; contbg. editor Saturday Evening Post, 1957-64, editor-at-large, from 1965. Author: Trial of Ruth Snyder and Judd Gray, 1938, Some Like It Gory, 1940, Afternoon in the Attic, 1950, The Reluctant Surgeon: A Biography of John Hunter, 1960, Luce: His Time, Life and Fortune, 1968, Capone, 1971, Ardent Spirits: The Rise and Fall of Prohibition, 1973, Damned in Paradise: The Life of John Barrymore, 1977, Otto the Magnificent: The Life of Otto Kahn, 1989. Home: 165 W 66th St New York NY 10023-6508

KOBLIK, STEVENS S., academic administrator. Pres. Reed Coll., Portland, Oreg., 1992—. Office: Reed College Office of President 3203 SE Woodstock Blvd Portland OR 97202-8199*

KOBLINER, RICHARD, secondary school educator; b. Bronx, N.Y., May 29, 1935; s. Meyer and Celia (Kantner) K.; m. Suzanne, July 11, 1965. BA, CCNY, 1959, MS in Edn., 1962; postgrad., U. Wis. Cert. adminstr. and supr., social studies tchr., N.Y. Secondary sch. educator DeWitt Clinton, Bronx, N.Y., Hillcrest, Jamaica, N.Y., Cardozo, Bayside, N.Y.; mem. Nat. Coun. for Accreditation of Tchr. Edn.; supr., student tchr. Queens Coll., N.Y.C. Author: Handbook for the Teaching of Social Studies, Middle Ages Workbook, History of Black Americans; mem. adv. bd. Wall St. Jour.; classroom edit., social studies publs.; contbr. Ency. of N.Y.C. Mem. ASCD, AFT, N.Y. SUT, UFT (chair innovations com.), ATSS, NCSS. Home: 1826 Corporal Kennedy St Flushing NY 11360-1447

KOBLUK, MICHAEL D., municipal official; b. Trail, B.C., Can., Dec. 10, 1937. BA, Gonzaga U., 1969. Owner Am. Theater Prodns., N.Y.C., 1965-69; dir. opera house and convention ctr. City of Spokane (Wash.), 1974-79; dir. entertainment facilities, 1979—; dir. performance and visual arts Expo 74, Spokane, Wash., 1974. Entertainer The Chad Mitchell Trio, 1958-69. Recipient Disting. Svc. award State of Wash., 1974. Mem. Internat. Assn. Assembly Mgrs. (pres. 1990-91). Office: City of Spokane 334 W Spokane Falls Blvd Spokane WA 99201-0212*

KOBRAK, PETER MAX, educator; b. Dec. 1, 1936. BA, Oberlin Coll., 1959; PhD, Johns Hopkins U., 1971. Legis. asst. Office of Congressman William Steiger, Washington, 1967-69; prof. Western Mich. U., Kalamazoo, Mich., 1973—, dir. sch. pub. affairs and adminstrn., 1980-89. Ford Found. Nat. Ctr. Edn. grantee N.Y. State Gov's. Office for Nelson Rockefeller, 1966. E-mail: peter.kobrak@wmich.edu. Home: 1304 West Maple St Kalamazoo MI 49008

KOBRIN, LAWRENCE ALAN, lawyer; b. N.Y.C., Sept. 14, 1933; s. Irving and Hortense (Freezer) K.; m. Ruth E. Freedman, Mar. 5, 1967; children: Jeffrey, Rebecca, Debra. AB in History with honors, summa cum laude, Columbia U., 1954, JD, 1957. Bar: N.Y. 1957, U.S. Dist. Ct. (so. dist.) N.Y. 1958, U.S. Dist. Ct. (ea. dist.) N.Y. 1959, U.S. Ct. Appeals (2d cir.) 1959, U.S. Supreme Ct. 1966. Assoc. Cahill, Gordon, Reindel & Ohl, N.Y.C., 1958-59, Arthur D. Emil, N.Y.C., 1959-63; ptnr. Emil & Kobrin, N.Y.C., 1963-79, Milgrim, Thomajan, Jacobs and Lee, N.Y.C., 1979-83, Cahill Gordon & Reindel, N.Y.C., 1984—; bd. govs. Wurzweiler Sch. of Social Work, 1984—, vice-chmn., 1994-98; dir. UMB Bank and Trust Co., 1978-91; dir., treas. The Jewish Week, N.Y.C., 1992-96, chmn., 1996—. Notes editor Columbia U. Law Rev.; contbr. articles to law jours. V.p., assoc. treas., chmn. dist. com. Fedn. Jewish Philanthropies, N.Y.C., 1981-84, com. long range planning, 1985-86, com. inner city, 71-76; chmn. Ramaz Sch., N.Y.C., 1978-83; sec. to bd. Bar Ilan U., N.Y.C., 1972-80; pres. The Jewish Ctr., N.Y.C., 1987-90; dir. N.Y.C.-UJA-Fedn., chmn. communal planning com., 1988-91, chmn. com. on cmty. couns., 1996-98; v.p. Union Orthodox Jewish Congregations, 1968-74, dir., 1962—, chmn. campus com., 1962-66, chmn. Israel com., 1967-72, chmn. pub. com., 1972-78; pres. Massad Camps, 1971-77; mng. editor Tradition, 1961-64, editl. com. 1964—; bd. dirs. Am. Friends Pardes, 1991-96, Histadrut Ivrit, 1991—; pres. Ariel Am. Friends of Midrasha and United Instns., 1991-95, chmn., 1995—; sec. Beth Din of Am., 1994-96, chmn. exec. com., 1997—, exec. com. Orthodox Caucus, 1995—. Kent scholar, Stone scholar. Mem. Am. Coll. Real Estate Lawyers, Coop. Housing Lawyers Group (exec. com. 1972-80), N.Y. atty. gen. adv. com. 1972-80, Assn. Bar City of N.Y. (com. on philanthropic orgns. 1974-79, edn. and law com. 1985-88, com. on legal edn. 1988-91, com. on legal problems of elderly 1991-94), N.Y. County Lawyers Assn. (real property law sect., chmn. 1991-93), Nat. Assn. Coll. and Univ. Attys. (1971-79), N.Y. State Bar Assn. (com. coops and condominiums, com. fgn. investment real estate), Columbia Coll. Alumni Assn. (bd. dirs. 1990—, v.p. 1996-98), The Down Town Assn., Cream Hill Lake Assn., Phi Beta Kappa. Home: 15 W 81st St New York NY 10024-6022 also: 8 Popple Swamp Rd Cornwall Bridge CT 06754-1135 Office: Cahill Gordon & Reindel 80 Pine St Fl 17 New York NY 10005-1702

KOBS, JAMES FRED, advertising agency executive; b. Chgo., IL, June 27, 1938; s. Fred Charles and Ann (Ganser) K.; m. Nadine Schumacher, May 18, 1963; children: Karen, Kathleen, Kenneth. B.S. in Journalism, U. Ill., 1960. Copywriter Rylander Co., Chgo., 1960-62; mng. dir. Success Mag., Chgo., 1963-65; mail order mgr. Am. Peoples Press, Westmont, Ill., 1966-67; exec. v.p. Stone & Adler Advt., Chgo., 1967-78; chmn. Kobs & Brady Advt., Inc. (now Draft Direct Worldwide), Chgo., 1978-88; vice chmn. Kobs & Brady Advt., Inc. (now Draft Worldwide), Chgo., 1988; chmn. Kobs Gregory & Passavant, Chgo., 1989—; guest lectr. U. Wis., U. Ill., NYU; adj. prof. direct mktg. Northwestern U. Medill Sch. Journalism Grad. Program; internat. lectr. in field. Author: Profitable Direct Marketing, 2d edit., 1991, 24 Ways to Improve Your Direct Mail Results, 99 Proven Direct Response Offers; contbr. articles to periodicals. Recipient numerous local and nat. advt. awards. Mem. Direct Mktg. Assn. (dir., sec., mem. exec. com., trustee, recipient Silver and Gold Mailbox, Gold Medallion, Gold Echo, Ed Mayer award), Chgo. Assn. Direct Mktg. (past pres., Direct Marketer of Yr.), Boys and Girls Clubs of Chgo. (corp. bd.), Alpha Delta Sigma. Office: Kobs Gregory Passavant 205 N Michigan Ave Chicago IL 60601-5927

KOBUS, RICHARD LAWRENCE, architect, designer, executive; b. Chgo., Nov. 19, 1952. BS in Architecture, U. Ill., 1974; MArch, Harvard U., 1978. Registered architect, Mass., N.H., Maine, Ill., Pa., R.I., Ohio, N.J., Conn., Wash. Designer Metz, Train, Olsen & Youngren, Chgo., 1974-75, Shepley, Bulfinch, Richardson & Abbott, Boston, 1978-79; assoc. Skidmore, Owings and Merrill, Boston, 1979-83; pres., prin., founder Tsoi/Kobus & Assocs., Inc., Cambridge, Mass., 1983—; archtl. prin. healthcare acad., corp., and rsch. facilities U.S., Europe, Asia. Active U. Ill. Pres. Coun., 1995-99; bd. dirs. Boston Soc. Architects, 1996-98; pres., bd. dirs. Major's Cove Assn., Edgartown, Mass.; mem. Belmont Pub. Schs., Bus. Leaders Adv. Coun.; trustee Buckingham, Browne and Nichols, 1999—. Julia Amory Appleton fellow Harvard U., 1978-79; recipient Gov. Design award, 1986, Modern Healthcare Nat. Design award, 1988, 94, 98, PCI Design award, 1995, 98, AIA Honor Design award, 1994, 97, 98, 99, Am. Sch. and Univ. Archtl. Portfolio award, 1989, 90. Mem. AIA, Nat. Assn. Indsl. and Office Parks, Boston Soc. Architects (dir. 1997—), Urban Land Inst., Soc. for Campus and Univ. Planning, Billings Soc. Avocations: sailing, rowing, photography, auto racing. Office: Tsoi/Kobus & Assocs Inc PO Box 9114 One Brattle Square Cambridge MA 02238-9114

KOBYLARZ, JOSEPH DOUGLAS, secondary education educator; b. Garfield, N.J., Dec. 18, 1948; s. Joseph H. and Josephine (Rys) K.; m. Joyce Ann Metzger, July 15, 1978; children: Lauren Ann, Kristen Ann. BS, Northwestern State Coll., 1970; MA, Montclair State Coll., 1976. Cert. tchr. indsl. arts, coord. C.I.E., supr., prin., N.J. Tchr. Garfield Bd. Edn., 1970—, master tchr., 1974-76, dept. chmn., 1976—, adminstrv. asst. to the supt., 1991—; mem. Am. Indsl. Arts Safety Com., 1978-81, adv. Am. Indsl. Arts Student Assn., Garfield, 1980-85; adj. instr. Montclair State Coll., Upper Montclair, N.J., 1982-86; transcript reviewer Bennett Pub. Co., Peoria, Ill., 1985-87; mem. com. practitioners State N.J. Dept. Edn., 1996—. Co-author: (safety guide) New Jersey Industrial Arts Safety Manual, 1982; author (safety guide) Garfield District Safety Manual, 1981. County committeeman Garfield Dem. Orgn., 1972-75; bd. govs. Ocean Beach and Yacht Club, Lavallette, N.J., 1972-78, dir. beach security, 1989—; mem. Garfield Housing Authority, 1979-84, chmn., 1984; mem. Kinnelon Cmty. Edn. Adv. Com., 1994—, N.J. State Dept. Edn. Com. Practitioners, 1966—. Mem. Vocat. Edn. Assn. N.J. (rec. sec. 1982-88, pres.-elect 1986-87, pres. 1987-88, editor newsletter 1991, region I rep. to Am. Vocat. Assn. 1992—, focus and task force com. State Vocat. Safety Manual 1991-92), Am. Vocat. Assn. (N.J. rep. region I 1990-91), N.J. Vocat. Adminstrs. and Suprs. Assn. (pres. 1997-98, Supr. of Yr. 1993), Kinnelon Edn. Found., Phi Delta Kappa. Roman Catholic. Avocations: windsurfing, jogging, racquetball, hiking, wave riding. Home: 97 Miller Rd Kinnelon NJ 07405-3003 Office: Garfield High Sch 500 Palisade Ave Garfield NJ 07026-2546

KOBZA, DENNIS JEROME, architect; b. Ullysses, Nebr., Sept. 30, 1933; s. Jerry Frank and Agnes Elizabeth (Lavicky) K.; B.S., Healds Archtl. Engring., 1959; m. Doris Mae Riemann, Dec. 26, 1953; children—Dennis Jerome, Diana Jill, David John. Draftsman, designer B.L. Schroder, Palo Alto, Calif., 1959-60; sr. draftsman, designer Ned Abrams, Architect, Sunnyvale, Calif., 1960-61, Kenneth Elvin, Architect, Los Altos, Calif., 1961-62; partner B.L. Schroder, Architect, Palo Alto, 1962-66; pvt. practice architecture, Mountain View, Calif., 1966—. Served with USAF, 1952-56. Recipient Solar PAL award, Palo Alto, 1983, Mountain View Mayoral award, 1979. Mem. C. of C. (dir. 1977-79, Archtl. Excellence award Hayward chpt. 1985, Outstanding Indsl. Devel. award Sacramento chpt., 1980) , AIA (chpt. dir. 1973), Constrn. Specifications Inst. (dir. 1967-68), Am. Inst. Plant Engrs., Nat. Fedn. Ind. Bus. Orgn. Club: Rotary (dir. 1978-79, pres. 1986-87). Home: 3840 May Ct Palo Alto CA 94303-4545 Office: 2083 Old Middlefield Way Mountain View CA 94043-2401

KOBZA, JULIA COLLEEN, drafter, building designer; b. Grand Rapids, Mich., Sept. 21, 1966; d. Thomas Theodore K. and Joyce Colleen (Stephens) Kelly; m. Randy Thomas Van Blaricum, Oct. 12, 1985 (div. July 1992); children: Aimee Colleen, Codie Leigh. Student, Grand Valley State U., 1984-85, Northwestern Mich. Coll., 1994-95. Waitress Timberlanes Bowling Alley, Traverse City, Mich., 1991-92, 626 Family Restaurant, Traverse City, Mich., 1992; customer svs. Meijers, Traverse City, Mich., 1992; adminstrv. asst. MAM Contracting, Traverse City, Mich., 1991-92; office adminstr. Builders' Arch. Woodworking, Traverse City, Mich., 1992; acctg. asst. Brown Lumber, Traverse City, Mich., 1992-93; adminstrv. asst. Brown Mfg., Traverse City, Mich., 1993; owner, designer Art 'N' Texture Building Design, Traverse City, Mich., 1993. Planning commr. Elmwood Twp., Traverse City, 1997. Mem. NAFE, Mich. Soc. Planning Ofcls., Congress for New Urbanism, Bldg. Ofcls. Code Adminstrs. Internat. Avocations: reading, clarinet, family, volunteering.

KOCEN, LORRAINE AYRAL, accountant; b. Levittown, N.Y., July 20, 1956; d. Edward Joseph and Joan Dorothy (Destefanis) Ayral; m. Ross Kocen, Oct. 4, 1981; 1 child, Daniel. BS, Hofstra U., 1978; MBA, U. Minn., 1985. Engr. Sperry Systems Mgmt., Great Neck, N.Y., 1978-81; fin. analyst ITT Consumer Fin. Corp., Mpls., 1981-84; cost acct. Mercy Med. Ctr., Mpls., 1984-85, contr., 1985-86; bus. segments acct. GTE, Thousand Oaks, Calif., 1986-88, Cerritos project acct., 1988-90, Cerritos project adminstr., 1990-92, fin. adminstr., 1992-93, sr. sales adminstr., 1993-94, adminstr. mobile comms., 1994-96; fin. mgr. Blue Cross of Calif., Newbury Park, 1996-97; bus. analyst GTE, Newbury Park, 1997—. Asst. editor newsletter Healthcare Fin. Mgmt. Assn., Mpls., 1985-86. Mem. archtl. com. Foxmoor Hills Homeowners Assn., Westlake, Calif., 1989; bd. dirs. Parent Faculty Assn., 1998—. Office: GTE 851 Lawrence Dr Newbury Park CA 91320-2200

KOCH, ALBIN COOPER, lawyer; b. Pitts., Aug. 25, 1933; s. John Lester and Theodosia (Cooper) K.; m. Harriet W. Woodworth, June 24, 1960. B.A., Yale U., 1956; J.D., Harvard U., 1959. Bar: Calif., D.C., Mass. Assoc. Silverstein & Mullens, Washington, 1963-68, ptnr., 1968-72; ptnr. Agnew, Miller & Carlson, L.A., 1973-75; v.p., asst. gen. tax counsel Bank Am., San Francisco, 1976-80; ptnr. Morrison & Foerster, L.A., 1980-88, of counsel, 1989; of counsel Horgan, Rosen, Beckham & Coren, Toluca Lake, L.A., 1990-95; pvt. practice Law Office of Albin C. Koch, Glendale, Calif., 1995—; gen. counsel Mcpl. Consultants, Westlake Village, Calif., 1995—; mem. Calif. Franchise Tax Bd. adv. com. 1992-95. Chmn. Southwest Neighborhood Assembly, Washington, 1966-67; mem. Calif. bd. Common Cause, 1974-76; trustee Human Family Ednl. and Charitable Inst., 1974-79, bd. dirs. Pasadena Chamber Orch., 1983-87, pres. 1984-86; mem. vestry All Saints Episcopal Ch., Pasadena, 1985-89, jr. warden, 1988-89. Mem. ABA (chmn. tax sect. banking and savings com., vice chmn. urban, state and local govt. law sect. taxes and revenue com.), L.A. County Bar Assn. (chmn. tax sect. income tax com. 1982-83, chmn. tax sect. 1986-87, mem. exec. com. 1982-87), Calif. State Bar Assn. (exec com. tax sect. 1990-94. vice chair 1994). Home: 1506 E California Blvd Pasadena CA 91106-4104*

KOCH, BRUCE R., diplomat; b. Robesenia, Pa., Aug. 1, 1933; s. Mervyn R. and Sarah E. (Boyer) K.; m. Johanna Heinzel, Mar. 1, 1958; 1 child, Sigrid D. Assoc. degree in Chemistry, Wyomissing Polytech, 1954; BA in Polit. Sci., Ursinus Coll., 1961; MA in Internat. Affairs, George Washington U., 1971. Field officer Am. Embassy, Bonn, Germany, 1973-75; dep. cultural affairs officer Am. Embassy, London, 1975-77; counselor pub. affairs Am. Embassy, Prague, Czechoslovakia, 1978-81, Accra, Ghana, 1981-83, Lagos, Nigeria, 1985-88; min. counselor, 1987; counselor pub. affairs Am. Embassy, Belgrade, Yugoslavia, 1989-91; dir. European Affairs USIA, Washington, 1991-92, dir. African Affairs, 1992-94; dir. German-Am. Inst., Tuebingen, Fed. Rep. Germany; dir., mgr. U.S. Nat. Exhibit, Romania, 1969; asst. cultural affairs officer, Am. Embassy, Bucharest, Romania, 1966-68; br. info. officer, Am. Embassy Consulate Gen., Zagreb, Yugoslavia, 1962-65. Bd. dirs. World Affairs Coun. of Berks County, Pa.; pres. Susquehanna Valley chpt. People to People Internat., pres. East Coast Coun. PTIP; IRS vol. German-Am. Soc.; vol. tax counselor AARP Landis Valley Assoc. Recipient Youth Conservation award Pa. Fedn. Sportsmen, 1950; sr. rsch. scholar Atlantic Coun., Washington, 1984. Mem. U.S. Humane Soc., Nat. Wildlife Fedn., Nature Conservancy, Hawk Mt. Sanctuary, Nat. Wildflower Rsch. Ctr. Home and Office: CEE Consulting 105 E 3rd Ave Lititz PA 17543-2724

KOCH, CAROLE JACKSON, human resources executive; b. Evergreen Park, Ill., Feb. 25, 1951; d. Robert Lawrence Capman and Norma Gene (Benson) C.; m. Donald Charles Jackson, Sept. 24, 1976 (dec. Mar. 1984); m. Curtis Gerard Koch, Aug. 28, 1987. BA with honors, U. Ill., Chgo., 1972. Job analyst U. Ill., Chgo., 1973-76, personnel coordinator, 1976-80, assoc. personnel dir., 1980-83; dir. human resources U. Ill. Hosp. and Clinics, Chgo., 1983-96; assoc. hosp. dir./ dir. human resources U. Ill.-Chgo. Med. Ctr., 1996—. Mem. human resources coun. Met. Chgo. Healthcare Coun., 1987—. Mem. Am. Soc. Healthcare Human Resources Adminstrn., Soc. Human Resource Mgmt. Office: U Ill Hosp 1740 W Taylor St Rm 1400 Chicago IL 60612-7232

KOCH, CHARLES DE GANAHL, oil industry executive; b. Wichita, Kans., Nov. 1, 1935; s. Fred Chase and Mary Clementine (Robinson) K. B.S. in Gen. Engring, MIT, 1957, M.S. in Mech. Engring., 1958, M.S. in Chem. Engring., 1959. Engr. Arthur D. Little, Inc., Cambridge, Mass., 1959-61; v.p. Koch Engring. Co., Inc., Wichita, 1961-63, pres., 63-71, chmn., 1967-78; pres. Koch Industries, Inc., Wichita, 1966-74, chmn., 1967—; bd. dirs. Intrust Bank, N.A. Chmn., Inst. for Humane Studies; chmn. Mercatus Ctr., George Mason U. Mem. Mt. Pelerin Soc., Wichita Country Club, N.Y. Athletic Club. Office: Koch Industries PO Box 2256 4111 E 37th St N Wichita KS 67220-3298

KOCH, CHARLES JOSEPH, banker; b. Cleve., Oct. 29, 1919; s. Charles Frank and Mary (Cunat) K.; m. Elizabeth Rusch, May 7, 1945; children: Charles John, John David. B.S., Case Inst. Tech., 1941. Dir. space div. Martin Marietta Corp., Balt., 1941-67; mgr. advanced program McDonnell Douglas Corp., St. Louis, 1967-68; chmn. bd., chief exec. officer Charter One Bank, Fed. Savs. Bank, Cleve., 1980-87; chmn. bd. dirs. Charter One Bank, FSB, Cleve., 1988-95, chmn. emeritus, 1995—; instr. Johns Hopkins U., U. Md., 1943-47; Mem. adv. com. NASA, 1956-67. Adv. bd. St. Alexis Hosp.; bd. dirs. Am. Cancer Soc. Mem. Northeastern Ohio Savs. and Loan League (Treas., past pres.); Mem. Nat. Council Savs. Instns., Ohio Savs. and Loan League (past chmn., bd. dirs.), Am. Mgmt. Assn., Greater Cleve. Growth Assn., Sigma Xi, Phi Kappa Theta, Tau Beta Pi. Clubs: Rotarian. (Cleve.), Union (Cleve.), Clevelander (Cleve.), Cleve. Athletic (Cleve.), Shaker Heights Country (Cleve.). Office: Charter One Bank 1215 Superior Ave E Cleveland OH 44114-3299

KOCH, DAVID HAMILTON, chemical company executive; b. Wichita, Kans., May 3, 1940. BS in Chem. Engring., MIT, 1962, MS in Chem. Engring., 1963. Engr. Amicon Corp., Cambridge, 1963-64, Arthur D. Little, Inc., Cambridge, Mass., 1964-67, Halcon Internat., Inc., N.Y.C., 1967-70; with Chem. Tech Group of Koch Ind., Wichita, Kans., 1970—, exec. v.p., 1981—. Bd. trustees NYU Med. Ctr., N.Y.C.; gov. N.Y. Hosp., N.Y.C., chmn. devel. com.; trustee Meml. Sloan Kettering, N.Y.C., others; bd. dirs. Am. Mus. Natural History, N.Y.C., Aspen Inst., Colo., Earthwatch, Watertown, Mass., Inst. of Human Origins, Berkeley, Calif.; mem. bd. assocs. Whitehead Inst., Cambridge, Mass.; bd. overseers, WGBH, Channel 2, Boston; trustee Guggenheim Mus., N.Y.C., others; Libertarian Party Candidate for V.P. of U.S., 1980; bd. dirs. Reason Found., L.A., CATO Inst., Washington, Citizens for a Sound Economy, Washington. Mem. River Club (N.Y.), Racquet & Tennis Club (N.Y.), Explorers Club (N.Y.), numerous others. Avocations: skiing, tennis, golf. Office: Koch Engring 161 E 42nd St Fl 31 New York NY 10017-4011*

KOCH, DAVID VICTOR, librarian, administrator; b. Highland, Ill., Feb. 19, 1937; s. Victor Hugo and Eunice Louise (Matter) K.; m. Noel Janet Wyandt, July 15, 1959 (div. 1968); 1 child, John David; m. Carolyn Melvin, Mar. 21, 1970 (div. 1979); 1 child, Victor Louis; m. Loretta Marie Peterson, Aug. 25, 1979; 1 child, Elizabeth Louise. BA in Lit., DePauw U., 1959; MA in English and Modern Lit., So. Ill. U., 1963, postgrad.; postgrad., U. Cin. Reporter, columnist Dayton (Ohio) Jour. Herald newspaper, 1959-61; instr. dept. English Wright State U., Dayton, 1964-69; asst. rare books libr. Morris Libr., So. Ill. U., Carbondale, 1961-64, rare books libr., 1970-80, curator spl. collections, univ. archivist, 1980-91, dir. spl. collections and devel., 1991-96, assoc. dean spl. collections and devel. svcs., 1997—; mem. Midwest Archives Conf., 1980—; mem. Conf. of Editors of Learned Jours., 1974—; mem. univ. acad./student affairs com. So. Ill. U., Carbondale, 1984-86, univ. rsch. com., 1980-82, 97—, libr. affairs mgmt. com., 1991—, libr. affairs exec. com., 1991—, univ. libr. of the future com., 1992—; mem. adv. bd. Ill. State Archives, 1997—, Ill. State Hist. Records, 1997—. Editor: (with Joseph Katz and Dick Allen) The Mad River Review, 1965-68, (with Alan Cohn and Kenneth Duckett) ICarbS; contbr. articles to profl. jours. Home: 2800 W Sunset Dr Carbondale IL 62901-2046 Office: So Ill U Spl Collections Morris Libr Carbondale IL 62901-6632*

KOCH, DONALD LEROY, geologist, state agency administrator; b. Dubuque, Iowa, June 3, 1937; s. Gregory John and Josephine Elizabeth (Young) K.; m. Celia Jean Swede, July 5, 1962; children: Kyle Benjamin, Amy Suzanne, Nathan Gregory. BS, U. Iowa, 1959, MS in Geology, 1967, postgrad., 1971-73. Research geologist Iowa Geol. Survey, Iowa City, 1959-71, chief subsurface geology, 1971-75, asst. state geologist, 1975-80, state geologist and dir., 1980-86; state geologist and bur. chief Geol. Survey Bur., Iowa City, 1986. Contbr. articles to profl. jours. Fellow Iowa Acad. Sci. (bd. dirs. 1986-89); mem. Geol. Soc. Iowa (pres. 1969), Iowa Groundwater Assn. (pres. 1986), Sigma Xi. Lodge: Rotary. Avocations: bicycling, camping, chess, numismatics. Home: 1431 Prairie Du Chien Rd Iowa City IA 52245-5615 Office: Geol Survey Bur 109 Trowbridge Hall Iowa City IA 52242-1319

KOCH, DOUGLAS DONALD, ophthalmologist; b. Port Huron, Mich., May 28, 1951; s. Donald Allen and Helen Baptie (Webster) K. BA, Amherst Coll., 1973; MD, Harvard U., 1977. Diplomate Am. Bd. Ophthalmology. Intern St. Luke's Episcopal Hosp., Houston, 1977-78; resident in ophthalmology Baylor Coll. Medicine, Houston, 1978-81, assoc. prof. ophthalmology, 1982—; ophthalmologist Cullen Eye Inst., Houston. Mem. River Oaks Breakfast Club, Phi Beta Kappa, Alpha Omega Alpha. Office: Cullen Eye Inst 6565 Fannin St # Nc205 Houston TX 77030-2704

KOCH, EDNA MAE, lawyer, nurse; b. Terre Haute, Ind., Oct. 12, 1951; d. Leo K. and Lucille E. (Smith) K.; m. Mark D. Orton. BS in Nursing, Ind. State U., 1977; JD, Ind. U., 1980. Bar: Ind. 1980, U.S. Dist. Ct. (so. dist.) Ind. 1980. Assoc. Dillon & Cohen, Indpls., 1980-85; ptnr. Tipton, Cohen & Koch, Indpls., 1985-93, LaCava, Zeigler & Carter, Indpls., 1993-94, Zeigler Carter Cohen & Koch, Indpls., 1994—; leader seminars for nurses, Ind. U. Med. Ctr., Ball State U., Muncie, Ind., St. Vincent Hosp., Indpls., Deaconess Hosp., Evansville, Ind., others; lectr. on med. malpractice Cen. Ind. chpt. AACCN, Indpls. "500" Postgrad. Course in Emergency Medicine, Ind. Assn. Osteo. Physicians and Surgeons State Conv., numerous others. Mem. ABA, ANA, Ind. State Bar Assn., Indpls. Bar Assn., Am. Soc. Law and Medicine, Ind. State Nurses Assn. Republican. Office: Zeigler Carter Cohen & Koch 8500 Keystone Xing Ste 510 Indianapolis IN 46240-2461

KOCH, EDWARD I., former mayor, lawyer; b. N.Y.C., Dec. 12, 1924; s. Louis and Joyce K. Student, Coll. City N.Y.; LLB, NYU, 1948. Bar: N.Y. State 1949. Pvt. practice N.Y.C., 1949-64; democratic dist. leader Greenwich Village, 1963-65; sr. partner firm Koch Lankenau Schwartz & Kovner, N.Y.C., 1965-69; mem. N.Y.C. Council, 1967-68, 91st-92nd Congresses from 17th Dist. N.Y., 1969-72; mem. 93d-95th congresses from 18th Dist. N.Y., 1973-77, mem. appropriations com., sec. N.Y. Congl. del.; mayor N.Y.C., 1978-89; ptnr. Robinson Silverman Pearce Aronsohn and Berman, N.Y.C., 1990—. Author: Mayor, 1984, Politics, 1985, His Eminence and Hizzoner, 1989, All the Best, Letters from a Feisty Mayor, 1990, Citizen Koch, 1992, Ed Koch on Everything, 1994, Murder at City Hall, 1995, Murder on Broadway, 1996, Murder on 34th Street, 1997, The Senator Must Die, 1998; appears daily on nationally syndicated TV Show, The People's Court. Served with AUS, World War II. Office: Robinson Silverman Pearce Aronsohn & Berman 1290 Avenue Of The Americas New York NY 10104

KOCH, EDWARD RICHARD, lawyer, accountant; b. Teaneck, N.J., Mar. 25, 1953; s. Edward J. and Adelaide M. K.; m. Cora Susan Koch, Apr. 12, 1997, one child: Edward Peter. BS in Econs. magna cum laude, U. Pa., 1975; JD, U. Va., 1980; LLM in Taxation, NYU, 1986. Bar: N.J. 1980, U.S. Dist. Ct. N.J. 1980, U.S. Tax Ct. 1981, U.S. Ct. Claims 1981. Staff acct. Touche Ross & Co. (now Deloitte & Touche), Newark, 1975-77; assoc. Winne, Banta & Rizzi, Hackensack, N.J., 1980-82; tax atty. Allied Corp. (now Allied-Signal, Inc.), Morristown, 1982-87; asst. v.p. ChemBank (now Chase Manhattan), N.Y.C., 1987-90; tax mgr. Paul Scherer & Co. LLP, N.Y.C., 1990-97, ptnr., 1998—. Vice chmn. law and legis. com. U.S.A. Track and Field, Indpls., 1985-89—, chmn., 1989—, chmn. ins. com., 1984-88, bd. dirs., 1989—; pres. N.J. Athletics Congress, Red Bank, 1986-90; mem. Jury of Appeals, 1988, U.S. Olympic Men's Marathon Trials, Holy Family Sch. Edn. Coun., 1992-96; Olympic Track and Field ofcl., 1996. Mem. AICPA, N.J. Soc. CPAs, Am. Assn. Attys.-CPAs, N.J. State Bar Assn., N.J. Striders Track Club (chmn. 1981-96). Republican. Roman Catholic. Avocations: running, track and field. Home: 130 Grant St Haworth NJ 07641 Office: Paul Scherer & Co 335 Madison Ave Fl 9 New York NY 10017-4605

KOCH, EDWIN ERNEST, artist, interior decorator; b. Bronx, N.Y., Feb. 21, 1915; s. Henry Koch and Elsie Ziegenbalg. One-man shows include Mus. of Hudson Highlands, 1986; exhibited in group shows at Met. Mus. Art, 1952, Bklyn. Mus., 1953, Pa. Acad., 1953, NAD, 1958, Am. Watercolor Soc.; represented in permanent collections Butler Art Inst., Youngstown, Ohio. With AUS, 1942-46. Recipient Top Best in Show awrd Middle Town Art Soc., 1980's, Nat. Arts Club, 1989. Mem. Audubon Artists Am., Nat. Soc. Painters in Casein and Acrylic (bd. dirs. 1975-76), Painters and

Sculptors Soc. N.J. (v.p. 1978), Knickerbocker Artists, Artists Equity. Home and Studio: 109 Old Hoagerburgh Rd Wallkill NY 12589-3430

KOCH, GEORGE WILLIAM, lawyer; b. Cin., Apr. 8, 1926; s. George Earl and Lucille (Arnold) K.; m. Helen Lawton, July 29, 1950; children: Jorie, Danny, P.C., Bobby, Monte, Lucy. B.B.S., U. Cin., 1948, LL.B., J.D., 1950. Bar: Ohio 1950. Asst. city atty. Cin., 1950-54; assoc. dir. Ohio Council Retail Merchants, Columbus, 1954-59; dir. fed. affairs Sears, Roebuck & Co., Washington, 1959-65; pres., chief exec. officer Grocery Mfrs. Am., Inc., Washington, 1966-90; ptnr. Kirkpatrick Lockhart, 1990—; bd. dirs. Borden Chems. and Plastics Inc., Mc Cormick & Co. Chmn. Congl. Charity Tennis Tournament, Congl. Charity Golf Tournament. Served with USNR, World War II. Mem. Nat. Press Club, Union League, City Tavern Club, Congl. Country Club. Home: 10837 Stanmore Dr Potomac MD 20854-1521 Office: Kirkpatrick & Lockhart 1800 Massachusetts Ave NW Fl 2 Washington DC 20036-1800*

KOCH, JAMES VERCH, academic administrator, economist; b. Springfield, Ill., Oct. 7, 1942; s. Elmer O. and Wilma L. K.; m. Donna L. Stickling, Aug. 20, 1967; children: Elizabeth, Mark. BA, Ill. State U., 1964; PhD, Northwestern U., 1968. Research economist Harris Trust Bank, Chgo., 1966; from asst. prof. to prof. econs. Ill. State U., 1967-78, chmn. dept., 1972-78; dean Faculty Arts and Scis., R.I. Coll., Providence, 1978-80; prof. econs., provost, v.p. acad. affairs Ball State U., Muncie, Ind., 1980-86; pres. U. Mont., Missoula, 1986-90, Old Dominion U., Norfolk, Va., 1990—. Author: Industrial Organization and Prices, 2d edit, 1980, Microeconomic Theory and Applications, 1976, The Economics of Affirmative Action, 1976, Introduction to Mathematical Economics, 1979. Mem. Am. Econ. Assn., Econometric Soc., Am. Assn. Higher Edn., AAUP. Lutheran. Home: 5000 Edgewater Dr Norfolk VA 23508-1720 Office: Old Dominion U Office of President Norfolk VA 23529 *Survival in the 1990s, whether in higher education or in automobile production, demands and requires quality. Excellence must be our goal in all that we undertake. This is an attitude that must be instilled in the home, in our schools, and throughout society so that it permeates our lives.*

KOCH, JANE ELLEN, secondary school educator; b. Evansville, Ind., Sept. 11, 1947; d. Mason Irwin and Mary Louise (Westfall) Price; m. Donald Lawrence Koch, Dec. 26, 1970; children: Christopher Evan, Darren Nicholas. BA in Edn., U. Evansville, 1970, MA in Edn., 1973. English tchr. Princeton (Ind.) Cmty. H.S., 1970-72, North Posey H.S., Poseyville, Ind., 1972-76; English tchr., libr. New Harmony (Ind.) Sch., 1989—. Roman Catholic. Avocations: reading, organ, piano. Home: 176 N Cale Poseyville IN 47633-0532 Office: New Harmony Sch 1000 E St New Harmony IN 47631

KOCH, JOANNE ELLEN, guidance counselor; b. Paterson, N.J., Dec. 28, 1962; d. Walter Ernest and Karen Gambert. BA in Early Childhood Edn., William Paterson Coll., 1984, MA in Social Sci., 1987, MEd in Counseling, 1988, MEd in Ednl. Adminstrn., 1991. Cert. tchr., supr., dir. student pers. svcs., N.J. Tchr. St. Andrew Sch., Westwood, N.J., 1985-86; guidance counselor DePaul High Sch., Wayne, N.J., 1986-87; county 4-H agt. Rutgers Coop. Extension Svc., New Brunswick, N.J., 1987-88; guidance counselor High Point Regional High Sch., Sussex, N.J., 1988—. Leader seeing-eye pup project Bergen County 4-H Youth Devel. Program, Paramus, N.J., 1981—. Mem. N.J. Edn. Assn., Sussex County Guidance Assn., Kappa Delta Pi, Pi Lambda Theta. Avocations: swimming, bicycling, rollerblading, animals, travel.

KOCH, KATHERINE ROSE, communications executive; b. Pitts., Apr. 21, 1949; d. Irving Samuel Stapsy and Betty Ruth (Sachs) Blake; m. Stanley Christopher Brown, July 26, 1986; 1 child, Matthew. BFA, Rochester Inst. Tech., 1973. Instr. Ivy Sch. Profl. Art, Pitts., 1973-74; advt. dir. Buhl Optical Co., Pitts., 1974-77; pres., creative dir. Ambit Mktg. Comm., Ft. Lauderdale, Fla., 1977—; instr. Point Park Coll., Pitts., 1977-78. Bd. dirs., vice-chair mktg. and comms. United Way, Broward County, 1995-97, mem. exec. com., 1994—; mem. women's adv. bd. Columbia Plantation Gen. Hosp., 1993—; bd. dirs. Broward Alliance, Broward Coorinating Coun., 1994—. Mem. Greater Ft. Lauderdale Mktg. Alliance (chair 1993-94), Womens Exec. Club (pres. 1995-96), Tower Forum (bd. dirs. 1995-97). Office: Ambit Mktg Comm 2455 E Sunrise Blvd Ste 711 Fort Lauderdale FL 33304-3110*

KOCH, KATHLEEN DAY, lawyer; b. St. Louis, Nov. 27, 1948; d. Edward J. and Margaret (Beckmeier) D.; children: Stefan, Martha, Rebecca. Student, Concordia Coll., River Forest, Ill., 1966-69; BS in Edn., U. Mo., 1971; JD, U. Chgo., 1977. Bar: Ill. 1977, D.C. 1978. Atty. HUD, Washington, 1977-79, U.S. Merit Sys. Protection Bd., Washington, 1979-84; sr. atty. U.S. Dept. Commerce, Washington, 1984-87; assoc. counsel to pres. White House, Washington, 1987-88; gen. counsel Fed. Labor Rels. Authority, Washington, 1988-91; spl. counsel Office Spl. Counsel, Washington, 1991-97; chief OEEOA FBI, Washington, 1997—. Recipient Disting. Alumni award U. Mo., St. Louis, 1990. Office: FBI 935 Pennsylvania Ave NW Rm 7901 Washington DC 20535-0002

KOCH, KENNETH, poet, playwright; b. Cin., Feb. 27, 1925; s. Stuart J. and Lillian Amy (Loth) K.; m. Mary Janice Elwood, June 12, 1954 (dec. 1981); 1 child, Katherine; m. Karen Steinbrink, 1994. AB, Harvard U., 1948; MA, Columbia U., 1953, PhD, 1959. Lectr. Rutgers U., Newark, N.J., 1953-58, Brooklyn Coll., 1957-59; asst. prof. Columbia U., 1959-66, assoc. prof., 1966-71, prof. English and comparative lit., 1971—; dir. poetry workshop New Sch. for Soc. Rsch., 1958-66. Author: (poetry) Poems, 1953, Ko; or, A Season on Earth, 1959, Permanently, 1960, Thank You and Other Poems, 1962, Poems from 1952 and 1953, 1968, The Pleasures of Peace and Other Poems, 1969, When the Sun Tries to Go On, 1969, Sleeping with Women, 1969, The Art of Love, 1975, The Duplications, 1977, The Burning Mystery of Anna in 1951, 1979, Days and Nights, 1982, Selected Poems, 1950-1982, 1985, On the Edge, 1986, Seasons on Earth, 1987, Selected Poems, 1991, One Train, 1994, On the Great Atlantic Rainway, 1994, Straits, 1998; (fiction) Interlocking Lives, 1970, The Red Robins, 1975, Hotel Lambosa, 1993; (non-fiction) Wishes, Lies and Dreams: Teaching Children to Write Poetry, 1970, Rose, Where Did You Get That Red?: Teaching Great Poetry to Children, 1973 (Christopher Book award 1974, Ohioana Book award 1974), I Never Told Anybody: Teaching Poetry Writing in a Nursing Home, 1977, Les Couleurs des voyelles: Pour faire écrire de la poésie aux enfants, 1978, Desideri Sogni Bugie, 1980, (with Kate Farrell) Sleeping on the Wing, 1981, (with Farrell) Talking to the Sun, 1985, The Art of Poetry (criticism) 1996, Making Your Own Days/The Pleasures of Reading and Writing Poetry, 1998; (plays) Bertha and Other Plays, 1966, (a book of plays) The Gold Standard, 1996, A Change of Hearts, 1973, The Red Robins, 1979, One Thousand Avant-Garde Plays, 1988 (Nat. Book Critics Circle award nomination 1988); plays produced include Little Red Riding Hood, 1953, Bertha, 1959, The Election, 1960, Pericles, 1960, George Washington Crossing the Delaware, 1962, The Construction of Boston, 1962, Guinevere, or the Death of the Kangaroo, 1964, The Tinguely Machine Mystery, or the Love Suicides at Kaluka, 1965, The Moon Balloon, 1969, The Artist, 1972, A Little Light, 1972, The Gold Standard, 1975, Rooster Redivivus, 1975, The Art of Love, 1976, The Red Robins, 1978, The New Diana, 1984, A Change of Hearts, 1985, Popeye Among the Polar Bears, 1986, The Banquet, 1998; mem. bd. editors lit. mag. Locus Solus, 1960-62. Recipient Harbison award for teaching, 1970, Frank O'Hara prize for poetry, 1973, Nat. Inst. Arts and Letters award, 1976, Award of Merit for poetry Am. Acad. of Arts and Letters, 1986, Contbn. to Poetry award Fund for Poetry, 1992, Disting. Work award Merrill Found., 1992, Bollingen prize for poetry Yale Univ. Libr., 1995, Bobbitt Nat. prize fo poetry, Libr. of Congress, 1996; Fulbright fellow, 1950-51, 78, 82; Guggenheim fellow, 1961-61; Nat. Endowment for Arts grantee, 1966; Ingram Merrill Found. fellow, 1969. Home: 25 Claremont Ave New York NY 10027-6802 Office: Columbia U Hamilton Hall New York NY 10027

KOCH, LORETTA PETERSON, librarian, educator; b. Anna, Ill., Mar. 5, 1951; d. Vance G. and Dorothy M. (Cline) Peterson; m. David Victor Koch, Aug. 25, 1979; 1 child, Elizabeth; stepchildren: John, Victor. AB in in English with high honors, U. Ill., 1973, MS in LS, 1974; postgrad., So. Ill. U., Carbondale, 1976. Adult svcs. libr. Carbondale Pub. Libr., 1974-81; owner, operator L. Koch-Words, editing and word processing, Carbondale, 1981-85; rsch. asst. So. Ill. U., 1973, asst. humanities libr., 1985-86, libr. tech. asst. III humanities div., 1986-89, asst. humanities libr., 1989-92, acting humanities libr., 1992-93, humanities libr., 1993—, asst. prof. libr. affairs, 1989-95; assoc. prof. libr. affairs So. Ill. U., Carbondale, 1995—; mem. faculty exec. bd. So. Ill. U., 1989-91; participant confs. and workshops; presenter in field; field reader grant proposals Ill. Coop. Collection Mgmt. Coordinating Com., 1993. Contbr. articles to profl. publs. Divsn. coord. fund drive United Way, 1989, 90; room parent Lakeland Sch., 1993-94, Parrish Sch., 1994-95, 95-96, 96-97, Thomas Sch., 1998-99; asst. leader troop 813, Girl Scouts U.S.A., 1993-94. Mem. ALA (chmn. poster session abstracts booklet com. 1993-94), Assn. of Coll. and Rsch. Libr. (comm. com. women's studies sect. 1993-95), Libr. Adminstrn. and Mgmt. Assn. (using stats. for libr. evaluation com.), Reference and adult svcs. divsn. Ill. Libr. Assn. (nominations com. resources and tech. svcs. forum 1993-94), Margaret Atwood Soc., Midwest Assn. for Can. Studies, Assn. for Can. Studies in U.S., Beta Phi Mu. Home: 2800 W Sunset Dr Carbondale IL 62901-2046 Office: So Ill U Humanities Div Morris Libr Carbondale IL 62901

KOCH, MARGARET R., writer, artist, historian; b. Sacramento; d. Geroge James Rau and Callista Marie Martin; children: Edward James, Kathleen, Thomas C. Student, U. Calif., Berkeley. Mem. editl. staff Santa Cruz (Calif.) Sentinel, 1958-76. Author: Santa Cruz County, Parade of the Past, They Called It Home, Walk Around Santa Cruz, The Pasatiempo Story, Going To School in Santa Cruz County. Organizer, first pres. Santa Cruz Hist. Soc. Recipient 3 Mixed Media Watercolor awards Yavapai County Art Fair, 2 Watercolor awards Fort Verde Art Show. Mem. No. Ariz. Watercolo Soc., Pen Women, Santa Cruz Art League, Sedona Art Ctr.

KOCH, NANCY JOY, music educator, choral director, vocal coach; b. Wellsboro, Pa., May 15, 1940; d. Alvan Robert and Irene Mildred (Howells) K. BS in Music Edn., Mansfield State Coll., 1962; postgrad., Mich. U., 1963; MA in Voice, Trenton State Coll., 1972; Fellowship, Oberlin Conservatory, 1967; pvt. vocal study with Emile Renan, Manhattan Sch. Music, N.Y.C., 1968-81; postgrad., Pa. State U., 1989. Cert. music educator, Pa. Tchr. vocal music, choral dir. East Strousburg (Pa.) Jr. Sr. H.S. Area, 1962-68, McDonald Elem. Sch., Warminster, Pa., 1968-72; tchr. vocal music, choral dir. Log Coll. Jr. H.S., Warminster, Pa., 1972-89, dept. chairperson, 1976-80; tchr. vocal music Log Coll. Mid. Sch., Warminster, Pa., 1989—; choir dir. Warminster Presbyn. Ch., 1987-92; dept. chmn. Log Coll. Jr. H.S., Warminster, 1976-80; founder, dir. New Beginning Youth Cmty. Choral Group, 1976-86. Soprano soloist (Bach cantata) Oberlin-Robert Fountain Dir., 1967, Verdi Requiem, Trenton State Coll., 1972, Schubert Mass in G, Nativity Cath. Ch., 1996. Recipient Rockefeller Found. grant Oberlin Conservatory, 1967, 1st Place award-Log Coll. Vocal Ensemble, Music In The Pks., 1980-95, 97, 98, Cmty. Svc. award Hatboro YMCA, 1981, Overall Outstanding Trophy, Music In the Pks., 1989, 91-94, 98, Centennial/S.D. Tchr. of Yr. Achievement award, 1992. Mem. NEA, Pa. State Edn. Assn., Penn State Music Educators, Nat. Music Educators Assn., Pa. State Edn. Assn., Bucks County Music Educators, Bucks County Music Educators (treas. 1978-88), Order Ea. Star (Morning Light chpt. 312). Lutheran. Avocations: decorating, photography, gardening, choral performances for area nursing homes and cmty. orgns. Home: 1524 Mulberry Cir Warminster PA 18974-1871

KOCH, RANDALL GLORY, hospital administrator; b. Passaic, N.J., Oct. 12, 1970; s. Gilbert William and Geraldine (Abruscato) K. BA, William Paterson Coll., 1993; postgrad., Seton Hall U., 1993—. Registration supervisor Kennedy Hosp., Saddlebrook, N.J., 1988-92; patient acct. supervisor Englewood (N.J.) Hosp., 1992—. Mem. Am. Soc. Pub. Adminstrn., U.S. Golf Assn., Am. Soc. Notaries. Office: Englewood Hosp & Med Ctr 350 Engle St Englewood NJ 07631-1808

KOCH, RICHARD, pediatrician, educator; b. N.D., Nov. 24, 1921; s. Valentine and Barbara (Fischer) K.; m. Kathryn Jean Holt, Oct. 2, 1943; children: Jill, Thomas, Christine, Martin, Leslie. B.A., U. Calif. at Berkeley, 1958; M.D., U. Rochester, 1951. Mem. staff Children's Hosp., Los Angeles, 1952-75, 77-98, dir. child devel. div., 1955-75; dep. dir. Calif. Dept. Health, 1975-76; prof. pediatrics U. So. Calif., 1955-75, 77—; prof. clin. pediatrics U. So. Calif. Sch. of Medicine, L.A., 1958—; co-dir. Phenylketonuria Collaborative Study, 1966-82; med. dir. Spastic Children's Found., Los Angeles, 1980-85; mem. Project Hope, Trujillo, Peru, 1970; dir. Regional Center for Developmentally Disabled at Children's Hosp., Los Angeles, 1966-75; mem. research adv. bd. Nat. Assn. Retarded Citizens, 1974-76; mem. Gov.'s Council on Devel. Disabilities, 1981-83; bd. dirs. Down's Syndrome Congress, 1974-76; prin. investigator Maternal Phenylketonuria Project Nat. Inst. Child Health and Human Devel., Washington, 1985—. Author: (with James Dobson) The Mentally Retarded Child and his Family, 1971, (with Kathryn J. Koch) Understanding the Mentally Retarded Child, 1974, (with Felix de la Cruz) Downs Syndrome, 1975; contbr. articles to profl. jours. Recipient Albert L. Anderson award for outstanding health care profl., 1997, Homer Smith Rsch. award, 1998. Mem. Am. Assn. on Mental Deficiency (pres. 1968-69), Am. Acad. Pediatrics, Western Soc. Pediatric Research, Soc. for Study Inborn Errors Metabolism, Soc. Inborn Metabolic Disorders, Sierra Club (treas. Mineral King task force 1972). Rsch. on mental retardation and relation to pediatrics. Home: 2125 Ames St Los Angeles CA 90027-2902 Office: MPKU # 73 4650 W Sunset Blvd Los Angeles CA 90027-6062

KOCH, ROBERT, art educator; b. N.Y.C., Apr. 7, 1918; s. Millard Fillmore and Ella (Heidelberg) K.; m. Gladys Leah Rooff, Aug. 5, 1942; children: B'rak Elana Asher, Mitchell David. AB, Harvard U., 1939; MA, NYU, 1953; PhD, Yale U., 1957. Asst. instr. Queen's Coll., N.Y.C., 1951-53; grad. asst. Yale U., New Haven, 1953-56; asst. prof. So. Conn. State U., New Haven, 1956-59; lectr. U. Calif., Berkeley, 1960-61; assoc. prof. So. Conn. State U., New Haven, 1959-66, prof., 1966-79, prof. emeritus, 1979—. Author: Louis C. Tiffany, Rebel in Glass, 1964, Louis C. Tiffany's Glass, Bronzes, Lamps, 1971, Louis C. Tiffany's Art Glass, 1977; contbr. articles to profl. jours. Pres. Temple Shalom of Norwalk, Conn., 1966-69; hon. trustee Mark Twain Meml. 1st Lt. U.S. Army, 1942-45. Recipient Faculty Scholar award So. Conn. State U., 1973-74. Mem. Coll. Art Assn., AAUP. Democrat. Jewish. Avocations: collecting books, antiques. Home: 143 Hoyt St Apt 7G Stamford CT 06905-5746

KOCH, ROBERT LOUIS, II, manufacturing company executive, mechanical engineer; b. Evansville, Ind., Jan. 6, 1939; s. Robert Louis and Mary L. (Bray) K.; m. Cynthia Ross, Oct. 17, 1964; children: David, Kevin, Kristen, Jennifer. BSME, U. Notre Dame, 1960; MBA, U. Pitts., 1962; D of Tech. (hon.), Vincennes U., 1992. Registered profl. engr., Ind. V.p. Ashdee Corp., Evansville, 1962-68, pres., 1968-82; ptnr. Fesk Partnership, Evansville, 1964—; chmn., CEO Gibbs Die Casting Corp., Henderson, Ky., 1976—; pres., CEO Koch Enterprises, Inc., Evansville, 1982—; chmn., dir. UNISEAL, Inc., Evansville, 1984—; v.p., dir. Brake Supply Co., Evansville, 1986—; chmn. bd. Marco Sales, Inc., St. Louis, 1997—; exec. in residence U. So. Ind., Evansville, 1967; bd. dirs. CNB Bancshares, Inc., So. Ind. Gas & Electric Co., Sigcorp, Inc., Evansville, Bindley Western Industries, Indpls., So. Ind. Properties, Inc., Evansville, So. Ind. Minerals, Inc., N.Am. Green, Inc.; chmn. bd. dirs. Uniseal Rubber Products, Inc., Arnold, Mo., 1988-95; bd. dirs. Audubon Metals LLC. Inventor, patentee water purifier, drying oven, powder coating booth, electro painting system. Contr., dep. mayor City of Evansville, 1976-80; active Gov.'s Fiscal Policy Adv. Com., Indpls., 1978-89, Pres. Adv. Coun. Indiana Univ., 1992—, Purdue U., 1992—, parents exec. com., West Lafayette, 1985-88, sch. bd. nominating com., 1987-89; vice-chmn. bd. trustees U. Evansville, 1985-92, chmn. bd. trustees, 1993-96; pres. Signature Learning Ctr. Inc., Evansville, 1994—; vice-chmn. bd. trustees Evansville Mus. Arts and Scis., 1982-92; bd. dirs. SW Ind. Pub. Broadcasting, 1985-89, Pub. Edn. Found., Evansville, 1986-88, Hoosiers for Higher Edn., 1991—, Commit, Inc., Cmty. Alliance Found., 1991—, Ind. Colls. Ind., 1992—, Found. for Ind. Higher Edn., 1996—; treas. Vanderburgh County Rep. Com., Evansville, 1984-88; pres. Cath. Edn. Found., Evansville, 1978-82; chmn. Ind. Econ. Devel. Coun., 1991-92, Ind. Humanities Coun. Bus. Forum, 1999, United Way of Southwestern Ind. Campaign, 1998; co-chmn. Ind. Bus. Higher Edn. Forum, 1991-96; pres. Cath. Found. Southwestern Ind., 1992—. 1st lt. USAR, 1961-67. Recipient Challenger award Nat. Assn. Woodworking Machinery Mfrs., Louisville, 1980, Boy Scout's Disting. Citizen's award, 1991, Rotary Club Citizenship award, 1991, Sagamore of the Wabash, 1999; named Exec. of Yr. Profl. Secs. Assn., 1984, Knight of the Order of the Holy Sepulchre, 1996, Entrepreneur of Yr., Ind. Mfg., 1998. Mem. Metro Evansville C. of C. (bd. dirs. Met. 1983-96, named Bus. Person of Yr. 1998), Ind. C. of C. (bd. dirs., chmn. 1991—), Young Pres. Orgn., World Pres. Orgn., Evansville Country Club, Tri State Athletic Club, Ind. Acad. Avocations: golf, tennis, snow skiing. Home: 4120 Mulberry Pl Evansville IN 47714-0668 Office: Koch Enterprises Inc 10 S 11th Ave Evansville IN 47744-0001

KOCH, ROBERT MICHAEL, senior research scientist, consultant, educator; b. Mineola, N.Y., Apr. 19, 1964; s. Roy Arthur and Ellen Anne (Trimble) K.; m. Laureen Theresa Chase, July 6, 1991. BSME, Poly. U., Bklyn., 1986, PhD in Applied Mechanics, 1991. Profl. engr., R.I. Mech. engr. Vernitech Corp., Deer Park, N.Y., 1983-85; instr. Poly. U., Bklyn., 1986-91; sr. rsch. scientist Naval Undersea Warfare Ctr., Newport, R.I., 1991—; cons. Beltran, Inc., Bklyn., 1988-91; adj. prof. Roger Williams U., Bristol, R.I., 1993—. Teaching fellow Poly. U., 1986-90, rsch. fellow, 1987, 90. Mem. AIAA, ASME, ASA, N.Y. Acad. Scis., Sigma Xi. Republican. Roman Catholic. Achievements include research in undersea propulsion, underwater shock analysis, underwater structural acoustics, adaptive procedures in h-and p-version finite element analysis, rapid prototyping with stereolithography, probabilistic structural mechanics, ultrasonic wave propagation in elastic solids. Home: 18 Mcintosh Rd Portsmouth RI 02871-1263 Office: Naval Undersea Warfare Ctr Code 8232 Bldg 1302 Newport RI 02841

KOCH, RONALD PETER, retired biologist; b. Buffalo, Oct. 27, 1932; s. Karl W. and Marian Elizabeth (Andrews) K.; m. Loraine M. May, July 26, 1958; children: Edna E. Hoagland, Ronald P. Jr. BA in Biology, U. Buffalo, 1954, EdM in Secondary Sch. Tchg., 1955. Sci. tchr. Cleveland Hill H.S., Cheektowaga, N.Y., 1955-56; asst. dist. scout exec. Boy Scouts Am., Buffalo, 1959, dist. scout exec., 1960-64; dist. scout exec. Boy Scouts Am., Rochester, N.Y., 1964-66; asst. to chmn. biochemistry SUNY, Buffalo, 1966-69; rsch. analyst Roswell Park Cancer Inst., Buffalo, 1969-73; lab. technician Erie County Pub. Health Lab., Buffalo, 1975-94, ret., 1994. Author: Dress Clothing of the Plains Indians, 1977. Dist. positions Boy Scouts Am., Buffalo, 1966-74, dist. chmn., 1975-76, ecology-conservation dir. Nat. Camping Sch., N.E. region, 1977-99. With U.S. Army, 1956-58. Recipient Silver Beaver award Boy Scouts Am., 1974. Mem. SAR (chpt. pres. 1984-85), Mass. Soc. Mayflower Descendants, Huguenot Soc. N.Y., Sons Union Vets, Civil War. Lutheran. Avocations: nature study, American Indian studies, genealogy. Home and Office: 2778 George Urban Blvd Depew NY 14043-2150

KOCH, TAD HARBISON, chemistry educator, researcher; b. Mount Vernon, Ohio, Jan. 1, 1943; s. Justin Louis and Mary Fosdick (Grove) K.; m. Carol Ann Kuban, May 28, 1976. B.S., Ohio State U., 1964; Ph.D., Iowa State U., 1968. Asst. prof. chemistry U. Colo., Boulder, 1968-74, assoc. prof. chemistry, 1974-82, prof. chemistry, 1982—, chmn. dept. chemistry and biochemistry, 1983-86. Contbr. numerous articles to profl. jours.; patentee in field. With U.S. Army Med. Comd., 1998. Grantee NSF, 1985, 89, 92, NIH, 1985, 87, 93, 98, Coun. Tobacco Rsch., 1992, 96, Petroleum Rsch. Fund, 1997, Am. Cancer Soc., 1997. Mem. AAAS, Am. Chem. Soc., Am. Assn. Cancer Rsch., Am. Soc. Photobiology. Office: U Colo PO Box 215 Boulder CO 80309-0215

KOCH, WILLIAM I., energy company executive. CEO Oxbow Carbon & Minerals, West Palm Beach, Fla. Office: Oxbow Corp 1601 Forum Pl West Palm Beach FL 33401-8101*

KOCHANEK, PATRICK MICHAEL, pediatrician, educator; b. Detroit, July 1, 1954; s. Julius E. and Stella A. (Mrowiec) K.; m. Denise Marie Kochanek; children: Ashley, Stanton, Jillian. BS, U. Mich., 1976; MD, U. Chgo., 1980. Intern, then resident U. Calif., San Diego, 1980-83; fellow pediatric critical care medicine Children's Hosp. Nat. Med. Ctr., Washington, 1983-86; guest scientist Naval Med. Rsch. Inst., Bethesda, Md., 1983-86; asst. prof. U. Pitts., 1986-91, assoc. prof., 1991—, dir. Safar Ctr. for Resuscitation Rsch., 1994—; dir. pediatric critical care medicine rsch. Children's Hosp. Pitts., 1992—. Recipient Investigator award Soc. Critical Care Medicine, 1994—. Office: Safar Ctr Resuscitation Rsch 3434 5th Ave Pittsburgh PA 15260

KOCHAR, MAHENDR SINGH, physician, educator, administrator, scientist, writer, consultant; b. Jabalpur, India, Nov. 30, 1943; came to U.S., 1967, naturalized, 1978; s. Harnam Singh and Chanan Kaur (Khaturia) K.; m. Arvind Kaur, 1968; children: Baltej (Baj), Ajay (Jay). *Father, Harnam Singh, was superintendent of police in the Central Province, India. Brother, Hardit, retired colonel in the Indian Army. Brother, Pritam, a physician, retired additional director of health services, Maharashtra, India. Sister, Joginder, was a professor of economics. Sister, Amrit, a scholar of Hindi language, immigrated to the U.S., 1992. Brother, Gurcharan, lieutenant in the Indian Army, was killed in action, 1962. Wife, Arvind has been a radiologist for 25 years. Son, Baltej, earned Bachelors Degrees in Economics and Applied Sciences, University of Pennsylvania, MBA, Harvard University, 1997. Son, Ajay earned a BA in Psychology from Stanford University in 1999.* MB, BS, All India Inst. Med. Scis., New Delhi, 1965; MSc, Med. Coll. Wis., 1972; MBA, U. Wis., Milw., 1987. Diplomate Am. Bd. Internal Medicine, Nephrology and Geriatrics, Am. Bd. Family Practice, Am. Bd. Mgmt., Am. Bd. Clin. Pharmacology. Intern All India Inst. Med. Scis. Hosp., New Delhi, 1966-67, Passaic N.J. Gen. Hosp., 1967-68; resident in medicine Allegheny Gen. Hosp., Pitts., 1968-70; fellow in clin. pharmacology Milw. VA Med. Ctr., 1970-71, attending physician, 1973; fellow in nephrology and hypertension Milw. County Gen. Hosp., 1971-73, attending physician, 1973-95; attending physician St. Michael Hosp., Milw., 1974—, dir. hemodialysis unit, 1975-80; clin. asst. prof. medicine and pharmacology and toxicology Med. Coll. Wis., Milw., 1973-75, asst. prof., 1975-78, assoc. prof., 1978-84, prof., 1984—, assoc. dean continuing med. edn., 1985-86, assoc. dean grad. med. edn., 1987—, sr. assoc. dean acad. affairs, 1994-95; attending physician St. Joseph's Hosp., Milw., 1975—; chmn. medicine Northpoint Med. Group, Milw., 1974-75; dir. Milw. Blood Pressure Program, 1975-78; dir. Hypertension Clinic, Milwaukee County Downtown Med. and Health Services, 1975-79; chief hypertension. VA Med. Center, Milw., 1978—, asso. chief staff for edn., 1979—; exec. dir. Med. Coll. Wis. Affiliated Hosps. Inc., Milw., 1987—. Author: Hypertension Control, 1978, 2nd rev. edit., 1985; editor: Textbook of General Medicine, 1983, Concise Textbook of Medicine, 2d edit., 1990, 3d edit., 1998. Recipient Grad. of Last Decade award U. Wis., Milw., 1998. Fellow ACP/Am. Soc. Internal Medicine (pres., gov. Wis. chpt. 1994-98, mem. bd. regents 1997—, chmn. bd. govs. 1998-99), Am. Coll. Cardiology, Am. Acad. Family Physicians, Royal Coll. Physicians Can., Am. Coll. Clin. Pharmacology, Am. Heart Assn. (high blood pressure coun.), Royal Coll. Physicians (London), Am. Coll. Physician Execs.; mem. AMA, Am. Assn. Physicians from India (pres. Wis. chpt. 1995-97), Am. Fedn. Med. Rsch., Milw. Acad. Medicine (pres. 1996-97, pres.'s award 1998), Milw. County Med. Soc., Milw. Internist Club, Wis. State Med. Soc., Mensa, Highlander Elite Tennis Club, U. Club Milw. E-mail: kochar@mcw.edu. Home: 18630 Le Chateau Dr Brookfield WI 53045-4924 Office: Clement J Zablocki VA Med Ctr 5000 W National Ave # 14A Milwaukee WI 53295-0001

KOCH-EILERS, EVAMARIA WYSK, oceanographer, researcher; b. Porto Alegre, Brazil, May 11, 1961; came to U.S., 1985; d. Walter and Eva Margarethe Elsa Anna (Wysk) K. BS in Oceanography, U. Rio Grande, Brazil, 1984; MS in Botany, U. South Fla., 1988, PhD in Marine Sci., 1993. Rsch. asst. U. Rio Grande, 1980-85, U. South Fla., Tampa, 1985-89; biol. scientist Fla. Marine Rsch. Inst., St. Petersburg, 1988-89; rsch. scientist U. Conn./NOAA, Milford, 1993-95; asst. prof. Horn Point Lab., Cambridge, Md., 1995—. Contbr. to profl. publs. Mem. Brazilian Assn. Oceanography, Estuarine Rsch. Fedn., Am. Soc. Limnology and Oceanography, Sigma Xi. Achievements include development of first culture media for tissue culture of seagrasses. Office: Horn Point Lab PO Box 775 Cambridge MD 21613-0775

KOCHER, JUANITA FAY, retired auditor; b. Falmouth, Ky., Aug. 9, 1933; d. William Birgest and Lula (Gillespie) Vickroy; m. Donald Edward Kocher, Nov. 18, 1953. Grad. high sch., Bright, Ind. Cert. internal auditor and compliance officer. Bookkeeper Mchts. Bank and Trust Co., West Harrison, Ind., 1952-56, teller, asst. cashier, 1962-87, br. mgr., 1979-87, internal auditor, 1987-96, ret., 1996; bookkeeper Progressive Bank, New

Orleans, 1956-58; with proof dept. 1st Nat. Bank, Cin., Ohio, 1958-59; teller 1st Nat. Bank, Harrison, Ohio, 1959-62; bookkeeper Donald E. Kocher Constrn., Harrison, 1981—. Mem. Am. Bankers Assn., Ind. Bankers Assn. Home: 11277 Biddinger Rd Harrison OH 45030

KOCHER, MARGARET, technical writer; b. Salem, Mass., Feb. 6, 1921; d. J. Willard and Margaret (Mason) Helburn; m. Eric Kocher, Apr. 26, 1947; children: Eric Glenn, Terry, Christopher, Debra Margaret Mildred. BA cum laude, Harvard U., 1941; MA, Am. U., 1969. Lic. comml. pilot, instrument and instr. rating, FAA. Casting aide, stage mgr. The Theatre Guild, N.Y.C., 1941-42; sales pilot Republic Aviation, Farmingdale, N.Y., 1945; analyst, writer, crash injury rsch. Cornell Med. Ctr., N.Y.C., 1946-47; tech. and chief editor Vitro Engrng., Washington, 1956-59; rschr., writer Ctr. for Applied LInguistics, Washington, 1967-69; instr. linguistics Queens Coll., N.Y.C., 1970-72, Adelphi U., Garden City, N.Y., 1970-72; exec. sec. project 208 N.Y.C. Dept. Environ. Protection, 1976-80; writer N.Y. Inst. Tech., Old Westbury, 1981-82; pub. participation specialist Helen Neuhaus Assocs., N.Y.C., 1980-83; prin. Kocher Assocs., N.Y.C., 1982—. Author: Guide to Kuala Lumpur, 1955, Energy Information Guidance Manual, 1982, The World of Waste, 1988; co-author: Human Resources Directory, 1981. Chair bldg. and grounds com. Alley Pond Environ. Ctr., 1993-95; mem. nominating com. Citywide Recycling Adv. Bd., N.Y.C., 1991-93; bd. dirs. Alley Pond Environ. Ctr., N.Y., 1991—. Pilot, USAF, 1943-44. Recipient Cert. of Appreciation U.S. EPA, 1979, Earthling award for Lifetime Achievement, The City Club of N.Y., 1993. Mem. LWV (chair environ. com. N.Y.C. chpt. 1982-93, bd. dirs. Tri-State met. region 1986-98), Transp. Alternatives, Environ. Def. Fund, Nat. Resources Def. Coun., Nat. Wildlife Fedn., Nature Conservancy, Sierra Club. Avocations: bicycling, hiking, swimming, knitting, crossword puzzles.

KOCHERIL, ABRAHAM GEORGE, physician, educator; b. Alwaye, Kerala, India, Feb. 20, 1962; came to U.S., 1970; s. George Paul and Mary G. (Kallappara) K.; m. Elizabeth Kuruvilla, Jan. 3, 1988; children: George Stephen, Philip Abraham. AB, NYU, 1982, MD, 1986. Diplomate Am. Bd. Internal Medicine, Am. Bd. Cardiovascular Disease, Am. Bd. Clin. Cardiac Electrophysiology. Intern, resident, chief resident Miriam Hosp. Brown U., Providence, R.I., 1986-90; fellow Yale U., New Haven, Conn., 1990-93; dir. clin. electrophysiology, asst. prof. medicine Med. Coll. Ga., Augusta, 1993-95; head of cardiac electrophysiology Carle Clinic Assn., Urbana, Ill., 1995—; asst. prof. medicine U. Ill., Urbana, 1995—. Contbr. articles to profl. jours.; various TV appearances. Presdl. scholar N.Y.U., 1979-82. Fellow Am. Coll. Cardiology, ACP; mem. AMA, N.Am. Soc. Pacing and Electrophysiology, Phi Beta Kappa. Avocations: wine tasting, tae kwon do, impressionist paintings. Office: Carle Heart Ctr 602 W University Ave Urbana IL 61801-2530

KOCHHAR-LINDGREN, GRAY MEREDITH, humanities educator; b. Memphis, Jan. 15, 1955; s. Gray Meredith and June Queen (Thomason) Lindgren; m. Kanta Ann Kochhar, May 24, 1980; 1 child, Duncan. BA, U. Colo., 1977; MA in Religion, Yale Div. Sch., 1982; MA, U. N.C., Greensboro, 1987; PhD, Emory U., Atlanta, 1990. Dir. humanities The Am. Sch. in switzerland, Lugano, 1982-84; admissions staff Duke U., Durham, N.C., 1986-87; asst. prof. Emory U., Atlanta, 1990-91; lektor U. Regensburg, Germany, 1991-93; asst. prof. Temple U., Phila., 1994-98; faculty, chmn. accelerated degree Rosemont Coll., Phila., 1994—; asst. prof. Cen. Mich. U., 1998—. Author: Starting Time, 1995, Narcissus Transformed, 1993; contbr. articles to profl. jours. Named Tchr. of the Yr., Rosemont Coll., 1996-97; Carswell scholar Wake Forest U., 1973-75. Mem. MLA.

KOCHI, JAY KAZUO, chemist, educator; b. Los Angeles, May 17, 1927; s. Tsuruzo and Shizuko (Moriya) K.; m. Marion Kiyono, Mar. 1, 1959; children—Sims, Julia. Student, Cornell U., 1945; B.S., UCLA, 1949; Ph.D., Iowa State U., 1952. Faculty Harvard U., 1952-55; NIH fellow Cambridge U., Eng., 1956; mem. faculty Iowa State U., 1956; with Shell Devel. Co., 1957-61; mem. faculty dept. chemistry Case Western Res. U., Cleve., 1962-69; prof. Case Western Res. U., 1966-69; prof. chemistry Ind. U., Bloomington, 1969-74; Earl Blough prof. chemistry Ind. U., 1974-84; Robert A. Welch Disting. prof. chemistry U. Houston, 1984—; cons. chemist, 1964—. Mem. Am. Chem. Soc., Chem. Soc. (London), Nat. Acad. Scis., Sigma Xi. Achievements include research on mechanism of catalysis of organic reactions, organometallics, electrochemistry and photochemistry, time-resolved spectroscopy of reactive intermediates. Home: 4372 Faculty Ln Houston TX 77004-6601

KOCHTA, RUTH MARTHA, art gallery owner; b. N.Y.C., Jan. 5, 1924; d. Harry Joseph and Anna (Braun) Evers; m. Albert Emil Kochta, Nov. 7, 1948; children: Alan, Carol. Student, CUNY, Queens, 1965-68, Art Students League, 1970-75. Artist Queens, N.Y. and Lenox, Mass., 1965—; dir. Imperial Gallery, N.Y.C., 1981; owner, dir. Clark Whitney Gallery, Lenox, 1983—. Work exhibited at Nat. Acad., N.Y.C. 1969, Audubon Artists, N.Y.C. 1971, Heckscher Mus., Huntington, N.Y., 1972, Elizabet Ney Mus., Austin, Tex., 1972, Wadsworth Atheneum, Hartford, Conn., 1975, Philathea Mus., Ont., Can., 1976, New Britain (Conn.) Mus., 1978, Guild Gallery, N.Y.C. 1979, other exhibits. Recipient over 50 awards in various competitions. Home and Office: 25 Church St Lenox MA 01240-2504

KOCIOLKO, JOHN STEPHEN, town official; b. Chgo., Apr. 20, 1949; s. John Ellis and Helen Mary (Rapacz) K. BA with highest honors, DePaul U., 1970, MA with distinction, 1971; postgrad., Loyola U., 1972-74. Cert. assessing officer Ill. Property Assessment Inst. Manpower dir. Town of Cicero, Ill., 1975-77; town trustee Town of Cicero, 1977-81; state rep. State of Ill., Springfield, 1981-83; town trustee Town of Cicero, 1983-93, town assessor, 1993—; chmn. Cicero Police Aux. Bd., 1980-93; bd. dirs. Family Fed. Savs. of Ill., Cicero. Author newspaper column Cicero Observer, 1993-98. Mem. Grade Sch. Bd. of Edn., Cicero, 1976-77; pres. United Way/Cmty. Chest-Cicero, 1987—, Morton Coll. Found., Cicero, 1990-97; bd. dirs. United Way Suburban Chgo., 1994—, sec., 1997—; bd. dirs. Cicero unit Am. Cancer Soc.; chmn. Cicero Bicentennial Commn., 1975-76; del. Rep. Nat. Conv., 1988; presdl. elector Ill., 1988; lectr. on history and current events. Recipient Recognition award Am. Cancer Soc., 1993, Paul Harris award Cicero Rotary Club, 1994, Disting. Svc. award Morton Coll., 1995, Gov.'s award Cicero Cmty. Chest, 1996, Exceptional Svc. award Morton Coll. Found., 1997. Mem. Twp. Ofcls. of Ill., Twp. Assessors of Cook County, Cicero Plan Commn. (chmn. 1975-80), Cicero C. of C. (bd. dirs. 1993—, Disting. Citizen award 1992), Chgo. Civil War Roundtable, Hawthorne Businessman's Assn. (pres. 1985-87), Kiwanis of Cicero (pres. 1980-81), Rotary Club Cicero (hon.), KC, Blue Key, Delta Epsilon Sigma, Pi Gamma Mu. Republican. Roman Catholic. Avocations: astronomy, photography. Office: Town of Cicero 4937 W 25th St Cicero IL 60804-3435

KOCKROW, ELAINE ODEN, nurse educator, medical/surgical nurse, obstetrical nursing; b. Chariton, Iowa, July 5, 1935; d. Charles T. and Marjorie Elizabeth (Swanson) Oden; m. Donald R. Kockrow, Dec. 21, 1958; children: Anne Marie, Amy Lou, Donald Bradley. Diploma, Broadlawns Polk County Hosp., Des Moines, 1956; BS, U. Nebr., Kearney, 1978, MS, 1988. Staff nurse, head nurse, med.-surg. St. Mary's Hosp., North Platte, Nebr.; staff nurse, head nurse, obstetrics Luth. Hosp., North Platte; nurse educator Mid-plains Community Coll., North Platte. Nurse reviewer Comprehensive Review of Practical Nursing, 1990; co-editor: Foundations of Nursing, 1991, 2nd edit., 1995, 3rd edit., 1999. Home: 901 S Ash St North Platte NE 69101-6002

KOCORAS, CHARLES PETROS, federal judge; b. Chgo., Mar. 12, 1938; s. Petros K. and Constantina (Cordonis) K.; m. Grace L. Finlay, Sept. 22, 1968; children: Peter, John, Paul. Student, Wilson Jr. Coll., 1956-58; BS, DePaul U., 1961, JD, 1969. Bar: Ill. 1969. Assoc. Bishop & Crawford, 1969-71; asst. atty. Office of U.S. Atty. U.S. Dist. Ct. (no. dist.) Ill., Chgo., 1971-77, judge, 1980—; chmn. Ill. Commerce Commn., Chgo., 1977-79; ptnr. Stone, McGuire, Benjamin and Kocoras, Chgo., 1979-80; adj. prof. trial practice, evening div. John Marshall Law Sch., 1975—; various positions IRS, Chgo., 1962-69. With Army N.G., 1961-67. Mem. Chgo. Bar Assn., Fed. Criminal Jury Instrn. Com. 7th Cir., Beta Alpha Psi. Greek Orthodox. Office: US Courthouse 2588 Dirksen Bldg 219 S Dearborn St Chicago IL 60604-1802*

KOCSIS, JAMES PAUL, artist; b. Buffalo, Apr. 27, 1936. Grad., U. of the Arts, 1958. Illustrator children's books, 1961-68; illustrator, designer Random House Publ., 20th Century Fcx, 1967; pub. Kocsis catalogues, books, color prints and posters; instr. drawing and pictorial composition, lectr. U. of Arts, Phila., 1965-67; lectr. Kutztown State Tchrs. Coll., civic and social grps. Works included in pub. collections: Lessing J. Rosenwald, Nat. Gallery Art, Washington, Library of Congress, Washington, Albright-Knox Art Gallery, Buffalo, Victoria and Albert Mus., London, Kendal (Eng.) Mus., Bodleian Library Oxford U., Eng.; pvt. collections Her Royal Highness Elizabeth Queen of Eng., His Royal Highness Charles, Prince of Wales, Right Hon. Lord Kenneth Clark, Nancy and Ronald Reagan Presdl. Collection, White House, Lehigh Valley (Pa.) Hosp., 1989, Lehigh Valley Internat. Airport, Allentown, Pa., others; one-man shows Igneous Man Exhbn.1, Columbia (S.C.) Mus. Art, 1974, Crucifixion Exhbn.-Memory of Phila. Scourge Period 1972, U. of Arts, 1976, Igneous Man Exhbns. 2-31, Harvard U., 1976, Sydney (Australia) Opera House, 1979, Dhahran (Saudi Arabia) Cen. Library, 1982, Jilin U., Changchun, China, 1982, 13th Ann. Festival Arts, United World Coll SE Asia, 1984, Italsider Steel Co., Genoa and Alessandria, Italy, 1985, United World Coll. Adriatic, Trieste, Italy, 1985, United World Coll. So. Africa, Mbabane, 1985, Internat. Music & Art Festival, Glamorgan, Wales, 1985, U.S. Internat. U.-Europe, London, 1985, U. Glasgow, Scotland, 1985, James Joyce Mus., Dublin, Ireland, 1985, Kendal (Eng.) Mus., 1986, Internat. Pub. Rels. Conv., Harare, Zimbabwe, 1987, Trinity Coll. Oxford U., 1988, Imo State Libr., Owerri, Nigeria, 1989, Progress Bank of Nigeria Ltd., Lagos, 1989, Nat. Arts Theatre, Lagos, 1989, Freedom Hall, Martin Luther King, Jr. Ctr. Nonviolent Social Change and Atlanta-Fulton Pub. Libr., Atlanta, 1990, U.S. Mission to the UN, N.Y.C., 1991, UN, N.Y.C. (first Am. honored with one-man exhbn., 1991), Sopot, Poland, 1991, Gdansk, Poland, 1991, German-Am. Inst., Saarbrucken, Germany, 1992, Amerika Haus, Frankfurt, Germany, 1992, Zentral-Bibliothek, Cologne, Germany, 1993, Freie Universitat Berlin, Universitatbibliothek, Berlin, 1994, Igneous Man Exhbn./India, Gandhi Peace Found., New Delhi, 1995, Internat. India Ctr., New Delhi, 1995, Nat. Mus. and Libr. Casa Dela Cultura Ecuatoriana Benjamin Carrion, Quito, Ecuador, South Am., 1998, Benjamin Franklin Libr., Mexico City, 1998. Recipient Biannual award Am. Inst. Graphic Arts, 1968, Letters of Recognition Lord Kenneth Clark, 1981, Her Royal Highness Elizabeth, The Queen of Eng., His Royal Highness, Charles, Prince of Wales, 1983. Media: oil on linen; style and technique: creator of psychic impressionism; subject of book, monograph and mag. articles. Home and Office: PO Box 20782 Lehigh Valley PA 18002-0782

KOCZERA, ROBERT MICHAEL, state legislator; b. New Bedford, Mass., Nov. 25, 1953; s. Wladyslaw and Bertha (Olejarczyk) K.; m. Ann Borowiec, 1986; children: Gwendolyn, Elizabeth. BA, U. Mass., 1975; MPA, Suffolk U. City councillor, Ward 2 New Bedford, Mass., 1984-89; pres. New Bedford City Coun., 1987; rep. dist. 11 Mass. Ho. of Reps., Boston, 1989—. Treas. New Bedford Dem. Ward 2, 1976-80; mem. New Bedford Dem. Com., 1976—, del. Dem. State Conv., 1979-90, chmn. New Bedford Dem. Ward 2, 1980-86; mem. New Bedford Planning Bd., 1984-86. Mem. Mass. Legislators Assn., Lions Club. Home: 119 Jarry St New Bedford MA 02745-2518*

KODA-CALLAN, ELIZABETH, illustrator; b. Stamford, Conn., Sept. 26, 1944; d. Alexander John and Helen (Wojciehowski) Koda; m. J. Michael Callan, Aug. 14, 1971 (div. 1978); 1 dau., Jennifer Kristen. B.A. in Art, U. Dayton, 1966; postgrad Sch. Visual Arts, 1969-70, 72-75. Designer Glamour mag. Condé Nast Publs., N.Y.C., 1967-69; designer, art dir. CBS, N.Y.C., 1969-70; designer, illustrator Mademoiselle mag., N.Y.C., 1970-71; asst. to illustrator Visible Studio, N.Y.C., 1973-75; designer, art editor, assoc. art dir. Scholastic Inc., N.Y.C., 1975-81; illustrator Pushpin Lubalin Peckolick, N.Y.C., 1982-84; designer, assoc. art dir. Scholastic's Early Childhood Program Teaching Guides, 1981 (Am. Inst. Graphic Arts book design show award 1982); illustrator 200 Years of American Illustration, 1976. Author, illustrator children's books The Magic Locket, 1988, The Silver Slippers, 1989, The Good Luck Pony, 1990, The Tiny Angel, 1991, The Shiny Skates, 1992, The Cat Next Door, 1993, The Two Best Friends, 1994, The Queen of Hearts, 1995, The Storyteller, 1996, The Secret Diary, 1997, The Artist's Palette, 1998; creator Magic Charm Books series. Recipient illustration awards, Soc. Illustrators, 1975; Art Dirs. Show, Art Dirs. Club, 1980, Print Mag. N.Y. Regional Show, 1982; Graphis Annual, Zurich, Switzerland, 1983-84. Home and Office: 792 Columbus Ave Apt 6D New York NY 10025-5119

KODAKA, KUNIO, plastics company executive; b. Toyko, Apr. 4, 1932; s. Shintaro and Hana (Tonegawa) K.; m. Masako Kodaka, Oct. 10, 1959; children: Akiko, Ichiro. *Daughter Akiko Koh, BS and MS in 1985 after four years at MIT, is a nuclear engineer. Currently employed as Master Black Belt of General Electric Corporation, Japan. Married to Fumihiko Koh, nuclear engineer, employed in Toshiba Electric Corporation. Son Ichiro Kodaka BS 1988, MS 1990 from Columbia University is a mechanical engineer. He is president of Abante Corporation, Berkeley, California. Wife Masako retired from her position as vice president and treasurer of Yamaichi Capital Management Corporation, USA, 1996.* BS, Waseda U., Tokyo, 1955. V.p. gen. mgr. Achilles KCI Corp., N.Y.C., 1963-71; gen. mgr. internat. ops. Kohokoku Chem. Ind. Corp., Tokyo, 1971-77, bd. mem., 1973-77; pres., chief exec. officer HOP Industries Corp., Garfield, N.J., 1977-97; treas., dir. Have our Plastics Corp., Mississauga, Ont., Can., 1985-97; dir. Tashin Shoji Co., Ltd., Osaka, Japan, 1981-97; pres., CEO Tamerica Products, Inc., Ontario, Calif., 1994—; chmn. Abante Corp., Berkeley, Calif., 1996—. Mem. Haworth Country Club. Home: 10800 Beechwood Dr Rancho Cucamonga CA 91737-2430 Office: HOP Industries Corp 174 Passaic St Garfield NJ 07026-1355 Office: Tamerica Products Inc 1560 Archibald Ave Ontario CA 91761 also: Abante Corp 2607 7th St Berkeley CA 94710

KODALI, HARI PRASAD, electrical engineer; b. Guntur, India, July 14, 1949; came to U.S., 1982; s. Appiah Chowdary and Raja Ratnamma (Thottempudi) K.; m. Vijaya Lakshmi Tummala, Aug. 16, 1978; children: Sireesha, Deepa. BSEE, Sri Venkateswara U., Tirupathi, India, 1977; MSEE, George Washington U., 1995. Jr. engr. Maharashtra State Electricity Bd., Nagpur, India, 1978-81; telecommunications engr. Electronic Data Systems, Southfield, Mich., 1985; engr. Bechtel Power Corp., Gaithersburg, Md., 1986-88; elec. engr. Niagara Mohawk Power Corp., Syracuse, N.Y., 1988-94; sr. elec. engr. N.Y. Power Authority, Lycoming, N.Y., 1995—. Mem. IEEE. Hindu. Achievements include development of design basis to calculate thermal overload protection of safety equipment, development of fuse control program for nuclear power station.

KODIS, MARY CAROLINE, marketing consultant; b. Chgo., Dec. 17, 1927; d. Anthony John and Callis Ferebee (Old) K.; student San Diego State Coll., 1945-47, Latin Am. Inst., 1948. Controller, div. adminstrv. mgr. Fed. Mart Stores, 1957-65; controller, adminstrv. mgr. Gulf Mart Stores, 1965-67; budget dir., adminstrv. mgr. Diana Stores, 1967-68; founder, treas., controller Handy Dan Stores, 1968-72; founder, v.p., treas. Handy City Stores, 1972-76; sr. v.p., treas. Handy City div. W.R. Grace & Co., Atlanta, 1976-79; founder, pres. Hal's Hardware and Lumber Stores, 1982-84; retail and restaurant cons., 1979—. Treas., bd. dirs. YWCA Watsonville,1981-84, 85-87; mem. Santa Cruz County Grand Jury, 1984-85. Recipient 1st Tribute to Women in Internat. Industry, 1978; named Woman of the Yr., 1986. Mem. Ducks Unltd. (treas. Watsonville chpt. 1981-89). Republican. Home and Office: 2705 Robin Dr Virginia Beach VA 23454-1813

KODITSCHEK, THEODORE, historian, educator; b. Elizabeth, N.J., May 19, 1951; s. Paul and Leah (Kuselewitz) K.; m. Lee Ann Whites, Dec. 27, 1983 (div. Jan. 1996); 1 child, Sara Ann Whites-Koditshek. BA, Rutgers U., 1973; MA, PhD, Princeton U., 1981. Lectr. Princeton U., 1978-79; Harper fellow U. Chgo., 1979-80; asst. prof. U. Calif., Irvine, 1980-87, Worcester (Mass.) Poly., 1988-89; asst. prof. U. Mo., Columbia, 1989-91, assoc. prof., 1991-98. Author: Class Formation and Urban, Industrial Society, Bradford, 1750-1850, 1990. Mem. Am. Hist. Soc. (Herbert Baxter Adams prize 1991), N.Am. Conf. Brit. Studies. Avocations: music, bicycling, gardening. Office: U Mo Dept History 101 Read Hall Columbia MO 65211-7500

KODNER, MARTIN, art dealer, consultant; b. St. Louis, Nov. 25, 1934; s. Charles and Sofia K.; m. Penny Ann Worth. BS, St. Louis Coll. Pharmacy, 1956. Pres., dir. Kodner Gallery, St. Louis, 1974—; bd. dirs. Centerre Bank Ladue, St. Louis; mem. adv. bd. Boatmans Bank, Ladue, Mo.; expert cons. on Am. artists Oscar E. Berninghaus, Charles (Carl) Wimar. Contbr. articles to profl. jours. Mem. Jefferson Soc., Mo. Hist. Soc., St. Louis City Art Mus., Appraiser's Assn. Am., St. Louis Club, Lotos Club (N.Y.). Office: Kodner Gallery 9918 Clayton Rd Saint Louis MO 63124-1102

KODSI, SYLVIA ROSE, ophthalmologist; b. Boston, Nov. 13, 1962. BS, Stanford U., 1983; MD, NYU, 1987. Intern in internal medicine Beth Israel Med. Ctr., N.Y.C., 1987-88; resident in ophthalmology St. Vincent's Med. Ctr., N.Y.C., 1988-91; neuro-ophthalmology fellow Mayo Clinic, Rochester, Minn., 1991-92; pediat. ophthalmology fellow U. Minn., Mpls., 1992-93; attending physician in-charge pediat. ophthalmology L.I. Jewish Med. Ctr., New Hyde Park, N.Y., 1994—. Fellow Am. Acad. Ophthalmology; mem. Assn. Pediat. Ophthalmology and Strabismis, N.Y. Soc. Pediat. Ophthalmology and Strabismis. Office: 600 Northern Blvd Ste 214 Great Neck NY 11021-5200

KOEBEL, SISTER CELESTIA, health care system executive; b. Chillicothe, Ohio, Jan. 12, 1928. BS, Coll. of Mount St. Joseph, 1958; MHA, St. Louis U., 1964; D, U. Albuquerque, 1976. Asst. dir. nursing svcs. Good Samaritan Hosp. & Health Ctr., Dayton, Ohio, 1961-62; adminstrv. resident Providence Med. Ctr., Seattle, 1963-64; pres. St. Joseph Healthcare Corp., Albuquerque, 1964-85, Sisters of Charity Health Care Systems, Cin., 1985-96; hon. offcl. Cath. Health Care Initiatives, Cin., 1996—. Mem. Am. Hosp. Assn. (adv. coun., 1987-88), N.Mex. Hosp. Assn. (treas. 1968-69, v.p. 1970, pres. 1972). Office: 345 Neeb Rd Cincinnati OH 45233-5102*

KOEDEL, JOHN GILBERT, JR., retired forge company executive; b. Pitts., June 25, 1937; s. John Gilbert and Elizabeth Marie (Kramer) K.; m. Fay Birren, Dec. 21, 1963; 1 son, John III. BS in Commerce, Washington and Lee U., 1959. V.p. Pitts. Nat. Bank, 1960-68; various positions up to pres. Nat. Forge. Co., 1968-95; bd. dirs. The RCR Group, Inc., Nat. Forge Co. Served to sgt., U.S. Army, 1960-65. Mem. Fishing Bay Yacht Club, Conenango Club, Masons. Republican. Presbyterian. Avocations: sailing, wood working. Home: PO Box 877 Deltaville VA 23043-0877

KOEDEL, ROBERT CRAIG, minister, historian, educator; b. Tarentum, Pa., July 1, 1927; s. Theodore and Evelyn (Dagan) K.; m. Barbara Ellen Wood, Jan. 6, 1962. B.A., Wheaton Coll., Ill., 1949; M.Div., Pitts. Theol Sem., 1953; M.A., U. Pitts., 1964; postgrad., Temple U., 1964-70. Ordained to ministry Presbyn. Ch. U.S.A., 1953. Pastor Monaghan Presbyn. Ch., Dillsburg, Pa., 1956-59; asst. pastor Mt. Calvary Presbyn. Ch., Corapolis, Pa., 1959-60; assoc. pastor Dormont Presbyn. Ch., Pitts., 1960-64; mem. faculty Atlantic Community Coll., Mays Landing, N.J., 1966-92, prof. social sci., history, religion, 1978-92, chmn. dept. history, 1969-70, 78-79, asst. dean instrn., 1970-72; lectr. in history Stockton State Coll., 1985-86; clergyman Pitts. Presbytery. Author: South Jersey Heritage: A Social, Economic and Cultural History, 1977, God's Vine in This Wilderness: Religion in South Jersey to 1800, 1980, Following the Water: The Shellfish Industry in South Jersey, 1983, Ships and the Sea Down Jersey, 1989, Becoming a Presbyterian, 1993, Letters from Wheaton by a Forty-Niner, 1997; contbr. articles to profl. jours., articles to newspapers. Mem. Atlantic County Cultural and Heritage Adv. Bd., 1991. Served as chaplain USAF, 1953-56. N.J. Hist. Commn. research grantee, 1974, 84. Mem. United Teaching Professions, N.J. Hist. Soc. (trustee 1985-88), Atlantic County Hist. Soc. (editor jour. 1983-91), Gloucester County Hist. Soc., Pitts. Presbytery, Hist. Soc. Western Pa. (rsch. historian). Home: 1 Unger Ln Pittsburgh PA 15217-1018

KOEGEL, WILLIAM FISHER, lawyer; b. Washington, Aug. 18, 1923; s. Otto Erwin and Rae (Fisher) K.; m. Barbara Bixler, Feb. 2, 1946 (dec. 1968); children: John Bixler, Robert Bartlett; m. Ruth Swan Boynton, June 21, 1969 (dec. 1983); m. Irene Lawrence, Aug. 4, 1984. B.A., Williams Coll., 1944; LL.B., U. Va., 1949. Bar: N.Y. 1950. From assoc. to ptnr. Roger & Wells and predecessor firms, N.Y.C., 1949—, head litigation dept., 1977-88, sr. counsel, 1989—. Chmn. Scarsdale (N.Y.) Republican Town Com., 1965-71; pres. trustees Hitchcock Presbyn. Ch., Scarsdale, 1970-73, 78-79, 82-83. Served with AUS, 1943-45, ETO. Fellow ACTL; mem. ABA, N.Y. State Bar Assn., Bar Assn. City N.Y., Order of Coif. Clubs: Town (Scarsdale) (pres. 1976-77); Sky (N.Y.C.), Williams (N.Y.C.); Shenorock Shore, Fox Meadow Tennis, The Moorings. Home: 7 Chesterfield Rd Scarsdale NY 10583-1619 Office: Rogers & Wells 200 Park Ave New York NY 10166-0005

KOEGEN, ROY JEROME, lawyer; b. Spokane, Wash., Mar. 1, 1949; s. Frank J. and Jeanne (Bardsley) K.; m. Ann Martinelli, Aug. 28, 1970; children: Jennifer, Christopher. BA, Gonzaga U., 1971; JD, U. Calif., San Francisco, 1974. Bar: Calif. 1974, Wash. 1979, U.S. Supreme Ct. 1982. Assoc. Wilson, Jones, Morton & Lynch, San Mateo, Calif., 1974-78, Blair & Koegen, Spokane, 1978-80; ptnr. Preston, Thorgrimson, Ellis & Holman, Spokane, 1980-90, Perkins Coie LLP, Seattle, Spokane, 1990—. Author: Washington Municipal Financing Deskbook, 1992. Chmn. exec. com. Community Alcohol Ctr., Spokane, 1982-84, Century II Park Dist., Spokane, 1982-84; bd. dirs. Nature Conservancy. Mem. ABA, Wash. Bar Assn., Calif. Bar Assn., Nat. Assn. Bond Lawyers, The Nature Conservancy (bd. dirs.). Roman Catholic. Office: Perkins Coie LLP 221 N Wall St Ste 600 Spokane WA 99201-0826

KOEHL, CAMILLE JOAN, accountant; b. Chgo., Nov. 9, 1943; d. Alfonse James and Genevieve V. (Riche) Daurio; children: David A., Laura L., Robert M., Karen M. BS in Acctg., De Paul U., 1976; postgrad., Roosevelt U., 1987—. CPA, Ill.; CFP. Treas. Meritex Corp., Carpentersville, Ill., 1966-68; controller Di Com Corp., Glenview, Ill., 1968-73; v.p., treas. Ridge Road Co., Northbrook, Ill., 1982-87, Decker Gardens, Inc., Northbrook, 1979-87, S&L Engrng. Co., Northbrook, 1973-87; ptnr. HJS Constrn. Co., Barrington Hills, Ill., 1979—; pres. Lé Tan Ltd., Palatine, Ill., 1984—, CJK Enterprises Ltd., Lakemoor, Ill., 1985—; owner Camille J. Koehl & Assoc., Lakemoor, 1978—; pres. Koehl Constrn. and Devel. Corp., Lakemoor, 1990—, Pressing Matters Ltd., McHenry, Ill., 1990—. Mem. Internat. Bd. Cert. Fin. Planners, Ill. CPAs. Avocations: golf, reading. Home and Office: 2020 W Il Route 120 # A Mchenry IL 60050-1101

KOEHLER, FRANK JAMES, city manager; b. Phila., Sept. 1, 1952; s. Bernard James and Mildred Nadine (Crane) K.; m. Jean M. Mehorczyk, June 11, 1994. AA in Liberal Arts, Bucks County C. C., 1972; BA in Polit. Sci., Mansfield U., 1974; MA in Govt., Lehigh U., 1976; MBA in Fin., DePaul U., 1984. Mgmt. intern City of Bethlehem, Pa., 1975-76; adminstrv. asst. Township of Falls, Fallsington, Pa., 1976-78; assoc. planner Village of Homewood, Ill., 1978-80; asst. mgr. Vill. University Park, Ill., 1980-83; dir. econ. devel. Village of Romeoville, Ill., 1984-90; owner Mcpl. Consulting Svcs., Romeoville, 1990-93; comml. sales Honig Comml. Real Estate, Joliet, Ill., 1990-91; dir. econ. devel. Village of Riverdale, Ill., 1991-96; dir. Calumet Region Enterprise Zone, Riverdale, Ill., 1994-96; village adminstr. Village of Bourbonnais, Ill., 1996; bd. dirs. Southtowns Bus. Growth Corp., University Park, Calumet Region Indsl. Devel. Authority, Riverdale; mem. orgn. com. Southland Community Devel. Corp., Homewood, 1992. Fin. dir. Riverdale Centennial Com., 1992. Mem. Internat. City Mgmt. Assn., Am. Planning Assn., Ill. Devel. Coun. (bd. dirs. 1985-86), Ill. Jaycees (bd. dirs. 1980-81), Romeoville C. of C. (bd. dirs. 1985). Democrat. Roman Catholic. Avocations: golf, horseback riding, photography, baseball, football. Office: Village of Bourbonnais 700 Main St NW Bourbonnais IL 60914-2302

KOEHLER, GEORGE APPLEGATE, broadcasting company executive; b. Phila., July 23, 1921; s. Herbert Jacques and Mildred Warrington (Applegate) K.; m. Jane Marie Caputi, Feb. 20, 1944; children: Eric George, Gary Stephen. BA, U. Pa., 1942. Various positions WFIL Stas., Phila., 1945-55; sta. mgr. WFIL Radio and TV, 1955-68; gen. mgr. radio and TV div. Triangle Pubs., Inc., Phila., 1968-72; pres. Gateway Communications, Inc., Cherry Hill, N.J., 1970-84; vice chmn. bd Gateway Communications, Inc., 1985—; mem. planning com. Phila. Commn. on Human Rels., 1957; mem. Adv. Com. on Naval Affairs, 1968-70; pub. rels. chmn. United Fund, 1965. Trustee Meth. Hosp., Phila., 1962-97, Salem County C.C., 1996-98; mem. Com. Commn., United Meth. Ch., 1980-84; bd. dirs. Pennington (N.J.) Sch., 1973-80; elder Presbyn. Ch., 1992—. Capt. USAAF, 1942-45. Decorated D.F.C., Air medal with 3 oak leaf clusters; recipient Distinguished Service award Chapel of 4 Chaplains, 1969; named Man of Yr. TV and Radio Advt. Club, Phila., 1971; Broadcast Pioneer of Yr. Delaware Valley chpt. Broadcast Pioneers. Mem. Pa. Assn. Broadcasters (pres. 1958-59), ABC-TV Affiliates Assn. (adv. bd. 1967-71, chmn. 1970-71), Assn. Maximum Svc. Telecasters (bd. dirs. 1976—, sec.-treas. 1980-83, chmn. 1984-85, chmn. emeritus 1986), Religion in Am. Life (bd. dirs. 1986-87, inducted Phila. Broadcasting Hall of Fame 1994), Union League Club (Phila.), Rotary (pres. 1960), Alpha Delta Sigma. Republican. Presbyterian. Clubs: Union League (Phila.); Rotary (pres. 1960).

KOEHLER, HARRY GEORGE, real estate executive; b. Somerville, N.J., Jan. 10, 1954; s. Harry George and Lillian Elizabeth (Fischer) K.; m. Marylou Elizabeth Harrison, Aug. 21, 1976; children: Kristen, Kelly, Meghan. BS, Rutgers U., 1977; MCRP, U. Tex., 1985. Project mgr. Kupper Assocs., Piscataway, N.J., 1977-78; regional site planner JCPenney Co., Inc., N.Y.C. and Dallas, 1978-83; v.p. site planning May Realty Inc. (May Dept. Stores Co.), St. Louis, 1983—. Recipient Eagle Scout Boy Scouts Am., 1969; George H. Cook scholar Rutgers U., 1977. Mem. Alpha Zeta. Avocations: one-design sailing. Office: May Dept Stores Co 611 Olive St Saint Louis MO 63101-1721

KOEHLER, JOHN EDGET, entrepreneur; b. Olympia, Wash., June 8, 1941; s. Herman Richard and Frances (Schwartz) K.; divorced; 1 child, Andrew C.; m. Susan m. Fiske, Apr. 27, 1991, children: Matthew J., Margaret S. Student, MIT, 1963-64; BA, Yale U., 1963, MA, 1965, PhD, 1968. Economist, assoc. dept. head Rand Corp., Santa Monica, Calif., 1967-75; asst. dir. Congl. Budget Office, Washington, 1975-78; dep. to dir. cen. intelligence Intelligence Community Staff, Washington, 1978-81, dir., 1981-82; dir. resources planning space and communications group Hughes Aircraft Co., El Segundo, Calif., 1982-84; exec. v.p. Hughes Communications, Inc., El Segundo, Calif., 1984-86, pres., chief exec. officer, 1986-87; v.p. internat. Hughes Aircraft Co., L.A., 1987-88, v.p. telecomm. and space sector, 1988-92; pres., CEO Hughes Asia/Pacific, 1992-95; exec. v.p., COO Titan Corp., San Diego, 1995; pres. J. Koehler & Co., Inc., Del Mar, Calif., 1995—; sr. advisor RAND, Santa Monica, Calif., 1995—; pres., CEO, founder Tachyon, Inc., San Diego, 1997—. Co-author: The Matrix of Policy in the Philippines, 1971; contbr. articles on internat. econs. and nat. security issues to profl. jours. Recipient Nat. Intelligence Disting. Svc. medal Nat. Fgn. Intelligence Bd., 1981. Mem. Internat. Inst. for Strategic Studies. Democrat. Episcopalian. Avocations: tennis, skiing. Home: 3495 Caminito Daniella Del Mar CA 92014-4156 Office: 6224 Nancy Ridge Dr Ste 101 San Diego CA 92121

KOEHLER, MARILYN JOINER, principal, educator; b. Plano, Iowa, Dec. 19, 1937; d. Herbert Leo and Cloe Ellen Wells Joiner; m. David Koehler, Sept. 25, 1955; children: Darrell, Duane, Deanna; foster children: Norman, Mike. BS in Elem. Edn., Truman State U., 1973, MA in Spl. Edn., 1978, EdS, 1984; EdD, Drake U., 1994. Tchr. spl. edn. Davis County, Bloomfield, Iowa, 1973-85; supt., prin. Moulton (Iowa)-Udell Sch., 1985-89; prin. Garner (Iowa)-Hayfield Schs., 1989-95, Kirksville (Mo.)-R-111 Sch., 1995—; part-time asst. prof. Truman State U., Kirksville, 1982-83; adj. prof. William Woods, Fulton, Mo., 1997-98. Mem. Internat. Reading Assn., Sch. Adminstrs. of Iowa (v.p., pres.-elect, pres.), Phi Delta Kappa. Mem. Church of Brethren. Avocations: antiques, quilts, gardening. E-mail: marilynúk@kirksville.k12.mo.us.

KOEHLER, REGINALD STAFFORD, III, lawyer; b. Bellevue, Pa., Dec. 29, 1932; s. Reginald S. and Esther (Hawken) K.; m. Ann Ellsworth Rowland, June 15, 1956; children: Victoria Elizabeth Clark, Cynthia Rowland, Robert Steven. B.A., Yale U., 1956; J.D., Harvard U., 1959. Bar: N.Y. 1960, Calif., Fla., D.C. 1979, Wash. 1984, Oreg. 1985, Alaska 1985, U.S. Supreme Ct. 1973. Assoc. Davis Polk & Wardwell, N.Y.C., 1959-68; ptnr. Donovan Leisure Newton & Irvine, N.Y.C., 1968-84, Perkins Coie, Seattle, 1984—. Author: The Planning and Administration of a Large Estate, 1982, 5th edit. 1986. Chmn. bd. trustees Fred Hutchinson Cancer Rsch. Ctr. With U.S. Army, 1952-54. Fellow Am. Coll. Trust and Estate Counsel; mem. N.Y. State Bar Assn., Calif. Bar Assn., D.C. Bar Assn., Wash. Bar Assn., Oreg. Bar Assn., Alaska Bar Assn., Rainier Club, Chi Psi. Republican. Episcopalian. Office: Perkins Coie 1201 3rd Ave Fl 40 Seattle WA 98101-3099

KOEHLER, ROBERT BRIEN, priest; b. Hastings, Nebr., Aug. 26, 1950; s. Robert Joseph and Melba Deloris (Morey) K.; m. Terry Ellen Collins; children: Gregory, Michael, Louisa. BA cum laude, U. Dallas, 1972; postgrad., U. Wis., 1973; MDiv, Nashotah Ho., 1976. Chaplain DeKoven Found., Racine, Wis., 1976-81; curate Emmanuel Ch., Rockford, Ill., 1978-81; rector St. Raphael's Ch., Ft. Myers Beach, Fla., 1981-84; vicar Ch. Holy Cross, Burleson, Tex., 1984-87; canon to the ordinary Diocese of Ft. Worth, 1987-93; rector St. Luke's Ch., Ft. Myers, Fla., 1993—; exec. dir. Episc. Synod Am., Ft. Worth, 1991-93. Dist. chmn. Boy Scouts Am., Ft. Myers, 1993-96; trustee Nashotah (Wis.) House, 1994—; bd. dirs. Interfaith Vol. Care Givers, 1996—. Mem. SAR, Soc. Holy Cross, Soc. Colonial Wars, Ft. Worth Club, Ridglea Country Club. Office: St Luke's Ch 2635 Cleveland Ave Fort Myers FL 33901-5898*

KOEHN, SUSAN MICHELE, accountant; b. Canton, Ohio, June 8, 1971; d. David Michael and Lilly Ann Koehn. BBA in Acctg., Ohio U., 1993. CPA, Ohio. Acctg. mgr. GSO Am. Inc., Columbus, 1994-98; contr. Ohio Mulch, Columbus, 1998—. Avocation: skiing. Office: 2140 Advance Ave Columbus OH 43207-1722

KOEHN, WILLIAM JAMES, lawyer; b. Winterset, Iowa, Mar. 24, 1936; s. Cyril Otto and Ilene L. (Doop) K.; m. Francia C. Leeper, Sept. 6, 1958; children: Cynthia Rae, William Fredric, James Anthony. BA, U. Iowa, 1963, JD cum laude, 1963. Bar: Iowa 1963, U. S. Ct. Appeals (8th cir.) 1971, U.S. Ct. Appeals (10th cir.) 1972, U.S. Ct. Appeals (2d cir.) 1972, U.S. Ct. Appeals (5th cir.) 1977, U.S. Supreme Ct. 1971. Mem. Davis, Brown, Koehn, Shors & Roberts, P.C., Des Moines, 1963—; prof., lectr. in U.S., Can., Europe. Bd. editors Iowa Law Rev., 1961-63; contbr. articles to profl. jours. C0-founder Big Bros.-Sisters of Greater Des Moines, 1969, pres., 1976-77; chmn. Des Moines Friendship Commmn., 1970-71; bd. dirs. Greater Des Moines YMCA, 1983-90; co-chmn. Des Moines Bicentennial Commn., 1975-76; chmn. Environ. and Pub. Works Commn.; mem. adv. com. civil justice reform act, 1990; chmn. worldwide dispute resolution com., Lex Mundi, 1989-94, bd. dirs., 1992-96. Lt. USNR, 1958-61. Mem. ABA (environ. litigation sub-com., construction com., internat. lit. environ. commn.), Iowa State Bar Assn. (environ. coun. 1989-92, litigation com. 1992-95, proflism. com. 1994-98), Polk County Bar Assn., Iowa Trial Lawyers Assn., Order of Coif. Republican. Home: 9 Meadow Ln Cumming IA 50061-1015 Office: Fin Ctr 666 Walnut St Des Moines IA 50309-3904

KOEHNKE, DONNA R., federal agency administrator. AAS summa cum laude, No. Va. C.C., 1986. Notary pub. Info. asst. to mass media bur. chief FCC, 1983-88, sec., 1988-93; sec. U.S. Internat. Trade Commn., Washington, 1993—. Office: US Internat Trade Commn 500 E St SW Washington DC 20436

KOEHNLEIN, JOHN MARTIN, SR., minister, consultant; b. Phillipsburg, N.J., Mar. 27, 1951; s. C. Edgar Koehnlein (dec.) and Hilda Katherine (Martin) Asher; m. Suzanne Gaye Sproull, Aug. 23, 1980; children: Bennett, Shawn, Paula, Jay, John Jr. BA, Gettysburg Coll., 1973; MDiv, Luth. Theol. Sem., 1977, STM, 1989; MA, U. Iowa, 1994. Ordained to ministry Evang. Luth. Ch. in Am., 1977. Pastor Faith Luth. Ch., Oklahoma, Pa., 1977-79, Orkney Springs (Va.) Luth. Parish, 1983-91; interim pastor Hope Lutheran Ch., Brighton, Iowa, 1992-93, Gloria Dei Lutheran Ch., Iowa City, 1993; pastor Palestine Lutheran Ch., Huxley, Iowa, 1993-95, St. John's Lutheran Ch., Westminster, Md., 1995—; sem. cons., 1989—; dean Cen. Valley Luth. Conf., Shenandoah, Va., 1988-91; chmn. leadership support Luth. Ch., Salem, Va., 1984-89, mem. commn. on ministry, Salem, 1985-89, mem. continuing edn. com., Atlanta, 1988-89, Synod coun., Del.-Md. Synod ELCA, 1996—; chaplain Basye (Va.)/Bryce Mountain Lions, 1984-91, West Shenandoah Ruritan Club, Orkney Springs, 1984-91. Dir. Response, Woodstock, Va., 1984-86, Luth. Family Svcs. Va., Salem, 1985-88. Mem. Am. Soc. Ch. History, Soc. Holy Trinity, Am. Hist. Assn. Home: 789 Medinah Cir Westminster MD 21158-6127 Office: Saint John's Luth Ch 827 Leisters Church Rd Westminster MD 21157-6431

KOEKEMOER, CARL LODEWICUS, university official, business consultant; b. Pretoria, South Africa, June 8, 1948; s. Petrus Philippus and Olga Koekemoer; m. Annette Moelich, Nov. 9, 1974; children: Minette, Carlé, Lize-Marie. B Commerce, U. Pretoria, 1969, MBA, 1971; PhD, Rhodes U., South Africa, 1976; B Commerce with honours, Rand Afrikaans U., Johannesburg, South Africa, 1978. Econs. rschr. South African Dept. Commerce, Pretoria, 1969-70; market rsch. mgr. Market Rsch. Africa (Pty) Ltd., Johannesburg, South Africa, 1971-72; account dir. VZ divsn. Otm, 1972-73; dir. market rsch. De V & S div. Young & Rubicam, Cape Town, South Africa, 1973-75; sr. lectr. Ft. Hare U., Alice, 1975-76, Rand Afrikaans U., Johannesburg, 1977-78; dep. mng. dir. Mortimer Tiley Group div. BBDO, Johannesburg, 1979-86; prof. U. Pretoria, 1986-90; sr. lectr. Rand Afrikaans U., Johannesburg, 1977-78, chmn., dir. dept. bus. mgmt., 1990-95, dir. sch. for devel. of bus. leaders, 1995—; owner Checklist Mktg. Cons., 1986—; vis. prof. U. N.C. Kenan Flagler Bus. Sch., Chapel Hill, 1991; vis. prof. disting. lectr. series Calif. State U., 1996; mng. dir. RAA Sch. Advt., 1999—. Author: Print Media Advertising, 1978, Profit from Effective Advertising, 1991; author, editor: Marketing Communications Management, 1987, Promotional Strategy, Marketing Communications in Practice, 1998; co-author: Business Economics, 1991, Marketing Management, 1996. Recipient Loerie award Asom Advt. Awards, 1983, recipient best paper of conf. award Internat. Coun. for Small Bus., 1992. Mem. Inst. Mktg. (edn. bd. 1992—). Mem. Dutch Reformed Ch. Avocation: golf. Home: Northcliff, 12 De La Rey Rd, Johannesburg 2195, South Africa Office: Rand Afrikaans U, PO Box 524, Auckland Park 2006, South Africa

KOELKER, GAIL, family nurse practitioner; b. Wichita, Feb. 5, 1956; d. John Howard and Jean (McWilliams) K. BSN summa cum laude, Ariz. State U., 1986; MS in Nursing, U. Tex., Arlington, 1993. RN Tex.; cert. family nurse practitioner. Staff nurse El Dorado Hosp. and Med. Ctr., Tucson, 1986-88; traveling nurse Travcorp, Inc., Walden, Mass., 1988-90; nurse home health Health Corp., Inc., Dallas, 1990-94; family nurse practitioner Good Sheperd Med. Ctr., Longview, Tex., 1994—; facilitator chronic pain/chronic disease support group Hughes Springs, Tex., 1995—; clin. preceptor nurse practitioner program U. Tex. Sch. Nursing, Arlington, 1993—; lectr. in field. Mem. Am. Acad. Nurse Practitioners, Am. Coll. Nurse Practitioners, Tex. Nurse Practitioners, Sigma Theta Tau, Phi Kappa Phi. Home: RR 1 Box 344 Avinger TX 75630-9641 Office: Good Sheperd Med Clinic PO Box 1440 Hughes Springs TX 75656-1440

KOELLER, LYNN GARVER, public defender; b. Portsmouth, Ohio, Dec. 4, 1943; d. Stanley Wayne and Ruth Louise (Garver) Paulson; m. Michael Koeller, Sept. 6, 1964 (div. July 1980); children: Kristin Schmid, Mark. BS, U. Dayton, 1977, JD, 1980. Bar: Ohio, 1980, U.S. Dist. Ct., 1980. Assoc. Denny, Malloy & Cox, Dayton, Ohio, 1980-82; asst. pub. defender Montgomery County Pub. Defender Office, Dayton, 1982-95, chief pub. defender, 1995—. Mem. Dayton Bar Assn. (criminal law com.), Dayton Women's Bar Assn. Montgomery County Criminal Justice Coun., Barbara Jordon/Thurgood Marshall Roundtable. Home: 1314 Yankee Vineyards Dayton OH 45458-3116 Office: Montgomery County Pub Defender Office 301 W 3rd St # Ll Dayton OH 45402-1446

KOELLER, ROBERT MARION, lawyer; b. Quincy, Ill., Apr. 8, 1940; s. Marion Alfred and Ruth (Main) K.; m. Marlene Meyer, June 1962; children—Kristin, Katherine, Robert. A.B., MacMurray Coll., 1962; LL.B., Vanderbilt U., 1965. Bar: Ind. 1968. Asst. gen. csl. Nat. Homes Acceptance Corp., Lafayette, Ind., 1967-70; gen. csl., sec. Herff Jones Co., Indpls., 1970-74; ptnr. Warren, Snider, Koeller & Warren, Indpls., 1974-76; sole practice, Indpls., 1976—; mem. Coons, Maddox & Koeller, Indpls., 1993-96, Maddox, Koeller Hargett & Caruso, 1996—; dir. various cos. Mem. ABA, Ind. Bar Assn., Indpls. Bar Assn. Republican. Methodist. Office: Ste 190 7351 Shadeland Station Way Indianapolis IN 46256-3924

KOELMEL, LORNA LEE, data processing executive; b. Denver, May 15, 1936; d. George Bannister and Gladys Lee (Henshall) Steuart; m. Herbert Howard Nelson, Sept. 9, 1956 (div. Mar. 1967); children: Karen Dianne, Phillip Dean, Lois Lynn; m. Robert Darrel Koelmel, May 12, 1981; stepchildren: Kim, Cheryl, Dawn, Debbie. BA in English, U. Colo., 1967. Cert. secondary English tchr. Substitute English tchr. Jefferson County Schs., Lakewood, Colo., 1967-68; sec. specialist IBM Corp., Denver, 1968-75, pers. administr., 1975-82, asst. ctr. coord., 1982-85, office systems specialist, 1985-87, backup computer operator, 1987—; computer instr. Barnes Bus. Coll., Denver, 1987-92; owner, mgr. Lorna's Precision Word Processing and Desktop Pub., Denver, 1987-89; computer cons. Denver, 1990—. Editor newsletter Colo. Nat. Campers and Hikers Assn., 1992-94. Organist Christian Sci. Soc., Buena Vista, Colo., 1963-66, 1st Ch. Christ Scientists Thornton-Westminster, Thornton, Colo., 1994—; chmn. bd. dirs., 1979-80. Named to Pres.'s Club, Avon, 1997, 98, 99. Mem. NAFE, Nat. Secs. Assn. (retirement ctr. chair 1977-78, newsletter chair 1979-80, v.p. 1980-81), Am. Guild Organists, U. Colo. Alumni Assn., Avon Ind. Sales Rep and Pres. Club, Alpha Chi Omega (publicity com. 1986-88). Republican. Club: Nat. Writers. Lodge: Job's Daus. (recorder 1953-54). Avocations: needlepoint, piano, bridge, reading, golf.

KOELPIN, DANIEL HERBERT, religious association administrator; b. Aug. 22, 1945. BA, Northwestern Coll., 1967; STM, Wis. Luth. Sem., 1971. Adminstr. Wis. Evang. Luth. Synod, Milw. Office: 2929 N Mayfair Rd Milwaukee WI 53222

KOELSCH, WILLIAM ALVIN, history educator; b. Morristown, N.J., May 16, 1933; s. Alvin Charles and Alice Boniface (Smith) K. B.Sc., Bucknell U., 1955; M.A., Clark U., 1959; Ph.D., U. Chgo., 1966. Instr. to asst. prof. Fla. Presbyn. Coll., St. Petersburg, 1963-67; asst. prof. to prof. history and geography Clark U., Worcester, Mass., 1967—, univ. archivist, 1972-82, univ. historian, 1982—; commr. Mass. Archives Adv. Com., Boston, 1974—. Author/editor (with Barbara G. Rosenkrantz) American Habitat, 1973, (with Seymour Wagner) Freud in Our Time, 1988. Author: Incredible Day-Dream, 1984, Clark University, 1887-1987, 1987. Contbr. articles to profl. jours. Trustee Michael P. Quinn Scholarship Fund, 1969—; mem. nat. fin. com. Anderson campaign, 1980; mem. diocesan library and archives bd. Episcopal Diocese of Mass., 1981-86; bd. dirs. Bostonian Soc., 1984—; mem. Hist. Soc. Episcopal Ch. Served to 1st lt. U.S. Army, 1955-57. NSF grantee, 1970-72; Penrose Fund grantee, 1971; U. Trier-W. Ger. vis. prof., 1984. Fellow Am. Geog. Soc. (life); mem. Orgn. Am. Historians (life), Bostonian Soc. (life), History of Edn. Soc., History of Sci. Soc., Nat. Episcopal Historians Assn. Home: 34 Reed St Worcester MA 01602-4356 Office: Clark U 950 Main St Worcester MA 01610-1400

KOELTL, JOHN GEORGE, judge; b. N.Y.C., Oct. 25, 1945; s. John J. and Elsie (Bender) K. AB summa cum laude, Harvard U., 1967, JD magna cum laude, 1971. Bar: N.Y. 1972, U.S. Dist. Ct. (so. and ea. dists.) N.Y. 1975, U.S. Ct. Appeals (2d cir.) 1975, U.S. Supreme Ct. 1978, U.S. Ct. Appeals (5th and 11th cirs.) 1981, U.S. Ct. Appeals (4th cir.) 1992, U.S. Dist. Ct. (no. dist.) N.Y. 1982. Law clk. to Judge U.S. Dist. Ct. (so. dist.), N.Y.C., 1971-72; laew clk. to Justice Potter Stewart U.S. Supreme Ct., Washington, 1972-73; asst. spl. prosecutor Watergate Spl. Prosecution Force, Dept. Justice, Washington, 1973-74; assoc. Debevoise & Plimpton, N.Y.C., 1975-78, ptnr., 1979-94; judge U.S. Dist. Ct. (so. dist.), N.Y.C., 1994—. Contbr. articles to profl. jours. Mem. ABA (bd. editors jour. 1991-97, vice chmn. securities com. adminstrv. law sect. 1979-81, co-dir. divsn. publs. litigation sect. 1982-84, coun. mem. litigation sect. 1984-87, assoc. editor Litigation jour. 1975-78, exec. editor 1978-80, editor-in-chief 1980-82, chmn. 1st amendment com. 1987-89, chmn. spl. pubs. com. 1989-92, dir. divsn. publs. litigation sect. 1992-93), Coalition for Justice, Assn. Bar N.Y.C. (mem. com. on fed legislation 1976-78, sec. cts. 1978-81, mem. com. profl. and jud. ethics 1981-84, fed. cts. com. 1984-86, chmn. 1986-89, mem. com. on profl. responsibility 1991-94), N.Y. State Bar Assn., N.Y. County Lawyers Assn. (mem. fed. cts. com. 1984-87), Harvard Law Sch. Assn. N.Y. (v.p. 1993-94). Office: US Courthouse 500 Pearl St Rm 1030 New York NY 10007-1316

KOELZER, GEORGE JOSEPH, lawyer; b. Orange, N.J., Mar. 21, 1938; s. George Joseph and Albertina Florence (Graul) K.; m. Patricia Ann Kilian, Apr. 8, 1967; 1 son, James Patrick. AB, Rutgers U., 1962, LLB, 1964. Bar: N.J. 1964, D.C. 1978, N.Y. 1980, Calif. 1993. Assoc. Louis R. Lombardino, Livingston, N.J., 1964-66, Lum Biunno & Tompkins, Newark, 1971-73, Giordano, Halleran & McOmber, Middletown, N.J., 1973-74; asst. U.S. atty. for N.J. U.S. Dept. Justice, 1966-71; ptnr. Evans, Koelzer, Osborne & Kreizman, N.Y.C. and Red Bank, N.J., 1974-86, Ober, Kaler, Grimes & Shriver, N.Y.C., 1986-92, Lane Powell Spears Lubersky, L.A., 1993-97, Hancock, Rothert & Bunshoft, L.A., 1997—; adj. prof. Seton Hall U. Sch. Law, 1989-92; mem. lawyers adv. com. U.S. Ct. Appeals (3d cir.) 1985-87, vice chmn., 1986, chmn., 1987; mem. lawyers adv. com. U.S. Dist. Ct. N.J., 1984-92; permanent mem. Jud. Conf. of U.S. Ct. Appeals for 3d cir.; del. jud. conf. U.S. Ct. Appeals for 2d cir., 1987, 88, 89. Recipient Atty. Gen.'s award, 1970. Fellow Am. Bar Found.; mem. ABA (sect. litigation, co-chmn. com. on admirality and maritime litigation 1979-82, 89-90, mem. coun. sect. litigation 1985-88, chmn. 9th ann. meeting sect. litigation 1984, dir. divsn. IV procedural coms. 1982-85, dir. divsn. I adminstrn. 1988-89, mem. nominating com. 1982, 84, 87, advisor standing com. lawyer competence 1986—), Maritime Law Assn. U.S. (ABA relations com., fed. procedure com., vice chmn. com. on maritime fraud and crime 1989-94, chmn. 1994—, bd. dirs. 1998—), State Bar Calif., N.Y. State Bar Assn. (chmn. admirality com., comml. and fed. litigation sect. 1989-92), Assn. of Bar of City of N.Y. (admirality com. 1987-90), D.C. Bar Assn., L.A. County Bar Assn. (mem. fed. practice com. 1993—), Fed. BAr Assn. (mem. fed. practice com. 1994—), Fed. Bar Council, Comml. Bar Assn. (London), Assn. Average Adjustrs Gt. Britain, Assn. Average Adjusters U.S., Assn. Bus. and Trial Lawyers, L.A. World Affairs Coun. Roman Catholic. Republican. Clubs: Wig and Pen, Directors (London); Mid-Ocean (Bermuda), Jonathan Club (L.A.). Home: 521 S Orange Grove Blvd 100 Pasadena CA 91105-3504 Office: 515 S Figueroa St Los Angeles CA 90071-3301*

KOEN, BILLY VAUGHN, mechanical engineering educator; b. Graham, Tex., May 2, 1938; s. Ottis Vaughn and Margaret (Branch) K.; m. Deanne Rollins, June 3, 1967; children: Kent, Douglas. B.A. in Chemistry, U. Tex., 1961, B.S. in Chem. Engring., 1961; S.M. in Nuclear Engring., MIT, 1962, Sc.D. in Nuclear Engring., 1968; Diplome d'ingenieur en Genie Atomique, L'institut National des Scis. et Techniques Nucleaires, France, 1963. Asst. prof. mech. engring. U. Tex., Austin, 1968-71, assoc. prof., 1971-80, Minnie S. Piper prof., 1980, prof., 1981—; dir. Bur. Engring. Teaching U. Tex.-Austin, 1973-76; prof. Ecole Centrale, Paris, 1983; undergrad advisor mech. engring., 1988-92; vis. prof. Tokyo Inst. Tech., 1994 (summer); cons., lectr. in field. Author: Definition of the Engineering Method, 1985; contbr. articles to profl. jours. Bd. dirs. Oak Ridge Associated Univs., 1975-76. Recipient Standard Oil Ind. award, 1970, W. Leighton Collins Distinguished and Unusual Service awd., Am. Soc. for Engineering Education, 1992. Fellow Am. Soc. Engring. Edn. (v.p. 1987-93, Chester Carlson award 1980, Ben Dasher best paper award 1985, 86, Helen Plants award 1986, William Elgin Wickenden best paper award 1986, Olmsted award, dir. 1982-84, W. Leighton Collins award 1992, Centennial medallion 1993); mem. Am. Nuclear Soc., Tex. Soc. Profl. Engrs., N.Y. Acad. Sci., Association des Ingenieurs en Genie Atomique, Rotary Club (Austin; Internat. fellow 1962), Phi Beta Kappa, Sigma Xi (disting. lectr. 1981-83), Tau Beta Pi. Quaker. Achievements include developement of computer algorithm for calculation of nuclear system reliability. Office: U Tex Dept Mech Engring Etc 5160 Austin TX 78712*

KOENIG, ALLEN EDWARD, higher education consultant; b. L.A., Feb. 11, 1939; s. Edward and Eva (Barnes) K.; m. Judy Lynn Gill, June 8, 1969; children: Wendy, Jody, Mark. BA, U. So. Calif., Los Angeles, 1961; MA, Stanford U., 1962; PhD, Northwestern U., 1964. Asst. prof. speech Eastern Mich. State U., Ypsilanti, 1964-65, U. Wis.-Milw., 1965-67, Ohio State U., Columbus, 1967-69; dir. comm. AAUP, Washington, 1969-70; v.p. devel. Capital U., Columbus, 1970-74; exec. v.p. Marycrest Coll., Davenport, Iowa, 1974-75; assoc. dir. U. So. Calif.-Idyllwild Campus, 1975-76, exec. dir., 1976-79; pres. Emerson Coll., Boston, 1979-89, Chapman U., Orange, Calif., 1989-91; sr. assoc. Thomas H. Langevin & Assocs., 1992—; sr. cons. R.H. Perry & Assocs., 1993—; bd. dirs. Bay Bank Merrimack Valley, 1986-89; prof. cons. radio TV stas., Appalachia Ednl. Lab., Charleston, W.Va., 1967-69; mem. commn. on leadership devel. Am. Council on Edn., Washington, 1984-86; co-founder Registry Coll. & U. Pres., 1992; vis. prof. mass comm. Boston U., 1991-92. Sr. editor: The Farther Vision: Educational Television Today, 1967; editor: Broadcasting and Bargaining: Labor Relations in Radio and Television, 1970; editor Jour. Ednl. Broadcasting Rev., 1967-69; contbr. articles to profl. jours. Exec. bd. dirs. pres.'s steering com. Boston Pub. Schs., 1982-86; v.p., treas. Profl. Arts Consortium, Boston, 1984-85, pres., 1985-87, trustee, 1988-89; trustee Marycrest Coll., Davenport, 1982-86. Recipient 2 Broadcast Preceptor awards San Francisco State Coll., 1969, 71. Mem. NATAS (bd. govs. New Eng. chpt. 1980-84, pres. 1988-89), Am. Assn. Higher Edn., Assn. Ind. Colls. and Univs. in Mass. (exec. com. 1983-89), Mass. Corp. for Ednl. Telecommunications (chmn. 1989), Alpha Epsilon Rho, Alpha Kappa Delta.

KOENIG, BONNIE, international non-profit organization consultant; d. Bruce D. and Florence (Englander); m. Gerald N. Rosenberg. BA, Dickinson Coll., 1979; MA, Yale U., 1983. Program assoc. U.S. Dept. Commerce/ITA, Washington, 1983-85; exec. dir. Coun. Great Lakes Govs., Chgo., 1986-90, Zonta Internat., Chgo., 1990-95; pres. Going Internat. Assocs., 1995—. Mem. CIVICUS: World Alliance for Citizen Participation. Mem. Am. Soc. Assn. Execs., Chgo. Soc. Assn. Execs. (internat. sect. planning com.). Address: 11344 S Lothair Ave Chicago IL 60643-4134

KOENIG, ELIZABETH BARBARA, sculptor; b. N.Y.C., Apr. 20, 1937; d. Hayward and Selma E. (Rosen) Ulman; m. Carl Stuart Koenig, Sept. 10, 1961; children: Katherine Lee, Kenneth Douglas. BA, Wellesley Coll., 1958; MD, Yale U., 1962; postgrad., Art Students League N.Y., 1963-64, Corcoran Sch. Art, 1964-67. One-woman shows include St. John's Coll., Annapolis, Md., 1974, also solo retrospectives Lyman Allyn Mus., New London, Conn., 1978, Rotunda of Pan-Am. Health Orgn., Washington, 1978, Gallery Metayer, Paris, 1999; exhibited in group shows Itnernat. Dedication Nat. Bur. Stds., Gaithersburg, Md., 1966, Textile Mus., Washington, 1974-75, No. Va. Mus., Alexandria, 1975, Meridian House Internat., Washington, 1980; commd. works include Free Spirit marble carving Washington Hebrew Congregation, 1978, Monumental Torso bronze for grounds George Meany Ctr. for Labor Studies, 1982; represented in pvt. collectins, U.S. and Europe, 1965—. Recipient 1st prize sculpture Tri-State Regional Exhbn., Md., 1970, 2d and 3d prize sculpture, 1971. Mem. Artists Equity Assn. (v.p. Washington 1977-83), Art Students League N.Y. (life), Internat. Sculpture Ctr., New Arts Ctr. Avocations: reading, gardening. Home: 9014 Charred Oak Dr Bethesda MD 20817-1924

KOENIG, HAROLD MARTIN, former United States Navy surgeon general; b. Salinas, Calif., Feb. 28, 1940; m. Deena Prescott; children: Steven Fillmore, Scott Osborne, Grant Matthew. BS, Brigham Young U., 1962; MD, Baylor U., 1966. Diplomate Am. Acad. Pediatrics, Pediatric Hematology and Oncology. Commd. lt. USN, 1958, advanced through grades to vice adm.; gen. med. officer Fleet Activities, Sasebo, Japan, 1967-69; resident, fellow Naval Hosp., San Diego, 1969-73, head pediatric, hematology-oncology div., 1973-80; chief pediatrics Naval Regional Med. Ctr., Oakland, Calif., 1980-83; dir. med. svcs. Naval Hosp., Oakland, 1983-84; exec. officer Naval Hosp., Portsmouth, Va., 1984-85; comdg. officer Naval Hosp., San Diego, 1985-87, Naval Health Scis. Edn. and Tng. Command, Bethesda, Md., 1987-88; dir. health care ops. div. Office of Surgeon Gen./Naval Medicine, Washington, 1988-90; dep. asst. sec. def. Health Svcs. Ops., Office of Sec. Def., Washington, 1990-94; surgeon gen. USN, Washington, 1994-98; ret. USN, 1998. Contbr. articles to profl. jours. Decorated Def. Superior Svc. medal, Legion of Merit (2); recipient 4 other personal awards, Navy disting. svc. medal. Fellow Am. Acad. Pediatrics (chmn. mil. sect. 1982-84), Am. Soc. Hematology; mem. AMA, other med. socs. Home: 4933 Marlborough Dr San Diego CA 92116-2346 Office: Dept of the Navy 2300 E St NW Washington DC 20372-0001*

KOENIG, HAROLD PAUL, management consultant, ecologist, evangelist, writer; b. Mason City, Iowa, Apr. 22, 1926; s. Reuben Harold and Dorothea (Paule) K.; m. Barbara Anne Rucker, June 29, 1974; 1 child, Kimberley Anne. Student Navy V-12 officer tng., Ohio Wesleyan U., 1944-45; BS, Iowa State U., 1947; MS, Ill. Inst. Tech., 1956. Registered profl. engr., Iowa, Minn., Ill., Ind., Fla.; ordained to ministry Bapt. Ch., 1994. Chief engr. Grain Processing Corp., Muscatine, Iowa, 1948-50; engr. mgr. Standard Oil Co. Ind., Whiting, Ind., 1953-56; with Booz, Allen & Hamilton, Chgo. and Genoa, Italy, 1956-64; v.p. Dresser Industries, Inc., Dallas, 1964-67; founder, chmn., pres., chief exec. officer, bd. dirs. Ecol. Sci. Corp., Miami and Lugano, Switzerland, 1967-73, Tele-Optics, Inc., West Palm Beach, Fla., 1986-90; chmn., pres., chief exec. officer, bd. dirs. Unionam., Inc. subs. Windham Power Lifts, Elba, Ala., 1974-76; dir. gen. Matisa, S.A., Lausanne, Switzerland, 1977-78, Canron Pipe & Hydraulics, Montreal, Que., Can., 1978-80; chief operating officer, bd. dirs. Tel-Tech Devices, Inc., Ft. Lauderdale, Fla., 1984-86; chmn. H.P. Koenig Mgmt. Cons., Miami, 1980-84, Jupiter, Satellite Beach, Fla., 1990—; cert. trainer Evang. Explosion Internat., Ft. Lauderdale, 1981—, cert. Evang. Explosion lectr., West Palm Beach, 1991—; advisor Citizens Democracy Corps, Russia, 1996, 97, Ukraine, 1998. Author: Winning Against Satan-Applying Military Principles to Spiritual Warfare, 1991; also articles, lectures. Witness on environ. and ecol. matters U.S. Congress, Washington, 1969-71; adv. for founding Earth Day, 1970; mem. Citizens Democracy Corps, Khabarovsk, Sakhalin Island, Russia, 1996, Velikie Luki, Russia, 1997, Odessa and Nikolaev, Ukraine, 1998; adv. for Drug Treatment Fla., 1998-99; mem. Pres. Nixon's Com. on Environ. Quality, 1969-72; deacon Bapt. Ch., missionary to Kenya. Lt. comdr. USNR, 1943-46, 51-53, PTO. Recipient Meritorious Svc. award Govt. of Italy, 1962. Mem. Phi Gamma Delta (Golden Owl award), Gideon. Republican. Avocations: tennis, bridge, Christian witnessing, golf, Eagle scout. Home and Office: 341 Lanternback Island Dr Satellite Beach FL 32937-4708

KOENIG, JACK L., chemist, educator; b. Cody, Nebr., Feb. 12, 1933; s. John and Lucille (Ewart) K.; m. Jeanus Brosz, July 5, 1953; children: John, Robert, Stan, Lori. BS, Yankton Coll., 1955; MS, U. Nebr., 1957, PhD, 1959. Chemist E. I. DuPont, Wilmington, Del., 1959-63; prof. Case Western Res. U., Cleve., 1963—; program officer NSF, Washington, 1972-74. Author: Chemical Microstructure of Polymer Chains, 1982, Spectroscopy of Polymers, 1992; co-author: Physical Chemistry of Polymers, 1985, Theory of Vibrational Spectroscopy of Polymers, 1987. With U.S. Army, 1953-55. Recipient Disting. Lectr. award BASF, 1990, Internat. Rsch. award Soc. Plastics Engrs., 1991, Disting. Svc. award Cleve. Tech. Socs. Coun., 1991, Pioneer in Polymer Sci. award Polymer New Mag., 1991, ACS award in applied polymer sci. Am. Chem. Soc., 1997. Fellow Am. Physics Soc.; mem. Am. Chem. Soc. (award in applied polymer sci. 1997), Soc. Applied Spectroscopy. Achievements include research in characterization of polymers by spectroscopic methods. Office: Case Western Res U 10900 Euclid Ave # 7202 Cleveland OH 44106-1712

KOENIG, LOUIS WILLIAM, political science educator, author; b. Poughkeepsie, N.Y., May 28, 1916; s. Casper and Pauline (Graf) K.; m. Eleanor Margaret White, July 30, 1945; 1 child, Juliana. BA, Columbia U., 1938, MA, 1940, PhD, 1944; LHD (hon.), Bard Coll., 1960. Adminstrv. addt. Nat Resources Planning Bd., Washington, 1941; legis. analyst U.S. Bur. Budget, Washington, 1941-42; procedures analyst Office Price Adminstrn., Washington, 1943-44, assoc. adminstrv. history project, 1944-46; instr., asst. prof. Bard Coll., Annandale-on-Hudson, N.Y., 1944-50; assoc. prof., prof. polit. sci. NYU, N.Y.C., 1950-86, adj. prof., 1986—; mem. fgn. affairs task force Hoover Commn., Washington, 1948-49; intelligence analyst Dept. State, Washington, 1950; staff assoc., cons. Fund for Advancement Edn., Ford Found., N.Y.C., 1954-55; lectr. exec. seminars CSC, King's Point, N.Y., Oak Ridge, Tenn., U. Va., Charlottesville, 1964—; lectr. Nat. War U., Washington, 1966—, Air War Coll., 1965—; vis. prof. Columbia U., N.Y.C., 1965, 78, CUNY, 1968, C.W. Post Ct., L.I. U., Brookville, N.Y., 1986—; instr. non-fiction writing Bread Loaf Writers' Conf., Middlebury Coll., 1960; cons. program in polit. theory and constl. law Rockefeller Found., N.Y.C., 1962-63; cons. N.Y.C. Charter Revisin Commn., 1987-88; dir. seminar for coll. tchrs. NEH, Washington and N.Y.C., 1976, 77, 79, 81; dir. seminar on polit. parties, Robert A. Taft Inst., N.Y.C., 1982; commentator on presdl. inauguration, NBC-TV, 1969. Author: The Presidency and the Crisis: From the Invasion of Poland to Pearl Harbor, 1944, The Truman Administration, 1956, repub. 1979, The Presidency Today, 1956, The Invisible Presidency, 1960, The Chief Executive, 1964, 6th edit., 1996, Congress and the President, 1965, Bryan, A Political Biography of William Jennings Bryan, 1971, paperback edit. 1975, Toward a Democracy, 1973, An Introduction to Public Policy, 1986; co-author: Congress, the Presidency, and the Taiwan Relations Act, 1985; chmn. bd. editors Presdl. Studies Quar., 1972-94. Chmn. concerned Christian for social responsibility Cmty. Ch., Garden City, N.Y., 1968-74, chmn. bd. missions, 1976-80. Gilder fellow Columbia U., 1940. Mem. ASPA, Am. Polit. Sci. Assn., Phi Beta Kappa. Avocations: gardening, stamp collecting, travel. Home: 135 Chestnut St Garden City NY 11530

KOENIG, MARIE HARRIET KING, public relations director, fund raising executive; b. New Orleans, Feb. 19, 1919; d. Harold Paul and Sadie Louise (Bole) King; m. Walter William Koenig, June 24, 1956; children: Margaret Marie, Susan Patricia. Major in Voice, La. State U., 1937-39; Pre-law, Loyola U., 1942-43; BS in History, U. LaVerne, 1986. Adminstrv. asst. to atty. gen. State of La., New Orleans, 1940-44; contract writer MGM Studios, Culver City, Calif., 1944-46; asst. sec., treas. Found. for Ind., L.A., 1950-56, Found. for Social Rsch., L.A., 1950-56; dir. communications Incentive Rsch. Corp., L.A., 1969-78; rsch. supr., devel. dept. Calif. Inst. Technology, Pasadena, Calif., 1969; dir. funding devel. Rep. Party of L.A. County, South Pasadena, 1989-92. Author: Does the National Council of Churches Speak for You?, 1978; delivered lecture series on U.S. fgn. policy. Named Hon. Citizen Colonial Williamsburg Found., 1987; active Nat. Trust for Historic Preservation, 1986, Friends of the Huntington Libr., 1986, Town Hall of L.A., 1986—, Pasadena City Women's Club, 1982-84; past mem. Coun. Women's Clubs; charter mem. Nat. Mus. of Women in Arts; bd. mem. Pasadena Opera Guild; contbg. mem. L.A. World Affairs Coun., 1990, L.A. County Mus. Art, 1990; past pres., pub. chmn., Pasadene Rep. Women Federated; charter mem. Freedoms Found. at Valley Forge L.A. County Chpt., Autry Mus. Western Heritage, 1986, Women of L.A.; pres. Greater L.A. Women's Coun., Navy League of the U.S. Recipient Pres.'s award So. Calif. Motion Picture Coun., 1996, Cert. Recognition Calif. State Assembly, 1989, 95, Recognition of Excellence, Achievement and Commitment U.S. Ho. Reps., 1989, Cert. Merit Rep. Presdl. Task Force, 1986, Cert. Appreciation U.S. Def. Com., 1984, Hon. Freedom Fighter award U.S. Def. Com., 1985, Cert. Appreciation Am. Conservative Union, 1983, Cert. Commendation Rep. Cen. Com. L.A. County, 1972, Cert. Appreciation Eisenhower-Nixon So. Calif. Com., 1952; named Disting. Citizen of Yr. L.A. Area Coun. Boy Scouts Am. Mem. Women in Communication, Greater L.A. Press Club, World War II Meml. (charter). Republican. Avocations: reading, music, opera. Home: 205 Madeline Dr Pasadena CA 91105-3311

KOENIG, MARVIN, heavy manufacturing executive; b. 1932. BBA, Miami U., 1954; MBA, CCNY, 1960. Exec. v.p. United Indsl. Syndicate, Inc., N.Y.C., 1956-78; cons. N.Y.C., 1978-90; with, now exec. v.p. Renco Holdings, Inc., N.Y.C., 1980—. With U.S. Army, 1954-56. Office: Renco Group Inc 30 Rockefeller Plz Ste 4225 New York NY 10112-4225*

KOENIG, MICHAEL EDWARD DAVISON, information science educator; b. Rochester, N.Y., Nov. 1, 1941; s. Claremont Judson and Mary Fletcher (Davison) K.; m. Nancy Crane Packard, 1966 (div. 1976); children: Christopher Wells Bowen, Davison Packard; m. Luciana Marulli, Feb. 2, 1980. BA in Psychology, Yale U., 1963; MLS, U. Chgo., 1968, MBA, 1970; PhD in Information Sci., Drexel U., 1982. Info. svcs. mgr. Pfizer, Inc., Groton, Conn., 1970-74; info. ops. dir. Inst. Scientific Info., Phila., 1974-77, devel. dir., 1977-78; v.p. ops. Swets N.Am., Berwyn, Pa., 1978-80; assoc. prof. Columbia U., N.Y.C., 1980-85; v.p. info. mgmt. Tradenet, Inc., N.Y.C., 1985-88; prof., dean sch. libr. and info. sci. Dominican U., River Forest, Ill., 1988-95, prof., dean emeritus, 1995—; chmn. editl. bd. Third World Librs., 1991-96. Contbr. numerous peer reviewed articles to profl. jours. Lt. USNR, 1963-65. Mem. ALA (councilor 1993-97), Am. Soc. Info. Sci., Internat. Soc. Scientometrics and Informetrics (pres. 1995-97), Assn. Computing Machinery, Spl. Librs. Assn., Grolier Club, Caxton Club, Elizabethan Club. Home: 16 Buckwalter Farm Ln Phoenixville PA 19460-2317

KOENIG, ROBERT AUGUST, clergyman, educator; b. Red Wing, Minn., July 14, 1933; s. William C. and Florence E. (Tebbe) K.; BS cum laude, U. Wis., Superior, 1955; MA in Ednl. Adminstrn., U. Minn., 1965, PhD, 1973; MDiv magna cum laude, San Francisco Theol. Sem., 1969; postgrad. (John Hay fellow) Bennington Coll., summer, 1965; m. Pauline Louise Olson, June 21, 1962. Supr. music Florence (Wis.) H.S., 1955-56; dir. instrumental music Chetek (Wis.), public schs., 1958-62; tchr. instrumental music and humanities Palo Alto (Calif.) Sr. H.S., 1962-65; asst. to minister St. John's Presbyn. Ch., San Francisco, 1964-65; ordained to ministry Presbyn. Ch., 1970; minister Sawyer County (Wis.) larger parish, 1969-74; tchr. gen. music Jordan Jr. H.S., Palo Alto, 1966-69; instr., Coll. Edn., U. Minn., 1969-71; adminstrv. asst. to pres. Lakewood State C.C., White Bear Lake, Minn., 1971-72; asst. to exec. dir. Minn. Higher Edn. Coordinating Bd., St. Paul, 1972, coordinator commn. and personnel svcs., 1972-74; instr. Inver Hills C.C., Inver Grove Heights, Minn., 1974; minister First Presbyn. Ch. of Chippewa Falls (Wis.), 1974-85; sr. pastor Grove Presbyn. Ch., Danville, Pa., 1985-88, First Presbyn. Ch., South St. Paul, Minn., 1988-98; mem. study com. Presbytery of Chippewa, 1973-74, mem. ministerial relations com., 1974-77; adj. asst. prof. dept. ednl. adminstrn. U. Minn., Mpls., 1976-77; mem. faculty U. Wis. Extension, Eau Claire, 1977, chmn. 3d Ann. Bibl. Seminar, 1977, mem. faculty Communiversity, 1977-85; mem. internat. coordinating com. of ch. mission Synod of Lakes and Prairies, 1978-79; mem. ministerial relations com. Presbytery of No. Waters, 1977-82, chmn. ministerial relations com., 1981-82, moderator, 1983; chmn. Synod Designation Pastor Plan Cabinet 1982-84; chmn. Presbytery Council, 1982-84; chairperson Christian edn. com. Presbytery of Northumberland, 1987-88, mem. Presbytery council, 1987-88; mem. Christian edn. com. Synod of the Trinity, 1987-88, mem. Com. on Ministry, Presbytery of the Twin Cities Area, 1999—, Danville-Riverside Area Ministerial Assn., 1985-88, pres., 1987-88; mem. South St. Paul Ministerial Assn., 1988-98, pres., 1989-90. Bd. dirs. North Central Career Devel. Center, Mpls., 1978-84, chmn. fin. com., 1979-84, bd. dirs. devel. found., 1983-85; pres. Chippewa Valley Ecumenical Housing Assn., 1984-85. Served with U.S. Army, 1956-58; Korea. Lodges: Danville Elks; Wis. Masons (grand chaplain Wis. 1977-80, 83-85). Contbr. articles to profl. jours. Home: 6045 Bowman Ave E Inver Grove Heights MN 55076

KOENIG, ROBERT EMIL, clergyman; b. St. Louis, Aug. 31, 1919; s. Hermann Emil and Martha Ida (Baur) K.; m. Norma Caroline Evans, July 18, 1943; children: Elsa Koenig Weber, Robert, Richard, Martha Koenig Stone, Thea Koenig Burton, Laura Koenig Godinez. BS, U. Chgo., 1941; BD, Chgo. Theol. Sem., 1945; PhD, U. Chgo., 1953; DD, Elmhurst Coll., 1987. Pastor St. John's Evang. & Reformed Ch., Hinsdale, Ill., 1943-46; from instr. to assoc. prof. religion Elmhurst (Ill.) Coll., 1946-54; dir. curriculum Bd. Christian Edn., Phila., 1954-61; editor-in-chief United Ch. Bd. for Homeland Ministries, Phila., 1961-84; interim pastor St. Paul's United Ch. Christ, Fort Washington, Pa., 1985-87, Bethany United Ch. Christ, Phila., First United Ch. of Christ, Quakertown, Pa., St. Vincent United Ch. of Christ, Phoenixville, Pa., Collenbrook United Ch.; Brownback's United Ch. of Christ, Spring City; adj. prof. Christian edn. Lancaster (Pa.) Theol. Sem., 1988-89; cons., dir. Koenig Ch. Edn. Cons., Inc., Havertown, Pa., 1988—; adj. instr. Defiance Coll., 1995—. Mng. editor PRISM Mag., 1990—. Pres. Ardmore (Pa.) Jr. High Home and Sch. Assn., 1962-63; mem. Penn Wynne (Pa.) Libr. Bd., 1985-89; pres. Univ. Glee Club of Phila., 1987-88; mem. ElderNet, Lower Merion, Pa., 1986—, pres., 1988-89, treas., 1994-96. Democrat. Avocations: singing, playing violin, hiking. Home and Office: 566 Haverford Rd Havertown PA 19083-2642

KOENIG, RODNEY CURTIS, lawyer, rancher; b. Black Jack, Tex., Nov. 21, 1940; s. John Henry and Elva Marguerite (Oeding) K.; m. Mary Mishler, May 1, 1993; children: Erik Jason, Jon Todd. BA, U. Tex., 1962, JD with honors, 1969; postgrad., Auburn U., 1965-67. Bar: Tex. 1969, U.S. Dist. Ct. (so. dist.) Tex. 1970, U.S. Ct. Appeals (5th cir.) 1970, U.S. Tax Ct. 1980, U.S. Ct. Mil. Appeals 1986. Ptnr. Fulbright & Jaworski, LLP, Houston, 1969—; lectr. State Bar Tex., various univs., local estate planning councils; asst. prof. Auburn U., 1965-67. Contbr. articles to profl. jours. Pres. Houston Navy League, 1979-81; commr. Battleship Texas Commn.; Houston Saengerbund; bd. dirs. Houston divsn. Am. Heart Assn., Fayette Heritage Mus.; dir. Advanced Estate Planning and Probate Course, 1988; trustee Luck and Loessin Collection Trust, Luth. Found. of the S.W.; active Tex. Luth. U. Corp. With USN, 1962-67; served to capt. JAGC, USNR, 1967-89. Recipient Fed. Republic of Germany Order of Merit, 1994. Fellow Am. Coll. Trust and Estate Counsel, Coll. State Bar Tex. (charter); mem. ABA, Internat. Acad. Estate and Trust Law (academician), Tex. Judge Adv. Res. Officers Assn., German Texan Heritage Soc. (pres. 1997—), Res. Officers Assn., Sons of Republic of Tex., Wednesday Tax Forum (past chmn.), German Gulf Coast Assn. (pres. 1989-93), Bach Soc. (bd. dirs.), Houston Karneval Verein (prince 1994-95), USS San Jacinto Com. (treas.), Houstonian Club, Houston Ctr. Club, Frisch Auf Valley Country Club, Order of Coif, U.S. Naval Order, Phi Delta Phi, Omicron Delta Kappa. Lutheran. Home: 2720 University Blvd Houston TX 77005-3440 Office: Fulbright & Jaworski LLP 1301 Mckinney St Fl 51 Houston TX 77010-3031

KOENIGSBERG, ROBERT ALAN, neuroradiologist; b. Phila., Sept. 10, 1956; s. Abraham and Eleanor Marilyn (Teacher) K.; m. Bess Shira, Aug. 18, 1985; children: David Louis, Sarah Michelle. BA, Brandeis U., 1978; DO, Phila. Coll. Osteo. Medicine, 1982, MS, 1988. Diplomate Nat. Bd. Examiners for Osteo. Physicians, Am. Osteo. Bd. Radiology. Intern Met. Hosp., Phila., 1982-83; resident in diagnostic radiology Phila. Coll. Osteo. Medicine, 1984-87; resident in neurology Hahnemann U., Phila., 1983-84; fellow in neuroradiology L.I. Jewish Med. Ctr., New Hyde Park, N.Y., 1987-89; fellow interventional neuroradiology U. Ill., Chgo., 1994-95; asst. prof. radiology L.I. Jewish Med. Ctr., New Hyde Park, 1989-90; asst. prof. radiology Med. Coll. Pa., Phila., 1990-97, assoc. prof. of radiology, 1997—, dir. neuroradiology, 1992—, mem. stroke task force, 1992-93, mem. trauma com., 1992-93; fellow in interventional neuroradiology U. Ill., Chgo., 1994-95; mem. edtl. rev. com. Am. Osteo. Coll. Radiology, 1990-92, Am. Coll. Radiology, 1992; presenter Am. Soc. Neuroradiology, 1990, Radiol. Soc. N.Am., Chgo., 1990, others. Contbr. articles to profl. jours. Mem. Brandeis Alumni Admissions Coun., Phila., 1992—. Mem. Am. Soc. Neuroradiology, Am. Osteo. Coll. Radiology, Am. Osteo. Assn., Am. Coll. Radiology, Pa. State Radiol. Soc., Radiol. Soc. N.Am., Am. Roentgen Ray Soc., Brandeis U. Alumni Assn. Office: Hahneman Univ 3300 Henry Ave Philadelphia PA 19129-1191

KOENIGSBERG, ROBERTA GALE, lawyer, non-profit organization administrator; b. New York, NY, Apr. 5, 1957; d. Harry and Rae (Kaufman) K.; m. Joseph Giovannelli, Oct. 13, 1985; children: Daniel, Harrison. BA, Barnard Coll., N.Y.C., 1979; JD, NYU, N.Y.C., 1982. Bar: N.Y. 1983. Assoc. Proskauer Rose, N.Y.C., 1982-84, Rebell & Katzive, N.Y.C., 1984-89, McGuire, Kehl & Nealon, N.Y.C., 1989-94; dir. planning and new initiatives YAI, Nat. Inst. for People with Disabilities, N.Y.C., 1994—. Root Tilden scholar NYU Sch. Law, N.Y.C., 1979-82. Mem. N.Y. State Bar Assn., Assn. Bar City N.Y. (chair com. on legal issues affecting people with disabilities 1991-94, mem. com. on health law 1997-98), Phi Beta Kappa. Avocations: ice skating, reading, cooking. Home: 420 Riverside Dr New York NY 10025-7773 Office: YAI 460 W 34th St New York NY 10001-2320

KOENIGSKNECHT, ROY A., education administrator; b. Fowler, Mich., Dec. 27, 1942; s. Joseph I. and Katherine (Zimmermann) K.; m. Marilie A. Dani, Aug. 20, 1966; children: John, Adam, Amanda. AB in Psychology, Central Mich. U., 1964; MA in Speech and Lang. Pathology, Northwestern U., 1965, PhD in Communicative Disorders, 1968. Head speech and lang. pathology Northwestern U., Evanston, Ill., 1973-78, prof. speech and lang. pathology, 1975-85, chair communicative disorders, 1978-81, assoc. dean Grad. Sch., 1981-85; dean Grad. Sch. Ohio State U., Columbus, 1985-95; v.p. Ohio State U. Rsch. Found., Columbus, 1985-95; mem. Grad. Record Exams. Bd., 1991-95, NIH adv. bd. on deafness and other communicative disorders, 1990-95; cons. evaluator Commn. on Instns. Higher Edn., 1996—. Author: Developmental Sentence Analysis, 1974; Interactive Language Development, 1975. Contbr. articles to profl. jours. Mem. adv. coun. on grad. study Ohio Bd. Regents, Columbus, 1985-95; bd. dirs. Friends of Evanston Pub. Libr., 1984, Evanston Pub. Libr., 1985. Recipient Disting. Alumni award Central Mich. U., 1977; Fulbright fellow, 1982. Fellow Am. Speech-Lang. Hearing Assn. (exec. bd. 1986-91, pres. 1990), AAU Assn. Grad. Schs.), Com. on Instnl. Cooperation Grad. Deans (chair 1985-86), Nat. Assn. State U. and Land Grant Colls.- Coun. Rsch. Pol. and Grad. Edn. (exec. com. 1995-96). Avocations: golf; skiing. Home: 720 Gatehouse Ln Columbus OH 43235-1732 Office: Ohio State U 105 Pressey Hall Columbus OH 43210-1335

KOENIGSMARK, JOYCE ELYN SLADEK, geriatrics nurse; b. Chgo., Sept. 29, 1938; d. John E. and Elsie (Volman) Sladek; m. Jerry Koenigsmark, Sept. 12, 1959; children: Jeffrey, Joy, Jocelyn, Joletta, Janine. Diploma in nursing, Presbyn. Sch Nursing, Chgo., 1959. RN, Ill. Co-owner Hawthorne Pharmacy and Gift Shop, Wheaton, Ill., 1967-78; staff nurse Parkway Terrace Nursing Home, Wheaton, Ill., 1977-78; staff nurse med./surg. Cen. DuPage Hosp., Winfield, Ill., 1978-80, staff and charge nurse well baby nursery, 1980-85; staff and charge nurse, advanced clinician well baby nursery, mother-baby care, spl. care nursery Edward Hosp., Naperville, Ill., 1985-94; prin. Joyce Koenigsmark, Document Examiner, 1978-84, Joyce Koenigsmark, Master Graphoanalyst, 1978-86; staff nurse Alpha Christian Registry, Glen Ellyn, 1995-96, Wheaton Franciscan Sisters, Our Lady of Angels Convent Health Ctr., 1996-98. Mem. AWHONN (cert.), Internat. Graphoanalysis Soc. (life, sec. Ill. chpt. 1980, v.p. 1981, pres. 1982, cert. graphoanalyst, Master graphoanalyst, cert. document examiner, Ill. Graphoanalyst of Yr. 1983, Pres.'s citation of merit 1983).$D. Home: 1510 Center Ave Wheaton IL 60187-6102

KOENKER, DIANE P., history educator; b. Chgo., July 29, 1947; m. Roger Koenker; 1 child. AB in History, Grinnell Coll., 1969; AM in Comparative Studies in History, U. Mich., 1971, PhD in History, 1976. From asst. prof. to assoc. prof. in history Temple U., Phila., 1976-83; asst. prof. history U. Ill., Urbana-Champaign, 1983-86, assoc. prof., 1986-88, prof. history, 1988—, dir. Russian and East European Ctr., 1990-96, editor Slavic Rev., 1996—; vis. lectr. history U. Ill., Urbana-Champaign, 1975; vis. fellow Australian Nat. U., 1989; Fulbright-Hays Faculty Rsch. Abroad, 1993; active Study Group on Russian Revolution, Study Group on Internat. Labor and Working-Class History; lectr. in field. Author: Moscow Workers and the 1917 Revolution, 1981, paperback edit., 1986, (with William G. Rosenberg) Strikes and Revolution in Russia 1917, 1989, editor: Tret'ya Vserossiiskaya Konferentsiya Professional'nykh Soyuzov 1917, 1982, (with William G. Rosenberg and Ronald Grigor Suny) Party, State and Society in the Russian Civil War: Explorations in Social History, 1989, (with Ronald D. Bachman) Revelations from the Russian Archives, 1997; editor, translator: (with S.A. Smith) Notes of a Red Guard, 1993; mem. editl. bd. Cambridge Soviet Paperbacks; mem. adv. bd. Soviet Studies in History, 1986-89; book reviewer to numerous jours.; contbr. articles to profl. jours. Rsch. fellow Temple U., 1977, 82, Sr. fellow Russian Inst.-Columbia U., 1977-78, Individual fellow NEH, 1983-84, Rsch. fellow NEH, 1984-85, 94-95, MUCIA Exch. fellow Moscow State U., 1991; grantee Am. Coun. Learned Socs.-Social Sci. Rsch. Coun., 1977-78, Temple U., 1979-81, 82-83, William and Flora Hewlett Internat. Rsch. grantee, 1986, Nat. Coun. for Soviet and East European Rsch. grantee, 1989, IREX Travel grantee, 1993; recipient Fulbright-Hays Faculty Rsch. award for USSR, 1989, Arnold O. Beckman Rsch. Bd. award, 1990-91. Mem. Am. Hist. Assn. (mem. membership com. 1996-98), Am. Assn. Advancement Slavic Studies (bd. dirs. 1996—), Midwest Workshop of Russian and Soviet Historians, Assn. Women in Slavic Studies. Office: U Ill Slav Rev 57 E Armory Ave Champaign IL 61820-6601 also: U Ill Dept History 309 Gregory Hall 810 S Wright St Urbana IL 61801-3611

KOEPFINGER, JOSEPH LEO, utilities executive; b. Sewickley, Pa., May 6, 1925; s. Joseph P. and Mary M. (O'Hanlon) K.; m. Genevieve C. Strobel, Oct. 1, 1955; children: Nancy, Joseph, Margaret, Patricia, James, Paul. BSEE, U. Pitts., 1949, MSEE, 1953. Jr. devel. engr. Duquesne Light Co., Pitts., 1949-52, devel. engr., 1952-54, sr. devel. engr., 1954-57, project engr., 1957-61, sr. project engr., 1961-64, product and comml. engr., 1964-80, dir. project and comml. dept., 1980-85, dir. systems studies and rsch., 1985—; chmn. accredited std. com. C62 Am. Nat. Std. Inst.; bd. dirs. Maglev, Inc., Mehta Tech., Inc.; U.S. Tech. Adv. for IEC SC37A & 37B, 1979—, sec. for IEC TC 37, 1996—. Prin. writer standard Guide for Surge Withstand Capability Test, 1974. Pres. Moon Area Sch. Dist., Moon Twp., Pa., 1978-79. With U.S. Army, 1943-45, ETO. Fellow IEEE (mem. emeritus stds. bd., Charles P. Steimetz award 1989), IEEE Power Engring. Soc. (Excellence in Power Distbn. Engring. award 1998). Democrat. Roman Catholic. Home: 119 Windy Willow Dr Coraopolis PA 15108-2945

KOEPKE, DONALD HERBERT, retired mechanical engineer and real estate professional; b. Milw., Sept. 19, 1923; s. Herbert Hugo and Lillie (Kirchen) K.; B.A. in Bus., Valparaiso U., 1949; B.S. in Mech. Engring., Purdue U., 1951; m. Helena Koepke; children: Debora, Andrew, Thomas. Vice pres. dealer relations Valeer Industries, Inc., Mundelein, Ill., 1974-76; dir. engring. Respiratory Care, Inc., Arlington Heights, Ill., 1976-80; pres. Sorbets, Inc., Hampshire, Ill., 1980-83; pres. Liquorland Enterprises, Inc., Elgin, Ill., 1962-84, also dir.; chief engr. Rinn, Inc., Elgin, 1984-86; with real estate sales dept. Windsor Realty, Elgin, 1988-90. Active Elgin Choral Union. Served with U.S. Army, 1943-46. Cert. mfg. engr. Mem. Soc. Automotive Engrs., Soc. Mfg. Engrs., Anvil Club, Elgin Country Club, Lions. Republican. Lutheran. Contbr. articles to profl. jours.; patentee in field. Home: 532 N Melrose Ave Elgin IL 60123-3336

KOEPKE, JOHN ARTHUR, hematologist, clinical pathologist; b. Milw., Mar. 25, 1929; s. Elmer Paul and Meta Clara (Jennrich) K.; m. Evelyn Mae Lovekamp, June 18, 1955; children: Mary Evelyn, John Frederick, Mark David, James Robert. BA, Valparaiso U., 1951; MD, U. Wis., 1956; MS, Marquette U., 1964. Intern, resident in clin. pathology and internal medicine Milw. Hosp., 1956-60; mem. faculty U. Ky. Coll. Medicine, 1961-71, assoc. prof., 1965-71; dir. clin. pathology, prof. pathology U. Iowa, Iowa City, 1972-79; vice chmn. dept. U. Iowa, 1972-79; prof. pathology, assoc. prof. internal medicine Coll. Medicine, Duke U., Durham, N.C., 1979-94; dir.clin. transfusion svc. hematology lab. Duke U. Med. Ctr., 1979-88, prof. emeritus, 1994—; vis. scientist Karolinska Inst., Stockholm, 1967-68, Royal Postgrad. Med. Sch., London, 1978. Author 7 books in field; editor 7 books; bd. editors Am. Jour. Clin. Pathology, 1976—, Clin. and Lab. Hematology, 1978-94, Blood Cells, 1985-98; assoc. editor Cytometry, 1993—, Comms. in Clin. Cytometry, 1994-99, Lab. Hematology, 1994—; contbr. over 200 articles to profl. jours., 37 chpts. to books. Recipient Pres.'s award Valparaiso U., 1951, also Disting. Alumnus award, 1980. Fellow Am. Soc. Clin. Pathologists, Coll. Am. Pathologists; mem. AMA, Internat. Coun. for Standards in Hematology (secretariat 1978—, v.p. 1990-92, pres. 1992-94). Lutheran. Home: 3924 Saint Marks Rd Durham NC 27707-5015

KOEPP, DAVID, screenwriter. Screenwriter: (with Martin Donovan) Apartment Zero, 1989, Bad Influence, 1990, (with Daniel Petrie Jr.) Toy Soldiers, 1991, (with Donovan) Death Becomes Her, 1992, (with Michael Crichton) Jurassic Park, 1993, Carlito's Way, 1993, (with Stephen Koepp) The Paper, 1994, The Shadow, 1994.

KOEPP, DONNA PAULINE PETERSEN, librarian; b. Clinton, Iowa, Oct. 8, 1941; d. Leo August and Pauline Sena (Outzen) Petersen; m. David Ward Koepp, June 5, 1960 (div. June 1984). BS in Edn., U. Colo., 1967; MA in Libr., U. Denver, 1974; postgrad., U. Colo., 1984-85. Subject specialist govt. publs., map dept. Denver Pub. Libr., 1967-85; head govt. documents, map libr. U. Kans., Lawrence, 1985—; apptd. Fed. Depository Libr. Coun. to Pub. Printer, 1998—. Prodn. mgr. Meridian Jour., 1988-93, 96—; editor: Index and Carto-Bibliography of Maps, 1789-1969, 1995. Recipient Documents to the People award CIS/GODORT/ALA, 1999. Mem. Map & Geography Round Table of Am. Libr. Assn. (chmn. 1986-87, Outstanding Contbn. to Map Librarianship 1991), Govt. Documents Round Table of Am. Libr. Assn., Western Assn. Map Librs. (sec. 1983-84). Office: Univ Kans Librs 6001 Malott Hall Lawrence KS 66044-7564

KOEPPE, EUGENE CHARLES, JR., electrical engineer; b. Chgo., Sept. 15, 1955; s. Eugene Charles and Lucille (Luczak) K. BSEE, Ill. Inst. Tech., 1977, MSEE, 1984. Registered profl. engr.-in-tng., Ill. R & D engr. Teletype Corp., Skokie, Ill., 1977-85; tech. staff AT&T Bell Labs., Skokie, 1985-90; tech. staff AT&T Bell Labs., Naperville, Ill., 1990-96, feature engr. svc. cir. system, 1993-94; tech. staff Lucent Techs. (formerly Bell Labs.), Naperville, 1996—, dept. webmaster, 1997; cert. TEMPEST engr., 1986-88. Mem. IEEE, NSPE, Am. Radio Relay League, Mensa, Tau Beta Pi. Office: Lucent Techs PO Box 3033 2000 N Naperville Rd Naperville IL 60566-3033

KOEPPEL, GARY MERLE, publisher, art gallery owner, writer; b. Albany, Oreg., Jan. 20, 1938; s. Carl Melvin and Barbara Emma (Adams) K.; m. Emma Katerina Koeppel, May 20, 1984. BA, Portland State U., 1961; MFA, State U. Iowa, 1963. Writing instr. State U. Iowa, Iowa City, 1963-64; guest prof. English U. P.R., San Juan, 1964-65; assoc. prof. creative writing Portland (Oreg.) State U., 1965-68; owner, operator Coast Gallery, Big Sur, 1971—, Pebble Beach, Calif., 1986—, Maui, Hawaii, 1985—, Hana, Hawaii, 1991—, Lahaina, Hawaii, 1992; owner Coasst Pub. Co., Coast Seri

Graphics, Coast Advt., 1991—; editor, pub. Big Sur Gazette, 1978-81; producer, sponsor Maui Marine Art Expo., 1984-95, Calif. Marine Art Expo., Paris Marine Art Expo., Hawaiian Cultural Arts Expo., 1993; founder The Blue Movement, 1994; founder, pres. Global Art Expos, 1994, Planet Big Sur, 1996, Coast Constrn., 1998; founder ideasbank.com, 1999. Author: Sculptured Sandcast Candles, 1974, Henry Miller, The Paintings, 1991. Jr. asst. scoutmaster Boy Scouts Am.; master DeMolay, 1955; founder Big Sur Vol. Fire Brigade, 1975; chmn. coordinating com. Big Sur Area Planning, 1972-75; chmn. Big Sur Citizens Adv. Com., 1975-78. Mem. Internat. Soc. Appraisers, Am. Soc. Appraisers, Big Sur C. of C. (pres. 1974-75, 82-84), Big Sur Grange, Audubon Soc., Cousteau Soc., Phi Gamma Delta, Alpha Delta Sigma. Address: Coast Gallery PO Box 223519 Carmel CA 93922-3519

KOEPPEL, HARRY SAUL, interior designer, educator; b. Anniston, Ala., Feb. 6, 1942; s. Harry Saul Koeppel and Eula Jean (Griffen) Irish; m. Rita Ann Jezuit, Aug. 12, 1967; children: Brent Everett, Jill Christine. BFA, Syracuse U.; MA, SUNY New Paltz. Lic. interior designer, N.Y. Tchr. art N.Y. State Schs., 1964-73; furniture designer N.Y.C., 1972-74, interior designer, 1978-82; project mgr. N.Y. State Docs, 1983-95; interior design mgr. N.Y.C. Sch. Constrn. Authority, 1995—; design cons. N.Y.C., 1964—; instr. SUNY Albany, 1972—; profl. scouter Boy Scouts Am., 1974-78. Mem. Am. Soc. Interior Designers, Interior Design Soc. Home and Office: 501 Route 15 Elizaville NY 12523-1008

KOEPPEL, JOHN A., lawyer; b. Jersey City, Aug. 9, 1947; s. A.J. and Florence (McDonald) K.; m. Susan Lynn Rothstein, Nov. 12, 1972; children: Adam, Leah. BA in Govt. cum laude, U. Notre Dame, 1969; MA in Internat. Law, Tufts U., 1970; JD, U. Calif., San Francisco, 1976. Bar: Calif. 1976, D.C. 1980, U.S. Dist. Ct. (no. dist.) Calif. 1976, U.S. Supreme Ct. 1980. Assoc. Barfield, Barfield, Dryden & Ruane, San Francisco, 1976-80; from assoc. to shareholder Ropers, Majeski, Kohn & Bentley, San Francisco, 1980—; resident dir. Ropers, Majeski, Kohn, Bentley, Wagner & Kane, San Francisco, 1992-95, 97—; arbitrator San Francisco Superior Ct., 1979—; legal counsel San Francisco Jaycees, 1980-81, Amigos de los Americas, San Francisco, 1982-84, St. Francis Homes Assn., 1987-89, treas.; instr. Hastings Coll. Advocacy, San Francisco, 1988-91; lectr. U. Calif., San Francisco, 1990-95; sec. San Francisco Casualty Claims Assn., 1993-95. Active youth sports coaching San Francisco Sch., bd. dirs., 1997—. Mem. Nat. Bd. Trial Advocacy, Am. Bd. Profl. Liability Attys., Calif. State Bar (certificate of recognition for pro bono legal work, 1989), D.C. Bar, San Francisco Bar Assn. Avocations: running, skiing, hiking, camping, travel. Office: Ropers Majeski Kohn & Bentley 333 Market St Ste 3150 San Francisco CA 94105-3916

KOEPPEL, NOEL IMMANUEL, financial planner, securities and real estate broker; b. N.Y.C., Apr. 30, 1930; s. Eziel and Anna (Bodian) K.; divorced; children: Thomas Joseph, Elizabeth Mansfield, Roberta Sharon. BA, U. Wis., 1952; MBA, Wharton U. of Pa., 1957. CFP. V.p. E. Koeppel, Inc., Jamaica, N.Y., 1956-77; account exec. First Investors Corp., N.Y.C., 1977-79, Ross Stebbins Co., N.Y.C., 1980-82; account exec., CFP Advest Inc., Forest Hills, N.Y., 1982-83, Donald & Co. Securities Inc., Jersey City, N.J., 1983-90, Stuart Coleman Co. Inc., N.Y.C., 1990-97; account exec. Brill Sec. Inc., N.Y.C., 1998—. Lt. (j.g.) USN, 1952-56. Mem. Inst. CFPs, Metro N.Y. Inst. CFPs. Avocations: skiing, sailing, hiking, classical music and art. Home: 130 E End Ave New York NY 10028-7553 Office: Brill Sec Inc 152 W 57th St Fl 16 New York NY 10019-3310

KOEPPEN, RAYMOND BRADLEY, lawyer; b. Valparaiso, Ind., July 9, 1954; s. Raymond Carl August and Thelma Gleda (Moore) K.; m. Debra Gail Ray, Dec. 21, 1985. BS, Ball State U., 1976; MA, Kent (Ohio) State U., 1983; JD, Valparaiso U., 1983. Bar: Ind. 1984, Fla. 1984. Assoc. Sachs & Hess, P.C., Hammond, Ind., 1984-85, Lucas Holcomb Medrea, Merrillville, Ind., 1985; city atty. City of Valparaiso, 1985-88; ptnr. Clifford, Clauden, Alexa & Koeppen, Valparaiso, 1988-90, Douglas, Alexa, Koeppen and Hurley, Valparaiso, 1991—. Mem. com. Valparaiso Popcorn Festival, 1985-97; mem. Valparaiso Econ. Devel. Corp., 1986, 87; mem. Valparaiso C. of C.; bd. dirs. Boys and Girls Club of Porter County, 1986—, chmn. bd. dirs., 1995-97. Greek Ministry of Culture and Sci. scholar, 1975; Fulbright scholar U.S. Ednl. Found., 1976. Mem. ABA, Ind. State Bar Assn., Porter County Bar Assn., Fla. Bar Assn., Phi Alpha Theta, Pi Gamma Mu, Beta Theta Pi. Presbyterian. Avocations: golf, basketball, reading, running, community volunteering. Home: 2005 Beulah Vista Blvd Valparaiso IN 46383-2950 Office: Douglas Alexa et al PO Box 209 14 Indiana Ave Valparaiso IN 46383-5634

KOERBER, JOAN C., retired educator; b. Newark, Mar. 23, 1929; d. George Vincent and Catherine Rose (Donahue) Callanan; m. John Calvin Koerber, June 27, 1953; children: John C., Joanne C. BS in Elem. Edn., Newark State Coll., 1952; MA in Adminstrn., Kean Coll., Union, N.J., 1984. Tchr. 15th Ave Sch., Newark, 1952-71; tchr. Lincoln Sch., Newark, 1971-78, tchr. Chpt. I, 1978-79, coord. Chpt. I,, 1979-84, basic skills tchr., 1984-95, ret., 1995; summer sch. coord. Lincoln Sch., 1979-84; past pres. Kean Coll. Grad. Sch. Coun. Sec. Essex County PTA; rec. sec., dir. Crandon Lakes Country Club Inc. Property Owners Assn.; lector and eucharist minister Our Lady of Mt. Carmel Ch., Swartswood, N.J. Mem. ASCD, AAUW, PTA (hon. life), NEA, N.J. Edn. Assn., Essex County Edn. Assn., Newark Edn. Assn., Newark Tchrs. Union, N.J. State Columbiettes (supreme bd. dirs., past state pres.), Kappa Delta Phi (past pres.), Phi Delta Kappa (past pres.). Home: 17 N Bayberry Rd Newton NJ 07860-6570

KOERBER, JOHN ROBERT, computer programmer; b. L.A., Aug. 17, 1955; s. Thomas Joseph and Betty (Turner) Koerber; m. Kimberly Sue Rider, Mar. 15, 1986. BS, Yale U., 1977. Computer technician Tech Mart, Tarzana, Calif., 1977-79; programmer, ptnr. J&J Computer Svc., Northridge, Calif., 1979-80; sr. programmer Mitec Computer Bus. Systems, Chartsworth, Calif., 1980-87; sr. software engr. Dracon div. Harris Corp., Camarillo, Calif., 1987-88; programmer, cons. SALING Computer Systems, Chatsworth, 1988-99; programmer Music Reports, Inc., Burbank, Calif., 1999—. Mem. IEEE (affiliate, Commns. Soc.), Assn. for Computing Machinery. Democrat. Avocation: theatre pipe organ maintenance. Home: 6657 Franrivers Ave West Hills CA 91307-2816

KOERBER, LINDA RENÉ GIVENS, educator, counselor; b. Seattle, Mar. 9, 1948; d. David and Gladys (Hall) Givens; children: Andre, Dominic, Kendra Corr. AA, Ctrl. seattle Coll., 1973; BA, U. Wash., 1975; MEd, City U. Seattle, 1996. Tchr's. aid Seattle Sch. Dist., 1970-73, tchr., 1975-92, counselor, 1976-95; tchr. King County Juvenile Ct., 1977-82; trainer strengthening multi ethnic families and cmtys. Vol. Ctrl. Area Youth Club, Seattle, 1971, Ctrl. Area Sch. Coun., Seattle, 1972-73, Black Prisoners Forum, Seattle, 1970—; mem. Mayor's Commn. on Children and Youth, Seattle, 1994-99; foster parent Dept. Social and Health Svcs., Seattle, 1996, Casey Family Found. Mem. Am. Fedn. Tchrs. (chpt. organizer 1971). Baptist. Home: 7705 S Mission Dr Seattle WA 98178-3143

KOERBER, MARILYNN ELEANOR, gerontology nursing educator, consultant, nurse; b. Covington, Ky., Feb. 1, 1942; d. Harold Clyde and Vivian Eleanor (Conrad) Hilge; m. James Paul Koerber, May 29, 1971. Diploma, Christ Hosp. Sch. Nursing, Cin., 1964; BSN, U. Ky., 1967; MPH, U. Mich., 1970. RN, Ohio, S.C.; cert. gerontologist. Staff nurse premature and newborn nursery Cin. Gen. Hosp., 1964-65; staff nurse, hosp. discharge planner Vis. Nurse Assn., Cin., 1967-69; asst. dir. Vis. Nurse Assn., Atlanta, 1976-78; instr. Coll. Nursing, U. Ky., Lexington, 1970-71; supr. Montgomery County Health Dept., Rockville, Md., 1971-74; asst. prof. Coll. Nursing, U. S.C., Columbia, 1979-86, instr., 1987-89; alzheimer's project coord. S.C. Commn. on Aging, Columbia, 1988-90; dir. edn. and tng. Luth. Homes S.C., White Rock, 1988-91; grad. asst. U. S.C. Sch. of Pub. Health, 1991-94; trainer for homemakers home health aides S.C. Divsn. on Aging, 1991-97; coord. to train homemakers home aides nursing assts. State Pilot Program, DSS and Divsn. on Aging, 1993-95; Alzheimer's trainer office aging, nurse mgr. Beanfort-Jasper Comprehensive Health, 1998—; allied health program mgr. Tech. Coll. of the Lowcountry, 1998—; mem. utilization rev. bd. Palmetto Health Dist., Lexington, 1984—; test item writer, nurse aide cert. Psychol. Corp., San Antonio, 1989, 91, 92; bd. examiners Nursing Home Adminstrn. and Community Residential Care Facility Adminstr., chmn. of edn. com., Columbia, S.C., 1990-93; presenter gerontol. workshops and residential care facilities adminstrn. Contbg. editor: (handbook) Promoting Caregiver Groups, 1984; reviewer gerontology textbooks, 1983-91; contbr. tng. video and manuals on Alzheimers, 1988 (hon. mention Retirement Rsch. Found. 1989). Del. S.C. Gov. White House Conf. on Aging, Columbia, 1981; chmn. ann. mtg. S.C. Fedn. for Older Ams., Columbia, 1989-91; bd. dirs. Sr. Svcs. of Beaufort County, 1997—, Alzheimers Support Group, Beaufort, 1997—, v.p. 1998—. USPHS trainee, 1965-67, Adm. on Aging trainee, 1969-70. Mem. ANA (cert. gerontol. nurse, cmty. health nurse), S.C. Nurses Assn., So. Gerontol. Soc., Gerontol. Soc. Am., S.C. Gerontol. Soc. (treas. 1989-91, Rosamond R. Boyd award 1986, Pres. award Mid State Alzheimers Chpt., 1993), Soc. for Pub. Health Edn., Am. Soc. on Aging, Alzheimers Assn. (bd. dirs. Columbia chpt. 1988-93, sec. 1992, chmn. nominating com. 1991-92; bd. dirs. S.C. combined health appeal 1991-93), Nat. Coun. on Aging, Nat. Gerontol. Nursing Assn. Democrat. Unitarian Universalist. Avocations: interior decorating, wine tasting.

KOERBER, ROBERT CONRAD, company executive; b. Mar. 13, 1950. BSBA, Washington U., St. Louis, 1971; MBA in Fin. with honors, U. Mo., 1973. Pres. Apollo Golf, Chgo., 1989-93, Reynolds USA, Chgo., 1990-93, RK Indsl. Corp., Memphis, 1994-96; pres., CEO Waterfield Inc., Memphis, 1998—. Home: 3237 Club Breeze Dr Germantown TN 38125

KOERING, MARILYN JEAN, anatomy educator, researcher; b. Brainerd, Minn., Jan. 7, 1938; d. Clement J. and Vi K. (Holtkamp) K. BA, Coll. St. Scholastica, Duluth, 1960; MS, U. Wis.-Madison, 1963, PhD, 1967, postgrad., 1968. Instr. dept. anatomy U. Wis., 1963-64; asst. prof. George Washington U., Washington, 1969-73, assoc. prof., 1973-79, prof. anatomy, 1979—, dir. neurosci. program, 1990-94; vis. assoc. div. biology Calif. Inst. Tech., 1976; affiliate scientist Wis. Primate Research Ctr., Madison, 1975-78; guest worker Pregnancy Research br. Nat. Inst. Child Health and Devel., 1977-84; vis. prof. Jones Inst. for Reproductive Medicine, Eastern Va. Med. Sch., 1985-92. Mem. editorial bd. Biology of Reproduction, 1974-78; contbr. articles to profl. jours. Recipient Alumni award Coll. of St. Scholastica, 1989, Disting. Tchr. of Yr. award George Washington U. Med. Sch., 1996; NIH fellow, 1967-68; NIH grantee, 1969—. Mem. AAAS, Am. Assn. Anatomists, Soc. Study Reproduction. Office: George Washington U Med Ctr Dept Anatomy & Cell Biology 2300 I St NW Washington DC 20037-2336

KOESSEL, DONALD RAY, retired banker; b. Grand Rapids, Mich., May 15, 1929; s. Fred Christian and Erna Wilhelmina (Grein) K.; m. Jeannine C. Koessel; children: Martin, Kathryn. B.A., Yale U., 1951; M.B.A., Harvard U., 1955. Copywriter Grand Rapids Press, 1951-52; public relations rep. Smith Kline & French Labs., 1952-53; money market analyst Nat. Shawmut Bank of Boston, 1955-58; asst. sec. 1st Bank System, Mpls., 1958-62; asst. v.p. 1st Bank System, 1962-65; with 1st Nat. Bank Mpls., 1965-85, exec. v.p., 1975-85, chmn. trust com., 1979-85. Home: 630 Meadow Run Dr Fort Collins CO 80525-3756

KOESTEL, MARK ALFRED, geologist, photographer; b. Cleve., Jan. 1, 1951; s. Alfred and Lucille (Kemeny) K.; children: Jennifer Rose, Bonnie Leigh. BS, U. Ariz., 1978. Registered profl. geologist Wyo., Alaska, Ind.; registered environ. assessor, Calif. Sr. geologist Union Oil Co. of Calif., Tucson and Denver, 1978-86; mgr. geology Harmsworth Assocs., Laguna Hills, Calif., 1986-88; sr. project mgr. Applied GeoSystems, Irvine, Calif., 1988-90; cons. geologist, photographer Adventures in Geology/Outdoor Images, Chino, Calif., 1990—. Contbr. articles and photographs to profl. jours. and mags. N.Mex. state rep. Minerals Exploration Coalition, Tucson and Denver, 1982. Sci. Found. scholarship No. Ariz. U., 1969, Acad. Achievement scholarship, 1970, Disting. Scholastic Achievement scholarship, 1971. Mem. Am. Inst. of Profl. Geologists (cert.), Soc. of Mining Engrs., Aircraft Owners and Pilots Assn., Geol. Soc. of Am., Nat. Geographic Soc. Avocations: woodworking, photography, backpacking, travel, scuba. Home and Office: 13214 Breton Ave Chino CA 91710-5952

KOESTER, BERTHOLD KARL, lawyer, law educator, retired honorary German consul; b. Aachen, Germany, June 30, 1931; s. Wilhelm P. and Margarethe A. (Witteler) K.; m. Hildegard Maria Buettner, June 30, 1961; children: Georg W., Wolfgang J., Reinhard B. JD, U. Muenster, Fed. Republic Germany, 1957. Cert. Real Estate Broker, Ariz. Asst. prof. civil and internat. law U. Muenster, 1957-60; atty. Cts. of Duesseldorf, Fed. Republic Germany, 1960-82; v.p. Bank J. H. Vogeler & Co., Duesseldorf, 1960-64; pres. Bremer Tank-u., Kuehlschiffahrtsges.m.b.H., 1964-72; atty., trustee internat. corps., Duesseldorf and Phoenix, 1973-82, Phoenix, 1983—; of counsel Tancer Law Offices, Phoenix, 1978-86; prof. internat. bus. law Am. Grad. Sch. Internat. Mgmt., Glendale, Ariz., 1978-81; with Applewhite, Laflin & Lewis, Real Estate Investments, Phoenix, 1981-86, ptnr., 1982-86, Beucler Real Estate Investments, 1986-88, Scottsdale, Ariz.; chief exec. officer, chmn. bd. German Consultants in Real Estate Investments, Phoenix, 1989—; hon. consul Fed. Republic of Germany for Ariz., 1982-92; prof. internat. bus. law Western Internat. U., Phoenix, 1996—; chmn., CEO Arimpex, Inc., Phoenix, 1981—; bd. dirs. Ariz. Ptnrship for Air Transp., 1988-92; chmn. Finvest Corp., Phoenix, 1990—. Contbr. articles to profl. jours. Pres. Parents Assn. Humboldt Gymnasium, Duesseldorf, 1971-78; active German Red Cross, from 1977. Mem. Duesseldorf Chamber of Lawyers, Bochum (Fed. Republic Germany) Assn. Tax Lawyers, Bonn German-Saudi Arabian Assn. (pres. 1976-79), Bonn German-Korean Assn., Assn. for German-Korean Econ. Devel. (pres. 1974-78), Ariz. Consular Corps (sec., treas. 1988-89), Nat. Soc. Arts and Letters (Ariz. Valley of Sun chpt.), German-Am. C. of C., Phoenix Met. C. of C., Rotary (Scottsdale, Ariz.). Home: 6201 E Cactus Rd Scottsdale AZ 85254-4409 Office: PO Box 15674 Phoenix AZ 85060-5674

KOESTER, HELMUT HEINRICH, theologian, educator; b. Hamburg, Germany, Dec. 18, 1926; came to U.S., 1958; s. Karl and Marie-Luise (Eitz) K.; m. Gisela G. Harrassowitz, July 8, 1953; children: Reinhild, Almut, Ulrich, Heiko. Dr. theol., U. Marburg, Germany, 1954; Privatdozent, U. Heidelberg, Germany, 1956; Dr. theol. (hon.), U. Geneva. Ordained to ministry Luth. Ch., 1956; asst. pastor Hannover, Germany, 1951-54; teaching asst., then asst. prof. U. Heidelberg, 1954-56, 56-58, 59; mem. faculty Harvard U. Div. Sch., 1958-98, John H. Morison prof. N.T. studies, 1964-98, Winn prof. ecclesiastical history, 1968-98; vis. prof. U. Heidelberg, 1963, Drew U., 1966, U. Minn., 1990, Free U. Amsterdam, 1992. Author: Synoptische Ueberlieferung bei den Apostolischen Vaetern, in Texte und Untersuchungen, 1957, (with James M. Robinson) Trajectories through Early Christianity, 1971, Einfuehrung in das Neue Testament, 1979, Introduction to the New Testament, 1982, Ancient Christian Gospels, 1990, (with Francois Bovon) Genèse de l'écriture chrètienne, 1991, History, Religion and Culture of the Hellenistic Age, 1995; editor Harvard Theol. Rev., Hermeneia, Archaeol. Resources for New Testament Studies. Asso. trustee Am. Schs. Oriental Research, 1974-75; trustee William F. Albright Inst. Archaeol. Research, 1974-80. Served with German Navy, 1944-45. Guggenheim fellow, 1964-65; Am. Council Learned Socs. fellow, 1971-72, 78-79. Fellow Am. Acad. Arts and Scis.; mem. Soc. Bibl. Lit. (pres. 1990-91), Soc. Novi Testamenti Studiorum. Home: 12 Flintlock Rd Lexington MA 02420-1704 Office: 45 Francis Ave Cambridge MA 02138-1911

KOESTER, ROBERT GREGG, record company executive; b. Wichita, Kans., Oct. 30, 1932; s. Edward Albert and Mary (Frank) K.; m. Susan Buescher; children: Robert, Katherine. Student, St. Louis U., 1951-54. Organizer, propr. Blue Note Record Shop, St. Louis, 1952-58, Delmark Records, St. Louis, 1952—; founder Jazz Report mag., 1953, pub., 1953-60; owner Seymour's Jazz Mart, 1959-61; founder-owner Jazz Record Mart, 1961—; owner Collector's Record Mart, 1989-92, Riverside Studios, 1992—; pub., editor Blues News Bull., 1961-67. Publisher: Rhythm & News, 1970—; contbr. numerous articles, chpt. in book. Recipient Grand Prix du Disque Hot Club France, 1966, Internat. Critics Poll award Jazz mag., W.C. Handy award for best blues LP prodn., 1980, W.C. Handy award for Keepin' the Blues Alive, 1990, cert. of appreciation for exceptional contbn. to music City of Chgo., 1992, 93, Blues Retailer of Yr. award Nat. Blues Found., 1996, Best Blues CD of Yr. Indie award, 1997; inducted into Blues Hall of Fame, 1996, Nat. Blues Found. Hall of Fame (classics of Blues Album). Mem. Nat. Assn. Ind. Record Distbrs. and Mfrs. (charter mem.), Jazz Inst. Chgo. (charter mem.). Office: 4121 N Rockwell St Chicago IL 60618-2822 Office: 444 N Wabash Ave Chicago IL 60611-5622 *I have managed to afford myself the luxury of making my living in the music business where my daily occupation is with the music that I have loved since my early teen years so that I enjoy my work far beyond any other occupation that I might otherwise have chosen.*

KOESTERER, LARRY J., pharmacist; b. Belleville, Ill., Dec. 13, 1956; s. Edward John and Antionette Catherine (Meister) K.; m. Sandra J. Meyers, Jan. 5, 1991. BS in Pharmacy, St. Louis Coll. Pharmacy, 1974; MBA, Webster U., St. Louis, 1989. Registered pharmacist, Mo., Ill. Pharmacy intern Meml. Hosp., Belleville, 1976-79; staff pharmacist St. Elizabeth's Hosp., Belleville, 1979-88, ops. coord., 1988-89; dir. pharmacy St. Louis Children's Hosp., 1989-94; regional dir. Owen Healthcare, St. Louis, 1995-99; dir. pharm. svcs. Sisters of Mercy Health Sys., St. Louis, 1999—; bd. dirs. Child Health Corp., pharmacy com. 1994; bd. dirs. Pediat. Pharmacy Advocacy Group, 1994. Bd. dirs. Second Generation Swing, Belleville, 1979—. Mem. Rho Chi. Roman Catholic. Office: Sisters of Mercy Health Sys 2039 N Geyer Rd Saint Louis MO 63131

KOETSER, DAVID, export company executive; b. Amsterdam, The Netherlands, July 22, 1906; came to U.S., 1939; s. Joseph and Mathilda Pauline (Hollander) K. Grad., Lyceum, Amsterdam, 1926. Owner Music Pub. Co., Amsterdam, 1935-39; exec. sec. The Netherlands C. of C., 1947-56; owner D.K. Co., Inc., San Francisco, 1957-84. Contbr. articles to profl. jours. Moderator U.S. Small Bus. Adminstrn., Score workshops, San Francisco, 1987—. Staff sgt. CIC, 1942-45, ETO. Mem. Holland Am. Soc. (treas. 1950—), World Trade Club (entertainment com. 1960—), Internat. Exporters Assn. (pres. 1965, recipient Pres. E award). Avocation: travel. Home and Office: PO Box 257 Lafayette CA 94549-0257

KOFF, HOWARD MICHAEL, lawyer; b. Bklyn., July 25, 1941; s. Arthur and Blanche Koff; m. Linda Sue Bright, Sept. 10, 1966; 1 son, Michael Arthur Bright. B.S., NYU, 1962; J.D., Bklyn. Law Sch., 1965; LL.M. in Taxation, Georgetown U., 1968. Bar: N.Y. 1965, D.C. 1966, U.S. Supreme Ct. 1969, U.S. Ct. Appeals (2d, 3d, 4th, 5th, 7th, 9th and D.C. cirs.), U.S. Dist. Ct. (no. dist.) N.Y. 1981. Appellate atty. Tax Div., U.S. Dept. Justice, Washington, 1965-69; tax supr. Chrysler Corp., Detroit, 1969-70; chief tax counsel Conn. Gen. Life Ins. Co., Hartford, Conn., 1970-77; chief tax counsel Rohm & Haus Co., Phila., 1977-78; ptnr. Dibble, Koff, Lane, Stern and Stern, Rochester, N.Y., 1978-81; pres. Howard M. Koff, P.C., Albany, N.Y., 1981—; lectr. tax matters. Mem. pub. adv. coun. N.Y. State Ethics Commn. Recipient Founders Day award NYU, 1962; Lawyers Coop. award for gen. excellence Lawyers Coop. Pub. Co., 1965. Mem. Fed. Bar Assn. (past pres. Hartford County chpt.), ABA (past chmn. subcom. com. on partnerships tax sect.), Albany County Bar Assn., Estate Planning Council Eastern N.Y., Albany Area C. of C. Republican. Jewish. Clubs: Rotary, Colonie Guilderland N.Y. Editor-in-chief Bklyn. Law Rev., 1964-65; charter mem. editorial adv. bd. Jour. Real Estate Taxation; contbr. articles to legal jours. Home: 205 Bentwood Ct W Albany NY 12203-4905 Office: 600 Broadway Albany NY 12207-2205

KOFF, ROBERT HESS, foundation administrator; b. Chgo., June 5, 1938; s. Arthur Karl and Dorothy (Hess) K. BA, U. Mich., 1961; MA, U. Chgo., 1962, PhD, 1966. Lic. psychologist, Calif. Instr., counselor S. Shankman Orthogenic Sch. U. Chgo., 1961-64; tchr. U. Chgo. Lab. Sch., 1963-64; instr. U. Ill., Champaign, 1964, U. Chgo., 1964-66; vis. scientist, Lab. for Hypnosis Rsch., asst. prof. Stanford (Calif.) U., 1966-72; prof., dean Roosevelt U., Chgo., 1972-79; univ. dean SUNY, Albany, 1979-92; program dir., v.p. Danforth Found., St. Louis, 1992—; vis. scholar Oxford U., Eng., 1965; chmn. N.Y. State Ednl. Conf. Bd., Albany, 1981-92. Mem. Nat. Adv. Coun. on Edn. of Disadvantaged Children, Washington, 1979-82, Gov.'s Adv. Commn. on Children and Youth, Albany, 1981-92. Mem. APA (com. chmn.), Am. Ednl. Rsch. Assn., Nat. Register Health Svc. Providers in Psychology. Office: 211 N Broadway Saint Louis MO 63102-2733

KOFF, SHIRLEY IRENE, writer, church administrator; b. Oakland, Calif., Aug. 31, 1948; d. Lawrence Ray and Stella Pauline (Durham) Butler; m. Robert Allen Koff, June 12, 1971; children: Jennifer, Katherine. BA, Calif. State U., 1971, MA, 1972. Adj. prof. Pellissippi State U., Knoxville, 1989-93; asst. mgr. Adolfo II, Pigeon Forge, Tenn., 1994-98; supr. Oneida Silversmiths; poet, writer; tchr. adult religious edn. classes and seminars. Tchr., lay min., bd. dirs. First Assembly of God Ch., Sevierville, 1996-99; core group leader, founding mem. Wellspring Congregation, United Meth. Ch., 1999—. Mem. AAUW, Mensa. Democrat. Avocations: writing, speaking, teaching. Home: 1214 Amber Ln Sevierville TN 37862-6101

KOFFEL, MARTIN M., engineering company executive; b. 1939. MS, MBA, Stanford U., 1971. With Homestake Mining Co., 1974-81, Cooper Labs., Inc., 1981-84, Gilette Corp., 1984-86, Cooper Vision Inc., 1986-88; chmn. bd., pres., CEO URS Corp., San Francisco, 1989—. Active adv. coun. McLaren Sch. Bus., U. San Francisco; trustee Am. Enterprise Inst. Pub. Policy, Washington. Office: URS Corp 100 California St Ste 500 San Francisco CA 94111-4510*

KOFFEL, WILLIAM BARRY, lawyer; b. Cleve., Jan. 28, 1948; s. William Kelly and Marilyn (Barry) K.; m. Dorothy Marion Koffel, Feb. 24, 1973; children: William, Jonathan, Benjamin. BA magna cum laude, Boston Coll., 1970; JD cum laude, Suffolk U., 1977. Bar: Mass. 1977, U.S. Dist. Ct. Mass. 1978. Compliance officer U.S. Dept. Labor, Boston, 1970-77, trial atty., 1978-81; atty. Foley, Hoag & Eliot, Boston, 1981—. Active Metro West Leadership Conf., Framingham, Mass., 1990. Mem. ABA, Mass. Bar Assn. (chair labor & employment law sect. 1992-93). Avocations: skiing, hiking. Home: 129A Brook St Framingham MA 01701-3953 Office: Foley Hoag & Eliot One Post Office Sq Boston MA 02109

KOFFLER, HERBERT, health plan administrator, educator; b. Columbus, Ohio, July 7, 1940; s. Joseph and Esther Koffler; m. Michelle Ann Rudman, Dec. 29, 1965; children: evan Douglas, Joshua Adam. BS in Zoology, U. Cin., 1962, MD, 1966; postgrad., Ariz. State U., 1989-91; MS in Adminstrv. Medicine, U. Wis., 1993. Diplomate Am. Bd. Pediatrics, Am. Bd. Neonatology. Instr. in pediatrics U. Cin., 1969-70, 72-74, U. Calif., Davis, 1971-72; assoc. prof. pediatrics U. N.Mex., Albuquerque, 1974-78, dir. newborn svcs. divsn. neonatology, 1976-88, assoc. prof. pediatrics and ob-gyn., 1978-88, prof. pediatrics and ob-gyn., 1988-95, prof. emeritus, 1995, clin. prof. family and cmty. medicine, 1995-97; asst. dir. managed care svcs. U. N.Mex. Hosp., Albuquerque, 1992-95; med. dir. Prudential HealthCare, Albuquerque, 1995-97, Presbyn. Salud, Albuquerque, 1997-99; v.p. med. affairs for neonatology Paradigm Health Corp., Concord, Calif., 1999—; mem. cons. staff pediatrics Presbyn. Hosp., Albuquerque, 1974-95, Lovelace Hosp., Albuquerque, 1974-95. Author: (with R. Coen) Primary Care of the Newborn, 1987. Bd. dirs. Chaparral Home and Adoption Svcs., Family and Children Svcs., Albuquerque, 1984, Ronald McDonald Charities, Albuquerque, 1987—. Maj. USAF, 1970-72. Herb Koffler Day proclaimed in his honor State of N.Mex. and U. N.Mex., 1995. Mem. Am. Acad. Pediatrics, Am. Coll. Physician Execs., Western Soc. for Pediatrics Rsch., Greater Albuquerque Med. Assn. (alternate del., del. 1992—), Phi Delta Epsilon. Home: 41 Agua Sarca Rd Placitas NM 87043-9405 Office: Paradigm Health Corp Ste 300 1001 Galaxy Way Concord CA 94520

KOFFLER, STEPHEN ALEXANDER, investment banker; b. Providence, R.I., Sept. 22, 1942; s. Irving I. and Jessie Lillian (Seltzer) K.; m. Enid Freya Mellion, June 15, 1963; children: Samara Rachel, Debra Lyn. BMetE, Rensselaer Poly. Inst., 1964, MS, 1967, PhD, 1968. Security analyst Auerbach Pollak & Richardson, N.Y.C., 1968-70; asst. v.p. investment banking A.G. Becker, Inc., N.Y.C., 1970-72; v.p., treas. Mattel, Inc., Hawthorne, Calif., 1972-74; sr. v.p., chief fin. officer Audio Magnetics, Inc., Gardena, Calif., 1974-75; cons. Koffler & Co., L.A., 1975-81; mng. dir. Becker Paribas, Inc., L.A., 1981-84, Merrill Lynch, L.A., 1984-91; exec. v.p., dir. investment banking dvsn. Sutro and Co., Inc., L.A., 1991-94; mng. dir. Smith Barney Inc., L.A., 1994-96; pres. Koffler & Company, L.A., 1996—. Bd. dirs. L.A. Music Ctr. Opera, 1989-96. Mem. Am. Soc. for Metals, Nat. Assn. Securities Dealers Inc. (mem. corp. fin. com. 1994-95), Riviera Tennis Club, Regency Club, Teton Pines Country Club. Avocations: tennis, golf, hiking, opera. Office: Koffler & Co 11755 Wilshire Blvd Ste 2370 Los Angeles CA 90025-1569

KOFFLER, WARREN WILLIAM, lawyer; b. N.Y.C., July 21, 1938; s. Jack and Rose (Conovich) K.; m. Barbara Rose Holz, June 11, 1959; m. Jayne Audri Goetzel, May 15, 1970; children: Kevin, Kenneth, Caroline. B.S., Boston U., 1959; J.D., U. Calif.-Berkeley, 1962; LLD, NYU, 1972. Bar: D.C. 1962, N.Y. 1963, U.S. Dist. Ct. D.C. 1963, Fla. 1980, Va. 1981, Pa. 1982. Atty. FAA, Washington, 1964; pvt. practice law, Washington, 1964, 78—, Hollywood, Palm Beach, and Miami, Fla., 1978—; atty. Fed. Home Loan Bank Bd., Washington, 1964-66; ptnr. Koffler & Spivack, Washington, 1967-77. Mem. ABA, Inter-Am. Bar Assn., Fed. Bar Assn., D.C. Bar Assn., Fla. Bar Assn., Va. Bar Assn., Assn. Trial Lawyers Am., Brit. Inst. Internat. and Comparative Law, Univ. Club (Washington), Bankers Club (Miami). Office: 11440 Us Highway 1 Palm Bch Gdns FL 33408-3226 also: 1730 K St NW Washington DC 20006-3868

KOFFMAN, ALEXANDRA, medical/surgical nurse; b. N.Y.C., Mar. 21, 1956; d. Nikita and Alice May (Juenger) Roodkowsky; m. Howard Koffman, June 6, 1977; children: Lauren, Mitchell. Diploma, Framingham (Mass.) Union Hosp., 1977; grad., St. Joseph's Coll., Windham, Maine, 1992; post-grad., Boston U. Cert. med-surg. nursing, hospice nursing. Staff nurse Mass. Gen. Hosp., Boston, 1978-81; nurse liaison New Eng. Sinai Hosp., Stoughton, Mass., 1989-90, Jewish Meml. Hosp., 1988-90; clin. nurse Norwood (Mass.) Hosp., 1981-90; critical care rsch. assoc. Boston U. Med. Ctr., 1991-93; nurse Hospice of Boston, 1991—, Neoponset Valley Hospice, 1993-94; with Staff Builders, 1995-98; clin. project mgr. OMS Inc., 1998—. Home: 65 Poskus St Stoughton MA 02072-2719

KOFINK, WAYNE ALAN, minister; b. Chgo., Apr. 21, 1949; s. Lawrence Howard and Catherine Elizabeth (Szlavik) K. MusB, Roosevelt U., 1971; MDiv, Luth. Sch. Theology, Chgo., 1976; BA in Philosophy, Fla. Internat. U., 1981, MS Adult Edn., 1985, EdD, 1991; postgrad., Westminster Choir Coll., 1982, St. Thomas U., 1984-85. Ordained to ministry Evang. Luth. Ch. in Am., 1977. Choir dir. Ascension Luth. Ch., Chgo., 1971-73; pastor Messiah Evang. Luth. Ch., Miami, Fla., 1977-98; lectr. religious studies Fla. Internat. U., Miami, 1986-98; interim pastor St. Thomas Luth. Ch., Miami, 1993; pastor Our Saviour Luth. Ch., Ocala, Fla., 1998—; sec., v.p. Luth. Campus Ministry of Dade County, Miami, 1979-85; mem. Fla. Synod Worship Consultation, Tampa, 1988—; trustee Guardian Shepherd Luth. Sch., Coral Gables, Fla., 1990-98; adj. South Fla. Ctr. for Theol. Studies, Miami, 1995-98 ; chair Dade-Monroe conf. Evangelical Luth. Ch. Am., 1996-98. Editor (newsletter) Doxology, 1986-87; contbr. articles to profl. jours. Mem. adv. com. Miami-Coral Pk. Adult Edn. Ctr., 1988-93; mem. Marion Oaks Civic Assn. Mem. Soc. Bibl. Lit., Liturgical Conf., Spiritual Dirs. Internat., Am. Soc. Ch. History, Greater Ocala Ministerial Assn. Home: 2901 SW 41st St Apt 2702 Ocala FL 34474-7431 Office: Our Saviour Luth Ch 260 Marion Oaks Ln Ocala FL 34473 *God gives every person the ability to make a positive contribution to life. The difference our particular gifts and opportunities allow us to make may seem insignificant in a world needing radical transformation, but we must do what is in our power. Success isn't determined by the size of the results, but by loving faithfulness.*

KOFMEHL, KENNETH THEODORE, political science educator; b. Spokane, Wash., Jan. 31, 1920; s. Theodore August and Gladys (MacKenzie) K.; m. Jerrie Lorraine McGhee, May 22, 1985. BA in Polit. Sci., U. Idaho, 1941; MA in Polit. Sci., Columbia U., 1949, PhD in Polit. Sci., 1956. Vis. instr. U. Kans., Lawrence, 1955-56, vis. asst. prof., 1956-57; asst. prof. Purdue U., Lafayette, Ind., 1957-62; assoc. prof. Purdue U., Lafayette, 1962-67, prof. Polit. Sci., 1967-90, prof. emeritus, 1990—; cons. subcom. on Constitution, U.S. Senate Judiciary com., Washington, 1966-80, com. on Sci. and Pub. Policy, NAS, Washington, 1964, select com. on Coms., U.S. House Reps., Washington, 1973. Author: Professional Staffs of Congress, 1962, 2d rev. edit., 1969, 3rd rev. edit., 1977; contbr. articles to profl. jours. Panelist congl. debate Tippecanoe County Sta. WASK-AM, Lafayette, 1976; moderator LWV and Ind. Commn. on Humanities discussion group on Mondale-Dole debate, West Lafayette, 1976. Capt. U.S. Army, 1942-46, PTO. Decorated Bronze Star medal with two oak leaf clusters, 1945; recipient undergrad. tchg. award Std. Oil Found., 1969; named Outstanding Alumnus U. Idaho, 1991. Mem. Phi Eta Sigma, Phi Beta Kappa, Blue Key, Omicron Delta Kappa, Pi Sigma Alpha, Phi Gamma Delta. Democrat. Presbyterian. Avocations: birdwatching, swimming, hiking, bicycling, reading. Home: 400 N River Rd Apt 1129 Lafayette IN 47906-3136

KOFORD, STUART KEITH, electronics executive; b. North Hollywood, Calif., Oct. 25, 1953; s. Kenneth Harold and Theresa (Sutton) K.; m. Gail Anne Joerger, Dec. 28, 1985; 1 child, Michael Anne. BSME, Mich. Tech. U., 1976. Engr. Motorola, Schaumburg, Ill., 1976-77, sr. engr., 1977-79; engring. project mgr. Amphenol, Cicero, Ill., 1979-80, mgr. R & D, 1980-82; mgr. engring. Amphenol, Broadview, Ill., 1982—; pres. Koford Engring., Lisle, Ill., 1982; ptnr., sec.-treas. Micro-Lungo, 1998. Contbr. articles to profl. jours.; patentee in field. Mem. IEEE (program com. Electronic Components Conf. 1979-91), Soc. Plastic Engrs., ASME, Electronic Connector Study Group (program chmn. 1982-84). Republican. Avocation: slot car racing (World Champion 1989). Home: 1239 Cheshire Ave Naperville IL 60540-5724 Office: Koford Engring 1948 University Ln Lisle IL 60532-2150

KOFRANEK, ANTON MILES, floriculturist, educator; b. Chgo., Feb. 5, 1921; s. Antonin J. and Emma (Rehorek) K.; children—Nancy, John A. B.S., U. Minn., 1947; M.S., Cornell U., 1949, Ph.D., 1950. Asst. prof. to prof. U. Calif., Los Angeles, 1950-68; prof. hort. dept. U. Calif., Davis, 1968-87, ret. prof. emeritus, 1987; vis. prof. U. Wageningen, Netherlands, 1958, Cornell U., 1966, Hebrew U., Rehovot, Israel, 1972-73, Lady Davis fellow, 1980; vis. prof. Glasshouse Crops Research Inst., Littlehampton, U.K., 1980, AID, Egypt, 1978-82, FAO-UN, India, 1985. Co-author: (with Hartmann, Rubatzky and Flocker) Plant Science—Growth, Development and Utilization of Cultivated Plants, 2d edit., 1981; co-editor: (with R. A. Larson) U. Calif. Azalea Manual, 1975; contbr. articles to profl. jours. Served with AUS, 1942-45, ETO; Served with AUS, PTO. Recipient rsch. awards of merit Calif. State Florist Assn., 1966, Garland award 1974; named Young Man of Yr. Westwood Jr. C. of C., 1956; recipient rsch. and tchg. award Soc. Am. Florists, 1993. Fellow Am. Soc. Hort. Sci (dir., sectional chmn. 1973-74); mem. Sigma Xi, Pi Alpha Xi. Office: U Calif-Davis Dept Environ Hort Davis CA 95616 *Always give dollar value for the work you promise to perform.*

KOGA, MARY, artist, photographer, social worker; b. Sacramento, Aug. 10, 1920; d. Hisakichi Harry and Tsugime (Yoneda) Ishii; m. Albert M. Koga, June 28, 1947. BA, U. Calif., Berkeley, 1942; MA (Sch. Social Service Adminstrn. scholar), U. Chgo., 1947; MFA, Art Inst. Chgo., 1973. With Family Service Bur., United Charities of Chgo., 1947-52; chief psychiat. social worker Med. Sch. Northwestern U., 1952-58; asst. prof. clin. social work Sch. Social Service Adminstrn. U. Chgo., 1959-69; instr. photography dept. Columbia Coll., Chgo., 1973-80; prin. Mary Koga: Photographs, 1979—. Contbr. to Women of Photography, 1975, Family of Children, 1977, Chicago: The City & Its Artists, 1945-78, How to Create a Photo Essay, What a Story, 1995, others; one-woman shows include Sch. of Art Inst. Chgo., 1971, Evanston Art Center, 1972, Shado Gallery, 1977, Utah State U., 1979, Pitts. Film-makers Gallery, 1983, J.B. Speed Art Mus., 1985, Truman Coll., 1985, Knox Coll. Art Gallery, 1986, Ill. Wesleyan U. Art Gallery, 1988, Rutgers U., 1988, Adams Gallery, 1990, Catskill Ctr. for Photography, 1990, Smith-Barney Gallery, N.Y.C., 1991, Camera Club of N.Y., 1991, Art Mus. S. Tex., Corpus Christi, 1992, Chgo. Cultural Ctr., 1993, Nat. Louis U., Evanston, Ill., 1994, Noyes Cultural Arts Ctr., Evanston, 1995, Viewpoint Gallery, Sacramento, Calif., 1997, Arts Club Washington, 1998; group shows include, Art Inst. Chgo., 1973, 84, 85, Smithsonian Traveling Exhbn., 1975, U. Mich., 1978, San Francisco Mus. Modern Art, 1975, 78, others; represented in permanent collections: San Francisco Mus. Modern Art, Art Inst. Chgo., Mus. Contemporary Photography, Chgo., Exchange Nat. Bank, Seagram Co., Kimberley Clark Corp., Knox Coll. Art Dept., Sioux City (Iowa) Art Ctr., Art Mus. S. Tex., Balch Inst., Phila.; also numerous pvt. collections. Ill. Arts Coun. grantee, 1975, 79, 84, Nat. Endowment Arts grantee, 1982, Chgo. Office Fine Arts/Community Arts Assistance grantee, 1988-90. Mem. NASW, Japan Am. Soc. Chgo., Inc. (bd. dirs. 1960—), soc. Photog. Edn., Friends of Photography, Photog. Soc., Arts Club of Chgo. Home and Studio: 1254 W Elmdale Ave Chicago IL 60660-2523

KOGA, ROKUTARO, physicist; b. Nagoya, Japan, Aug. 18, 1942; came to U.S., 1961, naturalized, 1966; s. Toyoki and Emiko (Shinra) K.; m. Cordula Rosow, May 5, 1981; children: Evan A., Nicole A. BA, U. Calif., Berkeley, 1966; PhD, U. Calif., Riverside, 1974. Rsch. fellow U. Calif., Riverside, 1974-75; rsch. physicist Case Western Res. U., Cleve., 1975-79, asst. prof., 1979-81; physicist Aerospace Corp., L.A., 1981-96, sr. scientist, 1996—. Contbr. articles to profl. confs. Mem. IEEE, Am. Phys. Soc., Am. Geophys. Union, N.Y. Acad. Scis., Sigma Xi. Achievements include research on gamma-ray astronomy, solar neutron observation, space scis.; charged particles in space and the effect of cosmic rays on microcircuits in space. Home: 7325 Ogelsby Ave Los Angeles CA 90045-1356 Office: Aerospace Corp Space Environ and Tech Ctr Los Angeles CA 90009

KOGAN, GERALD, state supreme court justice; b. Bklyn., May 23, 1933; s. Morris and Yetta (Weinstein) K.; m. Irene Vulgan, Nov. 17, 1955; children: Robert, Debra, Karen. BBA, JD, U. Miami, Coral Gables, Fla., 1955. Bar: Fla. 1955. Sole practice Miami, Fla., 1955-60, 67-80; asst. state's atty. Dade County, Fla., 1960-67, chief prosecutor homicide and capital crimes sect., 1960-67; judge criminal div. Fla. 11th Jud. Cir. Ct., Miami, 1980-87, adminstrv. judge criminal div., 1984-87; justice Supreme Ct. Fla., Tallahassee, 1987—, chief justice, 1996—; adj. prof. law Nova U. Law Sch., U. Miami Sch. Law, Fla. State U. Sch. Law; mem. faculty Am. Acad. Jud. Edn. Served with CIC, AUS, 1955-57. Mem. ABA, Fla. Bar, Dade County Bar Assn. Office: Supreme Ct Fla 500 S Duval St Tallahassee FL 32399-6556*

KOGAN, RICHARD JAY, pharmaceutical company executive; b. N.Y.C., June 6, 1941; s. Benjamin and Ida K.; m. Susan Linda Scher, Aug. 29, 1965. BA, CCNY, 1963; MBA, NYU, 1968. V.p. planning and adminstrn. pharm. divsn. Ciba-Geigy Ltd., Summit, N.J., 1975-76; pres. Can. pharm. ops. Ciba-Geigy Ltd., Can., 1976-79, pres. U.S. pharm. divsn., 1979-82; exec. v.p. pharm. ops. Schering-Plough Corp., Madison, N.J., 1982-86, pres., COO, 1986-95; pres., CEO Schering-Plough Corp., Madison, 1996-98, chmn. bd. dirs., CEO, 1999—; bd. dirs. Colgate-Palmolive Co., The Bank of N.Y. Co., Inc.; vice chmn. bd. trustees St. Barnabas Med. Ctr. and Corp.; bd. trustees NYU. Mem. Council Fgn. Rels., The Bus. Roundtable. Office: Schering-Plough Corp One Giralda Farms Madison NJ 07940-1010

KOGELNIK, HERWIG WERNER, electronics company executive; b. Graz, Austria, June 2, 1932; came to U.S., 1960; naturalized, Jan. 1992; s. Sepp and Siglinde K.; m. Christa Muller, Mar. 7, 1964; children—Christoph N., Florian A., Andreas M. Dipl.-Ing., Tech. U. Vienna, 1955, Dr.techn., 1958; D.phil., Oxford U., 1960. Mem. research staff Bell Labs., Murray Hill, N.J., 1961-67; head coherent optics research dept. Bell Labs., Holmdel, N.J., 1967-76; dir. electronics research lab. Bell Labs., 1976-83; dir. photonics research lab. Bell Labs. Lucent Technologies, 1983—. Contbr. articles in field to profl. jours. Chmn. Monmouth (N.J.) Arts Found., 1973-76; past trustee N.Y. Mus. Holography. Recipient Johann Joseph Ritter von Prechtl medal Tech. U., Vienna, Austria, 1990; hon. fellow St. Peter's Coll., Oxford U., 1992. Fellow IEEE (David Sarnoff award 1989, Quantum Electronics award 1991), Optical Soc. Am. (pres. 1989, Frederic IVES medal 1984), NAS, NAE; mem. AAAS, Am. Phys. Soc., Am. Inst. Physics (past gov.), Seabright Lawn Tennis & Cricket Club (pres. 1994—). Patentee in field of lasers, holography, electronics and optical comm. Home: 27 N Ward Ave Rumson NJ 07760-1913 Office: Bell Labs Lucent Technologies Photonics Rsch Lab Holmdel NJ 07733

KOGER, FRANK WILLIAMS, federal judge; b. Kansas City, Mo., Mar. 20, 1930; s. C.H. and Lelia D. (Williams) K.; m. Jeanine E. Strawhacker, Mar. 19, 1954; children: Lelia Jane, Mary Courtney. AB, Kansas City U., 1951, LLB, 1953; LLM, U. Mo., Kansas City, 1966. Staff judge adv. USAF, Rapid City, S.D., 1953-56; ptnr. Reid, Koger & Reid, Kansas City, 1956-61, Shockley, Reid & Koger, Kansas City, 1961-86; U.S. bankruptcy judge U.S. Dept. Judiciary, Kansas City, 1986—; chief judge 8th Cir. Bankruptcy Appellate Panel, 1997—; adj. prof. law sch. U. Mo., Columbia, 1990—, U. Mo.-Kansas City, 1992—. Author: (manual) Foreclosure Law in Missouri, 1982, Missouri Collection Law, 1983; author, co-editor: Bankruptcy Handbook, 1992; editor: Bankruptcy Law, 1990. Bd. dirs. Jackson County Pub. Hosp., Kansas City, 1974-79, St. Lukes Hosp., Kansas City, 1970—; chair subcom. Jackson County Charter Transition Com., Kansas City, 1978-79. Capt. USAF, 1953-56. Recipient Shelley Peters Meml. award Am. Inst. Banking, Kansas City, 1986. Fellow Am. Coll. Bankruptcy Judges; mem. Nat. Conf. Bankruptcy Judges (dir. 1990-93, sec. 1994-95, pres.-elect 1995-96, pres. 1996-97), Comml. Law League Am. (pres. 1983-84). Avocations: contract bridge, gardening. Office: US Bankruptcy Ct 811 Grand Blvd Kansas City MO 64106-1904

KOGGE, PETER MICHAEL, computer scientist, educator; b. Washington, Dec. 3, 1946; s. Roy and Louise (McGrath) K.; m. Mary Ellen Clarke, June 12, 1971; children: Peter Michael, Mary Elizabeth, Timothy McGrath. BSEE, U. Notre Dame, 1968; MS in Systems Info. Scis., Syracuse U., 1970; PhDEE, Stanford U., 1973. Jr. engr. IBM, Owego, N.Y., 1968-72, staff engr., 1972-74, adv. engr., 1974-76, sr. engr., 1976-81, mem. sr. tech. staff, 1981-93; IBM fellow, 1993; McCourtney prof. computer sci. U. Notre Dame, Ind., 1994—; adj. prof. computer scis. SUNY, Binghamton, 1977-94; past mem. rev. com. NSF Computing Divsn.; program chair 6th Symposium on Frontiers of Massively Parallel Computation, 1996; disting. vis. scientist NASA Jet Propulsion Lab., 1997; program com. Supercomputing, 1998, 99, Internat. Symposium on Computer Arch., 1999; program vice chair 7th Symposium on Frontiers of Massively Parallel Computation, 1999. Author: Architecture of Pipelined Computers, 1980, Architecture of Symbolic Computers, 1991; editor conf. proc. Internat. Conf. on Parallel Processing, 1988. Recipient IBM Outstanding Innovation awards for Space Shuttle, IOP, 3838 Array Processor, AI Parallel Processor, Pres.'s award for patents, Daniel L. Slotnick award for most original paper Internat. Conf. Parallel Processing, 1994, Outstanding Computer Sci. and Engring. Dept. Instrn., 1999. Fellow IEEE; mem. Assn. for Computing Machinery, Am. Assn. Artificial Intelligence, IBM Acad. Tech. Roman Catholic. Office: U Notre Dame Dept Computer Sci and Engring 384 Fitzpatrick Hl Engrng Notre Dame IN 46556-5637

KOGUT, JOHN ANTHONY, retail/wholesale executive; b. Lackawanna, N.Y., Dec. 8, 1942; s. John J. and Rose J. (Gaj) K.; m. Deborah A. Hillman; children: David J., Robert J., Katherine A., Lindsey A., Kimberly M. B.S. in Pharmacy, U. Buffalo, 1965; M.B.A., Syracuse U., 1978. Pharmacist, mgr. Fay's Drug Co., Liverpool, N.Y., 1969-75, v.p., 1975-82, sr. v.p., 1982-89, pres., 1989-95; pres. Health Mart divsn., v.p. Franchise Svcs. FoxMeyer Corp., 1995-96; pres. Health Mart Divsn., v.p. mktg. McKesson Corp., 1996-99; pres. pharmac ops. Cmty. Health Svcs., Inc., Chgo., 1999—; mem. N.Y. State Bd. Pharmacy, 1987-95. Served to capt. U.S. Army, 1966-69. Mem. Am. Pharm. Assn., Pharm. Soc. of State N.Y., Am. Mgmt. Assn., Nat. Assn. Chain Drug Stores (pharmacy affairs com. chmn. 1982-83), N.Y. State Bd. Pharmacy. Republican. Roman Catholic.

KOGUT, KENNETH JOSEPH, consulting engineer; b. Chgo., Dec. 3, 1947; s. Joseph Henry and Estelle Theresa (Swiercz) K.; student Lewis Coll., 1966-68; BME, U. Detroit, 1971, ME, 1972, postgrad, 1972—; m. Darlene Agnes Jedlicka, June 15, 1974. Mech. engr. Fluor Pioneer Inc., Chgo., 1972-73, cons. engr., 1973-75; project mgr. Engring. Corp. Am., Chgo., 1976-77; sr. cons. pub. utilities DeLoitte, Haskins & Sells, Chgo., 1977-79; individual practice as energy and mgmt. cons., 1979—. Registered profl. engr., Ill.; cert. energy mgr. Sloan fellow, 1971-73; recipient award Pres.'s Program for Energy Efficiency, Corporate Energy Mgmt. award, 1981, Regional Energy Profl. Devel. award, 1984, Regional Energy Engr. of Yr. award, 1987, Ill. Energy award, 1988, Illiana Energy Mgmt. Exec. of Yr. award Assn. Energy Engrs. 1992, 96, Excellence in Engring. award Am. Soc. Heating Refrigeration & Air-Conditioning Engrs. Ill. chpt., 1994. Mem. Am. Nuclear Soc., Nat., Ill. socs. profl. engrs., Assn. Energy Engrs. (pres Chgo. chpt. 1985, pres. Ill. chpt. 1990-93, regional v.p. 1993-95, dir. chpt. devel., 1996, internat. pres-elect 1997, internat. pres. 1998), Environ. Engrs. and Mgrs. Inst., Demand-Side Mgmt. Soc., Exec. Hosp. Engrs. Soc. Ill., Energy Svcs. Mktg. Soc., Blue Key, Tau Beta Pi, Pi Tau Sigma, Polish Nat. Alliance. Author: Energy Management for the Community Bank. Address: 5232 170th Pl Oak Forest IL 60452-4450

KOGUT, MAURICE DAVID, pediatric endocrinologist; b. Bklyn., July 7, 1930; s. Nat and Etta K.; m. June Patricia Wenzel, May 9, 1959; children: Melissa, Pamela, Stacy. B.A., N.Y. U., 1951, M.D., 1955. Diplomate Am. Bd. Pediatrics, Am. Bd. Pediatric Endocrinology. Pediatric intern and resident Bellevue Hosp., N.Y.C., 1955-57; chief resident in pediat. Children's Hosp. L.A., 1959-60, fellow in pediatric endocrinology, 1960-62, head div. endocrinology and metabolism, 1970-80, asso. head dept. pediat., 1975-80, program dir. clin. rsch. ctr., 1967-79; asst. prof. pediat. Sch. Medicine, U. So. Calif., 1965-68, asso. prof., 1968-73, prof. pediat., 1973-80; prof. pediat., chmn. dept. pediat. Sch. Medicine, Wright State U., Dayton, Ohio, 1980-98, emeritus prof., 1998—; v.p. for med. affairs Children's Med. Center, Dayton, 1980-97. (recipient CINE/65 Golden Eagle film award for med. film 1965). Served as capt. M.C. USAF, 1957-59. USPHS fellow, 1960-62. Mem. Am. Acad. Pediatrics, Am. Acad. Med. Dirs., Soc. for Pediatric Research, Assn. Med. Sch. Pediatric Chairmen, AAAS, AMA, Am. Fedn. Clin. Research, Am. Diabetes Assn., Endocrine Soc., Am. Pediatric Soc., Lawson Wilkins Pediatric Endocrine Soc., Alpha Omega Alpha.

KOHAN, CAROL E., historial site administrator; b. Kingston, N.Y.. BA, Union Coll., Schenectady, N.Y., 1974; MA, 1980. Curator Regional Pk. Svc., Iowa City, 1986-90, Martin Van Buren Birthplace Site, Kinderhook, Nev., 1990-93; supt. Herbert Hoover Nat. Hist. Site, West Branch, Iowa, 1993—. Office: Herbert Hoover Nat Hist Site Parkside Dr and Main St West Branch IA 52358*

KOHAN, DENNIS LYNN, international trade educator, consultant; b. Kankakee, Ill., Nov. 22, 1945; s. Leon Stanley and Nellie (Foster) K.; m. Julianne Johnson, Feb. 14, 1976 (dec. Sept. 1985); children: Toni, Bart, Elyse; m. Betsy Burns, Mar. 8, 1986; 1 child, David. BA, Ill. Wesleyan U., 1967; MPA, Gov.'s State U., 1975; postgrad., John. Marshall Law Sch., 1971-74. Police officer Kankakee County, 1967-75; loan counselor, security officer Kankakee Fed. Savs. & Loan, Kankakee, 1975-76; mgr. Bank Western, Denver, 1976-85; mgr. real estate lending dept. Cen. Savs., San Diego, 1985-87; maj. loan work-out officer Imperial Savs., San Diego, 1987-88; cons. Equity Assurance Holding Corp., Newport Beach, Calif., 1987-88; compliance officer Am. Real Estate Group and New West Fed. Savs. and Loan, Irvine, Calif., 1988-90; co-founder Consortium-Real Estate Asset Cons., Costa Mesa, Calif., 1990-91; investigator, criminal coord. Resolution Trust Corp., Newport Beach, Calif., 1991-94; instr. for Internat. Trade Anhui Inst. Fin. and Trade, Bengbu, People's Republic of China, 1994-95; instr. Guangzhou Inst. Fgn. Trade, People's Republic of China, 1995—; owner Kohan Internat. Bus. Forensics, 1995—; instr. U. No. Colo. Coll. Bus., Greeley, 1981-85; chmn. bd. North Colo. Med. Ctr., Greeley, 1983-85; pres. bd. Normedco, Greeley, 1984-85. Vol. cons., chmn. ARC, Colo., 1979-85; campaign mgr. Donley Senatorial campaign, Colo., 1982, Kinkade City Coun. campaign, Colo., 1983; chmn. Weld County Housing Authority, 1981. Staff sgt. U.S. Army, 1969-71, Vietnam. Mem. Nat. Assn. Realtors, Shriners, Kiwanis.

KOHAN, LOIS RAE, community health nurse; b. Paterson, N.J., Feb. 2, 1945; d. Raymond Cornelius and Margaret Gavina (Phillips) Englishman; m. Raymond Roy Kohan, Oct. 16, 1966; children: Jeffrey, Glenn, Sharon, Kevin, Craig. Diploma, Hackensack (N.J.) Sch. Nursing, 1966. Substitute sch. nurse Hillsdale (N.J.) Pub. Schs., 1976-80; physical assessment nurse Physical Measurements, Inc., Caldwell, N.J., 1978-81; pvt. duty nurse Charles Blando Family, Oradell, N.J., 1980-85, At Home Nursing Agy., Thells, N.Y., 1985-87; pub. health nurse Dumont (N.J.) Bd. Health, 1987-91, Hillsdale (N.J.) Bd. Health, 1992—. Den leader Boy Scouts Am., Hillsdale, 1975-85; counselor, dir., founder Helping Hand Food Pantry, Hillsdale, 1992—; mem. Drug Alliance Force, Hillsdale, 1996-97; adv. bd. Bergen County Juvenile Fire Prevention Program, Paramus, N.J., 1994-97;. Recipient Hillsdalean award Mayor and Coun. Hillsdale, 1992, Mayor's award Mayor and Coun. Hillsdale, 1995. Mem. N.J. State Nurses Orgn., Nurses Alumni Hackensack Med. Ctr., Bergen County Mcpl. Nurses Assn., Hillsdale Woman's Club. Methodist. Avocations: walking, hiking, tennis, gardening, crafts. Home: 45 Carlyle Pl Hillsdale NJ 07642-2805

KOHEL, RUSSELL JAMES, geneticist; b. Omaha, Nov. 30, 1934; married; 3 children. BS, Iowa State U., 1956; MS, Purdue U., 1958, PhD, 1959. Supervisory rsch. geneticist Argrl. Rsch. Svc. USDA, College Station, Tex., 1959—. Fellow Am. Soc. Agronomy; mem. Am. Soc. Plant Physiologists, Am. Genetic Assn., Genetics Soc. Am. Office: USDA So Crops Rsch Lab 2765 F&B Rd College Station TX 77845-9593

KOHL, BENEDICT M., lawyer; b. 1931. A.B., Brown U., 1952; LL.B. cum laude, Harvard U., 1955. Bar: D.C. 1955, U.S. Supreme Ct. 1962, N.J. 1963. Partner Lowenstein, Sandler, Kohl, Fisher & Boylan, Roseland, N.J.; atty. interpretative div. Office Chief Counsel, IRS, 1957-60, Office of Tax Legis. Counsel, U.S. Treasury Dept., 1960-62. Nat. v.p. Am. Jewish Com., former N.J. pres.; former trustee Overlook Hosp. Mem. ABA, N.J. State, Essex County bar assns. Office: Lowenstein Sandler Kohl et al 65 Livingston Ave Ste 9 Roseland NJ 07068-1725

KOHL, DAVID, dean, librarian; b. Grand Island, Nebr., July 31, 1942; s. D. Franklin and La Vern Harriet (De Long) K; m. Marilyn L. Kohl, Sept. 28, 1969 (div. 1986); 1 child: Nathaniel F. BA cum laude, Carleton Coll., 1965; ThM Divinity Sch., U. Chgo., 1967, DMn, 1969, MA, 1972. Asst. dir. Admission and Aid U. Chgo., 1969-72; Social Scis. reference librarian Washington State U., Pullman, 1972-77, head cir. circulation, 1977-80; undergrad librarian U. Ill., Urbana, 1980-86; asst. dir. Pub. Svcs. U. Colo., Boulder, 1986-91, head Norlin Libr., 1989-91; dean, univ. libr. U. Cin., 1991—; dir. U. Cin. Digital Press, 1996—; assoc. prof. U. Ill. Urbana Libr. Sch., 1984-86, Emporia State U., 1991-92, Ind. U., Bloomington, 1992, U. Ky., 1994—. Author: Handbooks for Library Management (6 vols.), 1984-86, 12 Years 'Til 2000, 1990; review editor RQ Reference Tools, 1988—; contbr. articles to profl. jours. Relief houseparent for Learning Disabled Student Whitman County Mental Health, Pullman, Wash., 1973-75; Koinonia House Bd. (pres. 1979-80), Pullman, 1975-81; mem. bd. Mental Health Found., Boulder County, 1986-91. Rockefeller fellow Rockefeller Found., 1965-66; Disciples House scholar Disciples Divinity House, Chgo., 1965-69. Mem. ALA (v.p., pres. reference and adult svc. divsn. 1993—), Libr. Guild. Presbyterian. Avocation: jogging. Home: 2929 Courtropes Ln Cincinnati OH 45244-3807 Office: Univ of Cincinnati Langsam Libr Mail Location 33 Cincinnati OH 45221-0033

KOHL, HAROLD, missionary, educator; b. Linden, N.J., Dec. 13, 1923; s. Herman and Martha (Sperber) K.; m. Beatrice Minniebelle Wells, Mar. 21, 1946; children: Loren, Loretta, Lyndon. BA, Monmouth Coll., 1962; MA in Edn., NYU, 1968, postgrad., 1974; ThD in English Bible, Internat. Bible Inst., 1980. Ordained to ministry Assemblies of God Ch., 1948. Pastor, evangelist Assemblies of God Ch., W.Va., Md., 1944-50; pres. youth ministries Potomac Dist. Coun. Assemblies of God Ch., 1947-48; fgn. missionary Assemblies of God Ch., Colombo, Sri Lanka, 1950-56; pastor Assemblies of God Ch., N.J., 1956-61; missionary, tchr., educator Assemblies of God Ch., Far East, Pacific, Europe, 1961-94; ednl. cons. Assemblies of God Ch., Far East, Pacific, 1980-83; assoc. pastor Hayfield (Va.) Assembly of God, 1995—; pres. Bethel Bible Coll., Manila, 1963-68; pres., founder Far East Advanced Sch. Theology (now Asia Pacific Theol. Sem., Baguio City, The Philippines), Manila, 1964-73; adj. prof. Baguio City, 1991—; dean coll. divns. Internat. Corr. Inst. (now named ICI U.), Brussels, 1973-78, Belgium, 1983-88, Rhode St. Genese, Belgium, 1988-99, mem. external faculty, Brussels/Irving, Tex., 1988-94. Mem. Soc. Pentecostal Studies, Religious Edn. Assn., Phi Delta Kappa, Phi Theta Kappa. Republican. Avocations: photography, reading, walking. Home: 429 Superior Ave Winchester VA 22601-4253 *In a truly successful and satisfying life, the will of God is always paramount. At the heart of every personal decision there must be unreserved cooperation with the holy and wise will of God.*

KOHL, HERBERT, professional sports team executive, former senator; b. Milw., Feb. 7, 1935. BA, U. Wis., 1956; MBA, Harvard U., 1956. Owner Milw. Bucks (NBA), part owner Milw. Brewers; U.S. senator from Wis., 1989—; pres. Herbert Kohl Investments; state chmn. Dem. Party, Wis., 1975-77; mem. com. on aging, Appropriations Com., Senate Dem. Steering & Coordination Com., Com. on Judiciary, 1989; ranking minority mem. Jud. subcom. on Terrorism, Tech. & Govt. Info. With USAR, 1958-64. Office: US Senate 330 Hart Senate Office Bldg Washington DC 20510-4903 also: Milw Bucks Bradley Ctr 1001 N 4th St Milwaukee WI 53203-1314*

KOHL, KATHLEEN ALLISON BARNHART, lawyer; b. Ft. Leavenworth, Kans., Jan. 11, 1955; d. Robert William and Margaret Ann (Snowden) Barnhart. BS, Memphis State U., 1978; JD, Loyola U., New Orleans, 1982. Bar: La. 1982, U.S. Dist. Ct. (ea. dist.) La. 1982, U.S. Dist. Ct. (no. dist.) Tex. 1985, U.S. Ct. Appeals (5th cir.) 1986, U.S. Ct. Appeals (11th cir.) 1988, U.S. Supreme Ct. 1994. Assoc. Garrity & Webb, Harahan, La., 1982; revenue officer IRS, Dallas, 1984; sr. trial atty. EEOC, Dallas, 1984-86; sr. criminal enforcement counsel U.S. EPA, Dallas, 1986-91, chief water enforcement sect., office regional counsel, 1991-92; dep. dir. criminal enforcement counsel divsn. U.S. EPA, Washington, 1992-93, dir. criminal enforcement counsel divsn., 1993-94; sr. criminal enforcement counsel U.S. EPA, Dallas, 1994—; spl. asst. U.S. atty. (spl. assignment from U.S. EPA), U.S. Atty.'s Office, Montgomery, Ala., 1988-89; vis. instr. Fed. Law Enforcement Tng. Ctr., Glynco, Ga., 1987—; adj. prof. environ. crimes seminar Cornell U. Law Sch., spring 1993, environ. law Sch. Law Tex. Wesleyan U., fall 1998; instr. EPA Nat. Acad., 1997—. Vol. instr. New Orleans Police Acad., 1981. Mem. La. Bar Assn. Office: EPA 1445 Ross Ave Ste 1200 Dallas TX 75202-2733

KOHL, LINDA WEIR, city official; b. June 1, 1958. BA in Polit. Sci., SUNY, Fredonia, 1980; MPA, SUNY, Albany, 1982. Councilwoman Town of Penfield (N.Y.), 1992—.

KOHLER, DEBORAH DIAMOND, dietitian, food service executive; b. Queens, N.Y., Nov. 5, 1960; d. Morris and Susan Erika (Pottasch) Diamond; m. Michael Henry Kohler, July 31, 1988; children: Joshua, Jacob, Abigail. BS, Mich. State U., 1982. Registered dietitian. Res. clin. dietitian South Nassau Cmty. Hosp., Oceanside, N.Y., 1982; clin. dietitian Southampton (N.Y.) Hosp., 1982-84; chief dietitian Allentown (Pa.) Osteo. Med. Ctr., 1984-86, food svc. dir., 1986—; food svc. dir. St. Luke's Quakertown (Pa.) Hosp., 1996—; computer cons. dist. area Marriott Internat., Allentown, 1991—. Mem. Am. Dietetic Assn., Lehigh Valley Dietetic Assn. Jewish. Avocations: volleyball, bowling, raising children, baseball fan, pinochle. Home: 5750 Woodcrest Dr Coopersburg PA 18036-2312

KOHLER, EDITH A., senior citizen's organization executive; b. Middletown, Ohio, Sept. 25, 1936; d. Elmer Van and Mona Bair; m. Dale Martin Kohler, June 9, 1956; children: Lynne A., Martin D. A.Fine Arts, Miami U., Oxford, Ohio, 1979. Pres. Middletown Fine Arts Ctr., 1979-81; dir. Spring Arts Festival, Middletown, 1982; devel. dir. Ohio Presbyn. Retirement Svcs., Monroe/Columbus, 1982-86, United Ch. Homes, Beavercreek, Ohio, 1986-87; exec. dir. Middletown Area Sr. Citizens, 1987-94; gerontologist Ohio Assn. Sr. Ctrs., Columbus, 1995—. Bd. trustees, sec., chmn. pers. com. Careview Home Health Affiliated Middletown Reg. Hosp., 1987-97; exec. bd., bd. trustees Ohio Presbyn. Retirement Svcs., Monroe and Columbus, 1990—; auction chmn. Mt. Pleasant Retirement Cmty., Monroe, 1998; art auction chmn. Middletown Fine Arts Ctr., 1982-83; program chmn., exec. com. Salvation Army Aux., Middletown, 1994—; pub. editor Midfest Internat., Middletown, 1983-84. Presbyterian. Avocations: golf, bridge, reading. Home: 1904 Antrim Ct Middletown OH 45042-2901

KOHLER, FRED CHRISTOPHER, tax specialist; b. Cleve., Oct. 21, 1946; s. Fred Russell and Ruth Mary (Harris) K. BS (Austin scholar), Northwestern U., 1968; MBA (Faville fellow), Stanford U., 1970. Sr. analyst adminstrv. svcs. dissn. Arthur Andersen & Co., San Francisco, 1970-75; fin. systems analyst, sr. cost acct. Hewlett Packard Co., Palo Alto, Calif., 1975-77, internat. mktg. systems adminstr., 1977-80, sr. planning and reporting analyst corp. hdqrs., 1980-86, fin. planning and reporting mgr., 1986-90, tax mgr., 1990-92; sr. tax mgr. Hewlett Packard Co., 1992—. Mem. World Affairs Coun. No. Calif., Commonwealth Club, Churchill Club, Northwestern U. Alumni Club No. Calif., Stanford U. Alumni Assn., Beta Gamma Sigma. Home: 1736 Oak Creek Dr Apt 211 Palo Alto CA 94304-2112 Office: 3000 Hanover St Palo Alto CA 94304-1112

KOHLER, FREDERICK WILLIAM, JR., pharmacist; b. Passaic, N.J., Apr. 28, 1955. Student, U. Toledo, U. Md.; BS in Pharmacy, Temple U., 1981, MS in Pharmacology, 1985, PhD in Pharmacology, 1990. Registered pharmacist, N.J., Pa. Instr. pharmacology Temple U. Sch. Dental Hygiene, Phila., 1982-84; teaching asst. anatomy, pharmacy, pharmacology labs. Temple U. Sch. Pharmacy, Phila., 1982-87, tchg. assoc. in pharmacology, 1987-90, instr. pharmacology, 1990-95; dir. Michael and Charles Barnett Meml. Lab. Lab. Mitochondrial Disease Biochemistry, 1991-95; lectr. Gwynedd-Mercy Coll., Gwynedd Valley, Pa., 1995-96; med. info. projects mgr. Zeneca Pharms., Wilmington, Del., 1996-99, sr. mgr. med. info. projects, 1999—; pharmacist RXD PHarmacies, Inc., Collingswood, N.J., 1985—; dir. undergrad. pharmacology lab. Temple U. Sch. Pharmacy, 1986-95, admissions com. mem., 1987-95, coord. grad. seminar, 1989-93, grad. rsch. com. for PhD candidate, 1990-95, dir. pharmacology grad. rsch. data analysis and computer programming, 1990-95, chmn. tchg. evaluation and recognition com., 1991-93, disciplinary com. mem., 1992, grad. thesis reading com. for MS candidate, 1993; collection devel. com. Temple U. Health Sci. Libr., 1990-95; cons. Law Offices Reuss, Cavaglarao & Kaspar, 1995; ind. contractor Target Rsch. Assocs., Scotch Plains, N.J., 1995; cons. Dept. Atty. Gen. of Commonwealth of Pa., 1995. Recipient Furst award Am. Coll. Toxicology, 1987, Upjohn Pharmacy Rsch. award, 1990. Mem. AAAS, Am. Assn. Coll. Pharmacy, Am. Pharm. Assn., Mid-Atlantic Pharmacology Soc., Mid. Atlantic Reprodn. and Teratology Assn., Mid. Atlantic Soc. Toxicology, Montgomery County Pharm. Assn., Rotary, Sigma Xi, Rho Chi, Kappa Psi (faculty advisor 1991-95). Avocations: computers, electronics, music, photography, softball. Office: Zeneca Pharmaceuticals 1800 Concord Pike PO Box 15437 Wilmington DE 19850-5437

KOHLER, HERBERT VOLLRATH, JR., diversified manufacturing company executive; b. Sheboygan, Wis., Feb. 20, 1939; s. Herbert Vollrath and Ruth Miriam (DeYoung) K.; m. Linda Elizabeth Karger, Sept. 23, 1961; children: Laura Elizabeth, Rachel DeYoung, Karger David. Grad., The Choate Sch., 1957; B.S., Yale U., 1965. With Kohler Co., Wis., 1965—; gen. supr. warehouse div. Kohler Co., 1965-67, factory systems mgr., 1967-68, v.p. operations, 1968-71, exec. v.p., 1971-72, chmn. bd., chief exec. officer, 1972—, pres., 1974—, dir., 1967—; dir. Harnishchfeger Corp. Mem. adv. bd. John Michael Kohler Arts Ctr., from 1972; bd. dirs., v.p. Friendship House, from 1959; bd. dirs. Kiddies Camp Corp., from 1972; trustee Lawrence U., from 1973; pres. bd. dirs. Kohler Found., from 1968. Served with U.S. Army, 1957-58. Mem. NAM (dir. 1973—), Sheboygan C. of C., Am. Horse Show Assn., Am. Morgan Horse Assn. Republican. Episcopalian. Club: Sheboygan Economic (pres. 1973-74). Office: Kohler Co 444 Highland Dr Kohler WI 53044-1500*

KOHLER, KARL EUGENE, architect; b. Washington, Oct. 26, 1932; s. Frederick Leslie and Nora (Gibson) K.; m. Betty Jane Sampson, June 13, 1954; children: Mark Allen Eric Leslie, Janis Lynn, James Robert. BS in Bldg. Design, Va. Polytech. Inst., 1954, MS in Architecture, 1957. Cert. architect Va., Md., D.C., Pa., W.Va., N.C.; cert. Class A Contractor. Asst. instr. architecture Va. Polytech. Inst., Blacksburg, 1956-57; apprentice architect William N. Denton Jr. Architects, Washington, 1957-61; architect Beery & Rio Architects, Annandale, Va., 1961-63; prin. Kohler Mizner Daniels Architects, Vienna, Va., 1963-68, Kohler Daniels Assoc. Architects, Vienna, 1968-77; pres., treas. Kohler Daniels Harrell Architects, Vienna, 1977-80; pres. Karl E. Kohler Assoc. Architects, Vienna, 1980-96, v.p., 1996—; pres., treas. 301 Plaza, Inc., 1967-85, Kohler Enterprises, Inc., 1985—; chmn. bd. dirs. Windmill Point Marine Resorts, White Stone Va., 1979-90; gen. ptnr. The Coves at Wilton Creek Ltd., 1987—. Prin. works include Statler Hilton Hotel, Williamsburg, Va., 1968, 307 Condominium Office Complex, Vienna, 1975, JKJ Chevrolet, Vienna, 1976, 301 Office Complex, Vienna, 1979, The Coves at Wiolton Creek, 1987-94; featured in numerous profl. jours., newspapers, mags. Treas. Mill Creek Park Civic Assn., 1962, pres., 1963-64; deacon Calvary Hill Bapt. Ch., 1966-68; bd. dirs. Fairfax County (Va.) Jr. Achievement, 1975-77. 1st lt. corps. engrs. U.S. Army, 1954-56. Recipient Merit award Fairfax County Exceptional Design awards program 1987, Comml. award for Excellence No. Va. Bldg. Industry Assn. (2), 1987, Premier Builder award Homecraft Corp., 1988, Beautification award City of Fairfax, 1989, Hon. Mention Va. Masonry Coun., 1989, award of Excellence James City Planning Commn., 1991. Mem. AIA (Excellence in Architecture award Va. chpt. 1989, Excellence in Design award cedar shake and shingle bur.), No. Va. AIA (Assoc. award Notice Spl. Recognition 1989, Assoc. Young award Excellence 1990, award of Merit 1990, 91, 92, Excellence in Architecture award 1992, Excellence in Design award 1993, 94), Vienna Sertoma Club (bd. dirs. 1965-67), Vienna C. of C. (bd. dirs. 1970-72), Fairfax County C. of C., Northumberland County C. of C., Va. Hist. Soc., Tower Club No. Va., Tau Sigma Delta. Avocations: golf, boating. Home: 474 Coan Haven Rd Lottsburg VA 22511-2630

KOHLER, LAURA E., public relations executive; married; 2 children. Grad., Duke U., 1984; MFA, Cath. U., 1987. Past tchr. Chgo. Pub. Schs.; past corp. team facilitator; past mgr. Nat. Players, Washington; past residence mgr. Olney (Md.) Theatre; founder Address Unknown, Chgo.; past exec. dir. Kohler Found., Inc.; v.p. comm. Kohler Co., 1994—. Office: Kohler Co 444 Highland Dr Kohler WI 53044-1500*

KOHLER, MAX ADAM, consulting hydrologist, weather service administrator; b. Lincolnville, Kans., Sept. 6, 1915; s. John Henry and Martha Augusta (Gilbert) K.; m. Estella Anna Pospisil, Feb. 6, 1939; children: Donna, Max Adam, II, Kathryn. B.S. in Physics, U. N.Mex., 1939. Registered profl. engr., D.C. Draftsman Soil Conservation Service and Indian Service, Albuquerque, 1936-39; field insp. Nat. Weather Service, Roswell, N.Mex. and Los Angeles, 1940-41; hydrologist Nat. Weather Service, Washington, 1941-51, chief hydrologist, 1951-71, assoc. dir., 1971-73; pres. Commn. Hydrology, World Meteorl. Orgn., 1960-68; cons. UN, Yugoslavia, 1953, East Africa, 1962, 72, World Met. Orgn., N.Y., Geneva, Switzerland, 1974-75. Co-author: Applied Hydrology, 1949; Hydrology for Engineers, 1958, 2 edit, 1975, 3 edit, 1981; contbr. articles to profl. jours. Recipient meritorious award U.S. Dept. Commerce, 1949, Gold Medal citation U.S. Dept. Commerce, 1959, Distinguished Service award U.S. Dept. Commerce, 1962, Engr. award Wash. Acad. Scis., 1951, Hydrology prize Internat. Assn. Hydrological Scis., 1986. Fellow Am. Geophys. Union (pres. sect. hydrology 1968-70); mem. Nat. Acad. Engring. (civil engr. peers com. 1983-86), ASCE (life), Am. Meteorol. Soc. (council mem. 1972-75). Home: 3530 Twin Branches Dr Silver Spring MD 20906-1466

KOHLER, PETER OGDEN, physician, educator, university president; b. Bklyn., July 18, 1938; s. Dayton McCue and Jean Stewart (Ogden) K.; m. Judy Lynn Baker, Dec. 26, 1959; children: Brooke Culp, Stephen Edwin, Todd Randolph, Adam Stewart. BA, U. Va., 1959; MD, Duke U., 1963. Diplomate Am. Bd. Internal Medicine and Endocrinology. Intern Duke U. Hosp., Durham, N.C., 1963-64, fellow, 1964-65; clin. assoc. Nat Cancer Inst., Nat Inst. Child Health and Human Devel., NIH, Bethesda, Md., 1965-67, sr. investigator, 1968-73, head endocrinology service, 1972-73; resident in medicine Georgetown U. Hosp., Washington, 1969-70; prof. medicine and cell biology, chief endocrinology divsn. Baylor Coll. Medicine, Houston, 1973-77; prof., chmn. dept. medicine U. Ark., 1977-86, interim dean, 1985-86; chmn. Hosp. Med. Bd., 1980-82, chmn. council dept. chmn., 1979-80; prof., dean Sch. Medicine, U. Tex., San Antonio, 1986-88; pres. Oreg. Health Scis. U., Portland, 1988—; cons. endocrinology merit rev. bd. VA, 1985-86; mem. endocrinology study sect. NIH, 1981-85, chmn., 1984-85; mem. bd. sci. counselors NICHD, 1987-92, chair, 1990-92; mem. Nat. Adv. Rsch. Resources Coun., NIH, 1998—; chair task force on health care delivery AAHC, 1991-92; Inst. Medicine bd. dirs. Standard Ins. Co., HealthChoice, Assn. Acad. Health Ctrs., (chair elect 1997-98), OHSU bd. Northwest Health Found., 1997— ; mem. adv. bd. Loaves and Fishes, 1989; mem. Gov.'s adv. com. Commn. on Tech. Edn., 1989—; chair Oreg. Health Coun., 1993-95; mem. bd. govs. Am. Bd. Internal Medicine, 1987-93, mem. endocrinology bd., 1983-91, chmn., 1987-91, 97. Editor: Current Opinion in Endocrinology and Diabetes, 1994—, Diagnosis and Treatment of Pituitary Tumors, (with G. T. Ross), 1973, Clinical Endocrinology, 1986; assoc. editor: Internal Medicine, 1983, 87, 90, 94, 98; contbr. articles to profl. jours. Bd. dirs. Portland C. of C., 1997—. With USPHS, 1965-68. NIH grantee, 1973—; Howard Hughes Med. Investigator, 1976-77; recipient NIH Quality awrds, 1969, 71, Disting. Alumnus award Duke Med. Sch., 1992, MRF Mentor award, Med. Rsch. Found., 1994, Humanitarian award Am. Lung Assn., 1996, Jewish Nat. Fund Tree of Life award, 1998. Fellow ACP; mem. AMA (William Beaumont award 1988), Inst. Medicine, Am. Soc. Clin. Investigation, Am. Fedn. Clin. Rsch. (nat. coun. 1977-78, pres. so. sect. 1976), So. Soc. Clin. Investigation (coun. 1979-82, pres. 1983, Founder's medal 1987), Am. Soc. Cell Biology, Assn. Am. Physicians, Am. Diabetes Assn., Endocrine Soc. (coun. 1990-93), Raven Soc., Phi Beta Kappa, Sigma Xi, Alpha Omega Alpha, Omicron Delta Kappa, Phi Eta Sigma. Methodist. Office: Oreg Health Scis U Office of Pres 3181 SW Sam Jackson Park Rd Portland OR 97201-3011

KOHLER, WILLIAM CURTIS, sleep specialist, neurologist; b. Wharton, N.J., May 22, 1942; s. Walter Henry and Elizabeth (Curtis) K.; m. Barbara Bauman, Sept. 1, 1962; children: Jonathan, Kristina, Elizabeth. AB, Oberlin Coll., 1964; MD, U. Fla., 1968. Diplomate Am. Bd. Pediats., Am. Bd. Neurology with spl. competence in child neurology, Am. Bd. Electroencephalography and Neurophysiology, Am. Bd. Sleep Medicine. Asst. prof. pediatrics U. Fla., Gainesville, 1973-76; neurologist Tallahassee Neurol. Clinic, 1976-94, Billings (Mont.) Clinic, 1994-96, The Sleep Ctr. of Mont., Billings, 1996—; med. dir. The Sleep Ctr. at St. Vincent, 1996—; staff neurologist Wilford Hall Med. Ctr., USAF, San Antonio, 1973-75; from clin. asst. to clin. assoc. prof. pediatric neurology U. Tex., San Antonio, 1973-75; cons. child neurology Divsn. Children's Med. Svcs. Fla., Tallahassee, 1973-94; med. dir. Lancaster Youth Devel. Ctr., Trenton, Fla., 1975-76. Bd. dirs. United Cerebral Palsy Assn., 1977-84, Big Bend Epilepsy Assn., 1977-92. Recipient Humanitarian Svc. award United Cerebral Palsy Assn., Physician's Recognition award, AMA. Fellow Am. Acad. Pediatrics, Am. Acad. Neurology, Am. Sleep Disorders Assn.; mem. Am. Med. EEG Assn., Am. Epilepsy Soc., Child Neurology Soc. Office: The Sleep Ctr of Montana 1233 N 30th St Billings MT 59101-0127

KOHLHEPP, EDWARD JOHN, financial planner; b. Phila., Aug. 11, 1943; s. Edward H. and Helen Kathleen (Egan) K.; m. Elizabeth A. Bretschneider, June 21, 1969; children: Edward Joseph, Karen Ann, Mary Beth. BS in Acctg., LaSalle U., 1967; MBA in Mgmt., Temple U., 1969. Cert. pension cons.; CLU, CFP; registered prin. NASD; chartered fin. cons.. Instr. Bucks County C.C., Newtown, Pa., 1969-72, asst. prof., 1976-79, assoc. prof., 1979-83, sr. assoc. prof., 1983-86; sec.-treas. Lincoln Investment Planning, Inc., Jenkintown, Pa., 1972-75; cons. Neil G. Kyde, Inc., Yardley, Pa., 1975-79; v.p. William L. Marshall Assocs., Inc., Doylestown, Pa., 1979-80; pvt. practice as fin. planner, 1980-87; pres. Van Buren & Kohlhepp, Ltd., 1987-94; prin. Manchester Benefits Group, Ltd., 1994-98; pres. Manchester Advisers, 1994-98, Manchester Fin. Svcs., 1994-98, Kohlhepp Investment Advisors, 1998—; adj. faculty Bucks County C.C. Mem. Internat. Assn. Fin. Planning, Inst. CFPS, Am. Acad. Actuaries, Am. Soc. Pension Actuaries, Bucks County Estate Planning Coun., Beta Gamma Sigma, Beta Alpha. Home: 29 Woods End Dr Doylestown PA 18901-9461 Office: 150 E State St Doylestown PA 18901

KOHLHORST, GAIL LEWIS, librarian; b. Phila., Dec. 5, 1946; d. Richard Elliott and Lucille (Lampkin) Lewis; m. Allyn Leon Kohlhorst, Feb. 14, 1974; 1 child, Jennifer Marion. B.A. in Govt, Otterbein Coll., Westerville, Ohio, 1969; M.S. in L.S, Cath. U. Am., 1977. Info. classifier U.S. Ho. of Reps. Commn. on Internal Security, Washington, 1969-70; adminstrv. asst. Office of Gen. Counsel, GSA, Washington, 1971-76; chief tech. services sect. GSA Libr., Washington, 1976-79; chief GSA libr., 1979-88; acting chief, div. info. and libr. svcs. U.S. Dept. Interior, Washington, 1988-89; chief libr. svcs. br. GSA, Washington, 1989-96; chief mgmt. analysis FDA, Rockville, Md., 1996; dir. mgmt. sys. and policy FDA, Rockville, 1996—. Author: Art and Architecture: An Annotated Bibliography, 1986, Total Quality Management: An Annotated Bibliography, 1990, 91, 93, Federal Librarians Round Table, ALA, Yearbook, 1989, Federal Librarian, 1991-94; contbr. Calendar Commn. on the Bicentennial for the U.S. Constn. Recipient Outstanding Performance awards, 1973, 75, 76, 79, 81-86, 88-89, 91-96, Spl. Achievement awards, 1982-84, Commendable Svc. award, 1984, Nat. Capital Performance award, 1985, Meritorious Svc. award, 1992, Disting. Svc. award, 1995, Dep. Commr.'s Spl. Achievement award, 1999. Mem. ALA (Fed. Libr.'s Achievement award 1995), Fed. Libr. Round Table (pres. 1990-91, membership chair 1994-96), Fed. Libr. and Info. Ctr. (observer 1984-96, exec. bd. 1992-94, chair 1994, membership and governance com.), Fed. Pre-Conf. on the White House Conf. on Librs. and Scis. (del. 1990), Fedlink Adv. Coun. (chair exec. adv. coun. 1988-90), Pub. Employees Roundtable (bd. dirs. 1994-96), D.C. Libr. Assn., United Meth. Women (mem. Dulin outreach com. 1994-96, pres. Joshua's Way 1995-96), Beta Phi Mu. Methodist. Home: 1830 Opalocka Dr Mc Lean VA 22101-5445 Office: FDA 5600 Fishers Ln Rockville MD 20852-1750

KOHLMAN, NANCY ANN (ZEIGENFUSE), medical/surgical nurse; b. Balt., Oct. 7, 1947; d. Irvin Freeman and Hazel Rosetta (May) Zeigenfuse. Diploma, Luth. Hosp. Sch. Nursing, 1968. Staff nurse Long Beach (Calif.) Meml. Hosp., 1971-72, Greater Balt. Med. Ctr., Towson, Md., 1972—. Lt. (j.g.) USNR, 1969-71.

KOHLMEIER, LOUIS MARTIN, JR., newspaper reporter; b. St. Louis, Feb. 17, 1926; s. Louis Martin and Anita (Werling) K.; m. Barbara Anne Wilson, Nov. 15, 1958; children—Daniel Kimbrell, Ann Werling. B.Journalism, U. Mo., 1950. Staff writer Wall St. Jour., St. Louis and Chgo., 1952-57, Washington, 1960—; staff writer St. Louis Globe-Democrat, 1958-59. Author: The Regulators Watchdog Agencies and the Public Interest, 1969. Served with AUS, 1950-52. Recipient Nat. Headliners Club award nat. reporting, 1959, Sigma Delta Chi award Washington corr., 1964, Pulitzer prize nat. reporting, 1964. Home: # 105 11400 Strand Dr Apt 105 Rockville MD 20852-2942

KOHLOSS, FREDERICK HENRY, consulting engineer; b. Ft. Sam Houston, Tex., Dec. 4, 1922; s. Fabius Henry and Rowena May (Smith) K.; m. Margaret Mary Grunwell, Sept. 9, 1944; children: Margaret Ralston, Charlotte Todesco, Eleanor. B.S. in Mech. Engring, U. Md., 1943; M.Mech. Engring., U. Del., 1951; J.D., George Washington U., 1949. Mem. engring. faculty George Washington U., Washington, 1946-50; devel. and standards engr. Dept. Def., 1950-51; chief engr. for mech. contractors Washington, 1951-54, Cleve., 1954-55; chief engr. for mech. contractor Honolulu, 1955-56, cons. engr., 1956-61; pres. Frederick H. Kohloss & Assocs., Inc., Cons. Engrs., Honolulu, 1961-91; chmn. Lincolne, Scott & Kohloss Inc, Cons. Engrs., Honolulu, 1991-97, sr. cons., 1997—. Contbr. to publs. in field. Served with U.S. Army, 1943-46. Fellow ASME, ASHRAE, Chartered Inst. Bldg. Svcs. Engrs., Instn. Engrs. Australia, Australian Inst. Refrigeration, Air Conditioning, Heating, Soc. Mil. Engrs.; mem. IEEE (sr.), NSPE. Clubs: Oahu Country (Honolulu). Home: 1645 Ala Wai Blvd Penthouse 1 Honolulu HI 96815 Office: 201 Merchant St Ste 2310 Honolulu HI 96813-2926

KOHLSTEDT, JAMES AUGUST, lawyer; b. Evanston, Ill., June 1, 1949; s. August Lewis and Deloris (Weichelt) K.; m. Patricia Ann Lang, Oct. 8, 1977; children: Katherine, Matthew, Lindsey, Kevin. BA, Northwestern U., 1971; JD, MBA, Ind. U., 1976. Bar: U.S. Dist. Ct. (no. dist.) Ill. 1976, U.S. Tax Ct. 1978. Tax specialist Peat Marwick, Mitchell & Co., Chgo., 1976-77; assoc. Bishop & Crawford Ltd., Oak Brook, Ill., 1977-83, 1984-85; ptnr. Arnstein, Gluck, Lehr & Milligan, Oak Brook, 1985-87, Keck, Mahin and Cate, Oak Brook, 1987-96; ptnr. McBride Baker & Coles, 1996—, mem. mgmt. com., 1997; chair McBride Baker & Coles Trade and Profl. Assn. Practice Group. Bd. dirs. Nat. Entrepreneurship Found., Bloomington, Ind., 1981-92, Camp New Hope Devel. Bd., Oak Brook, 1983; mem. sch. bd. Lyons Twp. H.S. Dist. 204, La Grange , Ill., 1985-97; pres. Hinsdale (Ill.) Cmty. House Coun., 1991-94; mem. area leadership com. Superconducting Super Collider, 1987-88; mem. citizens adv. com. on edn. to U.S. Congressman Harris Fawell, 1986-93; bd. dirs. Ill. Corridor Partnership for Excellence in Edn., 1988-94; mem. planned giving com. Elmhurst Coll., 1986—; mem. citizens adv. panel U.S. Army ROTC Cadet Command, 1991-94; bd. dirs. Ill. Math and Sci. Acad. Alliance, 1989—; del. White House Conf. Travel and Tourism, 1995; mem. allied adv. bd. midwest chpt. Am. Soc. Travel Agents, 1995; Collegiate Edn. adv. com. Dept. Def., 1995. Recipient Outstanding Young Citizen of Chgo. award 1987. Mem. ABA, Ill. Travel and Tourism Assn., Ill. Bar Assn., DuPage Estate Planning Coun., Oak Brook Jaycees (pres. 1984—, chmn. bd. 1985, trustee 1985-86), Beta Gamma Sigma. Republican. Lutheran. Office: McBride Baker & Coles 500 W Madison St 40th Fl Chicago IL 60661-2511

KOHLSTEDT, SALLY GREGORY, history educator; b. Ypsilanti, Mich., Jan. 30, 1943. BA, Valparaiso U., 1965; MA, Mich. State U., 1966; PhD, U. Ill., Urbana, 1972. Asst. prof. Simmons Coll., Boston, 1971-75; assoc. prof. to prof. Syracuse (N.Y.) U., 1975-89; prof. history of sci. U. Minn., Mpls., 1989—; dir. Ctr. for Advanced Feminist Studies, 1997—; vis. prof. history of sci. Cornell U., 1989, Amerika Inst. U. Munich, 1997; lect. univs. in U.S. and abroad; mem. nat. panels. Author: The Formation of the American Scientific Community: AAAS, 1848-1860, 1976; editor: (with Margaret Rossiter) Historical Writing on American Science, Osiris, 2d Series, 1, 1985, (with R.W. Home) International Science and National Scientific Identity: Australia between Britain and America, 1991, The Origins of Natural Science in the United States: The Essays of George Brown Goode, 1991, (with Barbara Haslett et al.) Gender and Scientific Authority, 1996, (with Helen Lonino) The Women, Gender, and Science Question, 1997; contbr. articles to profl. jours.; mem. editl. bd. Signs, 1980-88, 90-93, Sci., 1980-81, News and Views: History of Am. Sci. Newsletter, 1980-86, Sci., Tech. and Human Values, 1983-90, Syracuse Scholar, 1985-88, chair, 1988; assoc. editor Am. Nat. Biography, 2d edit., 1988—, consulting edit., 1993—; reviewer books, articles, proposals for NSDF, NEH, U. Chgo. Press, numerous other pub. cos.; editor sci. biography series Cambridge U., 1997—. NSF grantee, 1969, 78-79, 84, 93-95, Smithsonian Instn. predoctoral fellow, 1970-71, Danforth Assoc., 1975-82, Syracuse U. grantee, 1976, 82, Am. Philos. Soc. rsch. grantee, 1977, Haven fellow Am. Antiquarian Soc., 1982, Fulbright Sr. fellow U. Melbourne, Australia, 1983, Woodrow Wilson Ctr. fellow, 1986, Smithsonian Instn. Sr. fellow, 1987. Fellow AAAS (nominating com. 1980-83, 96—, sect. chair 1986, bd. dirs. 1998—), Am. Hist. Assn. (profl. com. 1974-76, rep. U.S. Nat. Archives Adv. Coun. 1974-76), Berkshire Conf. Women Historians (program com. 1974), Forum on the History Sci. in Am. (coord. com. 1980-86, chair 1985, 86), History of Sci. Soc. (sec. 1978-81, coun. 1982-84, 89-91, 94-96, com. on publs. 1982-87, chair nominating com. 1985, women's com. 1972-74, vis. lectr. 1988-89, chair edn. com. 1989, pres. 1992, 93), Internat. Congress for History of Sci. (U.S. del. 1977, 81, vice chair 1985) Orgn. Am. Historians (chair com. on status of women 1983-85, endowment fund drive, auction subcom. 1990-91). Lutheran. Home: 4140 Edmund Blvd Minneapolis MN 55406-3646

KOHL-WELLES, JEANNE ELIZABETH, state senator, sociologist, educator; b. Madison, Wis., Oct. 19, 1942; d. Lloyd Jr. and Elizabeth Anne (Sinness) K.; m. Kenneth D. Jenkins, Apr. 15, 1973; children: Randall Hill, Brennan Hill, Terra Jenkins, Kyle Jenkins, Devon Jenkins; m. Alexander Sumner Welles, Nov. 10, 1985. BA, Calif. State U., Northridge, 1965, MA, 1970; MA, UCLA, 1973, PhD, 1974. Tchr. L.A. Sch. Dist., 1965-70; lectr. Calif. State U., Long Beach, 1973-85; vis. asst. prof. U. Calif., Irvine, 1974-77; So. Calif. mgr. Project Equity/U.S. Dept. Edn., 1978-84; asst. dean, coord. women's programs U. Calif., Irvine, 1979-82; lectr. Calif. State U., Fullerton, 1982-85; lectr. U. Wash., Seattle, 1985—, chair senate higher edn. com., 1999—; asst. prof. Pacific Luth. U., Tacoma, Wash., 1986-88; state legislator from 36th dist. Wash. Ho. of Reps., Olympia, 1992-94, majority whip, 1993-94; mem. Wash. Senate, Olympia, 1994—; Wash. State Senate, 1998; chair Senate Higher Edn. COm., 1999—. Author: Growing Up Equal, 1979, Explorations in Social Research, 1993, Student Study Guide-Marriage and the Family, 1993, 94, 95, 97, 98; contbr. articles to profl. jours. Bd. dirs. Com. for Children, Seattle, 1986-91, Queen Anne Cmty. Coun., Seattle, 1988-93, Stop Youth Violence, Wash., 1993—, Queen Anne Helpline, Seattle, 1992—, Youth Care, 1996—; mem. Wash. State Sentencing Guidelines Commn., 1995—, Wash. State Child Care Coord. Com., 1995—; mem. Gov.'s Task Force on Higher Edn., 1995-96. Grantee U.S. Dept. Edn., 1988-89, 90-91. Home: 301 W Kinnear Pl Seattle WA 98119-3732 Office: Wash State Senate PO Box 40436 Olympia WA 98504-0436

KOHLWEY, HEATHER LOUISE, landscape architect, artist; b. Monroe, Wis., Aug. 12, 1968; d. Merlin Joseph Casey and Jenny Leah Elmer. BS in Landscape Architecture, U. Wis., 1993. Horticulture intern U. Wis., Platteville, 1988-89; landscape designer McKay Nursery Co., Waterloo, Wis., 1993; landscape architect Quality Cons. Svcs., Madison, Wis., 1995-96; pvt. practice landscape design Rio, Wis., 1997—; artist Rio, 1993—; libr. aide Rio (Wis.) Mid/H.S., 1998—. Commd. The Koch House, 1995. Project leader 4-H, Mt. Horeb, Wis., 1984-87. Mem. Am. Soc. Landscape Archs. Avocations: gardening, crocheting, bird watching. Home: W5130 Cowgill Rd Rio WI 53960-9305 Office: 411 Church St Rio WI 53960

KOHN, A. EUGENE, architect; b. Phila., Dec. 12, 1930; s. William Bernard and Hannah (Steinberg) K.; m. Diane Barnes; children: Brian, Steve, Laurie. BArch, U. Pa., 1953, MArch, 1957. Registered architect Ala., Calif., Colo., Conn., Del., D.C., Fla., Ga., Idaho, Ill., Kans., Ky., Md., Mass., Mich., N.J., N.Y., N.C., Ohio, Okla., Pa., Tenn., Tex., Va., Wis., Minn., U.K., Japan; lic. profl. planner, N.J. With Nolan Swinburne, 1957-60; project designer, project mgr. Nolan & Swinburne, Architects, Phila., 1958-60; project designer, studio designer head Vincent G. Kling Architects, Phila., 1960-64; designer Kahn & Jacobs Architects, N.Y.C., 1964-65; dir. design Welton, Becket & Assocs., N.Y.C., 1965-67; pres., prin. John Carl Warnecke & Assocs., N.Y.C., Los Angeles, San Francisco, 1967-76; founder, pres. Kohn Pedersen Fox Assocs. PC, Architects and Planners, N.Y.C., 1976—; mem. archtl. review panel N.Y. Port Authority; guest lectr. Bucknell U., U. Ky., UCLA, U. Pa., Miami U., Oxford, Ohio, Kent State U., U. Tenn., N.Y. Inst. Tech., Clemson U., Pa. State U., U. Fla., Washington U., St. Louis, U. Chgo., Ill. Inst. of Tech., U. Wis., Pratt U., Harvard U., Kuala Lumpur, Australia, New Zealand, Japan, Russia, Hong Kong; mem. com. on art gallery and Brit. art ctr. Yale U.; speaker in field; archtl. critic various univs. Former bd. dirs. Sheltering Arms Children Svc., Archtl. League, Chgo. City Ballet; chmn. bd. overseers U. Pa., also trustee, Columbia U. Grad. Sch. Arch. and Planning, also adv. bd. MS in Real Estate Devel.; trustee Silvermine Art Guild; mem. Wharton Real Estate Adv. Bd.; active United Way; bd. adv. Yale U. com. on the Art Gallery and Brit. Arts Ctr.; bd. trustees Mus. for African Art, N.Y.C. Lt. comdr. USN, 1953-56. Recipient Receiving the Flame of Truth award Fund for Higher Edn., 1987, GSA award; Theopolis Parsons Chandler fellow. Fellow AIA (pres. N.Y. chpt. 1987-88, honor design awards, 1962, 84, 87, internat. steering com.); mem. Royal Inst. Brit. Architects, Urban Land Inst. (trustee), N.Y. Bldg. Congress, N.Y. State Assn. Architects, Nat. Council of Archtl. Registration Bds., Mcpl. Arts Soc. N.Y., Phila. C. of C., Octagon Soc. of the AIA, City Club N.Y., Tau Sigma Delta. Club: University (N.Y.C.). Avocations: painting, music, tennis, golf, skiing. Home: 14 Sutton Pl New York NY 10022-3058 Office: Kohn Pedersen Fox Assocs PC 111 W 57th St New York NY 10019-2211*

KOHN, ALAN J., zoology educator; b. New Haven, Conn., July 15, 1931; s. Curtis and Harriet M. (Jacobs) K.; m. Marian S. Adachi, Aug. 29, 1959; children: Lizabeth, Nancy, Diane, Stephen. AB. in Biology, Princeton U., 1953; PhD in Zoology, Yale U., 1957. Asst. prof. zoology Fla. State U., Tallahassee, 1958-61; asst. prof. zoology U. Wash., Seattle, 1961-63, assoc. prof. zoology, 1963-67, prof., 1976-98, prof. emeritus, 1998—; Bd. dirs. Coun. Internat. Exchange Scholars, Wash., 1986-90. Author: A Chronological Taxonomy of Conus, 1758-1840, 1992, (with F.E. Perron) Life History and Biogeography: Patterns in Conus, 1994, (with D. Röckel and W. Korn) Manual of the Living Conidae, 1995, (with others) The Natural History of Enewetak Atoll, 1987; editor: (with F.W. Harrison) Microscopic Anatomy of Invertebrates, vol. 5, Mollusca I, 1994, vol. 6 II, 1997; mem. editl. bd. Am. Zoologist, 1973-77, Am. Naturalist, 1976-78, Malacologia, 1974—, Jour. Exptl. Marine Biology and Ecology, 1981-84, Coral Reefs, 1981-87, Am. Malacological Bull., 1983—; contbr. articles to profl. jours. Sr. postdoctoral fellow Smithsonian Inst., 1990, John Simon Guggenheim fellow, 1974-75, Nat. Rsch. Coun. fellow, 1967; numerous rsch. grants NSF, 1960-94. Fellow AAAS, Linnean Soc. London; mem. Internat. Soc. Reef Studies, Soc. for Integrative and Comparative Biology (treas. 1971-74, pres. 1997-98), Am. Soc. Limnology & Oceanography, Am. Soc. Naturalists, Ecol. Soc. Am., Am. Malacol. Union (pres. 1982-83), Soc. Systematic Zoology, Marine Biol. Assn. India, Brit. Ecol. Soc., Marine Biol. Assn. U.K., Malacol. Soc. London, Malacol. Soc. Japan, Australian Coral Reef Soc., Pacific Sci. Assn., Hawaiian Acad. Scis., Sigma Xi (pres. U. Wash. chpt. 1971-72). Home: 18300 Ridgefield Rd NW Shoreline WA 98177-3224 Office: U Wash Dept Zoology Seattle WA 98195-1800

KOHN, DAVID LUPO, legislative staff member; b. Chgo., Apr. 3, 1960; s. Arnold Lupo and Shirlee Rice Kohn; m. Julie Anne Partridge, Sept. 3, 1993; 1 child, Keith. BA, DePaul U., 1982; MA, Northwestern U., 19983. Prodr., engr. WEEF Radio, Highland Park, Ill., 1978-82; pub. affairs dir. WKRS Radio, Waukegan, Ill., 1983-85; press sec. U.S. Congressman John Porter, Deerfield, Ill., 1985—. Publicity chmn. Lake County Toys for Tots Campaign, USMC, Waukegan, 1988-90; dir. West Shore Pk. Corp., Mundelein, Ill., 1995—; bd. mem. Diamond Lake Sch. Dist. 76 Bd. Edn., Mundelein, 1998—; campaign mgr. Porter for Congress Com., Deerfield, 1995—. Republican. Jewish. Avocations: playing the drums and piano. E-mail: dkohn162@aol.com and David.Kohn@mail.house.gov. Fax: 847-940-7143. Home: W86 Circle Dr Mundelein IL 60060-3402 Office: Congressman John Porter Ste 200 102 Wilmot Rd Deerfield IL 60015

KOHN, HAROLD ELIAS, lawyer; b. Phila., Apr. 5, 1914; s. Joseph C. and Mayme (Rumm) K.; m. Edith Anderson, Dec. 30, 1946; children: Amy, Ellen, Joseph Carl. AB, U. Pa., 1934, LLB, 1937; LLD (hon.), Temple U., 1990. Bar: Pa. 1938, D.C. 1972. Pres. Kohn, Swift & Graf, P.C., Phila.; spl. counsel transit matters City of Phila., 1952-53, 56-62; counsel to gov. State of Pa., 1972; mem. bd. Southeastern Pa. Transp. Authority, 1972-77; mem. Pa. Jud. Inquiry and Rev. Bd., 1973-77; mem. Pa. Supreme Ct. Continuing Legal Edn. Bd., 1992-97; bd. consultors Villanova U. Law Sch. Trustee Temple U., U. of Arts; bd. dirs. Wilma Theatre, Moss Rehab. Hosp., Phila. Geriatric Ctr.; treas., bd. dirs. Kohn Found.; pres., bd. dirs. Arronson Found., Lavine Found.; past bd. dirs. Phila. Psychiat. Ctr.; trustee, mem. exec. com. Phila. Fedn. Jewish Agys.; past mem. exec. com. United Jewish Appeal; past v.p., bd. dirs. Phila. chpt. ACLU. Mem. ABA, Pa. Bar Assn., Phila. Bar Assn., D.C. Bar Assn., Internat. Acad. Trial Lawyers, Jud. Conf. 3d Cir., Am. Law Inst., Order of Coif, Phi Beta Kappa. Office: Kohn Swift & Graf PC 1101 Market St Ste 2400 Philadelphia PA 19107-2926

KOHN, JAMES PAUL, engineering educator; b. Dubuque, Iowa, Oct. 31, 1924; s. Harry Theodore and Kathryn (Piepel) K.; m. Mary Louise McGovern, Aug. 30, 1958; children: Kathleen, Kevin, Mary Louise. B.S. in Chem. Enging, U. Notre Dame, 1951; M.S., U. Mich., 1952; Ph.D., U. Kans., 1956. Chem. engr. Reilly Tar & Chem. Corp., Indpls., 1946-51; mem. faculty U. Notre Dame, 1955—, prof., 1964-95, prof. emeritus, 1995—; dir. Solar Lab. for Thermal Applications, 1973—; cons. Am. Oil Co., summer 1958, Imagineering Interprises, 1957-65, Hills-Morrow, 1966-70, Frito Lay Corp., 1982—, South Bend Energy Conservation Commn., 1983—, sec. 1986—. Served with U.S. Army, 1943-46. Decorated Bronze star, Purple Heart; recipient Faculty award U. Notre Dame, 1983, Outstanding Tchr. of Yr. award, 1987, Outstanding Faculty mem. minority engring. program, 1995, Spl. Presdl. award Notre Dame, 1995; Donald L. Katz award Gas Processors Assn., 1988. Fellow AIChE; mem. AAAS, Am. Chem. Soc., Sigma Xi. Republican. Roman Catholic. Patentee removal acidic gaseous components from natural gas. Home: 17684 Waxwing Ln South Bend IN 46635-1387 Office: U Notre Dame Dept Chem Enging Notre Dame IN 46656

KOHN, JEAN GATEWOOD, medical facility administrator, physician, retired; b. Chgo., July 8, 1926; d. Gatewood and Esther Lydia (Harper) Gatewood; m. Martin M. Kohn, Feb. 10, 1951; children: Helen, Joel, Michael, David. BS, U. Chgo., 1948, MD, 1950; MPH, U. Calif., Berkeley, 1973. Diplomate Am. Bd. Pediatrics. Physician Permanente Med. Group, San Leandro, Calif., 1953-60; pediatric cons. Calif. Children Svcs., 1961-72; lectr. maternal and child health U. Calif., 1973-91; med. advisor rehab. engring. ctr. Packard Children's Hosp. at Stanford, Calif., 1976-97, med. dir. child prosthetic clinic, 1977-97, ret., 1997; asst. neurologic diagnostic ctr. U. Calif., San Francisco, 1960-72; pediatric cons. Project HOPE, Nicaragua, 1966, Peru, 1962; pediatric cons. sch. pub. health U. Hawaii, Okinawa, 1975. Contbr. chpts. to books and articles to profl. jours. Mem. adv. panel State of Calif. Dept. Spl. Edn., Calif. Children Svcs.; bd. dirs. Mental Health Assn., United Cerebral Palsy Assn., Head Start, San Mateo County, 1993—. Recipient Lyda M. Smiley award Calif. Sch. Nurses Orgn., 1987. Fellow Am. Acad. Pediats., Am. Acad. Cerebral Palsy and Devel. Medicine; mem. Project HOPE Alumni Assn. (pres. 1988-92).

KOHN, JOSEPH JOHN, mathematician, educator; b. Prague, Czechoslovakia, May 18, 1932; came to U.S., 1945, naturalized, 1953; s. Otto and Emilie (Schwarz) K.; m. Anna DiCapua, Dec. 15, 1966; children: Edward, Emma, Alicia. S.B., Mass. Inst. Tech., 1953; M.A., Princeton, 1954, Ph.D., 1956; hon. degree, U. Bologna, 1990. Instr. Princeton U., 1956-57; mem. Inst. Advanced Study, 1957-58, 62-63, 76-77, 80-81, 88-89; mem. faculty Brandeis U., 1958-68, prof. math., 1965-68, chmn. dept., 1964-68; prof. math. Princeton, 1968—, chmn. dept., 1973-76, 93-96; vis. prof. U. Florence, Italy, 1972-73, Harvard U., 1996-97; mem. U.S. pure and applied math. del. to People's Republic of China, 1976; chmn. com. math. NRC, mem. Bd. Math. Scis. Editor: Annals of Mathematics, 1977-88, University Series in Mathematics; contbr. articles to profl. jours. Bd. dirs. Am., Czech and Slovak Edn. Fund. Recipient L.P. Steele prize, 1979, Bolzano medal Czechoslovak Union Mathematicians and Physicists, 1990, first degree medal Union of Czech Mathematicians and Physicists, 1993; named NSF fellow, 1954, Sloan fellow, 1964, Guggenheim fellow, 1976-77. Mem. NAS, Am. Acad. Arts and Scis., Am. Math. Soc. (trustee 1976-81), Czechoslovak Soc. Arts and Scis. (v.p. 1992-94). Home: 32 Sturges Way Princeton NJ 08540-5335

KOHN, JULIEANNE, travel agent; b. Detroit, Apr. 15, 1946; d. Ralph Merwin and Jane Tacke (Meyers) K.; BA, Heidelberg Coll., Tiffin, Ohio, 1968; postgrad. Eastern Mich. U., 1969-70; diploma Inst. Cert. Travel Agts., 1979. Travel agt. Am. Express Co., Detroit, 1970-73, Thomas Cook Inc., Detroit, 1973-75; mgr. Island Traveller, Grosse Ile, Mich., 1975-76; pres., owner Flying Suitcase, Inc., Grosse Ile, 1976—; owner Tri-Kohn Investments, Grosse Ile, Mich., 1983—; ptnr. Gifts of the World, Gross Ile, Mich., 1993—. Mem. Trenton Soroptomists Club, Am. Soc. Travel Agts., Inst. Cert. Travel Agts. (life). Episcopalian. Club: Grosse Ile Golf and Country, Grosse Ile Exchange Club. Home: 8063 Colony Dr Apt 23 Grosse Ile MI 48138

KOHN, KAREN JOSEPHINE, graphic and exhibition designer; b. Muskegon, Mich., Jan. 8, 1951; d. Herbert George and Catherine Elizabeth (Johnson) K.; m. Robert Joseph Duffy Jr., July 10, 1982; children: Megan Kathleen, Sarah Evelyn. BFA cum laude, U. Mich., 1973; MFA, Sch. Art Inst., Chgo., 1975. Free-lance designer Chgo., 1976-77; designer Stevens Exhibits, Chgo., 1977-78; artist-in-residence Chgo. Coun. Fine Arts, 1978-79; designer Chgo. Hist. Soc., 1979-81, dir. design, 1981-84; prin. Karen Kohn & Assocs. Ltd., Chgo., 1985—. Work appeared in Mus. News, Kraft Gen. Foods hdqrs. Recipient Superior Achievement award for temporary exhbn. Congress of Ill. Hist. Socs. and Mus., 1985, Superior Achievement award for permanent exhbn., 1989, Cert. Excellence Strathmore Graphics Gallery, 1990, award of Merit Ill. Assn. Bus. Comm., 1993, Motorola Pinnacle award, 1994. Mem. Am. Assn. Mus. (Distinctive Merit awards 1982-84, 92), Am. Ctr. Design, Chgo. Women in Pub. (1st prize Individual Excellence in Design 1995, 97, 1st prize in sci. and tech. publs. 1995, 1st prize Self Pub. Books 1996, 98, 1st prize Juveniile Non-fiction 1998, 1st prize Brochures 1998, 2d prize Brochures Acad. Jours. 1999).

KOHN, LIVIA, educator; b. Hoiheim, Germany, Mar. 14, 1956; came to U.S., 1986; d. Adalbert and Eva-Maria Knaul; m. Detlei Kohn, Sept. 2, 1986 (Jan. 1999). PhD, Bonn U., Germany, 1980; Dr.habil, Goettingen U., Germany, 1990. Asst. prof. Boston U., 1988-92, assoc. prof., 1992—; bd. dirs. Chinesiche Medizin, Meunchen, Germany, Japan Taoist Soc., Tokyo, Kyoto Ctr Japanese Studies, Stanford, Calif. Author: Seven Steps to the Tao: Sima Chengzhhen's Zuowanglun, 1987, Taoist Meditation and Longevity Techniques, 1989, Taoist Mystical Philosophy: The Scripture of Western Ascension, 1991, Early Chinese Mysticism: Philosophy and Soetriology in the Taoist Tradition, 1992, The Taoist Experience: An Anthology, 1993, Laughing at the Tao: Debates Among Buddhists and Taoists in Medieval China, 1995; editor: Lao-tzu and the Tao-te-ching, 1998. Mem. Royal Scottish Country Dance Soc. Office: Boston U Dept Religion 745 Commonwealth Ave Boston MA 02215

KOHN, RICHARD H., historian, educator; b. Chgo., Dec. 29, 1940; s. Henry L. and Kate K.; m. Lynne Holtan, Aug. 15, 1964; children: Abigail, Samuel. A.B., Harvard U., 1962; M.S. in History, U. Wis., 1964, Ph.D. in history, 1968. Asst. prof. history CCNY, 1968-71; from asst. prof. to prof. Rutgers U., New Brunswick, N.J., 1971-84; Harold Keith Johnson vis. prof. mil. history U.S. Army Mil. History Inst., Army War Coll., Carlisle Barracks, Pa., 1980-81; chief Office Air Force History, USAF, Washington, 1981-91; adj. prof. Nat. War Coll., Washington, 1985-90; from assoc. prof. to prof. history U. N.C., Chapel Hill, 1991—, chair, curriculum in peace, war and defense, 1992—; expert witness U.S. Indian Claims Commn., Washington, 1974; cons. to various def. and hist. agys. and orgns., 1972—; vis. scholar strategic studies Johns Hopkins U. Sch. Advanced Internat. Studies, 1991; exec. sec. Triangle Inst. for Security Studies, 1992—; bd. visitors Air Univ. USAF, 1996—. Author: Eagle and Sword: The Federalists and the Creation of the Military Establishment in America, 1783-1802, 1975; coauthor: The Exclusion of Black Soldiers from the Medal of Honor in World War II, 1997; editor (reprint series) The American Military Experience, 1979; editor: The U.S. Military under the Constitution of the United States, 1789-1989, 1991; co-editor: (books) Air Superiority in World War II and Korea, 1983, Air Interdiction in World War II, Korea, and Vietnam, 1986, Strategic Air Warfare, 1988; contbr. articles to profl. jours., chpts. to books. Recipient cert. for patriotic civilian service Dept. of Army, 1981, 96, Organizational Excellence award Dept. Air Force, 1990, Exceptional Civilian Svc. award Dept. Air Force, 1991. Fellow Inter-Univ. Seminar on Armed Forces and Soc. (exec. coun. 1977-87); mem. Air Force Hist. Found. (Pres.' award 1987), Am. Antiquarian Soc., Am. Hist. Assn. (coun. 1986-89), Orgn. Am. Historians (Binkley-Stephenson award 1973, pub. history com. 1989-92, chair 1991-92), Soc. for Mil. History (trustee 1981-89, 95-99, parliamentarian 1982-89, pres. 1989-93), World War II Studies Assn. (bd. dirs. 1985-88, 91-94). Office: U NC Curriculum Peace War Defense CB # 3200 Chapel Hill NC 27599-3200

KOHN, RITA, author, playwright, journalist, educator; b. South Fallsburg, N.Y., Oct. 10, 1933; d. William and Molly Tevelowitz; m. Walter S.G. Kohn, June 19, 1955; children: Sharon Ruth, Martin Steven, Thomas David. BS summa cum laude, Buffalo State Coll., 1955; MS, Ill. State U., Normal, 1968. Cert. tchr., N.Y. Tchr. Tonawanda (N.Y.) Jr. H.S., 1955-56, Metcalf Lab. Sch., Normal, 1963-68, 78-79; from instr. to asst. prof. Ill. State U., Normal, 1969-73, 87-88, dir. mktg., CEPS, 1980-83; dir. continuing edn. Butler U., Indpls., 1983-84; adj. prof. journalism Ind. U., Indpls., 1984—; coord. Always A People Project, Ind. Humanities Coun., NEH, Indpls., 1988-91, 93; editor Ohio River Valley Books, Univ. Press. of Ky., Lexington, 1991—; columnist, feature writer NUVO News Weekly, Indpls., 1997—; cons. Indpls. Children's Mus., 1988-93, Corn Belt Libr. Sys., Normal, 1974-79; cons. to Office of Devel., Ill. Wesleyan U., Bloomington, 1967-74. Author: (picture book) Spring Planting, 1995; playwright: Necessities, 1984, numerous other publs. Precinct committeeman, asst. committeeman Dem. Party, Normal, 1960s-80s; vol. Ind. Repertory Theatre, Phoenix Theatre, Civic Theatre, Indpls., 1983—; bd. dirs., vol. Indpls. Hebrew Congregation, 1983—. Recipient Spirit of Philanthropy award Ind. U.-Purdue U., 1996, Mitzvah award Indpls. Hebrew Congregation, 1996, others; Land Salzburg rsch. grantee, 1982. Mem. Authors Guild, Dramatists Guild, The Drama League, Soc. Profl. Journalists, Soc. Childrens Book Writers and Illustrators, Hoosier Folklore Soc., Ind. Theatre Assn. Avocations: reading, gardening, travel, volunteering.

KOHN, ROBERT SAMUEL, JR., real estate investment consultant; b. Denver, Jan. 7, 1949; s. Robert Samuel and Miriam Lackner (Neusteter) K.; m. Eleanor B. Kohn; children: Joseph Robert, Randall Stanton, Andrea Rene. BS, U. Ariz., 1971. Asst. buyer Robinson's Dept. Store, L.A., 1971; agt. Neusteter Realty Co., Denver, 1972-73, exec. v.p., 1973-76; pres. Project Devel. Svcs., Denver, 1976-78, pres., CEO, 1978-83; pres. Kohn and Assocs., Inc., 1979-83; pres. The Burke Co., Inc., Irvine, Calif., 1983-84, ptnr., 1984-91; sr. mktg. assoc. Iliff, Phoenix, 1992-94; owner RSKJ, Inc., 1992-97. Mem. Bldg. Owners and Mgrs. Assn. (pres. 1977-78, dir. 1972-78, dir. S.W. Conf. Bd. 1977-78), Denver Art Mus., Denver U. Libr. Assn., Central City Opera House Assn., Inst. Real Estate Mgmt., Newport Beach Tennis Club. Republican. Jewish.

KOHN, ROGER ALAN, surgeon; b. Chgo., May 1, 1946; s. Arthur Jerome and Sylvia Lee (Karlen) K.; m. Barbara Helene, Mar. 30, 1974; children: Bradley, Allison. BA, U. Ill., 1967; MD, Northwestern U., 1971. Diplomate Am. Bd. Ophthalmology. Internship UCLA, 1971-72; residency Northwestern U., Chgo., 1972-75; fellowship U. Ala., Birmingham, 1975, Harvard Med. Sch., Boston, 1975-76; chmn. dept. ophthalmology Kern Med. Ctr., Bakersfield, Calif., 1978-87; asst. prof. UCLA Med. Sch., 1978-82, assoc. prof., 1982-86, prof., 1986—. Author: Textbook of Ophthalmic Plastic and Reconstructive Surgery, 1988; contbr. numerous articles to profl. jours.; author chpts. in 16 additional textbooks; patentee in field. Bd. dirs. Santa Barbara (Calif.) Symphony, 1990—. Capt. USAR, 1971-77. Name applied to med. syndrome Kohn-Romano Syndrome. Mem. Am. Soc. Ophthalmic Plastic and Reconstructive Surgery (cert.), Santa Barbara Ophthalmologic Soc. (pres. 1998), Pacific Coast Ophthal. Soc. (bd. dirs. 1986—, 1st v.p. 1990), Santa Barbara Ophthalmologic Soc. (pres. 1998). Jewish. Avocations: guitar, tennis. Office: 525 E Micheltorena St Ste 201 Santa Barbara CA 93103-4212

KOHN, SHALOM L., lawyer; b. N.Y.C., Nov. 18, 1949; s. Pincus and Helen (Roth) K.; m. Barbara Segal, June 30, 1974; children: David, Jeremy, Daniel. B.S. in Acctg. summa cum laude, CUNY, 1970; J.D. magna cum laude, Harvard U., 1974, M.B.A., 1974. Bar: Ill. 1975, U.S. Dist. Ct. (no. dist.) Ill. 1975, U.S. Ct. Appeals (7th cir.) 1976, U.S. Supreme Ct. 1980, N.Y. 1988, U.S. Dist. Ct. (so. dist.) N.Y. 1988. Law clk. to chief judge U.S. Ct. Appeals (2d cir.), N.Y.C., 1974-75; assoc. Sidley & Austin, Chgo., 1975-80, ptnr., 1980—. Contbr. articles to profl. jours. Mem. exec. com. Adv. Coun. Religious Rights in Eastern Europe and Soviet Union, Washington, 1984-86; bd. dirs. Brisk Rabbinical Coll., Chgo., 1980—. Mem. ABA, Chgo. Bar Assn. Office: Sidley & Austin 1 First Natl Plz Chicago IL 60603-2003 also: 875 3rd Ave New York NY 10022-6225

KOHN, WALTER, educator, physicist; b. Vienna, Austria, Mar. 9, 1923; m. Mara Schiff; children: J. Marilyn , Ingrid E. Kohn Katz, E. Rosalind. BA, U. Toronto, Ont., Can., 1945, MA, 1946, LLD (hon.), 1967; PhD in Physics, Harvard U., 1948; DSc (hon.), U. Paris, 1980; PhD (hon.), Brandeis U., 1981, Hebrew U. Jerusalem, 1981; DSc (hon.), Queens U., Kingston, Can., 1986, Fed. Inst. of Tech., Zurich, 1994, U. Wuerzburg, 1995, Tech. U. Vienna, 1996; PhD (hon.), Weizmann Inst., Israel, 1997. Indsl. physicist Sutton Horsley Co., Can., 1941-43; geophysicist Koulomzine, Que., Can., 1944-46; instr. physics Harvard U., Cambridge, Mass., 1948-50; asst. prof. physics Carnegie Mellon U., Pitts., 1950-60, assoc. prof. physics, 1953-57; prof. physics U. Calif., San Diego, 1960-79, chmn. dept. physics, 1961-63; dir. Inst. for Theoretical Physics, U. Calif., Santa Barbara, 1979-84; prof. dept. physics U. Calif., Santa Barbara, 1984-91, prof. of physics emeritus, rsch. prof. of physics, 1991—; rsch. physicist Ctr. for Quantized Electronic Structures, U. Calif., Santa Barbara, 1991—; vis. scholar U. Pa., U. Mich., U. Wash., U. Paris, U. Copenhagen, U. Jerusalem, Imperial Coll., London, ETH, Zurich, Switzerland; cons. Gen. Atomic, 1960-72, Westinghouse Rsch. Lab., 1953-57, Bell Telephone Labs., 1953-66, IBM, 1978; mem. or chmn. rev. coms. Brookhaven Nat. Labs., Argonne Nat. Labs., Oak Ridge Nat. Labs., Ames Lab., Tel Aviv U. (physics dept.), Brown U., Harvard U., U. Mich., Simon Frazer U., Tulane U., Reactor Divsn. NIST, Gaithersburg, Md.; chmn. S.D. divsn. Acad. Senate, 1968-69; dir. NSF Inst. Theoretical Physics, U. Calif. Santa Barbara, 1979-84; mem. senate rev. com. U. Calif. Management Nat. Labs., 1986-89; adv. bd. Statewide Inst. Global Conflict and Cooperation, 1982-92; mem. bd. govs. Weizmann Inst. of Sci., 1997—. Contbr. over 200 sci. articles and revs. to profl. jours. With inf., Can. Army, 1944-45. Recipient Buckley prize, 1960, Davisson-Germer prize, 1977, Nat. Medal of Sci., 1988, Feenberg medal, 1991, Niels Bohr/UNESCO Gold Medal, 1998, Nobel prize in chemistry, 1998; Lehman fellow Harvard U., 1946-46, fellow Nat. Rsch. Coun., 1950-51, sr. fellow NSF, 1958, Guggenheim fellow, 1963, sr. postdoctoral fellow NSF, 1967. Fellow AAAS, Am. Phys. Soc. (counselor-at-large 1968-72), Am. Acad. Arts and Scis.; mem. NAS, Internat. Acad. Quantum Molecular Scis., Am. Philos. Soc. Achievements include research on electron theory of solids and solid surfaces. Office: U Calif Dept Physics Santa Barbara CA 93106

KOHN, WILLIAM IRWIN, lawyer; b. Bronx, N.Y., June 27, 1951; s. Arthur Oscar and Frances (Hoffman) K.; m. Karen Mindlin, Aug. 29, 1974; children: Shira, Kinneret, Asher. Student, U. Del., 1969-71; BA with honors, U. Cin., 1973; JD, Ohio State U., 1976. Bar: Ohio 1976, U.S. Dist. Ct. (no. dist.) Ohio 1982, Ind. 1982, U. S. Dist. Ct. (no. and so. dists.) Ind. 1982, D.C. 1992, U.S. Supreme Ct., 1992, Ill. 1994; cert. Bus. Bankruptcy Law Am. Bankruptcy Bd. Cert. Ptnr. Krugliak, Wilkins, Griffith & Dougherty, Canton, Ohio, 1976-82, Barnes & Thornburg, Chgo., 1982—; adj. prof. law U. Notre Dame, Ind., 1984-90. Author: West's Indiana Business Forms, West's Indiana Uniform Commercial Code Forms; contbr. articles to profl. jours. Bd. dirs. Family Svcs., South Bend, 1985-94, Jewish Fedn., Highland Park United Way. Mem. ABA (bus. bankruptcy subcom.), Am. Bankruptcy Inst. (insolvency sect., bd. dirs.), Ill. Bar Assn., Chgo. Bar Assn., Comml. Law League. Office: Barnes & Thornburg 2610 Madison Plz 200 W Madison St Chicago IL 60606-3414*

KOHNE, RICHARD EDWARD, retired engineering executive; b. Tientsin, China, May 16, 1924; s. Ernest E. and Elizabeth I. (Antonenko) K.; m. Gabrielle H. Vernaudon; children: Robert, Phillip, Daniel, Paul, Renee. B.S., U. Calif., Berkeley, 1948. Structural engr. hydro projects Pacific Gas & Electric Co., San Francisco, 1948-55; cons. engr. Morrison-Knudsen Engrs., Inc., San Francisco, 1955—, regional mgr. for Latin Am., then v.p., 1965-71, exec. v.p. world-wide ops. in engring. and project mgmt., 1971-79, pres., chmn., chief exec. officer, 1979-88; chmn., chief exec. officer Morrison-Knudsen Internat. Co., Inc., San Francisco, 1988-90, chmn. emeritus, 1990—. Decorated Chevalier Nat. Order of Leopold (Zaire). Mem. ASCE, U.S. Com. Large Dams, Cons. Engrs. Assn. Calif., World Trade Club (San Francisco). Democrat. Roman Catholic. Home and Office: 1827 Doris Dr Menlo Park CA 94025-6101

KOHNSTAMM, ABBY E., marketing executive; married; 2 children. BA, Tufts U.; MA in Edn., NYU, MBA. V.p. corp. mktg. Internat. Bus. Machines Corp., Armonk, N.Y.; bd. dirs. Overseers Arts & Sci. Tufts U., IBM Credit Corp. Mem. Assn. Nat. Advertisers. Avocations: family acitivies, music, theater. Office: Internat Bus Machines Corp New Orchard Rd Armonk NY 10504-1722*

KOHR, ROLAND ELLSWORTH, retired hospital administrator; b. Middletown, Ohio, Dec. 22, 1931; s. Roland Meredith and Mildred (Brandeberry) K.; m. Hilda Scherz, Sept. 6, 1952; children: Linda Kohr Harper, Roland Meredith, Jeffrey Stuart. BS, U. Cin., 1954; MS in Health Adminstrn., Northwestern U., 1959. Resident and adminstrv. asst. Bethesda Hosp., Cin., 1958-60; adminstr. William S. Major Hosp., Shelbyville, Ind., 1961-66; pres. Bloomington (Ind.) Hosp., 1966-95; past chmn. bd. dirs. So. Ind. Med. Group, Inc., Bloomington Convalescent Ctr., Inc.; asst. prof., vis. lectr. Sch. Pub. and Environ. Affairs, Ind. U.; bd. dirs. Children's Organ Transplant Assn., Evergreen Inst., VHA-Tri-State Inc., Indpls. Contbr. hosp. adminstrn. articles to profl. jours.; mem. editl. bd. Trustee mag. Past pres. United Way of Bloomington and Monroe County; bd. dirs. Cmty. Found. of Bloomington and Monroe County, Inc. Named for disting. svc. Shelbyville C. of C., 1966, Ind. Hosp. Assn., 1987, Sagamore of the Wabash, Gov. of State of Ind.; Paul Harris fellow Rotary Internat.; hon. Ky. col. Fellow Am. Coll. Healthcare Execs.; mem. Bloomington and Monroe County C. of C. (bd. dirs.), Rotary (Bloomington chpt. pres. 1987-88, bd. dirs. Bloomington Rotary Found. 1988—), Ind. Hosp. Assn. (past chmn. bd. dirs.), Masons, Am. Hosp. Assn. (coun. on governance). Avocations: photography, scuba. Home: 2989 N Bankers Dr Bloomington IN 47408-1021 Office: Bloomington Hosp PO Box 1149 625 W 2nd St Bloomington IN 47403-2317

KOHRING, DAGMAR LUZIA, fundraiser, consultant; b. Lage, Germany, Mar. 8, 1951; came to U.S., 1966; d. Wilfried and Luzia W. (Knichel) K.; m. Arthur Gingrande Jr., Dec. 29, 1976 (div. June 1982). BA, Am. U., 1972, MA, 1974. Cert. fundraising exec. Asst. dir. devel. Harvard Art Mus., Cambridge, 1981-83; campaign officer Harvard U., Cambridge, 1983-85; sr. cons., campaign dir. C.H. Benz Assocs., Westfield, N.J., 1985-88; v.p., sen. cons. Brakeley, John Price Jones, Inc., Stamford, Conn., 1988-93; pres., CEO, Internat. Fundraising & Mgmt. Cons., Inc., Boston and Bonn, 1993-97; ind. counsel in philanthropy, 1998—. Nat. Endowment for Arts fellow, 1983. Mem. Nat. Soc. Fundraising Execs., Harvard Club, Women in Devel. of Greater Boston. Home and Office: 36 Hancock St Boston MA 02114-4117

KOHRING, VICTOR H., state legislator, construction executive; b. Waukegan, Ill., Aug. 2, 1958; s. Heinz H. and Dolores E. Kohring. *Kohring moved to Alaska with his family in 1963 from the Chicago area at the age of four. Driving the Alaska-Canada Highway, three thousand miles later they* *settled in the community of Chugiak. Nine months thereafter, the Kohring family survived the 1964 Great Alaska Earthquake, the strongest quake ever recorded in North American history. Rep. Kohring was actively involved in athletics in his youth. While at Anthony J. Dimond High School in Anchorage, he won two Most Valuable Player Awards in basketball, was selected to the All-Anchorage All-Star Basketball Team and lead his team to the Alaska High School State Basketball Championship in 1976.* AAS in Bus. Adminstrn., Matanuska-Susitna C.C., Palmer, Alaska, 1985; BA in Mgmt. Sci., Alaska Pacific U., 1987, MBA, 1989. State legislator Ho. of Reps., Dist. 26 Wasilla and Peters Creek/Chugiak, 1994, re-elected 1996, 98—; mem. ho. fin. com. Ho. of Reps., 1994, 96, 98—; chmn. house budge subcoms. for dept. edn., 1995-96, adminstrn., 1995-96, environ. conservation, 1997-98, cmty. and regional affairs, 1997-98, commerce and econ. devel., 1997-98, law, 1999—, natural resources, 1999—; constn. exec., 1978—; real estate developer, 1978-82; owner South Ctrl. Bldg. Maintenance. *Rep. Kohring, BA 1987, MBA 1989, Alaska Pacific University, is currently a third-term state legislator and represents Wasilla and Chugiak in the Alaska State Legislature. He is a member of the House of Finance Committee, and is Chairman of the Departments of Law and Natural Resources Budget Committees. Rep. Kohring was appointed by Governor Walter J. Hickel to the Alaska Housing finance Corporation Board of Directors in 1991 and 1993, where he served as vice-chairman. Rep. Kohring is a regular guest columnist in newspapers throughout Alaska, and is currently in the process of publishing a book containing a five-year accumulation of writings.* Bd. dirs. Alaska Housing Fin. Corp., Anchorage, 1991-94; vice chmn., mem. Iditarod Trail Com.; mem. Matanuska-Susitna Borough Econ. Devel. Commn., 1993-94; with Wasilla Planning and Utilities Commn., 1991-94; chmn., mem. Alaska del. Rep. Nat. Conv., Dallas, 1984, dist. del. rep., 1984, 86, 90, 92; treas. Rep. Party Alaska, Mat-Su, 1990, fin. chmn., 1990-91. Mem. NRA (life), Nat. Fedn. Ind. Bus., Christian Businessman's Assn., Greater Wasilla C. of C., Chugiak-Eagle River C. of C., Anthony J. Dimond H.S. Alumni Assn., Pioneers of Alaska. Republican. Home: PO Box 870515 Wasilla AK 99687-0515 Office: Alaska Ho of Reps State Capitol Bldg Juneau AK 99801

KOHRMAN, ARTHUR FISHER, pediatrics educator; b. Cleve., Dec. 19, 1934; s. Benjamin Myron and Leah (Fisher) K.; m. Claire Hoffenberg, Nov. 10, 1955; children: Deborah, Benjamin, Ellen, Rachel. BA, BS, U. Chgo., 1955; MD, Western Res. U., 1959. Diplomate Am. Bd. Pediatrics. Lic. Ill., Mich., Ind. Intern Cleve. Met. Gen. Hosp., 1959-60; resident in pediatrics Western Res. U., Cleve., 1960-62; post doctoral fellow Stanford U., Palo Alto, Calif., 1965-68; asst. prof. to prof. Mich. State U., East Lansing, 1968-81, assoc. chmn. dept. human devel., 1968-78, assoc. dean Coll. Human Medicine, 1977-81; prof., assoc. chmn. dept. pediatrics U. Chgo., 1981-96; pres. La Rabida Children's Hosp. and Research Ctr., Chgo., 1981-96; prof. pediatrics, assoc. chmn. Northwestern U. Sch. Medicine and Children's Meml. Hosp., Chgo., 1997—; Congl. fellow Office Tech. Assessment, U.S. Congress, 1980-81; pres. Children's Hospice Internat., 1983-86; chmn. instl. rev. bd. U. Chgo., 1986-96. Contbr. numerous scholarly articles to profl. jours. Served to capt. USAF, 1962-65. Recipient Outstanding Service award Am. Diabetes Assn. Mich. chpt., 1977. Fellow Am. Acad. Pediatrics (chmn. com. on bioethics 1990-94); mem. Am. Pediatric Soc., Ambulatory Pediatric Assn., Soc. Pediatric Rsch., Lawson Wilkins Pediatric Endocrine Soc., Alpha Omega Alpha. Office: Childrens Meml Hosp 2300 N Childrens Plz Chicago IL 60614-3394

KOHRT, CARL FREDRICK, manufacturing executive, scientist; b. Normal, Ill., Dec. 18, 1943; s. Carl Fred and Catherine Elizabeth (Traughber) K.; m. Margaret Lynne McCartney; children: Kristopher Alan, Brian Douglas, Jason Ivor. BS, Furman U., 1965; PhD, U. Chgo., 1971; MS, MIT, 1991. Postdoctoral fellow James Frank Inst., U. Chgo., 1970-71; sr. scientist rsch. labs. Eastman Kodak, Rochester, N.Y., 1971-76, rsch. lab. head, 1977-79, asst. div. dir. rsch. labs., 1979-84, asst. to vice chmn. Kodak office, 1984-85, div. dir. electronic rsch. labs., 1985-87, dir. rsch. photographic rsch. labs., 1987-90; Kodak's mem. of Sloan fellow program MIT, Cambridge, 1990-91, gen. mgr. health scis. divsn., 1991-95; exec. v.p., asst. COO, 1995-98, exec. v.p., asst. COO, chief tech. office, 1998—; bd. dirs. Patient Info. Sys., Inc. Contbr. articles to profl. jours.; patentee in field. Chmn. sustaining membership Boy Scouts Am., Rochester, 1988, scoutmaster, Pittsford, N.Y., 1976-88, mem. exec. bd. Otetiana coun., 1997—; chair Community Needs Study, Greece, N.Y., 1973. Woodrow Wilson fellow (hon.), 1965; NSF Grad. fellow, 1965-70. Mem. Indsl. Rsch. Inst. (alt. rep.). Presbyterian. Avocations: backpacking, whitewater canoeing, music. Office: Eastman Kodak Co Kodak House I 321 Java Rd North Point NY 14650-0001

KOHUT, ROBERT IRWIN, otolaryngologist, educator; b. Chgo., Nov. 29, 1932; s. Emil and Ruth Irene Kohut; m. Joanne Kay Hughes, Dec. 26, 1953 (dec. Oct. 1982); children: James, Paul, Robert, John; m. Frances Irene Speas, June 6, 1983. BA, Wittenburg Coll., 1956; MD, U. Chgo., 1960. Diplomate Am. Bd. Otolaryngology (bd. dirs. 1979). Intern U. Chgo., 1961-62, resident in otolaryngology, 1962-65, NIH fellow, 1965-66, instr. in otolaryngology, 1965-66; assoc. prof. U. Fla., Gainesville, 1966-68, 1968-71, assoc. prof., acting chmn., 1971-72; prof., chief otolaryngology U. Calif., Irvine, 1972-79; prof., chmn. otolaryngology Wake Forest U. Sch. Medicine, Winston-Salem, 1979-98, prof. emeritus, 1998—; mem. study sect. Nat. Insts. Neurol. and Communicative Disorders and Stroke/NIH, Bethesda, Md., 1981-86; cons. NASA, 1982-84; mem. adv. bd. nat. Inst. Deafness and Other Comm. Disorders, 1991-94. Contbr. numerous chpts. to books and articles to profl. jours.; editor otology divsn. Head and Neck Surgery-Otolaryngology; mem. editorial bd. Am. Jour. Otology, 1992—, Am. Jour. Otolaryngology, 1982—, Archives of Otolaryngology, 1980—, Laryngoscope, 1976—. With USAF, 1950-53. Recipient Norvel Pierce award Chgo. Laryngological Soc., 1965, Basic Rsch. award Acad. Ophthalmology and Otolaryngology, 1968. Mem. ACS, Soc. Univ. Otolaryngologists (pres. 1978-79), Barany Soc., Am. Laryngological, Rhinological and Otological Soc. (exec. coun. 1987-90, Edmund Fowler award 1974, Guest of Honor, So. sect. 1996), Am. Broncho-Esophagological Ass., Am. Neurotology Assn., Otosclerosis Study Group, Am. Otological Soc. (sec.-treas. 1987-92, pres.-elect 1992-93, pres. 1993-94), Assn. Acad. Depts. Otolaryngology, Pacific Coast Oto-Ophthalmol. Soc., Forsyth County Med. Soc., N.C. Med. Soc., N.C. Soc. Otolaryngology Head and Neck Surgery (v.p. 1985, pres. 1986-87), Assn. for Rsch. in Otolaryngology, Am. Acad. Otolaryngology-Head and Neck Surgery, Am. Soc. Head and Neck Surgery, Internat. Fedn. Oto-Rhino-Laryngological Soc. (chmn. standing com. edn.), others. Avocations: fishing, hunting, sailing. Office: Wake Forest U Sch Medicine Dept Otolaryngology Medical Center Blvd Winston Salem NC 27157-1034

KOIDE, FRANK TAKAYUKI, electrical engineering educator; b. Honolulu, Dec. 25, 1935; s. Sukeichi and Hideko (Dai) K.; children: Julie Anne M., Cheryl Lynne K. BSEE, U. Ill., 1958; MEE, Clarkson U., Potsdam, N.Y., 1961; PhD (NIH predoctoral fellow), U. Iowa, 1966. Publs. engr. to electronics engr. Collins Radio Co., Cedar Rapids, Iowa, 1958-61; tchr. Cedar Rapids Adult Edn. Sch., 1960-61; lab. instr. U. Iowa Coll. Medicine, 1963-64; asst. prof. Iowa State U., 1966-69; prin. biomed. engr. Tech., Inc., San Antonio, 1968-69; mem. faculty U. Hawaii, 1969—, prof. elec. engring. and physiology, 1974—; cons. in field. Author papers, reports in field. NASA-Am. Soc. Engring. Edn. Space systems Design Inst. fellow, 1967; NSF Digital and Analogue Electronics Inst. fellow U. Ill., 1972. Mem. IEEE. Office: U Hawaii Dept Electrical Engring 2540 Dole St Honolulu HI 96822-2303

KOIVO, ANTTI JAAKKO, electrical engineering educator, researcher; b. Ilmajoki, Finland, Apr. 9, 1932; s. Niilo J. and Elma S. (Lahti) Koivuniemi; m. Anne Pihlak, Apr. 19, 1969 (div.); children: Lilli S., Allan. Diploma engring., Finland Inst. Tech., 1956; PhD in Elec. Engring., Cornell U., 1963. From asst. to full prof. Purdue U., Lafayette, Ind., 1965—; vis. rschr. Finnish Acad. Sci., AIST, Ministry Internat. Trade and Industry of Japan, Armstrong Lab. of Wright-Patterson AFB, Wright Lab. of Tyndall AFB, U. Hannover, Germany. Contbr. articles on to profl. jours.; numerous conf. presentations. Office: Purdue U Dept Elec/Computer Engring West Lafayette IN 47907

KOJAC, JEFFREY STANLEY, military officer; b. L.A., Nov. 30, 1967. BA, St. John's Coll., Annapolis, Md., 1989; cert., Amphibious Warfare Sch., 1992, Marine Aviation Tactics Sch., 1997, MIT, 1998. Commd. 2d lt. USMC, 1989, advanced through grades to maj., 1999; instr. Marine Corps Comm.-Electronics Sch., 1993-96; comdr. Tactical Air Ops. Ctr., 1997-99; staff writer Commandant of the Marine Corps, 1999. Contbr. articles, revs. to U.S. Naval Inst. Procs., Mil. Rev., Airpower Jour., Parameters, Talon, Marine Corps Gazette, Naval War Coll. Rev., Joint Force Quar. Participant Pacific Coun. on Internat. Policy, L.A., 1995-96. Recipient Navy Commendation medal, USMC, 1996, 99, Navy Achievement medal, 1998. Mem. U.S. Naval Inst., U.S. Strategic Inst., Marine Corps Assn.

KOJIMA, TAKESHI, law educator, arbitrator, writer; b. Yokohama, Japan, Sept. 1, 1936; s. Buzaemon and Maki Kojima; m. Shigeko Niwa, May 3, 1966; children: Natsuko, Haruka. BA, Chuo U., Tokyo, 1959, LLM, 1961, LLD, 1978; qualified lawyer, Inst. Legal Tng. and Rsch., Tokyo, 1963. Rschr. U. Mich., Ann Arbor, 1966-68; asst. prof. law Chuo U., 1960-64, assoc. prof., 1964-71, prof., 1971—, councilor, 1995—, chmn. grad. sch., 1997—; vis. prof. U. Florence, Italy, 1974, Columbia U., N.Y.C., 1988; guest prof. Aix-Marseille (France) U., 1983, Frankfurt (Germany) Goethe U., 1991-92; examiner nat. jud. exam. Ministry Justice, Tokyo, 1984-90, acting chmn. Study Commn. on Issue Fgn. Lawyers (with Ministry Justice, Japan Fedn. Bar Assns.), 1992-94, chmn. Study Commn. on Representation in Internat. Arbitration (with Ministry Justice, Japan Fedn. Bar Assns.), 1994-95; chmn. Study Commn. on Fgn. Lawyers (with Ministy Justice, Japan Bar Assns.), 1996—, acad. councillor Ctr. Internat. Civil & Comml. Law, 1996—; trustee Ctr. Automobile Product Liability, 1995—; chmn. study commn. on issue fgn. lawyers Ministry of Justice, Japan Fedn. Bar Assns., 1996—; legis. coun. Ministry of Justice, 1997—; expert mem. coun. for screening newly founded univs. and other schs., Ministry Edn., 1990-95; dir. Japan Inst. Comparative Law, Tokyo, 1987-90. Co-author: Access to Justice, Vol. I, 1978, Small Claims Courts, 1991; editor: Perspectives on Civil Justice and ADR, 1990, The Grand Design of America's Justice System, 1995; contbr. articles to profl. jours. Spl. arbitrator Ctrl. Tribunal, Ministry Constrn., Tokyo, 1990—; spl. mem. coun. on indsl. structure Ministry Internat. Trade and Industry, Tokyo, 1991-94; mem. Nat. Tribunal Constrn. Procurement, Office of Prime Min., Tokyo, 1991-96; insp. Govtl. Sch. Insp., Ministry Edn., Tokyo, 1993—, chmn. collaborators conf. for rsch. legal edn. reform; coun. legis. on civil procedure, Ministry Justice, 1997—. Mem. Japanese Assn. Civil Procedure Law (pres. 1995-98), Japanese Assn. Pvt. Law (bd. dirs. 1983-87), Japan Legal Aid Assn. (mng. trustee 1993—), Japan Negotiation Assn. (v.p. 1993—), Japan Assn. Lawyers (trustee 1975—), Japanese-Am. Assn. for Legal Studies (councilor 1991—), Am. Law Inst. Buddhist. Avocations: golf, travel. Home: 1013 Shinyoshida-machi, Yokohama Kohoku 223, Japan Office: Chuo U, 742-1 Higashinakano, Hachioji Tokyo 192-03, Japan

KOK, FRANS JOHAN, investment banker; b. Zaandam, Netherlands, May 14, 1943; came to U.S., 1963; s. Cornelis and Aaf K.; m. Mary M. Shirley, Dec. 23, 1971. BA in Econ., Occidental Coll., L.A., 1967; MA in Econs., Calif. State U., L.A., 1969; MBA, Insead, Fontainebleau, France, 1971, Harvard U., 1972. Assoc. Booz, Allen & Hamilton, Washington, 1974-78; chief economist EPA, Washington, 1978-80; CFO, co-founder Long Lake Energy Corp., N.Y.C., 1980-83; mng. dir. Ferris, Baker-Watts, Inc., Balt., 1983-89, 1st Nat. Bank Md., Balt., 1989-94; chmn., CEO, Johan Hekelaar, Inc., Chevy Chase, Md., 1994—; bd. dirs. Mindersoft, Inc., Herndon, Va. Home: PO Box 1256 Purcellville VA 20134-1256

KOKE, RICHARD JOSEPH, author, exhibit designer, museum curator; b. N.Y.C., Sept. 19, 1916; s. Joseph and Emily Josephine (Chevrolet) K.; m. Mary A. Kimbley, Jan. 1, 1955. Student, Art Students League, 1935, Cooper Union Art Inst., 1935-37; A.B., NYU, 1941; M.A., Columbia U., 1947. Historian, Bear Mountain (N.Y.) Trailside Hist. Mus., 1935-37; curator Stony Point (N.Y.) Battlefield Mus., summers 1937-41; research cons. Hudson Valley Survey, 1946-47; historian Saratoga Nat. Hist. Park, 1947; curator mus. N.Y. Hist. Soc., 1947-83, curator emeritus, 1983—; conducted archaeol. investigations on Revolutionary War mil. sites in Highlands of the Hudson, N.Y., 1935-41. Author: Accomplice in Treason; Joshua Hett Smith and the Arnold Conspiracy, 1973, Corridor Through the Mountains, 1998; editor: Scenic and Historic America, 1938; contbr. mags. and revs.; compiler American Landscape and Genre Painting in the New York Historical Society, 3 vols., 1982. Served with AUS, 1942-45; art dir, in charge cartographic dept. M.C. 1942-44; battlefield history research analyst. hist. sect. Hdgrs. 1944-45; engaged in collection and editing of mil. data pertaining to tactical operations Am. forces, preparation ofcl. army histories of Services of Supply, 1st, 3d, 7th, 9th, 15th armies World War 11, Western European Front. Recipient 1st prize hist. essay contest sponsored by Colonial Dames of N.Y., 1940. Home: PO Box 700 Peru NY 12972-0700 Office: 170 Central Park W New York NY 10024-5152

KOKEN, M. DIANE, commissioner, state; b. Lancaster, Pa., Dec. 29, 1952; d. James E. Koken and Helen Sotiro; m. John K. Herr III; children: Kathryn, Rebecca. BS magna cum laude, Millersville U., 1972; JD, Villanova U., 1975. Counsel, v.p., corp. sec. Provident Mutual Ins. Co., Harrisburg, Pa., 1975-97; acting commr. Pa. Ins. Dept., Harrisburg, 1997—. Bd. dirs. endowments and capital campaign com. Millersville U. Mem. ABA, Internat. Claims Assn., Am. Coun. Life Ins. (state v.p.), Am. Life Ins. Counsel, Am. Corp. Counsel Assn., Am. Trial Lawyers Assn., Phila. Bar Assn. Office: Pa Insurance Dept 1326 Strawberry Sq Harrisburg PA 17120-0046*

KOKKO, JUHA PEKKA, physician, educator; b. Helsinki, Finland, Mar. 26, 1937; came to U.S., 1949; s. U. Pentti and Kirsti (Taskinen) K.; m. Nancy Radford, June 21, 1961; children: Kenneth E., Karl R. BA, Emory U., 1959, MD, 1964, PhD, 1964. Intern in medicine Johns Hopkins Hosp., Balt., 1964-65, resident, 1965-66; clin. assoc. Nat. Heart Inst., Bethesda, Md., 1966-69, chief resident, NIH, 1968-69; asst. prof. medicine U. Tex. Health Sci. Ctr., Dallas, 1969-72, assoc. prof., 1972-74, prof., 1974-86, chief nephrology dept., 1973-86; prof., chair medicine dept. Emory U. Sch. Medicine, Atlanta, 1986-99; Asa G. Candler prof. medicine, assoc. dean clin. rsch. Emory U. Sch. Medicine, 1999—. Author: Fluids and Electrolytes. Chmn. Planning and Zoning Com., Addison, Tex., 1975-80, Airport Commn., Addison, 1984-86. Comdr. USPHS, 1966-69. Fellow ACP; mem. Am. Soc. Nephrology (pres. 1984-85), So. Soc. Clin. Investigators (pres. 1989-90), Assn. Profs. Medicine. Lutheran. Office: Emory U Dept Medicine H153 Emory Hosp 1364 Clifton Rd NE Atlanta GA 30322-1059

KOKOTOVIC, PETAR V., electrical and computer engineer, educator; b. Mar. 18, 1934. Dipl.Eng., U. Belgrade, Yugoslavia, 1958, Magistar (Elec. Engring.), 1963; Candidate of Tech. Scis., Russian Acad. Scis., Moscow, 1965. Prof. elec. engring. U. Ill., Urbana, 1966-91, Grainger prof. emeritus, 1991—; prof. elec. and computer engring. U. Calif., 1991—; dir. Ctr. for Control Engring. and Computation. Recipient Quazza medal Internat. Fedn. Automatic Control, 1990, IEEE Control Sys. Field award, 1995. Fellow IEEE (Engring., Outstanding AC Transactions Paper award 1982-83, Axelby Outstanding Paper award 1991-92, H. Bode Prize lecture 1991); mem. NAE. Office: University of California Electrical & Comp Eng Dept Santa Barbara CA 93106

KOKOWSKI, PALMA ANNA, nurse consultant; b. New Brighton, Pa., Aug. 15, 1947; d. William M. and Steffa A. (Zaleski) Mangine; m. Clifford M. Kokowski, Oct. 2, 1971; 1 child, Bonnie A. RN, South Side Hosp., Pitts., 1968. RN. W.Va., Pa., Md., Ohio; cert. disability mgmt. specialist; cert. rehab. RN. cert. case mgr., Rehab. Nursing Certification Bd. Real estate sales Marsh Realty, Pitts.; staff nurse South Side Hosp., 1968-73; field nurse Upjohn Healthcare Svcs., Pitts., 1975-77, field supr., 1977-78, field nurse rehab., 1978-81, rehab. coord., 1981-82; charge nurse Greater Pitts. Guild for Blind, Bridgeville, Pa., 1977-79; med. and rehab. specialist Champion Claim Svc., Pitts., 1982-87; owner, rehab. nurse cons. Palma Kokowski Rehab., Library, Pa., 1988—. Mem. ANA, Pa. Nursing Assn., NARPPS, Assn. Rehab. Nurses (treas. 1982), Western Pa. Assn. Rehab. Nurses, Am. Acad. Nurse Life Care Planners, Pa. Claims Assn. Home and Office: Palma Kokowski Rehab 1188 Mike Reed Dr Library PA 15129-9457

KOLA, ARTHUR ANTHONY, lawyer; b. New Brunswick, N.J., Feb. 16, 1939; s. Arthur Aloysius and Blanche (Raym) K.; m. Jacquelin Lou Draper, Sept. 3, 1960; children—Jill, Jean, Jennifer; m. Anna Molnar, Apr. 15, 1977. AB, Dartmouth Coll., 1961; LLB, Duke U., 1964. Bar: Ohio 1964, U.S. Dist. Ct. (no. dist.) Ohio 1969, U.S. Ct. Appeals (6th cir.) 1971, U.S. Supreme Ct. 1972. Assoc. Squire, Sanders & Dempsey, Cleve., 1964-65, assoc., 1968-74, ptnr., 1974-94; pvt. practice Kola Law Office, Cleve., 1994—; asst. prof. law Ind. U., Bloomington, 1967-68; instr. labor law Case Western Res. U., Cleve., 1976. Bd. visitors Duke U. Sch. Law, 1985—. Served to capt. U.S. Army, 1965-67. Mem. Ohio Bar Assn., Cleve. Bar Assn. (chmn. labor and employment law sect. 1993-94), Am. Arbitration Assn. (bd. dirs. 1991-97). Office: Kola Law Office Corp Plz I Ste 100 6450 Rockside Woods Blvd S Cleveland OH 44131-2230

KOLAK, DANIEL, philosopher; b. Zagreb, Croatia, June 30, 1955; s. Miro Kolak and Rajka (Ivosevic) Ungerer; m. Wendy Zentz, July 28, 1991; 1 child, Julia. BA, U. Md., 1978, MA, 1981, PhD, 1986. Instr. Univ. Coll., Md., 1983-86; asst. prof. Towson (Md.) State U., 1986-87, U. Wis., Oshkosh, 1987-89; asst. prof. William Paterson U., Wayne, N.J., 1989-95, prof., chmn., dir. Cognitive Sci. Lab., 1995—; theatrical dir. Source Theater, Washington, 1980-85, composer, musician, 1980-85; musician with various jazz artists, including Dizzy Gillespie, Charlie Byrd, 1976—. Author: (books) In Search of Myself: Life, Death and Personal Identity, 1999, Lovers of Wisdom, 1996, In Search of God: The Language and Logic of Belief, 1994, Wisdom Without Answers, 1995, Self, Cosmos, God, 1993, From the Presocratics to the Present, 1998; editor: (books) The Experience of Philosophy, 1995, From Plato to Wittgenstein, 1994, Self and Identity, 1991, Wittgenstein's Tractatus, 1998; composer film score: Forsaken Cries: The Case of Rwanda, 1997. Office: William Paterson U Dept Philosophy Wayne NJ 07470

KOLAKOWSKI, DIANA JEAN, county commissioner; b. Detroit, Aug. 28, 1943; d. Leo and Genevieve (Bosh) Zyskowski; m. William Francis Kolakowski, Jr., Oct. 22, 1966; children: Wiliam Francis III, John. BS, U. Detroit, 1965. Lab. asst. chemistry dept. U. Detroit, 1961-65; rsch. chemist Detroit Inst. Cancer Rsch., Mich. Cancer Found., 1965-70; substitute tchr. Warren (Mich.) Consol. Schs., 1979-81; mem. Macomb County Bd. Commrs., Mt. Clemens, Mich., 1983—; vice chmn. Macomb County Bd. Commrs., Mt. Clemens, 1993-95, chmn., 1995-97; dir. S.E. Mich. Transp. Authority, Detroit, 1983-85; trustee Macomb County Ret. System, Mt. Clemens, 1988-91, 92-95; chmn. Macomb County Planning Commn., 1991-96; del. S.E. Mich. Coun. Govts., Detroit, 1987—, vice chmn., 1995-99, chmn. 1999-2000; chmn. Regional Transit Coord. Coun., 1995-97; bd. dirs. Creating a Healthier Macomb, 1996—, Macomb Bar Found., 1996—. Contbr. articles to sci. jours. Trustee Myasthenia Gravis Found., Southfield, Mich., 1964-71; dir. Otsikita coun. Girl Scouts Am., 1995-96; mem., sec. Sterling Heights (Mich.) Bd. Zoning Appeals, 1978-83; mem. Macomb County Dem. Exec. Com., Mt. Clemens, 1982—, 10th and 12th Dem. Congl. Dist. Exec. Com., Warren, 1982—, del. 1996 Dem. Nat. Conv.; mem. behavioral medicine adv. coun. St. Joseph Hosp. GM scholar U. Detroit, 1961-65; named Woman of Distinction Macomb County Girl Scouts U.S.A., 1996; recipient Leadership award Cath. Social Svcs. Macomb, 1997, Polish Pride award Polish Am. Citizens for Equity, 1997, Excellence in County Govt. award, 1997, others. Mem. Nat. Assn. Counties, Mich. Assn. Counties, Mich. Assn. Planning Ofcls., Am. Polish Cultural Ctr., Polish Am. Congress, Alpha Sigma Nu. Roman Catholic. Avocations: singing, piano, crossword and jigsaw puzzles. Home: 33488 Breckenridge Dr Sterling Heights MI 48310-6082 Office: Office Bd Commrs Macomb Co Adminstrn Bldg 1 S Main St 9th Fl Mount Clemens MI 48043-8607

KOLANOSKI, THOMAS EDWIN, financial company executive; b. San Francisco, Mar. 1, 1937; s. Theodore Thaddeus and Mary J. (Luczynski) K.; m. Sheila O'Brien, Dec. 26, 1960; children: Kenneth John, Thomas Patrick, Michael Sean. BS, U. San Francisco, 1959, MA, 1965. Cert. fin. planner; registered rep. Educator, counselor, administr. San Francisco Unified Sch. Dist.; adminstr. Huntington Beach (Calif.) Union, 1969-79; v.p. fin. svcs. Waddell & Reed, Inc., Ariz., Nev., Utah, So. Calif., 1979-94; retired Waddell & Reed, Inc., 1994; investment cons. Foothill Securities Inc.; personal fin. planner. Fellow NDEA, 1965. Mem. Nat. Assn. Secondary Sch. Prins., Internat. Assn. of Fin. Planners, Nat. Assn. Securities Dealers. Republican. Roman Catholic. Avocation: fly fishing. Fax: 714-434-9425. Home: 1783 Panay Cir Costa Mesa CA 92626-2348

KOLANSKY, HAROLD, physician, psychiatrist, psychoanalyst; b. Carbondale, Pa., Aug. 15, 1924; s. Abe and Miriam (Raker) K.; m. Elsa Harwitz, June 8, 1948; children: Jeffrey, Betta, Daniel. Student, U. Scranton, 1942-44; MD cum laude, Georgetown U., 1948. Rotating intern Walter Reed Army Hosp., Washington, 1948-49; resident Coatesville (Pa.) VA Hosp. and Deans' Com. Program, Phila., 1949-52; practice medicine specializing in psychiatry and psychoanalysis Phila., 1952—, Elkins Park, Pa., 1959—; clin. assoc. prof. psychiatry U. Pa. Sch. Medicine, 1972-77, clin. prof., 1977, 91—, mem. steering com. Psychoanalytic Cluster, 1991—, chair steerimg com. Psychoanalytic Cluster, 1997—; prof. psychiatry and human behavior Jefferson Med. Coll., Thomas Jefferson U., Phila., 1977-91, dir. sect. child and adolescent psychoanalysis, 1980-90, dir. sect. psychoanalysis, 1982-90; mem. psychiatry staff Albert Einstein Med. Ctr., 1952-69, 82—, sr. attending, 1983—, dir. divsn. child psychiatry, 1955-69, acting chmn. dept. psychiatry, 1968-69, dir. child psychiatry fellowship, 1960-69, dir. ctr. for psychoanalysis, 1991—, mem. exec. com., tng. com. and curriculum com., 1991—; mem. faculty Inst. Phila. Assn. Psychoanalysis, 1960—, chmn. administrv. bd., 1966-69, dir. divsn. childrn and adolescent psychoanalysis, 1975-84, tng. and supervisory analyst, 1976—, chmn. tng. analyst com., 1982-83, 93-94, 95-96, chmn. curriculum com., 1982-88, dir. consultation and evaluation divsn., 1988-89, mem. ednl. com., 1989-94, mem. ednl. com., vice chmn., 1997, mem. ednl. com., 1997—, vice-chmn., 1997—, chmn. faculty com., 1997—, chmn., liaison com. med. edn., 1994—; mem. staff psychiatry Phila. Psychiat. Ctr., 1952-81; pres. Regional Coun. Child Psychiatry, Pa., S.E. N.J., Del., 1967-68, 72-73, chmn. exec. com., 1970-73; chmn. med. bd. Ea. State Sch. and Hosp., Trevose, Pa., 1966-69; asst. prof. psychiatry Hahnemann Med. Coll. and Hosp., Phila., 1952-60; mem. Pa. Task Force on Mental Health Children, 1971-74; vis. prof. psychiatry U. P.R. Sch. Medicine, 1982—; mem. steering com. psychoanalytic cluster U. Pa. Sch. Med., 1991—, chmn., 1997—. Contbg. author to numerous texts on psychoanalysis and psychiatry including: A Handbook of Child Psychoanalysis, 1968, Behavior Pathology of Childhood and Adolescence, 1973, Controversy in Psychiatry, 1978, Prognosis, 1981; contbr. numerous articles on child and adult psychiatry and psychoanalysis to profl. jours. Capt. M.C., U.S. Army, 1950-51, Korea. Recipient 1st prize biochemistry Georgetown U., 1945, Robert Waelder award for Teaching Excellence in Psychiatry Thomas Jefferson Med. Coll., 1987, Dedication to Edn. award, 1990, award for teaching excellence dept. psychiatry Albert Einstein Med. Ctr., 1993, award for tchg. excellence, 1996; 1st pl. U.S. in Surgery Nat. Bd. Med. Examiners, 1948. Fellow Am. Psychiat. Assn., Am. Acad. Child Psychiatry (chmn. com. continuing med. edn. 1974-82, citation for developing continuing med. edn. program 1976, councillor), Phila. Coll. Physicians; mem. AMA, Phila. Assn. Psychoanalysis (bd. dirs. 1984-86, pres. 1984-86, Gerald Pearson Prize award 1960), Assn. Child Psychonalysis, Phila. Psychiat. Soc., Internat. Psychoanalytic Assn., Am. Psychoanalytic Assn. (exec. counselor 1969-73, 77-82, fellow bd. profl. standards 1983-89, 1992-98, mem. com. on child and adolescent analysis 1984-90, 99, acting fellow bd. on prof. standards 1989, mem. univ. and med. edn. com. 1995—, budget and fin. com. 1996-98), Pa. Med. Soc., Phila. County Med. Soc.

KOLAR, JANET BROSTRON, physician assistant, medical technologist; b. St. Louis, Jan. 8, 1937; d. William Olaf and Susan Ann (Dzurovcin) B.; m Robert Joseph Kolar, Sept. 21, 1957 (div. June 1976); children: John Alexander, Elizabeth Susan Hinn, Paul Daniel, Peter Nicholas. Diploma in med. tech., Century Coll. Med. Tech., 1955; diploma in physicians asst. program, St. Louis U., 1976. Bd. cert. physician asst. Biochem. rsch. technologist Argonne Cancer Rsch. Hosp., Chgo., 1955-60; cyto technician, biochem. rsch. technologist dept. medicine U. Chgo. Hosp., 1960-62, supr. surg. biochem. lab., rsch. asst. dept. surgery, 1962-65; med. technologist Overland (Mo.) Med. Ctr., 1967-89; medication counselor, physicians asst. Lipid Rsch. Ctr., Wash. U. Sch. of Medicine, St. Louis, 1976-83; physician asst., coord. cardiovascular risk reduction ctr. St. Louis U. Med. Ctr., 1983-85; physician asst. VA Med. Ctr., St. Louis, 1985-90; physician asst. in gen. surgery Barnes-Jewish-Christian Health System, St. Louis, 1990—; mem. adv. subcom. to intervention com. NIH-Coronary Primary Prevention Trial, 1981-83. Contbr. articles to profl. jours. Co-chairwoman childhood edn. Women's Internat. League Peace and Freedom, St. Louis, 1970-73; vol. enrichment program children's folk music Flynn Park Sch., University City, Mo., 1972-73; vol. children's folk music Countryside Montessori Sch., Creve Coeur, Mo., 1968-71. Mem. Mo. Acad. Physician Assts. VA Physicians Asst., Epsilon Omicron Mu. Avocations: folk guitar, dancing, drag racing, cooking, needlework. Office: Barnes Jewish Christian Health System 216 S Kingshighway Blvd Saint Louis MO 63110-1026

KOLAR, MARY JANE, trade and professional association executive; b. Benton, Ill., Aug. 9, 1941; d. Thomas Haskell and Mary Jane (Sanders) Burnett; m. Otto Michael Kolar, Aug. 13, 1966; children: Robin Lynn, Deon Michael. BA with high honors, So. Ill. U., 1963, MA with highest honors, 1964. Tchr. pub. schs. Benton and Zeigler, Ill., 1960-63; grad. asst. and grad. fellow So. Ill. U., Carbondale, 1963-64; instr. Ridgewood High Sch., Norridge, Ill., 1964-67, Maine Twp. High Sch., Des Plaines, Ill., 1967-70; freelance writer plumbing, heating & cooling industry couns. Chgo., 1970-71; ednl. coord. Am. Dietetic Assn., Chgo., 1971-72; dir. profl. devel. Am. Dental Hygienists Assn., Chgo., 1972-78; dir. Learning Ctr. div. Am. Coll. Cardiology, Bethesda, Md., 1978-80; dir. edn. Nat. Moving and Storage Assn., Alexandria, Va., 1980-82; exec. dir. Women in Communications, Inc., Austin, Tex., 1982-84, Altrusa Internat., Chgo., 1984-87, Assn. Govt. Accts., Alexandria, Va., 1987-90, Bus./Profl. Advt. Assn., Alexandria, 1991-92, Am. Assn. Family and Consumer Scis., Alexandria, 1992-96; pres., CEO The Alexandria Group, Inc., 1996—; cons. spkr. various profl. assn., ednl. instns. and fed. ays.; dir. project taking charge adolescent pregnancy prevention program, 1993-95. Contbr. articles to profl. jours. and assn. mags., chpts. to books. Mem. adv. council Accrediting Commn. Assn. of Ind. Colls. and Schs., 1980-88; treas. Pub. Employees Roundtable, 1988-90, Hollin Hills Civic Assn., 1989-90. Fellow Am. Soc. Allied Health Professions (dir. 1978-79), Am. Soc. Assn. Execs. (cert., mem. Key Profl. Assn. coun. 1994-96, rsch. com. 1996—, strategic leadership forum com. 1996-97, awards com. 1992-93, univ. affairs commn. 1986-92, chair 1990-91, found. bd. 1987-91, chmn. edn. sect. 1982-83, bd. dirs. 1983-86, chair higher edn. task force 1990-91, chair fellows 1987, peer rev. com. 1997—, Educator of Yr. award 1978, Key award 1990), Greater Washington Soc. Assn. Execs. (edn. com. 1979-82, CEO com. 1990-92, 94-96, vice chair 1995-96, mem. strategic planning com. 1994-95, exec. search com. 1994-96); mem. Future Home Makers Am. (bd. dirs. 1992-96), Alexandria C. of C. (assn. coun. 1990-96, steering com. 1993-96), Women in Comm. (newsletter editor, legis. and career reentry chair, chair ERA task force, dir. Washington profl. chpt. 1981-83, program com. Chgo. chpt. 1984-86), So. Ill. U. Alumni Assn. (bd. dirs. 1984-89, v.p. 1986-89, presdl. search com. 1986-87). Office: 526 King St Ste 423 Alexandria VA 22314-3143 *Being a professional means many things. It means adhering to an ethical code, having high standards of quality, striving toward excellence through basic and ongoing preparation for the profession I have chosen to practice. It means having goals and being willing to contribute to solving the social, economic and political problems of the society of which I am a part. Professionalism is more than acceptance of responsibility, more than doing one's duty, more than being good at what one does. Professionalism requires a commitment to what you do and to the future. It carries with it obligation and risk. It necessitates service to the profession—a willingness to be a leader—and a desire to meet the needs of others.*

KOLAROV, KRASIMIR DOBROMIROV, computer scientist, researcher; b. Sofia, Bulgaria, Oct. 16, 1961; came to the U.S., 1987; s. Dobromir Krastev and Margarita Georgieva (Kurukafova) K.; m. Janet Louise Barba, July 4, 1990; children: April, Kathryn, Sonia, Elena. BS in Math. with honors, U. Sofia, Bulgaria, 1981, MS in Ops. Rsch. with honors, 1982, MA in English, 1982; MS in Mech. Engring., Stanford U., 1990, PhD in Mech. Engring., 1993. Rschr. Bulgarian Acad. Scis., Sofia, 1982-83; rsch. assoc., vis. prof. Inst. Mechanics and Biomechanics, Bulgarian Acad. Scis., Sofia, 1983-87; tchg. asst. Stanford (Calif.) U., 1988-92; mem. rsch. staff Interval Rsch. Corp., Palo Alto, Calif., 1992—; vis. prof. Inst. for Civil Engring., Sofia, 1983-86; lectr. H.S. U., Sofia, 1985; reviewer Jour. Robotic Sys., Palo Alto, 1991—, others. Contbr. articles to profl. jours. Mem. IEEE, Assn. for Computing Machinery, Soc. for Indsl. and Applied Math. Avocations: bridge, travel, skiing, bicycling, flying. Office: Interval Rsch Corp 1801 Page Mill Rd # C Palo Alto CA 94304-1216

KOLATCH, ALFRED JACOB, publisher; b. Seattle, Jan. 2, 1916; s. Sander and Yetta (Jacobs) K.; m. Thelma Rubin, June 16, 1940; children: Jonathan, David. BA, Yeshiva U., 1937; Rabbi, Jewish Theol. Sem., 1941. Ordained rabbi, 1941; rabbi Columbia, S.C., 1941-43, Kew Gardens, N.Y., 1946-48; founder, pres. Jonathan David Pubs., Middle Village, N.Y., 1949—. Author: These Are the Names, 1948 Who's Who in the Talmud, 1964, The Name Dictionary, 1967, Jewish Information Quiz Book, 1967, The Family Seder, 1968, Names for Pets, 1971, JD Dictionary of First Names, 1980, Jewish Book of Why, 1981, Complete Dictionary of English and Hebrew First Names, 1984, The Second Jewish Book of Why, 1985, Today's Best Baby Names, 1986, This Is the Torah, 1987, The New Name Dictionary, 1989, The Jewish Home Advisor, 1990, The Jewish Child's First Book of Why, 1992, The Jewish Mourner's Book of Why, 1992, Classic Bible Stories for Jewish Children, 1994, The Jewish Heritage Quiz Book, 1995, Great Jewish Quotations, 1996, Let's Celebrate Our Jewish Holidays, 1997, A Child's First Book of Jewish Holidays, 1997, Best Baby Names for Jewish Children, 1998, What Jews Say About God, 1999. Served as chaplain U.S. Army, 1943-46. Mem. Rabbinical Assembly, Assn. Jewish Chaplains (past pres.), Mil. Chaplains Assn. (past v.p.). Home: 72-08 Juno St Forest Hills NY 11375-5930 Office: 68-22 Eliot Ave Middle Village NY 11379

KOLATCH, MYRON, magazine editor; b. Bklyn., Sept. 26, 1929; s. Philip S. and Rebecca (Langberg) K.; m. Francine Ruth Miller, Jan. 28, 1951; children: Barry Steven, Jonathan Lee, Sari Elana. B.A., N.Y. U., 1950, postgrad in English, 1950-51. Mem. staff New Leader, 1953—, mng. editor, 1960-61, exec. editor, 1961—. Bd. dirs. Tamiment Inst. Served with AUS, 1951-53. Home: 186-22 Radnor Rd Jamaica NY 11432-5829 Office: 275 7th Ave New York NY 10001-6708

KOLATTUKUDY, PAPPACHAN ETTOOP, biochemist, educator; b. Cochin, Kerala, India, Aug. 27, 1937; came to the U.S., 1960; m. Marie M. Paul. BS, U. Madras, 1957; B in Edn., U. Kerala, 1959; PhD, Oreg. State U., 1964. Prin. jr. high sch. India, 1957-58, high sch. chemistry tchr., 1959-60; asst. biochemist Conn. Agrl. Experiment Sta., New Haven, 1964-69; assoc. prof. Wash. State U., Pullman, 1969-73, prof. biochemistry, 1973-80, dir. inst. biol. chemistry, 1980-86; dir. Ohio State Biotech. Ctr., Columbus, 1986-95, dir. neurobiotech. ctr., dir. med. biotech., 1995—; cons. Analabs, New Haven, Allied Chem. Corp., Solvay, N.Y., Genencor Corp., South San Francisco, Calif., Monsanto Co., St. Louis; mem. Overseas Adv. Com., India; mem. Edison Bio-Tech. Ctr., Cleve., trustee; mem. adv. com. to MUCIA on Sci. and Tech., Nat. Agrl. Biotech. Consortium; Ohio rep. to Midwest Plant Biotech. Consortium. Contbr. over 300 articles to profl. jours.; patentee in field. Recipient Golden Apple award Wash. State Apple Commn., President's Faculty Excellence award Wash. State U.; grantee NIH, NSF, Am. Heart Assn., Am. Cancer Soc., DOE. Mem. Fedn. Am. Socs. for Exptl. Biology, Am. Soc. Plant Physiologists, Am. Soc. Microbiology. Home: 2301 Hoxton Ct Columbus OH 43220-4739 Office: Ohio State Neurobiotech Ctr 1060 Carmack Rd Columbus OH 43210-1002

KOLAYA, MARGARET HELEN BOUTWELL, librarian; b. Concord, N.H., Apr. 15, 1947; d. Harvey B. and Margaret A. Boutwell; m. John L. Kolaya, June 20, 1970; children: Lauren B., Timothy A. BA in History, Bucknell U., 1969; MLS, Rutgers U., 1979. Manuscripts asst. Yale U. Libr., New Haven, 1969-70; head libr. The Wardlaw-Hartridge Sch., Edison and Plainfield, N.J., 1983-96; supervising libr. Rockwood Meml. Libr., 1996-97; bd. dirs. Literacy Vols. Am. Bd. dirs. Hist. Soc. Plainfield, 1973-97, pres., 1987-88; bd. dirs. Catherine Webster Home, Inc., Plainfield, 1993—, Clark Pub. Libr., 1997—. Mem. ALA, N.J. Libr. Assn., Third N.J. Regiment (Brigade of the Am. Revolution), Lions Club. Home: 1081 Oakland Ave Plainfield NJ 07060-3411 Office: Clark Pub Libr 303 Westfield Ave Clark NJ 07066

KOLB, CHARLES CHESTER, humanities administrator; b. Erie, Pa., Sept. 4, 1940; s. John Christian and Edna Lucille (Church) K.; m. Joy Bilharz, June 3, 1972 (div. Mar. 1991); 1 child, Nancy Gwenyth; m. P. Jean Drew, July 20, 1991; 1 child, Catherine Claire Fraley. BA in History, Pa. State U., 1962, PhD in Archaeology and Anthropology, 1979. Instr. anthropology Pa. State U., University Park, 1966-69, Bryn Mawr (Pa.) Coll., 1969-73; from instr. to asst. prof. anthropology Pa. State U., Erie, 1973-84; dir. rsch. and grants Mercyhurst Coll., Erie, 1984-89, asst. dir. Hammermill Libr., 1989; humanities administr. program officer divsn. state programs NEH, Washington, 1989-91, program officer divsn. preservation and access, 1991-96, sr. program officer, 1997—; manuscript reviewer Holt, Rinehart and Winston, Inc., 1977-89, Prentice-Hall, Inc., 1979-85, William C. Brown, Pubs., 1982-85, U. Tex. Press, 1988—, U. Utah Press, 1991—, U. Press of Fla., 1994—, AltaMira Press/Sage, 1995—, U. Pa. Mus. Applied Sci. Ctr. Archaeology, 1996—, Dover Pub., 1996—; grant proposal reviewer NEH, 1981-89, NSF, 1982—, Wenner-Gren Found. for Anthropol. Rsch., 1987-89; co-founder, ann. symposium co-organizer Ceramic Studies Interest Group, 1986—. Author: Marine Shell Trade and Classic Teotihuacan, 1987; editor: A Pot for All Reasons, 1988, Ceramic Ecology, 1988, 89, 97; contbr. articles to profl. jours., chpts. to books; book and film reviewer Sci. Books and Films, 1977—; manuscript reviewer Am. Antiquity, 1978—, Current Anthropology, 1979—, Ancient Mesoamerica, 1990—, Ethnohistory, 1995—, Jour. Material Culture, 1995—, Hist. Archaeology, 1995—, L.Am. Antiquity, 1995—, Jour. Archaeological Sci., 1998—; abstractor Ceramic Abstracts, 1990-96, Art and Archaeology Technical Abstracts, 1996—; regional editor La Tinaja: Newsletter of Archaeol. Ceramics, 1991—; N.Am. corr. Old Potter's Almanack, 1992—; reviewer Choice, 1992—. Mem. Commonwealth Pa., Gov.'s Conf. on Librs. and Info. Systems, 1989. Mem. Am. Ceramic Soc., Am. Chem. Soc., Am. Ethnological Soc., Am. Soc. Ethnohistory, Archaeol. Inst. Am., Assn. Field Archaeology, Coun. Mus. Anthropology, Materials Rsch. Soc., Prehist. Ceramic Rsch. Group, Soc. Am. Archaeology, Soc. Archaeol. Scis. (life, assoc. editor for archaeol. ceramics Bull. 1997—), Soc. Hist. Archaeology, Soc. Med. Anthropology, Soc. Am. Archivists, Register Profl. Archaeologists, U.S. Naval Inst. (life), Nat. Railway Hist. Soc., N.Y. State Archaeol. Assn., Paleopathology Assn., Pearl Harbor History Assocs. (life), Alpha Kappa Delta, Phi Kappa Phi, Pi Gamma Mu, Sigma Xi. Achievements include rsch. in tech. and cultural interpretations of archaeol. ceramics by using physiochem. analyses and petrographic microscopy, ceramics from Afghanistan, Ctrl. Asia, Mexico, Guatemala, East Africa, Great Lakes Basin. Home: 1005 Pruitt Ct SW Vienna VA 22180-6429 Office: NEH Divsn Preservation & Access 1100 Pennsylvania Ave NW Washington DC 20004-2501

KOLB, CHARLES EUGENE, research corporation executive; b. Cumberland, Md., May 21, 1945; s. Charles Eugene and Doris Helen (McFarland) K.; m. Susan Marie Foote, Aug. 19, 1965; children: Craig E., Amy C. BS, MIT, 1967; MA, Princeton U., 1968, PhD, 1971. Sr. rsch. sci. Aerodyne Rsch. Inc., Burlington, Mass., 1971-74; prin. rsch. sci. Aerodyne Rsch. Inc., Bedford, Mass., 1975-76, dir. Ctr. Chem. and Environ. Physics, 1977-79, tech. dir. applied scis. div., 1979-80, dir. applied scis. div., v.p., 1981-84; exec. v.p. and dir. rsch. Aerodyne Rsch. Inc., Billerica, Mass., pres., chief exec. officer; 1985—; assoc. in atmospheric chemistry Harvard U., 1976-85, rsch. affiliate Spectroscopy Lab. MIT, 1981-92, rsch. affiliated dept. aeronautics and astronautics MIT, 1993. Editor: Geophys. Rsch. Letters, 1996-99; mem. editl. bd. Internat. Jour. Chem. Kinetics, 1990-92; author book chpts.; contbr. numerous articles to profl. jours. Fellow Optical Soc. Am., Am. Phys. Soc.; mem. AAAS, Am. Chem. Soc. (chmn.-elect northeastern sect. 1990, chmn. 1991, trustee, 1994-96, Creative Advances in Environ. Sci. and Tech. award 1997), Am. Geophys. Union, Combustion Inst., Union of Concerned Scientists, MIT Alumni Assn. (Bronze Beaver award 1987, Lobdell award 1981). Home: 8 Stearns Rd Bedford MA 01730-1077 also: 46 Oak Grove Ave East Falmouth MA 02536-7431 Office: Aerodyne Rsch Inc 45 Manning Rd Billerica MA 01821-3976

KOLB, DAVID ALLEN, psychology educator; b. Moline, Ill., Dec. 12, 1939; s. John August and Ethel May (Petherbridge) K.; 1 son, Jonathan Demian. AB cum laude, Knox Coll., 1961; PhD, Harvard U., 1967; ScD (h.c.), U. N.H., 1984; PhD (h.c.), Internat. Mgmt. Ctr., Buckingham, 1988; LittD (h.c.), Franklin U., 1994; DHL (h.c.), SUNY, 1996. Asst. prof. organizational psychology MIT, Cambridge, 1965-70, assoc. prof., 1970-75; prof. organizational behavior and mgmt. Case Western Res. U., Cleve., 1976—, deWindt Prof. Leadership and Enterprise Devel. Weatherhead Sch. Mgmt., 1992-97, chmn. dept., 1984-90; vis. prof. mgmt. London Grad. Sch. Bus., 1971; dir. Devel. Research Assos., 1966-80; mgmt. cons., U.S., Australia, N.Z., Indonesia, Singapore, Malaysia, Thailand, Japan. Author: Experiential Learning: Experience as the source of learning and development, 1984; co-author: Organizational Behavior: An Experiential Approach, 6th edit, 1995, Organizational Behavior: A Book of Readings, 6th edit, 1995, Changing Human Behavior: Principles of Planned Intervention, 1974, Innovation in Professional Education: Steps on Journey from Teaching to Learning, 1995. Woodrow Wilson fellow, 1962. Mem. Am. Psychol. Assn., Internat. Assn. Applied Social Scientists (charter), Soc. Intercultural Edn., Tng. and Research (charter), Council Advancement of Experiential Learning (Research Excellence award 1984, Morris T. Keaton Adult and Experiental Learning award 1991), Nat. Ctr. on Adult Learning (coun. mem. 1988—). Office: Case Western Res U Dept of Chmn Cleveland OH 44106

KOLB, DEREK ANDREW, information systems specialist; b. Rochester, N.Y., July 14, 1964. BS in MIS, St. John Fisher Coll., 1986. Cert. netware engr.-intranetware; cert. network expert-CNX, Microsoft cert. profl. systems engr.; CISCO cert. network assoc. CCNA; CISCO cert. design assoc. CCDA; project mgmt. cert. program PMCE. Customer engr. JWP/Eastman Kodak, Rochester, 1990-92; PC specialist Prudential Bank, Atlanta, 1992-93; mgr. info. sys. Zoo Atlanta, 1993—. Mem. IEEE, IEEE Computer Soc., Network Profl. Assn., Nat. Computer Security Assn, Project Mgmt. Inst. Home: 2575 Delk Rd SE Apt 1440D Marietta GA 30067-6526 Office: Zoo Atlanta 800 Cherokee Ave SE Atlanta GA 30315-1440

KOLB, DOROTHY GONG, elementary education educator; b. San Jose, Calif.; d. Jack and Lucille (Chinn) Gong; m. William Harris Kolb, Mar. 22, 1970. BA with highest honors, San Jose State U., 1964; postgrad., U. Hawaii, Calif. State U., L.A.; MA in Ednl. Tech., Pepperdine U., 1992. Cert. in elem. edn., edn. for mentally retarded, edn. for learning handicapped pre-sch., adult classes, resource specialist. Tchr. Cambrian Sch. Dist., San Jose, Calif., 1964-66, Ctrl. Oahu Sch. Dist., Wahiawa, Hawaii, 1966-68, Montebello (Calif.) Unified Sch. Dist., 1968—. Recipient Very Spl. Person award Calif. PTA, 1998; Walter Bachrodt Meml. scholar. Mem. Pi Lambda Theta, Kappa Delta Pi, Pi Tau Sigma, Tau Beta Pi.

KOLB, FELIX OSCAR, physician; b. Vienna, Austria, Nov. 12, 1921; arrived in U.S., 1938; s. Leon and Hilde (Grunwald) K.; m. Susan L. Goldberger, July 1, 1966; children: Lisa F., Marc E. AB, U. Calif., Berkeley, 1941; MD, U. Calif., San Francisco, 1943. Diplomate Am. Bd. Internal Medicine, Am. Bd. Endocrinology and Metabolism. Intern San Francisco Gen. Hosp., 1943-44; clin. asst. U. Calif. Med. Ctr., San Francisco, 1946-47; med. resident VA Hosp., U. Calif., San Francisco, 1947-49, New Eng. Ctr. Hosp., Boston, 1949-50; grad. asst. Mass. Gen. Hosp., Boston, 1950-51; attending physician U. Calif. Hosp., San Francisco, 1952—; asst. chief, assoc. chief, sr. dept. of medicine Mt. Zion Hosp., San Francisco, 1952-98, emeritus, 1998—; clin. prof. medicine U. Calif., San Francisco, 1969—, asst. assoc. dir. metabolic rsch. unit, 1952-85; pvt. practice in endocrinology and metabolism San Francisco, 1952—; cons. physician Shriners Hosp., San Francisco, VA Hosp., San Francisco, Children's Hosp., San Francisco, Letterman Hosp., San Francisco, Marshal Hale Hosp., San Francisco, Calif. Pacific Med. Ctr., San Francisco. Co-author, author 3 text book chpts.; contbr. numerous articles to profl. jours.; editl. bd. Metabolism, Reviewer for Ann. and Arch. Internal Medicine, Calcified Tissue Internat. Capt. U.S. Army, 1944-46. Fellow ACP; mem. AMA, Calif. Med. Assn., San Francisco Med. Assn., Am. Diabetes Assn., Endocrine Soc., Am. Fedn. for Clin. Rsch., We. Soc. for Clin. Rsch., Am. Soc. Internal Medicine, Calif. Soc. Internal Medicine, San Francisco Soc. Internal Medicine, Am. Soc. for Bone and Mineral Rsch., Alpha Omega Alpha (sec.-treas. 1955-56), Phi Delta Epsilon. Democrat. Jewish. Avocation: piano, golf. E-mail: FOKolb@pol.net. Fax: (415) 383-1013. Home: 9 Starboard Ct Mill Valley CA 94941-3210 Office: 2100 Webster St San Francisco CA 94115-2373

KOLB, GWIN JACKSON, language professional, educator; b. Aberdeen, Miss., Nov. 2, 1919; s. Roy Rolly and Nola Undine (Jackson) K.; m. Ruth Alma Godbold, Oct. 11, 1943; children: Gwin Jackson II, Alma Dean. BA, Millsaps Coll., 1941; MA, U. Chgo., 1946, PhD, 1949; LHD, Millsaps Coll., 1991. Editorial asst. Modern Philology, 1946-56; mem. faculty U. Chgo., 1949-89, prof. English, 1961-77, Chester D. Tripp prof. humanities, 1977-89, emeritus, 1990—, chmn. dept., 1963-72, chmn. coll. English staff, 1958-60, head humanities sect. in coll., 1960-62; vis. assoc. prof. Northwestern U., winter 1958, Stanford U., spring 1960; vis. prof. U. Wash., summers 1967, 73, Ohio State U., spring 1987, Peking U., fall 1994, U. Evansville, winter, spring 1996, Huntingdon Coll., winter, spring 1997, U. Ga., winter 1998. Co-author: Dr. Johnson's Dictionary, 1955, Reading Literature: A Workbook, 1955; editor: (Samuel Johnson) Rasselas and Other Tales, 1990; co-editor: A Bibliography of Modern Studies Complied for Philological Quarterly, 1951-65, 3 vols., 1962, 72, Modern Philology, 1973-89, Approaches to Teaching the Works of Samuel Johnson, 1993. Served with USNR, 1942-45. Frederick A. and Marion S. Pottle fellow Beinecke Libr. Yale U., 1993; recipient Quantrell award U. Chgo., 1955, Medal of Honor U. Evansville, 1992, Alumni award Millsaps Coll., 1967; Guggenheim fellow, 1956-57; grantee Am. Coun. Learned Socs., 1961-62. Mem. MLA, Midwest MLA (pres. 1964-65), Johnson Soc. Ctrl. Region (pres. 1965-66), Nat. Coun. Tchrs. English (bd. dirs. coll. sect. 1966-68), Am. Soc. 18th Century Studies (exec. bd. 1973-76, pres. 1976-77), The Johnsonians, Assn. Depts. English (pres. 1968), Caxton Club, Quadrangle. Home: 5819 S Blackstone Ave Chicago IL 60637-1855

KOLB, HAROLD HUTCHINSON, JR., English language educator; b. Boston, Jan. 16, 1933. BA in English with honors, Amherst Coll., 1955; MA in Am. Studies, U. Mich., 1960; PhD in British and Am. Lit., Ind. U., 1968. Instr. English Valparaiso U., 1960-62; teaching assoc. Ind. U., 1962-65; from asst. prof. to prof. English U. Va., Charlottesville, 1967—; dir. Ctr. for Liberal Arts U. Va., Charlottesville, 1984—; project dir. NEH, 1972-76, 85-90, 90—; dir. Canadian Judicial Writing Program, 1981-84; guest prof. Am. studies U. Bonn, 1982. Author: The Illusion of Life-American Realism as a Literary Form, 1969, A Field Guide to the Study of American Literature, 1976, A Writer's Guide: The Essential Points, 1980, A Handbook for Research in American Literature and American Studies, 1994; contbr. articles to scholarly publs. Naval aviator, 1955-59. Recipient Armstrong prize in English, Amherst Coll., 1952, James A. Work prize U. Ind., 1965, Guggenheim fellowship, 1970-71, Faculty Leadership award Am. Assn. Higher Edn., Carnegie Found. for Advancement of Teaching and Change mag., 1986, Citation for Leadership in Rejuvenation of Secondary and Elem. Edn., Va. Bd. Edn., 1987, Phillip E. Frandson award for Innovation and Creative Programming, Nat. U. Continuing Edn. Assn., 1988, Outstanding Faculty award Va. Coun. Higher Edn., 1988. Mem. MLA (chmn. del. assembly steering com. 1984-85). Office: U Va English Dept Bryan Hall Charlottesville VA 22903

KOLB, JOHN, automotive executive. CEO Holman Enterprises, Pennsauken, N.J. Office: Holman Enterprises PO Box 1400 Pennsauken NJ 08109-0400*

KOLB, JOHN JOSEPH, art educator; b. Winnipeg, Can., Nov. 12, 1951; came to U.S., 1958; s. Harold J. and Catherine M. Kolb; m. Linda M. Ackland, June 14, 1980; children: Ingrid A., Britta M. BS, Bemidji (Minn.) State U., 1977; MA, Mankato (Minn.) U., 1979; MFA, U. N.D., 1983. Comml. artist Dept. Natural Resources, Bemidji, 1976; art tchr., coach St. Francis (Minn.) Schs., 1977-78; art tchr., camera club Westbrook (Minn.) Schs., 1979-80; art tchr., coach Soux Falls (S.D.) Schs., 1980-86; cons., 1986-87; art tchr. N.W. Iowa C.C., Sheldon, 1988—; asst. cross country and track coach U. Sioux Falls, 1996—; dir. Sioux River Ann. Internat. Art Competition, 1983. Represented in permanent collections S.D. Meml. Art Ctr., Brookings, Dahl Fine Art Ctr., Rapid City, S.D., Civici Fine Arts Ctr., Sioux Falls, Mount Marty Coll., Yankton, S.D., Nobles County Art Ctr., Worthington, Minn., Bemidji State U., Albert Lea Art Ctr., Minn., U. Sioux Falls. Bd. dirs. Sioux Falls Figure Skating Club, 1997—. Sgt. USAF, 1970-74. Mem. USA Weightlifting. Democrat. Roman Catholic. Home: 624 E 28th St Sioux Falls SD 57105

KOLB, JOYCE DIANA, artist, educator; b. Detroit, Nov. 28, 1942; d. David Victor and Jean (Silber) Howell; m. Gary Jack Kolb, June 15, 1963; 1 child, Michael Daniel. BFA, Corcoran Sch. Art, Washington, 1981. Legal sec. Advance Mortgage Co., Detroit, 1961-63; profl. artist Arnold, Md., 1981—; founder, facilitator Healing Through Art, Arnold, 1995—; facilitator Natural Healing, Inc., Severna Park, Md., 1997—, Unity By-the-Bay, Severna Park, 1996—, Psyche's WEll, Easton, Md., 1998—, Art Inst. Gallery, Salisbury, Md., 1998—, Sunrise Assisted Living, Severna Park, 1998—, Innersource, Annapolis, Md., 1998—; art educator home sch. for children Arnold, 1996—; founder, facilitator Healing Through Art workshops, Arnold, 1995—. Exhibited sculpture, Flint, Mich., 1976 (3-Dimension Design award 1976), painting, Glen Echo, Md., 1981 (artist-in-residence 1981); represented in permanent collection Nat. Mus. of Women in Arts, Washington. Recipient 1st pl. award 23d Invitational Art Exhibit, Towson Bus. Assn., 1990, Best of Show Annapolitan Gallerie, 1994. Mem. Women's Caucus for Arts (participating artist D.C. chpt. Beijing 1996), Md. Fedn. Art, Corcoran Alumni Assn. Avocations: promoting positive energy, traveling, friends, animal lover, appreciation of outdoors. Office: Healing Through Art PO Box 163 Arnold MD 21012

KOLB, KEITH ROBERT, architect, educator; b. Billings, Mont., Feb. 9, 1922; s. Percy Fletcher and Josephine (Randolph) K.; m. Jacqueline Cecile Jump, June 18, 1947; children: Brooks Robin, Bliss Richards. Grad. basic engring., US Army Specialized Training Rutgers U., 1944; BArch cum laude, U. Wash., 1947; MArch, Harvard U., 1950. Registered architect, Wash., Mont., Idaho, Calif., Oreg., Nat. Council Archtl. Registration Bds. Draftsman, designer various archtl. firms Seattle, 1946-54; draftsman, designer Walter Gropius and Architects Collaborative, Cambridge, Mass., 1950-52; prin. Keith R. Kolb, Architect, Seattle, 1954-64, Keith R. Kolb Architect & Assocs., Seattle, 1964-66; ptnr. Decker, Kolb & Stansfield, Seattle, 1966-71, Kolb & Stansfield AIA Architects, Seattle, 1971-89; pvt. practice Keith R. Kolb FAIA Architects, Seattle, 1989—; instr. Mont. State Coll., Bozeman, 1947-49; asst. prof. arch. U. Wash., Seattle, 1952-60, assoc. prof., 1960-82, prof., 1982-90, prof. emeritus, 1990—. Design architect Dist. II Hdqrs. and Comm. Ctr., Wash. State Patrol, Bellevue, 1970 (Exhbn. award Seattle chpt. AIA), Hampson residence, 1970 (nat. AIA 1st honor 1973, citation Seattle chpt. AIA 1980), Acute Gen. Stevens Meml. Hosp., 1973, Redmond Pub. Libr., 1975 (jury selection Wash. coun. AIA 1980), Tolstedt residence, Helena, Mont., 1976, Herbert L. Eastlick Biol. Scis. Lab. bldg. Wash. State U., 1977, Redmond Svc. Ctr., Puget Sound Power and Light Co., 1979, Computer and Mgmt. Svcs. Ctr., Paccar Inc., 1981 (curatorial team selection Mus. History and Industry exhbn. 100th anniversary of AIA 1994), Seattle Town House, 1960 (curatorial team selection Mus. History and Industry exhbn. 100th anniversary of AIA 1994), Comm. Tower, Pacific N.W. Bell, 1981 (nat. J.F. Lincoln bronze), Forks br. Seattle 1st Nat. Bank, 1981 (commendation award Seattle chpt. AIA 1981, nat. jury selection Am. Architecture, The State of the Art in the '80's 1985, regional citation Am. Wood Coun. 1981), Reg. ops. Control Ctr. Sacramento Dist. Corps Engrs. McChord AFB, Wash., 1982, Puget Sound Blood Ctr., 1983-88, expansion vis./dining/recreation facilities Wash. State Reformatory, Monroe, 1983, Univ. Sta. P.O., U.S. Postal Svc., Seattle, 1983, Guard Towers, McNeil Island Corrections Ctr. Wash., 1983, Magnolia Queen Anne Carrier Annex, U.S. Postal Svc., Seattle, 1986, Tolstedt residence, Seattle, 1987, Maxim residence, Camano Island, Wash., 1991, Carmean residence alterations/additions, Seattle, 1995, 96, 97. Pres. Laurelhurst Community Club, Seattle, 1966. Served with U.S. Army, 1943-45, ETO. Decorated Bronze Star medal ETO; recipient Alpha Rho Chi medal; selected Am. Architects, Facts on File, inc., 1989. Fellow AIA (dir. Seattle chpt. 1970-71, sec. Seattle chpt. 1972, Wash. state coun. 1973, pres. sr. coun. Seattle chpt. 1994-96, trustee Seattle Archtl. Found. 1994-96, Citation award Seattle chpt. for a Seattle 1960 Town House, 1990); mem. U. Wash. Archtl. Alumni Assn. (pres. 1958-59), Phi Beta Kappa, Tau Sigma Delta. Home and Office: 3379 47th Ave NE Seattle WA 98105-5326

KOLB, KEN LLOYD, writer; b. Portland, Oreg., July 14, 1926; s. Frederick Von and Ella May (Bay) K.; m. Emma LaVada Sanford, June 7, 1952; children: Kevin, Lauren, Kimrie. BA in English with honors, U. Calif., Berkeley, 1950; MA with honors, San Francisco State U., 1953. Cert. jr. coll. English tchr. Freelance fiction writer various nat. mags., N.Y.C., 1951-56; freelance screenwriter various film and TV studios, Los Angeles, 1956-81; freelance novelist Chilton, Random House, Playboy Press, N.Y.C., 1967—; instr. creative writing Feather River Coll., Quincy Calif., 1969; minister Universal Life Ch. Author: (teleplay) She Walks in Beauty, 1956 (Writers Guild award 1956), (feature films) Seventh Voyage of Sinbad, 1957, Snow Job, 1972, (novels) Getting Straight, 1967 (made into feature film), The Couch Trip, 1970 (made into feature film), Night Crossing, 1974, contbr. fiction and humor to nat. mags. and anthologies. Foreman Plumas County

Grand Jury, Quincy, 1970; chmn. Region C Criminal Justice Planning commn., Oroville, Calif., 1975-77; film commr. Plumas County, 1986-87. Served with USNR, 1944-46. Establishment Ken Kolb Collection (Boston U. Library 1969). Mem. Writers Guild Am. West, Authors Guild, Mensa, Phi Beta Kappa, Theta Chi. Democrat. Club: Plumas Ski (pres. 1977-78). Avocations: skiing, tennis, traveling. Home and Office: PO Box 30022 Cromberg CA 96103-3022 *The true measure of success is not the attainment of great wealth or a position of power over others, but the quality of one's own life. I'm grateful for the money and honors I've had from writing, but more important to me is my ongoing love affair with my wife and the loving friendship of my grown children. I believe in God and a sense of humor as guiding principles, but I can't explain either one.*

KOLB, NATHANIEL KEY, JR., architect; b. Sherman, Tex., Aug. 17, 1933; s. Nathaniel Key and Nelcine (Dial) K.; m. Catherine Conner, Nov. 24, 1958; children: Nathaniel Key, Mary Catherine, Amy Monica, Peter Paul, John Conner, Elizabeth Dial. BArch, Tex. A&M U., 1957; MArch, U. Pa., 1960. Registered architect, Tex. With CRSS, Houston, 1955-58, Vincent G. Kling, Phila., 1958-61, William B. Tabler, N.Y.C., 1961-63; chmn. bd., pres. Omniplan, Inc., Dallas, 1963—; instr. Tex. A&M Univ., Coll. Station, 1957-58; adj. asst. prof. Columbia U., N.Y.C., 1961-62; bd. dirs. Fidelity Bank, Dallas, 1985-98; mem., chmn. Urban Design Task Force, Dallas, 1974-83; dir., mem. exec. com. Greater Dallas Planning Coun., 1982-85; mem. adv. coun. Ryan Real Estate Coun., U. Tex., Arlington, 1985-88; bd. dirs. Peacock Alley. Chmn. Hist. Landmarks Com., Dallas, 1977-79; pres., dir. Dallas Ballet, 1982-87. Fellow AIA; mem. Tex. Soc. Architects, Dallas chpt. AIA (dir. 1976-80, pres. 1979), Dallas Club (pres., dir. 1980-86). Office: Omniplan 2611 N Haskell Ave # 16 Dallas TX 75204-2904

KOLB, RICHARD MAURICE, sports writer, sportscaster; b. Washington, Feb. 17, 1951; s. Maurice Woodrow and Dorothy Evelyn (Taylor) K.; m. Diane Marie Buczkowski Falcone, July 4, 1976 (div. Oct. 1990); 1 child, Michael Richard. Student, U. Md., 1969-71; AA, Prince George's Coll., 1971; AS, No. Va. Coll., 1978. Lic. radio operator, D.C. Pub. info. news specialist USDA, Washington, 1977-78; sports writer Tampa (Fla.) Tribune, 1988-89; pub. rels. dir. Brewster Tech. Ctr., Tampa, 1991; editor Sports Tampa Bay, 1993; sports columnist Bowl Mag., Washington, 1990—, Bowling World, Dublin, Calif., 1991—, Pinbuster, St. Petersburg, Fla., 1993—, Across the Lanes, San Antonio, 1996—; radio sports anchor WTAN, Clearwater, Fla.; writer-photographer Bowling Digest, Chgo., 1998—. Columnist Sports Time mag., 1999—. Mem. Young Dems. of Am., College Park, Md., 1970-79. Recipient Best Sports Writer and Sportscaster, Tampa Tribune's Top Ten Awardd, 1994, Best Feature Story award Bowling Mag., 1998. Mem. Bowling Writers Assn. Am. (Bowler of Mo. com. 1997—), Young Am. Bowling Alliance (mem. collegiate bowling poll 1995—), Fla. Press Club. Democrat. Avocations: photography, videos, exercising, bowling, golf. Home: 5677 Sailfish Dr Lutz FL 33549-7108

KOLBE, JAMES THOMAS, congressman; b. Evanston, Ill., June 28, 1942; s. Walter William and Helen (Reed) K. BA in Polit. Sci., Northwestern U., 1965; MBA in Econs., Stanford U., 1967. Asst. to coordinating architect Ill. Bldg. Authority, Chgo., 1970-72; spl. asst. to Gov. Richard Ogilvie Chgo., 1972-73; v.p. Wood Canyon Corp., Tucson, 1973-80; mem. Ariz. Senate, 1977-83, majority whip, 1979-80; mem. 99th-106th Congresses from 5th dist. Ariz., 1985—; mem. appropriations com. 99th-105th Congresses from 5th dist. Ariz., 1987—, chmn. appropriations subcom. on treasury, postal svc. and ge, 1997—. Trustee Embry-Riddle Aero. U., Daytona Beach, Fla.; bd. dirs. Community Food Bank, Tucson; Republican precinct committeeman, Tucson, 1974—. Served as lt. USNR, 1968-69, Vietnam. Republican. Methodist. Office: US Ho of Reps 2266 Rayburn Washington DC 20515-0305

KOLBE, JOHN WILLIAM, newspaper columnist; b. Evanston, Ill., Sept. 21, 1940; s. Walter William and Helen (Reed) K.; m. Mary Bauman, Feb. 24, 1990; stepchildren: Erin Simmons, James Simmons; children by previous marriage: Karen, David. BS in Journalism, Northwestern U., 1961; MA in Polit. Sci., U. Notre Dame, 1962. Feature writer, polit. reporter Rockford (Ill.) Register-Republic, 1964-68; press aide Ogilvie for Gov. campaign, Chgo., 1968; asst. press sec. Office Gov., Springfield, Ill., 1969-73; polit. reporter, columnist Phoenix Gazette, 1973-97; polit. columnist Arizona Republic, 1997—. Elder Valley Presbyn. Ch., Scottsdale, Ariz., 1978-81; bd. dirs. Morrison Inst., Ariz. State U., Tempe, 1982-97. Lt. (j.g.) USNR, 1962-64. Recipient Best Column of Yr. award Ariz. Press Club, 1976, 80, 84. Office: Arizona Republic 200 E Van Buren St Phoenix AZ 85004-2238

KOLBE, KARL WILLIAM, JR., lawyer; b. Passaic, N.J., Sept. 29, 1926; s. Karl William Sr. and Edna Ernestine (Rumsey) K.; m. Barbara Louise Bogart, Jan. 28, 1950 (dec. Aug. 1992); children: Kim E., William B., Katherine B.; m. Patricia L. Coward, Apr. 30, 1994. BA, Princeton U., 1949; JD, U. Va., 1952. Bars: N.Y. 1952, D.C. 1976. Ptnr. Reid & Priest, N.Y.C., 1966-92, of counsel, 1993—; dir. Bessemer Trust Co. (N.A.), N.Y.C., 1977-97, Carolinas Cement Co., World Trade Corp.; vice-chmn. The friends of Thirteen Inc. Bd. dirs. N.J. Ballet Co., West Orange, 1970-98, Ocean Liner Mus., 1992—. Served with USN, 1944-46. Mem. ABA (chmn. pub. utility law sect. 1984-85). Republican. Episcopalian. Clubs: Univ. (N.Y.C.); Metro. (Washington). Home: PO Box 278 111 Old Chester Rd Essex Fells NJ 07021-1625 Office: Thelen Reid & Priest 40 W 57th St New York NY 10019-4097

KOLBECK, SISTER ANN LAWRENCE, school principal; b. Salem, S.D., Jan. 10, 1935; d. Lawrence Bernard and Nora Jeannette (Dunn) K. BA in Sociology, Cardinal Stritch Coll., Milw., 1973; MA in Adminstrn., Loyola Marymount U., L.A., 1987. Tchr. for mentally retarded St. Coletta Sch., Jefferson, Wis., 1956-74; tchr. Hanna Boys Ctr., Sonoma, Calif., 1975-77, St. Benedict Sch., Montebello, Calif., 1978-84; prin. St. Benedict Sch., 1985—. Office: St Benedict Sch 217 N 10th St Montebello CA 90640-4604

KOLBERT, JACK, foreign language educator, French literature educator, humanities educator; b. Perth-Amboy, N.J., Apr. 25, 1927; s. Robert S. and Sophie (Burstein) Kolbert-Kroop; m. Ruth M. Katz; children: Harry Jules, Shelley Robert. BA magna cum laude, U. So. Calif., 1948, MA; postgrad., U. Calif., Berkeley, 1949-51; PhD, Columbia U., 1957. Lectr. French Columbia U., N.Y.C., 1951-52; instr. French, Spanish Wesleyan U., Middletown, Conn., 1954-55; from asst., assoc. prof. to prof. Romance langs. U. Pitts., 1955-65, chmn. dept. of Romance and Modern langs., 1960-65; prof. U. N.Mex., Albuquerque, 1965-77; vis. prof. Pomona Coll., Claremont, Calif., 1970-71; pres. Monterey (Calif.) Inst. of Internat. Studies, 1977-80; dir. external rels. Calif. Acad. of Scis., San Francisco, 1980-82; div. chmn. Piedmont Community Coll., Charlottesville, Va., 1982-85; dept. chmn. Susquehanna U., Selinsgrove, Pa., 1985-92, prof., 1992-96, prof. emeritus, 1996—; cons. City of Pitts. and Forest Hills Schs., Allegheny County, Pa., 1956-66; cons. Holmes & Meier Publs., N.Y.C., 1985—; hon. fellow, mem. bd. advisors Inst. of Am. Univs., Aix-en-Provence, France; vis. prof. U. Kansas, 1968, Calif. State U., L.A., 1971, Am. Inst. Univs., Aix-En-Provence, France, 1995; cons. Dept. Edn. Commonwealth of Pa., 1985-96. Author: Edmond Jaloux, Critique, 1962, The World of A. Maurois, 1986 (Choice Book award 1987); co-author: L'Art de Michel Butor, 1970, Vols. I and II French for Elementary Teachers, 1958, 60, Elie Wiesel: Cinders of the Past, Flames of the Future, 1999; editl. bd. profl. jours.; contbr. more than 500 articles and reviews to profl. jours. Hon. Consul Gen. French Republic, N.Mex., No. Calif., 1965-80; pres. City Coun. Albuquerque, 1974-77; bd. dirs. St. Joseph's Med. Ctr., Albuquerque, 1974-77, Albuquerque C. of C., 1974-77; co-chmn. Commonwealth of Va. Lang. Com., Richmond, 1983-85. Fulbright fellow, Pre, Post Doctoral Fulbright fellow, Paris, 1953-54, 63-64, Ford fellow, Ford Found., 1954-55, Camargo Found. fellow, France, 1992-93, fellow Cerisy-La-Salle Found. Elie Wiesel, 1995; decorated knight and officer Acad. Palms, French Govt., Paris, knight Nat. Order of Merit, French Govt., Paris; named Pa. Lang. Prof. of Year, 1987. Mem. MLA (hon., life), Am. Assn. Tchrs. of French (bd. mem. 1967-75, hon. life). Democrat. Jewish. Avocations: classical music, gymnastics, travel, lecturing. Home: PO Box 271 Selinsgrove PA 17870-0271

KOLBERT, KATHRYN, lawyer, educator; b. Detroit, Apr. 8, 1952; d. Melvin and Rosalie Betty (Frank) K.; children: Samuel Kolbert-Hyle, Kate Kolbert Hyle. BA, Cornell U., 1974; JD, Temple U., 1977. Bar: Pa. 1977, U.S. Dist. Ct. (ea. dist.) Pa. 1977, U.S. Ct. Appeals (3d cir.) 1977, U.S. Supreme Ct. 1985, U.S. Dist. Ct. N.D. 1991, U.S. Ct. Appeals (5th cir.) 1991, U.S. Ct. Appeals (10th cir.) 1994, U.S. Ct. Appeals (8th cir.) 1994. Atty. Community Legal Svcs., Phila., 1977-79, Women's Law Project, Phila., 1979-88; co-founder, dir. policy Women's Agenda, Phila., 1984-88; v.p., litigator Ctr. for Reproductive Law & Policy, N.Y.C., 1992-97; atty. pvt. practice, Wyndmoor, Pa., 1997—; cons. Planned Parenthood Fedn., N.Y.C., 1988-89, Nat. Abortion Rights Action League, Washington, 1987; cons. reproductive freedom project ACLU, N.Y.C., 1988-89, state coordinating counsel, 1989-92; v.p. Ctr Reproductive Law & Policy, N.Y., 1992; lectr. dept. women's studies U. Pa., 1978-86, 90-91, lectr. Sch. Law, 1989-91, sr. rsch. adminstr. Annenberg Pub. Policy Ctr., 1998; Open Soc. Inst. fellow, 1998. Exec. prodr. (radio series on constnl. law) Justice Talking; contbr. chpts. to books. Founder, Commn. to Elect Women Judges, Women Judges Pac, Phila, 1984; bd. dirs. Com. to Elect the Cosey 5, Phila. Recipient Dedicated Advocacy award Nat. Abortion Rights Action League Pa., 1986, Pa. Coalition Against Domestic Violence, 1986, Luth. Settlement House Women's Program, 1987, Am. Dem. Action award, 1989, honoree Women's Way, 1991; named One of 100 Most Influential Lawyers in Am., Nat. Law Jour. Democrat. Jewish.

KOLDA, THOMAS JOSEPH, non-profit organization executive; b. Chgo., Dec. 1, 1939; s. Amos Joseph and Cecilia Marie (Baxa) K.; m. Gail Judith Kettler, June 30, 1962; children: Brian Joseph, Jeffrey Thomas. BA, Coe Coll., 1961, MA, 1984; PhD in Adminstrn. and Fin. Mgmt., Columbia Pacific U., 1986. Cert. fund raising exec. Dir. devel./pub. rels. Mt. Mercy Coll., Cedar Rapids, Iowa, 1965-69; v.p. delve. St. Mary's Coll., Orchard Lake, Mich., 1969-71; dir. devel. Roman Catholic Diocese, Tucson, 1971-74; dir. devel./pub. rels. The Pontifical Coll. Josephinum, Columbus, Ohio, 1975-77; dir. trusts and estates Ohio State U. Devel. Fund, Columbus, 1977-85; v.p. devel. Coe Coll., Cedar Rapids, Iowa, 1985-87; dir. trusts and estates Marquette U., Milw., 1987-92; pvt. practice cons. fin. and charitable gift planning, 1992-98; exec. dir. univ. rels. U. Wisc., Whitewater, 1999—. Mem. Nat. Soc. Fund Raising Execs. (past pres. Ctrl. Ohio chpt.), Internat. Assn. Fin. Planning (bd. dirs. 1991-95), Coun. Advancement and Support Edn., Nat. Com. on Planned Giving. Home: 800 W Main St Whitewater WI 53190

KOLDE, BERT, professional basketball team executive. Vice chmn. Portland Trail Blazers. Office: Portland Trail Blazers One Center Ct Ste 200 Portland OR 97227*

KOLDE, RICHARD ARTHUR, insurance company executive, consultant; b. Pomona, Calif., Jan. 25, 1944; s. Arthur and Rosemary (Decker) K.; children: Nicole Rochelle, Eric Christian, Katarina R. Lic. CPCU. AA, Mt. San Antonio Coll., 1963; BS, U. So. Calif., 1965; AS, Mira Costa Coll., 1979. Asst. mgr., mgr. Lord Rebel Ind., Montclair, Costa Mesa and Carlsbad, Calif., 1971-74; agt. Conn. Mut. Life Ins. Co., San Diego and Carlsbad, 1974-77; pres., owner Investment Assocs., Carlsbad, 1977-82, 93—; mng. gen. agt. E.F. Hutton Life Ins. Co., San Diego, 1982—; cons. Hansch Fin. Group, Laguna Hills, Calif., 1984; cons., recruiter Ky. Gen. Life Ins. co., 1990-92; mng. gen agt. N.W. Life of Can. Ins. Co, 1991—. Bd. dirs. Boys Club Am., Carlsbad, 1980-84, adv. bd., 1984—; bd. dirs. YMCA, Pomona, 1960-64. Served with USAF, 1966-71. Decorated Outstanding Unit award, Small Arms Expert award, Security 1 & 2 Protection of Pres. U.S. award; named Largest Producing Mng. Gen. Agt. in Nation, E.F. Hutton Life Co., 1982, 83. Mem. Nat. Assn. Life Underwriters (legis. officer 1974—), Calif. Assn. Life Underwriters, Internat. Assn. Fin. Planners (Mem. of Yr. award 1977), U.S. Gymnastics Fedn. (coaching credentials, ofcl. judge collegiate level), VFW, Phi Sigma Beta. Republican. Lodge: Rotary.

KOLE, JULIUS S., lawyer; b. Chgo., July 27, 1953; s. Jack H. and Ruth (Rakowsky) K.; m. Dorie Elrod, June 27, 1976; children: Ryan, Frederick, Abby. BS in Fin., U. Ill., Chgo., 1975; JD, John Marshall Law Sch., 1978. Bar: Ill. 1978. Asst. pub. defender Cook County Pub. Defender, Chgo., 1978-80; prin. Law Offices of Julius S. Kole, Buffalo Grove, Ill., 1980—. Fellow Ill. State Bar Assn., Lake County Bar Assn. Jewish. Avocations: sports, reading, motorcycling. Office: 750 W Lake Cook Rd Ste 135 Buffalo Grove IL 60089-2075

KOLEAN, BONITA LAMAE, artist, educator; b. Holland, Mich., Feb. 21, 1940; d. John and Lamae (Schippa) K.; m. D.A. Drennen, Oct. 30, 1998. BA, U. Ctrl. Mich., 1962; MA, U. Mich., 1968, Purdue U., 1978; MFA, Fla. State U., 1980. Tchr. Garden City (Mich.) Pub. Schs., 1962-66; crisis tchr. Washtenaw Sch. Dist., Ann Arbor, Mich., 1966-69; tchr., counselor Copper Country Sch. Dist., Hancock, Mich., 1969-74; tchr. Tippecanoe Pub. Schs., West Lafayette, Ind., 1974-75; art tchr. Cairo Am. Coll., Egypt, 1975-76, Leon County Pub. Schs., Tallahassee, 1978-80; drawing tchr. Fla. State U., Tallahassee, 1980, Lemoyne Art Ctr, Tallahassee, 1983; art tchr. Thomas County Pub. Schs., Thomasville, Ga., 1980-98. Illustrator: Building a Legacy, 1995; one woman show Thomasville Cultural Ctr., 1998; exhibited in group shows at Thomasville Cultural Ctr., 1999, Fla. State U. Mus. Fine Arts, 1999. Recipient 2d pl. award Gadsden Arts Coun., 1997, Best of Show award Thomasville Art Guild, 1996. Mem. Nat. Art Edn. Assn., Art League Tallahassee, LeMoyne Art Ctr.

KOLEHMAINEN, JAN WALDROY, professional association administrator; b. Virginia, Minn., July 8, 1940; s. John Ilmari and Astrid Irene (Petrell) K.; m. Katherine Lorene MacDanel, June 18, 1966; children: Lynn Kristine, Mark Daven. BA, Heidelberg Coll., 1962; MA, Bowling Green U., 1965. Asst. dir. admissions Syracuse U., N.Y., 1965-68; dir. admissions St. Xavier Coll., Chgo., 1968-72; dir. med. soc. rels. AMA, Chgo., 1972-80; dir. interspty. affairs Minn. Med. Assn., Mpls., 1980-82; exec. dir. Am. Acad. Neurology, Mpls., 1982-99; ret., 1999. Mem. Am. Soc. Assn. Execs., Minn. Soc. Assn. Execs. (bd. dirs. 1989-93, sec.-treas. 1991-93), Am. Assn. Med. Soc. Execs. (bd. dirs. 1984-88), Profl. Conv. Mgrs. Assn. (bd. dirs. 1992-93). Avocations: tennis; fishing; reading. Office: Am Acad Neurology 1080 Montreal Ave Saint Paul MN 55116-2311

KOLEILAT, BETTY KUMMER, middle school educator, mathematician; b. Houston, Aug. 18, 1948; d. Will Ernest and Nellie Kummer; m. Bashir M. Koleilat, Jan. 12, 1973; 1 child, Farah. BS in Edn., U. Houston, 1970, MEd in Adminstrn., 1973, EdD in Curriculum and Instrn., 1994. Cert. elem. and mid. sch. math. tchr., Tex.; cert. in mid.-mgmt., TEx. Elem. educator, math. specialist, asst. prin. Houston Ind. Sch. Dist., 1970-78; mid. math. tchr., team leader Singapore Am. Sch., 1978-80; tchr. 1st grad Spring Ind. Sch. Dist., Houston, 1980-85, gifted tchr. 3d to 5th grades, 1985-90; tchr. math. Aldine Ind. Sch. Dist., Houston, 1990-96; asst. prin. for curriculum/magnet program, Drew Acad.; presenter Coun. for Advancement of Math. Tchg., 1984-99; mem. Tex. Essential Knowledge and Skills Math Writing Team, Tex. Edn. Agy., 1995-97. Contbg. author: Helping Your Child at Home...With Mathematics, 1991. Recipient Austin High PTA Scholarship, 1966, Harris County PTA Scholarship, 1966, Tchr. Initiative Project award Spring Ind. Sch. Dist., 1983, 84, Link Elem. PTA Scholarship, 1990, Outstanding Math. Educator award, 1994-95. Mem. ASCD, Nat. Coun. Tchrs. Math. (Arithmetic Tchr. Tchg. Math. in the Middle articles referee Reston chpt. 1987-99, materials reviewer 1995-99). Avocations: tennis, bridge.

KOLEK, ROBERT EDWARD, lawyer; b. Chgo., June 1, 1943; s. Joseph Stanley and Mary Lillian (Heteniak) K.; m. Linda Lee Bernicchi, Aug. 27, 1966; children: Kimberley M., Robert E. Jr. BBA, Loyola U., Chgo., 1965, JD, 1968. Bar: Ill. 1968. Law clk. to Hon. Thomas Kluczynski, Ill. Supreme Ct., Chgo., 1968-70. Mem. ABA, Chgo. Bar Assn. Roman Catholic. Avocation: photography. Office: Schiff Hardin & Waite 6600 Sears Tower Chicago IL 60606-6473

KOLESAR, PETER JOHN, business and engineering educator; b. N.Y.C., Nov. 25, 1936; s. John Michael and Agnes (Vajda) K.; m. Nicole Bordat, May 30, 1969 (div. 1981); children: Lara, Alexandre; m. Miriam Larsson, June 18, 1988; 1 child, Angelica. B.A., Queens Coll., 1959; B.S. in Indsl. Engring., Columbia U., 1959, M.S., 1962, Ph.D., 1964. Systems analyst Procter & Gamble, Cin., 1959-61; lectr. Imperial Coll., London, 1964-65; asst. prof. Sch. Engring. Columbia U., N.Y.C., 1965-70, prof. Grad. Sch. Bus., 1975—, rsch. dir. Dening Ctr. Quality Mgmt., 1990; sr. analyst Rand Corp., N.Y.C., 1971-74; examiner Malcolm Baldrige Nat. Quality Award, 1990-91; cons. in field. Assoc. editor Mgmt. Sci.; contbr. articles to profl. jours. Recipient Systems Sci. prize NATO, 1976. Fellow AAAS; mem. Ops. Research Soc. Am. (council 1980-83, Lanchester prize 1976), Inst. Mgmt. Scis., Am. Statis. Assn., Am. Soc. Quality Control. Home: 410 Riverside Dr New York NY 10025-7974 Office: Columbia U 408 Uris Hall New York NY 10027

KOLESKE, JOSEPH VICTOR, chemical engineer, consultant; b. Stratford, Wis., Jan. 23, 1930; s. Joseph John and Mary Helen (Jilek) K.; m. Mary Anne Casey, Nov. 3, 1951; children: Robert Casey, Krista Koleske Killmeier. BS in Chem. Engring., U. Wis., 1958; MS, Inst. Paper Chemistry, Appleton, Wis., 1960, PhD, 1963. Corp. rsch. fellow Union Carbide Corp., South Charleston, W.Va., 1963-88; sr. cons. Consolidated Rsch. Inc., Kingsford, Mich., 1988—; short course lectr. radiation chemistry, N.D. State U., 1996—. Author: Free Radical Radiation Curing, 1997, Alkylene Oxides and Their Polymers, 1990, Poly Ethylene Oxide, 1976, Poly Vinyl Chloride, 1969, Cationic Radiation Curing, 1991, others; editor: ASTM Paint and Coating Testing Manual, 1995; mem. editl. rev. bd. Jour. Coatings Tech., 1979—; contbr. chpts. to books and more than 100 articles to profl. jours.; patentee in fields of chemistry, polymer blends, and coatings. With USAF, 1950-54. Recipient Interstab Award, U. So. Miss., 1981, Award for Sci. Achievement, Am. Chem. Soc., 1978. Mem. ASTM (editor Paint and Coating Testing Manual 1995), Radtech Internat., Fedn. Socs. for Coating Techs., Serra of Charleston. Roman Catholic. Avocations: philately, writing, reading. Home and Office: 1513 Brentwood Rd Charleston WV 25314-2307

KOLESON, DONALD RALPH, retired college dean, educator; b. Eldon, Mo., June 30, 1935; s. Ralph A. and Fern M. (Beanland) K.; children—Anne, David, Janet. B.S. in Edn., Central Mo. State U., 1959; M.Ed., So. Ill. U., 1973. Mem. faculty So. Ill. U., Carbondale, 1968-73; dean tech. edn. Belleville (Ill.) Area Coll., 1982-93; ret. 1993. Mem. Am. Vocat. Edn. Assn., Am. Welding Assn., Nat. Assn. Two-Year Schs. of Constrn. (pres. 1984-85). Clubs: Masons; Shriners, Jesters.

KOLFF, WILLEM JOHAN, internist, educator; b. Leiden, Holland, Feb. 14, 1911; came to U.S., 1950, naturalized, 1956; s. Jacob and Adriana (de Jonge) K.; m. Janke C. Huidekoper, Sept 4, 1937; children: Jacob, Adriana P., Albert C., Cornelis A., Gualtherus C.M. Student, U. Leiden Med. Sch., 1930-38; M.D. summa cum laude, U. Groningen, 1946; MD (hon.), U. Turin, Italy, 1969, Rostock (Germany) U., 1975, U. Bologna, Italy, 1983; DSc (hon.), Allegheny Coll., Meadville, Pa., 1960, Tulane U., 1975, CUNY, 1982, Temple U., 1983, U. Utah, 1983; D. of Tech. Scis. (hon.), Tech. U. Twente, Enschede, The Netherlands, 1986; DSc (hon.), U. Athens, 1988, Aix-Marseille II, 1993. Internist, head med. dept. Mcpl. Hosp., Kampen, Holland; dir. divsn. artificial organs Cleve. Clinic Found., 1950-67; privaat docent, dept. medicine U. Leiden, 1950-67; prof. surgery U. Utah Coll. Medicine, Salt Lake City, 1967—, Disting. prof. medicine and surgery, 1979—, prof. internal medicine, 1981—, dir. Kolff's Lab., 1986—, dir. Inst. Biomed. Engring., dir. divsn. artificial organs, 1967-86, ret. Patent for ventricular assist device and method of manufacturing, collapsible artificial ventricle and pumping shell, ventricular assist device with volumne displacement chamber, electrohydraulic heart with septum mounted pump, muscle and air powered left ventricular assist device. Decorated commandeur Orde Van Oranje Netherlands, 1970; Orden de Mayo al Merito en el Grade de Gran Official Argentina, 1974; recipient Landsteiner medal for establishing blood banks during German occupation in Holland, Netherlands Red Cross, 1942, Cameron prize U. Edinburgh, Scotland, 1964, Gairdner prize Gairdner Found., 1966, Valentine award N.Y. Acad. Medicine, 1969, 1st Gold medal Netherlands Surg. Soc., 1970, Leo Harvey prize Technion, Israel, 1972, Sr. U.S. Scientist award Alexander Von Humboldt Found., 1978, Austrian Gewerbeverein's Wilhelm-Exner award, 1980, John Scott medal City of Phila., 1984, Japan prize Japan Found. Sci. and Tech., 1986, Rsch. prize Netherlands Royal Inst. Engrs., 1986, 1st Jean Hamburger award Internat. Soc. Nephrology, 1987, 1st Edwin Cohn-De Laval award World Apheresis Assn, 1990, Fed. prize Fedn. Sci. Med. Assn., 1990, Father of Artificial Organs award and medal Internat. Soc. Artificial Organs, 1992, Christopher Columbus Discovery award in biomed. rsch. NIH, 1992, Legacy of Life award LDS Deseret Found., 1995, Lifetime Achievement award, Ahmedabad, India, 1996; named to Nat. Inventors Hall of Fame, 1985, 95, named to On the Shoulders of Giants Hall of Fame, Cleve., 1989, one of Utah's Most Disting. Achievers, 1996. Mem. AMA (Sci. Achievement award 1982), AAUP, Am. Physiol. Soc., Soc. Exptl. Biology and Medicine, AAAS, NAE (City of Medicine award 1989), ACP, N.Y. Acad. Scis., Am. Soc. Artificial Internal Organs, Nat. Kidney Found., European Dialysis and Transplant Assn., Austrian Soc. Nephrology (hon.), Academia Nacional de Medicine (Colombia, hon.), Rotary. Achievements include development of artifical kidney for clinical use, 1943, of heart-lung machine, 1949, of first membrane oxygenator, 1955, of disposable twin-coil kidney, 1956, of balloon pump, 1962, of wearable artificial kidney (WAK), 1981; development of artificial heart, 1958, human implantation, Dr. Barney Clark, 1982; patentee in field. Home: 1 Lauren Ln Westmont Johnstown PA 15905-4398*

KOLINSKY, MICHAEL ALLEN, emergency physician; b. Phila., Dec. 23, 1947; s. Maurice and Lenore (Rose) K.; m. Barbara Victorine, June 20, 1981; children: Nicole, Daniel, Samuel. BA, U. Wis., 1970; MD, Rush U., 1979. Diplomate Am. Bd. Emergency Medicine. Staff physician emergency dept. River Parishes Hosp., LaPlace, La., 1982-85; co-med. dir. emergency dept. Meadowcrest Hosp., Gretna, La., 1985-92; co-med. dir. City of New Orleans Emergency Med. Svcs., 1987—; med. dir. emergency dept. Tulane U. Med. Ctr., New Orleans, 1992—. Fellow Am. Acad. Emergency Medicine. E-mail: kolinsky@mailhost.tcs.tulane.edu. Office: Tulane Med Ctr Emergency Dept 1415 Tulane Ave New Orleans LA 70112-2600

KOLKER, ALLAN ERWIN, ophthalmologist; b. St. Louis, Nov. 2, 1933; s. Paul P. and Jean K.; m. Jacquelyn Krupin, Dec. 8, 1957; children: Robin, Marci, David, Scott. AB, Washington U., St. Louis, 1953, MD, 1957. Diplomate Am. Bd. Ophthalmology. Intern St. Louis Children's Hosp., 1957-58; resident in ophthalmology Washington U./Barnes Hosp., 1960-65; staff, faculty Washington U., 1964—, prof. ophthalmology, 1974—; ophthalmologist Eye Health Care Assocs., 1996—; glaucoma com. Prevent Blindness Am.; bd. dirs. Am. Bd. Ophthalmology, 1994-98. Author: (with J. Hetherington) Becker and Shaffer's Diagnosis and Therapy of the Glaucomas, 3d, 4th, 5th edit., 1983; contbr. numerous articles to profl. jours. Served with USPHS, 1958-60. NIH spl. fellow, 1963-65; grantee, 1969-80; 1st Disting. Alumni award Washington U., 1990; glaucoma fellow Washington U., 1963-64. Mem. AMA, Assn. Rsch. in Vision and Ophthalmology, Am. Acad. Ophthalmology (mem. coun. 1986-92, trustees 1994-98), Am. Bd. Ophthalmology (dir. 1994-98), Am. Ophthal. Soc., Am. Glaucoma Soc. (founding, pres. 1992-94), Mo. Ophthal. Soc. (pres. 1986-87), St. Louis Med. Soc. Home: 176 Plantation Dr Saint Louis MO 63141-8352 Office: 633 Emerson Rd Saint Louis MO 63141-6731

KOLKER, ROGER RUSSELL, insurance executive; b. Guttenberg, Iowa, Aug. 14, 1929; s. Russell Edward and Olina Colby (Schwab) K.; m. Suzanne Chaddock Griffin, June 9, 1954; children: Roger Russell, Karolyn, Sara. Student, U. Iowa, 1947-50; B.S., U.S. Mil. Acad., 1954. C.L.U., 1966. Field sales dir. Mut. of N.Y., Chgo., 1964-66; dir. mgmt. tng. Mut. of N.Y., N.Y.C., 1966-68; regional v.p. Mut. of N.Y., Atlanta, 1968-71; exec. v.p. N. Am. Life Ins. Co., Mpls., 1971-77; exec. v.p. Monumental Life Ins. Co., Balt., 1978-79, pres., chief exec. officer, 1979-83; chmn., pres., chief exec. officer Monumental Gen. Ins. Group, Inc., Balt., 1983-84; pres., chmn., chief exec. officer Monumental Gen. Ins. Co., Balt., 1983-84; bd. dirs. Equitable Bancorp N.A., Balt., French/Bray, Inc. Bd. dirs. Balt. Symphony Orch.; bd. dirs. South Balt. Gen. Hosp. Mem. Gen. Agts. and Mgrs. Assn., Balt. Life Underwriters Assn., Am. Coll. Life Underwriters (sponsor Gold Key Soc.), Legal Mut. Liability Ins. Soc. Md. (bd. dirs.). Lutheran. Home: PO Box 510124 Key Col Bch FL 33051-0124 Office: The Kolker Consultancy 511 Chatterton Rd Lutherville Timonium MD 21093-1929

KOLKEY, DANIEL MILES, judge; b. Chgo., Apr. 21, 1952; s. Eugene Louis and Gilda Penelope (Cowan) K.; m. Donna Lynn Christie, May 15, 1982; children: Eugene, William, Christopher, Jonathan. BA, Stanford U., 1974; JD, Harvard U., 1977. Bar: Calif. 1977, U.S. Dist. Ct. (ea. dist.) Calif. 1978, U.S. Dist. Ct. (cen. dist.) Calif. 1979, U.S. Ct. Appeals (9th cir.) 1979, U.S. Dist. Ct. (no. dist.) Calif. 1980, U.S. Supreme Ct. 1983, U.S. Dist. Ct. Ariz. 1992, U.S. Dist. Ct. (so. dist.) Calif. 1994. Law clk. U.S. Dist. Ct. judge, N.Y.C., 1977-78; assoc. Gibson Dunn & Crutcher, L.A., 1978-84, ptnr., 1985-94; counsel to Gov., legal affairs sec. to Calif. Gov. Pete Wilson,

1995-98; assoc. justice Calif. Ct. Appeals, 3rd Appellate Dist., Sacramento, 1998—; arbitrator bi-nat. panel for U.S.-Can. Free Trade Agreement, 1990-94; commr. Calif. Law Revision Commn., 1992-94, vice chair, 1993-94, chair, 1994; mem. Blue Ribbon Commn. on Jury Sys. Improvement, 1996. Contbr. articles to profl. publs. Co-chmn. internat. rels. sect. Town Hall Calif., L.A., 1981-90; chmn. internat. trade legis. subcom., internat. commerce steering com. L.A. Area C. of C., 1983-91, mem. law and justice com., 1993-94; mem. adv. coun., mem. exec. com. Asia Pacific Ctr. for Resolution of Internat. Bus.Disputes, 1991-94; bd. dirs. L.A. Ctr. for Internat. Comml. Arbitration, 1986-94, treas., 1986-88, v.p., 1988-90, pres., 1990-94; assoc. mem. ctrl. com. Calif. Rep. Party, 1983-94, mem. ctrl. com., 1995-98, dep. gen. coun. credentials com., Rep. Nat. Convention, 1992, alt. Calif. Delegation, 1992, Calif. del., 1996; mem. L.A. Com. on Fgn. Rels., 1983-95, Pacific Coun. Internat. Policy, 1999—; gen. counsel Citizens Rsch. Found., 1990-94. Master Anthony Kennedy Inns. of Ct., 1996—. Mem. Am. Arbitration Assn. (panel of arbitrators, arbitrator large complex case dispute resolution program 1993-94), Chartered Inst. Arbitrators, London (assoc. 1986-94), Friends of Wilton Park So. Calif. (chmn. exec. com. 1986-94, exec. com. 1986—). Jewish. Office: Ct of Appeal 3rd Appellate Dist 914 Capitol Mall Sacramento CA 95814-4906

KOLKO, GABRIEL, historian, educator; b. Paterson, N.J., Aug. 17, 1932; s. Philip and Lillian Kolko; m. Joyce Manning, June 11, 1955. B.A., Kent State U., 1954; M.S., U. Wis., 1955; Ph.D, Harvard U., 1962. Assoc. prof. U. Pa., 1964-68; prof. history SUNY-Buffalo, 1968-70; prof. history York U., Toronto, Ont., Can., 1970-92, Disting. research prof., 1986-92, prof. emeritus, 1992—. Author: Wealth and Power in America, 1962, The Triumph of Conservatism, 1963, Railroads and Regulations, 1965, The Politics of War, 1968, The Roots of American Foreign Policy, 1969, The Limits of Power, 1972, Main Currents in Modern American History, 1976, Anatomy of a War, 1985, Confronting the Third World, 1988, Century of War, 1994, Vietnam, Anatomy of a Peace, 1997; contbr. articles to profl. jours. Fellow Social Sci. Research Council, 1963-64; Guggenheim fellow, 1966-67; fellow Am. Council Learned Socs., 1971-72; Killam fellow, 1974-75, 82-84. Fellow Royal Soc. Can. Home: Wittenburgergracht 53, 1018 MX Amsterdam The Netherlands

KOLL, RICHARD LEROY, retired chemical company executive; b. Muscatine, Iowa, Mar. 16, 1925; s. Charles C. and Emma (Schafer) K.; m. Patricia Ann Grunder, Jan. 2, 1955; children: Craig, Christine, Cary. BSME, U. Iowa, 1951. Plant mgr. Grain Processing Corp., Muscatine, Iowa, 1971-72, v.p., 1972-77, sr. v.p., 1977-90, mem. exec. com., bd. dirs., 1989-90, ret., 1990. With USMC, 1944-46. Mem. Elks, Univ. Athletic Club (Iowa City), Geneva Golf and Country Club (Muscatine, Iowa), Seminole Lakes Country Club (Punta Gorda, Fla.). Home: 1750 Jamaica Way Apt 323 Punta Gorda FL 33950-5170 also: 1317 Oakland Dr Muscatine IA 52761-5511

KOLLAER, JIM C., real estate executive, architect; b. Amarillo, Tex., Jan. 5, 1943; s. Walter W. and Margaret M. Kollaer; m. Sally Ann Hawkins, Aug. 6, 1966; 1 son, Andrew N. Student, Amarillo (Tex.) Coll., 1960-62, La. State U., 1962-65; B.Arch., Tex. Tech U., 1969. Lic. architect, Tex.; lic. broker, Tex. V.p., dir. urban design RKA Inc. Assoc., Dallas, 1969-75; v.p., dir. mktg. CRS Inc., Houston, 1977-80, sr. planner, 1975-76, assoc., 1976-77; pres. Houston div. Henry Miller Co., Houston, 1980-85; pres. Henry S. Miller/Grubb & Ellis, 1985-89, Kollaer Internat., 1989-90; pres., CEO Greater Houston Partnership, 1990—; past chmn. Tex. Bus. Hall of Fame; cons. and lectr. in field. Sr. fellow Am. Leadership Forum. Fellow Soc. Internat. Bus. Fellows; Fellow AIA; mem. Assn. C. of C. Execs., Tex. Soc. Architects, Urban Land Inst., Tex. Assn. Realtors, Nat. Assn. Realtors, Soc. Mktg. Profl. Svcs., Coun. for Urban Econ. Devel. Republican. Presbyterian. Office: Greater Houston Partnership 1200 Smith St Ste 700 Houston TX 77002-4400

KOLLAR, MARK PATRICK, newsletter editor; b. Gary, Ind., Mar. 6, 1958; s. Louis Edward and Madge Elizabeth (Dougherty) K.; 1 child, Samuel Thomas. BA in English Lit., DePauw U., Greencastle, Ind., 1980; MA in English Lit., U. Chgo., 1981. Fin. reporter Knight-Ridder Fin. News, N.Y.C., 1993-95; editor IDD Enterprises, N.Y.C., 1993-95, 1995—. Mem. N.Y. Fin. Writers. Office: IDD Enterprises LP 18th Fl Two World Trade Ctr New York NY 10048

KOLLAR-KOTELLY, COLLEEN, district judge. BA, Cath. U., 1965, JD, 1968. Dist. judge U.S. Dist. Ct. D.C., 1997—. Office: 333 Constitution Ave NW Washington DC 20001

KOLLER, BERNEDA JOLEEN, library administrator; b. Marion, S.D., Dec. 23, 1935; d. Theodore Jacob Poppe and Clara Johanna Goertz; m. Dennis Eugene Koller, May 8, 1955; children: Kim Denise, Kerry Tay, Kecia Rae. BA, Augustana Coll., 1974; postgrad., U. S.D., 1976-77. Cert. pub. libr. mgmt., S.D. Sec. Turner County Soil Conservation Dist., Parker, S.D.; tchr. Freeman (S.D.) Pub. H.S., 1974-81; sec. State Farm Ins., Freeman, 1982-90; libr. dir. Freeman Pub. Libr., 1990—; spkr. hist. lectrs., 1984—. Author: (book) Ironic Point of Light, 1994; columnist Freeman Courier, 1983-88. Pres. Parker (S.C.) Alumni Assn., 1959; sec. S.D. Assn. German-Russians, Pierre, 1989—; dir. Musicals at Schmeckfest, Freeman, 1976, 82, 86; mem. Am. Hist. Soc. of Germans from Russia, Lincoln, Nebr., 1986—, German Russian Hist. Soc., Bismarck, N.D., 1994—; pres. Homestead chpt. Am. Hist. Soc. of Germans from Russia, Fremman and Yankton, 1988—; historian, sec., chairperson Dorcas Soc., Freeman, 1976-96; tour guide Freeman Devel. Corp., 1997—; pres., sec., mem. Freeman Area Arts Coun. and Freeman Area Arts Alliance, 1998—; ch. del. Wellspring Wholistic Care Ctr., Freeman, 1997—. Recipient Best Local Column award S.D. Press Assn., 1985. Mem. S.D. Libr. Assn. Democrat. Mennonite. Avocations: writing genealogy, traveling, knitting, guitar. Fax: (605) 925-7127. E-mail: bkoller@gwtc.net. Office: Freeman Pub Libr 185 E 3d St Freeman SD 57029

KOLLER, KAREN KATHRYN, social services administrator; b. Lorain, Ohio, June 23, 1949; d. Harry Charles and Lavonne Rita (Ball) K. BA, Adrian (Mich.) Coll., 1971; MBA, Baldwin Wallace Coll., Berea, Ohio, 1977. Mgr. Harry C. Koller, Acct., Lorain, Ohio, 1974-79; sec.-treas. Credit Bur. of Lorain, Inc., 1971-79, Haytotter, Inc., 1979-80; ops. mgr. Lorain br. Credit Bur. Toledo, 1979-83; owner Karen Koller Bookkeeping, Lorain, 1979-95; ptnr. Crackabee Shelties, Lorain, 1980-95, K & K Co., Lorain, 1979-88; comptroller Neighborhood House Assn. of Lorain County, Inc., 1985-94; acct. Amethyst Inc., Columbus, 1995—. Treas. Erie Shores council Girl Scouts U.S., Lorain, 1987-93, bd. dirs., 1982-93; chmn. City of Lorain Adv. Bd. for Disabled, 1988; campaign chmn. Mem. Lorain Bus. and Profl. Women (treas. 1979-80), AAUW, Quota, Delta Mu Delta.

KOLLER, LOREN D., veterinary medicine educator; b. Pomeroy, Wash., June 16, 1940; s. Edwin C. and Doris K. (Shelton) K.; m. Kathleen Noel Ringness, Sept. 7, 1963; children: Susan E., Michael D., Christopher L. DVM, Wash. State U., 1965; MS, U. Wis., 1969, PhD, 1971. Head diagnostic and comparative pathology Nat. Inst. Environ. Health Scis., Research Triangle Park, N.C., 1971-72; rsch. assoc. dept. vet. medicine Oreg. State U., Corvallis, 1972-76, assoc. prof., 1976-78, prof., 1995—, dean Coll. Vet. Medicine, 1985-95; assoc. prof., asst. dean Dept. Vet. Medicine, U. Idaho, Moscow, 1978-81, assoc. prof., assoc. dean, 1981-82, prof., assoc. dean, 1982-85; research asst. Dept. Vet. Sci. U. Wis., Madison, 1968-71; assoc. veterinarian Blue Cross Vet. Clinic, Corvallis, 1965-66. Contbr. articles to profl. jours., chpts. to books. Served to capt. M.C., U.S. Army, 1966-68. Grantee NIH, USDA, Dow Chem. Co., EPA, FDA, Merck Sharp & Dohme, Warner-Lambert, Pew Found. Fellow Acad. Toxicol. Sci.; mem. AVMA, NAS (mem. com. toxicology), Am. Assn. Vet. Immunologists, Soc. Toxicology, Soc. Toxicologic Pathologists, Assn. Vet. Med. Colls., Oreg. Vet. Med. Assn.

KOLLER, SHIRLEY LEAVITT, sculptor; b. Youngstown, Ohio, Apr. 6, 1921; d. Benjamin Harrison and Rose (Cohen) Leavitt; m. Herbert Richard Koller Mar. 7, 1943 (wid. June 1988); children: Donald Lee, Susan Koller Van Horne, Laura Frances. Diploma, Cleve. Inst. of Art, 1942; BS, Western Res. U., Cleve., 1942; MFA, The Am. U., 1972. Lectr. No. Va. C.C., Alexandria, Va., 1977-92; curator of art AAAS, 1997—; lectr. to sr. citizens Jewish Cmty. Ctr. of Greater Washington, Rockville, md., 1990, 95, Washington Hebrew Congregation, Washington, 1995; appearance on Peter Jennings/ABC World News Tonight, 1991, Arlington Cable, 1990, Voice of Am. Radio, 1992; adj. faculty Md. Coll. of Art & Design, 1991-93; vis. artist Fairfax County Pub. Schs., 1982-85; visual art specialist, Fillmore Arts Ctr., Washington, 1977-81. Artist: (3-D wall installation) The Joy of Transportation, 1989-90 (comm. 1989); writer: (newsletter) Eye Wash, 1990-92; curator art exhibit installations, 1989—; one-person shows include Gate House Gallery, Washington, 1994, Mansion Art Gallery, Rockville, 1993, Fridholm Fine Arts Gallery, Asheville, N.C., 1991, O Street Studios, Washington, 1990, AAAS/Atrium Gallery, Washington, 1989-90, others; exhibited in group shows at Gallery 10, Washington, 1998, Tri-State Sculptors Ednl. Assn., Washington, 1997, Associated Artists of Winston-Salem, N.C., 1996, Tri-State Sculptors Conf. Exhbn., U. S.C., Spartenburg, 1996, ARTS 901 E Street, Washington, 1996, AAAS Exhibit, Washington, 1995-96, Newhouse Ctr. for Contemporary Art, S.I., N.Y., 1995-96, Mill River Gallery, Ellicott, Md., 1999, Tysons Galleria II, Vienna, Va., 1999, Washington Sculptors Group, 1998, 99, others; work collected at Ballston Metro Sta., Arlington, Va., First Am. Bank, Va. Commonwealth U., U. Md., AAAS/Washington, Akin Group, Law Offices, Washington, IBM Rsch. Hdqtrs., Durham, N.C., others. Recipient Editor's Choice award Internat. Libr. Photography, 1998. Mem. Tri-State Sculptors Ednl. Assn. (life mem. 1994), Washington Sculptors Group. Democrat. Jewish. Avocations: travel, lecturing, gourmet cooking. Home: 2700 Virginia Ave NW Washington DC 20037-1908

KOLLER, WILLIAM CARL, neurology educator; b. Milw., July 12, 1945; m. Vicki Royse Koller; children: Todd, Chad, Kyle. BS, Marquette U., 1968; MS, Northwestern U., Chgo., 1971, PhD, 1974, MD, 1976. Diplomate Am. Bd. Psychiatry and Neurology, 1982. Instr. Northwestern Med. Sch., Chgo., 1975-77, Rush Med. Coll., Chgo., 1976-80; asst. prof. Neurology U. Ill., Chgo., 1980-82; staff neurologist VA Med. Ctr., Chgo., Ill., 1980-82; assoc. prof. Neurology Loyola U. Stritch Sch. of Medicine, Chgo., Ill., 1982-86; staff neurologist VA Med. Ctr., Hines, Ill., 1982-87; prof. Neurology Loyola U. Stritch Sch. of Medicine, Chgo., 1986-87; prof., chmn. U. Kans. Med. Ctr., Kansas City, 1987-99; prof. U. Miami, 1999—; cons. Merrill-Marion Dow Pharm., Kansas City, 1991—; dir. Am. Parkinson Disease Assn., Kansas City, 1987—; chmn. Internat. Tremor Found., 1988—; mem. Med. Adv. Bd. DuPont, Wilmington, 1991—. Author: Tremor, 1990; editor: Handbook of Parkinson's Disease, 1987, 92. Fellow NIH Predoctoral, Nat. Inst. Health, 1968-74, Pillsbury Co., 1979-80. Mem.Am. Acad. Neurology, Am. Neurol. Assn., Soc. for Neuroscience, Kans. Neurol. Soc., Cen. Soc. Neurology, Am. Soc. for Neurologic Investigation, Behavioral Neurology Soc., Internat. Med. Soc. Motor Disturbances, Assn. U. Prof. Neurology, So. Clin. Neurol. Soc. Office: Nat Parkinson Found Neurology 1501 NW 9th Ave Bob Hope Rd Miami FL 33136-1494*

KOLLMEYER, KENNETH ROBERT, surgeon; b. Berwyn, Ill., Feb. 1, 1947. BS in Biology-Chemistry, Randolph-Macon Coll., 1969; PhD in Physiology, U. Cin., 1973; MD cum laude, U. Colo., 1977. Diplomate Am. Bd. Surgery, Am. Bd. Gen. Vascular Surgery. Rsch. asst. Cardiac Rsch. Lab., Sch. Medicine U. So. Calif., L.A., 1967; head lab divsn. thoracic and cardiovascular surgery Med. Ctr. Va., Richmond, 1968-69; NIH rsch. fellow dept. clin. physiology Nat. Asthma Ctr., Denver, 1973-74; intern in surgery Parkland Meml. Hosp., Dallas, 1977-78, resident in surgery, 1978-80, chief resident in surgery, 1980-81; fellow in vascular surgery, instr. dept. surgery U. Tex. Southwestern Med. Sch., Dallas, 1981-82, clin. asst. prof. surgery, 1982—; dir. S.W. Vascular Lab., Dallas, 1982—; attending vascular surgeon Meth. Med. Ctr., Dallas, 1982—, chief gen. surgery, 1997—; mem. staff Charlton Meth. Hosp., St. Paul Med. Ctr., Parkland Meml. Hosp., Med. City Hosp.; teaching asst. dept. physiology U. Cin. Coll. Medicine, 1972-73; chmn. Doctors Care PA, Dallas; presenter in field. Contbr. articles to profl. publs. Fellow ACS; mem. AMA, Tex. Med. Assn., Tex. Surg. Soc., Dallas County Med. Soc., Dallas Soc. Gen. Surgeons, Soc. for Non-Invasive Vascular Tech., Nat. Hon. Biol. Soc., Parkland Surg. Soc., Alpha Omega Alpha. Office: Dallas Surgical Group Meth Med Ctr Pavilion II 221 W Colorado Blvd Ste 625 Dallas TX 75208-2345

KOLLSTEDT, PAULA LUBKE, communications executive, writer; b. Cin., Aug. 27, 1946; d. Elmer George and Mary Margaret (Kelly) Lubke; m. Stephen Leonard Kollstedt, Jan. 21, 1968; children: Kelly, Lance, Stacey, Jonathan. BA, Xavier U., 1968, MEd, 1982. Cert. secondary tchr., Ohio. Editor, writer Shillito's Dept. Store, Cin., 1966-69; freelance writer, Cin., 1969-74; pub. info. coord. Prince William County Parks and Recreation Com. (Va.), 1974-75; communications coord. City of Cin. Recreation Com., 1975-78; cons. Warner Amex Cable Television, Cin., 1982-84, Moellers Assocs., Cin., 1982-84; writer Cin. Enquirer, 1982-83; executive communication specialist Gen. Electric Aircraft Engines, 1984-87, employee communication specialist 1987-90, mgr. communication 1990—; speaker Cin. Preschool Coops., 1981, Cin. Women's Conf., 1984, lectr., presenter workshops on self-esteem for parents, 1975-86; lectr. bus. communications, 1992—. Author: Surviving the Crisis of Motherhood, 1982; contbr. articles to newspapers; writer, producer multi-media presentation Communication Cincinnati, (Unique Program award Ohio Parks and Recreation), 1978. Mem. Women in Communications (v.p. programs 1981-82, v.p. corp. sponsorship 1998, 99, Gt. Lakes regional 1st pl. award 1984, 86, 87, 88, 95, recipient Nat. Clarion awards 1990, 98, Gem award 1992, Communicator of Yr., 1992). Recipient Prism award Pub. Rels. Soc. Am., 1983, 85, 86, 87, 88, 92, 94, 95, 96, Pres.' award 1995, 97, 98, Bronze Quill award Internat. Assn. Bus. Communicators, 1986, 87, 88, 90, 92, 95, 96, 97, 98, Silver Quill award Internat. Assn. Bus. Communicators, 1989. Roman Catholic. Home: 5391 Haft Rd Cincinnati OH 45247-7419 Office: GE Aircraft Engines 1 Neumann Way # J4 Cincinnati OH 45215-1915

KOLMAN, MARK HERBERT, lawyer; b. Balt., Aug. 24, 1946; s. Lester Norman and Jeannette (Carmel) K.; m. Susan Dellheim, July 26, 1998; 1 child, Margaret Carmel. BA in History, Bucknell U., 1968; JD, U. Md., 1971. Bar: Md. 1972, D.C. 1991, U.S. Dist. Ct. Md. 1980, U.S. Ct. Appeals (4th cir.) 1980, U.S. Supreme Ct. 1980, U.S. Dist. Ct. D.C. 1991. Asst. state's atty. City of Balt., 1971-75, County of Balt., Towson, Md., 1975-80; asst. fed. defender Pub. Defender's Office, Balt., 1980; asst. U.S. atty. Balt., 1980-84; assoc. Gordon, Feinblatt, Rothman, Hoffberger & Hollander, Balt., 1984-86; ptnr. Gordon, Feinblatt, Rothman, Hoffberger & Hollander, 1986-91, chmn. litigation dept., 1991; ptnr. Anderson Kill Olick & Oshinsky, P.C., Washington, 1991-96, Dickstein Shapiro Morin & Oshinsky, Washington, 1996—. Trustee Md. chpt. Leukemia Soc. Am., 1987-91; mem. adv. bd. Greenebaum Cancer Ctr.; bd. dirs. Nat. Coalition for Cancer Survivorship, 1993-95. Mem. ABA, Fed. Bar Assn. (chmn. bd. govs. 1990-91, pres. Md. chpt. 1994-95, 4th cir. officer 1995-96), Md. Bar Assn., Balt. County Bar Assn., Md. State's Attys. Assn. (bd. dirs. 1976-91), Md. Trial Lawyers Assn., Md. Criminal Def. Attys. Assn. Avocations: golf, swimming, scuba. Home: 9775 Polished Stone Columbia MD 21046-2800 Office: Dickstein Shapiro Morin Oshinsky 2101 L St NW Washington DC 20037-1526

KOLMIN, KENNETH GUY, lawyer; b. N.Y.C., Oct. 22, 1951; s. Frank William and Edith Kolmin; m. Suzan L. Frumm, Sept. 3, 1978; children—Stephen Todd, Jennifer Dana, Robert Scott. BS summa cum laude, SUNY-Albany, 1973; MS, Syracuse U., 1975, JD cum laude, 1975. Bar: Ill. 1976, U.S. Dist. Ct. (7th dist.) Ill. 1976, U.S. Tax Ct. 1980, U.S. Supreme Ct. 1985; CPA, Ill. Tax cons. Arthur Young and Co., Chgo., 1976-79; atty. Shefsky Saitlin & Froelich, Chgo., 1979-81; ptnr. Rooks Pitts & Poust, Chgo., 1981-84, Schwartz & Freeman, 1984-96, Sonnenschein, Nath & Rosenthal, Chgo., 1996—. Contbr. articles to profl. jours. Mem. ABA, AICPA, Ill. Bar Assn., Ill. Soc. CPAs. Home: 975 Eastwood Rd Glencoe IL 60022-1122 Office: Sonnenschein Nath & Rosenthal 8000 Sears Tower Chicago IL 60606

KOLODEY, FRED JAMES, lawyer; b. LaCoste, Tex., Mar. 5, 1936; s. Raymond and Mamie V. (Newman) K.; children: Trecia Anne Estep, Michele Leigh; m. Halen Gable McIntosh, June 10, 1989. B.A., Tex. Christian U., 1962; LL.B., So. Methodist U., 1964. Bar: Tex. 1964. Since practiced in Dallas; ptnr. Kolodey & Thomas, 1975-83, of counsel, 1983-94; of counsel Thomas, Sheehan & Culp, 1994—; pres. Dallas Jr. Bar Assn., 1969. Comments editor: Southwestern Law Jour, 1963-64. Mem. dist. hearing office panel Dallas Community Coll., 1974, Democratic precinct chmn., 1968-73. Mem. Tex., Dallas bar assns., Delta Theta Phi (pres. 1963, Nat. award 1964), Alpha Chi, Pi Sigma Alpha. Home: 540 Mariah Bay Dr Rockwall TX 75032-7671

KOLODINSKY, RICHARD HUTTON, lawyer; b. Perth Amboy, N.J., Aug. 31, 1952; s. William Alexander and Helen (Kulpinsky) K.; m. Betty Mangino, 1975 (div. 1978); m. Alison Kolodinsky, June 20, 1981; 1 child, Chris. BA, Rutgers U., 1974, JD, 1977. Bar: Fla. 1978, N.J., Penn., U.S. Dist. Ct. (no. and mid. dists.) Fla., U.S. Dist. Ct. N.J., U.S. Ct. Appeals (11th cir). Atty. Ctr. Fla. Legal Svc., Daytona Beach, 1977-81; partner Kolodinsky, Berg, Seitz & Tresher, Daytona Beach, 1981—, New Smyrna Beach, 1981—; Fla. Gov.'s appointee to Judicial Nominating Commn., Daytona Beach, 1997. Bd. dirs. Atlantic Ctr. for Arts, New Smyrna Beach, Fla., 1990-94, 98—, Unitarian Universalist Ch., Ormond Beach, Fla., 1991-94; cmty. svc. vol. NAACP, 1992. Mem. Leading Am. Attys., Fla. Bar Assn. (grievance com., bd. mem., chair), Academy Fla. Trial Lawyers (bd. dirs., Eagle Talon), Volusia County Bar Assn. (bd. dirs.). Democrat. Avocations: tennis, sailing. E-Mail: KBSandT@worldnet.att.net. Office: Kolodinsky Berg Seitz Tresher 707 E 3rd Ave New Smyrna Beach FL 32169-3101

KOLODNER, RICHARD DAVID, biochemist, educator; b. Morristown, N.J., Apr. 3, 1951; s. Ignace Izack and Ethel (Zelnick) K.; m. Karin Ann Gregory, Aug. 6, 1983 (div. May 1991). BS, U. Calif., Irvine, 1971, PhD, 1975; MS (hon.), Harvard U., 1988. Rsch. fellow Harvard U. Med. Sch., Boston, 1975-78; asst. prof. Dana Farber Cancer Inst. and Harvard U. Med. Sch., Boston, 1978-83, assoc. prof., 1983-88, prof. biochemistry, 1988-97; chmn. divsn. cellular molecular biology Dana-Farber Cancer Inst., Boston, 1991-94, head x-ray crystallography lab., 1991-97, chmn. divsn. of human cancer genetics, 1995-97; prof. medicine, mem. Cancer Ctr. U. Calif. Med. Sch., San Diego, 1997—; mem. Ludwig Inst. for Cancer Rsch., San Diego, 1997—. Editor PLASMID jour., 1986-95; assoc. editor Cancer Rsch., 1995—, Cell, 1996—; mem. editl. bd. Molecular Cellular Biology, 1999—, Jour. Biol. Chemistry, 1999—; contbr. articles to sci. jours. Recipient Jr. Faculty Rsch. award Am. Cancer Soc., 1981, Faculty Rsch. award, 1984, Merit award NIH, 1993, Charles S. Mott prize GM Cancer Rsch. Found., 1996; rsch. grantee Am. Cancer Soc., 1980-82, grantee NIH, 1978—. Fellow Am. Acad. Microbiology; mem. Am. Soc. for Biochemistry and Molecular Biology, Am. Soc. for Microbiology, Genetics Soc. Am., Am. Assn. Cancer Rsch. Home: 13468 Kibbings Rd San Diego CA 92130-1231 Office: Ludwig Inst for Cancer Rsch CMME 3080 9500 Gilman Dr La Jolla CA 92093-5003

KOLODNY, ABRAHAM LEWIS, physician; b. Norfolk, Va., July 2, 1917; s. William and Jennie (Eisenberg) K.; m. Mildred Fiske, Aug. 10, 1942; children: William (dec.), David Greene, Sukie, Douglas Merrill, Peggy Lee. Grad., U. Va., 1941. Intern South Balt. Gen. Hosp., 1941-42; residency Ashburn Army Arthritis Ctr., McKinney, Tex., 1944-46; with Arthritis Clinic/Sinai Hosp., Balt., 1948-70; chief, rheumatology N. Charles Hosp., Balt., 1951-90; co-chief, rheumatology Franklin Square Hosp., Balt., 1970-95; commr. Md. Commn. Rheumatic Diseases, 1987-91; ret., 1999; pres. North Charles Gen. Hosp., 1963-67; staff mem. Franklin Sq. Hosp., 1970-95; state commr. Arthritis and Related Diseases, 1986-91; ret. chief rheumatology Homewood Hosp. Ctr.; formerly active Johns Hopkins Med. Health Systems. Contbg. author textbooks in field, articles to profl. jours. Maj. U.S. Army, 1942-47, CBI. Decorated Bronze Star, Combat Med. badge, Presdl. Unit citation, Victory medal, Chinese Victory medal, others. Fellow Am. Coll. Rheumatology, N.Y. Acad. Scis.; mem. AMA, Am. Soc. Clin. Pharmacology, Md. Arthritis Found. (bd. dirs. 1975-91), Md. Soc. for Rheumatic Diseases (co-founder), So. Med. Assn. Home: PO Box 964 Brooklandville MD 21022

KOLODNY, DEBRA RUTH, labor management consultant; b. N.Y.C., Aug. 21, 1960; d. Sidney and Irma (Smith) K.; m. Kenneth Seward Seibert, May 6, 1995. BS, Cornell U., 1981; JD, U. Pa., 1985. Bar: D.C. 1985, Pa. 1985. Lawyer Fed. Election Commn., Washington, 1985-86; asst. counsel negotiations Nat. Treas. Employees Union, Washington, 1986-87, dir. coop. efforts, 1988-92; consulting assoc. Restructuring Assocs., Inc., Washington, 1992-94; labor mgmt. cons. Washington, 1995—; coord. workplace participation programs Svc. Employees Internat. Union, Washington, 1996; spkr. at numerous confs. Contbr. articles to profl. jours. Nat. coord., lobbyist BiNet USA, 1992-94, 96-98, mem. adv. bd., 1998—; mem. bd. dirs. Interfaith Alliance Montgomery County, 1998-99, v.p., 1999—; prison minister Adelphi Friends, Md., 1991-93; steering com. DC BiNetwork, Washington, 1989-92; co-founder core group AmBi, Washington, 1991-93. Mem. Assn. Quality and Participation (bd. dirs. 1991-94), Washington Bar Assn., Fabrangen Havurah. Democrat. Jewish. Avocations: bicycling, swimming, singing, dancing. Home and Office: 631 Ritchie Ave Silver Spring MD 20910-5240

KOLODNY, EDWIN HILLEL, neurologist, geneticist, medical administrator; b. Boston, Mar. 15, 1936; s. Myer Zeman and Naomi Lillian (Zalkind) K.; m. Roselyn Leinwand, May 31, 1958; children: Nancy, Leonard Benjamin, Robin, Noah Jacob. AB cum laude in Econs., Harvard Coll., 1957; MD with honors, NYU, 1962. Diplomate Am. Bd. Psychiatry and Neurology, Am. Bd. Med. Genetics. Intern, resident in internal medicine Bellevue Hosp., N.Y.C., 1962-64; resident in neurology Mass. Gen. Hosp., Boston, 1964-67; spl. fellow lab. neurochemistry Nat. Inst. Neurol. Diseases, Bethesda, Md., 1967-70; asst. prof. neurology Harvard Med. Sch., Boston, 1970-76, assoc. prof. 1976-85, prof., 1985-91; Bernard and Charlotte Marden prof., chmn. dept. neurology NYU Med. Ctr., N.Y.C., 1991—; vice-chmn. exec. com. Med. Bd. Tisch Hosp., N.Y., 1993-97; chmn., 1997—; vis. prof. Weizmann Inst. Sci., Rehovot, Israel, 1988, 1990; assoc. dir. Eunice Kennedy Shriver Ctr. Mental Retardation, Inc., Waltham, Mass., 1976-83, acting dir., 1983-84, dir., 1984-90; assoc. neurologist Mass. Gen. Hosp., Boston, 1976-87, neurologist, 1988-91; chmn. com. Research Ctrs. Forward Planning Mental Retardation, Nat. Inst. Child Health and Human Devel., 1983-84; cons. pres.' com. Mental Retardation, 1982; adv. genetic services Dept. Pub. Health Mass., 1977-80; mem. Mass. Nat. Inst. Health Centennial Com., 1987-88, profl. adv. bd. Internat. Rett Syndrome Assn., 1986-94, sci. adv. bd. United Leukodystrophy Found., 1986-94, sci. med. adv. com. Canavan Found, 1994—. Mem. editorial bd. Annals of Neurology, 1984-89. Contbr. articles to profl. jours. Mem. sci. adv. bd. Nat. Tay Sachs and Allied Diseases Assn., 1970—; v.p., trustee Temple Emanuel, Newton, Mass., 1983-89; trustee Hebrew Coll., Brookline, Mass. Recipient Solomon A. Berson Medical Alumni Achievement award clin. sci. NYU Sch. Med., 1993. Fellow Am. Acad. Neurology (S. Wier Mitchell award 1970); mem. Am. Assn. Neuropathology (Moore award 1975), Am. Neurol. Assn., Am. Soc. Human Genetics, Am. Soc. Neurochemistry, Child Neurology Soc., Harvard Varsity Club (Cambridge), NYU, Alpha Omega Alpha. Avocations: Judaica, photography. Home: 110 Bleecker St Apt 24D New York NY 10012-2106 Office: NYU Med Ctr 550 1st Ave New York NY 10016-6481

KOLODNY, RICHARD, finance educator; b. Jersey City, May 13, 1943; s. Harry and Mildred Kolodny; m. Alene Judith Kolodny, Feb. 2, 1969. BSBA, Northwestern U., 1965; MBA, NYU, 1967, PhD, 1972. Asst. prof. fin. SUNY, Binghamton, 1972-76, assoc. prof. fin., 1976-78; assoc. prof. fin. U. Md., College Park, 1978-82, prof. fin., 1982—, chair dept. fin., 1989-98; cons. in field. Assoc. editor Fin. Mgmt., Jour. Acctg. Pub. Policy; contbr. articles to profl. jours. Grantee NSF, 1978-82, U. Md., 1980, 85; PhD fellow NYU; recipient research awards SUNY-Binghamton, 1975, 76, 77. Mem. Am. Fin. Assn., Fin. Mgmt. Assn., Ea. Fin. Assn. (bd. dirs. 1984-88), So. Fin. Assn. Office: Univ of Maryland Coll of Business & Mgmt College Park MD 20742

KOLODNY, STANLEY CHARLES, oral surgeon, air force officer; b. N.Y.C., Feb. 22, 1923; s. Aaron and Lea (Stern) K.; m. Mary Kathryn Leigh, Feb. 22, 1947; children: Kathleen, Carter Leigh, Stanley Charles. B.A., U. Tex., 1944; D.D.S., Baylor U., 1947; M.S., U. Ill., 1961. Diplomate: Am. Bd. Oral and Maxillofacial Surgery. Commd. 1st lt. USAF, 1951, advanced through grades to maj. gen., 1981; cons. in oral surgery Surgeon Gen. U.S. Air Force, 1966; chmn. dept. oral surgery Wilford Hall USAF Med. Center, San Antonio, 1969-75; dir. dental services Wilford Hall USAF Med. Center, 1975-77; asst. surgeon gen. for dental services Bolling AFB, Washington, 1979-82; clin. prof. dept. surgery U. Tex. Dental Br., Houston, 1969-77; clin. asso. prof. dept. surgery U. Tex. Med. Sch., San Antonio, 1969-77. Contbr. chpt. to book, articles to profl. jours. Bd. dirs. Am. Cancer Soc., 1970-77. Decorated D.S.M., Legion of Merit with oak leaf cluster, Air Force Commendation medal; recipient cert. of achievement for outstanding oral surgery USAF. Fellow Am. Coll. Dentists, Am. Assn. Oral and Maxillofacial Surgeons; mem. ADA, Soc. Air Force Clin. Surgeons. Home: 6401 Red Bud Dr Flower Mound TX 75022-5859

KOLODZEI, NATALIA A., art foundation administrator, art historian; b. Moscow, Jan. 8, 1974; d. Tatiana A. and Alexander D. Kolodzei. BA in Art History with honors, State U. N.J., 1998. Exec. dir. Kolodzei Art Found., Inc., Cin., 1991—; mem. adv. bd. Russian Am. Forum, N.Y., 1995—. Named Hon. Citizen of State of Okla., Gov. of Okla., 1993. Mem. Am. Assn. for Advancement of Slavic Studies, Internat. Salon Soc. (ambassador 1996—), Internat. Art Fund, Golden Key Nat. Honor Soc., Phi Beta Kappa. Fax: (732) 545-8428. E-mail: kolodzei@iname.com. Home: 123 S Adelaide Ave Apt 1N Highland Park NJ 08904-1615

KOLODZIEJ, EDWARD ALBERT, political scientist, educator; b. Chgo., Jan. 4, 1935; s. Albert Stanley and Anna Caroline (Chudzik) K.; m. Antje Heberle, Aug. 15, 1959; children: Peter, Andrew, Matthew, Daniel. BS summa cum laude, Loyola U., Chgo., 1956; MA, U. Chgo., 1957, PhD, 1961. Analyst nat. security fgn. affairs div. Congl. Research Service, Library of Congress, Washington, 1960-62; asst. prof. polit. sci. U. Va., Charlottesville, 1962-67, assoc. prof., 1967-73, chmn. dept. govt. and fgn. affairs, 1967-69, prof. polit. sci., 1973-83; head dept. U. Ill., Urbana, 1973-77, dir. Office Arms Control, Disarmament and Internat. Security, 1983-86, research prof. polit. sci., 1983—, elected univ. scholar, 1988; cons. in field. Author: The Uncommon Defense and Congress, 1966, French International Policy under de Gaulle and Pompidou: The Politics of Grandeur, 1974, Making and Marketing Arms: The French Experience and Its Implications for the International System, 1987; editor: American Security Policy, 1979, Security Policies of Developing States, 1981, Limits of Soviet Power in the Developing World, 1987, Security and Arms Control: Guide to National and International Policy-Making, 2 vols., 1989, Cold War as Cooperation, 1991, Coping with Conflict After the Cold War, 1996; mem. editl. bd. Internat. Studies Quar., Defence and Peace Econs., Contemporary Security Policy, European Security; contbr. articles on fgn. and security policy and decision-making to profl. jours., U.S., Europe; also contbg. author books. Mershon Postdoctoral fellow nat. security Ohio State U., 1964-65, Rockefeller Postdoctoral fellow in internat. rels., Paris, 1965-66, Ford Found. fellow in social sci., 1969-71, Fulbright Rsch. fellow, 1986; NSF grantee, 1971, Deutscher Akademischer Austauschdienst grantee, 1975, Ford Found. Internat. Arms Control Competition grantee, 1976, Ctr. for Advanced Study, U. Ill., 1979, 95—, Rockefeller Found. grantee, 1980, grantee NEH, 1981, Woodrow Wilson Ctr., 1987, U.S. Inst. Peace grantee, 1987, 91, grantee Ford Found., 1993; recipient Burlington award for outstanding tchg. and scholarship, 1985. Mem. Council Fgn. Relations N.Y., Am., Midwest internat. polit. sci. assns., Internat. Studies Assn. Home: 711 W University Ave Champaign IL 61820-3919 Office: U Ill Dept Polit Sci Urbana IL 61801*

KOLSTAD, ALLEN C., state official; b. Chester, Mont., Dec. 24, 1931; s. Henry B. & Mabel (Webb) K.; m. Iva Matteson, 1951; children: Cedric A., Chris A., Cheryl D., Corrine F. Student, Concordia Coll., Moorhead, Minn. Mont. state rep., dist. 19, 1969-75, state senator, dist. 5,, 1975-88, pres. pro tem. 1979-84, lt. gov., 1989—; precinct committeeman, 1962-66; chmn. Liberty County Rep. Com., 1967-68. Mem. Jaycees, Shriners, Masons. Republican. Lutheran. Office: Office of Lt Gov Capitol Sta Rm 207 Helena MT 59601

KOLSUN, BRUCE ALAN, special education educator; b. Pitts., Apr. 9, 1952; m. Cynthia Phillips, May 26, 1979; children: Stacey Elizabeth, Phillips Bruce. AA, Allegheny Community Coll., 1973; BA in Psychology, W.Va. U., 1975; MA in Spl. Edn., Duquesne U., 1978; Ednl. Specialist degree, W.Va. Grad. Coll., 1996. Cert. W. Va. specific learning disabilities, mentally impaired and behavior disorder K-12, edn. administrn. K-12. Tchr. specific learning disabilities/mentally impaired Randolph County Sch., Elkins, W.Va., 1978-79; dir. edn. W.Va. Dept. Correction, Huttonsville, 1979-85; specific learning disabilities/mentally impared tchr. Tygart Valley H.S., 1988095; prin. Homestead Elem. Sch., Dailey, W.Va., 1995—; instr. adult basic edn. Randolph County Schs., 1987-88, learning disabilities diagnostician, 1985-88, acting supr. spl. edn., 1987-88; instr. psychology Alderson-Broaddus Coll., Philippi, W.Va., 1985; clin. supr. for learning disabilities W.Va. U., Morgantown, 1986-87; dir. Braille project W.Va. Corrections and Dept. Edn., Huttonsville, 1982-83; tchr. specific learning disabilities Upshur County Schs., Buckhannon, W.Va., 1979-81; edn. cons. W.Va. Dept. Corrections, 1986. Chmn. Randolph County Rep. Exec. Com., Elkins, 1991; vice chmn. State of W.Va. Young Reps.; co-dir. W.Va. Young Reps. Alumni; elected to Elkins City Coun., 1993—, chmn. pers. com., mem. pub. safety and bldg. coms. Mem. W.Va. Univ. Alumni Assn., Duquesne Univ. Alumni Assn. Avocations: sports, running, skiing, sports cars. Home: 220 Sylvester Dr Elkins WV 26241-3044 Office: Homestead Elem Sch PO Box 158 Dailey WV 26259-0158

KOLTNOW, PETER GREGORY, engineering consultant; b. N.Y.C., Apr. 14, 1929; s. Harry George and Fay (Richman) K.; m. Dorothy D. Witter, Oct. 27, 1950; children: Nan Koltnow Chase, Nina Koltnow. B.S., Antioch Coll., 1951; M.S., U. Calif. at Berkeley, 1956. Engr. City of Dayton, Ohio, 1953-55; traffic engr. County of Fresno, Calif., 1956-62, Auto Club of So. Calif., 1962-67; dir. urban div. Automotive Safety Found., Washington, 1967-69; dir. urban div. Hwy. Users Fedn., 1970-71, v.p., 1971-74, pres., 1974-84; counselor to pres. Am. Trucking Assns., 1985-90; guest lectr. various univs., 1965—; chmn. Transp. Research Bd., 1979. Contbr. articles to profl. jours. Pres. Candlelighters, 1970-71; bd. dirs. ATA Found. With Ordnance Corps, U.S. Army, 1951-53. Recipient Disting. Service award Transp. Research Bd., 1982. Mem. ASCE (James Laurie prize 1984). Unitarian. Home and Office: 9210 Fernwood Rd Bethesda MD 20817-3316

KOLTUN, FRANCES LANG, editor, publisher, broadcaster; b. N.Y.C.; d. Samuel and Rebecca (Lang) K. BA magna cum laude, Bklyn. Coll., 1942; MA, Columbia U., 1945. Editor Am. Girl Mag., N.Y.C., 1945-48, Charm Mag., N.Y.C., 1948-58, Mademoiselle Mag., N.Y.C., 1958-72; owner, pres. Frances Koltun Enterprises Ltd., N.Y.C., 1972—; radio and TV broadcaster NBC, N.Y.C., 1970-75; writer and performer Travel Today, a radio program syndicate with 400 stas.; bd. dirs. Travel Industry Assn., Washington. Author: Frances Koltun's Complete Book for the Intelligent Woman Traveler, 1967; editor, pub. of ann. supplement A Fifth Avenue Christmas, other spl. newspaper supplements; pub., editor A Matter of Wit mag., 1998—. Named as A Woman of Accomplishment Wings Club, N.Y.C., 1981. Mem. Trends, Women's Forum.

KOLVE, V. A., English literature educator; b. Taylor, Wis., Jan. 18, 1934; s. Amos and Gunda (Lien) K. BA, U. Wis., 1955; BA with honors, Oxford U., 1957, MA, 1962, D Philosophy, 1962. From asst. prof. to assoc. prof. English Stanford (Calif.) U., 1962-69; prof. English U. Va., Charlottesville, Va., 1969-78, Commonwealth prof. English, 1979-86, chmn. dept. English, 1979-81; Found. prof. English UCLA, 1986—; Guggenheim Found. ednl. adv. bd., 1988—; The Alexander Lectures, U. Toronto, 1993, The Clark Lectures, Cambridge U., 1994. Author: The Play Called Corpus Christi, 1966, Chaucer and The Imagery of Narrative, 1984; author, editor: (with Glending Olson) Norton Critical Edition: Chaucer: The Canterbury Tales, 1989. 1st lt. U.S. Army, 1959. Recipient Brit. Coun. Humanities prize, 1985, Harbison Teaching award Danforth Found., 1972, UCLA Disting. Teaching award, 1995, Disting. Faculty award, 1999; Jenkins Rsch. fellow Oxford U., 1958-62, Guggenheim fellow, 1968, Sr. fellow Ctr. Advanced Studies in Visual Arts, Nat. Gallery, 1984, fellow Ctr. Advanced Study in Behavioral Scis., Stanford U., 1985; Rhodes scholar, 1955-58. Fellow Medieval Acad. Am. (pres. 1992); mem. MLA (chair exec. com. Chaucer divsn. 1973-77, 86-90, James Russell Lowell prize 1985), New Chaucer Soc. (trustee 1988-92, pres. 1994-96), Early English Text Soc., AAUP, Phi Beta Kappa. Democrat. Home: 2034 Outpost Dr Los Angeles CA 90068-3726 Office: UCLA Dept Of English Los Angeles CA 90024

KOLZ, BEVERLY ANNE, publishing executive; b. Newark, Ohio, Dec. 25, 1946; d. Willard Joseph and Lydia Marie (Gaze) K. BA, Ohio Dominican Coll., 1968; MBA, U. Iowa, 1991. Prodn. editor Merrill Pub., Columbus, Ohio, 1968-69, series editor, 1969-75, media buyer, 1975-76, prodn. buyer, 1976-78, mng. editor, 1978-80, adminstrv. editor, 1980-85, exec. editor, 1985-86; v.p., dir. of ops. and prodn. William C. Brown Pub. Co., Dubuque, Iowa, 1986-91; corp. v.p. ops. William C. Brown Comm., Inc., Dubuque, 1991-92; exec. v.p., gen. mgr. William C. Brown Pubs., Dubuque, 1992-94, CEO, pres., 1995-97; prin. Simon and Kolz Pub., Dubuque, 1997—. V.p. Altrusa, Columbus, 1985-86. Mem. Am. Ednl. Rsch. Assn., Women in Comm. (pres. 1979-80, 92-93), Chgo. Women in Pub. (Pub. Woman of Yr. 1993), Am. Assn. Pubs. (exec. coun. higher edn. divsn. 1992-97), Nat. Assn. Coll. Stores (bd. trustees 1994-95), Dubuque Area C. of C.(small bus. coun.). Avocations: biking, reading, golf, walking. Office: Simon and Kolz Publishing 1631 Main St Dubuque IA 52001-4512

KOMANDO, KIMBERLY ANN, computer company executive, radio and television host; b. Union, N.J.. BS in Computer Info. Systems, Ariz. State U., 1985. Mktg. rep. IBM, Phoenix, 1984-85; major account rep. AT&T, Phoenix, 1985-87; pres. The Komando Corp., Ariz./Fla., 1991—; mgr. UNISYS, Phoenix, 1987-91; pres. WestStar Talk Radio Network, 1998—; domestic and internat. mktg. cons.; speaker in field. Author: 401 Great Letters, 1993, 1,001 Komputer Answers, 1995, CyberBucks, 1996, Dummies 101: Creating Web Pages, 1997; editor Popular Mechanics mag.; talkshow and weekly radio show host; internationally syndicated radio talk show host; internationally weekly syndicated columnist L.A. Times; contbr. articles to profl. jours. Avocations: competitive bicyclist, golf, tennis, art. Office: The Komando Corp 2711 N 24th St Ste 100 Phoenix AZ 85008-1051

KOMANSKY, DAVID H., financial services executive; b. 1939. Grad., U. Miami, 1965. Comptr. Colonial Press, Miami, Fla., 1966-68; with Merrill Lynch & Co., N.Y.C., 1968—, exec. v.p., 1990-92, dir., 1991—, exec. v.p. debt markets, 1992-93, exec. v.p. debt and equity markets, 1993-95, pres., COO, 1995-96; CEO Merrill Lynch & Co., 1996; chmn., CEO Merrill Lynch & Co., Inc., 1997—. Office: Merrill Lynch & Company World Financial Center, North Tower 250 Vesey St Fl 4 New York NY 10080-0002*

KOMAR, VITALY, artist; b. Moscow, Sept. 11, 1943. Student, Stroganov Inst. Art and Design, Moscow, 1967. Ptnr. Komar & Melamid Studio, N.Y.C., 1965—; instr. visual art Moscow Regional Art Sch., 1968-76. Exhibitions include Wadsworth Atheneum, Hartford, Conn., 1978, Mus. Modern Art, Oxford Eng., Mus. Decorative Art, Paris, 1985, Neuen Gesellschaft für Gildende Kunst, Berlin, 1988, Bklyn. Mus., 1990, Alternative Mus., N.Y.C., 1994, Storefront for art and architecture, N.Y.C., 1995, Ukraine State Mus., Kiev, 1995, Mus. Modern Art, Cologne, Germany, 1997; exhibited in group shows at Met. Mus. Art, N.Y.C., 1982, 84, Chrysler Mus., Norfolk, Va., 1983, Sydney, Australia, 1986, Kassel, Germany, 1987, Solomon R. Guggenheim Found., 1987, FIAC, Paris, 1989, Bklyn. Mus., 1990, Venice Bienalle, 1997; represented in permanent collections Whitney Mus. Am. Art, N.Y.C., Stedeliyk Mus., Amsterdam, The Netherlands, Guggenheim Mus., Mus. Modern Art, Met. Mus. Art; commns. include mural Unity, 1st Interstate Bank Bldg., L.A., 1993, murals Liberty as Justice, N.Y., Bronx Housing Ct., 1994-98. Grantee Nat. Endowment Arts, 1982. Office: Komar & Melamid Studio 53 Lispenard St New York NY 10013-2501

KOMAROFF, ANTHONY LEADER, physician; b. Milw., June 7, 1941; s. Michael I. and Lillian J. (Leader) K.; m. Lydia Villa, June 18, 1970. AB, Stanford U., 1963; MD, U. Wash., 1967. Intern Cambridge Hosp., Cambridge, 1967-8; resident Beth Israel Hosp., Boston, 1970-72, asst. physician, 1971-79; sr. physician Brigham & Women's Hosp., Boston, 1992—, chief div. gen. medicine, 1982-97, sr. physician, 1992—; editor-in-chief Harvard Med. Publs., 1997—; mem. nat. adv. coun. Reg. Med. Programs, Dept. HEW, Washington, 1971-76. Contbr. over 270 articles to profl. jours. Lt. col. USPHS, 1968-70. Grantee, HEW, Dept. Health and Human Svcs., 1976—. Achievements include development of field of clinical algorithms; applications of computers in medical care; studies of common illnesses. Office: Harvard Health Publs 10 Shattuck St Boston MA 02115

KOMAROFF, STANLEY, lawyer; b. Bklyn, Apr. 1, 1935; s. William Ralph and Fanny (Wein) K.; m. Rosalyn Steinglass, Dec. 25, 1960; children: William Charles, Andrew Steven. BA, Cornell U., 1956, JD, 1958. Bar: N.Y. 1959. Assoc. Proskauer Rose LLP, N.Y.C., 1958-68, ptnr., 1968—, chmn., 1991-99. Mem. rev. and planning coun. N.Y. State Hosp., 1982-92; trustee Beth Israel Med. Ctr., 1984—; bd. dirs. Edmond de Rothschild Found., Club Med, Inc., 1984-95, Overseas Shipholding Group, Inc., Westhampton Beach Performing Arts Ctr.; chmn. ann. fund Cornell U. Law Sch., 1991-93. 1st lt. USAR, 1958. Mem. N.Y. State Bar Assn., Assn. of Bar of City of N.Y., N.Y. County Lawyers Assn., Order of Coif, Sunningdale Country Club, Phi Kappa Phi. Home: 910 Park Avenue Apt 5-S New York NY 10021-4168 Office: Proskauer Rose LLP 1585 Broadway New York NY 10036-8200

KOMATER, CHRISTOPHER JOHN, artist; b. South Bend, Ind., Nov. 16, 1965; s. Rudolph Andrew and Mary Frances (Napolitan) K. BFA, San Francisco Art Inst., 1987. Curator exhbn. Millenium Coming: The New Degenerate Art Show, 1995; co-curator Bottom's Up exhbn. Lab Gallery, San Francisco, 1998; one-man show 509 Cultural Ctr., San Francisco, 1997, Patricia Sweetow Gallery, 1997, 99; exhibited in group shows Haines Gallery, San Francisco, 1991, Jan Kesner Gallery, L.A., 1994, Oliver Art Ctr., Calif. Coll. Arts and Crafts, Oakland, Calif., 1994, Capp Street Project, San Francisco, 1996, Refusalon, San Francisco, 1997, Patricia Sweetow Gallery, San Francisco, 1997, 99. pres. bd. dirs. The Lab Gallery, San Francisco, 1995—, mem. curatorial com., 1994—; bd. dirs. Secession Gallery, San Francisco, 1990-95, mem. adv. bd., 1995—. Regional Visual Arts fellow Western States Art Fedn./Nat. Endowment Arts, 1994; recipient artist residency award Villa Montalvo Ctr. for Arts, 1994; San Francisco Arts Commn. Market Street Art in Transit grantee, 1998. E-mail: www.chriskomater.com. Home and Studio: 4303 20th St San Francisco CA 94114-2816

KOMATSU, S. RICHARD, architect; b. San Francisco, May 5, 1916; s. Denzo and Tome (Fujimoto) K.; m. Chisato Frances Kuwata, Aug. 6, 1943; children: Richard Shigeto, Kathryn Kay. BArch, U. Calif., Berkeley, 1938; cert. in interior design, San Francisco Archtl. Club, 1939; cert. in machine design, Lawrence Inst. Tech., Detroit, 1944. Registered architect, Calif.; cert. architect Nat. Coun. Archtl. Registration Bds. Landscape planner Golden Gate Internat. Expn., San Francisco, 1938-39; designer/architect Charles F. Strothoff, Architect, San Francisco, 1939-42, 46-52; asst. project engr. Fed. Pub. Housing Authority, Detroit, 1944; designer Harley, Ellington & Day, Architects, Detroit, 1944; assoc./architect Donald L. Hardison & Assocs., Richmond, Calif., 1952-57; sec./prin. Hardison and Komatsu Assocs., San Francisco, 1957-79; pres./prin. Hardison Komatsu Ivelich & Tucker, San Francisco, 1979-88, cons., 1988—; pvt. practice cons. S. Richard Komatsu, Architect, El Cerrito, Calif., 1988—; invited speaker nat. conv. Nat. Assn. Home Builders, Chgo., 1966, confs. ASCE, San Francisco, 1972, Calif. and Nev. Water Pollution Control Assn., South Lake Tahoe, Calif., 1972; vis. archtl. adviser Cogswell Coll., San Francisco, 1981-82. Prin. works include 47 water treatment plants and related facilities, East Bay Mcpl. Utility Dist., 1964-84 (Gov.'s award 1974), Advanced Wastewater Treatment Plant, Clark County Sanitation Dist., Las Vegas, Nev., 1979, South Valley Water Reclamation Facility, Midvale, Utah, 1987, East Bank Wastewater Treatment Plant, Metairie, La., 1988, main office complex, Turlock (Calif.) Irrigation Dist., 1988, 24 water treatment plants and related facilities, Contra Costa Water Dist., Concord, Calif., 1967-88 (Concord award 1972), pre-design of 6 water reclamation plants, 3 pumping plants, 1 dechlorination facility for Clean Water Program Greater San Diego, 1990-92; design advisor adminstrn., ops., and lab. bldg., wastwater treatment plant City of Santa Rosa, Calif., administrn. bldg. Dublin San Ramon (Calif.) Svcs. Dist., plant ops. ctr. Delta Diablo Sanitation Dist., Calif., 1991-92; contbr. articles to jours. in field. Bd. dirs. Richmond (Calif.) Art Ctr., 1956-60, City of Richmond Ballet Co., 1956-60; mem. El Cerito Planning Commn., 1962-75, chmn., 1966-67; mem. El Cerrito Design Rev. Bd., 1969-78, chmn., 1973-77; mem. Contra Costa chpt. Japanese Am. Citizens League, 1950—, pres., 1957, bd. dirs., 1956-60 (silver pin achievement award 1966). Master sgt. Mil. Intelligence Svc., U.S. Army, 1944-46. Recipient Eminent Conceptor award Consulting Engrs. Assn. Calif., 1974, Cons. Engrs. award Fairfield-Suisun Wastewater Mgmt. Facilities, 1978, AIA award Student Ctr. Complex U. Calif., 1978, Gold Nugget award Southeast Water Pollution Control Plant, 1984. Fellow (emeritus) AIA (East Bay chpt., bd. dirs. 1968-69, chmn. numerous coms.); mem. Am. Water Works Assn. (cert. life mem., invited speaker various confs.). Republican. Presbyterian. Avocations: water color painting, archtl. delineating, golf. Address: 1323 Devonshire Dr El Cerrito CA 94530-2572 *I was blessed with perseverence, thirst for knowledge and a will to nurture aptitude. However, my humble environment did not allow optimism for a meaningful future until an unexpected scholarship gave me the means to advance to a university. Still, adversities had be overcome: World War II, the unconstitutional internment, military service and racial discrimination. Perhaps in spite of these, the meaningful accomplishments have been achieved with God and family, and the inspiring people who guided, encouraged and supported me.*

KOMEN, LEONARD, lawyer; b. St. Louis, May 31, 1943; s. Meyer and Yetta (Ellman) K.; m. Sandra Gail Cytron, June 8, 1969; children: Douglas Steven, Matthew Todd. BA, U. Mo., 1965, JD, 1970. Bar: Mo. 1970, U.S. Dist. Ct. (ea. dist.) Mo. 1971, U.S. Supreme Ct. 1973, U.S. Ct. Appeals (8th cir.) 1985, U.S. Claims Ct. 1992, U.S. Ct. Appeals (3d cir.) 1995. Assoc. Susman, Willer & Rimmel, St. Louis, 1970-74; assoc. Susman Schermer Rimmel & Parker, St. Louis, 1974-77, ptnr., 1977-80; prin., v.p. Selner, Glaser, Komen, Berger & Galganski, P.C., St. Louis, 1980-96; prin. mgr. Komen, Berger & Cohen, L.C., 1996—; ct.-apptd. trustee, examiner, receiver U.S. Bankruptcy Ct., 1988—. bd. dirs. Zeta Beta Tau Frat. Inc., 1984—, nat. sec., 1989-90, nat. v.p., 1990-92, nat. pres., 1992-94; mem. supervisory bd. Nat. Interfraternity Coun. Legal Advocacy Fund, 1993-98. Pres. Creve Coeur Hockey Club Inc., St. Louis, 1987-88, bd. dirs., 1989-93; coord. Parkway North Hockey Club, 1989-91; pres., bd. dirs. Roswell Messing Ednl. Found., 1989—; bd. dirs. Zeta Beta Tau Centennial Found. 1990-98. Recipient Merit citation Zeta Beta Tau Frat., Inc., 1977, 91, 92. Mem. ATLA, Comml. Law League Am., Met. St. Louis Bar Assn., Lawyers Assn. Jewish. Home: 14385 Stablestone Ct Chesterfield MO 63017-2502 Office: Komen Berger & Cohen 222 S Central Ave Ste 1100 Saint Louis MO 63105-3576

KOMER, ROBERT WILLIAM, government official, consultant; b. Chgo., Feb. 23, 1922; s. Nathan A and Stella (Deiches) K.; m. Geraldine M. Peplin, Nov. 3, 1961 (dec.); children: Douglas Robert, Richard Donen, Anne Elizabeth. S.B. magna cum laude, Harvard U., 1942, M.B.A., 1947; student, Nat. War Coll., 1956-57. With Directorate of Intelligence and Office Nat. Estimates, CIA, 1947-60; sr. staff mem. Nat. Security Council, 1961-65; dep. spl. asst. to Pres. for nat. security affairs, 1965-66, spl. asst. to Pres., 1966-67; dep. to comdr. USMACV for CORDS, 1967-68; ambassador to Turkey, 1968-69; sr. social sci. researcher Rand Corp., Washington, 1969-77; adviser to sec. def. for NATO affairs, 1977-79; undersec. for policy U.S. Dept. Def., Washington, 1979-81; vis. fellow George Mason U., Fairfax, Va., 1981-82; adj. prof. George Washington U., 1981-84; bd. advs. Coun. on Fgn. Rels.; bd. visitors Nat. Def. U , 1964-70, cons. Rand Corp. 1982—. Author: Maritime Strategy or Coalition Defense? 1984, Bureaucracy at War, 1986; contbr. numerous articles to newspapers and profl. publs. Served to 1st lt. AUS, 1943-46; lt. col. Res. Decorated Bronze Star; Nat. Order Vietnam; Vietnam Gold Economy medal; Vietnam Croix de Guerre; Revolutionary Devel. medal (Vietnam); Grand Cross, German Order of Merit; recipient Presdl. Medal of Freedom; Disting. Honor award State Dept.; medal and oak leaf cluster for Disting. Public Service Dept. of Def. Mem. Phi Beta Kappa. Democrat. Home: 900 N Taylor St Apt 1407 Arlington VA 22203-1889 Office: RAND Corp 2100 M St NW Washington DC 20037-1207

KOMERATH, NARAYANAN MENON, aerospace engineer; b. Thrissur, Kerala, India, June 3, 1956; m. Padma Komerath. B Tech. in Aeronautical Engring., Indian Inst. Tech., Madras, 1978; MS in Aerospace Engring., Ga. Inst. Tech., 1979, PhD in Aerospace Engring., 1982. Postdoctoral fellow aerospace engring. Ga. Inst. Tech., Atlanta, 1982-83, rsch. engr., 1983-85, asst. prof., 1985-90, assoc. prof., 1990-94, prof. aerospace engring., 1994—; engring. cons. Lockheed-Ga. Co., Marietta, 1985-88, Southwire Co., Carrollton, Ga., 1992-93; chmn. SCV, Inc., Alpharetta, Ga., 1994—; dir. John J. Harper Wind Tunnel, Ga. Inst. Tech., Atlanta, 1990—. Contbr. articles to profl. jours. Fellow AIAA (assoc., nat. tech. com. on aerodynamic measurement 1995—); mem. Am. Helicopter Soc. (nat. tech. com. on aerodynamics 1994-96), Am. Soc. Engring. Edn., Soc. Exptl. Mechs., Amnesty Internat., Sigma Xi. Achievements include patents for spatial cross-correlation velocimeter, stagnation point vortex controller, and wind driven dynamic manipulator. Office: Ga Inst Tech Sch Aerospace Engring Atlanta GA 30332-0150

KOMISAR, DAVID DANIEL, retired university provost; b. N.Y.C., July 20, 1917; s. Jacob and Yetta (Jacobson) K.; m. Beatrice Liebman, Aug. 15, 1940 (dec. Sept. 1981); children—Jack Lloyd, June Diana; m. Molly Komisar, Nov. 1984. B.S.S., Coll. City N.Y., 1937, M.S., 1940; postgrad., U. Glasgow, 1945, Sorbonne, 1946; Ph.D., Columbia U., 1953. With Civil Service, N.Y.C., 1939-42; indsl. personnel work, 1943-44; counselor vocational rehab. U.S. Army, 1943-46; dir. guidance Mohawk Coll., 1946-48; dir. guidance, chmn. dept. psychology Champlain Coll., State U. N.Y., Plattsburg, 1948-53; chmn. dept. psychology U. Hartford, 1953—, pres. univ. faculty senate, 1964-65; dean U. Hartford (Sch. Arts and Scis.), 1966-67, dean of faculties, 1967-70, v.p. acad. affairs, 1970-71, provost, 1972-80, Univ. prof., 1980-84, prof. and provost emeritus, 1984—; mem. Conn. Civil Service Commn., 1980-84; pres. Emeriti Assn., 1989-91; cons. Palm Beach County Mental Health Assn., 1991—; Project dir. research in mental retardation Office Vocat. Rehab., Dept. Health, Edn. and Welfare, 1964-65, psychosocial com. social rehab. services, 1968-74; head New Eng. Conf. Mental Retardation, 1960, Conn. Task Force on Mental Retardation, 1960-61; Conn. rep. Nat. Def. Edn. Act, 1960-61; research fellow U.S. Office Vocational Rehab., 1962-63; Conn. Citizens Com. on State Welfare, 1967-69; mem. standing com. accreditation Conn. Commn. High Edn., 1969-75. Contbr. articles on testing, therapy, vocational selection to profl. jours. Co-chmn. Citizens Charter Com. Hartford, 1959; mem. bd. Hartford Jewish Cmty. Ctr., 1955-63, v.p., 1963-78, life officer 1978—; mem. bd. Mental Health Assn., 1959-62; bd. dirs. Inst. of New Dimensions, Palm Beach Cmty. Coll., 1994—. Recipient rsch. grant for study residential care retarded children HEW, 1965-69, Disting. Svc. medal U. Hartford, 1990, Univ. medal U. Hartford, 1991; elected to Townsend Harris Hall of Fame, 1998. Mem. Conn. Valley Assn. Psychologists (past pres.), Am. Psychol. Assn., Conn. Psychol. Assn. (council; pres.), Nat. Vocational Guidance Assn., Am. Personnel and Guidance Assn., Sigma Xi. Clubs: Connecticut Valley Torch (past pres.), Probus (past pres.) (Hartford).

KOMISARJEVSKY, CHRISTOPHER P.A., public relations executive; b. 1946. BS in Polit. Sci., MBA; postgrad. German Lit./Internat. Affairs, U.S./Europe. Hill and Knowlton, Inc., 1972-92, Pres., CEO Europe, Mid. East and Africa ops., CEO Carl Byoir & Assocs.; pres., CEO Gavin Anderson & Co. Omnicom, 1992-95; pres., CEO Burson-Marsteller U.S., N.Y.C., 1995-99; CEO Burson-Marsteller Worldwide, N.Y.C., 1999—; chmn. Burson-Marsteller Global Corp. Practice, 1995-99. Contbr. articles to profl. jours.; lectr. at Spain's Instituto de Empresa, Switzerland's Internat. Inst. for Mgmt. Devel., N.Y.U. Grad. Sch. Bd. dirs. several non-profit orgs.; trustee EQ Advisors Trust. Capt. U.S. Army, 1967-72 (Vietnam). Recipient Ellis Island Medal of Honor, 1996. Office: Burson Marsteller 230 Park Ave New York NY 10003-1566*

KOMISSARCHIK, EDWARD, computer scientist; b. Moscow, Russia, July 5, 1949; came to U.S., 1990; s. Alexander and Riva (Zilberstein) K.; m. Stella Mnatsakanian, Sept. 5, 1969; 1 child, Julia. M in Math., Lomonosov U., Moscow, 1971; PhD of Computer Sci., Inst. Cybernetics, Russia, 1978. Rsch. scientist Inst. Control Scis., Acad. Scis., Moscow, 1971-77, Inst. Sys. Studies, Acad. Scis., Moscow, 1977-90; assoc. prof. computer sci. Inst. Radio Electronics and Automation, Moscow, 1978-90; pres., chief tech. officer Accent, Inc., San Francisco, 1993-96; dir. Aspect Telecomm., San Jose, 1999. Contbr. articles to profl. jours. Mem. IEEE, ACM, Internat. Platform Assn., Russian Math. Soc., Scientists Club. Avocations: public speaking, medieval history, tennis. Home: 2452 Melendy Dr San Carlos CA 94070-3623

KOMIVES, PAUL J., federal judge; b. 1932. AB, U. Detroit, 1954; JD, U. Mich., 1958. Bar: Mich. 1958, D.C. 1958, U.S. Ct. Appeals (6th cir.) 1961, U.S. Ct. Appeals (D.C. cir.) 1961, U.S. Supreme Ct. 1963. Asst. U.S. atty. U.S. Dist. Ct. (ea. dist.) Mich., 1961-66; spl. prosecutor Mich. Cir. Ct., Detroit, 1966-67; pvt. practice, 1967-71; magistrate judge U.S. Dist. Ct. (ea. dist.) Mich., Detroit, 1971—; adj. prof. Detroit Coll. Law, 1972—; adj. prof. Wayne State U. Law Sch., Detroit, 1998—. Fax: (313) 234-5497. Office: US Dist Ct Ea Dist Mich 629 US Courthouse 231 W Lafayette Blvd Detroit MI 48226

KOMIYA, NOBORU, psychology educator; b. Sakai, Osaka, Japan, May 5, 1966; came to U.S., 1991; s. Kazuyuki and Akiko (Yamane) K. B Gen. Edn., U. Osaka, Sakai, 1990; MS, Frostburg State U., 1994; PhD, U. Mo., 1999. Grad. asst. Frostburg (Md.) State U., 1993-94; psychologist II, North Ctrl. Human Svc. Ctr., Minot, N.D., 1994-95; tchg. asst. U. Mo., Columbia, 1995-97, grad. instr., 1997-98; predoctoral intern psychology consortium So. Miss. State U., Hattiesburg, 1998-99. Robert S. Daniel tchg. fellow U. Mo.-Columbia, 1997. Mem. APA (multi-cultural scholar divsn. 17, 1997).

KOMM, KERMIT MATTHEW, software engineer; b. LaGrange, Ill., Apr. 9, 1964; s. Charles Paul and Dorothy Anna Jean (Groves) K. BS in Elec. Engring., UCLA, 1986. Dir. ops. Leviathan Devel., L.A., 1986-90; software engr. FortuNet, Las Vegas, Nev., 1991; v.p. software engring. Future Techs., Las Vegas, 1991-95; v.p. engring. Innovation Mgmt. Group, Las Vegas, 1995—. Author: (software) My-T-Mouse, 1993, Joystick-to-Mouse, 1995, My-T-Soft AT, 1998, The Magnifier, 1998. Avocations: travel, driving, hiking. Office: Innovation Mgmt Group Inc 4425 E Sahara Ave Ste 9 Las Vegas NV 89104-6357

KOMMEDAHL, THOR, plant pathology educator; b. Mpls., Apr. 1, 1920; s. Thorbjorn and Martha (Blegen) K.; m. Faye Lillian Jensen, June 2, 1924; children: Kris Alan, Siri Lynn, Lori Anne. B.S., U. Minn., 1945, M.S., 1947, Ph.D., 1951. Instr. U. Minn., St. Paul, 1946-51, asst. prof. plant pathology, 1953-57, assoc. prof., 1957-63, prof., 1963-90, prof. emeritus, 1990—; asst. prof. plant pathology Ohio Agrl. Research and Devel. Ctr., Wooster, 1951-53, Ohio State U., Columbus, 1951-53; prof. Univ. Coll., U. Minn., St. Paul, 1990—; cons. botanist and taxonomist Minn. Dept. Agr., 1954-60, Sci. Mus. Minn., 1990—; 7th A.W. Dimock lectr. Cornell U., 1979; external assessor U. Pertanian Malaysia, 1994—. Author: Pesky Plants, 1989; co-author: Scientific Style and Format, 1994; editor Minn. Fulbright newsletter, 1993—, Procs. IX Internat. Congress Plant Protection, 2 vols., 1981, Corn Disease newsletter, 1970-76; assoc. editor The Boghopper, 1996—; cons. editor McGraw Hill Ency. Sci. and Tech., 1972-78; editor-in-chief Phytopathology, 1964-67; sr. editor: Challenging Problems in Plant Health, 1982, Plant Disease Reporter, 1979; contbr. articles to profl. jours. Bd. mem. Park Bugle, 1998—. Recipient Elvin Charles Stakman award, 1990, Award of Merit, Gamma Sigma Delta, 1994; Guggenheim fellow, 1961, Fulbright scholar, 1968. Fellow AAAS, Am. Phytopathol. Soc. (councilor 1958-60, pres. 1971, publs. coord. 1978-84, Disting. Svc. award 1984, 93, sci. adv. 1984—, mem. adv. bd. office internat. programs 1987-93, editor Focus 1981—); mem. Am. Inst. Biol. Scis., Bot. Soc. Am., Coun. Biology Editors, Internat. Soc. Plant Pathology (councilor 1971-78, sec.-gen. and treas. 1983-88, treas. 1988-93, editor newsletter 1983-93), Mycol. Soc. Am., Minn. Acad. Sci., N.Y. Acad. Scis., Weed Sci. Soc. Am. (award of excellence 1968), Fulbright Assn. (Minn. chpt., editor newsletter 1995—). Baptist. Home: 1666 Coffman St Apt 322 Saint Paul MN 55108-1340 Office: U Minn 495 Borlaug Hall 1991 Upper Buford Cir Saint Paul MN 55108-6030

KOMP, BARBARA ANN, marketing communications executive; b. La Porte, Ind., Nov. 3, 1954; d. Gerald Lee and Betty Mae (Schelin) K. BA in Elem. Edn., Ball State U., 1977; cert. in lang. arts/reading competencies, 1977. Quality control insp. Foreman Mfg. Co., Rolling Prairie, Ind., 1978-80; quality control inspector Weil-McLain Co., Michigan City, Ind., 1980-81, jr. quality control engr., 1981-84, tech. writer, 1984-88, mgr. tech. pubs., 1988-97, mktg. comms. specialist, 1997—. Advisor Jr. Achievement, Michigan City, 1982-84; mem. bd. dirs. Mich. City YMCA, 1992-93, Christmas-in-April, Michigan City, chair in-kind donations com., 1993-95, bd. sec. 1994-95. Mem. Soc. for Tech. Communication (Tech. Manual Achievement award 1986, Tech. Manual Achievement award 1986, Tech. Manual Merit award 1990, 92, 93, 96, Tech. Manual Excellence award 1996). Avocations: jazz aerobics, photography, volleyball. Office: Weil-McLain A Marley Co 500 Blaine St Michigan City IN 46360-2388

KOMPALA, DHINAKAR SATHYANATHAN, chemical engineering educator, biochemical engineering researcher; b. Madras, India, Nov. 20, 1958; came to U.S., 1979; s. Sathyanathan and Sulochana Kompala; m. Sushila Viswamurthy Rudramuniappa, Nov. 18, 1983; children: Tejaswi Dina, Chytanya Robby. BTech., Indian Inst. Tech., Madras, 1979; MS, Purdue U., 1982, PhD, 1984. Asst. prof. chem. engring. U. Colo., Boulder, 1985-91, assoc. prof., 1991—; vis. assoc. chem. engring. Calif. Inst. Tech., 1991-92; vis. prof. Internat. Ctr. Biotech., Osaka U., Japan, 1999. Editor Cell Separation Sci. and Tech., 1991; contbr. articles to profl. jours. Recipient NSF Presdl. Young Investigators award, 1988-93; NSF Biotech. Rsch. grantee, 1986-89, 89-92, 95-99; Dept. Commerce rsch. grantee, 1988; The Whitaker Found. grantee, 1990-93. Mem. Am. Inst. Chem. Engrs., Am. Chem. Soc. (program chair biochem. tech. divsn. 1993). Office: U Colo PO Box 424 Boulder CO 80309-0424

KOMPASS, EDWARD JOHN, consulting editor; b. Jersey City, Dec. 22, 1926; s. Edward F. and Margaret A. (Doran) K.; m. Amelia M. Heubel, Sept. 22, 1951; children: Christine (Mrs. Kevin Scully), Daniel E., Andrew J., Timothy M., Matthew P., Julie A. (Mrs. Matthew Wilhm). Degree in mech. engring., Stevens Inst. Tech., 1951. Jr. engr. Intelectron Inc., N.Y.C., 1951-52; engr. De Florez Co., N.Y.C., 1952-54; asst. editor control engring., McGraw-Hill Pub. Co., N.Y.C., 1954-60, assoc. editor, 1960-65; mng. editor control engring., Dun-Donnelley Pub. Corp., N.Y.C., 1965-72; editor control engring., Tech. Pub., Barrington, Ill., 1972-86; editorial dir. control engring. Cahners Publ., 1986-87, cons. editor, 1987—, forum discussions moderator, control engring online, 1997; co-organizer ann. advanced control confs. Purdue U., Lafayette, Ind., 1974-77, 79-93; conf. dir. Internat. Control. Engring. Expn. and Conf., Chgo., 1992-94; mem. adv. coun. Indsl. Automation Conf., 1994, 95, 96. Editor, contbr. profl. articles and editorials to jours.; editorial advisor Detroit Engr. With USNR, 1944-46. Recipient 19th Ann. Crain award Assn. Bus. Pubs., 1987. Mem. IEEE, Am. Soc. Bus. Paper Editors, Instrument Soc. Am., Engring. Soc. Detroit, Am. Legion, VFW, Rotary Internat., Beta Theta Pi. Roman Catholic. Home and Office: 678 Cobb Hill Rd Lincoln VT 05443-9699

KOMUNYAKAA, YUSEF (JAMES WILLIE BROWN, JR.), poet; m. Mandy Sayer. BA, U. Colo., 1975; MA, Colo. State U., 1978, U. Calif., Irvine, 1980. Assoc. prof., then prof. Afro-Am. Studies Ind. U., Bloomington, 1987-98; prof. creative writing, counsel in the humanities Princeton (N.J.) U., 1997—; vis. prof. Ind. U., Bloomington, 1985. Author: Lost in Bone-Wheel Factory, 1979, Dien Cai Dau, 1988, Magic City, 1992, Neon Vernacular: New and Selected Poems, 1993 (Kingsley Tufts Poetry award 1994, Pulitzer Prize for poetry 1994), Ploughshares Spring, 1997, Thieves of Paradise, 1998. Office: Princeton U Creative Writing Program 185 Nassau St Princeton NJ 08544*

KONCAR, GEORGE ALAN, secondary education educator; b. Kenton, Ohio, Oct. 1, 1950; s. George Jr. and Wilma Faye (Hufford) K.; m. Jody Ann Kasler, Aug. 12, 1972; children: Glenda Ann, Jessica Renee. BA, Capital U., Bexley, Ohio, 1972; MS in Math., Ohio U., Athens, 1988. Cert. tchr., Ohio. Tchr. Hilliard (Ohio) City Schs., 1972-73, Maysville Local Schs., South Zanesville, Ohio, 1973—. Recipient Outstanding Svc. award Kiwanis, 1984, Outstanding Local Treas. award Ohio Edn. Assn., 1989. Mem. Maysville Edn. Assn. (pres. 1993-98). Lutheran. Avocation: military history. Home: 112 Juanita Dr Zanesville OH 43701-6235 Office: Maysville HS 2805 Pinkerton Rd Zanesville OH 43701-8594

KONCHALOVSKY, ANDREI, film director; b. USSR, Aug. 20, 1937; came to U.S., 1980.; s. Sergei Mikhalkov; m. Vivianne Mikhalkov. Dir. feature films The First Teacher, 1965, Asya's Happiness, 1967, Siberiade, 1980, Runaway Train, 1980, Tango and Cash, 1989, The Inner Circle, 1991, Ryaba, My Chicken, 1994, Lumiere et Compagnie, 1995, also films in Soviet Union. Recipient Emmy award for Outstanding Individual Achievement in Directing a Miniseries or Spl. for The Odyssey, 1996. Office: CAA 9830 Wilshire Blvd Beverly Hills CA 90212-1825

KONCHAN, KENNETH JOSEPH, humanities educator; b. Cleve., Jan. 3, 1941; s. Joseph Lawrence and Eileen Catherine (McLean) K.; m. Linda Susan Phillips, Dec. 2, 1992. BA in History, Hiram Coll., 1963; postgrad., Akron U., 1967; MA in Humanities, John Carroll U., 1992. Cert. tchr. Ohio. Tchr., coach Valley Forge H.S., Parma City (Ohio) Sch. Dist., 1964—; humanities instr. Cuyahoga C.C., Parma, 1997—; owner, operator North Coast Basketball Camp, Oberlin, Ohio, 1987—; planning com., presenter Ohio Dept. Edn., Global Inst., Columbus, 1996—; lectr. Ohio Coun. on Holocaust Edn., Kent State U., 1997—. Active forum on Bosnia UN, 1995; advisor Sun Newspapers Cmty. Adv. Bd., Cleve., 1989—. Study grant Nat. Endowment for Humanities, 1995; fellowship in Germany Armonk Inst., 1996, Alumni fellowship, 1998; scholar Martha Hollen Jennings Found., 1979. Mem. Ohio Coun. for Social Studies, Ohio Basketball Coaches Assn., Greater Cleve. Basketball Coaches Assn. (Coach of Yr. 1994). Republican. Roman Catholic. Avocations: travel, basketball, research, reading, writing. Home: 7545 Creekwood Dr North Royacton OH 44133 Office: Valley Forge HS 9999 Indpedence Blvd Parma Heights OH 44130

KONDO, EDWARD SHINICHI, plant pathologist, researcher; b. Victoria, B.C., Can., Sept. 5, 1939; m. Jeanne D. Sabourin, 1970; children: Christine, Michelle. BSc in Forestry, U. Toronto, Ont., Can., 1964, MSc in Forestry, 1966, PhD in Plant Pathology, 1970. Rsch. officer dept. environment Can. Forestry Svc., Sault Ste. Marie, Ont., 1969-71, rsch. scientist forest pathology, 1971-82, dir. Forest Insect and Disease Survey, 1983-88, dir. Biorational Control Agts. Program, 1988-90, dir. gen. Forest Pest Mgmt. Inst., 1990-95; dir. gen. Natural Resources Can. Can. Forestry Svc., Sault Ste. Marie, 1996—; adj. prof. forestry U. Toronto, 1972-74. Achievements include research in vascular wilt tree diseases; Dutch elm disease; urban forestry; tree and fungus physiology, mycology, chemotherapy of tree diseases. Office: Canadian Forest Svc, Great Lakes Forestry Ctr, 1219 Queen St E POB 490, Sault Sainte Marie, ON Canada P6A 5M7

KONDRACKI, EDWARD JOHN, lawyer; b. Elizabeth, N.J., Sept. 27, 1932; s. John and Catherine Chudio (Saas) K.; m. Barbara Terese Caruso; children: Carol Ann, Maryanne, Christopher. BSEE, N.J. Inst. Tech., 1959; JD with honors, George Washington U., 1963. Bar: Va. 1964, U.S. Dist. Ct. D.C. 1964, U.S. Dist. Ct. (ea. dist.) Va. 1964, U.S. Ct. Appeals (fed. cir.) 1983, U.S. Ct. Claims 1976, U.S. Ct. Customs and Patent Appeals 1976. Patent atty. Gen. Electric Co., Washington, 1959-63; dir. Kerkam, Stowell Kondracki & Clarke, P.C. and predecessor, Arlington, Va., 1963-65; ptnr., 1965—; dir. Patmark Paralegal Svcs., 1975-90; treas. SOC Enterprises, 1989-90, chn., 1990—. Author: Trademarks-Servicemarks, Use, Usage and Protection, 1981, Proper Use of Trademarks and Servicemarks, 1982, Common Pitfalls Encountered in Patenting Inventions, 1983, Copyright Protection of Computer Software. Served with USN, 1951-55. Mem. ABA, Am. Intellectual Property Law Assn., Internat. Assn. Protection Indsl. Property, Va. Bar Assn., Internat. Trademark Assn., Washington Patent Lawyers Club, D.C. Bar Assn. (chmn. com. internat. affairs 1973), Gt. Falls Hist. Soc., Marmota Farm Assn., KC, Tau Beta Pi, Eta Kappa Nu, Omicron Delta Kappa, Phie Eta Sigma. Office: 5203 Leesburg Pike Falls Church VA 22041-3401

KONDYLIS, COSTAS ANDREW, architect; b. Bujumbura, Burundi, Apr. 17, 1940; came to U.S., 1967; s. Andrew and Vassiliki (Kalogreas) K.; m. Gretchen Barnes, Feb. 22, 1969 (div. 1976); 1 child, Katherine; m. Lori Neuner, Jan. 2, 1979; 1 child, Alexia. MArch, U. Geneva, 1967; M in Urban Design, Columbia U., 1969. Registered arch., N.Y., N.J., Conn. Arch. Davis Brody & Assocs., N.Y.C., 1967-80; ptnr. Philip Birnbaum & Assocs., N.Y.C., 1980-89; pres. Costas Kondylis Archs., PC, N.Y.C., 1989-93, C.K. Arch., PC, N.Y.C., 1993—. Bd. dirs. Greek Orthodox Cathedral, N.Y.C., 1993-94. Recipient Lifetime Achievement award N.Y. Soc. Archs., 1996. Mem. AIA. Avocations: travel, bicycling, photography. Home: 157 E 81st St # 7A New York NY 10028-1844 also: 500 N Main St Southampton NY 11968-2831 Office: CK Architect PC 3 W 18th St New York NY 10011-4610 also: 500 N Main St Southampton NY 11968-2831*

KONECK, JOHN MICHAEL, lawyer; b. Mpls., Aug. 16, 1953; s. Robert W. and Bernice V.; m. Debra K. Plotz, Aug. 16, 1980; 1 child, Robert John. BS, N.D. State U., 1975; J.D., Yale Law Sch., Mpls., 1978. Bar: N.D. 1978, Minn. 1979. Jud. law clk. N.D. Supreme Ct., Bismarck, 1978-79; ptnr. Fredrikson & Byron, Mpls., 1979—; mem. Minn. Bd. Legal Cert., Supreme Ct. Minn., 1994—, chairperson, 1996—; mem. Vol. Lawyers Network; assoc. prof. William Mitchell Coll. Law, 1997—. Mem. ABA (chair litigation and dispute resolution, com. of sect. real property, probate and trust law 1995-98, chief editor newsletter of litigation and dispute resolution com. 1991-93, vice chair 1991-95), Minn. State Bar Assn. (mem. real property cert. coun. 1990—, rules of profl. conduct com.), State Bar Assn. N.D., Hennepin County Bar Assn. (co-chair rules of profl. conduct com. 1994-96). Office: Fredrikson & Byron 1100 International Ctr 900 2nd Ave S Ste 1100 Minneapolis MN 55402-3397

KONER, PAULINE, dancer, choreographer, author; b. N.Y.C., June 26, 1912; d. Samuel and Ida (Ginsberg) K.; m. Fritz Mahler, May 23, 1939 (dec. 1973). Student, Columbia U., 1928-30; studies with Michel Fokine, studies with Michio Ito, studies with Angel Cansino; DFA (hon.), R.I. Coll., 1985. Faculty dance div. Juilliard Sch., 1986—; lectr. dance workshop, Tokyo, 1965; mem. faculty Sch. Performing Arts, N.Y.C., N.C. Sch. Arts, Winston-Salem; adj. prof. Bklyn. Coll., 1975-79; guest tchr. modern dance Internat. Ballet Seminar, Copenhagen, 1971, 72, Am. Dance Ctr., N.Y.C., 1972; lectr. and guest artist many leading univs. in U.S.; performed under auspices State Dept. in Mex., S.Am., Europe; artist-in-residence N.C. Sch. Arts, Winston-Salem, 1965-76; tchr. choreographer workshop Cultural Ctr. of Philippines, 1973; dir. Pauline Koner Dance Consort, 1976-82; nat. adjudicator Am. Coll. Dance Festival, Kennedy Ctr., 1981; guest lectr. U. Arts, Phila., 1991, 92, 93; staged Farewell for dancer Margie Gillis, 1995; mem. Fulbright workshop, Japan, 1965; lectr. tour WSIS, India and Korea, 1967. Performed at White House, 1967; conducted choreography workshops Nat. Assn. Regional Ballets, 1968; staged ballet Dayton (Ohio) Civic Ballet, 1969, Alvin Ailey Repertory Co., 1969, Atlanta Ballet Co., 1969; filmed TV broadcasts of numerous performances; premiere: The Farewell, 1962, Solitary Songs, Am. Dance Festival, 1975, Pauline Koner Dance Consort, 1976-82, A Time of Crickets, Am. Dance Festival, 1976, Mosaic, Dance Umbrella Series, 1977, Cantigas, Am. Dance Festival, 1978, Flight Riverside Festival, 1980; resident dancer Riverside Dance Festival, 1979-81; solo concerts in N.Y.C., 1930—, Near East, 1932, Russia, 1935, Riverside Co., 1980-82; guest artist Jose Limon Co., 1945-60; guest artist, tchr. Jacob's Pillow Dance Festival, intermittently 1945-70; dir. Pauline Koner Dance Co., 1947-64; performed Farewell, Tokyo, 1965, Montreal, 1996; guest choreographer Nat. Sch. Dance, Rome, 1960-63, Nat. Ballet Chile, 1961; performer, tchr. Conn. Coll. Sch. Dance, 1948-60; pioneer TV dance CBS, 1946; artist-in-residence: U. Ill., 1984, Alvin Ailey Repertory Co., 1984; choreographer: Solitary Songs at Alvin Ailey Repertory Co., 1984; author: (autobiography) Solitary Song, 1989, Elements of Performance, 1993; contbr. articles to books and mags.; State Dept. tour of India, Singapore and Korea, 1967; restaged Poéme for N.C. Sch. Art, 1991, Concertino for Dance-Fusion, Phila., 1991; spl. coaching Jacobs Pillow, 1991; solo performance The Farewell for Margie Gillis, 1995. Recipient Dance Mag. award, 1963, Citation award De La Torre Bueno Awards Com., 1990; named Balasar Aswati/Ann Dewey Beinecke chair for disting. tchg. at Am. Dance Festival, 1998; Nat. Endowment of Arts grantee, 1969, 75, 77-78, 79. Avocations: music, swimming. *I am a humanist. As a creative artist I search for basic truths. I try to capture the poetry, the humour, the agony of the human condition, to know and experience compassion. Compassion is essential for communication and communication is a key to survival.*

KONG, LAURA S. L., geophysicist; b. Honolulu, July 23, 1961; d. Albert T.S. and Cordelia (Seu) K.; m. Kevin T.M. Johnson, Mar. 3, 1990. ScB, Brown U., 1983; PhD, MIT/Woods Hole Oceanog. Inst., 1990. Grad. rschr. Woods Hole (Mass.) Oceanog. Instn., 1984-90; postdoctoral fellow U. Tokyo, 1990-91; geophysicist Pacific Tsunami Warning Ctr., Ewa Beach, Hawaii, 1991-93; seismologist U.S. Geol. Survey Hawaiian Volcano Obs., 1993-95; rschr. U. Hawaii, Honolulu, 1996—; mem. Hawaii Earthquake adv. bd., 1994—; mem. equal opportunity adv. bd. Nat. Earth Svc. Pacific Region, Honolulu, 1992-93, Asin-Am.-Pacific Islander spl. emphasis program mgr., 1992-93; legis. rschr. Hawaii Senate, 1996-98. Contbr. articles to profl. jours.; spkr., editl. reviewer in field. Rsch. fellow Japan Govt.-Japan Soc. for Promotion of Sci., 1990; recipient Young Investigator grant Japan Soc. for Promotion of Sci., 1990. Mem. Am. Geophys. Union, Seismol. Soc. Am., Hawaii Ctr. for Volcanology, Assn. Women in Sci., Sigma Xi. Avocation: sports. Office: U Hawaii Hawaii Inst Geophysics 2525 Correa Rd Honolulu HI 96822-2219

KONICEK, MICHAEL, city official; m. Paula Konicek; children: David, John. B Chem. Engring., Ohio State U., 1966, MSChemE, 1966. Rsch. engr. ohio, 1966-69; sr. rsch. engr. Monsanto Rsch. Corp., 1969-72; R & D group leader, tech. supt., staff engr. Diamond Shamrock, mgr. R & D and market devel., mgr. bus. devel., 1972-82; mgr. bus. devel. Eltech Sys. Corp., 1982-84; v.p., ptnr. Lectranator Corp., 1984-87; tech. mgr. Lectranator Corp. subs. Olin Corp., 1987-90; dir. pub. utilities City of Cleve., 1990—; bd. dirs. N.E. Ohio Regional Sewer Dist., 1994—. Office: Cleve Dept Pub Utilities 1201 Lakeside Ave Cleveland OH 44114-1132*

KONIECZNY, SHARON LOUISE, insurance company executive; b. Madison, Minn., July 2, 1952; d. Frank H. and Elenore A. (Mikkelson) K. Student, Dakota Wesleyan U., 1970-71, U. Minn., 1971-72. CLU. Sales rep. Advance Schs., Bloomington, Minn., 1972; sales agt. ITT Life Ins., Mpls., 1973-75, mktg. auditor, 1975-76, supr. new bus., 1976-79, mgr. UND Issue, 1979-81, asst. v.p. new bus., 1981-83, asst. v.p.sales support, 1983-87, v.p., sales mktg., 1987-94; nat. dir. new bus. devel. ITT Life Ins., 1994-95; v.p. mktg. Minn. Chamber Bus. Svcs., St. Paul, 1995—. Mem. United Way, Mpls. (vice chmn. 1984-85, chmn. 1985). Mem. Nat. Assn. Life Underwriters (gen. agt. mgmt. conf.), Nat. Assn. Health Underwriters, Am. Mktg. Assn., Nat. Assn. Ins. Women, Soc. Ins. Trainers and Educators, Internat. Assn. Fin. Planners, Minn. Assn. Health Underwriters (bd. dirs.). Lutheran. Avocations: woodworking, swimming, reading, fishing. Home: 12610 50th Ave N Minneapolis MN 55442-2060

KONIGSBERG, ALLEN STEWART See ALLEN, WOODY

KONIGSBERG, ROBERT LEE, electrical engineer; b. N.Y.C., May 23, 1921; s. Max and Rose (Saper) K.; m. Helen Mae Aronson, June 11, 1950; children: Richard L., Jane F. BEE, Cooper Union, 1942; MAdE, NYU, 1948; MSE, Johns Hopkins U., 1954. Test/standardization engr. Western Electric Co., Kearny, N.J., 1942-46, product engr. filter dept., 1946-47; electronics engr. telemetering group Fairchild Engine & Aircraft Corp., Farmingdale, N.Y., 1947; electronic engr. radar component design DeMornay Budd Co., Bronx, N.Y., 1948; electronics engr. telemetering instrumentation Glenn L. Martin Co., Balt., 1948-51; rsch. assoc. radiation lab. Johns Hopkins U., Balt., 1951-56, prin. profl. staff engr. Applied Physics Lab., Laurel, Md., 1956-88, ret., 1988; part time cons., 1989—; part-time instr. engring. Johns Hopkins U., 1965-71. Contbr. articles to profl. jours. Recipient Group Achievement award to MAGSAT Project Team NASA, 1979, Group Achievement award to AMPTE Project Team NASA, 1985. Mem. IEEE, Sigma Xi, Tau Beta Pi. Democrat. Jewish. Avocations: amateur radio; tennis. Home: 2218 Ridgemont Dr Finksburg MD 21048-1717

KONIGSBURG, ELAINE LOBL, author; b. N.Y.C., Feb. 10, 1930; d. Adolph and Beulah (Klein) Lobl; m. David Konigsburg, July 6, 1952; children—Paul, Laurie, Ross. BS, Carnegie Mellon U., 1952; postgrad., U. Pitts., 1952-54. Author: juveniles Jennifer, Hecate, Macbeth, William McKinley and Me, Elizabeth, 1967 (Newbery Honor Book), From The Mixed-Up Files of Mrs. Basil E. Frankweiler, 1967 (Newbery medal 1968), About the B'nai Bagels, 1969, (George), 1970, Altogether, One at a Time, 1971, A Proud Taste for Scarlet and Miniver, 1973 (Nat. Book award nominee), The Dragon in the Ghetto Caper, 1974, The Second Mrs. Giaconda, 1975, Father's Arcane Daughter, 1976, Throwing Shadows, 1979 (Am. Book award nominee), Journey to an 800 Number, 1981, Up From Jericho Tel, 1986, Samuel Todd's Book of Great Colors, 1990, Samuel Todd's Book of Great Inventions, 1991, Amy Elizabeth Explores Bloomingdale's, 1992, T-backs, T-shirts, COAT and Suit, 1993, TalkTalk, 1995, The View From Saturday, 1996 (Newbery medal 1997). Recipient Newbery medal, 1997.

KONING, HANS (HANS KONINGSBERGER), author; b. Amsterdam, The Netherlands, July 12, 1924; came to U.S., 1951; s. David and Elizabeth (Van Collen) K.; m. Henriette Waterland; 1 child, Ellen; m. Elizabeth Sutherland Martinez; 1 child, Tessa; m. Kathleen Scanlon; children: Christina, Andrew. Student, U. Amsterdam, 1939-41, 46, U. Zurich, 1941-43, Sorbonne U., 1946. Editor Amsterdam, weekly, 1947-50; radio dir. Indonesia, 1950-51. Author: Aquarel of Holland, 1950, The Golden Keys, 1956, The Affair, 1958, An American Romance, 1960, A Walk with Love and Death, 1961 (also film script 1968), I Know What I'm Doing, 1964, Love and Hate in China, 1966, The Revolutionary, 1967 (also film script 1970), Along the Roads of the New Russia, 1968, The Future of Che Guevara, 1971, The Almost World, 1972, Death of a Schoolboy, 1974, The Petersburg-Cannes Express, 1975 (also film script 1981), Columbus, His Enterprise, 1976, A New Yorker in Egypt, 1976, The Kleber Flight, 1981, DeWitt's War, 1983, America Made Me, 1983, Nineteen Sixty-Eight, A Personal Report, 1987, Acts of Faith, 1988, The Iron Age, 1990, Columbus: His Enterprise (new version), 1991, To the North Pole, 1994, The Conquest of America, 1994, Pursuit of a Woman on the Hinge of History, 1998; (plays) The Blood-Red Cafe, 1958, Hermione, 1962, A Day in the Life of Alexander Herzen, 1977, A Woman of New York, 1981, (film) Wind in the Pines, 1961; author essays, polit. articles for nat. mags.; translator: (from Dutch) Maria Dermout, 1958, 3d edit., 1983, (from French) Carlo Coccioli, 1958. With Brit. Army, 1943-46. Home and Office: c/o Peter Matson Sterling Lord Agy 65 Bleecker St New York NY 10012-2420 *In the arts, the only genuine sucess must be truthfulness to oneself. This may, now more than ever, entail financial sacrifice in the short run, but in the long run it bringS fulfilment.*

KONING, HENDRIK, architect; came to the U.S., 1979; BArch, U. Melbourne, Australia, 1978; MArch II, UCLA, 1981. Lic. architect Calif., 1982, contractor, 1984; registered architect, Australia; cert. Nat. Coun. Archtl. Registration Bds. Prin. in charge of tech., code, and prodn. issues Koning Eizenberg Architecture, 1981—; v.p. Koning Eizenberg Architecture, Santa Monica, Calif., 1990—; instr. UCLA, U. B.C., Harvard U., MIT; lectr. in field. Exhbns. incl. "House Rules" Wexner Ctr., 1994, "The Architect's Dream Houses for the Next Millenium", The Contemporary Arts Ctr., 1993, " Angels & Franciscans", Gagosian Gallery, 1992, "Conceptual Drawings by Architects", Bannatyne Gallery, 1991, Koning and Eizenberg Projects Grad. Sch. Architecture & Urban Planning UCLA, 1990, others; prin. works include Digital Domain renovation and screening rm., Santa Monica, Lightstorm Entertainment offices and THX theater, Santa Monica, Gilmore Bank addition and remodel, L.A., 1548-1550 Studios, Santa Monica, (with RTA) Materials Rsch. Lab. U. Calif., Santa Barbara, Ken. Edwards Ctr. Cmty. Svcs., Santa Monica, Peck Park Cmty. Ctr. Gymnasium, San Pedro, Calif., Sepulveda Recreation Ctr. Gymnasium, L.A., (Nat. Concrete /Masonry award 1996, AIA Calif. Coun. Honor award 1996, AIA L.A. Chpt. Merit Award, 1997, L.A. Bus. Coun. Beautification awrd 1996, AIA/SFV Design award 1995), PS# 1 Elem. Sch., Santa Monica, Famers Market additions and master plan, L.A. (Westside Urban Forum prize 1991), Stage Deli, L.A., Simone Hotel, L.A. (Nat. Honor award AIA 1994), Boyd Hotel, L.A. Cmty. Corp. Santa Monica Housing Projects, 5th St. Family Housing, Santa Monica, St. John's Hosp. Replacement Housing Program, Santa Monica, Liffman Ho., Santa Monica, (with Glenn Erikson) Electric Artblock, Venice (Beautification award L.A. Bus. Coun. 1993), 6th St. Condominiums, Santa Monica, Hollywood Duplex, Hollywood Hills (Record Houses Archtl. Record 1988), Calif. Ave. Duplex, Santa Monica, Tarzana Ho. (Merit award L.A. chpt. AIA 1991, Merit Award AIA Calif. Coun., 1998, Sunset Western Home awards 1993-94), 909 Ho., Santa Monica (Merit award L.A. chpt. AIA 1991), 31st St. Ho., Santa Monica (Honor award AIACC 1994, Record House 1995, Nat. AIA Honor award 1996), others. Recipient 1st award Progressive Architecture, 1987; named one of Domino's Top 30 Architects, 1989. Fellow AIA (juror San Diego design awards 1992, panelist honor awards 1994, Calif. coun. spl. awards 1997, nat. interior design awards 1997), Royal Australian Inst. Archs.; mem. Nat. Trust for Hist. Preservation, So. Calif. Assn. Non-Profit Housing, L.A. Conservancy. Office: Koning Eizenberg Architecture 1548 18th St Santa Monica CA 90404-3404*

KONINGSBERGER, HANS See KONING, HANS

KONIOR, JEANNETTE MARY, elementary school educator; b. Bronx, N.Y., Jan. 7, 1947; d. Stephen Louis and Frieda Anna (Schmautz) Sirko.; m. Richard Henry Drago, Nov. 13, 1971 (div. Mar., 1985); 1 child, Christina Angelina; m. John Anthony Konior, Feb. 20, 1993; stepchildren: John Adalbert, Joseph Anthony. AA in Social Sci., Orange County C.C., Middletown, N.Y., 1983; BS in Elementary Edn., SUNY, New Paltz, 1985, MS in Elementary Edn., Secondary English, 1993. Cert. tchr. elementary, secondary English, N.Y. Sec. M.W. Kellogg Co., N.Y.C., 1964-69; legal sec. Kaye, Scholar et al., N.Y.C., 1969-72; records coord. Orange & Rockland Utilities, Pearl River, N.Y., 1975-76; personal sec. Hercules, Inc., Middletown, 1976-82; substitute tchr. various dists., Orange County, N.Y., 1986-87; tchr. Archdiocese of N.Y. Most Precious Blood Sch., Walden, N.Y., 1987—; student tchr. advisor Most Precious Blood Sch., 1992—, editor-in-chief Yearbook, 1988—, dir. Christmas Play, 1987, coord. various classroom plays, 1987—. Vol. religious edn. tchr. St. Matthew's Ch., Bklyn., 1969-70, Mt. Carmel Ch., Middletown, 1973-83, St. Mary's Ch., Montgomery, N.Y., 1992-93, St. John's Ch., Woodstock, N.Y., 1994—; chmn. membership com. Village on Green I Homeowners' Assn., Middletown, 1980-81, v.p., sec., 1981-82, pres., 1982-84; mem. Parents without Ptnrs., 1990-91. Avocations: dressmaking, swimming, boating, walking, reading, writing. Office: Most Precious Blood Sch 180 Ulster Ave Walden NY 12586-1095

KONISHI, MASAKAZU, neurobiologist, educator; b. Kyoto, Japan, Feb. 17, 1933. BS, Hokkaido U., Japan, 1956, MS, 1958, LLD (hon.), 1991; PhD in Zoology, U. Calif., Berkeley, 1963. Postdoctoral Alexander von Humboldt Found. fellow, 1963-64, Internat. Brain Rsch. Orgn. and UNESCO fellow, 1964-65; asst. prof. zoology U. Wis., 1965-66; asst. prof. to assoc. prof. biology Princeton (N.J.) U., 1970-75; prof. biology Calif. Inst. Tech., Pasadena, 1975-79, Bing Prof. behavioral biology, 1979—; mem. Salk Inst., 1991—. Assoc. editor Jour. Neurosci., 1980-89, sect. editor, 1990-93; mem. editorial adv. bd. Jour. Comparative Physiology. Recipient Elliot Coues award Am. Ornithologists Union, 1983, F.O. Schmitt prize, 1987, Internat. prize for biology Japan Soc. for Promotion Sci., 1990, honoris causa Hokkaide Univ., 1991. Recipient David Sparks award in Integrative Neurophysiology U. Ala., 1992, Charles A. Dana award for Pioneering Achievements in Health and Edn., 1992, Sci. Writing prize Acoustical Soc. Am., 1994. Office: Calif Inst Tech Div Biology 1200 E California Blvd Pasadena CA 91125-0001*

KONISKY, JORDAN, microbiology educator; b. Providence, Apr. 8, 1941; s. George Martin and Norma Virginia (Storti) K.; m. Judith Esther Wax, June 25, 1967; children: Daniel L., David M. BA, Providence Coll., 1963; PhD, U. Wis., 1968. Asst. prof. U. Ill., Urbana, 1970-75, assoc. prof., 1975-81, prof., 1981—, chmn. dept. microbiology, 1984-89, dir. Sch. Life Scis., 1989-94, dir. Biotech. Ctr., 1995-96; vice provost for rsch. and grad. studies Rice U., Houston, 1996—, prof. biochemistry and cell biology, 1996—; postdoctoral fellow NIH, 1968-70, Yale U.; cons. in field. Contbr. articles to profl. jours. Recipient Research Career Devel. award NIH, 1975-80. Fellow AAAS; mem. Am. Soc. Microbiology, Fedn. Am. Socs. Exptl. Biology, Am. Acad. Microbiology, Am. Chem. Soc. Jewish. Office: Rice U Off Vice Provost Rsch Grad Stud MS13 Houston TX 77025

KONKEL, HARRY WAGNER, civic volunteer, retired career officer; b. Jackson, Wyo., July 11, 1935; s. Maurice and Beatrice Helen (Nelle) Wagner; m. Susan Donnell Konkel, June 3, 1960; children: James Donnell Konkel, Susan Konkel. Student, U. Wyo., 1953; BS, U.S. Naval Acad., 1958; BS in Elec. Engring., Naval Postgrad. Sch., 1965; MA, Naval War Coll., 1974. Commd. ensign USN, 1958, advanced through ranks to capt., 1979, ret., 1985, elecs. material officer, comms. officer, weapons officer USS Trathen, 1959-63, engr. officer USS Richard E. Byrd, 1965-67; asst. fleet elecs. maintenance officer US Atlantic Fleet USN, Norfolk, Va., 1967-70; exec. officer USS Keppler USN, 1970-71, commdr. USS Laffey, 1971-72, commdr. USS DAmato, 1972-73, engr. officer USS America, 1978-79, head availabilities sect., maintenance policy and progamming branch Ships Maintencance and Modernization Divsn. Office Chief of Naval Opers., 1979-81, commdr. USS Yellowstone, 1982-84; dir. electronic and spl. warfare divsn. Naval Electronic Systems Command, 1974-77; head surface ship fleet modernization program design mgmt. divsn. Naval Sea Systems Command, 1984; dep. dir. ship maintenance and modernization divsn., head ships maintenance and modernization branch Office of Chief of Naval Ops., 1984-85. Bd. trustees Gunston Sch., Centreville, Md., 1981-91, Gould Acad., Bethel, Me., 1987-93; bd. dirs. Humane Soc. Hancock County, Findlay, Ohio, 1986-87; nat. dir. Navy League US, 1989-97, Portland Mus. Art, fellow 1993-96, trustee, 1996—; pres. Osher Libr. Assocs., Osher Map Libr., 1995-98, USNA Blue and Gold, 1994—. Decorated Legion of Merit, Meritorious Svc. medal with one gold star, Navy Commendation Medal with two gold stars. Mem. Am. Soc. Naval Engrs., Am. Inst. Conservation of Historic and Artistic Works, Am. Philatelic Soc., Am. Numismatic Assn., Am. Orchid Soc., U. Wyo. Alumni Assn., US Naval Acad. Alumni Assn., Naval Postgrad. Sch. Alumni Assn., Naval War Coll. Aluni Assn., US Naval Inst., Navy League US, Retired Officers Assn., Surface Navy Assn. (lifetime plankowner mem.), USS DAmato Assn., USS Laffey Assn., USS Trathen Assn., Army-Navy Country Club, Bohemian Club, Woodlands Club, Portland Country Club. Republican. Episcopalian. Avocations: golf, stamp and coin collecting. Home: 71 Carroll St Portland ME 04102-3522

KONKEL, MARY SUSAN, library administrator; b. Portland, Oreg., Jan. 7, 1957; d. William Eugene Konkel and Carole Barbara Lehman; m. Steven Andrew Balcken, Dec. 19, 1981; 1 child, Dianna Lynn Balcken. BA in Spanish and Portuguese, U. Wis., Milw., 1979, MLS, 1981; MA in Comm. Studies, Governors State U., University Park, 1992. Libr. tech. asst. U. Wis., Milw., 1976-81, original cataloger, acad. specialist, 1982-85; fieldworker Am. Geog. Soc. Collection, Milw., 1980-81; head monographic cataloging unit, asst. libr. U. Cin., 1985-87; head cataloging, libr., univ. prof. Governors State U., 1987-92; head cataloging, asst. prof. bibliography U. Akron, Ohio, 1992-98, assoc. prof. bibliography, 1999—; pres. Online Audiovisual Catalogers, Inc., 1994-95, mem. cataloging policy com., 1989-93; presenter in field. Contbr. articles to jours. in field. Vol. Inventure Pl. Nat. Inventors Hall of Fame Mus., Akron, 1995—; bd. dirs. Suburban Libr. Sys., Burr Ridge, Ill., 1989-92; trustee Richton Park (Ill.) Pub. Libr., 1989-92; founding mem. YMCA Trailblazers Oreg. Trail Bunkhouse, 1993-96. Mem. ALA, Assn. Coll. and Rsch. Librs., Assn. Libr. Collections and Tech. Svcs., Acad. Libr. Assn. Ohio (pres. 1998-99, bd. dirs. 1995-97, chair pub. rels. com. 1996-97). Avocations: camping, mall shopping, movies, music, reading. Office: Univ Akron Bierce Libr 176A Akron OH 44325-1712

KONKOWSKI, DEBORAH ANN, mathematics educator; b. Akron, Ohio, Mar. 3, 1955; d. Daniel J. and Dorothea A. K. BS in Physics, Harvey Mudd Coll., 1977; PhD in Physics, U. Tex., 1983. Asst. prof. U.S. Naval Acad., Annapolis, Md., 1987-91, assoc. prof., 1991-97, prof., 1997—; vis. assoc. prof. U. London, 1995. Contbr. articles to profl. jours. NSF grantee, 1989—, U.S. Naval Acad., 1987-89; Rsch. fellow U.Md., College Park, 1983-85, U. London, 1985-87. Mem. AAAS, Am. Phys. Soc., Am. Math. Soc., Math. Assn. Am., N.Y. Acad. Scis., Internat. Soc. Gen. Relativity & Gravitation. Office: U S Naval Acad Dept Math Annapolis MD 21402

KONNER, JOAN WEINER, university administrator, educator, publisher, broadcasting executive, television producer; b. Paterson, N.J., Feb. 24, 1931; d. Martin and Tillie (Frankel) Weiner; children: Rosemary, Catherine; m. Alvin H. Perlmutter. Student, Vassar Coll., 1948-49; BA, Sarah Lawrence Coll., 1951; MS, Columbia U., 1961. Editorial writer, columnist, reporter Hackensack (N.J.) Record, 1961-63; producer, reporter WNDT Ednl. Broadcasting Corp., N.Y.C., 1963-65; producer, writer, reporter NBC News, N.Y.C., 1965-77; exec. producer nat. pub. affairs programs WNET Ednl. Broadcasting Corp., N.Y.C., 1977-78, v.p. programming WNET, 1981-84, exec. producer, 1984-86; exec. producer Bill Moyers' Jour., 1978-81; pres. Pub. Affairs TV, Inc.; exec. producer Bill Moyers' series for PBS, 1986-88; prof. broadcast and journalism, dean Grad. Sch. Journalism Columbia U., N.Y.C., 1988-97, pub. Columbia Journalism Rev., 1988-99; bd. dirs. Providence Jour. Past trustee Columbia U. Rockland Ctr. for Arts, Sarah Lawrence Coll. Recipient 12 Emmy awards NATAS, Columbia-du Pont award, Peabody award, Gavel award ABA, Edward R. Murrow award, others. Mem. Dirs. Guild, Writers Guild, Soc. Profl. Journalists, Newspaper Women's Club of N.Y.C., Century Assn., Cosmopolitan Club. Office: Columbia U Grad Sch Journalism Journalism Bldg New York NY 10027

KONNYU, ERNEST LESLIE, former congressman; b. Tamasi, Hungary, May 17, 1937; came to U.S., 1949; s. Leslie and Elizabeth Konnyu; m. Lillian Muenks, Nov. 25, 1959; children: Carol, Renata, Lisa, Victoria. Student, U. Md., 1960-62; BS in Acctg., Ohio State U., 1965. Mem. Calif. Assembly, Sacramento, 1980-86, 100th Congress from 12th Calif. dist., 1987-89; owner Premier Printing, San Jose, Calif., 1990—; CEO Konnyu Fins. and Taxes, Inc.; chmn. Assembly Rep. Policy Com. of State Assembly, Sacramento, 1985-86; vice chmn. Assembly Human Svcs., Sacramento, 1980-86; vice chmn. Policy Rsch. Com., Sacramento, 1985-86. Mem. Rep. State Cen. Com., Calif., 1977-88, Rep. Cen. Com., Santa Clara County, Calif., 1980-88; mem. adv. bd. El Camino Hosp., Mountain View, Calif., 1987-89. Served to maj. USAF, 1959-69. Recipient Nat. Def. Medal, 1968, Disting. Service award U.S. Jaycees, 1969, Nat. Security award Am. Security Council Found., 1987; named lifetime senator U.S. Jaycees, 1977. Mem. Am.- Hungarian C. of C. (v.p. 1995-97). Republican. Roman Catholic. Avocations: politics, golf.

KONO, JEAN E., nursing educator; b. Marshalltown, Iowa, Oct. 20, 1941; d. Harold and Helen I. (Melton) Bailey; m. Frederick L. Kono, June 8, 1963; children: Matthew D., Kristine H. Diploma, Mercy Hosp., 1962; BSN, Mary Crest Coll., 1977; postgrad., U. Iowa, Coll. nursing. Head nurse, mental health St.Luke's Hosp., Cedar Rapids, Iowa; child therapist Vera French Mental Health Ctr., Davenport, Iowa; nurse mgr., mental health Mercy Hosp., Davenport, Iowa; clin. instr. Eastern Iowa Coll., Bettendorf, Iowa. Mem. APNA, Iowa Nurses Assn. (bd. dirs., dist. 6 pres.).

KONO, TETSURO, biochemist, physiologist, educator; b. Tokyo, Japan, May 17, 1925; s. Ichiro and Hiroko (Sasaki) K.; m. Seiko Kanda, Dec. 18, 1961; children: Michiko, Masahiro, Kenji. B.A., U. Tokyo, 1947, Ph.D., 1958. Research assoc. Johns Hopkins U., Balt., 1958-59; research asso. Vanderbilt U., Nashville, 1959-60; mem. faculty Vanderbilt U., 1963—, prof. physiology, 1974-85; prof. molecular physiology and biophysics, 1985-92, prof. emeritus molecular physiology and biophysics, 1992—; instr. Univ. Tokyo, 1960-63. Contbr. articles to profl. jours. NIH grantee, 1961-92. Mem. Am. Diabetes Assn. Am. Soc. Biol. Chemists, Sigma Xi. E-mail: tetsuro.kono@vanderbilt.edn. Home: 505 Belair Way Nashville TN 37215-6108 Office: Vanderbilt Med Sch Dept Molecular Physiol 209 Oxford House Nashville TN 37232

KONOPINSKI, VIRGIL JAMES, industrial hygienist; b. Toledo, Ohio, July 11, 1935; s. Mack and Mary Veronica (Jankowski) K.; m. Joan Mary Wielinski, June 27, 1964; children—Ann Marie, Carol Sue, Peter James. BS in Chem. Engring., U. Toledo, 1956; MS in Chem. Engring., Pratt Inst., 1960; MBA, Bowling Green State U., 1971. Registered profl. engr., Ohio, Ind., Calif.; cert. indsl. hygienist; cert. safety profl. Assoc. engr. Owens Illinois, Toledo, 1956, 60; real estate developer, Grand Rapids, Ohio, 1961; chem. engr. USPHS, Cin., 1961-64; sr. environ. engr. Vistron Corp., Lima, Ohio, 1964-67; environ. specialist, asst. to dir. environ. control Owens Corning Fiberglas, Toledo, 1967-72; gen. mgr. Midwest Environ. Mgmt., Maumee, Ohio, 1972-73; staff specialist, indsl. hygienist Williams Bros. Waste Control., Tulsa, Okla., 1973-75; dir. div. indsl. hygiene and radiol. health Ind. State Bd. Health, Indpls., 1975-87, exec. v.p. ACT of Ind., Indpls., 1987-89; sr. cons. Occusafe, 1990-91; regional safety engr., human resources analyst/safety U.S. Postal Svc., 1991— ; bd. dir. IOSHA indsl. hygiene, 1975-83; cons. indoor air, radon, occupational health, Zionsville, 1987-91, Cary, 1991—, ; lectr. With USNR, 1956-59. Mem. Am. Indsl. Hygiene Assn., Am. Conf. Govtl. Indsl. Hygienists, Am. Soc. Safety Engrs., Naval Res. Assn., Ret. Officers Assn. Republican. Roman Catholic. Contbr. articles to profl. jours. Home: 14 Fairfield Ln Cary IL 60013-1946 Office: 4th Flr 244 Knollwood Dr Fl 4 Bloomingdale IL 60108-2208

KONRAD, ADOLF FERDINAND, artist; b. Bremen, Germany, Feb. 21, 1915; came to U.S., 1925, naturalized, 1931; s. Roman and Katherine Heidientje (Engelken) K.; m. Adair Watts, Apr. 26, 1980. Student, Newark Sch. Fine and Indsl. Art, 1930-34, Cummington (Mass.) Sch., 1936-37; DFA, Kean U., 1971. Tchr., advisor N.J. State Council on Arts, 1971-74; artist-in-residence Everhart Mus., Scranton, Pa., 1973, Somerset County Coll. (now Raritan Valley Coll.), Somerville, N.J., 1977-80; lectr., panelist. One-man shows include Newark Mus., 1966, Everhart Mus., Scranton, Pa., 1973, Mus. Fine Arts, Springfield, Mass., 1973, Montclair Art Mus. and N.J. State Mus., Trenton, 1980, The Newark Mus., 1997; represented in permanent collections Newark Mus., Montclair Art Mus., Mus. Fine Arts, Everhart Mus., N.J. State Mus., NAD, N.Y.C., Newark Public Library, The Forbes Collection, N.Y.C, Ct. Gen. Sessions Painting Collection, Washington, CIBA Geigy, Basle, Switzerland, AT&T, Bedminster, N.J., Crum & Forster Ins. Co., Morristown, N.J., Bell Labs. Murray Hill, N.J., N.J. Public Service, Newark, Schering-Plough Corp., Liberty Corner, N.J., Geraldine R. Dodge Found., Morristown, N.J.; mural executed N.J. Vets. Meml. Home, Paramus, 1986; retrospective exhbn. The Morris Mus., Morristown, N.J., 1992, Hunterdon Art Mus., Clinton, N.J., 1996. Louis Comfort Tiffany fellow, 1937; Tiffany Found. fellow, 1961; resident fellow Yaddo, Saratoga Springs, 1956; winner grand prize Atlantic City Fine Arts Festival, 1961, 63; first prize Montclair Art Mus. Ann. Exhbn., 1963; Andrew Carnegie prize NAD Ann., 1967; Audience Choice award Marietta (Ohio) Coll., 1969; Gov.'s citation; N.J. Symphony Ann. Arts award, 1969; David Humphreys Meml. prize Allied Artist of Am., 1971; Artist of Year award Art Educators N.J., 1973; Fellowship award in Painting N.J. State Council on Arts, 1982. Mem. Associated Artists N.J. (pres. 1960-65), Artists Equity Assn. N.J. (pres. 1952-60, NAD (academician; Thomas B. Clark prize 1956). Home: 183 Buttermilk Bridge Rd Asbury NJ 08802-1011

KONRAD, AGNES CROSSMAN, retired real estate agent, retired educator; b. Rutland, Vt., Nov. 26, 1921; d. Warren Julius and Susan Anna (Cain) Crossman; children: Suzanne Martha, Dianna Marie; m. Henry Konrad, Nov. 27, 1954. Assoc. degree in Edn., Castelton Coll., 1943; BS in Edn., Castelton State Coll., 1952; postgrad., SUNY, New Paltz, 1969-70, Fla. Atlantic U., 1973; Graduate, Realtors Inst. Fla., 1981. Cert. realtor; grad. Realtors Inst. Tchr. 1st to 8th grades Pittsford (Vt.) Pub. Schs., 1943-44, tchr. 1st grade, 1950-52; tchr. 3d grade Ralph Smith Sch.-Hyde Park (N.Y.) Ctrl. Schs., 1952-69, Violet Ave. Sch.-Hyde Park Sch. Sys., 1969-73; realtor assoc. Four Star Realty of Boca Raton (Fla.), 1974-93; ret., 1993. Mem. AAUW, N.Y. State Ret. Tchrs. Assn. (life), Castleton Vt. State Coll. Alumni. Avocations: oil painting, acrylic art, traveling, reading. Home: 1229 SW 13th St Boca Raton FL 33486-5307

KONRAD, PETER ERICH, neurosurgeon; b. Rockford, Ill., May 6, 1961; s. Erich and Gertraud (Heinig) K.; m. Stephanie Ann Myers, Nov. 26, 1994. BA, Rockford Coll., 1983; MS, Purdue U., 1985, PhD, 1988; MD, Ind. U., 1991. Diplomate Am. Bd. Neurol. Surgery. Intern surgery Ind. U. Med. Ctr., Indpls., 1991-92; resident Vanderbilt U. Med. Ctr., Nashville, 1992-97, asst. prof. neurosurgery, 1998—, asst. prof. biomed. engring., 1998—; chief neurosurgery VA Hosp., Nashville. Reviewer Jour. Spinal Disorders, 1995—; contbr. articles to profl. jours. Mem. AMA, Congress Neurol. Surgeons, Phi Beta Kappa, Sigma Xi. Avocations: underwater photography, sailing, woodworking. Office: Dept Neurosurgery Rm T4224 Vanderbilt Univ Med Ctr Nashville TN 37232

KONSCHNIK, DAVID MICHAEL, lawyer; b. Weston, Pa., Apr. 21, 1948; s. Frank Joseph and Margaret (Broyan) K.; m. Maureen Anne Talty, June 26, 1970; children: Katherine Erin, David Michael Jr. BS, Georgetown U., 1970, JD, 1975; MA in Teaching, Howard U., 1971. Bar: Md. Ct. Appeals 1975, D.C. Ct. Appeals 1980. Teaching intern Urban Tchr. Corps., Washington, 1970-71; math. tchr. Ballou Sr. High Sch., Washington, 1971-76; atty. advisor sect. of fin. proceedings ICC, Washington, 1976-79, atty. advisor office of commr. Clapp, 1979-82, atty. advisor sect. of rates, office of proceedings, 1982, atty. advisor office of commr. Gradison, 1982-85, chief of staff, 1985-90, dir. office of procs., 1990-95; dir. office of procs. Surface Transp. Bd., Washington, 1996—. Roman Catholic. Home: 3510 Horseman Way Davidsonville MD 21035-2423 Office: Surface Transp Bd 1925 K St NW Washington DC 20423-0001

KONSELMAN, DOUGLAS DEREK, lawyer; b. Tampa, Fla., Oct. 3, 1958; s. Derek Konselman and Linda (Horton) Fisher. BA in Biology, U. South Fla., 1981; JD, Loyola U., New Orleans, 1984; LLM, Georgetown U., 1996. Bar: Fla., 1984, N.J. 1985, N.Y. 1985, D.C. 1985, U.S. Supreme Ct. 1986. Ptnr. Konselman & Co., Washington, 1991-96; mng. ptnr. Konselman & Ptnrs., N.Y.C., 1996—; mem. Practicing Law Inst., N.Y.C., 1985—. Contbr. articles to law jours. Bd. dirs. Boca Raton (Fla.) Mus. Art, 1987, Market Square West, 1995-98. Mem. Am. Corp. Counsel Assn., Am. Soc. Internat. Law, Fgn. Law Soc., Soc. for Internat. Devel., Asia Soc., Mensa. Republican. Presbyterian. Avocations: foreign languages, Russian, French, German. Office: 801 Pennsylvania Ave NW Washington DC 20004-2617

KONSIS, KENNETH FRANK, forester, educator; b. Danville, Ill., Dec. 3, 1952; s. Frank John and Regina Ann (Stefaniak) K.; m. Lorna Jean Wiesemann, May 6, 1978. AS, Danville Area Community Coll., 1972; BS in Forestry, So. Ill. U., 1974. Park ranger Vermilion County Conservation Dist., Danville, 1974-84, dist. forester, 1984-87, rsch. forester, instr. in outdoor edn., 1987-91, dep. dir., 1991-92, exec. dir., 1992—; state del. Ill. Conservation Congress, 1993, 94, 97; mem. Lake Vermilion Water Quality Coalition, 1996—, Vermilion River Ecosys. Partnership, 1997—. Mem. VOTEC Agr. and Horticulture Adv. Com.; mem. citizen's adv. com. Dept. Natural Resources and Environ. Scis., U. Ill., 1993—. Mem. Ill. Native Plant Soc. (pres. 1986-93, exec. com. 1986—), Internat. Walnut Coun. (nat. meeting program chair 1998, v.p. 1998, pres. 1999), Ill. Woodland Owners and Users Assn., Ill. Lake Mgmt. Assn. (charter), Am. Chestnut Soc., Soc. Am. Foresters (comms. chair 1997-98), Ill. Walnut Coun. (v.p. 1991-92, pres. 1992-93, regional bd. dirs. 1989-92, treas. 1994—), Ill. Tree Farm Com., Shiitake Growers' Assn. Wis., Am. Forestry Assn., Interstate 74 Corridor Planning Com., Ill. Assn. Conservation Dists. (v.p. 1995-96, pres. 1996—, Ill. trails and greenways coun. 1997—), Danville Halo Project (nat. resources com.). Roman Catholic. Avocations: photography, gardening, travel, biking, nature. Home: 234 S Walnut St Westville IL 61883-1664 Office: Vermilion Co Conserv Dist Conservation Dist 22296-A Henning Rd Danville IL 61834-5336

KONSKI, JAMES LOUIS, civil engineer; b. N.Y.C., Nov. 4, 1917; s. Herbert D. and Ruby (Louis) K.; children: Alexander (dec.), Christina, Marguerite. B.S. in Civil Engring., U. Mo., 1950, M.S. in Civil Engring., 1951; PhD, European Inst. Cycle Engring., Essex, England, 1985. Registered profl. engr., N.Y., Ky., R.I., Kans. registered profl. surveyor. Engr., Bur. Yards and Docks, Washington, 1951; structural engr. Sanderson & Porter, N.Y.C., 1951-52; field engr. Ebasco Services, Inc., Owensboro, Ky., 1952-53; chief structural engr. Berger Assos., Syracuse, N.Y., 1953-54, Endman, Anthony & Hosley (formerly Berger Assos.), Syracuse, 1954-57; pres. Konski Engrs. Profl. Corp., Syracuse, 1957—; prin. Konski Engrs. Internat., 1965—; cons. engr. U.S. Trade Mission to Africa, 1965, to Far East, 1970; speaker Met. Assn. Urban Designers and Environ. Planning Conf., Eng., 1974, Netherlands, 1975. Contbr. articles to profl. jours. Served with USMC, 1939-46; maj. Res. ret. Recipient Honor Award for Disting. Service in Engring., U. Mo., 1986. Fellow ASCE (v.p. 1972-73, nat. dir. 1966-70), Am. Cons. Engrs. Council (past chpt. pres.); mem. Internat. Assn. Bridge and Structural Engrs., NSPE (past chpt. pres., Engr. of Yr. award Cen. N.Y. chpt., 1991), Am. Concrete Inst., Prestressed Concrete Inst., Am. Congress Surveying and Mapping, Am. Mil. Engrs., Am. Water Works Assn., Am. Road Builders Assn., Am. Soc. Photogrammetry, League Am. Wheelman (area rep. 1967-77), U.S. Cycling Fedn., Am. Coll. Sports Medicine, Internat. Randonneurs (dir. USA/Can.), Sigma Xi, Tau Beta Pi, Chi Epsilon, Pi Mu Epsilon. Participant Paris-Breast-Paris Bicycle Race, 1975, 79, 83, 87; directed Internat. Randonneurs (U.S.), 401 Man Cycle Team, France, 1991, 95). Office: Old Engine House #2 727 N Salina St Syracuse NY 13208-2510

KONSLER, GWEN KLINE, oncology and pediatrics nurse; b. Ithaca, N.Y., July 11, 1959; d. Donald E. and Katherine (Schillroth) Kline; m. Thomas Konsler, Jr., 1983. BSN, U.N.C., 1981. Staff nurse pediatrics U. N.C. Hosps., Chapel Hill, 1981-84, edn. clinician, 1984-87, pediatric oncology nurse, 1986—; nursing coord. Camp Carefree, 1987-97; chmn. rsch. subcom. N.C. Cancer Pain Initiative, 1991-94. Mem. Assn. Pediatric Oncology Nurses (charter N.C. chpt.), Oncology Nursing Soc., Sigma Theta Tau. Home: 3623 Hawk Ridge Rd Chapel Hill NC 27516-5736

KONSTAN, DAVID, classics and comparative literature educator, researcher; b. N.Y.C., Nov. 1, 1940; s. Harry and Edythe (Wahrman) K.; m. Pura Nieto; children: Eve Anna, Geoffrey Theodore. Instr. Bklyn. Coll., 1965-67; prof. Wesleyan U., Middletown, Conn., 1967-87; prof. classics and comparative literature Brown U., Providence, R.I., 1987—. Author: Epicurean Psychology, 1973, Roman Comedy, 1983, Simplicius Physics 6, 1989, Sexual Symmetry, 1994, Greek Comedy and Ideology, 1995, Friendship in The Classical World, 1997, Philodemus on Frank Criticism, 1998. Mem. Am. Philol. Assn. (pres. 1999). Avocation: cooking. Home: 92 Ivy St Providence RI 02906-2515 Office: Brown U 48 College St Providence RI 02912-9021

KONSTAN, MICHAEL WILLIAM, pediatric pulmonologist, researcher; b. Akron, Ohio, Feb. 5, 1956; s. Louis M. and Billie (Mamas) K. BA magna cum laude, Case We. Res. U., 1978, MD, 1982. Diplomate Am. Bd. Pediat., Am. Bd. Pediat. Pulmonology. Intern then resident Childrens Hosp. Buffalo, 1982-85; pediatric pulmonary fellow Univ. Hosps. Cleve., 1985-88, attending staff, 1988—; med. dir. pediat. bronchoscopy lab. Rainbow Babies and Childrens Hosp, Cleve., 1992—; co-dir. Cystic Fibrosis Ctr. Rainbow Babies and Childrens Hosp., Cleve., 1993-97, co-med. dir. pulmonary function lab., 1998—, dir. Cystic Fibrosis Ctr., 1998—; clin. tutorial instr. Case We. Res. U. Sch. Medicine, 1990; physician advisor Scandipharm, Inc.; mem. sci. adv. bd. Alpha 1 Biomeds., Inc., 1995-96, Datalog, Inc., 1997—; clin. asst. instr. pediat. SUNY Buffalo Sch. Medicine, 1982-85; asst. then assoc. prof. pediat. Case We. Res. U. Sch. Medicine, 1988—; cons. in field; mem. data review com. Glaxo, Inc., 1993-96; chmn. data safety monitoring bd. Burroughs Wellcome, 1994-95; ad hoc grant reviewer med. biochemistry study sect. NIH, 1995; ad hoc grant reviewer Swiss Nat. Sci. Found., 1995; ad hoc pulmonary panel reviewer USFDA, 1996—; lectr. in field. Author: (with others) Clinics in Chest Medicine: Cystic Fibrosis, 1998, Cystic Fibrosis in Adults, 1998, others; mem. editl. bd. Pediat. Pulmonology, 1994—; reviewer numerous profl. jours.; contbr. articles to profl. jours. Bd. trustees Cleve. chpt. Cystic Fibrosis Found., 1980-82; active Nat. Cystic Fibrosis Found., 1991—, ad hoc grant reviewer rsch. and rsch. tng. com., ad hoc grant reviewer clin. rsch. com. 1991-93, mem. clin. rsch. com., 1994—, ad hoc grant reviewer rsch. devel. program, 1994; ad hoc grant reviewer Can. Cystic Fibrosis Found., 1996—; external reviewer Cochrane Cystic Fibrosis Group, 1996—. Recipient Harry Shwachman Clin. Investigator award Cystic Fibrosis Found., 1988-91; fellow No. Ohio Lung Assn., 1978; grantee numerous orgns. Mem. Am. Acad. Pediat., Am. Coll. Chest Physicians, Am. Fedn. Clin. Rsch., Am. Thoracic Soc., Soc. Pediat. Rsch., Phi Beta Kappa. Greek Orthodox. Avocation: sailing. Fax: 216-844-3267. E-mail: mwk3@po.cwru.edu. Home: One Bratenahl Pl # 1408 Bratenahl OH 44108 Office: Rainbow Babies and Childrens Hosp Pediat Pulmonary Div 11100 Euclid Ave Cleveland OH 44106

KONSTANTINOV, TZVETAN KRUMOV, musician, concert pianist, educator; came to U.S., 1979; s. Krum Christov and Maria Apostolov (Veselkov) K.; m. Lee-Ann Larson, Mar. 7, 1980; children: Alexander, Christian. MusM, Bulgarian State Conservatoire, Sofia, Bulgaria, 1974; postgrad., Hochschule Fur Musik, Vienna, Austria, 1979. Prof. Bulgarian State Conservatoire, Sofia, 1974-77, Levine Sch. Music, Washington, 1984-89, George Washington U., Washington, 1989—; bd. dirs. Met. Chorus. Am. debut at Meany Hall, Seattle, 1980; performer TV documentary including Music To Promote Democracy, 1990, Spotlight, 1988, Capital Concerts, 1989, Voice of Am., TV broadcast performance, 1999. Organizer extensive tours throughout Europe and U.S. Recipient Diploma for Highest Achievements Fifth All-Bulgarian Competition, 1969, Laureate Second Nat. Competition, 1970. Mem. AAUP, Am. Liszt Soc., Am. Assn. for Promoting Bulgarian Culture, Am. Beethoven Soc., Friday Morning Music Club. Avocations: arts, hiking, languages, history, jogging. Home: PO Box 554 Mc Lean VA 22101-0554 Office: George Washington U Dept Music Washington DC 20052

KONSTANTINOVSKAIA, VALERIA, puppeteer, puppet maker, sculptor, educator; b. Kirovo, Russia, Aug. 23, 1934; came to U.S., 1991; d. Konstantin Konstantinovsky and Lidia Mironovich Mikhilova; m. Boris Belov, Jan. 4, 1960 (dec. Oct. 1991); 1 child, Anton. EdM, Tchr. Coll., Moscow, 1955. Cert. tchr. Tchr. ESL U. Samarkand, Uzbekistan, 1955-58, Saratov, Russia, 1958-66; translator, editor Moscow, 1966-76, tchr. ESL, 1976-80; tchr. ESL Moscow Arts U., 1980-84; puppet theater dir., mgr., tchr. Cultural Ctr., Moscow, 1980-91; ESL tchr. Westbrook (Maine) Schs., Maine, 1993—; puppeteer, puppet maker, instr., founder Puppets 'R' Us Theater, Portland, Maine, 1991—; pres. Arts for All Ednl. Internat. Non-Profit Corp., Portland, 1993—; founder Biddeford (Maine) Hist. Museums, Mus. of Old Am. Life Style, Hall of Fame of Maine, Biddeford, 1997, Mus. Puppetry, Biddeford, 1998. Sculptor, vis. artist to schs., hosps., group homes, cmty. ctrs.;

pres. More Museums for Maine (internat. non-profit corp.), Portland, 1996—. Avocations: craft making, skiing, dancing. Home and Office: Puppets 'R' Us Theater PO Box 106 Biddeford ME 04005-0106

KONTNY, VINCENT L., rancher, engineering executive; b. Chappell, Nebr., July 19, 1937; s. Edward James and Ruth Regina (Schumann) K.; m. Joan Dashwood FitzGibbon, Feb. 20, 1970; children: Natascha Marie, Michael Christian, Amber Brooke. BSCE, U. Colo., 1958, DSc honoris causa, 1991. Operator heavy equipment, grade foreman Peter Kiewit Son's Co., Denver, 1958-59; project mgr. Utah Constrn. and Mining Co., Western Australia, 1965-69, Fluor Australia, Queensland, Australia, 1969-72; sr. project mgr. Fluor Utah, San Mateo, Calif., 1972-73; sr. v.p. Holmes & Narver, Inc., Orange, Calif., 1973-79; mng. dir. Fluor Australia, Melbourne, 1979-82; group v.p. Fluor Engrs., Inc., Irvine, Calif., 1982-85, pres., chief exec. officer, 1985-87; group pres. Fluor Daniel, Irvine, Calif., 1987-88, pres., 1988-94; pres. Fluor Corp., Irvine, 1990-94, vice chmn., 1994; ret., 1994; purchased Last Dollar Ranch, Ridgway Co. 1989, Centennial Ranch, Colona Co., 1992, owner Double Shoe Cattle Co. Contbr. articles to profl. jours. Mem. engring. devel. coun., U. Colo.; mem. engring. adv. coun., Stanford U. Lt. USN, 1959-65. Republican. Roman Catholic. Club: Cet. (Costa Mesa, Calif.). Avocation: snow skiing.

KONTOS, GEORGE JOHN, JR., cardiothoracic surgeon; b. Chgo., May 26, 1958; s. George John and Helen (Vlasis) K.; m. Sherry Knox Reed, Mar. 14, 1957. Student, Western Ill. U., 1975-77; BA, Northwestern U., 1979; MD, Loyola U., Maywood, Ill., 1982. Diplomate Am. Bd. Surgery, Am. Bd. Thoracic Surgery. Intern, then resident in gen. surgery Mayo Clinic, Rochester, Minn., 1982-85, 86-87, chief resident dept. surgery, 1987-88; fellow Cardiac Surg. Rsch. Lab. Johns Hopkins Hosp., Balt., 1985-86; resident in cardiothoracic surgery U. Ala., Birmingham, 1988-90, fellow in congenital heart surgery, 1990-91, instr. surgery, 1990-91; cardiothoracic surgeon Midwest Cardiovascular Ctr., Sioux Falls, S.D., 1992—; presenter at profl. confs. Contbr. articles to profl. jours.; guest reviewer Transplantation, Jour. Applied Physiology, 1991-92. Fellow ACS (assoc.); mem. AAAS, AMA, N.Y. Acad. Scis., Am. Coll. Cardiology, Soc. Thoracic Surgeons, Mayo Alumni Assn., Priestly Soc., Johns Hopkins Med. and Surg. Assn., Am. Chem. Soc., Phi Beta Kappa, Phi Eta Sigma. Office: Midwest Cardiovascular Ctr 1200 S 7th Ave Ste 100 Sioux Falls SD 57105-0912

KONTOS, HERMES APOSTOLOU, dean; b. Lefka, Cyprus, Dec. 13, 1933; married; 3 children. MD, U. Athens, 1958; PhD, Med. Coll. Va., 1967. Resident Nocosia (Cyprus) Gen. Hosp., 1959; intern Md. Gen. Hosp., 1959-60; jr. asst. resident Med. Coll. Va., Richmond, 1960-61, asst. resident, 1961-62, rsch. fellow, 1962-64, from instr. medicine to asst. prof., 1964-70; from assoc. prof. medicine to prof. Va. Commonwealth U., Med. Coll. Va., Richmond, 1970, from co-chmn. divsn. cardiology to chmn., 1977-86, 86-91, vice chmn. dept. internal medicine, 1984-91, acting chmn. dept. internal medicine, 1988, 93, acting chmn. dept. pathology, 1991-93, interim dean sch. medicine, 1993-94, dean sch. medicine, 1994-95, dean sch. medicine, sr. assoc. v.p. health svcs., 1995-97; v.p. health scis., dean Sch. Medicine, Va. Commonwealth U., Richmond, 1997—. Office: Va Commonwealth U Office VP Health Scis PO Box 980549 Richmond VA 23298-0549

KONVITZ, MILTON RIDBAZ, law educator; b. Safad, Israel, Mar. 12, 1908; came to U.S., 1915, naturalized, 1926; s. Rabbi Joseph and Welia (Ridbaz-Willowski) K.; m. Mary Traub, June 18, 1942; 1 son, Josef. BS, NYU, 1928, AM, 1930, JD, 1930; PhD (Sage fellow in philosophy 1932-33), Cornell U., 1933; LittD, Rutgers U., 1954, Dropsie U., 1975; DCL, U. Liberia, 1962; LHD, Hebrew Union Coll-Jewish Inst. Religion, 1966, Yeshiva U., 1972; LLD, Syracuse U., 1971, Jewish Theol. Sem., 1972. Bar: N.J. 1932. Practice law Jersey City and Newark, 1933-46; lectr. on law and pub. adminstrn. NYU, 1938-46; asst. gen. counsel NAACP Legal Def. and Edn. Fund, 1943-46; mem. faculty New Sch. for Social Rsch., 1944-46; prof. indsl. and labor rels. N.Y. State Sch. Indsl. and Labor Rels., Cornell U., 1946-73; prof. Law Sch. Cornell U., 1956-73, prof. emeritus, 1973—; vis. prof., assoc. dir. Truman Ctr. for Peace Rsch., Hebrew U., 1970; dir. Liberian Codification of Laws project, 1952-80; gen. counsel Newark Housing Authority, 1938-43, N.J. State Housing Authority, 1943-45; Pub. rep. Nat. War Labor Bd. region 2, 1943-46; mem. enforcement commn. and hearing commn. Wage Stablzn. Bd., 1952-53; chmn. nat. com. study of Jewish Edn. in U.S., 1958-59; faculty Salzburg (Austria) Seminar Am. Studies, 1952; panel Fed. Mediation and Conciliation Svc., N.Y. Mediation Bd., Am. Arbitration Assn., N.Y. State Pub. Employment Rels. Author: On the Nature of Value: Philosophy of Samuel Alexander, 1946, The Alien and the Asiatic in American Law, 1946, Constitution and Civil Rights, 1946, Civil Rights in Immigration, 1953, Bill of Rights Reader, 1954, Fundamental Liberties of a Free People, 1957, A Century of Civil Rights, 1961, Expanding Liberties: Freedom's Gains in Postwar America, 1966, Religious Liberty and Conscience, 1968, Judaism and Human Rights, 1972, Judaism and the American Idea, 1978, Torah and Constitution, 1997; founding editor: Industrial and Labor Relations Rev. (vols. 1-5), 1947-52, Liberian Code of Laws (5 vols.), 1958-60, Liberian Code of Laws Revised, 1973—, Liberian Law Reports (27 vols.); chmn. editl. bd. Midstream Mag.; chmn. adv. editl. bd. Jour. Law and Religion; co-editor: Jewish Social Studies, 1975-93; cofounder: Judaism Mag.; mem. editl. bd. Ency. Judaica. Chmn. Hebrew Culture Found., 1956-95; mem. commn. for reorgn. World Zionist Orgn. Decorated comdr. Order Star of Africa, grand band (Liberia); recipient NYU Washington Sq. Coll. Disting. Alumni award, 1964, Mordecai ben David Disting. award Yeshiva U., 1965, Morris J. Kaplun internat. prize for scholarship Hebrew U., 1969, Tercentenary medal Jewish Community of Essex County, N.J., 1954; Ford Found. Faculty fellow, 1952-53, Guggenheim fellow, 1953-54, Fund for the Republic fellow, 1955, Inst. Advanced Study fellow, 1959-60, Ctr. Advanced Study Behavioral Scis. fellow, 1964-65, NEH fellow, 1975-76. Fellow Am. Acad. Arts and Scis.; mem. AAUP (mem. coun. 1961-64), ACLU (mem. nat. com.), Am. Philos. Assn., Am. Acad. Jewish Rsch., Law and Soc. Assn., Indsl. Rels. Rsch. Assn., Workers Def. League (mem. adv. bd.), Am. Jewish League for Israel (mem. adv. bd.), Internat. Assn. Jewish Law, Internat. Assn. Jewish Lawyers and Jurists, Order of Coif, Phi Beta Kappa. Home: 150 Norwood Ave Oakhurst NJ 07755-1604

KONWIN, THOR WARNER, financial executive; b. Berwyn, Ill., Aug. 17, 1943; s. Frank and Alice S. (Johnson) K.; m. Carol A. Svitak, Aug. 2, 1967 (div. Feb. 1990); 1 child, Christopher Vernon; m. Virginia Colburn, May 21, 1993. AA, Morton Jr. Coll., 1966; BS, No. Ill. U., 1967; MS, Roosevelt U., 1971. Acct. Beckerman & Terrill, CPA's, Chgo., 1967-68; cost acct. Sunbeam Corp., Chgo., 1968-72; controller Gen. Molded Products, Inc., Chgo., 1972-75, Sunbeam Appliance Co., Chgo., 1975-81; chief fin. officer Bear Med. System, Inc., Riverside, Calif., 1981-84, Bird Products Corp., Palm Springs, Calif., 1984—; gen. ptnr., 1985—; pres. B&B Ventures Ltd., Riverside, 1987—; chief exec. officer Med One Fin. Group, Salt Lake City; pres. Tags Antiques, Inc., Palm Springs; bd. dris. Bird Med. Techs., Inc., Palm Springs, Bird Products Corp., Palm Springs, Bird Internat., Inc., Riverside, B&B Ventures, Inc., Riverside, Equilink, Inc. Riverside, Stackhouse, Inc., Riverside, Med One Fin. Group, Salt Lake City; CEO Equitable Inc., Palm Springs, Calif., 1990—; adv. coun. U. Calif. Grad. Bus. Sch., Riverside, 1988—; CEO Entertainment Leader Inc., Cathedral City, Calif., 1995—. Served with U.S. Army, 1969-71. Home: 45500 Verde Santa Palm Desert CA 92260 Office: 68845 Perez Rd Ste 30 Cathedral City CA 92234-7254

KONZ, GERALD KEITH, retired manufacturing company executive; b. Racine, Wis., Apr. 3, 1932; m. Marianne Bubolz; children: Richard C., Brenda S. BS in Econs., U. Wis., 1957, LLB, 1960. V.p. in charge corp. tax dept. S.C. Johnson & Son, Inc., Racine, 1982-98, chmn. bd. trustees pension trust, employee profit sharing and savs. plan, 1982-98; bd. dirs. Johnson Family Funds, Inc., Racine; mem. adv. bd. Venture Investors, Inc., Madison, Wis., 1997—. Bd. dirs. YMCA, Racine, Wis., 1988-98; treas. St. Catherines H.S. Found., Racine, Wis., 1994-97, pres., 1997—. Mem. ABA, Tax Execs. Inst. (pres. Wis. chpt. 1972), Wis. Bar Assn., Racine-Kenosha Estate Planning Coun. (pres. 1980). Office: SC Johnson & Son Inc 1525 Howe St Racine WI 53403-2237

KOO, GEORGE PING SHAN, business consultant; b. Changting, China, June 4, 1938; came to the U.S., 1949, naturalized, 1955; s. Ted Swei Yen and Pei-Fen (Yang) K.; m. May Jen, May 5, 1962; children: Denise, Douglas, Alyssa. BS, MIT, 1960, MS, 1962; DSc, Stevens Inst. Tech., 1969; MBA, U. Santa Clara, 1975. Mgr. Allied Chem. Corp., 1963-71; assoc. dir. SRI Internat., 1972-78; v.p. Chase Manhattan Bank, 1978-79; mng. dir. Bear-Stearns China Trade, 1979-82; v.p. Bear-Stearns & Co., 1982-83; pres. Microelectronic Bus. Internat., Inc., Mountain View, Calif., 1983-85; v.p. Tiara Computer Sys., Inc., 1985-86; mng. dir. internat. svcs. H&Q Tech. Ptnrs., Inc., 1987; mng. dir., CEO Internat. Strategic Alliances, Inc., 1988-99, chair, 1990-93; dep. dir. Pacific Rim svcs. Deloitte & Touche LLP, San Jose, Calif., 1999—; bd. dirs. Aeolus-Thomson Corp., Shiyan, Hubei, China; cons. on Asian Fin. and Alliances, Santa Clara, Calif. Human rels. commr. City of Mountain View, 1994-98. Mem. Asian Am. Mfrs. Assn. (chmn. 1996-97, mem. com. of 100 1997—, dir. com. of 100 1998—). Home: 1819 Van Buren Cir Mountain View CA 94040-4054

KOOB, CHARLES EDWARD, lawyer; b. Kansas City, Mo., Aug. 31, 1944; s. Charles H. and Adeline (Meinert) K.; m. Pamela Ann Nabseth, June 26, 1971; children: Jason Wyeth, Peter Nabseth. BA, Rockhurst Coll., 1966; JD, Stanford U., 1969. Bar: Calif. 1970, N.Y. 1972, U.S. Dist. Ct. (so. and ea. dists.) N.Y. 1973, U.S. Ct. Appeals (2d cir.) 1975, U.S. Ct. Appeals (5th cir.) 1979, U.S. Supreme Ct. 1988, U.S. Ct. Claims 1988, U.S. Ct. Appeals (3d cir.) 1985. Assoc. Simpson, Thacher & Bartlett, N.Y.C., 1970-76, ptnr., 1976—. Mem. ABA, N.Y. State Bar Assn., Calif. Bar Assn. Office: Simpson Thacher & Bartlett 425 Lexington Ave Fl 15 New York NY 10017-3954

KOOB, ROBERT DUANE, chemistry educator, educational administrator; b. Graetinger, Iowa, Oct. 14, 1941; s. Emil John and Rose Mary (Slinger) K.; m. E. Yvonne Ervin, June 9, 1960; children—Monique, Gregory, Michael, Angela, Julie, Eric, David. B.A. in Edn., U. No. Iowa, 1962; Ph.D. in Chemistry, U. Kans., 1967. From asst. prof. to prof. chemistry N.D. State U., Fargo, 1967-90, chmn. dept. chemistry, 1974-78, 79-81, dir. Water Inst., 1975-85, dean Coll. Sci. and Math., 1981-84, v.p., 1985-90, interim pres., 1987-88; v.p. for acad. affairs, sr. v.p. Calif. Poly. State U., San Luis Obispo, 1990-95; pres. U. No. Iowa, Cedar Falls, 1995—, prof., 1995—; cons. TrnasAlta, Edmonton, Alta., Can., Alta. Rsch. Coun., Mitre Corp., Washington; bd. dirs. State Bank Fargo, Fagro Cass County Econ. Devel. Corp.; chair bd. dirs. Cal Poly Found.; chair Iowa Coordinating Coun. for Post-H.S. Edn., 1996-97. Contbr. articles to profl. jours. Vice pres. Crookston Diocesan Sch. Bd., Minn., 1982; pres. elem. sch. bd. St. Joseph's Ch., Moorhead, Minn., 1982, parish council, 1983; pres. bd. Shanley High Sch., Fargo, 1985. Grantee in field. Mem. Iowa Assn. Coll. Pres. (pres. 1996—). Roman Catholic. Avocations: reading; flying; sailing; racquet sports; water skiing. Office: Univ of Northern Iowa 1222 W 27th St Cedar Falls IA 50613-4800*

KOOGLE, TIM, communications executive. MS in Engr., Stanford U. Pres. Intermec Corp.; corp. v.p. Western Atlas Inc.; with Motorola Inc.; chmn., CEO Yahoo! Corp., Santa Clara, Calif., 1999—; chmn. bd. dirs. AIM. Office: Yahoo! Corp 3400 Central Expy Ste 201 Santa Clara CA 95051-0703*

KOOIMA, LINDA KAY, neonatal and pediatrics nurse; b. Rock Valley, Iowa, Aug. 26, 1948; d. Thomas and Frances Mae (Harmelink) K.; m. Orlando Sabas Arroyo, Apr. 12, 1976; children: Annie Josephine, Solomon Jordan. Dipl. nursing, Northwestern U., 1969; BA in Spanish, S.D. State U., 1988. RN, Ill., S.D., Ariz., Calif., Fla. Critical care nurse Children's Meml. Hosp., Chgo., 1969-70; nurse neonatal ICU, Moffitt Hosp. U. Calif., San Francisco, 1970-76; clinic nurse S.D. State U., Brookings, 1985-88; mother and baby nurse Santa Barbara (Calif.) Cottage Hosp., 1988-89; neonatal nurse Santa Ana (Calif.) Hosp. and Med. Ctr., 1990, Hoag Presbyn. Meml. Hosp., Newport Beach, Calif., 1991; pediatric camp nurse Camp Gulliver, Coral Gables, Fla., 1993-95; utilization rev. nurse Initial Health Care, Miami, 1995-98; travel nurse mother/baby Star-Med Co., 1998-99. Mem. Assn. Camp Nurses. Republican. Avocation: scuba diving. Home: 13890 SW 100th Ln Miami FL 33186-6869

KOOISTRA, WILLIAM HENRY, clinical psychologist; b. Grand Rapids, Mich., May 20, 1936; s. Henry P. and Marguerite (Brinks) K.; m. Jean Heynen, Aug. 24, 1957 (div. Dec. 1984); children: Kimberly Lynn, William Peter, Kristin Jean, Allison Carol; m. Carol Sue Smitter, Mar. 9, 1985. BA, Calvin Coll., 1957; PhD, Wayne (Mich.) State U., 1963. Diplomate Am. Bd. Profl. Psychology, Am. Bd. Forensic Examiners. Intern psychology Lafayette Clinic, Detroit, 1961-62; chief psychologist Pine Rest Christian Hosp., Grand Rapids, Mich., 1964-67; clin. psychologist Kooistra, Jansma, Teitsma, DiNallo & Van Hoek, Grand Rapids, 1967—; instr. Wayne State U., 1959-63, Hope Coll., Holland, Mich., 1964, Calvin Coll., Grand Rapids, 1964-81, Grand Valley State U., 1987-92. Founder Project Rehab., Grand Rapids, 1968, bd. dirs., 1969—, pres., 1972-74; mem. Kent County Dem. Exec. Com., 1969-73, 79-82, 86—, mem. governing bd. Fountain Street Ch., 1989-95, pres. 1994; rep. 3d dist. Presl. Electoral Coll., 1992. Mem. Am. Psychol. Assn. (council rep. 1982-85), Am. Soc. Psychologists in Pvt. Practice (sec. 1973-75), Mich. Psychol. Assn.(pres. 1979), Mich. Soc. Forensic Psychology, Grand Rapids Area Psychol. Assn (pres. 1968). Avocations: golf, tennis, sailing. Home: 2946 Cascade Rd SE Grand Rapids MI 49506-1965 Office: 3330 Claystone St SE Grand Rapids MI 49546-7716

KOOKEN, JOHN FREDERICK, retired bank holding company executive; b. Denver, Nov. 1, 1931; s. Duff A. and Frances C. K.; m. Emily Howe, Sept. 18, 1954; children: Diane, Carolyn. MS, Stanford U., 1954, PhD, 1961. With Security Pacific Nat. Bank-Security Pacific Corp., L.A., 1960-92; exec. v.p. Security Pacific Corp., L.A., 1981-87; chief fin. officer Security Pacific Corp., Los Angeles, 1984-92, vice chmn., 1987-92; bd. dirs. The Centris Group, Inc., Golden State Bancorp., Pacific Gulf Properties Inc.; lectr. Grad. Sch. Bus. U. So. Calif., 1962-67; chmn. Bank Adminstrn. Inst., 1989-90. Pres. bd. dirs. Children's Bur., L.A., 1981-84; bd. dirs. United Way, L.A., 1982-89, Huntington Meml. Hosp., Pasadena, 1985—, chmn., 1999—; bd. dirs. So. Calif. Healthcare Systems, 1993—. Lt. (j.g.) USNR, 1954-57. Mem. Fin. Execs. Inst. (pres. Los Angeles chpt. 1979-80, dir. 1981-84).

KOOMEN, CORNELIS JAN, telecommunications, micro and consumer electronics executive; b. Zaandam, The Netherlands, Sept. 25, 1947; s. C.J. and G. (Dykman) K.; m. Jantiena Catharina de Jong; children: Casper Jan, Jeroen. MS, Tech. U., Delft, The Netherlands, 1972, PhD, 1982. Rschr. RVO/TNO, The Hague, The Netherlands, 1973-74, Philips Rsch. Labs., Eindhoven, 1974-83; system engr. Philips Telecommunications and Data Systems, Hilversum, The Netherlands, 1983-84; software coord. Philips Electronics, Eindhoven, 1984-86; mgr. Philips Rsch. Labs., Eindhoven, 1987-89; IC exec., tech. mgr., dir. Philips Telecom. and Data Systems, Hilversum, 1989-90; dir. Philips Comm. Systems, Hilversum, 1990-91; dir., v.p. Philips Semiconductors, Eindhoven, 1991-94, exec. v.p., 1995-98; chmn. Philips Semiconductors, N.Am., 1996-98; pres. digital video group Philips Consumer Electronics, Palo Alto, Calif., 1996-98; prof. Tech. U., Eindhoven, The Netherlands, 1984—; module dir. Found. Toptech Studies, Delft, 1987-92. Author: The Design of Communicating Systems; editor Internat. Fedn. of Info. Processing Computer Hardware Description Langs. conf. proc., 1985-87; patentee in field; contbr. articles to profl. jours. Chmn. Cultural Com., Waalre, The Netherlands, 1977-81. Named Prof. Bahlerprice, Royal Inst. Engrs., 1986. Mem. IFIP WG 10.2, Soc. for Gen. Edn. (chmn. 1985-88). Avocations: aguarel painting, sailing, tennis. Home: 15415 Via Caballero Monte Sereno CA 95030-2101 Office: Philips Consumer Electronics 1804 Embarcadero Rd Palo Alto CA 94303-3318

KOON, RAY HAROLD, management and security consultant; b. Little Mountain, S.C., Nov. 19, 1934; s. Harold Clay and Jessie Rae (Epting) K.; m. Bertha Mae Gardner, Aug. 19, 1958; children: Shari Madilyn Koon Goode, Schyler Michele Koon Richards, Kamela Suzanne Koon Scott. BSBA, Old Dominion U., 1957; postgrad., Columbia (S.C.) Coll., 1957-58. Lic. pvt. pilot. Supr. office svcs. FBI, Norfolk, Va., 1953-61, Las Vegas, Nev., 1961-62; agt. State Gaming Control Bd., Carson City, Nev., 1962-64, coord., 1967-80, chief of investigations, 1980-83; prodn. control mgr. Colite Industries, Inc., West Columbia, S.C., 1964-67; pres. Assoc. Gaming Consultants, Las Vegas, 1983; dir. gaming surveillance Hilton Hotels Corp., Beverly Hills, Calif., 1983-86; pres. JRJ Enterprises, Las Vegas, 1986-88, Assoc. Cons. Enterprises, Las Vegas, 1983—; pres. Assoc. Gaming Cons., Las Vegas, 1983—, CEO, 1990—; past sec. Sta. KNIS-FM. Editor, pub. Ray Koon's Gaming/Gram, 1986—; columnist Casino Gaming Internat., 1990-92. Chief vols. Warren Engine Co. 1, Carson City Fire Dept., 1962-83; mem. Carson City Sheriff's Aero Squadron, 1983—, past comdr.; past mem. exec. bd. Nev. Bapt. Conv. With U.S. Army, 1957-59. Mem. Nev. Arbitration Assn. (bd. dirs. 1986-90), Las Vegas C. of C. (mem. commerce crime prevention and legis. action coms. 1989-90), Zelzah Shrine Aviation Club (past comdr.), Nat. Intelligence and Counterintelligence Assn. (bd. dirs. 1995—), Assn. Former Intelligence Officers, Toastmasters, Masons. Republican. Avocations: flying, do-it-yourself projects. Office: Assoc Cons Enterprises 3271 S Highland Dr Ste 705A Las Vegas NV 89109-1051

KOONCE, JEFFERSON MICHAEL, psychologist, university official, consultant; b. New Orleans, Sept. 8, 1937; s. William Wood and Gladys Edwina (Germann) K.; m. Virginia Darlene Koonce, Dec. 12, 1969; 1 child, Stuart Speight. BS, Tulane U., 1959, MS, 1961; PhD, U. Ill., 1974. Lic. psychologist, Colo. Commd. officer USAF, 1961, advanced through grades; asst. prof. dept. psychology and leadership USAF Acad., Colo., 1967-69, assoc. prof., prof., chief human factors engring. divsn., 1974-81; human performance engr. Flight Dynamics Lab., Wright-Paterson AFB, Ohio, 1970-71; ret., 1981; prof., head human factors engring. program U. Mass., Amherst, 1981-88; prof.mech.-indsl. engring., acting head Aviation Rsch. Lab., U. Ill. Inst. Aviation, Champaign-Urbana, 1988-92; dir., chief scientist Ctr. Applied Human Factors in Aviation U. Ctrl. Fla., Orlando, 1992—; dir. aviation sys. and human factors Tech. Sys., Inc., Wiscasset, Maine, 1987—; mem. airway scis. rsch. adv. bd. Embry-Riddle Aero. U., 1989-92; CEO, Global Tng. Sys., Inc., Sarasota, Fla., 1994—; cons. tng. sys. divsn. Flight Safety Internat., Daytona Beach, Fla., 1997—; cons. to numerous agys. Author: Human Factors in the Training of Pilots; editor monograph Human Factors Soc.; editor, cons. editor, reviewer Jour. Human Factors, Jour. Applied Psychology ScycSCAN, Soc. Automotive Engrs., Internat. Jour. Aviation Psychology, Jour. Aviation, Aerospace Edn. and Rsch., Internat. Jour. Indsl. Engring., Mil. Psychology, Jour. Applied Psychology; contbr. over 70 articles to profl. jours., also chpts. to books. Recipient cert. for sutstanding svc. Soc. Automotive Engrs., 1989, Jerome H. Ely award Human Factors and Ergonomics Soc., 1991; sr. faculty rsch. grantee Am. Soc. for Engring. Edn., 1987, 88. Fellow APA (pres. divsn. 21 1961-95), Am. Psychol. Soc. (charter); mem. Assn. Aviation Psychologists, Airplane Owners and Pilots Assn., Golden Key (hon.), Elks, Sigma Xi (pres. Pikes Peak chpt. 1977-79, U. Mass. chpt. 1985-86), Tau Beta Pi, Alpha Pi Mu, Phi Kappa Phi. Lutheran. Avocations: golf, fly fishing, ballroom dancing, piloting aircraft. Home: 336 Caddie Dr Debary FL 32713-4511 Office: U Ctrl Fla Ctr Applied Human Factors in Aviation Orlando FL 32816-1780

KOONCE, JOHN PETER, investment company executive; b. Coronado, Calif., Jan. 8, 1932; s. Allen Clark and Elizabeth (Webb) K.; B.S., U.S. Naval Acad., 1954; postgrad. U. So. Calif., 1957, U. Alaska, 1961, U. Ill., 1968-69; M.S. in Ops. Research, Fla. Inst. Tech., 1970; postgrad. Claremont Grad. Sch., 1970; m. Marilyn Rose Campbell, Sept. 21, 1952; children—Stephen Allen, William Clark, Peter Marshall. Indsl. engr. Aluminum Co. Am. Lafayette, Ind., 1954-56; electronic research engr. Autonetics Div. N.Am. Aviation, Downey, Calif., 1956-57; systems field engr. Remington Rand Univac, Fayetteville, N.C., 1957-59; project engr. RCA Service Co., Cheyenne, Wyo., 1959-60, project supr., Clear, Alaska, 1960-62, project supr., Yorkshire, Eng., 1962-64, re-entry signature analyst, Patrick AFB, Fla., 1964-66; mem. tech. staff TRW Systems Group, Washington, 1966-68; mgr. ops research systems analysis Magnavox Co., Urbana, Ill., 1968-69; tech. advisor, EDP, to USAF, Aerojet Electro Systems Co., Azusa, Calif., Woomera, Australia, 1969-72; investment exec. Shearson Hammill, Los Angeles, 1972-74; investment exec. Reynolds Securities, Los Angeles, 1974-75; v.p. investments Shearson Hayden Stone, Glendale, Calif., 1975-77; v.p. accounts Paine, Webber, Jackson & Curtis Inc., Los Angeles, 1977-82; pres. Argo Fin. Corp., Santa Monica, Calif., 1982-83, Fin. Packaging Corp., Flintridge, Calif., 1983—; fin. lectr. Princess Line Cruise Ships; tchr. investments Citrus Coll., Azusa, Calif., Claremont (Calif.) Evening Sch. Vice pres. Claremont Republican Club, 1973, pres., 1974. Chmn., Verdugo Hosp. Assos., 1979. Recipient Merit certificate RCA, 1966. Mem. Nat. Assn. Security Dealers, L.A. Philharmonic Bus. and Profl. Com., Navy League U.S., Naval Acad. Alumni Assn., La Can. Flintridge Tournament Roses Assn. (patron), Clubs: Masons (master 1987, pres. dist. officers assn., 32d degree), Shriner (Al Malaikah Temple), Kiwanis (pres. La Canada chpt. 1995-96), Marbella Golf & Country (founding mem.). Host, commentator, Sta. KWHY-TV, Los Angeles, (weekly) West of Wall Street, 1986-87; contbr. articles to bus. jours. Home: 415 Foxenwood Dr Santa Maria CA 93455-4228 Office: 15233 Ventura Blvd Ste 404 Sherman Oaks CA 91403-2218

KOONCE, NEIL WRIGHT, lawyer; b. Kinston, N.C., July 8, 1947; s. Harold Wright and Edna Earle (Regan) K.; m. Virginia Gayle Evans, Feb. 27, 1993; children: Channing, Carl Younger, Ginny Younger. A.B., U. N.C., 1969; J.D., Wake Forest U., 1974; postgrad. exec. program U. Va., 1983. Bar: N.C. 1973, U.S. Dist. Ct. (mid. dist.) N.C. 1975, U.S. Ct. Appeals (4th cir.) 1978, U.S. Supreme Ct. 1981. Atty., Cone Mills Corp., Greensboro, N.C., 1974-81, sr. atty., 1981-85, asst. gen. counsel, 1985-87, gen. counsel, 1987—, v.p., 1989—. Bd. dirs. Family and Children's Services, Greensboro, 1981-89, S.C. Energy Users Com., Columbia, S.C., 1984-89, Carolina Utility Customer's Assn., Raleigh, 1983-90, 94—; bd. dirs. N.C. Found. for Research and Econ. Edn., 1986-87, 93—; bd. dirs. Electricity Consumers Resource Coun., Washington, 1987-92—, vice chmn., 1990, chmn., 1991; bd. dirs. N.C. Citizens for Bus. and Inustry, Raleigh, 1991-96, Met. YMCA, Greensboro, N.C., 1991-95, Salvation Army Boys and Girls Clubs, Greensboro, 1996—, S.C. Mfrs. Alliance, 1998—, N.C. Textile Mfrs. Assn., 1998—. Served with AUS, 1970-71. Mem. Greensboro Bar Assn., N.C. Bar Assn., ABA, N.C. Textile Mfrs. Assn. Democrat. Presbyterian. Lodge: Rotary (sec. 1983-86, bd. dirs. 1985-90, pres. 1988). Home: 200 Irving Pl Greensboro NC 27408-6510 Office: Cone Mills Corp 3101 N Elm St Greensboro NC 27408-3184

KOONIN, STEVEN ELLIOT, physicist, educator, academic administrator; b. Bklyn., Dec. 12, 1951. BS, Calif. Inst. Tech., 1972; PhD, MIT, 1975. Asst. prof. Calif. Inst. Tech., Pasadena, Calif., 1975-78; assoc. prof. Calif. Inst. Tech., Pasadena, 1978-81, prof., 1981—, v.p., provost, 1995—; cons. Inst. for Def. Analysis, MITRE Corp., Lawrence Livermore Nat. Lab., Oak Ridge Nat. Lab. Author: Computational Physics, 1985, Computational Nuclear Physics, vol. 1, 1991, vol. 2, 1993. Recipient Green Prize for Creative Scholarship, Calif. Inst. Tech., 1972, Assoc. Students Teaching award Calif. Inst. Tech., 1975-76, Sr. U.S. Scientist award Humboldt Found., 1985-86, Fusion Power Assocs. Leadership award, 1994, E.O. Lawrence award U.S. Dept. Energy, 1998; Alfred P. Sloan fellow, 1977-81. Fellow AAAS, Am. Acad. Arts and Scis., Am. Phys. Soc. (chmn. APS divsn. nuclear physics 1988-89, exec. bd. dirs. 1994-96). Office: Calif Inst Tech Office of Provost 206-31 Pasadena CA 91125

KOONS, ELEANOR (PEGGY KOONS), clinical social worker; b. Sarasota, Fla., July 26, 1927; d. James Lee and Odessa (Dobbs) Swafford; m. Nelson A. Koons, Dec. 27, 1945. BA in Human Resources, Eckerd Coll., 1986; MSW, U. So. Fla., 1988. Lic. clin. social worker. Indsl. nurse Electro-Mech. Rsch. Co., Sarasota, Fla., 1963-65; office mgr. Koons Constrn. Co., Sarasota, 1970-80; day treatment counselor Manatee Community Mental Health Ctr., Bradenton, Fla., 1980-81, day treatment counselor geriat. residential treatment sys., 1981-82, community liaison, counselor, 1982-83; office mgr. Koons Constrn. Co., 1983-88; hospice intern Hospice S.W. Fla., 1987-88, sr. social svc. counselor, 1988-92; pvt. practice Sarasota, 1992—; presenter Nat. Hospice Assn. Conf., Detroit, Fla. Hospice Symposium, Ocala, Fla. Assn. Pediatric Tumor Programs, State Conf., Clearwater, others. Mem. spl. adv. bd. Storytelling World; contbr. articles to Bereavement Mag., Reminisce Extra, Tales from Heart and Home. Recipient Retired Social Worker of Yr. award Tampa Bay (Fla.) Unit; Grad. record fellow U. So. Fla. Mem. NASW (co-chairperson 1993-94), ACA. Home: 80 Larkspur Ln Cullowhee NC 28723

KOONS, IRVIN LOUIS, design and marketing executive, graphic artist, consultant; b. Harrisburg, Pa., Mar. 14, 1922; s. Frank and Rose (Silver) K.; m. Leah Fay, Dec. 25, 1949; children: Adam, Jonathan, Joshua. Grad., Pratt Inst., 1942, New Sch., N.Y., 1946; student and instr., Ecole Des Beaux Arts, Fontainebleau, France, 1948-50; student, others schs. in France, Switzerland and Italy, 1947-49. Designer, chief exec. officer Irv Koons Assocs. (subs. Saatchi and Saatchi Worldwide, since 1983), N.Y.C., 1950-89; sr.

advisor to adminstr. UN Devel. Program, N.Y.C., 1989—; sr. advisor Div. for Pvt. Sector in Devel. and UNISTAR, UNDP; founder, co-dir. Internat. Design Assistance Commn., 1984—; sr. advisor to adminstr. UN Devel. Programme, 1989—; past cultural attache, spl. cons. U.S. Dept. State, India; dir. 1st internat. packaging exhbn. USIA; tchr. various art schs.; advisor Inferential Focus Forum; lectr. mktg. NYU, U. Pa., Columbia U., U. Tel Aviv, Northwestern U. and others in Eng., Holland, France, Switzerland, Brazil, India. Exhibited paintings and drawings in group shows in U.S. and France, represented in permanent collections including Mus. Modern Art, Cooper Hewitt Nat. Design Mus., the Jewish Mus., Yeshiva U. Mus.; complete collection of works on 7,000 slides plus several thousand sketches and finished itmes at Hagley Mus. and Libr., Wilmington, Del.; slides also available on CD-Rom; prin. works include Life of Moses series, 1975-78, stained glass wall for Fedn. Jewish Philanthropies, 1975, series coord. Torah ornaments for Temple Emmanuel, N.J., 1986; designed stage sets for traveling shows of original broadway casts: Harriette, Three Sisters, Blythe Spirit, Springtime for Henry, others; illus. many books and mags. including Ladies Home Jour., Good Housekeeping, Forturne, Seventee, Sports Illustrated; designer 1st Daily offset newspaper in world, Middletown Daily Record, 1956 (Ayer Cup best design 1957, 58), redesign Washington Star, 1969; cons. editor Graphis Packaging, Switzerland, 1970; art critic The Statesman newspaper, India, 1946; contbr. articles on mktg. to profl. jours.; subject one-man articles in mags. including Graphis, Idea, 1976, others; 40-min. multi-image show of life and work produced by PDC, 1982. Founder, co-dir. Internat. Design Assistance Commn.; bd. dirs., mem. exec. com. Found. for Future Generations; bd. dirs. Temple Emanuel, Englewood N.J., 1987; trustee Art Ctr. No. N.J., Englewood, 1960-68; contbr. logo and trade mark designs to various non-profit civic orgns. including Am. Cancer Soc., Fedn. Jewish Philanthropies, World Hunger, Sloan-Kettering Meml. Hosp., United Cerebral Palsy, Jewish Theol. Sem., many others. Served with inf. U.S. Army, 1942-46, CBI. Recipient numerous awards including Clio awards, 1976, 77, 81, Gold Clio award, 79, 84, 88, Best ann. report design, 1957, 59, 61, Silver award Variety Store Merchandisers, 1967, Gold award Variety Store Merchandisers, 1970, Gold award Internat. Folding Carton Competition, 1964, Gold award Paperboard Packaging Council, 1974, awards N.Y. Art Dir.'s Club, 1958, 59, 63, 76, 77, 79 (2), awards Am. Inst. Graphic Arts, 1955, 58, 59, 60 (3), 61, 65 (2), 72, awards Package Design Mag., 1963, 64, 65, 66, 67, 68, 70 (3), Gold awards Package Design Council, 1977, 79, 80 (2), 87 (2); Best of Best 1985 (2); Desi award 1981, Indsl. Design awards, 1968, 75, Package of Yr. award, 1968, Nat. Printing award, 1981, Communication Arts awards, 1960, 64, 66, 67, 71, Best Bottle of Yr. award, 1975, awards Soc. Illustrators, 1959, 68, awards N.J. Art Dir.'s Club, 1962, 65 (3), 68, awards NYU, 1973, 74, Pratt. Inst. Alumni Achievement award, 1998, many others. Mem. Package Designers Coun. (Person of Yr. 1982, bd. dirs. 1962—), Indsl. Design Soc. Am., Packaging Inst., Am. Inst. Graphic Arts, Am. Soc. Profl. Cons. Avocations: collecting historical packages, rewriting and illustrating legends, fables and fairy tales. Home: 213 Engle St Tenafly NJ 07670-2139 Office: Irv Koons Assocs 213 Engle St Tenafly NJ 07670-2139

KOONS, JEFF, artist; b. York, Pa., 1955. One person shows include New Mus. Contemporary Art, N.Y., 1980, Internat. With Monument, N.Y., 1985, Feature Gallery, N.Y., 1985, Daniel Weinberg Gallery, L.A., 1986, MCA, Chgo., 1988, Sonnabend Gallery, N.Y., 1988, 91, Max Hetzler Gallery, Cologne, Germany, 1988, 91, Donald Young Gallery, Chgo., 1988, Venster Gallery, Rotterdam, The Netherlands, 1989, Lehmann Gallery, Lausanne, Switzerland, 1992, Christophe Van de Weghe, Brussels, 1992, San Francisco Mus. Modern Art, 1992, 93, Walker Art Ctr., Mpls., 1992, Stedelijk Mus., Amsterdam, 1992, Mus. Contemporary Art, Sydney, 1996, Per Skarstedt Fine Art Gallery, N.Y.C., 1996; exhibited in group shows at P.S. 1, Long Island City, N.Y., 1981, Annina Nosei Gallery, N.Y., 1981, Barbara Gladstone Gallery, N.Y., 1981, Renaissance Soc., Chgo., 1982, 85, Espace Lyonnais d'Art Contemporain, Lyon, France, 1982, Artists Space, N.Y., 1983, LACE, L.A., 1983, White Columns, N.Y., 1984, Hallwalls, Buffalo, 1984, Features Gallery, Chgo., 1985, Whitney Mus., N.Y., 1985, 87, 89, 90, Michael Kline Gallery, N.Y., 1985, Galerie Crousel-Hussenot, Paris, 1985, New Mus., N.Y., 1985, Fundacion Caixa de Pensiones, Madrid/Barcelona, 1985, ICA, Boston, 1985, 88, Prospect Gallery, Frankfurt, Germany, 1985, Centro Reina Sofia, Madrid, 1987, Saatchi Collection, London, 1987, 88, LACMA, L.A., 1987, Centre Pompidou, Paris, 1987, John & Marble Ringling Mus. Art, Sarasota, Fla., 1987, Carnegie Internat., Pitts., 1988, Ctr. Nat. des Art Plastiques, Paris, 1988, MCA, Chgo., 1988, Kunsthalle, Dusseldorf, Germany, 1988, Roseum, Malmo, 1988, MOCA, L.A., 1989, Kunstverein, Hamburg, 1989, Kunsthalle, Basel, Switzerland, 1989, Mus. Modern Art, N.Y.C., 1989, 90, Biennale, Venice, Italy, 1990, Mus. Haus Lange and Mus. Haus Esters, Krefeld, 1990, Pharmakon, Tokyo, 1990, Biennial, Sydney, 1990, Thaddaeus Ropac Gallery, Salzburg, Austria, 1990, Stedelijk Mus., Amsterdam, 1990, Israel Mus., Tel Aviv, 1990, Deste Found., Athens, Greece, 1990, Mus. Art, Indpls., 1991, Martin-Gropius-Bau, Berlin, 1991, Mus. voor Hedendaagse Kunst, Hertogenbosch, The Netherlands, 1992, Anthony d'Offay Gallery, London, 1992, Musee d'Art Contemporain Pully/Lausanne, 1992, Ctr. Curatorial Studies Mus., Bard Coll., Annondale-on-Hudson, N.Y., 1996-97. Studio: 600 Broadway Fl 2 New York NY 10012-3206*

KOONTS, JONES CALVIN, retired education educator; b. Lexington, N.C., Sept. 19, 1924; s. Harvey Hill and Elsie (Tussey) K.; m. Cortlandt Morper, Sept. 6, 1953; children: Carlisle Woodson, Camille Walton. A.B. in History and English magna cum laude, Catawba Coll., Salisbury, N.C., 1945; M.A. in Sociology, George Peabody Coll., Vanderbilt U., Nashville, 1949, Ph.D. in Edn., 1958; Lit.D., Catawba Coll., 1979. Tchr. English and social studies Boyden High Sch., Salisbury, 1945-48; dir.-asst. student teaching George Peabody Coll., 1951-52; mem. faculty Erskine Coll., Due West, S.C., 1949-90, prof. edn., 1949-90, prof. emeritus, 1990—, chmn. dept. edn., 1949-87; tchr. adult edn. Abbeville (S.C.) County Community Ctr., 1955; tchr. grad. courses Coastal Carolina Coll., U. S.C., 1971-78; also Clemson U., 1956; postdoctoral researcher UCLA, 1977. Author: (poetry) Since Promontory, 1967, Straws in the Wind, 1968, Under the Umbrella, 1971, A Slice of the Sun, 1976, A Stone's Throw, 1986, Lines: Opus 8, 1994; editor: (poetry) Green Leaves in January, 1972, Inklings, 1983. Rep. S.C. Bd. Edn., 1966-71; bd. commrs. Piedmont Tech. Coll., 1972-75; alumni bd. dirs. Catawba Coll., 1966; bd. advisers Gardner-Webb Coll., 1981-89; bd. dirs. Due West Retirement Ctr., 1993—. Jesse H. Jones scholar, 1951; Algernon Sydney Sullivan scholar, 1951; fellow Council So. Univs., 1957-58; Peabody-Harvard scholar, 1960; Fulbright grantee, 1964; fellow, seminarist Worcester Coll., Oxford U., Eng., 1985; recipient Disting. Service key Phi Delta Kappa. Mem. N.C. Edn. Assn. (chpt. sec. treas. 1946-47), S.C. Assn. Student Teaching (founder, 1st pres. 1955-56), S.C. Council Tchr. Edn., S. Atlantic Philosophy Edn. Soc., Poetry Soc. S.C. (bd. dirs., William Gilmore Simms poetry prize 1973, Unicorn Poetry prize 1974, Lyric Poetry prize, 1975, Elizabeth B. Coker Poetry award 1977), Nat. Assn. Tchr. Educators (del S.C.), Am. Assn. Colls. for Tchr. Edn. (rep. S.C.), S.C. Assn. Colls. for Tchr. Edn. (pres. 1979-80), Acad. Am. Poets, Asso. Ref. Presbyterian. Home: PO Box 163 Due West SC 29639-0163 *My philosophy of life is from Salutation to the Dawn, written in Sanskrit: "Yesterday is but a dream, tomorrow only a vision; but today well lived makes every yesterday a dream of happiness and every tomorrow a vision of hope".*

KOONTZ, ALFRED JOSEPH, JR., financial and operating management executive, consultant; b. Balt., Mar. 6, 1942; s. Alfred J. and Mary Agnes (Valis) K.; m. Kay Francis Frank, Aug. 4, 1962; children—Debbie Kay, Denise Marie, Stacey Lynn, Alfred Joseph, III. BSBA, Pa. State U., 1964. CPA, Md. Mgr. Price Waterhouse & Co., Balt., 1964-73; sr. mgr. Price Waterhouse & Co., N.Y.C., 1973-74, Morristown, N.J., 1974-75; v.p. fin Piper Aircraft Corp., Lock Haven, Pa., 1975-80; sr. v.p. fin. Piper Aircraft Corp., 1980-85, sr. v.p. fin., treas., 1985-86; exec. v.p., chief operating officer Piper Aircraft Corp., Vero Beach, Fla., 1987-88; pres., dir. Piper Acceptance Corp., Lakeland, Fla., 1985-88; sr. v.p. fin. and adminstrn., treas., bd. dirs. Todd Shipyards Corp., Seattle, 1988-91; exec. v.p., CFO Pay'N Pak Stores Inc., Bellevue, Wash., 1992-93; pres. Alfred J. Koontz & Assoc., Vero Beach, 1993—; co-owner, CFO Pub. Telecomm. Providers, Inc., Vero Beach, 1993-97; co-owner, operator A&K Enterprises of Vero, Inc., 1994—; client rels. exec. Diamond Tech. Ptnrs., Inc., Chgo., 1998—; CFO Wannabe's, LLC, 1999—. Prodr. (film) Wannabe's. Mem. AICPA, Md. Assn. CPAs, Inst. Mgmt. Accts. Home: 1790 Sand Dollar Way Vero Beach FL 32963-2723 Office: PO Box 4434 Vero Beach FL 32964

KOONTZ, BRAD MATTHEW, accountant; b. Bedford, Pa., Oct. 7, 1970; s. Bruce Edward and Carla Jean (Pencil) K. BS in Acctg., Pa. State U., 1992. CPA, Pa. Assoc. Coopers & Lybrand LLP, Washington, 1992-94, sr. assoc., 1995; audit mgr. Ritchey, Ritchey & Koontz, Bedford, Pa., 1995—. Mem. Friends of Senator Jubelirer of Bedford County, 1997—. Mem. AICPA, Pa. Assn. CPAs, Bedford Area Jaycees (treas. 1996—), Bedford County C. of C. Republican. Mem. United Ch. of Christ. Avocation: turkey hunting. Home: 229 N Davidson St Apt 3D Bedford PA 15522-1218 Office: Ritchey Ritchey & Koontz 336 E Pitt St Bedford PA 15522-1439

KOONTZ, CARL LENNIS, II, investment counselor; b. Oct. 28, 1942; s. Carl Lennis and Jessie Marie (Rhodes) K.; m. Rose Marie Catalano, May 6, 1978. BS, U. Tenn., 1964, MS magna cum laude, 1968. Quality control analyst Ford Motor Co., Cin., 1965-66; mgmt. trainee Abbott, Procter & Paine, Richmond, Va., 1968-70; v.p. pesion cons. Paine, Webber, N.Y.C., 1970-76; asst. v.p. Scudder, Stevens & Clark, N.Y.C., 1976-78, v.p. investments, 1978-85, mng. dir., 1985-87; v.p. Scudder, Stevens & Clark of Can., Toronto, Ont., 1984-87, Smith Barney Capital Mgmt., 1987-92; v.p. investment policy com. Capital Mgmt. Assocs., N.Y.C., 1992, sr. v.p., 1993; pres. Capital Mgmt. Mid-Cap Fund, 1994, co-head equity investments, 1996, co-chief investment officer, mng. dir., 1998; pres. Capital Mgmt. Small-Cap Fund, 1998. With U.S. Army ANG, 1965-70. Fellow Fin. Analysis Fedn. (chartered fin. analyst); mem. Investment Counsel Assn. Am. (chartered investment counselor), N.Y. Soc. Security Analysts, Madison Ave. Sports Car Driving and Chowder Soc., Holland Lodge, Univ. Club, Antique Automobile Club Am., Pontiac Oakland Club Internat. Avocations: antique cars, model railroading, photography, swimming, tennis. Home: 373 Middlesex Rd Darien CT 06820-2518

KOONTZ, CHRISTINE MILLER, research faculty; b. Miami, Fla., May 24, 1949; d. Wilson Averre and Dorothy Elizabeth (Miller) K.; m. Thomas A. Lynch, Mar. 27, 1982 (div. Sept. 1992); children: Katelyn Koontz, Thomas Averre Koontz. BS, Fla. State U., 1980, MLS, 1981, PhD, 1990; chmn., Save the Old Capitol Campaign. Gen. supr. spl. svcs. Amtrak, Washington, 1973-74; gen. supr. train and yard svcs. Amtrak, Oakland, Calif., 1974-75; coord. creative dept. Hoefer, Dietrich & Brown Advt., San Francisco, 1976-77; prodn. asst. William Cook Advt., Jacksonville, Fla., 1977-78; pub. info. asst. Dept. of State, State of Fla., Tallahassee, 1977-78; spl. svcs. coord. Gubernatorial Campaign, Bruce Smathers, State of Fla., Tallahassee, 1978; account exec. Snowhite Advt., Tallahassee, 1978-79, WOWD Radio FM, Tallahassee, 1979-80; asst. dir. S.W. Ga. Regional Libr., Bainbridge, 1981-83; asst. in rsch. Fla. Resources and Environ. Analysis Ctr., Fla. State U., Tallahassee, 1990—; presentations various orgns. and univs.; developer materials and bibliography mktg. unit Fla. State U. Sch. Libr. and Info. Scis., 1986-91, adj. prof., 1993—, developer materials and bibliography storytelling unit Coll. Edn., 1988—; storyteller presch. and elem. and pub. libr. presentations, 1988—, Fla. Folklife Festival, 1989—, developed and taught non-profit Mktg. of Info. and Librs. Fla. State Univ. Sch. of Libr. and Info. Studies, 1996-97. Author: Library Facility Siting and Location Handbook; contbr. articles to profl. jours., chpts. to books. Mem. bd. Tallahassee Cold Nights Shelter, Inc., 1992— (Vol. of Yr. award 1994); Olympic Torch bearer, 1996. Grantee Ga. Endowment for Humanities, 1982-83, Brown Bag Film Festival, 1983, Carroll Preston Baber Rsch. award, 1992-93, Dept. of Edn. Librs. and Lifelong Learning, 1996—, Inst. Mus. and Libr. Scis., 1998—, Internat. Fedn. Libr. Agys., 1999—. Office: Fla State U Fla Resrces/Environ Analysis Ctr C2200 University Ctr Tallahassee FL 32306

KOONTZ, DEAN RAY, writer; b. Everett, Pa., July 9, 1945; s. Raymond and Florence (Logue) K.; m. Gerda Ann Cerra, Oct. 15, 1966. BS, Shippensburg U., 1966, LittD (hon.), 1989. Tchr. Appalachian Poverty Program, Saxton, Pa., 1966-67, Mechanicsburg (Pa.) Sch. Dist., 1967-69; freelance writer Orange, Calif., 1969—. Author of over 59 novels including Star Quest, 1968, The Fall of the Dream Machine, 1969, Fear That Man, 1969, Anti-Man, 1970, Beastchild, 1970 (Hugo award nomination 1971), Dark of the Woods, 1970, The Dark Symphony, 1970, Hell's Gate, 1970, The Crimson Witch, 1971, A Darkness in My Soul, 1972, The Flesh in the Furnace, 1972, Starblood, 1972, Time Thieves, 1972, Warlock, 1972, A Werewolf Among Us, 1973, Hanging On, 1973, The Haunted Earth, 1973, Demon Seed, 1973, rev. edit., 1997, After the Last Race, 1974, Nightmare Journey, 1975, Night Chills, 1976, The Vision, 1977, Whispers, 1980, Phantoms, 1983, Darkfall, 1984, Twilight Eyes, 1985, Strangers, 1986, Watchers, 1987, Lightning, 1988, Servants of Twilight, 1989, The Bad Place, 1990, Cold Fire, 1991, Hideaway, 1992, Dragon Tears, 1993, Mr. Murder, 1993, Winter Moon, 1994, Dark Rivers of the Heart, 1994, Strange Highways, 1995, Intensity, 1996, Santa's Twin, 1996, Fear Nothing, 1997, Tick Tock, 1997, Sole Survivor, 1997, others under pseudonyms David Axton, Brian Coffey, Deanna Dwyer, K.R. Dwyer, John Hill, Leigh Nichols, Anthony North, Richard Paige, and Owen West. Office: William Morris Agy 1325 Avenue Of The Americas New York NY 10019-6026*

KOONTZ, ELDON RAY, management and financial consultant; b. Randolph County, Ind., Oct. 20, 1913; s. Irvin Delbert and Martha Caroline (Farmer) K.; m. Florence Gloria Gustus, Jan. 20, 1944; children: Rebecca Anne Koontz Stumm, Stephen Wickey Koontz. AB in Econs., Earlham Coll., 1938; Diploma in Bus. Adminstrn., Alexander Hamilton Inst., N.Y.C., 1956. Chief cost acct. and spl. assignments, Crosley Div. Avco Mfg. Corp., Richmond, Ind.; asst. to pres. F.C. Russell Co., Cleve.; controller, asst. sec. Pacific Mercury Electronics, Joplin, Mo.; sr. mgmt. engr. Bell Aerosystems Co., Wheatfield, N.Y.; controller, asst. sec. Fleet of America, Inc., Buffalo, N.Y.; asst. to pres., acting gen. mgr. Tycodyne Industries, Inc./Lakeside Mfg. Co., Lackawanna and Honeoye, N.Y.; chmn., pres. E.R. Koontz & Assocs., Inc., Williamsville, N.Y., 1970—; mng. dir. Koontzco Internat. div. E.R. Koontz & Assocs., Inc., 1990—; exec. dir. Troika Sys. Engring. Group div. E.R. Koontz & Assocs., Inc., 1993—. Contbg. author: Mergers and Acquisitions Procedures, 1987. Treas. First English Luth. Ch., Richmond, Ind., 1950-55; v.p. Cen. Presbyn. Ch., Buffalo, N.Y., 1979-85; mem. The Chapel, Amherst, N.Y., 1986. Capt. U.S. Army, 1943-45. Mem. Richmond Accts. Assn. (pres. 1951-52), Nat. Assn. Cost Accts. (assoc. dir. for publs. Dayton, Ohio 1951-55), Nat. Assn. Mergers and Acquisitions Cons. (bd. dirs., sec. 1973-83), Internat. Assn. Mergers and Acquisitions Cons. (bd. dirs., sec. 1974-83), Am. Fin. Assn. (charter), Am Legion, Amherst C. of C., Rotary (Rotarian of Yr. North Amherst chpt. 1990). Republican. Avocations: golf, fishing. Home: 52B Williamsburg Sq Williamsville NY 14221-6431 Office: ER Koontz and Assocs Inc PO Box 182 Buffalo NY 14221

KOONTZ, LAWRENCE L., JR., state supreme court justice; b. Roanoke, Va, Jan. 25, 1940. BS, Va. Polytech. U., 1962. Asst. commonwealth's atty. Roanoke, 1967-68; judge Va. Juvenile & Domestic Rels. Dist. Ct., 1968-76, Va. Cir. Ct. (23rd cir.), 1976-85, Ct. Appeals of Va., 1985-95, Supreme Ct. of Va., 1995—. Mem. ABA. Office: PO Box 687 Salem VA 24153-0687

KOONTZ, LISA ELAINE, speech-language pathologist; b. Marion, Ind., Sept. 15, 1950; d. William Benton and Margaret Ruth Trees; m. Stanley Thomas Koontz, July 19, 1969; children: Randi Kathleen, Erin Marie. BS, Ball State U., 1972, MA, 1975. Lic. speech-lang. pathologist Ind. State Bd. Health, Ind. Profl. Grade Pub. Sch. Tchrs. Cert. Speech-lang. pathologist Mississinewa Comty. Schs., Gas City, Ind., 1972-97, Carey Svcs., Marion, Ind., 1996—; pvt. practice Upland, Ind., 1972—. Adult leader 4-H, Upland, 1987—; organizer, leader Upland Labor Day Charity Car Show, 1992—. Mem. NEA, Ind. Speech and Hearing Assn., Ind. State Tchrs. Assn., Mississinewa Tchrs. Assn. (pres., v.p., sec., treas.). Home: 4520 S 900 E Upland IN 46989-9791

KOOP, CHARLES EVERETT, surgeon, educator, former surgeon general; b. Bklyn., Oct. 14, 1916; s. John Everett and Helen (Apel) K.; m. Elizabeth Flanagan, Sept. 19, 1938; children: Allen van Benschoten, Norman Apel, David Charles Everett, Elizabeth. AB, Dartmouth Coll., 1937, DSc (hon.), 1989; MD, Cornell U., 1941; DSc in Medicine, U. Pa., 1947, DSc (hon.), 1990; LLD (hon.), Ea. Bapt. Coll., 1960, Phila. Coll. Osteo. Medicine, 1979, LaSalle Coll., 1983, Colby-Sawyer Coll., 1988, Princeton U., 1989, Hahnemann U., 1989, U. Miami, 1991, U. Cin., 1991; MD (hon.), U. Liverpool, Eng., 1968; LHD (hon.), Wheaton Coll., 1973, Phila. Theol. Sem., 1980, Chgo. Med. Sch., 1988, Brown U., 1990; DSc (hon.), Gwynedd Mercy Coll., 1978, Washington and Jefferson Coll., 1979, Marquette U., 1983, Ea. Mich. U., 1985, N.Y. Med. Coll., 1985, Ball State U., 1987, Kirskville Coll. Osteo. Med., 1988, Albany Med. Coll., 1988, Colby Coll., 1988, Yeshiva U., 1988, Phila. Coll. Pharmacy and Sci., 1988, Baylor Coll. Medicine, 1988, U. Mass., Boston, 1989, Brandeis U., 1990, Northwestern U., 1990, U. New England, 1991; D. Pub. Svc. (hon.), George Washington U., 1991; DPH, Cedar Crest Coll., 1995; D in Humanities, So. Utah U., 1997; LLD, Med. Coll. Pa., 1997. Diplomate Am. Bd. Surgery, Nat. Bd. Med. Examiners. Intern Pa. Hosp., Phila., 1941-42; fellow in surgery U. Pa. Hosp., Phila., 1942-47; fellow in pediat. surgery Children's Hosp., Boston, 1946; surgeon-in-chief Children's Hosp. of Phila., 1948-81; with U. Pa. Sch. Medicine, 1942-85, prof., 1959-85; former dep. asst. sec. for health HHS; surg. gen. of U.S., 1981-89; former dir. internat. health USPHS, from 1982; chair Safe Kids Nat. Campaign, Washington; dir. Elizabeth De Camp McInery prof. surgery C. Everett Koop Inst. Dartmouth-Hitchkock Med. Ctr., Hanover, N.H., 1993—; cons. USN, 1964-81; sr. scholar the C. Everett Koop Inst. at Dartmouth; dir. Ready to Learn Program Carnegie Found., 1993-95. Author: Visible and Palpable Lesions in Children, 1976, The Right to Live, The Right to Die, 1976, rev. edit., 1980, Smoking: The New Book of Knowledge, 1989; (with E. Koop) Sometimes Mountains Move, 1979; (with F. A. Schaeffer) Whatever Happened to the Human Race?, 1979, Koop: The Memoirs of America's Family Doctor, 1991, (with T. Johnson) Let's Talk, 1992; editor surgery sect. Jour. Clin. Pediatrics, 1961-64; mem. editorial bd. Zeitschrift fur Kinderchirurgie and Grenzgebiete, 1964-81; editor in chief: Jour. Pediatric Surgery, 1965-77; editorial cons. Japanese Jour. Pediatric Surgery and Medicine, 1970-81; chmn. editorial bd. PHS Reports, 1982-89; mem. editorial adv. bd. Tobacco Control: An Internat. Jour.; contbr. publs. in surg. physiology, biomed. ethics, physiology of surg. neonate, tech. advances in pediatric surgery. Bd. dirs. Med. Assistance Programs, Inc., Brunswick, Ga., Friends Nat. Libr. of Medicine, Nat. Health Mus. Inc. (pres.); bd. dirs., chmn. sci. adv. com. Biopure; chmn. Patient Med. Edn., 1993-96, Patient Med. Record, Inc., 1997—. Decorated chevalier Legion of Honor (France); Order Duarte, Sanchez and Mella (Dominican Republic); recipient medal City of Marseille, Presbyn. Man of Yr. award Presbyn. Social Union Phila., 1975, Super Achiever of Yr. award Phila. chpt. Juvenile Diabetes Found., 1975, Man of Yr. award Jewish Community Chaplaincy Svc. Phila., 1975, Copernicus medal Polish Surg. Soc., 1977, Gold medal Children's Hosp. Phila., 1981, Sec. of Health of Commonwealth of Pa. award, 1981, Thomas Linacre award Nat. Fedn. Cath. Physicians Guild, 1981, Key to City of St. Louis, 1985, Award of Distinction Alumni Assn. Cornell U. Med. Coll., 1988, Humanitarian Svc. award City of Boston, 1989, Harry S. Truman award City of Independence, Mo., 1990, Daniel Webster award Dartmouth Coll., 1990, John Wiley Jones Disting. Lectr. award Rochester Inst. Tech., 1990, NAS Public Welfare medal, 1990, Tyler prize U. So. Calif., 1991, Albert Schweitzer prize Johns Hopkins U., 1991, Person of Yr. award Nat. Hosp. Orgn., 1991, others; named Hon. Citizen, City of Balt., 1985; C. Everett Koop Hon. Lectr. medal named in his honor Anchor & Caduceus Soc., 1991, C. Everett Koop Health Adv. award named in his honor Am. Soc. for Health Care Mktg. and Pub. Rels, Gustav O. Lienhard award Inst. Medicine, 1992, Presdl. medal of Freedom, 1995, Heinz Found. award, 1995; Disting. scholar to Carnegie Found. for advancement of teaching. Fellow ACS, Am. Acad. Pediatrics (William E. Ladd Gold medal), Royal Coll. Surgeons Eng. (hon.), Royal Coll. Physicians and Surgeons of Glasgow (hon.); mem. AMA, Am. Surg. Assn., Royal Soc. Medicine, Soc. U. Surgeons, Brit. Assn. Pediatric Surgeons (Dennis Browne Gold medal), Internat. Soc. Surgery, Assn. Mil. Surgeons U.S. (pres. 1982, 87, Founders medal), Societé Française de Chirurgie Infantile, Deutschen Gesselschaft für Kinderchirugi, Societé Suisse De Chirurgie Infantile, Sigma Xi. Office: Dartmouth Coll Dartmouth-Hitchkock Med Ctr C Everett Koop Inst Hanover NH 03755

KOOPMAN, WILLIAM JAMES, medical educator, internist, immunologist; b. Lafayette, Ind., Aug. 19, 1945; s. William James and Barbara Mary (Morehouse) K.; m. Lilliane Kathryn Desimone, June 15, 1968; children: Benjamin, Anna, Rebecca, Steven. BA, Washington and Jefferson U., 1967; MD, Harvard U., 1972. Diplomate Am. Bd. Internal Medicine. Intern/resident in medicine Mass. Gen. Hosp., Boston, 1972-74; rsch. fellow NIH, Bethesda, Md., 1974-77; from asst. prof., assoc. prof. to prof. medicine specializing in rheumatology and clin. immunology U. Ala., Birmingham, 1977—, Howard L. Holley prof. medicine, 1988-95, dir. Multipurpose Arthritis Ctr., 1983-96; chmn. Dept. Medicine, 1995—; mem. nat. adv. coun. Nat. Inst. Arthritis, Musculo-skeletal and Skin Diseases, 1987-90; chmn. bd. sci. counselors, NIH, NIAMS, 1991-95. Editor: Arthritis and Rheumatism jour., 1985-90, Arthritis and Allied Conditions, 13th ed.; contbr. more than 250 articles to profl. jours. Recipient Carol Nachman Rsch. prize Fed. Republic Germany, 1982. Fellow ACP (master), Am. Coll. Rheumatology (pres. Southeastern region 1986-87, treas. 1992-94, 2nd v.p. 1994-95, pres.-elect 1995-96, pres. 1996-97); mem. ACP (master), Am. Soc. Clin. Investigation (pres. 1990-91), Assn. Am. Physicians, Am. Assn. Immunologists, Inst. of Medicine, Birmingham Area C. of C. Presbyterian. Avocations: fishing, gardening. Office: U Ala Sch Medicine DERB 1808 7th Ave S # Bdb420 Birmingham AL 35233-1912

KOOPMANN, GARY HUGO, educational center administrator, mechanical engineering educator; b. Howells, Nebr., May 8, 1939; s. Hugo Martin and Elsie (Hledik) K.; m. Barbara Bogue, May 26, 1972; children: Hannah, Eve. BS, U. Nebr., 1962; MS, Cath. U., 1966, PhD, 1969. Cert. engr., Tex. Rsch. scientist U.S. Naval Rsch. Lab., Washington, 1962-66; postdoctoral fellow Inst. Sound and Vibration, Southampton, Eng., 1969-70, univ. lectr., 1970-76; prof. U. Houston, 1976-87; dir. Ctr. Acoustics & Vibrations Pa. State U., State Coll., 1988—, prof. mechanical engring., 1988—; vis. prof. DFVLR, Berlin, 1982-83. Patentee noise reduction system, TRC suspension sim. Fellow Am. Soc. Mechanical Engrs. (editor jour.), Acoustical Soc. Am. Quaker. Avocation: music. Office: Pa State U Ctr Acoustics & Vibration 157 Hammond Bldg University Park PA 16802-1400*

KOPAC, ANDREW JOSEPH, manufacturing executive; b. Hackensack, N.J., May 21, 1947; s. Andrew S. and Mary C. (Spacek) K.; m. Patricia Ann Leoniy, June 7, 1970; children: Andrew, Jeffrey. BA, Rutgers U., New Brunswick, 1969; AAS in Mgmt., Middlesex County Coll., Woodbridge, 1981, AAS in Mktg., 1982. Quality control supr. Delco-Remy, New Brunswick, N. J., 1972-74, gen. foreman quality control, 1974-76; quality engr. Delco-Remy div. Gen. Motors, New Brunswick, 1976-81, gen. supr. mfg., 1988-90; supt. quality control Delco-Remy div. Gen. Motors, Fitzgerald, Ga., 1983-85; supt. quality control Delco-Remy div. Gen. Motors, Kans., 1985-86, supt. material control, 1991-93; pers. dir. Delco-Remy/Delphi Energy and Engine Mgmt. Systems, 1993—. With U.S.Army 1969-71. Decorated Bronze Star medal; recipient Frank M. Chambers award, Middlesex County Coll., 1981-82. Mem. Am. Legion, VFW. Roman Catholic. Avocations: coaching, youth soccer, coaching youth baseball, golf, gardening. Home: 12209 Haskins St Overland Park KS 66213-4835

KOPEC, JOHN WILLIAM, research scientist; b. Chgo., Nov. 5, 1936; s. John Frank and Marie Eva (Wreshnig) K.; m. Jean Elois Prather, Dec. 28, 1958 (div. June 1977); children: Brian More, Vaune Estra. AA, Chgo. City Coll., 1974; student, Ill. Inst. Tech., Chgo., 1974-80. Systems analyst Motorola, Chgo., 1959-61; asst. exptl. engr. Ill. Inst. Tech. Rsch. Inst., Chgo., 1961-68, extpl. engr., 1968-74; lisison engr. Ill. Inst. Tech. Rsch. Inst., Chgo. and Geneva, Ill., 1974-81; supr. Riverbank Acoustical Labs., Ill. Inst. Tech. Rsch. inst., Chgo. and Geneva, Ill., 1986-94, lab. mgr., 1994—; ret. Riverbank Acoustical Labs., Ill. Inst. Tech. Rsch. inst., Chgo. and Geneva, 1998. Author: The Sabines at Riverbank, 1997; contbr. articles to Jour. Acoustical Soc. Am.; paper reviewer, contbr. articles Internat. Noise Control Engrs. With USAF, 1955-59. Fellow Acoustical Soc. Am. (chmn. archives and history 1992-94, sec. tech. com. 1991-94, mus. curator 1985-98); mem. ASTM (chmn. awards com., sec. E 33.01 1980-98 , appreciation award 1994), N.Y. Acad. Scis., Soc. Automotive Engrs. (task group, paper reviewer), Can. Acoustical Soc. Achievements include one of first smokeless fires for firefighters of U.S. Navy and U.S. Air Force; one of first to discover ionization of turbulent flow in a hypersonic wind tunnel; discovered Wallace Clement Sabine files previously thought destroyed; developed one of first rapid transit speech noise floor's, also an industrial colored noise floor map. Home: 5206 S Lotus Ave Chicago IL 60638-1632

KOPEL, DAVID BENJAMIN, lawyer; b. Denver; s. Gerald Henry and Dolores B. Kopel; m. Deirdre Frances Dolan, Apr. 5, 1987. BA in History, Brown U., 1982; JD, U. Mich., 1985. Bar: Colo. 1986, N.Y. 1986, U.S. Dist. Ct. (ea. and so. dists.) N.Y. 1986, U.S. Ct. Appeals (2d cir.) 1986, U.S. Dist. Ct. Colo. 1988, U.S. Ct. Appeals (10th cir.) 1988, U.S. Supreme Ct., 1991,

U.S. Ct. Appeals (D.C. cir.) 1997. Assoc. Sullivan & Cromwell, N.Y.C., 1985-86; asst. dist. atty. Manhattan Dist. Atty., N.Y.C., 1986-88; asst. atty. gen. Colo. State Atty. Gen., Denver, 1988-92; rsch. dir. Independence Inst., Golden, Colo., 1992—. Mem. Order of Coif. Democrat. Avocations: skiing, ham radio.. Office: Independence Inst Ste 185 14142 Denver West Pkwy Golden CO 80401-3119

KOPELMAN, JOSHUA MARC, information company executive; b. Boston, Apr. 17, 1971; s. Richard Eric and Carol Fran (Fialkov) K.; m. Rena Marcy Cohen, Aug. 13, 1995. BS in Econs., U. Pa., 1993. Analyst PolyVentures, Farmingdale, N.Y., 1990-91; bus. devel. assoc. Telebase Systems, Wayne, Pa., 1991-92; exec. v.p., co-founder Infonautics Corp., Wayne, Pa., 1992—. Home: 921 Honeysuckle Ln Wynnewood PA 19096-1649 Office: Infonautics Corp 900 W Valley Rd Ste 1000 Wayne PA 19087-6884

KOPELMAN, LEONARD, lawyer; b. Cambridge, Mass., Aug. 2, 1940; s. Irving and Frances Estelle (Robbins) K.; m. Carol Hunsberger. B.A. cum laude, Harvard U., 1962, J.D., 1965. Bar: Mass. 1966. Assoc. Warner & Stackpole, Boston, 1965-73; sr. ptnr. Kopelman and Paige, Boston, 1974—; lectr. Harvard U., 1965—; permanent master Mass. Superior Ct., 1971—; hon. consul gen. of, Finland, Mass., 1975—; U.S. del. Soc. for Internat. Devel.; Chmn. Mass. Jud. Selection Com. for the Fed. Judiciary, 1971—; chief counsel AAUP. Trustee Cathedral of the Pines, 1972; pres. Hillel Found. of Cambridge, Inc., 1973—; trustee Faulkner Hosp., 1974—, Parker Hill Med. Ctr., 1976—; dir. gen. Consular Corps Coll. NEH grantee, 1975. Mem. ABA (exec. coun. 1969—), Mass. Bar Assn. (chmn. mcpl. law sect.), Am. Judges Assn., Mass. C. of C. (pres. 1974-77), Harvard Faculty Club, Algonquin Club (pres.), Harvard Club, Union Club, Hasty Pudding Club, St. Botolph Club. Home: 33 Yarmouth Rd Chestnut Hill MA 02467-2815 Office: Kopelman and Paige 31 St James Ave Boston MA 02116-4101

KOPELMAN, RICHARD ERIC, management educator; b. N.Y.C., May 31, 1943; s. Seymour H. and Leona L. (Quint) K.; m. Carol Fialkov, June 7, 1970; children: Joshua Marc, Michael Adam. BS, U. Pa., 1965, MBA, 1967; DBA, Harvard U., 1974. Instr. bus. C.C. Phila., 1967-69; instr. mgmt. Baruch Coll./CUNY, N.Y.C., 1973-74, asst. prof., 1974-77, assoc. prof., 1978-80, prof., 1981—; cons. in field; corp. dir. Aleph Null Corp., 1979-88, Applied Photonics, Inc., 1986-91, Infodex Sys., Inc., 1986-88, EMS Devel. Corp., 1992-96; pres. Cube One, Inc., 1998—; acad. dir. MS in Indsl. Rels. program Baruch/Cornell U., 1985-97, acad. co-dir. Baruch exec. MS in Indsl. Rels. program, 1994—. Author: The Management of Productivity: A Practical People-Oriented Perspective, 1986; mem. editl. rev. bd. Jour. Social Behavior and Personality, 1985-89, Nat. Productivity Rev., Jour. Orgnl. Behavior Mgmt., Perceptions, 1991-94, Jour. Psychology, 1999—; contbr. numerous articles to profl. and acad. jours. Bd. dirs. Day Care Council, Nassau County, 1979-82; Nassau Symphony Orch., 1984-85. Recipient Teaching award Baruch Coll., 1987, Teaching Excellence award, 1989, 91, 92, 93; William B. Harding fellow Harvard U. Mem. APA, Acad. Mgmt., Decision Scis. Inst., Soc. for Human Resource Mgmt. (accredited pers. diplomate, sr. profl. in human resources), Am. Compensation Assn., Met. N.Y. Assn. for Applied Psychology (sec. 1986-87, treas. 1987-88, v.p. 1988-89, pres. 1989-90), Sigma Iota Epsilon. E-mail: rekopelman@managingperformance.com. Home: 65 Colgate Rd Great Neck NY 11023-1501 Office: Baruch Coll Zicklin Sch Bus/Dept Mgmt 17 Lexington Ave New York NY 10010-5518

KOPELSON, ARNOLD, film producer; b. New York, NY, Feb. 14, 1935. B.S., N.Y.U.; J.D., N.Y. Law Sch., 1959. Prodr. (film) Foolin' Around, 1980, Platoon, 1986 (Acad. awd Best Picture), Triumph of the Spirit, 1989, Out for Justice, 1991, Falling Down, 1993, The Fugitive, 1993 (Acad. award nom Best Picture), Outbreak, 1995, Seven, 1995, Eraser, 1996, Murder at 1600, 1997, Mad City, 1997, The Devil's Advocate, 1997, U.S. Marshals, 1998; exec. prodr. (film) Lost and Found, 1979, The Legacy, 1979, Night of the Juggler, 1980, Final Assignment, 1980, Dirty Tricks, 1981, Model Behavior, 1984, Warlock, 1989, Fire Birds, 1990. *

KOPEN, DAN FRANCIS, surgeon, consultant; b. Kingston, Pa., Aug. 14, 1948; s. Francis and Maryann (Kumiega) K.; m. Kathleen Elizabeth Roberts; children: Krystin, Derek, Kaytlin. BS in Chemistry, Wilkes Coll., 1970; MD, Milton S. Hershey Med. Ctr., 1974. Diplomate Am. Bd. Surgery. Resident in surgery Washington U., St. Louis, 1975-80, fellow in surgery, 1976-77; clin. asst. in surgery Washington U. Sch. Medicine, St. Louis, 1980-82; staff surgeon Wyoming Valley Health Care System, Kingston, Pa., 1984—; pres. Northeastern Surg. Group, Kingston, 1986—, AIDS Awareness Com. of Luzerne County, 1990—. Pub. Padakami Press, 1991—; contbr. articles to profl. jours. Bd. mem. Am. Cancer Soc., Wyoming Valley, Pa., 1985—, Wilkes Coll., Wilkes-Barre, 1987—, United Way Wyoming Valley, 1994—, N.E. Pa. ARC, 1996—; physicians com. United Way of Wyoming Valley, 1988. Fellow ACS, Am. Soc. Abdominal Surgeons, Am. Soc. Breast Surgeons; mem. AMA, Pa. Med. Soc., Am. Burn Assn., Am. Chem. Soc., Pa. Coun. for Humanities, Luzerne County Med. Soc. (bd. dirs. 1989—, v.p. 1999), Harrel Soc. of Milton S. Hershey Med. Ctr. of Pa. State U., Milton S. Hershey Med. Ctr. of Pa. State U. Alumni Assn. (bd. dirs. 1991—, pres. 1998-99), bd. visitors, Milton S. Hershey Med. Ctr., 1999—, Am. Chemistry Soc. (div. medicinal chemistry). Roman Catholic. Avocations: reading, jogging. Office: 534 Wyoming Ave Kingston PA 18704-3742

KOPENHAVER, LILLIAN LODGE, journalism educator; b. Linden, N.J., Jan. 25, 1941; d. Thomas J. and Angela T. (Wolczanski) Lodge; m. David Arthur Kopenhaver. BA, Glassboro (N.J.) State Coll., 1962; MA, U. Wis., 1967; EdD, Nova U., 1980. Cert. English and journalism tchr., N.J., Fla. Tchr. English and journalism Brick Twp. High Sch., Bricktown, N.J., 1962-67; asst. prof. humanities Ocean County Coll., Toms River, N.J., 1967-71; asst. prof. journalism Miami-Dade Community Coll., Fla., 1971-73; dir. student activities Fla. Internat. U., Miami, 1971-73, asst. v.p. student affairs, 1976-78, dir. pub. relations, 1978-81, assoc. dean, prof. sch. Journalism/Mass Comm., 1981—; corp. bd. Student Press Law Ctr., 1976—; reporter, editor Ocean County Daily Observer, Toms River, 1962-68; pres. Student Press Law Ctr., Washington, 1987-89; cons. in field. Author: (with J. W. Click) College Media Advising: Ethics and Responsibilities, 3d edit., 1993; contbr. articles on pub. rels. and press law to profl. jours. Recipient Gold Key award Columbia Scholastic Press Assn., 1980, Pioneer award Nat. Scholastic Press Assn., 1983, Gold Medallion award Fla. Scholastic Press Assn., 1986, Fla. Internat. U. Outstanding Faculty Svc. award,1996 ; named to C.C. Journalism Assn. Hall of Fame, 1994. Mem. Coll. Media Advisers (pres. 1975-79, dir. Spring Coll. Media Conv., N.Y. 1983—, Disting. Svc. award 1987, Svc. Achievement award 1989, Hall of Fame 1994), Soc. Profl. Journalists (chmn. profl. devel. com. 1983-94, chmn. internat. journalism com. 1994-98, Outstanding Svc. award 1986, Wells Meml. Key 1987), Assn. Edn. Journalism and Mass Comm. (pres.elect 1997-98, pres. 1998-99 chmn. coun. affiliates 1987-88, chair adv. bd. 1988-89, chair newspaper divsn. 1991-92, chair pubs. com. 1992-95, vice-chair teaching standards com. 1992-93, chair membership com. 1995-96, Disting. Svc. award 1990, others), Pub. Rels. Soc. Am., Women in Comm., Inc., Greater Miami Soc. Profl. Journalists (bd. dirs. 1981-94), Miami Internat. Press Club (founding bd. mem. 1986-88). Home: 2642 Nassau Dr Miramar FL 33023-4625 Office: Fla Internat U Sch Journalism/Mass Comm North Miami FL 33181

KOPENHAVER, PATRICIA ELLSWORTH, podiatrist. Student, Columbia U., 1950-53; BA, George Washington U., 1954; MA, Columbia U., 1956; Dr. Podiatric Medicine, N.Y. Coll. Podiatric Medicine, 1963, postgrad., 1980; LLD (hon.), Barry U., 1998. Diplomate Nat. Bd. Podiatry Examiners. Pvt. practice podiatry Greenwich, Conn., 1964—; mem. staff Laurelton Convalescent Hosp., Greenwich; trustee N.Y. Coll. Podiatric Medicine, 1998. Bd. dirs. Monmouth Opera Guild, 1965; trustee Monmouth Opera Festival, 1966, v.p., 1964; mem. Greenwich Arts Coun.; program chmn. Greenwich Women's Rep. Club, 1983-84, 4th dist. rep., 1984-85, 87—; trustee N.Y. Coll. Podiatric Medicine, 1998—. Recipient Hosp. Fund award for med. research translations ARC, Alumni award of distinction N.Y. Coll. Podiatric Medicine, 1997; scholarship named in her honor N.Y. Coll. Podiatric Medicine, 1997. Mem. AAUW (v.p. 1991, pres. Greenwich br. 1992-94, bd. dirs. 1996), NOW, Conn. Podiatric Med. Assn., Hist. Soc., Asian Soc., Fairfield Podiatry Assn., Am. Assn. Women Podiatrists (charter pres. 1969-78), Acad. Podiatry, Am. Podiatry Coun., UN Assn. U.S.A., Acad. Podiatric Medicine (chmn. nominating com. 1981, 1st v.p. 1983-84, chmn. fundraising 1984-85, chmn. women's issues 1985, chmn. cmty. edn. 1989), Am. Acad. Sports Medicine, Am. Acad. Podiatric Sports Medicine (assoc. 1989), George Washington U. Alumni Assn., Columbia Alumni Assn., Fairfield County Alumni Assn. Columbia U., Coast Soc. of Founders Barry U. (treas. 1998), Nat. Fedn. Rep. Women, Bruce Mus., Nature Conservancy, Federated Garden Clubs Conn., St. Mary Ladies Guild, Greenwich Gardeners, Womans' Club (ways and means com. 1989, pres.), English Speaking Union, Soroptimists Internat. Am. (pres. Greenwich br. 1990—, bd. dirs. 1997-98), Inc. (vice chmn. program com. 1985—, regional med. scholarship chmn. 1987, med. scholarship chmn. N.E. region 1988, program dir. 1988—, pres. Greenwich br. 1990-92), Toastmasters, Travel Club (program com. 1984—), Soroptimist (bd. dirs. 1997—), Pi Epsilon Chi. Home: 2 Sutton Pl S New York NY 10022-3070 Office: 8 Dearfield Dr Greenwich CT 06831-5348

KOPF, GEORGE MICHAEL, ophthalmologist; b. Chilton, Wis., Oct. 20, 1935; s. George and Mary (Schmid) K.; m. Sandra Mary Nolte, Dec. 29, 1962; children: Karen, Jennifer, Nancy. B.S., U. Wis.-Madison, 1958, M.D., 1961. Diplomate Am. Bd. Ophthalmology. Intern Luther Hosp., Eau Claire, Wis., 1961-62; resident in surgery Milw. County Hosp., 1962-63; resident in ophthalmology Detroit Gen. Hosp., 1965-68; practice medicine specializing in ophthalmology, Zanesville, Ohio, 1968—; mem. med. staff Bethesda Hosp., Zanesville; mem. med. Staff Good Samaritan Med. Ctr., Zanesville, pres., 1978, sec. bd. dirs., 1986-96. Served to capt. USAF, 1963-65. Fellow Am. Acad. Ophthalmology, ACS; mem. Ohio Ophthal. Soc. (pres. 1976-77), Muskingum County Acad. Medicine (pres. 1983), Ohio State Med. Assn. Republican. Roman Catholic. Lodges: Elks, Rotary, Avocations: tennis, swimming, hiking, reading, travel. Home: 2950 Ash Meadows Blvd Zanesville OH 43701-9081 Office: Ophthalmologists Inc 2315 Maple Ave Zanesville OH 43701-2028

KOPF, RANDI, family/oncology nurse practitioner, lawyer; b. Jersey City, Mar. 30, 1953; d. Soloman and Sydell Kopf. BS, Cornell U., 1975, SUNY, Stony Brook, 1978; MS, SUNY, Stony Brook, 1978; JD, U. Md., Balt., 1989. Bar: Md., 1989, D.C., 1991; cert. family nurse practitioner. Pvt. practitioner allergy and dermatology, 1982-83, pvt. cons. practice as oncology nurse practitioner; legal intern Office of Gen. Counsel, NIH, 1988; legal assoc., health svcs. group Nixon, Hargrave, Devans & Doyle, Washington, 1990-93; prin. atty., founder Kopf HealthLaw Group, Bethesda, Md., 1995; pvt. law practice, 1995—; lectr., cons. Am. Cancer Soc.; mem. faculty Georgetown U., U. Md., Adelphi U.; nat. lectr. on med. legal topics. Author: Handbook of Nursing Physical Assesment, 1987, Before You Sign...Managed Care Contract Review for Health Care Providers, 1996; editor, contbg. author Jour. Nursing Law, 1993—; contbr. articles to nat. profl. jours. Recipient Alumni award for Outstanding Volunteerism, Cornell U., 1998. Mem. D.C. Bar Assn., Md. Bar Assn., Am. Hosp. Atty. Assn., Chesapeake Nurse Atty. Assn. (pres., bd. dirs.), Am. Health Lawyers Assn.

KOPF, RICHARD G., federal judge; b. 1946. BA, U. Nebr., Kearney, 1969; JD, U. Nebr., Lincoln, 1972. Law clk. to Hon. Donald R. Ross U.S. Ct. Appeals (8th cir.), 1972-74; ptnr. Cook, Kopf & Doyle, Lexington, Neb., 1974-87; U.S. magistrate judge, 1987-92; fed. judge U.S. Dist. Ct. (Nebr. dist.), 1992—. Mem. ABA, ABA Found., Nebr. State Bar, Nebr. State Bar Found. Office: US Dist Ct 586 US Courthouse 100 Centennial Mall N Lincoln NE 68508-3859

KOPIDAKIS, EMMANUEL G., general surgeon; b. Iraklion, Crete, Greece, Apr. 15, 1931; s. George and Victoria K.; m. Marianna; children: George, Thomas. MD, Athens U. Med. Sch., 1956. Diplomate Am. Bd. Surgery. Dir. surgery Evangelismos Hosp., Iraklion, 1965-68; surgeon John F. Kennedy Med. Ctr., Edison, N.Y., 1968—. Med. officer Greek Army, 1957-59. Avocation: painting. Office: Kopidakis and Kopidakis 98 James St Ste 101 Edison NJ 08820-3903*

KOPIS, F. JAN, real estate broker; b. Chgo., Dec. 21, 1942; s. Frank John and Marie Melvina (Herrmann) K.; m. Carol Ann Brune, June 1, 1965 (div. May, 1976); children: Kelly Sue, Casey Marie; m. Lois Jean Whermann, June, 1978. BA, U. Dayton, 1964. Lic. real estate broker; cert. residential specialist, Grad. Realtor Inst. Exec. tng. Marshall Field & Co., Oak Brook, Ill., 1964-67; mgr., owner The Music Shop, Downers Grove, Ill., 1967-78; real estate broker Re/Max Enterprises, Downers Grove, 1978—. Commr., pres. dist. of Downers Grove Park, Ill., 1975-85; councilman Village of Downers Grove, 1985-93. Recipient Gold medal Nat. Sports Found., 1984; named Citizen of the Yr., Village of Downers Grove, 1993. Mem. Downers Grove C. of C. (chmn. bd. dirs. 1996—), C. of C. Ambs. (past chmn.), Argonne Nat. Lab. Regional Consortium (village liaison 1986-92), Lions (past pres.). Avocation: tennis.

KOPLAN, JEFFREY POWELL, physician; b. Boston, Jan. 3, 1945; s. Samuel R. and Kate G. K.; m. Carol R. Bassuk, May 18, 1969; children—Adam, Kate. B.A., Yale Coll., 1966; postgrad., Tufts U., 1966-68; M.D., Mount Sinai Sch. Medicine, N.Y.C., 1970; M.P.H., Harvard U., 1978. Diplomate Am. Bd. Internal Medicine, Am. Bd. Preventive Medicine. Intern, resident Montefiore Hosp. and Med. Ctr., Bronx, N.Y., 1970-72; epidemic intelligence service officer Ctr. for Disease Control, Atlanta, 1972-74, med. officer Office of Program Planning, 1978-82, asst. dir. pub. health practice, 1982-88; dir. Nat. Ctr. Chronic Disease Prevention and Health Promotion, Atlanta, 1989-94; asst. surgeon gen., 1989-94; exec. v.p., dir. Prudential Ctr. for Health Care Rsch., Atlanta, 1994-95; pres., 1995-98; vis. prof. community health Emory U., 1986—; resident Stanford U. Hosp, Calif., 1974-75; med. epidemiologist Calif. State Dept. Health, Berkeley, 1975, Caribbean Epidemiology Ctr., Port of Spain, Trinidad, 1975-77; dir. Ctrs. for Disease Control and Prevention, Atlanta, 1998—; cons. World Bank, Washington, AID, Washington. Contbr. articles to profl. jours. With USPHS, 1970-94. Recipient Order of Bifurcated Needle WHO, 1979; Saul Horowitz award Mt. Sinai Sch. Medicine, 1983; Commendation medal USPHS, 1984. Fellow ACP, Am. Coll. Epidemiology; mem. Assn. Tchrs. Preventive Medicine, Am. Pub. Health Assn., Soc. Med. Decision Making. Office: Prudential Ctr Health Care Rsch 8th Fl 2859 Paces Ferry Rd NW Fl 8 Atlanta GA 30339-5701

KOPLEWICZ, HAROLD SAMUEL, child and adolescent psychiatrist; b. Bklyn., Jan. 12, 1953; s. Joseph and Romana (Magid) K.; m. Linda Jane Sirow, June 22, 1980; children: Joshua, Adam, Sam. BS, U. Md., 1973; MD, Albert Einstein Coll. of Medicine, 1978. Diplomate Am. Bd. Psychiatry and Neurology, Am. Bd. Child Psychiatry. Med. dir. preschool hyperactivity program N.Y. State Psychiat. Inst., N.Y.C., 1982-85, med. dir. children's anxiety clinic, 1983-86; dir. gen. residency tng. child psychiatry Columbia Coll. Physicians and Surgeons, N.Y.C., 1985-86; chief divsn. child and adolescent psychiatry Schneider Children's Hosp. and Hillside Hosp. of L.I. Jewish Med. Ctr., N.Y.C., 1986-96; editor Youth Mental Health Update, 1989-96; assoc. prof. psychiatry Albert Einstein Coll. Medicine, N.Y.C., 1991-96; prof. clin. psychiatry and pediatrics, vice chmn. psychiatry NYU Sch. Medicine, 1996—; dir. child and adolescent divsn. NYU Med. Ctr./Bellevue Hosp. Ctr., N.Y.C., 1996—; dir. NYU Child Study Ctr. NYU Sch. Medicine, N.Y.C., 1997—; cons. Riverdale Cmty. Ctr., 1981-86, The Dalton Sch., 1991-96, The N.Y. Infirmary, 1991, The Family Acad., 1991-96, Jewish Child Care Assn., 1992-96, Health Edn. Task Force, Roslyn Sch. Dist., 1993-96; dir. Nat. Child Mental Health Inst., 1999. Author: It's Nobody's Fault: New Hope and Help for Difficult Children and Their Parents, 1996; editor NYU Child Study Ctr. Letter, 1996—; editor-in-chief: Jour. Child and Adolescent Psychopharmacology, 1998—; editor: Childhood Revealed: Art Expressing Pain, Discovery, and Hope; mem. adv. bd. Parents Mag., 1996—. Bd. dirs. Raoul Wallenberg New Leadership Soc., 1983-87, Cmty. Mainstreaming Assocs., 1990; chmn. Simon Wiesenthal Ctr., 1984-86; commr. N.Y. State Commn. for Study of Youth Crime and Violence and Reform of the Juvenile Justice Sys., 1993-96; prin. investigator Developing Innovative Mental Health Care Delivery for Adolescents, Hewlett-Woodmere Sch. Dist., 1992; adv. bd. Our Children's Found., 1996-97. Recipient award Lowenstein Found., 1986, Hulse award N.Y. Coun. Child and Adolescent Psychiatry, 1995, Exemplary Psychiatrist award Nat. Alliance Mentally Ill., 1997,. Fellow Am. Acad. Child and Adolescent Psychiatry (Reiger award 1997), Am. Psychiat. Assn.; mem. Soc. Profs. Child and Adolescent Psychiatry, Am. Bd. Psychiatry and Neurology (examiner 1988-98), Nat. Bd. Med. Examiners (mem. psychiatry com. 1993-96), Nat. Found. Depressive Illness (nat. bd. dirs. 1992—), Mental Health Assn. of N.Y. (profl. adv. bd.). Fax: 212-263-0484. E-mail: harold.koplewicz@med.nyu.edu. Office: NYU Child Study Ctr (NB21E7) 550 1st Ave New York NY 10016-6481

KOPLIK, MICHAEL R., durable goods company executive. Sales manager Castle & Overton Inc., N.Y.C., 1957-1960; dir., v.p. Perry H. Koplik & Sons Inc., N.Y.C., 1960-78, pres., CEO, 1978—. Office: Perry H Koplik & Sons Inc 505 Park Ave New York NY 10022-1106*

KOPLIK, PERRY H., durable goods company executive. Exec. v.p. Castle & Overton Inc., N.Y.C., 1932-1960; prin. Perry H. Koplik & Sons Inc., N.Y.C., 1960—, chmn. Office: Perry H Koplik & Sons Inc 505 Park Ave New York NY 10022-1106*

KOPLIN, DONALD LEROY, health products executive, consumer advocate; b. Greenleaf, Kans., Dec. 31, 1932; s. Henry G. Koplin and Edith Mary Stevens; m. Patricia Joynes, June 2, 1962 (div. Aug. 1974); children: Marie Claire, Marie Joelle (adopted); m. Joan Freudenthal, June 28, 1997. Student, U. San Diego, 1956-59, 67-68. Electronics test insp. Gen. Dynamics, San Diego, 1956-59; cryptographer Dept. of State, Washington, 1959-67; communications program officer Dept. of State, France, Angola, Madagascar, Qatar, India, Oman, Benin and the Bahamas, 1977-86; tech. writer Ryan Aero. Corp., San Diego, 1967-68; comml. dir., tech. advisor, pub. rels. officer Societe AGM, San Francisco, Athens, Greece, Antananarivo and Morondava, Dem. Republic of Madagascar, 1968-72; founder, dir. Soc. Bells, Cyclone & Akai, Antananarivo, 1972-74; founder, ptnr., assoc. editor Angola Report, Luanda, 1974-75; polit. reporter Angola Report, Reuters, AP, UPI Corr., BBC, Luanda; supr. Tex. Instruments, Lubbock, 1976-77; exec. Dial A Contact Lens, Inc., La Jolla, Calif., 1986-90, Assn. for Retarded Citizens, San Diego, 1991-92, Club Med, Copper Mountain, Colo., 1992-94; CEO Vient Inc., 1994-97, Koplin Kollection Fine Arts Gallery, La Jolla, Calif., 1996-98. Active San Diego Zool. Soc. With USN, 1951-55, Korea. Mem. Am. Fgn. Svc. Assn. Republican. Roman Catholic. Avocation: writing. Home: 6718 Evergreen Ave Oakland CA 94611-1518

KOPLINSKI, SARAH E. PRUITT, college development director; b. Canton, Ill., Dec. 4, 1972; m. Trent Koplinski. BA in Pub. Adminstrn./Polit. Sci., Blackburn Coll., 1995. Mktg. coord. Jr. Achievement, Indpls., 1995-96; devel. officer Blackburn Coll., Carlinville, Ill., 1996-98, dir. devel., 1998—. Mem. Jr. C. of C. (sec. 1997—). Roman Catholic. Avocations: running, reading. Office: Blackburn Coll 700 College Ave Carlinville IL 62626-1454

KOPLOVITZ, KAY, communication network executive; b. Milw., Apr. 11, 1945; d. William E. and Jane T. Smith; m. William C. Koplovitz Jr., Apr. 17, 1971. BS, U. Wis., 1967; MA in Communications, Mich. State U., 1968. Radio and TV producer, dir. Sta. WTMJ-TV, Milw., 1967; editor Communications Satellite Corp., Washington, 1968-72; dir. community services UA Columbia Cablevision, Oakland, N.J., 1973-75; v.p., exec. dir. UA Columbia Satellite Services Inc., Oakland, 1977-80; founder, chmn., ceo USA Networks and Sci-Fi Channel, N.Y.C., 1980-98; CEO Koplovitz & Co., N.Y.C., 1998—. Mem. bd. overseers NYU Grad. Sch. Bus., 1984-87; bd. dirs. Nat. Jr. Achievement, 1986—. Recipient Outstanding Alumnus award Mich. State U. Grad. Sch. Bus., 1985, Outstanding Corp. Social Responsibility CUNY, 1986, Women Who Run the World award Sara Lee Corp., 1987, Muse award N.Y. Women in Film and TV, 1992, Ellis Island medal of honor, 1993, Crystal award Women in Film, 1993; named to Broadcasting Mag. Hall of Fame, 1992. Mem. Nat. Cable TV Assn. (bd. dirs. 1984—), Advt. Coun. Inc. (chmn. 1992-93, bd. dirs. 1985—), Internat. Coun., Nat. Acad. TV Arts and Scis. (chmn. 1994-95, bd. dirs. 1984-93), Women in Cable (founding bd. dirs., membership chmn. 1979-80, v.p. 1981-82, pres. 1982-83), Cable Advt. Bur. (bd. dirs., exec. com., treas. 1981-87, Chmn.'s award for leadership 1987), Nat. Acad. Cable Programming (bd. dirs. 1984-87), Com. of 200, Womens Forum, N.Y.C. Partnership (bd. dirs. 1987—). Avocations: tennis, skiing, travel. Office: Kpolovitz & Co Rm 515-w 237 Park Ave Ste 2100 New York NY 10017*

KOPP, CHARLES GILBERT, lawyer; b. Hartford, Conn., Jan. 10, 1933; s. Henry and Grace (Goldberg) K.; m. Ann Weiss, June 10, 1962 (div. 1963). BA, Amherst Coll., 1955; JD, U. Pa., 1960. Bar: Pa. 1961. Sr. counsel Wolf, Block, Schorr and Solis-Cohen, Phila., 1960—. Contbr. articles to profl. jours. Commr. Delaware River Port Authority, 1986-87; co-chmn. select com. of U.S. Embassy, Bern, Switzerland, 1985; mem. Pa. Gov.'s Spl. Tax Commn., 1980; bd. dirs. Pennsylvanians for Effective Govt., Harrisburg, 1987; mem. Pa. Electoral Coll., 1988; mem. adv. bd. region I, Resolution Trust Corp., 1990-93; mem. coun. The Pa. Soc.; bd. dirs Thomas Jefferson U. Hosp.; mem. adv. bd. PNC, Phila. 1st lt. USAF, 1955-57. Recipient Pop Warner Gold Football award, 1988. Mem. ABA, Pa. Bar Assn., Phila. Bar Assn., The Union League of Phila., Philmont Country Club (Huntingdon Valley, Pa., pres. 1976-78), Pyramid Club. Republican. Jewish. Home: 210 W Rittenhouse Sq Apt 3306 Philadelphia PA 19103-5780 Office: Wolf Block Schorr and Solis-Cohen SE Corner 15 And Chestnut T Philadelphia PA 19122

KOPP, DAVID EUGENE, manufacturing company executive; b. St. Louis, Apr. 21, 1951; s. Doyle Eugene and Irene Audrey (Gloyeske) K. BA in English, U. South Fla., 1975. Supr. Titleist Golf Co., Escondido, Calif., 1979-80; supr. Imed Corp., San Diego, 1980-82, process engr., 1982-83, sr. process engr., 1983-85; area mgr. Husky Injection Molding Systems Inc., Newport Beach, Calif., 1985-91; dir. sales Tech C.B.I. Inc., Scottsdale, Ariz., 1991-93; exec. v.p. Top-Seal Corp., Phoenix, 1993-97, v.p., gen. mgr., 1997—. Mem. Soc. Plastic Engrs. (affiliate, bd. dirs., student liaison person Canoga Park, 1985-87). Republican. Roman Catholic. Avocations: golf, music, sports, running, tennis. Home: 9980 N 106th St Scottsdale AZ 85258-9203 Office: Top-Seal Corp 2236 E University Dr Phoenix AZ 85034-6805

KOPP, DEBRA LYNN, manufacturing engineer, consultant; b. Bunker Hill AFB, Ind., Aug. 24, 1964; d. Dennis Frank and Elaine Mary (Mayer) Mathis; m. Bruce Alan Kopp, Sept. 28, 1964 (div. 1993). BS in Indsl. Engring., Ariz. State U., 1986; MS in Indsl. Engring., Stanford U., 1989. Cert. Am. Prodn. and Inventory Control Soc. Mfg. engr. Amdahl Corp., Sunnyvale, Calif., 1986-90; engr. Applied Physics Lab., Johns Hopkins U., Laurel, Md., 1991-93; prin. mem. technical staff Amecom dvsn. Litton Systems, Inc., College Park, Md., 1993; cons., assoc. Synergistek Assocs., Round Lake Beach, Ill., 1992; cons., co-founder, pres. ITM, Inc., Durham, N.H., 1993-96; strategic bus. mgr. Dell Computer Corp., Austin, Tex., 1996—. Contbr. articles to conf. procs. Mem. Inst. Indsl. Engrs. (sr.), Surface Mount Tech. Assn. (arrangements chmn. Capital chpt. 1992, v.p. 1993, pres. 1994), Inst. for Interconnective and Packaging Electronic Cirs. (reliability coms. 1992—). Republican. Roman Catholic. Achievements include research on alternatives to tin-lead solder in electronic assemblies; surface mount technology design and processing with expertise in reflow technologies, especially vapor phase soldering, solder joint reliability studies to determine void and grain structure effects. Office: Dell Computer Corp 1 Dell Way Round Rock TX 78682-0001

KOPP, EUGENE HOWARD, electrical engineer; b. N.Y.C., Oct. 1, 1929; s. Jacob and Fanny (Lipschitz) K.; m. Claire Bernstein, Aug. 31, 1950; children: Carolyn, Michael, Paul. B.E.E., CCNY, 1950, M.E.E., 1953; Ph.D. in Engring, UCLA, 1965. Registered profl. engr., Calif. Project engr. Polarad Electronics Corp., Long Island City, N.Y., 1950-53, Kaye Halbert Corp., Culver City, Calif., 1953-55; chief engr. Precision Radiation Instruments, Inc., Los Angeles, 1955-58; mem. faculty sch. engring. Calif. State U., Los Angeles, 1958-74; assoc. prof. Calif. State U., 1962-66, prof., 1966-74, dean engring. Sch., 1967-73; v.p. acad. affairs West Coast U., Los Angeles, 1973-79; sr. scientist Hughes Aircraft Co., 1980-85, mgr. research and devel., 1985-93, dir. advanced programs, 1994-95; v.p. mobile satellites Hughes Electronics Corp., 1996-97, chief scientist comml. satellites, 1998—; lectr. evening divsn. CCNY, N.Y.C., 1950-53; lectr. UCLA, 1979-91. Vis. research fellow U. Leeds, Eng., 1966-67. Mem. IEEE, AIAA, Tau Beta Pi, Eta Kappa Nu, Pi Tau Sigma. Office: Hughes Electronics Corp PO Box 1351 South Pasadena CA 91031-1351

KOPP, EUGENE PAUL, lawyer; b. Charleston, W.Va., Nov. 20, 1934; s. Eugene Alexander and Virginia Elizabeth (King) K.; m. Katherine Patricia

Rogers, July 1, 1967; 1 son, Eugene Paul. B.A., U. Notre Dame, 1957, M.A., 1958; J.D., W. Va. U., 1961. Bar: W. Va. 1961, D.C. 1977, Tex. 1980. Law clk. U.S. Dist. Ct. W. Va.,1961-62; trial atty. Dept. Justice, Washington, 1962-69; dep. dir. USIA, 1973-77, acting dir., 1976-77; assoc. gen. counsel Champlin Petroleum Co., Ft. Worth, 1977-81; v.p. Washington affairs Union Pacific Corp., Washington, 1981-87; dep. dir. U.S. Info. Agy., 1989-93; exec. dir. MFJ Task Force, 1993-94; of counsel Clarendon Assocs., Inc., 1995-97, Ruddy and Muir, 1998—; cons. Nat. Security Council, Washington, 1981, mem. transition team, 1980. Mem. W.Va. Bar Assn., Tex. Bar Assn., D.C. Bar Assn. Roman Catholic. Clubs: Belle Haven Country; Metropolitan (Washington). Home: 508 Cathedral Dr Alexandria VA 22314-4706

KOPP, GEORGE PHILIP, JR., minister; b. Cin., July 17, 1927; s. George Philip and Ann Elizabeth (Suffield) K.; m. Janet Marie Thompson Schultz, Oct. 13, 1956. BA, Heidelberg Coll., 1950; BD, Eden Sem., 1955, MDiv, 1969. Ordained to ministry United Ch. of Christ, 1955. Pastor St. John's Ch., Middlebrook, Va., 1955-60, 83-85, ret.; commd. ensign USN, 1954, advanced through grades to lt. comdr., 1976, served as chaplain; ret., 1976, ret., 1976; dir. Ctr. Atlantic Conf. United Ch. Christ, 1983-88. With USN, 1945-51, USNR, 1952. Home and Office: 308 Valley View Dr Staunton VA 24401-2101

KOPP, RICHARD EDGAR, electrical engineer; b. Bklyn., July 12, 1931; s. Edgar A. and Anna M. (Barto) K.; m. Elaine Hecker, June 14, 1953; children: Debra, Richard (dec.), Lisa, Barbara. BEE, Poly. Inst. Bklyn., 1953, MS, 1957, DEE, 1960. Rsch. engr. Grumman Aerospace Corp., Bethpage, N.Y., 1953-58, head computing rsch. group, 1958-65, head systems rsch. lab., 1965-70, dir. systems scis. rsch., 1970-89, dir. sci. adv. bd., 1989-90, pvt. cons., 1990—; mem. adv. com. Poly. Inst. Imaging Scis.; adj. prof. Poly. Inst. Bklyn.,, 1961-70. Contbr. articles to profl. jours. Fellow AIAA (assoc.); mem. IEEE (sr.), U.S. Power Squadron, Mariners Landing Golf and Country Club. Home: 205 Sherwood Dr Huddleston VA 24104-3351

KOPP, ROBERT WALTER, lawyer; b. Boston, Feb. 21, 1935; s. Robert A. and Marie (Powers) K.; m. Carol A. Rosenberger, Aug. 22, 1959; children: Robert A., Christopher F., J. Brian, David W., Karen A. BS in Physics, Holy Cross Coll., 1957; LLB, Georgetown U., 1963. Bar: N.Y. 1963. Sr. ptnr. Bond, Schoeneck & King, Syracuse, N.Y., 1963—; gen. counsel Pay Bd. Econ. Stabilization Program Phase II, Washington, 1972-73. Lt. (j.g.) USN, 1957-62. Fellow Am. Bar Found., Coll. Labor and Employment Law (founding); mem. ABA (coun. sect. labor and employment law 1980-88, sect. governance liaison 1989-90, 94—, sect. del. to ho. of dels. 1990-93), N.Y. State Bar Assn. Roman Catholic. Home: 217 Brattle Rd Syracuse NY 13203-1320 Office: Bond Schoeneck & King 1 Lincoln Ctr Fl 18 Syracuse NY 13202-1324

KOPP, WENDY, teaching program administrator; b. Austin, Tex., June 29, 1967. B.A., Princeton U., 1998; degree (hon.), Conn. Coll., Drew U. Pres. and founder Teach For America, 1989—. Bd. dirs. New Tchr. Project, The Learning Project, Kipp Acad. Recipient Nat. Acad. fellow, 1990, Jefferson Award for Pub. Svcs., Woodrow Wilson award, 1993, Aetna's Voice of Conscience award, 1994, Citizen Activist award, 1994, Kilby Young Innovator award; named to Time Mag. Roster of Am. Most Promising Leaders Under 40, 1994, Woman of Yr. Glamour mag., 1990. Office: Teach For America 315 W 36th St 6th Fl New York NY 10018

KOPPE, WILLIAM PAUL, deputy sheriff; b. Chgo., May 7, 1949; s. Paul John and Dolores Imelda (Pritchett) K.; m. Cathy Urbaniak, Sept. 10, 1977; children: Carrie Jane, David William. BSBA, U. San Francisco, 1971. Dep. sheriff Cook County, Chgo., 1985—; world advisor, grandmaster Han Chakyo Universal Taekwondo, Wheeling, Ill., 1991-96. German-Greek liaison United Hellenic Voters of Am., Addison, Ill. With U.S. Army, 1983. Named Knight of the Blessed Virgin Mary, Cath. Ch., 1997; recipient degree of Wing Chun, Jun Fan, Calif., 1960's. Mem. Am. Legion, Teamsters, U. San Francisco Alumni Assn., Von Steuben, German-Am. Nat. Congress. Republican. Avocations: martial arts, writing, bowling, internet. Home: 8970 N Parkside Ave Apt 401 Des Plaines IL 60016-5514 Office: Cook County Sheriff Daley Ctr 50 W Washington St Chicago IL 60602-1305

KOPPEL, AUDREY FEILER, electrologist, educator; b. N.Y.C., Sept. 25, 1944; d. Jules Eugene and Lee (Gibel) Feiler; m. Mark Alyn Koppel, May 28, 1967; children: Jason, Seth. B.A., Bklyn. Coll., 1972; diploma in electrolysis Hoffman Inst., 1975; postgrad. George Washington U., 1984, Essex Community Coll., 1984, Kree Inst., 1980. Lic. esthetician cosmotologist; cert. Dermablend Corrective Cosmetics Paramedical Tng. program, Advanced Aesthetics Paramedical Skin Care & Camouflage application, cert. paramedical skin care Dermablend Corp. for Corrective Cosmetics. Electrologist, Bklyn., 1976, Glemby Internat., N.Y.C., 1976-78, Island Electrolysis, Manhasset, N.Y., 1982-84; registrar, supervising instr. Kree Inst., N.Y.C., 1978-82; pres. North Shore Electrolysis, Manhasset, 1982-84; dir., electrologist Bklyn. Studio, 1982—; pres. Ray Internat., 1986—. Editor, author pamphlet Glossary for Electrolysis, 1985; contbr. articles to profl. jours. Active Greater N.Y. coun. Boy Scouts Am., 1977-84; flag lt. Bklyn. Power Squadron; chmn. hosp. and med. coms. Share, 1993-94. Mem. Am. Electrology Assn. (v.p. 1984—, edn. chmn. 1984—, continuing edn. coord. 1985, chmn. pub. rels. com. 1989—), Nat. Esthetic Rehab. Assn., N.Y. Electrolysis Assn. (corr. sec. 1983-85, pres. 1985-90, bd. trustee 1990-94, advisor 1990-94), Internat. Guild of Electrologists (merit award 1978), Soc. Clin. and Med. Electrologists, Aesthetics Internat. Assn. Democrat. Jewish. Clubs: U.S. Power Squadron (flag lt.), Bklyn. Yacht. (v.p. ladies aux. 1989-90, pres. 1990-94). Avocations: boating, swimming, music. Office: Bklyn Studio of Electrolysis 2376 E 16th St Ste 1 Brooklyn NY 11229-4471 also: 82 Norwood Ave Deal NJ 07723-1374

KOPPEL, TED, broadcast journalist; b. Lancashire, Eng., 1940; came to U.S., 1953; m. Grace Anne Dorney; 4 children. B.A. in Liberal Studies, Syracuse U.; M.A. in Mass Communications Rsch. and Polit. Sci., Stanford U. News corr., writer Sta.-WMCA, N.Y.C., 1963; with ABC News, 1963—, former gen. assignment corr., former corr. Vietnam; diplomatic corr. Hong Kong Bur. ABC News, Washington; chief Miami, Fla. Bur. ABC News, 1968, chief Hong Kong Bur., 1969-71, chief diplomatic corr., 1971-80; anchorman ABC News Nightline, 1980—, also editl. mgr., 1980—. Corr. for TV spls. including: The People of People's China, 1973, Kissinger: Action Biography, 1974, Second to None, 1979, The Koppel Reports, 1988-90; author The Wit and Wisdom of Adlai Stevenson, 1965, (with Marvin Kalb) novels In The National Interest, 1977; Nightline: History in the Making, 1996. Recipient Sol Taishoff award for excellence in broadcasting, Nat. Press Found., 1984, 2 George Polk award for network TV reporting, 18 Emmy awards Acad. TV Arts and Scis., 3 George Foster Peabody awards, 8 duPont-Columbia awards, 7 Overseas Press Club awards, 2 Ohio State U. awards, 2 Soc. Profl. Journalism awards, numerous others. Office: Nightline 1717 Desales St NW Washington DC 20036-4401*

KOPPELMAN, CHAIM, artist; b. Bklyn., Nov. 17, 1920; s. Samuel and Sadie (Mondlin) K.; m. Dorothy Myers, Feb. 13, 1943; 1 child, Ann. Student, Bklyn. Coll., 1938, Am. Artists Sch., 1939; student Aesthetic Realism, with Eli Siegel, 1940-78; student, Art Coll. Western Eng., Bristol, 1944, Ecole des Beaux-Arts, Rheims, 1945, Art Students League, 1946, Amedée Ozenfant Sch., 1946-49; student Aesthetic Realism, with Ellen Reiss, 1978—. Art instr. N.Y. U., 1947-55, N.Y. State U., New Paltz, 1952-58; instr. Sch. Visual Arts, N.Y.C., 1959—; cons. Aesthetic Realism Found., N.Y.C., 1971—. Author: This is the Way I See Aesthetic Realism, 1969; illustrator: Definition, 1972; contbr. articles to profl. jours.; Bibliographies of his work The Indignant Eye (Ralph Shikes), 1969, The New Humanism (Barry Schwartz), 1974, The Art of the Print (Fritz Eichenberg), 1976, American Prints and Printmakers (Una Johnson), 1980, Hilla Rebay: In Search of the Spirit in Art (Joan Lukach), 1983; one man shows include Asso. Am. Artists Gallery, 1973, Terrain Gallery, N.Y.C., 1974, 83, Warwick (Eng.) Gallery, 1975, Merida Rapp Graphics, Louisville, 1985, Print Club, Phila., others; group shows include Purdue U., 1972, Utah State U., 1972, Arte Fiera, Bologna, 1978, NAD, N.Y.C., 1983, Print Club, Phila., 1988, Alternative Mus., N.Y.C., 1988, Art Mus., Bogota, 1996; represented in permanent collections Victoria and Albert Mus., London, Mus. Fine Arts, Caracas, Venezuela, Mus. Modern Art, N.Y.C., Met. Mus. Art, N.Y.C., Library of Congress, Washington, Los Angeles County Mus. Art, Phila. Mus. Art, Guggenheim Mus., others. Served with USAF, 1942-45. Decorated Bronze Star; recipient N.Y. State Creative Artists Pub. Svc. award, 1976, prize Soc. Am. Graphic Artists, Fabri prize Nat. Acad. Ann., 1989, Cook prize, 1998; Louis Comfort Tiffany grantee, 1956, 59. Mem. Nat. Acad. Design. Home and Office: 498 Broome St New York NY 10013-2213 *I learned from Eli Siegel, the great American poet and critic, the most important thing an artist can know-this Aesthetic Realism statement: "All beauty is a making one of opposities and the making one of opposites is what we are going after in ourselves." Every artist is trying to put together opposites such as sameness and difference, warm and cool, freedom and order, and every person and artist is trying to put these same opposites together in his life.*

KOPPELMAN, DOROTHY MYERS, artist, consultant; b. N.Y.C., June 13, 1920; d. Harry Walter and May (Chalmers) M.; m. Chaim Koppelman, Feb. 13, 1943; 1 child, Ann. Student Bklyn. Coll., 1938-42, Am. Artists Sch., 1940-42, Art Students League, 1942; student of Aesthetic Realism with Eli Siegel, 1942-78, Ellen Reiss, 1978—. Instr. Art Bklyn. Coll., 1952-75; dir. Terrain Gallery, N.Y.C., 1955-83; dir. Visual Arts Gallery, Sch. Visual Arts, 1961-62; pres. Aesthetic Realism Found., 1973-85, cons., 1973—; instr. Nat. Acad. Sch. of Design, 1988-89, 96, 98; one woman shows include Terrain Gallery, 1961, Rina Gallery, Jersey City, 1963, Atlantic Gallery, 1999; exhibited in group shows at Mus. Modern Art, N.Y.C., 1962, Balt. Mus., 1962, Bklyn. Mus., 1962, N.J. State Mus., Jersey City, Butler Art Inst., Youngstown, Ohio, San Francisco Art Inst., 1961-62, 65, Nat. Acad. Ann., 1986, 90, Swiss Inst., N.Y.C., Susan Teller Gallery, N.Y.C., 1993, 95, Drawing Ctr., N.Y.C., Audubon Soc. ann., N.Y.C., 1995-96, Chuck Levitan Gallery, N.Y.C., 1996, Washington Square East Gallery, N.Y.C., 1992, 96, Am. Soc. Contemporary Artists Anns., 1994-96, 97, 98, Atlantic Gallery, 1998; represented in permanent collections Hampton Inst., Nat. Mus. Women in the Hearts, Mus. Jewish Family, Durham, N.C., Savannah Coll. Art and Design; co-author: Aesthetic Realism: We Have Been There - Six Artists, 1969. Illustrator Children's Guide to Parents (by Eli Siegel), 1971. Tiffany grantee for painting, 1965; recipient Theresa Lindner award for painting ASCA, 1996. Home: 498 Broome St New York NY 10013-2213 Office: Aesthetic Realism Found Inc 141 Greene St New York NY 10012-3201

KOPPELMAN, LEE EDWARD, regional planner, educator; b. N.Y.C., May 19, 1927; s. Max and Madelyn Judith (Eisenberg) K.; m. Constance E. Lowinger, June 18, 1948; children: Leslie, Claudia, Laurel, Keith. BEE, CCNY, 1950; MS, Pratt Inst., 1964; D in Pub. Adminstrn., NYU, 1970; LLD, L.I. U., 1978; DHL, Dowling U., 1991. Cert. landscape architect, N.Y.; cert. profl. planner, N.J. Cons. on site planning and landscape architecture, 1950-60; dir. planning Suffolk County Planning Dept., 1960-88; exec. dir. L.I. Regional Planning Bd., 1965—; leading prof. polit. sci., dir. ctr. regional policy studies SUNY, Stony Brook, 1967—; adj. prof. environ. scis. Syracuse U., 1976-83; cons. U.S. Dept. Housing and Urban Devel., 1972-78, UN on Land Use and Coastal Zone Planning; mem. Coastal Zone Mgmt. Adv. Com., 1973-75, Nassau/Suffolk Comprehensive Health Planning Council, Melville, N.Y., 1973-76, Nat. Shoreline Erosion Adv. Panel, 1974-81; exec. dir. tax relief on L.I. Bi-County State Commn., 1991-92; adv. coun. Schs. of Art, Architecture and Planning Cornell Univ., 1995—. Co-author: Planning Design Criteria, 1968 (3rd edit. 1981), Housing: Planning and Design, 1974, A Methodology to Achieve the Integration of Coastal Zone Science and Regional Planning, 1974, The Urban Sea: Long Island Sound, 1976, Site Planning Criteria, 1978, Long Island Comprehensive Waste Treatment Management Plan, Vols. 1 and 2, 1979, Time Saver Standards for Site Planning, 1982, Long Island Segment of the Nationwide Urban Runoff Program, 1982, Financing Government on Long Island, 1992, The Long Island Comprehensive Special Groundwater Protection Area Plan, 1992, Airport Joint Use Feasibility Study: Calverton Airport, 1993, Financing Government on Long Island, working paper, vols. 1, 2, and 3, 1993, Groundwater and Land Use Planning Experience from North America, 1996. Recipient cert. of tribute Temp. State Commn. on Water Resources Planning, 1964, career achievement medal Engrng. and Archtl. Alumni CCNY, 1977, Disting Alumnus award NYU, 1985, medal of honor L.I. Assn., 1987, Lone Eagle award Pub. Rels. Soc. Am., 1987, Disting. Leadership award nat. honors program Am. Planning Assn., 1989; named Citizen of Yr. L.I. chpt. Nat. Soc. Profl. Engrs., 1983. Mem. Am. Inst. Architects (hon.), Am. Inst. Planners, N.Y. State County Planners Assn. (pres. 1967-68), Internat. Fedn. Planning and Housing, Assn. Architecture and Engrins., Sigma Xi. Home: 2 Dune Ct East Setauket NY 11733-1527 Office: SUNY Ctr Regional Policy Studies Stony Brook NY 11794-4395

KOPPELMAN, MURRAY, investment banker; b. N.Y.C., July 7, 1931; s. Isidore and Ruth (Pisetzky) K.; m. Sarah Levy, 1957 (div. 1972); children: Lisa, Suzanne, Janet; m. Alison Mary Wharton, Nov. 21, 1976 (div. 1998); m. Ellen Irene Kaplan, May 23, 1999. BS in Acctg., Bklyn. Coll., 1957. CPA, N.Y. Ptnr. Triebwasser and Koppelman CPAs, N.Y.C., 1960-68; exec. v.p., COO D.H. Blair and Co., Inc., N.Y.C., 1968-84; pres., CEO Eastlake Securities, Inc., N.Y.C., 1984—; pres. Stamford Advisors, Inc., N.Y.C., 1975-91. Trustee, exec. com. Bklyn. Coll. Found., 1986; bd. dirs., adv. com. Neighborhood Housing Svcs. N.Y.; pres. Am. Ort Fedn., 1991; dir. exec. com., sec., asst. treas. Anti-Defamation League. With U.S. Army, 1952-54. Named Man of Yr., Am. Ort Fedn., 1987, Alumnus of Yr., Bklyn. Coll., 1994, recipient Presdl. medal, 1995; recipient Ellis Island Medal of Honor, 1996. Mem. N.Y. State Soc. CPA's, Friars Club. Avocations: youth career counseling, tennis, travel, running. Home: 812 5th Ave New York NY 10021-7253 Office: Eastlake Securities Inc 575 Lexington Ave New York NY 10022-6102

KOPPENAAL, RICHARD JOHN, psychology educator; b. Milw., Mar. 27, 1930; s. Peter John and Bernice Icelyne (Hagerty) K.; m. Lois Helen Cohen, Mar. 3, 1951 (div. June 1987); children: Ross Selden, Peter John; m. Barbara Ann Freitas, 1997. BA, U. B.C., Vancouver, Can., 1955, MA, 1956; PhD, McGill U., Montreal, Que., Can., 1958. Prof. U. Man., Winnipeg, Can., 1958-63; vis. prof. Northwestern U., Evanston, Ill., 1963-64; prof. NYU, N.Y.C., 1964—, chmn. psychology, 1982-87, dean Coll. Arts and Scis., 1986-93, dean Gallatin Coll., 1993-98. Contbr. articles to profl. jours. Office: NYU 6 Washington Pl New York NY 10003-6634

KOPPES, STEVEN NELSON, science writer, editor; b. Manhattan, Kans., Aug. 28, 1957; s. Ralph James and Mary Louise (Nelson) K.; m. Susan Camille Keaton, May 18, 1984. BS in Anthropology cum laude, Kans. State U., 1978; MS in Journalism, Kans. U., 1982. Rsch. asst. dept. anthropology Kans. State U., Manhattan, 1979; reporter The Morning Sun, Pittsburg, Kans., 1981-83; co-mgr. Doc's B.R. Others Restaurant, Tempe, Ariz., 1983-85; info. specialist Ariz. State U. New Bur., Tempe, 1985-87, asst. dir., 1987-96, interim dir., 1996-97; sci. writer-editor Office Rsch. Comms. U. Ga., Athens, 1997-98; sci. writer U. Chgo. News Office, 1998—; cons. Ariz. Sci. Ctr., 1995-96. Contbr. to Ariz. State U. Rsch. Mag., 1984—; contbr. articles to profl. jours. Bd. dirs. Children's Mus. of Metro Phoenix, 1988. Recipient Excellence award Internat. Assn. Bus. Communicators, 1991-92, Merit award, 1989-93, Disting. Tech. Comm. award Soc. Tech. Comm. Phoenix Chpt., 1994-95, Excellence award Coun. for the Advancement and Support of Edn. Dist. III, 1998, Spl. Merit award, 1998, Awd. of Excellence, Counc. for the Advancement and Support of Edn. Dist. III, Spec. Merit Awd., Case Dist. III, 1998. Mem. Nat. Assn. Sci. Writers, Ariz. Archaeol. Soc. (bd. dirs. Phoenix chpt. 1987-88), Rio Salado Rowing Club (charter mem. 1995-97). Avocations: long-distance running, backpacking, outdoor photography. Office: U Chgo News Office 5801 S Ellis Ave Rm 200 Chicago IL 60637

KOPPETT, LEONARD, columnist, journalist, author; b. Moscow, Russia, Sept. 15, 1923; s. David and Marie (Dvoretskya) Kopeliovitch; m. Suzanne Silberstein, Apr. 24, 1964; children: Katherine, David. B.A., Columbia U., 1946. Sportswriter, columnist N.Y. Herald Tribune, 1948-54, N.Y. Post, 1954-63, N.Y. Times, 1963-78, 88-91, Sporting News, 1967-82; exec. sports editor Peninsula Times Tribune, 1980-81, editor, 1982-84, editor emeritus, 1984-93; free-lance columnist, 1978—; tchr. journalism Stanford (Calif.) U., 1977-81, 97-98, San Jose State U., 1988-89. Books include A Thinking Man's Guide to Baseball, 1967, 24 Seconds to Shoot, 1969, The N.Y. Times Guide to Spectator Sports, 1970, The New York Mets, 1970, The Essence of the Game is Deception, 1974, Sports Illusion, Sports Reality, 1981, The New Thinking Fan's Guide to Baseball, 1991, The Man in the Dugout, 1993, Koppett's Concise History of Major League Baseball, 1998. Served with U.S. Army, 1943-45. Named to writer's wing Baseball Hall of Fame, 1992, Basketball Hall of Fame, 1994. Mem. Baseball Writers Assn. Am., Profl. Football Writers, Authors Guild. Democrat. Jewish.

KOPPUS, BETTY JANE, retired savings and loan association executive; b. Toledo, June 14, 1922; d. Carl Emerson and Hilda Sarah (Semlow) K.; student pub. schs. With United Savs. and Loan Assn. (now Standard Fed.), Toledo, 1940—, asst. sec., 1943, treas., 1943-73, sec., 1973-78, v.p. 1978-84. Former trustee, sec. Lutheran Social Service Northwestern Ohio; mem. St. Mark Luth. Ch. Mem. Toledo C. of C. (past treas., trustee), Toledo Area Govt. Research Assn. (past treas., dir.), Mgmt. Forum N.W. Ohio, Beta Sigma Phi. Clubs: Zonta (Toledo I), Brandywine Country, River Road Garden. Address: 5709 Chardonnay Dr Toledo OH 43615-7312

KOPROSKI, ALEXANDER ROBERT, real estate executive; b. Stamford, Conn., Apr. 6, 1934; s. Alexander J. and Gladys J. (Kryger) K.; m. Patricia A. Velliquette; children: Lisa, Susan, Gregory, Beth. Student, U. Conn., 1952-54; BS in Mktg. and Fin., Tri-State U., Angola, Ind., 1959. Lic. real estate broker, Conn., N.Y. Comml. and indsl. broker S.H. Silberman, Inc., Stamford, 1960-73; owner, CEO, comml. and indsl. broker Al Koproski Realty, Stamford, 1973—; mem. Coastal Mgmt. Adv. Com. Past pres. Holy Name Home and Sch. Assn.; past chmn. Poles for Ford Com., Kosciuszko Park Meml. Com., Southea. Conn. Pulaski Meml. Com., Hartford; past mem. Stamford Bicentennial Commn., Resource Recovery Task Force, Polish Am. Affairs Coun., Mayor's South End Adv. Com., Stamford C.E.T.A. Manpower Program; mem. Stamford Hist. Soc.; mem. South End Revitalization Com., Stamford, 1996—; past chmn. lay adv. bd., past chmn. 75th ann. yr. book Holy Name of Jesus Cath. Ch.; past bd. dirs. Polish Am. Congress Conn., Polish Am. Cen. Com. Stamford; bd. dirs. Polish Slavic Info. Ctr., Stamford, 1975—, Am. Ctr. Polish Culture, Washington, 1990—; mem. Polish studies adv. com. Ctrl. Conn. State U., 1994; chmn. Little League, Dialdowo, Poland, nat. dir. Polish Nat. Youth Baseball Found., 1997. With U.S. Army, 1955-57. Named Citizen of Yr., Polish Am. World, N.Y.C., 1978, Layman of Yr., Stamford Kiwanis Club, 1979; recipient Krzyżem Kawalerskim Orderu Zasługi Rzeczypospolitej Polskiej medal Govt. of Poland, 1994, Ellis Island Medal of Honor, 1998. Mem. Stamford Bd. Realtors, Am. Coun. Polish Cultural Clubs (nat. fundraising chmn. Washington project), Kosciuszko Found. (co-chmn. nat. coun.), Polish Am. Cultural Soc. (historian, Citizen of Yr. 1975), Am. Assn. Mil. Order of Malta, Exch. Club, Holy Name Athletic Club (pres., CEO, Citizen of Yr. 1982), Polish Am. Bus. and Profl. Club (past pres.), Oceanview Beach and Tennis Club (past treas.). Republican. Roman Catholic. Avocations: swimming, fundraising, travel. Home: 222 Ocean Dr E Stamford CT 06902-8134 Office: Polish Slavic Info Ctr PO Box 631 36 Pulaski St Stamford CT 06902-6826

KOPROWSKA, IRENA, cytopathologist, cancer researcher; b. Warsaw, Poland, May 12, 1917; came to U.S., 1944; d. Henryk and Eugenia Grasberg; m. Hilary Koprowski, July 14, 1938; children: Claude, Christopher. BA, Popielewska/Roszkowska, Warsaw, 1934; MD, Warsaw U., 1939. Cert. Am. Bd. Pathology, Internat. Bd. Cytology. Intern in medicine Villejuif Lunatic Asylum, Seine, France, 1940; asst. pathologist Rio de Janeiro City Hosp., Miguel Couto, Brazil, 1942-44; rsch. fellow dept. pathology Cornell U. Med. Coll., N.Y.C., 1945-46, rsch. asst. dept. pharmacology, 1949-50, rsch. fellow dept. of anatomy, 1949-54; rsch. fellow applied immunology Pub. Health Rsch. Inst. of The City of N.Y., 1946-47; asst. pathologist N.Y. Infirmary for Women and Children, N.Y.C., 1947-49; asst. prof. dept. pathology SUNY Downstate Med. Ctr., Bklyn., 1954-57; assoc. prof. pathology, dir. cytology lab./Sch. Cytotech. Hahnemann Med. Coll., Phila., 1957-64, prof. pathology dir. cytology lab., sch. cytotechnology, 1964-70; prof. pathology, dir. cytology lab. Temple U. Sch. Med., Phila., 1970-87, prof. emerita, 1987—; cons. WHO, Switzerland, Egypt, Iran, Latin Am., India, 1960-85, Armed Forces Inst. Pathology, Air Force Cytology Rescreen Project, 1979-80. Author: Woman Wanders Through Life and Science, 1997; contbr. articles on cancer rsch. to profl. and sci. jours. Named Woman Physician of Yr., Polish Am. Med. Assn., 1977; grantee USPHS-Nat. Cancer Insts., 1954-75, rsch. grantee Bender Co., Vienna, Austria, 1983-89. Fellow Am. Soc. Clin. Pathologists (emeritus), Coll. Am. Pathologists (emeritus), Coll. Physicians of Phila., Internat. Acad. Cytology (hon.), Internat. Acad. Pathology (emeritus); mem. Am. Assn. for Cancer Rsch. Inc. (emeritus), Am. Assn. Pathologists Inc. (emeritus), Am. Med. Women's Assn., Am. Soc. Cytology (life, Papanicolaou award 1985), Am. Soc. Exptl. Pathology, Argentinian Soc. Cytology (hon.), Path. Soc. Phila. Avocations: reading, writing. Home: 334 Fairhill Rd Wynnewood PA 19096-1804

KOPROWSKI, HILARY, microbiologist, educator; b. Warsaw, Poland; s. Pawel and Sarah (Berland) K.; m. Irena Grasberg; children: Claude Eugene, Christopher Dorian. BA, Nikolaj Rej Gymnasium of Luth. Congregation, Warsaw; MD, U. Warsaw; grad., Warsaw Conservatory Music and Santa Cecilia Acad., Rome; DSc (hon.), Ludwig-Maximilian U., Munich, Widener Coll.; D of Medicine and Surgery, U. Helsinki, Finland; MD (hon.), U. Uppsala, Sweden; LittD (hon.), Thomas Jefferson U.; DMS (hon.), U. Lublin, Poland, Univ. Coll. Dublin. Rsch. asst. dept. exptl. and gen. pathology U. Warsaw, 1936-39; staff Yellow Fever Rsch. Svc., Rio de Janeiro, 1940-44; staff rsch. divsn. Am. Cyanamid Co., 1944-46; asst. dir. viral and rickettsial rsch. Lederle Lab., Pearl River, N.Y., 1946-57; dir. Wistar Inst., Phila., 1957-91, prof., 1957-93, prof. laureate, 1993—; Wistar Inst. prof. of rsch. medicine U. Pa., 1957—; prof. microbiology and immunology Thomas Jefferson U., Phila., 1992—; dir. Ctr. Neurovirology, Inst. of Biotechnology and Advanced Molecular Medicine, 1992—; cons. WHO, 1950—; mem. microbiology study sect. NIH, 1956-60; mem. PAHO; mem. adv. com. Nat. Multiple Sclerosis Soc., 1970-78; mem. immunobiology adv. com. NIH, USPHS, 1975-76; mem. bd. sci. counselors div. cancer etiology Nat. Cancer Inst., 1982-86, chmn., 1987-90; mem. biol. response modifiers program decision network com. NIH, 1985-87; mem. immunobiol. adv. com. NIH, USPHS, 1975-76. Co-editor: Methods in Virology, Viruses and Immunity, Current Topics in Microbiology and Immunology, 1965—. Hon. trustee Kosciuszko Found., 1993—. Decorated commandeur Order du Mérite pour la Rch. et l'Invention, chevalier Order Royal De Lion Belgium, comdr. Order of The Lion of Finland, 1995, officer Order of the Polish Republic, Chevalier Legion d'honneur The French Govt., 1997, Great Order of Merit, Pres. Poland, 1998; recipient Alvarenga prize Coll. Physicians Phila., 1959, Alfred Jurzykowski Found. Polish Millenium prize, 1966, Felix Wankel Tierschutz prize, 1979, Alexander Von Humboldt Sr. U.S. Scientist award, Phila. Cancer Rsch. award Phila. Cancer Club, 1989, San Marino award, 1989, John Scott award, Nicolaus Copernicus medal Polish Acad. Scis., 1989, The Phila. award, 1990, John Scott award, 1990; Hon. trustee Kosciuszko Found., 1993; Fulbright scholar Max Planck Inst. für Verhaltensphysiologie, Seewiesen, Fed. Republic Germany, 1971. Fellow AAAS, N.Y. Acad. Medicine, Phila. Coll. Physicians; mem. Nat. Acad. Arts and Scis., Yugoslavian Acad. Scis., Polish Acad. Scis., Russian Acad. Med. Scis., Finnish Acad. Arts and Scis., N.Y. Acad. Scis. (pres. 1959, trustee 1960-72), Nat. Acad. Scis. Achievements include development of first oral polio vaccine which ultimately led to elimination, in 1992 of polio from the Americas; development of new rabies vaccine for humans, reducing the number of injections and of oral vaccine in bait for immunization of wildlife; research on mechanism of damage of cells in brain in neurotropic virus infection; development of first monoclonal antibody for treatment and cure of colorectal cancer. Office: The Wistar Inst 3601 Spruce St Philadelphia PA 19104-4265 also: Thomas Jefferson U M-85 Jefferson Alumni Hall 1020 Locust St Philadelphia PA 19107-6731

KORAB, ARNOLD ALVA, engineering executive; b. Penns Grove, N.J., June 15, 1917; s. Harry Emil and Lydia Maria (Toykalla) K.; m. Evelyn Marr Stevens, June 16, 1939 (dec. Oct. 1972); children: William, Anne; m. Helen Norine Schlossnagel, Dec. 30, 1973. BSME, U. Md., 1938; degree in Aero Engrng., Calif. Inst. Tech., 1943. Registered profl. engr. Md., D.C. Engr. Office of James Posey, Balt., 1938-40, Pub. Bldg. Adminstrn., G.S.A., Washington, 1940-43; cons. engr. Redmile, Korab & Wood, Inc., Washington, 1946-57; chmn. Ellenco, Inc., Brentwood, Md., 1957—; bd. dirs. Ellenco, Inc., Brentwood; prtnr. Korab Assocs., Brentwood, 1958—. Lt. comdr. USN, 1943-46, PTO. Mem. NSPE, Nat. Fire Protection Assn., Mil. Order of World Wars, Rotary Internat., Masons, Shriners, Pi Tau Sigma. Episcopalian. Avocations: reading, investing, sailing, bridge.

KORAL, ALAN MAX, lawyer; b. N.Y.C., July 10, 1941; s. Max and Sylvia (Stoffman) K. AB with highest honors, U. Rochester, 1962; postgrad.,

Princeton U., 1962-65; JD, U. Chgo., 1975. Bar: Ill. 1975, N.Y. 1977, U.S. Dist. Ct. (no. dist.) Ill. 1975, U.S. Dist. Ct. (so. dist.) N.Y. 1978, U.S. Dist. Ct. (no. dist.) N.Y. 1981, U.S. Dist. Ct. (ea. dist.) N.Y. 1986, U.S. Ct. Appeals (11th cir.) 1987, U.S. Ct. Appeals (2nd cir.) 1990, U.S. Ct. Appeals (3d and 4th cirs.) 1995. Assoc. Vedder, Price, Kaufman & Kammholz, Chgo., 1975-76; assoc. Vedder, Price, Kaufman, Kammmholz & Day, N.Y.C., 1976-81, ptnr., 1982—. Author: Conducting the Lawful Employment Interview, 1st edit., 1984, 4th edit., 1992, Employee Privacy Rights, 1988. Mem. N.Y. State Human Rights Adv. Coun., N.Y.C., 1985. Recipient Cmty. Svc. award Bar Assn. Human Rights Greater N.Y., 1988. Mem. ABA, N.Y. State Bar Assn., Assn. of Bar of City of N.Y. Office: Vedder Price Kaufman & Kammholz 805 3rd Ave New York NY 10022-7513

KORAL, MARIAN, writer; b. Washington, Pa., Jan. 31, 1954; d. Charles Oscar and Grace Regina (Cook) Skoog; m. Enis Osman Koral, Sept. 8, 1990. BA, U. Pitts, 1975. Pub. rels. asst. City of Pitts., 1975-76; English tchr. Centro-Colombo Am., Bogota, Colombia, 1977-78, Point Park Coll., Pitts., 1978, Berlitz, Pitts., 1979-82; adminstrv. asst. U. Pitts., 1982-86, alumni editor, 1997—; writer U. Pitts. Med. Ctr., 1986-97. Mem. Coun. for the Advancement and Support of Edn. Avocations: travel, photography, reading.

KORAN, DENNIS HOWARD, publisher; b. L.A., May 21, 1947; s. Aaron Baer and Shirley Mildred (Kassan) K.; m. Roslynn Ruth Cohen, Apr. 6, 1979; 1 child, Michael; stepchildren: Jeff, Beth, Judy. Student, U. Leeds, Eng., 1966-67, UCLA, 1979-80; BA, U. Calif., Berkeley, 1980; postgrad., Loyola U., L.A., 1982-84, 86-89. Co-founder, co-editor Cloud Marauder Press, Berkeley, 1969-72, Panjandrum/Aris Books, San Francisco, 1973-81; founder, editor Panjandrum Books, San Francisco, 1971—, Panjandrum Press, Inc., San Francisco, 1971—; substitute tchr. L.A. Unified Sch. Dist., 1997—; co-dir. poetry reading series Panjandrum Books, 1972-76. Author: (book of poetry) Vacancies, 1975, After All, 1993; (with Mike Koran) Refrigerator Poems: Variations on 24, 48 & 120 Words, 1997; editor Panjandrum Poetry Jour., 1971—; co-editor Cloud Marauder, 1969-72; author poetry pub. various jours. Liaison between U.S. Govt. and Seminole Indians VISTA, Sasakwa, Okla., 1969-70. Nat. Endowment for Arts Lit. Pub. grantee, 1974, 76, 79, 81, 82, 84, Coord. Coun. for Lit. Mags., 1971-80, grantee Lit. Pub. Calif. Arts Coun., 1985-86, L.A. Cultural Arts Found., 1986. Mem. Lovers of the Stinking Rose, Poets and Writers. Avocations: rare book collecting, travel, athletics, stamp and coin collecting. Office: Panjandrum Books 6156 Wilkinson Ave North Hollywood CA 91606-4518

KORANDO, DONNA KAY, journalist; b. Chester, Ill., Mar. 31, 1950; d. Samuel L. and Dorothy L. (Meyer) K.; m. James J. Heidenry, Nov. 28, 1981; children: Reid Samuel, Rachel. BA, So. Ill. U., 1972; MSL, Yale U., 1980. Tchr. journalism Lincoln H.S., Manitowoc, Wis., 1972-73; copy editor St. Louis Post-Dispatch, 1973-77, editorial writer, 1977-86, editor commentary page, 1986—. Mem. Lafayette Square Restoration Com., St. Louis, 1981—. Mem. Assn. Opinion Page Editors (bd. dirs.). Roman Catholic. Avocations: children, literature. Office: St Louis Post Dispatch 900 N Tucker Blvd Saint Louis MO 63101-1099*

KORANYI, ADAM, mathematics educator; b. Szeged, Hungary, July 13, 1932; came to U.S., 1957, naturalized, 1963; s. Jeno and Vilma (Szigethy) K.; m. Anna Eiben, Mar. 16, 1968; children—Peter, Daniel. Diploma, U. Szeged, 1954; Ph.D., U. Chgo., 1959. Instr. Harvard, 1959-60; asst. prof. U. Calif. at Berkeley, 1960-64; vis. asst. prof. Princeton, 1964-65; faculty Belfer Grad. Sch. Sci., Yeshiva U., N.Y.C., 1965-79; prof. math. Belfer Grad. Sch. Sci., Yeshiva U., 1968-79, Washington U., St. Louis, 1979-85; Disting. prof. Lehman Coll. CUNY, 1985—. Contbr. articles to profl. jours. Mem. Am. Math. Soc. Home: 26 Royden Rd Tenafly NJ 07670-1010 Office: CUNY Lehman Coll Bronx NY 10468

KORB, ELIZABETH GRACE, nurse midwife; b. Wilmington, N.C., Mar. 1, 1951; d. Carl Wilhelm Bissenger Korb and Betty Jane Stroup; m. Joel Vincent LeFebvre, May 19, 1973 (div. June 1976); m. James Clinton Queen, June 22, 1984; 1 child, James Michael Andrew Queen. BSN, U. N.C., Greensboro, 1973; MSN, U. Utah, 1980. Cert. nurse midwife. Staff nurse, instr. New Hanover Meml. Hosp., Wilmington, N.C., 1973-76; staff nurse Meml. Mission Hosp., Asheville, N.C., 1976-78, LDS Hosp., Salt Lake City, 1978-79; practising nurse midwife Dr. Michael Watson, Bamberg, S.C., 1980, Fletcher (N.C.) Ob-Gyn. Assocs., 1981-83, Nurse-Midwifery Assocs., Fletcher, 1983-85, Asheville (N.C.) Women's Med. Ctr., 1985-86, 88; practising nurse midwife, clin. coord. Regional Perinatal Assocs., Asheville, 1986-88; perinatal clin. coord., practicing nurse midwife Mountain Area Health Edn. Ctr., Asheville, 1988—; clin. preceptor Cmty.-Based Nurse-Midwifery Edn. Program, 1993—, East Carolina U. Nurse-Midwifery Edn. Program, 1993—; mem. mgmt. team Mountain Area Perinatal Substance Abuse Program, 1993—; bd. dirs. Mary Benson House, Asheville; mem. adv. panel Emory U., Nurse Midwifery in Pub. Sector, Atlanta, 1988—; mem. strategic planning group for women's and children's svcs. Mission-St. Joseph's Health Sys., 1998—. mem. birth defects task force WNC, 1998—; mem. mission St. Joseph. Named to Outstanding Young Women of Am., 1982; recipient Profl. award March of Dimes, Asheville, 1993. Mem. ANA, Nat. Perinatal Assn., N.C. Perinatal Assn. (bd. dirs. 1988-93), N.C. Nurses Assn., Am. Coll. Nurse Midwives (N.C. del. legis. conf. 1993, 94, nominating com. 1981-82), Internat. Childbirth Edn. Assn., Phi Kappa phi, Sigma Theta Tau. Democrat. Lutheran. Avocations: exercise, swimming, fishing, sewing. Office: Mountain Area Health Edn Ctr Ob-Gyn 60 Livingston St Ste 100 Asheville NC 28801-4400

KORB, LAWRENCE JOHN, metallurgist; b. Warren, Pa., Apr. 28, 1930; s. Stanley Curtis and Dagna (Pedersen) K.; B.Chem.Enging., Rensselaer Poly. Inst., Troy, N.Y., 1952; m. Janet Davis, Mar. 30, 1957; children: James, William, Jeanine. Sales engr. Alcoa, Buffalo, 1955-59; metall. engr. N. Am. Rockwell Co., Downey, Calif., 1959-62; enging. supr. metallurgy Apollo program Rockwell Internat. Co., Downey, 1962-66, enging. supr. advanced materials, 1966-72, enging. supr. metals and ceramics space shuttle program, 1972-88; cons., 1988—; mem. tech. adv. com. metallurgy Cerritos Coll., 1969-74. Served with USNR, 1952-55. Registered profl. engr., Calif. Fellow Am. Soc. Metals (chmn. aerospace activity com. 1971-76, judge materials application competition 1969, handbook com. 1978-83, chmn. handbook com. 1983, chmn. publs. coun. 1984). Republican. Author articles, chpts. in books. Home: 251 S Violet Ln Orange CA 92869-3740

KORB, LAWRENCE JOSEPH, government official; b. N.Y.C., July 9, 1939; s. Joseph Anthony and Katherine Veronica K.; children: Mary Katherine, Karen, Julia, Lawrence Jr. B.A., Athenaeum Ohio, Norwood, 1961; M.A., St. John's U., Jamaica, N.Y., 1962; Ph.D., SUNY, Albany, 1969. Asst. prof. polit. sci. U. Dayton, 1969-71; asso. prof. govt. USCG Acad., 1971-75; prof. mgmt. U.S. Naval War Coll., 1975-70; adj. prof. Georgetown U., 1980-93; resident dir. def. policy studies Am. Enterprise Inst. Public Policy Studies, 1980-81; asst. sec. for manpower, res. affairs and logistics Dept. Def., Washington, 1981-85; v.p. Raytheon Co., 1985-86; dean U. Pitts., 1986-88; sr. fellow The Brookings Inst., 1988-98; v.p./Maurice R. Greenberg chair/dir. studies Coun. Fgn. Rels., N.Y.C., 1999—. Author: The Joint Chiefs of Staff: The First Twenty-Five Years, 1976, The Fall and Rise of the Pentagon, 1979, American National Security Policy and Progress, 1993. Served with USN, 1962-66, Vietnam. Mem. Council Fgn. Relations, Nat. Acad. Pub. Adminstrn., Aspen Strategy Group. Republican. Roman Catholic. Office: Coun Fgn Rels Harold Pratt House 58 E 68th St New York NY 10021 *The foundation of good public policy is the free and open competition of ideas.**

KORB, ROBERT WILLIAM, former materials and processes engineer; b. Warren, Pa., Mar. 12, 1929; s. Dallas Weigand and Evelyn Eleanor (Peterson) K.; m. Diane Marie Anderson, Oct. 14, 1964 (div. 1972); 1 child, Karen; m. Setsu Campbell, Aug. 9, 1980; children: Theresa Campbell, Mark Campbell, Laura Campbell. BS in Chemistry, U. Nev., 1951. Chemist Rezolin, Inc., Santa Monica, Calif., 1956-57; mem. tech. staff Hughes Aircraft Co., Culver City, Calif., 1957-64; mem. tech. staff Hughes Aircraft Co., Fullerton, Calif., 1971-74, group head materials enging., 1974-79, sect. head materials and processes enging., 1979-93; mem. tech. staff TRW Systems, Redondo Beach, Calif., 1964-71; ret., 1993. Contbr. articles to profl. jours.; patentee flexible cable process. 1st lt. USAF, 1951-56. Mem. Inst. for Interconnecting and Packaging Electronic Circuits (co. rep.), Soc. for Advancement Materials and Process Engring. Republican. Avocations: golf, skiing, tennis, photography. Home: 31222 Calle Bolero San Juan Capistrano CA 92675-5392

KORB, WILLIAM BROWN, JR., manufacturing company executive; b. Warren, Pa., Apr. 27, 1940; s. William Brown and Helen (Haslett) K.; m. Dorothy Wendell Trout, June 11, 1962; children: Karen Michel, David Wendell, Christine Leigh. B.S. in Indsl. Engring, Pa. State U., 1962; grad., Advanced Mgmt. Program, Harvard U., 1979. With Reliance Electric Co. div. Exxon, 1962-86, gen. mgr. mech. group, Mishawaka, Ind., 1977-79; operating v.p., Cleve. Reliance Electric Co. div. Exxon, Cleve., 1979-86; pres., CEO, bd. dirs. Gilbarco, Inc., Greensboro, N.C., 1987—; bd. dirs. Avery, India, Beijing Chang Gi Petroleum Equipment Corp., Guest Svcs. Inc.. GEC Inc., Cambrex Corp.; bd. advisors Wachovia Bank of N.C., Greensboro. Bd. visitors N.C. Agrl. and Tech. State U., Greensboro Coll.; trustee Moses Cone Health System. Club: Greensboro Country. Home: 2704 Lake Forest Dr Greensboro NC 27408-3805 Office: Gilbarco Inc PO Box 22087 Greensboro NC 27420-2087

KORBA, ROBERT W., communications executive; b. 1943. BA, U. Nebr., Omaha, 1965, JD, 1968. Of counsel Lifetime Security Life Ins., Denton, Tex., 1971-72; ptnr. Foxter & Korba, Inc. PC, Denton, Tex., 1972-73; gen. counsel LSL Corp., Denton, Tex., 1973; pres., CEO Sammons Enterprises, Inc., Dallas, 1973—. With U.S. Army, 1968-71. Office: Sammons Enterprises Inc 5949 Sherry Ln Ste 1900 Dallas TX 75225-8015*

KORBITZ, BERNARD CARL, retired oncologist, hematologist, educator, consultant; b. Lewistown, Mont., Feb. 18, 1935; s. Fredrick William and Rose Eleanore (Ackmann) K.; m. Constance Kay Bolz, June 22, 1957; children: Paul Bernard, Guy Karl. B.S. in Med. Sci., U. Wis.-Madison, 1957, M.D., 1960, M.S. in Oncology, 1962; LL.B., LaSalle U., 1972. Asst. prof. medicine and clin. oncology, U. Wis. Med. Sch., Madison, 1967-71; dir. medicine Presbyn. Med. Ctr., Denver, 1971-73; practice medicine specializing in oncology, hematology, Madison, 1973-76; med. oncologist, hematologist Radiologic Ctr. Meth. Hosp., Omaha, 1976-82; practice medicine specializing in oncology, hematology, Omaha, 1982-95, ret., 1995; sci. advisor Citizen's Environ. Com., Denver, 1972-73; mem. Meth. Hosp., Omaha, 1977—; dir. Bernard C. Korbitz, P.C., Omaha, 1983-96; bd. dirs., pres. B.C. Korbitz P.C., ret., 1996. Contbr. articles to profl. jours. Webelos leader Denver area Council, Mid. Am. Council of Nebr. Boy Scouts Am.; bd. elders King of Kings Luth. Ch., Omaha, 1979-80; bd. elders St. Mark Luth. Ch., Omaha, 1993-98; mem. People to People Del. Cancer Update to People's Republic China, 1986, Eastern Europe and USSR, 1987; mem. U.S. Senatorial Club, 1984, Republican Presdl. Task Force, 1984. Served to capt. USAF, 1962-64. Named Medford (Wis.) H.S. Athletic Hall of Fame, 1997. Fellow ACP, Royal Soc. Health; mem. Am. Soc. Clin. Oncology, Am. Soc. Internal Medicine, AMA, Nebr. Med. Assn., Omaha Med. Society, Omaha Clin. Soc., Phi Eta Sigma, Phi Beta Kappa, Phi Kappa Phi, Alpha Omega Alpha. Avocations: photography, fishing, travel. Home: 9024 Leavenworth St Omaha NE 68114-5150

KORBMAN, JACK SOLOMAN, cantor, educator; b. Newark, N.J., Mar. 30, 1936; s. Abraham and Celia K.; m. Barbara Kopf, July 4, 1982; children: Jeffrey, Mark, Barry. BS, Upsala Coll., 1958; MA, Seton Hall U., 1963. Cert. pub. sch. adminstr. N.J. Tchr. Newark (N.J.) Bd. Edn., 1958-76, adminstr., 1976-96; cantor Temple A.A.B.C., Irvington, N.J., 1965-85, Temple Adath Shalom, Parsippany, N.J., 1985—. Author: The Magic Pencil, 1989; composer. Mem. Am. Soc. Jewish Music, N.J. Assn. Communal Workers. Avocations: piano, antiques. Office: Temple Adath Shalom 841 Mountain Way Morris Plains NJ 07950-1132

KORBMAN, MEYER HYMAN, rabbi, public school administrator; b. Newark, Oct. 30, 1925; s. Abraham and Celia Korbman; m. Mildred Penn, Dec. 17, 1950; children: Marc, Riva, David. BA, Yeshiva U., 1949; MA, Seton Hall U., 1954. Ordained rabbi, 1952. Rabbi Congregation Beth El, Hightstown, N.J., 1951-70, Temple Israel, Union, N.J., 1970—; v.p. pub. schs. Newark, 1974-95; mem. Coun. Congregations and Chs., Union, 1970—. Trustee Rabbinical Coll., N.J., 1952-54, Jewish Fedn., Union, 1970—; trustee, exec. bd. Grad. Inst. Talmudical Studies, 1954; apptd. mem. Sr. Citizens Adv. Commn., Union, 1976—. With U.S. Army, 1944-46. Recipient cert. of merit Newark Bd. Edn., 1978, Citizen of Yr. award B'nai Brith, 1986, award Union County Bd. of Chosen Freeholders, 1986, citation Union Twp., 1986, Gen. Assembly citation State of N.J., 1986, Notable Am. award of merit, 1987, cert. recognition Union Twp. Bd. Edn., 1987, Golden Circle award Israel Histadrut Found., 1988. Mem. NEA, Union County Bd. Rabbis, Essex County Bd. Rabbis, Newark Reading Resource Assn. (pres. 1969-72), City Adminstrs. and Suprs. Assn., Right to Read (N.J. bldg. dir. 1970-72), Internat. Reading Assn. Home: 2454 Ogden Rd Union NJ 07083-6526 Office: Temple Israel of Union 2372 Morris Ave Union NJ 07083-5785 *Life is so tenuous that it would be most prudent to live it in such a way as to leave good memories to those who come after us.*

KORC, MURRAY, endocrinologist; b. Gunsburg, Fed. Republic of Germany, Apr. 3, 1947; came to U.S., 1960; m. Antoinette Korc. BA, Bklyn. Coll., 1968; MD, Albany (N.Y.) Med. Coll., 1974. Intern, then resident Albany Med. Ctr. Hosp., 1974-77; endocrinology fellow U. Calif., San Francisco, 1977-79; from prof. to chief divsn. endocrinology, diabetes and metab U. Calif., Irvine, 1989—. Office: U Calif Div Endocrinology Med Sci I # C240 Irvine CA 92697

KORCHIN, JUDITH MIRIAM, lawyer; b. Kew Gardens, N.Y., Apr. 28, 1949; d. Arthur Walter and Mena (Levisohn) Goldstein; m. Paul Maury Korchin, June 10, 1972; 1 son, Brian Edward. BA with high honors, U. Fla., 1971, JD with honors, 1974. Law clk. to judge U.S. Dist. Ct., 1974-76; assoc. Steel, Hector & Davis, Miami, Fla., 1976-81; ptnr. Steel, Hector & Davis, Miami, 1981-87, Holland and Knight, Miami, 1987—. Author, exec. editor U. Fla. Law Rev., 1973-74. Mem. U. Fla. Law Ctr. Coun., 1980-83; pres. alumni bd. U. Fla. Law Rev., 1983; bd. dirs. Fla. Film & Rec. Inst., 1982-84. Recipient Trail Blazer award The Women's Com. of 100, 1988. Fellow Am. Bar Found.; mem. ABA (sect. alternative dispute resolution, vice chmn. 1994-95, co-chmn. fed. ct. mediation com. 1995), Am. Arbitration Assn. (employment law panel, southeast 1993—), CPR Inst. for Dispute Resolution (nat. panelist 1994—), Dade County Bar Assn. (bd. dirs. 1981-82, treas. 1982, sec. 1983, 3d v.p. 1984, 2d v.p. 1985, 1st v.p. 1986, pres. 1987), Nat. Assn. Women Bus. Owners (adv. coun. 1987-88), Fla. Assn. Bank Women (TV panelist greater Miami chpt. 1987), Fla. Bar Assn. (vice chmn. jud. nominating procedures com. 1982, civil procedure rules com. 1984-89, 93-95), Fla. Bar Found. (subcom. legal assistance for poor 1988-90), Rabbinical Assn. Greater Miami (TV panelist Still Small Voice 1987), Dist. XI Health and Human Svcs. Bd. (gov.'s appointee 1993-95, vice chmn. 1993, 94), Greater Miami C. of C. (com. profl. devel. 1988-90), City Club (bd. dirs. 1988-93), Order of Coif, Phi Beta Kappa, Phi Kappa Phi. Office: Holland & Knight PO Box 015441 701 Brickell Ave Ste 3000 Miami FL 33131-2898

KORCHNAK, LAWRENCE CHARLES, educational administrator, consultant, writer; b. New Kensington, Pa., July 5, 1946; s. Joseph B. and Mary (Farina) K.; m. Karen Hornick Korchnak, May 16, 1970; 1 child, Lawrence Daniel. BA, Georgetown U., 1968; MS in Edn., Duquesne U., 1974; PhD, U. Pitts., 1987. Tchr., basketball coach St. Vincent Prep. Sch., Latrobe, Pa., 1968-70; tchr., counselor St. Mary of the Mount H.S., Pitts., 1970-76; dir. of edn. Median Sch., Pitts., 1983-85; vocat. guidance coord., drug & alcohol coord., counselor Hopewell Area Sch. Dist., Aliquippa, Pa., 1976-86; instr. Pa. State Beaver, Monaca, Pa., 1990—; adminstr., profl. devel. coord. Beaver (Pa.) Area Sch. Dist., 1986-98; asst. supt. Hampton Township Sch. Dist., 1998—; cons. Ednl. Support Svcs., Aliquippa, 1987—; lectr. U. Pitts. Grad. Sch. Edn., 1988—; continuing edn. adv. bd. Pa. State U., Beaver, 1993—; student assistance adv. bd. Prevention Project, Monaca, Pa., 1990—; sch. attendance task force Beaver County, 1996—; mem. Teen Pregnancy Task Force of Beaver County; mem. Allegheny County Student Assistance Coordinating Coun., 1998—; mem. Hampton Alliance for Ednl. Excellence, 1998—, Spl. Edn. Family Tng. Task Force, 1999—. Author: Case Law and Common Sense, 1998, Important Legal Issues..., 1987, Focus on Careers, 1978; contbr. articles to profl. publs. Mem. Managed Care Task Force, Beaver County, 1996—, Drug and Alcohol Planning Coun., Beaver County, 1991-96, chair, 1994-98; exec. bd. dirs. Drs. Ars Millenium, Pitts., 1996—. Mem. ASCD, Pa. Assn. for Supervision and Curriculum Devel. (legis. com. 1986—, pre-conf. inst. chair 1996-97, Svc. award 1994-98), Nat. Assn. of Secondary Sch. Prins., Pa. Assn. of Elem. and Secondary Sch. Prins. (legis. liason 1986-98), Pa. Sch. Bds. Assn., Middle Level Prins. of Beaver County (pres., v.p. 1994-98), Pa. Assn. of Student Assistance Profls., Pa. Assn. Pupil Svcs. Adminstrs. Avocations: numismatic research, writing, antiquities. Home: 103 N Brodhead Rd Aliquippa PA 15001-1705 Office: Hampton Township Sch Dist Mt Royal Blvd Allison Park PA 15101

KORCHYNSKY, MICHAEL, metallurgical engineer; b. Kiev, Ukraine, Apr. 11, 1918; came to U.S., 1950, naturalized, 1956; s. Michael and Jadwiga (Zdanowicz) K.; m. Taisija Lapin, Nov. 22, 1951; children—Michael, Marina, Roksana. Dipl. Ing. in Metals Tech., Tech. U. Lviv, 1942. Lectr. Tech. U. Lviv, 1942-44; chief engr. C.E., U.S. Army, Fed. Republic Germany, 1945-50; research metallurgist Union Carbide Co., Niagara Falls, N.Y., 1951-61; research supr. Jones & Laughlin Steel Corp., Pitts., 1962-68; dir. product research Jones & Laughlin Steel Corp., 1969-72; dir. alloy devel. metals div. Union Carbide Co., N.Y.C., 1973-77, Pitts., 1978-86; cons., prin. Korchynsky and Assocs., Pitts., 1986—; lectr. Niagara U., 1957-58. Author, patentee in field of alloy design and processing tech. of a family of microalloyed high-strenght low alloy steel. Union Carbide sr. fellow, 1979. Fellow Am. Soc. Metals Internat. (Andrew Carnegie lectr. 1973, W.H. Eisenman medal 1984, F.C. Bain award 1986); mem. AIME (Howe meml. lectr. 1983, Robert Earll McConnell engring. achievement award 1991, mem. Iron and Steel Soc.), SAE Internat., Am. Iron and Steel Inst. (medalist), Acad. Engring. Scis. of Ukraine, Ukrainian Technol. Soc. Home: 2770 Milford Dr Bethel Park PA 15102-1763

KORDASH, DOROTHY MAE, artist; b. St. Joseph, Mo., Sept. 7, 1927; d. Perle Elisha and Carrie Allene (Womach) Reece; m. James A. Kordash, Apr. 20, 1956. Art studies, various workshops, U.S., Can., Eng. Acctg. clk. Interstate Bakeries, Kansas City, Mo., 1946-50; adminstrv. clk. Ford Motor Co., Lenexa, Kans., 1951-82; freelance artist Leawood, Kans., 1972—; treas. Art Images Gallery, Kansas City, 1982-86. One-woman shows at Grand Opening, Macy's Dept. Store, Overland Park, Kans., 1975, Arte Ctr., Plano, Tex., 1997; exhibited with Knickerbocker Artists, Salmagundi Club, N.Y.C., 1983; contbr. paintings to Pub. TV Art Auction, Kansas City, 1985-90; artist commemorative bicentennial book Johnson County, Kans., 1975, invitation cover Truman Med. Ctr., Kansas City, 1988; represented in permanent collections including Ford Motor Co., Claycomo, Mo., Volume Shoe Co., Topeka. Mem. Kans. Watercolor Soc. (signature, Purchase awards 1973, 75, 77, 83), Greater Kansas City Art Assn. (Best of Show award 1983), Art-A-Fair Laguna Beach (exhibitor, Best Abstract award 1997, 98). Avocation: photography. Home and Studio: 8624 Reinhardt Ln Leawood KS 66206-1455

KORDONS, ULDIS, lawyer; b. Riga, Latvia, July 9, 1941; came to U.S., 1949; s. Evalds and Zenta Alide (Apenits) K.; m. Virginia Lee Knowles, July 16, 1966. AB, Princeton U., 1963; JD, Georgetown U., 1970. Bar: N.Y. 1970, Ohio 1978, Ind. 1989. Assoc. Whitman, Breed, Abbott & Morgan, N.Y.C., 1970-77, Anderson, Mori & Rabinowitz, Tokyo, 1973-75; counsel Armco Inc., Parsippany, N.J., 1977-84; v.p., gen. counsel, sec. Sybron Corp., Saddle Brook, N.J., 1984-88, Hillenbrand Industries Inc., Batesville, Ind., 1989-92; pres. Plover Enterprises, Cin., 1992-95; of counsel Case Law Offices, Cin., 1996-97; pres. Kordons & Co., LPA, Cin., 1998—. Lt. USN, 1963-67. Mem. N.Y. Bar Assn., Ohio Bar Assn., Ind. Bar Assn.

KORE, ANITA MAUREEN, veterinary toxicologist; b. Milw., Wis., Sept. 7, 1961; d. Alexander V. Kore and Brigita (Ekmanis) Kore-Kakulis. BS, U. Wis., 1983, DVM, 1987; PhD, U. Ill., Champaign-Urbana, 1992. Cert. Am. Bd. Vet. Toxicology; Vet. lic., Wis. Resident in vet. toxicology Nat. Animal Poison Control Ctr., Urbana, Ill., 1987-90; vet. toxicologist Wis. Animal Health Lab., Madison, 1992—; adj. asst. prof. Dept. Comparative Bioscis., Madison, 1995—. Author: (with others) Current Veterinary Therapy, XI, 1992; contbr. articles to profl. jours. Interdisciplinary Environ. Toxicology scholar Inst. Environ. Studies U. Ill., Champaign-Urbana, 1989-92. Mem. Am. Assoc. Vet. Lab. Diagnostics, Wis. Vet. Med. Assn., Wis. Sci. Profls. Home: 5702 Piping Rock Rd Madison WI 53711-3419 Office: Wisconsin Animal Health Lab 6101 Mineral Point Rd Madison WI 53705-4457

KOREC, JACEK, corporation executive; b. Warsaw, Poland, Aug. 27, 1951; s. Anatol and Natalia (Galazka) K.; m. Alicja Lawnicka, Nov. 27, 1971; 1 child, Bartosz. MS, Tech. U., Warsaw, 1974, DSc, 1978. Sci. asst. Inst. Tech. Elec. Materials, Warsaw, 1974-81; Alexander von Humboldt fellow Rheinisch Westfalische Tech. Hochschule, Aachen, Germany, 1981-83; asst. Rheinish Westfalische Tech. Hochschule, Aachen, Germany, 1983-86; rschr. Allgemeine Elec. Ges. Rsch. Inst., Frankfurt, Germany, 1986-88; sr. mgr. Daimler-Benz AG Rsch. Inst., Frankfurt, 1988-96; project leader Siliconix, Santa Clara, Calif., 1991-96; mem. adv. bd. Power Semiconductor Rsch. Ctr., N.C. State U., Raleigh, 1991-96; mem. program com. Internat. Conf., Internat. Symposium Power Semiconductor Devices, 1993, 96, 97, publicity chmn., 1997. Contbr. articles to profl. jours.; patentee in field. Avocations: guitar, fishing, sailing.

KOREMAN, DOROTHY GOLDSTEIN, physician, dermatologist; b. Bklyn., Nov. 1, 1940; d. Benjamin and Ida (Krenick) Goldstein; m. Neil M. Koreman, Aug. 16, 1964; children: Elizabeth Koreman Landau, Robert Stephen. BA, Bklyn. Coll., 1961; MD, SUNY, Bklyn., 1965. Diplomate Am. Bd. Dermatology. Intern pediatrics Kings County Hosp. Ctr., Bklyn., 1965-66; resident dept. dermatology Wayne State U. Sch. Medicine, Detroit, 1966-69; clin. instr. dermatology Sch. Medicine Wayne State U., Detroit, 1969-71; asst. clin. prof. dermatology U. Miami, 1971-75, assoc. clin. prof. dermatology, 1975-82, clin. prof. dermatology and cutaneous surgery, 1982—; chief of staff Ami Palmetto Gen. Hosp., Hialeah, 1990-91. Mem. North Dade Bd., Greater Miami Jewish Fedn., 1975—. Mem. Miami Dermatol. Soc. (pres. 1978-79). Avocations: traveling, cooking, reading, skiing, needlepoint. Office: 7100 W 20th Ave Ste 107 Hialeah FL 33016-1813

KOREN, EDWARD BENJAMIN, cartoonist, educator; b. N.Y.C., Dec. 13, 1935; s. Harry L. and Elizabeth (Sorkin) K.; m. Catherine Curtis Ingham; children: Nathaniel, Alexandra, Benjamin. B.A., Columbia U., 1957; student, Atelier 17, Paris, 1957-59; M.F.A., Pratt Inst., 1964; D.H.L. (hon.), Union Coll., 1984. Cartoonist New Yorker mag., N.Y.C., 1962—; mem. faculty Brown U., 1964—, asso. prof. art, 1969-77, adj. assoc. prof., 1977—; mem. bd. advisors Swann Collection Caricature and Cartoon. One-man travelling exhbn. Art Gallery, SUNY, Albany, 1982; exhibited in group shows including Expn. Dessins d'Humeur, Soc. Protectrice d'Humeur, Avignon, France, 1973, Biennale Illustration, Bratislav, Czechoslovakia, 1973, Art from the New York Times, Soc. Illustr., N.Y.C., 1973, Art from the New Yorker, Grolier Club, 1975, Terry Dintinfass Gallery, N.Y.C., 1975-77, 79, 91, Virginia Lynch Gallery, 1992, 94; work appears in Fogg Mus., Princeton U. Mus., RISD Mus., Fitzwilliam Mus., Swann Collection Cartoon and Caricature; contbr.: drawings to various publs. including The Nation, Time mag., Newsweek mag., Fortune mag., N.Y. Times, Sports Illustrated mag., Vogue mag., Vanity Fair mag.; illustrator: Don't Talk to Strange Bears, 1969, The People Maybe, 1974, Cooking for Crowds, 1975, Noodles Galore, 1977, How to Eat Like a Child, 1978, Dragons Hate to be Discrete, 1978, Teenage Romance, 1981, Do I Have to Say Hello?. 1989, A Dog's Life, 1995, The Hard Work of Simple Living: A Daybook for the Sustainable Hedonist, 1998; author, illustrator: Behind The Wheel, 1972; author: Do You Want to Talk About It?, 1977, Are You Happy?, 1978, Well, There's Your Problem, 1980, Caution, Small Ensembles, 1983, What About Me?, 1989, Quality Time, 1995, The Hard Work of Simple Living, 1998. John Simon Guggenheim fellow, 1970-71. Mem. Author's League, Soc. Am. Graphic Artists.

KOREN, EDWARD FRANZ, lawyer; b. Eustis, Fla., Aug. 6, 1946; s. Edward Franz Sr. and Frances (Boyd) K.; m. Louise Poole, June 19, 1970; children: Daniel Edward, Susan Louise. BSBA, U. Fla., 1971, JD, 1974. Bar: Fla. 1975, U.S. Dist. Ct. (mid. dist.) Fla. 1977, U.S. Supreme Ct. 1980, U. S. Ct. Appeals (11th cir.) 1981, U.S. Tax Ct. 1985, U.S. Ct. Claims 1986. Instr. tax U. Fla., Gainesville, 1974-75; assoc. Holland & Knight, Lakeland, Fla., 1975-79; ptnr. Holland & Knight, Lakeland, 1980—, chmn. trusts and estates dept., 1983—; adj. prof. graduate tax program U. Fla., Gainesville, 1996. Author: Estate and Personal Financial Planning, 1988, 11th edit.,

1999; contbr. articles to profl. jours. Capt. U.S. Army, 1971-72. Fellow Am. Coll. Trust and Estates Counsel (mem. estate and gift tax and bus. planning com., bd. regents 1997—), Am. Coll. Tax Counsel, Am. Bar Found.; mem. ABA (real property, probate and trust law sect., mem. exec. coun. 1995—, chmn. marital deduction com. 1991-95), Fla. Bar Assn. (chmn. real property, probate and trust law sect. 1988-89, chmn. tax sect. 1990-91, active various sects. and coms.), Am. Assn. Attys. and CPAs, Fla. Inst. CPAs, Order of the Coif, Tampa Club, Lakeland Yacht and Country Club, Centre Club. Republican. Presbyterian. Home: 114 Hickory Creek Dr Brandon FL 33511-8012 Office: Holland & Knight 92 Lake Wire Dr PO Box 32092 Lakeland FL 33802-2092

KOREN, ISRAEL, electrical and computer engineering educator; s. Zahava Koren; children: Yuval, Yaron. BSc, Technion/Israel Inst. Tech., Haifa, 1967, MSc, 1970, DSc, 1975. Asst. prof. elec. and computer engring. U. Calif., Santa Barbara, 1976-78, U. So. Calif., L.A., 1978-79; sr. lectr. Technion/Israel Inst. Tech., Haifa, 1979-85, head VLSI Sys. Rsch. Ctr., 1985-86; prof. elec. and computer engring. U. Mass., Amherst, 1986—; vis. prof. U. Calif., Berkeley, 1982-83; cons. Tolerant Sys., San Jose, Calif., 1986, Digital Equipment Corp., Hudson, Mass., 1991, Intel, Haifa, 1992, AMD, Austin, Tex., 1994, IBM, 1995—. Author: (textbook) Computer Arithmetic Algorithms, 1993; editor, co-author: Defect and Fault Tolerance in VLSI, 1989. Fellow IEEE, Computer Soc. of IEEE, Japan Soc. for Promotion of Sci.; mem. Assn. Computing Machinery (mem. spl. interest group on computer architecture 1990—). Office: U Mass Dept Elec and Computer Engring Amherst MA 01003

KORENIC, LYNETTE MARIE, librarian; b. Berwyn, Ill., Mar. 29, 1950; d. Emil Walter and Donna Marie (Harbutt) K. m. Jerome Dennis Reif, Dec. 31, 1988. BS in Art, U. Wis., 1977, MFA, 1979, MA in LS, 1981, MA in Art History, 1984. Asst. art libr. Ind. U., Bloomington, 1982-84; art libr. U. Calif., Santa Barbara, 1984-88, head Arts Libr., 1988—. Author articles. Mem. Art Librs. Soc. N.Am. (sec. 1983-84, v.p. 1989, pres. 1990), Beta Phi Mu. Office: U Calif Arts Libr Santa Barbara CA 93106

KORETSKY, SIDNEY, internist, educator, paper historian; b. Chelsea, Mass., Dec. 30, 1921; s. Harry and Rachel (Greenfield) K.; m. Elaine Ruth Stern, Feb. 22, 1953; children: Peter Austin, David Stuart, Donna Monel. AB, Harvard U., 1943; MD, Jefferson Med. Coll., 1946. Intern Springfield (Mass.) Hosp., 1946-47; resident Boston City Hosp., 1949-52, New England Med. Ctr., Boston, 1952-53; clin. instr. in medicine Tufts U. Sch. Medicine, Boston, 1953—; pvt. practice internist Boston, 1953—; sr. physician Beth Israel Deaconess Med. Ctr., Boston, 1992—; rschr. in heart disease, Beth Israel Deaconess Med. Ctr., 1953-68. Contbr. numerous articles to profl. med. jours.; editor, graphic designer, photographer: The Goldbeater of Mandalay, 1991, and other books dealing with the history of hand papermaking. Former pres. Greater Boston Med. Soc. Capt., U.S. Army Med. Corps, 1947-49, Korea, Japan. Mem. AMA, Internat. Assn. Paper Historians, Dard Hunter Paper History Soc., Mass. Med. Soc., Mass. Horticultural Soc., Harvard Club of Boston. Avocations: horticulture, high adventure travel, photography. Home and Office: 756 Washington St Brookline MA 02446-2151

KOREY-KRZECZOWSKI, GEORGE J. M. KNIAZ, university administrator, management consultant; b. Kielce, Poland, July 13, 1921; came to Can., 1951; s. Antoni-Marian Kniaz and Zofia-Emilia Wanda (Chmielewska) Korczak-Krzeczowski; m. Irene-Marie Latacz, July 15, 1944; 1 child, Andrew George. LL.M., Jagellonian U., Cracow, Poland, 1945; postgrad., Acad. Polit. and Social Sci., Warsaw, Dept. Internat. Law, U. Bucharest, Rumania; LL.D., U. Freiburg, Fed. Republic Germany, 1949; D.Sc. in Econs., U. Tubingen, Fed. Republic Germany, 1950; grad. Inst. Ednl. Mgmt., Harvard U., 1975; recipient 10 hon. doctorate degrees. Dir. Dept. Ministry Culture and Arts, Poland, 1945; v.p. Coun. Arts and Scis, Kielce, Poland, 1945; press attache Polish embassy, Bucharest; vice-counsul of Poland Polish embassy, cultural counsellor of embassy, 1946; dir., prof. Polish Inst., Bucharest, 1947; consul of Poland Bucharest, 1947, econ. advisor of embassy, 1947; counselor Ministry Fgn. Affairs, Warsaw, 1947; consul of Poland Berlin, 1948-50, Baden-Baden, Fed. Republic Germany, 1948-50; head Econ. and Restitution Mission, 1949-50; asst. supr. indsl. engring. dept. and contract estimating dept. Canadair Ltd., Montreal, Que., Can.; asst. mng. dir., contr. Damar Products of Can. Ltd., Montreal, Around-the World Shoppers Club (Can.) Ltd., Montreal; v.p., mng. dir. Schlemm Assocs. Ltd.; pvt. practice mgmt. cons.; pres. Pan-Am. Mgmt. Ltd.; dean bus., v.p. Ryerson Poly. Inst., 1971, exec. v.p., dean external programs, 1973-77, pres., 1974-75; prof., pres. Can. Sch. Mgmt., Toronto, Ont., 1976—; pres. Northland Open U., 1976-84, Korey Internat. Ltd., Toronto, 1980; disting. vis. prof. bus. adminstrn. Fla. Atlantic U.; prof. bus. adminstrn. Polish U., London; internat. prof. strategic mgmt. IMC, Buckingham, Eng.; former pres. Ryerson Applied Research Ltd.; v.p. and dir. York-Ryerson Computing Ctr.; dir. Can. Ops., Can. Textile Cons.-Ltd., Werner Mgmt. Cons. (Can.) Ltd., indsl. and econ. devel. div. Werner Mgmt. Cons. Inc., N.Y.C.; mng. dir. Werner Assocs., Inc. Author: Siedemnasta Wiosna, 1938, Globorze, 1939, Internationale Rechtsverhaeltnisse Polens im Gebiete des Strafrechts, 1949, Plannung in der Polnischen Landwirtschaft, 1950, Liryki Nostalgiczne, 1974, New Role for the Canadian Economy in the Age of World Food Shortage, 1975, Lunch w Sodomie, 1976, Korey's Stubborn Thoughts, 1980, University Without Walls, 1980, Tree of Life, 1982, Wszedzie i Nigdzie Poetry, Paris, 1991, Natretne Mysli, 1994, Wiatry Zycia, 1995, Dojrzala Pogoda, 1995; author articles on mgmt., econ. planning, internat. affairs, fgn. markets and mktg.; contbr. to publs. including: Industrial Canada, Can. Textile Jour., Jour. Mktg.; guest lectr. radio and TV. Decorated companion Brit. Inst. Mgmt., bailiff-grand cross of justice and grandmaster, prin. king of arms Sovereign Order St. John of Jerusalem, knight Grand Cross of Most Venerable Order of Golden Fleece, knight Imperial Order of Heraklian Crown, knight Mil. Constantinian Order St. George, knight Guard of Honor of Apostolic Throne, Patriarchate of Alexandria, knight grand cross Mil. Order St. Agatha di Paterno; cross of Polish Home Army, 1939-45; Polish mil. medal for World War II; hon. citizen City of Winnipeg. Fellow Royal Econ. Soc., Royal Soc. Arts, N.Y. Acad. Scis., Can. Internat. Acad. Humanities and Social Scis. (pres.); mem. Inst. Mgmt. Cons. Que. and Ont., Acad. Mktg. Sci. (U.S.), Am. Mgmt. Assn., Acad. Mgmt. (U.S.), World Assn. Univs. and Colls., Inter-Am. Research Inst., Acad. Internat. Bus., Brit. Inst. Mgmt. (companion), Can. Council Internat. Cooperation (dir.), Can. Inst. Pub. Affairs, European Found. Mgmt. Devel., Internat. Inventors Assn., Polish Inst. (U.K.), Can. Assn. Univ. Bus. Officers, Can. Polish Congress (pres. nat. council 1960-69), other orgns. Roman Catholic. Office: Can Sch Mgmt, 335 Bay St Ste 1120, Toronto, ON Canada M5H 2R3

KOREZ, JOHN JOSEPH, chemical executive; b. Queens, N.Y., Apr. 22, 1964; s. Harold and Barbar K.; m. Hope J., July 7, 1990; children: Casey, Shea, Paige. BS, L.I. U., 1986. Mgmt. tng. program, comml. lending tng. program Chem. Banking Corp., N.Y.C., 1986-90; v.p., treas., sec. Andrews Paper & Chem. Co., Inc., Port Washington, N.Y., 1990—; dir. Andrews Paper & Chem. Co., Inc.; semi-profl. football def. end Bklyn. Mariners, 1988-90. Republican. Roman Catholic. Avocations: horses, running, weight lifting, golf. Office: Andrews Paper & Chem Co Inc PO box 509 1 Channel Dr Port Washington NY 11050

KORF, GENE ROBERT, lawyer; b. Greenville, S.C., June 2, 1952; s. Norman and Paula (Heller) K.; m. Madeline Jane Hammer, June 20, 1976; children: Scott, Neil. BA summa cum laude, Hunter Coll., 1974; JD, Bklyn. Law Sch., 1977; LLM in Taxation, NYU, 1983. Dir. Korf & Rosenblatt, Morristown, N.J. Prodr. (mus. rev.) And the World Goes Round (Drama Desk award 1990, 91, Outer Critics Cir. award 1990, 91), The Kentucky Cycle, 1993 (Tony award nominee 1994). Trustee Roundabout Theatre Co., 1993—, Harold Wetterberg Found., 1991—, Blanche and Irving Laurie Found., 1991—, Schulman Family Found., 1993. Jewish. Office: Korf & Rosenblatt 89 Hdqrs Plz North Tower 14th Fl Morristown NJ 07960-1734

KORF, LEONARD LEE, theater arts educator; b. Chgo., Jan. 31, 1917; s. William Milton and Eva (Lewin) K.; m. Claire Jean Prinz, Aug. 15, 1949; children: William Milton II, Kerry Lee, Geoffrey Leonard. BA, UCLA, 1949; diploma, Harvard U., 1945; MA, UCLA, 1957, PhD, 1972; diploma, Harvard U. Lifetime tchg. credential, Calif. Prof. theatre arts, chmn. dept. Fullerton (Calif.) Coll., 1952-56, Cerritos (Calif.) Coll., 1956-82; CEO Korfco, Inc., Whittier, Calif., 1983—. Screen writer The AAF Comes of Age, 1945, The Lifemaker, 1956; exec. editor Ednl. Theatre News, 1956-93; book and theatre reviewer L.A. Times, 1972-73; rev. editor Calif. Ednl. Theatre Assn., L.A., 1993—; lead actor Space Chase. Maj. USAF, 1941-46. Decorated Disting. Flying Cross with two clusters USAF, 1943-44, Air medal with 5 clusters USAF, 1943-44. Fellow Am. Theatre Fellow Kennedy Ctr. (life); mem. Am. Theatre Assn. (bd. mem., pub. rels. dir. 1970-71), So. Calif. Ednl. Theatre Assn. (pres. 1975-76). Democrat. Agnostic. Avocation: national table tennis champion. Home and Office: Korfco Inc 9811 Pounds Ave Whittier CA 90603-1616

KORF, RICHARD PAUL, mycology educator; b. Bronxville, N.Y., May 28, 1925; s. Frederick and Evelyn F. (Krug) K.; m. Kumiko Tachibana, June 27, 1959; children: Noni, Mia, Ian, Mario. BSc, Cornell U., 1946, PhD, 1950. Lectr. botany U. Glasgow, Scotland, 1950-51; asst. prof. Cornell U., Ithaca, N.Y., 1951-55, assoc. prof., 1955-61, prof. mycology, 1961-92, chmn. theatre arts, 1985-86, prof. emeritus, 1992—; Fulbright rsch. prof. Yokohama (Japan) Nat. U., 1957-58; cons. prof. U. Ryukyus, Ryukyu Islands, 1969; adjunktvikar U. Copenhagen, 1973; Fulbright rsch. scholar U. Louvain, Belgium, 1972-73; dir. Exe Island Biol. Sta., Portland, Ont., 1973—; mem. sci. coun. Academia Sinica, Beijing, China, 1985-90. Editor Mycotaxon, 1974-91; book rev. editor Mycologia, 1972-80; corr. editor Mycological Rsch., 1996-98; mem. editl. bd. Persoonia, 1987—, Mycosystema, 1988-94. State vice chair Liberal party, N.Y., 1968. Sr. postdoctoral fellow NSF, Yokohama, 1957; recipient SUNY Chancellor's award for excellence in teaching, 1992. Fellow Br. Mycol. Soc. (Centennial); mem. Internat. Mycol. Assn. (nomenclature chmn. 1971-84), Internat. Assn. Plant Taxonomy (mem. gen. com. 1975-91); Mycol. Soc. Am. (pres. 1971, Disting. Mycologist Award 1991). Avocations: acting, contract bridge, naturism. Home: 316 Richard Pl Ithaca NY 14850-3129 Office: Cornell U Plant Pathology Plant Sci Bldg Ithaca NY 14853

KORFF, PHYLLIS G., lawyer; b. N.Y.C., 1943. BA, Bklyn. Coll., 1964; EdM, Boston U., 1967; JD, NYU, 1981. Bar: N.Y. 1982. Ptnr. Skaden, Arps, Slate, Meagher & Flom, N.Y.C., 1990. Office: Skadden Arps Slate Meagher & Flom 919 3rd Ave New York NY 10022-3902*

KORFF, YITZCHOK AHARON, rabbi; b. Boston, Aug. 30, 1949; s. Nathan and Helen (Pfeffer) K.; children: Kimberlee A., Yaakov Yisroel, Dovid Yehoshua, Mordechai, Boruch. BJE, Hebrew Coll., 1968; BA, Columbia U., 1969; DD, Rabbinical Acad., 1971; JD, Bklyn. Law Sch., 1972; MA in Internat. Rels., Fletcher Sch. Law and Diplomacy, Tufts U.-Harvard U., 1973, MA in Law and Diplomacy, 1975; PhD in Internat. Law, Tufts U.-Harvard U., 1976; grad. resident Divinity Sch., Harvard U., 1975; LLM, Boston U., 1980. Bar: Mass. 1974, U.S. Dist. Ct. Mass. 1975, U.S. Tax Ct. 1976, U.S. Ct. Appeals (1st cir.) 1976, U.S. Supreme Ct. 1978, D.C. 1980, U.S. Ct. Internat. Trade, 1981. Ptnr. Hill, Livingstone & Assocs. and Enterprise Internat., Inc., Boston, 1974-81, Lewenberg & Korff, Boston, 1974-94; rabbi Beth Sholom, Hull, Mass., 1969-71, Charles River Pk. Synagogue, Boston, 1971-74, Beth Sholom, Providence, 1974-75, Temple Aliyah, Needham, Mass., 1975-83, Congregation B'nai Jacob, Newton, Mass., 1983—; Zvhil-Mezbuz Rebbe Zvhil-Mezbuz Beis Medrash, Boston and Newton, Mass., 1993—; spl. cons. to dist. atty. Norfolk County, Mass., 1975-85; spl. asst. to atty. gen. Commonwealth of Mass., Boston, 1977-85; judge Rabbinical Ct. Justice, Boston, 1975—; hon. consul Austria, dir. Austrian Consulate, Boston, 1987—; sr. v.p., bd. dirs. Viacom, Inc., N.Y.C., 1987-94, Viacom Internat., N.Y.C., 1987-94; pres. Nat. Amusements Inc., Dedham, 1988-94, pres., mng. dir. Nat. Amusements (UK) Ltd., Dedham, 1987-94; bd. dirs. Coun. on Religion and Law, Boston, 1978-84; bd. dirs., mem. exec. com. Nat. Assn. Theatre Owners, 1988-94. Owner, pub. The Jewish Advocate, The Jewish Times, Guide to Jewish Boston and New England, Boston, 1990—. Mem. Friends of Fletcher Sch. Law and Diplomacy, Boston, 1974-94, Boston Consumers Coun., 1975-80; trustee Dana Farber Cancer Inst., Boston, 1990-95; bd. visitors Hebrew Coll. Boston, 1990—; Jewish chaplain City of Boston, 1974—. Mem. Am. Arbitration Assn., Harvard U. Club (Boston). Office: 15 School St Boston MA 02108-4307

KORG, JACOB, English literature educator; b. N.Y.C., Nov. 21, 1922; s. Reuben and Mary (Lehrman) K.; m. Cynthia Stewart, Jan. 21, 1952; 1 dau., Nora Francis. B.A., CCNY, 1943; M.A., Columbia U., 1947, Ph.D., 1952. Instr. English Bard Coll., 1947-49, CCNY, 1950-55; from asst. prof. to prof. U. Wash., Seattle, 1955-68; prof. English U. Wash., 1970-91, prof. emeritus, 1991—; prof. English U. Md., 1968-70; vis. prof. Nat. Taiwan U., 1960. Author: George Gissing, A Critical Biography, 1963, Dylan Thomas, 1965, Language in Modern Literature, 1979, rev. edit., 1992, Browning and Italy, 1983, Ritual and Experiment in Modern Poetry, 1995, also articles, revs.; editor: London in Dickens' Day, 1960, George Gissing's Commonplace Book, 1962, The Force of Few Words, 1966, Twentieth Century Views of Bleak House, 1968, Poetry of Robert Browning, 1971; co-editor: George Gissing on Fiction, 1978; mem. editl. bd. Victorian Poetry, 1979—, Nineteenth-Century Lit., 1983-95, Rivista di Studi Vittoriani. Served with AUS, 1943-46. Mem. MLA, Assn. Literary Scholars and Critics. Home: 6530 51st Ave NE Seattle WA 98115-7741 Office: Univ Wash Dept English Seattle WA 98195

KORGAN, MICHELLE LEE, restaurateur; b. Portland, Oreg., May 29, 1973; d. Milton Eugene and Carol Lee (Codr) K. Grad., Whitman Coll., Walla Walla, Wash., 1998. Restaurant mgr. The Chase Co., Portland, 1990-92; pastry chef The Strudel House, Portland, 1992-93; restaurant owner Pangea, Walla Walla, 1995-98; mgr. Heceta Lightstation Bed and Breakfast, Yachats, Oreg., 1998—; restaurant cons. The Chase Co., 1990-92. Avocations: writing, directing, biking. Office: Heceta Lightstation Bed and Breakfast 92072 Hwy 101 S Yachats OR 97498

KORINOW, IRA LEE, rabbi; b. Newton, Mass., Feb. 14, 1951; s. Maurice and Freida (Pecker) K.; m. Gail Lynne Jaffe, Feb. 20, 1977; children: Morry Lev, Doron Ephraim, Raanan Meir. BA in Religion, Boston U., 1973; MA in Hebrew Lit., Hebrew Union Coll., 1976, cert. crisis counseling, 1989. Ordained rabbi, 1978. Prin. Rodeph Sholom Religious Sch., N.Y.C., 1975-77; rabbi Temple B'nai Israel, Laconia, N.H., 1977-78, North Shore Congregation Israel, Glencoe, Ill., 1978-81, Temple Emanu-El, Haverhill, Mass., 1981—. Bd. dirs. Union Coun. for Soviet Jews, Washington, 1984-87, Action for Soviet Jewry, Waltham, Mass., 1983-88; founder, chmn. Greater Haverhill Citizens' Civil Rights Commn., 1991—. Mem. Nat. Conf. Soviet Jewry (bd. dirs. 1985-88), Ctrl. Conf. Am. Rabbis (Soviet Jewry conf. 1981-87, Gerut com. 1991—), N.E. Region Ctrl. Conf. Am. Rabbis (treas. 1989-91, sec. 1991-93, v.p. 1993-97, pres. 1997-99), Rabbinical Assembly (corr. 1991—), Mass. Bd. Rabbis (sec. 1985-87, treas. 1987-89, v.p. 1989-95, pres. 1995-97), Greater Haverhill Clergy Assn. (pres. 1989-92), Coalition for the Advancement Jewish Edn., Rotary. Home: 23 Singingwood Dr Haverhill MA 01830-1452 Office: Temple Emanu-El 514 Main St Haverhill MA 01830-3293

KORMAN, EDWARD R., federal judge; b. N.Y.C., Oct. 25, 1942; s. Julius and Miriam K.; m. Diane R. Eisner, Feb. 3, 1979; children: Miriam M., Benjamin E. B.A., Bklyn. Coll., 1963; LL.B., Bklyn. Law Sch., 1966; LL.M., NYU, 1971. Bar: N.Y. 1966, U.S. Supreme Ct. 1972. Law clk. to judge N.Y. Ct. Appeals, 1966-68; assoc. Paul, Weiss, Rifkind, Wharton and Garrison, 1968-70; asst. U.S. atty. Eastern Dist. N.Y., N.Y.C., 1970-72; asst. to solicitor gen. of U.S., 1972-74; chief asst. U.S. atty. Eastern Dist. N.Y., 1974-78, U.S. atty., 1978-82; ptnr. Stroock & Stroock & Lavan, N.Y.C., 1982-84; prof. Bklyn. Law Sch., 1984-85; U.S. dist. judge Eastern Dist. N.Y., 1985—. Chmn. Mayor's Com. on N.Y.C. Marshals, 1983-85; mem. Temporary Commn. of Investigation of State of N.Y., 1983-85. Jewish. Office: US Dist Ct US Courthouse 225 Cadman Plz E Brooklyn NY 11201-1818

KORMAN, HARVEY HERSCHEL, actor; b. Chgo., Feb. 15, 1927; s. Cyril Raymond and Ellen (Blecher) K.; m. Donna Ehlert, Aug. 27, 1960; children: Maria Ellen, Christopher Peter; m. Deborah Fritz, Sept. 18, 1982; children: Katherine, Laura. Student, Wright Jr. Coll., Chgo., Goodman Theatre, 1946-50. Actor: TV series The Danny Kaye Show, 1963-67, Carol Burnett Show, 1967-77, The Tim Conway Show, 1980-81, Mama's Family, 1983-84, Leo and Liz in Beverly Hills, 1986, The Nutt House, 1989; appeared in films Lord Love a Duck, 1966, The Last of the Secret Agents, 1966, Three Bites of an Apple, 1967, Don't Just Stand There, 1968, April Fools, 1969, Blazing Saddles, 1974, Huckleberry Finn, 1974, High Anxiety, 1978, Americathon, 1979, First Family, 1980, Herbie Goes Bananas, 1980, History of the World, Part I, 1981, Trail of the Pink Panther, 1982, The Invisible Woman, 1983, Curse of the Pink Panther, 1983, The Long Shot, 1986, Munchies, 1987, Betrayal of the Dove, 1993, Radioland Murders, 1994, (voice) The Flintstones, 1994, Dracula: Dead and Loving It, 1995, Jingle All the Way, 1996; TV films: Three's a Crowd, 1969, Suddenly Single, 1971, The Love Boat, 1976, Bud and Lou, 1978, Carpool, 1983, The Invisible Woman, 1983, Alice in Wonderland, 1985, Gideon's Web, 1998. Served with USNR, 1945-46. Recipient Emmy awards, 1969, 71, 72, 74. *

KORMAN, JAMES WILLIAM, lawyer; b. Washington, Apr. 29, 1943; s. Milton D. and Bernice (Rosensweig) K.; m. Barbara Dale Lewis, June 11, 1967; 1 child, Katherine Bernice. AB, Coll. William & Mary, 1965; JD, George Washington U., 1968. Bar: Va. 1968, D.C. 1970, U.S. Supreme Ct. 1972, U.S. Ct. Appeals (4th cir.) 1974, U.S. Dist. Ct. (ea. dist.) Va. 1975. Assoc. Kinney, Smith and Barham, Arlington, Va., 1968-73, ptnr., 1973-78; mng. prin. Bean, Kinney & Korman, Arlington, 1979—; neutral case evaluator Fairfax Cir. Ct., 1995—; mem. Va. Bar Coun., 1983-89, 98—, 10th dist. grievance com., 1978-81; mem. adv. bd. Bank of Arlington, Va., 1977-78; lectr. various civil litigation topics continuing legal edn.; contbg. atty. Mathew Bender's Fed. Practice Forms, 1978; panelist Va. Conf. Nat. Assn. Bank Women, 1984; adj. prof. George Mason U. Law Sch., 1996—; mem. faculty Va. State Bar Profl. Course, 1998—. Contbr. articles to profl. jours. Bd. dirs. No. Va. Jewish Cmty. Ctr., 1985-91; mem. adv. bd. Sch. Contemporary Edn., Springfield, Va., 1985-91; mem. Va. Commn. on Women and Minorities in the Law, 1988-92. Capt. USAR, 1972-74. Recipient Meritorious Svc. award Legal Aid Bur., 1968, Adult Leadership award Boy Scouts Am., 1972. Fellow Am. Acad. Matrimonial Lawyers (cert. arbitrator, Va. chpt. v.p. 1996—); mem. ABA, ATLA, Va. State Bar (pro bono steering com. 1992-93), Arlington Bar Assn. (pres. 1981-82, bd. dirs. 1977-81), Arlington Bar Found. (bd. dirs. 1990—), Va. Trial Lawyers Assn. (jud. task force 1998—), Plaintiffs Bar Ltd. Democrat. Avocations: racquetball, collecting polit. buttons. Home: 2450 N Wakefield Ct Arlington VA 22207-3554 Office: Bean Kinney & Korman 2000 14th N St Ste 100 Arlington VA 22201-2552

KORMAN, JESS J., advertising executive, writer, producer; b. N.Y.C.; s. Rubin and Beatrice K. B.A., NYU. Freelance TV writer, playwright, 1963-69; v.p., assoc. creative dir. J. Walter Thompson Co., N.Y.C., 1969-77; sr. v.p., exec. creative dir. J. Walter Thompson Co., Los Angeles, 1978-81; freelance writer TV, films, 1980-83; sr. v.p., creative dir. Benton & Bowles, Inc., N.Y.C., 1983-86; pres., creative dir. Air Korman Inc. Creative Avt. Services, N.Y.C., 1987—. Writer numerous TV shows, plays, radio, TV commls. and videos. Mem. Writers Guild Am. Office: Ste 907 419 Park Ave S New York NY 10016-8410

KORMAN, LEWIS J., entertainment/media company executive, lawyer; b. N.Y.C., Feb. 18, 1945; s. Irving D. and Sylvia (Margolies) K.; m. Sharon G. Weiss, Aug. 20, 1967; children: Eric Andrew, Raina Allison. BS in Indsl. and Labor Rels., Cornell U., 1966; JD cum laude, NYU, 1969. Bar: N.Y. 1970. Assoc. Kaye, Scholer, Fierman, Hays & Handler, N.Y.C., 1969-77, ptnr., 1978-79; founding ptnr. Gelberg & Abrams, N.Y.C., 1979-84, cons., 1984-87; gen. ptnr. Delphi Film Assocs. Partnerships, N.Y.C., 1982-86; sr. exec. v.p. Tri-Star Pictures, Inc., N.Y.C., 1987; COO, chmn. motion picture group Columbia Pictures Entertainment, Inc., 1988-89; pres. Savoy Pictures Entertainment, Inc., 1990-96; vice chmn. R.A.B. Holdings, Inc., 1997—; pres. Delphi Film Enterprises, Ltd., 1997—. Mem. Acad. Motion Pictures Arts and Scis. (exec. br.), Assn. Bar City of N.Y., Order of the Coif. Office: RAB Holdings Inc 444 Madison Ave Ste 601 New York NY 10022-6903

KORMAN, NATHANIEL IRVING, research and development company executive; b. Providence, Feb. 23, 1916; s. William and Tillie (Jacobs) K.; m. Ruth C. Kaplan, Apr. 6, 1941; children—Michael, Robert. BS summa cum laude, Worcester Poly. Inst., 1937; MS (Coffin fellow), MIT, 1938; PhD, U. Pa., 1958. Dir. advance mil. systems RCA Corp., 1958-67; chmn. radar panel U.S. R&D Bd., 1948-56; lectr. U. Pa. Evening Grad. Sch., 1967-68; cons. in field Color Sci., 1968-83; pres. Ventures R&D Group; cons. to Satellite Wholesales of N.Mex., 1991—. Author: The Evolution of Human Society, 1998; patentee in field. Mem. Citizens Com. for Better Schs., Moorestown, N.J., 1958. Recipient Merit award RCA, 1951. Fellow IEEE; mem. Sigma Xi. Home: 5700 Teakwood Trl NE Albuquerque NM 87111-6225

KORMONDY, EDWARD JOHN, university official, biology educator; b. Beacon, N.Y., June 10, 1926; s. Anthony and Frances (Glover) K.; m. Peggy Virginia Hedrick, June 5, 1950 (div. 1989); children: Lynn Ellen, Eric Paul, Mark Hedrick. BA in Biology summa cum laude, Tusculum Coll., 1950, DSc (hon.), 1997; MS in Zoology, U. Mich., 1951, PhD in Zoology, 1955. Teaching fellow U. Mich., 1952-55; instr. zoology, curator insects Mus. Zoology, 1955-57; asst. prof. Oberlin (Ohio) Coll., 1957-63, assoc. prof., 1963-67, prof., 1967-69, acting assoc. dean, 1966-67; dir. Commn. Undergrad. Edn. in Biol. Scis., Washington, 1968-72; dir. Office Biol. Edn., Am. Inst. Biol. Scis., Washington, 1968-71; mem. faculty Evergreen State Coll., Olympia, Wash., 1971-79, interim acting dean, 1972-73, v.p., provost, 1973-78; sr. profl. assoc., directorate sci. edn. NSF, 1979; provost, prof. biology U. So. Maine, Portland, 1979-82; v.p. acad. affairs, prof. biology Calif. State U., Los Angeles, 1982-86; sr. v.p., chancellor, prof. biology U. Hawaii, Hilo/West Oahu, 1986-93; pres. U. West L.A., 1995-97. Author: Concepts of Ecology, 1969, 76, 83, 96, General Biology: The Integrity and Natural History of Organisms, 1977, Handbook of Contemporary World Developments in Ecology, 1981, International Handbook of Pollution Control, 1989, (textbook) Biology, 1984, 88, Fundamentals of Human Ecology, 1998; contbr. articles to profl. jours. Served with USN, 1944-46. U. Ga. postdoctoral fellow radiation ecology, 1963-64; vis. research fellow Center for Bioethics, Georgetown U., 1978-79; research grantee Nat. Acad. Scis., Am. Philos. Soc., NSF, Sigma Xi. Fellow AAAS; mem. Ecol. Soc. Am. (sec. 1976-78), Nat. Assn. Biology Tchrs. (pres. 1981), N.Am. Assn. Environ. Edn., Soc. Calif. Acad. Scis. (bd. dirs. 1985-86, 93-97, v.p. 1995-96), Sigma Xi, Phi Kappa Phi.

KORN, BARRY PAUL, equipment and vehicle leasing company executive; b. N.Y.C., May 27, 1944; s. Nat and Judith K.; children: Lisa Michele, Suzanne Leslie, Amy Beth. BBA in Acctg., CCNY, 1966; MBA in Fin., CUNY, 1969. Assoc. E.M. Warburg, Pincus & Co., Inc., N.Y.C., 1964-70; treas., sec. Interstate Brands (formerly DPF Inc.), Hartsdale, N.Y., 1970-75; pres. Barrett Capital Group, Mamaroneck, N.Y., 1975—, dir. ARC Westchester chpt., 1991—, Trustee Westchester Arts Coun., 1990—. Mem. Am. Assn. Equipment Lessors (bd. dirs. 1974-77), Fin. Execs. Instr. (pres. Westchester chpt. 1976-77, bd. dirs. Conn./West chpt. 1989-92), Computer Dealers and Lessors Assn. (treas. 1971-72, bd. dirs. 1979-84, chmn. industry practices com. 1979-82, v.p. 1982-84). Office: 930 Mamaroneck Ave Mamaroneck NY 10543-1629

KORN, DAVID, educator, pathologist; b. Providence, Mar. 5, 1933; s. Solomon and Claire (Liebman) K.; m. PhoebeRichter, June 9, 1955 (div. Dec. 1993); children: Michael Philip, Stephen James, Daniel Clair; m. Carol Scheman, Dec. 24, 1997. BA, Harvard U., 1954, MD, 1959. Intern Mass. Gen. Hosp., Boston, 1959-60, resident in Pathology, 1960-61; rsch. assoc. NIH, 1961-63, asst. pathologist, 1963-68; mem. staff Lab. Biochem. Pharmacology; prof. pathology Sch. Medicine, Stanford (Calif.) U., 1968-97, chmn. dept. pathology Sch. Medicine, 1968-84; physician-in-chief pathology Stanford Hosp., 1968-84, dean Sch. Medicine, 1984-95, v.p., dean, 1986-95; cons. pathology Palo Alto VA Hosp., 1968-84; sr. v.p. biomed. and health scis. rsch. Assn. Am. Med. Colls., 1997—; sr. surgeon USPHS, 1961-66; mem. cell biology study sect. NIH, 1973-77, chmn., 1976-77; mem. bd. sci. counselors, divsn. cancer biology and diagnosis Nat. Cancer Inst., 1977-82, chmn., 1980-82; chmn. Nat. Cancer Adv. Bd., 1984-91; disting. scholar in residence Assn. Am. Med. Colls., 1995-97; sr. fellow sci. and health policy Assn. Acad. Health Ctrs., 1995-97. Mem. editorial bd. Human Pathology, 1969-74, assoc. editor, 1974-88; mem. editorial bd. Jour. Biol. Chemistry, 1973-79. Recipient Young Scientist award Md. Acad. Sci., 1967. Mem. Am. Soc. Biochemistry Molecular Biology, Am. Soc. Investigative Pathology. Fedn. Am. Soc. Exptl. Biology (bd. dirs., mem. exec. com.), Inst. of Medicine. Home: 4018 Chancery Ct NW Washington DC 20007-2140 Office: AAMC 2450 N St NW Washington DC 20037-1167

KORN, EDWARD DAVID, biochemist; b. Phila., Aug. 3, 1928; s. Joel and Carrie (Goldman) K.; m. Muriel Evelyn Fisher, June 23, 1950; children: Elizabeth Gail Korn Schoenherr, Sarah Harris Korn Gilchrist. BA, U. Pa., 1949, PhD, 1954. Scientist Nat. Heart, Lung, Blood Inst., Bethesda, Md., 1954-69; vis. scientist Cambridge (Eng.) U., 1958-59, 69-70; prof. FAES Grad. Program, Bethesda, 1966-76; head sect. on cell biology Nat. Heart Lung and Blood Inst., Bethesda, 1969—, chief lab. of cell biology, 1974—, sci. dir., 1989-99. Editor: (book series) Methods in Membrane Biology, 1974-79; assoc. editor Jour. Biol. Chemistry, 1977-93; contbr. numerous sci. articles to jours. in field, 1953—. Recipient Superior Svc. award USPHS, 1980, Presdl. Meritorious Exec. Rank award, 1987; Mider lectr. NIH, 1985. Mem. NAS, Am. Soc. for Biochemistry and Molecular Biology, Biophys. Soc., Am. Soc. Cell Biology, Found. Advanced Edn. in Scs. (bd. dirs. 1977-92). Office: NIH Bldg 10 Rm 7N-214 MSC 1668 Bethesda MD 20892

KORN, HENRY, museum administrator; b. Sept. 19, 1945. AB, Johns Hopkins U., 1968. Exec. dir. Lower Manhattan Cultural Coun., N.Y.C., 1978-80; arts commn. dir. City of Santa Monica, Calif., 1986-90; cultural affairs mgr. City of Irvine, Calif., 1990-93; pres., CEO, mus. dir. Guild Hall of East Hampton, N.Y., 1993-99; dir. art and culture City of Beverly Hills, Calif., 1999—. Author: Muhammad Ali Retrospective, 1976, Difficult Act to Follow, 1982, Marc Chagall, 1984. Fiction fellow Nat. Endowment for the Arts, 1977. Office: 455 N Rexford Dr Beverly Hills CA 90210

KORN, JESSICA SUSAN, education educator, researcher, ambassador; b. L.A., Aug. 16, 1968; d. Lester B. and Carolbeth (Goldman) K. BA in Sociology, UCLA, 1990, MA in Edn., 1992, PhD of Edn., 1996. Actor Curb-Esquire Films, Burbank, Calif., 1984; exec. asst. Korn Capital Group, Inc., L.A., 1991; tchg. asst. Grad. Sch. Edn. and Info. Studies UCLA, 1995, rsch. analyst Grad. Sch. Edn. and Info. Studies, 1992-96, postdoctoral fellow Higher Edn. Rsch. Inst., 1996—, tchg. assoc., 1997; rsch. scientist, affiliate asst. prof. U. Wash., 1997—; internat. election observer Orgn. for Security and Cooperation in Europe, 1997, 98. Contbr. articles to profl. jours. Jr. assoc. Big Sisters Am., L.A., 1994—. Mem. AAUW, Am. Ednl. Rsch. Assn., Assn. Study of Higher Edn., Assn. for Instnl. Rsch., Nat. Coun. Rsch. on Women, Screen Actors Guild Am. Avocations: working with rape and other trauma survivors, humanitarian aid, travel, writing, yoga, acting. Office: Univ Wash 400 NE Campus Pky Rm 453 Seattle WA 98195-5387

KORN, LESTER BERNARD, business executive, diplomat; b. N.Y.C., Jan. 11, 1936. BS with honors, UCLA, 1959, MBA, 1960; postgrad., Harvard Bus. Sch., 1961. Mgmt. cons. Peat, Marwick, Mitchell & Co., L.A., 1961-66, ptnr., 1966-69; founder, CEO Korn/Ferry Internat., L.A., 1969-91, chmn. emeritus, 1991—; U.S. amb. and U.S. rep. Econ. and Social Coun. UN, 1987-88; chmn., founder Korn Tuttle Capital Group, Inc., 1991; alt. rep. 42d and 43d UN Gen. Assembly; chmn., CEO Korn Tuttle Capital Group, Inc., 1991; bd. dirs. Continental Am. Properties, Music Ctr. Operating Co. L.A., Tenet Healthcare Corp., RAND-Ctr. for Russian and Eurasian Studies; mem. U.S. Presdl. Del. to Observe Elections in Bosnia, 1996. Author: The Success Profile, 1989. Trustee UCLA Found.; bd. overseers and bd. visitors Anderson Grad. Sch. Mgmt., UCLA; trustee, founding mem. Dean's Coun. UCLA; mem. adv. coun. Am. Heart Assn.; spl. advisor, del. UNESCO Intergov. Conf. on Edn. for Internat. Understanding, Coop., Peace, 1983; adv. bd. Women in Film Found., 1983-84; chmn. Commn. on Citizen Participation in Govt., State of Calif., 1979-82; bd. dirs. John Douglas French Found. for Alzheimer's Disease; mem. Republican Nat. Exec. Fin. Com., 1985, Pres.'s Commn. White House Fellowships, Republican Eagles; hon. chairperson 50th Am. Presdl. Inaugural, 1985; co-chmn. So. Calif. region NCCJ; mem. U.S. Presdl. Del. to observe elections in Bosnia, 1996. Recipient Alumni Profl. Achievement award UCLA, 1984, Superior Honor award U.S. Dept. State, 1988, Neil H. Jacoby Internat. award, 1990, Internat. Citizen of Yr. award Internat. Visitors Coun., 1991; Korn Convocation Hall at UCLA dedicated in his honor, 1995. Mem. AICPAs, Calif. Soc. CPAs, Am. Bus. Conf. (founding mem.), Coun. Am. Ambs., Prodrs. Guild of Am., Hillcrest Country Club, Regency Club, Rockefeller Ctr. Club. Office: Korn Tuttle Capital Grp 1800 Century Park E Ste 210 Los Angeles CA 90067-1505

KORN, MICHAEL JEFFREY, lawyer; b. Jersey City, Dec. 22, 1954; s. Howard Leonard and Joyce Ellen (Blumenkranz) K.; m. Pamela Ann VanZandt, May 29, 1983; children: David Harold, Suzanne Faye. BA, U. Va., 1976; JD, U. Fla., 1979. Bar: Fla. 1980, U.S. Dist. Ct. (no. and mid. dists.) Fla., U.S. Ct. Appeals (5th and 11th cirs.). Jud. law clk. Fla. 1st Dist Ct. Appeal, Tallahassee, 1980-81; assoc. Boyer, Tanzler & Boyer, Jacksonville, Fla., 1981-84; pvt. practice Jacksonville, 1984-87; ptnr. Prom, Korn & Zehmer, P.A., Jacksonville, 1987—, Korn & Zehmer, P.A., Jacksonville, 1995—; mem. Fla. Appellate Ct. Rules Com., 1990—. Bd. dirs. North Fla. coun. Camp Fire, 1983-86, Jacksonville Jewish Fedn., 1985—, v.p., 1994—; bd. dirs. Youth Leadership Jacksonville, 1989-93; bd. dirs. Jacksonville Cmty. Coun., 1989-94, 96-98, pres., 1995; Mandarin Comty. Club, Jacksonville, 1988-91; cmty. adv. bd. WJCT-TV, Jacksonville, 1996—, vice-chmn., 1998-99. Recipient Young Leadership award Jacksonville Jewish Fedn., 1992. Mem. Fla. Bar (litig, appellate and health law sects.), Jacksonville Bar Assn. (fee arbitration cir. 1987-90, CLE chair 1995-96, 97—), Acad. Fla. Trial Lawyers. Democrat. Jewish. Avocations: recreational basketball, reading, golf. Office: Korn & Zehmer PA Ste 200 6620 Southpoint Dr S Jacksonville FL 32216-0940

KORN, NEAL MARK, painter, art educator; b. Nyack, N.Y., May 11, 1957; s. Jacob and Sylvia Korn; m. Patsy Anne Trine, Oct. 25, 1985; 1 child, Sasha Jaye. AA, Palm Beach Jr. Coll., Lake Worth, Fla., 1978; BS in Art, Bklyn. Coll./SUNY, 1983; MA in Studio Art, Kean U., 1998. Exhibited in group shows Night Gallery, N.Y.C., 1987, La Mama's La Galleria, N.Y.C., 1988, 89, Ape Gallery, N.Y.C., 1990, 92, Art et Industrie Gallery, N.Y.C., 1991, 148 Gallery, N.Y.C., 1992, 93, 94, 95, City Without Walls, N.J., 1995, 96, Art Alliance, N.J., 1995, 96, 97, 98, Art Ctr. No. N.J., 1998, Aljira, N.J., 1996, Audart, N.Y.C., 1996, N.J. Ctr. for Visual Arts, 1997, Watchung Arts Ctr., N.J., 1997, William Paterson U., N.J., 1998, Gallery of South Orange, N.J., 1999, Kean U., N.J., 1998, Joan Prats Gallery, N.Y.C., 1998, Liquid Gallery, N.J., 1999, others. Recipient Shaw award for painting Bklyn. Coll., 1982, Best of Oil Painting-Book, Rockport Pubs., 1996, other awards; Heart Grant for Art, 1998. Address: 912 Pennsylvania Ave Union NJ 07083-6930

KORN, PETER A., city manager; b. N.Y.C., Sept. 16, 1939; s. Samuel S. and Sylvia (Sachs) K.; m. Marian Bell, Dec. 24, 1967; 1 child, Sheryl Robin. B.B.A., CCNY, 1961; M.G.A., U. Pa., 1962. Exec. asst. City of Rochester, N.Y., 1962-64, budget dir., 1964-69, city mgr., 1980-85; mgr. City of Long Beach, N.Y., 1970-71; adminstr. Jersey City, 1972-75, Broward County, Fla., 1975-76; prof., asst. to pres. Nova U., Ft. Lauderdale, Fla., 1976-80; v.p. electronic tng. div. Kodak Corp., Rochester, 1986-87, cons. state and local services, electronic tng. div., 1987-89; prof. pub. adminstrn. SUNY, Brockport, 1987-90; city mgr. City of Peoria, Peoria, Ill., 1990-96, City of New Rochelle, N.Y., 1996—. Author: Financing City and Schools in Yonkers NY, 1976. Mem. Internat. City Mgmt. Assn., Am. Soc. Pub. Adminstrn. Jewish. Avocations: gardening; boating.

KORN, STEVEN ERIC, medical publisher; b. N.Y.C., Apr. 1, 1944; s. Otto and Melanie (Ungar) K.; Deborah Dee, Aug. 24, 1975; 3 children. BA with honors, NYU, 1965. V.p. Intercontinental Med. Book Corp. (subs. Grune & Stratton), N.Y.C., 1965-70; chmn. bd. Futura Pub. Co., Mt. Kisco, N.Y., 1970—. Mem. N.Y. Acad. Scis. Office: Futura Pub Co PO Box 418 135 Bedford Rd Armonk NY 10504-1937

KORNATOWSKI, SUSAN CAROL, elementary education educator; b. Constableville, N.Y., Apr. 21, 1955; d. Anthony John and Estella Helen (Ward) K. BA, SUNY, Potsdam, 1977; MA, Cortland State U., 1984. Cert. elem. edn. tchr., N.Y. 2nd grade tchr. Adirondack Central Sch., West Leyden, N.Y., 1983—. Active PTA. Named to SUNY Potsdam Alumni Sports Hall of Fame, 1990, Excellent Tchr. of Yr., 1997. Mem. West Leyden Free Reading Ctr. (librarian 1982-83, treas. 1983—). Roman Catholic. Avocations: ceramics, knitting, sewing, sports, volleyball. Home: PO Box 121 West Leyden NY 13489-0121 Office: West Leyden Elem Sch Fish Creek Rd West Leyden NY 13489

KORNBERG, ALAN WILLIAM, lawyer; b. N.Y.C., Dec. 11, 1952; s. Peter and Selma (Borden) K. AB, Brandeis U., 1974; JD, NYU, 1977. Bar: N.Y. 1978, D.C. 1993. Assoc. Milbank, Tweed, Hadley & McCloy, N.Y.C., 1977-86, ptnr., 1986-90; ptnr. Paul, Weiss, Rifkind, Wharton & Garrison, N.Y.C., 1990—; Fellow Am. Coll. Bankruptcy, 1995; adj. instr. law Yeshiva U., N.Y.C., 1984-85. Bd. dirs. Lubovitch Dance Found., Inc., 1988-98, Photographers & Friends United Against AIDS, 1989-92, Classical Action, 1993-98. Mem. ABA, N.Y. Bar Assn., Assn. of Bar of City of N.Y., Akin Hall Assn. Home: 71 E 77th St New York NY 10021-1834 Office: Paul Weiss Rifkind Wharton & Garrison Rm 200 1285 Avenue Of The Americas New York NY 10019-6065

KORNBERG, ARTHUR, biochemist; b. N.Y.C., N.Y., Mar. 3, 1918; s. Joseph and Lena (Katz) K.; m. Sylvy R. Levy, Nov. 21, 1943 (dec. 1986); children: Roger, Thomas Bill, Kenneth Andrew; m. Charlene Walsh Levering, 1988 (dec. 1995). BS, CCNY, 1937, LLD (hon.), 1960; MD, U. Rochester, 1941, DSc (hon.), 1962; DSc (hon.), U. Pa., U. Notre Dame, 1965, Washington U., 1968, Princeton U., 1970, Colby Coll., 1970; LHD (hon.), Yeshiva U., 1963; MD honoris causa, U. Barcelona, Spain, 1970. Intern in medicine Strong Meml. Hosp., Rochester, N.Y., 1941-42; commd. officer USPHS, 1942, advanced through grades to med. dir., 1951; mem. staff NIH, Bethesda, Md., 1942-52, nutrition sect., div. physiology, 1942-45; chief sect. enzymes and metabolism Nat. Inst. Arthritis and Metabolic Diseases, 1947-52; guest research worker depts. chemistry and pharmacology coll. medicine NYU, 1946; dept. biol. chemistry med. sch. Washington U., 1947; dept. plant biochemistry U. Calif., 1951; prof., head dept. microbiology, med. sch. Washington U., St. Louis, 1953-59; prof. biochemistry Stanford U. Sch. Medicine, 1959—, chmn. dept., 1959-69, prof. emeritus dept. biochemistry, 1988—; Mem. sci. adv. bd. Mass. Gen. Hosp., 1964-67; bd. govs. Weizmann Inst., Israel. Author: For the Love of Enzymes, 1989; contbr. sci. articles to profl. jours. Served lt. (j.g.), med. officer USCGR, 1942. Recipient Paul-Lewis award in enzyme chemistry, 1951; co-recipient of Nobel prize in medicine, 1959; recipient Max Berg award prolonging human life, 1968, Sci. Achievement award AMA, 1968, Lucy Wortham James award James Ewing Soc., 1968, Borden award Am. Assn. Med. Colls., 1968, Nat. medal of sci., 1979. Gairdner Foundation International Awards, 1995. Mem. Am. Soc. Biol. Chemists (pres. 1965), Am. Chem. Soc., Harvey Soc., Am. Acad. Arts and Scis., Royal Soc., Nat. Acad. Scis. (mem. council 1963-66), Am. Philos. Soc., Phi Beta Kappa, Sigma Xi, Alpha Omega Alpha. Office: Stanford U Sch of Med Dept Biochemistry Beckman Ctr Rm B400 Stanford CA 94305-5307

KORNBERG, SIR HANS LEO, biochemist; b. Herford, Germany, Jan. 14, 1928; s. Max and Margarete (Silberbach) K.; m. Monica Mary King, Oct. 6, 1956 (dec. June 1989); children: Julia Margaret, Rachel Elizabeth, Jonathan Paul, Simon Alexander; m. Donna Haber, July 28, 1991. B.Sc., U. Sheffield, 1949, Ph.D., 1953, D.Sc. (hon.), 1979; M.A., Oxford U., 1958, D.Sc., 1961; Sc.D. (hon.), U. Cin., 1974; Sc.D., Cambridge U., 1975; D.Sc. (hon.), Warwick U., 1975, Leicester U., 1979, Bath U., 1980, Strathclyde U., 1985, South Bank U., 1994, Leeds U., 1995, La Trobe U., 1997; D.U. (hon.), Essex U., 1979; M.D. (hon.), Leipzig U., 1984; LLD (hon.) Dundee U., 1999. John Stokes research fellow U. Sheffield, 1951-53; Commonwealth Fund fellow Yale U., U. Calif., Berkeley, Pub. Health Research Inst., N.Y., 1953-55; mem. sci. staff M.R.C. cell metabolism rsch. unit, Oxford, 1955-60; prof. biochemistry U. Leicester, 1960-75; Sir William Dunn prof. biochemistry Cambridge (Eng.) U., 1975-95, fellow Christ's Coll., 1975—, Master, 1982-95; lectr. Worcester Coll., Oxford, 1958-60; Leeuwenhoek lectr. Royal Soc., 1972; Weizmann Meml. lectr., Rehovot, 1975; mem. Sci. Rsch. Coun., 1967-72, chmn. sci. bd., 1969-72; mem. U.G.C. Biol. Sci. Com., 1967-76; U.K. rep. NATO-ASI Panel, 1970-76, chmn., 1974-75; chmn. Royal Commn. on Environ. Pollution, 1976-81; mem. Agrl. Rsch. Coun., 1981-84; mem. Priorities Bd. for Rsch. and Devel. in Agr., 1984-90; chmn. adv. com. on Genetic Modification, 1986-95. Mng. trustee Nuffield Found., 1972-93; gov. Hebrew U. Jerusalem, 1976-97, hon. gov., 1997—; sci. gov. Weizmann Inst. Sci., Rehovot, Israel, 1981-90, emeritus gov., 1990—; trustee Marine Biol. Lab., Woods Hole, Mass., 1982-87, 88-93, Wellcome Trust, 1990-92; gov. Wellcome Trust Ltd., 1992-95; bd. dir. U.K. Nirex Ltd., 1986-95; pres. Biochem. Soc. U.K., 1990-95, Assn. Sci. Edn., 1991-92; Internat. Union of Biochemistry and Molecular Biology, 1991-94. Recipient Colworth medal Biochem. Soc., 1963, Otto Warburg medal German Biochem. Soc., 1973; created knight bachelor, 1978; hon. fellow Worcester Coll., Oxford, 1981, Brasenose Coll., Oxford, 1982, Wolfson Coll., Cambridge, 1990. Fellow Royal Soc. (council 1975-77), Inst. Biology (v.p. 1970-72), Royal Soc. Arts, Royal Coll Physicians (London) (hon.), Am. Acad. Microbiology; hon. mem. Am. Soc. Biochemistry and Molecular Biology, Am. Acad. Arts & Scis. (fgn. assoc.), German Soc. Biol. Chemists, Japanese Biochem. Soc.; mem. NAS (fgn. assoc.), Am. Philos. Soc., German Acad. Scis. (Leopoldina), Italian Nat. Acad. Sci. (Lincei), Phi Beta Kappa. Author: (with Hans Krebs) Energy Transformations in Living Matter, 1957; contbr. articles to profl. jours. Office: The University Professors Boston U 745 Commonwealth Ave Boston MA 02215-1401

KORNBERG, ROGER DAVID, biochemist, structural biologist; b. St. Louis, Apr. 24, 1947; s. Arthur and Sylvy Ruth (Levy) K.; m. Yahli Deborah Lorch, Sept. 18, 1984; children: Guy Joseph, Maya Lorch, Gil Lorch.adr. BS, Harvard U., 1967; PhD, Stanford U., 1972. Mem. sci. staff MRC Lab. Molecular Biology, Cambridge, Eng., 1974-75; asst. prof. biol. chemistry Harvard Med. Sch., Cambridge, Mass., 1976-77; prof. cell/structural biology Stanford (Calif.) U., 1978—, chmn. dept., 1984-92. Contbr. articles to profl. jours. Recipient Eli Lilly award, 1981, Passano award, 1982, Ciba-Drew award, 1990, Harvey prize Technion, 1997. Mem. NAS. Office: Stanford U Dept Structural Biology Fairchild Bldg D-123 Stanford CA 94305-5400

KORNBERG, WARREN STANLEY, science journalist; b. N.Y.C., June 21, 1927; s. Murray and Helen (Blumberg) K.; m. Felice Sher, June 15, 1952; children: Lisa, Jena, Eva. BA, Adelphi Coll., 1950; MA, Columbia, 1952; postgrad., U. Mo., 1954-55. Reporter Fall River (Mass.) Herald News, 1955-58, Boston Herald, 1958-59, Washington Post, 1960-61; Washington corr.-sci. editor McGraw Hill Publs., Washington, 1962-66; editor Sci. News, Washington, 1966-70; writer syndicated column Warren Kornberg on Science, 1969-70; sci. editor pub. affairs NSF, Washington, 1970-75, editor Mosaic, 1975-93; book editor Physics Today, 1993—. Home: PO Box 153 Garrett Park MD 20896-0153

KORNBLUM, JOHN CHRISTIAN, ambassador; b. Detroit, Feb. 6, 1943; s. Samuel Christian and Ethelyn (Tonkin) K.; m. Helen Sen, Sept. 10, 1987; children: Alexander Christian, Stephen John. BA, Mich. State U., 1964; postgrad., Georgetown U., 1967-69. Officer-in-charge Berlin and Ea. affairs Bonn, 1970-73; mem. policy planning staff Dept. State, 1973-75, officer-in-charge European regional polit. affairs, 1977-79; polit. advisor U.S. Mission, Berlin, 1979-81; dir. Office Ctrl. European Affairs Dept. State, 1981; U.S. minister and dep. commandant Berlin, 1985; dep. U.S. rep. to North Atlantic Treaty Orgn. Brussels, 1987; amb., U.S. rep. to Conf. on Security and Coop. in Europe, 1991, asst. sec. state European and Canadian affairs, 1996, amb. to Fed. Rep. Germany, 1997—; mem. U.S. Del. to Quadripartite Negotiations, Berlin, 1970-72; coord. Belgrade meeting of CSCE, 1977; chmn. U.S. Del. to Helsinki Follow-up Meeting of CSCE, 1992; head U.S. Del. to Conf. on Security and Coop. in Europe, Vienna, Austria, 1992; sr. dep. asst. sec. state European Affairs, 1994. Decorated Knight's Cross, Fed. Republic of Germany, 1991, Order Merit Rep. Austria, 1994; recipient Disting. Alumni award Mich. State U., 1999; named Hon. Citizen Sarajevo, 1997, Hon. Knight, Aachen (Germany) Carnival Assn., 1999. Methodist. Avocations: music, sports, gardening, traveling. Office: Am Embassy PSC 120 Box 1001 APO AE 09265

KORNBREKKE, RALPH ERIK, colloid chemist; b. Bklyn., Nov. 22, 1951; s. Henning Norman and Esther (Pedersen) K.; m. Annette Elizabeth Kingman, Aug. 17, 1974. BS, Rensselaer Poly. Inst., 1974, PhD, 1981. Chemist Petroleum Action Inc., Rensselaer, N.Y., 1974-75, Rensselaer Rsch. Corp. Internat., Latham, N.Y., 1975-76; sr. rsch. chemist The 3M Corp., St. Paul, 1980-84; project leader Std. Oil of Ohio, Warrensville Hts., 1984-87; rsch. chemist IV The Lubrizol Corp., Wickliffe, Ohio, 1987-90, sr. rsch. chemist, 1990-91, rsch. scientist, 1991-97; prin. rsch. scientist The Lubrizol Corp., Wickliffe, 1998—; session chmn. Am. Chem. Soc. Nat. Meeting Colloid Div., N.Y.C., 1986; chmn. the Interface Sci. chpt. of 3M Tech. Forum, St. Paul, 1982-84; staff mem. NBS Molton Salts Data Ctr., Troy, 1975-76. Contbr. articles to profl. jours.; patentee in field. Pres. Oakwood Lustre Townhome Assn., Oakdale, Minn., 1981-84; judge Reg. Sci. Fair, Mpls., Cleve., 1981—; team capt. Cleve. Orch. Campaign Fund Raising, 1988-90. N.Y. State Regents scholar 1970; named J. Willard Gibbs Rsch. fellow, 1979-80. Fellow Am. Inst. Chemists; mem. AAAS, Internat. Assn. Colloid and Interface Scientists, Am. Chem. Soc., Soc. Automotive Engrs., Soc. Tribologists and Lubrication Engrs., Sigma Xi, Phi Lambda Epsilon. Achievements include discovery of stochastic nature of emulsion-type inversion process, complex nature of wetting near the critical point, special expertise surfactant interactions at solid-liquid interfaces, nonaqueous colloidal properties regarding dispersions and lubrication. Home: 8340 Tulip Ln Chagrin Falls OH 44023-4675 Office: The Lubrizol Corp 29400 Lakeland Blvd Wickliffe OH 44092-2298

KORNEGAY, HORACE ROBINSON, trade association executive, former congressman, lawyer; b. Asheville, N.C., Mar. 12, 1924; s. Marvin Earl and Blanche Person (Robinson) K.; m. Annie Ben Beale, Mar. 25, 1950; children: Horace Robinson, Kathryn Elder Kornegay Cozort, Martha Beale Kornegay Howard. B.S., Wake Forest U., 1947, J.D., 1949. Bar: N.C. 1949, D.C. 1979, U.S. Supreme Ct 1959. Practice in Greensboro; asst. solicitor Superior Ct. Guilford County, 1951-53; dist. solicitor 12th Solicitorial Dist., 1955-60; mem. 87th-90th Congresses from 6th Dist. N.C.; v.p., counsel The Tobacco Inst., Washington, 1969-70; pres., exec. dir. The Tobacco Inst., 1970-81, chmn., 1981-86; counsel Adams Kleemeier Hagan Hannah & Fouts, Greensboro, N.C., 1987—; bd. dirs. Greensboro Mcht. Assn. Pres. Guilford Young Dem. Club, 1952, N.C. Young Dem. Clubs, 1953-54; chmn. bd. visitors Sch. Law, Wake Forest U., 1979-93; past chmn. adminstrv. bd. Concord-St. Andrew's United Meth. Ch., Bethesda, Md.; mem. adminstrv. bd. West Market St. United Meth. Ch., Greensboro. With AUS, 1943-46. Decorated Purple Heart, Bronze Star, Combat Inf. badge; recipient Americanism award Anti-Defamation League, B'nai B'rith, Washington, 1985. Mem. ABA, Fed. Bar Assn., N.C. Bar Assn. (chmn. dispute resolution com. 1989-92), Greensboro Bar Assn. (pres. 1992-93), D.C. Bar Assn., Am. Judicature Soc., Wake Forest Univ. Lawyers Alumni Assn. (past pres.), SAR (trustee), Alpha Sigma Phi Edn. Found. (trustee), Am. Legion, VFW, Royal Brit. Legion (hon.), Greensboro Country Club, Congl. Country Club, Greensboro City Club, Masons, Shriners, Rotary, Alpha Sigma Phi. Home: 12 St Augustine Sq Greensboro NC 27408-3834 Office: Adams Kleemeier Hagan Hannah & Fouts 701 Green Valley Rd # 3463 Greensboro NC 27408-7096

KORNEL, LUDWIG, medical educator, physician, scientist; b. Jaslo, Poland, Feb. 27, 1923; came to U.S., 1958, naturalized, 1970; s. Ezriel Edward and Ernestine (Karpf) K.; m. Esther Muller, May 27, 1952 (div. 1996); children: Ezriel Edward, Amiel Mark; m. Barbara Konaszewska, Mar. 18, 1997. Student, U. Kazan Med. Inst., USSR, 1943-45; MD, Wroclaw (Poland) Med. Acad., 1950; PhD, U. Birmingham, Eng., 1958. Intern Univ. Hosp., Wroclaw, 1949-50, Hadassah-Hebrew U. Hosp., Jerusalem, 1950-51; resident medicine Hadassah-Hebrew U. Hosp., 1952-55; Brit. Council scholar, Univ. research fellow endocrinology U. Birmingham, 1955-57, lectr. medicine, 1956-57; fellow endocrinology U. Ala. Med. Ctr., 1958-59, from asst. prof. to prof. medicine, 1961-67; dir. steroid sect. U. Ala. Med. Center, 1962-67, assoc. prof. biochemistry, 1965-67; postdoctoral trainee in steroid biochemistry U. Utah, 1959-61; prof. medicine U. Ill. Coll. Medicine, Chgo., 1967-71; dir. steroid unit Presbyn.-St. Lukes Hosp., Chgo., 1967-93, assoc. biochemist, 1967-70, sr. biochemist on sci. staff, 1970-71; attending physician Presbyn.-St. Lukes Hosp., 1967-71; prof. medicine and biochemistry Rush Med. Coll., 1970-93; prof. emeritus of internal medicine and biochemistry Rush Med. Coll., Chgo., 1993—; sr. attending physician, sr. scientist Rush-Presbyn.-St. Lukes Med. Ctr., 1971-96, dir. steroid hypertension rsch. lab., 1971-95; sr. endocrinologist KHK Endocrinology and Diabetes Outpatient Clinic, Jerusalem, Israel, 1996-98; hon. guest lectr. Polish Acad. Sci., Warsaw, 1965; vis. prof. Kanazawa (Japan) U., 1973, 82, 88, 93. Mem. editl. bd. Clin. Physiol. Biochemistry, 1975-94, Endocrinology, 1994-98; co-editor: Yearbook of Endocrinology, 1986-90; co-author: Ency. of Human Biology, 1991, 96; contbr. articles on endocrinology and steroid biochemistry to profl.jours.; contbr. chpts to textbooks. Recipient Physicians Recognition award AMA, 1969, 73, 76, 81, 86, Outstanding New Citizen award Citizenship Council Met. Chgo., 1970. Fellow Am. Coll. Clin. Pharmacology and Chemotherapy, Nat. Acad. Clin. Biochemistry (bd. dirs. 1982-86), Royal Soc. health; mem. AMA, AAAS, AAUP, Endocrine Soc., Am. Fedn. Clin. Rsch., N.Y. Acad. Scis., Am. Physiol. Soc., Cen. Soc. Clin. Rsch., Israel Soc. for Biochemistry and Molecular Biology, Am. Acad. Polit. and Social Scis., Fedn. Am. Socs. for Exptl. Biology (nat. corr. 1975—), Fedn. Israel Socs. for Exptl. Biology, Sigma Xi. Home: 9 Haportzim St, Jerusalem 93662, Israel Office: KHK Outpatient Clinic, 8 Hanania St, Jerusalem Israel *Nothing can be accomplished without a sense of purpose. A long-term goal in life is a sine qua non for creative productivity. When the latter is channeled towards achieving a better understanding of various phenomena around us, the process of learning is at its best and a progress in scientific investigation ensues.*

KORNER, JULES GILMER, III, judge; b. Washington, July 27, 1922; s. Jules Gilmer and Susan Leonard (Brown) K.; m. Jean McKee, Sept. 19, 1943; children: Jules Gilmer, Catherine Korner Ett. BA, U. Va., 1943; JD, 1947. Bar: Va. 1947, D.C. 1948, U.S. Tax Ct. 1948, U.S. Ct. Appeals (4th cir.) 1949, U.S. Ct. Appeals (3rd cir.) 1951, U.S. Supreme Ct. 1951, Md. 1953, U.S. Ct. Appeals (10th cir.) 1960. Ptnr. Korner Doyle Worth & Crampton and predecessor firm Blair Korner Doyle & Worth, Washington, D.C., 1947-70; sr. ptnr. Pope Ballard & Loos, Washington, D.C., 1970-81; judge U.S. Tax Ct., 1981—; adj. prof. Georgetown U. Law Sch., 1963-68. Contbr. articles to profl. jours. Chmn. bd. trustees House of Mercy, 1979-80; pres. bd. trustees Maret Sch., 1969-72. Served as lt. USNR, 1943-60. Mem. ABA (sec. taxation com.), D.C. Bar Assn., Phi Delta Phi, Kappa Sigma. Office: US Tax Ct 400 2nd St NW Washington DC 20217

KORNFELD, LAWRENCE, theatre director, educator; b. N.Y.C., May 21, 1930; s. Murry William and Lily (Friedman) K.; m. Margaret Marie Zipse, Oct. 16, 1965; 1 child, Sarah Elizabeth Ciabattari. BA, Adelphi U., 1951. Gen. mgr., asst. dir. The Living Theater, 1957-61; res. dir., co-founder The Judson Poets Theater, 1961-78; prof. Sch. Drama Yale U., New Haven, 1982-83; dean Purchase Theatre Arts and Film, SUNY, 1983-86; prof. theatre arts Purchase Coll., 1986—; artistic dir., co-founder Theater for the New City, 1970-72; dir. theatre program The N.Y. State Coun. on the Arts, 1974-76. Dir. of over 120 Broadway, off-Broadway and regional prodns. including You're The Top (A Review), Vieux Carre, Under Milkwood, Three History Plays, The Service for Joseph Axminster, The Price, The Love Cure, Storm Craft Warnings, Savage Love, Purgatory, Peace, Listen to Me, Like a Hill, Jonah, Anthony and Cleopatra, others. With U.S. Army, 1952-54. Recipient 3 Obie awards, 2 Showbusiness awards, N.E.T. award, Vernon Rice award, N.Y. Drama Desk award. Home: 7A 2d Pl Brooklyn NY 11231 Office: Purchase Coll Huderson Hill Rd Purchase NY 10577

KORNFELD, ROSALIND HAUK, research biochemist; b. Dallas, Aug. 2, 1935; d. Walter L. and Margaret (Wallace) Hauk; m. Stuart A. Kornfeld, June 11, 1959; children: Katherine, Stephen Kerry, Carolyn. BS, George Washington U., 1957; PhD, Washington U., 1961. Post-doctoral rsch. fellow dept. biol. chemistry Washington U., St. Louis, 1961-63; staff fellow NIH, Bethesda, Md., 1963-65; rsch. instr. dept. medicine Washington U., St. Louis, 1965-69, rsch. asst. prof., 1969-71, rsch. assoc. prof., 1971-78, assoc. prof. biochemistry and medicine, 1978-81, prof. medicine and biol. chemistry, 1981—; Mem. com. on cancer immunobiology Nat. Cancer Inst., Bethesda, 1975-78, physiol. chemistry study sect. NIH, Bethesda, 1980-83. Editorial bd. Jour. of Biol. Chemistry, 1981-86; contbr. articles to profl. jours. Named scholar of the Leukemia Soc. Am., Washington U. Sch. Medicine, 1971-76. Mem. Am. Soc. Biochemistry and Molecular Biology, Am. Soc. Hematology, The Soc. for Glycobiology, Clayton Twp. (Mo.) Dem. Club (pres. 1974-76), Phi Beta Kappa. Democrat. Office: Washington U Sch Medicine PO Box 8125 Saint Louis MO 63156-8125

KORNFELD, STUART A., hematology educator; b. St. Louis, Mo., Oct. 4, 1936. AB, Dartmouth Coll., 1958; MD, Washington U., 1962. Rsch. asst. biochemistry dept. sch. medicine Washington U., St. Louis, 1958-62, from instr. to asst. prof. medicine, 1966-70, from asst. to assoc. prof. biochemistry, 1968-72, prof. medicine dept. internal medicine, 1972—, prof. biochemistry, co-dir. divsn. hematology and oncology, 1976—, dir. divsn. oncology, 1973-76; intern med. ward Barnes Hosp., 1962-63, asst. resident, 1965-66; rsch. assoc. nat. inst. arthritis and metabolic disease NIH, 1963-65; faculty rsch.

assoc. Am. Cancer Soc., 1966-71; mem. cell biology study sect. NIH, 1974-77; mem. bd. sci. counselors Nat. Inst. Arthritis, Diabetes & Digestive & Kidney Disease, 1983-87; mem. sci. rev. bd. Howard Hughes Med. Inst., 1986—; mem. bd. sci. advisers Jane Coffin Childs Meml. Fund. Res., 1987—; Jubilee lectr. Biochemistry Soc., 1989. Assoc. editor Jour. Clin. Investigation, 1977-81, editor, 1981-82; assoc. editor Jour. Biol. Chemistry, 1982-87; author 145 publs. Recipient Borden award, 1962, Rsch. Career Devel. award NIH, 1971-76; named Harden Medallist, Biochemistry Soc., 1989, Passano Found. laureate, 1991. Mem. NAS (mem. inst. medicine), Am. Soc. Clin. Investigation (counselor 1972-75), Am. Soc. Hematology, Am. Soc. Biol. Chemists, Assn. Am. Physicians (sec. 1986—), Am. Acad. Arts and Sci., Am. Chem. Soc., Sigma Xi. Achievements include research in the structure, biosynthesis and function of glycoproteins, especially those which are found on the surface of normal and malignant cells, targeting of newly synthesized acid hydroloses to lysosomes. Office: Washington U Sch Med Dept Internal Medicine 660 S Euclid Ave Saint Louis MO 63110-1010*

KORNFIELD, NATHANIEL RICHARD, computer engineer educator; b. Phila., Mar. 3, 1924. BSEE, U. Pa., 1951, MSEE, 1954, PhD, 1964. Design engr. rsch. divsn. Burroughs corp., 1951-54; sect. mgr. computer divsn. RCA, 1954-58; dept. mgr. computer divsn. Philco-Ford, 1958-63; prof., dean engring. Widener U., 1963-89, prof. emeritus Sch. Engring., 1989—. Fellow IEEE (v.p. area activities and tech. interest group, chmn. test tech. technical com., chmn. edn. subcom., com. on pub. policy, awards com., sec., chair planning com., tech. activities bd. Computer Soc., chmn. planning com. internat. test conf., Centennial medal 1984, Computer Soc. Meritorious Svc. award, Computer Soc. Honor Roll award, Phila. Sect. award 1988, Oustanding Contbn. award Computer Soc.). Office: Widener Univ Sch Engring 1 University Pl Chester PA 19013-5792

KORNGOLD, ALVIN LEONARD, broadcasting company executive; b. N.Y.C., Nov. 28, 1924; s. Samuel and Sadelle (Samisch) K.; m. Joyce Singer, Jan. 10, 1954; children: Susan Korngold Osherow, Wendy Ellen Korngold Roseman, Ben Alan. AB, NYU, 1943, JD, 1948; certificate, U. Cambridge, Eng., 1946. Bar: N.Y. 1948, U.S. Dist. Ct. (so. dist.) N.Y. 1948, U.S. Ct. Appeals (2nd cir.) 1950, U.S. Dist. Ct. Conn. 1953, U.S. Supreme Ct. 1956, U.S. Dist. Ct. (ea. dist.) N.Y. 1964, Ariz. 1967, U.S. Ct. Appeals (D.C. cir.) 1968, U.S. Ct. Dist. Ct. Ariz. 1970. Practiced in N.Y.C., 1948-65; spl. asst. dist. atty. Queens County, N.Y., 1951-52; spl. dep. atty. gen. N.Y. State, 1952; pres. Sta. KEVT, Tucson Radio, Inc., 1966-81, All Spanish Network, Tucson, 1972-78; licensee, owner Sta. KAMX, Albuquerque, 1971-78, Sta. KWFM, Tucson, 1970-81, Sta. KLAV, Frontier Broadcasting Inc., Las Vegas, 1976-83, Sta. WWAM, Savannah, Ga., 1983; chmn. Caribbean Broadcast Systems Ltd.; chmn. stas. ZHIT-FM, ZWAVE-FM, ZGOLD-FM, Tortola, Brit. Virgin Islands; dir. Gold Medal Motion Picture Studios, N.Y.C., 1954-59, New Haven Clock & Watch Corp., 1964-66. Contbr. articles to profl. jours. Co-chmn. Vets. for Truman, 1948; dir. Dem. N.Y. Lawyers for Kennedy, 1960; Rep. candidate for County Atty. Tucson, 1968; col., a.d.c. Gov. N.Mex., 1978. Served to cpl. U.S. Army, 1943-46, ETO. Mem. ABA, N.Y. Bar Assn., Tau Kappa Alpha. Home: PO Box 3059, Road Town, Tortola British Virgin Islands also: 2751 S Ocean Dr Hollywood FL 33019-2721

KORNHAUSER, HENRY, advertising executive; b. Vienna, Austria, May 26, 1932; came to U.S., 1939, naturalized, 1953; s. George Harry and Ernestine (Kallman) K.; children: Steven, Richard, Edith. BA, CCNY, 1953. V.p. Ted Bates, N.Y.C., 1956-63; sr. v.p. Cunningham & Walsh, N.Y.C., 1963-69; pres. Dusenberry, Ruriani & Kornhauser, N.Y.C., 1970-74, Clyne Co., N.Y.C., 1974-80; chmn. Kornhauser & Calene, Inc., N.Y.C., 1980-88; with Ptnrs. & Shevack, N.Y.C., 1988-98; v.p. advt. Church & Dwight, N.Y.C., 1998—. Mem. Am. Assn. Advt. Agys., Friar's Club. Club: Friars. Home: Dean Road Hope NJ 07844 Office: Church & Dwight Co 469 N Harrison St Princeton NJ 08540-3510*

KORNHAUSER, KENNETH RICHARD, funeral director, executive; b. N.Y.C., Oct. 6, 1947; s. Martin and Gladys (Tuchman) K.; m. Ann Rona Morris, July 4, 1976; children: Evan Jason, Craig Morris. BS, Jacksonville U., 1969; MS, L.I. U., 1973; postgrad. in edn., N.Y.U., 1973-76; diploma, Am. Acad. McAllister Inst., 1977. Cert. corrective therapist, 1973. Phys. edn. tchr. Andrew Jackson High Sch., St Albans, N.Y., 1969-73; dean of boys Andrew Jackson High Sch., St Albans, 1973-76; assoc. prof., dir. spl. phys. edn. Queens Coll., Flushing, N.Y., 1973-75; athletic trainer U.S. Merchant Marine Acad., Kings Point, N.Y., 1975-76; pres. I.J. Morris, Inc., Bklyn., 1976—, IJM Computer Sys., Inc., Hempstead, N.Y., 1985-95, Monuments by I.J. Morris, Inc., Bklyn., 1989—, I.J. Morris of Fla., Inc., 1993—. Bd. dirs. Suffolk Y-JCC, Commack, N.Y., 1986—; pres. Temple Beth Torah, Westbury, N.Y., 1992-94; bd. dirs. Gurwin Jewish Geriatric Ctr., Commack, 1989—, Theodore Roosevelt coun. Boy Scouts Am., 1991—, Metro N.Y. region United Synagogue Conservative Judaism, 1993—, Suffolk Assn. Jewish Ednl. Svcs., 1993—, United Jewish Cmty. Ctrs. of L.I., 1993; bd. govs. Rabbinical Coll. of the Jewish Theol. Sem. of Am., N.Y., 1995—. Named Man of Yr., Suffolk County region Women's Am. Orgn. Rehab. Tng., 1987. Mem. Jewish Funeral Dirs. Am. (bd. govs.), Masons, Knights of Pythias, Nat. Eagle Scout Assn. (mem. exec. bd. Nassau chpt. 1990), Old Westbury Golf and Country Club (N.Y., bd. govs.). Republican. Avocations: golf, tennis, skiing, juggling, photography. Home: 90 Wheatley Rd Old Westbury NY 11568-1212 Office: IJ Morris Inc 21 E Deer Park Rd Dix Hills NY 11746-4814

KORNHEISER, ANTHONY I., journalist; b. N.Y.C., July 13, 1948; s. Ira James and Estelle R. Kornheiser; m. Karril Fox, May 7, 1972; children: Elizabeth, Michael. B.A., Harpur Coll., 1970. Reporter Newsday, Long Island, N.Y., 1970-75; reporter New York Times, N.Y.C., 1976-79; reporter, columnist Washington Post, 1979—. Author: The Baby Chase, 1983, Pumping Irony, 1995, Bald As I Wanna Be, 1997; contbr. articles to popular mags. including Sports Illustrated, Esquire, ESPN Mag.; author syndicated humor column; radio and TV commentator, Washington; participant ESPN Sports Reporters program; host nationally syndicated daily program, ESPN radio. Recipient best feature story award AP Sports Editors, 1977, 81, front page award N.Y. Newspaper Guild, 1980, best feature story award Best Sports Stories Competition, 1978, best column award U.S. Basketball Writers, 1988, Washington Mag. Best Columnist award, 1991-98, best columnist award Am. Assn. Sunday and Features Editors, 1992, 94, best talk show host Washington, 1996. Avocations: reading, gardening. Office: Washington Post 1150 15th St NW Washington DC 20071-0002

KORNICKER, LOUIS S., museum curator; b. N.Y.C., May 23, 1919; s. Howard and Lena (Cohen) K.; m. Beatrice Nyman; children—Lance, Steven, William. B.S., U. Ala., 1941, B.S. in Chem. Engring., 1942; M.A., Columbia U., 1954, Ph.D., 1957. Tech. group supr. Hercules Powder Co., Chattanooga, 1942-45; sr. process engr., pilot plant supt. Cities Service Refining Co., Lake Charles, La., 1945-48; sec., treas. Uncle Sam Chem. Co., N.Y.C., 1948-57; asst. dir. Inst. Marine Sci., U. Tex., Port Aransas, 1957-60; geologist Office Naval Research, Chgo., 1960-61; prof. oceanography Tex. A. and M. U., College Station, 1961-64; curator dept. invertebrate zoology Smithsonian Inst., Washington, 1964—; adj. prof. biology George Washington U., 1968—. Author: Antarctic Ostracoda (Myodocopina), 1975, Research: Revision, Distribution, Ecology and Ontogeny of the Ostracode Subfamily Cyclasteropinae, 1981, Antarctic and Subantarctic Myodocopina (Ostracoda), 1993. Assoc. editor: Biology and Paleobiology of Ostracoda, 1975; mem. editorial bd. Palaeogeography, Palaeoclimatology and Palaeoecology, 1960-87; mem. bd. assoc. editors Antarctic Research Series, Am. Geophys. Union, 1978-90. Mem. Soc. Systematic Zoology, Crustacean Soc., Sigma Xi. Office: Smithsonian Instn Nat Mus Natural History Washington DC 20560

KORNREICH, EDWARD SCOTT, lawyer; b. Bklyn., Apr. 18, 1953; s. Lawrence and Selma (Rosenblatt) K.; m. Shirley Werner, Feb. 28, 1982; children: Mollie, Davida, Lawrence. BA magna cum laude, Columbia U., 1974; JD, Harvard U., 1977. Appellate atty. Legal Aid Soc., N.Y.C., 1977-79; assoc. atty. Rosenman & Colin, N.Y.C., 1979-84; v.p., legal affairs/gen. counsel St. Luke's-Roosevelt Hosp. Ctr., N.Y.C., 1984-87; mem. Garfunkel Wild & Travis P.C., Great Neck, N.Y., 1987-90; ptnr. Proskauer Rose LLP, N.Y.C., 1990—; mem. joint com. on health care decisions near end of life ABA and Hastings Ctr., 1992-95. Trustee Postgrad. Ctr. Mental Health, N.Y.C., 1992—. Mem. Am. Health Lawyers Assn., Assn. of Bar of City of N.Y. (mem. com. on medicine and law 1985-88, chairperson health law com. 1991-94, mem. AIDS com. 1986-97), Phi Beta Kappa. Jewish. Avocations: running (completed N.Y.C. Marathon 1978, 83, 86, 95, 97). Office: Proskauer Rose LLP 1585 Broadway New York NY 10036-8200

KORNS, LEOTA ELSIE, writer, mountain land developer, insurance broker; b. Canton, Okla., Jan. 19, 1916; d. James Abraham and Ida Agnes (Engel) Klopfenstine; m. Richard Francis Korns, July 1, 1943 (wid. Dec. 17, 1988); 1 child, Michael Francis. BS, Pitts. State U. of Kans., 1966. Sec. various firms, Kans. City, Mo., 1937-45; cons. Electrolux Corp., St. Paul, 1946-49; sec. health, safety and waste IAEA, Vienna, Austria, 1959-60; tchr. Montezuma-Cortez H.S., Cortez, Colo., 1966-67; ins. agent Korns Ins. Agy., Durango, Colo., 1968—; owner, pres. Korns Investments, Inc., Durango, Colo., 1970—; bd. dirs. LaPlata County Landowners Assn., Durango, 1981-87; authored and instr. women's history course, U. N.Mex., Albuquerque, Ft. Lewis Coll., Durango, and Mesa (Ariz.) C.C., 1970-75; also spkr. in field. Author: (novel) Yesterday Should Have Been Over, 1965; (play) Angry Young Men, 1957; writer numerous short stories including The Combine, 1960. Convenor, mem. NOW, Durango, 1970—; precinct capt. La Plata County Rep. Party, 1981—. Mem. Ink Slingers Writing Group, Unity Sch. Christianity, Trimble Hot Springs. Avocations: mountain walking, swimming, piano, cross-country skiing. Home: 556 2d Ave Durango CO 81301-5604

KORNWASSER, JOSEPH K., ; married; 2 children. BS in Fin. and Bus., UCLA, 1968, JD, 1972. Mng. ptnr. K&F Comml. Properties/Kornwasser & Friedman Shopping Ctr., 1979-97; gen. ptnr. P&K Assocs., 1983-93; pres., CEO, bd. dirs. Price REIT, Inc., 1993-98; sr. exec v.p. Kimco Realty Corp., L.A., 1998—; chmn. bd. dirs. Nat. Bank of Calif.; bd. dirs. adv. com. N.Y. Stock Exch. Past chmn. area devel. Vitalize Fairfax com., L.A.; past mem. City of L.A. Econ. Coun.; bd. dirs. Echo-Nat. Inst. Health, N.Y.C. Mem. ABA, L.A. County Bar Assn., Calif. Bd. Realtors, Urban Land Inst., Internat. Coun. Shopping Ctrs., Nast. Assn. Real Estate Investment Trusts. Fax: (213) 937-8175. Office: 145 S Fairfax Ave 4th Fl Los Angeles CA 90036

KORNYLAK, HAROLD JOHN, osteopathic physician; b. Jersey City, Feb. 16, 1950; s. Andrew Thomas and Lucille Bertha (Reilly) K.; children: Laura, Michael. BS in Physics with honors, Stevens Inst. Tech., 1971; MA, Maharishi Internat. U., 1977; MS, Maharishi European Rsch. U., 1977; DO, U. New Eng., 1983. Mem. indsl. R & D staff Kornylak Corp., Hamilton, Ohio, 1971-73, mgr. data processing, 1974-79; researcher Maharishi European Rsch. U., Weggis, Switzerland, 1973-74; intern Mich. Osteo. Med. Ctr., Detroit, 1983-84; staff physician Indian Health Svc., USPHS, San Carlos, Ariz., 1984-87, St. Louis Orthopedic Sports Medicine Clinic, 1987-88; pvt. practice Virginia Beach, Va., 1989—; cons. in systems analysis; instr. Atlantic U., Virginia Beach, 1989—, Harold J. Reilly Sch. Massotherapy, Virginia Beach, 1989—. Mem. Am. Osteo. Assn., Am. Acad. Osteopathy, Am. Acad. Med. Acupuncture, Cranial Acad., Va. Osteo. Med. Assn. Avocations: sailboarding, backpacking, Tantra yoga, meditation, whitewater kayaking. Home and Office: 1432 E Bay Shore Dr Virginia Beach VA 23451-3760

KOROBKIN, BARRY JAY, architect; b. N.Y.C., Dec. 9, 1949; s. Raymond Lawrence and Leanore Anne (Kaplan) K.; m. Laura Hanft, Aug. 27, 1977; children: Rachel Tess, Robert Benjamin. BA magna cum laude, Williams Coll., 1971; MArch, Harvard U., 1976. Registered architect, Mass., N.Y., Fla. Planner M. Paul Friedberg and Assocs., N.Y.C., 1972; architect Herman Hertzberger, Amsterdam, The Netherlands, 1976-77; lectr. Harvard Grad. Sch. Design, Cambridge, Mass., 1977-79; ptnr. KJA Architects, Somerville, Mass., 1979-89, Linden Properties Inc., Somerville, 1983—; prin. Korobkin Assocs., Somerville, 1990—. Author: Images for Design, 1974; prin. works include Eldridge House, 1981 (AIA award 1982, Mass. Gov.'s award 1987), Maxim House, 1984 (New England AIA award 1987). Recipient AIA medal Harvard U. Grad. Sch. Design, 1976; Sheldon fellow Harvard U., 1977. Mem. AIA (chmn. housing com. 1987-90, rsch. fellow 1973), Boston Soc. Architects (bd. dirs. 1990-92), Phi Beta Kappa. Democrat. Office: Korobkin Assocs 288 Walnut St Newton MA 02460-1947

KOROLOGOS, TOM CHRIS, government affairs consultant, former federal official; b. Salt Lake City, Apr. 6, 1933; s. Chris T. and Irene (Kolendrianos) K.; m. Carolyn Joy Goff, June 16, 1960; children—Ann, Philip Chris, Paula. B.A., U. Utah, 1955; M.S. (Grantland Rice Meml. fellow 1957; Pulitzer traveling fellow 1958), Columbia, 1958. Reporter Salt Lake Tribune, 1950-56, 59-60; reporter N.Y. Herald Tribune, 1958; account exec. David W. Evans & Assos., Salt Lake City, 1960-62; asst. to Senator Wallace Bennett of Utah, Washington, 1962-71; dep. asst. Pres. Nixon, 1971-74; asst. to Pres. Ford, 1974-75; cons. Timmons and Co., Washington, 1975—; dir. congl. rels. Pres.-Elect Reagan; former chmn. U.S. Adv. Commn. Pub. Diplomacy. Former chmn. bd. trustees Am. Coll. of Greece; former mem. bd. dirs. Internat. Media Fund; mem. Internat. Broadcasting Bd. Govs., 1995—. With USAF, 1956-57. Recipient Disting. Alumnus award U. Utah, 1989. Mem. Ahepa. Greek Orthodox. Home: 2209 N Oak Ct Arlington VA 22209-1130 Office: Timmons & Co 1850 K St NW Ste 850 Washington DC 20006-2241

KORONES, SHELDON BERNARR, physician, educator; b. N.Y.C., Apr. 26, 1924; s. Samuel Aaron and Estelle (Goldstein) K.; m. Judith Ann Kest, June 15, 1952; children: David N., Susan Gifford. BS, U. Tenn., 1944; MD, U. Tenn., Memphis, 1947. Diplomate Am. Bd. Pediatrics, Am. Bd. Neonatal/Perinatal Medicine. Intern Boston City Hosp., 1948-49; asst. resident pediat. Babies Hosp., N.Y.C., 1950-51, 53-54; asst. in pathology Children's Med. Ctr., Boston, 1949-50; asst. clin. prof. pediat. U. Tenn., 1961-68, assoc. prof. newborn svcs. dept. pediats., 1968-72, prof. pediats., dir. newborn svcs., 1972-89, prof. ob-gyn., 1982-89, alumni disting. svc. prof. pediat. ob-gyn., 1989—; project dir., prin. investigator collaborative perinatal project NIH, Bethesda, 1960-75; dir. newborn ctr. Regional Med. Ctr. Memphis, 1968—; perinatal adv. com. State Tenn., 1974—, chmn. subcom. standards regionalization perinatal care, 1975—, subcom. liaison, legis. funding and cmty. edn., 1979—, subcom. perinatal transp., 1979-86, gov.'s task force prevention mental retardation, 1980-83, gov.'s task force healthy children, 1983-86, subcom. follow-up, 1983-86, subcom. evaluation, 1983-86, subcom. med. home., 1983-86, task force child devel. standards dept. human svcs., 1984-86; med. svc. adv. com. March of Dimes, 1974-78, edn. adv. com., 1979-1987, exec. com. west Tenn. chpt., 1986-92; bd. examiner oral exams maternal and fetal medicine Am. Bd. Ob-Gyn., Chgo., 1975; study panel bur. med. devices diagnostic products FDA, 1976-93; prin. investigator Nat. Heart, Lung, Blood Inst., Bethesda, Md., 1976-83, Coop. Multictr. Network Neonatal Intensive Care Rsch., Bethesda, 1986—; profl. edn. rsch. com. Am. Lung Assn. Tenn., 1977-81; pres.-elect med. staff Regional Med. Ctr. Memphis, 1982-83, pres. 1983-84; adv. bd. Office Drug Policy, Memphis, 1991; subcom. ob-gyn. newborn svcs. TLC Family Care Healthplan, Memphis, 1994—; mem. perinatal com. devel. clin. practice guidelines TennCare, First Mental Health, Inc., 1996; spkr., cons. in field. Author: High Risk Newborn Infants: The Basis for Intensive Nursing Care, 1972, 4th edit., 1986, Spanish translation, 1979, Russian translation, 1981; co-author: Neonatal Decision Making, 1993; author, co-author: (chpts.) Synopsis of Pediatrics, 1963, 6th edit., 1984, Resuscitation of the Newborn, 3d edit., 1973, Iatrogenic Problems in Neonatal Intensive Care, 1976, Current Diagnosis, 1977, Standards and Recommendations for Hospital Care of Newborn Infants, 6th edit., 1977, Current Therapy in Obstetrics and Gynecology, 1980, 83, Assisted Ventilation of the Newborn, 1981, The Use of Computers in Perinatal Medicine, 1982, Parent-Baby Attachment in Premature Infants, 1983, Infant Stress under Intensive Care, 1985, Gynecology and Obstetrics, Vol. 2, 1985, Teratogen Update: Environmentally Induced Birth Defect Risks, 1986, Assisted Ventilation of the Neonate, 1988, 3d edit., 1996, Comprehensive Pediatrics, 1990; author: (introduction) Planning and Design for Perinatal and Pediatric Facilities, 1977; editor Ross Labs., Columbus, Ohio, 1975-82, Perinatal Press, U. Tenn., Memphis, 1976-78, Brentwood Pub. Corp., L.A., 1977-88, Am. Baby Hosp. Network Adv. Bd., 1984—, Jour. Perinatology-Neonatology, 1988—, Am. Baby Mag., 1992—; reviewer C.V. Mosby Co., 1976-77, 81, 83, J.B. Lippincott Co., 1979, Williams and Wilkins Co., 1981, Polymorph films, 1985, Pediats., 1974—, New Eng. Jour. Medicine, 1975—, Am. Jour. Ob-gyn., 1979, 92, 97, Jour. Pediats., 1997, Pediat. Nephrology, 1997, 98, Pediat. Infectious Disease Jour. 1997, 98, others; contbr. over 240 articles to profl. publs. Bd. dirs. Memphis Orch. Soc., 1961-70. With USPHS, 1951-53. Named Citizen of Yr. Newspaper Guild Memphis, 1974, Who's Who in Medicine, Memphis Mag., 1984-88, Top Doctors, 1996; recipient Myrtle Wreath award Hadassah, 1976, Contribn. to Perinatal Medicine commendation Commr. Pub. Health Tenn., 1978, Cmty. Svc. award Nat. Conf. Christians and Jews, 1982, City Coun. Memphis, 1982, L.M. Graves Meml. Health award Mid-South Med. Ctr. Coun., Inc., 1984, Cert. Appreciation, Gov. Lamar Alexander, 1986, Key to City Memphis, Mayor Richard Hackett, 1988, Alumni Svc. award U. Tenn. Nat. Alumni Assn., 1989, Themis award March of Dimes, 1991, Meritorious Svc. commendation State Tenn. Ho. of Reps., 1992, Person of Vision award Alliance for Blind Visually Impaired, 1994, Meritorious Svc. award Tenn. Hosp. Assn., 1995; Sheldon B. Korones Chair Neonatology U. Tenn. Coll. Medicine named in his honor, 1989; grantee NIH, 1960-75, 71-75, 85-88, Merck, Sharpe and Dohme, 1970-73, Tenn. Dept. Health, 1970—, Memphis Regional Med. Program, 1972-75, Tenn. Dept. Human Svcs., 1972—, March of Dimes, 1973-80, Nat. Heart, Lung, Blood Inst., 1976-83, Nat. Inst. Child Health Human Devel., 1986-91, 91-96, 96—. Fellow Am. Coll. Ob-Gyn. (assoc.); mem. So. Soc. Pediat. Rsch., Am. Acad. Pediats. (com. fetus and newborn 1969-75, liaison com. perinatal health Am. Coll. Ob-Gyn. 1965-74, rep. to joint com. newborn hearing Am. Speech Hearing Assn., Am. Acad. Ophthalmology Otolaryngology 1969-75, task force on circumcision 1973-74), Tenn. chpt. Pediatrician of Yr. 1994), Tenn. Pediat. Soc., Memphis Pediat. Soc., Am. Pediat. Soc., Tenn. Perinatal Assn. (bd. dirs. 1983—), Russian Perinatologists Assn. (hon. pres. 1996), Nat. Assn. Perinatal Social Workers (hon. 1980), Sigma Xi, Alpha Omega Alpha. Office: U Tenn 853 Jefferson Ave Rm 201 Memphis TN 38103-2807

KOROS, WILLIAM JOHN, chemical engineering educator; b. Omaha, Aug. 31, 1947; s. William Alexander and Mary Ellen (Roth) K.; m. Ann Marie Teahan, Dec. 19, 1970. BSChemE, U. Tex., 1969, MSChemE, 1975, PhDChemE, 1977. Registered profl. engr., Tex. Chem. engr. E.I. DuPont, Wilmington, Del., 1969-71, cons., 1982—; engr. E.I. DuPont, Camden, S.C., 1971-73; research asst. U. Tex., Austin, 1973-77; asst. prof. chem. engring. N.C. State U., Raleigh, 1977-80, prof., 1980-83; prof. chem. engring. U. Tex., Austin, 1983—, B.F. Goodrich prof. material engring., 1986—, chmn. chem. engring., 1993-97. Editor in chief Jour. Membrane Sci.; mng. editor Membrane Quar. Recipient Sigma Xi Research award, 1980, Young Investigators award NSF, 1983, Alcoa Found Research award N.C. State U., 1983. Mem. Am. Chem. Soc., Am. Inst. Chem. Engrs. Office: U Tex Dept Chmn Engring Code C0400 Austin TX 78712-1062*

KOROT, BERYL, artist; b. N.Y.C., Sept. 17, 1945; d. George and Frieda (Braunstein) K.; m. Steve Reich, May 30, 1976; 1 child, Ezra. Student, U. Wis., 1963-65; BA, Queens Coll., 1967. chief, co-founder Radical Software, 1970-73; co-editor Video Art, 1976. Freelance artist, N.Y.C.; one-woman and group shows include Dachau (4 channel video work) Text and Commentary, (5 channel video work, weavings, drawings), Kitchen, N.Y.C., 1975, Everson Mus. Art, Syracuse, N.Y., 1975, 77, Documenta 6, Kassel, Germany, 1977, Videopoints, Mus. Modern Art, N.Y.C., 1978, Mickery Theatre, Holland, 1978, Whitney Mus., N.Y.C., 1980, San Francisco Art Inst., 1981, Leo Castelli Gallery, N.Y.C., 1977, Mus. Fine Arts, Montreal, Can., 1979, Whitney Mus., N.Y.C., 1980, Long Beach Mus. Art, 1988, Jewish Mus., N.Y.C., 1988, Video Skuptur, Kunstverein, Koln, 1989, (with Steve Reich) The Cave, 1993, (video installation) Reina Sofia Mus., Madrid, 1993-94, Dusseldorf Kunsthalle, Whitney Mus. of Am. Art, Carnegie Mus. of Art, ICC Gallery, Tokyo, 1997, Hindenburg, 1998, Bklyn. Acad. Art, 1998, Mass. Coll. Art, 1999; (paintings) John Weber Gallery, N.Y.C., 1986, Jack Tilton Gallery, 1987, Carnegie Mus. Art, 1990. Artist fellow NEA, 1975, 77, 79, N.Y. State Coun. on Arts, 1978, Creative Artist Pub. Svc., 1975, 79, Guggenheim fellow, 1995; grantee Rockefeller Found., 1989, 98, Andy Warhol Found., 1991, NEA, 1991-92. Home and Studio: 258 Broadway New York NY 10007-2315

KOROTKIN, FRED, writer, philatelist; b. Duluth, Minn., Oct. 25, 1917; s. Morris and Ethel (Billert) K. B.A., U. Minn., 1949. Writer-instr. Palmer Writers Sch., Mpls., 1961-66; editor Finance & Commerce, and Daily Market Record, Mpls., 1966-67; stamp editor Mpls. Star, 1970-74, White Bear Press, 1976, Minn. Suburban Newspapers, Inc., 1983-85, The EnterpriSe, 1988-89, Post Publs. Weekend, 1989-91; Mem. philatelic adv. panel Am. Revolution Bicentennial Commn., 1971-74, Am. Revolution Bicentennial Adminstrn., 1974, philatelic advisor, 1974-76; regional rep. Interphil '76, 1974-76, USO, AARP, So. Poverty Law Ctr./Klanwatch Project. Contbr. revs., articles to popular mags., newspapers. Pres. North High Alumni Assn., Mpls., 1946-47; mem. nat. adv. bd. The Generation After; assoc. Simon Wiesenthal Ctr. for Holocaust Studies; mem. St. Louis Park Centennial Commn., 1985-86; charter mem. U.S. Holocaust Meml. Mus., U.S. World War II Meml.; founding mem. F.D.R. Meml. Recipient Disting. Topical Philatelist Hall of Fame award and invited to sign Disting. Topical Philatelist scroll of honor, 1962, Silver medal for Keeping Posted column in Mpls. Star Am. Philatelic Soc.-Chgo. Philatelic Soc. Conv., 1974, Silver award for Keeping Posted column in Post Publs. Weekend, sponsored by Coun. Philatelic Orgns., 1989, True Grit award, 1997, 98. Mem. Am. Topical Assn. (founding pres. chpt. 1957-61, nat. pres. 1968-70, 70-72, dir., nat. adv. com.), Internat. Philatelic Press Club (gov.), Internat. Assn. Philatelic Journalists, Am. Philatelic Soc. (speakers' bur. 1977—, writers unit), New Zealand Stamp Collector's Club Inc. (hon., anonymously donated annual Fred Korotkin Cup for best thematic entry 1966—), Christchurch Philatelic Soc., Inc., Royal Philatelic Soc. New Zealand, Collectors Club N.Y., Manuscript Soc., Statue of Liberty-Ellis Island Found. Inc. (charter), Nat. Com. To Preserve Social Security, Am. United for Separation of Ch. and State, Holocaust Survivors Assn. USA (nat. adv. bd.), Keren Or, Inc., Jerusalem Instn. for the Blind, Internat. Platform Assn., People for the Am. Way, DAV (life; comdr. Mpls. chpt. No 1, 1986), Paralyzed Vets. Am. (hon.). Home: 4925 Minnetonka Blvd Apt 512 Minneapolis MN 55416-2271 also: PO Box 11053 Minneapolis MN 55411-0053 *Ever since I was a youngster I've tried to determine what character traits help make a person successful. I've come to believe that the most important combination is still confidence in self, stick-to-itiveness, and that other winning ingredient which can be called aim, direction or goal.*

KOROTKIN, MICHAEL PAUL, lawyer; b. N.Y.C., Oct. 5, 1937; m. Marcia Ellen, Aug. 28, 1960; children: Darryl, Alan, Alyssa. AB, Duke U., 1959; LLB, NYU, 1962. Bar: N.Y. 1963. Ptnr. Kramer, Levin, Naftalis & Frankel LLP, N.Y.C., 1973—. Office: Kramer Levin Naftalis & Frankel LLP 919 3rd Ave New York NY 10022-3902

KORPAL, EUGENE STANLEY, banker, former army officer; b. St. Louis, Sept. 1, 1931; s. Stanley Anthony and Mary Ann (Bronakowski) K.; m. Lily M. Alder, July 17, 1954; children: Teresa Kaye, Karla Jeannine. B.S., U. Mo., 1953. Commd. officer U.S. Army, 1954; advanced through grades to maj. gen.; served with inf. div. U.S. Army, Hawaii and Vietnam, 1964-67; comdr. 1st Bn., 29th Arty. Ft. Carson, Colo., 1969-70; comdr. 3d Bn., 319th Arty. Vietnam, 1970-71; comdr. 3d Inf. Div. Arty. Ger., 1973-75; asst. div. comdr. 25th Inf. Div. Schofield Barracks, Hawaii.; comdg. gen. Ft. Sill, Okla., 1985-87; adv. dir., v.p. Ft. Sill Nat. Bank, 1987—. Decorated DSM, Legion of Merit with oak leaf cluster, Bronze Star, Air medal, others. Mem. Assn. U.S. Army, Field Arty. Assn.

KORS, R. PAUL, search company executive; b. Pontiac, Mich., June 12, 1935; s. Ralph Dewey and Lydia Elizabeth (Shavlik) K.; m. Carol Jayne Kullick, July 17, 1966; children: Kristen Patricia, Shannon Elizabeth. BBA, U. Mich., 1958; MBA, U. So. Calif., 1965. Salesman Nalco Chem. Co., Los Angeles, 1958-66; investment mgr. Dean Witter & Co., Los Angeles, 1966-73; sr. assoc. Korn Ferry Internat., Los Angeles, 1973-74; v.p. Korn Ferry Internat., Houston, 1974-77, v.p., mgr., 1977-78; founder, pres., chief exec. officer Kors Montgomery Internat., Houston, 1978—. Served to 1st lt. U.S. Army, 1958. Mem. World Tech. Exec. Network (bd. dirs. 1985—). Clubs: Houston Racket, Galveston Country. Avocations: skiing, golf, tennis, films, reading. Home: 14306 Heatherfield Dr Houston TX 77079-7407 Office: Kors Montgomery Internat 1980 Post Oak Blvd Ste 2280 Houston TX 77056-3808

KORSCH, BARBARA M., pediatrician; b. Jena, Germany, Mar. 30, 1921; came to U.S., 1937; widowed; 1 child. BA, Smith Coll., 1941; MD, Johns Hopkins U., 1944. Cert. Am. Bd. Pediats. Asst. resident Bellevue Hosp., 1945, Mary Imogene Basset Hosp., 1946; asst. resident N.Y. Hosp., 1947, fellow Inst. Child Devel., 1948-49; asst. pediats. Med. Coll. Cornell U., 1949-50, from instr. to assoc. prof., 1950-61; assoc. clin. prof. preventive medicine

Sch. Medicine UCLA, 1961-64; assoc. prof. U. So. Calif., L.A., 1964-69, prof. pediats. Sch. Medicine, 1969—; George Armstrong lectr. Ambulatory Pediat. Assn., 1973; Katherine D. McCormick Disting. lectr. Stanford U., 1977; Kathy Newman Meml. lectr. Tulane U., 1987; asst. outpatient pediatrician N.Y. Hosps., 1949-50, asst. attending pediatrician, 1950-55, clin. dir. pediat. outpatient dept., 1950-61, assoc. attending pediatrician, 1955-61; pediat. cons. Dept. Health, N.Y., 1949-51, Hosp. Spl. Surgery, 1955-61, Gen. Pediat. Childrens Hosp., L.A., 1961-65, Med. Ctr., U. So. Calif., 1969-74; coord. pediat. rehab. program Nat. Found. Infantile Paralysis, 1953-61; pediat. dir. Obs. Clinic Children L.A., 1961-64; assoc. attending pediatrician Cedars Lebanon Hosp., 1961—; vis. prof. numerous U.S. and fgn. univs., 1973-89; hon. staff mem. dept. pediats. Cedars-Sinai Med. Ctr., 1976—. Author: Intelligent Patients Guide to the Doctor-Patient Relationship, 1997; contbr. articles to profl. jours. Chmn. coun. Bayer Inst. for Health Comm., 1989-98. Recipient Disting. Career award Ambulatory Pediat. Assn., 1991. Mem. Inst. Medicine-NAS, Am. Acad. Pediats. (C. Anderson Aldrich award 1988, Genesis award for med. ethics 1998), Am. Pediat. Soc., Soc. Behavioral Pediats. (pres. 1985), Soc. Pediat. Rsch., Sigma Xi. Office: Childrens Hosp Divsn Gen Pediats MB # 76 4650 W Sunset Blvd Los Angeles CA 90027-6062*

KORSCHOT, BENJAMIN CALVIN, investment executive; b. LaFayette, Ind., Mar. 22, 1921; s. Benjamin G. and Myrtle P. (Goodman) K.; m. Marian Marie Schelle, Oct. 31, 1941; children: Barbara E. Korschot Haehlen, Lynne D. Korschot Gooding, John Calvin. BS, Purdue U., 1942; MBA, U. Chgo., 1947. V.p. No. Trust Co., Chgo., 1947-64; sr. v.p. St. Louis Union Trust Co., 1964-73; exec. v.p. Waddell and Reed Co., Kansas City, Mo., 1973-74, pres., 1974-79, vice-chmn. bd., 1979-85; pres. Waddell & Reed Investment Mgmt. Co., 1985-86; chmn. bd. Waddell & Reed Asset Mgmt. Co., 1973-86; pres. United Group of Mut. Funds, Inc., Kansas City, Mo., 1974-85, chmn., 1985-86; vice-chmn. Roosevelt Fin. Group, St. Louis, 1968-91, chmn. adv. bd., 1991-92; treas. Helping Hand of Goodwill Industries, 1993-95, chmn. investment com., 1995—; bd. dirs., investment com. Mo. United Meth. Found., 1995—; chmn. bd. govs. Investment Co. Inst., 1980-82; chmn. bd. Fin. Analyst Fedn., 1978-79;. Contbr. articles on investment fin. to profl. publs.; author autobiography, 1997. Mem. Civic Coun. Greater Kansas City, Mo., 1974-85; chmn. fin. com. ARC Retirement Sys., 1986-87. With USN, 1942-45, 50-52. Mem. Inst. CFAs, Fin. Execs. Inst., Kansas City Soc. Fin. Analysts, Indian Hills Country Club. Republican. Home: 101 NW Hackberry St Lees Summit MO 64064-1477 *A happy Christian home environment, the adversity of the depression of the 30's, the challenges of competitive sports, the desire to achieve knowledge, recognition and responsibilities, a devoted wife and three children who made our marriage most meaningful have been the dominant influences of my life.*

KORSGAARD, CHRISTINE MARION, philosophy educator; b. Chgo., Apr. 9, 1952; d. Albert and Marion Hangaard (Kortbek) K.; m. Timothy David Gould, June 1980 (div. Sept. 1984). BA, U. Ill., 1974; PhD, Harvard U., 1981. Instr. Yale U., New Haven, 1979-80; asst. prof. U. Calif., Santa Barbara, 1980-83; from asst. prof. to prof. U. Chgo., 1983-91; prof. Harvard U., Cambridge, Mass., 1991—, chair philosophy dept., 1996—; vis. assoc. prof. Berkeley, 1989, UCLA, 1990; Tanner lectr. human values, 1992. Author: The Sources of Normativity, 1996, Creating the Kingdom of Ends, 1996; editor: (with Andrews Reath and Barbara Herman) Reclaiming the History of Ethics: Essays for John Rawls, 1997; contbr. chpts. to books, articles to profl. jours. Whiting fellow, 1978-79; Ctr. for Human Values fellow, 1995-96. Mem. Am. Philos. Assn., N.Am. Kant Soc., Hume Soc., Am. Soc. for Polit. and Legal Philosophy.

KORSGREN, MARY LOUISE, home care nurse; b. Wayne, Mich., Mar. 8, 1943; d. Jesse Eugene and Jennie (DeMascio) Bugard; m. Richard Charles Korsgren, Nov. 5, 1966; 1 child, Stephen Daniel. LPN, McPherson Sch., 1965. LPN, Mich. LPN, staff nurse med.-surg., ob-gyn. McPherson Cmty. Health Ctr., Howell, Mich., 1965-92; home care nurse McPherson Hosp., Howell, 1992—. Roman Catholic. Avocations: crocheting, homemade jams and jelly, baking, gardening. Office: Home Care McPherson Hosp 620 Byron Rd Howell MI 48843-1002

KORSHAK, YVONNE, art historian; b. Chgo., May 30, 1936; d. Donald Korshak and Irma B. Jaffe; m. Robert J. Ruben; 1 child, Karin. BA cum laude, Radcliffe Coll., Cambridge, Mass., 1958; MA, U. Calif. Berkeley, 1966; PhD, U. Calif., 1973. Asst. prof. U. Md., College Park, 1972-74, Fordham U., N.Y.C., 1974-75; from asst. prof. to prof. Adelphi U., Garden City, N.Y., 1975—, chairperson Dept. Art and Art History, 1978-81, dir. honors program, dir. mus. studies, 1979—; project dir. seminar on the modern condition NEH, 1990. Author: Frontal Faces in Attic Vase Painting, 1987, co-editor: Selections from Permanent Collection, 1983. Recipient Pres.'s award for excellence in teaching, 1990. Mem. Coll. Art Assn. Am., Archaeological Inst. Am., Long Island Art Historians Assn., American Soc. for Eighteenth Century Studies, American Philological Assn. Office: Adelphi U Dept Art And Art History Garden City NY 11530

KORSMEYER, STANLEY JOEL, pathologist, educator. MD, U. Ill., 1976. Sr. investigator Nat. Cancer Inst., Bethesda, Md., 1979-86; assoc. prof. internal medicine & immunology Howard Hughes Med. Inst., Sch. Medicine, Washington U., St. Louis, 1986-90; former prof. medicine and pathology Washington U. Med. Ctr., St. Louis, 1990—, former chief molecular oncology, 1992—; mem. Investigative Howard Hughes Med. Inst., Chevy Chase, Md. Recipient Clowes Meml. award Eli Lilly Co., 1997, Charles S. Mott prize for cancer rsch. GM; Cancer Rsch. grantee Bristol-Myers Squibb Found., 1997. Mem. NAS, Am. Soc. Clin. Investigation. Achievements include discovery of genes that initiate apoptosis and another gene that prevents it. Office: Dana Farber Cancer Inst 44 Binney St Boston MA 02115*

KORST, HELMUT HANS, mechanical engineer, educator; b. Vienna, Jan. 4, 1916; came to U.S., 1948; married, 1942; 4 children. Diploma in Engring., Vienna Tech. U., 1941, Dr. Tech. Sci., 1947, Golden Dr. diploma, 1997. Rsch. engr. Maschinenfabrik Augsburg-Nurnberg AG, Germany, 1941-45; asst. prof. mech. engring. Vienna Tech. U., 1945-48, vis. lectr. gas dynamics, 1948-49; from assoc. prof. to prof. mech. engring. U. Ill., Urbana, 1949-84, head dept. mech. and indsl. engring., 1962-74, prof. emeritus, 1984—; chair naval air power engring. USN Postgrad. Sch., Monterey, Calif., 1979; Ebaugh Chair Mech. Engring. U. Fla., Gainesville, 1984; pvt. practice cons. Urbana, 1956—; vis. prof. Kans. State U., Manhattan, 1950, Va. Poly. Inst. and State U., Blacksburg, 1954; design specialist Gen. Dynamics Convair, Ft. Worth, 1955; propulsion specialist Rocketdyne div. N.Am. Aviation, 1960, 65-68; cons. GE, 1959, Adv. Group Aeronautical R & D NATO, 1964, U.S. Missile Command, 1971—. Sr. postdoctoral fellow NSF, 1957; recipient ASEE Centennial medal 1993, Daniel Guggenheim medal in aviation, 1994. Fellow ASME, AIAA; mem. Am. Soc. Engring. Edn., Sigma Xi. Research on internal and external aerodynamics, jet and rocket propulsion, and heat transfer. Address: 3 Eton Ct Champaign IL 61820-7602

KORSTAD, JOHN EDWARD, biology educator; b. Woodland, Calif., July 4, 1949; s. Vernon E. and Jeanette (Beard) K.; m. Sally Diane Steffen, July 29, 1972; children: Shauna, Sarah, Joya, Janna. BA, BS, Calif. Luth. U., Thousand Oaks, 1972; MS, Calif. State U., Hayward, 1979, U. Mich., 1979; PhD, U. Mich., 1980. Postdoctoral fellow SINTEF, Trondheim, Norway, 1987-88; prof. biology Oral Roberts U., Tulsa, 1980—; asst. dir., dir. collegiate acad. Okla. Acad. Sci., 1984-89. Bd. dirs. MEND Pregnancy Crisis Ctr. and Young Life, Broken Arrow, Okla., 1991—. Fulbright fellow in aquaculture rsch., Norway, 1993-94; named Carnegie Found. Prof. of Yr. for Okla., 1996. Mem. Am. Soc. Limnology and Oceanography, World Aquaculture Soc., Catfish Farmers of Okla., Am. Assn. of Zool. Parks and Aquariums (advisor marine fishes adv. com. 1991—), Beta Beta Beta (advisor). Republican. Avocations: scuba diving, snow skiing, outdoor sports, basketball. Office: Oral Roberts U Dept Biology Tulsa OK 74171

KORT, BETTY, secondary education educator. English tchr. Hastings (Nebr.) Sr. High Sch. Named Nebr. State English Tchr. of Yr., 1993. Office: Hastings Sen High Sch 1100 W 14th St Hastings NE 68901-3064*

KORTE, LEON LEE, accountant, educator; b. Hampton, Iowa, Apr. 25, 1952; s. Leuie and Ruth (Westendorf) K.; m. Solveig Sperati, Dec. 5, 1952; children: Kendra Marie, Kirsten Leigh. BA, Northwestern Coll., Orange City, Iowa, 1975; MBA, Ohio U., 1979; PhD, U. Nebr., 1992. CPA, cert. mgmt. acct. Revenue auditor Iowa Dept. Revenue, Waterloo, 1975-77; instr. Wayne (Nebr.) State Coll., 1979-83, U. Nebr., Omaha, 1983-87; internal auditor Occidental/Nebr. Fed. Savs. Bank, Omaha, 1988-90; assoc. prof. acctg. U. S.D., Vermillion, S.D., 1992—; dir. Inst. Rural Banking, Vermillion. Treas. Vermillion Area Arts Coun., 1994-96, Luther Ctr. Campus Coun., Vermillion, 1995-97; v.p. Trinity Luth. Ch., Vermillion, 1997, pres., 1998, treas., 1999. Mem. Inst. Mgmt. Accts. (pres. Siouxland chpt. 1995-96), Am. Acctg. Assn. (com. mem. 1995-96). Avocations: biking, genealogy. Office: U SD Vermillion SD 57069

KORTEBEIN, STUART ROWLAND, orthopedic surgeon; b. Evanston, Ill., Apr. 17, 1930; s. Rowland J. and Grace K.; m. Alice C. Johnson, July 10, 1954; children: William, David. AA, North Park Coll., 1950; BS, Wheaton Coll., 1952; postgrad., North Park Theol. Sem., 1952-53; MD, Loyola U., 1957; JD, Jefferson Coll. Law, 1983. Diplomate Nat. Bd. Med. Examiners, Am. Bd. Orthopaedic Surgery. Intern Akron (Ohio) Gen. Hosp., 1957-58, resident, 1961-64; resident Hines (Ill.) VA Hosp., 1960, Northwestern U., Chgo., 1964; pvt. practice medicine specializing in orthopedic surgery Arlington Heights, Ill., 1965-88; mem. orthopedic surgeon staff U.S. Naval Regional Med. Ctr., Memphis, 1986-96; pvt. practice medicine specializing in orthopedic surgery Milw., 1988—; chief dept. orthopedic surgery U.S. Naval Hosp., Great Lakes, Ill., 1987; mem. orthopaedic surgeon staff Sinai-Samaritan Med. Ctr., Milw., 1988—; attending surgeon N.W. Cmty. Hosp., Arlington Heights, 1965-90, chief orthopedics, 1976; v.p. Magnetrans Rsch. and Devel. Corp., 1972-84, Window Well Protectors, Inc., McHenry, Ill., 1983-86; coord. med. cons. Compusoft Corp., Darien, Ill., 1984—, Pomsoft Corp., Willowbrook, Ill.; instr. emergency medicine technician course Haper Coll., 1973-84; vis. instr. police self-def. tactics Oakton Cmty. Coll., 1984-88. Water safety instr. ARC, 1949-54; aux. police officer City of Rolling Meadows, Ill., 1984-89; bd. dirs. Chicagoland Drug Prevention Program, 1971-84; choir dir. First Bapt Ch., Twenty Nine Palms, Calif., 1959-60, tech. advisor Jubo-Kai Internat., 1977—. Lt. M.C., USNR, 1958-60. Mem. Am. Acad. Orthopaedic Surgeons, Physicians Martial Arts Assn., Soc. Black Belts Am., Christian Med. Soc., Wis. Orthopaedic Soc., State Med. Soc. of Wis., Milw. Orthopaedic Soc., Hakko-Ryu Jitsu Fed., Jiu Jitsu Black Belt Fedn. Am. (pres. Ill., rep. 1971-74), Oikiru-Ryu Jitsu (Sandan instr. 1977-85), U.S. Judo Assn. (Sho Dan life mem.). Office: 2455 N 124th St Brookfield WI 53005-4630

KORTH, FRITZ-ALAN, lawyer; b. Ft. Worth, Aug. 29, 1938; s. Fred and Vera (Connell) K.; m. Penne Percy, Dec. 15, 1965 (div. 1997); children: Fritz-Alan Jr., Maria Eleanor, James Frederick. AB, Princeton U., 1961; LLB cum laude, U. Tex., 1964; HHD (hon.), U. Americas, 1982. Bar: Tex. 1964, D.C. 1964. Asst. sec. OKC Corp., Dallas, 1964-65; partner firm Korth & Korth, Washington, 1965—; pres. Wilmar Corp., Port Chester, N.Y., 1980—; dir. Wilmar Corp., 1974—; founder, sec., bd. dirs. Women's Nat. Bank, Washington, 1978-85, chmn. bd. First WNB Corp., 1982-85; bd. dirs. Trans Leisure Corp., N.Y.C., 1970-75, chmn. bd., 1973-75; bd. dirs. Del Norte Tech., Inc., Dallas., 1969—, chmn., 1982-98, vice chmn. bd. dirs., 1998—; bd. dirs. Del Norte Tech. Ltd., Swindon, Eng. Registrar St. John's Episcopal Ch., Washington, 1968-70, vestryman, 1970-74, treas., 1973-77; chmn. fin. com., mem. diocesan coun. Episcopal Diocese Washington, 1973-77; trustee, treas. Cathedral chpt. Washington Nat. Cathedral, 1977-84; pres. U. Americas Found., 1969-84; bd. assocs. U. Americas, Puebla, Mex., 1969—; bd. dirs. Travelers Aid Soc. Washington, 1969-86, pres., 1973-75; dir. Southwestern Exposition and Livestock Show, 1987—; charter commr. U.S.-Mex. Commn. for Ednl. and Cultural Exch., 1991-97; pres. AMMA Found., Inc., 1994—, dir. 1989. Mem. ABA, Inter-Am. Bar Assn., D.C. Bar, Tex. Bar Assn., Am. Law Inst., Am. Soc. of Most Venerable Order of Hosp. of St. John of Jerusalem, Phi Delta Phi. Clubs: Met. (Washington), Chevy Chase (Washington); Steeplechase (Ft. Worth); Princeton (N.Y.C.); Gymkhana Club (Mauritius). Office: Korth & Korth 1700 K St NW Ste 501 Washington DC 20006-3897

KORTH, PENNE PERCY, ambassador; b. Hattiesburg, Miss., Nov. 3, 1942; m. Fritz-Alan Korth, Dec. 15, 1965 (div. 1997); children: Fritz-Alan Jr., Maria Korth Chieffalo, James Frederick. Sr. Washington assoc., client liaison and rep. trust and estate div. Sotheby's, 1986-89; amb. to Mauritius, Port Louis, 1989-92; pres. Firestone and Korth Ltd., Washington, 1993-97; commr. U.S. Adv. Commn. Pub. Diplomacy, 1997—; bd. dirs. Chevy Chase Bank; rep. Sotheby's Internat., 1997—. Bd. dirs. Meridian Internat. Ctr., Coun. of Am. Ambs., Van Cliburn Found., Marjorie Merriweather Post Found., Washington, 1995—; co-chmn. Am. Bicentennial Presdl. Inauguration, 1988-89. Mem. Assn. for Diplomatic Studies and Tng. (bd. dirs. 1996—), Sulgrave Club. Home: 2540 Massachusetts Ave NW Washington DC 20008-2832 Office: Chevy Chase Bank Pvt Banking 8401 Connecticut Ave 9th fl Chevy Chase MD 20815-5889

KORTSHA, GENE XHEVAT, industrial hygienist; b. Shkoder, Albania, Feb. 16, 1924; came to the U.S., 1955; s. Xhevat Zeqir and Seadet Kortsha; m. Margaret Walther, Apr. 7, 1958; children: Dennis, Duane, Anna Maria. BA in Chemistry, Wayne State U., 1960, MS in Occupational and Environ. Health, 1972. Inspector pub. health Health Sect., Shkoder, 1948-50; jr. indsl. hygiene engr. GM Corp., Detroit, 1960-61, indsl. hygiene engr., 1961-68, sr. indsl. hygiene engr., 1968-74, mgr. field ops., 1974-76, corp. dir. indsl. hygiene, 1976-89; cons. in field, Shelby Twp., Mich., 1989—; advisor Wayne State U., Detroit, 1980—, U. Mich., Ann Arbor, 1980-95, Internat. Occupational Hygiene Assn., London, 1987-99; bd. dirs. Fultz Sch., Washington. Fellow Am. Indsl. Hygiene Assn. (Cummings lectr. 1990). Home: 6774 Canterbury Ct Shelby Township MI 48316-3412

KORVER, GERRY R(OZEBOOM), purchasing executive; b. Orange City, Iowa, June 17, 1952. BA, Northwestern Coll., 1977. Gen. mgr. purchasing K-Products, Inc., Orange City, 1978—; bd. trustees Northwestern Coll. Trustee Northwestern Coll. Mem. Nat. Assn. Purchasing Mgmt. (cert.). Avocation: athletics. Home: 1602 Albany Ave NE Orange City IA 51041-2039 Office: K-Products Inc Industrial Air Park Orange City IA 51041

KORWEK, ALEXANDER DONALD, management consultant; b. Madison, Ill., Feb. 20, 1932; s. Alexander and Constance (Gulewicz) K.; m. Katherine Moore, Oct. 24, 1954 (div. Nov. 1974; dec.); children: Alexander D., Brian P., Lizabeth E.; M. Judith Joy, Jan. 11, 1975; 1 child, Theodore Sofianos. BSBA, Washington U., St. Louis, 1962; MBA, U. Utah, 1967. C.D.P., 1962. Asst. sec., asst. treas. Hoechst (Hystron) Fiber, N.Y.C., 1966-72; v.p. fin. Reeves/Teletape, N.Y.C., 1972-76; prin. A.D. Korwek Cons., North Babylon, N.Y., 1975-77; bus. mgr., chief fin. officer Queens Coll., CUNY, Flushing, N.Y., 1977-79; mng. dir. ASCE, N.Y.C., 1979-81; sec., gen. mgr., chief exec. officer United Engring. Trustees, N.Y.C., 1981-90; prin. A.D. Korwek Mgmt. Cons., 1990—; exec. sec. Engring. Found., N.Y.C., 1981-90, Engring. Socs. Library, N.Y.C., 1981-90; sec. Daniel Guggenheim Medal Bd., N.Y.C., 1981-90, John Fritz Medal Bd., N.Y.C., 1981-90, Frank F. Aplan Award Bd., N.Y.C., 1989-90. Author: Cost Estimating Relationships, 1967, A Dissertation on Management, 1978; author manuals in field. Commr. Norwalk-Wilton Conv. and Visitors Bur., Conn., 1985; vol. bd. bank mem., bd. instr. Volusia/Flagler United Way, Fla., 1992-95; bd. dirs. Marineland Found., Inc., 1988—. Recipient award of Appreciation Queen's Coll. Student Body, 1979. Mem. ASCE, IAJBBSC (bd. dirs. dist. 10 1989-90), Coun. of Engr. and Sci. Soc. Execs., N.Y. Soc. Assn. Execs., N.Y. Acad. Sci., Assn. for a Better N.Y., N.Y.C. C. of C., Conn. Specialty Club (pres. Norwalk 1985-90), Elks (treas. lodge # 2709 1992-94). Avocations: decanter collecting; golf; philately; numismatics.

KORY, MICHAEL A., graphics computer animator; b. L.A., May 8, 1959; s. Irving L. and Shirley (Kahan) K. Student, U. Calif., San Diego, 1976-79; BA, UCLA, 1983. Tech. dir. Digital Prodns., L.A., 1983-84, Omnibus, L.A., 1984-87; creative tech. dir. Homer & Assocs., L.A., 1987-94, WunderFilm Design, L.A., 1994-96; 3D dept. supr., CG supr. Cinesite, L.A., 1996-98; faculty Am. Film Inst., L.A., 1997—; instr. UCLA, 1998. Dir., designer animated short: Why Do You Think They Call Him Bonehead, 1990 (1st Pl. Montreal Animation Film Festival, 1st Pl. Truevision Competition). Recipient Emmy awards, 1996, 98, 4 Emmy award nominations, 1996. Mem. L.A. SIGGRAPH, Visual Effects Soc. Address: 2055 N Gramercy Pl Los Angeles CA 90068-3616

KORZEC, PATRICIA ANN, museum administrator; b. Ware, Mass., Sept. 9, 1953; d. Edward and Bertha (Broton) Sablak. BA, Anna Maria Coll., Paxton, Mass., 1975. Cert. museum programmer. Dir. gallery Xanadu Gallery Folk Art Internat., San Francisco, 1990-92; dir. Bowers Kidseum, Santa Ana, Calif., 1992-96; exec. dir. Riverside Youth Mus., 1997—; docent MH De Young Mus., San Francisco, 1988-93; storyteller. Author (short story) The Magic Moment, 1995. Bd. dirs., adv. Bowers Singles for the Arts, 1995—. Recipient Earthwatch Folk Art Bali award Arensberg Found., 1995. Mem. Bead Soc. Orange County (founding com.), Collector's Coun. Roman Catholic. Home: 4541 Mission Inn Ave Riverside CA 92501-3034

KORZENIK, ARMAND ALEXANDER, lawyer; b. Hartford, Conn., Oct. 31, 1927; s. Bernard and Dorothy (Goldman) K.; m. Ursula Guttmann, June 30, 1956; children: Peter Brent, Jeffrey Dean, Andrea Diane. A.B. magna cum laude, Harvard Coll., 1951; J.D., Harvard U., 1951; LL.M., Yale U., 1952. Bar: Conn. 1951, U.S. Supreme Ct. 1959. Practiced in Hartford, 1951—; asst. corp. counsel Hartford, 1966-72; counsel Hartford Redevel. Agy., 1966-68, Hartford Bd. Edn., 1968-72; instr. bus. law Hartford Inst. Accounting, 1974-75. Editor: Amicus Curiae, 1956-59; bd. editors: Conn. Bar Jour., 1971-79. Mem. Hartford Bd. Edn., 1953-59, Hartford Zoning Bd. Appeals, 1960-66, Hartford Dem. Town Com., 1985-92; justice of peace, Hartford, 1960-73, 84—; Mayor's rep. to Libr. Bd., 1989-91; bd. dirs. YMCA, Boy Scouts Am., PTA, Urban League, Am. Youth Hostels, Jr. C. of C.; founder Blue Hills Civic Assn., West End Civic Assn., Hartford. With USAF, 1946-48, 50; brig. gen. Conn. Air Nat. Guard, 1953-82. Mem. Conn. Bar Assn. (ho. of dels. 1975-78, 89-90, exec. com. gen. practice sect. 1983—, chmn. 1997—), Hartford County Bar Assn. (editor Bar-Fly 1976-78), Conn. Criminal Def. Lawyers Assn., Phi Beta Kappa. Democrat. Club: Harvard of No. Conn. Home: 120 Terry Rd Hartford CT 06105-1111 Office: 436 Farmington Ave Hartford CT 06105-4423

KORZENIK, SIDNEY S., lawyer; b. N.Y.C., Jan. 12, 1909; s. Adolph and Sally (Seiden) K.; m. Emily Faust K., June 23, 1949; children: David, Jeremy, Deborah, Joshua. BA, Harvard U., 1929; MA, Columbia U., 1931; LLB, NYU, 1939. Bar: N.Y., Federal Bar, U.S. Supreme Ct. Pvt. practice N.Y.C., 1946—; with N.Y. State Unemployment Adv. Coun., 1936-41; mem. U.S. Govt. Mgmt.-Labor Textile adv. com.; mem. gen. arbitration coun. of Textile Industry; counsel to various apparel, textile and fur interest orgns., including Nat. Knitted Outerwear Assn., Fedn. Apparel Mfrs., Knitted Textile Assn., Am. Transfer Printing Inst., others; formerly adj. asst. prof. NYU Law Sch.; advisor to govt. textile trade missions; adviser in field. Bd. dirs. Ednl. Found. of Fashion Inst. of Technology, N.Y.C. With U.S. Army, 1941-46. Mem. Phi Beta Kappa. Home: 120 Carthage Rd Scarsdale NY 10583-7202

KOS, HEATHER ANNE, management consultant; b. Jackson, Mich., Dec. 7, 1970; d. David Garrett Kos and Vonnie Maurine (Scott) Petersen; m. Andrew Dustin Dondlinger, July 18, 1997. BA in Acctg. with highest honors, Mich. State U., 1993; MBA, DePaul U., Chgo., 1997. CPA, Ill.; cert. mgmt. acct. 2d yr. tax assoc. Price Waterhouse, Detroit, 1993-94; cost mgr. Bimba Mfg. Co., Monee, Ill., 1994-97; ABM cons. Navistar Internat., Chgo., 1997—. Mem. aux. bd. Make-A-Wish Found., Chgo., 1996—; active Big Bros./Big Sisters Chgo., 1997. Recipient Helene Ramanauskas-Marconi award, 1996; recipient scholarships. Mem. NAFE, AICPA, Ill. Assn. CPAs, Mich. Assn. CPAs, Delta Mu Delta (Gold Medallion award 1996). Home: 1409 W Cuyler Ave Apt 3E Chicago IL 60613-1975 Office: Navistar Internat 455 N Cityfront Plaza Dr Chicago IL 60611-5503

KOSAKOW, JAMES MATTHEW, lawyer; b. New London, Conn., Apr. 12, 1954; s. Leonard Louis and Lois Ann (Rosen) K.; m. Yvonne Manijeh Bokhour, June 4, 1978; 1 child, Jonathan Daniel. BA, Conn. Coll., 1976; JD, Yeshiva U., 1984. Bar: N.Y. 1985, Conn. 1985, D.C. 1985, Fla. 1991, U.S. Dist. Ct. (so. and ea. dists.) 1985, U.S. Tax Ct. 1993. Assoc. Vittoria & Forsythe, N.Y.C., 1986-92, Gregory and Adams, Wilton, Conn., 1992-94; pvt. practice N.Y.C. and Westport, Conn., 1994-97; ptnr. Kove & Kosakow, LLC, 1997—; vice-chancellor Cambridge Theol. Seminary, Carthage, Ill., 1996—; guardian and litem N.Y. County Surrogate's Ct., N.Y.C., 1987—, Norwalk Probate Ct., 1993—; lectr. in field; arbitrator BBB, N.Y.C., 1988-89. Contbr. articles to profl. jours. Trustee, bd. dirs. Internat. Nursery Sch., Queens, N.Y., 1987-89; mem. estates & trusts specialty group lawyers divsn. United Jewish Appeal-Fedn. Jewish Philanthropies of N.Y., Inc., 1990-94; commr. Wilton Water Commn., 1995-96, Wilton Fire Commn., 1996—; ptnr. Creative Philanthropic Resources, 1995—; chmn. membership com. Mid-Fairfield Substance Abuse Coalition, 1995-96; dir. The Art Tree Source, Inc., 1995—; adv. com. The Unicorn Archive. Mem. N.Y. Bar Assn. (legis. com., trusts and estates sect. 1987—), Conn. Bar Assn. (elder law com.), Fla. Bar (real property, probate and trust law, out-of-state mem. rels. com. 1994—), Assn. of Bar of City of N.Y., Exch. Club (bd. dirs. Wilton club). Office: 25 Ford Rd Westport CT 06880-1261 also: 122 E 42d St New York NY 10168

KOSALKA, TERESA MARIE, elementary education educator; b. Milw., May 15, 1965; d. Patrick Joseph and Mary Virginia (Titler) Hurley; m. Robert William Kosalka, June 18, 1988; children: Ryan Alexander, Kyle Andrew, Danielle Alexandra, Jacqueline Ann. BA, Buena Vista Coll., 1987. Admitting clk. Meth. Hosp., Omaha, 1987-89; tchr. jr. high St. Ann's Sch., Omaha, 1987-88, Blessed Sacrament Sch., Lincoln, 1988-89; tchr. aid Boystown (Nebr.)-Wegner Sch., 1988-90; unit clk. U. Nebr. Med. Ctr., Omaha, 1990-95, Bergan Mercy Hosp., 1994—; tchr. jr. high All Sts. Sch., Omaha, 1990-91; mem. spl. tng. Project Wild and Aquatic, 1990, Boystown Motivational System, 1988, 89. Roman Catholic. Home: 6615 S 163d St Omaha NE 68135

KOSANAVICH, LISA A., interior designer, industrial designer; b. Ill., May 21, 1963; d. Philip Stephen and Maureen Virginia (Dulian) K. BS, Ill. State U., 1985. Interior designer Mitchell Internat., Northfield, Ill., 1985-87, Perkins & Will, Chgo., 1987, Integrated Planning & Design, Lombard, Ill., 1987-88, Bus. Office Sys. Inc., Elk Grove Village, Ill., 1988-95; corp. accounts mgr., sr. interior designer Bus. Office Sys. Inc., Chgo., 1995—; corp. account mgr., sr. interior designer Bus. Office Sys. Inc., Elk Grove Village, Ill., 1995—; project mgr. The Gunlocke Co., Chgo., 1995. Mem. Ill. Interior Design Assn. (coms.). Rep. Roman Cath. Avocations: snow skiing, walking, reading, travel. Home: 403 N Grove Ave Oak Park IL 60302-2025

KOSAR, JOHN E., architectural firm executive. BS in Architecture, U. Cin., 1962. Lic. architect 10 states. Pres. Burt Hill Kosar Rittelmann Assocs., Washington, Pitts., Phila., Butler, Pa. and Boston; pres. DPRCG. Trustee Penn's S.W. Assn.; judge Inc. Mag. and Arthur Young & Co. competitions, 1990, 93, 94. Recipient Entrepreneur of Yr. award Inc. Mag. and Arthur Young & Co., 1989, Disting. Svc. award Butler County Bus. Community, 1991. Mem. Pitts. C. of C. (bd. dirs.). Office: Burt Hill Kosar Rittelmann Assoc 400 Morgan Ctr Butler PA 16001

KOSARAJU, S. RAO, computer science educator, researcher; b. Pedapulivarru, Guntur, India, Feb. 20, 1943; came to U.S., 1966; s. Punnaiah and Dhanalakshmi K.; m. Padmaja Valluripalli, Aug. 20, 1970; children: Sheela, Akhila. B.E., Andhra U., (India), 1964; M.Tech., Indian Inst. Tech., Kharagpur, 1966; Ph.D., U. Pa., 1969. Vis. asst. prof. computer sci. Johns Hopkins U., Balt., 1969-70, asst. prof., 1970-75, assoc. prof., 1975-77, prof., 1977—, Kouwenhoven prof., 1981-87; Compere and Marcella Loveless prof. Purdue U., West Lafayette, Ind., 1986-87; Edward J. Schaefer prof. Johns Hopkins U., Balt., 1987—. Contbr. articles to profl. jours.; assoc. editor Jour. Computer Langs., 1976-89, Theory of Computing Systems, 1976—, Jour. Computer and System Scis., 1981—, Information and Computation, 1983-91. Fellow IEEE, Assn. for Computing Machinery; mem. Soc. Indsl. and Applied Math. (mng. editor SIAM Jour. on Computing 1980-89, assoc. editor 1975—). Home: 4 Woodward Ct Reisterstown MD 21136-1835 Office: Johns Hopkins U Dept Computer Sci Baltimore MD 21218

KOSASKY, HAROLD JACK, fertility researcher; b. Winnipeg, Man., Can., Oct. 19, 1927; s. Jack and Lillian (Resnick) K.; m. Shirley Anne Johnston, Sept. 3, 1955; children: Julia, Leah, Robert. BA, U. Manitoba, Can., 1948; MD, U. Manitoba, 1953. Diplomate Am. Bd. Ob-gyn.; lic. Coll Physicians and Surgeons Can., Med. Coun. Can., Ky. State Bd. Health, Idaho State Bd. Health, Mass. Bd. Registration in Medicine. Intern Deer Lodge VA and Grace Hosps., Winnipeg, Man., Can., 1952-53; resident in gen. surgery Col.

Belcher Hosp., Calgary, Alta., Can., 1953-54; resident in psychiatry Warren (Pa.) State Hosp., 1955-56; jr. asst. resident, asst. resident, sr. resident in ob-gyn. Chgo. Lying-In Hosp., 1956-59; exch. fellow in ob-gyn. Newcastle Gen. Hosp., U. Durham, Eng., 1959-60; asst. and assoc. prof. U. Louisville Sch. Med., 1961-65; asst. and assoc. in ob-gyn. various hosps., Boston, 1966-81; gynecologist and obstetrician Boston Hosp. for Women, 1965-81; gynecologist Brigham & Women's Hosp., Boston, 1981—; instr. ob-gyn. Harvard U., 1965—; cons. Ovutime, Boston, 1972—; pres. Saltime Co., 1994, chmn. 1999; asst. vis. surgeon Boston City Hosp., 1967-69; mem. Ky. Govs. Task Force on Mental Retardation, 1964-65, Com. on Malignancy, chmn., 1963-65. Contbr. numerous articles to profl. jours.; co-inventor Ovutime; inventor Saltime Ovulation group of instruments. Fellow ACS, Royal Coll. Surgeons of Can. (cert.), Royal Soc. Health, Boston Obstetric Soc. (emeritus); mem. AAAS, Gen. Med. Coun. Gt. Britain (lic.), Royal Coll. Obstetricans and Gynecologists, Assn. Prof. Ob-gyn., Louisville Obstet. and Gynecol. Soc. (sec., treas. 1962-65), Louisville Med. Forum (v.p.). Episcopalian. Club: Harvard. Office: 25 Boylston St Chestnut Hill MA 02467-1710

KOSC, GREG, umpire; b. Bridgeport, Conn., Apr. 27, 1949. BBA, U. Tex., El Paso; grad., Al Somers Sch., 1972. Former umpire We. Carolina League, Fla. Instrnl. League, Carolina League, So. League, Pacific Coast League, Puerto Rican Winter League; umpire maj. league baseball Am. League, N.Y.C., 1976—; with Umpires Union, Phila. Avocation: weightlifting. Office: Am League 350 Park Ave New York NY 10022 also: Umpires Union 1735 Market St Philadelphia PA 19103

KOSCHMANN, J. VICTOR, history educator, academic program director. Student, Lewis and Clark Coll., 1960-62; BA in Social Scis., Internat. Christian U., Tokyo, 1965; MA in Internat. Studies, Sophia U., Tokyo, 1971; PhD in History, U. Chgo., 1980. Translator, assoc. editor Japan Interpreter, Tokyo, 1971-77; Asian studies instr. Sophia U., Tokyo, 1975-76; social sci. lectr. U. Chgo., 1978-80; asst. prof. Japanese history Cornell U., Ithaca, N.Y., 1980-86, assoc. prof. Japanese history, 1986-94, prof. Japanese history, 1994—, dir. East Asia program; Fulbright fellow, vis. rsch. assoc. Faculty of Law and Politics, Rikkyo U., Tokyo, 1983-84; vis. lectr. Internat. U. Japan, Niigata, 1983-84; vis. prof. Kyoto Ctr. for Japanese Studies, 1990-91; guest prof. Faculty of Lit., U. Kyoto, 1990-91; vis. rschr. Tokyo U. of Fgn. Studies, 1995-96; cons. CBS News, N.Y. Times, Tokyo Broadcasting Sys.; manuscript and proposal reader for numerous instns., including Cambridge U. Press, Princeton U. Press, Cornell U. Press, Calif. U. Press, N.C. U. Press, Cornell East Asia Papers series, Sociol. Forum, East Asia Cultures Critique, Jour. Asian Studies, Pacific Affairs, Jour. Japanese Studies, Columbia East Asian Inst., Social Scis. and Humanities Rsch. Coun. Can., NEH, among others; lectr., panel mem., participant NEH Seminar on Japanese Intellectual History, Hawaii, 1976, SSRC/ACLS, Monterey, 1978, Assn. for Asian Studies conv., Toronto, 1981, Cornell U., 1981, 82, 83, 85, 87, 88, 89, U. Chgo., 1982, 85, McGill U., Montreal, 1982, Harvard U., 1983, U. Calif., Berkeley, 1983, Hokkaido Nat. U., Sapporo, Japan, 1984, Japan Fgn. Svc. Tng. Inst., Tokyo, 1984, U. Seiji Kenkyukai, Atami, Japan, 1984, Rikkyo U. Internat. Symposium, Tokyo, 1985, Am. Hist. Assn., N.Y.C., 1985, San Francisco, 1989, Assn. Asian Studies, Boston, 1987, Chgo., 1990, Duke U., 1988, Smithsonian Instn., Airlie, Va., 1988, Sweet Briar Coll., 1989, Harvard U., 1989, U. Calif., San Diego, 1989, Columbia U., 1989, SUNY, Binghamton, 1990, Hokkaido *., 1991, U. Mich., 1993, Princeton U., 1994, U. Wash., 1995, Heidelberg, 1995, Rikkyo U., Tokyo, 1996, UCLA, 1997, others. Author: The Mito Ideology: Discourse, Reform and Insurrection in Late Tokugawa Japan, 1790-1864, 1987, Revolution and Subjectivity in Postwar Japan, 1997; editor: Authority and the Individual in Japan: Citizen Protest in Historical Perspective, 1978, Conflict in Modern Japanese History: The Neglected Tradition, 1982, International Perspectives in Yanagita Kunio and Japanese Folklore Studies, 1985; contbr. articles to profl. jours. Fellow U. Chgo., 1976-79, Ctr. for far Eastern Studies, 1978, 1979-80, Japan Found., 1979, 95-96, Cornell U., 1985-86; grantee Social Sci. Rsch. Coun., 1983, 83-84, NEH, 87, 88, 92, 1983, Japan-U.S. Edn. Commn., 1983-84, Cornell U., 1984, 85, 91, Japan Found., 1989, 94, Assn. for Asian Studies, 1985. Office: Cornell Univ Hist Dept 320 McGraw Hall Ithaca NY 14853-7601*

KOSCIELAK, JERZY, scientist, science administrator; b. Lodz, Poland, Sept. 6, 1930; s. Jozef and Regina (Pokrzywa) K.; m. Anna Kitaszewska, 1969 (div. 1974); 1 child, Katarzyna. MB, Med. Acad., Warsaw, Poland, 1953, MD, 1960, DrSci, 1966. Asst. dept. physiol. chemistry Med. Acad., Warsaw, 1950-51; asst. and sr. asst. dept. biochemistry Inst. of Hematology, Warsaw, 1951-67; rsch. fellow Harvard Coll., Cambridge, 1964-65; head immunochem. lab. Inst. of Hematology, Warsaw, 1968-69, head dept. biochemistry, 1969—; sci. sec. Inst. of Hematology, Warsaw, 1969-97, dir., rsch. 1997—, prof., 1973—. Editor-in-chief Acta Haematologica Polonica jour., 1976-85; contbr. articles to profl. jours. Mem. Polish Biochem. Soc. (chmn. Warsaw divsn. 1967-69), Forum of Carbohydrates Coming of Age (FCCA), Polish Acad. Sci., N.Y. Acad. Scis., Internat. Glycoconjugate Orgn. (Polish rep. 1988—, pres. 1993-95), Found. for Glycobioloby Glyco XII (founder, pres. 1993—). Avocation: history. Office: Inst of Hematology, Chocimska 5, 00957 Warsaw Poland

KOSHI, ANNIE K., education educator, researcher; b. Changanacherry, Kerala, India, Apr. 30, 1934; came to U.S., 1969; d. Chacko Varkey and Thresiakutty (Thottacher) Thollairam; m. Mathew Koshi, Dec. 28, 1978; children: Sarita, Anita, Mathew. MA, DePaul U., 1971; MEd, Columbia U., 1976, EdD, 1977. Sr. lectr. Assumption Coll., Changanachery, Kerala, India, 1958-69; adj. lectr. CUNY, N.Y.C., 1971-77; assoc. prof. City Coll., 1982—; tchr. L.D. Brandeis H.S., N.Y.C., 1977-82. Author: Discoveries, 1992. Named Outstanding Cmty. Leader Edn. Fedn. Kerala Assn. N. Am., 1994. Mem. Asian-Am. Higher Edn. Coun. (bd. dirs. 1995—), soc. Indian Academics in Am. (culture com. 1990—, sec. 1992-94, chair membership 1994-96). Avocation: walking. Home: 2621 Palisade Ave Apt 10H Bronx NY 10463-6110 Office: City Coll 138th St at Convent Ave New York NY 10031

KOSHLAND, DANIEL EDWARD, JR., biochemist, educator; b. N.Y.C., Mar. 30, 1920; s. Daniel Edward and Eleanor (Haas) K.; m. Marian Elliott, May 25, 1945; children: Ellen, Phyllis, James, Gail, Douglas. BS, U. Calif., Berkeley, 1941; PhD, U. Chgo., 1949; PhD (hon.), Weizmann Inst. Sci., 1984; ScD (hon.), Carnegie Mellon U., 1985; LLD (hon.), Simon Fraser U., 1986; LHD (hon.), Mt. Sinai U.; LLD (hon.), U. Chgo., 1992; PhD (hon.), U. Mass., 1992. Chemist Shell Chem. Co., Martinez, 1941-42; research asso. Manhattan Dist. U. Chgo., 1942-44; group leader Oak Ridge Nat. Labs., 1944-46; postdoctoral fellow Harvard, 1949-51; staff Brookhaven Nat. Lab., Upton, N.Y., 1951-65; affiliate Rockefeller Inst., N.Y.C., 1958-65; prof. biochemistry U. Calif., Berkeley, 1965-97, prof. molecular biology, 1997—, chmn. dept., 1973-78; fellow All Souls, Oxford U., 1972; Phi Beta Kappa lectr., 1976; John Edsall lectr. Harvard U., 1980, William H. Stein lectr. Rockefeller U., 1985; Robert Woodward vis. prof. Harvard U., 1986; G. N. Lewis lectr. U. Calif., Berkeley. Author: Bacterial Chemotaxis as a Model Behavioral System, 1980; mem. editl. bd. jours. Accounts Chem. Rsch., Jour. Chemistry, Jour. Biochemistry; editor jour. Procs. NAS, 1980-85; editor Sci. mag., 1985-95. Recipient T. Duckett Jones award Helen Hay Whitney Found., 1977, Nat. Medal of Sci. NSF, 1990, Merck award Am. Soc. Biochemistry and Molecular Biology, 1991; Guggenheim fellow, 1972; recipient Clark Kerr award U. Calif., 1994, Lasker Found. award, 1998. Mem. NAS, Am. Chem. Soc. (Edgar Fahs Smith award 1979, Pauling award 1979, Rosentiel award 1984, Waterford prize 1984), Am. Philos. Soc., Am. Soc. Biol. Chemists (pres.), Am. Acad. Arts and Scis. (coun.), Acad. Forum (chmn.), Japanese Biochem. Soc. (hon.), Royal Swedish Acad. Scis. (hon.), Alpha Omega Alpha (hon.). Home: 3991 Happy Valley Rd Lafayette CA 94549-2423 Office: U Calif Dept Molecular Cell Biology 329 Stanley Hall # 3206 Berkeley CA 94720-3206

KOSHY, VETTITHARA CHERIAN, chemistry educator, technical director and formulator; b. Kumbanad, Kerala, India, Jan. 5, 1952; came to U.S., 1984; s. Vettithara and Mariamma Cherian; m. Valsamma Koshy, Jan. 31, 1983; children: Rincy Mary, John Cherian. BSc in Chemistry, Kerala U., India, 1973; MSc in Chemistry, Ravishankar U., India, 1975, PhD in Chemistry, 1983; MS in Econ. Aspects of Chemistry, U. Detroit, 1992. Rsch. fellow chemistry Ravishankar U., Raipur, 1976-81; lectr., head dept. chemistry J.M. Patel Coll., 1981-83; lectr. dept. chemistry D.B. Sci. Coll., Gondia (India) Edn. Soc., India, 1983-84; group leader and evening supr. in R & D Widger Chem. Corp., Warren, Mich., 1984-87; mgr. automotive divsn., R & D Croda Caourep Corp., Westland, Mich., 1987-89; dir. R & D, quality control and mfg. Autotek, inc., Farmington Hills, Mich., 1989-94; pres. Koshy Speciality Products, Inc., Bloomfield Hills, Mich., 1994—; engr. Dale Packaging Inc., Livonia, Mich., 1994-95; sr. chemist Novamax Techs. (U.S.) Inc., Warren, 1995-96; tech. mgr. Henkel Corp. Novamax Techs., 1996-98; sr. rsch. scientist Henkel Surface Techs., Madison Heights, 1998—. Contbr. articles to Jour. Chem. Engring., Croatica Chemica Acta, Indian Acad. Scis., Nat. Acad. Scis. Sci. Letters, among others. Pres. sci. assn. J.M. Patel Coll., Bhandara, India, 1981-82; pres. chem. soc. Ravishankar U., Raipur, 1977-78, pres. rsch. scholars assn., 1979-81. Recipient numerous grants. Mem. Am. Chem. Soc., Am. Inst. Chemists, Soc. Automotive Engrs. (assoc.), Fedn. Kerala Assns. N.Am. (region 7 v.p. 1998—). Achievements include development of a formula for a universal sealer for automotive application. Home: 7030 White Pine Dr Bloomfield Hills MI 48301-3715 Office: Henkel Surface Techs 32100 Stephenson Hwy Madison Heights MI 48071-5514

KOSINSKI, RICHARD ANDREW, public relations executive; b. Chgo., Aug. 12, 1951; s. Andrew Ignatius and Olga Sophia (Janusz) K.; m. Susan M. Mark, Oct. 13, 1974 (div. June 1985). BS, Loyola U. Chgo., 1974; MPA, Roosevelt U., 1979. From dir. parents assocs. to dir. dental devel. Loyola U. Chgo., 1976-79; assoc. dir. devel. Am. Fund for Dental Health, Chgo., 1979-80; dir. devel. & pub. rels. Niles Twp. Sheltered Workshop, Skokie, Ill., 1985-88; assoc. exec. dir. Leukemia Soc. Am., Chgo., 1988-93; mgr. major gifts Prevent Blindness Am., Schaumburg, Ill., 1993-97; dir. devel. Youth Found. Skokie (Ill.) Park Dist., 1997—. Mem. svc. and rehab. com. Am. Cancer Soc., 1986-88. Recipient Tribute U.S. Ho. of Reps., 1986. Roman Catholic. Avocations: travel, photography, writing. Home: 838 Mcintosh Ct Apt 208 Prospect Heights IL 60070-2252

KOSKELLA, LUCRETIA C., real estate broker, appraiser; b. Newburgh, N.Y., Aug. 29, 1928; d. Vincent George and Josephine Anita (Gross) Canadé; m. John Archie Koskella, June 13, 1954 (div. May 1961); 1 child, Judith Ann. Grad. h.s., Newburgh. Lic. real estate, N.Y., lic. real estate broker, N.Y., lic. real estate appraiser, N.Y. Real estate salesperson, 1961-71, real estate broker, 1971—; chair adv. bd. real estate appraisal L.K.R.B., Newburgh, 1971—; active C.L.E.A.N. Chadwick Lake, Newburgh, 1980-96. Contbr. poetry to mags. Charter mem., organizer Scenic Hudson, Newburgh, 1980-96; Orange County Rep. committeewoman Rep. Party, 1980-92; campaign mgr., chmn., coord. local, state, and nat. campaigns, N.Y., 1980-96; publicist senate campaigns, Orange County and Newburgh, 1980-96; mem. exec. bd., speechwriter, spkr. Orange County Rep. Com., 1992-94; active Orange County Chpt. N.Y. Fedn. Rep. Women; vol. Am. Cancer Soc., Heart Assn., March of Dimes, PTA, Am. Diabetes Assn. Recipient Dedication Contest winner Water and Light Poetry Mag., 1994. Mem. NRA, NOW, Nat. Mus. Women in Arts, N.Y. State Sheriffs Assn. (bus. mem.). Avocations: golf, art, writing poetry, swimming, computers, skeet shooting. Home and Office: 19 Pat Rd Newburgh NY 12550-7219

KOSKI, DONNA FAITH, poet; b. Wildwood, N.J., Aug. 18, 1935; d. Sebastian and Mildred (Shastany) Rossitto; m. Paul A. Koski, May 5, 1968 (div. June 1982); children: Danita Joy, Darla Jean, Deanna Rene, Deena Marie, Charles Ray. Student, San Diego Jr. Coll., 1955-58, Mesa Jr. Coll, San Diego, 1993. With Pacific Telephone, San Diego, 1954-68; credit clk. Norwich (Conn.) Gas & Lights, 1968-70; clk. Navy Exch., New London, Conn., 1969-70; front desk clk. Del Webb's, San Diego, 1971-72; payroll clk. U.S.I.U., San Diego, 1974-76; facility mgr. Price Costco, San Diego, 1978-94, Price Enterprises, Inc., San Diego, 1994-97, Price Smart Vacations (Costco Travel), 1997—. Author poetry: The Power of Love, 1995, Nights in Sedona, 1995, Faces in the Clouds, 1994. Vol. Nat. Multiple Sclerosis Soc., San Diego, 1995, React-Telecom. Emergency, San Diego, 1985-93, Perot Hdqrs., San Diego, 1992, 96, Social Svcs., San Diego, 1980-82. Recipient Editor's Choice award Nat. Libr. of Poetry, 1995, Accomplishment of Merit, Creative Arts and Sci., 1994, 1st Place Browning Competition award Iliad Press, 1998, Presdl. Recognition award, 1998, Outstanding Achievement in Poetry award Famous Poets Soc., 1998, Pres. Recognition award for literary excellence, 1999. Mem. Internat. Soc. Poets, Internat. Soc. Authors and Artists, Nat. Autor's Registry (Pres.'s recognition award for lit. excellance 1999), Moose Lodge. Unity Ch. Avocations: poetry, computer Internet, music. Home: 3190 Atlas St San Diego CA 92111-5025 Office: Price Smart (Costco Travel) 4649 Morena Blvd San Diego CA 92117-3650

KOSKI, WALTER S., chemistry educator, scientist; b. Phila., Dec. 1, 1913; s. Bruno and Helen (Laskowska) Stankiewicz; m. Helen Ireton Tag, May 11, 1940; children—Carol Lee, Ann Louise, Nancy Cheryl, Phyllis Ireton. Ph.D., Johns Hopkins, 1942. Research chemist Hercules Powder Co., 1942-43; group leader Los Alamos Sci. Lab., 1944-47; physicist Brookhaven Nat. Lab., 1947-48; asso. prof. Johns Hopkins, 1947-55; prof. chemistry Johns Hopkins (Grad. Sch.), 1955—, B.N. Baker prof. chemistry, 1975—, chmn. dept., 1958-69. Fellow Am. Phys. Soc.; mem. Am. Chem. Soc. (merit award Md. sect), Phi Beta Kappa. Office: Johns Hopkins U 3400 N Charles St Baltimore MD 21218-2680

KOSKINEN, JOHN ANDREW, federal government executive; b. Cleve., June 30, 1939; s. Yrjo Alfred and Irja (Danska) K.; m. Patricia Salz, June 15, 1963; children: Jeffrey, Cheryl. BA magna cum laude, Duke U., 1961; JD cum laude, Yale U., 1964; postgrad., Cambridge U., Eng., 1964-65. Bar: Calif. 1965, Conn. 1972. Clk. to presiding justice U.S. Ct. Appeals, Washington, 1965-66; lawyer Gibson, Dunn & Crutcher, L.A., 1966-67; spl. asst. to dep. exec. dir. Nat. Adv. Commn. Civil Disorders (also called Kerner Commn.), Washington, 1967-68; legis. asst. to Mayor John Lindsay N.Y.C., 1968-69; adminstrv. asst. to Senator Abraham Ribinoff Conn., 1969-73; v.p. Palmieri Co., Washington, 1973-77, pres., chief operating officer, 1977-79, pres., chief exec. officer, 1979-94; dep. dir. for mgmt. Office of Mgmt. and Budget, Washington, 1994-97; asst. to Pres., chmn. President's Coun. on Year 2000 Conversion, Washington, 1998—. Mem. Pres.'s Mgmt. Improvement Coun., 1979-80; bd. dirs. Nat. Captioning Inst., 1979-91, chmn., 1986-87, vice-chmn., 1979-86; trustee Coop. Assistance Fund, 1982-93; trustee Duke U., 1985-97, vice chmn. 1993-94, chmn. 1994-97; chmn. Washington 1994 World Cup Commn., 1989-94, Washington Olympic Football Organizing Com., 1993-94; vice chmn. Am. Soccer League, 1987-91. Fellow Nat. Acad. Pub. Adminstrn.; mem. Duke U. Gen. Alumni Assn. (pres. 1980-81), Phi Beta Kappa. Avocations: soccer, tennis, music. Office: Office Mgmt and Budget OEOB Rm 115 Washington DC 20503

KOSKO, SUSAN UTTAL, legal administrator; b. N.Y.C., Oct. 8, 1954; d. Sheldon and Jane Louise (Kaufmann) Uttal; m. James J. Kosko, July 6, 1996. BA, Clark U., 1976; cert. paralegal, Inst. Paralegal Tng., Phila., 1978. Legal asst. Winthrop, Stimson, Putnam & Roberts, N.Y.C., 1978-80; legal coord. Schroder Real Estate Corp., N.Y.C., 1980-83; legal asst. supr. real estate svcs. dept. Cravath, Swaine & Moore, N.Y.C., 1983-89; sr. legal asst. real estate dept. Rackemann, Sawyer & Brewster, Boston, 1989-90; sr. legal asst. leasing and real estate depts. Goulston & Storrs, Boston, 1990-97; contracts adminstr. Cabletron Systems, Inc., Rochester, N.H., 1997-99; v.p. ops. Nonpareil Software, New Durham, N.H., 1999—. Mem. Clark U. N.Y. Young Alumni Assn. (steering com.). Democrat. Jewish. Avocations: pottery, piano, photography, cycling, gourmet cooking. Office: Nonpareil Software Inc 39 N Shore Rd New Durham NH 03855-2113

KOSLER, SONJA RAYE, political consultant, artist; b. Helena, Mont., Oct. 15, 1946; d. Clayton S. and Geraldine Mary (Mueller) Christianson; m. Garrett G. Alberts, Nov. 5, 1963 (div. apr. 1971); 1 child, Teresa Lynn; m. David R. Kosler, June 19, 1981. Student, N.D. State U., 1964, Mesa C.C., San Diego, 1973-74, U. Calif., San Diego, 1976. Merchandise acctg. mgr. Handyman, San Diego, 1972-79; asst. contr. Dixieline Lumber, San Diego, 1979-83; owner Sonja's House, San Diego, 1983-85; contr. Leisure Time Sports, El Cajon, Calif., 1985-86; chmn. bd., treas. Christianson Asphalt Products, Fargo, 1986-95; owner Sonja R. Kosler, Strategist, Dent, Minn., 1995—. Mem. LWV; chmn. City of Fargo Planning Commn., 1995-96, mem., 1991-95; mem. steering com. Close Up Intergenerational Forum, Fargo, 1992-94; mem. Gov.'s Employment & Tng. Forum, Bismarck, 1989-92; chmn. N.D. State Gaming Commn., 1993-94, mem., 1990-93; sr. mentor Page Found., Moorhead, Minn., 1994-95; cand. N.D. State Legis., 1990, 92; dir. Mus. E. Otter Tail County, Otter Tail County Democrat Farm Labor. Mem. Am. Planning Assn., Assn. Gen. Contrs., Nat. Assn. Women in Constrn. (dir., pres. 1987-95), Southgate Exch. Club (dir., pres. 1989-95). Avocations: gardening, politics, cooking, papier mache art, storytelling. Office: RR 1 Box 429 Dent MN 56528-9766

KOSLOW, SALLY, editor-in-chief. Editor-in-chief McCall's mag., N.Y.C., 1994—. Office: McCalls 375 Lexington Ave New York NY 10017-5514

KOSLOW, STEPHEN HUGH, science administrator, pharmacologist; b. N.Y.C., Oct. 14, 1940; s. Julius and Lillian (Kaye) K.; m. Diane Heisler, Aug. 18, 1962; children: Karin, James. BS, Columbia U., 1962; PhD, U. Chgo., 1967. Internat. postdoctoral fellow Swedish Med. Rsch. Coun., Karolinski Inst., 1968-69; pharmacologist, chief neurobiology unit St. Elizabeth's Hosp., Washington, 1970-77; chief biol. rsch. sect. Clin. Rsch. Br., Rockville, Md., 1975-81; chief div. Extramural Rsch. Neurosci. Rsch. Br. NIMH, Rockville, 1981-85, chief div. Basic Scis. Neurosci. Rsch. Br., 1985-88, acting dir. div. Basic Brain and Behavioral Scis., 1988-89, dir. divsn. Basic Brain and Behavioral Scis., 1990-92; dir. divsn. Neurosci. and Behavioral Sci. NIMH-NIH, Rockville, 1992-96, dir. divsn. Basic and Clin. Neurosci. Rsch., 1996-99; assoc. dir., dir. office neuroinformatics NIMH, Rockville, Md., 1999—; project dir. NIMH-CRB Collaborative Program on Psychobiology of Depression-Biol. Study, 1975-85; mem. adv. bd. Tourette Syndrome Assn., Bayside, N.Y., 1984; chair fed. coordinating com. on the Human Brain Project, 1991—. Mem. editl. bd. Neuropsychopharacology, 1987-92, Critical Revs. in Neurobiol., 1991—, Human Brain Mapping, 1993—, Psychopharm. Bull., 1989-99, Neuroimage, 1995—; series editor Progress in Neuroinformatics Rsch., Neuroimage, 1995—, CNS Drug Revs., 1995—. Recipient NIMH Quality Increase award, 1977-78, Health Adminstr.'s award for Meritorious Achievement, 1986, Pub. Health Svc. Spl. Recognition award, 1992, Alumni Achievement award U. Chgo. Club of Washington, 1995, two Dir.'s awards NIH, 1996 ; Swedish Med. Rsch. Coun. internat. postdoctoral fellow, 1968-69, Spl. NATO fellow, 1969. Fellow AAAS, Am. Coll. Neuropsychopharmacology; mem. Am. Soc. for Neurochemistry, Am. Soc. Pharmacology and Exptl. Therapeutics, Collegium Internat. Neuro Psychopharmacologium, Soc. for Neurosci., Soc. Biol. Psychiatry. Fax: 301-443-1867. E-mail: koz@helix.nih.gov. Office: NIMH Rm 6167 MSC 9613 6001 Executive Blvd Bethesda MD 20892-9613

KOSLOWITZ, KAREN, councilwoman; children: Heidi, Marcia. Legis. aide Congressman Gary Ackerman, 1983-85, Councilman Arthur Katzman, 1985-88; spl. asst., Queens ombudsman City Coun. Pres. Andrew Stein; councilwoman Dist. 22 City of N.Y., 1991—; mem. aging, civil svc. and labor, gen. welfare coms., chmn. consumer affairs com. N.Y. City Coun. Office: 11821 Queens Blvd Forest Hills NY 11375-7201

KOSMOSKI, MARY LOU TERESA, special education educator; b. Perth Amboy, N.J., Mar. 14, 1962; d. Benjamin Walter and Frances Dolores Kosmoski. BA, Georgian Ct. Coll., Lakewood, N.J., 1984, MEd, 1995. Cert. elem. tchr., N.J.; cert. handicapped tchr., N.J. Tchr. 2d grade Holy Spirit Sch., Perth Amboy, N.J., 1984-85; tchr. 3d grade Sacred Heart Sch., South Amboy, N.J., 1985-90; tchr. 1st grade St. Mary Sch., South Amboy, N.J., 1990-92; substitute tchr. South Amboy Elem. Sch., 1993, tchr. 1st and 4th grades resource rm., 1994—; tchr. 6th thru 8th grades resource rm. South Amboy Mid. Sch., 1993-94; isntr. drawing and watercolor Matawan (N.J.) Student Enrichment Program, 1989—; presenter workshops. Contbr. article to profl. jour. Georgian Ct. Coll. dean's scholar, 1982-84. Mem. ASCD, Nat. Assn. Mediation in Edn., Nat. Coun. Tchrs. English, N.J. Edn. Assn., N.J. Maths. Coalition, Delta Tau Kappa (Gamma Kappa chpt.). Roman Catholic. Avocations: oil painting, watercolors, needle point, reading, exercise. Home: 12 Kearney Ave South Amboy NJ 08879-1011 Office: South Amboy Elem Sch John St South Amboy NJ 08879

KOSNER, EDWARD A(LAN), magazine editor and publisher; b. N.Y.C., July 26, 1937; s. Sidney and Annalee (Fisher) K.; m. Alice Nadel, Feb. 1, 1959; children: John Robbins, Anthony William; m. Julie Baumgold, Nov. 19, 1978; 1 dau., Lily. B.A., CCNY, 1958. Rewriteman, asst. city editor N.Y. Post, 1958-63; assoc. editor Newsweek Mag., N.Y.C., 1963-67; gen. editor Newsweek Mag., 1967-69, nat. affairs editor, 1969-72, asst. mng. editor, 1972, mng. editor, 1973-75, editor, 1975-79; editor New York Mag., N.Y.C., 1980-93; pub. New York Mag., 1986-91; pres. New York Mag., N.Y.C., 1991-93; editor-in-chief Esquire Mag., N.Y.C., 1993-97; editor N.Y. Sunday Daily News, N.Y.C., 1998—. Recipient various journalism awards. Mem. Am. Soc. Mag. Editors (pres. 1984-86, exec. com.), Century Club. Home: 180 E 79th St New York NY 10021-0437

KOSOKOFF, JEFFREY EUGENE, librarian; b. Springfield, Oregon, Apr. 19, 1964; s. Stephen Arnold Kosokoff and Sandra (Poll) Polishuk. BA in Philosophy, U. Calif., Santa Cruz, 1987; MA in History Philosophy Sci., Ind. U., 1994, MLS, 1994. English instr. Inner Mongolia's Tchrs. U., Hohhot, People's Republic China, 1982; tchg. asst. U. Calif., Santa Cruz, 1984-87; rsch. asst. Oreg. Health Sci. U., Portland, 1988-90; assoc. instr. Ind. U., Bloomington, 1991-93, reference asst., 1993-94, web adminstr., 1994-95; info. tech. libr. Conn. Coll., New London, 1995-97; reference libr. DePaul Univ., Chgo., 1997-99, elec. rsch. coord., 1999—; cons. Wooster (Ohio) Coll., 1994, 95; advisor Mid-Peninsula Libr. Coop., Iron Mtn., Mich., 1995. Co-author: Internet Skills for Information Networking, 1995. Asst. campaign dir. Barbara Roberts Gov. Oreg., 1990. Mem. ALA, Assn. Coll. Rsch. Librs. (leadership com. 1997-), Beta Phi Mu. Office: DePaul University 2350 N Kenmore Ave Chicago IL 60614-3210

KOSOVICH, DUSHAN RADOVAN, psychiatrist; b. Trepca, Niksic, Yugoslavia, Dec. 23, 1926; came to U.S., 1967, naturalized, 1972; s. Radovan Dj and Djurdja K. (Bacovic) K.; children—Jasmine, Nicholas. M.D., Belgrade U., 1954, postgrad., 1954-57; certificate, Am. Inst. for Psychoanalysis and Postgrad. Center, 1972. Resident in neuropsychiatry Belgrade, Yugoslavia, 1954-57; resident in psychiatry Bellevue Med. Center, N.Y.C., 1957-59, McGill U., Montreal, Que., Can., 1965-67; founder, chief neuropsychiatric service for inpatient and outpatients Gen. Hosp., Titograd, Montenegro, Yugoslavia, 1960-65; staff psychiatrist Bellevue Med. Center, N.Y.C., 1967-73; dir. inpatient psychiat. service Lincoln Hosp., Bronx, N.Y., 1973-75; chief inpatient services Methodist Hosp., Bklyn., 1975-76, acting dir. psychiat dept., 1976-78, dir., 1978-84; pvt. practice N.Y.C., 1984—; clin. asso. prof. dept. psychiatry Downstate Med. Center, State U. N.Y., 1975—; Psychoanalyst Karen Horney Psychoanalytic Inst., N.Y.C. Author: Stress, 1989, Optimistic Psychoanalysis, 1989; contbr. articles to profl. jours. Served with Yugoslavian Army, 1944-46. Recipient City of Titograd award for best sci. achievement, 1964. Fellow Assn. for Advancement Psychoanalysis, Karen Horney Psychoanalytic Inst. and Ctr., Am. Acad. Psychoanalysis; mem. Am. Acad. Clin. Psychiatrists, N.Am. Acad. for Auricular Medicine, Am. Acad. Psychiatry and Law, World Psychiat. Assn., Am. Yugoslav Med. Soc. Home: 524 E 72nd St Apt 41A New York NY 10021-9806 Office: 233 E 50th St New York NY 10022-7718

KOSOWICZ, FRANCIS JOHN, concert organist; b. Lowell, Mass., July 20, 1946; s. Stanley Marion and Mildred Helen (Lavigne) K.; m. Augusta Benning Blundon, Sept. 15, 1985. Student, Harvard U., 1960-64, Manhattanville Coll., 1963-66, Iona Coll., 1964-66, U. Mass., 1971-73, U. Salamanca, Spain, 1983; MusM, Lancashire Sch. of Music, Blackpool, Eng., 1988; studies with numerous master tchrs. including Charles A. MacGrail, Edgar Hilliar, E. Power Biggs, William Harms, Richard Casper, Walter Ehret,, Montserrat Torrent, Guy Bovet. Dir. music St. Catherine's Ch., Graniteville, Mass., Chapel of Peace, Kings Point, Bermuda, Holy Trinity Chapel, Gia Le, Socialist Republic of Vietnam; artist-in-residence St. Joseph's Abbey, Spencer, Mass., Holy Ghost Monastery, Conyers, Ga., Christian A. Herter Ctr., Boston; cons. U.S. Dept. Def., Washington, 1970, Cabin Creek (W.Va.) Quilts. Author, editor: Book of Worship for United States Forces, 1974; contbr. articles to profl. jours.; solo organist La Sonora Tecolutla, Veracruz, Mex., 1975-76, Cathedral of Most Holy Trinity, Hamilton, Bermuda, Cathedral of Redemption, Hue, Socialist Republic of Vietnam, Cathedrale Met., Guadalajara, Mex., Catedrale Nueva, Salamanca, Cathedral, Ciudad Rodrigo, Spain, other recitals in U.S., Can., Mex., Europe, Australia, Oceania; composer: Wedding for Organ, 1967, Imperial Suit, 1975, Carillon Snow Piece, 1975; performer All-Bach Organ Concert commemorating Bach's 303d Birthday, Christ Ch. Cathedral, Nassau, The Bahamas, Mar. 21, 1988. Advisor to Pres. of U.S., Washington, 1968; founder Roane Arts and Humanities Council, Inc., Spencer, W.Va., 1977, The Jehan Alain Found., Romainmotier and Geneva, Switzerland; co-founder, treas. The Roane County Humane Authority/Soc., 1990-93. With USN, 1966-72, Vietnam. Decorated 3 Bronze Stars; recipient Gold Medal Ministry of Culture, People's Republic of China, 1993. Mem. Am. Musicological Soc., Organ Hist. Soc., Consociatio Internationalis Musicae Sacrae, Universa Laus, Am. Guild Organists (state chmn. W.Va. 1980-85), Royal Coll. Organists, Royal Can. Coll. Organists, Southeastern Hist. Keyboard Soc. (life). Home: 13C Harmony Rt Spencer WV 25276-9306

KOSOWSKY, DAVID I., retired biotechnical company executive; b. N.Y.C., Feb. 27, 1930; m. Ingrid M. Mehlstaeubl; children: Michael, Richard P., Steven A. BEE summa cum laude, CUNY, 1951; SM, MIT, 1952, ScD, 1955. Chmn. emeritus Damon Corp., Needham Heights, Mass.; speaker, lectr. on policy developments and trends in the health care industry. Patentee in field. Mem. Corp. MIT, mem. vis. com. dept. biology; trustees Beth Israel Hosp., U. Hosp., New Eng. Aquarium, Children's Hosp.; mem. exec. group Harvard Med. Ctr. bd. trustees; mem. Corp. Joslin Diabetes Ctr., Inc., Corp. Mus. Sci.; mem. Commn. on Acad. Health Ctrs., Economy of New Eng. for the New Eng. Bd. of Higher Edn. Mem. N.Y. Acad. of Scis., IEEE, Sigma Xi, Tau Beta Pi, Eta Kappa Nu, Order of St. John, Knights of Malta. Home: 403D Dedham St Newton MA 02459-3300

KOSS, LEOPOLD G., physician, pathologist, educator; b. Gdansk, Poland, Oct. 2, 1920; came to U.S., 1947, naturalized, 1952; s. Abram and Rose (Merenholc) Kon; m. Lydia Palla; children: Michael S., Andrew C., Richard P. M.D., U. Berne, Switzerland, 1946. Intern, Lincoln Hosp., N.Y.C., 1947-48; tng. pathology St. Gallen, Switzerland, 1946-47, Kings County Hosp., Bklyn., 1949-52; instr. pathology L.I. (N.Y.) U. Coll. Medicine, 1949-52; mem. staff Meml. Hosp. Cancer and Allied Diseases, N.Y.C., 1952-70, attending pathologist, 1961-70, chief cytology service, 1961-70; pathologist-in-chief Sinai Hosp. Balt., 1970-73; prof., chmn. dept. pathology Montefiore Hosp., Med. Ctr. Albert Einstein Coll. Medicine, Bronx, N.Y., 1973-92, prof., chair emeritus, 1993—; hon. prof. pathology Severance Med. Coll., Seoul, Korea, 1956; assoc. mem. Sloan-Kettering Inst. Cancer Research, N.Y.C., 1957-70; assoc. prof. pathology Sloan-Kettering div. Postgrad. Sch. Med. Scis., Cornell U., 1957-70; prof. pathology Jefferson Med. Coll., Phila., 1970-73; clin. prof. pathology U. Md. Med. Sch., 1971-73; vis. pathologist James Ewing Hosp., N.Y.C., 1952-60; former cons. pathologist N.Y. State Dept. Health, Hosp. Spl. Surgery, N.Y.C.; cons. pathologist Walter Reed Army Med. Ctr., Nassau County Med. Ctr. Author: Diagnostic Cytology and Its Histopathologic Bases, 4th rev. edit. 1992, Tumors of the Urinary Bladder, 1975, Supplement, 1984, Aspiration Biopsy: Cytologic Interpretation and Histologic Bases, 2nd rev. edit. 1992; editor: Advances in Clinical Cytology, Vol. I, 1981, Vol. II, 1984, Papillomaviruses and Human Diseases, 1987, Errors and Pitfalls in Diagnostic Cytology, 1997, Introduction to Gunecolgie Cytopathology, 1999; contbr. articles to profl. jours. and chpts. to books also monographs. Served to maj. M.C., AUS, 1955-57. Recipient Wien award Papanicolaou Cancer Inst., 1963, Alfred P. Sloan award cancer rsch., 1964, Fred Stewart award, 1984, Vandenbergne-Hill award, 1984, Meritorious medal U. Brussels, 1987, Jurzykowski award, 1991. Fellow AAAS, Royal Coll. Pathologists (hon.), Am. Soc. Clin. Pathology, Coll. Am. Pathologists, Internat. Acad. Cytology (Goldblatt award 1962, Kazumasa Masubuchi Life-Time Achievement award in clin. cytology, 1995); mem. AMA, Am. Soc. Exptl. Path. (Gold Cane award 1993), James Ewing Soc., Am. Soc. Cytology (pres. 1962, Papanicolaou award 1966), Internat. Acad. Pathology (Maude Abbott lectr. 1989), N.Y. Pathology Soc. (pres. 1985-87, Middleton-Goldsmith lectr. 1992), N.Y. State Soc. Pathology (Lansky-Ratner award 1989), Royal Acad. Medicine Spain (corr.), Brit. Soc. Clin. Cytology (hon.), Korean Med. Assn., Mex. Soc. Cytology, Argentinian Soc. Cytology, Japanese Soc. Pathology, Polish Soc. Pathology, Peruvian Soc. Ob-Gyn., German Acad. Sci. (Leopoldina), Internat. Soc. of Urol. Pathology (pres. 1991-94, F.K. Mostofi Disting. Svc. award 1995), Am. Soc. for Colposcopy and Cervical Pathology (Disting. Svc. award 1996). Office: Montefiore Medical Ctr 111 E 210th St Bronx NY 10467-2401

KOSSAETH, TAMMY GALE, intensive care nurse; b. San Antonio, Feb. 18, 1969; d. Kenneth Roland and Hermina Marie (Hilzfelder) K. BSN, U. Tex., San Antonio, 1991. RN, Tex.; cert. BLS instr.; cert. ACLS; cert. cardiac rehab.; cert. med.-surg. nurse. Staff nurse surg. ICU Audie L. Murphy VA Hosp., San Antonio, 1991—. Mem. Women's Internat. Bowling Congress (local league pres. and league sec. 1994-95, 95-96, 96-97, 97-98, 98-99). Roman Catholic. Avocations: reading, sewing, crafts, traveling, horseback riding. Home: 12379 W Fm 471 # 3 San Antonio TX 78253-4808

KOSSAK, SHELLEY, think-tank executive. Wash. office contact Population Resource Ctr., Washington, D.C., 1990—. Office: Population Resource Ctr 1725 K St NW Ste 1102 Washington DC 20006-1401*

KOSSEL, CLIFFORD GEORGE, retired philosophy educator, clergyman; b. Omro, Wis., Apr. 22, 1916; s. George C. and Sarah (Haigh) K. A.B., Gonzaga U., 1940, M.A., 1941; Ph.D., U. Toronto, 1945; Th.L., Alma Coll., 1949. Assoc. prof. Gonzaga U., Spokane, 1950-63, prof. philosophy, 1963-87, emeritus, 1988, chmn. dept. philosophy, 1966-69, dean Sch. Philosophy and Letters, 1958-71; sabbatical leave to Oxford, Eng. and Florence, Italy, 1969-70. Bd. editors Communio: Internat. Cath. Rev., 1974-93; contbr. profl. jours. Mem. Am. Cath. Philos. Assn., Jesuit Philos. Assn. (past pres.). Office: Gonzaga U Philosophy Dept Spokane WA 99258

KOSSIAKOFF, ALEXANDER, chemist; b. St. Petersburg (formerly Leningrad), Russia, June 26, 1914; m. Arabelle Davies, Feb. 18, 1939; children: Tanya Ann, Anthony. B.S. in Chemistry, Calif. Inst. Tech., 1936, postdoctoral fellow, 1939; Ph.D. in Chemistry, Johns Hopkins U., 1938. Instr. chemistry Catholic U. Am., 1939-42; tech. aide Office Sci. Research and Devel.; also Nat. Def. Research Council, Washington, 1942-43; dep. dir. research Allegany Ballistics Lab., George Washington U., Cumberland, Md., 1944-46; with Applied Physics Lab., Johns Hopkins U., Silver Spring, Md., 1946—; asst. dir. tech. ops., asso. dir. Applied Physics Lab., Johns Hopkins U., 1961-66, head surface missile systems dept., 1965-69, dep. dir., 1966-69, dir. lab., 1969-80, chief scientist, 1980—, chmn. MS Tech. Mgmt./MS Sys. Engring. program, Sch. Enring.; Chmn. launching and handling panel research and devel. bd. U.S. Dept. Def., 1948-51; cons. Tech. Adv. Panel on Aeros., 1954-60; mem. com. on nat. labs. Office Sci. and Tech., 1969-73. Contbr. articles to profl. jours. Bd. dirs. Montgomery Gen. Hosp., 1979-85; mem. Gov.'s Sci. Adv. Council, 1979—. Recipient Navy Disting. Public Service award, Def. Dept. medal for disting. public service, Pres.'s Cert. of Merit, other awards. Fellow Am. Inst. Chemists; mem. AAAS, INCOSE, Phi Beta Kappa, Sigma Xi, Tau Beta Pi, Phi Lambda Upsilon. Club: Cosmos. Home: 120 Haviland Mill Rd Brookeville MD 20833-2308 Office: Johns Hopkins Rd Laurel MD 20723

KOSSIN, SANFORD MARSHALL, illustrator; b. L.A., June 4, 1926; s. Leo and Clara Kossin; m. Josephine Koscomb, May 21, 1954; children: David, James. Student, Jepson Sch. Art, L.A., 1946-50. Freelance illustrator N.Y.C., 1952—; drawing instr. Parsons Sch. Art, N.Y.C., 1977-87; advanced illustraton instr. Pratt Inst., Bklyn., 1988-90. Illustrator paper back book covers Bantam Books, Pocket Books, New Am. Libr., Ballantine Books, 1950's-1985, children's books Houghton Mifflin Pubs., 1975-85, mags. including Readers Digest, Saturday Eve Post, Good Housekeeping, Boys Life, Harper Collins Pubs., Life Mag., 1963. Sonarman 2nd class USNR, 1944-46, PTO. Mem. Soc. Illustrators (life, Best Illustration of Yr. ann. exhbn. 1956-80), NCS Berndt Toast Gang. Avocations: cartooning, portrait painting, watercolor painting. Home and Office: Sandy Kossin Illustration 143 Cow Neck Rd Port Washington NY 11050-1143

KOSSLER, WILLIAM JOHN, physics educator; b. Charleston, S.C., Mar. 26, 1937; s. William John and Lois Covil (Gordon) K.; m. Margaret O'Neil; children: Neil, William, Paul. BS, MIT, 1959; PhD, Princeton U., 1964. Grad. asst. Princeton (N.J.) U., 1962-64; asst. prof. MIT, Cambridge, Mass., 1966-69; asst. prof. Coll. William & Mary, Williamsburg, Va., 1969-70, assoc. prof., 1970-78, prof. physics, 1978—. Author: Low Magnetic Fields in Anisotropic Super Conductors, 1995; contbr. articles to profl. jours. Fellow Am. Phys. Soc. Avocation: sailing. Home: 496 Burnham Rd Williamsburg VA 23185 Office: Coll William & Mary Physics Dept Williamsburg VA 23187-8795

KOSSLYN, STEPHEN M., psychologist educator; b. Santa Monica, Calif., Nov. 30, 1948; s. S. Duke and Rhoda (Rosenberg) K.; m. Robin S. Rosenberg, Mar. 28, 1982; children: Justin Lewis, David Alan, Nathaniel Solté. BA in Psychology, UCLA, 1970; PhD in Psychology, Stanford U., 1974. Asst. prof. of Psychology The Johns Hopkins Univ., 1974-77; assoc. prof. of Psychology Harvard Univ., 1977-81; rsch. affiliate of the Ctr. for Cognitive Sci. M.I.T., 1980-94; assoc. prof. of Psychology Brandeis Univ., 1981-82; prof. of Psychology Harvard Univ., 1983—; co-dir. James S. McDonnell Found. Summer Inst. in Cognitive Neuroscience, 1987; assoc. psychologist in neurology Mass. Gen. Hosp., 1990—; vis. asst. prof. psychology U. Calif., Berkeley, 1976; vis. prof. psychology The Johns Hopkins U., 1982-83, Matre de Conference, Coll. de France, 1997-98; cons. Consulting Statisticians, Inc., 1977-83; gov. bd. Cognitive Sci. Soc., 1989-95. Author: Image and Mind, 1980, Ghosts in the Mind's Machine, 1983, Wet Mind: The New Cognitive Neuroscience, 1992, Image and Brain, 1994, Elements of Graph Design, 1994; editor: (with others) Tutorials in Learning and Memory: Essays in Honor of Gordon H. Bower, 1983, Quantitative Analyses of Behavior, Vol. 9: Computational and Clinical Approaches to Pattern Recognition and Concept Formation, 1989, An Invitation to Cognitive Science: Visual Cognition and Action, 1990, Essays in Honor of William K. Estes, 1992, Frontiers in Cognitive Neuroscience, 1992, The Neuropsychology of Mental Imagery, 1996; contbr. articles to profl. jours. Recipient Boyd R. McCandless Young Scientist award divsn. 7 APA, 1978, Initiatives in Rsch. award NAS, 1983, Cattell award for sabbatical leave, 1991, J-L Signoret prize Fondation Ipsen/Am. Acad. Arts and Scis., 1995. Mem. AAAS, APA, Am. Psychol. Soc., Mass. Neuropsychol. Soc., Cognitive Sci. Soc., Psychonomic Soc., Soc. for Neurosci., Am. Acad. Arts and Scis., Soc. Exptl. Psychologists. Avocations: classical music, ice skating, science fiction. Office: Harvard U 33 Kirkland St Cambridge MA 02138-2044

KOSSUTH, SELWYN BARNETT, trade association consultant; b. Johannesburg, Republic of S. Africa, Aug. 16, 1937; arrived in Can., 1980; s. Barnett Reginald and Lyrice Beryl (Israel) K.; m. Philippa Kathleen Holford, July 4, 1964; children: Guy Barnett, Donald Graham, Robert Stephen. B in Commerce cum laude, U. Stellenbosch, South Africa, 1958; MA in Law, Oxford (Eng.) U., 1960. Barrister, Eng. Various mktg. positions, S.Am., regional co-ordinator, London Shell Internat. Petroleum Co., Ltd., 1961-66; personnel and indsl. rels. mgr. Massey-Ferguson, Republic S. Africa, 1967; with distbn., export sales and mktg. staff African Explosives and Chem. Industries, Republic S. Africa, 1968-70; ptnr. Whitehead, Morris and Kossuth, Mgmt. Cons., Republic S. Africa, 1970-72; various mgmt. positions, head non-tech. personnel, sec. to exec. com., mng. dir., Brazil Anglo Am. Corp., 1972-77; dir. adminstrn. Brascan-Brazil, 1977; pres. Hochschild Group, Toronto, Ont., Can., 1978-81; v.p., dir., corp. fin. Nesbitt Thomson Deacon Inc., Toronto, 1981-89; exec. dir. Ont. Securities Commn., Toronto, 1989-91; pres., CEO Investment Funds Inst. Can., 1991—; cons. Bd. Investment Funds Inst. of Can., 1994—; past chmn. Ont. dist. coun. Investment Dealers Assn. Can.; dir. Royal Mutual Funds Can., Glen-Ardith Frazer Corp., Can., Casmyn Corp. Team capt. corp. fund raising Toronto Symphony; fund raiser Salvation Army. Rhodes scholar, 1958. Mem. Vincents Club (Oxford), Nat. Club, Mississauga Golf and Country, Wanderers Golf Club, Trafalgar Golf and Country Club, Blue Mountain Golf Club, Rotary (past pres. Port Credit club). Avocations: golf, curling, skiing. Home: 1200 Walden Circle Unit 58, Missussauga, ON Canada L5J 4J9 Office: 4 King St W Ste 1310, Toronto, ON Canada M5B 1X8

KOST, WAYNE L., business executive; b. Chgo., Feb. 8, 1951; m. Denice Lee Eslinger, Nov. 24, 1979. B.S., Northwestern U., 1973; M.P.A., Syracuse U., 1974. Adminstrv. asst. Chgo. Crime Commn., 1973; staff asso. Va. Mcpl. League, Richmond, 1975-77; dir. inst. affairs Am. Public Works Assn., Chgo., 1977-79; exec. dir. Am. Soc. Quality Control, Milw., 1980-82; sr. v.p. Philip Crosby Assocs., Winter Park, Fla., 1982-85; mng. dir. Crosby Assocs. Internat., Brussels, 1985-87; dir. Can. Region Crosby Assocs. Internat., Winter Park, 1987-89, pres. Ams. div., 1989-95; CEO Internat. Computer Negotiations, Inc., Winter Park, 1995-97; pres. Philip Crosby Assocs. II, Inc., Winter Park, Fla., 1997—; lectr. public adminstrn. Golden Gate U., 1976-78. Bd. dirs. Nat. Council YMCAs, 1970-73, Ill. Commn. on Children, 1969-73; chmn. Gov.'s Com. on Age of Majority, 1972. Gov.'s fellow, 1972. Mem. Am. Soc. Assn. Execs., Nat. Soc. YMCA Youth Govs. Office: PO Box 2687 Winter Park FL 32790-2687

KOSTECKE, B. WILLIAM, utilities executive; b. Caro, Mich., Aug. 1, 1925; s. Steve and Stella (Telewiek) K.; m. Lo Rayne M. Smith, Mar. 25, 1950; children: Diane, Keith. B.S., U.S. Mcht. Marine Acad., 1947, Mich. State U., 1951. Controller Miller Brewing Co., Milw., 1963-66, treas., chief financial officer, 1966-70, pres., 1970-72; v.p., treas., dir. Wis. Gas Co., Milw., 1972-88; v.p., treas., sec., dir. WICOR, Inc., Milw., 1980-88. Gen. chmn. Milw. Nat. Alliance Businessmen, 1972. Recipient Dean Mellencamp award U. Wis., Milw., 1967, Outstanding Profl. Achievement award Kings Point Alumni Assn., 1972. Mem. Financial Execs. Inst. Clubs: Blue Mound Golf and Country. Home: 10708 N Fairway Cir Thiensville WI 53092-5106

KOSTELANETZ, BORIS, lawyer; b. St. Petersburg, Russia, June 16, 1911; came to U.S., 1920, naturalized, 1925; s. Nachman and Rosalia (Dimschetz) K.; m. Ethel Cory, Dec. 18, 1938; children: Richard Cory, Lucy Cory. B.C.S., N.Y. U., 1933, B.S., 1936; J.D. magna cum laude, St. John's U., 1936, LL.D. (hon.), 1981. Bar: N.Y. 1936; CPA, N.Y. With Price, Waterhouse & Co., C.P.A.'s, N.Y.C., 1934-37; asst. U.S. atty. So. Dist. N.Y.; also confidential asst. to U.S. atty, 1937-43; spl. asst. to atty. gen. U.S., 1943-46; chief war frauds sect. Dept. Justice, 1945-46; spl. counsel com. investigate crime in interstate commerce U.S. Senate, 1950-51; ptnr. Kostelanetz Ritholz Tigue & Fink, N.Y.C., 1946-89, of counsel, 1990-94; of counsel Kostelanetz & Fink, N.Y.C., 1994—; instr. acctg. N.Y. U., 1937-47, adj. prof. taxation, 1947-69; Mem. com. on character and fitness Appellate div. Supreme Ct. N.Y., 1st dept., 1974—, chmn., 1985—. Author: (with L. Bender) Criminal Aspects of Tax Fraud Cases, 1957, 2d edit., 1968, 3d edit., 1980; Contbr. articles to legal, accounting and tax jours. Chmn. Kefauver for Pres. Com. N.Y. State, 1952. Recipient Meritorious Svc. award NYU, 1954, John T. Madden Meml. award, 1969, Pietas medal St. John's U., 1961, medal of honor, 1983, James Madison award, 1988, Torch of Learning award Am. Friends of Hebrew U. Law Sch., 1979, N.Y.U. Presdl. citation, 1990, N.Y. State Bar Assn. Fifty-Yr. Lawyer award, 1990. Fellow Am. Coll. Trial Lawyers, Am. Coll. Tax Counsel, Am. Bar Found.; mem. ABA (coun. sect. taxation 1978-81, ho. of dels. 1984-89), Fed. Bar Assn., Internat. Bar Assn., Soc. King's Inn, Ireland (hon. bencher 1995), N.Y. State Bar Assn., N.Y. State CPAs, N.Y. County Lawyers Assn. (v.p. 1966-69, pres. 1969-71, bd. dirs. 1958-64, 66-69, 71-74, chmn. judiciary com. 1965-69), Assn. of Bar of City of N.Y., NYU Sch. Commerce Alumni Assn. (pres. 1951-52), NYU Alumni Fedn. (pres. 1989-92), St. John's U. Law Sch. Alumni Assn. (pres. 1955-57), India House. Home: 37 Washington Sq W New York NY 10011-9181 Office: Kostelanetz & Fink 230 Park Ave New York NY 10169*

KOSTELANETZ, RICHARD, writer, media and visual artist; b. N.Y., May 14, 1940; s. Boris and Ethel (Cory) K. AB with honors, Brown U., 1962; postgrad. (Fulbright scholar), King's Coll., U. London, 1964-65; MA, Columbia U., 1966. Program assoc. thematic studies John Jay Coll. CUNY, 1972-73; sr. staff Inl. U. Writers' Conf., 1976; vis. prof. English and Am. studies U. Tex. at Austin, 1977; guest Mishkenot Sha'ananim, Jerusalem, 1979, 86, DAAD Berliner Kunstlerprogramm, 1981-83. Co-propr. Assembling Press, 1970-82; lit. dir. The Future Press, 1976—; propr. Words and Music (ASCAP), 1982—; Archae Editions, 1978— guest artist WXXI-FM, Rochester, 1975, 76, Synapse, Syracuse U., 1975, Cabin Creek Ctr. for Work and Environ. Studies, 1978, Electronic Music Studio of Stockholm, 1981, 83, 84, 86, 88, Bklyn. Coll. Ctr. for Computer Music, 1984, Dennis Gabor Lab. Mus. of Holography, 1985, 89, Exptl. TV Lab., Owego, N.Y., 1985, 86, 87, 89, 90, 91, Real Art Ways, 1988, Film/Video Arts, 1989. Author: Music of Today, 1967, The Theatre of Mixed Means, 1968, 81, Master Minds: Portraits of Contemporary American Artists & Intellectuals, 1969, Visual Language, 1970, In the Beginning, 1971, The End of Intelligent Writing, 1974; 2d edit. as Literary Politics in Am, 1977; I Articulations/Short Fictions, 1974, Recyclings, vol. 1, 1974, complete text, 1984, Openings & Closings, 1975, Extrapolate, 1975, Come Here, 1975, Modulations, 1975, Portraits from Memory, 1975, Constructs, 1976, Rain Rains Rain, 1976, Numbers: Poems and Stories, 1976, Numbers Two, 1977, Illuminations, 1977, One Night Stood, 1977, Grants & the Future of Literature, 1978, Constructs Two, 1978, Tabula Rasa, 1978, Inexistences, 1978, Wordsand, 1978, Twenties in the Sixties, 1979, "The End" Appendix, 1979, "The End" Essentials, 1979, And So Forth, 1979, Exhaustive Parallel Intervals, 1979, More Short Fiction, 1980, Metamorphosis in Arts, 1980, The Old Poetries and the New, 1981, Autobiographies, 1981, Reincarnations, 1982, Turfs/Arenas/Fields/Pitches, 1983, American Imaginations, 1983, Epiphanies, 1983, Autobiographien New York Berlin, 1986, Prose Pieces/After Texts, 1987, The Old Fictions and the New, 1987, The Grants-Fix, 1987, Conversing with Cage, 1988, On Innovative Music(ian)s, 1989, Unfinished Business, 1990, The New Poetries and Some Olds, 1991, Politics in the African-American Novel, 1991, Constructs Three, 1991, Constructs Four, 1991, Constructs Five, 1991, Constructs Six, 1991, Fifty Untitled Constructivist Fictions, 1991, Intermix, 1991, Flipping, 1991, Published Encomia, 1991, Solos, Duets, Trios & Choruses, 1991, On Innovative Art(ist)s, 1992, A Dictionary of the Avant-Gardes, 1993, 2d edit., 1999, Wordworks: Poems New & Selected, 1993, On Innovative Performance(s), 1994, One Million Words of Booknotes 1958-1993, 1996, Minimal Fictions, 1994, Crimes of Culture, 1995, Fillmore East: Recollections of Rock Theater Twenty-Five Years After, 1995, Radio Writings, 1996, Openings, 1997, Thirty Years of Critical Engagements with John Cage, 1997. An ABC of Contemporary Reading, 1995, John Cage (Ex)plain(ed), 1996, 3-Element Stories, 1998, Vocal Shorts: Collected Performance Texts, 1998, Which Witch?, 1999, Political Essays, 1999; numerous others, works included various anthologies.; editor, contbr.: On Contemporary Literature, 1964, 69, The New American Arts, 1965, Twelve from the Sixties, 1967, The Young American Writers, 1967, Beyond Left & Right: Radical Thought for Our Times, 1968, Imaged Words & Worded Images, 1970, Moholy-Nagy, 1970, 91, John Cage, 1970, 91, Possibilities of Poetry, 1970, Social Speculations, 1971, Human Alternatives: Visions for Us Now, 1971, Future's Fictions, 1971, Seeing Through Shuck, 1972, Breakthrough Fictioneers, 1973, The Edge of Adaptation, 1973, Essaying Essays, 1975, Language & Structure, 1975, Younger Critics in North America, 1976, Esthetics Contemporary, 1977, 88, Assembling Assembling, 1978, Visual Literature Criticism, 1979, Text-Sound Texts, 1980, Scenarios, 1980, The Yale Gertrude Stein, 1980, A Critical Assembling, 1980, Aural Literature Criticism, 1981, American Writing Today, 1981, The Avant-Garde Tradition in Literature, 1982, Gertrude Stein Advanced, 1990, Merce Cunningham, 1992, 98, John Cage: Writer, 1993, Writings About John Cage, 1993, Nicolas Slonimsky: The First 100 Years, 1994, A Portable Baker's Biographical Dictionary of Musicians, 1995, Another E.E. Cummings, 1998, Writing on Glass, 1997, Classic Essays on 20th Century Music, 1996, A B. B. King Companion, 1997; A Frank Zappa Companion, 1997, others; composer: Praying to the Lord, 1977, 81, Invocations, 1981, 84, The Gospels/Die Evangelien, 1982, The Eight Nights of Hanukah, 1983, New York City, internat. version, 1984, Am. version, 1987, A Special Time, 1985, Baseball: Americas' Game, 1988, 2nd edit., 1998, Onomatopoeia, 1988, Kaddish, 1990, Acoustic Fiction I: Ululation, 1992, No, I'm Not Richard Kostelanetz, 1993; producer numerous audiotapes, films, videotapes, extended radio features for stas. in Australia, Fed. Republic Germany, Sweden, U.S.; filmmaker: (with others) Openings & Closings, 1978, Constructivist Fictions, 1978, Epiphanies, 1981-94, Ein Verlorenes Berlin/A Berlin Lost/Berlin Perdu/Ett Forlorat Berlin/El Berlin Perdido/Berlin Scheinena Jother, 1984-88 (prizewinner Ann Arbor, Mich., Film Festival); video art: Three Prose Pieces, 1975, Kinetic Writings, 1989, Video Strings, 1989, Stringsieben, 1989, Turfs/Grounds/Lawns, 1989, Invocations, 1988, Seductions, 1988, The Gospels Abridged, 1988, Relationships, 1988, Two Erotic Videotapes, 1988, Two Sacred Texts, 1988, Partitions, 1986, Onomatopoeia, 1989, Kaddish, 1991, Video Poems, 1994, Video Stories, 1994, Openings & Closings, 1975, Partitions, 1986, Video Writing, 1987, Declaration of Independence, 1979, Epiphanies, 1980, Home Movies Reconsidered, 1992; contbg. editor: Pushcart Prize; writer, narrator: Camera Three, WCBS-TV, 1974; co-founder, compiler Assembling, 1970-82; co-pub., editor: Precisely, A Critical Jour., 1977—; contbr. articles, poems, revs., photographs and essays to mags.; numerous group exhbns. visual poetry, visual fiction, audiotapes, videotapes, films, holograms and numerical art; comprehensive exhbn.: Wordsand, at Simon Fraser U., U. Alta., Cornell Coll., Vassar Coll., U. N.D., Calif. State U., Bakersfield, Dade County C.C., Miami, Fla., 1978-81; retrospectives of video art: Anthology Film Archives, 1994, Bumbershoot, Seattle, 1991, Festival de la Baite, Geneva, 1989, U. of S.C., 1978. Woodrow Wilson fellow, 1962-63, Pulitzer fellow in critical writing, 1965-66, fellow Guggenheim Meml. Found., 1967-68, Fund for Investigative Journalism, 1980, Vogelstein Found., 1980, Internat. fellow Columbia U., 1963-64, Editors fellow CCLM, 1983; Visual Arts grantee Nat. Endowment of Arts, 1976, 78, 79, 85, 86, 90, Media Arts grantee Nat. Endowment of Arts, 1981, 82, 84, 91; N.Y. State Regents scholar, 1963-64, Am. Pub. Radio Program Fund, 1984; recipient Standard award ASCAP, 1983-92, 94— (annually). Mem. Nat. Coalition Ind. Scholars, Internat. Assn. Art Critics, Soc. for Origination of Horspiel in Am., Phi Beta Kappa. Address: PO Box 444 Prince St New York NY 10012-0008 *To do what has not been done in several domains and in the course of that adventure to discover new possibilities in art, in writing, and in myself.*

KOSTELNIK, MICHAEL C., career officer. BS in Mech. Engring., Tex. A&M U., 1969; MS in Indsl. and Mgmt. Engring., U. Iowa, 1970; student pilot tng., Vance AFB, Okla., 1970-71; RF-4C upgrade tng., 18th Tactical Reconnaissance, Shaw AFB, S.C., 1971-72; postgrad., U. Fla., 1981; student, Indsl. Coll. Armed Forces, 1986, Def. Sys. Mgmt. Coll., 1989, U. N.H., 1993, Syracuse U., 1996, Johns Hopkins U., 1996. Commd. 2d lt. USAF, 1969, advanced through grades to maj. gen., 1996; stationed at Royal Air Force, Alconbury, Eng., 1972-75; various pilot assignments, 1975-77; squadron ops. officer, F-4 and F-15 test pilot 3246th Test Wing, Eglin AFB, Fla., 1977-81; stationed at Hdqs. USAF, Washington, 1981-85; dir. combined test forces 6510th Test Wing, Edwards AFB, Calif., 1986-87; comdt. USAF Test Pilot Sch., Edwards AFB, 1987-89; stationed at Wright-Patterson AFB, Ohio, 1989-93; vice comdr. Warner Robins Air Logistics Ctr., Robins AFB, Ga., 1993-94; various positions Pentagon, Washington, 1994-95; dir. plans Hdqs. Air Force Materiel Command, Wright-Patterson AFB, 1995-97, vice comdr., 1997; comdr. Air Force Devel. Test Ctr., Air Force Materiel Command, Eglin AFB, 1997-98, Air Armament Ctr., Air Force Material Command, Eglin AFB, 1998—. Decorated D.S.M., Legion of Merit. Office: AAC/CC 101 W D Ave Ste 117 Eglin AFB FL 32542-5495

KOSTELNY, ALBERT JOSEPH, JR., lawyer; b. Phila., July 11, 1951; s. Albert Joseph and Margaret (Naile) K. BA, U. Pa., 1973, MA, 1974; JD, Fordham U., 1979. Bar: N.Y. 1980, U.S. Dist. Ct. (so. dist.) N.Y. 1983, U.S. Ct. Claims 1983, U.S. Supreme Ct. 1983, U.S. Ct. Internat. Trade 1985, U.S. Ct. Appeals (2d cir.) 1985. Atty. N.Y. State Divsn. Human Rights, N.Y.C., 1980-81, sr. atty., 1981-89, acting chief adminstrv. law judge, 1989-91, adjudication counsel to commr., 1990-98, supr. atty., dir. prosecutions unit, 1998—. Mem. ABA, N.Y. State Bar Assn., N.Y. County Lawyers Assn., Assn. Trial Lawyers Am. Republican. Roman Catholic. Office: NY State Div Human Rights 55 W 125th St New York NY 10027-4516

KOSTER, ELAINE LANDIS, publishing executive; b. N.Y.C.. BA, Barnard Coll., 1962. Pres., pub. Dutton Signet, N.Y.C.; head Elaine Koster Literary Agy. LLC, N.Y.C. Office: Elaine Koster Literary Agy LLC 55 Central Park W Ste 6 New York NY 10023-6003

KOSTER, EMLYN HOWARD, geologist, educator; b. Suez Canal Zone, Egypt, Mar. 18, 1950; arrived in England, 1953, Canada, 1971, came to U.S., 1996; s. Douglas Albert and Dorothy Muriel (Roberts) K.; m. Maryse Remillard, June 22,1974; children: Veronique Justina, Simon Emlyn. BSC with spl. honours in Geology, U. Sheffield, Eng., 1971; PhD in Geology, U. Ottawa, 1977. Rsch. scientist terrain scis. divsn. Geological Survey of Can., Ottawa, 1973-74; cons. Geo-Analysis Ltd., Ottawa, 1975-76; asst. prof. dept. geology Concordia U., Montreal, Can., 1976-77; asst. prof. dept. geological scis. U. Saskatchewan, Saskatoon, Can., 1977-80; rsch. officer, project mgr. Alberta Geological Survey, Alberta Rsch. Coun., Edmonton, Can., 1980-86; dir. Royal Tyrrell Mus. of Palaeontology, Drumheller and Field Sta., Dinosaur Provincial Park, UNESCO World Heritage Site, Alberta, 1986-91; dir. gen. Ontario Sci. Centre, Agy. Govt. Ontario, Toronto, 1991-96; pres., CEO Liberty Sci. Ctr., N.J., 1996—; mem. Can.-China Dinosaur Expedition to Gobi Desert, 1987; vis. prof. U. Buenos Aires, 1988; bd. dirs. Challenger Ctr. Space Sci. Edn., Alexandria, Va., 1993—, Assn. of Sci. Tech. Ctrs., Wash., 1995—, Internat. Space Theater Consortium, San Diego, 1997—; pres. Geog. Assn., 1996-97; spkr. in field. Contbr. papers in sci. jours.; author numerous field guidebooks, book reviews; many interviews in field; internat. speaker at more than 125 sci. confs., assn. events, convs., workshops. Recipient Tracks award Can. Soc. Petroleum Engrs., 1984, Chevalier dans l'Ordre des Palmes Academiques award Govt. of France, 1995. Mem.

Hudson County C. of C. (trustee 1997—); fellow Explorers Club. Avocations: ecology, culture, tourism. Office: Liberty Sci Ctr Liberty State Pk Jersey City NJ 07305-4600*

KOSTERE, KIM MARTIN, psychologist, consultant; b. Detroit, Jan. 22, 1954; d. Walter Thomas and Shirley Marian (Goebel) K. BA, Mercy Coll., 1977; MA, Ctr. Humanistic Studies, Detroit, 1983; PsyS, Ctr. Humanistic Studies, 1986; PhD, Union Inst., Cin., 1989. Therapist Metro T.A.G., Livonia, Mich., 1978-81, Highland Waterford Ctr., Waterford, Mich., 1981-83; psychologist, v.p. substance abuse svcs. Square Lake Counseling Ctr., Bloomfield Hills, Mich., 1983-90; psychologist, co-dir. Counseling Ctr., P. C., Bloomfield Hills, Mich., 1991-99; cons., 1999—; co-founder, dir. Ont. (Can.) NLP Inst., 1979-80. Author: A Brief Account of the Center for Humanistic Studies, 1987; co-author: Get the Results You Want, 1987, Maps, Models and the Structure of Reality, 1989, Utilizing the Metaphor: An Ericksonian/NLP Approach, 1992. Democrat. Roman Catholic.

KOSTIC, PETAR JOVAN, physicist; b. Zemun, Serbia, Nov. 20, 1953; s. Jovan Petar and Mira Branko (Sever) K. BS in Elec. Engring., Physics, U. Belgrade, 1980, MS in Elec. Materials, 1985, PhD, 1988. Rschr., asst. scientist Serbian Acad. Sci., Belgrade, 1981-87; vis. scientist Argonne (Ill.) Nat. Lab., 1987-88; asst. scientist U. Belgrade, 1988-91; vis. scientist, asst. scientist Argonne Nat. Lab., 1991-96; vis. rschr. U. Calif., Santa Cruz, 1997—. Mem. Am. Physics Soc., Materials Rsch. Soc. E-mail: petar@physics.ucsc.edu. Office: U Calif Dept Physics Santa Cruz CA 95064

KOSTKA, ELMER BOHUMIL, secondary school educator; b. Chgo., Nov. 16, 1922; s. Vincent and Anastasia (Flemer) K.; m. Mildred Musil, June 26, 1954. BS, U. Ill., 1949, MS, 1950. Tchr. indsl. edn. Chgo. Bd. Edn., 1950-88; chmn. tech. dept. Steinmetz H.S., Chgo., 1959-68, editor yrbook., 1964-68. Sgt. U.S. Army Air Corps, 1942-45. Mem. Am. Legion. Avocations: collecting books, coins and stamps. Home: 16154 Pine Dr Tinley Park IL 60477-6311

KOSTKA, JANICE ELLEN, company executive; b. Chgo., Aug. 25, 1940; d. Nicholas Jr. and Sylvia Helen (Lissy) Smicklas; m. Roger Denis Kostka, Aug. 15, 1959; children: Joseph Nicholas, Laura Ann. Grad. high sch. Cert. hazardous material employee, 1997. Staff asst. sec. Sears, Roebuck & Co., Chgo., 1958-62; staff sec. IBM, River Forest, Ill., 1962-64; sec., statis. typist Rights Temps, Elmhurst, Ill., 1979-84; sec., tech. typist Secs., Inc., Oak Brook, Ill., 1979-84; realtor, sales assoc. Long Realty, Westmont, Ill., 1981-82, 89-90; owner, office mgr., sec. Kostka Bros., Inc., Chgo., 1964-89; asst. hazardous materials and safety regulations coord. Kostka, Inc., Chgo., 1990—. Author: (manual) Do-It-Yourself Credit Repair, 1993. Bd. dirs. Oak Brook Civic Assn., 1978-79; mem. State of Ill. Gov.'s Small Bus. Environ. Task Force, Springfield, 1994. Mem. Automotive Wholesalers of Ill. (Appreciation award 1995). Avocations: golf, crafts, travel, investments.

KOSTKA, RONALD WAYNE, marketing consultant; b. Chgo., Sept. 13, 1931; s. James V. and Marie (Zvolanek) K.; m. Madonna Lou Miller, June 8, 1957 (div. Dec. 1980); children: Paul, Daniel, Jane; m. Irene Mary Harnett, Sept. 14, 1991. BS in journalism, U. Ill., Urbana, 1957. Reporter Champaign News Gazette, Champaign, Ill., 1956-57; copy editor Mpls. Tribune, Mpls., 1957-58; pub. rels. mgr. 3M Co., St. Paul, Minn., 1958-92; cons. mktg. Pub. Rel., Minnetonka, Minn., 1992—. Contbr. articles to profl. jours. Firearms safety instr. State of Minn., Minnetonka, 1967-77; docent Planes of Fame Air Museum, Eden Prairie, Minn., 1994—. Staff Sgt. USAF, 1951-55, Korea. Decorated Air medal (4 OLC), Purple Heart, Hwarang (Republic of Korea). Mem. DAV, Nat. Muzzle Loading Rifle Assn., NRA, Soc. of Profl. Jours. (cert 1957), Nat. Wildlife Fed., Minnetonka Game & Fish Club. Avocations: canoeing, hunting, competitive skeet shooting. Home: 1004 Sunset Dr S Minnetonka MN 55305-1164

KOSTOFF, RONALD NEIL, aerospace scientist; b. Phila., Apr. 26, 1938; s. David and fannie (Weisbrod) K. BSME, Drexel U., 1961; MA, Princeton U., 1963, PhD, 1967. Mem. tech. staff Bell Labs, Murray Hill, N.J., 1966-75; divsn. head Dept. Energy, Washington, 1975-83; dir. tech. assessment Office of Naval Rsch., Arlington, Va., 1983—. Editor Rsch. evaluation, 1994, Scientometrics, 1996, Jour. Tech. Transfer, 1997; editl. bd. Scientometrics, 1995—, Jour. Tech. Transfer, 1996—; reviewer R&D Mgmt., 1993—, IEEE Trans. on Engring. Mgmt., 1996—; contbr. articles to profl. jours. Achievements include patent on database tomography; pioneered aerobraking subfield of orbit to orbit transfer; invented Wake Shield for high vacuum in low orbit. Home: 3713 S George Mason Dr Apt 602W Falls Church VA 22041-3732 Office: Office of Naval Rsch 800 N Quincy St Arlington VA 22217-0002

KOSTOULAS, IOANNIS GEORGIOU, physicist; b. Petra, Pierias, Greece, Sept. 12, 1936; came to the U.S., 1965, naturalized, 1984; s. Georgios Ioannou and Panagiota (Zarogiannis) K.; m. Katina Sioras Kay, June 23, 1979; 1 child, Alexandra. Diploma in physics, U. Thessoloniki, Greece, 1963; MA, U. Rochester, 1969, PhD, 1972; MS, U. Ala., 1977. Instr. U. Thessaloniki, 1963-65; tchg. asst. U. Ala., 1966-67, U. Rochester, 1967-68; guest jr. rsch. assoc. Brookhaven Nat. Lab., Upton, N.Y., 1968-72; rsch. physicist, lectr. UCLA, U. Calif.-San Diego, 1972-76; sr. rsch. assoc. Mich. State U., East Lansing, 1976-78, Fermi Nat. Accelerator Lab., Batavia, iLL., 1976-78; rsch. staff mem. MIT, Cambridge, 1978-80; sr. sys. engr., physicist Hughes Aircraft Co., El Segundo, Calif., 1980-86; sr. physicist electro-optics and space sensors Rockwell Internat. Corp., Downey, Calif., 1986-96, Boeing Corp., Downey, 1996-98; scientist Raytheon Sys. Co., El Segundo, Calif., 1998—. Contbr. articles to profl. jours. With Greek Army, 1961-63. Rsch. grantee U. Rochester, 1968-72. Mem. Am. Phys. Soc., Los Alamos Sci. Lab. Exptl. Users Group, Fermi Nat. Accelerator Lab. Users Group, High Energy Discussion Group Brookhaven Nat. Lab., Pan Macedonian Assn., Save Cyprus Coun. L.A., Sigma Pi Sigma, Hellenic U. Club, Ahepa Lodge. Home: 2404 Marshallfield Ln # B Redondo Beach CA 90278-4406 Office: Raytheon Sys Co Mail Code EO/E1/A117 2000 E El Segundo Blvd El Segundo CA 90245-4501

KOSTRUBALA, MARK ANTHONY, writer; b. Chgo., Aug. 13, 1968; s. Bart John and Berniece (Keteris) K. BA in English, U. Iowa, 1990. Front desk mgr. Oaklawn (Ill.) Park Dist., 1991-92; night auditor Hyatt Hotels, Oakbrook, Ill., 1991—. Author: (novel) Dark Legacy, 1996. Avocations: historical researcher, treasure hunting, scuba diving, running. Home: 10227 S Kostner Ave Oak Lawn IL 60453-4210 Office: Hyatt Hotels 2815 Jorie Blvd Oak Brook IL 60523-2161

KOSTRZEWA, RICHARD MICHAEL, pharmacology educator; b. Trenton, N.J., July 22, 1943; s. John Walter and Wladyslosa (Wnuk) K.; m. Florence Agnes Palmer, Sept. 4, 1965; children: Theresa, Richard, Joseph, Maria, Krystyna, Thomas, John Palmer, Francis, Roseanna, Monica. BS, Phila. Coll. Pharmacy and Sci., 1965, MS, 1967; PhD, U. Pa., 1971. Rsch. pharmacologist VA Hosp., New Orleans, 1971-75; asst. prof. pharmacology Tulane Med. Ctr., New Orleans, 1972-76; asst. prof. physiology La. State U. Med. Ctr., New Orleans, 1975-78; assoc. prof., then prof. pharmacology East Tenn. State U. Med. Sch., Johnson City, 1978—; vis. prof. Silesian Acad. Medicine, Katowice, Poland, 1997—. Author: Pharmacology, 1995, Highly Selective Neurotoxins, 1998; editor-in-chief Neurotoxicity Resh.; mem. editl. adv. bd. Peptides, 1980—, Nutritional Neurosci., 1997—, Amino Acids, 1998—; contbr. articles to profl. pubs. Recipient Rsch. award East Tenn. state U. Found., 1981. Fellow Japan Soc. Promotion of Sci., 1996; mem. Am. Soc. Pharmacology, Soc. Neurosci., Internat. Brain Rsch. Orgn. Roman Catholic. Achievements include NIMH project on tardive dyskinesia, Scottish Rite project on schizophrenia. Office: East Tenn State Univ PO Box 70577 Johnson City TN 37614-0577

KOSTYO, JACK LAWRENCE, physiology educator; b. Elyria, Ohio, Oct. 1, 1931; s. Louis and Matilda (Thomasko) K.; m. Shirlianne Guth, June 10, 1953; children: Cecile A., Louis C. AB, Oberlin Coll., 1953; PhD, Cornell U., 1957; MD (hon.), U. Göteborg, 1978. NRC fellow Harvard Med. Sch., Boston, 1957-59; asst. prof., then prof. physiology Duke U., 1959-68; prof., chmn. dept. physiology Emory U., Atlanta, 1968-79; prof. physiology U. Mich. Med. Sch., Ann Arbor, 1979-94, chmn. dept. physiology, 1979-85, active prof. emeritus in internal medicine, 1995—, chmn. dept., 1979-85; assoc. dir. Mich. Diabetes Rsch. and Tng. Ctr., Ann Arbor, 1986-97, dir. grants program, 1997—; mem. endocrinology study sect. NIH/USPHS, 1967-71, internat. and coop. projects study sect., 1992-96; mem. physiology test com. Nat. Bd. Med. Examiners, 1974-77, mem. comprehensive part II com., 1986-91, U.S. Med. Licensure Examination Step 2 Com., 1990-91. Editor in chief Endocrinology, 1978-82; sect. editor Ann. Rev. Physiology, 1982-86; mem. editorial bd. Growth Regulation, 1990—; contbr. articles to profl. jours. Mem. adv. bd. Searle Scholars. Recipient Lederle Med. Faculty award, 1961, Ernst Oppenheimer Meml. award Endocrine Soc., 1969. Mem. Endocrine Soc. (editl. bd., coun., chmn. awards com.), Am. Physiol. Soc. (editl. bd., coun., chmn. standing com. on edn., mem. coun. of endocrinology and metabolism sect., chmn. endocrinology and metabolism sect. 1990-91, rep. to Coun. Acad. Socs. of Assn. Am. Med. Colls., mem. AAAS sect. on med. scis., editor Handbook of Physiology sect. 7, Endocrinology, vol. 5), Soc. for Exptl. Biology and Medicine (editl. bd.), Internat. Union Physiol. Scis. (commn. on med. edn.), Assn. Chmn. Depts. Physiology (pres. 1979, coun.), Am. Diabetes Assn., Coun. Acad. Socs. (adminstrv. bd. 1983-86), Sigma Xi. Home: 1100 Hwy 98 E Unit B304 Destin FL 32541-3307 Office: Mich Diabetes Rsch-Tng Ctr U Mich Med Sch 1331 E Ann St Rm 0580 Ann Arbor MI 48109

KOSTYO, JOHN FRANCIS, lawyer; b. Findlay, Ohio, Feb. 9, 1955; s. Albert Robert and Mary Agnes (Welsh) K.; m. Shirley Ann Allgyre, June 9, 1984. BA in Polit. Sci. and Philosophy magna cum laude, John Carroll U., 1978; JD, Case Western Res. U., 1981. Bar: Ohio 1981, U.S. Dist. Ct. (no. dist.) Ohio 1982, U.S. Dist. Ct. (ea. dist.) Mich. 1991, U.S. Supreme Ct. 1991, U.S. Dist. Ct. (so. dist.) Mich. 1992, U.S. Dist. Ct. (we. dist.) Mich. 1992. Assoc. Weasel & Brimley, Findlay, 1981-89; ptnr. Brimley, Kostyo & Elliott, L.P.A., Findlay, 1989-91, Brimley & Kostyo Co., L.P.A., Findlay, 1991, Brimley, Kostyo & Lather Co., L.P.A., 1991-93, Brimley & Kostyo Co. L.P.A., 1993—; v.p. Mid-Am. Title Agy., Inc., Findlay, Ohio, 1989—; lectr. contracts and negotiable instruments U. Findlay, 1981-84, sr. lectr. 1984-96. Mem. ABA (corp. banking and bus. law, litigation div.), Ohio Bar Assn., Toledo Bar Assn., Findlay/Hancock County Bar Assn., Alpha Sigma Nu. Roman Catholic. Clubs: Rockwell Springs Trout. Lodge: Elks, K.C. (4th degree). Avocations: sports, comml. trans., books, theater. Home: 462 Penbrooke Dr Findlay OH 45840-7472 Office: Brimley & Kostyo Co LPA 320 S Main St Findlay OH 45840-3353 also: MidAm Title Agy Inc 100 E Main Cross St Findlay OH 45840-4861

KOSTYRA, RICHARD JOSEPH, advertising executive; b. Winnipeg, Man., Can., Nov. 4, 1940; came to U.S., 1980; s. Joseph and Ann K.; m. Juleinne E. Lynden, Aug. 4, 1961 (div.); 1 son, Corwin Gregory; m. 2d Lorraine T. Antoniello, Sept. 19, 1981. With J. Walter Thompson, Toronto, Ont., Can., 1959-63, media dir., 1966-73, sr. v.p., dir. diversification, 1973-76; sr. v.p., gen. mgr. J. Walter Thompson, Montreal, Que., Can., 1976-80; exec. v.p., media dir. J. Walter Thompson, N.Y.C., 1980-92; exec. v.p., U.S. dir. Media Services, 1987; pres. and founder Media First Internat., Inc., N.Y.C., 1993—; bd. dirs. J. Walter Thompson Can., 1965-76. Office: Media First Internat Inc 205 Lexington Ave New York NY 10016-6022

KOSUB, JAMES ALBERT, lawyer; b. San Antonio, Jan. 8, 1948; s. Ernest Pete and Lonie (Doege) K.; divorced; 1 child, James Jr.; m. Jane Stevens Cain, Aug. 11, 1979; children: Kathryn, Nicholas (dec.). Student, East Carolina U., 1970, San Antonio Coll., 1971-72; BS, SW Tex. State U., 1974; JD, St. Mary's U., San Antonio, 1977. Bar: Tex. 1978, U.S. Dist. Ct. (we. dist.) Tex. 1980, U.S. Ct. Appeals (5th cir.) 1981, U.S. Dist. Ct. (so. dist.) 1986, U.S. Supreme Ct. 1988, U.S. Dist. Ct. (no. and ea. dists.) Tex. 1990. Ptnr. Kosub & Langlois, San Antonio, 1978-79, Kosub, Langlois & Van Cleave, San Antonio, 1979-83; mng. ptnr. Kosub & Langlois, San Antonio, 1983-86; sr. ptnr. James A. Kosub, San Antonio, 1986-94; pvt. practice Eldorado, Tex., 1994—. Bd. dirs. Judson Ind. Sch. Bd. Trustees, Converse, Tex., 1975-81, Bexar County Fedn. Sch. Bds., San Antonio, 1977-80. Sgt. USMC, 1966-70. Fellow Tex. Bar Found., San Antonio Bar Found.; mem. ABA (EEOC liaison com. San Antonio chpt. 1987-93), San Antonio Bar Assn. (bd. dirs. 1990-92, sec. 1992-93), Fed. Bar Assn. 5th Cir. Bar Assn., Coll. of State Bar of Tex., State Bar of Tex. (coun. labor and employment sect. 1993—, sec. 1997-98, vice chair 1998-99). Episcopalian. Avocations: carpentry, gardening, golf. Office: 105 S Main Eldorado TX 76936-0460

KOSZARSKI, RICHARD, film historian, writer; b. N.Y.C., Dec. 18, 1947; s. Casimir and Janina (Orzechowski) K.; m. Diane Kaiser, 1975; 1 child, Eva. BA, Hofstra U., 1969; MA, NYU, 1974, PhD, 1977. Lectr. Sch. Visual Arts, N.Y.C., 1974-84, NYU, 1976, 97, Columbia U., N.Y.C., 1980-86; historian Astoria Motion Picture & TV Found., N.Y.C., 1977-81; curator of film Am. Mus. Moving Image, N.Y.C., 1981-92, exhbn. curator Masterpieces of Moving Image Tech., 1988, head collections and exhbns., 1992-96, sr. historian, 1996-97; asst. prof. English Rutgers U., 1998—. Author: (books) Hollywood Directors 1914-40, 1976, The Rivals of D.W. Griffith, 1976, Hollywood Directors 1941-76, 1977, Universal Pictures: 65 Years, 1977, The Man You Loved to Hate, 1983, The Astoria Studio and Its Fabulous Films, 1983, An Evening's Entertainment: The Age of the Silent Feature Picture, 1915-1928, 1990; (documentary films) Roger Corman, Hollywood's Wild Angel, 1978, The Man You Loved to Hate, 1979; editor-in-chief Film History, An Internat. Jour., N.Y.C., 1986—. Rsch. associateship Am. Film Inst., 1971, 72; rsch. grantee Am. Coun. Learned Socs., 1978; recipient Nat. Film Book award Nat. Film Soc., 1984, award Prix Jean Mitry, 1991. Mem. Polish Inst. Arts and Scis., Antique Wireless Assn., Domitor, Assn. Moving Image Archivists.

KOT, MARTA VIOLETTE, artist, art educator; b. Hartford, Conn., Nov. 27, 1963; d. Edward Anthony and Maria (Czermak) Kot. Fulbright student, Royal U. of Malta, 1985; BA in Graphic Design/Art, Ctrl Conn. State U., 1985; pvt. art studies Studio Antoine Camilleri, Valletta, Malta, 1985; pvt. art studies, Studio Adam Wsiolkowski, Cracow, Poland, 1988; studied with Zbylut Grzywacz, Cracow, 1988; MS in Adminstrn., Supervision and Curriculum Devel., Ctrl Conn. State U., 1988; cert. in Polish Art History, Jagiellonian U., Cracow, Poland, 1988; MA in Studio Art and Environ. Art, NYU, 1990; student, Acad. de la Grande Chaumiere, Paris, 1990-93; cert. French lang. and Civilization, U. Paris, Sorbonne, 1992; cert. Polish lang., Cath. U. of Lublin, Poland, 1993; EdM in Art and Art Edn., Tchrs. Coll., Columbia U., 1997; postgrad. in Polish lang., Warsaw U., 1997; postgrad., Columbia U. Cert. art educator, N.Y. Art educator summer art program Consolidated Sch. Dist. City of New Britain, 1977; art cons. gifted and talented programs Consol. Sch. Dist. of City of New Britain, Conn., 1987-88; art educator summer art program Consolidated Sch. Dist. City of New Britain, 1997; art tchr. Harlem Sch. of Arts, N.Y.C., 1997—; art educator LaGuardia H.S. of Music and Art and Performing Arts, N.Y.C., 1996-97; art tchr. parent/toddler program Henry Street Settlement/Arbor Arts Ctr., N.Y.C., 1997; collaborator with artist Charles Searles Harlem Sch. of the Arts, N.Y.C., 1996, art cons., educator Totem Spirits project, 1996; prin., chair dept. music and art Internat. Am. Sch., Warsaw, 1997-98; supr. tchr. coll. dept. art and humanities Columbia U., 1998—; invited artist lectr. New Britain Mus. Am. Art, Conn., 1996, Nat. Mus. of Fine Arts, Malta and Macy Gallery, Tchr. Coll. Columbia U., 1997, Macy Gallery, Tchrs. Coll. Columbia U., 1996, Marymount Manhattan Coll., N.Y.C., 1998, 99; curator CCSU Elihu Brritt, 1997, Macy Gallery, N.Y.C., 1997; Annenberg art cons. PS153, N.Y.C., 1998—; art specialist project arts PS129, N.Y.C., 1999; art educator Silvermine Art Sch., New Caanan, Conn., 1999. One-woman shows include 80 Washington Sq. East Galleries, N.Y.C., 1990, Conn. Ho. of Reps., Hartford, 1995, City Hall, New Britain, Conn., 1996, Macy Gallery, N.Y.C., 1996, Cen. Conn. State U. Elihu Burritt Libr., 1996, New Britain Pub. Libr., 1997, Nat. Mus. Fine Arts, Malta, 1997, Harlem Sch. of the Arts, N.Y.C., 1997, City of N.Y. Divsn. of Legal Affairs, 1997, Tchrs. Coll., Columbia U., 1997, New Britain City Hall, 1997, CCSU Elihu Burritt Libr. Spl. Collections Gallery, Conn., 1998, Lab. Gallery, Ctr. Contemporary Art, Warsaw, 1999; exhibited in group shows at Slocumb Gallery, Tenn., 1985, Ctrl. Conn. State U., New Britain, 1982, 84-88, Macy Art Gallery, N.Y.C., 1994-97, Presdl. Inauguration, Tchrs. Coll., Columbia U., 1994, Nat. Arts Club, N.Y.C., 1995, Pumphouse Gallery, Hartford, 1995, Student Lounge Tchrs. Coll., Columbia U., 1996, Bklyn. Brewery, John Jay Gallery, N.Y.C., 1996, MMC Gallery, N.Y.C., 1997, Hudson River Barge Mus., Red Hook, N.Y., 1997, others. Corp. mem. Boys and Girls Club, New Britain; bd. dirs. Camp Schade Program Affiliated United Way, New Britain. Recipient award for graphic design Advt. Club Greater Hartford, 1984, mural project (with Dave Burke) Incarnation Ctr. for Children with AIDS Tamarand Found., N.Y.C., 1995. Mem. ASCD, AAUW, Coll. Art Assn., Nat. Art Edn. Assn., Bklyn. Waterfront Artists Coalition, Kappa Delta Pi. Home: PO Box 2697 New Britain CT 06050-2697

KOTAK, MARNI, marketing administrator, visual artist; b. Norwood, Mass., Nov. 20, 1974; d. Edwin Adolph and Lydia Jeanette (LaPointe) K. BA in Linguistics/Art, Bard Coll., 1996. Mktg. asst. Manhattan Studios, N.Y.C., 1997-87; mktg. mgr. Virtual Growth Inc., N.Y.C., 1998—. Exhibited art works at W.A.F.E. Festival, 1998, Holland Tunnel Centennial Exhbn., 1998, Stephan Gang Gallery, 1998; curator/artist art exhbn. Operation Greenhouse Prairie Exhbn., 1998. Dir. art programs Ind. Friends of McCarren Park, Bklyn., 1997—; curator Operation Grenhouse Inc., Bklyn., 1998; devel. asst. Woven Spaces Inc., Bklyn., 1998. Nat. Security edn. Program scholar, India, 1994. Mem. N.Y. New Media Assn., World Wide Web Artists Consortium. Avocations: listening to music, taking walks in the park, cooking. Home: 352 Bedford Ave Brooklyn NY 11211 Office: Virtual Growth Inc 118 W 22d St New York NY 10011

KOTAS, ROBERT VINCENT, research physician, educator; b. Buffalo, Nov. 26, 1938; s. Vincent John and Regina Agnes (Hadynka) K.; m. Ilona Rae Fielding, Mar. 2, 1968; children: Nicole, Timothy, Robert, Rebecca. B.S., Canisius Coll., 1959; M.D., U. Buffalo, 1963. Diplomate: Am. Acad. Pediatrics. Research assoc. McGill U., 1969-70; intern Buffalo Children's Hosp., 1963-64; resident in pediatrics Johns Hopkins Hosp., Balt., 1964-66; asst. prof. pediatrics U. Okla. Med. Sch., 1970-72, dir. newborn services, 1970-72; dir., div. devel. physiology; career investigator W.K. Warren Med. Research Center, Tulsa, 1972-76; sci. dir. W.K. Warren Med. Research Center, 1976-80; dir. William and Natalie Warren Med. Inst., Tulsa, 1980-83; chief pediatrician Ella Austin Health Ctr., San Antonio, 1989-95, med. dir., 1993-95; lab. dir., 1993-95; pediatrician UTHSC-SA Primary Care Cmty. Pediat., San Antonio, 1995-98, Minor Emergency Ctr., San Antonio, 1998—; assoc. Fernando A. Guerra, MD, San Antonio, 1998—; mem. staffs Santa Rosa Hosp., San Antonio, St. Rose Hosp., San Antonio, Bapt. Health System, Meth. Healthcare System; clin. prof. pediat. U. Okla. Med. Sch., Tulsa, 1977—; assoc. prof. pediat. U. Tex. Health Sci. Ctr., San Antonio, 1983-98, dir. rsch. devel., 1993-94, also med. dir.; guest scientist Nat. Inst. Child Health and Human Devel., Bethesda, Md., 1975-77, also cons.; cons. Am. Lung Assn., others; cons. pediatrician San Antonio Ind. Sch. Dist. Contbr. articles to profl. jours. and books. Served as capt. USAF, 1966-68. Recipient continuing edn. awards AMA; Best M.D. Written Book award Am. Med. Writers Assn., 1980; Mosby scholar, 1963; grantee NIH, 1969-70, 75-79, 84-88; grantee USPHS, 1968-69, 91-95; others. Fellow Am. Coll. Obstetricians and Gynecologists (assoc.); mem. Johns Hopkins Med. and Surg. Assn., So. Soc. Pediatric Rsch., Soc. Pediatric Rsch., Am. Physiol. Soc., Soc. Gynecol. Investigation. Office: Fernando A Guerra MD 401 W Commerce St # 500 San Antonio TX 78207-3165 *Grateful for the excitement of impending discovery which characterizes my work with its promise of surprise in the midst of daily routine, I am indebted for the guidance and inspiration that my present and past associates have given me to deal effectively with the diversity and perversity of experience.*

KOTCHER, RAYMOND LOWELL, public relations executive; b. N.Y.C., Nov. 19, 1951; s. Richmond and Elaine (Germain) K.; m. Betsy Kasper, Sept. 10, 1978; children: Maris, Gregory. BS, SUNY, Geneseo, 1973; MS in Comm., Boston U., 1983. Account exec. Burson Marsteller, N.Y.C., 1978-79; v.p., mgmt. supr. J. Walter Thompson Co., N.Y.C., 1979-82; v.p. Ketchum Pub. Rels., N.Y.C., 1982-84; exec. v.p. G.S. Schwartz & Co., N.Y.C., 1984-85; exec. v.p., chief U.S. ops. pres. pub. rels. divsn. Ketchum Comm., N.Y.C., 1986—, also bd. dirs.; pres., CEO Ketchum PR, N.Y.C., 1990—; pres., sr. ptnr. Ketchum PR Worldwide, N.Y.C. Mem. exec. com. Boston U. Coll. Comm., 1988—. Mem. Pub. Rels. Soc. Am., Princeton Club, Board Room Club, Old Westbury Country Club. Avocations: tennis, sailing, golf. Office: Ketchum Pub Rels 292 Madison Ave New York NY 10024*

KOTCHIAN, SARAH, municipal government official. MEd, Harvard U., 1977; MPH, U. Wash., 1985. Dir. dept. environ. health City of Albuquerque, 1982—. Office: City of Albany Environ Health Dept PO Box 1293 Albuquerque NM 87103

KOTEEN, JACK, management consultant, writer; b. N.Y., Aug. 22, 1919; s. Meyer and Eva (Gitlin) K.; m. Gloria Rogoff, Oct. 9, 1949; children: Glenn Michael, Douglas Evan. BA, NYU, 1940, attended John Hopkins Sch. for Advanced Internat. Studies. Mgmt. analyst Exec. Office of Pres. Fed. Govt. Agy., 1941-42; dir. devel. adminstrn., chief African tech. assist. in pub. and bus. adminstrn. in agy. for internat. devel. U.S. Dept. State, 1955-74; v.p. Assocs. for Mgmt. and Evaluation, 1975-79; ind. cons., 1980-90; dir. Strategic Mgmt. Ctr., 1991—; instr. U. Md., Am. U., USDA. Author: (book) Strategic Management in Public and Non-profit Organizations, 1989, 91, 2d edit., 1997. Chair bd. dirs. Internat. Program for Human Resources Devel., Bethesda, Md., 1981-85. 1st Lt. Army Air Corps, 1942-45. Named Hon. Paramount Chief Mpelle People, N. Liberia, 1960; recipient Superior Honor award U.S. Dept. of State, 1974. Avocations: African art, golf. Home: 66 Northwoods Cir Boynton Beach FL 33436-7417

KOTEFF, ELLEN, periodical editor; b. Harvey, Ill.; d. Walter Peter and Florence (Walz) K. BS in Journalism, U. Fla., 1977. Editor Palm Beach (Fla.) Daily News, 1977-90; met. editor Daily Record, Parsippany, N.J., 1990-92; exec. editor Nation's Restaurant News, N.Y.C., 1992—. Office: Nations Restaurant News 425 Park Ave New York NY 10022-3506

KOTELLY, GEORGE VINCENT, editor, writer, electrical engineer; b. Boston, Aug. 27, 1931; s. James Visar and Pauline (Plaha) K.; m. Shirley Elizabeth Mullo, June 14, 1959; children—Kenneth James, William John, Douglas George, Joanne Elizabeth. B.S.E.E., Tufts U., 1953. Publs. engr. Raytheon, Burlington, Mass., 1970-73; tech. writer USM Corp., Beverly, Mass., 1973-75; engring. writer Analogic, Wakefield, Mass., 1975-77; tech. editor Computer Design Mag., Littleton, Mass., 1977-79; sr. editor Edn. Mag., Boston, 1979-83; editor-in-chief Mini-Micro Systems Mag., Cahners Pub. Co., Boston, 1983-88; mng. editor Lightwave Jour. PennWell Pub. Co., Westford, Mass., 1988-89; sr. editor Lincoln Lab. MIT, Lexington, 1989-91; editor COMDEX Preview and Show Daily The Interface Group, Needham, Mass., 1991-93; exec. editor Lightwave Jour. PennWell Pub. Co., Nashua, N.H., 1993-97, Vision Systems Design Mag., 1997—. Contbr. numerous articles to tech. jours. Sgt. U.S. Army, 1954-56. Mem. IEEE. Republican. Mem. Albanian Orthodox Ch. Avocations: golf; bowling; chess; jogging; baseball. Home: 12 Scotch Pine Ln Merrimack NH 03054-3900

KOTEN, JOHN A., retired communications executive; b. Indpls., May 21, 1929; s. Roy Y. and Margaret (Neerman) K.; m. Catherine M. Hruska, Nov. 22, 1952; children: John, Mark, Sarah. BA, North Cen. Coll., Naperville, Ill., 1951, LLD (hon.), 1991; postgrad., Northwestern U., 1953; LLD (hon.), Quincy Coll., 1990. Supr. field advt. Montgomery Ward, Chgo., 1951-52; asst. dir. pub. rels. Am. Osteo. Assn., Chgo., 1952-53; editorial asst. Ill. Bell Tel. Co., Chgo., 1955-56, editor Telebriefs newsletter, 1956-57, supr. info., 1957-59, supr. comml. staff, 1959-60; supr. news svc. and advt. Ill. Bell Tel. Co., Springfield, 1960-62, dist. comml. mgr., 1962-63; supr. pub. info. AT&T, N.Y.C., 1963, supr. customer rels., 1963-64; mgr. div. traffic Ill. Bell Tel. Co., Chgo., 1965-66, mgr. pub. rels., 1966-68, asst. v.p. civic affairs, 1968-69, asst. v.p. Chgo. ops., 1969-70; gen. mgr. upstate area Ill. Bell Tel. Co., Joliet, 1970-71; dir. state regulatory matters AT&T, Lisle, Ill., 1971-72; asst. v.p. pub. rels. Ill. Bell Tel. Co., Chgo., 1972-74; dir. pub. rels. AT&T, N.Y.C., 1974-75; v.p. pub. rels. N.J. Bell Telephone Co., Newark, 1975-77, Ill. Bell Telephone Co., Chgo., 1977-80; v.p. corp. communications Ill. Bell Telephone Co., 1980-87; sr. v.p. corp. communications Ameritech Corp., Chgo., 1987-92, ret., 1992; pres. The Wordsworth Group, Barrington Hills, Ill. Trustee Chgo. Symphony Orch., 1985-97, life trustee, 1997—; trustee Joint Coun. on Econ. Edn., N.Y.C.; trustee Am. Coun. Arts, 1987-98, treas., 1991-93; v.p. Ill. Arts Alliance, Chgo., 1986-91; trustee Arthur W. Page Soc., 1985—, pres., 1985-87; pres. Ameritech Found., Chgo., 1987-94; vice chmn. Am. Arts Alliance, Washington, 1983-92; bd. dirs. Am. Symphony Orch. League, Washington, 1982-94, Gt. Books Found., Chgo., 1991—, chmn. exec. com.; trustee SOS Children's Internat. Villages, Ill., 1996—; trustee Assoc. Colls. Ill., Chgo., 1986-96, life trustee, 1997—; trustee Nat. Cultural Alliance, 1990-98; bd. visitors Medill Sch. Journalism, Northwestern U., 1988-94; assoc. trustee Wordsworth Trust, Eng., 1988; mem. corp. coun. Bus. Com. for Arts, 1988-96; mem. bd. overseers Curtis Inst. Music, Phila.,

1997—; life trustee North Ctrl. Coll., Ill., 1997—. Mem. Pub. Rels. Soc. Am., Conf. Bd. Corp. Communications Coun., Chgo. Advt. Club (bd. dirs. 1978-82), Ind. Soc., Pub. Affairs Coun., Brookings Coun., Chgo. Club, Tavern Club, Econs. Club, Chgo. Yacht Club. Home and Office: The Wordsworth Group 271 Otis Rd Barrington IL 60010-5123

KOTHARI, RAVI, science educator; b. Calcutta, India. B of Engring., Birla Inst. Tech., India, 1986; MS, La. State U., 1988; PhD, W.Va. U., 1991. Assoc. prof. U. Cin., 1992—. Mem. editl. bd. Pattern Analysis and Applications; reviewer profl. jours.; contbr. sci. papers to jours. including Neural Computation, Phys. Rev. B, IEEE Transactions on Biomed. Engring. Recipient Rsch. Funding award Whitaker Found., 1997. Mem. IEEE, Internat. Neural Network Soc. E-mail: ravi.kothari@uc.edu. Office: U Cin PO Box 210030 Cincinnati OH 45221-0030

KOTHE, CHARLES ALOYSIUS, lawyer; b. Jersey City, Oct. 12, 1912; s. Charles A. and Lillian (Hansen) K.; m. Janet Fleming, Feb. 19, 1937; children: Diane, Charles F., James R., David J. Student, Bucknell U., 1930-33; AB, U. Tulsa, 1934; scholarship, U. Heidelberg, Germany; JD with honors, U. Okla., 1938. Bar: Okla. 1938. Staff counsel Mid-Continent Petroleum Co., Tulsa, 1939-41; gen. counsel Macnick Co., Tulsa, 1941-43; v.p. indsl. rels. NAM, N.Y.C., 1959-65; atty., v.p., dir. Coburn Optical Industries, 1966-76; dir. T.D. Williamson Co.; of counsel Pray, Walker, Jackman Law Firm, Tulsa, 1990—; mem. faculty labor law dept. Tulsa Law Sch., 1939-60; dean indsl. rels. dept. Okla. Sch. Acctg., 1960-65; founding dean O.W. Coburn Law Sch.; mem. Faculty Univ. Ctr. at Tulsa, 1989—; mem. panel Am. Arbitration Assn., Fed. Mediation and Conciliation Svc.; spl. cons., 1966-90, EEO Commn., 1980-85; chmn. Pub. Employees Rels. Bd., 1989—; mem. Fed. Svc. Impasses Panel, 1991-95. Author: Industrial Relations in the Non-Union Plant, 1960, NLRB and the Rights of Management, 1966; Editor: Tale of 22 Cities, 1964. Co-founder, 2d pres. Effective Citizens Orgn., 1957; mem. Tulsa Civil Svc. Commn., 1980-85. Named Citizen of Year Tulsa, 1946. Mem. ABA (10th Circuit councilman 1940), Okla. Bar Assn. (chmn. labor law section), U.S. Jr. C. of C. (v.p. 1956), Okla. Jr. C. of C. (pres. 1955), Tulsa Jaycees (pres. 1954), Jr. Bar Conf. Okla. (pres. 1946), U. Tulsa Alumni Assn. (pres. 1957, distinguished alumnus 1974), Order of Coif, Tulsa Club, So. Hills Country Club, Nat. Lawyers Club, Masons, Shriners, Sigma Alpha Epsilon, Phi Delta Phi, Beta Gamma Sigma. Home: 4180 Oak Rd Tulsa OK 74105-4245 Office: 900 Oneok Bldg 100 W 5th St Tulsa OK 74103-4240*

KOTHS, JAY SANFORD, floriculture educator; b. Taylor, Mich., July 22, 1926; s. George William Koths and Elva Herman; m. Margaret Louise Edwards; children: Kirston, Gwen, Kim. BS, Mich. State U., 1948; MS, Purdue U., 1950; PhD, U. Mass., 1967. Comml. greenhouse mgr., Boone, Iowa, Bloomington, Ill. and Milw., 1950-55; prof. floriculture, extension floriculturist U. Conn., Storrs, 1955-86, emeritus prof., 1986—; cons. in field. Editor Conn. Greenhouse Newsletter, 1964-87. Contbr. numerous articles to profl. jours. Served with USN, 1945-46. Fellow Am. Soc. Hort. Sci. (chmn. floriculture working group 1978-81, extension awardee); mem. Am. Soc. Agronomy, Internat. Soc. Hort. Sci., Sigma Xi, Beta Alpha Sigma, Gamma Sigma Delta. Republican. Avocations: antiques, tennis. Home: 409 N Eagleville Rd Storrs Mansfield CT 06268-1810 Office: U Conn PO Box 67U Storrs Mansfield CT 06268-0067

KOTIN, PAUL, pathologist; b. Chgo., Aug. 13, 1916; s. Elias and Rose (Spunt) K.; m. Pauline H. Stephan, Dec. 12, 1970; children: Joel Tepper, David Bernard. B.S., U. Ill., 1937, M.D., 1940. Intern Deaconess Hosp., Chgo., 1939-40; resident pathology Deaconess Hosp., 1940-41; pvt. practice pathology and internal medicine San Luis Obispo, Calif., 1946-48; researcher pathology U. So. Calif., 1949-50; med. microbiologist Los Angeles County Hosp., 1950-51, attending staff pathologist, 1951-62; mem. faculty U. So. Calif., 1951-62, prof. pathology, 1959-60, Paul Pierce prof. pathology, 1960-62; chief carcinogenesis studies br. Nat. Cancer Inst., 1962-63, asso. dir. for field studies, 1963-64, sci. dir. for etiology, 1964-66; dir. div. environ. health scis. NIH, 1966-69; dir. Nat. Inst. Environ. Health Scis., 1969-71; v.p. for health scis., dean Sch. Medicine, Temple U., Phila., 1971-74; sr. v.p. health, safety and environment Johns-Manville Corp., 1974-81; Edgar Allen Meml. lectr. Yale Sch. Medicine, 1957; vis. prof. oncology U. Wis., 1959-60; vis. prof. pathology U. N.C., also Duke U., 1967-71; Harry Shay Meml. lectr. Temple U., 1964; Sappington Meml. lectr. Am. Occupational Medicine Assn., Anaheim, Calif., 1979, Gehrmann lectr., Nashville, 1981; chmn. Gordon Research Conf. Cancer, 1965, Beryllium Industry Sci. Adv. Com., 1995—; adj. prof. pathology U. Colo., 1974—; Cons. air pollution med. program, div. spl. health service USPHS, 1958-62; mem. sci. adv. bd. Council Tobacco Research-U.S.A., 1952-65; adv. com. r.r. diesel gases and dust Calif. Pub. Utilities Commn., 1956-62; adv. com. research pathogenesis cancer Am. Cancer Soc., 1962-65; pathology study sect. NIH, 1962-66, lung cancer task force, 1967-68; corr. mem. permanent European com. Research Chronic Hazards, 1960—; cancer prevention com. UICC, 1962-66, com. on exptl. design and methodology in carcinogenesis, 1967-70; sci. com. Inst. Occupational and Environ. Health, Quebec. Asbestos Mining Assn., 1966-75; mem. Fed. Com. Pest Control, 1964-71; program com. Tenth Internat. Congress, 1967-70; mem. Expert Panel on Carcinogenicity, 1962-70, Nat. Environ. Health Scis. Center, 1965, Nat. Adv. Com. Occupational Safety and Health, 1975-78, Armed Forces Epidemiol. Bd., 1976-80. Editorial adv. bd.: Cancer Research, 1957-61, Internat. Rev. Exptl. Pathology, 1968—; editorial bd.: AMA Archives Pathology, 1965-71, Environ. Research, 1966—, Am. Jour. Pathology, 1971-82; Contbr. articles to med. jours. Served with AUS, 1941-46. Recipient Superior Service award HEW, 1966, Disting. Service award, 1969; Sr. postdoctoral fellow NSF, 1959-60; named Alumnus of Yr. U. Ill. Coll. of Medicine, 1990. Fellow Coll. Am. Pathologists, N.Y. Acad. Scis., Am. Acad. Occupational Medicine; mem. AMA (com. research on tobacco and health 1966-78), Am. Assn. Cancer Research (dir.), Am. Assn. Pathologists and Bacteriologists, AAAS, Am. Indsl. Hygiene Assn. (hon.), Am. Occupational Medicine Assn. (Knudsen award 1981), Sigma Xi, Alpha Omega Alpha. Home: 1521 E Crown Ridge Way Tucson AZ 85737-7104

KOTKIN, DAVID See COPPERFIELD, DAVID

KOTKOV, BENJAMIN, clinical psychologist; b. Boston, Apr. 8, 1910; s. Moses and Annie (Hopner) K.; m. Sally B., Jan. 28, 1941; children: Ralph, Frank. AB, Cornell U., 1929; MA, Harvard U., 1934; PhD, Ottawa U., Ont., Can., 1954. Diplomate Am. Bd. Clin. Psychology, Am. Bd. Profl. Psychology, Am. Bd. Med. Psychotherapists, Am. Bd. Disability Cons., Am. Bd. Prescribing Psychologists, Am. Coll. Forensic Examiners, Serious Mental Illness, Am. Coll. Advanced Practice Psychologists, Internat. Coll. Prescribing Psychologists in Serious Mental Illness, Am. Coll. Advanced Practicing Psychologists; cert. Am. Soc. Clin. Hypnosis. Staff to chief Nerve Clinic, New Eng. Med. Ctr., Boston, 1934-42, VA Mental Hygiene Unit, Boston, 1946-52; chief psychologist Mental Hygiene Clinics, State of Del., 1952-53; clin. exec. Child Guidance Ctr., Brattleboro, Vt., 1954-64; staff to prof. and faculty head Windham Coll., Putney, Vt., 1964-76; pvt. practice Brattleboro, 1976—; internat. adv. bd. Acad. of Psychoanalysis, Germany, 1969—. Contbr. numerous articles to profl. jours. Lt. U.S. Army, 1942-46. Recipient Editor's award Internat. Jour. Profl. Hypnosis, 1977, medallion Acad. Psychosomatic Medicine, 1979, Membership Leader award Vt. Lions, 1993-94, Outstanding Premier Leadership award in psychopharmacology, 1998; NEA grantee, 1956-57. Fellow Am. Psychol. Soc., Internat. Soc. Profl. Hypnosis, Acad. Sci. Hypnotherapy, Am. Assn. Applied and Prevention Psychology, Acad. Clin. Psychology; mem. AAUP (emeritus), APA (life), Am. Philos. Assn., Soc. Personality Assessment (life), Vt. Psychol. Assn. (pres. 1968-69, chmn. cert. bd. 1974-76), New Eng. Soc. Clin. Hypnosis (pres. 1988), DAV (life), Lions (pres. 1973-74, 84-85, 94-97), Elks. Home and Office: 70 Orchard St Brattleboro VT 05301-2678

KOTLER, MARTIN JOSEPH, painter; b. Newark, Oct. 24, 1953; s. Edward and Rosalyn Kotler. BFA in Painting and Sculpture cum laude, Md. Inst. Coll. Art, 1975; MFA in Painting, Am. U., 1980. Tchr. Md. Inst. Coll. Art, 1974-76; tchr. dept. art Am. U. Coll. Arts and Sci., 1979; tchr. drawing and painting Am. U., 1979; grad. and undegrad. intern supr. Nat. Mus. Am. Art, 1984—; lectr. in field. One-man shows include Govinda Gallery, Washington, 1980, 81, Anton Gallery, Washington, 1982, 84, Fendrick Gallery, Washington, 1987, 89, South Ea. Ctr. Contemporary Art, Winston-Salem, N.C., 1988, Barbara Fendrick Gallery, N.Y., 1990, Addison/Ripley Gallery, Washington, 1992-98, Reynolds Gallery, Richmond, Va., 1994, 95, 98; group exhbns. include Md. Inst. Coll. Art, Balt., 1974, Huber/Pollner Gallery, Washington, 1979, Anton Gallery, Washington, 1983, 84, Watkins Gallery, Washington, 1984, Fendrick Gallery, Washington, 1985, Zenith Gallery, Washington, Washington Studio Sch. Gallery, 1986, 87, 89, Aetna Inst. Gallery, Hartford, Conn., 1988, Fine Arts Gallery, Washington, 1989, Foster Gallery, Eau Clair, Wis., 1990, Middendorf Gallery, Washington, 1991, Gallery K, Washington, 1991, Reynolds Gallery, Richmond, Va., 1993, U. Md., College Park, 1995, Marsha Mateyka Gallery, 1996, Washington Studio Sch., 1996, Artists' Mus. Galllery, Washington, 1997; represented in permanent collection U.S. Dept. State, Md. Inst., Coll. Art, Watkins Gallery, Smithsonian Instn., Balt. Mus. Art, L.A. County Mus. Art, Fogg Mus., Met. Mus. Art. Recipient Painting fellowship Am. U., 1979-80.

KOTLER, RONALD LEE, physician, educator; b. Pitts., June 10, 1956; s. Milton and Marion (Oppenheimer) K.; m. Jane Ellyn Cobin, Feb. 20, 1982; children: Jennifer, Rachel, Drew. BA, Emory U., 1978; MD, U. Pa., 1982. Diplomate Am. Bd. Internal Medicine, Am. Bd. Pulmonary Disease, Am. Bd. Critical Care Medicine, Am. Bd. Sleep Medicine. Intern Pa. Hosp., Phila., 1982-83, resident, 1983-85; fellow pulmonary disease Hosp. U. Pa, Phila., 1985-87; clin. assoc. in medicine U. Pa. Sch. Medicine, Phila., 1987-88, clin. asst. prof., 1988-95, 97—; clin. asst. prof. Thomas Jefferson U., Phila., 1994—; co-dir. hosp. sleep lab. Pa. Hosp., Phila., 1991—. Contbr. articles to profl. jours. Lectr. City Phila. Dept. Health, Phila., 1988, 89, Pa. Hosp., 1995. Fellow ACP, Am. Coll. Chest Physicians; mem. Am. Thoracic Soc., Phi Beta Kappa, Omicron Delta Kapp, Alpha Omega Alpha. Avocation: tennis. Office: Casey Lugano Kotler Assocs 700 Spruce St Ste 500 Philadelphia PA 19106-4027

KOTLER, STEVEN, investment banker; b. N.Y.C., Jan. 9, 1947; s. Louis and Etta (Smeltzer) K.; BBA, CCNY, 1967; m. Carolyn Miller, Sept. 26, 1973; children: William, Thomas. Vice pres. N.Y. Hanseatic Corp., N.Y.C., 1967-74; with Schroder Wertheim & Co. Inc., N.Y.C., 1974—, gen. ptnr., 1979—, mng. dir., 1981—, pres. 1987—, CEO, 1996—; chmn. exec. com., dir. Moore Med. Corp., Del Labs., Inc.; mem. exec. com. Schroders plc, also bd. dirs.; bd. govs. Am. Stock Exch.; trustee Columbia Grammar and Prep. Sch; mem. coun. The Woodrow Wilson Internat. Ctr. for Scholars; mem. infrastructure & housing tadk force N.Y.C. Partnership, N.Y.C. C. of C. Served with USAR, 1967-72.

KOTLER, WENDY ILLENE, art educator, social studies educator, grants coordinator; b. Chgo., Mar. 4, 1947; d. Robert and Florence (Rabin) Abrams; m. Neil G. Kotler, Dec. 17, 1971; 1 child, Jena Julianne. BFA, U. Ill., 1969; MEd, U. Va., 1982, PhD, 1991. Cert. NK-12 art tchr., gifted and talented edn., mid., elem. and secondary sch. supr. and prin. Tchr. Sch. Dist. 109 and 23, Cook County, Ill., 1969-71; tchr. art, supr. Supervisory Union 32, N.H., 1972-74; tchr., curriculum developer Austin (Tex.) Ind. Sch. Dist., Hanover, N.H., 1974-75; staff devel. trainer, program developer Fairfax County (Va.) Pub. Schs., 1975-76, tchr., curriculum developer, 1979-85, program coord., art and mid. sch. resource tchr., 1985-92; mem. adj. faculty No. Va. Ext., U. Va., Fairfax, 1985—; adj. faculty George Mason U., ; program developer, tchr. trainer Regional Ctr. for Ednl. Tng., Wilson Mus., Dartmouth Coll., Hanover, N.H., 1972-74; workshop presenter in field to regional, state, nat. and sch. confs.; curriculum and instrn. cons.; adj. faculty George Mason U. Contbr. articles to profl. publs. Recipient commendation for profl. excellence Fairfax County Pub. Schs., 1989, 92. Mem. NEA, ASCD, NCSS, Va. Edn. Assn., Fairfax Edn. Assn., Nat. Art Edn. Assn. (Southeastern Elem. Art Educator of Yr. award 1991, Nat. Elem. Art Educator of Yr. award 1992), Va. Art Edn. Assn. (bd. dirs. 1989, 93, Va. Elem. Art Tchr. of Yr. award 1989, cert. of commendation 1990), No. Va. Art Edn. Assn. (pres. 1993, No. Va. Art Tchr. of Yr. award 1988, 89), Phi Delta Kappa. Home: 200 S Abingdon St Arlington VA 22204-1333

KOTLOWITZ, ALEX, writer, journalist. Student, Wesleyan U. Former prodr. segments TV series MacNeil/ Lehrer NewsHour; former reporter The Wall Street Jour.; former contbr. NPR. Author: There Are No Children Here: The Story of Two Boys Growing Up In the Other America, 1991 (Helen Bernstein award Excellence Journalism N.Y. Pub. Libr. 1992), The Other Side of the River: A Story of Two Towns, a Death and America's Dilemma, 1998 (Heartland prize for nonfiction Chgo. Triune 1998); contbg. writer The New Yorker. Recipient George Polk award TV reporting Long Island U. Journalism dept. work on MacNeil/Lehrer NewsHour, 1984, Robert F. Kennedy award Coverage of Disadvantaged.

KOTLOWITZ, ROBERT, writer, editor; b. Paterson, N.J., Nov. 21, 1924; s. Max and Debra (Kaplan) K.; m. Carol Naomi Leibowitz, Oct. 15, 1950; children—Alexander William, Daniel Justin. B.A., Johns Hopkins, 1947; preparatory diploma, Peabody Conservatory Music, 1941. Asso. editor Pocket Books, Inc., 1950-55, Discovery, 1952-55; mgr. press and information RCA Victor Records, 1955-60; sr. editor Show mag., 1960-64; sr. editor Harper's mag., 1965-67, mng. editor, 1967-71; sr. v.p., dir. programming Sta. WNET/ Channel 13, N.Y.C., 1971-91, editorial advisor, 1991—; guest lectr. Queen's Coll., 1954-55; author monthly column Performing Arts, 1966—. Author: novel Somewhere Else, 1972, The Boardwalk, 1977, Sea Changes, 1986, His Master's Voice, 1992, Before Their Time, 1997; Contbg. editor: Atlantic Monthly, 1971-74; Contbr. nat. publs. Served with inf. AUS, 1943-46. Recipient Edward Lewis Wallant award for novel, 1972, Nat. Jewish Book award, 1972, Nat. Emmy award, 1973; sr. fellow Freedom Forum, Columbia U., 1993; fellow Am. Acad., Berlin, 1998. Mem. Century Assn. Home: 54 Riverside Dr New York NY 10024-6509

KOTOK, ALAN, publishing association executive; b. Buffalo, N.Y., June 21, 1945; s. Theodore and Rhoda (Natowitz) K.; m. Sharon Rose Bandy, Oct. 11, 1976. BA, U. Iowa, 1967; MS, Boston U., 1969. Cert. systems prof. Rsch. analyst U.S. Info. Agy., Washington, 1969-75, rsch. and devel. officer, 1975-79, systems analyst, 1979-81, dir. planning and devel., 1982-85; dir. computer svcs. Aurora Assocs., Inc., Washington, 1985-87; pres. Overseas Technology, Inc., Arlington, Va., 1987-90; v.p. electronic business Graphic Comms. Assn., Alexandria, Va., 1990—; adv. bd. Internat. Approval Svcs., Clev., 1993-97. Co-author: Print Communications and the Electronic Media Challenge, 1996; editor: GCA Bar Code Reporter Jour., 1990-94, Graphic Communications Today, 1996—; contbg. editor: EDI World jour., 1992—; contbr. articles to jours. Jefferson fellow Am. U., 1981-82. Mem. Am. Soc. Quality, Nat. Assn. Sci. Writers, Internat. Trade Assn. No. Va., Am. Fgn. Svc. Assn. Avocations: running (mem. D.C. Roadrunner's Club). E-mail: akotok@gca.org. Office: Graphic Comms Assn 100 Daingerfield Rd Alexandria VA 22314-2886

KOTOSKE, ROGER ALLEN, artist, educator; b. South Bend, Ind., Jan. 4, 1933; s. Michael and Louise (Gallo) K.; 1 child, Tamara. Student, U. Notre Dame, 1950-52; B.F.A., U. Denver, 1955, M.A., 1956. instr. Fitzsimons Army Hosp., Denver, 1956-58, U. Denver, 1958-68; mem. faculty U. Ill., 1968—; now assoc. prof. Vice pres., artist Denver Nat. Sculpture Symposium, 1968. One man shows James Yu Gallery, N.Y.C., 1974, Hiestand Gallery, Miami U., Oxford, Ohio, 1978, Hilton Center for Performing Arts, St. Louis, 1979, group shows include, Galex Nat. 23, Galesburg, Ill., 1989, Greater Midwest Internat. III, Warrensburg, Mo., 1988, SUNY, Potsdam, 1975, Grey Gallery, N.Y.C., 1976, Illinois Painters III, 1980; exhibited in group show U. Del., Newark, 1986, U. of Ill. Faculty Internat. Exchange Exhbn., Chinese Fine Arts Mus., Beijing, China, 1987, Art Yard, Denver, 1996; represented in permanent collections Rock Hill Nelson Gallery, Kansas City, Mo., SUNY, Oswego, Denver Art Mus., others. Ford Found. grantee, 1975-78. Home: 1611 W White St Champaign IL 61821-3017

KOTSAY, MARK STEVEN, baseball player; b. Woodler, Calif., Dec. 2, 1975. Student, Calif. State U., Fullerton. Ctr. field, right field Fla. Marlins, 1996—; mem. U.S. Olympic Baseball Team, 1996. Recipient Golden Spikes award USA Baseball, 1995; named Most Outstanding Player Coll. World Series, 1995; tied for Ea. League for double plays by outfielder with four, 1997. Office: Florida Marlins 2267 NW 199th St Miami FL 33056-2600

KOTT, BEVERLY PARAT, financial counselor; b. Chgo., Sept. 7, 1936; d. Louis Joseph and Marie Elizabeth (Katich) Parat; m. Russell Kott; children: Vinson V., Donna M., James L., Michael A. Grad., Life Underwritr Tng. Coun., Washington, 1977. Mem. mgmt. ea. region Met. Life Ins. Co., Balt., 1977; ins. broker, 1979-85; pres. Kott & Assocs. Fin. Counseling Svc., Joppa, Md., 1985—; fin. counselor coop. extension svc. U. Md., Bel Air, 1987—, mem. Harford extension adv. coun., 1988-93; dir. Prison Ministry, 1983—; lay minister Roman Catholic Ch., 1995—. Commr. Harford County Commn. for Women, Bel Air, 1981-87; v.p. Joppa Friends of the Libr., 1988—; mem. Rumsey Island Civic Assn., 1980—; dir. Joppatowne Civic Assn., Joppa, 1990—, Padre Rio Rosary Makers, 1993—, Postal Adv. Coun., 1992—; sec. Harford County Libr. Coun., 1999—. Named one of Most Beautiful People, Harford County, 1990. Mem. Hunt Valley Bus. and Profl. Woman's Club (charter), Aux. VFW (pres. 1988-90, legis., youth, publicity and cancer aid coms. 1989, 90), Mensa Internat. Roman Catholic. Avocations: chess, bridge, writing, travel, volunteering. Home: 661 Towne Center Dr Joppa MD 21085-4439

KOTT, DAVID RUSSELL, lawyer; b. Trenton, N.J., Jan. 22, 1952; s. Maurice G. and Ruth (Shulman) K.; m. Lauren Handler, Aug. 24, 1980; children: Emily R., Adam J. BA, Am. U., 1973; JD, Rutgers U., 1977. Bar: N.J. 1977, U.S. Dist. Ct. N.J. 1977, U.S. Ct. Appeals (3d cir.) 1980, N.Y. 1984, U.S. Dist. Ct. (so. and ea. dists.) N.Y. 1985; cert. civil trial atty. Law clk. to justice N.J. Supreme Ct., Morristown, 1977-78; from assoc. to ptnr. McCarter & English LLP, Newark, 1978—; sustaining mem. Product Liability Adv. Coun. Mem. ABA, Am. Bd. Trial Advocates, N.J. Bar Assn., Essex County Bar Assn., Assn. Def. Trial Lawyers Attys., Trial Lawyers N.J., Fedn. Ins. and Corp. Attys., Def. Rsch. Inst., The Newark Club, Club at World Trade Ctr. Republican. Jewish. Office: McCarter & English LLP 4 Gateway Ctr 100 Mulberry St Newark NJ 07102-4004

KOTT, JOSEPH, transportation executive, consultant, educator; b. Detroit, July 15, 1947; s. Joseph Frank and Catherine Marie (Szydloski) K.; m. Katherine Babette Kitto, Sept. 28, 1973; children: Paul, Andrew, Amy. BA, Wayne State U., 1976; M of Regional Planning, U. N.C., 1979. Planner Orange County, Hillsborough, N.C., 1979-80; transp. planner N.C. Dept. Transp., Raleigh, 1980-84, Ill. Commerce Commn., Springfield, Ill., 1984-86; planning coord. So. Ill. Sch. Medicine, Springfield, 1986-88; sr. transp. planner Androscoggin Valley Coun. Govts., Auburn, Maine, 1989-91; transp. planning mgr. Greater Portland (Maine) Coun. Govts., 1992-98; chief transp. ofcl. City of Palo Alto, Calif., 1999—; adj. prof. cmty. planning & devel. Muskiw Sch. Pub. Svc. U. So. Maine, Portland, 1997. Chair Auburn Maine Planning Bd., 1995-98, mem., 1992-98; adv. com. So. Maine Rideshare, Portland, 1993-98, Kids & Transp., Portland, 1994-98, Portland Area Clean Cities, 1996-98; bd. dirs. Western Maine Transp. Svcs., Mexico, 1994-98. Inst. Transp. Sys. scholar, Washington, 1997, Eno Transp. Found. Can. Transit Studies Mission scholar, Washington, 1996; recipient Maine Environ. Citizen Yr. Natural Resources Coun. Maine, Augusta, 1995. Mem. AICP, Am. Planning Assn., Inst. Transp. Engrs. Democrat. Roman Catholic. Avocations: jogging, cross-country skiing, hiking. Home: 815 Santa Fe Ave Albany CA 94706 Office: City of Palo Alto 250 Hamilton Ave Palo Alto CA 94303

KOTTAS, JAMES ALAN, computer scientist; b. Buffalo, Feb. 8, 1961; s. Walter Edward and Delphine Jane (Aguglia) K.; m. Cynthia Darlene Bone, Oct. 11, 1992; children: Joel Edward, Jason Robert. BSEE, Carnegie-Mellon U., 1983; MSEE, MIT, 1986, PhDEE, 1991. Rsch. scientist Symbus Tech., Inc., Brookline, Mass., 1991-94; chief scientist Miros, Inc., Wellesley, Mass., 1994—; cons. Cambridge, Mass., 1988-90, West Newton, Mass., 1992-94. Mem. IEEE, Internat. Neural Network Soc., Sigma Xi, Eta Kappa Nu, Tau Beta Pi. Achievements include co-invention of system, method and application for the recognition, verification and similarity ranking of facial or other object patterns, co-authorship of Prēdix Market Analysis System, creation of first neural network model to include adaptable time delays. Avocations: hockey, cycling, tennis, golf, family activities. Office: Miros Inc 572 Washington St Ste 18 Wellesley MA 02482-6418

KOTTAS, JOHN FREDERICK, business administration educator; b. Hampton, Va., Apr. 18, 1940; s. Harry and Johnny (Edwards) K.; m. Betty Ann Hokenson, Aug. 7, 1965; children: John Bohlin, Ellen Elizabeth, Katherine Caroline, Paul Frederick. B.S., Purdue U., 1962; M.S., Northwestern U., 1964, Ph.D., 1968. Lectr. Wharton Sch., Univ. Pa., Phila., 1966-68; asst. prof. Sch. Bus. Adminstrn., Univ. N.C., Chapel Hill., 1968-73; adj. asso. prof. Boston Univ. Overseas Grad. Program, Heidelberg, W. Ger., 1973-74; asso. prof. coordinator mgmt. sci. and info. systems Sch. Bus. Adminstrn., Univ. Mo., St. Louis, 1974-79; Zollinger prof. bus. adminstrn. Coll. of William and Mary, Williamsburg, Va., 1979—; presented three-day mgmt. seminar on Inventory Mgmt. and Control at numerous univs., U.S. and Can., 1976-78; cons. in field. Co-author: Production/Operations Management: Contemporary Policy of Managing Operating Systems, 1972, Cases and Applications in Lotus 1-2-3 (for DOS), 1995, Cases and Applications in Lotus 1-2-3 (for Windows), 1996, Cases and Applications in Microsoft EXCEL 5.0, 1996; contbr. articles to various publs. NDEA fellow, 1962-65; Walter P. Murphy fellow, 1962. Mem. Inst. Decision Scis., Inst. for Ops. Rsch. and Mgmt. Scis. Home: 109 Maxwell Pl Williamsburg VA 23185-5523 Office: Coll of William and Mary Sch Bus Adminstrn Williamsburg VA 23187

KOTTICK, EDWARD LEON, music educator, harpsichord maker; b. Jersey City, June 16, 1930; s. Hyman W. and Frieda M. (Stoller) K.; m. Gloria Astor, May 10, 1953; children: Judith, Janet. AB, NYU, 1953; MA, Tulane U., 1959; PhD, U. N.C., Chapel Hill, 1962. Trombonist New Orleans Philharm., 1955-57; asst. prof. music Alma Coll., Mich., 1962-65; vis. prof. music U. Kans., Lawrence, 1965-66; assoc. prof. music U. Mo.-St. Louis, 1966-68; prof. music U. Iowa, Iowa City, 1968-92, prof. emeritus, 1992. Author: The Unica in the Chansonnier Cordiforme, No. 42 of Corpus Mensurabilis Musicae, 1967, Tone and Intonation on the Recorder, 1974, The Collegium: A Handbook, 1977, The Harpsichord Owner's Guide, 1987, (with G. Lucktenberg) Early Keyboard Instruments in European Museums, 1997; contbr. articles to profl. jours. With U.S. Army, 1953-55. U. Iowa grantee, 1975, 80, 85, 90, summer fellow, 1976; Galpin Soc. grantee, 1978. Mem. Am. Mus. Instrument Soc. (bd. govs. 1986-90, Am. Musicol. Soc. (chpt. sec. 1961-62, chpt. program com. 1964-66, chair com. 1972-73, 96-97, mem. nat. com. Collegium Musicum 1973-75), Fellowship Makers and Restorers of Hist. Instruments, Galpin Soc., Guild Am. Luthiers, Midwestern Hist. Keyboard Soc., Midwestern Hist. Keyboard Soc. (bd. dirs. 1980-90, 94-97). Home: 502 Larch Ln Iowa City IA 52245-3434

KOTTLER, RAYMOND GEORGE MICHAEL, economist, researcher; b. Washington, Dec. 11, 1966. Diplomas, Goethe Inst., Staufen, Fed. Republic Germany, 1986, Tech. U. Dresden, German Dem. Republic, 1988, U. Vienna, Austria, 1988; BA in Econs., German, Rutgers U., 1989. Mgmt. trainee Met. Life Ins. Co., N.Y.C., 1989-90; environ. info. systems coord. Johnson & Johnson, New Brunswick, N.J., 1990-92; asst. economist Fed. Res. Bank N.Y., 1993-96; fin. analyst, client svcs. coord. Fed. Res. Bank of N.Y. - Rsch. and Market Analysis Group, 1996—. Mem. Rutgers First Aid Squad, 1985-89, crew chief, ambulance driver, 1987-89; cons. Literacy Vols. Am.-N.J., East Brunswick, N.J., 1991-93; mem. pres.'s com. on edn. for civic leadership/cmty. svc. CECL project, Rutgers U., 1988-91, co-chair pres.'s mng./promoting diversity com. task force CACP, 1990-91; co-chair cmty. svc. com. Rutgers Alumni Assn., 1991-94; mem. Rep. Presdl. Task Force, Rep. Senatorial Com., Rep. Presdl. Roundtable; nominee Rep. Senatorial Com. Inner Circle. Scholar Fed. Republic Germany Acad. Exch. Program, 1986, German Dem. Republic Fgn. Ministry, 1988, Austrian Ministry Sci. and Rsch., 1988, Merrill Lynch Disting. scholar, 1985-89, Garden State Disting. scholar, 1985-89; honoree Rep. Wall of Honor, Washington, 1993; recipient Ronald Reagan Eternal Flame of Freedom award, 1994, Legion of Merit medal, Legion of Honor. Mem. Rutgers Alumni Assn. (bd. dirs. 1988—, reunion chair 1989—, Rutgers Loyola Sons/Loyal Daus. award 1999, Rutgers Class of 1931 award 1999), Cap and Skull Soc., Phi Sigma Iota, Delta Phi Alpha, Omicron Delta Epsilon. Republican. Roman Catholic. Avocations: camping, swimming, boating, outdoor activities, gardening.

KOTTLOWSKI, FRANK EDWARD, geologist; b. Indpls., Apr. 11, 1921; s. Frank Charles and Adella (Markworth) K.; m. Florence Jean Chriscoe, Sept. 15, 1945; children: Karen, Janet, Diane. Student, Butler U., 1939-42; AB, Ind. U., 1947, MA, 1949, PhD, 1951. Party chief Ind. Geology Survey, Bloomington, summers 1948-50; fellow Ind. U., 1947-51, instr. geology, 1950; adj. prof. N.Mex. Inst. Mining and Tech., Socorro, 1970-95; econ. geologist N.Mex. Bur. Mines and Mineral Resources, 1951-66, asst. dir., 1966-68, 70-74, acting dir., 1968-70, dir., 1974-91, state geologist, 1989-91, dir. emeritus, state geologist emeritus, 1991—; geologic cons. Sandia Corp., 1966-72. Contbr. articles on mineral resources, stratigraphy and areal geology to tech. jours. Mem. Planning Commn. Socorro, 1960-68, 71-78, chmn., 86-90; mem. N.Mex. Energy Resources Bd.; chmn. N.Mex. Coal Surface Mining Commn.; sec. Socorro County Democratic Party, 1964-68. Served to 1st lt. USAAF, 1942-45. Decorated D.F.C., Air medal; recipient Richard Owen Disting. Alumni award in Govt. and Industry, U. Ind., 1987. Fellow AAAS, Geol. Soc. Am. (councilor 1979-82, mem. exec. com. 1981-82, Disting. Svc. award coal geology divsn., Cady Coal Geology award 1996); mem. AIME, Am. Assn. Petroleum Geologists (hon.; dist. rep. 1965-68, editor 1971-75, pres. energy minerals divsn. 1987-88, Disting. Svc. award), Assn. Am. State Geologists (pres. 1985-86), Soc. Econ. Geologists, Am. Inst. Profl. Geologists (Pub. Svc. award 1986), Am. Commn. Statigraphic Nomenclature (past sec., chmn.), Cosmos Club, Rotary Internat. (Paul Harris fellow), Sigma Xi. Home: 703 Sunset St Socorro NM 87801-4657 Office: NMex Bur Mines NMex Tech 801 Leroy Pl Socorro NM 87801-4681

KOTTMEYER, MARTIN S., farmer, writer; b. Breese, Ill., Aug. 11, 1953; s. Martin and Alvera (Woker) K. AS, Kaskaskia Coll., Centralia, Ill., 1973. Engaged in farming Carlyle, Ill., 1970s—. Contbr. articles to Magonia, The Reall News, Ency. of the Paranormal, others. Recipient Dr. Alexander Imich award Soc. for Enlightenment and Transformation of UN, 1995. Mem. Rational Exam. Assn. of Lincoln Land. Avocations: UFO culture, science fiction, bad movies. Home: 10501 Knolhoff Rd Carlyle IL 62231-3523

KOTUK, ANDREA MIKOTAJUK, public relations executive, writer; b. New Brunswick, N.J., Oct. 19, 1948; d. Michael and Julia Dorothy (Muka) Mikotajuk. BA, Douglass Coll., Rutgers U., 1970. Pub. relations asst. Wall St. Jour. Newspaper Fund, Princeton, N.J., 1970; editorial asst. Redbook mag., N.Y.C., 1970-71; asst. pub. relations dir. Children's Aid Soc., N.Y.C., 1971-75; assoc. pub. relations dir. Planned Parenthood, N.Y.C., 1975-80; pres. Andrea & Assocs., N.Y.C., 1980—. Writer publicist for non-profit agys.; contbg. editor Arts Mag., 1970-75. Office: Andrea & Assocs 112 E 23rd St New York NY 10010-4518

KOTULAK, RONALD, newspaper science writer; b. Detroit, July 31, 1935; s. John and Mary (Roman) K.; m. Jean Bond, May 6, 1961 (dec. July 1974); chidren: Jeffrey, Kerry, Christopher; m. Donna Clausonthue, July 19, 1980; stepchildren: Paul, Lisa. Student, Wayne State U., 1953-54; BJ, U. Mich., 1959. Mem. staff Chgo. Tribune, 1959—, sch. bd. reporter, 1961-63, writer, 1965—. Recipient 1st pl. sci. writing award ADA, 1966, 1st pl. med. writing award AMA, 1968, 1st pl. Howard Blakeslee sci. writing award Am. Heart Assn., 1968, 1st prize Russell L. Cecil award Arthritis Found., 1969, 1st pl. Claude Bernard Sci. Journalism award Nat. Soc. Med. Rsch., 1971, James T. Brady award Am. Chem. Soc., 1974, Lifeline award Am. Health Found., 1976, Edward Scott Beck award Chgo. Tribune, 1965, 76, 91, 93, Outstanding Achievement award U. Mich., 1978, Robert T. Morse Writers award Am. Psychiat. Assn., 1982, 89, Helen Carringer Nat. Mental Health Journalism award Nat. Mental Health Assn., 1988, Excellence in Journalism award Am. Aging Assn., 1992, Pulitzer Prize for explanatory journalism, 1994, others. Mem. Nat. Assn. Sci. Writers (pres. 1972-73). Home: 737 N Oak Park Ave Oak Park IL 60302-1536 Office: The Chicago Tribune 435 N Michigan Ave Chicago IL 60611-4066*

KOTZ, SAMUEL, statistician, educator, translator, editor; b. Harbin, China, Aug. 28, 1930; s. Boris and Guta (Kahana) K.; m. Roselyn Greenwald, Aug. 6, 1963; children—Tamar Ann, Harold David, Pauline Esther. MSc with honors, Hebrew U., Jerusalem, 1956; PhD, Cornell U., 1960; Dr. honoris causa, U. Athens, 1995, Bowling Green State U., 1997. Rschr. Israel Meterol. Service, 1954-58; lectr. Bar-Ilan U., Israel, 1960-62; postdoctoral Ford fellow U. N.C., 1962-63; asso. prof. U. Toronto, 1963-67; prof. math. Temple U., 1967-79; prof. stats. U. Md., College Park, 1979-97; disting. scholar-tchr. U. Md., 1984-85; disting. vis. prof. Bucknell U., 1977, Guelph (Can.) U., 1987; hon. prof. Harbin Inst. Tech., 1987; Eugene Lukacs disting. rsch. prof. Bowling Green (Ohio) State U., 1992; vis. prof. U. Luleå, Sweden, 1993, 95, Hong Kong U., 1994, U. Copenhagen, summer 1996, U. South Brittany, Vannes, France, 1998; vis. prof. econs. and fin. St. Petersburg (Russia) U., summer 1995; vis. rschr. Internat. Statis. Inst., The Hague, summer 1996, U. Paul Sabatier, Toulouse, France, summer 1998, U. York, Eng., U. Salford, Eng.; vis. scholar George Washington Univ., 1997—. Author, editor 30 books, 4 Russian-English profl. dictionaries, also numerous rsch. papers; translator 18 books; co-editor-in-chief Encyclopedia of Statistical Sciences, 9 vols. and supplement, 1982-89, editor-in-chief update vols. 1-3, 1994-98; co-editor-in-chief Breakthroughs in Statistics, 3 vols., 1995-98; editor: Leading Statistical Personalities, 1997; mem. editl. bd. Soviet Jour. Applied Math. Stats., Jour. Quality Rsch. and Tech.; coord. editor Jour. Statis. Planning and Inference. Served with Israeli Army, 1950-52. Fellow Am. Statis. Assn., Inst. Math. Stats., Royal Statis. Soc., Washington Acad. Scis. (hon.); mem. Internat. Statis. Inst. (elected mem.). Office: George Washington U Dept Ops Rsch Washington DC 20052

KOUBEK, RICHARD JOHN, engineering educator; b. Berwin, Ill., Sept. 10, 1959. BA in Theology, Chemistry, Oral Roberts U., 1981; BA in Psychology, Northeastern Ill. U., 1982; MS in Indsl. Engring., Purdue U., 1985, PhD in Indsl. Engring., 1987. Rsch. asst. Human-Computer Interaction Lab. Northeastern Ill. U., 1983-84; NSF rsch. asst. Sch. Indsl. Engring. Purdue U., W. Lafayette, Ind., 1984-85, NEC rsch. fellow, 1986-87, from asst. prof. to assoc. prof., 1991-97; asst. prof. human factors engring. Wright State U., Dayton, Ohio, 1988-91, prof., chair biomedical and human factors engring., 1997—. Editor: (with W. Karwowski) Manufacturing Agility and Hybrid Automation - I, 1996; (with G. Salvendy, M. J. Smith) Design of Computing Systems: Cognitive Considerations, 1997, Design of Computing Systems: Social and Ergonomic Considerations, 1997; referee Internat. Jour. Human Factors Mfg., 1990—, mem. editl. bd., 1993—; referee Internat. Jour. Human-Computer Studies, 1990—, Knowledge Acquisition, 1991—, Ergonomics, 1991—, Behaviour and Info. Tech., 1991—, Behavior Rsch. Methods, Instruments and Computers, 1994—, Internat. Jour. Computer-Integrated Mfg., 1995—; book rev. editor Internat. Jour. Human-Computer Interaction, 1990-92, referee, 1991—, mem. editl. bd., 1993—; chpt. reviewer Handbook of Industrial Engineering, 1991; proposal reviewer NSF, 1992—, NASA, 1994—, Office Naval Rsch., 1995—; mem. editl. bd. Theoretical Aspects Ergonomics, 1998—; co-editor Internat. Jour Cognitive Ergonomics, 1995—; contbr. articles and papers to profl. jours. Mem. Am. Soc. Engring. Edn., Human Factors Soc., Inst. Indsl. Engrs. Home: 631 Valleyview Point Springboro OH 45066 Office: Wright State U Dept Biomed & Human Factors Russ Engring Ctr Dayton OH 45435

KOUCHOUKOS, NICHOLAS THOMAS, surgeon; b. Grand Rapids, Mich., Dec. 26, 1936; s. Thomas Paul and Antoinette (Karver) K.; m. Judith Buell, Aug. 24, 1966; children—Nicholas Thomas, Robert Buell, Thomas Paul. Student (James B. Angell scholar), U. Mich., 1954-57; MD cum laude, Washington U., 1961. Diplomate Am. Bd. Thoracic Surgery (bd. dirs. 1989-96). Intern Barnes Hosp., Washington U. Med. Ctr., St. Louis, 1961-62; asst. resident in surgery Barnes Hosp., Washington U. Med. Ctr., 1962-65, chief adminstrv. resident, 1965-66; sr. clin. trainee in surgery USPHS, 1966-67; asst. in surgery Sch. Medicine Washington U., St. Louis, 1961-65; instr. surgery Sch. Medicine Washington U., 1965-67, John M. Shoenberg prof. cardiovascular surgery, 1984-96, vice chmn. dept. surgery, 1993-96; research fellow surgery Sch. Medicine, U. Ala., Birmingham, 1967-68; instr. surgery Sch. Medicine, U. Ala., 1967-69, advanced trainee thoracic and cardiovascular surgery, 1968-70, asst. prof. surgery, 1969-71, assoc. prof., 1971-74, prof., vice-dir. div. thoracic and cardiovascular surgery, 1974-81, John W. Kirkin prof. cardiovascular surgery, 1981, clin. prof., 1981-84; cardiovascular surgeon-in-chief Jewish Hosp. of St. Louis, 1984-96, surgeon in chief, 1988-96; mem. cardiovascular research study com. Am. Heart Assn., 1977-79; surgery study sect. USPHS, Bethesda, Md., 1977-80; vice chmn. dept. surgery Washington U. Sch. Medicine, St. Louis, 1991-96; ad hoc cons. Specialized Centers in Research Arteriosclerosis, Nat. Heart and Lung Inst., Bethesda, 1971-72, mem. ad hoc rev. com. for collaborative studies on coronary artery surgery, 1973-75, surgery A study sect., 1976-77; mem. merit rev. bd. in cardiovascular studies VA, Washington, 1976-78. Editorial bd. Jour. Cardiac Rehab., 1979-84, Current Topics in Cardiology, 1977-92, Circulation, 1978-81, 86-88, Cardiology Update, 1979-92, Annals Thoracic Surgery, 1980-89, Cardiosat, 1984-92; assoc. editor Jour. Thoracic and Cardiovascular Surgery, 1996-98. Fellow ACS, Southeastern Surg. Congress, Am. Coll. Cardiology (asst. treas., finalist Young Investigators award 1962); mem. AMA (asst. treas. 1997-99, sec. 1999—), AAUP, Am. Assn Thoracic Surgery, Am. Surg. Assn., Assn. Clin. Cardiac Surgeons, Assn. Acad. Surgery, Internat. Surg. Soc., St. Louis Met. Med. Soc., John Kirklin Soc., Soc. Thoracic Surgeons (treas. 1992-97, v.p. 1998, pres. 1999), St. Louis Thoracic Surg. Soc. (pres. 1993-95), So. Thoracic Surg. Assn., So. Surg. Assn., Soc. Univ. Surgeons, Soc. Vascular Surgery, Internat. Cardiovascular Soc., Phi Beta Kappa, Alpha Omega Alpha. Home: 25 Picardy Ln Saint Louis MO 63124-1606 Office: Mo Bapt Hosp 3009 N Ballas Rd Ste 266C Saint Louis MO 63131-2308

KOUCKY, FRANK LOUIS, geology educator, archeogeology researcher; b. Chgo., June 24, 1927; s. Frank Louis Sr. and Ella (Harshman) K.; m. Virginia Ruhl, Sept. 10, 1949; children: Frank Louis III, David, Walter, Jonathan. BPh, U. Chgo., 1949, MS, 1953, PhD, 1956. Instr. U. Ill., Chgo., 1949-55; asst. prof. Mont. Sch. of Mines, Butte, 1955-58, U. Ill., Urbana, 1958-60; assoc. prof. U. Cin., 1960-72; prof. Coll. of Wooster, Ohio, 1972-92; ret., 1992; vis. prof. field camp U. Ill., Sheridan, Wyo., summers 1958-72; vis. prof. U. Swansea, Wales, 1968, MIT, Cambridge, Mass., 1978, 83, Am. Ctr. for Oriental Rsch., Ammon, Jordan, 1987; mem. archaeol. excavation in Cyprus, Jordan, Israel. Contbr. articles to profl. jours. With U.S. Army, 1945-47. Danforth fellow, 1965—, Bucher fellow U. Cin., 1968, NEH fellow, 1987. Fellow AAAS, Geol. Soc. Am., Ohio Acad. Sci.; mem. Mineral. Assn. Can., Geochem. Soc., Soc. Econ. Geologists, Am. Schs. of Oriental Rsch., Sigma Xi (pres. 1990-91). Avocatins; archaeogeology, metallurgy. Home: 122 W Easton Rd Burbank OH 44214-9746

KOUCKY, JOHN RICHARD, metallurgical engineer, manufacturing executive; b. Chgo., Sept. 21, 1934; s. Frank Louis and Ella (Harshman) K.; m. Beverly Irene O'Dell, Aug. 16, 1958 (dec. May 1990); children: Deborah, Diane; m. Beverly Kay Cummins, Apr. 27, 1991 (dec. Jan. 1996); m. Mary Ann Hubbard, Jan. 4, 1997. BS in MetE., U. Ill., 1957; MBA, Northwestern U., 1959. Metallurgist, asst. plant mgr. Fansteel Metall. Corp., North Chicago, Ill., 1957-64; supr. production engring. cen. foundry div. Gen. Motors Corp., Saginaw, Mich., 1964-67; asst. gen. mgr. Marion (Ind.) Malleable Iron, 1967-68; mgr. production engring. tech., plant mgr., v.p. engr. Wagner Castings Co., Decatur, Ill., 1968-79, 83-91; v.p., gen. mgr. Pa. mall iron div. Gulf & Western, Lancaster, 1979-82; v.p. tech. Wagner Laser Techs., 1989-94; v.p. Decatur Mfg. Co., 1993-95, 300 Below, Inc., Decatur, 1993—. Served to 1st lt. U.S. Army, 1957-58. Mem. Am. Soc. Metals (local chmn. 1976—), Am. Foundrymans Soc. (local vice chmn. 1968—), Ductile Iron Soc. (nat. bd. dirs. 1983—), Iron Castings Soc., Soc. Automotive Engrs., U. Ill. Dept. Materials Sci. Alumni Assn. (bd. dirs. 1983—, Loyalty award 1986), Gray Iron Founders Assn., Soc. for Advancement Material and Process Engring., Country Club Decatur, Decatur Tennis Club (pres. 1976-78), Decatur Racquet Club. Republican. Avocations: tennis, golf, bridge, gardening. Home: 1625 Martin Dr Decatur IL 62521-5805 Office: 300 Below Inc 2101 E Olive St Decatur IL 62526-5138

KOUFAX, SANDY, retired baseball player; b. Bklyn., Dec. 30, 1945. Baseball player Bklyn. Dodgers, 1955-57, L.A. Dodgers, 1958-61; broadcaster NBC, 1966-73. Named to Baseball Hall of Fame, 1972; recipient Cy Young award, Nat. League Most Valuable Player, 1963; selected to Nat. League All-Star Team, 1966-73; mem. World Series Champions, 1959, 63, 65; pitched no-hitter, 1962, 63, 64, pitched perfect game, Sept. 9, 1965. *

KOUGH, ROBERT HAMILTON, retired clinical hematologist, consultant; b. Harrisburg, Pa., Feb. 19, 1921; s. Harry Milton and Olive Jane (Smith) K.; m. Nancy Jane Trunnell, June 18, 1943; 1 child, Elizabeth Trunnell Beiler. BS, Pa. State U., 1942; MD, U. Pa., 1945. Diplomate Am. Bd. Internal Medicine, Am. Bd. Hematology. Intern Hosp. of U. Pa., Phila., 1945-46; med. resident, Am. Cancer Soc. fellow in hematology Hosp. U. Pa., Phila., 1955-58; from asst. instr. to assoc. in pharmacology U. Pa. Med. Sch., Phila., 1949-52; mem. med. staff Carlisle (Pa.) Hosp., 1952-55; assoc. in hematology Geisinger Med. Ctr., Danville, Pa., 1958-65; head hematology Geisinger Med. Ctr., 1965-74, dir. dept. hematology and oncology, depts. medicine, 1974-86, sr. cons. in hematology and oncology, 1986-91; mem. various coms. Geisinger Med. Ctr., 1959-91; affiliate Leukemia Group B Cancer Control Program, Cornell U., N.Y.C., 1974-78, Eastern Cooperative Oncology Group, Fox Chase, Pa., 1977-86, Mayo Clinic, 1986-87, North Ctrl. Cancer Treatment Group, Mayo Clinic, 1986-91; clin. prof. medicine Pa. State U., Hershey, 1975-87. Prin. author: Anemias Case Studies, 1981; contbr. articles to profl. jours. Active Mid Atlantic Oncology Program, 1984-86; corp. mem. Pa. Blue Shield, Camp Hill, 1972-87, mem. dental affairs com., 1977-79, med. affairs com., 1973-79, med. rev. com. 1980-86, corp. bd. nominating com., 1982-85, mem. profl. adv. coun., alt., 1985-86; bd. dirs. Capital Blue Cross, Harrisburg, Pa., 1969-93, hon. dir., 1993; cons. drug-related patient needs Dept. Health, Edn. and Welfare, NIH, Rockville, Md., 1971, med. surg. task force Dept. Health Commonwealth of Pa., Harrisburg, 1981; Pa. Liaison Coun. for Internal Medicine, 1980-87. Lt. (j.g.) M.C., USN, 1946-49. Recipient awards Pa. State chpt. Alpha Epsilon Delta, Phi Sigma Phi. Fellow ACP (life mem., regional planning com. 1964, program com. 1978, 79, 82, gen. chmn. 1981, book reviewer Annals of Internal Medicine 1964-74, manuscript reviewer Socioecons. 1981); mem. AAAS, AMA, Am. Cancer Soc. (chmn. profl. rels. com. Montour county unit 1959-64, Crusade award 1963), Am. Group Practice Assn. (editl. adv. com. Group Practice 1966-73), Am. Med. Writers Assn. (ad hoc com. on awards 1959), Am. Soc. Clin. Oncology, Am. Soc. Internal Medicine (ho. of dels. 1980-85, reference com. D 1980, meetings com. 1978-83, survey com. 1976, manpower pool 3d party payors 1980), Assn. Cmty. Cancer Ctrs. (Washington) (instl. rep. 1978), Am. Soc. Hematology, Pa. Med. Soc. (med. svcs. com. 1964-72, profl. liability commn. 1979-85, malpractice ins. task force 1966-71, Dept. Pub. Assistance com. 1966, profl. liability appeal com. 1986, pub. policy com. 1984, internal medicine adv. com. 1980-84, contbg. editor Pa. Medicine 1970-84), Pa. Soc. Internal Medicine (med. svcs. com. 1973-80, chmn. 1975-79, membership com. 1980-86, chmn. 1980-86, legis. com. 1981-83, peer rev. com. 1980-86, program chmn. 1978-79, chmn. nominating com. 1980, pres. 1979-80), Pa. Soc. Hematology and Oncology (organizing com. 1964-81, exec. com. 1982-95, pres. 1986-87), Montour County Med. Soc. (chmn. com. on comprehensive health planning 1970, censor, pres.-elect 1971-72, pres. 1972-73), Phila. Hematology Soc., Phi Eta Sigma, Phi Kappa Phi, Phi Beta Kappa, Alpha Omega Alpha. Republican. Lutheran. Achievements include pioneering rsch. with others in human vols. on the ctrl. control of respiration, cerebral blood flow and oxygen toxicity at 1 atm and 3.5 atm O2 partial press; author of 1st authenticated report of an unprovoked attack, with a bite, by a rabid insectivorous bat, alerting public to the insectivorous bat as a significant reservoir of rabies in spite of rarity of an obvious bite and in spite of fact that the method of transmission from bat to man and animals is not obvious; rsch. on recognition of membrane abnormalities of erythrocytes in myeloproliferative disorders by Merocyanine 540.

KOUPAL, RAYMOND, newspaper publishing executive. With Mpls. Star & Tribune, Minn., 1970-77, Morristown Daily Record, N.J., 1977-80, The Bulletin Co., Phila., 1980-82; v.p., cfo The Hartford Courant Co., Conn., 1982—. Office: The Hartford Courant Co 285 Broad St Hartford CT 06115-3785*

KOURI, DONALD JACK, chemist, educator; b. Hobart, Okla., July 25, 1938; s. Eddie and Theresa LaJuan (Williams) K.; m. Shirley Ann Stewart, Apr. 9, 1965; children: Lisa Renee, David Matthew. BA, Okla. Bapt. U., 1960; MS, U. Wis., 1962, PhD, 1965. Postdoctoral fellow Joint Inst. Lab Astrophysics, U. Colo., 1965-66; asst. prof. chemistry Midwestern U., Wichita Falls, 1966-67; asst. prof. chemistry U. Houston, 1967-71, assoc. prof., 1971-73, prof., 1973—, Disting. Univ. prof., 1987-96, Cullen Disting. prof. chemistry, physics; vis. lectr. U. Ill., 1972; vis. scientist Inst. für Strömungsforschung, Göttingen, Fed. Republic Germany, 1973-74. Recipient U.S. Sr. Scientist award Alexander von Humboldt Found., 1973-74, Southwestern Tex. sect. award Am. Chem. Soc., 1981, Sigma Xi Rsch. award, 1995; fellow A.P. Sloan Found., 1972-74, Weizmann Inst., 1973, Inst. for Advanced Studies, Hebrew U. Jerusalem, 1978-79; Guggenheim Found., 1978-79. Fellow Am. Phys. Soc. (exec. com. mem., sec.-treas. Few Body Topical group); mem. IEEE, ASCAP, Am. Chem. Soc., Am. Assn. Physics Tchrs. Democrat. Baptist. Office: U Houston Dept Chemistry 4800 Calhoun Rd Houston TX 77004-2610

KOURIDES, IONE ANNE, endocrinologist, researcher, educator; b. N.Y.C., Sept. 1, 1942; d. Peter T. and Anne E. (Spetseris) K.; m. Charles G. Zaroulis, Nov. 30, 1974; children: Anna Larisa, Andrew, Christina, Peter. BA, Wellesley Coll., 1963; MD, Harvard U., 1967. Diplomate Am. Bd. Internal Medicine, Am. Bd. Endocrinology and Metabolism. Intern Jewish Hosp., Wash. U., St. Louis, 1967-68; resident Montefiore, Albert Einstein Med. Sch., Bronx, N.Y., 1968-69; fellow Beth Israel, Harvard U., Boston, 1970-72; assoc. prof. medicine Cornell U. Med. Coll., N.Y.C., 1981—; sr. assoc. med. dir. Pfizer Pharms., N.Y.C., 1990—. Mem. editorial bd. Endocrinology, Jour. Clin. Endocrinol Metabolism, also others; contbr. over 100 articles to sci. jours., chpts. to books. Mem. nat. campaign Harvard Med. Sch., Boston, 1986-92; nat. bd. dirs. Philoptochos Soc. Greek Orthodox Archdiocese. Grantee NIH, 1979-84. Fellow ACP; mem. Am. Soc. Clin. Investigation, Am. Assn. Physicians, Am. Thyroid Assn. (coms.), Endocrine Soc. (coms.). Achievements include discovery of alpha-secreting pituitary tumors; demonstrated that measurement of amniotic fluid thyroid stimulating hormone can be used to diagnose hypthyroidism in utero. Home: 1070 Park Ave New York NY 10128-1000 Office: Pfizer Pharms 235 E 42nd St New York NY 10017-5755

KOURIDES, PETER THEOLOGOS, lawyer; b. Istanbul, Turkey, July 24, 1910; came to U.S., 1912, naturalized, 1931; s. Theologos and Zafiro (Gurlides) K.; m. Anna E. Spetseris, Aug. 4, 1938; children—Ione A., P. Nicholas. B.A., Columbia, 1931, J.D., 1933; HHD (hon.), Hellenic Coll., 1985. Bar: N.Y. 1933. Mem. firm Seward, Raphael & Kourides, N.Y.C., 1935—; gen. counsel Greek Archdiocese of North and South Am., 1938-96; trustee Hellenic Cathedral City N.Y., 1938-98; trustee, counsel St. Basil's Acad., Garrison, N.Y., 1946-97, United Greek Orthodox Charities, 1965-70; counsel World Conf. Religion for Peace, 1970-82; counsel for Am. affairs to Ecumenical Patriarchate of Eastern Orthodox Ch., Istanbul, 1949-72; dir., counsel Hellenic Am. C. of C., 1955—; dir. Atlantic Bank N.Y., 1974-97; Counsel, consulate gen. of Greece in N.Y., 1963-90; nat. sec. Greek War Relief Assn., 1941-46; rep. Greek Archdiocese of North and South Am. at enthronement Athenagoras I, Istanbul, 1949; pres. Hellenic U. Club, 1951-52. Author: The Evolution of the Greek Orthodox Church in America and its Current Problems, 1959, The Centennial History of the Archdiocesan Cathedral of the Holy Trinity, 1992. Nat. v.p. Order of Ahepa, 1960; mem. gen. bd. Nat. Council Chs., 1960-82, v.p., 1969-72; counsel Columbia U. Cancer Clinic in Greece, 1965-70; del. 3d Assembly World Council Chs., New Delhi, India, 1961, 4th Assembly, Uppsala, Sweden, 1968, 5th Assembly, Nairobi, Kenya, 1975, World Conf. Religion on Peace, Kyoto, Japan, 1971; mem. internat. affairs com. World Council Chs., 1968-74; trustee Hellenic Coll., Brookline, Mass., 1968-97, Modern Greek Library, Columbia, 1958-80. Decorated Gold Cross Order of Phoenix by King Constantine II Greece, 1967, Titular Archon Megas Nomophylax by Ecumenical Partriarchate of Eastern Orthodox Ch., 1968, grand comdr. Knights of Holy Sepulchre Jerusalem Patriarchate of Eastern Orthodox Ch., 1961. Mem. ABA, N.Y. Bar Assn., Consular Law Soc., Am. Judicature Soc., Columbia Alumni Assn. Home: 46 Groton St Forest Hills NY 11375-5921 Office: 110 E 59th St New York NY 10022-1304

KOURLIS, REBECCA LOVE, judge; b. Colorado Springs, Colo., Nov. 11, 1952; d. John Arthur and Ann (Daniels) Love; m. Thomas Aristithis Kourlis, July 15, 1978; children: Stacy Ann, Katherine Love, Aristithis Thomas. BA with distinction in English, Stanford U., 1973, JD, 1976; LLD (hon.), U. Denver, 1997. Bar: Colo. 1976, D.C. 1979, U.S. Dist. Ct. Colo. 1976, U.S. Ct. Appeals (10th cir.) 1976, Colo. Supreme Ct., U.S. Ct. Appeals (D.C. cir.), U.S. Claims Ct., U.S. Supreme Ct. Assoc. Davis, Graham & Stubbs, Denver, 1976-78; sole practice Craig, Craig, Colo., 1978-87; judge 14th Jud. Dist. Ct., Denver, 1987-94; arbiter Jud. Arbiter Group, Inc., 1994-95; justice Colo. Supreme Ct., 1995—, 1995—; water judge divsn. 6, 1987-94; lectr. to profl. groups. Contbr. articles to profl. jours. Chmn. Moffat County Arts and Humanities, Craig, 1979; mem. Colo. Commn. on Higher Edn., Denver, 1980-81; mem. adv. bd. Colo. Divsn. Youth Svcs., 1988-91; mem. com. civil jury instructions, 1990-95, standing com. gender & justice, 1994-97, chair jud. adv. coun., 1997—, chair com. on jury reform, 1996—; co-chair com. on atty. grievance reform, 1997—; mem. long range planning com. Moffat County Sch., 1990; bd. visitors Stanford U., 1989-94, Law Sch. U. Denver, 1997—; bd. dirs. Kent Denver Sch., 1996—. Fellow Am. Bar Found., Colo. Bar Found.; mem. Am. Law Inst., Rocky Mountain Mineral Found., Colo. Bar Assn. (bd. govs. 1983-85, mineral law sect. bd. dirs. 1985, sr. v.p. 1987-88), Dist. Ct. Judges' Assn. (pres. 1993-94), N.W. Colo. Bar Assn. (Cmty. Svc. award 1993-94). Office: State Jud Bldg 2 E 14th Ave Rm 415 Denver CO 80203-2115

KOURLIS, THOMAS A., state commissioner; m. Rebecca Kourlis; 3 children. BS in Fin., U. Denver. Owner, operator cattle and sheep ranch, Craig, Colo., 1973—; commr. Colo. Dept. Agr., Lakewood, 1994—. Mem. Colo. Sheep and Wool Bd.; mem. N.W. Coordinated Resource Mgmt. Steering Com.; mem. Colo. Rangeland Reform Working Group; a founder Habitat Partnership Program. Mem. Soc. Range Mgmt. (award for excellence in grazing mgmt.), Colo. Woolgrowers Assn. (pasat v.p.), Am. sheep Industry Assn. (past bd. dirs.). Office: Colo Dept Agr 700 Kipling St Ste 4000 Lakewood CO 80215

KOURY, AGNES LILLIAN, real estate owner and manager; b. Denver, Oct. 16, 1935; d. John Joseph and Lucy Maria (Plomteaux) K.; m. William L. May, July 21, 1958 (div. 1961); 1 child, Tia Leslie Koury. BSBA, U. Denver, 1958; protocol cert., Southeastern U., 1964; paralegal cert., Georgetown U., 1978; MA, Marymount U., 1991. Registered profl. realtor, Va. Com. sec. N.Mex. Ho. of Reps., Santa Fe, 1959; contracts sec. Atomic Energy Commn., Albuquerque, 1959-63; ptnr. legal sec. Sughrue, Rothwell, Washington, 1963-65; legal asst. McClure & Trotter, Washington, 1965-67; case worker U.S. Ho. of Reps., Washington, 1968; adminstrv., rsch. asst. Harvard U., Washington, 1969-73; asst. mgr. Koury's Real Estate, Sant Fe, 1974-85; owner, mgr. various realty properties, Santa Fe and Arlington, 1985—. Pres. Yorktown Condominium, Arlington, 1972-74, bd. dirs.; treas. Birches Homeowners Assn., Arlington, 1987-90; chmn., vol. spkrs. bur. Hospice of No. Va., Arlington, 1993—, mem. spkrs. bur., 1985—, mem. 20th anniversary com., 1996-97, chmn. Tree of Lights event, 1999; bd. dirs. Arlington Symphony Assn., 1990—, chmn. music scholarship competition for no. Va. high sch. students, 1994—, chmn. artistic and edn. com., 1997. Mem. Delta Sigma Epsilon, Phi Gamma Nu (Outstanding Mem. 1958). Roman Catholic. Avocations: travel, writing, poetry, playing piano, picture puzzles. Home and Office: 4741 23rd St N Arlington VA 22207-3408

KOUSPARIS, DIMITRIOS, oil consulting company executive; b. Greece, May 16, 1949; came to U.S., 1973; s. John and Vicky Kousparis; m. Helen Pritzos, Dec. 26, 1976; children: Vicky, Johnny, Andy. BS, U. Athens, Greece, 1973; MS, U. Okla., 1975; PhD, U. Tulsa, 1979. Cons. Rsch. Ctr. Amoco Prodn. Co., Tulsa, 1976-78; interpreter geophysicist Conoco Inc., Houston, 1979-80, dir. exploratory wells, 1987-89, area geophyicist, 1989-90, economist, 1990-93; interpreter geophysicist Conoco, London, 1980-84; chief geophysicist Conoco, The Netherlands, 1984-87; founder, pres. Strategic Petroleum Investment Cons. Enterprise Inc., Katy, Tex., 1993—; dir. Greek lang. sch. Nea Vassileiada, 1992-95. Founder, pres. Nea Vassileiada, Hellenic ednl. and religious orgn., Houston, 1992, 93, 94, 95, 96; co-founder St. Basil the Great Greek Orthodox Ch., Houston, pres., 1993, 94. Mem. Soc. Exploration Geophysicists, Am. Assn. Petroleum Geologists.

KOUSSA, HAROLD ALAN, insurance account executive; b. Central Falls, R.I., June 20, 1947; s. Harold Albert and June Joann (John) K. BSEngring. Sci., U. R.I., 1969; MBA Fin., U. Hartford, 1975; MS in Engring. Sci. Nuclear Engring., Rensselaer Poly. Inst., 1977. Lic. property and casualty prodr., Conn. Reactor engring. asst. Conn. Yankee Atomic Power Co., Haddam Neck, 1969-75, reactor engr., 1975-77; staff nuclear engr. Am. Nuclear Insurers, Farmington, Conn., 1977-79, sr. staff nuclear engr., 1979-81, prin. engr., 1981-82; mgr. ops., 1982-89, account exec., 1989-93, cons., 1993-94; account exec. Indsl. Risk Insurers, Hartford, Conn., 1994-97; account mgr., sen. account exec. Arkwright, Waltham, Mass., 1997—. Mem East Hampton Rep. Town Com., 1982-88; del. Conn. Rep. Conv., 1982, 84, 86; mem. East Hampton Water Pollution Control Authority, 1982-88, vice chmn., 1984-85, chmn., 1985-88. Comdr. USNR, qualified engring. duty officer, 1982—. Recipient Navy Commendation medal, Navy Achievement medal, 2nd Navy Achievement medal, 3d award Navy Achievement medal, Nat. Defense Svc. medal, Mil. Outstanding Vol. Svc. medal, Armed Forces

Res. medal. Mem. ASME, Am. Nuc. Soc., Am. Soc. Naval Engrs., U.S. Naval Inst., Navy League U.S., Naval Res. Assn., Res. Officers Assn., Masons, U. R.I. Fast Break Club. Home: 26 Meadowlark Dr Windsor CT 06095-1533

KOUSSER, J(OSEPH) MORGAN, history educator; b. Lewisburg, Tenn., Oct. 7, 1943; s. Joseph Maximillian and Alice Holt (Morgan) K.; m. Sally Ann Ward, June 1, 1968; children: Rachel Meredith, Thaddeus Benjamin. AB, Princeton U., 1965; M.Phil., Yale U., 1968, PhD, 1971; MA, Oxford U., Eng., 1984. Instr. Calif. Inst. Tech., Pasadena, 1969-71; assoc. prof. Calif. Inst. Tech., Padadena, 1975-79, prof., 1979—; vis. prof. U. Mich., Ann Arbor, 1980, Harvard U., Cambridge, Mass., 1981-82, Oxford U., 1984-85, Claremont Grad. Sch., 1993; expert witness Minority Voting Rights Cases; researcher. Author: Shaping of Southern Politics, 1974, Colorblind Injustice: Minority Voting Rights and the Undoing of the Second Reconstruction, 1999. Guggenheim Found. fellow, 1984-85, Woodrow Wilson Ctr. fellow, 1984-85; grantee NEH, 1974, 82. Mem. Orgn. Am. Historians, Am. Hist. Assn., Social Scis. History Assn., So. Hist. Assn. Democrat. Avocation: running. Office: Calif Inst of Tech 228-77 Caltech Pasadena CA 91125

KOUTAS, SAMUEL DEMETRIOS, human resources executive; b. Royal Oak, Mich., Sept. 24, 1930; s. James Samuel and Angeline (Xenos) K.; m. Bess Hatzopoulos, Oct. 23, 1960; children: James Samuel, Dina Elizabeth. BS in Mktg., Wayne State U., Detroit, 1952; BS in Naval Sci., U.S. Naval Acad., Annapolis, Md., 1956. Mgr. GE, 1960-91; dep. to mayor Town of Fairfield, Conn., 1991-97; mem. exec. com. bd. dirs. Bridgeport (Conn.) Econ. Devel. Corp., 1985-91. Bd. dirs. Chgo. Cosmpolitan Chamber, Discovery Mus., Bridgeport, 1982-92, Greater Bridgeport Symphony, 1985—. Lt. USN, 1952-60, capt. Res. ret. Mem. U.S. Naval Inst. Avocations: reading, tennis, walking. Home: 2979 Burr St Fairfield CT 06430-1853

KOUTROULIS, ARIS GEORGE, artist, educator; b. Athens, Greece, May 14, 1938; came to U.S., 1953; s. George Aris and Julia (Eftimiades) K.; m. Mary Ann Schmid, 1964 (div. 1973); m. Jill Warren, July 4, 1982; 1 child, Georgina. BFA, La. State U., 1961; Master Printer, Tamarind Lithography Workshop, L.A., 1964; MFA, Cranbrook Acad. Art, Bloomfield Hills, Mich., 1966. Chmn. bd. Willis Gallery, Detroit, 1970-71; pres. Common Ground of the Arts, Detroit, 1969-72; guest artist Ox-Bow Summer Sch. Art, Saugatuck, Mich., 1973; co-dir. Ox-Bow Summer Sch. Art, Saugatuck, 1975; assoc. prof. art Wayne State U., 1966-75; head painting dept. Ctr. Creative Studies, Detroit, 1975-81; prof., chmn. Fine Arts Dept. Ctr. Creative Studies, 1981—. exhibited one-man shows Hanamura Gallery, Detroit, 1966, Montgomery Mus. Fine Arts, Ala., 1966, Va. Poly. Inst., 1968, Baton Rouge Gallery, 1968, Wayne State U., 1969, Mich. Council for Arts, 1969, Gertrude Kasle Gallery, Detroit, 1970, Detroit Artists Market, 1973, Klein-Vogel Gallery, Detroit, 1974, Detroit Inst. Arts, 1976, Gloria Cortella Gallery, N.Y.C., 1977, Gallery Renaissance, Detroit, 1980, Haber-Theodore Gallery, N.Y.C., 1980, OK Harris Gallery, N.Y.C., 1980, 81, 82, 83, 85, 87, 90, 92, 98, Mich. Traveling Exhbn., 1981, Cantor/Cemberg Gallery, Birmingham, Mich., 1982, 88, Dubins Gallery, L.A., 1984, Nimbus Gallery, Dallas, 1986, Argo Gallery, Athens, Greece, 1988, Argo Gallery, Cypres, 1991, 94, OK Harris Works of Art, Birmingham, Mich., 1991, Art Gallery Registry Resort, Naples, Fla., 1992, Bell Gallery, B'haui, 1995, Ctr. Gallery, Detroit, 1996; exhibited group shows Decorative Arts Ctr., N.Y.C., 1973, Detroit Inst. Arts, 1974, Bykert Gallery, N.Y.C., 1974, Bklyn. Mus., 1977, Brooks Meml. Art Gallery, Memphis, 1977, La. State U. Gallery, 1978, Tyler Sch. Art, Temple U., 1978, Mus. Fine Arts, Springfield, Mass., 1978, Van Doren Gallery, San Francisco, 1978, Consulate Gen. Greece, N.Y.C., 1978, Landmark Gallery, N.Y.C., 1978, Cranbrook Mus. Art, Bloomfield Hills, Mich., 1979, Detroit Inst. Arts, 1980, Mus. Fine Arts Tampa, 1987, 51st nat. mid-yr. exhbn. Butler Inst. Am. Art, Youngstown, Ohio, 1987, Flint Mus. of Art. Mich., 1989, Japan Expo, Tokyo, 1989, Ctr. Gallery Ctr. Creative Studies, Detroit, 1989, 95, 97; represented in pub. collections including Mus. Modern Art, Nat. Gallery Art, Detroit Inst. Arts, L.A. County Mus. Art, Cranbrook Mus. Art, Detroit Engring. Soc., Detroit Pub. Libr., U. Mich. Art Mus., Anglo-Am. Mus., Amon Carter Mus. Western Art, Ft. Worth, UCLA Grunwald Graphic Arts Found., Ball State U. Art Mus., Vores Mus., Athens, The Goulandis Mus. Modern Art, Andros, Greece; represented in corp. collections; commd. Standard Oil Corp., San Ramon, Calif., Arbor Drugs, Inc., Bracewell/Patterson, Washington, Mich. Found. for Arts, Detroit Engring. Soc., Art for Detroit, City of Detroit, WDIV-TV4, Detroit, Tampa Mus. Collection, Criterion Ctr., N.Y.C., Masco Corp., Taylor, Mich. Address: PO Box 307 Denver NY 12421-0307

KOUTS, HERBERT JOHN CECIL, physicist; b. Bisbee, Ariz., Dec. 18, 1919; s. Oliver Allen and Lillian (Niemeyer) K.; m. Hertha Pretorius, Feb. 2, 1942; children: Anne Elizabeth, Catherine Jennifer; m. Barbara Stokes, Mar. 27, 1974; stepchildren: Francis Spitzer, Michael Spitzer, Daniel Spitzer. B.S., La. State U., 1941, M.S., 1946; Ph.D., Princeton U., 1952. With Brookhaven Nat. Lab., Upton, L.I., N.Y., 1950-73, 77-89; sr. scientist, asso. div. head Brookhaven Nat. Lab., 1958-73, chmn. dept. nuclear energy, 1977-88; mem. Def. Nuclear Facilities Safety Bd., U.S. Govt., Washington, 1989—; dir. div. reactor safety rsch. AEC, Washington, 1973-75; dir. Office Nuclear Regulatory Rsch., U.S. Nuclear Regulatory Commn., Washington, 1975-76; mem. adv. com. reactor physics AEC, 1956-63, mem. adv. com. reactor safeguards, 1962-66; mem. European Am. Adv. Com. for Reactor Physics to European Nuclear Energy Agy., 1962-68; mem. internat. nuclear safety adv. group to IAEA, 1985-92. Served with USAAF, 1942-45. Recipient E. O. Lawrence award AEC, 1963, Disting. Service award, 1975; Disting. Service award NRC, 1976, Sec. Energy's Gold medal for achievement, 1999. Mem. Am. Nuclear Soc. (Theos Thompson award in nuclear reactor safety 1983), N.Y. Acad. Scis., Center Moriches Audubon Soc., Nat. Acad. Engring. Home: 249 S Country Rd Brookhaven NY 11719-9704 Office: Defense Nuclear Facilities Safety Board 625 Indiana Ave NW Ste 7000 Washington DC 20004-2923

KOUTSKY, DEAN ROGER, advertising executive; b. Omaha, Nov. 17, 1935; s. John Lewis and Ann Helen (Swan) K.; m. Kathryn Junette Strand; children: Linda, Lisa. BFA, Mpls. Coll. Art and Design, 1957. Art dir. Knox Reeves Advt., Inc., Mpls., 1958-65; v.p., exec. art dir. BBDO, Inc., Mpls., 1965-70; v.p., assoc. creative dir. Campbell-Mithun, Inc., Mpls., 1970-80, sr. v.p., creative dir., 1980-83, exec. v.p., exec. creative dir., 1983-85, vice chmn., 1985-89; exec. cons. Campbell-Mithun Esty, Inc., Mpls., 1989-90; ptnr., mgr. Harmon Ct., 1991-97; bd. trustees Mpls. Coll. Art and Design, 1982-90, chmn., bd. trustees, 1985-89, adj. prof. advt./design divsn., 1995—. Office: 2005 James Ave S Minneapolis MN 55405-2404

KOUVEL, JAMES SPYROS, physicist, educator; b. Jersey City, May 23, 1926; s. Spyros and Ifegenia (Cassianos) K.; m. Audrey Lumsden, June 26, 1953; children: Diana, Alexander. B.Engring., Yale U., 1946, Ph.D., 1951. Research fellow U. Leeds, Eng., 1951-53, Harvard, 1953-55; physicist Gen. Electric Co. Research and Devel. Center, 1955-69; prof. physics U. Ill.-Chgo., 1969—; vis. scientist Atomic Energy Rsch. Establishment, Harwell, Eng., 1967-68; vis. prof. U. Paris, Orsay, France, 1981; cons. Argonne (Ill.) Nat. Lab., 1969-89, mem. rev. com., 1970-72, vis. scientist, 1973-74; mem. materials rsch. adv. com. NSF, 1980-82, mem. materials rsch. groups spl. emphasis panel, 1993; mem. evaluation panel NRC, 1981-85. Author papers in field.; Editor: Magnetism Conf. proc, 1965-67; editorial bd.: Jour. Magnetism and Magnetic Materials, 1975—. Served with USNR, 1944-46. Guggenheim fellow, 1967-68; NSF rsch. grantee, 1973-96. Fellow Am. Phys. Soc., AAAS. Home: 223 N Euclid Ave Oak Park IL 60302-2107 Office: U Ill Physics Dept Chicago IL 60607-7059

KOUWENHOVEN, GERRIT WOLPHERTSEN, museum director; b. Mt. Kisco, N.Y., May 8, 1939; s. John Atlee and Eleanor Warren (Hayden) K.; m. Ellen Mather Davis, June 17, 1961; children: Derek Gerritsen, Kirsten Elizabeth. BA in English, U. Colo., 1962, postgrad., 1962-64; postgrad., Seattle Pacific U., 1975-76, Antioch, 1981-82. Human rights intern Eleanor Roosevelt Meml. Found., 1964-65; field rep., investigator equal opportunities divsn. State of Wis. Indsl. Commn., 1964-66; from employment specialist to asst. dir. Seattle Urban League, 1966-73; pvt. practice campaign cons., 1973-75; tchr. English, chair dept. English LaConner (Wash.) High Sch., 1976-78; tchr. English Arlington (Vt.) Meml. High Sch., 1978-79; pvt. practice rschr., 1979-80; dean Ethan Allen C.C., Manchester Center, Vt., 1981-82; with Friends of Hildene, Inc., Manchester, Vt., 1983—, exec. dir., 1986—. Mem. chancel choir First Congl. Ch., Manchester, 1979—, chair stewardship, 1980-82, 91-93, bd. trustees, 1981-84, 91-94, co-chair bicentennial steering com., 1983-84, bd. deacons, 1985-88, 96-99, chair, 1986, chair search com., 1986-88, 1996-98; trustee Dorset (Vt.) Players, Inc., 1983-91, treas., 1986-91; bd. trustees Long Trail Sch., Dorset, 1988-98, vice chair, 1989-90, 96-97, chair, 1990-96; bd. trustees Am. Theatre Works, Inc., Dorset, 1990-94, chair fin. com., 1992-94; bd. dirs. Preservation Trust Vt., Windsor, 1991—, v.p., 1993, pres., 1994—; bd. trustees United Counseling Svc. Bennington County, Inc., 1992—, sec., 1994—, v.p., 1995—, pres., 1996—, Bennington County Mental Health Fund, 1994-98; mem. allocation com. United Way Bennington County, 1992-95; bd. dirs. Vt. Conf. United Ch. of Christ, 1998—. Recipient Cmty. Svc. award Manchester C. of C., 1994. Mem. Dorset Nursing Assn. (bd. dirs. 1997—, sec. 1997—), Lions (Manchester chpt., bd. dirs. 1984-94, sec. 1984-88, pres. 1991-93). Office: Hildene Rte 7 S PO Box 377 Manchester VT 05254

KOUYMJIAN, DICKRAN, art historian, Orientalist, educator; b. Tulcea, Romania, June 6, 1934; came to U.S. (parents Am. citizens), 1939; s. Toros S. and Zabelle I. (Calusdian) K.; m. Angèle Kapoïan, Sept. 16, 1967. BS in European Cultural History, U. Wis., 1957; MA in Arab Studies, Am. U., Beirut, 1961; PhD in Near East Lang. and Culture, Columbia U., 1969. Instr. English Columbia U., N.Y.C., 1961-64; dir. Am. Authors, Inc., N.Y.C., 1965-67; asst. prof. and asst. dir. Ctr. for Arabic Studies Am. U., Cairo, 1967-71; assoc. prof. history Am. U. Beirut, 1971-75; prof. art history Am. U., Paris, 1976-77; prof. history and art, dir. Armenian Studies program Calif. State U., Fresno, 1977—; dir. Sarkis and Meline Kalfayan Ctr. for Armenian Studies, Calif. State U., Fresno, 1990—; Fulbright disting. lectr., prof. Armenian and Am. Lit., Yerevan (Armenia, USSR), 1987; cons. archaeology UNESCO, Paris, 1976; prof., chairholder Armenian Sect., Inst. Nat. des Langs. et Civilisations Orientales, U. Paris, 1988-91; 1st incumbent Haig & Isabel Berberian endowed chair Armenian Studies Calif. State U., Fresno, 1989—, 2nd incumbent William Saroyan endowed chair of Armenian studies U. Calif., Berkeley, 1996-97. Author: Index of Armenian Art, part I, 1977, part II, 1979, The Armenian History of Ghazar P'arpetzi, 1986, Arts of Armenia, 1992; co-author: (with A. Kapoïan) The Splendor of Egypt, 1975; author and editor: William Saroyan: An Armenian Trilogy, 1986, William Saroyan: Warsaw Visitor and Tales of the Vienna Streets, 1990; editor: (books) Near Eastern Numistatics, Iconography, Epigraphy and History, 1974, Essays in Armenian Numismatics in Honor of C. Sibilian, 1981, Armenian Studies: In Memoriam Haïg Berbèrian, 1986; editl. bd. Armenian Rev., 1974—, Ararat Lit. mag., 1975—, Revue des Etudes Armèniennes, 1978—, NAASR Jour. Armenian Studies, Jour. of the Soc. for Armenian Studies, 1995—; contbr. articles to profl. jours. Served with U.S. Army, 1957. Recipient St. Sahaq and St. Mesrob medal His Holiness Karekin I, Catholics of All Armenians, 1996, Outstanding Prof. award Am. U., Cairo, 1968-69, 69-70, Outstanding Prof. of Yr. award Calif. State U., 1985-86, Hagop Kevorkian Disting. Lectureship in Near Eastern Art and Civilization, NYU, 1979; Fulbright fellow, USSR, 1986-87; grantee NEH, Paris, 1980-81, 95, Bertha & John Garabedian Charitable Found., 1994-99. Mem. Am. Oriental Soc., Am. Numismatic Soc., Mid. East Studies Assn. (charter), Coll. Arts Assn., Soc. Armenian Studies (charter, pres. 1985-86, 92-94), Sociéte asiatique (Paris), Medieval Acad., Internat. Assn. of Armenian Studies, Mid. East Medievalist, Assn. Paléographique Internat., Phi Kappa Phi (nat. scholar Fresno chpt. 1998, Univ. Scholar award chpt. 962 1999). Avocations: music, film, bibliophile. Home: 30 rue Chevert, 75007 Paris France Office: Calif State U Armenian Studies Program 5245 N Backer Ave # Pb4 Fresno CA 93740-8001

KOUYOUMJIAN, CHARLES H., diversified financial services company executive; b. Cambridge, Mass., Nov. 20, 1940; s. Housep J. and Victoria M. (Madenjian) K.; m. Donna A. Daniels; children: Joseph, Charles. BS in Bus. Adminstrn., Boston U., 1963; postgrad., Boston Coll., 1969-71. Dir. purchasing Allis Chalmers Mfg. Co., Boston, 1968; investment broker Hornblower & Weeks Hemphill Noyes Inc., Boston, 1969-71; v.p., resident mgr. Hornblower & Weeks Hemphill Noyes Inc., Springfield, Mass., 1971-76; regional hdqrs. Hornblower & Weeks Hemphill Noyes Inc., Boston, 1976-77; v.p., resident mgr. Paine Webber, Inc., Boston, 1977-79, regional sales mgr. Fla. divsn., 1980-81, v.p. spl. accounts dept., 1983-85; dir. Asset Mgmt. Group, nat. hdqrs. Paine Webber, Inc., N.Y.C., 1982-83; pres., CEO Empire Nat. Securities, Buffalo, 1985-88, Charles Assocs., 1988—. Mem. camp com. Springfield YMCA, 1973-76; bd. dirs. Health Care Found. Western Mass., 1973-74. Served to capt. USAF, 1963-67. Mem. Boston Options Soc. (chmn.), Springfield C. of C. (bd. dirs. 1973-75), Nat. Assn. Securities Dealers (mem. quotation com. 1975-76), Boston Fin. Rsch. Assocs., Boston U. Alumni Assn. (bd. dirs.), Boston Investment Club, Boston Stockbrokers Club, Securities Industry Assn., Newsomen Soc. U.S. and Gt. Britain, Internat. Assn. Fin. Planning, Bond Club of Boston, Bond Club of Buffalo. Home: 616 Lewis Wharf Boston MA 02110-3915 Office: Charles Assocs 125 Middlesex Tpke Bedford MA 01730-1409

KOUYOUMJIAN, ROBERT G., electrical engineering educator; b. Apr. 26, 1923. BS in Physics, Ohio State U., 1948, PhD in Physics, 1953. Prof. emeritus dept. elec. engring. Ohio State U.; mem. URSI Commn. B. Fellow IEEE (Fellow award, Disting. Lectr., Centennial medal 1984); mem. Sigma Xi, Eta Kappa Nu, Sigma Pi Sigma. Office: Ohio State U Dept of Elec Engring 2015 Neil Ave Dept Of Columbus OH 43210-1210*

KOVAC, MICHAEL G., engineering educator; b. June 9, 1941. BSEE, U. Notre Dame, 1963; MS, Northwestern U., 1968, PhD, 1970. Dean coll. engring. U. South Fla., Tampa, 1986—. Fellow IEEE (mem. admission and advancement com.). Office: Univ So Florida Coll Engring Deans Office 4202 E Fowler Ave ENB 118 Tampa FL 33620*

KOVACEK, DUANE MICHAEL, secondary school educator; b. Lake Forest, Ill., Oct. 31, 1948; s. Albert G. and Katherine (Macinovich) K.; m. Kathy Ann Whitton, July 22, 1972 (dec. Sept., 1988); children: Kristin Ann. AA, Amundson-Mayfair Jr. Coll., 1969; BA, Western Ill. U., 1970; MA, Roosevelt U., 1977. Cert. secondary shc. tchr., spl. reading tchr., adminstr./supr., Ill. Computer operator Abbott Labs., North Chicago, Ill., 1971-72; tchr., coach, lang. arts liaison, drama dir. North Chicago H.S., 1972—; tournament mgr. Warhawk Forensics Program, North Chicago, 1972—. Block capt. Neighborhood Watch Program, Gurnee, Ill., 1990—; prodr. performing arts/flower show Ptnrs. in Progress, North Chicago, 1985—. Named Tchr. of Yr., North Chicago VFW, 1990, Chicagoland Educator of Month, Coca Cola, 1995, Educator of Week, Chgo. Sun Times, 1997. mem. Ill. Speech and Theater Assn. (contbr. to newsletter), Scotie Orgn. (commr. 1988-92), Nat. Coun. Tchrs. English, Croatian Fraternal Union Am., We. Ill. U. Alumni Assn. Avocations: fishing, gardening, amateur theater, television production, travel. Home: 1050 Ferndale Ave Gurnee IL 60031-2273 Office: North Chicago HS 1717 17th St North Chicago IL 60064-2052

KOVACEVIC, BRENDA L., sales administrator; b. Massillon, Ohio, Feb. 12, 1962; d. George Lewis and Marjorie Alice (Hockenberry) Gortney; m. William Kovacevic, July 27, 1985; 1 child, Layla. BS in Materials Sci., Northwestern U., 1984; MS in Elec. Engring., Santa Clara U., 1991; postgrad., Heriot-Watt U., Scotland, 1996—. Dir. strategic mktg. Gahtoo Tech. Vol. Silicon Valley Ball Found. Mem. IEEE. Avocations: jazz trumpet, skiing. Home: 927 Wilmington Way Redwood City CA 94062-4068

KOVACEVICH, RICHARD M., banker. BA, Stanford U., 1965, MBA, 1967. Exec. v.p. Kenner div. Gen. Mills, Inc., Mpls., 1967-72; prin. Venture Capital, 1972-75; v.p. consumer services Norwest Corp., Mpls., from 1975, then sr. v.p. N.Y.C. banking group, then exec. v.p., mgr. N.Y.C. bank div., then exec. v.p.. mem. policy com., vice-chmn., chief operating officer banking group, from 1986, now pres., chief oper. officer, vice chmn., also dir., chmn., CEO, 1996—, now chmn., CEO; pres., CEO Norwest Svcs. Inc., Mpls., 1999—. Office: Norwest Svcs Inc 255 2d Ave S Minneapolis MN 55479*

KOVACH, ANDREW LOUIS, administrative executive; b. Greensboro, Pa., Feb. 4, 1948; s. Andrew and Pauline (Nassar) K.; m. Cindy Juliani, Nov. 28, 1970; 1 child: Courtney. BS in Indsl. Engineering, W.Va. U., 1969. Engr. DuPont, Martinville, Va., 1970-73; supt. engr. Allied Corp., Syracuse, N.Y., 1973-75; mgr. employee rels. Allied Corp., Morristown, N.J., 1976-80, mgr. orgnl. devel., 1980; dir. human resources Allied Corp., N.Y.C., 1981-82, dir. comml. devel., 1983-87; ptnr. Thomas Andrew Assoc., Morristown, N.J., 1987—; sr. v.p. human resources, info. systems Morristown Meml. Hosp., 1988-96; v.p. human resources and shared svcs. Atlantic Health Sys., Florham Park, N.J., 1996—; bd. dirs. Morris County Rides; chmn. bd. Morristown Meml. Physician Hosp. Orgn. Mem. pers. com., mem. ethics com. Morris Twp.; co-compliance officer Atlantic Health Sys. Mem. Indsl. Engring. Adv. Orgn., Morristown Club, Park Ave. Club. Presbyterian. Office: Atlantic Health System 325 Columbia Tpke Florham Park NJ 07932-1212

KOVACH, BARBARA ELLEN, management and psychology educator; b. Ann Arbor, Mich., Dec. 28, 1941; d. Harry Arnold and Margaret Mayne (Buell) Lusk; m. Craig Randall Duncan, Dec. 28, 1963 (div. 1973); children: Deborah Louise, Mark Randall; m. Randall Louis Kovach, May 2, 1981; 1 child, Jennifer Elizabeth. *Great grandparents traveled west to Montana in the 1800s, eventually settling in the western United States. They had two children, one of whom was grandfather Lloyd Buell, a 1903 graduate of MIT. Married Eleanor Newcomb and lived in Chile, South America. Their eldest child, Margaret Mayne Bell, is Barbara's mother. She married Harry Lusk, doctor and Chief of Staff at Hollywood Presbyterian Hospital. They had three children. Barbara also had three children. Deborah is a senior manager in an Austin research firm. Mark, has developed strong abilities in sales. Jennifer, still in high school, participates in swimming, singing and tutoring.* BA magna cum laude, Stanford U., 1963, MA, 1964; PhD, U. Md., 1973. Asst. prof. psychology U. Mich., Dearborn, 1973-77, assoc. prof., 1977-82, prof., 1982-84, chair Dept. Behavioral Scis., 1980-83; dean Univ. Coll. Rutgers U., New Brunswick, N.J., 1984-88, prof. mgmt. and psychology, 1984—, dir. leadership devel. program, 1988—; pres. Leadership Devel. Inst., Princeton, N.J., 1990—; cons. Rochester (N.Y.) Products-GM, Grand Rapids, Mich., 1982-87, Ford Motor Co., Dearborn, 1981-82, Mich. Bell Telephone, 1980-81, Rockwell Internat., Troy, Mich, 1993-97, Meritor Automotive, Troy, 1997—, Johnson & Johnson, 1995-97. *Over twenty-five years in the academic world has brought Barbara from early studies in mathematics, history and French, to the fortunate position of combining teaching of organizational behavior in its various guises with active consulting with major companies, primarily in the automobile industry, where she draws the raw material for her research and writing. She is head of the Leadership Development Program in the School of Business at Rutgers University, and head of the Leadership Development Institute in Princeton, New Jersey. She is author of numerous books and articles and is completing requirements for a license as a clinical psychologist in New Jersey.* Author: Sex Roles and Personal Awareness, 1978, 90, Power and Love, 1982, Organizational Synch, 1983, Adolescent Experience, 1983, The Flexible Organization, 1984, Survival on the Fast Track, 1988, 93, Organization Gameboard, 1989, Leaders in Place, 1994, More About Survival on the Fast Track, 1996; producer (videotape series) Keys to Leadership I, 1991-93, II, 1993-94, III, 1995-97; contbr. articles to profl. jours. Daniel E. Prescott fellow U. Md., 1972; recipient Susan B. Anthony and Faculty Recognition awards U. Mich., 1980. Mem. Am. Psychol. Assn., Acad. Mgmt., Organizational Devel. Network, Phi Beta Kappa. Republican. Episcopalian. Home: 19 Woodland Dr Princeton NJ 08540-1313 Office: Rutgers U Sch of Bus 94 Rockafeller Rd Piscataway NJ 08854

KOVACH, BILL, educational foundation administrator; b. Greeneville, Tenn., Sept. 16, 1932; s. John and Olga (Sicos) K.; m. Lynne Marie Stamm, Jan. 11, 1956; children: Teresa, David, Charles, John. BS, East Tenn. State U., 1959. Gen. assignment Press-Chronicle, Johnson City, Tenn., 1959-61; reporter Nashville Tennessean, 1961-68, N.Y. Times, N.Y.C., 1968-79; Washington bur. chief N.Y. Times, Washington, 1979-86; editor Atlanta Jour.-Constitution, 1986-88; curator Nieman Found., Harvard U., 1989—; lectr. Ball State U., Muncie, Ind., 1981; mem. internat. adv. bd. Warsaw Ind. Press Ctr.; mem. adv. bd. Africa News; mem. adv. com. Ctr. for Pub. Integrity; chmn. Com. Concerned Journalists. Co-author: Warp Speed: America in the Age of Mixed Media; contbr. to Assignment America, 1984, The Art of Writing Non-Fiction, 1986. Adv. bd. The Com. to Protect Journalists. With USN, 1951-55. Stanford Profl. Journalism fellow, 1967-68, NSF grantee, 1959. Mem. AAAS. Office: Nieman Found One Francis Ave Cambridge MA 02138

KOVACH, DORIS ANNE, critical care nurse; b. Doniphan, Mo., July 18, 1945; d. Samuel H. and Mary Catherine (Martin) Leonard; m. Mickey L. Kovach, Apr. 25, 1964; children: Mickey D., Margie Thomas, Pamela Day. AD, Three Rivers Community Coll., Poplar Bluff, Mo., 1981. RN, Mo.; cert. ACLS. Staff nurse emergency rm. AMI Lucy Lee Health Care Sys., Poplar Bluff, 1981-83; staff nurse CCU AMI Lucy Lee Hosp., Poplar Bluff, 1983-87, nurse mgr. CCU, 1987-93, 1st interventional radiology nurse, 1993—, part-time x-ray interventional nurse, 1992-93, procedure nurse, 1994-99; procedure nurse Tenet (formerly AMI Lucy Lee Hosp.), Poplar Bluff, 1999—. Mem. AACCN, ARNA.

KOVACH, EUGENE GEORGE, government official, consultant; b. Irvington, N.J., May 18, 1922; s. Eugene John and Hortense Marie (Telmany) K.; m. Mary Eleanor Frenning, Apr. 11, 1950; children—George Eugene, Mary Edith, Katherine Eleanor, Christine Marie, John Peter. B.S., Wayne U., 1943, M.S., 1944; M.A., Harvard U., 1948, Ph.D., 1949. Mem. faculty, research organic chemistry Colgate U., 1950-51, U. Fla., 1949-54; sci. adviser to comdr. U.S. Naval Forces, Germany, 1954-57; with NSF, 1958, State Dept., Washington, 1959-70; acting dir. Office Gen. Sci. Affairs, 1966-70; dep. asst. sec.-gen. for sci. affairs NATO, Brussels, Belgium, 1970-76, Div. Policy Research NSF, 1976-78; dir. Office Advanced Tech., Dept. State, 1978-82; cons. Dept. State, 1982—; alt. U.S. rep. NATO Sci. Com., 1982-95. Capt. USNR, 1944-45. Recipient Wayne U. Disting. Alumnus award, 1961. Mem. Am. Chem. Soc., AAAS, Sigma Xi. Home: 4118 Aspen St Chevy Chase MD 20815-5059 Office: US Dept of State Washington DC 20520

KOVACH, GEORGE DANIEL, writer; b. Fairfield, Calif., Dec. 29, 1951; s. George Elmer and Margaret Evelyn (Shaner) K.; m. Anne Marie Pleskovic, Jan. 23, 1980 (dec. Apr. 1993); children: Aria, Aura. Grad. high sch., Monaca, Pa. Author/writer ASCAP, N.Y.C., 1978—; one-man theater Verseary Prodns., various locations, 1969—; Shakespearean poet Lundonia House, London, 1984—; rec. artist Eastern Recording, Richmond, Va., 1977-78; Shakespearean actor Coun. of the Arts, Trenton, N.J., 1985—; poet, actor Renaissance Faire, Mt. Hope, Pa.; artist in residence at several schs. Author: Passion of a Peasant, 1978, Three Dreams of Obsession, 1983, Tales and Legends of Immortality, 1983, Blessed Be Thine...and Other Verses, 1989, Graveless, 1992, Poetry and Tales for the Little Ones, As Night Now Enters, George and the Jester, Candleberry Tale, Enchanted Melody, Love and the Wind, Poet and the Poetess, The Tale of Woodland Shire, Tale Bearer's Whimsical Tale, Omen from a Stranger, Rune of Rose Lee, Mistress of the Ravens, When White Roses Turn Brown, Mr. Velvet Ears, The Adventures of Thicket Hollow, Other Side of Darkness, Octobering Haunt, Among Tallowing Embers, Anytime! Bedtime! Rhymes!, From the Heart, A Basket Full of Six Tales, Fairytales of the Wintry Kind, Festoon Balloons, Forevermore!, Bough of Amenity, Quest for the Devil's Bones, Lore of Elizabeth Ann, Battlefields and Drum Sticks, From The Edge of Time, Words of The Spirits, Of Midnight Tales Obsessed, Allow Thy Candle to Light Up Your Moon; feature writer Smile Mag.; rec. artist: She's Crying My Tears, No One. Recipient Golden Poet award World of Poetry Press, 1989, 90, 91, 92, Outstanding Poet of 1994, 95 award, Nat. Libr. of Poetry, Man of the Year award, Internat. Biog. Ctr., Cambridge, Eng., 1996, Internat. Man of Yr., Order of Internat. Fellowship, 1996; Five Hundred Leaders of Influence Man of Yr., 1996; Platinum Record, 1996. Mem. ASCAP, Internat. Platform Assn., Men's Inner Cir. of Achievement. Avocations: travel, fund raising, guest speaking. Address: 328 William St Apt A Downingtown PA 19335-2562

KOVACH, JOHN STEPHEN, oncologist, research center administrator; b. Cleve., Oct. 11, 1936; s. John and Irene Ann (Cherosky) K.; m. Barbara C. H. Summerskill, Apr. 29, 1978; children: Alexandra, Elizabeth. BA, Princeton U., 1958; MD, Columbia U., 1962. Intern Presbyn. Hosp., Coll. Physicians and Surgeons Columbia U., 1962-63, med. resident, 1963-65; fellow hematology Coll. Physicians and Surgeons Columbia U., 1965-66; med. officer USPHS, lab. chem. biology Nat. Inst. Arthritis and Metabolic Diseases NIH, Bethesda, Md., 1966-68, biochemist lab. chem. biology, 1968-72; vis. resident div. med. oncology Mayo Clinic, Rochester, Minn., 1972-73, assoc. prof. oncology Mayo Med. Sch., 1976-81, cons. med. oncology, 1976—, chmn. div. devel. oncology rsch., 1976-86, prof. oncology Mayo

Med. Sch., 1981—, chmn. dept., 1986-94, dir. Mayo Comprehensive Cancer Ctr., 1986-94, George M. Eisenberg prof. oncology Mayo Med. Sch., 1989; dir. City of Hope NCI-designated Cancer Ctr., Duarte, Calif., 1994—, exec. v.p. for med. and sci. affairs Nat. Med. Ctr., 1994—; assoc. prof. medicine Coll. Physicians and Surgeons, N.Y.C., 1973-76; dep. dir. clin. oncology Cancer Rsch. Ctr. Columbia U., N.Y.C., 1973-76, attending physician Presbyn. Med. Ctr., 1973-76; mem. support rev. com. Cancer Ctr. Nat. Cancer Inst., Bethesda., 1988—. Surgeon USPHS, 1966-68. Mem. Am. Assn. Cancer Insts. (bd. dirs. 1988-90, pres. 1994—), Am. Soc. Clin. Oncologists, Am. Assn. Cancer Rsch., Am. Soc. Microbiology. Office: City of Hope 1500 Duarte Rd Duarte CA 91010-3000*

KOVACH, JOSEPH WILLIAM, management consultant, psychologist, educator; b. Hammond, Ind., Oct. 4, 1946; s. William Charles and Florence (Miotke) K. BA in Speech, St. Joseph Coll., Whiting, Ind., 1969; MA in Psychology, Roosevelt U., 1974; PhD, Ill. Inst. Tech., 1981; PhD in Clin. Psychology, Chgo. Sch. Profl. Psychology, 1986. Lic. sch. psychologist, Ill., Ind., Mo.; cert. marriage & family therapist, Ind. Asst. corp. merchandising mgr. Kroch's & Brentano's, Chgo., 1965-70; regional ops. mgr. Interstate Dept. Stores, Inc., Highland, Ind., 1971-73; prof. and chmn. divsn. social and behavioral scis. Calumet Coll. St. Joseph, Whiting, Ind., 1984—; dir. Ednl. Rsch. Exch., Calumet City, Ill., 1988—; pres. Joseph W. Kovach and Assocs., Ltd., Calumet City, 1969—; dir. Buzan Centre Ltd. of Chgo., 1992—; sr. cons. Calumet City Youth Svc. Bur., 1973-75; supr. Loyola U. Med. Ctr., Maywood, Ill., 1980-83, Northwestern Meml. Hosp., 1973-83, rsch. assoc., 1979-81; pre-doctoral intern Chgo. Read Mental Health Ctr., 1983-84, asst. program dir., 1988-89; sch. psychologist intern Sch. Dist. 163, Park Forest, Ill., 1986; grad. asst. Roosevelt U., Chgo., 1970-71; rsch. assoc. Northwestern U. Med. Sch., 1974-76, Loyola U. Med. Ctr., Maywood, 1976-78; adj. mem. faculty Thornton C.C. (name now South Suburban Coll.), South Holland, Ill., 1976, 97—, Purdue U. Calumet, Hammond, Ind., 1976-89; presenter Internat. Conf. of The Role of Social Science in the Devel. of Education, Business and Government Entering the 21st Century, Kaunas, (Lith.), 1998, 24th Internat. Congress on Arts and Comm., Oxford, Eng.; organizer First USA Mind Sports Championships. *Whether in front of a camera, on the radio, from behind a podium, or sitting in a chair, Professor Dr. Kovach has spent over thirty years working with the human condition. From consulting with business leaders to students, he is a world authority on whole brain thinking strategies and planning, learning techniques, and creativity, for the 21st century. He frequently speaks on stimulating and developing our natural genius. He is a columnist and has authored numerous articles, position papers, and books. As a visionary, he is paragidm shifter and an architect of the possibility. He was one of the original co-organizers for the first USA Memory Championships.* Columnist: Bus. in Rev./The Times, Munster, Ind., Executive Excellence and Personal Excellence, Provo, Utah., Talking to the Boss, Skokie, Ill. Bd. dirs. Milton H. Erickson Inst. No. Ill.; co-founder, bd. dirs. Internat. Acad. for Study of Virtual Reality; trustee Calumet Coll. St. Joseph. Mem. APA, Midwest Psychol. Assn., Ill. Sch. Psychologists Assn. Office: PO Box 113 Calumet City IL 60409-0113

KOVACH, ROBERT LOUIS, geophysics educator; b. L.A., Feb. 15, 1934; s. Nicholas Arthur and Stefania Teresa (Rüssler) K.; m. Linda Elly Heyn, Dec. 23, 1960; children: Denise Lynn, Dianne Yvonne, John Robert, Robert John. Geophysical Enging Degree, Colo. Sch. Mines, 1955; MA, Columbia U., 1959; PhD, Calif. Inst. Tech., 1962. Registered geophysicist, Calif. Sr. scientist Jet Propulsion Lab., Pasadena, Calif., 1961-63; asst. prof. Calif. Inst. Tech., Pasadena, 1963-65; asst. prof. Stanford (Calif.) U., 1965-66, assoc. prof., 1966-70, prof. geophysics, 1970—; prin. investigator Apollo Moon Seismic Expts., 1996-76; cons. DOE, 1996-97. Author: Earth's Fury, 1995, Conflict with the Earth, 1997. Lt. U.S. Army, 1956-58. Fellow John Simon Guggenheim Found., 1971; recipient Exceptional Sci. Achievement award NASA, 1973. Fellow Geol. Soc. Am.; mem. Am. Geophysical Union (pres. seismology sect. 1976-78), Can. Well Logging Soc., Seismol. Soc. Am., Soc. Exploration Geophysicists. Office: Dept Geophysics Stanford University Stanford CA 94305

KOVACH, RONALD, footwear manufacturing executive; b. N.Y.C., Dec. 22, 1946; s. Edward Joseph and Louise Christine (Ragno) K.; m. Linda Cathrine Clark, May 5, 1969; children: Meredith Alexa, Matthew Alexander. BA with honors, U. Calif., Riverside, 1968, MA, 1970; postgrad., UCLA, 1970-74. Asst. v.p. Big 5 Sporting Goods, El Segundo, Calif., 1972-91; dir., founder Eagle Claw Saltwater Fishing Schs., Huntington Beach, Calif., 1989—; ind. cons. to sporting goods industry Huntington Beach, 1992—; bd. dirs. Penn Fishing U.; lectr., condr. seminars, Huntington Beach, 1985—; frellance photojournalis, Huntington Beach, 1985—; co-owner FX (fishing expeditions outdoor apparel); bd. dirs. Advt. Maj. Footwear Co.; cons. in field; host Fishing Expdns. on Outdoor Channel. Author: Bass Fishing in California: Secrets of the Western Pros, 1985, Trout Fishing in California: Secrets of the Top Western Anglers, 1987, Saltwater Fishing in California: Secrets of the Pacific Experts, 1989, Serious Bass Fishing: Winning Secrets of Advanced Bass Anglers, 1994, The Serious Pacific Angler: Advanced Secrets of The Eagle Claw Fishing School, 1994; host: Fishing Expeditions Sta. XTRA-sports Radio, L.A.; host: Fishing Expdns. TV; co-host: World of Big Game Fishing Show ESPN-TV; contbr. numerous articles to various publs. Organizer Proposition 132, Calif. anti-gill net initiative, 1990. Calif. State scholar U. Calif., 1970; rsch. NIMH fellow UCLA, 1972. Mem. Internat. Game Fish Assn., Nat. Resource Def. Coun., Calif. Trout, Bass Anglers Sportsman Soc., Outdoor Writers Assn. Am., Outdoor Writers Calif., United Anglers, Pacific Offshore Rsch. Found., Scripps Inst. Oceanography. Avocations: fishing, travel, racquetball. Home: 17911 Portside Cir Huntington Beach CA 92649-4931 Office: 7351 Heil Ave Ste D Huntington Beach CA 92647-4534

KOVACHEVICH, ELIZABETH ANNE, federal judge; b. Canton, Ill., Dec. 14, 1936; d. Dan and Emilie (Kuchan) Kovachevich. AA, St. Petersburg Jr. Coll., 1956; BBA in Fin. magna cum laude, U. Miami, 1958; JD, Stetson U., 1961. Bar: Fla. 1961, U.S. Dist. Ct. (mid. and so. dists.) Fla. 1961, U.S. Ct. Appeals (5th cir.) 1961, U.S. Supreme Ct. 1968. Rsch. and adminstrv. aide Pinellas County Legis. Del., Fla., 1961; assoc. DiVito & Speer, St. Petersburg, Fla., 1961-62; house counsel Rieck & Fleece Builders Supplies, Inc., St. Petersburg, 1962; pvt. practice law St. Petersburg, 1962-73; judge 6th Jud. Cir., Pinellas and Pasco Counties, Fla., 1973-82, U.S. Dist. Ct. (mid. dist.) Fla., St. Petersburg, 1982-96; chief judge U.S. Dist. Ct. (mid. dist.) Fla., Tampa, 1996—; chmn. St. Petersburg Profl. Legal Project-Days in Court, 1967; chmn. Supreme Ct. Bicentennial Com. 6th Jud. Circuit, 1975-76. prodr., coord. TV prodn. A Race to Judgement. Bd. regents State of Fla., 1970-72; legal advisor, bd. dirs. Young Women's Residence Inc., 1968; mem. Fla. Gov.'s Comm. on Status of Women, 1968-71; mem. Pres.'s Comm. on White House Fellowships, 1973-77; mem. def. adv. com. on Women in Service, Dept. Def., 1973-76; Fla. conf. publicity chmn. 18th Nat. Republican Women's Conf., Atlanta, 1971; lifetime mem. Children's Hosp. Guild, YWCA of St. Petersburg; charter mem. Golden Notes, St. Petersburg Symphony; hon. mem. bd. of overseers Stetson U. Coll. of Law, 1986. Recipient Disting. Alumni award Stetson U., 1970, Woman of Yr. award Fla. Fedn. Bus. and Profl. Women, 1981, ann. Ben C. Willard Meml. award, Stetson Lawyers Assn., 1983, St. Petersburg Panhellenic Appreciation award, 1964, Mrs. Charles Ulrick Bay award, St. Petersburg Rotary award, St. Petersburg Quarterback Club award, Pinellas United Fund award in recognition of concern and meritorious effort, 1968, Woman of Yr. award Beta Sigma Phi, 1970, Am. Legion Aux. Unit 14 Pres. award cmty. svc., 1970, Dedication to Christian Ideals award and Man of Yr. award KC Dists. 20-21, 1972. Mem. ABA, Fla. Bar Assn., Pinellas County Trial Lawyers, Assn. Trial Lawyers Am., Am. Judicature Soc., St. Petersburg Bar Assn. (chmn. bench and bar com., sec. 1969). Office: US Dist Ct 801 N Florida Ave Tampa FL 33602-4509*

KOVACHY, EDWARD MIKLOS, JR., psychiatrist; b. Cleve., Dec. 3, 1946; s. Edward Miklos and Evelyn Amelia (Palenscar) K.; m. Susan Eileen Light, June 21, 1981; children: Timothy Light, Benjamin Light. BA, Harvard U., 1968, JD, 1972, MBA, 1972; MD, Case Western Reserve U., 1977. Diplomate Nat. Bd. Med. Examiners. Resident in psychiatry Stanford U. Med. Ctr., Stanford, Calif., 1977-81; pvt. practice psychiatry mediator mgmt. cons. Menlo Park, Calif., 1981—. Columnist The Peninsula Times Tribune, 1983-85. Trustee Mid-Peninsula H.S., Palo Alto, Calif., 1990—; mem. gift com. Harvard Coll. Class of 1968, 25th reunion chmn. participation, San Francisco, 1993, 30th reunion chmn. participation, West Coast, 1998. Mem. Am. Psychiat. Assn., Physicians for Social Responsibility, Assn. Family and Conciliation Cts., No. Calif. Psychiat. Soc. Presbyterian. Avocations: personal activism, musical comedy, athletics. Office: 1187 University Dr Menlo Park CA 94025-4423

KOVACIC, WILLIAM EVAN, law educator; b. Poughkeepsie, N.Y., Oct. 1, 1952; s. Evan Carl and Frances Katherine (Crow) K.; m. Kathryn Marie Fenton, May 18, 1985. AB with honors, Princeton U., 1974; JD, Columbia U., 1978. Bar: N.Y. 1979. Law clk. to sr. dist. judge U.S. Dist. Ct. Md., Balt., 1978-79; atty. planning office bur. competition FTC, Washington, 1979-82, atty. advisor to commr., 1983; assoc. Bryan, Cave, McPheeters & McRoberts, Washington, 1983-86; prof. George Mason U. Sch. Law, Arlington, Va., 1986-99, George Washington U. Law Sch., 1999—; cons. in field; mem. U.S. Senate Judiciary Subcom. on Antitrust and Monopoly, Washington, 1975-76. Contbr. legal articles to profl. jours. Assoc. Father Ford Found. Columbia U. Cath. Campus Ministry, N.Y.C. 1985—. Harlan Fiske Stone fellow Columbia U., 1976-78. Mem. ABA (antitrust law and pub. contract law sects.), Fed. Bar Assn. Roman Catholic. Avocations: hiking, camping, photography. Home: 7575 Dunquin Ct Clifton VA 20124-1840

KOVACIK, NEAL STEPHEN, hotel and restaurant executive; b. Toledo, Mar. 2, 1952; s. Albert Joseph and Phyllis (Lesinski) K.; m. Denise Reichert, Apr. 20, 1974 (div. June 1976). Student, Bowling Green State U., 1971-72, U. Toledo, 1973-74, Owens Tech. Coll., 1975. Dir. food and beverages Motor Inn of Perrysburg, Ohio, 1976-78; v.p. food and beverage ops. Bennett Enterprises, Perrysburg, 1978-82, v.p. hotel and restaurant ops., 1982—. Bd. dirs. Greater Toledo Office of Tourism and Convs., 1994—. Recipient Food and Beverage Dir. of Yr. award Holiday Inns. Inc. and Internat. Assn. Holiday Inns, 1976. Mem. Northwestern Ohio Restaurant Assn. (bd. dirs. 1980-84), Toledo Hotel and Motel Assn. Democrat. Roman Catholic. Avocations: art, wildlife photography. Home: 9640 Monclova Rd Monclova OH 43542-9709 Office: Bennett Enterprises Corp 27476 Holiday Ln Perrysburg OH 43551-3345

KOVACIK, THOMAS L., chief operating officer and safety director Toledo; b. Toledo, Ohio, Aug. 9, 1947. BS in Chemistry, Bowling Green State U., 1969, MA, 1971. Chemist water treatment City of Toledo, 1967-69, chief chemist water plant, chief chemist, dir. pollution control, dir. pub. utilities, 1982-89; pres. Envirosafe, Toledo, 1989-92, Great Lakes N-Viro, 1992-94; cons. Toledo, 1994-96; COO, safety dir. City of Toledo, 1996—. Office: City of Toledo Ste 2200 1 Govt Ctr Toledo OH 43604

KOVACS, AIMEE, conference speaker, minister; b. Laredo, Tex.; d. Arturo and Hilaria; m. James Kovacs; six stepchildren and 1 son. BS, U. Tex.; M in Bibl. Counseling, Friends Internat. Christian U., D in Ministry in Dance, PhD. Cert. tchr. Tex. and N.J.; cert. min. Eagles House, N.Y. Mktg. staff Abbington Assocs., N.J.; tchr. N.J. Sch. Sys.; min. The Eagle House, N.Y.C.; pres. Kingdom Glory, Inc., West Long Branch, N.J.; pres. World Wide Dominion Dancers, N.J.; mem. mktg. staff Abbington Assocs., N.J. Author: Dancing Into The Anointing, 1996; choreographer (dance concert) World of Dance, 1967, (play) Monmouth Players; writer, dir. (play) Comedy of Teachers, 1975; prodr. (video) World of Dance, 1998. Team mother West Long Branch (N.J.) Sports, 1984-87; art appreciation vol. West Long Branch Elem., 1987; class mother Rumson Country Day Sch., 1988; choreographer UN, N.Y., 1993; mothers club Christian Bros. Acad., Lincroft, 1995-96; vol. Children of the World Found., 1998. Named Sweetheart, Pan Am. Student Forum, Tex., 1962, Ms. Sail Boat Race, Atlantic Highlands Yacht Club, 1976, Mrs. West Long Branch, Mrs. N.J. Internat. Pageant, 1996, Mrs. Colts Neck, Mrs. N.J. Internat. Pageant, 1997, Mrs. Monmouth County, Mrs. N.J. Internat. Pageant, 1998; Martin High Choir scholar, Laredo, Tex., 1962. Mem. Battle Ground Country Club, Elisha House, B. Hinn Ptnrs. Republican. Avocations: golf, sailing, skiing, dancing, gardening. Home: PO Box 40 West Long Branch NJ 07764-0040 Office: Kingdom Glory Inc PO Box 40 West Long Branch NJ 07764-0040

KOVACS, BEATRICE, library studies educator; b. Seekirchen, Austria, June 2, 1945; came to U.S., 1948; d. Lorand and Helen (Magyary-Kossa) K.; m. Thomas Gordon Basler, Apr. 20, 1969 (div. 1979); m. Louis Edward Mitchum, Jan. 10, 1994. AB in English, Syracuse U., 1966; MLS, Rutgers State U., 1967; DLS, Columbia U., 1983. Libr. Nassau Acad. Medicine, Garden City, N.Y., 1967-70; cataloger, asst. acquisitions libr. Augusta (Ga.) Regional Libr., 1974-78; collection devel. libr. Med. Coll. Ga., Augusta, 1978-80; acct. specialist Readmore Publs., N.Y.C., 1982-83; chief collection devel. U. N.Mex. Med. Ctr. Libr., Albuquerque, 1984-85; asst. prof. U. N.C., Greensboro, 1985-91, assoc. prof., 1991—; vis. instr. Pratt Inst. Grad. Sch. Libr., Bklyn., 1982-83; adj. prof. U. N.C. Chapel Hill Sch. Info. and Libr. Sci., 1997-98. Author: Decision-Making Process for Library Collections, 1990, ALA Fingertip Guide to National Health-Information Resources, 1995; co-author: Health Sciences Librarianship, 1977, Using Science and Technology Information Resources, 1991; contbr. articles to profl. jours. Bishop scholarship Med. Libr. Assn., 1966. Mem. ALA, Southeastern Libr. Assn., N.C. Libr. Assn., Spl. Librs. Assn., N.C. Spl. Librs. Assn. (pres. 1992-93), Assn. Libr. & Info. Sci. Educators. Office: Univ N C Greensboro PO Box 26171 Sch Of Education Greensboro NC 27402-6171

KOVACS, LASZLO, cinematographer; b. Hungary, May 14, 1933; came to U.S., 1957, naturalized, 1963; s. Imre and Julia K. M.A., Acad. Drama and Motion Picture Arts of Budapest, Hungary, 1956. lectr. at univs., film schs. Dir. photography for numerous motion pictures including Hell's Angels on Wheels, 1967, A Man Called Dagger, 1968, Psych-Out, 1968, The Savage Seven, 1968, Single Room Furnished, 1968, Targets, 1968, That Cold Day in the Park, 1969, Easy Rider, 1969, Alex in Wonderland, 1970, Getting Straight, 1970, Five Easy Pieces, 1970, The Last Movie, 1971, The Marriage of a Young Stockbroker, 1971, The King of Marvin Gardens, 1972, Pocket Money, 1972, Slither, 1972, Steelyard Blues, 1972, What's Up Doc?, 1972, Huckleberry Finn, 1973, Paper Moon, 1973, A Reflection of Fear, 1973, Freebie and the Bean, 1974, For Pete's Sake, 1974, At Long Last Love, 1975, Shampoo, 1975, Harry and Walter Go to New York, 1976, Baby Blue Marine, 1976, Nickelodeon, 1976, New York, New York, 1977, The Last Waltz, 1978, Paradise Alley, 1978, F.I.S.T., 1978, Heart Beat, 1979, The Runner Stumbles, 1979, Butch and Sundance: The Early Days, 1979, Inside Moves, 1980, The Legend of the Lone Ranger, 1981, Frances, 1982, The Toy, 1982, Crackers, 1982,, Ghostbusters, 1983, Mask, 1985, Legal Eagles, 1986, Little Nikita, 1988, Say Anything, 1989, Shattered, 1991, Radio Flyer, 1992, Ruby Cairo, 1992, The Next Karate Kid, 1993, The Scout,, 1993, Free Willy 2, 1994, Copycat, 1994, Multiplicity, 1995, My Best Friends Wedding, 1996; freelance cinematographer for motion pictures and TV commls. Mem. Acad. Motion Picture Arts and Scis., Am. Soc. Cinematographers. Office: Mirisch Agency Ste 700 10100 Santa Monica Blvd Los Angeles CA 90067*

KOVACS, ROSEMARY, newpaper editor. BS in Journalism, Bowling Green State U., 1968. Mng. editor prodn. The Plain Dealer, Cleve., 1990—. Named to Bowling Green State U. Journalism Hall of Fame, 1988. Mem. Press Club of Cleve. (pres.). Office: Plain Dealer Pub Co 1801 Superior Ave Cleveland OH 44114-2198*

KOVAK, ELLEN B., public relations firm executive; b. N.Y.C., Nov. 28, 1948; m. Stanley Kovak, Apr. 20, 1971; 1 child, Janet (J.J.). B.A., Skidmore Coll.; postgrad., Brown U. Sr. acct. supr. Creamer Dickson Basford, Inc., N.Y.C., 1977-80; exec. v.p. Lobsenz-Stevens Inc., N.Y.C., 1980-85; pres. Kovak-Thomas Pub. Relations, Inc., N.Y.C., 1985-96, Kovak Likiy, 1997—. Mem. Pub. Relations Soc. Am., Am. Horse Show Assn. Avocation: horseback riding (show and own hunter horses). Office: Kovak Likiy Communications LLC 387 Danbury Rd Wilton CT 06897-2529

KOVAL, DON O., electrical engineering educator; b. Pickle Crow, Ont., Can., Mar. 20, 1942; s. Peter and Katherine Koval. BE, U. Sask., Saskatoon, 1965, MSc, 1969, PhD, 1978. Distbn. subtransmission design engr. Sask. Power Corp., Regina, 1965-66; distbn. spl. studies engr. B.C. Hydro & Power Authority, Vancouver, 1967-79; prof. elec. enging. U. Alta., Edmonton, 1980—. Fellow IEEE (chmn. Gold Book 1991—, Ralph H. Lee prize paper 1991), Am. Biog. Inst. (life, commemorative medal of honor 1991), Internat. Biog. Assn. (life); mem. Internat. Assn. Sci. and Tech. for Devel. (Zurich, bd. dirs. 1990—), Assn. Profl. Engrs. (B.C.), Assn. Profl. Engrs. and Geologists of Province Alta., Internat. Inst. for Advanced Studies in Systems Rsch. and Cybernetics (Baden-Baden, Fed. Republic Germany, bd. dirs. 1990—). Home: 155 Marion Dr, Sherwood Park, AB Canada T8A 2G9 Office: Dept Elec Enging, Univ of Alta, Edmonton, AB Canada T6G 2G7

KOVALA, KATHLEEN ANN, small business owner, educator; b. Ishpeming, Mich., Dec. 3, 1940; d. John William and Jennie Mathilda (Ruuska) Prusi; m. Charles J. Arnold Kovala; children: Wendy, Bridget, Janice, Steven, Michael. Grad., Negaunee (Mich.) H.s., 1958. Instr. Nicolet Coll., Rhinelander, Wis., 1977—; pres. Finnishing Touches Inc., Rhinelander, 1990—. Bd. dirs. Am. Cancer Soc., 1980-87, St. Mary's Hosp. Aux., 1980-85, Rhinelander Area Recreation and Conv. Ctr., 1990; pres. Rhinelander Country Club Ladies, 1983, Northwood Cmty. Concert Assn., Rhinelander, 1984-87. Recipient 1st pl. award Wis. State Exhbn., 1984, 85, 86. Mem. No. Decorative Artists (Peoples Choice award 1982), Mpls. Decorative Artists, Nat. Tole and Decorative Soc. Avocations: golf, cross country skiing, travel. Office: Finnishing Touches Inc 919 Arbutus St Rhinelander WI 54501-3902

KOVALCIK, PAUL JEROME, surgeon; b. Buffalo, Apr. 16, 1943; s. Jerome G. and Dorothy I. (Kalinowski) K.; m. Janet I. Howe, Jan. 13, 1968; children: Julia, Peter, John, Matthew, Andrew. BA, CUNY, Flushing, 1965; MD, Georgetown U., 1969. Diplomate Nat. Bd. Med. Examiners, Am. Bd. Surgery, Am. Bd. Colon and Rectal Surgery; ATLS instr. Commd. ensign USN, 1969, advanced through grades to capt., 1984, ret. Med. Corps, 1989; intern medicine and surgery Naval Hosp., Boston, 1969-70, resident gen. surgery, 1970-73; resident gen. surgery Naval Regional Med. Ctr., Portsmouth, Va., 1973-74; fellow colon and rectal surgery Lahey Clinic, Boston, 1974-75; assoc. prof. surgery Ea. Va. Med. Sch., 1980—, Uniformed Svcs. U. Health Scis., 1986—; head dept. gen. surgery Naval Hosp. Portsmouth, 1985-87; cons. Naval Hosp. Portsmouth; chmn. CME com. Portsmouth Gen. Hosp.; chmn. ethics com. Maryview Hosp., Portsmouth; chmn. surg. endoscopy com. Chesapeake (Va.) Gen. Hosp.; assoc. examiner Am. Bd. Colon and Rectal Surgery; vis. prof. Greenville (S.C.) Hosp. System, 1984, U. S.C., Columbia, 1984, W.Va. U. Med. Ctr., Charleston, 1986, East Carolina U., Greenville, 1991, 93; lectr. Georgetown U., Washington, 1985, U.S. Naval Hosp., Guantanamo Bay, Cuba, 1986, U.S. Naval Hosp., Roosevelt Roads, P.R., 1987, U.O.A. Mid-Atlantic Regional Conf., 1987, Acute Combat Symposium Tidewater chpt. AMSUS, Norfolk, 1987, Trauma Symposium Naval Hosp., Roosevelt Roads, 1988, Thomas Jefferson U. Med. Sch., 1988, 90, Acute Combat Trauma Symposium, Norfolk, 1988, Piedmont Soc. Colon and Rectal Surgeons, Williamsburg, Va., 1990, Sardestin, Fla., 1992, Kiawah Island, S.C., 1993, Joseph F. Mulach Med. Lectr. Series St. Clair Hosp., Pitts., 1991, Student Cancer Conf. Ea. Va. Med. Sch., Norfolk, 1994; Thordur Thordarson Meml. lectr., Reykjavik, Iceland, 1987; pres. Portsmouth Acad. Medicine, 1998—. Contbr. numerous articles to med. jours. Fellow Am. Coll. Surgeons, Am. Soc. Colon and Rectal Surgery; mem. AMA, Am. Soc. Colon and Rectal Surgeons (chmn. self-assessment com. 1988-92, recert. com., mem.-at-large to exec. coun. 1992—), Soc. Am. Gastrointestinal Endoscopic Surgeons (founder), Va. Surg. Soc., Lahey Clin. Alumni Assn. Republican. Roman Catholic. Avocations: fishing, tennis, gardening, travel. Home: 4762 River Shore Rd Portsmouth VA 23703-1518 Office: 3101 American Legion Rd Ste 15 Chesapeake VA 23321-5655 also: 667 Kinsborough Sq Ste 300 Chesapeake VA 23320

KOVALY, JOHN JOSEPH, consulting engineering executive, educator; b. McKeesport, Pa., June 12, 1928; s. Joseph and Mary (Demko) K.; m. Joan P. Misiewicz, June 16, 1957; children: Pamela Jane, Kurt David. B.S., Muskingum Coll., 1950; M.S., U. Ill., 1953. Research assoc. Coordinated Sci. Lab., U. Ill., Urbana, 1951-55; adv. research engr. Sylvania Electronic Products, Inc., Waltham, Mass., 1958-65; cons. engr., program mgr. Raytheon Co. Patriot Missile Sys. Enging. Svcs., Bedford, Mass., 1965-95; lectr. Northeastern U., 1956-58, UCLA, 1977-87. Author: Synthetic Aperture Radar, 1976; contbr. articles profl. jours. Served to lt. U.S. Navy, 1955-58. Named to Hall of Fame, McKeesport High Sch., 1988. Fellow IEEE (pres. Boston sect. Aerospace and Electronic Systems Group 1972 contbn. award). Home: 3 Tubwreck Dr Dover MA 02030-1808

KOVARSKY, JOEL SEVERIN, rheumatologist, small business owner; b. Chgo., Aug. 16, 1947; s. Irving and Esther (Rabinovitz) K.; m. Deborah Barricks, Aug. 17, 1969; children: Lee B., Ian M. BS, U. Iowa, 1969, MD, 1972. Diplomate Am. Bd. Internal Medicine, Am. Bd. Rheumatology. Intern Duke U. Med. Ctr., Durham, N.C., 1972-73; fellow in rheumatology Duke U. Med. Ctr., Durham, 1974-76, jr. asst. resident in medicine, 1976-77; asst. resident neurology Strong Meml. Hosp., U. Rochester, N.Y., 1973-74; chief rheumatology William Beaumont Arym Med. Ctr., El Paso, Tex., 1977-79; rheumatologist Diagnostic Clinic Houston, 1979-80; asst. prof. medicine Baylor Coll Medicine, Houston, 1980-85, clin. asst. prof. medicine, 1985-96; pvt. practice Houston, 1985-96, Danville, Va., 1996—; dir. rheumatology Danville Regional Med. Ctr., 1996—; asst. cons. prof. med. Duke U. Rheumatology, 1998—; owner The Prime Meridian: Antique Maps and Books, 1998—; asst. clin. prof. medicine Tex. Tech. U., Lubbock, 1977-79; cons. Meth. St. Luke's Episcopal Hosp., Houston, 1980-96; lectr. in field. Contbr. articles to profl. jours., chpts. to books. Mem. mus. adv. coun. Harwood Found., U. New Mexico, Taos, 1993-97. Maj. U.S. Army, 1977-79. Recipient Army Commendation medal, 1979. Fellow Am. Coll. Rheumatology; mem. Tex. Med. Assn., Med. Soc. Va., Mystery Writers Am. Jewish. Avocations: book collecting, racquetball, skiing. Office: 159 Executive Dr Ste A Danville VA 24541-4160

KOVATCH, JAK GENE, artist; b. Los Angeles, Jan. 17, 1929; s. Jack and La Vinia Blanche (Abernathy) K.; m. Carol Jean Wilhelm, Dec. 24, 1967; 1 son by previous marriage, Jason. Student, UCLA, 1946, Chouinard Art Inst., 1947-49, Calif. Sch. Art, L.A., 1949-50, U. So. Calif., 1951, L.A. City Coll., 1955-56, Art Students League, N.Y.C., 1972, 75. Student asst. Lynton Kistler Studio, L.A., 1952-53; staff animation dept. Walt Disney Prodns., Inc., Burbank, Calif., 1953; instr. drawing and anatomy Famous Artists Schs., Westport, Conn., 1957-59; tchr. Roger Ludlowe H.S., Fairfield, Conn., 1959-60; extension instr. N.Y.C. Coll., 1959-60; instr. sculpture Fairfield U., 1967; mem. faculty U. Bridgeport, Conn., 1962-94, Ethyl prof. design, 1988-94, assoc. prof. dept. design, 1978-88, prof. design, 1988-94; mem. faculty Silvermine Sch. of Art, New Canaan, Conn., 1994—; vis. faculty mem. Aldrich Mus. Contemporary Art, Ridgfield, Conn., 1999; fellow Mellon Found.; Vis. Faculty Program Yale U., 1979-83; guest lectr. anatomy and figure drawing, 1953—. Stage designer for, Benjamin Zemach, L.A., 1953-54, freelance illustrator, N.Y.C., 1957-58; exhibited in some 600 group shows including Taipei Fine Arts Mus., Taiwan, R.O.C., 1987, 91, Tokyo Met. Mus., Japan, 1985-87, Barbican Arts Ctr., London, 1989, Legislative and State Office Bldgs., Hartford, 1991, Salford Mus., Eng., 1989, Inst. Tech. Aeroespacial, Sao Jose dos Campos, Brasil, 1987, U. Hawaii, 1985, Mus. Modern Art, Wakayama, Japan, 1987, Northeastern U., Boston, 1999; represented in permanent collections Fogg Mus. Art, Cambridge, Mass., Library of Congress, Joseph Hirshhorn Collection, Greenwich, Conn., Fairfield Art Collection, John Slade Ely House Collections, New Haven, Bicentennial Art Collection, Westport (Conn.) Town Hall, U. Miss., Albert Dorne Collection, N.Y.C., others; artist project grant from Conn. Commn. on Arts, Hartford, 1984-85. Selection com. State of Conn. Commn. on Arts, Percent for Art Program, Hartford, 1987-88. Recipient award Boston Mus. Fine Arts, 1954, Wadsworth Atheneum, Hartford, Conn., 1958, 79, Mus. Art, Sci. and Industry, Bridgeport, 1962-63, 65-66, 75, 77, 79, 81-84, 22 awards Fairfield (Conn.) U., 1973-95, award New Haven Paint and Clay Club, 1976, 78, 81, 89-90, 97-98, spl. recognition award Print Club Albany, Schenectady Mus., 1992, John Taylor Arms Meml. award Audubon Artists, Inc., Nat. Arts Club, N.Y.C., 1993, etching award Stamford (Conn.) Mus., 1994, Painting award New Britain Mus. Am. Art, 1997, more than 135 others. Mem. Boston Printmakers, N.Y. Artists Equity Assn., Audubon Artists (bd. dirs. for graphics 1995), Conn. Acad. Fine Arts, Greenwich Art Soc., L.A. Printmaking Soc., Phila. Print Club, Silvermine Guild Artists (trustee 1979-83), Westport-Weston Arts Coun., Graphic Arts Coun. N.Y. Home: 34 Sasco Creek Rd Westport CT 06880-6341 Office: Silvermine Sch of Art Inc 1037 Silvermine Rd New Canaan CT 06840-4398 *I consider my concept of Image Continuum to be a significant consequence of 40 years of painting and printmaking. Six basic components form the foundation of this concept: 1. Use of former images to create new ones; 2. Repetition of a theme (subject matter and symbols repeated); 3. Use of modules; 4. Use of storyboards and grids; 5. Structuring forms transparently; 6. Use of abstraction, animation, distortion. An integral part of Image Continuum is persis-*

tent use of multiple images. This means of expression may be directly related to my personal impatience with dwelling too long on one image or idea. I have been able to temper this drive for immediacy and rapid image development by using images in a series or storyboard format.

KOVEL, RALPH M., author, antiques expert; b. Milw.; s. Lester and Dorothy K.; m. Terry Horvitz; children: Lee R., Karen. Attended, Ohio State U. Pres., chmn. U.S. Brands, Inc.; pres. Lucayan Aquaculture, Freeport, Bahamas; v.p., treas. Antiques, Inc.; trustee WVIZ-TV, Western Res. Hist. Soc., Cleve., Cleve. Pops Orch., Inc.; past tchr. course in antiques Western Res. U., John Carroll U.; Hiram fellow. Appeared radio and TV discussion programs, subject of antiques; writer: (with Terry Kovel) syndicated column Kovels Antiques and Collecting, 1955—, Ask the Experts, House Beautiful, 1979—, Medio, CD-Rom Mag., 1995; editor: monthly newsletters Kovels on Antiques and Collectibles, 1974—, Kovels Sports Collectibles, 1992-97; Know Your Antiques, Pub. Broadcasting Libr., 1969—; syndicated TV series Kovels on Collecting, 1981, 87, Collector's Journal, 1989-93; author: (with Terry Kovel) Kovels' Dictionary of Marks-Pottery and Porcelain, 1953, rev. edit., 1995, Directory of American Silver, Pewter and Silver Plate, 1958, American Country Furniture, 1780-1875, 1963, Kovels Know Your Antiques, rev. edit., 1993, Kovels Antiques and Collectibles Price List, 31th edit., 1999, Kovels American Art Pottery, 1993, The Kovels Bottle Price List, 11th edit., 1999, Kovels Price Guide for Collector Plates, Figurines, Paperweight and Other Ltd. Editions, 1978, Kovels Collector's Guide to American Art Pottery, 1974, Kovels Know Your Collectibles, 1981, Kovels Book Antique Labels, 1982, Kovels Depression Glass and Dinnerware Price List, 6th edit. 1998, Kovels Illustrated Price Guide to Royal Doulton, 2d edit., 1984, Kovels Organizer for Collectors, rev. edit., 1983, Kovels Collectors Source Book, 1983, Kovels New Dictionary of Marks Pottery and Porcelain, 1850 to the Present, 1986, Kovels Advertising Collectibles Price List, 1986, Kovels Guide to Selling Your Antiques and Collectibles, rev. edit., 1990, Kovels American Silver Marks 1650 to Present, 1989, Kovels Antiques and Collectibles Fix-It Source Book, 1990, Kovels Picture-a-Day Collectibles Calendar, 1990, 91, Kovels Quick Tips: 799 Helpful Hints on How to Care For Your Collectibles, 1995, Kovels Guide to Selling, Buying and Fixing Your Antiques and Collectibles, 1995; (video tape series) Collecting With the Kovels, 1995—, Art Pottery I, Art Pottery II, The Label Made Me Buy It, 1998, Kovel's Yellow Pages, 1999, also articles. Former mem. rev. and allocations com. United Torch Fund, Cleve.; past pres. E. End Neighborhood Settlement House; past chmn. adv. com. Woodhill Homes; past bd. dirs. Soc. Collectors, Silver Mus. Religious Art. Recipient Lane Bryant award, 1966; Peirce Award for Outstanding community svc. Sta. WVIZ-TV, 1980. Mem. Union League Club (Chgo.), Oakwood Club (Cleve.). Office: PO Box 22200 Cleveland OH 44122-0200

KOVEL, TERRY HORVITZ (MRS. RALPH KOVEL), author, antiques authority; b. Cleve.; d. Isadore and Rix Horvitz; m. Ralph Kovel; children: Lee R., Karen. BA, Wellesley Coll., 1950. Tchr. math. Hawken Sch. for Boys, Shaker Heights, Ohio, 1961-71; now pres. Antiques Inc.; past tchr. course in antiques Western Res. U., John Carroll U.; radio and TV discussion programs on antiques. Writer: (with Ralph Kovel) syndicated column Kovels Antiques and Collecting, 1955—, Ask the Experts, House Beautiful, 1979—; editor: monthly newsletters Kovels on Antiques and Collectibles, 1974—, Kovels Sports Collectibles, 1992-97; TV series Know Your Antiques, Pub. Broadcast Library, 1969—; syndicated TV Series Kovels on Collecting, 1981, 87, Collector's Journal, 1989-93; author: (with Ralph Kovel) Kovels' Dictionary of Marks-Pottery and Porcelain, 1953, rev. edit., 1995, Directory of American Silver, Pewter and Silver Plate, 1958, American Country Furniture, 1780- 1875, 1963, Kovels' Know Your Antiques, rev. edit, 1993, Kovels' American Art Pottery, 1993, Kovels' Antiques and Collectibles Price List, 31st edit., 1999, Kovels' Know Your Collectibles, 1981, Kovels' Bottle Price List, 11th edit., 1999, Kovels' Organizer for Collectors, 1978, revised, 1983, Kovels' Price Guide for Collector Plates, Figurines, Paperweights and Other Limited Editions, 1978, Kovels' Collector's Guide to American Art Pottery, 1974, Kovels' Price Guide to Depression Glass and Dinnerware, 6th edit., 1998, Kovels' Illustrated Price Guide to Royal Doulton, 2d edit., 1984, Kovels' Collectors' Source Book, 1983, Kovels' New Dictionary of Marks Pottery and Porcelain, 1850 to the Present, 1986, Kovels' Advertising Collectibles Price List, 1986, Kovels' Guide to Selling Your Antiques and Collectibles, 1987, 2d edit., 1990, Kovels' Book of Antique Labels, 1982, Kovels' American Silver Marks 1650 to the Present, 1989, Kovel's Antiques and Collectibles Fix-It Source Book, 1990, Kovels' Picture-a-Day Collectibles Calendar, 1990, 91, Kovels' Guide to Selling, Buying and Fixing Your Antiques and Collectibles, 1995, Kovels' Quick Tips: 799 Helpful Hints on How To Care for Your Collectibles, 1995; (videotape series) Collecting With the Kovels, Art Pottery I, Art Pottery II, 1995—, The Label Made Me Buy It, 1998, Kovels' Yellow Pages, 1999; contbr. articles on antiques, numerous publs. Trustee Hiram Coll., 1989-99; bd. mem. Shaker Hist. Soc. Hiram fellow; recipient Peirce award for outstanding cmty. svc. Sta. WVIZ-TV, 1980, Cleve. Emmy award for best entertainment, 1971, Cleve. Emmy award for cultural affairs programming, 1987; Laurel Sch. Alumanae of Yr. Office: 22000 Shaker Blvd Cleveland OH 44122-2644

KOVELESKI, KATHRYN DELANE, retired special education educator; b. Detroit, Aug. 12, 1925; d. Edward Albert Vogt and Delane (Bender) Vogt; BA, Olivet (Mich.) Coll., 1947; MA, Wayne State U., Detroit, 1955; m. Casper Koveleski, July 18, 1952; children: Martha, Ann. Tchr. schs. in Mich., 1947-88; tchr. Garden City Schs., 1955-56, 59-88, resource and learning disabilities tchr., 1970-88, ret. 1988. Sec. bd. Christian edn. Congl. Ch., 1988-89, 96-99, chmn., 1988-90, mem. Mem. BPW (Woman of Yr. 1985-86 Garden City), Mich. Assn. Ret. Sch. Pers., Wayne Hist. Soc. (trustee 1998—, sec.-treas. 1998-99), Wayne Garden Club, Wayne Lit. Club (past pres., treas. 1988-89, co-historian 1998—), Sch. Masters Bowling League (v.p. 1984-88), Odd Couples Bowling League (pres. 82-83, treas. 1995-97, 1998—), Savvy Wayne Srs. Investment Club.

KOVTYNOVICH, DAN, civil engineer; b. Eugene, Oreg., May 17, 1952; s. John and Elva Lano (Robie) K. BCE, Oreg. State U., 1975, BBA, 1976. Registered profl. engr., Calif., Oreg. V.p. Kovtynovich, Inc., Contractors and Engrs., Eugene, 1976-80, pres., chief exec. officer, 1980—. Apptd. to State of Oreg. Bldg. Codes and Structures Bd., 1996—. Fellow ASCE; mem. Am. Arbitration Assn. (arbitrator 1979—), N.W. China Coun., Navy League of U.S., Eugene Asian Coun. Republican. Avocations: flying, skiing, fishing, hunting. Office: Kovtynovich Inc PO Box 898 Lake Oswego OR 97034-0143

KOWAL, RUTH ELIZABETH, library administrator; b. Amherst, Mass., Mar. 16, 1948; d. Alfred Alexander and Mary Arandale (Tomlinson) Brown; m. Harold F. Kowal, June 19, 1989; children: Elizabeth Ann, Susannah Terry. BS, Syracuse U., 1970; MLS, Simmons Coll., 1971. Reference libr. Falmouth (Mass.) Pub. Libr., 1971-74; sch. libr. Nauset High Sch., Eastham, Mass., 1974-75; asst. dir. Plymouth (Mass.) Pub. Librs., 1975, dir., 1976-83; exec. dir. Southeastern 3R's, Highland, N.Y., 1983-86; regional adminstr. Ctrl. Mass. Libr. System, Worcester, 1987-91, Ea. Mass. Libr. System, Boston, 1991-97; regional adminstr. Boston Pub. Libr., 1997—, asst. dir., 1997—; instr. Northeastern U., Boston, 1980-83, SUNY, Albany, 1984-86. Mem. ALA. Office: Boston Pub Libr Regional Svcs Office Boston MA 02117

KOWALCZYK, KIM JAN, editor, writer; b. Ellwood City, Pa., Aug. 20, 1952; d. Joseph and Josephine A. (Alexander) Januszkiewicz; m. Frank Joseph Kowalczyk, Aug. 26, 1972; children: Tanya Marie, Kelly Ann, Christopher Michael. BA in Gen. Arts and Sci., Pa. State U., 1989, postgrad., 1989-90. Office mgr. Ginther Wycoff Group, Denver, 1983-85; asst. to pres. Linguex Internat., Denver, 1985-86; sec., dir. engring. Locus, Inc., State College, Pa., 1987-89; tech. editor, writer Locus, Inc., Kaman Scis., State College, 1989-90; manuscript editor, writer Am. Philatelic Soc., State College, 1990—; freelance editor, writer, Denver, State College, Pa., 1987—; cons. editor Real Time Devices, State College, 1990, Peter Jehrio Enterprises, State College, 1991-93, State College area YMCA, 1992-95. Editor The Battles of George S. Patton's Lowest Ranks, 1996-97; author, editor: (videos) Fish Day in Bellefonte, 1990, The Last Cruise, 1990, Welcome to Union Cemetery, 1996. Mem. State College Area H.S. Swim Team Boosters, sec., 1994-95; mem. YMCA swim team boosters, v.p., 1994-95. Mem. Kiwanis. Republican. Roman Catholic. Avocations: painting, drawing. Home: 504 N Burrowes St State College PA 16803-3506 Office: Am Philatelic Soc 100 Oakwood Ave State College PA 16803-1607

KOWALEWSKI, MICHAEL JOHN, educator; b. San Francisco, Nov. 2, 1956; s. Edward John and Suzanne Marie (Thome) K.; m. Catherine Anne Oates, June 25, 1983; children: Nicholas Edward, Sarah Marie, Kevin Eugene. BA, Amherst Coll., 1978; MA in English, Rutgers U., 1982, PhD in English, 1986. Asst. prof. Princeton (N.J.) U., 1986-91; asst. prof. Carleton Coll., Northfield, Minn., 1991-95, assoc. prof., 1995—. Editor: Temperamental Journeys: Essays on the Modern Literature of Travel, 1992, Deadly Musings: Violence and Verbal Form in American Fiction, 1993, Popular Classics of American Literature, 1996; editor: Reading the West: New Essays on the Literature of the American West, 1996, Gold Rush: A Literary Exploration, 1997. Mem. MLA, Assn. for Study of Lit. and Environ. (adv. bd. 1994—), Western Lit. Assn. (v.p. 1996-97, pres.-elect 1997-98, pres. 1998-99), Calif. Studies Assn., Book Club of Calif. Roman Catholic. Avocations: travel, photography, book collecting, outdoor sports. Office: Carleton Coll English Dept Northfield MN 55057

KOWALKE, KIM H., music educator, musicologist, conductor, foundation executive; b. Monticello, Minn., June 25, 1948; s. Henry O. and Mayta M. (Schmidt) K.; m. Elizabeth Jane Keagy; 1 child, Kyle William Henry. BA, Macalester Coll., 1970; MA, Yale U., 1972, MPhil, 1974, PhD, 1977. Asst. prof. music Occidental Coll., L.A., 1977-82, assoc. prof., 1982-86; prof. music, dept. chair Eastman Sch. Music U. Rochester, N.Y., 1986—. Author: Kurt Weill in Europe, 1979 (Field prize 1978), Accounting for Success: Musinderstanding Die Dreigroschenoper (Deems-Taylor award 1990), Kurt Weill Modernism and Popular Culture, 1995 (Irving Lowens prize 1995); editor: A New Orpheus: Essays on Kurt Weill, 1986 (Deems-Taylor award 1987), A Stranger Here Myself: Kurt Weill Studien, 1993, Speak Low: The Letters of Kurt Weill and Lotte Lenya, 1996 (Freedley award 1997, Deems-Taylor award 1997), For Those We Love: Hindemith, Whitman, and 'An American Requiem'", 1997 (Irving Lowens prize 1998, Deems-Taylor award 1998); founding mem. editl. bd. Kurt Weill Edit., 1992—; contbr. articles to music and theater jours. Pres. bd. trustees Kurt Weill Found. for Music, N.Y.C., 1981—. Staff sgt. N.G., 1970-77. Recipient Graves Commn. award, Pomona Coll.; Martha Baird Rockefeller fellow, 1976, Whiting fellow, 1976-77, Am. Coun. Learned Socs. fellow, 1979. Mem. Am. Musicol. Soc. (coun. 1984-87, program com., 50 com.), Sonneck Soc., Internat. Brecht Soc. Presbyterian. Avocations: tennis, bridge, running. Office: U Rochester Eastman Sch Music 26 Gibbs St Rochester NY 14604-2505

KOWALSKI, KAZIMIERZ, computer science educator, researcher; b. Turek, Poland, Nov. 7, 1946; came to U.S., 1986; naturalized, 1994; s. Waclaw and Helena (Wisniewska) K.; m. Eugenia Zajaczkowska, Aug. 5, 1972. MSc, Wroclaw (Poland) U. Tech., 1970, PhD, 1974. Asst. prof. Wroclaw U. Tech., 1970-76, assoc. prof., 1976-86; assoc. prof. Pan Am. U., Edinburg, Tex., 1987-88; prof. computer sci. Calif. State U.-Dominguez Hills, Carson, 1988—, chmn. computer sci. dept., 1998—; lectr. U. Basrah, Iraq, 1981-85; cons. XXCal, Inc., L.A., 1987-91; conf. presenter in field; rsch. fellow Power Inst. Moscow, USSR, 1978; info. sys. tng. UNESCO, Paris, 1978. Co-author: Principles of Computer Science, 1975, Organization and Programming of Computers, 1976; also articles. Recipient Bronze Merit Cross, Govt. of Poland, 1980, Knights' Cross of the Order of Merit Republic of Poland, 1997. Mem. IEEE Computer Soc., The N.Y. Acad. Scis., Assn. for Computing Machinery, Assn. for Advancement of Computing in Edn., Am. Assn. for Artificial Intelligence, Mensa, Sigma Xi. Avocations: travel, puzzles. Home: 3836 Weston Pl Long Beach CA 90807-3317 Office: Calif State U 1000 E Victoria St Carson CA 90747-0001

KOWALSKI, KENNETH LAWRENCE, physicist, educator; b. Chgo., July 24, 1932; s. Florian Lawrence and Emily Helen (Sinoga) K.; m. Audrey Bellin; children—Eric Clifford, Claudia Gail. B.S., Ill. Inst. Tech., 1954; Ph.D. (Universal Match Found. fellow), Brown U., 1963. Aero. research scientist Lewis Research Center, NACA, 1954-57; research asso. in physics Brown U., summer 1962, Case Inst. Tech., Cleve., 1962-63; asst. prof. physics Case Inst. Tech., 1963-67, asso. prof., 1967-73; asso. prof. Case Western Res. U., 1967-73, prof., 1973—, exec. officer dept. physics, 1970-71, chmn. dept. physics, 1971-76; vis. prof. Inst. Theoretical Physics U. Louvain, Belgium, 1968-69; scientist-in-residence Argonne Nat. Lab., 1986-87, User Fermilab, 1993—. Author: (with S.K. Adhikari) Dynamical Collision Theory and It's Applications, 1991; editor: (with W.J. Fickinger) Modern Physics in America, 1988; contbr. articles to profl. jours. NSF grantee, 1972-96. Mem. Am. Phys. Soc. Achievements include rsch. on theoretical physics. Home: 2275 S Overlook Rd Cleveland Heights OH 44106-3141 Office: Case Western Res U Dept Physics 10900 Euclid Ave Dept Physics Cleveland OH 44106-1712

KOWALSKI, RICHARD SHELDON, hospital administrator; b. Detroit, Feb. 18, 1944; s. Richard Joseph and Margaret Lucile (Sheldon) K.; m. Doris Kay Smith, Nov. 20, 1982; children: Renée Marie, Jerrod Patrick, Sterling Prescott. BBA, Ea. Mich. U., 1966; MS in Health Adminstrn., Trinity U., San Antonio, 1971. Adminstrv. asst. Univ. Hosp.-U. Wash., Seattle, 1969-70; med. facilities cons. Ill. Dept. Health, Des Moines, 1970-72; asst. adminstr. Mercy Hosp., Cedar Rapids, Iowa, 1972-79; chief exec. officer St. Mary Med. Ctr., Galesburg, Ill., 1979—; mem. coun. for govt. rev. Crescent Counties Found. for Med. Care, Naperville, Ill., 1986—; bd. dirs. Assn. Venture Corp., Naperville; chmn. bd. dirs. United Health Properties, Galesburg, 1985—; mem. adv. bd. Physician Hosp. Inst.; mem. comty. bd. Norwest Bank. Bd. dirs. Econ. Devel. Coun., Galesburg, 1986—, Knox County Devel. Corp., 1986; mem. strategic planning steering com. City of Galesburg, 1986—. Named hon. alumnus Grad. Program in Hosp. and Health Adminstrn., U. Iowa, 1990. Fellow Am. Coll. Healthcare Execs.; mem. Ill. Hosp. Assn. (pres. region 1-B, bd. dirs. 1987—, Disting. Leadership award 1986), Galesburg Area C. of C. (chmn. 1990), Soangetaha Country Club (bd. dirs. 1990), Rotary. Avocations: golf, tennis. Office: St Mary Med Ctr 3333 N Seminary St Galesburg IL 61401-1251

KOWALSKI, STEPHEN WESLEY, chemistry educator; b. Bayonne, N.J., June 24, 1931; s. Steve J. and Anna (Gillack) K.; m. Evelyn L. Geiger, Apr. 2, 1955 (div. Apr. 1971); children: Lillian Ann, Kathryn Lynn, Kristina Eve, Stephen Edward; m. Barbara A. Soffe, Aug. 7, 1971; children—Brian Ashley, Scott William. B.S., Fairleigh Dickinson U., 1953; M.A., N.Y. U., 1954, Ph.D., 1964. Research chemist, cons. Shulton, Inc., Clifton, N.J., 1953-56; instr. chemistry Upsala Coll., East Orange, N.J., 1953-54; guest lectr. Upsala Coll., 1954-65; instr. sci. N.Y. U., 1954-55; tchr. sci. Kearny (N.J.) High Sch., 1955-56; research chemist Hoffman LaRoche, Nutley, N.J., 1956-57; prof., chmn. physics-geosci. dept. Montclair State U., Upper Montclair, N.J., 1956—; also chmn. physics-geosci. dept. Montclair State Coll.; prof. emeritus, 1995—; guest lectr. Fairleigh Dickinson U., 1955-69; coordinator, supr. AID Summer Sci. Insts., India and Ohio State U., 1966, NSF-AID Summer Sci. Insts., India, 1967; sci. coordinator master of arts in teaching program Fairleigh Dickinson U., 1968; vis. prof., cons. Interam U. P.R., 1983-84; internat. speaker on sci. in consumer edn.; mem. nat. edn. adv. com. Consumers Union. Author: Floridation of Polyethylenes, 1955, Chromotographic Separation of Xanthophylls, 1957, Laboratory Manual in Consumer Science, 1972, Consumer Science Text and Laboratory Manual, 1975, revised edit., 1978; contbr.: book Flavor Chemistry, 1959. Bd. dirs. N.J. Consumers League, 1964-67, Montclair Athletic Commn.; sr. asso. Danforth Found., 1961—. Finished 3rd in archery, World Masters Games, Brisbane, Australia, 1994, 3rd in archery, U.S. Sr. Olympics, Baton Rouge, La., 1995, 5th in archery U.S. Sr. Olympics, Tucson, Ariz., 1997, 1st in archery in N.J. Masters State Championship, 1998. Mem. Am. Chem. Soc. (nat. com. confs. and insts., div. chem. edn. 1968—), N.E.A., N.J. Edn. Assn. (chmn. higher edn. com. 1968-70), Nat. Sci. Tchrs. Assn. (com. establishing goals sci. literacy), N.J. Sci. Tchrs. Assn., Assn. N.J. Coll. and Univ. Profs. (founder 1969), AAAS, Phi Delta Kappa (life). Club: Elk. Patentee permeability of polyethylene, floridation. Home: 23 Dwyer Rd Wayne NJ 07470-3543 Office: Montclair State University Montclair NJ 07043-1624
God works in strange ways. But whatever happens always happens for the best even though it may be hard to accept at the moment.

KOWARSKI, ALLEN AVINOAM, endocrinologist, educator; b. Tel Aviv, Dec. 30, 1927; s. Hanoch and Sima (Tkazh) K.; m. Hanna Rose Zas, Mar. 24, 1950; children: David, Ruth. Student, Hebrew U., Jerusalem, 1946-47, MD, 1955; student, U. Lausanne (Switzerland) Med. Sch., 1949-52. Academic physician Hebrew U., 1955-62; instr., fellow Johns Hopkins U., Balt., 1962-68, asst. prof., 1968-72, assoc. prof., 1972-81; prof. U. Md., Balt., 1981—; pres. Kay Labs., Inc., 1974—. Patentee in field; contbr. over 170 articles to profl. jours.; inventor nonthrombogenic blood withdrawal sys., nonthrombogenic glucose monitor; discovered DAWN phenomenon in diabetes and bioinactive growth hormone syndrome (Kowarski syndrome), also integrated concentration of growth hormone method for diagnosis of growth hormone deficiency. Grantee NIH, 1979-97, McNeil Pharm., 1984-86, DuPont Critical Care, 1985-90, Genentech Found. for Growth & Devel., 1994-95, Lilly Rsch. Lab. 1996-98. Mem. Am. Pediat. Soc., Soc. Pediat. Rsch., Lawson-Wilkins Pediat. Endocrine Soc., The Endocrine Soc., Am. Fedn. Clin. Rsch., Am. Diabetes Assn. (Diabetes Rsch. award 1983, Charles H. Best medal for disting. svc. 1994). Office: Kay Labs Inc 2405 Sugarone Rd Baltimore MD 21209

KOWEL, STEPHEN THOMAS, electrical engineer, educator; b. Phila., Nov. 20, 1942; s. Abraham and Anna (Forman) K.; m. Janis Zoltan, June 7, 1970; children: Ann, Eugene, Rose. BSEE, U. Pa., 1964; PhD in Elec. Engring., 1968; MSEE, Poly. Univ., 1966. Rsch. assoc. U. Pa., Phila., 1968-69; asst. prof. elec. and computer engring. Syracuse (N.Y.) U., 1969-74, assoc. prof., 1974-79, prof., 1979-84; prof. elec. engring. and computer sci. U. Calif., Davis, 1984-90, vice-chair dept., 1986-90, dir. organized rsch. program on polymeric ultrathin film systems, 1988-90; chmn. elec. and computer engring. U. Ala., Huntsville, 1990-97, dir. PhD program in optical sci. and engring., 1992-97, interim dean engring., 1997-98, dir., lab. for integrated computing and optoelectric systems, 1998-99, prof elec. and computer engring., 1998-99; dean engring. U. Cin., 1999—; vis. prof. Cornell U., Ithaca, N.Y., 1982-83; cons. in field. Contbr. articles to profl. jours.; patentee in field. Grantee NASA, USAF, U.S. Army, NSF, Advanced Rsch. Projects Agy. Fellow OSA, IEEE (Centennial medal 1984); mem. AAAS, AAUP, Am. Soc. Engring. Edn., Soc. for Optical Engring., Sigma Xi. Home: 11370 Brittany Woods Ln Cincinnati OH 45249 Office: Univ Cin Coll Engring PO Box 210018 Cincinnati OH 45221-0016

KOWIT, STEVE MARK, poet, educator; b. New York City, NY, June 30, 1938. MA, San Francisco State Coll., 1968; MFA, Warren Wilson Coll., 1992. Prof. Southwestern Coll., Chula Vista, Calif., 1990—. Author: Passionate Journey, In the Palm of the Hand, The Poet's Portable Workshop, 1995, The Maverick Poets, 1984, Lurid Confessions, 1984, The Dumbbell Nebula, 1999. Fellowship NEA; recipient Paumanok Prize Atlanta Rev. Prize, 1996. Home: PO Box 184 Potrero CA 91963 Office: Dept English Southwestern Coll 900 Otay Lakes Rd Chula Vista CA 90101

KOYANIS, MELINDA T., publishing executive, lawyer; b. Bridgeport, Conn., Aug. 9, 1951; d. Elward Austin and Katherine (Lennon) Thompson; 1 child, Aristos. BA, Boston U., 1975; JD, Suffolk U., 1994. Bar: Mass. 1994. Lab asst. hematology Children's Hosp. Med. Ctr., Boston, 1977-83; editl. asst. Little, Brown & Co., Boston, 1981-83; permissions coord. Houghton Mifflin Co., Boston, 1983-87, subs. rights assoc., 1987-89, mgr. children's rights, 1989-91, rights & permission supr., 1991-94; mgr. copyright & permissions Harvard Univ. Press, Cambridge, Mass., 1994-97, dir. intellectual property, 1997—. Mem. Vol. Lawyers for the Arts, Boston, 1994—. Mem. Assn. Am. Pubs. (mem. rights & permissions adv. com. 1986-94, copyright com. 1994—), Assn. Am. Univ. Presses (mem. copyright com. 1994—). Home: 5 Chetwynd Rd Cambridge MA 02140-2601 Office: Harvard Univ Press 79 Garden St Cambridge MA 02138-1423

KOYM, ZALA COX, elementary education educator; b. San Antonio, July 21, 1948; d. Bruce Meador and Ruby Esther (Jordan) Cox; m. Charles Raymond Koym, July 5, 1969; children: Carol Ann, Cathy Lynn, Suzie Kay. BS in Edn., SW Tex. State U., 1970. Cert. supervision of tchr. effective practices. Elem. tchr. Schertz (Tex.)-Cibolo Ind. Sch. Dist., Schertz, Tex., 1970-71; substitute tchr. Alamogordo (N.Mex.) Pub. Schs., 1973-75; elem. tchr. Round Rock (Tex.) Ind. Sch. Dist., 1983-96, asst. prin., 1988-91, mentor tchr., 1993-96; 3-4th grade multiage tchr. Ft. Sam Houston Elem., San Antonio, Tex., 1996-98; 3rd grade tchr. Silver Creek Elem., Azle, Tex., 1998—; textbook advisor State of Tex., 1989; chair, coord. 5th grade level Round Rock Ind. Sch. Dist., 1986-90, 2d grade level chair, 1990-93; sci. lab. coord. Robertson Elem., Old Town Elem, 1983-89; Ft. Sam Houston Dist. Improvement Coun., 1996-97, campus gifted and talented com. 1997-99, dir. campus spelling bee, 1998-99, campus sci. coord., 1999; presenter in field. Active PTA, 1981-96, v.p. programs, 1994-95, PTO, 1996—, site-based decision making campus rep., 1993-95; dir. vacation Bible sch. FUMC, 1984-87, scholarship com., 1992-94; neighborhood capt. March of Dimes, 1990, Am. Heart Assn., 1994-95; mem. Campus Student Assistance Program Team, 1990-96, Old Town Bldg Leadership Team, 1991-92. Mem. ASCD, Assn. Tex. Profl. Educators (campus rep. 1998-99), Phi Delta Kappa (sec. 1991-93, assoc. historian 1994-95, v.p. programs 1995-96). Home: 2316 Walter Smith Rd Azle TX 76020-4333 Office: Fort Sam Houston Elem Rt 1 Box 672 3370 Nursery Rd San Antonio TX 78234-1479

KOZAK, HARLEY JANE, actress; b. Wilkes-Barre, Pa., Jan. 28, 1957; d. Joseph Aloysius and Dorothy (Taraldsen) K.; m. Gregory Aldisert, 1997. Cert., NYU, 1980. Appeared in films Parenthood, 1989, Arachnophobia, 1990, The Taking of Beverly Hills, 1990, The Favor, 1990, Necessary Roughness, 1991, All I Want for Christmas, 1991, Magic in The Water, 1995, TV series Harts of the West, 1993-94, Bringing Up Jack, 1995, You Wish, 1997. Office: United Talent Agy 9560 Wilshire Blvd Fl 5 Beverly Hills CA 90212-2400

KOZAK, JOHN W., lawyer; b. Chgo., July 25, 1943; s. Walter and Stella (Palka) K.; m. Elizabeth Mathias, Feb. 3, 1968; children: Jennifer, Mary Margaret, Suzanne. BSEE, U. Notre Dame, 1965; JD, Georgetown U., 1968. Bar: Ill. 1968, D.C. 1968. Patent advisor Office of Naval Research, Corona, Calif., 1968-69; assoc. Leydig, Voit & Mayer, Ltd. (and predecessor firms), Chgo., 1969-74, ptnr., 1974—, chmn. mgmt. com., 1982-91; mem. United Charities Legal Aid Soc., 1989—. Mem. ABA, Am. Intellectual Property Assn., Licensing Execs. Soc., Chgo. Intellectual Property Law Assn., University Club (Chgo.), Law Club (Chgo.), Winter Club (Lake Forest, Ill.), Knollwood Club (Lake Forest). Office: Leydig Voit & Mayer Ste 4900 2 Prudential Pla Chicago IL 60601

KOZBERG, DONNA WALTERS, rehabilitation administration executive; b. Milford, Del., Jan. 1, 1952; d. Robert Glyndwr and Gailey Ruth (Bedorf) Walters; m. Ronald Paul Kozberg, June 8, 1974; 1 child, Mariel Gailey. BA, U. Fla., 1973, M in Rehab. Counseling, 1974; MFA, CUNY, 1979; MBA, Rutgers U., 1986. Cert. rehab. counselor. Rehab. counselor Office Vocat. Rehab., N.Y.C., 1975-81; area dir. Lift, Inc., Staten Island, N.Y., 1981-83; ea. region dir. pub. relations, advt. Lift, Inc., Mountainside, N.J., 1983-85, v.p., 1985—, v.p., chief fin. officer, 1988, exec. v.p., 1991-93, pres., 1993; cofounder, mng. dir. Expert Strategies, Inc., Mountainside, N.J., 1992—; self-employed writer, editor, 1975—; adv. bd. Rutgers Exec. Master Bus. Adminstrn. Contbr. articles to profl. jours.; assoc. editor Parachute mag., 1978; editor-in-chief (newsletter) Counselor Adv, 1980. Pres. Com. on Employment of People with Disabilities; trustee Ctr. for Creative Living; bd. dirs. N.J. Adv. Coun. for Independent Living, adv. panel NYU. Mem. Nat. Rehab. Assn. (Spl. citation 1974, grantee 1973), Nat. Rehab. Adminstrs. Assn., Nat. Rehab. Counselors Assn., N.J. Rehab. Counselors Assn. (pres. 1996), Poets and Writers. Avocations: tennis, English lit. Home: 45 Dug Way Watchung NJ 07060-6011 Office: Lift Inc PO Box 1072 Mountainside NJ 07092-0072

KOZBERG, RONALD PAUL, health and human services administrator; b. N.Y.C., Apr. 8, 1951; s. Raymond and Muriel (Tolmas) K.; m. Donna Lynn Walters, June 8, 1974; 1 child, Mariel Gailey. BA, Gomes Coll., 1973; M of Rehab. Counseling, U. Fla., 1974; M of Pub. Health, Columbia U., 1986. Cert. rehab. counselor. Program dir. South Beach Psychiat. Ctr., S.I., N.Y., 1974-76; dir. rehab. svcs. Bklyn. Developmental Ctr., 1976-85; dir. stds. and compliance Bronx Developmental Svcs., 1985-91; pres. Expert Strategies, Inc., Mountainside, N.J., 1991—; technology com. chairperson Union County Edn. Coun., Westfield, N.J., 1993—. Author: The Do's and Dont's of Interviewing, 1992. Recipient Dean's Coun. award Dean of Health Related Professions, 1974. Mem. Nat. Rehab. Adminstrs. Assn. (N.E. regional bd. mem. 1982), Nat. Rehab. Counselors Assn. (N.Y. state sec., treas. 1981-82), Nat. Rehab. Assn. (pres., Spl. Citation 1974), Am. Pub. Health Assn.

Avocations: golf, tennis, photography. Home: 45 Dug Way Watchung NJ 07060-6011 Office: Expert Strategies Inc PO Box 4264 Warren NJ 07059-0264

KOZBERG, STEVEN FREED, psychologist; b. Mpls., Apr. 30, 1953; s. Martin L. and Lois (Bix) K. BA, Macalester Coll., 1975; MA, U. Minn., Duluth, 1978; PhD, U. Wis., 1981. Lic. psychologist, Minn. Rsch. asst. dept. counseling and guidance U. Wis., Madison, 1978-79, tchg. asst., 1980-81; rsch. asst. Guidance Inst. for Talented Students, 1979-80; counseling psychologist, asst. prof. psychology Carleton Coll., Northfield, Minn., 1981-88; counseling psychologist, lectr. psychology Carleton Coll., Northfield, 1988-92, counseling psychologist, sr. lectr. psychology, 1992-95, sr. lectr. psychology, 1995—; pvt. practice Mpls., 1995—; staff psychologist divsn. child and adolescent psychiatry, dept. psychiatry U. Minn., 1997-99. Mem. APA, Am. Psychol. Soc., Minn. Psychol. Assn., Soc. Rsch. on Adolescence, Midwestern Psychol. Assn., Phi Kappa Phi. Home: 5121 Tifton Dr Minneapolis MN 55439-1464 Office: Lake Pointe Corporate Ctr 3100 W Lake St Ste 465 Minneapolis MN 55416-4500

KOZBIAL, RICHARD JAMES, elementary education educator; b. Toledo, Nov. 11, 1933; s. Phillip and Bernice Bronislawa (Durka) K.; m. Jane Ardys Verny, July 8, 1961 (dec. Nov. 1983); children: Ardys Jane, Beth Lynne. EdB, U. Toledo, 1957, EdM, 1976. Tchr. Toledo Pub. Schs., 1956-58, 1962-84, Van Dyke Sch. Dist., Warren, Mich., 1958-62; intern tchr. cons. Toledo Pub. Schs., 1984-87, cons., 1987-93; supr. student tchrs., course facilitator U. Toledo, 1987-97, vis. prof., 1997-99, mem. faculty, 1997-99; ESL tchr. Szeged, Hungary, 1993-95; supr. alt. plan U. Toledo, 1993-99, vis. prof., 1997—, instr. integrated social studies/lang. arts/reading block, 1996-99; mem. textbook selection coms. Toledo Pub. Schs.; instr. student tchr. tng. programs Toledo U., 1962-84; instr. student tchr. tng. Bowling Green State U., 1962-84, Mich. State U., 1958-59; organizer Multi-Cultural Awareness Workshop Toledo Elem. Tchrs. Internat. Inst., 1986-90; organizer Outdoor Edn. Program; participant Multi Unit Edn. Plan; mem. U. Toledo Internat. Edn. Com., 1997-98. Author Spelling Curriculum Guide Toledo Pub. Schs., 1968; prodr. (TV programs) WGTE Famous Ams. Born in Feb., Israel. Up with People Host Family, Ohio Arab Affairs Coun., 1989—, YCMA, ISS, USIA Host Family, 1986—; mem. Planned Parenthood N.W. Ohio, Toledo Mus. Modern Art, Nat. Trust Historic Preservation, 1988—; vestry mem. Trinity Episc. Ch., 1984-87, sesquicentennial com., chmn. music; baritone soloist Canterbury Choir; bereavement vol. Hospice N.W. Ohio, Nat. Hospice Assn.; exec. bd. Toledo/Poznan Alliance (Dozynki com. chmn. 1993—); mem. Bedford Polish Culture Club, 1989-99; sponsor, coord. host families Zulu Choir, Durham, South Africa, Poznan (Poland) Nightengales. Named Outstanding Your Educator, Toledo C. of C., 1965-66; Jennings Founder scholar, 1979-80; recipient Miss Peach award Toledo Blade, 1963, Award of Excellence, 1983, Internat. Inst. Hall of Fame Disting. Svc. award, 1994, Letter of Commendation, Gov. of Ohio, 1994. Mem. Am. Fedn. Tchrs., Ohio Fedn. Tchrs., Toledo Fedn. Tchrs. (life), Internat. Inst. Inc. (life, chmn. edn. com., bd. dirs. 1985-91, pres. 1988-89), Assn. Two Toledos (bd. dirs., 1st v.p. 1990-91), U. Toledo Alumni Assn. (life), U. Mich. Alumni Assn., Am. Assn. Ret. Persons, Lucas County Ret. Tchrs. (life), Mid. East Affairs Coun. (bd. dirs.), Ellis Island Found., Smithsonian Assocs., Nat. Coun. Sr. Citizens, Toledo Sister Cities Internat. (bd. dirs., chmn. entertainment Masked Bash 1996, com. English lang. camp for students from Poland 1995, 96, chmn. host families), Am. Ctr. Polish Culture, Inc., Greenpeace, Phi Delta Kappa, Kappa Delta Pi (various offices including corr. sec., treas., v.p., pres., Point of Excellence award 1992). Democrat. Avocations: gardening, travel, reading, stained glass, calligraphy, phys. fitness, folk dancing. Home: 3823 Grantley Rd Toledo OH 43613-4218

KOZELKA, EDWARD WILLIAM, seed and feed company executive; b. Monona, Iowa, July 19, 1912; s. William Frank and Elizabeth (Tayek) K.; student Loras Coll., 1929-31; m. Beulah Annette Gunderson, Feb. 24, 1941; 1 dau., Gail Kathleen. Gen. mgr. Hall Roberts' Son, Postville, Iowa, 1932-46, v.p., gen. mgr., 1946-75, treas., 1975—; salesman Schiedel Real Estate, Postville, 1984—; dir. Postville State Bank. Mem. Postville City Coun., 1960-61; pres. Postville Hist. Soc., 1975-78; treas. Upper Explorerland Resource, Conservation and Devel. Com., 1969-87; chmn. Upper Explorerland Regional Planning Commn., 1971-80; chmn. N.E. Iowa River Basin Com., 1976-79; mem. Iowa Policy Adv. Coun. on Water Quality, 1976-82; mem. citizens adv. coun. Dept. Transp., 1977-87; mem. NE Iowa Water Resource Bd., 1986-87, Allamakee County Econ. Devel. Com., 1988-95, Allamakee County E-911 Bd., 1990-92, planning and fin. com. Postville Hosp., 1959-60; chmn. bldg. com. Postville Hosp., 1960-61; co-chmn. fund raising com. Postville Good Samaritan Center, 1968; bd. dirs. Big 4 Fair, 1946-74; mem. adv. council Area Aging Com., 1983-92. Recipient Disting. Service award Jaycees, 1966; hon. future farmer FFA. Mem. Iowa Seed Dealers Assn. (pres. 1972), Iowa Grain and Feed Assn., Western Seed Dealers Assn. Republican. Roman Catholic. Clubs: Kiwanis, Postville Comml. Home: 520 Wilson St Unit 12 Postville IA 52162-8590 Office: PO Box 396 Postville IA 52162-0396

KOZINSKI, ALEX, federal judge; b. Bucharest, Romania, July 23, 1950; came to U.S., 1962; s. Moses and Sabine (Zapler) K.; m. Marcy J. Tiffany, July 9, 1977; children: Yale Tiffany, Wyatt Tiffany, Clayton Tiffany. AB in Econs. cum laude, UCLA, 1972, JD, 1975. Bar: Calif. 1975, D.C., 1978. Law clk. to Hon. Anthony M. Kennedy U.S. Ct. Appeals (9th cir.), 1975-76; law clk. to Chief Justice Warren E. Burger U.S. Supreme Ct., 1976-77; assoc. Covington & Burling, Washington, 1979-81; asst. counsel Office of Counsel to Pres., White House, Washington, 1981; spl. counsel Merit Systems Protection Bd., Washington, 1981-82; chief judge U.S. Claims Ct., Washington, 1982-85; judge U.S. Ct. Appeals (9th cir.), 1985—; lectr. law U. So. Calif., 1992. Office: US Ct Appeals Ste 200 125 S Grand Ave Pasadena CA 91105-1652*

KOZITKA, RICHARD EUGENE, retired consumer products company executive; b. Staples, Minn., Apr. 30, 1934; s. Michael V. and Luella H. (Drews) K.; m. Mary Elizabeth Juneau, Sept. 27, 1969; children: Michael Arthur, Laura Juneau. BA in Journalism, U. Minn., 1956. Program dir. Jr. Achievement of Chgo., 1961-63; mgr. publ./employee communications The Quaker Oats Co., Chgo., 1963-72, dir. employee and audio visual communications, 1972-78, v.p. corp. adminstrv. svcs., 1978-95. Trustee Luth. Social Svcs. Ill. Served with U.S. Army, 1957-61. Mem. Westmoreland Country Club (Wilmette, Ill.), Chgo. Curling Club (Northbrook, Ill.), Univ. Club Chgo., Pelican Strand Country Club (Naples, Fla.). Lutheran. Home: 1023 Franz Dr Lake Forest IL 60045-3649

KOZLIK, MICHAEL DAVID, lawyer; b. Omaha, Apr. 20, 1953; s. Otto John and Ella Mae (Slightam) K.; m. Emily C. Cunningham, Sept. 30, 1983; children: John E., Caroline C. BS in Bus., Creighton U., 1975, JD, 1979. Bar: Nebr. 1979, U.S. Dist. Ct. Nebr. 1979, U.S. Dist. Ct. Appeals (8th cir.) 1979, U.S. Tax Ct. 1991; CPA, Nebr. Acct. Peat Marwick, Omaha, 1979-84; v.p. fin. Emelco, Omaha, 1984-86; assoc. Nelson Morrow, Omaha, 1986-88; shareholder Schmid Mooney, Omaha, 1988-97, Croker Huck, Omaha, 1997—; mem. Nebr. CPA Ethics Comm., 1984-85, Nebr. CPA Edn. Comm., 1988—. Contbr. articles to mags. Bd. dirs. County Health Dept., Omaha, 1986—, Hugh O'Brien Found., Omaha, 1989—, Nebr. ACC Decathlon. Recipient Leadership Omaha award Omaha C. of C., 1989; named One of Ten Outstanding Young Omahans Jaycees, 1990, 92. Mem. Omaha Bar Assn., Nebr. Bar Assn., Optimists (pres. 1989-90, honor award 1990). Republican. Avocations: hunting, fishing, billiards, geneology. Home: 5122 Nicholas St Omaha NE 68132-1434 Address: Croker Huck DeWitt Anderson &c Gonderinger 1250 Commerical Federal Tower 2120 S 72nd St Omaha NE 68124-2303

KOZLOFF, LLOYD M., university dean, educator, scientist; b. Chgo., Oct. 15, 1923; s. Joseph and Rose (Hollobow) K.; m. Judith Bonnie Friedman, June 16, 1947; children—James, Daniel, Joseph, Sarah. B.S., U. Chgo., 1943, Ph.D., 1948. Asst., then assoc. prof. biochemistry U. Chgo., 1949-61, prof., 1961-64; prof. microbiology U. Colo., Denver, 1964-80, chmn. dept. microbiology, 1966-76, assoc. dean, prof., 1976-80; dean, prof. U. Calif., San Francisco, 1981-91, prof., dean emeritus, 1991—; career investigator USPHS, U. Chgo., 1962;. Founding editor Jour. Virology, 1966-76; contbr. articles to profl. jours., chpts. to books. Chmn. bd. dirs. Proctor Fund., 1981-91; v.p. San Francisco Alliance for Mental Illness, 1993-96; pres. emeritus U. Calif. San Francisco Faculty Assn., 1996—. With USN, 1944-46. Commonwealth Fund fellow, 1953, Lederle Found. fellow, 1954. Fellow AAAS, Am. Acad. Microbiol. (hon.); mem. Am. Soc. Biol. Chemistry, Am. Soc. Microbiology (head virology sect. 1974-76), Am. Chem. Soc., N.Y. Acad. Sci. Home: 2106 Jackson St # 6 San Francisco CA 94115-1551 Office: U Calif Grad Divsn San Francisco CA 94114-2732

KOZLOSKI, LILLIAN TERESE D., history of aerospace technology educator; b. Pitts., Sept. 11, 1934; d. Andrew and Juliana (Yevchak) Dzmura; m. Joseph Kozloski, May 22, 1956; children: Lisa, Cynthia, Charles, Christopher, Dolores Anne. AS, Mt. Aloysius Coll., 1954; BIS, George Mason U., 1981. Mus. technician Smithsonian Air & Space Instn., Washington, 1981-85, mus. specialist, 1985-95, ret., 1995; lectr. U.S. Space Gear Enterprises, Spotsylvania, Va., 1996—; cons. Smithsonian Instn., Washington, 1996, N.Y. Times, 1996; lectr. on living and working in space. Author: U.S. Space Gear History of Space Suit Technology, 1994; contbr. articles to profl. publs. Mem. AAUW, Am. Assn. Mus., N.Y. Acad. Scis., Soc. for History of Tech. Roman Catholic. Achievements include categorization and study of Nat. Air and Space Mus. collection of space suits; collected and organized space suit into loan collections and preservation and study collection. Home: 5035 Ridge Rd Spotsylvania VA 22553-6334

KOZLOWSKI, BETTE MARIE, accountant; b. Camden, N.J., Apr. 2, 1959; d. Joshua Ashley and Doris Annette (Saunders) Tobey. BS with honors in Acctg., Pa. State U., 1981. CPA, Conn. Staff acct. Ernst and Whinney, Hartford, Conn., 1981-83; mid-Atlantic dir. univ. rels. KPMG LLP, Phila., 1983—. Fin. sec. St. Matthews United Meth. Ch. Mem. AIPCA, Jules Link Inst. Accts., Pa. State U. Alumni Assn., Friends of the Libr. U.S. (treas.), Nat. Assn. of Coll. Employers, Am. Acctg. Assn., Ea. Assn. Coll. and Univ. Bus. Officers, Golden Key Nat., Beta Gamma Sigma, Beta Alpha Psi, Phi Mu. Republican. Methodist. Avocations: golf, running, gardening. Office: KPMG LLP 1600 Market St Philadelphia PA 19103-7240

KOZLOWSKI, DOROTHY, health center administrator; b. Feb. 10, 1950; d. Walter and Sophia (Bodziak) K. BSN, Rutgers U., 1977; MSAN, Seton Hall U., 1980. Cert. adult health nurse practitioner, N.J. Mem. faculty Mountainside Hosp. Sch. Nursing, Montclair, N.J., 1978-86; dir. Willets Health Ctr. Rutgers U. N.J., clin. prof.; clin. prof. Seton Hall U.; adj. faculty mem. Fairleigh Dickinson U., Rutherford, N.J., 1990-91, Bloomfield (N.J.) Coll., 1994-96; bd. dirs. Interested Nurses for Polit. Action Coalition, 1980-90. Contbr. articles to profl. jours. Fellow Am. Coll. Health Assn. (rep. to Nat. Alliance Nurse Practitioners, sec. exec. com., mem. spl. interest group for nurse practitioners, mem. task force on nat. health objectives for Yr. 2010, legal case reviewer 1995—); mem. Nat. Alliance Nurse Practitioners (rep. to dept. health and human svcs. divsn. nursing consortium on alcohol and drug abuse 1992), Mid. Atlantic Coll. Health Assn. (pres-elect 1996, pres. 1997), N.J. Coll. Health Assn. (vice chmn. med.-surg. divsn. 1981-85, del. to ANA conv. 1986-89, vice chmn. primary care nurse practitioner forum 1987-89). Avocations: antiques, photography. Home: 204 Ayliffe Ave Westfield NJ 07090-2204

KOZLOWSKI, L. DENNIS, manufacturing company executive; b. Irvington, N.J., Nov. 16, 1946; s. Leo Kelly and Agnes (Kozell) K. BS, Seton Hall U., 1968; MBA, Rivier Coll., 1976. V.p. fin. Grinnell Fire Protection Systems Divsn., Providence, 1976-81; v.p., CFO Ludlow Corp. subs. Tyco Labs., Needham, Mass., 1981-82; pres., CEO Grinnell Corp., 1982—; pres., COO Tyco Labs., Inc., 1989-92, CEO, 1992—, chmn. bd. dirs., 1993—; bd. dirs. Thiokol Corp., Atlantic Bank and Trust Co. Bd. regents Seton Hall U. Office: Tyco Internat Ltd 1 Tyco Park Exeter NH 03833-2923*

KOZLOWSKI, RONALD STEPHAN, librarian; b. Chgo., Oct. 18, 1937; s. Stephan James and Helen Marie Beck (Tancula) K.; m. Barbara Hartlein, Aug. 8, 1964; children: Ann, Keith, Ellen, Brent. BS in Edn, Ill. State U., 1961; MA in LS, Rosary Coll., 1968. Audiovisual libr. Triton Jr. Coll., River Grove, Ill., 1968-69; br. libr. Evansville (Ind.) Pub. Librs., 1969-70; asst. dir. Evansville (Ind.) Pub. Libraries, 1971-74; head reference and acquisitions dept. Ind. State U., Evansville, 1970-71; dir. West Fla. Regional Libr., Pensacola, 1974-77, Louisville Free Pub. Libr., 1977-83, Pub. Libr. Charlotte and Mecklenburg County, N.C., 1983-86; exec. dir. Cuyahoga County Pub. Libr., Cleve., 1986-89; dir. Miami-Dade Pub. Libr. System, Miami, Fla., 1989-1993; adminstr. Anne Arundel County Pub. Libr., Annapolis, Md., 1993—; del. White House Conf. on Librs. Mem. ALA, Md. Libr. Assn., Southeastern Libr. Assn. Home: 1160 Jeffery Dr Crofton MD 21114-1315 Office: Anne Arundel County Libr 5 Harry S Truman Pkwy Annapolis MD 21401-7084

KOZLOWSKI, THOMAS JOSEPH, JR., lawyer, trust company executive; b. Norristown, Pa., July 29, 1950; s. Thomas Joseph Sr. and Mary Elisa (Alvarez) K.; m. Michelle Mary Champagne, Jan. 9, 1971; children: Brian Christopher, Scott Michael, Mark Daniel. BSBA in Acctg., Georgetown U., 1971, JD, 1979; MBA, George Washington U., 1975. Bar: D.C. 1979, Va. 1980; CPA, Va. Sr. acct. Touche Ross & Co., Washington, 1972-75; dir. internal audit Pentagon Fed. Credit Union, Arlington, Va., 1975-77; supervisory acct. Snyder, Newrath & Co., Washington, 1977-79; v.p., sec. Owens & Co., Inc., Arlington, 1979-86; sr. v.p. fin. Realty Investment Co., Inc., Silver Spring, Md., 1986-89; sr. v.p., treas. The Selzer Group, Inc., N.Y.C., 1989-93; pres. The Collector's Gallery Of Va. Inc., Alexandria, 1992-96; sr. v.p., sr. trust officer family office group Merrill Lynch Trust Co., Princeton, N.J., 1993—; bd. dirs. Owens & Co., Alexandria, Va. Editor Jour. Law and Policy in Internat. Bus., 1976-79. Arbiter Fairfax County (Va.) Consumer Protection Commn., 1977-95; treas. Commonweal Found., Inc., Silver Spring, 1986-89; bd. dirs. Residential Youth Services, Inc., Alexandria, 1981-89, treas., 1982-84, v.p., 1984-85; treas. Coplex Found., N.Y.C., 1989-93. Fellow D.C. Inst. CPAs; mem. ABA, AICPA, D.C. Bar Assn., Va. State Bar Assn., Inst. Mgmt. Acctg. (cert. mgmt. acctg., cert. disting. performance 1975). Democrat. Roman Catholic. Avocations: reading, photography. Office: Merrill Lynch Trust Co 800 Scudders Mill Rd Plainsboro NJ 08536

KOZMA, ADAM, electrical engineer; b. Cleve., Feb. 2, 1928; s. Desire and Vera (Nagy) K.; m. Eileen Marie Somogyi, Oct. 24, 1956 (dec. Jan. 1978); children: Paul A. (dec.), Peter A.; m. Rebecca Chelius, Feb. 6, 1993. BSME, U. Mich., 1952, MS in Engring.-Instrumentation Engring., 1964; MS in Engring. Mechanics., Wayne State U., 1961; PhDEE, U. London, 1968. Design engr. US Broach Co., Detroit, 1951-57; rsch. engr. Inst. Sci. & Tech., Willow Run Labs. U. Mich., Ann Arbor, 1958-69; gen. mgr. Electro Optics Ctr. Harris, Inc., Ann Arbor, 1969-73; sr. rsch. engr. radar div. Environ. Rsch. Inst. Mich., Ann Arbor, 1973-75, mgr. elec. and electromagnetics dept., 1975-76, mgr. tech. staff, 1976-77, v.p., dir. radar div., 1977-85, v.p., corp. devel., 1985-86; v.p., dir. def. electronics engring. div. Syracuse (N.Y.) Rsch. Corp., 1986-88; head intelligence systems dept. MITRE Corp., Bedford, Mass., 1988-89, head advanced systems dept., 1990-93; adj. prof. Coll. Engring. U. Mich., Ann Arbor, 1993—; cons. Conductron Corp., Ann Arbor, 1966, IBM, Endicott, N.Y., 1967-68, U.S. Army Missile Command, Huntsville, Ala., 1974-76, Mitre Corp., 1993—; lectr. various univs.; engring. cons., 1993—. Co-author: Hologram Visual Displays (Motion Picture TV Engrs. honorable mention 1977); patentee in field. With U.S. Army, 1946-47. Fellow IEEE (life), Optical Soc. Am.; mem. Aero. and Electronics Systems Soc. of IEEE (radar systems panel 1984—, bd. govs. 91-93), Geoscience and Remote Sensing Soc. of IEEE, Am. Def. Preparedness Assn. (chmn. various coms. avionics sect. 1975-88, Ordnance medal 1984), Soc. Photo-Optical Instrumentation Engrs., Sigma Xi. Lutheran. Avocations: tennis, skiing, bicycling. Home and Office: 2996 Appleway Ann Arbor MI 48104-1808

KOZMA, HELENE JOYCE MARIE, adult educator; b. Bridgeport, Conn.; d. Ernest A. and Helen C. (Skurski) K. BA in English, Adelphi U.; MBA in Bus. Mgmt., Sacred Heart U., 1986, postgrad., 1990. Cert. English and bus. tchr., Conn. Tchr. bus. Town of Stratford, Conn., 1986-87, 92, 96, Acad. of Our Lady of Mercy, Milford, Conn., 1987-88; Gateway Comty./Tech. Coll., New Haven, Conn., 1994—; tchr. Sacred Heart U., 1998—, St. Vincent Coll., 1998—, Gateway Cmty. Coll. Eucharistic min. Holy Name of Jesus Ch., 1991, lectr., reader, 1991, catechist tchr., 1990-91; min. Secular Franciscan Order, Coun. of Holy Spirit Fraternity, 1991-94; mem. Stratford town com., 1995-97; bd. dirs. Stratford Libr. Assn., 1995-97. Mme. Nat. Coun. Tchrs. of English, Shakespeare Guild, Toastmasters (charter, treas. 1984, adminstrv. v.p. 1986).

KOZMA, KAREN JEAN, nurse, educator; b. Detroit, June 29, 1957; d. Donald Lee and Barbara Jean (Lines) P.; m. George Kozma, June 7, 1986 (div. June 1996); children: Jeminii, Marie. AS in Nursing, Central Fla. C.C., Ocala, 1980; BA in Finance, U. S. Fla., Tampa, 1990, MBA in Mgmt., 1993; postgrad., U. S. Fla. and La. State U.; PhD in Bus. Adminstrn., Walden U., Mpls., 1997. Pres., owner KKKonsultants, Sarasota, 1990—; asst. prof. Va. Intrnat. Coll., Bristol, 1999—; adj. on-line instr. N.H. Coll.; adj. prof. Manatee Coll., 1996-99, U. South Fla., 1999. With U.S. Army, 1976-77. Republican. Avocations: traveling to foreign countries. Home and Office: PO Box 21193 Sarasota FL 34276-4193

KOZMETSKY, GEORGE, computer science educator; b. Seattle, Oct. 5, 1917; s. George and Nadya (Omelan) K.; m. Ronya Keosiff, Nov. 5, 1943; children: Gregory Allen, Nadya Anne (Mrs. Michael Scott). BA, U. Wash., 1938; MBA, Harvard U., 1947, DCCS, 1957. Instr. Harvard U., 1947-50; asst. prof. Carnegie-Mellon U., Pitts., 1950-52; mem. tech. staff Hughes Aircraft Co., Los Angeles, 1952-54; dir. computer, controls lab. Litton Co., Los Angeles, 1954-59; v.p., asst. gen. mgr. electronic equipment div. Litton Co., 1959-60; exec. v.p. Teledyne Corp., Beverly Hills, Calif., 1960-66; prof. mgmt. and computer sci., dean Coll. Bus. Adminstrn. and Grad. Sch. Bus., U. Tex. at Austin, 1966-82, exec. assoc. for econ. affairs univ. system, 1966—; Leatherbee lectr. Harvard U., 1967; vis. scholar U. Wash., 1968, Walker-Ames prof., 1970. Author: Financial Reports of Labor Unions, 1950, (with Simon and Guetzkow) Centralization Versus Decentralization in Organizing the Controller's Department, 1954, (with Paul Kircher) Electronic Computers and Management Control) 1956, (with Ronya Kozmetsky) Making It Together, 1981, Transformational Management, 1985; (with Gill and Smilor) Financing and Managing Fast-Growth Companies, 1985, Creating the Technopolis, 1988; (with Matsumoto and Smilor) Pacific Cooperation and Development, 1988, (with Peterson and Albaum) Modern American Capitalism, 1990, (with Yue) Global Economic Competition, 1997. With AUS, 1942-45. Decorated Silver Star, Bronze Star with oak leaf cluster, Purple Heart; recipient of Nat. Medal of Tech., Nat. Sci. Found., 1993. Fellow AAAS; mem. Inst. Mgmt. Sci. (chmn. bd., pres.), Assn. Advancement of Med. Instrumentation, Brit. Interplanetary Soc., Am. Soc. Oceanography. Home: PO Box 2253 Austin TX 78768-2253 Office: IC2 Institute U Tex at Austin 1301 W 25th St Ste 300 Austin TX 78705

KOZODOY, NEAL, magazine editor; b. Boston, Apr. 4, 1942; s. Peter H. and Marion (Seder) K.; m. Ruth Lurie, June 7, 1964; children—Sarah Naomi, Peter, Elizabeth. B.A., Harvard U., 1963; B.H.L., Hebrew Coll., Boston, 1963; M.A., Columbia U., 1966. Mem. editorial staff Commentary mag., N.Y.C., 1966—, exec. editor, 1968-90, editor, 1990-95; chief editor Commentary mag., 1995—; editor Library Jewish Studies, 1970-95; vis. lectr. Jewish Theol. Sem., 1974-75, Yale U., 1976; cons. President's Commn. Campus Unrest, 1970, NEH, 1976-82, U.S. Dept. Edn., 1985-88, Office of Nat. Drug Control Policy, 1989-90. Sec. Com. for the Free World, 1981-90. Woodrow Wilson fellow, 1964-65; Danforth fellow, 1965-67. Office: Commentary Am Jewish Com 165 E 56th St New York NY 10022-2709

KOZOL, JONATHAN, writer; b. Boston, Sept. 5, 1936; s. Harry Leo and Ruth (Massell) K. BA, Harvard U., 1958; Rhodes scholar, Magdalen Coll., Oxford U., 1958-59. Tchr. Boston pub. schs., 1964-65, Newton pub. schs., 1966-68; dir., trustee Store-front Learning Center, 1968-74; vis. lectr. Yale U., 1969, numerous univs., 1971-97; prof. edn. Trinity Coll., 1980; cons. U.S. Office Edn., 1965-66; inst. Ctr. for Intercultural Documentation, Cuernavaca, Mex., 1969, 70, 74. Author: Death At An Early Age, 1967 (Nat. Book award, 1968), Free Schools, 1972, The Night Is Dark and I Am Far From Home, 1975, Children of the Revolution, 1978, Prisoners of Silence, 1980, On Being A Teacher, 1981, People of the Book, 1982, Alternative Schools, 1983, Illiterate America, 1985, Rachel and Her Children, 1988 (Robert F. Kennedy Book award, 1989), Savage Inequalities, 1991 (New Eng. Book award, 1992, Amazing Grace, 1995 (Anisfield-Wolf Book award, 1996); corr.: Los Angeles Times, USA Today, 1982-83; contbr. to N.Y. Times Book Rev., 1968-85; reporter-at-large The New Yorker mag., 1988. Trustee New Sch. for Children, Roxbury, Mass.; bd. dirs. Nat. Literacy Coalition, 1980-83. Recipient Olympia Thousand Dollar award, 1962, Lannan Literary award, 1994; Saxton fellow in creative writing Harper & Row, 1964; Guggenheim fellow, 1970, 84; Field Found. fellow, 1972; Ford Found. fellow, 1974; Rockefeller Found. fellow, 1978, fellow in humanities, 1983. Mem. P.E.N., Nat. Coalition for the Homeless, Fellowship of Reconciliation. Address: PO Box 145 Byfield MA 01922-0145 *My concerns are the education, health and housing of low income children.*

KOZSUCH, MILDRED JEANNETTE, librarian, archivist; b. Lynnville, Tenn., Dec. 3, 1928; d. Kenneth Carl and Minnie Kate (Schott) Spaulding; m. Paul James Kozsuch, Aug. 28, 1951 (div. Nov. 1959); 1 child, James Sandhi. BA, West Liberty State Coll., 1950; MA, East Tenn. State U., 1969. Tchr. Mt. Pleasant (Ohio) H.S., 1950-51; libr. clk. East Tenn. State U., Johnson City, 1956-60; libr., archivist, 1968-85; tchr., libr. Kingsport (Tenn.) City Schs., 1960-68; libr., archivist (part time) Milligan Coll. (Tenn.), 1991-98. Editor: Historical Reminiscenses of Carter County, Tenn., 1985. Co-chair Washington County Bicentennial Commn., Jonesborough, Tenn., 1993-96; vol. libr. First Christian Ch., Johnson City, Tenn., 1961-88. Mem. Tenn. Archivists, Watauga Assn. Genealogists (v.p.), Jonesborough Geneal. Soc., (v.p.), Washington County Hist. Assn. (pres., v.p., editor Washington County Hist. Assn. Speeches 1987-1988), Boone Tree Libr. Assn., Tenn. Hist. Soc., East Tenn. Hist. Soc. Avocations: local history, genealogy, collecting postcards and books, collecting data for writing books. Home: 546 Matson Rd Jonesborough TN 37659-5767

KOZUCH, JULIANNA BERNADETTE, librarian, educator; b. Wallis, Tex., Feb. 16, 1921; d. Felix Joseph and Agnes Mary (Vrana) K. BA in English, Our Lady of the Lake U., San Antonio, 1951; MEd, Our Lady of the Lake U., 1961, MLS, 1972. Joined Sisters of Divine Providence order, Roman Cath. Ch., 1936; cert. tchr., Tex., Okla., La. Tchr. Sts. Cyril & Methodius, Granger, Tex., 1940-41, St. John's Sch., Fayetteville, Tex., 1941-42, 55-56, St. Ferdinand's Sch., San Fernando, Calif., 1942-43, Immaculate Conception, Houston, 1943-52, St. Joseph Meml., Enid, Okla., 1952-55, St. Mary's Sch., Natchitoches, La., 1956-57, St. Francis Sch., Iota, La., 1957-58, St. Joseph's Sch., Abilene, Tex., 1958-59, St. Genevieve, Lafayette, La., 1959-61, St. Peter and Paul Sch., New Braunfels, Tex., 1961-63, St. Pius, Pasadena, Tex., 1963-65, St. Anne's, Houston, 1965-70, Meml. High, Lafayette, La., 1972-73; tchr., libr. St. Mary's Sch, San Antonio, Tex., 1970-72, St. Augustine, Laredo, Tex., 1973-77; with bookstore Our Lady of Lake U., San Antonio, 1977-78, ref. libr., 1978-85; head libr. Worden Sch., San Antonio, 1985—; mem. ethnic affairs Tex. Cath. Conf., 1978—, treas., 1982—; speaker Tex. Inst. Texan Cultures, 1983; translator for Czechoslovakia refugees, 1981—, Dr. Denton Belk; interviewed on Channel 36 TV, 1982, Channel 12, 1979, 82. Mem. math. textbook com. Galveston (Tex.) Houston Diocese, 1968-70; rep. religious women Bishop's Coun., Corpus Christi (Tex.) Diocese, 1976-77; docent Luth. Youth Conf., Inst. Texan Cultures, 1983. Recipient Disting. Svc. award Bayanihan Dance Troupe, 1977, Margil award Tex. Cath. Conf. on Cmty. Ethnic Affairs, 1985, Papal medal, 1987. Mem. AAUP (sec. 1979-82), Nat. Coun. Math. Tchrs., Nat. Cath. Libr. Assn. (treas. Houston chpt. 1968-70, treas. San Antonio chpt. 1970-72, Community Leader of Am. award 1969), Tex. Libr. Assn., Bexar County Libr. Assn. (membership com. 1970-72), Teenage Libr. Assn. (bd. dirs Houston chpt. 1968-70), Southwestern Libr. Assn., Our Lady of the Lake U. Assn. (sec. San Antonio chpt. 1980-82, historian 1982—), Our Lady of the Lake Sisters Orgn. (social com. 1978-79), Czech-Am. Cultural and Edn. Found. (bd. dirs. 1982—, Svc. award 1987). Democrat. Roman Catholic. Home: 602 SW 24th St San Antonio TX 78207-4620 Office: Our Lady of the Lake U 411 SW 24th St San Antonio TX 78207-4666

KRA, ETHAN EMANUEL, actuary; b. Port Chester, N.Y., Mar. 26, 1948; s. Michael Aaron and Bessie (Shragowitz) K.; m. Madeline Rollhaus, Jan. 4, 1976; children: Joseph, Rachel, Joshua. BA summa cum laude, MA, Yale U., 1969, M of Philosophy in Math., 1973, PhD, 1974. Enrolled actuary. Prize teaching fellow Yale U., New Haven, 1972-73; with Prudential Ins. Co., Newark, 1973-77, asst. actuary, 1977; with William M. Mercer, Inc., N.Y.C., 1977—, prin., 1984-89, mng. dir., 1989-94, mng. dir. and chief actuary-retirement, 1994—; lectr. in field. Author: Infinitary Forcing for Languages with the Q-Quantifier, 1974; contbr. articles to profl. jours. Trustee Young Israel West Orange, N.J., 1987-89. Fellow Woodrow Wilson Found., 1969, NSF, 1969-72. Fellow Soc. Actuaries (pension sect. coun. 1991-94, chair

1993-94, bd. govs. 1997—), Conf. Cons. Actuaries; mem. Assn. Pvt. Pension and Welfare Plans (ret. and investment policy com. 1993—), Am. Acad. Actuaries (pension practice coun. 1993-94, 97—, pension com. 1994—), Phi Beta Kappa. Jewish. Avocation: bridge. Office: William M Mercer Inc 1166 Avenue Of The Americas New York NY 10036-2708

KRA, PAULINE SKORNICKI, French language educator; b. Lodz, Poland, July 30, 1934; came to U.S., 1950, naturalized, 1955; d. Edward and Nathalie Skornicki; m. Leo Dietrich Kra, Mar. 10, 1955; children: David Theodore, Andrew Jason. Student, Radcliffe Coll., 1951-53; BA, Barnard Coll., 1955; MA, Columbia U., 1963, PhD, 1968; MA, Queens Coll., 1990. Lectr. Queens Coll., CUNY, 1964-65; asst. prof. French, Yeshiva U., N.Y.C., 1968-74, assoc. prof., 1974-82, prof., 1982-99, prof. emerita, 1999—; programmer/analyst Ctr. Advanced Tech. Columbia U., N.Y.C., 1998—. Author: Religion in Montesquieu's Lettres persanes, 1970; contbr. articles to profl. jours. Mem. MLA, Am. Assn. Tchrs. French, Am. Soc. 18th Century Studies, Société Francaise d'étude du XVIII Siècle, Soc. Montesquieu, Assn. for Computers and Humanities, Assn. for Lit. and Linguistic Computing, Phi Beta Kappa. Home: 10914 Ascan Ave Forest Hills NY 11375-5370

KRABBE, JEROEN AART, actor; b. Amsterdam, Dec. 5, 1944; s. Maarten and Margreet (Reiss) K.; m. Herma van Geemert, Dec. 31, 1965; children: Martyn, Jasper, Jakob. Student, Acad. of Fine Arts, Amsterdam, 1980, Acad. of Dramatic Arts, Amsterdam, 1965. Actor Rosenberg (Marion) Office, L.A. Actor: (films) Soldier of Orange, 1978, The Fourth Man, 1982 (Best Actor award), No Mercy, 1987, The Living Day Lights, 1987, A World Apart, 1988, Crossing Delancey, 1988, Melancholia, 1989, Till There Was You, 1990, The Prince of Tides, 1991, Robin Hood, 1991, Kakda, King of the Hill, 1992, The Fugitive, 1993, Farinelli, 1994, Immortal Beloved, 1994, Blood of a Poet, 1995, Business for Pleasure, 1996, Dangerous Beauty, 1996, (TV miniseries) Dynasty, 1991, Cinderella: Only Love (tv miniseries), 1998, Left Luggage, 1998, Jesus, 1999; dir., actor (film) Left Luggage, 1997. Recipient Imagfic '84 award, Madrid, 1984, Vittorio de Sica prize, Sorrento, 1983, Anne Frank prize, Amsterdam, 1985, Rotterdams Golden Heart award, 1986-87, Golden Calf award for life achievement Dutch Film Festival, 1996, The Rembrandt award for life achievement Veronica Broadcasting Corp., 1998, Berlin, Blue Angel award, 1998, Emden, Best Film of Festival; comdr. Order of the Dutch Lion. Office: Marion Rosenberg 8428 Melrose Pl Ste C West Hollywood CA 90069-5308

KRABBENHOFT, KENNETH LESTER, radiologist, educator; b. Sabula, Iowa, Jan. 7, 1923; s. Lester Henry and Bessie Grant (Thompson) K.; m. Gloria Darlene Eriksen, June 17, 1944; children: Kenneth Lester, Douglas Harold, Karen Ann Krabbenhoft Graham. BA, State U. Iowa, 1943, MD, 1946. Diplomate Am. Bd. Radiology. Intern Harper Hosp., Detroit, 1946-47, resident in radiology, 1949-52, assoc. radiologist, 1952-57, radiologist, 1957—; practice medicine specializing in radiology Birmingham, Mich., 1957—; prof., chmn. dept. radiology Wayne State U., Detroit, 1969-84; chief radiology Detroit Receiving Hosp.-Univ. Health Center, 1980-84; cons. radiologist VA Hosp., Allen Park, Mich., Children's Hosp. Mich., Crittenton Gen. Hosp., Herman Kiefer Hosp., Nat. Cancer Inst.; mem. Nat. Cancer Adv. bd.,, 1970-73; pres. Affiliated Radiologists, Inc., Detroit, 1973-85, Detroit Gen. Hosp. Rsch. Corp., 1974-82; mem. Environ. Radiation Exposure Adv. Com., 1975-78; trustee Am. Bd. Radiology, 1971-93, sec., exec. dir., 1981-93, assoc. exec. dir., 1993-95; treas. Am. Bd. Med. Specialists, 1981-85; alt. del. Internat. Congress Radiology. Cons. editor: Am. Jour. Roentgenology, 1975-81. Served to lt. (j.g.), M.C. USNR, 1947-49. Recipient Disting. Alumnus award M.D. Anderson Cancer Ctr., 1988; Nat. Cancer Inst. grantee, 1971-75; Nat. Cancer Inst. Specialized Cancer Center grantee, 1973-75. Fellow Am. Coll. Radiology (Gold medal 1989); mem. Detroit Acad. Medicine, Detroit Med. Club, AMA (vice chmn. sect. council 1969-71), Mich., Wayne county med. socs., Mich. Radiol. Soc. (pres. 1969-70), Am. Radium Soc., Am. Roentgen Ray Soc. (Silver medal 1962, Gold medal 1983), AAAS, Radiol. Soc. N.Am., Chicago Radiol. Soc. (hon., Gold medal 1992), Inter-Am. Coll. Radiology, Friends of Detroit Public Library, Founders Soc. Detroit Inst. Art, State Hist. Soc. Iowa, Mich. Hist. Soc., Lost Lakes Woods Assn., Sigma Xi, Alpha Omega Alpha. Clubs: Masons. Exhibited portable radioactive istopes for radiography at Smithsonian Inst., 1964-67. Home: 52 Oxford Blvd Pleasant Ridge MI 48069-1111

KRABILL, ROBERT ELMER, osteopathic physician; b. Wayland, Iowa, June 4, 1934; s. Robert H. and Amanda (Wyse) K.; m. Ellen Savage, Sept. 1, 1963; children: Keith Andrew, Angela Kay, Valerie Ann, Kelly Dawn. BS, Iowa Wesleyan Coll., 1961; DO, Kirkville (Mo.) Coll. Osteo. Medicine, 1966. Diplomate Am. Bd. Family Practice. Intern Cuyahoga Falls (Ohio) Gen. Hosp., 1966-67, mem. staff, 1967—; gen. practice osteo. medicine Uniontown, Ohio, 1967—; sec., treas. gen. practice dept. Cuyahoga Falls Gen. Hosp., 1985-86. Named one of Outstanding Young Men of Am., U.S. Jaycees, 1969. Mem. Am. Osteo. Assn., Ohio Osteo. Assn., Am. Coll. Gen. Practitioners Osteo. Medicine and Surgery. Mennonite. Home: 3733 N Vista St NW Uniontown OH 44685-8496 Office: 13017 Cleveland Ave NW PO Box 399 Uniontown OH 44685-0399

KRACKE, ROBERT RUSSELL, lawyer; b. Decatur, Ga., Feb. 27, 1938; s. Roy Rachford and Virginia Carolyn (Minter) K.; m. Barbara Anne Pilgrim, Dec. 18, 1965; children: Shannon Ruth, Robert Russell, Rebecca Anne, Susan Lynn. Student Birmingham So. Coll.; BA, Samford U., 1962; JD, Cumberland Sch. Law, 1965 . Bar: Ala. 1965, U.S. Tax Ct. 1971, U.S. Supreme Ct. 1971; individual practice law Birmingham, Ala., 1965—; pres. Kracke, Thompson & Ellis, 1980—. Deacon Ind. Presbyn. Ch., Birmingham, 1973-76, elder, 1999—, pres. adult choir, 1968—, Housing Agy. Retarded Citizens; pres. Ala. chpt. Nat. Voluntary Health Agys.; mem. exec. com. legal counsel Birmingham Opera Theatre, 1983-95; bd. dirs. Ala. Assn. Retarded Citizens, Jefferson County Assn. Retarded Citizens, 1983-91, pres.-elect, 1994-96, pres. 1996-98, past pres., 1998—; coord. com. mem. Nat. Conv. of the ARC of U.S., 1999—; bd. dirs., founding pres. Birmingham chpt. Juvenile Diabetes Found., bd. dirs. The ARC of Ala., 1996-98, Found. of ARC, 1998—. With USNR, 1955-61. Mem. Birmingham (exec. com., chmn. law libr., law day 1976, history and archives com.), Ala. Bar Assn., ABA (award merit law day 1976), Am. Judicature Soc., Ala. Hist. Assn., So. Hist. Assn., The Club, Phi Alpha Delta (pres. chpt. 1964-65), Rotary (pres. Shades Valley club 1988-89, Paul Harris fellow, sec. dist. 686 1990-91, dist. coord. comm., bd. dir., sec. ednl. found.), Sigma Alpha Epsilon. Editor, Birmingham Bar Bull., 1974—; bd. editors Ala. Lawyer, 1980-86; contbr. articles to profl. publs. Home: 4410 Briar Glen Dr Birmingham AL 35243-1743 Office: Kracke Thompson & Ellis Lakeview Sch Bldg 808 29th St S Birmingham AL 35205-1004

KRAEHE, ENNO EDWARD, history educator; b. St. Louis, Dec. 9, 1921; s. Enno and Amelia Roth (Henckler) K.; m. Mary Alice Eggleston, May 25, 1946; children: Laurence Adams, Claudia. BA, U. Mo., 1943, MA, 1944; PhD, U. Minn., 1948. Instr. history U. Del., 1946-48; asst. prof. history U. Ky., 1948-50, asso. prof., 1950-63, prof., 1963-64; prof. U. N.C., 1964-68; prof. U. Va., 1968-71, Commonwealth prof., 1971-77, William W. Corcoran prof., 1977-91, William W. Corcoran prof. emeritus, 1991—; vis. prof. U. Mo., 1946, U. Va., 1955, U. Tex., 1955, U. Minn., 1963; U.S. Dept. State Specialist in, Germany, 1953; mem. regional selection com. Woodrow Wilson fellowship Found., 1959-60; mem. Sr. Fulbright-Hayes History Screening Com., 1970-73. Author: Metternich's German Policy Volume I: The Contest with Napoleon 1799-1814, 1963; author: Volume II: The Congress of Vienna, 1814-1815, 1983; editor: The Metternich Controversy, 1971; mem. editl. bd. Ctrl. European History, 1967-72, Austrian History Yearbook, 1969-74; contbr. entries and articles to encys. and hist. jours., U.S. and Europe. Active Charlottesville Com. on Fgn. Rels.; mem. Nat. Coordinating Com. for Promotion of History, mem. policy bd., 1985-88; mem. Met. Opera Guild, Friends of Ky. Ctr. Recipient Best Book award Phi Alpha Theta; Fulbright scholar Austria, 1952-53; Guggenheim fellow, 1960-61, Am. Coun. Learned Socs. fellow, 1969, 73, resident fellow Rockefeller Ctr. in Bellagio, 1983; grantee NEH, 1973, 80, 83, NEH Libr. Preservation Screening Com., 1988. Mem. Am. Hist. Assn., Conf. Group for Ctrl. European History (mem. exec. bd. 1966-68), German Studies Assn. (mem. exec. coun. 1985—), So. Hist. Assn. (chmn. European sect. 1974, 75, Disting. Svc. award European sect.), Colonnade Club, Blue Ridge Swimming Club, Phi Beta Kappa. Episcopalian. Home: 130 Bennington Rd Charlottesville VA 22901-2653

KRAEMER, ALFRED ROBERT, school librarian; b. N.Y.C., Dec. 25, 1948; s. Philip George and Bernadette (Klein) K.; m. Alice Palmer McCall, Dec. 29, 1989; children: Sarah McCall, Philip Joseph. BA, Beloit Coll., 1973; MSLS, U. N.C., 1978; MA, N.C. State U., 1983; PhD, U. N.C., Greensboro, 1997. Cert. pub. libr., N.C.; lic. elem. and secondary tchr., N.C. Libr. asst. Duke Med. Ctr., Durham, N.C., 1976-78; English tchr. Patterson Sch., Lenoir, N.C., 1978-80; asst. prof. English St. Mary's Coll., Raleigh, N.C., 1980-88; asst. dir. tchg. fellows N.C. State U., Raleigh, 1989-92; sch. libr. Guilford County Schs., Greensboro, N.C., 1995–; Mem. Com. on Mission in Higher Edn., Raleigh, 1994--. Author: Malory's Grail Seeders and 15th Century English Hagiography, 1999. With USN, 1967-70. Mem. MLA, ALA. Democrat. Episcopalian. E-mail: kraemea@guilford.k12.nc.us.

KRAEMER, DAVID C., theology educator; b. Newark, Oct. 23, 1955; s. Paul William and Phyllis (Ferster) K.; m. Susan L. Boxerman, July 21, 1955; children: Talia, Liviya. BA, Brandeis U., 1977; MA, Jewish Theol. Sem., N.Y.C., 1978, PhD, 1984. Asst. prof. theology Jewish Theol. Sem., 1984-90, assoc. prof. theology, 1990-94, prof. theology, 1994—; cons. The Jewish Mus., N.Y.C., 1990-92, Heritage/WNET, N.Y.C., 1997. Author: Reading the Rabbis, 1996, Responses to Suffering, 1995, The Mind of the Talmud, 1990; editor: The Jewish Family, 1989, The Meanings of Death in Rabbinic Judaism, 1999. Assn. Jewish Studies, Soc. Bibl. Lit. Democrat. Jewish. Avocations: cooking, family care, pet care, running. Office: Jewish Theological Seminary 3080 Broadway New York NY 10027-4650

KRAEMER, JAY ROY, lawyer; b. St. Louis, Sept. 7, 1948; s. Jerome and Miriam J. (Lewin) K.; m. Ruth Joanne Wallerstein, Aug. 8, 1971; children: Julia, Jennifer. BA, George Washington U., 1970, JD, 1973. Bar: Md. 1973, D.C. 1974, U.S. Ct. Appeals (4th cir.) 1974, U.S. Supreme Ct. 1981, U.S. Ct. Appeals (fed. cir.) 1982. Law clk. U.S. Dist. Ct. Md., Balt., 1973-74; assoc. Fried, Frank, Harris, Shriver & Jacobson, Washington, 1974-81, ptnr., 1981—; adj. prof. Georgetown U. Law Ctr., 1997—. Mem. ABA, Md. Bar Assn., D.C. Bar Assn., Internat. Nuclear Law Assn. Office: Fried Frank Harris Shriver & Jacobson 1001 Pennsylvania Ave NW Washington DC 20004-2505

KRAEMER, KENNETH LEO, architect, urban planner, educator; b. Plain, Wis., Oct. 29, 1936; s. Leo Adam and Lucy Rose (Bauer) K.; m. Norine Florence, June 13, 1959; children: Kurt Randall, Kim Rene. BArch, U. Notre Dame, 1959; MS in City and Regional Planning, U. So. Calif., 1964, M of Pub. Adminstrn., 1965, PhD, 1967. From instr. to asst. prof. U. So. Calif., Los Angeles, 1965-67; asst. prof. U. Calif., Irvine, 1967-71, assoc. prof., 1971-78, prof., 1978—, dir. Pub. Policy Research Orgn., 1974-92, dir. Ctr. for Rsch. on Info. Tech. and Orgns., 1992—; cons. Office of Tech. Assessment, Washington, 1980, 84-85; pres. Irvine Research Corp., 1978—. Author: Management of Information Systems, 1980, Computers and Politics, 1982, Dynamics of Computing, 1983, People and Computers, 1985, Modeling as Negotiating, 1986, Data Wars, 1987, Wired Cities, 1987, Managing Information Systems, 1989, Asia's Computer Challenge, 1998. Mem. Blue Ribbon Data Processing Com., Orange County, Calif., 1973, 79-80, Telecomm. Adv. Bd., Sacramento, 1987-92. Mem. Am. Soc. for Pub. Adminstrn. (Disting. Research award 1985), Internat. Conf. on Info. Systems, Am. Planning Assn., Assn. for Computing Machinery. Democrat. Roman Catholic. Club: Notre Dame. Office: U Calif Ctr Rsch Info Tech & Orgns Berkley Pl N Ste 3200 Irvine CA 92697

KRAEMER, LILLIAN ELIZABETH, lawyer; b. N.Y.C., Apr. 18, 1940; d. Frederick Joseph and Edmee Elizabeth (de Watteville) K.; m. John W. Vincent, June 22, 1962 (div. 1964). BA, Swarthmore Coll., 1961; JD, U. Chgo., 1964. Bar: N.Y. 1965, U.S. Dist. Ct. (so. dist.) N.Y. 1967, U.S. Dist. Ct. (ea. dist.) N.Y. 1971. Assoc. Cleary, Gottlieb, Steen & Hamilton, N.Y.C., 1964-71; assoc. Simpson Thacher & Bartlett, N.Y.C., 1971-74, ptnr., 1974—; mem. vis. com. U. Chgo. Law Sch., 1988-90, 91-94, 97—. Bd. mgrs. Swarthmore Coll., 1993—. Fellow Am. Coll. Bankruptcy; mem. Lawyers Alliance for N.Y. (bd. dirs. 1996—), Assn. of Bar of City of N.Y. (mem. various coms.), Coun. on Fgn. Rels., N.Y. State Bar Assn., Order of Coif, Phi Beta Kappa. Democrat. Episcopalian. Avocations: travel, reading, word games. Home: 2 Beekman Pl New York NY 10022-8058 also: 62 Pheasant Ln Stamford CT 06903-4428 Office: Simpson Thacher & Bartlett 425 Lexington Ave Fl 15 New York NY 10017-3954

KRAEMER, MICHAEL FREDERICK, lawyer; b. N.Y.C., Jan. 21, 1947; s. Jerome W. and Honey (Dunner) K.; m. Ross Shepard, June 21, 1970; 1 child, Jordan Harriet. BA cum laude, Amherst Coll., 1969; JD, U. Pa., 1972. Bar: Pa. 1972, U.S. Dist. Ct. (ea. dist.) Pa. 1972, N.J. 1973, U.S. Dist. Ct. N.J. 1973, U.S. Ct. Appeals (3d cir.) 1974, U.S. Ct. Appeals (2d cir.) 1980, U.S. Ct. Appeals (4th and 7th cirs.) 1981, U.S. Ct. Appeals (6th cir.) 1990. Assoc. Astor & Weiss, Phila., 1972-75, Pechner, Sacks, Dorfman, Rosen & Richardson, Phila., 1975-76; ptnr. Kleinbard, Bell & Brecker, Phila., 1976-85, White and Williams, LLP, Phila., 1985—. Bd. dirs. Ctr. City Residents Assn., Phila., 1976-78; Served to 2d lt. USAR, 1972-73. Recipient Disting. Svc. award Amherst Coll. Alumni Coun., 1994. Mem. Phila. Bar Assn. (profl. responsibility com. 1972-84, labor and employment law com. 1985—), Amherst Alumni Assn. Phila. (pres. 1977-79), Indsl. Rels. Rsch. Assn. Club: Germantown Cricket (Phila.). Office: White and Williams LLP 1800 One Liberty Pl Philadelphia PA 19103-7395

KRAEMER, SYLVIA KATHARINE, government official, historian; b. Neisse, Silesia, Germany, Feb. 24, 1944; came to U.S., 1948; d. Thomas Paramore and Dorothea Freihube (Kraemer) Doughty; m. Russell Inslee Fries, Apr. 11, 1970 (div. Nov. 1991); children: Thomas Mount, Gwyneth Buchanan. BA in English, Hollins Coll., 1965; PhD in History, Johns Hopkins U., 1969. Instr. Johns Hopkins U., Balt., 1969; asst. prof. history Vassar Coll., Poughkeepsie, N.Y., 1969-70, So. Meth. U., Dallas, 1970-73; rsch. assoc. prof. U. Maine, Orono, 1975-78; mem. vis. faculty Bangor (Maine) Theol. Sem., 1981-83; chief historian NASA, Washington, 1983-89, dir. Office Spl. Studies, 1989-98, mem. adv. coun., 1981-83, dir. policy devel., 1998—. Author: Urban Idea in Colonial America, 1977, NASA Engineers in the Age of Apollo, 1992; also essays. Mem. Maine Humanities Coun., 1979-83; cons. on edn. issues, Va., 1993—. Fellow Coun. Humanities, So. Meth. U., 1973; rsch. grantee NSF, 1978-80. Fellow Internat. Acad. Astronautics; mem. Women in Aerospace, Exec. Women in Govt., Soc. for History in Fed. Govt. (exec. coun. 1988-91, James Madison award 1989), AAUW. Avocations: visual arts, writing, gardening. Office: NASA 300 E St SW Washington DC 20546-0005*

KRAFFT, JOHN M., English educator, editor; b. Springfield, Ohio, Sept. 1, 1951; s. Friedrich G. and June (Swisher) K.; m. Sharon Beighey, Dec. 18, 1871. BA, Miami U., Oxford, Ohio, 1973; MA, SUNY, Buffalo, 1976, PhD, 1978. Vis. asst. prof. W.Va. U., Morgantown, 1977; from instr. to assoc. prof. Suffolk County C.C., Selden, N.Y., 1978-90; from asst. prof. to assoc. prof. English Miami U., Hamilton, Ohio, 1990—; co-founder Pynchon Notes, 1979, co-editor, 1979—; sr. acad. supr. Program for Internat. Pynchon Studies, U. London, 1997—. Andrew Mellon fellow CUNY Grad. Ctr., 1988. Mem. MLA, Coun. of Editors of Learned Jours., Soc. for Study of Narrative Lit. Home: 3585 Freeman Ave Hamilton OH 45015-1754 Office: Miami U Hamilton 1601 Peck Blvd Hamilton OH 45011-3316

KRAFKA, MARY BAIRD, lawyer; b. Ottumwa, Iowa, Jan. 4, 1942; d. Glenn Leroy and Alice Erna (Krebill) B.; m. Jerry Lee Krafka, Oct. 14, 1962; children: Lisa Krafka Piper, Gregory D., Jeffrey A., Amy Krafka Pittman. BA in English and Human Rels., William Penn Coll., Oskaloosa, Iowa, 1990; JD, U. Iowa, 1993. Bar: Iowa 1993. Vol. lawyer Legal Svcs. Corp., Ottumwa, 1993-94; pvt. practice, Ottumwa, 1994—. Mem. AAUW, ABA, Iowa Bar Assn., Wapello County Bar Assn., PEO Sisterhood (Iowa chpt. HC 1973). Lutheran. Avocations: sewing, walking and running, interior designing, church activities, reading. Home: 931 W Mary St Ottumwa IA 52501-4904 Office: 101 S Market St Ste 203 Ottumwa IA 52501-2933

KRAFT, ARTHUR, academic dean; b. Eden, N.Y., May 7, 1944; s. Arthur Brauer and Mary Jane (Forti) K.; m. Joan Marie Brown, Sept. 3, 1966; children: Arthur G., Stephen Michael, Leigh Judith. BS, St. Bonaventure U., 1966; MA, SUNY, Buffalo, 1969, PhD, 1970. Asst. prof. Ohio U., Athens, 1969-72, assoc. prof., 1972-75; prof. U. Nebr., Lincoln, 1975-77, assoc. dean Coll. Bus., 1977-83; dean Coll. Bus. and Econs. W.Va. U., Morgantown, 1983-87; dean sch. bus. Rutgers U., New Brunswick, N.J., 1987-93; dean Sch. Mgmt. Ga. Inst. Tech., Atlanta, 1993—. Pension adv. com. Monongalia County Hosp., Morgantown, 1985-87. Recipient NASA fellowship Stanford U., 1973, fellowship Sears-Roebuck Fellowship Found, Washington, 1974-75; named Outstanding Young Individual Jaycees, Lincoln, 1978. Mem. Am. Econ. Assn., Am. Assembly of Collegiate Schs. of Bus. (visitation com. 1977—, continuing accreditation com. 1987, bus. accreditation com. 1995—), North Ctrl. Assn. (evaluator 1986-87), Beta Gamma Sigma. Avocations: trivia, sports.

KRAFT, BURNELL D., agricultural products company executive; b. Chester, Ill., July 24, 1931; s. Herman F. and Ella Kraft; m. Shirley Ann Huch, Dec. 30, 1950; children: Jon B., Julie Ann Kraft Schwalbe. BS, So. Ill. U., 1956. Acct., mcht. Tabor and Co., Decatur, Ill., 1956-59, v.p., 1959-61, exec. v.p., 1961-70, pres., 1970-75; with Archer Daniels Midland Co. (merged with Tabor and Co.), Decatur, 1975-84, corp. v.p., 1984-94, group v.p., 1994-97, sr. v.p., 1997—, pres. ADM/GROWMARK River System div., 1985—, pres. Collingwood Grain div., 1989-94; bd. dirs. Alfred C. Toepfer Internat., United Grain Growers. Trustee Millikin U., Decatur, 1983-95, chmn. trustees, 1990-94; bd. dirs. Decatur Meml. Hosp., 1970-80. With U.S. Army, 1952-53, Korea. Mem. N.Am. Export Grain Assn., Nat. Feed Grains Council, Nat. Grain and Feed Assn., St. Louis Mchts. Exchange, Chgo. Bd. Trade, Decatur C. of C. (past bd. dirs.), Phi Kappa Phi, Beta Gamma Sigma. Republican. Lutheran. Clubs: Decatur, Country Club Decatur (bd. dirs. 1974-78). Avocations: aviation, golf, boating, tennis. Office: Archer Daniels Midland Co 4666 Faries Pkwy PO Box 1470 Decatur IL 62525-1820

KRAFT, C. WILLIAM, JR., federal judge; b. Phila., Dec. 14, 1903; s. C. William and Wilhelmina J. (Doerr) K.; m. Frances V. McDevitt, June 27, 1942; 1 child, C. William III. A.B., U. Pa., 1924, LL.B., 1927, J.D., 1930. Bar: Pa. 1927. Trial lawyer Kraft, Lippincott & Donaldson, Media, Pa., 1928-55; dist. atty. Delaware County, Pa., 1944-52; judge U.S. Dist. Ct., Phila., 1955-70; sr. judge U.S. Dist. Ct., 1970—. Mem. ABA, Pa. Bar Assn. Home and Office: Island House 200 Ocean Lane Dr Apt 602 Key Biscayne FL 33149-1447

KRAFT, DONALD BOWMAN, advertising agency executive; b. Seattle, Mar. 20, 1927; s. Warren E. and Beulah (Bowman) K.; m. Mary Jo Erickson, Dec. 20, 1973; children: Daniel, Karen Kraft VanderHoek, Berkeley, Erika. BA, U. Wash., 1948. Pres. Kraft Advt., Seattle, 1948-54; v.p. Honig Cooper, Seattle, 1954-59; pres., chief exec. officer Kraft Smith Advt., Seattle, 1959-84, Evans, Kraft Advt., Seattle, 1984-87; chmn. emeritus EvansGroup, Publics, Seattle, 1998—; chmn. Evans Group, Inc., Salt Lake City, 1989—. Bd. dirs. KCTS Assn., Public TV, Seattle, 1982-90. Served with USN, 1945-46. Recipient Man and Boy award Boys Club Am., 1960; named Young Man of Yr., Seattle Jaycees, 1962. Mem. Am. Assn. Advt. Agys. (chmn. we. region 1962-64, nat. sec.-treas. 1970-71, mem. nat. govt. relations com. 1983-86), Affiliated Advt. Agys. Internat. (internat. pres. 1967-68, Albert Emery Mgmt. Excellence award 1984, 92), Young Pres.'s Orgn Alumni (chmn. Pacific NW chpt. 1980-81), Greater Seattle C. of C. (bd. dirs.). Republican. Methodist. Clubs: Wash. Athletic (pres. 1987-88), Rainier (pres. 1990-91), Seattle Tennis, Broadmoor Golf, Rotary Seattle (pres. 1973-74, Paul Harris fellow 1974). Home: 1569 Parkside Dr E Seattle WA 98112-3719 Office: Evans Group Inc 5th Fl 190 Queen Anne Ave N Seattle WA 98109-4900*

KRAFT, ELAINE JOY, community relations and communications official; b. Seattle, Sept. 1, 1951; d. Harry J. and Leatrice M. (Hanan) K.; m. Lee Somerstein, Aug. 2, 1980; children: Paul Kraft, Leslie Jo. BA, U. Wash., 1973; MPA, U. Puget Sound, 1979. Reporter Eastside Jour., Bellevue, Wash., 1972-76; editor Jour./Enterprise Newspapers, Wash. State, 1976; mem. staff Wash. State Senate, 1976-78, Wash. Ho. of Reps.,1978-82, pub. info. officer, 1976-78, mem. leadership staff, asst. to caucus chmn., 1980—; ptnr., pres. Media Kraft Communications; mgr. corp. info., advt. and mktg. communications Weyerhaeuser Co., 1982-85; dir. comms. Weyerhaeuser Paper Co., 1985-87; dir. cmty. rels. N.W. region Coors Brewing Co. 1987-95; comms. dir. King County exec. King County Ct. House, 1996—. Recipient state and nat. journalism design and advt. awards. Mem. Nat. Fedn. Press Women, Women in Comms., Wash. Press Assn. Home: 14329 SE 63d St Bellevue WA 98006-4802 Office: King County Courthouse 516 3d Ave Seattle WA 98104-2312

KRAFT, GEORGE HOWARD, physician, educator; b. Columbus, Ohio, Sept. 27, 1936; s. Glen Homer and Helen Winner (Howard) K.; children: Jonathan Ashbrook, Susannah Mary. AB, Harvard U., 1958; MD, Ohio State U., 1963, MS, 1967. Diplomate Am. Bd. Phys. Medicine and Rehab., Am. Bd. Electrodiagnostic Medicine. Intern U. Calif. Hosp., San Francisco, 1963-64, resident in phys. medicine and rehab., 1964-65; resident in phys. medicine and rehab. Ohio State U., Columbus, 1965-67; assoc. U. Pa. Med. Sch., Phila., 1968-69; asst. prof. U. Wash., Seattle, 1969-72, assoc. prof., 1972-76, prof., 1976—; chief of staff U. Wash. Med. Ctr., Seattle, 1993-95; dir. electrodiagnostic medicine U. Wash. Hosp., 1987—, dir. Multiple Sclerosis Ctr., 1982—; co-dir. Muscular Dystrophy Clinic, 1974—; assoc. dir. rehab. medicine Overlake Hosp., Bellevue, Wash., 1989—; bd. dirs. Am. Bd. Electrodiagnostic Medicine, 1993—, chmn., 1996—. Co-author: Chronic Disease and Disability, 1994, Living with Multiple Sclerosis: A Wellness Approach, 1996; cons. editor: Phys. Medicine and Rehab. Clinics, 1990—, EEG and Clin. Neurophysiology, 1992-96; assoc. editor Jour. Neurol. Rehab., 1988—, Muscle and Nerve, 1998—; contbr. articles to profl. jours. Sci. peer rev. com. C Nat. Multiple Sclerosis Soc., N.Y.C., 1990-96, chmn., 1993-96, med. adv. bd., 1991—; bd. sponsors Wash. Physicians for Social Responsibility, Seattle, 1986—. Rsch. grantee Rehab. Svcs. Adminstrn., 1976-81, Nat. Inst. Handicapped Rsch., 1984-88, Nat. Multiple Sclerosis Soc., 1990-92, 94-95, Nat. Inst. Disability and REhab. Rsch., 1998—. Fellow Am. Acad. Phys. Medicine and Rehab. (pres. 1984-85, Zeiter award 1991); mem. Am. Assn. Electrodiagnostic Medicine (pres. 1982-83), Assn. Acad. Physiatrists (pres. 1980-81), Am. Acad. Clin. Neurophysiology (pres. 1995-97), Am. Acad. Neurology, Internat. Rehab. Medicine Assn., Alpha Omega Alpha. Episcopalian. Office: U Wash Dept Rehab PO Box 356490 Seattle WA 98195-6490

KRAFT, GERALD, economist; b. Detroit, July 1, 1935; s. Jule and Shirley (Schwartz) K.; m. Sandra Doris Johnson, Aug. 7, 1955; children: Michael Stanton, Lynn Barbara. Student, U. Chgo., 1951-52; BA, Wayne U., 1955; MA, Harvard U., 1957. Mng. dir. Harvard U. Statis. Lab., Cambridge, Mass., 1957-58; prin. United Rsch. Inc., Cambridge, 1958-61; sr. rsch. assoc. Sys. Analysis and Rsch. Corp., Boston, 1961-64, Regional and Urban Planning Implementation, Inc., Cambridge, 1964-65; pres., dir. Charles River Assocs. Inc., Boston, 1965-92, sr. v.p., 1993; pres. The GSK Group, Ltd., 1994—; chmn. Modern Broadcast Prodns.; lectr. MIT, Harvard U., U. Pa.; mem. planning com., dir. Maritime Transp. Rsch. Bd., NRC, 1976-79; mem. Group I Coun., mem. coms. Transp. Rsch. Bd., 1977-80; pres. Transp. Rsch. Forum, 1977, v.p. program, 1976; chmn. 2nd Internat. Tungsten Symposium, 1982. Author: (with others) The Role of Transportation in Regional Economic Development, 1971; co-author: Report of Task Force on Transp. to Sci. Adv. panel to Com. on Pub. Works, U.S. Ho. of Reps, 1974; contbr. articles to profl. jours. Trustee, dir., fin. com., exec. com., former chmn. budget subcom., asst. treas. Beth Israel Hosp.; past dir. Beth Israel Corp.; trustee, fin. com., patient care and quality com. Beth Israel Deaconess Med. Ctr.; past dir. Med. Care Boston, Inc.; fin. com. Commonwell, Inc.; mem. Harvard U. Grad. Sch. Arts & Scis., adv. com. grad. student life Harvard U.; adv. bd. Medifile, Inc. Mem. AAAS, Am. Econ. Assn., Econometric Soc., Am. Statis. Assn., Inst. Mgmt. Scis., Ops. Rsch. Soc. Am., Internat. Wine and Food Soc., Confrerie des Chevaliers du Tastevin (past chef du protocole, comdr.), Grand Sénéchal Sous-Commanderie de Mass., Harvard Club Boston, Univ. Club, Rotary (past bd. dirs., trustee student aid fund), Fine Wine Coun. Mass. (bd. dirs.), Beefeater Club, Wine and Food Soc. Boston (gov., past chmn., past pres.), Chaine des Rotisseurs, Confraternita Enogastronomica Toscana, Phi Beta Kappa. Home: 60 Scotch Pine Rd Weston MA 02493-1405

KRAFT, HENRY R., lawyer; b. L.A., Apr. 27, 1946; s. Sylvester and Freda (Shochat) K.; m. Terry Kraft, July 21, 1968; children: Diana, Kevin. BA in History, San Fernando Valley State Coll., 1968; JD, U. So. Calif., 1971. Bar: Calif. 1972, U.S. Dist. Ct. (ctrl. dist.) Calif. 1985, U.S. Ct. Appeals (9th cir.) 1998, U.S. Dist. Ct. (so. and no. dists.) Calif 1998. Dep. pub. defender San

Bernardino (Calif.) County, 1972-78; pvt. practice, Victorville, Calif., 1979-96; city atty. Victorville, 1987—; of counsel Best Best & Krieger LLP, Victorville, 1996-98; assoc. Parker, Covert & Chidester, Tustin, Calif., 1999—; atty. City of Barstow, Calif., 1980-97; instr. Victor Valley Coll., Victorville, 1986—. Atty. Barstow Community Hosp., 1980-88. Mem. FBA, San Bernardino Bar Assn. (fee dispute com., jud. evaluation com.), High Desert Bar Assn. (pres., v.p., sec. 1979-81), Calif. Soc. Health Care Attys., League Calif. Cities, Am. Arbitration Assn. (panel neutral arbitrators). Democrat. Jewish. Avocations: bicycling, travel, wine enthusiast. Office: Parker Covert & Chidester East Bldg 17862 E 17th St Ste 204 Tustin CA 92780-2164

KRAFT, IRVIN ALAN, psychiatrist; b. Huntington, W.Va., Nov. 20, 1921; m. Shirley Goldin, July 4, 1951; children: Karen Kraft Pennebaker, Joanna Kraft Katz, Elizabeth Kraft Schmachtenberger, Mark. BS, NYU, 1943, MD, 1949. Diplomate Am. Bd. Psychiatry and Neurology, Am. Bd. Child Psychiatry. Chief psychiatry Tex. Children's Hosp., Houston, 1958-65; prof. mental health U. Tex. Sch. Pub. Health, Houston, 1975-91; emeritus prof. mental health U. Tex., Houston, 1991—; assoc. clin. prof. pediatrics Baylor Coll. Medicine, Houston, 1977—, clin. prof. psychiatry, 1977—; clin. prof. psychiatry U. Tex. Sch. Medicine, Houston, Galveston; med. dir. Tex. Inst. Family Psychiatry, Houston, 1964-79; dir. Houston Heart Assn., 1969-70; med. dir. Adult Adolescent Rehab. Ctr., Houston, 1982-85; chmn. subcom. Mental Health Needs Coun., Houston, 1988-89. Author: (with others) Adolescent Group Psychotherapy, 1989, Bibliography of Child and Adolescent Psychiatry, 1990; co-editor: Child Group Psychotherapy: Future Tense, 1986; mem. editorial bd. Jour. Child and Adolescent Group Therapy, 1989—. Mem. drug prevention com. High Sch. for Health Professions, Houston, 1989-90; mem. Tex. House Rep. Com. on Edn., 1974. N.Y. Acad. Scis. fellow, 1971—; recipient Gold award Am. Acad. Pediatrics, 1969, cert. of award Am. Group Psychotheraphy Assn., 1970. Life fellow Am. Acad. Child and Adolescent Psychiatry, Am. Acad. Psychoanalysis, Am. Psychiat. Assn., Houston Group Psychotherapy Soc., Southwestern Group Psychotherapy Soc., Houston Psychiat. Soc., Tex. Soc. Psychiat. Physicians, Tex. Soc. of Child and Adolescent Psychiatry, Am. Orthopsychiatry Assn. Fax: 713-850-1522. Home: 2423 Gramercy Blvd Houston TX 77030-3105 Office: 3100 Weslayan St Ste 260 Houston TX 77027-5752

KRAFT, KAREN ANN, secondary school educator; b. Bklyn., June 27, 1964; d. Michael John and Barbara Ann (DeMaio) Miele; m. John L. Kraft, June 17, 1989; children: Taylor Michael, Mason Genaro. BS, North Tex. State U., 1986; MA in Edn., U. North Tex., 1990. Lic. provisional tchr. English and Spanish, gifted and talented, Tex. Tchr. Westwood H.S., Palestine, Tex., 1987-88, Allen (Tex.) H.S., 1988-93, Coppell (Tex.) H.S., 1993—; tchr. Nat. Honor Soc. Faculty Coun., Allen, 1989-93; student coun. sponsor Coppell H.S., 1994-97; facilitator Student Mentorship Course. Mem. ASCD, Nat. Coun. Tchrs. English, Tex. Assn. for Gifted and Talented. Roman Catholic. Home: 1303 Laguna Vista Way Grapevine TX 76051-2829

KRAFT, KENNETH HOUSTON, JR., insurance agency executive; b. Chgo., Apr. 2, 1934; s. Kenneth Houston and Elizabeth (Preston) K.; m. Ruth Neely, Aug. 11, 1956 (div. Sept. 1979); children: Katherine Elizabeth, Carolyn Ruth, Kenneth Houston III; m. Kathleen Hartung, Mar. 16, 1985. BS in Fin., Purdue U., 1956. Pres., chmn. bd. Kraft Ins. Agy., Inc., Winter Park, Fla., 1960—, KHK Fin. Corp., Winter Park, 1974—; chmn. bd. Echo Pub. Co., Sulfur Springs, Tex., 1970—; bd. dirs. NationsBank Ctrl. Fla.; sr. mem. bd. dirs., mem. exec., fin., comml. loan, audit and examining coms. Barnett Bank Cen. Fla., Orlando, 1965-98; founding dirs. Goodings Groceries of Fla., Altamonte Springs, Fla., Schwartz Electro-Optics, Orlando, Internat. Laser Sys., Orlando, Princeton Fin. Corp., Orlando, Falcon Aviation, Orlando, TV-9 Inc., ABC affiliate, Orlando, First Ctrl. Corp., Orlando, Inglewood Daily News, Inglewood Citizen Co., L.A. Bd. dirs. Winter Park C. of C., 1965-70, Orange County chpt. ARC, Orlando, 1963-65, Orange County chpt. United Way, Winter Park, 1970-72, Winter Park YMCA, 1972-75, citrus grower Kraft Groves, 1966—; mem. Fla. Citrus Mut., Lakeland, 1966—, Com. of 100 of Orange County, Inc., Orlando, 1983—; meml. bd. trustees Winter Park Hosp., 1969-88, also exec. com., compensation com., chmn. long range planning com.; chmn. Winter Park Cmty. Trust Fund, 1981-92; mem. grievance com. 9th Jud. Cir., 1987-90; active Boy Scouts Am., Crummer Grad. Sch. Bus., Winter Park, Fla. Lt. (j.g.) USNR, 1956-58. Named Outstanding Young Man of Winter Park, Winter Park Jaycees, 1970. Mem. Ctrl. Fla. Assn. Ins. Agts. (pres. 1963-64), Fla. Assn. Ins. Agts., Nat. Assn. Ins. Agts., So. Grand Bank Owners Assn., Lake Region Packaging Assn., U.S. Naval Inst., U.S. Navy League, Purdue U. Alumni Assn. (pres. coun., dirs. cir. Krannert Grad. Sch. Mgmt., Deans Club Sch. Sci.), Gold Club Purdue Musical Orgn., MVP John Purdue Club, Country Club of Orlando (pres. 1994-95), U. Club, Citrus Club, Captiva Island Yacht Club, Useppa Island Club, Masons, Rotary (bd. dirs. Winter Park Club 1968-74), Sigma Chi, Delta Delta. Republican. Presbyterian. Home: 231 Chelton Cir Winter Park FL 32789-6004 also: 1765 Venus Dr Samibal FL Office: Kraft Ins Agy Inc PO Box 1443 Winter Park FL 32790-1443

KRAFT, MICHAEL EUGENE, political science educator; b. L.A., Nov. 18, 1943; s. Louis and Pearl (Wiener) K. BA, U. Calif., Riverside, 1966; MA, Yale U., 1967, PhD, 1973. Asst. prof. Vassar Coll., Poughkeepsie, N.Y., 1973-76; asst. prof. U. Wis., Green Bay, 1977-79, assoc. prof., 1979-82, prof., 1982—; vis. disting. prof. Oberlin (Ohio) Coll., 1984-85, U. Wis., Madison, 1987-88. Author: Environmental Policy and Politics, 1996; author, editor: Technology and Politics, 1988, Public Reactions to Nuclear Waste, 1993, Environmental Policy, 4th edit., 1999, Toward Sustainable Communities, 1999. Bd. dirs. Lake Mic. Fedn., Chgo., 1986-97. Yale U. fellow, 1966-69, Mem. AAAS, Am. Polit. Sci. Assn., Western Polit. Sci. Assn., Phi Beta Kappa. Avocations: computers, running, music. Office: U Wis Pub & Environ Affairs 2420 Nicolet Dr Green Bay WI 54311-7001

KRAFT, RICHARD JOE, sales executive; b. Toppenish, Wash., Apr. 20, 1944; s. Joseph Nian and Rose Goldie (Merrick) K.; m. Karolyn Idell Keyes, Oct. 9, 1963 (div. 1982); children: Craig J., Jeffrey Eugene; m. Margaret Celeste Porter, Apr. 9, 1983. Student, Yakima Valley Coll., 1962-63; student, U. Wash., 1964-70. Project engr. Gray & Osborne Consulting Engrs., Seattle, 1965-76; project engr., constrn. cons. Pool Engring., Ketchikan, Alaska, 1976-81; project mgr. Cape Fox Corp., Ketchikan, 1982; project engr. Buno Constrn., Woodinville, Wash., 1983, Straiger Engring. Svcs., Ketchikan, Sitka, Alaska, 1984; owner Kraft Constrn. Svcs., Kirkland, Wash., 1984-85; dir. mcpl. projects ESM, Inc., Renton, Wash., 1985-86; estimator Active Constrn., Inc., Gig Harbor, Wash., 1987; sr. sales engr. Advanced Drainage Systems, Inc., Woodinville, 1987-93; with Ty-Matt, Inc., Ketchikan, 1993-94; owner Kraft Constrn. Svcs., Ketchikan, 1994—; storm sewer/sanitary specification subcom. Am. Pub. Works Assn., Wash. state chpt., 1985-93. Pres. Snohomish (Wash.) Camp, Gideons Internat., 1990-91; pres. exec. com. Maltby (Wash.) Congl. Ch. Mem. Utility Contractors Assn. Wash. (bd. dirs. 1990-92). Mem. Christian Ch. Avocations: old cars, outdoor sports activities. Home and Office: PO Box 1168 Wrangell AK 99929-1168

KRAFT, RICHARD LEE, lawyer; b. Lassa, Nigeria, Oct. 14, 1958; m. Tanya Kraft, July 14, 1984; children: Devin, Kelsey. BA in Fgn. Svc., Baylor U., 1980, JD, 1982. Bar: N.Mex. 1982, U.S. Dist. Ct. N.Mex., U.S. Ct. Appeals, U.S. Supreme Ct. Assoc. Sanders, Bruin & Baldock, Roswell, N.Mex., 1982-87, ptnr., 1987-98; ptnr. Kraft & Stone, LLP, Roswell, 1998—. Vol. lawyer Ea. N.Mex. U. Roswell, 1984—; bd. dirs. Roswell YMCA, 1983-87, Crimestopper, 1991-94; pres. Roswell Mens Ch. Basketball League; participant Roswell Mens Ch. Softball League; asst. chair legal div. United Way Drive, 1990. Recipient Outstanding Contribution award N.Mex. State Bar, 1987. Mem. ABA, N.Mex. Trial Lawyers Assn., N.Mex. Bar Assn. (bd. dirs. young lawyers div. 1983-91, pres. 1986-87, chmn. membership com., bar commr. 1986-87, 91—, pres. 1998-99, Outstanding Young Lawyer award 1990), Chaves County Bar Assn. (chair law day activities, chair ann. summer picnic com., rep. bench and bar com.), Roswell Legal Secs. Assn. (hon.), Roswell C. of C. (participant and pres. Leadership Roswell, exec. dir., bd. dirs. 1991-97), Sertoma (bd. dirs. Roswell club 1989-91). Baptist. Office: Kraft & Stone LLP Ste 1250 400 N Pennsylvania Ave Roswell NM 88201-1250

KRAFT, ROBERT ALAN, history of religion educator; b. Waterbury, Conn., Mar. 18, 1934; s. Howard Russell and Marian Augusta (Northrop) K.; m. Carol Lois Wallace, June 11, 1955; children: Cindy Lee Shapiro, Scott Wallace, Todd Alan, Randall Jay. B.A. summa cum laude, Wheaton Coll., 1955, M.A., 1957; Ph.D., Harvard U., 1961. Teaching fellow Harvard U., 1959-61; asst. lectr. U. Manchester, Eng., 1961-63; asst. prof. religious studies U. Pa., Phila., 1963-68, assoc. prof., 1968-76, prof., 1976—, acting chmn. dept. religious studies, 1972-73, chmn., 1977-84, chmn. grad. program in religious studies, 1973-75, 76-84, 97—, Moritz and Josephine Berg prof., 1992—, acting grad. chmn., 1994-95, 96-97; vis. lectr. Luth. Theol. Sem., 1965-66; coord. Phila. Sem. on Christian Origins, 1963—; mem. Rev. Standard Version Bible Com., 1972—; bd. advisors Ancient Bibl. Manuscript Ctr. for Preservation and Rsch., Claremont, Calif., 1978—; mem. series adv. bd. Berlin Akademie, 1971—; bd. dirs. Dead Sea Scrolls Found. Contbr. articles and revs. to profl. publs. U Pa. faculty fellow, summers 1965, 67, 73; Guggenheim fellow, 1975-76; Am. Council Learned Socs. fellow, 1975-76; Am. Council Learned Socs. travel grantee, 1970; Nat. Endowment for Humanities project grantee, 1978-79, 80-81, 82-94, Ctr. for Judaic Studies fellow, 1995-96. Mem. Soc. Bibl. Lit. (sec. Mid-Atlantic sect. 1965-69, pro-tem N.T. book editor Jour. Bibl. Lit. 1965-66, 70, editor Monograph series 1967-72, editor Pseudepigrapha series 1973-78), Studiorum Novi Testamenti Societas (editorial bd. 1973-76), Internat. Orgn. Septuagint and Cognate Studies (exec. com. 1969—), N.Am. Patristics Soc., Am. Soc. Papyrologists, Assn. for Computers and Humanities. Office: 227 Logan Hall U Pa Philadelphia PA 19104-6304 *To be critical in evaluating the work of others is not very difficult; the ability to evaluate one's own work critically is something to be cultivated.*

KRAFT, ROBERT ARNOLD, retired medical educator, physician; b. Seattle, Mar. 27, 1924; s. Vincent Irving and Blanche (Palmer) K.; m. Robby Lee Roberson, June 12, 1949; children: Angela Kraft Cross, Peter, Darius. BA, U. Wash., 1948, MD, 1954. Diplomate Am. Bd. Pathology, Am. Bd. Nuclear Medicine. Intern USPHS Hosp., Staten Island, N.Y., 1954-55; resident in Pathology Tacoma (Wash.) Gen. Hosp., 1958-60, U. Calif., San Francisco, 1960-62; staff pathologist Peninsula Hosp., Burlingame, Calif., 1962-90, dir. nuclear medicine, 1965-90; asst. clin. prof. nuclear medicine and pathology U. Calif., San Francisco, 1962-90; bd. dirs. Am. Bd. Nuclear Medicine, L.A., 1990-95. Capt. USAF, 1943-45, ETO. Decorated Disting. Flying Cross. Fellow Am. Coll. Nuclear Physicians (regent 1985-91), Coll. Am. Pathologists; mem. Am. Coll. Nuclear Physicians (pres. Calif. chpt. 1972-73), Soc. Nuclear Medicine (trustee 1982-85), South Bay Pathology Soc. (pres. 1966-67). Avocations: golf, astronomy, mining history, orchids. Home: 971 Baileyana Rd Hillsborough CA 94010-6173

KRAFT, ROBERT K., professional sports team executive; b. Brookline, Mass., July 5, 1941; m. Myra Kraft; 4 children. Grad., Columbia U.; MBA, Harvard U. Owner Foxboro (Mass.) Stadium; chmn. Chestnut Hill Mgmt.; pres. New England TV Corp., 1986-91; with Rand-Whitney Group, Inc., Worcester, Mass.; founder Internat. Forest Products, 1972; pres. Internat. Forest Products Group Cos.; chmn. Carmel Container Systems, Ltd., Israel; owner New England Patriots, 1994—; mem. exec. com. Dana Farber Cancer Inst.; trustee Columbia U.; bd. dirs. Harvard Sch. Bus. Mem. bd. overseers Boston Symphony Orch., Boston Mus. Sci. Avocations: golf, tennis. Office: New England Patriots Foxboro Stadium 60 Washington St Foxboro MA 02035-1388*

KRAFT, ROBERT PAUL, astronomer, educator; b. Seattle, June 16, 1927; s. Victor Paul and Viola Eunice (Ellis) K.; m. Rosalie Ann Reichmuth, Aug. 28, 1949; children—Kenneth, Kevin. B.S., U. Wash., 1947, M.S., 1949; Ph.D., U. Calif.-Berkeley, 1955; DSc (hon.), Ind. U., 1995. Postdoctoral fellow Mt. Wilson Obs., Carnegie Inst., Pasadena, Calif., 1955-56; asst. prof. astronomy Ind. U., Bloomington, 1956-58, Yerkes Obs., U. Chgo., Williams Bay, Wis., 1958-59; staff Hale Obs., Pasadena, 1960-67; prof., astronomer Lick Obs., U. Calif., Santa Cruz, 1967-92; astronomer, prof. emeritus, 1992—; acting dir. Lick Obs., 1968-70, 71-73, dir., 1981-91; dir. U. Calif. Observatories, 1988-91; chmn. Fachbeirat, Max-Planck-Inst., Munich, Fed. Republic Germany, 1978-88; bd. dirs. Cara corp. (Keck Obs.), Pasadena, 1985-91; bd. dirs. AURA, 1989-92. Contbr. articles to profl. jours. Jila vis. fellow U. Colo., Nat. Bur. Stds., Boulder, 1970; Fairchild scholar Calif. Inst. Tech., Pasadena, 1980, Tinsley prof. U. Tex., 1991-92; Henry Norris Russell lectr. Am. Astron. Soc., 1995; recipient Disting. Alumnus award Coll. Arts and Scis., U. Wash., 1995. Mem. Nat. Acad. Sci., Am. Acad. of Arts and Scis., Am. Astron. Soc. (pres. 1974-76, Warner prize 1962, Russell prize lectr. 1995), Internat. Astron. Union (v.p. 1982-88, pres.-elect 1994-97, pres. 1997—), Astron. Soc. Pacific (bd. dirs. 1981-87), Royal Astron. Soc. (fgn. assoc.). Democrat. Unitarian. Avocations: contract bridge; art appreciation; classical music; opera; eonology. Office: U Calif Lick Observatory Santa Cruz CA 95064

KRAFT, SCOTT COREY, correspondent; b. Kansas City, Mo., Mar. 31, 1955; s. Marvin Emanuel and Patricia (Kirk) K.; m. Elizabeth Brown, May 1, 1982; children: Kate, Kevin. BS, Kans. State U., 1977. Staff writer AP, Jefferson City, Mo., 1976-77, Kansas City, 1977-79; corr. AP, Wichita, Kans., 1979-80; nat. writer AP, N.Y.C., 1980-84; nat. corr. L.A. Times, Chgo., 1984-86; bur. chief L.A. Times, Nairobi, Kenya, 1986-88, Johannesburg, South Africa, 1988-93, Paris, 1993-96; dep. fgn. editor L.A. Times, 1996-97, nat. editor, 1997—. Recipient Disting. Reporting in a Specialized Field award Soc. of the Silurians, 1982, Peter Lisagor award Headline Club Chgo., 1985, Feature Writing finalist Pulitzer Prize Bd., 1985, Sigma Delta Chi award, 1993. Office: LA Times Nat Editor Times Mirror Square Los Angeles CA 90053

KRAFT, WILLIAM ARMSTRONG, retired priest; b. Rochester, N.Y., Apr. 13, 1926; s. William Andrew and Elizabeth Ruth (Armstrong) K. BA, St. Bernard Coll., 1947; ThM, Immaculate Heart Theol. Coll., 1951; D of Ministry, Claremont Sch. of Theology, 1981. Ordained priest Roman Cath. Ch., 1951. Dir. and founder of Newman Apostolate Diocese of San Diego, Calif., 1951-63; dir. of pub. rels. Diocese of San Diego, 1956-63, dir. of cemeteries, 1964-70, exec. dir. of devel., 1979-91; founding pastor St. Therese of Child Jesus Parish, San Diego, 1956-70, Good Shepherd Parish, San Diego, 1970-77; pastor St. Charles Borromeo Parish, San Diego, 1977-79; bd. dirs. Cath. Charities, San Diego; bd. of consultors Diocese of San Diego, 1985-91, mem. Presbyteral Coun., 1985-91, mem. bldg. commn., 1977-91. Bd. dirs. Am. Nat. Red Cross, San Diego, 1956-63, Legal Aid Soc., San Diego, 1956-65, Travelers' Aid Soc., San Diego, 1956-65; mem. Presdl. Task Force, Washington, 1984—; spl. dep. San Diego County Sheriff, 1964—. Named Prelate of Honor to Pope, Pope John Paul II, Vatican City, 1985, Knight Comdr. of Equestrian, Order of The Holy Sepulchre, Latin Patriarcii, Jerusalem, 1984, Knights of Columbus 4th degree. Mem. Benevolent and Protective Order of Elks, Univ. Club Atop Symphony Towers, Nat. Cath. Conf. for Total Stewardship (bd. dirs.), Nat. Cath. Devel. Conf., Nat. Soc. Fund Raising Execs. (cert.). Republican. Avocations: music appreciation, swimming. Home: 6910 Cibola Rd San Diego CA 92120-1709

KRAFTSON, RAYMOND HARRY, business executive; b. Delaware County, Pa., June 20, 1940; s. Harry A. and Elisabeth (Hallstrom) k.; m. Marguerite Knewstub; children: Donald W., Marguerite O., Audrey E., Michele S. BA, U. Pa., 1962; JD, Coll. of William and Mary, 1967. Trial atty. SEC, Washington, 1967-68; counsel Ringe, Peet & Mason, Phila., 1968-70, Monsanto Co., St. Louis, 1970-71; sr. v.p., gen. counsel Life of Pa. Fin. Corp., Phila., 1972-78; sr. staff counsel INA Corp., Phila., 1978-80; v.p., gen. counsel, dir. Safeguard Scientifics, Inc., Wayne, Pa., 1980-90; pres. Ailes Communications Inc., N.Y.C., 1990-91, The J.D. Group, Ltd., Villanova, Pa., 1991-95; pres. and CEO PulseGroup Inc., Bryn Mawr, Pa., 1995—; bd. dirs. Hoffman Surgical Equipment Co., Conshohocken, Pa. Mng. editor William and Mary Law Rev., 1966-67. Pres. Gladwyne Montessori Sch., 1986-88; v.p., trustee The Baldwin Sch., Bryn Mawr, 1987-91; vestry mem. St. David's Ch., 1988-94, The Am. Missionary Fellowship, 1992—; bd. chmn. Urban Equity Ptnrs., 1996—. Mem. Nat. Assn. Corp. Dirs., Merion Cricket Club (Haverford), The Racquet Club (Phila.), Phila. Club. Republican. Episcopalian. Avocations: antique and classic boats and cars. Office: Pulse Group Inc 932 County Line Rd Bryn Mawr PA 19010-2502

KRAFVE, ALLEN HORTON, management consultant; b. Superior, Wis., Jan. 26, 1937; s. Richard Ernest and Frances Virginia (Horton) K.; m. Lois Anne Reed, Aug. 15, 1959; children—Bruce Allen, Anne Marie, Carol Elizabeth. BSME, U. Mich., 1958, MBA, 1960, MSME, 1961. Asst. prof. mech. engring. San Jose State U. (Calif.), 1961-65; various positions including quality control mgr. Ford Motor Co., Dearborn, Mich., 1965-77; engring. mgr. Kysor/Cadillac, Cadillac, Mich., 1977-82; mgmt. cons., Lake City, Mich., 1982—; pres. Lark Homes, Inc., 1979—; area mktg. dir. Lindal Cedar Homes, 1985-94. Co-author: Reliability Considerations in Design, 1962, internat. conf. paper, 1961. Bd. dirs. Crooked Tree coun. Girl Scouts U.S., Traverse City, Mich., 1983. Mem. ASME, Soc. Automotive Engrs., Am. Soc. Engring. Edn. Republican. Methodist. Home: 1725 S Duck Point Rd Lake City MI 49651-8646 Office: Allen H Krafve Cons 2604 Sunnyside Dr Cadillac MI 49601-8749

KRAG, OLGA, interior designer; b. St. Louis, Nov. 27, 1937; d. Jovica Todor and Milka (Slijepcevic) Golubovic. AA, U. Mo., 1958; cert. interior design UCLA, 1979. Interior designer William L. Pereira Assocs., L.A., 1977-80; assoc. Reel/Grobman Assocs., L.A., 1980-81; project mgr. Kaneko/Laff Assocs., L.A., 1982; project mgr. Stuart Laff Assocs., L.A., 1983-85; restaurateur The Edge, St. Louis, 1983-84; pvt. practice comml. interior design, L.A., 1981—, pres., R.I., 1989—. Mem. invitation and ticket com. Calif. Chamber Symphony Soc., 1980-81; vol. Westside Rep. Coun., Proposition 1, 1971; asst. inaugural presentation Mus. of Childhood, L.A., 1985. Recipient Carole Eichen design award U. Calif., 1979. Mem. Am. Soc. Interior Designers, Inst. Bus. Designers, Phi Chi Theta, Beta Sigma Phi. Republican. Serbian Orthodox. Home and Office: 700 Levering Ave Apt 10 Los Angeles CA 90024-2797

KRAHEL, THOMAS STEPHEN, account executive; b. Bklyn., Oct. 4, 1947; s. John Frank and Anna (Trusz) K.; m. Jill Susan Friedl, June 12, 1969; children: Bryan Thomas, Audrey Gerda, Leah Ann, Eric Jourdan. PhB, Bklyn. Coll., 1970; MA in Banking and Mgmt. with honors, Adelphi U., 1980. Asst. treas. Chase Manhattan Bank, N.Y.C., 1970-82; sales mgr. Glossit Mfg., Northport, N.Y., 1982-84; mktg. rep. Executone of L.I., Hauppauge, N.Y., 1984-85; account exec. Fin. Mktg. Corp., N.Y.C., 1985-86, UARCO, Inc., N.Y., N.Y., 1986-96, Standard Forms, Inc., N.Y., 1996-97, Neopost, Woodbury, N.Y., 1997—; instr. Dale Carnegie Courses. Co-founder, treas. Tuscany Gardens Assn., Great Neck, N.Y., 1970-80; counselor L.I. Youth Guidance Program; deacon, elder 1st Presbyn. Ch. Northport, N.Y. Mem. Mensa, Couples Club (pres. Great Neck, 1976-77), Delta Mu Delta. Democrat. Presbyterian. Home: 16 West St Northport NY 11768-1246

KRAHL, ENZO, retired surgeon; b. Fiume, Italy, Apr. 22, 1924; came to U.S., 1951, naturalized, 1955; s. Massimiliano and Camilla (Aub) K.; m. Anne Katharine Ferbstein, June 14, 1958; children—Edward Alexander, Katharine Frances. M.D., U. Florence, Italy, 1948. Diplomate Am. Bd. Surgery. Asst. dept. surgery U. Rome, 1948-51; fellow in vascular surgery Columbia Presbyn. Med. Ctr., N.Y.C., 1951-52; fellow in surgery Columbia Presbyn. Med. Ctr., 1954-55; resident in surgery St. Vincent's Hosp., N.Y.C., 1952-54; chief resident in surgery Akron City Hosp., Ohio, 1957-58; dir. grad. edn. Akron Gen. Hosp., 1959-60; practice medicine specializing in surgery Akron, 1958-60, Superior, Wis., 1960-84; ret., 1984; mem. staff Superior Meml. Hosp., also bd. dirs.; founder Superior Clinic, 1964; past dir. Blue Cross-Blue Shield United of Wis. Contbr. articles to med. jours. Past v.p. Duluth-Superior Symphony; past mem. exec. com. bd. dirs. Health Systems Agy. Western Lake Superior. Served as capt. M.C., U.S. Army, 1955-57. Recipient United Fund award, 1965, cert. of merit N.Y.C. CD, 1953. Mem. Wis. State Med. Soc., Italian Heritage Soc., Am. Bridge League, Marshwood Country Club, AAD Temple Club, Masons, Shriners. Jewish. Home: 15 Cotton Xing Savannah GA 31411-2504

KRAHMER, DONALD LEROY, JR., lawyer; b. Hillsboro, Oreg., Nov. 11, 1957; s. Donald L. and Joan Elizabeth (Karns) K.; m. Suzanne M. Blanchard, Aug. 16, 1986; children: Hillary, Zachary. BS, Willamette U., 1981, MM, 1987, JD, 1987. Bar: Oreg. 1988. Fin. analyst U.S. Bancorp, Portland, 1977-87; intern U.S. Senator Mark Hatfield, 1978; legis. aide State Sen. Jeannette Hamby, Hillsboro, Oreg., 1981-83, State Rep. Delna Jones, Beaverton, Oreg., 1983; bus. analyst Pacificorp, Portland, 1987; mgr. mergers/acquisitions Pacificorp Fin. Svcs., Portland, 1988-89; dir. Pacificorp Fin. Svcs., 1990; CEO, pres. Atkinson Group, Portland, 1991—; ptnr. Black Helterline, Portland, 1991—; bd. dirs., sec. Marathon Fin. Assocs., Portland, 1989; bd. dirs. Self-Enhancement, Inc.; chmn. Willamette Forum; bd. dirs. Oreg. Entrepreneur Forum, 1993—, editor, 1993, chmn. adv. bd., 1995, chmn. bd., 1998; founder co-chmn. Oreg. Emerging Bus. Initiative, 1997—; bd. dirs. Concordia Univ. Found., 1995-97. Treas. Com. to Re-Elect Jeannette Hamby, 1986; bd. dirs. fin. com./devel. com. Am. Diabetes Assn., Portland, 1990-96; founder Needle Bros., 1994; chmn. Atkinson Grad. Sch. Devel. Com., Salem, 1989-92; Bd. Vis. Coll. Law, Willamette U., 1997—; mem. adv. bd. Ctr. for Law and Entrepreneurship, U. Oreg. Sch. Law, 1997—; founder Conf. of Entrepreneurship, Salem, 1984, chmn. Entrepreneurship Breakfast Forum, Portland, 1993; chmn., founder Oreg. Conf. on Entrepreneurship and Awards Dinner, 1994-99, sr. v.p., 1999—; mem. exec. com., bd. dirs. Cascade Pacific Coun. Boy Scouts Am., 1998—, chmn. cmty. fund. dir., 1997; vice chmn. Govs. Coun. on Small Bus., State of Oreg. Recipient Pub.'s award Oreg. Bus. Mag., 1987, Founders award Willamette U., 1987, award Scripps Found., 1980, Bus. Jour. 40 Under 40 award, 1996. Mem. ABA, Oreg. Bar Assn. (chmn. exec. com., fin. instns. com. sec., exec. com., bus. law sect., chmn. 1999, sec. 1998), Multnomah County Bar Assn., Washington County Bar Assn., Assn. for Corp. Growth, Oreg. Biosci. Assn., Portland Soc. Fin. Analysts, Japan-Am. Soc. Oreg., Assn. Investment Mgmt. and Rsch., City Club, Software Assn. of Oreg., Oreg. Biotech. Assn., Multnomah Athletic Club, Arlington Club. Republican. Lutheran. Home: 16230 SW Copper Creek Dr Portland OR 97224-6500 Office: Black Helterline 1200 Union Bank Calif Tower 707 SW Washington St Portland OR 97205-3536

KRAHN, THOMAS FRANK, photographer; b. Racine, Wis., Feb. 14, 1941; s. Marvin Carl and Marie Mattie (Myers) K. Diploma, Control Data Inst., 1972; Doctorate (hon.), United World Assembly, 1984. Pres. Puget Sound Pub. Group, Everett, Wash.; photographer Arcturus Studio, Everett. Author: (novels) Atkar, The Norseman, 1998, Atkar in Africa, 1999, Adventure at Whiterood, (novellas) The Boy on the Horse, 1994, The Naked Prey, 1994, Die Wolfenkindern, Vols. 1-3, 1994, The Indian Affair, 1998, The Dry Creek Canyon Incident, 1998, Something Lives Under the Porch, 10 Miles Hard, 1998, H.M.S. Futility, 1999, High Wind to Jamaica, Treasure of San Padre Island, 1999, The Northgate Affair, (nonfiction) Gay Ethics, Vols. 1 and 2, Vessels of Silver and Gold, 1994, Children and Chicanery, A Biblical Approach to Modern Gay Living, 1989, The Complete Number Line and Introduction to the Algebraic Celestial Sphere, 1998, (booklets) The Seven Days of Wonder, 1996, How Do I Love Thee, 1996, (plays) The Doughnut, The Dumpster, Witness for the Defense, Oz-Mosis (Oz Twenty Years Later), The Mystery of Edmund O'Shay, Every Man's Folly, also stories, poems; composer various works for piano, organ, vocal ensembles and solo works. Pres. First All-Everett Foto Flea Market, 1996-97. Recipient Cert. of Appreciation KCTS 9 TV Sta., 1991, award Exec. Coun. Selection Com., Everett C.C., 1988-89. Mem. Hist. Everett Theater Soc., Everet Photo Club (pres. 1996-99), Tau Alpha Epsilon. Avocations: writing, composing. Home: 1321 Chestnut St Apt 1 Everett WA 98201-5203 Office: Arcturus Studio 1321 Chestnut St Apt 1 Everett WA 98201-5203

KRAHNKE, BETTY ANN, county official; b. Washington, Sept. 27, 1942; d. Richard George Jr. and Mary (McLaughlin) Fletcher; m. Wilson Norris Krahnke, July 11, 1964; children: Carolyn, Catherine, Margaret. BA in Political Sci. with highest honors, U. Calif., Santa Barbara, 1964; postgrad., Johns Hopkins U., 1964-65. Councilwoman Dist. 1, Rockville, Md., 1990—. Columnist The Planning Game, The Montgomery Jour.; moderator Montgomery Week in Review, Montgomery Cmty. TV. Mem. Montgomery County Planning Bd., 1979-87; vol. coord. Congresswoman Connie Morella's re-election campaign, 1988; Bush del. Rep. Nat. Conv., 1988, 92; chmn. Citizen's Coord. Com. on Friendship Heights; active mem. LWV; former exec. v.p. Montgomery County Hist. Soc.; former mem. coun. Montgomery United Way, 1986-96; elected mem. Montgomery County Coun., 1990, 94, chair Coun. pub. safety com., coun. health & human svcs. com., chair coun. govt.'s com. on noise abatement at Nat. and Dulles Airport; mem. Nat. Assn. County Ofcls. land use and environ. com.; treas., mem. bd. dirs. Nat. Orgn. to insure a Sound-Controlled Environment. Mem. Chevy Chase

Kiwanis. Office: Office County Coun Coun Office Bldg 6th Fl 100 Maryland Ave Rockville MD 20850-2322*

KRAICHNAN, ROBERT HARRY, theoretical physicist, consultant; b. Phila., Jan. 15, 1928; s. Robert Maxwell and Anna (Maximon) K.; m. Carol Gebhardt, May 22, 1954 (div. 1988); 1 child, John; m.Judy Ellen Moore, June 30, 1989. BS in Physics, MIT, 1947, PhD in Theoretical Physics, 1949. Mem., asst. to Albert Einstein Inst. Advanced Study, Princeton, N.J., 1949-50; mem. tech. staff Bell Telephone Labs., 1950-52; rsch. assoc. Columbia U., N.Y.C., 1952-56; rsch. assoc. Courant Inst. NYU, 1956-58, sr. rsch. scientist Courant Inst., 1958-62; pvt. practice physicist, 1962-80; pres., prin. Robert H. Kraichnan, Inc., Santa Fe, 1980—; adj. assoc. prof. dept. grad. physics NYU, 1956-57; assoc. in physics Woods Hole (Mass.) Oceanographic Inst., 1960-70; rsch. affiliate meteorology MIT, 1963—; contractor Office Naval Rsch., 1962-80, NASA, 1967-69; cons. Naval Rsch. Lab., 1957-59, Inst. for Space Studies, NASA, 1961-69, Inst. fro Def. Analyses, 1967-70, Los. Alamos Nat. Lab., 1979—, Princeton U., 1987—. Contbr. over 100 articles to sci. jours. Recipient ADION medal Observatoire de Nice; grantee NSF, 1970—. Fellow AAAS, Am. Phys. Soc. (Otto Laporte award 1993, Lars Onsager Meml. prize 1997). Avocations: mountain hiking, violin, carpentry.

KRAININ, JULIAN ARTHUR, film director, producer, writer, cinematographer; b. N.Y.C., Jan. 24, 1941; s. David A. and Anne N. (Wineblatt) K.; BS, Allegheny Coll., 1962, HHD (hon.), 1993; MFA, Columbia U., 1965; m. Martha Wineblatt, June 17, 1967; 1 child, Todd Philip. Producer spl. projects Westinghouse Broadcasting Co., N.Y.C., 1967-69, also producer, dir., writer, 1967—; v.p., exec. producer Krainin/Sage Prodns., Inc., N.Y.C., 1969-80, also dir., writer, 1969-80; pres. Krainin Prodns., Inc., N.Y.C., 1976—; nat. lectr. motion pictures at various univs. and colls., 1967—; cons. on films U. Mass., 1973; juror Mid-West Film Makers and Graphic Arts Festival, 1971-72, Nat. Emmy Awards, 1975-82, 85-90, Dirs. Guild of Am. Awards, 1987-90; mem. journalism adv. bd. Queens Coll., 1987-90; bd. dirs. Bklyn. Ctr. For Families in Crises, 1986-90. Recipient numerous awards and citations including Acad. award, 1973, Emmy award, 1969, Chgo. Internat. Film Festival award, 1969, 77, 78, Florence Internat. Film Festival award, 1969, Cine Golden Eagle awards, 1969, 72, 73, 74, 76, 78, Photog. Soc. Am. award, 1968, Venice Film Festival award, 1970, Moscow Internat. Film Festival award, 1970, Cindy award Producers Assn. Am., 1971, 76, San Francisco Internat. Film Festival award, 1972, Am. Film Festival award, 1974, 76, 78, Tel Aviv Internat. Film Festival award, 1970, Atlanta Internat. Film Festival award, 1969, 72, Festival of Ams. award, 1976, N.Y. Internat. Film and TV Festival award, 1969, 72, Gabriel award, 1968-70, Oberhausen Internat. Film Festival award, 1969, Columbus Film Festival award, 1973, Mannheim Internat. Film Festival award, 1969, U.S. Indsl. Film Festival award, 1973, Ohio State award, 1967, N.Y. Film Festival at Lincoln Center award, 1970. Mem. Writers Guild Am., Acad. Motion Picture Arts and Scis., Photog. Soc. Am., Dirs. Guild Am. (award 1973), Bklyn. Psychiatric Crises Ctr. (bd. dirs.), 1983—. Major films include: The Reluctant Revolution, 1968; Exit to Nowhere, 1967; Promises to Keep, 1967; The March, 1965; Nowhere Fast, 1968; Hide and Seek, 1966; (with Jacques Cousteau) Oceans: The Silent Crisis, 1972; Art Is (Acad. award nomination); hon. film screenings White House and Mus. Modern Art 1972), 1972; The Other Americans (Emmy award), 1969; Princeton: A Search for Answers (Acad. award), 1973; The American Experiment, 1974; Going Metric, 1975; To America, 1976; The Broken Silence, 1976; The World of James Michener: Hawaii Revisited, 1977; The World of James Michener: The South Pacific; End of Eden? (hon. screening Mus. Modern Art), 1978; (with Ed Asner) The Writer, 1980; The Making of an Opera, 1980; Luciano Pavarotti At Home, 1980; La Gioconda Mini-Series, 1980; Heritage: Civilization and the Jews (Peabody and Christopher awards), 1981-82, also PBS series; CBS Reports; Don't Touch That Dial!: The Making of a Television Series (Emmy nominee, TV Guide citation), 1982; The Smithsonian Quadrangle: A View from the Castle, 1984; America Undercover: The Wrong Man, 1985-86; (with Tom Peters) The Power of Excellence, 1987; co-author: (with Abba Eban) Heritage: Civilization and the Jews, Disaster at Silo 7, 1988, Memory and Imagination, New Pathways to the Library of Congress, 1990; documentary film: The Television Quiz Show Scandal, 1991, Queen's College, 1993, (feature film) Quiz Show, 1994, (four Academy award nominations), The Unabomber: Deadly Mail!, 1996, The Thousand Acre Universe, 1996, George Wallace, 1997, Golden Globe, Humanitas, Cable Ace, Peabody Awds, John Glenn: Return to Space. Avocations: skiing, physics, poetry. Office: Krainin Prodns Inc 8 Century Rd Palisades NY 10964-1503

KRAIZER, SHERRYLL A., health services and interpersonal violence prevention educator; b. San Antonio, June 12, 1948; d. Faye Burton and Phyllis Anne (Ringer) Graves; m. Alvin T. Kraizer, July 30, 1978; children: Charles, Ben. BS in Edn./Spl. Edn., Emporia State U., 1969, MS in Edn./Psychology, 1970; postgrad., U. Minn., 1973; PhD in Edn., The Union Inst., 1991. Pres., exec. dir. Coalition for Children, 1983—; presenter confs. in field; expert witness on child abuse, instnl. abuse, stds. and practices. Author: The Safe Child Book, 1985, 2d edit., 1995; author (tng. programs) The Safe Child Program (pre-K-grade 3), 1989, 2d edit., 1994, Dating Violence: Prevention and Intervention, 1991, Domestic Violence Prevention and Intervention, 1991, Reach, 1992, Challenge, 1992, Recovery, 1992. Recipient Nat. Prog. award Child Abuse Prevention Coun., Houston, 1989, rsch. grant Nat. Ctr. on Child Abuse and Neglect, 1987, prog. devel. grant Small Bus. Adminstrn., 1988, Violence Against Women Act grantee, 1996—. Mem. Internat. Soc. Prevention of Child Abuse and Neglect, Nat. Assn. Prevention of Child Abuse and Neglect, Am. Profl. Soc. on Abuse of Children. Office: Coalition for Children PO Box 6304 Denver CO 80206-0304

KRAJEWSKI, JOAN L., councilwoman; b. Phila.. Investigator Phila. Dept. Revenue, 1972-79; councilwoman dist. 6 City of Phila., 1992—, majority leader; chmn. standing com., appropriations com., vice chair pub. safety com., mem. law and govt., labor and civil svc., legis. oversight and transp., pub. utilities coms. Phila. City Coun. Pres. Local 1660 Sch. Bd. Employees, Dist. Coun. 13, Am. Fedn. State, County and Mcpl. Employees' Union, 1977-79. Named one of 500 Best Councilperson, Phila. Mag., 1986, 87, 90, 91. Office: City Hall Rm 591 Philadelphia PA 19107-3290*

KRAJICEK, MARK ANDREW, lawyer; b. Montreal, Que., Can., Dec. 1, 1958; s. Alexander J. and Emily P. (Ovsenny) K.; m. Lori Diane Lalonde, June 1, 1985; children: Kimberly, Ryan. B of Commerce, Queen's U., Kingston, Ont., Can., 1980; LLB, McGill U., Montreal, 1983, BCL, 1984; MBA, U. Toronto, Ont., Can., 1995. Bar: N.Y., Ont. Lawyer Keyser, Mason, Ball, Lewis, Mississauga, Ont., 1986-90; legal counsel, sec. Philips Electronics Ltd., Toronto, Ont., 1990-91; sec. Philips Can. Ltd., Toronto, 1990-91, MEL Def. Systems Ltd., Stittsville, Ont., 1990-91, Philips Med. Systems Can. Ltd., Toronto, 1990-92; sec., dir. Philips Can. Ltd., Toronto, 1992—; gen. counsel, sec., dir. Philips Electronics Ltd., Toronto, 1992—; sec., dir. Philips Electron Optics Can. Ltd., Toronto, 1997—. Mem. ABA, Law Soc. Upper Can., Can. Bar Assn., N.Y. State Bar Assn. Home: 11 Goswell Rd, Toronto, ON Canada M9A 1G2 Office: Philips Electronics Ltd, 601 Milner Ave, Toronto, ON Canada M1B 1M8

KRAJICK, KEVIN RUDOLPH, journalist; b. Camp Kilmer, N.J., Aug. 10, 1952; s. Rudolph Adam and Katherine Sarah (Distin) K.; m. Ruby Jean Kipniss, Sept. 8, 1996. BA in Comparative Lit. cum laude, Columbia U., 1976, MS in Journalism, 1977. Assoc. editor Police and Corrections mags., N.Y.C., 1978-84; nat. editor Nat. Law Jour., N.Y.C., 1984-85; assoc. editor Newsweek, N.Y.C., 1988-96; freelance author N.Y.C., 1981—. Contbr. articles to Aububon, Smithsonian, Sci., Natural History, Discover, Nat. Geographic, N.Y. Times, others. Recipient Walter Sullivan award for excellence in sci. journalism Am. Geophys. Union, 1998, Brook award for agrl. writing Calif. Poly. U., 1998; Sci. Writing fellow Marine Biol. Lab., 1996. Mem. Nat. Assn. Sci. writers. Home: 245 W 104th St Apt 14B New York NY 10025-4280

KRAKAUER, DAVID, musician, educator; b. N.Y.C., Sept. 22, 1956. BA, Sarah Lawrence Coll., 1978; MusM, Juilliard Sch., 1980; cert., Paris Conservatoire, 1977. Clarinetist Apsen Wind Quintet, N.Y.C., 1981-89, Continuum, N.Y.C., 1981-92; mem. faculty Vassar Coll., Poughkeepsie, N.Y., 1983-93; clarinet soloist Klezmatics, N.Y.C., 1989-96; mem. clarinet and chamber music faculty Manhattan Sch. Music, N.Y.C., 1990—, Mannes Coll. Music, N.Y.C., 1993—; mem. clarinet faculty Aaron Copland Sch. Music, Queens (N.Y.) Coll., 1995—; leader, clarinetist David Krakauer's Klezmer Madness!, 1994—; clarinetist N.Y. Philomusica, 1981—. Featured artist CD Klezmer N.Y., 1998, (with Kronos Quartet) The Dreams of Prayers of Isaac the Blind, 1997, others; composer suite A Klezmer Tribute to Sidney Bechet, 1997. Recipient award Marlboro Music Festival, 1978-92, Lado 1st prize Concert Artists Guild, 1985, Chamber Music award Naumburg Found., 1984. Avocations: backpacking. Office: Trillum Prodns 345 Riverside Dr Apt 6A New York NY 10025-3430

KRAKAUER, THOMAS HENRY, museum director; b. Buffalo, Sept. 6, 1942; m. Janet MacColl, Dec. 20, 1968; 1 child, Alan Henry. AB, U. Rochester, 1964; MS, U. Miami, 1966; PhD, U. Fla., 1970. Asst. prof. biology Hollins Coll., Hollins College, Va., 1970-74; natural sci. chmn. Sci. Mus. Va., Richmond, 1974; sr. resident assoc. biology Hollins Coll., 1976-85; exec. dir. Sci. Mus. Assn. of Roanoke (Va.) Valley, 1976-85, N.C. Mus. Life and Sci., Durham, 1985—; adj. asst. prof. Va. Poly. Inst. and State U., Blacksburg, 1973. Bd. dirs. Assn. Sci.-Tech. Ctrs., Triangle Land Conservancy; bd. dirs., pres. Grassroots Sci. Mus. Named Conservation Educator of Yr. Va. Wildlife Fedn., 1978, Profl. Svc. award N.C. Mus. Coun., 1998. Mem. Assn. Sci.-Tech. Ctrs. (v.p. 1987, 95), Va. Assn. Mus. (past pres.), Am. Assn. Mus. Home: 128 White Horse Run Bahama NC 27503-8980 Office: NC Mus Life and Sci PO Box 15190 Durham NC 27704-0190

KRAKER, DEBORAH SCHOVANEC, special education educator; b. Enid, Okla., May 28, 1960; d. Charles Raymond and Marcella Ruth (Mack) Schovanec; m. Kevin Mark Kraker, July 10, 1987. BS, U. Ctrl. Okla., 1982; postgrad., Okla. State U., Stillwater, 1995—. Cert. tchr. spl. edn., learning disability/mentally handicapped. Customer svc. mgr. Skaggs, Oklahoma City, 1982-92; tchr. spl. edn. Edmond (Okla.) Pub. Schs., 1993—; tchr. Francis Tuttle Vocat. Tech. Ctr., Oklahoma City, 1993, 94, 95, mem. adv. bd., 1993-96. Mem. adv. bd. Francis Tuttle Vocat. Tech. Ctr., 1993—. Mem. NEA, Okla. Edn. Assn. (del. nat. assembly 1996), Edmond Assn. Classroom Tchrs. (v.p. 1997-98), Coun. for Exceptional Children, Assn. Classroom Mems. (exec. bd.), Okla. Commn. Tchr. Preparation (mem. portfolio rev. team, mem. accreditation rev. team), Learning Disabilities Assn., Kappa Delta Pi. Republican. Roman Catholic. Avocations: reading, sewing, cooking, collecting antiques. Home: 2721 Berkshire Way Oklahoma City OK 73120-2704

KRAKOFF, ROBERT LEONARD, publishing executive; b. Pitts., May 4, 1935; s. Frank and Della (Zionts) K.; m. Sandra Gusky, June 22, 1958; children: Roger, Hope, Reed. BS with honors, Pa. State U., 1957; MBA, Harvard U., 1959. Staff v.p. mktg. planning TransWorld Airlines, N.Y.C., 1963-70; v.p., contr. consumer product div. Singer, N.Y.C., 1970-71; staff v.p. strategic planning RCA, N.Y.C., 1971-72; pres. Am. Internat. Travel Svc., Boston, 1972-73, Cahners Travel Group, N.Y.C., 1973-74, Cahners Expn. Group, N.Y.C., 1974-86; exec. v.p., chief oper. officer Reed Pub. U.S.A., Newton, Mass., 1986-89, pres., chief oper. officer, 1989-91, chmn., CEO, 1991-96; chmn., CEO Advanstar, Inc. (formerly Advanstar Holdings, Inc.), Boston, 1996—; bd. dirs. Reed Elsevier, 1990-96. With USAR, 1957-63. Office: Advanstar Inc 545 Boylston St Boston MA 02116

KRAKOW, AMY GINZIG, public relations, advertising, and marketing executive, writer; b. Bklyn., Feb. 25, 1950; d. Nathan and Iris (Minkowitz) Ginzig. BA, Bklyn. Coll., 1971, postgrad., 1974. Copy mgr. U.S. News & World Report, N.Y.C., 1977-80; promotion mgr. Sta. WINS, N.Y.C., 1980-82; promotion dir. CBS Mags., N.Y.C., 1982-84, The Village Voice, N.Y.C., 1984-85, N.Y. Woman (Am. Express Pub.), N.Y.C., 1987-89; cons. Silverman Collection, Santa Fe, 1985—; owner, mgr. AG Krakow & Assocs. Inc./AgitProp, Inc., N.Y.C.; sem. leader Radcliffe Pub. workshop, 1986-92, Mag. Pubs. Congress, 1989; bd. dirs. Body Sculpt. Author: Total Tattoo Book, 1994; prodr. Festival of Street Entertainers, N.Y.C., 1984-93, Albuquerque, 1980, Obies-Off-Broadway Theater Awards, 1984-86; creator, prodr. Ann. Coney Island Tattoo Festival, 1986-93, The Psychedelic Festival, 1988; exec. dir. Radio Creative Mercury Awards, 1991-93; curator American Style: New York's Tattoo Roots, South St. Seaport Mus., 1995. Bd. dirs. Sideshows by Seashore, Coney Island, U.S.A., Bklyn., 1985-92, City Lor e, N.Y.C., 1987—, Princeton Bio Ctr., 1991-93. Recipient BPA award, 1981, Addy award, 1985, AAF Crystal Prism award, 1994. Mem. Advt. Women N.Y. Fax: 212-343-3629.

KRAKOWER, BERNARD HYMAN, management consultant; b. N.Y.C., May 11, 1935; s. David and Bertha (Glassman) K.; m. Sondra Joan Fishbein, Apr. 14, 1968; children: Lorna, Victoria, Ariela Shauna. BA in Advt., UCLA, 1959, cert. in real estate, 1966, cert. in indsl. relations, 1972; MBA, Pepperdine U., 1979. Loan officer Lytton Fin. Corp., L.A., 1961-65; mgmt. cons. James R. Colvin & Assocs., L.A., 1965-67; sr. indsl. rels. rep. Sci. Data Systems (Xerox), 1967-68; dir. ops. Tratec, Inc., L.A., 1968-70; chmn. Krakower/Brucker Internat., Inc., Los Angeles, 1970-88; sr. ptnr. Krakower Finnegan Assocs., L.A., 1988-90; pres. Krakower Group, Inc., 1990—; bd. dirs. Columbia Nat. Bank, Santa Monica, Calif. Mem. citizens liaison com. L.A. Dept. Recreation and Parks, 1973; apptd. commr., v.p. L.A. County-wide Citizens Planning Coun. by L.A. County Bd. Suprs., 1988-97, v.p., 1991-93, pres. 1993-97; pres., bd. dirs. L.A. Bus. Coun. past chmn. bd.; mem. bd. visitors Pepperdine U. Graziadio Sch. Bus. and Mgmt., 1997—; mem. Santa Barbara Region C. of C., Santa Barbara Region Econ. Cmty. Project, 1997; mem. bd. Santa Babara Newcomers, 1999. Office: 233 Wilshire Blvd Ste 600 Santa Monica CA 90401-1207

KRAKOWER, TERRI JAN, biochemist, researcher; b. Houston, Mar. 9; d. Sidney and Delores K. BS in Biochemistry and Biophysics, U. Houston, 1979; postgrad., U. Calif., Davis, 1980; PhD in Chemistry, U. Tex., 1990. Grad. student asst. State of Calif. Air Resources Bd., Sacramento, 1981, 82; environ. quality specialist State of Tex. Air Control, Austin, summer 1984; predoctoral fellow, tchg. and rsch. U. Tex., Austin, 1987-90; staff fellow Boston Biomed Rsch. Inst., Boston, 1990-92; postdoctoral rsch. fellow Harvard Med. Sch., Boston, 1990-91; rsch. assoc. Baylor Coll. Medicine, Houston, 1993-94; postdoctoral fellow dept. biochemistry U. Tex. Health Sci Ctr., San Antonio, 1994-96; sci. com. specialist and coord. IBIDS database NIH, Bethesda, 1998—; nutritional biochemist Offices Dietary Supplements and Dir., NIH, Bethesda, Md., 1998—; major contbr. to Calif. document leading to first regulation of air emissions from class I hazardous waste disposal in U.S., State of Calif. Air Resources Bd., Sacramento, 1981, 1982; organic and biochem. lab. instr. U. Tex., Austin, 1986. Vol. Mus. of Sci., Boston, 1992; vol. radio prodr., v.p. Radio Prodrs. Guild, WEBR, Fairfax County Access Corp. Recipient scholarship U. Calif, Davis, 1980; grantee: Tex. Pub. Edn. grants, U. Tex., 1986-89; named predoctoral rsch. fellow Nat. Inst. Alcohol and Alcohol Abuse, through Inst. for Neurosci., U. Tex., Austin, 1988-89. Mem. Am. Chem. Soc., Am. Soc. Biochemistry and Molecular Biology. Achievements include isolation of monoclonal antibody that recognizes monoamine oxidase A and B in human tissue, and first monoclonal antibody that recognizes rodent monoamine oxidase A. Home: 101 Westcott St Houston TX 77007-7044

KRAL, WILLIAM GEORGE, lawyer; b. Bronx, N.Y., Oct. 16, 1946; s. Michael Abraham and Eleanor Helen (DeFilippo) K.; m. Mary Margaret Schuman, Dec. 28, 1970; children: Marianne, Elizabeth, Emily. BA, Manhattan Coll., 1968; JDL, Bklyn. Law Sch., 1974. Bar: N.Y. 1975, U.S. Supreme Ct. 1981. Assoc. D'Amato, Costello & Shea, N.Y.C., 1974-79; ptnr. Costello & Shea, N.Y.C., 1980-85; founding ptnr. Kral, Clerkin, Redmond & Ryan, N.Y.C., 1985—; founder, pres. Adirondack Alarm Systems Inc., Ticonderoga, N.Y., 1983—; co-founder, dir. N.Y. Home Brew Inc., Floral Park, 1992—, North County Collectibles, Moria, N.Y., 1991—; co-founder Angels Watch Inc., N.Y. With U.S. Army, 1969-70. Republican. Roman Catholic. Avocations: history, chess, antique arms collecting. Office: Kral Clerkin Redmond & Ryan 69 E Jericho Tpke Mineola NY 11501-3197 also: 43 Maple Ave Morristown NJ 07960-7506 also: 170 Broadway New York NY 10038-4154

KRALEWSKI, JOHN EDWARD, health service administration educator; b. Durand, Wis., May 20, 1932; s. Joseph and Esther (Hetrick) K.; m. Marjorie L. Gustafson; Apr. 22, 1957; children: Judy, Ann, Sara. BS in Pharmacy, U. Minn., 1956, MHA, 1962, PhD, 1969. Asst. prof. U. Minn., Mpls., 1965-69, prof., 1978—; prof. U. Colo., Denver, 1969-78. Contbr. articles to profl. jours. 1st lt. USAF, 1957-60. Kellogg fellow Kellogg Found., 1962-65, Valencia (Spain) Acad. Medicine fellow, 1993. Mem. APHA, Assn. Health Svcs. Rsch. Avocation: oenology. Office: U Minn Health Svc Rsch 420 Delaware St SE Box 729 Minneapolis MN 55455-0374

KRALJEVIC, VLADIMIR, producer; b. Valpovo, Croatia, Apr. 8, 1943; s. Stanko K. and Jelka (Zadravec) Kraljevic; children: Brando, Kristian, Virginia. Grad., Bakar (Croatia) Nautical Sch., 1964; student, Sorbonne U., Paris, 1967-68, Sommelier Soc., N.Y.C., 1970. Model Carita, Paris, 1968; maitre d' Russian Tea Room, N.Y.C., 1970-72, Hampshire House, N.Y.C., 1972-78, The Four Seasons, N.Y.C., 1983, Tavern on the Green, N.Y.C., 1984-87; pres., owner Veritas Stella, Ltd., Pelham, N.Y., 1989-98; cons. to Ivana Trump, 1997-99, Globus Group, Zagreb, Croatia, 1997-99; lic. broker in Croatia Playboy, 1995-97, Cosmopolitan, 1996-98, Miss Universe, 1996-97, Penthouse, 1998; ptnr. with Hotel Intercontinental Zagreb, 1999. Prodr. (film) Gospa, 1993-94; exec. prodr. Miss Universe Croatia, Zagreb, 1996-97, nat. dir., 1998-99; pub. (book) Ivana Trump's, The Best is Yet to Come, 1999. 3rd officer Yugoslav Merchant Marine, Rijeka, 1962-66. Co-author: (screenplay) Porthole to Paradise, 1992; named Outstanding Contbr. to Internat. Film Cannes Film Festival, 1995. Roman Catholic. Avocations: painting, classic Mercedes Benz, swimming, sailing, yacht-building.

KRALLINGER, JOSEPH CHARLES, entrepreneur, business advisor, author; b. Lancaster, Pa., May 29, 1931; s. Ferdinand and Mathilde (Meyer) K.; m. Hilde Eisenhauer, Oct. 1, 1955; children—Joanne, Diane, Robert. BS in Econs. cum laude, Franklin and Marshall Coll., 1953. C.P.A. Auditor GAO, Denver, 1953; auditor Army Audit Agy., 1953-55; ptnr. Arthur Andersen & Co., Phila., 1955-76; v.p. strategic planning and acquisitions, chief fin. officer Berwind Corp., Phila., 1976-88; cons. Palm Desert, Calif., 1988—; dir., bus. advisor and investor various indsl., health care, mining, oil and gas cos., 1976—; cons. in field. Author: An Auditor's Approach to Statistical Sampling, 5 vols., 1967-72, Strategic Planning Workbook, 1989, 2d edit., 1993, How to Acquire the Perfect Business for Your Company, 1991; Planeacion Estrategica Practica, 1991; Mergers and Acquisitions: Managing the Transactions, 1997; contbr. articles to profl. jours. Bd. dirs. alumni coun. Franklin and Marshall Coll., Lancaster, 1969-75; pres., tchr. religious edn. St. Genevieve Cath. Ch., Flourtown, Pa., 1971-76; bd. dirs. Whitemarsh Twp. Citizens Coun., Plymouth Meeting, Pa., 1972-75; hon. life mem., past chmn. bd. dirs. Phila. chpt. Am. Cancer Soc. Recipient Nat. Vol. award Am. Cancer Soc., 1985, Crusade award Am. Cancer Soc., 1985, Teaching award St. Genevieve Ch., 1985, Cert. Merit Inst. Mgmt. Accts., 1998. Mem. AICPA (statis. sampling com.), Pa. Inst. CPAs, Nat. Assn. Accts. (past pres. Phila. chpt.), Planning Forum (past pres. Phila. chpt.), Soc. Children's Book Writers and Illustrators, Ironwood Country Club (bd. dirs. 1991-93). Avocations: golf, racquet sports, writing, reading. Home and Office: 48-872 Mariposa Dr Palm Desert CA 92260

KRAM, MARK LENARD, hydrogeologist, environmental geochemist; b. L.A., July 8, 1961; s. Albert and Marjorie (Chudner) K. BA in Chemistry, U. Calif., Santa Barbara, 1983; MS in Geology, San Diego State U., 1988. Cert. ground water profl. Geochemist Marine Sci. Inst. U. Calif., Santa Barbara, 1984; geochronologist San Diego State U. Found., 1985-86; material specialist Decisive Testing, San Diego, 1987; geochemist Naval Ocean Sys. Ctr., San Diego, 1986-88; hydrogeologist Naval Facilities Engrng. Svc. Ctr., Pt. Hueneme, Calif., 1989—, site characterization and analysis penetrometer sys. field project mgr., 1991-97, lead internal groundwater cons., 1990—. Author: We CAN Change the World, 1991; co-author: Practical Handbook of Soil, Vadose Zone, and Ground-Water Contamination: Assessment, Prevention, and Remediation, 1994, Natural Attenuation General Data User's Guide, 1999; editor: (govt. document) United States Air Force Remediation Handbook for POL-Contaminated Sites, 1994; contbr. articles to Applied Organometallic Chemistry, others. Founder, chmn. Student Environ. Action, San Diego State U., 1986, chmn., 1987, vice-chmn., 1988; tech. reviewer Surfrider Found., Santa Barbara, 1991—. Mem. ASTM. Achievements include discovery of method for in-situ delineation of volatile organic contaminant/dense non-aqueous phase liquid contaminant plumes using cone penetrometer deployed laser spectroscopy; invention of high resolution piezocone for determining hydrogeologic parameters controlling fate and transport of contaminants in groundwater. Office: 1734 Castillo St Santa Barbara CA 93101

KRAM, SHIRLEY WOHL, federal judge; b. N.Y.C., 1922. Student, Hunter Coll., 1940-41, CUNY, 1940-47; LLB, Bklyn. Law Sch., 1950. Atty. Legal Aid Soc. N.Y., 1951-53, 1962-71; assoc. Simons & Hardy, 1954-55; pvt. practice law, 1955-60; judge Family Ct., N.Y.C., 1971-83; judge U.S. Dist. Ct. (so. dist.) N.Y., N.Y.C., 1983-93, sr. judge, 1993—. Author: (with Neil A. Frank) The Law of Child Custody, Development of the Substantive Law. Office: US Dist Ct US Courthouse 40 Foley Sq Rm 2101 New York NY 10007-1502*.

KRAMBERG, ROSS, arts administrator; b. N.Y.C., Apr. 29, 1955; s. Harold and Marilyn (Lief) K. BA in Theatre, Bklyn. Coll., 1980. House mgr. Bklyn. Ctr. for Performing Arts at Bklyn. Coll., 1976-78, assoc. artistic dir., program mgr., 1978-80; pub. rels. assoc. Jacob's Pillow Dance Festival, 1980; exec. asst. to exec. dir. The Joffrey Ballet, N.Y.C., 1981; company mgr. The Paul Taylor Dance Co., N.Y.C., 1982-89, gen. mgr., 1990, co-exec. dir., 1991, exec. dir., 1992—; bd. dirs. Paul Taylor Dance Found., Inc. Bd. dirs. Broadway Cares/Equity Fights AIDS, 1994-98. Office: Paul Taylor Dance Co 552 Broadway New York NY 10012-3922

KRAMEK, ROBERT E., United States Coast Guard officer; m. Patricia Havard; children: Tracy, Joseph, Suzanne, Nancy. BS in Engring. with honors, USCG, 1961; postgrad., U. Mich., Johns Hopkins U., U. Alaska; MS in Naval Architecture and Marine Engring., Mech. Engring., Engring. Mgmt.; degree with highest distinction, U.S. Naval War Coll., Newport, R.I.; diploma Capstone program, Nat. Defense U. Inst. of Higher Defense Studies. Commd. ensign U.S. Coast Guard, 1961, advanced through grades to admiral, 1994, ret., 1998. Recipient 2 Disting. Svc. medals U.S. Coast Guard, 2 Legion of Merit awards, Meritorious Svc. medal, 4 Commendation medals, Achievement medal, Unit Commendations award, Meritorious Unit Commendation awards, Spl. Ops. Ribbon with Silver Star, Humanitarian Svc. medal with Bronze Star, Sea Svc. Ribbon with Bronze Star. Avocations: physical fitness. Office: Dept Transp US Coast Guard 2100 2nd St SW Washington DC 20593-0001

KRAMER, ALAN SHARFSIN, lawyer; b. N.Y.C., Apr. 28, 1934; s. Michael and Alene (Sharfsin) K. B.A., Dickinson Coll., 1956; LL.B., Columbia, 1962, J.D., 1969. Bar: N.Y. 1962. Practice in N.Y.C., 1962-69, 73—; sr. v.p. Am. Medicorp, Inc., N.Y.C., 1969-72; individual practice, 1974-78; pres. Alan S. Kramer (p.c.), 1978—; sr. mng. dir. Bear, Stearns & Co., Inc., 1990-96. Editor: Columbia Law Rev, 1960-62. Mem. nat. council Salk Inst. Served with M.I. AUS, 1956-58. Mem. Assn. of Bar of City of N.Y. Home: 315 E 86th St New York NY 10028-4714 Office: 65 E 55th St New York NY 10022-3219

KRAMER, ALEX JOHN, dentist; b. Aurora, Ill., Dec. 21, 1939; s. Roy Edward and Frances (Astromskis) K.; m. Phyllis Rose Gonsky, July 15, 1967 (div. Sept. 1978); m. Brenda Jean Schillinger, Sept. 12, 1981; children: Ian Alexander, Elizabeth Katherine. Student, Marquette U., 1957-60; DDS, U. Ill., Chgo., 1964. Gen. practice dentistry Montgomery, Ill., 1966-88, Ashland, Wis., 1988-91; priv. practice craniofacial pain Duluth, Minn., 1991-94; gen. dental practice Duluth, 1994—. Mem. exec. bd. Two Rivers Boy Scouts Am., St. Charles, Ill., 1969-79, asst. scout master Troop #9, Voyageurs Area Coun., Boy Scouts Am., Duluth Minn., 1995—. Lt. Dental Corps USNR, 1964-66. Master Internat. Coll. Craniomandibular Orthopedics; mem. ADA, Am. Assn. Maxillofacial Orthopedics, Ill. State Dental Assn., Chgo. Dental Soc., Wis. State Dental Assn., No. Wis. Dental Assn., Am. Acad. Gnathological Orthopedics, Am. Soc. Gen. Dentistry, Dentafacial Orthopedics Study Club Mo., Am. Assn. Functional Orthodontics, Internat. Acad. Orthomolecular and Preventive Medicine, Am. Acad. Pain Mgmt. (diplomate), Minn. State Dental Assn., U. Ill. Alumni Assn. (life), Pershing Rifles Hon. Mil. Frat., Psi Omega. Republican. Methodist. Club: Aurora (Ill.) Country. Lodge: Optimists. Avocations: boating, skiing, diving, fishing, hiking. Home: 54 E Kent Rd Duluth MN 55812-1420 Office: 1601 Woodland Ave Duluth MN 55803-2629

KRAMER, ALEXANDER GOTTLIEB, financial director; b. DesPlaines, Ill., Sept. 21, 1964; s. Gottlieb G. and Norma L. Kramer. BA in Econ.

Devel. and Internat. Rels., Lake Forest Coll., 1987; M in Internat. Fin., Am. Grad. Sch. Internat. Mgmt., Glendale, Ariz., 1990. Asst. to dir. parliamentary affairs Spanish Parliament, Madrid, 1985-87; intern to chief polit. consular U.S. Dept. State, Rabat, Morocco, 1987-88; project mgr. H. Shapiro & Assocs., Inc., Chgo., 1988-90; dir. fin. and logistics Pacific Inter-Trade Corp., Westlake Village, Calif., 1990-93; fin. dir. Export SBDC Sr. Counsel Internat., L.A., 1993-95; head trade fin. group Am. Honda Motor Co., Torrance, Calif., 1995-99; dir. fin. Latin Am. Case Capital Corp., Lincolnshire, Ill., 1999—; prof. internat. fin., UCLA, 1991—; mem. adv. bd. Bestone Group, Hong Kong and Shanghai; bd. dirs. Export Mgrs. Assn. Calif. Mem. Fgn. Trade Assn. (bd. dirs.). Avocations: international development, tennis, Latin American art. Office: Case Capital Corp 100-2W-SE 475 Half Day Rd Lincolnshire IL 60006

KRAMER, ALLAN FRANKLIN, II, botanical garden official, researcher; b. N.Y.C., Dec. 10, 1950; s. Walter Frederick and Dorothea (Russell-Hurley) K. AB, Coll. of Holy Cross, 1972; MS, Pratt Inst., 1979. Sr. document analyst Aspen Systems Corp., N.Y.C., 1979-81, team leader analyst, 1981-83, mgr. rsch. staff, 1983-86; sr. editor Bus. Guides, Inc. div., sr. rsch. mgr. Lebhar-Friedman, Inc., N.Y.C., 1987-91; conservator Bklyn. Botanic Garden, 1991—. Mem. exec. com. Bklyn. Bot. Garden Aux., 1991—, v.p., 1993-95, pres. 1995-97; mem. pres.'s coun. Coll. Holy Cross, class chmn.; dir. Park Slope Geriatric Ctr, dir. Vol. Svcs. Opportunity Project, Brooklyn Conservatory of Music, chmn. devel. com., mem. exec. bd.; mem. Prospect Park Coun. The Woodlands Coun., New Leadership Coun., United Hosp. Fund; trustee Bklyn. Bot. Garden 1995-97; dir. Park Slope Vol. Ambulance Corps. Fellow Bklyn. Mus., Roebling Soc., Bklyn. Hist. Soc.; mem. Soc. Scholarly Pub., Am. Soc. Info. Sci., Spl. Librs. Assn., Am. Assn. Bot. Gardens and Arboreta, New Eng. Soc. in City of Bklyn. (v.p., dir.), Hundred Yr. Assn. N.Y., Royal Oak Found., Friendly Sons of St. Patrick (chmn.), Soc. Old Bklyn. (life), Battle of Bklyn. Conservancy (dir.), Assn. St. George the Martyr (Knight), Greek Order of St. Dennis of Zante, Montauk Club (pres.), Mcpl. Club Bklyn., Surf Club of Quogue, English Speaking Union, Beta Phi Mu (life). Avocations: sailing, travel, antiquing. Home: 35 Prospect Park W Brooklyn NY 11215-2370 Office: Bklyn Botanic Garden 1000 Washington Ave Brooklyn NY 11225-1008

KRAMER, ANDREW JOSEPH, clergyman; b. Greensburg, Pa., May 31, 1954; s. Andy and Genevieve (Fultz) K.; m. Sandra Lee Hoy, June 7, 1975; children: Lauren Rae, Jenna Marie. BA in History summa cum laude, Grove City Coll., 1975; MDiv cum laude, Pitts. Theol. Sem., 1979. Ordained to ministry Presbyn. Ch. USA, 1979. Sales clk. H. Kimball Sportswear for Men, North Huntingdon, Pa., 1969-72; indsl. engr. Ft. Pitt Steel Casting, McKeesport, Pa., 1975-77; pastor 1st United Presbyn. Ch., Brilliant, Ohio, 1979-85; assoc. pastor 1st United Presbyn. Ch., Belleville, Ill., 1985—; bd. dirs., sec., treas. Uni-Pres Kindercottage, East St. Louis, Ill., 1985-96; developer, advisor Deacons Dental Grants Program, Belleville, 1992—; cons. ptnr. Belleville AmeriCorps Program, 1994—. Founder, pres. bd. dirs. Abraham Lincoln Neighborhood Assn., Belleville, 1993—; coach West Pointe Lightning Select Soccer Team, Belleville, 1996—; developer, bd. dirs. Neighbors for Renewal in Belleville, Inc., 1997—. Recipient Citizen of Yr. award Brilliant Lions Club, 1984 co-recipient Mildred Hagedorn award Giddings-Lovejoy Presbytery Coun. of Aging, 1993. Mem. Sundowner Club, Elks. Avocations: fishing, sports, reading. Home: 34 Char Claire Dr Belleville IL 62226-1527 Office: 1st United Presbyn Ch 1303 Royal Heights Rd Belleville IL 62223-5400

KRAMER, ANDREW MICHAEL, lawyer; b. N.Y.C., Nov. 2, 1944; s. Irving and Ida (Kaplan) K.; m. Cheryle Lynn Safran, June 21, 1966; children: Howard, Jennifer; m. Nita Lynne Albert, Mar. 13, 1983; children: Samantha, Stephanie. BA cum laude, Mich. State U., 1966; JD cum laude, Northwestern U., 1969. Bar: Ill. 1969, D.C. 1977, U.S. Ct. Appeals (4th cir.) 1977, U.S. Ct. Appeals (5th cir.) 1972, U.S. Ct. Appeals (6th cir.) 1972, U.S. Ct. Appeals (7th cir.) 1970, U.S. Ct. Appeals (11th cir.) 1982, Ohio 1990. Assoc. firm Seyfarth, Shaw, Fairweather & Geraldson, Chgo., 1969-73; ptnr. Seyfarth, Shaw, Fairweather & Geraldson, Washington, 1974-83, Jones, Day, Reavis & Pogue, Washington and Cleve., 1983—; exec. dir. Ill. Office Collective Bargaining, Springfield, 1973-74. Contbr. articles to profl. jours. Mem. ABA, Chgo. Bar Assn., D.C. Bar Assn., Congressional Country Club (Md.), Standard Club (Chgo.), Firestone Country Club, Union Club (Cleve.), Pepper Pike Club (Cleve.). Office: Jones Day Reavis & Pogue 51 Louisiana Ave NW Washington DC 20001

KRAMER, ANTHONY FERDINAND, real estate company executive; b. Chgo., Apr. 18, 1940; s. Ferdinand and Stephanie (Shambaugh) K.; m. Mary Christine Kramer, Feb. 10, 1969 (div. Dec. 1984); children: Timothy Shambaugh, Thomas Walker; m. Linda Sue Murray, Apr. 10, 1987; children: Stephanie Shepperd, Stephen Capps. BA, Colby Coll., 1962; M.City Planning, Harvard U., 1964. Chief adminstrv. officer Draper & Kramer, Chgo., 1967—; chmn. bd. Tipperay Corp., Denver, Colo., 1989-91. Bd. dirs. Near South Planning Bd., Chgo., 1988—, vice-chmn., 1999—; bd. dirs. Sch. dist. 86, Hinsdale, 1997—; bd. dirs., treas. Consol. Sch. Dist. 180, Burr Ridge, Ill., 1989-97, Duncan YMCA; bd. overseers Colby Coll., Waterville, Maine, 1989-97; bd. trustees Found. for Excellence, Burr Ridge, 1993—, chmn. 1999—. Lt. USNR, 1964-67. Mem. U.S. Coast Guard Aux., Chgo. Yacht Club, Ruth Lake Country Club, Lambda Alpha Internat. United Ch. of Christ. Avocations: scuba diving, skiing, flying, boating. Home: 411 Westminster Dr Burr Ridge IL 60521-8338 Office: Draper & Kramer 33 W Monroe St Chicago IL 60603-5300

KRAMER, BARNETT SHELDON, oncologist; b. Balt., July 29, 1948; s. Mervin and Muriel Hannah (Woolf) K.; m. Ruth Solomon, June 25, 1972; 1 child, Jeremy. Student, Johns Hopkins U., 1966-69, MPH, 1991; MD, U. Md., 1973. Intern Washington U., St. Louis, 1973-74, med. resident, 1974-75; fellow Nat. Cancer Inst., Bethesda, Md., 1975-78, sr. investigator, 1986-90, assoc. dir., 1990-96, dep. dir. Divsn. Cancer Prevention and Control, 1996-97, dep. dir., Divsn. Cancer Prevention, 1997—; asst. prof. U. Fla., Gainesville, 1978-83, assoc. prof., 1983-86; prof. medicine Uniformed Svcs. U. Health Scis., Bethesda, Md., 1989-90, clin. prof. medicine, 1990—. Co-editor: (with P. Greenwald and D. Weed) Cancer Prevention and Control, 1995; (with J. Gohagan and P. Prorok) Cancer Screening Theory and Practices, 1999; assoc. editor Jour. Nat. Cancer Inst., 1988-94, editor-in-chief, 1994—; mem. editl. bd. Physicians Data Query, 1988—, chmn. bd. cancer prevention and screening, 1992—; contbr. articles to profl. publs., chpts. to books. With USPHS, 1975-78. Fellow ACP; mem. Am. Soc. Clin. Oncologists, Am. Assn. Cancer Rsch., Alpha Omega Alpha, Delta Omega. Avocation: fountain pen collecting. Office: Nat Cancer Inst DCP Bldg 31 Rm 10A49 31 Center Dr Bethesda MD 20892-2580

KRAMER, BARRY ALAN, psychiatrist; b. Phila., Sept. 9, 1948; s. Morris and Harriet (Greenberg) K.; m. Paulie Hoffman, June 9, 1974; children—Daniel Mark, Steven Philip. B.A. in Chemistry, NYU, 1970; M.D., Hahnemann Med. Coll., 1974. Resident in psychiatry Montefiore Hosp. and Med. Ctr., Bronx, N.Y., 1974-77; practice medicine specializing in psychiatry, N.Y.C., 1977-82; staff psychiatrist L.I. Jewish-Hillside Med. Ctr., Glen Oaks, N.Y., 1977-82; asst. prof. SUNY, Stony Brook, 1978-82; practice medicine specializing in psychiatry, L.A., 1982—; asst. prof. psychiatry U. So. Calif., 1982-89, assoc. prof. clin. psychiatry, 1989-94, prof. clin. psychiatry U. So. Calif. U. Hosp., 1994-98; ward chief Los Angeles County/U. So. Calif. Med. Ctr., 1982-98; med. dir. ECT, Cedars Sinai Med. Ctr., 1998—; cons. Little Neck Nursing Home (N.Y.), 1979-82, L.I. Nursing Home, 1980-82; dir. ECT U. So. Calif. Sch. Medicine, 1990. Reviewer: Am. Jour. Psychiatry, Hospital and Community Psychiatry; mem. editorial bd. Convulsive Therapy; contbr. articles to profl. jours., papers to sci. meetings. NIMH grantee, 1979-80; fellow UCLA/U. So. Calif. Long-Term Gerontology Ctr., 1985-86. Fellow Am. Psychiat. Assoc.; mem. AMA, Assn. Convulsive Therapy (editorial bd.), Soc. Biol. Psychiatry, Calif. Med. Assn., L.A. Med. Assn., Am. Assn. Geriatric Psychiatry, Gerontol. Soc. Am., So. Calif. Psychiat. Soc. (chair ETC com.). Jewish. Office: Cedars Sinai Med Ctr Thalians 223 W 8730 Alden Dr Los Angeles CA 90048 also: PO Box 5792 Beverly Hills CA 90209-5792

KRAMER, BERNARD, physicist, educator; b. N.Y.C., Nov. 12, 1922; s. Jack and Mollie (Miller) K.; m. Miriam Adelman, Aug. 4, 1946; children—Matthew, Jesse. B.S., CCNY, 1942; Ph.D., N.Y.U., 1952. Physicist Internat. Tel. & Tel. Corp., 1942-47; lectr. Bklyn. Coll., 1947-49; research asst., then research asso. N.Y.U., 1949-68; mem. faculty Hunter Coll., 1952—, prof. physics, 1966-86, chmn. dept., 1960-71, prof. emeritus, 1986—; vis. prof. Munich Inst. Tech., Fed. Republic Germany, 1959-60; vis. scientist Princeton U., 1973-74; research collaborator Brookhaven Nat. Lab., 1980; vis. scholar U. Del., 1981. Author articles luminescence and photoconductivity. Mem. Am. Phys. Soc., Sigma Xi. Home: 115 Carnation St Bergenfield NJ 07621-3803

KRAMER, BURTON, graphic designer, educator; b. N.Y.C., June 25, 1932; s. Sam and Ida (Moore) K.; m. Irene Margarite Therese Mayer, Feb. 22, 1961; children: Gabrielle Kimberly, Jeremy Jacques. BS in Graphic Design, Ill. Inst. Tech., Chgo., 1954; postgrad. (Fulbright scholar), Royal Coll. Art, London, 1955-56; M.F.A., Yale U., 1957. Designer Will Rurtin, N.Y.C., 1957-58; asst. art dir. Arch. Record, N.Y.C., 1959; Pres., creative dir. Kramer Design Assocs., Ltd., Toronto, 1967—; designer Geigy Chem. Corp., N.Y.C., 1959-61; dir. corp. graphics Clairtone Sound Corp., Toronto, 1967; chief designer Halpern Advt., Zurich, Switzerland, 1961-65; instr. Ont. Coll. Art & Design, 1978—; guest lectr. Rochester Inst. Tech., 1976, 81, designer-in-residence, 1981; vis. lectr. U. Cin., 1980; guest lectr., Arnhem, The Netherlands, 1994, Mexico City U. Autonoma, 1995; spkr. 1st Internat. Biennial of Symbols/Logotypes, Ostend, Belgium, 1994. Book designer The Art of Norval Morrisseau, 1979, Passionate Spirits, 1980; author Can. sect. Trademarks and Symbols of the World, 1973; co-author: Report on Canadian Road Sign Graphics, 1968; work pub. in numerous nat. and internat. jours., annuals and books; contbr. articles to profl. jours.; major works include signing-info. sys. CBC Broadcast Ctr., Toronto, IBM Tng. Ctr., Centenary Hosp., Scarborough, St. Lawrence Ctr. for Arts, Eaton Ctr., Erin Mills New Town, Mississauga, Metro Ctrl. YMCA, Copps Coliseum, Union Sta.; designer visual identity programs for CBC, N.Am. Life Assurance, Can. Imperial Bank Commerce, Reed Paper, ONEX Packaging Inc., Gemini, Vincor Internat., Can. Sys. Group, Nat. Rsch. Coun. Can., Centrestage, Royal Ont. Mus., Teknion Furniture Sys., Inc., Decoustics, Chartwell I.R.M., Scarborough Bd. Edn., Ont. Edn. Comm. Authority, Can. Crafts Coun., Ont. Guild Crafts, Zoomit Corp. Recipient Gold medal Internat. Typographic Composition Assn., 1971, gold medal Art Dirs. Club Toronto, 1973, medal Leipzig BookFair. Fellow Soc. Graphic Designers Can. (past pres.); mem. Alliance Graphique Internat., Royal Can. Acad. Arts, Nat. Yacht Club. Home: 101 Roxborough St W, Toronto, ON Canada M5R 1T9 Office: 103 Dupont St, Toronto, ON Canada M5R 1V4

KRAMER, CAROL GERTRUDE, marriage and family counselor; b. Grand Rapids, Mich., Jan. 14, 1939; d. Wilson John and Katherine Joanne (Wasdyke) Rottschafer; m. Peter William Kramer, July 1, 1960; children: Connie R. Kramer Sattler, Paul Wilson Kramer. AB, Calvin Coll., 1960; MA, U. Mich., 1969; PhD, Holy Cross Coll., 1973; MSW, Grand Valley State U., 1985. Diplomate Internat. Acad. Behavioral Medicine, Counseling and Psychotherapy; cert. addictions/substance abuse counselor, Mich.; cert. hypnotherapist/psychotherapist. Elem. tchr. Jenison (Mich.) Pub. Sch., 1960-65; sch. social worker Grand Rapids Pub. Sch., 1964-81; pvt. practice marriage and family counselor Grand Rapids, 1973—; v.p. Human Resource Assocs., Grand Rapids, 1983-88; pres. bd. dirs. Telecounseling, 1996—; guest lectr. Calvin Coll., Mich. State U., Grand Valley State U., 1975-85. Co-author: Parent Involvement Program, 1993, Stop Sexual Abuse for Everyone, 1996. Ruling elder 1st Presbyn. Ch., Grand Rapids, 1975-78; mem. Gerald R. Ford Rep. Women, Grand Rapids, 1980-87; co-chair pastoral rels. com. Gun Lake Community Ch., 1989-91, v.p. consistory, 1991-93; apptd. mem. State Mich. Bd. Marriage Counselors, 1985-87. Named one of Outstanding Young Women in Am., 1974; recipient Meritorious Svc. award Kent County Family Life Coun., 1983. Fellow Am. Assn. Marriage and Family Therapist; mem. NASW, Mich. Assn. Marriage Counselors (awards com. 1988, chmn. 1991, nominations com. 1992-95), Kent County Family Life Coun. (pres. 1975), Voters Against Sexual Abuse (pres., bd. dirs. 1992—). Home: 12622 Park Dr Wayland MI 49348-9085 Office: Psychology Ctr 2059 Lake Michigan Dr NW Grand Rapids MI 49504-4742

KRAMER, CECILE E., retired medical librarian; b. N.Y.C., Jan. 6, 1927; d. Marcus and Henrietta (Marks) K. B.S., CCNY, 1956; M.S. in L.S., Columbia U., 1960. Reference asst. Columbia U. Health Scis. Library, N.Y.C., 1957-61, asst. librarian, 1961-75; dir. Health Scis. Libr. Northwestern U., Chgo., 1975-91; asst. prof. edn. Northwestern U., 1975-91, prof. emeritus, 1991—; instr. library and info. sci. Rosary Coll., 1981-85 ; cons. Francis A. Countway Library Medicine, Harvard U., 1974. Pres. Friends of Libr., Fla. Atlantic U., Boca Raton. Fellow Med. Libr. Assn. (chmn. med. sch. librs. group 1975-76, editor newsletter 1975-77, instr. continuing edn. 1966-75, mem. panel cons. editors Bull. 1987-90, disting. mem. Acad. Health Info. Profls. 1993—); mem. Biomed. Comm. Network (chmn. 1979-80). Home: 9184 Flynn Cir Apt 4 Boca Raton FL 33496-6675

KRAMER, CHARLES HENRY, psychiatrist; b. Oak Park, Ill., May 31, 1922; s. Charles Henry and Martha (Ball) K.; m. Jeannette Ross, Sept. 15, 1945; children: Dan, Judy, Doug, Greg, Chip, David. B.S., U. Ill., 1944, M.D., 1945; grad., Inst. Psychoanalysis, Chgo., 1967; LLD, Valparaiso U., 1991. Diplomate: Am. Bd. Psychiatry and Neurology. Intern Cook County Hosp., Chgo., 1945-46, U. Ill. Hosp., Chgo., 1946-47; resident Chanute AFB Hosp., Ill., 1951-53, Elgin (Ill.) State Hosp., 1953-54, Inst. Juvenile Research, Chgo., 1955-59; pvt. practice medicine and surgery Palatine, Ill., 1947-51; pvt. practice psychiatry Oak Park, 1954-94; founder Family Inst. Chgo., 1968, pres., 1968-86; dir. family studies Inst. Psychiatry, Northwestern Meml. Hosp., 1975-86; prof. psychiatry and behavioral scis. Northwestern U. Med. Sch., 1975-92, prof. emeritus, 1992—; founder, pres. Plum Grove Nursing Home, 1953-83, Kramer Found., 1961-94, Kramer Enterprises, 1980-88; cons. mental health orgns. Author: Basic Principles of Long-Term Patient Care, 1976, Becoming a Family Therapist, 1980. Served with U.S. Army, 1943-45; Served with USAF, 1951-53. Recipient Better Life awards Ill. and Am. Nursing Home Assns., 1970. Fellow Am. Psychiat. Assn. (life); mem. Am. Family Therapy Assn. (incorporator, founding dir.), Am. Assn. Marriage and Family Therapy (approved supr. and fellow), Ill. Coun. Child and Adolescent Psychiatry, Mich. Psychiat. Soc., Chgo. Psychoanalytic Soc., Sigma Xi. Home: 2160 Amelia Pl Ann Arbor MI 48104-6305

KRAMER, CONSTANCE ANN, songwriter; b. Aug. 1, 1945; d. Isadore Arthur and Evelyn Antoinette (Hart) K.; m. Jerry Preston Raepdale, June 2, 1966 (div. 1979). BA in Psychology, Bklyn. Coll., 1995. In teletype dept. All Metal Nuts & Bolts Factory, Garden City, N.Y., 1965-66; receptionist Isadore Arthur Kramer, M.D., Hempstead, N.Y., 1966, 76-83; file clk. Ashforth Real Estate Corp., N.Y.C., 1967; with Vantage Press, Inc., N.Y.C., 1994—. Mem. Animals & The Environment, 1980—, Farm Sanctuary, 1993—, Ctr. Marine Conservation, 1994—, Friends of Animals, United Animal Nats., In. Def. of Animals, 1993—, Physicians Com. for Responsible Medicine, 1994, The Fund for Animals, 1995, The Gorilla Found., 1995, Doris Day Animal League, The Nature Conservancy. Avocations: singing, dancing, swimming, painting, bicycling. also: Doris Day Animal League Ste 100 227 Massachusetts Ave NE Washington DC

KRAMER, DALE VERNON, retired English language educator; b. Mitchell, S.D., July 13, 1936; s. Dwight Lyman and Frances Elizabeth (Corbin) K.; m. Cheris Gamble Kramarae, Dec. 21, 1960; children: Brinlee, Jana. B.S., S.D. State U., 1958; M.A., Case Western Res. U., 1960, Ph.D., 1963. Instr. English Ohio U., Athens, 1962-63, asst. prof., 1963-65; asst. prof. U. Ill., Urbana, 1965-67, assoc. prof., 1967-71, prof. English, 1971-96; prof. emeritus, 1997—; acting head English dept. U. Ill., Urbana, 1982, 86-87, assoc. dean Coll. of Arts & Scis., 1992-95; chmn. bd. editors Jour. English and Germanic Philology, 1972-95; assoc. vice provost, prof. English, U. Oreg., 1990. Author: Charles Robert Maturin, 1973, Thomas Hardy: The Forms of Tragedy, 1975, Thomas Hardy: Tess of the d'Urbervilles, 1991; editor: Critical Approaches to the Fiction of Thomas Hardy, 1979, Thomas Hardy, The Woodlanders, 1981, 85, Thomas Hardy, The Mayor of Casterbridge, 1987, Critical Essays on Thomas Hardy: The Novels, 1990, The Cambridge Companion to Thomas Hardy. Served to capt. U.S. Army, 1958-66. Mem. Center for Advanced Study, 1971; Am. Philos. Soc. grantee, 1969, 86, NEH grantee, 1986. Congregationalist.

KRAMER, DANIEL JONATHAN, lawyer; b. Cin., Dec. 20, 1957; s. Milton and Fradie (Ehrlich) K.; m. Judith L. Mogul, June 10, 1984; children: Ilona, Hannah, Joshua. BA magna cum laude, Wesleyan U., Middletown, Conn., 1980; JD, NYU, 1984. Bar: N.Y. 1985, U.S. Dist. Ct. (so. and ea. dists.) N.Y. 1985, U.S. Ct. Appeals (2d cir.) 1989. Assoc. Cravath, Swaine & Moore, N.Y.C., 1985-86; law clk. to Chief Judge Wilfred Feinberg, U.S. Ct. Appeals for 2d Cir., N.Y.C., 1986-87; assoc. Schulte Roth & Zabel LLP, N.Y.C., 1987-92, ptnr., 1993—; mem. pro se discretionary panel U.S. Ct. Appeals for 2d Cir., 1988—. Author: Federal Securities Litigation: Commentary and Forms, A Deskbook for the Practitioner, 1997; contbr. articles to law jours. and newspaper. Bd. dirs. Leukemia Soc., N.Y.C., 1995-98. Mem. ABA, Assn. Bar City N.Y. Office: Schulte Roth & Zabel LLP 900 3rd Ave Fl 19 New York NY 10022-4774

KRAMER, DONALD, insurance executive; b. N.Y.C., Nov. 17, 1937; s. Lawrence and Ruth Kramer; m. Elizabeth Gunderssen, June 1, 1982; children: Lauren Kramer Grau, Kim, Morten E., Christian Hoybye. BA in Econs., CUNY Bklyn. Coll., 1958; MBA, NYU, 1964. Chartered Fin. Analyst. Chmn. NAC RE Corp., Greenwich, 1984-93, Nat. Am. Ins. Co. Calif., Rancho Dominguez, 1986-91, Kramer Capital Cons. Inc., Greenwich, 1975-91, KCC Capital Mgrs., Greenwich, 1986-93; gen. ptnr. KCC Ptnrs. L.P., Greenwich, 1986-93; chmn. KCP Holding Co., Rancho Dominguez, Calif., 1986-91; pres., dir. Carteret Fed. Savs. Bank, Morristown, N.J., 1991-93; pres. Tempest Reins. Co. Ltd., Hamilton, Bermuda, 1993-99; bd. dirs. Nat. Benefit Life Ins. Co., N.Y.C.; vice chmn., dir. Ace Ltd, Bermuda, 1996—. Contbr. articles to jours. in field. Dir. Bklyn. Coll. Found. Mem. N.Y. Soc. Securities Analysts, Assn. for Investment Mgmt. and Rsch., Old Oaks Club (Purchase, N.Y.). Office: Ace Ltd, 30 Woodbourne Ave, Hamilton HM08, Bermuda

KRAMER, DONOVAN MERSHON, SR., newspaper publisher; b. Galesburg, Ill., Oct. 24, 1925; s. Verle V. and Sybil (Mershon) K.; m. Ruth A. Heins, Apr. 3, 1949; children: Donovan M. Jr., Diana Sue, Kara J. Kramer Cooper, Eric H. BS in Journalism, Pub. Mgmt., U. Ill., 1948. Editor, publisher, ptnr. Fairbury (Ill.) Blade, 1948-63, Forrest (Ill.) News, 1953-63; ptnr. Gibson City (Ill.) Courier, 1952-63; pres., publisher, editor Casa Grande (Ariz.) Valley Newspapers, Inc., 1963—; mng. ptnr. White Mt. Pub. Co., Show Low, Ariz., 1978—. Wrote, edited numerous articles and newspaper stories. Many award-winners including Sweepstakes award in Ill. and Ariz. Mem., chmn. Econ. Planning and Devel. Bd. State of Ariz., Phoenix, 1976-81; pres. Indsl. Devel. Authority of Casa Grande, 1977—; founding pres. Greater Casa Grande Econ. Devel. Found., exec. bd. dirs., 1982-99 (Lifetime Achievement award 1994); gov. apptd. bd. mem. Ariz. Dept. Transp., 1992-97, chmn., 1997; adv. bd. dept. journalism U. Ariz. With USAAF, WWII, PTO. Recipient Econ. Devel. plaque City of Casa Grande, 1982. Mem. Ariz. Newspapers Assn. (pres. 1980, Master Editor-Pub. 1977, Hall of Fame, 1998), Cmty. Newspapers Ariz. (pres. 1970-71), Inland Newspapers Assn., Newspapers Assn. Am., Ctrl. Ariz. Project Assn., Nat. Newspapers Assn., Greater Casa Grande C. of C. (pres. 1981-82, Hall of Fame 1991), Soc. Profl. Journalists. Republican. Lutheran. Avocations: hiking, fishing, nature studies, travel, health awareness, econ. devel., military history.

KRAMER, EDWARD GEORGE, lawyer; b. Cleve., July 15, 1950; s. Archibald Charles and Katherine Faith (Porter) K.; m. Roberta Darwin, June 15, 1974. BS in Edn., Kent State U., 1972; JD, Case Western Res. U., 1975. Bar: Ohio 1975, U.S. Dist. Ct. (no. dist.) Ohio 1975, U.S. Ct. Appeals (6th cir.) 1980, U.S. Supreme Ct. 1980. Assoc. dir. The Cuyahoga Plan of Ohio, Cleve., 1975-76; exec. dir. The Housing Advs., Inc., Cleve., 1976—; sr. ptnr. Kramer & Assocs., LPA, Cleve., 1981—; spl. counsel atty. gen. State of Ohio, Columbus, 1983-95; pres. Atty. Svcs., Inc., 1987—, ASI Info. Sys.; dir. Housing Law Clinic, 1989-95; dir. Fair Housing Law Clinic, 1995—; adj. lectr. Cleve. State U., 1991-94, adj. prof., 1994—; alt. consumer rep., FTC, Washington, 1976-77; cons. HUD, Washington, 1978-80, joint select com. sch. desegregation, Ohio Gen. Assembly, Columbus, 1979; mem. visitors com., Case Western Res. U. Sch. Law, Cleve., 1977-83; mem., chmn. Ford Motor Consumer Appeals Bd., 1989-93; bd. advisors Brownstone Pub. Author: How to Settle Small Claims: A Guide to The Use of Small Claims Courts, 1973, (with others) A Guide to Regional Housing Opportunities, 1979, (with Buchanan) Mobile Home Living: A Guide to Consumers' Rights, 1979; contbr. articles to legal jours. Chmn. Ohio Protection and Advocacy System for Developmentally Disabled, Columbus, 1978-80; trustee Muscle Disease Soc., Cleve., 1979-81; sec. Cuyahoga County Housing and Econ. Devel. com., Cleve., 1983—; mem. Cleve. Mayor's Com. on Employment of Handicapped, 1978-79; mem. fair housing adv. bd. John Marshall Law Sch. Named Disting. Recent Grad. Case Western Reserve U. Law Alumni Assn., 1985; Roscoe Pound fellow. Mem. ABA (sect. on urban state & local govt. law, com. on housing and urban devel., forum on constrn. industry), ACLU (litigation com.), Cleve. Bar Assn. (trustee 1995-98, vice chmn. com. on homeless, chmn., vice-chmn., law sch. liaison), Nat. Audubon Assn., Nat. Employment Lawyers Assn., Practicing Law Inst. (assoc.), Assn. Trial Lawyers Am. (employment rights sect., 2d vice chair, newsletter editor), Assn. Am. Law Schs. (com. on clin. legal edn.), Nat. Trust for Hist. Preservation, Nat. Platform Assn., Planetary Soc., Boat Club Nautica, Palm Beach Club (London), Old River Yacht Club, Cleve. Grays, Masons, Tyrian (worshipful master), Order of Eastern Star (James A Garfield chpt.). Democrat. Mem. United Ch. Christ. Avocations: softball, scuba diving, collecting coins and stamps, chess, reading. Office: Kramer & Assocs, LPA 3214 Prospect Ave E Cleveland OH 44115-2614

KRAMER, EDWARD JOHN, materials science and engineering educator; b. Wilmington, Del., Aug. 5, 1939; s. Edward Noble and Irma (Nemetz) K.; m. Gail Allen Woodford, Aug. 24, 1963; children: Eric Woodford, Jeanne Noble. BChemE, Cornell U., 1962; PhD, Carnegie-Mellon U., 1967. Asst. prof. dept. materials sci. and engring. Cornell U., Ithaca, N.Y., 1967-72, assoc. prof., 1972-79, prof., 1979-88, Samuel B. Eckert prof. materials sci. and engring., 1988-97; prof. dept. materials & chem. engring. U. Calif., Santa Barbara, 1997—; vis. scientist Argonne (Ill.) Nat. Lab., 1974-75; vis. prof. Akademie der Wissenschaften Inst. Metallphysik, Göttingen, Germany, 1979, Ecole Poly. Federale de Lausanne, Switzerland, 1982, Johannes Gutenberg U., Mainz, Germany, 1987-88. Contbr. over 250 articles to sci. jours. Recipient U.S. Sr. Scientist award Alexander von Humboldt Stiftung, 1987-88, Swinburne award Inst. Materials, U.K., 1996; NATO fellow, 1966-67, John Simon Guggenheim Found. fellow, N.Y.C., 1988. Fellow AAAS, Am. Phys. Soc. (High Polymer Physics prize 1985); mem. NAE, Materials Rsch. Soc., Am. Chem. Soc., Böhmische Phys. Soc. Avocation: masters swimming. Office: Univ Calif Materials Dept Engring II Santa Barbara CA 93106

KRAMER, ELISSA LIPCON, nuclear medicine physician, educator; b. N.Y.C., Feb. 22, 1951; d. Jules and Esther Ruth (Wagner) L.; children: Rachel, Aaron. BA, U. Pa., 1973; MD, NYU, 1977. Diplomate Am. Bd. Nuc. Medicine, Am. Bd. Radiology. Ob-gyn. intern Bellevue Hosp. Ctr./NYU Med. Ctr., 1977-78, resident in radiology, 1978-80, fellow in nuc. medicine, 1980-82; asst. prof. clin. radiology NYU, 1982-89, assoc. prof. clin. radiology, 1989-96, prof. clin. radiology, 1996—; assoc. prof. radiology Cornell U. Med. Ctr., Ithaca, N.Y., 1989-90; assoc. Sloan-Kettering Cancer Ctr., N.Y.C., 1989-90; assoc. dir. nuc. medicine Tisch Hosp., N.Y.C., 1989—; assoc. attending physician Tisch Hosp., 1990—, Bellevue Hosp., N.Y.C., 1990—. Author, editor: (book) Clinical SPECT Imaging, 1995; contbr. articles to profl. jours. Nat. Cancer Inst./NIG Rsch. grantee, 1993—. Mem. Am. Coll. Radiology, Am. Assn. Women Radiologists, Radiology Soc. N.Am., Soc. Nuc. Medicine (mem. brain imaging coun. 1982—, mem. bd. dirs. 1992-93). Office: NYU Med Ctr Divsn Nuc Med 560 1st Ave New York NY 10016-6402

KRAMER, EUGENE LEO, lawyer; b. Barberton, Ohio, Nov. 7, 1939; s. Frank L. and Portia I. (Acker) K.; m. JoAnn Stockhausen, Sept. 19, 1970; children: Martin, Caroline, Michael. AB, John Carroll U., 1961; JD, U. Notre Dame, 1964. Bar: Ohio 1964. Law clerk U.S. Ct. Appeals (7th cir.), Chgo., 1964-65; ptnr. Squire, Sanders & Dempsey, Cleve., 1965-91, Roetzel & Andress, A Legal Profl. Assn., Cleve. and Akron, Ohio, 1992-97; cons. Ohio Constl. Revision Commn., Columbus, 1970-74. Trustee Citizens League Greater Cleve., 1984-90, 93—, Citizens League Rsch. Inst., 1995-97, St. Ann Found., 1990-92, Consultation Ctr. for Diocese of Cleve., 1990-96, Lyric Opera Cleve., 1995—, Regina Health Ctr., 1997—; past pres. HELP Found, Inc., HELP, Inc., Cleve., 1981-92, Playhouse Sq. Assn., Cleve., 1980-84; pres. N.E. Ohio Transit Coalition, 1992—; mem. policy com. Build-Up Greater Cleve. Program, 1982-98, Build-Up Lorain County Program, 1998—; mem. Greater Cleve. Growth Assn. Recipient Disting. Leadership award HELP, Inc., 1986, Pioneer achievement award HELP--Six Chimneys, Inc., 1986, Disting. Svc. award Assn. Retarded Citizens, Cuyahoga County, 1990. Mem. ABA, Ohio State Bar Assn. (chmn. local govt. law com. 1986-90), Akron Bar Assn., Cleve. Bar Assn., The Clifton Club (Lakewood, Ohio, bd. dirs. 1986-89), The Union Club of Cleve. Democrat. Roman Catholic. Avocations: music, theater, sports, travel. Home and Office: 1422 Euclid Ave Ste 706 Cleveland OH 44115-2001

KRAMER, FERDINAND, mortgage banker; b. Chgo., Aug. 10, 1901; s. Adolph F. and Ray (Friedberg) K.; m. Stephanie Shambaugh, Dec. 22, 1932 (dec. Feb. 1973); children: Barbara Shambaugh Kramer Bailey, Douglas, Anthony; m. Julia Wood McDermott, Aug. 19, 1975. PhB, U. Chgo., 1922. Engaged in real estate bus. and mortgage banker Chgo., 1922—; with Draper & Kramer, Inc., Chgo., 1922—; chmn. bd. Draper & Kramer, Inc., 1944-95, chmn. emeritus, 1995—; dir., mem. exec. com. Chgo. 21 Corp.; Program supr. Div. Def. Housing Coordination (and successor Nat. Housing Agy.), Washington, 1941-42; past pres. Met. Housing and Planning Council, Chgo., Actions, Inc.; past mem. Pres.'s Com. Equal Opportunity in Housing. Past chmn. steering com. United Negro Fund; mem. vis. com. dept. design and visual arts Harvard, 1963-64; life trustee U. Chgo. Recipient citation of merit U. Chgo. Alumni Assn., 1947, Individual Disting. Housing and Redevel. Svc. award Nat. Assn. Housing Ofcls., 1952, Disting. Alumnus award, 1982, Alumni Svc. medal, 1997, Disting. Pub. Svc. award Union League Club, Chgo., 1994. Mem. Chgo. Mortgage Bankers Assn. (past pres.), Mortgage Bankers Assn. Am., Nat. Assn. Housing Ofcls., Chgo. Assn. Commerce and Industry. Clubs: Chicago, Quadrangle, Standard, Tavern, Mid-Town Tennis, Commercial (Chgo.). Home: 1115 S Plymouth Ct Apt 511 Chicago IL 60605-2038

KRAMER, FRANK RAYMOND, classicist, educator; b. Baraboo, Wis., Jan. 2, 1908; s. Chris Edward and Mabel (Shaw) K.; m. Hetty Louise Eising, Dec. 20, 1935; children: Bryce Allen, Anita Louise (Mrs. James Cyril Shew). *Frank's maternal ancestors (Shaws) migrated from Ayrshire, Scotland to Connecticut before 1777. His grandfather Henry Waggoner Shaw settled in Sauk County, Wisconsin. Frank's paternal grandfather Christian Kramer migrated from the Palatinate, Germany (Kirchheimbolanden and Kaiserslautern) to Sauk County in 1865. Hetty's maternal lineage (King-Loomer) extends to the barons confronting King John and beyond to Charlemagne. Emigrating from Devonshire, England, the Loomers settled in Connecticut before 1687. Her paternal ancestors were from Alten Hagen, Prussia; her grandfather John Eising migrated to Waukesha County, Wisconsin, in the mid-1850's.* B. Humanities, U. Wis., 1929, M.A. in Greek and Latin, 1931, Ph.D., 1936. Mem. faculty Heidelberg Coll., Tiffin, Ohio, 1938-78; prof. classics Heidelberg Coll., 1944-78; asso. in residence U. Wis., 1948-49, 51-52; vis. prof. Ohio State U., summer 1962, prof. classics, 1978-79; research Am. Sch. Classical Studies, Athens, 1965. Author: Voices in the Valley, Mythmaking and Folk Belief in the Shaping of the Middle West, 1964; also articles; contbr. American National Biography. Grantee Wis. Com. Study Am. Civilization, 1948-49, 51-52; Grantee Social Sci. Research Council, 1951. Mem. Am. Philol. Assn., Classical Assn. Middle West and South, Ohio Classical Conf. (pres. 1948-49), Phi Alpha Theta, Eta Sigma Phi. Democrat. Mem. United Ch. Christ. Home: 192 Saint Francis Ave Apt 24 Tiffin OH 44883-4413 *The effort to develop perspectives has been a guiding principle of my life. Shaped in the course of a career in Classics, these perspectives have helped me to distinguish the significant in scholarship from the trivial, to differentiate between long-range values and temporary advantage, and to discriminate between ethical focus and, e.g., cultic distortion. And at least part of this principle is the realization that not to take oneself too seriously may help put these perspectives themselves into perspective.*

KRAMER, FRANKLIN DAVID, lawyer; b. Liberty, N.Y., Nov. 13, 1945; s. Solomon and Carolyn Bertha (Cohen) C.; m. Noël Anketell, May 30, 1970; children: Katherine Anketell, Christopher Anketell. BA, Yale U., 1967; JD, Harvard U., 1971. Bar: N.Y. 1972, D.C. 1972, Supreme 1976. Law clk. assoc. judge U.S. Ct. Appeals (2d cir.), N.Y.C., 1971-72; assoc. Shea & Gardner, Washington, 1972-77, ptnr., 1982—; spl. asst. to asst. sec. def. Dept. Def., Washington, 1977-79, prin. dep. asst. to asst. sec. def. for internat. security affairs, 1979-81. Contbr. articles to profl. jours. Mem. ABA, Internat. Inst. Strategic Studies, Am. Arbitration Assn. (comml. arbitrator). Democrat. Jewish. Home: 3555 Springland Ln NW Washington DC 20008-3119 Office: Shea & Gardner Ste 800 1800 Massachusetts Ave NW Washington DC 20036-1872

KRAMER, GEORGE P., lawyer; b. Holyoke, Mass., Feb. 22, 1927; m. Elizabeth M. Truax, Oct. 13, 1973; children: Alice S. Truax, R. Hawley Truax, Charles W. Truax. A.B., Harvard U., 1950, LL.B., 1953; student, Sorbonne, 1948. Bar: N.Y. 1954. Assoc. Watson Leavenworth Kelton & Taggart, N.Y.C., 1953-59, partner, 1960-65; partner Conboy, Hewitt, O'Brien & Boardman, N.Y.C., 1965-86, Hunton & Williams (merger Conboy, Hewitt, O'Brien & Boardman), N.Y.C., 1986—; lectr. Practising Law Inst.; Pres. Mergers Co., Inc., N.Y.C.; bd. dirs. Burleson Corp.; vis. com. Peabody Mus. of Harvard U., 1974-80; mem. N.Y. Cotton Exch., N.Y. Bd. Trade. Author: Misleading Trademarks and Consumer Protection. Trustee Hancock Shaker Village, 1982—; trustee Harvard U. Law Sch. Assn. of N.Y., 1985-89, v.p. 1987-89. Served to ensign USNR, 1945-46. Recipient Congl. Antarctic medal, 1977. Mem. ABA, Internat. Bar Assn., Assn. Bar City N.Y. (sec. 1963-65, exec. com. 1970-74, chmn. various coms.), Am. Law Inst., U.S. Internat. Trademark Assn. (dir. 1975-78), Assn. Internationale pour la Protection de la Propriete Industrielle, Harvard U. Alumni Assn. (bd. dirs. 1983-89), Mass. Speleological Soc. (pres.), Antarctican Soc., Am. Polar Soc., Century Assn., Harvard Club (sec. 1972-83, 88-90, bd. mgrs. 1983-86), Harvard Faculty Club. Home: 151 E 79th St New York NY 10021-0417 Office: Hunton & Williams Fl 43 200 Park Ave New York NY 10166-0091

KRAMER, GERHARDT THEODORE, architect; b. New Orleans, Oct. 26, 1909; s. Gotthilf Mathias and Antonette (Smrcka) K.; m. Ravenna Evelyn Ross, July 10, 1935 (dec. Mar. 1995); children: Gayle (Mrs. Gerald Grommet), Ross. B.Arch., Tulane U., 1930; M.Arch., Cornell U., 1932; LL.D. (hon.), Concordia Sem., 1978. Asso. in architecture Middle Am. Research Inst., Tulane U., 1933-41; with Douglass V. Freret, New Orleans, 1941-42, Hugo K. Graf, St. Louis, 1946-53; prin. Kramer & Assos., St. Louis, 1953-56, Kramer & Harms, Inc., St. Louis, 1956-94; v.p. Concordia Hist. Inst., St. Louis, 1961-69, pres., 1970-81; v.p. Heritage/St. Louis, 1970-74; pres. Landmarks Assn. St. Louis, Inc., 1960-62, 65-67, 68-71, exec. dir., 1974-78, sec., 1978-79; commr. Tower Grove Park, St. Louis, 1973-92; mus. dir. Kirkwood History House, 1978-81. Bd. dirs. Chatillon-DeMenil House Found., St. Louis, 1972-87, Robert Campbell House Found., 1976-89; mem. Mo. Adv. Coun. Hist. Preservation, 1978-81; v.p. Eugene Field House Found., 1981-85; vice chmn. Kirkwood Landmarks Comm., 1981-88; mem. Met. Zool. Park and Mus. Dist. Bd., 1982-89; pres. Concordia Luth. Kirkwood, 1953-54. With USNR, 1942-69, capt. St. Louis Brigade, ret. Fellow AIA (pres. St. Louis chpt. 1958-59, Mo. preservation coord. 1970-72, pres. Mo. coun. archs. 1973). Lutheran. Home: 727 S Laclede Station Rd S Webster Groves MO 63119

KRAMER, GORDON, mechanical engineer; b. Bklyn., Aug. 1937; s. Joseph and Etta (Grossberg) K.; m. Ruth Ellen Harter, Mar. 5, 1967 (div. June 1986); children: Samuel Maurice, Leah Marie; m. Eve Burstein, Dec. 17, 1988. BS Cooper Union, 1959; MS, Calif. Inst. Tech., 1960. With Hughes Aircraft Co., Malibu, Calif., 1959-63; sr. scientist Avco Corp., Norman, Okla., 1963-64; asst. div. head Batelle Meml. Inst., Columbus, Ohio, 1964-67; sr. scientist Aerojet Electrosystems, Azusa, Calif., 1967-75; chief engr. Beckman Instrument Co., Fullerton, Calif., 1975-82; prin. scientist McDonnell Douglas Microelectronics Co., 1982-83, Kramer and Assocs., 1983-85; program mgr. Hughes Aircraft Co., 1985-96; ret., 1996; cons. Korea Inst. Tech. NSF fellow, 1959-60. Mem. IEEE. Democrat. Jewish. Home: 153 Lake Shore Dr Rancho Mirage CA 92270-4055

KRAMER, GORDON EDWARD, manufacturing executive; b. San Mateo, Calif., June 22, 1946; s. Roy Charles and Bernice Jeanne (Rones) K.; BS in Aero. Engring., San Jose State Coll., 1970; m. Christina Hodges, Feb. 14, 1970; children: Roy Charles, Charlena. Purchasing agent Am. Racing Equipment, Brisbane, Calif., 1970-71, asst. to v.p. mktg., 1971-72; founder, pres. Safety Direct Inc., hearing protection equipment, Sparks, Nev., 1972—; dir. Hodges Transp., Condor Inc.; mem. adv. bd. to pres. Truckee Meadows Community Coll., 1991—. Named Nev. Small Businessperson of Yr., Nev. Small Bus. Adminstrn., 1987, Bus. Person of Yr. Sparks Community C. of C., 1987. Mem. Am. Soc. Safety Engrs., Safety Equipment Distributors Assn., Indsl. Safety Equipment Assn., Nat. Assn. Sporting Goods Wholesalers, Nat. Sporting Goods Assn., Nev. State Amature Trapshooting Assn. (dir. 1978-79), Pacific Internat. Trapshooting Assn. (Nev. pres. 1979-80, 80-81), Nev. Mfrs. Assn. (dir. 1992—), Advanced Soccer Club (pres.1985-86). Republican. Methodist. Rotary Club (pres. Spark Club 1988-89). Office: Safety Direct Inc 56 Coney Island Dr Sparks NV 89431-6335

KRAMER, HELENE G., political and civic association executive; b. Newark, Aug. 9, 1946; d. Victor and Sylvia (Weissman) Kaufman; m. Louis Weinner, Dec. 19, 1992; children: Lauren Weinreb, Stuart Kramer. Student, Edison C.C., Manatee C.C., Sarasota County Vocat. Ctr., Fairleigh Dickinson U.; grad., Eastern Sch. Physicians Aides. Lab. technician Rockland State Hosp., Orangeburg, N.Y., 1965-67; supr. blood bank, serology Nyack (N.Y.) Hosp., 1967-74; adminstr. religious sch. Monroe (N.Y.) Temple, 1977-78; tchr. pre-sch. Temple Beth Shalom Nursery Sch., Sarasota, 1978-81, Camp Maccabee, divsn. Jewish Fedn., Sarasota, 1978-81; program dir. Sarasota-Manatee Jewish Fedn., 1981-88; exec. dir. Jewish Fedn. Lee and Charlotte Counties, Ft. Myers, 1988-95; v.p. trusts No. trust Bank, Ft. Myers, 1995-97; campaign dir. Jewish Fedn. Greater New Orleans, 1997—; mem. nat. com. Conversations on Health, Robert Wood Johnson Foun., Coun. of Jewish Fedns., Assn. Jewish Cmty. Orgns. personnel; mem., office holder local county coms. on health and health svcs.; speaker numerous panels, workshops and media events; coord. Missions to Israel, Jewish inmate visitations Charlotte Correctional Inst., cultural and ednl. programs for Jewish cmty., others. Avocations: photography, exercise, bicycling, reading. Office: Jewish Fedn Greater New Orleans 3500 N Causeway Blvd Metairie LA 70002-3527

KRAMER, JAY HARLAN, physiologist, researcher, educator; b. Bklyn., Dec. 26, 1952; s. Albert and Blossom K.; m. Aisar Atrakchi, Apr. 18, 1993; 1 child, Evan. BA with honors, Northeastern U., 1976; MS, Lehigh U., 1979, PhD, 1982. Clin. lab. technician Boston Med. Lab., Waltham, Mass., 1974-75; rsch. asst. Lehigh U., Bethlehem, Pa., 1979-81; rsch. assoc. Med. Coll. Va., Richmond, 1982-83; sr. rsch. assoc. Okla. Med. Rsch. Found., Oklahoma City, 1983-85; rsch. assoc. George Washington U., Washington, 1985-86, asst. rsch. prof. medicine, 1986-90, assoc. rsch. prof., 1990—, adj. assoc. prof. physiology, 1991—, assoc. rsch. prof. physiology, 1998—; lectr. physiology George Washington U., Washington, 1987-89; cons. Squibb & Sons, Princeton, N.J., 1989, mem. George Washington U. Instl. Animal Care and Use Com., 1988—, mem. Basic Sci. Faculty Assembly and Inst. Biomed. Scis., 1996—. Contbr. more than 45 articles to profl. jours.; article referee profl. jours. Mem. basic sci. faculty assembly coun. George Washington U., 1992-94. Grad. sch. scholar Lehigh U., 1980; named one of Outstanding Young Men of Am., Jaycees, 1981, 82. Mem. Am. Heart Assn., Am. Physiol. Soc., N.Y. Acad. Scis. (invited speaker 1993, presenter various nat. scientific meetings), Internat. Soc. for Heart Rsch., Internat. Soc. for Free Radical Rsch., Soc. for Exptl. Biology and Medicine, Acad. Honor Soc., Phi Sigma. Achievements include first to demonstrate relationship between toxic free radical prodn. and severity of ischemia in heart; first to demonstrate superoxide anion prodn. in postischemic heart using ESR spin trapping; first to demonstrate free radical prodn. in regionally ischemic canine and postischemic swine heart models; first to demonstrate that excessive neuropeptide release during dietary magnesium restriction leads to reduced tolerance of animal hearts to ischemia/reperfusion injury; developed non-invasive ESR spin trapping technique for free radical detection; demonstrated occurrance of potentially toxic free radicals in human heart following open heart surgery. Office: George Washington U Dept Medicine 2300 I St NW Washington DC 20037-2336

KRAMER, JOEL ROY, journalist, newspaper executive; b. Bklyn., May 21, 1948; s. Archie and Rae (Abramowitz) K.; m. Laurie Maloff, 1969; children—Matthew, Elias, Adam. B.A., Harvard U., Cambridge, 1969. Editor-in-chief Harvard Crimson; reporter Sci. Mag., Washington, 1969-70; free lance writer Washington, 1970-72; from copy editor to news editor, exec. news editor, asst. mng. editor Newsday, L.I., N.Y., 1972-80; exec. editor Buffalo Courier-Express, 1981-82; exec. editor Star Tribune, Mpls., St. Paul, 1983-91, pub., pres., 1992-98; sr. fellow Sch. Journalism and Mass Comms., U. Minn., Mpls., 1998—; bd. dirs. Harvard Crimson Inc., 1969—, World Press Inst. Chmn. bd. Mpls. Children's Theatre Co., 1994-96. Co-recipient Pulitzer prize for Pub. Service, Newsday (The Heroin Trail), 1973; Best Legal Writing on Large Daily award N.Y. Bar Assn., 1974. Mem. Am. Soc. Newspaper Editors, Newspaper Assn. Am. Address: Sch Journalism U Minn 111 Murphy Hall 206 Church St SE Minneapolis MN 55455*

KRAMER, JOHN PAUL, entomologist, educator; b. Elgin, Ill., Mar. 13, 1928; s. Rutherford Hayes and Anna Maria (Burita) K.; m. Jean Kent Simpson, June, 1957 (div. 1973); children: Philip Simpson, Katherine Jean. B.S., Beloit (Wis.) Coll., 1950; M.S., U. Mo., 1952; Ph.D., U. Ill., 1958. Asst. prof. entomology N.C. State U., 1958-59; asso. entomologist Ill. Natural History Survey, Urbana, 1959-65; with Cornell U., 1965-90, prof. insect pathology dept. entomology, 1975-90, prof. emeritus, 1990—; WHO traveling cons., 1962, NSF vis. scientist, Japan, 1967; mem. study sect. for tropical medicine and parasitology NIH, 1966-68; vis. scientist Inst. Arctic Biology in Alaska, 1972; vis. prof. entomology Ohio State U., Columbus, 1984. Contbr. articles to profl. jours. Served to 1st lt. U.S. Army, 1952-54. Decorated Bronze Star., Korean Svc. medal with 2 battle stars; NSF fellow, 1967; NIH research grantee, 1959-72; Office of Naval Research grantee, 1971-74; WHO research grantee, 1979-82; U.S. Dept. Agr. research grantee, 1980-90. Mem. Soc. Invertebrate Pathology, N.Y. Entomol. Soc., Am. English Spot Rabbit Club, Am. Cavy Breeders Assn., Am. Rabbit Breeders Assn., N.Y. State Rabbit Breeders Assn. (pres. 1989-90), Taughannock Area Rabbit Breeders Assn. (pres. 1983-84, 91-96), Am. Netherland Dwarf Rabbit Breeders Assn., Nat. English Rabbit Club Gt. Britain, Empire State English Spot Rabbit Club, N.Y. State Cavy Fanciers Club (v.p. 1973-75). Republican. Unitarian-Universalist. Home: 115 Hanshaw Rd Ithaca NY 14850-2207 Office: Cornell Univ Dept Entomology 3142 Comstock Hall Ithaca NY 14853-2601*

KRAMER, KAREN SUE, mind-body psychologist; b. L.A., Sept. 6, 1942; d. Frank Pacheco Kramer and Velma Eileen (Devlin) Moore; m. Stewart A. Sterling, Dec. 30, 1965 (div. 1974); 1 child, Scott Kramer Sterling. BA, U. Calif., Berkeley, 1966; MA, U.S. Internat. U., 1976; PhD, Profl. Sch. Psychology, 1980. Psychometrist U. Calif. Counseling Ctr., Berkeley, 1966-67; social worker Alameda County Welfare Dept., Oakland, Calif., 1967-69; vol. coord. San. Diego County Probation Dept., 1971-73; officer San Diego County Probation Dept., 1973-76; counselor and coord. clin. and outreach programs Western Inst., San Diego, 1976-77; program coord. and counselor Women's Resource Ctr., Oceanside, Calif., 1977-78; pvt. practice psychology San Diego, 1978-81; planner/analyst San Diego County Dept. Health Svcs., 1979-81; prof. psychology Nat. U., San Diego, 1979-81; social svcs. program cons. Calif. Dept. Social Svcs., Emeryville, 1981-83; affirmative action officer State Compensation Ins. Fund, San Francisco, 1983-87; cmty. psychologist Calif. Dept. Mental Health, 1987-89; pvt. practice psychology Berkeley, 1990—; personal analyst State Comp. Ins. Fund, 1989-91; regional property mgr. State Compensation Ins. Fund, San Francisco, 1991-95; prof. Nat. U. San Diego, 1979-81; pres. North County Coun. Social Concerns, Vista, Calif., 1977-78; advisor USMC Camp Pendleton Human Svcs., 1977-79; mem. adv. bd. Chinatown Resources Devel. Ctr., San Francisco, 1984-87, San Francisco Rehab., 1984-87; bd. dirs. Network Cons. Svcs., Napa, Calif.; founder Qi Gong in China-Ednl. Svcs., 1994; pub. chmn. Intuition Network Conf., 1997; advisor Calif.-Hawaii Inst., 1998—; asst. prof. Am. Coll. Traditional Chinese Medicine, S.F., 1999. Editl. advisor (website) Alternative Medicine, 1998. Mem. Calif. Peer Counselors Assn. (adv. bd. 1987-90), Calif. Prevention Network (bd. dirs. 1989-93, editl. advisor jour. 1992-93). E-mail: karenúkramer@compuserve.com.

KRAMER, KENNETH BENTLEY, federal judge, former congressman; b. Chgo., Feb. 19, 1942; s. Albert Aaron and Ruth (Pokrass) K.; children: Kenneth Bentley, Kelly J. BA magna cum laude in Polit. Sci., U. Ill., 1963; JD, Harvard U., 1966. Bar: Ill. 1966, Colo. 1969. Dep. dist. atty. El Paso County, Colo., Colorado Springs, 1970-72; pvt. practice law Colorado Springs, 1972-78; mem. Colo. Ho. of Reps., 1973-78, 96th-99th Congresses from 5th Colo. Dist., 1978-86; asst. sec. Dept. Army, Washington, 1988-89; assoc. judge U.S. Ct. of Appeals for Vets. Claims, Washington, 1989—. Bd. visitors U.S. Air Force Acad., 1979-86; bd. dirs. Pikes Peak Mental Health Ctr., 1976-78, Mountain Valley chpt. March of Dimes, 1983-85, U.S. Space Found., 1983-91; founder U.S. Space Found.; commr. Nat. Coun. on Uniform State Laws, 1977-78. Capt. U.S. Army, 1967-70. Recipient Disting. Civilian Svc. medal. Mem. Phi Beta Kappa. Office: US Ct Appels for Vets Claims 625 Indiana Ave NW Washington DC 20004-2901

KRAMER, LAWRENCE STEPHEN, journalist; b. Hackensack, N.J., Apr. 24, 1950; s. Abraham and Ann Eve (Glasser) K.; m. Myla F. Lerner, Sept. 3, 1978; children: Matthew Lerner, Erika. B.S. in Journalism, Syracuse U., 1972; M.B.A., Harvard U., 1974. Reporter San Francisco Examiner, 1974-77; reporter Washington Post, 1977-80; exec. editor Trenton Times, N.J., 1980-82; asst. to exec. editor Washington Post, 1982, asst. mng. editor, 1982-86; exec. editor San Francisco Examiner, 1986-91; pres. Datasport Inc., San Mateo, Calif., 1991-94; v.p. Data Broadcasting Corp., San Mateo, 1994-97; pres., CEO CBS.Marketwatch.com., San Francisco, 1997—. Recipient W.R. Hearst Found. award 1971-72, Gerald Loeb award 1977. Mem. Soc. Profl. Journalists. Home: 8 Auburn Ct Belvedere Tiburon CA 94920-1349*

KRAMER, LINDA KONHEIM, curator, art historian; b. N.Y.C., Nov. 8, 1939; d. Clarence John and May (Sternberg) Konheim; m. Samuel R. Kramer, Apr. 24, 1977; 1 child, Nicholas Clarence. BA in Fine Arts and Art History, Smith Coll., 1961; BFA in Painting and Graphic Design, Yale U., 1963; MA in 19th and 20th Century European and Am. Art, NYU, 1968, postgrad. Program adminstr. Solomon R. Guggenheim Mus., 1973-76; cataloger modern drawings Sotheby Park-Bernet, N.Y.C., 1980-82; expert in modern drawings Sotheby's N.Y., 1982-85; curator prints and drawings, dept. head Bklyn. Mus., 1985-94; tchr. Sch. Visual Arts, N.Y.C., 1977-80, Manhattanville Coll., summer 1995, 96; exec. dir. Nancy Graves Found., N.Y.C., 1996—; mem. adv. bd. Coll. Fine Arts, West Wash. U., Bellingham, 1987-95. Author pamphlets and catalogs; contbr. articles to profl. jours. Grantee Nat. Mus. Act, 1976, 78; Jane and Morgan Whitney fellow Met. Mus. Art, 1995-96. Mem. Am. Assn. Mus., Print Coun. Am., Art Table, Coll. Art Assn. Home: 372 Central Park W New York NY 10025-8240

KRAMER, LORNE C., protective services official. BA in Pub. Mgmt., U. Redlands, 1977; MPA with honors, U. So. Calif., 1979; Advanced Exec. Cert., Calif. Law Enforcement Coll., 1987; grad., Nat. Exec. Inst., 1993. Comdr. L.A. Police Dept., 1963-91; chief police Colorado Springs (Colo.) Police Dept., 1991—; Cons., instr. drugs and gangs Nat. Inst. Justice, Office Juvenile Justice U.S. Dept. Justice. Active Colo. State DARE Adv. Bd.; bd. dirs. Ctr. Prevention Domestic Violence, Pikes Peak Mental Health. Mem. Colo. Assn. Chiefs Police (bd. dirs., major cities rep.), Internat. Assn. Chiefs Police (juvenile justice com.), Police Exec. Rsch. Forum. Office: PO Box 2169 Colorado Springs CO 80901-2169

KRAMER, MARY ELIZABETH, health services executive, state legislator; b. Burlington, Iowa, June 14, 1935; d. Ross L. and Geneva M. (McElhinney) Barnett; m. Kay Frederick Kramer, June 13, 1958; children: Kent, Krista. BA, U. Iowa, 1957, MA, 1971. Cert. tchr., Iowa. Tchr. Newton (Iowa) Pub. Schs., 1957-61; tchr. Iowa City Pub. Schs., 1961-67, tchr., asst. supt., 1971-75; dir. pers. Younkers, Inc., Des Moines, 1975-81; v.p. Wellmark, Inc., Des Moines, 1981—; mem. Iowa State Senate, Des Moines, 1990-96, pres., 1997—. Bd. dirs. Polk County Child Care Rsch. Ctr., Des Moines, 1986-96, YWCA, Des Moines, 1989-94; mem. Olympic adv. com. Blue Cross and Blue Shield Assn., Chgo., 1988-92. Named Mgr. of Yr. Iowa Mgmt. Assocs., 1985, Woman of Achievement YWCA, 1986, Woman of Vision Young Women's Resource Ctr., 1989. Mem. Soc. Human Resource Mgmt. (Profl. of Yr. 1996), Iowa Mgmt. Assn. (pres. 1988), Greater Des Moines C. of C. (bd. dirs. 1986-96), Nexus, Rotary Internat. Republican. Presbyterian. Avocations: music, public speaking. Home: 1209 Ashworth Rd West Des Moines IA 50265-3546 Office: Wellmark Inc 636 Grand Ave Des Moines IA 50309-2502 also: Iowa State Senate State Capitol Des Moines IA 50319

KRAMER, MARY LOUISE, journalist; b. Grand Rapids, Mich., Apr. 18, 1953; d. Vincent Paul and Solina Josephine (Langhals) K. BS, Grand Valley State U., 1979. Asst. city editor, reporter Grand Rapids Press, 1974-82; city editor Greenwich (Conn.) Time, 1982-83; assignment editor Ann Arbor (Mich.) News, 1983-86; city editor Kalamazoo (Mich.) Gazette, 1986-89; assoc. pub., editor Crain's Detroit Bus., 1989—; chair Leadership Detroit, 1991-92. Named Internat. Woman of Yr. Women in Internat. Trade, 1991, Role Model of Yr. Alternatives Girls, 1996. Mem. Detroit Athletic Club (bd. dirs.), Women's Econ. Club (adv. com., 30 Most Dynamic Women 1992). Office: Crain's Detroit Bus 1400 Woodbridge St Detroit MI 48207-3110

KRAMER, MEYER, lawyer, editor, clergyman; b. Russia, Feb. 4, 1919; came to U.S., 1927, naturalized, 1933; s. Chaim and D'vorah (Kotzin) K.; m. Rose Schnabel, Dec. 22, 1944; children: Doniel, Rena, Tamar, Shira. B.A., Yeshiva Coll., 1940; postgrad., Rabbi Isaac Elchanan Theol. Sem., 1941; LL.B., U. Pa., 1944. Bar: Pa. 1944; ordained rabbi, 1941. Law clk. Superior Ct. Pa., 1944-45; atty. Opinion Writing Office, SEC, 1945-46; lectr. U. Pa. Law Sch., 1947-69; rabbi Adath Zion, Phila., 1951-67, Beth Tefilath Israel, Phila., 1967-72, Bustleton-Somerton Synagogue, Phila., 1972-75; editorial cons. The Orchard, 1988—; dir. Office Periodicals, Am. Law Inst-Am. Bar Assn., Phila., 1972-84, dir. Office Publs., 1984-87; bd. dirs. Gratz Coll., Beth Jacob Schs., Phila., Talmudical Yeshiva Phila., Hapoel-Hamizrachi, Phila. Author: (with A. Leo Levin) Conservative Ketubah; editor Ali-ABA CLE Rev., 1972-84, ALI-ABA Course Materials Jour., 1976-84, CLE Register, 1979-84; assoc. editor Jewish Horizon, 1960-62, Practical Lawyer, 1972-84. Mem. Rabbinical Coun. Phila. (pres. 1966-68, 90-92), Rabbinical Coun. Am., Rabbinic Alumni Yeshiva U. (v.p. 1960-68). Home: 1401 Ocean Ave Brooklyn NY 11230-3971

KRAMER, MICHAEL STUART, pediatric epidemiologist; b. N.Y.C., July 8, 1948; arrived in Can., 1978; s. George and Beatrice (Jacobs) K.; m. Claire Yael Sasportas, June 14, 1981; children: Eric, Elise, Philippe. BA, U. Chgo., 1969; MD, Yale U., 1973; intern in pediat., Yale New Haven (Conn.) Hosp., 1973-74, resident in pediat., 1974-76. Diplomate Am. Bd. Pediatrics, Am. Coll. Epidemiology. Fellow clin. epidemiology Yale U., 1976-78; asst. prof. faculty medicine McGill U., Montreal, Que., Can., 1978-82, assoc. prof., 1982-87, prof., 1987—; com. mem. U.S. Inst. of Medicine/NAS, Washington, 1986—; vis. scientist Nat. Perinatal Epidemiology Unit, Oxford, Eng., 1991-92; cons. WHO, Geneva, 1984—, Nat. Health Rsch. Scientist, Nat. Health R & D Program, Can., 1992-97; disting. scientist Med. Rsch. Coun., Can., 1997—. Author: Clinical Epidemiology and Biostatistics, 1988, Nutrition During Pregnancy, 1990, Adverse Events Associated With Childhood Vaccines, 1994. Violinist:New Haven Symphony, 1969-73, I Medici di McGill, Montreal, 1990-94. Nat. Health Rsch. scholar, 1982-88; recipient Prix d'excellence Insvc. Clubs Coun. Que., Montreal, 1987, Chercheur Boursier Sr. FRSQ, Que., 1988-91, Rsch. award Ambulatory Pediatric Assn., 1993. Mem. Soc. Pediatric Rsch. (coun. mem. 1986-89), Soc. Epidemiol. Rsch., Ambulatory Pediatric Assn. (rsch. award 1993), Soc. Pediatric and Perinatal Epidemiol. Rsch. (pres. 1997-98). Avocations: chamber music (violin), skiing, hiking, tennis, squash. Office: McGill U, 1020 Pine Ave, Montreal, PQ Canada H3A 1AZ

KRAMER, NORMA DOMENICA ANDREA, artist; m. Vernon V. Kramer, 1966. Student, Traphagen, 1946-47, Pratt Inst., N.Y.C., 1948-50, CCNY, 1951-52, Art Students League, 1979-87, Nat. Acad. Design, N.Y.C., 1988-89. In mdse. mgmt., sales, design Henri Bendel, Mainbocher, Macy's, N.Y.C., 1946-50; publs. mgr. Met. Mus. of Art, N.Y.C., 1951-58; editl. asst., exhbn. asst., registrar Am. Fedn. Arts., N.Y.C., 1958-65; poet, asst. to Harold Rosenberg, art critic, bull. editor, campaigns mgr., dir. rsch. The Advt. Coun., N.Y.C., 1965-89. One-man shows include 3 Arts Club Homeland, Balt., 1998, Pearl Gallery, Balt., 1999; exhibited in group shows at Nat. Inst. Architects, 1949, Met. Mus. Art, 1957, Epiphany Ch., N.Y.C., 1983, Am. Watercolor Soc., 1984, Nat. Acad. Design, 1988, Cork Gallery, Lincoln Ctr., 1986, Nat. Arts Club, 1987, Pearl Gallery, 1996—, Old Forge Art Ctr., 1985, Art Dirs. Club, 1999, Hubbard Telescope Space Ctr., John /Hopkins; represented in permanent collections. Recipient award Traphagen, 1947, 1st prize Pratt Inst., 1950, concours prizes, purchase award Art Students League, 1984-87, Award of Excellence for solo watercolor exhbt., 2d Ave. Fair., N.Y.C., 1980, 2d Prize award Rose Soc. Md., 1998, Solo Exhbt. award

Barts Club Homeland. Mem. Three Arts Club of Homeland, Art Students League (life), Am. Watercolor Soc. (assoc.), Balt. Watercolor Soc. Home: 116 W University Pkwy Baltimore MD 21210-3305 Gallery Rep: The Pearl Gallery 815 W 36th St Baltimore MD 21211-2508

KRAMER, PAMELA KOSTENKO, librarian; b. Chgo., Mar. 5, 1944; d. Barry Michael and Helene (Ullrich) Kostenko; m. Claude Richard Kramer, Aug. 17, 1966. AB, U. Ill., 1966; MALS, Rosary Coll., 1973. Tchr. English United Twp. H.S., East Moline, Ill., 1966-70, audiovisual libr., 1970-76; instr. Marycrest Coll., Davenport, Iowa, 1973-75; libr. United Twp. H.S., 1976-81, libr., audio visual dept. head, 1981-87; asst. libr. Libertyville (Ill.) High Sch., 1987-92; asst. libr. Barrington (Ill.) H.S., 1992; dep. exec. dir. Am. Assn. Sch. Librs., 1993-97; owner Pamela K. Kramer and Assocs., Sch. Libr. Cons., 1997—; sch. libr. cons. Trustee River Bend Libr. Sys., 1986-87. Author audiovisual software revs. for Previews mag. Sch. Libr. Jour., 1973-80; contbr. articles to Ill. Librs. mag. and Ill. English Bull. mag. Edmund J. James scholar, 1962-66. Mem. ALA, NEA, ASCD, Ill. Sch. Libr. Media Assn. (state pres. 1990-91, editor ISLMA news 1992—), Ill. State Libr. (adv. com. 1991-94, chair subcom. Interlibr. cooperation 1993-94), Ill. Libr. Assn., Ill. Edn. Assn., Am. Assn. Sch. Librs., Delta Kappa Gamma, Beta Phi Mu. Home: 326 Stillwater Ct Wauconda IL 60084-2908

KRAMER, PAUL R., lawyer; b. Balt., June 6, 1936; s. Phillip and Lee (Labovitz) K.; m. Janet Amitin, Sept. 1, 1957; children: Jayne, Susan, Nancy. BA, Am. U., 1959, JD, 1961. Bar: Md. 1961, D.C. 1962, U.S. Supreme Ct. 1965, U.S. Ct. Appeals (6th cir.) 1992, U.S. Dist. Ct. 1963, U.S. Ct. Appeals (4th cir.) 1964, U.S. Ct. Appeals (9th cir.) 1996. Staff atty., dep. dir. Legal Aid Agy. Fed. Pub. Defender's Office, Washington, 1962-63; asst. U.S. atty. Dist. Md., 1963-69; dep. U.S. atty. Md. Balt., 1969-83; exec. bd. Balt. area coun. Boy Scouts Am., 1970-83, adv. counsel to exec. bd., 1983—; instr. U. Md. Sch. Law, 1975-80; assoc. prof. law Villa Julie Coll., 1976-80; assoc. professorial lectr. George Washington U., 1979; instr. Nat. Coll. Dist. Attys., 1979; permanent mem. 4th cir. fed. jud. conf. Mem. ABA, Fed. Bar Assn. (pres. Md. chpt. 1973-74, nat. dep. sec. 1981-82, nat. sec. 1982-83, nat. cir. v.p. 1973-81, 86-87, cir. officer 4th cir. 1992-93, v.p. 4th cir. 1996—, chmn. nat. cir. v.p. 1978-80, nat. coun. 1973—, jud. selection com. 1971-79, 88—, faculty Fed Practice Inst. 1981-86, strategic long range planning com. 1995-96), Md. Bar Assn. (subcom. litig. dist. ct. 1990—), Balt. Bar Assn. (jud. selection com. 1992—, chair judiciary sub-com. on policy 1993-94, chair criminal law com. 1994-95, grievance commn. Md. 1993—, drug ct. com. 1994-95, dist. ct. com. 1990—), Nat. Assn. Criminal Trial Attys., Md. Trial Lawyers Assn., Md. Criminal Def. Atty.'s Assn., U.S. Atty. Alumni Assn., Masons (past master). Office: 231 Saint Paul Pl Baltimore MD 21202-2028

KRAMER, PAULA LEE, occupational therapist, educator; b. N.Y.C., May 16, 1952; d. Samuel Maurice and Rosalia (Antman) K. BS, NYU, 1973, MA, 1977, PhD, 1993. Staff occupl. therapist N.Y.C. Bur. for Handicapped Children, 1973-75; sr. occupl. therapist St. Vincent's Hosp., N.Y.C., 1975-81; asst. prof. Kean Coll. N.J., Union, 1981-84, assoc. prof., 1984-93, prof., 1993—; cons. Our Place Sch., S.I., N.Y., 1986-88, Toddler and Infant Programs for Spl. Edn., S.I., 1989—; cons. Agy. for Functional Living, 1994; chair dept. occupl. therapy Kean Coll. of N.J., 1983—, mem. accreditation coun. for occupl. therapy edn. Co-author: Occupational Therapy, 1993, Frames of Reference for Pediatric Occupational Therapy and Evaluation: Obtaining and Interpreting Data, 1998, 2d edit., 1999. Bd. trustees Presbyn. Homes N.J., 1993—. Recipient Merit award Kean Coll., 1988, 89. Fellow Am. Occupl. Therapy Assn. (Merit award 1985, Svc. award 1993, 95, 99), Am. Assn. for Mentally Retarded (exec. bd. N.J. chpt. 1985-88), N.J. Occupational Therapy Assn. (award of merit for contbns. to edn. 1990). Office: Kean Coll NJ 311 Willis Hall Union NJ 07083

KRAMER, PETER ROBIN, computer company executive; b. N.Y.C., Sept. 29, 1951; s. Morris and Ruth (Soloway) K.; m. Gerry Festo, Aug. 25, 1985. BA in Fine Arts, SUNY, Stony Brook, 1973; MFA, L.I. U., 1975. Dir., gen. ptnr. Doll & Richards Gallery, Boston, 1979-81; v.p. and dir. Zoom Telephonics, Inc., Boston, 1977—. Bd. dirs. Cambridge Art Assn., 1983-86, pres. 1986-88. Avocations: old houses, fine arts, antiques, tennis, golf.

KRAMER, RICHARD JAY, gastroenterologist; b. Morristown, N.J., Mar. 31, 1947; s. Bernard and Estelle (Mishkin) K.; m. Leslie Fay Davis, June 28, 1970; children: Bryan Jeffrey, Erik Seth Davis. Student, UCLA, 1965-68; MD, U. Calif., Irvine, 1972. Diplomate Am. Bd. Internat. Med., Am. Bd. Gastroenterology. Intern Los Angeles County Harbor Gen. Hosp., Torrance, Calif., 1972-73; resident Santa Clara Valley Med. Ctr., San Jose, Calif., 1973-76; fellow gastroent. Stanford (Calif.) U. Hosp., 1976-78; pvt. practice, San Jose, 1978—; clin. assoc. prof. of medicine Stanford (Calif.) U., 1984—; chmn. med. dept. Good Samaritan Hosp., San Jose, 1988-90. Pres. Jewish Family Service Bd., San Jose, 1974. Recipient Regents scholarship U. Calif., 1965, 68, Mosby Book award, Mosby Books, Inc., Irvine, Calif., 1972. Mem. Am. Coll. Physicians, Calif. Med. Soc., Santa Clara County Med. Soc., No. Calif. Soc. Clin. Gastroenterologists, Internat. Brotherhood Magicians, Mystic 13 (pres. 1986-87, San Jose), Masons, Alpha Omega Alpha. Democrat. Jewish. Avocations: magic, piano, tennis, traveling. Office: 2505 Samaritan Dr Ste 401 San Jose CA 95124-4013

KRAMER, ROBERT, dean; b. Davenport, Iowa, Aug. 17, 1913; s. Robert and Juanita (Mapes) K.; m. Mary Rainey Gaston, Mar. 22, 1941; children: Mary Elizabeth Kramer Helsinger, Lucy Mapes Kramer Keefe, Robert Gaston. A.B. cum laude, Harvard U., 1935, LL.B magna cum laude, 1938. Bar: D.C. 1938, N.Y. 1947. Atty. NLRB, 1938-40; antitrust div. Dept. Justice, 1941-42; asso. Paul, Weiss, Wharton & Garrison, N.Y.C., 1946-47; prof. law Duke U., 1947-59; vis. prof. law Stanford U., 1950, U. Wis., 1956, U. N.C., 1957, NYU, 1958, Northwestern U., 1959; asst. atty. gen. Office Legal Counsel, Dept. Justice, 1959-61; dean Nat. Law Center, George Washington U., Washington, 1961—. Author: (with C.L.B. Lowndes and J. McCord) Federal Gift and Estate Taxes, 1974; editor: Law and Contemporary Problems, 1947-56, Jour. Legal Edn., 1948-55; Am. editor: Business Law Rev., 1952-55. Served to lt. col. AUS, 1942-46. Decorated Legion of Merit. Mem. Am. Law Inst., Assn. Am. Law Schs. (exec. com. 1959). Democrat. Episcopalian. Home: Collington # 1101 10450 Lottsford Rd Mitchellville MD 20721-2734 Office: 720 20th St Washington DC 20052

KRAMER, SHERRI MARCELLE, business and community development consultant; b. Phila., Apr. 14, 1954; d. Irvin and Rhoda Pearl (Levin) K.; m. Peter MacPhee, Oct. 18, 1997. Student, Montgomery C.C., 1971-73; BA, Rutgers U., 1975; paralegal asst., U. Md., 1977; MA in Bus. Adminstrn., Am. World U., 1999. Asst. to counsel U.S. Senator Jacob K. Javits, Washington, 1974-77; legis. asst. U.S. Senator Orrin G. Hatch, Washington, 1977-78; asst. project dir. Coun. Exceptional Children, Reston, Va., 1978-79; sr. legis. analyst Alliance Am. Insurers, Chgo., 1979-83; dir. legis. monitoring Ins. Svcs. Offices, N.Y.C., 1983-86; pres. Kramer Consulting, Ltd., Tampa, Fla., 1986-87; asst. dir. Tampa Jewish Fedn., 1987-89; assoc. exec. dir. Jacksonville (Fla.) Jewish Fedn., 1989-92; exec. dir. Ronald McDonald House of Jacksonville, 1992, Kramer Cons., Ltd., 1993, Dynamic Bus. Solutions, Milton Mills, N.H., 1992—; dir. Dept. Econ. & Cmty. Devel., Farmington, N.H., 1998—; legis. and technical cons. Voc-Ed Handbook for Disabled, Univ. Wis., 1980; instr. Women's Bus. Ctr., Portsmouth, N.H., 1996-98; exec. bd. mem. York County Devel. Corp., 1996—; adv. com. on bus. adminstrn. York County Tech. Coll., Wells, Maine, 1996—. Co-author: Retraining Special Educators in Career Education, 1979. Del., Hillsborough County Human Rights Commn., Tampa, 1987-89, Interfaith Coun. Jacksonville, 1989-92; trustee Hillel Found. U. South Fla., Tampa, 1988-89; mem. Mayor's Coun. Reconciliation, 1992; bd. dirs. Jewish Family Svcs. Mem. NCCJ, NAFE, N.H. Econ. Devel. Assn., Assn. Jewish Communal Orgns. Profls., Orgn. for Rehab. and Tng., Yorks C. of C., Sanford-Springvale C. of C., Women's Bus. Devel. Corp., Anti-Defamation League, Nat. Soc. Fundraising Execs., Montgomery County C.C. Alumni Assn. (bd. dirs. 1973-81). Avocations: dogs, travel, politics. Home: PO Box 203 Milton Mills NH 03852-0203

KRAMER, SIDNEY B., publisher, lawyer, literary agent; b. N.Y.C., 1915; s. Louis and Mildred (Hindin) K.; m. Esther Schlansky, Nov. 23, 1939; children: Wendy Beth Kramer Posner, Mark William. BS, NYU, 1936; JD, Bklyn. Law Sch., St. Lawrence U., 1939. Bar: N.Y. 1940, Conn. 1962, U.S. Supreme Ct. 1975. Practice in N.Y.C., 1940-45, Westport, Conn., 1963—; sr. v.p., dir. Bantam Books, Inc., N.Y.C., 1945-67; founder (1950), mng. dir. Corgi Books, London, 1960-62; pres., dir. Remarkable Bookshop, 1960-95; pres. New Am. Library, N.Y.C., 1967-72, MEWS Books Ltd., Westport, Conn., London, Eng., 1975—; mng. dir., cons. Cassell & Collier Macmillan Pubs. Ltd., London, 1973-74; chmn. Nat. Assn. Paperback Pubs., 1945-67. Occasional contbr.: N.Y. Times. Chmn. Democratic Town Com., also justice peace, Westport, 1960-64, 84—; chmn. Save Westport Now, 1981—. Mem. Conn. Bar Assn. Home: 20 Bluewater Hl Westport CT 06880-6504 Office: 25 Queensgate Gardens, London SW7 5QL, England

KRAMER, STEVEN G., ophthalmologist; b. Chgo., Feb. 28, 1941; s. Paul and Maria Kramer; m. Anne Crystal Kramer, Dec. 26, 1961 (div.); children: Janice Lynn, Kenneth David; m. Bernadette E. Coatar, June 30, 1974 (div.); children: Daniel Steven, Susan Mary; m. Susan E. Garrett, Jan. 17, 1997. BA in Biology, U. Chgo., 1967; MD, Case Western Res. U., 1965; PhD, U. Chgo., 1971. Cert. assoc. examiner Am. Bd. Ophthalmology; lic. ophthalmologist, Calif., Wash. Instr. ophthalmology U. Chgo., 1968-71; chief of ophthalmology Madigan Army Med. Ctr., Tacoma, 1971-73; chief of ophathlmology VA Med. Ctr., San Francisco, 1973-75; prof. ophthalmology, chmn. U. Calif., San Francisco, 1975—, dir. Beckman Vision Ctr., 1988—; mem. various coms. VA Hosp., San Francisco, 1973—; mem. exec. med. bd. sch. medicine U. Calif., 1975—, mem./chmn. various coms., 1975—, mem. clin. dept. chmn. group, 1975—, mem. governing bd. continuing med. edn. program, 1984-85, mem. clin. rev. working group, 1985-86, pres.-elect med. staff, 1985, pres., 1986-88, mem. chancellor's governance group, 1986—, mem. adv. group devel. spine svcs., 1992—; v.p. That Man May See, Inc., 1975—, bd. trustees, 1975—, campaign cabinet mem. for Vision Rsch. Ctr., 1983—; sec., bd. govs. Francis Proctor Found. for Rsch. in Opthalmology, 1975—; mem. Rsch. to Prevent Blindness, Inc., N.Y., 1976—, ad hoc adv. com., 1976-77; NIH mem. vision rsch. program com. NEI, 1978-82, chmn., 1980-82; site visit chmn. U. Wash., Seattle, 1979, Mass. Eye and Ear Infirmary, Boston, 1980, dept. neurobiology Harvard Med. Sch., Boston, 1980; mem. joint program and planning bd. sch. medicine U. Calif./Mt. Zion, 1985-88; mem. courtesy staff San Francisco Gen. Hosp.; lectr. in field. Editor, editl. bd. therapeutics rev. sect. Survey of Ophthalmology, 1977-84, diagnostic and surg. techniques sect., 1984—; sci. referee Am. Jour. Ophthalmology, 1967-81, editl. bd., 1981—; editl. bd. Ophthalmic Soc.; sci. referee Life Scis.; editor CMA Ophthalmology Epitomes, Western Jour. Medicine, 1976-77; med. adv. bd. Nat. Soc. to Prevent Blindness, 1979—; editor sect. cornea and sclera Yearbook of Ophthalmology, 1982. Mem. legis. com. for State of Calif., 1977; bd. dirs. Found. for Glaucoma Rsch., 1980—. Maj. U.S. Army, 1971-73. USPHS Spl. fellow in ophthalmologic rsch., 1970; VA Hosp. Rsch. Program grantee; NIH grantee, That Man May See grantee. Mem. AMA, ACS, Am. Acad. Ophthalmology, Am. Intra-Ocular Implant Soc., Assn. for Rsch. in Vision and Ophthalmology, Pacific Coast Oto-Ophthalmology Soc., Frederick C. Cordes Eye Soc., Calif. Med. Assn. (sci. adv. panel 1974—, adv. panel on ophthalmology subcom. for accreditation 1976-77, 78), Calif. Assn. Ophthalmology (adv. cons.), Assn. Univ. Profs. of Ophthalmology (chmn. resident placement svc. com., mem. ophthalmology resident and fellowship edn. com.), No. Calif. Soc. to Prevent Blindness (med. adv. bd.), Pan Am. Assn. Ophthalmology, Am. Congress, San Francisco Ophthal. Round Table, Rsch. to Prevent Blindness, Inc., Retinitis Pigmentosa Internat. Soc. (founding mem., sci. adv. bd.), Castroviejo Corneal Soc., Internat. Cornea Soc., Internat. Soc. Refractive Keratoplasty, Calif. Cornea Club, Ophthalmologic Hon. Soc. of Am. Ophthal. Soc., Phi Beta Kappa, Alpha Omega Alpha, Sigma Xi. Achievements include patents on surg. instrument tray; multi-compartmentalized bottle; instrument for cataract extraction through small incision; bottle closure; reminder closure; surg. instrument; internally sterile pulsatile irrigator, others. Office: U Calif Beckman Vision Ctr 10 Kirkham St # K-301 San Francisco CA 94143-0730

KRAMER, WEEZIE CRAWFORD, broadcast executive. Student, U. Ky., 1977, Wheaton Coll. Sales/local sales mgr. WKQQ, Lexington, Ky., 1977-80; local sales mgr. WHBQ, Memphis, 1980-81; gen. sales mgr. KBPI/KNUS, Denver, 1981-85, WFYR, Chgo., 1985-88; gen. sales mgr. WMAQ All News 67, Chgo., 1988-94, sta. mgr., 1994, v.p., gen. mgr., 1994—. Office: WMAQ-AM 455 N Cityfront Plaza Dr Chicago IL 60611-5503*

KRAMER, WILLIAM DAVID, lawyer; b. Anniston, Ala., Feb. 2, 1944; s. John Robert and Janice Marian (Dye) K.; m. Johanna Scalzi, Dec. 1, 1973; children: Elizabeth Annemarie, David MacLaren. Student, Case Western Res. U., 1959-60; AB in Govt. with honors magna cum laude, Oberlin Coll., 1965; JD, M in Pub. Adminstrn., Harvard U., 1969. Bar: Mass. 1969, D.C. 1973, U.S. Ct. Appeals (D.C. cir.) 1974, U.S. Dist. Ct. D.C. 1976, U.S. Ct. Appeals (10th cir.) 1978, U.S. Ct. Internat. Trade 1983, U.S. Ct. Appeals (fed. cir.) 1983. Assoc. dir. Gov.'s Com. on Law Enforcement and Adminstrn. Criminal Justice, Boston, 1969-71, dep. dir., 1971-73; assoc. Squire, Sanders & Dempsey, Washington, 1973-79, ptnr., 1979-92; ptnr. Baker & Botts, Washington, 1992—; mem. internat. law sect. D.C. Bar. chmn. bd. dirs. Children's Chorus of Washington, 1995-97, mem. adv. bd., 1997—. Mem. Phi Beta Kappa. Office: Baker & Botts LLP Ste 1200 1299 Pennsylvania Ave NW Washington DC 20004-2400

KRAMISH, ARNOLD, physicist, historian, author; b. Denver, June 6, 1923; s. John I. and Sarah (Kaitz) K.; m. Vivian Ruth Raker, Aug. 19, 1952; children: Pamela, Robert. B.S., U. Denver, 1945; A.M., Harvard U., 1947. With Manhattan Project, 1944-46, AEC, 1946-51; sr. staff mem. Rand Corp., Santa Monica, Calif., 1951-68; v.p. Inst. for the Future, Washington, 1968-70; sci. attache U.S. Mission to UNESCO, Paris, 1970-73; counselor for sci. and tech. affairs U.S. Mission to OECD, Paris, 1974-76; sci. research R & D Assocs., Arlington, Va., 1976-81; ind. tech. cons., 1981—; assoc. Global Bus. Access Ltd., 1991—; prof. UCLA, 1965-66, London Sch. Econs., 1967-68; adj. prof. internat. studies U. Miami, Fla., 1969; fellow Woodrow Wilson Internat. Ctr. for Scholars, 1982-83; Rockefeller scholar, Bellagio, Italy, 1984; pres. Tech. Analysis Internat., 1983—. Author: Atomic Energy for Your Business, 1956, Atomic Energy in the Soviet Union, 1959, The Peaceful Atom in Foreign Policy, 1963, The Future of Non-Nuclear Nations, 1970, The Griffin, 1986; also numerous articles, book chpts. Sci. advisor European Cmty., 1960-62. With AUS, 1943-46. Carnegie fellow Coun. on Fgn. Rels., 1958-59; John Simon Guggenheim fellow, 1966-67; Rsch. fellow Inst. for Strategic Studies, London, 1966-67; Sr. fellow Global Access Inst., 1994—. Patentee nuclear radiometer. Home: 2065 Wethersfield Ct Reston VA 20191-3629 Office: PO Box 2621 Reston VA 20195-0621

KRAMM, DEBORAH ANN, data processing executive; b. Pasadena, June 24, 1949; d. Donald F. and Mary (Roach) Coonan; m. Kenneth R. Kramm, Dec. 20, 1969; children: Deidre Lyn, Jonathan Russel. BA, U. Calif.-Irvine, 1971; MS, Mich. Tech. U., 1981. Math. asst. NASA-Jet Propulsion Lab., Pasadena, 1967-70; library asst. U. Calif. Irvine Libr., 1967-71; rsch. assoc. animal behavior lab. Mich. Tech. U. , Houghton, 1971-80; programmer/analyst Shell Oil Co., Houston, 1981-85, corp. auditor EDP, 1985-87, team leader systems analyst, 1987-88, group leader SLA, 1988-90, supr. resource planning and adminstrn., 1990-91, adminstrv. contd. product devel. ctr.-design ctr., 1991-93, bus. analyst sr. systems analyst, 1993-96, engagement mgr., 1996-97, mgr. engagement svcs., 1998—; chmn. bd. MMARK, Houston, 1983-85. Contbr. articles to profl. jours.; Designer (program application software) Shell Point-of-Sale Terminal, 1982-85. Treas. KFHS Orch., 1986-88; co-leader Boy Scouts Am., Houston, 1981-83. AAUW scholar, 1980, Calif. State scholar, 1967-71. Mem. NAFE, AAUW (pres. br. 1975-81). Club: Shell Data Processors, Houston Bus. Forum (pres. bd. dirs.). Home: 5814 Pinewilde Dr Houston TX 77066-2324 Office: Shell Svc Internat 1500 Old Spanish Trl Houston TX 77054-1818

KRAMM, DEBORAH LUCILLE, lawyer; b. Milw.; d. Hartzell McDonald and Alice Lucille (Johnson) K. Student, Trinity Coll., Deerfield, Ill., 1971-73; BS, Bradley U., 1974; JD, New Eng. Sch. of Law, 1977; postgrad., Georgetown U., 1978. Bar: N.Y. 1982, Ill. 1980, Mass. 1978. Trademark atty. U.S. Trademark Office, Washington, 1977-78; assoc. Hume, Clement, Willian, Brinks & Olds, Chgo., 1978-81; atty. Avon Products, Inc., N.Y.C., 1981-84; atty. Tiffany & Co., N.Y.C., 1981-84, v.p., sec., 1984-85; counsel Am. Brands, Inc., Old Greenwich, Conn., 1986-95; of counsel Rudnick & Wolfe, Washington, 1996—. N.Y. bd. dirs. Nat. Found. for Advancement for Arts, 1987-91; chmn. Martha Graham Guild, 1988—; trustee Martha Graham Ctr. for Contemporary Dance, Inc., N.Y.C., 1989—. Curt Tiege scholar, 1973. Mem. U.S. Trademark Assn. (bd. dirs. 1984-87), Cosmetic, Toiletry and Fragrance Assn. (chmn. trademark com. 1984). Office: Rudnick & Wolfe 203 N La Salle St Chicago IL 60611

KRAMPF, JOHN EDWARD, lawyer; b. Glens Falls, N.Y., Sept. 11, 1947; s. Charles Edward and Judith Carolyn (Strempel) K.; children: Alison Seelye, Emily Christine, Charles Alexander; m. Christine Ellen Bancheri, May 2, 1981. BA, Duke U., 1969; JD, U. Pa., 1972. Bar: Pa. 1972, U.S. Ct. Appeals (3d cir.), U.S. Dist. Ct. (ea., we. and mid. dists.) Pa. Assoc. Morgan, Lewis & Bockius LLP, Phila., 1972-79; ptnr. Morgan, Lewis & Bockius, Phila., 1979—. Editor: Employer's Guide to Pennsylvania Labor Laws and Regulations, 1990, Employer's Guide to N.J. Labor Laws and Regulations, 1990, Employer's Guide to Delaware Labor Laws and Regulations, 1989, Federal Employer Relations Laws and Regulations, 1991. Bd. dirs. Gilpin Hall Residential Care Facility, Wilmington, Del., 1978—; mem. bd. visitors Duke U. Coll. Arts and Scis. Mem. ABA, Pa. Bar Assn., Phila. Bar Assn., Nat. Assn. Coll. and Univ. Attys., Nat. Assn. Water Cos. Office: Morgan Lewis & Bockius LLP 1701 Market St Philadelphia PA 19103-2903*

KRAMPITZ, BARBARA E.M., library director; b. Springfield, Mass., Jan. 20, 1934; d. Fritz and Helen Rose Maier; m. David F. Krampitz, July 10, 1954; children: Karyn N., D. Dane, Marta L. BA, CUNY, Flushing, 1977; MLS, L.I. U., 1980. Cert. libr., N.Y. Libr. Westbury (N.Y.) Meml. Pub. Libr., 1980—, asst. dir., 1994-95, dir., 1996—; adv. bd. mem. Libr. Svcs. and Tech. Act Grants, Nassau County, N.Y., 1997-99; presenter in field. Mem. ALA, N.Y. Libr. Assn., Nassau County Libr. Assn. Office: Westbury Meml Pub Libr 445 Jefferson St Westbury NY 11590

KRANE, STEPHEN MARTIN, physician, educator; b. N.Y.C., July 15, 1927; s. Daniel Golden and Bessie (Berman) K.; m. Cynthia Ramin, June 28, 1952; children: David Alan, Peter Jay, Ian Matthew, Adam. A.B., Columbia U., 1946, M.D., 1951; A.M. (hon.), Harvard U., 1968; M.D. (hon.), U. Geneva, 1989. Intern to chief resident in medicine Mass. Gen. Hosp., Boston, 1951-57, chief arthritis unit, 1961, physician, 1969; research fellow Washington U., St. Louis, 1956; asst. in medicine Harvard U. Med. Sch., Boston, 1958, prof., 1972-87, Persis, Cyrus and Marlow B. Harrison prof. clin. medicine, 1987—. Contbr. articles to profl. jours. Served with USNR, 1945-46. Recipient Kappa Delta award Orthopedic Rsch. Soc., 1977, Herberden medal Herberden Soc., London, 1980; named Guggenheim fellow Oxford U., 1973-74. Fellow ACP, AAAS, Am. Acad. Arts and Scis., Am. Coll. Rheumatology (master, Disting. Investigator award 1995); mem. Am. Soc. Clin. Investigation, Assn. Am. Physicians, Am. Fedn. Clin. Rsch., Am. Soc. Biol. Chemistry, Molecular Biology, Soc. Bone Mineral Rsch., Endocrine Soc. Home: 101 Windsor Rd Newton MA 02168 Office: Mass Genl Hosp Boston MA 02114*

KRANE, STEVEN CHARLES, lawyer; b. Far Rockaway, N.Y., Jan. 20, 1957; s. Harry and Gloria (Christle) K.; m. Faith Marston, Oct. 1, 1983; children: Elizabeth Jordan, Cameron Marston. BA, SUNY, Stony Brook, 1978; JD, NYU, 1981. Bar: N.Y. 1982, U.S. Dist. Ct. (so. and ea. dists.) N.Y. 1982, U.S. Ct. Appeals (2d and 6th cirs.) 1987, U.S. Supreme Ct. 1987. Ptnr. Proskauer Rose LLP, N.Y.C.; law clk. to Assoc. Judge Judith S. Kaye N.Y. Ct. Appeals, N.Y.C. and Albany, 1984-85; lectr. in law Columbia U. Sch. Law, N.Y.C., 1989-92; vis. prof. Ga. Inst. of Tech., 1994-96; mem. departmental disciplinary com. Appellate divsn. 1st Jud. dept. Supreme Ct. N.Y., 1996—, spl. trial counsel, 1991-93. Editor articles, NYU Jour. Internat. Law and Politics, 1980-81. Securities Inst. NYU fellow, 1980-81; recipient Vol. Counsel award Legal Aid Soc., 1984. Fellow N.Y. Bar Found.; mem. N.Y. Bar Assn. (com. on stds. of atty. conduct, chmn. 1999—, com. on profl. ethics 1990-94, spl. com. to rev. the code of profl. responsibility 1992-95, chmn. 1995-99, vice chair spl. com. on future of the profession 1997—, ho. of dels. 1996—, spl. com. on mass disaster response 1997—, com. on multidisciplinary practice and the legal profession 1998—, exec. com. 1998—, mem.-at-large, exec. com. 1998—), Assn. of Bar of City of N.Y. (com. on profl. and jud. ethics 1990-93, chmn. 1993-96, sec 1985-88, com. on profl. responsibility, chmn. subcom. provision legal svcs. 1985-88, com. on fed. cts. 1996—, chmn. del. to N.Y. State Bar Assn. ho. dels. 1997-98), Am. Law Inst., Phi Beta Kappa, Pi Sigma Alpha. Republican. Avocations: military history, meteorology, Boston Red Sox baseball. Office: Proskauer Rose LLP 1585 Broadway New York NY 10036-8299

KRANIS, MICHAEL DAVID, lawyer, judge; b. N.Y.C., Aug. 17, 1955; s. Herbert and Mildred (Swartz) K.; m. Patricia Ann Pagano, Sept. 29, 1989. BA, SUNY, Albany, 1977; JD, Union U., 1980. Bar: N.Y. 1981, U.S. Dist. Ct. (so. and ea. dists.) N.Y. 1983. Law clk. to hon. judge Robert C. William N.Y. Supreme Ct., Monticello, 1980-82; prin. Michael D. Kranis, P.C., Poughkeepsie, N.Y., 1982-88; ptnr. Coombs, Kranis & Wing, Poughkeepsie, 1988-94; sole practitioner Poughkeepsie, 1995—; asst. corp. counsel City of Poughkeepsie, 1983-85, hearing officer, 1985—; adj. prof. D.C. C.C., Poughkeepsie, 1984-87; judge Town of Pleasant Valley, N.Y., 1988-97; gen. counsel Grace Smith House, Inc., Poughkeepsie, 1983-95; adj. prof. Marist Coll., 1993. Mem. exec. com. Dutchess County Rep. Com., Pleasant Valley, 1997, Jud. Nominating Com., Dutchess County, 1987, 97—; mem. exec. com.D.C. Republican Com.; mem. Pleasant Valley Planning Bd., 1986-88; bd. dirs., chmn., vice chmn. Task Force for Child Proection, Inc.; mem. bd. dirs. Dutchess County Economic Devel. Corp. Mem. N.Y. State Bar Assn. (del.), Dutchess County Bar Assn. (pres.,treas., v.p. 1996, pres.-elect 1997, chmn. fee dispute com., chmn. bar endowment, v.p.), Dutchess County Magistrates Assn., N.Y. State Magistrates Assn., Rotary (pres., bd. dirs. Pleasant Valley chpt. 1985-96, Paul Harris fellow 1987). Office: PO Box 4978 Poughkeepsie NY 12602-4978

KRANITZ, THEODORE MITCHELL, lawyer; b. St. Joseph, Mo., May 27, 1922; s. Louis and Miriam (Saferstein) K.; m. Elaine Shirley Kaufman, June 11, 1944; children—Hugh David, Karen Gail and Kathy Jane (twins). Student, St. Joseph Jr. Coll., 1940-41; BS in Fgn. Svc., Georgetown U., 1948, JD, 1950. Bar: Mo. 1950, U.S. Supreme Ct. 1955. Pres., sr. ptnr. Kranitz & Kranitz, PC, St. Joseph, 1950—. Author articles in field. Pres. St. Joseph Comty. Theatre, Inc., 1958-60; bd. dirs. United Jewish Fund St. Joseph, 1957—, pres., 1958-63; sec. Boys' Baseball St. Joseph, 1964-68; trustee Temple Adath Joseph, 1970-74, 77-80; bd. dirs. B'nai Sholem Temple, 1976—, Lyric Opera Guild Kansas City, 1980-91; founder, pres. St. Joseph Light Opera Co., Inc., 1989-90; mem. St. Joseph Postal Customers Adv. Coun., 1993—, chmn., 1993-95; mem., sec. St. Joseph Downtown Assn., 1995-97. Mem. Mo. Bar, St. Joseph Bar Assn. (pres. 1977-78), Am. Legion, Air Force Assn., B'nai B'rith (dist. bd. govs. 1958-61). Home: 2609 Gene Field Rd Saint Joseph MO 64506-1615 Office: Kranitz & Kranitz PC Boder Bldg 107 S 4th St PO Box 968 Saint Joseph MO 64502-0968

KRANKING, MARGARET GRAHAM, artist; b. Dec. 21, 1930; d. Stephen Wayne and Madge Williams (Dawes) Graham; m. James David Kranking, Aug. 23, 1952; children: James Andrew, Ann Marie Kranking Eggleton, David Wayne. BA summa cum laude (Clendenin fellow), Am. U., 1952. Asst. to head publs. Nat. Gallery Art, Washington, 1952-53; profl. artist, 1966—; tchr. art Woman's Club, Chevy Chase (Md.), 1976-88, 98—; guest instr. Amherst Coll., 1985, The Homestead, Hot Springs, Va., 1997. One-woman shows include Spectrum Gallery, Washington, 1974, 76, 78, 79, 83, 85, 87, 90, 92, 95, 97, Philip Morris, U.S.A., Richmond, Va., 1982, 83, 86, Forence (S.C.) Mus., 1991, Lombardi Cancer treatment Ctr., Washington, 1992, Capital Gallery, Frankfort, Ky., 1993, Acad. Arts, Easton, Md., 1999, Warm Springs (Va.) Gallery, 1997, 98; group shows include: Balt. Mus., 1974, 76, Corcoran Gallery Art, Washington, 1952, 72, USIA Traveling Exhbt., C.Am., 1978-79, AARP Traveling Exhbn., 1986; represented in permanent collections U. Va., Philip Morris U.S.A., USCG, AT&T, Freddie Mac, Florence Mus., S.C., Navy Fed. Credit Union Hdqs., Vienna, Va.; traveling exhbn. Nat. Watercolor Soc., Watercolor U.S.A., Am. Watercolor Soc., Am. Artist mag., North Light mag., Adirondacks Nat. Exhbn. of Am. Watercolor, Artitude 7th Internat. Art Competition, N.Y., Shada Gallery, Riyadh, Saudi Arabia, Belle Grove Plantation Invitational, Middletown, Va., Strathmore Hall Arts Ctr., North Bethesda, Md., Wash. Woman mag., Am. Speech-Lang. Hearing Assn., mag., Govt. House, Annapolis, Montgomery Coll. Invitational, Md.; ofcl. artist USCG; contbr. reproductions and text to numerous books. Recipient George Gray award USCG Art Program, N.Y., 1991, 98. Mem. Nat. Watercolor Soc., M.W. Watercolor Soc., Southwe. Watercolor Soc., Ga. Watercolor Soc., So. Watercolor Soc., Washington Watercolor Assn., Potomac Valley Watercolorists (pres. 1981-83), Spectrum

Gallery Washington. Roman Catholic. Home: 3504 Taylor St Chevy Chase MD 20815-4022

KRANSELER, LAWRENCE MICHAEL, lawyer; b. Newton, Mass., Oct. 28, 1958; s. Arthur Sheldon and Barbara Joan (Siegel) K.; m. Wendy Kranseler; children: Alex, Jenna. BS in Econs., Boston Coll., 1980; MBA, JD, U. Pa., 1984. Bar: Mass. 1985, U.S. Dist. Ct. Mass. 1985. Assoc. Hale and Dorr, Boston, 1984-89; supervising sr. counsel Hasbro, Inc., Pawtucket, R.I., 1989-95, mng. atty., 1995—; vol. mentor UCAP Mentoring Program. Bd. dirs., mem., vol. Big Brother/Big Sister Assn.; fundraising capt. Am. Heart Assn., Combined Jewish Philanthropies; coach Town of Sharon Baseball, Town of Sharon Soccer. Recipient James E. Shaw Meml. award Pres. Boston Coll., 1980. Mem. ABA, Mass. Bar Assn., Boston Bar Assn., Phi Delta Phi. Home: 30 Sentry Hill Rd Sharon MA 02067-1522 Office: Hasbro Inc 1027 Newport Ave Pawtucket RI 02861-2500

KRANTZ, JUDITH TARCHER, novelist; b. N.Y.C., Jan. 9, 1928; d. Jack David and Mary (Brager) Tarcher; m. Stephen Falk Krantz, Feb. 19, 1954; children: Nicholas, Anthony. BA, Wellesley Coll., 1948. Fashion publicist Paris, 1948-49; fashion editor Good Housekeeping mag., N.Y.C., 1949-56; contbg. writer McCalls, 1956-59, Ladies Home Jour., 1959-71; contbg. west coast editor Cosmopolitan mag., 1971-79. Author: Scruples, 1978, Princess Daisy, 1980, Mistral's Daughter, 1982, I'll Take Manhattan, 1986, Till We Meet Again, 1988, Dazzle, 1990, Scruples Two, 1992, Lovers, 1994, Spring Collection, 1996, The Jewels of Tessa Kent, 1998.

KRANTZ, KERMIT EDWARD, physician, educator; b. Oak Park, Ill., June 4, 1923; s. Andrew Stanley and Beatrice H. (Cibrowski) K.; m. Doris Cole Krantz, Sep. 7, 1946; children: Pamela (Mrs. Richard Huffstutter), Sarah Elizabeth, Kermit Tripler. BS, Northwestern U., 1945, BM, 1947, MS in Anatomy, 1947, MD, 1948; LittD (hon.), William Woods Coll., 1971. Diplomate Am. Bd. Ob-Gyn. Intern ob-gyn. N.Y. Lying-In Hosp., 1947-48; asst. resident, asst. ob-gyn. Cornell U. Med. Coll., N.Y. Lying-In Hosp., N.Y. Hosp., 1948-50; fellow, resident in ob-gyn Mary Fletcher Hosp., Burlington, Vt., 1950-51; dir. Durfee Clinic, 1952-55; instr., then asst. prof. U. Vt. Coll. Medicine, 1951-55; asst. prof. U. Ark. Med. Sch., 1955-59; prof., chmn. dept. ob-gyn. U. Kans. Med. Ctr., 1959-90, Univ. Disting. prof., 1990-94, prof. anatomy, 1963—, lectr. history medicine, 1959—, dean clin. affairs, 1972-74, chief staff, 1972-74, obstetrician and gynecologist in chief, 1959-90, assoc. to exec. vice chancellor for facilities devel., 1974-83; univ. disting. prof. emeritus ob/gyn. and anatomy U. Kans., 1994—; cons. in field. Author numerous articles in field. Mem. Nat. Adv. Child Health and Human Devel. Council, NIH, 1974-76. Bowen-Brooks fellow N.Y. Acad. Medicine, 1948-50; recipient Found. award South Atlantic Assn. Obstetricians and Gynecologists, 1950, Found. award Am. Assn. Obstetricians and Gynecologists, 1950, Wyeth-Ayerst Pub. Recognition award 1st Am. Assn. Prof. of Gynecology and Obstetrics, 1988; named Outstanding Prof. in Coll. of Medicine Nu Sigma Nu, 1955; Robert A. Ross lectureship award Armed Forces Dist. meeting Am. Coll. Obstetricians and Gynecologists, 1972, Outstanding Civilian Service medal U.S. Army-Dept. Def., 1985; Charles A. Durham Meml. lectr. Ann. Session Tex. Med. Assn., 1978; Markle scholar med. sci., 1957-62; Kermit E. Krantz Soc. established at U. Kans. Med. Ctr., 1982. Founding fellow Am. Coll. Obstetricians and Gynecologists (Kermit E. Krantz Lectureship award established 1973, Outstanding Dist. Services award 1978, 82); fellow ACS, Am. Coll. Ob-Gyn (life); mem. Am. Assn. Anatomists, Am. Fedn. Clin. Research, AMA, Am. Med. Writers Assn., Am. Fertility Soc., AAUP, Soc. Exptl. Biology and Medicine, Aerospace Med. Assn., Endocrine Soc., Soc. Gynecologic Investigation, Central Assn. Obstetricians and Gynecologists, N.Y. Acad. Medicine, N.Y. Acad. Sci., Kans. Med. Soc., Assn. Mil. Surgeons U.S. (sustaining), Kans. Obstet. Soc., Sigma Xi, Alpha Omega Alpha. Home: 6711 Overhill Rd Shawnee Mission KS 66208-2263 Office: U Kans Med Ctr Kansas City KS 66160-7316

KRANTZ, LINDA LAW, librarian; b. Princeton, N.J., June 19, 1943; d. Harold Bell and Ruth Workman Law; m. David Walter Krantz, July 29, 1967. Student, Mt. Union Coll., 1961-63; BA in French Lit., U. Rochester, 1965; MLS, Rutgers State U., 1967. Libr. asst. Fine Hall Libr. Math. and Physics Princeton U., summers 1962-66; cataloger NASA Lewis Rsch. Ctr., Cleve., 1967; reference libr. sci.-tech. Cleve. Pub. Libr., 1968-69; reference libr. Wright State U. Libr., Dayton, Ohio, 1969-73; libr. dir. Rockbridge Regional Libr., Lexington, Va., 1974—; reference libr. Princeton Pub. Libr., 1996-97. Violin player Rockbridge Orch., Lexington, Va., 1975-96, Allegheny-Highlands Symphony Orch., 1997—. Mem. ALA, Va. Libr. Assn. (legis. co-chair 1997-99), Lexington Rotary Club (founder, bd. mem., Paul Harris fellow 1996), Omicron Delta Kappa. Avocations: music, nature, reading, cats, electronics. E-mail: lkrantz@cfw.com and lkrantz@lib.rang.gen.va.us. Home: 151 Elliots Hill Ln Lexington VA 24450-7203 Office: Rockbridge Regional Libr 138 S Main St Lexington VA 24450

KRANTZ, MELISSA MARIANNE, public relations company executive; b. Cornwall, N.Y., Sept. 19, 1954; d. Abraham and Jane (Steinheimer) K.; m. David Michael Fleisher, Nov. 19, 1978; children: Jenny Rachel, Sara Rose. BA in Polit. Sci., SUNY Coll., Purchase, 1976. Account exec. Pub. Interest Pub. Relations, Inc., N.Y.C., 1975-77; assoc. Kekst & Co., N.Y.C., 1977-83, ptnr., 1983-91; v.p. corp. comm. JWP Inc., 1991-92; pres. Krantz Group, Inc., 1992-99; sr. v.p., chief comm. officer Repuglic N.Y. Corp., 1999—. Trustee Bet Am Shalom Synagogue, White Plains, N.Y., 1985-87, Mazon; bd. dirs. Project Ezra, N.Y.C., 1986-95, VISIONS; bd. dirs. BBB Met. N.Y., Inc., 1988—, mem. exec. com., 1989—. Democrat. Jewish. Home: 15 Franklin Ln Harrison NY 10528-1105

KRANTZ, PALMER E., III, parks and recreation director; b. Columbia, S.C., Jan. 27, 1950. BS in Zoology, Clemson U., 1972. Various mgmt. positions Riverbanks Zool. Park and Bot. Garden, Columbia, 1973-76, exec. dir., 1976—. Chmn. bd. visitors Clemson U.; past pres. bd. dirs. Children's Hosp. at Richland Meml., River Alliance; past pres. U. S.C. Mem. Internat. Union Dirs. Zool. Gardens-World Zoo Orgn. (pres.), Am. Zoo and Aquarium Assn. (past pres., accreditation commn., ethics bd.), Rotary Club of Columbia. Fax: 803/253-6381. E-mail: imcmickn@riverbanks.org. Office: Riverbanks Zoo and Garden 500 Wildlife Pkwy PO Box 1060 Columbia SC 29210*

KRANTZ, SANFORD BURTON, physician; b. Chgo., Feb. 6, 1934; s. Max and Fannie (Orenstein) K.; m. Sandra R. Goldstein, Dec. 28, 1958; children—Michael David, Marcy Sharon, Alan Thomas, Sarah Ann. A.B., U. Chgo., 1954, B.S., 1955, M.D., 1959. Intern U. Chgo. Hosps., 1959-60; asst. resident medicine, 1960-63; NATO postdoctoral fellow biochemistry U. Glasgow, 1964-65; asst. prof. medicine U. Chgo. Hosps. and Argonne Cancer Research Hosp., Chgo., 1965-68; asst. chief hematology service clin. center NIH, Bethesda, Md., 1968-70; chief hematology VA Hosp., Nashville, 1970—, Vanderbilt Med. Sch., Nashville, 1970-98; asso. prof. medicine Vanderbilt U., 1970-74, prof. medicine, chief hematology, 1974—. Author: (with L.O. Jacobson) Erythopoietin and the Regulation of Erythropoiesis, 1970. Recipient Joseph A. Capps prize for med. research, 1964; USPHS postdoctoral fellow, 1962-64; NATO postdoctoral fellow, 1964; Leukemia Soc. scholar, 1965-68; NIH grantee, 1971—. Fellow A.C.P.; mem. Am. Fedn. Clin. Research, Am. Soc. Clin. Investigation, Assn. Am. Physicians, AAAS, Am. Soc. Hematology, Internat. Soc. Exptl. Hematology, Central Soc. Clin. Research, Am. Soc. Exptl. Pathology, So. Soc. Clin. Investigation (pres. 1985-86, Founders medal 1998), Sigma Xi. Home: 300 Estbury Ct Nashville TN 37215-5801

KRANTZ, STEVEN GEORGE, mathematics educator, writer; b. San Francisco, Feb. 3, 1951; s. Henry Alfred and Norma Oliva (Crisafulli) K.; m. Randi Diane Ruden, Sept. 7, 1974. BA, U. Calif., Santa Cruz, 1971; PhD, Princeton U, 1974. Asst. prof. UCLA, 1974-81; assoc. prof. Pa. State U., University Park, 1981-84, prof., 1984-86; prof. dept. math. Washington U., St. Louis, 1986—; cons. editor CRC Press, 1988—. Studies in Advanced Math. book series, Am. Math. Soc. book series; founder, mng. editor Jour. Geometric Analysis; Author: Function Theory of Several Complex Variables (monograph), 1982, 2d edition, 1992, Complex Analysis: The Geometric Viewpoint, 1990, Real Analysis and Foundations, 1991, Partial Differential Equationsand Analysis, 1992, A Primer of Real Analytic Functions, 1992, Geometric Analysis and function Spaces, 1993, How to Teach Mathematics, 1993, 2nd edit., 1999, A Tex Primer for Scientists, 1995, the Elements of Advanced Mathematics, 1995, Techniques of Problem Solving, 1996, Function Theory of One Complex Variable, 1997, A Primer of Mathematical Writing, 1996; (with H. R. Parks) The Geomery of Domains in Space, 1999, Contemporary Issues in Mathmatics Edn., 1999, A Handbook of Complex Variables, 1999, A Panorama of Harmonic Analysi, 1999; contbr. numerous rsch. articles to profl. publs. Recipient Disting. Tchg. award, UCLA Alumni Found., 1979:NSF rsch. grantee, 1975—, Kemper grantee, 1994. Fellow Richardson Australian Nat. U., 1995; mem. Am. Math. Soc. (prin. organizer summer rsch. inst. 1989), Math. Assn. Am. (Chauvenet prize, Beckenbach prise 1994), Textbook Authors Assn.

KRANWINKLE, CONRAD DOUGLAS, lawyer; b. Elgin, Ill., Oct. 27, 1940; s. Conrad David and Helen Elvira (Walgren) K.; m. Susan Hall Warren, Aug. 24, 1962; children: Mark Conrad, Jane Shafer. BA, Northwestern U., 1962; JD, U. Mich., 1965. Bar: Calif. 1966, U.S. Dist. Ct. (ctrl. dist.) Calif. 1966, U.S. Ct. Appeals (9th cir.) 1966, N.Y. 1995. Law clk. to chief justice U.S. Supreme Ct., Washington, 1966-67; ptnr. Munger, Tolles & Olson, L.A., 1967-88, O'Melveny & Myers, L.A. and N.Y.C., 1989—; mng. ptnr. O'Melveny & Myers, 1996—; vis. prof. law U. Mich., winter 1993; bd. dirs. Fremont Geh Corp., L.A. Pres. Poly. Sch. Bd. Trustees, Pasadena, Calif., 1986-88; mgr. Rep. Gubernatorial campaign, Calif., 1973-74; chmn. U.S. Senate campaign, Calif., 1978. Mem. Am. Law Inst., Calif. C. of C. (bd. dirs. 1990-94), Calif. Club, Valley Hunt Club, River Club. Office: O'Melveny & Myers 153 E 53rd St Ste 5400 New York NY 10022-4611

KRANYIK, ELIZABETH ANN, secondary education educator; b. Bridgeport, Conn., Nov. 15, 1957; d. Andrew Ladislaus and Marion Irene (Slater) K.; m. Charles Edward Porzelt III, Nov. 28, 1992; children: Charles Edward Porzelt IV, Marial Elizabeth Porzelt. BS summa cum laude, Western Conn. State U., 1979; MA, Fairfield U., 1989. Cert. h.s. tchr., gen. sci. endorsement, Conn. Tchr., program coordinator Fairfield (Conn.) Elem. Summer Sch., 1973-85; tchr. St. Maurice Sch., Stamford, Conn., 1980-82, Our Lady of Lourdes Sch., Melbourne, Fla., 1982-85, St. Pius X Sch., Fairfield, 1985-87, Bridgeport Pub. Schs., 1988-93, Bridgeport Regional Vocat. Aquaculture Sch., 1993—; freelance tutor; cons., tchr. Mill River Wetlands Prog., Fairfield, 1985-87, honors tchr., 1991; cons. Ocean Classroom, Bridgeport, Conn., 1989-90, NASA Newest Scholar, 1991, Sound Educators Assn., 1992—. Vol., tour guide H.M.S. Rose Found., Bridgeport, 1985—. Mem. Nat. Sci. Tchrs. Assn., Alliance Francais (Merit award 1979), Sound Educators Assn., Southeastern New Eng. Marine Educators, Phi Delta Kappa. Congregationalist. Avocations: nature study, reading, swimming, carpentry. Home: 129 Jockey Hollow Rd Monroe CT 06468-1270

KRANZ, KENNETH LOUIS, human resources company executive, entrepreneur; b. Evanston, Ill., July 7, 1946; s. Kenneth Louis Sr. and Florence A. (Knapton) K.; m. Susan Emilie Mueller, Apr. 3, 1976. BA, Tarkio Coll., 1969. Cert. compensation profl.; lic. IRS enrolled agt., adminstrv. svc. mgr., life and health agt. Cost acct. Fluid Power, Wheeling, Ill., 1969-71; cost acct. Wells Lamont Corp., Chgo., 1971-74, sr. cost acct., 1974-76, asst. mgr. cost, audit, 1977-80, asst. mgr. taxes, employee benefits, 1980-81, mgr. taxes, employee benefits, 1981-84; benefits mgr. Keeler Brass Co., Grand Rapids, Mich., 1984-86, employee benefits and compenstion mgr., 1986-90; human resources mgr. GRM Industries, Grand Rapids, 1990-92; co-owner Profl. Benefits Svcs., Inc., Grand Rapids, 1992-95; pres. MagnaCare Group Inc., Grand Rapids, 1995—. Mem. Home Health Svcs. (treas. 1986-90), Internat. Soc. Pre-Retirement Planners, West Mich. Compensation Assn., Am. Compensation Assn., Human Resource Mgmt. Assn., Life Underwriters Assn. Republican. Lutheran. Avocations: numismatics, all sports. Office: MagnaCare Group Inc 6147 28th St SE Ste 14 Grand Rapids MI 49546-6934

KRANZOW, RONALD ROY, lawyer; b. Chgo., Aug. 4, 1931; s. Roy Ludwig and Elsie Emma (Hennig) K.; m. Joan Carole Stromberg, June 7, 1952; children: Susan, Kenneth, Jill. Student, De Paul U., 1949-52, Syracuse U., 1952-53, Trinity U., 1953-54, Roosevelt U., 1956, John Marshall Law Sch., 1956-59; JD, Golden Gate U., 1961. Bar: Calif. 1961, Tex. 1977, U.S. Ct. Appeals (9th cir.) 1961, U.S. Ct. Appeals (2d cir.) 1969, U.S. Ct. Appeals (8th cir.) 1976, U.S. Ct. Appeals (fed. cir.) 1982. Sales corr. Internat. Cellucotton Products Co., Chgo., 1949-52; sales asst. Kaiser Aluminum & Chem. Corp., Oakland, Calif., 1956-61, trademark counsel, 1961-68; trademark counsel PepsiCo Inc., Purchase, N.Y., 1968-74, asst. gen. counsel, 1976-86; assoc. gen. counsel PepsiCo Inc., Purchase, 1986-96; v.p., legal counsel Frito-Lay Inc., Dallas, 1974-89, sr. v.p., legal counsel, 1989-95; assoc. gen. counsel Frito-Lay, Inc., Dallas, 1995-96. Contbr. articles to profl. jours. Trustee Grace Presbyn. Village, Dallas, 1995-96. Mem. ABA, Dallas Bar Assn. (chmn. antitrust and trade regulation sect. 1990-91), Am. Intellectual Property Law Assn., U.S. Trademark Assn. (chmn., com. mem. 1965—, pres., chmn. bd. dirs. 1977-78), Internat. Trademark Assn. (neutral trademark and unfair competition panel 1994—). Republican. Presbyterian. Avocations: church teaching, sports, reading.

KRARAS, GUST C., hotel executive; b. Terpsithea, Greece, Mar. 4, 1921; came to U.S., 1938; s. Christ I. and Ypapanti (Contos) K.; m. Stella Dialectos, Apr. 28, 1946; children: Christ, Angel, Ypapanti. *Gus and Stella Kraras started their family business in Wildwood, N.J., 1955. They developed their holdings from a small restaurant, now owning several motels and restaurants with their entire family. As an offshoot of this beginning, their son, Chris, founded a nationally known tour packaging company called White Star Tour and Travel that operates thousands of tours a year to destinations all over the U.S. and Canada from their different offices. In addition, the Kraras family owns several real estate developments, banquet facilities, and other small businesses throughout Pennsylvania and New Jersey.* Owner-operator Lorraine Hotel & Restaurant, Wildwood, N.J., 1955-73, White Star Motel, Wildwood, 1972—; owner-operator Nantucket Motel, Wildwood, 1973—, White Star Tours, Reading, Pa., 1975—; owner Two Mile Landing, Wildwood, 1982—; owner-operator Beach Terrace Motor Inn, Wildwood, 1985—, Rusty Rudder Restaurant, Wildwood, 1985—, Mansion Heights Assocs., Birdsboro, Pa., 1986—; owner-operator G.C.M., Reading, 1980—, Hopewell Heights, Birdsboro, 1988—. *Gus and Stella's son, Chris, was instrumental in developing the family business. He founded a nationally known travel company called White Star Tour and Travel, and along with Gus and Stella's daughters Angel and Partricia and their husbands, Mauro Cammarano and Bernard Donahue, and Chris's wife, Ann, the entire family broadened their business interests to include real estate developments, banquet facilities, building companies, and additionall motels and restaurants. Their grandson, Dean, joined the business five years ago and is also intimately involved, rounding out three generations of family business endeavors.* Editor hist. jours., 1954, 70, 75, 89. Pres. St. Constantine Ch., St. Helen Ch., Reading, 1958-59, 77, chpt. 61 Am. Hellenic Ednl. Progressive Assn., Reading, 1957; dist. gov. 5th dist. AHEPA, N.J., Del., 1981-82. With OSS, 1943-45, ETO. Mem. Nat. Tour Assn., Archon Depoutatos of Ecumenical Patriarchate of Constantinople, Masons, Shriners. Democrat. Greek Orthodox. Office: White Star Tours Inc 26 E Lancaster Ave Reading PA 19607-2693

KRASEAN, THOMAS KARL, historian; b. South Bend, Ind., Feb. 21, 1940; s. William Henry and Rose Ercelia (Mariottini) K.; m. Arleen Ruth Llewellyn, June 19, 1965 (div. Oct. 1970); children: Thomas Karl, David William, Elizabeth Rose; m. Liliane Siahou, Nov. 4, 1972. AA, Kellogg Community Coll., 1960; student, U. Ala., 1960-61; BA, East Mich. U., 1963; MA, Western Mich. U., 1965. Cert. in fund raising mgmt., 1996. Field rep. Ind. State Libr., Indpls., 1965-69, state archivist, 1969-70; dir. Byron Lewis Libr., Vincennes (Ind.) U., 1970-77; field rep. Ind. Hist. Soc., Indpls., 1977-82, dir. field svcs. divsn., 1982-92, dir. cmty. rels. divsn., 1992-97, dir. devel. and membership svcs., 1997—; rep. Ind. Am. Revolution Bicentennial Commn., 1971-77; mem. Adv. Com. Historic Preservation, 1972-73, Adv. Com. Ind. Hist. Bur., 1980—; chmn. George Rogers Clark Trail Found., 1972-74; founder, pres. Old N.W. Corp., 1973-77; bd. dirs. Ind. Adv. Com. Nat. Hist. Publs. and Records Commn., 1979-97. Mem. White River Park Task Force, Indpls., 1981-83. Mem. Am. Assn. State and Local History (state chmn. awards com. 1981-92, regional chmn. awards com. 1988-92, nominating com. 1992-95), Soc. Am. Archivists, Midwest Archives Conf. (charter), Ind. Hist. Soc. (adv. coun. Ind. Jr. Hist. Soc. 1971—), Ind. Oral History Roundtable (charter), Soc. Ind. Archivists (founder, sec., treas. 1972-92), Civil War Roundtable (pres. 1970-71, 79-80, 93-94), Battle Creek (Mich.) Civil War Roundtable (life), Indpls. Lit. Club (pres. 1989, treas. 1991—), Contemporary Club Indpls. (bd. dirs. 1998—), Sagamore of the Wabash. Republican. Roman Catholic. Avocations: travel, book collecting. Home: 6038 Castlebar Cir Indianapolis IN 46220-4107 Office: Ind Hist Soc 315 W Ohio St Indianapolis IN 46202-3299

KRASLOW, DAVID, retired newspaper publishing executive, reporter, author, consultant; b. N.Y.C., Apr. 16, 1926; s. Frank and Goldie (Sirota) K.; m. Bernice Schonfeld, Sept. 18, 1949; children: Ellen Anne, Karen Leah, Susan Beth. BA in Journalism, U. Miami, Fla., 1948. Washington corr. L.A. Times, 1963-66, news editor Washington bur., 1966-70, chief Washington bur., 1970-72; asst. mng. editor Washington Star-News, 1972-74; chief Washington bur. Cox Newspapers, 1974-77; pub. Miami News, 1977-88, sports writer, 1947-48; successively sports writer, reporter, Washington corr. Miami Herald, 1948-63; panelist news program Sta. WPBT-TV, Miami, 1979-91; v.p. Cox Newspapers, Miami, 1989-91. Co-author: A Certain Evil, 1965, The Secret Search for Peace in Vietnam, 1968. Life trustee, mem. acad. affairs com., athletic adv. com. U. Miami; mem. Orange Bowl Com.; bd. dirs. Greater Miami Tennis Found., Inc., Internat. Oceanographic Found., U. Miami. With USAAF, 1944-46. Recipient George Polk award, 1969; Raymond Clapper award, 1969; Dumont award, 1969; Nieman fellow Harvard U., 1961-62. Mem. Gridiron Club (Washington). Jewish.

KRASNA, ALVIN ISAAC, biochemist, educator; b. N.Y.C., June 23, 1929; s. Selig and Esther (Finer) K.; m. Elaine C. Cohen, Feb. 27, 1955; children—Susan Roni, Gary Marc, Allen Selig. B.A., Yeshiva Coll., 1950; Ph.D., Columbia U., 1955. Mem. faculty Columbia U., 1956—, prof. biochemistry, 1970—, acting chmn., 1977-78, 88-90, vice chmn., 1978-88, 90—. Contbr. to profl. jours. Predoctoral fellow NSF, 1953; Guggenheim fellow, 1962; research grantee NSF; research grantee NIH; research grantee Am. Cancer Soc.; research grantee AEC, Dept. Energy. Mem. Am. Chem. Soc., Am. Assn. Biol. Chemists, AAAS, Harvey Soc., Am. Soc. Microbiology, Sigma Xi. Home: 6 Arbor Dr New Rochelle NY 10804-1101 Office: 630 W 168th St New York NY 10032-3702

KRASNE, CHARLES A., food products executive; b. 1932. BS, Yale U., 1952; MBA, Harvard U., 1954. With Kradale Foods, White Plains, N.Y., 1954—, CEO. Office: Kradale Foods 65 W Red Oak Ln White Plains NY 10604-3616*

KRASNER, DANIEL WALTER, lawyer; b. N.Y.C., Mar. 18, 1941; s. Nathan and Rose Krasner; m. Ruth Pollack, Dec. 20, 1964; children: Jonathan, Lisa, Noah, Rebecca. BA, Yeshiva Coll., 1962; LLB, Yale U., 1965. Bar: N.Y. 1966, U.S. Dist. Ct. (so. dist.) N.Y. 1967, U.S. Supreme Ct. 1978. Assoc. Pomerantz Levy Houdek & Block, N.Y.C., 1965-76; sr. ptnr. Wolf Haldenstein Adler Freeman & Herz, N.Y.C., 1977—. Vice chmn. Westchester Day Sch., Mamaroneck, N.Y., 1979-86; v.p., trustee Bd. Jewish Edn., N.Y.C., 1981—. Democrat. Avocations: tennis, golf, sailing. Office: Wolf Haldenstein Adler Freeman & Herz 270 Madison Ave New York NY 10016-0601

KRASNER, MICHAEL ALAN, political science educator; b. Hot Springs, S.D., July 2, 1943; s. George David and Alice (Doress) K.; m. Deborah Jane Shapiro, June 16, 1974; children: Abigail Judith, Elizabeth Sara. AB, U. Chgo., 1964; PhD, Columbia U., 1977. Program analyst Office Econ. Oppty., Washington, 1967-68; adj. lectr. Lehman Coll. CUNY, Bronx, 1967-68; adj. lectr. Hunter Coll. CUNY, N.Y.C., 1968-69; half-time lectr. Queens Coll., CUNY, Flushing, N.Y., 1970-72, instr., 1972-74, asst. prof., 1974-77, assoc. prof. polit. sci., 1977—; vis. prof., rsch. fellow U. Aarhus, Denmark, 1985-86, Fulbright exch. prof., 1983-84; exch. prof. U. Paris, 1994; cons., trainer, evaluator U.S. Postal Svc., N.Y.C. and Boston, 1989—; cons. Townsend Harris H.S., Queens, 1996—; cons., project dir. Ctr. for Applied Rsch. in Social Scis., Bklyn., 1978-83. Author: Going For It: How to Organize a Grassroots Campaign, 1992; co-author: American Government: Structure and Process, 1982; contbr. articles to profl. publs. Commentator WBAI-FM, N.Y.C., 1978-91; county bd. mem. Vt. Progressive Coalition, Brattleboro, 1990—; vice chair Queens Coll. chpt. Profl. Staff Congress, 1996—, co-dir. Taft Inst. for Govt., 1996—; guest tchr. Brattleboro Union H.S., 1995—. Tng./rsch. grantee U.S. Inst. of Peace, 1992-93. Mem. Internat. Peace Rsch. Inst. Jewish. Avocations: swimming, writing fiction, camping. Home: 192 Taylor Rd Putney VT 05346-9023 Office: CUNY Queens Coll Dept Polit Sci 65-30 Kissena Blvd Flushing VT 11367

KRASNEY, RINA SUSAN, school librarian; b. Phila., Mar. 15, 1950; d. Myron and Lillian (Shiman) K. BA, Douglass Coll., 1971; MLS, Rutgers U., 1973. Libr. Austin (Tex.) C.C., 1977-80, U. Mo., St. Louis, 1980-85, St. Louis Pub. Libr., 1985-86, Ferguson-Florissant Sch. Dist., St. Louis, 1986—. Mem. NEA. Home: 8260 Audrain Dr Saint Louis MO 63121-4504

KRASNO, RICHARD MICHAEL, educational organization executive, educator; b. Chgo., Jan. 20, 1942; s. Louis R. K. and Adeline G. (Glassman) Kaplan; children: Jeffrey Patrick, Eric Peter; m. Carin Blucher. BS, U. Ill., 1965; PhD, Stanford U., 1970; LittD (hon.), Coll. St. Rose, 1983; LLD (hon.), Sacred Heart U., 1984. Asst. prof. ednl. psychology U. Chgo., 1970-74; program advisor Brazil Ford Found., Rio de Janeiro, 1974-77; program advisor Latin Am. Ford Found., N.Y.C., 1977, program advisor Mid.-East & Africa, 1978-80; deputy asst. sec. of edn. U.S. Dept. Edn., Washington, 1980-81; exec. v.p. Inst. Internat. Edn., N.Y.C., 1981-83, pres., CEO, 1983-98; pres. Monterey (Calif.) Inst. Internat Stud, 1998—; commr. U.S.-Brazil Fulbright Commn., 1975-77, U.S. Nat. Commn. UNESCO, 1983; chmn. Internat. Transition Team Dept. Edn., 1979, 80; mem. U.S.-Mex. Bilateral Commn., 1980, 84; sr. Fulbright lectr., 1973-74. Contbr. articles to profl. jours. Trustee Laspau, Cembridge, Mass., 1980-82, Ctr. applied Linguistics, Washington, 1982-85. Nat. Defense Edn. fellow U.S Govt., 1967-68. Mem. Coun. Fgn. Rels., Century Assn., Cosmos Club. Office: Monterey Inst Internat Studies 425 Van Buren St Monterey CA 93940-2623

KRASNOW, ERWIN GILBERT, lawyer; b. Bklyn., Jan. 8, 1936; s. Charles and Etta (Simowitz) K.; m. E. Judith Levine, Sept. 6, 1960 (dec. July 1994); children: Michael Andrew, Catherine Beth; m. Jane Gasperini, Nov. 25, 1995. A.B. summa cum laude, Boston U., 1958; J.D., Harvard U., 1961; LL.M., Georgetown U., 1965. Bar: Mass. 1961, D.C. 1963, U.S. Dist. Ct. Mass. 1961, U.S. Ct. Appeals (D.C. cir.) 1963, U.S. Ct. Appeals (4th cir.) 1978, U.S. Ct. Appeals (5th cir.) 1982, U.S. Ct. Appeals (11th cir.) 1982, U.S. Supreme Ct. 1965. Research asst. Law Sch. Harvard U., Cambridge, Mass., 1961; adminstrv. asst. to Congressman Torbert H. Macdonald, U.S. Ho. of Reps., Washington, 1962-64; ptnr. Kirkland and Ellis, Washington, 1964-76; sr. v.p. and gen. counsel Nat. Assn. Broadcasters, Washington, 1976-84; ptnr. Verner, Liipfert, Bernhard, McPherson & Hand, Washington, 1984—; vis. prof. Ohio State U., 1974; disting. vis. lectr. Temple U., 1976; adj. prof. Am. U., 1975, Law Ctr. Georgetown U., 1984; professorial lectr. Grad. Sch. Arts and Scis. George Washington U., 1982, 83, Sch. Law Cath. U. Am., 1982; adj. prof. Grad. Sch. Arts and Scis. Georgetown U., 1998, bd. dirs. Broadcast Capital Fund, Inc. (formerly Minority Broadcast Investment Fund), 1978—, treas., 1979-92, vice chmn., 1993—; govt. industry adv. council Ctr. for Telecommunications Studies, George Washington U., 1980-84; adv. bd. Inst. for Communications Law, Sch. Law, Cath. U. Am., 1982—; bd. advisors Communications Media Ctr., N.Y. Law Sch., 1982—; adv. com. UCLA Communications Law Program, 1983-85. Co-author: The Politics of Broadcast Regulation, 1973, 2d edit. 1978, 3d edit. 1982; co-author: A Candidate's Guide to the Law of Political Broadcasting, 1977, 2d edit. 1980, 3d edit. 1984; Buying and Building a Broadcast Station.3d edit., 1987; 100 Ways to Cut Legal Fees and Manage Your Lawyer, 1988, Radio Financing: A Guide for Lenders and Investors, 1990, Insider's Guide to Radio Acquisition Contracts, 1992; editor: National Association of Broadcasters Legal Guide to FCC Broadcast Rules, Regulations and Policies, 1977; contbr. articles, writings to publs. in field; bd. editors Fed. Communications Bar Jour., 1973-75; editorial adv. bd. Jour. of Broadcasting, 1972-85, Telematics and Informatics, 1982—; adv. com. COMM/ENT Law Jour., 1983—. Mem. ABA (vice chmn. agy. adjudication com. 1974-77, chmn. communications law com. adminstrv. law sect. 1980-81), Fed. Bar Assn. (pres. Capitol Hill chpt. 1963-64, dep. co-chmn. communications law com. 1967-69, co-chmn., 1970-71), Fed. Communications Bar Assn. (exec. com. 1976-79, 84-85, treas. 1984-85), Capitol Hill Bar Assn. (past pres.), Boston U. Alumni Club Washington (pres. 1967-70), Boston U. Nat. Alumni Assn.

(bd. dirs. 1966-68, regional v.p. 1971, 73), Phi Beta Kappa. Home: 3307 Q St NW Washington DC 20007-2717 Office: Verner Liipfert Bernhard McPherson & Hand 901 15th St NW Ste 700 Washington DC 20005-2327

KRASNOW, JORDAN PHILIP, lawyer; b. Malden, Mass., May 14, 1944; s. Louis and Roslyn (Packer) K.; children: Laura, Joshua, Abbey, Abigail. AB, Clark U., 1965; JD magna cum laude, Boston U., 1968. Bar: Mass. 1970. Law clk. to Presiding Justice Mass. Superior Ct., Boston, 1968-69; assoc. atty. Peabody & Arnold, Boston, 1969-71; assoc. atty. Gaston Snow & Ely Bartlett, Boston, 1971-75, ptnr., 1975-86; officer, dir. Goulston & Storrs, Boston, 1986—; co-mng. dir., 1994-97; lectr. Mass. Continuing Legal Edn., Boston, 1975-85; adv. com. Boston U. Real Estate Program, 1988—; charter mem. Greater Boston Real Estate Bd.-Real Estate Fin., 1989. Mem. Mayor's Adv. Com. Housing Linkage, Boston, 1984. Recipient Disting. Achievement award B'nai B'rith Realty Unit, 1995. Fellow Mass. Bar Found.; mem. Mass. Bar Assn., Boston Bar Assn., B'nai Brith (trustee realty unit New Eng. chpt.). Jewish. Avocations: travel, sports. Home: 94 Beacon St Apt 2 Boston MA 02108-3329 Office: Goulston & Storrs 400 Atlantic Ave Boston MA 02110-3333

KRATE, NAT, artist; b. N.Y.C., Aug. 26, 1918; s. Samuel and Ida (Tuchschneider) K.; m. Helen Levy Krate, May 26, 1923; children: Iris Ann, David, Riva. Attended, WPA Art Sch., N.Y.C., 1934-35, Pratt Inst., N.Y.C., 1935-36, Art Students League, 1936-38, 46-47, Syracuse U., 1943-44. Art dir. Erland Advtg. Agy., N.Y.C., 1946-48; creative dir. Krate/Basch Advtg. Agy., N.Y.C., 1948-61; owner & dir. Nat Krate Co. Inc., N.Y.C. and Pittsfield, Mass., 1961-80; mem. adv. bd. Sarasota (Fla.) Art Assn., 1989-91, Longboat Key (Fla.) Art Ctr., 1986-88; art instr. Ringling Sch. of Art and Design, Sarasota, Fla., 1989-90. Solo exhbns. include Becket Art Gallery, Mass., 1978, Welles Gallery, Lenox, Mass., 1981, Ana Sklar Gallery, Bal Harbor, Fla., 1985, Foster Harmon Galleries Am. Art, Sarasota, Fla., 1986, 89, 92, 94, Arvida Gallery, Longboat Key, 1986, Longboat Key Art Ctr., Fla., 1989, Anna Howard Galleries, Washington, Conn., 1992, Lee County Alliance of the Arts, Ft. Myers, Fla., 1994, Donn Roll Galleries, Sarasota, 1994, 96, Hang-Up Gallery, Sarasota, 1998; group exhbns. include Soc. for the Four Arts, Palm Beach, Fla., 1989, 90, 91, 95, Fla. Figure Show, Brevard Mus., Melbourne, Fla., 1993, 43d Ann All Fla. Boca Raton Mus., Fla., 1994-95, Fla. Artist Group, Mus. Arts & Science, Daytona Beach, Fla., 1994, 4th Biennial Exhbn., Huntsville Mus., Ala., 1994, Mickelson Gallery, Washington, 1994-95, Mobile Mus. of Art, Ala., 1996, Mus. Contemporary Art, Jacksonville, Fla., 1998, Hunter Mus. Am. ARt, Chattanooga, 1998, Venice (Fla.) Art Ctr., 1997, Lee County Alliance of Arts, Ft. Myers, Fla., 1997, Ridge Art Assn., Winter Haven, Fla., 1997-98, 99, Hang-Up Gallery, Sarasota, 1998, Jacksonville (Fla.) Mus. Contemporary Art, 1998. Mem. Longboat Key Art Ctr., Sarasota Visual Art Ctr., Mus. of Arts and Scis., Daytona Beach, Fla., Sarasota County Arts Coun.; co-founder, mem. bd. dirs. Pub. Interest Com., Longboat Key, 1985-95; adv. cons. various candidates for pub. office, 1986-95. Staff sgt. U.S. Army, 1941-45. Mem. Am. Artists Profl. League, Inc., Knickerbocker Artists U.S.A., Fla. Artists Group, The Salmagundi Club. Home: 4737 Sweetmeadow Cir Sarasota FL 34238-3398

KRATHEN, DAVID HOWARD, lawyer; b. Phila., Nov. 17, 1946; s. Morris S. and Lillian E. K.; m. Francine Ellen, Oct. 21, 1973; children: Richard, Stefanie, Michael. BBA, U. Miami, Fla., 1969, JD, 1972. Bar: Fla. 1972, D.C. 1972, N.Y. 1984, Colo. 1989, U.S. Supreme Ct. 1976. Atty. advisor ICC, Washington, 1972-73; asst. pub. defender 17th Jud. Cir., Ft. Lauderdale, Fla., 1973-74; ptnr. Glass, Krathen, Rastatter, Stark & Tarlowe, Ft. Lauderdale, 1974-78, Krathen & Sperry, P.A., Ft. Lauderdale, 1978-84, David H. Krathen, P.A., 1984—; pvt. practice Law Offices of David Krathen, 1996—; mem. Fla. Bar Grievance Com. 17 C, 1982-85, 1988-91, vice chmn., 1985, 89-90, chmn. 1990-91; mem. Jud. Adminstrn., Selection and Tenure Com., 1982-85, 4th Dist. Ct. of Appeal Jud. Nominating Commn., 1983-87, chmn. 1986-87; mem. jud. nominating commn. 17th Jud. Cir., 1991-95, chmn., 1994-95; apptd. by Fla. Gov. to State Ethics Commn., 1995-99. Mem. Acad. Fla. Trial Lawyers (diplomate), Broward County Bar Assn. (bd. dirs. 1988-89), Broward Med. Assn. (mem. com. joint med. legal 1997—), Broward County Trial Lawyers Assn. (bd. dirs. 1983-84, sec. 1984-85, v.p. 1985-86, pres. 1987-88), Assn. Trial Lawyers Am., Fla. Bar (bd. cert. civil trial lawyer 1984—), Nat. Bd. Trial Advocacy (bd. cert. civil trial advocate 1986—), Am. Bd. Trial Advocacy (advocate 1989—, sec. Ft. Lauderdale chpt. 1991-92, pres.-elect 1993-95, pres. 1995-96). Office: 888 E Las Olas Blvd Ste 200 Fort Lauderdale FL 33301-2239

KRATHWOHL, DAVID READING, education educator emeritus; b. Chgo., May 14, 1921; adopted by Marie (Reimold) K.; m. Helen Jean Abney, Dec. 20, 1943; children: James D. (dec. Nov. 1967), David A., Ruth Anne Krathwohl Cleghorn, Kristin Jeanne. B.S., U. Chgo., 1943, M.S., 1947, Ph.D., 1953. Asst. dir. unit on evaluation Bur. Ednl. Research, Coll. Edn., U. Ill., 1949-55, instr., 1949-53; asst. prof., 1953-55; asso. prof. Mich. State U., 1955-58, prof., 1958-65, research coordinator, 1955-63; chmn. Psychol. Found. Edn., 1960-63; dir. Bur. Ednl. Research, 1963-65; dean Sch. Edn. Syracuse (N.Y.) U., 1965-76; prof. Sch. Edn., Syracuse (N.Y.) U., 1965-91, Hannah Hammond prof. edn., 1982-91, Hannah Hammond prof. emeritus, 1991—; chmn. bd. trustees Eastern Regional Inst. for Edn., 1966-71. Author: (with others) Taxonomy of Educational Objectives: Cognitive Domain, 1956, Affective Domain, 1964, Social and Behavioral Science Research: A New Framework for Conceptualizing, Implementing and Evaluating Research Studies, 1985, How to Prepare a Research Proposal, 3d edit., 1988, Methods of Educational and Social Science Research: An Integrated Approach, 2d edit., 1998. Served with USAAF, 1943-46. Fellow Center for Advanced Study in Behavioral Scis., 1980-81. Fellow AAAS, Am. Psychol. Assn. (v.p. ednl. psychology div.); mem. Am. Ednl. Rsch. Assn. (pres.), Am. Psychol. Soc. Home: 9 Thornwood Ln Fayetteville NY 13066-2529 Office: Syracuse U Sch Of Education Syracuse NY 13244

KRATKA-SCHNEIDER, DOROTHY MARYJOHANNA, psychotherapist; b. New Britain, Conn., Apr. 29, 1934; d. Josef Matthew and Mari Catherine (Stifl) Kratka; m. Warren Andrew Schneider, Apr. 26, 1975. BS in Nursing, Columbia U., 1960; MSW, Fordham U., 1969; EdD in Counseling Psychology, U. San Francisco, 1983. RN, Conn.; bd. cert. diplomate in clin. social work. Instr. pub. health nursing U. Conn., Storrs, 1963-64; participant Voter Registration Drive, Greenwood, Miss., 1965; pub. health nurse Jesuit Med. Mission Bd., Tanzania, East Africa, 1965-67; chief psychiat. social worker Knickerbocker Hosp., N.Y.C., 1969-74; coordinator social services Rockefeller U. Hosp., N.Y.C., 1974-77; asst. prof. Calif. State U., Sacramento, 1985-88, assoc. prof., 1985-88; counseling psychologist VA, San Francisco, 1987-89; psychologist, social worker Dept. Transp., 1989-93; pvt. practice Corte Madera, Calif., 1993—; bd. dirs. Nat. Assn. Soc. Work Referral Service, San Francisco, 1984-86. Bd. dirs. Health Systems Adv. Com., San Francisco, 1978; mem. Cath. Charities Bd. for Aging, San Francisco, 1985, bd. dirs., 1983-85. NIMH grantee, 1967-69. Mem. APA, Internat. Assn. Profl. Counselors and Psychotherapists (diplomate psychotherapy), NASW (diplomate in clin. social work), Register for Clin. Social Workers of NASW, Amnesty Internat., Kappa Delta Pi. Democrat. Roman Catholic. Avocations: hiking, watercolors, flying, swimming. Office: 240 Tamal Vista Blvd Corte Madera CA 94925-1132 Office: Diablo Med Plz Ste 200 Novato CA 94947

KRATOCHVIL, BYRON GEORGE, chemistry educator, researcher; b. Osmond, Nebr., Sept. 15, 1932; came to Can., 1967; s. Frank James and Mabel Louise (Schneider) K.; m. Marianne Spain; children: Susan, Daniel, Jean, John. BS, Iowa State U., 1957, MS, 1959, PhD, 1961. Asst. prof. chemistry U. Wis.-Madison, 1961-67; assoc. prof. chemistry U. Alta., Edmonton, Can., 1967-71, prof. chemistry, 1971-98; prof. emeritus U. Alta., Edmonton, 1998—; dept. chmn. U. Alta., Edmonton, Can., 1989-95, assoc. v.p. rsch., 1996-98—; sr. advisor, v.p. rsch. U. Alta., Edmonton, 1998—. Co-author: (with W.E. Harris) Chemical Analysis, 1969, Chemical Separations and Measurements, 1974, Introduction to Chemical Analysis, 1981; analytical editor Can. Jour. Chemistry, Ottawa, Ont., 1985-88, sr. editor, 1988-93; contbr. numerous articles to sci. jours. Recipient merit award Iowa State U. Alumni, 1990. Fellow AAAS, Chem. Inst. Can. (bd. dirs. 1977-80, Fisher Lectr. award 1990); mem. Am. Chem. Soc. Office: U Alta Dept Chemistry, Chemistry Centre, Edmonton, AB Canada T6G 2G2

KRATOCHVIL, L(OUIS) GLEN, lawyer; b. Highland, Wis., Oct. 11, 1922; s. John A. and Emma (Pusch) K.; m. Evelyn Gregory, Sept. 12, 1946; 1 son, Louis Glen Jr. LLB, U. Wis., 1951; JD. Bar: Wis. 1951, Tex. 1952, U.S. Dist. Ct. (so. dist.) Tex. 1956, U.S. Ct. Appeals (5th cir.) 1956, U.S. Supreme Ct. 1956, U.S. Dist. Ct. (ea. dist.) Tex. 1961. Landman Shell Oil Co., Houston, 1951-52; assoc. firm Murphy & Crystal, Houston, 1953-55; asst. U.S. atty. So. Dist. Tex., 1955-57; pvt. practice Houston, 1957—. Pres. McGregor Terr. Civic Club, Houston, 1954, Young Rep. Club U. Wis., 1950. Lt. USNR, 1941-46, PTO. Mem. ABA, Fed. Bar Assn., Tex. Bar Assn., Wis. Bar Assn., Houston Bar Assn., Maritime Law Assn., U. Wis. Alumni Assn. (pres. Houston chpt. 1972-73), Brazos River Club (treas. 1970—), Lions (pres. 1955), Phi Alpha Delta (chief justice 1950). Home: 302 Kickerillo Dr Houston TX 77079-7412 Office: Kratochvil and Powell 9601 Katy Fwy Houston TX 77024-1342

KRATOVIL, JANE LINDLEY, think tank associate, developer/fundraiser; b. Boston, Nov. 25, 1952; 1 child, Lindley. BA, Lynchburg Coll., 1974. Various positions U.S. Ho. of Reps., Washington, 1974-77, The Pittston Co., Greenwich, Conn., 1977-79; assoc. dir. City Sports Mgmt. Inc., Washington, 1979-82; adminstrv. asst. to spl. asst. to pres. for adminstrn. The White House, Washington, 1982-85; exec. asst. to gen. and dep. gen. counsel U.S. Dept. Treasury, Washington, 1985-88; exec. dir., sec. Eisenhower World Affairs Inst., Washington, 1988—. Office: 1620 Eye St NW Ste 703 Washington DC 20006-4005

KRATT, PETER GEORGE, lawyer; b. Lorain, Ohio, Mar. 7, 1940; s. Arthur Leroy and Edith Ida (Dietz) K.; m. Sharon Amy Maruska, June 15, 1968; children—Kevin George, Jennifer Ivy. B.A., Miami U., Oxford, Ohio, 1962; J.D., Case Western Res. U., 1966. Bar: Ohio 1966. Atty. Cleve. Trust Co., 1966-74; assoc. counsel AmeriTrust Co., 1974-84, sec., assoc. counsel, 1985-87, sec., sr assoc. counsel, 1987-92; v.p., mgr. personal trust adminstrn. Huntington Trust Co., 1993—. Mem. Am. Soc. Corp. Secs., Ohio Bar Assn. Methodist. Lodges: Rotary, Lions. Avocations: hiking, gardening.

KRATTENMAKER, THOMAS JOHN, public relations executive; b. Mpls., June 27, 1960; s. Thomas Louis K. and Cecelia (Nistler) Daline; m. Carolyn Marie Gretton, June 22, 1994; 1 child, Holland Elene. BA, U. Minn., 1983; postgrad., U. Pa., 1996—. Reporter Orange County Register, Santa Ana, Calif., 1983-87; reporter Associated Press, Mpls., 1987-88, Trenton, N.J., 1988-90; sr. writer Princeton (N.J.) U. Comm. Office, 1990-95; pub. rels. dir. Swarthmore (Pa.) Coll., 1995—; mem. pub. rels. com. Annapolis Group of Leading Liberal Arts Colls. Contbr. articles to various mags. Mem. Coun. Advancement & Support of Edn., Coll. & Univ. Pub. Rels. Assn. Pa. Democrat. Unitarian. Avocations: basketball, internet, guitar. Office: Swarthmore Coll 500 College Ave Swarthmore PA 19081-1390

KRATZ, CHARLES E., JR., library director; b. Balt., Apr. 22, 1951; s. Charles Edward Sr. and Catherine Mary (Hudson) K. BA in History, U. Notre Dame, 1973, MA in History, 1974; M of Libr. Sci., U. Md., 1976. Asst. head of public svcs. U. Mo. Libr., Kansas City, 1979-80, head of public svcs., 1980-82; assoc. dir. Rider U., Lawrenceville, N.J., 1982-85; asst. dean of public svcs. Hofstra U., Hempstead, N.Y., 1985-91; libr. dir. U. Scranton (Pa.) Libr., 1991—; v.p. to pres. bd. trustees PALINET, 1997-99. Author: (with others) Facts & Figures, 1987, Training Issues and Strategies, 1990, Staff Development: A Practical Guide, 1992; contbr., editor: The Personnel Manual: An Outline for Libraries, 1994; editor: Library Personnel Consultants List, 1990, Training Issues in Changing Technology, 1986; contbr. articles to profl. jours. Mem. ALA, LAMA (pres. 1997—), ACRL (coms.), LITA (coms.). Roman Catholic. Avocations: theatre, skating, sports. Home: 12 Eaglesmere Cir East Stroudsburg PA 18301-3141

KRATZ, HOWARD RUSSEL, physicist, researcher; b. Mattoon, Wis., Nov. 2, 1916; s. Samuel H. and Clara A. (Jones) K.; m. Mary K. Bunsa, June 2, 1942; children: Marilyn Kratz Locker, William H. BA, Ripon Coll., 1938; PhD, U. Wis., 1942. Tchg. asst. U. Wis., Madison, 1938-41; rsch. asst. Princeton (N.J.) U., 1941-42; mem. staff Metall. Lab., U. Chgo., 1942-44; mem. staff Los Alamos (N.M.) Sci. Lab., 1944-46, GE Rsch. Lab., Schnectady, N.Y., 1946-59, Gen. Atomic, San Diego, 1959-72; sr. scientist Sys., Sci., and Software, San Diego, 1972-79; ret., 1979—. Contbr. articles to Phys. Revue, Rev. Sci. Instruments, Jour. Optical Soc. Am., Jour. Am. Instrument Soc. Recipient 1972 best paper award Am. Instrument Soc., 1973. Mem. Am. Phys. Soc., Sigma Xi. Democrat. Unitarian. Home: 102 Spanish Oak Ln Hendersonville NC 28791-2906

KRAUS, EILEEN S., bank executive. Grad. magna cum laude, Mt. Holyoke Coll.; MA, Trinity Coll.; D Comml. Sci. (hon.), U. Hartford, 1995. Chmn. - Conn. Fleet Bank, Hartford, Conn.; pres. Career Search Resources; v.p. human resources planning and devel. Shawmut Nat. Corp., vice chmn., bd. dirs.; bd. dirs. Best Food, Kaman Corp., Stanley Works, Yankee Energy Sys. Mem. exec. com., v.p. Bushnell Meml. Hall; bd. dirs. Cmty. Econ. Devel. Found., Inc.; bd. dirs. Yale New Haven Hosp. Named Conn. Bus. Leader of Yr., Hartford Courant, 1990; recipient Leadership award to women in bus. New Eng. Coun., 1993, Woman of Merit award Conn. Valley Coun. Girl Scouts U.S., 1994. Mem. Greater Hartford C. of C. (chmn.). Office: Fleet Bank 777 Main St Hartford CT 06115-2303

KRAUS, HENRY, retired physician, educator; b. Akron, Ohio, Apr. 12, 1923; s. Charles Morton and Gertrude (Gibans) K.; m. Esther Elizabeth Mackey, July 7, 1946; children: Charles Thomas, Thomas Henry, Anne Elizabeth, James Douglas. Cert., Harvard U., 1943; MD, Case Western Res. U., 1947. Diplomate Am. Bd. Internal Medicine. Intern in medicine Univ. Hosps. Cleve., 1947-48, asst. resident in medicine, 1948-49; fellow in cardiology Thorndike lab. Boston City Hosp., 1949-50; sr. resident in medicine West Roxbury Vets. Hosp., Boston, 1950-51; sr. attending physician Akron Gen. Med. Ctr., 1956-91, chief of medicine, 1958-62; assoc. clin. prof. medicine Northeastern Ohio U. Coll. of Medicine, Rootstown, 1980-91; ret., 1991; bd. of trustees Akron Gen. Med. Ctr., 1972—, mem. exec. com., 1972-88; bd. dirs. PIE Ins. Co., Cleve. Bd. dirs. Pioneer Western Life Ins. Co., 1959-76. 1st lt. USMC, 1953. Mem. ACP, Mayflower Club (Akron), Alpha Omega Alpha. Republican. Avocations: photography, travel, skiing, woodworking. Home: 395 Delaware Ave Akron OH 44303-1233

KRAUS, HERBERT MYRON, public relations executive; b. Cleve., Sept. 21, 1921; s. Joseph Emil and Eva (Meyers) K.; m. Barbara Cohen, Sept. 9, 1945 (div. Jan. 1, 1955); 1 child, Gale Ann Kraus Bier; m. Catherine Eugenia Capraro, Mar. 5, 1955; 1 child, Claudia Willa Kraus Piper. BA, U. Ill., 1941. Pub. rels. assoc. Nat. Jewish Hosp., Chgo., 1948-51; dir. pub. rels. State of Israel Bond Dr., Chgo., 1951-54; pvt. practice Chgo., 1954-73; pres. Manning, Selvage & Lee of Chgo., 1973-82; pvt. practice Chgo., 1982-85; pres. Kraus Dunham Nikolich P.R., Chgo., 1986-88; sr. counselor Weiser Walek Group, Chgo., 1989-92, Fin. Rels. Bd., Chgo., 1992—; instr. pub. rels. Columbia Coll., Chgo. Co-chmn. John Fischetti Cartoon Awards Com., Chgo., 1957—, Comms. Chgo. XV, 1989; pres. Friends of WFMT, Inc., 1989-90; bd. dirs. Victory Gardens Theatre, Chgo., 1978-95, Am. Jewish Com., Chgo., 1989—; del. Rep. Nat. Conv., Detroit, 1980. Recipient Alschuler award for comty. svc. Am. Jewish Com., 1995. Fellow Pub. Rels. Soc. Am.; mem. Am. Names Soc. (bd. dirs. 1990-93), Am. Friends of Czech Republic, Chgo. Press Vets., Chgo. TV Acad., Publicity Club Chgo. (pres. 1989-90), Chgo. Headline Club. Avocations: theatre, travel, humor writing, poker. Home: 415 W Aldine Ave Apt 7A Chicago IL 60657-3601

KRAUS, JOHN D., electrical engineer, educator; b. Ann Arbor, Mich., June 28, 1910; married; 2 children. BS, U. Mich., 1930, MS, 1931, PhD in Physics, 1933. Asst. physics U. Mich., Ann Arbor, 1931-32, rsch. assoc. dept. engring. rsch., 1934-35, rsch. physicist, 1936-37; rsch. physicist Physicist Rsch. Co., 1937-38; ind. rschr. and cons. Ann Arbor, 1938-40; physicist Naval Ordinance Lab., 1940-43; rsch. assoc. Radio Rsch. Lab. Harvard U., Cambridge, Mass., 1943-46; prof. elec. engring. Ohio State U., 1946—, dir. Radio Obs., 1952-80, Taine G. McDougal prof. elec. engring. and astronomy emeritus, 1970—. Author several textbooks in field. Fellow IEEE (Centennial medal 1984, Sullivant medal 1970, Edison medal 1984, 85, Heinrich Herz medal 1990, chmn. Detroit sect. 1940, bd. editors IRE 1940-55); mem. NAE, Am. Astron. Soc., Am. Phys. Soc. Address: 1854 Home Rd Delaware OH 43015-8924

KRAUS, JOHN DELBERT, investment advisor; b. Pitts., Dec. 7, 1960; s. John Millard and Lois Marie (Cooper) K.; m. Pamela Fay Pfeil, Sept. 7, 1985; children: Joshua, Matthew, Jacob. BA in Acctg., Duquesne U., 1983. CFA. Cons. William M. Mercer Co., Pitts., 1984-89; dir. asset mgmt. Allegheny Fin. Mgmt., Pitts., 1989—; speaker at profl. meetings, 1990—. Mem. Pitts. Soc. Fin. Analysts, Internat. Assn. for Fin. Planning, Am. Assn. Individual Investors. Avocations: photography, gardening. Office: Allegheny Fin Group Ltd 3000 Mcknight East Dr Pittsburgh PA 15237-6439

KRAUS, JOHN WALTER, former aerospace engineering company executive; b. N.Y.C., Feb. 5, 1918; s. Walter Max Kraus and Marian Florance (Nathan) Sandor; m. Janice Edna Utter, June 21, 1947 (dec. Feb. 1981); children: Melinda Jean Kraus Peters, Kim Kohl Kraus; m. Jean Curtis, Aug. 27, 1983. BS, MIT, 1941; MBA, U. So. Calif., 1972. Registered indsl. engr., Calif. From indsl. engr. to indsl. engring. mgr. TRW, Inc., Cleve., 1941-61; spl. asst. Atomics Internat., Chatsworth, Calif., 1961-65; br. chief McDonnell Douglas Astronautics Co., Huntington Beach, Calif., 1966-74; sr. mgr. McDonnell Douglas Space Systems Co., Huntington Beach, Calif., 1983-93; pres. Kraus and DuVall, Inc., Santa Ana, Calif., 1975-83; retired, 1993; cons. Tech. Assocs. So. Calif., Santa Ana, 1974-75. Author: (handbook) Handbook of Reliability Engineering and Management, 1988. Mem. Nat. Def. Industries Assn. (formally Am. Def. Preparedness Assn., life, chmn. tech. div. 1954-57), Nat. Soc. Profl. Engrs. (life), Oasis Sailing Club (commodore 1996—). Republican. Avocations: sailing, reading, gardening. Home: 2001 Commodore Rd Newport Beach CA 92660-4307

KRAUS, KATHLEEN, acting director public safety, Pittsburgh. BA in Polit. Sci., Wesleyan U., Ohio, 1975; MPA, Pa. State U., 1976. Performance auditor City of Pittsburgh, 1982-91; sr. rsch. analyst Pub. Safety Dept., Pitts., 1991-94, acting dir., 1994—. Office: Pub Safety Dept Pub Safety Bldg 100 Grant St Pittsburgh PA 15219-2021*

KRAUS, MARGERY, consultant; b. Franklin, N.J., May 20, 1946; d. Soland Lily (Cvern) Rosen; B.A. in Polit. Sci., Am. U., 1967, M.A. in govt., 1970; m. Stephen Kraus, Sept. 4, 1966; children: Lisa, Evan, Mara. With Close Up Found., Arlington, Va., 1971-84, v.p., 1976-84; exec. v.p. APCO Assocs., Inc., Washington, 1984-88 , pres. and CEO, 1988—; bd. dirs. Internat. Mgmt. and Devel. Inst.; cons., speaker in field. Chmn. bd. Children's Rsch. Inst., Children's Nat. Med. Ctr.; bd. dirs. Close Up Found., End Hunger Network, Pub. Affairs Coun., The Acad. Marshall Found. Home: 9609 Whitecedar Ct Vienna VA 22181-5423 Office: APCO Assocs. 1615 L St NW Ste 900 Washington DC 20036-5623*

KRAUS, MICHAEL JOHN, English language and literature educator; b. Milw., Dec. 8, 1955; s. Martin Ewald and Jane (Ditter) K.; m. Linda Louise Flanigan, July 20, 1991. BA, Marian Coll., 1985; MA, U. Wis., Milw., 1988, postgrad., 1989—. Writing and rsch. lab. dir. Marian Coll., Fond du Lac, Wis., 1986-88, asst. prof., 1988—, chair human rels., 1989-92, co-chair English dept., 1990—, mem. values task force, 1991—; cons. in field. Mem. Fond Du Lac Human Rels. Coun., 1990-93. Recipient Wis. Libr. Honorarium, 1989, Underkofler Teaching Excellence award Wis. Power & Light. Mem. ACLU, MLA, Wis. Humanities Com., Nat. Coun. Tchrs. English, Amnesty Internat., Greenpeace, Delta Epsilon Sigma. Roman Catholic. Avocations: reading, traveling, music, sports, collecting. Office: Marian Coll 45 S National Ave Fond Du Lac WI 54935-4621

KRAUS, NORMA JEAN, industrial relations executive; b. Pitts., Feb. 11, 1931; d. Edward Karl and Alli Alexandra (Hermanson) K. BA, U. Pitts., 1954; postgrad. NYU , 1959-61, Cornell U., 1969-70. Pers. mgr. for several cos., 1957-70; corp. dir. personnel TelePrompter Corp., N.Y.C., 1970-73; exec. asst., speech writer to lt. gov. N.Y. State, Office Lt. Gov., Albany, 1974-79; v.p. human resources, labor relations and stockholder relations Volt Info. Scis., Inc., N.Y.C., 1979—. Co-founder, Manhattan Women's Polit. Caucus, 1971, N.Y. State Women's Polit. Caucus, 1972, vice chair N.Y. State Women's Polit. Caucus, 1978; bd. dirs. Ctr. for Women in Govt., 1977-79. Lt. (s.g.) USNR, 1954-57. Pa. State Senatorial scholar, 1950-54. Mem. Women's Econ. Roundtable. Democrat. Avocations: politics, women's rights. Office: Volt Info Scis Inc 47th Fl 1221 Avenue of the Americas New York NY 10020-1579

KRAUS, PETER LEO, librarian; b. Mineola, N.Y., June 18, 1968; s. Leo Emil Kraus and Barbara Luise (Hausser) Kessler; m. Kristin Louise Borden, July 22, 1995. BA in History, Fla. State U., 1991, MS in Library Sci., 1993. Rsch. asst. Ctr. for Local Govt. U. North Fla., Jacksonville, 1991-92; libr. N.Y. Pub. Libr., N.Y.C., 1994-99; libr. Marriott Libr., U. Utah, Salt Lake City, 1999—. Mem. ALA, Am. Assn. Coll. and Rsch. Librs., Spl. Librs. Assn., Am. Assn. Law Librs. Office: U Utah Marriott Libr Dept Documents & Microforms Salt Lake City UT 84112

KRAUS, SHERRY STOKES, lawyer; b. Richmond, Ky., Aug. 11, 1945; d. Thomas Alexander and Callie (Ratliff) Stokes; m. Eugene John Kraus, Aug. 27, 1966. Student, U. Ky., 1962-64; BS, Roosevelt U., 1966; JD cum laude, Albany Law Sch., 1975; LLM in Taxation, NYU, 1981. Bar: N.Y. 1976, U.S. Dist. Ct. (we. dist.) N.Y. 1976, U.S. Tax Ct. 1986. Law clk. U.S. Tax Ct., Washington, summer 1974; law clk. 4th dept. appellate divsn. N.Y. State Supreme Ct., Rochester, 1975-77; assoc. Nixon, Hargrave, Devans & Doyle, Rochester, 1977-81, 83-84, Harter, Secrest & Emery, Rochester, 1984-86; pvt. practice Rochester, 1986—; faculty grad. tax program Sch. Law, NYU, N.Y.C., 1981-82; prin. tech. adv. to assoc. chief counsel - tech. IRS, Washington, 1983-84; mem. N.Y. State Tax Appeals Adv. Panel on Practice & Procedure, 1998—. Articles editor ABA Tax Articles Periodical, The Tax Lawyer, 1984-88; mng. editor NYU Tax Articles Periodical, NYU Tax Law Rev., 1981-82; lead articles editor Tax Articles Periodical, Albany Law Rev., 1973-75; contbr. articles to profl. jours. David J. Brewer scholar Albany Law Sch., 1973. Mem. ABA, N.Y. State Bar Assn. (tax sect. exec. com. 1984—), Monroe County Bar Assn. (treas. 1990-92), Monroe County Bar Found. (pres. 1994-95), Justinian Soc. Avocations: watercolors, guitar, dulcimer. Office: 513 Times Square Bldg Rochester NY 14614-2078

KRAUS, STEVEN GARY, lawyer; b. Newark, Aug. 22, 1954; s. Leon Judah Kraus and Rose (Cohen) Turchin; m. Jane Susan Sukoneck, June 29, 1980; children: Adam. AB, Brandeis U., 1976; JD, Rutgers U., 1979. Bar: N.J. 1979, Pa. 1979, U.S. Dist. Ct. N.J. 1979. Jud. law sec. to assignment judge Charles A. Rizzi, Superior Ct. N.J., Camden, 1979-80; assoc. Kavesh & Basile, Vineland, N.J., 1980-81, Bennett & Bennett, West Orange, N.J., 1981-82; pvt. practice, Watchung, N.J., 1982—. Mem. ABA, N.J. State Bar Assn. Home: 17 Regent Cir Basking Ridge NJ 07920-1900 Office: 40 Stirling Rd Watchung NJ 07060-5903

KRAUSE, CHARLES JOSEPH, otolaryngologist; b. Des Moines, Apr. 21, 1937; s. William H. and Ruby I. (Hitz) K.; m. Barbara Ann Steelman, June 14, 1962; children—Sharon, John, Ann. B.A., State U. Iowa, 1959, M.D., 1962. Diplomate: Am. Bd. Otolaryngology. Intern Phila. Gen. Hosp., 1962-63; resident in surgery U. Iowa, 1965-66, resident in otolaryngology, 1966-69; fellow dept. plastic surgery Marien Hosp., Stuttgart, W. Ger., 1970; asst. prof. otolaryngology U. Iowa, 1969-72, asso. prof., 1972-75, vice chmn. dept. otolaryngology, 1973-77, prof., 1975-77; prof., chmn. dept. otolaryngology U. Mich. Med. Sch., Ann Arbor, 1977-92; chief clin. affairs U. Mich. Hosps., Ann Arbor, 1986-89; asst. dean for clin. affairs U. Mich., 1986-89, sr. assoc. dean U. Mich. Med. Sch., 1992-96; chief clin. affairs, 1992-95, sr. assoc. hosp. dir., 1995-96, prof. dept. otolaryngology, 1996—. Author book in field; contbr. chpts. to books, articles to profl. jours. Served to capt. USAF, 1963-65. Fellow Am. Soc. Head and Neck Surgery (coun. 1980-83, chmn. rsch. com. 1980-83, pres. 1987-88); mem. AMA, Am. Acad. Otolaryngology Head and Neck Surgery (bd. dirs. 1987-93, sec.-treas. 1987-93, pres.-elect 1995, pres. 1996), Am. Acad. Facial Plastic and Reconstructive Surgery (regional v.p.1977-80, chmn. rsch. com. 1977-80, pres. 1981-82), A.C.S. (adv. coun. otolaryngology 1979-83), Assn. Head and Neck Oncologists Gt. Britain (corr. mem.), Am. Assn. Cosmetic Surgeons, Assn. rsch. in Otolaryngology, Washtenaw County Med. Soc. (exec. com. 1979-82), Mich. State Med. Soc., Mich. Otolaryngol. Soc., Am. Acad. Depts. Otolaryngology, Soc. Unit. Otolaryngologists, Walter P. Work Soc. (pres. 1987), Am. Cancer Soc. (med. adv. com. Washtenaw County unit), Am. Laryngol., Rhinol. and Otol. Soc., Am. Laryngol. Assn., Centurions of Deafness Rsch. Found., Am. Bd. Otolaryngology (bd. dirs 1984—, exam. com. chair 1993—, pres.-elect 1996-98, pres. 1998-2000). Republican. Presbyterian. Home: 3100 Hunting

Valley Dr Ann Arbor MI 48108 Office: U Mich 1904 Taubman Ctr 1500 E Medical Ctr Dr Ann Arbor MI 48109-0600

KRAUSE, CHESTER LEE, publishing company executive; b. Iola, Wis., Dec. 16, 1923; s. Carl and Cora E. (Neil) K. Grad. high sch., Iola. Ind. contractor, 1946-52; chmn. bd. Krause Publs., Inc., Iola, 1952-95. Co-editor: Standard Catalog of World Coins. Chmn. bldg. fund drive Iola Hosp., 1975-80; active Village Bd., 1963-72, Assay Commn., 1961, Marshfield Clinic Nat. Adv. Coun., 1992-96. With AUS, 1943-46. Named Wis. Small Businessman of Yr. Wis. Small Bus. Adminstrn. Adv. Coun., 1990; Melvin Jones fellow, 1989; recipient Meguiar award, 1995, Friend of Automotive History award Soc. Automotive Historians, 1995. Mem. Soc. of Automobile Historians (Friends of Automobile Historians 1995), Am. Numis. Assn. (medal of merit, Farren Zerbe award, Hall of Fame, Lifetime Achievement award), Can. Numis. Assn. Home: 290 E Iola St Iola WI 54945-9620 Office: 700 E State St Iola WI 54945-9642 *To publish on time, all the time.*

KRAUSE, DOROTHY SIMPSON, fine artist, educator; b. Mobile, Ala., Sept. 22, 1940; d. Edwin Holland and Ethel Alberta (Simmons) Tuthill; m. Richard Alan Krause, July 7, 1978; 1 child, Laura Simpson Flynn. BA in Painting with honors, Montevallo U., 1960; MA in Art Edn., U. Ala., 1962; EdD in Art Edn., Pa. State U., 1968. Assoc. prof. Va. Commonwealth U., 1969-74; dir. grad. art programs Mass. Coll. Art, Boston, 1974-75, dean grad. and continuing edn., 1975-82, v.p. adminstrn. and fin., 1982-85, prof. computer graphics, 1985—; corp. curator Iris Graphics, Bedford, Mass., 1992—; cons. to Kodak, Concord, Digital Equipment Corp., Burlington, Mass.; artist-in-residence Digitial Atelier, NMAA Smithsonian Instn., 1997; mem. Do While Studio. Represented in mus. collection Nat. Mus. Am. Art, Washington, 1997, DeCordova Mus., Lincoln, Mass., Zimmerlie Mus., Rutgers, Spencer Mus., Lawrence, Kans. Mem. Boston Visual Artist Union, Women's Caucus for Art, Coll. Art Assn. Home: PO Box 421 Marshfield Hills MA 02051

KRAUSE, HARRY DIETER, law educator; b. Görlitz, Germany, Apr. 23, 1932; came to U.S., 1951, naturalized, 1954; s. Renatus and Ellen (Abel-Musgrave) K.; m. Eva Maria Disselnkötter, Aug. 30, 1957; children: Philip Renatus, Thomas Walther, Peter Herbert. Student, Freie U., Berlin, 1950-51; B.A., U. Mich., 1954, J.D., 1958. Bar: Mich. 1959, D.C. 1959, Ill. 1963, U.S. Supreme Ct. 1963. With firm Covington & Burling, 1958-60; with Ford Motor Co., Dearborn, Mich., 1960-63; asst. prof. to prof. law U. Ill., Champaign, 1963-82, Alumni Disting. prof. law, 1982-89, Max L. Rowe prof. law, 1989-94, tchg. prof. emeritus, 1994—; Fulbright prof. U. Bonn, Germany 1976-77; vis. assoc. Ctr. Socio-Legal studies, 1977; vis. fellow Wolfson Coll. Oxford (Eng.) U., 1984; U.S. Del. to Hague Conf. on Pvt. Internat. Law Treaty on Internat. Adoptions, 1990-93; commr. Uniform State Laws, Ill., 1991-97; reporter Uniform Parentage Act, 1969-73, Rev. Uniform Adoption Act, 1979-84, Uniform Putative Fathers Act, 1985, Nat. Conf. Commrs. on Uniform State Laws; mem. Internat. Acad. Comparative Law Rapporteur U.S., Uppsala, 1966, Teheran, 1974, Budapest, 1978, Caracas, 1983, Sydney, 1986, gen. rep. Athens, 1994; cons. on family law and social legis. to fed. and state legis., jud. and exec. commns.; vis. prof. law U. Mich., 1981, U. Miami, 1987; Culverhouse prof. Stetson U., 1991. Author: Illegitimacy: Law and Social Policy, 1971, Family Law: Cases and Materials, 1976, 4th edit., 1998, Kinship Relations, 1976, Family Law in a Nutshell, 1977, 3d edit., 1995, Child Support in America: The Legal Perspective, 1981; law editor: (with R. Walker et. al.) Inclusion Probabilities in Parentage Testing, 1983, Family Law (West's Blackletter Series), 1988, 2d edit., 1996, International Library of Essays in Law and Legal Theory: Family Law I: Society and Family, 1992, Family Law II: Cohabitation, Marriage and Divorce, 1992, Child Law: Parent, Child and State, 1992; bd. editors Mich. Law Rev., 1957-58, Family Law Quar., 1971—, Jour. Legal Edn., 1988-91, Am. Jour. Comparative Law, 1991—, and others. With U.S. Army, 1954-56. Recipient von Humboldt Found. rsch. prize, 1992; Guggenheim fellow, 1969-70; assoc. Ctr. Advanced Study U. Ill., 1970, 79; German Marshall Fund U.S. fellow, 1977-78; Hewlett fellow, Australia, 1984; German Acad. Exch. Svc. fellow, 1985. Mem. ABA (past mem. coun. sect. family law, com. chmn.), Am. Law Inst. (adviser family law project 1990—), Ill. Bar Assn. (past mem. coun. sect. on family law, internat. law), Am. Assn. Comparative Study of Law (dir. 1980—), Internat. Soc. Family Law (v.p. 1973-77, exec. coun. 1977-97), Order of Coif. Home: 903 Silver St Urbana IL 61801-6336 Office: U Ill Coll Law Champaign IL 61820

KRAUSE, HEATHER DAWN, data processing executive; b. Kansas City, Kans., May 6, 1956; d. Jack E. Firth and Bonnie Jo (Reeves) Cupps; m. Kerry Murray Krause, May 23, 1981. Cert., Kansas City Skill Ctr., 1980. Cert. drafting tchr.; cert. in bus. supervision; cert. in Novell Netware system adminstrn. Assoc. drafter Black & Veatch, Kansas City, Mo., 1980; technician mech. design Wilcox Electric, Kansas City, 1980; network adminstr. Smith & Loveless, Inc., Lenexa, Kans., 1980—; owner Digital Design Technologies, Kansas City, Mo., 1989—; tech. editor Que Books Macmillan Computer Pub., 1994—; instr. Longview C.C., Lee's Summit, Mo., 1987-93. Mem. NAFE, Heartland Windows User Group, Phi Theta Kappa. Democrat. Avocations: camping, fishing, hiking, skiing, web site development. Home: PO Box 11319 Kansas City MO 64112-0319

KRAUSE, HELEN FOX, physician, otolaryngologist; b. Boston, Mar. 20, 1932; d. Nathan and Frances Lena (Rich) Fox; children: Merrick Eli, Beth Riva Harper, Kim Debra Codd. BS, U. Maine, 1954; MD, Tuft U., 1958. Diplomate Am. Bd. Otolaryngology. Intern Health Ctr. Hosps. Pitts., 1958-59; resident Eye & Ear Hosp., Children's Hosp., VA Hosp., 1959-62; pvt. practice Pitts., 1962—; mem. otolaryngology adv. bd. U.S. Pharmacopea, 1991-96, chmn., 1995—; bd. govs. Am. Acad. Otolaryngology H & N Surgery, 1982-89, 90—; clin. assoc. prof. U. Pitts. Sch. Medicine, Pa. State U. Hershey Med. Coll.; vis. prof. Pan Hellenic Otorhinolaryngology Soc., Crete, Greece, 1993, Panama, Argentina, 1998, China, Hong Kong, 1999; pres., dir. 1st World Congress of Otorhinolaryngologic Allercy, Endoscopy and Laser Surgery, Athens, 1998. Author, editor: Otolaryngic Allergy and Immunology, 1989; lectr., vis. prof. Singapore, Bangkok, Hong Kong (multiple tng. programs 1990); contbr. chpts. to books and articles to profl. jours. Pres. North Hills Jewish Community Ctr., Pitts., 1973-74; cons. North Allegheny Sch. Bd., Pitts., 1977; lectr. North Allegheny Sr. High Sch., Wexford, 1979-84; chmn. Desert Storm Project, North Hills Bus. and Profl. Women, 1991. Rsch. scholar Jackson Meml. Labs., Bar Harbor, Maine, 1954; recipient Disting. Svc. award Pa. Acad. Otolaryngology, 1993, Hon. Achievement award Am. Acad. Otolaryngology Head and Neck Surgery, 1993. Fellow ACS, Am. Acad. Otolaryngologic Allergy (pres. 2984-85), Svc. award 1990, cert. appreciation 1991, Pres.'s award 1997, Spl. Achievement award 1997), Am. Acad. Facial Plastic and Rsch. Surgery; mem. Pa. Acad. Otolaryngology (pres. 1989-90), Internat. Soc. Otorhinolaryngic Allergy and Immunology (pres. 1995-98), Pitts. Otological Soc. (pres. 1983-85), Phi Beta Kappa, Phi Kappa Phi. Office: 9104 Babcock Blvd Ste 4110 Pittsburgh PA 15237-5818

KRAUSE, JAMES R., urologist; b. Cleve., Dec. 8, 1945; s. George R. and Sophie C. Krause; m. June 15, 1969; children: Jonathan, Karen. BA, U. Pa., 1968; MD, Case Western Res. U., 1972. Diplomate Am. Bd. Urology. Pvt. practice, St. Petersburg, 1977—. Contbr. articles to med. jours. Mem. Pinellas County Med. Soc. (bd. dirs. 1985-87). Office: St Petersburg Suncoast Med Group 1099 5th Ave N Saint Petersburg FL 33705

KRAUSE, JERRY (JEROME RICHARD KRAUSE), professional basketball team executive; b. Chgo., Apr. 6, 1939; s. Paul and Gertrude (Sherman) K.; m. Sharon Bergofsky, Oct. 16, 1969 (div. 1971); m. Thelma Frankel, July 1, 1979; children: Stacy, David. Student, Bradley U., 1957-61. Dir. scouting Balt. Bullets Basketball Club, 1962-65, 67-69; dir. scouting Chgo. Bulls Basketball Club, 1969-72, v.p. basketball ops., 1985—; dir. scouting Phoenix Suns Basketball Club, 1972-75; gen. mgr. Portland Baseball Club, Pacific Coast League, 1966; scout Cleve. Indians Baseball Club, 1967-72, Oakland (Calif.) Athletics Baseball Club, 1973-75; dir. scouting Los Angeles Lakers Basketball Club, 1977-79; supr. Midwestern scouting Seattle Mariners Baseball Club, 1977-79; spl. assignment scout Chgo. White Sox Baseball Club, 1979-85. Contbr. articles to profl. jours. Named Exec. of Yr. NBA, 1988, named to Bradley U. Athletic Hall of Fame, 1992. Mem. Nat. Basketball Assn. (competition com., Exec. of Yr. 1988). Office: Chgo Bulls 1901 W Madison St Chicago IL 60612-2459*

KRAUSE, JOHN L., optometrist; b. Portland, Oreg., Oct. 26, 1917; m. Nancy D., Sept. 30, 1942; children: Diana L., Karen L., Ronald L. O.D., Ill. Coll. Optometry, 1947. Practice optometry, Niles, Ill., 1956-88; USAF Med. Service liaison officer, Northwestern U. Med. Sch., Chgo., 1964-91. Author: Sight Check Your Child, 1961, Holiday Fax, 1991, Win-Win, Inc., 1994; contbr. articles to nat. mags.; patentee card holder, 1967. Bd. overseers S.E. Univ. Coll. Optometry, North Miami Beach, Fla., 1993; liaison to optometry Nat. Alliance Mental Health, 1993. Mem. ins. coun. City Tamarac, Fla., 1995—; ombudsman State of Fla., Broward County, 1996—. Served with U.S. Army, 1941-45, to lt. col. USAF, ret., 1970. Decorated Bronze Star with cluster. Mem. Am. Optometric Assn., Ill. Optometric Assn., Am. Optometric Found., Am. Interprofl. Assn., Armed Forces Optometric Soc., Air Force Assn., Ret. Officers Assn., Fla. Pub. Health Assn. (chmn.-elect vision sect. 1992), Fla. Ret. Optometrists Assn. (pres. 1993-95), Kappa Phi Delta, Phi Theta Upsilon, Phi Mu Delta. Avocations: golf, stamp collecting, autographs. Home: 7270 Fairfax Dr Tamarac FL 33321-4305

KRAUSE, LOIS RUTH BREUR, chemistry educator; b. Paterson, N.J., Mar. 26, 1946; d. George L. and Ruth Margaret (Farquhar) Breur; m. Bruce N. Pritchard, 1968 (div. May 1982); children: John Douglas, Tiffany Anne,; m. Robert H. Krause, June 16, 1990. Student, Keuka Coll., 1964-65; BS in Chemistry cum laude, Fairleigh Dickinson U., 1980, MAT summa cum laude, 1994; postgrad., Stevens Inst. Tech.; PhD, Clemson U., 1996. With dept. R & D UniRoyal, Wayne, N.J., 1966-68, Jersey State Chem. Co., North Haledon, 1968-69, Inmont, Clifton, N.J., 1969; from chemist to sr. analyst Lever Bros., Edgewater, N.J., 1976-80; process engr. Bell Telephone Labs., Murray Hill, N.J., 1980-84, RCA, Somerville, N.J., 1984-86; sr. engr. electron beam lithography ops. Gain Electronics Corp., Somerville, 1986-88; ind. tech. cons. Pritchard Assocs., Budd Lake, N.J., 1988-92; tchr. of math. and scis. Mt. Olive bd. Edn. (temporary assignments), 1990-92; tchr. chemistry Morris Hills Regional Dist., 1992-93; instr. chemistry, vis. asst. prof. edn. Clemson U., 1994-95, instr. chem. labs., 1994-96, vis. asst. prof. edn., 1995-96, vis. asst. prof. chemistry, 1996-98, lectr. phys. scis. dept. geol. scis., 1998—; faculty fellow Clemson U., 1999—; presenter workshops and profl. papers for profl. confs. Author: How We Learn and Why We Don't: Student Survival Guide, 1999; contbr. articles to profl. jours.; patentee package design. Troop leader, trainer, cons. Bergen County council Girl Scouts U.S., 1969-80, troop leader Morris Area council, 1980-83, head com. Mt. Olive twp., 1980-81; den leader, den leader coach, trainer Boy Scouts Am., 1973-76. Peter Sammartino scholar, 1994. Fellow Am. Inst. Chemists; mem. IEEE (sr., Components, Hybrids and Mfg. Tech. Soc. semicondr. tech. subcom. electronic components conf. program com. 1981-86), NRA (life mem., endowment mem.), AAAS, ASCD, APA, AAUW, Am. Soc. Quality Control, Soc. Women Engrs., Am. Chem. Soc., Assn. Women in Sci., N.Y. Acad. Scis., Nat. Sci. Tchrs. Assn., Nat. Woodlot Owners Assn., Arbor Day Found., Mensa, Marine Corps League Aux., Clan Farquharson U.S.A. (asst. commr. for S.C. 1997-98, commr. Carolinas region 1998—, clan genealogist 1999—), 2d Amendment Found. (life), Clan Stewart Soc. of Am., Catawba Valley Scottish Soc. (life patron), Scottish Am. Mil. Soc. (color guard), Phi Omega Epsilon, Phi Delta Kappa (editor Clemson Kappan), Alpha Epsilon Lambda. Republican. Episcopalian. Achievements include work in ultra fine line electron beam lithography, statis. process control, rsch. in learning and cognition; designed graduate course of student centered instruction. E-mail: krause@clemson.edu. Home: 303 Cherokee Hills Dr Pickens SC 29671-8619 Office: Clemson U 442 Brackett Hall Clemson SC 29634-1908

KRAUSE, MANFRED OTTO, physicist; b. Stuttgart, Germany, Mar. 11, 1931; came to U.S., 1960, naturalized, 1970; s. Friedrich Bernhard and Friedel Ernstine K.; m. Josephine Winifred Cammer, Dec. 26, 1963. B.S., Technische Universitat Stuttgart, 1954, diploma in physics, 1957, Ph.D., 1960. Sr. physicist Wm. H. Johnston Labs., Inc., Balt., 1960-63; sr. scientist Oak Ridge Nat. Lab., 1963-95; cons. Oak Ridge, 1995—; exch. prof. U. Paris, 1975. Contbr. articles on electron, charge and x-ray spectrometry to sci. publs., chpts. to books. Recipient Alexander von Humboldt award, 1975-76. Fellow Am. Phys. Soc.; mem. AAAS, Smithsonian Instn., Natural History Soc., Audubon Soc. Discoverer x-ray spectrometry based on photoelectric effect, 1971. Home: 125 Baltimore Dr Oak Ridge TN 37830-7837 Office: PO Box 2008 Oak Ridge TN 37831-6201

KRAUSE, MARJORIE N., biochemist, computer scientist; b. Chgo., July 25, 1937; d. Robert Mortimer Krause and Eleanor Driese. *By the age of 18, Marj Krause's maternal great grandfather, Earnest Wehmhoeffer, had immigrated from Germany to America and had set up a wagon shop. Marj Krause's paternal great grandfather, Robert Krause, from Prussia, was also among the early settlers in the region and was a recognized leader in reorganizing the community into what is now known as Glenwood, Illinois.* BS, Mich. State U., 1959; MS, Cleve. State U., 1986. Cert. tchr., Mich.; cert. medical technologist in hematology Am. Soc. Clinical Pathologists. Technician Dartmouth Coll., Hanover, N.H., 1960-66, U. Vt., Burlington, 1966-70; technologist Case We. Res. U., Cleve., 1971-75, 89-93, U. Hosps., Cleve., 1975-79; lab technologist, med. technologist Cleve. Clinic Found., 1979-89; computer lab technician Lakeland C.C., Kirtland, Ohio, 1996-97, 99—; narrator Sea World Cleve., Aurora, Ohio, 1998; judge youth sci. fair Ohio Acad. Scis., Columbus, Ohio, 1995, 96. Vol. Cleve. Orch., 1972—, Playhouse Sq. Found., Cleve., 1988—. Recipient Cert. Recognition, Playhouse Sq. Found., 1995, 96, 98. Avocations: natural history, bird watching, opera, theater, classical music. Home: 4285 River St Apt 219 Willoughby OH 44094

KRAUSE, RICHARD MICHAEL, medical scientist, government official, educator; b. Marietta, Ohio, Jan. 4, 1925; s. Ellis L. and Jennie Mae (Waterman) K. B.A., Marietta Coll., 1947, D.Sc. (hon.), 1978; M.D., Case Western Res. U., 1952; D.Sc. (hon.), U. Rochester, 1979, Med. Coll. Ohio, Toledo, 1981, Hahnemann Med. Coll. and Hosp., 1982; LLD (hon.), Thomas Jefferson U., 1982. Rsch. fellow dept. preventive medicine Case Western Res. U., 1950-51; intern Ward Med. Service, Barnes Hosp., St. Louis, 1952-53; asst. resident Ward Med. Service, Barnes Hosp., 1953-54; asst. physician to hosp. Rockefeller Inst., 1954-57, asst. prof., assoc. physician to hosp., 1957-61; prof. epidemiology Sch. Medicine, Washington U., St. Louis, 1962-66; assoc. prof. medicine Sch. Medicine, Washington U., 1962-65, prof. medicine, 1965-66; assoc. prof., physician to hosp. Rockefeller U., 1966-68, prof., sr. physician, 1968-75; dir. Rockefeller U. (Animal Rsch. Ctr.), 1974-75, Nat. Inst. Allergy and Infectious Diseases, NIH, HEW, Bethesda, Md., 1975-84; USPHS surgeon, 1975-77, asst. surgeon gen., 1977-84; dean Emory U. Sch. Medicine, Atlanta, 1984-89, Robert W. Woodruff prof. medicine, 1984-89; mem. program com. Inst. Medicine, 1986-87; sr. sci. adv. Fogarty Internat. Ctr. NIH, Bethesda, 1989—; Bd. dirs. Mo.-St. Louis Heart Assn., 1962-66, mem. research com., 1963-66; mem. exec. com. council on rheumatic fever and congenital heart disease Am. Heart Assn., 1963-66, chmn. council research study com., 1963-66, mem. assn. research com., 1963-66, mem. policy com., 1966-70; mem. commn. streptococcal and staphylococcal diseases U.S. Armed Forces Epidemiol. Bd., 1963-72, dep. dir., 1968-72; bd. dirs. N.Y. Heart Assn., 1967-73, chmn. adv. council on research, 1969-71, mem. dirs. council, 1973-75; cons., mem. coccal expert com. WHO, 1967—; mem. steering com. Biomed. Sci. Scientific Working Group, WHO, 1978; mem. infectious disease adv. com. Nat. Inst. Allergy and Infectious Disease, NIH, 1970-74; bd. dirs. Royal Soc. Medicine Found., Inc., 1971-77, treas., 1973-75; bd. dirs. Allergy and Asthma Found. Am., 1976-77, Lupus Found. Am., 1977-79. Assoc. editor: Jour. Immunology, 1963-71; sect. editor: Viral and Microbial Immunology, 1974-75; editor: Jour. Exptl. Medicine, 1973-75; adv. editor, 1976-84; mem. editorial bd. Bacteriological Revs, 1969-73, Infection and Immunity, 1970-78, Immunochemistry, 1973-80, Clin. Immunology and Immunopathology, 1976-78; contbr. numerous articles to profl. jours. Served with U.S. Army, 1944-46. Decorated Gumhuria medal Egypt; recipient Disting. Service medal HEW, 1979; C. William O'Neal Disting. Am. Service award; Robert Koch Medal in Gold, Berlin, 1985; Sr. U.S. Scientist award Alexander Von Humboldt Found., Fed. Republic Germany, 1986. Mem. U.S. Nat. Acad. Scis., Inst. Medicine, Assn. Am. Physicians, Am. Acad. Allergy, Am. Soc. Biol. Chemists, Am. Soc. Clin. Investigation, Am. Assn. Immunologists, Am. Soc. Microbiology, Harvey Soc., Am. Coll. Allergists, AAAS, Infectious Diseases Soc. Am., Royal Soc. Medicine, Practitioner's Soc. N.Y., Am. Epidemiol. Soc. Clubs: Century Assn. (N.Y.C.); Cosmos (Washington). Rsch. on pathogenesis and epidemiology of streptococcal diseases; immunochem. studies on streptococcal antigens; immunogenetics; recognition of rabbit antibodies with molecular uniformity, genetics of immune response. Home: 4000 Cathedral Ave NW Apt 413B Washington DC 20016-5268 Office: NIH Fogerty Internat Ctr Rm 202 16 Center Dr Bldg 16 Bethesda MD 20892-6705

KRAUSE, SONJA, chemistry educator; b. St. Gall, Switzerland, Aug. 10, 1933; came to U.S., 1939; d. Friedrich and Rita (Maas) K.; m. Walter Walls Goodwin, Nov. 27, 1970. BS, Rensselaer Poly. Inst., 1954; PhD, U. Calif.-Berkeley, 1957. Sr. phys. chemist Rohm & Haas Co., Phila., 1957-64; vol. U.S. Peace Corps, Nigeria, 1964-65; asst. lectr. Lagos U.; asst. prof. Gondar Health Coll. U.S. Peace Corps, Ethiopia, 1965-66; vis. asst. prof. U. So. Calif., Los Angeles, 1966-67; chemistry faculty Rensselaer Poly. Inst., Troy, N.Y., 1967—; prof. Rensselaer Poly. Inst., 1978—; mem. coun. Gordon Rsch. Conf., 1981-83; mem. com. on polymers and engrng. NRC, 1992-94; sabbatical Inst. Charles Sadron, Ctr. Rsch. on Macromolecules, Strasbourg, France, 1987. Author: (with others) Chemistry of Environment, 1978; editor: Molecular Electro-Optics, 1981; mem. editorial adv. bd. Macromolecules, 1982-84. Bd. dirs. Nat. Plastics Ctr. and Mus., Leominster, Mass., 1996—. Fellow Am. Phys. Soc. (coun. divsn. biol. physics 1980-93); mem. IUPAC (assoc.), Am. Chem. Soc. (chmn. ea. N.Y. sect. 1981-82, councillor 1991-95, adv. bd. petroleum rsch. fund 1979-81, assoc. mem. com. on edn. 1993-95, assoc. mem. internat. com. 1996), Biophys. Soc. (coun. 1977), N.Y. Acad. Scis., Sigma Xi (pres. Rensselaer Poly Inst. chpt. 1984-85). Office: Rensselaer Poly Inst Dept Chemistry Troy NY 12180

KRAUSE, STEVEN ALBERT, writer; b. Wausau, Wis., Apr. 24, 1951; s. Albert and Jean (Otto) K. BS in Biology, U. Wis., Stevens Point, 1974. Freelance writer popular pubs. Author: Wines From the Wilds, 1982, 96, In Search of the Wild Dewberry, 1983, reprinted as Drinks From the Wilds, 1996. Home: 1313 Emter St Wausau WI 54401-6122

KRAUSE, THOMAS EVANS, record promotion and radio consultant; b. Mpls., Dec. 17, 1951; s. Donald Bernhard and Betty Ann (Nokleby) K.; m. Barbara Ann Kaufman, Aug. 17, 1974 (div. Apr. 1978); m. Nicole Michelle Purkerson, Aug. 13, 1988; children: Andrew Todd Evans, Allison Michelle. Student, Augsburg Coll., 1969-73; BA, Hastings Coll., 1975. Lic. 3d class with broadcast endorsement FCC. Air personality Sta. KHAS Radio, Hastings, Nebr., 1974-75; air personality, news dir. Sta. KWSL Radio, Sioux City, Iowa, 1975-76; asst. program dir. Sta. KISD Radio, Sioux Falls, S.D., 1976-78; music dir. Sta. KVOX Radio, Fargo, N.D., 1978; program dir. Sta. KPRQ Radio, Salt Lake City, 1978-79; air personality Sta. KIOA Radio, Des Moines, 1980; program dir., ops. mgr. Sta. KKSS Radio, Sioux Falls, 1981-83; program dir. Stas. KIYS/KBBK Radio, Boise, Idaho, 1983-87; program dir., ops. mgr. Sta. WSRZ AM/FM Radio, Sarasota, Fla., 1988-90; owner, cons. Tom Evans Mktg., Seattle, 1990—; editor., pub. Northwest Log, Seattle, 1991-96; mgr. neverMAN, 1994—; co-founder Sta. KCMR Radio, Augsburg Coll., Mpls., 1973; TV show coord./host Z-106 Hottraxx, Sarasota, 1988-90; air personality/guest disc jockey various radio stas., Pacific N.W., 1990—; host Am. Music Report. Sta. KIX-106 Radio, Canberra, Australia, 1992; instr. Sta. KGRG-FM and KENU-AM, Green River Coll., Auburn, Wash., 1994—. Contbr. articles to various trade publs., mags. Bd. judges Loyola U. Marconi Awards, Chgo., 1992-93; bd. dirs. Habitat for Humanity, Snohomish County, Wash., 1992-96, Martin Luther King Day Celebration, Sarasota County, Fla., 1989-90, Shoreline/So. County YMCA, 1992-95; dist. coord. Carter for Pres., Nebr. 1st Dist., 1975-76; hon. chair March of Dimes Walk Am., Sioux Falls, 1977; head coach Beavers Baseball Club, 1999—; media vol., MC or spokesperson M.S. Soc., MDA, Am. Diabetes Assn., Human Soc., others. Mem. Free Methodist Ch. Avocations: sports, films, science fiction, photography, travel. Office: Tom Evans Mktg 16426 65th Ave W Lynnwood WA 98037-2710

KRAUSE, TIMOTHY GILBERT, English educator; b. Chippewa Falls, Wis., July 17, 1969; s. Gregory Mitchem and Donna Mae (Ripienski) K.; m. Kimberly Catherine Taft, June 18, 1994. BS in Acctg., St. Johns U., 1991; MA in English, St. Cloud State U., 1993; postgrad., Purdue U., 1997. Acct. St. Johns U., Collegeville, Minn., 1988-97; pvt. practice West Lafayette, Ind., 1995-97; pub. affairs counselor Cargill, Inc., Mpls., 1997—; cons. Mpls. Pub. Libr.; instr. Princeton Rev., Chgo., 1994-96; educator St. Cloud (Minn.) State U., 1991-93, Purdue U., West Lafayette, Ind., 1993-97; lectr. Richard Hadley Profl. Devel., West Lafayette, 1996; presenter in field. Author: (textbook) Wired Resumes; reviewer IEEE Profl. Comm., 1996—, Tech. Comm. Quar., 1997—; contbr. articles to profl. jours. Mem. MLA, Nat. Coun. Tchrs. English, Assn. for Bus. Comm. (book rev. editor 1997-98), Rhetoric Soc. Am., Conf. on Coll. Composition and Comm., Alliance for Computers & Writing, Phi Kappa Phi. Avocations: web design, fishing. Home: 5441 Scott Ave N Crystal MN 55429 Office: Cargill Inc PO Box 5625 Pub Affairs Minneapolis MN 55440

KRAUSE, WALTER, retired economics educator, consultant; b. Portland, Oreg., Jan. 12, 1919. PhD, Harvard U., 1945. John F. Murray prof. internat. bus. and econs. emeritus U. Iowa, Iowa City, 1987—. Mem. Phi Beta Kappa. Home: Walden Pl 315 2423 Walden Rd Iowa City IA 52246-4130

KRAUSE, WERNER WILLIAM, plastics company executive; b. Milw., Jan. 16, 1937; s. Erhard Werner and Mary T. (Kojis) K.; m. Susan Mary Kramer, Mar. 29, 1958; children: Patricia, David, Steven. BBA, U. Wis., Milw., 1958; MBA, U. Chgo., 1971. CPA. Sr. auditor Arthur Andersen & Co., Milw., 1958-61; mgr. corp. cost acctg. Jewett & Sherman & Co., Milw., 1961-62; sr. fin. analyst Miller Brewing Co., Milw., 1962-66; mgr. capital planning Allis Chalmers, W. Allis, Wis., 1966-72; sr. v.p. fin. Vinyl Plastics Inc., Sheboygan, Wis, 1972-93, sr. v.p., 1993-95; bd. dirs. Sheboygan Devel. Corp.; v.p. Woodhaven Enterprises, Sheboygan, 1981—. Bd. dirs. U. Chgo. Grad. Sch. Bus., 1986-90, Sheboygan County Med./Industry Coalition, 1986-91; co-chmn. Sheboygan Water Quality Task Force, 1986-90; bd. dirs. Sheboygan City YMCA, 1989—, treas., 1989-93; bd. dirs. Manitowoc Maritime Mus., 1991-94. Mem. Associated Industries and Mfrs. (bd. dirs. 1981-87), Soc. Plastics Industry (vice chmn. fin. com. 1987), Planning Execs. Inst., Sheboygan Yacht Club, Rotary. Republican. Lutheran. Avocations: sailing, woodworking.

KRAUSE, WILLIAM AUSTIN, engineering executive; b. Lennox, Calif., Nov. 16, 1930; s. William August and Grace Olive (Davies) K.; m. Judith M.; children: Kenneth R., Michael W., Richard R., William R. A.A., Pasadena City Coll., 1950; B.S. in Engring., U. Calif.-Berkeley, 1952. Registered profl. engr., Mont., La., N.Mex., Fla., Miss., Tex., Calif., Del., Ky., Okla., Ala., Colo., Ill., Kans., Mich., W.Va.; also The Netherlands. Supt., mgr. constrn. operations C.F. Braun Co., Alhambra, Calif., 1952-63; gen. mgr. Lummus Co., Bloomfield, N.J., 1963-69; pres., chief exec. officer J.F. Pritchard & Co., Kansas City, Mo., 1969-73, Internat. Systems and Controls Process Group, Houston, 1969-73; pres. Sigma-Chapman, Inc., Houston, 1973-86; chmn. Omnipure, Inc., Houston, 1975-86; pres. Chapman Engrs. Inc., 1973-90, also bd. dirs.; chmn. Chapman Engrs. Internat. Inc., 1988-89; pres. Krause, Inc., 1990—; dir., mem. audit and exec. coms. Camco, Inc., Houston. Patentee in field. Mem. Young Pres.'s Orgn. (dir. 1973-77, chmn. exec. com. 1975-76, sec. Kansas City chpt. 1971-72), World Pres. Orgn., ASME, Am. Inst. Chem. Engrs. (lectr. project mgmt.), AIME, Nat., Calif., Tex. socs. profl. engrs., Calif. Alumni Assn., Univ. Club (Houston, bd. govs.). Home and Office: 10 S Briar Hollow Ln Unit 93 Houston TX 77027-2891

KRAUSEN, ANTHONY SHARNIK, surgeon; b. Phila., Feb. 22, 1944; s. B.M. and Kay S. (Sharnik) K.; m. Susan Elizabeth Park, Sept. 6, 1970; children: Nicole, Allison. Student, Germantown Acad., 1949-61; BA, Princeton U., 1965; MD, U. Mich., 1969. Intern Presbyn. Med. Ctr., Denver, 1969-70; resident St. Joseph Hosp., Denver, 1970-71, Barnes Hosp., St. Louis, 1972-76; with Milw. Med. Clinic, 1976—, head dept. facial plastic surgery, 1984—; mem. staffs Columbia, St. Michael, St. Mary Hosp., Oankee. Pres. Contemporary Art Soc., Milw. Art Mus., 1983; bd. dirs. Friends of Art. Served with U.S. Army Nat. Guard, 1970-76. Fellow ACS, Am. Acad. Cosmetic Surgery, Am. Acad. Facial Plastic and Reconstructive Surgery, Am. Acad. Otalaryngology; mem. Nat. Neurofibramatosis Soc. (med. advisor Wis. chpt. 1985-92), Wis. Otolaryngological Soc. Clubs: Ivy (Princeton, N.J.), Town Club (Milw.). Office: 3003 W Good Hope Rd Milwaukee WI 53209-2042

KRAUSER, JANICE, special education educator; b. Chgo., Apr. 30, 1951; d. John Francis and June (Fogle) K. BS, U. Tenn., 1973; MEd, Fla. Atlantic U., 1979. Tchr. John Sevier Elem. Sch., Knoxville, Tenn., 1973-76;

substitute tchr. Broward County Schs., Ft. Lauderdale, Fla., 1976-78; tchr. Broward Estates Elem. Sch., Ft. Lauderdale, 1978-79, Attucks Mid. Sch., Hollywood, Fla., 1979-81; tchr., spl. edn. specialist South Broward High Sch., Hollywood, 1981-92; spl. edn. specialist New River Middle Sch., Ft. Lauderdale, 1992—; selected mem. Fla. Spkrs. Bur.; state-wide design team mem. of inclusion materials for sch.-based adminstrs.; mem. Fla. Comprehensive Sys. Pers. Devel. Co-author: (curriculum) Fundamental Math I and II, Consumer Math, Applied English I, II, and III, Fundamental English I, II, III; published photographer. Zone chmn. U.S.Water Polo, Colorado Springs, 1984-92, 98—, bd. dirs. 1998—; treas. Fla. Water Polo, 1982-97; dist. del. U.S. Masters Swimming, 1987-95; mem. internat. congress Internat. Swimming Hall of Fame, Ft. Lauderdale, 1994—, (bd. dirs. 1989-93); water polo referee VII World Master's Swimming Championships, Casablanca, Morocco, 1998. Named Swimming Coach of Yr. Hollywood Sun-Tattle, 1984-85, Head Water Polo Coach U.S. Olympic Festival, 1986, 90; selected to Pine Crest Sch. Athletic Hall of Fame, 1998, U.S. Water Polo Hall of Fame, 1998. Mem. ASCD, Coun. Exceptional Children, Fla. Atlantic U. Alumni Assn., Pine Crest Alumni Assn. (bd. dirs. 1993—, sec. 1995-97, v.p. 1999—), Broward Libr. Found., Phi Delta Kappa; v.p. Broward County Coun. for Exceptional Children, 1998—. Avocations: needlepoint, reading, sewing, volunteering. Home: 1610 NE 43rd St Oakland Park FL 33334-5509

KRAUSER, PETER B., lawyer, political party executive; b. Phila., May 5, 1947. BA, Northwestern U.; JD, U. Pa. Atty. Thompson, Hine & Flory, Largo, Md., 1988-94, Krauser & Taub, Largo, 1994-98; chmn. Md. State Dem. Party, 1997—. Mem. Assn. Dem. Chairs (chmn. 1997—). Office: Krauser & Taub 9200 Basil Ct Ste 300 Largo MD 20774

KRAUSER, ROBERT STANLEY, health care executive; b. N.Y.C., Aug. 24, 1937; s. Benjamin and Eva (Ferester) K.; m. Mary Kay Edwards, June 12, 1977; children: Robert Edwards, Kathryn Edwards. *Wife, Mary Kay, cum laude Carlow College, 1959, is senior vice president of merchandising for Bali Company, a division of Sara Lee Corporation and has received numerous awards in the intimate apparel industry, including the 1992 Femmy Award. Son, Robert, a 1997 graduate of Greenwich High School, received the Thomas H. Chandris award for exemplary "humanitarian spirit, friendliness and concern for others". He was captain of the varsity hockey team and MVP 1996, member of the varsity lacrosse team and chamber singers, class vice president and is currently a member of the Colgate University Class of 2001. Daughter Kathryn is a captain of the Greenwich High School varsity tennis team, student government and girls' chorus.* BA, U. Vt., 1958; MS, Columbia U., 1959. Rschr., portfolio analyst Merrill, Lynch, Pierce et al, N.Y.C., 1961-63; dir. spl. situations rschr. Orvis Bros., N.Y.C., 1964-66; dir. rsch. Amott, Baker, N.Y.C., 1966-69; v.p. rsch. counsel Bruns, Nordemann & Rea, N.Y.C., 1970-75; v.p. rsch. assoc. Rosenkrantz, Ehrenkrantz, N.Y.C., 1976-77; investment banker Herzfeld & Stern, Stamford, Conn., 1978-82; chmn., pres. Viral Response Sys., Inc., Greenwich, Conn., 1983—. Patentee in field. With U.S. Army, 1959, res. Recipient Certificate of Recognition Eli Whitney Mus., 1987. Mem. Nat. Assn. Chain Drug Stores, Am. Mensa (Philanthropic award 1987), Inventors Assn. Conn. (Inventor of Yr. 1988), U.S. Tennis Assn. (ranked 1995), Landmark Club, East Hampton Tennis Club (mixed doubles champ 1972), Armonk Tennis Club, Grand Slam Tennis Club (singles champ 1977, 78). Republican. Avocations: tennis, skiing, swimming, travel, medical reading. Home: 444 Taconic Rd Greenwich CT 06831-2850 Office: Viral Response Sys Inc 34 E Putnam Ave Greenwich CT 06830-5425

KRAUSHAR, JONATHAN POLLACK, communications and media consultant; b. Kew Gardens, N.Y., Apr. 26, 1948; s. Leo and Evelyn (Pollack) K.; m. Linda Marie Pekarski, Apr. 20, 1980; children: Matthew, Elizabeth. BA in English, U. Wis., 1969; MBA in Mktg. and Internat. Bus., NYU, 1981. Reporter The Hudson Dispatch, Union City, N.J., 1970, The Record, Hackensack, N.J., 1970-72; assoc. prodr. Sta. WPIX-TV News, N.Y.C., 1973, Sta. WCBS-TV News, N.Y.C., 1974-76; spl. projects supr. Philip Morris Internat., N.Y.C., 1976-82; v.p. Ailes Comms., Inc., N.Y.C., 1982, sr. v.p., 1984, pres. corp. comms. group, 1990, pres., 1991-95; pres. Jon Kraushar and Assocs., Inc., N.Y.C., 1996—; freelance writer N.Y. Times, N.Y.C., 1972-76, Washington Post, Washington, 1972-76. Author: (with Roger Ailes) You Are the Message, 1988; inventor (video) Electronic Resume, 1982. Media adviser Reagan/Bush Campaign, N.Y.C., 1984, Bush/Quayle Campaign, N.Y.C., 1988, Forbes for Pres., 1996. Recipient Feature Writing award N.J. Press Assn., 1972; pub. affairs reporting fellow Washington Journalism Ctr., 1974; fed. grantee U. Wis. Dept. Behavioral Disabilities, 1969. Mem. Internat. Assn. Bus. Communicators (bd. dirs. N.Y. chpt., chmn. main event spkrs. program 1983-85), Econ. Club, Union League Club (N.Y.). Republican. Jewish. Avocations: in-line skating, swimming, water sports. Office: Jon Kraushar and Assocs Inc 440 Park Ave S New York NY 10016-8012

KRAUSKOPF, KONRAD BATES, geology educator; b. Madison, Wis., Nov. 30, 1910; s. Francis Craig and Maude Luvan (Bates) K.; m. Kathryn Isabel McCune, Jan. 1, 1936; children—Karen Hyde, Frances Conley, Karl, Marion Foerster. A.B. in Chemistry, U. Wis., 1931; Ph.D. in Chemistry, U. Calif.-Berkeley, 1934; Ph.D. in Geology, Stanford U., 1939; Ph.D. (hon.), U. Wis., 1972. Instr. chemistry U. Calif., Berkeley, 1934-35; asst. to full prof. geology Stanford U., Calif., 1939-76; chmn. geology dept. Stanford U., 1972-76; geologist U.S. Geol. Survey, Menlo Park, Calif., 1943-88; chief geog. sect. U.S. Army F.E.C., Tokyo, 1947-48; prof. geology emeritus Stanford U., 1976—; cons. Woodward-Clyde, Arthur D. Little, Aerospace Corp, Phillips Petroleum, EPA, NRC, Dept. Energy 1954—. Author: Introduction to Geochemistry, 1967—, The Third Planet, 1974, Radioactive Waste Disposal and Geology, 1988; co-author: (with A. Beiser) Fundamentals of Physical Science, 1941-74, The Physical Universe, 1960—. Recipient Ian Campbell medal Am. Geol. Inst., 1984. Fellow Geol. Soc. Am. (pres. 1967, Day medal 1961); mem. NAS, Geochem. Soc. (pres. 1970, Goldschmidt medal 1982), Soc. Econ. Geologists, Am. Geophys. Union, Am. Philos. Soc., Am. Inst. Profl. Geologists (hon.). Democrat. Home: Stanford U Pearce Mitchell Pl #13 Stanford CA 94305-2115 Office: Stanford U Dept Geology & Environ Scis Stanford CA 94305-2115

KRAUSS, ALISON, country musician; b. July 23, 1971. Albums include Too Late to Cry, 1987, Two Highways, 1989, I've Got That Old Feeling, 1990, Every Time You Say Goodbye, 1992, I Know Who Holds Tomorrow, 1994 (Bewst Southern, Country or Bluegrass Gospel album Grammy award), Now That I've Found You, 1995; (with Union Sta.) So Long So Wrong, 1997. Recipient Female Vocalist of Yr. award Internat. Bluegrass Music Assn., 1990-91, 93, 95, Entertainer of Yr. award, 1991, 95, Rising Video Star of Yr.-Europe award Country Music TV, 1995, Single of Yr. award Country Music Assn., 1995, Vocal Event of Yr., 1995, Horizon award, 1995, Female Vocalist of Yr., 1995, Best New Country Artist Tour award Pollstar, 1995, Americana Artist of Yr. award Gavin, 1995, Country Artist of Yr. Rolling Stone, 1995, Best Bluegrass Recording Grammy award, 1992, Best Country Collaboration with Vocals Grammy award, 1995, Best Female Country Vocal Performance Grammy award, 1996, Bluegrass/Old-Time Music Album award, 1996, Best Female Vocalist, 1996, Best Country Instrumental Performance Grammy award, 1998, Best Bluegrass Album Grammy award, 1998, Best Country Performance by a Duo or Group with Vocals Grammy award, 1998. Office: Myers Media 250 W 57th St Ste 307 New York NY 10107-0398*

KRAUSS, BOB, newspaper columnist, author; b. Plainview, Nebr., Jan. 14, 1924; s. Frederick F. and Matilda (Kraushaar) K.; m. Betty Ann Mickelsen, May 27, 1957 (div. 1980); 1 child, Ginger Ann; stepchildren: Robert Mickelsen, Richard Mickelsen. BA, U. Minn., 1950. Reporter Watertown Pub. Opinion, S.D., 1950-51; reporter Honolulu Advertiser, Hawaii, 1951-53, columnist, 1953—. Author: Here's Hawaii, 1960, Bob Krauss' Travel Guide to the Hawaiian Islands, 1963, Grove Farm Plantation, 1965, High Rise Hawaii, 1970, Historic Waianae, 1973, The Island Way, 1975, Kauai, 1978, McInerny, 1981, Detective Jardine, 1983, Keneti, South Sea Adventures of Kenneth Emory, 1988, Tides of Change, 1989, Our Hawaii, The Best of Bob Krauss, 1990, Birth by Fire, 1992, Johnny Wilson, First Hawaiian Democrat, 1994; editor: A Children's History of Hawaii, 1973, A Child's History of America, 1976, An Exceptional View of Life, 1977. Pres. Falls Clyde Maritime Mus., 1963-68; trustee Hawaii Maritime Ctr., 1982—. With USN, 1943-46, PTO. Recipient Disting. Historian award Hawaiian Hist. Soc., 1992. Mem. Honolulu Press Club (pres. 1955). Office: Honolulu Advertiser Inc PO Box 3110 Honolulu HI 96802-3110*

KRAUSS, CARL F., lawyer; b. St. Louis, Mar. 22, 1936; s. Frederick Emanuel and Jewell Edith (Bell) K.; m. Gladys Weber, July 27, 1972; children: Kenneth F., Stephen W. AB in Econs./Bus. Administrn., Knox Coll., 1958; JD, U. Mo., 1961. Bar: Mo. 1961, Kansas 1981, Tex. 1989. Assoc. Morrison & Hecker, Kansas City, Mo., 1961-67, ptnr., 1967-81; ptnr. Morrison & Hecker, L.L.P, Overland Park, Kans., 1981—. Bd. editors Mo. Law Review. Founding mem. Overland Park Econ. Devel. Coun., 1986. Mem. ABA, Mo. Bar Assn., Kansas Bar Assn., Tex. Bar Assn., Johnson County Bar Assn., Kansas City Met. Bar Assn., Overland Park C. of C. (dir. 1991-97). Avocation: farming. Home: 1608 E Frontier Ln Olathe KS 66062-2243 Office: Morrison & Hecker LLP 9 Corporate Woods 450 9200 Indian Creek Pkwy Overland Park KS 66210-2002

KRAUSS, GEORGE, metallurgist; b. Phila., May 14, 1933; s. George and Berta (Reichelt) K.; m. Ruth A. Oeste, Sept. 10, 1960; children: Matthew, Jonathan, Benjamin, Thomas. B.S. in Metall. Engring., Lehigh U., 1955; M.S., MIT, 1958, Sc.D., 1961. Registered profl. engr., Colo., Pa. Devel. metallurgist Superior Tube Co., Collegeville, Pa., 1955-56; prof. Lehigh U., Bethlehem, Pa., 1963-75, Colo. Sch. Mines, Golden, 1975—; dir. Advanced Steel Processing and Products Research Ctr., 1984-93; Amax Found. prof., 1975-90; prof. dept. metall. engring. Colo. Sch. Mines, Golden, 1990-92, John Henry Moore prof., 1992-97, Univ. prof. emeritus, metallurg. cons., 1997—. Author: Principles of Heat Treatment of Steel, 1980, Steels: Heat Treatment and Processing Principles, 1990, Tool Steels, 5th edit., 1998; editor: Deformation Processing and Structure, 1984,, Carburizing: Processing and Performance, 1989; editor Jour. Heat Treating, 1978-82; co-editor Fundamentals of Microalloying Forging Steels, 1987; contbr. articles profl. jours. NSF fellow Max Planck Inst. fur Eisenforschung, 1962-63; recipient Adolf Martens medal, Wiesbaden, 1990, Disting. Alumni award Lehigh U., 1993, George R. Brown gold medal, 1998; named Outstanding Educator, Colo. Sch. Mines, 1990. Fellow ASM, Japan Soc. Promotion Sci.; mem. AIME, Iron and Steel Soc.-AIME (disting. mem. 1993), Iron and Steel Inst. Japan (hon.), Am. Soc. Materials Internat. (trustee 1991-94, v.p. 1995-96, pres. 1996-97, C.S. Barrett silver medal 1998, Bodeen Heat Treating Achievement award 1999, A.E. White Disting. Tchr. award 1999), Internat. Fedn. Heat Treatment (pres. 1989-91). Home: 3807 S Ridge Rd Evergreen CO 80439-8517 Office: Colo Sch Mines Dept Metall Engring Golden CO 80401

KRAUSS, HERBERT HARRIS, psychologist; b. Phila., June 13, 1940; s. Leon and Ethel Sarah (Cohen) K.; m. Beatrice Joy Osgood, Aug. 26, 1965; children: Michael Conal, Daniel Avram. BS, Pa. State U., 1961, MS, 1962; PhD, Northwestern U., 1966. Lic. psychologist, N.Y. Intern in med. psychology U. Oreg. Med. Sch., 1962-63; asst. prof. psychiatry, psychology U. Kans. Med. Sch., Kansas City, Kans., 1966-67; asst. prof. psychiatry, psychology, chief psychologist in child psychiatry Ohio State U. Coll. Medicine, Columbus, 1967-69; assoc. prof. psychology U. Ga., Athens, 1969-71; prof. psychology Hunter Coll., CUNY, N.Y.C., 1971—, chair dept. psychology, 1992—; dir. rehab. rsch. Internat. Ctr. for the Disabled, N.Y.C., 1984—; cons. Managed Health Network, N.Y.C., 1979-90, PhD Program, NYU, rehab. counselling, 1991—; adj. assoc. prof. psychiatry Cornell Med. Sch., N.Y.C., 1978—; assoc. attending psychologist Payne Whitney Clinic, N.Y. Hosp., 1978—; ptnr. Health Resources Mgmt. Co-author: Living with Anxiety and Depression, 1974; co-editor: Between Survival and Suicide, 1976, A Provider's Guide to Psychiatric Services in the General Hospital, 1986, The Aging Workforce: A Guide for University Administrators, 1992; co-editor Internat. Jour. Group Tensions, 1995—; cons. editor Jour. Individual Psychology, 1996—. Cons. Irvington, N.Y. Drug Coun., 1983; coach football and wrestling Irvington Sunnysiders, 1978-83, soccer Am. Youth Soccer Orgn., Houston, 1976-78. Named Outstanding Teacher Psychology, N.Y. Psychol. Assn., 1972. Mem. APA, N.Y. Acad. Scis., Ea. Psychol. Assn., Internat. Organ for Study of Group Tensions (v.p.), Am. Coun. on Germany, Am. Evaluation Assn., Cornell Club, Sigma Xi. Home: 520 Grand Ave Newburgh NY 12550-1929 Office: Hunter Coll 695 Park Ave New York NY 10021-5024

KRAUSS, JOHN LANDERS, public policy, urban affairs consultant, mediator; b. Orange, N.J., Oct. 20, 1948; s. George Howard Jr. and Shirley (Landers) K.; m. M. Elizabeth Wood, May 23, 1976 (div. Sept. 1988); m. Eleanor C. Werbe, June 29, 1991. BA with honors in Polit. Sci., Colo. Coll., 1971; JD, Ind. U., Indpls., 1976. Bar: Ind. 1976, U.S. Dist. Ct. (so. dist.) Ind. 1976, U.S. Ct. Appeals (7th cir.) 1979, U.S. Supreme Ct. 1986; cert. mediator. Spl. asst. to gov. Office of Gov. of Ind., Indpls., 1971-72; dep. dir. Greater Indpls. Progress Com. Inc., Indpls., 1972-73, exec. dir., 1973-81; dir. dept. met. devel. City of Indpls., 1981-82, dep. mayor, 1982-91; sr. fellow Ind. U. Ctr. for Urban Policy and Environment, Indpls., 1991—; mediator Ind. Dept. Edn., 1998—, U.S. Postal Svc., 1998—; mediator and fact finder Ind. Edn. Employment Rels. Bd., 1991—; exec. dir. Ind. Adv. Commn. on Intergovtl. Rels., 1995—; assoc. Kettering Found., Dayton, Ohio, 1997—; mem. state adv. bd. Ind. Small Bus. Devel. Ctrs.; co-chmn. Charles L. Whistler Award Com.; bd. dirs. Nyhart Co., Inc.; cons. U.S. Govt. projects in Ukraine, Morocco, Russia, Estonia, Turkey and South Africa. Trustee Indpls. Mus. Art, Ptnrs. for Livable Comtys., Washington; bd. dirs. Indpls. Project, Inc., Ind. Swiss Found., Ind. Convention and Vis. Assn.; past mem. exec. com., bd. dirs. Eiteljorg Mus. Am. Indian and Western Art; past mem. exec. com. Pan Am. Games Organizing Com., 1987; past vice chmn. Greater Indpls. Progress Com., Inc.; past mem. exec. com. Indpls. Econ. Devel. Corp., Commn. for Downtown, Inc.; dir. Gov.'s Gambling Impact Study Commn., 1998-99; founding dir. and v.p. Ind. Sports Corp. Ford Found. Venture grantee for ind. rsch. Mem. AIA (past bd. dirs. Indpls. chpt.), Soc. Individuals in Dispute Resolution, Am. Soc. Pub. Adminstrn. (pres. Ind. chpt. 1992-94, bd. dirs. Ind. chpt.), Soc. for Human Svcs. Mgmt., Am. Arbitration Assn. (comml. panel mediators and arbitrators 1998—), Ind. Comty. Devel. Soc. (bd. dirs.), Contemporary Club Indpls., Dramatic Club, Indpls. Com. on Fgn. Rels., Sagamore of the Wabash, State of Ind., Pi Gamma Mu. Office: Ind U Ctr Urban Policy/Envn 342 N Senate Ave Indianapolis IN 46204-1708

KRAUSS, JUDITH BELLIVEAU, nursing educator; b. Malden, Mass., Apr. 11, 1947; d. Leo F. and Dorothy (Conners) Belliveau; m. Ronald L. Krauss, Sept. 5, 1970; children: Jennifer Leigh, Sarah Elizabeth. BS, Boston Coll., 1968; MSN, Yale U., 1970. RN, Conn. Clinical specialist Conn. Mental Health Ctr., New Haven, 1971-73; clin. instr. Yale Sch. Nursing, New Haven, 1971-73; asst. prof. rsch. Yale U. Sch. Nursing, New Haven, 1973-78, assoc. dean, 1978-85; prof., dean Yale U. Sch. Nursing, New Haven, Conn., 1985-98, prof. mental health policy, 1998—; cons. pharm. and pub. cons., sch., govt. agys. Author: The Chronically Ill Psychiatric Patient and the Community, 1982 (Am. Jour. Nursing Book of Yr. 1982); editor Archives of Psychiat. Nursing, 1986—; mem. editorial bd. Issues in Mental Health Nursing, Psychiat. Rehab., Psychiat. Nursing Forum, Psychiat. Svcs.; contbr. articles to profl. jours. Am. Nurses Found. scholar, 1978; recipient Chamberlain award Soc. Edn. and Rsch. in Nursing, 1994; named Disting. Alumna Yale Sch. Nursing, 1984; Am. Acad. Nursing/Inst. of Medicine sr. scholar in residence, 1998—. Mem. ANA (Disting. Contbn. to Psychiat. Nursing award 1992), Am. Acad. Nursing, Conn. Nurses Assn. (mem. cabinet on edn. 1987-89, bd. dirs. 1988-91, rep. to ANA house of dels. 1988-91, Josephine Dolan award 1989), Sigma Theta Tau (Disting. Lectr. award 1987), Delta Mu (Founders award 1987). Avocations: tennis, golf, reading mystery novels. Office: Yale U Sch Nursing PO Box 9740 New Haven CT 06536-0740

KRAUSS, LEO, urologist, educator; b. N.Y.C., Nov. 5, 1928; s. Moe and Marie (Shapiro) K.; m. Harriet Powell, Dec. 4, 1955; children: Robert, Jennifer. BA summa cum laude, Syracuse U., 1948; MD, NYU, 1953. Diplomate Am. Bd. of Urology. Attending urologist N. Shore U. Hosp., Plainview, N.Y., 1963—, Manhasset, N.Y., 1987—; chief of urology Syosset (N.Y.) Comty. Hosp., 1963-78; urologist pvt. practice, Plainview, 1963—; consulting urologist USAF, Plattsburgh, N.Y., 1961-63, VA Hosp., Tupper Lake, N.Y., 1961-63; asst. prof. urology SUNY, Stony Brook, 1976—. Contbr. articles and abstracts to profl. jours. Bd. dirs. Long Island Cancer Coun., Huntington, N.Y., 1977-79. Capt. USAF, 1954-56, Korea. Named Attending Urologist of Yr., Nassau County Med. Ctr., E. Meadow, N.Y., 1981. Fellow Am. Coll. Surgeons; mem. AMA, N.Y. State Urolog. Soc., Am. Assn. Clin. Urologists, Am. Fedn. for Clin. Rsch., Am. Urolog. Assn., Phi Beta Kappa, Alpha Omega Alpha. Avocations: tennis, travel, reading. Home: 33 Orchard Dr Woodbury NY 11797-2827 Office: Leo Krauss MD PC 875 Old Country Rd Plainview NY 11803-4942

KRAUSS, MICHAEL EDWARD, linguist; b. Cleve., Aug. 15, 1934; s. Lester William and Ethel (Sklarsky) K.; m. Jane Lowell, Feb. 16, 1962; children: Marcus Feder, Stephen Feder, Ethan, Alexandra, Isaac. Bacc. Phil. Islandicae, U. Iceland; BA, U. Chgo., 1953, Western Res. U., 1954; MA, Columbia U., 1955; Cert. d'études supérieures, U. Paris, 1956; PhD, Harvard U., 1959. Postdoctoral fellow U. Iceland, Reykjavik, 1958-60; rsch. fellow Dublin Inst. Advanced Studies, Ireland, 1956-57; vis. prof. MIT, Cambridge, 1969-70; prof. linguistics Alaska Native Lang. Ctr., U. Alaska, Fairbanks, 1960—, dir., 1972—, head Alaska native lang. program, 1972—; panel mem. linguistics NSF. Author: Eyak Dictionary, 1970, Eyak Texts, 1970, Alaska Native Languages: Past, Present and Future, 1980; editor: In Honor of Eyak: The Art of Anna Nelson Harry, 1982, Yupik Eskimo Prosodic Systems, 1985; mem. editorial bd.: Internat. Jour. Am. Linguistics, Arctic Anthropology; edited dictionaries and books in Alaska Eskimo and Indian langs. Halldor Kiljan Laxness fellow Scandinavian-Am. Found., Iceland, 1958-60, Fulbright fellow Leningrad, USSR, 1990; Fulbright study grantee Iceland, 1958-60; grantee NSF, 1961—, NEH, 1967; named Humanities Forum, 1981; recipient Athabaskan and Eyak rsch. award NSF, 1961—. Mem. Linguistics Soc. Am. (chair com. endangered langs. and preservation 1991-95), Am. Anthropol. Assn., Soc. Study Indigenous Langs. of the Ams. (pres. 1991). Jewish. Office: U Alaska Alaska Native Lang Ctr Fairbanks AK 99775

KRAUSS, MITCHELL E., journalist; b. N.Y.C., Sept. 17, 1930; s. Murray Dewey and Frances (Lutz) K.; m. Elisabeth Woodward, July 4, 1957; children: Jennifer, David. BA, NYU, 1951; MA, U. Pa., 1953. Newscaster Sta. WQXR, N.Y.C., 1950-51; newscaster, announcer Sta. WFLN, Phila., 1951-56; reporter, news exec. Sta. WIP, Phila., 1956-60; news broadcaster, exec., dir. news Radio N.Y. Worldwide, 1960-66; TV news anchor, host Channel 13, N.Y., 1966-72; news corr. CBS News, N.Y.C. and Cairo, 1972-97; lectr. on role fo media in society, world affairs and history of broadcasting to world affairs orgns., civic clubs, schs. and corps. Candidate Bd. Reps., Stamford, Conn., 1968. Sgt. U.S. Army, 1953-55. Recipient George Foster Peabody award, 1964, AP award, 1958, Broadcast award ohio State, 1988. Mem. Econ. Broadcasters Assn. (past pres.), Radio-TV News Analysts Assn. (past pres.), Forum for World Affairs (chmn. 1992-97), Ambs. Roundtable (chmn. 1991—), Overseas Press Club (award 1972), Fgn. Press Club (pres. 1982-83), Sigma Delta Phi. Democrat. Jewish. Avocations: travel, gardening, book collecting.

KRAUSZ, MICHAEL, philosopher, educator; b. Geneva, Switzerland, Sept. 13, 1942; s. Laszlo and Susan Beate (Strauss) K.; m. Constance Frances Costigan. BA, Rutgers U., 1965; spl. studies, London Sch. Econs., 1963-64. Acting chmn. dept. Bryn Mawr Coll., Pa., 1983-84, chmn. dept., 1993—; vis. asst. prof. Am. U., Washington, 1973-74; vis. prof. lectr. Georgetown U., 1977-79, Hebrew U., Jerusalem, 1978, Swarthmore Coll., 1980-81, Haverford Coll., 1981-82, U. Nairobi, 1985; disting. vis. prof. Am. U. in Cairo, 1980; spl. lectr. U. Oxford, 1987, 88, 89; chmn. external rev. com. Dept. Philosophy, Swarthmore Coll., 1987, Smith Coll., 1990; rsch. assoc. to vice prin. Linacre Coll., Oxford U., 1988, vis. sr. mem., 1986-90; vis. sr. mem. Linacre Coll., 1986-90, 98, 99; vis. prof. Indian Inst. Advanced Studies, Shimla, India, 1992, U. Ulm, 1997; co-dir. Confs. on Philosophy of Human Studies, 1981-88, chmn., 1988-94, Greater Phila. Referee NEH, 1978, 82, Jour. Aesthetics and Art Criticism, 1986, Nous, 1996, others; author: Rightness and Reasons: Interpretation in Cultural Practices, 1993; co-author: (with Rom Harré) Varieties of Relativism, 1995; editor: The Interpretation of Music, 1993; co-editor: The Concept of Creativity in Science and Art, 1981, Relativism: Cognitive and Moral, 1982, Rationality, Relativism, and the Human Sciences, 1986, Jewish Identity, 1993, Interpretation, Relativism & the Metaphysics of Culture, 1999; editor series in Philosophy of History and Culture, The Netherlands, 1986—; Greater Phila. Philosophy Consortium Series, Philosophy in the Global Context, 1995—; author revs., papers. Founder, pres., assoc. artistic dir. Phila. Chamber Orch., 1984; bd. dirs. Solisti N.Y., 1987-88. Fellow Royal Soc. Arts, London, 1973—, Andrew Mellon, Aspen Inst. Humanitic Studies, 1977-78, Ossabaw Found., 1978, 80; grantee Ford Found., 1971, Bryn Mawr Coll., 1973-74, 76, 85-86, 89, Alfred Sloan Found., 1986; hon. fellow Tata Energy Rsch. Inst., New Delhi. Fellow Ctr. Study Developing Soc.; mem. Am. Philos. Assn., Am. Soc. Aesthetics (program chmn. ea. div. 1987—, chmn. steering com. ea. div. 1989-90, program chmn. nat. div. 1991, mem. Am. steering com.), World Congress Philosophy, 1998, fellow, Ctr. for the study of Developing Soc., Delhi, 1998, 99. Jewish. Avocations: 16 art shows natl., internatl., music (violin and conducting). Office: Bryn Mawr Coll Dept Philosophy Bryn Mawr PA 19010

KRAUT, JOEL ARTHUR, ophthalmologist; b. Jersey City, July 21, 1937; s. Alan and Lillian Betty (Kravitz) K.; m. Cathy Jane Kleven, June 30, 1963; children: David Terence, Amy Melissa. AB cum laude, Princeton U., 1958; MD, Columbia U., 1962. Diplomate Am. Bd. Ophthalmology. Intern Boston U. Med. Ctr., 1962-63; resident in ophthalmology NYU-Bellevue Med. Ctr., N.Y.C., 1963-66; chief ophthalmology USAF Hosp., Tachikawa, Japan, 1966-68; pvt. practice specializing in ophthalmology Brookline, Mass., 1968—; asst. prof. Ophthalmology Harvard Med. Sch., 1996—; clin. assoc., clin. instr. ophthalmology Harvard U. Med. Sch.; clin. instr. ophthalmology Tufts U. Sch. Medicine, 1968-91, clin. assoc. prof. ophthalmology, 1991—, assoc. surgeon ophthalmology, 1981-91, surgeon in ophthalmology, 1991—; dir. Low Vision Ctr., Mass. Eye & Ear Infirmary, 1968—, med. dir. Rehab. Ctr., bd. surgeons, 1993—, pres. eye staff, 1994-96, pres. med. staff, 1995-96, bd. dirs.; mem. med. staff Beth Israel Deaconess Med. Ctr., 1991—; bd. dirs. physiol. optics dept. ophthalmology Tufts-New Eng. Med. Ctr., 1968-73; cons. U.S. 5th Air Force, Japan, 1966-68; ophthalmology adv. com. Tufts U. Health Plan; spl. gift com. Princeton U. Contbr. articles to med. and profl. jours. Chmn. United Way campaign, 1973; bd. dirs. Boston Aid to Blind, 1987—(Man of Vision award 1996); mem. adv. bd. Mass. Commn. for Blind, 1988-94. Cane scholar, 1954-58, St. John-Princeton scholar, 1958-62; U. Calif. Rsch. fellow, 1960. Fellow ACS; mem. Royal Soc. Medicine, Am. Acad. Ophthalmology (state councillor 1998—, mem. low vision rehab. com. 1995—, honor award 1991), New Eng. Ophthal. Soc. (mem. com. nomination 1997—), Mass. Ophthal. Soc., Nat. Assn. Visually Handicapped (adv. b. 1991—), Soc. Geriatric Ophthalmology, Intraocular Lens Soc., New Eng. Implant Soc. (sec. 1979-81, pres. 1981-83), Mass. Med. Soc. Greater Boston, Med. Soc., Mass. Soc. Eye Physicians and Surgeons (exec. bd. 1988—, recorder 1991-94, treas. 1995-96, pres.-elect 1996, pres. 1996-1998.), Hazel Hotchkiss Wightman Tennis Club, du Bailliage de la Chaine des Rotissurs, Princeton U. Club (spl. gifts com. 1992-93, 96-98), Phi Beta Kappa, Sigma Xi. Office: 16 Webster St Brookline MA 02446-4938

KRAUTER, AARON JOSEPH, farmer, state senator; b. Dickinson, N.D., July 21, 1956; s. Adam Robert and Ann Christine (Grundhauser) K.; m. Cynthia Marie Nordquist, June 28, 1986; children: Emily Christine, Mitchell Aaron, Hannah Marie. BSEd., U. Mary, Bismarck, 1978, BSBA, 1981. Music instr. Cooperstown (N.D.) High Sch., 1978-79; store mgr. Best Product, Inc., Bismarck, 1979-85; ops. mgr. Best Product, Inc., Richmond, Va., 1985-87; farmer Regent, N.D., 1987—; mem. N.D. Senate, 1990—. Mem. N.D. Gov.'s Coun. on Children and Youth, Bismarck, 1989-94, N.D. Gov.'s Coun. on Phys. Fitness and Health, 1992-94; mem. agronomy seed adv. bd. N.D. State U., 1991—, mem. ext. adv. coun., 1991—; chair N.D. Senate Dem. Caucus, 1993-97; asst. minority leader, 1997—. Recipient Know Your State award N.D. Bar Assn., 1974, Excellence in Govt. award Assn. Counties, 1993, Flemming Fellow Leadership award Ctr. for Policy Alternatives, Washington, 1995. Mem. KC, Elks. Democrat. Roman Catholic. Home and Office: HC 1 Box 27 Regent ND 58650-9721*

KRAUTHAMMER, CHARLES, columnist, editor; b. N.Y.C., Mar. 13, 1950; s. Shulim and Thea K.; m. Robyn Trethewey; 1 child, Daniel. BA, McGill U., 1970; postgrad., Balliol Coll. Oxford U., 1970-71; MD, Harvard U., 1975. Diplomate Am. Bd. Psychiatry and Neurology. Resident in psychiatry Mass. Gen. Hosp., Boston, 1975-78; sci. advisor Dept. HHS, Washington, 1978-80; speech writer V.P. Walter Mondale, Washington, 1980-81; sr. editor The New Republic, Washington, 1981-88; essayist Time Mag., 1983—; syndicated columnist The Washington Post, 1984—. Author: Cutting Edges, 1985; contbr. sci. articles to psychiat. jours. Recipient Nat.

Mag. award Am. Soc. Mag. Editors, 1984, Pulitzer prize for commentary, 1987, Commonwealth scholarship British Coun., Oxford, 1970-71. *

KRAVATH, ALAN WOLFE, education evaluator; b. N.Y.C., Sept. 27, 1939; s. Reuben and Fanny (Tannenbaum) K.; m. Carla Friedman, June 11, 1967; children: Gabriel, Daniel (dec.). BA in English, CCNY, N.Y.C., 1965; MS in Spl. Edn., L.I. U., Bklyn., 1993. Cert. tchr. spl. edn., tchr. English, N.Y. Assoc. editor RSI Mag., N.Y.C., 1963-67; account exec. Creamer-Dickson-Basford Pub. Rels., N.Y.C., 1967-71; nat. dir. pub. info. United Svc. Orgns., Washington, 1971-77; evaluation educator, tchr. N.Y.C. Bd. Edn., 1987—. Founder, pub. (booklet) Westchester Media Directory, 1984. Pub. rels. advisor pub. rels. adv. com. New Rochelle (N.Y.) Bd. Edn., 1977. Mem. East Yonkers Kiwanis (sec. 1984-87). Home: 37 Wildwood Rd New Rochelle NY 10804-4712 Office: PS 150 920 E 167th St Rm 114 Bronx NY 10459-2317

KRAVCHUK, ROBERT SACHA, management educator, financial consultant; b. Stamford, Conn., July 4, 1955; s. Sacha and Estelle Helen (Wachowski) K.; m. Natalie Marie Kuzma, June 24, 1978; children; Elisabeth Aasta, Timothy Robert. BA, BS cum laude, U. Conn., 1977; MFA, U. Hartford, 1979; MBA, Columbia U., 1980; MA, Syracuse U., 1987, PhD, 1989. Cert. internal auditor, mgmt. acct. group ins. underwriter Conn. Gen. Life Ins. Co., Hartford, 1977-79; sr. control analyst CIGNA Corp., Hartford, 1981-82, clah flow product mgr., 1982-83; assoc. Booz, Allen & Hamilton, N.Y.C., 1984-86; instr. Le Moyne Coll., 1988-89; asst. prof. pub. adminstrn. U. Hartford, 1990-93; undersec. office policy & mgmt. State of Conn., Hartford, 1991-93; resident budget advisor Govt. of Ukraine, 1993-94; fin. advisor Fedn. Bosnia-Hercegovina, Sarajevo, 1995-96; asst. prof. polit. sci. U. Conn., 1994-98; assoc. prof. sch. pub. & environ. affairs Ind. U., Bloomington, 1998—; adj. prof. William Paterson Coll., Wayne, N.J., 1980; adj. instr. Le Moyne Coll., Syracuse, N.Y., 1986-88, U. Hartford, 1989-90. Co-author: Politics and Society in Ukraine, 1999. Mem. State Senate Reps. Office, Hartford Conn., 1989-90. Doctoral fellow Maxwell Sch. Citizenship and Pub. Affairs, Syracuse U., 1986-89. Fellow Life Mgmt. Inst.; mem. Am. Soc. pub. Adminstrn., Am. Polit. Sci. Assn. Republican. Roman Catholic. Home: 3809 Lauras Way Bloomington IN 47401-8827 Office: Ind U Sch Pub & Environ Affairs SPEA 410-D Bloomington IN 47405-2100

KRAVEC, CYNTHIA VALLEN, microbiologist; b. Newark, Sept. 8, 1951; d. William George and Elizabeth Irene (VanAllen) K. BS, Syracuse (N.Y.) U., 1974; MS, Seton Hall U., S. Orange, N.J., 1980; MBA, Monmouth Coll., W. Long Branch, N.J., 1986. Registered microbiologist. Sr. technician GIBCO/Invenex, Millburn, N.J., 1974-79; rsch. scientist Wampole Labs. div. Carter-Wallace Inc., East Windsor, N.J., 1979-90; scientist Roche Diagnostic Systems subsidiary Hoffmann-LaRoche, Inc., Nutley, N.J., 1990-98, Schering-Plough, Kenilworth, N.J., 1998—. Contbr. articles to profl. jours. Mem. Am. Soc. Microbiology, Tissue Culture Assn., Soc. of Indsl. Microbiology. Home: 1006 Coolidge St Westfield NJ 07090-1215 Office: Schering-Plough Rsch Inst 2015 Galloping Hill Rd Kenilworth NJ 07033-1300

KRAVEC, FRANCES MARY, elementary education educator; b. Slovakia, Sept. 26, 1948; came to U.S., 1949; d. Emerick Andrew and Martha Mary (Jancosek) K. BS, California (Pa.) U., 1970, MS, 1971. Cert. elem. tchr., Pa. Phys. edn. tchr. Charleroi (Pa.) Area Sch. Dist., 1970-71, kindergarten tchr., 1971—. Writer: kindergarten reading curriculum. Mem. Charleroi Elem. PTA. Mon Valley Consortium grantee, 1988, 91, 93, 94. Mem. NEA, Pa. State Edn. Assn., Charleroi Area Edn. Assn. Democrat. Roman Catholic. Avocations: photography, sewing, travel. Home: 479 Charles St Charleroi PA 15022-1006 Office: Charleroi Elem Ctr Fecsen Dr Charleroi PA 15022

KRAVETZ, CHERYL DUPREE, reporter; b. Atlanta, Feb. 5, 1948; d. Thomas Felder and Florence Elsie May (Jones) DuPree; m. Robert Rosamond, June 3, 1973 (div. May 1991); 1 child, Kimberly Dawn Rosamond; m. Jay Norman Kravetz, Apr. 21, 1995. Reporter Palm Beach Jewish World, The Lake Worth (Fla.) Herald, The South Fla. Newspaper Network, Wellington, Fla.; book reviewer, author interviews for classic bookshop, Palm Beach, Fla. Book reviewer, interviewer of authors Classic Bookshop, Palm Beach Website. Recipient Outstanding Media Coverage award Phi Delta Kappa, 1987, Excellence in Comm. award Am. Cancer Soc., 1988, 1st Pl. Media Competition award, 1990, Citizenship award Civitan Club, 1993. Home: 226 S B St Lake Worth FL 33460-4037 Office: The Forum Newspaper Group Forum Newspaper Group 11320 Fortune Cir # G-32 Wellington FL 33414-8742

KRAVETZ, NATHAN, educator, author; b. N.Y.C., Feb. 11, 1921; s. Louis and Anna (Thau) K. m. Evelyn Cottan, Dec. 10, 1944; children: Deborah Ruth, Daniel. BEd with hons., UCLA, 1941, MA, 1949, EdD, 1954. Cert. tchg., adminstrn., Calif. Tchr. Walnut Creek (Calif.) Elem Sch., 1941-42; tchr., prin. L.A. Unified Sch. Dist., 1946-64; prof. Hunter/Lehman Coll., CUNY, N.Y.C., 1964-76, prof. emeritus, 1979; prof. internat. and gifted edn., dean Calif. State U., San Bernardino, 1976-91, prof. emeritus, 1991; vis. prof. U. S.C., 1985-87, UCLA, 1989, Calif. State U., Northridge, 1998—; fgn. svc. officer U.S. Dept. State, Lima, Peru, 1958-60; staff officer UNESCO, Paris, 1969-72, cons. Venezuela, 1968; cons. Ford Found., Chile, 1964, UN Devel. Program, S.Am., 1973-74; cons. U.S. AID, Pakistan and Indonesia, 1974-75, Benin, 1977, Guatemala, 1992, Thailand, 1999. Author 9 children's books; editor Borgo Press, Calif., 1990-95. With USAAF, 1942-46. Univ. fellow Harvard U., 1951-52; grantee Fulbright Found., Argentina, 1980. Jewish. Avocations: reading history.

KRAVITCH, PHYLLIS A., federal judge; b. Savannah, Ga., Aug. 23, 1920; d. Aaron and Ella (Wiseman) K. BA, Goucher Coll., 1941; LLB, U. Pa., 1943; LLD (hon.), Goucher Coll., 1981, Emory U., 1998. Bar: Ga. 1943, U.S. Dist. Ct. 1944, U.S. Supreme Ct. 1948, U.S. Ct. Appeals (5th cir.) 1962. Practice law Savannah, 1944-76; judge Superior Ct., Eastern Jud. Circuit of Ga., 1977-79, U.S. Ct. Appeals (5th cir.), Atlanta, 1979-81; judge U.S. Ct. Appeals (11th cir.), 1981—, sr. judge, 1996—; mem. Jud. Conf. Standing Com. on Rules, 1994—. Trustee Inst. Continuing Legal Edn. in Ga., 1979-82; mem. Bd. Edn., Chatham County, Ga., 1949-55; mem. coun. Law Sch., Emory U., Atlanta, 1985—; mem. vis. com. Law Sch., U. Chgo., 1990-93; bd. visitors, Ga. State U. Law Sch., 1994—; mem. regional rev. panel Truman Scholarship Found., 1992—. Recipient Hannah G. Solomon award Nat. Coun., Jewish Women, 1978, James Wilson award U. Pa. Law Alumni Soc., 1992. Fellow Am. Bar Found.; mem. ABA (Margaret Brent award 1991), Savannah Bar Assn. (pres. 1976), State Bar Ga., Am. Judicature Soc. (Devitt award com. 1998—), Am. Law Inst, U. Pa. Law Soc. Office: US Ct Appeals 11th Cir 56 Forsyth St NW # 202 Atlanta GA 30303-2205

KRAVITT, JASON HARRIS PAPERNO, lawyer; b. Chgo., Jan. 19, 1948; s. Jerome Julius and Shirley (Paperno) K.; m. Beverly Ray Niemeier, May 11, 1974; children: Nikola Wedding, Justin Taylor Paperno. AB, Johns Hopkins U., 1969; JD, Harvard U., 1972; diploma in comparative legal studies, Cambridge U., Eng., 1973. Bar: Ill., U.S. Dist. Ct. (no. dist.) Ill. Assoc. Mayer, Brown & Platt, Chgo., 1973-78, ptnr., 1979—, co-chmn., 1998—; adj. prof. law Northwestern U., Evanston, Ill., 1994—, adj. prof. fin. Kellogg Sch. Mgmt., 1998—. Editor: Securitization of Financial Assets, 2d edit., 1996. Bd. dirs. Mus. Contemporary Art, Chgo., 1974-75; dir., chmn. The Cameron Kravitt Found., 1984—. Fellow Am. Coll. Comml. Lawyers; mem. ABA, Chgo. Coun. Lawyers, Chgo. Bar Assn., Econ. Club of Chgo. Home: 250 Sheridan Rd Glencoe IL 60022-1948 Office: Mayer Brown & Platt 190 S La Salle St Ste 3100 Chicago IL 60603-3441

KRAVITT, MARTIN KENNETH, architect; b. New Haven, Conn., Dec. 30, 1946; s. Charles and Doris (Gross) K.; m. Monica Pommier, Nov. 4, 1979; 1 child, Alexandra Kaye. BArch, Pratt Inst., 1970. Registered architect, N.Y., Conn., Pa. Campus planner N.Y. City C.C., Bklyn., 1968-73; project designer Heritage Devel. Corp., Somers, N.Y., 1973-74; sr. designer Rosenfield Assocs., N.Y.C., 1974-76; dir. architecture Hillman, Engrs., White Plains, N.Y., 1976-79; project architect Office Design Assocs., N.Y.C., 1979-80; prin. Martin Kravitt, Architects and Planners, Katonah, N.Y., 1980—. Prin. works include Katonah Village Libr., 1992, William Doyle House, 1995, Signal Electronics Co., 1995, Interfaith Coun. Housing and Master Plan, Ossining, N.Y., 1997, Village Hall, Police Headqtrs. & Ct., Pleasantville, N.Y., 1998, Restoration of Akin Hall Libr., 1999; photographer Mus. City of N.Y., 1973, N.Y. Mag., 1973. Mem. AIA (Westchester-Mid Hudson chpt., Honors award, 1995), N.Y. State Assn. Architects. Home and Office: 97 Edgemont Rd Katonah NY 10536-1702

KRAVITZ, EDWARD ARTHUR, neuroscientist; b. N.Y.C., Dec. 19, 1932; m. 1958; 2 children. BS, CCNY, 1954; PhD in Biochemistry, U. Mich., 1959. Fellow biochemistry Nat. Heart Inst., 1959-60; rsch. fellow neurophysiology and neuropharmacology Harvard Med. Sch., Boston, 1960-61, instr. neurophysiology and neuropharmacology, 1961-63, from asst. prof. to assoc. prof., 1963-69, prof. neurobiology, 1969-86, George Packer Barry Prof. neurobiology, 1986—; dir. program neurosci., Harvard Med. Sch., 1982-90; bd. trustees, exec. com., dir. neurobiology course Marine Biol. Lab., 1975-79; governing coun. Inst. Med., 1991-93; ectr. in field. Recipient Von Humboldt award, 1991, Guggenheim award 1992. Mem. Inst. Med. Rsch., Nat. Acad. Sci., Soc. Neurosci. (co-founder neurobiology of disease workshops), Am. Acad. Arts & Sci., Am. Soc. Biol. Chemists. E-mail: edward kravitz@hms.harvard.edu. Office: Harvard Med Sch Dept of Neurobiology 220 Longwood Ave Boston MA 02115-5701

KRAVITZ, ELLEN KING, musicologist, educator; b. Fords, N.J., May 25, 1929; d. Walter J. and Frances M. (Prybylowski) Kokowicz; m. Hilard L. Kravitz, Jan. 9, 1972; children: Julie Frances, Heather Frances; stepchildren: Kent, Kerry, Jay. BA, Georgian Ct. Coll., 1964; MM, U. So. Calif., 1966, PhD, 1970. Tchr. 7th and 8th grade music Mt. St. Mary Acad., North Plainfield, N.J., 1949-50; cloistered nun Carmelite Monastery, Lafayette, La., 1950-61; instr. Loyola U., L.A., 1967; asst. prof. music Calif. State U., L.A., 1967-71, assoc. prof., 1971-74, prof., 1974—; founder Friends of Music at Calif. State U., L.A., 1976. Author: Music in Our Culture, 1996; Jour. Arnold Schoenberg Inst., L.A.; jour. editor Vol. I, No. 3, 1977, Vol II, No. 3, 1978; author (with others) Catalog of Schoenberg's Paintings, Drawings and Sketches; mem. editl. adv. bd. Jour. Arnold Schoenberg Inst., 1977-87. Mem. Schoenberg Centennial Com., 1974, guest lectr., 1969—. Recipient award for masters thesis U. So. Calif., 1966. Mem. Am. Musicol. Soc., L.A. County Mus. Art, L.A. Music Ctr., Mu Phi Epsilon, Pi Kappa Lambda. Home: PO Box 5360 Beverly Hills CA 90209-5360

KRAVITZ, HILARD L(EONARD), physician; b. Dayton, Ohio, June 26, 1917; s. Philip and Elizabeth (Charek) K.; divorced; children: Kent C., Kerry, Jay; m. Ellen King, Jan. 9, 1972; 1 child, Julie Frances. BA, U. Cin., 1939, MD, 1943. Lic. physician, Calif., Ohio. Resident in internal medicine Miami Valley Hosp., VA Hosp., Dayton, 1946-49; practice medicine specializing in internal medicine Dayton, 1950-54, Beverly Hills and Los Angeles, Calif., 1955—; practice medicine specializing in internal medicine and cardiology Los Angeles, 1955—; attending physician Cedars-Sinai Med. Ctr., 1955—; cons., med. dir. Adolph's Ltd., Los Angeles, 1955-74; mem. exec. com. Reiss-Davis Clinic, Los Angeles, 1966-70; chmn. pharmacy and therapeutic com. Cent City Hosp., Los Angeles, 1974-79; mem. pain commn. service Dept. Health and Human Services, Washington, 1985-86. Patentee sugar substitute, 1959, mineral-based salt, 1978. V.p. Friends of Music Calif. State U., Los Angeles, 1979-81. Served to capt. U.S. Army, 1944-46, ETO. Decorated Bronze Star with oak leaf cluster; Fourragere (France). Mem. AMA, Calif. Med. Assn., Los Angeles County Med. Assn., Am. Soc. Internal Medicine, Calif. Soc. Internal Medicine (del. 1974). Jewish. Office: 436 N Bedford Dr Ste 211 Beverly Hills CA 90210-4312

KRAVITZ, LENNY, singer, guitarist. Albums: Let Love Rule, 1989, Mama Said, 1991, Are You Gonna Go My Way, 1993 (2 Grammy nominations), Circus, 1995, Five, 1998 (Grammy); Soundtrack Austin Powers, The Spy Who Shagged Me, 1999. Office: care CAA 9830 Wilshire Blvd Beverly Hills CA 90212-1825 also: Virgin Records 550 Madison Ave New York NY 10022-3211 also: Virgin Records 2100 Columbia Ave Santa Monica CA 90404*

KRAW, GEORGE MARTIN, lawyer, essayist; b. Oakland, Calif., June 17, 1949; s. George and Pauline Dorothy (Herceg) K.; m. Sarah Lee Kenyon, Sept. 3, 1983. BA, U. Calif., Santa Cruz, 1971; student, Lenin Inst., Moscow, 1971; MA, U. Calif., Berkeley, 1974, JD, 1976. Bar: Calif. 1976, U.S. Dist. Ct. (no. dist.) Calif. 1976, U.S. Supreme Ct. 1980, D.C., 1992. Pvt. practice, 1976—; ptnr. Kraw & Kraw, San Jose, 1988—; Mem. ABA, Nat. Assn. Health Lawyers, Inter-Am. Bar Assn., Union Internationale des Avocats. Office: Kraw & Kraw 333 W San Carlos St Ste 1050 San Jose CA 95110-2735

KRAWETZ, STEPHEN ANDREW, molecular medicine and genetics scientist; b. Fort Frances, Ont., Can., Sept. 17, 1955; s. Stephen and Michaelene (Medynski) K.; m. Lorraine Ruth St. John, Aug. 19, 1977; children: Rhochelle Tairaesa, Alexandra Renée. BS, U. Toronto, Ont., 1977, PhD, 1983. Tchr. Scarborough Bd. Edn., Ont., 1976-77; Alberta Heritage Found. Med. Rsch. postdoc. fellow U. Calgary, Alta., Can., 1983-89; asst. prof. rsch. ctr. for molecular biology Wayne State U., Detroit, 1989, asst. prof. molecular biology and genetics, 1989-92, asst. prof. obstetrics and gynecology and molecular biology and genetics, 1992-94, assoc. prof. ob/gyn. and molecular medicine and genetics, 1994—; biotech. cons., Calgary, 1985-89, Grosse Pointe Woods, Mich., 1989—; co-founder Genetic Imaging, Inc., 1988; mem. fetal therapy group Hutzel Hosp., Detroit, 1994—; mem. gene therapy group DMC, Detroit, 1997—. Mem. editl. bd. BioTechniques, Ag Biotech News and Info.; contbr. numerous articles to scholarly jours. Recipient B.C. Childrens Hosp. Rsch. award, Vancouver, 1984, Computer Applications in Molecular Biology award, IntelliGenetics Inc., Mountain View, Calif., 1988; Alta. Heritage Found. Med. Rsch. fellow, 1985-88. Mem. AAAS, Am. Soc. Human Genetics, Soc. for the Study of Reproduction, Internat. Soc. for Matrix Biology (founding mem.), Am. Soc. Gene Therapy. Achievements include development of splinkers for sequencing DNA, of a computer-based imaging system for biological data, of VPCS cloning vectors, of the basis of biological sequence alignment algorithm; one of the first to describe overlapping reading frames in eucaryotes; first detailed analysis of a mammalian protamine gene; first definition of sequence interpretation errors in the GenBank database; first to define a genic domain in human sperm; research in gene therapy targeted to the amelioration of human disease; showed that selective potentiation of our genome mediates cell-phenotype. Home: 805 Canterbury Rd Grosse Pointe MI 48236-1285 Office: Dept Ob-Gyn Ctr Molecular Med Genetics Detroit MI 48201

KRAYBILL, DONALD BRUBAKER, college provost; b. Mt. Joy, Pa., Sept. 24, 1945; s. Wilmer Garber and Helen (Brubaker) K.; m. Frances Mellinger, Sept. 3, 1966; children: Sheila Lynn, Joy Louise. BA in Sociology and Religion, Ea. Mennonite U., Harrisonburg, Va., 1967; MA in Sociology, Temple U., 1972, PhD in Sociology, 1975. Prof. sociology Elizabethtown (Pa.) Coll., 1971-96; provost Messiah Coll., Grantham, Pa., 1996—; dir. Young Ctr., Elizabethtown Coll., 1989-96. Author: The Upside-Down Kingdom, 1978, 90 (Nat. Religious Book award Religious Book Rev. 1979), The Riddle of Amish Culture, 1989, The Amish and the State, 1993 (Outstanding Acad. Book award Choice 1994), Amish Enterprise, 1995, also others. Sr. Rsch. fellow NEH, 1987. Office: Messiah Coll Grantham PA 17027

KREAGER, EILEEN DAVIS, administrative consultant; b. Caldwell, Ohio, Mar. 2, 1924; d. Fred Raymond and Esther (Farson) Davis. BBA, Ohio State U., 1945. With accounts receivable dept. M & R Dietetic, Columbus, Ohio, 1945-50; complete charge bookkeeper Magic Seal Paper Products, Columbus, 1950-53, A. Walt Runglin Co., L.A., 1953-54; office mgr. Roy C. Haddox and Son, Columbus, 1954-60; bursar Meth. Theol. Sch. Ohio, Delaware, 1961-86; adminstrv. cons. Fin. Ltd., 1986—; ptnr. Coll. Administrv. Sci., Ohio State U., 1975-80; seminar participant Paperwork Systems and Computer Sci., 1965, Computer Systems, 1964, Griffith Found. Seminar Working Women, 1975; pres. Altrusa Club of Delaware, Ohio, 1972-73. Del. Altrusa Internat., Montreal, 1972, Altrusa Regional, Greenbrier, 1973. Mem. AAUW, Assoc. Am. Inst. Mgmt. (exec. coun. of Inst. 1979), Am. Soc. Profl. Cons., Internat. Platform Assn., Ohio State U. Alumna Assn., Columbus Computer Soc., Innovation Alliance, Toastmasters Internat., Ohio State U. Faculty Club, Univ. Club Columbus, Capital Club, Delaware Country Club, Columbus Met. Club, Friends Hist. Costume & Textile Collection Ohio State U., Kappa Delta. Methodist. Home: PO Box 214 Columbus OH 43085-0214

KREBS, ARNO WILLIAM, JR., lawyer; b. Dallas, July 7, 1942; s. Arno W. and Lynette (Linnstaedter) K.; m. Peggy Sharon Stagg, Dec. 17, 1966; 1 child, Kirsten; m. Barbara Lyn Craig, Dec. 28, 1973. B.A., Tex. A&M U., 1964; LL.B., U. Tex., 1967. Bar: Tex. 1967, U.S. Dist. Ct. (so. dist.) Tex. 1968, U.S. Ct. Appeals (5th cir.) 1971, U.S. Ct. Appeals (11th cir.) 1981, U.S. Dist. Ct. (we. and no. dists.) Tex. 1981, U.S. Supreme Ct. 1983, U.S. Dist. Ct. (ea. dist.) Tex. 1984. Assoc. Fulbright & Jaworski, Houston, 1967-75, ptnr., 1975—. Contbr. articles to profl. jours. Mem. Tex. Assn. Def. Counsel, Internat. Assn. Def. Counsel, Houston Bar Assn., ABA, Tex. Aggie Bar Assn., Tex. Bar Found., Houston Bar Found., Tex. A&M U. 12th Man Found. (pres. 1988), Houston Ctr. Club. Lutheran. Office: Fulbright & Jaworski 1301 Mckinney St Fl 51 Houston TX 77010-3031 also: 2200 Ross Ave Ste 2800 Dallas TX 75201-2750

KREBS, CAROL MARIE, architect, psychiatric therapist; b. St. Louis, May 6, 1958; d. Festus John and Virginia (Klohr) K. B in Environ. Design, U. Kans., 1982; MA in Edn. Counseling, St. Louis U., 1995. Archtl. intern GSA, Kansas City, Mo., 1980-81, Old Post Office Renovation, St. Louis, 1980-81; free-lance archtl. designer St. Louis, 1981-84; archtl. designer Interior Space, St. Louis, 1984, Gina Ward and Assoc., St. Louis, 1984-85, Michael Fox and Assoc., St. Louis, 1985-86; mgr. facility design and constrn. Southwestern Bell Telephone, St. Louis, 1986-88; mgr. int. arch. and design exec. facilities Southwestern Bell Corp. Asset Mgmt., St. Louis, 1989-94; psychiat. therapist DePaul Health Ctr., St. Louis, 1994—, Comtrea, Inc.; therapist St. Mary's Health Ctr., Mo. Dept. Mental Health, Dept. of Developmental Disabilities, 1998—. Active Big sister Big Bros./Big Sisters of Greater St. Louis, 1986—; mem. Operation Food Search. Mem. AIA. Avocations: historic building rehabilitation, art and play therapy activities with children and adults. Home: 965 Cleveland Ave Saint Louis MO 63122-2606

KREBS, EDWIN GERHARD, biochemistry educator; b. Lansing, Iowa, June 6, 1918; s. William Carl and Louise Helena (Stegeman) K.; m. Virginia Frech, Mar. 10, 1945; children: Sally, Robert, Martha. AB in Chemistry, U. Ill., 1940; MD, Washington U., St. Louis, 1943, DSc (hon.), 1995; DSc honoris causa, U. Geneva, 1979; hon. degree, Med. Coll. Ohio, 1993; DSc (hon.), U. Ind., 1993, U. Ill., 1995; D honoris causa, U. Nat. De Cuyo, 1993. Intern, asst. resident Barnes Hosp., St. Louis, 1944-45; rsch. fellow biol. chemistry Wash. U., St. Louis, 1946-48; prof., chmn. dept. biol. chemistry Sch. Medicine U. Calif., Davis, 1968-76; from asst. prof. to prof. biochemistry U. Wash., Seattle, 1948-66, prof., chmn. dept. pharmacology, 1977-83, prof. biochemistry and pharmacology, 1984-91; investigator, sr. investigator Howard Hughes Med. Inst., Seattle, 1983-90, sr. investigator emeritus, 1991—; mem. Phys. Chemistry Study Sect. NIH, 1963-68, Biochemistry Test Com. Nat. Bd. Med. Examiners, 1968-71, rsch. com. Am. Heart Assn., 1970-74, bd. sci. counselors Nat. Inst. Arthritis, Metabolism and Digestive Diseases, NIH, 1979-84, Internat. Bd. Rev., Alberta Heritage Found. for Med. Rsch., 1986, external adv. com. Weis Ctr. for Rsch., 1987-91; mem. subgroup interconvertible enzymes IUB Spl. Interest Group Metabolic Regulation; internat. adv. bd. Advances in Second Messenger Phosphoprotein Rsch.; external adv. com. Cell Therapeutics Inc., Seattle; adv. bd. Kinetek, Vancouver, B.C. Mem. editorial bd. Jour. Biol. Chemistry, 1965-70; mem. editorial adv. bd. Biochemistry, 1971-76; mem. editorial and adv. bd. Molecular Pharmacology, 1972-77; assoc. editor Jour. Biol. Chemistry, 1971-93; mem. internat. adv. bd. Advances in Cyclic Nucleotide Rsch., 1972—; editorial advisor Molecular and Cellular Biochemistry, 1987—. Recipient Nobel Prize in Medicine or Physiology, 1992, Gairdner Found. award, Toronto, 1978, J.J. Berzelius lectureship, Karolinska Institutet, 1982, George W. Thorn award for sci. excellence, 1983, Sir Frederick Hopkins Meml. lectureship, London, 1984, Rsch. Achievement award Am. Heart Assn., Anaheim, Calif., 1987, 3M Life Scis. award FASEB, New Orleans, 1989, Albert Lasker Basic Med. Rsch. award, 1989, CIBA-GEIGY-Drew award Drew U., 1991, Steven C. Beering award, Ind. U., 1991, Welch award in chemistry Welch Found., 1991, Louisa Gross Horwitz award Columbia U., 1989, Alumni Achievement award Coll. Liberal Arts and Scis. U. Ill., 1992, Kaul Found. award for excellence, 1996; John Simon Guggenheim fellow, 1959, 66. Mem. NAS, Am. Soc. Biol. Chemists (pres. 1986, ednl. affairs com. 1965-68, councillor 1975-78), Am. Acad. Arts and Scis., Am. Soc. Pharmacology and Exptl. Therapeutics. Achievements include lifelong study of the protein phosphorylation process. Office: U Wash Dept Pharmacology PO Box 357370 Seattle WA 98195-7370

KREBS, GARY MICHAEL, editor, author; b. Bklyn., Aug. 24, 1967; s. David K. and Kay D. (Donenfeld) K. BFA in Dramatic Writing, NYU, 1989. Editor acquisitions Facts on File, Inc., N.Y.C., 1989-94; editor The Guinness Book of Records, N.Y.C., 1994-95; exec. editor Macmillan Books, 1996—; editor: The Guinness Book of Sports Records, 1995-96. Interviewee various TV and radio programs, including Live with Regis and Kathie Lee, Baywatch, What's New, others; author: The Rock and Roll Reader's Guide. Avocations: writing fiction, screenwriting, playwriting. Home: 173 Forest Rd Glen Rock NJ 07452-1916*

KREBS, HOPE PAULA, lawyer; b. Phila., Feb. 13, 1961; d. Robert Krebs and Lois Sheila (Ponnock) Krebs Panitch; m. Kim R. Kinser, May 17, 1992; 1 child, Lindsey Elizabeth Kinser. BS in Acctg., Drexel U., 1984; JD, Villanova (Pa.) U., 1987; LLM in Taxation, N.Y.U., 1992. Bar: N.Y. 1988, U.S. Tax Ct. 1988, Pa. 1998. Part-time acct. Morris J. Cohen & Co., Phila., 1980-84; law clerk Frank & Pollack, Phila., 1985-86; lawyer Gordon, Hurwitz, Butowsky et al, N.Y.C., 1987-90, Milgrim Thomajan & Lee P.C., N.Y.C., 1990-92, Varet & Fink P.C., N.Y.C., 1992-95, Piper & Marbury L.L.P., N.Y.C., 1995-97; sr. tax mgr. Ernst & Young L.L.P., Phila., 1997-98; ptnr. Duane, Morris & Heckscher L.L.P., Phila., 1998—; adj. prof. of law Villanova (Pa.) U., 1995—. Contbr. articles to profl. jours. Mem. bd. dirs. Sr. Citizens Judicare Project, 1997-98. Mem. ABA, NAFE, Internat. Fiscal Assn., Internat. Tax Inst., Am. Women's Econ. Devel. Corp., N.Y. State Bar Assn., Wall St. Tax Assn. Democrat. Jewish. Office: Duane Morris & Heckscher LLP One Liberty Pl Philadelphia PA 19103

KREBS, MARTHA, physicist, federal science agency administrator. PhD in Theoretical Physics, Cath. U. America, Washington, D.C., 1975. Staff dir. House subcommittee on energy development and applications, Washington, D.C., 1977-83; assoc. dir. planning and devel. Lawrence Berkeley Lab., 1983-93; dir. office of sci. Dept. of Energy, 1993—. Office: Office of Sci Dept Energy 1000 Independence Ave SW Washington DC 20585-0001

KREBS, MARY JANE SCHIRGER, psychiatric nurse specialist; b. Perth Amboy, N.J., June 2, 1948; d. John William and Eleanore Jean (Hydo) Schirger; m. Jeffrey Scott Krebs, Aug. 4, 1979; children: Derek Jon, Richard William. BS, Trenton (N.J.) State Coll., 1970; MA, NYU, 1977. Cert. clin. nurse specialist in psychiat./mental health nursing. Clin. nurse specialist in adult mental health N.Y. Hosp.-Cornell Med. Ctr., N.Y.C., 1977-83; rsch. assoc. dept. psychiatry Cornell U. Med. Coll., N.Y.C., 1984-87; psychiat. clin. nurse specialist Payne Whitney Clinic, N.Y.C., 1984-88; psychotherapist Assoc. Psychotherapists of Danbury, Conn., 1987-95; asst. dir. nursing Westchester div. N.Y. Hosp.-Cornell Med. Ctr., White Plains, 1988-94; dir. nursing Silver Hill Hosp., New Canaan, Conn., 1994-97; v.p. clin. svcs. Jackson Brook Inst., South Portland, Maine, 1997-99, Spring Harbor Hosp., South Portland, 1999—; nursing cons. Contbr. chpts. to books, articles to profl. jours; editor textbook in field. Mem. ANA, Conn. Nurses Assn., Sigma Theta Tau.

KREBS, ROBERT ALAN, lawyer; b. Pitts., Dec. 12, 1958; s. James Arthur and Helen Marie (McGrogan) K.; m. Elizabeth Ann Bedford, Apr. 20, 1985; 1 child, Stephen Vladimir. BA, Pa. State U., 1981; student, U. Exeter, U.K., 1981; JD, Capital U., 1984. Bar: Pa. 1984, D.C. 1989, U.S. Dist. Ct. (ea. dist.) Pa. 1990, U.S. Dist. Ct. (we. dist.) Pa. 1984, U.S. Dist. Ct. (no. dist.) Ohio 1990, U.S. Dist. Ct. (D.C.) 1989, U.S. Ct. Appeals (D.C. cir.) 1989, U.S. Ct. Appeals (3d cir.) 1986, U.S. Supreme Ct. 1988. Assoc. Henderson & Goldberg, Pitts., 1985-87, Messer Shilobod & Crenney, Pitts., 1987-89, Klett Lieber Rooney & Schorling, Pitts., 1989-91, Conte, Melton & D'Antonio, Conway, Pa., 1992—. Articles editor Capital Law Rev., 1983-84. Mem. Pa. Dem. State Com., 37th Dist. (elected 1994, re-elected, 1998), Allegheny County Dem. Com., Pitts., 1991—; vol. Pitts. Ctr. for Grieving Children, 1995, 96. Recipient Am. Jurisprudence award Lawyers Coop. Pub. Co., 1982. Mem. ABA, FBA, D.C. Bar Assn., Pa. Trial Lawyers Assn. (amicus curiae com. 1996—), Allegheny County Bar Assn. (fed. ct. sect. coun. 1996—), Capital U. Law Sch. Alumni Assn. (bd. dirs. 1995—, v.p. 1996—), Western Pa. Trial Lawyers Assn. (bd. govs. 1994—). Democrat.

Roman Catholic. Home: 3235 Comanche Rd Pittsburgh PA 15241-1138 Office: 300 9th St Conway PA 15027-1647

KREBS, ROBERT DUNCAN, transportation company executive; b. Sacramento, May 2, 1942; s. Ward Carl and Eleanor Blauth (Duncan) K.; m. Anne Lindstrom, Sept. 11, 1971; children: Robert Ward, Elisabeth Lindstrom, Duncan Lindstrom. B.A. with distinction, Stanford U., 1964; M.B.A., Harvard U., 1966. Asst. gen. mgr. So. Pacific Transp. Co., Houston, 1974-75; asst. regional ops. mgr. So. Pacific Transp. Co., 1975-76; asst. v.p. So. Pacific Transp. Co., San Francisco, 1976-77; asst. to pres. So. Pacific Transp. Co., 1977-79, gen. mgr., 1979, v.p. transp., 1979-80, v.p. ops., 1980-82, pres., 1982-83, also dir.; pres., chief operating officer Santa Fe So. Pacific Corp., 1983-88,-pres., CEO, 1988-96; chmn., pres., CEO Burlington Northern Santa Fe Corp (merger Santa Fe So. Pacific Corp and Burlington Northern), 1997-99; chmn., CEO Burling No. Santa Fe Corp., 1999—. Trustee John G. Shedd Aquarium, Northwestern Meml. Hosp., Chgo., Lake Forest Coll.; bd. dirs. Phelps Dodge Corp., No. Trust Co., Santa Fe Pacific Gold Corp., Ft. Worth Symphony Orch. Assn. Mem. Assn. Am. R.R.s (bd. dirs.), Stanford U. Alumni Assn., Phi Beta Kappa, Kappa Sigma. Clubs: Onwentsia (Lake Forest, Ill.), Burlingame, Calif., Pacific Union, World Trade, Bohemian, Chicago. Office: Burlington Northern Santa Fe Corp PO Box 961052 Fort Worth TX 76161-0052*

KREBS, ROBERT PRESTON, lawyer; b. Pascagoula, Miss., July 20, 1948; s. Edmund Ory and Dorothy Nell (Davis) K.; m. Cynthia Schaub, Aug. 7, 1971. BA, St. Joseph Sem. Coll., St. Benedict, La., 1970; JD, U. Miss., 1974. Bar: Miss. 1974. Asst. dist. atty. Jackson County, Pascagoula, 1976-77; pvt. practice Pascagoula, 1975-77; assoc. John G. Corlew Law Office, Pascagoula, 1977-80; ptnr. Corlew, Krebs & Hammond, P.A., Pascagoula, 1980-84; pres. Krebs & Williams, P.A., Pascagoula, 1984-96, Robert P. Krels, P.A., Pascagoula, 1997-96. Pres. J.C. Hist. Soc., Pascagoula, 1986-87, United Christian Outreach-Our Daily Bread, Pascagoula, 1986-87; chmn. J.C. Dem. Exec. Com., Pascagoula, 1976-83. Mem. ABA, Miss. State Bar Assn. (bar commr. 1986-89), Jackson County Bar Assn., Miss. Bar Found., Inc. Am. Judicature Soc., Am. Coll. Mortgage Attys., Jackson County Young Lawyers Assn. (pres. 1976-77), St. Joseph Sem. Coll. Alumni Assn. (pres. 1995-97). Roman Catholic. Avocations: Tai Chi, woodworking, gardening, guitar. Home: 903 Ford Ave Pascagoula MS 39567-4924 Office: Robert P Krebs PA 3003 Magnolia St PO Box 1959 Pascagoula MS 39568-1959

KREBS, ROCKNE, artist; b. Kansas City, Mo., Dec. 24, 1938; s. Arthur Sanford and Lorine (Fisher) Krebs; m. Nizette Brennan, Oct. 30, 1991; children: Heather, Rockne Brennan, Nizette Cameron. BFA, U. Kans., 1961. Exhbns. include Gallery of Modern Art, Washington, 1968, Corcoran Gallery Art, Washington, 1969, U.S. Pavilion Expo 70, Osaka, Japan, 1970, Art Inst. Chgo., 1970, L.A. County Mus., 1970, New Orleans Mus., 1971, Phila. Mus. Art, 1973, Omni-Internat. Complex, Atlanta, 1973-76, Walker Art Ctr., Mpls., 1974, Art Prk, Lewiston, N.Y., 1975, U.S. Bicentennial Exop Sci. and Tech. Kennedy Space Ctr., Cape Canaveral, Fla., 1976, Balt. Inner Harbor, 1977, Fort Worth Art Mus., 1978, Disneyland Hotel, Anaheim, Calif., 1979, The Mall, Washington, 1980, Cin. Contemporary Art Ctr., 1985, Meml. Art Gallery, Rochester, N.Y., 1987, U. Rochester (N.Y.), 1987, Okla. Art Ctr., 1988; executed laser and neon artwork Urban Scale-Pine Ave. and City of Long Beach, Calif., 1992, laser artwork Pegasus Cloud Projection at Downtown Plz., City of Sacramento, 1993, neon, laser, fiber optic and search lights artwork Red River Bridge, Shreveport, La., 1993-95, animated laser projection Olympics CNN Ctr., Atlanta, 1996. Pioneer use of lasers in art. Patentee in field. Lt. USN, 1961-64. Office: 1428 U St NW Washington DC 20009-3916

KREBS, SHERRY LYNN, elementary education educator; b. Seattle, May 26, 1951; d. Donald Eugene and Ailene Leda (Wine) Barngrover; m. Kenneth Marvin Krebs, Aug. 25, 1950; children: Camille Kathleen, Karl Josef. BA, Whitworth Coll., Spokane, Wash., 1973; MEd, Lesley Coll., Cambridge, Mass., 1996. Tchr. jr. high sch. phys. edn. Wenatchee (Wash.) Pub. Schs., 1973-80; bus. mgr. Wenatchee Valley Symphony, 1980-88; tchr. elem. music Wenatchee (Wash.) Pub. Schs., 1989—. Prodr./artist: (cassette tape music) Woodside: Dances and Dreams, 1994. Actor, musician, condr. Music Theater of Wenatchee, 1975—; music dir. Short Shakespeareans, Wenatchee, 1986-92. Recipient Christa MaCaulliff Excellence in Edn. award State of Wash. Legis., 1994, Excellence in Edn. award North Ctrl. Wash. E.S.D., 1994; Barbara Thomas Meml. scholar, 1993. Mem. NEA, ASCD, Wash. Edn. Assn., Wenatchee Edn. Assn. Avocations: quilting, canoeing, skiing, being with family and friends. Home: 1520 9th St Wenatchee WA 98801-1656 Office: Lincoln Elem Sch 1224 Methow St Wenatchee WA 98801-3552

KREBS, WILLIAM HOYT, company executive, industrial hygienist; b. Detroit, Apr. 6, 1938; s. William Thomas and Mary Louise (Hoyt) K.; m. Susan Kathryn Bartholomew, Aug. 8, 1964 (div. July 1976); children: Elizabeth Louise, William Thomas II; m. Jane Germer Meikle, June 18, 1983; stepchildren: David Andrew, Sarah Elizabeth. BS, U. Mich., 1960, MPH (IH), 1963, MS, 1965, PhD, 1970. Rsch. asst. U. Mich., Ann Arbor, 1962-63; indsl. hygienist Lumbermens Mut. Casualty Co., Chgo., 1963-64; indsl. hygienist GM Corp., Detroit, 1970-77, mgr. toxic materials control activity, 1977-81, dir. toxic materials control activity, 1981-90, dir. indsl. hygiene activity, 1990-93; v.p. Indsl. Health Scis., Inc., Grosse Pointe Park, Mich., 1993—; mem. asbestos adv. com. Mich. Occupational Health Standards Commn., Lansing, 1984—. Contbr. articles to profl. jours. Mem. Grosse Pointe Meml. Ch., Grosse Pointe Farms, 1954; mem. health and safety com. Detroit Area coun. Boy Scouts Am., 1980. Fellow Am. Indsl. Hygiene Assn. (hon. mem.; bd. dirs. 1976-79, v.p. 1986-87, pres. 1988-89); mem. AAAS, APHA, Mich. Indsl. Hygiene Soc. (pres. 1980-81), Brit. Occupational Hygiene Soc., Internat. Occupational Hygiene Assn. (v.p. 1990-91, pres. 1992-93), Internat. Commn. on Occpl. Health, Soc. Automotive Engrs. Presbyterian. Home: 1014 Bishop Rd Grosse Pointe MI 48230-1421 Office: Indsl Health Scis Inc 1014 Bishop Rd Grosse Pointe MI 48230-1421

KREBSBACH, KAREN ANTON, journalist; b. Fond du Lac, Wis., Oct. 21, 1957; d. Orville Edward and Evelyn Rose (Sukowaty) K. BA in Journalism, English, U. Wis., Eau Claire, 1980; M of Latin Am. Studies, Harvard U., 1991. Reporter, bur. chief, asst. met. editor, asst. Sunday editor The Middlesex News, Framingham, Mass., 1983-89; copy editor, fgn. desk The Boston Globe, Mass., 1989-90; reporter The Daily Jour., Caracas, Venezuela, 1991-92; mng. editor Bus. Venezuela, Caracas, 1992-93; editor Fgn. Svc. Jour., Washington, 1993-97; copy editor overseas copy desk The Wall Street Jour., N.Y.C., 1997-98; mng. editor Global Business, N.Y.C., 1998—; fellow Knight Ctr. for Fgn. Journalists, Bolivia, 1996. Recipient ACE award, 1993. Mem. Inter-Am. Press Assn., Women's Fgn. Policy Group. Home: 321 E 22nd St Apt 3C New York NY 10010-4803 Office: The Wall Street Jour 200 Liberty St New York NY 10281-1003

KREC, GEORGE FRANK, JR., fundraiser; b. Waukegan, Ill., Mar. 6, 1946; s. George Frank and Dorothy Hattie (Neuendorf) K.; m. Catherine Gentry, Aug. 26, 1967 (div.); m. Rosa L. Dudash, June 25, 1992; children: David, Lisa, Lonnie, Brian. BS, George Williams Col., 1968. Dist. exec. Northeast Ill. Area Council Boy Scouts of Am., Highland Park, Ill., 1968-74; exploring dir. Miami Valley Council Boy Scouts of Am., Dayton, Ohio, 1974-78; exploring dir. Greater Cleve. Council Boy Scouts of Am., Cleve., 1978-84, fin. dir. Greater Cleve. Council, 1984-87; devel. dir. Detroit Area Council Boy Scouts of Am., Detroit, 1987-90; devel. coord. Mich. Metro Girl Scout Council, Detroit, 1992-94; dir. fund devel. Presbyn. Villages of Mich., Redford, 1994—; fund devel. couns. Huron Valley Girl Scout Council, Ypsilanti, Mich., 1991. Dir. Mundelein (Ill.) Cmty. Credit Union, 1971-74. Mem. Nat. Soc. Fund Raising Execs. (cert. fund raising exec.), Planned Giving Roundtable (v.p.). Presbyn. Home: 17194 Birwood Ave Beverly Hills MI 48025-3242 Office: Presbyn Villages Mich 25300 W 6 Mile Rd Redford MI 48240-2105

KRECH, SHEPARD, III, anthropology educator. BA in Anthropology, Yale U., 1967; BLitt in Social Anthropology, Oxford U., 1969; PhD in Anthropology, Harvard U., 1974. Tchg. fellow Harvard U., 1970-71; from instr. to asst. prof. U. Mass., Boston, 1974-75; instr. Northeastern U., 1975; from asst. prof. to prof. George Mason U., 1975-88, coord. anthropology program, 1979-85; rsch. assoc. dept. anthropology Am. Mus. Natural History, 1982—; prof. anthropology Brown U., 1988—, dir. Haffenreffer Mus. of Anthropology,, 1988—. Author: Praise the Bridge That Carries You Over: The Life of Joseph L. Sutton, 1981, Indians, Animals and the Fur Trade, 1981, The Subarctic Fur Trade: Native Social and Economic Adaptations, 1984, A Victorian Earl in the Arctic, 1989, Native Canadian Anthropology and History: A Selected Bibliography, rev. edit., 1994, Passionate Hobby, 1994, The Ecological Indian, 1999, Collecting Native America, 1870-1960, 1999, others; editor Ethnohistory, 1982-92; mem. editl. bd. Rupert's Land Rsch. Ctr., 1985—; contbr. numerous articles to profl. publs. Trustee H.L. Ferguson Mus., N.Y., 1976-79; sec. Class of 1967 Yale U., 1982-92; bd. dirs. Mashantucket Pequot Tribal Mus., 1990-92. Fellow Nat. Endowment for Humanities, 1981-82, Woodrow Wilson Internat. Ctr., 1992-93, Nat. Humanities Ctr., 1993-94; grantee Wenner-Gren Found., 1971-72, Nat. Inst. Mental Health, 1971-72, Am. Philos. Soc., 1975, 78, 81, Nat. Endowment for Humanities, 1986, Grotto Found., 1986, others. Mem. AAAS, Am. Anthropol. Assn., Anthropol. Soc. Washington (treas. 1982-86), Am. Soc. Ethnohistory, others. Fax: 401-863-7588. Office: Brown U Box 1921 Dept Anthropology Providence RI 02912

KRECHEVSKY, ROBERT L., federal judge; b. 1922. Bar: Conn. Bankruptcy judge for Conn., U.S. Bankruptcy Ct., Hartford, 1978—. Office: US Bankruptcy Ct 450 Main St Rm 712 Hartford CT 06103-3002

KREDA, ALLAN JAY, journalist; b. Bklyn., May 26, 1965; s. Bert and Roberta (Sussman) K.; m. Claudia Pizzi, July 25, 1993. BA in Biology, Bklyn. Coll., 1987; M Journalism, Northwestern U., Evanston, Ill., 1988. Writer, editor AP, N.Y.C., 1989—. Mem. N.Y. Friars Club. Home: 276 1st Ave New York NY 10009-1819 Office: AP 50 Rockefeller Plz New York NY 10020-1605

KREDLO, THOMAS ANDREW, real estate appraiser; b. East Chicago, Ind., Jan. 27, 1952; s. Raymond Vincent and Marna Maude (Smith) K. BS, Ind. U., 1977. Loan officer Michigan City (Ind.) Savs. and Loan, 1978-81; assoc. appraiser Meyer & Assocs., Hillsboro, Oreg., 1981-85, Lamb, Hanson, Lamb, Seattle, 1985-93; staff appraiser Strategic Mortgage Svcs., Denver, 1993-96, Alpha Appraisal & Consulting, Renton, Wash., 1997—. Author of short stories. Mem. Ptarmigan Mountaineering Club. Democrat. Roman Catholic. Avocations: mountaineering, bicycling, walking, back packing. Office: Alpha Appraisal & Consulting 16711 163rd Pl SE Renton WA 98058-8273

KREEGEL, DREW A., plastic and reconstructive surgeon; b. Dec. 26, 1956. MD, U. Tenn., Memphis, 1984. Plastic surgeon Midsouth Plastic Surgery, P.A., Nashville, 1991—. Office: 5651 Frist Blvd Ste 712 Hermitage TN 37076

KREEK, LOUIS FRANCIS, JR., lawyer; b. Washington, Aug. 24, 1928; s. Louis F. and Esperance (Agee) K.; m. Gwendolyn Schoepfle, Sept. 12, 1970. BS, MIT, 1948; JD, George Washington U., 1952. Bar: D.C. 1952, U.S. Dist. Ct. D.C. 1952, U.S. Ct. Appeals (D.C. cir) 1952, Ohio 1955, N.Y. 1964, U.S. Dist. Ct. (so. and ea. dists.) N.Y. 1964, N.J. 1972. Patent examiner U.S. Patent Office, Washington, 1948-53; patent atty. Pitts. Plate Glass Co., Washington, 1953-54, Battelle Meml. Inst., Columbus, Ohio, 1954-56, Merck & Co., Inc., Rahway, N.J., 1956-60; divsn. patent counsel Air Reduction Co., Murray Hill, N.J., 1960-63; assoc. Kenyon & Kenyon, N.Y.C., 1963-66; patent atty. Johns-Manville Corp., Manville, N.J., 1967-68; sr. patent atty. Esso Rsch. and Engring. Co., Linden, N.J., 1968-73, ICI Ams. Inc, Wilmington, Del., 1973-85; assoc. Oldham, Oldham & Weber Co. (now Oldham & Oldham Co.), Akron, Ohio, 1985-94, of counsel, 1994—. Mem. ABA, Am. Intellectual Property Law Assn., N.Y. Intellectual Property Law Assn. (assoc.), Cleve. Intellectual Property Law Assn. (bd. dirs. 1991-92), Akron Bar Assn., MIT Alumni Assn. (bd. dirs. fund bd 1977-80, officers conf. com. 1981-84, chmn. 1983), MIT Club Del. Valley (pres. 1978-80), MIT Club NE Ohio (pres. 1986-89), Am. Diabetes Assn. (bd. dirs. Akron chpt. 1989-90), Akron Roundtable (bd. dirs. 1989-90), Kiwanis (pres. 1989-90, lt. gov. 1992-93). Home: 2321 Stockbridge Rd Akron OH 44313-4512

KREEK, MARY JEANNE, physician; b. Washington; d. Louis Francis and Esperance (Agee) K; m. Robert A. Schaefer, Jan. 24, 1970; children: Robert A., Esperance Anne. Med. rschr. NIH, Bethesda, Md., 1957-62; intern, resident Cornell N.Y. Hosp. Med. Ctr., N.Y.C., 1962-65, fellow, 1965-67; instr. medicine Cornell Med. Coll., 1966-67; acad. medicine specializing in internal medicine, endocrinology, gastroenterology, clin. pharmacology N.Y.C., 1966—; mem. staff N.Y.-Presbyn. Hosp-Weill Sch. Medicine of Cornell U., 1968-77, clin. asst. prof., asst. attending physician, now assoc. attending physician, adj. assoc. prof.; ast. prof. Rockefeller U., 1967-72, sr. rsch. assoc., physician, 1972-83, assoc. prof., physician, 1983-94, prof., sr. physician, head of lab., 1994—; head Ind. Lab. on Biology of Addictive Diseases, 1975-94, head of lab., 1994—; sr. physician Rockefeller U. Hosp., 1994—; mem. gen. medicine study sect. NIH, 1973-77; co-chmn. John E. Fogarty (NIH) Internat. Conf. Hepatotoxicity Due to Drugs and Chems., 1977, charter mem. peer rev. oversight group, 1996—; vis. prof. Pahlavi U., Shiraz, Iran, summer 1977; spl. adv. Nat. Inst. Drug Abuse, 1976-86, mem. Nat. Adv. Coun., 1991-95; mem. NIH Peer Rev. Oversight Group, 1996—; prin. investigator Rsch. Ctr. Biol. Basis Addictive Diseases, 1987—; mem. gastroenterology adv. com. FDA, 1975-79, 92-96, NIH Gen. Clin. NIH Gen. Rsch. Ctr. Study Sect., 1979-83, chmn., 1982-83; mem. exec. com. Coll. Problems Drug Dependence, 1982-87, 89-94, chmn. exec. com., 1985-87, chair sci. program com., 1991-96; fellow CPDD, 1992—; dir. NIH-NIDA Rsch. Ctr., 1987—. Recipient Borden Rsch. award, 1962, Career Scientist award Health Rsch. Coun. City N.Y., 1974-75, Dole/Nyswander award, Rsch. Scientist award NIH Gen. Clin. sect., 1978—, Mentor of Mentors award Am. Soc. Addiction Medicine, 1995, Assn. for Med. Edn. and Rsch. in Substance Abuse-Betty Ford award for outstanding rsch., 1996, R. Brinkley Smithers Disting. Scholar award Am. Soc. Addiction Medicine, 1999, Nathan B. Eddy award Coll. on Problems of Drug Dependence, 1999. Fellow ACP, Am. Coll. Neuropsychopharmacology, Am. Fedn. for Clin. Rsch.; mem. Shakespeare Soc. of Wellesley, Am. Gastroent. Assn., N.Y. Gastroent. Assn. (pres. 1987), Endocrine Soc., Am. Assn. Study Liver Diseases, Internat. Assn. Study Liver, Internat. Narcotic Rsch. Conf. Group (exec. com. 1993-97), Rsch. Soc. on Alcoholism, Soc. on Neurosci., Phi Beta Kappa, Sigma Xi. Home: 1175 York Ave New York NY 10021-7169 Office: Rockefeller U New York NY 10021

KREER, IRENE OVERMAN, association and meeting management executive; b. McGrawsville, Ind., Nov. 11, 1926; d. Ralph and Laura Edith (Sharp) Overman; m. Henry Blackstone Kreer, Dec. 22, 1946; children: Laurene (dec.), Linda Kreer Witt. BS in Speech Pathology, Northwestern U., 1948. Speech pathologist Chgo. pub. schs., 1947-49; staff asst., lectr. Art Inst. Chgo., 1962—; pres. Irene Overman Kreer & Assocs., Inc., Chgo., 1962—; frequent lectr. on art, arch., Chgo. area; TV appearances representing Art Inst. edn. programs. Past bd. dirs. Glenview (Ill.) Pub. Libr.; mem. The Art Inst. Chgo., Glenview Cmty. Ch., Field Mus., Chgo. Architecture Found., Smithsonian Assocs. Mem. Nat. Trust Hist. Preservation, Assn. Alumnae Northwestern U. (bd. dirs. 1975—), Delta Delta Delta. Republican. Avocations: travel, archaeology, tennis (ranked in women's singles and doubles, Chgo.).

KREESE, JOHN L., basketball coach; b. Apr. 17, 1943; m. Sue Sommer-Kreese, Dec. 28, 1985; children: John and Ryan (twins). BA in English, St. John's U., 1964, MS in Edn., 1970. Asst. varsity, jr. varsity head coach Christ the King H.S., 1964-65; asst. coach St. John's U., 1965-70, 1973-79; asst. coach, dir. player pers., chief scout N.Y. Nets, 1970-73; head coach Coll. Charleston, S.C., 1979—, athletics dir., 1984—; mem. southeast regional adv. com. NCAA Divsn. Basketball Tournament; lectr. in field. Coauthor: Attacking Zone Defense. Hon. chmn. Med. U. S.C. Hosp.'s Holiday Card Drive. Mem. Nat. Assn. Basketball Coaches (congressman). Office: Coll Charleston 30 George St Charleston SC 29401-1434*

KREFTING, ROBERT J(OHN), publishing company executive; b. Peoria, Ill., Apr. 29, 1944; s. Walter and Rebecca Juliana K.; m. Sally Ann Kingsmill, Aug. 27, 1978; children: Matthew, Nicholas; children by previous marriage: Gordon, Melissa, Sarah. BA magna cum laude with honors in History, Williams Coll., 1966. Subscription sales mgr. Time, Inc., N.Y.C., 1966-71; assoc. pub. Psychology Today, Del Mar, Calif., 1971-74; with CBS Publs., N.Y.C., 1974-83; v.p., group pub. spl. interest mags. CBS Publs., 1977-79, pres., 1979-83; pres. City Home Pub., Houston, 1984-85; exec. v.p. McCall Pub. Co., 1985-87; pres. Park Ave. Pub., N.Y.C., 1987-90, Holly Hill Pub., Katanah, N.Y., 1991-98; sr. v.p. Reader's Digest Assn., Pleasantville, N.Y., 1998—. Mem. Mag. Pubs. Assn., Young Presidents Orgn., Waccabuc Country Club, Sky Club, Phi Beta Kappa. Home: 4 Powder Hill Rd Waccabuc NY 10597 Office: Reader's Digest Assn Readers Digest Rd Pleasantville NY 10570

KREGEL, JAMES R., publishing executive; b. Grand Rapids, Mich., Apr. 18, 1950. BA, Mich. State U., 1972. Pres. Kregel Publs., Grand Rapids, Mich., 1989—. Office: Kregel Publs Box 2607 733 Wealthy St SE Grand Rapids MI 49503-5553*

KREGG, JUDITH LYNNE, accountant; b. Miami, Fla., June 1, 1947; d. Edward and Vernon Margurite (Davis) Malm; m. Gene Robert Kregg, Dec. 11, 1971 (div. Mar. 1977). A in Bus., Miami-Dade C.C., 1980. Staff acct. SONY Corp., N.Y.C., 1968-72, First Mortgage Investment, Miami Beach, Fla., 1975-78; regional contr. Smith Barney, Miami, Fla., 1978; staff acct. Fininvest Internat., Key Biscayne, Fla., 1979; chief acct. Transway Internat., Coral Gables, Fla., 1980-81; constrn. acct. Senior Corp., Miami Beach, 1981-85; dir. acctg. The Continental Cos., Coconut Grove, Fla., 1985-90; contr. Ireland Cos., North Miami, Fla., 1990; comml. acctg. mgr. Harbour Realty, Bay Harbor, Fla., 1991-94; contr. divsn. Carnival Resorts and Casinos Grand Bay Resort & Residencies, Coconut Grove, Fla., 1994—. Editor The SandDollar, 1991-96. Bd. dirs., 2d v.p., community coun. WLRN, South Fla.'s Pub. Radio & TV Sta., Miami, 1992-94. Recipient Cert. of Appreciation, WLRN, 1993. Mem. Ctr. for Orangutan and Chimpanzee Conservation (asst. editor Primapes newsletter 1995-97), Inst. Mgmt. Accts.(pres. Miami chpt. 1993-94, bd. dirs. 1991-92, nat. dir., 1996—, cert. of appreciation 1995, 97), Am. Orchid Soc., Coral Gables Orchid Soc., PEO Sisterhood (Miami Lakes Chpt. treas. 1992-93, pres. 1995-96, 98-99). Avocations: orchid culture, Victorian collectibles. Home: 2620 SW 23rd Ave Miami FL 33133-2322

KREHBIEL, FREDERICK AUGUST, II, electronics company executive; b. Chgo., June 2, 1941; s. John Hammond and Margaret Ann (Veeck) K.; m. Kay Kirby, Dec. 20, 1973; children: William Veeck, Jay Frederick. B.A., Lake Forest Coll., 1963. Export mgr., then v.p. internat. Molex Inc., Lisle, Ill., 1970-75, exec. v.p., dir., from 1976; vice chmn. and chief exec. officer Molex Co., 1988-93; chmn., CEO Molex, Inc., Lisle, Ill., 1993—; dir. Tellabs Inc., Molex, Inc., No. Trust Bank, Nalco Chem., DeVry, Inc. Trustee Inst. Internat. Edn., Chgo., Rush Med. Ctr., Chgo., Lyric Opera, Chgo., Chgo. Zool. Soc., Chgo. Hist. Soc., Mus. Sci. and Industry, Chgo., Chgo. Orch. Assn., World Wildlife, Washington. Mem. Hinsdale (Ill.) Golf Club, Chgo. Club, Casino Club (Chgo.), Chgo. Yacht Club, Racquet Club Chgo. Home: 505 S County Line Rd Hinsdale IL 60521-4725 Office: Molex Inc 2222 Wellington Ave Lisle IL 60532-3820

KREHBIEL, ROBERT JOHN, lawyer; b. Waukegan, Ill., Dec. 8, 1948. BA magna cum laude, Knox Coll., 1971; JD, Washington U., 1980. Bar: Mo. 1980, U.S. Dist. Ct. (ea. dist.) Mo. 1980, U.S. Dist. Ct. (we. dist.) Mo. 1992, Ill. 1981, U.S. Ct. Appeals (8th cir.) 1981, U.S. Supreme Ct. 1987. Mem. Evans & Dixon, St. Louis. Mem. Mo. Bar, Bar Assn. Met. St. Louis, Order of Coif, Phi Beta Kappa. Office: Evans & Dixon 1200 St Louis Pl 200 N Broadway Ste 1200 Saint Louis MO 63102-2749*

KREHTINKOFF-YARLOVSKY, NINA, nursing administrator; b. Flin Flon, Man., Can., Oct. 5, 1955; d. Vasyl Nicolov and Milka Georgi (Krehtinkoff) Yarlovsky; m. Jay Richard Fisherman, June 26, 1983 (div. Dec. 1996). BS, Roanoke Coll., 1977; postgrad., Autonomous U. Guadalajara, 1977-79; MS, Pace U. Grad. Sch. Nursing, 1982. Diplomate Am. Bd. Quality Assurance and Utilization Rev. Profls. Staff nurse oncology Yonkers (N.Y.) Gen. Hosp., 1982-83, Montefiore Med. Ctr., Bronx, N.Y., 1984-85; br. mgr., nursing supr. Staff Builders, Health Care Svcs., Inc., Flushing, N.Y., 1985-88; inpatient nurse mgr. Ritter-Scheuer Hospice, Bronx, 1988-90; supr. home care Jacob Perlow Hospice, Beth Israel Med. Ctr., N.Y.C., 1990; patient care mgr. Westmoreland Hospice, Greensburg, Pa., 1992-93; dir. clin. svcs. Olsten Kimberly Quality Care, Inc., White Plains, N.Y., 1993-94; utilization review supr. Staff Builders, Health Care Svcs., Inc., Washington, 1994-95; sr. utilization rev. nurse ADP Integrated Med. Solutions, Bethesda, Md., 1996—; presenter AIDS conf. Am. Bd. of Quality Assurance and Utilization Review Physicians (ABQAURP), diplomate, 1997—.

KREIDER, CLEMENT HORST, JR., neurosurgeon; b. Annville, Pa., Oct. 14, 1932; s. Clement Horst and Eleanor Lucille (Etter) K.; m. Yvonne Maria Vignone, Mar. 6, 1983; children: Clement H. III, John William H., George E. Etter; stepchildren: Michael A. Ketcham (dec. July 1997), David C. Ketcham. Student, Yale U., 1949-51, 53-54; BS, Bethany (W.Va.) Coll., 1957; MD, Temple U., 1963. Lic. physician, Pa., N.J. Intern Pa. Hosp., Phila., 1963-64; resident in gen. surgery Temple U. Hosp, Phila., 1964-65, resident in neurosurgery, 1965-69; pvt. practice neurosurgery Harrisburg, Pa., 1969-72, Ocean, N.J., 1972—; chief sect. neurosurgery Jersey Shore Med. Ctr., Neptune, N.J., 1972-96; sr. attending Monmouth Med. Ctr., Long Branch, N.J., 1972-99; full attending Riverview Med. Ctr., Red Bank, N.J.; cons. CentraState Med. Ctr., Freehold, N.J.; courtesy staff Med. Ctr. of Ocean County, Point Pleasant, N.J., Kimball Med. Ctr., Lakewood, N.J., Bayshore Cmty. Hosp., Holmdel, N.J.; clin. instr. surgery Hershey (Pa.) Med. Ctr., 1970-72, Hahnemann Med. Ctr., Phila., 1970-72. Contbr. articles to profl. jours.; mem. com. on pub. N.J. Medicine, Lawrenceville, 1985—. With U.S. Army, 1951-53. Fellow Stroke Coun., Am. Heart Assn.; mem. Congress of Neurol. Surgeons, Am. Assn. Neurol. Surgeons Joint Sect. on Cerebrovasc. Surgery, Med. Soc. N.J., N.J. Neurosurg. Soc., Monmouth County Med. Soc., Acad. Medicine of N.J. Avocation: boating. Office: West Shore Plaza 1398 Highway 35 Ocean NJ 07712-3522 also: Middletown Med Arts Plaza 370 Highway 35 Ste 103 Red Bank NJ 07701-5922

KREIDER, LEONARD EMIL, economics educator; b. Newton, Kans., Feb. 25, 1938; s. Leonard C. and Rachel (Weaver) K.; m. Louise Ann Pankratz, June 10, 1963; children: Brent Emil, Todd Alan, Ryan Eric. Student, Bluffton Coll., 1956-58; BA, Bethel Coll., 1960; student, Princeton U., 1960-61; MA, Ohio State U., 1962, PhD, 1968. Economist So. Ill. U., Carbondale, 1965-70; asst. prof. Beloit (Wis.) Coll., 1970—, prof., 1978, chmn. dept. econs. and mgmt., 1984-89, acting v.p. acad. affairs, 1987-88, Allen Bradley prof. econs., 1991—; chief of party Devel. Assocs., Asuncion, Paraguay, 1970; economist Deere and Co., 1973, Castle and Cooke, San Francisco, 1975-76, AmCore, Rockford, Ill., 1984, Rockford Meml. Hosp., 1990-91, Stone Container, San Jose, Costa Rica, 1996; cons. corps. and attys. Author: Development and Utilization of Managerial Talent, 1968; contbr. numerous articles, reports to profl. jours. Mem. Nat. Assn. Bus. Economists, Am. Econs. Assn., Am. Assn. Higher Edn., Soc. Internat. Devel. (pres. So. Ill. chpt. 1969), Indsl. Relations Research Assn. (elections com. 1974). Presbyterian. Home: 820 Milwaukee Rd Beloit WI 53511-5636 Office: Beloit Coll Dept Econ Mgmt Beloit WI 53511

KREIDER, SANDRA ANNE MILLER, medical/surgical nurse; b. Utica, Mich., Aug. 31, 1948; d. Maurice A. and Jennie C. (Brooks) Miller; children: Teresa, Catherine, Tara; m. Melvin L. Kreider. AS in Nursing, Pasco-Hernando C.C., New Port Richey, Fla., 1988. Staff nurse Citrus Meml. Hosp., Inverness, Fla.; case mgr., staff nurse ABC Home Health, Inverness, Fla., Vis. Nurses, New Port Richey, Fla.; intake coord. ABC Home Health, Port Richey, Fla.; patient car coord., nursing supr.; adminstr. ABC Home Health, Bayonet Point, Fla.; adminstr. ABC Home Health, Bayonnet Point, Fla.; case mgr. 1st Am. Homecare, Zephyr Hills, Fla.; staff nurse Homecare of East Tenn. Mem. West Pasco Community Svc. Coun. Mem. West Pasco C. of C. (health svcs. com.), COECHA of Pasco, Phi Theta Kappa. Home: 849 Bates Ln Kodak TN 37764-2305

KREIDLER, CHARLES W(ILLIAM), linguist, educator; b. Frankfort, Ky., Aug. 5, 1924; s. Christopher George and Elizabeth Allen (Best) K.; m. Carol Jane Kardos, Aug. 15, 1959; children: James Christopher, Julia Frances Hickey. AB in Spanish, U. Cin., 1948; MA in Linguistics, U. Mich., 1951, PhD, 1957. Teaching fellow U. Mich., Ann Arbor, 1953-54, asst. prof. English, 1959-63; instr., then asst. prof. modern langs. St. Peter's Coll., Jersey City, 1954-58; Fulbright lectr. in English Ctrl. Univ. Ecuador and U. Guayaquil, Quito, Ecuador, 1958-59; assoc. prof., then prof. linguistics Georgetown U., Washington, 1963-93, prof. emeritus, 1993—; Fulbright Prof. U. Sao Paulo, Brazil, 1990, Cath. U. of Asuncion, Paraguay, 1994; lectr. U. P.R., 1965, U. So. Calif., 1968; guest prof. U. Regensburg, Germany, 1975; cons. in field. Author: (with Allen Glatthorn and Ernest Heiman) The Dynamics of Language, 1971, The Pronunciation of English: A Course Book in Phonology, 1989, Describing Spoken English, 1997, Introducing English Semantics, 1998; contbr. articles to profl. jours. With USNR, 1943-46. Home: 4512 Verplanck Pl NW Washington DC 20016-2432

KREIG, ANDREW THOMAS, trade association executive; b. Chgo., Feb. 28, 1949; s. Albert Arthur and Margaret Theresa (Baltzell) K. AB, Cornell U., 1970; MSL, Yale U., 1983; JD, U. Chgo., 1990. Bar: D.C. 1991, Mass. 1991, Ill. 1991. Writer, editor Hartford (Conn.) Courant, 1970-84; media dir. Conn. House Spkr., Hartford, 1984; freelance author, journalist, lectr. Hartford and Chgo., 1985-89; law clk. U.S. Dist. Judge Mark L. Wolf, Boston, 1990-91; assoc. Latham & Watkins, Washington, 1991-93; v.p., comms. dir. Wireless Comms. Assn. Internat., Inc., Washington, 1993-96, v.p., gen. counsel, 1996, pres., 1997—; ethics com. Soc. Profl. Journalists, 1987-90. Author: Spiked: How Chain Management, 1987, 2d edit., 1988; editor Spectrum, 1994—; bd. editors Pvt. & Wireless Cable, 1994—, Wireless Internat., 1996—; contbr. articles to profl. jours. V.p. Residences Market Square, Washington, 1993-98. Ford Found. fellow Yale Law Sch., New Haven, 1982-83. Mem. Fed. Com. Bar Assn. (legis. com.). Home: PH8 701 Pennsylvania Ave NW Washington DC 20004-2608 Office: Wireless Comms Assn Ste 810 1140 Connecticut Ave NW Washington DC 20036-4010

KREILICK, ROBERT W., chemist, educator; b. Kalamazoo, Jan. 3, 1938; s. Herbert A. and Lenore K. K.; m. Willma J. Ham, Aug. 15, 1958; children: Christian J., Kelley G. AB, Washington U., 1959, PhD, 1964. Chemist Monsanto Chem., 1959-60; asst. prof. chemistry U. Rochester, N.Y., 1964-69; asso. prof. U. Rochester, 1969-71, prof., 1971-80, prof. chemistry, 1980—; founding ptnr. Adaptable Lab. Software, developed ASYST program language; cons. NIH. Contbr. chpts. to books, articles to profl. jours. Shell Oil fellow, 1962; NIH fellow, 1963; Alfred P. Sloan fellow, 1968; NIH grantee. Mem. AAUP, Am. Chem. Soc., Biophys. Soc., Sigma Xi. Office: U Rochester Dept Chemistry Rochester NY 14627*

KREILING, JEAN LOUISE, music educator; b. Middletown, N.Y., Mar. 29, 1955; d. Robert Taylor and Mary Louise (Lucas) K. BA in English, The Coll. of William & Mary, 1976; MA in English, U. Va., 1978; BA in Musicology, U. N.C., Greensboro, 1981; MA in Musicology, U. N.C., 1983, PhD in Musicology, 1986. Instr. english Western Carolina Univ., Cullowhee, N.C., 1978-79; tchr., adminstr. South Shore Conservatory of Music, Hingham, Mass., 1986-87; asst. prof. to prof. music Bridgewater (Mass.) State Coll., 1987-97, prof. music, 1997—. Contbr. articles to James Joyce Quar., Beethoven Newsletter, and Bridgewater Review. Fund raising vol. Nat. Public Radio, Chapel Hill, N.C., 1982-86, Boston, 1990; vol. tutor Mass. Coalition Adult Lit., Brockton, Mass., 1989-91. Mem. Am. Musicological Soc., Coll. Music Soc., Am. Brahms Soc., Mass. State Coll. Assn. Office: Bridgewater State Coll Dept of Music Bridgewater MA 02325

KREIMER, MICHAEL WALTER, financial planner, investment company official; b. N.Y.C., Aug. 29, 1963; s. Anthony Kreimer and Frieda (Gœbel) Rath; m. Madeline Louise Lawler, Dec. 31, 1992; children: Jillian Marie, Maximilian Walter. BS cum laude, SUNY, Albany, 1985. Lic. ins. agt., N.Y.; CFP. Assoc. v.p. McLaughlin, Piven, Vogel Inc., Jericho, N.Y., 1985-88; fin. planner, br. mgr. A.G. Edwards & Sons, Smithtown, N.Y., 1988—; agt. Ins. Dept. State of N.Y., 1989—. Cons (newsletter) Investing, 1992—. Fundraiser Big Bros./Big Sisters Suffolk, Commack, N.Y., 1989; mem. Nat. Parks Conservation Assn., Washington, 1992. Mem. Nat. Assn. Securities Dealers (lic.), Internat. Bd. Standards and Practices for CFPs (CFP mark 1993), Inst. CFPs (direct pub. awareness program 1994-97, L.I. chpt.), Smithtown C. of C. (assoc.), Southampton C. of C., Southampton C. of C., United Consumers Club. Republican. Roman Catholic. Avocations: tennis, skiing, golf, running. Home: 2 Abets Creek Path East Patchogue NY 11772 Office: AG Edwards & Sons 760 Montauk Hwy Water Mill NY 11976

KREIN, CATHERINE CECILIA, public relations professional, educator; b. N.Y.C., July 2, 1938; d. Timothy T. and Catherine A. (Lavery) Mitchell; m. Robert Krein, Apr. 18, 1970; 1 child, Karen Elise. BS, Fordham U., 1960; film cert., NYU, 1974; MA, Queens Coll., 1994. Various positions including prodr., editl. dir., writer CBS News, N.Y.C., 1963-86; chief spokesperson Bklyn. Dist. Atty., 1986-87; v.p. external affairs Molloy Coll., Rockville Centre, N.Y., 1987—, prof. broadcast journalism, 1997—. Mem. Coun. for Advancement and Support of Edn., Internat. Assn. Bus. Communicators, Nat. Acad. TV Arts and Scis., Pub. Rels. Soc. Am., Profl. Pub. Rels. of L.I., L.I. Coalition Fair Broadcasting, L.I. Communicators Assn. Home: 151-20 88th St Apt 6J Howard Beach NY 11414-2008

KREINDLER, PETER MICHAEL, lawyer; b. 1945. BA, Harvard U., 1967, JD, 1971. Bar: D.C. 1971, N.Y. 1989. Assoc. Hughes, Hubbard & Reed, 1975-77, ptnr., 1977-88; ptnr. Arnold & Porter, 1990-91; sr. v.p., gen. counsel and sec. AlliedSignal, Morristown, N.J., 1992—; sec. Allied-Signal, Morristown, N.J., 1995—. Office: Allied Signal Inc 101 Columbia Rd Morristown NJ 07962-2245*

KREINHEDER, HAZEL FULLER, genealogist, historian; b. Northampton, Mass., Aug. 27, 1935; d. John Herbert and Hazel Gertrude (Lamica) Fuller; m. Robert Frederick Kreinheder, Nov. 14, 1959; children: John Frederick, Paul Robert. BA, U. Mass., 1957. Lab. asst. dept. chemistry Amherst (Mass.) Coll., 1952-57; rsch. analyst Dept. Def., Fort George, Meade, Md., 1957-63; libr. staff mem. Columbia Hist. Soc., Washington, 1976-77; hist. rschr. Washington, 1977-81; staff genealogist DAR, Washington, 1981-85, corrections genealogist, 1985—, ethnic and minority genealogist, 1997—; hist./geneal. cons. Washington Perspectives, Inc., 1977-90. Co-author 3 booklets. Sec. Capitol Hill Restoration Soc., Washington, 1967-68, treas., 1968-70, co-chair hist. preservation com., 1976-79, chmn. house com., 1979-81, mem., 1966—; vol. rschr. joint com. Landmarks Nat. Capital, 1973-76; mem. Com. 100 Fed. City, 1978—, hist. preservation, 1978-81; mem. Oldest Inhabitants D.C., 1993—; mem. Bryan Sch. Neighborhood Assn., 1995—; vol. Prevention of Blindness Soc. Pre-Sch. Vision Screening Program, 1969-72; mem. Friends of the Libr./U. Mass.; charter mem. Friends of the Evergreens, Amherst, 1998—; mem. Nat. Bldg. Mus., 1999—; mem. Capitol Hill Babysitting Co-op, 1963-75, mem. exec. bd., 1966-68; mem. Circle-on-the-Hill, treas., 1964-65. Named Capitol Hill Citizen Yr. Capitol Hill Restoration Soc., 1970. Mem. DAR, NSDAR (life, nat. vice chmn.'s assn., vice chair patriot index com. 1992-95, vice chair minority rsch. Lineage Rsch. Com. 1998—, Mary Mattoon chpt. libr. 1996—), Orgn. Am. Historians, Nat. Geneal. Soc., Nat. Inst. on Geneal. Rsch. Alumni Assn., Am. Hist. Assn., Conn. Soc. Genealogists, Soc. Genealogie Que., Soc. Genealogique Canadienne-Francaise, No. N.Y. Geneal. Soc., New Eng. Hist. Geneal. Soc., Assn. Profl. Genealogists, U.S. Capitol Hist. Soc., Chi Omega. Republican. Lutheran. Avocations: civic activities, reading, needlework. Home: 113 Kentucky Ave SE Washington DC 20003-1447 Office: Nat Soc DAR 1776 D St NW Washington DC 20006-5303

KREININ, MORDECHAI ELIAHU, economics educator; b. Tel Aviv, Jan. 20, 1930; came to U.S., 1951, naturalized, 1960; m. Marlene Miller, Aug. 29, 1956; children: Tamara, Elana, Miriam. B.A., U. Tel Aviv, 1951; M.A., U. Mich., 1952, Ph.D., 1954. Asst. prof. econs. Mich. State U., East Lansing, 1957-59, assoc. prof., 1959-61, prof., 1961-90, univ. disting. prof. econs., 1990—; vis. prof. econs. UCLA, 1969, UN, Geneva, 1971-73, NYU, 1975, 93, 96, U. Toronto, 1978, others; vis. scholar Inst. Internat. Econs. Studies, U. Stockholm, 1978-80, U. B.C., summer, 1983, Monash U., Melbourne, Australia, 1987-94, NYU, 1993, 96, Copenhagen Bus. Sch., Denmark, 1994-95, Kobe (Japan) U., 1997, Ctr. Southeast Asian Studies, U. Singapore, 1998; adj. rsch. assoc. East-West Ctr., Honolulu, 1990—; world lectr. tours on behalf of U.S. Info. Svc., 1974-96; cons. to Dept. Commerce, 1964-66, Dept. State, 1972-74, UN Con. Rels, N.Y.C., 1965-67, Brockings Instn., 1972-75, C. Am. Common Market, 1972-75, Internat. Monetary Fund, 1976, East-West Ctr., Honolulu, 1987—; mem. internat. econs. rev. bd. NSF, 1981, 85; bd. mem. Internat. Trade & Fin. Assn., 1990—, pres. 1993. Author: Israel and Africa: A Study in Technical Cooperation, 1964, Alternative Commercial Policies—Their Effects on the American Economy, 1967, International Economics—A Policy Approach, 8th edit., 1998, Trade Relations of the EEC—An Empirical Investigation, 1974, International Commercial Policy: Issues for the 1990's, 1993, Contemporary Issues in Trade Policy, 1995, (with L. Officer) The Monetary Approach to the Balance of Payments: A Survey, 1978, Economics, 1983, 3d edit., 1999; editor: Can Australia Adjust?, 1988, International Commercial Policy: Issues for the 90's, 1993, Contemporary Issues in Trade Policy, 1995, The U.S.-Canada Free Trade Agreement, 1999; co-editor: Asia-Pacific Economic Linkages, 1997; contbr. articles to profl. jours. NSF fellow, 1964-73, Ford Found. fellow, 1960-61; recipient Disting. Faculty award Mich. State U., 1968, State of Mich. Collegiate award, 1984, Whitefield Winslow Faculty award, 1994. Mem. AAUP, Am. Econ. Assn., Midwest Econ. Assn., Western Econ. Assn., Royal Econ. Assn., Internat. Trade and Fin. Assn. (bd. dirs. 1991-94). Jewish. Home: 1431 Sherwood Ave East Lansing MI 48823-1851 Office: Mich State U Dept Econs East Lansing MI 48824

KREIS, JASON, professional soccer player; b. Omaha, Dec. 29, 1972. Student, Duke U. Midfielder Dallas Burn; U.S. Nat. Soccer Team debut 1996; finished 9th in MLS scoring, 1996, scored goal in all-star game; 3-time All-Am., Duke U. Office: US Soccer Fedn 1801-1811 S Prairie Ave Chicago IL 60616 and: Dallas Burn 2602 McKinney Ste 200 Dallas TX 75204*

KREIS, WILLI, physician; b. Switzerland, Nov. 3, 1924; came to U.S., 1961; naturalized citizen, 1992; s. Alfred and Lina (Kuratli) K.; m. Emily Lowndes, Dec. 8, 1962; children: Elizabeth, Katherine, Christopher, Rebecca. MD, U. Zurich, Switzerland, 1954; PhD, U. Basel, Switzerland, 1957. Rsch. mem. Sandoz, Ltd., Basel, 1958-61; rsch. assoc. Sloan-Kettering Inst., Rye, N.Y., 1961-64, assoc., 1964-69, assoc., head lab., 1969-81; assoc. prof. biochemistry Grad. Sch. Med. Scis., Cornell U., 1970-81, assoc. prof. pharmacology and exptl. therapeutics, 1980-81; assoc. rsch. prof. Med. Coll., Cornell U., N.Y.C., 1982-92, rsch. prof., 1992—; assoc. attending North Shore Univ. Hosp., Manhasset, N.Y., 1982-95, attending physician, 1995—; rsch. prof. NYU Sch. Medicine, 1997—. Contbr. numerous articles to profl. jours. Grantee NCI, ACS, Don Monti Meml. Rsch. Found., ICI Pharm., Merck Sharp Dohme, Janssen Rsch. Found. Mem. Am. Assn. for Cancer Rsch., Am. Soc. for Clin. Oncology, Am. Soc. for Clin. Pharmacology and Therapeutics, Am. Soc. Biol. Chemists, N.Y. Acad. Scis. Office: North Shore U Hosp Dept Medicine 300 Community Dr Manhasset NY 11030-3801

KREISBERG, JEFFREY I., medical educator, researcher. BS in Biology, SUNY, Albany, 1971; PhD in Exptl. Pathology, U. Md., 1975. Instr. dept. pathology Harvard Med. Sch., Boston, 1977-78, asst. prof. dept. pathology, 1978-80; asst. biologist dept. medicine Mass. Gen. Hosp., Boston, 1979-80; asst. prof. dept. pathology U. Tex. Health Sci. Ctr., San Antonio, 1980-83, assoc. prof. dept. medicine, 1983-89, assoc. prof. dept. pathology, 1983-89, prof. dept. medicine, prof. dept. pathology, 1989—, career scientist dept. VA dept. pathology, 1989—; mem. staff South Tex. VA Healthcare Sys., 1989—. Contbr. articles to profl. jours., chpts. to books. Recipient Rsch. award Am. Diabetes Assn., 1996. Office: U Tex Health Sci Ctr Dept Pathology 7703 Floyd Curl Dr San Antonio TX 78284-6200*

KREISBERG, NEIL IVAN, advertising executive; b. N.Y.C., Feb. 1, 1945; s. Leo and Lucille (Levy) K.; children: Andrew Jay, Tracy Michelle (dec.); m. Linda Gering, Sept. 24, 1986; children: William Gering, James Gering. BS,BA, Rider Coll., Trenton, N.J., 1966. With Grey Advt. Inc., N.Y.C., 1966—, v.p., mgmt. supr., 1974-79, sr. v.p., account mgmt., 1979-85, exec. v.p., 1985-93, exec. v.p., group dir., 1993—. Dir. Byran Hills Edn. Found. Mem. Brae Burn Country Club (gov., treas.). Jewish. Office: Grey Advt Inc 777 3rd Ave New York NY 10017-1401

KREISER, FRANK DAVID, real estate executive; b. Mpls., Sept. 20, 1928; s. Harry D. and Olive W. (Quist) K.; student U. Minn., 1950-51; m. Patricia Williams, Aug. 23, 1973; children: Sally, Frank David, Susan, Paul, Mark, Patti, Richard. Real estate developer 1960—; founder, owner Frank Kreiser Real Estate, Inc., Mpls., 1966-89, pres., 1979—; br. mgr. Merrill Lynch Realty, 1989-90, br. mgr., v.p. Burnet Realty, 1990-97; broker Coldwell Banker, 1998—; ptnr., founder B & K Properties Co., Mpls., 1976-96; chmn. bd., founder Transfer Location Corp., Atlanta, 1979-84 . Served with U.S. Army, 1948-50, Korea. Mem. Nat. Assn. Realtors, Mpls. Bd. Realtors (dir. 1972), Minn. Assn. Realtors, Realtors Nat. Mktg. Inst., Minn. Multi Housing Assn., Edina Country Club. Lutheran. Address: 5036 France Ave S Minneapolis MN 55410-2033

KREISMAN, ARTHUR, higher education consultant, humanities educator emeritus; b. Cambridge, Mass., June 7, 1918; s. Louis and Rose (Shechtell) K.; m. B. Evelyn Goulston, Apr. 20, 1940 (dec. July 1992); children: Peter Jon, Steven Alan, Richard Curt, James Bruce; m. Mamie Jewel Liles Tribble, July 17, 1994. AB, Brigham Young U., 1942; student, Harvard U., 1939; AM, Boston U., 1943, PhD, 1952; LittD (hon.), City U., 1988. Grad. asst. in English Boston U., 1942-43; instr. U.S. Armed Forces Inst., 1945; instr. So. Oreg. U., Ashland, 1946, asst. prof., 1947-51, assoc. prof., 1951-55, prof., 1955-81, chmn. dept. English, 1951-63, chmn. humanities div., 1955-69, dir. gen. studies, 1959-66, dean arts and scis., 1966-77, dir. curricular affairs, 1978-80, prof. emeritus, 1981—, appt. ofcl. univ. historian, 1985; co-founder with Evelyn Kreisman Edukon, Inc., 1982—; TV lectr. Network Ednl. TV, 1955-58; dir. Block Teaching Project, U.S. Office Edn., 1957-59, Nat. Def. Edn. Act Inst. for Advanced Study in English, 1966; cons. Fedn. Regional Accrediting Commns. in Higher Edn., 1974-75, Council on Postsecondary Accreditation, 1975-79, Chico (Calif.) State U., 1973-76, City U. Seattle, 1975—, Lincoln Meml. U., 1976, Marylhurst Edn. Center, 1976, Oreg. Inst. Tech., 1977-79, Sheldon Jackson Coll., 1979-83, Council on Chiropractic Edn., 1982, 83, Griffin Coll., 1990-91; mem. Gov.'s Adv. Com. on Arts and Humanities, 1966-69, 71-76; mem. task force human services Oreg. Ednl. Coordinating Council, 1972; mem. steering com. Oreg. Joint Com. for Humanities, 1972-74; chmn. Seminar Coll. Evaluators NW Assn. Schs. and Colls., U. Wash., 1977-84; mem. nat. adv. bd. on quality assurance in experiental learning Council on Advancement Experiental Learning, 1978-80; team leader Danforth Found. Workshop on Liberal Arts Edn., Colo. Coll., 1972. Author: Correspondence Courses for State System, American Literature, 1955, World Literature, 1956, Contemporary Literature, 1961, Reader's Guide to the Classics, 1961; Editor: Oregon Centennial Anthology, 1959; Contbr. poetry and articles to periodicals. Mem. Ashland City Coun., 1950-54; co-founder Rogue Valley Unitarian Fellowship, 1953; bd. dirs. Comty. Chest, Inst. Renaissance Studies, 1956-64, Friends of Libr., 1991-96, pres., 1994-96; mem. steering com. Learning in Retirement Program, 1993-94; chmn. bd. trustees Ashland Comty. Hosp., 1960-64; bd. dirs. So. Calif. U. for Profl. Studies, 1997-99; chmn. bd. dirs. North Ctrl. U., 1998-99. Recipient Bicentennial anniversary prize in humanities Columbia U., 1954, disting. svc. award Ashland Cmty. Hosp. Found., 1998; prize for excellence in teaching, 1966, Outstanding Service award Indsl. Coll. Armed Forces, 1976, Disting. Service award Alumni Assn., 1977; Ford Found. fellow in Oriental philosophy and religion Harvard, 1954. Mem. AAUP (past pres. Oreg. coun.), Nat. Coun. Tchrs. English (past pres. Oreg. coun.), Commn. of Pacific Assn. of Schs. and Colls. (elected 1994-95), N.W. Assn. Schs. and Colls. (examiner 1958—, trustee 1976-80, mem. comm. colls. 1972-80), Am. Legion (past post comdr.), Lambda Iota Tau, Phi Kappa Phi, Tau Kappa Alpha. Office: 1880 Green Meadows Way Ashland OR 97520-3683

KREITENBERG, ARTHUR, orthopedic surgeon, consultant; b. L.A., Apr. 24, 1957; s. Sam and Irene Dina (Deutsch) K.; m. Melissa Carr, Sept. 4, 1988; children: Elliot Moses, Zoe Rachel. B of Math. magna cum laude, UCLA, 1978; MD, U. Calif., San Diego, 1982; cert. bioengr., U. Calif., Irvine, 1984. Diplomate Am. Bd. Orthopedic Surgeons. Summer intern NASA, Houston, 1979; resident U. Calif., Irvine, 1982-87, chief resident, 1987-88, asst. clin. prof., 1989—; pvt. practice Beverly Hills, Calif., 1989—; assoc. clin. prof. U. Calif., Irvine, 1990—; expert med. reviewer Med. Bd. Calif., Sacramento, 1991—; med. examiner State of Calif., San Francisco, 1993—. Contbr. articles to profl. jours.; patentee in field. Bd. dirs., past pres. Calif. Handicapped Skiers, Big Bear, Calif., 1992—; med. officer Nat. Disaster Med. Systems, San Diego, 1994—. Astronaut selection finalist NASA, 1992, 94. Fellow ACS, Am. Acad. Orthopedic Surgeons; mem. AIAA. Avocations: parenthood, running, skiing. Office: 434 S San Vicente Blvd Los Angeles CA 90048-4108

KREITMAN, BENJAMIN ZVI, rabbi, Judaic studies educator; b. Warsaw, Poland, Dec. 25, 1920; came to U.S., 1925, naturalized, 1926; s. Jacob and Anna (Grabower) K.; m. Joyce Beth Krimsky, Aug. 7, 1956; children—Jamie, Jill. BA, Yeshiva U., 1939; MHL, Jewish Theol. Sem., 1942; MA, Vale U., 1951; DHL, Jewish Theol. Sem., 1952, DD (hon.), 1970; LHD (hon.), Hebrew Coll., Boston, 1997. Ordained rabbi, 1943. Rabbi Temple Israel, Wilkes-Barre, Pa., 1943; asst. rabbi Kehillat Israel, Brookline, Mass., 1947-48; rabbi Congregation Beth El, New London, Conn., 1948-52, Bklyn. Jewish Center, 1952-68, Congregation Shaare Torah, Bklyn., 1968-76; exec. v.p. United Synagogue Am., N.Y.C., 1976-89, exec. v.p. emeritus, 1989—; vis. prof. Judaic studies Bklyn. Coll., 1974-75, Jewish Theol. Sem., 1974-75. Cons. editor: (with others) Illustrated History of the Jews, 1962. Pres. Bklyn. Jewish Community Coun., 1973-776; mem. N.Y.C. Bd. Health, 1972-79; chmn. Bklyn. Borough's President's Commn. on Human Rels., 1963-70, Small Bus. Opportunities Corp. Bklyn., 1964-67. Chaplain USN, 1943-46. Mem. Zionist Orgn. for Conservative Judaism (exec. v.p. 1989—, vice chmn. 1989—), Rabbinical Assembly, World Coun. Synagogues (exec. vice chmn. 1989—), Am. Acad. Jewish Rsch., Assn. Coll. Profs., Assn. Jewish Chaplains Armed Forces (pres. 1), MERCAZ-Movement to Reaffirm Conservative Zionism. Home: 1612 Ditmas Ave Brooklyn NY 11226-6602 Office: 155 Fifth Ave New York NY 10010-6802

KREITZBERG, FRED CHARLES, construction management company executive; b. Paterson, N.J., June 1, 1934; s. William and Ella (Bohen) K.; m. Barbara Braun, June 9, 1957; children: Kim, Caroline, Allison, Bruce, Catherine. BSCE, Norwich U., 1957, DS in Bus. Adminstrn. (hon.), 1994. Registered profl. engr., Ala., Alaska, Ariz., Ark., Calif., Colo., Del., D.C., Fla., Ga., Idaho, Ill., Ind., Iowa, Kans., Ky., Md., Mass., Minn., Miss., Mo., Nebr., Nev., N.H., N.J., N.Mex., N.Y., Ohio, Okla., Oreg., S.C., S.D., Tenn., Va., Vt., Wash., W.Va., Wis., Wyo. Asst. supt. Turner Constrn. Co., N.Y.C., 1957; project mgr. Project Mercury RCA, N.J., 1958-63; schedule cost mgr. Catalytic Constrn. Co., Pa., 1963-65, 65—; cons. Meridien Engring., 1965-68; prin. MDC Systems Corp., 1968-72; chmn., CEO O'Brien-Kreitzberg Inc., San Francisco, 1972—; lectr. Stanford (Calif.) U., U. Calif., Berkeley. Author: Crit. Path Method Scheduling for Contractor's Mgmt. Handbook, 1971; tech. editor Constrn. Inspection Handbook, 1972; contbr. articles to profl. jours. Bd. dirs. Partridge Soc.; chmn. bd. trustees Norwich U. 2d lt. C.E., U.S. Army, 1957-58. Recipient Disting. Alumnus award Norwich U., 1987, Crystal Vision award Nat. Assn. Women in Constrn., 1997; named Boss of Yr., Nat. Assn. Women in Constrn., 1987; Kreitzberg Amphitheatre named in his honor, 1987, also Kreitzberg Libr. at Norwich U., 1992; Bay Area Discovery Mus.-Birthday Room and Snack Bar named in honor of Kreitzberg family, 1989. Fellow ASCE (Constrn. Mgr. of Yr. 1982); mem. Am. Arbitration Assn., Constrn. Mgmt. Assn. Am. (founding, bd. dirs.), Soc. Am. Value Engrs., Community Field Assn., Ross Hist. Soc., N.J. Soc. Civil Engrs., N.J. Soc. Profl. Planners, Project Mgmt. Inst., Constrn. Industry Pres. Forum. Avocations: running, bicycling, tropical fish. Home: 19 Spring Rd PO Box 1200 Ross CA 94957-1200 Office: O'Brien-Kreitzberg Inc 50 Fremont St Fl 24 San Francisco CA 94105-2230

KREITZER, LOIS HELEN, personal investor; b. Pitts., Feb. 2, 1933; d. Franklin and Helen Katherine (Leyda) Maroney; m. William Emil Kreitzer, Nov. 14, 1962. BS, Pa. State U., 1955. Stockbroker Parker Hunter (formerly McKelvy & Co.), Pitts., 1955-62; cons. Pitts., 1962-68, executrix of estates, 1968-82, personal investor, 1975—, shareholder activist, 1970—. Mem. AAUW (life, jrs. sec., v.p., pres. 1960-62), DAR (jrs. treas.-sec., v.p., pres. 1957-60), Pitts. Assn. Investors Corp. (life), Pa. State U. Alumni Assn. (life), Colonial Dames 17th Century (charter treas.), Pa. State Club of Allegheny County (pres. 1963), Coll. Club Pitts. (life, jr. v.p., pres. 1959-60), Soroptimists (life, v.p. Pitts. chpt. 1961). Republican. Presbyterian. Avocations: cooking, baking, theatre, traveling, walking.

KREITZMAN, RALPH J., lawyer; b. N.Y.C., Nov. 11, 1945; s. Emanuel M. and Hannah G. (Steinhardt) K.; m. Wendy A. Karpel, Nov. 24, 1968; children: Susan Beth, Emily Meg. BS in Acctg., Rider U., 1967; JD cum laude, Bklyn. Law Sch., 1970. Bar: N.Y. 1971, U.S. Dist Ct. (so. dist.) N.Y. 1971, U.S. Dist. Ct. (ea. dist.) N.Y. 1973, U.S. Ct. of Appeals (2nd cir.) 1975, U.S. Supreme Ct. 1976. Assoc. Hughes Hubbard & Reed LLP, N.Y.C., 1970-80; ptnr., chmn. real estate group Hughes Hubbard & Reed LLC, N.Y.C., 1980—. Chair planning bd., mem. archtl. review com. Village of Great Neck. Served with U.S. Army (Res.) 1968-74. Mem. ABA (real property law sect. and com. on fgn. investment in U.S. real estate), N.Y. State Bar Assn. (real property law sect., com. on comml. leases and com. on financings), Assn. of Bar of City of N.Y. (com. on real property law, chair environ. subcom., sublease subcom.). Office: Hughes Hubbard & Reed LLP 1 Battery Park Plz New York NY 10004-1482

KREIZINGER, LOREEN I., lawyer, nurse; b. Syracuse, N.Y., Apr. 16, 1959; d. David F. and Blanche L. (Heaney) Mosher; m. Kenneth R. Kreizinger, Aug. 30, 1985; 1 child, Katelyn Rose. Grad. in nursing, Crouse-Irving Meml. Hosp., Syracuse, 1981; BS in Bus. with honors, Nova U., 1987, JD, 1990. Bar: Fla. 1990; RN, N.Y., Fla. Nurse ICU and infants neonatal unit, Syracuse, Ft. Lauderdale, Fla., 1979-86; med. malpractice cons. Krupnick, Campbell et al, Ft.Lauderdale, 1986-90, assoc., 1990-92, of counsel, 1992—; pvt. practice, Ft.Lauderdale, 1992—; instr. adult intensive care Crouse-Irving Meml. Hosp., 1981-82; adj. prof. Nova U., Ft. Lauderdale, 1994—; seminar instr. legal aspects of nursing Fla. Bd. Nursing, 1990-92; guest spkr. TV talk show Med. Malpractice, 1991. Sec., bd. dirs. Shepherd Care Ministries, Hollywood, Fla., 1993, 94; mem. choir 1st Bapt. Ch. Ft. Lauderdale, 1994—. Mem. ABA (law and medicine com. 1990—), FBA, ATLA (spl. L-Trytophen com. 1991-94), Fla. Bar Assn., Fla. Assn. Women Lawyers, Fla. Acad. Trial Lawyers, Broward County Women Lawyers Assn., Broward County Trial Lawyers Assn., Phi Alpha Delta. Republican. Avocations: sailing, snow skiing, rollerblading. Office: 515 E Las Olas Blvd Ste 1150 Fort Lauderdale FL 33301-2281

KREJCI, ROBERT HARRY, non-profit organizations development consultant; b. Chgo., June 4, 1913; s. John and Johanna (Tischer) K.; m. Marian Hallock, Mar. 28, 1941 (dec. Aug. 1986); 1 child, Susan Ann Krejci Stevens. BS in Forestry with honors, Mich. State U., 1940. Dist. exec. Boy Scouts Am., Chgo., 1940-48, asst. scout exec., 1948-50; scout exec. Boy Scouts Am., Herrin, Ill., Huntington, W.Va., 1950-65; devel. cons. The Cumerford Corp., Kansas City, 1965-73; dir. western divsn. The Cumerford Corp., Ft. Lauderdale, Fla., 1974-78; devel. cons. in pvt. practice, San Diego, 1978-90; co-founder, pres. Philanthropy Coun., San Diego, 1987-93; dir. World War II Farm Labor Camp, State of Ill., 1942, 43. Author: How to Succeed in Fund Raising For Your Non-Profit Organization, 1989. Vol. organizer United Way, various cities, Ill., 1955, 56. Recipient George Washington medal Freedoms Found. at Valley Forge, 1953; named Vol. of Yr. Philanthropy Coun., 1996, Exemplar, Rancho Bernardo Rotary Found., 1995. Mem. Rotary Internat. (Paul Harris fellow). Avocations: travel, gardening, writing, collecting humor. Home: 16566 Casero Rd San Diego CA 92128-2743

KREJCI, ROBERT HENRY, aerospace engineer; b. Shenandoah, Iowa, Nov. 15, 1943; s. Henry and Marie Josephine (Kubicek) K.; m. Carolyn R. Meyer, Aug. 21, 1967; children—Christopher S., Ryan D. B.S. with honors in Aerospace Engring., Iowa State U., Ames, 1967, M.Aerospace Engring., 1971. Commd. 2d lt. U.S. Air Force, 1968, advanced through grades to capt., 1978; lt. col. Res.; served with systems command Space Launch Vehicles Systems Program Office, Advanced ICBM program officer; research assoc. U.S. Dept. Energy Lawrence Livermore lab.; dept. mgr. advanced tech. programs Strategic div. Thiokol Corp., 1978-84, mgr. space programs, 1984-85, mgr. Navy advanced programs, 1986—. Decorated A.F. commendation medal, Nat. Def. Service medal, Meritorious Svc. medal. Fellow AIAA. Home: 885 N 300 E Brigham City UT 84302-1310 Office: Thiokol Propulsion PO Box 707 Brigham City UT 84302-0707

KREJCSI, CYNTHIA ANN, textbook editor; b. Chgo., Dec. 28, 1948; d. Charles and Dorothea Bertha (Hahn) K.; m. Daniel Neil Ehlebracht, May 16, 1986 (div. Nov. 1988). BA, North Park Coll., 1970; postgrad. Nat. Coll. Edn., 1989—. Prodn. editor Ency. Brit., Chgo., 1970-71, style editor, 1971-72; asst. editor Scott, Foresman & Co., Glenview, Ill., 1972-77, assoc. editor, 1977, editor, 1978-84, sr. editor, 1984-95; sr. editor Benefic Press, Westchester, Ill., 1977-78; editl. mgr. Ligature, Chgo., 1995-96, Contemporary Books., Chgo., 1996; editl. dir. edn. divsn. NTC/Contemporary Pub., Lincolnwood, Ill., 1996—; bd. dirs. Camp Fire Boys and Girls, 1998—. Mem. ASCD, Nat. Council of Tchrs. of English, Internat. Reading Assn.,

Nat. Reading Conf., Assn. Ill. Mid. Schs. Home: 1425 Partridge Ln Arlington Heights IL 60004-7988 Office: NTC/Contemporary Pub Co 4255 W Touhy Ave Lincolnwood IL 60646-1933

KRELL, SUSAN MARIE, hospital administrator; b. New Brunswick, N.J., Mar. 21, 1971; d. Joakim and Arlene Krell; m. James George Fett, Aug. 3, 1997. BA, Lehigh U., 1993; MPH, NYU, 1998. Quality and resource data coord. St. Barnabas Med. Ctr., Livingston, N.J. Mem. Am. Coll. Healthcare Execs. (assoc.), St. John's Sr. Club (recording sec. 1989—), Phi Beta Kappa, Omicron Delta Kappa. Russian Orthodox.

KRELLWITZ, MARGIT C., nursing consultant; b. Oak Park, Ill., May 16, 1954; d. Guenter and Ilse (Heinemeier) K.; m. Robert M. Miller, Sept. 10, 1980; children: Jennifer Anne, Michelle Elizabeth, Jason Robert. BSN, Incarnate Word Coll., San Antonio, 1976; MSN, U. Tex., San Antonio, 1987. RN, Tex.; cert. nursing adminstr. Commd. officer U.S. Army Nurse Corps, 1976, advanced through grades to maj.; staff nurse, phys. medicine rehab. unit Villa Rosa Rehab. Ctr., San Antonio, 1976; staff nurse, med. ward Brooke Army Med. Ctr., San Antonio, 1976-78, staff nurse, emergency rm., 1978-80, instr., nursing edn. and tng. svc., 1980-82; asst. chief, evening/night supr. 130th Sta. Hosp., Heidelberg, West Germany, 1982-83; head nurse, emergency rm., outpatient dept. & ambulance sect 130th Sta. Hosp., Heidelberg, 1983-84; head nurse 546 Gen. Dispensary, Mannheim, West Germany, 1984-85; orientation officer Det 1 94th Gen Hosp., San Antonio, 1985-87; dir. nursing Thomason Hosp., El Paso, Tex., 1987-89; OER officer Det 1 44th Evac Hosp., El Paso, 1987-89; pvt. practice nursing cons. Corsicana, Tex., 1989-91; res. tng. officer VA Nursing Svc. jobsite 94th Gen. Hosp., Mesquite, Tex., 1989-91; pvt. cons. Ft. Smith, Ark., 1991—. Contbr. articles to profl. jours. Mem. USAR, 1985-91. Mem. Incarnate Word Coll. Alumni Assn., U. Tex. Health Sci. Ctr. Sch. Nursing Alumni Assn., Sigma Theta Tau.

KREMENTZ, JILL, photographer, author; b. N.Y.C., Feb. 19, 1940; d. Walter and Virginia (Hyde) K.; m. Kurt Vonnegut, Jr., Nov. 1979; 1 child, Lily. Student, Drew U., 1958-59; attended Art Students League. With Harper's Bazaar mag., 1959-60, Glamour mag., 1960-61; pub. relations staff Indian Industries Fair, New Delhi, 1961; reporter Show mag., 1962-64; staff photographer N.Y. Herald Tribune, 1964-65, staff photographer Vietnam, 1965-66; assoc. editor Status-Diplomat mag., 1966-67; contbg. editor N.Y. mag., 1967-68; corr. Time-Life Inc., 1969-70; contbg. photographer People mag., 1974—. Contbr. photography numerous U.S. and fgn. periodicals.; one-woman photography shows Madison (Wis.) Art Center, 1973, U. Mass., Boston, 1974, Nikon Gallery, N.Y.C., 1974, Del. Art Mus., Wilmington, 1975, Newark Mus., 1994; Staley-Wise Gallery, 1996, represented in permanent collections Mus. Modern Art, Library of Congress; photographer: The Face of South Vietnam (text by Dean Brelis), 1968, Words and Their Masters (text by Israel Shenker), 1974; photographer, author: Sweet Pea: A Black Girl Growing Up in the Rural South (foreword by Margaret Mead), 1969, A Very Young Dancer, 1976, A Very Young Rider, 1977, A Very Young Gymnast, 1978, A Very Young Circus Flyer, 1979, A Very Young Skater, 1979, The Writer's Image, 1980, How It Feels When a Parent Dies, 1981, How It Feels to be Adopted, 1982, How It Feels When Parents Divorce, 1984, The Fun of Cooking, 1985, Lily Goes to the Playground, 1986, Jack Goes to the Beach, 1986, Katherine Goes to Nursery School, 1986, Jamie Goes on an Airplane, 1986, Tanya Goes to the Dentist, 1986, Benjy Goes to a Restaurant, 1986, Holly's Farm Animals, 1986, Zachary Goes to the Zoo, 1986, A Visit to Washington, D.C., 1987, How It Feels to Fight For Your Life, 1989, A Very Young Skier, 1990, A Very Young Musician, 1990, A Very Young Gardener, 1990, A Very Young Actress, 1991, How It Feels to Live With a Physical Disability, 1992, The Writer's Desk, 1996, The Jewish Writer, 1998. Recipient Nonfiction award Washington Post/Children's Book Guild, 1984, ACCH Joan Fassler Meml. Book award, 1990, Equality, Dignity, Independence award Nat. Easter Seals, 1992. Mem. PEN. Address: care Alfred A Knopf Inc 201 E 50th St New York NY 10022-7703

KREMER, ANDREA, sports correspondent. Prodr., dir., on-air reporter This is the NFL NFL Films, 1984-89; contbg. reporter Phila. Eagles PreGame Show Sta. WIP-AM, Phila., 1988; Chgo.-based corr. SportsCenter, NFL Game Day, NFL Prime Mon. ESPN, 1989-94, L.A. corr. NBA Today, ESPN Radio, 1994—; reporter Super Bowls, 1985—; reporter NBA Finals, All-Star Game, Major League Baseball's All-Star Game and League Championship Series, NCAA bowl games, the NCAA Men's Basketball Tournament, Olympic basketball trials, and the PGA Championship; corr. several breaking news stories, and has provided investigative pieces on social issues relating to sports, such as sexual assault and domestic violence. Prodr. (one-hr. spls.) All-Pro Dream Team, All the Best, and Gift of Gab; contbr. ESPN's Outside the Lines series, conducts Sunday Conversations with leading sports personalities including Michael Jordan, Steve Young, David Robinson, Joe Montana, Phil Jackson, Jerry Rice, Charles Barkley, Mike Keenan, Don Shula, and John Elway, Reggie White; sub. host ESPN Up Close. Recipient Emmy nomination for writing and editing spl. Autumn Ritual, 1986. Office: ESPN ESPN Plaza Bristol CT 06010*

KREMER, EUGENE R., architecture educator; b. N.Y.C., Jan. 4, 1938; s. John and Ida (Applegreen) K.; m. Sara Lillian Kimmel, June 26, 1960; children: Michael, Ian. BArch, Rensselaer Poly. Inst., 1960; postgrad. U. Pa., 1960-61; MArch, U. Calif., 1967; grad. coll. mgmt. program, Carnegie Mellon U., 1991. Registered architect, N.Y., Kans. Architect, Ulrich Franzen assoc., N.Y.C., 1963-66; asst. prof. Washington U., St. Louis, 1967-70; lectr. Portsmouth Poly. Inst., Eng., 1970-71, Poly. Central London, 1971-72; dir. Inst. Environ Design, Washington, 1972-73; prof., head dept. architecture Kans. State U., Manhattan, 1973-85, 92-95, dir. program devel. Coll. Architecture and Design, 1985-92, asst. dean, 1988-90, dir. Boston Architecture and Design, summer 1983-90; vis. faculty mem. Czech Tech. U., Prague, 1999; mem. editl. bd. Jour. Arch. and Planning Research, College Station, Tex., 1983—; mem. State Bldg. Adv. Bd., Topeka, Kans., 1984-86, 92-95. Author: Careers in Architecture, 1967, Leadership Meetings in Environmental Design, 1973; author/editor newsletter Architecture Update, 1984-86, 92—; editor Architecture and Design News, 1990-92; contbr. Architects Handbook of Professional Practice, 13th edit., also articles to profl. publs. Chmn. Adv. Bd. Gifted, Talented, Creative, Manhattan, 1974-75; mem. Convocations Com., Manhattan, 1974-93, chmn., 1984-88, 90-93; mem. Truman Scholarship Com., Manhattan, 1980—; pres. Friends Kans. State Univ. Librs., Manhattan, 1985-86. Fellow AIA (Spl. Svc. award Kans. 1984, 88, 91, 94,98, Presdl. citation Kans. City 1993); mem. Environ. Design Rsch. Assn., Assn. Collegiate Schs. Architecture (treas. 1976-80, pres. 1981-82, Svc. award 1983), AIA Kans. (sec. 1989, v.p./pres.-elect 1990, pres. 1991, past pres. 1992, univ. liaison 1993—), AIA Flint Hills (pres., 1998); Golden Key (hon.), Tau Sigma Delta, Tau Beta Pi, SCARAB (hon.), Tau Epsilon Phi (pres. 1959-60). Avocations: reading, photography. Office: Kans State U Coll Architecture Planning and Design 211 Seaton Hall Manhattan KS 66506-2900

KREMER, HONOR FRANCES (NOREEN KREMER), real estate broker, small business owner; b. Ireland, Aug. 9, 1939; came to U.S., 1961; m. Manny Kremer, May 17, 1963; 1 child, Patrick David. BS, CUNY; MS, Baruch Coll. Group sec. Bentalls, Ltd., Kingston-On-Thames, Surrey, Eng., 1954-58, Cen. Secondary Sch., Hamilton, Ont., Can., 1959-61; office mgr. Aschner Assocs., N.Y.C., 1961-63; pub. rels. asst. McMaster U., Hamilton, 1963-64; office mgr. Packaging Components, N.Y.C., 1965-67; head acctg. Shaller Rubin Assocs., N.Y.C., 1967-72, v.p. fin. and adminstrn., 1972-79, sr. v.p., 1979-82, sr. v.p., mem. exec. com., 1982—, sec.-treas. multi-media div., 1972-75; pvt. practice bus. cons., 1986-89; sr. v.p., exec. v.p., fin. officer Lewis & Gace Med. Advt., N.Y.C., 1989-91; broker, owner Malone Kremer Realty, Leonia, N.J., 1991—; bus. cons., 1991—. Mem. Nat. Assn. Realtors, N.J. Assn. Realtors, Nat. Fedn. Bus. and Profl. Women (bd. dirs., v.p.), Advt. Fin. Mgmt. Group. Roman Catholic.

KREMER, S. LILLIAN, English educator; b. N.Y.C., June 30, 1939; d. Joseph and Rachel Kimmel; m. Eugene Kremer, June 26, 1960; children: Michael, Ian. BA, SUNY, Albany, 1959; MA, CUNY, Bklyn., 1964; PhD, Kans. State U., 1979. Prof. English Kans. State U., Manhattan, 1986—. Author: Witness Through the Imagination, 1989, Women's Holocaust Writing, 1999. Mem. MLA, Assn. for Jewish Studies, Am. Assn. Profs. Yiddish, Saul Bellow Soc., Bernard Malamud Soc. (co-dir.), Modern Jewish Studies and Yiddish (editl. bd.). Office: Kans State U Dept English Denison Hall Manhattan KS 66506

KREMERS, CAROLYN SUE, writer, musician, educator; b. Denver, Nov. 2, 1951; d. Richard Treakle and Patricia Sue (Willson) K. BA in English & Humanities with honors, Stanford U., 1973; BA in Flute Performance, Met. State Coll., 1981; MFA in Creative Writing, U. Alaska, 1991. Cert. secondary English lang. arts tchr., Alaska. Tchr. music and English various schs., Ill., Colo., Alaska, 1974-88; vis. asst. prof. English U. Alaska Fairbanks, 1991-92; asst. prof. devel. studies U. Alaska Fairbanks, Bethel, 1992-93; instr. English U. Alaska Fairbanks, 1993-97; asst. prof. English and creative writing Ea. Wash. U., 1997—; cons. Alaska State Writing Consortium, 1990—. Author: Place of the Pretend People: Gifts from a Yup'ik Eskimo Village, 1996; author numerous essays and poems. Individual Artist fellow Alaska State Coun. Arts, 1992. Avocations: flute playing, skiing, backpacking, running, bicycling. Office: Ea Wash Univ Creative Writing Program 705 W First Ave MS #1 Spokane WA 99201-3909

KREMKAU, PAUL, principal. Prin. Highland Upper Grade Ctrl. Sch., Libertyville, Ill., 1984—. Recipient Blue Ribbon Sch. award U.S. Dept. Edn., 1990-91. Office: Highland Mid Sch 310 W Rockland Rd Libertyville IL 60048-2739*

KREMPEL, ROGER ERNEST, public works management consultant; b. Waukesha, Wis., Oct. 8, 1926; s. Henry and Clara K.; m. Shirley Ann Gray, June 16, 1948; children: John, Sara, Peter. Student Ripon Coll., 1944, Stanford U., 1945; BCE, U. Wis.-Madison, 1950. Registered profl. engr., Wis., Colo.; registered land surveyor, Wis. Asst. city engr., Manitowoc, Wis., 1950-51; city engr. dir. pub. works, Janesville, Wis., 1951-75; dir. water utilities, pub. works Ft. Collins, Colo., 1975-84; dir. natural resources, streets and stormwater utilities, Ft. Collins, 1984-88; faculty affiliate Internat. Sch. for Water Resources, Colo. State U.; pub. works mgmt. cons., 1988—; lectr. various univ., coll., nat. confs. and seminars. Contbr. numerous articles to profl. pubs. Past pres. bd. Janesville YMCA. With U.S. Army, 1944-46. Recipient numerous tech. and profl. awards, Distin. Svc. citation U. Wis. Coll. Engring., 1989, Outstanding Leadership and Cmty. Devel. award Janesville C. of C., 1972. Fellow ASCE (life, Gov. Civil Engr. award 1984, Wis. Oustanding Civil Engring. Achievement award 1970); mem. NSPE, ASCE (Mgmt. award 1990), Am. Water Works Assn. (life), Am. Pub. Works Assn. (life mem., past pres. Colo. and Wis. chpts., past mem. rsch. found., Man of Yr. 1971, Nichols award 1984, Swearingen award 1988), Pub. Works Hist. Soc. (pres. 1993-95), Wis. Soc. Profl. Engrs. (past pres.), Am. Acad. Environ. Engrs. (diplomate, 1982-91), Colo. Engrs. Coun. (pres. 1990-91, honor award 1989).

KREMPL, ERHARD, mechanics educator, consultant; b. Regensburg, Germany, Mar. 5, 1934; came to U.S., 1964, naturalized, 1983; m. Johanna A. Wunderlich, Dec. 19, 1961 (dec.); children: Christiane C., Ralph D. Dipl. Ing., Technische Hochschule Muenchen, W. Germany, 1956, Dr.Ing., 1962. Instr., research engr. Technische Hochschule Muenchen, 1956-59, wissenschaftl asst., 1959-64; mechanics of materials engr. Gen Electric Co., Schenectady, 1964-68; assoc. prof. Rensselaer Poly Inst., Troy, N.Y., 1968-75, prof. mechanics, 1975-93, dir. Mechanics of Materials Lab., 1975—, head dept. mech. engring., aero. engring. and mechanics, 1987-96, Rosalind and John J. Redfern Jr. prof. engring., 1993—; vis. scientist Argonne Nat. Lab., Ill., 1974; Richard Merton guest prof. Institut für Statik und Dynamic der Luft und Raumfahrtkonstruktionen, Stuttgart, W.Ger., 1975-76. Author: (with Lai and Rubin) Introduction to Continuum Mechanics, 3d edit., 1993; contbr. numerous articles to profl. jours.; editor: Jour. Engring. Materials and Tech., 1981-84. Rsch. grantee NSF, Office Naval Rsch., NASA, Pressure Vessel Rsch. Com., Dept. Energy; Japanese Soc. Promotion Sci. fellow, 1984; Fulbright-Hayes grantee U. Innsbruck, Austria, 1985; recipient Sr. U.S. Scientist Humboldt award, 1993-94. Fellow ASME (chmn. materials div. 1977-78), Am. Acad. Mechanics; mem. ASTM, AAUP, Am. Soc. Engring. Edn., Soc. Engring. Sci. Office: Rensselaer Poly Inst Dept Mech Engring Dept Mech Engring Troy NY 12180-3590*

KREND, WILLIAM JOHN, secondary education educator; b. Chgo., Oct. 25, 1947; s. Patrick H. and Irene Krend; m. Marjorie J. Tow, Aug. 15, 1970; children: Andrew William, Kira Loren. BA, U. Calif., Santa Barbara, 1969; MA, Calif. State U., Fresno, 1978. Cert. secondary, community coll. tchr., Calif. Tchr. Avenal (Calif.) High Sch., 1970-73; tchr. history Lemoore (Calif.) High Sch., 1973—; faculty history West Hills Coll., Lemoore, 1978-86, 97—, Chapman U., Nas Lemoore, Calif., 1979—; curriculum cons. Kings County Office of Edn., Hanford, Calif., 1990-91. Contbr. articles to profl. jours.; contbr: World History supplement, 1990. Coord. History Day, Kings County, 1987—, Am. Youth Competition, 1992, We the People for Calif. 20th Congl. Dist., 1992—; bd. dirs. Avenal Recreation Com., 1973-74. Named Calif. State History Day Tchr. of Merit, 1997; CLIO Project/U. Calif.-Berkeley fellow, 1986, Calif. History Project/Calif. State U.-Fresno fellow, 1990, Ctr. for Energy Edn. fellow, 1994. Mem. Nat. Coun. for Social Studies (presenter), Calif. Coun. for Social Studies (bd. dirs. 1992—, no. cochmn. govt. rels. com., co-chair publs. com. 1995-96, conf. com. 1996-97, cochair profl. standards com. 1997-99), Calif. Hist. Soc., Nat. Geog. Soc., Calif. Fedn. Tchrs., San Joaquin Coun. for Social Studies (bd. dirs. 1991—, pres. 1995—). Avocations: travel, stamp collecting, photography, guitar playing. Home: 14230 16th Ave Lemoore CA 93245-9517 Office: Lemoore High Sch 101 E Bush St Lemoore CA 93245-3601

KRENDEL, EZRA SIMON, systems and human factors engineering consultant; b. N.Y.C., Mar. 5, 1925; s. Joseph and Tamara (Shapiro) K.; m. Elizabeth Spencer Malany, Aug. 20, 1950 (dec. Nov. 1983); children: David A., Tamara E. Krendel-Clark, Jennifer J. Hall; m. Janet Brownlee Allen, June 27, 1992. A.B., Bklyn. Coll., 1945; Sc.M. in Physics, MIT, 1947; A.M. in Social Relations, Harvard, 1949; M.A. honoris causa, U. Pa., 1971. From research engr. to sr. staff engr. Franklin Inst. Research Labs., 1949-55, lab. mgr., 1955-63, tech. dir., 1963-66, sr. adviser, cons., 1961; dir. Mgmt. Sci. Ctr., Wharton Sch. U. Pa., Phila., 1967-69, prof. ops. research and stats., Wharton Sch., 1966-90, prof. emeritus, 1990—, prof. systems engring. Sch. Engring. and Applied Sci., 1983-93; prin. scientist Systems Tech., Inc., Hawthorne, Calif., 1987—; mem. rsch. adv. com. on control guidance and nav. NASA, 1964-65; various coms. Hwy. Rsch. Bd., NRC, 1964-74; vis. lectr. NATO, 1968, 71; mem. roster of arbitrators Fed. Mediation and Conciliation Svc.; cons. govt. agys., industry, legal profession. Author: Unionizing the Armed Forces, 1977; contbr. articles to profl. publs. Mem. Phila. Mayor's Sci. and Tech. Adv. Council. Recipient Louis E. Levy Gold medal Franklin Inst., 1960. Fellow IEEE, AAAS, Am. Psychol. Assn., Am. Psychol. Soc., Human Factors Soc.; mem. Ergonomics Soc., Am. Arbitration Assn. (labor panel), Cosmos Club, Sigma Xi. E-mail: krendel@wharton.upenn.edu. Home: 211 Cornell Ave Swarthmore PA 19081-1933

KRENDL, KATHY, dean. Dean Ohio U. Coll. Comms., Athens, 1996—. Office: Ohio U Coll Comm 9 S College St Rm 483B Athens OH 45701-2905*

KRENEK, DEBBY, newspaper editor; d. Ernest Reed and Elizabeth Pendleton (Brown) K.; m. James C. Roberts Jr., Feb. 28, 1987; children: Christine Elizabeth Roberts, Taylor James Roberts. BJ, Tex. A&M Univ., 1978. Copy editor Corpus Christi (Tex.) Caller-Times, 1978-81; news editor Dallas Times Herald, 1981-85, asst. bus. editor, 1985-86, exec. news editor, 1986-87; dep. news editor N.Y. Daily News, 1987-88, dep. mng. editor, 1988-91, mng. editor, 1991-93, exec. editor, 1993-97, editor, 1997—. Named to Acad. of Women Achievers YWCA, N.Y., 1997. Avocations: photography, tennis, home renovation. Office: New York Daily News 450 W 33d St Fl 3 New York NY 10001-5806

KRENEK, MARY LOUISE, political science researcher, educator; b. Wharton, Tex., Dec. 8, 1951; d. George P. Jr. and Vlasta (Zahn) Krenek. AA, Wharton County Jr. Coll., 1972; BA, Tex. A&I U., Corpus Christi, 1974; MA, St. Mary's U., San Antonio, 1992; Czech lang. cert., Charles U., Prague, Czech Republic, 1994. Cert. secondary and elem. tchr., Tex. Polygraph examiner San Antonio, 1979-81; ind. contractor market, polit. and social rsch. San Antonio and Houston, 1982—; substitute tchr., tchr. San Antonio Ind. Sch. Dist., 1981-82, Houston Ind. Sch. Dist., 1991-98; instr. govt. Wharton County Jr. Coll., 1997—; assoc. J.C. Penney Co., Inc., 1994—. Del. Tex. Dem. Conv., 1971-72. 1st lt. U.S. Army, 1975-78, lt. col. USAR, 1978—. Mem. CESAT, Houston Czech Cultural Ctr., Nat. Assn. of Self-Employed, Res. Officers Assn. (sec.-treas. Alamo chpt., jr. v.p. Dept. Tex., sec. Greater Houston chpt., ROTC coord.), Women in Mil. Svc. for Am. Meml. Found. (charter), St. Mary's U. Alumni Assn., Am. Legion, Pi Sigma Alpha. Roman Catholic. Avocations: reading, writing, travel. Home: 10502 Fountain Lake Dr Stafford TX 77477-3728 also: PO Box 310 Egypt TX 77436-0310

KRENER, ARTHUR J., systems engineering educator; b. Bklyn., Oct. 8, 1942. BS, Holy Cross Coll., 1964, MS, 1967; PhD, U. Calif., Berkeley, 1971. Prof. math. U. Calif., 1943—. Fellow IEEE. Office: U Calif-Davis Dept Maths 660 Kerr Hall Davis CA 95616*

KRENS, THOMAS, museum director; b. N.Y.C., Dec. 26, 1946. BA in Polit. Economy with honors, Williams Coll., 1969; M in Art, SUNY, Albany, 1971, HHD (hon.), 1989; M in Pub. and Pvt. Mgmt., Yale U., 1984. Asst. prof. art Williams Coll., Williamstown, Mass., 1972-80, asst. prof. history art grad. program, 1977-80, adj. prof.; dir. Mus. Art Williams Coll. Mus. Art, Williamstown, Mass., 1981-88; cons. Solomon R. Guggenheim Mus., N.Y.C., 1986-88; dir. Guggenheim Mus. SoHo, N.Y.C., 1988—, The Peggy Guggenheim Collection, Venice, Italy, 1988—; dir., trustee Solomon R. Guggenheim Found. N.Y.C., 1988—; adv. com. mus. project NEA and Am. Fedn. Arts, Washington; adj. prof. art history Williams Coll., 1988-91, dir. artist in residence program, 1976-80; lectr. in field. Author: Jim Dine Prints: 1970-77, 1977, The Prints of Helen Frankenthaler, 1980, The Drawing of Robert Morris, 1982, Robert Morris: The Mind/Body Problem, 1994; exhbns. include Jim Dine Prints, 1970-77, 1976, The Prints of Helen Frankenthaler, 1980, The Drawing of Robert Morris: 1956-82, 1982, Refigured Painting: The German Image, 1960-88, The Great Utopia: The Russian and Soviet Avant-Garde, 1915-1932, Marc Chagall and the Jewish Theatre, Robert Morris: The Mind/Body Problem. Honorary Award: Doctor of Humane Letters, SUNY. Mem. Aspen Inst. Italia (bd. dirs.), Soc. Kandinsky/Ctr. Georges Pompidou, Gesellschaft fur Moderne Kunst am Mus. Ludwig (adv. bd.), Coun. Fgn. Rels., Assn. Art Mus. Dirs. (assoc.), AFA (adv. com.), Yale Univ. Coun. (com. on the art gallery and Brit. Art Ctr). Office: Solomon R Guggenheim Mus 1071 5th Ave New York NY 10128-0112*

KRENSKY, HARRY F., fund manager, educator; b. N.Y.C., July 1, 1963; s. Arthur P. and Doris H. Krensky; m. Linda M. Revithas, Sept. 15, 1991; 1 child, Cole Alexander. BA, Colby Coll., 1985; MSc, London Sch. of Econs., 1986; MBA, Columbia U., 1991. Mng. dir. Weston Group, N.Y.C., 1991-93; dir. emerging markets Bear Stearns, N.Y.C., 1993-96; dir. Deutsche Bank, N.Y.C., 1996-99, DB New World Fund, N.Y.C., 1997-99; mng. dir. Discovery Capitol, Westport, CT, 1999—; adj. prof. N.Y. U., 1999—; adv. bd. Toggle Inc., N.Y.C., 1996—. Mem. Assn. for Investment Mgmt. Rsch. Home: 57 Little Town Ln Bedford NY 10506

KRENTS, MILTON ELLIS, broadcast executive; b. Springfield, Mass., Dec. 22, 1911; s. Morris Joseph and Ethel Malufka (Kramer) K.; m. Irma Kopp, May 1, 1938; children: Lawrence, Harold, Elisabeth. B.S., N.Y. U., 1935. Jr. exec. trainee NBC, N.Y.C., 1935-39; dir. radio-TV Am. Jewish Com., 1936-69; TV programming cons. Assn. for Higher Edn. of N.E.A., 1965-68; radio, TV cons. Council Fin. Aid to Edn., 1960-65; exec. producer religious series directions ABC-TV Network, 1965-85; communications cons. Revson Found., 1979-80; adv. bd. Nat. Jewish Broadcast Archives, Jewish Mus., N.Y.C., 1987—. Originator, exec. prodr. radio and TV series The Eternal Light, Jewish Theol. Sem., NBC, 1945-89 (over 250 awards from 50 years of broadcasting on NBC radio and TV networks including Emmy award 1982, 83, 89, George Foster Peabody award for program excellence U. Ga. 1978, 80 83; radio cons. Coun. for Democracy, 1942-45, prodr. WWII NBC radio letters series Dear Adolf from H. Hayes, R. Massey, James Cagney, William Holden, J. Schildcraut for scripts Stephen Vincent Benet, 1944; radio and TV dir. Am. Jewish Tercentenary, 1954; co-prodr. Meet the Professor series, NEA, ABC-TV Network, 1972. Nat. chmn. William E. Wiener Oral History Library, Am. Jewish Comm., 1969-84, dir., 1985—; bd. dirs. NYU Alumni Fedn., 1979-85; co-founder Weiner Oral History Libr., 1969. Recipient Robert E. Sherwood award, 1958, Faith and Freedom Broadcasting award Religious Heritage Am., 1972, Red Ribbon award Am. Film Festival, N.Y.C., 1983, Nat. Daytime Emmy award, 1983, 86, Alumni Meritorious Svc. award and medal NYU, 1984, 40 yrs. svc. award Sta. WNBC, NBC,, 1985, Media Arts award and medal Nat. Found. for Jewish Culture, 1991, Emmy Lifetime Achievement award. Mem. NATAS (Lifetime Achievement in Broadcasting Emmy award 1990), Pub. Rels. Soc. Am., NYU Alumni Assn. (chmn. communications com. 1980-87, hon. chmn. 1987—), Broadcast Pioneers. Home: 141 E 89th St New York NY 10128-2318 Office: 165 E 56th St New York NY 10022-2709

KRENTZ, EUGENE LEO, university president, educator, minister; b. Edmonton, Alta., Can., June 16, 1932; came to U.S., 1958; s. Emil and Natalie (Martin) K.; m. Joyce Ann Triolet, Feb. 1, 1958; children—Paul, Cynthia, Tamara. B.Th., Concordia Theol. Sem., Springfield, Ill., 1958, B.D., 1971, M.Div., 1973; M.A., Eastern Mich. U., 1973; Ph.D., U. Mich., 1980; LHD (hon.), Dominican U., River Forest, Ill., 1995. Ordained to ministry Lutheran Ch. 1958. Pastor St. Paul Luth. Ch., Susanville, Calif., 1958-61; pastor Trinity Luth. Ch., St. Joseph, Mich., 1961-65; prof. Concordia Coll., Ann Arbor, Mich., 1965-83; pres. Concordia U., River Forest, Ill., 1983-95. Contbg. author: Concordia Pulpit, 1974, 78, 80, 83, 85; contbg. editor: Luth. Edn., 1983-95. Chmn. coll. divsn. United Way, Ann Arbor; mem. troop com. Boy Scouts Am., Ann Arbor; peer reviewer U.S. Dept. Edn.; bd. dirs. Fedn. Ind. Ill. Colls. and Univs., Concordia Mission Soc.; mem., past pres. Luth. Edn. Conf. N.Am. Recipient Servus Ecclaesiae Christi, Concordia Theol. Sem., Ft. Wayne, Ind., 1978, Servant of Christ award Condordia Coll., Bronxville, N.Y., 1995. Mem. Luth. Edn. Assn., Phi Delta Kappa. Avocations: tennis; sailing; skiing; reading; travel. Home: 36395 N Tara Ct Ingleside IL 60041-8576

KRENTZMAN, BEN Z., family physician; b. Louisville, Aug. 26, 1937; s. David and Edna Krentzman. BA in Biology, U. Louisville, 1959, MD, 1964. Diplomate Am. Bd. Family Practice. Physician The No-Diet Diet Program, Culver City, Calif. Author: Weight Control Handbook for Physicians, 1996; contbr. articles to profl. jours. Capt. U.S. Army, 1965-67. Avocation: computers.

KREPINEVICH, ANDREW F., organization administrator; b. Queens, N.Y., Feb. 13, 1950. BS, U.S. Mil. Acad., 1972; MPA, Harvard U., 1980, PhD, 1984. Formerly mem. faculty U.S. Mil. Acad., West Point, George Mason U., Johns Hopkins U. Sch. Advanced Internat. Studies; exec. secretariat, Sec. Def. Office Net Assessment Dept. Def., Washington; exec. dir. Ctr. for Strategic and Budgetary Assessments, Washington, 1995—; lectr. in field. Author: The Army and Vietnam, 1987 (Furniss award 1987); author project analyses; contbr. to Washington Post, L.A. Times, U.S. News and World Report, others. Office: CSBA # 912 1730 Rhode Island Ave NW Washington DC 20036-3113*

KREPS, JUANITA MORRIS, economics educator, former government official; b. Lynch, Ky., Jan. 11, 1921; d. Elmer M. and Cenia (Blair) Morris; m. Clifton H. Kreps, Jr., Aug. 11, 1944; children: Sarah, Laura, Clifton. AB, Berea Coll., 1942; MA, Duke U., 1944; PhD, 1948; hon. degrees, Bryant Coll., 1972, U. N.C. at Chapel Hill, Denison U., Cornell Coll., 1973, U. Ky., Queens Coll., St. Lawrence U., 1975, Wheaton Coll., 1976, Claremont Grad. Sch., Berea Coll., 1979, Tulane U., Colgate U., 1980, Trinity Coll., 1981, U. Rochester, Grove City Coll., 1984, Davidson Coll., 1990; hon. degree, Lenoir-Rhyne Coll., 1991, U. Notre Dame, 1992, Duke U., 1993, Western Md. Coll., 1982. Instr. econs. Denison U., 1945-46, asst. prof., 1948-50; mem. faculty Duke U., 1955-77, assoc. prof., 1962-68, prof. econs., 1968-77, James B. Duke prof., 1972-77, James B. Duke prof. emerita, 1979—, asst. provost, 1969-72, v.p., 1973-77, v.p. emerita, 1979—; sec. U.S. Dept. Commerce, 1977-79; mem. adv. com. Congl. Commn. for the Future of Worker Mgmt. Rels., Secs. of Commerce and Labor, 1993-94. Author: (with C.E. Ferguson) Principles of Economics, 2d rev. edit. 1965, Lifetime Allocation of Work and Income, 1971, Sex in the Marketplace: American Women at Work, 1971, Women and the American Economy, 1976; co-author: (with Richard Perlman and Gerald Somers) Contemporary Labor Economics,

1973; Editor: Employment, Income and Retirement Problems of the Aged, 1963, Technology, Manpower and Retirement Policy, 1966, Sex, Age and Work, 1975. Bd. dirs. Am. Coun. on Germany, Rsch. Triangle Found., Ednl. Testing Svc., 1972-77; mem. Nat. Manpower Policy Task Force; trustee Berea Coll., 1972-78, 80-98, Duke Endowment, 1979—, Nat. Humanities Ctr., 1983-86, U. N.C., Wilmington, 1993—, HumRRO, 1980-83, Coun. Fgn. Rels., 1983-89, Kenan Inst. Pvt. Enterprise of U. N.C., Chapel Hill, 1995—; pres. bd. overseers Tchrs. Ins. and Annuity Assn., 1992-96; bd. dirs. TIAA, 1968-72, 85-96, Coll. Retirement Equities Fund, 1972-77. Named to Presl. Commn. on Nat. Agenda for the 80's, 1979; recipient N.C. Pub. Svc. award, 1976, Stephen Wise award, 1978, Woman of Yr. award Ladies Home Jour., 1978, Duke U. Alumni award, 1983, Haskins award Coll. Bus. and Pub. Adminstrn., NYU, 1984, First Corp. Governance award Nat. Assn. Corp. Dirs., 1987, Dir.'s Choice Leadership award Nat. Women's Econ. Alliance Found., 1987, Disting. Meritorious Svc. medal Duke U. Alumni, 1987. Fellow Gerontol. Soc. (v.p. 1971-72), Am. Acad. Arts and Scis.; mem. AAUP, AAUW (Achievement award 1981), Am. Econ. Assn. (v.p. 1983-84), So. Econ. Assn. (pres. 1975-76), Indsl. Rels. Rsch. Assn. (exec. com.). Office: Duke U 115 E Duke Bldg Durham NC 27708-0768

KRESA, KENT, aerospace executive; b. N.Y.C., Mar. 24, 1938; s. Helmy and Marjorie (Boutelle) K.; m. Joyce Anne McBride, Nov. 4, 1961; 1 child, Kiren. BSAA, MIT, 1959, MSAA, 1961, EAA, 1966. Sr. scientist rsch. and advanced devel. divsn. AVCO, Wilmington, Mass., 1959-61; staff mem. MIT Lincoln Lab., Lexington, Mass., 1961-68; dep. dir. strategic tech. office Def. Advanced Rsch. Projects Agy., Washington, 1968-73; dir. tactical tech. office Def. Advanced Rsch. Project Agy., Washington, 1973-75; v.p., mgr. Rsch. & Tech. Ctr. Northrop Corp., Hawthorne, Calif., 1975-76; v.p., gen. mgr. Ventura divsn. Northrop Corp., Newbury Park, Calif., 1976-82; group v.p. Aircraft Group Northrop Corp., L.A., 1982-86, sr. v.p. tech. devel. and planning, 1986-87, pres., COO, 1987-90; chmn. bd., pres., CEO Northrop Grumman Corp., L.A., 1990—; bd. dirs. John Tracy Clinic; mem. Chief of Naval Ops. exec. panel Washington, Def. Sci. Bd., Washington, DNA New Alternatives Working Group, L.A., Dept. Aeronautics and Astronautics Corp. Vis. Com. MIT. Bd. dirs. John Tracy Clinic for the Hearing-Impaired, W.M. Keck Found., L.A. World Affairs Coun.; bd. govs. L.A. Music Ctr. Recipient Henry Webb Salsbury award MIT, 1959, Arthur D. Flemming award, 1975, Calif. Industrialist of Yr. Calif. Mus. of Sci. and Industry and the Calif. Mus. Found., 1996, Bob Hope Disting. Citizen award Nat. Security Indsl. Assn., 1996; Sec. of Def. Meritorious Civilian Svc. medal, 1975, USN Meritorious Pub. Svc. citation, 1975, Exceptional Civilian Svc. award USAF, 1987. Fellow AIAA; mem. Aerospace Industries Assn. (past bd. govs.), Naval Aviation Mus. Found., Navy League U.S., Soc. Flight Test Engrs., Assn. U.S. Army, Nat. Space Club, Am. Def. Preparedness Assn., L.A. Country Club. Office: Northrop Grumman Corp 1840 Century Park E Los Angeles CA 90067-2101

KRESGE, ALEXANDER JERRY, chemistry educator; b. Wilkes-Barre, Pa., July 17, 1926; married; 3 children. BA, Cornell U., 1949; PhD in Chemistry, U. Ill., 1953. Rsch. assoc. Purdue U., West Lafayette, Ind., 1954-55, MIT, 1955-57; assoc. chemist Brookhaven Nat. Lab., 1957-60; from asst. prof. to prof. chemistry Ill. Inst. Tech., Chgo., 1960-74, chmn. chem. group, 1974-78; prof. chemistry U. Toronto, Ont., Can., 1974-92, prof. emeritus, 1992—; vis. lectr. Bedford Coll., London, 1964-65, Mardi Gras lectr. La. State U., 1987; Mobay lectr. U. N.H., 1982; Nelson J. Leonard lectr. U. Ill., 1986, Frontiers in Chem. lectr. Wayne State U., 1992, Nakamoto lectr. Marquette U., 1995; vis. prof. Oxford U., 1965, U. Toronto, 1970-71, U. Mich., 1979, U. Lausanne, 1981, Tech. U. Denmark, 1982, U. San Paulo, 1984, Fed. U. Santa Catarina, 1984, Kyoto U., 1985; guest prof. MIT, 1965; vis. scientist Fritz Haber Inst., 1981, U. Goteborg, 1983; mem. Gordon Rsch. Conf. on Chemistry and Physics of Isotopes, vice chmn., 1967, chmn., 1968. Mem. editorial adv. bd. Isotopes in Organic Chemistry, Jour. Phys. Organic Chemistry. Fulbright scholar U. London, 1953-54; NSF sr. fellow, 1964-65, Guggenheim fellow, 1964-65, Killam fellow, 1984-86, Yamada fellow, 1985; recipient Morley medal of Cleve. sect. Am. Chem. Soc., Syntex award Chem. Inst. Can. Fellow Royal Soc. Can., Chem. Inst. Can.; mem. AAAS, Am. Chem. Soc., Royal Soc. Chemistry (Ingold lectr. 1995), Argentinian Soc. Organic Chemistry (hon.). Rsch. in reaction mechanisms, isotope effects, flash photolysis, acid-base catalysis and kinetics. Office: Dept Chemistry, Univ Toronto, Toronto, ON Canada M5S 3H6

KRESGE, BRUCE ANDERSON, retired physician; b. Detroit, Dec. 20, 1931; s. Stanley Sebastian and Dorothy Eloise (McVittie) K.; m. Peggy Ann Sale, June 14, 1952; children—Deborah Kresge McDowell, Katherine Kresge Lutey, Susan Kresge Drewes, Cynthia Kresge Furlong, Stephen. BA, Albion Coll., 1953; JD, Wayne State U., 1956. Intern Detroit Receiving Hosp., 1956-57; resident U. Mich. Hosp., 1959-60; pvt. practice Rochester, Mich., 1960-90; mem. staff St. Joseph Mercy Hosp., Pontiac, Mich., also; Pontiac Gen. Hosp., 1960-67, Crittenton Hosp., Rochester, 1967—. Pres. Rochester br. YMCA, 1975-77; trustee Kresge Found., 1967—, Crittenton Hosp., 1993—; hon. trustee Albion Coll., 1999—. With M.C., U.S. Army, 1957-59. Mem. AMA. Republican. Methodist. Home: 1071 N Lake Angelus Rd Lake Angelus MI 48326-1026

KRESIC, EVA, pediatrician; b. Zagreb, Croatia, July 20, 1935; came to U.S., 1969; d. Ignatz and Marta (Neumann) Klein; m. Mark Miljenko Kresic, July 26, 1956; children: Mladen, Daniela. MD, U. Zagreb, 1960. Resident in pediats. Mt. Sinai Hosp., Elmhurst, N.Y., 1970-72; fellow L.I. Jewish Hosp., New Hyde Park, N.Y., 1972-74; attending, clin. instr. Mt. Sinai, Elmhurst, 1972-77; pediatrician Health Ins. Plan-Queens/L.I. Med. Group, Flushing, N.Y., 1972—; Bd. cert. Am. Acad. Pediats. Fellow Am. Acad. Pediats. (bd. cert.); mem. N.Y. State Med. Soc., Queens Med. Soc., Queens Pediat. Soc. Republican. Jewish. Avocations: skiing, traveling, classical music, opera. Office: HIP-Queens LI Med Group 14015 Sanford Ave Flushing NY 11355-2557*

KRESS, ALBERT OTTO, JR., polymer chemist; b. Cullman, Ala., June 15, 1950; s. Albert Otto and Odell Pearl (Norris) K.; m. Ruth Jeanette Beach, Dec. 30, 1972 (div. Aug. 1978); children: Adrian Konrad, Katyna Ileana; m. Roby Lynn Rice, Apr. 14, 1984 (div. Oct. 1998); 1 child, Ashley Alan Rice Kress. BS, U. Montevallo, 1972; PhD, U. Ala., 1979. Rsch. scientist Hercules Chem. Corp., Wilmington, N.C., 1979-83; rsch. assoc. Clemson (S.C.) U., 1983-84; assoc. prof. U. Montevallo, Ala., 1984-86; rsch. assoc. U. So. Miss., Hattiesburg, 1986-88; sr. scientist Schering-Plough HealthCare Products Corp., Memphis, 1988-99, Urethane Specialist Cons., Cleveland, Tenn., 1999—. Contbr. articles to Jour. Organic Chemistry, Dissertation Abstracts Internat. B, Jour. Chem. Soc., Jour. Applied Polymer Sci. Recipient Dean's scholarship U. Ala., 1975. Mem. AAAS, Soc. Plastics Industry, Soc. Plastics Engrs., Am. Chem. Soc., Moose. Republican. Lutheran.

KRESS, NANCY, writer; b. Buffalo, Jan. 20; d. Henry Francis and Angelina (Canale) Koningisor; m. Michael Joseph Kress, July 14, 1973 (div. 1986); children: Kevin Michael, Brian Stephen. BS in Edn., SUNY, Plattsburgh, 1969; MEd, SUNY, Brockport, 1978, MA in English, 1979. Cert. tchr. N.Y. K-6 and English 7-12. Grade 4 tchr. Penn Yan (N.Y.) Schs., 1970-73; tchr. grade 9 English Holley (N.Y.) Ctrl. Schs., 1979-80; instr. SUNY, Brockport, 1980-83; copywriter Stanton & Hucko, Inc., Rochester, N.Y., 1984-89; freelance writer, 1990—. Author: (novels) An Alien Light, 1988, Beggars in Spain, 1993, Oaths & Miracles, 1996, Maximum Light, 1997; columnist Writer's Digest mag., 1992—. Winner 1997 Nebula awd for Flowers of Aulit Prison. Mem. Sci. Fiction Writers Am. (nebula awards for best short story 1985, best novella 1991, hugo award for best novella 1992). *

KRESS, WILLIAM F., manufacturing company executive. Pres. Green Bay (Wis.) Packaging. Office: Green Bay Packaging 1700 Webster Ct Green Bay WI 54302-1166*

KRESSEL, HENRY, venture capitalist; b. Vienna, Jan. 24, 1934; came to U.S., 1946, naturalized, 1955; s. Aaron and Hudi (Zauderer) K.; m. Bertha Horowitz, Sept. 16, 1956; children—Aron, Kim. B.S. magna cum laude, Yeshiva U., 1955; M.S., Harvard U., 1956; M.B.A., U. Pa., 1959, Ph.D. (David Sarnoff fellow), 1965. Engr. Solid State div. RCA, 1959-61, engring. leader, 1961-63, 65-66; mem. tech. staff RCA David Sarnoff Research Center, 1966-70, head semicondr. device research, 1970-78, dir. materials research lab., 1978-79; staff v.p. solid state research RCA David Sarnoff Research Center, Princeton, N.J., 1979-83; sr. v.p. E.M. Warburg, Pincus & Co., N.Y.C., 1983-84; mng. dir. E.M. Warburg, Pincus & Co., 1985—; regents lectr. U. Calif., San Diego, 1978-79; bd. dirs. Yeshiva U. Rsch. Inst.; cons. solar energy U.S. ERDA, 1975, USAF; adv. com. engring. NSF, 1996-99; engring. adv. coun. N.C. State U., 1985-88; mem. bd. dirs. several high tech. companies. Author: Semiconductor Lasers and Heterojunction LED's, 1977; editor: Characterization of Epitaxial Semiconductor Films, 1976, Semiconductor Devices for Optical Communication, 1980; assoc. editor: IEEE Jour. Quantum Electronics, 1978-81; chmn. coordinating com. Jour. Lightware Tech., 1981-82; contbr. numerous articles to sci. jours. Served with Fin. Corps U.S. Army, 1959. Recipient David Sarnoff award RCA, 1974, Revel award Yeshiva U., 1980. Fellow IEEE (pres. Lasers and Electro-optics Soc. 1978-79, Centennial award 1984, Sarnoff award 1985, Leos Svc. award 1992), Am. Phys. Soc.; mem. AIME, Nat. Acad. Engring. Patentee in field. Home: 529 Riverside Dr Elizabeth NJ 07208-2147 Office: E M Warburg Pincus & Co 466 Lexington Ave Fl 10 New York NY 10017-3147

KRESSEL, HERBERT YEHUDE, medical educator; b. Bklyn., Nov. 20, 1947. BA, Brandeis U., Waltham, Mass., 1968; MD, U. So. Calif., L.A., 1972. Diplomate Am. Bd. Radiology in diagnostic radiology; lic. physician, Calif., Pa., Wis., N.Y., N.J., Mass. Intern in medicine U. Wash. Hosp., Seattle, 1972-73; resident in radiology U. Calif., San Francisco, 1973-74, NIH fellow in diagnostic radiology, 1974-76, clin. instr. radiology, 1976-77, asst. prof., 1977-80, assoc. prof., 1980-85, prof., 1985-93; Miriam H. Stoneman prof. radiology Harvard Med. Sch., Boston, 1993—; attending physician GI radiology sect. dept. radiology Hosp. of U. Pa., 1977-82, dir. continuing edn., 1979-93, attending physician, chief MRI sect., 1982-93; radiologist-in-chief Beth Israel Deaconess Med. Ctr., Boston, 1996; pres., CEO Beth Israel Deaconess Med. Ctr., 1998—; mem. plan devel. adv. task force on magnetic resonance for 1986 HealthSystems Plan-Health Systems Agy. Southeastern Pa., Inc., 1985-87; dir. R.I. Magnetic Resonance Imaging Network, Providence, 1988-93; mem. sci. adv. com. for rsch. grants Am. Cancer Soc., 1990-93; task force chmn. Com. on Studies Involving Human Beings, U. Pa., 1985-92; mem. coun. for continuing med. edn. U. Pa., 1990-93. Mem. editl. bds. Radiology, 1985-91, Magnetic Resonance in Medicine, 1987—; editor Magnetic Resonance Ann., 1985-88, Magnetic Resonance Quar., 1988-94; patentee in field. Mem. bd. dirs. Coregroup, 1996. Recipient Sylvia Sorkin Greenfield award Am. Assn. Physicists in Medicine, 1993. Fellow Am. Coll. Radiology (Commn. on Magnetic Resonance 1987-90, com. on pub. rels. 1987—, com. MR stds. and accreditation 1987—, chmn. com. on MR clin. applications 1987, Commn. on Govt. Rels. 1992—), Soc. Magnetic Resonance in Medicine (trustee 1987, sci. program com. chmn. 1989-90, pres.-elect 1990-91, pres. 1991-92, Crues Kressel award sect. magnetic resonance technologists 1991, Silver medal 1994), Radiol. Soc. N.Am. (refresher course com. 1992-93), Am. Roentgen Ray Soc., Soc. Gastrointestinal Radiologists, Soc. Computed Body Tomography (rsch. com. 1990-93), Mass. Radiol. Soc., New Eng. Roentgen Ray Soc. Office: Beth Israel Hosp Dept Radiology 330 Brookline Ave Boston MA 02215-5491

KRESSLEY, GEORGE JOHN, JR., financial analyst; b. Washington, Sept. 8, 1951; s. George John and Margaret (Hyatt) K.; m. Catherine Hermina Gill, Dec. 22, 1973 (div. Feb. 1989); children: Matthew Joshua, Rebecca Lauren; m. C. Jean Wilfong, Aug. 15, 1992. BA, U. Md., 1973; MBA, U. N.C., 1983. Media rels. assoc. G.W. Univ. Hosp., Washington, 1974-80; asst. dir. media rels. D.C. Gen. Hosp., Washington, 1980-83; pres. The Greenwood Group, Takoma Park, Md., 1983-84; from new product analyst to internat. country analyst Eli Lilly & Co., Indpls., 1984-90; from N.Am. fin. mgr. to dist. sales mgr. Dow Elanco, Indpls., 1990-97; global fin. leader Dow Agroscis., Indpls., 1997—. Author: Magic Does the Trick, 1978, Skate Wall Mall, 1979. Mem. Inst. Mgmt. Accts. (cert.). Office: Dow Agrosci 9330 Zionsville Rd Indianapolis IN 46268-1053

KRESSLEY, LARRY, foundation administrator; b. Allentown, Pa., Aug. 2, 1949; s. Ralph T. and Marcella (Reiss) K. Grad., Goddard Coll.; MEd, Antioch Coll., 1976. Program officer Pub. Welfare Found., Washington, 1980, sr. program officer, 1981, exec. dir., 1991; project dir. Rural Am., Washington, 1982; mem. com. inclusiveness Coun. Founds. Vol. VISTA, Warren, Ark., 1969; trustee Goddard Coll. Mem. Nat. Network Grantmakers (co-chair bd. dirs., mem. steering com. working group funding lesbian gay issues), Washington Tegional Assn. Grantmakers (dir.). Home: 2500 Q St NW Apt 702 Washington DC 20007-4347 Office: Pub Welfare Found 2600 Virginia Ave NW Ste 505 Washington DC 20037-1977*

KRESTON, MARTIN HOWARD, advertising, marketing, public relations, and publishing executive; b. N.Y.C., May 27, 1931; s. Henry and Frances (Stoll) Kreizvogel; m. Audrey Elizabeth Muir, Aug. 20, 1960 (dec. Jan., 1992); children: Mark Bradley, Rebecca Sarah; m. Judith Kate Stern, Dec. 15, 1996. B.S. in Econs, Wharton Sch., U. Pa., 1953; postgrad., N.Y. U., Northwestern U. Asst. dept. mgr. R.H. Macy & Co., N.Y.C., 1953-54; mktg. supr., account exec. Edward H. Weiss & Co., Chgo., 1956-60; with Doyle Dane Bernbach Inc., N.Y.C., 1960-86, v.p., mgmt. supr., 1970-72, sr. v.p., mgmt. supr., 1972, group sr. v.p., 1972-86, exec. v.p., 1984-86, cons., 1986-88; exec. v.p. England & Co. Pub. Rels., 1988-89; pres., chief exec. officer Caggiano, Kreston & Siebel, N.Y.C., 1989-90; dir. mktg. optical group Jobson Pub. Corp., N.Y.C., 1990; N.E. sales dir. USA Today, N.Y.C., 1991-98. With U.S. Army, 1954-56. Mem. Univ. Club. Republican. Jewish. Home: 130 Hillside Ave Englewood NJ 07631-3024

KRETSCHMAR, WILLIAM EDWARD, state legislator, lawyer; b. St. Paul, Aug. 21, 1933; s. William Emanuel and Frances Jane (Peterson) K. BS, Coll. St. Thomas, 1954; LLB, U. Minn., 1961. Bar: N.D. 1961, U.S. Dist. Ct. N.D. 1961. Ptnr. Kretschmar & Kretschmar, Ashley, N.D., 1962—; mem. N.D. Ho. of Reps., Bismarck, 1972-98, speaker, 1988-90, N.D. Comsn. Uniform State Laws, 1987—; bd. dirs. N.W. G.F. Mut. Ins. Co., Eureka, S.D.; del. N.D. Constl. Conv., Bismarck, 1971-72. Mem. ABA, State Bar Assn. N.D., Lions (pres. local club 1972-73, 93-94), Jaycees (pres. local club 1967-68), Elks. Republican. Roman Catholic. Avocations: hunting, swimming, hiking, bicycling, skiing. Home: 201 E 3d St Venturia ND 58489-4015 Office: Kretschmar & Kretschmar 117 1st Ave NW Ashley ND 58413-7037

KRETSCHMER, FRANK FREDERICK, JR., electrical engineer, researcher, consultant; b. Phila., July 31, 1930; m. Shirley J. Kretschmer; children: Frank F. III, John, Diane, Linda, Thomas. BSEE, Pa. State U., 1957; MSEE, Drexel Inst. Tech., 1961; PhD, Johns Hopkins U., 1970. Asst. devel. engr. Burroughs Corp., Paoli, Pa., 1957-58; project engr. Bendix Radio Corp., Towson, Md., 1958-64; rsch. assoc. Johns Hopkins U., Balt., 1964-70; supervisory electronics engr. Naval Rsch. Lab., Washington, 1970-90, 90—; cons. in field. Author: Aspects of Radar Signal Processing, 1986; contbr. over 30 articles to profl. jours. and confs. With USN, 1948-52. Fellow IEEE (life). Achievements include over 20 patents in field.

KRETSCHMER, KEITH HUGHES, investor; b. Omaha, Oct. 20, 1934; s. John G. and Mary (Hughes) K.; m. Adine Williams, Oct. 1, 1960; children: Hugh, Dara, Kurt. A.A., Wentworth Acad., 1954; B.S., U. Nebr., 1956; student, UCLA, 1968. With J.G. Kretschmer & Co., Omaha, 1958-60; gen. agt. Lincoln (Nebr.) Life & Casualty, 1960-62; exec. v.p., sec.-treas. Automated Mgmt. systems, Kansas City, Mo., 1962-68; investment exec. Shearson, Hammill & Co., Los Angeles, 1968-75; gen. ptnr. Bear Stearns & Co., Los Angeles, 1975-85; sr. mng. dir. Bear Stearns & Co. Inc., Boston, 1985-91, spl. assoc. dir., 1991-92; mng. dir. Oppenheimer & Co., Inc., Boston, 1993-94, Oppenheimer Capital, 1995—; mem. stockholders com. Tosco Corp., Los Angeles, 1982. Author: Your Option, 1978. Advanceman Rep. Pres.'s Nixon and Ford, 1970-76; trustee Lighthouse Preservation Soc., 1986-88; active United Way Mass.; founding dir. Option Soc. So. Calif, 1974-85; bd. dirs. Pacific Palisades-Malibu YMCA, 1976-86, chmn. bd. dirs., 1980; bd. dirs. South Shore Art Ctr., Cohasset, Mass., 1988-97, pres., 1991-93; bd. dirs. World Affairs Coun. Boston, 1989-96. Served to maj. U.S. Army, 1956-58. Mem. The Explorers Club, Aircraft Owners and Pilots Assn., Experimental Aircraft Assn., Seaplane Pilots Assn., CEO Club Phila., Angel Flight, AERO Club New England, Vintage Sports Car Club Am., Doylestown C.C. Congregationalist. Lodges: Masons, Shriners. Avocation: pilot since 1952. Home: 6 Aster Ct Doylestown PA 18901-2618 Office: Oppenheimer Capital Oppenheimer Tower One World Fin Ctr New York NY 10281-1098

KRETZSCHMAR, WILLIAM ADDISON, JR., English language educator; b. Ann Arbor, Mich., Sept. 13, 1953; s. William Addison and Audrey June (Krauss) K.; m. Claudia Suzanne Miller. AB, U. Mich., 1975; MA in Medieval Studies, Yale U., 1976; PhD in English, U. Chgo., 1980. Instr. English Mundelein Coll., Chgo., 1977-82, dir. summer sch., 1979-81; asst. prof. English U. Wis., Whitewater, 1982-86; asst. prof. English U. Ga., Athens, 1986-89, assoc. prof., 1989-95, prof., 1995—, dir. linguistics program, 1996-99. Author: Introduction to Quantitative Analysis of Linguistic Survey Data, 1996; editor: Dialects in Culture (R.I. McDavid, Jr.), 1979, Handbook of the Linguistic Atlas of the Middle and South Atlantic States, 1993; editor: Linguistic Atlas Middle and South Atlantic States, Lunguistic Atlas North-Central States, 1984; editor Jour. English Linguistics, 1983-99, Empirical Linguistic Series, 1996-99; contbr. articles to profl. jours. Mem. MLA (regional del. 1983-86), Am. Dialect Soc., Linguistic Soc. Am., Medieval Acad. Am., Assn. Computers Humanities (bd. dirs. 1989—). Home: 125 Renfrew Dr Athens GA 30606-3936 Office: U Ga Dept English Athens GA 30602

KREUL, CAROL ANN, nurse; b. Dodgeville, Wis., Mar. 6, 1956; d. Norbert Francis and Rose Blanch (Winters) K. ADN, Madison (Wis.) Area Tech. Coll., 1981. RN, Wis.; cert. critical care, instr. ACLS. Staff nurse ICU Meml. Hosp. Iowa County, Dodgeville. Mem. AACN. Home: 506 Diagonal St Highland WI 53543-9709

KREUTER, GRETCHEN V., academic administrator; b. Mpls., May 7, 1934; d. Sigmund and Marvyl (Larson) von Loewe; m. Robert L. Sutton, 1993; children: David Karl, Betsy Ruth Rymes. BA, Rockford Coll., 1955; MA, U. Wis., 1958, PhD, 1961; LLD (hon.), Rockford Coll., 1992, Coll. St. Mary. Lectr. in Am. Studies Colgate U., Hamilton, N.Y., 1962-67; lectr. in history Coll. St. Catherine, St. Paul, 1969-71, Hamline U., St. Paul, 1971-72; prof. of history Macalester Coll., St. Paul, 1972-73, St. Olaf Coll., Northfield, Minn., 1975-80; asst. to pres. Coll. St. Catherine, St. Paul, 1980-84; asst. to v.p. acad. affairs U. Minn., Mpls., 1984-87; pres. Rockford Coll., Ill., 1987-92, Olivet (Mich.) Coll., 1992-93; sr. fellow Am. Coun. Edn., Washington, 1993-94; hon. fellow Inst. for Rsch. in Humanities U. Wis., Madison, 1994—; interim pres. Coll. of St. Mary, Omaha, 1995-96; mem., chmn. Minn. Humanities Coun., St. Paul, 1974-83; mem. Mich. Humanities Coun., 1993; bd. dirs. Nat. Assn. State Humanities Commn., Washington, 1984-86. Author: An American Dissenter, 1969 (McKnight prize 1978), Running the Twin Cities: editor: Women of Minnesota, 1977, 2d edit., 1998, Two Career Family, 1978, Forgotton Promise: Race and Gender Conflict on a Small College Campus: A Memoir, 1996. Bd. dirs. Kobe Coll. Corp., Rockford Mus. Ctr., ACE Commn. on Minorities in Higher Edn., 1991—, Mich. Humanities Coun., 1993—. Address: 2402 Kendall Ave Madison WI 53705-3845

KREUTZ, AUSTIN THOMAS, clergyman; b. Queensvillage, N.Y., July 11, 1952; s. Austin Edward and Elaine Ann (Macksood) K.; m. Monica Kay Phillips, May 18, 1975; children: Andrew Michel, John Austin. BA, Heidelberg Coll., 1976; MA, Ashland Theol. Sem., 1983; postgrad., Trinity Sem., 1992—. Ordained to ministry assemblies of God, 1982, Light of the World, 1994. Asst. pastor Calvary Temple, Royal Oak, Mich., 1982-83; sr. pastor New Life Assembly of God, Holland, Mich., 1983-88, Peekskill (N.Y.) Assembly of God, 1988-90, Light of the World, Yorktown, 1990—; exec. dir. Caring for the Homeless of Peekskill, 1990-92, projects Jan peek House/Noontime Meal Program; sr. pastor Light of the World Adirondack, 1993—. Pres., founder Holland (Mich.) Ministers Fellowship, 1986-88; bd. dirs. Prison Chaplins Saugatuck Dunes Correction, 1985-88. Mem. Peekskill Area Pastors Assn. (v.p. 1989-90). Home and Office: 32 Mcelwain Ave Cohoes NY 12047-2421

KREUTZBERG, DAVID W., lawyer; b. Edwardsville, Ill., May 20, 1953. BA summa cum laude, Ariz. State U., 1975, JD magna cum laude, 1978. Bar: Ariz. 1978, U.S. Dist. Ct. (Ariz. dist.) 1978. Law clk. to Hon. William E. Eubank Ariz. Ct. Appeals, Phoenix, 1978-79; ptnr. Squire, Sanders & Dempsey LLP, Phoenix, 1989. Mem. ABA (mem. bus. law sect.), State Bar Ariz., Maricopa County Bar Assn., Phi Beta Kappa. Office: Squire Sanders & Dempsey LLP Two Renaissance Sq 40 N Central Ave Ste 2700 Phoenix AZ 85004-4424

KREUZ, DANIEL EDWARD, city engineer; b. Toledo, Ohio, June 13, 1956; s. Norman Charles and Mary Eloise (Okuley) K.; m. Pamela Beth Gorney, May 16, 1980; children: Phillip, Matthew, Jeffrey. BS, U. Buffalo, 1978. Registered profl. engr., N.Y. Traffic engr. City of Buffalo, N.Y., 1985-88; engr. staff Buffalo Urban Renewal Agy., 1988-96; city engr. Buffalo, 1996-99. Home: 502 City Hall Buffalo NY 14202-7520

KREUZ, JEANETTE C., accountant, school official; b. Chgo.; d. Ronald B. and Joyce E. Jordan; m. Steven A. Kreuz, Mar. 28, 1987. BS in Acctg., DePaul U., 1983; MPA, Gov.'s State U., 1997, MBA, 1999. Fiscal officer Ctrl. Office City Colls. Chgo., 1983-88, fixed asset mgr., 1989-90, asst. dir. bus. and operational svcs. Daley Coll., 1990-97; personal tax acct. New Lenox, Ill., 1987—; acctg. supr. Dist. Office J. Sterling Morton H.S., Cicero, Ill., 1997—. Treas. Tinley Park (Ill.) Arts Alive Band, St. Gall Troop 697, Boy Scouts Am., Chgo., 1979-83; mem. sch. bd. St. Gall, 1983-84; ch. musician various Cath. chs., Chgo., 1983—. Grantee Ill. Arts Coun., 1998. Mem. ASPA, Ill. Assn. Sch. Bus. Ofcls. Avocations: music, reading, collecting dolls. E-mail: sax4516885@aol.com. Office: J Sterling Morton HS 2423 S Austin Blvd Cicero IL 60804

KREVANS, JULIUS RICHARD, university administrator, physician; b. N.Y.C., May 1, 1924; s. Sol and Anita (Makovetsky) K.; m. Patricia N. Abrams, May 28, 1950; children: Nita, Julius R., Rachel, Sarah, Nora Kate. B.S. Arts and Scis, N.Y. U., 1943, M.D., 1946. Diplomate: Am. Bd. Internal Med. Intern, then resident Johns Hopkins Med. Sch. Hosp., mem. faculty, until 1970, dean acad. affairs, 1969-70; physician in chief Balt. City Hosp., 1963-69; prof. medicine U. Calif., San Francisco, 1970—, dean Sch. Medicine, 1971-82, chancellor, 1982-93, chancellor emeritus, 1993—. Contbr. articles on hematology, internal med. profl. jours. Served with M.C. AUS, 1948-50. Mem. A.C.P., Assn. Am. Physicians. Office: U Calif San Francisco Sch Medicine San Francisco CA 94143-0296

KREWER, JULIE-ANN, scholar; b. N.Y.C., Oct. 21, 1951; d. Semyon Efimovitch and Elsa (Silberstein) K. BA, Harvard U., 1972; student, U. Pa. Scholar Univ. Pa., Phila., 1967—; rsch. asst. Hand Gym Inc., N.Y.C., 1967-85; A.A.S. candidate New Sch. Social Rsch., N.Y.C., 1995—. Mem. Congregation Beth Sholom, Long Beach, N.Y., 1996—. Félicitation Lycée-français de N.Y., 1958—. Mem. Pa. Club N.Y. Jewish. Avocations: crafts, piano, exhibiting artwork & photography. Home: 75 Freeport Ave Point Lookout NY 11569 Office: Ben Franklin Scholar 240 S 33rd St 310 Hayden Hall Philadelphia PA 13103

KREY, ANDREW EMIL VICTOR, minister; b. Bklyn., Nov. 2, 1948; s. Rudolf E.M. and Gertrude Emily (Berhrens) K.; m. Sally June Olson, Nov. 24, 1973; children: Heather, Benjamin. BA, Northeastern U., 1972; MDiv, Luth. Theol. Sem., 1976. Ordained to ministry Luth. Ch., 1976. Pastor Zion Luth. Ch., Bristol, Conn., 1976-90; chaplain New Eng. Seamen's Mission, Providence, 1990-94, Migrant Ops., Guantanamo Bay, Cuba, 1994-94; domestic maritime ministry cons. Evang. Luth. Ch. in Am., 1995—; chaplain, missionary Maritime Ministry So. New Eng., 1995—; dir. chaplaincy Seafarers Internat. House, N.Y.C., 1999—; chair 5 yr. plan for evangelism and stewardship Luth. Ch. Am., 1981-86; Luth. rep. Billy Graham So. New Eng. Crusade, Hartford, Conn., 1985; maritime ministry cons. Divsn. for Outreach Evangelical Luth. Ch. Am., Chgo., 1995—. officer-in-charge indoctrination course for Navy chaplains USCG, Governors' Island, N.Y.C., 1985-87; prod. and orig. concept play, the Last Supper, 1995-99, N.Y.C., 1999, Westbury, Ct. 1997-99. Chair Greater Bristol Social Concerns Com., 1985-90; coord. various youth programs, Bristol, 1979-90; founder Cen. Conn. Soup Kitchen, Bristol, 1981—. Lt. comdr. USNR, 1978-99, ret. Named to Outstanding Young Men Am., Conn. Jaycees, 1983; recipient Disting. Svc. award WFSB-TV3, 1984. Mem. Internat. Christian Maritime Assn., N.Am. Maritime Ministry Assn. (bd. dirs. 1991—), Luth. Assn. for Maritime Ministry (pres. 1991-97, natl. trng. coord., 1998—). Republican. Congregation resettled many refugees, 1976-90. Home: 140 Country Club Rd Waterbury CT 06708-3319 Office: Maritime Ministry of Southern New Eng PO Box 4049 New Haven CT 06525-0049 *The primary* *task of Christ's church is to proclaim Jesus as Saviour and Lord through evangelism, service and advocacy. Individual committed Christians allow the church to reach this goal.*

KREY, MARY ANN REYNOLDS, beer wholesaler executive; b. St. Louis, June 17, 1947; d. Frederick Curtis and Phyllis M. (Terry) R.; m. John F. Krey III (dec. Nov. 1986); 1 child, Laura Christine; m. Michael Van Lokeren, Apr. 15, 1994. BA, Washington U., St. Louis, 1969, MBA, 1988. Sec. Krey Distbg., St. Charles, Mo., 1978-80, v.p., 1980-86, pres., chief exec. officer, 1986—; bd. dirs. Laclede Gas Co., St. Louis, CPI Corp., Commerce Bancshares, Inc., Kansas City, Mo., Masco Corp. Mem. Mo. Clean Water Commn., Jefferson City, 1988—; bd. dirs. Arts and Edn. Coun. St. Louis, St. Louis Art Mus., Kids Under Twenty-One, World Affairs Coun., Variety Club, SBA Region VII, St. Louis Children's Hosp.; bd. dirs., trustee Washignton U. Recipient Leadership award YWCA, 1993; named Mo. Anheuser-Buscher wholesaler, 1989, Woman of Yr. Variety Club, 1994. Mem. Young Pres. Orgn., Regional Commerce and Growth Assn. (bd. dirs. 1990—), Jr. League St. Louis. Office: Krey Distbg 150 Turner Blvd Saint Peters MO 63376-1078

KREYCHE, GERALD FRANCIS, retired philosophy educator; b. Kenosha, Wis., June 19, 1927; s. Harold Joseph and Henrietta Fredericka (Oteman) K.; m. Eleanor Ann Okon, June 19, 1948. AB, DePaul U., 1949, AM, 1950; PhD cum laude, U. Ottawa, Can., 1958. Mem. faculty DePaul U., 1950-59, chmn. dept. philosophy, 1961-82, prof., 1965-89, prof. emeritus, 1989—; now also Danforth assoc.; Aquinas lectr. Alverno Coll., Milw., 1963; vis. prof. St. Mary's Coll., Minn., 1977; bd. advisors Univ. Press Am. Condr.: radio programs What Do You Think? ; also What's the Big Idea?, 1960; frequent appearances ednl. and comml. TV, also radio, 1958—; Author: Perspectives on God, 1972, Thirteen Thinkers; also articles religious publs.; Co-editor: Harbrace Philosophy series; Visions of the American West, 1988; sr. editor: Am. Thought; sect. editor: U.S.A. Today; bd. advisors: Philos. Research and Analysis; former editor-in-chief Listening: A Journal of Religion and Culture; referee Archives of Philosophy. With AUS, 1945-46. Recipient DePaul U. Distinguished Service award, 1969, Univ. award for excellence, 1984-85, Viam Sapientiae award, 1989. Mem. Am. Metaphys. Soc., Ill.-Ind. Am. Cath. Philos. Assn. (pres. 1960), Am. Cath. Philos. Assn. (pres. 1972-73), Chgo. Lit. Club (pres. 1986-87), Phi Kappa Theta, Phi Eta Sigma. Home: 15881 County Rd 28 Dolores CO 81323

KREYLING, EDWARD GEORGE, JR., railroad executive; b. St. Louis, June 1, 1923; s. Edward George and Mildred (Schroeder) K.; m. Mary Emily Gronemeyer, Sept. 4, 1943; children: Carol (Mrs. Robert D. Knight), Deborah Ann (Mrs. Hugh J. Risseeuw), Edward George III. BSBA, Washington U., St. Louis, 1947, MBA, 1954. Accountant Monsanto Chem. Co., 1947-50; chief statistician White Rodgers Elec. Co., St. Louis, 1950-54; dir. market research Laclede-Christy Co., St. Louis, 1954-55; with St. L.-S.F. Ry., 1955-69, dir. marketing, 1964-65, v.p. traffic and indsl. devel., 1965-69; v.p. traffic I.C. R.R., Chgo., 1969-70; exec. v.p. Penn Central Transp. Co., Phila., 1970-71; v.p. marketing So. Ry., 1971-79, sr. v.p. mktg. service, 1979-80, exec. v.p. mktg., 1981-82; v.p. mktg. services Norfolk So. Corp. (Va.), 1982-87, ret. Active Va. Beach. Sch. Bd., 1992-94; dir. Seton House, 1995-98, Va. Chrsitian Coalition, 1998—. Served with AUS, 1943-45. Mem. Nat. Freight Traffic Assn. Home: 11307 Stons Throw Dr Reston VA 20194

KRIBEL, ROBERT EDWARD, academic administrator, consultant physicist; b. Pitts., Sept. 17, 1937; s. Joseph P. and Helen M. K.; m. Ruth Ann Gropelli; children—Robert E., Karen A., Mark P., Gary P. B.S., U. Notre Dame, 1959; M.S., U. Calif., San Diego, 1966, Ph.D. in Physics, 1968. Research scientist Gen. Atomic, Inc., 1965-69; assoc. prof. physics Drake U., 1970-73; vis. assoc. prof. applied physics Cornell U., 1973-74; prof., head dept. physics James Madison U., 1974-78; prof., head dept. physics Auburn (Ala.) U., 1978-87, acting dean scis. and math., 1985-87, prof. physics, 1987-88; v.p. acad. affairs Jacksonville (Ala.) State U., 1988-92, prof. physics, 1992-93; dean natural scis. and math. Mesa State Coll., 1993-99; pres. REK Consulting Svcs., Auburn, Ala., 1999—. Contbr. articles to profl. jours. Served with U.S. Navy, 1959-62. Mem. Am. Phys. Soc., IEEE, Am. Assn. Physics Tchrs., Sigma Xi, Phi Kappa Phi. Home: 674 Ogletree Rd Auburn AL 36830 Office: REK Enterprises 674 Ogletree Rd Auburn AL 36830

KRICK, EDWIN HARRY, SR., medical educator, preventive medicine physician; b. Takoma Pk., Md., Aug. 13, 1935; s. Russell Kenneth and Flora Shaffer Parsons K.; m. Kay Saunders Kronquest, June 2, 1957 (dec. May 1982); children: Joylyn Marie Grant, Edwin Harry Krick Jr.; m. Beverly Kay Hardt, Oct. 9, 1983. BA in Chemistry, Atlantic Union Coll., 1957; MD, Loma Linda U., 1961, MPH, 1971. Diplomate Am. Bd. Internal Medicine, Am. Bd. Allergy and Immunology: Preventive Medicine, Nat. Bd. Medicine U.S. and Japan. Intern White Meml. Hosp., L.A., 1961-62; resident Loma Linda U. Med. Ctr., 1970-73; fellow in rheumatology and immunology Scripps Clinic and Rsch. Found., La Jolla, Calif., 1974-76; staff physician Tokyo Adventist Hosp., 1962-66; dir. Kobe Adventist Clinic Japan Mission Seventh-Day Adventists, 1966-70; instr. preventive medicine Loma Linda (Calif.) U., 1971-76, asst. prof. medicine, 1976-80, assoc. prof. medicine, 1980—; dir. preventive medicine Loma Linda U. Sch. Medicine, 1973-83, chief sect. rheumatology, 1977-84, dean Sch. Pub. Health, 1986-90, dir. rheumatology fellowship, 1993—. Treas. Loma Linda U. Sch. Medicine Alumni Assn., 1973-75, pres., 1979-80. Named Alumnus of Yr., Loma Linda U. Sch. Medicine Alumni Assn., 1988. Fellow ACP, Am. Coll. Rheumatology; mem. AMA, Calif. Med. Soc., San Bernardino County Med. Soc., Alpha Omega Alpha. Republican. Avocations: flying, amateur radio, hiking, white water rafting, fitness-jogging, running marathons. E-mail: edbevkrick@earthlink.net. Home: PO Box 2113 Redlands CA 92373 Office: Faculty Med Offices Loma Linda U 11370 Anderson St Loma Linda CA 92354

KRIDER, E. PHILIP, atmospheric scientist, educator; b. Chgo., Mar. 22, 1940; s. Edmund Arthur and Ruth (Abbott) K.; m. Barbara A. Reed, June 13, 1964 (div. Mar. 1983); children: Ruth Ellen, Philip Reed. BA in Physics, Carleton Coll., 1962; MS in Physics, U. Ariz., 1964, PhD in Physics, 1969. Resident rsch. assoc. NASA Manned Spacecraft Ctr. NAS, Houston, 1969-71; asst. rsch. prof. Inst. Atmospheric Physics U. Ariz., Tucson, 1971-75, asst. prof. dept. atmospheric scis., 1973-75, assoc. prof. dept. atmospheric scis., Inst. Atmos. Physics, 1975-80; exec. v.p., part-time chmn. Lightning Location and Protection, Inc., Tucson, 1976-83; adj. prof. dept. elec. engring. U. Fla., Gainesville, 1988—; prof. dept. atmospheric scis. Inst. Atmospheric Physics U. Ariz., 1980—, dir. Inst. Atmospheric Physics, head dept. atmospheric scis., 1986-95; pres. Internat. Commn. Atmospheric Electricity, 1992—; co-chmn. panel Earth's elec. environment geophysis study com. NAS, 1982-86; mem. panel weather support for space ops. NAS, 1987-88, geostationary platform sci. steering com. NASA, 1987—; mems. rep. Univ. Corp. for Atmospheric Rsch., 1986-95; mem. U.S. nat. com. Internat. Sci. Radio Union; mem. lightning and sferics subcom. Internat. Commn. on Atmospheric Electricity, 1976—; mem. aerospace corp. adv. team USAF Launch Vehicle Lightning/Atmospheric Elec. Constraints, Post Atlas/Centaur 67 Incident, 1987-89; sci. advisor Air Force Geophys. Lab., 1988; mem. lightning adv. com. U.S. Army Missile Command, 1986-87; lectr. in field. Author: (with others) Thunderstorms, 1983, Lightning Electromagnetics, 1990, Benjamin Franklin des Lumieres á nos Jours., 1991; contbr. numerous articles to profl. jours.; co-chief editor Jour. of Atmospheric Scis., 1990-92, editor, 1992-93; assoc. editor Jour. Geophys. Rsch., 1977-79; referee Jour. Geophys. Rsch., Geophys. Rsch. Letters, Jour. of Atmospheric Scis., Planetary and Space Sci. Fellow Am. Meteorol. Soc. (Outstanding Contbn. to Advance Applied Meteorology award 1985), Am. Geophys. Union (Smith medal selection com. 1994, com. on atmospheric and space electricity 1990—); mem. IEEE (Transactions Prize Paper award EMC Soc. 1982), Am. Assn. Physics Tchrs., Sigma Xi, Sigma Pi Sigma. Achievements include patents for All-Sky camera apparatus for time-resolved lightning photography, photoelectric lightning detector apparatus, transient event data acquisition apparatus for use with radar systems and the like, lightning detection system utilizing triangulation and field amplitude comparison techniques, thunderstorm sensor and method of identifying and locating thunderstorms. Office: U Ariz Dept Atmospheric Scis PO Box 210081 Tucson AZ 85721-0081*

KRIDER, MARGARET YOUNG, art educator; b. Pitts., Aug. 20, 1920; d. Thomas Smith and Josephine Bridget (Connolly) Y.; m. Robert Arthur Krider, May 12, 1945; children: Karen L., Ann Noel, Darcie Ellen Robbins. BFA in Art Edn., Carnegie-Mellon U., 1942; MEd in Art Edn., Edinboro U., 1969. Tchr. art West Homestead (Pa.) Pub. Sch., 1942-44, Mt. Oliver (Pa.) Pub. Sch., 1942-44; recreational worker Valley Forge Gen. Hosp. ARC, Phoenixville, Pa., 1944-45; assoc. prof. Villa Maria Coll., Erie, Pa., 1950-87; adj. instr. Pa. State U. Behrend Campus, Erie, Pa., 1981-87; presenter papers Ea. Arts Conv., N.Y.C., 1962, Kutztown (Pa.) State U., 1967, U. Pa. Art Conf., Pitts., 1980; condr. workshops Peterborough State Coll., Toronto, Ont., Can., 1972-73; presenter in field, 1962—. Exhibited in one and two-man shows incl. Chautauqua Art Gallery, William Penn Meml. Mus., Butler Mus., Patterson Gallery, Glass Growers Gallery, Kada Gallery, Erie, Sycamore Gallery, Cummings Gallery, Schuster Gallery, juried and invitational shows incl. Erie Art Mus., Erie Summer Festivals, Agnon Fine Art and Crafts, Carlow Coll. Pa. Women's Art, Bruce Gallery, Forum Gallery, Kada Gallery; contbr. articles to art jours. Bd. dirs., sec. Arts Coun. Erie, Pa., 1974-76, Erie Civic Ballet Co., 1970-75; bd. dirs. Erie County Hist. Soc., 1988-94; active LWV, 1950s; Girl Scout leader Cathedral Grade Sch., Erie, 1956-66; hist. restoration advisor Battles Mus., Girard, Pa., 1993-98. Recipient Community award Florence Crittenton Home, 1991; named Outstanding Tchr. Villa Maria Coll. Presdl. Award, 1987, Outstanding Art Educator PAEA, 1989. Mem. AAUW (bd. dirs., chair 1967-90, Found. Ednl. award 1984, Outstanding Woman finalist 1992), Women's Round Table, Nat. Art Edn., Northwestern Pa. Artists Assn. (chair membership), Pa. Soc. Art Edn., Erie County Hist. Soc. (hon., life), Delta Kappa Gamma (chmn. Book Alive). Republican. Roman Catholic. Home: 6130 Mistletoe Ave Fairview PA 16415-2702

KRIDLER, JAMIE BRANAM, children's advocate, social psychologist; b. Newport, Tenn., Jan. 23, 1955; d. Floyd A. and Mary Leslie (Carlisle) Branam; m. Thomas Lee Kridler, Mar. 19, 1989; children: Brittani Audra, Houston Scott, Clark Eaton, Sabrina Morrow. BS, U. Tenn., 1976, MS, 1977; PhD, Ohio State U., 1985; cert. retailing, profl. modeling, Bauder Fashion Coll., Atlanta, 1973. Fashion coord. Bill's Wear House, Newport, Tenn., 1969-77; buyer Shane's Boutique, Gatlinburg, Tenn., 1977-78; instr. Miami U., Oxford, Ohio, 1978-81; asst. prof. U. Tenn., Knoxville, 1985-89; mktg. dir. Profitt's Dept. Stores, Alcoa, Tenn., 1989-90; mktg. cons. Kridler & Kridler Mktg., Newport, Tenn., 1990-93; children's advocate Safe Space, Newport, Tenn., 1993-95; adj. faculty U. Tenn., Knoxville, 1990-94, Walters State Coll., Morristown, Tenn., 1990-96, Carson Newman Coll., Jefferson City, Tenn., 1993-94; prof. East Tenn. State U., 1996—; founding mem. Cmty. House Coop., 1995—; mem. Nation Funding Collaborative on Violence Prevention; participant Children's Defense Fund, Washington, 1992—; founding mem. Cmty. House Co-op; mem. Gov.'s Prevention Initiative and Family Needs Task Force. Costume designer Newport Theatre Guild: Guys and Dolls, Carousel, Fiddler on the Roof, Music Man, Crimes of the Heart, Rumors, Come Back to the Five and Dime, Jimmy Dean, Oliver, The Odd Couple, The Sunshine Boys, Harvey, Miami U. Dance Theatre, Ice Show. Bd. dirs. Safe Space, 1991-92; v.p. Newport Theatre Guild, 1991-92, pres., 1992-96, bd. dirs., 1990-97; dir. Cast and Crew Youth Theatre; creator Looking Glass Players. Named Outstanding Tchr., Miami U., Oxford, 1981, Outstanding Educator, U. Tenn., Knoxville, 1989; recipient numerous grants from univ. and non-profit orgns. Mem. NAACP, Lioness Club, Kappa Omicorn Nu. Democrat. Lutheran. Avocations: Yogi exercise, fashion design, dance, family activities. Home: 112 Woodlawn Ave Newport TN 37821-3031

KRIEBEL, CHARLES HOSEY, management sciences educator; b. Tarrytown, N.Y., Nov. 6, 1933; s. Nelson Stearly and Elizabeth Grace (Hosey) K.; m. Jan Lilly McAuley, June 7, 1961; children: Paul Charles, Susan, James McAuley, Carl Nelson. BS in Econs., U. Pa., 1959, MA in Stats., 1961; PhD in Indsl. Mgmt., MIT, 1964. Instr. Wharton Sch. Fin., U. Pa., Phila., 1959-61; asst. prof. Sloan Sch., MIT, Cambridge, 1963-64, Grad. Sch. Indsl. Adminstrn., Carnegie-Mellon U., Pitts., 1964-67; assoc. prof. Grad. Sch. Indsl. Adminstrn., Carnegie-Mellon U., 1967-70, prof., 1970—, head dept indsl. mgmt., 1981-86; dir. strategic tech. Met. Life, N.Y.C., 1987-88; cons. McKinsey & Co., Inc., N.Y.C., Rand Corp., Santa Monica, Calif., Gulf Oil Corp., Pitts., Imperial Tobacco, Montreal, Que., Can., Mellon Bank (N.A.), Pitts., LTV STeel Co., Inc., Gen. Reins Corp., N.Y.C., Industrikonsulent I.K.O., Copenhagen, Westinghouse Electric Corp., Pitts., U.S. Steel Corp., Pitts., Rockwell Internat., Pitts., Am. Mgmt. Sys., Fairfax, Va., HAL Inst. Computer Tech., Osaka, Japan, other indsl. firms; rep. NAS; mem. adv. bd. NSF, 1985-88. Mem. editorial bd.: Internat. Fedn. Info. Processing, 1971—; editorial cons. Prentice-Hall, Inc., 1967-80; contbr. over 100 articles to profl. jours. With Signal Corps, U.S. Army, 1954-56. Fulbright-Hays advisor, 1965-79; Ford Found. fellow MIT, 1964. Fellow AAAS; mem. Assn. Computing Machinery (nat. lectr.), Inst. Mgmt. Scis. (dept. editor Mgmt. Sci.), Ops. Rsch. Soc. Am., Am. Econ. Assn., Am. Statis. Assn., Econometric Soc., N.Y. Acad. Scis., Info. Systems Rsch. (sr. editor bd.), Delta Kappa Epsilon (pres. 1959). Home: 108 Silent Run Rd Fox Chapel Pittsburgh PA 15238 Office: Carnegie-Mellon U Grad Sch Indsl Admin Pittsburgh PA 15213

KRIEBEL, MAHLON EDWARD, physiology educator, inventor; b. Garfield, Wash., Nov. 18, 1936; s. Louise (Bowen) K.; m. Monika Büsing, Feb. 18, 1980. BS, Wash. State U., 1958; MS, U. Wash., 1964, PhD, 1967. Postdoctoral fellow Albert Einstein Coll. Medicine, Yeshiva U., N.Y.C., 1967-69; prof. physiology SUNY Health Sci. Ctr., Syracuse, 1969—; vis. prof. U. Konstanz, Germany, 1977-78, U. Calif., Irvine, 1979-84, U. Graz, Austria, 1993. Author: (book and software) Manual for CHAOS, 1990; World of CHAOS, 1992; inventor CHAOS machine, CHAOS water dropper. Vol. Sci. Mus., Syracuse. Recipient von Humboldt prize Max Planck Inst., Göttingen, Germany, 1986; grantee NIH, 1971-91, Marine Biol. Lab., 1962, 63. Achievements include research in transmitter release at nerve-muscle junction; development of hypothesis that release is through channe. Avocations: woodworking, writing. Home: 202 Hillsboro Pkwy Syracuse NY 13214-2025 Office: SUNY Syracuse Health Science Ctr 750 E Adams St Syracuse NY 13210-2306*

KRIEG, DOROTHY LINDEN, soprano, performing artist, educator; b. Moline, Ill.; d. Carl Victor Lundin and Maybelle Eugenia (Bohman) Linden; m. Eugene D. Krieg, Nov. 24, 1949; m. John C. Ludke, Feb. 1, 1996. Studied piano, voice, pvt. instrs., from 1932; student, Am. Conservatory, 1938-44; studied, opera and oratorio with numerous Maestri. Tchr. Midwestern Conservatory, Chgo., 1947-49; pvt. practice teaching singing Chgo., 1952-94, L.A., 1994—; past treas. Nat. Assn. Tchrs. Singing Chgo. Began singing career in vaudeville at age 4; later appeared with Midwest Opera Co.; artist Moments of Opera show, Colosimo's and on TV; appearances in Chgo. area include supper clubs Singer's Rendevous, Caruso's, Singing Sorinis, Pucci's, Black Forest in Three Lakes, Wis., Northernaire Showboat in Three Lakes, Wis., ballrooms Drake Hotel, Conrad Hilton Hotel, Blackstone Hotel, others, polit. convs., USO shows; concert artist Chgo. Symphony Orch., from 1950's appearing at Orch. Hall, on tour and on TV with condrs. Fritz Reiner, Rafael Kubelic, George Schick, others; soprano soloist ann. performances Messiah, Marshall Field Choral Soc., 27 yrs., Bryn Mawr Community Ch., Chgo., 17 yrs., Chgo. Temple, 10 yrs., other chs. and temples throughout Chgo.; soloist major oratorio socs. including Swedish Choral Club, Apollo Club, Rockefeller Chapel Choir, Collegium Musicum, St. Louis Bach Soc., Cornell Coll., Calvin Coll., Testor Chorus, Rockford, Ill.; soloist U.S. premieres Vivaldi's Gloria and Handel's Psalm 112, Orch. Hall with Chgo. Symphony; female soloist Chgo. Swedish Glee Club, Chgo. Swedish Male Chorus, Schwaebisher Saengerbund, Chgo. Master Bakers Chorus, Combined German Male Choruses at Civic Opera Ho., others; tchr. voice prodn., phrasing, stage deportment, coach opera, oratorio, English, French and Italian lit., German lieder. 1st pl. winner West Side div. Chicagoland Music Festival Contest, 1939; named Western Springs Music Club scholar. Mem. Seal Watch (Can., Magdalen Islands), Greenpeace, Internat. Fund Animal Welfare, Internat. Soc. Animal Rights, People for Ethical Treatment of Animals, Whale Adoption Project. Avocations: cats, gemology, stero and video recording, Swedish culture. Address: 15459 Celtic St Mission Hills CA 91345-1303

KRIEGER, ABBOTT JOEL, neurosurgeon; b. N.Y.C., Apr. 29, 1939; m. Marsha Tomback; children: Lloyd, Lara, Dana. BA, Bklyn. Coll., 1959; MD, N.Y. Med. Coll., 1963; DMS in Pharmacology, Columbia U., 1970. Diplomate Am. Bd. Neurol. Surgery. Intern in surgery Montefiore Hosp., N.Y.C., 1963-64; resident in surgery, then in neuropathology Montefiore Hosp. and Med. Center, 1964-65; resident in neurol. surgery Albert Einstein Coll. Medicine, 1966-67, 70-71, resident in neurology, 1968; chief neurosurgery VA Hosp., Pitts., 1971-73; asst. prof. neurosurgery U. Pitts. Sch. Medicine, 1971-73; prof., chief program dir. neurosurgery N.J. Med. Sch., Univ. Medicine and Dentistry, Newark, 1974-94; pvt. practice Livingston, N.J., 1994—; attendent St. Barnabas Med. Ctr., Beth Israel Hosp. Contbr. articles to med. jours. Served with USMCR, 1956-62. Fellow ACS; mem. Soc. Neurol. Surgeons, Congress Neurol. Surgeons, Am. Assn. Neurol. Surgeons, N.J. Neurosurg. Soc. Home: 49 Nottingham Rd Short Hills NJ 07078-2036 Office: 22 Old Short Hills Rd Livingston NJ 07039-5605

KRIEGER, ALEX, architecture and design educator; b. Vilnuis, Lithuania, Feb. 17, 1951; came to U.S. 1960; s. Isaac and Haya (Segal) K.; m. Anne Mackin, Sept. 11, 1988, 1 child, Isara. B in Architecture, Cornell U., 1974; M in City Planning/Urban Design, Harvard U., 1977. Registered architect Mass., Conn.; cert. Nat. Coun. Archtl. Registration Bds. Architect and planner Skidmore Owings & Merrill, Boston, 1977-79; prof. architecture and urban design Harvard Grad. Sch. Design, 1978—; assoc. Moshe Safdie and Assocs., Boston, 1980-82; prin. Chan, Krieger & Assocs., Inc., Cambridge, Mass., 1985—; dir. urban design program Harvard Grad. Sch. Design, 1990-98, chmn. dept. urban planning and design, 1998—; vis. prof. Rice U., U. Miami, U. Ark., Kansas State U., Miami U. of Ohio, Boston Archtl. Ctr., 1984-92; cons. Groupe Cardinal Hardy, Peter Rose Architects, 1992; commr. Boston Civic Design Commn., 1988—; lectr. in the field. Principal works include: Loeb Fellows Residence Hall Remodeling Harvard U., 1987, Photographic Resource Ctr., Boston U., 1985, Housing Design Guidelines, Boston Pub. Facilities Dept., 1987, Travilah Quarry New Town Master Plan, Potomac, Maryland, 1988-90, Main St. Master Plan, Village of Roslindale, Mass., 1987, New Seabury Master Plan, Village of Roslindale, Mass., 1987, New Seabury Master Plan and Town Ctr., Mass., 1989—, Harvard Med. Sch. Master Plan, Boston, 1989-90, Ctrl. Artery Master Plan Boston Redevelopment Authority, 1989-91, Harvard U. AIDS Inst. Boston, 1989-90, Master Plan and Design Review, Capital Ctr. Commn., Providence, R.I., 1990—, CN Railyards Devel. Montreal, Canada, 1991, Old Port Montreal Master Plan, Canada, 1991, Discovery Mus., Bridgeport, Conn., 1990—, Beth Israel Hosp. Ctr., Boston, 1990—, Downtown East and U.S. Courthouse Urban Design Study, Mlps. Minn., 1991-92, Completion Charles River Esplanade, 1992—, North Harvard Yard Master Plan, Cambridge, 1992, U. Minn. Master Plan, 1992-93, Francois-Xavier Bagnoud Ctr. for Health and Human Rights, Boston, 1992-93, No. Tama Dist. Urban Design Plan, Tokyo, Japan, 1992-93, Downtown Master Plan Worcester Ma., 1993—; editorial bd. contbg. author New American Vitruvius, 1993; contbr. to profl journs. and mags. Cons. Boston Redevelopment Authority, 1992. Recipient AIA Henry Adams Achievement award Cornell U., 1974, Gold Medal award Coun. Advancement and Support of Edn., 1986, Internat. Design Honor award W. Hollywood Civic Ctr., 1987, Design Excellence award New England Regional Coun. AIA, 1986, Ruby Brunner award, 1991; Thomas Eggers Travellinf fellow Cornell U., 1975, Skidmore & Owings & Merrill Found Educators fellowship, 1988; Hon. mention Roosevelt Island Internat. Housing Design Competition, 1975, Santa Barbara Art Mus. Nat. Design Competition, 1983, Ariz. Hist. Soc. Mus. Nat. Design Competition, 1985, PPG Nat Glass Blocks Awards Program, 1988; recipient Progressive Architecture citation Ctrl. Artery Master Plan, 1992, Old Port Montreal Master Plan, 1992. Mem. Am. Inst. Architects, Am. Planning Assn. also: Harvard University Grad Sch Design/Dept Urban Plan 48 Quincy St Cambridge MA 02138-3000*

KRIEGER, BRUCE PHILLIP, medical educator; b. Erie, Pa., May 31, 1952; s. Mortimer G. and Adele (Berger) K.; m. Deborah Ann Larson, Aug. 15, 1983; children: Jori, Ashley, Jonathan. BA in Philosophy, U. Mich., 1973; MD, U. Pitts., 1977. Diplomate Am. Bd. Internal Medicine with subspecialties in pulmonary disease and critical care medicine. Fellow in pulmonary medicine U. Calif., San Diego, 1980-84; asst. prof. medicine U. Miami, Fla., 1985-90; assoc. prof. medicine U. Miami, 1990-95, prof. of medicine, 1996—; mem. med. adv. bd. Fla. Medicare, Jacksonville, 1993-95; cons. Blue Cross/Blue Shield, Washington, 1996—; med. dir. respiratory therapy programs, Miami-Dade C.C., Miami, 1997—. Author: (books) Economics of Mechanical Ventilation, 1994, Non-invasive Respiratory Monitoring, 1989, Asthma in the Elderly, 1997. Bd. dirs. Colony Theater, Miami Beach, Fla., 1985-87. Recipient Armour Pharm. award Am. Respiratory Care Found., Dallas, 1986, Cmty. Svc. award Am. Lung Found. of South Fla., Miami, 1987; named One to Watch, South Fla. Mag., Miami, 1987. Fellow Am. Coll. Chest Physicians, Am. Thoracic Soc.; mem. Fla. Thoracic Soc. (treas. 1993—), Fla. Soc. Critical Care Medicine (pres. 1992-93), Am. Coll. Chest Physicians (pres. Fla. chpt. 1991-94). Avocations: tennis, boating, music. Office: Dept Medicine Mt Sinai Med Ctr 4300 Alton Rd Miami Beach FL 33140-2800*

KRIEGER, IRVIN MITCHELL, chemistry educator, consultant; b. Cleve., May 14, 1923; s. William I. and Rose (Brodsky) K.; m. Theresa Melamed, June 9, 1965; 1 dau., Laura. B.S., Case Inst. Tech., 1944, M.S., 1948; Ph.D., Cornell, 1951. Rsch. asst. Case Inst. Tech., Cleve., 1946-47; teaching fellow Cornell U., Ithaca, N.Y., 1947-49; instr. Case Western Res. U., 1949-51, asst. prof., 1951-55, assoc. prof., 1955-68, prof., 1968-88, prof. emeritus, 1988—; dir. Center for Adhesives, Sealants and Coatings, 1983-88; vis. prof. U. Bristol, 1977-78; cons. for chem. firms; prof. invité Ecole Nat. Supérieure de Chimie de Mulhouse, 1987, Louis Pasteur U., Strasbourg, France, 1989. Contbr. articles to profl. jours. Served as ensign USNR, 1943-46. NSF fellow Université Libre De Bruxelles, 1959-60; sr. fellow Weizmann Inst., 1970. Mem. Am. Chem. Soc., Am. Inst. Chem. Engrs., AAUP, Soc. Rheology (pres. 1977-79, Bingham medalist 1989). E-mail: imk@po.cwru.edu. Home: 3460 Green Rd Apt 101 Beachwood OH 44122-4076 Office: Case Western Reserve U Cleveland OH 44106

KRIEGER, MARCIA SMITH, judge; b. Denver, Mar. 3, 1954; d. Donald P. Jr. and Marjorie Craig (Gearhart) Smith; m. Michael S. Krieger, Aug. 26, 1976 (div. July 1988); children: Miriam Anna, Matthias Edward; m. Frank H. Roberts, Jr., Mar. 9, 1991; stepchildren: Melissa Noel Roberts, Kelly Suzanne Roberts, Heidi Marie Roberts. BA, Lewis & Clark Coll., 1975; postgrad., U. Munich, 1975-76; JD, U. Colo., 1979. Bar: Colo. 1979, U.S. Dist. Ct. Colo. 1979, U.S. Ct. Appeals (10th cir.) 1979. Assoc. Mason, Reuler & Peek, P.C., Denver, 1976-83, Smart, DeFurio Brooks, Eklund & McClure, Denver, 1983-84; ptnr. Brooks & Krieger, P.C., Denver, 1984-88, Wood, Ris & Hames, P.C., Denver, 1988-90; pvt. practice U.S. Bankruptcy Court, 10th Circuit, Denver, 1990-94, judge, 1994—; lectr. U. Denver Grad. Tax Program, 1987—, Colo. Soc. CPA's, Denver, 1984-87, Colo. Continuing Legal Edn., Denver, 1980—, Colo. Trial Lawyers Assn., Denver, 1987—. Contbr. articles to profl. publs. Vestry person Good Shepherd Episcopal Ch., Englewood, 1986—, judge and coach for H.S. mock trial. Mem. Colo. Bar Assn., Arapahoe Bar Assn., Arraj Inn of Ct. (v.p.), Nat. Conf. Bankruptcy Judges, Littleton Adv. Coun. for Gifted and Talented education. Republican. Avocations: international relations, travel, marksmanship. Office: US Custom House 721 19th St Denver CO 80202-2500

KRIEGER, MURRAY, English language educator, author; b. Newark, Nov. 27, 1923; s. Isidore and Jennie (Glinn) K.; m. Joan Alice Stone, June 15, 1947; children: Catherine Leona, Eliot Franklin. Student, Rutgers U., 1940-42; M.A., U. Chgo., 1948; Ph.D. (Univ. fellow), Ohio State U., 1952. Instr. English Kenyon Coll., 1948-49, Ohio State U., 1951-52; asst. prof., then asso. prof. U. Minn., 1952-58; prof. English U. Ill., 1958-63; M.F. Carpenter prof. lit. criticism U. Iowa, 1963-66; prof. English, dir. program in criticism U. Calif. at Irvine, 1966-85; prof. English UCLA, 1973-82; univ. prof. U. Calif., 1974-94; univ. rsch. prof., 1994—; co-dir. Sch. Criticism and Theory U. Calif., 1975-77, dir., 1977-81, hon. sr. fellow, 1981—; assoc. mem. Ctr. Advanced Study, U. Ill., 1961-62; dir. U. Calif. Humanities Rsch. Inst., 1987-89; mem. adv. bd. Internat. Sch. Theory in Humanities, Santiago de Compostela, Spain, 1997—. Author: The New Apologists for Poetry, 1956, The Tragic Vision, 1960, A Window to Criticism: Shakespeare's Sonnets and Modern Poetics, 1964, The Play and Place of Criticism, 1967, The Classic Vision, 1971, Theory of Criticism: A Tradition and Its System, 1976, Poetic Presence and Illusion, 1979, Arts on the Level, 1981, Words About Words About Words: Theory, Criticism and the Literary Text, 1988, A Reopening of Closure: Organicism Against Itself, 1989, Ekphrasis: The Illusion of the Natural Sign, 1992, The Ideological Imperative: Repression and Resistance in Recent American Theory, 1993, The Institution of Theory, 1994; editor: (with Eliseo Vivas) The Problems of Aesthetics, 1953, Northrop Frye in Modern Criticism, 1966, (with L.S. Dembo) Directions for Criticism: Structuralism and its Alternatives, 1977, The Aims of Representation: Subject/

Text/History, 1987. Served with AUS, 1942-46. Recipient rsch prize Humboldt Found., Fed Republic Germany, 1986-87, medal U. Calif. at Irvine, 1990; Guggenheim fellow, 1956-57, 61-62; Am. Coun. Learned Socs. postdoctoral fellow, 1966-67; grantee NEH, 1971-72; Rockefeller Found. humanities fellow, 1978; resident scholar Rockefeller Study Ctr., Bellagio, 1990. Fellow Am. Acad. Arts and Scis. (council and exec. com. 1987-88); mem. MLA, Internat. Assn. Univ. Profs. English, Acad. Lit. Studies. Home: 407 Pinecrest Dr Laguna Beach CA 92651-1471 Office: U Calif Dept English Irvine CA 92697

KRIEGER, ROBERT EDWARD, publisher; b. Chgo., Apr. 6, 1925; s. Nicholas Francis and Clara Maude (Larson) K.; m. Maxine Donalda Spooner, June 21, 1947; children: Robert Edward, Donald Eric, Thomas Eliot. Formerly exec. with multi-corp. book and pub. firms; chmn. bd. dirs. Krieger Pub. Co., Inc., Malabar, Fla., 1969—. Chmn. Tech. R&D Authority, 1988-92. Mem. ALA, Internat. Assn. Ind. Pubs., So. Pubs. Assn., Scholarly Pubs. Assn., Masons. Republican. Methodist. Office: Krieger Pub Co PO Box 9542 Melbourne FL 32902-9542

KRIEGER, ROBERT LEE, JR., human resource/management consultant, educator, writer, travel/meeting planner, political analyst; b. Louisville, Nov. 13, 1946; s. Robert Lee and June Elise (Waters) K. BBA, U. Memphis, 1968, MBA, 1969. Cert. pers. cons.; cert. travel planner; cert. mgmt. cons. Adminstrv. asst. to mayor City of Memphis, 1969-72; dir. devel. programs U. Memphis, 1972-74; cons. pvt. practice, Memphis, 1974-76; exec. v.p. Randall Howard & Assocs., Memphis, 1976-95, pres. KR Internat. Inc., 1995—; mem. faculty U. Memphis Coll. Bus., 1984—; worldwide travel cons. and meeting planner, 1962—; keynote spkr. numerous profl. groups. Trustee, life mem. Republican Presdl. Task Force, Washington, 1980—; mem. Rep. Nat. Adv. Com., Washington, 1972—, Rep. Regional Steering Com.; mem. U.S. Olympic Soc., Boulder, Colo., 1968—. Recipient U.S. Treasury award U.S. Dept. Treasury, 1971; Nat. Presdl. medal of Merit, Rep. Presdl. Task Force, 1984; Rep. Legion of Merit; Pres.'s award Memphis Cotton Carnival Assn., 1968-85. Mem. Data Processing Mgmt. Assn., Am. Mgmt. Assn., Am. Film Guild, Met. Opera Guild, U.S. Navy League, Nat. Wildlife Fedn., Alpha Delta Sigma, Sigma Delta Chi. Episcopalian. Clubs: Mensa, U. Memphis Alumni. Avocations: writing, bowling, movies and photography, travel, public speaking. Home: 2948 Dalebrook St Memphis TN 38127-8316

KRIEGER, SANFORD, lawyer; b. N.Y.C., Nov. 4, 1943; s. Harry and Ruth Krieger; m. Carol B. Bachenheimer, Aug. 19, 1967; 1 child, Paul Matthew. BA cum laude, Cornell U., 1965; JD cum laude, Harvard U., 1968. Bar: N.Y., U.S. Supreme Ct., U.S. Dist. Ct. (so. dist.) N.Y. Legal adviser to Ethiopian Govt., 1968-70; assoc. Simpson Thacher & Bartlett, N.Y.C., 1970-73; assoc. Fried Frank Harris Shriver & Jacobson, London, 1973-75, ptnr., N.Y.C., 1977—; dir. corps. Mem. ABA, Assn. Bar City of N.Y. Office: Fried Frank Harris Shriver & Jacobson 1 New York Plz Fl 22 New York NY 10004-1980

KRIEGER, THEODORE KENT, poet; b. Charles City, Iowa, Sept. 26, 1950; s. Dale Theodore and Beverly (Clapp) K.; m. Elaine Marie Dorwin, Aug. 2, 1974 (div. July 1979). Diploma, Am. Sch. Photography, Lombard, Ill., 1973; BA in English cum laude, N.W. Mo. State U., 1977. Newspaper reporter, photographer Charles City Press, 1977-80, Atchison County Mail, Rock Port, Mo., 1983; freelance writer Charles City, 1983—; security guard Guard Sys., Ltd., Charles City, 1985-86; ind. sales agt. Author: (book of poems) Bearing It Alone, 1979 (Voices Internat. award 1981); contbr. poetry to anthologies. Grantee Author's League, 1982. Mem. Author's Guild. Roman Catholic. Avocations: photography, reading. Home: 403 8th Ave Charles City IA 50616-2309

KRIEGLER, ARNOLD MATTHEW, management consultant; b. Omaha, July 29, 1932; s. Matthew and Mildred Elsie (Svoboda) K.; m. Joan Willey, June 6, 1999; children: Kurt, Karen. BSc in Bus. and Engring. Adminstrn., U. Nebr., Omaha, 1955; postgrad., U. Iowa, 1957-58. Chief draftsman Ballantye Electronics, Omaha, 1948-55; various mgmt. positions Collins Radio div. Rockwell Internat., Cedar Rapids, Iowa, 1957-76; dir. mfg. electronics ops. Rockwell Internat., Dallas, 1976-78, dir. prodn. ops. Collins Transmission Systems div., 1978-88; mgmt. cons. AMK Assocs., Plano, 1988—; mem. com. on computer aided mfg. NAS, Washington, 1978-81; mem. engring. scis. curriculum adv. com. U. Tex., Dallas, 1988—. 1st lt. USAF, 1955-57. Recipient Exec. of Yr. United Way, Cedar Rapids, 1973. Mem. Nat. Mgmt. Assn. (instr. 1977—, chpt. dir. 1978-79, Silver Knight Mgmt. 1989), Inst. Indsl. Engrs. (chpt. pres. 1973-74), Theta Chi (chpt. pres. 1954-55). Republican. Presbyterian. Avocations: golf, music. Home and Office: 3605 Seltzer Dr Plano TX 75023-5809

KRIEGSMAN, ALAN M., retired critic; b. N.Y.C., Feb. 28, 1928; s. Harry Pickel and May (Cohn) K.; m. Sali Ann Ribakove, Nov. 28, 1957. Student, MIT, 1945-46; BS, Columbia U., 1951, MA, 1953. Lectr. in music Columbia U., N.Y.C., 1955-60; music and performing arts critic San Diego Union, 1960-65; asst. to the pres. Juilliard Sch., N.Y.C., 1965-66; music and performing arts critic Washington Post, 1966-74, dance critic, 1974-96, critic emeritus, 1996; advisor-cons. vis. com. on arts and humanities, MIT, 1976-86; vis. lectr. Dance Critics Conf., Am. Dance Festival; adjudicator Pulitzer Prize juries in music, criticism, feature writing, 1980-94; bd. dirs. Choo-San Goh & H. Robert Magee Found., 1996—. Contbr. articles on performing arts to various publs. Mem. leadership group nat. dance/media project UCLA, 1999. With U.S. Army, 1946-47. Fulbright scholar U. Vienna, 1956-57; recipient Pulitzer prize in Criticism, 1976. Mem. Dance Inst. Washington (bd. dirs. 1996—), Dance Critics Assn. (bd. dirs. 1996-98), Cunningham Dance Found. (bd. dirs. 1999—). Democrat. Jewish. Avocations: piano, mathematics, science. Fax: (309) 907-4682. E-mail: amkmike@ibm.net. Home: 4701 Willard Ave Apt 1013 Chevy Chase MD 20815-4622

KRIEGSMAN, SALI ANN, arts administrator, artistic director, writer, consultant; b. N.Y.C., Apr. 16, 1936; d. Aaron and Charlotte (Pomeranz) Ribakove; m. Alan M. Kriegsman, Nov. 28, 1957. MA, Goddard Coll., 1976. Rsch. assoc. Scripps Clinic and Rsch. Found., La Jolla, Calif., 1961-65; exec. editor Am. Film Inst., Washington, 1969-74; asst. prof. George Washington U., Washington, 1979-80; dance cons. Smithsonian Instn., Washington, 1981-84; dir. dance program NEA, Washington, 1986-95; exec. dir. Jacob's Pillow Dance Festival, Becket, Mass., 1995-98; writer An Evening of Dance, In Performance at the White House, Sta. WETA-TV, 1998; mem. arts acad. adv. com. Coll. Bd., 1996-97; mem. nat. dance and media project leadership group UCLA, 1996-99. Author: Modern Dance in America: The Bennington Years, 1981; contbg. author: International Encyclopedia of Dance, 1998. Bd. dirs. Mass. Mus. Contemporary Art, 1995-97; pres. Dance Heritage Coalition, 1999—. Recipient Flo-Bert award N.Y. Com. To Celebrate Nat. Tap Dance Day, 1997, Oklhamoa City U. Preservation of Heritage Am. Dance award, 1999.

KRIENS, SCOTT G., information technology executive. BA, Calif. State U., Hayward. CEO Juniper Networks, Inc., Mountain View, Calif., 1996—. Office: Juniper Networks Inc 385 Ravendale Dr Mountain View CA 94043

KRIER, JAMES EDWARD, law educator, author; b. Milw., Oct. 19, 1939; s. Ambrose Edward and Genevieve Ida (Behling) K.; m. Gayle Marian Grimsrud, Mar. 22, 1962; children: Jennifer, Amy; m. Wendy Louise Wilkes, Apr. 20, 1974; children: Andrew Wilkes-Krier, Patrick Wilkes-Krier. B.S., U. Wis., 1961, J.D., 1966. Bar: Wis. 1966, U.S. Ct. Claims 1968. Law clk. to chief justice Calif. Supreme Ct., San Francisco, 1966-67; assoc. Arnold & Porter, Washington, 1967-69; acting prof., then prof. law UCLA, 1969-78, 80-83; prof. law Stanford U., Calif., 1978-80; prof. law U. Mich. Law Sch., Ann Arbor, 1983—, Earl Warren DeLano prof., 1988—; cons. Calif. Inst. Tech., EPA; mem. Nat. Acad. Scis. Pesticides Panel, 1972-75, Com. on Energy and the Environment, 1975-77. Author: Environmental Law and Policy, 1971, (with Stewart) 2d edit., 1978; (with Ursin) Pollution and Policy, 1977; (with Dukeminier) Property, 1981, 4th edit., 1998; contbr. articles to profl. jours. Served to lt. U.S. Army, 1961-63. Mem. Artus, Order of Coif, Phi Kappa Phi. Office: U Mich Law Sch 625 S State St Ann Arbor MI 48109-1215

KRIER, JOSEPH ROLAND, chamber of commerce executive, lawyer; b. Port Washington, Wis., Apr. 15, 1946; m. Cyndi Taylor. BA, U. Tex., 1968, JD, 1971. Bar: Tex. 1971. Assoc. real estate sect. Bracewell & Patterson, Houston, 1971-73; ptnr., mem. corp. and comml. litigation sect. Groce, Locke & Hebdon, 1973-83; ptnr. Grieshaber & Roberts, San Antonio, 1983-87; pres. The Greater San Antonio C. of C., 1987—; head JK & Assocs., 1983-87. Mem. centennial commn. U. Tex.; mem. Tex. Higher Edn. Coordinating Bd.; coordinating chmn. task force Target '90: Goals for San Antonio project; past pres., bd. dirs. San Antonio Amateur Sports Found.; past chmn., bd. dirs. Arts Coun. San Antonio; founder, bd. dirs. San Antonio Winston Sch.; bd. dirs. Ctr. for Multiple Handicapped Children, Tex. Soc. for the Prevention of Blindness, San Antonio Cmty. Radio Corp., San Antonio chpt. Tex. Execs., Tex. Bus. Hall of Fame; bd. visitors M.D. Anderson Cancer Clinic, co-chmn. Annual Gift Campaign South Tex., 1987; mem. adv. bd. Tex. Lyceum. Fellow Tex. Bar Assn.; mem. San Antonio Bar Assn., Omicron Delta Kappa. Office: The Greater San Antonio C of C PO Box 1628 602 E Commerce St San Antonio TX 78205-2620*

KRIESBERG, LOUIS, sociologist, educator; b. Chgo., July 30, 1926; s. Max and Bessie (Turner) K.; m. Lois Ablin, Aug. 23, 1959; children: Daniel A., Joseph A. PhB, U. Chgo., 1947, MA, 1950, PhD, 1953. Instr. sociology sch. gen. studies Columbia U., N.Y.C., 1953-56; Fulbright rsch. scholar U. Cologne, Germany, 1956-57; sr. fellow in law and behavior scis. U. Chgo., 1957-58; sr. study dir. Nat. Opinion Rsch. Ctr., 1958-62; assoc. prof. dept. sociology, 1962-67; assoc. prof. dept. sociology Syracuse (N.Y.) U., 1962-67, prof., 1967-97, prof. emeritus, 1997—, dir. program on analysis and resolution conflicts, 1985-94, Maxwell prof. social conflict studies, 1994-97, Maxwell prof. emeritus social conflict studies, 1997—. Author: Mothers in Poverty, 1970, Social Inequality, 1979, Social Conflicts, 1973, rev. edit., 1982, International Conflict Resolution, 1992, Constructive Conflicts, 1998; editor: Social Processes in International Relations, 1968, Research in Social Movements, Conflicts, and Change, vols. 1-14, 1978-92, Intractable Conflicts and Their Transformation, 1989, Timing the De-escalation of International Conflicts, 1991. Active Syracuse Area Middle East Dialogue Group; commr. Human Rights Commn. Syracuse and Onondaga County. Grantee U.S. Inst. Peace, MacArthur Found., Hewlett Found. Fellow Am. Sociol. Assn. (chmn. peace and war sect. 1990-91, award for Disting. Career 1993), Internat. Peace Rsch. Assn. (co-chmn. internat. conflict resolution 1989-94), Internat. Studies Assn. (chmn. peace studies sect. 1998-99), Internat. Sociol. Assn. (rsch. com. 1, exec. com. 1982-86), Internat. Soc. Polit. Psychology (governing coun. 1992-94), Soc. for Study Social Problems (pres. 1983-84, Lee Founders award 1990), Ea. Sociol. Soc. (exec. com. 1977-81, Peace Studies Assn. ann. award 1995). Jewish. Avocations: sculpture, swimming. Home: 164 Summerhaven Dr East Syracuse NY 13057-3115 Office: Analysis Resolution Conflicts Syracuse U Syracuse NY 13244-1090

KRIESBERG, SIMEON M., lawyer; b. Washington, June 4, 1951; s. Martin and Harriet M. K.; m. Martha L. Kahn, Jan. 9, 1994. AB, Harvard U., 1973; M in Pub. Affairs, Princeton U., 1977; JD, Yale U., 1977. Bar: D.C. 1977, U.S. Dist. Ct. D.C. 1978, U.S. Ct. Appeals (D.C. cir.) 1978, U.S. Ct. Internat. Trade 1979, U.S. Ct. Appeals (Fed. cir.) 1981, U.S. Supreme Ct. 1982. Assoc. Leva, Hawes, Symington, Martin & Oppenheimer, Washington, 1977-83; sr. counsel internat. trade Sears World Trade Inc., Washington, 1983-85, v.p., gen. counsel, 1985-87; ptnr. Mayer Brown & Platt, Washington, 1987—; professorial lectr. Nitze Sch. Advanced Internat. Studies, Johns Hopkins U., 1991-93; mem. binat. dispute resolution panel under U.S.-Can. Free Trade Agreement, 1990-92; guest scholar Brookings Inst., 1992-93; mem. roster of dispute resolution panelists under NAFTA, 1996—. Mem. editorial adv. com. Internat. Legal Materials, 1991-97; article and book rev. editor Yale Law Jour., 1976-77. Officer or dir. Washington Hebrew Congregation, 1980-94, Jewish Cmty. Coun. Greater Washington, 1986-94, Interfaith Conf. of Met. Washington, 1989—, D.C. Jewish Cmty. Ctr., 1994—, Mid-Atlantic coun. Union Am. Hebrew Congregations, 1994—. Recipient Pro Bono Svc. award Internat. Human Rights Law Group, 1991, Lawrence L. O'Connor medal Sears, Roebuck and Co., 1984. Mem. ABA, Am. Law Inst., Am. Soc. Internat. Law, D.C. Bar. Office: Mayer Brown & Platt 1909 K St NW Washington DC 20006-1106

KRIESE, CHARLES (CHUCK), tennis coach; b. Indpls., 1950; 3 children. BS, Tenn. Tech. Coll., 1972, MS in Health & Phys. Edn., 1975. Coach tennis Pt. Washington Tennis Acad., N.Y., 1972-73; head coach Clemson (S.C.) U., 1975—. Author: Total Tennis Training, 1988, Winning Tennis, 1993, Youth Tennis, 1995. Named Coach Yr. ACC, So. Tennis, Intercollegiate Tennis Coach's Assn., 1981; recipient nat. award U.S. Profl. Tennis Assn., 1981, 86; inducted into S.C. Tennis Hall Fame, 1983, Tenn. Tech. Coll. Hall Fame, 1985. Office: Clemson U PO Box 31 Clemson SC 29633-0031*

KRIGER, PETER WILSON, healthcare administrator; b. San Francisco, Jan. 22, 1936; s. Peter Clark and Dorothy Margaret (Noethig) Wilson; children: Peter W., Marilyn, Nicole. Student, Humboldt State Coll., Arcata, Calif., 1965-72; AA with honors, Coll. of Redwoods, 1972; BA in Health Adminstrn., Antioch U., San Francisco, 1985; cert., U. Calif., Berkeley, 1967, Cornell U., 1968. Adminstr. Klamath-Trinity Hosp., Hoopa, Calif., 1961-66; asst. adminstr. St. Joseph Hosp., Eureka, Calif., 1966-75, adminstr., exec. v.p., 1975-83, pres., CEO, 1983-91; adminstr. Eureka Internal Medicine, 1992—; mem. hosp. rels. com. Blue Cross Calif., 1986-91, bd. dirs., 1988-91, mem. audit com., 1989-91; pres. No. Redwood Empire Hosp. Conf., 1966-68, 88; mem. health occupations adv. com. Coll. of Redwoods, 1972-76. Mem. Humbold County Hist. Soc.; treas., chmn. budget and fin. com. Humboldt-Del Norte unite Am. Cancer Soc., 1978; bd. dirs. Calif. affiliate Am. Heart Assn., 1976; mem. Rhododentron Festival Com., 1984-88, chmn. awards and judging, 1986-88; bd. regents St. Bernard H.S., 1987-89, chmn., 1988-89; mem. AIDS Task Force, County of Humboldt, 1989-91. Served with Med. Svc. Corps, U.S. Army. George H. Walker fellow, 1989. Fellow Am. Coll. Healthcare Execs.; mem. Am. Hosp. Assn. (ho. of dels. 1982-86), Calif. Hosp. Assn. (bd. dirs. 1983-86), Hosp. Coun. No. Calif. (bd. dirs. 980-86, exec. com. 1981-82, chmn. fin. and econs. com. 1982-83), Cath. Health Assn. (rural hosp. study group 1988-90), Rotary Club of Eureka (bd. dirs. 1987-89, chmn. blood bank com. 1983-84, 91-92). Avocations: gardening, camping, canoeing, railcar operator, bicycling. Home: 1928 Greenbriar Ln Eureka CA 95503-6535 Office: Eureka Internal Medicine 2280 Harrison Ave Ste B Eureka CA 95501-3200

KRIKEN, JOHN LUND, architect; b. Calif., July 5, 1938; s. John Erik Nord and Ragnhild (Lund) K.; m. Anne Girard (div.); m. Katherine Koelsch, Aug. 8, 1988. BArch, U. Calif., Berkeley, 1961; MArch, Harvard U., 1968. Ptnr. Skidmore, Owings and Merrill, San Francisco, 1970—; tchr. Washington U., St. Louis, 1968, U. Calif., Berkeley, 1972, Rice U., Houston, 1979; design advisor, chief architect Ho Chi Minh City, Vietnam, 1994—; mem. design rev. bd. Port San Francisco, 1995—. Mem. Bay Conservation and Devel. Commn., Calif., 1984—; mem. Arts Commn. City and County of San Francisco, 1989-95; mem. design rev. bd. Berkeley campus U. Calif., 1986-92; bd. dirs. San Francisco Planning and Rsch., 1995—.Vice chair, Eng. and Des. Advisory Panel (EDAP) for the rebuilding pf San Francisco Bay Bridge, 1997—. Fellow AIA; mem. Am. Inst. Cert. Planners, Sunday Afternoon Watercolor Soc. (founding mem.), Lambda Alpha Internat. Office: Skimore Owings & Merrill 1 Front St San Francisco CA 94111-5325

KRIKORIAN, ABRAHAM DER, biochemistry and cell biology educator; b. Worcester, Mass., May 5, 1937. PhD, Cornell U., 1965. Rsch. assoc. Lab. for Cell Physiology, Growth and Devel. Cornell U., Ithaca, N.Y., 1965, asst. prof. div. biol. scis., 1965-66, assoc. prof., 1972-73; asst. prof. dept. biol. scis. SUNY, Stony Brook, 1966-71, assoc. prof. dept. biology, 1971-81, assoc. prof. dept. biochemistry, 1981-83, prof. dept. biochemistry and cell biology, 1983—; vis. scientist U. Philippines, Los Banos, 1979; guest biologist dept. biology Brookhaven Nat. Lab., Upton, N.Y., 1968—; past mem. sci. adv. bd. United AgriSeeds, Inc., Champaign, Ill.; mem. Biotech. Coun. Sci. Advisors, Brazil; mem. Internat. Adv. Bd. for Agrl. Biotech. and Chemistry, Kathmandu, Nepal. Western Hemisphere editor Annals of Botany, 1976-82; mem. editorial bd., contbr. articles to Am. Soc. Gravitational and Space Biology Bull., 1987—; mem. editorial bd. Jour. Ethnopharmacology, 1979—, Phytomorphology, 1991—, Indian Acad. Scis., 1985-91; bd. reviewing editors In Vitro Cellular & Devel. Biology, 1991—; plant sci. book rev. cons. Quar. Rev. Biology, 1966—; contbr. numerous articles to profl. publs. including AIAA Bull., Annals of Botany, In Vitro, Am. Jour Botany, others. Fellow AAAS; mem. Internat. Plant Growth Substances Assn., Am. Soc. Plant Physiologists, Bot. Soc. Am., Am. Soc. Pharmacognosy, Scandinavian Soc. Plant Physiology, Internat. Soc. Plant Morphologists, Soc. Econ. Botany, Internat. Palm Soc., History of Sci. Soc., Internat. Assn. Rsch. Plantains and Bananas, Soc. Devel. Biology, Internat. Assn. Plant Tissue Culture, Plant Growth Regulator Soc. Am., Tissue Culture Assn., Sigma Xi, Rho Chi, Phi Kappa Phi, Gamma Alpha. Achievements include research in physiological, morphological and biochemical aspects of plant growth and development, plant cell and tissue, control of morphogenesis and secondary metabolism in cultured cells and tissues of higher plants, gravitational plant biology, biotechnology as it relates to higher plants, economic botany, ethnopharmacology. Office: SUNY Dept Biochem Cell Biol Stony Brook NY 11794-5215

KRIKORIAN, VAN Z., lawyer; b. Framingham, Mass., Feb. 7, 1960; s. George O. and Agnes A. (Kalousdian) K.; m. Priscilla A. Dodakian, June 1, 1985; children: Ani, Sarah, Lena, George. BA in Internat. Affairs, George Washington U., 1981; JD, Georgetown U., 1984. Bar: Vt. 1985, D.C. 1986, U.S. Tax Ct. 1987, N.Y. 1994, U.S. Ct. Internat. Trade 1996. Law clk. Hon. Jerome Niedermeier U.S. Dist. Ct., civlington, Vt., 1984-85; assoc. Gravel & Shea, Burlington, Vt., 1985-88; dir. govt. and legal affairs Armenian Assembly Am., Washington, 1988-92; counsellor, dep. rep. to UN Rep. of Armenia, N.Y.C., 1992; counsel Patterson, Belknap, Webb & Tyler, LLP, N.Y.C., 1993-98; ptnr. Vedder, Price, Kaufman & Kammhol, 1998—; adj. prof. comml. law St. Michael's Coll., Winooski, Vt., 1987-88. Contbr. more than 20 articles to profl. jours. Ofcl. U.S. del. to Moscow Conf. on Security and Cooperation in Europe, 1991; vice chair fin. com. Dole for Pres., Washington, 1995. Mem. ABA, Assn. of the Bar of the City of N.Y., D.C. Bar Assn., Vt. Bar Assn., U.S.-Armenian Bus. Coun. (chmn. 1996—), Armenian Assembly Am. (trustee, chmn. bd. dirs. 1998—). Office: Vedder Price Kaufman & Kammholz 805 3rd Ave New York NY 10022-7513

KRIKOS, GEORGE ALEXANDER, pathologist, educator; b. Old Phaleron, Greece, Sept. 17, 1922; came to U.S., 1946; s. Alexios and Helen (Spyropoulou) K.; m. Aspasia Manoni, June 22, 1949; children: Helen, Alexandra, Alexios. DDS, U. Pa., 1949; PhD, U. Rochester, 1959; PhD (hon.), U. Athens, Greece, 1981. Asst. prof. pathology U. Pa. Sch. Dentistry, 1958-61, assoc. prof., 1961-67, prof., 1967-68, chmn. dept., 1964-68; assoc. prof. oral pathology U. Pa. Grad. Sch., 1962-68, prof. oral pathology, 1968; prof. pathobiology Sch. Dentistry, U. Colo., Denver, 1968-75, chmn. dept. pathobiology, 1968-73, prof. oral biology, 1975-86, clin. prof. oral biology, 1986-91, prof. oral biology emeritus, 1991—; asst. dean basic sci. affairs Sch. Dentistry, U. Colo., 1973-75, asso. dean oral biology affairs, 1975-76; vis. prof. Sch. Dentistry, U. Athens, 1980-81; mem. dental study sect. NIH, 1966-70; mem. cancer com. Colo.-Wyo. Regional Med. Program, 1970-72; cons. oral pathology Denver VA Hosp., 1970-72. Served with AUS, 1949-54. Mem. Am. Soc. Investigative Pathology, Internat. Assn. Dental Rsch., Sigma Xi. Home: 350 Ivy St Denver CO 80220-5855

KRIMENDAHL, HERBERT FREDERICK, II, investment banker; b. Cin., Oct. 28, 1928; s. Herbert F. and Mary Bess (Christian) K.; m. Constance Kathryn McCown, Sept. 21, 1957 (dec. Sept. 1989); children: Elizabeth Knowles, Nancy Christian; m. Emilia Alice Saint Amand, Feb. 4, 1999. BA, Ohio State U., 1950; MBA, Harvard U., 1952. Assoc. Goldman, Sachs & Co., N.Y.C., 1953-62, ptnr., 1963-87; ltd. ptnr., 1987—; chmn. Petrus Ptnrs. Ltd., N.Y.C., 1992—; bd. dirs. A.T. Cross, Lincoln, R.I. Trustee Philharm. Symphony Soc. N.Y., 1977—, pres., 1989-96, The James Madison Coun. of Libr. of Congress, Ohio State U. Found., 1998—. Mem. River Club, Maidstone Club, The Brook, Links Club, Jupiter Island Club. Office: Petrus Ptnrs Ltd 630 Fifth Ave Ste 3170 New York NY 10111-0100

KRIMM, SAMUEL, physicist, educator; b. Morristown, N.J., Oct. 19, 1925; s. Irving and Ethel (Stein) K.; m. Marilyn Marcy Neveloff, June 26, 1949; children: David Robert, Daniel Joseph. B.S., Poly. Inst. Bklyn., 1947; M.A., Princeton U., 1949, Ph.D., 1950. Postdoctoral fellow U. Mich., Ann Arbor, 1950-52; mem. faculty U. Mich., 1952—, prof. physics, 1963—; mem. Macromolecular Rsch. Ctr., 1968—; mem. biophysics rsch. divsn. U. Mich., 1962—, chmn. biophysics research div., 1976-86, dir. program in protein structure and design, 1985-94, assoc. dean research Coll. Lit., Sci. and Arts,, 1972-75; chmn. infrared spectroscopy Gordon Rsch. Conf., 1968; mem. NAS/NRC NBS Polymers divsn. Evaluation Panel, 1973-76, chmn., 1975-76; mem. materials rsch. adv. com. NSF, 1981-86, chmn., 1984; mem. DOE Coun. on Material Scis., 1986-89; mem. program adv. com. Internat. Conf. on Raman Spectroscopy, 1984-86, mem. exec. com., 1988-90; Fraser Price Meml. lectr., 1988; disting. lectr. Inst. Materials Sci. U. Conn., 1995; mem. com. on promoting rsch. collaboration NAS/IOM, 1987-89; cons. B.F. Goodrich, 1956-86, Allied 1963-93, Monsanto, 1987-92; vis. prof. U. Mainz, 1983, U. Paris, 1991. Author papers on vibrational spectroscopy, x-ray diffraction studies of natural and synthetic polymers, potential energy function devel.; mem. editorial bd. Jour. Polymer Sci. Polymer Physics Edn., 1967—; Biopolymers, 1973—; Macromolecules, 1968-71; Jour. Macromolecular Sci.-Rev. Macromolecular Chemistry, 1983-92. Served with USNR, 1944-46. Recipient Humboldt award, 1983; U. Mich. Disting. Faculty Achievement award, 1986; Textile Research Inst. fellow, 1947-50; NSF sr. postdoctoral fellow, 1962-63; sr. fellow U. Mich. Soc. Fellows, 1971-76. Fellow AAAS, Am. Phys. Soc. (High Polymer Physics prize 1977, chmn. div. biol. physics 1979, div. councilor 1981, exec. com. 1983, planning com. 1992); mem. Am. Chem. Soc., Am. Crystallographic Assn., Biophys. Soc., Coblentz Soc. (hon., bd. mgr. 1967-70). Office: U Mich Dept Physics 930 N University Ave Ann Arbor MI 48109-1055

KRINER, SALLY GLADYS PEARL, artist; b. Bradford, Ohio, Jan. 29, 1911; d. Henry Walter and Pearl Rebecca (Brubaker) Brant; m. Leo Louis Kriner, Feb. 28, 1933; children—Patricia Staab, Jane Palombo. Grad. Arsenal Tech. sch. Indpls.; student Ind. U.-Indpls., 1954, Herron Sch. Art, Indpls., 1958. Exhibited in one woman shows Hoosier Salon, Indpls., 1960, Village Art Gallery, Southport, Ind., 1967, 70, 73, Brown County Art Guild, Nashville, Ind., 1970, 74, 77, 80, 83, 87, 92; group shows include South Side Art League, Indpls., 1959-74, Indpls. Art League, 1959-64, Brown County Art Guild, 1969—, Hoosier Salon, 1961, 65, 67, 68, 73, 75, 76, 77, 82, 86, 87, 91, 95, Frames and Things Gallery, 1995; represented in permanent collections Riley Hosp., Indpls., others. Founder Southside Women's Symphony Com., Indpls., 1958; treas. Perry Twp. Republican Club, Ind., 1960-65; pres. State Assembly Women's Club, 1965-67; bd. dirs. ARC, Indpls., 1942-45, Southside Civic Orgn., Indpls., 1954, Clowes Hall Women's Com., Indpls., 1963. Recipient citation ARC, 1946; citation Marion County Meritorious Service Award, 1959; citation Greater Southside Civic Orgn., 1961; Art award Kappa Kappa Kappa, 1967, 68, 70, 71. Fellow Indpls. Art League Found. (numerous awards 1960-66); mem. Southside Art League, Inc. (pres. 1964-65, numerous awards 1964-75, founder), Ind. Artists Club, Inc. (Purchases award 1978), Ind. Heritage Arts, Inc., Rutland Art Assn., Brown County Art Guild (pres. 1980-83, v.p. 1983—), Ind. fedn. Arts Clubs (bd. dirs. 1963-73), Ind. Artist (chmn. prize fund 1974-75), Consignment and appraisal of fine arts, Hoosier Salon, Indpls. Mus. Arts, Nat. Soc. Arts and Letters, Nat. Mus. Women in Arts, Hoosier Group Women in Arts, Oil Painters of America (Master of Art award for contbg. to heritage Brown County Indiana Art Colony 1997). Presbyterian. Avocation: growing flowers. Home and Studio: 394 E Freeman Ridge Rd Nashville IN 47448-8871

KRINGEL, JEROME HOWARD, lawyer; b. Milw., Apr. 2, 1940; s. Lester E. and Irene A. (Kreutzer) K.; m. Mary Kathleen McAuliffe, Sept. 8, 1962; children: Anne, Mary Karen, Jennifer, Elisabeth, Katherine. AB, Marquette U., 1962; postgrad., U. Heidelberg, Germany, 1963; LLB, Yale U., 1966. Bar: Wis. 1966, U.S. Dist. Ct. (ea. dist.) Wis. 1966, U.S. Ct. Appeals (7th cir.) 1966. Ptnr., coord. bus. practice Michael, Best & Friedrich, Milw., 1966—. Trustee Shorewood (Wis.) Village Bd., 1974-80. Mem. ABA, Wis. Bar Assn. (chmn. bus. law sect. 1990-91), Milw. Bar Assn. Office: Michael Best & Friedrich LLP 100 E Wisconsin Ave Ste 3300 Milwaukee WI 53202-4108

KRINGEL, JOHN G., health products company executive; b. Manila, Philippines, Mar. 14, 1939; came to U.S., 1940; s. John Robert and Martha (Cunningham) K.; m. Marcia Kayleen Miller, Nov. 17, 1962 (div. Aug. 1985); children: John G. Jr., Kirk M.; m. Mary Elizabeth Naes, Aug. 16, 1985. BS, St. Lawrence U., 1960; MBA, U. Pa., 1967. Gen. mgr. U.S. med. div. Corning Glass Works, 1970-1977; exec. v.p. Am. Optical Vision Care subs. of Warner-Lambert Corp., Southbridge, Miss., 1977-80; v.p. corp. planning Abbott Labs, North Chicago, Ill., 1980-81, pres. Sorenson div., 1981-83, pres. hosp. products div., 1983—; bd. dirs. NAVIX Rachaloy, Inc., Pacific Pharm., Inc. Trustee Lakeland Health Svcs., Highland Park, Ill., 1990; bd. dirs. Arden Shore, Lake Bluff, Ill., 1988—, Ill. Northeast coun. Boy Scouts Am., 1991—, Am. Soc. Hosp. Pharmacists Found., 1992—. Republican. Avocation: athletics. Office: Abbott Labs AP-30 200 Abbott Park Rd North Chicago IL 60064-3537*

KRINSKY, CAROL HERSELLE, art history educator; b. N.Y.C., June 2, 1937; d. David and Jane (Gartman) Herselle; m. Robert Daniel Krinsky, Jan. 25, 1959; 2 children. BA, Smith Coll., 1957; MA, NYU, 1960, PhD, 1965. Mem. faculty NYU, 1965—, assoc. prof. art history, 1973-78, prof., 1978—. Author: Vitruvius de Architectura, 1521. 1969, Rockefeller Center, 1978, Synagogues of Europe, 1985, rev. edit., 1996, Gordon Bunshaft of Skidmore, Owings & Merrill, 1988, Europas Synagogen, 1988, Contemporary Native American Architecture, 1996; contbr. articles to profl. jours. Bd. dirs. Internat. Survey Jewish Monuments, Syracuse, N.Y., 1981—, Soc. Archtl. Historians, 1978-80, 86-89, The Mac Dowell Colony, Inc., 1989—, Jewish Heritage Coun. World Monuments Fund; co-chair seminar on the city Columbia U., 1993-95. Am. Coun. Learned Socs. grantee, 1981, Nat. Endowment for the Arts grantee, 1993; recipient Arnold Brunner award N.Y.C. chpt. AIA, 1990. Fellow Soc. Archtl. Historians (pres. 1984-86, pres. N.Y.C. chpt. 1977-79); mem. Coll. Art Assn., Planning History Group, Am. Urban History Assn., Women's City Club, Century Assn., Phi Beta Kappa. Office: NYU Dept Fine Arts 100 Washington Sq E New York NY 10003-6688

KRINSKY, MARY MCINERNEY, lawyer; b. Oklahoma City, l, Dec. 12, 1946; d. Henry B. and Lucille L. (Walker) McInerney; m. William L. Krinsky, Oct. 31, 1970; children: David M., Benjamin H. BS, Iowa State U., 1967; MPh, PhD, Yale U., 1971; JD, U. Mont., 1977. Bar: Conn. 1978, U.S. Patent Office 1986. Rsch. assoc. Cornell U., Ithaca, N.Y., 1971-74; researcher hist. legal documents North Haven (Conn.) Hist. Soc., 1979-88; assoc. St. Onge, Steward, Johnston & Reens, Stamford, Conn., 1988-94, ptnr., 1994-97; pvt. practice New Haven, Conn., 1997—. Contbr. articles to sci. jours. Mem. Am. Intellectual Property Law Assn., Conn. Patent Law Assn. Avocation: writing. Office: 79 Trumbull St New Haven CT 06511-3708

KRINSKY, ROBERT DANIEL, consulting firm executive; b. Bklyn., Jan. 24, 1937; s. Milton and Josephine E. (Bachrach) K.; m. Carol M. Herselle, Jan. 25, 1959; children: Alice E., John D. BA, Antioch Coll., 1957. Various actuarial positions The Segal Co., N.Y.C., 1954-65, v.p. to exec. v.p., 1966-82, pres., 1982-93, chmn., 1994—; mem. working com. Nat. Coordinating Com. for Multi-employer Pension Plans, Washington, 1982—. Trustee Antioch U., Yellow Springs, Ohio, 1983—, chmn., 1993—; trustee Moses L. Parshelsky Found., 1982—; bd. dirs. Harbor Festival Found., N.Y.c., 1983-87. Asst. health svc. officer USPHS, 1959-61. Fellow Conf. Actuaries in Pub. Practice; mem. Am. Acad. Actuaries, Soc. Actuaries (assoc.), Assn. Pvt. Pension and Welfare Plans (bd. dirs. 1982—, chmn. 1988-89), Nat. Dance Inst. (bd. dirs. 1987—, chmn. 1988-89, 93—), Century Assn. Office: The Segal Co 1 Park Ave New York NY 10016-5895

KRINSLY, STUART Z., lawyer, manufacturing company executive; b. N.Y.C., May 19, 1917; m. Charlotte Wolf, Aug. 18, 1944; children: EllinJane, Joan Susan. BA, Princeton U., 1938; LLB, Harvard U., 1941. Bar: N.Y. 1941. Asst. U.S. atty. So. Dist. N.Y., 1942-45; mem. firm Schlesinger & Krinsly, 1945-57; sec. Sun Chem. Corp., N.Y.C., 1957-65, v.p., gen. counsel, 1965-76, sr. v.p., gen. counsel, 1976-78, exec. v.p., gen. counsel, 1978-82, also bd. dirs.; sr. exec. v.p., gen. counsel Sequa Corp., N.Y.C., 1982—; also bd. dirs.; bd. dirs. Chock Full O'Nuts Corp. Mem. Beach Point Club, Princeton Club N.Y. Home: 1135 Greacen Point Rd Mamaroneck NY 10543-4612 Office: Sequa Corp 200 Park Ave Fl 44 New York NY 10166*

KRIPKE, KENNETH NORMAN, lawyer; b. Toledo, Feb. 16, 1920; s. Maurice and Celia (Vine) K.; m. Derril Kanter, Nov. 4, 1945; children: Teri Schwartz, Marcie K. Gaon. Student, Ohio State U., 1937-41; LL.B., U. Colo., 1948. Bar: Colo. 1949, U.S. Ct. Appeals (10th cir.) 1954, U.S. Ct. Appeals (5th cir.) 1965, U.S. Supreme Ct. 1967, U.S. Ct. Appeals (8th cir.) 1974. Mem. firm Kripke & McLean, 1953-58, Kripke, Hoffman & Carrigan (and successors), 1965-73; pvt. practice law Denver, 1991-95; ptnr. Kripke, Epstein & Lawrence (P.C.), Denver, 1980-90; mem. nominating com. 9th Jud. Cir., 1976-78, standing com. on rules civil procedure Colo. Supreme Ct., 1978-93; guest speaker Internat. Congress Hosp. Laws, Tel Aviv, 1985. Treas. Denver Allied Jewish Fedn., 1978-84; chmn. Denver civil rights com. Anti-Defamation League B'nai Brith, 1976-82; mem. nat. law com. Anti-Defamation League, 1980—, chair mountain state region, 1990-92; commr. Denver Pub. Safety Rev. Commn., 1992-95; mem. San Diego Citizens' Rev. Bd. on Police Practices, 1996-97. With USAAF, 1942-46. Recipient Kenneth Norman Kripke Ann. award for Lifetime Achievement Colo. Trial Lawyers Assn., 1996. Fellow Internat. Soc. Barristers (emeritus); mem. ABA (discovery subcom. litigation sect. 1982-93), Colo. Bar Assn. (bd. dirs. lend-a-lawyer program 1990-92), Assn. Trial Lawyers Am. (past bd. govs., past exec. adv. com., chmn. conv. 1962, 69), Western Trial Lawyers Assn. (sec. 1971-72, v.p. 1973, pres. 1974-75), Colo. Trial Lawyers Assn. (pres. 1958), Pub. Justice Found. (pres. 1986-89), Internat. Assn. Jewish Lawyers and Jurists. Office: 5310 Renaissance Ave San Diego CA 92122-5632

KRIPOWICZ, ROBERT S., energy administrator. BS in Chemistry cum laude, Lafayette Coll., 1963; MBA, U. Pitts., 1970. Chemist Dupont; mgr. fin. planning and budgeting NUMEC (sub. ARCO); mgr. constrn. contracts Consolidated Edison of N.Y.; mgr. R&D programs Mech. Tech. Inc.; staff House interior and related agencies subcom. Com. on Appropriations, Washington; staff dir. house energy subcom. Com. on Sci. and Tech.; dep. asst. sec. bldg. techs. Dept. of Energy, 1995, acting dep. asst. sec. House liaison, 1995, prin. dep. asst. sec. for fossil energy, 1996—. With U.S. Army. Office: Dept of Energy Office of Pub Affairs 1000 Independence Ave SW Washington DC 20585-0002

KRIPPAEHNE, MARION LARSEN, medicine educator; b. Missoula, Mont., June 22, 1923; d. Martin Isadore and Mathilda (Johansen) Larsen; m. William Wonn Krippaehne, Nov. 17, 1949; children: William Jr., Thomas, Joanne, Carol, Richard, Suzanne, Robert. BS, U. Wash., 1944; MD, U. Oreg., 1948. Intern, then resident Emanuel Hosp., Portland, 1948-50; resident, then fellow exptl. medicine divsn. U. Oreg., Portland, 1950-52; from clin. instr. to prof. medicine Oreg. Health Scis. U., Portland, 1953-88, prof. medicine emeritus, 1988—.

KRIPPNER, STANLEY CURTIS, psychologist; b. Edgerton, Wis., Oct. 4, 1932; s. Carroll Porter and Ruth Genevieve (Volenberg) K.; m. Lelie Anne Harris, June 25, 1966; stepchildren: Caron, Robert. BS, U. Wis., 1954; MA, Northwestern U., 1957, PhD, 1961; PhD (hon.), U. Humanistic Studies, San Diego, 1982. Diplomate Am. Bd. Sexology. Speech therapist Warren Pub. Schs. (Ill.), 1954-55, Richmond Pub. Schs. (Va.), 1955-56; dir. Child Study Ctr. Kent (Ohio) State U., 1961-64; dir. dream lab. Maimonides Med. Ctr., Bklyn., 1964-73; prof. of psychology Saybrook Grad. Sch., San Francisco, 1973—; adj. prof. psychology Calif. Inst. Human Sci., 1994—; vis. prof. U. P.R., 1972, Sonoma State U., 1972-73, U. Life Scis., Bogota, Colombia, 1974, Inst. for Psychodrama and Humanistic Psychology, Caracas, Venezuela, 1975, West Ga. Coll., 1976, John F. Kennedy U., 1980-82, Inst. for Rsch. in Biopsychophysics, Curitiba, Brazil, 1990; adj. prof. Calif. Inst. Integral Studies, 1991-97; lectr. Acad. Pedagogical Scis., Moscow, 1971, Acad. Scis., Beijing, 1981, Minas Gerais U., Belo Horizonte, Brazil, 1986-87. Author: (with Montague Ullman) Dream Telepathy, 1973, rev. edit., 1989, Song of the Siren: A Parapsychological Odyssey, 1975; (with Alberto Villoldo) The Realms of Healing, 1976, rev. edit., 1987, Human Possibilities, 1980, (with Alberto Villoldo) Healing States, 1987; (with Jerry Solfvin) La Science et les Pouvoirs Psychiques de l'Homme, 1986, (with Joseph Dillard) Dreamworking, 1988, (with David Feinstein) Personal Mythology, 1988, (with Patrick Welch) Spiritual Dimensions of Healing, 1992, (with Dennis Thong and Bruce Carpenter) A Psychiatrist in Paradise, 1993, (with David Feinstein) The Mythic Path, 1997, (with Andre de Carvalho) Sonhos Exoticos, 1998; editor: Advances in Parapsychological Research, Vol. 1, 1977, Vol. 2, 1978, Vol. 3, 1982, Vol. 4, 1984, Vol. 5, 1987, Vol. 6, 1990, Vol. 7, 1994, Vol. 8, 1997, Psychoenergetic Systems, 1979, Dreamtime and Dreamwork, 1990; co-editor: Galaxies of Life, 1973, The Kirlian Aura, 1974, The Energies of Consciousness, 1975, Future Science, 1977, Broken Images, Broken Selves, 1997; mem. editl. bd. Alternative Therapies in Health and Medicine, Jour. Humanistic Psychology, Jour. Transpersonal Psychology, Jour. Indian Psychology, Dream Network, Humanistic Psychologist; contbr. 500 articles to profl. jours. Bd. dirs., adv. bd. Acad. Religion and Phys. Rsch., Survival Rsch. Found., Hartley Film Found., Inst. for Multilevel Learning, Humanistic Psychology Ctr. N.Y., Joseph Plan Found. Recipient Svc. to Youth award YMCA, 1959, Citation of Merit Nat. Assn. Creative Children and Adults, 1975, Cert. Recognition Office Gifted and Talented, U.S. Office Edn., 1976, Volker medal South Africa Soc. Psychical Rsch., 1980, Bicentennial medal U. Ga., 1985, Charlotte Bühler award, 1992, Dan Overlade Meml. award, 1994, Humanist of Yr. award Ch. of Humanism, 1996, Career Achievement award Parapsychological Assn., 1998. Fellow APA (pres. divsn. 32, 1980), Am. Soc. Clin. Hypnosis, Am. Psychol. Soc., Soc. Sci. Study Religion, Soc. Sci. Study Sexuality, Western Psychol. Assn.; mem. AAAS, Am. Soc. Psychical Rsch., Am. Ednl. Rsch. Assn., Am. Counseling Assn., Internat. Council Psychologists, Assn. for Study of Dreams (pres. 1993-94), Soc. for the Anthropology Consciousness, Com. for Study Anomalistic Rsch., Inter-Am. Psychol. Assn., Assn. Humanistic Psychology (pres. 1974-75), Assn. Transpersonal Psychology, Internat. Soc. Hypnosis, Internat. Soc. for Study of Dissociation, Nat. Assn. for Gifted Children, Sleep Rsch. Soc., Soc. Sci. Exploration, Biofeedback Soc. Am., Coun. Exceptional Children, Soc. Accelerative Learning and Tchg., Soc. Gen. Sys. Rsch., Swedish Soc. Clin. and Exptl. Hypnosis, Western Psychol. Assn., Internat. Soc. Gen. Semantics, Menninger Found., Nat. Soc. Study of Edn., Parapsychol. Assn. (pres. 1983), Soc. Clin. and Exptl. Hypnosis, World Future Soc. E-mail: skrippner@saybrook.edu. Home: 79 Woodland Rd Fairfax CA 94930-2153 Office: Saybrook Grad Sch 450 Pacific Ave Rm 300 San Francisco CA 94133-4611

KRISCH, ALAN DAVID, physics educator; b. Phila., Apr. 19, 1939; s. Kube and Jeanne (Freiberg) K.; m. Jean Peck, Aug. 27, 1961; 1 child, Kathleen Susan. AB, U. Pa., 1960; PhD, Cornell U., 1964. Instr. Cornell U., 1964; mem. faculty U. Mich., Ann Arbor, 1964—; assoc. prof. high energy physics U. Mich., 1966-68, prof., 1968—; vis. prof. Niels Bohr Inst., Copenhagen, 1975-76; trustee Argonne Nat. Lab., 1972-73, 80-82, chmn. zero gradient syncrotron users group, 1973-75, 78-79, chmn. internat. com. for high energy spin physics symposia, 1977-94, past chmn., 1995—, chmn. organizing com. conf. on particle and nuclear physics intersections, 1983-86, mem., 1987-91, hon. mem., 1994—; chmn.-elect, chmn. IUCF Users Group, 1997—; spokesperson NEPTUN-A Expt. at 400 GeV UNK accelerator in Russia, 1989—, SPIN collaboration Fermilab, 1991-95, SPIN at HERA collaboration DESY in Germany, 1996-99. Fellow NSF, 1963, Guggenheim Found., 1971-72, Denmark Nat. Bank, 1975-76. Fellow Am. Phys. Soc.; mem. AAAS. Achievments include discovery of heavy elementary particles, of structure within the proton, of scaling in inclusive reations, of spinning core within proton, of large spin forces in violent proton collisions, of precise confirmation of large spin forces; invention of inclusive reactions; development of first high energy spin-polarized proton beam, of first strong focusing spin-polarized proton beam; demonstration of "Siberian snake" technique for accelerating spin-polarized beams. Office: U Mich Randall Lab Ann Arbor MI 48109-1120

KRISE, JACK CLOYDE, JR., treasurer; b. Cleve., Mar. 14, 1957; s. Jack C. and Edith J. K.; m. Karen A. Krise, June 14, 1986; children: Kelli, Ryan, Shannon. BS Mgmt., Dyke Coll., Cleve., 1980; degree in edn., Cleve. State U., 1981; degree in pub. fin., Kent State U., 1989. Cert. mcpl. fin. adminstr. Mgr. Bowson Enterprises, Parma Hts., Ohio, 1983-84; dep. auditor Cuyahoga County, Cleve., 1985; councilman City of Parma, Ohio, 1979-85, treas., 1986—. Co-author: Debt Policy Handbook, 1998; editor Treasury Notes, 1993-94. Dem. ward leader Cuyahoga County Dem., Parma, 1994—, mem. exec. com., 1979—, mem. ctrl. com., 1978—; pres. Parma Lions, 1981. Mem. Mcpl. Fin. Officer Assn., Mcpl. Treas. Assn. USA (treas. 1997-98, bd. dirs. 1993-97), Ohio Mcpl. Treas. Assn. (pres. 1991-92). Roman Catholic. Office: City of Parma 6611 Ridge Rd Parma OH 44129-5530

KRISE, THOMAS WARREN, military career officer, English language educator; b. Fort Sam Houston, Tex., Oct. 27, 1961; s. Edward Fisher and Elizabeth Ann (Bradt) K.; m. Patricia Lynn Love, Sept. 5, 1987. BS, USAF Acad., 1983; MSA, Cen. Mich. U., 1986; MA, U. Minn., 1989; PhD, U. Chgo., 1995. Commd. 2d lt. USAF, 1983, advanced through grades to lt. col.; dep. missile comdr. 742d Strategic Missile Squadron, Minot AFB, N.D., 1983-85, missile crew comdr., 1985-86, ICBM flight comdr., 1986-87; mem. English faculty USAF Acad., Colorado Springs, 1989-92, 97—; sr. mil. fellow Inst. for Nat. Strategic Studies, 1995-97; vice-dir. Nat. Def. U. Press, 1995-97; dir. English major program USAF Acad., 1997—; dir. core lit. program, 1998—; exec. officer Air Force Humanities Inst., 1997—; visiting prof., U. of the West Indies, Mona, Jamaica, 1999—. Asst. editor War, Literature and the Arts, 1991-92, assoc. editor, 1998—; gen. editor: McNair Papers monograph series, 1995-97, Caribbeana: An Authority of English Literature of the West Indies, 1657-177 (U. of Chgo. Press, 1999); contbr. articles to profl. jours.. Adult literacy tutor Coalition for Adult Literacy, Colorado Springs, 1989-91, literacy tutor trainer, Adult Literacy Network, Colorado Springs, 1991-92. Fulbright Fellow, 1999; recipient Pres.' Student Leadership award U. Minn., 1989; Summer Inst. grant Nat. Endowment for the Humanities, Johns Hopkins U., 1990, Seiler Rsch. grant F.J. Seiler Rsch. Lab., A.F. Systems Command, 1991, Rsch. grant Faculty Rsch Com., 1998, 99, Rsch. grant USAF Inst. Nat. Security Studies, 1998, 99, CBS Bicentennial Narrators scholarship, 1994. Mem. SAR (Pikes Peak chpt. pres. 1991-92), Toastmasters Internat. (U. Minn. chpt. pres. 1988-89), MLA, Am. Soc. for 18th Century Studies, Soc. for 18th Century Am. Studies (sec.-treas. 1995—), Colorado Springs Adult Literacy Network (pres. 1991-92), Assn. of Grads. USAF Acad. (bd. dirs. 1991-95, Chgo. chapter pres. 1993-95), Army and Navy Club (Washington), Royal Air Force Club (London), Phi Kappa Phi. Episcopalian. Avocations: travel, sailing, writing, hiking. Home: 2635 Edenderry Dr Colorado Springs CO 80919-3868 Office: Dept English and Fine Arts 2354 Fairchild Dr Ste 6d45 U S A F Academy CO 80840-6299

KRISHER, BERNARD, foreign correspondent; b. Frankfurt, Germany, Aug. 9, 1931; s. Joseph and Fella (Solnica) K.; m. Akiko Yaginuma, May 1, 1960; children: Deborah, Joseph. BA, Queens Coll.; postgrad. in advanced internat. reporting program, Columbia U., 1961-62. Staffwriter, then asst. editor mag. N.Y. World-Telegram & Sun, 1955-61; corr. Newsweek, 1963—; bur. chief Newsweek, Tokyo, 1968-80; corr. Fortune, 1981-83; chief editorial advisor Focus Weekly Mag. Shincho-sha Pub. Co., Tokyo, 1981-97; editorial advisor Dohosha Pub. Co., Kyoto and Tokyo, 1984-98; editor at large Japan Avenue, 1991-94; editor at large Asia Wired mag., 1993-98; pub. The Cambodia Daily, Phnom Penh, 1993—; editl. dir. Future Book series Tachibana Pub. Co., Tokyo, 1998—; hon. research assoc., vis. scholar East Asian Research Ctr., Harvard U., 1978-79; Far East rep. The Media Lab. MIT, 1987—. Author: (with Alan Levy) Draftee's Confidential Guide, 1957, Interview, 1976, The Plus and Minuses of Being Japanese, 1978, Harvard Diary, 1979, How Harvard Sees Japan, 1979, We Who Lived in Japan, 1986, (with King Norodom Sihanouk) Charisma and Leadership, 1990. Founder, vol. chmn. Japan Relief for Cambodia, 1992—; vol. chmn. Am. Assistance for Cambodia, 1993—, Internet Appeal for N. Korean Flood Victims, 1995—; hon. chmn. Sihanouk (free charity) Hosp.- Ctr. of Hope, Phnom Penh, Cambodia, 1996—. Ford Found. fellow Advanced Internat. Reporting Program Columbia U., 1961-62. Mem Coun. Fgn. Rels., Signet Soc., Player's Club. Home: 4-1-7-605 Hiroo, Shibuya-ku, Tokyo 150-0012, Japan

KRISHNA, GOPAL, scientist, pharmacokineticist; b. Kanpur, India; came to U.S., 1990; s. Hari V. and Urmila Dhariyal; m. Shalini Dumka. BS, Jadavpur U., Calcutta, India, 1990; PhD, Va. Commonwealth U., 1996. Tchg. asst. Va. Commonwealth U., Richmond, Va., 1990-92, rsch. asst., 1992-96; sr. scientist Schering-Plough, Kenilworth, N.J., 1996-98, assoc. prin. scientist, 1999—; sec. grad. student orgn. Va. Commonwealth U., Richmond, 1994; mem. rsch. com. PharmD candidate. Co-author: Pharmacokinetic/Pharmacodynamic Analysis, 1996; editor Pharmacokinetics/Biopharmaceutics Web Page; author papers in field; reviewer manuscripts in field. Mem. AAAS, Am. Assn. Pharm. Scientists (Outstanding Paper award 1996), Am. Chem. Soc., N.Y. Acad. Sci., Rho Chi. Achievements include rsch. interests in gastrointestinal absorption and metabolism of drugs in humans; in vitro model to predict oral absorption and metabolism in humans; pharmacokinetic and pharmacodynamic data analysis and modeling; cytochrome P450's; intestinal intubation or regional absorption studies in humans; gamma-scientigraphy studies; in vitro-in vivo correlations; deconvolution to assess rate of absorption; phase I, II, and bioequivalence studies; use of culture cell model, Caco-2, and ussing chamber to study drug transport; p-glycoprotein mediated durg efflux; high-througout absorption screening methods; mathematical modeling and simulation of pharmacokinetic data; oral drug absorption. Home: 304 Cinder Rd Edison NJ 08820-3355 Office: Schering Plough Rsch Inst K15-3700 2015 Galloping Hill Rd Kenilworth NJ 07033-1300

KRISHNAMACHARI, SADAGOPA IYENGAR, mechanical engineer, consultant; b. Chidambaram, Tamil Nadu, India, Sept. 14, 1944; came to U.S., 1982; s. Renga Iyengar and Alamelu Sadagopan; m. Lalitha Ramanujam, June 2, 1969; children: Sriram, Parashar. BS in Math., U. Madras, India, 1963, BSME, 1966; MS in Mechanics, Ill. Inst. Tech., 1984. Engr. Bharat Heavy Elecs. Ltd., Tiruchi, Tamil Nadu, 1967-73, sr. engr., 1973-77, mgr. nuclear engring., 1977-82; mgr. product design and devel. L.J. Broutman & Assocs., Chgo., 1984-91, 1991-96; ind. cons. Pioneer Techs., Naperville, Ill., 1996—; industry rep. Indian Boiler Regulatory Bd., 1976-77; mem. vis. faculty dept. mech. engring. Ill. Inst. Tech., Chgo., 1985—; bd. dirs. Soc. Plastics Engrs. PD3. Author: Applied Stress Analysis of Plastics--A Mechanical Engineering Approach, 1992. Founder classical music sch. for children, Tiruchi, 1978. Mem. ASME (sr.), Soc. Plastics Engrs. (bd. dirs. PD3 divsn., editor SPE/PD3), Soc. Exptl. Mechanics. Hindu. Achievements include pioneered capabilities for stress analysis of pressure vessels, piping, thermal and mechanical design of nuclear heat exchangers, components made of non-metallic materials; development of stress analysis of non-metallic materials. Office: Pioneer Techs 1507 Branford Ln Naperville IL 60564-6120

KRISHNAMURTHY, SRIRAM, planner; b. Sengottai, India, Feb. 24, 1964; s. Ramaswamy and Pravathy K.; m. Sonya Christian, Feb. 13, 1993; 1 child, Eisha. B of Engring., U. Madras, Coimbatore, India, 1985; M, U. So. Calif., 1990, PhD, 1993. Temp. planner So. Calif. Assn. Govts., L.A., 1993, Met. Transp. Authority, L.A., 1993-94; assoc. prof. Kern Coun. Govts., Bakersfield, Calif., 1994—; adj. prof. Calif. State U., Bakersfield, 1998—. Contbr. articles to profl. jours. Mem. Am. Soc. Pub. Adminstrn., Am. Planning Assn. Independent. Home: 3504 Rancho Sierra Bakersfield CA 93306-1822 Office: Kern Coun Govts 1401 19th St Ste 300 Bakersfield CA 93301

KRISHNAN, KRISHNASWAMY RANGA RAMA, psychiatrist; b. Madras, India, Apr. 22, 1956; came to U.S., 1981; s. N. Krishnaswamy and Sulochana (Govinda) Reddy; m. Sripriya Chithamoor, May 21, 1987; children: Vaishnavi, Prahlad. MBBS, U. MAdras, 1978. Sr. house officer Queen Elizabeth Hosp., Barbados, West Indies, 1980-81; asst. prof. Duke U., Durham, N.C., 1984-89, assoc. prof., 1989-95, head divsn. biol. psychiatry, 1989—, dir. program, 1989—, prof. psychiatry, 1995—; chair dept. psychiatry and behavioral medicine Duke U. Med. Ctr., 1998—; mem. NIMH Review Com., Washington, 1990—. Author: Chronic Pain: Brain Imaging in Clinical Psychiatry, 1988; contbr. articles to profl. jours. Recipient Laughlin award Am. Coll. Psychiatry, 1984, Rafaelsen award CINP, 1988, Doreman award Psychosomatics, 1990. Mem. Am. Psychiat. Assn., Am. Coll. Neuropsychopharmacology, Nat. Bd. Med. Examiners. Achievements include application of magnetic resonance imaging/spectroscopy in affective disorders. Office: Duke U Med Ctr PO Box 3950 Durham NC 27715-3018

KRISKO, MARY ELLEN, primary school educator; b. Danville, Ill., Dec. 6, 1942; d. Joseph C. and Nina F. Payne; m. Robert M. Krisko; children: Jonathan Christopher, Nathaniel Robert. BA, Lake Forest Coll., 1964; MS in Botany/Morphology, U. Ill., 1970; postgrad., U. Wyo., 1982—, Kennedy-Western U. Cert. tchr. Wyo. Tchr. 7-12 East Bridgewater H.S., 1964-68; instr. dept. sci. Almo C.C., Greeley, Colo., 1970-72; asst. to the provost U. Northern Colo., Greeley, 1970-72; tchr. Washakie County Sch. Dist. No. 1, Worland, Wyo., 1984—; instr. Ctrl. Wyo. Coll., Riverton, Wyo., 1980, 82, 87, 95, 98, 99. Mem. Big Horn Basin Found.; bd. trustees Hot Springs County Meml. Hosp. Found.; chmn. Hot Springs County Mus. Bd., Hot Springs County Recreation Bd.; bd. dirs. Hot Springs County C. of C., First Bapt. Ch.; reading is fundamental coord. Hot Springs County Schs. Named State of Wyo. Tchr. of Yr. 1998, State of Wyo. Disting. Educator, 1997, Tchr. of Yr. State Sch. Bd. Assn., 1997, Am. Legion Educator of Yr. 1997, Eduator of Week Wyo. State Dept. of Edn., 1997; recipient Toshiba Laptop Learning Challenge award, 1999, Presdl. award for Excellence, 1997; Wyo. Innovative grant, 1993. Mem. NEA, Nat. Sci. Tchrs. Assn., Wyo Edn. Assn., Worland Edn. Assn., Delta Kappa Gamma, Kappa Delta Pi. E-mail: mkrisko@trib.com. Home: 1415 Valley View Dr Thermopolis WY 82443

KRISLOV, MARVIN, federal government lawyer; b. Balt., Aug. 24, 1960; s. Joseph and Evelyn (Moreida) K.; m. Amy Ruth Sheon, Aug. 25, 1993; children: Zachary Jacob, Jesse Harris. BA in Econs. summa cum laude, Yale U., 1982; BA/MA in Modern History, Oxford (Eng.) U., 1985; JD, Yale U., 1988. Bar: Calif. 1988, D.C. 1989. Law clk., Judge M.H. Patel U.S. Dist. Ct. (no. dist.) Calif., San Francisco, 1988-89; trial atty. U.S. Dept. Justice, Civil Rights Divsn., Washington, 1989-93; spl. asst. U.S. atty. U.S. Atty.'s Office, Washington, 1989-90; spl. counsel Office of Counsel to the Pres., Washington, 1993-94, asst. counsel, 1994, assoc. counsel, 1995-96; dep. solicitor U.S. Dept. Labor, Washington, 1996-98, acting solicitor, 1997-98; v.p., gen. counsel U. Mich., Ann Arbor, 1998—; adj. prof. law, George Washington U. Law Sch., Washington, 1991-93. Alderman, New Haven Bd. Aldermen, 1982-83. Rhodes scholar, 1983. Phi Beta Kappa. Office: U Mich 4010 Fleming Adminstrn Bldg Ann Arbor MI 48109-1340

KRISS, GARY W(AYNE), Episcopal priest; b. Balt., Dec. 29, 1946; s. Warren B. and Margaret L. (Austin) K. AB cum laude, Dartmouth Coll., 1968; MDiv, Yale U. Divinity Sch., 1972; postgrad. studies, The Gen. Theol. Sem., N.Y.C., 1972, St. George Coll., Jerusalem, 1978. Ordained to ministry Episcopal Ch. as deacon, 1972, as priest 1972. Chaplain to the congregation Cathedral Ch. of St. Paul, Burlington, Vt., 1972-74; coord. Rock Point (Vt.) Summer Confs., 1973-77; vicar St. Mark's, St. Luke's Parishes, Castleton and Fair Haven, Vt., 1974-78; asst. to dean The Cathedral of All Saints, Albany, N.Y., 1978-79; canon precentor The Cathedral of All Saints, Albany, 1979-84, dir. inst. Christian studies, 1979-84; dean Cathedral of All Saints, Albany, 1984-91; dean and pres. Nashotah (Wis.) House, 1992—; bd. dirs. Brookhaven Home for Boys, Chelsea, Vt., 1975-79, Albany Collegiate Interfaith Ctr., 1982-90, pres. 1984-90; Episcopal campus priest, SUNY, Albany, 1980-84; bd. dirs. Capital Area Coun. of Chs., Albany, N.Y., 1989-91, chmn. of Faith and Learning Commn.; The Living Ch. Found., 1994—. Bd. dirs. Samaritan Shelters, Glenmont, N.Y., 1979-91, The Child's Hosp., Albany, 1986-90, Child's Nursing Home, Albany, 1987-91, pres. 1990-91. Home and Office: Nashotah House 2777 Mission Rd Nashotah WI 53058-9790

KRISS, PATRICIA ANNE, health services executive; b. Syracuse, N.Y., Oct. 14, 1947; d. John Casimir and Annette Elizabeth (Burns) Miod; m. Gary Frederick Kriss, June 21, 1969. BA in Fine Arts and Edn., Coll. of New Rochelle, 1969. Psychiat. geriatric therapist N.Y. Hosp./Cornell U., White Plains, 1971-74; cmty. affairs coord. Assn. Vis. Nurse Svcs., White Plains, 1975-77; dir. pub. rels. and devel. St. Joseph's Med. Ctr., Yonkers, N.Y., 1977-82; chief devel. officer Lawrence Hosp., Bronxville, N.Y., 1982-90; devel. dir. Whitby Sch., Greenwich, Conn., 1990-94; asst. exec. dir. Stamford (Conn.) Orch., 1994; dir. cmty. affairs Vis. Nurse Svcs. of Conn., Bridgeport, 1994-98; found. exec. dir. Nursing & Home Care, Wilton, Conn., 1998—; pres. Kristal Inkwell Cons., South Salem, N.Y., 1977—; lectr. in field. One woman show at Syracuse, 1975; exhibited in Second Ch., 1987; contbr. articles to Greenwich Mag., cartoons to Saturday Review. Organizer Afghanistan surgery effort Americares, Bronxville, N.Y., 1988; Stephen min. Second Congl. Ch., Greenwich, 1996—; chmn. conservation adv. coun. Town of Lewisboro, 1988-93; outreach chmn. Guatemala Heart Team, Greenwich, 1993; chmn. Conservation Adv. Coun., Lewisboro, 1988-93; mem. Wetlands Commn., Lewisboro, 1990-95. N.Y. Regents scholar, 1965; recipient Blue Ribbon Union Carbide Art Show, 1968; fellow Tchrs. Coll. Columbia U., 1969, Healthcare Mktg. award, 1996, 1997. Mem. St. Andrew's Soc., bd. dirs. Ridgefield Guild Artists. Avocations: birdwatching, conservation, cycling, triathlon, antiques. Home: 169 Laurel Rdg South Salem NY 10590-2407 Office: Nursing Home Care Inc 180 School St PO Box 489 Wilton CT 06897-0489

KRISS, ROBERT J., lawyer; b. Cleve., Dec. 15, 1953. BA summa cum laude, Cornell U., 1975; JD cum laude, Harvard U., 1978. Bar: Ill. 1978, U.S. Dist. Ct. (no. dist.) Ill. 1978, U.S. Ct. Appeals (7th cir.) 1983, U.S. Dist. Ct. (no. dist. trial bar) Ill. 1982, U.S. Ct. Appeals (5th cir.) 1984. Ptnr. Mayer, Brown & Platt, Chgo.; presenter in field. Chmn. consent degree task force Chgo. Park Dist., 1986-87; bd. dirs. Chgo. Legal Assistance Found., 1996—. Mem. Nat. Inst. Trial Advocacy (faculty midwest regional program 1988-91, 94), Winnetka Caucus (chmn. schs. candidate selection com. 1997). Office: Mayer Brown & Platt 190 S La Salle St Ste 3100 Chicago IL 60603-3441

KRISSEL, SUSAN HINKLE, university official; b. Miami, Nov. 21, 1947; d. Jack Boyd and Carolyn (Frates) Hinkle; m. Richard Krissel, Mar. 19, 1972; children: John Boyd, Carolyn Frates. BA, U. Miami, 1970, MEd, 1977. Grad. admissions counselor Fla. Internat. U., Miami, 1971-74, budget coord. external degree program, 1974-78, transcript officer, 1978-82; owner, dir. Southeastern Consolidated Industries, Inc., 1982—. Bd. dirs. Jr. League Miami, 1985-86, Beaux Arts, U. Miami, Coral Gables, 1980-84, Parents Assn. Trinity Episcopal Sch., Miami, 1988-91; pres. Woman's Cancer Assn., U. Miami, 1980-81, Palmer Trinity Parents Assn., 1992-93; trustee Palmer Trinity Sch., 1992-93. Mem. The Flamingo Forum, Y.P.O. Episcopalian. Avocations: reading, boating, travel, needlepoint, golf. Home: 8750 SW 63rd Ct Miami FL 33143-8069

KRIST, BETTY JANE, mathematics educator, researcher; b. Buffalo, Dec. 4, 1946; d. Thomas James and Agnes (Ruchaczewska) K. BS, SUNY, 1968, MS, 1971; EdD, SUNY, Buffalo, 1980. Cert. permanent secondary math. tchr., N.Y. Rsch. assoc. Nat. Inst. Edn., SUNY, Buffalo, 1976-80, co-dir. Gifted Math. Program, 1980—, adj. assoc. prof. edn., 1985—; tchr. math. West Seneca (N.Y.) Schs., 1968-76, 78-80; assoc. prof. math. and computer sci. D'Youville Coll., Buffalo, 1980-87; prof. math. State U. Coll., Buffalo, 1987—, chmn. math. dept., 1991-97; mem. adv. coun. Sci. Svc., Washington, 1987-90; dir. math. N.Y. State Summer Inst. for Sci. and Math., Albany, 1989-90; mem. steering com. math. alert program SUNY. Co-author: Using Calculators in Mathematics ll, 12, 1980, Providing Opportunities for Gifted Students in Mathematics K-12, 1987; editor Math. Tchr., 1986-88; contbr. articles to math. jours. Speaker schs. in western N.Y., 1980—. Named Tchr. of Yr., West Senaca Schs., 1976, Outstanding Alumnae Grad. Sch. Edn. SUNY, Buffalo, 1994. Mem. ASCD, AAAS, Nat. Coun. Tchrs. Math. (editorial chmn. 1986-88, contbr. to yearbooks 1982, 85, 88), Math. Assn. Am. (founding mem. Strengthening Underrepresented Minorities Math. Achievement 1991—), Nat. Coun. Suprs. Math., Computing Educators League, Assn. Math. Tchrs. N.Y. State, AAUW (bd. dirs. Buffalo chpt. 1986-87). Democrat. Mem. United Ch. of Christ. Avocations: skiing, cooking, gardening. Home: 116 Iris Ave West Seneca NY 14224-2747

KRIST, GARY MICHAEL, writer; b. Jersey City, May 23, 1957; s. Harold Charles and Winifred Joyce (Braddon) K.; m. Elizabeth Yen-Tsen Cheng, Oct. 2, 1983; 1 child, Anna Chang-Yi. AB in Comparative Lit., Princeton U., 1979. adv. editor Hudson Rev., N.Y.C., 1990—; judge Bennett Awards in Lit., N.J. Coun. for the Arts Fellowships. Author: The Garden State, 1988, paperback edit., 1989, translation 1990, Bone by Bone, 1994, translation 1995, Bad Chemistry, 1998, translations, 1998; author of short stories; contbr. articles to profl. jours. Recipient Sue Kaufman prize for first fiction Am. Acad. Arts and Letters, N.Y.C., 1989; Fulbright fellow, U. Konstanz, Germany, 1979; Creative Writing fellow Nat. Endowment for the Arts, Washington, 1989. Mem. PEN-USA, Nat. Book Critics Cir. Home: 7207 Bybrook Ln Chevy Chase MD 20815-3162

KRISTENSEN, JOHN, church organization administrator; b. Copenhagen, Jan. 2, 1948; arrived in Can., 1951; s. Magnus and Anna (Christensen) K.; m. Janet Mary Morris, Aug. 28, 1971; children: David, Joel, Evan. Honors BSc, U. Western Ont., London, Can., 1971. Ordained to ministry Apostolic Ch. in Can., 1981. Ops. rsch. analyst Govt. of Can., Ottawa, Ont., 1971-74; sys. cons. Quasar Sys., Ottawa, 1974-78; cons. Eco-Sys., Montreal, Que., Can., 1976-81, v.p., 1979-81; min. Apostolic Ch. in Can., Montreal, 1981-94, gen. sec., 1988-94, pres., 1994—. Home and Office: The Apostolic Church, 685 Park St S, Peterborough, ON Canada K9J 3S9

KRISTENSEN, MARLENE, early childhood education educator; b. Baudette, Minn., Sept. 1, 1932; d. Glenn Edward and Frances Emma (Wilson) Munson; m. Robert A. Kristensen, June 5, 1955; children: Mary Kristensen-Quinlan, Debra Kristensen-Anderson. BA, Concordia Coll., Moorhead, Minn., 1954; student, Everett Community Coll., 1973, Edmonds Community Coll., 1974—; postgrad., Cen. Wash. U. From asst. dir. to dir. Lynnwood (Wash.) Day Care, 1974-84; kindergarten tchr. Edmonds (Wash.) Sch. Dist., 1957-58; tchr. trainer Children's World Learning Ctr., Edmonds, 1984-93; ret., 1993; honor roll tchr., 1987-91. Mem. tchrs.' adv. bd. Weekly Reader Publs., 1991-93. Mem. ASCD, Nat. Assn. for Edn. Young Children.

KRISTIANSEN, MAGNE, electrical engineer, educator; b. Elverum, Norway, Apr. 14, 1932; came to U.S., 1958, naturalized, 1967; s. Martin and Ella (Sobye) K.; m. Aud Bohn, July 6, 1957; children: Sonja Bohn, Eric Bohn. B.S. in Elec. Engring., U. Tex., Austin, 1961, Ph.D. (Ford Found. fellow), 1967. Registered profl. engr., Tex. Rsch. engr. U. Tex., Austin, 1964-66; faculty Tex. Tech U., Lubbock, 1966—, prof., 1971—, P.W. Horn prof., 1977—, C.B. Thornton prof., 1990—, dir. plasma lab., 1966—, dir. pulsed power lab., 1980—; v.p. rsch. and engring. Enfitek, Inc., Lubbock, 1987-90; v.p. R & D Integrated Tech. Inc., Lubbock, 1990-98; cons. def. products divsn. Varo, Inc., Garland, Tex., 1970-71; cons. Aerospace Corp., El Segundo, Calif., 1974-76, BDM Corp., Albuquerque, 1975-76, 85-87, Palisades Inst., N.Y. and NRC, 1977, Rockwell Internat., 1978, Maxwell Labs., 1979-83, LaJolla Inst., 1979, NASA, 1979, Norwegian Rsch. Coun., 1980, Sci. Applications, Inc., 1983-88, 91-92, Lawrence Livermore Nat. Lab., 1983-95, McDonnell Douglas, 1986, LTV Missiles and Electronics Group, 1987-89, NEA-Lindberg A/S, 1988, Physics Internat. Co., 1992-97, Rocket Rsch. Co., 1992, Swedish Def. Rsch. Inst., 1992—; Hazeltine Ocean Sys., 1995, Lockheed Martin, 1995-96, Integrated Technologies, Inc., 1998—; collaborator Los Alamos Nat. Lab., 1974-95, others; contractor DNA, 1986-97, NASA, 1990—, Wright Aeronautical Labs., 1994—. Co-author: An Introduction to Controlled Thermonuclear Fusion, 1977, Russian, Japanese, Chinese translations, 1980-81, Rotating Mirror Cameras, 1997; co-editor: Advances in Pulsed Power Technology, 1984—. Contbr. articles to profl. jours. Mem. USAF Sci. Adv. Bd., 1981-85. Served with Royal Norwegian Air Force, 1950-58. Recipient Meritorious Civilian Svc. award USAF, 1985, Excellence award Halliburton Found., 1994; grantee State of Tex., 1966-85, 88-94, NSF, 1967-87, AEC, 1968-71, Air Force Office Sci. Rsch., 1968—, Army Rsch. Lab., 1994—, Dept. Energy, 1978-79; sr. fellow in sci. NATO, 1975, fellow Japan Soc. for Promotion Sci., 1979. Fellow IEEE (life, Pulsed Power Conf. Peter Haas award 1987, Nuclear and Plasma Sci. Soc. Merit award 1991), Am. Phys. Soc.; mem. AAAS, Russian Acad. Scis. (fgn. mem., Ural sect.), Am. Soc. Engring. Edn., Sigma Xi, Tau Beta Pi, Eta Kappa Nu, Phi Kappa Phi. Home: 3105 78th St Lubbock TX 79423-1815 Office: Tex Tech U Dept Elec Engring Lubbock TX 79409-3102

KRISTOF, KATHY M., journalist; b. Burbank, Calif., Feb. 4, 1960; d. Joseph E. and Frances S. Kristof; m. Richard R. Magnuson, Jr., Jan. 4, 1986; 2 children. BA, U. So. Calif., L.A., 1983. Reporter L.A. Bus. Jour., 1984-88, Daily News, Woodland Hills, Calif., 1988-89, L.A. Times, 1989—; syndicated columnist L.A. Times Syndicate, 1991—. Author: Kathy Kristof's Complete Book of Dollars and Sense, 1997; contbr. articles to mags. and profl. jours. Recipient John Hancock Fin. Svcs. award, 1992, Personal Fin. Writing award ICI/Am. U., 1994, Consumer Adv. of Yr., Calif. Alliance for Consumer Edn., 1998. Mem. Soc. Bus. Editors and Writers. Office: Los Angeles Times Times-Mirror Sq Los Angeles CA 90053

KRISTOF, LADIS KRIS DONABED, political scientist, author; b. Cernauti, Romania, Nov. 26, 1918; came to U.S., 1952, naturalized, 1957; s. Witold and Maria (Zawadzki) Krzysztofowicz; m. Jane McWilliams, Dec. 29, 1956; 1 son, Nicholas. Student, U. Poznan, Poland, 1937-39; BA, Reed Coll., Portland, Oreg., 1955; MA, U. Chgo., 1956, PhD, 1969. Regional exec. dir. Sovromlemn, Romania, 1948; sales mgr. Centre du Livre Suisse, Paris, France, 1951-52; lectr. U. Chgo., 1958-59; assoc. dir. Inter-Univ. Project History Menshevism, N.Y.C., 1959-62; mem. faculty dept. polit. sci. Temple U., 1962-64; research fellow Hoover Instn., Stanford U., 1964-67; faculty polit. sci. U. Santa Clara, 1967-68; asso. Studies Communist System, Stanford, 1968-69; mem. faculty polit. sci. U. Waterloo, Ont., Can., 1969-71; prof. polit. sci. Portland (Oreg.) State U., 1971-89, prof. emeritus, 1990—; vis. prof. U. Wroclaw, Poland, 1990, U. Iasi, Romania, 1991, U. Punjab, India, 1992. Author: The Nature of Frontiers and Boundaries, 1959, The Origins and Evolution of Geopolitics, 1960, The Russian Image of Russia, 1967, The Geopolitical Contours of the Post-Cold War World, 1992; also articles in Romania; co-author, co-editor: Revolution and Politics in Russia, 1972. Active Internat. YMCA Center, Paris, 1950-52, NAACP, Chgo., 1957-59, Amnesty Internat., Portland, 1975—. Served with Corps Engrs. Romanian Army, 1940-43. Fulbright scholar Romania, 1971, 84. Mem. Am. Polit. Sci. Assn., Assn. Am. Geographers, Am. Assn. for Advancement of Slavic Studies, Internat. Polit. Sci. Assn., Western Slavic Assn. (pres. 1988-90), Am.-Romanian Acad. Arts and Scis. (v.p. 1995—). Home: 23050 NW Roosevelt Dr Yamhill OR 97148-8336 Office: Portland State Univ Dept Polit Sci Portland OR 97207 *War, want and concentration camps, exile from home and homeland, these have made me hate strife among men, but they have not made me lose faith in the future of mankind. Personal experience, including my own unsteady progress through life, has taught me to beware of man's capacity for plain stupid, irrational, as well as consciously evil behavior, but it also has taught me that man has an even greater capacity for recovery from lapses. In a short thrust of planned, wisely guided activity he is able to climb to higher levels of material and intellectual achievement than he ever reached before. In short, I remain a rationalist and an optimist at a time when the prophets of doom have the floor. My query is, if man has been able to create the arts, the sciences and the material civilization we know in America, why should he be judged powerless to create justice, fraternity and peace.**

KRISTOF, NICHOLAS DONABET, journalist; b. Chgo., Apr. 27, 1959; s. Ladis K.D. and Jane (McWilliams) K.; m. Sheryl WuDunn; children: Gregory, Geoffrey, Caroline. BA, Harvard U., 1981; BA and MA in Law, U. Oxford, Eng., 1983; diploma in Arabic, Am. U. in Cairo, 1983-84; student, Taipei Lang. Inst., 1987-88. Econs. reporter N.Y. Times, N.Y.C., 1984-85, fin. corr. L.A. bur., 1985-86, chief Hong Kong bur., 1986-87, chief Beijing bur., 1988-93, chief Tokyo bur., 1995—; vis. fellow East-West Ctr., 1993; vis. scholar Linfield Coll., 1994. Author: (with S. WuDunn) China Wakes: The Struggle for the Soul of a Rising Power, 1994. Recipient Pulitzer prize for fgn. reporting, 1990, George Polk award for fgn. reporting L.I. U., N.Y., 1990, Hal Boyle award Overseas Press Club, 1990, Citations for Excellence, 1994, 96; Rhodes scholar, 1981-83. Avocations: travel, reading, running. Office: New York Times Fgn Desk 229 W 43rd St New York NY 10036-3959

KRISTOFF, KARL W., lawyer; b. Buffalo, Mar. 31, 1942. BA, SUNY, Buffalo, 1965; JD, John Marshall Law Sch., 1968. Bar: Ill. 1968, U.S. Supreme Ct. 1974, N.Y. 1976. Ptnr., chair edn. law practice group Hodgson, Russ, Andrews, Woods & Goodyear, Buffalo. Mem. editorial bd. The John Marshall Jour. Practice and Procedure, 1968, active, 1967. Asst. adjutant gen. for air N.Y. Air Nat. Guard. Mem. Am. Arbitration Assn. (comml. panel arbitrators), Nat. Pub. Employer Labor Rels. Assn., Nat. Coun. Sch. Attys., N.Y. State Assn. Sch. Attys., N.Y. State Pub. Employer Labor Rels. Assn. Office: Hodgson Russ Andrews Woods & Goodyear One M&T Plz Ste 2000 Buffalo NY 14203-2391

KRISTOFFERSON, KARL ERIC, writer; b. Jacksonville, Fla., Mar. 3, 1929; s. Gustave Edward and Oma Nancy (Reynolds) K.; m. Barbara Elaine Dalton, Jan. 22, 1954; children—Karol, Paul, Scott. A.A., Jacksonville U., 1961; B.S. with honors in Journalism, U. Fla., 1963. Engring. writer Pratt & Whitney Aircraft Co., West Palm Beach, Fla., 1963; publs. supr. Ling-Temco-Vought Ops. and Boeing Co., Kennedy Space Ctr., Fla., 1964-72; chief pub. affairs IRS Dist. Hdqrs., Greensboro, N.C., 1972-74; senior writer, editor NASA Pub. Affairs, Kennedy Space Ctr., 1974-88, news chief, 1988-93; freelance writer for TV, motion pictures and maj. nat. mags. and publs., 1960—; regular assignment writer Reader's Digest; corr. Titusville Star Advocate, 1995—Fla. Today, 1995—. Served with USAF, 1950-53, Korea. Decorated Air medal; recipient Apollo, Skylab, Apollo-Soyuz, Voyager, Space Shuttle Achievement awards NASA, 1969-93, Aviation Space Writers' Assn. award for articles writing, 1974. Mem. Canaveral Press Club.

KRISTOL, DANIEL MARVIN, lawyer; b. Wilmington, Del., July 7, 1936; s. Abraham Louis and Pearl Cecile (Oltman) K.; m. Katherine Fairfax Chinn, Nov. 4, 1968; children—Sarah Douglas, Susan Fairfax. B.A., U. Pa., 1958, LL.B., 1961. Bar: Del. 1961, U.S. Dist. Ct. Del. 1962. Assoc., ptnr. Killoran & VanBrunt, Wilmington, Del., 1961-76; dir. Prickett, Jones, Elliott & Kristol, P.A. and ptnr. predecessor Prickett, Ward Burt & Sanders, Wilmington, 1976—; pub. defender Ct. Common Pleas, Wilmington, 1966-69; asst. solicitor City of Wilmington, 1970-73; spl. counsel Div. Housing State of Del., 1972-87, gen. counsel Del. State Housing Authority, 1973—. Served with USAR, 1964-67. Mem. ABA, Del. State Bar Assn. (chmn. real and personal property com. 1974-78, chmn. world peace through law com. 1980-81), Am. Coll. Real Estate Lawyers. Republican. Jewish. Clubs: Wilmington (Del.) Country; Greenville (Del.) Country, Mill Reef (Antigua, W.I.), Wilmington Club. Office: PO Box 1328 Wilmington DE 19899-1328

KRISTOL, IRVING, social sciences educator, editor; b. N.Y.C., Jan. 22, 1920; s. Joseph and Bessie (Mailman) K.; m. Gertrude Himmelfarb, Jan. 18, 1942; children: William, Elizabeth. BA, CCNY, 1940; LittD, Franklin and Marshall Coll., 1972; LLD, U. Dallas, 1974, Kenyon Coll., 1977. Mng. editor Commentary mag., 1947-52; co-founder, co-editor Encounter mag., 1953-58; editor The Reporter mag., 1959-60; exec. v.p. Basic Books Inc., N.Y.C., 1961-69; co-editor The Pub. Interest mag., 1965—; mem. faculty NYU, 1969-88; John M. Olin prof. social thought Grad. Sch. Bus. Adminstrn. NYU, 1979-88; sr. fellow Am. Enterprise Inst., 1987—. Author: On the Democratic Idea in America, 1972, Two Cheers for Capitalism, 1978, Reflections of a Neoconservative, 1983, Neoconservatism: The Autobiography of an Idea, 1995; editor: (with Stephen Spender and Melvin Lasky) Encounters, 1963, (with Daniel Bell) Confrontation: The Student Rebellion and the University, 1969, Capitalism Today, 1971, The Crisis of Economic Theory, 1981, (with Nathan Glazer) The American Commonwealth, 1976, (with Paul Weaver) The Americans, 1976, (with Moran, Barnes, Mertes and Oduber) Third World Instability, 1985; contbr. numerous articles. Mem. Pres.'s Commn. on White House Fellowships, 1981-84, Nat. Council on the Humanities, 1972-77. Served with U.S. Army, 1944-46. Fellow Am. Acad. Arts and Scis. Mem. Council Fgn. Relations. Club: Century Assn. Office: Public Interest Mag National Affairs Inc 1112 16th St NW Ste 530 Washington DC 20036-4821

KRISTOL, WILLIAM, editor, publisher; b. Dec. 23, 1952; s. Irving Kristol and Gertrude Himmelfarb; m. Susan Scheinberg, Dec. 28, 1975; children: Rebecca Louise, Anne Elizabeth, Joseph Max. AB, Harvard U., 1973, PhD, 1979. Instr., then asst. prof. polit. sci. U. Pa., Phila., 1978-83; asst. prof. pub. policy Harvard U., Cambridge, Mass., 1983-85; spl. asst., chief of staff Dept. Edn., Washington, 1985-89; campaign mgr. Alan Keyes for Senate, Md., 1988; domestic policy advisor Office of V.P., Washington, 1989, chief of staff to v.p., 1989-93—; dir. Bradley Project of 90s, Washington, 1993; chmn. Project for the Rep. Future, Washington, 1993-95; editor, pub. The Weekly Standard, Washington, 1995—. Jewish. Office: 1150 17th St NW Ste 505 Washington DC 20036-4621

KRITCHEVSKY, DAVID, biochemist, educator; b. Kharkov, Russia, Jan. 25, 1920; came to U.S., 1923, naturalized, 1929; s. Jacob and Leah (Kritchevsky) K.; m. Evelyn Sholtes, Dec. 21, 1947; children—Barbara Ann, Janice Eileen, Stephen Bennett. BS, U. Chgo., 1939, MS, 1942; PhD, Northwestern U., 1948. Chemist Ninol Labs., Chgo., 1939-46; postdoctoral fellow Fed. Inst. Tech., Zurich, Switzerland, 1948-49; biochemist Radiation Lab., U. Calif. at Berkeley, 1950-52, Lederle Lab., Pearl River, N.Y., 1952-57, Wistar Inst., Phila., 1957—; prof. biochemistry Sch. Vet. Medicine U. Pa., Phila., 1965—; prof. emeritus, 1992—; prof. biochemistry Sch. Medicine U. Pa., 1970-92, chmn. grad. group molecular biology, 1972-84; mem. USPHS study sect. Nat. Heart Inst., 1964-68, 72-76; chmn. rsch. com. Spl. Dairy Industry Bd., 1963-70; mem. food and nutrition bd. NAS, 1976-82. Author: Cholesterol, 1958, also numerous articles.; editor: (with G. Litwack) Actions of Hormones on Molecular Processes, 1964; co-editor: (with R. Paoletti) Advances in Lipid Research, 1963-89, (with P. Nair) 1973, Bile Acids, 1971; Western Hemisphere editor Atherosclerosis, 1978-90, cons. editor, 1990—. Recipient Rsch. Career award Nat. Heart Inst., 1962, Herman award Am. Soc. Clin. Nutrition, 1992, Disting. Svc. award U. N.C. Inst. Nutrition, 1993, Auenbrugger medal U. Graz, Austria, 1994, SUPELCO/AOCS award, 1996, Lifetime Achievement award Am. Inst. for Cancer Rsch., 1996. Fellow AAAS, Am. Inst. Nutrition (pres. 1979, Borden award 1974), Am. Coll. Nutrition (award 1978); mem. Am. Soc. Biol. Chemists, Am. Chem. Soc. (award Phila. sect. 1977), Soc. Exptl. Biology and Medicine (pres. 1985-87), Arteriosclerosis Coun., Am. Heart Assn. (spl. recognition coun. on atherosclerosis 1993), Am. Soc. Oil Chemists (chmn. methods com. 1963-64), Internat. Soc. Fat Rsch. Achievements include research on role vehicle when cholesterol and fat produces atherosclerosis in rabbits, effects of saturated and unsaturated fat, deposition of orally administered cholesterol in aorta of man and rabbit, caloric restriction and cancer. Home: 136 Lee Cir Bryn Mawr PA 19010-3724 Office: Wistar Inst 36th And Spruce St Philadelphia PA 19104-4268

KRITIKOS, HARALAMBOS N., electrical engineering educator; b. Tripoli, Greece. PhD, U. Pa., 1961. Prof. elec. engring. U. Pa. Mem. IEEE (assoc. editor transactions 1986, 88, exec. editor 1981-85). Address: 200 S 33rd St Philadelphia PA 19104-6314

KRITZER, PAUL ERIC, media executive, communications lawyer; b. Buffalo, May 5, 1942; s. James Cyril and Bessie May (Biddlecombe) K.; m. Frances Jean McCallum, June 20, 1970; children: Caroline Frances, Erica Hopkins. BA, Williams Coll., 1964; MS in Journalism, Columbia U., 1965; JD, Georgetown U., 1972. Bar: U.S. Supreme Ct. 1978, Wis. 1980. Reporter, copy editor Buffalo Evening News, 1964, 69, 70; instr. English Augusta (Ga.) Coll., 1968-69; law clk. Office of FCC Commr., Washington, 1971, MCI, Washington, 1972; counsel U.S. Ho. of Reps., Washington, 1972-77; assoc. counsel Des Moines Register & Tribune, 1977-80; editor, pub. Waukesha (Wis.) Freeman, 1980-83; legal v.p., sec. Jour. Communications Inc., Milw., 1983—; bd. dirs. Jour. Communications, Inc., Milw. Trustee Carroll Co., Waukesha, 1981-89; producer Waukesha Film Festival, 1982; bd. dirs. Des Moines Metro Opera, Inc., 1979-80; bd. dirs. Milw. Youth Symphony Orch., 1992—, pres. 1994-97; bd. dirs. Milw. Symphony Orch., 1997—; bd. dirs. United Performing Arts Fund, 1994-97. With U.S. Army, 1965-68. Presbyterian. Avocations: bridge, gardening. Home: 211 Oxford Rd Waukesha WI 53186-6263 Office: Jour Communications Inc 333 W State St PO Box 661 Milwaukee WI 53201-0661

KRITZMAN, LAWRENCE DAVID, humanities educator; b. N.Y.C.; s. Melvin M. and Margy (Rosenstein) K.; m. Janie L. Kritzman; 1 child, Jeremy. BA, U. Wis., 1969; AM, Middlebury Coll., 1970; PhD, U. Mich., 1976. Lectr. Rutgers U., New Brunswick, N.J., 1976-77, asst. prof., 1977-82, assoc. prof., dir. grad. studies, 1982-87; prof. French civilization Ohio State U., Columbus, 1987-89; prof. French & comparative lit. Dartmouth Coll., Hanover, N.H., 1989—, Edward Tuck prof. French, 1994—, chair comparative lit. dept., 1992-95; Ted and Helen Geisel Third Century prof. in the humanities Dartmouth Coll., 1995—; chair Com. for Future of French Studies, French Embassy, N.Y., 1991—; vis. prof. U. Mich., Ann Arbor, 1991, 93, Duke NEH Inst., 1986, 90, Northwestern NEH Inst., assoc. dir., 1995; vis. prof. Stanford U., 1999. Author: Destruction/Découverte, 1980, Rhetoric of Sexuality and Literature of French Renaissance, 1991; editor: Fragments, 1981, France Under Mitterand, 1984, Foucault: Politics, Philosophy, Culture, 1988, Le Signe et le Texte, 1989, Auschwitz & After: Race, Culture & The Jewish Question in France, 1995, The Columbia History of 20th Century French Thought, 1999-2000; mem. editl. bd. Etudes Montaignistes, 1988, Montaigne Studies, Early Modern Culture, Studies in 20th Century Literature, Contemporary French Civilization Sites; gen. editor: European Perspectives, 1989—, Columbia U. Press; adv. editor Publs. of MLA, Substance; mem. adv. bd. French Politics and Society; contbr. numerous articles to profl. jours., chpts. to numerous books. Chair Com. for Future of French Studies in U.S.; dir. Edward Morot-Inst. of French Cultural Studies, 1994; dir. 1997, Inst. French Cultural Studies, 1989. Recipient Chevalier de l'Ordre des Palmes Academics, French Govt., 1991; Officier des Palmes des Palmes Academics, 1994; sr. fellow Am. Coun. Learned Soc., 1989; Andrew W. Mellon Found. grant Duke U., 1980. Mem. MLA, Am. Coun. French Social and Cultural Affairs, Nat. Writer's Union, Am. Comparative Lit. Assn., Acad. Lit. Studies. Home: 19 Abbottsford Rd Brookline MA 02446-3105 Office: Dept French Dartmouth Coll Hanover NH 03755

KRIVIT, JEFFREY SCOT, surgeon; b. Aug. 15, 1955; m. Mary Hoyme, July 6, 1986; children: Bradley, Alex, Elyse, Hanna. BS, U. Ill., 1977, MD, 1981. Resident Ill. Eye & Ear Infirmary, Chgo., 1982-86; physician Carle Clinic Assoc., Urbana, Ill., 1986-89, Linn Head & Neck Surgery, Cedar Rapids, Iowa, 1989-92, Cedar Rapids ENT, 1992-96, Ea. Iowa ENT, Cedar Rapids, 1996—; chief surgery St. Luke's Hosp., Cedar Rapids, 1995-96. Fellow Am. Rhinol. Soc., Am. Acad. Otolaryngology Head & Neck Surgery, Am. Soc. Head & Neck Surgery, Am. Acad. Facial Plastic & Reconstructive Surgery, Am. Coll. Surgeons; mem. AMA, Linn County Med. Soc., Iowa Med. Soc. Office: PCI ENT Dept 2d Fl 600 7th St SE Fl 2D Cedar Rapids IA 52401-2112

KRIVKOVICH, PETER GEORGE, advertising executive; b. Bad Ischl, Austria, Oct. 25, 1946; came to U.S., 1953; s. George M. Krivkovich and Ada (Kalenkiewicz) Bajor; m. Linda J. Monken, Aug. 30, 1970; children: Peter A., Alexis C. BS, U. Ill., 1969; postgrad., Loyola U., Chgo., 1972-73. Advt. asst. Kemper Ins. Co., Chgo., 1969-71; account exec. Nader-Lief, Chgo., 1971-72; account mgr. Leo Burnett, Chgo., 1972-73; ptnr. Hackenberg, Normann, Krivkovich, Chgo., 1973-80; pres. Cramer-Krasselt, Chgo., 1981-86; pres., COO Cramer-Krasselt, Chgo./Milw./Orland, 1987-98, pres., CEO, chmn. bd., 1999—; mem. Nat. Advt. Rev. Bd. Bd. dirs. Manufactures Bank and Off The Street Club and Prentice Hosp. Named One of 100 Best and Brightest Advt. Execs. of Yr. Advt. Age mag., 1986, Midwest Advt. Exec. of Yr. Adweek mag., 1987. Mem. Am. Assn. Advt. Agys. (chmn. Chgo. chpt. 1992, 93, regional bd. govs. 1996, 97, nat. bd. govs. 1998, 99), Direct Mktg. Assn. (nat. bd. dirs.), Chgo. Assn. Direct Mktg., Chgo. Advt. Club, Glenview (Ill.) C. of C., Tavern Club, Exec. Club. Office: Cramer-Krasselt 225 N Michigan Ave Ste 800 Chicago IL 60601-7690

KRIVOSHIK, ANDREW PETER, engineer; b. Elizabeth, N.J., Feb. 20, 1968; s. Peter Enoch and Elizabeth Elsie Krivoshik; m. Susan Elise Lyon, Aug. 10, 1991; 1 child, Amy Elise. BSE with honors, Princeton (N.J.) U., 1990; MD-PhD, U. Ill., 1999. Registered profl. engr., Ill. Tech. cons. KEA Inc., Elizabeth, N.J., 1983-90; technician IBM TJ Watson, Yorktown Heights, N.Y., 1988, 89; Univ. fellow U. Ill., Urbana, 1990-91, 98-99, Nat. Inst. on Drug Abuse fellow, 1993-98; elec. item writer Nat. Coun. of Examiners for Engring. and Surveying, 1996—. Contbr. articles to profl. jours. Recipient rsch. svc. award USPHS, 1993-98; USPHS fellow NIH, 1991-93. Mem. NSPE, IEEE, Biophys. Soc., Cum Laude Soc., Tau Beta Pi. Office: Mayo Clinic U Ill 524 Burrill Hall 200 1st St SW Rochester MN 55905

KRIZ, GEORGE JAMES, agricultural research administrator, educator; b. Brainard, Nebr., Sept. 20, 1936; s. George Jacob and Rose Agnes Kriz; m. Patricia Elizabeth Kelly (div. Feb. 1989); children: Rosalie Sue, Richard Patrick, Thomas George; m. Rhoda Mae Whitacre, June 23, 1989. BS in Agrl. Engring., Iowa State U., 1960, MS in Agrl. Engring., 1962; PhD, U. Calif., Davis, 1965. Lectr. U. Calif., Davis, 1965; asst. prof. agrl. engring. N.C. State U., Raleigh, 1965-68, assoc. prof., 1968-72, prof., 1972—, assoc. dept. head, 1969-73, asst. rsch. dir., 1973-81, assoc. rsch. dir., 1981—. Fellow Am. Soc. Agrl. Engring. (bd. dirs. 1983-85, found. trustee 1986-94, 96-97, pres. 1995-96, presdl. citation 1988, 91); mem. Coun. Agrl. Scis. and Tech. Avocation: gardening, walking. Office: NC State U Box 7643 100 Patterson Hall Raleigh NC 27695-7643

KRIZEK, RAYMOND JOHN, civil engineering educator, consultant; b. Balt., June 5, 1932; s. John James and Louise (Polak) K.; m. Claudia Stricker, Aug. 1964; children—Robert A., Kevin J. BE, Johns Hopkins U., 1954; MS, U. Md., 1961; PhD, Northwestern U., 1963. Instr. U. Md., College Park, 1957-61; rsch. asst. civil engring. Northwestern U., Evanston, Ill., 1961-63, asst. prof. civil engring., 1963-66, assoc. prof. civil engring., 1966-70, prof. civil engring., 1970, chmn. dept. civil engring., 1980-92, dir. Master of Project Mgmt. program, 1994—, Stanley F. Pepper chair prof., 1987—; cons. to industry. Editor books; contbr. numerous articles to profl. jours. Served to lt. U.S. Army, 1955-57. Decorated Palmes Academiques (France), 1993; recipient Hogentogler award ASTM, 1970; named disting.

vis. scholar NSF, 1972. Mem. ASCE (pres. Geo Inst. 1997-98, Huber Rsch. prize 1971, Karl Terzaghi award 1997, Ill. sect. Civil Engr. of Yr. 1998), Internat. Soc. Soil Mechanics and Geotech. Engring., Spanish Acad. Engring. (corr.). Roman Catholic. Home: 1366 Sanford Ln Glenview IL 60025-3165 Office: Dept Civil Engring Northwestern U 2145 Sheridan Rd Evanston IL 60208-3109

KRIZER, JODI, performing arts executive. Mng. dir. Bill T. Jones/Arnie Zane Dance Co., N.Y.C., exec. dir. Office: Bill T Jones/Arnie Zane Dance Co Arnie Zance Dance Co 853 Broadway Ste 1706 New York NY 10003-4703*

KROB, MELANIE GORDON, writer; b. Houston, June 19, 1970; d. Robert Allen and Connie Marshall Gordon; m. Adam Nelson Krob, May 16, 1998. BA, U. of the South, 1992; PhD, Tulane U., 1998. Tchg. asst. Tulane U., New Orleans, 1992-98. Exch. fellow Freie U., Berlin, 1995-96, Mellon fellow Mellon Found., Tulane U., 1997; rsch. grantee Deutscher Akademischer Austausch Dienst, Berlin, 1998, German Exile Rsch. grantee U. So. Calif., L.A., 1999.

KROCHALIS, JEANNE ELIZABETH, English language educator; b. Enterprise, Ala., Mar. 4, 1944; d. Edmund Leonard and Jeanne Marie (Brown) K. AB, Mt. Holyoke Coll., 1965; MPhil, Oxford U., 1968; MA, Harvard U., 1969, PhD, 1973. Vis. prof. Catholic U. Am., Washington, 1974, U. Pitts., 1985-86; asst. prof. U. Pa., Phila., 1973-80; vis. asst. prof. Bucknell U., Lewisburg, Pa., 1980-81; assoc. prof. Pa. State U., State College, 1981—; assoc. editor The Chaucer Review, University Park, Pa., 1985—. Author: (CD ROM) The Road to Compostela for Windows, 1998; (book) (with Alison Stones) The Pilgrim's Guide to Santiago da Compostela, 1998; contbr. articles to profl. jours. Discussion leader Pa. Humanities Coun., 1998. Huntington Library fellow, 1977, Humanities fellow Dartmouth Coll., 1991; recipient NEH stipend, Florence, Italy, 1994. Mem. APICES, Medieval Acad. Am., Medieval Latin Assn. N.Am., Friends of Rd. to Santiago, Early Books Soc. Avocations: cooking, travelling, book collecting. Office: Pa State U 3550 7th Street Rd New Kensington PA 15068-1765

KROCHALIS, RICHARD F., municipal government official. BS in Environ. Sys. Engring., Cornell U.; M in City and Regional Planning, Harvard U. Dir. Dept. of Constrn. and Land Use, Seattle, 1992—; examiner Wash. State Quality Award Bd., 1995-96. Bd. dirs. Sustainable Seattle; active Cornell U. Alumni Affairs; mem. coun. Cornell U., 1991-98. Mem. Urban Land Inst., Am. Planning Assn., Am. Inst. Cert. Planners, Wash. State City Planning Dir.'s Assn. (v.p.). Office: City of Seattle Dexter Horton Bldg 710 2nd Ave Ste 700 Seattle WA 98104-1712*

KROCK, CURTIS JOSSELYN, pulmonologist; b. Fort Smith, Ark., Oct. 11, 1935; s. Frederick Henry and Hazel Armiger (Josselyn) K.; m. Ruth Leone Johnson, Apr. 27, 1968; children: Eric Gregory, Lynn Alyson. BA, Stanford U., 1957; MD, Johns Hopkins U. Sch. Medicine, 1961. Diplomate Am. Bd. Internal Medicine, Am. Bd. Pulmonary Medicine. Intern Barnes Hosp., St. Louis, 1961-62, resident in internal medicine, 1963-65; resident in pathology Johns Hopkins U. Sch. Medicine, Balt., 1962-63; pulmonary fellow Duke U., Durham, N.C., 1965-66; pvt. practice Holt-Krock Clinic, Ft. Smith, Ark., 1966-72; pvt. practice Carle Clinic, Urbana, Ill., 1972—, also bd. dirs., 1978-80, chief medicine dept., 1996—; clin. asst. prof. U. Ill., Urbana, 1976—. Capt. U.S. Army, 1966-68, Denver, Colo. Fellow ACP; mem. Sierra Club, Sigma Xi. Avocations: violinist, reading. Home: 2125 Lynwood Dr Champaign IL 61821-6606 Office: Carle Clin 602 W University Ave Urbana IL 61801-2530

KROCKMAN, ARNOLD FRANCIS, publisher, advertising executive; b. N.Y.C., Sept. 4, 1945; s. Arnold W. and Alice Frances (Nowack) K.; m. Lorraine Edith Strunck, Jan. 19, 1980; 1 child, Alicia Lorraine. BA, Fordham U., 1970; MFA, Pratt Inst., 1973. Editor Studio Photography Mag., Melville, N.Y., 1977-78; assoc. editor Billboard Publs., N.Y.C., 1978-79; photographer Wagner Internat. Photos, N.Y.C., 1979-81; editor PR Newswire, N.Y.C., 1988-89; mgr. Fidata, Fort Lee, N.J., 1982-86; pub. AK Publs., East Rutherford, N.J., 1990—; v.p. Meadowlands Advt. Agy., East Rutherford, 1991-93; mktg. mgr. North Am. Thermal, Lyndhurst, N.J., 1992-94. Mem. N.Am. Book Dealers Exch., Mensa. Office: AK Publs PO Box 352 East Rutherford NJ 07073-0352

KROEBER, KARL, English language educator; b. Oakland, Calif., Nov. 24, 1926; s. Alfred Louis and Theodora Quinn (Kracaw) K.; m. Jean Taylor, Mar. 21, 1953; children—Paul Demarest, Arthur Romeyn, Katharine. AA, Coll. of Pacific, Stockton, Calif., 1945; AB, U. Calif., Berkeley, 1947; MA, Columbia U., 1951, PhD, 1956. Asst. prof. U. Wis.-Madison, 1956-61, asso. prof., 1961-63, prof., 1963-70; asso. dean U. Wis.-Madison (Grad. Sch.), 1963-65; prof. English and comparative lit. Columbia U., N.Y.C., 1970—, chmn. dept. English and comparative lit., 1973-76, Mellon prof. humanities, 1987. Author: Romantic Narrative Art, 1960, The Artifice of Reality, 1964, Studying Poetry, 1965, Backgrounds to British Romantic Literature, 1968, Styles in Fictional Structure, 1971, Romantic Landscape Vision, 1975, Images of Romanticism, 1978, Traditional Literatures of the American Indian, 1981, rev. edit. 1997, Wordsworthian Scholarship and Criticism, 1973-84, 1986, British Romantic Art, 1986, Romantic Fantasy and Science Fiction, 1988, Retelling/Rereading, 1992, Romantic Poetry: Recent Revisionary Criticism, 1993, Native American Persistence and Resurgence, 1994, Ecological Literary Criticism, 1994, Artistry in Native American Myths, 1998; emeritus editor Studies in American Indian Literatures; mem. editorial bd. The Wordsworth Circle, Native American Bibliography Series, Studies in English Lit., Boundary 2, European Romantic Review. Served with USNR, 1944-46. Named Disting. Scholar, Keats-Shelley Assn., 1991; Fulbright Rsch. grantee Italy, 1960-61, U.S. Office Edn. Rsch. grantee, 1965-66; Guggenheim fellow, 1966-67; NEH fellow, 1991. Mem. MLA, Internat. Assn. Univ. Profs. English, N.Am. Soc. Study of Romanticism, Jane Austen Soc. N.Am., Acad. Lit. Studies, Byron Soc., Assn. for Study of Native Am. Lit., Keats-Shelley Assn. Home: 226 St Johns Pl Brooklyn NY 11217-3406 Office: Columbia U Dept English & Comparative Lit New York NY 10027

KROEGER, ARTHUR, university chancellor, former government official; b. Naco, Alta., Can., Sept. 7, 1932; s. Heinrich and Helena (Rempel) K.; m. Gabrielle Jane Sellers, May 7, 1966 (dec.); children: Alexandra, Kate. BA with honors, U. Alta., 1955; BA, Oxford U., Eng., 1958; LLD (hon.), U. Western Ontario, Can., 1991, U. Calgary, Can., 1995. Fgn. service officer Can. Dept. External Affairs, 1958-71, treasury bd. secretariat, 1971-75, dep. minister Indian and No. affairs, 1975-79; dep. minister transport Can., Ottawa, Ont., 1979-83; sec. Ministry of State for Econ. Devel., Ottawa, Ont., 1983-84; spl. advisor to clk. Privy Council, 1984-85, dep. minister Regional Indsl. Expansion, 1985-86, dep. minister of Energy, Mines and Resources, 1986-88, dep. minister employment & immigration, 1988-92; chancellor Carleton U., Ottawa, Can., 1993—; vis. fellow Queen's U., Kingston, Ont., 1994—; vis. prof. U. Toronto, 1993-94; chmn. Pub. Policy Forum, Ottawa, 1992-94. Program chmn. Gov. Gen.'s Study Conf., 1995; chmn. Can. Policy Rsch. Networks; bd. dirs. The Parliamentary Ctr., Social Rsch. and Demonstration Corp., Transparency Internat., Can. Ctr. for Mgmt. Devel.; mem. adv. bd. Alta. N.E. G&S; mem. Nat. Stats. Coun.; mem. Panel on Voluntary Sector Governance, 1997-99. Decorated officer Order of Can.; recipient Pub. Svc. Outstanding Achievement award, 1989; Rhodes scholar, 1955. Mem. Can. Assn. Rhodes Scholars (exec. mem., pres. 1995-97). Club: Five Lakes Fishing. Home: 245 Springfield Rd, Ottawa, ON Canada K1M 0L1

KROEGER, LIN J., management consultant; b. Wilmington, Del., Mar. 24, 1952; s. John F. and Janice (Eddy) K. BA in Interdisciplinary Studies, Coll. William and Mary, 1974; MA in English, Villanova U., 1977; MA in Theater Arts, Cornell U., 1980. Tchr. Chevy Chase H.S., Bethesda, Md., 1974-75, Ewing H.S., Trenton, N.J., 1975-77; profl. specialist, course mgr. Arthur Andersen & Co., St. Charles, Ill., 1979-81; ind. mgmt. cons., pres. The Comm. Link Co. Inc., N.Y.C., N.J., 1982-94; ind. cons., 1994-96; sr. mgr. Andersen Cons., Change Navigation Leadership Team, N.Y.C., 1996-99; pres. PWD Cons., Inc., 1999—. Author: A Pragmatist Answers Questions About Making Presentations, 1994, The Complete Idiot's Guide to Business Presentations, 1997. Com. mem., spkr. Edn. Com. of Morris County C. of C. (N.J.), 1984-86. Mem. Inst. Mgmt. Cons. (cert.), N.Y. Human Resources Planners, Human Resource Planning Soc. Office: Andersen Cons 1345 Avenue Of The Americas New York NY 10105-0302

KROEHLER, RALPH S., association executive; b. Chgo., Mar. 6, 1930; s. Henry G. and Laura S. K.; m. Marjorie A. Engel, Aug. 29, 1952; 1 child, Beth A. Student, Elmhurst Coll., 1947-50. Cert. fundraising exec. Dist. exec. Boy Scouts Am., Freeport, Ill., 1956-60, Allegan, Mich., 1960-63; fin. dir. Boy Scouts Am., Grand Rapids, Mich., 1963-67, asst. scout exec., 1967-69; scout exec., CEO Boy Scouts Am., Waukegan, Ill., 1969-71, Janesville, Wis., 1971-80, Peoria, Ill., 1980-95; fundraising cons., Peoria, 1995—. Bd. dirs. Peoria City Beautiful, 1982-88. Mem. Nat. Soc. Fundraising Execs. (del. to nat. assembly 1992-95, pres. Ctrl. Ill. chpt. 1994-95, Outstanding Fundraising Exec. 1993), Rotary Club Peoria (pres. Beloit chpt. 1979-80). Mem. United Ch. of Christ. Avocations: Civil War research, genealogy, photography. Home: 6910 N Rockvale Dr Peoria IL 61614-2341

KROEKER, LISA DAWN, secondary education educator; b. Enid, Okla., Feb. 17, 1972; d. Lowell James and Linda Lee (Smith) K. Student, Phillips U., Enid, 1990-91; BA, Northwestern Okla. State U., 1995. Cert. secondary tchr., Okla. Tchr. drama, debate and speech Ponca City (Okla.) H.S., 1995-98; prof. speech, forensics and debate Cowley County C.C., Arkansas City, Ark., 1998—. Disciples of Christ scholar Phillips U., 1990, Phillips Acting Talent scholar, 1990, Acting Talent scholar Northwestern Okla. State U., 1991-94. Mem. Okla. Edn. Assn., Okla. Speech Theatre Comm. Assn., Okla. Fine Arts Camp, Alpha Psi Omega. Democrat. Avocations: reading, crafting, watching movies. Home: 2600 N 5th St Apt 111 Ponca City OK 74601-1648 Office: Cowley County Cmty Coll 125 S 2d St Arkansas City KS 67005

KROEMER, HERBERT, electrical engineering educator; b. Weimar, Ger., Germany, Aug. 25, 1928. Diplom-Physiker, Gottingen U., Ger., 1951, Dr. rer. nat., 1952; Doctorate (hon.), Tech. U. Aachen (Ger.), 1985, U. Lund, 1998. Prof. elec., computer engring. U. Calif. mem. NAE, IEEE (J.J. Ebers award 1973, Jack Morton award 1986), Am. Phys. Soc. Office: U Calif Elec-Computer Engring Dept Santa Barbara CA 93106

KROENER, WILLIAM FREDERICK, III, lawyer; b. N.Y.C., Aug. 27, 1945; s. William Frederick Jr. and Barbara (Mitchell) K.; m. Evelyn Somerville Bibb, Sept. 3, 1966; children: William F. IV (dec.), Mary Elizabeth, Evangeline Alberta, James Mitchell. AB, Yale Coll., 1967; JD, Stanford U., 1971, MBA, 1971. Bar: Calif. 1972, N.Y. 1979, D.C. 1983. Assoc. Davis Polk & Wardwell, N.Y.C. and London, 1971-79, ptnr., N.Y.C., 1979-82, Washington and N.Y.C., 1982-94; gen. counsel Fed. Deposit Ins. Corp., Washington, 1995—; lectr. law sch. Stanford (Calif.) U., 1993-94, George Washington U. Law Sch., Washington, 1994—, Washington Coll. Law, Am. U. Law Sch., Washington, 1996—. Mng. editor Stanford Law Rev., 1970-71. Mem. governing bd. St. Albans Sch., 1991-95; mem. finance com. Protestant/Episcopal Cathedral Found. (Wash. Nat. Cathedral), 1992-95; mem. bd. visitors Stanford U. Law Sch., 1983-92, mem. dean's adv. coun., 1992-93, nat. chair Stanford Law Fund, 1990-92; dir. and gen. counsel Kenwood Citizens Assn., Inc., 1993-94. Mem. ABA, Am. Law Inst., Assn. of Bar of City of N.Y., N.Y. Law Inst., Yale Club, Kenwood Golf Club. Republican. Episcopalian. Home: 6412 Brookside Dr Chevy Chase MD 20815-6649 Office: FDIC 550 17th St NW Washington DC 20429-0001

KROENERT, ROBERT MORGAN, lawyer; b. Kansas City, Mo., July 19, 1939; s. Robert Andrew and Marion Leona (Morgan) K.; m. Susan Aldrich, Aug. 18, 1962; children: Kathleen Susan, Ann Elizabeth, Robert Aldrich. BS, U. Kans., 1961; JD, U. Mich., 1964. Bar: Mo. 1964, U.S. Dist. Ct. (we. dist.) Mo. 1965, U.S. Ct. Appeals (8th cir.) 1984, U.S. Ct. Appeals (5th, 10th and D.C. cirs.) 1986, U.S. Supreme Ct. 1991. Assoc. Morrison & Hecker L.L.P., Kansas City, 1964-69; ptnr. Morrison & Hecker, Kansas City, 1969—. Bd. dirs. Guadalupe Ctr., Inc., Kansas City, 1978-87; mem. adv. bd. greater univ. fund, U. Kans., Lawrence, 1985-88; Mem. fin. com. Johnson County Rep. Com., 1987-90, Mo. Supreme Ct. Disciplinary Com. for Jackson County, 1992—, divsn. chair, 1995-97; mem. coun. Colonial Congregtional Ch., 1990-93, moderator, 1991-93. Mem. Mo. Bar, Kansas City Met. Bar Assn., Internat. Assn. Def. Counsel, Mo. Orgn. Def. Lawyers, Lawyers Assn. Kansas City (bd. dirs., pres.), Kansas City Club, Mission Hills Country Club, Rotary. Avocation: golf. Office: Morrison & Hecker LLP 2600 Grand Blvd Ste 1200 Kansas City MO 64108-4606

KROENKE, STAN, sports association administrator; b. Cole Camp, Mo.; m. Ann Kroenke; children: Whitney, Josh. Degree, U. Mo., grad. degree. Chmn., owner The Kroenke Group, Columbia, Mo.; vice chmn., owner St. Louis Rams; bd. dirs. Wal-Mart Stores, Inc., Cmty. Investment Partnership I and II, St. Louis, Boone County Nat. Bank, Columbia, Ctrl. Bancompany, Jefferson City, Mo. Trustee Coll. of the Ozarks; mem. strategic devel. bd. U. Mo. Sch. Bus.; trustee Mo. Basketball Hall of Fame. Office: St Louis Rams 1 Rams Way Earth City MO 63045-1525*

KROESEN, FREDERICK JAMES, retired army officer, consultant; b. Phillipsburg, N.J., Feb. 11, 1923; s. Frederick James K. and Jean Ursula (Shillinger) Kroesen; m. Rowene Wilder McCray, Mar. 4, 1944; children: Karen McCray Kroesen Klare, Frederick J. III, Gretchen McCray Kroesen Tackaberry. BS in Agr., Rutgers U., 1944, LHD (hon.), 1983; BA in Internat. Affairs, George Washington U., 1962, MA in Internat. Affairs, 1966. Enlisted U.S. Army, 1942, commd. 2d lt., 1944; served with 63d Infantry div. U.S. Army, Europe; advanced through grades to gen. U.S. Army, 1976; served with 187th Airborne Regimental Combat Team, Korean War, 1953-55; instr. U.S. Army War Coll., 1962-65; mem. staff asst. chief of staff for force devel. U.S. Army, 1965-68, 70-71; served with Americal Div. Vietnam War, 1968 and 1971, comdr. Div., 1971; dep. comdr. XXIV Corps. U.S. Army, 1971-72, comdr. 1st Regn. Asst Command, VN, 1972, comdr. 82d Airborne Div., 1972-74, comdr. VII Corps., 1975-76, comdr. U.S. Army Forces Command, 1976-78, vice chief of staff U.S. Army, 1978-79; comdr.-in-chief U.S. Army in Europe, 1979-83; comdr. NATO Cen. Army Group Heidelberg, Germany, 1979-83; ret., 1983; pvt. cons. in internat. security affairs; former mem. Army Sci. Bd.; chmn. emeritus Mil. Profl. Resources, Inc. Decorated Def. D.S.M., Army D.S.M. with oak leaf cluster, Purple Heart with 2 oak leaf clusters, Silver Star with oak leaf cluster, Legion of Merit with 2 oak leaf clusters, D.F.C., Bronze Star with V and 2 oak leaf clusters, combat inf. badge with two stars; recipient Mil. Order of World War Disting. Svc. medal, 1985, Americanism award Am. Legion, 1993, State of N.J. Disting. Svc. medals, 1983, 95; named to Rutgers Hall Disting. Alumni, Rutgers Loyal Son. Fellow Inst. Land Warfare (sr.), Assn. U.S. Army; mem. U.S. Army War Coll. Alumni Assn. (former pres.), U.S. Army War Coll. Found. (past bd. dirs.), 63d Div. Assn., 82d Div. Assn., Amcl Div. Vets. Assn., Rakkasan Assn., Soc. French Legion of Honor, Soc. Rhin et Danube, Delta Upsilon. Home: 1250 S Washington St # 223 Alexandria VA 22314-4455

KROFT, GLENN VINCENT, painter; b. Lansing, Mich., Apr. 23, 1965; s. Glenn Aldro and Julie Ann (Murphy) K.; m. Vanessa Lynn Hoage, Oct. 21, 1995; children: Aria Lajauette, Jenna Lajauette, Renee Taresa. Grad. H.S., Ithaca, N.Y. Painter Paint Am., East Herkimer, N.Y., 1990; entrepreneur K-T Enterprises, Herkimer, 1998. Author: On My Way From Home, 1998. Avocation: chain rotations. Home: 124 Main St Apt 1 East Herkimer NY 13357

KROFT, STEVE, news correspondent, editor; b. Kokomo, Ind., Aug. 22, 1945; s. Fred and Margaret K.; m. Jennet Conant, June 29, 1991; 1 child, John Conant. BS, Syracuse U., 1967; MS in Journalism, Columbia U., 1975. Reporter Sta. WSYR-TV, Syracuse, N.Y., 1972-74; investigative reporter Sta. WJXT-TV, Jacksonville, Fla., 1975-77; reporter Sta. WPLG-TV, Miami, Fla., CBS News, N.Y.C., 1980-81; corr. S.W. bur. CBS News, Dallas, 1981-83; corr. Cen. Am. bur. CBS News, Miami, 1983-84; corr. CBS News, London, 1984-86; prin. corr. W. 57th program CBS News, N.Y.C., 1986-89, corr., co-editor 60 Minutes, 1989—. Trustee Syracuse U. Sgt. U.S. Army, 1970-71; Vietnam. Recipient Ohio State award Ohio Stte U., 1979, 92, 94, Emmy awards, 1982 (2), 84, 90, 93 (2), Arents award Syracuse U., 1992, George Foster Peabody award, 1992. Office: CBS News 60 Minutes 555 W 57th St New York NY 10019-2925*

KROGH-JESPERSEN, MARY-BETH, academic administrator; b. Schenectady, N.J., Aug. 10, 1949; d. George Henry and Barbara V. (Norton) Baillie; m. Karsten Krogh-Jespersen, Dec. 20, 1975; children: Erik, Sheila Ann, Michelle Grace. BA in Chemistry, Northeastern U., 1972; MBA, Pace U., 1990; PhD in Chemistry, NYU, 1976. Lectr. in chemistry Rutgers U., New Brunswick, N.J., 1979-81; prof. Pace U., N.Y.C., 1981-92, chair dept. chemistry, 1990-92; dean coll. of sci. Rochester (N.Y.) Inst. Tech., 1992-95; vice provost Rowan Coll., Glassboro, N.J., 1995-96; assoc. v.p. for acad. affairs Richard Stockton Coll., Pomona, N.J., 1996—. Contbr. articles to profl. jours. Mem. Am. Chem. Soc., Am. Phys. Soc. Roman Catholic. Office: Richard Stockton Coll Jim Leeds Rd Pomona NJ 08240

KROGIUS, TRISTAN ERNST GUNNAR, international marketing consultant, lawyer; b. Tammerfors, Finland, Apr. 13, 1933; came to U.S., 1939; s. Helge Lorenz and Valborg Isolde (Antell) K.; m. Barbara Jane Brophy, Aug. 29, 1952; children—Ferril Anne, Lars Anthony, Karin Therese, Eric Lorenz, Marian Elaine, Rebecca Kristina. B.A., U. N.Mex., 1954; M.A., Calif. State U.-Los Angeles, 1962; student Advanced Mgmt. Program, Harvard U., 1980; JD, Western State U., 1990. Bar: Calif. 1991. With Scott Paper Co., Phila., 1960-65, Hunt-Wesson Foods, Fullerton, Calif., 1965-75; pres. Hunt-Wesson Foods Can., Ltd., Toronto, Ont., 1969-71, pres. frozen and refrigerated foods div., 1971-75; pres., chief exec. officer Dalgety Foods, Salinas, Calif., 1975-78; v.p., gen. mgr. food div. Tenneco West, Inc., Bakersfield, Calif., 1978-80, pres., chief exec. officer, 1981-87; pres. Landmark Mgmt., Inc., 1987-88; ptnr. The Cons. Co., South Laguna, 1988-90, Internat. Mktg. Consultancy, 1990—; adj. prof. Western State U. Coll. of Law, 1992-97. Bd. dirs. South Coast Med. Ctr., Laguna Beach, Calif., 1969-74, pres., CEO, 1974; bd. dirs. South Sierra coun. Boy Scouts Am., 1981-87, Calif. State Coll. Found., Bakersfield, 1983-87, Found. for 21st Century, 1987-90; mgr. elder abuse program Pub. Law Ctr., 1992-93. Capt. USMC, 1954-60. Recipient World Food award Ariz. State U., Tempe, 1982. Republican. Episcopalian.

KROGSTAD, JACK LYNN, accounting educator; b. Harlan, Iowa, Jan. 27, 1944; s. Chester Milo and Geraldine Elizabeth (Archibald) K.; m. Nancy Ellen Coffin, June 18, 1967; children: Kristine Ellen, Brian Lynn. BS, Union Coll., 1967; MBA, U. Nebr., 1971, PhD, 1975. Staff acct. Trachtenbarg & Grant CPAs, Lincoln, Nebr., 1967-68; asst. prof. U. Tex., Austin, 1975-78; assoc. prof. Kans. State U., Manhattan, 1978-80; John P. Begley prof. acctg. Creighton U., Omaha, 1980-96, prof. acctg., 1997—; vis. assoc. prof. U. Mich., Ann Arbor, 1980; dir. rsch. Nat. Commn. Fraudulent Fin. Reporting, 1985-87. Editor: Auditing: A Journal of Practice and Theory; contbr. articles to profl. jours. With U.S. Army, 1968-70. Recipient Disting. Faculty Svc. award Creighton U., 1988; Arthur Anderson & Co. doctoral fellow, 1974-75, Paton Acctg. Ctr. rsch. fellow, 1980. Mem. AICPA, Nebr. Soc. CPAs (Acctg. Educator of Yr. award 1983), Am. Acctg. Assn. (regional v.p. 1984-85, auditing sect. chmn. 1984-85, Outstanding Auditing Educator award 1994), Beta Gamma Sigma, Beta Alpha Psi. Republican. Seventh-Day-Adventist. Home: 56717 Deacon Rd Pacific Junction IA 51561-4169

KROH, MARK SINCLAIR, educational administrator; b. Manchester, Md., May 12, 1969; s.Loren Henry Kroh and Elizabeth (Hook) Irish; m. Kari Ann Behers, July 19, 1995. BA with honors in Art History, Bucknell U., 1994. Coord. continuing edn. Bradley Acad. for Visual Arts, York, Pa., 1995-97, dir. continuing edn., 1997—. Bd. dirs. Yorkarts, 1997—. Mem. Agrl. and Natural Lands Trust, Multiple Sclerosis Found., Advt. Club Ctrl. Pa. Avocations: permaculture, restoration. Office: Bradley Acad for Visual Arts 1409 Williams Rd York PA 17402-9012

KROHA, BRADFORD KING, electronics manufacturing corporation executive; b. Rochester, N.Y., Dec. 16, 1926; s. George Frederic and Neva Alice (Smy) Kroha; m. Nona Jane Hobbs, June 15, 1979; children: Nancy, Judy, Sally, Jane, Robert. B.E.E., Yale U., 1947; B.S. in Indsl. Adminstrn., 1948; postgrad., Harvard U. Grad. Sch. Bus. Adminstrn., 1952. Gen. mgr. Can. Motorola Ltd., Toronto, Ont., 1969-72; dir. internat. subs. Motorola Inc., Schaumburg, Ill., 1972-77, asst. gen. mgr. communications internat. div., 1977-79, v.p., gen. mgr. European communications div., 1979-85; v.p., dir. communications sector sourcing Motorola Inc., 1985-88; ret., 1988. Served with USNR, 1944-46. Mem. Barrington Hills Country Club, Club PGA West. Republican. Presbyterian. Home: 101 Lakeside Ct Barrington IL 60010-6953*

KROHN, CLAUS DANKERTSEN, insurance company executive; b. Oslo, Jan. 7, 1923; came to U.S., 1950; s. Dankert and Marie (Skjolden) K.; m. Madeline M. Moore, Oct. 10, 1954; 1 child, Christina Marie. Student, Oslo Katedralskole, Norway, 1947; student, Oslo U., 1947-49; MBA, Ind. U., 1951. Cons. Samvirke Ins. Co., Oslo, 1953-54; asst. sec. Manhattan Life Ins. Co., N.Y.C., 1954-59; sys. mgr. Raytheon Co., Andover, Mass., 1959-62; v.p. sys. Ohio Nat. Life Ins. Co., Cin., 1962-76, sr. v.p., 1977-88, also bd. dirs. Fellow Am. Scandinavian Found., 1950. Mem. LOMA/Life Ins. Assn. (adv. coun.), Den Gode Hensight Club (Bergen, Norway). Republican. Lutheran. Avocations: skiing, fishing. Home: 2324 Madison Rd Cincinnati OH 45208-2671

KROHN, FRANKLIN BERNARD, marketing specialist, educator; b. Erie, Pa., July 1, 1933; s. Lewis Harry and Marian (Post) K.; m. Alice Lester Krohn, July 4, 1954 (div. Mar. 1969); children: Debra, Robert, Lynette; m. Inez Claire Judelsohn, Aug. 23, 1973. BA, SUNY, Buffalo, 1971, MA, 1974, PhD, 1977. Disting. Svc. prof. bus adminstrn. and mktg. SUNY, Fredonia, 1978—; bd. dirs. Small Bus. Inst., SUNY, Fredonia, 1986—. Contbr. articles to profl. jours. Chmn. Brocton (N.Y.) Tourism Promotion Group, 1987-88. Served with U.S. Army, 1954-56. Recipient DeWitt Clinton Masonic award Lake Shore Lodge 851, 1988, Chancellor's award SUNY, 1987, Robert A. Beck Ethics Journalism award, 1992, 95, SUNY Disting. Svc. Prof. award, 1993, Pres. award for Excellence in Tchg. SUNY, Fredonia, 1999; Sam M. Walton Free Enterprise fellow Students in Free Enterprise, 1995—. Mem. Am. Mktg. Assn. (bd. dirs. Buffalo/Niagara chpt. 1984-90), Assn. for Bus. Communication, Assn. Mktg. Educators, Internat. Soc. for Gen. Semantics, Sml. Bus. Inst. Directors' Assn. (region II v.p. 1993-94). Home: 136 Old Mill Rd Brocton NY 14716-9630 Office: SUNY Dept Bus Adminstrn Fredonia NY 14063

KROHN, KENNETH ALBERT, radiology educator; b. Stevens Point, Wis., June 19, 1945; s. Albert William and Erma Belle (Cornwell) K.; 1 child, Galen. BA in Chemistry, Andrews U., 1966; PhD in Chemistry, U. Calif., 1971. Acting assoc. prof. U. Wash., Seattle, 1981-84, assoc. prof. radiology, 1984-86, prof. radiology and radiation oncology, 1986—, adj. prof. chemistry, 1986—; guest scientist Donner Lab. Lawrence Berkeley (Calif.) Lab., 1980-81; radiochemist, VA Med. Ctr., Seattle, 1982—; affiliate investigator Fred Hutchinson Cancer Rsch. Ctr., 1997—. Contbr. articles to profl. jours.; patentee in field. NDEA fellow; recipient Aebersold award, 1996. Fellow AAAS; mem. Am. Assn. for Cancer Rsch., Am. Chem. Soc., Radiation Rsch. Soc., Soc. Nuclear Medicine, Acad. Coun., Sigma Xi. Home: 550 NE Lakeridge Dr Belfair WA 98528-8720 Office: U Washington Imaging Rsch Lab PO Box 356004 Seattle WA 98195-6004

KROHNKE, DUANE W., lawyer; b. Keokuk, Iowa, June 29, 1939; s. Ward Glenn and Marian Frances (Brown) K.; m. Mary Alyce Luschen, June 25, 1963; children: Alan Duane, Brian Douglas. BA, Grinnell (Iowa) Coll., 1961, Oxford U., 1963; MA, Oxford U., 1970; JD, U. Chgo., 1966. Bar: N.Y. 1967, Minn. 1970, U.S. Supreme Ct. 1970, U.S. Ct. Appeals (2d cir.) 1967, U.S. Ct. Appeals (8th cir.) 1970, U.S. Ct. Appeals (D.C.) 1974, U.S. Dist. Ct. (so., ea. dists.) N.Y. 1967, U.S. Dist. Ct. Minn. 1970. Assoc. atty. Cravath, Swaine, Moore, N.Y.C., 1966-70; assoc. atty. Faegre & Benson, Mpls., 1970-73, ptnr., 1974—. Editorial bd. U. Chgo., 1964-66. Co-chair Bicentennial com. U.S. Dist. Ct. Minn. dist., Mpls., 1986-88; elder Westminster Presbyn. Ch., Mpls., 1985-91; trustee United Theol. Seminary, New Brighton, Minn., 1988-98. Recipient Alumni award Grinnell Coll., 1982; Rhodes scholar Rhodes Trustees, Oxford, Eng., 1961-63; Mecham scholar U. Chgo., 1963-66. Mem. ABA, Minn. State Bar Assn. (co-chair antitrust sect. 1982-84, co-chair ethics/standards of practice com. of conflict mgmt. and dispute resolution sect. 1995-96, chair-elect conflict mgmt. and dispute resolution sect. 1996-97, chair conflict mgmt. and dispute resolution sect. 1997-98), Fed. Bar Assn., Minn. Human Rights Advocates (vol. award 1991), Order of Coif, Phi Beta Kappa. Avocations: reading, cultural events, exercise. Office: Faegre & Benson 2200 Northwest Ctr 90 S 7th St Ste 2200 Minneapolis MN 55402-3901

KROIS, AUDREY, artist; b. Boston, Mar. 14, 1934; d. Henry and Lillian Marie (Mueller) Haeberle; m. Richard Gamage, May 14, 1966 (div. Mar. 1975); m. Joseph E. Krois Jr., June 17, 1978. BA, Syracuse U., 1956; MSW,

Columbia U., 1958; postgrad., Fashion Inst. Tech., 1964-66, Art Students League, 1973-76. Social worker Pleasantville (N.Y.) Cottage Sch., 1958-62; cons. to UNICEF UN, Bangkok, Thailand, 1963; supr. vol. program Henry St. Settlement, N.Y.C., 1964-66; dir. cmty. devel. program Anti Poverty Funding, N.Y.C., 1966-68; supervising dir., asst. v.p., cons. Divsn. Homemaker, Home Health Care, G.H.I., Inc., N.Y.C., 1969-78. One-woman shows at Clayton Liberatore Gallery, Bridgehampton, N.Y., 1995, 96, South Palm Beach Town Hall Gallery, 1998, Southampton Town Hall, 1998; exhibited in group shows at Access to the Arts, Jamestown, N.Y., 1981, Embroiders Guild and Abigail Adams Smith Mus., N.Y.C., 1982, Arrowmont Sch., Gatlinburg, Tenn., 1982, Gayle Willson Gallery, Southampton, N.Y., 1983, 88, Discovery Art Gallery, Glen Cove, N.Y., 1989, Decatur House, Washington, 1990, Mus. Am. Quilter Soc., Paducah, Ky., 1992, Vanderbilt Mus., Centerport, N.Y., 1992, 94, Wellspring Gallery, Santa Monica, Calif., 1993, 94, Aullwood Audubon Ctr., Dayton, Ohio, 1996 (Best of Show). Recipient 2d Pl. award Brookhaven Arts and Humanities Coun., 1997, 2d Pl. award East End Arts Coun., 1998. Mem. South Fork Craft Assn., Southampton Artists Assn. (bd. dirs. 1990-96, fin. dir. 1992-93, pres. 1994, Award of Excellence in Watercolor, 1994, 95, 96), Godoman Design Gallery (Award of Merit in Watercolor 1993), Palm Beach Watercolor Soc., Armory Art Ctr. Fla. Home: PO Box 2482 Palm Beach FL 33480-2482 also: PO Box 960 Southampton NY 11969-0960

KROL, JOHN A., retired diversified chemicals executive; b. Gilbertsville, Mass., Oct. 16, 1936; m. Janet Ruth Valley, Sept. 12, 1938; children: Cynthia, Deborah. BS, MS in chemistry, Tufts U., 1958, MS in Phys. Chemistry, 1959. With textile fibers sect. of DuPont Chestnut Run Rsch. Lab., Wilmington, Del., 1963-65; mktg. rep. Centre Road Office, Wilmington, Del., 1965-66, supr. indsl. tech. mktg., 1966-69; mktg. mgr. N.Y.C., 1969-70; mktg. mgr. industrial fibers Akron, Ohio, 1970-72; regional mktg. mgr. Textile Fibers, Wynnewood, Pa., 1972-73; product mgr. Dacron, Wilmington, Del., 1973-75; mfg. supt. Dacron, Old Hickory, Tenn., 1975-77; asst. plant mgr. mfg. DuPont, Old Hickory, Tenn., 1975-78; mktg. dir. DuPont Carpet Fibers and FIberfill divsn., Wilmington, 1978-80, dir., 1980-83; v.p. fibers DuPont DeNemours & Co., Wilmington, 1983-86, v.p. agrl. products dept., 1986-87; group v.p. agrl. products, 1987-90; sr. v.p. fibers DuPont DeNemours & Co., Wilmington, 1990-91, vice chmn., 1992—, dir.; chmn. DuPont DeNemours & Co., 1997—; bd. dirs. Mead Corp., Nat. Assn. Manufactures, Del. Art Mus.; bd. trustees Tufts Univ., Univ. Del., Elwyn Inst. Handicapped; corp. liaison bd. Am. Chemical Soc. Served to lt. USN, 1959-63. Mem. Nat. Agrl. Chems. Assn. (bd. dirs. 1987—). Republican. Roman Catholic. Clubs: Radley Run Country (West Chester, Pa.) (bd. govs.), Rodney Sq. (Wilmington), Wilmington Country, Bonita Bay Country (Naples, Fla.). Avocations: golf, skiing, squash, tennis. Home: 1001 General Stevens Dr West Chester PA 19382-8037 Office: DuPont 1007 N Market St Fl 2 Wilmington DE 19801-1229*

KROL, JOHN CASIMIR, city manager, municipal planner; b. Chelmsford, Essex, Eng., June 1, 1949; came to U.S., 1951; s. Fortunat and Stanislawa (Kosowicz) K.; m. Linda Sue Wright, Jan. 2, 1971; children: Pamela, Suzanne, Michael. BS, Clarkson Coll. Technol., 1971; MS, SUNY, Buffalo, 1977. Planner St. Lawrence County, Canton, N.Y., 1971-74, county adminstrv. asst., 1984-85; sr. planner Town of Amherst, Williamsville, N.Y., 1974-77; planning dir. Clinton County, Plattsburg, N.Y., 1977-79, City of Ogdensburg(N.Y.), 1979-83; city mgr. City of Ogdensburg (N.Y.), 1987—; planning commr. Broome County, Binghamton, N.Y., 1986-87. Bd. dirs Soc. United Helpers, Ogdensburg, 1983-84, Ogdensburg Boys and Girls Club, 1990-93, Ogdensburg Minor Hockey Assn., 1993-97; co-chair annual city fund drive Am. Cancer Soc., Ogdensburg, 1982. Mem. Am. Inst. Cert. Planners, Mcpl. Mgmt. Assn. N.Y. State (dir. 1987-92, pres. 1992-93), Internat. City Mgrs. Assn., St. Lawrence County C. of C. (bd. dirs. 1988-94), Greater Ogdensburg C. of C. (bd. dirs. 1992-97). Presbyterian. Home: 515 John St Ogdensburg NY 13669-2007 Office: City of Ogdensburg 330 Ford St Ogdensburg NY 13669-1626

KROL, JOSEPH JOHN, JR., career officer; b. Washington, Pa., 1944; m. Carolyn Krol. Grad., U.S. Naval Acad., 1967. Commd. 2d lt. USN, 1967, advanced through grades to rear admiral, 1983; various divsn. officer assignments USS Nathanael Greene, 1969-72; navigator, ops. officer USS Andrew Jackson, 1972; navigation br. head Fleet Readiness & Tng. Br. Strategic Sys. Project Office, Washington; exec. officer USS Phoenix, 1979-82; commdg. officer USS Norfolk, 1983-85, USS Oklahoma City, 1985-87, Submarine Squadron 8, Norfolk, Va., 1990-91; spl. asst. to dir. Naval Nuclear Propulsion Program U.S. Dept. Energy, 1987-90; nuclear program mgr., head submarine detailer Bur. Naval Pers., Washington, 1991-93; chief staff Atlantic Fleet Submarine Force, 1993-98; dir. Deep Submergence Br. OPNAV; comdr. submarine group 7 Japan, 1998—. Office: USN 2000 Navy Pentagon Washington DC 20350-2000*

KROL, NANCY ANN, critical care nurse; b. Buffalo, Mar. 2, 1949; d. Walter S. and Dorothy M. (Bojanek) K. Diploma in nursing, Sisters of Charity Hosp., Buffalo, 1970. RN, N.Y.; CCRN. Staff nurse neonatal surg. ICU, Sisters of Charity Hosp., staff nurse surgery-recovery rm., charge nurse ICU; charge nurse, preceptor Buffalo Gen. Hosp.; mem. nursing edn. study group to Australia and New Zealand, 1986; apptd. panel mem. Nat. Practitioner Data Bank, 1997. Co-author play for Internat. Critical Care Conf., Niagara Falls, N.Y., 1994 (videotaped for edn. use 1995); contbr. articles to nursing newsletter. Mem. AACN (cert., nominations com. 1988 Western N.Y. chpt., publs. com. 1989. Home: 137 Pierce St Buffalo NY 14206-3328

KROLIK, JULIAN HENRY, astrophysicist, educator; b. Detroit, Apr. 4, 1950; m. Elaine F. Weiss, Oct. 9, 1983; children: Theodore, Abigail. BS, MIT, 1971; PhD, U. Calif., Berkeley, 1977. Mem. Inst. for Advanced Study, Princeton, N.J., 1977-79; postdoctoral scientist MIT, Cambridge, Mass., 1979-81; rsch. assoc. Harvard U., Cambridge, Mass., 1981-84; asst. prof. Johns Hopkins U., Balt., 1984-86, assoc. prof., 1986-91, prof., 1991—. Office: Johns Hopkins Univ Dept Of Physics Astron Baltimore MD 21218

KROLL, ARTHUR HERBERT, lawyer, educator, consultant; b. N.Y.C., Dec. 2, 1939; s. Abraham and Sylvia Kroll; m. Lois Handmacher, June, 1964; children: Douglas, Pamela. BA, Cornell U., 1961; LLB cum laude, St. John's U., 1965; LLM in Taxation, NYU, 1969. Bar: D.C. Assoc. Patterson, Belknap, Webb & Tyler, N.Y.C., 1965-72, ptnr., 1972-1990; ptnr. Pryor, Cashman, Sherman & Flynn, N.Y.C., 1990-95; CEO KST Consulting Group, Inc.; adj. prof. U. Miami Sch. Law, NYU; lectr. numerous confs.; mem. adv. bd. Bur. Nat. Affairs Tax Mgmt., Inc., Practising Law Inst. Tax Adv. Bd., U. Miami Inst. Estate Planning, Bus. Laws, Inc.; mem. adv. com. NYU Ann. Inst. on Fed. Taxation. Author Executive Compensation, 3 vols., Compensating Executives; monthly newsletter Family Bus. Profl.; mem. bd. contbg. editors and advisers Corporate Taxation; mem. editl. adv. bd. Jour. Compensation and Benefits. Mem. ABA (subcom. exec. compensation), Am. Pension Conf. (mem. steering com.). Office: KST Consulting Group Inc 50 1/2 E 64th St New York NY 10021

KROLL, BARRY LEWIS, lawyer; b. Chgo., June 8, 1934; s. Harry M. and Hannah (Lewis) K.; m. Jayna Vivian Leibovitz, June 20, 1956; children: Steven Lee, Joan Lois Kroll Dolgin, Nancy Maxine Kroll Richardson. A.B. in Psychology with distinction, U. Mich., 1955, J.D. with distinction, 1958. Bar: Ill. 1958. Since practiced in Chgo.; assoc. firm Jacobs & McKenna, 1958-66, Epstein, Manilow & Sachnoff, 1966-68, Schiff, Hardin, Waite Dorschel & Britton, 1968-69; partner firm Wolfberg & Kroll, 1970-74, Kirshbaum & Kroll, 1972-74; of counsel Jacobs, Williams & Montgomery, Ltd., 1973-74; partner Jacobs, Williams & Montgomery Ltd., 1974-85, Williams & Montgomery Ltd., 1985—; faculty John Marshall Law Sch., Chgo., 1969-73; atty. for petitioner in U.S. Supreme Ct. decision Escobedo vs Ill., 1964, guest lectr. before groups, 1964—; mem. legal and legis. com. Internat. Franchise Assn., 1976-80. Asst. editor: Mich. Law Rev, 1957-58. Chmn. Park Forest Bd. Zoning Appeals, 1971-78. Served to capt. AUS, 1959-62. Named Outstanding Young Man Park Forest Jr. C. of C., 1966. Mem. Ill. Bar Assn., Chgo. Bar Assn. (chmn. legis. com. 1974-75), Ill. Appellate Lawyers Assn. (treas. 1978-79, sec. 1979-80, pres. 1981-82), Bar Assn. 7th Fed. Circuit, Order of Coif, Tau Epsilon Rho, Alpha Epsilon Pi. Jewish (trustee congregation 1966-70, 72-75, 90—, pres. men's club 1965-66). Home: 1440 N State Pky Chicago IL 60610-1564 Office: Williams & Montgomery 20 N Wacker Dr Chicago IL 60606-2806

KROLL, C(HARLES) DOUGLAS, minister; b. Florence, S.C., June 19, 1949; s. Clifford Carl and Martha Kurtain (Gasque) K.; m. Lana Gale Gerling, May 1, 1976; children: Timothy, Matthew. BS, USCG Acad., 1971; MDiv, Luther Theol. Sem., 1980; MA, U. San Diego, 1985. Ordained to ministry Luth. Ch.-Mo. Synod, 1980. Assoc. pastor Faith Luth. Ch., Saginaw, Mich., 1980-81; instr. Luth. High Sch., San Diego, 1984-85; dean of chapel Luth. High Sch., LaVerne, Calif., 1985-86; pastor St. Paul's Luth. Ch., Pomona, Calif., 1986-99; chaplain US Naval Reserve, various cities, 1981-96, Old Baldy Coun. Boy Scouts Am., Ontario, Calif., 1986—; chmn. Nat. Luth. Com. on Civic Youth Agys., 1990-93; dir. Scouting in the Luth. Ch. conf., 1991. Author: A History of Navy Chaplains Serving With the Coast Guard, 1982; contbr. articles to profl. jours. Mem. religious relationships com. Boy Scouts Am., 1991—. Recipient Lamb award Luth. Coun. USA, 1987, Silver Beaver award Boy Scouts Am., 1989. Mem. Am. Legion (chaplain 1990-91). Home: 524 W Foxpark Dr Claremont CA 91711-3630

KROLL, DENNIS EDWARDS, industrial engineering educator; b. Chgo., June 7, 1947; s. Witold Charles and Lillian Mary (Zwic) K.; m. Susan Ann Michalski, May 26, 1973 (div. Dec. 1979); children: Steven Edward, Brian Christopher; m. Karen Elizabeth Wood, Jan. 13, 1990 (div. Sept. 1994). BS in Indsl. Engring., Bradley U., 1970; MS in Indsl. Engring., U. Wis., 1973; PhD, U. Ill., 1989. Devel. engr. Western Electric Co., Chgo., 1970-74; plant mgr. Junis Mfg. Co., Franklin Park, Ill., 1974-75; sr. indsl. engr. Sunbeam Appliance Co., Chgo., 1975-76; sr. mfg. engr. Victor Comptometer, Chgo., 1976; indsl. engr. Methode Mfg., Rolling Meadows, Ill., 1976-77; planning engr. Western Electric div. AT&T Tech., Lisle, Ill., 1977-81; assoc. prof. indsl. engring. Bradley U., Peoria, Ill., 1981—. Founding editor Jour. Indsl. Engring. Design, 1995—; contbr. articles to profl. jours., chpts. to books. Precinct committeeman Peoria Rep. Com., 1981-82; mem. bd. West Peoria (Ill.) Street Light Dist., 1991-95; founding alderman City of West Peoria, 1993—; mem. Peoria Water Adv. Com., 1999—. Recipient lab. devel. award Soc. Mfg. Engrs., 1990, Simulation Lab. Devel. award St. Francis Med. Ctr., 1995. Mem. Soc. Mfg. Engrs. (sr.), Inst. Indsl. Engrs. (sr.; cert. sys. integrator, chpt. pres. 1982-83, 94-95), Am. Legion, Planetary Soc., Am. Soc. for Engring. Edn. (IE Divsn. webmaster, sec., newsletter eidtor). Roman Catholic. Avocations: fishing, gardening, cooking, history. Office: Bradley U IMET Morgan 110 1501 W Bradley Ave Peoria IL 61625-0002

KROLL, NATHAN, film producer, director; b. N.Y.C., Nov. 5, 1911; s. Samuel-Louis Kroll and Sarah Silverstein; m. Lucy Rosengardt, Nov. 5, 1939 (div. 1974); 1 child, Stephen Robert; m. Claire Birsh Merrill, Aug. 7, 1982; children: Philip Merrill, Lucy Merrill. Student, The Juilliard Sch. Music, 1926. Concert violinist, 1925-32; film producer, dir. Kroll Prodns. Inc., N.Y.C. Producer/dir. (films) The Guns of August (1st prize at Am. Film Festival for the following) Pavarotti at Juilliard, The World of Carl Sandburg, A Dancer's World, Casals Master Class Series, Appalachian Spring; (1st prizes for the following TV films), Heifetz Master Class Series, Segovia Master Class Series, Who's Afraid of Opera? with Joan Sutherland; (TV spls.) Masterpieces and Music, One Man's Triumph (Peabody Awards); Helen Hayes-Portrait of an American Actress (Emmy Award); (multimedia) Lillian Gish and the Movies, The Segovia Legacy, 1990; (miniseries) Commodore Perry and the Opening of Japan, 1993; condr., composer radio-TV. Served with USAF, 1942-45. The Juilliard Sch. Music fellow, 1926. Avocations: tennis, music, historical research. Home and Office: Kroll Prodns Inc 247 Martling Ave Tarrytown NY 10591-4707

KROLL, PAUL BENEDICT, auditor; b. Ft. Ord, Calif., Oct. 24, 1954; s. Harry Gardner and Jane Ellen (Cornwell) K.; 1 child, Dane Garcia. BA, Kans. Wesleyan U., 1977; MS, Emporia State U., 1979, MBA, 1983; cert. tchr., Washburn U., 1990. Cert. tchr., Kans., Tex. Pension adminstr. Kansas City (Mo.) Life Ins., 1980-82; actuary Victory Life Ins. Co., Topeka, 1983-85; actuarial analyst Security Trust Life Ins., Macon, Ga., 1985-87; policy examiner Kans. Ins. Dept., Topeka, 1987-88; adj. instr. math. Highland (Kans.) C.C., 1991-93; premium auditor Mountain States Mus. Cos., Albuquerque, 1993—; owner Kroll Ins. Transl. Author: The Student's T Distribution, 1979. Mem. Ins. Inst. Am. (assoc. premium auditor). Avocations: short wave listening, bird watching, tennis. Home and Office: 7516 Pecos Trl NW Albuquerque NM 87120-2826

KROLL, SANDRA L., healthcare facility administrator; b. Cleve., June 2, 1938; d. Gustave and Ruth (Davis) Donner; m. Charles Chung, Apr. 12, 1966 (dec. July 1994); m. Michael Kroll, Feb. 17, 1997. AAS in Nursing, Cuyahoga C.C.; MPH in Health Svcs. Adminstrn., Honolulu U., 1997. Staff nurse emergency dept. Kaiser Permanente Med. Care Program, Honolulu, supr., grant coord. family practice program, supr. med. subspecialty clinics, clin. supr., clinic supr. Hawaii Kai Clinic; clinic supr. Kaiser Permanente Med. Care Program, Hawaii Kai Clinic, 1984-97; clin. supr. Kailua Clinic, 1997; analyst/cons., infomatics & clin. support svcs. Kaiser Permanente, Honolulu, 1998-99. Past. pres. Am. Cancer Soc.; rsch. bd. dirs. Am. Biog. Inst.; trustee Temple Emanu-El, Honolulu. Mem. ANA (cert. nursing adminstr., Nat. Disting. Svc. Registry), Hawaii Nurses Assn. (past pres.), Hawaii Kai Bus. and Profl. Women (past pres.), East Honolulu Pub. Health Nurses (chair adv. com.), Hawaii Horse Show Assn. (bd. dirs.), Hawaii Combined Tng. Assn. (bd. dirs.), Oahu Quarter Horse Assn. (past pres.). Home: 4814 Aukai Ave Honolulu HI 96816-5209 Office: 801 Dillingham Blvd Honolulu HI 96817-4582

KROLL, SOL, lawyer; b. Russia, Aug. 10, 1918; m. Ruth Saslow; children: Gerald, Judy, Elise, Elliott. LLB, St. John's U., 1942. Bar: N.Y. 1942, U.S. Supreme Ct. 1956. Former U.S. counsel to Assn. Francaise des Socs. D'Assurances Transports; former mem. com. of interfraud task force N.Y. Ins. Dept. *Mr. Kroll has been listed in Who's Who in Law, Who's Who in New York, and Who's Who in United States.* Contbr. articles on Am. ins. law to various ins. mags. Mem. ABA, Fed. Bar Assn., N.Y. State Bar Assn., Internat. Assn. Ins. Counsel, Industry Adv. Com. on Ins.; bd. govs. Internatl. Ins. Soc. Home: 600 Cantitoe St Bedford NY 10506-1107 Office: 110 E 59th St New York NY 10022

KROLOPP, RUDOLPH WILLIAM, retired industrial designer, consultant; b. Chgo., June 7, 1930; s. Rudolph and Emma (Nice) K.; m. Dorcas S. Hall; children: Jacqueline, Mark, Joseph, Sharon, Lizabeth, John, Jennifer. BFA, U. Ill.-Champaign, 1956; postgrad., Lake Forest Coll., Ill., 1974-78. Staff designer Motorola Consumer Products, Chgo., 1956-59, chief designer, 1959-62, mgr. indsl. design communication div., 1962-82, dir. indsl. design, 1982-97, mem. patent com., 1981-97, chmn. corp. graphic standards council, 1983-97; assoc. prof. indsl. design. U. Ill. Chgo. 1984. Patentee in field. Instr. phys. fitness Oak Park YMCA, Ill., 1967; instr. cardiovascular health Buehler YMCA, Palatine, Ill., 1968—, bd. dirs., 1980—, chmn. program com., 1980—, sec. bd. dirs., 1983-84. Served with USMC, 1948-52. Recipient Master Design award Product Engring. Mag., 1961, Weson Design award Western Electronic Conv., 1970, Design Excellence award Indsl. Design Mag., 1972, Design Engring. award Nat. Marine Electronics Assn., 1972, Good Design award Hannover Fair, Germany, 1978, Nekkei Design award, 1990, Internat. Design award, 1991, Corp. award for good design, 1992, Design Excellence award, 1996, Idea Design award, 1997, Good Design award Hannover Fair, 1997. Fellow Indsl. Designers Soc. Am. (chmn. fellowship awards com. 1996, program chmn., sec., regional v.p., chmn. nat. nominating com., Spl. award 1993). Roman Catholic. Club: Parkers SAC (Chgo.) (pres. 1962-65). Home: 103 Golfview Rd Lake Zurich IL 60047-1290

KROM, RUUD ARNE FINCO, surgeon; b. Padang Brahrang, Indonesia, May 29, 1941; came to U.S., 1985; s. Herman Christoph and Catherina Dirkje (van Offeren) K.; m. Jeannette Cornelia Treels, Oct. 16, 1982; 1 child, Russell John. MD, U. Utrecht, The Netherlands, 1968; PhD, U. Leiden, The Netherlands, 1976. Cert. Dutch Bd. Specialists. Resident Diaconnessenhuis Utrecht (The Netherlands), 1969-70, U. Hosp. of Leiden (The Netherlands), 1971-74; fellow Colo. Med. Ctr., Denver, 1976-77; chef de clinique St. Lucas Hosp., Amsterdam, The Netherlands, 1975-76; prof. Mayo Med. Sch., Rochester, Minn., 1986—, head Liver Transplant Program Mayo Clinic, 1985—; bd. dirs. LifeSource (upper Midwest organ procurement orgn.), 1988—. Contbr. articles to profl. jours. Recipient Tilanus award Soc. for Physics, Medicine and Surgery, 1981, medal for outstanding contbn. to medicine Dutch Med. Soc., 1987. Fellow ACS; mem. Am. Soc. Transplant Surgeons, Internat. Transplantation Soc., European Soc. for Organ Transplantation, Internat. Biliary Assn. Office: Mayo Clinic and Found 200 1st St SW Rochester MN 55905-0002*

KROMBEIN, KARL VONVORSE, entomologist; b. Buffalo, May 26, 1912; s. Louis Henry and Gertrude (Hoeffler) K.; m. Dorothy Carpenter Buckingham, Dec. 11, 1942; children: Kristin, Kyra, Karlissa. Student, Carnegie Inst. Tech., 1929-31, Canisius Coll., 1931-32; BS, Cornell U., 1934, MA, 1935, PhD, 1960; PhD in Zoology, U. Peradeniya, Sri Lanka, 1980. Research entomologist Bur. Entomology and Plant Quarantine, Dept. Agr., 1941-51, investigations leader Insect Identification and Parasite Introduction Research br., 1951-65; chmn. dept. entomology Smithsonian Instn., Washington, 1965-71, sr. entomologist, 1971-80, sr. scientist, 1980-93, emeritus, 1993—; cons. to surgeon gen. USAF, 1972-79, emeritus, 1979—; rsch. assoc. Archbold Biol. Sta., 1992—. Author, editor: (with others) Hymenoptera of America North of Mexico-Synoptic Catalog, 1951, Catalog of Hymenoptera in America North of Mexico, 3 vols, 1979; author: Trap-nesting Wasps and Bees: Life Histories, Nests and Associates, 1967; contbr. articles to profl. jours. Served from 1st lt. to maj. AUS, 1942-46, PTO; col. USAF Res. Decorated Legion of Merit, Air Force Commendation medal; named Chief Biomed. Scientist; grantee Am. Philos. Soc., 1952, 55, 59; grantee NSF, 1963; grantee Smithsonian Research Found., 1967, 69, 70, 73; prin. investigator Ceylon Insect Project. Fellow AAAS (councillor 1970-73), Entomol. Soc. Am. (governing bd. 1970-72), Entomol. Soc. Washington (hon., past pres., past editor, Festschrift vol. "Contbns. on Hymenoptera and assoc. insects dedicated to Karl V. Krombein" 1996); mem. Washington Biologists Field Club (hon., past pres.), Am. Entomol. Soc. (hon.), Cosmos Club, Sigma Xi, Sigma Phi Epsilon. Unitarian. Home: 1425 Highwood Dr Mc Lean VA 22101-2519 Office: Smithsonian Instn Washington DC 20560

KROMER, ANN MARIE, artist; b. Cin., Mar. 20, 1938; d. Albert David and Jane (Busch) Castellini; m. Frank Pierce Kromer, May 2, 1964; children: John, Edward, Elizabeth, James. BS, Marygrove Coll., 1960. Color seperator Gibson Greeting Cards, Cin., 1960-61; artist Mailway Advt., Cin., 1961-62; prodn. artist Long Advt., San Francisco, 1962-64; freelance graphic artist, painter, 1965-75; painter Ridgefield, Conn., 1975—. Art included in The Best of Acrylic Painting, 1996, The Best of Oil Painting, 1996, Postmarked Kentucky, 1989, Artist Mag., 1999, Water Color Expressions, 1999, Art of the Northeast, 1999; 13 solo exhbn. Recipient 1st in Mixed Media award Richter Art Ctr., 1st in Acrylic; finalist Arts for the Park, 1997. Mem. Catherine Lorillard Wolfe Art Club (Salmagundi award 1993, Lovell award 1994, DeCozen award 1997), Ridgefield Guild Artists (First in Acrylic 1996), Rowayton Art Ctr. (First in Oil, Mixed Media 1996, First in Acrylic 1997), Kent Art Assn. (Art of Merit award 1995). Avocations: gardening, travel, flower arranging, walking. Home and Office: 40 Beechwood Ln Ridgefield CT 06877-5803

KROMER, JOHN, city official. Grad., Haverford (Pa.) Coll.; postgrad., Temple U. Sr. assoc. Urban Ptnrs.; acting dir. Phila. Housing Authority, 1993, mem. Bd. Commrs., 1992-94; dir. City of Phila. Office Housing and Cmty. Devel., 1992—. Office: Office Housing & Cmty Devel Pub Info Dept 1234 Market St 17th Floor Philadelphia PA 19107-3721*

KROMIDAS, LAMBROS, cell biologist, physical scientist, toxicologist; b. Chios, Greece, Nov. 25, 1956; came to U.S., 1969.; s. George and Maria (Moutafi) K. BA, NYU, 1980; MS, St. John's U., 1984, PhD, 1990. Tchg. asst. St. John's U., Jamaica, N.Y., 1981-87; rsch. fellow St. John's U., Jamaica, N.Y., 1988-90; fellow dept. physiology Med. Coll. Cornell U., N.Y.C., 1990-92; physical scientist U.S. Dept. Energy, N.Y.C., 1992-96; sr. toxicologist Avon Products, Inc., Suffern, N.Y., 1996—; environ. field worker U.S. Dept. Energy, N.Y.C., 1991. Contbr. articles to profl. jours. Rsch. vol. Mt. Sinai Sch. of Medicine, N.Y.C., 1983-84. Valergakis grantee, 1986. Mem. N.Y. Acad. Scis., Soc. Toxicology (Neurotoxicology Splty. award 1990), Hellenic U. Club of N.Y. Achievements include demonstration of methyl mercury disruption of the cytoskeleton and protection of glutathione against toxicity of methyl mercury. Fax: (914) 369-2898. E-mail: lambros.kromidas@avon.com. Office: Avon Products Inc Dept Toxicology Avon Pl Suffern NY 10901

KROMINGA, LYNN, cosmetic and health care company executive, lawyer; b. L.A., May 16, 1950; d. Dale E. and Phyllis M. Krominga; m. Amnon Shiboleth, Apr. 9, 1992; 1 child, Karen Lee Shiboleth. BA in German, U. Minn., 1972, JD, 1974. Bar: Minn. 1974, N.Y. 1976. Assoc. firms in Mpls. and N.Y.C., 1974-77; assoc. counsel Am. Express Co., N.Y.C., 1977-80; sr. internat. counsel Revlon, Inc., N.Y.C., 1981-92, v.p. law, 1988-92, gen. counsel to exec. com., 1991-92, pres. licensing div., 1992-98, mem. exec. com., 1993-94; 97—, exec. v.p. bus. devel., 1998—. Mem. ABA, Internat. Bar Assn., Cosmetic, Toiletry and Fragance Assn. (vice chmn. govt. rels. com. 1991-92), Am. Arbitration Assn. (corp. counsel com. 1986-92; panel of arbitrators for large complex cases 1993-94, internat. panel of arbitrators 1997—), Phi Beta Kappa. Home: 325 E 50th St New York NY 10022-7901 Office: Revlon 625 Madison Ave New York NY 10022-1894

KRONAUER, LISA ELLIOTT, art director; b. Boston, July 17, 1962; d. Charles Kindred and Ann Whitney (Whiting) Elliott; m. Brad Jeffrey Kronauer, July 6, 1991; children: Paige Whiting, Nicole Hayward. A in Occupl. Studies, Pratt Manhattan, 1984. Art dir. Kronauer Design Assocs., Madison, Conn., 1990—. Home and Office: 5 Deveron Dr Madison CT 06443-3467

KRONE, IRENE, product consultant; b. N.Y.C., Oct. 12, 1940; d. Frederick Wilhelm and Gertrude (Gottschlich) Beckmann; m. Helmut Krone, Nov. 14, 1970; 1 child, Kathryn Maria. BS, Chestnut Hill Coll., 1962; postgrad., Sch. Visual Arts and Interior Design, 1962-64, NYU, 1967-68. Market rsch. analyst, then licensing mgr. Celanese Corp., N.Y.C. and Brussels, 1962-67; v.p. product devel. Doyle Dane Bernbach, N.Y.C., 1967-79; pres. I. Krone Assocs. Inc., N.Y.C., 1979—. Pres., founder Stop Traffic Offenses Program, N.Y.C., 1982—. Home: 1 E 62nd St New York NY 10021-7232 Office: 767 3rd Ave New York NY 10017-2023

KRONE, JULIE, jockey; b. Benton Harbor, Mich., July 24, 1963; d. Don and Judy Krone. Profl. jockey Tampa Bay (Fla.) Downs, others, 1981—; first female jockey to win a Triple Crown race; first woman to win 5 races in a day at Saratoga, N.Y.; leading woman jockey in U.S., 1986-88; leading woman jockey money won, 1986—; winningest female jockey in history with nearly 3,400 victories. Author: (with Nancy Ann Richardson) Riding for My Life, 1995. Winner of 19 Grade I races including $77 Million in purses; races won include Cornhusker Handicap, AK-Star Ben Racetrack, Omaha, 1988, Flower Bowl Handicap, Belmont Park, 1988, Modesty Stakes, Arlington Park, Ill., 1989, Budweiser Md. Classic, Pimlico, 1989, Belmont Stakes, Elmont, N.Y., 1993, The Molson Million, Toronto, Can., 1995, The Meadowlands Cup, East Rutherford, N.J., 1995, The Ill. Derby, Chgo., 1995, N.J. Derby, Cherry Hill, 1992, 94, 95; first rode in Ky. Derby, 1991; recipient Comeback award Am. Sportscasters Assn., 1994, ESPY Award winner female athlete of yr., 1993. Office: care Jockeys' Guild 250 W Main St Ste 1820 Lexington KY 40507-1733

KRONE, RAY BEYERS, civil and environmental engineering educator, consultant; b. Long Beach, Calif., June 7, 1922; s. Ray Bell and Vera Harriet (Beyers) K.; m. Charlotte Jane Baldrige, June 18, 1946; children: Charlotte Ann Krone Nelson, Ray Baldrige. BS in Soil Sci., U. Calif., Berkeley, 1950, MS in Sanitary Engring., 1957, PhD in Sanitary Engring., 1962. Soil scientist, staff sanitary engr., assoc. rsch. engr. U. Calif., Berkeley, 1950-64; assoc. prof. U. Calif., Davis, 1964-72, prof., 1972-88, prof. emeritus, 1988—, assoc. dean engring., 1972-88; cons. Ray B. Krone & Assoc., Davis, 1981—; cons. to com. tidal hydraulics U.S. Army Corps Engrs., Vicksburg, Miss., 1975—; mem. bd. cons. Phila. Dist. USACE, 1972-74. 1st lt. USAAC, 1943-45. Fellow AAAS; mem. ASCE (life, Einstein award 1991, Moffatt-Nichol award 1991), NAE, Am. Geophys. Union, Estuarine Rsch. Fedn. Avocations: flying, photography. Office: U Calif Dept Civil/Environ Engring Davis CA 95616

KRONEGGER, MARIA ELISABETH, French and comparative literature educator; b. Graz, Austria, Sept. 23, 1932; came to U.S., 1962, naturalized, 1968; d. Karl and Josefine (Sparovitz) K. Grad., Karl-Franzens U., Austria, 1960; postgrad., U. Sorbonne, Paris, 1953-55; MA in English and Am. Lit.,

Kans. U., 1958; PhD in French and Humanities, Fla. State U., 1960. Instr. French, German and humanities Fla. State U., 1958-60; mem. faculty Internat. Coll., St. Gallen, Switzerland, 1961-62; asst. prof. Hollins Coll., Va., 1962-64; asst. prof. French and comparative lit. Mich. State U., East Lansing, 1964-67, assoc. prof., 1967-70, prof., 1970—. Author: James Joyce and Associate Image Makers, 1968, Impressionist Literature, 1973, The Life Significance of French Baroque Poetry, 1988; editor: Phénoménologie et Littérature: L'origine de l'oeuvre d'art, Hommages à A.-T. Tymieniecka, 1986, Phenomenology and Aesthetics: Approaches to Comparative Literature and the Other Arts, 1990, Dordrecht (Kluwer) vol. XXXIII of book series Analecta Husserliana, 1990; editor: Esthétique Baroque et Imagination Créatrice, 1997, Allegory Old and New in Literature, the Fine Arts, Music and Theatre, and its Continuity in Culture, 1994; co-editor: Life, The Human Quest for an Ideal, 1996, Life Differentiation and Harmony: Vegetal, Animal, Human, Analecta Husseliana LVII, 1998; contbr. more than 135 articles on 17th and 20th century French and English lit., lit. and the fine arts, lit. and phenomenology to scholarly publs., anelecta Husseliana LVII, 1998. Bd. dirs. World Inst. Phenomenology, 1980—; pres. Internat. Soc. Phenomenology and Lit., Internat. Soc. Phenomenology, Fine Arts and Aesthetics; exec. v.p. World Inst. for Advanced Phenomenological Rsch. and Learning. Fulbright scholar, 1957-60; Ford Found. grantee, 1965-66. Mem. MLA, AAUP, Am. Soc. Aesthetics, Am. Comparative Lit. Assn., Semiotic Soc. Am., Chinese Comparative Lit. Assn., Internat. Soc. for Phenomenology and Lit. (pres. 1985—), Internat. Comparative Lit. Assn., Internat. Soc. Civilization, Internat. Semiotic Soc., South Atlantic MLA, Société Paul Claudel, Am. Assn. Tchrs. French, Fédération Internationale de Langues et Littératures Modernes, Gold Key Soc. (hon., Rsch. award). Roman Catholic. Home: 1324 Chartwell Carriage N Stonelake East Lansing MI 48823 Office: Mich State U Old Horticulture East Lansing MI 48824 *Only where there is emotion there is art, where there is art there is life, where there is life there is hope, where there is hope, there is redemption.*

KRONEN, JERILYN, psychologist; b. N.Y.C., July 17, 1947; d. Morris and Hester (Engel) Levy; m. Kenneth Kronen, Apr. 11, 1976; children: Ari, Joshua. PhD, Yeshiva U., 1982; cert. in psychotherapy & psychoanalysis, N.Y.U., 1988. Lic. psychologist, N.Y. Tchr. Pub. Sch. 119, N.Y.C., 1969-72; sch. psychologist Bd. Coop. Edn. Svc., N.Y.C., 1972-82; pvt. practice N.Y.C., 1982—; mem. faculty Resolve, N.Y.C., 1989—; adj. clin. supr. Ferkauf-Yeshiva U., N.Y.C., 1989—; lectr. in field. Bd. dirs. Couples Club Kehilat Jeshurun Synagogue, N.Y.C., 1989-91, adoption resource person, 1990—; liaison mem. Lower Sch. Ramaz, N.Y.C., 1990-92. Mem. APA, Div. 39 Psychoanalysis. Home and Office: 137 E 36th St Ste 14 New York NY 10016-3528

KRONENBERG, JACALYN (JACKI KRONENBERG), nurse administrator; b. N.Y.C., July 21, 1949; d. Martin Jerome and Joyce (Weinberg) Jacobs; m. Robert Kronenberg, Jan. 23, 1971 (div.); 1 child, Joshua Louis. BA, William Paterson Coll. of N.J., 1971; ADN, Phoenix Coll., 1977. RN, Calif.; cert. IV nurse, chemo, ACLS, PALS. Asst. charge nurse Phoenix Gen. Hosp.; nurse Ariz. State Crippled Children's Hosp., Tempe; maternal, child nurse Desert Samaritan Hosp., Mesa, Ariz.; nurse mgr. PPS Inc., Phoenix, Med-Pro 2000, Phoenix; clin. nurse II Phoenix Children's Hosp.; nurse mgr. adolescent unit Shriners Hosp., L.A.; nurse mgr. pediatrics, oncology, gynecology, med./surg. Santa Monica (Calif.) Hosp. Med. Ctr., 1993-94; dir. nurses, dir. patient care svcs. NMC Homecare, Anaheim, Calif., 1994; dir. med./surg. svcs. and staffing, nursing office/supr. Midway Hosp. Med. Ctr., L.A., 1995; dir. patient care svcs., dir. nursing edn. Children's Home Care Infusion Svcs. & Pediatrics, Children's Home Care, L.A., 1995—; clin. nurse II UCLA Med. Ctr., 1998—; cons. Kronenberg & Kronenburg Cons., Redondo Beach, Calif.; quality improvement specialist Bellflower (Calif.) Med. Ctr., 1998—; mem. joint rsch. project on pediatric cystic fibrosis and human growth factor U. Calif., Irvine; rschr. in field; cons. Kronenberg & Kronenberg Cons. Homecare, 1996—. Mem. Oncology Nursing Soc., IV Nursing Soc., Pediatric Nursing Soc. Home: 332B Calle Miramar Redondo Beach CA 90277-6347

KRONENBERG, RICHARD SAMUEL, physician, educator; b. Chgo., Aug. 7, 1938; s. Frank Paul and Ruth Ida (Zaretzsky) K.; m. Carole Marie Hurd, Oct. 13, 1963; children: Karen, Marilyn, Brenda. BA, Northwestern U., 1960, MD, 1963. Intern Parkland Meml. Hosp., Mpls., 1967-68, resident in internal medicine, 1968; rsch. fellow Cardiovascular Rsch. Inst. U. Calif., San Franciso, 1968-70; asst. prof. medicine U. Minn., 1970-74, assoc. prof., 1974-79, prof., dir. pulmonary div., 1979-84; prof. U. Tex. Health Sci. Ctr., Houston, 1984—; prof. medicine, exec. v.p. for clin. affairs U. Tex. Health Ctr., Tyler, 1984—; reviewer subsplty. programs in internal medicineAccreditation Coun. Grad. Med. Edn., Chgo., 1985—. Mem. editorial rev. bd. The Asbestos Monitor, Nat. Asbestos Coun. Jour., 1990-93; contbr. chpts. to books. Capt. USAF, 1965-67. Recipient Rsch. Career Devel. award NIH, 1973-78. Fellow ACP, Am. Coll. Chest Physicians; mem. Nat. Asbestos Coun. (bd. dirs. 1990-93), Asbestos Disease Assn. (pres. 1990-93), Ctrl. Soc. Clin. Rsch. Avocation: bicycling. Home: 5615 Cedar Hill Cir Tyler TX 75703-3912 Office: U Tex Health Ctr PO Box 2003 Tyler TX 75710-2003

KRONENFELD, JUDY ZAHLER, humanities educator, writer; b. N.Y.C., July 17, 1943; d. Samuel and Stella (Jupiter) Zahler; m. David Brian Kronenfeld, June 21, 1964; children: Daniel Aaron, Mara Gianna. BA in English summa cum laude, Smith Coll., 1964; MA in English Lit., Stanford U., 1966, PhD in English Lit., 1971. Asst. prof. English Purdue U., West Lafayette, Ind., 1976-77; lectr. U. Calif., Irvine, 1978-79; lectr. Creative Writing Dept. U. Calif., Riverside, 1984—; vis. asst. prof. English U. Calif., Riverside, 1980-81, 88-89, Irvine, 1984, 85-87. Author: (poetry) Shadow of Wings, 1991, (critical study) King Lear and The Naked Truth: Rethinking the Language of Religion and Resistance, 1998; contbr. articles to profl. jours. Leverhulme Trust Fund fellow, 1968. Mem MLA, Renaissance Soc. Am., Assn. Lit. Scholars and Critics, Phi Beta Kappa. Home: 3314 Celeste Dr Riverside CA 92507 Office: U Calif Creative Writing Dept Riverside CA 92521-0318

KRONER, FRED L., journalist; b. Champaign, Ill., Nov. 16, 1955; s. James Carlton and Naomi Ruth Kroner; m. Dee Siddens, Aug. 21, 1976 (div. Nov. 1996); 1 child, Devin Richard; m. Emoly Moon, June 6, 1999; m. Emily Sue Moon, June 6, 1999. BS, U. Ill., 1978. Sportswriter Champaign Courier, 1974-78, Bloomington (Ill.) Pantagraph, 1978-81, Champaign News-Gazette, 1981—. Contbg. author: Cascade of Memories, 1998; author booklets and newspaper series. Coach, Little League Baseball, Champaign, 1982-86, Summer League Basketball, Sullivan, Ill., 1990-93; guest commentator WDAN Radio, Danville, 1995—. Recipient awards AP, 1985, 89; named Newsman of Yr., Ill. Wrestling Coaches Assn., 1984, 88. Mem. Soc. Profl. Journalists, Ill. Press Assn., Nat. Sportswriters and Sportscasters Assn. Methodist. Avocations: gardening, writing poetry. Email: ItsFred586@aol.com. Home: 105 S Division Box 778 Mahomet IL 61853 Office: Champaign-Urbana News-Gazette 15 Main St Box 677 Champaign IL 61824

KRONFOL, ZIAD ANIS, psychiatrist, educator, researcher; b. Beirut, Mar. 29, 1949; came to U.S., 1974; s. Anis and Inam (Ardati) K.; m. Rima Naja, Mar. 26, 1983; children: Zeina, Sara. BS, Am. U. Beirut, 1970, MD, 1974. Diplomate Am. Bd. Psychiatry and Neurology. Intern Am. U. Beirut, 1973-74, instr. psychiatry, 1977-79; resident in psychiatry U. Iowa, Iowa City, 1974-77, asst. prof., 1982-85; rsch. fellow U. Mich., Ann Arbor, 1979-82, assoc. prof. psychiatry, dir. psychoimmunology, 1986—; staff psychiatrist, rsch. dir. adult inpatient psychiatry U. Mich. Med. Ctr., Ann Arbor, 1986-95; chief consultation/liaison psychiatry VA Med. Ctr., Iowa City, 1984-85; cons. intensive psychiat. cmty. care VA Med. Ctr., Ann Arbor, 1995-99; staff psychiatrist amb. divsn. U. Mich. Med. Ctr., Ann Arbor, 1995—, rsch. dir., psycho-oncology program 1999—; presenter at profl. confs. Contbr. to profl. publs. Grantee NIMH, 1987-94, NIAAA, 1988-93, Nat. Alliance for Rsch. on Schizophrenia and Depression, 1997—. Mem. AAAS, Am. Psychiat. Assn., Soc. Biol. Psychiatry, N.Y. Acad. Scis., Am. Psychosomatic Soc., Soc. Neurosci., Internat. Soc. Neuroimmunomodulation (charter). Home: 1220 Severn Ct Ann Arbor MI 48105-2863 Office: Univ Mich Med Ctr 1500 E Medical Center Dr Ann Arbor MI 48109-0722

KRONICK, BARRY, lumber company executive; b. 1935. Furman Lumber, Billerica, Mass., 1957—, Pres., 1990—. Office: Furman Lumber 32 Manning Rd Billerica MA 01821-3915

KRONIK, JOHN WILLIAM, Romance studies educator; b. Vienna, Austria, May 18, 1931; came to U.S. 1939, naturalized 1944; s. Bernard and Melanie (Hollub) K.; m. Eva Kronik, Dec. 26, 1955; children—Theresa J., Geoffrey B. B.A., Queens Coll., 1952; M.A., U. Wis., 1953, Ph.D., 1960; D.H.L., Ill. Coll., 1979. Asst. prof. Romance lang. Hamilton Coll., Clinton, N.Y., 1958-63; assoc. prof. Spanish, U. Ill., Urbana, 1963-66; prof. Romance studies Cornell U., Ithaca, N.Y., 1966—; vis. prof. Columbia U., 1968, Middlebury Coll., Vt., 1979, 80, 86, 91, Brigham Young U., 1982, U. Colo., 1989, U. Calif., Berkeley, 91, U. Calif., Irvine, 1994, UCLA, 1999; cons. NEH, 1973—, Guggenheim Found., 1988—; corporator Internat. Inst. in Spain, Madrid, 1972—. Author: La farsa y el teatro espanol, 1971; co-editor: La familia de Pascual Duarte, 1961, Textos y Contextos de Galdos, 1994, Intertextual Pursuits: Lit. Mediations in Modern Spanish Narrative, 1998; series editor Prentice-Hall, 1962-75; mem. editorial bd. MLA, N.Y.C., 1983-85; editor PMLA, 1985-92, Anales Galdosianos, 1986-90; contbr. articles to profl. jours. With U.S. Army, 1953-55. Fulbright fellow, 1960-61, 1987-88; Rockefeller Found. research residency, 1975; Guggenheim fellow, 1983-84; Am. Council Learned Socs. grantee, 1983-84. Mem. MLA, Internat. Assn. Hispanists, Internat. Galdos Assn. (pres.), Am. Assn. Tchrs. Spanish and Portuguese. Home: 1020 Highland Rd Ithaca NY 14850-1448 Office: Cornell U Dept Romance Studies Ithaca NY 14853-3201

KRONISH, RICHARD MARK, sports association executive; b. Bronx, N.Y., Oct. 1, 1961; s. William C. and Lillian B. (Hollinger) K. Student, CUNY, 1979-83. Chief exec. officer Kronish Sports Enterprises, N.Y.C., 1981—. Author: NHL Draft Guide, 1985, 15th rev. edit., 1999. Com. mem. N.Y. County Dem. Com., 1995-97. Democrat. Jewish. Avocations: poetry, music, sports cards, billiards, politics. Home: 521 E 14th St New York NY 10009-2917

KRONMAN, ANTHONY TOWNSEND, law educator, dean; b. 1945; m. Nancy I. Greenberg, 1982. B.A., Williams Coll., 1968, Ph.D., 1972; J.D., Yale U., 1975. Bar: Minn. 1975, N.Y. 1983. Assoc. prof. U. Minn., 1975-76; asst. prof. U. Chgo., 1976-79; vis. assoc. prof. Yale U. Law Sch., New Haven, 1978-79, prof., 1979—, Edward J. Phelps prof. law, 1985—, dean, 1994—. Editor: (with R. Posner) The Economics of Contract Law, 1979 (with F. Kessler and G. Gilmore) Cases and Materials on Contracts, 1986; past mem. editorial bd. Yale Law Jour.; author: Max Weber, 1983, The Lost Lawyer, 1993. Danforth Found. fellow, 1968-72. Fellow ABA, Am. Acad. Arts and Scis.; mem. Selden Soc., Conn. Bar Assn. (Cooper fellow), Coun. on Fgn. Rels. Office: Yale Law Sch PO Box 208215 New Haven CT 06520-8215

KRONMAN, CAROL JANE, lawyer; b. Passaic, N.J., Mar. 25, 1944; d. Robert M. and Helen (Harris) K.; children: Audrey Jane, Heather Sue. AB, Cornell U., 1965; MA, Columbia U., 1966; JD, Yeshiva U., 1980. Bar: N.Y. 1981, N.J. 1981, Fla. 1981, U.S. Dist. Ct. N.J. 1981, U.S. Dist. Ct. (so. dist.) N.Y. 1984, U.S. Supreme Ct. 1990, U.S. Dist. Ct. (ea. dist.) N.Y. 1991. Asst. prof. William Paterson Coll., Wayne, N.J., 1967-69; treas. Capital Theatre Inc., N.J., 1977-83; coord. paralegal studies Montclair State Coll., N.J., 1982-83, prof., 1982-85; ptnr. Kronman & Kronman P.A., Totowa, N.J., 1981-85; ptnr. N.J. office Max E. Greenberg, Cantor & Reiss, South Hackensack, N.J., 1986-89; of counsel Budd, Larner, Gross, Rosenbaum, Greenberg & Sade, 1989-90; gen. counsel office of Mayor Office of Constrn. City of N.Y., 1991-94; lectr. N.J. Inst. for Continuing Legal Edn., 1987, Constrn. Failure and Disaster Super conf. Conf. Mgmt. Corp., N.Y.C., 1988; assoc. Hosp. Joint Diseases, N.Y.C. Author: Different Types of Contracts, 1987; pub. The Kronman Letter, Update for Insurance and Bond Providers, Producers and Users, 1995—; contbr. articles to profl. jours. Recipient Svc. award in engring. and industry Am. Orgn. Rehab. through Tng. Fedn., 1993, Svc. award in real estate and constrn., 1994, Spl. Recognition award Profl. Women in Constrn., 1993; noted for Spl. Presentation for Committment to Excellence in Rsch., Hosp. for Joint Diseases, N.Y. Hosp. Mem. Orgn. Rehab. through Tng. (bd. dirs. real estate and constrn. industry divsn., nat. bd. dirs., Svc. award), N.J. Bar Assn., N.Y. State Bar Assn., Fla. Bar Assn., Stern Coll. Profl. Women in Constrn. (bd. dirs.). Home: 2 Sutton Pl S Apt 3A New York NY 10022-3070 Office: 1040 1st Ave Ste 124 New York NY 10022-2902

KRONMAN, JOSEPH HENRY, orthodontist; b. N.Y.C., Apr. 4, 1931; s. Jacob and Anna Rita (Dick) K.; m. Arlene Brenda Wice, Mar. 30, 1961; children: David Arthur, Bruce Edward, Lisa Sue. B.S. in Biology, NYU, 1952, D.D.S., 1955; cert. in orthodontics, Columbia U. Sch. Dentistry, 1959; Ph.D. in Anatomy, Med. Coll. Va., 1962. Postdoctoral fellow Med. Coll. Va., 1959-61; mem. faculty Tufts U. Sch. Dental Medicine, Boston, 1962-94; prof. orthodontics Tufts U. Sch. Dental Medicine, 1968-94, prof. anatomy, 1983-94, dir. postdoctoral studies, 1964-70, dir. continuing edn., 1982-88, asst. to dean Grad. Sch. Arts and Scis., 1964-69; pvt. practice orthodontics, 1963-78, prof. emeritus, 1994; prof. orthodontics Nova S.E. U., 1997—; cons. VA, 1966-68. Mem. editorial bd. Jour. Oral Surgery, Oral Medicine, Oral Pathology. Served to capt. Dental Corps U.S. Army, 1955-57, Korea. Recipient Oscar award Internat. Assn. Inventors and Compagnie 12 Pub., Paris, 1986. Fellow Internat., Am. colls. dentists; mem. ADA, Mass. Dental Soc., Internat. Assn. Dental Research, AAUP, Am. Assn. Orthodontists, Am. Assn. Anatomists, N.Y. Acad. Scis., Internat. Soc. Craniofacial Biology, AAAS, Mass. Assn. Orthodontists, Am. Assn. Dental Schs., Sigma Xi, Omicron Kappa Upsilon. Jewish. Co-inventor GK-101 caries removal agent, applicator (caridex), hydron root canal filling material and delivery system, root canal irrigation system, orthodontic headgear attachment. Home: 11755 Caracas Blvd Boynton Beach FL 33437-4081

KRONSCHNABEL, GERALD LEO, sales executive; b. Appleton, Wis., May 5, 1931; s. Clarence Frank and Dorothy Magdalin (Huhn) K.; m. Darlene Mary Doughty, June 2, 1951; children: Robert, Patricia, Jean, Mary. Student, St. Norbert Coll., 1977-79, U. Wis., Sales, 1980. Dairy farmer Outagamie County, Wis., 1950-56, Waukesha County, Wis., 1956-63; tech. foreman Bruce Berg, Inc., Waukesha, Wis., 1963-65; farm mgr. Talisman Hill Farm, Greenleaf, Wis., 1965-75, Deer Lake Farm, St. Croix Falls, Wis., 1975-79; area sales dir. Germania Dairy Automation, Waunakee, Wis., 1979-89; regional mktg. mgr. Germania Dairy Automation, Waunakee, 1989-96, nat. sales coord., 1996—; mem. adv. bd. N.E. Wis. Tech. Coll., Green Bay, Wis., 1982-86. Inventor in field. Religious instr. St. Marys Parish, Greenleaf, Wis., 1965-75, St. Joseph Parish, St. Croix Falls, 1975-79, St. Boniface Parish, DePere, Wis., 1979-87. Roman Catholic. Avocation: Intarsia. Home: 1 Waywood Cir Madison WI 53704-6484 Office: Germania Dairy Automation 606 Cooper Rd Waunakee WI 53597-1464

KRONSCHNABEL, ROBERT JAMES, manufacturing company executive; b. Green Bay, Wis., Jan. 13, 1935; s. Cyril E. and Margaret (Bierman) K. m. Catherine G. Murray, June 27, 1959; children: Frederick, Nina, Erich, Liesl, Mara. BSME, Marquette U., 1958; MBA, Harvard U., 1963. Field svc. engr. A.C. Electronics div. GM, Milw., 1958-61; mgr. materials Clark Contr. div. A.O. Smith, Cleve. and Lancaster, S.C., 1963-65; v.p., sr. cons. MSI, Appleton, Wis., 1965-67; plant mgr. Allis Chalmers, Port Washington, Wis., 1967-77, Simplicity Mfg. Co., Lexington, S.C., 1970-73; dir. mfg. bearings div. TRW, Jamestown, N.Y., 1977-79; v.p. mfg. bldgs. div. Butler Mfg. Co., Kansas City, Mo., 1979-83, v.p. corp. mfg., 1983-88; pres. Skylight div. Butler Mfg. Co., Garland, Tex., 1988-91; pres. grain sys. divsn. CTB, Inc., Kansas City, 1991—; mem. prison industries bd. Mo. Dept. Corrections, Jefferson city, 1986-88. Chmn. bd. dirs. Prime Health, Kansas City, 1980-88; bd. regents Rockhurst Coll., Kansas City, 1985—. Mem. Harvard Bus. Sch. Club. Republican. Roman Catholic. Avocations: gardening, golf, fishing. Office: CTB Grain Sys 7400 E 13th St Kansas City MO 64126-2339

KRONSTEIN, WERNER J, lawyer; b. Heidelberg, Germany, Dec. 12, 1930; came to U.S., 1935; s. Heinrich D. and Kate (Brodnitz) K.; m Ilse Marie Engel, Feb. 10, 1962; 1 child, Phillip D. A.B., Georgetown U., 1953, L.L.B., 1956. Bar: 1956. Law clk. U.S. Ct. Appeal for D.C. Circuit, Washington, 1956-57; ptnr. Arnold & Porter, Washington, 1957—; trustee, Internat. Law Inst., Washington, 1983—, vice chmn., 1989—. Mem. bd. contbg. editors advisers Securities Regulation Law Jour. Contbr. articles to profl. jours. Roman Catholic. Office: Arnold & Porter 555 12th St NW Washington DC 20004-1206

KRONZER, LANCE, city auditor, Richmond, Virginia. BA in Liberal Arts, St. Mary's Coll., Ind., 1962; MBA, Wayne State U., 1979. Cert. CPA. Staff auditor City of Detroit, 1980-89; dep. city auditor City of St. Louis, 1989-91; auditor City of Ft. Myers, Fla., 1995-97, City of Richmond, Va., 1991-95, 97—. Mem. AICPA, NALGA, VLGAA. Office: Office City Auditor City Hall Ste 506 900 E Broad St Richmond VA 23219-1907*

KROPF, SUSAN J., cosmetics company executive; married. BA in English, St. John's U.; MBA in Fin., NYU. Adminstrv. asst. Avon Products, Inc., N.Y.C., 1970, various mgmt. positions, 1970-85, v.p. purchasing and package devel., 1985-90, v.p., sr. officer product devel., 1990-92, v.p. R&D and mfg., 1992-97, sr. v.p. global ops. and bus. devel., 1992-97, exec. v.p., 1998—; bd. dirs. Green Point Savs. Bank. Mem. Cosmetic Exec. Women, Fashion Group Internat. Office: Avon Products Inc 1251 Avenue Of The Americas New York NY 10019-5374*

KROPOTOFF, GEORGE ALEX, civil engineer; b. Sofia, Bulgaria, Dec. 6, 1921; s. Alex S. and Anna A. (Kurat) K.; came to Brazil, 1948, to U.S., 1952, naturalized, 1958; BS in Engring., Inst. Tech., Sofia, 1941; ext. courses in computer sci. U. Calif., 1968; Registered profl. engr., Calif.; m. Helen P., July 23, 1972. With Std. Eletrica S.A., Rio de Janeiro, 1948-52, Pacific Car & Foundry Co., Seattle, 1952-64, T.G. Atkinson Assocs., Structural Engrs., San Diego, 1960-62, Tucker, Sadler & Bennett A-E, San Diego, 1964-74, Gen. Dynamics-Astronautics, San Diego, 1967-68, Engring. Sci., Inc., Arcadia, Calif., 1975-76, Incomtel, Rio de Janeiro, Brazil, 1976, Bennett Engrs., structural cons., San Diego, 1976-82; project structural engr. Hope Cons. Group, San Diego and Saudi Arabia, 1982-84; cons. structural engr. Pioneered engring. computer software. Warrant officer U.S. Army, 1945-46. Fellow ASCE; mem. Structural Engrs. Assn. San Diego (assoc.), Soc. Am. Mil. Engrs., Soc. Profl. Engrs. Brazil. Republican. Russian Orthodox. Home: 7430 Park Ridge Blvd Apt E San Diego CA 92120-2252

KROPP, DAVID ARTHUR, retired landscape architect; b. Chgo., Apr. 30, 1933; s. Roy Paul and Elfriede Marie (Kreis) K. BS, Ill. Inst. Tech., 1956. Owner, pres. Kropp Co., Plainfield, Ill., 1971—; guest lectr. various univs. Author: The Prairie Annual, 1975. Recipient Bradfod Williams award for profl. writing, 1976. Mem. United Ch. of Christ.

KROPP, STACY ANNE, small business owner; b. Bklyn., Jan. 22, 1964; d. Alan Marc and Sheila Harriet (Friend) G.; 1 child, Ryan. Student, Suffolk C.C., 1981, Valencia C.C., 1982. Lic. real estate agt., Fla., 1986. Pres., owner Account Mgmt. Svcs. Inc., Hollywood, Fla.; gen. mgr. Gen. Accounts Svc., Inc., Miami, Fla.; pres., owner KC & Co., Inc., Davie, Fla.; ops. mgr. Color All Techs., Pompano Beach, Fla.; CEO Gold Power Supplements, Ft. Lauderdale, Fla. Mem. NAFE, Nat. Assn. Self-Employed, Nat. Nutritional Foods Assn., Greater Miami Credit Assn., Am. Collectors Assn., Fla. Collectors Assn., Women in Network. Home: 14130 Langley Pl Fort Lauderdale FL 33325-6413

KROPSCHOT, RICHARD HENRY, retired physicist, science laboratory administrato; b. Kalamazoo, May 25, 1927; s. Henry J. and Della (Burdorf) K.; m. Claire Mills, June 23, 1950; children: Susan, Anne. BS in Physics, Mich. State U., 1948, MS in Physics, 1950, PhD in Physics, 1958. Rsch. scientist N.Am. Aviation, Downey, Calif., 1950-51; physicist Nat. Bur. Standards, Boulder, Colo., 1951-79; dir. Office Basic Energy Scis., Dept. Energy, Washington, 1979-85; assoc. lab. dir. energy scis. Lawrence Berkeley (Calif.) Lab., 1985-90; liaison officer Office of Pres. U. Calif., Oakland, 1990-97, ret.; adj. prof. U. Colo., Boulder, 1969-79; cons. Cryogenic Engring., 1998—. Author: Technology of Liquid Helium, 1968; former editor Cryogenics, London, Rev. Sci. Instruments; contbr. articles to profl. jours. With USN, 1945-46, PTO, ETO. Recipient Gold medal U.S. Dept. Commerce, 1954, sci. fellow, 1976-77; recipient Disting. Svc. award U.S. Dept. Energy. Fellow Am. Phys. Soc. Presbyterian.

KROSNICK, JOEL, cellist; b. New Haven, Apr. 3, 1941; s. Morris Yale and Estelle (Crossman) K.; m. Dinah Straight, 1983. B.A., Columbia Coll., 1970; D.F.A., Mich. State U. Co-founder Group for Contemporary Music, Columbia U., 1962; asst. prof. music U. Iowa, 1963-66; cellist Iowa Quartet, 1963-66; asst. prof. U. Mass., 1966-70; artist in residence Calif. Inst. Arts, 1970-74; cellist Juilliard String Quartet, N.Y.C., 1974—; artist-in-residence Mich. State U., Library of Congress; mem. faculty Juilliard Sch., 1974—. Appeared in solo recitals, N.Y.C., London, Hamburg, Munich, Amsterdam, Belgrade, Berlin, Library of Congress, Washington; premiere performances include solo works by Ralph Shapey, Solo works by, Milton Babbitt, Mario Davidovsky, Charles Wuorinan, Donald Martino, M.W. Karlins, Gerhard Samuel, Mel Powell, Elliott Carter, Morton Subotnick, others; presented The Cello: A 20th Century Retrospective, at Juilliard Sch., Library of Congress, 1984; 3 concert series Carnegie Recital Hall, 1985-86; rec. artist, Columbia, CRI, Orion and Nonesuch records. Office: Juilliard String Quartet care Colbert Artists Mgmt 111 W 57th St Ste 1416 New York NY 10019-2211*

KROSSER, HOWARD S., aerospace company executive, retired congressman; b. Bklyn., Dec. 2, 1936; s. Samuel and Celia (Wexler) K.; m. Roslyn Elaine Rosenthal, Apr. 30, 1939; children: Scott A., Barry I. BS in Engring., Rutgers Coll., 1959; MS in Indsl. Mgmt., Ga. Inst. Tech., 1970; postgrad., Harvard U., 1985. Engr., engring. supr. Picatinny Arsenal, Dover, N.J., 1959-66; br. mgr., engr. Prodn. Modernization Agy., Dover, 1966-73; divsn. engring. mgr. Army Prodn. Agy., Dover, 1973-78; program mgr. Army Tank Command, Warren, Mich., 1978-85; dir. lab. Army Armament R & D Ctr., Dover, 1985-86, tech. dir., 1986-88; v.p., gen. mgr. Hercules Aerospace, Wilmington, Del., 1988-89; pres. Hercules Def. Electronic Systems Inc., Wilmington, 1990-94; chmn. bd. dirs., pres. Alliant Def. Electronics Sys. Inc., Clearwater, Fla., 1994-96; v.p. smart weapons sys. Alliant Techsys., Inc., Mt. Arlington, N.J., 1996—. Mem. Army Sci. Bd., Washington, 1990-93. Recipient Meritorious Civilian Svc. award U.S. Army, 1986, Exceptional Civil Svc. award, 1988. Mem. Assn. of U.S. Army, Am. Def. Preparedness Assn. (Leslie Simon award 1988). Office: Alliant Techsys Inc 100 Stierli Ct Ste 112 Mount Arlington NJ 07856-1312

KROSTAG, DIANE THERESA MICHAELS, clinical informatics analyst; b. Wilkes-Barre, Pa., Apr. 13, 1959; d. William Adam Michaels and Theresa J. Zielinski Stauber; m. William Joseph Krostag, Oct. 20, 1979. AAS in Nursing, Luzerne County Community Coll., Nanticoke, Pa., 1979; student, U. N.Mex., Albuquerque, 1987-90, Nat. Am. U., Rio Rancho, Albuquerque, 1997—. Staff nurse pediatrics U. Hosp., Albuquerque, 1979-80, staff nurse newborn nursery, 1980-81, asst. head nurse newborn nursery, 1981-85; charge nurse pediatric clinic U. Hosp.-Children's Hosp. N.Mex., Albuquerque, 1985-92; clin. info. specialist Shared Med. Systems Action System Univ. Hosp., Albuquerque, N. Mex., 1992-95; clin. informatics analyst Cerner Carenet Order Mgmt. System, Albuquerque, 1995—. Recipient Disting. Nurse award Univ. Hosp., 1989. Mem. ANA, Am. Nursing Informatics Assn., N.Mex. Nurses Assn., Balloon Fedn. Am., Albuquerque Aerostat Ascension Assn. Avocation: pvt. pilot hot air balloon. Home: 77 Arizona Sunset Rd NE Albuquerque NM 87124-2538

KROTINGER, MYRON NATHAN, lawyer; b. N.Y.C., Oct. 31, 1914; s. Benjamin A. and Anna M. (Perlo) K.; m. Ada S. Segal, Nov. 14, 1953; children: Andrew S., Jonathan H. BA, NYU, 1933; MA, Columbia U., 1935, LLB, 1937. Bar: N.Y. 1937, Ohio 1938, U.S. Dist. Ct. (no. dist.) Ohio 1944, U.S. Dist. Ct. (so. dist.) N.Y. 1948, U.S. Ct. Appeals (2d cir.) 1948, U.S. Ct. Appeals (4th and 6th cirs.) 1958, U.S. Supreme Ct. 1963. Assoc. Ulmer, Berne & Gordon, Cleve., 1937-39; atty. corp. reorgn. div., regional interpretive atty. SEC, Cleve., 1939-45; pvt. practice N.Y.C., 1945-48, Cleve., 1948-54; ptnr. Lane, Krotinger & Santora, Cleve., 1954-70, Van Aken & Bond, Cleve., 1988—; of counsel Burke, Haber & Berick, Cleve., 1970-88; instr. antitrust law and trade regulation Case Western Res. U., Cleve., 1951-70; panelist Practicing Law Inst., 1967-77. Contbr. articles to profl. publs. Trustee The Park Synagogue, Cleve., 1952—, Cleve. Inst. Art, 1986—; pres. Cleve. Art Assn., 1985-87. Mem. ABA, Fed. Bar Assn. (pres. 1978-79), Ohio State Bar Assn. (chmn. antitrust confs. 1973, 74), Cuyahoga County Bar Assn., Cleve. Bar Assn., Union Club, City Club, English Speaking Union. Avocation: fly fishing. Home: 2703 Coventry Rd Cleveland OH 44120-1307 Office: Van Aken & Bond 629 Euclid Ave Ste 1000 Cleveland OH 44114-3054

KROTIUK, WILLIAM JOHN, mechanical engineer; b. Bklyn., July 7, 1948; s. William John and Regina Helen (Chrzanowski) K.; m. Claire Elise

Guglielmelli, Oct. 20, 1973; 1 child, Elise Marie. BSME cum laude, Poly. U., Bklyn., 1970; MME, Poly. U., 1978; postgrad., Rensselaer Poly. Inst., 1970-71; MS in Nuclear Engring., Columbia U., 1972. Registered profl. engr., N.Y. R&D project engr. Combustion Engring., Windsor, Conn., 1970-71; supr. applied physics Ebasco Svcs., Inc., N.Y.C., 1972-85; prin. rsch. engr. Battelle Pacific Northwest Labs., Richland, Wash., 1985-87; staff engr. design Lockheed Martin, N.J., Pa., 1988-99; sr. tech. mgr. Dynatherm Corp. Inc., Hunt Valley, Md., 1999—; instr., organizer profl. symposia. Author, editor: Thermal-Hydraulics for Space Power, Propulsion and Thermal Management, 1990; contbr. articles, reports to profl. publs. Mem. ASME (reviewer fluids divsn. 1978—), AIAA (reviewer Jour. Thermophysics and Heat Transfer), Am. Nuclear Soc., Pi Tau Sigma, Tau Beta Pi. Avocations: model railroading, woodworking, gardening. Office: Dynatherm Corp. Inc. 1 Beaver Ct Hunt Valley MD 21030-1784

KROTKI, KAROL JOZEF, sociology educator, demographer; b. Cieszyn, Poland, May 15, 1922; emigrated to Can., 1964; s. Karol Stanislaw and Anna Elzbieta (Skrzywanek) K.; m. Joanna Patkowski, July 12, 1947; children—Karol Peter, Jan Jozef, Filip Karol. BA (hons.), Cambridge (Eng.) U., 1948, MA, 1952; MA, Princeton U., 1959, PhD, 1960. Civil ser. Eng., 1948-49; dep. dir. stats. Sudan, 1949-58; vis. fellow Princeton U., 1958-60; rsch. adviser Pakistan Inst. Devel. Econs., 1960-64; asst. dir. census rsch. Dominion Bur. Stats., Can., 1964-68; prof. sociology U. Alta., 1968-83, prof., 1983-91, prof. emeritus, 1991—; vis. prof. U. Calif., Berkeley, 1967, U. N.C., 1970-73, U. Mich., 1975, U. Costa Rica, 1993; coord. program socio-econ. rsch. Province Alta., 1969-71; cons. in field. Author 14 books; contbr. articles to profl. jours. Served with Polish, French and Brit. Armed Forces, 1939-46. Decorated 9 wartime medals; recipient Achievement award Province of Alta, 1970, Commemorative medal for 125th Ann. of Can., 1992; hon. citizen Gizalki, Poland, 1994; grantee in field. Fellow Am. Statis Assn., Royal Soc. Can. (v.p. 1986-88), Acad. Humanities and Social Scis. (v.p. 1984-86, pres. 1986-88); mem. Fedn. Can. Demographers (v.p. 1977-82, pres. 1982-84), Can. Population Soc., Assn. des Demographes du Que., Soc. Edmonton Demographers (founder, pres. 1990-96, hon. advisor), Ctrl. and E. European Studies Soc. (pres. 1986-88), Population Assn. Am., Internat. Union Sci. Study Population, Assn. Internat. des Demographes de Langue Francaise, Internat. Statis. Inst., Royal Statis. Soc. Roman Catholic. Home: 10137 Clifton Pl, Edmonton, AB Canada T5N 3H9 Office: U Alta, Dept Sociology, Edmonton, AB Canada T6G 2H4

KROTO, HAROLD WALTER, chemistry researcher, educator; b. Oct. 7, 1939; s. Heinz and Edith K.; m. Margaret Henrietta Hunter, 1963; 2 children. Student, U. Sheffield, 1958-64. Postdoctoral fellow NRCC, 1964-66; rsch. scientist Bell Tel. Labs., N.J., 1966-67; lectr. U. Sussex, Brighton Sussex, Eng., 1968-77, reader, 1977-85, prof. chemistry, 1985-91, Royal Soc. Rsch. prof., 1991—; chmn. Vega Sci. Trust. Contbr. 280 articles to profl. jours. Created knight, 1996; recipient award Sunday Times Book Jacket Design Competition, 1964, Tilden lectr., 1981-82, Internat. New Materials prize Am. Phys. Soc., 1992, Italgas prize for innovation in chemistry, 1992, Longstaff medal Royal Soc. Chemistry, 1993, Hewlett Packard Europhysics prize, 1994, Science pour L'art prize Moet Hennessy Louis Vuitton, 1994; co-recipient Nobel prize in chemistry, 1996. Office: U Sussex, Sch Chem Phys & Environ Sci, Brighton Sussex BN1 9QJ, England

KROTO, JOSEPH JOHN, secondary educator; b. Washington, June 9, 1947; s. Joseph J. and Tillie (Leavitt) K.; m. Faith Gail Eisner, Aug. 17, 1969; children: Joseph John III, Stacey Gabrielle. BS in Math., U. Md., 1970; MS in Edn., Johns Hopkins U., 1996. Cert. sci. tchr., prin., Md. Sci. tchr. Potomac Sr. H.S., Oxon Hill, Md., 1970-75; chair dept. sci. Eleanor Roosevelt Sci. and Tech. H.s., Greenbelt, Md., 1976-86; coord. sci., math. and tech. program Nicholas Orem Mid. Sch., Hyattsville, Md., 1986-88; coord. Biotech. Ctr. Fairmont Hts. H.S., Capitol Heights, Md., 1988-92; chmn. dept. sci. and tech. Western Sch. Tech. and Environ. Sci., Balt., 1992—; dir. Ctr. for Space Sci. Tech., Goddard Space Flight Ctr., Greenbelt, summer 1984; instr. biotech. workshops for tchrs. Author: Selected Abstracts, 1985-88; contbr. articles to profl. jours. Founder, chair No. Area Sci. Tchr. Coords. Adv. Group, Prince George's County, Md., 1978-81; mem. negotiating team Prince George's County Educators vs. Bd. Edn., 1980-82; established corp. sponsorship Kids for Sci., Prince George's county, 1988. Recipient Outstanding Educator award Prince George's County Pub. Schs., 1985, Excellence in Edn. award Am. Soc. Microbiology, 1983, NSF award, 1986, others; grantee NSF, 1989, Eisenhower Staff/Curriculum Devel., Met. Heart Guild, others. Mem. NEA, ASCD, Nat. Assn. Sci. Tchrs., Nat. Sci. Leadership Assn., Md. State Tchrs. Assn. Democrat. Jewish. Home: 1420 Crockett Ln Silver Spring MD 20904-5478 Office: Western Sch Tech 100 Kenwood Ave Baltimore MD 21228-3610

KROUSE, GEORGE RAYMOND, JR., lawyer; b. Atlantic City, Sept. 30, 1945; s. George R. and Viola (Rogers) K.; m. Susan Naylor, Aug. 7, 1967; children: Geoffrey, Alison. AB cum laude, Brown U., 1967; JD with distinction, Duke U., 1970. Bar: N.Y. 1971, U.S. Ct. Mil. Appeals 1971, U.S. Dist. Ct. (so. and ea. dists.) N.Y. 1975. Assoc. Simpson Thacher & Bartlett, N.Y.C., 1970-71, 75-78, ptnr., 1978—. Articles editor Duke Law Jour. Mem. bd. visitors Sch. Law, Duke U., Durham, N.C., 1986-92, chmn., 1997—; mem. nat. devel. coun. Duke U., 1994—. Capt. USAF, 1971-75. Recipient Air Force Commendation medal, 1973, Meritorius Svc. medal 1975. Mem. ABA, N.Y. State Bar Assn., Assn. of Bar of City of N.Y. (com. on corps. 1985-88, com. art law 1990-93), Order of Coif, Montclair Golf Club. Avocation: golf. Home: 4 Erwin Park Montclair NJ 07042-3018 Office: Simpson Thacher & Bartlett 425 Lexington Ave Fl 15 New York NY 10017-3954

KROUSE, HELENE JUNE, nursing educator; b. Bklyn., Mar. 24, 1955; d. Sidney and Gertrude Kempner; m. John H. Krouse, May 6, 1979; children: Beth Melissa, Daniel Jacob. BS cum laude, SUNY, Bklyn., 1976; MS, U. Rochester, 1979; PhD, Boston Coll., 1984. Cert. adult nurse practitioner, cert. otorhinolaryngology nurse. Staff nurse Downstate Med. Ctr., Bklyn., 1976-77; instr. in nursing Hunter Coll.-Bellevue Sch. Nursing, N.Y.C., 1979-80; asst. prof., coord. med.-surg. nursing Emmanuel Coll., Boston, 1980-84; asst. prof. nursing Boston Coll., Chestnut Hill, Mass., 1984-89; adult nurse practitioner Mass. Eye and Ear Infirmary, Boston; adminstr., nurse practitioner to Ear, Nose, Throat, Sinus and Allergy practice, Ormond Beach, 1989—; assoc. prof. U. North Fla., Jacksonville, 1995-97, acting chairperson dept. nursing, 1996-97; assoc. prof. U. Fla., 1997—; faculty fellow Boston Coll., 1988, rsch. fellow, 1987. Contbr. articles on otolaryngology, compliance and decision makingto profl. pubs., also chpts. to books. Recipient Ednl. award ENT divsn. Smith and Nephew Inc., 1998, First Place in Ann. Videotape Contest, Soc. Otorhinolaryngology-Head and Neck Nurses; grantee U. Rochester Alumni Seed Found., 1978-79, Emmanuel Coll., 1981-83; So. Nursing Rsch. Soc./Am. Nurses Found. scholar, 1998. Mem. Oncology Nurse Soc., So. Nursing Rsch. Soc., Soc. Otorhinolaryngology and Head-Neck Nurses, Inc. (chair nat. rsch. com.), Sigma Theta Tau (Clin. Rsch. award 1986-87). E-mail: kroushj.valencia@shands.ufl.edu. Office: U Fla Coll Nursing Orlando Urban Campus PO Box 3028 Orlando FL 32802-3028

KROUT, BOYD MERRILL, psychiatrist; b. Oakland, Calif., Jan. 31, 1931; s. Boyd Merrill and Phoebe Lenore (Colby) K.; m. Helena Luise Keel, Aug. 25, 1965. AB, Stanford U., 1951, MD, 1955. Diplomate Am. Bd. Psychiatry and Neurology. Intern San Francisco Hosp., 1954-55; resident Boston U. Hosps., 1958-60, Boston Va Hosp., 1960-61; asst. to clin. prof. UCLA Sch. Medicine, 1961-95, vis. prof., 1995—; chief physician Harbor/UCLA Med. Ctr., Torrance, 1961-95. Capt. USAF, 1955-58. Fellow Am. Psychiat. Assn., So. Calif. Psychiat. Soc. (councillor 1988-91), Am. Psychiat. Soc.; mem. L.A. County Med. Soc. Republican. Office: Harbor/UCLA Med Ctr PO Box 8 Torrance CA 90507-0008

KRPATA, RICHARD MARTIN, state agency administrator; b. Rockville, Conn., Aug. 22, 1955; s. Edward Joseph and Nancy Jean Davis. BS, U. Mass., 1977. Mgr. Interstate United, Middletown, Conn., 1978-82, Victorian Too, Hamden, Conn., 1982-83, Daka Internat., Bridgeport, Conn., 1983-85; constrn. mgr. Am. Constructors, Hebron, Conn., 1985-87; owner, pres. Burgundy Constrn., Windsor, Conn., 1987-90; asst. dept. of Revenue State of Conn., Hartford, 1992—. Campaigner Rowland for Gov., Hartford 1994, Dole for Pres., Hartford and N.H., 1996. Avocations: golf, house restoration. Home: 200 Swamp Rd Coventry CT 06238-1437 Office: State of Conn Dept of Revenue 25 Sigourney St Dept Of Hartford CT 06106-5001

KRSUL, JOHN ALOYSIUS, JR., lawyer; b. Highland Park, Mich., Mar. 24, 1938; s. John A. and Ann M. (Sepich) K.; m. Justine Oliver, Sept. 12, 1958; children: Ann Lisa, Mary Justine. BA, Albion Coll., 1959; JD, U. Mich., 1963. Bar: Mich. 1963. Assoc. Dickinson Wright PLLP, 1963-71; ptnr. Dickinson Wright PLLP, Detroit, 1971—. Asst. editor: U. Mich. Law Rev, 1962-63; editorial bd. ABA Jour., 1996—. Recipient Disting. Alumnus award Albion Coll., 1984; Sloan scholar, 1958-59; Fulbright scholar, 1959-60; Ford. Found. grantee, 1964. Fellow Am. Bar Found. (life, chmn. Mich. chpt. 1988-89); mem. ABA (sect. gen. practice, chmn. 1989-90, exec. coun. 1984-91, ho. of dels. 1979—, chmn. standing com. on membership 1983-89, tort and ins. practice sect., exec. coun. 1991-94, chmn. fin. com. 1993-94, bd. govs. 1991—, exec. com. 1993-94, 96—, treas. 1996—), Detroit Bar Assn. (dir. 1971-80, pres. 1979-80), Detroit Bar Assn. Found. (dir. 1971-84, pres. 1979-80), State Bar Mich. (commr. 1973-83, pres. 1982-83), Mich. State Bar Found. (trustee 1982-83, 85—, chmn. fellows 1986-87), Fellows of Young Lawyers Am. Bar (bd. dirs. 1977-86, chmn. bd. 1984-86, pres. 1983-84), Am. Judicature Soc. (dir. 1971-79, exec. com. 1973-74), Nat. Conf. Bar Pres. (exec. coun. 1986-89), Am. Bar Endowment (bd. dirs. 1996—), Am. Bar Ins. Cons. Inc. (bd. dirs. sec. 1988-95), Sixth Cir. Jud. Conf. (life), Orchard Lake Country Club, Detroit Club, Phi Beta Kappa, Omicron Delta Kappa, Phi Eta Sigma, Delta Tau Delta. Home: 7094 Huntington Dr Sawyer MI 49125-9319 Office: Dickinson Wright PLLC 500 Woodward Ave Ste 4000 Detroit MI 48226-3416

KRUCENSKI, LEONARD JOSEPH, secondary education educator; b. Buffalo, June 15, 1931; s. Stanislous and Anna Victoria (Pyzanowska) K.; m. Estelle Ann Gaik, Oct. 19, 1957; children: Leonard S., Brian M., William G. BS cum laude, SUNY, Buffalo, 1976, MS in Edn., 1980. Electronics technician Bell Aero Space Inc., Niagara Falls, N.Y., 1953-62, Moog Valve Inc, East Aurora, N.Y., 1962-69; engring. aid Cornell Aero. Labs. Inc., Buffalo, 1969-75; jr. engr. Kistler Instruments Inc., Clarence, N.Y., 1975-79; tchr. electronics Buffalo Pub. Sch. System, 1979—. Recipient 85th Anniversary Alumni Disting. Svc. award Hutchinson Cen. Tech. High Sch., 1989. Mem. ASCD, NEA, Am. Vocat. Assn., Nat. Assn. Indsl. and Tech. Tchr. Educators, N.Y. State Occupational Edn. Assn., Vocat. Tech. Guild Buffalo, Buffalo Tchrs. Fedn. Avocations: woodworking, philately. Home: 176 Lorelee Dr Tonawanda NY 14150-4325 Office: Hutchinson Cen Tech High Sch 256 S Elmwood Ave Buffalo NY 14201-2339

KRUCKEBERG, ARTHUR RICE, botanist, educator; b. Los Angeles, Mar. 21, 1920; s. Arthur Woodbury and Ella Muriel K.; m. Mareen Schultz, Mar. 21, 1953; children—Arthur Leo, Enid Johanna; children by previous marriage—Janet Muriel, Patricia Elayne, Caroline. B.A., Occidental Coll., Los Angeles, 1941; postgrad., Stanford U., 1941-42; Ph.D., U. Calif.-Berkeley, 1950. Instr. biology Occidental Coll., 1946; teaching asst. U. Calif.-Berkeley, 1946-50; mem. faculty U. Wash., Seattle, 1950—; prof. botany U. Wash., 1964-88, emeritus, 1988—, chmn. dept., 1971-77; cons. in field. Co-founder Wash. Natural Area Preserves system, 1966. Served with USNR, 1942-46. Mem. Wash. Native Plant Soc. (founder 1976), Calif. Bot. Soc. Rsch. edaphics of serpentines, flowering plants. Home: 20312 15th Ave NW Shoreline WA 98177-2166 Office: U Wash PO Box 351330 Seattle WA 98195-1330

KRUCZEK, MIKE, coach; b. Mar. 15, 1953; m. Leigh Kruczek; children: Kelly, Garrett. BA, Boston Coll., 1976. Profl. football player Pitts. Steelers, 1976-81, Washington Redskins, 1981-82; asst. coach Fla. State U., 1982-84; asst. coach Jacksonville (Fla.) Bulls U.S. Football League, 1984; asst. coach U. Ctrl. Fla., Orlando, 1984-97, coach, 1998—. Office: Univ Ctrl Fla Athletics Dept PO Box 163555 Orlando FL 32816-3555*

KRUEGEL, PATRICK FERDINAND, purchasing agent; b. Bern, Switzerland, July 22, 1967; came to U.S., 1993; s. Marius Andre and Charlotte Catherine (Frieden) K. BABA, Bus. Sch., Bern, 1987; MA in Hospitality Mgmt., Hospitality Mgmt. Sch., Thun, Switzerland, 1990. Night auditor Hotel Christiania, Gstaad, Switzerland, 1987-88; asst. mgr. food and beverage Restaurant Moevenpick, Zurich, Switzerland, 1991-92; purchasing agt. Novartis Nutrition, Mpls., 1993—. Cpl. Swiss Army, 1987-91. Avocations: sports, travel, movies, music, reading. Home: 4130 Upton Ave N Minneapolis MN 55412-1522 Office: Novartis Nutrition Corp PO Box 370 Minneapolis MN 55440

KRUEGER, ALAN DOUGLAS, communications company executive; b. Little Rock, Dec. 24, 1937; s. Herbert C. and Estelle B. Krueger; m. Betty Burns, Apr. 4, 1975; children: (by previous marriage) Scott Alan, Dane Kieth, Kip Douglas, Bryan Lee. Student, U. Ill., 1956, Wright Coll., 1957-58. Project engr. Motorola, Inc., Chgo., 1956-64; service mgr., field tech. rep. Motorola, Inc., Indpls., 1964-67; pres. Comm. Maintenance, Inc., Indpls., 1967-68, Comm. Unltd., Inc., Indpls., 1968—. Recipient Friend of the Child award, 1995. Mem. Indpls. Zoologian Soc., Specialized Mobile Radio Wireless Operator Network. Methodist. Club: Elks. Home: 6242 N 575 E Franklin IN 46131-8759 Office: Comm Unltd Inc 4545 Southeastern Ave Indianapolis IN 46203-2307

KRUEGER, ANNE O., economics educator; b. Endicott, N.Y.. BA, Oberlin (Ohio) Coll., 1953; MS, U. Wis., 1956, PhD, 1958; PhD, Georgetown U., 1992; PhD (hon.), Hacettepe U., Ankara, Turkey, 1990, Monash U., 1995. Asst. prof. econs. U. Minn., St. Paul, 1959-63, assoc. prof. econs., 1963-66, prof. econs., 1966-82; v.p. econs. and rsch. The World Bank, Washington, 1982-86; art and scis. prof. econs. Duke U., Durham, N.C., 1987-95; prof. dept. econs. Stanford (Calif.) U., 1993—, dir. Ctr. Rsch. Econ. Devel. and Policy Reform, 1996—; bd. dirs. Nordson Corp., Westlake, Ohio, Western Digital, Irvine, Calif.; mem. vis. com. Econs. Dept. Harvard U., 1990-98; sr. non-resident fellow Brookings Inst.; rsch. assoc. Nat. Bur. Econ. Rsch. Author: Trade Policies and Developing Nations, 1995, Economic Policies at Cross Purposes, 1993, Economic Policy Reform in Developing Countries, 1992, The Political Economy of Agricultural Pricing Policy, Vol. 5: A Synthesis of the Political Economy in Developing Countries, 1992; co-author (with O. Aktan): Swimming Against the Tide: Turkish Trade Reform in the 1980s, 1992; editor: (with R.H. Bates) Political and Economic Interactions in Economic Policy Reform, 1993, The World Trade Orgnaization as an International Institution, 1998. Mem. N.Y. State Regents Commn. on Higher Edn., 1992-93. Recipient Robertson prize NAS, 1984, Bernhard Harms prize Inst. for World Economy, Kiel, 1990, Enterprise award Kenan Inst., 1990, Seidman prize, 1994. Fellow AAAS, Econometric Soc. (award 1981); mem. NAS (chmn. com. rsch. 1998-92,Am. Econ. Assn. (chmn. commn. on grad. edn. in econs. 1989-90, v.p. 1977, pres.-elect 1995, pres. 1996, rep. to Internat. Econ. Assn. and mem. IEA exec. com. 1992-98, v.p. Internat. Econ. Assn. 1994-98). Office: Stanford U Dept Econs Stanford CA 94305

KRUEGER, ARLIN JAMES, physicist; b. Lamberton, Minn., Oct. 22, 1933; s. Rudolph August and Mathilda E. (Pooch) K.; B.A., U. Minn., 1955, postgrad., 1956-58; Goddard research and study fellow, Colo. State U., 1976-78, Ph.D., 1984; m. Susan J. Peacock, Dec. 28, 1978; children: Sandra, Timothy, Terry. Physicist, Naval Weapons Center, China Lake, Calif., 1959-69; physicist-astrophysicist Goddard Space Flight Center, Greenbelt, Md., 1969—, developer of rocket and satellite instruments: sensor sci. Nimbus-7 Total Ozone Mapping Spectrometer (TOMS), 1975-93, Rocoz Optical Rocket Ozonesonde, 1961-79, Volcanic Ash Mapper (VOLCAM), 1998; mem. com. extension U.S. Standard Atmosphere; instrument scientist U.S.-USSR Meteor 3/TOMS mission, U.S. Earth Probe/TOMS mission; prin. investigator Japanese ADEOS/TOMS mission, NASA Earth Sys. Scis. Pathfinder, Volcanic Ash Monitor (VOLCAM) Satellite Program, NASA Airborne Antarctic Ozone Experiment/TOMS Real-Time Support, NASA Airborne Arctic Experiment/TOMS Real time Support; co-investigator Earth Observing System Volcanic Eruption Investigation, Rsch. on Antarctic Ozone Hole; adv. volcanic hazards panel Office Fed. Coord. of Meteorology; invited lectr. Nat. Inst. Polar Rsch., Tokyo, AT&T Bell Labs., U.S. Naval Acad., Goddard Space Flight Ctr. Engring. Colloquium, Gordon Rsch. Conf. on Volcano-Climate, Fermi Sch. Physics, Italy, Russian Acad. Scis., Moscow; Quaternary Rsch. Lectr U. Wash.; invited participant and speaker sci. workshops and confs. Recipient NASA Exceptional Scientific Achievement medal. Research on stratospheric ozone, remote sensing from satellites, volcanic eruptions, volcanic aviation hazards, atmosphere of Mars. Mem. Am. Meteorol. Soc., Internat. Assn. Meteorology and Atmospheric Physics (internat. ozone commn.), Am. Geophys. Union, AAAS, Sigma Xi. Contbr. articles to profl. publs. Office: Goddard Space Flight Ctr Code # 916 Greenbelt MD 20771

KRUEGER, ARTUR W. G., international business consultant; b. Neuendorf, Ger., Jan. 16, 1940; came to U.S., 1975; s. Werner Georg and Charlotte (Klein) K.; Betriebswirt grad., Wirtschafts-Akademie, Bremen, Ger., 1968; MS in Bus. Policy, Columbia U., 1978. Mktg. exec., gen. mgr., Rosenthal A.G. Subsidaries in Spain, Scandinavia and U.S., 1970-79; pres. Am. European Cons. Co. Inc., Houston, 1980—; lectr. in field. Mem. Am. Mgmt. Assn., Space Found., Columbia Bus. Assocs., Internat. Bus. Council, Marine Tech. Soc., Instrument Soc. Am., Houston World Trade Assn., Norwegian-Am. C. of C., U.S. C. of C., German Am. C. of C., Swiss Am. C. of C., French Am. C. of C. Office: Am European Cons Co Inc PO Box 19686 Houston TX 77224-9686

KRUEGER, BONNIE LEE, editor, writer; b. Chgo., Feb. 3, 1950; d. Harry Bernard and Lillian (Soyak) Krueger; m. James Lawrence Spurlock, Mar. 8, 1972. *Husband James L. Spurlock, Chicago, Illinois, is a publisher at Associated Publications, Inc., and has been since 1978. Prior to this, Mr. Spurlock served as an editor at Playboy Enterprises, Inc., and as a reporter at the Chicago Daily News.* Student, Morraine Valley Coll., 1970. Adminstrv. asst. Carson Pirie Scott & Co., Chgo., 1969-72; traffic coord. Tatham Laird & Kudner, Chgo., 1973-74; traffic coord. J. Walter Thompson, Chgo., 1974-76, prodn. coord., 1976-78; editor-in-chief Assoc. Pubs., Chgo., 1978—, Sophisticate's Hairstyle Guide, 1978—, Sophisticate's Beauty Guide, 1978—, Complete Woman, 1981—; pub., editorial svcs. dir. Sophisticate's Black Hair Guide, 1983—, Sophisticate's Soap Star Styles, 1994-95. Mem. Statue of Liberty Restoration Com., N.Y.C., 1983; campaign worker Cook County State's Atty., Chgo., 1982; poll watcher Cook County Dem. Orgn., 1983; mem. Chgo. Architecture Found. Mem. Soc. Profl. Journalists, Am. Health and Beauty Aids Inst. (assoc. mem.), Lincoln Park Zool. Soc., Landmarks Preservation Coun. of Ill., Art Inst. Chgo., Chgo. Hist. Soc., Mus. Contemporary Art, Peta, Headline Club, Sigma Delta Chi. Lutheran. Office: Complete Woman 875 N Michigan Ave Chicago IL 60611-1803 *I approach my life like one would approach the climbing of a mountain—plenty of faith, determination, self criticism, hard work and the joy and knowledge that the top is there for everyone to reach, if you pursue it with a combination of fervor, patience and love.*

KRUEGER, CANDICE JAE, assistant principal; b. Milw., Jan. 24, 1946; d. William Elmer and June Marie (Nelson) K. BA in English, U. No. Colo., 1967; MA in Edn. Curriculum and Instrn., Boise State U., 1989; Ednl. Specialist, U. Idaho, 1994. Tchr. English Grant Joint Union Sch. Dist., Sacramento, 1967-69, Sch. Dist. #11, Colorado Springs, Colo., 1969-74, Meridian (Idaho) Sch. Dist. #2, 1974-94, Sch. Dist. #422, Cascade, Idaho, 1994-95; asst. prin. Mountain Home (Idaho) Sch. Dist. #193, 1995—. Newsletter editor Idaho Coun. Tchrs. English, 1990-93; contbr. poetry to profl. jours. Vol., race coord. Ronald McDonald House, Boise, 1989—; start line dir. Idaho Women's Fitness Celebration, Boise, 1996, Hallando House, Cath. Diocese of Denver, Colorado Springs, 1970-74; coach Little League, Boise, 1990-92. Mem. AAUW, ASCD, N.W. Women in Edn. (treas.). Republican. Episcopalian. Avocations: hiking, cycling, writing poetry. Home: 2310 Smith Ave Boise ID 83702-0349 Office: Mountain Home High School 300 S 11th E Mountain Home ID 83647-3263

KRUEGER, CHARLES CONRAD, fishery science educator; b. Mpls., Jan. 14, 1952; s. Conrad Paul and Frances (Dahl) K.; m. Sharon Louise Thompson, Aug. 3, 1974. B.S. with distinction, U. Minn., 1974, Ph.D., 1979; M.S., Iowa State U., 1976. Research fellow U. Minn., St. Paul, 1979, research assoc., 1980-81; Gt. Lakes sport fisheries specialist Wis. Dept. Natural Resources, Madison, 1981-83; asst. prof. fisheries Cornell U., Ithaca, N.Y., 1984-89, assoc. prof., 1990—. Contbr. articles to profl. jours. grantee Gt. Lakes Fishery Commn., 1979; Minn. sea grantee, 1981, U.S. Fish Wildlife Svc., U.S. G.S., N.Y., Minn., Wisc.. Mem. Am. Fisheries Soc., Soc. for Conservation Biology, Internat. Assn. Great Lakes Rsch., Sigma Xi, Phi Kappa Phi, Gamma Sigma Delta. Office: Cornell U Dept Natural Resources Fernow Hall Rm 206-D Ithaca NY 14853-0188*

KRUEGER, CHRISTINE MARIE, assistant principal; b. Gary, Ind., May 11, 1957; d. Arthur John and Edna Eloise (Klepser) K. BS in Edn., Murray State U., 1979, MA in Reading, 1988. Cert. adminstr., supr., Ky. Learning disabilities tchr. McNabb Elem., Paducah, Ky., 1980, St. Mary Elem., Paducah, 1980-87, Paducah Mid. Sch., 1987-94; vocat. edn. tchr. Paducah Middle Sch., 1994-96, asst. prin., 1996—; chairperson Positive Environ. Project, Paducah, 1988-93; area dir. Ky. Spl. Olympics, Frankfort, Ky., 1984-96. Pres. Plays Rely on People Support/Market House Theatre, Paducah, 1985-87; clk. ch. session First Presbyn. Ch., Paducah, 1988; coach Ky. Spl. Olympics Internat., Paducah, 1987, 91, world games coach, 1995. Named Ambassador of Good Will, State Ky., Frankfort, 1987, Outstanding Vol., Western Ky. Mental Health, Paducah, 1989, Paducah Mid. Tchr. of Yr., Ky. Dept. Edn. and Paducah Ind. Schs., Frankfort, 1990; recipient Extra Mile award Paducah Area C. of C., 1989. Mem. Ky. Edn. Assn., Paducah Edn. Assn. (spl. edn. rep. 1991-92, instr. for crisis prevention/intervention inst. 1993—, chmn. insvc. com. 1994—). Avocations: walking, music, decorating, family time.

KRUEGER, DARRELL WILLIAM, university president; b. Salt Lake City, Feb. 9, 1943; s. William T. and E. Marie (Nelson) K.; m. Verlene Terry, July 1, 1965 (dec. Jan., 1969); 1 child, William; m. Nancy Leane Jones, Sept. 2, 1969; children: Tonya, Amy, Susan. BA summa cum laude, So. Utah State Coll., 1967; MA in Govt., U. Ariz., 1969, PhD in Govt., 1971. Asst. prof. polit. sci. N.E. Mo. State U., Kirksville, 1971-73, v.p. acad. affairs, dean of instrn., 1973-89; pres. Winona (Minn.) State U., 1989—; facilitator The 7 Habits of Highly Effective People, 1993; mem. adv. bd. U.S. Bank, Rochester, Minn., 1989—. Mem. Gamehaven Coun. Boy Scouts Am., 1989—. Recipient Outstanding Alumnus award, So. Utah State, 1992. Mem. Am. Assn. State Colls. and Univs., Am. Assn. Higher Edn., Rotary, Phi Beta Kappa. Mem. LDS Ch. Avocations: running, golf. Home: 1411 Heights Blvd Winona MN 55987-2519 Office: Winona State U Somsen 201 8th & Johnson Winona MN 55987

KRUEGER, EUGENE REX, academic program consultant; b. Grand Island, Nebr., Mar. 30, 1935; s. Rudolph F. and Alma K.; m. Karin Schubert, June 9, 1957; children: Eugene Eric, Richard Kevin, Kristina. Student, Kans. State U., 1952-53; B.S. in Physics, Rensselaer Poly. Inst., 1957, M.S. in Math, 1960, Ph.D. in Applied Math, 1962. Research physicist IBM, 1957-58; research fellow Army Math. Research Center, U. Wis., 1962-63; prof. U. Colo., Boulder, 1965-74; vice chancellor, prof. Oreg. State System of Higher Edn., Eugene, 1974-82; exec. cons. Control Data Corp., 1982-85, v.p., 1985-89; exec. dir. tech.-based engring. edn. consortium William C. Norris Inst., 1989-96, v.p., 1996-97; adj. prof. computer sci. U. Minn., 1989-94; chmn. seminar for dirs. of acad. computing facilities, 1969-82; pres. Krueger & Assocs., 1989—; cons. on computer graphics computing facility mgmt.; dir. various research grants and contracts; interim pres. Christian Heritage Coll., 1998. Contbr. research papers in field to publs. Mem. Sigma Xi, Phi Kappa Phi.

KRUEGER, JAMES A., lawyer; b. Sept. 21, 1943; s. A.A. and Margaret E. (Hurley) K.; m. Therese Eileen Connors, Aug. 2, 1968; 1 child, Colleen. BA cum laude, Gongaza U., 1965; JD, Georgetown U., 1968; LLM, NYU, 1972. Bar: Wash. 1969, U.S. Supreme Ct. 1972, U.S. Tax Ct. 1972, U.S. Dist. Ct. (we. dist.) Wash. 1980, U.S. Ct. Appeals (9th cir.) 1982. Mem. staff U.S. senator from Wash., 1967-68; assoc. Kane, Vandeberg & Hartinger, Tacoma, 1972-76; ptnr. Kane, Vandeberg, Hartinger & Walker, Tacoma, 1976-90; shareholder Vandeberg Johnson & Gandara, Tacoma, 1990—; spl. dist. counsel Wash. State Bar Assn., 1984-94; adj. prof. law, U. of Puget Sound, 1974-76. Contbr. chpt. to Representing the Close Corporation, 1979, Partnership Agreements, 1981, Planning for the Small Business Enterprise, 1982, The Partnership Handbook, 1984. Chmn. bd. Cath. Cmty. Svcs. of Pierce and Kitsap Counties, 1983-84; bd. dirs. United Way of Pierce County, 1973-82, 99—. Capt. U.S. Army, 1968-72. Decorated Bronze star. Mem. ABA, Wash. State Bar Assn. (spl. dist. counsel), Tacoma-Pierce County Bar

Assn. Roman Catholic. Office: 1201 Pacific Ave Ste 1900 Tacoma WA 98402-4315

KRUEGER, JOHN ANTHONY, biomedical engineer, musician; b. Brookfield, Wis., June 20, 1968; s. Russell James and Jackie (Hilma) Krueger; children: James Russell, John Anthony. BS, U. Wis.; MS, U. Minn. Musician Cross Reference, Milw., 1985-96; biomed. engr. Heyer Schulte NeuroCare, 1995—; media editor Elmbrook Ch., Waukesha, Wis., 1986-96, actor, 1986-99, photographer, 1986-97, media cons., 1986-95. Appeared in numerous prodns. as actor or musician; mem. Milw. Symphony Chorus, 1996-98; 4 patents in field. High sch. youth worker Elmbrook Ch, 1990-99. Mem. Nat. Ski Patrol, Profl. Assn. Diving Instrs., Golden Key, Pi Tau Sigma, Theta Tau (co-founder), Tau Beta Pi. Home: 17900 Anthony Ln Brookfield WI 53045-2408

KRUEGER, JOHN CHARLES, financial planner, investment advisor; b. St. Louis, Oct. 5, 1951; s. Edward Rice and Frances (Lingel) K.; m. Mary Jo Holtz, Apr. 20, 1979; children: Kimberly Ann, Eric John. BS in Bus., U. Miss., 1974; MBA, U. Phoenix, 1987. CLU; cert. fin. planner; chartered fin. cons.; registered investment advisor. With Aetna Life Ins., Phoenix, 1975-76; fin. planner, investments advisor Krueger Fin. Services Inc., Phoenix, 1976—; guest instr. Ariz State U., 1983-86; lectr. and coordinator cable TV programs on fin., Ariz., 1983, 84; adj. faculty mem. Coll Fin. Planning, Denver, 1984—. Guest instr. in fin. planning. City of Phoenix Retirement Ctr., 1984—, City of Mesa (Ariz.) Retirement Ctr., 1984, City of Tempe (Ariz.) Retirement Ctr., 1984-85. Mem. Inst. Cert. Fin. Planners (past pres. greater Phoenix chpt.), Am. Soc. CLU's. Republican. Avocation: tennis. Home: 2159 E La Vieve Ln Tempe AZ 85284-3543 Office: Krueger Fin Svcs 7776 S Pointe Pkwy W Ste 136 Phoenix AZ 85044-5402

KRUEGER, KATHLEEN SUSAN, special education administrator; b. Cape Girardeau, Mo., Jan. 21, 1951; d. Robert Settle and Myldred Frances (Jones) K. BS in Edn., Athens Coll., 1973; MEd, Ala. A&M U., 1980. Classroom tchr. Limestone County Schs., Athens, Ala., 1973-74; spl. edn. tchr. Huntsville (Ala.) City Schs., 1974-95, spl. edn. coord., 1995—; mem. city-wide policy com. Huntsville City Schs., 1987-89, profl. devel. coord., 1986-95, dept. chair for spl. edn., 1993-95. Bd. dirs. H-Vote, Huntsville, 1989; vol. ARC, 1981-82; tchr. Sunday Sch., First United Meth. Ch., Huntsville, 1983-85, sec., 1985-86, mem. choir, 1985-89, hon. treas. for State of Ala., 1988. Mem. NEA (PAC), Ala. Edn. Assn., Huntsville Edn. Assn. (bldg. rep. 1992-95, treas. 1989, sec. 1992-93), Coun. for Exceptional Children, Ala. Coun. for Sch. Adminstrn. and Supervision, Phi Delta Kappa, Phi Mu (membership chair 1970-71, treas. 1971-72). Home: 7801 Regent Pl SW Apt 8 Huntsville AL 35802-1471 Office: Huntsville City Schs 200 White St Huntsville AL 35801

KRUEGER, KENNETH JOHN, corporate executive, nutritionist, educator; b. L.A., Jan. 29, 1946; s. Charles Herbert and Adelaide Marie K.; m. Ellen Santucci, June 16, 1979 (div. 1989); children: Kenneth, Michael, Scott, David. BA in Humanities, U. So. Calif., 1968; MS in Edn. (Psychology), Mt. St. Mary's Coll., 1972. English tchr. Corcoran (Calif.) High Sch., 1968, Charter Oak High Sch., Covina, Calif., 1969-90; nutrition and exercise instr. Mt. San Antonio Coll., Walnut, Calif., 1974-90; pres. Mega Group, Ltd., 1990, The Krueger Group, Malibu, Calif., 1991—; exec. Overnite Express, L.A., Calif., 1993, Calif. Parcel Express, Encino, 1994-95; nutritionist Swiss Nat. Team, 1995-99; phys. edn. tchr. Hiram Johnson H.S., Sacramento, Calif., 1995-96; adj. prof. phys. edn. Sierra Coll., Rocklin, Calif., 1996; health instr. L.A. City Coll., 1996-97, West L.A. Coll., 1998; swim coach Mt. San Antonio Coll., Walnut, Calif., 1974-77; coach, v.p. Trojan Swim Club, Newport Beach, Calif., 1978-90; bd. dirs. Nutrition and Exercise Cons., Tustin, Calif.; nutrition and exercise dir. Health Am., 1987-90; chmn., nutrition and fitness com. Internat. Eating Disorders Com., 1988; U.S. nat. team nutritionist for (FINA) World Cup 1988 Champions; recruiter Club Med, Paris, 1976-78; program coord. Pacific Am. Inst., San Francisco, 1983; asst. coach Vevey Natation, Switzerland, 1972-73; asst. swim coach Swiss Nat. Team, 1968, 85; chief marshall U.S. Olympic Swim Trials, Irvine, 1980, linguistics chmn. protocol U. So. Calif. Venue, L.A. Olympic Com., 1983-84; mem.-at-large long distance com. U.S. Swimming, Colorado Springs, 1987-91, coach So. Calif. Long Distance Swimming, 1987-89; del. chief, coach and swimmer So. Calif. Swimming for Internat. Crossing of Lake Geneva, sponsored by Internat. Olympic Com., Switzerland, 1987; meet dir. U.S. 25K Long Distance Swimming Championships/FINA World Cup Trials, Long Beach, Calif., 1988, U.S. 25K Swim Championships, Long Beach, 1989. Author: Reflections and Refractions, 1973; contbr. articles to internat. profl. nutrition and sport jours. Bd. dirs. U.S.A. Athletes Hall of Fame, 1991-92. Recipient NCAA All Am. award U. So. Calif., 1966, NCAA Nat. Champ award, 1966, U.S. Masters Swimming Champion, 1972 and annually 1974-81, Internat. Sr. Olympics Champion, 1972 and annually 1974-85; recipient commendations U.S. Congress, Calif. Senate, L.A. County Bd. Suprs; inducted into U.S.A. Athletes Hall of Fame. Mem. KC. Republican. Roman Catholic. Avocations: sports, reading. Office: The Krueger Group 6158 Trancas Rd Malibu CA 90265-3120

KRUEGER, LARRY EUGENE, import export company executive, lawyer; b. Pasco, Wash., Apr. 22, 1944; s. Albert H. and Mabel K. (Mosgaard) K.; m. Barbara Kay Strunk, Apr. 9, 1966; children: Kelli Kay, Eric Alan. AA magna cum laude, Columbia Basin Coll., 1965; BA in Edn. magna cum laude, Gonzaga U., 1966, JD, 1971; ME in Counseling, Whitworth Coll., 1982. Bar: Wash. 1972, U.S. Dist. Ct. (ea. dist.) Wash. 1973. Pvt. practice Deer Park, Wash., 1973-76, Spokane, Wash., 1978—; rep. west coast CMA, Inc., Honolulu; CEO, owner N.W. Investment and Trade, 1992-93, The Country Connection. 1st trustee Wooden Trust, 1999—; owner Krueger Mediation and Facilitation Svcs., 1998—; legal dir. County Homes Kiwanis Club, Spokane; leader 5th dist. Rep. Ctrl. Com, Spokane, 1973-76; pres. South Hill of Spokane Kiwanis Club, 1997-98; bd. dirs. Family Counseling Svc., Spokane, 1978-98, Kiwanis Club of South Hill Spokane Divsn. 46; mem. Coun. of Twelve Chs., 1987-99. Capt. USAR, 1963-73. Pasco Kiwanis scholar, 1965, Gonzaga U. Law Sch. scholar, 1966-67; named to Outstanding Young Men of Am. U.S. Jaycees, 1979. Mem. Wash. State Bar Assn., Wash. State Trial Lawyers Assn., ABA, Am. Trial Lawyers Assn., Spokane County Bar Assn., Phi Theta Kappa, Phi Alpha Delta, Kappa Delta Pi, Eagles. Home: 102 E Weile Ave Ste 2 Spokane WA 99208-5434 Office: PO Box 18589 Spokane WA 99228-0589

KRUEGER, RALPH ARTHUR, motel and food executive; b. Cleve., Apr. 14, 1952; s. Daniel and Florence (Myer) K. AA, Adirondack Community Coll., Glen Falls, N.Y., 1983; BS, Hudson Valley C.C. Dept. mgr./inventory Telescope Furniture Co., Granville, N.Y., 1970-82; owner, mgr. Pine Grove Motel, Diner and Bakery, Granville, 1979-89, Park Enterprises, Granville, 1987—, Valley Food Ct., Granville, 1988-89; owner Eagles Nest Homes of Granville, N.Y., 1990-93; parts mgr. SAAB, SUBARU, 1990-97, Yamaha, 1997-98; mgr. Cumberland Farms, 1998—; real estate sales rep., 1991—. Editor, pub.: Border Rider News, 1987-92. Treas. Heritage Days Village of Granville, 1986; trustee Congl. Ch., 1985—. Recipient Scouters Key award Boy Scouts Am., 1984, dist. award of merit, 1985, Leaders Woodbadge-Honor Campers award, 1985. Mem. Internat. Media and Info. Coun. (co-chmn. 1988), Internat. Snowmobile Coun. (Va.), Border Riders Snowmobile Club (pres. 1974-76, 87-90), Washington County Assn. Snowmobile Clubs (pres. 1983-87, treas. 1990-95, Washington County coord. 1990-94), Granville C. of C., Wakpominee Order of Arrow. Republican. Avocations: snowmobiling, camping, pipe organ restoration.

KRUEGER, RAYMOND ROBERT, lawyer; b. Portage, Wis., Aug. 29, 1947; s. Earl Andrew and Catherine Virginia (Klenert) K.; m. Barbara Bowen, June 21, 1969; children: Lindsey, Michael. BA in Econs., U. Wis., 1969, JD, 1972. Bar: Wis. 1972. Assoc. Charne, Glassner, Tehan, Clancy & Taitelman S.C., Milw., 1973-79, shareholder, 1979-91; shareholder Charne Clancy Krueger Pollack & Corris S.C., Milw., 1991-92; ptnr. Michael, Best & Friedrich, Milw., 1992—; presenter numerous seminars. Chmn. Georgia O'Keeffe Found., Abiquiu, N.Mex., 1989—; trustee Village of Whitefish Bay, Wis., 1989—; mem. Milwaukee River Revitalization Coun., 1988—, vice chair, 1989-96, chair. 1996—; mem. Milw. Art Mus. Bldg. Com., 1996—. Capt. USAF, 1969-78. Mem. ABA (natural resources sect.), State Bar Wis. (environ. law sect.), Milw. Bar Assn. (environ. law sect.), Environ. Law Inst. Avocation: visual arts. Office: Michael Best & Friedrich 100 E Wisconsin Ave Ste 3300 Milwaukee WI 53202-4108

KRUEGER, RICHARD ARNOLD, technology executive; b. St. Paul, Feb. 13, 1949; s. Richard Earnest and Shirley Mae (Popp) K.; m. Diane Susan Schiller, Apr. 14, 1973; children: Melissa, Ryan, Alisha. BA, Winona State Coll., 1971; MA in Teaching, Coll. of St. Thomas, 1973; MPA, Harvard U., 1992; PhD, U. Minn., 1997. Program dir. Midway YMCA, St. Paul, 1971-72; tchr. Lakeville (Minn.) Pub. Schs., 1973-79; dir. Staples (Minn.) Tchr. Ctr., 1979-82; owner Computer Networx, Inc., Staples, 1983-89; mem. Minn. Ho. of Reps., St. Paul, 1983-94, asst. majority leader, 1987-90, chair internat. trade and tech. com., 1989-90, speaker pro tempore, 1991-92, chair state govt. fin., 1993-94; info. mgmt. cons., Staples, 1990-94; pres. Minn. High Tech. Assn., Inc., Eagan, 1994—. Contbr. articles to profl. publs. Named Outstanding Alumnus, Winona State U., 1990; recipient Top Tech. Legis. Group award Am. Electronic Assn., 1992, Top Pub. Sector award Med. Alley, 1993. Mem. Democrat Farm Labor Party. Lutheran. Avocations: swimming, reading. Home: 11605 177th St W Lakeville MN 55044-7676 also: High Tech Assn Inc 655 Lone Oak Dr Eagan MN 55121

KRUEGER, ROBERT CHARLES, ambassador, former senator, former congressman; b. New Braunfels, Tex., Sept. 19, 1935; s. Arlon E. and Faye (Leifeste) K.; m. Kathleen Tobin Krueger; children: Mariana, Sarah, Christian. BA, So. Meth. U., 1957; MA, Duke U., 1958; M.Litt., Oxford (Eng.) U., 1961, D.Phil., 1964; D.Litt. (hon.), U. St. Thomas. From instr. to assoc. prof. English Duke U., 1961-72; vice provost, dean Trinity Coll. Arts and Scis., Duke U., 1972-73; chmn. bd. Comal Hosiery Mills, 1973-75; ptnr. Krueger Brangus Ranch, 1974-86; mem. 94th-95th Congresses from 21st Tex. dist.; U.S. ambassador-at-large, coord. for Mex. affairs, 1979-81; pres. Krueger Assocs., 1981-91; Bentsen prof. govt.-bus. rels. Lyndon B. Johnson Sch., U. Tex., 1985-86; Tsanoff prof. pub. affairs Rice U., 1986-88; Disting. lectr. So. Meth. U., 1989-91; U.S. senator from Tex., 1993-94; amb. to Burundi Am. Embassy, 1994-96, amb. to Botswana, 1996—; special rep. of secretary of state Southern Africa Development Community, 1998—. Author: The Poems of Sir John Davies, 1975; contbr. articles to profl. jours. and newspapers. Commr. Tex. R.R. Commn., 1991-93. Mem. Tex. Philos. Soc. (pres. 1993), Blue Key, Phi Beta Kappa. Office: PO Box 311717 New Braunfels TX 78131-1717 Office: US Embassy Gaborone Dept of State Washington DC 20521-2170*

KRUEGER, ROBERT EDWARD, manufacturing executive, mechanical engineer; b. L.A., Mar. 26, 1922; s. Edward Jr. and Ida Viola (Herren) K.; m. Elizabeth Westerfors, Sept. 10, 1949; children: Karen Elizabeth, Clarence Frederick (dec.), Roger Carl (dec.), Bruce Wayne, Glen Herren. Student, L.A. City Coll., 1939-40, Calif. Inst. Tech., 1940-43, 46-47, Yale U., Harvard U., MIT, Army Electronics Tng. Ctr., 1943-44; BSME, Stanford U., 1950, MBA, 1952. Lic. fed. firearms dealer and ammunition mfr. Bur. Alcohol, Tobacco and Firearms. Trainee Douglas Aircraft Co., Santa Monica, Calif., summers 1941-43; staff mem. Los Alamos (N.Mex.) Sci. Lab., 1947-49; chief engr. Rutishauser Corp., Pasadena, Calif., 1952-53; asst. to pres. Unitek Corp., El Monte, Calif., 1953-55; sales mgr. Donner Sci. Co., Concord, Calif., 1955-57, Shand & Jurs divsn. Gen. Precision Equipment Corp., Berkeley, 1957-58; v.p. sales Advanced Instruments, Richmond, Calif., 1958-60; sales mgr. Gilliland Instruments, Oakland, Calif., 1960-62; ptnr. Krueger & Smith, Berkeley, 1969-72; founder, pres. Tetra Valves, Inc., Berkeley, 1972-78; owner, propr. Krueger Mfg.-Engring., Lafayette, Calif., 1962—. Author or co-author books, manuals, other works; patentee in field. Donor portraits of U.S. Pres. George Bush and Barbara Bush, White Ho., Washington, 1995, portrait of U.S. Pres. George Bush, Nat. Portrait Gallery, Washington, 1995; v.p. Calif. Rep. Assembly, 1983-84. With USAAF, 1942-47; with USAFR, 1947-53. Mem. IEEE (life), AAAS, ASTM, NRA (life, endowment), Am. Soc. for Metals Internat. (life), Am. Def. Preparedness Assn. (life), James Smithson Soc./Smithsonian Instn. (Patron award Benefactors Cir. 1991), Nat. Mus. Am. Indian (charter), Colonial Williamsburg Found. (assoc.), Calif. Rifle and Pistol Assn. (life). Pantheist. Avocations: U.S. national heritage, art collections, political activity, travel, photography. Home: 1084 Via Roble Lafayette CA 94549-2925 Office: Krueger Mfg-Engring 1084 Via Roble Lafayette CA 94549-2925

KRUEGER, ROBERT WILLIAM, management consultant; b. Phila., Nov. 16, 1916; s. Robert Henry and Frieda (Lehmann) K.; m. Marjorie Evelyn Jones, July 26, 1941; children: Arlene R. Krueger Pappan, Diane L. Krueger Lane. PhD in Physics, UCLA, 1942. Research engr. Douglas Aircraft Co., Santa Monica, Calif., 1942-46; asst. chief missiles div. RAND Corp., Santa Monica, 1946-53; missle systems cons. L.A., 1953-54; pres. Planning Research Corp., L.A., 1954-73, Profl. Services Internat., 1973—; founder Profl. Svcs. Coun., 1970, bd. dirs. Chmn. 59th Dist. Republican Central Com., 1960-61; pres. 59th Dist. Rep. Assembly, 1960-61; mem. Calif. Rep. Central Com., 1962-66; Trustee U. Calif. Los Angeles Found. Mem. Am. Phys. Soc. Home and Office: 1016 Moraga Dr Los Angeles CA 90049-1621

KRUEGER, RONALD, aerospace engineer; b. Calw, Ger., Nov. 28, 1958; s. Roman Hupalo and Margit Evelin Nassi Krueger. Abitur, Kepler Gymnasium, Pforzheim, 1978; Diplom Ingenieur, U. Stuttgart, 1989, DSc, 1996. Asst. U. Stuttgart, 1989-96; NRC rsch. assoc. Langley Rsch. Ctr. NASA, Hampton, Va., 1997—. With German Army, 1978-79. Mem. AIAA (sr.), ASTM, Deutsche Gesellschaft für Luft- und Raumfahrt Lilienthal-Oberth e.V. DGLR. Home: 117 Signature Way Apt 436 Hampton VA 23666-5968 Office: NASA Langley Rsch Ctr Mail Stop 188E Hampton VA 23681-0001

KRUEGER, WILLIAM WAYNE, III, lawyer; b. Houston, Apr. 2, 1960; s. William Wayne Jr. and Ida Graciela (Preciado) K.; m. Lydia Scott Blocker, Nov. 25, 1989; children: Christopher Wayne, Elizabeth Ashley, Sarah Whitney. BA in Acctg., Tex. A&M U., 1984; JD, Baylor U., 1985. Bar: Tex. 1986, U.S. Dist. Ct. (ea., we., so., and no. dist.) Tex., U.S. Ct. Appeals (5th cir.), U.S. Supreme Ct. Assoc. Clark, West, Keller, Butler & Ellis, Dallas, 1985-87, Fanning, Harper & Martinson, Dallas, 1987-91; sr. assoc. Ludlum & Ludlum, Austin, Tex., 1991-93; shareholder Wright & Greenhill P.C., Austin, 1993-95; ptnr. Fletcher & Springer L.L.P., Austin, 1995—; Contbr. articles to profl. jours. Vol. Legal Aid, Austin, 1993—, Habitat for the Humanities, Austin, 1993—. Mem. ABA, State Bar Tex. (adv. bd. evidence com. 1996-97), Tex. Assn. Def. Counsel, State Bar Coll. Law, Tex. Young Lawyers Assn., Austin Young Lawyers Assn., Am. Judicature Soc., Travis County Bar Assn., Knights of Columbus, Phi Delta Phi. Roman Catholic. Avocations: family, jogging, reading. Office: Fletcher & Springer LLP 823 Congress Ave Ste 510 Austin TX 78701-2429

KRUG, DOUGLAS EDWARD, emergency physician; b. Chelsea, Md., June 8, 1953; s. Edward Thatcher and Joan Marie (Gettell) K.; m. Lorraine Anne Schmidt, June 22, 1980; children: Ryan, Courtney, Kaitlin. AB, Colgate U., 1975; MS, Georgetown U., 1976, MD, 1980. Intern Tucson Med. Ctr., 1980-81; resident in emergency medicine Emory U. Affiliated Hosps., Atlanta, 1983-85; physician WellStar Kennestone Hosp., Marietta, Ga., 1985—; pvt. practice, Marietta, 1985—. Fellow Am. Coll. Emergency Physicians. Office: Kennestone Emergency Group 677 Church St NW Marietta GA 30060-1101*

KRUG, FRED ROY, film and television director and producer; b. Bern, Switzerland, Aug. 30, 1929; came to U.S., 1951; s. Adalbert and Margot Panchaud de Bottens-Krug; m. Rosemary Wehner, Feb. 25, 1956; 1 child, Vivian Evelyn. BA, Columbia Coll., L.A., 1962, postgrad., 1963. Freelance cinematographer, writer Europe and U.S., 1945-63; dir. Sta. KLYD-ABC TV, 1963; film and VTR dir. Sta. KCOP-TV, L.A., 1963-68; v.p. prodn. Bill Burrud Prodns., Los Angeles, 1968-72; producer, dir. Walt Disney Prodns., Burbank, Calif., 1972-74, Fred R. Krug Prodns., Hollywood, Calif., 1974—. Contr. articles to film mags. and profl. jours.; contbr. regular columns to European and U.S. newspapers; producer, dir. (TV series) The Wonderful World of Disney, NBC, various news, pub. affairs and mus. shows for U.S. Army, radio and TV; producer, dir., cinematographer (TV series) Animal World, ABC, NBC, and CBS, The American West, The Challenging Sea, World of Women, Wild Kingdom; producer (spl.) Population Explosion, syndication; numerous TV commls. and promotional films in U.S. Europe, C.Am., Frency Polynesia; cinematographer "CHiPS", MGM; producer (feature film) Pacific Internat. Enterprises, 1977-79; assoc. producer Across the Great Divide; exec. producer Mountain Family Robinson. Mem. Hollywood adv. coun. Salvation Army, 1984-85; bd. dirs. Bob Hope USO Club, Hollywood, 1984-87. Pilot, US Air Force Aux. CAP, maj., 1988—. Served in U.S. Army, 1953-56. Mem. Dirs. Guild Am., Producers Guild Am., Rotary (Paul Harris fellow 1987, v.p. Hollywood club 1987-88, pres. Santa Ynez Valley club 1996-97). Avocation: flying. Home: Ranchito de los Ciervos 3398 Calzada Ave Santa Ynez CA 93460-8703

KRUG, JOHN CARLETON (TONY KRUG), college administrator, library consultant; b. Evansville, Ind., Nov. 27, 1951; s. John Elmer and Mary Ellen K.; m. Anna Marie Waters, July 3, 1983. BA, Ind. State U., 1972, MLS, 1973; PhD, So. Ill. U., Carbondale, 1985. Ordained to ministry Bapt. Ch. Exec. dir. Olney (Ill.) Carnegie Pub. Libr., 1973-74; assoc. dean Wabash Valley Coll., Mt. Carmel, Ill., 1974-84; mem. Com. for U.S. Depository State Plan, Springfield, Ill., 1982-84; dir. librs. Maryville Coll., St. Louis, 1984-88; dir. info. svcs. Bethany (W.Va.) Coll., 1988-97; dean libr. svcs. Carson Newman Coll., Jefferson City, Tenn., 1997—; coord. libr. activities, Appalachian Coll. Assn.; sec. pro-tem Ill. Basin Coal Mining Manpower Council, Mt. Carmel, 1974-79; mem. governing bd. exec. com. Higher Edn. Ctr. Cable TV, 1986-88; conf. speaker Kans. State U., 1982. Author: Libraries Using/Planning for Microcomputers, 1986; also computer programs. V.p. bd. dirs. Wabash Area Vocat. Enterprises, Mt. Carmel, 1978-81; mem. bd. edn. Wabash Cmty. Unit, Mt. Carmel, 1980-83; mem. exec. com. Cmty. Edn. and Arts Assn., Carbondale, 1983-84; mem. visual arts adv. com. Ill. Arts Coun., Chgo., 1982-84; pastor Hopewell United Meth. Ch., Bridgeport, Ill., 1976-77; minister Terre Haute (Ind.) 1st Bapt. Ch., 1972—; elder Gateway Christian Ch., 1986-88; bd. dirs. Fair Haven Christian Sch., 1986-88; pres. T3-Tchrs., Tech., Tomorrow; bd. dirs. Christian Coll. Librs., 1995-97. Mem. So. Bapt. Libr. Assn., Assn. Christian Librs. Office: Stephens-Burnett Meml Libr Carson-Newman Coll Jefferson City TN 37760

KRUG, KAREN-ANN, healthcare financial executive, accountant; b. Riverdale, N.D., Apr. 22, 1951; d. C. and Elsie (Eide) K.; m. C. Scott James, Aug. 19, 1978. BS, N.D. State U., 1980; MBA, U. Phoenix, 1996. CPA. Mgr. proof transit 1st Nat. Bank Grand Forks, N.D.; sr. acct. Leo E. Bell & Assocs., Grand Forks, 1978-80; dir. project rev. Agassiz Health Systems Agy., Grand Forks, 1980-82; sr. adminstrv. asst. St. Mary's Hosp., Reno; dir. planning and devel. St. Mary's Health Care Corp., Reno, 1982-87; contr. Pacific Presbyn. Med. Ctr., San Francisco, 1987-89; corp. contr. Daughters of Charity Nat. Healthcare Sys. Seton Med. Ctr., Daly City, Calif., 1989-93; CFO, v.p. fin. Howard Cmty. Hosp., Kokomo, Ind., 1994-97; adminstr. fin., CFO St. Anthony Med. Ctr., Rockford, Ill., 1997—; bd. dirs. Rock River Pvt. Industry Coun., Rockford. Vol. Jr. Achievement, Reno, 1984-87, Project Literacy U.S., San Francisco, 1987-88. Fellow Healthcare Fin. Mgmt. Assn. (cert. managed care profl. 1995, chair Pressler Managed Care com. 1996, cet. mgr. Pt. Accts. 1996, HFMA Jour. editl. bd. 1996, forum adv. com. 1997); mem. AICPA (bd. trustees Benevolent Fund 1983-93), Calif. Soc. CPAs (healthcare com. 1989-93, chair 1991-93), Delta Gamma (treas. San Francisco alumni chpt. 1992-93).

KRUGER, BARBARA, artist, art critic; b. Newark, Jan. 26, 1945. Student, Syracuse U., Parsons Sch. Design, N.Y.C., Sch. Visual Arts, N.Y.C. Illustrator Condé Nast Publs., N.Y.C., 1967-68, chief designer Mademoiselle mag., 1968-72; film critic Artforum; vis. artist Calif. Inst. Art, Art Inst. Chgo., U. Calif., Berkeley; arranger collections Pictures and Promises, The Kitchen, N.Y.C., 1981, Artists' Use of Lang., Franklin Furnace, N.Y.C., 1983, Creative Perspectives in Am. Photography, Hallwall's Gallery, Buffalo, 1983. Author: Picture/Readings, 1979, No Progress in Pleasure, 1982; one-woman shows Crousel/Hussenot Gallery, Paris, 1987, Monika Spruth Gallery, Cologne, Germany, 1987, 90, Nat. Art Gallery, Wellington, New Zealand, 1988, Mary Boone Gallery, N.Y.C., 1989, Galerie Bebert, Rotterdam, The Netherlands, 1989, Fred Hoffman Gallery, Santa Monica, Calif., 1989, Duke U. Mus. Art, Durham, N.C., 1990, Whitney Mus. Modern Art, Mus. Contemporary Art, Chgo., Mus. Contemporary Art, L.A., 1999, numerous others; exhibited in group shows Whitney Mus. Am. Art, N.Y.C., 1973, 82, 83, 85, 87, 89, Castello di Rivoli, Turin, Italy, 1989, Pa. Acad. Fine Arts, Phila., 1989, Denver Art Mus., 1989, Mus. 20th Century, Vienna, Austria, 1989, Ctr. Georges Pompidou, Paris, 1989, Mus. Contemporary Art, L.A., 1989, Rheinhalle, Cologne, 1989, Frankfurt (Germany) Kunstverein and Schirn Kunsthalle, 1989, also numerous others; work represented in various publs. Grantee Creative Artists Svc. Program, 1976-77, Nat. Endowment Arts, 1983-84. Office: Mary Boone Gallery 745 Fifth Ave New York NY 10151-2928

KRUGER, BARBARA, audiologist, speech and language pathologist; b. Corpus Christi, Tex., Aug. 16, 1944. BA in Psychology cum laude, CUNY, 1967, MA in Speech Pathology, 1970, PhD in Audiology and Hearing Sci., 1975. Asst. prof. audiology, dir. hearing rsch. lab. Columbia U., N.Y.C., 1975-78; asst. prof. otolaryngology, dir. audiology and speech lang. pathology Albert Einstein Coll. Medicine, Montefiore Med. Ctr. Yeshiva U., Bronx, N.Y., 1978-87; cons. Kruger Assocs., Commack, N.Y., 1987—; dir. Audiology and Comm. Svcs., 1987—; founder, bd. dirs. The Hearing Care Group; adj. prof. Columbia U., 1979-82; chmn. earphone calibration Internat. Electrotech. Commn., Am. Nat. Standards Inst.; cons. Albert Einstein Coll. of Medicine, Kennedy Ctr., 1987-90; apptd. N.Y. State Hearing and Dispensing Adv. Bd. in Dept. of State, 1999—. Spencer Found. grantee, 1974-78, Am. Otological Soc. grantee, 1978-79, Rose M. Badgeley Residuary Charitable Trust grantee, 1981-84; recipient Program Project award NIH, 1984-86. Fellow Am. Speech-Lang. Hearing Assn., Am. Acad. Audiology; mem. Assn. L.I. Speech-Lang. Hearing Assn. Home and Office: 37 Somerset Dr Commack NY 11725-1636

KRUGER, CHARLES HERMAN, JR., mechanical engineering educator; b. Oklahoma City, Oct. 4, 1934; s. Charles H. and Flora K.; m. Nora Nininger, Sept. 10, 1977; children—Sarah, Charles III, Elizabeth, Ellen. S.B., M.I.T., 1956, Ph.D., 1960; D.I.C., Imperial Coll., London, 1957. Asst. prof. MIT, Cambridge, 1960; research scientist Lockheed Research Labs., 1960-62; prof. mech. engring. Stanford (Calif.) U., 1962—, chmn. dept. mech. engring., 1982-88, sr. assoc. dean engring., 1988-93, vice provost, dean rsch. and grad. policy, 1993—; vis. prof. Harvard U., 1968-69, Princeton U., 1979-80; mem. Environ. Studies Bd. NAS, 1981-83; mem. hearing bd. Bay Area Air Quality Mgmt. Dist., 1969-83. Co-author: Physical Gas Dynamics, 1965, Partially Ionized Gases, 1973, On the Prevention of Significant Deterioration of Air Quality, 1981; assoc. editor: AIAA Jour, 1968-71; contbr. numerous articles to profl. jours. NSF sr. postdoctoral fellow, 1968-69. Mem. AIAA (medal, award 1979), ASME, Am. Phys. Soc. Office: Stanford U Bldg 10 Stanford CA 94305-2061

KRUGER, GUSTAV OTTO, JR., oral surgeon, educator; b. N.Y.C., Sept. 28, 1916; s. Gustav Otto and Anna Charlotte (Mellquist) K.; m. Helyn E. Hollingsworth, Apr. 12, 1947; children: Deborah Ann (Mrs. M. Henry King III), Tristram Coffin, Abigail Hollingsworth Imus. BS, George Washington U., 1938, AM, 1939; DDS, Georgetown U., 1939, ScD (hon.), 1977. Diplomate Am. Bd. Oral and Maxillofacial Surgery (pres. 1964). Intern Johns Hopkins Hosp., 1939-40; fellow Mayo Found., 1940-42, 45-48; mem. faculty Georgetown U. Sch. Dentistry and Grad. Sch., 1948-87, prof. oral surgery, chmn. dept., 1948-87, prof. emeritus, 1987—, assoc. dean, 1966-82; chief dental dept. Georgetown U. Hosp., Washington, 1948-82; cons. VA hosps., Martinsburg, W.Va. and Washington, U.S. Naval Hosp., Bethesda, D.C. Gen. Hosp., Washington; cons. to Pres.'s physician, 1960-64; cons. Walter Reed Army Med. Ctr.; mem. cancer tng. com. Nat. Cancer Inst., USPHS, 1967-71, chmn., 1969-71. Author: Textbook of Oral and Maxillofacial Surgery, 1959, 6th edit., 1984; contbr. articles to profl. jours. Capt. Dental Corps AUS, 1942-45, CBI, PTO. Recipient Arnold K. Maislen award N.Y. U., 1970; Simon P. Hullihen award W.Va. Soc. Oral Surgeons and W.Va. Med. Ctr., 1980; named Man of Year Georgetown U. Alumni Assn., 1961, Disting. Svc. award, 1992. Fellow AAAS, Am. Coll. Dentists (chmn. D.C. sect. 1969-71), Internat. Coll. Dentists (chmn. D.C. sect. 1967-70); mem. ADA (chmn. oral surgery sect. 1961, mem. rev. commn. on advanced edn. in oral surgery 1965-71, chmn. commn. 1969-71), D.C. Dental Soc. (pres. 1960, Sterling V. Mead award 1989), Am. Assn. Oral and Maxillofacial Surgeons (program chmn. 1961, 79th Ann. Meeting dedication 1997), Middle Atlantic Soc. Oral and Maxillofacial Surgeons (pres. 1952), Am. Acad. Oral Pathology, Am. Acad. Oral and Maxillofacial Radiology, Internat. Assn. Dental Research, Am. Coll. Oral and Maxillofacial Surgeons (Harry Archer award 1992), Wash. Dental Study Club (pres. 1993), Kiwanis (co-chmn. orthop. com. 1971-86), Xi Psi Phi, Sigma Gamma Epsilon, Omicron Kappa Upsilon. Home: 6806 Bradgrove Cir Bethesda MD 20817-3001

KRUGER, JEROME, materials science educator, consultant; b. Atlanta, Feb. 7, 1927; s. Isaac and Sarah (Stein) K.; m. Mollee Coppel, Feb. 20, 1955; children: Lennard, Joseph. BS, Ga. Inst. Tech., 1948, MS, 1949; PhD, U. Va., 1952. With Naval Rsch. Lab., Washington, 1952-55; with Nat. Bur. Standards, Commerce Dept., Washington, 1955-83; group leader Corrosion and Electrodeposition Nat. Bur. Standards, Commerce Dept., 1966-83; prof. Johns Hopkins U., 1984—, chmn. materials sci. and engring., 1986-88; cons. Argonne Nat. Lab., Lockheed, Balt. Gas & Electric, Teletech Thompson, Dalton & DeRose, Mueller Brass, S.W. Rsch. Inst., Dickenson, Wright, Moon, Van Dusen & Freeman, Hainess, Dickey & Pierce, W.O. Snead, J.M. Huber Corp.; Jerome Kruger vis. scholar U. Va., 1998. Divisional editor Jour. Electrochem. Soc., 1966-83; subject area editor: Ency. of Materials Sci. and Engring.; also editor books; contbr. articles to tech. jours., chpts. to book. DuPont fellow U. Va., 1951-52; recipient Silver medal Commerce Dept., 1962, Gold medal, 1972; Blum award Nat. Capitol sect. Electrochem. Soc., 1966, Foley award, 1999; Samuel Wesley Stratton award Nat. Bur. Standards, 1982; Presdl. rank of Meritorious Exec. of Sr. Exec. Svc., 1982; U.R. Evans award Inst. Corrosion (U.K.), 1991, Hon. fellow, 1996; establishment of Jerome Kruger vis. scholar program at U. Va., 1998, 1st invited scholar, 1999. Fellow Electrochem. Soc. (treas. 1982-86, hon. mem. 1987, Outstanding Achievement award 1977, Olin Palladium medal 1995), Nat. Assn. Corrosion Engrs. (bd. dirs. 1983-86, W.R. Whitney award 1976, Jerome Kruger award in corrosion sci., Balt.-Washington sect., 1997); mem. Am. Inst. Conservation, Internat. Corrosion Coun. (1st v.p. 1984-87, pres. 1987-90), Fedn. Materials Socs. (pres. 1977), Sigma Xi, Tau Beta Pi. Jewish. Home: 619 Warfield Dr Rockville MD 20850-1921 Office: Johns Hopkins U Dept Materials Sci and Engring Baltimore MD 21218

KRUGER, KENNETH, architect; b. Newark, Aug. 13, 1928; s. Rudolph Robert and Clarise Estelle (Goldman) K.; m. Elinor Margaret Kane, July 22, 1978; children: Jonathan, Karen, Kai. BArch, MIT, 1951, MS, 1953, postgrad., 1964; MArch, Harvard U., 1952; postgrad., U. Rome, 1955. Registered arch., Mass., N.J., N.Y.; cert. Nat. Coun. Archtl. Registration Bds.; registered profl. engr., Mass., N.J., Calif. Archtl. designer Carl Koch & Assoc., Cambridge, Mass., 1953-54; structural designer Frank Grad, Paris, 1955; arch. Marcel Breuer & Assocs., N.Y.C., 1956-57; structural engr. Simpson & Stratta, San Francisco, 1959-60, Chin & Hensolt, San Francisco, 1961-62, Internat. Engring. Co., Rio de Janeiro, 1963; arch., engr. Kenneth Kruger, Boston, 1964-68, Kruger Kruger Albenberg Archs. & Engrs., Cambridge, Mass., 1969—; instr. arch. MIT, Cambridge, 1952-53. Overseas fellow MIT, 1952, Rotch prize, 1951; Fulbright scholar, 1954-55. Mem. ASCE, AIA, Am. Soc. Home Inspectors (v.p. 1991, Pres.'s award 1991, exec. com. 1991-93, dir.-at-large 1988-90, 92-94, chmn. bylaws com. 1992-94; dir. New Eng. chpt. 1982), Boston Soc. Archs. (dir., commr. 1974-77), Boston Soc. Civil Engrs., Boston Assn. Structural Engrs., Constrn. Specification Inst., Sigma Xi, Alpha Epsilon Pi. Avocations: skiing, tennis, squash, backpacking, biking. Office: Kruger Kruger Albenberg 67 Grozier Rd Cambridge MA 02138-3314

KRUGER, KENNETH CHARLES, architect; b. Santa Barbara, Calif., Aug. 19, 1930; s. Thomas Albin and Chleople (Gaines) K.; m. Patricia Kathryn Rasey, Aug. 21, 1955; children: David, Eric. B.Arch., U. So. Calif., 1953. Registered architect, Calif. Pres. Kruger Bensen Ziemer, Santa Barbara, 1960-90; part-time instr. architecture dept. Calif. Poly., San Luis Obispo, 1993-95; part-time architect, 1993—; regent Calif. Archtl. Found., 1997—. Bd. dirs. United Boys & Girls Club; bd. trustees, corp. sec. Unitarian Ch. Fellow AIA; mem. Archtl. Found. Santa Barbara (pres. 1987-89). Democrat. Home: 1255 Ferrelo Rd Santa Barbara CA 93103-2101

KRUGER, VIRGINIA JOY, health facility administrator lecturer; b. Fergus Falls, Minn., July 15, 1946; d. Henry and Delora (Christensen) Erickson; m. Jerry Paul Kruger, Apr. 30, 1969; three children. BS in Edn., N.D. State U., 1968. Home econs. tchr. Warren (Minn.) H.S., 1968-73; nutritionist Warren Cmty. Hosp., 1973-91; devel. dir. North Valley Health Ctr., Warren, 1990—; pub. rels. specialist Regional Soil Conservation Svc., Thief River Falls, Minn., 1986-88; dir. Red River of the North Resource Area, Thief River Falls, 1988-91; media cons. Agrl. Utilization Rsch. Inst., Crookston, Minn., 1989-92; motivational speaker, 1985—. Creator seminars "So You Want to Fund Raise?", 1996, Reflections of the Heart. Pres. Grace United Meth. Ch., Warren, 1992; bd. dirs. Godel Meml. Libr., Warren, 1970-79. Mem. Nat. Soc. Fund Raising Execs., Minn. Agrl. Women, Rural Health Care Roundtable, Nat. Spkrs. Assn. Home: RR 1 Box 76 Warren MN 56762-9756

KRUGLE, MARIE, health facility administrator; b. Pitts., Feb. 26, 1961; d. James M. and Clare J. (Wilson) Valente; m. Wilbert A. Krugle, Oct. 1, 1988. BSN, Duquesne U., 1983. Staff nurse VA Med. Ctr., Pitts., 1983-87, head nurse, 1987-88, office nurse, 1988, nurse mgr. Three Rivers Orthopedics, 1989-91, patient care coord., 1991-92, nurse mgr., 1992-93, clin. preceptor, 1993-94, orthopedic case mgr., 1994-95, surg. clin. nurse reviewer, 1995-98, orthopedic nurse coord., 1998—. Named Outstanding Young Woman in Am., 1987.

KRUGMAN, RICHARD DAVID, physician, university administrator, educator; b. N.Y.C., Nov. 28, 1942; s. Saul and Sylvia (Stern) K.; m. Mary Elizabeth Kerber, July 9, 1966; children: Scott, Joshua, Todd, Jordan. AB, Princeton U., 1963; MD, NYU, 1968. Resident U. Colo. Sch. Medicine, Denver, 1968-71; staff assoc. Nat. Inst. Health, Bethesda, Md., 1971-73; asst. prof. U. Colo. Sch. Medicine, 1973-78, assoc. prof., 1978-87, prof. of pediatrics, 1988—, dean, 1992—. Author: The Battered Child, 5th edit., 1997; editor: (jour.) Child Abuse/Neglect, 1986—. Chmn. U.S. Adv. Bd. Child Abuse and Neglect, Washington, 1989-91; dir. Kempe Nat. Ctr. for Prevention and Treatment of Child Abuse and Neglect, Denver, 1981-92. Recipient C. Henry Kempe award Nat. Conf. on Child Abuse, 1989, St. Geme award U. Colo. Sch. Medicine, 1992, 98; Paul Harris fellow Rotary Internat., Sydney, Australia, 1992. Mem. Internat. Soc. Prevention of Child Abuse and Neglect (pres. 1992-94), Am. Acad. Pediatrics (Ray Helfer award 1995, Brandt Steele award 1996), Am. Pediatric Soc. Office: U Colo Sch Medicine 4200 E 9th Ave Denver CO 80262

KRUGMAN, STANLEY LEE, international management consultant; b. N.Y.C., Mar. 2, 1925; s. Harry and Leah (Greenberg) K.; m. Helen Schorr, June 14, 1947; children: Vicky Lee, Thomas Paul; m. Carolyn Schambra, Sept. 17, 1966; children: David Andrew, Wendy Carol; m. Gail Jennings, Mar. 17, 1974. B Chem. Engring., Rensselaer Poly. Inst., 1947; postgrad., Poly. Inst. Bklyn., Columbia U., 1947-51. Process devel. engr. Merck & Co., Rahway, N.J., 1947-51; sr. process and project engr. C.F. Braun & Co., Alhambra, Calif., 1951-55; with Jacobs Engring. Co., Pasadena, Calif., 1955-76; from chief engr. to v.p. engring. and constrn. to v.p. gen. mgr. to exec. v.p. to pres., also dir.; exec. v.p., dir. Jacobs Engring. Group Inc., Pasadena, Calif., 1974-82; pres., dir. Jacobs Constructors of P.R., San Juan, 1970-82; pres. Jacobs Internat. Inc., 1971-82, Jacobs Internat. Ltd., Inc., Dublin, Ireland, 1974-82; dep. chmn. Jacobs LTA Engring., Ltd., Johannesburg, South Africa, 1981-82; pres. Krugman Assocs., 1982—; internat. mgmt. cons. Served to lt. (j.g.) USNR, 1944-46, PTO. Mem. Am. Inst. Chem. Engrs., Am. Chem. Soc. Presbyterian. Patentee in field. Home and Office: 24452 Portola Rd Carmel CA 93923-9327

KRUGMAN, STANLEY LIEBERT, science administrator, geneticist; b. St. Louis, June 8, 1932; s. Bernard and Della (Goldberg) K.; m. Judith Raechel Alfend, Jan 28, 1958; children: Mark Bernard, Jeffrey Jon. BS in Forestry, U. Mo., 1955; MF, U. Calif., Berkeley, 1956, PhD in Plant Physiology, 1961. Rsch. aide U. Calif., 1956-61, rsch. assoc., 1961-62; rsch. physiologist U.S. Forest Svc., 1962-64, project leader, 1964-71; staff geneticist U.S. Forest Svc., Washington, 1971-80, staff dir., 1980-95; sr. for specialist, pvt. cons. World Bank Natural Resources, Washington, 1995—; cons. in field. Editor: Seeds of Woody Plants, 1974, Advances in Reproductive Biology, 1974, Management Biosphere Reserves, 1979, Advances in Forest Physiology, 1980. Recipient Sci. medal USSR, 1995, Czech Republic, 1995. Fellow AAAS, Soc. Am. Foresters (William Schlich medal 1990); mem. Internat. Union Forestry Orgn. Jewish. Office: 6515 Dryden Dr Mc Lean VA 22101-4627

KRUIDENIER, DAVID, newspaper executive; b. Des Moines, July 18, 1921; s. David S. and Florence (Cowles) K.; m. Elizabeth Stuart, Dec. 29, 1948; 1 child, Lisa. BA, Yale U., 1946; MBA, Harvard U., 1948; LLD, Buena Vista Coll., 1960, Simpson Coll., 1963; LittD, Luther Coll., 1990; DHL, Drake U., 1990. With Mpls. Star and Tribune, 1948-52; with Des Moines Register and Tribune, 1952-85, pres., pub., 1971-78, chief exec. officer, 1971-85, chmn., chief exec. officer, 1982-85; with Cowles Media Co., 1983-93, pres., chief exec. officer, 1983-84, chmn., chief exec. officer, 1984-85, chmn., 1985-97. Pres. Gardner and Florence Call Cowles Found.; trustee Drake U., Menninger Found., Des Moines Art Ctr., Grinnell Coll. Greater Des Moines Found. With USAAF, 1942-45. Decorated Air medal with three clusters, D.F.C. Mem. Coun. on Fgn. Rels. , Des Moines Club, Mpls. Club, Sigma Delta Chi, Beta Theta Pi, Beta Gamma Sigma. Home: 3409 Southern Hills Dr Des Moines IA 50321-1318 Office: 715 Locust St Des Moines IA 50309-3703

KRUIZENGA, RICHARD JOHN, retired energy company executive; b. Spring Lake, Mich., Sept. 25, 1930; s. Richard James and Kathryn Ella K.; m. Margaret Helene Feldmann, Sept. 6, 1952; children: Derek Diedrich, Meg Froelich. B.A. in Econs, Hope Coll., 1952; Ph.D. in Econs, M.I.T., 1956. Chief economist Exxon Corp., 1966-69; logistics mgr. Esso Eastern, 1969-71; v.p. Esso Sekiyu, Tokyo, 1971-72; chmn. Esso Australia, 1972-77, Esso Prodn. Malaysia, Inc., 1977-80; v.p. corp. planning Exxon Corp., 1981-92; sr. fellow Inst. for the Study of Earth and Man, So. Meth. U., 1993-96, pres., 1997—. Trustee Com. for Econ. Devel., Inst. for Study of Earth and Man/So. Meth. U.; mem. MIT Corp. Devel. Com.

KRUKOWSKI, LUCIAN, philosophy educator, artist; b. N.Y.C., Nov. 22, 1929; s. Stefan Krukowski and Anna Belcarz; m. Marilyn Denmark, Jan. 14, 1955; 1 child, Samantha. BA, CUNY, 1952; BFA, Yale U., 1955; MS, Pratt Inst., 1958; PhD, Wash. U., St. Louis, 1977. Faculty mem. Pratt Inst., N.Y.C., 1955-69; dean Sch. Fine Arts Wash. U., 1969-77, prof. philosophy, 1977—, chmn. dept. philosophy, 1986-89. Author: Art and Concept, 1987, Aesthetic Legacies, 1992; contbr. articles to publs.; artist 10 one-person shows, 1960-92, outdoor murals for copr. bldgs., 1972, 83. Served to cpl. USMC, 1952-54. Mem. Am. Soc. for Aesthetics, Am. Philos. Assn. Avocations: hiking, climbing. Home: 665 S Skinker Blvd Apt 10D Saint Louis MO 63105-2350 Office: Washington U Dept of Philosophy 1 Brookings Dr Dept Of Saint Louis MO 63130-4899

KRULAK, CHARLES CHANDLER, marine officer; b. Quantico, Va., Mar. 4, 1942; s. Victor Harold and Amy (Chandler) K.; m. Zandra Lynn Meyers, June 27, 1964; children: David Chandler, Todd Cameron. BS, U.S. Naval Acad., 1964; MS, George Washington U., 1973; advanced mil. course, Amphib. War Sch., 1968, Army Command and Gen. Staff, Coll., 1976, Nat. War Coll., 1982. Commd. 2d lt. USMC, 1964, advanced through grades to brigadier gen., 1989; rifle co. comdr. USMC, Vietnam, 1965-66, 69-70; bn. comdr. USMC, Hawaii, 1983-85; mil. asst. Asst. Sec. Def. for Command, Control, Comm. and Intelligence, Washington, 1986-87; dep. dir. White House Mil. Office, Washington, 1987-89; brigade comrd. and asst. divsn. comdr. USMC, N.C., 1989-91, force svc. support group comdr., 1989-90; force svc. support comdr., brigade comdr. USMC, 1990-91; dir. pers. mgmt., pers. procurement Hdqtrs. Marine Corps, 1991-92; comdg. gen. MCCDC, Quantico, Va., 1992-94; comdr. marine forces, Pacific and comdg. gen. Fleet Marine Forces, Pacific, Camp Smith, Hawaii, 1994-95; commandant USMC, 1995—. Contbr. articles to Marine Corps Gazette. Decorated D.S.M., Def. D.S.M., Silver Star, Bronze Star with combat V (3), Purple Heart (2). Avocations: running, reading. Office: 2 Navy Annex HQ USMC Washington DC 20380-1775*

KRULAK, VICTOR HAROLD, newspaper executive; b. Denver, Jan. 7, 1913; s. Morris and Besse M. (Ball) K.; m. Amy Chandler, June 1, 1936; children: Victor Harold Jr., William Morris, Charles Chandler. B.S., U.S. Naval Acad., 1934; LL.D., U. San Diego. Commd. 2d lt. USMC, 1934; advanced through grades to lt. gen.; service in China, at sea, with USMC (Fleet Marine Forces), 1935-39; staff officer, also bn. regimental and divsn. comdr. World War II, World War II; chief staff (1st Marine Div. Korea); formerly comdg. gen. (Marine Corps Recruit Depot), San Diego; formerly spl asst. to dir., joint staff counterinsurgency and spl. activities (Office Joint Chiefs Staff); comdg. gen. Fleet Marine Force Pacific, Pacific, 1964-68; ret., 1968; v.p. Copley Newspaper Corp., 1968-79; pres. Words Ltd. Corp., San Diego. Trustee Zool. Soc. San Diego. Decorated D.S.M., Navy Cross, Legion of Merit with 3 oak leaf clusters, Bronze Star, Air medal, Purple Heart (2) U.S.; Cross of Gallantry; Medal of Merit Vietnam; Distinguished Service medal (Korea), Order of Cloud and Banner, Republic of China. Mem. U.S. Naval Inst., U.S. Marine Corps Assn., Am. Soc. Newspaper Editors, InterAm. Press Assn., U.S. Strategic Inst. (chmn.). Home: 3665 Carleton St San Diego CA 92106-2163 Office: Words Ltd 3045 Rosecrans St San Diego CA 92110-4827

KRULEE, GILBERT KOREB, computer scientist, educator; b. Cambridge, Mass., June 1, 1924; s. Max I. and Sadie (Koreb) K.; m. Dorsey Parker, July 7, 1956 (dec. 1970); m. Carolyn Sherwood Hall, Nov. 7, 1970; children: Catherine, Sarah, Margaret. BS in Chem. Engring., MIT, 1944, PhD in Indsl. Econs., 1950. Rsch. assoc. U. Mich., Ann Arbor, 1950-54; asst. prof. Tufts U., Medford, Mass., 1954-56; from asst. prof. to assoc. prof. Case Inst. Tech., Cleve., 1956-60; from assoc. prof. to prof. computer sci. Northwestern U., Evanston, Ill., 1960—. Fellow APA; mem. Assn. Computing Machinery. Home: 1305 Grant St Evanston IL 60201-2624 Office: Northwestern U Dept Computer Sci Sheridan Rd Evanston IL 60208

KRULEWICH, LEONARD M., lawyer; b. N.Y.C., Jan. 10, 1947; s. Wallace and Maxine K.; m. Helen Dworetzky, Sept. 2, 1973; children: Sara Heide, David Samuel. BA, Hofstra U., 1969; JD, Suffolk U., 1972; LLM, Boston U., 1977. Bar: Mass. 1972, U.S. Dist. Ct. Mass. 1972, N.Y. 1973, U.S. Supreme Ct. 1979, U.S. Ct. Appeals (1st cir.) 1984. Assoc. Cohn, Riemer & Pollack, Boston, 1974-78; ptnr. Krulewich & Arnowitz, Boston, 1979-81, Karger, Krulewich & Arnowitz, Boston, 1981-87; of counsel Silverman & Kudisch, Boston, 1987-89; pvt. practice Boston, 1989—. Mem. ABA, Mass. Bar Assn., Boston Bar Assn., Comml. Law League Am. (bd. govs., pres. N.E. region 1981-82), Comml. Law Found. (1st v.p.). Avocations: tennis, cooking, running. Office: 50 Staniford St Boston MA 02114-2517

KRULFELD, RUTH MARILYN, anthropologist, educator; b. N.Y.C., Apr. 15, 1931; m. Jacob Mendel Krulfeld, Aug. 28, 1964; 1 child, Michael David. BA cum laude, Brandeis U., 1956; PhD, Yale U., 1974. Field rschr. micro-geog. rsch. farms, Singapore, Malaya, 1951-53; anthrop. rschr., Jamaica, 1957, Costa Rica, Nicaragua, Panama, 1958, Lombok, Indonesia, 1960-62, 93; anthrop. rschr. S.E. Asian refugees to U.S., 1981—; anthrop. rschr., N.E. Thailand, 1993; asst. prof. anthropology, dir. grad. students George Washington U., Washington, 1964-72, 93-97, assoc. prof., 1973-76, prof., 1976—, chmn. dept. anthropology, 1984-87, founder spl. grad. program in internat. world devel., prof. anthropology, internat. affairs; mem. Judaic studies com. George Washington U.; bd. dirs. No. Va. Humanities Coun.; rschr. S.E. Asian refugees, 1981-94, Laotian refugees in U.S., 1981—, also rsch. on culture change in villages in Indonesia. Co-author: Power, Ethics, and Human Rights: Anthropological Studies of Refugee Research and Action, 1998; contbr. articles to profl. jours.; edit. bd. com. on refugees and immigrants. Bd. dirs. No. Va. Regional Humanities Coun. Currier scholar Yale U., 1958; Ford fellow, 1960-62; grantee Found. for Study of Man, 1957, Am. Coun., 1963, Cotlow faculty rsch. grantee, 1992-93, faculty rsch. grantee George Washington U., 1992-93, rsch. grantee Va. Found. for Humanities and Pub. Policy, 1995-96; recipient Banneker award Ctr. for Washington Area Studies, 1996. Mem. Anthrop. Soc. Washington, Am. Anthrop. Assn. (nominating com., com. on refugee issues gen. anthropology divsn., vice chair com. on refugees issues 1992-94, gen. anthropology divsn. 1993-94, exec. bd. com. refugees and immigrants 1994-99, CORI editl. bd. 1998-99, Cori award for best paper on refugees issues 1992, Pedagogical Rsch. and Innovative Devel. in Edn. award 1994). Jewish. Office: George Washington U Dept Anthropology Washington DC 20052 *Perhaps the major attitudes that have motivated my work have been a deep respect for my fellow human beings, and a need to learn from them, to experience their wondrous creativity, ability and diversity; as an anthropologist, to understand as much about human societies as I could, and as an educator, to ignite this enthusiasm and wonder in my students, to encourage them to go beyond our present understanding and abilities.*

KRULIK, BARBARA S., director, curator; b. N.Y.C., June 13, 1955; d. Herbert Arnold and Irene Sylvia (Lichterman) K. BA in Art History, Pa. State U., 1976, MA, 1999. Asst. to dir. NAD, N.Y.C., 1976-77, acting dir., 1977-78, coord. exhbns., 1978-83, asst. dir., 1983-89, interim dir., 1989-90, dep. dir., 1990-92; assoc. dir. Forum Gallery, N.Y.C., 1992-94; dir. Grad. Sch. Figurative Art New York Acad. Art, N.Y.C., 1994-97; ind. curator, author, cons., 1997—; lectr. in mus. mgmt. Reinhardt Acad., Amsterdam. Author, editor exhbn. catalogues. Mem. Am. Assn. Mus. (curators and registrars coms.), Internat. Coun. on Mus. E-mail: bskrulik@sprynet.com.

KRULITZ, LEO MORRION, financial executive; b. Wallace, Idaho, June 15, 1938; s. John Morrion and Myrtle (Parker) K.; m. Donna Eileen Ristau, June 18, 1960; children—Cynthia, Pamela. B.A., Stanford U., 1960; J.D. cum laude, Harvard U., 1963; M.B.A., Stanford U., 1969. Bar: Idaho bar 1963, Ind. bar 1969, D.C. bar 1978, U.S. Supreme Ct. bar 1978. Ptnr. firm Moffatt, Thomas, Barrett & Blanton, Boise, Idaho, 1963-67; v.p., treas. Irwin Mgmt. Co., Columbus, Ind., 1969-77; solicitor Dept. of the Interior, Washington, 1977-79; gen. counsel Cummins Engine Co., Columbus, Ind., 1979-80, v.p., 1980-92; pres. Cummins Fin., Inc., 1984-92, Cummins Cash and Info. Svcs., Inc., 1988-92; pres., CEO Saunders, Inc., Birmingham, Ala., 1992-93; pres., CEO, dir. Parkland Mgmt. Co., Cleve., 1994—; endowment trustee Euclid Ave. Christian Ch., 1995—; dir. Horvitz Newspapers, Inc., Bellevue, Wash., 1994—; trutee Lois U. Horvitz Found., 1998—; exec. dir. H.R.H. Family Found., 1994-98; treas. Irwin-Sweeney-Miller Found., Columbus, 1976-77; dir. L'Enfant Plaza Properties, Washington, 1974-77; mem. U.S. delegation Soviet Union Conf. on Environ. Law, 1978. Mem. Bartholomew Consol. Sch. Bd., 1982-88. Mem. Idaho Bar Assn., Ind. Bar Assn., D.C. Bar Assn., Harvard Club (N.Y.C.), Union Club (Cleve.). Democrat. Home: 20900 Colby Rd Shaker Heights OH 44122 Office: 1001 Lakeside Ave E Ste 900 Cleveland OH 44114-1172

KRULL, EDWARD ALEXANDER, dermatologist; b. Oakville, Conn., Oct. 25, 1929; s. Alexander and Marian (Ruppert) K.; m. Joan Marie Adams, Sept. 7, 1955; children: Alisa M., Lael Adams, Edward Alexander. Student, Yale U., 1948-51, MD, 1955. Diplomate Am. Bd. Dermatology (bd. dirs. 1984-94, v.p. 1992-93, pres. 1994), Am. Bd. Med. Spltys. (chmn. dermatology sect. 1992-94). Intern San Francisco City-County Hosp., 1955-56; with Madigan Gen. Hosp., 1959-60; resident Henry Ford Hosp., Detroit, 1960-63, staff physician dept. dermatology, 1965-76, chmn. dept., 1976-97; dermatology practice Grand Rapids, Mich., 1963-65; bd. dirs. Skin Cancer Found., 1977-80, Found. Internat. Dermatologic Edn., 1980-82; mem. residence rev. com. in dermatology, 1984-94, chmn., 1987-94. Mem. editl. bd. Jour. Dermatol. Surgery and Oncology, 1976-79, assoc. editor, 1993-96. Bd. govs. Henry Ford Hosp., trustee, 1986-94, mem. exec. com. bd. trustees, 1986-94, mem. fin. com. bd. trustees, 1986-94. Capt. M.C., U.S. Army, 1957-59, Iran. C.S. Livingood Lectures, 1998. Mem. AMA, Am. Dermatol. Assn. (pres. 1995-96), Am. Coll. Mohs Micrographic Surgery and Cutaneous Oncology, Am. Acad. Dermatology (hon.; editl. bd. jour. 1979-84, chmn. various task forces, bd. dirs. 1982-86, exec. com. bd. dirs. 1984-86, v.p. 1986-87, coun. sci. assembly 1991-95, chmn. 1995-96, Bronze award exhibit, 1969, Gold medal 1996), Mich. Dermatol. Soc. (sec.-treas. 1973-75, pres. 1976-77), Mich. State Med. Soc. (sec. dermatology sect. 1972-73, pres. 1973-74), Wayne County Med. Soc. (Profl. Achievement award 1997), Am. Soc. Dermatologic Surgery (pres. 1982, bd. dirs. 1973-76, 78-82, chmn. edn. coordinating com. 1978-82, Leon Goldman Achievement award 1988), Assn. Profs. Dermatology (bd. dirs. 1988-89), Assn. Acad. Dermatologic Surgeons (pres. 1988-89). Episcopalian. Avocations: tennis, trout fishing, golf. Home: 422 University Pl Grosse Pointe MI 48230-1638 Office: Henry Ford Hosp Dept Dermatology 2799 W Grand Blvd Dept Detroit MI 48202-2689

KRULL, JEFFREY ROBERT, library director; b. North Tonawanda, N.Y., Aug. 29, 1948; s. Robert George and Ruth Otilie (Fels) K.; m. Alice Marie Hart, Apr. 12, 1969; children: Robert, Marla. BA, Williams Coll., Williamstown, Mass., 1970; MLS, SUNY, Buffalo, 1974. Cert. profl. libr., N.Y., Ohio, Ind. Traffic mgr. New England Tel. Co., Burlington, Vt., 1970-71; tchr. Harrisburg (Pa.) Acad., 1971-72; reference libr. Buffalo and Erie County Pub. Libr., 1973-76; head libr. Ohio U., Chillicothe, 1976-78; dir. Mansfield-Richland County Pub. Libr., Ohio, 1978-86, Allen County Pub. Libr., Ft. Wayne, Ind., 1986—; mem. exec. com. Ft. Wayne Area Libr. Svc. Authority, 1986-90, v.p., 1989; mem. exec. com. Ind. Coop. Libr. Svcs. Authority, 1992—, pres., 1994-95; mem. Online Computer Libr. Ctr. Pub. Libr. Adv. Coun., 1994-97; pres. Ft. Wayne Area INFONET, 1995—. Pres. Three Rivers Literacy Alliance, 1997—; trustee Ohionet, Columbus, 1984-86. Mem. ALA, Pub. Libr. Assn. (pres. met. librs. sect. 1990-91, statistical report adv. com.), Libr. Adminstrn. and Mgmt. Assn. (sec. libr. orgn. and mgmt. assn. 1996-97), Ohio Libr. Assn. (bd. dirs. 1985-86), Ind. Libr. Fedn. (vice chmn. legis. com. 1987—), Beta Phi Mu (pres. Fort Wayne area InfoNet 1995—). Home: 3017 Oak Borough Run Fort Wayne IN 46804-7808 Offices: Allen County Pub Libr PO Box 2270 900 Webster St Fort Wayne IN 46802-3602

KRULL, KATHLEEN, juvenile fiction and nonfiction writer; b. Ft. Leonard Wood, Mo., July 29, 1952; d. Kenneth Owen and Helen (Folliard) K.; m. Loyal D. Cowles, Dec. 14, 1974 (div. May 1982); m. Paul W. Brewer, Oct. 31, 1989; stepchildren: Jacqui, Melanie. BA in English magna cum laude, Lawrence U., 1974. Editl. asst. Harper & Row, Evanston, Ill., 1973-74; assoc. editor Western Pub./Golden Books, Racine, Wis., 1974-79; mng. (acquiring) editor Raintree Pubs., Milw., 1979-82; sr. editor Harcourt Brace Jovanovich, San Diego, 1982-84; freelance writer and reviewer children's books, 1984—; frequent speaker at confs., workshops and univs. Author: Golden Everything Workbook Series, 1979, Beginning To Learn (24 books transl. into 5 langs. 1979-82), Sometimes My Mom Drinks Too Much, 1980 (Outstanding Social Studies Trade Book award 1980), Trixie Belden and the Hudson River Mystery, 1979, Twelve Keys to Writing Books That Sell, 1989, Songs of Praise, 1989, Alex Fitzgerald, TV Star, 1990, Alex Fitzgerald's Cure for Nightmares, 1991, Gonna Sing My Head Off; American Folk Songs for Children, 1992, World of My Own (4 books 1994, 95), Lives of the Musicians: Good Times, Bad Times...And What the Neighbors Thought, 1993, Maria Molina and the Days of the Dead, 1994, Lives of the Writers: Comedies, Tragedies (And What the Neighbors Thought), 1995, V is for Victory: America Remembers World War II, 1995, Lives of the Artists, 1995, Wilma Unlimited, 1996, Wish You Were Here, 1997, Lives of the Athletes, 1997, Lives of the Presidents, 1998; also articles and revs. Recipient Celebrate Literacy award Greater San Diego Reading Assn., 1994, also numerous awards for writing, including Boston Globe/Horn Book honor award, PEN West children's lit. award, 1994, nonfiction award So. Calif. Coun. on Lit. for Children and Young People, ALA Notable Book awards, Tchrs.' Choice award Internat. Reading Assn., Best Book of 1993 award Pubs. Weekly. Mem. Soc. Children's Book Writers and Illustrators (bd. dirs. 1995—, Golden Kite honor award for nonfiction). Avocations: quilting, gardening, singing, playing piano, travel. Office: care Harcourt Brace & Co Children's Books 525 B St Ste 1900 San Diego CA 92101-4495*

KRUMBOLTZ, JOHN DWIGHT, psychologist, educator; b. Cedar Rapids, Iowa, Oct. 21, 1928; s. Dwight John and Margaret (Jones) K.; m. Helen Brandhorst, Aug. 22, 1954 (div. Aug. 1986); children: Ann, Jennifer; m. Betty Lee Foster, Nov. 8, 1987. BA, Coe Coll., Cedar Rapids, 1950; MA, Columbia Tchrs. Coll., 1951; PhD, U. Minn., 1955; PhD (hon.), Pacific Grad. Sch. Psychology, 1991. Counselor, tchr. W. Waterloo (Iowa) H.S., 1951-53; from teaching asst. to instr. U. Minn., 1953-55; from asst. prof. ednl. psychology to assoc. prof. Mich. State U., 1957-61; faculty Stanford U. Sch. Edn., 1961-66, prof. edn. and psychology, 1966—; vis. sr. research psychologist Ednl. Testing Service, 1972-73; fellow Ctr. for Advanced Study in Behavioral Scis., 1975-76, Advanced Study Ctr., Nat. Ctr. for Research in Vocat. Edn., Ohio State U., 1980-81; vis. colleague dept. psychology Inst. Psychiatry, U. London, 1983-84. Author: (with others) Learning to Study, 1960; (with Helen B. Krumboltz) Changing Children's Behavior, 1972; editor: Learning and the Educational Process, 1965, Revolution in Counseling, 1966; (with Carl E. Thoresen) Behavioral Counseling: Cases and Techniques, 1969, Counseling Methods, 1976; (with Anita M. Mitchell and G. Brian Jones) Social Learning and Career Decision Making, 1979; (with Daniel A. Hamel) Assessing Career Development, 1982; contbr. articles to profl. jours. With USAF, 1955-57. Recipient Eminent Career award Nat. Career Devel. Assn., 1994; Guggenheim fellow, 1967-68. Mem. Am. Psychol. Assn. (pres. div. counseling psychology 1974-75), Am. Ednl. Research Assn. (v.p. div. E. 1966-68), Am. Personnel and Guidance Assn. (Outstanding Research award 1959, 66, 68, Disting. Profl. Services award

1974, Leona Tyler award 1990). Home: 933 Valdez Pl Stanford CA 94305-1008

KRUMM, CHARLES FERDINAND, electrical engineer; b. Macomb, Ill., Aug. 3, 1941; s. Harold F. and Jean Dunlap (Burns) K.; m. Patricia L. Kosanke, Dec. 9, 1967; children: Jennifer, Frederick. AS, Grand Rapids Jr. Coll., 1961; BSEE, U. Mich., 1963, MSEE, 1965, PhD, 1970. Sr. scientist Raytheon Co., Waltham, Mass., 1969-76; mem. tech. staff Hughes Rsch. Labs., Malibu, Calif., 1976-77, sect. head, 1977-79, asst. dept. mgr., 1979-81, dept. mgr., 1981-86, lab. mgr., 1986-89; program mgr. Hughes Radar and Comm. Sys., El Segundo, Calif., 1989-96; product line mgr. Hughes GaAs Operation, Torrance, Calif., 1996; divsn. mgr. Hughes Microelectronics Divsn., Newport Beach, Calif., 1996-98; v.p., dep. mgr. ctrs. excellence and strategic components, sensors, and elec. sys. segment Raytheon Sys. Co., 1998-99; gen. mgr. Raytheon RF Components, Andover, Mass., 1999—. Home: 3223 Monte Carlo Dr Thousand Oaks CA 91362-4604

KRUMM, ROSS W., federal judge. Chief bankruptcy judge U.S. Dist. Ct. (we. dist.) Va., Harrisonburg, Va., 1986—. Fax: (540) 433-6390. Office: US Dist Ct (we dist) Va PO Box 191 Harrisonburg VA 22801

KRUMP, GARY JOSEPH, lawyer; b. Breckenridge, Minn., June 27, 1946; m. Mary Kay Chermak; children: Adam, Jonathon. BA, N.D. State U., 1968; JD, U. Minn., 1971, postdoctoral, 1972; cert. in health care, So. Ill. U., Edwardsville, 1978, MBA, 1980; grad. cert., George Washington U., 1981; grad., Army Command & Gen. Staff Coll. Bar: Minn. 1971, U.S. Ct. Mil. Appeals 1972, U.S. Supreme Ct. 1975, D.C. 1977. Commd. 2nd lt. U.S. Army, 1970, advanced through grades to capt., 1971, capt. with JAGC, 1972-76, chief internat. law-Japan, 1974-76; chief adminstrv. law Walter Reed Army Med. Ctr., 1976-77; sr. staff atty. office of gen. counsel VA, Washington, 1978-83, nat. coord. med. care recovery program, 1979, dep. asst. gen. counsel, 1983-87, assoc. dep., asst. sec. for acquisitions, 1988-89; v.p., gen. counsel JSA Healthcare Corp., 1989-91; dir., corp. sec. DKH Healthcare; dir. Office of Real Property Mgmt. Office Real Property Mgmt., U.S. Dept. VA, Washington, 1991-92, dep. asst. sec. acqusitions and materiel mgmt., 1992—, acting asst. sec. acquisitions and facilities, 1992-95; VA environ. exec., 1994—; mem. faculty Ctrl. Mich. U., U. Va.; apptd. to career Fed. Sr. Exec. Svc.; gen. counsel, dir. Soccerama Assn., Inc., 1987-93; bd. dirs. JSA Healthcare Inc., 1989-91, JSA Internat., Inc., 1989-91, VA; sec. DKH Healthcare, Inc., 1990-91; prin., dir., gen. counsel ISG, Inc., 1991-97; dir., gen. counsel Am. Health Group, Inc., 1993-97; mem. Interagy. Com. on Supply Mgmt. Steering Group, Nat. Performance Rev. Com. on Reinventing VA; chair Interagy. Procurement Reform Working Group, 1993-95; chair interagy. contracts group GSA; mem. Interagy. Contracts Adv. Group; chair nat. conf. reinventing small bus. partnerships VA, 1993; chair interagy contracts group GSA, mem. adv. group; apptd. Pres.' Com. for Purchase from Blind and Other Severely Disabled, 1992—; com. chmn. Subcom. on Procurement Reform, 1996-97, elected com. chair, 1996—; mem. nat. adv. bd. Fed. Prison Industries, 1995—, chair subcom. administrn.; VA environ. exec., 1994—; bd.trustees Leadership VA, 1992-95; mem. Fed. Environ. Execs. Task Force, 1994—; mem. Interagy. Com. on Stds. Policy, 1995—, VA Stds. Exec., 1994—, VA Metrics Exec., 1994—; mem. Interagy. Electronic Commerce Task Force, 1994—; departmental co-chair Combined Fed. Campaign VA, 1994; chair VA Departmental Environ. Adv. Group, 1994—; bd. dirs. VA Dept., 1992-95; chmn. bd. dirs. VA Supply Fund, 1993—. Sec. Vets. Affairs Commendation, 1989, 95; mem. Ctr. for Pub. Resources Nat. Procurement Com., 1986-89, Adminstv. Conf. U.S. Alternative Disputes Resolution Symposium, 1988. Served to lt. col. JAGC, USAR, 1976—. Fellow Nat. Contract Mgrs. Assn. (bd. advisors 1989-90, 93—, com. internat. contracting 1995—); mem. ABA (vice chair com. on pub. contract law 1997—), Fed Bar Assn. (nat. chmn. tort law com., health and human svcs. coun. chmn. 1980-81, chmn. Nat. Tort Conf. 1979, editor Tort Law Newsletter 1978-81, Superior Svc. awards 1979, 81), Nat. Forensic Ctr., Am. Coll.-Legal Medicine (assoc.), Internat. Soc. Mil. Law and Law of War, Internat. Legal Soc., Res. Officers Ass. (life), Mid-Atlantic Token Kai, Japanese Sword Soc. U.S., Fed. Acquisition Inst. Policy Bd., Fed. Procurement Coun., Contract Svcs. Assn. (procurement com. 1989-91), Interagency Med. Procurement Mgmt. Com., Gov. Procurement Tng. (adv. com.), Interagency Procurement Career Mgmt. Com., VFW (life), Fed. Real Property Execs. (interagy. adv. coun. 1991-93), VFW (life), Vets. of Am., Am. Legion, Beta Gamma Sigma, Tau Kappa Epsilon. Home: 13812 Town Line Rd Silver Spring MD 20906-2112 Office: US Dept Vets Affairs Acquisitions and Material Mgmt 810 Vermont Ave NW Washington DC 20420-0001

KRUPA, PATRICIA ANN, retired nurse, consultant; b. Floral Park, N.Y., Nov. 3, 1937; d. James Joseph and Jessie M. (Steinmann) Hynes; m. John W. Krupa, Nov. 5, 1960; children: John W. III, James J., Daniel C. Diploma, St. Johns Episc. Sch. Nursing, Bklyn., 1959; student, Nassau Community Coll., Garden City, N.Y.; BS in Community Mental Health, N.Y. Inst. Tech., Greenvale, 1992. Lic. nurse, N.Y., S.C. Rehab. nurse Jordan Rehab., Carle Place, N.Y., 1981-85; family counselor Plainview (N.Y.) Alcohol Rehab., 1989-90; discharge planner Winthrop U. Hosp., Mineola, N.Y., 1987-91; with Community Long Term Care, Mt. Pleasant, S.C., 1991-99; ret.; mem. adv. bd. Berkley County Adult Protective Svcs.; co-chmn. Low Country Aids Svcs. Mem. N.Y. State Hospice Assn., St. John's Episcopal Hosp. Sch. Nursing Alumnae, Psi Chi. Home: 2049 Country Manor Dr Mount Pleasant SC 29466-7409

KRUPANSKY, BLANCHE, retired judge; b. Cleve., Dec. 10, 1925; d. Frank and Ann K.; m. Frank W. Vargo, Apr. 30, 1960. AB, Flora Stone Mather Coll., 1943-47; JD, Case Western Res. U., 1948, LLM, 1966. Bar: Ohio 1949. Gen. practice law, 1949-61, 83-84; asst. atty. gen. State of Ohio; asst. chief counsel Ohio Bur. Workmen's Compensation; judge Cleve. Mcpl. Ct., 1961-69; judge Common Pleas Ct. Cuyahoga County, 1969-77, Ct. Appeals Ohio 8th Appellate Dist., 1977-81; justice Supreme Ct. Ohio, 1981-83; judge 8th Dist. Ct. Appeals, 1983-95, chief justice, 1991; ret., 1995; vis. com. Case Western U. Law Sch., 1974-78, bd. govs., 1975-76. Recipient Outstanding Jud. Service award Supreme Ct. Ohio, 1972-76, Law Book scholar award Cuyahoga Women's Polit. Caucus, 1981, outstanding contbn. to law award Ohio Assn. Civil Trial Attys., 1982, Disting. Alumna award, 1982, Disting. Service award Women's Space, 1982, award Democratic Women's Caucus, 1983, award Women's Equity Action League Ohio, 1983; Personal Achievement and Community Svc. award Case We. Res. U., 1988, Margaret Ireland award Women's City Club, 1984; named Woman of Achievement Inter-Club Council Cleve., 1969; inducted into Ohio Women's Hall of Fame, 1981. Mem. Nat. Assn. Women Lawyers, Nat. Assn. Women Judges, Ohio Bar Assn. (Cronise Lutes award 1997), Bar Assn. Greater Cleve., Cuyahoga County Bar Assn., Cleve. Women Lawyers, LWV, Ohio Ctrs. of Appeals Assn., Ohio Assn. Attys. Gen., Ohio Appellate Judges Assn., Soc. of Benchers (chair 1994-95), SAR (Silver Medal award 1995). Republic. Roman Catholic. Club: Woman's City (Woman of Achievement award 1981) (Cleve.).

KRUPANSKY, ROBERT BAZIL, federal judge; b. Cleve., Aug. 15, 1921; s. Frank A. and Anna (Lawrence) K.; m. Marjorie Blaser, Nov. 13, 1952. BA, Western Res. U., 1946, LLB, 1948, JD, 1968. Bar: Ohio 1948, Supreme Ct. Ohio 1948, Supreme Ct. U.S 1948, U.S. Dist. Ct. (no. dist.) Ohio 1948, U.S. Ct. Appeals (6th cir.) 1948, U.S. Ct. Customs and Patent Appeals 1948, U.S. Customs Ct. 1948, ICC 1948. Pvt. practice law Cleve., 1948-52; asst. atty. gen. State of Ohio, 1951-57; mem. Gov. of Ohio cabinet and dir. Ohio Dept. Liquor Control, 1957-58; judge Common Pleas Ct. of Cuyahoga County, 1958-60; sr. ptnr. Metzenbaum, Gaines, Krupansky, Finley & Stern, 1960-69; U.S. atty. U.S. Dist. Ct. (no. dist.) Ohio, Cleve., 1969-70, U.S. dist. judge, 1970-82; judge, now sr. judge U.S. Ct. Appeals (6th cir.), Ohio, 1982—; spl. counsel Atty. Gen. Ohio, 1964-68; adj. prof. law Case Western Res. U. Sch. Law, 1969-70. 2d lt. U.S. Army, pilot USAAC, 1942-46; col. USAF Res. ret. Mem. ABA, Fed. Bar Assn., Ohio Bar Assn., Cleve. Bar Assn., Cuyahoga County Bar Assn., Am. Judicature Soc., Assn. Asst. Attys. Gen. State Ohio. Office: US Ct Appeals US Courthouse 201 Superior Ave NE Rm 328 Cleveland OH 44114-1201*

KRUPINSKI, CHRISTINE MARGARET, artist; b. Esslingen, Germany, Dec. 22, 1951; d. John Francis and Elfriede Gertrude (Klose) Newman; m. Dennis Krupinski, Mar. 19, 1977 (dec. Nov. 1995); children: Matthew, Kathleen, Andrew. One woman exhibns. include Shirlington Artist's Guild, Va., 1994, Gallery Okuda Internat., Washington, 1996, Fishscale & Mousetooth Gallery, Manassas, Va., 1997, Market St. Bar and Grill Hyat Regency, Reston, Va., 1997, Glass Growers Gallery, Erie, Pa., 1997, The Art League, Alexandria, Va., 1998; group shows include Va. Watercolor Soc., 1992, 93, 94, 95, 96, 97, 98, Brea (Calif.) Civic and Cultural Ctr., 1992, 93, 97, 98, Kirkpatric Gallery, 1992, 94, 95, 96, Miss. Mus. Art, Jackson, 1993, 94, 95, 96, 98, Neville Pub. Mus., Green Bay, Wis., 1993, 94, 95, 98, World Trade Ctr., New Orleans, 1993, 94, 95, 97, John Hopkins U. Gallery, Balt., 1993, 94, 95, Pitts. Watercolor Soc., 1993, 94, Perry House Galleries, Alexandria, Va., 1993, 94, Torpedo Factory Art League Gallery, Alexandria, 1993, 94, 95, 96, 97, 98, W.Va. Watercolor Soc., 1994, 96 (Best in Show), We. Colo. Ctr. for the Arts, Grand Junction, 1994, 95, 98, Wire Grass Mus. Art, Dothan, Ala., 1994, 95, 97, Tex. Watercolor Soc., San Antonio, 1994, 95, 96, 97, So. Watercolor Soc., 1994, 95, 96, 97, 98, Parkersburg (W.Va.) Art Ctr., 1994, 95, Red River Watercolr Soc., Fargo, N.D., 1994, 95, Phila. Watercolor Club, 1994, 95, Pa. Watercolor Soc., 1994, 95, N.W. Watercolor Soc., 1994, Keenan Ctr. Gallery, Lockport, N.Y., 1994, New Eng. Watercolor Soc., Boston, 1994, 95, Missoula (Mont.) Mus. Art, 1994, 95, Salmagundi Club, N.Y.C., 1994, 95, 96, 97, 98, Nat. Arts Club, N.Y.C., 1994, 95, 97, 98, Foothills Art Ctr., Golden, Colo., 1995, 97, 98, others; permanent collections include Time Life Books, Eat'n Park Restaurants, Cellular Telecomms. Industry Am.; featured in Artist's mag., Am. Artist, others. Recipient Grumbacher award Miss. Watercolor Soc., 1993, Juror's award Nat. Watercolor Okla. Exhibn., 1993, 3rd place Pitts. Watercolor Soc. Aqueous Open, 1993, Merit award Niagara Frontier Watercolor Soc., 1994, Spl. award of 500 prints We. Colo. Watercolor Soc., 1994, Equal award The Art League (2) 1994, (2) 95, (3) 96, 97, Hon. Mention The Art League, 1994, 95, Merit award Mid-Atlantic Regional Watercolor Soc., 1994, 95, Hon. Mention Arts coun. Fairfax County, 1995, Juror's Mention Nat. Watercolor Okla. Exhibn., 1995, Bd. Dirs. award We. Colo. Watercolor Soc., 1995, Strathmore Paper award Allied Artists of Am., Inc., 1997, Past Pres.'s award Watercolor Soc. Ala., 1997, Purchase award Watercolor USA, 1997, numerous others; named Best in Show Arts Coun. Farifax County, 1994, 96, W. Va. Watercolor Soc., 1996. Fellow Am. Artist's Profl. League (Maitland award 1994, Pres.'s award 1995, Medal of Honor 1997, Am. Artist's Profl. Fund award 1998); mem. Am. Watercolor Soc. (signature), Nat. Watercolor Soc. (signature), Ga. Watercolor Soc. (signature, Touring Exhibn. 1993), Ky. Watercolor Soc. (signature, Touring exhibn. 1993, 96, Purchase award 1995, 96, Merit award 1997), Midwest Watercolor Soc. (signature, Merit award 1997), N.E. Watercolor Soc. (signature, Merit award 1993, 96, 98), Okla. Watercolor Soc. (signature), Pa. Watercolor Soc. (signature), Potomac Valley Watercolorists, So. Watercolor Soc. (signature, Hal P. Moore award 1994, Dr. Jim congleton award 1995, George P. Shook Meml. award 1997. Merit award 1998), Tex. Watercolor Soc. (signature, Juror's Choice award 1995, Touring Exhibn. 1995), Va. Watercolor Soc. (signature, Merit award 1993, 94, 95, 96, 97), Watercolor West (signature, Founder's award 1993). Home: 10602 Barn Swallow Ct Fairfax VA 22032-3150

KRUPMAN, WILLIAM ALLAN, lawyer; b. Cleve., Aug. 14, 1936; s. Joel and Betty (Button) K.; m. Anne deLemos, June 19, 1960; children: Pamela, Theodore, Sally. BA, Amherst Coll., 1958; LLB, U. Mich., 1961; LLM in Labor Law, N.Y.U., 1962. Bar: Ohio 1961, N.Y. 1962. Ptnr. Jackson, Lewis, Schnitzler & Krupman, N.Y.C., 1962-75, mng. ptnr., 1975—. Author: Winning NLRB Elections, 1997. Bd. dirs. Children's Village, Dobbs Ferry, N.Y. Mem. N.Y. State Bar Assn. Home: 11 Cooper Rd Scarsdale NY 10583-2801 Office: Jackson Lewis Schnitzler & Krupman 101 Park Ave Fl 37 New York NY 10178-3898

KRUPNIK, VALERY EFIMOVICH, embryologist, writer; b. Moscow, Russia, Oct. 23, 1958; came to U.S., 1990; s. Epim P. and Sofia L. (Meltzer) K.; m. Vera A. Cherkasova, March 25, 1978 (div. 1989); 1 child, Maria Cherkasova. MSc., Moscow State U., 1981; PhD, Inst. Biotech., Russia, 1988. Lab. tech. Inst. Organ Transplantation, Moscow, 1975-76; jr. scientist Inst. Biotech., Moscow, 1981-85, sr. scientist, 1985-90; fellow Mass. Gen. Hosp., Boston, 1991-95, Mass. Eye Ear Infirmary, Boston, 1995-96, Beth Isreal Deaconess Med. Ctr., Boston, 1996—. Contbr. articles to profl. jours., stories to literary jours. Fight for Sight fellow Nat. Soc. Prevent Blindness, 1992. Home: 203 3rd St Apt 3 Cambridge MA 02141-2137 Office: Beth Isreal Deaconess Med Ctr 330 Brookline Ave Boston MA 02215-5400

KRUPP, BARBARA D., artist; b. Elyria, Ohio, July 1, 1942; d. Edward G. and Wilma Mary Nuhn; m. James L. Krupp, July 27, 1942; children: Rory, Rolf, Rachelle, Rodney. X-ray technician Elyria Meml. Hosp., 1969-74; ptnr. The Rockport (Mass.) Collection, 1983-92; owner Barbara Krupp Gallery, Rockport, Mass., 1983-89. Exhibited in group show Ariel Gallery, N.Y.C., 1990, Raiford Gallery, Roswell, Ga., 1997-98, 99; represented in permanent collections Musee des Duncan, Paris, Art Expo, N.Y., Art Expo Calif., L.A., Barbara Krupp Gallery, also numerous pub. and pvt. collections. Recipient Bronze medal, Salon d'Aout. Mem. Rockport Art Assn. Roman Catholic. Home and Office: 4915 Rte 20 PO Box 277 Wakeman OH 44889-0277

KRUPP, CLARENCE WILLIAM, lawyer, personnel and hospital administrator; b. Cleve., June 20, 1929; s. William Frederick and Mary Mae (Volchko) K.; m. Janice Margaret Heckman, June 28, 1952; children: Bruce, Carolyn. B.B.A. cum laude, Cleve. State U., 1958, LL.B., 1959, LL.M., 1963; LL.D. (hon.), 1974. Bar: Wis. 1972. Dir. indsl. relations and indsl. engring. Buxbaum Co., Canton, Ohio, 1963-66; mgr. indsl. relations Trane Co., La Crosse, Wis., 1966-73; dir. personnel-labor relations environ. products div. ITT, Phila., 1973; v.p. indsl. relations, gen. counsel G. Heileman Brewing Co., La Crosse, 1973-76; atty., v.p. human resources-risk control, sec. Good Samaritan Hosp., Dayton, Ohio, 1976-80; mgr. compensation and benefits State of Ariz., Phoenix, 1980-83; personnel adminstr., land mgmt. agt. Salt River Project, 1983-94; Indian and sch. land specialist, 1992—; chmn., pres. C.W. Krupp P.C., 1986—; cons. on labor relations, 1969, 81-83, 88—. Contbr. articles to profl. jours. Mcpl. arbitrator, La Crosse, 1976; pres., mem. La Crosse Bd. Edn., 1969-72; mem. Wis. Gov.'s Task Force on Edn., 1972-73, Ohio Little White House library del.; mem. Ariz. Spinal Injury Panel, 1984—. Served with U.S. Army, 1951-53. Named Outstanding Ariz. State Profl. Employee, 1982, Employee of Quarter, 1990, 91. Mem. Am. Bar Assn. (forum hosp. on law, labor law sect.), Am. Corp. Counsel Assn., Nat. Notary Assn., Wis Bar Assn. (Continuing Edn. award 1972), Am. Assn. Hosp. Attys., Ariz. Assn. Industries (healthcare com. 1983-97, chmn. legis. subcom. 1983-97), Am. Soc. Law and Medicine, Dayton C. of C., Electric League of Ariz. (ins. advisor 1985-97), Internat. Right of Way Assn. (regional cons. Native Am. land rights 1998—). Democrat. Roman Catholic. Club: Rotary. Home and Office: 8701 E Via De La Gente Scottsdale AZ 85258-4040 *Understand and be tolerant of the views of others. With that insight your decisons will be respected and your judgment both honored and sought.*

KRUPP, EDWIN CHARLES, astronomer; b. Chgo., Nov. 18, 1944; s. Edwin Frederick and Florence Ann (Olander) K.; m. Robin Suzanne Rector, Dec. 31, 1968; 1 son, Ethan Hembree. BA, Pomona Coll., 1966; MA, UCLA, 1968, PhD (NDEA fellow, 1970-71), 1972. Astronomer Griffith Obs., Los Angeles Dept. Recreation and Parks, 1972—, dir., 1976—; mem. faculty El Camino Coll., U. So. Calif., extension divs. U. Calif.; cons. in edni. TV Community Colls. Consortium; host teleseries Project: Universe. Author: Echoes of the Ancient Skies, 1983, The Comet and You, 1986 (Best Sci. Writing award Am. Inst. Physics 1986), The Big Dipper and You, 1989, Beyond the Blue Horizon, 1991, The Moon and You, 1993, Skywatchers, Shamans & Kings, 1996; editor, co-author: In Search of Ancient Astronomies, 1978 (Am. Inst. Physics-U.S. Steel Found. award for Best Sci. Writing 1978), Archaeoastronomy and the Roots of Science; editor-in-chief Griffith Obs., 1984—; contbg. editor Sky & Telescope, 1993—. Mem. Am. Astron. Soc. (past chmn. hist. astronomy divsn.), Astron. Soc. Pacific (past dir., recipient Klumpke-Roberts outstanding contbns. to the public understanding and appreciation of astronomy award 1989, G. Bruce Blair medal for contbns. to Pub. Astronomy 1996), Internat. Astron. Union, Explorers Club, Sigma Xi. Office: Griffith Observatory 2800 E Observatory Rd Los Angeles CA 90027-1255

KRUPP, FRED D., lawyer, environmental agency executive; b. Mineola, N.Y., Mar. 21, 1954; s. Arthur L. and Rosalind (Mehr) K.; m. Laurie Louise Devitt, Aug. 21, 1982; children: Alexander Mehr, Zachary Devitt, Jackson O'Connor. B.S., Yale U., New Haven, 1975; J.D., U. Mich., Ann Arbor, 1978. Ptnr. Albis & Krupp, New Haven, 1978-83; ptnr. Cooper, Whitney, Cochran & Krupp, New Haven, 1984; exec. dir. Environ. Def. Fund, 1984—; gen. counsel Conn. Fund for the Environment, New Haven, 1978-84. Mem. Pres.'s Commn. on Environ. Quality, 1991-92; mem. Pres.'s Coun. on Sustainable Devel., 1993—; mem. Pres.s' Adv. Com. Trade Policy and Negotiations, 1994—; bd. dirs. League of Conservation Voters, H. John Heinz III Ctr. for Sci., Econs. and Environment, Ind. Sector, Nat. Environ. Edn. and Tng. Found. Helen De Roy fellow U. Mich. Law Sch. 1986. Office: Environ Def Fund 257 Park Ave S New York NY 10010-7304*

KRUPSKA, DANYA (MRS. TED THURSTON), theater director, choreographer; b. Fall River, Mass., Aug. 13, 1921; d. Bronislaw and Anna (Niementowska) Krupski; m. James M. Hanrihan (div. 1953); 1 child, Brion; m. Ted Thurston, May 27, 1954 (dec. July, 1994); 1 child, Tina Lyn. Student, Lankenau Sch. for Girls, Phila.; studied with, Ethel Phillips Dance Studio, Catherine Littlefield Ballet Studio, L. Egorova, Paris, Mikhail Mordkin, N.Y.C. and Phila.; studied, Aubrey Hitchens Studio, N.Y.C., Bobby Lewis Dir.'s Studio, N.Y.C. Performed concerts and toured in Poland, Roumania, Balkan Countries, Hungary, Vienna, Palestine, 1929-36; joined Phila. Ballet (Littlefield) for European tour, 1937, Chgo. Opera Season, 1938, Am. Ballet (Ballanchine), N.Y.C., 1938; soloist Broadway prodn.: Frank Fay Show, Radio City Music Hall Ballet; leading role on nat. tour: Johnny Belinda 1941; soloist in: Chouve Souris, 1943; lead dancer in role of Laurie in Dream Ballet, 1st Nat. Co. of Okla., later Broadway Co., 1945; asst. to choreographer Agnes de Mille on Rodgers and Hammerstein prodn.: Allegro; asst. A. de Mille on ballet prodn.: Fall River Legend, opera prodn.: Rape of Lucrece, Broadway prodns.: Girl in Pink Tights, Gentlemen Prefer Blonds, Paint Your Wagon; assisted Michael Kidd on Broadway prodn.: Can Can; original choreographer Broadway prodn.: Most Happy Fella (Tony award nomination), Seventeen, 1st Shoestring Revue, Carefree Heart, Happiest Girl in the World (Tony award nomination), Her First Roman, 1968, Apollo and Miss Agnes; choreographer Met. Opera prodn.: The Gypsy Baron; choreographer Italian mus.: Rugantino, 1962; choreographer: TV Salute to the Peace Corps, 1965; guest choreographer: Zorba, Nat. Theatre, Reykjavik, Iceland, 1971, Sondheims Musical "Company" for Stora Teatern, Gothenburg, Sweden, 1971, Fantastiks, Little Theatre, Gothenburg, 1971, Okla. Nat. Theatre, Reykjavik, 1972, No No Nanette, Malmö Stadsteater, Sweden, 1973, Richard Rodger's Prodn. of Rex, Broadway, N.Y.C., 1976, Showboat, Malmö Stadsteater, 1976, Empress of China, Cin. Playhouse, 1984; dir., choreographer: Porgy and Bess, Malmö Stadsteater, Sweden, 1973, Bernstein's The Mass, Malmö Stadsteater, 1975, Chicago, Det Danske Teater, Denmark, 1977, Our Man in Havana, Poland, 1977, Cabaret, Helsingborg Stadsteater, Sweden, 1978, Guys and Dolls, Aarhus Teater, Denmark, 1978, Once Upon a Mattress, Nat. Theater Reykjavik, Iceland, 1981, Animalen, Malmö Stadsteater, Sweden, 1985, Papushko, Colonade Theatre, N.Y.C., 1985; producer, dir.; choreographer: The King and I, Malmö Stadsteater, Sweden, 1984; produced, directed, choreographed Sound of Music, Malmo Stadsteater, Sweden, 1990; directed, choreographed Lerner and Loewe lost musical Day before Spring, N.Y.C., 1990; dance and mus. staging How it Was Done in Odessa, Walnut St. Theatre, Phila., 1991; writing and preparing concert version of Our Man In Havana, Eng., 1997—; dir. mus. prodns., N.Y. City Center; Most Happy Fella, 1959, Showboat, 1961, Fiorello, 1962 (also White House prodn. for gov.'s conf. 1968); choreographer for TV Buick Hour, 1952, Colgate Comedy Hour, 1953, Omnibus; dir. U.S. Steel Theatre Guild Prodns; (ballets) Outlook for Three (Ellington), Pointes on Jazz (Brubeck), Am. Ballet Theatre. Mem. Actors Equity Assn., Soc. Stage Dirs. and Choreographers (exec. bd. mem.), Actors Studio (playwrights and dirs. unit), Dramatist's Guild. Office: PO Box 1958 New York NY 10101-1958*

KRUSE, ANN GRAY, computer programmer; b. Oklahoma City, Jan. 4, 1941; d. Floyd and Bernice Florence (Follansbee) Gray; A.B., Randolph Macon Woman's Coll., 1963; M.B.A., U. Chgo., 1973; m. Roy Edwin Kruse, Mar. 20, 1971 (dec.). Programming mgr. Ind. Info. Controls, Valparaiso, Ind., 1966-67; systems programmer Nat. Bus. Lists, Inc., Chgo., 1968-69, Am. Steel Foundries, Hammond, Ind., 1970-73; engr. applications programming Bell Helicopter Textron, Fort Worth, 1974-76; lead systems programmer Harris Data Communications, Dallas, 1976-81; sr. systems programmer Lone Star Gas Co., Dallas, 1981-82; sr. software specialist Raytheon Sys. Co., Dallas, 1982—. Republican. Episcopalian. Home: 6128 Black Berry Ln Dallas TX 75248-4909 Office: PO Box 660023 Dallas TX 75266-0023

KRUSE, CHARLES THOMAS, lawyer; b. Tulsa, Sept. 26, 1963; s. Joseph Daniel and Judith Sue (Holleman) K.; m. Jennifer Jones, May 20, 1989; 1 child, Charles Thomas Jr. BA, Emory U., 1985; JD, Vanderbilt U., 1989. Bar: Tex. 1989, U.S. Dist. Ct. (so. dist.) Tex. 1990, U.S. Ct. Appeals (5th and 8th cirs.) 1991; bd. cert. civil trial law Tex. Bd. Legal Specialization. Law clk. to Hon. Ricardo H. Hinojosa U.S. Dist. Ct. (so. dist.) Tex., McAllen, Tex., 1989-90; assoc. Fulbright & Jaworski, Houston, 1990-91; ptnr. McDade & Fogler, Houston, 1992-95; counsel to ptnr. King & Spalding, Houston, 1995—. Contbr. articles and papers to profl. publs. Bobby Jones scholar U. St. Andrews, 1985-86. Fellow Tex. Bar Found., Houston Bar Found.; mem. ABA, Houston Bar Assn., Houston Young Lawyer Assn. Republican. Roman Catholic. Home: 3727 Westerman St Houston TX 77005-1135 Office: King & Spalding 1100 Louisiana St Ste 3300 Houston TX 77002-5217

KRUSE, CYNTHIA SARA, nursing consultant; b. Dubuque, Iowa, Apr. 21, 1953; d. Edward M. and Kathleen C. (Hohmann) K. ADN, N.E. Iowa Community Coll., Calmar, 1974; diploma, Am. Inst. Paralegal Studies, 1988, U. Phoenix, 1991. Pediatric charge nurse Xavier Hosp., Dubuque, 1974-78; nursing supr. Stonehill Care Ctr., Dubuque, 1978-79; clin. nurse ob./gyn., gu/ent/opth., med. and surg. Desert Samaritan Hosp., Mesa, Ariz., 1979-89; nurse paralegal Broening, Oberg, Woods, Wilson and Cass, P.C., Phoenix, 1988-91; clin. nurse med./surg. and PACU Mesa (Ariz.) Gen. Hosp., 1991-92; clin. surg. nurse Chandler (Ariz.) Regional Hosp., 1992-93; med. claims reviewer Advantage Health Plan, Tempe, Ariz., 1993-94; freelance med.-legal cons., 1994—; med. eligibility assessor for long term care benefits State of Ariz., AHCCCS-ALTCS, 1995—.

KRUSE, DAVID LOUIS, II, transportation company executive; b. Frederick, Okla., Feb. 23, 1944; s. David Louis and Jewell Merlene (Dugan) K.; m. Beth Michele Newton, Feb. 6, 1944; children: Julie Lynn, William Bradley. BSME, U. Kans., 1967; MS in Indsl. Mgmt., Cen. Mo. State U., 1976. Registered profl. engr., Mo. Engr. Trans World Airlines, Kansas City, Mo., 1967-76, mgr. engine shop, 1976-78, dir. power plant engring., 1978-81, staff v.p. maintenance ops., 1981-85; v.p. maintenance and engring. Am. Airlines, Tulsa, 1985-89, sr. v.p. maintenance and engring., 1989—; mem. engring. sch. adv. bd. U. Kans., 1997—. Mem. adv. bd. Tulsa Econ. Devel. Found., 1987—; trustee St. Francis Healthcare Sys., 1994—, Hillcrest Med. Ctr., 1994-96, St. Francis Hosp., 1995—. With U.S. Army, 1967-73. Recipient Outstanding Achievement award U.S. Missile Command, 1969. Mem. Air Transport Assn., Okla. State C. of C. (bd. dirs. 1991-94), Tulsa C. of C. (bd. dirs. 1986—, exec. bd. 1988-92, 94—), Cedar Ridge Country Club. Republican. Avocations: golf, water sports. Home: 10012 S Louisville Ave Tulsa OK 74137-5221 Office: Am Airlines PO Box 582809 MD112 Tulsa OK 74158-2809

KRUSE, DIANE VIEWING, college library director; b. Nov. 10, 1937. BA, U. Ariz., 1981; MLS, So. Conn. State U., 1988. Circulation libr. U. Hartford, Conn., 1988-89; asst. libr. Wadsworth Atheneum, Hartford, 1989-91; curatorial, mus. specialist U. Ariz., Tucson, 1991-92; libr. dir. Pima County C.C., Tucson, 1998—. E-mail: viewing@azstarnet.com. Home: HC 1 Box 627 Tucson AZ 85736-1012

KRUSE, JAMES JOSEPH, merchant banker; b. St. Petersburg, Fla., Dec. 5, 1932; s. Charles Edward and Mary Joyce (Cappelen) K.; 1 child, Erika Leigh. BA, U. Fla., 1957; M.S., Fla. State U., 1958; postgrad., Aspen Inst. Humanistic Studies, 1977; Advanced Mgmt. Program, Harvard U., 1983. Mem. nat. hdqrs. staff Phi Delta Theta frat., Oxford, Ohio, 1958-60; mem. staff R.B. Troutman, Jr. (entrepreneur and investor), Atlanta, 1960-61; staff dir. Kennedy-Johnson campaign State of Ga., 1960-61; exec. dir. Plans for Progress, Pres.'s Com. on Equal Employment, Washington, 1961-63; asst. to pres. Textron, Inc., Providence, 1963-72; corp. sec. Textron, Inc., 1972-74, v.p., corp. sec., 1973-74, exec. v.p., corp. sec., 1974-78, sr. v.p. adminstrn., 1978-84; sr. v.p., ptnr. G. William Miller and Co. Inc., Providence, 1984-92; of counsel G. William Miller & Co., Inc., 1993—; pres. Kruse & Co., Inc., Warwick, R.I., 1993—; chmn. Profl. Facilities Mgmt., 1990—; chmn. adv. bd. Topsider Homes; mem. adv. bd. Investec Strategies, Inc.; bd. dirs. CNL Am. Properties Fund, Gateway Am. Bank. Pres. coun. Providence Coll., 1982—; bd. dirs. Providence Performing Arts Ctr.; trustee R.I. Coll. Found. Served with AUS, 1953-55. Recipient Presdl. citation for equal employment work, 1963, Vice Presdl. citation for equal employment work, 1966. Mem. Newport Country Club, Knight of St. Gregory. Roman Catholic. Home and Office: 5207 31st Ave S Gulfport FL 33707-5623 also: Ste 114 494 Woonasquatucket Ave North Providence RI 02911-1629

KRUSE, JOHN ALPHONSE, lawyer; b. Detroit, Sept. 11, 1926; s. Frank R. and Ann (Nestor) K.; m. Mary Louise Dalton, July 14, 1951; children: Gerard, Mary Louise, Terence, Kathleen, Joanne, Francis, John, Patrick. BS, U. Detroit, 1950, JD cum laude, 1952. Bar: Mich. bar 1952. Ptnr. Alexander, Buchanan & Conklin, Detroit, 1952-69, Harvey, Kruse, PC, Detroit, 1969—; Guest lectr. U. Mich., U. Detroit, Inst. Continuing Legal Edn.; city atty. Allen Park, Mich., 1954-59; twp. atty., Van Buren Twp., Mich., 1959-61. Co-founder Detroit Cath. Radio. Past pres. Palmer Woods Assn.; mem. pres.'s cabinet U. Detroit; mem. product liability adv. coun. Providence Hosp.; bd. dirs. Providence Hosp. Found. Legatus. Named one of 5 Outstanding Young Men in Mich., 1959, Outstanding Alumnus, U. Detroit Sch. Law, 1989, Humanitarian award Neuromuscular Inst. 1988. Mem. Detroit Bar Assn., State Bar Mich. (past chmn. negligence sect.), Assn. Def. Trial Counsel (bd. dirs. 1966-67), Am. Judicature Soc., Internat. Assn. Def. Counsel, Equestrian Order of the Holy Sepulchre, Cath. Campaign for Am. Roman Catholic. Club: Detroit Golf (past pres.). Home: 5569 Hunters Gate Dr Troy MI 48098-2342 Office: 1050 Wilshire Dr Ste 320 Troy MI 48084-1526 *Start each day with a simple petition - Lord help me to do your will today. End each day in thanks for his divine guidance. Prayer is to the soul as exercise is to the body. Neglect neither!.*

KRUSE, PAMELA JEAN, lawyer; b. Miami, Fla., June 3, 1950; d. Robert Emil and Irma G. Kruse. BS, Mich. State U., 1973, MA, 1975, PhD, 1979; JD, U. Mich., 1985. Bar: Mich. 1986. Grad. asst. Mich. State U., East Lansing, 1976-77, asst. intramural dir., 1977-79, labor rels. rep., 1979-81, asst. dir. labor rels., 1981-82; resident mgr. 719 Oakland, Ann Arbor, Mich., 1982-83; rsch. asst. Law Sch. U. Mich., Ann Arbor, 1982-85; jud. clk. U.S. Dist. Ct. (we. dist.) Mich., 1985-86; assoc. Clary, Nantz, Wood, Hoffius, Rankin & Cooper, Grand Rapids, Mich., 1986-91; with Village Bike Shops, 1991—. Bd. dirs. Babe Zaharias Golf Tournament, Am. Cancer Soc., 1987-91. Recipient Gold and Silver medals U.S. Pan Am. Team, Winnipeg, Man., Can., 1967, Silver medal U.S. Olympic Team, Mexico City, 1968; holder world records swimming 400 meters freestyle, 1967, 200 meters freestyle, 1967, 440-yard freestyle, 1966; inducted to Greater Fort Lauderdale Sports Hall of Fame, 1979. Mem. ABA, State Bar Mich. (exec. coun. young lawyers sect. 1987-90), Grand Rapids Bar Assn. (chairperson, exec. bd. dirs. young lawyers sect. 1987-91), Mich. Pub. Employer Labor Rels. Assn. (bd. dirs. 1981-82, chmn. manual revision com. 1982), Mich. State U. Alumni Assn. (1st v.p., bd. dirs. 1988-89), U.S. Olympians, Phi Delta Kappa, Kappa Alpha Theta.

KRUSE, PAUL ROBERT, retired librarian, educator; b. What Cheer, Iowa, Feb. 26, 1912; s. Carl Fred and Phoebe (Mumby) K.; m. Esther Moe, June 3, 1939 (div.); 1 son, Robert Leroy; m. Carolyn Rector, June 12, 1980 (dec. Sept. 1995). A.B., John Fletcher Coll., 1933; B.S. in L.S, U. Ill., 1940; Ph.D., U. Chgo., 1958. Librarian John Fletcher Coll., University Park, Iowa, 1932-33, Bolles Sch., Jacksonville, Fla., 1934-38; reference librarian Jacksonville Pub. Library, 1938-42; reference asst. in charge reference collections Library of Congress, Washington, 1942-45; established library for UN Conf., San Francisco, 1945; instr. Library Sch., Catholic U., Washington, 1943-48; bibliographer Ency. Brit., 1946-47; editor Who Knows and What, A.N. Marquis Co., 1949; vis. asst. prof. Library Sch., U. So. Calif., 1950, George Peabody Coll., 1950-51; reorganized library for Rollins Coll., Winter Park, Fla., 1951-52; vis. asso. prof. Library Sch., U. Ill., 1952-53; asso. prof. Library Sch., U. Denver, 1954-55; librarian Golden Gate U., San Francisco, 1955-63; assoc. prof. Sch. Library and Info. Scis., Univ. N. Tex., Denton, 1965-77; Fulbright lectr., library advisor U. Tehran, 1962-64, U. Ceylon, 1964-65; library cons. U.S. AID, Universidad Santa Maria la Antigua, Panama, 1968. Author: The Story of The Encyclopaedia Britannica, 1768-1943; Editor: Index for Lend Lease: Weapon for Victory, 1944; compiler bibliographies for: Ten Eventful Years, Ency. Brit, 1947, Profiles of Special Libraries, 2d edit, 1981; cons.: Pergamum Press, 1978; Contbr. articles to profl. jours. Active community and profl. theatre groups. Mem. ALA, Spl. Librs. Assn. (conf. chmn. 1961), Masons, Shrine. Republican. Methodist. Home: 2450 Aurora Ave N Apt 310 Seattle WA 98109-2269

KRUSE, PAUL WALTERS, JR., physicist, consultant; b. Hibbing, Minn., Nov. 24, 1927; s. Paul Walters and Marie Rae (Gibson) K.; m. Margaret Mary Fitzpatrick, Jan. 23, 1954; children—Paul II, Robert, John, Mary, Margaret, Charles, Thomas, Catherine, William. B.S., U. Notre Dame, 1951, M.S., 1952, Ph.D., 1954. Physicist Farnsworth Electronics Co., Ft. Wayne, Ind., 1954-56; sr. rsch. scientist Honeywell Corp. Tech. Center, Bloomington, Minn., 1956-59; prin. rsch. scientist Honeywell Corp. Tech. Center, 1959-60, staff scientist, 1960-69, sr. staff scientist, 1969-77, prin. staff scientist, 1977-79, prin. rsch. fellow, 1979-83; chief rsch. fellow Honeywell Corp. Sci. and Tech., 1983-86, Honeywell Sensor and System Devel. Ctr., 1987-93; cons., 1993—; chief scientist Infrared Solutions, Inc., Mpls., 1994-98; panel mem. Pres.'s Sci. Adv. Com., 1969-72; mem. Army Sci. Adv. Panel, 1965-77, Army Sci. Bd., 1978-82, 85-90; com. mem. Nat. Materials Adv. Bd., NRC-NAS, 1971-72, Adv. Bd. on Mil. Pers. Supplies, 1969-71; mem. planning com. 3d Internat. Photoconductivity Conf., 1968-69; chmn. Army ERADCOM Tech. Com., 1976; mem. com. on chem. and biol. sensor tech. NRC-Nat. Acad. Scis., 1982-84. Author: (with McGlauchlin and McQuistan) Elements of Infrared Technology, 1961; contbr. articles to profl. jours.; mem. editorial adv. bd.: Optics Letters, 1977-79, Infrared and Millimeter Waves, 1978-89 , Infrared Physics, 1986—; patentee in field. Bd. dirs. Benilde High Sch., 1970-74. Recipient H.W. Sweatt award for outstanding sci. accomplishment, 1966, Alan Gordon Meml. award Soc. Photo-Optical Instrumentation Engrs., 1981, Outstanding Civilian Service medal Dept. of Army, 1983; selected by sec. def. for Joint Civilian Orientation Conf. 37, 1967. Fellow Am. Phys. Soc., Optical Soc. Am., AIAA (assoc.); mem. Am. Electronics Assn. (sci. and tech. com. 1990-93), Notre Dame Club Minn. (pres. 1974-75), Notre Dame Alumni Assn. (dir. 1979-82). Home: 6828 Oaklawn Ave Minneapolis MN 55435-1627

KRUSE, ROSALEE EVELYN, accountant, auditor; b. Muscatine, Iowa, Aug. 23, 1953; d. Burr Arthur Beeding and Mary Ellen (Phillips) McGourty; m. Michael Raymond Kruse, May 20, 1972 (div. Oct. 1997); children: Lauretta Kathleen Kruse Tkaczyk, Matthew William Kruse. A in Gen. Studies, Muscatine C.C., 1986; BBA, U. Iowa, 1988; M of Acctg., St. Ambrose U., 1993. CPA, Iowa. Acct. Rock Island (Ill.) Arsenal, 1989-96, auditor, 1996-98, accountant, 1998; acctg. supr. Accountemps, 1999—; acctg. instr. Am. Inst. Commerce, 1989; adj. prof. St. Ambrose U., 1996. Mem. AICPA, Am. Soc. Mil. Comptrs. (chairperson chpt. competition 1991-92, treas. 1993-94, 1st v.p. 1994-95, scholarship chair 1997-98), Iowa Soc. CPAs (membership com. 1995-96, auditing stds. and acctg. prin. com. 1996-98, pub. and profl. rels. com. 1996-97, info. tech. com. 1999—), Inst. Mgmt. Accts (program roster com. Illowa chpt. 1995-96, acad. rels. and edn. project student affairs com. 1996-97, fin. and adminstrn. 1997-98, pres.-elect 1997-98, pres. 1998-99, pub. rels. 1999—, regional coun. exec. 1998—, MIG 1999—), Inst. Internal Auditors (bd. govs. 1996-99, pres. 1999—). Methodist. Home: Apt 422 3511 Jersey Ridge Rd #422 Davenport IA 52807-2283

KRUSE, THELMA MERLE, library director; b. Topeka, Kans., Aug. 3, 1941; d. Clifton Bryan and Merle Virginia K.; m. Lanson Brice Carney, June 1, 1962; children: Benjamin, Matthew, Rachel, Nathan. BA, U. Kans., 1963; MLS, U. Wash., 1976. From reference libr. to asst. dir. Anchorage (Alaska) Municipal Libr., 1977-88; dir. Plymouth (Mass.) Pub. Libr., 1988-93, Timberland Regional Libr., Olympia, Wash., 1993—; bd. dirs. The Evergreen St. Coll. Friends, Olympia. Reviewer Scholarship com. Evergreen St. Coll., Olympia, 1997—. Mem. Am. Libr. Assn. (com. chair, sec., Wash. chpt. program presenter), Rotary (Olympia chpt. com. chair on literacy 1994—). Avocations: remodeling historical houses, travel. E-mail: tkruse@timberland.lib.wa.us. Home: 223 Jorgensen Rd Onalaska WA 98570 Office: Timberland Regional Library 415 Airdustrial Way SW Olympia WA 98501

KRUSE, WILBUR FERDINAND, architect; b. Selden, Kans., Nov. 4, 1922; s. John Arnold and Kathryn (Zimmerman) K.; m. Mary Teresa Armstrong, Sept. 5, 1949; children: William, Karen, Katherine, Teresa, Peter, Thomas, Ann, Joan. Elem. tchr. cert., Fort Hays Tchrs. Coll., 1942; student, Tex. A&M Mil. Coll., 1943; BS in Arch., Kans. State U., 1949. Assoc. architect Glen H. Thomas & A.B. Harris Architects, Wichita, Kans., 1948-57; owner Wilbur F. Kruse Architects and Assocs., Wichita, 1957-67; owner Kruse Architects and Cons., Wichita, 1967—; owner K Industries. Patentee screened veneer vent for masonry, 1986; prin. works include Kans. Vocat. Correctional Tng. Ctr., Topeka, 1983, also numerous jails, detention ctrs, chs., and schs., Wichita Century II Auditorium Complex. Bd. dirs. Cmty. Corrections Wch/Sedgwick Co., Wichita, 1979-83, Kans. chpt. Arthritis Found., 1985-89, Serra Internat. Found., 1998—; advisor to Arthritis Water Exercise Club Inc., 1984-90; regional dir. #9 U.S. and Can. Coun., 1995-97, sec. 1997-99. Lt. USAF, 1942-45, ETO. Decorated 3 battle stars, pres. unit citation, air medal, 3 clusters; recipient Cert. Appreciation Kans. Dept. Corrections, Topeka, 1983, Honor award for Marshall County govt. complex State Soc. Engrs. Mem. Sierra Internat. Club, 1979—, pres. Wichita Club, 1988, gov. Dist. 12, 1993, reg. dir. #9, US and Canada Counc., 1995-97, sec., US and Canada Counc., 1997-99. Roman Catholic. Avocation: travel. Home: 1641 Womer St Wichita KS 67203-1537 Office: Kruse Architects and Cons 1337 N Meridian Ave Wichita KS 67203-4641

KRUSICK, MARGARET ANN, state legislator; b. Milw., Oct. 26, 1956; d. Ronald J. and Maxine C. K. BA, U. Wis., 1978; postgrad., U. Wis., Madison, 1979-82. Legal asst. Milw. Law Office, 1973-78; teaching asst. U. Wis., Milw., 1978-79; staff mem. Govs. Ombudsman Program for the Aging & Disabled, Madison, Wis., 1980; administrv. asst. Wis. Higher Edn. AIDS Bd., Madison, 1981; legis. aide Wis. Assembly, Madison, 1982-83, state rep., 1983—. Author: Wisconsin Youth Suicide Prevention Act, 1985, Wisconsin Nursing Home Reform Act, 1987, Wisconsin Truancy Reform Act, 1988, Elder Abuse Fund, 1989, Stolen Goods Recovery Act, 1990, Fair Prescription Drug Pricing Act, 1994, Anti-Graffiti Act, 1996, Caregiver Criminal Background Checks and Abuse Prevention Ace, 1998, Child Abuse Prosecution Act, 1998, Nursing Home Staffing and Forfeiture Reform Act, 1998. Mem. St. Gregory Great Cath. Ch., Milw., 1960—, Dem. Party, Milw., 1980—, Layton Park Assn.; bd. dirs. Alzheimer's Disease Assn., 1986-88. Named Legislator of Yr. award Wis. Sch. Counselors, Madison, 1986, Wis. County Constnl. Officers Legislator of Yr., 1999; recipient Sr. Citizen Appreciation Allied Coun. for Sr. Milw., 1987, Crime Prevention award Milw. Police Dept., Milw., 1988, Cert. Appreciation, Milw. Pub. Sch., 1989, Friends of Homecare award, 1989, Environ. Decades' Clean 16 award, 1986-90, 95-96, Badger State Sheriff's Law and Order award, 1993, Appreciation award Coalition of Wis. Aging Groups, 1998. Mem. Jackson Park Neighborhood Assn., U. Milw. Alumni Assn. (trustee 1986-90). Home: 3426 S 69th St Milwaukee WI 53219-4037 Office: Wis Assembly State Capitol Madison WI 53702

KRUSKAL, JOSEPH B., mathematician, statistician, researcher; b. N.Y.C., Jan. 29, 1928; s. Joseph B. and Lillian Rose (Vorhaus) K.; m. Rachel Solomon, May 24, 1953; children: Joyce, Benjamin. PhB, U. Chgo., 1948, BS, 1948, MS, 1949; PhD, Princeton U., 1954. Mem. analytical rsch. group Princeton U., 1954-56; rsch. instr. dept. math. U. Wis., Madison, 1956-58; asst. prof. dept. math. U. Mich., Ann Arbor, 1958-59; mem. tech. staff Bell Labs., Murray Hill, N.J., 1959-93; ofcl. visitor dept. stats. Cambridge (Eng.) U., 1966; vis. prof. dept. stats. Yale U., New Haven, 1967-68. Author: Multidimensional Scaling; co-author: Time Warps, String Edits, and Macromolecules. Founder, 1st prs. Fair Housing Com. of Maplewood and South Orange; bd. dirs. ACLU of N.J. Fellow AAAS, Am. Statis. Assn.; mem. Psychometric Soc. (pres.), Classification Soc. N.Am. (pres.). Democrat. Jewish. Office: Bell Labs Lucent Techs 600 Mountain Ave Murray Hill NJ 07974

KRUSKAL, MARTIN DAVID, mathematical physicist, educator; b. N.Y.C., Sept. 28, 1925; m. 1950; 3 children. BS, U. Chgo., 1945; MS, NYU, 1948, PhD in Math., 1952. Rsch. scientist Plasma Phys. Lab., Princeton U., 1951-61, prof. astrophys. sci., 1961—, prof. math., 1981—, emeritus, 1989—; David Hilbert prof. math. Rutgers U., New Brunswick, N.J., 1989—; trustee Soc. for Indsl. & Applied Math., 1985-91, Math. Scis. Edn. Bd. of NRC, 1986-89, Ext. Adv. Com., Ctr. for Nonlinear Studies, Los Alamos Nat. Lab., 1980—. Recipient Dannie Heineman Math. Phys. prize, 1983, Potts Gold medal Franklin Inst., 1986, Nat. Medal Sci. NSF, 1993, John von Neumann prize Soc. Indsl. and Applied Math., 1994; sr. fellow NSF, 1959-60, Weizmann Inst. Sci., 1973-74, fellow Jap. Soc. Promition Sci., 1979. Mem. AAS, Am. Math. Soc. (Gibbs lectr. 1979), Math. Assn. Am., Am. Phys. Soc. (fellow), Nat. Acad. Scis. (chmn. sect. of applied math. scis. 1990-93, award in Applied Mathematics and Numerical Analysis, NAS, 1989), Royal Soc. London (fgn. mem.). Home: PO Box 49 Arroyo Seco NM 87514-0049 Office: Rutgers U Dept Math Hill Ctr Busch Campus New Brunswick NJ 08903

KRUTSICK, ROBERT STANLEY, retired science center executive; b. Lansford, Pa., Dec. 6, 1942; s. John Jacob and Mary Ann (Novak) K.; m. Charlotte Ann Harper, Feb. 18, 1977; children: Robert Steven, Laurie, Tracy, Andrew, Daniel. BS, Pa. State U., 1966; M in Local and State Govt., U. Pa., 1967. Sr. v.p., treas. Univ. City Sci. Ctr., Phila., 1978-88, acting pres., 1988-90, exec. v.p., 1988-97. Supr. Upper Merion Twp., King of Prussia, Pa., 1989; pres. Upper Merion Pk. and Historic Found., 1997—; mem. Upper Merion Twp. Planning Commn., 1998—; bd. dirs. Cradle of Liberty coun. Boy Scouts Am. Mem. Upper Merion Area Edn. Found., Optimist Club. Republican. Roman Catholic. Avocations: tennis, golf, basketball. Home: 210 Cedar Pl Wayne PA 19087-2170

KRUTTER, FORREST NATHAN, lawyer; b. Boston, Dec. 17, 1954; s. Irving and Shirley Krutter. BS in Econs., MS in Civil Enging., MIT, 1976; JD cum laude, Harvard U., 1978. Bar: Nebr. 1978, U.S. Supreme Ct. 1986, N.Y. 1991. Antitrust counsel Union Pacific R.R., Omaha, 1978-86; sr. v.p. law, sec. Berkshire Hathaway Group, Omaha, 1986—. Co-author: Impact of Railroad Abandonments, 1976, Railroad Development in the Third World, 1978; author: Judicial Enforcement of Competition in Regulated Industries, 1979; contbr. articles Creighton Law Rev. Mem. ABA, Phi Beta Kappa, Sigma Xi. *

KRYGIER, MICHAEL ROBERT, mechanical engineer; b. Detroit, Apr. 11, 1970; s. John Walter and Connie Mae (Usher) K.; m. Susan Marie Scovera, May 11, 1996. AS, Schoolcraft C.C., Livonia, Mich., 1991; BSME, Lawrence Tech. U., 1994. Mech. engr. Gen. Motors Corp., Livonia, Mich., 1987-88, Detroit Diesel, 1988; owner KLK Enterprises, Livonia, Mich., 1986-94; mech. inspector Detroit Testing Lab., Inc., Warren, Mich., 1994-96, certification prog. supr., 1996-98; certification mgr. Detroit Testing Lab., Inc., Warren, 1998—; mech. engr. Lawrence Tech. U. Formula Soc. Automotive Engrs. Project, Southfield, Mich., 1992-94; interviewed by Dateline, NBC-TV, 1994. Co-author: Test Method for the Coefficient of Restitution on Softballs & Baseballs, 1995; contbr. articles, papers to profl. jours.; inventor drive train design. performed home and garden repairs and svcs. sr. citizen activity ctr., Livonia, Mich., 1988-94. Mem. NSPE, ASTM, NRPA, Mich. Soc. Prof. Engrs., Soc. Automotive Engrs. Office: Detroit Testing Lab Inc 7111 E 11 Mile Rd Warren MI 48092-2709

KRYS, SHELDON JACK, retired foreign service officer, career minister; b. N.Y.C., June 15, 1934; s. Martin and Anna K.; m. Doris M., May 24, 1964; children—Wendy M., Madeleine S., Susan Jennifer. N.D., U. Md., College Park, 1955; grad., Nat. War Coll., Washington, 1977; PhD (hon.), St. John Fisher Coll., 1996. Newscaster Radio Sta. KRSD, Rapid City, S.D., 1955-57; dir., producer Radio Sta. WWDC, Washington, 1957-59; prin. Chris Sheldon Pub. Relations, Washington, 1959-61; cons. to dir. FMCS, Washington, 1961-62; ednl. and cultural affairs officer, dir. reception ctrs. Dept. State, Washington, 1962-64; mgmt. officer Dept. State, London, Eng., 1965-66, spl. asst. to ambassador, 1966-69; dir. personnel Latin Am. Dept. State, Washington, 1969-74; adminstrv. counselor Dept. State, Belgrade, Yugoslavia, 1974-76; fgn. svc. insp. Dept. State, Washington, 1977-79, exec. dir. Bur. Near Eastern and South Asian Affairs, 1979-83, dep. dir. mgmt. ops., 1983-84, exec. asst. to under sec. for mgmt., 1984-85; amb. to Trinidad and Tobago, 1985-88, exec. sec. Laird Commn., 1987, asst. sec. state adminstrn. and info. mgmt., 1988-89, asst. sec. state diplomatic security, 1989-92; diplomat-in-residence George Washington U., Washington, 1992-93; cons. internat. and intergovtl. affairs Fletcher, Heald & Hildreth, P.L.C., Roslyn, Va., 1994—. Mem. nat. adv. bd. George Foster Peabody Awards, 1990-95, chmn. bd. 1993-95, chmn. emeritus 1997, chmn. editl. bd. Fgn. Svc. Jour., 1994-96; bd. dirs. Sr. Living Found., 1997—, Washington Inst. Fgn. Affairs, 1998—. Recipient Meritorious Honor award, Disting. Honor award, Superior Honor award Dept. State, Presdl. Meritorious Service award. Mem. Armed Forces Comm. and Electronics Assn. (bd. dirs. 1991-92), Nat. War Coll. Alumni Assn., Am. Fgn. Svc. Assn., Am. Broadcast Pioneers, Broadcast Found., City Tavern Club. Avocations: gardening, nature watching, tennis. Office: Fletcher Heald & Hildreth PLC 1300 17th St N 11th Fl Arlington VA 22209-3801

KRYSL, MARILYN, English educator; b. Feb. 26, 1942; d. Richard Rudolph and Edith Evelyn (Peterson) K.; 1 child, Riva Sweetrocket. MFA, U. Oreg., 1968. Prof. English U. colo., Boulder, 1972—. Author of poems. Mem. Poetry Soc. Am., Acad. Am. Poets. Office: U Colo Boulder CO 80309

KRYTER, KARL DAVID, research scientist; b. Indpls., Oct. 13, 1914; s. George David and Mary Matilda (Christoph) K.; m. Grace Irene Brown, June 21, 1946; children: Dianne, Victoria (Mrs. Myron I. Liebhaber), Kathryn (Mrs. Richard A. Rendon). A.B., Butler U., 1939; Ph.D., U. Rochester, 1942. Rsch. tchr. fellow Harvard U., Cambridge, Mass., 1942-46; asst. prof. Washington U., St. Louis, 1946-48; dir. human resources research labs. Air Force Cambridge Rsch. Ctr., 1948-57; head dept. psychoacoustics Bolt Beranek & Newman, Inc., Cambridge, Mass., 1957-65; dir. Sensory Scis. Rsch. Ctr., Menlo Park, Calif., 1965-76; staff scientist Stanford Rsch. Inst., Menlo Park, 1976-85; adj. prof. San Diego State U., 1990—; chmn. bd. Acousis Co., Santa Barbara, Calif.; tchr. Colby Coll., 1960-63, MIT, 1958-59; adviser U.S. Pres.'s Office for Sci. and Tech., 1968-70; mem. SST environ. study com. Dept. Interior, 1969; past chmn. coun. com. hearing and bioacoustics NAS-NRC, 1960. Author: The Effects of Noise on Man, 1970-85, Handbook of Hearing and the Effects of Noise, 1994. Recipient Disting. Svc. award in sci. Am. Speech and Hearing Assn., medal U. Liege, Belgium. Fellow APA (coun. reps. 1966-69), Soc. Enging. Psychologists (pres. 1965, Franklin V. Taylor award), Acoustical Soc. Am. (coun., pres. 1972). Home: 1515 San Antonio Creek Rd Santa Barbara CA 93111-1319

KRYZAK, LINDA ANN, educational administrator; b. Oak Park, Ill., Nov. 3, 1951; d. Eugene Joseph and Helen (Vlahos) K.; children: Melissa Lynn, Heather Rae. BS in Edn., No. Ill. U., 1973, MS in Edn., 1977; cert. advanced study in ednl. tech., Nat.-Louis U., 1998. Cert. gen. adminstr., elem. tchr., spl. edn., early childhood spl. edn. tchr., social/emotional disordered tchr., learning disabled, educable and trainable mentally handicapped, supervisory endorsements. Dir. career/life tng., rsch. project leader, ednl. cons. Grove Sch., Lake Forest, Ill., 1974-81; pvt. practice Addison, Ill., 1981-82; tchr. spl. edn. Sch. Dist. 83, Franklin Park, Ill., 1982-85; coord. spl. edn. Leyden Area Spl. Edn. Coop., Franklin Park, Ill., 1985-94; prin. South Elem. Sch., Franklin Park, Ill., 1994-99; dir. instrn. and tech. South Elem. Sch., Franklin Park, 1999—; founder Creative Learning Choices, 1992—. Pub. speaker on computers, assistive technology, software and integration of spl. edn. students into regular classrooms, 1988—. Mem. Ill. Computing Educators, Ill. Prins. Assn., Nat. Assn. Elem. Prins.

KRZYSZTOFOWICZ, ROMAN, systems engineering and statistical science educator, consultant; b. Cieszyn, Poland, Sept. 27, 1947; came to U.S., 1974; naturalized, 1985; s. Janusz and Irena (Rogozinska) K.; m. Liana Balayan, May 27, 1995; son, Arman; daughter Nayiri. MS with highest distinction, Cracow (Poland) Tech. U., 1970; PhD, U. Ariz., 1978. Research engr. Inst. for Meteorology and Water Resources, Cracow, 1970-72, head computer ctr., 1972-74; lectr. Chief Tech. Orgn., Cracow, 1973-74; asst. prof. systems engring. U. Ariz., Tucson, 1978-79; asst. prof. civil engring. MIT, Cambridge, Mass., 1979-82; assoc. prof. systems engring. U. Va., Charlottesville, Va., 1982-86; prof. systems engring. U. Va., Charlottesville, 1986—, dir. grad. program systems engring., 1984-89, assoc. dir. ctr. for risk mgmt. engring. systems, 1987-88, prof. statistics, 1995—; lectr. George Washington U., 1982-83, NATO Advanced Study Inst., Tucson, 1985, Deauville, France, 1993, Coop. Program for Operational Meteorology, Edn. and Tng., Boulder, Colo., 1993—; rep. NSF in coop. rsch. initiatives with Brazil and Poland, 1991; reviewer proposals NSF, 1980—, Natural Scis. and Engring. Rsch. Coun. Can., 1987—; rschr. Nat. Weather Svc., 1992, 1995; expert on flood forecasting, Commn. for Hydrology, World Meteorological Orgn., 1997—; reviewer articles for numerous jours. Editor Jour. of Hydrology, 1996—; mem. editorial adv. bd. Stochastic Hydrology and Hydraulics, 1990—, Control and Cybernetics, 1994—; contbr. articles to profl. jours., chpts. to books, entries to Systems and Control Ency., Concise Ency. Environ. Systems, Ency. Ops. Rsch. and Mgmt. Sci., Ency. of Sci. and Tech. Recipient Prof. W. Wierzbicki award Polish Soc. Civil Engrs. and Technicians, 1970, rsch. awards NSF, 1978—, Presdl. Young Investigator award Pres. of U.S., 1984. Mem. IEEE, Am. Statis. Assn., Soc. for Judgment and Decision Making, Internat. Inst. Forecasters, Inst. for Ops. Rsch. and the Mgmt. Scis., Am. Geophys. Union, Am. Water Resources Assn., Am. Meteorological Soc., Tau Beta Pi (Eminent Engr. award 1985). Republican. Armenian Catholic. Avocations: opera, theater, skiing, sailing, hiking. Office: U Va Dept of Systems Engring Thornton Hall Charlottesville VA 22903-2442 *Education is a launchpad to a rewarding life. Research demands passion and endurance. The challenge for me as an academician is to turn learners into thinkers, to bring about in students a transition from acquiring knowledge to creating new knowledge, to graduate scientists and engineers who not merely perpetuate today's technology but invent a better one. For it is the creative element that uplifts the individual and benefits mankind.*

KRZYZAN, JUDY LYNN, automotive executive; b. Buffalo, Sept. 1, 1951; d. James Lambert and Janet Lucille (Grabau) McKellar; m. Ronald Edward Krzyzan, Dec. 21, 1974 (div. Jan. 1989); 1 child, Brian Edward. Student, Erie C.C., 1969-70. With counter and delivery M & H Auto Supply, Orchard Park, N.Y., 1973-75; parts counter person Crest Dodge Inc., Orchard Park, 1975-81; parts mgr. Case Chrysler Plymouth, Hamburg, N.Y., 1981-87, Mancuso Chrysler Plymouth, Hamburg, 1987-91, Transitowne Dodge, Williamsville, N.Y., 1991—; supr. Profl. Inventory Assn., N.H., 1976-85. Named Mopar Parts Master, 1996. Mem. Chrysler Parts and Svc. Mgrs. Guild (v.p., sec. 1986-87, 89-92), The Greater Buffalo Auto Body Guild. Avocations: scuba diving, horseback riding, downhill skiing, cross-country skiing, trap shooting. Home: 2801 Creek Rd Hamburg NY 14075 Office: Transitowne Dodge 7408 Transit Rd Williamsville NY 14221-6091

KRZYZANOWSKI, RICHARD L(UCIEN), lawyer, corporate executive; b. Warsaw, Poland, Mar. 25, 1932; came to U.S., 1967, naturalized, 1972; s. Andrew and Mary K.; children: Suzanne, Peter, Christine. BA, U. Warsaw, 1956; ML, U. Pa., 1960; PhD, U. Paris, 1962. Bar: Pa. With Crown Cork & Seal Co., Inc., Phila., 1967—, dir., exec. v.p. gen. counsel, 1990—. Trustee John Paul II Found., Vatican, Rome, Italy; exec. trustee, founder Krzyzanowski Found., Phila. Office: Crown Cork & Seal Co Inc 1 Crown Way Philadelphia PA 19154-4599

KRZYZEWSKI, MIKE, university athletic coach. Head coach U.S. Mil. Acad., West Point, N.Y., 1975-80, Duke U. Blue Devils, Durham, N.C., 1980—. Named Nat. Coach of Yr., 5 times. Coached team to NCAA Divsn. I Championship, 1991, 92, 2nd place, 1986, 90, 94. Office: Duke Univ Cameron Indoor Stadium Durham NC 27708-0556*

KSANSNAK, JAMES E., service management company executive; b. Hazleton, Pa., Mar. 13, 1940; s. Edward J. and Helen (Holodick) K.; m. Valerie M. Anderson, June 9, 1962 (div. 1986); children—Keith, Janet, Linda; m. Suzanne M. Teefy, Feb. 21, 1987. B.S. magna cum laude in Acctg., St. Joseph's U., Phila., 1962. C.P.A. With Arthur Andersen & Co., Phila., 1962-86; sr. mem. staff Arthur Andersen & Co., 1964-67, mgr., 1967-71, ptnr., 1971-79, mng. ptnr., 1979-86; sr. v.p. ARAMARK Corp. (formerly ARA Svcs., Inc.), Phila., 1986-87, sr. v.p., CFO, 1987-91, exec. v.p., CFO, 1991-97, vice chmn., 1997—; also bd. dirs.; mem. chief administrv. officer's coun. Conf. Bd., 1992—; bd. dirs. CSS Industries, Inc., Advanta Corp., PJM Interconnection, LLC. Contbr. articles to profl. jours. Mem. Cmty. Leadership Seminar, 1972, trustee, bd. dirs., 1984; treas., bd. dirs. Ambler (Pa.) Youth Svcs., 1974-79; bd. dris., mem. exec. com. Phila.

YMCA, 1974-94, chmn. fin. com., chmn. ann. meeting, city fundraising chmn., 1974-83, maj. gifts chmn., 1984-87, chmn. 1987-91; mem. exec. com. Phila. Urban Affairs Coalition, 1978-95; bd. dirs. Greater Phila. Internat. Network, 1980-86, INROADS-Phila., Inc., 1981-90, Am. Cancer Soc., 1994-96, Thomas Jefferson U., 1994—, Main Line Health Sys., 1996—; mem. Mayor's Com. on Literacy, Phila., 1984-85; mem. fin. com., exec. com. Presbyn.-U. Pa. Med. Ctr., 1981-90, chmn. found., 1986; vice chmn. United Way, 1982; trustee Coll. Bus., St. Joseph's U., 1982-85. Recipient alumni award St. Joseph's U., 1980; named Profl. of Yr., Phi Chi Theta, 1981. Mem. AICPA, Pa. Inst. CPAs (chmn. tech. meetings 1970, chmn. coop. with attys. 1972, exec. comm. Phila. chpt. 1980-82), Planning Execs. Inst. (chmn. bd. 1981, Neil Denen award 1984), Union League, Sunnybrook Golf Club, Loxahatchee Golf Club, Knights of Malta. Republican. Roman Catholic. Home: 914 Latimer St Philadelphia PA 19107-5758 Office: ARAMARK Corp 1101 Market St Ste 45 Philadelphia PA 19107-2988

KSIENSKI, AHARON ARTHUR, electrical engineer; b. Warsaw, Poland, June 23, 1924; came to U.S., 1951, naturalized, 1959; s. Isreal and Rebecca K.; married; children—David, Ruth. B.E. in Mech. Engring, Inst. Mech. Engring., London, 1947; M.Sc. in Elec. Engring, U. So. Calif., 1952, Ph.D., 1958. Sr. staff engr., head antenna dept. research staff Hughes Aircraft Co., Culver City, Calif., 1958-67; prof. elec. engring., tech. dir. communication systems electrosci. lab. Ohio State U., 1967-76, prof. elec. engring., chmn. communication and propagation com. electrosci. lab., 1976-87, prof. emeritus, 1987—; bd. dirs. Ohio State U. Research Found., 1975-79; cons. in field. Editor trans., revs. in field. Recipient Brabazon award Inst. Electronic and Radio Engrs., London, 1967, 76. Fellow IEEE; mem. Internat. Union Radio Sci. (chmn. commns. B and C 1972-75). Home: 1780 Lynnhaven Dr Columbus OH 43221-1410 Office: 1320 Kinnear Rd Columbus OH 43212-1156

KU, CHARLOTTE, professional association administrator. BA, Am. U. Sch. Internat. Svc., 1971; MA, Fletcher Sch. Law, Diplomacy, 1972, MALD, 1973; summer scholar, Beijing Normal U., China, 1982; PhD, Fletcher Sch. Law, Diplomacy, 1984. Rsch. asst. Office Legal Affairs UN, N.Y.C., 1974; staff mem. Office U.S. Senator Alan Cranston, Washington, 1974-78; dir. rsch. and publs. Children's Rights Group, San Francisco, 1978-82; program mgmt. cons. San Francisco Found., 1982-84; asst. prof. govt. and fgn. affairs U. Va., Charlottesville, 1984-88; vis. prof. Johns Hopkins U., SAIS Nanjing Ctr., China, 1988-89; adminstrv. and programs dir. Am. Soc. Internat. Law, Washington, 1990-92, dep. exec. dir., 1992-93, exec. v.p., exec. dir., 1994—. Contbr. articles to profl. jours.; presenter at internat. confs. on internat. law studies. Chair Acad. Coun. on United Nations System. Grantee Asia-Pacific Ednl. Fund , 1985, European Comty. Visitor, 1988; named Guest scholar Acad. Sinica, Taiwan, 1990. Mem. Am. Polit. Sci. Assn., Am. Soc. Internat. Law, Coun. on Fgn. Rels., Internat. Studies Assn. (publs. com. 1992-95), Am. Coun. Learned Socs. (exec. com. mem. conf. of adminstrv. officers), Am. Assn. Law Schs. (pub. mem. membership rev. com.). Office: Am Soc Internat Law 2223 Massachusetts Ave NW Washington DC 20008-2847

KU, DAVID NELSON, medical educator; b. St. Louis, Mar. 15, 1956. BA, Harvard U., 1978; MS, Ga. Inst. Tech., 1982, PhD, 1983; MD, Emory U., 1984. Dir. vascular lab Hyde Park Cmty. Hosp., Chgo., 1985-86; from asst. prof. to assoc. prof. Ga. Inst. Tech., Atlanta, 1986-95, prof., 1995-98, Regents prof., 1998—; assoc. prof. Emory U., Atlanta, 1991-97, prof., 1997—; mem. adv. bd., exec. bd., mech. engring. faculty recruiting com. Ga. Inst. Tech., 1996—; chair tenure com. Coll. Engring. Ga. Inst. Tech., 1996—. Assoc. editor Jour. Vascular Investigation, 1994—, Jour. Biomech. Engring., 1995—. Mem. chorus Atlanta Symphony Orch., 1989-90. Mem. ASME (Larson award 1996), AMA, Am. Coll. Angiology, Sigma Xi. Office: Ga Inst Tech Mech Engring Atlanta GA 30332-0405

KU, JENTUNG, mechanical and aerospace engineer; b. Hsinchu, Republic of China; came to U.S., 1974; m. Jung-Chen and Chun-Yin (Hsieh) K.; m. Shu-Mei Chen, Aug. 17, 1979; children: Lisa, Daniel, Brian. BS, Tsing Hua U., Hsinchu, 1972; MS, Purdue U., 1976, PhD, 1980. Rsch. asst. Purdue U., West Lafayette, Ind., 1976-80; mem. tech. staff Advanced Tech. Ctr., Bendix Corp., Columbia, Md., 1980-83; section head/program mgr. OAO Corp., Greenbelt, Md., 1983-91; sr. engr. NASA Goddard Space Flight Ctr., Greenbelt, Md., 1991—. Contbr. articles on heat transfer and thermal control systems to profl. jours.; pioneer in developing capillary pumped loop heat transport systems (2 Tech. Innovation awards NASA). Bd. dirs. Columbia Chinese Bapt. Ch., 1991—. Mem. ASME, AIAA, Am. Nuclear Soc., Tau Beta Pi, Phi Tau Phi. Baptist. Avocation: tennis. Home: 14208 Bradshaw Dr Silver Spring MD 20905-6503 Office: NASA Goddard Space Flight Ctr Greenbelt MD 20771

KUBA, JOHN ALBERT, mortician; b. Cedar Rapids, Iowa, Apr. 14, 1940; S. Edward Rudolph and Josephine Marie (Barta-Letovsky) K. Student, Coe Coll., Cedar Rapids, 1958-59, Tex. A&I U., 1959-61, Washington U., St. Louis, 1961-62; grad., Wis. Inst. Mortuary Sci., 1963. Ptnr., owner E&J Homes Ltd., Kuba Funeral Homes, Cedar Rapids, 1963-94; trustee Czech Nat Cemetery, Cedar Rapids, 1966-81, fin. sec., 1981-94; owner Velvet Feed Bag Restaurant, 1979-84, Czech Village Shirt, ETC Shop, 1991, founder. Author: Cooking in America, 1971. V.p. Linn County Hist. Mus. Assn., Cedar Rapids, 1966-69, Czech Fine Arts, 1970-75; fin. sec. Linn County Dem. Ctrl. Com., 1970-74; vol. San Antonio AIDS Found.; docent Inst. Texan Cutures, San Antonio Conservation Soc.; mem. Bexar County Czech Heritage Soc., Victoria County Czech Heritage Soc., Unity Found., S.A. Equal Right Polit. Caucus; sec. Minn.-Iowa dist. Civitan Internat. Spl. Olympics, South Bend, Reno-Tahoe, Mpls.-St. Paul. Recipient Outstanding Lt. Gov. Civitan Internat., 1989-90, Outstanding Community Svc. and Humanitarian award Modern Woodmen of Am., 1990. Mem. Czechoslovak Soc. Am. Franternal Life Assn. (pres. 1964-67, sec.-treas. 1971—, Fraternalist of Yr. 1991), Western Fraternal Life (sec. 1986-89), K.C. (past faithful navigator 4 degrees), 16th Ave Merchants Assn. (sec.), Minowa Dist. Civitan (gov. 1980-81, fellow 1991, dist. honor key 1991), Tex. Czech Heritage Soc., Victoria County Czech Heritage Soc., Bexar County Czech Heritage Soc., Lodge Jr. Am. Czech #388 (pres., sec., treas., sec.-treas., fin. sec.), Cath. Order of Foresters, K.C., Moose Lodge, Eagles, Elks, Cath. Workman, Cedar Rapids Sokol, Fedn. of Czech Groups, Czech Heritage Found., Linn County Hist. Soc., Czech Fine Arts, W.F.L.A., Alamo Bus. Coun. San Antonio, Assn. for the Mentally Disabled, Civitan Club. Roman Catholic. Avocations: archaeology, gourmet cooking, travel, gardening, mystery reading. Home: PO Box 716 Helotes TX 78023-0716

KUBALE, BERNARD STEPHEN, lawyer; b. Reedsville, Wis., Sept. 5, 1928; s. Joseph and Josephine (Novak) K.; m. Mary Thomas, Apr. 21, 1956; children: Caroline, Catherine, Anne. BBA, U. Wis., 1950, LLB, 1955; LLD (hon.), St. Norbert Coll., 1985. Bar: Wis. 1955; CPA, Wis. Acct. John D. Morrison and Co., Marquette, Mich., 1950-51; atty., ptnr. Foley and Lardner, Milw., 1955—, chmn. mgmt. com., 1985-94; bd. dirs. Banta Corp., Menasha, Wis., Green Bay Packers, Wis.E.R. Wagner Mfg. Co., Milw., Wausau (Wis.) Homes, Consol. Papers, Inc., Wisconsin Rapids, Wis. Chmn. bd. dirs. St. Norbert Coll., DePere, Wis., 1980-84, Children's Hosp. Wis., Milw., 1982-91. 1st lt. USAF, 1951-53. Mem. ABA, AICPAs, Wis. Inst. CPAs, Wis. Bar Assn., Milw. Bar Assn., Chenequa Country Club, Milw. Country Club, The Milw. Club. Republican. Roman Catholic. Avocations: fishing, skiing, baseball. Home: 2649 E Shorewood Blvd Milwaukee WI 53211-2457 Office: Foley & Lardner 1st Wisconsin Ctr 777 E Wisconsin Ave Ste 3800 Milwaukee WI 53202-5367

KUBAS, GREGORY JOSEPH, research chemist; b. Cleve., Mar. 12, 1945; s. Joseph Arthur and Esther (Polcyn) K.; m. Jean Henry, Dec. 22, 1973; children: Kelly Richmond (dec. 1997), Sherry Richmond. BS, Case Inst. Tech., 1966; PhD, Northwestern U., 1970. Postdoctoral fellow Princeton (N.J.) U., 1971-72; postdoctoral fellow Los Alamos (N.Mex.) Nat. Lab., 1972-74, mem. staff, 1974—; lab. fellow, 1987—. Contbr. articles to profl. jours. Recipient E.O. Lawrence Meml. award US Dept. Energy, 1994. Mem. Am. Chem. Soc. (Inorganic Chemistry award 1993, E.O. Lawrence award 1994). Home: 29 Camino Cielo Santa Fe NM 87501-8614 Office: Los Alamos Nat Lab MS-J514 Los Alamos NM 87545

KUBE, HAROLD DEMING, retired financial executive; b. Buffalo, Wyo., June 16, 1910; s. Carl Christen and Inez (Mather) K.; m. Shirley Smith; children: Robert Ford, Thomas Smith. BS, U. Nebr., 1932; MBA, Harvard U., 1934. Owner Beef Cattle Farm, Warrenton, Va., 1950—; co-owner Resources Devel. Assocs., 1965-80; dir. emeritus Jefferson Savs. and Loan Assn., Warrenton, 1980—, Greater Washington Investors, Inc., 1987—; bd. dirs. A & K Land and Cattle Corp., Warrenton. Co-author: Manufacturing Distribution in U.S., 1938. With USN, 1944-46. Mem. Am. Econ. Assn. Episcopalian. Avocation: golf. Home and Office: 6470 Beverleys Mill Rd Broad Run VA 20137-2101

KUBIAK, JOHN MICHAEL, academic administrator; b. Pulaski, Wis., Jan. 15, 1935; s. Anton Joseph and Genevieve (McGuire) K.; m. Mary Dee Neville, Aug. 5, 1966; children: Michelle Jo, Leslie A. Welsh, Robert N. Welsh. BS in Mil. Engring., U.S. Mil. Acad., 1958; MBA, Washington U., St. Louis, 1976, M Data Processing, 1977; PhD, St. Louis U., 1981. Commd. 2d lt. USAF, 1958, advanced through grades to col., 1979; prof. aerospace studies Cornell U., Ithaca, N.Y., 1983-86; retired USAF, 1986; exec. dir. Emaudi Ctr. Internat. Studies, Cornell U., 1986-96; ret., 1997—. Decorated Legion of Merit (2), Air Force Commendation Medals (2), Air Medals (2). Mem. Air Force Assn., Rotary (pres. Boulder City 1998-99), Beta Gamma Sigma, Order Daedalians. Republican. Avocations: gardening, golf, aviation.

KUBIDA, JUDITH ANN, museum administrator; b. Chgo., Aug. 29, 1948; d. William and Julia Ann (Kun) K.; m. Benjamin Kocolowski, Nov. 22, 1980. Attended, Southeast Coll. Adminstrn. asst. in vis. svcs. and sci. and edn. depts. Mus. Sci. and Industry, Chgo., adminstrv. asst. in vis. svcs. and sci. and edn. depts. Columnist monthly community newspaper Pullman Flyer. Vice-pres. pub. rels. Hist. Pullman Found., Hist. Pullman Dist., Chgo., editor quarterly newsletter Update, create publicity brochures, liaison with Ill., Chgo. Film Offices, publ. chmn., mem. annual house tour com., prodr. commemorative plate. Democrat. Home: 11334 S Langley Ave Chicago IL 60628-5126 Office: Hist Pullman Found Hotel Florence 11111 S Forrestville Ave Chicago IL 60628-4649

KUBIDA, WILLIAM JOSEPH, lawyer; b. Newark, Apr. 3, 1949; s. William and Catherine (Gilchrist) K.; m. Mary Jane Hamilton, Feb. 4, 1984; children: Sara Gilchrist, Kathleen Hamilton. BSEE, USAF Acad., 1971; JD, Wake Forest U., 1979. Bar: N.C. 1979, U.S. Patent Office 1979, Ind. 1980, U.S. Dist. Ct. (no. dist.) Ind. 1980, U.S. Dist. Ct. (so. dist.) Ind. 1980, U.S. Ct. Appeals (7th cir.) 1981, U.S. Dist. Ct. Ariz. 1982, U.S. Ct. Appeals (9th and fed. cirs.) 1982, Ariz. 1982, Colo. 1990, U.S. Dist. Ct. Colo. 1990, U.S. Ct. Appeals (10th cir.) 1990. Patent and trademark atty. Lundy and Assocs., Ft. Wayne, Ind., 1979-81; patent atty. Motorola, Inc., Phoenix, 1981-85; intellectual property counsel Nippon Motorola, Ltd., Tokyo, 1985-87; ptnr. Lisa & Kubida, Phoenix, 1987-89; engring. law counsel Digital Equipment Corp., Colorado Springs, Colo., 1989-92; of counsel Holland & Hart, Denver, Colorado Springs, 1992-93, ptnr., chmn. intellectual property practice group, 1993—. 1st lt. USAF, 1971-76. Mem. Am. Intellectual Property Law Assn. (computer software sect.), Japan Am. Soc. Colo. (bd. dirs.), Licensing Exec. Soc. (Pacific Rim subcom.), Country Club Colo., Mensa, Intertel, Phi Delta Phi. Republican. Presbyterian. Home: 4165 Regency Dr Colorado Springs CO 80906-4368

KUBIET, LEO LAWRENCE, newspaper advertising and marketing executive; b. Apr. 11, 1924; s. Joseph J. and Laura Agnes (Bucy) K.; m. Mary Jean Metz, Sept. 14, 1946; children: Lawrence Michael, Martin Alan. BA in Journalism and English, Fairmont State Coll., 1949; postgrad., U. Mich., 1950, Wayne State U., 1952, U. Detroit, 1953. With The News, Detroit, 1950-68; retail advt. mgr. St. Petersburg (Fla.) Times and Evening Ind., 1968-70, advt. mgr., 1970-75, advt. dir., 1975-76, corp. dir., 1976-89, v.p. advt., 1986-87, sr. v.p., 1987-89; dir. Modern Graphic Arts Fla. Trend Mags., Inc. divsn. Semit Corp.; charter and hon. mem. advt. adv. council U. Fla., 1978—, hon. life, 1995—; bd. dirs. U. Fla. Found., chmn. Campaign Fund, Coll. Journalism, 1989-93; bd. govs. St. Petersburg Area C. of C., 1979-83; bd. dirs. Fla. Orch., 1988-89, Hall of Fame Bowl, 1987-91; mem. fund raising com. St. Anthony's Hosp. Found., 1991-93; bd. dirs. Tampa Bay Coun., Nat. Assn. Investors Corp., 1995-99. Bd. dirs. Pt. Brittany Condo Two Corp., 1999-2001. With 59th Seabees USN, 1942-46. Mem. Internat. Newspaper Advt. and Mktg. Execs. (hon. life, past pres.), So. Region Adv. Coun., Am. Press Inst., St. Petersburg Advt. Fedn. (bd. dirs. Silver medal 1977), St. Petersburg Sales and Mktg. Execs., Inc. (past pres.), Newspaper Advt. Bur. Am. Newspaper Pubs. Assn. (plans com.), Advt. Agy. Rev. Com., Fla. Lottery Commn., St. Petersburg Yacht Club, Pt. Brittany Yacht Club, Lakewood Country Club, Commerce Club of Pinellas County (past pres.). Roman Catholic. Avocations: boating, travel, tennis, golf, computers. Home: Point Brittany Bldg 2 5108 Brittany Dr S Apt 308 Saint Petersburg FL 33715-1525

KUBILUS, NORBERT JOHN, information technology executive; b. Newark, Oct. 6, 1948; s. Vity Leo and Ursula Eva (Yarusavage) K.; m. Linda J. Ferri, July 23, 1988; 1 child from previous marriage, Jessica Leigh; 1 stepchild, James M. Feigert. ScB cum laude, Seton Hall U., 1970; MS, Rensselaer Poly. Inst., 1973. Rsch. asst. Rensselaer Poly. Inst., Troy, N.Y., 1971-72; systems programmer, analyst RAPIDATA, Fairfield, N.J., 1972-76, mgr. quality assurance, 1976-78, mgr. corp. support svcs., 1978-79, dir. software devel., 1979-80, asst. v.p. ops. adminstrn., 1980-81; v.p., COO network svcs. divsn. NDC, Fairfield, 1981-83; sr. v.p. info. systems and tech. Ednl. Testing Svc., Princeton, N.J., 1983-86, mng. ptnr., Norda Group, Yardley, Pa., 1986-88; v.p., COO Optimal Solutions, Inc., Hoboken, N.J., 1987-91; v.p., chief info. officer BCM, Inc., Plymouth Meeting, Pa., 1991-94; v.p. ops. Leading Hotels of the World, Ltd., N.Y.C., 1994-96; mng. ptnr. Kubilus Ferri & Assocs., Yardley, Pa., 1996—; reviewer Reston (Va.) Pub. Co.; adj. prof. N.J. Inst. Tech., 1976-84; nat. lectr. Assn. Computing Machinery, 1976-80; vis. prof. computer sci. Coll. of N.J., 1997—. Author: Developing Computer-Based Accounts Receivable, 1981, Manager's Guide to Distributed Data Processing, 1982, How to Implement Management Information Systems, 1983, How to Select Small Business Computer Software, 1984, Business Use of the Internet, 1997; contbr. articles to profl. jours. Treas. Cedar Grove (N.J.) Jaycees, 1977; bd. dirs. Gathering Internat. Families Together, 1983-86. Decorated Order of Cross and Crescent, 1970; NSF tng. grantee, 1972; recipient Physics medal Seton Hall U., 1970, Tech. Leadership award Hewlett Packard Corp., 1993; Faculty fellow Coll. N.J., 1998. Mem. Assn. Computing Machinery, Contingency Planning Exch., Design Fin. Officers Group (vice-chmn. 1992-93, chair 1993-94), Digital Equipment Computer Users Soc. (U.S. exec. bd. 1977-81), Assn. Info. Tech. Profls. (legis. network 1985-93, bd. dirs. 1988-91, Individual Performance award 1987, 89, 90, 98), Planning Forum, Inst. Cert. Computer Profls. (life, cert. data processor, cert. systems profl., cert. computing profl., cert. amb. 1980-82, N.J. state dir. 1989-90), Am. Mgmt. Assn. (info. systems & tech. coun. 1985—, editor Management Handbook 3rd edition, chmn. Year 2000 Forum 1998—), Internat. Platform Assn., Small Bus. Assn. Del. Valley, Sigma Pi Sigma, Upsilon Pi Epsilon. Office: Kubilus Ferri & Assocs Ste 233 668 Stony Hill Rd Yardley PA 19067-4419

KUBISTAL, PATRICIA BERNICE, educational consultant; b. Chgo., Jan. 19, 1938; d. Edward John and Bernice Mildred (Lenz) Kubistal. AB cum laude, Loyola U., Chgo., 1959, AM, 1964, AM, 1965, PhD, 1968; postgrad. Chgo. State Coll., 1962, Ill. Inst. Tech., 1963, State U. Iowa, 1963, Nat. Coll. Edn., 1974-75. With Chgo. Bd. Edn., 1959-93, tchr., 1959-63, counselor, 1963-65, adminstrv. intern, 1965-66, asst. to dist. supt., 1966-69, prin. spl. edn. sch., 1969-75, prin. Simpson Sch., 1975-76, Brentano Sch., 1975-87, Roosevelt High Sch., 1987, Haugan Sch., 1989, Cook County Juvenile Temporary Detention Ctr. Sch., Jones Met. High Sch. Bus. and Commerce, 1988-89, Cook County Juvenile Temporary Detention Ctr., 1989-90, adminstr. dept. spl. edn., 1990-93; supr. Lake View Evening Sch., 1982-92, ednl. cons. 1993—; lectr. Loyola U. Sch. Edn., Nat. Coll. Edn. Grad. Sch., Mundelein Coll., 1982-91, DePaul U.; coord. Upper Bound Program of U. Ill. Circle Campus, 1966-68. Book rev. editor of Chgo. Prins. Jour., 1970-76, gen. editor, 1982-90. Active Crusade of Mercy; mem. com. Ill. Constnl. Conv., 1967-69; mem. Citizens Sch. Com., 1969-71; mem. edn. com. Field Mus., 1971; ednl. advisor North Side Chgo. PTA Region, 1975; gov. Loyola U., 1961-87. Recipient Outstanding Intern award Nat. Assn. Secondary Sch. Prins., 1966, Outstanding Prin. award Citizen's Shc. Com. of Chgo., 1986; named Outstanding History Tchr., Chgo. Pub. Schs., 1963, Outstanding Ill. Educator, 1970, one of Outstanding Women of Ill., 1970, St. Luke's-Logan Sq. Community Person of Yr., 1977; NDEA grantee, 1963, NSF grantee, 1965, HEW Region 5 grantee for drug edn., 1974, Chgo. Bd. Edn. Prins.' grantee for study robotics in elem. schs.; U. Chgo. adminstrv. fellow, 1984. Mem. Ill. Personnel and Guidance Assn., NEA, Ill. Edn. Assn., Chgo. Edn. Assn., Am. Acad. Polit. and Social Sci., Chgo. Prins. and Adminstrs. Assn. (pres. aux.), Nat. Council Adminstrv. Women, Chgo. Coun. Exceptional Children, pres. St. Matthews Parish Coun., 1995-98, Loyal Christian Benevolent Assn., Kappa Gamma Pi, Pi Gamma Mu, Phi Delta Kappa, Delta Kappa Gamma (parliamentarian 1979-80, pres. Kappa chpt. 1988-90, Lambda state editor 1982-92, chmn. Lambda state comm. com. 1992, Internat. Golden Gift Fund award), Delta Sigma Rho, Phi Sigma Tau. Home and Office: 5111 N Oakley Ave Chicago IL 60625-1829

KUBLER, FRANK LAWRENCE, lawyer; b. Pensacola, Fla., July 4, 1957; s. Frank Martin and Esther Helen (Flora) K. AA, Miami-Dade Jr. Coll., 1978; BS in Mech. Engring., U. Miami, Coral Gables, Fla., 1981, BA in History, 1982, JD, 1986. Bar: Fla. 1986, U.S. Cir. Ct. (11th cir) 1988, U.S. Cir. Ct. (fed. cir.) 1989, U.S. Patent Office 1987. Assoc. Dominik, Stein, Saccocio, Reese, Colitz & Van der Wall, Miami Lakes, Fla., 1986-90; pres. Law Office of Frank L. Kubler, Miami Lakes, 1990—; cons. Oltman, Flynn & Kubler, Ft. Lauderdale, Fla., 1990-96, ptnr., 1996—. Mem. Inter-Am. Law Rev., 1985. Mem. Patent Law Assn. South Fla. (v.p. 1993-94, pres. 1994-95), Mensa, Rotary (dir. 1992-94, chmn. scholarship com. 1994-95), Tau Beta Pi. Office: 915 Middle River Dr Ste 415 Fort Lauderdale FL 33304-3561

KÜBLER-ROSS, ELISABETH, physician; b. Zurich, Switzerland, July 8, 1926; came to U.S., 1958, naturalized, 1961; d. Ernst and Emma (Villiger) K.; m. Emanuel Robert Ross, Feb. 7, 1958; children: Kenneth Lawrence, Barbara Lee. M.D., U. Zurich, 1957; D.Sc. (hon.), Albany (N.Y.) Med. Coll., 1974, Smith Coll., 1975, Molloy Coll., Rockville Centre, N.Y., 1976, Regis Coll., Weston, Mass., 1977, Fairleigh Dickinson U., 1979; LL.D., U. Notre Dame, 1974, Hamline U., 1975; hon. degree, Med. Coll. Pa., 1975, Anna Maria Coll., Paxton, Mass., 1978; Litt.D. (hon.), St. Mary's Coll., Notre Dame, Ind., 1975, Hood Coll., 1976, Rosary Coll., River Forest, Ill., 1976; L.H.D. (hon.), Amherst Coll., 1975, Loyola U., Chgo., 1975, Bard Coll., Annandale-on-Hudson, N.Y., 1977, Union Coll., Schenectady, 1978, D'Youville Coll., Buffalo, 1979, U. Miami, Fla., 1976; D.Pedagogy, Keuka Coll., Keuka Park, N.Y., 1976. Rotating intern Community Hosp., Glen Cove, N.Y., 1958-59; rsch. fellow Manhattan State Hosp., 1959-62; resident Montefiore Hosp., N.Y.C., 1961-62; fellow psychiatry Psychopathic Hosp., U. Colo. Med. Sch., 1962-63; instr. psychiatry Colo. Gen. Hosp., U. Colo. Med. Sch., 1962-65; mem. staff LaRabida Children's Hosp. and Rsch. Ctr., Chgo., 1965-70; asst. prof. psychiatry, asst. dir. psychiatric consultation and liaison service Billings Hosp., U. Chgo., 1965-71; chief cons. and rsch. liaison sect. LaRabida Children's Hosp. and Rsch. Ctr., 1969-70; med. dir. Family Service and Mental Health Ctr. S. Cook County, Chicago Heights, Ill., 1970-73; pres. Ross Med. Assos. (S.C.), Flossmoor, Ill., 1973-77; pres., chmn. bd. Shanti Nilaya Growth and Health Ctr., Escondido, Calif., 1977—; consulting psychiatrist Chicago Lighthouse for the Blind, 1965-71; consultant Peace Corps, 1965-71, Illinois State Psychiatric Inst., 1965-71; mem. numerous adv., cons. bds. in field. Author: On Death and Dying, 1969, Questions and Answers on Death and Dying, 1972, Death: The Final Stage, 1974, To Live Until We Say Goodbye, 1978, Working It Through, 1981, Living With Death and Dying, 1981, Remember The Secret, 1981, On Children and Death, 1985, AIDS: The Ultimate Challenge, 1988, On Life After Death, 1991, Death is of Vital Inportance: On Life, Death and Life After Death, 1994, The Wheel of Life: Autobiography, 1997; contbr. chpts. to books, articles to profl. jours. Recipient Teilhard prize Teilhard Found., 1981; Golden Plate award Am. Acad. Achievement, 1980; Modern Samaritan award Elk Grove Village, Ill., 1976; named Woman of the Decade Ladies Home Jour., 1979; numerous others. Mem. AAAS, Am. Holistic Med. Assn. (founder), Am. Med. Women's Assn., Am. Psychiat. Assn., Am. Psychosomatic Soc., Assn. Cancer Victims and Friends, Ill. Psychiat. Soc., Soc. Swiss Physicians, Soc. Psychophysiol. Research, Second Attempt at Living. Address: PO Box 6168 Scottsdale AZ 85261-6168

KUBO, EDWARD HACHIRO, JR., prosecutor; b. Honolulu, July 9, 1953; s. Edward H. and Rose M. (Coltes) K.; children: Diana K., Dawn M., Edward H. III. BA in Polit. Sci., U. Hawaii, 1976; JD, U. San Diego, 1979. Bar: Hawaii 1979. Dep. pros. atty. Honolulu City Prosecutor's Office, 1980-83, 85-90; assoc. Carlsmith & Dwyer, Honolulu, 1983-85; asst. U.S. atty. U.S. Atty.'s Office, Honolulu, 1990—; instr. Honolulu Police Dept. Acad., Waipahu, Hawaii, 1986-89; lectr. U.S. Dept. Justice, Lincoln, Neb., 1997, Pearl Harbor Police Acad., 1995, Western State Vice Investigators Assn. Conf., Houston, 1997, Las Vegas, 1998; spkr. teleconf. U.S. Dept. Justice Violence Against Women Act, 1998, Hawaii Bar Assn. H.S. Mock trial adv., 1996-98. Co-author: Concurrent Jurisdiction for Cilil RICO, 1987. Recipient Nat. Art medal (France), 1992, Cert. of Appreciation, U.S. Immigration and Naturalization Svc., 1992, Drug Enforcement Adminstrn., 1997, Plaque of Appreciation, U.S. Border Patrol, 1995, cert. appreciation Bureau Alcohol, Tobacco & Firearms, 1999. Mem. Hawaii Bar Assn., Order of Barristers.

KUBO, GARY MICHAEL, advertising executive; b. Chgo., Aug. 15, 1952; s. Robert S. and Hideko (Nishimura) K.; m. Harriet Davenport, June 14, 1975; children: Michael J., R. Scott. BS, Ill. State U., 1974. Rsch. project dir. Foote, Cone & Belding Communications, Chgo., 1974-76, account rsch. supr., 1976-79, rsch. mgr., 1979-80; assoc. rsch. dir. Young & Rubicam, Chgo., 1980-83; ptnr., group rsch. dir. Tatham, Laird & Kudner Advt., Chgo., 1983-89; v.p., dir. strategic planning and rsch./Midwest, Bozell, Inc., Chgo., 1989-91; sr. v.p., dir. strategic planning and rsch./Midwest, 1991-93; sr. v.p. dir. strategic planning rsch. Ogilvy & Mather, Chgo., 1993-95; prin. The KUBO Group, Ltd., Chgo., 1995—. Bd. Dirs. Chgo. Coun. Urban Affairs, 1992—. Mem. Advt. Rsch. Found., Am. Mktg. Assn. (speaker 1983-84, exec. bd.). Avocations: racquet sports, running, music. Home: 2129 Scarlet Oak Ln Lisle IL 60532-2855

KUBO, ISOROKU, mechanical engineer; b. Tokyo, May 16, 1942; came to U.S., 1977; s. Shogo and Sono (Ito) K.; m. Mary Ann Stone, Mar. 17, 1974; children: Tomiko J., Yukari J., Kiyokaz J., Yuri J. PhD in Aero./Mech., Cornell U., 1974; MBA, Ind. U., 1987. Engr. Komatsu Ltd., Tokyo, 1965-73, asst. chief engr., 1973-77; rsch. assoc. Applied Rsch. Lab., Pa. State U., State College, 1977-79; group leader Cummins Engine Co., Columbus, Ind., 1979-82, tech. advisor, 1982-88, dir., 1988-97; gen. mgr. Kombassan Holding Rsch. and Devel., 1997—. Recipient Spl. Scholarship Japan Scholarship Assn., 1961-65; Cornell U. fellow, 1969. Mem. ASME, Soc. Automotive Engrs. (assoc.), Sigma Xi, Beta Gamma Sigma. Achievements include patents for gas lubricated piston ring assembly, a Nox reduction method and integrated diesel-rankine system; patent pending for solar energy system.

KUBOTA, GAYLORD, museum director. Exec. dir. Alexander & Baldwin Sugar Mus., Puunene, Hawaii. Office: Alexander & Baldwin Sugar Mus PO Box 125 Puunene HI 96784-0125

KUBOTA, MITSURU, chemistry educator; b. Eleele, Hawaii, Sept. 25, 1932; s. Giichi and Kiyono (Naskashima) K.; m. Jane Kinue Taketa, June 30, 1956; children: Lynne K., Keith N. BA, U. Hawaii, 1954; MS, U. Ill., 1957, PhD, 1960. Prof. chemistry Harvey Mudd Coll., Claremont, Calif., 1959—; vis. prof. U. Venice, Italy, 1988, Cambridge (Eng.) U., 1989. 1st lt. U.S. Army, 1954-56. Faculty fellow NSF, 1966, career devel. award, 1981; Fulbright advanced rsch. fellow, Sussex, Eng., 1973, Spl. fellow NIH, 1974. Fellow Royal Soc. Chemistry, AAAS, Am. Chem. Soc. (rsch. award 1992); mem. Sigma Xi. Office: Harvey Mudd Coll 301 E 12th St Claremont CA 91711-5901

KUBY, RONALD L., lawyer; b. Cleve., July 31, 9156; s. Donald Joseph Kuby and Ruth Miller; m. Marilyn Vasta; 1 child, Emma Sojourner. BA, U. Kans., 1979; JD magna cum laude, Cornell U., 1983. Assoc. Kunstler & Kuby, N.Y.C., 1994-95, Law Office William M. Kunstler, N.Y.C., 1984-94; ptnr. Law Office Ronald L. Kuby, N.Y.C., 1996—. Contbr. articles to profl. jours. Mem. adv. bd. N.Y. Civil Liberties Union, 1999—. Recipient Thurgood MArshall award N.Y. City Bar Assn., 1998. Communist. Office: 740 Broadway 5th Fl New York NY 10003-9518*

KUBZANSKY, PHILIP EUGENE, environmental and organizational psychologist; b. Bklyn., Aug. 11, 1928; s. Joseph and Libby (Kolko) K.; m.

Judith Linda Sagarin, Apr. 15, 1962; children: Jessica Rose, Michael Samuel, Laura Diane. B.S. in Social Sci, CCNY, 1950; Ph.D., Duke U., 1954. Postdoctoral fellow community mental health Mass. Gen. Hosp., 1956-57; chief psychologist Boston City Hosp., 1957-60; research asso. Harvard Med. Sch., 1957-74, lectr., 1974-79; mem. faculty Boston U., 1960—, prof. psychology, 1967—, dean Grad. Sch. Arts and Scis., 1966-75; vis. scholar Sch. Architecture, MIT, 1974, 81, 90, Sch. Environ. Studies Univ. Coll., London, 1975; Cons. VA, Naval Med. Research Inst., Judge Baker Guidance Center, City of Boston Parks and Recreation Dept., Polaroid Corp., Digital Equipment Corp., Raytheon Corp., Merrimack Coll.; mem. alcoholism and alcohol problems rev. group NIMH, 1967-71, chmn., 1970-71; mem. exec. com. Council Grad. Schs. in U.S., 1971-74; mem. steering com. for study quality in grad. edn. Council Grad. Schs.-Ednl. Testing Service, 1974-76; mem. tng. rev. com. Nat. Inst. for Alcohol Abuse and Alcoholism, 1976-80. Contbr. articles to sci. jours. Served with AUS, 1954-56. Mem. APA, Am. Psychol. Soc., Environ. Design Rsch. Assn. Home: 12 Inis Cir West Newton MA 02465-2408 Office: Boston U Psychology Dept 64 Cummington St Boston MA 02215-2407

KUC, JOSEPH A., education educator, consultant; b. N.Y.C., Nov. 24, 1929; s. Peter and Helen (Dubec) K.; m. Karola Ingrid Maywald, July 17, 1991; children: Paul D., Rebecca R., Miriam A. BS, Purdue U., 1951, MS, 1953, PhD, 1955. Asst. prof. Purdue U., West Lafayette, Ind., 1955-59, assoc. prof., 1959-63, prof., 1963-74; prof. U. Ky., Lexington, 1974-95, prof. emeritus, 1995—. Contbr. numerous articles to profl. jours. Pres. Cen. Ky. ACLU, Lexington, 1977-79. Mem. Am. Chem. Soc., Am. Phytopathol. Soc., Am. Soc. Plant Physiologists, Am. Soc. for Biochemistry and Molecular Biology, N.Y. Acad. Sci., Phytochem. Soc., Ky. Acad. Sci., Sigma Xi. Avocations: hiking, gardening, conversation. Home and Office: 700 Front St Apt 1202 San Diego CA 92101-6061

KUCERA, DANIEL WILLIAM, retired bishop; b. Chgo., May 7, 1923; s. Joseph F. and Lillian C. (Petrzelka) K. BA, St. Procopius Coll., 1945; MA, Catholic U. Am., 1950, PhD, 1954. Joined Order of St. Benedict, 1944, ordained priest Roman Cath. Ch., 1949. Registrar St. Procopius Coll. and Acad., Lisle, Ill., 1945-49, St. Procopius Coll., Lisle, 1954-56; acad. dean, head dept. edn. St. Procopius Coll., 1956-59, pres., 1959-65; abbot St. Procopius Abbey, Lisle, 1964-71; pres. Ill. Benedictine Coll. (formerly St. Procopius Coll.), Lisle, 1971-76; chmn. bd. trustees Ill. Benedictine Coll. (formerly St. Procopius Coll.), 1976-78; aux. bishop of Joliet, 1977-80; bishop of Salina Kans., 1980-83; archbishop of Dubuque Iowa Iowa, 1983-95; ret., 1995. Mem. KC (4 degree).

KUCERA, HENRY, linguistics educator; b. Trebarov, Czechoslovakia, Feb. 15, 1925; came to U.S., 1949, naturalized, 1953; s. Jindrich and Marie (Kral) K.; m. Jacqueline M. Fortin, Oct. 6, 1951; children: Thomas Henry, Edward James. MA, Charles U., Prague, Czechoslovakia, 1947, PhDr, 1991; PhD, Harvard U., 1952; MA ad eundem, Brown U., 1958; DSc (hon.), Bucknell U., 1984; PhilD (hon.), Masaryk U., Brno, Czechoslovakia, 1990. Asst. prof. fgn. langs. U. Fla., 1952-55; mem. faculty Brown U., 1955—, prof. Slavic langs. and linguistics, 1963—, prof. cognitive sci., 1981-90, Fred M. Seed prof. linguistics and cognitive scis., 1982—, chmn. dept. Slavic langs., 1965-68, head resident fellow of the Coll., 1956-66; mem. Ctr. for Cognitive Sci., 1977-85, exec. com., 1980-86; mem. Ctr. for Neural Studies, 1973-90, exec. com., 1977-90; dir. Inst. for Cognitive and Neural Research, 1981-88; fellow Russian Rsch. Ctr., Harvard U., 1952, 79-87, rsch. assoc. Slavic dept., 1977-79; rsch assoc. MIT, 1960-63; vis. prof. U. Mich., 1967, U. Calif. at Berkeley, 1969; vis. scholar U. Vienna, 1968-69; pres. Lang. Software Systems, Inc., 1982—. Author: The Phonology of Czech, 1961, (with W.N. Francis) Computational Analysis of Present-Day American English, 1967, (with G. Monroe) A Comparative Quantitative Phonology of Russian, Czech and German, 1968, Computers in Linguistics and in Literary Studies, 1975, (with K. Trnka) Time in Language, 1975, (with W.N. Francis) Frequency Analysis of English Usage, 1982; also linguistic and lit. articles.; Editor: American Contributions to the Sixth International Congress of Slavists, 1968. Bd. dirs. Internat. Inst. Providence, 1960-67; bd. adminstrn. Howard Found., 1977-95; mem. R.I. Com. for Humanities, 1986-90. Ford fellow, 1954-55; Howard Found. fellow, 1960-61; Guggenheim fellow, 1960-61; sr. fellow NEH, 1968-69; Am. Council Learned Socs. fellow, 1969-70. Hon. fellow Linguistic Soc. of Czech Acad. Scis.; mem. MLA, Linguistic Soc. Am., Assn. Computational Linguistics, Cognitive Sci. Soc., Czechoslovak Soc. Arts and Scis. in Am. (v.p. 1980-82), Am. Assn. Tchrs. Slavic and Ea. European Langs., Prague Linguistic Circle (hon.), Phi Beta Kappa. Home: Freedom Shores Rd Freedom NH 03836

KUCHAN, ANTHONY MARK, psychologist, educator; b. Canton, Ill., Apr. 21, 1930; s. Anthony Mark Sr. and Loraine Vesta (Walker) K.; m. Martha Katherine VeDepo, May 9, 1953; children: Mark, Cathryn, Christine, Susanne, Jeanne. BA, St. Ambrose Coll., 1952; MA, Bradley U., 1955; PhD, Purdue U., 1964. Lic. psychologist, Wis. Jr. engr. Caterpillar Tractor Inc., Peoria, Ill., 1952-54; psychometrist Bradley U. Guidance Ctr., 1954-55; tchg. asst. psychol. clinic Purdue U., West Lafayette, Ind., 1955-57; intern in psychology Galesburg (Ill.) State Rsch. Hosp., 1957-58, psychologist adolescent unit, 1958-60; instr. psychology Marquette U., Milw., 1960-64, asst. prof. psychology, 1964-97; cons. St. Charles Youth and Family Svcs., Milw., 1964—; assoc. dean grad. sch. Marquette U., 1967-72, chair dept. psychology, 1977-87; psychol. cons. Wis. Province, Soc. of Jesus, 1979—; cons. faculty mem. Wis. Sch. of Profl. Psychology, 1978—, House of The Good Shepherd/Cedarcrest girl's residence, 1965-72. Pres. coun. St. Catherine Parish, Milw., 1971-73, 90-91, lector and communion distributor, 1968—. Fellow Wis. Psychol. Assn. (ethics com. chair 1976-89, ombudsman/profl.issues com. 1989—, Disting. Profl. Svc. award 1984); mem. APA, AAUP (chpt. pres. 1975-76), Nat. Register Health Svc. Providers in Psychology, Wis. Psychol. Assn., Brown Deer Tennis Team (capt. 4.0 state league 1990—), Alpha Sigma Nu-Nat. Jesuit Hon. Soc. (chpt. pres. 1996—). Roman Cath. Avocations: tennis, fishing, gardening, piano. Home: 5760 W Green Brook Dr Brown Deer WI 53223-2333 Office: Marquette Univ Dept Psychology PO Box 1881 Milwaukee WI 53201-1881

KUCHAR, THEODORE, conductor, academic administrator, musician; b. N.Y.C.. Music dir., condr. Boulder (Colo.) Philharm. Orch., 1987—; prin. violist leading orchs. Cleve. and Helsinki, Finland; soloist, chamber musician Australia, Europe, New Zealand, U.S., Russia, festivals including Blossom, Edinburgh, Kuhmo, Tanglewood, others; dir. orchestral studies U. Colo., 1996—; artistic dir., prin. condr. Nat. Symphony Orch. Ukraine; artistic dir. Australian Festival Chamber Music, 1990—; past music dir. Queensland Philharm. Orch., Brisbane, Australia, W. Australian Ballet, Perth. Muscian Penderecki's String Trio, N.Y.C., 1994; music dir., condr. recordings with Nat. Symphony Orch. and Ukrainian Chamber Orch. including Lyatoshynsky's Symphonies Nos. 2 and 3 (Best Internat. Recording of Yr. 1994), others; music dir., condr. worldwide tours. Paul Fromm fellow, 1980; recipient bronze medal for his work in promoting that country's music Finnish Govt., 1989. Office: Boulder Philharm Orch 2590 Walnut St Ste 6 Boulder CO 80302-5700*

KUCHAREK, WILMA SAMUELLA, minister; b. Johnson City, N.Y., Sept. 19, 1954; d. Samuel and Wilma Kucharek; m. Thomas Drobena, Dec. 27, 1980; children: Thomas Samuel, Joshua Michael. BA, Valparaiso U., 1976; MDiv, Luth. Theol. Sem., 1982, STM, 1985. Parish deaconess Trinity Luth. Ch., Merrillville, Ind., 1976-78; vice pastor Ascension Luth. Ch., Binghamton, N.Y., 1978-79; pastor Holy Emmanuel Luth. Ch., Mahanoy City, Pa., 1982-86; pastor St. John's Luth. Ch., St. Clair, Pa., 1982-86, Nanticoke, Pa., 1983-86; pastor Holy Trinity Luth. Ch., Torrington, Conn., 1986—; chaplain USAF Aux.-CAP, 1983—; chair Learning Ministries Slovak Zion Synod, 1987-96; mem. planning group Evang. Luth. Ch. Am. Region 7, 1988—; co-chair internat. rels. com. Evang. Luth. Ch. Am.-Slovak Zion Synod, 1995—, dean ea. conf., 1995—, asst. to bishop, 1996—. Co-author: Heritage of the Slavs, 1976. Mem. ARC (bd. dirs. 1986-91), Slavic Heritage Inst. (dir., editor of Slovo), New Eng. Luth. Hist. Soc. (sec. 1991—). Office: Slavic Heritage Inst PO Box 1003 Torrington CT 06790-1003

KUCHARO, DONALD DENNIS, JR., manufacturer's representative; b. Des Moines, Mar. 25, 1946; s. Donald Dennis and Billie Wenonah (Stanford) K.; m. Carole Lee Toran, Sept. 11, 1971; children—Brian Neal, Bradley Alan, Stephen Grant. B.S.E.E., U. Iowa, 1969. Sales rep. Montgomery Elevator Co., Moline, Ill., 1970-73; v.p. Donald D. Kucharo Co., Davenport, Iowa, 1973-82, pres., 1982—; safety cons., leader product seminars. Republican. Unitarian. Club: Lindsay Park Yacht, U. Chgo., Davenport Country. Home: 2753 Nichols Ln Davenport IA 52803-3620 Office: PO Box 727 Bettendorf IA 52722-0013

KUCHEMAN, CLARK ARTHUR, religion educator; b. Akron, Ohio, Feb. 7, 1931; s. Merlin Carlyle and Lucile (Clark) K.; m. Melody Elaine Frazer, Nov. 15, 1986. BA, U. Akron, 1952; BD, Meadville Theol. Sch., 1955; MA in Econs., U. Chgo., 1959, PhD, 1965. Instr., then asst. prof. U. Chgo., 1961-67; prof. Claremont (Calif.) McKenna Coll., 1967—, Claremont Grad. Sch., 1967—. Co-author: Belief and Ethics, 1978, Creative Interchange, 1982, Economic Life, 1988; contbg. editor: The Life of Choice, 1978; contbr. articles to profl. jours. 1st lt. USAF, 1955-57. Mem. Am. Acad. Religion, Hegel Soc. Am., N.Am. Soc. for Social Philosophy. Democrat. Mem. United Ch. of Christ. Home: 10160 60th St Riverside CA 92509-4745 Office: Claremont McKenna Coll Dept Philosophy and Religon Pitzer Hall 850 Columbia Ave Claremont CA 91711-6420 *Education and life itself have the same purpose, and, borrowing words from G. W. F. Hegel, "...the final purpose of education is liberation and the struggle for a higher liberation still."*

KUCHERA, MICHAEL LOUIS, osteopathic physician, educator, author; b. Kirksville, Mo., June 25, 1955; s. William Arthur and Natalie Ione (Zange) K.; m. Eva Maria Stahl, Nov. 18, 1978; children: Katherine, Jennifer, Tiffany, David. BA History, BS in Zoology, Iowa State U., 1976; DO, Kirksville Coll. Osteo. Medicine, 1980. Diplomate Nat. Bd. Osteo. Examiners; cert. in osteo. manipulative medicine. Intern Richmond Heights (Ohio) Gen. Hosp., 1980-81; fellow in electromyography Cleve. Clin. Found., 1981; asst. prof. Kirksville Coll. Osteo. Medicine, 1981-87, assoc. prof., 1987-92, prof., 1992—, chmn. dept. osteo. manipulative medicine, 1987-98; co-dir. osteo. manipulative medicine residency program Kirkville Coll. Osteo. Medicine, 1989-98, dean, v.p. for acad. affairs, 1998—; co-dir. family practice-osteo. manipulative medicine integrated residency Northeast Mo. Regional Health Ctr., 1997—; dir. Nat. Levitor Ctr., Kirksville, 1983—; cons. Inst. for Gravitational Strain Pathology, Inc., Rangeley, Maine, 1982—; vice chmn. bd., chmn. long range com. Mo. Arthritis Adv. Bd., Jefferson City, 1983-94, chmn., 1994-96; chmn. Job Raising Task Force Mo., 1992-93; cons. Nat. Osteo. Bd. Examiners, 1985—, chmn., 1990-98; nat. faculty sponsor Undergrad. Acads. Osteopathy, Indpls., 1987-93; mem. Ednl. Coun. on Osteo. Principles, coll. rep. 1987—, chmn. 1997—. Clk. of vestry Trinity Episcopal Ch., Kirksville, 1982-87, 91-93; bd. dirs., mem. ednl. com. N.E. Mo. Regional Arthritis Ctr., Kirksville, 1984—; bd. dirs. Still Nat. Osteo. Mus., 1995—. Fellow Am. Acad. Disability Evaluating Physicians, Am. Acad. Osteopathy (chmn. undergrad. acads. 1987-93, bd. govs. 1990—, bd. trustees 1993-98, chmn. postgrad. stds. and evaluation com. 1992-96, Louisa Burns rsch. com., vis. clinician ednl. spkr., pres.-elect 1995, pres. 1996-97); mem. Am. Osteo. Assn. (vice chmn. bur. rsch. 1991-93, chmn. outcomes rsch. 1993—, pres.'s task force on enhancing osteo. principles and practice/osteo. manipulative treatment 1994-95, internat. com. 1996—, faculty Osteo. Med. Edn. Leadership Conf. 1994-97), N.Am. Acad. Musculoskeletal Medicine (mem. bd. councillors 1991-92), Am. Assn. Orthop. Medicine (bd. dirs. 1993—, chmn. edn. com.), Am. Assn. Electrodiagnostic Medicine, Internat. Back Pain Soc., Internat. Fedn. Musculoskeletal/Manual Medicine (N.Am. rep. 1997—), Cranial Acad. (bd. dirs. 1996—), Mo. Assn. Osteo. Physicians and Surgeons (bd. dels. 1990-93, 96-97, Mo. medallion of honor 1995), Australian Osteo. Assn., Thousand Hills Physicians Network (v.p. 1991-92), N.E. Mo. Osteo. Assn. (pres. 1985-86), Sigma Xi. Republican. Avocations: computer programming, trumpet, reading, collecting angel artwork. Home: 2 Fairlane Kirksville MO 63501-1926 Office: Kirksville Coll Osteo Medicine 800 W Jefferson St Kirksville MO 63501-1443

KUCHLER, JOSEPH ALBERT, surgeon; b. Feb. 20, 1948. BS, St. Joseph's U., 1970; MD, Jefferson Med. Sch., 1974. Attending surgeon Our Lady of Lourdes Med. Ctr., Camden, N.J., 1980—, Cooper Hosp., Camden, 1980—, West Jersey Health Sys., Marlton, N.J., 1980—. Home: 2 Tanbark Ct Voorhees NJ 08043-1544

KUCHMENT, ANNA M., journalist; b. Moscow; d. Mark M. Kuchment and Valeria M. Vilker-Kuchment. BA, Columbia U., 1994, MS, 1999. Rschr. Newsweek, N.Y.C., 1996-99; writer Newsweek Internat., N.Y.C., 1999—. Office: Newsweek 251 W 57th New York NY 10019

KUCHNER, EUGENE FREDERICK, neurosurgeon, educator; b. N.Y.C., Nov. 19, 1945; s. Morton H. and Edna Estelle (Marks) K. m. Joan Ruth Freedman, Sept. 2, 1968; children: Marc Jason, Eric Benjamin. AB, Johns Hopkins U., 1967; MD, U. Chgo., 1971. Diplomate Am. Bd. Neurol. Surgery, Am. Bd. Med. Examiners. Resident in surgery Yale U. Sch. Medicine, New Haven, 1971-72; resident in neurosurgery Montreal (Que., Can.) Neurol. Inst., McGill U., 1972-76, spine fellow, 1976; neurosurgeon SUNY Sch. Medicine, Downstate, 1976-79, Stony Brook, 1979—; mem. staff North Shore U. Hosp.-Cornell U. Med. Ctr., Univ. Hosp., Stony Brook, Nassau County Med. Ctr., St. John's Hosp.; cons. in field. Contbr. articles to profl. publs.; specialist in microsurgery, magnetic resonance imaging, spinal trauma, pituitary surgery. Recipient K.G. McKenzie Meml. award Royal Coll. Physicians and Surgeons Can., 1976, Open Scholarship award Johns Hopkins U., yearly, 1963-66, Scholarship award U. Chgo., yearly, 1967-70; NSF fellow, 1968, Blackman-Hoffman Found. fellow, 1969-70, USPHS fellow, 1969. Mem. ACS, AMA, Am. Assn. Neurol. Surgeons, Congress Neurol. Surgeons, N.Y. Acad. Scis., L.I. Neurosci. Acad., Suffolk Acad. Medicine, Montreal Neurol. Ins. Fellows Soc., N.Y. State Neurosurg. Soc., N.Y. State Med. Soc., N.Y. State Soc. Surgeons, Am. Coll. Med. Quality, Healthcare Info. and Mgmt. Sys. Soc., Am. Epilepsy Soc., Am. Soc. Neuroimaging (cert. neuroimager and computerized tomography, magnetic resonance imaging), Internat. Platform Assn., Philharm.-Symphony Soc. N.Y., Nat. Alumni Schs. (chmn. com. Johns Hopkins U.), Yale Surg. Soc., Assn. Yale Alumni in Medicine, Sterling Assn. Yale U. Alumni, Princeton Club N.Y., Wilson Ctr. Assocs., Johns Hopkins Club, Sigma Xi. Office: Stony Brook Med Ctr PO Box 721 Stony Brook NY 11790-0721

KUCHTA, JOHN ALBERT, manufacturing executive; b. Chgo., June 3, 1955; s. John and Janet Mary (Ivancak) K.; BS in Math., Northwestern U., 1982. Work coord. Continental Ill. Nat. Bank & Trust Co., Chgo., 1974-78; lab. technician Kasar Labs., Chgo., 1975-76, supr. quality control, 1976-77; supr. weights and measures Bell Chem. Co., Chgo., 1977-78, quality control chemist, 1978-82, mgr. shipping, receiving, distbn., 1982-94; prodn. coord. Bowne, 1994-95; warehouse mgr. Nation Pizza, Schaumberg, Ill., 1995-97; shipping foreman Unity Mfg. Co., Chgo., 1998—. Conductor and performer comty. theatre. Mem. Alpha Sigma Lambda. Roman Catholic. Home: 8032 N Wisner St Niles IL 60714-2435 Office: 1260 N Clybourn Ave Chicago IL 60610-1708

KUCHTA, JOHN ANDREW, management consultant; b. Bristol, Conn., June 24, 1943; s. John Stephen and Mildred (Reich) K.; m. Irene Barbara Levins, Sept. 16, 1965; children: Michelle Rachel, Tamara-Jean. AB, Brown U., 1965; MS, Fairleigh Dickinson U., 1983. Auditor Westinghouse Electric Co., Bloomfield, N.J., 1965-67; plant acct. Westinghouse Electric Co., Randolph, N.J., 1967-69; mgr. cost control Westinghouse Electric Co., Short Hills, N.J., 1969-71; account mgr. USV Pharm., Tuckahoe, 1971-74; mgr. inventory control Revlon Health Care, Tuckahoe, 1974-79; dir. material mgmt. Hudson Pharm., West Caldwell, N.J., 1979-84; cons. Gross & Assocs., Woodbridge, N.Y., 1984-86, 88—; dir. material mgmt. Superpharm Inc., Central Islip, N.Y., 1986-87. Author: How To Save Warehouse Space: 149 Tested Techniques, 1996. Mem. Am. Prodn. and Inventory Control Soc. (cert.), Warehouse Edn. and Rsch. Coun., Inst. Mgmt. Cons. (cert., bd. dirs.). Home: 15 Pawnee Ave Oakland NJ 07436-3007 Office: Gross & Assocs 167 Main St Woodbridge NJ 07095-2104

KUCHTA, RONALD ANDREW, art museum director, magazine editor, curator; b. Lackawanna, N.Y., June 23, 1935; s. Andrew and Clara May (Barnes) K.; m. Sique Stoll, Oct. 1, 1970 (div. 1974). BA, Kenyon Coll., 1957; MA, Western Res. U., 1961; postgrad. in mgmt., Cornell U., 1979. Curator Chrysler Mus., Provincetown, Mass., 1961-68, Santa Barbara (Calif.) Mus. Art, (Calif.), 1968-74; dir. Everson Mus. Art, Syracuse, N.Y., 1974-95; editor Am. Ceramics mag., 1995Ô; art editor Point of Contact mag., 1994; assoc. Loveed Fine Arts, N.Y.C., 1995; adj. prof. Syracuse U., 1974-95; trustee Fondo del Sol, Washington, 1974Ô, Nat. Conf. Educators of Ceramic Arts, 1986, Quarry Rd. Sculpture Pk., Cazenovia, N.Y.; founding dir. Syracuse China Ctr. for Study of Am. Ceramics; chmn. Urban Arts Commn., Syracuse; juror Mino '89 Internat. Competition for Ceramics, Gifu, Japan, 1989, Concorso Internat. della Ceramica d'Arte, Faenza, Italy, 1990, Biennale Nat. de Ceramique, Trois Rivieres, Que., Can., 1992, 2d Cairo Internat. Biennale Ceramics, 1994, Mainline Art Ctr., Phila., 1997, San Angelo (Tex.) Ceramic Nat., 1998; mem. adv. bd. Watershed Ctr. North Edgecomb, Maine; lectr. U. Regina, Sask., Can., Mimar Sinan U., Istanbul, Turkey, Alta. Coll. Art, Calgary, Calif. Conf. Advancement of Ceramic Art, Davis, Nat. Mus. History, Taipei, Taiwan, 1993, Japan Soc., N.Y.C., 1994; chmn. exhbn. com. Longhouse Found., East Hampton, L.I., 1994, Czech Ceramic Design Ctr., Cesky Krumlov, Czech Rep., 1996, Internat. Acad. Ceramics, Nagoya, Japan, 1996, Nat. Arts Club, N.Y.C., Bard Coll., N.Y.C., 1997; lectr. Cleve. Museum of Art, Stetson U., DeLand, Fla., Washington U., St. Louis, 1997, Santa Barbara City Coll., 1998; curator Enigmatic Visions/Sublime Forms Contemporary Japanese, 1998, Ceramic Longhouse Res., Easthampton, L.I.; lectr. Cotta Terra Symposium, Deruta, Italy, 1998, Konstfack U., Coll. of Arts, Crafts, and Design, Stockholm, 1998, Royal Coll. of Art, London, 1998; keynote spkr. Craft Futures Conf., Victoria and Albert Mus., London, 1998. Author: Mayan fugurines, 1971, Modern Mexican Art, 1972, Provincetown Painters, 1975, Interior Vision, 1971, Batuz: Works in Paper, 1981, Robert Beauchamp: An American Expressionist, 1984, The Elegial and the Primordial: Ceramics at the End of the Twentieth Century, 1997; publisher: A Century of Ceramics in the U.S., 1979, American Ceramics: Collection of Everson Museum of Art, 1989; translator: Pre-Hispanic Art: Time and culture, 1997. With U.S. Army, 1958-60. Mem. Internat. Acad. Ceramics, Nat. Arts Club, Phi Kappa Sigma. Democrat. Episcopalian. Home: 60 Sutton Pl S New York NY 10022-4168 Office: Am Ceramics Mag 9 E 45th St New York NY 10017-2425

KUCHYNSKI, MARIE, physician; b. Cleve., Sept. 23, 1964; d. Harry Gregory and Albina (Guarnera) K.; m. K. William Burdick. BA, Case Western Reserve U., 1986, MD, 1990. Diplomate Am. Bd. Internal Medicine; bd. cert. Rheumatology. Intern U. Hosps. Cleve., 1990-91, resident, 1991-93; physician pvt. practice, Elyria, Ohio, 1995-98; pvt. practice Brunswick, Ohio, 1998—; mem. utilization mgmt. com. Cleve. Health Network, 1996-98; med. advisor Tri-City Lupus Project. Rheumatology fellow U. Hosps. Cleve., 1993-95. Mem. AMA, Am. Coll. Physicians, Am. Coll. Rheumatology, Cleve. Soc. Rheumatology, Phi Beta Kappa. Democrat. Roman Catholic. Avocations: gardening, crafts, piano. Home: 29760 Westminister Dr North Olmsted OH 44070-5069 Office: Univ Primary Care Practice 3824 Center Rd Brunswick OH 44212

KUCIC, JOSEPH, management consultant, industrial engineer, network engineer, security specialist; b. Mali Losing, Croatia, qugoslavia, Dec. 21, 1964; came to U.S., 1967, naturalized, 1974; s. Roman Kucic and Esterina (Karcic) Milevoj; m. Gia Michelle Bonavisa, Sept. 11, 1992; children: Ann Marie, Jillian Michelle. AAS, Coll. of Aeronautics, 1984; BS, Thomas A. Edison State Coll., 1986; B in Tech., N.Y. Inst. Tech., 1986; MBA, St. John's U., Jamaica, N.Y., 1989. Workload planner Butler Aviation-Newark, Inc., Newark, 1984-85; tech. planner N.Y. Airlines, Flushing, N.Y., 1985-86; product support engr. United Techs.-Pratt & Whitney, East Hartford, Conn., 1986; indsl. engr. Montefiore Med. Ctr., Bronx, 1986-88; sr. work mgmt. analyst Bank Leumi Trust Co., N.Y.C., 1988-89; sr. methods analyst Salomon Bros., Inc., N.Y.C., 1989-92; mgmt. cons. United Mgmt. Techs., N.Y.C., 1992-93; sr. sys. analyst Met. Hosp. Ctr. N.Y.C. Health & Hosp. Corp. Metro. Hosp. Ctr., 1993; dir. info. svcs. N.Y.C. Health & Hosp. Corp. Bronx Mcpl. Hosp. Ctr., 1993-94; project mgr. Montefiore Med. Ctr., Bronx, N.Y., 1994-96, ANS Co. Sys. Inc.,, Elmsford, N.Y., 1996; mgr. infrastructure planning, divsn. of Am. Online ANS Comms., Inc., 1996-97; mgr. KPMG Peat Marwick, Hawthorne, N.Y., 1997-98; sr. mgr. KPMG LLP, N.Y.C., 1998—; spkr. in field. Contbr. articles to profl. jours. Mem. AIAA, IEEE (assoc.), SAE (affiliate), Inst. Indsl. Engrs. (chpt. pres. 1988-89, chmn. bd. N.Y.C. chpt. 1989-90, bd. govs. 1988-92, Cert. of Recognition, 1988), MBA Execs., Coll. Aeronautics Alumni Assn. (pres. 1990-92), St. John's U. Coll. Bus. Adminstrn. Alumni Assn. (bd. dirs. 1991-93), The Wings Club (N.Y.C.), Tau Alpha Pi. Democrat. Roman Catholic. Avocation: tennis. Home: 1542 Silver St Bronx NY 10461-2407 Office: KPMG Peat Marwick LLP 345 Park Ave 27th Flr New York NY 10154

KUCIJ, TIMOTHY MICHAEL, engineer, musician, minister; b. Whittier, Calif., Sept. 2, 1954; m. Paulina V. Jimenez, 1979. BA in Music, Calif. State Poly. U., Pomona, 1978; ThM cum laude, Christian Bible Coll., 1983; studied with Frank Sanucci, Edward D. Berryman, Thurla Wallis, Kathreen Prout, Eddy L. Manson, Henry Charles Smith, Joseph P. Free, Ronald Gearman, 1964-78; student, Sherwood Music Conservatory, Chgo., 1965-68; grad. studies, Cen. Bapt. Theol. Sem., Maranatha Bapt. Bible Coll. Lic. Bapt. minister, 1982. Tech. writer Honeywell Inc., West Covina (Calif.) and Mpls., 1977-84; hydromech. reliability engr. Advanced Systems div. Northrop Corp., Pico Rivera, Calif., 1984-86; sr. engr. quality and reliability Swedlow, Inc., Garden Grove, Calif., 1986-88, mgr., quality assurance, composites div., 1988-90, quality assurance staff specialist, 1990-92; div. quality assurance engr. Rexroth Corp. (Piston Pump Divsn.), Fountain Inn, S.C., 1992-94; sr. quality engr. Hi-Shear Corp., Torrance, Calif., 1996-98; quality sys. mgr. TRW Automotive, Kinetic Parts Ops., Harbor City, Calif., 1998—; lectr. tech. and engring.; tchr. piano, organ and composition, 1971-81; active pulpit supply local Bapt. chs., So. Calif., S.C. Performer (pipe organ) Wiltern Theater, L.A., 1966-68, Busch-Reisinger Mus., Harvard U., Cambridge, Mass., 1972, 73, 74; composer over 40 piano compositions including Persistence and The Storm, Remembrance, Purity, Your Song, Yearning, Compassion, A Little Jingle, A Familiar Song, Images, Paulina, Afterthought, Blue Fragrance, Sunset, Then, Piano Lesson #1, Chase, Unrest, Nebulae, Distress, Retrograde, Frolic, The Happy Whistler, The Little Toy March, Hope, Teardrops, Reminisce, Wind Chimes, A Place Somewhere, Rainbows, The Bicentennial Rag, The Pulsar Rag, Dazzling Fingers, The Butterfly Rag, first 25 original pieces written in honor of Am. bicentennial; compositions (score-books and recs.) housed in numerous librs. including L.A. County Libr., St. Louis Pub. Libr., Atlanta-Fulton County Libr., The Masters's Coll. Libr., Calif. State Poly. U. Libr., Denver Pub. Libr., Smithsonian Instn. Collection of Recordings, Washington, Archive of Contemporary Music, N.Y.C., Phila. Free Libr., Juilliard Sch. Music Libr., Calif. Bapt. Coll. Libr., Biola U. Libr., N.Y. Pub. Libr., Cleve. Pub. Libr., Boston Pub. Libr., Harvard U. Libr., among others; debut 1966; records for KRC Records, 1993— including A Place Somewhere, 1995, LifeSongs, 1995; concertized nationally (piano, pipe organ); scored comprehensive piano arrangements Jesus Loves Me, Over the Rainbow; songwriter Jesus Is the Answer, O Jesus; editor: The Golden State Baptist, 1995-96; contbr. articles to newspapers and jours. Bd. dirs. Garden Grove Symphony Orch., 1989-90; asst. to pastors local Bapt. chs. in Tex., Ga., Wis., Minn. and Calif., 1978-82; pastor Victory Bapt. Ch., Pine City, Minn., 1982-83; music dir., Bible tchr. Calvary Bapt. Ch., La Verne, Calif., 1988-92, mem. sch. bd., ch. coun., 1989-92; music dir., youth dir. Covina Bapt. Temple, 1985-87; pastor First Missionary Bapt. Ch., Gardena, Calif., 1994-96. Named one of Outstanding Young Men in Am., U.S. Jaycees, 1980; recipient First prize So. Calif. Organ Competition, 1966, Performer's certificate, 1967, Disting. Alumnus award Calif. State Poly. U., 1989. Mem. Am. Composer's Forum, Creation Rsch. Soc., Am. Soc. for Quality, Majority Text Soc., Broadcast Music, Inc. Republican. Home: 2239 W 236th Pl Torrance CA 90501-5950

KUCINICH, DENNIS J., congressman; 1 child, Jackie. Student, Cleveland State U.; BA, Case Western Reserve U., MA. Pres. K Comm., Cleve.; v. pres. sales and mktg. Town and Country Printing, Cleve.; councilman City of Cleve., 1969-73, clk. of mcpl. ct., 1975-77, mayor, 1977-79; senator State of Ohio; mem. 105th-106th Congress from 10th Ohio dist., 1997—, mem. edn. and the workforce, govt. reform & oversight coms. Named Outstanding Pub. Official, Internat. Eagles. Office: US Ho of Reps 1730 Longworth Washington DC 20515-3510*

KUCINICH-HORN, SANDRA LEE MCCARTHY, secondary education educator; b. Cleve., Mar. 26, 1950; d. Daniel T. and Pauline (Patrick) McCarthy; m. Dennis J. Kucinich, Jan. 15, 1977 (div. Aug. 1986); 1 child, Jacqueline Faith; m. C. Edward Horn, Aug. 29, 1992. BS, Bowling Green U., 1972; postgrad., Otterbein Coll., 1995—. Cert. English/speech edn. grades 7-12. Tchr. John Marshall H.S., Cleve., 1972-74, Berea (Ohio) City Schs., 1974-77; performer, guest interviewer Equity Actress/WKYC News, Cleve., 1980-83; reporter WJMR, Fredericktown, Ohio, 1989-90; tchr.

Worthington (Ohio) City Schs., 1993—; asst. to dir. Worthington Kilbourne Repertory Theatre, Columbus, 1994-97; advisor WKHS News, Columbus, 1996-97. Active First Lady of Cleve., 1978-79, Women City Club, Cleve., 1978-79; organizer Year of the Child, YWCA, Cleve., 1979. Recipient Golden Apple award Ashland Oil, Columbus, 1996. Mem. ASCD, Nat. Coun. Tchrs. English. Avocations: theatre and vocal performing, journalism. Office: Worthington Kilbourne HS 1499 Hard Rd Columbus OH 43235-5970

KUCKELMAN, BRIAN THOMAS, architect; b. Kansas City, Kans., Aug. 11, 1954; s. Paul J. and Bernice J. (Neeley) K.; m. Pamela J. Uhlmeyer, July 6, 1979; children: Crystal, Tyler, Michelle. BA in Architecture, U. N.Mex., 1977. Draftsman McHugh/Grenfell Architects, Santa Fe, N.Mex., 1977-79; project architect Architectural Svcs., Hilo, Hawaii, 1979-84; project mgr. Pace Constrn., Tucson, 1984-89, Doubletree Hotels Corp., Phoenix, 1989-94; v.p. facility devel. Meta Assocs., Louisville, 1994-96; v.p. design and constrn. Omni Hotels, Irving, Tex., 1996—. Membership v.p. Lehua Jaycees, Hilo, 1984. Republican. Roman Catholic. Office: Omni Hotels 420 Decker Dr Irving TX 75062-3952

KUCZMARSKI, SUSAN SMITH, management consulting company executive; b. Portland, Oreg., Apr. 24, 1951; d. Fernando Martin and Bula Grace (Weddle) Smith; m. Thomas Dale Kuczmarski, Aug. 21, 1976; children: John Thomas, James Smith, Thomas Michael. BA, Colo. Coll., 1973; MIA, Columbia U., 1975, MEd, 1978, EdD, 1979. Instr. U. Ill., Chgo., 1976-77, Nat.-Louis U., Evanston, Ill., 1986-88; lectr. Rosary Coll., River Forest, Ill., 1977-78; asst. prof. Concordia U., River Forest, 1977-79; edn. dir. Constl. Rights Found., Chgo., 1979-81; assoc. dir. devel., instr. Northwestern U., Evanston, 1981-84; exec. v.p. Kuczmarski & Assocs., Chgo., 1984—; instr. Colo. Coll., Colorado Springs, 1998; trustee Edward Lowe Found., Cassopolis, Mich., 1986-96. Author, editor: Youth and Society: Rights and Responsibilities, 2d edit., 1980; co-author: Values-Based Leadership: Rebuilding Employee Commitment, Performance, and Productivity, 1995; book rev. editor Jour. Internat. Affairs, 1973-75. Vol. Harlem Tutorial Program, N.Y.C., 1973-74; trustee Chgo. City Day Sch., Chgo., 1996—. Internat. House fellow, 1974, Columbia U. Sch. Internat. Affairs fellow, 1974-75, Columbia U. internat. fellow, 1975-76. Mem. Com. on Fgn. Affairs, Kappa Alpha Theta. Republican. Roman Catholic. Avocation: foreign travel. Office: 1165 N Clark St Chicago IL 60610-2702

KUCZWARA, THOMAS PAUL, postal inspector, lawyer; b. Dec. 21, 1951; s. Stanley Leo and Eleanore (Pawelko) K.; m. Diana Lynn Rychtarczyk, Sept. 8, 1979; 1 child, Paul Stanley. BA, Loyola U., Chgo., 1973; JD, U. S.C., 1976. Bar: Ill. 1976, U.S. Dist. Ct. (no. dist.) Ill. 1982. Assoc. Doria Law Offices, Chgo., 1977-78; asst. corp. counsel City of Chgo., 1978-80; asst. city atty. City of Aurora, Ill., 1980-82; postal insp. U.S. Postal Inspection Svc., Salt Lake City, 1982-85; regional insp. atty. cen. region U.S. Postal Inspection Svc., Chgo., 1985—. Mem. St. Bartholomew's Parish Coun., Chgo., 1978; vol. atty. Lawyers for Creative Arts, 1978. Ill. state scholar, 1969. Mem. Sierra Club, Pi Sigma Alpha. Roman Catholic. Office: US Postal Inspection Svc Ops Support Group 222 S Riverside Plz # 1250 Chicago IL 60606-6100

KUCZYNSKI, PEDRO-PABLO, investor; b. Lima, Peru, Oct. 3, 1938; s. Maxime and Madeleine Louise (Godard) K.; married; 3 children. B.A. (Coll. scholar), Exeter Coll., Oxford (Eng.) U., 1959; M.P.A. (John Parker Compton fellow), Princeton U., 1961. Economist World Bank, 1961-67, sr. economist, 1971-73; dep. dir.-gen. Central Res. Bank Peru, 1967-69; sr. economist Internat. Monetary Fund, Washington, 1969-71; v.p., partner Kuhn, Loeb & Co. Internat., N.Y.C., 1973-75; dir. dept. econs. Internat. Finance Corp., Washington, 1975-77; pres., chief exec. officer Halco Mining Inc., Pitts., 1977-80; minister of energy and mines Peru, 1980-82; chmn., mng. dir. First Boston Internat. Co., N.Y.C., 1982-92; pres., CEO Westfield Capital Ltd., Miami, Fla., 1992—; pres., CEO The Latin America Enterprise Fund L.P.; bd. dirs. ROC Taiwan Fund, Siderurgica Argentina S.A., BHP Tintaya Peru; chmn. Edelnor, Peru. Author: Peruvian Democracy under Economic Stress: an Account of the Belaunde Administration, 1963-68, 1977, The Latin American Debt Question, 1988. Mem. Am. Econ. Assn., Univ. Club (Washington), Pitts. Golf Club, Racquet and Tennis Club. Home: 2 Grove Isle Dr Miami FL 33133-4119 Office: Westfield Capital Ltd 2665 S Bayshore Dr Miami FL 33133-5448*

KUDELKA, JAMES, choreographer, artistic director; b. Newmarket, Ont., Can.. Student, Nat. Ballet Sch., Toronto. Dancer Nat. Ballet of Can., Toronto, 1972-81, artist in residence, 1992-96; prin. dancer Les Grands Ballets Canadiens, Montreal, 1981-84; resident choreographer Les Grands Ballets Canadiens, 1984-90; works created for San Francisco and Joffrey Ballets, Am. Ballet Theatre, Birmingham Royal Ballet; artistic dir. Nat. Ballet Can., 1996—. Ballets choreographed include: (for Nat. Ballet of Can.) Sonata, 1973 (Jean A. Chalmers award for Choreography), A Party, 1976, Washington Square, 1977, The Rape of Lucrece, 1980, Playhouse, 1980, All Night Wonder, 1981, Pastorale, 1990, The Miraculous Mandarin, 1993, The Actress, 1994, Spring Awakening, 1994, The Nutcracker, 1995, The Four Seasons, 1997, Swan Lake; (for Les Grands Ballets Canadiens) Genesis, 1982, In Paradisum, 1983, Alliances, 1984, Le Sacre du Printemps, 1987, La Salle des Pas Perdus, 1988, Concerto Grosso, 1988; (for American Ballet Theatre) Cruel World, 1994, States of Grace, 1995; (for San Francisco Ballet) Dreams of Harmony, The End, Terra Firma, Some Women and Men; (for Birmingham Royal Ballet) Le Baiser de la fée; (for Toronto Dance Theatre) Fifteen Heterosexual Duets; (for Montreal Danse) Six Tableaus for the Sexually Challenged; other choreography includes Passage, 1981, Intimate Letter, 1981, Hedda, 1983, Court of Miracles, 1983, Musings, 1991. Office: The National Ballet of Canada, 470 Queens Quay W, Toronto, ON Canada M5V 3K4*

KUDENOV, JERRY DAVID, zoology educator; b. Lynwood, Calif., Dec. 19, 1946; s. William and Marion Kudenov; m. Kathryn Anne Brown, May 30, 1969; children: Peter Alexander, Michael William. BA, U. Calif., San Diego, 1968; MS, U. Pacific, 1970; PhD, U. Ariz., 1974. Research scientist Ministry for Conservation, Melbourne, Australia, 1974-79; asst. prof. zoology U. Alaska, Anchorage, 1980-82, assoc. prof., 1982-86, prof., 1987—, chmn. dept. biol. sci., 1986-90, SEM lab. mgr., 1999—; vis. asst. prof. U. So. Calif., Los Angeles, 1979-80. Assoc. editor Am. Geophys. Union Antarctic Rsch. Series, 1994-97. Mem. AAAS, Am. Soc. Zoologists, Sci. Research Soc. N. Am., Biol. Soc. Wash., So. Calif. Acad. Scis. (bd. dirs. 1980), Internat. Polychaete Assn., Microscopical Soc. of Am. Avocation: fishing. Home: 3930 Alitak Bay Cir Anchorage AK 99515-2366 Office: U Alaska Anchorage Dept Biol Scis 3211 Providence Dr Anchorage AK 99508-4614

KUDER, ARMIN ULRICH, lawyer; b. Phila., Nov. 14, 1935; s. David Dennis and Ethel Rose (Strasburger) K.; m. Patricia A. Hipple, June 28, 1959 (div. Mar. 1968); children: Carlyn Elizabeth, Eric David, Keith Ulrich; m. Adrienne A. Allison, Aug. 25, 1989. AB, Lafayette Coll., 1956; LLB, Harvard U., 1959. Bar: D.C. 1959, Md. 1987, U.S. Ct. Mil. Appeals 1962, U.S. Dist. Ct. Md. 1968. Assoc. Coles & Goertner, Washington, 1963-65, Mehler, Smollar et al., Washington, 1965-67; ptnr. Smollar & Kuder, Washington, 1967-68, Kuder, Sherman et al., Washington, 1968-78, Kuder, Smollar & Friedman P.C., Washington, 1978—; lectr. continuing legal edn., various locations. Chmn. Nat. Health Agencies, NCAC, 1977-78, Ctr. Marine Conservation, Washington, 1981-83, NIMH human subjects rev. panel, 1978-83, Hyde Sch., Bath, Maine, 1984-87; vice chmn. Arthritis Found., Atlanta, 1979-80, 90-92, chmn., 1992-94; pres. Arthritis and Rhuematism Internat., 1996-98, treas., 1998—; mem. steering group The Bond and Joint Decade, Lund, Sweden, 1999—; chmn. New Art Assn., Washington, 1986-87; sec. Combined Health Appeal, Washington, 1984. Served to lt. comdr. JAGC, USNR, 1959-63. Fellow Am. Acad. Matrimonial Lawyers, Internat. Acad. of Matrimonial Lawyers; mem. ABA, D.C. Bar Assn. (trustee client security fund 1984-92, chmn. 1991-92, hearing com. chmn. bd. on profl. responsibility 1985-91), Md. Bar Assn. Office: Kuder Smollar & Friedman PC 1925 K St NW Washington DC 20006-1105

KUDISH, DAVID J., financial executive; b. N.Y.C., Aug. 10, 1943; s. L. Ben and Nellie D. (Kaufman) K.; children: Lisa, Seth, Debra. BS, U. Rochester, 1965; MS, U. Minn., 1967; postgrad., Harvard. U., 1996. With Dean Witter & Co., Inc., N.Y.C., 1968-73; with Oppenheimer & Co., N.Y.C., 1973-74; ptnr., dir. investment services Hewitt Assocs., Lincolnshire, Ill., 1974-82; pres., mng. dir. Stratford Adv. Group, Inc., Chgo., Ill., 1982—; pres. Stratford Investment Group, Inc., 1983—; investment cons. pension, endowment and charitable funds. Editor Benefits Quar. Active Mayor's Energy Task Force, City of Chgo.; gov. mem. Sustaining Fellows, Art Inst. Chgo., Contemporary Art Cir. of Mus. Contemporary Art; benefactor Lyric Opera of Chgo.; mem. gala com. Chgo. Abused Women's Coalition; mem. nat. bd. dirs. Com. for Accuracy in Mid. East Reporting in Am.; mem. Jewish Cmty. Rels. Coun., Jewish Fedn. Met. Chgo.; mem. exec. bd. Chgo. chpt. Am. Jewish Com. With USAF, 1968, Air NG, 1968-73. Minn. Mining and Mgr. fellow U. Minn., 1967; NSF grantee, 1967. Mem. Tau Beta Pi, Sigma Alpha Mu. Republican. Jewish. Clubs: Standard. Home: 1325 N Astor St Chicago IL 60610-2113

KUDLACZ, MICHAEL S., career officer; b. Omaha. BS in Criminal Justice, U. Nebr., Omaha, 1971; student, Squadron Officer Sch., 1974; M in Sociology, Pepperdine U., 1977; student, Air Command and Staff Coll., 1983, Indsl. Coll. Armed Forces, 1989. Commd. 2d lt. USAF, 1971, advanced through grades to maj. gen., 1999; stationed at Beale AFB, Calif., 1972-76, Ellsworth AFB, S.D., 1976-79; RF-4C asst. flight comdr./flight comdr., asst. ops. officer 91st Tactical Reconnaissance Squadron, Bergstrom AFB, Tex., 1980-81; wing and base airspace mgr. then chief current ops. div. 67th Tactical Reconnaissance Squadron, Bergstrom AFB, Tex., 1981-82; chief programs and requirements div. Hdqs. Strategic Air Command, Offutt AFB, Nebr., 1983-84, chief officer assignments div., dep. chief staff personnel, 1984-85; comdr. 62d Bombardment Squadron, Barksdale AFB, La., 1985-86; chief aircrew tng. div. Hdqs. Strategic Air Command, Offutt AFB, Nebr., 1986-87, exec. officer dep. chief of staff ops., 1987-88; chief N. Am. br. joint staff J-5 Pentagon, Washington, 1989-91, various assignments, 1997-98; various comdr. assignments USAF, 1991-97; dir. ops. and tng., dep. chief of staff air and space ops. Hdqs. USAF, Pentagon, Washington, 1998—. Decorated Legion of Merit, Air medal. Address: HQ USAF/XOO 1480 Air Force Pentagon Washington DC 20330-1480

KUDO, EMIKO IWASHITA, former state official; b. Kona, Hawaii, June 5, 1923; d. Tetsuzo and Kume (Koga) Iwashita; m. Thomas Mitsugi Kudo, Aug. 21, 1951; childrne: Guy J.T., Scott K., Candace F. BS, U. Hawaii, 1944; MS in Vocat. Edn., Pa. State U., 1950; postgrad., U. Hawaii, U. Oreg. Tchr. jr. & sr. h.s., Hawaii, 1945-51; instr. home econs. edn. U. Hawaii Tchrs. Coll., Honolulu, 1948-51, Pa. State U., State College, 1949-50; with Hawaii Dept. Edn., Honolulu, 1951-82, supr. sch. lunch svc., 1951-64, home econs. edn., 1964-68, adminstr. vocat.-tecy. edn., 1968-78; dep. supt. State Dept. Edn., Honolulu, 1978-82, cons. Am. Samoa vocat. edn. state plan devel., 1970-71; vocat. edn. U. Hawaii, 1986; internat. secondary program devel. Ashiya Ednl. Sys., Japan, 1986-91; cons. to atty. gen. mental health svcs. for children and adolscents State of Hawaii, 1994; chief planner devel. State of Hawaii Children & Adolscents Mental Health Svcs. Implementation Plan, 1994-95; state coord. industry-labor-edn., 1972-76; mem. nat. task force edn. and tng. for minority bus. enterprise, 1972-73; mem. steering com. Career Info. Ctr. Project, 1973-78; co-dir. Hawaii Career Devel. Continuum project, 1971-74; mem. Nat. Accreditation and Instl. Eligibility Adv. Coun., 1974-77, cons., 1977-78; mem. panel Internat. Conf. Vocat. Guidance, 1978, 80, 82, 86, 88; state commr. edn. commn. of the states, 1982-90; mem. Hawaii edn. coun., 1982-90. Author handbooks and pamphlets in field. Dir. Dept. Parks and Recreation, City and County of Honolulu, 1982-84; bd. dirs. Honolulu Neighborhood Housing Svcs., 1991—; exec. bd. Aloha coun. Boy Scouts Am., 1978-88; bd. trustees St. Louis H.S., 1988-95; mem. Gov.'s Commn. on Sesquicentennial Observance of Pub. Edn. in Hawaii, 1990-91; mem. Commn. State Rental Housing Trust Fund, 1992-98; mem. steering com. Hawaii Long Term Care Coalition, 1992—. Japan Found. Cultural grantee, 1977; Pa. State U. Alumni fellow, 1982. Mem. ASCD, NEA, Am. Assn. Retired Persons (mem. state legis. com. 1990-92), Pa. State U. Disting. Alumni, Western Assn. Schs. and Colls. (accreditation team mem. Ch. Coll. of Hawaii 1972-73), Am. Vocat. Assn., HAwaii Vocat. Assn., Hawaii Edn. Assn. (trustee 992—), Hawaii State Ednl. Officers Assn. (Konawaena H.S. Hall of Fame 1997), Am. Hawaii Family Consumer Sci. Assn., Hawaii Assn. Curriculum & Devel., Am. Tech. Edn. Assn., Hawaii Recreation and Park Assn., Omicron Nu, Pi Lambda Theta, Phi Delta Kappa, Delta Kappa Gamma. Home and Office: 217 Nenue St Honolulu HI 96821-1811

KUDO, IRMA SETSUKO, not-for-profit executive director; b. Ica, Peru, Feb. 25, 1939; arrived in U.S., 1944; d. Seiichi and Angelica (Yoshinaga) Higashide. Asst. dir. coun. annual session ADA, Chgo., 1971-80; exec. dir. Am. Assn. of Endodontists, Chgo., 1980—. Recipient Warren Wakai medal Japan Endodontic Assn., 1992. Mem. ADA Alumni Assn. Student Clinicians (hon.), Am. Assn. Endodontists (hon.), Am. Soc. of Assn. Execs., Profl. Conv. Mgmt. Assn., Assn. Forum Chicagoland. Office: Am Assn of Endodontists 211 E Chicago Ave Ste 1100 Chicago IL 60611-2687*

KUDRAVETZ, DAVID WALLER, lawyer; b. Sumter, S.C., Feb. 2, 1948; s. George and Barbara (Waller) K.; m. Eleanor McCrea Snyder, June 21, 1969; 1 child, Julia McCrea. BS, U. Va., 1971, JD, 1974. Bar: Va. 1974, U.S. Tax Ct. 1974; CPA, Va. Assoc. Robert M. Musselman, Charlottesville, Va., 1974; ptnr. Carwile & Kudravetz, Charlottesville, Va., 1975-78, McClure, Callaghan & McCallum, Charlottesville, Va., 1979-81, McCallum & Kudravetz, P.C., Charlottesville, Va., 1982—; instr. fed. income taxation U. of Va. Sch. Continuing Edn., 1975-79. Mem. AICPA, Va. State Bar Assn., Charlottesville-Albemarle Bar Assn., Am. Assn. Atty.-CPAs, Va. Soc. CPAs. Home: PO Box 162 Earlysville VA 22936-0162 Office: McCallum & Kudravetz PC 250 E High St Charlottesville VA 22902

KUDRLE, ROBERT THOMAS, economist, educator; b. Sioux City, Iowa, Aug. 23, 1942; s. Chester John and Helen Marguerite (Crakes) K.; m. Venetia Hilary Mary Thomas, July 20, 1970; children: Paul John Reginald, Thomas David Chester. AB, Harvard U., 1964, AM, 1969, PhD, 1974; MPhil., U. Oxford, Eng., 1967. Grad. rsch. assoc. Ctr. Internat. Affairs Harvard U., Cambridge, Mass., 1969-71; instr. Tex. A & M Univ., College Station, 1971-72; asst., assoc. prof. Humphrey Inst. U. Minn., Mpls., 1972-83, asst., assoc. dir. Ctr. Internat. Studies, 1972-82, prof. Humphrey Inst., 1983—, dir. MA program pub. affairs, 1984-86, dir. Freeman Ctr. Internat. Econ. Policy, 1990-97, assoc. dean rsch. Humphrey Inst., 1992-96; cons. U.S. Dept. Justice, U.S. AID, Urban Inst., UN Ctr. Transnat. Corps., Consumer and Corp. Affairs Can., WHO, others. Author: Agricultural Tractors: A World Industry Study, 1975; co-author State Evaluation of Foreign Sales Efforts, 1988; co-editor Reducing the Cost of Dental Care, 1983, The Industrial Future of the Pacific Basin, 1984, Jour. Internat. Studies Quarterly, 1980-84, 85; mem. editorial bd. Internat. Political Economy Yearbook, 1983—, Jour. Health Politics, Policy & Law, 1981-92; contbr. articles to profl. jours., chpts. to texts. First v.p. UN Assn. Minn., Mpls., 1976-78, mem. adv. coun., 1978-88. Graduate prize fellow Harvard U., 1967-69, Pew Faculty fellow in Internat. Affairs Harvard U., 1990-91; Nuffield Coll. studentship, Oxford, Eng., 1966-67; Rhodes scholar, Oxford, Eng., 1964-67. Mem. Assn. Pub. Policy Analysis and Mgmt. (instl. rep. 1988-97), Internat. Studies Assn. (v.p. 1998-99), Am. Econ. Assn., Harvard Club Minn. Avocations: running, gardening. Home: 4650 Fremont Ave S Minneapolis MN 55409-2263 Office: Humphrey Inst Pub Affairs 301 19th Ave S Ste 300 Minneapolis MN 55455-0429*

KUDROW, LISA, actress; b. Encino, Calif., July 30, 1963. BS in Biology, Vassar Coll., Poughkeepsie, N.Y. TV appearances include Bob, Cheers, Coach, Newhart, Flying Blind, Mad About You, 1991-99, Friends, 1994—; appeared in (films) The Carazysitter, 1995, Romy and Michele's High School Reunion, 1997, Clockwatchers, 1997, The Opposite of Sex, 1998, Hercules (voice) 1998, Analyze This, 1998, Hanging Up, 1999. *

KUDSK, KENNETH ALLAN, surgeon; b. Chgo., May 27, 1949; s. Kenneth and Hildegard Amanda (Toepel) K.; divorced. BA, U. Wis., 1971; MD, U. Ill., Chgo., 1975. Diplomate Am. Bd. Surgery, Am. Bd. Surg. Critical Care. Intern Ohio State U., Columbus, 1975-76, resident in surgery, 1977-79, 81-83; fellow in trauma San Francisco Gen. Hosp., 1979-81; co. dir. trauma svcs. Ohio State U., 1983-87, dir. nutrition support svcs., 1984-87, asst. prof. surgery, 1983-87; mem. staff Regional Med. Ctr., Memphis; assoc. prof. surgery U. Tenn., 1987-93, dir. surg. rsch., 1988—, assoc. prof. anesthesiology, 1989, dir. surg. rsch., 1989—, prof. surgery 1993—, prof. emergency medicine, 1994—; dir. nutrition support svcs. William F. Bowld Hosp., Memphis, 1995—; dir. surg. intensive care Regional Med. Ctr., Memphis, 1991—, nutrition support svcs. Contbr. over 200 articles to profl. jours., chpts. to books in field. Fellow ACS; mem. Am. Surg. Assn., Am. Assn. for Surgery of Trauma, Am. Soc. for Parenteral and Enteral Nutrition, Assn. for Acad. Surgery, Shock Soc., Surg. Infection Soc., S.E. Surg. Congress, Soc. Internat. de Chirurgie, Ea. Assn. for the Surgery of Trauma, Soc. of Mucosal Immunology, Soc. Critical Care Medicine, Soc. for Surgery of Alimentary Tract, Soc. Univ. Surgeons, So. Surg. Assn. Lutheran. Home: 1554 Harbert Ave Memphis TN 38104-5033 Office: U Tenn Med Group Inc 956 Court Ave Ste E228 Memphis TN 38163-2814

KUEBLER, CHRISTOPHER ALLEN, pharmaceutical executive; b. Hamilton, Ohio, Oct. 31, 1953; s. William E. and E. Dean (Morgan) K.; children: Megan, Lauren. BS, Fla. State U., 1975. Various sales and product mgmt. positions E.R. Squibb & Sons, Princeton, N.J., 1976-84; mgr. product devel. Monsanto Health Care, St. Louis, 1985-86; group product mgr. Abbott Pharms., Abbott Park, Ill., 1986-89; v.p. mktg. and sales Abbott Pharms., Abbott Park, 1989-93; corp. v.p. European operation Abbott Internat., Abbott Park, 1993-95; pres., chmn., CEO Covance Inc., Princeton, 1995—; bd. mem. Nat. Pharm. Coun., Washington; mem. mktg. steering com. Pharm. & Rsch. Mfrs. Assn., Washington. Office: Covance Inc 210 Carnegie Ctr Princeton NJ 08540-6233*

KUEBLER, DAVID WAYNE, insurance company executive; b. New Orleans, Apr. 18, 1947; s. Royce Matthew and Rosemary (West) K.; m. Bonnie Nadine Burton; children: Kendra Leigh, Krystal Lynn, Kira Louise. B. in Bus. Mgmt., Loyola U., New Orleans, 1969. Lic. ins. broker, investment mgr., CLU. Asst. mgr. Winn-Dixie, Inc., New Orleans, 1962-69; account exec. Travelers Ins. Co., St. Louis, 1969-74; sr. account exec. Gen. Am. Life., St. Louis, 1974-76; dist. mgr. Guardian Life Ins., New Orleans, 1976-81; pres. Profl. Planners, Inc., Kenner, La., 1981—; asst. chief of staff civil mil. ops. 377 Taacom, New Orleans, 1987. Coach girls athletics, Metairie, La., 1987. Col. USAR. Mem. Internat. Assn. Fin. Planners, Nat. Assn. Life Underwriters, New Orleans Assn. Life Underwriters, Million Dollar Round Table, Met Plus Group Millionaires. Democrat. Roman Catholic. Avocation: coaching girls softball and basketball. Home: 29 Chateau Haut-brion Dr Kenner LA 70065-2062 Office: Profl Planners Inc PO Box 640877 Kenner LA 70064-0877

KUECHLE, JOHN MERRILL, lawyer; b. Mpls., Dec. 18, 1951; s. Harry Bronson and Virginia (McClure) K.; m. Nancy Anderson, June 20, 1976; 1 child, David Michael. AB magna cum laude, Occidental Coll., 1974; JD cum laude, Harvard U., 1977. Bar: Calif. 1977. Assoc. Mitchell, Silberberg & Knupp, L.A., 1977-83, ptnr., 1983—. Mem. Phi Beta Kappa. Republican. Episcopalian. Avocations: masters track and field, orienteering, rock climbing. Home: 10733 Ranch Rd Culver City CA 90230-5458 Office: Mitchell Silberberg & Knupp 11377 W Olympic Blvd Los Angeles CA 90064-1625

KUEHL, ALEXANDER EDWARD, physician, health facility administrator, medical educator, writer; b. St. John, Nfld., Can., Aug. 12, 1944; came to U.S., 1945; s. Frederick George and Olivia Kendall (Dwyer) K.; 1 child, Kendall Ann Warsaw. BA, Johns Hopkins U., 1966, MPH, 1976; MD, Syracuse U., 1970. Bd. cert. in orthopaedic surgery; bd. cert. in emergency medicine. Intern Univ. Hosp., Syracuse, 1970-71, resident, 1971-73; resident Johns Hopkins Hosp., 1974-78; fellow in emergency med. svc. and trauma Univ. Hosp., Balt., 1978-79; dir. med. affairs Md. Inst. Emergency Med. Svcs., Balt., 1979-81; v.p. N.Y.C. Health & Hosps. Corp., 1981-89; assoc. prof. Cornell Med. Coll., N.Y.C., 1989—; chairperson N.Y.C. Regional Coun., 1988-89, N.Y.C. Med. Adv. Com., 1995-97; med. dir. CVPH Emergency Care Ctr. Author: (textbook) Medical Director's Handbook, 1989, Prehospital Systems and Medical Oversight, 1993. Chmn. Mayoral Transition (Health), N.Y.C., 1993. Lt. col. USAR. Fellow ACS, Am. Acad. Emergency Med. Dispatch (pres. 1994-99), Am. Coll. Emergency Physicians; mem. Nat. Assn. Emergency Med. Svc. Physicians (founding mem., bd. dirs. 1986-97. Stewart award 1990), Pub. Health Honor Soc. Johns Hopkins U. Home: 6 Rocky Edge Rd Morristown NY 13664 Office: 186 Rugar St Plattsburgh NY 12901

KUEHL, HANS HENRY, electrical engineering educator; b. Detroit, Mar. 16, 1933; s. Henry Martin and Hilde (Schrader) K.; m. Anna Meidinger, July 25, 1965; children—Susan, Michael. B.S., Princeton U., 1955; M.S., Calif. Inst. Tech., 1956, Ph.D., 1959. Asst. prof. elec. engring. U. So. Calif., 1960-63, assoc. prof., 1963-72, prof., 1972—, chmn. dept. elec. engring., electrophysics, 1987-98; cons. Hughes Aircraft Co., Culver city, Calif., 1975, Deutsch Co., Los Angeles, 1973. Contbr. articles to profl. jours. Recipient U. So. Calif. Teaching Excellence award, 1964, Haliburton award U. So. Calif., 1980; Outstanding Faculty award Eta Kappa Nu, Los Angeles, 1977. Fellow IEEE; mem. Am. Phys. Soc., Internat. Sci. Radio Union. Avocations: tennis; racquetball. Office: U So Calif Elec Engring Dept PHE 622 mc 0271 Los Angeles CA 90089

KUEHLER, JACK DWYER, engineering consultant; b. Grand Island, N.B., Aug. 29, 1932; married. BS, Santa Clara U., 1954, MS, 1974; DSc, Clarkson U., 1989. Assoc. engr. San Jose rsch. lab IBM Corp., 1958-67, dir. Raleigh (N.C.) comm. lab, 1967-70, dir. San Jose and Menlo Park devel. labs, 1970-72, v.p. gen. prodn. divsn., 1972-74, v.p. devel., 1974-77, pres. system prodn. divsn., 1978-70, v.p., pres. gen. tech. divsn., 1980-81, sr. v.p., 1982, group exec., tech. group, 1982-88, vice-chmn. bd., 1988-89, pres., 1989-93; ret., 1993, ind. cons., 1993—; asst. group exec. systems devel. Data Processing Prodn. Group, 1977-78, info. systems and tech. group exec., 1981, mem. corp. mgmt. bd., 1985, bd. dirs., 1986, exec. v.p., 1987; bd. dirs. Olin Corp., Nat. Assn. Mfrs., Aetna, Inc. Fellow IEEE, Am. Acad. Arts and Sci.; mem. NAE. Office: PO Box 11130 Telluride CO 81435

KUEHN, CARL PETER, information technology consultant, statistician; b. Neenah, Wis., May 16, 1966; s. Hasso Manfred and Alide (Koppenstein) K.; m. JoDee Stahlecker, Aug. 13, 1994. BS, U. Wis., 1988; postgrad., George Washington U., 1989-91; MS, Am. U., 1993. Statistician Bur. Labor Stats./U.S. Dept. Labor, Washington, 1989-94; prin. Am. Mgmt. Systems, Inc., Golden, Colo., 1994—, recruiter, 1995—. Patron Close UP Washington, Westminster, Colo., 1997; group Bible study leader Gethsemane Luth. Ch., 1995—. Avocations: running, skiing, games of strategy and chance, investing. Office: Am Mgmt Sys 14033 Denver West Pkwy Golden CO 80401-3107

KUEHN, DAVID LAURANCE, music academy administrator; b. San Marcos, Tex., Oct. 26, 1940; m. Susan Eileen Travis, June 8, 1963; children: Michael Paul, Barbara Loring. MusB, U. North Tex., 1962; MS, U. Ill., 1964; MusArtsD, Eastman Sch. Music, 1974. Instr. music U. Wis., Eau Claire, 1965-67; instr. music U. North Tex., Denton, 1967-71, asst. prof., 1971-76, assoc. prof., 1976-80, asst. dean Sch. Music, 1975-80; prof., chmn. dept. music Calif. State U., Long Beach, 1980-85; prof., dean Conservatory of Music U. Mo., Kansas City, 1985-93; pres. Music Acad. of the West, Santa Barbara, Calif., 1993—; mem. edn. com. Chamber Music Am., 1984—; vis. evaluator North Cen. Assn. Schs. and Colls., 1986-93. Editor: (books) 60 Musical Studies for Tuba, Books 1 and 2, 1969, 28 Advanced Studies for Tuba, 1972; co-author: (book) A Guide To Successful Instrumental Conducting, 1992. Pres. Kansas City Am. Arts Festival, 1988; bd. dirs. Ojai Festival, Kansas City Civic Orch., 1985-93, Lyric Opera of Kansas City, 1987-93. Fulbright Scholar, 1964-65. Mem. Nat. Assn. Schs. Music (mem. accreditation com. 1988-93). Office: Music Acad of the West 1070 Fairway Rd Santa Barbara CA 93108-2899

KUEHN, GEORGE E., lawyer, beverage company executive; b. N.Y.C., June 19, 1946; m. Mary Kuehn; children: Kristin, Rob, Geoff. BBA, U. Mich., 1968, JD, 1973. Bar: Mich. 1974. Assoc. Hill, Lewis et al, Detroit, 1974-78; ptnr. Butzel, Long et al, Detroit, 1978-81; exec. v.p., gen. counsel, sec. The Stroh Brewery Co., Detroit, 1981—. With U.S. Army, 1969-71. Office: The Stroh Brewery Co 100 River Place Dr Detroit MI 48207-4291

KUEHN, JAMES MARSHALL, newspaper editor; b. Mobridge, S.D., May 23, 1926; s. Christ A. and Selma (Brandon) K.; m. Phyllis Yvonne Larson, Apr. 3, 1950; children—Douglas James, Deborah Kay, Diana Lisa. B.A., U.S.D., 1949. State editor Rapid City (S.D.) Jour., 1949-54, wire editor, 1954-58, mng. editor, 1958-66, exec. editor, 1966-73, v.p.-editor, 1973-86. Vice pres. Rapid City Library Bd., 1969-73; dir. Mt. Rushmore Nat. Meml.

Soc., 1991—. Served with C.E. AUS, 1945-46. Mem. Rapid City C. of C. (v.p. 1970-73), S.D. C. of C. (dir. 1978-81), Lambda Chi Alpha. Republican. Lutheran. Lodge: Kiwanis (pres. 1973-74).

KUEHN, KLAUS KARL ALBERT, ophthalmologist; b. Breslau, Germany, Apr. 1, 1938; came to U.S., 1956, naturalized, 1971; s. Max and Anneliese (Hecht) K.; m. Eileen L. Nordgaard, June 22, 1961 (div. 1972); children: Stephan Eric, Kristina Annette; m. Lynda O. Hubbs, Oct. 2, 1974. Student, St. Olaf Coll., 1956-57; BA, BS, U. Minn., 1961; MD, 1963. Diplomate Am. Bd. Ophthalmology. Resident in ophthalmology UCLA Affiliated Hosps., 1968-71; practice medicine specializing in ophthalmology, San Bernardino, Calif., 1971—; chief ophthalmology dept. San Bernardino County Med. Ctr., 1979-80; assoc. clin. prof. ophthalmology Jules Stein Eye Inst. and UCLA Med. Ctr., 1978-81. Served to capt. U.S. Army, 1963-64. Fellow Am. Acad. Ophthalmology; mem. AMA, Calif. Med. Assn., Calif. Assn. Ophthalmology (bd. dirs.). Office: 902 E Highland Ave San Bernardino CA 92404-4007

KUEHN, RICHARD ARTHUR, telecommunications consultant; b. Cleve., Jan. 31, 1939; s. Arthur John and Alice (Schilling) K.; m. Cynthia Louise Shideler, Dec. 31, 1984. BBA, Case Western Res. U., 1960. V.p. Warwick Communications, Cleve., 1957-62; pres. RAK Assocs., Cleve., 1962—. Author: Cost Effective Telecommunications; editor Telecom. Info. Mgmt. Jour., 1999; columnist Bus. Communications Rev., 1974—; contbr. 100 articles to profl. jours. Mem. Soc. Telecommunication Cons. (founder). Home and Office: RAK Assocs 17894 Clifton Park Ln Cleveland OH 44107-1027

KUEHN, ROBERT JOHN, JR., air force officer; b. Yakima, Washington, Oct. 24, 1944; s. Robert John and Mary Mafalda (Salatino) K.; m. Elizabeth Muller Hochenedel, Aug. 8, 1970; 1 child, Robert John, III. BA in Polit. Sci. U. Wash., 1967; MBA, U. N.D., 1975. Commd. 2d lt. U.S. Air Force, 1967, advanced through grades to col., 1988; aircraft maintenance officer 416 Tactical Fighter Squadron, Phu Cat AB, Vietnam, 1968-69; plans staff officer Hdqrs. 5th Air Force, Tokyo, 1969-72; ICBM ops., staff officer 321 Strategic Missile Wing, Grand Forks AFB, N.D., 1972-77; instr., curriculum chief Squadron Officer Sch., Montgomery, Ala., 1977-81; plans, programming officer Hdqrs. U.S. Air Force, Washington, 1982-84; mil. asst. for policy planning Office Asst. Sec. Def./Internat. Security Affairs, Washington, 1984-85; mil. asst. for planning and programs Office Asst. Sec. Def. (comptroller), Washington, 1985-88; deputy comdr. for resource mgmt., 36 Tactical Fighter Wing, 1988-89; comdr. 36 Combat Support Group, 1989-97; pgram mgr., v.p. NASA Support Svcs., 1998—. Contbr. articles to profl. jours. Group devel. cons. Cath. Social Services, Montgomery, 1981-82; council pres. St. Elizabeth Parish, Montgomery, 1978; scoutmaster Troop 894 Boy Scouts Am., Annandale, Va., 1986-88, scouting area dist. commr., Bitbrug, Fed. Rep. of Germany, 1988-89. Decorated Bronze Star, Legion of Merit. Mem. Air Force Assn., Soc. Am. Mil. Engrs., Am. Soc. Mil. Comptrollers (Outstanding Author award 1988). Roman Catholic. Avocations: fitness, gardening, music. Office: Marshall Space Flight Ctr. PO Box 9262 Huntsville AL 35812-0262

KUEHN, RONALD L., JR., natural resources company executive; b. Bklyn., Apr. 6, 1935; m. Allison Spencer, June 7, 1986; children: Kathleen, Kelly, Erin, Coleen, Shannon, Caroline, Ronald L. III. B.S., Fordham U., 1957, LL.B., 1964. Bar: N.Y. 1964. Assoc. Hughes, Hubbard & Reed, N.Y.C., 1964-68; exec. v.p., gen. counsel Allied Artists Pictures, N.Y.C., 1968-70; v.p., gen. counsel, sec. So. Natural Resources, Inc., Birmingham, Ala., 1970-79, exec. v.p., 1979-81; pres., chief operating officer Sonat Inc., 1982-83, pres., 1982—, chief exec. officer, 1983—, chmn., 1986—, also bd. dirs.; bd. dirs. Transocean Offshore, Inc., Sonat Exploration Co., So. Natural Gas Co., Union Carbide Corp., AmSouth Bancorp., Protective Life Corp., Praxair Inc., The Dun & Bradstreet Corp.; trustee Tuskegee U., So. Rsch. Inst. Trustee Boys Club Am.; bd. dirs. area council Boy Scouts Am.; mem. pres.'s council U. Ala.-Birmingham. 1st lt. U.S. Army, 1958-59. Mem. ABA, N.Y. State Bar Assn., Assn. of Bar of City of N.Y., Fed. Energy Bar Assn., Newcomen Soc. of U.S., Bretton Woods Com., Gas Rsch. Inst. (bd. dirs.), Interstate Natural Gas Assn. (bd. dirs.), Nat. Petroleum Coun. Roman Catholic. Office: Sonat Inc 1900 5th Ave N Birmingham AL 35203-2610

KUEHNE, BENEDICT P., lawyer; b. Merced, Calif., Mar. 24, 1954; s. Ben and Jean T. K. B.A. cum laude, U. Miami, 1974; J.D. cum laude, 1977; postgrad., Fla. Atlantic U., 1979-81. Bar: Fla. 1977, D.C. 1978, U.S. Dist. Ct. (so. and mid. dists.) Fla. 1977, U.S. Dist. Ct. (so. dist.) Ala. 1983, U.S. Ct. Appeals (5th cir.) 1977, U.S. Ct. Appeals (4th cir.) 1980, U.S. Ct. Appeals (7th and 11th cir.) 1981, U.S. Ct. Appeals (9th and D.C. cirs.) 1982, U.S. Ct. Appeals (2nd cir.) 1984, U.S. Supreme Ct. 1981. Asst. atty. gen. State of Fla., West Palm Beach, 1977-79; spl. asst. state atty. 15th Jud. Cir., 1978-90; sr. assoc. Bierman, Sonnett Shohat & Sale, P.A., Miami and Ft. Lauderdale, Fla., 1980-87; ptnr. Sonnet Sale & Kuehne, P.A., 1987-93, Sale & Kuehne, P.A., 1993—; adj. instr. law U. Miami, 1987-88, Miami Dade Cmty. Coll., 1987-89; lectr. in field. Contbr. articles to profl. jours. Cmty. organizer United Way, 1987; mem. adv. bd. U. Miami Moot Ct., 1987-90; bd. dirs. Dem. Forum, Fla., 1987—, Legal Svcs. Greater Miami, Inc., 1992-98; gen. counsel Fla. Young Dems., 1986-87, pres., 1986-87; pres. Dade County Young Dems., Fla., 1982-83, bd. dirs., 1983-84; spl. counsel Biden for Pres. Campaign, 1987; dep. counsel Dade County Democratic Exec. Com., 1989-95; mem. exec. com. Alliance for Ethical Govt., 1998—. Named one of Outstanding Young Mem of Am., 1980, 82. Mem. Fla. Bar Assn. (exec. coun. criminal law sect., chair 1994-95, chair criminal cert. com. 1990-93, appelate cert. com. 1995—, chair-elect coun. sects. 1999—), Fla. Criminal Def. Attys. Assn. (chmn. brief bank com., Cert. of Merit 1984), Pub. Interest Law Bank (Award of Merit 1984), Dade County Bar Assn. (pres. 1998-99), Fla. Assn. Criminal Def. Lawyers (charter mem., bd. dirs., pres. 1990-91), Greater Miami Jewish Fedn. (atty.'s divsn.), U. Miami Iron Arrow Honor Soc., Metro-Miami Action Plant Trust (parliamentarian 1998—), Nat. Eagle Scout Orgn., U. Miami Law Alumni Assn. (pres. 1992-93, Thomas Davison svc. award 1985, 98), U. Miami Gen. Alumni Assn. (bd. dirs. 1987, pres. 1995—, Outstanding Law Alumnus award 1989, Outstanding Svc. award 1989, bd. trustees 1994—98), Coconut Grove Assn. (bd. dirs. 1982—). Home: PO Box 113405 Miami FL 33111-3405 Office: Sale & Kuehne PA 100 SE 2nd St Ste 3550 Miami FL 33131-2150

KUEHNE, CARL W., food products executive. CEO, pres. Am. Foods Group, Dakota Pork Industries. Office: Am Foods Group PO Box 8547 Green Bay WI 54308

KUEHNERT, DEBORAH ANNE, medical center administrator; b. Raleigh, N.C., Nov. 21, 1949; d. Eldor Paul and Lila Catherine (Gilbert) K. Student, Valparaiso (Ind.) U., 1967-69; BS in Biology, Lenior Rhyne Coll., Hickory, N.C., 1977. Cert. med. technologist. Rsch. asst. Strong Meml. Hosp., Rochester, N.Y., 1967-68; lab. technician Richard Baker Hosp., Hickory, N.C., 1969-76; med. technician, shift supr. Glenn R. Frye Hosp., Hickory, 1977-83; lab. tech. dir. Frye Regional Med. Ctr., Hickory, 1983-85, adminstrv. dir. lab. svcs., 1986-92; sr. tech. dir. lab. svcs. Al-Fanateer Hosp., Jubail, Saudia Arabia, 1993; med. technologist lab. Chinle (Ariz.) Health Care Facility, Navajo Indian Reservation USPHS Hosp., 1993; instr. microbiology Catawba Valley Tech. Coll., Hickory, 1977-94, Lenoir Rhyne Coll., Hickory, 1978-94; chief tech. lab. No. Area Armed Forces Hosp., Hafr Al Batin, Saudi Arabia, 1994-96; staff Relief Inc., Houston, 1996—; cons. Frye Physicians, Hickory, 1985—; lab. cons. Am. Med. Internat., New Orleans, 1986, Lake City, Fla., 1984-85; cons. Med. Lab. Observer, Chgo., 1989; spkr. in field; lab. regional rep. before Congl. Com., Washington. Recipient Svc. of Appreciation award Govt. Saudi Arabia, 1996. Mem. Am. Soc. Clin. Pathologists, N.C. Soc. Blood Bankers, Chi Beta Phi. Lutheran. Avocations: guitar, piano, hiking, traveling, reading. Home: 58 Penny Ln Hickory NC 28601-9346 Office: CODH Redmond OR 97756

KUEHNLE, KENTON LEE, lawyer; b. Chgo., Nov. 10, 1945; s. Robert Louis and Mary Caroline (Recktenwald) K.; m. Sherry L. Esposito, June 6, 1970; children: Robert, Amanda, Matthew. BA, Augustana Coll., 1967; JD, Duke U., 1970. Bar: Ohio 1970, U.S. Dist. Ct. (so. dist.) Ohio 1971. Assoc. Dunbar, Kienzle & Murphey, Columbus, Ohio, 1970-77; ptnr. Loveland, Callard & Clapham, Columbus, 1977-80, Scott, Walker & Kuehnle, Columbus, 1980-86, Thompson, Hine & Flory, Columbus, 1986—; mem., lectr. standard forms com. Columbus Bd. Realtors; instr. paralegal program Capital U. Law Sch. Co-author: (seminar book) Foreclosure Law, 1989-98, Title Insurance Endorsements, 1991-97, Commercial Leasing, 1994-97, Condominium Law, 1981-97, Use of Internet for Real Estate Lawyer, 1997; contbr. articles to profl. jours. Mem. Augustana Coll. Alumni Bd., Rock Island, Ill., 1986-89; trustee Madison Plains Schuolarship Found., Madison County, Ohio, 1986—; elder First Presbyn. Ch., Grove City, Ohio, 1990-93; pres. Computer Users Group, Columbus, 1985-86. Mem. ABA (sect. real property, probate and trust law 1973—, com. on condominium and coop. housing 1977—), Columbus Bar Assn. (chmn. real property com. 1976-78, chmn. micro computer subcom. 1986-87, 92-94, lectr. for bar assn. seminars), Ohio State Bar Assn. (bd. govs. real property sect. 1979-82, 90—, chmn. 1997—, editor state real property sect. newsletter 1995—, chmn. subcom. to rev. condominium statute 1980-81, lectr. continuing legal edn. programs), Am. Coll. Real Estate Lawyers, Coun. Ethics in Econs., Honesty in Bus., Legal Profession Task Force, Joseph Fletcher Lawyers Conf. (ann. ethics conf., spkr. selection chair). Avocations: computer programming, baseball, theology. Home: 11325 Big Plain Circleville Rd Orient OH 43146-9301 Office: Thompson Hine & Flory 10 W Broad St Ste 700 Columbus OH 43215-3435

KUELBS, JOHN THOMAS, lawyer; b. Springfield, Minn., Sept. 8, 1942; s. Alois Nicholas and Lucille Marie (Neudecker) K; m. J. Michele Norton; children: Susan, Thomas. BA, St. John's U., Collegeville, Minn., 1965; JD, Creighton U., 1973. Bar: Nebr. 1973, Calif. 1980, U.S. Ct. Claims, U.S. Ct. Appeals (9th circuit), U.S. Ct. Appeals (D.C. circuit), U.S. Supreme Ct. Sr. counsel Ford Aerospace, Newport Beach, Calif., 1976-78, divsn. counsel, 1978-81; group counsel Hughes Aircraft, El Segundo, Calif., 1981-86, staff v.p., asst. gen. counsel, 1986-88; v.p., assoc. gen. counsel Hughes Aircraft, L.A., 1988-94; sr. v.p., gen. counsel Hughes Aircraft, Arlington, Va., 1994-98; sr. v.p. legal Raytheon Sys. Co., Arlington, 1998-99, sr. v.p. acquisition policy, 1999—. Col. (ret.) JAGC, U.S. Army, 1976. Mem. ABA (pub. contract law sect. coun. 1992-94, coun. officer 1994-96, sec. pub. contract law sect. chair 1996-97), FBA, Calif. Bar Assn., Nebr. Bar Assn.; fellow ABA Pub. Contract Law Assn., Nat. Contract Mgmt. Assn. Office: Raytheon Corp Ops Ste 1500 1100 Wilson Blvd Arlington VA 22209

KUENNE, ROBERT EUGENE, economics educator; b. St. Louis, Jan. 29, 1924; s. Edward Sebastian and Margaret (Yochum) K.; m. Janet Lawrence Brown, Sept. 7, 1957; children: Christopher Brian, Carolyn Leigh Jeppsen. Student, Harris Jr. Coll., St. Louis, 1941-42; B.J., U. Mo., 1947; A.B., Washington U., St. Louis, 1948, A.M., 1949; A.M., Harvard, 1951, Ph.D., 1953; Ph.D. (hon.), Umea U., 1985. Asst. prof. econs. U. Va., 1955; mem. faculty Princeton (N.J.) U., 1956—, assoc. prof., 1960-69, prof. econs., 1969—; cons. U.S. Naval War Coll., 1954, 55, Inst. Def. Analyses, Arlington, Va., 1968—, Inst. for Energy Analysis, Washington, 1978-82; vis. prof. mil. systems analysis U.S. Army War Coll., 1967-85; mem. sci. and mgmt. adv. com. U.S. Army Computer Systems Command. Author: The Theory of General Economic Equilibrium, 1963, The Attack Submarine: A Study in Strategy, 1965, The Polaris Missile Strike: A General Economic Systems Analysis, 1966, Monopolistic Competition Theory: Studies in Impact, 1967, Microeconomic Theory of the Market Mechanism, 1968, Eugen von Böhm-Bawerk, 1971, Rivalrous Consonance, 1986, Economics of Oligopolistic Competition, 1992, General Equilibrium Economics, 1991, Economic Justice in American Society, 1993, Price and Nonprice Rivalry in Oligopoly: The Integrated Battleground. Served with AUS, 1943-46. Named Oliver Ellsworth Bicentennial preceptor, 1975-60; fellow European Econs. and Fin. Ctr., U. London, 1992—. Mem. Princeton Club (N.Y.C.), Harvard Club (Phila.). Home: 63 Bainbridge St Princeton NJ 08540-3901 Office: Princeton U Dept Econs Princeton NJ 08544

KUENNEN, THOMAS GERARD, journalist; b. St. Louis, June 30, 1953; s. George Glennon and Earline (Doherty) K.; m. Anne L. Gillette, Sept. 10, 1988; 1 child, Madeline Livingston. BJ, U. Mo., 1975. Copy editor Macon (Ga.) Telegraph & News, 1976-77; news editor Mascoutah (Ill.) Herald, and related newspapers, 1977-79; pub. rels. assoc. Booker Assocs., Inc., St. Louis, 1979-80, Fru Con Corp., St. Louis, 1980-81; assoc. editor Rock Products Mag., Chgo., 1981-84; editor Roads & Bridges Mag., Des Plaines, Ill., 1984-95; prin., editor Expressways Pub. Project, Wheeling, Ill., 1995—; mem. editl. com. Am. Bus. Press, N.Y.C., 1984-85. Recipient Jesse H. Neal award Am. Bus. Press, 1983, Svc. award La. Associated Gen. Contractors, 1990, Editl. Excellence award Am. Soc. Bus. Press Editors, 1998. Mem. Constrn. Writers Assn. (bd. dirs. 1985-86, 95-99, Robert F. Boger award 1985, 93, 95, 98), Nat. Asphalt Pavement Assn. (Hot Mix Hall of Fame), Women in Comm. (treas. 1983-84, Cub's Cup 1985). Roman Catholic. Office: Expwys Publishing 925 N Milwaukee Ave Ste 224B Wheeling IL 60090-1869

KUENSTER, JOHN JOSEPH, magazine editor; b. Chgo., June 18, 1924; s. Roy Jacob and Katheryn (Holechek) K.; m. Mary Virginia Maher, Feb. 15, 1947 (dec. Feb. 1983); m. Suely Brazão, July 1, 1995. Editor The Columbian, Chgo., 1948-57; staff writer Chgo. Daily News, Chgo., 1957-65; dir. devel. and pub. relations Mercy Hosp., Chgo., 1965-66; sr. writer The Claretians, Chgo., 1966—; editor Baseball Digest, Evanston, Ill., 1969—; exec. editor Century Pub. Co., Evanston. Author: Cobb to Catfish, (booklets) The Police, Money, Mission in Guatamala, Honesty, Is it the Best Policy?; co-author: To Sleep with the Angels. Mem. Baseball Writers' Assn. Am. Roman Catholic. Office: Baseball Digest Century Publishing Co 990 Grove St Evanston IL 60201-4370

KUENZLER, EDWARD JULIAN, ecologist and environmental biologist; b. West Palm Beach, Fla., Nov. 11, 1929; s. Edward and Flora Caroline (Jeske) K.; m. Jutta Gertraud Koslowski, Sept. 4, 1965; children—Doreen Friederika, Dirk Edward. BS with high honors, U. Fla., 1951; MS, U. Ga., 1954, PhD, 1959. Assoc. scientist Woods Hole (Mass.) Oceanographic Inst., 1959-65; assoc. prof. environ. scis. and engring. U. N.C., Chapel Hill, 1965-71, prof. environ. biology, 1972-92, prof. emeritus, 1992—, program dir. environ. chemistry and biology, 1980-83, dep. chmn. dept. environ. scis. and engring., 1984-87, program dir. aquatic and atmospheric scis., 1990-92, adv. com. environ. scis. and engring., 1980-87, 90-92; mem. curriculum in marine scis., 1968-92, chmn. curriculum in marine scis., 1968-71, 72-73, mem. curriculum in ecology, 1971-92, joint appointment dept. botany, 1969-75; Mem. N.C. Gov.'s Tech. Coordinating Com., 1968-70, N.C. Comml. and Sports Fisheries Adv. Com., 1975-77; program dir. for biol. oceanography NSF, 1971-72; mem. panel NAS, 1974-75; tchr. grad. courses phytoplankton ecol., oceanography, biol. oceanography, chem. oceanography, limnology, wetland ecol., 1967-91; dir. grad. rsch., 1984-87; cons. and mem. adv. panels in field. Contbr. articles on phytoplankton ecology, water quality, elemental cycling in estuarine, freshwater and wetland ecosystems to profl. jours. Bd. dirs. White Cross Recreation Assn., 1981-83, 93-95, treas., 1993-95; chmn. fin. com. Orange Chapel United Meth. Ch., 1988-98, treas. Men's Club, 1986—; mem. Bingham Twp. Adv. Coun., 1994—. 1st lt. USAF, 1954-57, res., 1957-60, capt., 1960. Named to U. Fla. Hall of Fame, 1951; grantee AEC, 1962-70, NOAA Office Sea Grants, 1971-76, Office Water Rsch. and Tech., U.S. Geol. Survey-N.C. Water Resources Rsch. Inst., 1970-89, EPA, 1987-90. Mem. Ecol. Soc. Am., Am. Soc. Limnol. and Oceanog. Estuarine Rsch. Fedn., N.C. Acad. Sci. (treas. 1982-85), Elisha Mitchell Sci. Soc. (pres. 1979-81), Soc. Wetland Scientists, Phycol. Soc. Am., N.C. Herpetol. Soc., Nat. Assn. Scholars, Phi Beta Kappa, Sigma Xi. Republican. Home: 6015 Old Greensboro Rd Chapel Hill NC 27516-8516

KUERLEY-SCHAFFER, DAWN RENEE, medical/surgical nurse; b. Bay City, Mich., June 8, 1959; d. Edward J. and Leaella Mae (Jacob) Kuerley; m. Michael B. Schaffer, May 30, 1986; 1 child, Randi Lea. Lic. practical nurse, Bay Practical Nurse Ctr., 1980; ADN, Alpena C.C., 1986. RN, Mich., La. Practical nurse Tawas St. Joseph Hosp., Tawas City, Mich., 1984-86, staff nurse, 1986-88; nurse 1st asst. in gen. surgery Fay E. Seppala MD PC, New Orleans, 1988-94; RN, clinic head nurse neurosurgery Tulane U. Med. Ctr., New Orleans, 1994-98; RN, 1st asst. dept. neurosurgery Children's Hosp., New Orleans, 1998—. Clark Sawyer meml. scholar. Mem. Assn. Oper. Rm. Nurses (cert. oper. rm. nurse), Alpena C.C. ADN Alumni Assn. (past pres.). Office: Children's Hosp 200 Henry Clay New Orleans LA 70118

KUERTI, ANTON EMIL, pianist, composer; b. Vienna, 1938; s. Gustav and Rosi (Jahoda) K.; m. Kristine Bogyo, Sept. 13, 1973; children: Julian, Rafael. MusB, Cleve. Inst. Music, PhD (hon.), 1996; diploma, Curtis Inst., 1959; PhD (hon.), York U., 1985, Laurentian U., 1985, Cleve. Inst. Music, 1996. Soloist, N.Y. Philharmonic, Cleve. Orch., Detroit Orch., Phila. Orch., Buffalo Orch., San Francisco Symphony, Denver Orch., over 25 appearances with, Toronto Symphony and Nat. Arts Ctr. Orch. (Ottawa), tours worldwide including Soviet Union, Far East, Australia, Latin Am., numerous TV appearances, radio broadcasts; recs. include complete cycle Beethoven Sonatas and Concerti and complete Schubert Sonatas; founder, Festival of Sound, Parry Sound, Ont.; composer: Linden Suite for piano, 1970, String Quartet, 1972, (violin sonata) Epomeo Symphony, 1975; Piano Man Suite and Piano Concerto, 1985, Clarinet Trio, 1989, Concertino, 1994, Jupiter Concerto, 1995; contbr. numerous articles to mags. and revs. Recipient Leventritt award, 1957, Juno award Canadian Grand Prix de Disque, 1985, Toronto Arts award, 1997. Mem. Amnesty Internat., Can. Scientists and Scholars, Order of Can. (officer). Address: 20 Linden St, Toronto, ON Canada M4Y 1V6 *In the arts, success can mean fame and money; or it can mean the satisfaction of having extracted the noblest, most profound expression the individual is capable of. The more one pursues the fame and money, the more elusive the inner satisfaction is likely to be. If I have had some success, it is because of my deep belief in music, one of man's supreme achievements, and perhaps his purest. It is capable of transforming and fulfilling the listener, and helping him become a new, better person. Even stronger is its effect on the performer. Only one thing matters more to me: the pursuit of peace and the preservation of this deeply endangered planet.*

KUERTI, ROSI, educator; b. Vienna, Austria, July 8, 1905; d. Karl and Betty Jahoda. PhD, U. Vienna, 1928. Tchr. U. Istanbul, Turkey, 1937-38, Buckingham Sch., Cambridge, Mass., England, 1938-39; prof. Hathaway Brown Sch., Cleve., 1939-40, Case Western Res. U., Cleve.; tchr. John Raper Sch., Cleve. Home: 2181 Ambleside Dr Cleveland OH 44706

KUESEL, THOMAS ROBERT, civil engineer; b. Richmond Hill, N.Y., July 30, 1926; s. Henry N. and Marie D. (Butt) K.; m. Lucia Elodia Fisher, Jan. 31, 1959; children—Robert Livingston, William Baldwin. B. Engring. with highest honors, Yale U., 1946, M. Engring., 1947. With Parsons, Brinckerhoff, Quade & Douglas, 1947-90; project mgr. Parsons, Brinckerhoff, Quade & Douglas, San Francisco, 1967-68; ptnr., sr. v.p. Parsons, Brinckerhoff, Quade & Douglas, N.Y.C., 1968-83, chmn. bd., dir., 1983-90; cons. engr., 1990—; vice chmn. OECD Tunneling Conf., Washington, 1970; mem U.S. Nat. Com. on Tunneling Tech., 1972-74; chmn. Geotech. bd. Nat. Rsch. Coun., 1988-89. Contbr. 60 articles to profl. jours.; designer more than 120 bridges, 135 tunnels and numerous other structures in 36 states and 20 fgn. countries, most recent L.A. Metro, 1982-98, Geo Coleman Bridge Replacement, Yorktown, Va., 1991-95, Boston Ctrl. Artery and Harbor Tunnel, 1994—, Boston Ocean Outfall Tunnel, 1988-90, Cumberland Gap Tunnel, Ky. and Tenn., 1986-90, Jamuna River Bridge, Bangladesh, 1985-95, Trans Koolau Tunnel, Hawaii, 1985-90, Ft. McHenry Tunnel, Balt., 1978-85, Rogers Pass Rwy. Tunnel, B.C., 1981-85, Glenwood Canyon Tunnel, Colo., 1981-88, subways Boston, N.Y., Balt., Wash., Atlanta, Pitts., San Francisco, Seattle, L.A., Caracas, Singapore and Taipei. Fellow ASCE; mem. Nat. Acad. Engring., Internat. Assn. for Bridge and Structural Engring. Brit. Tunnelling Soc., Yale Sci. and Engring. Assn., Am. Underground Construction Assn. (hon. mem.), The Moles, Yale Club N.Y.C., Wee Burn Club, Farmington Club, Tau Beta Pi.

KUETHE-STRUDTHOFF, DENISE LARAE, librarian; b. Waterloo, Iowa, Jan. 18, 1958; d. Wendall Harold and Rochelle Frances (Duecker) K.; m. David Otto Strudthoff, Oct. 17, 1987. BA in Edn., Upper Iowa U., 1979; MA, U. No. Iowa, 1994. Tchr. bus. Scranton (Iowa) Schs., 1980-83; head dept. sec. studies Am. Inst. Commerce, Cedar Falls, Iowa, 1985-87, acad. dean, 1989-92; grad. asst. U. No. Iowa, Cedar Falls, 1992-93; media dir. Iowa Valley Schs., Marengo, 1993-99; adj. prof. sch. libr. media studies U. No. Iowa, Cedar Falls, 1999—. Mem. Yalsa Intellectual Freedom Com. Mem. ALA, AAUW, Iowa Reading Assn., Iowa Ednl. Media Assn. Democrat. Lutheran. Avocations: reading, crocheting, travel, gardening. Home: 12392 Springfield Dr Postville IA 52162 Office: U Ho Iowa Rod Libr Cedar Falls IA 50614

KUFELD, WILLIAM MANUEL, lawyer; b. Hunter, N.Y., Aug. 4, 1922; s. Max and Carrie (Hausdorff) K.; m. Frieda Chesir, Apr. 9, 1949; 1 son, David J. Student, Bklyn. Coll., 1938-40; B.B.A., Coll. City N.Y., 1940-42; LL.B., N.Y. U., 1949, LL.M., 1952. Bar: N.Y. bar 1949. Since practiced in N.Y.C.; partner firm Carb, Luria, Cook & Kufeld, 1959—; adj. prof. law N.Y. U., 1962-77; lectr. Practicing Law Inst. Pres. Congregation of Young Israel of Fifth Ave., N.Y.C., 1962-65, North Shore Hebrew Acad., Great Neck, N.Y., 1969-73. Served to 1st lt. USAAF, 1943-46. Recipient Alumn. Meritorious Achievement award N.Y.U., 1965. Mem. Assn. Bar City N.Y., N.Y. State Bar Assn., N.Y. County Lawyers Assn., N.Y. U. Law Alumni Assn. (pres. 1970-71). Home: 22 Hawthorne Ln Great Neck NY 11023-2023 Office: 521 5th Ave New York NY 10175-0003*

KUFELDT, GEORGE, biblical educator; b. Chgo., Nov. 4, 1923; s. Henry and Lydia (Dorn) K.; m. Kathryn Rider, July 24, 1943 (dec. July 1956); children: Anita Kay Kufeldt Shelton, Kristina Sue Kufeldt Schmidt; m. Claudena Eller, June 21, 1957 (dec. Sept. 1978); m. Lydia Borgardt, Aug. 12, 1980. AB, Anderson Coll., Ind., 1945, ThB, 1946, MDiv, 1953; PhD, Dropsie U., 1974. Ordained to ministry Ch. of God, 1948. Pastor Ch. of God, Homestead, Fla., 1948-50, Ch. of God, Cassopolis, Mich., 1954-57, Ch. of God, Lansdale, Pa., 1957-61; prof. O.T. and Hebrew, Anderson U., 1961-90, prof. emeritus O.T., 1990—. Contbr. to Wesleyan Bible Commentary, vol. II, 1968, Nelson's Expository Dictionary of the Old Testament, 1980, Educating for Service, 1984, The Genesis Debate, 1986, Listening to the Word of God, 1990, Zondervan One-Vol. Bible Commentary, 1991. Dropsie U. fellow, 1961, 63; Land of the Bible Workshop grantee NYU, 1966. Mem. Nat. Assn. Profs. of Hebrew, Am. Hellenic Ednl. Progressive Assn. (pres., Achievement award 1990) , Am. Hist. Soc. Germans from Russia (life, bd. dirs. 1991-98). Home: 907 N Nursery Rd Anderson IN 46012-2721

KUFFEL, EDMUND, electrical engineering educator; b. Poland, Oct. 28, 1924; s. Franciszek and Marta (Glodowska) K.; m. Alicja, Oct. 4, 1952; children: Anna, John, Richard, Peter. BSc, U. Coll., Dublin, 1953, MSc, 1954, PhD, 1959; DSc, U. Manchester, 1967. Rsch. engr. Met. Vickers Electric Co., Manchester, Eng., 1954-60; mem. faculty elec. engring. U. Manchester Inst. Sci. and Tech., 1960-68; head of elect. engring. U. Windsor, Ont., Can., 1970-78; prof. elec. engring. U. Man., Winnipeg, Can., 1968-70, head of elec. engring., 1978-79; dean of engring. U. Man., Winnipeg, Can., 1979-89, prof. elec. engring., dean emeritus, 1989—; cons. various mfrs. high voltage cables; bd. dirs. Man. Hydro Elec. Bd., 1978-96; cons. prof. Xi'an Jiaotong U., People's Rep. China, 1986—. Author or co-author over 150 pub. tech. papers on high voltage engring. Fellow IEEE, Can. Acad. Engring. Home: 2661 Knowles Ave, Winnipeg, MB Canada R2G 2K7 Office: U Manitoba, Fac Engring, Winnipeg, MB Canada R3T 2N2

KUFFNER, GEORGE HENRY, dermatologist, educator; b. S.I., N.Y., Aug. 22, 1949; s. George Henry and Wilmouth Anne (Clendenin) K.; m. Lynne Diane Blakeslee, May 17, 1975; children: Kevin, Todd A. BA, Johns Hopkins U., 1971, MD, 1975. Intern U. Hosps. Cleve., 1975-78, resident, 1978-81; staff dermatologist Wooster (Ohio) Clin., LLC, Cleve. Clinic Found., 1981—; asst. clin. prof. dermatology U. Hosps. Cleve., 1981—. Contbr. articles to profl. jours. Fellow Am. Acad. Dermatology; mem. AMA, Ohio Med. Assn., Ohio Dermatology Assn., Cleve. Dermatology Soc. Methodist. Avocations: swimming, piano, reading, video/stero electronics, travel. Office: Wooster Clin LLC Cleve Clinic Reg Practice 1740 Cleveland Rd Wooster OH 44691-2204

KUFNER, SHARON KAY, women's health nurse; b. Manitowoc, Wis., Feb. 12, 1956; d. Paul James Jr. and Lois Jean (Dreger) Mrotek. BSN, U. Wis., Eau Claire, 1979; MS, U. Wis., Madison, 1988. RN, Wis. Staff nurse nursery Theda Clark Regional Med. Ctr., Neenah, Wis., 1980-86, Meriter Hosp., Madison, 1986-87; rsch. asst. Sch. Nursing U. Wis., Madison, 1987-88; clin. nurse specialist maternal-newborn Theda Clark Regional Med. Ctr., Neenah, Wis., 1988-90; staff Clin. Rsch. Ctr., Kimberly Clark Corp., Neenah, Wis., 1990—; nursing educator assoc. degree program Fox Valley Tech. Coll., Appleton, Wis., 1991—. Michele K. Del Monte Meml. scholar. Mem. Wis. Assn. Perinatal Care, Wis. Assn. Lactation Cons., Internat. Lactation Cons. Assn., Sigma Theta Tau.

KUGLER, ROBERT B., federal judge; b. 1950. BA, U. Syracuse, 1975; JD, Rutgers U., 1978. Bar: N.J. 1978. Law clk. to Hon. John F. Gerry, U.S.

Dist. Ct. for Dist. N.J., 1978-79; asst. prosecutor Camden County, 1979-81; dep. atty. gen. spl. prosecution sect. N.J. Dept. Law and Pub. Safety, 1981-82; ptnr. Moss, Power & Kugler, 1982-92; magistrate judge for N.J., U.S. Magistrate Ct., Camden, 1992—. Mem. ABA, N.J. Bar Assn., Burlington County Bar Assn., Camden County Bar Assn. Office: Mitchell Cohen Courthouse One John F Gerry Plz Camden NJ 08102

KUGLITSCH, MAUREEN ROSE, maternal/child health nurse; b. Racine, Wis., Sept. 29, 1944; d. John Edward and Elizabeth Rose (Larsen) Hall; m. John Frances Kuglitsch, August 26, 1967; children: Paul David, Mark Patrick. Diploma in nursing, St. Mary's Sch. Nursing, 1966; BSN cum laude, U. Wis., Oshkosh, 1978, MSN, 1992. RN, Wis., Minn.; cert. family nurse practitioner, ANCC. Pediatric nurse St. Mary's Hosp., Rochester, Minn., 1972-73; exec. dir., co-founder Pregnancy Health Line, Inc., Fond-du-Lac, Wis., 1978-88; patient educator Healthdyne Perinatal Svc., Milw., 1988—; home health care nurse St. Agnes Hosp., Fond-du-Lac, Wis., 1990-92; family nurse practitioner Mt. Carmel Health and Rehab. Ctr., Milw., 1993-97, Oconomocow (Wis.) Meml. Hosp., 1998—. Named Woman of the Year, Fond-du-Lac Bus. and Profl. Women's Club, 1983; recipient Faith in Dialogue award, Marian Coll. of Fond-du-Lac, 1984. Mem. ANA, Wis. Nurses Assn. (bd. dirs., v.p. local chpt. 1982-83), Wis. Assn. for Perinatal Care, Sigma Theta Tau. Home: 5055 S Loftus Ct New Berlin WI 53151-7550

KUH, CHARLOTTE VIRGINIA, economist; b. Apr. 13, 1944; d. Peter Greenebaum and Frederica Angela (Coerr) K.; m. Roy Radner, Jan. 22, 1978; children: Siobhan, Frederica, Michael Edwin. BA magna cum laude, Radcliffe Coll., 1967; MPhil (Univ. fellow), Yale U., 1969, PhD (Dept. Labor grantee), 1976. Rec. sec.-treas. Econometric Soc., New Haven, 1970-75; acting asst. prof. engrng. econ. systems Stanford U., 1974-76; asst. prof. Harvard U. Grad. Sch. Edn., 1976-79; staff mgr., dist. mgr. AT&T Corp., 1979-87; exec. dir. grad. records exams program Ednl. Testing Svc., 1987-95; exec. dir. Office of Sci. and Engring. Personnel Nat. Rsch. Coun., 1995—; mem. rev. panel NSF, 1979, 81, mem. adv. panel policy research and sci. resourcestudies, 1983-87; mem. rev. panel Nat. Inst. Edn., 1978-85; mem. com. study nat. needs for biomed. and behavioral research personnel NRC, 1980-85, mem. adv. panel Office Sci. and Engring. Personnel, 1983-90, mem. panel on stats. on supply and demand for precoll. sci. and math. tchrs., com. on nat. stats., 1986-89, mem. com. Women in Sci. and Engring. NRC, 1991—, vice chair, 1993—, mem. com. to study strategies to strengthen excellence of the N.I.H. Intramural Research Program, Inst. of Medicine, 1988; cons. in field. Author articles in field. Grantee Carnegie Coun. Higher Edn., Ford Found., Spencer Found. Mem. Am. Econ. Assn., Econometric Soc. Office: Natl Research Council 2101 Constitution Ave NW Washington DC 20418-0007*

KUH, ERNEST SHIU-JEN, electrical engineering educator; b. Peking, China, Oct. 2, 1928; came to U.S., 1948, naturalized, 1960; s. Zone Shung and Tsia (Chu) K.; m. Bettine Chow, Aug. 4, 1957; children: Anthony, Theodore. BS, U. Mich., 1949; MS, MIT, 1950; PhD, Stanford U., 1952; DEng (hon.), Hong Kong U. Sci. and Tech., 1997. Mem. tech. staff Bell Tel. Labs., Murray Hill, N.J., 1952-56; assoc. prof. elec. engring. U. Calif., Berkeley, 1956-62, prof., 1962—, Miller rsch. prof., 1965-66, William S. Floyd Jr. prof. engring., 1990—, William S. Floyd Jr. prof. engring. emeritus, 1993—, chmn. dept. elec. engring. and computer sci., 1968-72, dean Coll. Engring., 1973-80; cons. IBM Rsch. Lab., San Jose, Calif., 1957-62, NSF, 1975-84; mem. panel Nat. Bur. Stds., 1975-80; vis. com. Gen. Motors Inst., 1975-79, dept. elec. engring. and computer scis. MIT, 1986-91; mem. adv. coun. elec. engring. dept. Princeton (N.J.) U., 1986—; mem. bd. councilors sch. engring. U. So. Calif., 1986-91; mem. sci. adv. bd. Mills Coll., 1976-80. Co-author: Principles of Circuit Synthesis, 1959, Basic Circuit Theory, 1967, Theory of Linear Active Network, 1967; Linear and Nonlinear Circuits, 1987. Recipient Alexander von Humboldt award, 1980, Lamme medal Am. Soc. Endring. Edn., 1981, U. Mich. Disting. Alumnus award, 1970, Berkeley citation, 1993, C & C prize Japanese Found. for Computers and Comm. Promotion, 1996, 1998 EDAC, Phil Kaufman award; Brit. Soc. Engring. and Rsch. fellow, 1982. Fellow IEEE (Edn. medal 1981, Centenial medal 1984, Circuits and Systems Soc. award. 1988), AAAS; mem. NAE, Acad. Sinica, Chinese Acad. Scis. (fgn. mem.), Sigma Xi, Phi Kappa Phi. Office: U Calif Elec Engring & Computer Sci Depts Berkeley CA 94720

KUH, JOYCE DATTEL, education administrator; b. Greenville, Miss., Mar. 10, 1937; d. Milton Joseph and Hannah (Marks) Dattel; m. Richard Henry Kuh, Jul. 31, 1966; children: Michael Joseph, Jody Ellen. BA, Newcomb Coll. Tulane U., 1959. Asst. to treas. Dynatech. Corp., Cambridge, Mass., 1959-63; editorial asst. McCall's Mag., N.Y.C., 1963-64; asst. editor Ladies's Home Jour., N.Y.C., 1964-73; freelance writer, editor N.Y.C., 1973-89; dir. of devel. Grace Ch. Sch., N.Y.C., 1989—. Del. Dem. County Com., N.Y.C., 1993—; bd. trustees The Dome Project. Jewish. Avocations: opera, skiing, gardening, traveling. Home: 14 Washington Pl New York NY 10003-6609 Office: Grace Ch Sch 86 4th Ave New York NY 10003-5232

KUH, RICHARD HENRY, lawyer; b. N.Y.C., Apr. 27, 1921; s. Joseph Hellmann and Fannie Mina (Rees) K.; m. Joyce Dattel, July 31, 1966; children: Michael Joseph, Jody Ellen. BA, Columbia Coll., 1941; LLB magna cum laude, Harvard U., 1948. Bar: N.Y. 1948, U.S. Dist. Ct. (so. dist.) N.Y. 1948, U.S. Dist. Ct. (ea. dist.) N.Y. 1967, U.S. Supreme Ct. 1968. Assoc. firm Cahill, Gordon & Reindel, 1948-53; asst. dist. atty. N.Y. County Dist. Attys. Office, 1953-64, dist. atty., 1974; pvt. practice law N.Y.C., 1966-71; ptnr. firm Kuh, Goldman, Cooperman & Levitt, N.Y.C., 1971-73, Kuh, Shapiro, Goldman, Cooperman & Levitt, P.C., N.Y.C., 1975-78, Warshaw Burstein Cohen Schlesinger & Kuh, N.Y.C., 1978—; adj. prof. NYU Law Sch. Author: Foolish Figleaves, 1967; mem. bd. editors: Harvard Law Rev, 1947-48; mem. adv. bd.: Contemporary Drug Problems, 1975—, Criminal Law Bull, 1976—; contbr. articles to popular and profl. jours. Trustee Temple Israel, N.Y.C., 1975-84, Grace Ch. Sch., 1981-85. With U.S. Army, 1942-45, ETO. Walter E. Meyer Research and Writing grantee, 1964-65. Mem. ABA (chair criminal justice sect. 1983-84, chair spl. com. on evaluation jud. performance 1983-90, ho. dels. 1988-93, mem. jud. evaluation adv. com. Nat. Ctr. State Cts. 1990-91, chair 1st nat. conf. gun violence 1994), Assn. Bar City N.Y., Am. Bar Found., Harvard Law Sch. Assn. N.Y. (trustee 1989-92), Harvard Club (mem. admissions com. 1998—), Phi Beta Kappa. Democrat. Jewish. Home: 14 Washington Pl New York NY 10003-6609 Office: 555 5th Ave New York NY 10017-2416

KUHAR, JUNE CAROLYNN, retired fiberglass manufacturing company executive; b. Chgo., Sept. 20, 1935; d. Kurt Ludwig and Dorothy Julia (Lewand) Stier; m. G. James Kuhar, Feb. 5, 1953; children: Kathleen Lee, Debra Suzanne. Lic. real estate salesperson. Student William Rainey Harper Coll., Chgo. Engaged in fiberglass mfg., 1970—; sec.-treas. Q-R Fiber Glass Industries Inc., Rolling Meadows, Ill., 1970—. Leader Girl Scouts U.S.; mem. Civil Def. Disaster and Rescue Team, 1965-70, Rolling Meadows Golden Yrs. Coun., Arlington Heights Concerned People Helping to Understand Multiple Sclerosis; chmn. benefit fashion show William Rainey Harper Coll.- Sch. of Fashion Design, 1983. Mem. Multiple Sclerosis Soc., Nat. Fedn. Ileitis and Colitis, Bus. and Profl. Women N.W., Bus. and Profl. Woman's Club (pres. 1984—), Am. Legion Aux., Women in the Arts (charter). Home: 2303 Meadow Dr Rolling Meadows IL 60008-1546

KUHBACH, ROBERT GERDES, lawyer; b. New Haven, Conn., May 21, 1947; s. Arend Gerdes and Muriel Ruth (Dinger) K.; m. E. Sherrell Andrews, Nov. 5, 1977; children: Allison Meryl, Courtney Heather. BA in Econs., Yale U., 1969; JD, U. Mich., 1972. Bar: N.Y. 1974. Assoc. Breed, Abbott & Morgan, N.Y.C., 1973-79; atty., sr. atty., gen. counsel Gen. Host Corp., Stamford, Conn., 1980-89; sr. v.p., exec. v.p., dir., gen. counsel, sec. Sudbury, Inc., Cleve., 1989-92; v.p., gen. counsel, sec. Dover Corp., N.Y.C., 1993—. Capt. U.S. Army, 1971-78. Recipient S. Anthony Benton award U. Mich. Law Sch., Ann Arbor, 1972. Mem. ABA, Am. Soc. Corp. Secs., Am. Corp. Coun. Assn., Bar Assn. of City of N.Y. Office: Dover Corp 280 Park Ave New York NY 10017-1216*

KUHI, LEONARD VELLO, astronomer, university administrator; b. Hamilton, Ont., Can., Oct. 22, 1936; came to U.S., 1958; s. John and Sinaida (Rose) K.; m. Patricia Suzanne Brown, Sept. 3, 1960 (div.); children: Alison Diane, Christopher Paul; m. Mary Ellen Murphy, July 15, 1989. BS, U. Toronto, 1958; PhD, U. Calif., Berkeley, 1964. Carnegie postdoctoral fellow Hale Obs., Pasadena, Calif., 1963-65; asst. prof. U. Calif., Berkeley, 1965-69, assoc. prof., 1969-74, prof., 1974-89, chmn. dept. astronomy, 1975-76, dean phys. scis. Coll. Letters and Sci., 1976-81, provost, 1983-89; sr. v.p. for acad. affairs, provost U. Minn., Mpls., 1989-91, prof. astronomy, 1989—, chmn. dept. astronomy, 1997—; vis. prof. U. Colo., 1969, Coll. de France, Paris, 1972-73, U. Heidelberg, 1978, 80-81; bd. dirs. Am. Inst. Physics. Contbr. articles to profl. jours. Recipient Alexander von Humboldt Sr. Scientist award, 1980-81; NSF research grantee, 1966—. Fellow AAAS; mem. Am. Astron. Soc. (treas. 1987, 96—), Astron. Soc. Pacific (pres. 1978-80), Internat. Astron. Union, Assn. Univ. for Rsch. Astronomy (chair bd. dirs.), Sigma Xi. Office: U Minn Dept Astronomy 116 Church St SE Minneapolis MN 55455-0149

KUHL, DAVID EDMUND, physician, nuclear medicine educator; b. St. Louis, Oct. 27, 1929; s. Robert Joseph and Caroline Bertha (Waldemar) K.; m. Eleanor Dell Kasales, Aug. 7, 1954; 1 son, David Stephen. AB, Temple U., Phila., 1951; MD, U. Pa., 1955; LHD (hon.), Loyola U. Chgo., 1992. Diplomate: Am. Bd. Radiology, Am. Bd. Nuclear Medicine (a founder; life trustee 1977—). Intern, then resident in radiology Sch. Medicine and Hosp. U. Pa., 1955-56, 58-63, mem. faculty, 1963-76, prof. radiology, 1970-76, vice chmn. dept., 1975-76, chief div. nuclear medicine, 1963-76; prof. radiol. scis. UCLA Sch. Medicine and Hosp., 1976-86, chief div. nuclear medicine, 1976-84, vice-chmn. dept., 1977-86; prof. internal medicine and radiology, chief div. nuclear medicine U. Mich. Sch. Medicine, Ann Arbor, 1986—; Disting. faculty lectr. in biomed. rsch. U. Mich. Med. Sch., 1992, Henry Russel lectr., 1998; mem. adv. com. Dept.Energy, NIH, Internat. Commn. on Radiation Units and Measures; mem. sci. adv. bd. Max Planck Inst., Cologne. Mem. editorial bd. various jours.; contbr. articles to med. jours. Served as officer M.C. USNR, 1956-58. Recipient Research Career Devel. award USPHS, 1961-71, Ernst Jung prize for medicine Jung Found., Hamburg, 1981, Emil H. Grubbe gold medal Chgo. Med. Soc., 1983, Berman Found. award peaceful uses atomic energy, 1985, Steven C. Beering award for advancement med. sci. Ind. U., 1987, Disting. Grad. award U. Pa. Sch. Medicine, 1988, William C. Menninger Meml. award ACP, 1989, Javits Neuroscience Investigator award NIH, 1989. Fellow Am. Coll. Radiology, Am. Coll. Nuclear Physicians, Nat. Inst. for Med. and Biol. Engring.; mem. Assn. Am. Physicians, Am. Epilepsy Soc., Assn. Univ. Radiologists, Radiol. Soc. N.Am. (ann. orator 1982, Outstanding Rschr. award 1996), Soc. Nuclear Medicine (Nuclear Pioneer citation 1976, Herman L. Blumgart, M.D. Pioneer award 1979, Disting. Scientist award 1981, ann. lectr. 1991, George Charles de Hevesy Nuclear Medicine Pioneer award 1995, Benedict Cassen Prize for Rsch. 1996), Am. Heart Assn. (fellow coun. circulation), Am. Neurol. Assn. (Foster Elting Bennett Meml. lectr. 1981), Rocky Mountain Radiol. Soc., Soc. Neurosci., Inst. Medicine Nat. Acad. Scis., Sigma Xi, Alpha Omega Alpha. Office: U Mich Hosp Divsn Nuc Medicine 1500 E Medical Center Dr Ann Arbor MI 48109-0005

KUHL, JOHN R., JR., state legislator; b. Apr. 19, 1943; s. John R. and Myrtle (Wombacker) K.; m. Jennifer Knapp; children: John R. III, Christopher, James Whitney. BS, Union Coll.; JD, Syracuse U., 1969. Bar: N.Y. Formerly legal counsel Steuben County Social Svc. and Hwy. Dept.; formerly asst. atty. Steuben County, N.Y.; formerly county atty., village atty., Prattsburgh; formerly town atty. Rathbone and Pulteney; now in practice of law; mem. N.Y. State Assembly, 1980-86; mem. N.Y. State Senate, 1986—, chmn. agr. standing com., 1987-99, chmn. edn. com., 1999—; mem. banks com., health com., housing, constrn. and cmty. devel. com., commerce, econ. devel. and small bus., crime victims, crime and correction, fin., higher edn., transp. standing com.; former state chmn. Am. Legis. Exch. Coun.; chmn. Legis. Coun. on Dairy Industry Devel.; mem. agr., food policy and rural devel. com. Nat. Conf. State Legislatures, also vice chmn. wine indsl. task force; mem. State Coun. on Agrl. Devel. and Innovation. Mem. Senate select com. on interstate cooperation; mem. exec. com. Steuben Area coun. Boy Scouts Am. Mem. N.Y. Bar Assn., Steuben County Bar Assn., Rotary, Elks, Moose, Bath and Branchport Rod and Gun Club. Office: NY State Senate Rm 310 Legislative Office Bldg Albany NY 12247*

KUHL, PATRICIA K., science educator; b. Mitchell, S.D., Nov. 5, 1946; d. Joseph John and Susan Mary (Schaeffer) K.; m. Andrew N. Meltzoff, Sept. 28, 1985; 1 child, Katherine. BA, St. Cloud (Minn.) State U., 1967; MA, U. Minn., 1971, PhD, 1973. Postdoctoral research assoc. Cen. Inst. for Deaf, St. Louis, 1973-76; research assoc. U. Wash., Seattle, 1976-77, asst. prof., 1977-79, assoc. prof., 1979-82, prof. speech, language, hearing, 1982—, William P. and Ruth Gerberding univ. prof., 1997—, dept. chair, 1994—; gov. bd. Am. Inst. Physics, 1994-96; trustee Neurosci. Rsch. Found., 1994—; bd. dirs. Wash. Tech. Ctr., U. Wash., 1994-96; invited presenter White House Conf. on Early Learning and the Brain, 1997. Editor Jour. Neurosci., 1989-96. Recipient Women in Research citation Kennedy Council, 1978, Virginia Merrill Bloedel Scholar award, 1992-94. Fellow AAAS, Am. Psychol. Soc., Acoustical Soc. Am. (assoc. editor Jour. 1988-92, chair medals and awards, 1992-94, v.p. 1997, Silver medal 1997, pres. 1999—); mem. Am. Acad. Arts and Scis. Office: U Wash Dept Speech & Hearing Sciences 1417 NE 42nd St # 354875 Seattle WA 98105-6247

KUHL, PAUL BEACH, lawyer; b. Elizabeth, N.J., July 15, 1935; s. Paul Edmund and Charlotte (Hetche) K.; m. Janey Mae Stadheim, June 24, 1967; children: Alison Lyn, Todd Beach. BA, Cornell U., 1957; LLB, Stanford U., 1960. Atty. Law Offices of Walter C. Kohn, San Francisco, 1961-63, Sedgwick, Detert, Moran & Arnold, San Francisco, 1963—; pro tem judge, arbitrator San Francisco Superior Ct., 1989—. Served to lt. USCG, 1961. Mem. ABA, Am. Coll. Trial Lawyers, Am. Bd. Trial Advocates, Def. Rsch. Inst., No. Calif. Assn. Def., San Francisco Trial Lawyers Assn., Am. Arbitration Assn. (mem. arbitration panel), Tahoe Tavern Property Owners Assn. (sec. 1979-81, pres. 1981-83), Lagunitas Country Club (v.p. 1995-97). Avocations: tennis, reading. Home: PO Box 1434 Ross CA 94957-1434 Office: Sedgwick Detert Moran & Arnold 1 Embarcadero Ctr Ste 1600 San Francisco CA 94111-3716

KUHL, RONALD WEBSTER, marketing executive; b. Chgo., Dec. 12, 1938; s. Robert Emerson and Kathleen (Webster) K.; m. Mary Walls, Sept. 28, 1968; children: David Douglas, Kevin Lathrop. BS in Econs., U. Pa., 1960; MBA, Harvard U., 1964. Account exec. Young & Rubicam Advt., N.Y.C., 1964-71; v.p. mgmt. supr. Young & Rubicam Advt., San Francisco, 1988-90; mgr. promotion and design The First Ch. of Christ Scientist, Boston, 1971-75; account exec. BBDO Advt., San Francisco, 1975-77; acct. supr. Ketchum Communications, San Francisco, 1977-80; dir. mktg. ComputerLand Corp., Hayward, Calif., 1985-88; v.p. mktg. communications Ventura Software Inc., San Diego, 1990-92; v.p. mktg. Castelle, Santa Clara, Calif., 1992-94; v.p. advt. and mktg. svcs. Interactive Video Enterprises, San Ramon, Calif., 1994-96; v.p. mktg. and svcs. NetSoft, Irvine, Calif., 1996-98; v.p. mktg. E-Centric, Walnut Creek, Calif., 1998—. 1st lt. U.S. Army, 1960-62. Avocations: antique collecting, tennis, swimming, travel. Office: Randolphscom 1280 Boulevard Way Walnut Creek CA 94596

KUHL, WILLIAM BERNARD, landscape architect; b. Chgo., Feb. 17, 1944; s. Otto Andrew and Mar (Kremelberg) K.; m. Rena Agnes Sarro, Sept. 2, 1970; children: Dana Nichole, Alex Andrew. B in Landscape Architecture, Syracuse U., 1967; BLA, N.Y. State Coll. Environ. Sci., 1967; postgrad., NYU. Registered architect, Conn., Fla., Md., Mass., N.J., N.Y., N.C., Ohio, Pa., S.C., Tex., Va. Landscape architect N.Y. State Dept. Transp., Babylon, 1967-68; assoc. M. Paul F. Friedberg & Assocs., N.Y.C., 1968-72; prin. Balsley, Balsley, Kuhl, N.Y.C., 1972-76, Balsley Kuhl, N.Y.C., 1976-81, William B. Kuhl, N.Y.C., 1981—; adj. prof. dept. urban landscape architecture CCNY, 1970-72; vis. lectr. Rutgers U., SUNY Syracuse, N.J. Inst. Tech., Nat. Parks Assn. Seminar. Works include landscape design for Pope John Paul II's Mass in Central Park, 1995; contbr. articles to profl. jours. Pres. Mental Health Assn. Nassau County, Hempstead, N.Y., 1996—; bd. dirs. Garden City (N.Y.) Cmty. Found., archtl. design rev. bd., 1989-96; chmn. design com. Gateway Citizens Com.; mem. Urban Design Task Force N.Y.C. Recipient more than 60 nat., state, city and mcpl. design awards including 5 nat. honor awards presented by first ladies Roslyn Carter, Nancy Reagan and Hillary Rodham Clinton. Fellow Am. Soc. Landscape Architects (pres. N.Y. chpt. 1975-77, nat. trustee 1995—, exec. com.); mem. Nat. Trust Hist. Preservation, N.Y. State Coun. Landscape Architects (chmn. ann. awards program 1993—, dir., past pres. 1976-77), Parks Coun. Bd. Dirs. (past treas. 1977-81), Kiwanis. Roman Catholic. Avocations: fly fishing, photography, painting, golf, boating. Home: 69 Pine St Garden City NY 11530-6320 Office: 126 5th Ave Rm 3C New York NY 10011-5606

KUHLER, DEBORAH GAIL, grief therapist, former state legislator; b. Moorhead, Minn., Oct. 12, 1952; d. Robert Edgar and Beverly Maxine (Buechler) Ecker; m. George Henry Kuhler, Dec. 28, 1973; children: Karen Elizabeth, Ellen Christine. BA, Dakota Wesleyan U., 1974; MA, U. N.D., 1977. Cert. grief therapist; lic. profl. counselor, S.D. Outpatient therapist Ctr. for Human Devel., Grand Forks, N.D., 1975-77; mental health counselor Community Counseling Services, Huron, S.D., 1978-88, 91-93; owner, dir. bereavement svcs. Kuhler Funeral Home, Huron, 1978—; adj. prof. Huron U., 1979-83, 90—; mem. from dist. 23 S.D. Ho. Reps., Pierre, 1987-90; mem. House Judiciary com., chair House Health and Welfare Com., Pierre, 1990. Active Beadle County Rep. Women, 1st United Meth. Ch. Named Young Alumnus of the Yr., Dakota Wesleyan U., 1989, Bus. and Profl. Women, 1989. Mem. ACA, AAUW (Achievement in Politics award 1987), PEO, Am. Mental Health Counselors Assn., Assn. for Death Edn. and Counseling, Phi Kappa Phi. Avocations: reading, breadmaking, sewing, piano. Home: 1360 Dakota Ave S Huron SD 57350-3660

KUHLER, RENALDO GILLET, museum official, scientific illustrator; b. Teaneck, N.J., Nov. 21, 1931; s. Otto August and Simonne L. (Gillet) K. BA, U. Colo., 1961. Curator of history, illustrator exhibit, miniature diorama preparator Ea. Wash. State Hist. Soc. Mus., Spokane, 1962-67; mus. illustrator N.C. State Mus. Natural History, Raleigh, 1969—; designer, executor of art work for sci. illustrations, awards, brochures, pamphlets and periodicals Dept. Agr. and Mus., N.C., 1972-74; designer 36 illustrations for Handbook of Reptiles and Amphibians of Florida, Part 1 (Ray E. Ashton), 1981; contbr. many illustrations Atlas of Freshwater Fishes of North America (David Lee), Endangered Threatened and Rare Fauna of N.C. (Ross, Rohde and Lindquist), Distribution Survey of N.C. Mammals (Lee, Funderburg and Clark); Endangered Threatened and Rare Fauna of N.C., part 1 (Mary K. Clark), Potential Effect of Oil Spills on Seabirds, etc. (Lee and Socci), Poisonous Snakes of N.C. (William M. Palmer), Reptiles of North Carolina (William M. Palmer and Alvin Braswell); gen. illustrator: American Firearms and the Changing Frontier (Waldo E. Rosebush); also contbr. to jours. and bulls.; currently working on skull illustrations for Mammals of North Carolina (Mary Kay Clark); calligrapher; creator wood handicrafts; violin maker, 1949. *Renaldo Kuhler has completed 30 years of professional service as of April 1, 1999. He si also working with an independent filmmaker, brett Ingram, who is making a documentary film on Renaldo Kuhler showing his in interview with friends and his various activities.* Renaldo Kuhler has completed 30 years of professional service as of April 1, 1999. He is also working with an independent filmmaker, Brett Ingram, who is making a documentary film on Renaldo Kuhler showing him in interview with friends and his various activities. Mem. Nat. Trust Hist. Preservation, Nat. Smokers Alliance. Democrat. Avocations: experimenting with laminated paper and models of ships and trains, carburator fittings for smoking pipes, designer hiking and summer office suits. Home: Apt 3 510 Tilden St Raleigh NC 27605-1524 Office: NC State Mus Natural Scis 210 N Salisbury St Raleigh NC 27603-1358

KUHLMAN, GLORIA JEAN, mental health and geriatric nurse, educator; b. Wichita, Nov. 9, 1949; d. Virgil D. and Gladys (Plett) Coleman; m. Thomas A. Kuhlman, Sept. 12, 1969; 1 child, Jeffrey Paul. Diploma, St. Francis Sch. Nursing, Wichita, 1974; BSN, Wichita State U., 1976, MN, 1979; D. in Nursing Sci., U. Calif., San Francisco, 1992. Cert. community coll. instr. Prof., clin. coord. Ohlone Coll., Fremont, Calif., 1979—. Mem. NLN, Alzheimers Disease Assn., Am. Soc. on Aging, Gerontol. Soc. Am., Calif. Coun. on Gerontology and Geriatrics, Nat. Coun. on Aging. E-mail: gkuhlman@ohlone.cc.ca.us. Home: 674 Giraudo Dr San Jose CA 95111-2680 Office: Ohlone Coll 43600 Mission Blvd Fremont CA 94539-5847

KUHLMAN, JAMES WELDON, retired county extension education director; b. Amarillo, Tex., Feb. 13, 1937; s. Herman and Alma Marie (Gerdsen) K.; m. Ann Bullock Davis, Dec. 23, 1967; children: Lisa Ann, Jennifer Shawn. BS, West Tex. State U., Canyon, 1959; MS, U. Nebr., 1962. Tchg. West Tex. State U., Canyon, 1958-59; grad. asst. U. Nebr., Lincoln, 1959-62; county ext. agt. U. Nebr., Kearney, 1962-67, Buffalo County ext. agt., chair, 1967-72; Worth County ext. dir. Iowa State U., Northwood, 1972-81; Cerro Gordo County ext. edn. dir. Iowa State U., Mason City, 1981-97; ret., 1997; farmer, Randall County, Tex., 1955—, Buffalo County, Nebr., 1955-97; spkr. various civic clubs, 1980—, flower garden Buchart Gardens in Victoria, Can., 1990-99. Author: The History of the Nance Hereford Ranch, 1996, The Block Pasture, 1998. Mem., past pres., past treas. No. Iowa Figure Skating Club, Mason City, 1984—; active Mason City Iowa Conv. and Visitors Bur. With U.S. Army Res., 1961-67. Recipient Disting. Pres. award Sertoma Club Internat., Kearney, Nebr., 1966, Top award Lions Club Internat., Northwood, Iowa, 1979. Mem. Nat. Assn. County Agrl. Agts. (mem. nat. com., voting dir. 1984, 90, Disting. Svc. award 1984), Nat. Assn. Ret. Fed. Employees (pres. local chpt. 1998—), Am. Hereford Assn., Iowa Hereford Assn. (dir. 1991—), Nebr. Hereford Assn., Holstein Assn. Am., North Ctrl. Geneology Club (past vice chair, pres. 1999), Rotary Club Mason City (com. chair 1988, 97—), Mason City C. of C. (agr. com. 1981—, chmn. regional issues com. 1990-91), Iowa State U. Ext. Assn. (dir. 1980s), Nat. Assn. Ret. Fed. Emoloyees (pres. chpt. 1999). Presbyterian. Avocations: cattle breeding and cattle history of Hereford breed, genealogy research, writing, art, photography. Home: 722 N Hampshire Ave Mason City IA 50401-2440

KUHLMAN, KIMBERLY ANN, clinical dietician; b. Toledo, June 30, 1954; d. James Gilbert and Jane Marie (Konczal) Schramm; m. Carl Edwin Kuhlman Jr., May 23, 1981; children: Eric, Christopher. BS in Pub. Health, U. Toledo, 1977; BS in Dietetics, Bowling Green State U., 1978; MEd in Health Edn., U. Toledo, 1988. Cert. diabetes educator. Dietetic intern Good Samaritan Hosp., Cin., 1979; dietitian, tchr. The Toledo Hosp., 1980, clinical dietitian, 1981-83, nutrition support dietitian, 1983-86; dietitian Alcohol Treatment Ctr., Toledo, 1986-87; clin. dietitian Coop. Care Unit, Toledo Hosp., 1987-88; mem. faculty W.W. Knight Family Practice, Toledo, 1988-94, Mercy Coll. N.W. Ohio, 1995—; chief clin. dietitian Mercy/St. Charles Hosp., 1995-97, diabetes educator, Endocrine & Diabetes Care Ctr., 1997—; guest lectr. Toledo Pub. Schs., 1983-84, guest speaker pvt. industry coun., 1989—; instr. Health Aware program Toledo Hosp. Community Health Project, 1980-83; mem. adv. com. Mercy Health Ptnrs. Diabetes Edn. Network. Author: (fact sheet) Home Prental Nutrition; (booklet) Pediatric Nutrition, A Guide to Sensible Eating; reviewer (nutrition pieces) Am. Acad. of Family Physicians Found., 1996—. Mem. Toledo Art Mus., Toledo Zoo, Toledo Bot. Garden; treas. Presch. Nutrition Coun. N.W. Ohio, Toledo, 1986-89, Am. Cancer Soc. Babe Zaharias Classic; Cub Scout leader Boy Scouts Am.; bd. trustees Sunset House. Recipient Patient Care award Am. Acad. Family Physicians, Soc. Tchrs. Family Medicine, Patient Care Mag., 1994. Mem. Nutrition Educators of Health Profls. Practice Group, Sports and Cardiovascular Nutritionists Practice Group of Am. Dietetics Assn., Toledo Dietetic Assn. (chmn. regulations com. 1986-88, co-chmn. membership com. 1983-84, chmn. 1984-85), Toledo Hosp. Corp. Wellness Planning Com., Ann. Conf. on Patient Edn. for AAFP (planning com.), Soc. Tchrs. of Family Medicine, Am. Assn. Diabetes Educators (pres.-elect Toledo chpt. 1998-99, pres. 1999—). Lutheran. Avocation: golf. Home: 4264 River Rd Toledo OH 43614-5528

KUHLMAN, WALTER EGEL, artist, educator; b. St. Paul, Nov. 16, 1918; s. Peter and Marie (Jensen) K.; m. Nora McCants; 1 son, Christopher; m. Tulip Chestman, April 9, 1979. Student, St. Paul Sch. Art; BS, U. Minn., 1941; postgrad., Tulane U., Académie de la Grand Chaumière, Paris, Calif. Sch. Fine Arts. mem. faculty U. Calif. Sch. Fine Arts, Stanford, U. Mich., Santa Clara (Calif.) U., U. N.Mex., Sonoma State U., Rohnert Park, Calif., (prof. emeritus, 1988—). One person shows include U. N.Mex., Walker Art Center, Mpls., The Berkshire Museum, Mass., La Jolla Museum of Contemporary Art, Calif., Santa Barbara Mus. of Art, Calif., San Francisco Mus. of Modern Art, 1958, New Arts Gallery, Houston, 1959-61, Roswell Mus. Palace of Legion of Honor, Calif., 1956, 59, 61, 62, 64, San Francisco Mus. Art, De Saisset Mus., Jonson Gallery U. N.Mex., 1963, 64, 65, Charles Campbell Gallery, San Francisco, 1981, 83, 85, Djurovich Gallery, Sacramento, The Carlson Gallery, San Francisco, 1989, Gump's Gallery, San Francisco, 1976, 1992, University Gallery, Sonoma State U., Natsoulis Gallery Davis, Calif., Albuquerque Mus. Fine Arts, 1994, George Krevsky Fine

Arts, San Francisco, 1994, 96, Robert Green Gallery, Mill Valley, Calif.; group shows include N.Y. World's Fair, St. Paul Gallery, WPA Exhibition, Lawson Galleries, San Francisco, A 1948 Portfolio: 16 Lithographs (Diebenkorn, Lobdell, Hultberg), All Annual Invitational Exhibitions, San Francisco Mus. Modern Art, 1948-58, Petit Palais Mus., Paris, San Francisco Mus. Modern Art, III Biennial of Sao Paulo, Museo de Arte Moderna, Brazil, L.A. County Mus., Mus. Modern Art, Rio de Janiero, San Francisco Mus. Modern Art, 1955, 57, 66, 76, 96, Graham Found., Chgo, L.A. County Mus., Calif. Palace of the Legion of Honor, Virginia Mus. Fine Arts, Richmond, Stanford U., Gallery, Roswell Mus., 1961, 62, Univ. Art Mus., Austin, Texas Santa Fe Mus. Fine Arts, NM, Ca. Palace of Legion of Honor, Richard L. Nelson Gallery, UC Davis, Natsoulis Gallery, Northern California Figuration Expositions Art USA, 1992, 93, 94, George Krevsky Fine Art, San Francisco, Art Mus. Santa Cruz, Calif., 1993, Pasquale Ianetti Art Galleries, San Francisco, 1994, Robert Green Fine Arts, Mill Valley, Calif. 1994, 95, Acad. Arts and Letters, N.Y. 1995; permanent Collections include: The Phillips Collection, Washington, Nat. Gallery Am. Art, Washington, Walker Art Ctr., Washington, San Francisco Mus. Modern Art, Brit. Mus., Met. Mus. Art, NAD, N.Y., others. Recipient Maestro award Calif. Arts Coun., Outstanding Calif. Working Artist and Tchr. award; fellow Tiffany Found., Graham Found., Cummington Found. Mem. Nat. Acad. Design N.Y. Studio: Indsl Ctr Bldg Studio 335 480 Gate 5 Rd Sausalito CA 94965-1461

KUHLMANN, FRED MARK, lawyer; b. St. Louis, Apr. 9, 1948; s. Frederick Louis and Mildred (Southworth) K.; m. Barbara Jane Nierman, Dec. 30, 1970; children: F. Matthew, Sarah Ann. AB summa cum laude, Washington U., St. Louis, 1970; JD cum laude, Harvard U., 1973. Bar: Mo. 1973. Assoc. atty. Stolar, Heitzmann & Eder, St. Louis, 1973-75; tax counsel McDonnell Douglas Corp., St. Louis, 1975-82, corp. asst. sec., 1977-88, corp. counsel fin. matters, 1982-87, assoc. gen. counsel, 1984-87, staff v.p., 1985-87; exec. v.p. McDonnell Douglas Health Systems Co. div. McDonnell Douglas Corp., Hazelwood, Mo., 1987-88, pres., 1988-89; pres. McDonnell Douglas Systems Integration Co. div. McDonnell Douglas Corp., Hazelwood, Mo., 1989-91; v.p., gen. counsel, sec. McDonnell Douglas Corp., St. Louis, 1991-92, sr. v.p. adminstrn., gen. counsel, sec., 1992-95, sr. v.p., gen. counsel, 1995-97; of counsel Bryan Cave, St. Louis, 1997-99; pres. Sys. Svc. Enterprises, St. Louis, 1999—; bd. dirs. Republic Health Corp., Dallas, 1988-90; mem. governing bd. Luth. Med. Ctr., 1989-95, chmn., 1990-92. Bd. dirs. Luth. Charities Assn., 1982-91, sec. 1984-86, chmn. 1986-89; elder Lutheran Ch. of Resurrection, 1977-80; mem. Regents Coun. Concordia Sem., 1981-84; chmn. cub scout pack 459 Boy Scouts Am., 1984-86; bd. dirs. Luth. High Sch. Assn., 1978-84, 91-97, pres. 1992-97, long range planning com. 1990-92, chmn. alumni assn. 1981; chmn. north star dist. Boy Scouts Am., 1990-93; bd. dirs. Mcpl. Theatre Assn., St. Louis, 1991—; chmn. long range planning com. St. Paul's Luth. Ch., 1988-91, 98—, pres., 1996-97; bd. dirs., mem. exec. com. United Way of Greater St. Louis, 1994-97, chmn. Vanguard divsn., 1994-97; mem. amb. coun. Luth. Family and Children's Svcs. of St. Louis, 1998—. Recipient Disting. Leadership award Luth. Assn. for Higher Edn., 1981. Mem. ABA, Mo. Bar Assn., Bar Assn. Met. St. Louis, Bellerive Country Club, Phi Beta Kappa, Omicron Delta Kappa. Republican. Avocations: tennis, golf, racquetball. Home: 1711 Stone Rdg Trails Dr Saint Louis MO 63122-3546 Office: Sys Svc Enterprises 795 Office Pky Saint Louis MO 63141*

KUHLMANN-WILSDORF, DORIS, physics and materials science educator; b. Bremen, Germany, Feb. 15, 1922; came to U.S., 1956.; d. A. Friedrich and Elsa S. (Dreyer) K.; m. Heinz G.F. Wilsdorf, Jan. 4, 1950; children: Gabriele, Michael. BS in Physics, U. Göttingen, Germany, 1944, MS, 1946, PhD in Materials Sci., 1947; DS in Physics-Materials Sci., U. Witwatersrand, South Africa, 1954. Postdoctoral fellow U. Göttingen, 1947-48; postdoctoral fellow in physics U. Bristol, Eng., 1949-50; lectr. physics U. Witwatersrand, Johannesburg, South Africa, 1950-56; from assoc. prof. metall. engring. to prof. U. Pa., Phila., 1957-63; prof. engring. physics U. Va., Charlottesville, 1963-66, univ. prof. applied sci., 1966—. Editor 4 materials sci. books; contbr. articles to profl. jours. Recipient J. Shelton Horsley award Va. Acad. Sci., 1966, Americanism medal DAR, 1966, Heyn medal German Metall. Soc., 1988, Achievement award Soc. Women Engrs., 1989, Ragnar Holm Sci. Achievement award IEEE, 1991. Fellow Am. Soc. Metals Internat. (life), Am. Phys. Soc.; mem. Am. Soc. Women Engrs. (life), Am. Soc. Engring. Edn. (medal for excellence 1965, 66), AIME Metall. Soc., Nat. Acad. Engring. Office: U Va Dept Physics Charlottesville VA 22901

KUHN, ALBERT JOSEPH, English educator; b. Dowell, Ill., Apr. 4, 1926; s. Albert and Elizabeth (Furjes) K.; m. Roberta Marshall, June 12, 1949; children—William, Frederick. B.A., U. Ill., 1950; Ph.D., Johns Hopkins, 1954. Mem. faculty Ohio State U., 1954—, chmn. English dept., 1964-71, prof. English, 1965, provost, v.p. acad. affairs, 1971-79, dir. Univ. Honors, 1985-89, professor emeritus, 1989—. Contbr. to Romantic Bibliography, 1963, also articles.; editor: Three Sentimental Novels, 1970, Victorian Literature and Society, 1984. Mem. region VIII Woodrow Wilson Selection Com., 1961-68; mem. research bd. Children's Hosp., 1973-77; trustee Battelle Meml. Inst. Found., 1975-79. Served with USNR, 1944-46. Recipient Disting. Svc. award Ohio State U., 1991. Mem. MLA, North Cen. Assn. Colls. and Schs. (cons.-evaluator), Kit Kat Club (Columbus), Phi Beta Kappa, Phi Kappa Phi. Home: 35 Webster Park Ave Columbus OH 43214-3512

KUHN, BOWIE K., lawyer, former professional baseball commissioner, consultant; b. Takoma Park, Md., Oct. 28, 1926; m. Luisa Hegeler; four children. B.A., Princeton, 1947; LL.B., U. Va., 1950. Bar: N.Y. 1951, U.S. Supreme Ct. 1972. With firm Willkie, Farr & Gallagher, N.Y.C.; legal counsel several baseball clients, 1950-69, rep. Maj. League club owners in negotiations with Maj. League Players Assn., 1968, commr. pro tempore of baseball, 1969, commr., 1969-84; of counsel Willkie, Farr & Gallagher, 1984-87; former ptnr. Myerson & Kuhn, N.Y.C., 1988-89; pres. The Kent Group Inc., Ponte Vedra Beach, Fla., 1990—, Sports Franchises, Inc., Milford, Conn., 1992—. Author: Hardball: The Education of a Baseball Commissioner, 1987. Office: The Kent Group Inc 136 Teal Point Ln Ponte Vedra Beach FL 32082-1935

KUHN, HANS HEINRICH, chemist; b. Uzwil, St. Gallen, Switzerland; came to U.S., 1957; d. Werner and Gretchen (Haeberle) K.; m. Edith Lilly Peyer, Aug. 28, 1954; children: Johann Heinrich, Barbara Edith. Degree in Chem. Engring., Swiss Fed. Inst. Tech., Zürich, 1949, Doctor in Sci. Tech., 1954. Postdoctoral researcher Swiss Fed. Inst. Tech., Zürich, 1954-57; rsch. chemist Dewey & Almy, Div. W.R. Grace, Cambridge, Mass., 1957-60; group leader Deering Milliken Rsch. Co., Spartanburg, S.C., 1960-61, sect. leader, 1961-65, dep. mgr., 1965-80; sr. scientist Milliken Rsch. Co., Spartanburg, S.C., 1980-95; rsch. fellow Milliken Rsch. Co., Spartanburg, 1995—. Contbr. articles to profl. jours. Consul of Switzerland for S.C. and N.C., Spartanburg, 1970-94. Recipient Olney medal Am. Assn. Textile Chemists and Colorists, 1997. Mem. Am. Chem. Soc., New Swiss Chem. Soc., Rotary. Presbyterian. Home: 176 W Park Dr Spartanburg SC 29306-5045 Office: Milliken Rd 920 Milliken Rd Spartanburg SC 29303-4906

KUHN, HOWARD ARTHUR, engineering executive, educator; b. Pitts., Dec. 6, 1940; s. Howard E. and Selma W. (Schulze) K.; m. Beverly A. Burke, Dec. 23, 1961; children: Amy Van Zant, Jeffrey, David, Stephen. BS, Carnegie-Mellon U., 1962, MS, 1963, PhD, 1966. Registered profl. engr., Pa. Prof. engring. Drexel U., Phila., 1966-74; prof. engring. U. Pitts., 1975-89, adj. prof., 1989—; dir. freshman engring. program, U. Pitts, 1981-88, industrial advisory com.; cons. engr. Deformation Control Tech., Pitts., 1980-88; tech. dir. Concurrent Techs. Corp., 1988, tech. v.p., 1989-92, v.p., chief tech. officer, 1992—; bd. dirs. Pitts. Tech. Coun. Author: Powder Forging, 1990; editor: Powder Metallurgy Processing, 1978; inventor powder metallurgy forging, aluminum plate rolling improvements. Pres. PTA, Gibsonia, Pa., 1976-77; mem. Civic Adv. Com., Gibsonia, 1978-82; chmn. Laurel Highlands Cancer Program, bd. dirs. Johnstown Chiefs Hockey Team, 1995—; dir. advanced tech. programs Cambria County Area C.C., 1994-96, bd. trustees C.C., 1996—. Fellow Am. Soc. Materials Internat. (chmn. mfg. technology, nominating com., Zay Jeffries award, Edgar C. Bain award, Campbell lecture selection com.); mem. ASME, Am. Powder Metallurgy Inst., Soc. Mfg. Engrs. Democrat. Methodist. Home: 128 McCaffrey Ln Johnstown PA 15905-5713 Office: 100 CTC Dr Johnstown PA 15904-3374

KUHN, JAMES E., judge; b. Hammond, La., Oct. 31, 1946; s. Eton Percy and Mildred Louise (McDaniel) K.; m. Cheryl Aucoin, Dec. 27, 1969; children: James M., Jennifer L. BA, Southeastern La. U., 1968; JD, Loyola U. of South, 1973. Bar: La. 1973, Colo., 1995, U.S. Supreme Ct. 1978. Asst. dist. atty. 21st Jud. Dist. La., 1980-90; judge 21st Jud. Dist. Ct., Livinston, St. Helena, Tangipahoa, 1990-95; judge Ct. Appeals (1st cir.) Baton Rouge, 1995—; instr. history, govt. and criminal justice Southeastern La. U., Hammond, 1991—; mem. appellate ct. performance and standards com. La. Supreme Ct.; lectr. in field. Founder For Our Youth; past bd. dirs. La. Coun. Child Abuse, past sec.-treas. Conf. of Ct. Appeal Judges for State of La. Recipient Am. Jurisprudence award Loyola Law Sch. Mem. ABA, La. State Bar Assn. (Professionalism and Quality of Life com.), 21st Jud. Bar Assn., Livingston Parish Bar Assn., Delta Theta Phi. Home: 8178 Hermitage Dr Denham Springs LA 70726-6224

KUHN, JILL MARIE, school psychologist; b. Utica, Apr. 27, 1973; d. Glenn Francis and Loreen Katherine (Martin) K. BA, N.Y. state tchg. cert., SUNY, Potsdam, 1995; MA, cert. advanced studies, East Carolina U., 1998. Cert. in elem. edn., N.Y. state. Tchr.'s asst. Rome (N.Y.) City Sch. Dist., 1995, sch. psychologist intern, 1997-98, sch. psychologist Denti Elem. Sch., 1998—; resident asst. SUNY, Potsdam, 1993-95; resident advisor East Carolina U., Greenville, 1995-96, grad. asst., 1995-97; ednl. diagnostician Psychol. Resources, Greenville, 1996-97. Co-author: (book chpt.) American Psychological Association Medical Reference, 1996. Patricia Endrikat scholar for sch. psychologists East Carolina U., 1995. Mem. Nat. Assn. Sch. Psychologists (Rsch. award 1997). Avocations: running, weight training, golf. Home: 2550 King Rd Sauquoit NY 13456-3306 Office: Denti Elem Sch 1001 Ruby St Rome NY 13440

KUHN, KATHLEEN JO, accountant; b. Springfield, Ill., Aug. 9, 1947; d. Henry Elmer and Norma Florene (Niehaus) Burge; m. Gerald L. Kuhn, June 22, 1968; children: Gerald Lynn, Brett Anthony. BS in Bus., Bradley U., 1969. CPA, Ill. Controller Byerly Music Co., Peoria, Ill., 1969-70; staff acct. Clifton Gunderson & Co., Columbus, Ind., 1970-71; acct. Dept. of Transp., State of Ill., Springfield, 1972-76; acct. Gerald L. Kuhn & Assocs., Springfield, 1976-78, ptnr., 1979—, quality control mgr., 1990—; grad. asst. in Dale Carnegie courses, 1979-80. Writer, editor co. policy guideline, 1979-80; editor co. quality control manual, 1990. Recipient Attendance award Continuing Profl. Edn. for Accts., 1979—. Pianist Trinity Lutheran Ch. Mem. Am. Inst. CPAs, Springfield Art Assn., Ill. Soc. CPAs, Am. Woman's Soc. CPAs, Nat. Bus. & Motivational Assn. Lutheran. Clubs: Olympic Swim, Metro. Federated Jr. Women's. Home: 2511 Westchester Blvd Springfield IL 62704-5406 Office: 2659 Farragut Dr Springfield IL 62704-1462

KUHN, MATTHEW, engineering company executive; b. Sacalaz, Banat, Romania, Mar. 19, 1936; came to U.S., 1967; s. Peter and Katherine (Gerres) K.; m. Betty Jane Ritchie, Aug. 20, 1966; children: Andrew Jason, Andrea Suzanne. BASc in Engring. Physics, Queen's U., Kingston, Ont., Can., 1962; MASc, U. Waterloo, Ont., 1963, PhDEE, 1967, D of Engring. (hon.), 1985; postgrad., Brown U., 1967-68. Supr. MTS Bell Tel. Labs., Murray Hill, N.J., 1968-73; mgr. adv. tech. BNR Ltd., Ottawa, Ont., 1973-80, dir. corp. devel., 1980-85; asst. v.p. BNR Inc., Research Triangle Park, N.C., 1985-89; pres. Microelectronics Ctr. of N.C., Research Triangle Park, 1989-94, EconTech Cons. & Rsch. Mgmt. Svcs., 1994—; adj. prof. engring. mgmt. Duke U., 1997—; presenter numerous profl. meetings. Contbr. articles to profl. jours. Mem. N.C. Bd. Sci. & Tech., 1991-94; chmn. adv. coun. Queen's U., 1983-84; chmn. engring. adv. coun. Duke U., Durham, N.C., 1989-94. Fellow IEEE (editor spl. issue Electron Devices Jour. Optoelectronics 1975). Roman Catholic. Achievements include discovery of quasi-static method measurement technique for integrated circuit development; co-development first generation fiber optics technology. Home: 2 Whisper Ln Chapel Hill NC 27514-1635 Office: EconTech PO Box 16864 Chapel Hill NC 27516-6864 *It is sometimes necessary to disagree but never to be disagreeable.*

KUHN, MERRILY A., nursing educator; b. Buffalo, June 16, 1945; d. Norbert and Audrey (Nihart) K. BSN, D'Youville Coll., 1967; MS, Canisius Coll., 1973; PhD in Rsch., Evaluation and Physiology, SUNY, Buffalo, 1981, MSN, 1983. RN, CCRN. Staff nurse Mercy Hosp., Buffalo, 1967; staff, asst. head nurse Dover (N.J.) Gen. Hosp., 1967-68; faculty adult health All Souls Hosp. Sch. Nursing, Morristown, N.J., 1968-69; instr. critical care cardiovascular/respiratory Millard Fillmore Sch. Nursing, Buffalo, 1969-77; asst. prof. D'Youville Coll., Buffalo, 1977-81; asst. prof. pathophysiology/pharmacology SUNY Grad. Nursing Sch., Buffalo, 1981-84; edn. dir. Ednl. Svcs., Hamburg, N.Y., 1980—; assoc. prof. Daemen Coll., Buffalo, 1992—; cons. in intensive care nursing, pharmacology and complementary therapies throughout U.S. and Can.; nurse, coord., programdesigner for telephone lectr. network series Comm. in Learning, Buffalo, 1976-79; presenter in field. Author: Pharmacotherapeutics: A Nursing Process Approach, 1986, 4th edit., 1998, Manual of IV Drugs, 1996, 2d edit., 1998, Manual of Critical Care Nursing, 1996, Complementary Therapies for the Health Care Provider, 1999; (games) Critical Care Challenge, 1990, 93, NCLEX Challenge Game, 1990; 2 Computer Packages IV Fast Facts and PO Fast Facts, 1992; mem. editl. bd. Critical Care Nurse, 1982-93, Jour. N.Y. State Nurses Assn., 1993—; contbr. articles to profl. jours. Bd. dirs. N.Y. State Soc. Critical Care Medicine, 1982-83, Blue Cross Western N.Y., 1980-99; pres. cardiovascular Clin. Specialist Group, 1984, v.p., 1985; mem., coun. nurses Am. Heart Assn. Named Outstanding Young Woman of Am., 1978, 80-95. Mem. ANA, AACN (editor clin. issues 1992), ANA Coun. Computer Application, N.Y. State Nurses Assn. (chmn. edn. com. dist. 1 1995—), Am. Assn. Coun. Nurse Researchers, Hypertension Control Bd. Western N.Y. (bd. dirs. 1977-92), Sigma Theta Tau. Home: 6748 Boston State Rd Hamburg NY 14075-6607

KUHN, MICHAEL, motion picture company executive. Law degree, Cambridge U., Eng. Solicitor Supreme Ct., 1974; atty. Denton, Hall & Burgin, London; legal advisor Polygram U.K., London, 1974-78, dir., 1978-83; gen. counsel Polygram Internat., London, 1983-87, sr. v.p., 1987-93; pres. Polygram Filmed Entertainment, Beverly Hills, Calif., 1991-93; exec. v.p. Polygram Holding Inc., N.Y.C., 1993—; bd. mgmt. Polygram N.V., 1993—; pres., CEO Polygram Filmed Entertainment, Beverly Hills. Office: Polygram Filmed Entertain 9333 Wilshire Blvd Beverly Hills CA 90210-5408

KUHN, PAUL HUBERT, JR., investment counsel; b. Chattanooga, Sept. 7, 1943; s. P. Hubert and Pauline Anna (Byrnes) K.; m. Jeanne Bartlett Elmore, June 7, 1966 (dec. 1996); children—Katherine, Christopher. BA, Vanderbilt U., 1965; MBA, Ind. U., 1971. Chartered investment counselor. V.p., prin. Stein Roe & Farnham, Chgo., 1971-89; v.p. Stein Roe Spl. Fund, Chgo., 1983-89; mng. ptnr. Davidson Ptnrs. Investment Counsel, Nashville, 1989—; prnt. J.C. Bradford & Co. Bd. dirs. Augustana Hosp., Chgo., 1980-83, USO of Chgo.; pres. Lincoln Park Renewal Corp., Chgo. Served to lt. USN, 1965-69. Mem. Assn. Investment Mgmt. and Rsch., Nashville Soc. Fin. Analysis (bd. dirs. 1997—), Nat. Orgn. Reform Marijuana Laws (bd. dirs. 1997—), Phi Beta Kappa, Omicron Delta Kappa. Republican. Roman Catholic. Clubs: Tavern (Chgo.) (bd. govs.), Woman's Athletic Club of Chgo. (hon.), Nashville City. Mem. Investment Analysis Soc., Tavern Club (Chgo.)(bd. govs.), Nashville City Club, Phi Beta Kappa, Omicron Delta Kappa. Republican. Roman Catholic. Office: Davidson Ptnrs Investment Counsel 330 Commerce St Nashville TN 37201-1805 Home: 104 Savoy Cir Nashville TN 37205-5013

KUHN, ROBERT HERMAN, city and county official, engineer; b. Canton, Ill., Apr. 10, 1946; s. Orval Jesse Sr. and J. Nellie (Gallien) K.; m. Marlene Elizabeth Shuffer, May 29, 1971; children: Jesse, Regina. BS, U. Ill., 1969, MS, 1975. Registered profl. engr., Mich., Ill. Engr. Crawford, Murphy & Tilley, Springfield, Ill., 1965-68; cons. Grt. Basin Engring., Ogden, Utah, 1973; pub. works engr. City of Bloomington, Ill., 1974; asst. city engr. City of Muskegon, Mich., 1975-78; asst. dir. pub. works County of Muskegon, 1978-85, dir. pub. works and utilities, 1985—; pres. K&S Component Cars, Muskegon, 1978-82; owner BoMar Commodities, Muskegon, 1982—; mem. Solid Waste Planning Bd., 1988-89, Muskegon County Dept. Pub. Works Bd., 1989-96; founder, chmn. Muskegon Internet Coun. Originator and author: City of Muskegon's Internet Home Page. Speaker, facilitator Pre-Cana Marriage Preparation Seminars, 1972—; mem. exec. bd. St. Francis deSales Parish Coun., 1985-88, Muskegon County Cooperating Chs., 1989-92; mem. Charter Study Co., 1979; guitarist ecumenical religious retreats Muskegon Correctional Facilities. With USAF, 1969-73, Panama Canal. Decorated Meritorious Svc. medal; recipient Govt. award Am. City and County Mag., 1987; named One of Outstanding Young Men Am., 1971, Recycler of Yr. Mich. Recycling Coalition, 1989; Harry H. Gunther scholar U. Ill., 1965-69. Mem. ACSE, ASPA, Am. Pub. Works Assn., Am. Water Works Assn., Nat. Assn. Fleet Mgrs., Solid Waste Assn. N.Am. Roman Catholic. Avocations: contemporary gospel guitar, basketball, coaching, motivational speaker. Home: 3080 W Sherman Blvd Muskegon MI 49441-1154 Office: City of Muskegon Pub Svc 1350 E Keating Ave Muskegon MI 49442-6183

KUHN, ROBERT MITCHELL, rubber company executive; b. N.Y.C., May 9, 1942; s. Robert M. and Marie (Mildenberger) K.; m. Edda Clorinda Barsotti, Sept. 7, 1968; children—Marisa A., Michele T. B.A. in Psychology, Alfred U., 1964; M.B.A., NYU, 1970. Various fin. and operational positions Singer Co., Stamford, Conn., 1970-75, United Techs., Hartford, Conn., 1975-82; exec. v.p., dir. Armstrong Rubber Co., New Haven, 1982; pres. Dayco Products, Inc., Dayton, Ohio, 1986—; bd. dirs. Copolymer Rubber & Chem. Corp., Baton Rouge. Served to capt. USMC, 1964-68, Vietnam. Republican. Roman Catholic. Home: 9 Christmas Tree Ln Southport CT 06490-1313 Office: Goss Graphics Systems 700 Oakmont Ln Westmont IL 60559-5551

KUHN, ROSEANN, sports association administrator. Staff mem. Women's Internat. Bowling Congress, Greendale, Wis., 1974-96, exec. dir., 1996—. Office: Womens Internat Bowling Congress (WIBC) 5301 S 76th St Greendale WI 53129-1128

KUHN, RYAN ANTHONY, information industry investment banker; b. Framingham, Mass., Sept. 15, 1947; s. Robert Anthony Kuhn and Julia (Scott) McMillan; m. Cynthia Lynn DeVore, June 4, 1988; 1 child, Ryan R. BA in Psychology, Trinity Coll., Hartford, Conn., 1970; MBA, Harvard U., 1979. Mgr. corp. acquisitions McGraw-Hill, N.Y.C., 1979-85; sr. assoc. venture capital Golder, Thoma & Cressey, Chgo., 1985-86; pres. Reid Psychol. Systems, Chgo., 1986-90, Lilly Pulitzer, Chgo., 1990-93; prin. Kuhn & Assocs., Chgo., 1990—. Contbr. articles to profl. publs. and mags.; guest spkr. TV and radio talk show. Bd. dirs. Infant Welfare Soc. Chgo., Harvard Bus. Sch. of Chgo. Republican. Episcopalian. Office: Kuhn and Assocs 205 W Wacker Dr Ste 500 Chicago IL 60606-1212

KUHN, WILLIS EVAN, II, lawyer, mediator; b. Indpls., July 20, 1948; s. Theodore Roosevelt and Theresa Anne (Lupinacci) K.; m. Virginia Katherine Williams, Apr. 12, 1983; children: William Franklin, Virginia Anne. BA, Vanderbilt U., 1970; JD with honors, U. Tex., 1973. Bar: Tex. 1973; cert. mediator. Assoc. Johnson & Gibbs, Dallas, 1973-75, Moore & Peterson, Dallas, 1975-80; ptnr. Baker, Smith & Mills, Dallas, 1980-85, Kuhn & Fishman, Dallas, 1985-90, Hopkins & Sutter, Dallas, 1990-93; pvt. practice Dallas, 1993—. Counselor, v.p. Trinity Presbyn. Ch., Plano, Tex., 1990—; mem. Dallas So. Meml. Assn., 1992—. Mem. State Bar Tex., Dallas Bar Assn., Dallas Athletic Club, Order of Coif, Phi Kappa Psi. Republican. Avocations: golf, history. Home: 4118 Briargrove Ln Dallas TX 75287-6601 Office: 5550 LBJ Fwy Ste 400 Dallas TX 75240-6228*

KUHNS, CRAIG SHAFFER, business educator; b. Spokane, Wash., Apr. 14, 1928; s. Theodore Lewis and Audrey Grace (Shaffer) K. BS, U. Calif., Berkeley, 1950, BA, 1954, MBA, 1955. Analyst Standard Oil Co. of Calif., San Francisco, 1955-57; bus. educator U. Calif./San Jose State U., 1958-63, City Coll. of San Francisco, 1963—; adj. faculty U. San Francisco, 1977-90. 1st lt. U.S. Army, 1951-52, col. Mil. Intelligence USAR, 1953-80, col. AUS, ret. Mem. Calif. Alumni Assn., U.S. Army War Coll. Alumni Assn., Res. Officers Assn., Japan Soc. Republican. Avocation: travel. Home: 8 Locksley Ave Apt 8A San Francisco CA 94122-3850 Office: City Coll of San Francisco 50 Phelan Ave San Francisco CA 94112-1821

KUHNS, LARRY J., horticulturist, educator. Prof. ornamental horticulture Pa. State U., University Park. Recipient Outstanding Extension educator award, 1992. Office: Dept of Horticulture Tyson Bldg The Penn State U University Park PA 16802*

KUHNS, NANCY EVELYN, minister; b. Coaldale, Pa., June 5, 1947; d. Calvin Joseph and Helen Mary (Gerber) K.; m. Rodney W. Miller (div. 1975). BS in Bible, United Wesleyan Coll., 1969; MS in Early Childhood Edn., Marywood Coll., 1982; MDiv, Lancaster (Pa.) Theol. Sem., 1987. Ordained to ministry United Ch. of Christ, 1988. Organist, choir dir. Zion Stone Ch. of Snyder's, New Ringgold, Pa., 1976-86; pastor Rebersburg (Pa.) Charge United Ch. of Christ, 1987—; Gen. Synod Del., 1993, 95; dir. day care ctr. Jim Thorpe and Lehighton, Pa., 1976-86. Bd. dirs. Pa. Cen. Conf., United Ch. of Christ, 1991-93, chair ch. and ministry com., 1996-99. Home: PO Box 156 Rebersburg PA 16872-0156

KUHRAU, EDWARD W., lawyer; b. Caney, Kans., Apr. 19, 1935; s. Edward E. and Dolores (Hardman) K.; m. Janiece Christal; children: Quentin, Clayton. BA, U. Tex., 1960; JD, U. So. Calif., 1965. Bar: Calif. 1966, Wash. 1968, Alaska 1977. With Perkins Coie (and predecessor firms), Seattle, 1968—, ptnr., 1973—. Editor-in-chief Wash. Real Property Deskbook; contbr. articles to profl. jours. With USAF, 1955-58. Mem. ABA, Wash. Bar Assn., Am. Coll. Real Estate Lawyers, Pacific Real Estate Inst. (pres., founding trustee), Order of Coif, Seattle Yacht Club. Office: Perkins Coie 1201 3rd Ave Fl 40 Seattle WA 98101-3000

KUHRMEYER, CARL ALBERT, manufacturing company executive; b. St. Paul, May 12, 1928; s. Carl and Irma Luella (Lindeke) K.; m. Janet E. Pedersen, Oct. 31, 1953; children: Karen Graden, John, Paul. BSME, U. Minn., 1949. Registered profl. engr., Minn. Design engr. Magney, Tusler & Setter, St. Paul, 1950-51; with 3M Co., St. Paul, 1951-93, successively product devel. engr., machine devel. engr., project leader, copy machine prodn. supr., process engring. and contracting supr., process engring. mgr., project mgr., until 1964, tech. dir., 1964-66, div. v.p., 1967-70, corp. group v.p., 1970-80, corp. v.p., 1980-93; bd. dirs., chmn. bd. Product Level Control, Eagan, Minn., 1995—; bd. dirs. 1-800-TAKE-OFF, North Palm Beach, Fla. Patentee in field. Mem. nat. adv. coun. Nat. Multiple Sclerosis Soc., 1973—; trustee United Theol. Sem., St. Paul, 1986—; bd. dirs. Minn. Protestant Found., St. Paul, 1987—, pres., 1997—; bd. dirs. Minn. Pvt. Coll. Fund, St. Paul, 1986-95, St. Paul Winter Carnival Assn., 1987-93, chmn., dir., 1990-91; bd. dirs., v.p. Family Resources Devel. Inc., St. Paul. Mem. St. Paul C. of C. (bd. dirs. 1988-95, chmn. bd. 1993), Minn. Club (bd. dirs. 1994—), White Bear Yacht Club (bd. dirs. 1995-97), North Oaks Country Club (bd. dirs. 1981-83, pres. 1983), Osman Temple. Mem. United Church of Christ. Office: 3050 Minnesota World Trade Ctr 30 7th St E Saint Paul MN 55101-4914

KUHRT, SHARON LEE, nursing administrator; b. Denver, July 20, 1957; d. John Wilfred and Yoshiko (Ueda) K. BSN, Loretto Heights Coll., 1982; MSN, Regis U., 1992. RN, Colo., Mass., Maine. RN level III Porter Meml. Hosp., Denver, 1981-87; transport supr. Kapiolani Med. Ctr. for Women & Children, Honolulu, 1987-89; dir. patient care unit Aspen Valley Hosp., Colo., 1989-91; dir. clin. practice Ctrl. Maine Med. Ctr., Lewiston, 1991—. Mem. ANA (cert. in pediat. nursing and nursing adminstrn.). Home: 27 Chandler Mill Rd New Gloucester ME 04260-4041

KUIPER, DOUGLAS SCOTT, insurance executive; b. Grand Rapids, Mich., Sept. 15, 1960; s. David Alan and Mary Ann (Oosterhouse) K.; m. Barbara Ann Bredeweg, Aug. 23, 1985; children: Staci Lynn, Matthew James. BS, Grand Valley State U., 1982. Chartered life underwriter, chartered fin. cons. Agt. Kuiper Ins. Svcs., Grand Rapids, 1982-83; employee benefits specialist Shield Ins. Agy., Grand Rapids, 1983-88; pres. Shield Benefit Adminstrs., Grand Rapids, 1989-98; sr. acct. exec. Shield Benefit Adminstrs., 1999—, Nat. City Ins. Group, Inc., Grand Rapids, 1999—. Mem. Nat. Assn. Life Underwriters, Nat. Assn. Health Underwriters, Western Mich. Chpt. CLUs and ChFCs (membership com. 1987-88), Western Mich. Estate Planning Coun., Grand Rapids Assn. Life Underwriters. Republican. Avocations: skeet shooting, bicycling, snowmobiling, hunting. Fax: (616) 235-1334. Office: Nat City Ins Group Inc 945 Forest Hill Ave SE Grand Rapids MI 49546

KUIVINEN, NED ALLAN, pathologist; b. Mt. Vernon, Ohio, May 19, 1936; s. Thomas Oscar and Pauline Ruthella (Pealer) K.; m. Deborah Berle Miller, Feb. 5, 1972; children: David Joseph, Matthew Thomas. BS, Ohio State U., 1958, MD, 1962. Diplomate Am. Bd. Pathology. Pathologist St. Joseph's Hosp., Phoenix, 1969-98; dir. clin. lab. W. O. Boswell Meml. Hosp., Sun City, Ariz., 1970-98; pathologist D. E. Webb Meml. Hosp., Sun City, Ariz., 1988-98; dir. clin. lab. Vencor Hosp. Phoenix, Youngtown, Ariz., 1990-92, ret., 1998. Lt. comdr. U.S. Navy, 1966-68. Fellow Am. Soc. Clin. Pathology, Coll. Am. Pathology; mem. Ariz. Med. Assn., Ariz. Soc. Pathologists (pres. 1993-95). Avocations: musical instruments, windsurfing, skiing. Home: 4757 E Valley Vista Ln Paradise Vly AZ 85253-4068 Office: Pathology Assocs Ltd 49 E Thomas Rd Ste 101 Phoenix AZ 85012-3104

KUJALA, WALFRID EUGENE, musician, educator; b. Warren, Ohio, Feb. 19, 1925; s. Arvo August and Elsie Fannie (Ojajarvi) K.; m. Sherry Henry, Dec. 29, 1989; children by previous marriage: Stephen, Gwen, Daniel. MusB, Eastman Sch. Music, 1948, MusM, 1950. Flutist Rochester Philharm. Orch., 1948-54; soloist, flutist, piccoloist Chgo. Symphony Orch., 1954—; prof. flute Northwestern U., Evanston, Ill., 1962—; vis. prof. of flute Shepherd Sch. Music, Rice U., 1995-97. Author: The Flutist's Progress, 1970, The Flutist's Vade Mecum of Scales, Arpeggios, Trills and Fingering Technique, 1995; consulting editor Flute Talk Mag., 1991—; contbr. articles to profl. jours.; performed world premiere of Concerto for Flute by Gunther Schuller with Chgo. Symphony Orch., conducted by Sir Georg Solti, 1988. Served with AUS, 1943-45, ETO, PTO. Recipient Exemplar of Music Teaching award Northwestern U., 1992. Mem. Nat. Flute Assn. (past pres., Lifetime Achievement award 1997). Office: Sch Music Northwestern U Evanston IL 60208

KUJAWA, LORRAINE FRANCES, elementary educator; b. Bklyn., Dec. 15, 1942; d. Alexander and Lillian (Simchik) K. Student, Bloomsburg (Pa.) Coll., 1965; MEd, Eindboro (Pa.) U., 1973. Tchr. Susquenita Sch. Sys., Marysville, Pa., 1965-66, Ctrl. Dauphin Sch. Sys., Harrisburg, Pa., 1966-97. Editor Harrisburg Area Women's News, 1978-81, Lavender Letter, 1982-92 (outstanding svc. awards 1987, 92); corr. Shippensburg Sentinel. Mem. various coms. Women's Ctr.; mem. fin. com. Ctrl. Pa. Women's Chorus. Recipient award for excellence in edn. PTA, Harrisburg, Pa., 1997. Mem. NEA, Harrisburg Arts Factory. Unitarian-Universalist. Avocations: writing, poetry, gardening, painting, travel. Home: 125 Pugh Dr Shippensburg PA 17257-9297

KUJAWSKI, ELIZABETH SZANCER, art curator, consultant; b. N.Y.C., Feb. 7, 1951; d. Henryk and Irene (Zilz) Szancer; m. Nathan Kujawski, Mar. 25, 1973; children: Melissa, Stephanie. BA cum laude in Art History and Italian, Douglass Coll., 1972; MA in Art History, Queens Coll., 1975. Info. asst. Whitney Mus. Am. Art, N.Y.C., 1972-75; asst. curator Collection of Nelson A. Rockefeller, N.Y.C., 1975-79; asst. dir. SKT Galleries, Inc., N.Y.C., 1979-82; prin., art curator, cons. Elizabeth S. Kujawski-Curatorial Cons., N.Y.C., 1982—. Mem. Nat. Assn. Corp. Art Mgmt., Assn. Profl. Art Advisors (pres. 1998-2000), Art Table, Inc. Avocations: tennis, piano, travel. Office: 767 5th Ave Ste 4200 New York NY 10153-0023

KUK, MICHAEL LOUIS, protective services official; b. Clinton, Iowa, Jan. 11, 1949; s. Louis and Mary Ann (Popdan) K. MS, Columbia Pacific U., 1988; PhD Religion, Univeral Life Ch. U., 1999. Cert. emergncy med. tech., safety splst., fire officer IV, inspector II, Instr. II, HazMat tech., fire and arson investigator. Firefighter, emergency med. tech. Clinton (Iowa) Fire Dept., 1972-76; fire safety tech. Olin Chems., Lake Charles, La., 1976-81; fire chief PPG Industries, Westlake, La., 1979-81, Ward 1 Fire Dist., Moss Bluff, La., 1976-85; CEO, founder On Fire Cons., Clinton, 1985-89; fire chief Savanna (Ill.) Army Depot, 1989—. Author: M.A.C.I. Modifications, 1993, 97; contbr. articles to profl. jours. Guest spkr. Fire Svc. Caucus, Washington, 1997. With U.S. Army, 1969-71; civilan firefighter, 1998. Recipient Purple Heart of Firefighting, Internat. Fire Inst., 1992; named Firefighter of Yr. VFW, 1982, 83, 84. Mem. Internat. Assn. Fire Chiefs, Musicians Union #67. Roman Catholic. Avocations: music, collecting firefighting memorabilia. Home: 652 8th Ave S Clinton IA 52732-5608 Office: Savanna Army Depot Activity 3700 Army Depot Rd Savanna IL 61074-9636

KUKLA, EDWARD RICHARD, rare books and special collections librarian, lecturer; b. Detroit, Jan. 31, 1941; s. Stanley Frank and ClaraBelle (Morton) K. BA, Wayne State U., 1962; MA, U. Mich., 1963, M.L.S., 1973. Teaching fellow U. Mich., Ann Arbor, 1963-66; asst. instr. Mich. State U., 1970-72; media mobile librarian State Library Mich., 1972; asst. librarian rare books and manuscripts Greenfield Village and Henry Ford Mus., Dearborn, Mich., 1974-78; rare books and spl. collections librarian Wash. State U., Pullman, 1979-86; head spl. collections dept., Mpls. Pub. Library, 1987—, Mpls. Athenaeum librarian; educator, lectr. rare books, history of books and printing, book collecting; reviewer NEH. Recipient Mich. Jr. Acad. Sci., Arts, and Letters membership, 1958, C. Allen Harlan Scholarship Fgn. Lang. medal of distinction. Mem. ALA, Am. Film Inst. (charter), Assn. Coll. and Research Libraries (rare books sect., 1990 local arrangements com.), U. Mich. Sch. Library Sci. Alumni Assn., Am. Contract Bridge League, Am. Cut Glass Assn., Am. Film Inst. (charter), Am. Swedish Inst., Haviland Collectors Internationale Found., Pickard Collectors Club (charter), Walker Art Ctr., Inst. Arts, Mpls. Friends of Libr. Assn., Mpls. Libr. Staff Assn., Minn. Library Assn., Phi Beta Kappa, Sigma Delta Pi, Beta Phi Mu. Clubs: Ampersand, U. Mich. Union (life), Book Club Washington. Author: Un estudio critico sobre Altazor de Vicente Huidobro, 1963; The Scholar and the Future of the Research Library Revisited, 1973; The Struggle and the Glory: A Special Bicentennial Exhibition, 1976. Home: 2439 3rd Ave S Apt C-11 Minneapolis MN 55404-3518 Office: Mpls Pub Library/Info Ctr 300 Nicollet Mall Minneapolis MN 55401-1925

KUKLA, JON (KEITH), historian, museum director; b. Hustisford, Wis., Oct. 20, 1948; s. James George and Marion Ruth (Woelm) K.; m. Jeanette Margita Vos, May 30, 1970 (div. Dec. 1991); children: Amy Marie, Jennifer Anne; m. Kathryn Fay Prechter, Oct. 30, 1993; 1 child, Elizabeth Ross. AB in History with honors, Carthage Coll., 1970; MA in History, U. Toronto, Ont., Can., 1971, PhD in History, 1980. Rsch. asst. State Archivist of Va., 1973-74; editor Va. Cavalcade mag. Va. State Libr., 1974-76; dir. publs. Va. State Libr. and Archives, 1976-90; curator collections Hist. New Orleans Collection, 1990-92, dir., 1992-98; writer, 1998—; tchr. U. Richmond, Va. Commonwealth U., U. New Orleans; vis. instr. history Carthage Coll., 1973; chair Planning Com. for the La. Purchase Bicentenary; hist. advisor Spkr. of Ho. of Dels., and Gen. Assembly's Joint Subcom. on 200th Anniversary of Capitol of Va., 1984-90; hist. advisor Citizens Adv. Coun. Interpreting and Furnishing Exec. Mansion Va., 1985-90; mus. cons. Yorktown Victory Ctr., Jamestown-Yorktown Found., 1989-93, co-dir. summer inst. Bill of Rights secondary and mid.-sch. tchrs., 1992, co-dir. summer inst. New Orleans through its Sources, 1997; exhbn. evaluator La. State Mus., 1991; exhbn. curator Over Here! The New Orleans Home Front in World War II, 1992; mem. prize jury 3d ann. mus. prize Am. Assn. Mus., 1992; mem. vis. com. visual arts dept. Loyola U., 1993—, chair curriculum subcom., 1994; mem. Jamestown Rediscovery Adv. Com., 1993—; spkr. in field. Author: Speakers and Clerks of the Virginia House of Burgesses, 1643-1776, 1981, Political Institutions in Virginia, 1619-1660, 1989, (with Elizabeth R. Herbener) The General Assembly of Virginia, 11 January 1978-27 April 1989: A Register of Members, 1990; editor, contbr.: The Bill of Rights: A Lively Heritage, 1987; editor The Wonder and Terror of Clarence John Laughlin in Haunter of Ruins, 1997, Bill Russell: Good String in Jazz Scarpbook, 1998; prodr. (documentary) The Long Weekend, 1993, Brothers in Art, 1996; mem. adv. coun. Biographical Dictionary of Early Pennsylvania Legislators, 1984-90; mem. editorial adv. bd. Va. Mag. History and Biography, 1982-84; The Papers of Sir William Berkeley, 1989—; contbr. chpts. to books and articles to profl. jours. Mem. history news svc., state rev. bd. Va. Hist. Landmarks Commn., 1979-86, vice-chair, 1980-83, 87, chair, 1983-86; mem. gov.'s planning com. bicentennial of U.S. Constn. U. Va. Inst. Govt., 1982-85; mem. selection com. Va. Ctr. Humanities, 1986-87; mem. steering com. La. Ctr. Book, 1993-95; bd. dirs. Va. Co. Found., 1989-92, mem. exec. com., 1989-90. Travel-to-Collections grantee NEH, 1984; fellow U. Toronto, 1970-71. Mem. Am. Hist. Assn. (mem. program com. 1987, Michael Kraus rsch. grantee 1991-92), Nat. Trust Hist. Preservation, Va. Hist. Soc., La. Hist. Soc. (chair by-laws com. 1993, chair Kemper and Leila Williams prize com. 1994—), La. Assn. Mus. (mem. coun. 1991-93), So. Hist. Assn. (mem. program com. 1985, mem. membership com. 1992), Assn. Documentary Editing (dir. publs. 1979-80, mem. coun. 1979-80, mem. publs. com. 1981-83, mem. edn. com. 1986-87). Lutheran. Avocations: swimming, sailing. Office: Hist New Orleans Collection 533 Royal St New Orleans LA 70130-2113*

KUKLIN, ANTHONY BENNETT, lawyer; b. N.Y.C., Oct. 9, 1929; s. Norman B. and Deane (Cable) K.; m. Vivienne May Hall, Apr. 4, 1964; children: Melissa, Amanda. AB, Harvard U., 1950; JD, Columbia U., 1953. Bar: N.Y. 1953, D.C. 1970. Assoc. Dwight, Royall, Harris, Koegel & Caskey, N.Y.C., 1955-61; assoc. Paul, Weiss, Rifkind, Wharton & Garrison, N.Y.C., 1961-69, ptnr., 1969-95, counsel, 1995—; lectr. in Law, Columbia Law Sch., 1997—; bd. dirs. Chgo. Title & Trust Co., Chgo. Title Ins. Co., 1986-96. Contbr. articles to legal jours. Mem. ABA (chmn., sec. real property, probate and trust law 1987-88), Internat. Bar Assn. (chmn. div. one 1985-88), N.Y. State Bar Assn. (chmn. sect. real property 1981-82), Assn. of Bar of city of N.Y., Am. Coll. Real Estate Lawyers (pres. 1981-82), Anglo-Am. Real Property Inst. (chmn. 1989), Am. Coll. Constrn. Lawyers. Home: 22 Pryer Ln Larchmont NY 10538-4022 Office: Paul Weiss Rifkind Wharton & Garrison Ste # 4200 1285 Ave of Ams Fl 22 New York NY 10019-6065

KUKLINSKI, JOAN LINDSEY, librarian; b. Lynn, Mass., Nov. 28, 1950; d. Richard Jay and M. Claire (Murphy) Card; m. Walter S. Kuklinski, June 17, 1972. BA cum laude, Mass. State Coll., Salem, 1972; MLS, U. R.I., 1976. Classified librarian U. R.I. Extension Divsn. Libr., Providence, 1974-75, U. R.I. Cataloging Dept., Kingston, 1975-79; original cataloger Tex. A&M U. Libr., College Station, 1979-82; cataloger Goldfarb Libr., Braindeis U., Waltham, Mass., 1982-83; automation coord. Goldfarb Libr., Braindeis U., Waltham, 1983-85; exec. dir. Minuteman Libr. Network, Framingham, Mass., 1985-96, C/W Mars, Inc., Paxton, Mass., 1996—. Mem. Town of South Kingstown (R.I.) Women's Adv. Commn., 1977-79; trustee Princeton (Mass.) Pub. Libr., 1994—; mem. strategic planning com. for libr. svc. in yr. 2000 Mass. Bd. Libr. Commrs. Mem. ALA (resources and tech. svcs. divsn. 1980-85), Mass. Librs. Assn., New Eng. Libr. Assn., Libr. Info. Tech. Assn., Assn. Specialized Libr. and Coop. Groups (NELINET Bd. 1994—), Am. Contract Bridge League, Delta Tau Kappa. Office: C/W Mars Inc 1 Sunset Ln Paxton MA 01612-1105

KUKLOK, KEVIN B., career officer; b. Fargo, N.D., Dec. 20, 1946; m. Diana Lynn Roper; children: Nicole, Bryce. BS in Chem. Engring., U. N.D., 1968; MBA, U.S. Internat. U., San Diego; grad., Naval Aviation Flight Tng., Pensacola, Fla., 1969, Amphibious Warfare Sch., 1979. Commd. 2nd lt. USMC, 1968, advanced through grades to maj. gen., 1997; assigned to UH-1E helicopter transition HML-267, 1969; with HML-367, 1970-71; forward air contr. 2nd Bn. 7th Marines; with 4th Marine Aricraft Wing with HMA-773, Santa Ana, Calif., 1973-76; tng. officer CH-46 helicopter with HMM-766 Selfridge ANG Base, Mount Clemens, Mich.; with S-1 and maintenance dept. HMM-774, Norfolk, Va.; comdg. officer H&MS-41 Det B, 1986-88, HMM-764, 1988-92; dep. comdr., mobilization coord. MAG-46; dir. readiness and safety 4th Marine Aircraft Wing MARRESFOR, New Orleans; comdg. gen. Reserve Marine Air Ground Task Force East Command Element, Camp Lejeune, N.C., 4th Marine Aircraft Wing, New Orleans. Decorated Air medal with Numeral 66. Office: 4th Marine Aircraft Wing 4400 Dauphine St New Orleans LA 70146 also: Hdqs Marine Corps Divsn Pub Affairs Washington DC 20380-1775*

KUKOC, TONI, professional basketball player; b. Croatia, Sept. 18, 1968. Forward Chicago Bulls. Named European Player of the Yr., NBA Sixth Man of the Yr., 1995-96. Avocations: yachting, fishing, tennis, golf, movies. Office: Chicago Bulls 1901 W Madison St Chicago IL 60612*

KUKOVICH, ALLEN GALE, legislator, lawyer; b. Greensburg, Pa., Sept. 5, 1947; s. Albert Francis and Catherine Thelma (Heasley) K.; m. Nancy Ruth Egeberg, Nov. 23, 1991; 1 child, Alexandra Gale. BA in Polit. Sci., Kent State U., 1969; JD, Duquesne U., 1973. Bar: Pa. 1973. Pvt. practice, 1973-77; state legislator State of Pa., 1977—; pvt. practice North Huntingdon, Pa., 1995—. Bd. dirs. Americans for Dem. Action, Childrens Trust Fund; pres. Pa. Inst. on Pub. Policy; Sta. QED-TV bd. dirs. Pub. Broadcasting. Mem. Pa. Bar Assn. (legal svcs. to the pub. com.), Westmoreland County Bar Assn. Office: Senate Box 203039 185 Capitol Bldg Harrisburg PA 17120*

KUKURA, RITA ANNE, elementary school educator; b. Tulsa, July 18, 1947; d. James Albert and Carmen Alberta (Parsons) Hayden; m. Joel Richard Graft, Oct. 28, 1967 (dec. Apr. 1969); m. Raymond Richard Kukura, Dec. 18, 1971 (div. 1981); children: Tiffany Carmen Noel, Austin Raymond. BS, Kent State U., 1971; MS, Okla. State U., 1991. Cert. early childhood, nursery, elem. tchr., Okla., spl. edn. tchr. for emotionally disturbed. Tchr. kindergarten Southlyn Elem. Sch., Lyndhurst, Ohio, 1971-73; elem. tchr. Wakefield Acad., Tulsa, 1981-83, tchr. kindergarten, 1983-87; reg. early intervention coord. Okla. Dept. Edn., Tulsa, 1990-92; tchr. devel. delayed children, coord. integrated program Child Devel. Inst. Children's Med. Ctr., Tulsa, 1992-93; tchr. elem. sch. Prue (Okla.) Schs., 1993-95, Tulsa Pub. Schs., 1995—; manuscript reviewer for profl. orgns., 1989-91; mem. human rights com. Ind. Opportunities of Okla., 1995—; Oklahoma Edn. Assn. Leadership Acad., 1998; del. Okla. Edn. Assembly, 1995; grant reviewer for spl. grants State Dept. Edn., 1996; presenter and lectr. in field. Den leader Cub Scouts Am., Tulsa, 1984-88; com. mem. Boy Scouts Am., Tulsa, 1984-88; vol. office worker Met. Tulsa Citizen Crime Commn., 1986; adv. com. Latchkey Project, Tulsa County, 1985; ad hoc task force on day care Interagy, Coord. Coun., 1989-91; nat. rep. Tourette Syndrome Assn. to Nat. Broadcasting Assn. AERho, 1990-93; mem. resource com. Ronald McDonald House, 1990-92, vol. Tulsa area, 1991-97, STARBASE, 1993—, Drug Edn. for Youth, 1994; mem. adv. bd. Tulsa Regional Coordinating Coun. for Svcs. to Children and Youth and Families, 1991-92; planning com. symposium Magic Coun. Girl Scouts Am., 1991-93; lt. sr. mem. Tulsa Composite Squadron CAP, 1992-94; active Human Rights Com. for Ind. Opportunities, 1995—; presenter numerous confs.; workshop participant Alternatives to Violence Project, 1996. Recipient Den Leader Tng. award Boy Scouts Am., 1988. Mem. AAUW (bd. dirs. Tulsa county chpt. 1991-93, mem., 1997—), Nat. Assn. Early Childhood Tchr. Educators, Nat. Tourette Syndrome Assn. (state pres. 1987-92, state dir. 1992-93, hon. mem. bd. dirs. 1993, area coord., fundraiser 1988-90), Gold Star Wives Am., Tulsa Classroom Tchrs. Assn. (bldg. del. 1997-98), Okla. Edn. Assn. (leadership acad. 1998), Okla. Edn. Assn. (mem. resolution com. 1998—), Kappa Delta Pi, Omicron Nu, Alpha Epsilon Rho (hon. mem. S.W. region 1990-93), Phi Delta Kappa. Roman Catholic. Avocations: piano, excercising, reading. Office: Anderson Elem Sch 1921 E 29th St N Tulsa OK 74110-1728

KULAKOWSKI, BOHDAN TADEUSZ, mechanical engineering educator; b. Piotrkow Trybunalski, Poland, June 23, 1942; came to U.S., 1979; s. Tadeusz and Krystyna (Kolacinska) K.; m. Barbara Elzbieta Gluszkiewicz, Oct. 29, 1964; children: Dorota Anna Smith, Dominik. MS in Engring., Warsaw (Poland) Tech. U., 1966; PhD, Polish Acad. Scis., Warsaw, 1972. Rsch. asst., rsch. assoc., then head rsch. group Inst. Glass and Ceramics, Warsaw, 1965-74; head process control div. Computer Ctr. for Bldg. Industry, Warsaw, 1975-79; assoc. prof. mech. engring. Pa. State U., University Park, 1979-91, prof., 1991—, dir. Pa. Transp. Inst., 1992—; bd. dirs. Transp. Safety Rsch. Alliance, Pitts., 1992—; cons. Micromation Sys. Inc., Airline Pilots Assn., ins. cos.; univ. liaison Transp. Rsch. Bd., Washington, 1994—. Author: (with J.L. Shearer) Dynamic Modeling and Control of Engineering Systems, 1990; editor: Vehicle-Road Interaction, 1994; contbr. articles to profl. jours. Recipient premiere tchg. award Pa. State U. Engring. Soc., 1994; UN Econ. Commn. for Europe fellow U. York, Eng., 1974; Fulbright scholar, 1979. Mem. ASME, ASHRAE, Am. Soc. for Engring. Edn., Soc. Automotive Engrs., Pi Tau Sigma (hon.). Achievements include design of Pennsylvania Transportation Institute drag sled tester to measure slip resistance of walking surfaces. Office: Pa State U Pa Transp Inst 201 Rsch Office Bldg University Park PA 16802*

KULAS, FREDERICK JOHN, computer company executive; b. Hanover, N.J., June 27, 1951; s. Walenty William and Liliane Maria (Cailliatte) K.; m. Mary Catherine Rodock, July 19, 1987. BSME, Worcester Poly. Inst., 1973; MBA, Harvard U., 1977; grad., GE Mfg. Mgmt. Program, 1975. Registered Engr. in Tng., Mass. Mfg. mgr. GE, Schenectady, N.Y., 1973-74, Plainville, Conn., 1974-75; mktg. rep. IBM Corp., Waltham, Mass., 1977-80; product mktg. mgr. Digital Equipment Corp., Hudson, Mass., 1980-82; product mgr. Digital Equipment Corp., Stow, Mass., 1982-84; mktg. mgr. Digital Equipment Corp., Westborough, Mass., 1984-87, mktg. programs mgr., 1987-89; mktg. mgr. Digital Equipment Corp., Marlborough, Mass., 1989-92; software bus. mgr. Digital Equipment Corp., Stow, 1992-95, sys. bus. mgr., 1995-98; software bus. mgr. Compaq Computer Corp., Stow, 1998—. Class agt. ann. alumni fund Worcester Poly. Inst. Mem. Harvard Bus. Sch. Club Boston, Pi Tau Sigma. Republican. Roman Catholic. Avocations: tennis, golf, photography, music. Home: 9 Travis Dr Framingham MA 01702-6131 Office: Compaq Computer Corp 40 Old Bolton Rd Stow MA 01775-1215

KULCINSKI, GERALD LAVERNE, nuclear engineer, educator; b. La Crosse, Wis., Oct. 27, 1939; s. Harold Franklin and June Kramer K.; m. Janet Noreen Berg, Nov. 25, 1961; children: Kathryn, Brian, Karen. BS in Chem. Engring., U. Wis., 1961, MS in Nuclear Engring., 1962, PhD in Nuclear Engring., 1965. Rschr. Los Alamos (N.Mex.) Nuclear Lab., 1963; lectr. Ctr. Grad. Study, Richland, Wash., 1965-71; sr. rsch. sci. Battelle Northwest Lab., Richland, 1965-71; prof. U. Wis., Madison, 1972—, dir. Fusion Tech. Inst., 1973-75, 79—, Grainger Prof. Nuclear Engring., 1984—; vis. sci. Karlsruhe (Germany) Nuclear Rsch. Ctr., 1977, Bechtel Corp., San Francisco, 1989, 95; active Gov. Energy Policy Task Force, Wis., 1980; U.S. del. to Internat. Tokamak Reactor Project, Vienna, Austria, 1979-81; mem. adv. panel INTOR, 1987; mem. numerous review panels, including Los Alamos Nat. lab., Sandia Nat. Lab., Argonne Nat. Lab. Assoc. editor: Fusion Engring. and Design. Recipient Curtis W. McGraw Rsch. award Engring. Rsch. Com. Am. Assn. Engring. Edn., 1978, John Randle Grumman Achievement award Grumman Aircraft Corp., 1987, Leadership Fusion award Fusion Power Assocs., 1992, NASA Pub. Svc. medal, 1993, Disting. Faculty award Wis. Alumni Assn., 1994, Big 10 Centennial award, 1995. Fellow Am. Nuclear Soc. (sec. Richland sect. 1970, student advisor Wis. chpt. 1972-73, chmn. 2nd topical meeting on fusion tech. 1976, bd. dirs. 1987-90, Outstanding Achievement award 1980); mem. Nat. Acad. Engring. Home: 6013 Greentree Rd Madison WI 53711-3125 Office: U Wis 1500 Johnson Dr Madison WI 53706-1609

KULESZA, CHESTER STEPHEN (BUD KULESZA), finance executive; b. Elizabeth, N.J., Jan. 12, 1947; s. Chester S. and Mary Ellen (Sales) K.; m. Kathleen Marie Hickman, June 14, 1969; children: Kevin Michael, Marie Kathleen. AAS in Acctg., Middlesex County Coll., Edison, N.J., 1969; BS in Commerce, Rider U., 1973. Cert. mgmt. acct. Inst. Mgmt. Accts., cert. fin. mgmt. With fin./acctg. depts. Johnson & Johnson, New Brunswick, N.J., 1969-73; asst. contr. ITT Automotive Morton Frozen Foods, Charlottesville, Va., 1973-81; sr. fin. mgr. RJR Delmonte Frozen Foods, San Francisco, 1981-83; v.p., contr. ITT Automotive Bus. & Consumer Comm., Raleigh, N.C., 1983-86; CFO, contr. ITT Automotive Electromech. Components, Fountain Valley, Calif., 1986-90; sr. v.p. fin. ITT Automotive-Worldwide, Auburn Hills, Mich., 1990—; presenter XV World Congress of Accountancy, 1997. Author of book foreword: The Practice Analysis of Management Accounting, 1996; contbr. articles to profl. jours. Chmn. acctg. and fin. adv. bd. Oakland U., Rochester, Mich., 1994—; mem. bus. adv. curriculum com. Detroit Coll. of Bus., Dearborn, Mich., 1996—; mem. acctg. accreditation com. Internat. Assn. Mgmt. Edn., St. Louis, 1997; lay leader, mem. adminstrv. bd., fin. com. Howarth United Meth. Ch., Lake Orion, Mich., 1997. With U.S. Army, 1964-67. Honoree Beta Gamma Sigma, 1997. Mem. Inst. Mgmt. Accts. (nat. pres. 1999—, bd. dirs.), Fin. Execs. Inst. (chair acad. rels. com. Detroit chpt. 1995—), Beta Alpha Psi (hon.). Republican. Avocations: accounting education, wine tasting, gourmet cooking, travel, choir. Home: 10301 Rhett Butler Dr Austin TX 78739 Office: ITT Automotive 3000 University Dr Auburn Hills MI 48326-2356

KULICH, ROMAN THEODORE, healthcare administrator; b. Benton Harbor, Mich., Mar. 1, 1953; s. Roman and Helen (Gadumski) K.; m. Janet Kay Zuhl, Sept. 14, 1974; children: Andrew Joseph, Stephanie Ann. BBA magna cum laude, Mich. State U., 1974. CPA, Mich. Sr. auditor Ernst & Ernst, Detroit, 1975-77; controller Sinai Hosp. of Detroit, 1977-81, dir. finance, 1981-84; dir. finance Health Alliance Plan, Detroit, 1984-86, v.p. adminstrn. and finance, 1986-91, group v.p., chief operating officer, 1991-95; pres., CEO Healthcare Okla., Okla. Health Alliance, 1995, Select Care, Troy, Mich., 1996—; mem. President's adv. coun. Walsh Coll.; mem Young President's Orgn.; bd. dirs. Select Care, Inc., Select Care, HMO, Select Care Re. Tiscornia Found. Scholarship winner, St. Joseph, Mich., 1971. Fellow Health Care Fin. Mgmt. Assn. (pres. East Mich. chpt. 1990-91); mem. AICPA, Mich. Assn. CPAs, Greater Detroit Area Health Coun. (bd. dirs.), Met. Affairs Coalition (bd. dirs.), Detroit Regional C. of C. (bd. dirs.). Avocations: family activities, reading, boating, piano. Home: 2834 Pheasant Ring Dr Rochester Hls MI 48309-2857 Office: Select Care 2401 W Big Beaver Rd Ste 700 Troy MI 48084-3303

KULICK, ELLIOT DAVID, information technology specialist; b. N.Y.C., Jan. 4, 1964; s. Allan Elias and Sandra Francine Kulick; m. Joy Nadine Wurtzel, Sept. 7, 1998. BA, SUNY, Fredonia, 1986; MA in HUman Resource Devel., Webster U., Geneva, 1990, MA in Internat. Rels., 1990. Cert. Novell engr. Pres. Intelligent Interactive Solutions, N.Y.C., 1991-95; instr. tech. Touro Coll., N.Y.C., 1995-96; sys. engr. Pride Techs., N.Y.C., 1996-97; mgr. ctr. tech. Westcom Svcs. Corp., N.Y.C., 1997-98; mgr. info. tech. Entex Info. Svcs., Norwalk, Conn., 1998—; mgr. promotion Westchester County Bus. Jour., 1997. Me. Rep. Nat. Com., Washington, 1990—. Avocations: computres, reading, intellectual bantor, antiques, motorcycles. Office: Entex Info Svcs 101 Merritt Norwalk CT 06851

KULICK, RICHARD JOHN, computer scientist, researcher; b. New Kensington, Pa., Mar. 27, 1949; s. John Anthony and Anna Teresa (Tuzik) K. BS, Pa. State U., 1971; MBA, U. Md., 1973. Project acct. PPG Industries, Inc., Ford City, Pa., 1973-75; programmer analyst Allegheny Ludlum Steel Corp., Brackenridge, Pa., 1975-77, systems analyst, 1977-82, sr. systems analyst, 1982, sr. MIS planner, 1982-86; system design specialist Allegheny Ludlum Corp., Brackenridge, 1986-91; mgmt. info. systems assoc. Allegheny Ludlum Corp., Vandergrift, Pa., 1991—. Author: Heuristic Coil Slitting Optimization, 1986, (manual) Data Modeling Standards, 1988, Information Systems Integration Strategy, 1989. Mem. Computer Soc. of IEEE, Nat. Systems Programmers Assn., Assn. for Computing Machinery (voting), Tech. Coun. on Software Engring., Datamation High Tech. Panel, Compu Panel, IDC Corp. Computing Coun., Smithsonian Assocs., U.S. Tennis Assn., Racquet Club Pitts., Pa. State U. Club Alle-Kiski Valley. Avocations: music, reading, stamp collecting, running, fine art. Home: 483 Lillian Rd Leechburg PA 15656-8220 Office: Allegheny Ludlum Corp 132 Lincoln Ave Vandergrift PA 15690-1249

KULICKE, C(HARLES) SCOTT, business executive; b. Phila., Sept. 28, 1949; s. Frederick William, Jr., and Ruth (West) K.; m. Danielle Volckmar, Aug. 1, 1980; children: Ruth, Max. Robert. B.S. in Econs., U. Pa., 1972. Mgr. Far East ops. Kulicke & Soffa Industries, Inc., Horsham, Pa., 1973-75, product mgr., 1975-78, exec. v.p., 1978-80, pres., chief exec. officer, 1980-84, chmn., chief exec. officer, 1984—. Office: Kulicke & Soffa Industries 2101 Blair Mill Rd Willow Grove PA 19090-1795

KULIK, LEWIS TASHRAK, dentist; b. N.Y.C., Mar. 5, 1946; s. Arthur and Miriam (Zevin) K.; m. Loretta Margaret Smyth, Sept. 17, 1978; children: Jeanneil, Nicole Loretta. Student, Bklyn. Coll., 1963-66; DDS Coll. of Dentistry, NYU, 1970. Intern Bronx-Lebanon Hosp. Ctr., N.Y., 1970-71; clin. asst. prof. Coll. of Dentistry NYU, 1981-86; pvt. practice N.Y.C., 1971—; cons. N.Y. State Office of Profl. Discipline, 1981-84; chmn. profl. discipline com. N.Y. State Bd. for Dentistry, 1988-91; steering com. North East Reg. Bd. Dental Examiners, Washington, 1992-95; mem. N.Y. State Bd. for Dentistry Lic. & Disciplinary panel, 1994—. Mem. editorial bd. N.Y. Jour. Dentistry, 1981-83, Ea. Dental Soc. Jour., 1981-83. Vice-chmn. co-founder Trees for Rye, N.Y., 1991-92; mem. N.Y. State Bd. for Dentistry, 1984-94, mem. lic. and discipline panel, 1994—. Fellow Acad. Gen. Dentistry, Internat. Coll. Dentists, Am. Coll. Dentists, Royal Soc. Medicine, Pierre Fauchard Acad.; mem. ADA, Dental Soc. State N.Y., N.Y. County Dental Soc., Ea. Dental Soc., Am. Prosthodontic Soc., Am. Assn. Dental Examiners, North East Regional Bd. Dental Examiners, Rotary Club of N.Y. (bd. dirs. 1990-96, 1st v.p. 1996-97, pres. elect 1997, pres. 1998-99). Republican. Jewish. Avocations: philately, numismatics, gardening, fishing, table tennis. Office: 30 Central Park S Rm 12B New York NY 10019-1628

KULIK, ROSALYN FRANTA, food company executive, consultant; b. Wilmington, Del., Aug. 29, 1951; d. William Alfred and Virginia Louise (Ellis) Franta. BS in Voc. Home Econs. Edn., Purdue U., 1972, MS in Foods and Nutrition, 1974; postgrad. in advanced mgmt. program, Harvard Bus. Sch., 1990. Registered dietitian. Home economist Kellogg Co., Battle Creek, Mich., 1974-75, nutrition and consumer specialist, 1975-77, mgr. advt. to children, 1977-79, corp. adminstrv. asst., 1979, dir. nutrition, 1979-82, dir. nutrition and analytical services, 1982, v.p. nutrition and chemistry, 1983, v.p. quality and nutrition, 1983-87, v.p., asst. to chmn., 1987-88; exec. v.p., gen. mgr. Fearn Internat., Franklin Park, Ill., 1988-90; cons., 1991—; chmn. tech. com. Grocery Mfrs. Am., Washington, 1985-87, mem. tech. com. planning group, 1982-88; trustee Internat. Life Scis. Inst., Washington, 1982-88; v.p. Internat. Life Scis. Inst. Nutrition Found., Washington, 1985-88, exec. com., 1985-88; mem. of corp. Culinary Inst. Am.; co-founder and sec. Nutrition in Complementary Care Dietetic Practice Group Am. Dietetic Assn. Contbr. articles on food sci. and nutrition to profl. jours. Bd. dirs. State Arthritis Found., County Vol. Ctr. Recipient Ada Decker Malott Meml. scholarship, Purdue U., 1970, disting. alumna Purdue U. Sch. of Consumer and Family Sci. Fellow Am. Dietetic Assn.; mem. Inst. Food Technologists, Am. Dietetic Assn., Phi Kappa Phi, Gamma Sigma Delta, Omicron Nu, Alpha Omicron Pi (mem. Phi Upsilon chpt.). Republican. Lutheran. Avocations: music, church work, travel, Jr. League volunteerism.

KULIKOVSKAYA, SVETLANA ROMANOVNA, artist, costume designer, self-employed; b. Kineshma Ivanovskaya, Russia, Dec. 1, 1950; came to U.S., 1989; d. Roman I. and Alevtina N. (Smirnova) Ivanova; m. Vladimir A. Kulikovsky, Feb. 19, 1971 (dec. Sept. 1982); 1 child, Roman V. Student, Tech. U., Vilnius, Lithuania, 1970-74, Salt Lake Cmty. Coll., 1990-92; BA, Westminster Coll., 1994. Ballet actress Union of Orchestras and Ensembles, Vilnius, Lithuania, 1976-82, costumer, 1982-87; pvt. practice Vilnius, Lithuania, 1987-89; instr. Hawthorne U., 1992-94, The Sch. of Fashion Design, Boston, 1999. *Svetlana Romanovna Kulikovskaya is experienced as both a craft and business oriented person, though she was trained as an artist. She has a personal vision and philosophy for her designs and paintings and a strong desire to make them aesthetically comprehensible for an audience. She has received the Award of Merit from Manhattan Art International Magazine, 1995, and an award from the Musee Des Beaux Arts d'unet Artiste De'L'Annee, 1997. Her work has been displayed in a number of publications, including Boston Time (Russian edition newspaper), 1996, Book Art Press, New York, 1997, Institute International D'Arts Plastic Du Janan, 1997.* Mem. AAUW, Amnesty Internat., Women Caucus Arts, Nat. Mus. Women in Arts. Russian Orthodox. Home: 185 Elm St # 1 Cambridge MA 02139-1426

KULIKOWSKI, CASIMIR ALEXANDER, computer science educator; b. Hertford, Herts, Eng., May 4, 1944; came to U.S., 1961; s. Victor A. and Isabel S. (Tuckett) K.; m. Christine A. Wilk, May 31, 1969; children: Michael Edward, Victoria Anne. BE with honors, Yale U., 1965, MS, 1966; PhD, U. Hawaii, 1970. From asst. prof. to assoc. prof. Rutgers U., New Brunswick, N.J., 1970-77, prof., 1977-97, chmn. dept. computer sci., 1984-90, dir. Lab. Computer Sci. Rsch., 1985-96, bd. govs. prof., 1997—; mem. bd. sci. counselors Nat. Libr. Medicine, Bethesda, 1984-87; mem. biomed. libr. rev. com. NIH, 1994-99, chair, 1997-99. Author: A Practical Guide to Designing Expert Systems, 1984, Computer Systems that Learn, 1992; editor: Artificial Intelligence Expert Systems and Languages in Modeling & Simulation, 1988; mem. editl. bd. Methods Info. in Medicine, 1999—, Jour. Am. Med. Informatics Assn., 1993-98, Computers in Biology and Medicine, 1980—. Pres. Highland Park (N.J.) Residents Assn., 1983-88. Fellow AAAS, IEEE, Am. Assn. Artificial Intelligence, Am. Coll. Med. Informatics; mem. NAS Inst. Medicine. Office: Rutgers U Dept Computer Sci Hill Ctr Busch Campus New Brunswick NJ 08903

KULIN, KEITH DAVID, cinematographer; b. Bogota, N.J., Jan. 24, 1948; s. Joseph Julius and Ava L. (Finestone) K.; m. Mary Mulroy, Nov. 24, 1993. BA, Ramapo Coll. N.J., 1973. News photographer Ridgewood Newspapers, Paramus, N.J., 1967; desk asst. TV news CBS Inc., N.Y.C., 1975-77, newsreel photographer, 1977-84, documentary photographer, 1984-98; prodr., editor A Few Minutes With Andy Rooney, 1998—; staff documentary cinematographer for 60 Minutes, West 57th, CBS Reports, 48 Hours, Saturday Night with Connie Chung, other CBS news programs. Contbr. photography to Ridgewood newspapers, N.Y. Times, Womens World, 1966-75. Served with U.S. Army, 1968-70, Vietnam. Recipient Outstanding Photog. Achievement award Eastman Kodak Co., 1985, Spot News and Feature News awards, 1967; nominee Emmy award, 1985. Mem. Internat. Brotherhood Elec. Workers, TV and Radio Working Press Assn. Avocations: computers, still photography. Home: 202 Maple Dr Wyckoff NJ 07481-2317 Office: CBS News 555 W 57th St New York NY 10019-2925

KULINSKI, STEPHEN EDWARD, interior designer; b. Balt., Aug. 20, 1955; s. Paul Dominic and Christine (Armstrong) K.; m. Fredricka Strumpf, Aug. 6, 1983. B in Design, U. Fla., 1977; MBA, U. North Fla., 1983. Sr. designer Reynolds, Smith & Hills, Jacksonville, Fla., 1977-80, project mgr., 1980-83; project dir. Gresham, Smith & Ptnrs., Nashville, 1983-84, dir. interior architecture, 1984—, assoc., 1985-88, sr. assoc., 1988—, dir. comml. architecture, 1990, prin., 1994—, dir. mktg., 1997—. Mem. bd. visitors U. Tenn., Knoxville, bd. dirs. 1994—, mem. bd. visitors U. Fla., Gainsville, mem. Nashville Young Leaders Coun., Bldg. Owners and Mgrs. Assn., Nat. Assn. Indsl. and Office Parks, Nashville C. of C., Rotary. Republican. Home: 6743 Pennywell Dr Nashville TN 37205-3055 Office: Gresham Smith and Ptnrs 511 Union St Nashville TN 37219-1733

KULIS, ELLEN MAE, elementary education educator; b. Punxsutawney, Pa., Jan. 19, 1943; d. John Williams and Julia (Knopick) Johnson; m. Raymond Edward Kulis, July 2, 1983. BS in Elem. Edn., Ind. U., Pa., 1966; MS in Elem. Edn., Clarion U., Pa., 1970; principalship, Penn State U., University Park, Pa., 1988. First grade tchr. Ridgway Sch. Dist., Ridgway, Pa., 1966-67; head start tchr. Jefferson County, Syskesville, Pa., summers 1967-70; first grade tchr. Punxsutawney Areas Schs., Punxsutawney, Pa., 1970-85, third grade tchr., 1985—; co-op tchr. Ind. U., Pa., 1979-90. Asst. Encore Group, Punxsutawney, Pa., 1978-81; mem. Sodality, 1958-64, Newman Ctr., Indiana, Pa., 1983-90. Mem. PTO, PSEA, NEA, PAEA, RAEA, Delta Kappa Gamma. Democrat. Byzantine Catholic. Home: 921 Lilac St Indiana PA 15701-3332

KULKA, J(OHANNES) PETER, retired physician, pathologist; b. Vienna, Austria, Feb. 7, 1921; came to U.S., 1933; s. Ernest Walter and Anna Maria (Jolles) K. AB, Cornell U., 1941; MD, Johns Hopkins U., 1944. Diplomate Am. Bd. Pathology. Intern in pathology Strong Meml. Hosp., Rochester, N.Y., 1944-45; asst. resident in pathology Mass. Gen. Hosp., Boston, 1945-47; instr. anatomy Harvard U. Med. Sch., Boston, 1947-49, instr. pathology, 1949-52, clin. assoc., asst. clin. prof., assoc. clin. prof., 1952-70, clin. fellow in psychiatry, 1970-73; resident in psychiatry, then clin. fellow in psychiatry McLean Hosp., Belmont, Mass., 1970-74; child psychiatry trainee South Shore Mental Health Ctr., Quincy, Mass., 1973-74; pathologist Robert B. Brigham Hosp., Boston, 1955-58, 61-70, assoc. dir. grad. tng. grant, 1961-68; chmn. med. staff Robert B. Brigham Hosp., Boston, Mass., 1965-67; assoc. in pathology Peter Bent Brigham Hosp., Boston, 1955-58, asst. in medicine, 1958-61; clin. instr. medicine, gen. physician Health Svc., Tufts U., Medford, Mass.; mem. courtesy staff Lawrence Meml. Hosp., Medford, 1975-79. Mem. editl. bd. Arthritis and Rheumatism, 1960-68; contbr. articles to med. jours. Capt. M.C., U.S. Army, 1953-55. Avocations: camping, canoeing, skiing. Home: PO Box 316 Lincoln MA 01773-0316

KULKARNI, KUMAR BALAKRISHNA, automotive engineer; b. Bangalore, Karnataka, India, June 6, 1961; came to the U.S., 1986; s. Balakrishna R. and Kamala (Sunkad) K.; m. Asha Pendyalam, May 28, 1993; children: Kaushal, Anshul. BME, Bangalore U., 1984; MS, U. Toledo, 1989. Foreman Hindustan Aeronautics Ltd., Bangalore, 1984-86; sr. engr. EGS, Inc., Dearborn, Mich., 1989-95; tech. specialist Ford Motor Co., Dearborn, 1995—; cons. engr. Ford Motor Co., Dearborn, 1990-95. Mem. ASME. Avocations: travel, reading. Home: 4989 S Ridgeside Cir Ann Arbor MI 48105-9447 Office: Danou Tech Ctr Ste 1300 Cube 13G20 Southfield Rd Allen Park MI 48101

KULL, BRYAN PAUL, business information/technology executive, real estate investor; b. Newark, Jan. 23, 1960; s. Paul and Joan Lorraine (Schell) K.; m. Lindsay Fairfield Patton, Nov. 26, 1983; children: Taylor Bryan, Kathryn. BS in Mgmt., Keene (N.H.) State Coll., 1982; MBA in Mktg., So. Ill. U., 1987. Sales rep. Warner-Lambert Co., Morris Plains, N.J., 1982-84; key account mgr. Clorox Co., Oakland, Calif., 1984-86; div. mgr. Alberto-Culver Co., Melrose Park, Ill., 1986-89; area mgr. Schering-Plough Corp., Memphis, 1989-90; nat. sales mgr. Shering-Plough Healthcare, Liberty Corner, N.J., 1991-94; v.p. spl. mkts. Sunshine Biscuits, Inc., Woodbridge, N.J., 1994-96; v.p. client svc. sales Info. Resources, Inc., Fairfield, N.J., 1997—. Mem. Triathlon Fedn., Davis, Calif., 1988-89. Mem. Assn. MBA Execs., Nat. Assn. Chain Drug Stores (assoc.), Pres.'s Club at Schering-Plough. Republican. Presbyterian. Avocations: golf, tennis, skiing, cycling, wine collecting. Office: Information Resources Inc 100 Passaic Ave Fairfield NJ 07004-3580

KULL, JOSEPH, government administrator; b. New Brunswick, N.J., July 29, 1947; s. Joseph and Yolanda (Tegyi) K.; m. Patricia Donnellon, Sept. 12, 1970; children: Matthew, Courtney, Joseph L., Kevin. BS, Mt. St. Mary's Coll., Md., 1969; MBA, George Mason U., 1976. CPA; cert. govt. fin. mgr. Sr. auditor Arthur Andersen & Co., N.Y.C., 1969-72; auditor Cost of Living Coun., 1972-73; from sys. acct. to compt. CAB, Washington, 1973-84; dir. budget divsn. NSF, Arlington, Va., 1984-91, dir. Office of Budget, Fin. and Award Mgmt., 1991—, CFO, 1992—; acctg. and auditing policy com. Fed. Acctg. Stds. Adv. Bd.; CFO liaison Acctg. and Auditing Police Com., Budget Officers Adv. Coun., JFMIP; mem. OMB Budget Officers Adv. Coun., CFO Coun., chmn. com. on fin. statements and stds., liaison, govt.-wide fin. statements audit task force; adj. lectr. acctg. No. Va. C.C., 1978—. Mem. AICPA, Assn. Govt. Accts. Office: Nat Sci Found Nat Science Bd 4201 Wilson Blvd Arlington VA 22230-0002*

KULLAS, ALBERT JOHN, management and systems engineering consultant; b. Webster, Mass., May 5, 1917; s. Albert J. and Mary (Piechowiak) K.; m. Joyce M. Gladue, Jan. 31, 1942; children: Michael, Daniel, Mark, James. B.S. in Civil Engring., Worcester Poly. Inst., 1938; grad., Am. Mgmt. Assn., 1956; M.S. in Civil Engring., NYU, 1940; grad., Sloan Sch. Mgmt. Sr. Execs., MIT, 1973. With Martin Marietta Corp., 1940-82; structures mgr. Martin Marietta Corp., Balt., 1955-57; chief engr. Martin Marietta Corp., 1957, design engring. mgr., 1957-59, tech. devel. mgr., 1959-60, Dyna Soar and Gemini Launch vehicle tech. dir., 1960-62; research and engring. dir. Martin Marietta Corp., Denver, 1962-65, dir. tech. ops., 1965-66; dir. space sci., research, adv. tech. Martin Marietta Corp., 1966-67, dir. Voyager program, 1967-68, dir. Planetary Systems, 1968, dir. Viking project, div. v.p., 1969-72, div. v.p. ops. rev., 1972-73, v.p. data systems, 1973-82; mgmt. and systems engring. cons. Littleton, Colo., 1982—; pres. Albert J. Kullas, Inc.; mem. rsch. and tech. panel space vehicles NASA, 1968-78; chmn. bd. Biax Corp., 1987-90; bd. dirs. The Highlands, Inc., 1998—, 1st v.p., 1999—. Contbr. articles to profl. jours. Mem. rsch. adv. coun. Colo. State U., 1971—; treas. Porter Hosp. Found., 1980-85, 1st v.p., 1986-88, pres., 1988-90, v.p., 1990-93, active, 1993—; bd. dirs. Colo. Jud. Inst., 1980-91, chmn., 1984-86; mem. exec. com. Rocky Mountain Sci. Coun., 1964-65; bd. dirs. MIT Alumni Colo., 1990—. Recipient Robert H. Goddard award Worcester Poly. Inst., 1962. Fellow AIAA (award 1967); Asso. fellow (chmn. honors and awards com. 1973-81); mem. ASCE, Sigma Xi, Tau Beta Pi. Office: 5088 W Maplewood Ave Littleton CO 80123-6729 *I believe that being thorough, consistent, and persistent in pursuing one's convictions are necessary ingredients for personal and managerial success.*

KULLBERG, DUANE REUBEN, accounting firm executive; b. Red Wing, Minn., Oct. 6, 1932; s. Carl Reuben and Hazel Norma (Swanson) K.; m. Sina Nell Turner, Oct. 19, 1958 (dec. Sept. 1989); children: Malissa Ryan, Caroline Godellas; m. Susan Turley, Dec. 30, 1992; stepchildren: Betsy Holtzermann, Jane Holtzermann. BBA, U. Minn., 1954. With Andersen Worldwide, 1954-89, ptnr., 1967-89, mng. ptnr., Mpls., 1970-74, dep. mng. ptnr., Chgo., 1975-78, vice chmn. acctg. and audit practice worldwide, 1978-80, mng. ptnr., CEO, 1980-89, ret., 1989; bd. dirs. John Nuveen Co., Carlson Cos., Inc., Chgo. Bd. Options Exch. Life trustee Northwestern U., Art Inst. Chgo., U. Minn. Found., chmn. bd. trustees, 1993-95; chair, bd. dirs. Swedish Coun. Am. With U.S. Army, 1956-58. Decorated comdr. Royal Order of Polar Star (Sweden), 1989; recipient Legend in Leadership award Emory U., 1992, Regents award U. Minn., 1995, Outstanding Achievement award U. Minn., 1990. Mem. Chgo. Club, Comml. Club, Mpls. Club. Home: 179 E Lake Shore Dr Apt 1001 Chicago IL 60611-1306 also: 6444 N 79th St Scottsdale AZ 85250-7919

KULLBERG, GARY WALTER, advertising agency executive; b. White Plains, N.Y., Dec. 15, 1941; s. Walter George and Neva Virginia (Franz) K.; m. Audrey Ellen Greenwald, June 20, 1976; 1 child, Eric Alan. BS, U. R.I., 1963. Contr. WCD, Inc., N.Y.C., 1963-66; v.p., mgmt. supr. Ogilvy & Mather, N.Y.C., 1966-77; sr. v.p., account group head Wells, Rich, Greene, N.Y.C., 1977-83; CEO, CFO, co-founder Fredericks Kullberg Amato Pisacane, Inc., 1983-88; pres. Kullberg Amato Pisacane/ABP, Inc., 1987-89; pres., COO PanCom Internat. Corp., 1989-91; CEO PanCom Comm. Corp., 1991-93, Kullberg Cons. Group, N.Y.C., 1993—; guest spkr. univs. Mem. bd. advisors, chmn. mktg. and mktg. comm. com. Manhattan Salvation Army; mem. bus. adv. coun. U. R.I. Coll. Bus., vice-chmn., co-chair publicity com. Mem. West Point Soc. N.Y. (career adv. com.), Am. Numismatic Assn., N.Y. Athletic Club, Phi Gamma Delta. Home and Office: Kullberg Cons Group 171 Forge Rd North Kingstown RI 02852-1007

KULLBERG, JOHN FRANCIS, foundation administrator; b. Cranston, R.I., Apr. 16, 1939; s. Paul Frederick and Katherine Frances (Smith) K.; m. Karol Marie Runing, Sept. 15, 1979; children: Kathryn Marie, Kristen Frances, Evan Andrew. BA, Cath. U. Am., 1962; MA, U. R.I., 1967; postgrad., U. Ill., 1967-69; EdD, Columbia U., 1976. Chmn. dept. English, St. Raphael Acad., Pawtucket, R.I., 1962-64, Parkland Coll., Champaign, Ill., 1967-69; coordinator instrn. The Baldridge Reading Services, Greenwich, Conn., 1964-66; counselor Columbia Coll., Columbia U., N.Y.C., 1969-71; cons. The Dictaphone Corp., Rye, N.Y., 1969-71; dir. admissions, asst. dean Columbia U. Sch. Law, N.Y.C., 1971-77; postdoctoral fellow Office of Sec., Dept. HEW, Washington, 1977-78; pres. Am. Soc. Prevention Cruelty to Animals, N.Y.C., 1978-91; pres. Guiding Eyes for the Blind, Yorktown Hgts., N.Y., 1991-93, cons., 1993-94; exec. dir. The Humane Soc. Wildlife Land Trust, 1994—; advisor to N.Y. State Atty. Gen. on animal welfare legislation, 1974-77; bd. dirs. Soc. Animal Protective Legislation; lectr. in field. Author: The Communication Laboratory, 1971, also numerous essays; appearances in various TV and radio programs. Bd. dirs. Am. Soc. Prevention Cruelty to Animals, N.Y.C., 1976-78, N.Y. State Humane Assn., 1979-81, Am. Humane Assn., 1984-86, Global Tomorrow Coalition, 1981-86; chmn. bd. Nat. Coalition to Protect Our Pets, 1986-89. Kellogg fellow Columbia U., 1971-73; recipient Man of Yr. award East Manhattan C. of C., 1986; Disting. Alumnus award Teachers Coll., Columbia U., 1992. Home: 20653 Anndyke Way Germantown MD 20874-2881 Office: Humane Soc US Wildlife Land Trust 2100 L St NW Washington DC 20037-1525 *Leadership requires a prepared mind, an ability to recognize opportunities for influence and a willingness to sacrifice comfort and risk failure in their pursuit.*

KULLEN, SHIRLEY ROBINOWITZ, psychiatric epidemiologist, consultant; b. Balt., Sept. 6, 1922; d. Joseph and Rose (Collins) Robinowitz; m. Joseph Stephen Reff, Sept. 14, 1941 (div. 1958); children: Richard Brian, Robert Alan; m. Sidney Irving Margolis, Oct. 28, 1973 (dec. Dec. 1988); m. Sol Kullen, Jan. 10, 1993. BS, Am. U., 1959, MBA, 1961, PhD, 1972. Statistician NIMH, Bethesda, Md., 1964-72, health scientist adminstrn., 1972-93; cons. psychiatric epidemiologist, Chevy Chase, Md., 1993—; lectr. Am. U. Washington, 1961, 69, 70, 74, 87, seminar developer, 1987; lectr. Howard U., Washington, 1963-67. Bd. dirs. Jewish Cmty. Ctr. Greater Washington, Rockville, Md., 1979-90, Hebrew Home Washington, Rockville, 1980-85, Fed. Credit Union, Rockville, 1987-93. Mem. APHA (adv. bd. mental health sect. 1990-93), AAUW. Avocations: tennis, golf, ballet, music, writing. Home and Office: 5610 Wisconsin Ave Apt 1508 Chevy Chase MD 20815-4440

KULLER, JONATHAN MARK, lawyer; b. Paterson, N.J., Jan. 2, 1951; George and Muriel (Kaplan) K.; m. Mardi Risa Adelman, Oct. 8, 1977; children: Brett Louis, Devin Howard. BS, Livingston Coll., 1972; JD, Rutgers U., 1976. Bar: N.J. 1976, U.S. Dist. Ct. N.J. 1976, U.S. Supreme Ct. 1985. Law clk. to presiding judge N.J. Superior Ct., Hackensack, 1976-77; assoc. Miller & Platt, Paterson, 1977-78; ptnr. Markus, Kuller & Cohen, Parsippany, N.J., 1978-87, Blaustein & Wasserman, Woodbridge, N.J., 1987-98; spl. counsel L'Abbate, Balkan, Colavita & Contini, L.L.P., Livingston, N.J., 1998—. Mem. N.J. Bar Assn., Middlesex County Bar Assn., Comml. Law League Am. Democrat. Jewish. Avocation: tennis. Office: L'Abbate Balkan Et Al 7 Regent St Ste 711 Livingston NJ 07039

KULOK, WILLIAM ALLAN, entrepreneur, venture capitalist; b. Mt. Vernon, N.Y., July 24, 1940; s. Sidney Alexander and Bertha (Lembeck) K.; m. Susan B. Glick, June 26, 1965; children: Jonathan, Brian, Stephanie. BS in Econs., U. Pa., 1962. CPA, N.Y. Acct. David Kulok Co., N.Y.C., 1962-67; asst. to pres. Syndicate Mags., N.Y.C., 1967-70; founder Kulok Capital Inc., N.Y.C., 1970, pres., 1970—; pres. World Trade Ctr., West Palm Beach; bd. dir. Listcomp Corp., Mail Mgmt. Corp., Mag. Devel. Fund, Lazard Spl. Equities Fund, ASA Internat. Ltd., N.Y. Import/Export Ctr., Inc., Ctr. for Exec. Edn., Arts & Events, Inc.; lectr. Wharton Sch., U. Chgo., NYU. Pres. N.Y. Soc. Ethical Culture, 1978-80; vice chmn. bd. Ethical Culture Schs., 1979, chmn., 1982-86. Mem. AICPA, Sleepy Hollow Country Club, Loxahatchee Club, Tryall Golf and Beach Club (Jamaica, W.I.). Home: 116 Echo Dr Jupiter FL 33458-7716

KULONGOSKI, THEODORE RALPH, state supreme court justice; b. Nov. 5, 1940; married; 3 children. BA, U. Mo., 1967, JD, 1970. Bar: Oreg., Mo., U.S. Dist. Ct. Oreg., U.S. Ct. Appeals (9th cir.). Legal counsel Oreg. State Ho. of Reps., 1973-74; founding and sr. ptnr. Kulongoski, Durham, Drummonds & Colombo, Oreg., 1974-87; deputy dist. atty. Mulnomah County, Oreg., 1992—. State rep. Lane County (Oreg.), 1974-77, state senator, 1977-83; chmn. Juvenile Justice Task Force, 1994, Gov.'s Commn. Organized Crime; mem. Criminal Justice Coun.; exec. dir. Met. Family Svc., 1992; dir. Oreg. Dept. Ins. and Fin., 1987-91. Mem. Oreg State Bar Assn., Mo. Bar Assn. Office: Oreg Supreme Ct 1163 State St Salem OR 97310-1331

KULP, EILEEN BODNAR, social worker; b. Glens Falls, N.Y., Sept. 25, 1941; d. Joseph and Bertha Bodnar; m. Randolph Heath Kulp, June 5, 1961; children: Kimberly, Randolph Heath II, Kevin Joseph. B in Sociology, Hampton U., 1978; MSW, Norfolk State U., 1981. Lic. clin. social worker, Va.; diplomate in clin. social work Nat. Bd. Examiners; cert. addictions specialist. Social worker II adult chem. dependency Peninsula Hosp., Hampton, 1981-82, leader treatment team adolescent chem. dependency unit, 1982-84, sr. clinician adult chem. dependency unit, 1984-86, program coord. adult chem. dependency unit, 1986-88, dir. adult treatment programs, 1988-92; pvt. practice Newport News, Va., 1986-93; dir. new founds drug and alcohol programs Riverside Regional Med. Ctr., Newport News, 1994—; addictions profls. team People Exch. Program, Norway, Sweden, Germany, 1989—. Bd. dirs Hampton Count PTA's, pres., 1979-80; bd. dirs. Hampton City Schs. Bd. Edn., 1981-85, Safe Haven Home for Abused Children, 1993—, Commonwealth Va. Citizens Adv. Bd. Youth and Family Svcs., Dept. Corrections, 1989—; chmn. adv. bd. Hampton Juvenile and Domestic Rels. Ct., bd. dirs., 1984—. Mem. Va. Coun. Social Welfare (pres. Tidewater chpt. 1987-88), Nat. Assn. Social Workers, Va. Assn. Alcoholism and Drug Abuse Counselors, Am. Coun. Alcoholism, Hampton Mental Health Bd. (pres. 1988-89), Va. Soc. Clin. Social Workers, Va. Coun. PTA's (life), Acad. Cert. Social Workers (cert.), Alpha Kappa Mu. Roman Catholic. Avocations: jazz, classical music, theatre, traveling. Home: 26 Sarfan Dr Hampton VA 23664-1760

KULP, J. ROBERT, metal company executive; b. Buffalo, June 23, 1935; s. Joseph Francis Kulp and Mary Gertrude (O'Brian) Kulp O'Hearn; m. Suzanne Frances Schultz, Jan. 26, 1957; children: J. Robert Jr., Kaaren S., Kevin E., Kenneth C. BS in Bus., U. Buffalo, 1967; MBA, Canisius Coll., 1972. Sales Reynolds Metals Supply Co., Miami, Fla., 1957-58, Ryerson Steel Co., Buffalo, 1958-72; ptnr., v.p. Oehler Industries Inc., Buffalo, 1972-94; pres. Denler Metal Products, Buffalo, 1984—; bd. dirs. Erie County Industry Devel. Agy., Buffalo, 1980-86. Pres. Episcopal Charities bd., Buffalo, 1979-83; bd. regents Canisius Coll., Buffalo, 1980-84, 89-95, v.p., 1991-93, chmn., 1993-95; mem. pres.'s adv. coun. D'Youville Coll., Buffalo, 1987-92. Recipient Bernard J. Martin Outstanding M.B.A. award Canisius Coll., 1979, LaSalle medal. Mem. Fabricators and Mfrs. Assn. Internat. (treas., v.p. bd. dirs. 1991—, chmn. 1996), Am. Soc. Metals, Engring. Soc. Buffalo (bd. dirs. 1982-85), Frontier Metal Trades Assn. (pres. 1984-86), Canisius Coll. Alumni Assn. (pres. 1985, v.p. 1984), MBA Alumni Assn. (pres. 1979), Buffalo C. of C. (chmn. existing industries com. 1978-79), PGA Nat. Golf Club Palm Beach Gardens, Orchard Park Country Club (bd. dirs., sec. 1988-89, v.p. 1989-90), Beta Gamma Sigma. Republican. Roman Catholic. Avocations: golf, travel, reading, bridge. Home: 12 Briar Hill Rd Orchard Park NY 14127-3527 also: PGA Nat 12 Briar Hill Rd Orchard Park NY 14127-3527 Office: Denler Metal Products 333 Henderson Ave Tonawanda NY 14217-1538

KULP, JONATHAN B., elementary school educator; b. Norristown, Pa., July 18, 1937; s. Abraham Moyer and Frances Mann (Connelly) K.; m. Priscilla Lory June 20, 1959 (div. 1968); m. Carol Janice (Nabinger) Apr. 5, 1968; children: Julie E., Penny S. BA, Dickinson Coll., Carlisle, Pa., 1959; MA, Am. U., 1963. Cert. tchr., Pa. Tchr., coach The Mercersburg (Pa.) Acad., 1959-60; tchr., coach The Episcopal Acad., Merion, Pa., 1963—, head history dept., 1983-89, dir. curriculum and faculty devel., 1989-96, dean of faculty, 1996—; Adv. com. Project Cares, Extón, Pa., 1979-82; mem. Dodge Found. seminar on Women in History, Bryn Mawr, Pa., 1985-86; reader for Am. History Advanced Placement Program of Coll. Bds., Princeton, 1987; participant study mission Basic Edn. Leaders Study, China, Hong Kong, 1993; cons. in field. Active ARC, Montrose, Pa., 1974-96; mem. Downingtown Area Sch. Bd., Downingtown, Pa., 1975-79, pres. 1978-79; The Exton Chorale, Exton, Pa., 1976—, v.p., 1977-79, pres. 1981. Served with USAR, 1960-66. Cert. of Achievement Teaching fellow Commonwealth Partnership, 1986; Fellowship award, 1986; ind. study in humanities fellow Coun. for Basic Edn. and Nat. Endowment, 1987, Woodrow Wilson fellow in Am. History, 1989. Mem. ASCD, Ind. Sch. Tchrs. Assn. Phila. (chmn. history program 1985-88, profl. devel. chair 1991—), Nat. Interscholastic Swim Coaches Assn. Am., Coun. Basic Edn., Orgn. Am. Historians, Phila. Area Coun. for Women in Ind. Schs. (co-chmn. 1987-88, mem. exec. com. 1986-90). Republican. Avocations: swimming, tennis, walking, woodworking. Home: 1230 Street Rd Chester Springs PA 19425-1606 Office: The Episc Acad 376 N Latches Ln Merion Station PA 19066-1797

KULSKI, JULIAN EUGENIUSZ, architect, planner, educator; b. Warsaw, Poland, Mar. 3, 1929; came to U.S., 1948, naturalized, 1950; s. Julian Spitoslav and Eugenia Helena (Solecka) K; children: Helena E., Julian S., Stefan T.A. *Sir Julian E. Kulski joined the Underground Army when he was twelve and arrested by Gestapo, tortured, and sentenced to Auschwitz. After he was rescued, he joined the Commandos and fought in the Warsaw Uprising. He was captured, and sent to prisoner-of-war camp. After escaping, he went to Ireland. While at Portora Royal School, he won the Oxford and Cambridge certificate. His father, Julian S. Kulski, fought with Pilsudski Legions in World War I and 1920-21 Polish Soviet War. During World War II as Lord Mayor of Warsaw, he represented the Polish Government in Exile. He was a fierce protector of the Underground Army. His mother, Eugenia Solecka, descended from the King of Poland, Stanislaw Leszczynski, father-in-law of King of France Louis XV.* Student, Sch. Architecture Oxford (Eng.) U., 1947-48; BArch, Yale U., 1953, MArch, 1954; PhD, Warsaw Inst. Tech., 1966. Practice architecture, city planning Conn., 1954-59, Orlean, Va., 1959—; prof. architecture U. Notre Dame, South Bend, Ind., 1960-65; prof., dir. urban and regional planning George Washington U., Washington, 1965-67; prof., dir. city and regional planning Howard U., 1967-90; cons. World Bank, 1964-90; bd. dirs. Nat. Archtl. Accrediting Bd., 1971-76; chmn. accrediting com. Harvard U., 1972, 75, U. P.R., 1974, Pratt U., 1975, Carnegie-Mellon U., 1976, U. Va.1978. Author: Land of Urban Promise, 1967 (Book-of-Month award), Evolution of American Urban Systems, 1970, Architecture in a Revolutionary Era, 1971, Dying, We Live, 1979; contbr. numerous articles to profl. jours. Served with Polish Army, 1941-46. Decorated Home Army Cross, Army Cross (4), Combat medal (Poland); knight Order St. John of Jerusalem; recipient cert. of achievement Nat. Archtl. Accrediting Bd., 1973, 76. Fellow AIA; mem. Am. Planning Assn., Am. Inst. Cert. Planners, AAUP. Office: PO Box 69 Orlean VA 20128-0069 *My life has been guided by the following philosophy: It is hard to work for freedom, harder yet to die for it, and hardest of all to suffer for it.*

KULSTAD, GUY CHARLES, public works official; b. Feb. 28, 1930; s. John Marlyn and Anne Mildred (Boyd) Kulstad Ibison; m. Bonnie Jane Sherman, Aug. 28, 1955 (div. Aug. 1996); children: Anne Marie Kulstad Hurst, Mark, Alice Kulstad Krause. BS in Civil Engring., U. Calif., Berkeley, 1958. Registered profl. engr., Calif., Oreg., Wash., traffic engr., Calif., land surveyor, Oreg.; cert. c.c. instr., Calif. Engring. aid County Rd. Dept., L.A., 1951, asst. civil engr., 1953-58; dir. pub. wks. Benicia, Calif., 1958-59; dep. dir. pub. wks. Solano County, Calif., 1959-65; dir. pub. wks. Humboldt County, Calif., 1965-92; mgmt. cons., 1992—; gen. mgr. Humboldt Bay Wastewater Authority 1975, 82-89. Mem. Employer support of N.G. and Res. With AUS, 1951-53. Recipient Outstanding Svc. award North Bay chpt. Calif. Soc. Profl. Engrs., 1964, Boss of the Yr. award Arcata Jaycees, Recognition award Humboldt Toastmaster, Meritorious Leadership award, Surveyor award Calif. Land Surveyors Assn., Illmars Lagzdin award for engring. contbns., Guy C. Kulstad award Humboldt County Dept. Pub. Wks. Fellow ASCE; NSPE, mem. Nat. Soc. County Engrs., Calif. County Engrs., County Engrs. Assn. Calif., Commonwealth Club of Calif., Sons of Norway.

KULTERMANN, UDO, architectural and art historian; b. Stettin, Germany, Oct. 14, 1927; came to U.S., 1967, naturalized, 1981; s. Georg and Charlotte (Schultz) K.; m. Judith Danoff, May 10, 1975. Student, U. Greifswald, Germany, 1946-50; Ph.D. magna cum laude, U. Muenster, Germany, 1953. Curatorial asst. Kunsthalle, Bremen, Germany, 1954-55; art editor Bertelsmann Pubs., Guetersloh, Germany, 1955-56; program dir. Am. House, Bremen, Germany, 1956-59; dir. city art mus. Schloss Morsbroich, Leverkusen, Germany, 1959-64; dir. Morsbroicher Kunsttage, Leverkusen, Germany, 1961; lectr. Duesseldorfer Geschichts Verein, Duesseldorf, Germany, 1953, 62, Technische Hochschule, Braunschweig, Germany, 1962, Oslo U., 1963, Trondheim U., Harvard U., Yale U., U. Calif., Berkeley, UCLA, U. Pa., U. Minn., 1965—; prof. archtl. history Washington U., St. Louis, 1967-94, Ruth and Norman Moore Prof. of Architecture and Urbanism, 1986-94, prof. emeritus, 1994—; ednl. leader study tours with German architects to Japan, 1965, 67; participant 1st Internat. Congress African Culture, Salisbury, So. Rhodesia, 1962, 2d Biennale of Arab Art, Rabat, Morocco, 1976-77, Internat. Symposium for Islamic Architecture and Urbanism, Dammam, Saudi Arabia, 1980; lectr. U. Tel Aviv, U. Haifa, U. Jerusalem, 1972, U. Melbourne, U. Sydney, U. Calcutta, U. Bombay, 1977, U. Cairo, U. Beirut, 1978, U. Damascus, U. Khartoum, 1979, U. Buenos Aires, 1980, U. Kuala Lumpur, U. Singapore, U. Jakarta, U. Manila, U. Bangkok, U. Hong Kong, 1985, Tulane U., New Orleans, NYU, Achtl. Assn., London, 1989, U. N.Mex., Albuquerque, 1990, 93, Courtauld Inst., U. London, 1991, 92, Wallraff-Richartz-Mus., Cologne, U. Karlsruhe, 1991, U. Basel, Switzerland, German Architecture Mus., Frankfurt, 1992, U. Saarbruecken, others; mem. Architecture commn. Biennale Venice, 1979-82; ednl. leader Soviet-Am. Travelling Architecture Seminar, Moscow and Leningrad, 1987, Tashkent, Bukhara and Samarkand, all USSR, 1986-87; mem. jury Nat. U. in Al Ain, United Arab Emirates; ednl. leader Nat. Trust for Hist. Preservation Cruise, Copenhagen, Amsterdam, Rouen, Mont St. Michel, Bordeaux, Lisbon, 1989; participant in symposium The Translatability Between Cultures, Kyoto, Japan, 1992, Internat. Conf. Washington U., St. Louis; plenary speaker Am. Studies in Ideology Conf., U. Klagenfurt, Austria; guest speaker 1st World Wide Info. and Tech. Strategy Practitioner Meeting, St. Charles, Ill., 1993, and many other lectures; faculty seminar Pratt Inst. Brooklyn, 1994, Louvre, 1995, Bonn. U., 1995-96, Landau U., Mus. Schloss, Morsbroich, Leverkusen, Germany, 1996, Stiftung fuer Konkrete Kunst, Reutlingen, Germany, 1997, Middle Eastern Technical U., Ankara, Turkey, Jeu de Paume, Paris, 1998. Author: Architecture of Today, 1958, Hans und Wassili Luckhardt-Bauten und Projekte, 1958, Dynamische Architektur, 1959, New Japanese Architecture, 1960, New Architecture in Africa, 1963, Junge deutsche Bildhauer, 1963, New Architecture in the World, 1965, History of Art History, 1966, paperback edit., 1981, rev. edit., 1993, Japanese edit., 1996, Spanish edit., 1996, Italian edit., 1997, Korean edit., 1999, The New Sculpture-Assemblage and Environments, 1967, Gabriel Grupello, 1968, The New Painting, 1969, rev. edit., 1978, New Directions in African Architecture, 1969, Art and Life: The Function of Intermedia, 1970, (with Werner Hofmann) Modern Architecture in Color, 1970, Kenzo Tange: Architecture and Urban Design, 1970, paperback edits., 1978, 89, New Realism, 1972, Die Architektur im 20 Jahrhundert, 1977, 5th edit., 1987, Am. edit., 1993, Korean edit., 1998, Ernest Trova, 1978, I Contemporanei, Storia della Scultura nel Mondo, 1979, Architecture in the Seventies, 1980, Architects of the Third World, 1980, Zeitgenoessische Architektur in Osteuropa, 1985, Spanish edit., 1989, Kleine Geschichte der Kunsttheorie, 1987, Japanese edit., 1996, Korean edit., 1997, rev. 2d edit., 1998, Visible Cities-Invisible Cities-Urban Symbolism and Historical Continuity 1988, Kunst und Wirklichkeit-Von Fiedler bis Derrida-Zehn Annaeherungen, 1991, Die Maxentius-Basilika.Ein Schluesselwerk spaetantiker Architektur, 1996, Contemporary Architecture in the Arab States—Renaissance of a Region, 1999; editor: St. James Modern Masterpieces: The Best of Art, Architecture, Photography and Design Since 1945, 1998, Architektur der Welt, Verlag und Datenbank fuer Geisterwissenschaften, Weimar, 1996—, vol. VI Architecture in South and Central Africa in World Architecture: A Critical Mosaic 1900-2000, Beijing, China, 1999. Faculty mem. Nat. Humanities Faculty, Atlanta, 1986—. Recipient Disting. Faculty award Washington U., 1985. Mem. Croatian Acad. Scis. and Arts (corr.).

KULZICK, KENNETH EDMUND, retired lawyer, writer; b. Milw., July 20, 1927; s. Earl Joseph and Claire Agnes (Blask) K.; m. Patricia Louise Siekert, June 19, 1949; 1 child, Kate Kulzick Stafford. PhB, Marquette U., Milw., 1950; JD, UCLA, 1956. Bar: Calif. 1956, U.S. Dist. Ct. (no. and cen. dists.) Calif. 1956, U.S. Ct. Appeals (9th cir.) 1956. Teaching asst., researcher UCLA, 1953-56; asst. U.S. atty. (honor grad program) Dept. Justice, L.A., San Francisco, 1956-58; ptnr. Lillick, McHose & Charles, L.A., 1958-86, Liebig & Kulzick, L.A., 1987-91, Gipson, Hoffman & Pancione, L.A., 1991-94; media cons. specializing in dramatic documentaries, 1958—; media advisor League of Women Voters, L.A., 1986, 90; lectr. UCLA, 1987—. Contbr. articles to L.A. Lawyer mag., EMMY mag., Entertainment Law Reporter, others; bd. editors UCLA Law Rev., 1954-56. Served to lt. USN, 1950-53; Korea. Home: PO Box 1926 Eagle River WI 54521-1926 also (winter): 1520 Scenic Dr Felton CA 95018-9642

KUMANYIKA, SHIRIKI K., human nutrition and dietetics educator; b. Balt., Mar. 16, 1945; m. Christiaan B. Morssink; children: Chenjerai, Anoesjka. BA, Syracuse U., 1965; MS in Social Work, Columbia U., 1969; PhD in Human Nutrition, Cornell U., 1978; MPH, Johns Hopkins U., 1984. Asst. prof. nutrition Cornell U., Ithaca, N.Y., 1977-84; from asst. prof. to assoc. prof. epidemiology Johns Hopkins U. Sch. Hygiene and Pub. Health, Balt., 1984-89, asst. prof. internat. health, 1984-89; assoc. prof. nutritional epidemiology Pa. State U., University Park, 1989-92, prof. epidemiology, 1993-96; assoc. dir. for epidemiology Pa. State U. Coll. Medicine, Hershey, 1992-96; prof. epidemiology, prof. human nutrition and dietetics U. Ill. at Chgo., 1996—, head dept. human nutrition and dietetics, 1996—; chief of svc. U. Ill. Hosp. Nutritional Svcs., 1996—; adj. prof. epidemiology dept. health evaluation scis. Coll. Medicine, Pa. State U., Hershey, 1996—; mem. adv. bd. Women's Health Alliance. Contbr. articles to profl. jours. Bd. dirs. Nat. Black Women's Health Project, 1994—. Nat. Rural Ctr., 1978-82; active WHO. NIH grantee; recipient Corson medal Franklin Inst., 1997. Fellow Am. Coll. Epidemiology, Am. Coll. Nutrition; mem. AAUP, APHA, Am. Diabetes Assn., Am. Dietetic Assn., Am. Inst. Nutrition, Am. Soc. for Clin. Nutrition, Assn. Black Cardiologists, Internat. Soc. on Hypertension in Blacks, Nat. Med. Assn., N.Am. Assn. Study of Obesity, Soc. for Epidemiol. Rsch., Soc. for Nutrition Edn., Internat. Soc. and Fedn. Cardiology, others. Office: U Ill at Chgo Human Nutrition/Dietetics 1919 W Taylor St Rm 650 Chicago IL 60612-7246

KUMAR, ANIL, nuclear engineer; b. Agra, India, Aug. 3, 1952; came to U.S., 1988; s. Vedprakash and Satyawati (Sudhir) Parashar; m. Geeta Sharma, Nov. 29, 1979; children: Amitabh, Kishen. MSc in Physics, Agra U., 1973; PhD in Nuclear Engring., U. Bombay, India, 1981. Sci. officer Bhabha Atomic Rsch. Ctr., Bombay, 1974-81; sr. researcher Ecole Poly. Fed. Lausanne, Switzerland, 1982-88; devel. engr. UCLA, 1988-90, sr. devel. engr., 1990-99; dir. T.C. Rsch. Ctr., Culver City, Calif., 1998—. Contbr. articles to Jour. Fusion Energy, Nuclear Sci. and Engring., Fusion Tech., Fusion Engring. and Design, Atom Kern Energie, proc. internat. confs. and symposia. Mem. Am. Nuclear Soc., Am. Phys. Soc., Soc. Indsl. and Applied Math. Achievements include research in modified wigner rational approximation in neutronics, Boltzmann Fokker Planck transport equation, measurements of induced radioactivity and nuclear heating in fusion neutron environment, inertial confinement fusion, low activation materials, fusion reactor design, muon catalyzed fusion. Office: TC Rsch Ctr 4248 Overland Ave Ste 3 Culver City CA 90230-3701

KUMAR, ANITA, reporter; b. Charlottesville, Va., July 6, 1970; d. Shiv and Madhu (Bhatia) K. B in Govt. and Fgn. Affairs, U. Va., 1992. Reporter The Star Exponent, Culpeper, Va., 1992, The News and Advance, Lynchburg, Va., 1993-95, The News and Record, Greensboro, N.C., 1995-96, The St. Petersburg (Fla.) Times, 1996—; mng. editor The Cavalier Daily, U. Va., 1991-92. Recipient Journalism award Va. Bar Assn., 1996, 1st place for in-depth reporting Va. Press Assn., 1995, Excellence in Journalism award Va. Trial Lawyers Assn., 1995, others. Fellow Newspaper Assn. Am.; mem. Investigative Reports and Editors, N.C. Working Press, Cavalier Daily Alumni Assn. (bd. dirs. 1992—). Office: St Petersburg Times 710 Court St Clearwater FL 33756-5508

KUMAR, BANGAROSWAMY VIJAYA, neurologist; b. Feb. 18, 1961. MBBS, Madras Med. Coll., 1983. Neurologist NEA Clinic, Jonesboro, Ark., 1966—. Home: 2609 Greenbriar Dr Jonesboro AR 72401

KUMAR, KAPLESH, materials scientist; b. Lucknow, India, Nov. 9, 1947; came to U.S., 1970; s. Shiam and Vidya (Devi) Sunder; m. Savinder Kaur, May 27, 1974; children: Priyadarshini, Ruchira. B.Tech., Indian Inst. Tech., 1969; MS, Stevens Inst. Tech., 1971; ScD, MIT, 1975; JD magna cum laude, New Eng. Sch. Law, 1997. Bar: Mass. 1998; registered patent atty. Mem. tech. staff Charles Stark Draper Lab., Inc., Cambridge, Mass., 1975-80, chief materials devel. sect., 1980-88, chief materials sci. and tech. sect., 1988-91, prin. mem. tech. staff, 1992—; vis. lectr. IIM-ASM Internat., 1989; chmn. workshop on superconductivity and its applications to nat. needs, 1991; session chmn. Structures, Dynamics & Materials Conf., AIAA, 1996, 97. Author: (with others) Plasma Spraying: Theory and Applications, 1993; patentee in materials processing; pub. Applied Physics Review monograph, 1988; contbr. articles to profl. jours. Recipient Patent award Charles Stark Draper Lab., Inc., 1982, Outstanding Performance award, 1994, Invention Disclosure award NASA, 1983. Mem. ASM Internat. (mem. internat. materials revs. com. 1991—), AIAA (mem. materials tech. com. 1991-98), MIT Sangam Club for India Affairs (pres. 1972-73), India Assn. Greater Boston, Inc. (pres. 1995-97), IIT Soc. New Eng. (v.p. 1993-95), Indian Am. Forum for Polit. Edn. (pres. New Eng. chpt. 1998—). Achievements include research in intellectual property law; permanent and soft magnetic materials; structural materials; micromechanical devices, inertial instruments; subspecialties include materials; ceramics.

KUMAR, KRISHAN, management consultant company executive; b. Patiala, India, Aug. 17, 1944; came to U.S., 1970; naturalized, 1978; s. Sewa Ram and Savitri (Devi) Aggarwal; B.S.M.E. (Merit scholar), Birla Inst. Tech. and Sci., India, 1966; M.S.I.E., N.J. Inst. Tech., 1975; m. Saroj, July 23, 1969; children: Anuj, Amit. Engring. positions in U.S. and India, 1966-73; indsl. engr., then sr. indsl. engr. Berkey Photo, Inc., Clifton, N.J., 1973-76; assoc. Walter Frederick Friedman & Co., West Orange, N.J., 1977—, v.p., 1981-85; pres. Eskay Cons. Group, Edison, N.J., 1985—. Mem. Am. Inst. Indsl. Engrs. (sr.), Inst. Mgmt. Cons. (cert.), Coun. Logistics Mgmt., Am. Arbitration Assn. (panelist). Contbr. articles to profl. jours. Home and Office: 6 Vallata Pl Edison NJ 08820-1688

KUMAR, KRISHNA, physics educator; b. Meerut, India, July 14, 1936; came to U.S., 1956, naturalized, 1966; s. Rangi and Susheila (Devi) Lal; m. Katharine Johnson, May 1, 1960; children: Jai Robert, Raj David. BSc in Physics, Chemistry and Math., Agra U., 1953, MSc in Physics, 1955; MS in Physics, Carnegie Mellon U., 1959, PhD in Physics, 1964. Rsch. assoc. Mich. State U., 1963-66, MIT, 1966-67; rsch. fellow Niels Bohr Inst., Copenhagen, 1967-69; physicist Oak Ridge (Tenn.) Nat. Lab., 1969-71; assoc. prof. Vanderbilt U., Nashville, 1971-77; fgn. collaborator AEC of France, Paris, 1977-79; Nordita prof. U. Bergen, Norway, 1979-80; prof. physics Tenn. Tech. U., Cookville, 1980-83, 1983-99, prof. physics emeritus, 1999—; lectr. in field; cons. various rsch. labs. Author: Nuclear Models and the Search for Unity in Nuclear Physics, 1984, Superheavy Elements, 1989; contbr. articles to profl. jours., books. Sec. India Assn., Pitts., 1958-59; faculty advisor, assoc. mem. Triangle Fraternity, 1990—; deacon Presbyn. Ch., 1991-93; faculty advisor Indian Assn. of Cookeville, 1994-95. Recipient Gold medal Agra U., 1955; NSF rsch. grantee, 1972-75. Mem. Indian Phys. Soc., Am. Phys. Soc., Tenn. Acad. Scis., Internat. Cmty. Hospitality Assn. (pres. 1992-94), Planetary Soc., Rotary (Paul Harris fellow, bd. dirs. internat. coms. 1991-92), Phi Kappa Phi, Sigma Pi Sigma, Sigma Xi (bd. dirs. 1992-93, charter mem. chpt. installation 1994). Democrat. Home: 718 W 12th St Cookeville TN 38501-7788 Office: Tenn Tech U Box 5051 Cookeville TN 38505

KUMAR, PANGANAMALA RAMANA, electrical and computer engineering educator; b. Nagpur, Maharashtra, India, Apr. 21, 1952; came to U.S., 1973; s. Panganamala Bhavanarayana and Panganamala Kamala (Avasarala) Murthy; m. Devarakonda Jayashree Sundaram, Jan. 22, 1982; children: P. Ashwin, Shilpa P. BTech., Indian Inst. Tech., Madras, India, 1973; MS, Washington U., 1975, DSc, 1977. Asst. prof. dept. math. and computer sci. U. Md., Baltimore County, 1977-82, assoc. prof. dept. math. and computer sci., 1982-84; assoc. prof. dept. elec. and computer engring. and coordinated sci. lab. U. Ill., Urbana, 1985-87, prof. dept. elec. and computer engring., 1987—, rsch. prof. coordinated sci. lab., 1987—. Coauthor: Stochastic Systems, 1986; assoc. editor: Systems and Control Letters, 1984-93, Math. of Control, Signals and Systems, 1986—, SIAM Jour. on Control and Optimization, 1989-93, Jour. of Discrete Event Dynamic Systems: Theory and Application, 1993—; assoc. editor-at-large IEEE Trans. on Automatic Control, 1989-97; mem. editl. bd. Jour. on Adaptive Control and Signal Processing, 1986—, Math. Problems in Engring., 1995—; contbr. articles to profl. jours. Recipient Donald P. Eckman award Am. Automatic Control Coun., 1985. Fellow IEEE. Avocation: table tennis. Office: U Ill Coordinated Sci Lab 1308 W Main St Urbana IL 61801-2307

KUMAR, RAJENDRA, electrical engineering educator; b. Amroha, India, Aug. 22, 1948; came to U.S., 1980; s. Satya Pal Agarwal and Kailash Vati Agarwal; m. Pushpa Agarwal, Feb. 16, 1971; children: Anshu, Shipra. BS in Math. and Sci., Meerut Coll., 1964; BEE, Indian Inst. Tech., Kanpur, 1969, MEE, 1977; PhD in Electrical Engring., U. New Castle, NSW, Australia, 1981. Mem. tech. staff Electronis and Radar Devel., Bangalore, India, 1969-72; rsch. engr. Indian Inst. Tech., Kanpur, 1972-77; asst. prof. Calif. State U., Fullerton, 1981-83, Brown U., Providence, 1980-81; prof. Calif. State U., Long Beach, 1983—; cons. Jet Propulsion Lab., Pasadena, Calif., 1984-91. Contbr. numerous articles to profl. jours.; patentee; efficient detection and signal parameter estimation with applications to high dynamic GPS receivers; multistage estimation of received carrier signal parameters under very high dynamic conditions of the receiver; fast frequency acquisition via adaptive least squares algorithms. Recipient Best Paper award Internat. Telemetering Conf., Las Vegas, 1986, 10 New Technology awards NASA, Washington, 1987-91. Mem. IEEE (sr.), NEA, AAUP, Calif. Faculty Assn., Auto Club So. Calif. (Cerritos), Sigma Xi, Eta Kappa Nu, Tau Beta Pi (eminent mem.). Avocations: gardening, walking, hiking, reading. Home: 13910 Rose St Cerritos CA 90703-9043 Office: Calif State U 1250 N Bellflower Blvd Long Beach CA 90840-0001

KUMAR, RAJESH, biochemist researcher; b. Biwan, Haryana, India, Apr. 12, 1965; came to U.S., 1996; s. Om Parkash and Barfi Devi; m. Sandhya Sanghi, Nov. 22, 1997; 1 child, Partha Gupta. PhD, Panjab U., Chandigarh, India, 1994. Rsch. assoc. in biochemistry Inst. Microbial Tech., Chandigarh, 1994-96, U. Va., Charlottesville, 1996—. Contbr. articles to sci. jours. Mem. Am. Soc. Cell Biology. Avocations: swimming, computers, reading. Office: U Va 1300 Jefferson Park Ave Charlottesville VA 22908-0001

KUMAR, ROMESH, chemical engineer; b. Rajpura, India, Oct. 18, 1944; came to U.S., 1966; s. Kundan Lal and Pushpa (Wati) Agarwal; m. Kumkum Khanna, Feb. 22, 1976. B.S., Panjab U., India, 1965; M.S., U. Calif., Berkeley, 1968, Ph.D., 1972. Postdoctoral appointee Argonne (Ill.) Nat. Lab., 1972-73, asst. chem. engr., 1973-76, chem. engr., 1976—; also group leader Transp. Applications Chem. Tech. div. Argonne Nat. Lab.; tchr. fuel cell power sys. design and analysis for transp. applications. Contbr. to Weissberger's Techniques in Chemistry, 1975. Recipient Silver medal Panjab U., 1965. Hindu. Patentee in field. Home: 1549 Ceals Ct Naperville IL 60565-6148 Office: 9700 Cass Ave Argonne IL 60439-4803

KUMAR, SHAILENDRA, urologist, educator; b. Patna, Bihar, India, Oct. 7, 1941; m. Singh Meera; children: Yash, Pratish, Priya. MD, Patna Med. Coll., 1964. Urologist Howard U., 1970-73. Mem. Am. Urol. Assn., P.G. County Med. Assn. Office: 6510 Kenilworth Ave # 2200 Riverdale MD 20737

KUMAR, SURINDER, electrical engineering educator, consultant; b. Multan, Panjab, India, Aug. 26, 1945; arrived in Can., 1976; s. Lakhpat Rai and Parkash Vati; m. Suman Lata; children: Saket, Sumit. BSc, Dayanand Anglo Vedic Coll., Jullundur, India, 1964; B in Engring., Indian Inst. of Sci., Bangalore, India, 1967; M in Tech., Indian Inst. of Tech., Kanpur, India, 1971; PhD, Carleton U., Ottawa, Ont., Can., 1978. Sr. sci. officer Govt. of India, Delhi, 1967-69, 71-75; prin. sci. officer Govt. of India, Dehradun, 1978-82; v.p. rsch. SED Systems, Saskatoon, Sask., Can., 1982-87; Sid Buckwold rsch. prof. dept. elec. engring. U. Sask., Saskatoon, 1987—; cons. Andrew Corp., Dallas, 1987-90; founder, pres. Wavecom Electronics, Saskatoon, 1988—. Contbr. articles to profl. jours.; patentee communication systems. Mem. IEEE (sr.). Avocations: poetry, painting, hiking. Home: 222 Cardinal Crescent, Saskatoon, SK Canada S7L 6H8 Office: U Sask, WaveCom Electronics Inc, Dept Elec Engring, Saskatoon, SK Canada S7N 0W0 *Far too much time and effort is spent on strife and struggle between individuals, communities and nations and not enough on making the World better and more peaceful for everyone.*

KUMBLE, STEVEN JAY, lawyer; b. July 3, 1933; m. Barbara Kumble (div.); children: Charles Todd, Roger Glenn; m. Peggy Basten Vandervoort. BA, Yale U., 1954; JD, Harvard U., 1959; LLD (hon.), L.I. U., 1990. Bar: N.Y. 1960. Ptnr. Finley, Kumble, Wagner, Underberg, Manley & Casey, N.Y.C., 1968-87; of counsel Summit Rovins & Feldesman, N.Y.C., 1988-90; chmn. bd. dirs. Lincolnshire Mgmt., Inc., N.Y.C., 1985—. Vice chmn. bd. dirs. L.I.U., Greenvale, N.Y., 1984—, chm., 1982-94; trustee bd. Gov.'s Com. on Scholastic Achievement, N.Y.C., 1981—. 1st lt. U.S. Army, 1955-57. Mem. Assn. of Bar of City of N.Y., Phi Beta Kappa, Yale Club. Avocations: skiing, golf. Office: Lincolnshire Mgmt 780 3rd Ave 40th Fl New York NY 10017-2024

KUMIN, MAXINE WINOKUR, poet, author; b. Phila., June 6, 1925; d. Peter and Doll (Simon) Winokur; m. Victor Montwid Kumin, June 29, 1946; children: Jane Simon, Judith Montwid, Daniel David. AB, Radcliffe Coll., 1946, MA, 1948; LHD (hon.), Centre Coll., 1976, Davis and Elkins Coll., 1977, Regis Coll., 1979, New England Coll., 1982, Claremont Grad. Sch., 1983, U. N.H., 1984. Instr. Tufts U., Medford, Mass., 1958-61, lectr. English, 1965-68; scholar Radcliffe Inst. for Ind. Study, 1961-63; vis. lectr. U. Mass., Amherst, 1973, Princeton U., 1979, 81-82; adj. prof. Columbia U., 1975; Fannie Hurst prof. of literature Brandeis U., 1975, Wash. U., St. Louis, 1977; vis. sr. fellow, lectr. Princeton U., 1977; Carolyn Wilkerson Bell vis. scholar Randolph-Macon Woman's Coll., 1978; writer in residence Fla. Internat. U., 1998; poet in residence Bucknell U., 1983; vis. prof. MIT, 1984, U. Miami, 1995, Pitzer Coll., 1996, Fla. Internat. U., 1998; McGee prof. of writing Davidson Coll., 1997; master artist Atlantic Ctr. for Arts, New Smyrna Beach, Fla., 1984; staff mem. Bread Loaf Writers' Conf., 1969-71, 73, 75, 77; poetry cons. Library of Congress, 1981-82; elector The Poet's Corner, The Cathedral of St. John the Divine, 1990—; mem. staff Sewanee Writer's Conf., 1993-94. Author: (poetry) Halfway, 1961, The Privilege, 1965, The Nightmare Factory, 1970, Up Country: Poems of New England, 1972 (Pulitzer Prize for poetry 1973), House, Bridge, Fountain, Gate, 1975, The Retrieval System, 1978, Our Ground Time Here Will Be Brief, 1982, Closing the Ring, 1984, The Long Approach, 1985, Nurture, 1989, Looking for Luck, 1992, Connecting the Dots, 1996, Selected Poems 1960-1990, 1997; (novels) Through Dooms of Love, 1965, The Passions of Uxport, 1968, The Abduction, 1971, The Designated Heir, 1974; (essays) To Make A Prairie: Essays on Poets, Poetry, and Country Living, 1980, In Deep: Country Essays, 1987, Women, Animals and Vegetables: Essays and Stories, 1994; (short stories) Why Can't We Live Together Like Civilized Human Beings?, 1982; (juvenile) Sebastian and the Dragon, 1960, Spring Things, 1961, A Summer Story, 1961, Follow the Fall, 1961, A Winter Friend, 1961, Mittens in May, 1962, No One Writes a Letter to the Snail, 1962, (with Anne Sexton) Eggs of Things, 1963, Archibald the Traveling Poodle, 1963, (with Sexton) More Eggs of Things, 1964, Speedy Digs Downside Up, 1964, The Beach Before Breakfast, 1964, Paul Bunyan, 1966, Faraway Farm, 1967, The Wonderful Babies of 1809 and Other Years, 1968, When Grandmother Was Young, 1970, When Great-Grandmother Was Young, 1971, (with Sexton) Joey and the Birthday Present, 1971, (with Sexton) The Wizard's Tears, 1975, What Color Is Caesar?, 1978, The Microscope, 1984; contbr. poems to nat. mags. Recipient Lowell Mason Palmer award, 1960, William Marion Reedy award, 1968, Eunice Tietjens Meml. prize Poetry Mag., 1972, Borestone Mountain award, 1976, Radcliffe Coll. Alumnae Recognition award, 1978, Am. Acad. and Inst. Arts and Letters award for excellence in literature, 1980, Levinson award Poetry mag., 1987, The Poets' prize, 1994, Aiken Taylor Poetry prize, 1995, Centennial award Harvard Grad. Sch. Arts and Scis., 1996; grantee Nat. Endowment for the Arts, 1966; fellow Nat. Coun. on Arts and Humanities, 1967-68; fellow Acad. Am. Poets, 1986; fellow Woodrow Wilson, 1979-80, 91-93. Mem. Acad. Am. Poets (chancellor), Poetry Soc. Am., PEN Am., Authors Guild, The Writers Union. Address: Scott Waxman Agy Inc 1650 Broadway Ste 1011 New York NY 10019*

KUMM, WILLIAM HOWARD, energy products company executive; b. Bahia, Brazil, Feb. 6, 1931; s. Henry William and A. Joyce (Beale) K.; came to U.S., 1938, naturalized, 1949; B.A., Amherst Coll., 1952; cert. bus. adminstrn. McCoy Coll., Johns Hopkins U., 1959; m. Anne K. Gibson, July 11, 1953; children: John H., Elizabeth A., Katharine L. With Westinghouse Electric Corp., 1952-78, student, Pitts., 1952-53, jr. engr. AirArm div., Balt., 1953-54, sr. engr., 1955-60, supervisory engr. Westinghouse Surface div., Balt., 1961-62, supervisory engr. Systems Ops. div., 1962-65, mgr. advanced concept engring. sect. Westinghouse Ocean Research & Engring. Center, Annapolis, Md., 1965-69, subdiv. mgr., 1969-71; presdl. interchange exec. Pres.'s Commn. on Personnel Interchange, assigned NOAA, 1971-72; staff Nat. Adv. Com. on Oceans and Atmosphere, Washington, 1972; program mgr. submarine transp. project U.S. Maritime Adminstrn., 1972-73; mgr. marine programs Westinghouse Oceanic Div., 1973-78; pres., chief exec. officer Arctic Enterprises, Inc., 1978—, Arctic Energies Ltd., Trans Polar Shipping Co., Inc., Ottawa, Ont., Can., 1981—; exec. v.p. Agua Solar SA de CV, Mexico, 1993—; pres. H2otec Corp., Irvine, Calif., 1994—; participant joint Nat. Acad. Scis.-Nat. Acad. Engring. planning effort on Internat. Decade Ocean Exploration for Nat. Council on Marine Resources and Engring., 1968-69. Mem. Rural Area Devel. Bd., Carroll County, N.H., 1964-65; mem. Citizens Adv. Council on Edn., 1970-72; del. County Council PTAs, 1970, 71, treas. Cub Scout pack 332, Boy Scouts Am., Catonsville, Md., 1963-65; participant congl. office of Tech. Assessment Study of Marine Applications for Fuel Cell Tech., 1985. Registered profl. engr., Md. Mem. Soc. Naval Architects and Marine Engrs., Presdl. Interchange Exec. Assn. Participant Nat. Sci. Found., 1987. Patentee in field. Contbr. chpt. to Man Beneath the Sea, 1972. Home and Office: 511 Heavitree Ln Severna Park MD 21146-1010

KUMMER, FRED S., construction company executive; b. 1929. Student, U. Mo., 1952. Engr. William Ittner & Co., 1952-56; with Buckley Constrn. Co., Inc., 1957-59, Kummer Constrn. Co., Inc., from 1959; now pres., treas. HBE Corp., St. Louis. Office: Adam's Mark Hotels 11330 Olive St Rd Box 27339 Saint Louis MO 63141

KUMMER, GLENN F., manufactured housing executive; b. Park City, Utah, 1933. B.S., U. Utah, 1961. Sr. acct. Ernst & Ernst, 1961-65; trainee Fleetwood Enterprises Inc., Riverside, Calif., 1965-67, purchasing mgr., 1967-68, plant mgr., 1968-70, gen. mgr. recreational vehicle div., 1970-71, asst. v.p. ops., 1971-72, sr. v.p. ops., 1972-77, exec. v.p. ops., 1977-82, pres., 1982-98, dir., 1983—, chmn., CEO, 1998—. Office: Fleetwood Enterprises Inc PO Box 7638 3125 Myers St Riverside CA 92503-5544

KUMMER, WOLFGANG H., electrical engineer; b. Stuttgart, Germany, Oct. 10, 1925. BS, U. Calif., Berkeley, 1946, MS, 1947, PhD, 1954. Self-employed elec. engr.; mem. U.S. Comms. B & F, Internat. Sci. Radio Union; mem. evaluation panel NBS, Nat. Acad. Scis., 1975-81. Fellow IEEE (activities editor AP-S newsletter 1964-68, gen. chmn. AP-S internat. conv. 1971, chmn. antenna stds. subcom. 2.11 1971-77, adcom mem. AP-S 1972-79); mem. Antennas and Propagation Soc. (pres. 1975, chmn. 1985-86), Phi Beta Kappa, Tau Beta Pi, Eta Kappa Nu, Sigma Xi, Alpha Mu Gamma. Office: 1310 Sunset Ave Santa Monica CA 90405-5843

KUMMERFELD, DONALD DAVID, publisher; b. Gilroy, Calif., June 11, 1934; s. Theodore and Edith Aileen (Bowman) K.; m. Elizabeth Kubota Miller, Feb. 14, 1970; 1 dau., Theodosia W. B.A., Stanford U., 1956, M.A., 1958; M.A., Harvard U., 1960; postgrad., London Sch. Econs., 1961. Prin. examiner housing and urban devel. U.S. Bur. of Budget, Washington, 1961-68; sr. research officer Urban Inst. Washington, 1968-69; ptnr. Govt. Research Corp., Washington, 1969-71; v.p. 1st Boston Corp., N.Y.C., 1971-75; budget dir. City of N.Y., 1976-77, 1st dep. mayor, 1977; exec. dir. N.Y. State Emergency Fin. Control Bd., 1978; pres., chief operating officer News Am. Pub., Inc., 1978-85; chmn. Kummerfeld Assocs., 1985—; pres. Mag. Pubs. of Am. Inc., 1987—; bd. dirs. Sequa Corp., N.Y.C., Educap Inc., Washington, UN Devel. Corp., Internat. House, N.Y.C. Mem. CUNY Inst. Pub. Adminstrn., Grad. Ctr., Milano Grad. Sch., New Sch. U., N.Y.C., Fin. Control Bd. N.Y.C., 1985-90; chmn. Mayor's Task Force on Homeless, N.Y.C., 1986-87. Brookings Instn. fellow, 1965. Clubs: Harvard, Metropolitan (N.Y.C.). Office: Mag Pubs Am Inc 919 3rd Ave Fl Dave22D New York NY 10022-3902

KUMMEROW, ARNOLD A., superintendent of schools; b. Framingham, Mass., Mar. 25, 1945; s. Arnold A. Sr. and Elizabeth Patricia (Westfield) K.; m. Constance Booth, July 10, 1971. BME, Eastern Mich. U., 1968, MA, 1975; PhD, U. Mich., 1989. Cert. adminstrn., Mich. Instrumental music dir. Vandercook Lake Pub. Schs., Jackson, Mich., 1968-74; instrumental music dir., asst. prin., prin. L'Anse Creuse Pub. Schs., Mt. Clemens, Mich., 1975-89; asst. supt. curriculum and pers. Lincoln Consol. Schs., Ypsilanti, Mich., 1989-91; asst. supt. Ypsilanti Pub. Schs., 1991-93; mem. curriculum devel. staff Mich. Dept. Edn., 1993-94; supt. Carsonville-Port Sanilac (Mich.) Schs., 1994-97, Armada (Mich.) Area Schs., 1997—. Named Exemplary Sch. Prin., Mich. Dept. Edn. and U.S. Dept. Edn. Mem. AASA, MASA, ASCD. Home: 17201 Knollwood Dr Clinton Township MI 48038-2833 Office: Armada Area Schs 74500 Burk St Armada MI 48005-2700

KUMMINGS, DONALD DALE, English educator; b. Lafayette, Ind., July 28, 1940; s. Herman Wilhelm and Estelle Catherine (Easterwood) K.; m. Gail Nadine Savage, Mar. 23, 1963 (div. Aug. 1978); children: Kevin Scott (dec.), Jeremy William; m. Patricia Finnelly Larson, Mar. 21, 1987. BA, Purdue U., 1962, MA, 1964; PhD, Ind. U., 1971. Tchg. assoc. Purdue U., West Lafayette, Ind., 1963-64; instr. in English Adrian (Mich.) Coll., 1964-66; assoc. instr. Ind. U., Bloomington, 1966-70; asst. prof. English U. Wis.-Parkside, Kenosha, 1970-75, assoc. prof. English, 1975-85, prof. English, 1985—, chair dept. English, 1974-76, 91-94; book rev. editor Rutgers U., Camden, N.J., 1983-90; panelist, reviewer NEH, Washington, 1992-98; lectr. in field; book manuscript cons. Harcourt Brace Jovanovich, U. Tenn. Press, Susquehanna U. Press, U. Iowa Press, Houghton Mifflin, W.W. Norton, Oxford (Eng.) U. Press. Author: Walt Whitman, 1940-1975: A Reference Guide, 1982, The Open Road Trip: Poems, 1989; editor: Approaches to Teaching Whitman's "Leaves of Grass," 1990; co-editor: Walt Whitman: An Encyclopedia, 1998; contbr. over 115 articles to profl. jours. Mem. Honor Our Neighbors' Origins and Rights, 1991—. Named Wis. Prof. of Yr., Carnegie Found. for Advancement of Tchg., 1997. Mem. MLA (cons. reader 1993, 94), ACLU, Am. Lit. Assn., Acad. Am. Poets, Wis. Fellow of Poets, Walt Whitman Assn., Walt Whitman Birthplace Assn., Greenpeace. Avocations: travel, photography, jazz, racquetball. E-mail: kummings@uwp.edu. Office: U Wis-Parkside Dept English 900 Wood Rd Box 2000 Kenosha WI 53141

KUMMLER, RALPH H., chemical engineering educator; b. Jersey City, Nov. 1, 1940; s. Rudolph Frederick and Gertrude Annette (Kienast) K.; m. Jean Evelyn Helge, Aug. 25, 1962; children—Randolph Henry, Bradley Rolf, Jeffrey Ralf. B.S. in Chem. Engring., Rensselaer Poly. Inst., 1962; Ph.D., Johns Hopkins U., 1966. Chem. engr. Gen. Electric Space Scientist Lab., Valley Forge, Pa., 1965-69; assoc. prof. chem. engring. Wayne State U., Detroit, 1970-75, prof., 1975—, chmn. dept., 1974-93, dir. hazardous waste mgmt. programs, 1986—, assoc. dean rsch., 1997—. Editor Hazardous Materials Mgmt. Handbook; contbr. more than 150 articles to tech. publs.; co-patentee chem. innovations. Bd. dirs., past pres. Kirkwood Lake Assn. Fellow Am. Inst. Chemists, Engr. Soc. Detroit (Young Engr. of Yr. award 1975, Gold award 1990, Disting. Svc. award 1994, Horace Rackham Humanitarian award 1999); mem. AIChE (Svc. award 1981, Chem. Engr. of Yr. award 1981, past pres. Detroit chpt.), Am. Chem. Soc., Mich. Air and Waste Mgmt. Assn. (past pres.), Sigma Xi, Tau Beta Pi. Office: Wayne State U Dept Chem Engring Detroit MI 48202

KUMP, WARREN LEE, diagnostic radiologist; b. Jennings, Kans., June 30, 1926; s. Lee Robert and Hazel Jessie (Bobbitt) K.; m. Patricia Jeanne Burke, Oct. 16, 1950; children: Theresa, Lee, Mary, John. BA, U. Kans., 1947, MD, 1950. Diplomate Am. Bd. Radiology. Intern U. Ill., Chgo., 1950-51; med. officer USN/USMC, 1951-53; resident U. Minn., Mpls., 1953-56; staff radiologist North Meml. Med. Ctr., Mpls., 1957-96; chief radiology North Meml. Med. Ctr., 1965-91, chief of staff, 1974-75, trustee, 1982—, chmn. bd. dirs., 1993—; pres. Mpls. Radiology Assocs., 1965-91. Bd. dirs. Newman Found., 1955-60, St. Therese Found., New Hope, Minn., 1962-94; pres. St. Therese Charitable Svcs., New Hope, 1991-94. Fellow Am. Coll. Radiology; mem. AMA, Radiol. Soc. N.Am., Am. Roentgen Ray Soc., Minn. Radiol. Soc. (pres. 1974-75), Minn. Med. Assn. Roman Catholic. Avocations: reading, traveling, historical research. Office: Mpls Rad Assocs 604 Oakdale Med Bldg Minneapolis MN 55422

KUMTA, PRASHANT NAGESH, materials science educator, engineering educator, consultant; b. Madras, India, Aug. 17, 1960; arrived in U.S., 1984; s. Nagesh Shanker and Soomathee Nagesh (Marballi) K.; m. Ujwala Prashant Kamath, Dec. 20, 1994; 1 child, Tanay. BTech, Indian Inst. Tech., Bombay, 1984; MS, U. Ariz., 1987, PhD, 1990. Undergrad. rsch. asst. Indian Inst. Tech., Bombay, 1983-84; grad. work asst. Oreg. Grad. Ctr., Beaverton, 1984-85; grad. tchg. asst. U. Ariz., Tucson, 1985-87, grad. rsch. asst., 1987-88, grad. rsch. assoc., 1988-90; asst. prof. Carnegie Mellon U., Pitts., 1990-95, assoc. prof., 1995-99, prof., 1999—; prin. investigator Eveready Battery Co., Cleve., 1993—, Changs Ascending, Taiwan, 1996—, cons. 1998—; prin. investigator Jet Propulsion Lab., Pasadena, Calif., 1997—, Pitts. Plate Glass (PPG) Industries, 1998—; cons. Timo Industry, Pitts., 1992-93; mem. summer rsch. faculty Air Force Office, Washington, 1993. Author, editor: Role of Ceramics in Advanced Electrochemical Systems, 1996, Covalent Ceramics: Science and Technology of Non-Oxides, 1996, Chemical Processing Aspects of Electronic Ceramics, 1998; contbr. articles to profl. jours. Recipient Rsch. initiation award NSF, Washington, 1993; grantee NSF, Air Force Office, Army Rsch. Office, Advanced Rsch. Projects Agy., Washington, 1993—. Mem. Am. Ceramic Soc., Materials Rsch. Soc., Electrochem. Soc. Achievements include pioneering development of thio-sol-gel and hydrazide sol-gel processes to synthesize transition and rare-earth chalcogenides and nitrides, hydrozide sol-gel process to generate nitride ceramics, novel complexed precursor approaches to new non-oxide ceramics, patents pending related to development of novel processes to fabricate lithium-ion electrodes and new electrode materials, and new biomaterials for bone tissue engineering. Avocations: tennis, music, reading. Office: Carnegie Mellon U 4305 Wean Hall 5000 Forbes Ave Pittsburgh PA 15213-3890

KUN, JOYCE ANNE, secondary education educator, small business owner; b. Salem, Ohio, Oct. 20, 1946; d. Robert Malvern Slutz and Helen Roberta (Williams) Short; m. James Joseph Kun, June 10, 1978; 1 child, Jessica Erin. BS in Edn., Ohio U., 1969; MA in Tech., Kent State U., 1980. Cert. tchr., Ohio. Tchr. Ridgewood Local, West Lafayette, Ohio, 1970-71, Norton (Ohio) High Sch., 1971—; owner The Norton Pub, Norton, 1992—. Mem. NEA, Nat. Soc. DAR, Ohio Edn. Assn., Ohio Tech. Edn. Assn., N.E. Ohio Tech. Edn. Assn. (officer 1972-78), Norton Classroom Tchrs. Assn. (exec. bd.), Norton Grange, Barberton Moose Lodge, Epsilon Pi Tau. Lutheran. Avocation: bowling, golf, flower gardening. Office: The Norton Pub 4020 Cleve Mass Rd Norton OH 44203-5601 Home: 3500 Greenwich Rd Norton OH 44203-5567 Office: Norton High Sch 4128 Cleve Mass Rd Norton OH 44203-5633

KUN, KENNETH A., business executive; b. Bklyn., July 14, 1930; s. Elemer and Elizabeth (Strom) K.; m. Carolyn C. Kun, July 3, 1955; children: Michael Eric, Deborah Kun LoBello. BS in Chemistry, Bklyn. Coll., 1952; MS in Chemistry, Bklyn. Poly. Inst., 1955, Yale U., 1959; PhD in Chemistry, Yale U., 1961. Sr. rsch. chemist Rohm and Haas Co., Phila., 1961-66; from product mgr. to Far East regional indsl. product mgr. Rohm and Haas Co., Tokyo, 1966-72; regional mgr. sales, mktg., and tech. for Latin Am. Rohm and Haas Co., Miami, Fla., 1972-76; mgr. environ. and pollution control rsch. Rohm and Haas Co., Phila., 1972-78; dir. mktg. splty. chems. divsn. Church and Dwight Co., 1978-79; dir. rsch. splty. chems. divsn. Calgon Corp., 1979-81; v.p. rsch., devel. and engring., chief tech. officer Polychrome Corp., 1981-83; pres., CEO, bd. trustees Syracuse (N.Y.) Rsch. Corp., 1983-91; pres. Kun Assocs., Collegeville, Pa., 1991—. Author: Oxidation-Reduction Polymers, 1965, Electron-Transfer Polymers, 1966; contbr. articles to Jour. Am. Chem. Soc., Jour. Organic Chemistry, Jour. Polymer Sci., others; patentee in field. Bd. dirs. Cen. N.Y. Tech. Devel. Orgn.; chmn. Econ. Devel. Commn. Town of Dewitt, N.Y.; active N.Y. Econ. Devel. Commn., United Way Syracuse. Fellow Am. Inst. Chemists; mem. AAAS, ASTM, Am. Assn. Lab. Accreditation (bd. dirs., treas., exec. com.), Am. Chamber Commerce in Japan (chmn. licenses, patent, trademark com.), Am. Chem. Soc. (chmn. Syracuse sect.), Am. Mgmt. Assn., N.Y. Acad. Scis., Bklyn. Coll. Chemist's Assn., Yale Chemists Assn., Yale Sci. & Engring. Assn., Syracuse Chamber Commerce, Assn. Old Crows, Sigma Xi. Telefax: 610-409-9997. E-mail: kenakun@aol.com. Home and Office: 1754 Morgan Ln Collegeville PA 19426-2876

KUNC, JOSEPH ANTHONY, physics and engineering educator, consultant; b. Baranowicze, Poland, Nov. 1, 1943; came to U.S., 1978; s. Stefan and Helena (Kozakiewicz) K.; m. Mary Eva Smolska, May 24, 1979; 1 child, Robert. PhD, Warsaw Tech. U., 1974. Assoc. prof. Warsaw Tech. U., 1974-79; rsch. assoc. prof. U. So. Calif., L.A., 1980-84, assoc. prof., 1985-89, prof. dept. aerospace engring., dept. physics, 1990—; rsch. affiliate Jet Propulsion Lab., Calif. Inst. Tech., 1982-83; vis. scholar Inst. Theoretical Atomic and Molecular Physics, Harvard U., Cambridge, Mass., 1991; vis. scholar dept. high-temperature plasma Nat. Inst. for Nuclear Studies, Warsaw, 1991; vis. scholar atomic and plasma radiation divsn. Nat. Bur. Stds., Washington, 1979; cons. Nat. Tech. Systems, L.A., 1984-86, Phys. Optics Corp., Torrance, Calif., 1988—, Wolfsdorf and Assocs., L.A., 1991; mem. com. on liquid phase kinetics NRC, 1985-86; mem. Dept. Def. Adv. Group on Electron Devices, 1985—; mem. internat. adv. bd. Internat. Symposia Rarefied Gas Dynamics, 1994—; chmn. adv. bd. numerous sci. workshops and symposia. Author: (with others) Advances in Pulsed Power Technology, 1991, Progress in Astronautics and Aeronautics, vol. 116, 1989; contbr. over 200 articles to profl. jours., confs., symposia. Recipient award of merit Nat. Bur. Stds., 1979; fellow Nat. Bur. Stds., 1978, Harvard/Smithsonian fellow Inst. Theoretical Atomic and Molecular Physics, Harvard U., 1991. Fellow AIAA (assoc., mem. thermophysics com. 1994—, chmn. thermophysics publs. com. 1995—), Am. Phys. Soc.; mem. IEEE (sr.), Phi Beta Delta (co-founder Beta Kappa chpt.). Achievements include patent for heat release in micromechanical actuators and engines; principal investigator numerous government-sponsored research programs. Office: U So Calif University Park MC-1191 Los Angeles CA 90089-1191

KUNC, KAREN, artist, educator; b. Omaha, Dec. 15, 1952. BFA, U. Nebr., 1975; MFA, Ohio State U., 1977. Assoc. prof. printmaking U. Nebr., Lincoln, 1983—, gallery dir., 1988-91; vis. asst. prof. U. Calif., Berkeley, 1987; vis. artist, instr. Carleton Coll., Northfield, Minn., 1989; rsch. fellow Kyoto Seika U., Japan, 1993; vis. artist Icelandic Coll. Arts & Crafts, Rekyavik, 1995. One-woman show Columbus (Ohio) Mus. Art, 1983, Sheldon Meml. Art Gallery, Lincoln, 1984, Mus. Art, U. Iowa, City, 1994, Joslyn Art Mus., Omaha, 1995, Gallery APA, Nagoya, Japan, 1995, Kutna Hora, Czech Republic, 1996, Galleria Harmonia, Jyvasklya, Finland, 1996; exhibited in group shows San Francisco Mus. Modern Art, 1980, Honolulu Acad. Arts, 1985, Mednorodini Graficni Likovni Ctr., Ljubljana, Yugoslavia, 1987, Zimmerli Art Mus., Rutgers U., New Brusnwick, N.J., 1988, Greenville (S.C.) County Mus. Art, 1988, Calif. Palace Legion of Honor, San Francisco, 1989, Nat. Mus. Women in Arts, Washington, 1991, Elvehjem Mus. Art, U. Wis., Madison, 1993, 9th Seoul Internat. Print Biennale, 1994, Tama Art Mus., Japan, 1995, Graphicstudio Gallery, Tampa, Fla., 1996, Nat. Mus. Am. Art, Washington, 1997; represented in permanent collections Mus. of Modern Art, N.Y., Nat. Mus. Am. Art, Smithsonian Instn., Washington, Libr. Congress, Washington, Worcester (Mass.) Art Mus., Sheldon Meml. Art Gallery, U. Nebr., Nat. Art Libr., Victoria and Albert Mus., London, Mus. Modern Art, N.Y.C., Bklyn. Mus. Art, Fogg Art Mus. Harvard U.; commns. include woodcut print Madison Print Club, 1994, Benziger Winery Imagery Series, Glen Ellen, Calif., 1996, prints Zimmerli Art Mus., 1995, Rutgers Archives Printmaking Studios, 1995, artists book Nat. Mus. Women Arts, Washington, 1996; co-author, editor: Polish Prints: A Contemporary Graphic Tradition, 1989; author: Woodcut and the Contemporary Impressions, 1993; represented by Jane Haslem Gallery, Washington. Recipient 1st prize Graphica Atlaantica, Reykjavik, Iceland, 1987, purchase award U. Del., 1988, prize Machida City Mus. Graphic Art, Tokyo, 1993; fellow Nat. Endowment Arts, 1984, 96; Fulbright scholar, 1996. Mem. Nat. Acad. Design Mid-Am. Print Coun., Coll. Art Assn., Ctr. Book Arts, Calif. Soc. Printmakers, Boston Printmakers, Print Club. Office: Atrium Gallery 7638 Forsyth Blvd Saint Louis MO 63105-3404

KUNCE, AVON ESTES, vocational rehabilitation counselor; b. Sarasota, Fla., Apr. 20, 1927; d. William Breckinridge and Avon Mary (Zahlten) Estes; m. Henry Warren Kunce, May 26, 1948; children: Catherine Avon Hilton, Nancy Lynn Evers, Christopher Warren, Cynthia Tyree Kent, James Breckinridge. BEd in Secondary Edn., U. Miami, 1972; MS in Mgmt., Fla. Internat. U., 1977. Social worker State of Fla. Health & Rehab. Svcs., Miami, 1972-76; social and rehab. svcs. supr. State Disabled Adult Abuse Investigation Unit Adult Congregate Living Lic., Miami, 1976-82; med. disability specialist State of Fla. Health & Rehab. Svcs., Miami, 1982-89; sr. vocat. rehab. counselor State of Fla. Dept. of Labor, Miami, 1989—. Pres. LWV, Rockhill, Mo., 1955, mem., Miami, 1965-69; mem. South Dade Dem. Women's Club, Miami, 1967-69. Mem. ASPA, Nat. Assn. Disability Examiners, Nat. Rehab. Assn., Phi Lambda Pi, Gamma Theta Upsilon, Epsilon Tau Lambda, Pi Alpha Alpha. Democrat. Quaker. E-mail: kunce@ibm.net. Home: 5025 SW 74th Ter Miami FL 33143-6003

KUNDANIS, GEORGE, congressional aide; b. Chgo., Feb. 13, 1950; s. Ulysses George and Bessie (Kouzios) K. BA, Northwestern U., 1971; MA, U. Wis., 1972, PhD, 1982. Congl. fellow Am. Polit. Sci. Assocs., Washington, 1976-77; legis. asst. Rep. Thomas Foley, Washington, 1976-77; asst. to chmn. Dem. Caucus of House, Washington, 1977-80; floor asst. House Dem. Whip, Washington, 1981-86; asst. House Dem. Majority Leader, Washington, 1986-89; exec. dir. House Dem. Steering and Policy Com, Washington, 1989-94, sr. advisor to House Dem. Leader, 1995—. Democrat. Home: 2725 Ordway # 6NW Washington DC 20008-5048 Office: Office of the Leader H204 US Capitol Washington DC 20515

KUNDEL, HAROLD LOUIS, radiologist, educator; b. N.Y.C., Aug. 15, 1933; s. John A. and Emma E. (Tolle) K.; m. Alice Marie Pape, Mar. 28, 1958; children—Jean, Catherine, Peter. A.B., Columbia U., 1955, M.D., 1959; M.S., Temple U., 1963; M.A. (hon.), U. Pa., 1980. Diplomate Am. Bd. Radiology. Asst. to assoc. prof. Temple U., Phila., 1967-73, prof. radiology, 1973-80; Matthew J. Wilson prof. research radiology U. Pa., Phila., 1980—; dir. Pendergrass Diagnostic Imaging Labs., U. Pa., Phila., 1980—. Contbr. articles to profl. jours. Com. mem. Nat. Council Radiation Protection and Measurements. Served to capt. USAF, 1963-65. Fellow Am. Coll. Radiology; mem. Assn. Univ. Radiologists (Meml. award 1963, Stauffer award 1982), Radiol. Soc. N.Am. Honor award 1978), Am. Roentgen Ray Soc., Soc. Med. Decision Making, Soc. Thoracic Radiology, Alpha Omega Alpha. Lutheran.

KUNDLA, JOHN ALBERT, coach, retired; b. Star Junction, Pa., July 3, 1916. Student, U. Minn., 1939, ME, 1942. Head coach De La Salle (Minn.) H.S., 1946-68, Mpls. Lakers, 1947-59, U. Minn., 1960-69. Named to Basketball Hall of Fame, 1995. Achievements include coach of Championship Team, 1948, 50, 52-54, NBA, 1949, BBA.

KUNDTZ, JOHN ANDREW, lawyer; b. Cleve., June 23, 1933; s. Ewald E. and Elizabeth (O'Neill) K.; m. Helen Margaret Luckiesh, Aug. 31, 1957; children—John M., Helen E., Margaret L. B.S. in Social Studies, Georgetown U., 1955; J.D., Case Western Reserve U., 1958. Bar: Ohio 1958, U.S. Dist. Ct. (no. dist.) Ohio 1961. Ptnr. Falsgraf, Kundtz, Reidy & Shoup, Cleve., 1961-69; ptnr. Thompson Hine and Flory, Cleve., 1970-90; pvt. practice Cleve., 1990—; dir. Investment Advisors Internat., Inc., Cleve. Trustee Hathaway Brown Sch., Shaker Heights, Ohio, Chagrin River Land Conservancy, Chagrin Falls, Ohio, Cleve. Soc. for the Blind. 1st lt. USAF, 1958-60. Mem. ABA, Ohio State Bar Assn., Assn. Transp. Practitioners. Republican. Roman Catholic. Home: 32540 Creekside Dr Pepper Pike OH 44124-5224 Office: 3550 Lander Rd Ste 140 Cleveland OH 44124-5727

KUNDU, DEBABRATA, mechanical engineer; b. Calcutta, W. Bengal, India, Sept. 11, 1957; came to U.S., 1979; s. Charu Chandra and Chapala Bala (Mullick) K.; m. Madhuchhanda Ray, Feb. 21, 1990; 1 child, Debanjali Upasana. MME, U. Houston, 1984; PhD, U. Tex., Arlington, 1989. Registered profl. engr., Tex. Adj. instr. Fla. Inst. Tech., Melbourne, 1981; teaching fellow U. Houston, 1982-84; teaching asst. mech. engring. U. Tex., Arlington, 1985-89, teaching assoc. mech. engring., 1989; plant engr. IMCOA, Haltom City, 1989-91, dir. rsch. and devel., 1991-94; sr. engr. Rubatex Corp., Conover, N.C., 1995—; cons. IMCOA, Haltom City, 1986-89. Contbr. articles to profl. jours. Mem. Nat. Wildlife Found., 1991—. Recipient Nat. scholarship Bd. of Secondary Edn., Calcutta, India, 1974, Competitive scholarship U. Tex. at Arlington, 1985, Watamull scholarship, 1987. Mem. ASME, ASTM, Soc. Plastic Engrs., Sigma Xi. Hinduism. Achievements include establishment of correlations for heat transfer over a row of in-line cylinders placed between the parallel plates for different aspect ratios and Reynolds number; establishment of a correlation showing effects of shear strain, temperature of the polymer and the concentration of blowing agent on the viscosity of polyethylene; determination of the diffusion rate of isobutane from polythylene foam and the effect of the tempurature on the diffusion rate; developed polybutylene insulation foam, polypropylene insulation foam and continuous production of polyethylene foam using carbon dioxide as blowing agent; designed and developed new machines to manufacture new products; developed prototype and manufacturing of synthetic wine cork. Home: 8421 Golden Oak Ct Charlotte NC 28216-1692 Office: Rubatex Corp. 1004 Keisler Rd Conover NC 28613

KUNDU, MUKUL RANJAN, physics and astronomy educator; b. Calcutta, India, Feb. 10, 1930; came to U.S., 1959; s. Makhan Lal and Monoroma K.; m. Sept. 9, 1958; children: Krishna, Rina, Sanjit. BS (with first class honors), U. Calcutta, India, 1949, MS, 1951; DSc, U. Paris, 1957. Assoc. prof. Cornell U., Ithaca, N.Y., 1962-65, Tata Inst. Fund Rsch., Bombay, India, 1965-68; prof. U. Md., College Park, 1968—, dir. astronomy, 1978-85. Editor: Radio Physics of the Sun, 1980, Unstable Current Systems and Plasma Instabilities in Astrophysics, 1984, Energetic Phenomena on the Sun, 1989; author: Solar Radio Astronomy, 1965; mem. editorial bd. Solar Physics, 1967—. Named Nat. Acad. Sci. fellow, 1967, 74-75, 86, U.S. Sr. Scientist awardee Humbolt Found., 1978, Am. Phys. Soc. fellow, 1989. Fellow Am. Phys. Soc.; mem. Am. Astron. Soc., Am. Geophys. Union, Internat. Astron. Union, Internat. Union Radio Sci. Office: U Md Dept Astronomy College Park MD 20742

KUNER, CHARLES MICHAEL, minister; b. San Diego, Nov. 28, 1951; s. Joe Frank and Verna Irene (Landis) K.; m. Judith Lyn Jenkinson, June 16, 1973 (div. June 1985); m. Jennifer Slemmons, May 11, 1986; children: Ellen Claire, Emma Catherine. AA, San Diego Mesa Coll., 1972; BA, San Diego State U., 1974; MDiv, Princeton Theol. Sem., 1977. Ordained to ministry Presbyn. Ch., 1977. Asst. pastor 1st Presbyn. Ch., Valparaiso, Ind., 1977-80; interim pastor Ogden Dune (Ind.) Community Ch., 1980-81, Kouts (Ind.) Presbyn. Ch., 1981-82; assoc. pastor 1st Presbyn. Ch., Topeka, 1982—; chaplain Kans. Ho. Reps., Topeka, 1988—. Bd. dirs. Topeka Youth Project, 1987-88, Topeka Housing and Info., 1985-88, Topeka Festival Singers, 1989—. Paul Harris fellow Rotary, 1991. Mem. Rotary (pres. Topeka chpt. 1989-90). Democrat. Home: 11613 Bevenshire Rd Oklahoma City OK 73162-2031 *The variety of ways in which the church must "be there" for persons in society today is vast. It is the task of the church to work out ways in which to minister to those who are broken by the challenges and frustrations of life.*

KUNG, DAVID SHEAN-GUANG, plastic surgeon; b. Taipei, Taiwan, Republic China, Aug. 25, 1963; s. Luke C.S. and Patience M.U. Kung; m. Bonnie I.J. Lin, June 2, 1990. BA, Columbia Coll., 1984, DDS, 1989; MD, Harvard U., 1992. Intern in surgery Mass. Gen. Hosp., Boston, 1989, resident in surgery, 1992-95; resident in plastic surgery U. N.C., 1996-98, fellow in craniofacial surgery, 1998. Recipient Nat. Rsch. Svc. award NIH, 1986. E-mail: dskung@pol.net. Fax: 202-966-4639. Office: Ste 309 5100 Wisconsin Ave NW Washington DC 20016-4119

KUNG, FRANK F., biotechnology and life sciences venture capital investor; b. 1948. BS, Nat. Tsing Hwa U., Taiwan, 1970; MBA, U. Calif., Berkeley, 1983, PhD in Molecular Biology, 1976. Post doctoral rsch. scientist Univ. Calif., Berkeley, 1976-77; rsch. dir. Clin. Bio-Rsch., Emeryville, Calif., 1977-79; scientist, asst. to pres. Cetus Corp., Berkeley, Calif., 1979-81; dir. Cetus Immune Corp. (subs. of Cetus Corp.), Palo Alto, Calif., 1980-84; pres., CEO Genelabs Techs., Inc., Redwood City, Calif., 1984-95, chmn., 1984-96; chmn. BioAsia Investments, Palo Alto, Calif., 1996—. Office: BioAsia Investments 575 High St Ste 201 Palo Alto CA 94301-1648

KUNG, HAROLD HING-CHUEN, engineering educator; b. Hong Kong, Oct. 12, 1949; s. Shien C. and Kai Sau (Wong) K.; m. Mayfair Chu, June 12, 1971; children: Alexander, Benjamin. BS in chem. engring., U. Wis., 1971; PhD in chemistry, Northwestern U., 1974. Rsch. sci. ctrl. rsch. and devel. dept. E.I. duPont de Nemours & Co., Wilmington, Del., 1974-76; asst. prof. chem. engring. Northwestern U., 1976, asst. prof. chem. engring. and chemistry, 1977, assoc. prof., 1981, prof. chem. engring. and chemistry, 1985, chmn. chemical engring., 1986-92; dir. Ctr. for Catalysis and Surface Sci., 1993-97; chmn. Gordon rsch. Conf. on Catalysis, 1995; tech. advisor UNIDO Mission, 1995; John McClanahan Henske Disting. lectr. Yale U., 1996; mem. com. to rev. PNGV program Nat. Rsch. Coun., 1996, 97, 98; Olaf Hongen vis. prof. U. Wis., Madison, 1999. Author: Transition Metal Oxides, Surface Chemistry and Catalysis, 1989, Catalyst Modificaton-Selective Oxidation Processes, 1991; editor: Methanol Production and Use, 1994, Applied Catalysis A = General, 1996—. Japanese Soc. for Promotion of Sci. fellow, 1996. Mem. AIChE, Am. Chem. Soc., Chgo. Catalysis Club (program chair 1992, pres. 1993, Herman Pines award 1999), Catalysis Soc. (Paul H. Emmett award 1991, Robert L. Barwell lectr. 1999), Phi Lambda Epsilon. Patents include Photolysis of Water Using Rhodate Semiconductive Electrodes, and Oxidative Dehydrogenation of Alkanes to Unsaturated Hydrocarbons. Office: Dept of Chem Engring Northwestern University 2145 Sheridan Rd Evanston IL 60208-0834

KUNG, HSIANG-FU, health facility administrator; b. Chungking, China, Sept. 4, 1942; married; 2 children. BS, Nat. Chung-hsing U., 1963; PhD, Vanderbilt U., 1966. Fellow lab. biochemistry enzymes sect. NIH, 1969-70; sci. asst. Max-Planck Inst. Biology, 1970-71; rsch. fellow dept. biochemistry Roche Inst. Molecular Biology, 1971-73, asst. mem., 1973-80; rsch. fellow dept. molecular genetics rsch. divsn. Hoffman-La Roche Inc., 1980-81, sr. rsch. fellow, 1981-82, rsch. leader dept. molecular oncology, 1982-86; chief lab. biochemistry and physiology Nat. Cancer Inst., Frederick, Md., 1986—; vis. asst. prof. dept. biochemistry Coll. Medicine & Dentistry, N.J., 1971-73, 73-76; adj. prof. dept. zoology & physiology Rutgers State U., 1976-78. Mem. AAAS. Achievements include research in biochemical physiology. Home: 3392 Red Oak Ct Middletown MD 21769-6903 Office: Nat Cancer Inst Lab Biochemistry & Physiology Frederick Cancer R&D Center Bldg 567 Rm 152 Frederick MD 21702

KUNG, HSIANG-TSUNG, computer architect; b. Shanghai, China, Nov. 9, 1945; m. Ling-Ling Chang; 2 children. BS, Nat. Tsing Hua U., 1968; MA, U. N.Mex., 1970; PhD in Math., Carnegie Mellon U., 1974. Rsch. assoc. Carnegie Mellon U., 1973-74, from asst. prof. to prof. computer sci., 1974-92; William H. Gates prof. computer sci. and elec. engring. Harvard U., Cambridge, Mass., 1992—; archtl. cons. ESL, Inc., 1982; Guggenheim fellow, 1983-84. Mem. Nat. Acad. Engring., Acad. Sinica. Office: Harvard

U Divsn Engring & Applied Sci Pierce Hall 110 29 Oxford St Cambridge MA 02138-2901

KUNG, PANG-JEN, materials scientist, electrical engineer; b. I-Lan, Taiwan, May 13, 1959; s. Ching-Yu and A-Se (Yu) K.; m. Tzyy-Yun Tzeng, May 18, 1986; children: Naihau, Naiwei. MSChemE, Nat. Tsing Hua U., 1983; MSEE, Auburn U., 1988; MMetE, Carnegie Mellon U., 1991, PhD in Materials Sci., 1993; MBA, U. Conn., 1998. Jr. engr. Tatung Co., Taipei, Taiwan, 1979-80; teaching asst. Nat. Tsing Hua U., Hsin-Chu, Taiwan, 1981-82, rsch. asst., 1982-83; assoc. scientist Indsl. Tech. Res. Inst., Hsin-Chu, 1985-86; tchg. and rsch. asst. Auburn (Ala.) U., 1986-89; rsch. asst. Carnegie Mellon U., Pitts., 1989-91; staff rsch. asst. Los Alamos (N.Mex.) Nat. Lab., 1991-92, rsch. fellow, 1993-94; sr. scientist Advanced Fuel Rsch., Inc., East Hartford, Conn., 1995-97; chmn. Pioneer Techs., Inc., West Hartford, Conn., 1996—; chmn. acad. affairs Tatung Inst. Tech., Taipei, 1979-80; tech. info. editor Indsl. Tech. Rsch. Inst., Hsin-Chu, 1985-86; translator tech. articles Super Tech. Books Co., Taipei, 1986. Author, editor: Unit Operations in Chemical Engineering, 1986; contbr. articles to profl. jours. 2nd lt. Chinese Air Force, 1983-85. Recipient Editor's Choice award Nat. Poetry Assn., 1989, 90; Am.-Chinese Engr. scholar Am.-Chinese Assn. Engrs., 1980; Liang Ji-Duan fellow Carnegie Mellon U., 1991. Mem. AAAS, IEEE, SPIE, ASM, Am. Soc. Quality, Materials Rsch. Soc., Am. Vacuum Soc. (Paper award 1992), Soc. Info. Display, Beta Gamma Sigma. Achievements include research in diamond thin films and high Tc superconductors, superconducting quantum interference devices and biomagnetic systems, surface characterization and microstructural analysis, ferroelectric devices, giant magnetoresistive sensors, high-speed microelectronics, epitaxial heterostructures, in-process monitors, pulsed laser deposition, pyroelectric sensor arrays, gas sensors, plasma-enhanced chemical vapor deposition, x-ray imaging materials, digital radiographic systems. Office: Pioneer Tech Inc PO Box 270682 Hartford CT 06127-0682

KUNG, PATRICK CHUNG-SHU, biotechnology executive; b. Nanjing, China, July 10, 1947; came to U.S., 1969; s. Tao and Yuing (Li) K.; m. Rita Wu, Feb. 11, 1980; children: Julia, Calvin. BS, FuJen U., Taiwan, 1968; PhD, U. Calif., Berkeley, 1974. Rsch. fellow MIT, Cambridge, 1974-77; sr. rsch. fellow Ortho Pharm. Co., Raritan, N.J., 1978-81; v.p. rsch. Centocor Inc., Malvern, Pa., 1982-83; co-founder, exec. v.p. T Cell Scis., Inc., Cambridge, 1984-88, dir., 1989-98; CEO Phytoceutica, Inc., New Haven, 1998—; exec. bd. Coll. Letters and Scis. U. Calif., Berkeley, 1989-91; chmn., pres. Global Pharm. Ltd., Bermuda, 1994-98; bd. dirs. Asian Am. Bank and Trust Co., Boston, Ontogen Corp. Contbr. articles to profl. jours. Trustee Park Sch., Brookline, Mass., 1992-95. Recipient Philip Hoffman award Johnson & Johnson Co., 1979, Achievement award Chinese Inst. Engrs., 1988, Discoverers award U.S. Pharm. Mfrs. Assn., 1991, Thomas Alva Edison award N.J. Rsch. Coun., 1991. Mem. Am. Assn. Immunologists, N.Y. Acad. Scis., Soc. Chinese Bioscientists in Am. (pres. bio/pharm. scis. divsn. 1995). Office: T Cell Scis Inc 119 4th Ave Needham MA 02494-2725

KUNG, SHAIN-DOW, molecular biologist, academic administrator, educator; b. China, Mar. 14, 1935, came to U.S., 1971, naturalized, 1977; s. Chao-tzen and Chih (Zhu) K.; grad. Chung-Hsing U., Taiwan, China, 1958; Ph.D., U. Toronto, Can., 1968; m. Helen C.C. Kung, Sept. 5, 1964; children: Grace, David, Andrew. Research fellow Hosp. for Sick Children, Toronto, 1968-70; biologist UCLA, 1971-74; asst. prof. biology U. Md., Baltimore County, 1974-77, assoc. prof., 1977-82, prof., 1982-86, acting chmn. dept., 1982-84, assoc. dean arts and sci., 1985-86, prof. botany U. Md., College Park, 1986-93; hon. prof. Fudan U., 1986, Beijing Agrl. U., 1987; acting dir. U. Md. Ctr. for Agrl. Biotech, 1986-88, dir. 1988-93, acting provost Md. Biotech. Inst., 1989-91; dean Sch. Sci. Hong Kong U. Sci. and Tech., 1991-92, v.p. for acad. affairs, 1992-98. Author 3 books; editor 12 books; contbr. chpts. to books, articles to profl. jours. Recipient Philip Morris award for disting. achievement in tobacco sci., 1979, Outstanding Alumni award, 1990, Outstanding Svc. award, 1990; named Disting. Scholar, Nat. Acad. Sci., 1981; Fulbright grantee, 1982-83, grantee NSF, NIH. Mem. Am. Soc. Plant Physiologists, AAAS. Office: Hong Kong U Sci and Tech, Clear Water Bay, Kowloon Hong Kong

KUNIHOLM, BRUCE ROBELLET, university administrator; b. Washington, Oct. 4, 1942; s. Bertel Eric and Berthe Eugenie (Robellet) K.; m. Elizabeth Fairbank, June 29, 1968 (div. July 1987); children: Jonathan, Erin. AB in English, Dartmouth Coll., 1964; MA in History, Duke U., 1972, MA in Pub. Policy Sci., 1976, PhD in History, 1976. Instr. English Robert Acad./Robert Coll., Istanbul, Turkey, 1964-67; Coun. Fgn. Rels./NEH fellow Dept. State, Washington, 1979, internat. rels. officer policy planning staff, 1979-80; from instr. to lectr. policy studies and history Duke U., Durham, N.C., 1975-77, asst. prof. pub. policy studies and history, 1977-78, 80-84, assoc. prof. pub. policy studies and history, 1984-87, prof. pub. policy studies and history, 1987—, chmn. dept. public policy studies, 1989-94, dir. Terry Sanford Inst. Pub. Policy, 1989-94; vis. prof. Internat. Rels. Koc U., Istanbul, Turkey, 1995-96; prof. pub. policy studies and history, 1996—; vice-provost for acad. and internat. affairs, Duke U., Durham, N.C., 1996—; guest scholar Woodrow Wilson Internat. Ctr. Scholars, 1982; cons. NEH, USMC, Dept. State, U.S. Army, United Tech. Corp.; invited lectr. numerous orgns., colls., univs., fgn. countries including U.S. Senate Fgn. Rels.Com., CIA, State Dept., Chase Manhattan Bank, Harvard U., Brown U., Dartmouth Coll., Yale U., Princeton U., France, Eng., Germany, Italy, Kuwait, Saudi Arabia, Sudan, Can., Turkey, also others. Author: Origins of the Cold War in the Near East, 1980 (Stuart L. Bernath prize 1981), The Persian Gulf and United States Policy, 1984, The Palestine Problem and United States Policy, 1986; contbr. articles to profl. jours.; contbr. chpts. books. Capt. USMC, 1967-71, Vietnam. Decorated Bronze Star with V device; recipient Disting. Teaching award Trinity Coll., Duke U., 1989; rsch. grantee Harry S. Truman Libr., 1984, Duke U. Rsch. Coun., 1985-86, Inst. Turkish Studies, 1986-87, travel grantee Ctr. Soviet and East European Studies, 1991; Fulbright sr. rsch. fellow, Turkey, 1986-87, Woodrow Wilson Internat. Ctr. Scholars fellow Smithsonian Instn., 1986-87, sr. fellow Nobel Inst., Oslo, 1994. Mem. Am. Hist. Assn., Fulbright Fellows, Coun. Fgn. Rels., Orgn. Am. Historians, Soc. Historians Am. Fgn. Rels., Middle East Inst., Middle East Studies Assn., Internat. Inst. Strategic Studies, Phi Beta Kappa. Democrat. Avocations: triathlons, bluegrass banjo, wine. Home: 1719 Tisdale St Durham NC 27705-5631 Office: Duke U Office of Provost PO Box 90006 Durham NC 27708-0006

KUNIN, JACQUELINE BARLOW, art educator; b. Harrisburg, Pa., Apr. 20, 1941; d. Rodney Kipton and Marie (Trunk) Barlow; m. Richard Henry Kunin, June 17, 1967. BFA, Pratt Inst., 1963; MEd, Temple U., 1967. Comml. artist Dock and Kinney Co., N.Y.C., 1963-64; art libr. Norcross, Inc., N.Y.C., 1964; tchr. graphic arts Jones Jr. H.S., Phila., 1964-66; tchr. art John Bartram H.S., Phila., 1966-86; tchr. painting and drawing H.S. for Creative and Performing Arts, Phila., 1986—. Named Disting Tchr. White House Commn. Presdl. Scholars, Washington, 1994, Outstanding Educator award Phila. Coll. Textiles and Sci., 1997. Mem. AAUW, Pa. Art Edn. Assn., Victorian Soc. Am. (Phila. chpt. bd. dirs. 1986-96), Valley Forge Civic Assn. Avocations: painting, collecting American costumes 1850-1950.

KUNIN, MADELEINE MAY, ambassador to Switzerland, former governor; b. Zurich, Switzerland, Sept. 28, 1933; came to U.S., 1940, naturalized, 1947; d. Ferdinand and Renee (Bloch) May; children: Julia, Peter, Adam, Daniel. B.A., U. Mass., 1956; M.S., Columbia U., 1957; M.A., U. Vt., 1967; numerous hon. degrees. Newspaper reporter Burlington Free Press, Vt., 1957-58; guide Brussels World's Fair, Belgium, 1958; TV asst. producer Sta. WCAX-TV, Burlington, 1960-61; freelance writer, instr. English Trinity Coll., Burlington, 1969-70; mem. Vt. Ho. of Reps., 1973-78; lt. gov. State of Vt., Montpelier, 1979-82, gov., 1985-91; disting. vis. in Pub. Policy Bunting Inst., Cambridge, Mass., 1991-92, Dartmouth Coll., Hanover, N.H., 1992; dep. sec. edn. Dept. Education, Washington, D.C., 1993-96; U.S. amb. to Switzerland, 1996—; fellow Inst. Politics, Kennedy Sch. Govt., Harvard U., 1983; lectr. Middlebury Coll., St. Michael's Coll., 1984; disting. pub. policy visitor Rockefeller Ctr., Dartmouth Coll., 1992; pub. policy fellow Bunting Inst., Radcliffe Coll., Harvard U., 1991-92; Vt. Joint Fiscal Com., 1977-78; mem. exec. com. Nat. Conf. Lt. Govs., 1979-80; founder, pres. Inst. Sustainable Cmtys., Montpelier, Vt., 1991; mem. 3 person com. to recommend v.p. to Bill Clinton, co-chair nat. com. Women for Clinton, 1992. Author: Living a Political Life: A Memoir, 1994, The Big Green Book, 1976; contbr. articles to profl. jours., mags. and newspapers. Named Outstanding State Legislator, Eagleton Inst. Politics, Rutgers U., 1975; Montgomery fellow Dartmouth Coll., 1991. Fellow Am. Acad. Arts & Scis.; mem. Nat. Gov.'s Assn. (mem. exec. com.), Nat. Govs.' Conf. (chair com. on energy and the environ.), New Eng. Gov.'s Conf. (chairperson). Democrat.

KUNIN, RICHARD H., educational association administrator, artist; b. Stamford, Conn., May 28, 1944; s. Leonard and Ruth (Skigen) K.; m. Jacqueline April Barlow, June 17, 1967. BFA, Temple U., 1966; MEd, Lehigh U., 1971. Art tchr. Phila. Sch. Dist., 1967-85, asst. prin., 1985-96; exec. dir., founder Ctr. for Learning Through the Arts, Valley Forge, Pa., 1997—; cons. tchr. devel. workshops, Ctr. Learning Through the Arts, 1997—, cons. Phila. Arts in Edn. Ptnrs., Phila., 1997—; curriculum devel. cons. Inst. for Devel. of Edn. in the Arts, Camden, N.J., 1997—. Bd. dirs. Oak Lane Civic Assn., Phila., 1974-83, pres., 1983-84. Mem. Phi Delta Kappa. Office: Ctr Learning Through the Arts PO Box 974 Valley Forge PA 19482-0974

KUNISHIGE, LYNN LEIKO KIMURA, secondary education educator; b. Honolulu, Feb. 8, 1963; d. Donald Masayuki and Kay Yoshiko (Yamamoto) Kimura; m. Ray Kazuo Kunishige, Aug. 4, 1990. BS, Oreg. State U., 1985, MS, 1986. Tchr. math., computer sci. Punahou Sch., Honolulu, 1986—. Mem. Nat. Coun. Tchrs. Math., Internat. Coun. Computer Educators, Hawaii Coun. Tchrs. Math., Phi Kappa Phi. Avocations: needlework, golf. Office: Punahou Sch 1601 Punahou St Honolulu HI 96822-3399

KUNITZ, STANLEY JASSPON, poet, editor, educator; b. Worcester, Mass., July 29, 1905; s. Solomon Z. and Yetta Helen (Jasspon) K.; m. Helen Pearce, 1930 (div. 1937); m. Eleanor Evans, Nov. 21, 1939 (div. 1958); 1 dau., Gretchen; m. Elise Asher, June 21, 1958. A.B. summa cum laude, Harvard U., 1926, M.A., 1927; Litt.D. (hon.), Clark U., 1961, Anna Maria Coll., 1977, St. Mary's Coll., Md., 1994; L.H.D. (hon.), Worcester State Coll., 1980, SUNY, Brockport, 1987. Editor Wilson Library Bull., 1928-43; mem. lit. faculty Bennington Coll., 1946-49; prof. English Potsdam (N.Y.) State Tchrs. Coll., 1949-50; dir. seminar Potsdam Summer Workshop in Creative Arts, 1949-53; lectr. The New Sch., 1950-57; vis. prof. poetry U. Wash., 1955-56; vis. prof. English Queens Coll., 1956-57, Brandeis U., 1958-59; dir. poetry workshop Poetry Center YMHA, N.Y., 1958-62; Danforth vis. lectr. numerous Am. colls., 1961-63; lectr. Columbia, 1963-66, adj. prof. writing Grad. Sch. Arts, 1967-85; editor Yale Series Younger Poets, 1969-77; vis. prof. poetry Yale U., 1970, Rutgers U. at Camden, 1974; vis. prof., sr. fellow in humanities Princeton U., 1978, Vassar Coll., 1981; cons. poetry Libr. of Congress, 1974-76. Author: (verse) Intellectual Things, 1930, Living Authors, 1931, Authors Today and Yesterday, 1933, Junior Book of Authors, 1934, British Authors of the 19th Century, 1936, American Authors, 1600-1900, 1938, Twentieth Century Authors, 1942, First Supplement, 1955, Passport to the War, 1944, British Authors Before 1800, 1952, Selected Poems, 1928-1958, 1958, Poems of John Keats, 1964, European Authors, 1000-1900, 1967, The Testing-Tree, 1971, The Terrible Threshold, 1974, The Coat Without a Seam, 1974, A Kind of Order, A Kind of Folly: Essays and Conversations, 1975, The Poems of Stanley Kunitz 1928-1978, 1979, The Wellfleet Whale and Companion Poems, 1983; Next-To-Last Things: New Poems and Essays, 1985; The Essential Blake, 1987, Interviews and Encounters, 1993, Passing Through: The Later Poems, 1995, editor (with David Ignatow) The Wild Card, Selected Poems, Early and Late, of Karl Shapiro, 1998; translator: (with others) verse Antiworlds (A. Voznesensky), 1966, Antiworlds and The Fifth Ace, 1967, Stolen Apples (Y. Yevtushenko), 1971, (with Max Hayward) Poems of Akhmatova, 1973, Story Under Full Sail (A. Voznesensky), 1974; Editor, co-translator: Orchard Lamps (Ivan Drach), 1978. Served with AUS, 1943-45. Recipient Garrison medal for poetry Harvard, 1926, Oscar Blumenthal prize, 1941, Guggenheim fellow creative writing, 1945-46, Amy Lowell traveling fellow for poetry, 1953-54, Levinson prize for poetry, 1956, Harriet Monroe award U. Chgo., 1958, Pulitzer prize in poetry, 1959, Brandeis Creative Arts Poetry award, 1964, Lenore Marshall award for poetry, 1980, Nat. Endowment Arts sr. fellow, 1984, Bollingen prize, 1987, Montgomery fellow Dartmouth Coll., 1991, Centennial medal Harvard U., 1992, Nat. Medal Arts, 1993, Shelley Meml. award, 1995, Nat. Book award, 1995, award St. Botolph Club Found., 1996, Robert Frost medal Poetry Soc. Am., 1998, Courage Conscience award Peace Abbey, 1998; grantee Ford Found., 1958-59, Nat. Inst. Arts and Letters, 1959; named N.Y. State Poet, 1987-88, Walt Whitman Birthplace Poet, 1989. Mem. Acad. Am. Poets (fellowship award 1968, chancellor 1970-95); mem. AAAL (sec. 1985-88), Poets House N.Y. (founding pres. 1985-90), Fine Arts Work Ctr. in Provincetown (founding mem., bd. dirs. 1968—, medal for disting. svc. in arts 1997), Phi Beta Kappa. Home: 37 W 12th St New York NY 10011-8502*

KUNIYASU, KEITH KAZUMI, secondary education educator; b. Honolulu, Apr. 16, 1955; s. Hajime and Betty Mieko (Yamamoto) K. AA in Liberal Arts, U. Hawaii, Pearl City, 1978, AS in Graphic Arts, 1978; BS in Tech. Edn., Western Wash. U., 1982; MEd in Tech. Edn., Oreg. State U., 1987. Cert. vocat. adminstr. Instrumental music instr. Aiea (Hawaii) Intermediate Sch., 1978-88; spl. edn. instr. Highlands Intermediate Sch., Pearl City, 1983-84; visual comm. instr. Oak Harbor (Wash.) High Sch., 1982-83; photography instr. Olympic Coll., Bremerton, Wash., 1984-85; comm. techs. instr. North Kitsap High Sch., Poulsbo, Wash., 1984-93; instr. comm. techs. River Ridge High Sch., Lacey, Wash., 1993—; edn. rep. curriculum/competency validation com. Wash. State Supt. Pub. Instrn., Olympia, 1988-93; cons. Wash. State Assn. Vocat. Indsl. Clubs Am., 1990—; mem. Nat. Vocat. Indsl. Clubs of Am. Leadership Handbook Revision Team, 1995; pvt. woodwind instr., 1974-94; counselor, woodwind specialist Maui (Hawaii) Intermediate Select Band Camps, 1975-80; advisor Leeward C.C. Graphic Arts Club, Pearl City, 1978-80; sch. accreditation teams for various high schs. throughout Wash., 1988—; writing com. leadership curriculum Wash. State Supt. Instrn. Edn., Olympia, 1993—. Author: (pamphlet series) Care of Single Reeds, 1983, (brochures) Addressing Technology Education, 1988-92, Communication Technologies, 1995, What Is Hawk Communications?, 1995, VisCom Student Study Guide, 1987, 2nd edit., 1990, 3rd edit., 1993, 4th edit., 1996, From Goods to Services, 1988, Technology Education Facility, 1988, Communication Technologies at North Kitsap High School, 1989, Visual Communications, 1990, Bob's Law's (Robert's Rules of Order), 1995, 2nd edit., 1997. Organizer, pres. Pacific Islanders Club at Western Wash. U., Bellingham, 1981-82; organizer, bd. dirs. Leeward Fine Arts Coun., Pearl City, 1981-94. Named Advisor of Yr. Wash. State Assn. Vocat. Indsl. Clubs Am., 1993. Mem. NEA, Internat. Tech. Edn. Assn. (affiliate rep. 1990-94), Internat. Graphic Arts Educators Assn., Grapic Arts Tech. Found., Am. Vocat. Assn., Wash. Vocat. Assn., Wash. Tech. Edn. Assn., Vocat. Indsl. Clubs Am. (advisor, regional coord. 1990-93, 94-96). Avocations: travel, cooking, music, reading, working with young adults. Office: River Ridge H S 8929 Martin Way E Lacey WA 98516-5932

KUNJUKUNJU, PAPPY, insurance company financial executive; b. Punalur, Kerala, India, Aug. 26, 1939; came to U.S., 1974.; s. Varghese and Thankamma (Yohannan) Chacko; m. Kunjamma Zacharaiah, Dec. 31, 1971; children: Grace, Nancy, Samuel. B of Commerce, U. Ranchi, India, 1965; MBA, N.Y. Inst. Tech., 1976. CPA, N.Y.; cert. mgmt. acct. Cost. acct. Nat. Tobacco Co. India, Calcutta, 1964-68; exec. asst. Gen. Electric Co. of India (sub. of GEC/Eng.), Calcutta, 1968-69; mgr. mfg. div. GEC India, Coimbatore, 1969-74; examiner ins. dept. N.Y. State, N.Y.C., 1977-83, sr. examiner ins. dept., 1983-87; contr. Golden Eagle Mut. Life Ins. Corp., Bklyn., 1987-88, treas., 1988-89; v.p., treas. Golden Eagle Mutual Life Ins. Corp., Bklyn., 1989-97; dir. accounts Columbian Mutual Group, Binghamton, N.Y., 1997—. Mem. AICPA, Nat. Assn. Accts., Inst. Cost and Works Accts. India (assoc.), Fin. Mgmt. Assn. Mem. Assembly of God Ch. Home: 156 Bellevue Pl Yonkers NY 10703-1625 Office: Columbian Mutual Group Vestal Pkwy E Binghamton NY 13903

KUNKEL, DAVID NELSON, lawyer; b. Rochester, N.Y., Apr. 5, 1943; s. Frederick W. and Dorothy Jean (Smith) K.; m. Gayle Kellogg Van Dussen, Aug. 21, 1965; children: Jennifer Dawn, Nelson Charles. BA with high honors, U. Va., 1965; LLB, U. Pa., 1968. Bar: Pa. 1969, N.Y. 1972. Assoc. Montgomery, McCracken, Walker & Rhoads, Phila., 1968; Assoc. Nixon, Hargrave, Devans & Doyle, Rochester, N.Y., 1971-78, ptnr., 1978-95, sr. counsel, 1995; dir., exec. v.p., gen. counsel PSINet, Inc., Herndon, Va., 1995—. Mem. Bd. Edn. Bloomfield Ctrl. Sch., East Bloomfield, N.Y., 1982-85. Lt. USNR, 1969-71. Mem. ABA, Internat. Bar Assn. Office: PSINet Inc 510 Huntmar Park Dr Herndon VA 20170-5100

KUNKEL, GEORGIE BRIGHT, writer, retired school counselor; b. Chehalis, Wash.; d. George Riley and Myrtia (McLaughlin) Bright; m. Norman C. Kunkel, Apr. 25, 1946; children: N. Joseph D.C., Stephen Gregory, Susan Ann, Kimberly Janes Waligorska. BA in Edn., Western Wash. U., 1944; MEd, U. Wash., 1968. Tchr. pub. schs., Vader, Centralia, Seattle, Wash., 1941-67; counselor Highline Pub. Schs., Seattle, 1967-82; pvt. cons., Seattle, 1970—; sch. counselor rep. State of Art Conf., Balt., 1980. Author: (pseudonym Dorothy Bright) My Sex Secrets, 1989, Ho Do You Know You're Dying, 1991, Grandma's Holiday Greetings, 1992; editor Women and Girls in Edn., 1972-75; columnist Highline Times, Burien, Wash.; contbr. articles to profl. jours. Organizer Women and Girls in Edn., Wash. State, 1971; pres. Wash. State chpt. NOW, 1973; organizer, pres. Holmes Harbor Homeowners Assn.; pres. West Seattle Dem. Women's Club. Named Woman of Yr. in Wash. State, Women's Fedn. for World Peace, 1998; grantee Woen Adminstrs. Wash. State, 1971, Edn. Svc. Dist., Seattle, 1980. Mem. NEA (sec. pub. rels.), ACA (pres. state bf. 1982-83), Am. Sch. Counseling Assn. (pres. state divsn. 1980-81), Seattle Counselors Assn. (organizer, past pres. office exec., Counselor of Yr. award 1990), West Seattle C. of C., Past Pres. Assembly. Unitarian. Avocation: singing with Raging Grannies and Rolling Crones. Home and Office: 3409 SW Trenton St Seattle WA 98126-3743

KUNKEL, RICHARD LESTER, public radio executive; b. Syracuse, N.Y., Nov. 12, 1944; s. Lester DeLong Kunkel and Margaret Fanny Ralph; m. Mary Joan Goldsworthy, Aug. 10, 1968; children: Richard J., Charles J., Joseph B. BS, Syracuse U., 1967, MS, 1969. Lic. real estate broker, N.C. Program dir. Sta. WNBI, Northland Broadcasting, Park Falls, Wis., 1969-72; instr., prodn. dir. Sta. WMKY, Morehead (Ky.) State U., 1972-77; radio mgr. Maine Pub. Broadcasting Network, Orono, 1977-78; instr., sta. mgr. Sta. KNTU, U. North Tex., Denton, 1978-84; v.p., dean Southeastern Ctr. for Arts, Atlanta, 1985-88; gen. mgr., pres. Stas. KPBX-FM and KSFC-FM Spokane Pub. Radio Inc., Spokane, Wash., 1988—; cons., 1978—. With Army N.g., 1968-74. Recipient Addy award 1975. Avocations: photography, computers. Home: 18212 N Atlantic Rd Colbert WA 99005-9608 Office: KPBX and KSFC-Spokane Pub Radio 2319 N Monroe St Spokane WA 99205-4548

KUNKEL, ROBERT ANTHONY, business educator; b. Spring Valley, Ill., Mar. 14, 1961; s. Joseph Conrad and Louise Thelma (Stenbeck) K.; m. Erin Elizabeth Coates, Dec. 30, 1989. BS in Agr., U. Ill., 1983; MBA, Western Ill. U., 1989; MA in Econs., U. Tenn., Knoxville, 1993, PhD in Fin., 1994. Asst. county supr. Farmers Home Adminstrn., USDA, western Ill., 1983-86; county supr. Farmers Home Adminstrn., USDA, Macomb, Ill., 1986-88; asst. county supr. Farmers Home Adminstrn., USDA, Carthage, Ill., 1988-90; grad. asst. U. Tenn., Knoxville, 1990-94; asst. prof. fin. Minot (N.D.) State U., 1994-95, Western Ill. U., Macomb, 1995-97, Eastern Ill. U., Charleston, 1997—; mem. fin. com. Sisters of St. Francis, Clinton, Iowa, 1996—; bd. dirs. Western Ill. Credit Union, Macomb, 1996-97. Contbr. articles to profl. jours. Mem. fin. com. N.D. Region II Child Care Svcs., Minot, 1994-95. Fin. Mgmt. ASsn. Knoxville grad. fellow, 1994. Mem. Fin. Mgmt. Assn., Eastern Fin. Assn., Midwest Bus. Adminstrn. Assn. Roman Catholic. Avocations: golf, travel, sports, movies. Home: 5 Woodfield Ln Charleston IL 61920-3629 Office: Eastern Ill U Sch of Business Charleston IL 61920

KUNKLE, DAVID M., police chief. BS, U. Tex., Arlington, 1976, MA, 1994. Police chief Arlington (Tex.) Police Dept., 1985—. Office: PO Box 231 Arlington TX 76004-1065

KUNKLE, WILLIAM JOSEPH, JR., lawyer; b. Lakewood, Ohio, Sept. 3, 1941; s. William Joseph and Georgia (Howe) K.; m. Sarah Florence Nesti, July 11, 1964; children: Kathleen Margaret, Susan Mary. BA, Northwestern U., Evanston, Ill., 1963; Jd, Northwestern U., 1969. Bar: Ohio 1969, U.S. Dist. Ct. (no. dist.) Ill. 1969, Ill. 1969, U.S. Ct. Appeals (7th cir.) 1991, U.S. Supreme Ct. 1991. Process control engr. Union Carbide Corp., Cleve., 1964-65; prodn. supr. Union Carbide Corp., Greenville, S.C., 1965-66; assoc. Hauxhurst, Sharp, Mollison & Gallagher, Cleve., 1969-70; asst. pub. defender Cook County Pub. Defender, Chgo., 1970-73; asst. states atty. Cook County States Atty., Chgo., 1973-85; ptnr. Phelan, Cahill & Quinlan, Ltd., Chgo., 1985-96, Cahill, Christian & Kunkle, LTD., Chgo., 1996—; chmn. The Ill. Gaming Bd., 1990-93; dep. spl. outside counsel U.S. Ho. Reps., Washington, 1988-89; adj. prof. I.I.T. Chgo. Kent Sch. Law, 1980-84; instr. Nat. Inst. for Trial Advocacy, Chgo., 1978-82, 86; lectr. Nat. Coll. Dist. Attys., Houston, Denver, Chgo., Atlanta, Louisville, 1978-85, Nat. Law Enforcement Inst., San Francisco, Portland, Atlanta, Pitts., Boston, St. Louis, Chgo., 1983-85; 1st asst. states atty. of Cook County, 1983-85; spl. state's atty. 18th Jud. Cir., DuPage County, 1995—. Contbg. author: Punishment Prosecutor's Viewpoint, 1983, 1989, Trial Techniques Compendium, Nat. College of Dist. Attys. (2d, 3rd, 4th, 5th, 6th eds.). Recipient Disting. Faculty award Nat. Coll. Dist. Attys., 1980, Award for Prosecution Svc. Chgo. Assn. Commerce & Industry, 1981. Fellow Am. Coll. Trial Lawyers, ABA; mem. Internat. Soc. Barristers, Nat. Dist. Attys. Assn. (bd. dirs. 1984-85), Assn. Govt. Attys. in Capital Litigation (pres. 1983-84), Chgo. Bar Assn. (bd. mgrs. 1983-84), Ill. State Bar Assn. (LAWPAC trustee 1989-95), Internat. Assn. Gaming Attys., Chgo. Crime Commn. Republican. Avocations: golf, softball, carpentry, motorcycling. Office: Cahill Christian & Kunkle Ltd 224 S Michigan Ave Ste 1300 Chicago IL 60604-2589*

KUNKLER, ARNOLD WILLIAM, retired surgeon; b. St. Anthony, Ind., Nov. 18, 1921; s. Edward J. and Selma (Hasenour) K.; m. Muriel Helen Burns, May 22, 1954; children: Lisa, Arnold William, Carolyn, Christine, Phillip, Kevin. A.B., Ind. U., 1943, M.D., 1949. Diplomate Am. Bd. Surgery. Intern, Ind. U. Med. Ctr., Indpls., 1949-50; asst. resident in surgery, fellow vascular surg. research Ind. U. Med. Ctr., 1950-54, resident in surgery, 1954-55, faculty, 1955-94, clin. prof. surgery, 1976-94; ret., 1994; individual practice medicine specializing in gen. surgery, Terre Haute, Ind., 1955-94; dir. med. edn. Terre Haute Regional Hosp., 1970-79; staff Terre Haute Center Med. Edn.; chief of staff Terre Haute Regional Hosp., 1989-90. Contbr. articles to profl. jours. Pres. Terre Haute Med. Edn. Found., 1972-73, 78-81, bd. dirs., 1967-86; pres. community adv. council Terre Haute Center Med. Edn., 1976-80; treas. Wabash Valley Community Blood Program, 1974-78 ; trustee Terre Haute Regional Hosp., 1978-84 , chmn. bd., 1981-84. Served with U.S. Army, 1943-46, ETO. Fellow ACS (pres. Ind. chpt. 1980-81); mem. Ind. State Med. Assn. (com. med. edn. 1986-92), Vigo County Med. Soc., Pam. Am. Med. Assn., Pan Pacific Surg. Assn., Midwest Surg. Assn., Aesculapian Soc. Wabash Valley, Ind. Soc. Chgo., Rotary Club of Terre Haute, Sagamore of the Wabash, Skyline Club, Country Club of Terre Haute. Democrat. Roman Catholic. Home: 3515 Ohio Blvd Terre Haute IN 47803-1938 *Success and service are interdependent.*

KUNNEL, JOSEPH MATHEW, lawyer; b. Ernakulam, Kerala, India, May 3, 1963; came to U.S., 1991; s. Matthew and Annakutty Kunnel; m. Valsamma Thottumkal, Jan. 19, 1989; children: Nicole Ann, Jimmy M., Megan E. B.Com., U. Kerala, India, 1983; LLB, U. Gulberga, Karnataka, India, 1987; LLM, Widener U., Wilmington, Del., 1993. Bar: Pa. 1994. Pvt. practice Kerala, 1987-91; ptnr. Pasquarella & Kunnel, Phila., 1994—. Pres Malayalee Assn. of Phila., 1997—. Mem. ABA, Pa. Bar Assn. (exec. com. minority bar), Phila. Bar Assn., Am. Immigration Lawyers Assn., Dist. Bar Assn. Kerala (sec. 1988-90). Avocations: reading, writing, travel. Office: Pasquarella & Kunnel 1401 Walnut St Philadelphia PA 19102-3128

KUNNEMANN, NANCY BUSH, special education educator; b. Houston, Dec. 29, 1952; d. Joseph Herman Bush and Jacqueline Louise Richardson; m. Dennis Karl, June 11, 1977; children: Ryan Matthew, Michael Louis. BS in Spl. Edn., Western Ill. U., 1975; postgrad., Nat. Louis U., 1993. Cert. spl. edn. tchr., learning disabilities, behavior disorders, educationally handicapped, Ill.; cert. scotopic sensitivity screener Irlen Inst. Learning disabilities tchr. Hitchcock Sch., Wheaton, Ill., 1975-76; tchr. social studies, emotionally disturbed Grigsby Jr. H.S., Granite City, Ill., 1976-77; learning disabilities tchr. Serena (Ill.) H.S., 1977-79, Cmty. H.S. Dist. 99, Downers Grove, Ill., 1979-85; tchr. behavior disorders, mentally impaired, Cmty. H.S. Dist. 99, Downers Grove, 1990—, tchr. behavior disorders, inclusion facilitator,

1990—. Den leader Boy Scouts Am., Glen Ellyn, Ill., 1986-92; mem. PTA, Elem. Dist. 41, Glen Ellyn, 1986—, Glenbard Dist. 87, Glen Ellyn, 1996—, mem. booster club, 1996-98. Assistive Tech. grantee Sch. Dist. 99 Edn. Found., Downers Grove, 1995. Mem. Internat. Soc. for Tech. in Edn., Learning Disabilities Assn., Ill. Computing Educators. Democrat. Avocations: reading, computing, traveling, camping. E-mail: gannerk@aol.com. Home: 506 Carleton Ave Glen Ellyn IL 60137 Office: Cmty HS Dist 99 4436 Main St Downers Grove IL 60515

KUNOV, HANS, biomedical and electrical engineering educator; b. Copenhagen, Mar. 14, 1938; arrived in Can., 1967; s. Jens Christian and Ruth (Valeur) K.; m. Helle H.D. Jorgensen, Sept. 12, 1964 (div. 1972); children Mads Jacob, Niels Peter; m. D. Clare Lamb, Aug. 1, 1977. MASc, Tech. U. Denmark, Copenhagen, 1963, PhD, 1966. Registered profl. engr., Ont. Postdoctoral fellow Tech. U. Denmark, 1966-67; asst. prof. U. Toronto, Ont., Can., 1967-73, assoc. prof., 1973-82, prof., 1982—, dir. Inst. Biomed. Engring., 1989-99; dir. Elec. Engring. Consociates, Toronto, 1972—; pres. Artel Engring., 1975—; dir. rsch., co-founder Paul Madsen Med. Devices Ltd., Toronto, 1992-99; co-founder Electrobiologics Corp., 1995—; mem. grant selection com. Natural Scis. and Engring. Rsch. Coun., Ottawa, Ont., 1990-93. Contbr. numerous sci. papers and publs. Chmn. United Way, U. Toronto, 1991-92; mem. Big Bros. Met. Toronto, 1980—, dir., 1988-92. Recipient Big Brother of Yr. award Big Bros. Met. Toronto, 1985, 86, Irving Pomerantz award Big Bros. Met. Toronto, 1989. Mem. IEEE (assoc. editor BME Trans. 1991-93), Acoustical Soc. Am., Can. Med. Biol. Engring. Soc., Danish Engring. Soc. Achievements include development of novel audiometric techniques, of accurate mechano-acoustic models of human hearing and speech apparatus. Home: 4 Princeton Rd, Etobicoke, ON Canada M8X 2E2 Office: U Toronto, 4 Taddle Creek Rd, Toronto, ON Canada M5S 3G9

KUNSTADTER, GERALDINE SAPOLSKY, foundation executive; b. Boston, Jan. 6, 1928; d. Harry Herman and Nettie Sapolsky; m. John W. Kunstadter, Apr. 23, 1949; children: John W., Lisa, Christopher, Elizabeth. Student, MIT, 1945-48. Draftsman U. Chgo. Cyclotron Project, 1948; engring. asst. Gen. Electric Corp., Lynn, Mass., 1948-49; pres. Capricorn Investments Corp., 1971—; chmn., dir. A. Kunstadter Family Found., N.Y.C., 1966—; host family program dir. N.Y.C. Commn. for UN, 1971-86; pres. Nat. Inst. Social Scis., 1979-81. Bd. dirs. Friends of N.Y.C. Commn. for UN and Consular Corps, Bridge to Asia Found., Menninger Found., Atlantic Coun. of U.S., Internat. Devel. Enterprises, Inc., Yale-China Assn., Ballets Tech. Found., N.Y.C., Ctr. U.S.-China Arts Exch., Inst. World Affairs; mem. adv. coun. East Asian studies program MIT Sch. Arch.; mem. Peace Links Leadership Network, Overseas Devel. Coun., N.Y.-Beijing Friendship City Com.; mem. internat. hospitality com. Nat. Coun. Women; mem. Nat. Com. on U.S.-China Rels. Recipient Windham award, 1970, silver medal Nat. Inst. Social Sci., 1981. Mem. Inst. Current World Affairs, Coun. on Fgn. Rels., Am. Women's Club, Hurlingham Club, Lansdowne Club (London).

KUNTZ, CHARLES POWERS, lawyer; b. L.A., May 7, 1944; s. Walter Nichols and Katherine (Powers) K.; m. June Emerson Moroney, Dec. 23, 1969; children: Michael Nicholas, Robinson Moroney, Katie Moroney. AB with honors, Stanford U., 1966, JD, 1969; LLM, NYU, 1971. Bar: Calif. 1970, N.Y. 1970, U.S. Dist. Ct. (no. dist.) Calif. 1970, U.S. Ct. Appeals (9th cir.) 1970, U.S. Supreme Ct. 1979. Staff atty. project for urban affairs Office Econ. Opportunity, N.Y.C., 1969-71; dep. pub. defender Contra Costa County Pub. Defender's Office, Martinez, Calif., 1971-75; assoc. Treuhaft, Walker & Brown, Oakland, Calif., 1976-78; ptnr. Hirsch & Kuntz, San Rafael, Calif., 1979-85; pvt. practice San Rafael, 1985-89; ptnr. Coombs & Dunlap, Napa, Calif., 1989—. Mem. ABA, Calif. Attys. Consumer Justice, Napa County Bar Assn. Home: 1271 Monticello Rd Napa CA 94558-2019 Office: Coombs & Dunlap 1211 Division St Napa CA 94559-3372

KUNTZ, DIETER KURT, history educator, researcher, translator; b. Zweibruecken, Germany, Feb. 17, 1951; came to U.S., 1961; s. Kurt Hugo Kuntz and Louise Johanna (Gries) Willbourn; m. Anne Imelda Zimmerman, Oct. 11, 1974; children: Emma Elena, Rudi Paul. BA, Washburn U., 1973; MA, U. Kans., 1983, PhD, 1996. Instr. history U. Kans., Lawrence, 1985—; vis. asst. prof. History U. Iowa, 1999. Author: (book and study manual) Inside Hitler's Germany, 1992. Fulbright fellow, Bonn, Germany, 1986; James B. Pearson fellow Kans. Bd. Regents, 1986; Dwight Eisenhower fellow Eisenhower World Affairs Inst., 1990; Jerry Smith scholar Harry S Truman Found., 1986, Lila Atkinson Creighton scholar U. Kans., 1989. Mem. Phi Alpha Theta. Avocations: running, tennis, fishing, hiking, travel. Home: 2415 SW 10th Ave Topeka KS 66604-3946 Office: 3001 Wescoe Hall U Kans Dept History Lawrence KS 66045

KUNTZ, HAL GOGGAN, petroleum exploration company executive; b. San Antonio, Dec. 29, 1937; s. Peter A. and Jean (Goggan) K.; children: Hal Goggan, Peter, Michael B., Vesta. BS in Engring., Princeton U., 1960; MBA, Oklahoma City U., 1972. Line, staff positions Mobil Oil Corp., Dallas, Oklahoma City,, and New Orleans, 1963-74; co-founder, pres. CLK Corp., New Orleans and Houston, 1974—, IPEX Co., New Orleans, 1974—, CLK Investments I, II, III, and IV, 1979—; pres. Gulf Coast Exploration Co., New Orleans, 1979—, CLK Producing, CLK Oil and Gas Co., CLK Exploration Co., 1980—; bd. dirs. North Houston Bank. Mem. Mus. Fine Arts, Houston, 1978—; mem. condrs. cir. Houston Symphony, 1980; mem. governing bd. Houston Opera. With AUS, 1960-63. Mem. Am. Mgmt. Assn., Nat. Small Bus. Assn., Inter-Am. Soc., Soc. Exploration Geophysics, Am. Assn. Petroleum Geologists, Aircraft Owners and Pilots Assn., Houston C. of C., River Oaks C. of C., Petroleum Club, U. of Houston Club, Argyle Club, Order of Alamo, Coronado Club, Princeton Club, River Oaks Country Club, San Antonio Country Club. Republican. Roman Catholic. Avocations: golf, skiing, birdshooting. Office: CLK Co LLC 1001 Fannin St Ste 777 Houston TX 77002-6799

KUNTZ, JOEL DUBOIS, lawyer; b. Dennis, Mass., Feb. 5, 1946; s. Paul Grimley Kuntz and Harriette (Hunter) Ainsworth; m. Karan Judd, June 29, 1968; children: Matthew Christopher, Kristin Lara. BA, Haverford Coll., 1968; JD, Yale U., 1971; LLM in Taxation, NYU, 1980. Bar: Conn. 1972, Oreg. 1974. Assoc. Stoel, Rives, Boley, Jones & Grey, Portland, Oreg., 1974-79, ptnr., 1979-94; v.p., gen. counsel Entek Internat. LLC, Lebanon, Oreg., 1994—. Co-author: (with James S. Eustice) Federal Income Taxation of S Corporations, 1982, 3d edit., 1993; (with James S. Eustice, Charles S. Lewis III and Thomas P. Deering) Tax Reform Act of 1986: Analysis and Commentary, 1987; (with Robert J. Peroni) U.S. International Taxation, 1992. Capt. USMC, 1971-74. Mem. Am. Coll. Tax Counsel, Internat. Fiscal Assn. Democrat. Home: 3910 Lakeview Blvd Lake Oswego OR 97035-5549 Address: PO Box 39 Lebanon OR 97355-0039*

KUNTZ, LEE ALLAN, lawyer; b. Nashville, July 9, 1943; s. Irwin and Lucy (Kornman) K.; 1 child, Douglas. BA, Duke U., 1965; LLB, Columbia U., 1968. Bar: N.Y. 1968, U.S. Dist. Ct. (so. dist.) N.Y. 1973, U.S. Tax Ct. 1973. Assoc. Shearman & Sterling, N.Y.C., 1968-76, ptnr., 1976—, mng. ptnr., 1994-98; sr. ptnr. Real Estate Group Shearman & Sterling, 1988-93; mem. policy com. Shearman and Sterling, 1991—. Contbr. articles to profl. jours. Mem. ABA, Assn. Bar City N.Y. Office: Sherman & Sterling 599 Lexington Ave Fl C2 New York NY 10022-6069

KUNTZ, MARION LUCILE LEATHERS, classicist, historian, educator; b. Atlanta, Sept. 6, 1924; d. Otto Asa and Lucile (Parks) Leathers; m. Paul G. Kuntz, Nov. 26, 1970; children by previous marriage: Charles, Otto Alan (Daniels). BA, Agnes Scott Coll., 1945; MA, Emory U., 1964, PhD, 1969. Lectr. Latin Lovett Sch., Atlanta, 1963-66; mem. faculty Ga. State U., 1966—, assoc. prof., 1969-73, prof. Latin and Greek, 1973—, Regents' Prof., 1975—, chmn. dept. fgn. langs., 1975-84, research prof., 1984—, Fuller E. Callaway disting. prof., 1985—, alumni disting. prof., 1994. Author: Colloquim of the Seven About Secrets of the Sublime of Jean Bodin, 1975, Guillaume Postel, Prophet of the Restitution of All Things: His Life and Thought, 1981, Jacob's Ladder and the Tree of Life: Concepts of Hierarchy and the Great Chain of Being, 1987, Postello, Venezia e Il Suo Mondo, 1988, Venice, Myth and Utopian Thought, 1999; also scholarly articles; mem. editl. bd. Library of Renaissance Humanism. Named Latin Tchr. of Yr. State Ga., 1965; Semple scholar, 1965, Am. Classical League scholar, 1966, Gladys Krieble Delmas scholar, 1991; Am. Coun. Learned Socs. grantee, 1970, 73, 76, 81, 87, 90; recipient medal for excellence in Renaissance studies Pres. of Coun. Gen., Tours, France, 1995, Disting. Career Alumna award Agnes Scott Coll., 1995. Mem. Am. Philol. Assn., Renaissance Soc. Am. (coun. 1994—), Am. Soc. Aesthetics, Am. Cath. Philos. Assn., Soc. for Values in Higher Edn., Philosophy and Religion, Am. Soc. Ch. History, Am. Hist. Assn., Internat. Soc. Neo-Platonic Studies, Internat. Soc. Neo-Latin Studies, Soc. Christian Philosophers (exec. bd. 1987—), Sociètè des Seizièmistes, Medieval Acad. Sociètè de Culture Europèenne, Soc. Medieval and Renaissance Philosophy (exec. bd. 1988—), Soc. di Philosophique Medievale, Archaeol. Inst. Am., Am. Philological Assn., Classical Assn. Midwest and South (Semple award 1965), Am. Acad. Rome (sec.-treas. 1970-74), Friends of the Vatican Libr., Italia Nostra, Fondazione Ambiente Italiana, Amici di Querini-Stampalia Galleria e Biblioteca, Coun. Amici di Biblioteca Nazionale di San Marco, Italian Cultural Soc., Nat. Trust Hist. Preservation, Atlanta Hist. Soc., High Mus. of Art (patron), The Commerce Club, Friends of the Warburg Inst., World Monuments Fund, Phi Beta Kappa, Phi Kappa Phi, Omicron Delta Kappa. Roman Catholic. Home: Villa Veneziana 1655 Ponce De Leon Ave Atlanta GA 30307 also: Dorsoduro, 714 Venice Italy

KUNTZ, WILLIAM HENRY, lawyer, mediator; b. Indpls., Feb. 27, 1954; s. Herman William and Ethel Cleora (Stangle) K. BA in Chemistry, Purdue U. at Indpls., 1984; MS in Chemistry, Purdue U., Indpls., 1986; JD, Ind. U., Indpls., 1989. Bar: Ind. 1989, U.S. Dist. Ct. (so. and no. dists.) Ind. 1989, U.S. Patent Office 1992, U.S. Supreme Ct. 1993. Assoc. Urdal, Tarvin and Alexander, P.C., Connersville, Ind., 1989-90; dep. prosecutor County of Fayette, Connersville, 1990, chief dep. prosecutor, 1991-92; pvt. practice Indpls., 1992-94; chief dep. prosecutor Fayette County, Connersville, 1995-98; with Baker and Bodwell, P.C., Connersville, Ind., 1999—. Mem. ABA, Nat. Bar Assn., Ind. State Bar Assn. (bd. dirs. ADR sect. 1997—), Indpls. Bar Assn. (chmn. legal awareness com. 1996, chmn. law student liaison com. 1996), Fayette County Bar Assn. (sec.-treas. 1989-90), Marion County Bar Assn., Ind. Trial Lawyers Assn., Ind. Assn. Mediators (sec. 1993-94, 97—, pres.-elect 1994-95, pres. 1995-96), Soc. Profls. in Dispute Resolution, Acad. Family Mediators, Purdue U. Indpls. Sch. Sci. Alumni Bd. (v.p. 1998—). Home: 2065 Lick Creek Dr Indianapolis IN 46203-4922 Office: Bader and Bodwell PC County of Fayette 621 Central Ave Ste 1 Connersville IN 47331

KUNTZMAN, RONALD, pharmacology research executive; b. Bklyn., Sept. 17, 1933; s. Herman and Fanny Kuntzman; m. Bernice Russman, May 29, 1955; children: Fred, Gary. B.S., Bklyn. Coll., 1955; M.S., George Washington U., 1957, Ph.D. in Biochemistry, 1962. Biochemist lab. chem. pharmacology Nat. Heart Inst., NIH, Bethesda, Md., 1955-62; sr. biochemist Wellcome Research Labs.-Burroughs Wellcome & Co. U.S.A. Inc., Tuckahoe, N.Y., 1962-66, dep. head biochem. pharmacology dept., 1967-70; assoc. dir. dept. biochemistry and drug metabolism Hoffmann-La Roche Inc., Nutley, N.J., 1970-71, assoc. dir. biol. research, 1972-73, dir. therapeutics research, 1973-79, asst. v.p., 1974-81, dir. pharm. R & D, 1980-81, v.p. pharm. R&D, 1981-84, v.p. R&D, 1984-92; adj. prof. dept. chem. biology and pharmacognosy Rutgers U. Coll. Pharmacy, Piscataway, N.J., 1990—; adj. mem. Roche Inst. Molecular Biology, Nutley, N.J., 1992-96; mem. adv. coun. Nat. Orgn. for Rare Disorders, 1987-91; adj. prof. Rutgers U., 1990—. Mem. editl. bd. Biochem. Pharmacology, 1966-68, Neuropharmacology, 1970-78, Xenobiotica, 1970-84, Archives of Biochemistry and Biophysics, 1971-78, Life Scis., 1973-78; contbr. numerous articles to profl. jours. Mem. AAAS, Am. Soc. Pharmacology and Exptl. Therapeutics (editorial bd. jour. 1968-75, nominating com. 1972, chmn. div. nominating com. 1977, chmn. div. drug metabolism 1978-81, sec.-treas. 1981-83, coun. 1981-83, chmn. long-range planning com. 1987-92, exec. com. div. drug metabolism 1973-76, John Jacob Abel award 1969), Am. Soc. Biol. Chemists, Am. Coll. Neuropsychopharmacology, Soc. Toxicology, George Washington U. Alumni Assn. (Dist. Alumni Achievement award 1988), Roche Inst. of Molecular Biology (adj. 1992-96), Sigma Xi. Achievements include research on steroids and other normal body constituents which are metabolized by drug metabolizing enzymes; discovered P448, the hemoprotein inducible by hydrocarbon; demonstrated that DOPA-5HTP decarboxylase are the same enzyme. Address: 12 Augustine Ave Ardsley NY 10502-2203

KUNZ, CHARLES ALPHONSE, farm machinery manufacturing executive; b. Pitts., Aug. 28, 1955; s. James Thomas and Shirley Ann (Straub) K.; m. Pauline Postich, Aug. 11, 1979; children: Brennan Michael, Helen Louise. BSBA, Robert Morris Coll., Pitts., 1979. Shop mgr. A U Concrete & Pump, Zelienople, Pa., 1979-80; air traffic contr. FAA/Toledo Express Airport, Toledo, 1980-81; office mgr. Grand Builders, Pitts., 1981-83; telemktg. mgr. MCI, Pitts., 1983-84; mgmt. cons. Universal Scheduling Co., Bala Cynwyd, Pa., 1984-90; v.p. mfg. Monon (Ind.) Corp., 1990-95; plant mgr. AGCO Corp., Coldwater, Ohio, 1995—; bus. unit mgr. Twin Disc, Inc., Racine, Wis., 1997—. Committeeman Republican Party, Gibsonia, Pa., 1978-80; bd. dirs. Am. Youth Soccer Orgn., San Francisco, 1988-90, United Way, White County, Ind., 1990-95; advisor YMCA Hockey, Pitts., 1989-90. Mem. SAM (treas. 1976-79), Am. Prodn. and Inventory Control Soc., Am. Mktg. Assn., Am. Mgmt. Assn., Ducks Unltd., Sigma Nu. Roman Catholic. Avocations: hockey, golf, racquetball, drag racing. Home: 1212 Palamino Dr Racine WI 53402-2174 Office: 123 W Sycamore St Coldwater OH 45828-1853

KUNZ, MICHAEL LENNEY, archaeologist; b. Galveston, Tex., Sept. 1, 1942; s. Thomas John and Catherine Rita (Lenney) K.; m. Patricia Ann Allan, Jan. 28, 1965; children: Kelly Heather, Joshua Allan. BS in Anthropology, Ea. N.Mex. U., 1967. Instr. anthropology Ea. N.Mex. U., Portales, 1969-70; rsch. assoc. U. Alaska, Fairbanks, 1971-77; archaeologist, chief environ. monitor Bur. Land Mgmt., Fairbanks, 1977-80; archaelogist, quality assurance N.W. Alaskan Pipeline Co., Fairbanks, 1981-82; archaelogist Nat. Park Svc., Fairbanks, 1983-88, Bur. Land Mgmt., Fairbanks, 1989—; cons. Kunz & Assocs., Fairbanks, 1980—. Contbr. articles to profl. jours. Rsch. grantee Wenner-Gren Found., 1967, Sigma Xi, 1969, Bur. Land Mgmt., 1991—, Nat. Sci. Found./Mo. Univ. Rsch. Reactor, 1994. Mem. Soc. Profl. Archaelogists, Plains Anthropol. Soc., Soc. for Am. Archaeology, Alaska Anthropol. Assn. Achievements include rsch. on inland Paleo-Eskimos of No. Alaska; discovery and definition of No. Paleoindian tradition, peopling of N.Am.; Plesitocene faunal extinction; definitive rsch. on effects of Arctic environment on osidian hydration dating technique. Avocations: airplane pilot, hiking, camping, placer gold mining. Home: PO Box 80087 Fairbanks AK 99708-0087 Office: Bureau of Land Mgmt 1150 University Ave Fairbanks AK 99709-3899*

KUNZ, PHILLIP RAY, sociologist, educator; b. Bern, Idaho, July 19, 1936; s. Parley P. and Hilda Irene (Stoor) K.; m. Joyce Sheffield, Mar. 18, 1960; children: Jay, Jenifer, Jody, Johnathan, Jana. BS, Brigham Young U., 1961, MS cum laude, 1962; PhD (fellow), U. Mich., 1967. Instr. Eastern Mich. U., Ypsilanti, 1964, U. Mich., Ann Arbor, 1965-67; asst. prof. sociology U. Wyo., Laramie, 1967-68; prof. sociology Brigham Young U., Provo, Utah, 1968—; acting dept. chmn. Brigham Young U., 1973; dir. Inst. Geneal. Studies, 1972-74; cons. various ednl. and rsch. instns., 1968—; missionary Ch. Jesus Christ LDS, Ga. and S.C., 1956-58, mem. high coun., 1969-70, bishop; mission pres. La. Baton Rouge Mission, 1990-93. Author: 10 Critical Keys for Highly Effective Families, other books; contbr. articles on social orgn., family rels. and deviant behavior to profl. jours. Housing commr. City of Provo, 1984—. Served with AUS, 1954-56. Recipient Karl G. Maeser rsch. award, 1977. Mem. Am. Sociol. Assn., Rocky Mountain Social Sci. Assn., Am. Coun. Family Rels., Rural Sociol. Soc., Am. Soc. Criminology, Soc. Sci. Study of Religion, Religious Rsch. Assn., Sigma Xi, Phi Kappa Phi, Alpha Kappa Delta (Alcuin award 1997). Democrat. Home: 3040 Navajo Ln Provo UT 84604-4820 Office: Brigham Young Univ Dept Sociology Provo UT 84602

KUNZE, GEORGE WILLIAM, retired soil scientist; b. Warda, Tex., Sept. 16, 1922; s. John Paul and Hermine (Moerbe) K.; m. Flora Mae Rothmann, July 11, 1947; children: Brenda Kay, Wayne Lester. B.S., Tex. A&M U., 1948, M.S., 1950; Ph.D., Pa. State U., 1952. Mem. faculty Tex. A&M U., College Station, 1952—; asst. prof. Tex. A&M U., 1952-56, assoc. prof., 1956-60, prof. soil mineralogy, 1960-84, asso. dean Grad. Sch., 1967-68, dean, 1968-84, now ret.; cons. U. Alaska, 1963-66; cons. Bangladesh Agrl. U., 1970, Grad. Sch. Agrl. Scis., Castelar Argentina, 1972; mem. Fed. Adv. Com. on Affirmative Action in Employment Practices in Instns. of Higher Edn.; pres. Conf. So. Grad. Schs., 1980-81. Cons. editor Soil Science, 1958-84. Served with USAAF, 1943-45. Recipient Faculty Disting. Achievement award in research Tex. A&M U., 1966, in administration Tex. A.&M. U., 1984. Fellow Mineral. Soc. Am., AAAS, Am. Soc. Agronomy; mem., Clay Mineral Soc. Am (councilor). Lodge: Rotary. Home: PO Box 107 Warda TX 78960-0107

KUNZE, LINDA JOYE, educator; b. Grand Rapids, Mich., Mar. 27, 1950; d. Elon George and Lillian (Wolbers) Benaway; children: Christopher Russel, Jason Scott. BS, Grand Valley State U., Allendale, Mich., 1971, MEd, 1990. Substitute tchr. Kent Intermediate Sch. Dists., Grand Rapids, 1972-76, 85; instr. YWCA, Grand Rapids, 1972-77, youth svcs. dir., 1977-79; CETA tng. specialist Grand Rapids Pub. Schs., 1977-79; student intern Cen. Elem. Sch., Sparta, Mich., 1986; tchr. Sparta High Sch., 1986, Hastings (Mich.) Mid. Sch., 1986-87; dir. Northview Extended Day Care, Grand Rapids, 1988-95; tchr. Mich. Reformatory, Ionia, Mich., 1995-97, Ionia Temp. Facility, 1997—; cons. Forest Hills Pub. Schs., Grand Rapids, 1989, Rockford (Mich.) Pub. Schs., 1989-90, Godwin Pub. Schs., Grand Rapids, 1989—, Northview Child Care Network, Grand Rapids, 1989—. Cons. Citizens League/Child Care Task Force, Grand Rapids, 1988-89, Campfire Inc., Grand Rapids, 1988-89. Recipient Funding awards Fed. Govt., 1977, State Mich., 1988. Mem. Mich. Reading Assn., Mich. Assn. for Adult and Cmty. Educators, Nat. Assn. Edn. Young Children, Mich. Assn. Adult Basic Educators (founder). Avocations: volleyball, softball, camping, tennis, swimming. Home: 2182 Daylor Dr NE Grand Rapids MI 49525-1520 Office: Ionia Temp Facility 1755 Harwood Rd Ionia MI 48846-9457

KUNZE, OTTO ROBERT, retired agricultural engineering educator; b. Warda, Tex., May 27, 1925; s. John Paul and Hermine Amanda (Moerbe) K.; m. Alice Ruth Eifert, Aug. 5, 1951; children: Glenn, Allen, Charles, Karen. BS, Tex. A&M U., 1950; MS, Iowa State U., 1951; PhD, Mich. State U., 1964. Registered profl. engr., Tex. Agrl. and indsl. engr. Ctrl. Power and Light Co., San Benito, Tex., 1951-56; rsch. asst. agrl. engring. dept. Mich. State U., East Lansing, 1961-64; assoc. prof. agrl. engring. dept. Tex. A&M U., College Station, 1956-61, 64-69, prof. agrl. engring. dept., 1969-90, prof. emeritus agrl. engring. dept., 1990—; vis. prof. Nanjing (China) Coll. Food, Oil and Grain Econs., 1993; lectr. Tsukuba U., Japan, 93; cons. and vis. prof. Nat. Chung Hsing U. in Taichung and Nat. Taiwan U. in Taipei, Taiwan, 1994; lectr., cons. Internat. Conf. on Grain Drying in Asia, Bangkok, Thailand, 1995; engring. cons. Advanced Dryer Sys., Inc., Alachua, 1997, Farmers Rice Coop., Sacramento, 1992, Post Harvest Process and Food Engring. Ctr., G.B. Pant U., Pantnagar, India, 1985, Rice Process Engring. Ctr., Indian Inst. Tech., Kharagpur, 1975, Rice Tec, Alvin, Tex., 1996; lectr. on rice harvesting, Taichung, Taiwan, 1985, 87; lectr. U. P.R., Mayaguez, 1990; keynote spkr. P.R. sec. Am. Soc. Agrl. Engrs., Añasco, 1990; publ. coord. Rice Tech. Working Group, 1976-90. Contbr. chpts. to 4 books, more than 80 publs. in field of post harvest rice technology. Mem. A&M Consol. Bd. Equalization, College Station, 1969-71; mem. Tex. Air Control Bd., Austin, 1979-90; mem. pediatric scholarship com. M.D. Anderson Cancer Ctr., Houston, 1990—. With U.S. Army, 1944-46, ETO. Decorated 2 Bronze Stars, U.S. Army; recipient Outstanding Svc. award Rice Tech. Working Group, 1990; NSF faculty fellow, 1961-62. Fellow Am. Soc. Agrl. Engrs. (tech. dir., numerous coms.), Am. Assn. Cereal Chemists (assoc. editor), Sigma Xi (sec. 1969-70, chmn. 1970-71), Phi Kappa Phi (pub. rels. officer 1984-85). Lutheran. Home: 1002 Milner Dr College Station TX 77840-2215 Office: Tex A&M U Agrl Engring Dept College Station TX 77843

KUNZE, RALPH CARL, retired savings and loan executive; b. Buffalo, Oct. 31, 1925; s. Bruno E. and Esther (Graubman) K.; m. Helen Hites Sutton, Apr. 1978; children by previous marriage: Bradley, Diane Kunze Cowgill, James. BBA, U. Cin., 1950, postgrad., 1962-63; grad., Ind. U. Grad. Sch. Savs. and Loan, 1956, U. Calif., 1973. With Mt. Lookout Savs. & Loan Co., Cin., 1951-63, sec., mng. officer, 1958-63; with Buckeye Fed. Savs. & Loan Assn., Columbus, Ohio, 1963-77, exec. v.p., sec., 1967-70, pres., sec., vice chmn. bd. dirs., 1970-77; pres., chief operating officer, dir. Gate City Savs. and Loan Assn., Fargo, N.D., 1977-81; chief exec. officer, dir. United Home Fed., Toledo, 1981-91, also chmn. bd. dirs., 1985-91; ret., 1991; former trustee Ohio Savs. and Loan League, Toledo C. of C.; mem. investment adv. com. City of Toledo; mem. media contact group and legis. com. U.S. Savs. League. Mem. Toledo Com. 100, Toledo Zool. Soc., St. Vincent Hosp. Found.; past pres. Toledo Zoo; past pres. coun. Hope Luth. Ch.; pres. Toledo Neighborhood Housing Svcs., 1981-83; pres., chmn. pers. com. United Way Franklin County, Ohio; past pres. Ohio Soc. Prevention Blindness; bd. dirs. Revitalization Corp. Toledo, 1983-84, Bittersweet Farms, Artistic Cmty. of N.W. Ohio, Inc.; past mem., trustee Kidney Found. Northwestern Ohio and Luth. Social Svcs., Wesley Glen Retirement Meth. Ctr., Columbus, 1974-77. Served with USNR, 1944-45. Mem. Lambda Chi Alpha. Home: 2606 Emmick Dr Toledo OH 43606-2701

KUNZE, STEPHEN MICHAEL, management analyst; b. Boston, Mar. 22, 1963; s. David Paul and Judith (Orthman) K.; m. Carole Ann Ingallinera, Dec. 5, 1987; children: Lauren, Paul, Nicholas. BA, Providence Coll., 1985; MPA, Ind. U., 1987. Presdl. mgmt. intern IRS, Washington, 1987-89, fin. plan devel. chief, 1990-92, mgmt. support chief, 1992-93, chief budget ops., 1994-96, chief budget execution, 1996-97, sr. mgmt. analyst, 1997—. Coun. mem. Mother Seton Pastorial Coun., Germantown, Md., 1996—; mem. Roslindale Hist. Soc., 1984-87. Coun. for Excellence in Govt. fellow, 1996-97. Mem. KC (fin. sec. 1993-94). Avocations: skiing, coin collecting, writing children's stories.

KUNZEL, ERICH, JR., conductor, arranger, educator; b. N.Y.C., Mar. 21, 1935; s. Erich and Elisabeth (Enz) K.; m. Brunhilde Gertrud Strodl, Sept. 5, 1965. A.B. with distinction in Music, Dartmouth, 1957; postgrad., Harvard, 1957-58; A.M., Brown U., 1960; Litt.D., No. Ky. State U. Condr. Sante Fe Opera, 1957, 64, 65; music faculty Brown U., 1958-65; asst. condr. R.I. Philharmonic, 1963-65; resident condr. Cin. Symphony Orch., 1965-77; condr. Cin. Summer Opera, 1966, 73, Cin. Ballet Co., 1966-68; asso. prof. U. Cin. Coll.-Consevatory Music, 1965-71, chmn. opera dept., 1968-70; music dir. Philharmonia Orch., 1967-71, New Haven Symphony Orch., 1974-77, San Francisco Art Commn. Pops, 1981-83; condr. Cin. Pops Orch., 1977—; guest condr. Boston Symphony, Cleve. Orch., Boston Pops, Phila. Orch., San Francisco Symphony, Buffalo Philharmonic, Rochester Philharmonic, Pitts. Symphony, Atlanta Symphony, Pitts. Symphony Orch., Chgo. Symphony Orch., Interlochen Arts Festival, Dallas Symphony, Detroit Symphony, Toronto Symphony, Montreal Symphony, St. Louis Symphony, Nat. Symphony, Can. Opera Co., others. Editor, arranger choral works; recs. for Decca Gold Label, Atlantic Records, Telarc Internat., Vox Records, Caedmon Records, Pro Arte Records, Fanfare, MMG, MCA Classics Gold. Vice pres. Pierre Monteux Meml. Found., Met. Opera Guild. Recipient Grand Prix du Disque, 1989, Sony Tiffany award, 1989, Classical Record of Yr. award Japan, 1989, Grammy nomination, 1989, 91, 93, Disting. Alumnus award Phi Delta Theta Internat. Fraternity, 1996; named to Hon. Order Ky. Cols.; named Billboard Crossover Artist of Yr., 1988, 89, 90, 91. Mem. Am. Symphony Orch. League, Phi Delta Theta, Phi Mu Alpha Sinfonia, Delta Omicron. Office: Music Hall 1241 Elm St Cincinnati OH 45210-2231*

KUNZLER, JOHN EUGENE, physicist; b. Willard, Utah, Apr. 25, 1923; s. John Jacob and Freida (Meier) K.; m. Lois McDonald, Dec. 29, 1950; children: Carol Kunzler Blaine, Marilyn Kunzler Barker, Bonnie Kunzler Stein, Kim Kunzler Tomeo. B.S. in Chem. Engring, U. Utah; Ph.D., U. Calif., Berkeley. With AT & T Bell Labs., Murray Hill, N.J., 1952—; dir. electronic materials lab. AT & T Bell Labs., 1969-73, dir. electronic materials and device lab., 1973-79, dir. electronic materials, processes and devices lab., 1979-83, dir. magnetic bubble subsystems and common tech. support lab., 1983-85, dir. future devices study ctr., 1985-86; retired, 1986. Contbr. articles to profl. jours. Recipient John Price Wetherill medal Franklin Inst., 1964; Internat. prize for new materials Am. Phys. Soc., 1979; Kamerlingh Onnes medal, 1979. Fellow Am. Phys. Soc.; mem. Am. Chem. Soc., Nat. Acad. Engring., Sigma Xi, Tau Beta Pi, Alpha Chi Sigma. Patentee in field. Home: 80 Stephensburg Rd Port Murray NJ 07865-3204

KUO, FRANKLIN F., computer scientist, electrical engineer; b. Apr. 22, 1934; came to U.S., 1950, naturalized, 1961; s. Steven C. and Grace C. (Huang) K.; m. Dora Lee, Aug. 30, 1958; children: Jennifer, Douglas. BS, U. Ill., 1955, MS, 1956, PhD, 1958. Asst. prof. dept. elec. engring. Poly. Inst. Bklyn., 1958-60; mem. tech. staff Bell Telephone Labs., Murray Hill,

N.J., 1960-66; prof. elec. engring. U. Hawaii, Honolulu, 1966-82; exec. dir. SRI Internat., Menlo Park, Calif., 1982-94; v.p. Gen. Wireless Comm. Corp., 1994-98; sr. advisor W Channel Sys., 1998—; dir. info. systems Office Sec. of Def., 1976-77; liason scientist U.S. Office Naval Research, London, 1971-72; cons. prof. elec. engring. Stanford U., Calif., 1982—; vis. prof. U. Mannheim, Germany, 1995-96; mem. exec. panel Chief of Naval Ops., 1980-85. Author: Network Analysis and Synthesis, 1962, (2d edit.), 1966, Linear Circuits and Computations, 1973; co-author: System Analysis by Digital Computer, 1966, Computer Oriented Circuit Design, 1969, Computer Communications Networks, 1973, Protocols and Techniques in Data Communication Networks, 1981, Multimedia Communications, 1997; cons. editor, Prentice-Hall Inc., 1967—; mem. editorial bd. Future Generations Computer Systems; contbr. articles to profl. jours.; developer Alohanet packet broadcast radio network. Mem. Pres. coun. U. Ill.; adv. bd. Beckman Inst. Recipient Alexander von Humboldt Found. Rsch. award, 1994. Fellow IEEE; mem. The Internet Soc., Tau Beta Pi, Eta Kappa Nu. Home: 824 La Mesa Dr Portola Valley CA 94028-7421

KUO, JOHN TSUNGFEN, geophysicist, educator, researcher; b. Hangchow, Chejiang, China, Apr. 1, 1922; came to U.S., 1949; naturalized, 1967; s. Lee Chen and Che Chen (Ping) K.; m. Marilyn Dunlap, Apr. 14, 1957; children: Ping Andrea, Sonya Sue, J. David. BS in Geology, Physics and Math., U. Redlands, 1952, ScD (hon.), 1978; MS in Geophysics, Cal. Inst. Tech., 1954; PhD in Geophysics, Stanford U., 1958. Asst. prof. San Jose (Calif.) St. Coll., 1957-60; rsch. assoc. Stanford U., 1958-60; rsch. scientist Columbia U., N.Y.C., 1960-64, assoc. prof., 1964-67, prof., 1967-83, Vinton prof., 1983-85, Ewing and Worzel prof., 1985-92, Ewing and Worzel prof. emeritus, 1992—; participant DEEPSCAN, 1963; dir. Aldridge Lab. Applied Geophysics, 1964-92, Lamont-Doherty's Underground Geophys. Obs., Ogdensburg, N.J., 1967-77, Columbia U., Project Migration, Inversion, Diffraction and Scattering, 1979-89; disting. sr. vis. scholar U. Cambridge, Eng., 1970-71; vis. prof. U. Tex., Austin, 1977-78, Cornell U., N.Y., 1978, 92-97, Tech. U. Clausthal, Fed. Rep. of Germany, 1987; adj. prof. Cornell U., 1992-98; Columbia U. del. People's Republic of China, 1979; tech. adv. 20th Dist. Congressman, 1983—; hon. prof, co-dir. integrated basin studies Chengdu Inst. Tech., People's Republic of China, 1986; hon. prof. Acad. Sinica, 1979—, China U. Geoscis., Beijing, 1992; hon. sr. rschr. Inst. Geophysics, State Seismological Bur., People's Republic of China, 1995. Mem. editl. bd. Bollettino di Geofisica, Italy, 1985-89; contbr. over 120 articles to profl. jours. Danforth Tchg. fellow, 1957—, Sr. Postdoctoral fellow NSF, 1970; Rsch. grantee NSF, NASA, U.S. Geol. Survey, Office Naval Rsch., Air Force Office Sci. Rsch., Air Force Geophysics, U.S. Bur. Mines; recipient Alexander von Humboldt award for disting. U.S. sr. scientist, Fed. Republic Germany, 1986, Hon. Knight for Life award Knights Round Table Internat., 1993. Fellow Geol. Soc. Am., Royal Astron. Soc. U.K.; mem. Internat. Union Geodesy and Geophysics (fellow Assn. Geodesy, pres. permanent commn. for Earth tides 1979-87), Am. Geophys. Union (life, assoc. editor Geophysics Rev.), Soc. Exploration Geophysicists (rep.-at-large, com. mem., chmn. com.), Seismol. Soc. Am., Petroleum Exploration Soc. N.Y., Redlands Round Table (hon.), China Geophys. Soc. (fgn. corr.), Sigma Xi. Home: 11 Hoffman Ln Blauvelt NY 10913-1707 Office: Columbia U New York NY 10027

KUO, LIH, medical educator; b. Taipei, Taiwan, Aug. 28, 1957; came to U.S., 1983; BS in Biology, Tunghai Univ., Taichung, Taiwan, 1979; MS in Physiology, Nat. Taiwan U., 1983; DPhil, Med. Coll. Va., 1987. Rsch. asst. Dept. Physiology & Biophysics Nat. Def. Med. Ctr., 1979-81; tchg. asst. Dept. Physiology Nat. Taiwan U., 1981-83, Med. Coll. Va., Richmond, 1985-87; postdoctoral rsch. assoc. Dept. Med. Physiology Tex. A&M U., 1990-91; asst. prof. Tex. A&M U. Health Ctr., 1992-98, assoc. prof., 1998—; mem. exptl. cardiovascular scis. study sect. NIH, 1994-98; spkr. in field. Contbr. articles to profl. jours. Dr. Sun Yet Sen Scr. scholar Tunghai U., 1977-79, Ministry Edn. scholar Outstanding Student Coll. Medicine Nat. Taiwan U., 1981-83; A.D. Williams award Postdoctoral fellow Med. Coll. Va., 1983-85, Med. Coll. Va. Grad. fellow, 1985-87. Fellow Am. Heart Assn. (coun. circulation), Am. Physiol. Soc. (cardiovascular sect.); mem. Chinese Physiol. Soc., Microcirculatory Soc. (Grega-Zacharkow Young Investigator award 1990), Phi Kappa Phi. Office: Tex A&M U Dept Med Physiology College Station TX 77843-1114

KUO, PING-CHIA, historian, educator; b. Yangshe, Kiangsu, China, Nov. 27, 1908; s. Chu-sen and Hsiao-kuan (Hsu) K.; m. Anita H. Bradley, Aug. 8, 1946. A.M., Harvard U., 1930, Ph.D., 1933. Prof. modern history and Far Eastern internat. relations Nat. Wuhan U., Wuchang, China, 1933-38; editor China Forum, Hankow and Chungking, 1938-40; counsellor Nat. Mil. Council, Chungking, China, 1940-46, Ministry Fgn. Affairs, 1943-46; participated in Cairo Conf. as spl. polit. asst. to Generalissimo Chiang Kai-shek, 1943; during war yrs. in Chungking, also served Chinese Govt. concurrently in following capacities: mem. fgn. affairs com. Nat. Supreme Def. Council, 1939-46; chief, editorial and pubs. dept. Ministry Information, 1940-42, mem. central planning bd., 1941-45; tech. expert to Chinese delegation San Francisco Conf., 1945; chief trusteeship sect. secretariat UN, London; (exec. com. prep. commn. and gen. assembly), 1945-46; top-ranking dir. Dept. Security Council Affairs, UN, 1946-48; vis. prof. Chinese history San Francisco State Coll., summers 1954, 58; assoc. prof. history So. Ill. U., 1959-63, prof. history, 1963-72, chmn. dept. history, 1967-71, prof. emeritus, 1972—; sr. fellow Nat. Endowment for Humanities, 1973-74; Pres. Midwest Conf. Asian Studies, 1964. Author: A Critical Study of the First Anglo-Chinese War, with Documents, 1935, Modern Far Eastern Diplomatic History (in Chinese), 1937, China: New Age and New Outlook, 1960, China, in the Modern World Series, 1970; Contbr. to Am. hist. pubs. and various mags. in China and Ency. Brit. Decorated Kwang Hua medal A-1 grade Nat. Mil. Council, Chungking, 1941; Auspicious Star medal Nat. Govt., Chungking, 1944; Victory medal, 1945. Mem. Am. Hist. Assn., Assn. Asian Studies. Club: Commonwealth (San Francisco). Home: 8661 Don Carol Dr El Cerrito CA 94530-2752

KUO, WAY, industrial engineer, researcher; b. Taipei, Taiwan, Jan. 5, 1951; m. Suzanne Lee, July 13, 1951; children: Tiffany, Wendy. BS in Nuclear Engring., Nat. Tsing-Hua U., Taiwan, 1972; MS in Indsl. Engring., Kans. State U., 1978, MS in Stats., PhD in Engring., 1980. Tech. staff mem. Bell Labs., Holmdel, N.J., 1981-84; from asst. prof. to prof. Iowa State U., Ames, 1984-88, prof., chair indsl. and mfg. sys. engring., 1988-93; prof., head indsl. engring. dept. Tex. A&M U., College Station, 1993—; mem. adv. bd. NSF, Washington, 1990-92, Nat. Inst. Stds. and Tech., Washington, 1990-95. Co-author: Optimazation of Systems Reliability, 1985; editor: Quality through Engineering Design, 1993; contbr. numerous articles to profl. jours. Fellow IEEE, Am. Soc. Quality Control, Inst. Indsl. Engrs. Office: Texas A&M University Ind Eng Dept 241 Zachry College Station TX 77845

KUPCHAK, KENNETH ROY, lawyer; b. Forrest Hills, Pa., May 15, 1942; s. Frank V. and Anne B. (Ruzanic) K.; m. Patricia K. Geer, Jan. 27, 1967; children: Lincoln K., Robinson K. AB, Cornell U., 1964; BS, Pa. State U., 1965; JD in Internat. Affairs, Cornell U., 1971. Bar: Hawaii 1971, U.S. Dist. Ct. Hawaii 1971, U.S. Supreme Ct. 1988. Meteorology staff U. Hawaii, Honolulu, 1968; ptnr. Damon Key Leong Kupchak & Hastert, Honolulu, 1971—, also bd. dirs.; chief minority counsel 8th legis. Hawaii Ho. of Reps., Honolulu, 1974-75, legis. coord. Hawaii State Assn. Counties, Honolulu, 1988; bd. dirs. Fletcher Constrn. Co., N.Am. Ltd., Dinwiddie constrn. Co., San Francisco, Fletcher Gen. Ltd., Seattle; adj. prof. William S. Richardson Sch. of Law, U. Hawaii, 1993; mem. Honolulu Common Fgn. Rels., 1995—; vice chair bd. counselors Mid-Pacific Inst., 1993-95; bd. trustees Mid-Pacific Inst., 1995—, chmn. personnel com., vice chmn. edn. com.; lectr. on constrn. law. Co-author: Fifty State Construction Lien and Bond Laws, 1992, The Design/Build Process, 1997, A State-By-State Guide to Architect, Engineer and Contractor Licensing, 1998, A State-By-State Guide to Construction and Design Law, 1998; contbr. articles to profl. jours. Chair agenda com. C.Z.M. Statewide Adv. Com., Hawaii, 1980-92; pres., bd. dirs. Hawaii Cmty. Svc. Coun., Honolulu, 1982-88; trustee Moanalua Gardens Found., 1985-88, Operation Raleigh (N.C.) U.S.A., 1986-90; bd. dirs., chair program com. Hawaii Nature Ctr., 1989—; chair Hawaii State Commn. on Korean and Vietnam War Meml., 1992-95. Capt. USAF, 1964-68, Vietnam. Centennial fellow Pa. State U., 1996. Fellow Am. Coll. Constrn. Lawyers; mem. ABA (constrn. industry forum, dispute resolution steering com. 1994—, chair 1998—), Hawaii Bar Assn., Internat. Bar Assn., Am. Arbitration Assn. (panel arbitrators), USAF Assn. (v.p. Hawaii chpt. 1994-97), Cornell Law Alumni Assn. (exec. com. 1990-93), Cornell Club Hawaii (bd. dirs., chair scholarship com. 1994—), Oahu Country Club, Volcano Golf and Country Club. Avocations: lacrosse, hiking, photography. Office: 1600 Pauahi Tower 1001 Bishop St Honolulu HI 96813-3429

KUPCHAK, MITCHELL, professional sports team executive; b. Hicksville, N.Y., May 24, 1954; m. Claire Kupchak. MBA, UCLA, 1987. Basketball player Washington Bullets, 1976-81; basketball player L.A. Lakers, 1981-85, asst. gen. mgr., 1986-94, gen. mgr., 1994—; mem. U.S. basketball team World Univ. Games, 1973, Olympics, 1976. One of 20 players in NBA history to win a championship with 2 different clubs; recipient Gold medal World Univ. Games, 1973, Olympics, 1976. Office: LA Lakers PO Box 10 3900 W Manchester Blvd Inglewood CA 90306*

KUPCHICK, ALAN CHARLES, advertising executive; b. Bklyn., Apr. 8, 1942; s. Saul and Sylvia (Streifer) K.; 1 child from previous marriage: Seth; stepchildren from 2d marriage: Brian Rosson, Alexander Rosson; m. Janet Greenberg, Mar. 19, 1994. B.F.A., Pratt Inst., 1963. Asst. art dir. Grey Advt., Inc., N.Y.C., 1964-65; art dir. Grey Advt., Inc., 1965-71, creative supr., 1971-74, group creative dir., 1974-78, v.p., 1969-78; v.p., group creative dir. Wells-Rich-Greene Advt., Los Angeles, 1978-80; exec. v.p., dir. creative svcs. Grey Advt., Los Angeles, 1980-86, pres., exec. creative dir., 1986-95; vice-chmn., chief creative officer, 1995—; tchr. Sch. Visual Arts, Pratt Inst., Art Center Coll. of Design, L.A., Carson-Roberts creative course. Represented in Mus. of TV and Radio, Beverly Hills, Calif. Recipient awards Art Dirs. Club N.Y., awards Advt. Club N.Y., awards Am. TV Comml. Festival, awards Clio Festival, awards Cannes Film Festival; L.A. Art Dirs. Club awards, One Show awards. Club: Los Angeles Creative (bd. dirs. 1986-87). Office: Grey Advt Inc 6100 Wilshire Blvd Los Angeles CA 90048-5107

KUPCHYNSKY, JERRY MARKIAN, orchestra conductor, educator; b. Stryj, Ukraine, Sept. 12, 1928; came to U.S., 1946; s. Jaroslav and Cecilia Elizabeth (Jurkiv) K.; m. Jean Estelle Brown, June 29, 1957 (dec.); children: Melanie Jean, Stephanie Joy; m. Joan M. Rear, Sept. 13, 1997. B in Music Edn., Murray State U., 1951, MA in Edn., 1952; MEd, Rutgers U., 1961. Cert. tchr., supr., N.J. Tchr. music Pub. Schs., Shawneetown, Ill., 1954-57; tchr. music Pub. Schs., East Brunswick, N.J., 1957-68, supr. music, 1968-95; guest condr. youth orchs. various Eastern states, 1965—; founder, condr. Middlesex Youth Symphony Orch., 1961, Imperial Symphony Orch., 1979; founder, dir. Summer Conf. String Tchrs., 1964—; founder, chair East Brunswick Young Musicians Project, 1985—. Contbr. articles to profl. publs. Bd. dirs. East Brunswick Arts Commn., 1979, N.J. Teen Arts Festival, 1976, Alliance Arts Edn., 1977. With U.S. Army, 1952-54, Korea. Recipient N.J. Gov.'s award Arts Edn. for Disting. Leadership Music Edn., 1989, Cert. of Merit, N.J. Coun. on Arts, 1970; named to Order Ky. Cols., Commonwealth of Ky., 1978; selected for Wall of Hon., Brunswick Bd. Edn., 1998. Mem. N.J. String Tchrs. Assn. (Disting. Svc. award 1974, 78, 84, 89), Music Educators Nat. Conf., N.J. Music Educators Assn. (dir. Disting. Svc. award 1986), Am. String Tchrs. Assn. (nat. pres. 1976-78, Disting. Leadership award 1980), Nat. Sch. Orch. Assn. (nat. pres. 1984-86, Disting. Leadership award 1987, Merle J. Isaac Lifetime Achievement award 1994), N.J. Prins. and Suprs. Assn. Home: 38 Mason Ave East Brunswick NJ 08816-4837

KUPCINET, IRV, columnist; b. Chgo., July 31, 1912; s. Max and Anna (Paswell) K.; m. Essee Joan Solomon, Feb. 12, 1939; children: Karyn (dec.), Jerry Solomon. AB, Northwestern U., 1930-32; A.B., U. N.D., 1935. Columnist Chgo. Daily Times, 1935-43, Kup's Column, Chgo. Sun Times, 1943—; host TV program Kup's Show, Chgo., 1959—; commentator WBBM-TV, Chgo.; former commentator Chgo. Bears football broadcasts; spl. cons. in charge of columnists for War Fin. Divsn., drives U.S. Treasury Dept. V.p. Dr. Jerome D. Solomon Meml. Found.; originator, host Purple Heart Cruise. Recipient Emmy award, Peabody award, moderator TV show, numerous civic and profl. awards; Wabash Ave. Bridge, Chgo. renamed Irv Kupcinet Bridge, 1986. Mem. Newspaper Guild, Nat. Press Club (Washington), Chgo. Press Club, Tau Delta Phi. Office: Chgo Sun-Times 401 N Wabash Ave Chicago IL 60611-5642*

KUPEL, DOUGLAS EDWARD, historian; b. Long Beach, Calif., July 18, 1956; s. Frederick John and Nancy Kathryn (Eubank) K.; m. Maria Carmen Olivas, Nov. 27, 1991; 1 child, John Carlos. BA, U. Oreg., 1979; MA, U. Ariz., 1986; PhD, Ariz. State U., 1995. Archaeologist Regional Environ. Cons., San Diego, 1979-81, Calif. Dept. Transp., San Diego, 1981-84; historian Ariz. State Parks, Phoenix, 1986-88, City of Phoenix, 1988—; cons. historian Ryden Architects, Phoenix, 1990—; history instr. Maricopa County C.C. Dist., Phoenix, 1996—. Author: Indian and American Military Conflict, 1996. Pres. bd. dirs. Ariz. Preservation Found., Phoenix, 1988-94; fundraising capt. Phoenix Boys' Choir, 1994-96, treas., Friends of Arizona Archives, Phoenix, 1997—. Recipient Recognition award Ariz. Hist. Sites Rev. Commn., 1995, 97. Mem. Ariz. Hist. Soc. (James E. Officer award 1994), Soc. Profl. Archaeologists (cert.), Nat. Coun. for Public History, Soc. Hist. Archaeology, Nat. Trust for Hist. Preservation. Democrat. Avocations: golf, hiking. Office: City of Phoenix Law Dept 200 W Washington St Phoenix AZ 85003-1611

KUPEL, FREDERICK JOHN, counselor; b. Burbank, Calif., Apr. 22, 1929; s. Martin Charles and Lorene (Murray) K.; m. Nancy Kathryn Eubank, 1952 (div. 1979); children: James Frederick, Douglas Edward; m. Karen J. Jensen, 1980 (div. 1992); 1 stepchild, John Robert Jensen, Jr. Student, Claremont Men's Coll., 1948-50; B.A., U. Calif., Berkeley, 1951; M.A. in Psychology, Sonoma State U., 1980. Lic. profl. counselor. Acctg., fin. and mgmt. positions, 1951-66; acctg. and ops. exec. Evans Products Co., Portland, Oreg., 1967-71; v.p. fin. Columbia Corp., Portland, 1971-77, Plantronics, Inc., Santa Cruz, Calif., 1977-78; counselor Yellow Brick Rd. Program, Portland, 1975-76; cons., 1978-84; dir. bus. devel. and acquisitions ITT Communication Services, Inc., 1985-87; v.p. fin., chief fin. officer Bohemia, Inc., Eugene, Oreg., 1987-89; pres. Bus. Devel. Corp., Lake Oswego, Oreg., 1989-93; pvt. practice as counselor, 1990—. With AUS, 1946-47. Mem. Portland Indsl. Rotary (pres. 1999—). Office: Ste 314 6950 SW Hampton St Tigard OR 97223-8329

KUPER, ADAM JONATHAN, anthropologist, educator; b. Johannesburg, Transvaal, Republic of South Africa, Dec. 29, 1941; s. Simon Meyer and Gerty (Hesselson) K.; m. Jessica Sue Cohen, Dec. 16, 1966; children: Simon, Jeremy, Hannah. BA, U. Witwatersrand, Johannesburg, 1961; PhD, U. Cambridge, Eng., 1966; D (hons.), U. Gothenburg, Sweden, 1978. Lectr. in Social Anthropology Makerere U., Kampala, Uganda, 1967-70; lectr. in Anthropology U. Coll. U. London, 1970-76; prof. African Anthropology and Sociology U. Leiden, The Netherlands, 1976-85; prof. social anthropology, head human scis. dept. Brunel U., Middlesex, Eng., 1985—; mem. Inst. for Advanced Study, Princeton, N.J., 1994-95. Author: Kalahari Village Politics: An African Democracy, 1970, Anthropologists and Anthropology: The British School, 1922-72, 1973, 2d rev. ed. 1983, 3rd rev. ed. 1996, Changing Jamaica, 1976, Regionaal Vergelijkend Onderzoek in Afrika, 1977, Wives for Cattle: Bridewealth and Marriage in Southern Africa, 1982, South Africa and the Anthropologist, 1987, The Invention of Primitive Society: Transformations of an Illusion, 1988; editor: The Social Anthropology of Radcliffe-Brown, 1982, The Social Science Encyclopedia, 1985, 2nd edit., 1996, Current Anthropology, 1985-93, Conceptualizing Society, 1992, The Chosen Primate, 1994, Culture: The Anthropologist' Account, 1999, Among the Anthropologists, 1999; contbr. more than 90 articles to profl. jours. Avocations: cricket. Home: 16 Muswell Rd. London N10 2BG, England

KUPER, DANIELA F., writer, speaker; b. Chgo., June 18, 1950; d. Harry W. and Anne F. (Fisher) K.; children: Judah E., Sahra J. BA, So. Ill. U., 1971. Pres., creative dir. Kuper-Finlon Advt., Boulder, 1982-88; writer, spkr., 1988—. Contbr. fiction to newspapers and mags. Ucross Found. fellow, Djerassi Found. fellow. Mem. Colo. Author's League, Denver Ad Fedn., Boulder C. of C., Art Dirs. Club Denver (award 1985, 86).

KUPERMAN, FRANCES PERGERICHT, lawyer; b. Cleve., June 4, 1952; d. Joseph and Ann Pergericht; m. Roman G. Kuperman, Feb. 24, 1982; 1 child, Natalie Jill. BA magna cum laude, Case Western Res. U., 1974; JD, Washington U., St. Louis, 1978. Bar: N.H. 1979, Ill. 1981. Law clk. presiding justice U.S. Dist. Ct. No. Dist. Ill., Chgo., 1979-81; assoc. Jenner & Block, Chgo., 1981-83; asst. regional atty. Dept. Health and Human Svcs., Chgo., 1983-86; sr. counsel Office of Counsel to the Inspector Gen. Dept. Health and Human Svcs., Washington, 1996—. Topics editor Washington U. Law Quar., 1977-78. Mem. Phi Beta Kappa. Office: Office of Inspector Gen Dept Health and Human Svcs 330 Independence Ave SW Washington DC 20201

KUPERMAN, ROBERT IAN, advertising agency executive; b. Bklyn., Dec. 31, 1941; s. Morris and Gertrude Kuperman; m. Ellen Rose, June 6, 1973; children—Jason, Molly. B.F.A., Pratt Inst., 1963. Vice pres., sr. art dir. Doyle Dane Bernbach, N.Y.C., 1963-71; v.p., creative dir. Della Femina Travisano & Ptnrs., N.Y.C., 1971-73; sr. v.p., creative dir. Wells, Rich & Greene, N.Y.C. and Los Angeles, 1973-80, BBDO/West, Los Angeles, 1980-82; exec. v.p., exec. creative dir. Doyle Dane Bernbach/West, Los Angeles, 1982-87, exec. v.p., creative dir. Chiat/Day, Los Angeles, 1987-98, pres., CEO, 1998—; instr. Sch. Visual Arts, N.Y.C., 1968-74, Pratt Inst., Bklyn., 1966-68, Art Ctr., Los Angeles, 1975-79. Art dir. TV comml. 1949 Auto Show, 1970 (Clio Hall of Fame award 1979), Volkswagen advertisements, (now in Smithsonian Mus. Art), other TV commls. Recipient Gold medals N.Y. Art Dirs. Show, 1969, 71, Andy award Advt. Club N.Y., 1970, Clio awards for excellence in worldwide advt., 1970, 72, 74, 78, 83. Mem. Los Angeles Creative Club (co-founder, chmn. bd. dirs.), Los Angeles Advt. Club (bd. dirs. 1979). Office: TBWA Chiat/Day LA 5353 Grosvenor Playa Del Rey CA 90296*

KUPFER, CARL, ophthalmologist, science administrator; b. N.Y.C., Feb. 9, 1928; s. James and Hannah Kupfer; m. Muriel I. Kaiser, Dec. 9, 1969; children: Charles, Sarah. AB, Yale U., 1948; MD, Johns Hopkins U., 1952; DSc (hon.), U. Pa., 1982, SUNY, 1992. Diplomate Am. Bd. Ophthalmology. Intern, then resident Johns Hopkins U., 1952-55, 57-58; asst. prof. Harvard U. Med. Sch., Boston, 1960-66; prof., chmn. dept. ophthalmology U. Wash. Sch. Med., Seattle, 1966-69; dir. Nat. Eye Inst. NIH, Bethesda, Md, 1970—. Recipient Migel award Am. Found. for Blind, 1976, Pisart award Lighthouse for Blind, N.Y.C., 1984, Presdl. Rank award, 1991, Humanitarian award Lions Club Internat., 1992. Mem. Johns Hopkins Soc. Scholars, Inst. Medicine of NAS. Office: NEI/NIH Bldg 31 Rm 6A03 31 Center DR MSC 2510 Bethesda MD 20892-2510

KUPFER, DAVID J., psychiatry educator; b. N.Y.C., Feb. 14, 1941; s. Alex and Muriel (Greenfield) Kupferstein; m. Barbara Stern Burstin, June 1963 (div. Mar. 1975); m. Ellen Frank, June 1975; children: Andrea, Jeffrey, Deborah, Nancy, Erica, Tonia. BA magna cum laude, Yale U., 1961, MD, 1965. Diplomate Am. Bd. Psychiatry and Neurology. Med. intern Montefiore Hosp. Ctr., N.Y.C., 1965-66; clin. fellow in psychiatry Yale U. Sch. Medicine, New Haven, 1966-67; postdoctoral fellow, chief resident in psychiatry Dana Psychiat. Clinic, Yale-New Haven Hosp., 1969-70; asst. prof. Yale U. Sch. Medicine, New Haven, 1970-73; assoc. prof. psychiatry U. Pitts., 1973-75, prof., 1975—, chmn. dept., 1983—; dir. rsch. Western Psychiat. Inst. and Clinic Western Psychiat. Inst. and Clinic, Pitts., 1973—, Thomas Detre prof., chmn. dept. psychiatry, 1994—. Office: U Pitts Western Psychiat Inst & Clinic 3811 Ohara St Pittsburgh PA 15213-2593

KUPFERMAN, DAVID COBB, painter; b. Boston, Mar. 10, 1946; s. Lawrence Kupferman and Ruth Cobb; m. Beth Ann Fried, Feb. 24, 1993. Student, U. Wis., 1964-66; BS in Creative Intelligence, Maharishi European Rsch. U., Seelisberg, Switzerland, 1976. Apprentice to sculptor Mirko Harvard U., Cambridge, Mass. One-man shows include Greenfield Gallery, N.Y.C., 1971, Harvard U., 1971, Harold Ernst Gallery, Boston, 1974-76, French Libr. of Boston, 1976, Gallery of World Art, Newton, Mass., 1978, Visual Images Gallery, Wellfleet, Mass., 1984, 85, Newton Free Libr. Gallery, Mass., 1988, 99, Galerie Mourlot, Boston, 1992, Cataumet Art Ctr., Cape Cod, Mass., 1994, 96, Kendall Ctr. for Arts, Belmont, Mass., 1991, 97, Sswansborough Gallery,Wellfleet, 1995, 96, Thayer Acad., Braintree, Mass., 1997, Hodgell Gallery, Sarasota, Fla., 1997, 99, Gallery Szent-Gyorgyi, Falmouth, Mass., 1998, Hahn Gallery, Phila., 1999others; exhibited in group shows at Inst. Contemporary Art, Boston, 1974, 75, Midtown Gallery, N.Y.C., 1977, Wallace-Wentworth Gallery, Washington, 1985-87, Richard Green Gallery, N.Y.C., 1988-89, Galerie Keller, Paris, 1986, Allene LaPedes Gallery, Santa Fe, 1988-89, Jill George Gallery, London, 1991—, BostonFine Arts, 1993-94, Lydon Fine Arts, Chgo., 1993, DeCordova Mus., 1990-93, 98, Phila. Mus. Gallery, 1993, Cape Mus. Fine Art, Dennis, Mass., 1994-95, Danforth Mus. Art, Framingham, Mass., 1995-97, Mus. Fine Arts, Boston, 1997; represented in permanent collections at Cape Mus. Fine Arts, Danforth Mus. Art, Boston Pub. Libr., Provincetown (Mass.) Art Assn. and Mus., DeCordova Mus., Lincoln, Mass., Stamford Mus., Conn., Mass. Coll. Art, Boston; author, artist: Milkman Max, 1965; subject of TV documentary Impact: David Kupferman, 1994. Mass. Arts Lottery grantee, 1988. Home: 115 Irving St Watertown MA 02472-2705

KUPFERMAN, MEYER, composer; b. N.Y.C., July 3, 1926; s. Elias and Fanny (Hoffman) K.; m. Sylvia Kasten, June 16, 1946 (div.); 1 dau., Lisa; m. Pei-fen Chin, July 24, 1973. Student, Queens Coll., 1944-46. Co-dir. New Chamber Music Soc., 1946-48, Bolton Music Festival, Bolton Landing, N.Y., 1947-48; mem. forum group bd. N.Y. chpt. Internat. Soc. Contemporary Music, 1949-50; tchr. composition, chamber music, music for theatre Sarah Lawrence Coll., 1951—, prof. emeritus, 1955—, chmn. music dept., 1979; dir., founder Sarah Lawrence Improvisational Ensemble, 1967—; composer-in-residence Calif. Music Ctr., 1977-80; pres. Soundspells Prodns., 1986—; composer-in-residence N.Y. Virtuosi, 1997; condr. Monte Carlo Orch., 1999; concert lectr. Colgate U., 1996, SUNY-New Paltz, 1996. Composer: debut, Steinway Hall, N.Y.C., 1946, film scores Hallelujah the Hills, 1962, A X'mas Memory, 1966, Blast of Silence, 1960, Faces of America, 1965, Goldstein, 1964, Black Like Me, 1964, Cool Wind, 1961, Among the Paths to Eden, 1968; (operas) In a Garden, 1948, The Curious Fern, 1957, Voices for a Mirror, 1957, Draagenfut Girl, 1958, Doctor Faustus Lights the Lights, 1963, The Judgement, 1966-67, Prometheous, 1976, The Proscenium, 1991; symphony Symphony No. 10: FDR, 1982, Clarinet Concerto, 1984, Ode to Shreveport, 1985, Sound Phantoms, #8, 1983, Challenger (for large orch.), 1983, A Little Ivory Concerto, 1986, Jazz Symphony, 1988, Savage Landscape, 1989, Double Concerto for 2 clarinets and orch. commd. by Nassau Symphony for soloists Stanley and Naomi Druker, 4 Piano Retrospective on March 8, at Katheryn Bache Miller Theatre featuring premieres of Symphonic Odyssey, Vilnius, Lithuania, 1990, Red Sonata, Snow and In Quiet Measure, with pianists Morton Estrin, Kuzuko Hayami, Christopher Vassiliades and Svetlana Gorokhovich, 1992, Ice Cream Concerto, 1992, The Moor's Concerto, 1993, Fantasy Concerto for Violin and Orchestra, 1997, Strata for Solo Flute, N.Y.C., 1997, Percussion Symphony, Ithaca Percussion Ensemble, 1997, Quasar Symphony, Vilnius, 1997, Soun Phantoms # 8, Sinfonia Brevis II, Vilnius, 1997; chamber music Cycle of Infinities, 1962-67, Images of Chagall, 1988, (recs.) Images of Chagall, Jazz Symphony and Challenger with Lithuauian Nat. Philharm., Clarinet Concerto with Pro Arte Chamber Orch. of Boston; (choreographed by Martha Graham) ballet score O Thou Desire, 1977, Concerto for Guitar and Orch. premiered by Orquesta de Baja Calif., Chaccone Sonata premiered by Laurel Ann Mauer, Hexagon Skies for guitar and orch., Infinites Projection for small orch., winter symphony for orch., 1999; author: Atonal Jazz; commd. Concerto Brevis for Flute and Orch., Nat. Flute Assn., 1999: Concerto Brevis, A Faust Concerto. First recipient La Guardia Meml. award outstanding achievement field music, 1958, Music award Am. Acad. and Inst. Arts and Letters, 1981, Dutchess County Individual Artist's award, 1991; Nat. Endowment Arts grantee, 1974; Guggenheim fellow, 1974-75; Ford Found. grantee, 1975-76. Mem. ASCAP (mem. Deems Taylor Award com. of judges). *

KUPFERMAN, THEODORE R., former state justice, lawyer; b. N.Y.C., May 12, 1920; s. Samuel H. and Gertrude Kupferman; m. Dorothee Hering, Dec. 21, 1957 (dec. June 1969); children: Theodore R. Jr., Stephanie Elisabeth; m. Fran Liner, Sept. 12, 1975. BS, City Coll. N.Y.; LLB (Kent scholar, editor Law Rev.), Columbia U. Bar: N.Y., U.S. Supreme Ct. Law sec. presiding Judge D.W. Peck, appellate divsn. N.Y. State Supreme Ct., 1948-49; mem. legal dept. Warner Bros. Pictures, Inc., 1949-51, NBC, 1951-53; sec., v.p., gen. counsel Cinerama Prodns. Corp., 1953-59; ptnr. Kupferman & Price, 1959-66; counsel firm Battle, Fowler, Stokes & Kheel, N.Y.C., 1966-69; justice Supreme Ct., State of N.Y., 1969-70; assoc. justice Appellate Divsn., 1st Dept., 1971-96; counsel Tunick, Kupferman & Creadore; asst., then adj. prof. law N.Y. Law Sch., 1959-64; counsel, legis. asst. minority leader S.M. Isaacs, N.Y. City Coun., 1958-62. Editor-in-chief Comm. and the Law Quar., 1978—. Mem. N.Y. City Coun., 1962-66; mem. 89-90th Congress 17th Dist. N.Y.; past chmn. youth svcs. com., former bd.

dirs. YMCA, N.Y.C.; pres. Layman's Nat. Bible Com., 1975-80, chmn. bd., 1980-86; former bd. dirs. Practising Law Inst. Col. J.A.G. N.Y. State Guard. Recipient Finley award for mcpl. svc. Mem. ABA (past editor bull. sect. internat. and comparative law, Congl. affairs editor Internat. Lawyer), N.Y. State Bar Assn. (former chmn. judges speakers bur., spl. com. on cts. and community), Fed. Bar Coun. (pres. 1954-56, chmn. bd. dirs. 1956-60), Consular Law Soc. (past pres., trustee), Am. Arbitration Assn. (former mem. panel arbitrators), Theodore Roosevelt Assn. (pres. 1986-90), Acad. Polit. Sci., Internat. Radio and TV Soc., Med. Jurisprudence Soc. (pres.), City Club (past pres. N.Y.C. chpt.) Phi Beta Kappa (past pres. Gamma chpt., former mem. bd. dirs. Phi Beta Kappa Assocs.). Republican. Office: Tunick Kupferman & Creadore PC 425 Park Ave New York NY 10022-3506

KUPIETZKY, MOSHE J., lawyer; b. N.Y.C., May 17, 1944; s. Jacob Harry and Fanny (Dresner) K.; m. Arlene Debra Usdan, June 22, 1966; children: Jay, Jeff, Jacob. BBA cum laude, CCNY, 1965; LLB, Harvard U., 1968, JD magna cum laude, 1968. Bar: N.Y. 1969, Calif. 1970. Law clerk to Hon. William B. Herlands U.S. Dist. Ct., N.Y.C., 1968-69; assoc. Mitchell Silberberg & Knupp, L.A., Calif., 1969-74; ptnr. Mitchell Silberberg & Knupp, L.A., 1974-80; ptnr., prin. Hayutin Rubinroit Praw & Kupietzky, L.A., 1980-87; ptnr. Sidley & Austin, L.A., 1987—. Bd. dirs. Nat. Inst. Jewish Hospice, Beverly Hills, Calif., 1986—; mem. bd. advisors Graziadio Sch. Bus. and Mgmt. Pepperdine U., L.A., 1996-98. Mem. ABA, Beverly Hills Bar Assn., L.A. County Bar Assn. Office: Sidley & Austin 555 W 5th St Ste 4000 Los Angeles CA 90013-3000

KUPPERMAN, HENRY JOHN, lawyer; b. N.Y.C., May 18, 1957; s. Ben J. and Roma M. (Ash) K.; m. Rebecca Beauchamp, 1990; 1 child, Jonathan Andrew. BA, Johns Hopkins U., 1978; JD, St. John's U., 1982. Bar: N.Y. 1983, U.S. Ct. Appeals (3d cir.) 1983, Pa. 1984, Calif. 1987, U.S. Ct. Appeals (9th cir.) 1987, U.S. Supreme Ct. 1988; cert. fraud examiner. Student law clk. to judge U.S. Dist. Ct., N.Y.C., 1981-82; law clk. to chief judge U.S. Dist. Ct., Wilmington, Del., 1982-83; assoc. Drinker, Biddle & Reath, Phila., 1984-86; assoc. Brobeck, Phleger & Harrison, L.A., 1986-89, ptnr., 1990-93; gen. counsel, dir. West Coast ops. The Investigative Group, Internat., Inc., L.A., 1994—. Mem. ABA (co-chmn. subcom. on fed. local procedure 1986-88), Calif. Bar Assn. L.A. Bar Assn., Beverly Hills Bar Assn. Jewish. Office: The Investigative Group Internat Inc 725 S Figueroa St Ste 2400 Los Angeles CA 90017-5424 also: Kroll Assocs 300 S Grand Ave Ste 1300 Los Angeles CA 90071

KUPPERMAN, STEPHEN HENRY, lawyer; b. New Orleans, Sept. 17, 1953; s. Abraham Bernard and Jo-Ellyn (Levy) K.; m. Mara Rothstein, Oct. 18, 1980; children: Zachary Hart, Shane Levi, Jake Benjamin. BA, Duke U., 1974; JD, Tulane U., 1977. Bar: La. 1977, U.S. Dist. Ct. (ea. dist.) La. 1977, U.S. Dist. Ct. (mid. dist.) La. 1978, U.S. Dist. Ct. (we. dist.) La. 1981, U.S. Ct. Appeals (5th cir.) 1977, U.S. Ct. Appeals (11th cir.) 1982, U.S. Supreme Ct. 1980. Assoc. Stone Pigman Walther Wittmann & Hutchinson, New Orleans, 1977-81, ptnr., 1981—; adj. prof. Tulane Law Sch., 1988—; mem. Tulane Law Rev., 1975-77, adv. bd., 1992—. Articles editor Tulane Law Rev., 1976-77, mem., 1975-76; contbr. articles to law revs., profl. jours. Bd. dirs. Goodwill Industries, 1980-87, mem. adv. bd., 1987-91; bd. dirs. Jewish Family Svcs., New Orleans, 1978-93, treas., 1986, v.p., 1987-88, pres., 1989-90; bd. dirs. Jewish Fedn., New Orleans, 1989-93, 95—, treas., 1991-93; adv. bd. mem. Jewish Endowment Found., New Orleans, 1979—; mem. adv. bd. Tulane Continuing Legal Edn. Program, 1983—, B'nai B'rith Anti-Defamation League S. Ctrl. Region, 1987—, vice-chmn., 1991-95, chmn. 1995—; mem. Young Leadership Cabinet United Jewish Appeal, 1990-92; bd. dirs. Touro Infirmary Found., 1998—, Touro Synagogue, New Orleans, 1991—, sec., 1995-97, v.p., 1997—. Mem. ABA, La. Bar Assn. (continuing legal edn. com. 1986-88, disciplinary conduct com. 1995—), New Orleans Bar Assn. (mem. Inn of Ct. 1994—), Fed. Bar Assn. (bd. dirs. New Orleans chpt. 1989-94), Securities Industry Assn., Order of Coif. Democrat. Jewish. Office: Stone Pigman Walther Wittmann & Hutchinson 546 Carondelet St Ste 100 New Orleans LA 70130-3588

KUPPUSAMY, PERIANNAN, medical educator, medical researcher; b. Apr. 4, 1954; m. Lakshmi Kuppusamy; 2 children. BSc in Math., Physics and Chemistry, U. Madras, India, 1975, MSc in Chemistry, 1977; PhD in Electron Paramagnetic Resonance Spectroscopy, Indian Inst. of Tech., 1985. Lectr. dept. chemistry Pachaiyappa's Coll., Madras, India, 1978-80, asst. prof. dept. chemistry, 1985-86; tchr. fellow dept. chemistry Indian Inst. of Tech., Madras, 1980-85; rsch. fellow divsn. cardiology Johns Hopkins U. Sch. of Medicine, Balt., 1987-90, instr. medicine, 1990-92, asst. prof., 1992—. Mem. editl. rev. Shock, Stroke, Magnetic Resonance in Medicine; contbr. articles to profl. jours, chpts. to books. Tchr. fellow Univs. Grants Commn., Govt. of India, 1984, Fogarty fellow NIH, 1987; recipient Rsch. award Chesapeake Ednl. & Rsch. Trust, 1991. Mem. Am. Heart Assn. (Established Investigator award 1996), Am. Chem. Soc., N.Y. Acad. Scis., Biophys. Soc., Oxygen Soc. Home: 2910 Brightwater Ln Abingdon MD 21009-1829 Office: Johns Hopkins U Sch Medicine EPR Labs Divsn Cardiology 5501 Hopkins Bayview Cir # 14 Baltimore MD 21224-6821*

KUPSCH, WALTER OSCAR, geologist; b. Amsterdam, Netherlands, Mar. 2, 1919; emigrated to Can., 1950, naturalized, 1956; s. Richard Leopold and Elizabeth (Heuser) K.; m. Emmy Helene de Jong, Oct. 2, 1945; children—Helen Elizabeth, Yvonne Irene, Richard Christopher. M. Cand, U. Amsterdam, 1943; M.Sc., U. Mich., 1948, Ph.D., 1950, LLD (hon.), 1997. Asst. prof. geology U. Sask., Saskatoon, Can., 1950-56; assoc. prof. U. Sask., 1956-64, prof., 1964-86, emeritus prof., 1986—; dir. Inst. North Studies, 1965-73, Churchill River Study, 1973-76, Sask. Heritage Assocs. Ltd., 1973-76; bd. govs. Arctic Inst. N.Am., 1969-74, chmn., 1973-74; mem. Sci. Coun. Can., 1976-82; vice chmn. sci. adv. bd. N.W. Terrs., 1976-85; exec. dir. adv. com. Devel. of Govt. in N.W. Terrs., 1965-66; petroleum advisor to Govt. N.W. Terrs., 1980-85; mem. North Devel. adv. coun. to Govt. Sask., 1985-88; mem. BHP Diamond Mine Environ. Rev. Panel, N.W. Terrs., 1994-96. Contbr. articles to profl. jours. Served with Netherlands Army, 1939-40. Recipient Pub. Svc. award Commr. N.W.T., 1992, Order of Can., 1996. Fellow Royal Soc. Can., Geol. Soc. Am., Royal Can. Geographic Soc., Geol. Assn. Can., Arctic Inst. N.Am.; mem. Am. Assn. Petroleum Geologists, Sask. Geol. Soc. Home: 319 Bate Cr, Saskatoon, SK Canada S7H 3A6 Office: U Sask, Dept Geol Sci, Saskatoon, SK Canada S7N 0W0

KUPST, MARY JO, psychologist, researcher; b. Chgo., Oct. 4, 1945; d. George Eugene and Winifred Mary (Hughes) K.; m. Alfred Procter Stresen-Reuter Jr., Aug. 21, 1977. BS, Loyola U., 1967, MA, 1969, PhD, 1972. Lic. psychologist, Ill., Wis. Postdoctoral fellow U. Ill. Med. Ctr., Chgo., 1971-72; rsch. psychologist Children's Meml. Hosp., Chgo., 1972-89; assoc. prof. psychiatry and pediatrics Northwestern U. Med. Sch., Chgo., 1981-89; prof. pediatrics Med. Coll. Wis., Milw., 1989—, dir. pediatric psychology, 1995—; practice clin. psychology, Chgo., 1975-89, McHenry, Ill., 1987-89. Editor: (with others) The Child with Cancer, 1980; contbr. articles to profl. jours. V.p. McHenry County Mental Health Bd. Fellow APA; mem. Wis. Psychol. Assn., Soc. Pediatric Psychology. Office: Med Coll Wis Dept Pediats 8701 W Watertown Plank Rd Milwaukee WI 53226-3548

KURATKO, DONALD F., business management educator, consultant; b. Chgo., Aug. 27, 1952; s. Donald W. and Margaret M. (Browne) K.; m. Deborah Ann Doyle, Dec. 28, 1979; children: Christina Diane, Kellie Margaret. BA in Econs., John Carroll U., 1974; MS in Mortuary Sci. and Adminstrn., Worsham Coll., 1975; MBA in Mktg.-Mgmt., Benedictine U., 1979; DBA in Small Bus. Mgmt., Nova Southea. U., 1984. Lic. funeral dir., Ill.; prof. bus. Benedictine U., Lisle, 1979-83; prof., dir. entrepreneurship program Ball State U., Muncie, Ind., 1983—; disting. prof., Ball State U., 1990—; funeral dir. Kuratko Funeral Home, North Riverside, Ill., part-time, 1975—; cons. Kendon Assocs., Riverside, 1983—, Intrapreneurial Group, 1989—; dir. Pathologists Assocs., Acordia Ctrl. Ind., Inc. monument advisors; cons. Acordia, AT&T, GTE, United Techs., Ameritech, Union Carbide Corp. Author: Management, 1988, 3rd edit., 1991; Effective Small Business Management, 1986, 5th edit. 1998, Entrepreneurship, 1989, 4d edit. 1998, Intrapreneurship and Innovation in the Corporation, 1987; Entrepreneurial Strategy, 1994, The Entrepreneurial Decision, 1997, The Breakthrough Experience, 1998. Mem. editorial bd. Mid-Am. Bus. Jour., 1985—; consulting editor Entrepreneurship Theory & Practice Jour., Small Bus. Forum,. Contbr. articles in field to profl. jours . Named Outstanding Young Hoosier, Ind. Jaycees, 1985, one of Outstanding Young Men of Am., 1983, 84, recipient George Washington medal of Honor, 1987, Leavey Found. award 1988; named Disting. Teaching Professorship, 1990, Stoops Disting. Prof. Bus., 1990, Entrepreneur of Yr. in Ind., Ernst & Young, Inc. Mag. and Merrill Lynch, 1990, Excellence award N.F.I.B. Found., 1993, Nat. Outstanding Entrepreneurship Educator of the Year award, 1993, Kauffman Found. Entrepreneurship Educator award, 1994, Entrepreneural World of Differences award, 1998. Developed nationally-ranked entrepreneurship prgm., Top 20 Business Week, Top 25 Success Mag., Top 20 Entrpreneur Mag., Natl. Model Prog. Award, 1990; Natl. Model Prog. Award, grad. level, 1998; Mem. U.S. Assn. Small Bus. and Entrepreneurship (pres. 1993—), Nat. Acad. Mgmt., Internat. Council for Small Bus., Midwest Bus. Adminstrn. Assn. (pres. entrepreneurship divsn. 1992-93). Roman Catholic. Avocations: weightlifting, jogging. Home: 2309 N Kensington Way Muncie IN 47304-2484 Office: Ball State U Coll Bus Muncie IN 47306

KUREGEL, PATRICK FERDINAND, buyer; b. Bern, Switzerland, July 22, 1967; came to U.S., 1993; s. Marius André and Charlotte Catherine (Frieden) K. BABA, Bus. Sch., Bern, 1987; MBA in Hospitality Mgmt., Hospitality Mgmt. Sch., Thun, Switzerland, 1991. Night auditor Hotel Christiania, Gstaad, Switzerland, 1987-88; asst. mgr. Restaurant Moevenpick, Zurich, Switzerland, 1991-92; buyer Novartis Nutrition, Mpls., 1993—. Cpl. Swiss Army, 1987-93. Avocations: sports, travel, movies, music, reading. Home: 4130 Upton Ave N Minneapolis MN 55412-1522 Office: Novartis Nutrition Corp 5320 W 23rd St Saint Louis Park MN 55416-1657

KUREK, MICHAEL HENRY, music educator; b. Nashville, Sept. 23, 1955; s. Michael H. Sr. and Sarah Morse (Case) K.; m. Laurie Elizabeth Sterrett, Aug. 11, 1979; children: Andrew G., Timothy M. MusB, U. Tenn., 1977; MusM, U. Mich., 1981, D of Music Composition, 1985. Vis. asst. prof. Roosevelt U., Chgo., 1985-87, SUNY, Fredonia, 1987-88; assoc. prof. of composition Vanderbilt U., Nashville, 1988—; bd. dirs. John W. Work III Meml. Found., Nashville; bd. advisors Lexington Sinfonietta, Boston, 1995—; program annotator Nashville Symphony Orch., 1989—. Composer Concerto for Harp and Orchestra, 1994, String Quartet No. 2, 1995, Matisse Impressions, 1990; compact disc of compositions, 1996. Fellow MacDowell Colony, 1994, Fromm fellow Tanglewood Music Ctr., 1983; recipient Acad. Award in Music Am. Acad. Arts and Letters, 1994. Office: Vanderbilt Univ Blair Sch Music 2400 Blakemore Ave Nashville TN 37212-3406

KUREPA, ALEXANDRA, mathematician, educator; b. Zagreb, Yugoslavia, Dec. 31, 1956; came to U.S., 1985; d. Svetozar and Zora (Lopac) K.; m. Rodney Anthony Waschka II, June 24, 1988; children: Andre Kurepa Waschka, Lana Kurepa Waschka. BS, U. Zagreb, 1978, MS, 1982; PhD, U. North Tex., 1987. Asst. prof. math. U. Zagreb, 1987-88, Tex. Christian U., Ft. Worth, 1989-93; asst. prof. math. N.C. A&T State U., Greensboro, 1993-96, assoc. prof., 1996—. Author: Matematica 2, 1989; contbr. articles to profl. jours. Rsch. grantee UNESCO, 1988, 89, U.S. Dept. Edn., 1995—, Assn. Women in Math.-Nat. Security Agy., 1997-99, NSF, 1997—. Mem. Am. Math. Soc., Math. Assn. Am., Assn. for Women in Math., Nat. Coun. Tchrs. Math. Office: NC A&T State U Dept Math Greensboro NC 27411

KURFEHS, HAROLD CHARLES, real estate executive; b. Jersey City, Dec. 10, 1939; s. Harold Charles and Matilda Gertrude (Ruschman) K.; BS (Oaklawn Found. scholar), St. Peter's Coll., 1962; MBA, Wharton Sch., U. Pa., 1964; m. Linda Roberta Lepis, Aug. 1, 1964; children: Harold Charles III, Diane E., Robert C. Product mgr. Am. Brands, Inc., N.Y.C., 1958-62, 64-66; account exec. Benton & Bowles, N.Y.C., 1966-68; account mgr. Wells, Rich, Greene, Inc., N.Y.C., 1968-69; v.p., dir. marketing Meta-Language Products, Inc., N.Y.C., 1969-70; sr. account exec. McCaffrey & McCall, Inc., N.Y.C., 1970-71; dir. advt. Ethan Allen, Inc., N.Y.C., 1972-75; v.p., gen. mgr. retail/franchise div. N.Am. ops. Reed Ltd., Toronto, Ont., Can., 1975-76, also v.p., gen. mgr. fabric div. Reed Nat. Drapery Co., Sanderson, Can., 1975-76; pres. Fairfield Book Co. Inc., Harlin House, Ltd., Brookfield, Conn., 1977-83, dir. advt. and pub. rels., bd. dirs., mem. mktg. planning bd. Ethan Allen, Inc., Danbury, Conn., 1983-85; sr. comml. investment broker William Raveis Comml. Investment Real Estate, Danbury, Conn., 1985-96; sr. comml. investment broker Scalzo Realty, Inc., Bethel, Conn., 1996—; lectr. Western Conn. State U., 1985-86. Real estate chmn. United Way No. Fairfield County, Conn., 1990, 91; mem. policies and procedures com. lead mgmt. Conn. Econ. Resource Ctr., 1995-96; alt. mem. Brookfield Planning Commn., 1997, 98,99. Contbr. articles to profl. jours. Named Top Producer State of Conn., 1988, 1989, Broker of the Month Conn. Real Estate Jour., 1990, Broker of Yr. Scalzo Comml., 1998. Mem. NRA (life), Conn. Assn. Realtors (mem. comml.-investment divsn., regional treas. 1992, v.p. 1993, 94, pres. 1995-96, state dir. 1993, 94, 98, state sec. 1994, state v.p. 1995, state pres.-elect 1996, state pres. 1997), Lions Club (Brookfield), Wharton Grad. Club N.Y., Pi Sigma Phi. Home: 42 Obtuse Rd N Brookfield CT 06804-3140 Office: 6 Stony Hill Rd Bethel CT 06801-1028

KURFEHS, JOSEPH MORRIS, investment company systems manager; b. Jersey City, N.J., Sept. 21, 1965; s. Frederick Joseph and Maria (Linfante) K.; m. Debra Lynn Kubinak, Oct. 26, 1992; children: Casey Jo, Sydney Lynn. AS in Mgmt., Middlesex County Coll., Edison, N.J., 1989; BS in Mgmt. Sci., Kean U., 1995. Cert. LAN Mgr., Microsoft U. Tax specialist First Investors, Woodbridge, N.J., 1985-87; systems mgr. Prudential Investments, Edison, 1987—; cons. Dr. Kubinak, DDS, Metuchen, N.J., 1996—. Percussionist, Old Bridge (N.J.) Theater Guild, 1981-88; v.p. Italian Club, Old Bridge, 1982. Recipient Outstanding Sr. Indsl. Edn. award Madison Ctrl. H.S., Old Bridge; recipient Nebisco Art Gallery Expo award for fine art/woodworking, 1994. Mem. Internat. Sys. Security Assn., St. Lupo Soc. (Jersey City), Alpha Sigma Lambda. Republican. Roman Catholic. Avocations: computer games, drums, golf, woodworking. E-mail: Joseph.Kurfehs@Prudential.com.

KURFESS, THOMAS ROLAND, mechanical engineering educator; b. Des Plaines, Ill., May 18, 1964; s. Roland H. and Evelyn M. (Haschin) K.; m. Adriana D. Praddaude, May 28, 1988. SBME, MIT, 1986, SMME, 1987, SMEE and Computer Sci., 1988, PhD in Mech. Engring., 1989. Draper fellow The C. S. Draper Lab., Cambridge, 1985-89; asst. prof. Carnegie Mellon U., Pitts., 1989-94, assoc. prof., 1994; assoc. prof. Ga. Inst. Tech., Atlanta, 1994—. Mem. ASME (Pi Tau Sigma Medal, 1995), NSPE, Soc. Mfg. Engrs., Am. Soc. Engring. Edn., Pi Tau Sigma, Tau Beta Pi, Sigma Xi.

KURIAN, GEORGE THOMAS, publisher; b. Changanacherry, Kerala, India, Aug. 4, 1931; came to U.S., 1968; s. Thomas Kurian and Mary (Abraham) George; m. Annie Cyriack, Aug. 22, 1966; 1 child, Sarah Claudine. MA, Madras (India) Christian Coll., 1951. Dir. Indian Univs. Press, Madras, 1960-68; editor Clarence L. Barnhart, Bronxville, N.Y., 1968-71, Macmillan Inc., N.Y.C., 1971-72; pres. George Kurian Reference Books, Baldwin Place, N.Y., 1972—; bd. dirs. Fgn. Affairs Info. Svc., Baldwin Place, 1982—. Editor: Ency. of Third World, 1978 (ALA award 1978), World Press Ency., 1982, World Edn. ency., 1988 (ALA award 1988), Ency. of First World, 1990, Ency. of the Future, 1995, also 5 other encys. and 18 books. Mem. The Encyclopedists: Internat. Ency. Soc. (pres. 1990—), World Future Soc. Republican. Avocation: carpentry. Home: 3689 Campbell Ct Yorktown Heights NY 10598-1808 Office: George Kurian Reference Books PO Box 519 Baldwin Place NY 10505

KURIAN, PIUS, nephrologist, educator; b. Arpookara, Kerala, India, May 9, 1959; s. Pylo and Mariamma Kurian; m. Sally Kurian, May 11, 1986; children: Michelle Maria, Matthew Paul, Catherine Tresa. BSc, Kuriakose (India) Elias Coll., 1979; MB, BChir, Kottayam (India) Med. Coll., India, 1986. Diplomate Am. Bd. Internal Medicine, Am. Bd. Nephrology, Am. Bd. Forensic Examiners. Resident in internal medicine Nassau County Med. Ctr., East Meadow, N.Y., 1988-91; fellow in nephrology Nassau County Med. Ctr., East Meadow, 1991-94; attending physician in nephrology Mercy Med. Ctr. and Cmty. Hosp., Springfield, Ohio, 1994—; asst. prof. dept. medicine Wright State U., Dayton, Ohio, 1998; chief divsn. internal medicine Mercy Med. Ctr., Springfield, Ohio, 1999. Mem. ACP, AAAS, AMA, Am. Soc. Hypertension, Am. Soc. Nephrology, Am. Coll. Physicians Execs., Internat. Soc. Nephrology, Renal Physicians Assn., N.Y. Acad. Scis, Am. Diabetes Assn., Nat. Kidney Found. Roman Catholic. Office: 247 S Burnett Rd Springfield OH 45505-2639

KURIE, ANDREW EDMUNDS, mining geologist; b. Dallas, May 30, 1932; s. Charles Winfred and Katherine Doyle (Edmunds) K.; B.S. in Geology, Sul Ross State Coll., Alpine, Tex., 1954; M.A. in Geology, U. Tex. at Austin, 1956; m. Judith Ann Hankins, Feb. 14, 1970; children—Andrea, Mary Kay, Michael, Thomas, Teresa. Petroleum geologist Pure Oil Co., Fort Worth, 1956-63; geologist Utah State Dept. Hwys., Salt Lake City, 1964-67; mining geologist LaDomincia S.A. de C.V., Marathon, Tex., 1968-85, exploration supt., 1972-76, mgr. mines and exploration, 1977-85; cons. mining geologist, 1985-86; counselor Minas La Jabonera S.A. de C.V., Marathon, Tex., 1987—. Cert. profl. geologist. Fellow AAAS; mem. Geol. Soc. Am., Am. Assn. Petroleum Geologists, Am. Inst. Profl. Geologists, Explorers Club. Editor: West Tex. Geol. Soc. Membership Directory, 1962; contbr. articles to profl. jours. Home: Hwy 2627 Heath Crossing Marathon TX 79842-0386 Office: PO Box 386 Marathon TX 79842-0386

KURIEN, SANTHA T., psychiatrist; b. Perumpavoor, Kerala, India, June 15, 1945; came to U.S., 1973; d. Varghese and Mary (Thomas) Koshy; m. Thomas K. Kurien; children: Susan, Miriam. MD, Calicut Med. Coll., Kerala, India, 1970. Diplomate Am. Bd. Psychiatry and Neurology; cert. geriatric psychiatry; cert. addiction psychiatry, clin. psychopharmacology. Sr. house surgeoncy Vellore (Madras) Med. Coll., 1970-71; gen. med. practice St. Thomas Memorial Hosp., Vadasserikara, Kerala, India, 1971-72; psychiat. residency Fairfield Hills Hosp., Newtown, Conn., 1973-76; staff psychiatrist Fairfield Hills Hosp., Newtown, 1976-77, Danbury (Conn.) Hosp., 1977-82; psychiatrist pvt. practice, Danbury, 1982—; consulting psychiatrist Pope John Paul Ctr., Danbury, Conn., 1991—. Mem. Am. Psychiat. Assn., Am. Assn. Geriatric Psychiatry, New Haven County Med. Assn., Danbury Med. Soc., Assn. Kerala Med. Grads., Internat. Psychogeriatric Assn., Am. Soc. Clin. Psychopharmacology (cert.). Office: 27 Hospital Ave Ste 304 Danbury CT 06810-5954

KURIN, RICHARD, museum program director; b. Bronx, N.Y., Nov. 27, 1950; m. Allyn Bland; children: Danielle, Jaclyn. BA, SUNY, 1972; MA in Anthropology, U. Chgo., 1974; cert. in Urdu lang., U. Calif., Berkeley, 1974; PhD in Anthropology, U. Chgo., 1981. Vis. asst. prof. dept. anthropology So. Ill. U., Carbondale, 1981-84, asst. prof., 1984-85; program coord., curator, cons. Festival of India, Aditi & Mela Exhbns., Smithsonian Instn., Washington, 1984-85; chair 150th Anniversary Program Com. Smithsonian Instn., Washington, 1993—, chair deciduous group, 1997—, dep. dir. Ctr. for Folklife Programs & Cultural Studies, 1985-87, acting dir., 1987-90, dir., 1990—; professorial lectr. Johns Hopkins U., Paul Nitze Sch. Adv. Internat. Studies, 1985—; collector Am. Mus. Natural History, Punjabi Indian village artifacts, 1970; vis. instr. cmty. devel. program So. Ill. U., Carbondale, 1979-81; program coord. Indian Puppetry Program, Smithsonian Instn., 1980; cons. anthropologist Harza Engring. Co., UNDP and World Bank, Indus Basin Master Planning Project, 1977; ethnic tours mgr. divsn. performing arts On-Tour India Program, Pakistan Program, 1976; cons. anthropologist U. Karachi, U.S. HEW Family Planning Project, 1977; mem. adv. bd. Coun. Overseas Rsch. Ctrs., 1989; adj. prof. George Washington U., 1999—; presenter orgns., meetings and workshops. Author: Aditi: The Living Arts of India, 1986, Reflections of a Culture Broker: A View From the Smithsonian, 1997, Smithsonian Folklife Festival: Culture Of, By, and For the People, 1998; (film) Aditi: The Living Arts of India, 1986; lead writer, organizer: Iowa Folklife: Our People, Traditions and Communities, 1996-97; advisor film: Jerusalem: Gateways to the City, 1995, Hosay: Muslim Transnationalism in Trinidad, 1994—, White House Workers, 1994; edtl. advisor film Kathputli: An Indian Puppetry Tradition, 1986—; recs. Smithsonian Folkways Records, 1986—; contbr. articles to profl. jours., chpts. to books and encys. Bd. trustees, Smithsonian Sec.'s Rep., Libr. of Congress, Am. Folklore Ctr., 1989—; trustee Am. Pakistan Rsch. Orgn., 1989—; mem. Fairfax County Citizen Assn. Edn. Com., 1991—; chair com. on edn. and culture Culmore Area Citizen's Task Force, Fairfax County, Va., 1990-91; pres. Bailey's Elem. Sch. P.T.A., 1989-91, newsletter editor, 1992-95; chair model mid. sch. tech. com. Glasgow Mid. Sch., 1995-96. Recipient fellowships NDEA, Title VI, 1973, Fulbright-Hayes, HEW, 1976, Social Sci. Rsch. Coun., 1976, 83, Am. Inst. Pakistan Studies, 1983, Woodrow Wilson Ctr., 1988—; grantee, Smithsonian Instn., 1979, 86, 89, 90, 92, 95, 96, NEH, 1982, 1991—, Nat. Endowment Arts, 1987. Fellow Soc. Applied Anthropology; mem. Am. Folklore Soc., Am. Ethnological Soc., Assn. Asian Studies, Am. Anthropol. Assn. Office: Ctr Folklife Programs & Cultural Studies Smithsonian Instn MRC 914 Washington DC 20560-0914

KURIT, NEIL, lawyer; b. Cleve., Aug. 31, 1940; s. Jay and Rose (Rainin) K.; m. Doris Tannenbaum, Aug. 9, 1964 (div.); m. Donna Chernin, Aug. 24, 1986. BS, Miami U., Oxford, Ohio, 1961; JD, Case Western Res. U., 1964. Bar: Ohio 1964. Prin. Kahn, Kleinman, Yanowitz & Arnson Co., L.P.A., Cleve., 1964—. Co-author Handbook for Attorneys and Accountants, Jewish Community Fedn. Endowment Fund. Trustee, v.p. Montefiore Home, 1983-87; trustee Jewish Community Fedn. Cleve., 1983-86, 1990-95. Mem. ABA, Ohio State Bar Assn. Home: 2870 Courtland Blvd Cleveland OH 44122-2802 Office: Kahn Kleinman Yanowitz & Arnson Co LPA 2600 Tower at Erieview Cleveland OH 44114

KURK, MITCHELL, physician; b. N.Y.C., Aug. 25, 1931; s. Benjamin and Frieda (Steinbaum) K.; m. Marcia Carol Leon (dec. 1981); children: Hope, Nancy, Cindy. BS, MS, Columbia U., 1954; OD, Mass. Coll. Optometry, 1955; DO, Phila. Coll. Osteopathic, 1960; MD, U. Calif., 1962. Diplomate Am. Bd. Gen. Practice. Pvt. practice N.Y.C., 1962—; attending physician Peninsula Hosp. Ctr. Author: Prescription for a Long Life, 1997. Fellow Internat. Coll. Applied Nutrition, Am. Acad. Family Physicians; mem. Internat. Acad. Preventive Medicine, Am. Holistic Med. Assn., AMA, N.Y. State Med. Soc., Nassau County Med. Soc., Nassau Acad. Medicine. Republican.

KURLAND, HAROLD ARTHUR, lawyer; b. N.Y.C., Jan. 20, 1952; s. Jordan Emil and Anita (Siegel) K.; m. Christine Rogers, June 28, 1975; children: Thomas Philip, Andrew Rogers. AB, Dartmouth Coll., 1973; JD, Cornell U., 1976. Bar: N.Y. 1977, D.C. 1977, U.S. Dist. Ct. (we. dist.) N.Y. 1977, U.S. Dist. Ct. (no. dist.) N.Y. 1983, U.S. Dist. Ct. (no. dist.) Tex. 1981, U.S. Ct. Appeals (2nd cir.) 1980, U.S. Supreme Ct. 1980, U.S. Dist. Ct. (D.C. dist.) 1986, U.S. Ct. Appeals (D.C. cir.) 1986, U.S. Ct. Appeals (3d cir.) 1988, U.S. Dist. Ct. (mid. dist.) Pa., 1988, U.S. Dist. Ct. (ea. and so. dists.) N.Y. 1991. Assoc. Nixon, Hargrave, Devans & Doyle LLP, Rochester, N.Y., 1976-84, ptnr. 1985—; mediator, arbitrator Am. Arbitration Assn.; mem. adv. com. on civil practice N.Y. Office Ct. Adminstrn., 1988—, co-chair task force on reducing litig. cost and delay, 7th jud. dist., 1996—; chmn. bd. dirs. Rochester Philharm. Orch. Mem. ABA, N.Y. State Bar Assn., D.C. Bar Assn., Monroe County Bar Assn. (past chmn. cts. com., fed. ct. com., mem. exec. com., trustee), Rochester Inn of Ct. (pres., master). Democrat. Home: 154 Council Rock Ave Rochester NY 14610-3335 Office: Nixon Hargrave Devans & Doyle LLP Clinton Sq PO Box 1051 Rochester NY 14603-1051

KURLAND, LEONARD TERRY, epidemiologist educator; b. Balt., Dec. 24, 1921; s. Ellis M. and Sarah (Shein) K. BA, Johns Hopkins U., 1942, DrPH, 1951; MD, U. Md., 1945; MPH cum laude, Harvard U., 1948. Intern U. Md., 1945-46; with USPHS, 1946-64; assigned to NIMH, NIH, 1948-55; assigned to Nat. Inst. Neurol. Disease and Blindness, 1955-64, chief epidemiology br., 1955-64; fellow neurology Mayo Clinic, Rochester, Minn., 1952-53, rsch. asst. in neurology, med. statistics, 1953-55, prof., chmn. dept. med. statistics, epidemiology, 1964-86; prof. epidemiology Mayo Grad. Sch., Sch. Medicine, 1964-95; sr. cons. dept. health scis. rsch. Mayo Clinic, 1987-95; clin. asst. prof. neurology, Georgetown U., 1957-60; clin. prof. neurology Howard U., 1960-64; cons. NIH, FDA, WHO, Nat. Acad. Scis.; mem. geochemistry and health subcom. NRC, 1975-80, chmn. 1978-80; mem. Armed Forces Epidemiol. Bd., 1983-93; spl. asst. to dir pharmacovigilance and epidemiology FDA,, 1996-97. Sr. author: The Epidemiology of Neurologic and Sense Organ Disorders, 1973; co-editor: Motor Neurone Disease, 1969, Multiple Sclerosis East and West, 1982, The Post-Polio Syndrome: Advances in the Pathogenesis and Treatment, 1995; contbr. articles to med. jours. With AUS, 1943-45. Recipient Commanders award for pub. svc. Dept. of the Army, 1990, Disting. Svc. award Ho. Reps., 1992, Johns Hopkins Outstanding Alumnus award, 1995, James D. Bruce Meml. award in Preventive Medicine Am. Coll. Physicians, 1996, Alumnus Merit award Harvard U., 1999; named Disting. Alumnus Mayo Found., 1999. Fellow Am. Pub. Health Assn.; mem. Am. Acad. Neurology (past chmn. neuroepidemiology sect.), Am. Neurol. Assn., Am. Epidemiologic Soc. (pres. 1974), Internat. Epidemiologic Assn., Japanese Clin. Soc. Neurology (exec.

council), Nat. Multiple Sclerosis Soc. (Gold Sci. award 1966, Charcot award 1983, rsch. review panel), Soc. Scholars Johns Hopkins U. Achievements include research on epidemiology of trauma, vaccines and neurological diseases, medical record systems, epidemiology of dementia and other neurodegenerative diseases, genetics of diseases of nervous system and cancer. Office: Mayo Clinic Emeritus Ctr 200 1st St SW Rochester MN 55905-0002

KURLAND, STUART M., English language educator; b. Greensboro, N.C., Jan. 17, 1955; s. Jordan E. and Anita Kurland; m. Donna L. Ringle, Sept. 23, 1989; children: Michael, Alex. AB, Dartmouth Coll., 1977; MA, U. Chgo., 1978, PhD, 1984. Vis. asst. prof. Hamilton Coll., Clinton, N.Y., 1984-85, Emory U., Atlanta, 1985-86, Coll. William and Mary, Williamsburg, Va., 1986-87, St. John's U., Collegeville, Minn., 1987-88; asst. prof. English, Duquesne U., Pitts., 1988-93, assoc. prof., 1993—. Contbr. articles, revs. to profl. jours. Mem. Edgewood Fire Dept., 1989-92, Mt. Lebanon Vol. Fire Dept., 1993—. Office: Duquesne U English Dept 600 Forbes Ave Pittsburgh PA 15282

KURLANDER, CARL LITMAN, screenwriter; b. Chgo., Oct. 1, 1959; s. Donald Jay Kurlander and Jeanne (Cohen) Wechsler. Student, U. Bath, Eng., 1982; BA magna cum laude, Duke U., 1982. Screenwriter Columbia Pictures, Burbank, Calif., 1985, 88-89, Orion Pictures, L.A., 1986, Paramount Pictures, L.A., 1987, 20th Century Fox, NBC, 1989, Walt Disney Studios, 1990, Universal Studios, 1991; TV writer, prodr. NBC, Saved By The Bell, 1992-96, NBC USA High, 1997; supervising prodr. Hangtime, NBC, Burbank, Calif., 1997; co-exec. prodr., co-creator Malibu, CA NBC/Tribune, 1997—. Screenwriter St. Elmo's Fire, 1985, Universal Studios. Named MCA Universal Studios scholar, 1982. Mem. Writers Guild Am. Office: William Morris Agency Hollywood CA 90046

KURLANDER, NEALE, accounting and law educator, lawyer; b. Bklyn., Jan. 1, 1924; s. Sol and Eleanor Kurlander; m. Honey Wachtel, June 25, 1949; children: Harold M., Susan L. BS, Long Island U., 1948; JD, N.Y. Law Sch., N.Y.C., 1951; MBA, Adelphi U., 1967. Bar: N.Y. 1952; CPA, N.Y. V.p., chief fin. officer Profit Motivation Svcs., Inc., Garden City, N.Y., 1967-71; cons.-reviewer Ernst & Ernst, Garden City, 1967-72; lectr. Practicing Law Inst., N.Y.C., 1974; chmn. dept. acctng and law Adelphi U., Garden City, 1964-82; cons. Regent's External Degree, Albany, N.Y., 1974-87; pvt. practice law Old Westbury, N.Y., 1952—; pvt. practice acct., CPA Old Westbury, 1960—; prof. acctg. and law Adelphi U., Garden City, 1962—; profl. developer Harris, Kerr, Forster & Co., N.Y.C., 1969-71; treas. Fin. Execs. Inst., Long Island, N.Y., 1974-76, chmn. acad. rels., 1975—, bd. dirs. 1975—; faculty Found. for Acctg. Edn., 1975—, bd. trustees, 1976-79. Author: Basic Accounting, 1962, Auditing, Vol. I and II, 1978; contbr. articles to profl. jours. Cmdr. post 6081 VFW, Bklyn., 1953-54; mem. Bd. Elections, Nassau County, N.Y., 1964-70, Citizens' Adv. Com. N.Y. State Dept. Taxation, Albany, 1975-87, Bd. Appeals, Old Westbury, 1988-93; legis. adv. coun. N.Y. State Assembly 15th Dist., 1991-93. Recipient cert. Delta Mu Delta, 1982; named Outstanding Acctg. Educator, Found. for Acctg. Edn., N.Y., 1982, Acct. of Yr. Acctg. Soc., 1992. Mem. N.Y. State Soc. CPA's, AICPA, Am. Acctg. Assn., Nassau County Bar Assn., N.Y. State Assembly 15th Dist. (legis. adv. coun.). Avocations: reading, woodworking, traveling, walking, swimming. Home: 6 Kings Dr Old Westbury NY 11568-1108 Office: Adelphi U Depts Acctg & Law South Ave Garden City NY 11530

KURLINSKI, JOHN PARKER, physician; b. Buchanon, W.Va., Jan. 17, 1948; s. John Peter and Jean (Holloway) K.; m. Claire Sawyer, June 12, 1971; children: Joshua John, Ryan Edward, Seth Parker. AB cum laude, Williams Coll., 1970; MD, Johns Hopkins Sch. Medicine, 1974. Intern, then resident Johns Hopkins Hosp., Baltimore, 1974-77; fellowship neonatal/perinatal medicine U. Calif., San Diego, 1977-79; chief resident pediatrician Johns Hopkins Hosp., 1979-80; clin. assoc. prof. pediatrics U. Nev. Sch. Medicine, Reno, 1994—; vice chief of staff Sunrise Children's Hosp., Las Vegas, 1989-90, chief of staff, 1990-95; pediatrician, co-dir. neonatology S.W. Regional Neonatal Ctr. at Sunrise Hosp. and Med. Ctr., Las Vegas, 1980-93; vice chief pediatrics Sunrise Hosp., Las Vegas, 1983-90; dir. NICU Sunrise Children's Hosp., 1994—; bd. dirs. S.W. Regional Neonatal Ctr. Edn. Found.; chmn. bd. dirs. Sunrise Children's Hosp. Found.; mem. Med.-Legal Screening Panel, Nev., 1986—; many hosp. coms., 1980—. Bd. dirs. So Nev. chpt. March of Dimes, Las Vegas, 1984—. Mem. AMA, Am. Acad. Pediatrics (v.p. Nev. chpt. 1987-90, pres. 1990-93, coun. mem. dist. VIII sect. on perinatal pediatrics), Clark County Med. Soc., Las Vegas Pediatric Soc. (founding), Phi Beta Kappa. Avocations: rugby, skiing, hiking, camping. Home: 3322 Beam Dr Las Vegas NV 89139-5902 Office: Sunrise Childrens Hosp 3186 S Maryland Pky Las Vegas NV 89109-2317

KURN, NEAL, lawyer; b. Springfield, Mass., July 19, 1934; s. Samuel and Jane Etta (Freeman) K.; m. Barbara Agron, June 9, 1957; children: Jeffrey Howard, Sharon Ilene, Jennifer Rose. BSBA with high honors, U. Ariz., 1956, JD with honors, 1963. Bar: Ariz. 1963; cert. specialist tax, estate and trust law, Ariz.; CPA, Ariz. Staff mem. Price Waterhouse & Co., San Francisco, L.A. and Phoenix, 1956, 58-60; assoc., ptnr. Moore, Romley, Kaplan, Robbins & Green, Phoenix, 1963-71; ptnr. Powers, Ehrenreich, Boutell & Kurn, Phoenix, 1971-82; dir. Fennemore Craig, Phoenix, 1982—; adj. prof. law Ariz. State U., 1980-82. Editor-in-chief Ariz. Law Rev., 1962-63. Past chmn. tax adv. commn. Ariz. State Bd. Legal Specialization; bd. dirs. Ariz. Cmty. Found., 1986—, chmn. 1994-96; bd. dirs. Ariz. Bar Found., 1983-89, pres., 1988; bd. dirs. Jewish Fedn. Greater Phoenix, pres., 1977-79; bd. dirs. Nat. Law Ctr. Inter-Am. Free Trade, U. Ariz. Found., 1998—; bd. visitors U. Ariz. Law Sch.; v.p. coun. Jewish Fedn., 1988-90; chmn. Jewish Comty. Found. Greater Phoenix, . With U.S. Army, 1956-58. Fellow Am. Coll. Tax Counsel, Am. Bar Found., Am. Coll. Trusts and Estates Counsel; mem. ABA, State Bar Ariz. (past chmn. taxation sect., bd. govs. 1991-93), Maricopa County Bar Assn., Phi Kappa Phi, Beta Gamma Sigma. Democrat. Jewish. Office: Fennemore Craig 3003 N Central Ave Ste 2600 Phoenix AZ 85012-2913

KURNICK, NATHANIEL BERTRAND, oncologist-hematologist, educator, researcher; b. N.Y.C., Nov. 8, 1917; s. Jacob Kurnick and Celia (Levine) Zackheim; m. Dorothy Manheimer, Oct. 4, 1940 (dec. Dec. 1985); children: John E., Katherine (dec.), James T.; m. Sally Ann Kreeger, June 23, 1989. BA, Harvard U., 1936, MD, 1940. Diplomate Am. Bd. Internal Medicine, Am. Bd. Med. Oncology, Am. Bd. Hematology, Am. Bd. Med. Examiners. Intern Mt. Sinai Hosp., N.Y.C., 1941-42, chief resident internal medicine, 1946; asst. prof. medicine Tulane U. Med. Sch., New Orleans, 1949-54; chief hematology svc. VA Hosp., Long Beach, Calif., 1954-59, cons., 1954—; assoc. clin. prof. medicine U. Calif., L.A., 1954-64; clin. prof. medicine U. Calif., Irvine, 1964—; pvt. practice Long Beach, 1959-83; Bixby Hematology-Oncology Lab.; dir. Bixby Lab. Long Beach Cmty. Med. Ctr., 1982—; chmn. cancer activities, 1968-90, chmn. dept. medicine, 1966-68, chmn. dept. med. oncology and hematology, 1982-87; pres. Long Beach Soc. Internal Medicine, 1971; chmn. Franklin Thrift & Loan, Orange, Calif., 1988—. Contbr. articles to jours. in field. Trustee Garden Grove, Calif. Union High Sch.Dist., 1960-64. Capt. M.C., U.S. Army, 1942-46. Am. Cancer Soc./NRC fellow, 1946-47, Rockefeller Inst., 1946-47, Nobel Inst., 1947-49; NIH/Am. Cancer Soc. grantee, 1949-1972; Henry Hunter Workman rsch. fellow Harvard Med. Sch./Mass. Gen. Hosp., 1940-41. Fellow ACP; mem. Intern. Soc. Exptl. Hematology, Am. Soc. Hematology, Western Soc. Clin. Rsch., Cen. Soc. Clin. Rsch., Sigma Xi (fellow 1951). Democrat. Jewish. Avocations: sailing, skiing, travel. Office: Long Beach Cmty Med Ctr Bixby Hematology-Oncology Lab 1760 Termino Ave Ste G-20 Long Beach CA 90804-2182

KURNIT, SCOTT, telecommunications industry executive.

KURNIT, SHEPARD, advertising agency executive; b. Bronx, N.Y., Oct. 31, 1924; s. Samuel Philip and Frances (Lichtenstien) K.; m. Jeanette Zinsher, Aug. 1, 1945; children: Paul David, Richard Alan, Scott Philip. Scholar, Parsons Sch. Design, 1941-42. With Sterling Advt., N.Y.C., 1945, Harry Serwer Advt., N.Y.C., 1945-47, C.J. Herrick Assos., N.Y.C., 1947-49, Diamond Barnett Advt., N.Y.C., 1949; assoc. art dir. Morton Freund Advt., 1949; founder Kurnit Assocs., Inc., N.Y.C., 1950-54; pres. Kurnit, Geller Assocs., Inc., N.Y.C., 1954-56; exec. v.p. DKG, Inc. Calet Hirsch Kurnit & Spector (formerly Delehanty, Kurnit & Geller), N.Y.C., 1956-81, chmn., 1981-83; chmn. Ephron, Raboy, Tsao & Kurnit, Inc., N.Y.C., 1983-86; pres. Kurnit & Ptnrs. Inc., N.Y.C., 1986—; guest lectr. Columbia U., N.Y. Advt. Club. Founder East Meadow Com. Human Rights, 1964, pres., 1965; mem. Urban League, Great Neck Forum; bd. dirs. Am. Field Service Internat. Intercultural Exchange. Served with USAAF, 1943-45. Recipient numerous advt. awards; named one of Creative Leaders of Am. Advt., Wall Street Jour. Mem. Nat. Assn. Advt. Agys. (past pres. N.Y. chpt., gov. at large ea. region), Nat. Advt. Rev. Bd. (gov.), Met. Pres. Orgn., Fund for New Priorities in Am. Democrat. Home: 300 SE 5th Ave Boca Raton FL 33432-5058 Office: Kurnit & Ptnrs Inc 24 W 55th St New York NY 10019-5320

KURNOW, ERNEST, statistician, educator; b. Bklyn., Oct. 21, 1912; s. Harry and Sarah Malka (Shagaloff) K.; m. Joyce Litzky, Oct. 6, 1938; children: Ruth (Mrs. Jeffrey Jarrett), Susan Carol (Mrs. Leonard Weistrop), Alice Rose (Mrs. Claude Morin). B.S. cum laude, CCNY, 1932, M.S. in Edn, 1933; Ph.D., NYU, 1951. Tchr. N.Y.C. Bd. Edn., 1935-40, statistician, 1941-48; mathematician ordnance div. War Dept., 1940-41; mem. faculty NYU, 1948—, prof. econs., 1960-63, prof. bus. stats., chmn. dept., 1963-86, prof. emeritus bus. stats., adj. prof. bus. stats., 1986—, chmn. dept., 1963-76; chmn. doctoral program N.Y. U., 1976-85, dir. Careers in Bus. program, 1979-88; cons. N.Y. State Tax Structure Study Commn., 1959—, Mayor N.Y.C. Com. Mgmt. Survey, 1950-51, Turkish Ministry Finance, 1955-56; cons. temporary commn. Revision N.Y. State Constn., 1958; temporary commn. fiscal affairs N.Y. State Govt., 1953-54; cons. Tri-State Transp. Commn., 1964-66, 73-75; participant Brazilian capital markets program, 1968; study dir. Govs.' Spl. Commn. on Financing Mass Transp., 1970-71; cons. Commn. on Charter Revision, City of N.Y., 1973-74, Temporary Commn. on City Finances, 1975-76. Author: The Turkish Budgetary Process, 1956; also articles. Statistics for Business Decisions, 1959, Theory and Measurement of Land Rent, 1961. Recipient Gt. Tchr. award NYU Alumni Assn., 1974; Fulbright grantee to Greece, 1966-67; Kurnow Classroom established in his honor, NYU, 1993. Fellow Am. Statis. Assn.; mem. Internat. Statis. Inst. (elected), Am. Econ. Assn., Econometric Soc., Inst. Mgmt. Scis., Nat. Tax Assn., Am. Soc. Quality Control, Sphinx, Beta Gamma Sigma, Sigma Eta Phi, Delta Pi Sigma, Alpha Phi Sigma, Delta Sigma Pi. Jewish. Home: 3 Washington Square Vlg Apt 17I New York NY 10012-1810 Office: New York Univ Dept Stats Washington Sq N New York NY 10003-6635

KURODA, YASUMASA, political science educator, researcher; b. Tokyo, Apr. 28, 1931; came to U.S., 1951; s. Shohei and Take (Ishii) K.; m. Alice Kassis, Mar. 21, 1961 (div. Mar. 1995); children: Kamilla, Kamil; m. Miyoko Otaguro, Aug. 14, 1998. *Yasumasa Kuroda married Miyoko, who teaches an exercise program based on "chi" and other Eastern practices in Japan. She has taught exercise classes and lectured for corporations on health and wellness promotion. Miyoko used to sing professionally in Ginza when she was younger. Her daughter Miwa came to Hawaii to study in 1999. In 1998 Yasumasa's daughter Kamilla left her editor position at the North American Post in Seattle to assume an assistant editor position for the Business Examiner with an Olympia office located near her home. Kamil continues to fly for American Eagle as a captain in Dallas, Texas.* Student, Waseda U., 1951; BA, U. Oreg., 1956, MA, 1958, PhD, 1962. From instr. to asst. prof. polit. sci. Mont. State U., Bozeman, 1960-64; asst. prof. polit. sci. U. So. Calif., L.A., 1964-66; from assoc. to prof. polit. sci. U. Hawaii-Manoa, Honolulu, 1966-69; assoc. program officer advanced projects East-West Ctr., Honolulu, 1967-69; lectr. Japan-Am. Inst. Mgmt. Sci., Honolulu, 1973-90; pres. Election Svcs. Hawaii, Inc., 1996—; v.p. Minerva Rsch., Inc., Honolulu, 1981-96. Author: Reed Town, Japan, 1974, Chiho Toshi no Kenryokukozo, 1976, (with others) Palestinians Without Palestine, 1978; co-editor: Studies in Political Socialization in the Arab States, 1987, Japan in a New World Order: Contributing to the Arab-Israeli Peace Process, 1994, Japanese Culture in Comparative Perspective, 1997. Bd. of govs. Japanese Cultural Ctr. Hawaii, Honolulu, 1988—, program com., 1988—. Recipient Disting. Vis. Lectr. award SUNY, 1994; Rockefeller Found. grantee, 1963-64, Social Sci. Rsch. Coun. grantee, 1966-67, Toyota Found. grantee, 1984-87, 87-90; vis. rsch. fellow Harry S. Truman Rsch. Inst. of the Advancement of Peace, Hebrew U., 1992, Inst. Legal Studies, Kansai U., 1994. Mem. Am. Polit. Sci. Assn., Internat. Polit. Sci. Assn., Internat. Assn. Middle Ea. States (coll. of fellows 1986—). Democrat. Avocation: stamp collecting. Office: U Hawaii Dept Polit Sci Honolulu HI 96822

KUROPAS, MYRON BOHDON, elementary education educator; b. Chgo., Nov. 15, 1932; s. Stephen and Antoinette (Mehal) K.; m. Alexandra Waskiw, Oct. 24, 1964; children: Stephen, Michael. BS, Loyola U., 1953; MA, Roosevelt U., 1955; PhD, U. Chgo., 1974. Tchr. Chgo. Sch. System, 1956-65, asst. prin., 1965-70, prin., 1970-71; regional dir. ACTION, Chgo., 1971-77; spl. asst. to pres. Gerald R. Ford, Washington, 1976-77; legis. asst. Sen. Bob Dole, U.S. Senate, Washington, 1977; prin. DeKalb (Ill.) Sch. Dist. #428, 1977-80, tchr., 1980—; adj. prof. No. Ill. U., DeKalb, 1989—. Author: Ukrainians in America, 1972, The Ukrainian Americans: Roots and Aspirations, 1884-1954, 1991, Ukrainian-American Citadel: The First Hundred Years of the Ukrainian National Association, 1996. Recipient Human Rels. award Am. Jewish Com., 1978, Recognition of Svc. award Nat. Ctr. for Urban/Ethnic Affairs, 1982, Recognition of Svc. award Japanese Am. Citizens League, 1976, Spl. Commendation ACTION, 1976, Outstanding Performance award ACTION, 1975. Mem. Ukrainian Nat. Assn. (nat. v.p. 1978-90), Phi Delta Kappa. Republican. Ukrainian Catholic. Home: 107 Ilehamwood Dr Dekalb IL 60115

KUROSKY, ALEXANDER, biochemist, educator; b. Windsor, Ont., Can., Sept. 12, 1938; came to U.S., 1972; s. Peter and Stella (Gemper) K.; m. Anna Kinik, May 18, 1963; children: Lisa Kathryn, Tanya Kristine, Stephanie Ann. BSc, U. B.C., 1965; MSc, U. Toronto, 1969, PhD, 1972. Research technician Can. Dept. Agr., Harrow, Ont., Vancouver, B.C., 1959-64; chemist research and devel. Can. Breweries Ltd., Toronto, Ont., 1965-67; faculty Med. Br., U. Tex., Galveston, 1973—, assoc. prof., 1978-82, prof., 1982—. Contbr. articles to sci. pubs. Province of Ont. grad fellow, 1968-71; grantee Burkitt Found., NIH, Nat. Cancer Inst.; recipient Disting. Teaching award U. Tex. Med. Br. Grad. Sch., 1981. Mem. Am. Soc. Biochemistry and Molecular Biology, Am. Chem. Soc., AAAS, Can. Biochem. Soc., Am. Soc. Human Genetics, Sigma Xi (John G. Sinclair award 1988). Achievements include research on prohormone processing and structure, function and genetics of proteins. Home: 6605 Golf Crest Dr Galveston TX 77551-1821 Office: U Tex Med Br Dept Human Biol Chem and Genetics Galveston TX 77555

KURRELMEYER, LOUIS HAYNER, retired lawyer; b. Troy, N.Y., July 26, 1928; s. Bernhard and Lucy Julia (Hayner) K.; m. Phyllis A. Damon, June 14, 1952 (div. 1973); children: Ellen Laura, Louis Hayner, Nancy Snow; m. Martina Sophia Kluis, June 14, 1975. AB, Columbia U., 1949, LLB, 1953; MA in Econs., U. N.Mex., 1950. Bar: N.Y. 1953, D.C. 1968. Assoc. Debevoise, Plimpton, Lyons & Gates, N.Y.C., 1953-66; ptnr. Hale Russell & Gray, N.Y.C., 1967-75, counsel, 1976-85; counsel Winthrop, Stimson, Putnam & Roberts, Washington, 1985-96, ret. 1996. Author: The Potash Industry, 1951; contbr. to CPLR Forms and Guidance for Lawyers, 1963. U.S. panelist U.S.-Can. Free Trade agreement, 1989-92; asst. transp. adminstr. City of N.Y., 1966-67; v.p. Emerson Sch., N.Y.C., 1960-64, chmn., 1964-69; bd. dirs. Rice Meml. H.S., South Burlington, Vt., 1992-95; mem. Prudential Com. Fire Dist. No. 1, Shelburne, Vt., 1977-90, chmn., 1977-84; mem. Shelburne Sewer Commn., 1990-93, chmn., 1991-93, interim mgr., 1992-93; bd. commrs. Chittenden County Transp. Authority, 1991-97, treas., 1992-96; mem. Shelburne Selectboard, 1995. Decorated Knight 1st class Royal Swedish Order of North Star. Mem. ABA, D.C. Bar Assn. Home: 364 Clearwater Rd Shelburne VT 05482-7724

KURREN, BARRY M., federal judge. BA with highest honors, U. Hawaii, 1973, JD, 1977. Law clk. to Hon. Martin Pence U.S. Dist. Ct. Hawaii, 1977-78; with Goodsill Anderson & Quinn, 1978-80, Burke, Sakai, McPheeters, Bordner & Gilardy, 1980-91; judge U.S. Dist. Ct. (1st cir.) Hawaii; apptd. magistrate judge U.S. Dist. Ct. Hawaii, 1992; adj. prof. law William S. Richardson Sch. of Law, Hawaii, 1991-92; arbitrator Ct. Annexed Arbitration Program, 1st Jud. Cir., Hawaii, 1986-91. Mem. ABA, Am. Judicature Soc., Am. Arbitration Assn. (panel of arbitrators 1989-91), Fed. Magistrate Judges' Assn., Fed./State Jud. Coun., Am. Inn of Ct. (bencher), Hawaii State Bar Assn., Aloha Inn, Honolulu County Med. Soc. (med. practices com. 1987-90). Fax: (808) 541-3500. Office: C-232 US Courthouse 300 Ala Moana Blvd Honolulu HI 96850-0001

KURRUS, THOMAS WILLIAM, lawyer; b. Carmel, N.Y., May 13, 1947; s. Theo Hornsby and Jean Ellen (Cumming) K.; m. Desiree Ann Ross, Mar. 25, 1989. BS magna cum laude, U. Fla., 1975, JD, 1979. Bar: Fla. 1980, U.S. Dist. Ct. (no. dist.) Fla. 1980, U.S. Ct. Appeals (5th cir.) 1980, U.S. Dist. Ct. (mid. dist.) Fla. 1981, U.S. Ct. Appeals (11th cir.) 1981, U.S. Ct. Appeals (4th cir.) 1984, U.S. Supreme Ct. 1984. Assoc. Law Firm Larry G. Turner, Gainesville, Fla., 1981-83; ptnr. Turner, Kurrus & Griscti, Gainesville, 1983-88; prin. Law Offices of Thomas W. Kurrus, Gainesville, 1988—; mem. Fla. Supreme Ct. commn. on jury instructions, 1995. Contbr. articles to profl. jours. Mem. ACLU (Gainesville chpt. legal panel chmn. 1999), Nat. Assn. Criminal Defense Lawyers (Fla. chpt. bd. dirs., chmn. continuing legal edn. com., local legis. laison, pres. award 1993, appreciation award 1998). Avocations: fishing, art, horses. Office: PO Box 838 Gainesville FL 32602-0838

KURTH, LIESELOTTE, foreign language educator; b. Wuppertal, Germany; came to U.S., 1951; s. Otto and Emmi (Klammer) Voigt. MA, Johns Hopkins U., 1960, PhD, 1963. Asst. prof. German Johns Hopkins U., Balt., 1964-68, assoc. prof., 1968-73, prof., 1973-89, chmn. dept., 1980-87; prof. emeritus, 1989—. Author: Die Zweite Wirklichkeit, 1969, Perspectives and Points of View, 1974, Continued Existence, Reincarnation, and the Power of Sympathy in Classical Weimar, 1999; contbr. articles top profl. jours. and yearbooks; editor collections and edits. Gilman fellow, 1958-62; Gail fellow, 1962-63. Mem. MLA (mem. exec. com. South Atlantic br. 1982-84, pres. br. 1985-86), Lessing Soc., Goethe Soc. of N.Am., Phi Beta Kappa. Home: 800 Southerly Rd Apt 914 Towson MD 21286-8409 Office: Johns Hopkins U Dept German 34th and Charles Sts Baltimore MD 21218

KURTH, RONALD JAMES, university president, retired naval officer; b. Madison, Wis., July 1, 1931; s. Peter James and Celia (Kuehn) K.; m. Esther Charlene Schaefer, Dec. 21, 1954; children: Steven, Audrey, John, Douglas. BS, U.S. Naval Acad., 1954; MPA, Harvard U., 1961, PhD, 1970. Commd. ensign U.S. Navy, 1954, advanced through grades to rear adm., 1981; U.S. naval attache Moscow, 1975-77; comdg. officer NAS, Memphis at Millington, Tenn., 1977-79; mil. fellow Council Fgn. Relations, N.Y.C., 1979-80; exec. asst. to dep. chief naval ops. Dept. Navy, Washington, 1980-81, dir. Pol-Mil Policy and Current Plans, 1981-83, dir. Long Range Planning Group, 1983-84; U.S. def. attache Moscow, 1985-87; pres. U.S. Naval War Coll., Newport, R.I., 1987-90, Murray (Ky.) State U., 1990-94; dean acad. affairs Air War Coll., Maxwell AFB, Ala., 1994-98; pres. St. John's Northwestern Mil. Acad., Delafield, Wis., 1998—; teaching fellow Harvard U., Cambridge, Mass., 1969-70. Author: The Politics of Technological Innovation in the Navy, 1970. Mem. nat. adv. bd. Boy Scouts Am. Decorated Def. D.S.M., Navy D.S.M., Legion of Merit with 2 gold stars, Meritorious Svc. medal with gold star. Mem. Am. Acad. Polit. Sci., U.S. Naval Inst. (life), Naval War Coll. Found. (life), U.S. Naval Acad. Alumni, Harvard U. Alumni, Rotary. Episcopalian. Home: 505 Saint Johns Rd Delafield WI 53018-1440 Office: St John's Northwestern Mil Acad Delafield WI 53018 *Among those who know you, ponder whose respect you have and whose you do not. It will provide you with a measure of your worth.*

KURTY, JOHN THOMAS, secondary school administrator; b. Northampton, Mass., Jan. 12, 1957; s. John and Rita (Powers) K. BA, Colgate U., 1979; MA, Columbia U., 1981; EdD, Harvard U., 1988; MBA, Keller Grad. Sch. Mgmt., Chgo., 1997. Tchr. history The White Mountain Sch., N.H., 1981-83; tchr. English Kents Hill (Maine) Sch., 1983-85; dir. devel. Providence Country Day Sch., East Providence, R.I., 1988-90, dir. admission and fin. aid, 1990-92; dir. spl. programs Latin Sch. Chgo., 1993—; adj. prof. Nat.-Louis U., Chgo., 1997—; spkr. Ind. Sch. Assn. Ctrl. States, 1995, Nat. Assn. Ind. Schs., 1996, Nat. Mid. Sch. Assn., 1996; participant Woodrow Wilson History Inst., 1995; mem. ISACS Midwest diversity com., 1996—. Contbr. articles to profl. jours. Vol. Harvard Club Chgo., 1993—, United Way Chgo., 1993—, Ill. Math. and Sci. Acad., Aurora, 1993—. Mem. ASCD, Am. Ednl. Rsch. Assn., Nat. Mid. Sch. Assn., Ea. Ednl. Rsch. Assn., Chgo. Coun. Fgn. Rels., Appalachian Mountain Club. Avocations: international travel, horseback riding, Spanish, cooking, fishing. Home: 1122 N Clark St Apt 2407 Chicago IL 60610-7886 Office: Latin Sch Chgo 59 W North Blvd Chicago IL 60610

KURTZ, ALFRED BERNARD, radiologist; b. Albany, N.Y., May 1, 1944; s. Leonard David and Esther (Lederman) K.; m. Barbara Ellen, July 3, 1973; children: Dana, Liza, Amy. BA, NYU, 1966; MD, Stanford U., 1972. Diplomate Am. Bd. Radiology. Internal medicine intern Montefiore Hosp. and Med. Ctr., Bronx, N.Y., 1972-73, resident in internal medicine, 1973-74, resident in diagnostic radiology, 1974-77; fellow in ultrasound and body CT Jefferson Med. Coll., Thomas Jefferson Univ. Hosp., Phila., 1977-78, assoc. prof. ob/gyn, 1982-85; assoc. dir. Div. of U.S. and Radiol. Imaging, Phila., 1982-86, Body Computed Tomography, Thomas Jefferson U. Hosp., Phila., 1986-89, Div. Diagnostic U.S., Thomas Jefferson U. Hosp., Phila., 1986-89; prof. radiology Jefferson Med. Coll., Thomas Jefferson U. Hosp., Phila., 1983—, prof. ob/gyn., 1985—, vice chmn. dept. radiology, 1989—; fellowship ultrasound and body ct. Montefiore Hosp. and Med. Ctr., Bronx, N.Y., 1977-78; examiner oral bds. in ultrasound category Am. Bd. Radiology, 1985—; med. advisor Blue Shield of Pa., Phila., 1983—; mem. adv. com. Ctr. of Excellence in Biomed. Imaging, Phila., 1987—. Author: Ultrasound: The Requisites, 1995, Obstetrical Measurements in Ultrasound: A Reference Manual, 1988; editor: Atlas of Ultrasound Measurements, 1990; contbr. articles to profl. jours. Grantee Nat. Cancer Inst., NIH, 1993-96. Fellow Am. Inst. Ultrasound in Medicine (bd. govs. 1990-92, sec. 1993-97, pres.-elect 1999—), Am. Coll. Radiology (chmn. com. on edn. and tng. of commn. 1987-93, commn. on ultrasound 1987-93), Soc. Radiologists in Ultrasound (pres. 1991-93), Coll. Physicians Phila. Achievements include advancement of the ability of ultrasound to establish an accurate fetal age; establishment of ultrasound patterns for analysis of diffuse liver disease; advancement of ultrasound in evaluation of obstetrical and gynecologic problems including by intravaginal scanning and cross sectional imaging evaluation for ovarian cancer. Home: 1050 Indian Creek Rd Wynnewood PA 19096-3407 Office: Thomas Jefferson U Hosp 111 S 11th St Philadelphia PA 19107-5084

KURTZ, CHARLES JEWETT, III, lawyer; b. Columbus, Ohio, May 13, 1940; s. Charles Jewett, Jr. and Elizabeth Virginia (Gill) K.; m. Linda Rhoads, Mar. 18, 1983. BA, Williams Coll., 1962; JD, Ohio State U., 1965. Bar: Ohio 1965, D.C. 1967, U.S. Dist. Ct. (so. dist.) Ohio 1967, U.S. Dist. Ct. (no. dist.) Ohio 1976, U.S. Ct. of Appeals (6th cir) 1992. Law clk. to justice Ohio State Supreme Ct., Columbus, 1965-67; assoc. Porter, Wright, Morris & Arthur, Columbus, 1967-71, ptnr., 1972—, mng. ptnr. litigation dept., 1988-91, mem. directing ptnrs. com., 1988-89; mem. faculty Ohio Legal Ctr. Inst. Trustee Ballet Met., Columbus, 1990-94; vestry St. Albans Episcopal Ch., 1986-89. Mem. ABA, Am. Arbitration Assn. (mem. panel comml. arbitrators), Ohio Bar Assn. (mem. workers' compensation com.), Columbus Bar Assn. (sustaining mem.), Columbus Bar Found., Columbus Def. Assn. (pres. 1976), Athletic Club, Columbus Country Club, Capital Club. Office: Porter Wright Morris & Arthur 41 S High St Ste 2800 Columbus OH 43215-6194

KURTZ, DOLORES MAY, civic worker; b. Reading, Pa., Oct. 27, 1933; d. Harry Claude and Ethel Gertrude (Fields) Filbert; m. William McKillips Kurtz, Oct. 26, 1957. Cert. secretarial program, Pa. State U., 1980. Legal sec. Snyder, Balmer & Kershner, Reading, 1951-53; head teletype operator E.I. duPont de Nemours, Reading, 1953-56; exec. sec. Ford New Holland (Pa.) Inc. (formerly Sperry New Holland div. Sperry Corp.),, 1956-91, ret., 1991. Mem. Lancaster County Rep. Com., 1983-85; pres. New Holland Area Woman's Club, 1982-84; bd. dirs. Lancaster County Fedn. Women's Clubs, 1982—, 2d v.p., 1984-86, 1st v.p., 1986-88, pres. 1988-90; founding mem. Summer Arts Festival, New Holland, 1980—, bd. dirs., 1985-91; membership chmn. S.E. dist. Pa. Fedn. Women's Clubs, 1984-86; bd. dirs. Community Meml. Park Assn., New Holland, 1957-82; area rep., bd. dirs. Woman's Rep. Club Lancaster County, 1982-84; committeewoman New Holland Boro 1983-85; v.p. Lancaster-Lebanon Arthritis Found. Guild, 1992, pres., 1993. Recipient Outstanding Vol. for Pa. award Pa. Fedn. Women's Clubs, 1984, Woman in the Arts award, 1998. Mem. Gen. Fedn. Women's Clubs Pa. (conservation divsn. chmn. 1996-98), Gen. Fedn.

Women's Clubs Pa. (credentials com. 1998—). Methodist. Avocations: arts and crafts, travel, photography.

KURTZ, ELLEN R., journalist; b. Bklyn., May 22, 1934; d. George and Gertrude (Troiansky) Rabinowitz; m. Raymond J. Kurtz, June 26, 1954 (dec. May 1988); children: Jill A., Michael S., Jack L.; m. Sol T. Horowitz. BA, Bklyn. Coll., 1955. Tchr. N.Y.C. Pub. Schs., 1955-56; lectr. Weight Watchers of N.J., Livingston, 1969-83; owner, dir. Livingston Coll. Bd. Rev., 1975-83; mng. editor On the Scene, Livingston, 1984-86; editor Regional Weekly News, East Hanover, N.J., 1986; writer spl. sects. Star-Ledger, Newark, 1987—; cons. editor Hosp. News of N.J., Colonia, 1989-90; feature writer Drew U., Madison, N.J., 1996—, publicist Drew U. Ctr. for Holocaust Study, 1997—; instr. The Adult Sch. of the Chathams, Madison and Florham Park, 1999—. Contbr. articles to newspapers, mags. Essay contest judge B'nai Brith/Albert Adler Meml. Scholarship Fund, Livingston, 1987—; mem. Vols. for Israel, 1989. Mem. N.J. Press Women (office holder, com. chairperson, Communicator of Achievement award 1997), Livingston Writers' Group, Internat. Women's Writing Guild. Jewish. Avocations: travel, aerobics, reading, bowling. Home and Office: 27 Cherry Hill Rd Livingston NJ 07039-2435

KURTZ, EUGENE ALLEN, composer, educator, consultant; b. Atlanta, Dec. 27, 1923; s. Wilbur George and Annie Laurie (Fuller) K. BA in Mus., U. Rochester, 1947; MA in Mus., Eastman Sch. Mus., 1949; studied with Arthur Honegger and Darius Milhaud, Ecole Normale de Musique, Paris, 1949-51; studied with Max Deutsch, Paris, 1953-57. guest prof. composition U. Mich., Ann Arbor, 1967-68, 70-71, 73-74, 80-81, 88, Eastman Sch. Mus., Rochester, N.Y., 1975, U. Ill., Urbana, 1976, U. Tex., Austin, 1977-78, 85-86, Hartt Sch. Mus., Hartford, Conn., 1989; cons. Editions Jobert, Paris, 1972—; lectr. in field. Compositions include The Solitary Walker, 1964, Conversations for 12 Players, 1966, Ca...Diagramme Pour Orchestre, 1972, The Last Contrabass in Las Vegas, 1974, Mècanique, 1975, Logo, 1979, Five-Sixteen for piano, 1982, World Enough and Time, 1982, String Trio, Time and Again, 1984-85, From Time to Time for violin and piano, 1986-87, The Broken World for string quartet, 1993-94, Shadows on the Wind for 17 players, 1995-96, Icare for solo flute, 1997, also film scores and incidental music for radio, theatre and TV; commd. by U. Mich., 1958, Am. Cultural Ctr., Paris, 1966, Ministère de la Culture Français, 1972, 82, U. Nev., 1974, Radio France, 1975, 79, 85, Musical Arts Assn., Cleve., 1976. Sgt. inf. U.S. Army, 1942-46, ETO. NEA grantee, 1982-83; recipient Am. Acad. Inst. Arts and Letters award, 1992, French Acad. des Beaux-Arts award, 1997. Mem. Société des Auteurs, Compositeurs et Editeurs de Musique. Office: 6 Rue Boulitte, 75014 Paris France

KURTZ, HARVEY A., lawyer; b. Baraboo, Wis., July 9, 1950; s. Walter R. and Henrietta M. (Hinze) K.; m. Yvonne Larme, Jan. 28, 1978; children: Benjamin L., Leah L. BA, U. Wis., 1972; JD, U. Chgo., 1975. Bar: Wis. 1975, U.S. Dist. Ct. (ea. dist.) Wis. 1980. Atty. Whyte & Hirschboeck S.C., Milw., 1975-89, shareholder, 1981-89; ptnr. Foley & Lardner, Milw., 1989—. Mem. ABA, State Bar of Wis. Assn., Milw. Bar Assn. (chmn. employee benefits sect. 1993-94), Greater Milw. Employee Benefit Coun., Wis. Retirement Plan Profls. (pres. 1987-88), Internat. Pension and Employee Benefits Lawyers Assn., Kiwanis, Phi Beta Kappa. Home: 3927 N Stowell Ave Milwaukee WI 53211-2461 Office: Foley & Lardner Firstar Ctr 777 E Wisc Ave Milwaukee WI 53202

KURTZ, HOWARD, journalist, author; b. Bklyn., Aug. 1, 1953; s. Leonard and Marcia (Turetzky) K.; m. Mary Tallmer, June 20, 1979; children: Judy, Bonnie. BA in English, SUNY at Buffalo, 1974; MJ, Columbia U., 1975. Reporter Bergen Record, Hackensack, N.J., 1975-76, Washington Star, 1978-81, Washington Post, 1981—. Author: Media Circus: The Trouble with America's Newspapers, 1993; contbr. to The New Republic, Columbia Journalism Rev., Am. Journalism Rev., N.Y. Mag. Recipient Front Page award Washington-Balt. Newspaper Guild, 1982, 86, Mark Twain award AP, 1990, Best Media Critic in U.S. award Am. Journalism Rev., 1994. Office: The Washington Post 1150 15th St NW Washington DC 20071-0002*

KURTZ, JAMES EUGENE, freelance writer, minister; b. Altoona, Pa., June 28, 1928; s. Harry F. and Mildred (Sipes) K. LittD, Berean Coll., 1976; ThD, Ridgedale Theol. Sem., Chatanooga, 1974. Editorial writer Altoona Tribune, 1952-55; minister Jackson Park Ch., Chgo., 1957-58, First Congregational Ch., East Machias, Maine, 1991-93; advt. mgr. Pacific Flush Tank Co., Chgo., 1964-77; freelance news corr. Chgo., 1978-82; freelance corr. Joliet, Ill., 1987-88; pub.'s rep. Antioch Pub., Joliet, 1985-88. Editor Opinion mag., 1993—; editorial page editor Patriot Newspapers; contbr. articles to popular mags. Mem. Nat. Assn. Scholars, Soc. Profl. Journalists, Acad. Am. Poets. Home: PO Box 239 Peru IL 61354-0239

KURTZ, JEROME, lawyer, educator; b. Phila., May 19, 1931; s. Morris and Renee (Cooper) K.; m. Elaine Kahn, July 28, 1956; children: Madeleine, Nettie Kurtz Greenstein. BS with honors, Temple U., 1952; LLB magna cum laude, Harvard U., 1955. Bar: Pa. 1956, N.Y. 1981, D.C. 1982; CPA, Pa. Assoc. Wolf, Block, Schorr & Solis-Cohen, Phila., 1955-56, 57-63; ptnr. Wolf, Block, Schorr & Solis-Cohen, 1963-66, 68-77; tax legis. counsel Dept. Treasury, Washington, 1966-68; commr. IRS, 1977-80; ptnr. Paul, Weiss, Rifkind, Wharton & Garrison, 1980-90; prof. law NYU, 1991—, dir. grad. tax program, 1995-98; instr. Villanova Law Sch., 1964-65, U. Pa., 1969-74; vis. prof. law Harvard U., 1975-76; mem. adv. group to commr. IRS, 1976. Editor: Harvard Law Rev, 1953-55; contbr. numerous articles to profl. jours. Pres. Ctr. Inter-Am. Tax Adminstrn., 1980; bd. dirs. Common Cause, 1984-90, chmn. fin. com., 1985-88; bd. dirs. Nat. Capitol Area ACLU, 1990-91; mem. adv. bd. NYU Tax Inst., 1988-97, Little, Brown Tax Practice Series, 1994-96. Recipient Exceptional Service award Dept. Treasury, 1968, Alexander Hamilton award, 1980. Mem. ABA (chmn. tax shelter com. 1982-84), N.Y. Bar Assn. (exec. com. tax sect. 1981-82), Pa. Bar Assn., Phila. Bar Assn. (chmn. tax sect. 1975-76), Assn. of the Bar of the City of N.Y. (chmn. tax coun. 1993-95), Am. Law Inst. (cons. fed. inc. tax project taxation of pass through entities), Am. Coll. Tax Counsel, Beta Gamma Sigma. Home: 17 E 16th St New York NY 10003-3116 Office: NYU Sch Law 40 Washington Sq S New York NY 10012-1005

KURTZ, JOAN HELENE, pediatrician; b. N.Y.C., Apr. 23, 1937; d. Joseph G. and Catherine (Jacobs) Kurtz; m. Anthony M. Suriano, Oct. 15, 1960; children: Michael J., Anthony C., Catherine M. BA cum laude, NYU, 1958, MD, 1962. Diplomate Am. Bd. Pediatrics. Intern in pediatrics Bellevue Hosp., N.Y.C., 1962-63; resident in pediatrics Bronx Mcpl. Hosp. Ctr., N.Y., 1963-65; pvt. practice Carmel, N.Y., 1965-80; pediatrician Cigna Healthcare of Ariz., Phoenix, 1980—. Recipient Physicians Recognition award AMA, 1997. Fellow Am. Acad. Pediatrics; mem. Phoenix Pediatrics Soc., Phi Beta Kappa. Office: Cigna Healthcare of Ariz 12635 N 42nd St Phoenix AZ 85032-7689

KURTZ, KARL THEODORE, government executive; b. Oberlin, Ohio, Nov. 28, 1945; s. John W. and Edith M. (Davis) K.; m. Cecile C. Kurtz, June 7, 1967 (div. Sept. 1982); children: Eric J., Sarah C.; m. Janet L. Beardsley, Aug. 29, 1987; children: Emily L., Andrew S. AB, Oberlin Coll., 1967; PhD, Washington U., St. Louis, 1972. Congl. fellow Am. Polit. Sci. Assn., Washington, 1970-71; vis. prof. U. Ga., Athens, 1971-72; asst. dir. Nat. Legis. Conf., Lexington, Ky., 1972-74; dir. Nat. Conf. State Legislatures, Denver, 1975—. Contbr. articles to profl. jours. Regional selection panel Truman Scholarship Found., Denver, 1977—; mem., chair Bd. Adjustment, Boulder County, Colo., 1993-95; mem. Planning Commn., Boulder County, 1996—. Avocation: tennis. Home and Office: Nat Conf State Legislatures 1560 Broadway Ste 700 Denver CO 80202-5140

KURTZ, LARRY, corporate communications executive; m. Melissa Kurtz. AB in Econs., Princeton U.; postgrad., U. Mo. V.p., tech. group mgr. Burson-Marsteller, N.Y.C., Chgo., San Francisco and Houston, 1974-84; asst. dir. corp. comm. Crown Zellerbach Corp., San Francisco, 1984-86; dir. corp. comm. Chiron Corp., 1988-92; past v.p. corp. comm. Chiron Corp., Emeryville; v.p. corp. comm. McKesson HBOC, Inc., San Francisco, 1997—. Office: McKesson HBOC Inc 1 Post St Ste 3275 San Francisco CA 94104-5292

KURTZ, MAXINE, personnel consultant, lawyer; b. Mpls., Oct. 17, 1921; d. Jack Isadore and Beatrice (Cohen) K. BA, U. Minn., 1942; MS in Govt. Mgmt., U. Denver, 1945, JD, 1962; postdoctoral student, U. Calif., San Diego, 1978. Bar: Colo. 1962; U.S. Dist. Ct., Colo., 1992. Analyst Tri-County Regional Planning, Denver, 1945-47; chief rsch. and spl. projects Planning Office, City and County of Denver, 1947-66, dir. tech. and evaln. Model Cities Program, 1966-71; pers. rsch. officer Denver Career Svc. Auth., 1972-86, dir. pers. svcs., 1986-88, sr. pers. splst., 1988-90; pub. sector pers. cons., 1990-95, atty., 1990—, pers. and human resources cons., 1996-98; expert witness nat. com. on urban problems U.S. Ho. of Reps., U.S. Senate. Author: Law of Planning and Land Use Regulations in Colorado, 1966; co-author: Care and Feeding of Witnesses, Expert and Otherwise, 1974; bd. editors: Pub. Adminstrn. Rev., Washington, 1980-83, 88-92; editorial adv. bd. Internat. Pers. Mgmt. Assn.; prin. investigator: Employment: An American Enigma, 1979. Active Women's Forum of Colo.; Denver Dem. Com.; chair Colo. adv. com. to U.S. Civil Rights Commn., 1985-89, mem. 1989—. Sloan fellow, U. Denver, 1944-45; recipient Outstanding Achievement award U. Minn., 1971, Alumni of Notable Achievement award, 1994. Mem. ABA, Am. Inst. Planners (sec. treas. 1968-70, bd. govs. 1972-75), Am. Planning Assn., Am. Soc. Pub. Adminstrn. (nat. council 1978-81, Donald Stone award), Colo. Bar Assn., Denver Bar Assn., Order St. Ives., Pi Alpha Alpha. Jewish. Home and Office: 2361 Monaco Pky Denver CO 80207-3453

KURTZ, MELVIN H., lawyer, cosmetics company executive; b. N.Y.C., Mar. 31, 1936; s. Philip and Sadie (Brandt) K.; m. Sandra Koss, Dec. 21, 1958; children: Lisa Dawn, Glenn Michael, Jill Meredith. B in Chem. Engring., CCNY, 1959; JD, Fordham U., N.Y.C., 1963. Bar: N.Y. 1963, U.S. Patent and Trademark Office 1965, U.S. Ct. Appeals (3d cir.) 1967, U.S. Supreme Ct. 1967, U.S. Dist. Ct. (so. dist.) N.Y. 1976, U.S. Ct. Appeals (Fed. cir.) 1982. Assoc. Eyre, Mann & Lucas, N.Y.C., 1959-68; asst. gen. counsel Lever Bros. Co., N.Y.C., 1968-82; patent and trademark counsel Chesebrough-Pond's Inc., Greenwich, Conn., 1982-87, gen. counsel, v.p., sec., 1987—, also bd. dirs.; mem. trademark affairs pub. adv. com. Patent and Trademark Office. Bd. dirs. Stamford (Conn.) Symphony Orch. Mem. ABA, Internat. Patent and Trademark Assn., N.Y. State Bar Assn., N.Y. Patent Law Assn. Home: 93 Walworth Ave Scarsdale NY 10583-1140 Office: 33 Benedict Pl Greenwich CT 06830-5339

KURTZ, MYERS RICHARD, hospital administrator; b. Schaefferstown, Pa., June 18, 1924; m. Linda Bewan, Dec. 26, 1988; 1 child, Ronald Hayden; 1 stepchild, Erin B. Brown. B.S., U. Md., 1958; M.B.A., Ind. U., 1963. Served as enlisted man U.S. Army, 1942-51, commd. 2d lt., 1951; advanced through grades to lt. col. Med. Svc. Corps, 1965; mem. staff Army Surgeon Gen., Washington, 1963-67; ret., 1967; affiliation adminstr. NYU Med. Ctr., N.Y.C., 1967-69; exec. dir. Ephrata Community Hosp., Pa., 1969-76; supt. Longview State Hosp., Cin., 1976-79; asst. dir. Ohio Dept. Mental Health and Mental Retardation, Columbus, 1979-81; dir. Ohio Dept. Mental Health and Mental Retardation, 1981-82; sr. v.p. Cleve. Met. Gen. Hosp., 1982-83; supt., CEO Ctrl. State Hosp., Milledgeville, Ga., 1983-93; adminstr., CEO G. Pierce Wood Meml. Hosp., Arcadia, Fla., 1995-98; adj. asst. prof. dept. psychiatry U. Cin., 1977-83. V.p., bd. dirs. Coordinated Home Care Agy., Inc., Lancaster County; pres. Lancaster County Hosp. Coun.; bd. dirs. Pa. Hosp. Assn., Baldwin County United Way, 1986-91, Baldwin County Salvation Army; mem. adv. bd. Youth Devel. Ctr., 1984-91. Decorated Legion of Merit, Army Commendation medal with oak leaf cluster. Fellow Royal Soc. Health; mem. Am. Coll. Hosp. Adminstrs. (life diplomate), Am. Acad. Med. Adminstrs., Am. Hosp. Assn., Milledgeville-Baldwin County C. of C. (bd. dirs. 1984-87, exec. com. 1986—, treas. 1987—), Sigma Iota Epsilon, Rotary Internat. Home: 1799 Jackson Ct Fernandina Beach FL 32034-5616

KURTZ, MYRA BERMAN, microbiologist; b. N.Y.C., July 20, 1945; d. Milton Robert and Shirley (Letzter) Berman; m. Stuart Jacob Kurtz, Aug. 16, 1970; 1 child, Rachel Linda. AB, Goucher Coll., 1966; PhD, Harvard U., 1971. Rsch. assoc. SUNY, Albany, 1971-72; assoc. prof. microbiology Universidade Fed. de Sao Carlos, Brazil, 1972-74; rsch. assoc. Waksman Inst. Microbiology, Piscataway, N.J., 1975-76, asst. rsch. prof., 1976-82; sr. rsch. scientist E.R. Squibb & Sons, Princeton, N.J., 1982-87; sr. rsch. fellow Merck Rsch. Labs., Rahway, N.J., 1987-89, dir., 1989-95, sr. dir., 1995—; reviewer various jours. and granting orgns.; chmn. Gordon Rsch. Conf., 1992. Editor: Genetics of Candida; assoc. editor: Expl. Mycology Jour. (name changed to Fungal Genetics & Biology 1996), 1988—; contbr. articles to profl. jours. Del. Dem. Nat. Conv., Miami, Fla., 1970. Mem. AAAS, Am. Soc. for Microbiology. Avocations: cross-country skiing, hiking.

KURTZ, PAUL, publisher, philosopher, educator; b. Newark, Dec. 21, 1925; s. Martin and Sara (Lasser) K.; m. Claudine C. Vial, Oct. 6, 1960; children: Valerie L., Patricia A., Jonathan, Anne. BA, NYU, 1948; MA, Columbia U., 1949, PhD, 1952. Instr. Queens Coll., 1950-52; instr. philosophy Trinity Coll., Hartford, Conn., 1952-55; asst. prof. Trinity Coll., 1955-58, assoc. prof., 1958-59; assoc. prof. Vassar Coll., Poughkeepsie, N.Y., 1960-61; vis. prof. New Sch. Social Rsch., N.Y.C., 1960-65; assoc. prof. Union Coll., Schenectady, 1961-64, prof., 1964-65; vis. prof. U. Besancon, France, 1965; prof. philosophy SUNY, Buffalo, 1965-91, prof. emeritus, 1992—; moderator TV series. Author: (with Rollo Handy) A Current Appraisal of the Behavioral Sciences, 1964, Decision and the Condition of Man, 1965, The Fullness of Life, 1974, Exuberance, 1977, In Defense of Secular Humanism, 1983, A Skeptics Handbook of Parapsychology, 1985, The Transcendental Temptation, 1986, Forbidden Fruit, 1988, Eupraxophy, 1989, Philosophical Essays in Pragmatic Naturalism, 1990, The New Skepticism, 1992, Toward a New Enlightenment, 1994, The Courage To Become, 1997; editor: American Thought Before 1900, 1966, American Philosophy in the Twentieth Century, 1966, Sidney Hook and the Contemporary World, 1968, Moral Problems in Contemporary Society, 1969; co-editor: International Directory of Philosophy and Philosophers, 4th edit, 1978-81, Tolerance and Revolution, 1970, Language and Human Nature, 1971, A Catholic/Humanist Dialogue, 1972, The Humanist Alternative, 1973, Idea of a Modern University, 1974, The Philosophy of The Curriculum, 1975, The Ethics of Teaching and Scientific Research, 1977, University and State, 1978, Sidney Hook: Philosopher of Democracy and Humanism, 1983, Building A World Community, 1989, Challenges to the Enlightenment, 1994; mem. editorial bd.: The Humanist, 1964-78, editor, 1967-78; mem. editorial bd. Philosophers Index, 1969-85, Question, 1969-81; pres. Prometheus Books, 1970—; mem. editl. bd.: The Skeptical Inquirer, 1976—; editor-in-chief: Free Inquiry Mag., 1980—; pub. The Sci. Rev. of Alternative Medicine, 1997—. Chmn. Coun. for Secular Humanism, 1980—, Coun. on Internat. Studies and World Affairs, 1966-69; trustee Behavioral Rsch. Coun., Great Barrington, Mass.; bd. dirs. U.S. Bibliography of Philosophy, 1958-70, Univ. Ctrs. for Rational Alternatives, 1969-96; bd. dirs. Internat. Humanist and Ethical Union, 1968—, co-chmn., 1986-94; chmn. Com. for Sci. Investigation Claims of Paranormal, 1976—. With AUS, 1944-46. Behavioral Rsch. Coun. fellow, 1962-63, French Govt. fellow, 1965, John Dewey fellow, 1986-87; recipient Bertrand Russell Soc. award, 1988. Fellow AAAS; mem. Acad. Humanism (pres. 1995—, Internat. Humanist award 1999). Office: Prometheus Books Inc 59 John Glenn Dr Amherst NY 14228-2197 *Two passions have dominated my intellectual and professional life: (1) a commitment to critical intelligence—I am skeptical of the false beliefs and mythologies that have motivated other men and women—and (2) a belief in the importance of human courage, particularly in defending reason in society and in attempting to reconstruct ethical values so that they are more democratic and humane.*

KURTZ, ROBERT ARTHUR, finance company executive; b. Holyoke, Mass., June 16, 1943. BS in Fin., Am. Internat. Coll., Springfield, Mass., 1967; MBA in Fin., U. Okla., 1969. Sr. fin. analyst corp. treas. office Gulf Oil Internat., Pitts., 1969-71; with corp. fin. staff Humble Oil div. Exxon, Houston, 1971-73; account mgr. Merrill Lynch, Atlanta, 1973-75; personal and corp. fin. advisor Atlanta, 1975-77; pres., founder Internat. Trade and Mktg. Corp., Atlanta, 1977-84; chmn. Kray Fin. Corp., Atlanta, 1984—. Author: Diagnosing the Customer's Decision Strategy, 1994, Pick 'em Right the First Time, 1997. Mem. Soc. Neuro-Linguistic Programming (cert. trainer), Am. Assn. for Counseling and Devel. Lutheran. Home: 1630 Broadwell Oaks Dr Alpharetta GA 30004-1580

KURTZ, SHELDON FRANCIS, lawyer, educator; b. Syracuse, N.Y., May 18, 1943; s. Abraham Kurtz and Rosalyn (Bronstein) Stern; m. Alice Kaufman, June 22, 1968; children: Andrea, Emily. AB, Syracuse U., 1964, JD, 1967. Bar: N.Y. 1967, Iowa 1973. Assoc. Nixon, Mudge, Guthrie, Alexander & Mitchell, N.Y.C., 1967-69, Cleary, Gottlieb, Steen & Hamilton, N.Y.C., 1970-73; prof. U. Iowa Coll. Law, Iowa City, 1973-89, U. Va. Sch. Law, Charlottesville, 1979-80; dean Coll. Law, Fla. State U., Tallahassee, 1989-91; prof. Coll. Law U. Iowa, Iowa City, 1991—; prof. Coll. Med. U. Iowa. Author: (with Reimer) Iowa Estates: Taxation and Administration, 1975, Income and Estate Taxation of Decedents and Their Estates, 1977, Kurtz on Iowa Estates, 3 vols., 1981, 2d. edit., 2 vols., 1989, Problems, Cases and Materials on Family Estate Planning, 1983, (with Hood and Shors) Estate Planning for Shareholders of a Closely Held Corporation, 2 vols. and supplement, 1986, (with Hovenkamp) American Property Law, 1987, 3d edit., 1999, (with McGovern and Rein) Wills, Trusts and Estates, 1988, (with Boyer and Hovenkamp) The Law of Property, 1991; also articles. Recipient Burlington No. Teaching award U. Iowa, 1987. Mem. N.Y. State Bar Assn., Iowa Bar Assn., Am. Law Inst. Avocations: cooking, hiking. Office: U Iowa Coll Law Rm 446 Iowa City IA 52242

KURTZ, SWOOSIE, actress; b. Omaha; d. Frank and Margo (Rogers) K. Student, Acad. Music and Dramatic Arts, London, U. So. Calif. Appeared on TV series Mary, 1978, Love, Sidney, 1981-83 (nominated Best Actress in Comedy Series 1982-83), Sisters, 1991-96 (Emmy nominee Lead Actress in Drama 1993, 94, SAG award nominee 1995), ER, 1994, Suddenly Susan, 1996, 97, Touched by an Angel, 1997; (TV spls.) Uncommon Women and Others, Ah, Wilderness!, Fifth of July, The House of Blue Leaves, The Visit, Walking Through the Fire, The Mating Season; (TV films) Guilty Conscience, A Time to Live, Terror on Track 9, Baja, Oklahoma (Golden Globe nominee 1987), The Image (Emmy nominee, Ace award nominee), The Positively True Adventures of the Alleged Texas Cheerleader-Murdering Mom, And the Band Played On (Emmy award nominee 1994, Ace award nominee), Truman Capote's One Christmas, Betrayed: A Story of Three Women, A Promise to Carolyn, Harvey, Little Girls in Pretty Boxes, 1997, More Tales of the City, 1998, My Own Country, 1998; TV guest appearances on Kojak, Carol and Co. (Emmy award); (films) Slap Shot, 1977, The World According to Garp, 1982, Against All Odds, 1984, Wild Cats, 1986, True Stories, 1986, Vice Versa, 1988, Bright Lights, Big City, 1988, Dangerous Liaisons, 1988, Stanley and Iris, 1989, A Shock to the System, 1990, Reality Bites, 1994, Citizen Ruth, 1996, Liar, Liar, 1997; (theater) Ah Wilderness!, 1975, Children, 1976, Tartuffe, 1977 (Tony award nominee), A History of the American Film, 1978 (Drama Desk award), Uncommon Women and Others, 1978 (Obie award, Drama Desk award), Fifth of July, 1980-81 (Tony award, Drama Desk award, Outer Critics Circle award), Michael Bennett's Scandal, 1985, The House of Blue Leaves, 1986 (Tony award, Obie award), Who's Afraid of Virginia Woolf, 1980, Summer, 1980, Beach House, 1986, Hunting Cockroaches, 1987 (Drama Logue award nominee), Love Letters, 1989, Six Degrees of Separation, 1990, Lips Together, Teeth Apart, 1991. Recipient Emmy award Outstanding Guest Performer in Comedy or Drama series. Office: 1900 Ave Of Stars Ste 1640 Los Angeles CA 90067-4407*

KURTZ, THOMAS EUGENE, mathematics educator; b. Oak Park, Ill., Feb. 22, 1928; s. Oscar Christ and Helen (Bell) K.; m. Patricia Anne Barr, June 13, 1953 (div. Aug. 1973); children—Daniel Barr, Timothy David, Beth Louise; m. Agnes Seelye Bixler, June 10, 1974. B.A., Knox Coll., Galesburg, Ill., 1950; Ph.D., Princeton, 1956; DSc, Knox Coll., 1985. Mem. faculty Dartmouth, 1956-93, prof. math. and computer sci., 1966-93, chmn. Program in Computer and Info. Sci., 1966-93, dir. Kiewit Computation Ctr., 1959-75; dir. Office Acad. Computing, 1975-78. Author: Basic Statistics, 1963, (with J.G. Kemeny) Basic Programming, 1967, 2d edit., 1971, 3d edit., 1980, (with J.G. Kemeny) Structured Basic Programming, 1987. Trustee, chmn. coun. EDUCOM, 1974-78; chmn., bd. dirs. NERComp, Inc., 1970-78; trustee, vice chmn. Dartmouth Time Sharing Sys., Inc., 1972-78; chmn. X3J2 sub. com. Am. Nat. Standards Inst., 1974-84, convenor WG8 Internat. Standards Orgn. Basic Com., 1987-94; bd. dirs., vice chmn. True Basic, Inc., 1983—; mem. panel uses of computers in edn. Pres.'s Sci. Adv. Com., 1965-66. Democrat. Mem. United Ch. Christ. Co-designer BASIC computer lang. and Dartmouth time sharing system. Home: 3 Lakeview Dr Hanover NH 03755-3407

KURTZER, DANIEL, ambassador; b. Elizabeth, N.J.. BA, Yeshiva U., 1971; MA, Columbia, Columbia; PhD, Columbia, 1976. Dean Yeshiva Coll., Yeshiva U., N.Y.C., until 1979; joined Fgn. Svc., Dept. State, Washington, 1976, from 1979, with Bur. Internat. Orgn. Affairs, from 1976; 2d sec. for polit. affairs Am. Embassy, Cairo, 1979-82; 1st sec. for polit. affairs Am. Embassy, Tel Aviv, 1982-86; dep. dir. for Egyptian affairs Dept. State, from 1986, speechwriter, mem. sec.'s policy planning staff, until 1989, dep. asst. sec. for Nr. Ea. Affairs, 1989-94, prin. dep. asst. sec. for intelligence and rsch., 1994-97, acting asst. sec., 1997; amb. to Egypt, Am. Embassy, Cairo, 1997—. Office: Dept State US Amb to Egypt Washington DC 20521-7700*

KURTZKE, JOHN FRANCIS, SR., neurologist, epidemiologist; b. Bklyn., Sept. 14, 1926; s. John Ambrose and Teresa Rose (Knipper) K.; m. Margaret Mary Nevin, June 30, 1950; children: John Francis Jr., Catherine Kurtzke Brown, Elizabeth Kurtzke Siebert, Joan Kurtzke Brennan, Robert, James, Christine Kurtzke Hughes. BS summa cum laude, St. John's U., 1948; MD, Cornell U., 1952. Diplomate in neurology Am. Bd. Psychiatry and Neurology (asst. examiner, then examiner and sr. examiner in neurology 1964-96, cert. appreciation 1969, 90). Intern Kings County Hosp., Bklyn., 1952-53; resident in neurology VA Hosp., Bronx, N.Y., 1953-56; chief neurology service VA hosps. Coatesville, Pa., 1956-63, Washington, 1963-95; chief neuroepidemiology sect. VA Med. Ctr., Washington, 1995—; mem. faculty Jefferson Med. Coll., Phila., 1958-63, asst. prof. clin. neurology, 1963; mem. faculty Georgetown Med. Sch., Washington, 1963—, prof. neurology, 1968—, vice chmn. dept. neurology, 1976-95, prof. cmty. and family medicine, 1968-95; Disting. prof. neurology uniformed svcs. U. Health Scis., Bethesda, 1992—, USN med. student liaison officer, 1979-85; vis. prof. neurology and neuroepidemiology Temple U. Sch. Medicine, 1984-89; cons. neurology Nat. Naval Med. Ctr., Bethesda, 1966—, Surgeon Gen. Navy, 1970-97; mem. med. adv. bd. Nat. Multiple Sclerosis Soc., 1966-94, hon. mem., 1995—, mem. working group on design of clin. studies in multiple sclerosis, 1976-84, mem. exec. com., 1981-83; med. adv. bd. Internat. Fedn. Multiple Sclerosis Socs., 1972—,(hon. mem. 1998—), mem. specialist adv. group, 1991—; mem. com. multiple sclerosis World Fedn. Neurology, 1967—, com. neuroepidemiology, 1977—; chmn. epidemiology sect. NIH Epilepsy Adv. Com., 1973-76; med. rsch. program specialist for neurology and neurobiology VA Rsch. Svc., 1977-80; chmn. work group epidemiology HEW Commn. Control of Huntington's Disease, 1976-78; mem. naval exam. bd. Naval Med. Command, 1980-83; mem. Residency Rev. Com. Neurology, 1983-88, vice chmn., 1985-86, chmn., 1987-88; chmn. U.S. Naval Res. Med. Flag Coun., 1985-86; mem. instnl. rev. bd. Nat. Inst. Neurol. Diseases and Stroke, 1989-98; established investigator Nat. Multiple Sclerosis Soc., 1987—; mem. spl. panel Inst. Medicine, 1990. Author, co-author: Epidemiology of Multiple Sclerosis, 1968, Epidemiology of Cerebrovascular Disease, 1969, Epidemiology of Neurologic and Sense Organ Disorders, 1973, Neuroepidemiology, 1998, Psychiatry/Neurology, 1998, Practice Questions. Book One, 1998, Psychiatry Neurology, 1998, Book Two, 1998; mem. editl. bd. Neuroepidemiology, 1980—, Neurology, 1984-92, Stroke, 1986—, Jour. Clin. Epidemiology, 1988—, Jour. Neurol. Sci., 1990-96, Acta Neurologica Scandinavica, 1990-97; contbr. more than 400 articles to profl. jours., chpts. to books. Served with USN, 1944-46; rear adm. M.C., USNR, ret. 1986. Decorated Legion of Merit (2), Navy Commendation medal, Armed Forces Res. medal with gold hourglass; recipient cert. of merit Surgeon Gen. of Navy, 1969, Gold Bicennial medal Georgetown U., 1982, Sec.'s Disting. Career award Dept. Vets. Affairs, 1998, others. Fellow AAAS, ACP, Am. Acad. Neurology (chmn. sect. on neuro-epidemiology 1971-75, chmn. com. nat. needs in neurology 1981-85, subcom. nat. needs in neurology 1985-86, mem. work force task force 1997, John Jay Dystel prize for multiple sclerosis rsch. 1997), Am. Coll. Epidemiology, N.Y. Acad. Sci., Am. Coll. Preventive Medicine, Pan Am. Med. Assn. (coun. neurology sect.), Am. Heart Assn. (stroke coun. 1991—); mem. AAUP, AMA, So. Med. Assn., Assn. Mil. Surgeons (life), Am. Neurol. Assn. (chmn. bylaws ad hoc com. 1990-91), Am. Epidemiol. Soc., Internat. Epidemiol. Assn., Assn. Rsch. in Nervous and Mental Disease, Am. Public Health Assn., Soc. Epidemiol. Rsch., Am. Epilepsy Soc., Am. Soc. Microbiology, Internat. Stroke Soc., Senior Stroke Soc., Danish Neurol. Soc. (hon.), French Soc. Neurology (hon., fgn.), Soc. Med. Cons. to Armed Forces (com. on res. affairs 1980-83, com. on manpower 1984-98), German Soc. Neurology (hon.), Naval Res. Assn. (life), Naval Order U.S. (life), Res. Officers Assn. (life), Naval Inst. (life), Fleet Res. Assn. (life), Navy League (life), The Ret. Officers Assn. (life). Home: 7509 Salem Rd Falls Church VA 22043-3240 Office: VA Med Ctr 50 Irving

St NW Washington DC 20422-0001 *To be a physician demands recognition of the intrinsic value and dignity of human life while pursuing the goal of relieving pain and impairment due to disease or injury.*

KURTZMAN, NEIL A., medical educator; b. Bklyn., June 18, 1936; s. Louis S. and Roselie (Yegla) K.; m. Sandra Sabatini, Feb. 14, 1976; children from previous marriage: Jonathan, Laura. BA with honors, Williams Coll., 1957; MD, N.Y. Med. Coll., 1961. Intern Robert Packer Hosp., Sayre, Pa., 1961-62; resident Ohio State U. Hosp., Columbus, 1962-63; asst. chief med. services Nobel Army Hosp., Ft. McClellan, Ala., 1963-64; med. resident William Beaumont Gen. Hosp., El Paso, Tex., 1964-65, chief med. resident, 1965-66; fellow in nephrology U. Tex. Southwestern Med. Sch., Dallas, 1966-68; chief renal div. Brooke Army Med. Ctr., Ft. Sam Houston, Tex., 1969-72; prof., chief nephrology sect. U. Ill. Coll. Medicine, Chgo., 1972-84; Arnett prof. medicine Tex. Tech U. Health Scis. Ctr., Lubbock, 1985—, chief nephrology divsn., 1985-94, chief of staff univ. med. ctr., 1990-92, chmn. dept. internal medicine, 1985-98; mem. gen. medicine B study sect. Nat. Inst. Arthritis, Metabolic and Digestive Diseases, Bethesda, Md., 1978-83; mem. merit rev. bd. VA, Washington, 1979-82, chmn., 1981-82; mem. sci. adv. bd. Nat. Kidney Found., N.Y.C., 1981-92, chmn., 1988-90, v.p., 1990-92, pres., 1992-94; prin. investigator regulation urinary acidification NIH, Bethesda, 1978—. Author: Handbook of Urinalysis and Urinary Sediment, 1974, Pathophysiology of the Kidney, 1977; also more than 270 sci. papers, more than 600 sci. presentations; editor-in-chief Seminars in Nephrology, 1981—, Am. Jour. Kidney Diseases, 1997—; assoc. editor Am. Jour. Nephrology; mem. editorial bd. 7 sci. jours.; referee 16 sci. jours. Faculty advisor Alpha Omega Alpha, U. Ill., 1977-84, Tex. Tech U. Health Sci. Ctr., 1985—. Served to lt. col. U.S. Army, 1963-72. Decorated U.S. Army Meritorious Svc. award; recipient Pres.'s award Nat. Kidney Found., 1990, Outstanding Acad. Achievement award N.Y. Med. Coll., 1993, So. Soc. for Clin. Investigation's Founder's award, 1996, Tex. chpt. Am. Coll. Physicians Laureate award, 1996. Fellow AAAS; mem. Am. Physiol. Soc., Am. Soc. Clin. Investigation, Assn. Am. Physicians, Ctrl. Soc. Clin. Research, So. Soc. Clin. Investigation, Alpha Omega Alpha. Office: Tex Tech U Health Scis Ctr Sch of Medicine Lubbock TX 79430

KURTZMAN, RALPH HAROLD, retired biochemist, researcher, consultant; b. Mpls., Feb. 21, 1933; s. Ralph Harold, Sr. and Susie Marie (Elwell) K.; m. Nancy Virginia Leussler, Aug. 27, 1955; children: Steven Paul, Sue. BS, U. Minn., 1955; MS, U. Wis., 1958, PhD, 1959. Asst. prof. U. R.I., Kingston, 1959-62, U. Minn., Morris, 1962-65; biochemist U.S. Dept. Agriculture, Albany, Calif., 1965-97; ret., 1997; instr. U. Calif., Berkeley, 1981-82; cons. Bliss Valley Farms, Twin Falls, Idaho, 1983-84; pres. Santa Clara Valley Tex. Instrument PC Users' Group, 1991-92, editor, 1993-97; cons. in field. Editor Internat. Jour. Mushroom Scis., 1995—; inventor mushroom substrate (compost) preparation, 1982, decaffeination of beverages, 1973; contbr. articles to profl. jours. Chmn. Berkeley YMCA Camp Program Com., 1971-72; official Amateur Athletic Union (swimming), San Francisco, 1973-80; treas. Calif. Native Plant Soc., 1970. Mem. Am. Mushroom Inst., Mycological Soc. Am. (organizer symposium mushroom cultivation in Am. tropics 1998), Mycological Soc. Japan, Sigma Xi. Avocations: computers, wood working, photography. Home and Office: 445 Vassar Ave Berkeley CA 94708-1215

KURUVILLA, KOLLANPARAMPIL, electrical engineer; b. Kodukulanji, Kerala, India, July 20, 1943; came to U.S., 1988; s. Thomas and Susanna (Idicula) K.; m. Elizabeth Kuruvilla, Oct. 23, 1967 (dec. Jan. 1971); 1 child, Susan, m. Santha Mathew, Feb. 12, 1972; children: Babita Susan, Nandita, Oscar. BSc in Engring., Kerala U., 1965; MBA, Kennedy Western U., 1996; postgrad., Trinity Coll./Theol. Sem., Newburgh, Ind., 1998—. Lectr. in elec. engring. Mar. Athanasius Coll. Engring., Kerala, 1965-66; elec. engr., exec. engr. Kerala State Electricity Bd., Trivandrum, 1966-87; elec. engr. Zambia Electricity Supply Corp., Lusaka, 1972-75; chief power sta. Soiedade Hidroelectrico do Revue, Mininstry of Power, Chimoio, Mozambique, 1979-81; project engr., design engr. Southeastern Pa. Transp. Authority, Phila., 1989—. Author: In Nature's Lap, 1995, A Smell of Africa (Safe in his Arms), 1998; inventor in field of safety and security measures. Nat. assoc. Libr. of Congress. Named Citizen of Yr., Hutt River Province, Australia, 1994—. Mem. Instn. Engrs. India, Planetary Soc., Smithsonian Instn., Handi Ham Club. Avocations: reading, music, reading about nature, painting, amateur radio, writing. Home: 133A Dawn Dr Lansdale PA 19446-5251 Office: Southeastern Pa Transp Authority 1234 Market St Ste 13 Philadelphia PA 19107-3701

KURY, BERNARD EDWARD, lawyer; b. Sunbury, Pa., Sept. 11, 1938. AB, Princeton U., 1960; LLB, U. Pa., 1963. Bar: N.Y. 1964. Assoc. Dewey, Ballantine, Bushby, Palmer & Wood, N.Y.C., 1963-71, ptnr., 1971—. Home: 95 Horatio St New York NY 10014-1520 Office: Dewey Ballantine 1301 Avenue Of The Americas New York NY 10019-6022*

KURY, FRANKLIN LEO, lawyer; b. Sunbury, Pa., Oct. 15, 1936; s. Barney and Helen (Witkowski) K.; m. Elizabeth Heazlett, Sept. 14, 1963; children: Steven, David, James. Bar: Pa. 1962. Atty. Pa. Dept. Justice, Harrisburg, 1961-62; ptnr. Kury & Kury, Sunbury, 1963-80, Tive, Hetrick & Pierce, Harrisburg, 1981-82, Reed, Smith, Shaw & McClay, Harrisburg, 1983—. Mem. Pa. Ho. of Reps., Harrisburg, 1967-72, Pa. Senate, Harrisburg, 1973-80; del. at large Dem. Nat. Conv., San Francisco, 1984; bd. dirs. Pa. Environ. Coun., Hawk Mountain Sanctuary Assn. 1st lt. USAR, 1962-66. Mem. Am. Immigration Lawyers Assn., Pa. Bar Assn. (chmn. environ. sect. 1984, 1st award for Outstanding Contbn. to Profession of Environ. Law Practice 1993), Polish Nat. Alliance. Democrat. Avocation: golf. Office: Reed Smith Shaw & McClay PO Box 11844 213 Market St Harrisburg PA 17101-2132

KURYK, DAVID NEAL, lawyer; b. Balt., Aug. 24, 1947; s. Leon and Bernice G. (Fox) K.; m. Alice T. Lehman, July 8, 1971; children—Richard M., Robert M., Benjamin A. B.A., U. Md., 1969; J.D., U. Balt., 1972. Bar: Md. 1972, U.S. Dist. Ct. Md. 1973, U.S. Ct. Mil. Appeals 1973, D.C. 1974, U.S. Ct. Appeals (4th cir.) 1974, U.S. Supreme Ct. 1976, U.S. Ct. Appeals (Fed. cir.) 1982. Assoc. Harold Buchman, Esq., Balt., 1970-76; sole practice, Balt., 1976—. Served to sgt. USAF, 1967-73. Mem. ABA (products, gen. liability and consumer law com. 1976—, com. auto law 1977), Md. State Bar Assn., Bar Assn. Balt. City, Assn. Trial Lawyers Am., U. Balt. Alumni Assn., Zeta Beta Tau. Democrat. Jewish. Mem. bd. editors Md. Bar Jour., 1973-76. Home: 11200 S Springs Rd Lutherville MD 21093-3520 Office: Am Bldg 231 E Baltimore St Ste 702 Baltimore MD 21202-3415

KURZ, IRWIN, principal; b. N.Y.C., Oct. 10, 1946; s. Milton and Estelle (Weinstein) K.; m. Arlene J. Kurz, Dec. 22, 1968; 1 child, Gary. BA, Yeshiva U., 1968; MS, CUNY, 1971, cert. in Adminstrn., Supervision, 1973; student, Harvard U., 1998. Tchr. Pub. Sch. 289, Bklyn., 1968-80, asst. prin., 1980-81; asst. prin. Pub. Sch. 91, Bklyn., 1981-84; prin. Pub. Sch. 167, Bklyn., 1984-85, Pub. Sch. 161, Bklyn., 1986—; mem. registration review team N.Y.C. Bd. Edn., 1989; established Crown Sch. Law and Journalism, 1995; presenter title I dissemination project Mass. Dept. Edn., Hyannis, Mass., 1998; presenter reading strategies Sacramento, Calif., 1998; featured in Converge Mag., 1998; keynote spkr. Mass. Dept. Edn., Sturbridge, 1998; testified U.S. Congress on Endl. Reform, 1998; panelist Edn. Commn. of States, Denver, 1999. Appeared in articles Forbes mag., Education Week, Tchr. Mag., Converge Mag. Interviewed by Charles Kuralt on Sunday Morning, CBS-TV, 1990; named Outstanding Supr. of the Yr., Dist. 17 N.Y.C. Bd. of Edn., 1990; U. Pitts. fellow, 1999. Fellow U. Pitts., 1999; mem. ASCD, Am. Fedn. Sch. Adminstrs., Am. Fedn. Tchrs., Coun. Suprs., Adminstrs. Avocation: tennis. Office: Pub Sch 161 330 Crown St Brooklyn NY 11225-3000

KURZ, MITCHELL HOWARD, marketing communications executive; b. N.Y.C., Nov. 5, 1951; s. Robert Sydney and Lorraine Ruth (Wolosky) K.; m. Sandy Mitchell, Aug. 25, 1979; children: Zachary, Maxwell. BA, Dartmouth Coll., 1973; MBA, Harvard U., 1975. Acct. exec. Young & Rubicam, N.Y.C., 1976-77, v.p., account supr., 1978-80, sr. v.p., 1980-87, corp. sr. v.p., 1987-90; chmn. N.Am. Wunderman Worldwide, N.Y.C., 1990-91; pres., CEO worldwide Wunderman Cato Johnson, N.Y.C., 1992-97; pres., COO Young & Rubicam Advt., N.Y.C., 1997-98, chair client svcs., 1998-99; chmn., CEO Kurz and Friends, Westport, Conn., 1998—; bd. dirs. Young and Rubicam. Trustee Rheedlen Ctrs. for Children and Families, Town Sch., 1994—; bd. dirs. New Visions for Pub. Schs., 1994—, Teach for Am., 1996. Rufus Choate Scholar, Dartmouth Coll., 1971, 72, 73. Mem. Am. Mgmt. Assn., Pequot Runners, Phi Beta Kappa. Avocations: fin. markets, marathon running. Home: 95 Old Rd Westport CT 06880-4145 Office: Kurz and Friends 191 Post Rd W Westport CT 06880-6486*

KURZ, MORDECAI, economics educator; b. Nathanya, Israel, Nov. 29, 1934; came to U.S., 1957, naturalized, 1973; s. Moshe and Sarah (Kraus) K.; m. Lillian Rivlin, Aug. 4, 1963 (div. Mar. 1967); m 2d Linda Alice Cahn, Dec. 2, 1979. BA in Econs. and Polit. Sci., Hebrew U., Jerusalem, 1957; MA in Econs., Yale U., 1958, PhD in Econs., 1961; MS in Stats., Stanford U., 1960. Asst. prof. econs. Stanford U., 1962-63, assoc. prof., 1966-68, prof., 1969—, Joan Kenney prof. econs., 1997—, dir. econs. sect. Inst. for Math. Studies, 1971-89; sr. lectr. in econs. Hebrew U., 1963-66; cons. econs. SRI Internat., Menlo Park, Calif., 1963-78; spl. econ. advisor Can. health and Welfare Ministry, Ottawa, Ont., 1976-78; spl. econ. advisor Pres.'s Commn. on Pension, Washington, 1979-81; rsch. assoc. Nat. Bur. Econ. Rsch., 1979-82; Lady Davis vis. prof. Hebrew U., Jerusalem, 1993. Author: (with Kenneth J. Arrow) Public Investment, The Rate of Return and Optimal Fiscal Policy,1970, Endogenous Economic Fluctuations: Studies in the Theory of Rational Beliefs, 1997; co-editor Econ. Theory, 1997—. Bd. dirs. Ben-Gurion U. of the Negev, Israel, 1998—. Ford Found. faculty fellow Stanford U., 1973; Guggenheim Found. fellow Stanford U., Harvard U., Jerusalem, 1977-78; Inst. Advanced Studies fellow Hebrew U., Mt. Scopus, Jerusalem, 1979-80; prin. investigator NSF, 1969-93. Fellow Econometric Soc. (assoc. editor Jour. Econ. Theory 1976-90); mem. Am. Econ. Assn. Democrat. Jewish. Office: Stanford U Econs Dept Serra St at Galvez Stanford CA 94305-6702

KURZ, THOMAS PATRICK, lawyer; b. Stevens Point, Wis., Dec. 26, 1951; s. Edward Albert and Bertha Marie (Schmidt) K.; m. Debra Kay Gentz, Jan. 6, 1979; children: Natalie Jean, Thomas Patrick Jr. BA, U. Wis.-Madison, 1974; JD, Georgetown U., 1977. Bar: Wis. 1977, U.S. Dist. Ct. (ea. dist.) Wis. 1977, Ill. 1982, Tex. 1989. Assoc. Foley & Lardner, Milw. and Madison, 1977-82; atty. A.E. Staley Mfg. Co., Decatur, Ill., 1982-85; corp. counsel Staley Continental, Inc., Rolling Meadows, Ill, 1985-88; gen. counsel, asst. sec. Sysco Corp., Houston, 1988—. Mem. Georgetown Law Jour., 1975-76, editor, 1976-77. Recipient Eagle Scout award Samoset coun. Boy Scouts Am., 1967; Wis. honors scholar, 1970. Fellow Tex. Bar Found.; mem. ABA, Ill. Bar Assn., Wis. Bar Assn., State Bar Tex., Phi Beta Kappa. Roman Catholic. Home: 20010 Sky Hollow Ln Katy TX 77450-5218 Office: Sysco Corp 1390 Enclave Pkwy Houston TX 77077-2099

KURZBAN, IRA JAY, lawyer; b. Bklyn., May 9, 1949; s. Benjamin and Irene (Weiss) K.; m. Magda Montiel Davis, Apr. 15, 1989; children: Kathryn Montiel Davis, Paula Lindsay Davis, Magda Marie Davis, Sadie Bethany Kurzban, Benjamin Montiel Kurzban. BA, Syracuse U., 1971; MA, U. Calif., Berkeley, 1973, JD, 1976; hon. fellow, U. Pa. Law Sch., 1987. Bar: Calif. 1976, Fla. 1976, U.S. Ct. Appeals (5th cir.) 1978, U.S. Supreme Ct. 1980, U.S. Ct. Appeals (11th cir.) 1981. Ptnr. Kurzban Kurzban Weinger & Tetzeli P.A., Miami, Fla., 1977—; lectr. in field. Author: Kurzban's Immigration Law Sourcebook: A Comprehensive Outline and Reference Tool, 6th edit., 1998; contbr. articles to profl. jours. Founder Berkeley Law Found., 1976. Polit. sci. dept. fellow U. Calif., Berkeley, 1971, Kent fellow, 1974-77, law and soc. fellow U. Calif., Berkeley, 1975-76; recipient Tobias Simon pro bono svc. award, 1982. Mem. ABA (mem. coord. com. in immigration law), Am. Immigration Lawyers Assn. (south Fla. chpt. pres. 1980-81, nat. pres. 1987), Am. Inns of Ct. Office: Kurzban Kurzban Weinger & Tetzeli PA 2650 SW 27th Ave Fl 2 Miami FL 33133-3003

KURZDORFER, PETER JOHN, chess educator, writer; b. Buffalo, Dec. 30, 1949; s. Joseph and Elizabeth (Fernandez) K.; m. Kathleen R. Wing, May 21, 1994. Grad. h.s., Kenmore East, N.Y. Ch. organist various, Buffalo, 1964-69, 72-79, stock boy, 1968-69, ch. organist, 1982-84; laborer various, Buffalo and Lockport, N.Y., 1969-72; cellist, singer Kurzdorfer & Cady, Buffalo, 1978-79, 82-87; home health care aide Boston, San Diego, Buffalo, 1979-89; Bradford (Pa.) resident chess master Am. Chess Sch., 1989-97; owner, operator Kurzdorfer's Chess Svc., Bradford, 1997. Author endgame tutorials (CD-ROM) Chessmaster 5000 (Windows 95 software); co-author: (CD-ROM) How to Play Chess, Mindscape 1995, Zane, 1996; contbr. articles to jours. in field; columnist Bradford Jour., 1989-96; asst. editor Chess Life mage. , 1997—. Mem. Am. Chess Sch. (pres. 1992-96), U.S. Chess Fedn. (cert. nat. master, life master, coach, tournament dir.), Chess Journalists of Am. (judge 1992-95). Avocations: singing, piano. Home and Office: 649 South St Highland NY 12528-2234

KURZEJA, RICHARD EUGENE, professional society administrator; b. Hammond, Ind., July 12, 1935; s. Stanley A. and Helen E. (Stempkowski) K.; m. Dolores M. Michalak; children: Denise, Richard, Deanna. Student Purdue U., West Lafayette, Ind., 1953, Hartnett Coll., Hammond, Ind., 1955. With U.S. Ry. and Equip. Co., Blue Island, Ill., 1955-64; indsl. engr. Simmons Co., Munster, Ind., 1964-70; sales technician Melody-Olds-GMC Truck, Cedar Lake, Ind., 1970-72; sales mgr. Meidell GMC Truck, South Chicago Heights, Ill., 1972-86; truck broker, 1986-97; exec. sec. Internat. Buckskin Horse Assn., Shelby, Ind., 1971—, sec.-treas. Youth Scholarship Fund, 1988—; owner/operator Holiday Farm, Dyer, Ind., 1963-88, Equitara, Lowell, Ind., 1988—; v.p. Color Breed Coun., Inc., Ft. Worth, Tex., 1993—. Mem. Am. Quarter Horse Assn. (life), Mid-Am. Buckskin Assn. (life dir. 1965—), U.S. Dressage Fedn., Am. Youth Horse Coun. Roman Catholic. Home: 3517 W 231st Ave Lowell IN 46356-9211 Office: Internat Buckskin Horse Assn PO Box 268 Shelby IN 46377-0268 *No challenge in life is too great to try. The reward is in the effort put forth regardless of the end result. To deny the effort is to deny an experience and we all learn by experience.**

KURZENBERGER, DICK, health services executive; b. Ind., Nov. 26, 1949; children: Jon Ross, Blake Mead. BBA, Ft. Lauderdale U., 1970; MBA, U. Palm Beach, 1971. Asst. dir. St. Mary's Hosp., West Palm Beach, Fla., 1972-75; adminstr. The Hauser Clinic, Houston, 1975-79, Post Oak Psychiatry, Houston, 1979-86; asst. adminstr. Green Oaks Hosp., Dallas, 1986-88; div. adminstr. St. Joseph Hosp., Houston, 1988-90; exec. dir., chief exec. officer Greenwood Group, Houston, 1990-92; div. mgr. Kelsey Seybold Clinic, Houston, 1992-97; sr. v.p. western divsn. Greenwood Group Internat., Ft. Lauderdale, Fla., 1997—; CEO South Fla. Health Care Assn., Boca Raton, 1998—; pres., bd. dirs. Mental Health Assn. of Houston and Harris County, 1989-90; chmn. psychiat. sect. Greater Houston Hosp., 1988-90; del. dir. State Mental Health Bd., Austin, 1987-92. V.p. MHA Houston, 1982-86, Dallas, 1987; del. Mental Health Needs Coun., Houston, 1989-90. Recipient Vol. of Yr. award United Way, 1986, MM award M.M. Anderson, 1978, John Z. Rasco award, 1993, BBH Adminstr. of Yr. award, 1994. Mem. Tex. Hosp. Assn., Med. Group Mgmt. Assn. Home: 1920 S Ocean Dr Apt 901 Fort Lauderdale FL 33316-3739

KURZMAN, STEPHEN ALAN, accountant; b. Boston, Feb. 24, 1945; s. H. Edward and Gertrude (Blake) K.; B.S., Northeastern U., 1968; M.S., Bentley Coll., 1977; m. Marilyn Verna Baker, June 30, 1968; children—David Eric, Jessica Susan. Asst. to treas. Home Owners Fed. Savs. & Loan Assn., Boston, 1968-70; sr. acct. Martin D. Braver & Co., Chestnut Hill, Mass., 1970-73; tax supr. Laventhol & Horwath, Boston, 1973-76; ptnr. Kurzman, Scibetta & Dempsey, Canton, Mass., 1976—; adj. asst. prof. taxation Bentley Coll., 1978—, chmn. tax adv. bd., grad. tax program adv. com.; bd. dirs Congregation Mishkan Tefila. Chmn. IRS Dist. Dirs. Liaison Commn. for New Eng.; program chmn. Bentley Coll. Nat. Tax Conf.; active tax com. Smaller Bus. Assn. New Eng. Contbr. articles to profl. jours. Mem. AICPA (instr. 1982—), Mass. Soc. CPAs (past chmn. fed. tax com., bd. dirs., chmn. tax forum com., co-chmn. tax conf.), Bentley Coll. Alumni Assn., Beta Alpha Psi. Lodge: B'nai B'rith. Home: 8 David Rd Newton MA 02459-2712 Office: Kurzman Scibetta & Dempsey 1017 Turnpike St Canton MA 02021-2828

KURZWEG, ULRICH HERMANN, engineering science educator; b. Jena, Germany, Sept. 16, 1936; came to U.S., 1947, naturalized, 1952; s. Hermann Herbert and Erna Herta (Michaelis) K.; m. Sophia Speth, Dec. 21, 1963; 1 dau., Tina. B.S., U. Md., 1958; M.A. (Woodrow Wilson fellow 1958-59), Princeton U., 1959, Ph.D. in Physics, 1961. Sr. theoretical physicist United Tech. Research Labs., East Hartford, Conn., 1962-68; adj. assoc. prof. math. Rensselaer Poly. Inst., Hartford (Conn.) Grad. Center, 1964-68; mem. faculty U. Fla., Gainesville, 1968; prof. engrng. scis. U. Fla., 1968—. Contbr. numerous articles to sci. and tech. publs. Fulbright grantee, 1961-62; recipient Cert. of Recognition, NASA, 1984, award for excellence in undergrad. teaching U. Fla., 1991. Mem. AAAS, Am. Phys. Soc., N.Y. Acad. Scis., Sigma Xi. Home: 8407 NW 4th Pl Gainesville FL 32607-1414 Office: U Fla Dept Aerospace Engring Gainesville FL 32607

KURZWEIL, ARTHUR, publisher, writer, educator; b. N.Y.C., Aug. 10, 1951; s. Saul H. and Evelyn (Gottlieb) K.; (div. 1997); children: Pesha Malya, Miriam Golda, Moshe Yosef. BA, Hofstra U., 1971; MLS, Fla. State U., 1972. Libr. Plainfield (N.J.) Pub. Libr., 1972-74; freelance writer, 1974—; founding co-editor, co-pub. TOLEDOT: Jour. Jewish Genealogy, N.Y.C., 1976-79; editor Behrman House, West Orange, N.J., 1982-84; editor-in-chief Jewish Book Club, Northvale, N.J., 1985—; v.p. Jason Aronson Inc., Northvale, 1988—; lectr. Jewish Lecture Bur., N.Y.C., 1978-93, Sesil Lissberger, lecture and arts agy., Hillcrest, N.Y., 1984—; mem. faculty Midrasha Inst. for Jewish Studies, Whippany, N.J., 1988—. Author: From Generation to Generation: How to Trace Your Jewish Genealogy and Personal History, 1980, rev. edit., 1994, My Generations: A Course in Jewish Family History, 1984, (videotape) How to Trace Your Jewish Roots: A Journey with Arthur Kurzweil, 1995; contbg. author: The Jewish Catalog, 1976, The Third Jewish Catalog, 1978, The Jewish Almanac, 1977; co-editor: Behold a Great Image: Contemporary Jewish Experience in Photography, 1978, Ency. of Jewish Genealogy, 1991; editor: The Strife of the Spirit (Adin Steinsaltz), 1988, On Being Free (Adin Steinsaltz), 1995. Mem. adv. bd. B'nai B'rith Hillel, Hofstra U., Hempstead, N.Y., 1991—, Inst. for Contemporary Midrash, 1997—; bd. dirs. Elat Chayyim, 1997—. Recipient Disting. Humanitarian award Melton Ctr. for Judaic Studies, Columbus, Ohio, 1982. Mem. Assn. Jewish Book Pubs. (exec. bd. 1991—), Coalition for Advancement Jewish Edn., Jewish Book Coun. (pres. 1994-96), Aleph Soc. (bd. dirs. 1988—, founder, coord. Talmud Cir. Project 1993—), Beta Phi Mu. Avocations: collecting books, magician, genealogy. Office: Jason Aronson Inc 230 Livingston St Northvale NJ 07647-1731

KURZWEIL, EDITH, sociology educator, editor; b. Vienna; d. Ernest W. and Wilhelmine M. (Fischer) Weiss; m. Charles H. Schmidt, June 24, 1945 (div. 1958); children: Ronald J., Vivien A.; m. Mr. Kurzweil, Aug. 2, 1958 (dec. 1966); 1 child, Allen J. BA, Queens Coll., CUNY, 1967; MA, New Sch. Social Rsch., 1969, PhD, 1973. Asst. prof. sociology Hunter Coll., N.Y.C., 1972-75, Montclair State Coll., Upper Monclair, N.J., 1973-78; assoc. prof. sociology Rutgers U., Newark, 1979-85, prof. sociology, chmn., 1985-92; Disting. Olin. Prof. Adelphi U., 1993, univ. prof., 1994—; vis. prof. Goethe U., 1984. Author: The Age of Structuralism, 1980, Italian Entrepreneurs, 1983, The Freudians: A Comparative Perspective, 1989, Freudians and Feminists, 1995; editor: The Partisan Century: 60 Years of Partisan Review, 1996, (with others) Literature and Psychoanalysis, 1983, Writers and Politics, 1983, Cultural Analysis, 1984; exec. editor Partisan Rev., Boston, 1978-94, editor, 1994—; editl. bd. Psyche, 1990—, Psychoanalytic Books, 1996—; series editor Psychiatry and Psychology Transaction, 1995—. Mem. adv. bd. New Sch. Univ., 1998—. Rockefeller Humanities fellow, 1982-83, NEH fellow, 1987-88; NEH grantee, 1989-90, 91-92; NYCH grantee, 1995. Mem. Am. Sociol. Assn., Tocqueville Soc., Internat. Assn. History of Psychoanalysis, Internat. Sociol. Assn., Women's Freedom Network (bd. dirs. 1994—), P.E.N. Home: 1 Lincoln Plz New York NY 10023-7129 Office: Partisan Review 236 Bay State Rd Boston MA 02215-1403

KURZWEIL, HARVEY, lawyer; b. Bklyn., Mar. 23, 1945; s. Martin E. Kurzweil and Muriel (Krause) Kanow; m. Barbara Kramer, Aug. 17, 1969; children: David, Paul (dec.), Emily, Elizabeth. AB, Columbia Coll., 1966, JD, 1969. Bar: N.Y. 1970. Assoc. Dewey, Ballantine, Bushby, Palmer & Wood, N.Y.C., 1969-77, ptnr., 1977-90; ptnr. Dewey Ballantine, N.Y.C., 1990—, chmn. litigation dept., mem. mgmt. and exec. coms., 1990—. Bd. dirs. Vol. Lawyers for the Arts; trustee Menninger Found. Fellow Am. Bar Found.; mem. ABA, N.Y. State Bar Assn., D.C. Bar Assn., Assn. of Bar of City of N.Y. (trade regulation com. 1982-85), Univ. Club. Jewish. Avocations: sports cars, reading, gardening, sports. Home: 35 E 85th St New York NY 10028-0954 Office: Dewey Ballantine 1301 Avenue Of The Americas New York NY 10019-6022 also: 56 Hopper Farm Rd U Saddle Riv NJ 07458-1229*

KUS, JAMES STEDRY, geography educator, archaeologist; b. Cleve., Jan. 11, 1944; s. Alfred Otto and Dorothea Elizabeth (Sieferd) K.; m. Barbara Ann Roecker, Aug. 21, 1969 (div. Feb. 1985); children: James Alan, Elizabeth Ann; m. Claudia Ann Mader, July 18, 1989. BA, Case Western Res. U., 1965; MA, Mich. State U., 1965; PhD, UCLA, 1972. Prof. geography Calif. State U., Fresno, 1970—; prin. James S. Kus & Assocs., Clovis, Calif., 1986—. Contbr. articles to profl. jours. Mem. Fresno County Archaeol. Soc. (pres. 1990-92, 98-99, editor 1993-99, v.p. 1994-97). Home: 10528 E Sierra Ave Clovis CA 93611-9317 Office: Calif State U Fresno CA 93740

KUSAMA, YAYOI, sculptor, painter; b. Matsumoto-shi, Japan, Mar. 22, 1929; came to U.S., 1957, naturalized, 1963; Student, Kyoto (Japan) Arts and Crafts Sch., 1948-49. Pres. Japan Edn. Co., 1977—. Author: Manhattan Suicide Addict, 1978, Christopher Homosexual Brothel, 1983, Lost in Swapland, 1992, others; contbr. articles to mags. and newspapers; one-man shows include Aggregation One Thousand Boats, N.Y.C., 1963, Driving Image show, N.Y.C., 1964, Chrysler Mus., Provincetown, 1965, Castellane Gallery, N.Y.C., 1965, 66, Naviglio Gallery, Milan, Italy, 1966, 82 Thelen Gallery, Essen, Germany, 1966, Fillmore East Theatre Happening, 1968, Mus. Modern Art, N.Y.C., 1969, Fashion show Venice, Italy, 1971, The Haag, The Netherlands, 1971, Am. Ctr., Tokyo, 1980, Fuji Television Gallery, Tokyo, 1982, 84, 86, 88, 91, 94, Galerie Christian Cheneau, Paris, 1986, Musée des Beaux-Arts, Calais, 1986, Kitakyushu Mcpl. Mus., 1987, Musée Mcpl., Dôle, France, 1987, (retrospective) Ctr. for Internat. Contemporary Arts, N.Y.C., 1989, Mus. Modern Art, Oxford, London, 1989, Sogetsu Mus. Art, Tokyo, 1992, Niigata City Art Mus., 1992, Japan Pavilion Venezia Biennale, 1993, Galleria Valentina Moncada, Rome, 1993, Naviglio Venezia, 1993, Paula Cooper Gallery, N.Y.C., 1996, Robert Miller Gallery, N.Y.C., 1996, Baumgertner Galleries, Inc., Washington, 1997; group shows include Bklyn. Mus., 1955, 58, De Cordova Mus., Boston, 1960, 65, Riverside Mus., N.Y.C., 1960, Städtisches Mus., Schloss Morsbroish, Leverkusen, Germany, 1960, 61, Whitney Mus. Am. Art, N.Y.C., 1961, 62, Pitts. Mus., 1961, City Mus., Städtisches Mus., Trier, Germany, 1961, Nul Stedelijk Mus., Amsterdam, 1962, Inst. Contemporary Art, 1964, 65, Modern Art Gallery, Washington, 1965, Chrysler Mus., Provincetown, Mass., 1965, Mus. Modern Art, Stockholm, Sweden, 1966, Met. Mus., Tokyo, 1965, Mus. Modern Art, N.Y.C., 1966, Woman's Work-Am. Art, Phila., 1974, Improbable Furniture, U. Pa., 1977, Neich und Plastisch-Soft Art, Zurich, 1979, Nat. Mus. Art, Osaka, 1980, Nat. Mus. Modern Art, Tokyo, 1981, Yokohama City Gallery, 1982, Landmark Tower, Yokohama, 1993, Guggenheim Mus., 1994, Scream Against the Sky, San Francisco Mus. Modern Art, 1995, Otis Gallery, L.A., 1995, Ars 95, Helsinki, 1995, Louisiana Mus., Denmark, 1995, L.A. County Mus. Art, Mus. Modern Art, N.Y., Walker Art Ctr., 1998, Taipei Biennale, Taipei Art Fair, 1998, many others; represented in permanent collections Chrysler Mus., Stedelijk Mus., Amsterdam; organized, presented happenings worldwide. Invented infinity mirror room. Address: 1008 Ushigome Heim, 30-2 chome Haramachi Shinjuku-ku, Tokyo Japan

KUSE, JAMES RUSSELL, chemical company executive; b. Lincoln, Nebr., Aug. 20, 1930; s. Walter Herman and Gladys Katherine (Graham) K.; m. Shirley Rae Ernst, Sept. 27, 1953; children: Lynn Kuse Ehret, Carol Kuse Ehlen, Michael. B.S.Ch.E., Oreg. State U., 1955. Indsl. chems. salesman Ga.-Pacific Corp., Atlanta, 1967-68, mgr. splty. chem. div., 1968-70, mgr. chem. sales, 1970-74, mgr. coml. chems., 1974-76, v.p. chem. div., 1976-78, sr. v.p. chem. div., 1978-84; chmn. Ga. Gulf Corp., 1985—. Bd. dirs. Clark Coll., Atlanta, 1983. Served to cpl. U.S. Army, 1953-55. Mem. Am. Inst. Chem. Engrs., Am. Chem. Soc. Republican. Lutheran. Club: Capital City (Atlanta). Office: Georgia Gulf Corp Ste 595 400 Perimeter Center Ter NE Atlanta GA 30346-1264

KUSH, CHARLES ANDREW, III, telecommunications executive, entrepreneur; b. Somerville, N.J., Dec. 30, 1964; s. Charles A. Jr. and Barbara

A. (Zuris) K. BS in Mech. and Aerospace Engring., Rutgers U., 1987. Registered profl. engr. in tng., N.J. Prodn. engr. ITT Avionics, Clifton, N.J., 1987-88, project engr., 1988, program transition engr., 1988-89; pres. Creative Products, Middlesex, N.J., 1989—; info. mgr. AT&T, Piscataway, N.J., 1990-93, bus. mgr., 1994-97; portfolio mgr. Beechwood, Clark, N.J., 1997—. Recipient George R. Bolmer Meml. scholarship Bound Brook Rotary, 1983, Fisk Assocs. Engring. scholarship Fisk Assocs., 1983, Carl Rabke award for Citizenship and Scholarship, 1983, ITT Avionics Presdl. citations, 1988. Mem. ASME, AIAA, Nat. Soc. Profl. Engrs., Soc. Mfg. Engrs. (sr.), Internat. Platform Assn., Soc. Automotive Engrs., Assn. Old Crows, Nat. Mail Order Assn., Middlesex Borough Computer Com. Avocations: exercise, photography, travel, automobiles, boating.

KUSHEN, ALLAN STANFORD, retired lawyer; b. Chgo., Oct. 5, 1929; s. Barney and Ethel (Friedman) K.; m. Betty Cohen, Sept. 2, 1951; children: Annette Joyce, Robert Allan. BBA cum laude, U. Miami, Fla., 1952, LLB cum laude, 1952; LLM, NYU, 1955. Bar: Fla. 1952, N.Y. 1956. Atty. Schering Corp., Bloomfield, N.J., 1955-67; atty. counsel labs. divsn. Schering Corp., Bloomfield, 1967-69, atty. domestic ops. divsn., 1969-73; v.p., gen. counsel Schering-Plough Corp., Kenilworth, N.J., 1973-80; sr. v.p. pub. affairs Schering-Plough Corp., Madison, N.J., 1980-94; ret., 1994; adv. com. Allendale Ins. Co., N.Y., 1986-94; lectr. in field. Trustee Food and Drug Law Inst., 1972-94, Newark Mus., Am. Coun. for Arts. 1st lt. JAG, U.S. Army, 1952-54. Food and Drug Law Inst. fellow NYU, 1955. Mem. Phi Delta Phi, Omicron Delta Kappa, Iron Arrow. Home: 1 Raynor Rd West Orange NJ 07052-3004

KUSHEN, BETTY SANDRA, writer, educator; b. N.Y.C., Nov. 8, 1933; d. Moses and Betty (Cohen) Cohen; m. Allan Stanford Kushen; children: Annette Joyce, Robert Allan. BEd, U. Miami, 1954; MA, NYU, 1959, PhD, 1969. Author: (biography) Virginia Woolf and The Nature of Communion; assoc. editor Jour. Evolutionary Psychology; contbr. articles to Early Am. Lit., Lit. and Psychology, Am. Imago, Am. Writers Before 1800, Jour. Evolutionary Psychology. Mem. MLA, Virginia Woolf Soc. Jewish. Home: One Raynor Rd West Orange NJ 07052

KUSHINS, JOEL, communications executive. Exec. v.p., gen. mgr. TN Media, N.Y.C., 1994—. Office: TN Media 101 Park Ave New York NY 10178

KUSHLAN, JAMES A., biologist, research administrator, author, educator; b. Cleve., Oct. 11, 1947; m. Paula Frohring; children: Kristin, Philip. BS in Biology and Chemistry cum laude, U. Miami, 1969, MS in Biology, 1972, PhD in Biology, 1974; PhD (hon.), Thiele Coll., Greenville, Pa., 1996; DSc (hon.), John Cabot U., Rome, Italy. Rsch. biologist U.S. Dept. of Interior, 1975-84; dir. ctr. water resources studies Tex. A&M U., Commerce, 1986-88, assoc. prof. biology, 1984-87, prof. biology, 1987-88; prof. biology U. Miss., 1988-98, chmn. dept. biology, 1988-95; dir. Patuxent Wildlife Rsch. Ctr., 1995—; bd. dirs. Miss. Nature Conservancy, 1991-95, bd. dirs., Wetlands Internat., The Netherlands; bd. dirs. Wetlands Internat.-Americas, Can., Am. Ornithol. Union, Waterbird Soc., Ornithol. Coun.; policy coun. Am. Bird Conservancy . Author: (with J. Hancock) The Herons Handbook, 1984, Freshwater Fishes of Southern Florida, 1987, (with J. Hancock and M.P. Kahl) Storks, Ibises and Spoonbills of the World, 1992, Heron Conservation, 1999; contbr. chpts. to Environments of South Florida, Present and Past, 1974, Wading Birds, 1978, Rare and Endangered Biota of Florida, 1979, Crocodiles, 1982, Status and Management of Osprey and Eagles, 1983, Dictionary of Birds, 1985, Encyclopedia of Birds, 1985, Managing Cumulative Effects in Florida Wetlands, 1986, Ecosystems of Florida, 1990, The Rivers of Florida, 1991; editor Fla. Field Naturalist, 1981-86, Colonial Waterbirds, 1985-88; mem. editl. bd. Wetlands, 1982, assoc. editor, 1993-95; author 200 papers, revs., commentaries; contbr. articles to profl. jours. Active Maloy, Cmty. Improvement Assn., 1987, Tex. United Way Planning Coun., Oxford, Miss., 1991-92; trustee John Cabot U., Rome, 1992—; mem. policy coun. P & M Fohring Found., bd. dirs. Recipient Citizen award WIOD Radio, Miami, 1980; Paul Harris fellow Rotary Internat., 1989. Fellow Am. Ornithologists' Union (life, mem. coun., v.p., bd. dirs. 1994-97, v.p. 1998-99); mem. Soc. Wetland Scientist (life, assoc. editor), Colonial Waterbird Soc. (life, pres., v.p., editor jour.), Rotary (pres., dist. chair), Sigma Xi (chpt. pres. 1987-89). Achievements include research in ornithology, wetland sciences, international wetland and biodiversity conservation, and nature reserves. Office: PO Box 429 Annapolis MD 21404

KUSHLAN, SAMUEL DANIEL, physician, educator, hospital administrator; b. New Britain, Conn., Feb. 17, 1912; s. H. David and Bessie M. K.; m. Ethel Ross, June 24, 1934; children: Nancy Kushlan Wanger, David Ross. B.S., Yale U., 1932, M.D., 1935. Diplomate: Am. Bd. Internal Medicine with subsplty in gastroenterology. Intern New Haven Hosp., 1935-36, asst. resident, 1937; vol. research fellow Mass. Gen. Hosp., 1938; assoc. physician-in-chief Yale-New Haven Hosp., 1967-82, cons. to chief staff, 1982—; clin. prof. medicine Yale U., 1967—. Contbr. numerous articles to profl. jours. Chmn. bequest and endowment program Yale Med. Sch. Alumni Fund, 1977—. Named Physician of Yr. Conn. Digestive Disease Soc., 1975. Mem. Am. Gastroenterol. Assn., Am. Soc. Gastrointestinal Endoscopy, AMA, Conn. State Med. Soc., New Haven Med. Assn., Conn. Regional Soc. for Gastrointestinal Endoscopy, World Med. Assn., Assn. Yale Alumni in Medicine (pres. 1957-59), Yale Alumni Fund (bd. dirs. 1986-91), Sigma Xi, Alpha Omega Alpha. Office: Suite 1063 CB Yale-New Haven Hosp New Haven CT 06504 *Life must have Meaning.*

KUSHMA, DAVID WILLIAM, journalist; b. Phila., Oct. 27, 1954; s. John Joseph and Helen Elizabeth (Pusti) K.; m. Sandra Joe Cummins, June 2, 1989. BA in English, U. Pa., 1975; MA in Journalism and Mass Comm., U. Minn., 1977. Staff writer Phila. Bull., 1977-80; staff writer Detroit Free Press, 1980-87, editorial writer, 1987-92, assoc. editor, 1992-97; editl. page editor The Comml. Appeal, Memphis, 1997—. Mem. Am. Soc. Newspaper Editors, Nat. Conf. Editorial Writers. Office: The Comml Appeal 495 Union Ave Memphis TN 38103-3221

KUSHNER, AILEEN, medical/surgical nurse; b. Bklyn., Jan. 26, 1947; d. Harold and Gloria (Ostrofsky) Jarashow; divorced; Michelle, Adam, Brad. AS, SUNY, Farmingdale, 1983; student, SUNY, Stony Brook, 1988-89, Adelphi U., 1990-91, SUNY Regents Coll., 1993-96, Molloy Coll., 1997—. RN, N.Y. Staff nurse medicine, surgery Nassau County Med. Ctr., East Meadow, N.Y., 1983-89, med. head nurse, 1989-97, nurse liaison, case mgr. dept. phys. medicine and rehab., 1997—. Home: 3042 Lowell Ave Wantagh NY 11793-3221

KUSHNER, BRIAN HARRIS, pediatric oncologist; b. N.Y.C., July 8, 1951; s. William Isidore and Sheila Elaine (Kasselbranar) K.; m. Phyllis Debra Levinberg, Feb. 22, 1986; children: Sarah Lynn, Carolyn Joy. AB, Harvard U., 1972; MD, Johns Hopkins U., 1976. Diplomate Am. Bd. Pediatrics, Am. Bd. Pediatric Hematology-Oncology. Pediatric intern and resident Babies Hosp. of Columbia-Presbyn. Med. Ctr., N.Y.C., 1976-78; pediatric sr. resident N.Y. Hosp., N.Y.C., 1978-79; clin. fellow in pediatric hematology-oncology Children's Hosp., Boston, 1979-80; staff pediatrician Boston City Med. Clinics, North End Community Health Ctr., 1980-81; coord. in-patient svc., dir. ICU dept. pediatrics Lincoln Hosp., N.Y. Med. Coll., Bronx, 1982-83; clin. rsch. fellow in pediatric hematology-oncology Meml. Sloan-Kettering Cancer Ctr., N.Y.C., 1983-86, chief fellow dept. pediatrics, 1985-86, spl. fellow dept. pediatrics, 1986-87, clin. asst. pediatrician, 1987-92; asst. attending pediatrician dept. pediatrics N.Y. Hosp., N.Y.C., 1988—; asst. attending pediatrician Meml. Sloan-Kettering Cancer Ctr., N.Y.C., 1992—; staff physician Internat. Rescue Com., Khao-I-Dang Refugee Camp, Thailand, 1981; staff physician Oxfam Relief, Khiam, Lebanon, 1983; instr. in pediatrics Cornell U. Med. Coll., N.Y.C., 1987—, asst. prof. pediatrics, 1993—. Contbr. articles to Jour. Clin. Oncology, Jour. Pediatrics, Cancer, Blood, Leukemia, Med. Pediatric Oncology, Exptl. Cell Biology, others. Recipient Clin. Scholars Nat. Rsch. Svc. award, 1988-90, Career Devel. award Am. Cancer Soc., 1990-93; Am. Cancer Soc. grantee, 1993-95. Mem. Am. Acad. Pediatrics, Am. Assn. Cancer Rsch., Am. Soc. Clin. Oncology, Am. Soc. Hematology, Am. Soc. Pediatric Hematology-Oncology. Office: Meml Sloan Kettering Cancer Ctr 1275 York Ave # 299 New York NY 10021-6007

KUSHNER, DONN JEAN, microbiologist, children's author; b. Lake Charles, La., Mar. 29, 1927; arrived in Can., 1948; dual citizenship.; s. Sam and Lily (Donn) K.; m. Eva Milada Dubska, Sept. 15, 1949; children: Daniel Peter, Roland Joseph, Paul Joel. BSc in Chemistry, Harvard U., 1948; MSc, McGill U., 1950, PhD in Biochemistry, 1952. Postdoctoral fellow MGH Rsch. Inst., Montreal, Ont., Can., 1952-54; rsch. scientist Forest Insect Lab., Sault Ste. Marie, Ont., 1954-61, Nat. Rsch. Coun., Ottawa, Ont., 1961-65; assoc. prof. biology U. Ottawa, 1965-67, prof. biology, 1967-89, prof. emeritus biology, 1989—; prof. microbiology and botany U. Toronto, Ont., 1987-92, prof. emeritus microbiology and botany, 1992—; assoc. Can. Inst. Advanced Rsch., Toronto, 1987-93; invited lectr. in field; sabbaticals Nat. Inst. Med. Rsch., London, 1958-59, Pasteur Inst, Paris, 1972, McGill U., 1980-81, Cornell U., 1980-81, Inst. Jacques Monod, Paris, 1987. Author: The Witnesses and Other Stories, 1980, (children's books) The Violin-Maker's Gift, 1980 (Book of Yr. for Children award Can. Libr. Assn.), Dutch, German, Polish, French edit., 1983-87, Uncle Jacob's Ghost Story, 1984, German edit. 1987, A Book Dragon, 1987 (IODE Can. chpt. award, hon. mention Gov. Gen.'s award), The House of the Good Spirits, 1990, The Dinosaur Duster, 1992, A Thief Among Statues, 1993, French edit., 1994, The Night Voyagers, 1995, Life on Mars, 1998; editor: Microbial Life in Extreme Environments, 1978, Russian edit., 1982, Archives of Microbiology, 1986-94, Can. Jour. Microbiology, 1980-84; contbr. more than 160 articles to profl. jours. Fellow Am. Acad. Microbiology; mem. Can. Soc. Microbiologists (pres. 1980-81, award 1992), Ottawa Biol./Biochem. Soc. (award 1986), Am. Type Culture Collection (bd. sci. dirs. 1998—), Am. Soc. Biochemistry and Molecular Biology, Am. Soc. Microbiology, PEN, Writer's Union of Can., Can. Soc. of Children's Authors, Illustrators and Performers. Jewish. Avocations: music, playing violin and viola in chamber groups. Home: 63 Albany Ave, Toronto, ON Canada M5R 3C2 Office: Univ of Toronto, Dept of Botany, Toronto, ON Canada M5S 3B2

KUSHNER, EVA, academic administrator, educator, author; b. Prague, Czechoslovakia, June 18, 1929; d. Josef and Anna (Kafkova) Dubsky; m. Donn Jean Kushner, Sept. 15, 1949; children: Daniel Peter, Roland Joseph, Paul Joel. PhB, Coll. Marie de France, Montreal, 1946; BA, McGill U., 1948, MA, 1950, PhD in French Lit., 1956; D (hon.), Acadia U., 1988, United Theol. Coll., 1992, St Michael's U., 1993, U. Western Ont., 1996, U. Szeged, 1997. Lectr. French McGill U., Montreal, 1952-55, instr. French, 1956, 58, 61-62, 67-69, prof. French lang. and lit., 1976-87, chair dept. French, 1976-80; pres., vice chancellor Victoria U. U. Toronto, 1987-94, dir. ctr. comparative lit., 1994-95; sessional lectr. philosophy Sir George Williams U., 1952-53; lectr. U. Coll., London, 1958-59; lectr. Carleton U., 1961; asst. prof. French & comparative lit., 1963, assoc. prof., 1965, prof., 1969-76, chmn. comparative lit., 1965-69, 70-72, 75-76, adj. prof. lit., 1976-79; mem. exec. com. Can. Coun., 1975-81; v.p. Social Scis. & Humanities Rsch. Coun. Can., 1983-86; mem. adv. bd. Nat. Libr. Can.; pres. Humanities Rsch. Coun. Can. 1970-72; vice-chmn. George R. Gardiner Mus. Ceramic Arts, 1990-94. Author: Patrice de La Tour de Pin, 1961; Le Mythe d'Orphée dans la Littérature Française Contemporaine, 1961; Chants de Bohême, 1963; Rina Lasnier, Collection Ecrivains Canadiens d'Aujourd'Hui, 1964; Poètes d'Aujourd'Hui, 1969; Saint-Denys Garneau, 1967; François Mauriac, 1972, Japanese transl., 1976; co-author anthology Que. poetry, transl. into Hungarian, 1978, Polish, 1985; editor Renewals in the Theory of Literary History; co-editor/co-author: L'Avènement de l'Esprit Nouveau (1400-80), 1988, Théorie Littéraire: Problèmes et Perspectives, 1989, Histoire des Poétiques, 1997; editor, co-author La Problématique du Sujet chez Montaigne, 1995; co-dir. rsch. Renaissance vols. Histoire Comparée des Littératures de Langues Européennes; mem. editorial com. Can. Comparative Lit. Rev., Dalhousie French Studies, Etudes Montaignistes; mem. internat. adv. bd. Synthesis, Lit. Rsch., 1990-95; contbr. articles to profl. publs. Named Officer Order of Can., 1998. Fellow Royal Soc. Can. (v.p. 1980-82); mem. Academie Européenne des Lettres, des Sciences et des Arts, Am. Comparative Lit. Assn. (adv. bd.), Internat. Comparative Lit. Assn. (pres. 1979-82, co-editor proc. 7th and 9th ICLA Congress, 11th Congress, vols. IV-V, 1991, VI, 1992, VII-VIII, 1993, IX, 1994, X, 1995), Internat. Fedn. for Modern Langs. and Lits. (v.p. 1987-93, pres. 1996-99), MLA (del. assembly, chmn. 16th century French lit. divsn., mem. exec. coun. 1983-86, nominating com. 1986-88), Assn. Internat. des Études Françaises, Assn. Canadienne de Littérature Comparée (v.p. 1969-71), Internat. Assn. Neo-Latin Studies, Soc. Canadienne d'Études de la Renaissance, Assn. des Littératures Canadienne et Québecoise, Can. Soc. Semiotic Rsch., Assn. des Professeurs de Français des Universités Canadiennes, Renaissance Soc. of Am. (mem. coun. 1993-99). Office: Victoria Coll, 73 Queen's Park, Toronto, ON Canada M5S 1K7

KUSHNER, HAROLD JOSEPH, mathematics educator; b. N.Y.C., July 29, 1933; s. Hyman and Harriet Kushner; m. Linda Rosen, Sept. 20, 1960; children: Diana, Nina. BA, CCNY, 1955; MS, U. Wis.-Madison, 1956, PhD, 1958. Staff Lincoln Lab., Lexington, Mass., 1955-63, Rias, Balt., 1963-64; prof. applied math. Brown U., Providence, 1964—, dir. Lefschtez Ctr. Dynamical Systems, 1980—, chmn. div. applied math., 1988-91; cons. numerous govt. agys. and cos., 1964—. Author: Stochastic Stability and Control, 1967, Introduction to Stochastic Control Theory, 1972, Probability Methods for Approximations in Stochastic Control, 1977, Stochastic Approximation, 1978, Weak Convergence Methods and Applications to Stochastic Systems, 1984, Weak Convergence Methods and Singularly Perturbed Stochastic Control and Filtering Problems, 1991, Numerical Methods for Stochastic Control Problems in Continuous Time, 1992, Stochastic Approximation Algorithms and Applications, 1997. Recipient numerous grants U.S. govt. agys., 1964—, Louis E. Levy award Franklin Inst., 1994. Fellow IEEE (Control Systems award 1992); mem. Inst. Math. Stats., Soc. Indsl. and Applied Math., Ops. Rsch. Soc. Am., Inst. Mgmt. Sci. Home: 560 Lloyd Ave Providence RI 02906-5427 Office: Brown U Divsn Applied Math Providence RI 02912

KUSHNER, HAROLD SAMUEL, rabbi; b. N.Y.C., Apr. 3, 1935; s. Julius and Sarah (Hartman) K.; m. Suzette Estrada, Mar. 27, 1960; 1 child, Ariel. BA, Columbia U., 1955, MA, 1960; DHL, Jewish Theol. Sem., N.Y.C., 1972; DLH, U. Mass. Med. Ctr., 1987. Ordained rabbi 1960. Assoc. rabbi Temple Israel, Great Neck, N.Y., 1962-66; assoc. rabbi Temple Israel, Natick, Mass., 1966-90, rabbi laureate, 1991—. Author: When Bad Things Happen to Good People, 1981, When All You've Ever Wanted Isn't Enough, 1986, Who Needs God, 1990,To Life, 1993, How Good Do We Have To Be?, 1996. 1st lt. U.S. Army, 1960-62. Home: 20 Robinhood Rd Natick MA 01760-2553 Office: 145 Hartford St Natick MA 01760-3125 also: care Curtis Brown Ltd 10 Astor Pl New York NY 10003-6935

KUSHNER, HARVEY DAVID, management consultant; b. N.Y.C., Dec. 28, 1930; s. Morris K. and Hilda Kushner; m. Rose Rehert, Jan. 14, 1951 (dec. 1990); children: Gantt A., Todd R., Lesley K.; m. Patricia E. Sacks, Jan. 1997. BS in Engring., Johns Hopkins U., 1951. Assoc. engr. U.S. Navy Bur. Ships, 1951-53; mem. tech. staff Melpar Inc., 1953-54; with ORI Inc., 1955-88, pres., 1969-83; chmn. bd., CEO ORI, Inc., 1977-88; chmn. bd., pres. The ORI Group, Inc., 1985-88; v.p. Reliance Group Inc. (parent co. of ORI, Inc.), 1970-77; pres. Disclosure Inc., 1972-77; group pres., sr. v.p. Atlantic Rsch. Corp. parent co. of ORI Group, Inc., 1987-88; pres. Kushner Mgmt. Planning Corp., Bethesda, Md., 1988—; chmn. bd. trustees Maryland Venture Capital Trust, 1990—; cons. in bus. and tech. devel., mgmt. and orgn.; bd. dirs. CTA, Inc., MRJ Tech. Solutions, Inc., Stamet, Inc., Naviant Tech. Solutions Inc. Editor: If You've Thought About Breast Cancer. Chmn. Commn. Higher Edn. in Sci. and Tech., Montgomery County, Md., 1984-85, Md. Govs. High Tech. Roundtable, Annapolis, Md., 1983-86, United Way Campaign, Montgomery County, 1980, mem. exec. bd., 1981-85; bd. dirs. Suburban Md. High Tech. Coun., 1986-96, chmn. 1986-1991; chmn. bd. dirs. Rose Kushner Breast Cancer Adv. Ctr., 1990—; mem. nat. subcom. on breast cancer detection and control Am. Cancer Soc., 1991-95; mem. bd. vis. Sch. Pub. Affairs, U. Md., 1988-93, chmn., 1991-92; mem. nat. adv. coun. Sch. Engring. Johns Hopkins U., 1987—; mem. bd. vis. U. Md. Biotech. Inst., 1993—. Recipient Superior Pub. Svc. medal Dept. of Navy, 1988. Fellow N.Y. Acad. Scis.; mem. ASME, AAAS, IEEE (sr.), Nat. Security Indsl. Assn. (chmn. exec. com. 1987-88, chmn. anti-submarine warfare com. 1986-88, mem. bd. trustees 1982-97, vice-chmn. bd. trustees 1987-88, chmn. bd. 1988-89, Vice-Adm. Charles E. Weakley award 1991), Profl. Svcs. Coun. (bd. dirs. 1974—, v.p. 1983-88, chmn. bd. dirs. 1991-92), Inst. for Ops. Rsch. and the Mgmt. Scis., Am. Inst. Aerospace Sci., Nat. Def. Industry Assn. (trustee 1997—), Cosmos Club.

KUSHNER, JACK, physician executive; b. Montgomery, Ala., Dec. 5, 1939; s. Louis Harry and Rose (Feldman) K.; m. Annetta Esther Horwitz, June 21, 1964; children: Reyna, Eve. *In addition to his two children, Annetta and Jack, Dr. kushner has two grandchildren, Alison and Harrison.* BA, Tulane, 1960; MD, U. Ala., 1964; MGA, U. Md., 1990. Diplomate Am. Bd. of Neurosurgery. Intern George Washington U. Hosp., Washington, 1964-65; resident in surgery U. Mich., Ann Arbor, 1965-66; resident in neurosurgery Bowman Gray Sch. Medicine Wake Forest U., Winston-Salem, N.C., 1968-72; pvt. practice neurosurgery, Annapolis, Md., 1972-95; pres., CEO, Futuristic Instruments, Annapolis, 1995—; chmn., bd. dirs., CEO Futuristic Telmed, NY, Inc., 1998-99; speaker in field; bd. dirs. E-Global Telmed Solutions, 1999—. *Dr. Kushner has practiced medicine in one venue or another for thirty-five yearsand having practiced Neurosurgery for twenty-five years. After obtaining his Masters Degree in Finance, he started Futuristic Instruments. The company Futuristic Instruments became e-Futuristic Telmed Int., Inc. They have now merged with Millennium Health Solutions to become e-global Telmed Solutions, where he is CEO and Chairman of the Board of Directors. His company provides the technology and clinical applications for bringing tele-medicare and virtual reality surgical simulation to the world. This will transform the way health care is delivered and the manner in which surgeons are trained.* Author: Prepare To Tack: When Physicians Change Careers, 1995; contbr. articles to profl. jours. With U.S Army, 1966-68, Vietnam. Decorated Bronze Star. Fellow Am. Coll. of Surgeons (emerging tech. and edn. com.), Internat. Coll. of Surgeons; mem. Am. Assoc. Neurol. Surgeons, Congress of Neurol. Surgeons, So. Neurosurgical Soc., Pan Pacific Neurosurgical. Avocations: golf, tennis, yacht racing. E-mail: kushner20@aol.com. Fax: (410) 269-1457. Home: Ferry Farms 2030 Homewood Rd Annapolis MD 21402-1005

KUSHNER, JEFFREY L., manufacturing company executive; b. Wilmington, Del., Apr. 7, 1948; s. William and Selma (Kreger) K.; m. Carolyn Patricia Hypes, May 2, 1975; children: Tawnya Lynne. BBA summa cum laude, U. Hawaii, 1970; MBA, Columbia U., 1972. Sr. fin. analyst Black & Decker, Towson, Md., 1972-73; div. controller Black & Decker, Solon, Ohio, 1973-74; asst. div. controller Rockwell Internat., Pitts., 1974-75; div. contr. Carborundum Corp., Niagara Falls, N.Y., 1975-77; mgr. fin. planning United Techs. Corp., Hartford, Conn., 1977-80, corp. v.p. fin. planning, 1986-88, corp. v.p. asset mgmt., 1989-92; asst. contr. Sikorsky Aircraft, Stratford, Conn., 1980-82, div. controller, 1982-83, v.p. fin., chief fin. officer, 1983-85; v.p. fin. and adminstrn. MasterBrand Industries Inc., Deerfield, Ill., 1993-98; sr. v.p. fin. and CFO Lorillard Tobacco Co., 1998; exec. v.p., CFO Cookson Electronics, 1999—. Bd. dirs. ACR, Hartford. 1987-88. Recipient Bronfman Found. fellowship, 1970-71. Mem. Conf. Bd. (coun. 1987-88), Fin. Execs. Inst. Home: 1375 Saunders Rd Riverwoods IL 60015-1745

KUSHNER, LAWRENCE MAURICE, physical chemist; b. N.Y.C., Sept. 20, 1924; s. Hyman Tobias and Mary (Malkin) K.; children: Robb Adam, Leslie Meryl; m. Shirley Gayle Brown, June 24, 1972. B.S., Queens Coll., 1945; A.M., Princeton U., 1947, Ph.D., 1949. Teaching asst. Princeton U., 1947-48; with Nat. Bur. Standards, 1948-73, chief, metal physics sect., 1956-61, chief, metallurgy div., 1961-66; dep. dir. Inst. Applied Tech., 1966-68, dir., 1968, dep. dir. bur., 1969-73, acting dir., 1972-73; commr. Consumer Product Safety Commn., Washington, 1973-77; policy devel. Nat. Bur. Standards, 1977-80; mem. div. staff Mitre Corp., McLean, Va., 1980-85, cons. scientist, 1985-89; adj. prof. engring. and public policy Carnegie-Mellon U., 1981-91; lectr. chemistry Am. U., 1952-60; spl. asst. for legis. to asst. sec. of commerce for sci. and tech., 1964-65; mem. ad hoc internat. group metal physics OECD, 1961. Recipient Superior Accomplishment award Dept. Commerce, 1954, gold medal, 1968; Meritorious Svc. award Am. Nat. Standards Inst., 1973. Mem. Am. Phys. Soc., AAAS, Fed. Profl. Assn., Am. Chem. Soc., Washington Acad. Scis., ASTM (hon.), Sigma Xi (nat. pres. 1976, bd. dirs.). Spl. rsch. crystal properties, surface phenomena in chemistry and metallurgy, materials sci., product safety and environ. regulation, sci. and tech. policy, technol. innovation. Home: 20506 Beaver Ridge Rd Montgomery Village MD 20886-4326

KUSHNER, MARK JAY, physics and engineering educator; b. L.A., Dec. 21, 1952; s. Leonard Harry and Muriel (Chelin) K. BA, BS, UCLA, 1976; MS, Calif. Inst. Tech., 1977, PhD, 1979. Postdoctoral Calif. Inst. Tech., Pasadena, 1979-80; physicist Sandia Nat. Labs, Albuquerque, 1980-81, Lawrence Livermore (Calif.) Nat. Labs, 1981-83; dir. electron, atomic and molecular physics Spectra Tech., Bellevue, Wash., 1983-86; prof. U. Ill., Urbana, 1986—; chairperson Gaseous Electronics Conf., 1996-98. Assoc. editor Transactions Plasma Sci., 1989—; editl. bd. Plasma Sources Sci. and Tech., 1991—, Jour. Vacuum Sci. & Tech. A, 1998—; contbr. over 150 articles to tech. jours. Fellow IEEE, Am. Phys. Soc., Optical Soc. Am., Am. Vacuum Soc.; mem. Materials Rsch. Soc., Nat. Rsch. Coun.-Plasma Sci. Com., 1998—. Office: U Ill 1406 W Green St Urbana IL 61801-2918

KUSHNER, MICHAEL JAMES, neurologist, consultant; b. Hackensack, N.J., July 18, 1951; s. Samuel and Ruth Ellen (Paul) K.; m. Sarah Joan Warden, Aug. 14, 1976; children: Hunter Paul, Paul Macrae (dec.). BA in Physics, Yale U., 1973; MD, NYU, 1977. Diplomate Am. Bd. Psychiatry, Am. Bd. Neurology, Am. Bd. Med. Examiners; cert. Am. Bd. Electrodiagnostic Medicine, Am. Bd. Pain Medicine. Intern Parkland Meml. Hosp., U. Tex., Dallas, 1977-78; resident in neurology Neurol. Inst., Columbia-Presbyn. Med. Ctr., N.Y.C., 1978-81; rsch. assoc. U. Pa., Phila., 1981-83, asst. prof. neurology, 1983-90; attending physician Hosp. of U. Pa., Phila., 1983-90; with Wilson (N.C.) Neurology Ctr., 1992—; clin. asst. prof. East. Carolina U. Sch. Medicine, 1997—; dir. SPECT facility Hosp. of U. Pa., 1986-90, asst. dir. neurovascular lab., 1987-90; mem. sensory disorders and lang. study sect. NIH, Bethesda, Md., 1988-90; cons. Dupont Med. Products Div., Billerica, Mass., 1987—; staff neurologist Wilson (N.C.) Neurology Ctr.; legal medicine cons.; neurology physician advisor N.C. Blue Cross/Blue Shield; asst. prof. East Carolina U. Sch. Medicine; dir. Wilson Regional MRI Ctr. Contbr. numerous articles to profl. jours. Interviewer alumni schs. com. Yale U., Phila., 1984—. Fellow Am. Acad. Neurology, Am. Heart Assn. (stroke coun.); mem. AMA, Internat. Soc. for Blood Flow and Metabolism, N.C. Neurol. Soc. (pres. 1995-97), Yale of N.Y.C., Yale of Cen. N.C., Yale of N.C. Republican. Episcopalian. Avocations: oenology, travel, swimming, golf. Home: 1110 Salem St NW Wilson NC 27893-2137 Office: Wilson Neurology Ctr PO Box 3148 Wilson NC 27895-3148

KUSHNER, ROBERT ELLIS, artist; b. Pasadena, Calif., Aug. 19, 1949; s. Joseph and Dorothy (Browdy) K.; m. Ellen Saltonstall, Oct. 27, 1978; children: Max Saltonstall, Lila Saltonstall, Josef Nathaniel. BA, U. Calif., San Diego, 1971. One-man shows include DC Moore Gallery, N.Y.C., 1997, 98, Holly Solomon Gallery, N.Y.C., 1976, 79, 80, 82, 85, 87, 89-91, 94, Michael Lord Gallery, Milw., 1988-90, 93, Gallery Rudolf Zwirner, Cologne, Germany, 1982, 86, U. Colo. Art Gallery, Boulder, 1982, Am. Graffiti Gallery, Amsterdam, Netherlands, 1982, Studio Marconi, Milan, Italy, 1982, U. So. Calif. Helen Lindhurst Gallery, Los Angeles, 1982, James Mayor Gallery, London, 1978, 82, 86, 93, Castelli-Goodman-Solomon, East Hampton, N.Y., 1982, Whitney Mus., 1985, Inst. Contemporary Art, Phila., 1987-88, J.B. Speed Art Mus., Louisville, 1988, Aspen Art Mus., Colo., 1988, Wichita Art Mus., 1989, Staller Art Ctr., SUNY, Stony Brook, 1990, Am. Ctr. Tokyo, Osaka, Fukuoka and Sapporo, Japan, 1990-91, First Gallery, Moscow, 1991, Yoshiaki Inoue Gallery, Osaka, 1992, 94, 96, Gallery APA, Nagoya, Japan, 1994, 99, Midtown Payson Galleries, N.Y.C., 1992, 93, 95, Timothy Brown Fine Art, Aspen, Colo., 1992, 93, David Floria Gallery, Aspen, 1995, Hiroshima (Japan) Prefectural Mus., 1997, Lizan-Tops Gallery, East Hampton, N.Y., 1997, Bellas Artes, Santa Fe, 1997, N.J. Ctr. Visual Arts, Summit, N.J., 1998, Parchman Stremmel Gallery, San Antonio, Tex., 1998; exhibited numerous group shows including Whitney Mus. Am. Art, N.Y.C., 1975, 81, 82, 83, 85, Mus. Modern Art, N.Y.C., 1978, 80, 81, 83, 84, Albright-Knox Gallery, Buffalo, 1979, Bklyn. Mus., 1984, 86, Mpls. Inst. Arts, 1983, Phila. Inst. Contemporary Art, 1987, Sydney Art Mus., 1982, Venice Biennale, 1980, 84, Guggenheim Mus., Soho, N.Y., 1997, White Columns, N.Y., 1998; represented in permanent collections, Mus. Modern Art, Albright-Knox Mus., Buffalo, Tate Gallery, London, Whitney Mus. Am. Art, Met. Mus. Art, N.Y.C., Bklyn. Mus., Phila. Mus. Art, L.A. County Mus. Art, Balt. Mus. Art, Milw. Art Mus., Uffizzi Gallery, Florence; pub. commns. include Entex Bldg., Houston, 1985, 1270 Avenue of the Americas, Rockefeller Center, N.Y.C., 1991, Tower Place, Cin., 1991, Capital Group, L.A., 1996, Equitable Life Assurance Corp., N.Y., 1996, Royal Pines Golf Course, Kobe, Japan, 1996; artist numerous art performances, 1971-82; designer costumes, sets; author: (with Ed Friedman and Katherine Landman) The New York Hat Line, 1979; subj. of numerous publs. including Robert Kushner: Gardens of Earthly Delight, 1997. Office: DC Moore Gallery 724 5th Ave New York NY 10019-4106

KUSHNER, TODD ROGER, computer scientist, software engineer; b. Bethesda, Md., June 18, 1956; s. Harvey David and Rose Molly (Rehert) K.; m. Lea Louise Friedman, Nov. 11, 1990; children: Joshua Philip, Daniel Stuart. BS in Life Scis., MIT, 1976; MS in Computer Sci., U. Md., 1980, PhD in Computer Sci., 1982. Rsch. technician NIH, Bethesda, 1976-77; programmer Tech. Mgmt. Inc., Washington, 1977-78, GTE-Telenet, McLean, Va., 1978-79; grad. rsch. asst. U. Md., College Park, 1980-82, mem. rsch. staff, 1985-88; computer scientist SRI Internat., Menlo Park, Calif., 1982-83; sr. software engr. Vicom Sys. Inc., San Jose, Calif., 1983-85; sr. engr. Stanford Telecoms., Reston, Va., 1988-89; adv. programmer IBM Corp., Gaithersburg, Md., 1989-93; sr. scientist CTA Inc., Rockville, Md., 1993-96; mem. sr. software staff Lockheed Martin Fed. Systems, Denver, 1996—; adj. lectr. U. Santa Clara, Calif., 1983, U. Md., Gaithersburg, 1989-90, Johns Hopkins U., Gaithersburg, 1989-93; participant Software Process Interchange Network, McLean, Va., 1993—. Contbr. articles to profl. publs. Grad. fellow Air Force Office Sci. Rsch., 1980. Mem. IEEE Computer Soc., Assn. Computer Machinery. Democrat. Jewish. Avocations: swimming, racquetball, skiing, golf. Home: 6240 S Elmira Cir W Englewood CO 80111-5601 Office: Lockheed Martin Fed Systems PO Box 179 Denver CO 80201-0179

KUSHNER, TONY, playwright. Student, Columbia U., NYU. assoc. artistic dir. N.Y. Theatre Workshop, 1987; adj. faculty dramatic writing program NYU. Author: (plays) A Bright Room Called Day, 1990, Angels in America: A Gay Fantasia on National Themes Part I "Millenium Approaches," 1992 (Pulitzer Prize for drama 1993, Tony award Best Play 1993), Part II "Perestroika," 1993 (Tony award Best Play 1994), Slavs!, 1994; adaptor: The Illusion (Pierre Corneille), 1988; writer, dir.: Yes Yes No No: The Solice of Solstice, Apogee/Perigee, Bestial/Celestial Holiday Show, 1985, In Great Eliza's Golden Time, 1986. Recipient Writers award Whiting Found., 1990, AAAL award, 1994; NEA grantee 1985, 87, 93. *

KUSIAK, ANDREW, manufacturing engineer, educator; b. Kozia Wola, Poland, June 14, 1949; came to U.S., 1988; s. Stanislaw and Maria J. (Biernacka) K.; m. Anna B. Rakoczy, July 14, 1974; children: Derek, Dagmar E., Erik N.A. BS, Warsaw Tech. U., 1972, MS, 1974; PhD, Polish Acad. Scis., 1979. Project mgr. Inst. Mgmt. and Orgn., Warsaw, 1979-81; asst. prof. Tech. U. Nova Scotia, Halifax, 1982-85; assoc. prof. U. Manitoba, Winnipeg, 1985-88; prof., chair U. Iowa, Iowa City, 1988-95, prof., 1995—; cons. Rockwell Internat., Iowa City, 1989—, Motorola, Inc., Chgo., 1991—; editor in chief Chapman and Hall, London, 1990—; U.S. editor Taylor and Francis, London, 1990—; chmn. Artificial Intelligence Conf., London, 1990, Hybrid Systems Conf., Budapest, 1993, Prodn. Systems Conf., Winnipeg, 1987. Author: Intelligent Manufacturing, 1990, Engineering Design: Products, Processes, and Systems, 2000; editor: Intelligent Design, 1992, Artificial Intelligence, 1988, Expert Systems, 1988, Concurrent Engineering, 1993, 94, Handbook of Design Manufacturing and Automation, 1994. Active Iowa City Sci. Ctr., 1992. Recipient Publ. award Internat. Soc. for Productivity Enhancement, 1988, Outstanding Publ. award Inst. Indsl. Engrs., 1993. Mem. Ops. Rsch. Soc. Am., Soc. Mfg. Engrs. (sr., Publ. award 1990), Internat. Fedn. Automation and Control, Internat. Fedn. Info. Processing. Roman Catholic. Avocations: jogging, tennis. Home: 2629 Hickory Trl Iowa City IA 52245-3522 Office: U Iowa Dept Indsl Engring Iowa City IA 52242-1527

KUSKA, JOHN JOSEPH, JR., accountant; b. Balt., Feb. 27, 1953; s. John Joseph and T. Virginia (Branham) K.; 1 child, Jennifer L. BA magna cum laude, Lycoming Coll., 1975. CPA, Md.; registered rep. Staff acct. Deloitte & Touche (H & S), Balt., 1975-76; sr. acct. Henry E. Pear & Co., Laurel, Md., 1977-78; corp. sec. Nu-Homes, Inc., Columbia, Md., 1979-80; mgr. Barry S. Fishman & Assocs., Bethesda, Md., 1981-87; prin. John J. Kuska, Jr. & Co., Laurel, 1987—. Winner Durant Furey Meml. award (first in acctg. class) Lycoming Coll., 1975. Mem. AICPA, Md. Assn. CPAs. Republican. Avocations; bicycling, hunting. Office: 9342 Whiskey Bottom Rd Laurel MD 20723-1328

KUSMA, KYLLIKKI, lawyer; b. Tartu, Estonia, Dec. 8, 1943; came to U.S., 1951, naturalized, 1958; d. August and Helju (Traat) K.; B.F.A., Ohio U., 1966; M.A. (Vets. Rehab. Adminstrn. fellow), Ohio State U., 1967; J.D., Ohio No. U., 1976; M.L.T., Georgetown U., 1980. Bar: Ohio 1977, D.C. 1978. Speech and hearing therapist Lima (Ohio) Meml. Hosp., 1967-70, Tipp City (Ohio) Schs., 1970-74; atty.-adv. Office Chief Counsel, IRS, Washington, 1977-81; v.p., asso. tax counsel Security Pacific Nat. Bank, Los Angeles, 1981-83; ptnr. Brownstein Zeidman & Lore, Washington, 1983-95, Ernst & Young LLP, Columbus, Ohio, 1995—; instr. Wright State U., 1972-76. Author: (with others) Mortgage-Backed Securities Special Update: REMICs, 1988. Vol. local civic, polit. activities; contbr. articles to profl. jours. Mem. ABA, Columbus Bar Assn., Ohio Bar Assn., D.C. Women's Bar Assn., Phi Kappa Phi. Democrat. Office: Ernst & Young LLP 10 W Broad St Ste 2300 Columbus OH 43215-3400

KUSMIN, ELLYN SUE, music administrator; b. Boston, May 13, 1960; d. Murray and Phyllis (Nannis) K. BA, Oberlin Coll., 1982. Press assoc. Carnegie Hall, N.Y.C., 1982-83; gen. mgr. Sheldon Soffer Mgmt., N.Y.C., 1983-90; ops. mgr. N.Y. Philharmonic, N.Y.C., 1990-95; asst. to Maestro Andre Previn, N.Y.C., 1995—; freelance cons. Boston Symphony Orch., 1982—, mgmt. fellow Nat. Endowment for the Arts, Washington, 1987. Democrat. Jewish. Home: 101 W 81st St Apt 418 New York NY 10024-7228 Office: Manderville Enterprises 459 Columbus Ave # 249 New York NY 10024-5129

KUSNET, DAVID, speechwriter, commentator; m. Ruth Wattenberg, 1991; 1 child, Michael. BA in Polit. Sci., Yale U., 1973. Reporter Staten Island Advance, N.Y.C., 1972-74; speechwriter Am. Fedn. State, County and Mcpl. Employees, 1974-76; dir. pub. rels. Am. Fedn. State, County and Mcpl. Employees, Ill., 1976-77; pub. rels. troubleshooter Am. Fedn. State, County and Mcpl. Employees, 1977-82, field coord. pub. affairs dept., 1982-84; speechwriter Dem. Presdl. candidate Walter F. Mondale, 1984; dir. comm. People for the Am. Way, 1985-86, v.p., 1986-89; speechwriter Dem. Presdl. candidate Michael Dukakis, 1988; freelance writer, cons., 1989-92; chief speechwriter Dem. Presdl. candidate Bill Clinton, 1992; spl. asst. to Pres. Clinton for speechwriting Washington, 1993-94; cons. in field; vis. fellow Econ. Policy Inst., 1995. Author: Speaking American: How the Democrats Can Win in the Nineties, 1992; (with John J. Sweeney) American Needs a Raise, 1996; contbr. revs., articles newspapers, mags. E-mail: dkusnet@epinet.org. Office: Econ Policy Inst 1660 L St NW Ste 1200 Washington DC 20036-5632

KUSPIT, DONALD BURTON, art historian, art critic, educator; b. N.Y.C., Mar. 26, 1935; s. Morris and Celia (Schmukler) Kuspit Sigmund; m. Judith Clements Price, Mar. 22, 1962. BA in Philosophy with distinction, Columbia U., 1955; MA in Philosophy, Yale U., 1957; DPhil magna cum laude, U. Frankfort, 1960; PhD in Art History, U. Mich., 1971; DFA, Davidson Coll., 1993, San Francisco Art Inst., 1996; LHD (hon.), U. Ill., 1998. Asst. prof. Pa. State U., State College, 1960-66; assoc. prof. U. Windsor, Ont., Can., 1966-70; prof. U. N.C., Chapel Hill, 1970-78; Univ. Disting. prof. Rutgers U., New Brunswick, N.J., 1982-83; prof. art, chmn. dept. art SUNY-Stony Brook, 1978-83; editorial cons. UMI Rsch. Press, Ann Arbor, Mich., 1980-90; Andrew Dixon White prof. at large Cornell U., Ithaca, N.Y., 1991-97; editorial cons. Cambridge U. Press, 1991—; mem. overview com. visual arts sect. NEA, Washington, 1983-85. Author: Clement Greenberg, Art Critic, 1979, The Critic as Artist: The Intentionality of Art, 1984, Leon Golub: Existentialist/Activist Painter, 1985, The New Subjectivism: Art of the 1980's, 1988, Eric Fischl, 1988, Louise Bourgeois, 1989, Alex Katz: Night Paintings, The Dialectic of Decadence, 1993, The Cult of the Avant-Garde Artist, 1993, Signs of Psyche in Modern and Post-Modern Art, 1993, Albert Renger-Patzch, 1993, Primordial Presences: The Sculpture of Karel Appel, 1994, Idiosyncratic Identities: Artists at the End of Avant-Garde, 1996, Health and Happiness in Twentieth Century Avant-Garde Art, 1996, Dale Chihuly, 1997, Jamali, 1997, Joseph Raffael, 1998; contbg. editor Art in Am., 1978-92, Contemporanea, 1988-90, ArtForum, 1992—, Sculpture Mag., 1992—, New Art Examiner, 1993—; editor Art Criticism, 1984—. Younger humanist fellow NEH, 1973, critic fellow Nat. Endowment for Arts, 1977, Guggenheim fellow, 1977. Fellow Asian Cultural Coun.; mem. PEN, Coll. Art Assn. (Frank Jewett Mather award 1983), Am. Soc. Aesthetics, Internat. Assn. Art Critics (v.p. Am. sect. 1982-84), Am. Psychoanalytic Assn. Home: 38 W 26th St New York NY 10010-2012 Office: SUNY Dept Art Stony Brook NY 11794-5400

KUSS, JOSEPH, municipal official; b. Ill., Feb. 3, 1947. Acting pres. City of St. Louis, Bd. Pub. Svc., 1997-98; dep. city engr. City of St. Louis Bd. Pub. Svc., 1991—. Office: City of St Louis 301 City Hall 1200 Market St Saint Louis MO 63103-2826*

KUSSEL, WILLIAM FERDINAND, JR., lawyer; b. Norway, Mich., July 30, 1957; s. William F. and Mitzi (Markus) K.; m. Maria Salas, July 26, 1995. BS, St. Norbert Coll., 1979; JD, Southwestern U., 1984. Bar: Calif. 1985, D.C. 1985, Minn. 1986, Wis. 1989. Law clk. Wis. Cir. Ct., Marinette, 1982; law extern L.A. Dist. Atty.'s Office, 1983; pros. Menominee Indian Reservation, Keshena, Wis., 1986-92; program atty. Menominee Indian Tribe Wis., Keshena, 1992—. Mem. ABA, Calif. Bar Assn., Minn. Bar Assn., D.C. Bar Assn., Wis. Bar Assn. Avocations: photography, snowmobiling, boating, motorcycling. Office: Menominee Indian Tribe Office Program Atty PO Box 910 Keshena WI 54135-0910

KUSSEROW, RICHARD PHILLIP, government official, business executive; b. San Jose, Calif., Dec. 9, 1940; s. Roger Berthold and Eve W. (Larson) K.; m. Rebecca Kusserow, Sept. 14, 1985; 1 child, Carrie Elizabeth. BA in Polit. Sci, UCLA, 1963; MA in Govt., Calif. State U., L.A., 1964; postgrad., So. Meth. U., 1965, John Marshall Sch. Law, 1972, Harvard U., 1984. Cert. internal auditor, cert. govt. auditor; cert. govt. fin. mgr., cert. fraud examiner. Lectr. Calif. State U., L.A., 1963, 64; case officer CIA, 1968-69; spl. agt. supr. in white collar and organized crime FBI, 1969-81; insp. gen. U.S. Dept. HHS, 1981-92; mem. Pres.'s Coun. on Integrity and Efficiency, 1981-92, vice chmn., 1986-89, chmn. legislation com., 1982-85, 89-92; mem. Pres.' Council on Mgmt. Improvement, 1986-89, 91-92; chair Nat. Task Force of Implementation of Chief Fin. Officers Act, 1990-91; chmn. Chief Fin. Officers Task Force, 1991; pres. Strategic Mgmt. Sys., Inc., 1992—, Govt. Mgmt. Svcs., Inc., 1994—; pres., CEO Nat. Hotline Svc., 1995—; Presdl. appointee to Nat. Adv. Commn. on Law Enforcement, 1989; mem. CFOs Coun., 1990-92, Def. Procurement Round Table, 1993—; lectr. white collar crime, asset protection, health care, fraud and abuse, internal controls, corporate compliance programs, others; mem. Atty. Gen.'s Econ. Crime Coun., 1988-90; nat. chmn. Am. Compliance Inst., 1995. Author: Principles of Investigative Targeting, 1974; co-author: Management Principles for Asset Protection, 1986; contbr. articles on corp. compliance investigations, auditing and mgmt. to profl. jours. Pres. Nat. Honor Svc., 1996—. Capt. USMCR, 1964-68. Recipient Sec.'s Bronze medal for good govt., 1983, Outstanding Leadership award Pres. Coun. on Mgmt. Improvement, 1988, Cert. of Svc. Appreciation, Pres. of U.S., 1989, Donald L. Scantlebury award Assn. Govt. Accts., 1992; H. Horton Rontree Disting. lectr. in health law, 1990. Mem. Assn. Fed. Investigators (nat. pres. 1984-85, chmn. awards com. 1986-87), Soc. Former FBI Agts., Assn. Govt. Accts. (nat. task force on fed. fin. mgmt. 1983-88, pres. Balt. chpt. 1987, chmn. nat. profl. devel. conf. 1989, nat. pres. 1990, nat. leadership awards Boston chpt. 1985, No. Va. chpt., Washington chpt., D.C. chpt. 1985, Nat. Assn. 1987), Nat. Health Lawyers Assn., Nat. Health Care Anti-Fraud Assn. (pub. svc. award 1989), Inst. Internal Auditors (cert.), Am. Compliance Inst. (governing bd. 1996-99), Army-Navy Club. Presbyterian. Avocations: reading, travel, tennis.

KUSSROW, NANCY ESTHER, educational association administrator. BA, Valparaiso U., 1952; MA, U. N.C., 1954. Exec. dir. Nat. Assn. prins. of Schs. for Girls; ret., 1996.

KUSTERER, THOMAS, environmental planner; b. Balt., July 9, 1946; s. Edward Thomas and Anne Thelma (Ekas) K.; m. Janet Elizabeth Polunas, Sept. 16, 1972; children: David, Robert. BS, Loyola Coll., 1968, MBA, 1982; MS, Rutgers U., 1972. Instr. Balt. C.C., 1968-69; cons. Benedict (Md.) Estuarine Lab., 1971-72; planner Harford County (Md.) Govt., Bel Air, Md., 1972-84; natural resources mgr. Md. Dept. of the Environ., Balt., 1984-89; sr. environ. planner Montgomery County Govt., Rockville, Md., 1989—; mem. Md. Coastal Resources Adv. Com., 1984-88, Govs. Solid Waste Mgmt. Task Force, 1987, Md. Acid Deposition Adv. Com., 1984-88, nat. round table on unit pricing for solid waste collection and disposal U.S. EPA, 1992, nat. round table on full cost acctg. for solid waste mgmt. systems, 1994. Contbg. author/advisor: Pay As You Throw: Lessons Learned about Unit Pricing, 1994; contbg. author Developing Agreements on the Siting of Waste Management Facilties, 1994, Innovative Approaches to Siting Solid Waste Management Facilities, 1992; editor (newsletter) Md. Environ., 1986, 87; contbr. articles to profl. jours. Mgr. youth sports teams Parks and Recreation Depts., Howard and Balt. Counties, 1983-97; officer Md. Save Our Streams, Annapolis, 1973-76, Balt. County Growth Control, Perry Hall, Md., 1982-84; officer Hist. Ellicott City, Inc. Recipient Environtl. Svcs. award Pub. Technology Inst., 1991, Environtl. Merit award Take Pride in Am., 1990. Mem. Air and Waste Mgmt. Assn., Water Environment Fedn., Audubon Soc., Md. Sci. Ctr., Howard County Hist. Soc., Balt. Mus. Art. Democrat. Roman Catholic. Avocations: tennis, swimming, birding. Home: 3796 Dorsey Search Cir Ellicott City MD 21042-3753 Office: Montgomery County Govt 101 Monroe St Rockville MD 20850-2580

KUSTIN, KENNETH, chemist; b. Bronx, N.Y., Jan. 6, 1934; s. Alex and Mae (Marvisch) K.; m. Myrna May Jacobson, June 24, 1956; children—Brenda Jayne, Franklin Daniel, Michael Thorpe. B.Sc., Queens Coll., Flushing, N.Y., 1955; Ph.D., U. Minn., 1959. Postdoctoral fellow Max Planck Inst. for Phys. Chemistry, Göttingen, Germany, 1959-61; asst. prof. chemistry Brandeis U., Waltham, Mass., 1961-66, assoc. prof., 1966-72, prof., 1972-97, prof. emeritus, 1997—, chmn. dept. chemistry, 1974-77; prof. emeritus, 1997—; vis. prof. pharmacology Harvard U. Med. Sch., 1977-78; Fulbright-Hays lectr., 1978; program dir. NSF, 1985-86; adj. rsch. scientist U.S. Army, Natick RD&E Ctr., 1991—. Editor: Fast Reactions, vol. 16 of Methods in Enzymology, 1969; bd. editors Internat. Jour. Chem. Kinetics, 1983-90, Inorganic Chemistry, 1993-95; rsch. and publs. in field. Mem. AAAS, Am. Chem. Soc. (councilor 1983-85), Phi Beta Kappa.

KUSTURICA, EMIR, film director; b. Sarajevo, Yugoslavia, 1955. Films include: Do You Remember Dolly Bell?, 1981, When Father Was Away on Business, 1985 (Palme d'Or Cannes Internat. Film Festival, 1984), Time of the Gypsies, 1989, Arizona Dream, 1992 (Spl. Jury prize, Berlin, 1993), Underground, 1995 (Palme d'Or for best film Cannes Internat. Film Festival, 1995); dir. Chat noir, Chat blanc, 1997. Office: c/o October Films 65 Bleecker St New York NY 10012*

KUTA, JEFFREY THEODORE, lawyer; b. Oak Park, Ill., Aug. 30, 1947; s. Stanley Joseph and Helen Mary (Terpin) K.; m. Diane LaVerne Jancovic, June 22, 1969; children: Jonathan Paul, Joseph Anthony. BA with honors, U. Chgo., 1969, JD, 1972. Bar: Ill. 1972, U.S. Dist. Ct. (no. dist.) Ill. 1972. Assoc. Hopkins & Sutter, Chgo., 1972-76; assoc. to ptnr. Newman, Stahl & Shadur, Chgo., 1976-80; ptnr. Holleb & Coff, Chgo., 1981—; instr. Chgo. Kent Coll. Law, 1978-79; adj. prof. John Marshall Law Sch., 1996—. Sec. Chgo. Equity Fund, Inc., 1985—; sec. Nat. Equity Fund, Inc., 1987-89, sec. Cmty. Reinvestment Fund, Inc., 1997—. Mng. editor U. Chgo. Law Rev., 1971-72. Mem. ABA (mem. spl. com. on housing and urban devel. law 1987-91, editor ABA Jour. Affordable Housing and Cmty. Devel. Law 1991-93, mem. governing com. of forum on affordable housing and cmty. devel. law 1992-95, chmn. 1993-94), Chgo. Bar Assn. (chmn. mag. 1982-83), Chgo. Coun. Lawyers, U. Chgo. Alumni Assn. (v.p. 1973-76, chmn. law jour. 1973-76), Cliff Dwellers Club, Lambda Alpha Internat. Home: 442 W Melrose St Chicago IL 60657-3834 Office: Holleb & Coff 55 E Monroe St Ste 4100 Chicago IL 60603-5896

KUTCHINS, MICHAEL JOSEPH, aviation consultant, former airport executive; b. Chgo., IL, Dec. 1, 1941; s. Jack M. and Bernice L. K.; children: Bradley Charles, Scott Freeman. B.S., U. Ill., 1962. Accredited airport exec. Reporter Sta. WICD-TV, Danville, Ill., 1962-63, Sta. WSOY AM-FM, Decatur, Ill., 1963-65; bus. editor, reporter Sta. WSOC AM-FM-TV, Charlotte, N.C., 1965-67; adminstrv. asst. to mgr. Douglas Mcpl. Airport, Charlotte, 1968-71; asst. dir. aviation San Antonio Internat. Airport, 1971-81, dir. aviation, 1981-87; prin. Aviation Cons. Svcs., San Antonio, 1987—. Mem. Am. Assn. Airport Execs. (pres. 1985-86, pres. South Cen. chpt. 1976). Home & Office: 13426 Vista Del Rey San Antonio TX 78216-2233

KUTEMEYER, PETER MARTIN, industrial engineering executive; b. Freiburg, W. Germany, Nov. 19, 1938; came to U.S., 1954, naturalized, 1956; s. Martin Henry and Gertrude Barbara (Buechel) K.; m. Fresquez, June 25, 1961 (div. Aug. 1986); children: Michael, Kristina. BME with distinction, Ariz. State U., 1968, MS in Engring. Mechanics, 1969; MBA, U. Utah, 1977. Enlisted USAF, 1958, commd. 2d. lt. 1967, advanced through grades to capt., 1970; aero. engr., 1969-71, systems devel. engr., 1971-74, tech. liaison officer to W. German Fed. Govt., 1974-78; ret., 1978; indsl. mgr. Mining Progress, Inc., Highland Mills, N.Y., 1978-79, prodn. mgr., 1979-81; gen. mgr. Bischoff Environ. Systems div. Intertech Inc., Highland Mills, 1981-89; pres. PMK Enterprises, Inc., Wilmington, Del., 1989—; v.p., gen. mgr. Westfalia Ind. Equ. Inc., 1989-92. Mem. ASME, AIAA. Home: 5225 Pooks Hill Rd Apt 1020S Bethesda MD 20814-6718 Office: PMK Enterprises Inc # 543 2207 Concord Pike Wilmington DE 19803-2908

KUTER, KAY E., writer, actor; b. L.A., Apr. 25, 1925; s. Leo E. and Evelyn Belle (Edler) K. *The first Kuter to emigrate from Germany was Bernhard Kuter, in 1748. His sons were Revolutionary War captains under "Mad" Anthony Wayne. Maternal great-grandparents, Jessie McGill and Giovanni Maggginetti emigrated from Scotland and Switzerland, respectively, marrying and traveling to Salt Lake City by covered wagon in 1868. Jessie McGill Magginetti appeared with Harry Lauder at the Great Salt Lake Theatre, beginning family's theatrical tradition. Mother acted in silent films. Father was a pioneer motion picture art director, 1920-1965, designing over 300 films, and a founder, later president, of the Society of Motion Picture and Television Art Directors.* Student, Pomona Coll., 1943, UCLA, 1944; BFA in Drama, Carnegie Inst. Tech., 1949. Radio actor NBC, 1944; actor, 1944—. Actor in 198 musicals, off-Broadway, stock, repertory, touring, and Shakespearean stage prodns.; 45 feature films; more than 400 TV shows, including 7 yrs. as a series regular (Newt Kiley) in Green Acres and Petticoat Junction; voiceover actor for cartoon series Aladdin, The Little Mermaid, The Little Mermaid II, Prince Valiant, Biker Mice From Mars, Fantastic Four; in cartoon spls. Olympic Mascot Izzy, Annabelle's Wish, The Jungle Book: Mowgli's Story; in CD-ROMS The Beast Within, Ultima 9, Grim Fandango, The Curse of Monkey Island, Heretic II; in radio prodns. Getting Married, Treasure Island, Macbeth, Satanic Verses, Heartbreak House; author: Carmen Incarnate, 1946, Ships That Never Sailed, 1994, Hollywood Houdini, Picture Perfect World, 1995; voiceover spokesman Hershey's Kisses, 1989—; editor: The Jester, 1956-60, The Jester 35th Anniversary, 1960, 50th Anniversary, 1976; contbr. to Nat. Libr. Poetry anthologies, 1995, 96, 97; dir. more than 50 stage prodns. including Steve Allen's The Wake. Bd. dirs. Family Svc. of L.A., 1950-70. Mem. SAG (bd. dirs. 1970-73), ADA, AEA, AFTRA, ACLU, NOW, NARAL, Internat. Platform Assn., Book Publicists of So. Calif., Nat. Soc. Hist. Preservation, Smithsonian, Carnegie Mellon U. Westcoast Drama Alumni Clan (founding mem., officer, bd. dirs. 1968-80), Ephebian Soc., Internat. Soc. Poets (disting. mem.), Albert C. May Soc., Acad. Am. Poets, Andrew Carnegie Soc., Pacific Pioneer Broadcasters, Carnegie Mellon U. Alumni Assn. (regional v.p. 1976-79, Svc. award 1979), Masquers Club (bd. dirs. 1953-75, rec. sec. 1956-70, corr. sec. 1957-69. v.p. 1971-75), Actors' Fund of Am. (life mem.), others. Democrat. Avocations: composing, set design, piano. Home: 6207 Satsuma Ave North Hollywood CA 91606-3819

KUTKA, NICHOLAS, nuclear medicine physician; b. Czechoslovakia, Dec. 17, 1926; s. Vladimir and Agatha (Flenko) K.; m. Anna Cizmar, Aug. 14, 1965 (dec. Oct. 1996); children: Andrew, Gregory. MD, Comenius U., Bratislava, Czechoslovakia, 1951; PhD, Slovak Acad. Scis., Bratislava, 1962. Diplomate in internal medicine Postgrad. Edn. of Physicians; diplomate Am. Bd. Nuclear Medicine. Asst. prof. inst. physiology Comenius U., Bratislava, 1951; intern, resident in internal medicine Mil. Hosp., Bratislava, 1952-55; chief dept. inst. endocrinology Slovak Acad. Scis., Bratislava, 1956-69; tech. asst. Internat. Atomic Engery Agy., Bogota, Colombia, 1969-70; resident in nuclear medicine Duke U., 1971-73; asst. prof. radiology Baylor Coll. Medicine, Houston, 1973-95, assoc. prof. radiology, 1995—; dir. nuclear medicine Ben Taub Gen. Hosp., Houston, 1978-81; chief nuclear medicine service VA Med. Ctr., Houston, 1982-96, staff physician, 1996—; mem. med. staff univ. affiliated hosps. Houston, faculty Sch. Nuclear Medicine Tech.; fellow Internat. Atomic Energy Agy., Rome, 1962-63. Contbr. numerous articles to profl. jours; mem. editorial bd. Endocrinologia Experimentalis. Served with Health Service Czechoslovak Army, 1952-54. Recipient prize in nuclear medicine J.E. Purkyne, 1965. Mem. Harris County Med. Soc., Tex. Med. Assn., Soc. Nuclear Medicine, Am. Coll. Nuclear Physicians. Address: 2002 Holcombe Blvd #115 PO Box 20183 Houston TX 77225-0183

KUTLER, STANLEY IRA, history and law educator, author; b. Cleve., Aug. 10, 1934; s. Robert P. and Zelda R. (Coffman) K.; m. Sandra J. Sachs, June 24, 1956; children: Jeffrey, David, Susan, Andrew. BA, Bowling Green State U., 1956; PhD, Ohio State U., 1960. Instr. history Pa. State U., State College, 1960-62; asst. prof. San Diego State U., 1962-64; from asst. prof. to prof. U. Wis., Madison, 1964-80, E. Gordon Fox prof. Am. instns., law and history, 1980—; disting. exchange scholar to China Nat. Acad. Scis., 1982; Kenneth Keating lectr. Tel Aviv U., 1984; sr. Fulbright lectr. to Japan, 1977, to Israel, 1985, China, 1986; disting. vis. Fulbright scholar, Peru, 1987; Bicentennial prof. Tel Aviv U., 1985; cons. NEH, 1975—, The Constitution Project, 1985—; disting. chair Polit. Sci., U. Bologna, 1991; hist. cons. BBC/Discovery series Watergate, 1994. Author: Judicial Power and Reconstruction, 1968, Privilege and Creative Destruction, 1971, 2d edit., 1990, The American Inquisition, 1983, The Wars of Watergate: The Last Crisis of Richard Nixon, 1990, 92, Abuse of Power: The New Nixon Tapes, 1997; editor: Supreme Court and the Constitution, 1969, 3d edit., 1984, Looking for America, 1975, 80, The Encyclopedia of the Vietnam War, 1995, Encyclopedia of 20th Century America, 1995, American Perspectives: Historians on Historians, 1996, Watergate: The Fall of Richards Nixon, 1996, Dictionary of American History, 10 vols., 1996—; founding editor Rev. in Am. History, 1972-97; mem. adv. editor Greenwood Pub., 1968-73, Johns Hopkins U. Press, 1982—. Recipient Silver Gavel award ABA; fellow Sage Found., 1967-68, Emmy award, 1994, Peabody award, 1994; fellow Guggenheim Found., 1971-72, Rockefeller Found., 1979-80. Jewish. Office: U Wis Dept History Madison WI 53706

KUTNER, JANET, art critic, book reviewer; b. Dallas, Sept. 20, 1937; m. Jonathan D. Kutner, Jan. 15, 1961. Student, Stanford U., 1955-57; BA in English, So. Meth. U., 1959. Asst. dir. Dallas Mus. Contemporary Arts, 1959-61; art critic, book reviewer Dallas Morning News, 1970—; Dallas/Ft. Worth corr. ARTnews Mag., 1975—; mem. arts adv. panel Dallas Mcpl. Libr., 1981-91; mem. adv. bd. Arts Magnet H.S. of Dallas, 1980-92; mem. adv. com. Sch. Architecture and Environ. Design, U. Tex., Arlington, 1985-87; mem. long range planning com. Dallas Mus. Art, 1985-86; mem. visual arts and architecture adv. panel Tex. Com. on Arts, 1980-82. Contbr. articles to profl. jours.; juror various art exhbns. Bd. trustees Greenhill Sch., Dallas, 1980-81. Art critic's grantee Nat. Endowment for Arts, 1976-77, art critic's fellow Nat. Gallery Art, 1991—. Mem. Am. Assn. Museums, Dallas Mus. Art, Internat. Coun. Museums, ArtTable. Office: Dallas Morning News PO Box 655237 Dallas TX 75265-5237

KUTOSH, SUE, artist; b. Elizabeth, N.J., Dec. 25, 1947; d. Stephen and Irene (Ribecky) K. BFA, Carnegie-Mellon U., 1971; MA, Kent State U., 1973. One woman shows include Keane Mason Gallery, N.Y.C., 1978, West Broadway Gallery, N.Y.C., 1981, Kristen Richards Gallery, N.Y.C., 1983, N.Y. Botanical Gallery, Bronx, 1992, Montserrat Gallery, N.Y.C., 1996, Pleiades Gallery, N.Y.C., 1997; portraits included in books: The Films of Jane Fonda, 1981, Hispanic Hollywood, 1990, The Lavender Screen, 1993, Hollywood Babble On, 1994; art featured in book: New Art International, 1998-99. Recipient Daytime Emmy, 1993-94. Mem. United Scenic Artists, Local 829, Catharine Lorillard Wolfe Art Club, N.Y. Artists Equity, Nat. Assn. Women Artists. Avocation: photography. Home: 200 E 16th St Apt 2-d New York NY 10003-3708

KUTRZEBA, JOSEPH S., theatrical and film producer, director; b. Lodz, Poland, Oct. 11, 1927; came to U.S., 1950; s. Israel and Malka (Hakman) Fajwiszys; m. Valerie M. Hageman, Sept. 1955 (div. 1959); 1 child, Karen Janina; m. Michaela Lacher, Jan. 14, 1979; children: Marcus, Claudia Nina.

BA, U. Munich, 1950; MFA, Yale, 1956; PhD, NYU, 1974. Rschr., prodn. coord., dir., stage mgr. CBS-TV, N.Y.C., 1956-73; prodr., dir., writer, narrator UN Radio, N.Y.C., 1959-69; dir.-mem. Actors Studio, 1960-62; founder, prodr., artistic dir. Queens Playhouse, Flushing Meadows, N.Y., 1972-74, also mem. bd. dirs., pres.; faculty New Sch. for Social Rsch., N.Y.C., 1975-77; prodr.-dir. documentary film Children in the Holocaust, 1980; dir. 4 stage prodns., N.Y.C., 1995-97, (English & Polish versions) Helena: the Emigrant Queen, 1996 at La Mamma and Kosciuszko Found.; presented Shakespeare's Sonnets at St. Peter's Ch. Mem. citizens com. Study of N.Y. Theater, 1971-72; aux. mounted officer N.Y.C. Police Dept., 1974-77; founder (with others) Warsaw Ghetto Resistance Orgn.; exec. sec., dep. presiding officer Hidden Child Found. Served to lt. AUS, 1950-52, Korea. Tony award, Drama Desk award nominations for prodr. Best Broadway mus. The Lieutenant, 1975; recipient Bronze award Internat. Film and TV Festival of N.Y. for Children in the Holocaust, 1980. MacDowell Colony fellow, 1973. Mem. Dirs. Guild Am., Yale Alumni Assn. Avocations: tennis, skiing, horseback riding.

KUTSCHER, EUGENE BERNARD, educational administrator; b. N.Y.C., Aug. 19, 1947; s. Irving and Babette (Dreyfuss) K.; m. Robin Gerri Rochstein, June 23, 1974; children: Lauren Allison, Scott Jason. BA, Queens Coll., 1968, MA, 1972; postgrad., St. John's U., Jamaica, N.Y., 1976-82. Tchr. Brentwood (N.Y.) Pub. Schs., 1968-78; acting sch. adminstr. Brentwood East Jr. High Sch., 1975-78; lectr. in physics Queens (N.Y.) Coll., 1969-70; dist. chmn. sci. and health edn. Malverne (N.Y.) Pub. Schs., 1978-83, dist. coordinator computer services, 1981-83; dist. chmn. sci. Roslyn (N.Y.) Pub. Schs., 1983—, coordinator sci. research, 1983—; cons., frequent lectr. in field. Author: Physics Research Activities, 1988, Creative Science Activities, Grades 5-9, 1990, Environmental Science Activities, 1991; contbr. articles to profl. jours. V.p. bd. dirs. Zero Population Growth, Washington. Grantee N.Y. State Energy R&D, 1983-95. Mem. NSTA, Nat. Sci. Edn. Leadership Assn. (exec. com., del. Alliance for Environ. Edn. 1988-95, chair environ. edn. com. 1991—), N.Y. Sci. Suprs. Assn. (bd. govs. N.Y. State Sci. Honor Soc. 1991-93), Nassau County Sci. Edn. Leadership Assn., Sci. Tchrs. Assn. N.Y., Guitar Club N.Y.C. Jewish. Avocations: hiking, skiing, guitar and piano, camping. Office: Roslyn Pub Schs Adminstrn Bldg Roslyn NY 11576

KUTSCHER, RONALD EARL, retired federal government executive; b. Hebron, Nebr., Apr. 18, 1932; s. Earl Harvey and Doris Lillian (Zong) K.; m. Elizabeth Elin Granholm, Dec. 28, 1963; children: Laura Ingrid, Steven Ronald. BA, Doane Coll., 1955; postgrad., U. Ill., 1955-56. Economist Bur. Labor Stats., Washington, 1957-68, asst. chief for rsch. div. of econ. growth, 1968-76, asst. commr., 1976-82, assoc. commr., 1982-96. Contbr. articles to profl. jours. With U.S. Army, 1952-54. Mem. Am. Statis. Assn. (chair com. on coms. 1989-91, chair program com. 1985, Prize Best Econ. Forecast 1973). Lutheran. Avocations: photography, golf. Office: Bur Labor Stats 2 Massachusetts Ave NE Washington DC 20002-9997

KUTTLER, CARL MARTIN, JR., academic administrator; b. Daytona Beach, Fla., Jan. 31, 1940; s. Carl M. and Winona (Ellis) K.; m. Evelyn Flathmann, June 29, 1963; children—Cindy, Carl Martin III, Erika. AA, St. Petersburg Jr. Coll., 1960; BS in Mgmt., Fla. State U., Tallahassee, 1962; J.D., Stetson U., 1965. Bar: Fla. bar 1965. Research aide 2d Dist. Ct. Appeals, Lakeland, Fla., 1965-66; instr. St. Petersburg (Fla.) Jr. Coll., 1965-76, asst. to v.p. for adminstrn., 1966-67, dean. adminstrv. affairs, 1967-78, pres., 1978—; adj. instr., cons. grad. edn. program U. Tex., Austin; judge Templeton Prize in Religion. Co-author: 1,001 Exemplary Practices in America's Two-Year Colleges, 1994. Mem. pres.'s Coun. Div. Cmty. Colls., 1978—; candidate for Fla. Commr. Edn., 1974; mem. judging panel selecting outstanding high schs. in Am. for U.S. Sec. Edn.; apptd. by Pres. U.S. Nat. Adv. Coun. Ednl. Rsch. and Improvement; apptd. by U.S. Sec. VA to Adminstr.'s Ednl. Assistance Adv. Com. Named Most Disting. Alumnus Stetson U. Alumni Assn., 1978, 88, Hon. Father of C.C. Sys. in Russia, Assn. Edn. for Everybody, 1994, Outstanding C.C. Pres. in Am., Assn. of C.C. Trustees, 1998; recipient Disting. Floridian award Phi Theta Kappa, 1986, Nat. Disting. Coll. Pres. award, 1991, Internat. Leadership award, 1990, vis. scholar award, 1987, master tchr. award, 1988, 92, 93, U. Tex., Disting. pres.'s award PTK Fla., 1991, Alumnus award Fla. State U., 1981, 88, Liberty Bell award St. Petersburg Bar Assn., 1992, Werner Kubsch award for outstanding achievement in internat. edn. C.C. for Internat. Devel., Inc., 1997. Mem. Nat. Assn. Coll. and Univ. Attys., Am. Assn. C.Cs., Fla. Assn. Cmty. Colls., Fla. Bar Assn. Republican. Methodist. Home: 8336 40th Ave N Saint Petersburg FL 33709-3935 Office: St Petersburg Jr Coll PO Box 13489 Saint Petersburg FL 33733-3489

KUTTNER, BERNARD A., lawyer, former judge; b. Berlin, Ger., Jan. 13, 1934; s. Frank B. and Vera (Knopfmacher) K.; children: Karen M., Robert D., Stacey M. Gilby. AB cum laude, Dartmouth Coll., 1955; postgrad. U. Va. Law Sch., 1956; JD, Seton Hall U., 1959; postgrad. NYU. Bar: N.J. 1960, N.Y. 1982, D.C. 1982, U.S. Supreme Ct. 1964, U.S. Ct. Mil. Appeals., 1967; cert. civil trial lawyer, N.J., 1982. Assoc. Toner, Crowley, Woelper & Vanderbilt, 1959-62; sole practice, Newark, 1962-75; corp. counsel, Irvington, N.J., 1963-66; judge N.J. State Div. Tax Appeals., 1977-79; instr. civil litigation Montclair State Coll., 1979-82; del. Jud. Conf. N.J. Supreme Ct., 1974-81; vice chmn. Supreme Ct. N.J. Dist. Ethics Com., 1984-85, chmn., 1985-86. Contbr. articles to legal publs. Commr. Essex County (N.J.) Park Commn., 1973-79; appointed bd. on Trial Atty. Certification, N.J. Supreme Ct., 1986-90. Served to lt. comdr. USNR, 1964-74. Mem. Inst. for Ethical Behavior (pres. 1985—), ABA (co-editor trial techniques newsletter sect. on tort and ins. practice, chmn. trial techniques com. 1988-89, sect. on litigation), ATLA, D.C. Bar Assn., Irvington Bar Assn. (pres. 1968-70), Essex County Bar Assn. (chmn. 1973-75, com. trial and appellate litigation, judiciary com. 1972-75, treas. 1975-79, pres. 1980-81, products liability com. 1981—), Am. Counsel Assn. Jewish. Office: Kuttner Law Offices 24 Lackawanna Pl Millburn NJ 07041-1618

KUTTNER, DONNA HOLBERG, health education specialist; b. Houston, Sept. 14, 1945; d. L.R. and Melba Holberg; m. Charles H. Kuttner, Jan. 22, 1971; 1 child, Arwen Eve. MusB, U. Houston, 1968; EdM, Oreg. State U., 1988, MS, 1992, PhD, 1995. Cert. health edn. specialist. Tchr. elem. sch. Galveston (Tex.) Ind. Sch. Dist., 1968-70, Hitchcock (Tex.) Ind. Sch. Dist., 1970-73; tchr. music in pvt. practice San Francisco, 1973-76, Corvallis, Oreg., 1977-85; tchr. dept. edn. Oreg. State U., Corvallis, 1986-87, tchr. dept. pub. health, 1993, 95; cons. editor mental health divsn. State of Oreg., Salem, 1988-89; instrnl. designer Oreg. State Hosp., 1987-88; cons. health edn. Corvallis, 1996—; faculty Western Oreg. U., 1997-98; sec.-treas. Oreg. Alliance for Health Edn., 1996-99. Editor Oreg. jour. of Oreg. Alliance for Health PE recreation and dance, 1992-99; contbr. articles to profl. jours., (Corvallis Macintosh User Group newsletter) Mouse Droppings, 1990—. Bd. dirs. Corvallis Macintosh User Group, Corvallis, 1995-99. Mem. Am. Alliance for Health Physical Edn., Recreation and Dance, Am. Assn. Health Edn., Music Tchr. Nat. Assn. Avocations: stained glass, stichery, reading, writing, poetry.

KUTTNER, ROBERT LOUIS, editor, columnist; b. N.Y.C., Apr. 17, 1943; s. Arthur Paul Kuttner and Pauline M. Levy; m. Sharland Grace Trotter, Dec. 19, 1971 (dec. Nov. 1997); children: Gabriel A., Jessica A. AB, Oberlin Coll., 1965; MA, U. Calif., Berkeley, 1966; cert., London Sch. Econs., 1963-64; LLD (hon.), Swarthmore Coll., 1999. Asst. to I.F. Stone Washington, 1966, legis. asst. to Congressman W.F. Ryan, 1967-68; corr. program dir. Pacifica Radio, N.Y.C., 1968-71; editor The Village Voice, Washington, 1971-73; staff writer Washington Post, 1974-75; chief investigator Senate Banking Com., Washington, 1975-78; editor Working Papers, Mass., 1980-83; econs. writer, editor The New Republic, 1983-91; columnist Bus. Week, 1984—, Boston Globe and Washington Post Syndicate, 1985—; co-editor The Am. Prospect, 1989—; contbr. editor More Mag., Washington, 1973-78; lectr. Boston U., 1980-82, W. Colston Leigh Bur., N.J., 1987—; vis. prof. U. Mass., 1987-88, Brandeis U., Mass., 1991-92. Author: Revolt of the Haves, 1980, The Economic Illusion, 1984, The Life of the Party, 1987, The End of Laissez-Faire, 1991, Everything for Sale, 1997; nat. policy corr. New Eng. Jour. Medicine, 1996—. Exec. dir. Nat. Commn. on Neighborhoods, Washington, 1978; bd. dirs. Econ. Policy Inst. Washington, 1986—, Families USA, Boston, 1989—. Recipient Jack London award, United Steelworkers Am., 1982, John Hancock award, John Hancock Co., 1988, Paul Hoffman award UN Devel. Program, 1996, Sidney Hillman award Sidney Hillman Found., 1998; Woodrow Wilson fellow U. Calif., 1965-66, Kennedy fellow, Harvard U., 1979, fellow John Guggenheim Meml. Found., 1988; fellow McCormack Inst, 1987-88. Mem. Nat. Acad. Social Ins. Avocations: tennis, photography, writing poetry. Office: Am Prospect 6 University Rd Cambridge MA 02138-5731

KUTYNA, DONALD JOSEPH, air force officer; b. Chgo., Dec. 6, 1933; s. Frank A. and Isabel E. (Kmiec) K.; m. Lucille Mae Moellering, June 6, 1957; children: Dale J., Douglas J. Student, U. Iowa, 1951-53; BS, U.S. Mil. Acad., 1957; MA in Aero./Astronautics, MIT, 1965. Commd. 2d lt. USAF, 1957, advanced through grades to gen., 1990; pilot trainee Vance AFB, Enid, Okla., 1958; comdr. B-47 crew March AFB, Riverside, Calif., 1958; test pilot Edwards AFB, Calif., 1965-69; pilot 44th Tactical Fighter Squadron, Royal Takhli AFB, Thailand, 1969-70; planner R&D Pentagon, Washington, 1971-72; exec. officer Undersec. of Air Force, Washington, 1973-76; program mgr. Air Force Electronics Systems Div., Bedford, Mass., 1976-82; mgr. Dept. Def. Space Shuttle Program, L.A., 1982-84; dir. space systems Pentagon, Washington, 1984-86; vice comdr. Space Div., L.A., 1986-87; comdr. USAF Space Command, Peterson AFB, Colo., 1987-90; comdr.-in-chief N.Am. Aerospace Def. Command, U.S. Space Command, Peterson AFB, 1990-92; v.p. advanced space systems Lockheed Martin Corp. (formerly Loral Corp.), N.Y.C., 1993-99; v.p. space tech. Loral Space & Comm. Corp., N.Y.C., 1999—. Recipient Space award Nat. Geog. Soc., 1987, James V. Hartinger award Nat. Security Indsl. Assn., 1990. Mem. Air Force Assn. (Schriever award 1991). Avocations: skiing, surfing, fishing, hunting, antique cars.

KUTZ, KENNETH JOHN, retired mining executive; b. Elrose, Sask., Can., Nov. 16, 1926; came to U.S., 1957, naturalized, 1962; s. John and Leah (Lefevre) K.; B.S. summa cum laude in Geol. Engring., U. Sask., 1948; m. Nora M. Marchand, Nov. 10, 1948; children—Shirley Mae Kase, Gerald John. Surveyor Howe Sound Co., Britannia Beach, B.C., 1947-48, research engr., 1950-51, asst. chief engr., 1951-54, chief engr., maintenance supt., Snow Lake, Man., 1954-55, mine supt., Cobalt, Idaho, 1956-57; mine supt. Lakeview Mining Co. (Oreg.), 1958-59, Sunshine Mining Co., Kellogg, Idaho, 1960-61; mining engr. Texasgulf Inc., Moab, Utah, 1961-62, mine supt., 1963-65, tech. asst. to gen. mgr., 1965-66, tech. asst. to v.p. Potash div., Salt Lake City, 1966-68, adminstrv. asst., 1968-69, asst. to pres., mgr. Australian iron ore projects, 1969-73, v.p. Internat. div., 1973-82; pres. Texasgulf Minerals & Metals, 1983-90; pres. Texasgulf Panama, Pandora Mining (Pty.), 1983-90; ret., 1990. Registered Profl. engr., B.C., Oreg. Mem. AIME, Mining and Metall. Soc. Am. (past pres.), Can. Inst. Mining and Metallurgy (life), Australian Inst. Mining and Metallurgy, Mining Club N.Y. (bd. govs., past pres.), Innis Arden Golf Club, Collectors Club of N.Y. Republican. Roman Catholic. Author: Gold Fever, 1988, Nome Gold, 1991, Victoria Gold, 1993, California Gold, 1994, Black Gold, 1995, Klondike Gold, 1996, Untold Wealth, 1998; patentee in field. Home: 7 Whaling Rd Darien CT 06820-5930

KUURE, BOJAN MARLENA, operating room nurse; b. Jakobstad, Finland, Nov. 14, 1942; d. Anders Arne and Aina Viktoria (Back) Sundqvist; m. Arvo Antero Kuure, Nov. 3, 1965; 1 child, Saara Bojan. Diploma, Helsingfors Svenska Sjukvardsinstitut, Helsinki, Finland, 1964; specialty nursing in anesthia & surgery, Helsingfors Svenska Sjukvards, Helsinki, Finland, 1967-68; Aprubatur in Edn., U. Helsinki, 1972. Staff nurse U. Finland Hosp., 1964-67, specialty nurse, 1968-70; tchr. dir. Nursing Inst., Helsinki, 1970-72; oper. rm. nurse Island Hosp., Anacortes, Wash., 1972-83, surg. dir., 1983. Vol. Interplast, Inc., Healing the Children. Paul Harrison fellow Rotary Internat. Mem. Am. Assn. Oper. Rm. Nurses, Oper. Rm. Mgrs. Wash., Wash. State Coun. Peri-op Nursing, Wash. Orgn. Nurse Execs. Home: 1201 5th St Anacortes WA 98221-1709

KUWABARA, JAMES SHIGERU, research hydrologist; b. Honolulu, Apr. 26, 1953; s. Donald Shigeyuki and Setsue (Ogawa) K.; m. Rie Rita Kimura, June 6, 1982; children: Sara Mie, Annie Mako. BSCE, U. Hawaii, 1975; MS in Environ. Engring., Calif. Inst. Tech., 1976, PhD in Environ. Engring., 1980. Computer operator Computer Info. Svcs., Honolulu, 1971; engring. rschr. U. Hawaii, Honolulu, 1971-73; aquacultural rschr. Sea Grants Program, Honolulu, 1973-75; grad. rsch. fellow NSF, Pasadena, Calif., 1975-78; grad. rsch. asst. Calif. Inst. Tech., Pasadena, Calif., 1978-80; postdoctoral rsch. fellow Nat. Rsch. Coun., Menlo Park, Calif., 1980-82; rsch. hydrologist U.S. Geol. Survey, Menlo Park, Calif., 1982—; conf. chmn. West Coast Water Chem. Workshop, Stanford, 1986; final rev. panel Water Res. Rsch. Grants, Reston, Va., 1988-89; session organizer Estuarine Rsch. Conf., San Francisco, 1991; session moderator Am. Chem. Soc., Washington, 1992; coord. San Francisco Bay Toxic Substances Hydrology Program, 1994—. Editor Estuaries, 1993; contbr. chpts. to books; contbr. numerous articles to Geochimica et Cosmochimica Acta, Limnology and Oceanography, Science, and other profl. jours. Eagle scout rev. bd. Boy Scouts of Am., Honolulu, 1974-75. Hawaii State Acad. scholar U. Hawaii, 1972; recipient NSF Grad. fellowship Calif. Inst. Tech., 1975; Nat. Rsch. Coun. postdoctoral rsch. assoc. U.S. Geol. Survey, 1980. Mem. ASCE, Am. Inst. Chemists, Estuarine Rsch. Fedn., Phycological Soc. Am. Achievements include development of a larval culturing system of State of Hawaii's prawn industry; optimization of gametophytic culturing of giant kelp for biomass conversion program; design of toxicant introduction device, process-interdependent solute transport modeling. Office: US Geol Survey 345 Middlefield Rd # MS439 Menlo Park CA 94025-3591

KUWAYAMA, GEORGE, retired curator; b. N.Y.C., Feb. 25, 1925; s. Senzo and Fumiko Kuwayama; m. Lillian Yetsuko Yamashita, Dec. 5, 1961; children: Holly, Mark, Jeremy. B.A., Williams Coll., 1948; postgrad., NYU, 1948-54; M.A., U. Mich., 1956. Curator Oriental art L.A. County Mus. Art, 1959-70, sr. curator Far Ea. art, 1970-96, sr. curator emeritus, 1996—; lectr. U. So. Calif., UCLA; organizer spl. exhbns. Author: Far Eastern Lacquer, 1980, Shippo: The Art of Enameling in Japan, 1980, Chinese Ceramics in Colonial Mexico, 1997; author, editor: Japanese Ink Painting, 1983, The Quest for Eternity, 1987, Ancient Mortuary Traditions of China, 1991, New Perspective on the Art of Ceramics in China, 1992; author, co-editor: Imperial Taste, 1989; editor, author: The Great Bronze Age of China: A Symposium, 1983. Served with parachute inf. U.S. Army, 1944-46. Charles Freer scholar U. Mich., 1955-56; Inter-Univ. fellow Ford Found., 1957-58; rsch. travel grantee Nat. Endowment for Arts, 1974, 88. Mem. Assn. for Asian Studies, Am. Oriental Soc. (Louise Hackney fellow 1956), Coll. Art Assn., Japan Soc., Internat. House Japan, China Colloquium, Far Ea. Art Coun. Democrat. Methodist. Home: 1417 Comstock Ave Los Angeles CA 90024-5316 Office: LA County Mus Art 5905 Wilshire Blvd Los Angeles CA 90036-4597

KUWAYAMA, S. PAUL, physician, allergist, immunologist; b. Sapporo, Hokkaido, Japan, Nov. 8, 1932; s. Satoru and Chiyoko (Nishikawa) K.; m. Barbara Ann Dresback, June 29, 1974; children: David, Steven, Jason. BS, Hokkaido U., Sapporo, 1955, MD, 1959. Diplomate Am. Bd. Pediatrics, 1965, Am. Bd. Allergy & Immunology, 1972, Am. Bd. Pediatric Allergy, 1970; lic. Nat. Bd. Med. Examiners of Japan, 1960, Wis. State Bd. Med. Examiners, 1968, Ariz. State Bd. Med. Examiners, 1987, N.Mex. State Bd. Med. Examiners, 1987, Tenn. State Bd. Med. Examiners, 1992. Intern U.S. Naval Hosp., Seattle, 1959-60, St. Mary's Hosp., Milw., 1960-61; jr. resident in pediatrics Temple U. Sch. of Medicine, Phila., 1961-62; chief resident W.Va. U. Sch. of Medicine, Morgantown, 1962-63; postdoctoral fellow in immunology, sr. fellow in pediatric allergy The Children's Mercy Hosp.-U. Kans. Sch. of Medicine, Kansas City, 1964-65; staff pediatrician Atomic Bomb Casualty Commn. in Hiroshima, U.S. Nat. Acad. of Scis.-U.S. Atomic Energy Commn., 1966-67; sr. pediatric allergist, dept. immunobiology U. Kans. Sch. of Medicine, 1967-68; asst. clin. prof. pediatric allergy and immunology Med. Coll. Wis., Milw., 1970—. Contbg. author texts and forward to books. Fulbright scholar, 1960-63. Fellow Am. Acad. Pediatrics (sect. on allergy & immunology), Am. Coll. Allergy & Immunology, Am. Assn. Cert. Allergists, Am. Acad. Allergy, Asthma and Immunology, Am. Assn. Clin. Immunology and Allergy; mem. AMA, Fulbright Scholarship Grantee Alumni Assn., State Med. Soc. of Wis., Milw. Pediatric Soc. Office: 11035 W Forest Home Ave Hales Corners WI 53130-2541

KUYKENDALL, BENJAMIN LOREN, military officer; b. Pittsburg, Kans., Sept. 19, 1962; s. Ronald Loren and Hazel Ruth (Hyatt) K. BA in Polit. Sci., Mont. State U., 1988. With USMC, Camp Pendleton, Calif., 1982-85; welder Mont. Ready Mix, Bozeman, 1986-90; advanced through grades to capt. U.S. Army, 1991—; comdr. A/41st Engr. Battalion U.S. Army, Ft. Drum, N.Y., 1998—. Mem. Am. Mensa. Protestant. Avocations: sailing, running, boat design. Fax: (315) 772-0544. E-mail: bkuyken@ibm.net. Office: A/41st Engr Battalion 10632 S Riva Ridge Loop Fort Drum NY 13602

KUYKENDALL, JOHN WELLS, academic administrator, educator; b. Charlotte, N.C., May 8, 1938; s. James Bell and Emily Jones (Frazer) K.; m. Nancy Adams Moore, July 15, 1961; children—Timothy Moore, James Frazer. BA cum laude, Davidson Coll., 1959; BD cum laude, Union Sem., Richmond, Va., 1964; STM, Yale U., 1965; MA, Princeton U., 1972, PhD, 1975. Ordained to ministry Presbyterian Ch., 1965. Campus minister Presbyn. Ch., Auburn, Ala., 1965-70; faculty Auburn U., 1973-84; pres. Davidson (N.C.) Coll., 1984-97, pres. emeritus, prof. religion, 1997—. Author: (with others) Presbyterians: Their History and Beliefs, 1978, Southern Enterprize: The Work of Evangelical Societies in the Antebellum South, 1982; contbr. articles to profl. jours. Recipient Algernon Sydney Sullivan award Auburn U., 1982. Mem. Am. Soc. Ch. History, Phi Beta Kappa, Omicron Delta Kappa, Phi Kappa Phi. Democrat. Office: Davidson Coll PO Box 1719 Davidson NC 28036-1719

KUYKENDALL, STEVEN T., congressman; b. McAlester, Okla., Jan. 27, 1947; s. Henry and Frances (Campbell) K.; m. Janice E. Francis, Oct. 3, 1970; children: Kerry D., Brent T., Craig S. BS in Bus., Oklahoma City U., 1968; MBA, San Diego State U., 1974. Pres. Lockheed Mortgage Corp., 1981-84; prin. David Buxton Fin. Group, 1984-94; mem. 54th Assembly Dist., 1994-98, majority whip, vice chmn. utilities and commerce com., mem. banking and fin., local govt. and budget coms.; mem. U.S. Congress from 36th Calif. dist., 1999—; mem. armed svcs. com., mem. sci. com., mem. transp. and infrastructure com.; past pres., trustee Peninsula Edn. Found., 1988-93. mayor, coun. mem. City of Rancho Palos Verdes, Calif., 1991-94; legislator State of Calif., Sacramento, 1994—. Capt. USMC, 1968-73, Vietnam. Republican. Presbyterian. Office: Ho of Reps 512 Cannon HOB Washington DC 20515*

KUYPER, JOAN CAROLYN, foundation administrator; b. Balt., Oct. 22, 1941; d. Irving Charles and Ethel Mae (Pritchett) O'Connor; m. L. William Kuyper, Dec. 20, 1964; children: Susan Carol, Edward Philip. BA in Edn., Salisbury State U., 1963; postgrad. Columbia U., 1978; MA in Arts Mgmt. and Bus., NYU, 1988. Elem. sch. tchr. Prince Georges County Schs., Md., 1963-68; free lance singer, opera, oratorio, chamber music Amato Opera, N.Y.C., 1967-80; owner, mgr. Privette Artists' Registry, Placement Service for Singers, Teaneck, N.J., 1969-78; exec. dir. Teaneck Artists Perform-Chamber Music Series, 1975-80; program dir. Vols. in Arts & Humanities, Vol. Bur. Bergen County, N.J., 1978-81; dir. Bergen Mus. Art and Sci., 1981-83; cons. Am. Soc. Prevention-Cruelty to Animals, 1984, Am. Coun. for Arts, 1987; dir. ops. Isabel O'Neil Found. and Studio, 1984-85. Dir. vol. svcs. March of Dimes Birth Defects Found. of Greater N.Y., 1985-88; dir. chpt. devel. Huntington's Disease Soc. Am., 1988-91; bd. dirs Pro Arte Chorale and adv. bd. on arts, Teaneck, 1976-81; mgmt. cons. Girl Scouts U.S., 1992—; sr. counsel The Forbes Group. Mem. N.Y. Soc. Assn. Execs. (membership com. 1991-94, Cert. Assn. Execs. chair 1995-96, program planning com. 1996-98, chmn. profl. devel. com. 1998—), Am. Soc. Assn. Execs. (cert.), Assn. Mus., Mus. Coun. N.J., Am. Mktg. Assn. (bd. dirs. 1990-96), Assn. for Vol. Adminstrn. (author handbook), Nat. Soc. Fund Raising Execs., Orgnl. Devel. Network, SearchNet, Exec. Women in Golf Assn, Altrusa Club (bd. dirs. 1984-86, 90-93, 96—, pres. 1986-88), PEO, Phi Alpha Theta. Democrat. Presbyterian. Home: 345 W 58th St Apt 14X New York NY 10019-1142 also: 1275 Pebble Beach Rd Tobyhanna PA 18466-9119

KUZENSKI, JOHN C., educator; b. Mobile, Ala., Nov. 4, 1964; s. Kenneth F. and Sally T. K.; m. Kristine-Marie Miller, Feb. 29, 1996. BA, La. State U., 1985; MA, Miss. State U., 1987; PhD, U. Ga., 1993. Asst. prof. Vanderbilt U., Nashville, 1991-95, La. State U., Baton Rouge, 1995-96, The Citadel, Charleston, S.C., 1996—; cons. in field. Co-author: Politics, Parties and Race in Southern Politics, 1999, others; editor: David Duke and the Politics of Race in the South, 1995. Vol. ASPCA, Charleston, 1996-97, ARC, Baton Rouge, 1984-88. Recipient Outstanding Sr. award La. State U. Arts & Scis., 1985, Outstanding chpt. award Pi Sigma Alpha, 1996-97, 97-98. Office: The Citadel Dept Polit Sci Charleston SC 29409

KUZER, MINDY SUSAN, educator; b. N.Y.C., Sept. 18, 1951; d. Herbert and Lenore Gottlieb K. BA, SUNY, Buffalo, 1974; MS, U. Calif., Berkeley, 1979, PhD, 1984. Asst. prof. U. Minn., St. Paul, 1989-95, assoc. prof., 1995—. Recipient Future Leader award Inst. Life Scis.-Nutrition Found., Washington, 1992-93. Avocations: canoeing, backpacking, reading. Home: U Minn 1334 Eckles Ave Saint Paul MN 55108

KUZMA, GEORGE MARTIN, bishop; b. Windber, Pa., July 24, 1925; s. Ambrose and Anne (Marton) K. Student, Benedictine Coll., Lisle, Ill.; BA, Duquesne U., postgrad.; postgrad., U. Mich.; grad., SS Cyril and Methodius Byzantine Cath. Sem. Ordained priest Byzantine Cath. Ch., 1955. Asst. pastor SS Peter and Paul Ch., Braddock, Pa., 1955-57; pastor Holy Ghost Ch., Charleroi, Pa., 1957-65, St. Michael Ch., Flint, Mich., 1965-70, St. Eugene Ch., Bedford, Ohio, 1970-72, Annunciation Ch., Anaheim, Calif., 1970-86; rev. monsignor Byzantine Cath. Ch., 1984, titular bishop, 1986, consecrated bishop, 1987; aux. bishop Byzantine Cath. Diocese of Passaic, N.J., 1987-90; bishop Van Nuys, Calif., 1991—; judge matrimonial tribunal, mem. religious edn. commn., mem. commn. orthodox rels. Diocese of Pitts., 1955-69; judge matrimonial tribunal, vicar for religious Diocese of Parma, 1969-82; treas., bd. dirs., chmn. liturgical commn., mem. clergy & seminarian rev. bd., liaison to ea. Cath. dirs. religious edn., bd. dirs. diocesan credit union, chmn. diocesan heritage bd., chmn. diocesan ecumenical commn. Diocese of Van Nuys, 1982-86; vicar gen. Diocese of Passaic; episcopal vicar for Ea. Pa.; chmn. Diocesan Retirement Plan Bd.; pres. Father Walter Cizsek Prayer League; chaplain Byzantine Carmelite Monastery, Sugarloaf, Pa. Assoc. editor Byzantine Cath. World; editor The Apostle. With USN, 1943-46, PTO. Office: Byzantine Cath Eparchy of Van Nuys 8131 N 16th St Phoenix AZ 85020-3999

KUZMOWYCH, CHRYSTYNA PRYTULA, optometrist; d. Wasyl and Myroslawa (Ziniuk) Prytula; m. Truvor Vadym Kuzmowych, June 5, 1971. BS, Pa. Coll. of Optometry, 1968; BA, SUNY, Binghamton, 1967; O.D., Pa. Coll. of Optometry, 1971; Mgmt. Trainee, Group Health, Washington, 1986-94. Ind. contractor Great Falls, Va., 1997—; optometrist Group Health Assoc., Washington, 1972-86, 95-97; chief Group Health/Humana, Washington, 1986-95; panelist Optometric Coun. of D.C., U. of Md.; lectr. Am. Acad. of Optometry; participant Clek Study of Keratoconus, 1990; dir. Group Health Assoc. Ann., C.L. Seminar, 1987-94. Mem. AAUW, Nat. Mus. of Women in the Arts, Washington Performing Arts Soc., Ukrainian Nat. Women's League of Am., Nat. Symphony Orchestra, Va. Optometric Assn. (sec. 1978-80), D.C. Optometric Assn. (officer and exec. com. 1972-78). Avocations: music, gardening.

KUZNIECKY, RUBEN ITAMAR, neurologist, educator; b. Panama, Republic of Panama, Aug. 18, 1957; came to U.S., 1988; s. Salem and Sara Kuzniecky; m. Yvonne Zelenka, Dec. 11, 1983; children: Avi, Hannah, Joel. BS, David Wolfshon, Buenos Aires, 1975; MD, U. Buenos Aires, 1981. Diplomate Am. Bd. Psychiatry and Neurology. Intern CSS, Panama, 1981-83; resident McGill U., Montreal, Can., 1983-86, fellow in epilepsy, 1986-88; asst. prof. neurology U. Ala., Birmingham, 1988-92, assoc. prof., 1992-97, prof., 1997—; dir. Epilepsy Ctr., U. Ala., 1995—. Author: MR in Epilepsy, 1995. Avocations: classic music, opera. Office: U Ala Dept Neurology UAB Station Birmingham AL 35294

KUZNIK, SUSAN MARIE, management consultant; b. Cleve., Jan. 13, 1956; d. Joseph Stephen and Elizabeth Marie (Horvat) Rerko; m. Robert Joseph Kuznik, Sept. 22, 1979. BS, Cleve. State U., 1978; MS, Case Western Res. U., 1985; PhD, Clayton U., 1987; postgrad., Cleve. State U., 1998—. Info. system specialist Standard Oil of Ohio, Cleve., 1976-80, personnel devel. specialist, 1980-81, supr. sci. svcs., 1981-83, control assoc., 1983-84, sr. project mgr., 1984-85; pres. T.H.E. Assocs., Parma, Ohio, 1985—; adj. prof. Kent (Ohio) State U., 1985-86, Baldwin-Wallace Coll., Berea, Ohio, 1985-98, Ursuline Coll., 1990-92, Nova Southeastern U., 1990-92; assoc. cons. Daedalean Assocs., Rocky River, Ohio, 1986-96; chmn. The Paragon Ctr.,

North Ridgeville, Ohio, 1986-89; v.p. The Bart Brooks Ctr. for Ethics and Human Values, Houston, 1986-96; mem. exec. com. Ctr. for Profl. Ethics, Case Western Res. U., Cleve., 1989-96; thesis adv., guest lectr. Ursuline Coll., 1989-93; assoc. prof. Baldwin-Wallace Coll., 1998—. Mem. Am. Soc. for Tng. and Devel., Orgn. Devel. Network, World Future Soc., Cleve. World Trade Assn., Acad. Mgmt. Avocations: reading, sumi painting, ceramic design. Home and Office: 7544 Pleasant Run Dr Seven Hills OH 44131-5900

KVALSETH, TARALD ODDVAR, mechanical engineer, educator; b. Brunkeberg, Telemark, Norway, Nov. 7, 1938; married; 3 children. *Wife Amy Vetter Kvalseth has been an attorney with the Minnesota Attorney General's Office since 1990. She clerked for the Minnesota Supreme Court after receiving her JD from the University of Minnesota in 1989. Dr. and Mrs. Kvalseth's children are: Erik Olav, Lisbet May (married to Christopher Eric Kaiser) and Andrew Tor Oddvar (and Kirsten Margit, died in 1972).* B.S., U. Durham, King's Coll., Eng., 1963; M.S., U. Calif.-Berkeley, 1966, Ph.D., 1971. Research asst. engring. expt. sta. U. Colo., Boulder, 1963-64, teaching asst. dept. mech. engring.; mech. engr. Williams & Lane Inc., Berkeley, 1964-65; research asst. dept. indsl. engring. and ops. research U. Calif.-Berkeley, 1965-71, research fellow, 1973; asst. prof. Sch. Indsl. and Systems Engring. Ga. Inst. Tech., Atlanta, 1971-74; sr. lectr. indsl. mgmt. div. Norwegian Inst. Tech. U. Trondheim, 1974-79, head indsl. mgmt. div., 1975-79; assoc. prof. dept. mech. engring. U. Minn., Mpls., 1979-82, prof., 1982—; guest worker NASA Ames Research Ctr., Calif., 1973; mem. organizing com. 1st Berkeley-Monterey Conf. Timespan, Pay and Discretionary Capacity, 1973; mem. steering com. Internat. Conf. Human Factors in Design and Op. Ships, Gothenburg, Sweden, 1977; mem. bd. Norwegian Ergonomics Com., 1977-80; gen. session chmn. Conf. Work Place Design and Work Environ. Problems, Trondheim, 1978. Author book chpts., articles, presentations, reports in field; editor text books; mem. editl. bd., reviewer for numerous profl. jours., patentee in field. Mem. IEEE, AAAS, Inst. Indsl. Engrs. (sr.), Human Factors and Ergonomics Soc. (pres. upper Midwest chpt.), Nordic Ergonomics Soc. (coun. 1977-80), Internat. Ergonomics Assn. (gen. coun. 1977-80, v.p. 1982-85), Ergonomics Soc., Psychonomic Soc., Am. Psychol. Soc., Am. Statis. Assn., Sigma Xi. Lutheran. Club: Campus (U. Minn.). Home: 108 Turnpike Rd Minneapolis MN 55416-1149 Office: U Minn Dept Mech Engring Minneapolis MN 55455

KVAMME, MARK D., marketing professional. Programmer Apple Computer; founding mem., then internat. product mgr. in U.S. Apple France; founder, pres., CEO Internat. Solutions; dir. internat. mktg. Wyse Tech.; pres., chmn. CKS Group, Cupertino, Calif. Office: USWEB/CKS 10443 Bandley Dr Cupertino CA 95014-1912

KVAVIK, ROBERT BERTHEL, university administrator; b. Bklyn., May 5, 1942; s. Berthel and Ruth (Meland) K.; m. Karen Halladay, June 11, 1967. BA in Polit. Sci. with honors, Bklyn. Coll., 1964; MA, Stanford U., 1965, PhD, 1971. Dir. grad. studies U. Minn., Mpls., 1975-78, dir. Ctr. for Western European Studies, 1979-81, dir. for rsch. devel., 1982-86, asst. v.p. internat. edn., 1986-90, vice provost, 1992-95, assoc. v.p., 1995—. Author: Interest groups in Norwegian Politics, 1976; editor: Scandinavian Studies in America, 1989; contbr. articles to profl. jours. Bd. dirs. Minn. Internat. Ctr., Mpls., 1987-94; mem. Minn. Higher Edn. Coord. Bd., St. Paul, 1988-95; trustee Mpls. Found., 1988-91; mem., chmn. bd. Midwest Univs. Consortium for Internat. Activities, Columbus, Ohio, 1986—. NDEA Title VI grantee, 1979-85. Mem. Nat. Assn. State Univs. and Land Grant Colls. (chmn. internat. studies 1991-94), Soc. for Advancement of Scandinavian Study (pres.), Assn. of Internat. Edn. Adminstrs., Am. Polit. Sci. Assn., Coll. Bd. lutheran. Avocations: photography, fishing. Office: Morrill Hall 234 Church St SE Minneapolis MN 55455-0149

KVINT, VLADIMIR LEV, economist, educator, mining engineer; b. Krasnoyarsk, Siberia, Russia, Feb. 21, 1949; s. Lev V. Kvint and Lidia E. Adamskaya; children: Liza, Valeria. MS in Mining Engring., Inst. Non-Ferrous Metals, Krasnoyarsk, 1972; PhD in Managerial Econs., Inst. Nat. Economy, Moscow, 1975; D of Econs., Inst. Econs., Acad. Scis., Moscow, 1988; life-title: Prof. Pol. Economy, Inst. Economy, Acad. of Scis., Moscow, 1989; HHD, U. Bridgeport, 1997. Diplomate in mining engring. Asst. prof. Inst. of Non-Ferrous Metals, 1972; chief of dept. non-ferrous metals co., Norilsk, Russia, 1975-76; dep. chair, chief economist Automation of non-ferrous metals com., 1976-78; chief dept. sci.-tech. progress Siberian br. Acad. of Scis., Novosibirsk, 1978-82; part-time prof. various Russian univs., 1976-89; leading rschr., fellow Inst. Econs., Acad. Scis., Moscow, 1982-89; cons. GE, N.Y.C., 1989-94, Cable & Wireless, London, 1989-97, Pres. of the UN, 1997-98; vis. prof. Vienna (Austria) Econ. U., 1989-90; prof. Fordham Univ. Grad. Sch., N.Y.C., 1990—; disting. prof. Babson Coll., Babson Park, Mass., 1991; dir. emerging markets Arthur Andersen, 1992-97; adj. prof. NYU, 1995—; vice-chairperson Elbim Bank, Moscow, 1997—; bd. dirs. PLD Telecom., Inc., N.Y.C., Novy Holding, Bulgaria. Author: The Acceleration of Technological Development of Production, 1976, The Introduction and Use of Automation Systems, 1981, The Krasnoyarsk Experiment, 1982, Management of Scientific-Technical Progress, 1986, The Economic and Scientific-Technical Information, 1987, The Scientific Technological Development of Economy of Daghestan, 1988, The Barefoot Shoemaker: Capitalizing on the New Russia, 1993, A Different Perspective on Emerging Markets, 1995; co-author: Creating and Managing International Joint Ventures, 1996, Incorporating Global Risk Management in the Strategic Decision Making Process, 1997, International M&A, Joint Ventures and Beyond, 1997, The Global Emerging Market in Transition, 1999; editor-in-chief: Emerging Market of Russia: Sourcebook for Investment and Trade, 1997; contbr. articles to Forbes, Harvard Bus. Rev., others. Bd. dirs. USSR Exporters Assn., Moscow, 1988-90; mem. internat. com. Muhlenberg Coll., Allentown, Pa., 1992—; chmn. Summits Instl. Investors & Global Risk Management, World Econ. Devel. Congress, Washington, 1995-97. Recipient Silver medal for achievements in nat. economy USSR Main Nat. Com., Moscow, 1986; Jr. Boxing Champion of Russia, 1968. Fellow New Eng. Ctr. for Internat. and Regional Studies (hon.); mem. N.Y. Acad. Scis., Philos. Soc., Am. Econ. Assn., Russian Acad. Natural Scis. (life), Bretton Woods Com. (Washington), Internat. Acad. Emerging Markets (founder 1996—). Achievements include devel. of theory of regionalization of scientific tech. progress; evaluation of role of scientific-technical policy in devel. of regional economy; devel. of regional programs, developed a theory of emerging markets, developed a system of optimization models of strategies of companies in new emerging markets. Office: Fordham U 113 W 60th St Fl 6 New York NY 10023-7484 *In our life, we have to be prepared to face not only problems; we must also be prepared to face happiness. Those not prepared can lose the opportunity.*

KWAAN, JACK HAU MING, retired physician; b. Hong Kong, Apr. 9, 1928; came to U.S., 1953; s. Y.K. and Rose W. Kwaan; m. Min K. Ho, Feb. 11, 1973; children: Mary, Peter, Rebecca, Nicholas. MD, U. Hong Kong, 1952. Diplomate Am. Bd. Radiology, Am. Bd. Surgery, Am. Bd. Thoracic Surgery. Resident in radiology Roswell Park Meml. Inst., 1955-56; chief resident Peter Bent Brigham Hosp., 1956-57; rsch. fellow in radiology Harvard Med. Sch., Boston, 1956-57; sr. cancer rsch. radiol. therapist Roswell Park Meml. Inst., Buffalo, 1958-59; asst. prof. radiology U. Ky., Lexington, 1963-65; resident in surgery U. Calif., Irvine, 1965-68; rsch. fellow oncologic surgery M.D. Anderson Hosp., Houston, 1968-69; resident in thoracic U. Calif., Irvine, 1969-71, chief resident thoracic surgery, 1970, asst. prof. surgery, 1972-73; chief vascular surgery sect., co-dir. vascular surgery tng. program U. Calif. Irvine/Long Beach VA Med. Ctr., 1974-87; prof. surgery U. Calif., Irvine, 1983-87; sr. resident in thoracic surgery U. So. Calif./L.A. County Med. Ctr., 1971; staff thoracic cardiovasc. surgeon Long Beach VA Hosp., 1972-73; asst. chief dept. surgery Valley Med. Ctr., Fresno, Calif., 1973-74; prof. surgery U. Okla., Tulsa, 1987-93; ret., 1993; chief dept. surgery Valley Med. Ctr., Fresno, Calif., 1973-74; chief vascular surgery sect. Long Beach VA Med. Ctr., 1974-87; surgical cons. Kaiser Permanente Hosp. Contbr. articles to profl. jours. Fellow Am. Coll. Surgeons; mem. Brit. Med. Assn., Gen. Med. Coun. London (registrant), Assn. Mil. Surgeons of U.S. (life), Assn. VA Surgeons, Internat. Cardiovascular Soc. Home: PO Box 50183 Long Beach CA 90815-6183

KWAN, BENJAMIN CHING KEE, ophthalmologist; b. Hong Kong, July 12, 1940; came to U.S., 1959; s. Shun Ming and Lurk Ming (Lai) K.; m. Catherine Ning, Aug. 29, 1964; children: Susan San, David Daiwai. MD, Wash. U., St. Louis, 1967. Diplomate Am. Bd. Ophthalmology. Ptnr. So. Calif. Permanente Med. Ctr., Harbor City, 1976—, chief of svc. ophthalmology, 1976-88; clin. prof. dept. ophthalmology UCLA, 1995—. Chmn. winter blossom ball Chinese Am. Debutante's Guild, 1993. Capt. U.S. Army, 1969-71. Recipient Svc. award Asian Am. Sr. Citizens Svc. Ctr., 1993, Proclamation award Calif. Sec. of State, 1993, Svc. award East L.A. Chinese Everspring Sr. Assn., 1994. Fellow Am. Acad. Ophthalmology; mem. Chinese Am. Ophthal. Soc. (pres. elect 1997-99, pres. 1999, 2000, Svc. award 1994), Chinese Physician's Soc. So. Calif. (bd. dirs., pres. 1983, Svc. award 1983, 89), Orgn. Chinese Ams. (pres. L.A. chpt. 1986-87). Roman Catholic. Avocations: ballroom dancing, singing, snow skiing. Home: 6327 Tarragon Rd Rancho Palos Verdes CA 90275-5834 Office: 1050 Pacific Coast Hwy Harbor City CA 90710-3509

KWAN, MICHELLE, figure skater; b. Torrance, Calif., July 7, 1980. Student, Boston U. Recipient Skating Mag. Readers' Choice award for figure skater of the year, 1993-94, 95-96. Youngest World Champion in U.S. history; third youngest World Champion;victories include: World Junior Championships, 1994, 96, Hershey's Kisses Internat. Challenge, 1995, 96, Skate Am., 1995, Skate Can., 1995, Nations cup, 1995, U.S. Postal Svc. Challenge, 1995, State Farm U.S. Championships, 1996, Champions Series Final, 1996, others. Office: USFSA 20 1st St Colorado Springs CO 80906-3624*

KWASNICK, PAUL JACK, retail executive; b. N.Y.C., Apr. 8, 1925; s. Joseph and Dorothy (Ginsberg) K.; m. Selma Marcus, Sept. 7, 1947; children: Raymond, Diane, Robert. BBA, CCNY, 1947, MBA, 1957. Fin. exec. M.H. Fishman Co., Inc., N.Y.C., 1947-61; asst. sec.-treas. Zayre Corp., Natick, Mass., 1961-66; v.p., asst. sec.-treas. Zayre Corp., 1966-68, v.p., treas., 1968-72, sr. v.p., treas., 1972-73; exec. v.p., gen. mgr. Kings Dept. Stores, Inc., Newton, Mass., 1973-75; pres., chief operating officer Kings Dept. Stores, Inc., 1975-78, pres. retail div., chief operating officer, dir., mem. exec. com., 1981; chmn., pres., chief exec. officer, dir., mem. exec. com. Mars Stores, Inc., North Dighton, Mass., 1982-89; pres., chief exec. officer Landmark Advisors, Inc., Boston, 1989—; pres., chief exec. officer, chmn. Data Printer Corp., Malden, Mass., 1978-80, bd. dirs., 1967-83; regional dir., bd. dirs. Shawmut Community Bank, Framingham, Mass. Bd. dirs., asst. treas. Mass. Easter Seal Soc., 1986-88, treas., 1988-89, vice chmn., 1989-91, chmn. 1991-93; trustee Combined Jewish Philanthropies of Greater Boston, 1977—, The West Suburban YMCA, Newton, 1984—, chmn., 1991; dir. Mass. Coun. Compulsive Gambling, 1990-91. With AUS, 1943-46. Mem. Internat. Mass Retail Assn. (bd. dris. 1981-89, treas. 1986-89). Jewish. Office: Landmark Advisors Inc 110 Broad St Boston MA 02110-3033

KWESKIN, EDWARD MICHAEL, lawyer; b. Stamford, Conn., June 26, 1946; s. Sydney C. and Ethel (Jaffe) K.; m. Helen S. Truss, Aug. 17, 1969; children: Abigail, Adam. BA, U. Pa., 1968; JD with honors, George Washington U., 1971. Bar: Conn. 1971, U.S. Dist. Ct. Conn. 1971, U.S. Ct. Appeals (2d cir.) 1971, Pa. 1971, U.S. Dist. Ct. (ea. dist.) Pa. 1971, U.S. Supreme Ct. 1979. Staff atty. Cmty. Legal Svcs., Phila., 1971-73; assoc. Wofsey Rosen Kweskin & Kuriansky, Stamford, 1973-79, ptnr., 1979—; spl. master family law Superior Ct., State of Conn., 1995—; bd. dirs. Curtain Call, Inc., 1999—. Commr. Sixth Taxing Dist., Norwalk, Conn., 1993—; coach Little League 1990-95; pres. Temple Sinai, Stamford, 1994-96. Mem. ABA (mem. family law sect.), Conn. Bar Assn. (mem. exec. com. family law sect. 1997—), Stamford-Norwalk Regional Bar Assn. (past pres., past family law chmn.), U. Pa. Alumni Club of Fairfield County (pres. 1973-77, chmn. secondary sch. com. 1992—). Home: 3 Plant Ct Norwalk CT 06853-1824 Office: Wofsey Rosen Kweskin & Kuriansky 600 Summer St Stamford CT 06901-1490

KWETKAUSKIE, JOHN A., medical technologist; b. Elizabeth, N.J., June 25, 1947; s. Albert and Genevieve Kwetkauskie; m. Patricia Manning, May 13, 1972; children: Brian R., Lara A. BS in Life Scis., N.Y. Inst. Tech., 1970. Registered med. technologist. Med. technologist Geisinger Wyoming Valley Med. Ctr., Wilkes-Barre, Pa., 1974-96, Med. Transport, Inc., Hazleton, Pa., 1988—, Columbia Diagnostics, Inc., Canton, Mass., 1997-99, Greiner Vacuette N.Am., Bel Air, Md., 1999—; part-time EMT, end. coord. & designated officer Med. Transport, Inc., Hazleton, Pa., 1988—; EMT, instr. Pa. Dept. Health, Harrisburg, 1990—; adj. faculty Luzerne County C. C., 1994—, Lehigh Carbon County C.C., 1992—; cons. Ea. Safety Health, Inc., Nanticoke, Pa. Author: (instrn. manual) Prevention of Infectious Diseases - for EMS Providers, 1996. With U.S. Army, 1970-74, 90-91. Mem. Am. Med. Technologists, Nat. Assn. EMS Educators. Avocations: camping, boating, outdoor activities. Office: Greiner Vacuette NAm Ste 17A PO Box 943 260 Gateway Dr Bel Air MD 21014

KWIAT, DAVID MARK, educator, actor; b. Mpls., May 9, 1951; s. Joseph J. and Charlotte (Adler) K. BA summa cum laude, U. Minn., 1974; MFA, Fla. State U., 1976. Actor, dir. Actor's Theatre of St. Paul, Minn., 1978-80, 81-89; actor Ariz. Theatre Co., Tucson, 1980-81; prof. New World Sch. of the Arts, Miami, Fla., 1989—. Author: (play) John Barrymore: Confessions of an Actor, 1976; (poem) Flashpoint, 1996. Endowed tchg. chair, Miami-Dade Comty. Coll., 1996. Mem. Actors' Equity Assn., S. Fla. Theatre League, Fla. Assn. for Theater Edn. (bd. dirs. 1991-96), voting mem. Carbonell awards S. Fla. Entertainments Writers Assn., Miami, 1992-95, Phi Beta Kappa. Home: 11207 SW 114th Lane Cir Miami FL 33176-3863 Office: New World Sch of the Arts 300 NE 2d Ave Miami FL 33132

KWIATEK, KIM DAVID, emergency physician; b. Jersey City, July 25, 1952; s. Jack and Lottie (West) K.; m. Candace Rainar Kibbel, June 18, 1978; children: Keren Aviv, Oren Michael, Aliza Leia. BS, U. Cin., 1974, MD, 1977. Diplomate Am. Bd. Family Practice, Am. Bd. Emergency Medicine. Emergency dept. physician Piqua (Ohio) Meml. Hosp., 1978-85; physician emergency and internal medicine depts. Carmel Hosp., Haifa, Israel, 1980-81; emergency dept. physician Kettering Meml. Hosp., Dayton, Ohio, 1981—, Good Samaritan Hosp., Dayton, Ohio, 1989—, Grandview Hosp., Dayton, Ohio, 1997—; clin. instr. Wright State U. Dept. Emergency Medicine, Dayton, 1985—; chair edn. quality assurance bd. Kettering Hosp., 1994-97, chmn. dept. emergency medicine, 1998—. Med. dir. Wash. Twp. Fire & Rescue, Dayton, 1987—; rep. Montgomery City EMS Coun., Dayton, 1991-92; chmn. Young Execs. Divsn. United Jewish Campaign, Dayton, 1990-91; vol. physician Project Reach Out, Dayton, 1997—. Recipient Wasserman Young Leadership award, Dayton, 1992. Mem. Am. Acad. Family Physicians, Am. Coll. Emergency Physicians. Avocations: backpacking, piano, boating, medical ethics, reading. Home: 7505 Forest Brook Blvd Centerville OH 45459-4936 Office: care Kettering Hosp 3535 Southern Blvd Kettering OH 45429-1221

KWIK-KOSTEK, CHRISTINE IRENE, physician, air force officer; b. Lvov, Poland, Sept. 12, 1939; d. Karol Stanislaus and Leonarda Fryderica (Seniuk) Kostek; widowed; children: Christine, Catherine. Grad. summa cum laude, Med. Acad. Cracow, Poland, 1956-62; student primary aerospace medicine course, Brooks AFB, Tex., 1985; student chief of profl. staff course, Sheppard AFB, Tex., 1988. Diplomate Am. Bd. Emergency Medicine, Am. Bd. Internal Medicine, Poland; cert. Edni. Coun. Fgn. Med. Grads.; recert. Extended Allergy Care Provider. Intern. Med. Acad. Cracow, Poland, 1962-63; residency in internal medicine II-Clinic of Internal Diseases, Cracow, Poland, 1963-66, staff, 1966-69; gen. med. officer Gen. Hosp., Sokoto, Nigeria, 1969-72; intern. Frankford Hosp., Phila., 1972-73; house physician Holy Redeemer Hosp., Meadowbrook, Pa., 1973-74; emergency room physician John F. Kennedy Hosp., Phila., 1974-76, emergency room dir., 1976-78; commd. capt. USAF Med. Corps, 1978, advanced through grades to col., 1993; emergency rm., primary care physician USAF Clinic, Ramstein, West Germany, 1978-81; officer in charge Emergency Room and Gen. Practice Clinic, Peterson Field, Colo., 1981-84; primary care physician Malcolm Grow Med. Ctr., Andrews AFB, Md., 1984-88; chief clinic svcs. 63d Med. Group/SGH, Norton AFB, Calif., 1988-93; staff physician 60th Med. Group, Travis AFB, Calif., 1993-96, Occupl. and Environ. Health and Safety Svcs., Ft. George Meade, Md., 1996—; asst. tchr., sr. asst. tchr. Inst. Descriptive Anatomy, Cracow, 1963-69; emergency physician on call First Aid Sta., Cracow, 1966-69. Fellow Am. Coll. Emergency Physicians; mem. AMA, Am. Coll. Emergency Physicians, World Med. Assn., Am. Coll. Physician Execs. Avocations: photography, travel, gourmet cooking. Office: 694 Inteligence Group AIA Fort George G Meade MD 20755

KWILECKI, PAUL, photographer; b. Bainbridge, Ga., Feb. 24, 1928; s. Julian Gerard and Pearl K.; m. Charlotte Williford, June 13, 1952; children: Paul, Susan, Frances, Elizabeth. Author: Understandings, 1981, Lowly Wise, 1992; contbr.: Time-Life: Documentary Photography, 1982, Encyclopedia of Southern Culture, 1989; contbr. to profl. and popular publs.; one-man shows include Jacksonville (Fla.) Art Mus., Fine Arts Gallery Fla. State U., Tallahasse, Louise Jones Gallery Duke U., Durham, N.C., High Mus. Art, Atlanta, Madison (Ga.)-Morgan Mus., O.K. Harris Gallery, N.Y., Daytona Beach (Fla.) C.C., McIntosh Gallery, Atlanta, Albany (Ga.) Mus. Art, DuBois Gallery Lehigh U., Bethlehem, Pa.; group shows include Cummer Gallery Art, Jacksonville, Friends Photography, Carmel, Calif., Corcoran Gallery, Washington, Robert Freidus Gallery, N.Y., San Francisco Camerawork, Les Réncontres D'Arles, France, Aperture Gallery, N.Y., New Orleans Mus. Art, High Mus. Art, Atlnata, Macon (Ga.) Mus. Art Sci.; represented in permanent collections Mus. Modern Art, N.Y., High Mus. Art, Atlanta, Columbus (Ga.) Mus., Lyndhurst Found., Chattanooga, Tenn., Chase Manhatten Bank, N.Y., Nationsbank, Charlotte, N.C., Ga. Power Co., Atlanta, King & Spaulding, Atlanta, Albany Mus. Art., Duke U., Durham, others. NEA fellow, 1979, J.S. Guggenheim Found. fellow, 1981. Office: PO Box 5 Bainbridge GA 31718-0005

KWIRAM, ALVIN L., physical chemistry educator, university official; b. Riverhills, Man., Can., Apr. 28, 1937; came to U.S., 1954; s. Rudolf and Wilhelmina A. (Bilske) K.; m. Verla Rae Michel, Aug. 9, 1964; children: Andrew Brandt, Sidney Marguerite. BS in Chemistry, Walla Walla (Wash.) Coll., 1958, BA in Physics, 1958; PhD in Chemistry, Calif. Inst. Tech., 1963; DS (hon.), Andrews U., 1995. Alfred A. Noyes instr. Calif. Inst. Tech., Pasadena, 1962-63; research asso. physics dept. Stanford (Calif.) U., 1963-64; instr. chemistry Harvard U., Cambridge, Mass., 1964-67; lectr. Harvard U., 1967-70; asso. prof. chemistry U. Wash., Seattle, 1970-75; prof. U. Wash., 1975—, chmn. dept. chemistry, 1977-87, vice provost, 1987-88, sr. vice provost, 1988-90, vice provost for rsch., 1990—; bd. dirs. Seattle Biomed. Rsch. Inst., 1992—; mem. divsn. rev. com. Pacific N.W. Nat. Lab., Environ. and Health Scis. Divsn., 1998—; mem. adv. bd. for univ. connections U. Hawaii, 1999—. Contbr. numerous articles to sci. jours. Bd. dirs. Seattle Econ. Devel. Commn., 1988-92, Wash. Rsch. Found., 1989-94, Seattle-King County Econ. Devel. Coun., 1989-98, Helen R. Whiteley Found., 1997—; mem. vis. com. divsn. chemistry and chem. engring. Calif. Inst. Tech., 1991-96; chmn. adv. bd. Sch. Engring., Walla Walla Coll., 1992—. Recipient Eastman-Kodak Sci. award, U.-Industry Relations award Council for Chem. Research, 1986; Woodrow Wilson fellow, 1958; Alfred P. Sloan fellow, 1968-70; Guggenheim Meml. Found. fellow, 1977-78. Fellow AAAS (chmn.-elect, chmn., past chmn. sect. on chemistry 1991-94, mem. program com. 1994-98), Am. Phys. Soc.; mem. Am. Chem. Soc. (sec.-treas. div. phys. chemistry 1976-86, divsn. councilor 1986—; mem. com. on sci., chmn. subcom. on fed. funding for rsch. 1990-94), Coun. Chem. Rsch. (bd. dirs. 1980-84, chmn. 1982-83), Sigma Xi. Office: Univ Wash Office Provost 312 Gerberding Hall Seattle WA 98195-1237

KWOCK, ROYAL, architect; b. San Bernardino, Calif., Sept. 29, 1947; s. Eddie Sing and Jeanie K.; m. Irene L. Leau, June 26, 1983. BArch, Calif. Poly. U., 1972. Registered architect, Calif.; Cert. Nat. Coun. Archtl. Registration Bds. Draftsman Martinskis & Prodis, San Jose, Calif., 1973-74; intern architect, staff architect, assoc. Hawley, Stowers & Assoc., San Jose, 1974-83; project architect Winston & May, Santa Clara, Calif., 1983-86; prin. May & Kwock, Santa Clara, 1986-98, Ahearn & Kwock Archs., San Jose, 1998—. Bd. dirs. Youth Sci. Inst. Santa Clara Valley, 1985-95; mem. Nat. Trust Hist. Preservation, San Jose, 1984. Corp. mem. AIA (corr. mem. Interiors Commn. 1982-83), Kiwanis Club of West San Jose (bd. dirs. 1993, 98). Office: Ahearn & Kwock Archs 600 N 3rd St San Jose CA 95112

KWOLEK, STEPHANIE LOUISE, chemist; b. New Kensington, Pa., July 31, 1923; d. John and Nellie (Zajdel) K. BS, Carnegie-Mellon U., 1946; DSc (hon.), Worcester Poly. Inst., 1981, Clarkson U., 1977. Chemist E.I. duPont de Nemours & Co., Inc., Wilmington, Del., 1946-59; rsch. chemist E.I. duPont de Nemours & Co., Inc., Wilmington, 1959-67, sr. rsch. chemist, 1967-74, rsch. assoc., 1974-86, cons. in polymer chemistry, 1986—. Contbr. articles to profl. jours.; patentee in field. Recipient award for contbns. to Kevlar, Am. Soc.Metals, 1978, engring./tech. award Soc. Plastics Engrs., 1985; Harold deWitt Smith award ASTM, 1988, George Lublin Meml. award SAMPE, 1991, Medal of Excellence in Composite Materials, U. Del., 1992, Jack Kilby award Kilby Awards Found., 1994, Am. Innovation award Patent and Trademark Office, 1995, Achievement award Indsl. Rsch. Inst., Inc., 1996, Nat. Medal of Tech. award U.S. Dept. of Commerce Tech. Adminstrn., 1996, Perkin medal Soc. Chem. Industry, 1997, Commonwealth award Commonwealth Trust and PNC Bank, 1998, Lemelson-MIT Lifetime Achievement award, 1999; inducted into U. Akron Polymer Processing Hall of Fame, 1985, Nat. Inventors Hall of Fame, 1995, Dayton, Ohio Engring. and Sci. Hall of Fame, 1992, Women in Tech. Internat., 1996. Mem. Am. Chem. Soc. (Award for Creative Invention 1980), Am. Inst. Chemists (Chem. Pioneer award 1980), Franklin Inst. Phila. (Howard N. Potts medal 1976), Carnegie Mellon U. Alumni Assn. (merit award 1983, Disting. Achievement award 1998), DuPont Country (Wilmington), Sigma Xi, Phi Kappa Phi. Office: 312 Spalding Rd Wilmington DE 19803-2422

KWON, CHUL SOO, psychiatrist; b. Seoul, Korea, Sept. 10, 1948; m. Sung Hee Chung, Apr. 6, 1974; 1 child: Soon Jeong (Susan). MD, Seoul (Korea) Nat. U., Korea, 1974. Diplomate Am. Bd. Psychiatry. Intern Washington Hosp. Ctr., 1975-76, res. gen. surgery, 1976-77; res. psychiat. Johns Hopkins Hosp., Baltimore, Md., 1977-80; fellowship behavior sci. Johns Hopkins U., Baltimore, Md., 1977-80, asst. psyc., 1980-86; dir. partial hospitalization program North Charles Genl. Hosp., Baltimore, Md., 1981-88; med. dir. partial hospitalization program Homewood Hosp. Ctr., Baltimore, Md., 1988-91; med. dir. psychiat. partial hospitalization program Union Meml. Hosp., Baltimore, Md., 1991—; physician St. Joseph Med. Ctr., Towson, Md., 1991—, Church Hosp., Balt., 1991—, Maryland Gen. Hosp., Balt., 1991-98, Taylor Manor, Ellicott City, Md., 1987-98, JL Kernan Hosp., Balt., 1995—, Sheppard-Enoch Pratt Hosp., 1998—; instr. psyc., Johns Hopkins U., 1986-96. Mem. AMA, Am. Neuropsychiat. Assn., Johns Hopkins Med. and Surg. Assn., Md. Psychiat. Soc., Am. Acad. Clin. Psychiatrists, Am. Soc. Clin. Psychopharmacology (cert.), Internat. Psychogeriatric Assn., Korean Am. Med. Assn. Fax: 410-313-9641; 410-554-6603; E-mail: cskwon@jhu.edu. Home: 2908 Chainita Ct Ellicott City MD 21042-7625 Office: Union Meml Hosp Dept Psychiat. 201 E University Pkwy Baltimore MD 21218-2829

KWON, JOON TAEK, retired chemistry researcher; b. Kimpo, Kyunggi Do, Republic of Korea, Mar. 10, 1935; came to U.S., 1955; s. Young Tae and Byoung Soon (Kim) K.; m. Moon Ja You, Aug. 15, 1964; children: Howard Albert, Daphne Elsa. BS in Chemistry, U. Ill., 1957; MS in Chemistry, Cornell U., 1959, PhD in Chemistry, 1962; postdoctoral fellow, U. B.C., Vancouver, Can., 1962-64. Instr. II dept. chemistry U. B.C., 1964-65; assoc. rsch. chemist Chemcell Ltd., Edmonton, Alta., Can., 1965-66; rsch. chemist Celanese Corp., Summit, N.J., 1967-70; sr. rsch. chemist Lummus Co., Bloomfield, N.J., 1970-78; prin. rsch. chemist ABB Lummus Global Inc., Bloomfield, N.J., 1978-99. Co-author: Handbook of Chemical Production Process, 1986; contbr. articles to profl. jours. Disting. commr. and mem. Silver Beaver lodge Monmouth council 347 Boy Scouts Am., vigil mem. Order of the Arrow. Indsl. matching grantee Nat. Rsch. Coun., Ottawa, Can., 1966-67. Fellow Am. Inst. Chemists; mem. Royal Soc. Chemistry, Soc. Chem. Industry (N.Am. sect.), Am. Chem. Soc., Korean Chem. Soc. (life, rec. sec. N.Am. 1975-93), Korean Scientists and Engrs. in Am. (pres. N.J. chpt. 1976-77), Catalysis Soc. Met. N.Y.C., U. Ill. Alumni Assn. (life), Cornell U. Alumni Assn. Methodist. Achievements include patent for prodn. process for propylene oxide and 13 other patents in field of organometallic chemistry and process rsch. Home: 142 Derby Dr Freehold NJ 07728-2767

KWON, OJOUNG, computer scientist, educator, consultant; b. Taegu, South Korea, Apr. 18, 1955; came to U.S., 1982; s. Hun Sul Kwon and Suk Han Kim; m. Myounghie Kim, July 4, 1986; children: Eunice M., Daniel M., Ruth C.M. BSEE, Yeungnam U., Taegu, South Korea, 1978, MSEE, 1982; MBA, N.H. Coll., 1985; PhD, U. Ala., Tuscaloosa, 1991. Instr. Yeungnam Jr. Coll. of Tech., Taegu, 1982; grad. asst. N.H. Coll., Manchester, 1983-85; systems analyst Info. Resource Group, Inc., Contoocook, N.H., 1985; rsch. asst. Ala. Productivity Ctr. U. Ala., Tuscaloosa, 1989, rsch. asst. Artificial

Intelligence Lab., 1985-90; asst. prof. mgmt. info. systems Univ. Ill. at Springfield, 1991-96, assoc. prof. mgmt. info. sys., 1996—. Contbr. articles to profl. jours. and procs. With Korean Army, 1978-80. Recipient Competitive Scholarly Rsch. award, 1992, 93, 95, 96, 97, 98; U. Ala. Grad. Coun. rsch. fellow, 1988, Disting. Achievement award U. Ill., Springfield, 1993. Mem. Decision Sci. Inst., Korean Scientists and Engrs. Assn., Am. Assn. for Artificial Intelligence, Soc. of Computer Simulation, Internat. Assn. Knowledge Engrs., Inst. Mgmt. Sci., Beta Gamma Sigma, Mu Sigma Rho. Avocations: table tennis, tennis, audio systems, classical music. Office: Univ Ill Springfield Dept MIS L-109 Springfield IL 62794-9243

KWONG, DONALD, contracts administrator, consultant; b. Sacramento, Calif., Feb. 10, 1968; s. Dewey and Wai Ying (Chin) K. BA, U. Calif., Santa Cruz, 1991; DD, Universal Life Ch., 1996. Purchasing agt. U.S. Dept. Energy, Sacramento, 1991-93; procurement specialist PRC Environ. Mgmt., San Francisco, 1993-95; cons. San Jose MBDC, 1995-96; contracts adminstr. Aerotherm Corp., Mountain View, Calif., 1996-98; staff aide II City of Santa Clara, 1999—; mem. Industry Coun. for Small Bus. Devel., 1996-98, Dept. of Def. Small Bus. Coun., 1996-98. Editor: (literary jour.) Seaweed Soup, 1990-91. No. sec. Asian Pacific Caucus, Calif. Dem. Party, 1995-96; treas. Asian Pacific Dem. Club, San Francisco, 1995. Mem. Nat. Contract Mgmt. (chpt. v.p. 1994-95), Alumni Assn. U. Calif. Santa Cruz (life), Orgn. Chinese Ams. (bd. dirs. 1996—, sec. 1997-98, v.p. 1999—). Democrat. Office: City of Santa Clara Fin Dept 1500 Warburton Ave Santa Clara CA 95050

KWONG, EVA, artist, educator; b. Hong Kong, Feb. 9, 1954; came to the U.S., 1967; d. Tony and Ivory K.; m. Kirk S. Mangus, 1976; children: Una K., Jasper M. BFA, RISD, 1975; MFA, Tyler Sch. Art/Temple U., Phila., 1977. Vis. artist, 1977—; vis. faculty Cleve. (Ohio) Inst. Art, 1982-83; part-time faculty U. Akron, Ohio, 1987, 89, 95, Kent (Ohio) State U., 1990—; lectr. in field. Works in over 180 exhbns. Visual Arts Regional fellow Arts Midwest, Mpls., 1987, Visual Arts fellow Nat. Endowment for the Arts, Washington, 1988, Ohio Arts Coun., Columbus, 1988, 94, 99. Mem. Nat. Coun. on Edn. for the Ceramic Arts (dir.-at-large 1995-97). Office: Kent State Univ Art Dept Main St Kent OH 44242

KWORTNICK, LINDA MARIE, emergency nurse; b. Phila., Sept. 3, 1954; d. Robert Leroy and Mary Dolores (Murray) Schnee; m. William J. Kwortnick, Sept. 23, 1978; children: Angela Nicole, William Robert. Diploma, St. Josephs Hosp. Sch. Nursing, Phila., 1976. Cert. emergency nurse. Head nurse emergency dept. St. Mary Hosp., Phila., 1980-82; staff nurse Jeans Hosp., Phila., 1983—; nursing supr. Cheltenham York Rd. Nursing Home, Phila., 1985-86; relief nursing supr. Lawndale Hosp., Phila., 1989-92; ind. contractor Med. Tex. Industries, Inc., Phila., 1993—. First aid and CPR instr., Nat. Safety Coun., 1994-99. Mem. Emergency Dept. Nurses Assn. Home: 524 Robbins St Philadelphia PA 19111-5740

KYBAL, ELBA GÓMEZ DEL REY, economist, non-profit organization executive; b. Santa Fe, Argentina, Apr. 1, 1915; came to U.S., 1942; d. J. Ignacio and Concepción (del Rey) Gómez; m. Milic Kybal, July 16, 1950 (dec. July 1977); children: Cynthia, Alexander. *Milic's father , Vlastimil Kybal, was a scholar and professor and served in the Czech diplomatic service as an ambassador to Mexico. His mother, Ana Saenz Aguilar, was a painter who trained at Mexico's School Fine Arts. Milic, [illegible]or Juris Charles U., 1937, joined the Federal Reserve Bank, New York, and was an economist at the UN. Later he joined the Inter-American Development Bank, Washington D.C. as an advisor to the President and capital markets expert. Daughter Cynthia, BA 1975 Georgetown, MBA 1978 U. Virginia, is an advertising executive. She is married to Byron A. Grant. Son Alexander, BS 1977 U. Maryland, is a businessman.* BA in Internat. Rels., U. Litoral, Rosario, Argentina, 1940; MA in Econs., Harvard U., 1945, PhD in Econs., 1946. Economist Fed. Res. Bank, N.Y.C., 1946-47; economist, polit. affairs officer UN, N.Y.C., 1947-56; sr. economist Orgn. Am. States, Washington, head specialized conf., chief L.Am. econ. integration, dir. under secretariat for econ. and social affairs, 1956-80; cons. Argentine Govt., Buenos Aires, 1978. Contbr. articles to profl. jours. Advisor InterAm. com. of women OAS, Washington, 1960-80; vol. cons. Pan Am. Devel. Found., Washington, 1980-82; vol. Argentine, Ecuadorian and Peruvian Found., Washington, 1988-90; pres. Pan Am. Liaison Com. of Women's Orgns., 1995—; founder CEDA, Washington, 1970; bd. dirs. Gala Hispanic Theatre, Washington, 1997—. Named Vol. of the Yr., Pan Am. Devel. Found., 1981, Bus. and Profl. Women's Club, 1984. Mem. Phi Beta Kappa. Roman Catholic. Avocation: travel. Home: 2510 Virginia Ave NW Washington DC 20037-1904

KYGER, EDGAR ROSS, surgeon, educator; b. Kansas City, Mo., June 23, 1941; m. Mary K.; children: Caroline Boone, Christopher Boone, E. Ross IV. BS, Washington and Lee U., 1963; MD, U. Pa., 1967. Lic. surgeon, Tex., 1969. Intern Hosp. U. Pa., 1967-68, resident, 1968-73; resident St. Luke's Episcopal Hosp., 1973-74; attending surgeon Tex. Heart Inst., 1974-78; from asst. prof. to assoc. prof. surgery U. Tex. Med. Sch., Houston, 1974-78, clin. assoc. prof. surgery, 1978—; chief, thoracic, cardiovascular surgery Hermann Hosp., Houston, 1977-78, Woodland Hts. Hosp., Lufkin, Tex., Nacogdoches (Tex.) Meml. Hosp.; bd. dirs. Lufkin Nat. Bank, 1994—; med. dir. and bd. dirs. Hospice in the Pines, 1995—. Pres. Houston chpt. Am. Heart Assn., 1980; pres. bd. dirs., Tex. Affiliate of Am. Heart Assn., 1988-89; mem. corp. bd. Boys and Girls Clubs. Fellow Am. Coll. Cardiology, Am. Coll. Surgeons; mem. AMA, Tex. Med. Assn., Tex. Surgical Soc., Harris County Med. Soc., Denton A. Cooley Cardiovascular Surgery Soc., Assn. Acad. Surgery.

KYHL, ROBERT LOUIS, retired electrical engineering educator; b. Omaha, July 27, 1917; s. Louis Christian and Helen (Sadilek) K.; m. Edith Kettendorf, Sept. 13, 1943; 1 child, Alice Kyhl Brocoum. SB, U. Chgo., 1937; PhD in Physics, MIT, 1947. Rsch. assoc. W.W. Hansen Lab., Stanford U., 1947-54; rsch. staff Gen. Electric Rsch. Lab., Schenectady, 1954-56; rsch. assoc. radiation lab. MIT, 1941-45, prof. elec. engring., 1956-83, prof. emeritus, 1983—. Mem. Am. Phys. Soc., IEEE (Baker award 1956), Fedn. Am. Scientists. Home: 43 Malcolm Rd Jamaica Plain MA 02130-3439 Office: ELEC ENGRING MIT Cambridge MA 02139

KYHOS, M. GAITHER GALLEHER, private school educator; b. Durham, N.C., Sept. 17, 1955; d. Earl Potter Jr. and Martha Hungerford (Wheelwright) Galleher; m. Thomas Flynn Kyhos, Sept. 4, 1982; children: Jennifer Chalfant, Patrick Flynn, Justin Farleigh. BA in Polit. Sci. cum laude, St. Lawrence U., 1977. Layout and prodn. asst. Nat. Geographic Mag., Washington, 1977-80, illustrations rschr., 1980-82, sr. rschr., 1982-85, sr. rschr./writer, 1985-88, sr. rschr./compiler, 1988-94; asst. tchr., social studies-resource St. Patrick's Episcopal Day Sch., Washington, 1994-97, co-head tchr., 1997—; mem. internat. adv. bd. Sellinger Sch., Loyola Coll. in Md., Balt., 1992-96; presenter in field. Author map supplements for Nat. Geographic Mag. Bd. dirs. Lt. Joseph P. Kennedy Inst., Washington, 1993-95; Vice Presdl. advance person The White House, Washington, in Ivory Coast, 1991, in Estonia, 1992. Mem. Nat. Coun. for Social Studies, Spinal Cord Injury Network, Ednl. Alliance/Nat. Geog. Soc., So. Poverty Law Ctr. Avocations: travel, biking, yoga, reading, golf. Office: St Patrick's Episc Day Sch 4700 Whitehaven Pkwy NW Washington DC 20007-1554

KYHOS, THOMAS FLYNN, lawyer; b. Cheverly, Md., May 13, 1947. B.A. in Econs., DePauw U., 1969; J.D., Cath. U., 1973. Bar: Md. 1974, D.C. 1974, U.S. Tax Ct. 1974, U.S. Supreme Ct. 1978. sole practice, Washington, 1974—; pres. First Oxford Corp., Washington, 1976—. Mem. ABA, Md. Bar Assn., D.C. Bar Assn. Home: 5714 Massachusetts Ave Bethesda MD 20816-1929 Office: 3528 K St NW Washington DC 20007-3503

KYIN, SAW WILLIAM, chemist, consultant; b. Rangoon, Burma, Aug. 6, 1954; came to U.S., 1981; s. U. Shin Nga and Daw (Swa) Khin; m. Cynthia H. Hsuan-Hung, Jan. 30, 1975; children: Tim, Maureen., Michelle. BS, Rangoon Arts and Sci. U., 1977; MS, Western Ill. U., 1984. Dir. biotech. ctr. Genetic Engring. Facility, U. Ill., Urbana-Champaign, 1984-92; dir. molecular biology dept. Synthesis/Sequencing Facility, Princeton, N.J., 1992—. Mem. AAAS, Am. Chem. Soc., Am. Peptide Soc., Am. Soc. Mass Spectrometry, N.Y. Acad. Scis., Assn. Biomolecular Resource Facilities, Protein Soc. Office: Princeton Univ Dept Molecular Biology Washington Rd Princeton NJ 08544

KYKER, CHARLES CLINTON, pastor; b. Greensboro, N.C., Dec. 23, 1962; s. Dennis Clinton and Roberta Jean (McKay) K.; m. Julie Melissa White, Apr. 30, 1988; children: Mary Grace Caroline, Ashley Beth Mellisa, Molly Ann Beatrice. BA in Religion and Philosophy, Greensboro (N.C.) Coll., 1985; MDiv, Emory U., 1988; Th.M, Duke U., 1997; postgrad., Asbury Theol. Seminary, 1997—. Youth min. Unity United Meth. Ch., Thomasville, N.C., 1982-83, Asbury United Meth. Ch., Greensboro, 1983-85; assoc. pastor First United Meth. Ch., Buford, Ga., 1985-87, Fayetteville, Ga., 1987-88, Waynesville, N.C., 1988-90; pastor Centenary United Meth. Ch., Clemmons, N.C., 1990-97; lead pastor Christ United Meth. Ch., Hickory, N.C., 1998—; del. World Meth. Regional Sem., Ghana, West Africa, 1986-87, World Meth. Internat. Seminar, Atlanta, 1987, 250th Celebration of Aldersgate, Eng., 1988; cert. new world missioner, key event and new life herald, United Meth. Ch. Bd. of Discipline, Nashville, 1988. Author: Show Me the Way: Skits for the Young and Old, 1994. Student affiliate Atlanta Emergency Aid Ministry, 1986-87; bd. dirs. Haywood Christian Ministry, 1989-90. Sherman scholar Emory U., 1985-88, Beeson scholar, 1997—; recipient Hardee Christian svc. award, 1985. Mem. Clemmons Civic Club. Home: 1910 Twin Ponds Dr Hickory NC 28602-9281 Office: Christ United Meth Ch PO Box 10124 Hickory NC 28603

KYKER, CHRISTINE WHITE (CHRIS KYKER), human services consultant; b. Temple, Tex., Mar. 30, 1925; d. Labon Edmondson and Grace Mae (Wrye) White; m. Rex Paxton Kyker, Sept. 1, 1946; children: Jerilyn Kyker Pfeifer, Robert Paxton Kyker, Melinda Lea Kyker Fullerton, Jan Christi Kyker Bryan, Richard Morris Kyker. BA, Abilene Christian U., 1946, MS, 1959, MA, 1960. Lic. master social worker. Instr. Abilene (Tex.) Christian U., 1946-50, 1954-63; guest lectr. Hardin-Simmons U., Abilene, 1965-72; exec. dir. Abilene Assn. for Mental Health, 1963-74; dir. West Cen. Tex. Coun. of Govts., Area Agy. on Aging, Abilene, 1974-79; exec. dir. Tex. Dept. on Aging, Austin, 1979-84; program specialist family and children svcs. Tex. Dept. Human Svcs., 1984-86; pres., CEO Disability Resources, Inc., 1986-92; with Chris Kyker and Assocs., Cons., Abilene, 1992—; Tex. coord. White House Conf. on Aging, 1981; pres. Nat. Mental Health Assn., Staff Coun., 1974, Tex. Mental Health Assn. Staff Council, 1973, Tex. Assn. of Area Agy. Aging Dirs., 1976; lectr. in field. Mem. bd. visitors Abilene Christian U., 1986—; rep. Tex. Silver-Haired Legislation, 1992-94. Recipient Alumni award Abilene Christian U., 1980, Taylor County pathfinder award for pub. svc., 1990, Trail Blazer award Tex. Joint Conf. on Aging, 1997. Mem. Ch. of Christ. Address: PO Box 5996 Abilene TX 79608-5996

KYKER, JAMES CHARLES, engineering executive, computer programmer; b. Anadarko, Okla., Aug. 30, 1963; s. James David Kyker and Patricia Louise (Roberts) Drew; m. Sherri Lynn Wilcoxson, June 14, 1980; children: James G., Jonathan P., Jessica A. BS in Computer Sci., Okla. State U., 1993. Pvt. practice contract engr. Okla., 1991-93; contract engr. The Registry/Fidelity Investments, Dallas, 1993-94; dir. devel. Doug Carson and Assocs., Cushing, Okla., 1994—; v.p. tech. Doug Carson & Assoc., Cushing, 1997—. Vol. Multigraphics, Stillwater, 1993; mem. edn. found. com. Ednl. Found., Cushing, 1996-97. Office: Doug Carson and Assocs 1515 E Pine St Cushing OK 74023-9161*

KYL, JON L., senator; b. Oakland, Nebr., Apr. 25, 1942; s. John and Arlene (Griffith) K.; m. Caryll Louise Collins, June 5, 1964; children: Kristine Kyl Gavin, John Jeffry. BA, U. Ariz., 1964, LLB, 1966. Atty. Jennings, Strouss & Salmon, Phoenix, 1966-86; mem. 100th-103rd Congresses from 4th Ariz. dist., 1987-94; senator 106th Congress, Ariz., 1995—; mem. Appropriations Com., Jud. Com., Select Com. on Intelligence. Past chmn. Phoenix C. of C.; founding dir. Crime Victim Found., Phoenix Econ. Growth Corp.; past bd. dirs. Ariz. Acad.; past chmn. Young Rep.; gen. coun. Ariz. Rep. Party. Mem. Ariz. State Bar Assn. Office: US Senate 724 Hart Senate Bldg Washington DC 20515-0302

KYLE, CHESTER RICHARD, mechanical engineer; b. L.A., Nov. 18, 1927; s. Chester Raymond and Lorena Dale (Olson) K.; m. Joyce Sylvia; children: Scott D., Kelley L., Cova-Lee, Chester W. BSME, U. Ariz., 1951; MS in Engring., UCLA, 1964, PhD, 1969. Registered profl. engr., Calif. Prodn. engr. Shell Oil Co., Long Beach, Calif., 1951-57; prodn. supt. Internat. Petroleum Co., Talara, Peru, 1957-59; prof., mech. engr. Calif. State U., Long Beach, 1959-84; dir. Sports Equipment Rsch. Assocs., Weed, Calif., 1989—; pub., editor Cycling Sci., Mt. Shasta, Calif., 1989-91; bicycle design coord. U.S. Olympic Cycling Team, 1994-96; mem. sports equipment and tech. com. U.S. Olympic Com., Colorado Springs, Colo., 1984-88; cons. on solar cars U.S. DOE, 1993; cons. on aerodynamic sprinter's Nike. Sci. editor Bicycling, 1987-91; mem. editorial bd. Internat. Jour. Sports Biomechanics, 1988-92; contbr. articles to Sci. Am., Smithsonian, other profl. jours.; contbg. author/author books and publs. in field. Named Faculty fellow in sci. NSF, UCLA, 1967, Rsch. fellow U.S. Olympic Com., Long Beach, 1982-88, Fulbright prof., Lima, Peru, 1964-65; recipient Paul Dudley White award League Am. Bicyclists, 1995. Fellow Explorers Club (N.Y.); mem. Internat. Human Powered Vehicle Assn. (founder, bd. dirs. 1975—), L.A. Adventurer's Club (pres. 1986). Achievements include design of bicycles for medal winning U.S. Olympic team, clothing for U.S. track team, parts for World Solar Challenge winner Sunraycer, of world record setting U.S. streamlined bicycle, of Paul MacCready's Kramer prize winning Gossamer condor; research in human power vehicles; bicycle design for 1994-96 U.S. Olympic Cycling team; research in aerodynamic clothing U.S. Olympic teams 1999-2000. Home and Office: 9539 N Old Stage Rd Weed CA 96094-9516

KYLE, CORINNE SILVERMAN, management consultant; b. N.Y.C., Jan. 4, 1930; d. Nathan and Janno (Harra) Silverman; m. Alec Kyle, Aug. 29, 1959 (div. Feb. 1969); children: Joshua, Perry (dec.), Julia. BA, Bennington Coll., 1950; MA, Harvard U., 1953. Assoc. editor Inter-Univ. Case Program, N.Y.C., 1956-60; co-founder, chief editor Financial Index, N.Y.C., 1960-63; rsch. analyst McKinsey & Co., N.Y.C., 1963-64; sr. rsch. assoc. Mktg. Sci. Inst., Phila., 1964-67; founding ptnr. Phila. Group, 1967-70; sr. assoc. Govt. Studies and Systems, Phila., 1970-72, cons. program planning and control, Phila., 1972-78, sr. assoc. Periodical Studies Svc., 1978-81; v.p., dir. rsch. Total Rsch. Corp., Princeton, N.J., 1981-82; mgr. social rsch. The Gallup Orgn., Princeton, 1982-86; v.p., Response Analysis Corp., 1986-91; dir. rsch. Gallup Internat. Inst., 1991-97; assoc. Krog & Ptnrs., Inc., 1997—; lectr. rsch. methods Temple U., 1981-82; vis. prof. Fairleigh Dickinson U., 1990-91, 93; dir. Verbena Corp., N.Y.C. Contbr. numerous articles to profl. publs. Mem. adv. coun. to 8th Dist. city councilman, Phila., 1971-79; mem. 22d Ward Dem. Exec. Com., 1971-78, State Dem. Com., 1974-76; mem. Pa. Gov.'s Council on Nutrition, 1974-76; v.p. Miquon Upper Sch. Bd., Phila., 1977-78; trustee Princeton Regional Scholarship Found., 1982-85, pres., 1984-85; mem. bd. edn. Princeton Regional Sch. Dist., 1984-93, pres. 1987, 89; mem. exec. bd. Mercer County (N.J.) Sch. Bds. Assn., 1987-92, v.p., 1991-92; mem. exec. com. Princeton Community Dem. Orgn., 1992-97; mem. Princeton Regional Planning Bd., 1994—, chair, 1997—, Princeton Environ. Commn., 1994-97; chair Princeton Borough task force on consolidation, 1995, One Princeton, 1996—. Mem. Am. Polit. Sci. Assn., N.J. Assn. for Pub. Opinion Rsch. Home: 32 Randolph Pl West Orange NJ 07052-4808

KYLE, DIANE WAGMAN, librarian; b. York, Pa., Dec. 20, 1951; d. Leo A. and Mary Margaret (Dougherty) Wagman; children: Amy, Jonathan. BS, Millersville U., 1973. Cert. elem. tchr., libr. sci., Pa. Math. tchr. Selinsgrove (Pa.) Area Mid. Sch., 1973-88, libr., 1988-98; libr. Apollo-Ridge (Pa.) Sch. Dist., 1998—; trustee Pa. Trust, Lewisburg, 1985-98, Ctrl. Susquehanna Health Welfare Trust, Lewisburg, 1981-98, chair, 1984-85, sec. 1994-98. Active Jr. Womans Club of Milton, Pa., 1985-98, treas., 1989-94; outdoor chair Troop 605, Boy Scouts Am., 1989-93, com. chair, 1993-96; asst. leader, Girl Scouts U.S., Milton, 1990-93. Mem. Selinsgrove Area Edn. Assn. (faculty rep. 1979-85, treas. 1985-98), Pa. Sch. Librs. Assn., Pa. Mid. Sch. Assn. (rec. sec. 1991-94, pres. 1994-96, bd. dirs. 1990—), Delta Kappa Gamma (corr. sec. 1990-98). Democrat. Roman Catholic. Avocations: cross stitch, reading, downhill skiing, baseball. Home: RR 2 Box 405 Saltsburg PA 15681-9327 Office: Apollo-Ridge School District RD 1 Box 128 Saltsburg PA 15681

KYLE, GENE MAGERL, merchandise presentation artist; b. Phila., Oct. 11, 1919; d. Elmer Langham and Muriel Helen (Magerl) K. *Mother Muriel Helen was a dramatic soprano (studied at Curtis Institute, Philadelphia, PA, Lieder in Germany). She sang as a soloist in churches and theatre. She also sang with the Detroit Symphony Orchestra (Ossip Gabralowich, DSO Conductor). She had her own radio show on W.J.R. Detroit. Father Elmer Langham Kyle was an electrical engineer and a graduate of the University of Pennsylvania. He was a first lieutenant in the Army in World War I. He was a representative for coal companies out of Pennsylvania and Virginia. He wrote and transposed music for organ and two pianos* Student Center for Creative Studies, Detroit, 1938-45. Mdse. presentation artist D. J. Healy Shops, Detroit, 1946-50, Saks Fifth Ave., Detroit, 1950-58, J.L. Hudson Co., Detroit, 1958-84, Grosse Pointe, 1989-95; freelance merchandise presentations for windows, Grosse Pointe, Mich., 1989—, paper craft holiday shows Detroit Artist's Market Holiday show; tchr. workshop classes. Exhibited in group shows at Mich. Water Color Soc., 1944, 53, 74, Mich. Artists Exhbn., 1962, 64, Scarab Club, 1948-49, 52, Detroit Artists Market, 1946-97, Mich. Gallery, 1989-92, Coach House Gallery, 1980, 90, Cmty. House, Birmingham, Mich., 1993-94, First Fed. Mich. Bank, 1994, 95, Swann Gallery, 1996-97, Detroit Artists Market, 1997. Vol. presentation work. Recipient various art awards. Mem. Detroit Inst. Arts Founders Soc., Mich. Water Color Soc., Windsor Art Gallery.

KYLE, JOHN EMERY, mission executive; b. San Diego, July 7, 1926; s. John E. and Agnes (McDaniel) K.; m. Lois Ellen Rowland, June 8, 1947; children: Arlette Marie, Jayson Duane, Marcus Justin, Darlene Patricia. BS in Agriculture, Oreg. State U., 1950; BDiv, Columbia Theol. Sem., 1961, MDiv, 1971. Ordained to ministry Presbyn. Ch. in U.S., 1961. Sr. buyer Easwest Produce Co.-Safeway Stores Inc., San Francisco, 1951-57; pastor Presbyn. Ch. in U.S., Hazard, Ky., 1961-63; adminstr. Wycliffe Bible Translators, Manila, Philippines, 1964-73; coord. Mission to the World, Presbyn. Ch. in Am., Decatur, Ga., 1974-77, Wycliffe Bible Translators, Washington, 1977-79; missions dir. Intervarsity Christian Fellowship, Madison, Wis., 1979-88; exec. dir. Mission to World Presbyn. Ch. in Am., Atlanta, 1988-94; sr. v.p. Evang. Fellowship of Mission Agys., Norcross, Ga., 1994—; trustee Columbia Bible Coll. and Sem., 1982-86, Concerts of Prayer Internat., Mpls., 1988-99, Berkeley Hts., N.J., Overseas Missionary Fellowship, Robesonia, Pa., 1982-86, A.D. 2000 Movement, Colorado Springs, 1989—, Co mission, 1992-98. Author: Now This Generation, 1990; editor: The Unfinished Task, 1982, Finishing the Task, 1987, Urban Missions, 1988. Midshipman USNR, 1944-45. Recipient Presdl. Merit medal Pres. of Philippines. Mem. Evang. Fgn. Missions Assn. (trustee 1989-94), Nat. Assn. Evang., Assn. Ch. Missions Com., World Evang. Fellowship, Concerts of Prayer Internat. Home: 5747 Brooklyn Ln Norcross GA 30093-4117 Office: Evang Fellowship Mission Ag 5747 Brooklyn Ln Norcross GA 30093-4117

KYLE, RICHARD HOUSE, federal judge; b. St. Paul, Apr. 30, 1937; s. Richard E. and Geraldine (House) K.; m. Jane Foley, Dec. 22, 1959; children: Richard H. Jr., Michael F., D'Arcy, Patrick G., Kathleen. BA, U. Minn., 1959, LLB, 1962. Bar: Minn. 1962, U.S. Dist. Ct. Minn. 1992. Atty. Briggs & Morgan, St. Paul, 1963-68, 1970-92; solicitor gen. Minn. Atty. Gen. Office, St. Paul, 1968-70; judge U.S. Dist. Ct., St. Paul, 1992—. Pres. Minn. Law Rev., Mpls., 1962. Mem. Minn. State Bar Assn., Ramsey County Bar Assn. Republican. Episcopal. Office: US Dist Ct Federal Courts Bldg 316 Robert St N Saint Paul MN 55101-1495

KYLE, ROBERT ARTHUR, medical educator, oncologist; b. Bottineau, N.D., Mar. 17, 1928; s. Arthur Nichol and Mabel Caroline (Crandall) K.; m. Charlene Mae Showalter, Sept. 11, 1954; children: John, Mary, Barbara, Jean. AA, N.D Sch. Forestry, 1946; BS, U. N.D., 1948; MD, Northwestern U., 1952; MS, U. Minn., 1958. Diplomate Am. Bd. Internal Medicine; subsplty. Hematology. Fellow Mayo Grad. Sch., Rochester, Minn., 1953-59; clin. asst. Tufts U. Sch. Medicine, Boston, 1960-61; cons. internal medicine Mayo Clinic, Rochester, 1961—; prof. medicine and lab. medicine Mayo Med. Sch., Rochester, 1975—; pres. med. subjects unit Am. Topical Assn., Johnstown, Pa., 1976-81; chmn. standards, ethics and peer rev. orgn. Cancer & Acute Leukemia Group B, Scarsdale, N.Y., 1978-82; Robert A. Hettig lectr. in hematology Baylor U. Coll. of Medicine, Houston, 1984; Waldenström lectr., Stockholm, 1988; Redlich Meml. lectr Cedars-Sinai Med. Ctr., U. Calif., L.A.; vis. prof. St. Elizabeth's Med. Ctr., Tufts U. Sch. Medicine, Boston, 1998; bd. dirs. Waldenstrom's Macroglobulinemia Support Group. Author: The Monoclonal Gammopathies, 1976, Medicine and Stamps, vols. 1 and 2, 1980; author/editor: Neoplastic Disease of the Blood, 3rd edit., Myeloma: Biology and Management, 1995, 2nd edit. 1998. Chmn. bd. trustees First Presbyn. Ch., Rochester, Minn., 1967; chmn. Rochester Med. Ctr. Ministry, 1979-86. Capt. USAF, 1955-57. Named Disting. Topicl Philatelest, Am. Topical Soc., 1982; Recipient Waldenström award Internat. Workshop for Myeloma, Italy, 1991, Henry S. Plummer Distinguished Internist award Mayo Clin., 1995, Mayo Distinguished Clinician award 1996, Sioux award U. N.D., 1998; Bruce Wiseman lectr. Ohio State U., 1991, Kauffman Meml. lectr. Meml. Sloan Kettering Med. Ctr., N.Y.C., 1997; Clement Finch prof. U. Wash., 1993. Fellow ACP; mem. N.Y. Acad. Scis., Am. Soc. Hematology, Internat. Soc. Hematology (sec.-gen. Inter-Am. divsn. 1990), Am. Assn. Cancer Rsch., Internat. Myeloma Found. (chmn. scientific adv. bd. 1995), Phi Beta Kappa. Republican. Avocation: philately. Home: 1207 6th St SW Rochester MN 55902-1918 Office: Mayo Clinic & Hosps 200 1st St SW Rochester MN 55905-0002

KYLE, ROBERT CAMPBELL, II, publishing executive; b. Cleve., Jan. 6, 1935; s. Charles Donald and Mary Alice (King) K.; children: Peter F., Kit C., Scott G. BS, U. Colo., 1956; MA, Case Western Res. U., 1958; MBA, Harvard U., 1963, DBA, 1966. Ptnr. McLagan & Co., Chgo., 1966-67; founder, pres. Devel. Sys. Corp. (subs. Longman Group USA), Chgo., 1967-82; pres. Longman Group USA, Chgo., 1982-89; chmn., CEO Dearborn Pub. Group, Inc. (formerly Longman Group USA), 1989-98; chmn. CTS Fin. Pub., 1997—. Author: Property Management, 1979; co-author: Modern Real Estate Practice, 1967, How to Profit From Real Estate, 1988. Mem. dean's adv. coun. Coll. Bus. U. Colo., 1992—; trustee Mystic Seaport Mus., 1989—; dir. Chgo. Maritime Soc., pres. 1999—. Mem. Real Estate Educators Assn. (pres. 1981), Internat. Assn. Fin. Planning, Chgo. Book Clinic (dir.), Harvard Club N.Y., Econs. Club, Chgo. Yacht Club, San Diego Yacht Club, N.Y. Yacht Club. Avocations: yacht racing, tennis. Home: 605 W Madison St Apt 4510 Chicago IL 60661-2448 Office: 155 N Wacker Dr # 900 Chicago IL 60606-1719

KYLLONEN ROSE, JULIE FRANCES, college program administrator; b. Columbia, Mo., Aug. 18, 1943; d. Toimi Enoch Kyllonen and Frances Aileen Thompson; m. Charles Lincoln Rose, Aug. 17, 1972 (div. 1974). AA in Liberal Arts, Stephens Coll., 1963; AB in Polit. Sci., U. Mo., Columbia, 1965; MS in Fgn. Svc., Georgetown U., 1968. Clk.-typist US Peace Corps, Washington, 1965-67; jr. profl. Fgn. Census Rsch. Br. of U.S. Census Bur., Washington, 1967-68; office mgr. Teknekron Inc., Washington, 1968; archivist Eisenhower Presdl. Libr. Nat. Archives, Washington and Abilene, Kans., 1968-72; dir. admissions ELS Lang. Ctr., Oakland, Calif., 1974-78; program coord. for Sponsored Students Iowa State U., Ames, 1978-88; dir. internat. student affairs Western Ill. U., Macomb, 1988—; cons. Macomb Area Indsl. Devel. Corp., 1989-98; presenter and spk. in field, in9U.S. and internationally. Newsletter editor Friends of the Macomb Pub. Libr. Dist., 1994-98. Fulbright-Hays fellow U.S. Dept. of Edn., Egypt, 1988, Malone fellow Nat. Coun. U.S.-Arab Rels., Saudi Arabia, 1996; scholar Rotary Internat. Group Study Exch. program, Korea, 1994, scholar NAFSA, China, 1989. Mem. NAFSA (chair-elect Mid.-East Spl. Interest Group, newsletter editor 1991-95, cord. Nigerian Student Concerns 1980-85), Assn. of Internat. Educators, Soc. for Intercultural Edn., Tng. and Rsch., Macomb Area C. of C., Altrusa Internat. (bd. dirs. 1993-95), Univ. Women's Club (2d v.p. 1994-96), Delta Kappa Gamma. Avocations: fiber artist, weaver, mysteries, fashion design. E-mail: J-Rose@wiu.edu. Office: Western Ill U Office Internat Edn One Univ Cir Macomb IL 61455

KYLSTRA, JOHANNES ARNOLD, physician; b. Manado, Indonesia, Nov. 30, 1925; s. Jan Arnold and Johanna Leonore (Van Praag) K.; m. Carol S. Rous (dec.); children: Jan Andrew, Kimberly; m. Yvonne C. Alden. MD, U. Leiden, 1952, PhD, 1958. Asst. prof. physiology U. Leiden (Netherlands), 1961-63; vis. asst. prof. physiology SUNY, Buffalo, 1963-65; asst. prof. medicine and physiology Duke U., Durham, N.C., 1965-66; assoc. prof. medicine Duke U., 1966-72, prof. medicine, 1972-89, prof. emeritus medicine, 1989—, assoc. prof. physiology, 1972-89; TB control physician N.C. Dept. Environ., Health & Natural Resources, 1989-98. Contbr. numerous articles on respiratory physiology, liquid breathing and lung lavage to profl. jours. Served with Royal Netherlands Navy, 1955-58. Recipient Lockheed award Marine Technology Soc., 1970, Disting. Research award

Sigma Xi, 1974, Stover-Link award Undersea Med. Soc., 1979. Home: 3615 Ocean Dr Corpus Christi TX 78411-1342

KYNCL, JOHN JAROSLAV, pharmacologist; b. Prague, Czechoslovakia, Aug. 16, 1936; came to U.S. 1971; s. Jan Petr and Marie (Mikesova) K.; m. Mila Marie Tomaides, Mar. 4, 1961; children: Marketa Kyncl Leisure, John Anthony. PhD, Komensky U., Bratislava, 1963; ScC, Czech. Acad. Sci., 1967. Pharmacologist Rsch. Inst. for Biochemistry & Pharmacy, Prague, 1963-68; A. von. Humboldt fellow U. Heidelberg, Ger., 1968-71; rsch. fellow Cleveland Clinic Found., 1971-72; E. Volwiler rsch. fellow Abbott Labs., North Chicago, Ill., 1972—. Contbr. over 100 articles to profl. jours. Fellow Coun. for High Blood Pressure Rsch. Am. Heart Assn.; mem. Am. Hypertension Soc., Am. Endocrine Soc., Internat. Hypertension Soc. (Paris), FASEB. Achievements include over 20 patents including invention of terazosin (Hytrin) and terlipressin (Glypressin). Home: 800 Green Bay Rd Lake Bluff IL 60044-1807 Office: Abbott Labs Abbott Park Rd North Chicago IL 60064

KYOORE, PASCHAL BAYLON, foreign language educator; b. Nandom, Ghana; s. Germano and Monica (Kyiiripuo) K.; m. Martha Kamanda, Jan. 13, 1996. BA with honors, U. Ghana, Accra, 1980; MA, U. Bordeaux III, France, 1985, Diplome d'Etudes Approfondies, 1986; PhD, Ohio State U., 1991. Tchr. French and English Wa (Ghana) Secondary Sch., 1980-81; tchr. French Presbyn. Secondary Sch., Accra, 1981-83; assoc. prof. French Gustavus Adolphus Coll., St. Peter, Minn., 1991—. Author: The African and Caribbean Historical Novel in French: A Quest for Identity, 1996. Avocations: reading, writing, soccer, music, dance. Office: Gustavus Adolphus Coll 800 W College Ave Saint Peter MN 56082-1485

KYRIAZIS, ARTHUR JOHN (ATHANASIOS IOANNIS KYRIAZIS), lawyer; b. Thessaloniki, Greece, Nov. 2, 1958; came to U.S., 1960; s. George A. and Elpis (Halkedis) K.; m. Maria M. Zissimos, Aug. 31, 1986; children: Cassandra Hope, Michael John, George Athanasios II. AB, Harvard U., 1981; postgrad, Pepperdine U., 1982-83; JD cum laude, Temple U., 1985; postgrad., U. Pa., 1993-98, U. Pa. Bar: Pa. 1985, U.S. Dist. Ct. (ea. dist.) Pa. 1985, U.S. Bankruptcy Ct. (ea. dist.) Pa. 1985, U.S. Bankruptcy Ct. N.J., 1986, U.S. Dist. Ct. N.J. 1986, Calif. 1987, U.S. Dist. Ct. (ea. dist.) Calif. 1988, U.S. Ct. Appeals (3d cir.) 1991, U.S. Supreme Ct. 1994. Assoc. Cardillo & Corbett, N.Y.C., 1983; law clk. to Hon. Norma J. Shapiro U.S. Dist. Ct. (ea. dist.) Pa., 1984; assoc. Needleman Needleman Carey Stein & Kratzer, 1984-85; law clk. to Hon. James Gardner Colins Commonwealth Ct. Pa., Phila., Harrisburg, 1985-86; assoc. Rawle & Henderson, Phila. and Marlton, N.J., 1987-88, Lesser & Kaplin and predecessor firm, Phila., Blue Bell, Pa. and Marlton, N.J., 1988-89; prin. Kyriazis & Assocs., Phila., Cherry Hill, N.J. and Delaware County, Pa., 1989—; arbitrator Phila. Ct. Common Pleas, 1988—, Delaware County Ct. Common Pleas, 1993—; pro bono counsel Am. Assn. Univ. Students, 1989—. Author: (with H. Caldwell) Unchecked Discretion: The Buck Stops Here: Is There a Fourth Amendment at the International Borders of the United States, 1993, Whittier Law Rev. Pa. co-coord. Dukakis for Pres., 1987-88; del. Nat. Fin. Com., Dem. Conv., Atlanta, 1988, 1982 Dem. Mid-Term Conv., Phila.; mem. Young Lawyers for Dukakis, Hellenic Am. for Dukakis, Pa., 1987-88; founder Am. Assn. Univ. Students, Cambridge, Mass. and Phila., 1978-79, pres., 1990—; v.p. Hercules-Spartan Phila. chpt. 26 Am. Hellenic Progressive Edn. Assn., 1989-90, pres., 1990-91, bd. govs., 1987—; treas., shrager Common Pleas Judge, 1999. Mem. ATLA, ABA (young lawyers div., litigation and bus. law sect., bus., real estate sects.), Am. Hellenic Lawyers Assn. (treas. 1992-94), Phila. Bar Assn. (exec. com. young lawyers sect. 1988-90, fin. sec. exec. com. 1990, sec. exec. com. 1989, co-chmn. law related edn. com. 1988—, mem. bar edn. found. com. 1988—, mem. Bill Rights 200 coms., mem. fed. cts. 200 com., chmn. debate com. and mock trial 1987—, debate dir. fed. cts. 200 nat. high sch. debate tournament 1990—), Camden County Bar Assn. (young lawyers, pub. benefits, debtor-creditor relations), Pa. Bar Assn. (litigation, young lawyers jud. administrn.), N.J. Trial Lawyers Assn., Pa. Trial Lawyers Assn., Am. Arbitration Assn. (comml. arbitrator 1988—), State Bar Calif. (litigation, intellectual property, entertainment), Hellenic-Am. Lawyers Assn. (treas. 1992-96), Am. Assn. Univ. Students (legal counsel 1989—), Coll. Admissions Inst. Am. (adv. bd. 1992—), Hellenic Univ. Club (bd. trustees), Harvard Club (N.Y., Washington), Penn Club (N.Y.), Maxwell Football Club, Nat. Press Club, Harvard-Radcliffe Club Phila. (schs. com.), Maxwell Football Club, Penn Faculty Club. Republican. Greek Orthodox. Office: 1806 Garrett Rd Lansdowne PA 19050-1005 also: Woodland Falls Corp Park 336 Bay Ave Ste 503 Ocean City NJ 08226

KYRILLOS, JOSEPH M., state legislator; b. Middletown, N.J., Apr. 12, 1960. BA, Hobart Coll., 1982; MS, Boston U., 1983. Spl. asst. U.S. Sec. Interior, 1985-87; mem. dist. 13 N.J. State Assembly, 1987-91; senator dist. 13 N.J. State Senate, 1992—; senate majority conf. leader, mem. senate budget and appropriations com., mem. senate econ. growth com.; chmn. conservation, natural resources and energy com. N.J. State Assembly, appropriations com., edn. com., select com. on ocean and beach protection; dir. bus. stds. and ethics com. N.J. State Senate. host cable tv program Tour of N.J. Mem. Garden State Arts Ctr. Found., Count Basie Theater, Rainbow Found., Monmouth County Hist. Assn., Women's Ctr. of Monmouth County, Bayshore Sr. Day Ctr., Christian Ministry in the Nat. Parks, N.J. State Tourism Adv. Coun. Mem. No. Monmouth C. of C., Lions (Middletown club), Elks (Middletown club). Address: 1715 Highway 35 Middletown NJ 07748-1867*

KYTE, LYDIANE, retired botanist; b. L.A., Jan. 6, 1919; d. Aurele and Helen Scott (Douglas) Vermeulen; m. Robert McClung Kyte, June 2, 1939; children: Katherine Liu, Bobbin Cave, William Robert Kyte. BS, U. Wash., 1964. Supt. Weyerhaeuser Co., Rochester, Wash., 1972-77; lab mgr. Briggs Nursery, Olympia, Wash., 1977-80; owner Cedar Valley Nursery, Centralia, Wash., 1980—; cons. Internat. Exec. Service Corps, Brazil, 1987, Egypt, 1990. Author: Plants From Test Tubes: An Introduction to Micropropagation, 1983, 2d rev. edit., 1988, 3d edit., 1996. Mem. Internat. Plant Propagators' Soc., Internat. Assn. Plant Tissue Culture, Am. Assn. for Hort. Sci., Am. Assn. Univ. Women. Avocation: gardening. Home and Office: Cedar Valley Nursery 3833 Mc Elfresh Rd SW Centralia WA 98531-9510

KYTE, SUSAN JANET, lawyer; b. Riverhead, N.Y., Nov. 17, 1956; d. Bruce Whiteman Kyte and Barbara Jean (Clark) Goldberg. BA cum laude, Southampton Coll. divsn. L.I. U., 1978; JD, Capital U., 1984. Bar: Ohio, 1984. Assoc. atty. Matan & Smith, Columbus, Ohio, 1984-90; econ. devel. dir. City of Columbus, 1990-91; chief counsel, legis. dir. Ohio Sec. State, Columbus, 1991-95; pvt. practice Columbus, 1996—; del. Am. Coun. Young Polit. Leaders, Columbus, 1997; mgr. Drake for Congress, 1998. Vice-chair Franklin County Rep. Party, Columbus, 1992—; chair doorbell blitz, 1988-90; founder, 1st pres. Ohio Rep. Womens Campaign Fund, Columbus, 1994—, treas., 1997—; bd. dirs. Actors Theater, Columbus, 1996—; vol. Rinehart for State Treas., Columbus, 1982, Rinehart for Mayor of Columbus, 1983, Race for the Cure, Columbus, 1995—; coord. Franklin County coalitions Voinovich for Senate, Columbus, 1988, co-chair, 1997—; treas. Keep Ohio Working Ballot Issue Commn., 1997, Every Child Counts Ballot Issue Commn., 1998, Deters for Ohio's Future, 1998—; legal counsel Teater for Mayor, 1999; treas. Tanner for City Coun., 1999; co-mgr. Browell for Judge, Columbus, 1997—; policy com. Pryce for Congress, Columbus, 1992, 94; coord. Taft for Sec. of State, Columbus, 1990; trustee Cap City Young Rep., 1984-96; active Com. for 2000, 1993; asst. legal counsel Young Rep. Nat. Fedn., 1993-95; rep. Renews Congrl. Adv. Com., D.C., 1995, 97; v.p. Columbus Literacy Coun., Columbus, 1984-92; chair comm. com. Oktoberfest, Columbus, 1992-96; steering com. Kaleidoscope Conf. for Women, Columbus, 1994—. Mem. Nat. Fedn. Ind. Businesses, Assn. Polit. Cons., Ohio State Bar Assn., Coun. Govt. Ethics Lawyers, Ohio C. of C. (polit. affairs com. 1996—). Republican. Lutheran. Avocations: cooking, travel, reading, politics. Office: Ste 300 57 E Gay St Columbus OH 43215-3103

KYZAR, PATRICIA PARKS, maternity nurse; b. Locker, Tex., Feb. 3, 1937; d. Howard A. and Georgia (Sparkman) Parks; m. Bobby B. Kyzar, Mar. 17, 1956; children: Kymberly Ann, Katherine Mary, Karla Patricia. Diploma, Meth. Hosp. Sch. Nursing, Lubbock, Tex., 1957; BSN, Tex. Christian U., 1960; MSN, U. Ala., Birmingham, 1978; DS in Nursing, U. Ala., 1992. RN, Ala. Instr. U. North Ala., Florence, 1975-78, asst. prof., 1978-92, assoc. prof., 1992-94, prof., 1994—. Mem. ANA, Assn. Women's Health, Obstetric, and Neonatal Nursing, Sigma Theta Tau, Phi Kappa Phi. Home: 414 Russell St Florence AL 35633-1338 Office: U of North Alabama Florence AL 35630